Beckett®

THE #1 AUTHORITY ON COLLECTIBLES

BASKETBALL CARD PRICE GUIDE

NUMBER 33

THE HOBBY'S MOST RELIABLE AND RELIED UPON SOURCE™

Founder: Dr. James Beckett III • Edited by the staff of Beckett Basketball

Copyright © 2025 by Beckett Collectibles LLC

All rights reserved. No part of this book shall be reproduced in any form or by any means, electronic or mechanical, including photocopying, recording, or by any information or retrieval system, without written permission from the publisher.

Prices in this guide reflect current retail rates determined just prior to printing. They do not reflect for-sale prices by the author, publisher, distributors, advertisers, or any card dealers associated with this guide. Every effort has been made to eliminate errors. Readers are invited to write us noting any errors which may be researched and corrected in subsequent printings. The publisher will not be held responsible for losses which may occur in the sale or purchase of cards because of information contained herein.

BECKETT is a registered trademark of BECKETT COLLECTIBLES LLC, PLANO, TEXAS

Manufactured in the United States of America | Published by Beckett Collectibles LLC

BECKETT®

Beckett Collectibles LLC

2700 Summit Ave, Ste 100, Plano, TX 75074

1 (866) 287-9383 • beckett.com

First Printing ISBN: 978-1-953801-84-5

COVER PHOTO: GETTY IMAGES

CONTENTS

We're Always Buying!

Specializing in Buying Sports Cards/Memorabilia Collections:

Complete Set Runs, Player Collections, Graded, Raw, Modern, Autographs, Relics, Unopened Boxes/Sets, TCG/Pokémon, Vintage Cards, Memorabilia, and More!

Call: (631) 532-5797

Email: info@smrcollectibles.com

169A New Highway
Amityville, NY 11701

SMRCollectibles.com
SMRcollectibles

TRANSFORM YOUR CARD COLLECTION WITH

BECKETT'S TRUSTED GRADING

Why Submit to Beckett Grading Services?

- Subgrades option for Detailed Evaluation
- No Upcharges
- No Membership Fees
- No Minimum Quantity
- Includes Inner Sleeves for Maximum Protection
- Unmatched Authenticity and Quality

SCAN THE QR CODE TO SUBMIT NOW
or go to https://www.beckett.com/submit/cards/service

BECKETT®

HOW TO USE AND CONDITION GUIDE

Every year, this book gets bigger and better. This edition has been enhanced and expanded from the previous volume with the addition of new releases, updated prices and changes to older listings. The Beckett Basketball Card Price Guide has been successful where other attempts have failed because it is complete, current, and valid. The prices were added to the card lists just prior to printing and reflect not the author's opinions or desires, but the going retail prices for each card, based on the marketplace - sports memorabilia conventions and shows, sports card shops, online trading, auction results and other firsthand reports of realized sales.

What is the best price guide available on the market today? Of course, sellers will prefer the price guide with the highest prices, while buyers will naturally prefer the one with the lowest prices. Accuracy, however, is the true test. The Beckett Basketball Card Price Guide may not always have the highest or lowest values, but the accuracy of both our checklists and pricing - produced with the utmost integrity - has made it the most widely used reference book in the industry.

To facilitate your use of this book, please read the complete introductory section before going on to the pricing pages, paying special attention to the section on grading and card conditions, as the condition of the card greatly affects its value. We hope you find the book both interesting and useful in your collecting pursuits.

ADVERTISING

Within this Price Guide you will find advertisements for sports memorabilia material, mail order, and retail sports collectibles establishments. All advertisements were accepted in good faith based on the reputation of the advertiser. However, neither the author, publisher, the distributors, nor the other advertisers in this Price Guide accept any responsibility for any advertiser not complying with the terms of his or her ad.

HOW TO COLLECT

Each collection is personal and reflects the individuality of its owner. There are no set rules on how to collect cards. Since card collecting is a hobby or leisure pastime, what you collect, how much you collect, and how much time and money you spend collecting are entirely up to you. The funds you have available for collecting and your own personal taste should determine how you collect. It is impossible to collect every card ever produced. Therefore, beginners as well as intermediate and advanced collectors usually specialize in some way. One of the reasons this hobby is popular is that individual collectors can define and tailor their collecting methods to match their own tastes. Many collectors select complete sets from particular years, acquire only certain players, some collectors are only interested in the first cards or Rookie Cards of certain players, and others collect cards by team. Remember, this is a hobby, so pick a style of collecting that appeals to you.

UNDERSTANDING CARD VALUES

Why are some cards more valuable than others? Obviously, the economic laws of supply and demand are applicable to card collecting just as they are to any other field where a commodity is bought, sold or traded in a free, unregulated market. Supply (the number of cards available on the market) is less than the total number of cards originally produced since attrition diminishes that original quantity. Each year a percentage of cards is typically thrown away, destroyed or otherwise lost to collectors. This percentage is much, much smaller today than it was in the past because more and more people have become increasingly aware of the value of their cards. For those who collect only Mint condition cards, the supply of older cards can be quite small indeed. Until recently, collectors were not so conscious of the need to preserve the condition of their cards. For this reason, it is difficult to know exactly how many 1957-58 Topps are currently available, Mint or otherwise. It is generally accepted that there are fewer 1957-58 Topps available than 1970-71, 1978-79 or 1986-87 Fleer cards. If demand were equal for each of these sets, the law of supply and demand would increase the price for the least available sets. Demand, however, is never equal for all sets, so price correlations can be complicated. The demand for a card is influenced by many factors. These include the age of the card, the number of cards printed, the player(s) portrayed on the card, the attractiveness and popularity of the set and the physical condition of the card. In general, the older the card, the fewer the number of cards printed, the more famous, popular and talented the player, the more attractive and popular the set, and the better the condition of the card, the higher the value of the card will be. There are exceptions to all but one of these factors: the condition of the card. Given two cards similar in all respects except condition, the one in the best condition will always be valued higher. While those guidelines help to establish the value of a card, the countless exceptions and peculiarities make any simple, direct mathematical formula to determine card values impossible.

HOW THE PRICE GUIDE IS ORGANIZED

The Beckett Basketball Card Price Guide is listed alphabetically, followed by chronological order. Please note that for some brands, as a reflection of the secondary market, the manufacturer has been stripped from the set name. This includes, but is not limited to, the brands Exquisite Collection, Finest, SPx, SP Authentic, Stadium Club, Ultra, and Ultimate Collection. In other cases, "Upper Deck" has been shortened to "UD", as in UD Black, UD Glass, UD Choice, or UD Ionix.

WHAT THE COLUMNS MEAN

The LO and HI columns reflect a range of current retail selling prices and are listed in U.S. dollars. The HI column represents the typical full retail selling price while the LO column represents the lowest price one could expect to find through extensive shopping. Both columns represent the same condition for the card listed. Keep in mind that market conditions can change quickly up and down based on extreme levels of demand.

PRICING PREMIUMS

Some cards can trade at premium price levels compared to values listed in this issue. Those include but are not limited to cards of players who became hot since this book went to press, regional stars or fan favorites in high demand locally and memorabilia cards with unusually dramatic swatches or patches.

SET PRICES

A somewhat paradoxical situation exists in the price of a complete set vs. the combined cost of the individual cards in the set. In nearly every case, the sum of the prices for the individual cards is higher than the cost for the complete set. This is prevalent especially in the cards of the last few years. The reasons for this apparent anomaly stem from the habits of collectors and from the carrying costs to dealers. Today, each card in a set normally is produced in the same quantity as all other cards in its set. Many collectors collect only stars, superstars and particular teams. As a result, the dealer is left with a shortage of certain player cards and an abundance of others. He therefore incurs an expense in simply "carrying" these less-desirable cards in stock. On the other hand, if he sells a complete set, he gets rid of large numbers of cards at one time. For this reason, he generally is willing to receive less money for a complete set. By doing this, he recovers all his costs and makes a profit. The disparity between the price of the complete set and the sum of the individual cards also has been influenced by the fact that some of the major manufacturers now are pre-collating card sets. Since "pulling" individual cards from the sets involves a specific type of labor (and cost), the singles or star card market is not affected significantly by pre-collation. Set prices also do not include rare card varieties, unless specifically stated. Of course, the prices for sets do include one example of each type for the given set, but this is the least expensive variety.

MULTIPLIERS

Some parallel sets and lightly traded insert sets are listed with multipliers to provide values of unlisted cards. Multiplier ranges (i.e. 10X to 20X HI) apply only to the HI column. Example: If basic-issue card A or the insert card in question lists for 20 to 50 cents, and the multiplier is "20X to 40X HI", then the parallel version of card A or the insert card in question is valued at $10 to $20. Please note that the term "basic card" used in the Price Guide refers to a player's standard regular issue card. A "basic card" cannot be an insert or parallel card.

STATED ODDS AND PRINT RUNS

Odds of pulling insert cards are often listed as a ratio (1:12 - one in 12 packs). If the odds vary by pack type, they are generally listed separately. Stated print runs are also included in the set header lines or after the player's name for many serial numbered cards or for sets which the manufacturer has chosen to announce print runs. Stated odds and print runs are provided by the manufacturer based on the entire print run and should be considered very close estimates and not exact figures. The data provided in this book has been verified by Beckett to the best of our ability. Neither the stated odds nor print runs should be viewed as a guarantee by either Beckett or the manufacturer.

ONLY A REFERENCE

The data and pricing information contained within this publication is intended for reference only and is not to be used as an endorsement of any specific product(s) or as a recommendation to buy or sell any product(s). Beckett's goal is to provide the most accurate and verifiable information in the industry. However, Beckett cannot guarantee the accuracy of all data published. Typographical errors occasionally occur, and unverifiable information may reach print from time to time. Buyers and sellers of sports collectibles should be aware of this and handle their personal transactions at their own risk. If you discover an error or misprint in this book, please notify us via email at customerservice@beckett.com.

GLOSSARY/LEGEND

This glossary defines terms frequently used in the card collecting hobby. Many of these terms are also common to other types of sports memorabilia collecting. Some terms may have several meanings depending on use and context.

ASA - American Basketball Association
ACC - Accomplishment
ACO- Assistant Coach Gard
AL - Active Leader
ART - All-Rookie Team
AS - All-Star
ASA - All-Star Advice
ASW - All-Star Weekend
AUTO or AU - Autograph.
AW - Award Winner
B - Bronze
BC - Bonus card
BT - Beam Team or Breakaway Threats
CB - Collegiate Best
CBA - Continental Basketball Association
CL - Checklist card. Older checklist cards in Mint condition that have not been checked off are very desirable and command large premiums.
CO - Coach card
COMMON CARD - The typical card of any set; rt has no premium value accruing from subject matter, numerical scarcity, popular demand, or anomaly.
COR - Corrected card. A version of an error card that was fixed by the manufacturer.
CY - City Lights
DIE-CUT - A card will part of its stock partially cut for ornamental reasons.
DISC - A circular-shaped card
DP - Double Print. A card that was printed in approximately double the quantity compared to other cards in the same series.
ERR - Error card. A card with erroneous information, spelling, or depiction on either side of the card.
EXCH - An exchange card that is inserted into packs that can be redeemed.
FIN - Finals
FLB - Flashback
FPM - Future Playoff MVP's
FSL - Future Scoring Leaders
FULL SHEET - A complete sheet of cards that has not been cut into individual cards by the manufacturer. Also called an uncut sheet.
G - Gold
GQ - Gentleman's Quarterly
GRA - Grace
HL - Highlight card
HOF - Hall of Fame, or Hall of Famer (also abbreviated HOFer).
HOR - Horizontal pose on a card as opposed to the standard vertical orientation found on most cards.
IA - In Action card.
INSERT - A card of a different type, e.g., a poster, or any other sports collectible contained and sold in the same package along with a card or cards of a major set.
IS - Inside Stuff
JSY - card contains a jersey swatch
JWA - John Wooden Award
MAG - Magic of SkyBox cards
MC - Members Choice
MEM - Memorial
MO - McDonald's Open
MINI - A small card or stamp (the 1991-92 SkyBox Canadian set, for example)
MVP - Most Valuable Player
NNO - No card number on back
NY – New York
OLY - Olympic card
PANEL - An extended card that is composed of multiple individual cards
PC - Poster card
PF - Pacific Finest
POY - Player of the Year

We Buy Everything!

Kruk Cards is currently buying complete collections, inventories, and accumulations.
At Kruk Cards we sell everything so we have a need to buy everything.

We Can Really Use The Following Items

INSERTS AND ROOKIES
High end and low end graded and raw sets and partial sets

1950's 1960's 1970's
Vintage SETS & SINGLES ALL SPORTS especially HOCKEY

ALWAYS BUYING
Goudey's, T-Cards, Playballs, Caramels, and Regional Issues From ALL SPORTS and in ALL Conditions

Game Used Card Lots and Autographed Card Lots from ALL Major Sports

Set & Insert Set Deals From The 80's, 90's and 2000's From ALL Major Sports

UNOPENED CASES AND BOX DEALS
Boxes & Cases from the 1970's, 80's, 90's, 2000's to Present. Send us your list for an offer.

GAME USED JERSEYS
Including BP's, Bench Jackets, any game used equipment from all four sports especially BASEBALL

NON SPORT DEALS
Large Case and set deals especially

We Specialize in buying large accumulations!!

So if your collection is spread out between your basement, your attic, a storage shed, and a mini warehouse. We can make you an offer on the entire lot.

We have four buyers traveling the country looking for sports cards, non-sports cards and gaming cards.

Reach out if you'd like us to evaluate your collection!

www.krukcards.com

Check out our website for our available inventory!
We currently have over 75,000 eBay Auctions

eBay User ID: **Krukcards**

Sports Collectors Digest Krause Publications CUSTOMER SERVICE AWARD 30 Year

Kruk Cards
210 Campbell St.
Rochester, MI 48307
Email us:
George@krukcards.com
eric@krukcards.com
Hours: 8:00 AM - 5:30 PM EST
Phone: (248) 656-8803 • **Fax:** (248) 656-6547

HOW TO USE AND CONDITION GUIDE

CONDITION GUIDE

Much of the value of your card is dependent on the condition or "grade" of your card. Prices in this issue reflect the highest raw condition (i.e. not professionally graded by a third party) of the card most found at shows, shops, on the internet and right out of the pack for brand new releases. This generally means Near Mint-Mint condition for modern era cards. Use the chart below as a guide to estimate the value of your card in a variety of conditions using the prices found in this Price Guide. A complete condition guide follows. The most widely used grades are defined below. Obviously, many cards will not perfectly fit one of the definitions. Therefore, categories between the major grades known as in-between grades are used, such as Good to Very Good (G-Vg), Very Good to Excellent (VgEx), and Excellent-Mint to Near Mint (ExMt-NrMt). Such grades indicate a card with all qualities of the lower category but with at least a few qualities of the higher category. Unopened packs, boxes and factory-collated sets are considered Mint in their unknown state. Once opened, however, each card can be graded (and valued) by considering any defects that may be present although the card has never been handled.

Price Guide Percentage by Grade

	1933/34-1940/41	1951/52-1967/68	1968/69-1979/80	1980/81-1989/90	1990/91-Present
MT	300%+	300%+	250%+	125-150%	100-125%
NrMt-Mt	150-300%	150-250%	200%+	100%	100%
NrMt	100-150%	100%	100%	40-60%	30-50%
Ex-Mt	100%	50-75%	40-60%	25-40%	20-30%
Ex	50-75%	30-50%	20-40%	15-25%	10-20%
VG	30-50%	15-30%	10-20%	5-15%	5-10%
G/F/P	15-30%	5-15%	5-10%	5%	5%

GENERAL CARD FLAWS

CENTERING

Current centering terminology uses numbers representing the percentage of border on either side of the main design. Obviously, centering is diminished in importance for borderless cards.

SLIGHTLY OFF-CENTER (60/40)

A slightly off-center card is one that upon close inspection is found to have one border bigger than the opposite border. This degree once was offensive to only purists, but now some hobbyists try to avoid cards that are anything other than perfectly centered.

OFF-CENTER (70/30)

An off-center card has one border that is noticeably more than twice as wide as the opposite border.

BADLY OFF-CENTER (80/20 OR WORSE)

A badly off-center card has virtually no border on one side of the card.

MISCUT

A miscut card actually shows part of the adjacent card in its larger border and consequently a corresponding amount of its card is cut off.

CORNER WEAR

Corner wear is the most scrutinized grading criteria in the hobby.

CORNER WITH A SLIGHT TOUCH OF WEAR

The corner still is sharp, but there is a slight touch of wear showing. On a dark-bordered card, this shows as a dot of white.

FUZZY CORNER

The corner still comes to a point, but the point has just begun to fray. A slightly "dinged" corner is considered the same as a fuzzy corner.

SLIGHTLY ROUNDED CORNER

The fraying of the corner has increased to where there is only a hint of a point. Mild layering may be evident. A "dinged" corner is considered the same as a slightly rounded corner.

ROUNDED CORNER

The point is completely gone. Some layering is noticeable.

BADLY ROUNDED CORNER

The corner is completely round and rough. Severe layering is evident.

CREASES

A third common defect is the crease. The degree of creasing in a card is difficult to show in a drawing or picture. On giving the specific condition of an expensive card for sale, the seller should note any creases additionally. Creases can be categorized as to severity according to the following scale.

LIGHT CREASE

A light crease is a crease that is barely noticeable upon close inspection. In fact, when cards are in plastic sheets or holders, a light crease may not be seen (until the card is taken out of the holder). A light crease on the front is much more serious than a light crease on the card back only.

MEDIUM CREASE

A medium crease is noticeable when held and studied at arm's length by the naked eye, but does not overly detract from the appearance of the card.It is an obvious crease, but not one that breaks the picture surface of the card.

HEAVY CREASE

A heavy crease is one that has torn or broken through the card's picture surface, e.g., puts a tear in the photo surface.

ALTERATIONS

DECEPTIVE TRIMMING

This occurs when someone alters the card in order (1) to shave off edge wear, (2) to improve the sharpness of the corners, or (3) to improve centering— obviously their objective is to falsely increase the perceived value of the card to an unsuspecting buyer. The shrinkage usually is evident only if the trimmed card is compared to an adjacent full-sized card or if the trimmed card is itself measured.

OBVIOUS TRIMMING

Obvious trimming is noticeable and unfortunate. It is usually performed by non-collectors who give no thought to the present or future value of their cards.

DECEPTIVELY RETOUCHED BORDERS

This occurs when the borders (especially on those cards with dark borders) are touched up on the edges and corners with magic marker or crayons of appropriate color in order to make the card appear to be Mint.

MISCELLANEOUS CARD FLAWS

The following are common minor flaws that, depending on severity, lower a card's condition by one to four grades and often render it no better than Excellent-Mint: bubbles (lumps in surface), gum and wax stains, diamond cutting (slanted borders), notching, off-centered backs, paper wrinkles, scratched-off cartoons or puzzles on back, rubber band marks, scratches, surface impressions and warping. The following are common serious flaws that, depending on severity, lower a card's condition at least four grades and often render it no better than Good: chemical or sun fading, erasure marks, mildew, miscutting (severe off-centering), holes, bleached or retouched borders, tape marks, tears, trimming, water or coffee stains and writing.

GRADES

MINT (MT)

A card with no flaws or wear. The card has four perfect corners, 55/45 or better centering from top to bottom and from left to right, original gloss, smooth edges and original color borders. A Mint card does not have print spots, color or focus imperfections.

NEAR MINT-MINT (NRMT-MT)

A card with one minor flaw. Any one of the following would lower a Mint card to Near Mint-Mint: one corner with a slight touch of wear, barely noticeable print spots, color or focus imperfections. The card must have 60/40 or better centering in both directions, original gloss, smooth edges and original color border.

NEAR MINT (NRMT)

A card with one minor flaw. Any one of the following would lower a Mint card to Near Mint: one fuzzy corner or two to four corners with slight touches of wear, 70/30 to 60/40 centering, slightly rough edges, minor print spots, color or focus imperfections. The card must have original gloss and original color borders.

EXCELLENT-MINT (EXMT)

A card with two or three fuzzy, but not rounded, corners and centering no worse than 80/20. The card may have no more than two of the following: slightly rough edges, very slightly discolored borders, minor print spots, color or focus imperfections. The card must have original gloss.

EXCELLENT (EX)

A card with four fuzzy but definitely not rounded corners and centering no worse than 70/30. The card may have a small amount of original gloss lost, rough edges, slightly discolored borders and minor print spots, color or focus imperfections.

VERY GOOD (VG)

A card that has been handled but not abused: slightly rounded corners with slight layering, slight notching on edges, a significant amount of gloss lost from the surface but no scuffing and moderate discoloration of borders. The card may have a few light creases.

GOOD (G), FAIR (F), POOR (P)

A well-worn, mishandled or abused card: badly rounded and layered corners, scuffing, most or all original gloss missing, seriously discolored borders, moderate or heavy creases, and one or more serious flaws. The grade of Good, Fair or Poor depends on the severity of wear and flaws. Good, Fair and Poor cards generally are used only as fillers.

GLOSSARY/LEGEND

PROMOTIONAL SET - A set, usually containing a small number of cards, issued by a national card producer and distributed in limited quantities or to a select group of people, such as major show attendees or dealers with wholesale accounts. Also called a preview, prototype, promo, or test set.
OP - Quadruple Print. A card that was printed in approximately four times the quantity compared to other cards in the same series.
RC - Rookie Card. A player's first appearance on a regular issue card from one of the major card companies. With a few exceptions, each player has only one RC in any given set. A Rookie Card cannot be an All-Star, Highlight, In Action, League Leader, Super Action or Team Leader card. It can, however, be a coach card or draft pick card.
REGIONAL- A card issued and distributed only in a limited geographical area of the country.
REV NEG - Reversed or flopped photo side of the card. This is a common type of error card, but only some are corrected
RIS - Rising Star
ROY - Rookie of the Year
S - Silver
SA- Super Action card.
SAL - SkyBox Salutes
SERIES - The entire set of cards issued by a particular producer in a particular year, e.g., the 1978-79 Topps series. Also, within a particular set, series can refer to a group of (consecutively numbered) cards printed at the same time, e.g., the first series of the 1972-73Topps set (#1 through #132).
SET - One each of an entire run of cards of the same type, produced by a particular manufacturer during a single season. In other words, if you have a complete set of 1989-90 Fleer cards, then you have every card from #1 up to and including #132; i.e., all the different cards that were produced.
SHOOT - Shooting Star
SKED - Schedules
SP - Single or Short Print. A card which was printed in lesser quantity compared to the other cards in the same series (also see DP).
SS - Star Stats.
STANDARD SIZE - The standard size for sports cards is 2 1/2 by 3 1/2 inches. All exceptions, such as 1969-70 Topps, are noted in card descriptions.
STOCK - The cardboard or paper on which the card is printed.
STY - Style
SY - Schoolyard Stars
TC- Team card or team checklist card
TD - Triple Double.
TEAM CARD - A card that depicts an entire team, notably the 1989-90 and 1990-91 NBA Hoops Detroit Pistons championship cards and the 1991-92 NBA Hoops subset.
TEST SET - A set, usually containing a small number of cards, issued by a national producer and distributed in a limited section of the country or to a select group of people. Also called a promo or prototype set.
TFC - Team Fact card
TL - Team Leader
TO - Tip-off
TR - Traded card
TRIB - Tribune
TRV - Trivia
TT - Team Tickets card
UER - Uncorrected Error card
USA - Team USA.
VAR- Variation card. One of two or more cards from the same series, with the same card number (or player with identical pose, if the sense is unnumbered) differing from one another in some aspect, from the printing, stock or other feature of the card. This is often caused when the manufacturer of the cards notices an error in a particular card, corrects the error and then resumes the print run.
VERT - Vertical pose on a card
XRC - Extended Rookie Card. A player's first appearance on a card but issued in a set that was not distributed nationally nor in packs.
YB - Yearbook
20A - Twenty assist club
SOP - Fifty point club
6M - Sixth Man
! - Condition sensitive card or set

BECKETT

AUTHENTICATION SERVICES

Turning Your Basketball Signatures into Assets.

Scan the QR code to Submit Now

BECKETT®

The Gold Standard in Collecting

1996 A Question of Sport Who Am I
COMPLETE SET (100) 30.00 75.00
48 Magic Johnson 3.20 8.00

1970-71 ABA All-Star 5x7 Picture Pack
COMPLETE SET (12) 75.00 150.00
1 Rick Barry 20.00 40.00
2 John Brisker 5.00 10.00
3 George Carter 5.00 10.00
4 Mack Calvin 6.00 12.00
5 Joe Caldwell 6.00 12.00
6 Warren Jabali 7.50 15.00
7 Larry Jones 5.00 10.00
8 George Lehmann 5.00 10.00
9 Jim McDaniel 5.00 10.00
10 Bill Melchionni 7.50 15.00
11 John Roche 5.00 10.00
12 George Thompson 5.00 10.00

2012-13 Absolute
COMP.SET w/o SPs (100) 20.00 50.00
RETIRED PRINT RUN 499 SER.#'d SETS
AU RC PRINT RUN 199 TO 399 SER.#'d SETS
1 Kevin Love .75 2.00
2 Derrick Rose 1.25 3.00
3 LeBron James 6.00 15.00
4 Carmelo Anthony 1.25 3.00
5 Kevin Durant 3.00 8.00
6 Devin Harris .50 1.25
7 Blake Griffin .75 2.00
8 Andre Iguodala .75 2.00
9 Elton Brand .60 1.50
10 Rodney Stuckey .50 1.25
11 Brendan Haywood .50 1.25
12 Stephen Jackson .60 1.50
13 Paul Pierce 1.25 3.00
14 Ty Lawson .50 1.25
15 Dwight Howard 1.00 2.50
16 Jeremy Lin 1.25 3.00
17 Anderson Varejao .50 1.25
18 Derrick Favors .60 1.50
19 Jose Calderon .50 1.25
20 LaMarcus Aldridge .75 2.00
21 Tony Parker 1.25 3.00
22 Ersan Ilyasova .50 1.25
23 Zach Randolph .75 2.00
24 Kobe Bryant 6.00 15.00
25 Andrew Bogut .60 1.50
26 Andrei Kirilenko .60 1.50
27 Dirk Nowitzki 2.00 5.00
28 Deron Williams .60 1.50
29 Hakim Warrick .50 1.25
30 James Harden 1.50 4.00
31 Hedo Turkoglu .60 1.50
32 Channing Frye .50 1.25
33 Andre Miller .60 1.50
34 Joakim Noah .60 1.50
35 Rashard Lewis .75 2.00
36 Stephen Curry 6.00 15.00
37 Chris Paul 1.50 4.00
38 Wesley Matthews .50 1.25
39 Steve Nash 1.50 4.00
40 Josh Smith .50 1.25
41 Kevin Martin .60 1.50
42 Emeka Okafor .60 1.50
43 Gordon Hayward .75 2.00
44 Tyson Chandler .60 1.50
45 Russell Westbrook 1.25 3.00
46 Brandon Jennings .50 1.25
47 Marcin Gortat .50 1.25
48 Andrew Bynum .50 1.25
49 Brook Lopez .60 1.50
50 Manu Ginobili 1.50 4.00
51 Tyrus Thomas .50 1.25
52 Greg Monroe .50 1.25
53 Eric Gordon .60 1.50
54 DeMar DeRozan 1.00 2.50
55 Dwyane Wade 1.50 4.00
56 David West .60 1.50
57 Rudy Gay .75 2.00
58 Evan Turner .50 1.25
59 Shane Battier .60 1.50
60 Nick Collison .50 1.25
61 Daniel Gibson .50 1.25
62 DeMarcus Cousins .75 2.00
63 Kevin Garnett 2.00 5.00
64 Ricky Rubio .60 1.50
65 Roy Hibbert .60 1.50
66 DeAndre Jordan .60 1.50
67 Nicolas Batum .60 1.50
68 Al Horford .75 2.00
69 Al Jefferson .60 1.50
70 Carlos Boozer .60 1.50
71 Serge Ibaka .60 1.50
72 David Lee .50 1.25
73 Samuel Dalembert .50 1.25
74 Tyreke Evans .60 1.50
75 Jason Richardson .75 2.00
76 Goran Dragic .75 2.00
77 Danny Granger .50 1.25
78 Pau Gasol 1.25 3.00
79 Chris Bosh 1.00 2.50
80 Tim Duncan 2.00 5.00
81 Grant Hill 1.25 3.00
82 Jason Kidd 1.25 3.00
83 Danilo Gallinari .50 1.25
84 O.J. Mayo .50 1.25
85 Ryan Anderson .50 1.25
86 Joe Johnson .60 1.50
87 Marc Gasol .75 2.00
88 Darren Collison .50 1.25
89 Omer Asik .50 1.25
90 John Wall 1.00 2.50
91 Luol Deng .60 1.50
92 Monta Ellis .60 1.50
93 Ben Gordon .60 1.50
94 Thaddeus Young .50 1.25
95 DeShawn Stevenson .50 1.25
96 Ray Allen 1.25 3.00
97 Andrea Bargnani .50 1.25
98 Tayshaun Prince .75 2.00
99 Rajon Rondo 1.00 2.50
100 Amare Stoudemire .75 2.00
101 Kareem Abdul-Jabbar 4.00 10.00
102 Larry Bird 4.00 10.00
103 Rick Barry 1.00 2.50
104 David Robinson 2.00 5.00
105 Bob Cousy 2.00 5.00
106 Elgin Baylor 3.00 8.00
107 Scottie Pippen 3.00 8.00
108 Wes Unseld 1.50 4.00
109 Nate Thurmond 1.25 3.00
110 Dominique Wilkins 1.50 4.00
111 George Gervin 2.00 5.00
112 Bill Russell 4.00 10.00
113 James Worthy 2.00 5.00
114 Steve Kerr 1.25 3.00
115 Clyde Drexler 2.00 5.00
116 Sean Elliott 1.00 2.50
118 Kenny Smith 1.00 2.50
119 Shaquille O'Neal 4.00 10.00
120 Allan Houston 1.00 2.50
121 Dave Cowens 2.00 5.00
122 Karl Malone 2.00 5.00
123 Connie Hawkins 1.25 3.00
125 Yao Ming 2.50 6.00
126 Robert Horry 1.25 3.00
127 Jerry West 2.50 6.00
128 Muggsy Bogues 1.00 2.50
129 Darryl Dawkins .75 2.00
130 Kevin McHale 1.50 4.00
131 Chuck Person 1.00 2.50
132 Patrick Ewing 2.00 5.00
133 Dennis Rodman 3.00 8.00
134 Christian Laettner 1.25 3.00
135 Hakeem Olajuwon 2.50 6.00
136 George Mikan 4.00 10.00
137 John Starks 1.00 2.50
138 Nate Archibald 1.50 4.00
140 Bill Walton 2.00 5.00
141 Earl Monroe 1.50 4.00
142 Alonzo Mourning 2.00 5.00
143 Wilt Chamberlain 4.00 10.00
144 Gary Payton 1.50 4.00
145 Walt Frazier 2.00 5.00
146 Willis Reed 2.00 5.00
147 John Stockton 2.50 6.00
148 Julius Erving 3.00 8.00
149 Oscar Robertson 2.50 6.00
150 Moses Malone 2.00 5.00
151 Kyrie Irving AU/199 RC 75.00 200.00
152 Derrick Williams AU/199 RC 3.00 8.00
153 Quincy Acy AU/399 RC 3.00 8.00
154 Lavoy Allen AU/399 RC 3.00 8.00
155 Harrison Barnes AU/199 RC 6.00 15.00
156 Will Barton AU/399 RC 6.00 15.00
157 Bradley Beal AU/199 RC 25.00 60.00
158 J.Valanciunas AU/199 RC 6.00 15.00
159 B.Biyombo AU/249 RC 4.00 10.00
160 MarShon Brooks AU/299 RC 3.00 8.00
161 Alec Burks AU/249 RC 5.00 12.00
162 Jimmy Butler AU/299 RC 30.00 80.00
163 Norris Cole AU/249 RC 3.00 8.00
164 Jae Crowder AU/399 RC 6.00 15.00
165 Anthony Davis AU/199 RC 100.00 250.00
166 J.Cunningham AU/299 RC 3.00 8.00
167 A.Drummond AU/199 RC 8.00 20.00
168 Festus Ezeli AU/299 RC 3.00 8.00
169 Kim English AU/399 RC 3.00 8.00
170 Kenneth Faried AU/299 RC 4.00 10.00
171 A.Goudelock AU/399 RC EXCH 3.00 8.00
172 D.Green AU/399 RC 20.00 50.00
173 Evan Fournier AU/249 RC 5.00 12.00
174 Jordan Hamilton AU/399 RC 3.00 8.00
175 Jimmer Fredette AU/199 RC 5.00 12.00
176 Tobias Harris AU/249 RC 10.00 25.00
177 J.Harrellson AU/299 RC 3.00 8.00
178 John Henson AU/199 RC 4.00 10.00
179 Tyler Honeycutt AU/399 RC 3.00 8.00
180 Robert Sacre AU/399 RC 3.00 8.00
181 Justin Harper AU/399 RC 3.00 8.00
182 Johnson-Odom AU/399 RC 3.00 8.00
183 Reggie Jackson AU/399 RC 5.00 12.00
184 Bernard James AU/349 RC 3.00 8.00
185 Charles Jenkins AU/399 RC 3.00 8.00
186 John Jenkins AU/299 RC EXCH 3.00 8.00
187 JaJuan Johnson AU/299 RC 3.00 8.00
188 Ivan Johnson AU/399 RC 3.00 8.00
189 O.Johnson AU/399 RC 3.00 8.00
190 Terrence Jones AU/249 RC 3.00 8.00
191 Perry Jones AU/399 RC 3.00 8.00
192 Cory Joseph AU/349 RC 4.00 10.00
193 Kris Joseph AU/399 RC 3.00 8.00
194 Enes Kanter AU/249 RC 5.00 12.00
195 Kidd-Gilchrist AU/199 RC 4.00 10.00
196 Brandon Knight AU/199 RC 4.00 10.00
197 Jeremy Lamb AU/199 RC 5.00 12.00
198 Doron Lamb AU/399 RC 3.00 8.00
199 Malcolm Lee AU/399 RC 3.00 8.00
200 Kawhi Leonard AU/399 RC 100.00 250.00
201 Meyers Leonard AU/199 RC 4.00 10.00
202 Travis Leslie AU/399 RC 3.00 8.00
203 Jon Leuer AU/399 RC 3.00 8.00
204 DeAndre Liggins AU/399 RC 3.00 8.00
205 Shelvin Mack AU/299 RC 4.00 10.00
206 C.Fortson AU/399 RC 3.00 8.00
207 Kendall Marshall AU/249 RC 3.00 8.00
208 Fab Melo AU/249 RC 3.00 8.00
209 Khris Middleton AU/349 RC 15.00 40.00
210 Quincy Miller AU/399 RC 3.00 8.00
211 D.Miller AU/399 RC 4.00 10.00
212 E'Twaun Moore AU/299 RC 4.00 10.00
213 Mark.Morris AU/249 RC EXCH 5.00 12.00
214 Marc.Morris AU/249 RC EXCH 5.00 12.00
215 Darius Morris AU/399 RC 4.00 10.00
216 Arnett Moultrie AU/299 RC 3.00 8.00
217 Kevin Murphy AU/399 RC 3.00 8.00
218 A.Nicholson AU/249 RC 3.00 8.00
219 Kyle O'Quinn AU/399 RC 4.00 10.00
220 C.Parsons AU/249 RC 4.00 10.00
221 Miles Plumlee AU/349 RC 5.00 12.00
222 Austin Rivers AU/199 RC 5.00 12.00
223 T.Robinson AU/199 RC 3.00 8.00
224 Terrence Ross AU/199 RC 8.00 20.00
225 Jeremy Pargo AU/399 RC 3.00 8.00
226 Mike Scott AU/399 RC 4.00 10.00
227 Josh Selby AU/299 RC 3.00 8.00
228 T.Shengelia AU/299 RC 3.00 8.00
229 Iman Shumpert AU/299 RC 4.00 10.00
230 Chris Singleton AU/299 RC 4.00 10.00
231 Nolan Smith AU/249 RC 3.00 8.00
232 Greg Stiemsma AU/299 RC 3.00 8.00
233 Jared Sullinger AU/199 RC 3.00 8.00
234 Jeff Taylor AU/299 RC 3.00 8.00
235 Tyshawn Taylor AU/299 RC 3.00 8.00
236 Marquis Teague AU/299 RC 3.00 8.00
237 Isaiah Thomas AU/399 RC 6.00 15.00
238 Lance Thomas AU/399 RC 3.00 8.00
239 Trey Thompkins AU/399 RC 3.00 8.00
240 T.Thompson AU/199 RC EXCH 5.00 12.00
241 Klay Thompson AU/199 RC 100.00 250.00
242 Jeremy Tyler AU/349 RC 3.00 8.00
243 Jan Vesely AU/249 RC 3.00 8.00
244 Nikola Vucevic AU/299 RC 12.00 30.00
245 D.Waiters AU/199 RC 4.00 10.00
246 Kemba Walker AU/199 RC 12.00 30.00
247 Royce White AU/349 RC 3.00 8.00
248 Gustavo Ayon AU/299 RC 3.00 8.00
249 Tony Wroten AU/249 RC 3.00 8.00
250 Tyler Zeller AU/249 RC 3.00 8.00

2012-13 Absolute Spectrum Gold
*STARS: 2.5X TO 6X BASE HI
*RETIRED: 1.5X TO 4X BASE HI
STATED PRINT RUN 25 SER.#'d SETS
39 Steve Nash 6.00 15.00
81 Grant Hill 8.00 20.00
132 Patrick Ewing 10.00 25.00

2012-13 Absolute Frequent Flyer Autographs
STATED PRINT RUN 25 TO 149 SER.#'d SETS
1 Kobe Bryant/99 800.00 1,500.00
2 Blake Griffin/25 10.00 25.00
3 Kevin Durant/25 100.00 250.00
4 Vince Carter/25 60.00 150.00
5 Andre Iguodala/99 8.00 20.00
6 Josh Smith/99 4.00 10.00
7 Roy Hibbert/99 4.00 10.00
8 Russell Westbrook/49 60.00 150.00
9 LaMarcus Aldridge/99 10.00 25.00
10 Brandon Bass/149 4.00 10.00
11 Marcin Gortat/149 4.00 10.00
12 Chase Budinger/149 4.00 10.00
13 DeAndre Jordan/149 4.00 10.00
14 Brook Lopez/149 8.00 20.00
15 Hakim Warrick/149 4.00 10.00
16 Paul George/149 60.00 150.00
17 Carlos Boozer/99 6.00 15.00
18 Stephen Curry/99 600.00 1,200.00
19 Al Horford/99 8.00 20.00
20 Stephen Jackson/99 EXCH 4.00 10.00
21 Tyson Chandler/49 5.00 12.00
22 Andrew Bynum/49 4.00 10.00
23 Kendrick Perkins/149 EXCH 4.00 10.00
24 DeJuan Blair/149 EXCH 4.00 10.00
25 Anderson Varejao/142 4.00 10.00

2012-13 Absolute Frequent Flyer Materials
STATED PRINT RUN 10 TO 99 SER.#'d SETS
*PRIME: 1.25X TO 3X BASE HI
PRIME PRINT RUN ONE TO 25 SETS
1 Al Jefferson/74 3.00 8.00
2 Marc Gasol/74 5.00 12.00
3 John Wall/74 6.00 15.00
4 Derrick Rose/74 8.00 20.00
5 Rudy Gay/99 5.00 12.00
6 Tim Duncan/99 12.00 30.00
7 Wesley Johnson/99 3.00 8.00
8 Joel Anthony/99 3.00 8.00
9 Stephen Curry/99 40.00 100.00
10 Josh Smith/99 3.00 8.00
11 LeBron James/74 40.00 100.00
12 James Harden/74 12.00 30.00
13 Raymond Felton/74 3.00 8.00
14 Blake Griffin/74 5.00 12.00
15 Wesley Matthews/99 3.00 8.00
16 Nick Collison/99 3.00 8.00
17 Tyreke Evans/74 4.00 10.00
18 DeMar DeRozan/99 6.00 15.00
19 Kevin Martin/99 4.00 10.00
20 Danny Granger/99 3.00 8.00
21 Yao Ming/74 10.00 25.00
23 Anthony Mason/74 4.00 10.00
24 Shawn Kemp/49 8.00 20.00
25 Larry Johnson/49 6.00 15.00

2012-13 Absolute Frequent Flyer Materials Autographs
STATED PRINT RUN 49 TO 149 SER.#'d SETS
1 Al Jefferson/49 EXCH 5.00 12.00
2 Udonis Haslem/149 6.00 15.00
3 Tayshaun Prince/49 8.00 20.00
4 Kevin Love/49 8.00 20.00
5 Richard Hamilton/49 8.00 20.00
6 Channing Frye/99 5.00 12.00
7 LaMarcus Aldridge/74 8.00 20.00
8 Chris Bosh/49 10.00 25.00
9 Stephen Curry/74 600.00 1,200.00
10 Josh Smith/49 5.00 12.00
11 Brook Lopez/49 6.00 15.00
12 James Harden/49 EXCH 40.00 100.00
13 Chase Budinger/149 5.00 12.00
14 Blake Griffin/49 8.00 20.00
15 Wesley Matthews/74 5.00 12.00
16 DeJuan Blair/149 EXCH 5.00 12.00
17 Tyreke Evans/49 6.00 15.00
18 Zach Randolph/49 8.00 20.00
19 Kevin Martin/99 6.00 15.00
20 Danny Granger/49 5.00 12.00
21 Yao Ming/25 75.00 200.00
22 Xavier McDaniel/99 5.00 12.00
23 Jalen Rose/99 6.00 15.00
24 Dominique Wilkins/49 15.00 40.00
25 Larry Johnson/99 12.00 30.00

2012-13 Absolute Frequent Flyer Materials Autographs Prime
STATED PRINT RUN ONE TO 25 SER.#'d SETS
3 Tayshaun Prince/25 15.00 40.00
6 Channing Frye/25 10.00 25.00
16 DeJuan Blair/25 EXCH 10.00 25.00
18 Zach Randolph/25 15.00 40.00
19 Kevin Martin/25 12.00 30.00

2012-13 Absolute Heroes Autographs
STATED PRINT RUN 24 TO 99 SER.#'d SETS
1 Kobe Bryant/99 1,000.00 2,000.00
2 Calvin Murphy/49 12.00 30.00
3 Bill Russell/25 1,000.00 2,000.00
4 Rolando Blackman/99 8.00 20.00
5 Steve Nash/25 100.00 250.00
6 Steve Kerr/49 25.00 60.00
7 Michael Finley/49 10.00 25.00
8 Hakeem Olajuwon/25 75.00 200.00
9 Alonzo Mourning/25 60.00 150.00
10 Kevin Durant/49 100.00 250.00
11 Dave Cowens/49 15.00 40.00
12 Kareem Abdul-Jabbar/25 100.00 250.00
13 Robert Horry/49 15.00 40.00
14 James Worthy/25 30.00 80.00
15 David Robinson/25 75.00 200.00
16 John Stockton/25 75.00 200.00
17 Sam Jones/49 25.00 60.00
18 Derek Fisher/99 EXCH 12.00 30.00
19 Artis Gilmore/49 12.00 30.00
20 Isiah Thomas/49 20.00 50.00
21 Chris Mullin/99 12.00 30.00
22 Stephen Jackson/99 8.00 20.00
23 Gary Payton/25 40.00 100.00
24 Dominique Wilkins/25 25.00 60.00
25 Tyson Chandler/25 12.00 30.00
26 Nick Van Exel/49 15.00 40.00
27 Avery Johnson/99 12.00 30.00
28 Larry Johnson/99 15.00 40.00
29 Anfernee Hardaway/49 125.00 300.00
30 Tony Parker/25 30.00 80.00
31 Oscar Robertson/25 75.00 200.00
32 Magic Johnson/25 100.00 250.00
33 Larry Bird/25 100.00 250.00
34 Bill Laimbeer/99 10.00 25.00
35 Scottie Pippen/25 200.00 500.00
36 Muggsy Bogues/99 25.00 60.00
37 Willis Reed/49 40.00 100.00
38 Tim Hardaway/99 15.00 40.00
39 Dennis Rodman/25 125.00 300.00
40 John Starks/99 12.00 30.00
41 Vlade Divac/99 EXCH 10.00 25.00
42 Julius Erving/25 75.00 200.00
43 Grant Hill/25 50.00 120.00
44 Dikembe Mutombo/49 20.00 50.00
45 Andre Miller/49 8.00 20.00
46 Sean Elliott/99 10.00 25.00
47 Bruce Bowen/99 12.00 30.00
48 Jalen Rose/99 10.00 25.00
49 Bill Walton/49 25.00 60.00
50 Yao Ming/25 EXCH 200.00 500.00

2012-13 Absolute Hoopla Autographs
STATED PRINT RUN 25 TO 99 SER.#'d SETS
1 Blake Griffin/49 15.00 40.00
2 Aaron Brooks/99 4.00 10.00
3 Brook Lopez/49 6.00 15.00
4 Luol Deng/99 EXCH 4.00 10.00
5 Chase Budinger/99 4.00 10.00
6 Kyle Lowry/99 10.00 25.00
7 Ty Lawson/99 4.00 10.00
8 Greg Monroe/99 4.00 10.00
9 Antawn Jamison/99 4.00 10.00
10 Danny Granger/49 EXCH 4.00 10.00
11 Tyson Chandler/49 8.00 20.00
12 James Harden/99 EXCH 25.00 60.00
13 Rudy Gay/99 EXCH 4.00 10.00
14 Al Horford/49 5.00 12.00
15 Andre Miller/99 4.00 10.00
16 Monta Ellis/49 8.00 20.00
17 Tony Parker/25 25.00 60.00
18 DeMarcus Cousins/49 6.00 15.00
19 Josh Smith/49 5.00 12.00
20 DeAndre Jordan/99 5.00 12.00
21 Pau Gasol/25 25.00 60.00
22 Eric Gordon/49 5.00 12.00
23 Darren Collison/99 EXCH 4.00 10.00
24 Kobe Bryant/49 600.00 1,200.00
25 Ryan Anderson/99 4.00 10.00
26 Deron Williams/25 8.00 20.00
27 Marcin Gortat/99 4.00 10.00
28 Russell Westbrook/25 75.00 200.00
29 DeJuan Blair/99 EXCH 4.00 10.00
30 Avery Bradley/99 EXCH 4.00 10.00
31 Al Jefferson/49 4.00 10.00
32 Chris Paul/25 EXCH 40.00 100.00
33 Roy Hibbert/99 4.00 10.00
34 Joakim Noah/49 4.00 10.00
35 Kevin Love/25 10.00 25.00
36 Serge Ibaka/99 6.00 15.00
37 Derrick Favors/49 4.00 10.00
38 Andrew Bynum/25 6.00 15.00
39 Evan Turner/25 6.00 15.00
40 LaMarcus Aldridge/49 6.00 15.00
41 O.J. Mayo/99 4.00 10.00
42 Jrue Holiday/99 12.00 30.00
43 Steve Nash/25 60.00 150.00
44 Shane Battier/49 12.00 30.00
45 Kevin Martin/99 4.00 10.00
46 Goran Dragic/99 12.00 30.00
47 Chris Kaman/49 4.00 10.00
48 Arron Afflalo/99 4.00 10.00
49 Grant Hill/49 30.00 80.00
50 Ray Allen/25 60.00 150.00

2012-13 Absolute Iconic Autographs
STATED PRINT RUN 25 TO 99 SER.#'d SETS
1 Blake Griffin/25 EXCH 15.00 40.00
2 Steve Nash/25 50.00 120.00
3 Gerald Wallace/49 4.00 10.00
4 Chase Budinger/99 4.00 10.00
5 James Harden/49 50.00 120.00
6 Kevin Martin/99 4.00 10.00
7 Aaron Brooks/99 4.00 10.00
8 Luol Deng/99 EXCH 4.00 10.00
9 David Lee/99 4.00 10.00
10 Mario Chalmers/99 4.00 10.00
11 Boris Diaw/99 4.00 10.00
12 Paul George/99 60.00 150.00
13 Kendrick Perkins/99 4.00 10.00
14 Chris Paul/25 EXCH 60.00 150.00
15 Grant Hill/49 25.00 60.00
16 Ray Allen/25 60.00 150.00
17 Ty Lawson/49 4.00 10.00
18 Landry Fields/99 4.00 10.00
19 Carlos Boozer/99 4.00 10.00
20 Jason Kidd/25 25.00 60.00
21 DeAndre Jordan/99 4.00 10.00
22 Rodrigue Beaubois/99 4.00 10.00
23 Arron Afflalo/99 4.00 10.00
24 Kobe Bryant/99 1,000.00 2,000.00
25 Roy Hibbert/99 4.00 10.00
26 Deron Williams/25 4.00 10.00
27 O.J. Mayo/99 4.00 10.00
28 Jeff Teague/99 4.00 10.00
29 Andrew Bogut/99 4.00 10.00
30 Jose Calderon/99 4.00 10.00
31 Marcin Gortat/99 4.00 10.00
32 Carl Landry/99 4.00 10.00
33 LaMarcus Aldridge/49 10.00 25.00
34 Goran Dragic/99 12.00 30.00
35 Kevin Durant/25 150.00 400.00
36 Kris Humphries/99 4.00 10.00
37 Andrew Bynum/25 4.00 10.00
38 George Hill/99 4.00 10.00
39 Jrue Holiday/99 4.00 10.00
40 Brandon Bass/99 4.00 10.00
41 Hakim Warrick/99 4.00 10.00
42 Vince Carter/25 75.00 200.00
43 Anderson Varejao/99 4.00 10.00
44 Gordon Hayward/99 6.00 15.00
45 DeMarcus Cousins/48 8.00 20.00
46 Eric Bledsoe/99 6.00 15.00
47 Stephen Curry/99 800.00 1,500.00
48 Chris Bosh/25 12.00 30.00
49 Kevin Love/25 12.00 30.00
50 Andre Iguodala/49 6.00 15.00

2012-13 Absolute Iconic Materials
STATED PRINT RUN 10 TO 49 SER.#'d SETS
*PRIME: .75X TO 2X BASE HI
PRIME PRINT RUN 5 TO 25 SETS
1 Kevin Garnett/25 10.00 25.00
2 Dirk Nowitzki/25 10.00 25.00
3 David Lee/49 2.50 6.00
4 Derrick Rose/25 6.00 15.00
5 Tayshaun Prince/49 4.00 10.00
6 Serge Ibaka/49 3.00 8.00
7 John Wall/25 5.00 12.00
8 Al Horford/25 4.00 10.00
9 Raymond Felton/25 2.50 6.00
11 Russell Westbrook/25 6.00 15.00
12 Tony Parker/25 6.00 15.00
14 Marc Gasol/49 4.00 10.00
15 Kevin Durant/25 15.00 40.00
16 Tim Duncan/25 10.00 25.00
17 Paul Pierce/25 6.00 15.00
18 Dwyane Wade/25 8.00 20.00
19 Carmelo Anthony/25 6.00 15.00
20 LeBron James/25 30.00 80.00
21 David West/25 3.00 8.00
22 Kirk Hinrich/49 3.00 8.00
23 Amare Stoudemire/25 4.00 10.00
24 Al Jefferson/49 2.50 6.00
25 Linas Kleiza/49 2.50 6.00

2012-13 Absolute Iconic Materials Autographs
STATED PRINT RUN 25 TO 74 SER.#'d SETS
1 Raymond Felton/74 5.00 12.00
2 Kevin Durant/25 150.00 400.00
3 Kevin Love/25 10.00 25.00
4 Blake Griffin/25 20.00 50.00
5 Brandon Jennings/49 5.00 12.00
6 Chris Paul/25 EXCH 60.00 150.00
7 Tyson Chandler/49 10.00 25.00
8 LaMarcus Aldridge/49 10.00 25.00
9 Chris Bosh/25 15.00 40.00
10 James Harden/74 EXCH 75.00 200.00
11 Tony Parker/74 20.00 50.00
12 Al Jefferson/49 EXCH 5.00 12.00
13 Al Horford/74 12.00 30.00
14 Brook Lopez/49 8.00 20.00
15 Josh Smith/49 5.00 12.00
16 Deron Williams/25 12.00 30.00
17 Pau Gasol/25 40.00 100.00
18 Ty Lawson/74 5.00 12.00
19 Luol Deng/74 8.00 20.00
20 Carlos Boozer/74 8.00 20.00
21 Zach Randolph/74 10.00 25.00
22 Kyrie Irving/25 75.00 200.00
23 Danny Granger/74 5.00 12.00
24 Tristan Thompson/74 10.00 25.00
25 Tyreke Evans/74 EXCH 5.00 12.00

2012-13 Absolute Iconic Materials Autographs Prime
STATED PRINT RUN 5 TO 25 SER.#'d SETS
8 LaMarcus Aldridge/25 25.00 60.00
15 Josh Smith/25 12.00 30.00
18 Ty Lawson/25 6.00 15.00
19 Luol Deng/25 EXCH 15.00 40.00
20 Carlos Boozer/25 15.00 40.00

2012-13 Absolute Marks of Fame Autographs
STATED PRINT RUN 25 TO 149 SER.#'d SETS
1 Spud Webb/100 6.00 15.00
2 Dan Majerle/100 4.00 10.00
3 Paul Westphal/100 6.00 15.00
4 Glen Rice/100 4.00 10.00
5 World B. Free/100 4.00 10.00
6 Adrian Dantley/100 6.00 15.00
7 Wes Unseld/49 8.00 20.00
8 Mark Price/105 6.00 15.00
9 Larry Bird/49 60.00 150.00
10 Kenny Smith/49 6.00 15.00
11 Magic Johnson/49 60.00 150.00
12 Jeff Hornacek/100 4.00 10.00
13 Dan Issel/106 4.00 10.00
14 Charles Oakley/96 8.00 20.00
15 Michael Cooper/149 4.00 10.00
16 Fat Lever/108 4.00 10.00
17 Michael Finley/49 6.00 15.00
18 Dikembe Mutombo/128 12.00 30.00
19 Vin Baker/100 4.00 10.00
20 A.C. Green/105 8.00 20.00
21 Zydrunas Ilgauskas/100 4.00 10.00
22 Julius Erving/25 40.00 100.00
23 Jamal Mashburn/100 8.00 20.00
24 Hakeem Olajuwon/25 40.00 100.00
25 Darryl Dawkins/96 10.00 25.00
26 Dominique Wilkins/25 15.00 40.00
27 Detlef Schrempf/100 10.00 25.00
28 Gary Payton/99 25.00 60.00
29 Allan Houston/149 6.00 15.00
30 Mark Aguirre/100 4.00 10.00
31 Mark Jackson/99 4.00 10.00
32 Joe Dumars/100 8.00 20.00
33 Vernon Maxwell/149 4.00 10.00
34 Christian Laettner/25 10.00 25.00
35 Otis Birdsong/96 4.00 10.00
36 Sidney Moncrief/100 4.00 10.00
37 Kurt Rambis/100 5.00 12.00
38 Terry Porter/100 5.00 12.00
39 Lenny Wilkens/100 8.00 20.00
40 Bill Walton/100 20.00 50.00
41 John Paxson/100 4.00 10.00
42 Isiah Thomas/49 12.00 30.00
43 Kiki Vandeweghe/100 4.00 10.00
44 Vinny Del Negro/149 EXCH 5.00 12.00
45 Connie Hawkins/99 12.00 30.00
46 Rex Chapman/149 6.00 15.00
47 Kelly Tripucka/100 4.00 10.00
48 Shawn Bradley/149 EXCH 4.00 10.00
49 Bill Cartwright/100 4.00 10.00
50 Brent Barry/149 4.00 10.00

2012-13 Absolute Panini All-Stars
COMPLETE SET (18) 15.00 40.00
1 Carmelo Anthony 1.50 4.00
2 LeBron James 8.00 20.00
3 Blake Griffin 1.00 2.50
4 Dwyane Wade 2.00 5.00
5 Dwight Howard 1.25 3.00
6 Dirk Nowitzki 2.50 6.00
7 Kevin Durant 4.00 10.00
8 Kobe Bryant 8.00 20.00
9 Kevin Love 1.00 2.50
10 Karl Malone 1.50 4.00
11 Larry Bird 3.00 8.00
12 Magic Johnson 3.00 8.00
13 Julius Erving 2.50 6.00
14 Shaquille O'Neal 3.00 8.00
15 Yao Ming 2.00 5.00
16 John Stockton 2.00 5.00
17 Scottie Pippen 2.50 6.00
18 David Robinson 1.50 4.00

2012-13 Absolute Patches
STATED PRINT RUN 4 TO 25 SER.#'d SETS
1 Tony Parker/25 30.00 80.00
3 Amare Stoudemire/25 20.00 50.00
6 Tyrus Thomas/25 12.00 30.00
8 Brook Lopez/25 15.00 40.00
9 Derrick Rose/25 30.00 80.00
12 Manu Ginobili/25 40.00 100.00
13 LaMarcus Aldridge/25 20.00 50.00
16 Metta World Peace/25 15.00 40.00
17 Ty Lawson/25 12.00 30.00
20 George Hill/25 15.00 40.00
21 John Wall/25 25.00 60.00
22 David Lee/25 12.00 30.00
23 Kemba Walker/25 40.00 100.00
24 Tim Duncan/25 50.00 125.00
29 Deron Williams/25 15.00 40.00
30 Tristan Thompson/25 15.00 40.00
31 Raymond Felton/25 12.00 30.00
32 Danny Granger/25 12.00 30.00

2012-13 Absolute Private Signings
PSAM Alonzo Mourning 40.00 100.00
PSBC Billy Cunningham 20.00 50.00
PSBG Blake Griffin 15.00 40.00
PSBL Bob Lanier 15.00 40.00
PSDD Darryl Dawkins 15.00 40.00
PSGP Gary Payton 40.00 100.00
PSKJ Kevin Johnson 25.00 60.00
PSMP Mark Price 25.00 60.00
PSPG Pau Gasol 50.00 120.00
PSRR Rajon Rondo 40.00 100.00

2012-13 Absolute Star Gazing Jersey Number Materials
STATED PRINT RUN 10 TO 99 SER.#'d SETS
*PRIME: .75X TO 2X BASE HI
PRIME PRINT RUN ONE TO 25 SETS
1 Tim Duncan/99 15.00 40.00
2 Vince Carter/74 12.00 30.00
3 Dwyane Wade/99 12.00 30.00
4 Amare Stoudemire/74 6.00 15.00
5 Dirk Nowitzki/74 15.00 40.00
6 Paul Pierce/49 10.00 25.00
7 Derrick Rose/49 10.00 25.00
8 Kevin Garnett/74 15.00 40.00
9 Chris Paul/49 12.00 30.00
10 Kevin Durant/25 25.00 60.00
11 John Wall/99 8.00 20.00
12 Pau Gasol/49 10.00 25.00
14 Ricky Rubio/25 5.00 12.00
15 Marc Gasol/74 6.00 15.00
16 Carmelo Anthony/49 10.00 25.00
17 Joakim Noah/49 5.00 12.00
18 Al Jefferson/49 4.00 10.00
19 David West/49 5.00 12.00
20 Kevin Martin/74 5.00 12.00
21 Linas Kleiza/49 4.00 10.00
22 Manu Ginobili/25 12.00 30.00
23 Raymond Felton/49 4.00 10.00
24 Zach Randolph/49 6.00 15.00
25 LeBron James/49 50.00 125.00

2012-13 Absolute Team Tandem Materials
STATED PRINT RUN 25 TO 49 SER.#'d SETS
1 T.Duncan/T.Parker/49 15.00 40.00
2 D.Wade/L.James/25 50.00 125.00
3 Durant/Westbrook/25 25.00 60.00
4 D.Rose/L.Deng/25 10.00 25.00
5 J.Smith/A.Horford/49 6.00 15.00
6 T.Evans/J.Fredette/25 6.00 15.00
7 B.Griffin/C.Paul/25 12.00 30.00
8 P.Pierce/R.Rondo/25 10.00 25.00
9 Anthony/Stoudemire/25 10.00 25.00
10 D.Williams/B.Lopez/25 5.00 12.00
11 D.Granger/G.Hill/49 5.00 12.00
12 K.Thompson/D.Lee/49 40.00 100.00
13 Z.Randolph/M.Gasol/49 6.00 15.00
14 S.Hawes/J.Holiday/25 8.00 20.00
15 K.Bryant/M.Peace/49 50.00 125.00
16 Cartwright/E.Monroe/25 8.00 20.00
17 A.English/D.Issel/25 8.00 20.00
18 J.Stockton/K.Malone/25 12.00 30.00
19 T.Thompson/K.Irving/25 40.00 100.00
20 D.West/Hansbrough/25 5.00 12.00
21 E.Turner/T.Young/49 4.00 10.00
22 C.Boozer/D.Rose/25 10.00 25.00
23 Mourning/L.Johnson/25 10.00 25.00
24 A.Jefferson/Favors/25 5.00 12.00
25 T.Prince/B.Knight/49 6.00 15.00

2012-13 Absolute Team Tandem Materials Prime
*PRIME: 1X TO 2.5X BASE HI
STATED PRINT RUN 5 TO 25 SER.#'d SETS

2012-13 Absolute Team Trios Materials
STATED PRINT RUN 5 TO 25 SER.#'d SETS
7 Hywrd/Al/Favors/25 8.00 20.00
8 Manu/Dncn/Prkr/25 20.00 50.00
10 Morris/Frye/Dudley/25 8.00 20.00
12 Davis/DeMar/Klza/25 10.00 25.00
15 Tyler/Grngr/Hill/25 6.00 15.00
23 Harris/Jennings/Udrih/25 15.00 40.00
24 Miller/Ty/Faried/25 6.00 15.00
25 Nelson/Hedo/Davis/25 6.00 15.00

SUPERIOR SPORTS INVESTMENTS

Always Buying Unopened Boxes and Singles

Call us at: 682-706-8990

Text us pictures of your cards

Check Out Our Website for Our Huge Inventory of Graded Cards, Singles, Boxes and Supplies!

We have purchased thousands of collections

THIS YEAR!

WE BUY WHAT OTHERS DON'T!

Come visit our Super Store in Arlington Texas
2201 Brookhollow Plaza /Suite 145
Arlington, Tx 76006

www.superiorsportsinvestments.com

2009-10 Absolute Memorabilia
101-141 PRINT RUN 499 SER.#'d SETS
JSY AU RC PRINT RUNS LISTED IN CHECKLIST
1 Kobe Bryant 10.00 25.00
2 Dwight Howard 1.50 4.00
3 Rajon Rondo 1.50 4.00
4 Samuel Dalembert .75 2.00
5 LeBron James 10.00 25.00
6 Chris Andersen 1.25 3.00
7 Dwyane Wade 2.50 6.00
8 Chris Bosh 1.50 4.00
9 Steve Nash 2.50 6.00
10 LaMarcus Aldridge 1.25 3.00
11 Danilo Gallinari 1.00 2.50
12 Joakim Noah .75 2.00
13 Brook Lopez 1.25 3.00
14 Tony Parker 2.00 5.00
15 Deron Williams 1.00 2.50
16 Marc Gasol 1.25 3.00
17 Joe Johnson 1.25 3.00
18 Dirk Nowitzki 3.00 8.00
19 Chris Paul 2.50 6.00
20 Chris Kaman 1.00 2.50
21 Kevin Love 1.25 3.00
22 Danny Granger .75 2.00
23 Antawn Jamison 1.00 2.50
24 Trevor Ariza .75 2.00
25 Carmelo Anthony 2.00 5.00
26 Monta Ellis 1.00 2.50
27 Al Horford 1.25 3.00
28 Kevin Durant 5.00 12.00
29 Brandon Roy 1.50 4.00
30 Corey Maggette 1.00 2.50
31 Andre Iguodala 1.25 3.00
32 Ray Allen 2.00 5.00
33 Shaquille O'Neal 4.00 10.00
34 Jamal Crawford 1.25 3.00
35 Gerald Wallace 1.00 2.50
36 David West 1.00 2.50
37 Zach Randolph 1.25 3.00
38 Rodney Stuckey .75 2.00
39 Derrick Rose 2.00 5.00
40 Tim Duncan 3.00 8.00
41 David Lee .75 2.00
42 Amare Stoudemire 1.00 2.50
43 Aaron Brooks .75 2.00
44 Lamar Odom 1.00 2.50
45 Ben Wallace 1.50 4.00
46 J.J. Barea 1.25 3.00
47 Emeka Okafor 1.00 2.50
48 Brendan Haywood .75 2.00
49 Michael Beasley .75 2.00
50 Allen Iverson 2.50 6.00
51 Andrea Bargnani .75 2.00
52 Nene 1.00 2.50
53 Paul Pierce 2.00 5.00
54 Mo Williams 1.00 2.50
55 Jason Thompson .75 2.00
56 Russell Westbrook 2.50 6.00
57 Andrew Bogut 1.00 2.50
58 Al Jefferson .75 2.00
59 Devin Harris .75 2.00
60 Vince Carter 2.50 6.00
61 Jason Kidd 2.00 5.00
62 Kevin Garnett 3.00 8.00
63 Rudy Gay 1.25 3.00
64 Stephen Jackson 1.00 2.50
65 Luol Deng 1.00 2.50
66 Carl Landry .75 2.00
67 Baron Davis 1.00 2.50
68 Ben Gordon 1.00 2.50
69 Al Harrington 1.00 2.50
70 Carlos Boozer 1.00 2.50
71 Pau Gasol 2.00 5.00
72 Luke Ridnour 1.00 2.50
73 Josh Smith .75 2.00
74 Raymond Felton .75 2.00
75 Kendrick Perkins .75 2.00
76 Dahntay Jones .75 2.00
77 Kevin Martin 1.00 2.50
78 Shawn Marion 1.25 3.00
79 Marcus Camby 1.00 2.50
80 Jermaine O'Neal 1.25 3.00
81 Manu Ginobili 2.50 6.00
82 Richard Hamilton 1.25 3.00
83 Rashard Lewis 1.00 2.50
84 Jason Richardson 1.25 3.00
85 Jeff Green 1.00 2.50
86 Elton Brand 1.00 2.50
87 Mehmet Okur .75 2.00
88 O.J. Mayo .75 2.00
89 Caron Butler 1.00 2.50
90 Rasheed Wallace 1.50 4.00
91 Jason Terry 1.00 2.50
92 Ron Artest 1.25 3.00
93 Jason Williams 1.00 2.50
94 Hedo Turkoglu 1.00 2.50
95 Yao Ming 3.00 8.00
96 Chauncey Billups 1.50 4.00
97 Nate Robinson 1.00 2.50
98 Mike Dunleavy .75 2.00
99 Louis Williams 1.25 3.00
100 Juwan Howard 1.00 2.50
101 Jalen Rose 1.00 2.50
102 Chris Webber 1.50 4.00
103 David Robinson 2.50 6.00
104 Chuck Person 1.00 2.50
105 Alvan Adams .75 2.00
106 Larry Bird 5.00 12.00
107 Scottie Pippen 3.00 8.00
108 Connie Hawkins 1.50 4.00
109 Magic Johnson 5.00 12.00
110 Bill Laimbeer 1.25 3.00
111 Shawn Bradley .75 2.00
112 Kelly Tripucka .75 2.00
113 Robert Horry 1.00 2.50
114 Spud Webb 1.00 2.50
115 World B. Free 1.00 2.50
116 Tim Hardaway 1.25 3.00
117 Sean Elliott 1.00 2.50
118 Anfernee Hardaway 3.00 8.00
119 Paul Westphal 1.25 3.00
120 Pete Maravich 4.00 10.00
121 Willis Reed 2.00 5.00
122 Nate Thurmond 1.00 2.50
123 Mychal Thompson 1.25 3.00
124 Kenny Anderson 1.00 2.50
125 Jerry West 2.00 5.00
126 Marcus Thornton RC 1.50 4.00
127 Jonas Jerebko RC 1.50 4.00
128 Wesley Matthews RC 2.00 5.00
129 A.J. Price RC 1.25 3.00
130 David Andersen RC 1.25 3.00
131 Serge Ibaka RC 2.00 5.00
132 Garrett Temple RC 1.50 4.00
133 Derrick Brown RC 1.25 3.00
134 Sundiata Gaines RC 1.25 3.00
135 Chris Hunter RC 1.25 3.00
136 Jon Brockman RC 1.25 3.00
137 Danny Green RC 2.00 5.00
138 Marcus Landry RC 1.25 3.00
139 Lester Hudson RC 1.25 3.00
140 Patrick Mills RC 3.00 8.00
141 Dante Cunningham RC 1.25 3.00
142 B.Jennings JSY AU/499 RC 6.00 15.00
143 Jonny Flynn JSY AU/349 RC 4.00 10.00
144 S.Curry JSY AU/499 RC 2,000.00 4,000.00
145 Omri Casspi JSY AU/499 RC 4.00 10.00
146 J.Harden JSY AU/499 RC 300.00 600.00
147 Ty Lawson JSY AU/349 RC 5.00 12.00
148 Taj Gibson JSY AU/499 RC 5.00 12.00
149 T.Hansbrough JSY AU/499 RC 5.00 12.00
150 Chase Budinger JSY AU/499 RC 4.00 10.00
151 Sam Young JSY AU/299 RC 4.00 10.00
152 DeJuan Blair JSY AU/499 RC 5.00 12.00
153 Ter.Williams JSY AU/499 RC 4.00 10.00
154 D.Collison JSY AU/499 RC 6.00 15.00
155 T.Douglas JSY AU/499 RC 4.00 10.00
156 Wayne Ellington JSY AU/499 RC 5.00 12.00
157 Jrue Holiday JSY AU/499 RC 20.00 50.00
158 Eric Maynor JSY AU/499 RC 4.00 10.00
159 R.Beaubois JSY AU/349 RC 4.00 10.00
160 Austin Daye JSY AU/499 RC 4.00 10.00
161 Jodie Meeks JSY AU/499 RC 4.00 10.00
162 Jeff Pendergraph JSY AU/499 RC 4.00 10.00
163 Jordan Hill JSY AU/499 RC 4.00 10.00
164 DeMarre Carroll JSY AU/499 RC 5.00 12.00
165 Jeff Teague JSY AU/499 RC 5.00 12.00
166 T.Evans JSY AU/499 RC 5.00 12.00
167 J.Johnson JSY AU/349 RC 5.00 12.00
168 Earl Clark JSY AU/499 RC 4.00 10.00
169 G.Henderson JSY AU/499 RC 4.00 10.00
170 DaJuan Summers JSY AU/499 RC 4.00 10.00
171 Hasheem Thabeet JSY AU/499 RC 4.00 10.00
172 B.Griffin JSY AU/499 RC 40.00 100.00
173 B.J. Mullens JSY AU/499 RC 4.00 10.00
174 Taylor Griffin JSY AU/499 RC 4.00 10.00
175 J.Taylor JSY AU/299 RC 4.00 10.00
176 D.DeRozan JSY AU/499 RC 150.00 400.00

2009-10 Absolute Memorabilia Spectrum Gold
*GOLD: .6X TO 1.5X BASE HI
PRINT RUN 100 SER.#'d SETS

2009-10 Absolute Memorabilia Spectrum Platinum
*PLATINUM: 1.25X TO 3X BASE HI
PRINT RUN 25 SER.#'d SETS
118 Anfernee Hardaway 20.00 50.00

2009-10 Absolute Memorabilia Frequent Flyer
COMPLETE SET (19) 20.00 40.00
STATED PRINT RUN 100 SER.#'d SETS
1 Devin Harris .75 2.00
2 Elton Brand 1.00 2.50
3 Eric Gordon 1.00 2.50
5 Kobe Bryant 10.00 25.00
6 LeBron James 10.00 25.00
7 Kevin Martin 1.00 2.50
8 Shawn Marion 1.25 3.00
9 Vince Carter 2.50 6.00
10 DeMar DeRozan 5.00 12.00
11 Dwyane Wade 2.50 6.00
12 Nate Robinson 1.00 2.50
13 Allen Iverson 2.50 6.00
14 Amare Stoudemire 1.00 2.50
15 Gerald Wallace 1.00 2.50
16 Carmelo Anthony 2.00 5.00
17 Kevin Love 1.25 3.00
18 Ron Artest 1.25 3.00
19 Joe Johnson 1.25 3.00
20 Trevor Ariza .75 2.00

2009-10 Absolute Memorabilia Frequent Flyer Materials
STATED PRINT RUN 10 TO 100 SER.#'d SETS
1 Devin Harris/100 2.00 5.00
2 Elton Brand/100 2.50 6.00
3 Eric Gordon/100 2.50 6.00
5 Kobe Bryant/100 10.00 25.00
6 LeBron James/100 10.00 25.00
7 Kevin Martin/100 2.50 6.00
8 Shawn Marion/100 3.00 8.00
9 Vince Carter/100 6.00 15.00
10 DeMar DeRozan/100 12.00 30.00
11 Dwyane Wade/50 6.00 15.00
12 Nate Robinson/100 2.50 6.00
13 Allen Iverson/25 8.00 20.00
15 Gerald Wallace/100 2.50 6.00
16 Carmelo Anthony/100 5.00 12.00
17 Kevin Love/100 2.50 6.00
19 Joe Johnson/100 3.00 8.00

2009-10 Absolute Memorabilia Frequent Flyer Materials Jersey Number
STATED PRINT RUN 5 TO 25 SER.#'d SETS
1 Devin Harris/25 3.00 8.00
2 Elton Brand/25 4.00 10.00
3 Eric Gordon/25 4.00 10.00
5 Kobe Bryant/25 12.50 30.00
6 LeBron James/25 12.50 30.00
7 Kevin Martin/25 4.00 10.00
8 Shawn Marion/25 5.00 12.00
9 Vince Carter/25 10.00 25.00
10 DeMar DeRozan/25 75.00 200.00
11 Dwyane Wade/25 10.00 25.00
12 Nate Robinson/25 4.00 10.00
15 Gerald Wallace/25 4.00 10.00
16 Carmelo Anthony/25 8.00 20.00
17 Kevin Love/25 5.00 12.00
19 Joe Johnson/25 5.00 12.00

2009-10 Absolute Memorabilia Frequent Flyer Materials Jersey Number Signatures
STATED PRINT RUN 10 TO 25 SER.#'d SETS
1 Devin Harris/25 6.00 15.00
3 Eric Gordon/10 12.50 30.00
5 Kobe Bryant/25 100.00 250.00
17 Kevin Love/25 15.00 40.00

2009-10 Absolute Memorabilia Frequent Flyer Materials Signatures
STATED PRINT RUN 5 TO 25 SER.#'d SETS
1 Devin Harris/25 6.00 15.00
3 Eric Gordon/10 12.50 30.00
5 Kobe Bryant/25 800.00 1,500.00
10 DeMar DeRozan/25 75.00 200.00
17 Kevin Love/25 20.00 50.00

2009-10 Absolute Memorabilia Heroes
COMPLETE SET (14) 15.00 30.00
STATED PRINT RUN 100 SER.#'d SETS
1 Ray Allen 2.00 5.00
2 Rudy Fernandez .75 2.00
4 T.J. Ford .75 2.00
5 Brandon Jennings 1.25 3.00
6 Lamar Odom 1.00 2.50
7 Eric Gordon 1.00 2.50
8 Devin Harris .75 2.00
9 LeBron James 10.00 25.00
10 Russell Westbrook 2.50 6.00
11 Tyler Hansbrough 1.00 2.50
12 David Lee .75 2.00
13 Jason Kidd 2.00 5.00
14 Richard Hamilton 1.25 3.00
15 Kobe Bryant 10.00 25.00

2009-10 Absolute Memorabilia Heroes Materials
STATED PRINT RUN 50 TO 100 SETS
1 Ray Allen/100 5.00 12.00
2 Rudy Fernandez/100 2.00 5.00
4 T.J. Ford/100 2.00 5.00
5 Brandon Jennings/100 3.00 8.00
7 Eric Gordon/100 2.50 6.00
8 Devin Harris/100 2.00 5.00
9 LeBron James/100 8.00 20.00
10 Russell Westbrook/100 6.00 15.00
11 Tyler Hansbrough/100 2.50 6.00
12 David Lee/50 2.00 5.00
13 Jason Kidd/100 5.00 12.00
15 Kobe Bryant/100 8.00 20.00

2009-10 Absolute Memorabilia Heroes Materials Signatures
STATED PRINT RUN 5 TO 25 SER.#'d SETS
1 Ray Allen/25 20.00 50.00
4 T.J. Ford/25 6.00 15.00
5 Brandon Jennings/25 15.00 40.00
8 Devin Harris/25 6.00 15.00
10 Russell Westbrook/25 30.00 80.00
11 Tyler Hansbrough/25 10.00 25.00
13 Jason Kidd/25 12.00 30.00
15 Kobe Bryant/25 800.00 1,500.00

2009-10 Absolute Memorabilia Hoopla
COMPLETE SET (20) 25.00 50.00
STATED PRINT RUN 100 SER.#'d SETS
1 LeBron James 10.00 25.00
2 Dwyane Wade 2.50 6.00
3 Chris Paul 2.50 6.00
4 Kevin Durant 5.00 12.00
5 Dwight Howard 1.50 4.00
6 Gerald Wallace 1.00 2.50
7 Kobe Bryant 10.00 25.00
8 Steve Nash 2.50 6.00
9 Kevin Garnett 3.00 8.00
10 Dirk Nowitzki 3.00 8.00
11 Josh Smith .75 2.00
12 Chris Bosh 1.50 4.00
13 Carmelo Anthony 2.00 5.00
14 Brandon Roy 1.50 4.00
15 Derrick Rose 2.00 5.00
16 Tracy McGrady 2.50 6.00
17 Devin Harris .75 2.00
18 Tony Parker 2.00 5.00
19 Allen Iverson 2.50 6.00
20 Chris Andersen 1.25 3.00

2009-10 Absolute Memorabilia Hoopla Materials
STATED PRINT RUN 25 TO 100 SETS
1 LeBron James/100 10.00 25.00
2 Dwyane Wade/50 6.00 15.00
3 Chris Paul/100 6.00 15.00
4 Kevin Durant/100 12.00 30.00
5 Dwight Howard/100 4.00 10.00
6 Gerald Wallace/100 2.50 6.00
7 Kobe Bryant/100 10.00 25.00
9 Kevin Garnett/100 8.00 20.00
10 Dirk Nowitzki/100 8.00 20.00
11 Josh Smith/100 2.00 5.00
12 Chris Bosh/100 4.00 10.00
13 Carmelo Anthony/100 5.00 12.00
14 Brandon Roy/100 4.00 10.00
16 Tracy McGrady/100 6.00 15.00
17 Devin Harris/100 2.00 5.00
18 Tony Parker/50 5.00 12.00
19 Allen Iverson/25 8.00 20.00
20 Chris Andersen/100 3.00 8.00

2009-10 Absolute Memorabilia Hoopla Materials Jersey Number
STATED PRINT RUN 10 TO 25 SER.#'d SETS
1 LeBron James/25 15.00 30.00
2 Dwyane Wade/25 10.00 25.00
3 Chris Paul/25 10.00 25.00
5 Dwight Howard/25 6.00 15.00
6 Gerald Wallace/25 4.00 10.00
7 Kobe Bryant/25 15.00 30.00
11 Josh Smith/25 3.00 8.00
13 Carmelo Anthony/25 8.00 20.00
16 Tracy McGrady/25 10.00 25.00
17 Devin Harris/25 3.00 8.00
18 Tony Parker/25 8.00 20.00

2009-10 Absolute Memorabilia Hoopla Materials Jersey Number Signatures
STATED PRINT RUN 5 TO 25 SER.#'d SETS
7 Kobe Bryant/25 800.00 1,500.00
16 Tracy McGrady/25 20.00 40.00
17 Devin Harris/25 6.00 15.00
18 Tony Parker/25 15.00 30.00

2009-10 Absolute Memorabilia Hoopla Materials Signatures
STATED PRINT RUN 25 SER.#'d SETS
7 Kobe Bryant 800.00 1,500.00
16 Tracy McGrady 15.00 40.00
17 Devin Harris 6.00 15.00
18 Tony Parker 12.00 30.00

2009-10 Absolute Memorabilia Marks of Fame
COMPLETE SET (10) 15.00 30.00
STATED PRINT RUN 100 SER.#'d SETS
1 LeBron James 10.00 25.00
2 Kareem Abdul-Jabbar 4.00 10.00
3 Allen Iverson 2.50 6.00
4 Magic Johnson 5.00 12.00
5 Ray Allen 2.00 5.00
6 Dikembe Mutombo 2.00 5.00
7 Dirk Nowitzki 3.00 8.00
8 Bill Russell 4.00 10.00
9 Kobe Bryant 10.00 25.00
10 Mark Price 1.25 3.00

2009-10 Absolute Memorabilia Marks of Fame Materials
STATED PRINT RUN 25 TO 100 SETS
1 LeBron James/100 8.00 20.00
2 Kareem Abdul-Jabbar/100 12.00 30.00
3 Allen Iverson/25 8.00 20.00
4 Magic Johnson/100 8.00 20.00
5 Ray Allen/100 5.00 12.00
6 Dikembe Mutombo/100 6.00 15.00
7 Dirk Nowitzki/100 8.00 20.00
9 Kobe Bryant/100 8.00 20.00
10 Mark Price/100 4.00 10.00

2009-10 Absolute Memorabilia Marks of Fame Materials Signatures
STATED PRINT RUN 8 TO 25 SER.#'d SETS
4 Magic Johnson/25 40.00 100.00
5 Ray Allen/25 25.00 50.00
9 Kobe Bryant/25 800.00 1,500.00

2009-10 Absolute Memorabilia Materials Prime Spectrum
STATED PRINT RUN ONE TO 25 SER.#'d SETS
1 Kobe Bryant/25 25.00 60.00
2 Dwight Howard/25 8.00 20.00
3 Rajon Rondo/25 10.00 25.00
4 Samuel Dalembert/25 4.00 10.00
5 LeBron James/25 25.00 60.00
6 Chris Andersen/25 6.00 15.00
7 Dwyane Wade/25 12.00 30.00
8 Chris Bosh/25 8.00 20.00
10 LaMarcus Aldridge/25 6.00 15.00
11 Danilo Gallinari/25 5.00 12.00
12 Joakim Noah/25 4.00 10.00
13 Brook Lopez/25 6.00 15.00
15 Deron Williams/25 6.00 15.00
16 Marc Gasol/25 6.00 15.00
17 Joe Johnson/25 6.00 15.00
18 Dirk Nowitzki/25 10.00 25.00
19 Chris Paul/25 12.00 30.00
21 Kevin Love/25 6.00 15.00
22 Danny Granger/25 4.00 10.00
25 Carmelo Anthony/25 10.00 25.00
27 Al Horford/25 6.00 15.00
28 Kevin Durant/25 25.00 60.00
29 Brandon Roy/25 8.00 20.00
30 Corey Maggette/25 5.00 12.00
31 Andre Iguodala/25 6.00 15.00
32 Ray Allen/25 10.00 25.00
33 Shaquille O'Neal/25 20.00 50.00
35 Gerald Wallace/25 5.00 12.00
36 David West/25 5.00 12.00
38 Rodney Stuckey/25 4.00 10.00
40 Tim Duncan/25 15.00 40.00
41 David Lee/25 4.00 10.00
46 J.J. Barea/25 12.50 30.00
47 Emeka Okafor/25 5.00 12.00
51 Andrea Bargnani/25 4.00 10.00
53 Paul Pierce/25 10.00 25.00
56 Russell Westbrook/25 12.00 30.00
57 Andrew Bogut/25 5.00 12.00
58 Al Jefferson/25 4.00 10.00
59 Devin Harris/25 4.00 10.00
60 Vince Carter/25 12.00 30.00
61 Jason Kidd/15 10.00 25.00
62 Kevin Garnett/25 15.00 40.00
63 Rudy Gay/25 6.00 15.00
65 Luol Deng/25 5.00 12.00
67 Baron Davis/25 5.00 12.00
70 Carlos Boozer/25 5.00 12.00
73 Josh Smith/25 4.00 10.00
74 Raymond Felton/25 4.00 10.00
77 Kevin Martin/25 5.00 12.00
79 Marcus Camby/25 5.00 12.00
81 Manu Ginobili/25 8.00 20.00
83 Rashard Lewis/25 5.00 12.00
85 Jeff Green/25 5.00 12.00
86 Elton Brand/25 5.00 12.00
87 Mehmet Okur/25 4.00 10.00
88 O.J. Mayo/25 4.00 10.00
90 Rasheed Wallace/25 8.00 20.00
91 Jason Terry/25 5.00 12.00
94 Hedo Turkoglu/25 5.00 12.00
96 Chauncey Billups/25 8.00 20.00
98 Mike Dunleavy/25 4.00 10.00
102 Chris Webber/25 15.00 40.00
104 Chuck Person/25 5.00 12.00
105 Alvan Adams/25 4.00 10.00
106 Larry Bird/25 15.00 30.00
109 Magic Johnson/25 15.00 30.00
113 Robert Horry/25 10.00 25.00
124 Kenny Anderson/25 5.00 12.00
125 Jerry West/15 15.00 40.00

2009-10 Absolute Memorabilia NBA Icons
COMPLETE SET (15) 40.00 70.00
STATED PRINT RUN 100 SER.#'d SETS
1 Jerry West 5.00 12.00
2 Patrick Ewing 5.00 12.00
3 Scottie Pippen 8.00 20.00
4 Reggie Lewis 3.00 8.00
5 Alonzo Mourning 5.00 12.00
6 Karl Malone 4.00 10.00
7 Dominique Wilkins 5.00 12.00
8 Willis Reed 5.00 12.00
9 Tim Hardaway 3.00 8.00
10 George Mikan 10.00 25.00
11 George Gervin 4.00 10.00
12 John Stockton 5.00 12.00
13 Bob Lanier 4.00 10.00
14 Mark Aguirre 2.50 6.00
15 Mark Eaton 2.00 5.00

2009-10 Absolute Memorabilia NBA Icons Materials
STATED PRINT RUN 5 TO 100 SETS
2 Patrick Ewing/100 8.00 20.00
4 Reggie Lewis/100 10.00 25.00
6 Karl Malone/100 6.00 15.00
7 Dominique Wilkins/49 8.00 20.00
10 George Mikan/50 20.00 40.00
12 John Stockton/100 8.00 20.00
13 Bob Lanier/100 6.00 15.00
15 Mark Eaton/100 3.00 8.00

2009-10 Absolute Memorabilia Patches Jumbo Prime Spectrum
STATED PRINT RUN 25 SER.#'d SETS
1 Chris Paul 25.00 60.00
2 Danny Granger 8.00 20.00
3 Josh Smith 8.00 20.00
4 Marc Gasol 12.00 30.00
5 Kobe Bryant 100.00 250.00
6 Andre Iguodala 12.00 30.00
7 Kevin Garnett 30.00 80.00
8 Antawn Jamison 10.00 25.00
9 Raymond Felton 8.00 20.00
10 Marcus Camby 10.00 25.00

2009-10 Absolute Memorabilia Redemptions
EXCHANGES FOR FULL SIZE ITEMS
NNO Kobe Bryant Jersey/24 600.00 1,200.00
NNO Kobe Bryant Bsktbll/24 600.00 1,200.00

2009-10 Absolute Memorabilia Rookie Materials Jumbo Jersey Numbers Basketball
STATED PRINT RUN 25 SER.#'d SETS
142 Brandon Jennings 5.00 12.00
143 Jonny Flynn 3.00 8.00
144 Stephen Curry 500.00 1,000.00
145 Omri Casspi 3.00 8.00
146 James Harden 30.00 80.00
147 Ty Lawson 4.00 10.00
148 Taj Gibson 4.00 10.00
149 Tyler Hansbrough 4.00 10.00
150 Chase Budinger 3.00 8.00
151 Sam Young 3.00 8.00
152 DeJuan Blair 4.00 10.00
153 Terrence Williams 3.00 8.00
154 Darren Collison 5.00 12.00
155 Toney Douglas 3.00 8.00
156 Wayne Ellington 4.00 10.00
157 Jrue Holiday 15.00 40.00
158 Eric Maynor 3.00 8.00
159 Rodrigue Beaubois 3.00 8.00
160 Austin Daye 3.00 8.00
161 Jodie Meeks 3.00 8.00
162 Jeff Pendergraph 3.00 8.00
163 Jordan Hill 3.00 8.00
164 DeMarre Carroll 4.00 10.00
165 Jeff Teague 4.00 10.00
166 Tyreke Evans 4.00 10.00
167 James Johnson 4.00 10.00
168 Earl Clark 3.00 8.00
169 Gerald Henderson 3.00 8.00
170 DaJuan Summers 3.00 8.00
171 Hasheem Thabeet 3.00 8.00
172 Blake Griffin 20.00 50.00
173 B.J. Mullens 3.00 8.00
174 Taylor Griffin 3.00 8.00
175 Jermaine Taylor 3.00 8.00
176 DeMar DeRozan 75.00 200.00

2009-10 Absolute Memorabilia Rookie Materials Jumbo Jersey Numbers Basketball Signatures
STATED PRINT RUN 25 SER.#'d SETS
142 Brandon Jennings 20.00 50.00
143 Jonny Flynn 5.00 12.00
144 Stephen Curry 5,000.00 10,000.00
145 Omri Casspi 5.00 12.00
146 James Harden 75.00 200.00
147 Ty Lawson 6.00 15.00
148 Taj Gibson 6.00 15.00
149 Tyler Hansbrough 6.00 15.00
150 Chase Budinger 5.00 12.00
151 Sam Young 5.00 12.00
152 DeJuan Blair 6.00 15.00
153 Terrence Williams 5.00 12.00
154 Darren Collison 8.00 20.00
155 Toney Douglas 5.00 12.00
156 Wayne Ellington 6.00 15.00
157 Jrue Holiday 20.00 50.00
158 Eric Maynor 5.00 12.00
159 Rodrigue Beaubois 5.00 12.00
160 Austin Daye 5.00 12.00
161 Jodie Meeks 5.00 12.00
162 Jeff Pendergraph 5.00 12.00
163 Jordan Hill 5.00 12.00
164 DeMarre Carroll 5.00 12.00
165 Jeff Teague 6.00 15.00
166 Tyreke Evans 25.00 60.00
167 James Johnson 6.00 15.00
168 Earl Clark 5.00 12.00
169 Gerald Henderson 5.00 12.00
170 DaJuan Summers 5.00 12.00
171 Hasheem Thabeet 5.00 12.00
172 Blake Griffin 125.00 250.00
173 B.J. Mullens 5.00 12.00
174 Taylor Griffin 5.00 12.00
175 Jermaine Taylor 5.00 12.00
176 DeMar DeRozan 125.00 300.00

2009-10 Absolute Memorabilia Spectrum Signatures Gold
STATED PRINT RUN 20 TO 249 SETS
1 Kobe Bryant/99 400.00 800.00
14 Tony Parker/49 10.00 25.00
15 Deron Williams/49 4.00 10.00
21 Kevin Love/99 10.00 25.00
22 Danny Granger/49 3.00 8.00
31 Andre Iguodala/49 5.00 12.00
32 Ray Allen/49 15.00 40.00
43 Aaron Brooks/49 3.00 8.00
46 J.J. Barea/49 12.50 30.00
47 Emeka Okafor/49 4.00 10.00
51 Andrea Bargnani/49 3.00 8.00
56 Russell Westbrook/49 40.00 100.00
57 Andrew Bogut/49 5.00 12.00
59 Devin Harris/49 3.00 8.00
61 Jason Kidd/49 10.00 25.00
67 Baron Davis/49 6.00 15.00
70 Carlos Boozer/49 4.00 10.00
80 Jermaine O'Neal/49 5.00 12.00
82 Richard Hamilton/49 5.00 12.00
92 Ron Artest/49 15.00 40.00
96 Chauncey Billups/20 8.00 20.00
101 Jalen Rose/49 10.00 25.00
105 Alvan Adams/49 3.00 8.00
106 Larry Bird/49 30.00 80.00
107 Scottie Pippen/49 75.00 200.00
108 Connie Hawkins/49 8.00 20.00
109 Magic Johnson/49 30.00 80.00
110 Bill Laimbeer/99 6.00 15.00
111 Shawn Bradley/49 8.00 20.00
114 Spud Webb/49 6.00 15.00
115 World B. Free/49 5.00 12.00
116 Tim Hardaway/49 10.00 25.00
117 Sean Elliott/49 10.00 25.00
119 Paul Westphal/40 10.00 25.00
122 Nate Thurmond/99 6.00 15.00
125 Jerry West/49 25.00 60.00
126 Marcus Thornton/249 4.00 10.00
127 Jonas Jerebko/249 4.00 10.00
128 Wesley Matthews/249 5.00 12.00
129 A.J. Price/249 3.00 8.00
131 Serge Ibaka/249 5.00 12.00
133 Derrick Brown/99 3.00 8.00
134 Sundiata Gaines/249 3.00 8.00
136 Jon Brockman/249 3.00 8.00
137 Danny Green/249 5.00 12.00
138 Marcus Landry/249 3.00 8.00
139 Lester Hudson/249 3.00 8.00
140 Patrick Mills/99 8.00 20.00
141 Dante Cunningham/249 3.00 8.00

2009-10 Absolute Memorabilia Spectrum Signatures Platinum
*PLATINUM STARS: .5X TO 1.25X GOLD
*PLATINUM RCs: .6X TO 1.5X GOLD
STATED PRINT RUN 5 TO 25 SER.#'d SETS
1 Kobe Bryant/25 500.00 1,000.00
3 Rajon Rondo/25 20.00 50.00
71 Pau Gasol/25 25.00 50.00
121 Willis Reed/25 50.00 120.00

2009-10 Absolute Memorabilia Star Gazing
COMPLETE SET (35)
STATED PRINT RUN 100 SER.#'d SETS
1 LeBron James 100.00 250.00
2 Kobe Bryant 100.00 250.00
3 Brandon Jennings 1.50 4.00
4 Tyreke Evans 1.25 3.00
5 Carmelo Anthony 2.50 6.00
6 Dwyane Wade 3.00 8.00
7 Chris Bosh 2.00 5.00
8 Pau Gasol 2.50 6.00
9 Jonny Flynn 1.00 2.50
10 Stephen Curry 1,000.00 2,000.00
11 Jason Kidd 2.50 6.00
12 Tony Parker 2.50 6.00
13 Danny Granger 1.00 2.50
14 Deron Williams 1.25 3.00
15 Dwight Howard 2.00 5.00
16 Kevin Durant 20.00 50.00
17 Blake Griffin 10.00 25.00
18 Omri Casspi 1.00 2.50
19 Kevin Garnett 4.00 10.00
20 Ray Allen 2.50 6.00
21 Shaquille O'Neal 8.00 20.00
22 Brandon Roy 2.00 5.00
23 Monta Ellis 1.25 3.00
24 Chris Paul 3.00 8.00
25 Dirk Nowitzki 4.00 10.00
26 David Lee 1.00 2.50
27 Tim Duncan 4.00 10.00
28 Antawn Jamison 1.25 3.00
29 Joe Johnson 1.50 4.00
30 Amare Stoudemire 1.25 3.00
31 Chris Kaman 1.25 3.00
32 Zach Randolph 1.50 4.00
33 Andrea Bargnani 1.00 2.50
34 Brook Lopez 1.50 4.00
35 Derrick Rose 2.50 6.00

2009-10 Absolute Memorabilia Star Gazing Jumbo Jersey Numbers
STATED PRINT RUN 10 TO 25 SER.#'d SETS
1 LeBron James/25 600.00 1,200.00
2 Kobe Bryant/25 600.00 1,200.00
3 Brandon Jennings/25 5.00 12.00
4 Tyreke Evans/25 4.00 10.00
5 Carmelo Anthony/25 8.00 20.00
7 Chris Bosh/25 6.00 15.00
8 Pau Gasol/25 8.00 20.00
9 Jonny Flynn/25 3.00 8.00
10 Stephen Curry/25 2,000.00 4,000.00
11 Jason Kidd/25 8.00 20.00
13 Danny Granger/25 3.00 8.00
14 Deron Williams/25 4.00 10.00
15 Dwight Howard/25 6.00 15.00
16 Kevin Durant/25 125.00 300.00
17 Blake Griffin/25 20.00 50.00
18 Omri Casspi/25 3.00 8.00
19 Kevin Garnett/25 12.00 30.00
20 Ray Allen/25 8.00 20.00
21 Shaquille O'Neal/25 40.00 100.00
22 Brandon Roy/25 6.00 15.00
23 Monta Ellis/25 4.00 10.00
24 Chris Paul/25 10.00 25.00
25 Dirk Nowitzki/25 12.00 30.00
27 Tim Duncan/25 12.00 30.00
28 Antawn Jamison/25 4.00 10.00
29 Joe Johnson/25 5.00 12.00
33 Andrea Bargnani/25 3.00 8.00
34 Brook Lopez/25 5.00 12.00

2009-10 Absolute Memorabilia Star Gazing Jumbo Jersey Numbers Signatures
STATED PRINT RUN 10 TO 25 SER.#'d SETS
2 Kobe Bryant/25 1,500.00 3,000.00
3 Brandon Jennings/25 10.00 25.00
4 Tyreke Evans/25 8.00 20.00
8 Pau Gasol/25 30.00 60.00
9 Jonny Flynn/25 6.00 15.00
10 Stephen Curry/25 5,000.00 10,000.00
11 Jason Kidd/25 20.00 50.00
13 Danny Granger/25 10.00 25.00
14 Deron Williams/25 10.00 25.00
17 Blake Griffin/25 125.00 300.00
18 Omri Casspi/25 6.00 15.00
20 Ray Allen/25 50.00 120.00
33 Andrea Bargnani/25 6.00 15.00

2009-10 Absolute Memorabilia Star Gazing Jumbo Materials
STATED PRINT RUN 5 TO 25 SER.#'d SETS
1 LeBron James/25 15.00 40.00
2 Kobe Bryant/25 40.00 100.00
3 Brandon Jennings/25 5.00 12.00
4 Tyreke Evans/25 4.00 10.00
5 Carmelo Anthony/25 8.00 20.00
7 Chris Bosh/25 6.00 15.00
9 Jonny Flynn/25 3.00 8.00
10 Stephen Curry/25 1,000.00 2,000.00
11 Jason Kidd/25 8.00 20.00
13 Danny Granger/25 3.00 8.00
14 Deron Williams/25 4.00 10.00
15 Dwight Howard/25 6.00 15.00
16 Kevin Durant/25 12.00 30.00
17 Blake Griffin/25 20.00 50.00
18 Omri Casspi/25 3.00 8.00
19 Kevin Garnett/25 12.00 30.00
20 Ray Allen/25 10.00 25.00
21 Shaquille O'Neal/25 12.50 30.00
22 Brandon Roy/25 6.00 15.00
24 Chris Paul/25 10.00 25.00
25 Dirk Nowitzki/25 12.00 30.00
27 Tim Duncan/25 12.00 30.00
28 Antawn Jamison/25 4.00 10.00
29 Joe Johnson/25 5.00 12.00
33 Andrea Bargnani/25 3.00 8.00
34 Brook Lopez/25 5.00 12.00

2009-10 Absolute Memorabilia Star Gazing Materials
STATED PRINT RUN 10 TO 100 SER.#'d SETS
1 LeBron James/100 150.00 400.00
2 Kobe Bryant/100 150.00 400.00
3 Brandon Jennings/100 3.00 8.00
4 Tyreke Evans/100 2.50 6.00
5 Carmelo Anthony/100 5.00 12.00
6 Dwyane Wade/100 6.00 15.00
7 Chris Bosh/100 4.00 10.00
8 Pau Gasol/100 5.00 12.00
9 Jonny Flynn/100 2.00 5.00
10 Stephen Curry/100 1,000.00 2,000.00
11 Jason Kidd/100 5.00 12.00
12 Tony Parker/50 5.00 12.00
13 Danny Granger/100 2.00 5.00
14 Deron Williams/100 2.50 6.00
15 Dwight Howard/100 4.00 10.00
16 Kevin Durant/100 25.00 60.00
17 Blake Griffin/100 12.00 30.00
18 Omri Casspi/100 2.00 5.00
19 Kevin Garnett/100 8.00 20.00
20 Ray Allen/100 5.00 12.00
21 Shaquille O'Neal/100 15.00 40.00
22 Brandon Roy/100 4.00 10.00
23 Monta Ellis/100 2.50 6.00
24 Chris Paul/100 6.00 15.00
25 Dirk Nowitzki/100 8.00 20.00
26 David Lee/50 2.00 5.00
27 Tim Duncan/100 8.00 20.00
28 Antawn Jamison/100 2.50 6.00
29 Joe Johnson/100 3.00 8.00
31 Chris Kaman/25 2.50 6.00
33 Andrea Bargnani/100 2.00 5.00
34 Brook Lopez/100 3.00 8.00

2009-10 Absolute Memorabilia Star Gazing Materials Signatures
STATED PRINT RUN 25 SER.#'d SETS
2 Kobe Bryant 1,500.00 3,000.00
3 Brandon Jennings 10.00 25.00
4 Tyreke Evans 8.00 20.00
8 Pau Gasol 25.00 60.00
9 Jonny Flynn 6.00 15.00
10 Stephen Curry 5,000.00 10,000.00
11 Jason Kidd 15.00 40.00
12 Tony Parker 12.00 30.00
13 Danny Granger 10.00 25.00
14 Deron Williams 10.00 25.00
17 Blake Griffin 125.00 300.00
18 Omri Casspi 6.00 15.00
20 Ray Allen 20.00 50.00
33 Andrea Bargnani 6.00 15.00

2009-10 Absolute Memorabilia Team Quads TEAM Die Cut Materials
STATED PRINT RUN 25 TO 100 SER.#'d SETS
1 CP/DW/EO/PS 6.00 15.00
2 AB/CB/HT/JC 6.00 15.00
3 BG/RH/RS/TP 6.00 15.00
4 AM/BR/LA/RF 6.00 15.00
5 KG/PP/RR/RW 15.00 30.00
6 BD/CK/EG/MC 6.00 15.00
7 LJ/MW/SO/ZI 12.00 30.00
8 DH/JN/RL/VC 6.00 15.00
9 CA/CA/JS/N 6.00 15.00

2009-10 Absolute Memorabilia Team Tandems Materials
STATED PRINT RUN 100 SER.#'d SETS
1 D.West/E.Okafor 4.00 10.00
2 H.Turkoglu/J.Calderon 6.00 15.00
3 C.Andersen/Nene 6.00 15.00
4 A.Miller/R.Fernandez 4.00 10.00
5 R.Rondo/R.Wallace 8.00 20.00
6 B.Diaw/R.Felton 4.00 10.00
7 B.Lopez/D.Harris 4.00 10.00
8 S.O'Neal /Z.Ilgauskas 8.00 20.00
9 J.Nelson/R.Lewis 4.00 10.00

2009-10 Absolute Memorabilia Team Trios NBA Materials
STATED PRINT RUN 40 TO 100 SETS
1 Atlanta Hawks/100 6.00 15.00
2 Golden State Warriors/100 125.00 300.00
3 Memphis Grizzlies/100 5.00 12.00
4 Philadelphia 76ers/100 5.00 12.00

BECKETT BASKETBALL

DOUBLE DOWN & SAVE BIG

GET A 1-YEAR SUBSCRIPTION TO BOTH
BECKETT BASKETBALL + BECKETT BASEBALL

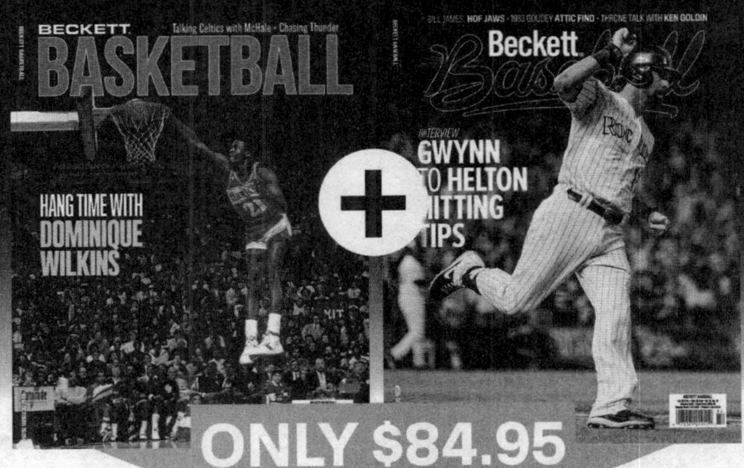

ONLY $84.95

SAVE 73% on the combined cover price
LIMITED TIME OFFER:
ACT NOW!

Subscribe online at www.beckettmedia.com/bkbb25
or Call us at 866-287-9383 (Mon - Fri, 9am - 6pm CDT)

JUST FILL IT ▸ CUT IT ▸ SEND IT

YES! Sign me up for a subscription to Beckett Basketball and Beckett Baseball for just $84.95
That's 24 issues for a total savings of $226.81 on the cover price.

Beckett Collectibles WHSL LBX Dept. #592 3451 Prescott Rd. Memphis, TN 38118

A85BKBB1

Method of Payment ☐ Check Enclosed ☐ Credit Card ☐ Money Order

Payment through Credit Card ☐ Visa ☐ MC ☐ AMEX ☐ Discover Name on Credit Card ____

Credit Card Number ☐☐☐☐☐☐☐☐☐☐☐☐☐☐☐☐ Expiration Date ___/___/___ CVV ☐☐☐

Subscriber Name: First ____ Middle ____ Last ____

Address ____

City ____ State ____ Zip ____

Phone ____ Email ____

Signature ____ Date ___/___/___

Allow 6 to 8 weeks for delivery of first issue. Outside U.S., add $140 per year for postage. Payment in U.S. funds only.

5 Boston Celtics/100 10.00 25.00
6 Minnesota Timberwolves/60 5.00 12.00
7 Oklahoma City Thunder/100 10.00 25.00
8 Utah Jazz/40 6.00 15.00
9 Houston Rockets/100 5.00 12.00

2009-10 Absolute Memorabilia Tools of the Trade Materials Prime Black Spectrum

STATED PRINT RUN ONE TO 25 SER.#'d SETS
*DOUBLE: .4X TO 1X BASE HI
DOUBLE PRINT RUN ONE TO 25 SETS
*TRIPLE: .6X TO 1.5X BASE HI
TRIPLE PRINT RUN ONE TO 25 SETS
2 Al Jefferson/25 4.00 10.00
3 Baron Davis/20 5.00 12.00
4 Brandon Roy/25 8.00 20.00
5 Carlos Boozer/25 5.00 12.00
8 D.J. Augustin/25 4.00 10.00
9 Elton Brand/25 5.00 12.00
10 Emeka Okafor/25 5.00 12.00
11 Kobe Bryant/25 20.00 50.00
12 LeBron James/25 20.00 50.00
15 Omri Casspi/25 4.00 10.00
16 Rajon Rondo/25 12.00 30.00
17 Ray Allen/25 8.00 20.00
20 Russell Westbrook/25 10.00 25.00
23 Stephen Curry/25 300.00 600.00

2009-10 Absolute Memorabilia Tools of the Trade Materials Prime Black Spectrum Jumbo

PRINT RUNS LISTED IN CHECKLIST
2 Al Jefferson/25 6.00 15.00
3 Baron Davis/25 12.00 30.00
5 Carlos Boozer/25 8.00 20.00
9 Elton Brand/25 8.00 20.00
10 Emeka Okafor/25 8.00 20.00
11 Kobe Bryant/25 60.00 150.00
15 Omri Casspi/25 6.00 15.00
16 Rajon Rondo/25 20.00 50.00
17 Ray Allen/25 15.00 40.00
20 Russell Westbrook/25 30.00 80.00
23 Stephen Curry/25 400.00 800.00

2009-10 Absolute Memorabilia Tools of the Trade Materials Red

STATED PRINT RUN 150 TO 249 SETS
*BLUE: .4X TO 1X BASE HI
BLUE STATED PRINT RUN 30 TO 100 SETS
2 Al Jefferson/249 2.00 5.00
3 Baron Davis/249 2.50 6.00
4 Brandon Roy/249 4.00 10.00
5 Carlos Boozer/249 2.50 6.00
7 Chris Kaman/150 2.50 6.00
8 D.J. Augustin/249 2.00 5.00
9 Elton Brand/249 2.50 6.00
10 Emeka Okafor/249 2.50 6.00
11 Kobe Bryant/249 12.00 30.00
12 LeBron James/249 10.00 25.00
14 Nene/249 2.50 6.00
15 Omri Casspi/249 2.00 5.00
16 Rajon Rondo/249 4.00 10.00
17 Ray Allen/249 5.00 12.00
20 Russell Westbrook/249 6.00 15.00
22 Shane Battier/249 3.00 8.00
23 Stephen Curry/249 100.00 250.00
24 T.J. Ford/249 2.00 5.00

2009-10 Absolute Memorabilia Retail Frequent Flyer

COMPLETE SET (20) 10.00 25.00
*RETAIL: .2X TO .5X HOBBY

2009-10 Absolute Memorabilia Retail Heroes

COMPLETE SET (15) 8.00 20.00
*RETAIL: .2X TO .5X HOBBY

2009-10 Absolute Memorabilia Retail Hoopla

COMPLETE SET (20) 10.00 25.00
*RETAIL: .2X TO .5X HOBBY

2009-10 Absolute Memorabilia Retail Marks of Fame

COMPLETE SET (10) 8.00 20.00
*RETAIL: .2X TO .5X HOBBY

2009-10 Absolute Memorabilia Retail NBA Icons

COMPLETE SET (15) 15.00 40.00
*RETAIL: .2X TO .5X HOBBY

2009-10 Absolute Memorabilia Retail Star Gazing

COMPLETE SET (35) 20.00 50.00
*RETAIL: .2X TO .5X HOBBY
10 Stephen Curry 200.00 500.00

2010-11 Absolute Memorabilia

COMP.SET w/o SPs (100) 25.00 60.00
ROOKIE PRINT RUN 499 SER.#'d SETS
JSY AU RC PRINT RUN 249 TO 499 SETS
EXCH.EXPIRATION 9/16/2012
1 Kevin Durant 3.00 8.00
2 Derrick Rose 1.50 4.00
3 Blake Griffin .75 2.00
4 Dwight Howard 1.00 2.50
5 Kobe Bryant 6.00 15.00
6 Dwyane Wade 1.50 4.00
7 Chris Paul 1.50 4.00
8 Deron Williams .60 1.50
9 Paul Pierce 1.25 3.00
10 Stephen Curry 12.00 30.00
11 Amare Stoudemire .75 2.00
12 Dirk Nowitzki 2.00 5.00
13 Steve Nash 1.50 4.00
14 LeBron James 6.00 15.00
15 Carmelo Anthony 1.25 3.00
16 Brandon Jennings .50 1.25
17 Kevin Love .75 2.00
18 Joakim Noah .75 2.00
19 Tyreke Evans .60 1.50
20 Monta Ellis .60 1.50
21 Kevin Martin .60 1.50
22 Tim Duncan 2.00 5.00
23 Joe Johnson .75 2.00
24 LaMarcus Aldridge .75 2.00
25 Brook Lopez .60 1.50
26 Ray Allen 1.25 3.00
27 Stephen Jackson .60 1.50
28 Pau Gasol 1.25 3.00
29 Michael Beasley .50 1.25
30 Danny Granger .50 1.25
31 Chris Bosh 1.00 2.50
32 Tony Parker 1.25 3.00
33 Jrue Holiday 1.00 2.50
34 Vince Carter 1.50 4.00
35 DeMar DeRozan 1.25 3.00
36 Daniel Gibson .50 1.25
37 Marc Gasol .75 2.00
38 David West .60 1.50
39 David Lee .50 1.25
40 Ben Gordon .60 1.50
41 Andrew Bogut .60 1.50
42 Rajon Rondo 1.00 2.50
43 Luis Scola .60 1.50
44 Caron Butler .60 1.50
45 Andray Blatche .50 1.25
46 Antawn Jamison .60 1.50
47 O.J. Mayo .50 1.25
48 Paul Millsap .60 1.50
49 Eric Gordon .60 1.50
50 Andre Iguodala .75 2.00
51 Al Horford .75 2.00
52 Kevin Garnett 2.00 5.00
53 Luol Deng .60 1.50
54 DeJuan Blair .50 1.25
55 Mike Dunleavy .50 1.25
56 Al Thornton .50 1.25
57 Lamar Odom .60 1.50
58 Andrea Bargnani .50 1.25
59 Jason Richardson .75 2.00
60 Russell Westbrook 1.25 3.00
61 Tracy McGrady 1.25 3.00
62 Gerald Wallace .60 1.50
63 Jamal Crawford .75 2.00
64 Al Jefferson .60 1.50
65 Marcus Camby .60 1.50
66 Jonny Flynn .50 1.25
67 Jeff Green .60 1.50
68 Trevor Ariza .50 1.25
69 Rudy Gay .75 2.00
70 Aaron Brooks .50 1.25
71 Jason Kidd 1.25 3.00
72 Danilo Gallinari .60 1.50
73 Ty Lawson .60 1.50
74 Elton Brand .60 1.50
75 Terrence Williams .50 1.25
76 Richard Jefferson .60 1.50
77 J.J. Redick .75 2.00
78 Chris Kaman .50 1.25
79 Gerald Henderson .50 1.25
80 Jeff Teague .50 1.25
81 Drew Gooden .60 1.50
82 Juwan Howard .60 1.50
83 Tyler Hansbrough .60 1.50
84 Derek Fisher .75 2.00
85 Boris Diaw .60 1.50
86 Anderson Varejao .50 1.25
87 Toney Douglas .50 1.25
88 Robin Lopez .50 1.25
89 Zach Randolph .75 2.00
90 Carl Landry .50 1.25
91 Rashard Lewis .60 1.50
92 Darren Collison .50 1.25
93 Sasha Vujacic .50 1.25
94 Nene .60 1.50
95 Shaquille O'Neal 3.00 8.00
96 Emeka Okafor .60 1.50
97 Brandon Roy 1.00 2.50
98 Josh Smith .50 1.25
99 Devin Harris .50 1.25
100 Rodrigue Beaubois .50 1.25
101 M.L. Carr 1.50 4.00
102 Patrick Ewing 2.50 6.00
103 World B. Free 1.25 3.00
104 Tim Hardaway 2.00 5.00
105 Sam Perkins 1.00 2.50
106 Kenny Smith 1.25 3.00
107 Walt Bellamy 2.00 5.00
108 Scott Skiles 1.25 3.00
109 Robert Reid 1.50 4.00
110 Mitch Richmond 2.00 5.00
111 Nick Anderson 1.25 3.00
112 Shawn Kemp 2.50 6.00
113 Gary Payton 2.50 6.00
114 John Stockton 2.50 6.00
115 Ron Harper 1.50 4.00
116 Elgin Baylor 3.00 8.00
117 Darryl Dawkins 1.50 4.00
118 Bernard King 2.00 5.00
119 Bill Laimbeer 1.25 3.00
120 Tree Rollins 1.00 2.50
121 Bill Sharman 1.50 4.00
122 Danny Manning 1.25 3.00
123 Charles D. Smith 1.50 4.00
124 Wilt Chamberlain 5.00 12.00
125 Dan Majerle 1.25 3.00
126 Jeff Hornacek 1.25 3.00
127 George McGinnis 1.50 4.00
128 John Starks 1.25 3.00
129 Toni Kukoc 1.50 4.00
130 Byron Scott 1.50 4.00
131 Gus Williams 1.00 2.50
132 Jalen Rose 1.25 3.00
133 Campy Russell 1.00 2.50
134 Elvin Hayes 2.00 5.00
135 Kurt Rambis 1.00 2.50
136 Jeremy Lin RC 6.00 15.00
137 Terrico White RC 1.00 2.50
138 Timofey Mozgov RC 1.25 3.00
139 Sherron Collins RC 1.00 2.50
140 Ishmael Smith RC 1.50 4.00
141 Pape Sy RC 1.00 2.50
142 Jeremy Evans RC 1.00 2.50
143 Tiago Splitter RC 1.25 3.00
144 Landry Fields RC 1.50 4.00
145 Solomon Alabi RC 1.00 2.50
146 Derrick Caracter RC 1.00 2.50
147 Hamady N'diaye RC 1.50 4.00
148 Gary Neal RC 1.25 3.00
149 Armon Johnson RC 1.00 2.50
150 Omer Asik RC 1.50 4.00
151 John Wall JSY AU/499 RC 30.00 80.00
152 Evan Turner JSY AU/299 RC 3.00 8.00
153 Derrick Favors JSY AU/499 RC 4.00 10.00
154 W.Johnson JSY AU/499 RC 2.50 6.00
155 D.Cousins JSY AU/499 RC 20.00 50.00
156 Ekpe Udoh JSY AU/499 RC 2.50 6.00
157 Greg Monroe JSY AU/499 RC 3.00 8.00
158 Al.Aminu JSY AU/399 RC 3.00 8.00
159 G.Hayward JSY AU/499 RC 20.00 50.00
160 Paul George JSY AU/499 RC 40.00 100.00
161 Cole Aldrich JSY AU/499 RC 2.50 6.00
162 Xavier Henry JSY AU/499 RC 2.50 6.00
163 Ed Davis JSY AU/499 RC 3.00 8.00
164 P.Patterson JSY AU/499 RC 3.00 8.00
165 Larry Sanders JSY AU/299 RC 2.50 6.00
166 Luke Babbitt JSY AU/499 RC 2.50 6.00
167 Kevin Seraphin JSY AU/249 RC 2.50 6.00
168 Eric Bledsoe JSY AU/499 RC 5.00 12.00
169 Avery Bradley JSY AU/499 RC 4.00 10.00
170 J.Anderson JSY AU/499 RC 2.50 6.00
171 Elliot Williams JSY AU/499 RC 2.50 6.00
172 Trevor Booker JSY AU/499 RC 2.50 6.00
173 Damion James JSY AU/299 RC 2.50 6.00
174 D.Jones JSY AU/299 RC 2.50 6.00
175 Q.Pondexter JSY AU/499 RC 2.50 6.00
176 J.Crawford JSY AU/499 RC 2.50 6.00
177 G.Vasquez JSY AU/499 RC 2.50 6.00
178 Daniel Orton JSY AU/499 RC 2.50 6.00
179 Lazar Hayward JSY AU/499 RC 2.50 6.00
180 Dexter Pittman JSY AU/499 RC 2.50 6.00
181 H.Whiteside JSY AU/499 RC 10.00 25.00
182 Andy Rautins JSY AU/499 RC 2.50 6.00
183 L.Stephenson JSY AU/499 RC 4.00 10.00
184 Devin Ebanks JSY AU/299 RC 2.50 6.00
185 Willie Warren JSY AU/299 RC 2.50 6.00

2010-11 Absolute Memorabilia Spectrum Gold

*GOLD 1-100: 1X TO 2.5X BASE HI
*GOLD 101-135: .5X TO 1.25X BASE HI
*GOLD 136-150: .6X TO 1.5X BASE HI
STATED PRINT RUN 100 SER.#'d SETS
136 Jeremy Lin 20.00 50.00

2010-11 Absolute Memorabilia Spectrum Platinum

*PLATINUM 1-100: 2X TO 5X BASE HI
*PLATINUM 101-135: 1X TO 2.5X BASE HI
*PLATINUM 136-150: 1X TO 2.5X BASE HI
STATED PRINT RUN 25 SER.#'d SETS
112 Shawn Kemp 75.00 150.00
113 Gary Payton 8.00 20.00

2010-11 Absolute Memorabilia Absolute Heroes

COMPLETE SET (15) 12.50 25.00
STATED PRINT RUN 399 SER.#'d SETS
*SPECTRUM: 1X TO 2.5X BASE HI
SPECTRUM PRINT RUN 100 SER.#'d SETS
1 Adrian Dantley 1.00 2.50
2 Alonzo Mourning 1.50 4.00
3 Bernard King 1.25 3.00
4 Bob Lanier 1.50 4.00
5 Detlef Schrempf 1.00 2.50
6 Glen Rice 1.00 2.50
7 Hakeem Olajuwon 2.00 5.00
8 Isiah Thomas 1.50 4.00
9 Karl Malone 2.00 5.00
10 Larry Bird 4.00 10.00
11 Larry Johnson 1.25 3.00
12 Magic Johnson 4.00 10.00
13 Mark Aguirre .75 2.00
14 Robert Parish 1.50 4.00
15 Toni Kukoc 1.00 2.50

2010-11 Absolute Memorabilia Absolute Heroes Materials

STATED PRINT RUN 25 TO 49 SER.#'d SETS
2 Alonzo Mourning/25 12.00 30.00
3 Bernard King/25 4.00 10.00
4 Bob Lanier/49 5.00 12.00
5 Detlef Schrempf/49 4.00 10.00
6 Glen Rice/49 3.00 8.00
7 Hakeem Olajuwon/49 6.00 15.00
8 Isiah Thomas/49 5.00 12.00
9 Karl Malone/49 6.00 15.00
10 Larry Bird/49 8.00 20.00
11 Larry Johnson/49 10.00 25.00
12 Magic Johnson/49 6.00 15.00
13 Mark Aguirre/49 2.50 6.00
14 Robert Parish/49 5.00 12.00
15 Toni Kukoc/49 5.00 12.00

2010-11 Absolute Memorabilia Absolute Heroes Materials Signatures

STATED PRINT RUN 5 TO 25 SER.#'d SETS
4 Bob Lanier/25 8.00 20.00
5 Detlef Schrempf/25 8.00 20.00
6 Glen Rice/25 8.00 20.00
8 Isiah Thomas/25 12.00 30.00
10 Larry Bird/25 50.00 120.00
11 Larry Johnson/25 20.00 50.00
13 Mark Aguirre/25 8.00 20.00
14 Robert Parish/25 10.00 25.00
15 Toni Kukoc/25 20.00 50.00

2010-11 Absolute Memorabilia Absolute Patches Jumbo Prime Spectrum

STATED PRINT RUN 5 TO 25 SER.#'d SETS
1 Bernard King/25 12.00 30.00
12 Robert Parish/25 20.00 50.00
13 Toni Kukoc/25 100.00 200.00

2010-11 Absolute Memorabilia Frequent Flyer

COMPLETE SET (20) 15.00 40.00
STATED PRINT RUN 399 SER.#'d SETS
*SPECTRUM: .6X TO 1.5X BASE HI
SPECTRUM PRINT RUN 100 SER.#'d SETS
1 LeBron James 8.00 20.00
2 Kobe Bryant 8.00 20.00
3 Blake Griffin 1.00 2.50
4 Nate Robinson .75 2.00
5 Shannon Brown .60 1.50
6 DeMar DeRozan 1.50 4.00
7 Dwight Howard 1.25 3.00
8 Vince Carter 2.00 5.00
9 Jason Richardson 1.25 3.00
10 Andre Iguodala 1.00 2.50
11 Josh Smith .60 1.50
12 Rudy Gay 1.00 2.50
13 Derrick Rose 2.00 5.00
14 Gerald Wallace .75 2.00
15 J.R. Smith 1.00 2.50
16 Amare Stoudemire 1.00 2.50
17 Corey Brewer .60 1.50
18 David Thompson 1.25 3.00
19 Clyde Drexler 2.00 5.00
20 Dominique Wilkins 2.00 5.00

2010-11 Absolute Memorabilia Frequent Flyer Materials Jersey Number

STATED PRINT RUN 5 TO 25 SER.#'d SETS
1 LeBron James/25 15.00 40.00
2 Kobe Bryant/25 15.00 40.00
3 Blake Griffin/25 4.00 10.00
5 Shannon Brown/25 2.50 6.00
6 DeMar DeRozan/25 6.00 15.00
7 Dwight Howard/25 5.00 12.00
11 Josh Smith/25 2.50 6.00
12 Rudy Gay/25 4.00 10.00
15 J.R. Smith/25 4.00 10.00
20 Dominique Wilkins/25 6.00 15.00

2010-11 Absolute Memorabilia Frequent Flyer Materials Jersey Number Signatures

STATED PRINT RUN 5 TO 25 SER.#'d SETS
2 Kobe Bryant/25 1,500.00 3,000.00
3 Blake Griffin/25 20.00 50.00
6 DeMar DeRozan/25 10.00 25.00
20 Dominique Wilkins/25 15.00 40.00

2010-11 Absolute Memorabilia Frequent Flyer Materials Signatures

STATED PRINT RUN 5 TO 25 SER.#'d SETS
2 Kobe Bryant/25 1,500.00 3,000.00
3 Blake Griffin/25 40.00 80.00
6 DeMar DeRozan/25 12.00 30.00
20 Dominique Wilkins/25 15.00 40.00

2010-11 Absolute Memorabilia Hoopla

COMPLETE SET (20) 15.00 40.00
STATED PRINT RUN 399 SER.#'d SETS
*SPECTRUM: .6X TO 1.5X BASE HI
SPECTRUM PRINT RUN 100 SER.#'d SETS
1 Andrew Bogut .75 2.00
2 Brook Lopez .75 2.00
3 Carmelo Anthony 1.50 4.00
4 Chauncey Billups 1.25 3.00
5 Chris Paul 2.00 5.00
6 Danilo Gallinari .75 2.00
7 Danny Granger .60 1.50
8 David Lee .60 1.50
9 Deron Williams .75 2.00
10 Dirk Nowitzki 2.50 6.00
11 Dwyane Wade 2.00 5.00
12 Gerald Wallace .75 2.00
13 Kobe Bryant 8.00 20.00
14 Kevin Durant 4.00 10.00
15 LeBron James 8.00 20.00
16 Monta Ellis .75 2.00
17 Derrick Rose 2.00 5.00
18 Rajon Rondo 1.25 3.00
19 Steve Nash 2.00 5.00
20 Tyreke Evans .75 2.00

2010-11 Absolute Memorabilia Hoopla Materials

STATED PRINT RUN 25 TO 49 SER.#'d SETS
1 Andrew Bogut/49 2.50 6.00
3 Carmelo Anthony/25 5.00 12.00
4 Chauncey Billups/49 4.00 10.00
5 Chris Paul/49 6.00 15.00
6 Danilo Gallinari/49 2.50 6.00
8 David Lee/49 2.00 5.00
9 Deron Williams/49 2.50 6.00
10 Dirk Nowitzki/49 8.00 20.00
11 Dwyane Wade/49 6.00 15.00
13 Kobe Bryant/49 12.00 30.00
14 Kevin Durant/49 12.00 30.00
15 LeBron James/49 10.00 25.00
17 Derrick Rose/49 6.00 15.00
18 Rajon Rondo/49 4.00 10.00
19 Steve Nash/49 6.00 15.00
20 Tyreke Evans/49 2.50 6.00

2010-11 Absolute Memorabilia Hoopla Materials Jersey Number

STATED PRINT RUN 5 TO 25 SER.#'d SETS
1 Andrew Bogut/25 3.00 8.00
3 Carmelo Anthony/25 6.00 15.00
4 Chauncey Billups/25 5.00 12.00
5 Chris Paul/25 8.00 20.00
8 David Lee/25 2.50 6.00
9 Deron Williams/25 3.00 8.00
10 Dirk Nowitzki/25 10.00 25.00
11 Dwyane Wade/25 8.00 20.00
13 Kobe Bryant/25 20.00 50.00
14 Kevin Durant/25 15.00 40.00
15 LeBron James/25 12.00 30.00
17 Derrick Rose/25 8.00 20.00
18 Rajon Rondo/25 5.00 12.00
20 Tyreke Evans/25 3.00 8.00

2010-11 Absolute Memorabilia Hoopla Materials Jersey Number Signatures

STATED PRINT RUN 5 TO 25 SER.#'d SETS
1 Andrew Bogut/25 15.00 40.00
13 Kobe Bryant/25 1,500.00 3,000.00
14 Kevin Durant/25 100.00 200.00

2010-11 Absolute Memorabilia Hoopla Materials Signatures

STATED PRINT RUN 5 TO 25 SER.#'d SETS
13 Kobe Bryant/25 1,500.00 3,000.00
14 Kevin Durant/25 100.00 200.00

2010-11 Absolute Memorabilia Marks of Fame

COMPLETE SET (10) 8.00 20.00
STATED PRINT RUN 399 SER.#'d SETS
*SPECTRUM: .75X TO 2X BASE HI
SPECTRUM PRINT RUN 100 SER.#'d SETS
1 Magic Johnson 4.00 10.00
2 John Stockton 1.50 4.00
3 Hakeem Olajuwon 2.00 5.00
4 Isiah Thomas 1.50 4.00
5 Kareem Abdul-Jabbar 3.00 8.00
6 Karl Malone 2.00 5.00
7 Moses Malone 1.50 4.00
8 Robert Parish 1.50 4.00
9 Scottie Pippen 2.50 6.00
10 Xavier McDaniel .75 2.00

2010-11 Absolute Memorabilia Marks of Fame Materials

STATED PRINT RUN 49 SER.#'d SETS
1 Magic Johnson 6.00 15.00
2 John Stockton 6.00 15.00
3 Hakeem Olajuwon 8.00 20.00
4 Isiah Thomas 6.00 15.00
5 Kareem Abdul-Jabbar 12.00 30.00
6 Karl Malone 8.00 20.00
7 Moses Malone 6.00 15.00
8 Robert Parish 6.00 15.00
9 Scottie Pippen 10.00 25.00
10 Xavier McDaniel 3.00 8.00

2010-11 Absolute Memorabilia Marks of Fame Materials Signatures

STATED PRINT RUN 5 TO 25 SER.#'d SETS
4 Isiah Thomas/25 15.00 40.00
8 Robert Parish/25 10.00 25.00

2010-11 Absolute Memorabilia Materials Prime Spectrum

STATED PRINT RUN ONE TO 25 SER.#'d SETS
3 Blake Griffin/25 6.00 15.00
9 Paul Pierce/25 10.00 25.00
13 Steve Nash/25 8.00 20.00
22 Tim Duncan/25 15.00 40.00
24 LaMarcus Aldridge/25 6.00 15.00
26 Ray Allen/25 8.00 20.00
29 Michael Beasley/25 4.00 10.00
32 Tony Parker/25 10.00 25.00
33 Jrue Holiday/25 8.00 20.00
35 DeMar DeRozan/25 10.00 25.00
38 David West/25 5.00 12.00
41 Andrew Bogut/25 5.00 12.00
43 Luis Scola/25 5.00 12.00
44 Caron Butler/25 5.00 12.00
47 O.J. Mayo/25 4.00 10.00
50 Andre Iguodala/25 6.00 15.00
51 Al Horford/25 6.00 15.00
52 Kevin Garnett/25 15.00 40.00
53 Luol Deng/25 5.00 12.00
54 DeJuan Blair/25 4.00 10.00
55 Mike Dunleavy/25 4.00 10.00
66 Jonny Flynn/25 4.00 10.00
71 Jason Kidd/25 10.00 25.00
73 Ty Lawson/25 4.00 10.00
74 Elton Brand/25 5.00 12.00
75 Terrence Williams/25 4.00 10.00
76 Richard Jefferson/25 5.00 12.00
77 J.J. Redick/25 6.00 15.00
78 Chris Kaman/25 4.00 10.00
79 Gerald Henderson/25 4.00 10.00
80 Jeff Teague/25 4.00 10.00
83 Tyler Hansbrough/25 4.00 10.00
85 Boris Diaw/25 5.00 12.00
87 Toney Douglas/25 4.00 10.00
94 Nene/25 5.00 12.00
95 Shaquille O'Neal/25 20.00 50.00
98 Josh Smith/25 4.00 10.00
99 Devin Harris/25 4.00 10.00
100 Rodrigue Beaubois/25 4.00 10.00
102 Patrick Ewing/25 15.00 40.00
105 Sam Perkins/25 4.00 10.00
110 Mitch Richmond/25 10.00 25.00
111 Nick Anderson/25 5.00 12.00
112 Shawn Kemp/25 75.00 200.00
114 John Stockton/25 15.00 40.00
118 Bernard King/25 8.00 20.00
126 Jeff Hornacek/25 5.00 12.00
129 Toni Kukoc/25 10.00 25.00
132 Jalen Rose/25 8.00 20.00
138 Timofey Mozgov/25 5.00 12.00

2010-11 Absolute Memorabilia NBA Icons

COMPLETE SET (15) 15.00 30.00
STATED PRINT RUN 399 SER.#'d SETS
*SPECTRUM: .75X TO 2X BASE HI
SPECTRUM PRINT RUN 100 SER.#'d SETS
1 Larry Bird 4.00 10.00
2 Kareem Abdul-Jabbar 3.00 8.00
3 Patrick Ewing 1.50 4.00
4 David Robinson 2.00 5.00
5 Gary Payton 1.50 4.00
6 John Stockton 1.50 4.00
7 Magic Johnson 4.00 10.00
8 Kevin Durant 4.00 10.00
9 Kobe Bryant 8.00 20.00
10 Amare Stoudemire 1.00 2.50
11 Rajon Rondo 1.25 3.00
12 Carmelo Anthony 1.50 4.00
13 Chris Bosh 1.25 3.00
14 Steve Nash 2.00 5.00
15 Deron Williams .75 2.00

2010-11 Absolute Memorabilia NBA Icons Materials

STATED PRINT RUN 25 TO 49 SER.#'d SETS
1 Larry Bird/49 12.00 30.00
2 Kareem Abdul-Jabbar/49 10.00 25.00
3 Patrick Ewing/49 8.00 20.00
4 David Robinson/49 6.00 15.00
6 John Stockton/49 5.00 12.00
7 Magic Johnson/49 6.00 15.00
8 Kevin Durant/49 12.00 30.00
9 Kobe Bryant/49 12.00 30.00
10 Amare Stoudemire/49 3.00 8.00
11 Rajon Rondo/49 4.00 10.00
12 Carmelo Anthony/25 5.00 12.00
13 Chris Bosh/49 4.00 10.00
14 Steve Nash/49 6.00 15.00
15 Deron Williams/49 2.50 6.00

2010-11 Absolute Memorabilia NBA Icons Materials Signatures

STATED PRINT RUN 5 TO 25 SER.#'d SETS
1 Larry Bird/25 50.00 120.00
8 Kevin Durant/25 100.00 200.00
9 Kobe Bryant/25 1,500.00 3,000.00

2010-11 Absolute Memorabilia Panini All Stars Rack Pack

1 Dwight Howard 2.50 6.00
2 Dwyane Wade 4.00 10.00
3 Kevin Garnett 5.00 12.00
4 LeBron James 15.00 40.00
5 Rajon Rondo 2.50 6.00
6 Amare Stoudemire 2.00 5.00
7 Derrick Rose 4.00 10.00
8 John Wall 6.00 15.00
9 Ray Allen 3.00 8.00
10 Chris Bosh 2.50 6.00
11 Paul Pierce 3.00 8.00
12 Shaquille O'Neal 8.00 20.00
13 Joakim Noah 2.00 5.00
14 Carmelo Anthony 3.00 8.00
15 Chris Paul 4.00 10.00
16 Kevin Durant 8.00 20.00
17 Kobe Bryant 15.00 40.00
18 Yao Ming 4.00 10.00
19 Andrew Bynum 1.25 3.00
20 Blake Griffin 2.00 5.00
21 Dirk Nowitzki 5.00 12.00
22 Manu Ginobili 4.00 10.00
23 Tim Duncan 5.00 12.00
24 Nene 1.50 4.00
25 Pau Gasol 3.00 8.00
26 Steve Nash 4.00 10.00
27 Bob Cousy 5.00 12.00
28 Elvin Hayes 2.50 6.00
29 Jerry West 4.00 10.00
30 John Havlicek 4.00 10.00
31 Kareem Abdul-Jabbar 6.00 15.00
32 Karl Malone 4.00 10.00
33 Larry Bird 8.00 20.00
34 Magic Johnson 8.00 20.00
35 Moses Malone 3.00 8.00

2010-11 Absolute Memorabilia Rookie Materials Jumbo Jersey Numbers Basketball

STATED PRINT RUN 25 SER.#'d SETS
151 John Wall 10.00 25.00
152 Evan Turner 4.00 10.00
153 Derrick Favors 5.00 12.00
154 Wesley Johnson 4.00 10.00
155 DeMarcus Cousins 12.00 30.00
156 Ekpe Udoh 3.00 8.00
157 Greg Monroe 4.00 10.00
158 Al-Farouq Aminu 4.00 10.00
159 Gordon Hayward 12.00 30.00
160 Paul George 25.00 60.00
161 Cole Aldrich 3.00 8.00
162 Xavier Henry 3.00 8.00
163 Ed Davis 4.00 10.00
164 Patrick Patterson 4.00 10.00
165 Larry Sanders 3.00 8.00
166 Luke Babbitt 3.00 8.00
167 Kevin Seraphin 3.00 8.00
168 Eric Bledsoe 6.00 15.00
169 Avery Bradley 5.00 12.00
170 James Anderson 3.00 8.00
171 Elliot Williams 3.00 8.00
172 Trevor Booker 3.00 8.00
173 Damion James 3.00 8.00
174 Dominique Jones 3.00 8.00
175 Quincy Pondexter 3.00 8.00
176 Jordan Crawford 3.00 8.00
177 Greivis Vasquez 3.00 8.00
178 Daniel Orton 3.00 8.00
179 Lazar Hayward 3.00 8.00
180 Dexter Pittman 3.00 8.00
181 Hassan Whiteside 6.00 15.00
182 Andy Rautins 3.00 8.00
183 Lance Stephenson 5.00 12.00
184 Devin Ebanks 3.00 8.00
185 Willie Warren 3.00 8.00

2010-11 Absolute Memorabilia Rookie Materials Jumbo Jersey Numbers Basketball Signatures

STATED PRINT RUN 25 SER.#'d SETS
151 John Wall 60.00 150.00
152 Evan Turner 8.00 20.00
153 Derrick Favors 10.00 25.00
154 Wesley Johnson 6.00 15.00
155 DeMarcus Cousins 20.00 50.00
156 Ekpe Udoh 6.00 15.00
157 Greg Monroe 8.00 20.00
158 Al-Farouq Aminu 8.00 20.00
159 Gordon Hayward 25.00 60.00
160 Paul George 60.00 150.00
161 Cole Aldrich 6.00 15.00
162 Xavier Henry 6.00 15.00
163 Ed Davis 8.00 20.00
164 Patrick Patterson 8.00 20.00
165 Larry Sanders 6.00 15.00
166 Luke Babbitt 6.00 15.00
167 Kevin Seraphin 6.00 15.00
168 Eric Bledsoe 12.00 30.00
169 Avery Bradley 10.00 25.00
170 James Anderson 6.00 15.00
171 Elliot Williams 6.00 15.00
172 Trevor Booker 6.00 15.00
173 Damion James 6.00 15.00
174 Dominique Jones 6.00 15.00
175 Quincy Pondexter 6.00 15.00
176 Jordan Crawford 6.00 15.00
177 Greivis Vasquez 6.00 15.00
178 Daniel Orton 6.00 15.00
179 Lazar Hayward 6.00 15.00
180 Dexter Pittman 6.00 15.00
181 Hassan Whiteside 12.00 30.00
182 Andy Rautins 6.00 15.00
183 Lance Stephenson 10.00 25.00
184 Devin Ebanks 6.00 15.00
185 Willie Warren 6.00 15.00

2010-11 Absolute Memorabilia Spectrum Signatures Gold

STATED PRINT RUN ONE TO 199 SER.#'d SETS
1 Kevin Durant/25 100.00 250.00
3 Blake Griffin/99 30.00 80.00
5 Kobe Bryant/25 1,500.00 3,000.00
8 Deron Williams/25 10.00 25.00
10 Stephen Curry/49 500.00 1,000.00
16 Brandon Jennings/99 4.00 10.00
18 Joakim Noah/99 8.00 20.00
19 Tyreke Evans/15 10.00 25.00
24 LaMarcus Aldridge/99 8.00 20.00
30 Danny Granger/99 4.00 10.00
31 Chris Bosh/25 20.00 50.00
33 Jrue Holiday/99 6.00 15.00
35 DeMar DeRozan/199 12.00 30.00
39 David Lee/99 4.00 10.00
40 Ben Gordon/199 4.00 10.00
44 Caron Butler/99 4.00 10.00
47 O.J. Mayo/49 4.00 10.00
51 Al Horford/49 4.00 10.00
54 DeJuan Blair/99 4.00 10.00
55 Mike Dunleavy/99 4.00 10.00
56 Al Thornton/199 4.00 10.00
57 Lamar Odom/99 8.00 20.00
58 Andrea Bargnani/99 4.00 10.00
60 Russell Westbrook/25 25.00 60.00
62 Gerald Wallace/199 4.00 10.00
64 Al Jefferson/25 4.00 10.00
70 Aaron Brooks/199 4.00 10.00
71 Jason Kidd/49 10.00 25.00
73 Ty Lawson/35 4.00 10.00
74 Elton Brand/25 5.00 12.00
75 Terrence Williams/99 4.00 10.00
77 J.J. Redick/99 5.00 12.00
78 Chris Kaman/99 4.00 10.00
79 Gerald Henderson/199 4.00 10.00
80 Jeff Teague/99 4.00 10.00
83 Tyler Hansbrough/99 4.00 10.00
84 Derek Fisher/99 8.00 20.00
85 Boris Diaw/199 4.00 10.00
87 Toney Douglas/199 4.00 10.00
88 Robin Lopez/99 4.00 10.00
89 Zach Randolph/99 4.00 10.00
90 Carl Landry/199 4.00 10.00
96 Emeka Okafor/99 4.00 10.00
97 Brandon Roy/99 4.00 10.00
99 Devin Harris/99 4.00 10.00
100 Rodrigue Beaubois/143 4.00 10.00
104 Tim Hardaway/49 8.00 20.00
105 Sam Perkins/99 4.00 10.00
121 Bill Sharman/99 4.00 10.00
122 Danny Manning/99 4.00 10.00
125 Dan Majerle/99 8.00 20.00
126 Jeff Hornacek/49 5.00 12.00
127 George McGinnis/49 4.00 10.00
128 John Starks/99 12.00 30.00
129 Toni Kukoc/25 20.00 50.00
130 Byron Scott/25 5.00 12.00
131 Gus Williams/99 4.00 10.00
133 Campy Russell/99 4.00 10.00
135 Kurt Rambis/49 6.00 15.00
136 Jeremy Lin/199 75.00 200.00
137 Terrico White/199 2.00 5.00
138 Timofey Mozgov/199 2.50 6.00
139 Sherron Collins/199 2.00 5.00
140 Ishmael Smith/199 3.00 8.00
142 Jeremy Evans/199 2.00 5.00
143 Tiago Splitter/199 2.50 6.00
144 Landry Fields/199 2.00 5.00
146 Derrick Caracter/199 2.00 5.00
149 Armon Johnson/199 2.00 5.00
150 Omer Asik/199 3.00 8.00

2010-11 Absolute Memorabilia Spectrum Signatures Platinum

*PLATINUM STARS: .6X TO 1.5X GOLD
*PLATINUM RCs: .75X TO 2X GOLD
STATED PRINT RUN ONE TO 25 SER.#'d SETS
3 Blake Griffin/25 50.00 120.00
57 Lamar Odom/25 10.00 25.00
72 Danilo Gallinari/25 6.00 15.00
77 J.J. Redick/25 10.00 25.00
92 Darren Collison/25 8.00 20.00
97 Brandon Roy/25 8.00 20.00
117 Darryl Dawkins/25 6.00 15.00
127 George McGinnis/25 8.00 20.00
128 John Starks/25 15.00 40.00
136 Jeremy Lin/25 300.00 600.00

2010-11 Absolute Memorabilia Star Gazing

COMPLETE SET (35) 30.00 60.00
STATED PRINT RUN 399 SER.#'d SETS
*SPECTRUM: .6X TO 1.5X BASE HI
SPECTRUM PRINT RUN 100 SER.#'d SETS
1 Kobe Bryant 8.00 20.00
2 Kevin Durant 4.00 10.00
3 Dwyane Wade 2.00 5.00
4 Amare Stoudemire 1.00 2.50
5 Dwight Howard 1.25 3.00
6 LeBron James 8.00 20.00
7 Pau Gasol 1.50 4.00
8 Rajon Rondo 1.25 3.00
9 Carmelo Anthony 1.50 4.00
10 Monta Ellis .75 2.00
11 Dirk Nowitzki 2.50 6.00
12 Derrick Rose 2.00 5.00
13 Kevin Martin .75 2.00
14 Russell Westbrook 1.50 4.00
15 Eric Gordon .75 2.00
16 Luis Scola .75 2.00
17 Michael Beasley .75 2.00
18 Rudy Gay 1.00 2.50
19 Deron Williams .75 2.00
20 Paul Pierce 1.50 4.00
21 Danny Granger .60 1.50
22 Paul Millsap .75 2.00
23 Kevin Garnett 2.50 6.00
24 Chris Paul 2.00 5.00
25 Brandon Roy 1.25 3.00
26 Kevin Love 1.00 2.50
27 Chris Bosh 1.25 3.00
28 Tony Parker 1.50 4.00
29 Steve Nash 2.00 5.00
30 Tyreke Evans .75 2.00
31 Joe Johnson 1.00 2.50
32 Ray Allen 1.50 4.00
33 Zach Randolph 1.00 2.50
34 Gerald Wallace .75 2.00
35 Brandon Jennings .60 1.50

2010-11 Absolute Memorabilia Star Gazing Materials Jumbo Jersey Number

STATED PRINT RUN 2 TO 25 SER.#'d SETS
1 Kobe Bryant/25 15.00 40.00
2 Kevin Durant/25 20.00 50.00
3 Dwyane Wade/25 10.00 25.00
5 Dwight Howard/25 6.00 15.00
6 LeBron James/25 15.00 40.00
7 Pau Gasol/25 8.00 20.00
8 Rajon Rondo/25 8.00 20.00
11 Dirk Nowitzki/25 12.00 30.00
12 Derrick Rose/25 10.00 25.00
14 Russell Westbrook/25 8.00 20.00
16 Luis Scola/25 4.00 10.00

19 Deron Williams/25 4.00 10.00
20 Paul Pierce/25 8.00 20.00
23 Kevin Garnett/25 12.00 30.00
24 Chris Paul/25 10.00 25.00
25 Brandon Roy/25 6.00 15.00
26 Kevin Love/25 5.00 12.00
27 Chris Bosh/25 6.00 15.00
28 Tony Parker/25 8.00 20.00
30 Tyreke Evans/25 4.00 10.00
31 Joe Johnson/25 5.00 12.00
35 Brandon Jennings/25 3.00 8.00

2010-11 Absolute Memorabilia Star Gazing Materials Jumbo Jersey Number Signatures

STATED PRINT RUN 5 TO 25 SER.#'d SETS
1 Kobe Bryant/25 1,500.00 3,000.00
2 Kevin Durant/25 75.00 200.00
14 Russell Westbrook/25 50.00 120.00
25 Brandon Roy/25 10.00 25.00
35 Brandon Jennings/25 12.50 30.00

2010-11 Absolute Memorabilia Star Gazing Materials

STATED PRINT RUN 5 TO 49 SER.#'d SETS
1 Kobe Bryant/49 10.00 25.00
2 Kevin Durant/49 12.00 30.00
3 Dwyane Wade/49 6.00 15.00
4 Amare Stoudemire/49 3.00 8.00
5 Dwight Howard/49 4.00 10.00
6 LeBron James/49 10.00 25.00
7 Pau Gasol/49 5.00 12.00
8 Rajon Rondo/49 4.00 10.00
9 Carmelo Anthony/25 5.00 12.00
11 Dirk Nowitzki/49 8.00 20.00
12 Derrick Rose/49 6.00 15.00
14 Russell Westbrook/49 5.00 12.00
16 Luis Scola/49 2.50 6.00
17 Michael Beasley/49 2.00 5.00
18 Rudy Gay/49 3.00 8.00
19 Deron Williams/49 2.50 6.00
20 Paul Pierce/49 5.00 12.00
23 Kevin Garnett/49 8.00 20.00
24 Chris Paul/49 6.00 15.00
25 Brandon Roy/49 4.00 10.00
26 Kevin Love/49 3.00 8.00
27 Chris Bosh/49 4.00 10.00
28 Tony Parker/49 5.00 12.00
29 Steve Nash/49 6.00 15.00
30 Tyreke Evans/49 2.50 6.00
31 Joe Johnson/49 3.00 8.00
32 Ray Allen/49 5.00 12.00
35 Brandon Jennings/49 2.00 5.00

2010-11 Absolute Memorabilia Star Gazing Materials Signatures

STATED PRINT RUN 5 TO 25 SER.#'d SETS
1 Kobe Bryant/25 1,500.00 3,000.00
2 Kevin Durant/25 60.00 120.00
14 Russell Westbrook/25 40.00 100.00
25 Brandon Roy/25 10.00 25.00
35 Brandon Jennings/25 8.00 20.00

2010-11 Absolute Memorabilia Team Quads TEAM Die Cut Materials

STATED PRINT RUN 100 SER.#'d SETS
1 Los Angeles Lakers 15.00 40.00
2 Boston Celtics 12.00 30.00
3 Dallas Mavericks 8.00 20.00
4 Orlando Magic 6.00 15.00
5 San Antonio Spurs 6.00 15.00

2010-11 Absolute Memorabilia Team Tandems Materials

STATED PRINT RUN 100 SER.#'d SETS
1 L.James/D.Wade 12.00 30.00
2 R.Rondo/P.Pierce 6.00 15.00
3 P.Gasol/K.Bryant 8.00 20.00
4 T.Parker/T.Duncan 4.00 10.00
5 R.Westbrook/K.Durant 10.00 25.00
6 S.Curry/D.Lee 6.00 15.00
7 D.Rose/J.Noah 10.00 25.00
8 B.Jennings/A.Bogut 4.00 10.00
9 C.Anthony/C.Billups 4.00 10.00
10 D.Nowitzki/J.Kidd 6.00 15.00

2010-11 Absolute Memorabilia Team Trios NBA Materials

STATED PRINT RUN 40 TO 100 SER.#'d SETS
1 Bryant/Gasol/Odom 10.00 25.00
2 Wade/James/Bosh 15.00 40.00
3 Pierce/Garnett/Rondo 12.00 30.00
4 Johnson/Smith/Horford 5.00 12.00
5 Anthony/Billups/Nene 5.00 12.00
6 Paul/West/Okafor 5.00 12.00
7 Curry/Biedrins/Lee/40 8.00 20.00
8 Rose/Noah/Deng 12.50 30.00
9 Nowitzki/Kidd/Terry 8.00 20.00
10 Williams/Kirilenko/Jefferson 5.00 12.00

2010-11 Absolute Memorabilia Tools of the Trade Materials Jumbo

STATED PRINT RUN ONE TO 99 SER.#'d SETS
1 Kevin Durant/99 15.00 40.00
2 Brandon Jennings/99 2.50 6.00
3 Derrick Rose/49 8.00 20.00
4 LeBron James/49 15.00 40.00
5 Kobe Bryant/49 30.00 80.00
6 Deron Williams/99 3.00 8.00
7 Amare Stoudemire/49 4.00 10.00
8 Jonny Flynn/99 3.00 8.00
9 Chris Paul/49 8.00 20.00
10 Gary Payton/49 6.00 15.00
11 Anfernee Hardaway/99 12.00 30.00
12 Brook Lopez/99 3.00 8.00
13 Blake Griffin/99 4.00 10.00
14 LaMarcus Aldridge/99 4.00 10.00
15 Rajon Rondo/49 6.00 15.00
16 Dan Majerle/49 6.00 15.00
17 Mark Price/49 8.00 20.00
18 Dwight Howard/99 5.00 12.00
19 Ben Gordon/25 3.00 8.00
20 Stephen Curry/49 30.00 80.00
21 Carmelo Anthony/49 6.00 15.00
22 Dennis Rodman/99 10.00 25.00
23 Paul Pierce/99 6.00 15.00
24 Kevin Love/99 5.00 12.00
25 David Robinson/49 8.00 20.00
26 Hakeem Olajuwon/49 8.00 20.00
27 Joakim Noah/25 5.00 12.00
28 Dwyane Wade/99 8.00 20.00
29 Charles Oakley/99 4.00 10.00
30 Alonzo Mourning/25 15.00 40.00
31 Dirk Nowitzki/99 8.00 20.00
32 Steve Nash/99 5.00 12.00

2010-11 Absolute Memorabilia Tools of the Trade Materials Jumbo Jersey Numbers

STATED PRINT RUN ONE TO 99 SER.#'d SETS
1 Kevin Durant/99 15.00 40.00
2 Brandon Jennings/99 2.50 6.00
3 Derrick Rose/25 8.00 20.00
4 LeBron James/49 25.00 60.00
5 Kobe Bryant/49 15.00 40.00
6 Deron Williams/99 3.00 8.00
7 Amare Stoudemire/49 4.00 10.00
8 Jonny Flynn/49 3.00 8.00
9 Chris Paul/25 8.00 20.00
10 Gary Payton/49 6.00 15.00
11 Anfernee Hardaway/99 12.00 30.00
13 Blake Griffin/99 4.00 10.00
14 LaMarcus Aldridge/99 4.00 10.00
15 Rajon Rondo/49 6.00 15.00
16 Dan Majerle/25 10.00 25.00
17 Mark Price/49 10.00 25.00
18 Dwight Howard/99 5.00 12.00
21 Carmelo Anthony/49 6.00 15.00
22 Dennis Rodman/49 10.00 25.00
23 Paul Pierce/99 6.00 15.00
24 Kevin Love/99 4.00 10.00
25 David Robinson/25 8.00 20.00
26 Hakeem Olajuwon/49 8.00 20.00
27 Joakim Noah/25 4.00 10.00
28 Dwyane Wade/99 8.00 20.00
29 Charles Oakley/25 4.00 10.00
30 Alonzo Mourning/25 15.00 40.00
31 Dirk Nowitzki/49 6.00 15.00
32 Steve Nash/99 4.00 10.00

2010-11 Absolute Memorabilia Tools of the Trade Materials Prime Black Double Spectrum

STATED PRINT RUN ONE TO 25 SER.#'d SETS
11 Anfernee Hardaway/25 30.00 80.00
13 Blake Griffin/25 25.00 60.00
14 LaMarcus Aldridge/25 8.00 20.00
17 Mark Price/25 15.00 40.00
23 Paul Pierce/25 12.00 30.00
29 Charles Oakley/25 10.00 25.00

2010-11 Absolute Memorabilia Tools of the Trade Materials Prime Black Spectrum

STATED PRINT RUN ONE TO 25 SER.#'d SETS
11 Anfernee Hardaway/25 25.00 60.00
13 Blake Griffin/25 25.00 60.00
14 LaMarcus Aldridge/25 8.00 20.00
17 Mark Price/25 10.00 25.00
23 Paul Pierce/25 10.00 25.00
29 Charles Oakley/25 6.00 15.00

2010-11 Absolute Memorabilia Tools of the Trade Materials Prime Black Triple Spectrum

STATED PRINT RUN ONE TO 25 SER.#'d SETS
8 Jonny Flynn/25 6.00 15.00
11 Anfernee Hardaway/25 20.00 50.00
13 Blake Griffin/25 30.00 80.00
14 LaMarcus Aldridge/25 10.00 25.00
17 Mark Price/25 15.00 40.00
23 Paul Pierce/25 15.00 40.00
29 Charles Oakley/25 15.00 40.00

2015-16 Absolute Memorabilia

101-160 PRINT RUN 999 SER.#'d SETS
161-200 PRINT RUN 999 SER.#'d SETS
1 Jonas Valanciunas .50 1.25
2 Deron Williams .50 1.25
3 Dwyane Wade 1.25 3.00
4 Harrison Barnes .50 1.25
5 Anthony Davis 1.50 4.00
6 DeAndre Jordan .50 1.25
7 Nikola Vucevic .50 1.25
8 Al Horford .60 1.50
9 Mason Plumlee .40 1.00
10 Kemba Walker .60 1.50
11 Kyle Lowry .60 1.50
12 Dirk Nowitzki 1.50 4.00
13 Goran Dragic .60 1.50
14 Klay Thompson 1.50 4.00
15 Jrue Holiday .75 2.00
16 Paul Pierce 1.00 2.50
17 Tobias Harris .50 1.25
18 Jeff Teague .40 1.00
19 DeMarcus Cousins .60 1.50
20 Nicolas Batum .40 1.00
21 Terrence Ross .50 1.25
22 Wesley Matthews .40 1.00
23 Giannis Antetokounmpo 3.00 8.00
24 Stephen Curry 5.00 12.00
25 Tyreke Evans .50 1.25
26 Jordan Clarkson .60 1.50
27 Victor Oladipo .60 1.50
28 Kyle Korver .50 1.25
29 Rajon Rondo .75 2.00
30 Derrick Rose 1.00 2.50
31 Gordon Hayward .60 1.50
32 Danilo Gallinari .50 1.25
33 Greg Monroe .60 1.50
34 Dwight Howard .75 2.00
35 Arron Afflalo .40 1.00
36 Kobe Bryant 5.00 12.00
37 Nerlens Noel .40 1.00
38 Evan Turner .40 1.00
39 Rudy Gay .60 1.50
40 Jimmy Butler 1.25 3.00
41 Rudy Gobert .75 2.00
42 Jusuf Nurkic .50 1.25
43 Jabari Parker .60 1.50
44 James Harden 1.25 3.00
45 Carmelo Anthony 1.00 2.50
46 Roy Hibbert .50 1.25
47 Robert Covington .50 1.25
48 Jared Sullinger .40 1.00
49 Kawhi Leonard 2.00 5.00
50 Joakim Noah .40 1.00
51 Trey Burke .40 1.00
52 Kenneth Faried .50 1.25
53 Michael Carter-Williams .40 1.00
54 Ty Lawson .40 1.00
55 Robin Lopez .40 1.00
56 Marc Gasol .60 1.50
57 Brandon Knight .40 1.00
58 Marcus Smart .75 2.00
59 LaMarcus Aldridge .60 1.50
60 Pau Gasol 1.00 2.50
61 Bradley Beal .75 2.00
62 Andre Drummond .60 1.50
63 Andrew Wiggins .75 2.00
64 Monta Ellis .50 1.25
65 Kevin Durant 2.50 6.00
66 Mike Conley .60 1.50
67 Eric Bledsoe .50 1.25
68 Bojan Bogdanovic .50 1.25
69 Manu Ginobili 1.25 3.00
70 Kevin Love .60 1.50
71 John Wall .75 2.00
72 Brandon Jennings .40 1.00
73 Kevin Garnett 1.50 4.00
74 Paul George 1.00 2.50
75 Russell Westbrook 1.00 2.50
76 Vince Carter 1.25 3.00
77 Tyson Chandler .50 1.25
78 Brook Lopez .60 1.50
79 Tim Duncan 1.50 4.00
80 Kyrie Irving 1.25 3.00
81 Marcin Gortat .40 1.00
82 Reggie Jackson .50 1.25
83 Ricky Rubio .50 1.25
84 Blake Griffin .60 1.50
85 Serge Ibaka .50 1.25
86 Zach Randolph .60 1.50
87 Damian Lillard 1.50 4.00
88 Joe Johnson .50 1.25
89 Tony Parker 1.00 2.50
90 LeBron James 5.00 12.00
91 Nene .50 1.25
92 Draymond Green .75 2.00
93 Zach LaVine 1.50 4.00
94 Chris Paul 1.25 3.00
95 Elfrid Payton .50 1.25
96 Chris Bosh .75 2.00
97 Gerald Henderson .40 1.00
98 Al Jefferson .40 1.00
99 DeMar DeRozan .75 2.00
100 Chandler Parsons .40 1.00
101 Bill Russell 2.50 6.00
102 Rick Fox .60 1.50
103 Dell Curry .60 1.50
104 Shareef Abdur-Rahim .60 1.50
105 Drazen Petrovic .75 2.00
106 Mitch Richmond 1.00 2.50
107 James Worthy 1.25 3.00
108 John Stockton 1.50 4.00
109 Allan Houston .60 1.50
110 Magic Johnson 3.00 8.00
111 Bob Cousy 1.25 3.00
112 Rik Smits .60 1.50
113 Dennis Johnson .60 1.50
114 Shawn Kemp 1.25 3.00
115 Elgin Baylor 1.50 4.00
116 Moses Malone 1.25 3.00
117 Jason Kidd 1.25 3.00
118 Julius Erving 2.00 5.00
119 Manute Bol .75 2.00
120 Allen Iverson 2.00 5.00
121 Chauncey Billups 1.00 2.50
122 Dennis Rodman 2.00 5.00
123 Robert Horry .60 1.50
124 Steve Kerr .75 2.00
125 Elvin Hayes 1.25 3.00
126 Tracy McGrady 1.25 3.00
127 Jerry Stackhouse .75 2.00
128 Karl Malone 1.25 3.00
129 Alonzo Mourning 1.25 3.00
130 Muggsy Bogues .60 1.50
131 Clyde Drexler 1.25 3.00
132 Rony Seikaly .60 1.50
133 Dikembe Mutombo 1.25 3.00
134 Steve Nash 1.25 3.00
135 Gary Payton 1.25 3.00
136 Will Chamberlain 3.00 8.00
137 Larry Bird 3.00 8.00
138 Jerry West 1.25 3.00
139 Anfernee Hardaway 2.00 5.00
140 Oscar Robertson 2.00 5.00
141 Damon Stoudamire .75 2.00
142 Scottie Pippen 2.00 5.00
143 Dino Radja .50 1.25
144 Michael Redd .50 1.25
145 Grant Hill 1.25 3.00
146 Yao Ming 2.00 5.00
147 John Havlicek 2.00 5.00
148 Latrell Sprewell .60 1.50
149 Antonio McDyess .60 1.50
150 Pete Maravich 2.00 5.00
151 David Robinson 1.50 4.00
152 Shaquille O'Neal 2.50 6.00
153 Dominique Wilkins 1.25 3.00
154 Mike Bibby .60 1.50
155 Hakeem Olajuwon 1.50 4.00
156 Tim Legler .50 1.25
157 John Starks .75 2.00
158 Louie Dampier .75 2.00
159 Baron Davis .60 1.50
160 Richard Hamilton .75 2.00
161 Justin Anderson RC .60 1.50
162 Frank Kaminsky RC .60 1.50
163 Jarell Martin RC .60 1.50
164 Devin Booker RC 15.00 40.00
165 Montrezl Harrell RC 2.00 5.00
166 Rashad Vaughn RC .60 1.50
167 Karl-Anthony Towns RC 4.00 10.00
168 Richaun Holmes RC 1.00 2.50
169 Nemanja Bjelica RC 1.00 2.50
170 Mario Hezonja RC .75 2.00
171 Bobby Portis RC 1.50 4.00
172 Justise Winslow RC 1.00 2.50
173 Larry Nance Jr. RC 1.25 3.00
174 Cameron Payne RC .60 1.50
175 Jordan Mickey RC .60 1.50
176 Sam Dekker RC .60 1.50
177 Pat Connaughton RC .60 1.50
178 D'Angelo Russell RC 2.50 6.00
179 Cliff Alexander RC .60 1.50
180 Willie Cauley-Stein RC .75 2.00
181 Rondae Hollis-Jefferson RC .75 2.00
182 Myles Turner RC 2.50 6.00
183 R.J. Hunter RC .60 1.50
184 Kelly Oubre Jr. RC 2.00 5.00
185 Anthony Brown RC .60 1.50
186 Jerian Grant RC .60 1.50
187 Jonathon Simmons RC .75 2.00
188 Jahlil Okafor RC .75 2.00
189 Joe Young RC .60 1.50
190 Emmanuel Mudiay RC .75 2.00
191 Tyus Jones RC .75 2.00
192 Trey Lyles RC .75 2.00
193 Chris McCullough RC .60 1.50
194 Terry Rozier RC 2.50 6.00
195 Rakeem Christmas RC .60 1.50
196 Delon Wright RC .75 2.00
197 Walter Tavares RC .60 1.50
198 Kristaps Porzingis RC 4.00 10.00
199 T.J. McConnell RC 5.00 12.00
200 Stanley Johnson RC .75 2.00

2015-16 Absolute Memorabilia Frequent Flyer Material Autographs

PRINT RUNS B/WN 40-99 COPIES PER
EXCHANGE DEADLINE 8/5/2017
*PRIME: .5X TO 1.2X BASIC
FRAD Adrian Dantley/65 6.00 15.00
FRAG A.C. Green/99 6.00 15.00
FRAG Aaron Gordon/49 6.00 15.00
FRAR Andre Roberson/99 4.00 10.00
FRBB Bojan Bogdanovic/99 5.00 12.00
FRBL Bill Laimbeer/99 6.00 15.00
FRBM Ben McLemore/49 4.00 10.00
FRCD Clyde Drexler/49 12.00 30.00
FRCL Carl Landry/99 4.00 10.00
FRDC DeMarre Carroll/99 4.00 10.00
FRDE Dante Exum/49 5.00 12.00
FRDM Dan Majerle/99 6.00 15.00
FRDM Donatas Motiejunas/99 4.00 10.00
FRDR Dino Radja/99 12.00 30.00
FRDS Dennis Schroder/99 6.00 15.00
FREK Enes Kanter/99 4.00 10.00
FREP Elfrid Payton/99 5.00 12.00
FRFE Festus Ezeli/99 4.00 10.00
FRGA G. Antetokounmpo/99 75.00 200.00
FRGH Gerald Henderson/99 4.00 10.00
FRGP Gary Payton/49 8.00 20.00
FRJC Jordan Clarkson/99 6.00 15.00
FRJD Joe Dumars/49 8.00 20.00
FRJE James Ennis/99 4.00 10.00
FRJK Jason Kidd/40 15.00 40.00
FRJN Jusuf Nurkic/99 5.00 12.00
FRJP Jabari Parker/49 10.00 25.00
FRJS John Starks/99 6.00 15.00
FRKA Kyle Anderson/99 4.00 10.00
FRKC Kentavious Caldwell-Pope/49 5.00 12.00
FRKV Keith Van Horn/99 5.00 12.00
FRKV Kiki Vandeweghe/99 5.00 12.00
FRLG Langston Galloway/99 4.00 10.00
FRMD Matthew Dellavedova/99 5.00 12.00
FRMF Michael Finley/49 6.00 15.00
FRMK Michael Kidd-Gilchrist/49 4.00 10.00
FRMM Mitch McGary/99 4.00 10.00
FRMP Mark Price/99 6.00 15.00
FRMS Marcus Smart/49 8.00 20.00
FRNM Nikola Mirotic/99 4.00 10.00
FRNS Nik Stauskas/99 4.00 10.00
FRNV Noah Vonleh/49 4.00 10.00
FRPB Patrick Beverley/99 4.00 10.00
FRPT P.J. Tucker/99 4.00 10.00
FRRA Rafer Alston/99 4.00 10.00
FRRA Ray Allen/49 10.00 25.00
FRRG Rudy Gobert/99 8.00 20.00
FRRH Roy Hibbert/99 5.00 12.00
FRRH Richard Hamilton/49 6.00 15.00
FRRK Ryan Kelly/99 4.00 10.00
FRRP Robert Parish/99 8.00 20.00
FRRS Ralph Sampson/49 5.00 12.00
FRSH Solomon Hill/99 4.00 10.00
FRSM Shabazz Muhammad/49 4.00 10.00
FRTA Tony Allen/99 4.00 10.00
FRTB Trey Burke/49 4.00 10.00
FRTG Taj Gibson/99 4.00 10.00
FRUH Udonis Haslem/99 4.00 10.00
FRVD Vlade Divac/99 6.00 15.00
FRVO Victor Oladipo/49 5.00 12.00
FRWC Wilson Chandler/99 5.00 12.00

2015-16 Absolute Memorabilia Frequent Flyer Materials

STATED PRINT RUN 99 SER.#'d SETS
*PRIME/20-25: .75X TO 2X BASIC
1 Anthony Davis 6.00 15.00
2 Jeff Teague 2.00 5.00
3 Brook Lopez 3.00 8.00
4 David Lee 2.00 5.00
5 Kemba Walker 3.00 8.00
6 Mason Plumlee 2.00 5.00
7 Elfrid Payton 2.50 6.00
8 Roy Hibbert 2.50 6.00
9 Aaron Gordon 3.00 8.00
10 Tony Allen 2.00 5.00
11 Avery Bradley 2.00 5.00
12 Joe Johnson 2.50 6.00
13 Chandler Parsons 2.00 5.00
14 Kenneth Faried 2.50 6.00
15 David West 2.50 6.00
16 Michael Kidd-Gilchrist 2.00 5.00
17 Eric Bledsoe 2.50 6.00
18 Serge Ibaka 2.50 6.00
19 Al Horford 3.00 8.00
20 Tony Wroten 2.00 5.00
21 Ben McLemore 2.00 5.00
22 Josh Smith 2.00 5.00
23 Chris Andersen 2.50 6.00
24 Kevin Love 3.00 8.00
25 Doug McDermott 2.50 6.00
26 Nick Young 2.00 5.00
27 George Hill 2.50 6.00
28 Shabazz Napier 2.00 5.00
29 Alex Len 2.00 5.00
30 Trey Burke 2.00 5.00
31 Boris Diaw 2.50 6.00
32 Jrue Holiday 4.00 10.00
33 Danilo Gallinari 2.50 6.00
34 Lance Stephenson 2.50 6.00
35 DeMar DeRozan 4.00 10.00
36 Paul Pierce 5.00 12.00
37 T.J. Warren 3.00 8.00
38 Goran Dragic 3.00 8.00
39 Andre Drummond 3.00 8.00
40 Tristan Thompson 2.00 5.00
41 Bradley Beal 4.00 10.00
42 Jusuf Nurkic 2.50 6.00
43 Danny Green 2.50 6.00
44 Deron Williams 2.50 6.00
45 Langston Galloway 2.00 5.00
46 Rajon Rondo 4.00 10.00
47 Taj Gibson 2.00 5.00
48 Greg Monroe 2.50 6.00
49 Andre Iguodala 3.00 8.00
50 Ty Lawson 2.00 5.00
51 Brandon Jennings 2.00 5.00
52 Kelly Olynyk 2.00 5.00
53 Dante Exum 2.50 6.00
54 Marcus Smart 4.00 10.00
55 Draymond Green 4.00 10.00
56 Reggie Jackson 2.50 6.00
57 Jared Sullinger 2.00 5.00
58 Terrence Ross 2.50 6.00
59 Andrew Bogut 2.50 6.00
60 Tyreke Evans 2.50 6.00
61 Toni Kukoc 3.00 8.00
62 Alonzo Mourning 5.00 12.00

2015-16 Absolute Memorabilia Freshman Flyer Jersey Autographs

PRINT RUNS B/WN 49-149 COPIES PER
EXCHANGE DEADLINE 8/5/2017
*PRIME: .5X TO 1.2X BASIC
FJAAB Anthony Brown/149 4.00 10.00
FJABP Bobby Portis/149 10.00 25.00
FJACM Chris McCullough/149 4.00 10.00
FJACP Cameron Payne/149 6.00 15.00
FJADB Devin Booker/149 200.00 500.00
FJADR D'Angelo Russell/149 15.00 40.00
FJADW Delon Wright/149 5.00 12.00
FJAEM Emmanuel Mudiay/149 5.00 12.00
FJAFK Frank Kaminsky/149 5.00 12.00
FJAJA Justin Anderson/149 4.00 10.00
FJAJG Jerian Grant/149 4.00 10.00
FJAJH Josh Huestis/149 4.00 10.00
FJAJM Jordan Mickey/149 4.00 10.00
FJAJM Jarell Martin/149 4.00 10.00
FJAJO Jahlil Okafor/149 5.00 12.00
FJAJR Josh Richardson/149 6.00 15.00
FJAJW Justise Winslow/149 6.00 15.00
FJAJY Joe Young/149 4.00 10.00
FJAKL Kevon Looney/149 12.00 30.00
FJAKO Kelly Oubre Jr./149 12.00 30.00
FJAKP Kristaps Porzingis/149 40.00 100.00
FJAKT Karl-Anthony Towns/149 40.00 100.00
FJAMH Mario Hezonja/149 5.00 12.00
FJAMH Montrezl Harrell/149 12.00 30.00
FJAMT Myles Turner/149 15.00 40.00
FJAPC Pat Connaughton/149 6.00 15.00
FJARC Rakeem Christmas/149 4.00 10.00
FJARH Richaun Holmes/149 6.00 15.00
FJARH Rondae Hollis-Jefferson/149 5.00 12.00
FJARH R.J. Hunter/149 4.00 10.00
FJARV Rashad Vaughn/149 4.00 10.00
FJASD Sam Dekker/149 4.00 10.00
FJASJ Stanley Johnson/149 5.00 12.00
FJATJ Tyus Jones/49 5.00 12.00
FJATL Trey Lyles/149 5.00 12.00
FJATR Terry Rozier/149 15.00 40.00
FJAWC Willie Cauley-Stein/149 5.00 12.00
FJAWT Walter Tavares/149 4.00 10.00

2015-16 Absolute Memorabilia Freshman Flyer Jumbo Jerseys

STATED PRINT RUN 99 SER.#'d SETS
*PRIME: 1.2X TO 3X BASIC
1 Karl-Anthony Towns 10.00 25.00
2 D'Angelo Russell 6.00 15.00
3 Jahlil Okafor 2.50 6.00
4 Kristaps Porzingis 8.00 20.00
5 Mario Hezonja 2.50 6.00
6 Willie Cauley-Stein 2.50 6.00
7 Emmanuel Mudiay 4.00 10.00
8 Stanley Johnson 2.50 6.00
9 Frank Kaminsky 2.50 6.00
10 Justise Winslow 3.00 8.00
11 Myles Turner 8.00 20.00
12 Trey Lyles 2.50 6.00
13 Devin Booker 25.00 60.00
14 Cameron Payne 3.00 8.00
15 Kelly Oubre Jr. 6.00 15.00
16 Terry Rozier 8.00 20.00
17 Rashad Vaughn 2.00 5.00
18 Sam Dekker 2.00 5.00
19 Jerian Grant 2.00 5.00
20 Delon Wright 2.50 6.00
21 Justin Anderson 2.00 5.00
22 Bobby Portis 5.00 12.00
23 Rondae Hollis-Jefferson 2.50 6.00
24 Tyus Jones 2.50 6.00
25 Jarell Martin 2.00 5.00
26 R.J. Hunter 2.00 5.00
27 Chris McCullough 2.00 5.00
28 Montrezl Harrell 6.00 15.00
29 Jordan Mickey 2.00 5.00
30 Anthony Brown 2.00 5.00
31 Rakeem Christmas 2.00 5.00
32 Richaun Holmes 2.50 6.00
33 Pat Connaughton 3.00 8.00
34 Josh Huestis 2.00 5.00
35 Joe Young 2.00 5.00
36 Josh Richardson 3.00 8.00
37 Walter Tavares 2.00 5.00
38 Kevon Looney 6.00 15.00

2015-16 Absolute Memorabilia Glass

EXCHANGE DEADLINE 8/5/2017
1 Kyrie Irving 20.00 50.00
2 James Harden EXCH 20.00 50.00
3 Chris Paul EXCH 20.00 50.00
4 Damian Lillard EXCH 25.00 60.00
5 Blake Griffin EXCH 10.00 25.00
6 Magic Johnson 40.00 100.00
7 Tim Duncan 40.00 100.00
8 Julius Erving 25.00 60.00
9 Kobe Bryant EXCH 60.00 150.00
10 Scottie Pippen EXCH 25.00 60.00
11 LeBron James 50.00 120.00
12 Andrew Wiggins EXCH 20.00 50.00
13 Stephen Curry 100.00 200.00
14 Kevin Garnett EXCH 25.00 60.00
15 Dwyane Wade EXCH 60.00 150.00
16 Larry Bird EXCH 40.00 100.00
17 Anthony Davis EXCH 40.00 100.00
18 Allen Iverson 40.00 100.00
19 Kevin Durant 40.00 100.00
20 Pete Maravich EXCH 25.00 60.00

2015-16 Absolute Memorabilia Heroes Autographs

PRINT RUNS B/WN 25-149 COPIES PER
EXCHANGE DEADLINE 8/5/2017
1 Rik Smits/149 5.00 12.00
3 Steve Kerr/99 8.00 20.00
4 Kobe Bryant/25 500.00 1,000.00
5 Artis Gilmore/49 8.00 20.00
6 Karl Malone/25 40.00 100.00
7 Rick Fox/49 5.00 12.00
8 Kyrie Irving/25 60.00 150.00
9 Robert Horry/99 5.00 12.00
10 Andrew Wiggins/25 30.00 80.00
11 Antoine Walker/149 5.00 12.00
12 Marcus Smart/49 10.00 25.00
13 Tim Hardaway/149 8.00 20.00
16 Anthony Davis/25 60.00 150.00
17 Jerry Stackhouse/99 6.00 15.00
18 Jabari Parker/25 40.00 100.00
19 Rolando Blackman/99 5.00 12.00
20 Dennis Rodman/25 50.00 120.00
21 Jo Jo White/149 6.00 15.00
22 Christian Laettner/49 5.00 12.00
23 Cedric Ceballos/149 4.00 10.00
24 Oscar Robertson/25 60.00 150.00
25 Robert Parish/49 8.00 20.00
26 Jerry West/25 30.00 80.00
27 Earl Monroe/99 8.00 20.00
28 Tom Chambers/25 12.00 30.00
29 Damon Stoudamire/149 6.00 15.00
30 Vince Carter/25 25.00 60.00

2015-16 Absolute Memorabilia Heroes Materials

STATED PRINT RUN 99 SER.#'d SETS
*PRIME/25: .75X TO 2X BASIC
1 Ray Allen 4.00 10.00
2 Dan Majerle 3.00 8.00
3 Shawn Bradley 2.00 5.00
4 Hakeem Olajuwon 6.00 15.00
5 James Harden 6.00 15.00
6 Kareem Abdul-Jabbar 10.00 25.00
7 LeBron James 25.00 60.00
8 Allen Iverson 5.00 12.00
9 Mark Jackson 2.50 6.00
10 Brad Daugherty 2.50 6.00
11 Richard Hamilton 3.00 8.00
12 Danny Manning 2.50 6.00
13 Walter Davis 2.00 5.00
14 Jamal Mashburn 2.50 6.00
15 John Wall 4.00 10.00
16 Kevin Duckworth 2.00 5.00
17 Marcin Gortat 2.00 5.00
18 Anfernee Hardaway 8.00 20.00
19 Michael Redd 2.50 6.00
20 Chris Mullin 4.00 10.00
21 Robert Parish 4.00 10.00
22 Adrian Dantley 3.00 8.00
23 Kobe Bryant 10.00 25.00
24 Jerry Stackhouse 3.00 8.00
25 Kevin Garnett 8.00 20.00
26 Larry Bird 12.00 30.00
27 Stephen Curry 25.00 60.00
28 Baron Davis 2.50 6.00
29 Moses Malone 5.00 12.00
30 Christian Laettner 2.50 6.00
31 Shane Battier 2.50 6.00
32 Gary Payton 5.00 12.00
33 Tim Duncan 8.00 20.00
34 John Starks 3.00 8.00
35 Kyle Lowry 3.00 8.00
36 Manute Bol 3.00 8.00
37 Tony Parker 5.00 12.00
38 Bill Laimbeer 3.00 8.00
39 Rafer Alston 2.00 5.00
40 Clyde Drexler 5.00 12.00

2015-16 Absolute Memorabilia Iconic Autographs

PRINT RUNS B/WN 25-149 COPIES PER
EXCHANGE DEADLINE 8/5/2017
1 Dan Issel/149 8.00 20.00
3 Cliff Hagan/99 6.00 15.00
4 Kareem Abdul-Jabbar/25 20.00 50.00
5 Paul Westphal/149 6.00 15.00
6 Shane Battier/99 6.00 15.00
7 Larry Nance/149 5.00 12.00
8 Kobe Bryant/25 600.00 1,200.00
9 Glen Rice/99 5.00 12.00
10 Magic Johnson/25 25.00 60.00
11 Dino Radja/149 4.00 10.00
12 John Wall/25 20.00 50.00
13 Zydrunas Ilgauskas/149 5.00 12.00
15 Rafer Alston/149 4.00 10.00
16 Byron Scott/49 6.00 15.00
18 Shaquille O'Neal/25 60.00 150.00
19 Kurt Rambis/149 5.00 12.00
20 Oscar Robertson/25 30.00 80.00
21 Eddie Jones/149 6.00 15.00
22 Andrew Wiggins/25 30.00 80.00
23 Alex English/149 8.00 20.00
24 Gary Payton/25 10.00 25.00
25 Dee Brown/149 4.00 10.00
26 Joe Dumars/49 8.00 20.00
27 Antoine Walker/149 5.00 12.00
28 Kevin Durant/25 50.00 120.00
29 Kenny Walker/149 4.00 10.00
30 Anthony Davis/25 40.00 100.00
31 Rony Seikaly/149 5.00 12.00
32 Kevin McHale/25 10.00 25.00
34 Rick Barry/49 8.00 20.00
35 Antonio McDyess/149 5.00 12.00
36 Dave Cowens/49 8.00 20.00
37 Bill Laimbeer/149 6.00 15.00
38 Dwyane Wade/25 EXCH 25.00 60.00
39 Dan Majerle/99 6.00 15.00

2015-16 Absolute Memorabilia Iconic Materials

STATED PRINT RUN 99 SER.#'d SETS
*PRIME/25: .75X TO 2X BASIC
1 Bernard King 4.00 10.00
2 John Stockton 6.00 15.00
3 Chris Webber 4.00 10.00
4 Larry Johnson 4.00 10.00
5 Danny Ainge 3.00 8.00
6 Mike Bibby 2.50 6.00
7 Jalen Rose 2.50 6.00
8 Reggie Lewis 3.00 8.00
9 Alex English 4.00 10.00
10 Shaquille O'Neal 5.00 12.00
11 Bobby Jackson 2.00 5.00
12 Karl Malone 5.00 12.00
13 Clifford Robinson 3.00 8.00
14 Mark Aguirre 2.50 6.00
15 Dikembe Mutombo 5.00 12.00
16 Patrick Ewing 5.00 12.00
17 Jason Kidd 5.00 12.00
18 Rick Fox 2.50 6.00
19 Alonzo Mourning 5.00 12.00
20 Toni Kukoc 3.00 8.00
21 Charles Oakley 2.50 6.00
22 Kevin McHale 5.00 12.00
23 Dan Issel 4.00 10.00
24 Michael Finley 3.00 8.00
25 Grant Hill 5.00 12.00
26 Ralph Sampson 2.50 6.00
27 Joe Dumars 4.00 10.00
28 Scottie Pippen 5.00 12.00
29 Antoine Walker 2.50 6.00
30 Yao Ming 8.00 20.00

2015-16 Absolute Memorabilia Marks of Fame

PRINT RUNS B/WN 25-149 COPIES PER
EXCHANGE DEADLINE 8/5/2017
1 Kevin Durant/25 75.00 150.00
2 Kenneth Faried/49 5.00 12.00
5 Jusuf Nurkic/99 5.00 12.00
6 Ron Harper/149 6.00 15.00
7 Tony Parker/25 15.00 40.00
8 Sean Elliott/125 5.00 12.00
9 Kobe Bryant/25 600.00 1,200.00
10 Michael Carter-Williams/49 4.00 10.00
11 Magic Johnson/25 25.00 60.00
12 Enes Kanter/99 4.00 10.00
13 John Wall/25 25.00 60.00
14 Dennis Rodman/25 12.00 30.00
15 Marcin Gortat/99 4.00 10.00
16 Adrian Dantley/149 6.00 15.00
17 Klay Thompson/25 25.00 60.00
18 DeMarre Carroll/149 4.00 10.00
19 Shaquille O'Neal/25 60.00 150.00
22 Frank Ramsey/99 6.00 15.00
24 Muggsy Bogues/149 5.00 12.00
26 Larry Nance/149 5.00 12.00
28 Kenny Anderson/149 5.00 12.00
29 Julius Erving/25 25.00 60.00
30 Bradley Beal/49 8.00 20.00

2015-16 Absolute Memorabilia NBA Stars Materials

STATED PRINT RUN 99 SER.#'d SETS
*PRIME/20-25: .75X TO 2X BASIC
1 Joakim Noah 2.00 5.00
2 Ricky Rubio 2.50 6.00
3 Chris Bosh 4.00 10.00
4 Victor Oladipo 2.50 6.00
5 DeMarcus Cousins 3.00 8.00
6 Klay Thompson 6.00 15.00
7 Dwight Howard 4.00 10.00
8 Manu Ginobili 6.00 15.00
9 Andrew Wiggins 4.00 10.00
10 Monta Ellis 2.50 6.00
11 Kawhi Leonard 10.00 25.00
12 Russell Westbrook 5.00 12.00
13 Chris Paul 6.00 15.00
14 Zach LaVine 8.00 20.00
15 Derrick Rose 5.00 12.00
16 Kyrie Irving 6.00 15.00
17 Dwyane Wade 5.00 12.00
18 Marc Gasol 3.00 8.00
19 Blake Griffin 4.00 10.00
20 Nicolas Batum 2.00 5.00
21 Kevin Durant 6.00 15.00
22 Tobias Harris 2.50 6.00
23 Damian Lillard 5.00 12.00
24 Zach Randolph 3.00 8.00
25 Dirk Nowitzki 8.00 20.00
26 LaMarcus Aldridge 3.00 8.00
27 Jimmy Butler 6.00 15.00
28 Mike Conley 3.00 8.00
29 Carmelo Anthony 5.00 12.00
30 Nikola Vucevic 2.50 6.00

2015-16 Absolute Memorabilia Next Day Autographs

EXCHANGE DEADLINE 8/5/2017
1 Karl-Anthony Towns 150.00 400.00
2 D'Angelo Russell 75.00 200.00
3 Jahlil Okafor 5.00 12.00
4 Kristaps Porzingis 125.00 300.00
6 Willie Cauley-Stein 5.00 12.00
7 Emmanuel Mudiay 5.00 12.00
8 Stanley Johnson 5.00 12.00
9 Frank Kaminsky 5.00 12.00
10 Justise Winslow 6.00 15.00
11 Myles Turner 40.00 100.00
12 Trey Lyles 5.00 12.00
13 Devin Booker 800.00 1,500.00
14 Cameron Payne 6.00 15.00
15 Kelly Oubre Jr. 40.00 100.00
16 Terry Rozier 40.00 100.00
17 Rashad Vaughn 4.00 10.00
18 Sam Dekker 4.00 10.00
19 Jerian Grant 4.00 10.00
20 Delon Wright 5.00 12.00
21 Justin Anderson 5.00 12.00
22 Bobby Portis 25.00 60.00
23 Rondae Hollis-Jefferson 5.00 12.00
24 Tyus Jones 5.00 12.00
25 Jarell Martin 4.00 10.00
27 R.J. Hunter 4.00 10.00
28 Chris McCullough 4.00 10.00
29 Montrezl Harrell 12.00 30.00

30 Jordan Mickey 4.00 10.00
31 Anthony Brown 4.00 10.00
32 Rakeem Christmas 4.00 10.00
33 Richaun Holmes 6.00 15.00
34 Pat Connaughton 6.00 15.00
35 Joe Young 4.00 10.00
37 Dakari Johnson 4.00 10.00
38 Tyler Harvey 4.00 10.00
40 Walter Tavares 4.00 10.00
46 Josh Richardson 6.00 15.00
47 Kevon Looney 40.00 100.00

2015-16 Absolute Memorabilia Team Quads Materials

STATED PRINT RUN 99 SER.#'d SETS
*PRIME/25: 1X TO 2.5X BASIC
TQCHI McDrmtt/Noah/Rose/Gbsn 8.00 20.00
TQCLE Jms/Love/Irvng/Thmpsn 40.00 100.00
TQGSW Brns/Curry/Igdla/Thmpsn 40.00 100.00
TQLAC Grffn/Jrdn/Paul/Rdck 10.00 25.00
TQSAS Dncn/Lnrd/Gnbli/Prkr 12.00 30.00

2015-16 Absolute Memorabilia Team Tandems Materials

STATED PRINT RUN 99 SER.#'d SETS
*PRIME/25: 1X TO 2.5X BASIC
TTATL A.Horford/J.Teague 3.00 8.00
TTBRK B.Lopez/J.Johnson 3.00 8.00
TTCHA A.Jefferson/K.Walker 3.00 8.00
TTCHI D.Rose/J.Butler 6.00 15.00
TTCLE K.Irving/L.James 15.00 40.00
TTDAL D.Nowitzki/C.Parsons 8.00 20.00
TTDEN D.Gallinari/K.Faried 2.50 6.00
TTDET A.Drummond/B.Jennings 3.00 8.00
TTGSW K.Thompson/S.Curry 25.00 60.00
TTHOU J.Harden/D.Howard 6.00 15.00
TTLAC C.Paul/B.Griffin 6.00 15.00
TTMEM M.Gasol/M.Conley 3.00 8.00
TTMIA C.Bosh/D.Wade 5.00 12.00
TTMIN A.Wiggins/Z.LaVine 8.00 20.00
TTOKL K.Durant/R.Westbrook 6.00 15.00
TTORL N.Vucevic/E.Payton 2.50 6.00
TTSAN M.Ginobili/T.Duncan 8.00 20.00
TTTOR K.Lowry/D.DeRozan 4.00 10.00
TTWAS B.Beal/J.Wall 4.00 10.00

2015-16 Absolute Memorabilia Team Trios Materials

STATED PRINT RUN 99 SER.#'d SETS
*PRIME/25: 1X TO 2.5X BASIC
TTRBOS Bradley/Sullinger/Smart 6.00 15.00
TTRCHI Rose/Butler/Noah 10.00 25.00
TTRCLE Love/James/Irving 40.00 100.00
TTRGSW Iguodala/Curry/Thompson 30.00 80.00
TTRLAL Clarkson/Bryant/Young 8.00 20.00
TTRMEM Conley/Randolph/Gasol 5.00 12.00
TTRMIA Chalmers/Bosh/Wade 5.00 12.00
TTRORL Harris/Gordon/Vucevic 5.00 12.00
TTRSAC McLemore/Collison/Cousins 5.00 12.00
TTRSAS Leonard/Duncan/Parker 10.00 25.00

2015-16 Absolute Memorabilia Tools of the Trade Jumbo Rookie Material Signatures

STATED PRINT RUN 99 SER.#'d SETS
EXCHANGE DEADLINE 8/5/2017
*PRIME: .5X TO 1.2X BASIC
TTJAB Anthony Brown 4.00 10.00
TTJBP Bobby Portis 12.00 30.00
TTJCM Chris McCullough 4.00 10.00
TTJCP Cameron Payne 10.00 25.00
TTJDB Devin Booker 200.00 500.00
TTJDR D'Angelo Russell 30.00 80.00
TTJDW Delon Wright 5.00 12.00
TTJEM Emmanuel Mudiay 5.00 12.00
TTJFK Frank Kaminsky 5.00 12.00
TTJJA Justin Anderson 4.00 10.00
TTJJG Jerian Grant 4.00 10.00
TTJJM Jarell Martin 4.00 10.00
TTJJM Jordan Mickey 4.00 10.00
TTJJO Jahlil Okafor 30.00 80.00
TTJJW Justise Winslow 20.00 50.00
TTJKL Kevon Looney 10.00 25.00
TTJKO Kelly Oubre Jr. 12.00 30.00
TTJKP Kristaps Porzingis 150.00 300.00
TTJKT Karl-Anthony Towns 150.00 300.00
TTJMH Mario Hezonja 10.00 25.00
TTJMH Montrezl Harrell 12.00 30.00
TTJMT Myles Turner 20.00 50.00
TTJPC Pat Connaughton 6.00 15.00
TTJRC Rakeem Christmas 4.00 10.00
TTJRH R.J. Hunter 4.00 10.00
TTJRH Rondae Hollis-Jefferson 5.00 12.00
TTJRV Rashad Vaughn 4.00 10.00
TTJSD Sam Dekker 4.00 10.00
TTJSJ Stanley Johnson 12.00 30.00
TTJTL Trey Lyles 5.00 12.00
TTJTR Terry Rozier 15.00 40.00
TTJWC Willie Cauley-Stein 10.00 25.00
TTJWT Walter Tavares 4.00 10.00

2015-16 Absolute Memorabilia Tools of the Trade Rookie Autograph Materials

STATED PRINT RUN 99 SER.#'d SETS
EXCHANGE DEADLINE 8/5/2017
*PRIME: .5X TO 1.2X BASIC
TTJCM Chris McCullough 4.00 10.00
TTJCP Cameron Payne 6.00 15.00
TTJDB Devin Booker 200.00 500.00
TTJDR D'Angelo Russell 25.00 60.00
TTJDW Delon Wright 5.00 12.00
TTJEM Emmanuel Mudiay 5.00 12.00
TTJFK Frank Kaminsky 10.00 25.00
TTJJA Justin Anderson 4.00 10.00
TTJJG Jerian Grant 4.00 10.00
TTJJM Jarell Martin 4.00 10.00
TTJJM Jordan Mickey 4.00 10.00
TTJJO Jahlil Okafor 20.00 50.00
TTJJR Josh Richardson 10.00 25.00
TTJJW Justise Winslow 6.00 15.00
TTJJY Joe Young 4.00 10.00
TTJKL Kevon Looney 12.00 30.00
TTJKO Kelly Oubre Jr. 12.00 30.00
TTJKP Kristaps Porzingis 50.00 120.00
TTJKT Karl-Anthony Towns 60.00 150.00
TTJMH Mario Hezonja 5.00 12.00
TTJMH Montrezl Harrell 12.00 30.00
TTJMT Myles Turner 10.00 25.00
TTJPC Pat Connaughton 6.00 15.00
TTJRC Rakeem Christmas 4.00 10.00
TTJRH Richaun Holmes 6.00 15.00
TTJRH R.J. Hunter 4.00 10.00
TTJRH Rondae Hollis-Jefferson 5.00 12.00
TTJRV Rashad Vaughn 4.00 10.00
TTJSD Sam Dekker 4.00 10.00
TTJSJ Stanley Johnson 5.00 12.00
TTJTL Trey Lyles 5.00 12.00
TTJTR Terry Rozier 15.00 40.00
TTJWC Willie Cauley-Stein 12.00 30.00

2015-16 Absolute Memorabilia Tools of the Trade Rookie Materials Dual

STATED PRINT RUN 125 SER.#'d SETS
*PRIME/49: .75X TO 2X BASIC
*PATCH/25: 1.2X TO 3X BASIC
1 Karl-Anthony Towns 12.00 30.00
2 D'Angelo Russell 5.00 12.00
3 Jahlil Okafor 5.00 12.00
4 Kristaps Porzingis 12.00 30.00
5 Mario Hezonja 2.50 6.00
6 Willie Cauley-Stein 2.50 6.00
7 Emmanuel Mudiay 4.00 10.00
8 Stanley Johnson 2.50 6.00
9 Frank Kaminsky 2.50 6.00
10 Justise Winslow 3.00 8.00
11 Myles Turner 8.00 20.00
12 Trey Lyles 2.50 6.00
13 Devin Booker 25.00 60.00
14 Cameron Payne 3.00 8.00
15 Kelly Oubre Jr. 6.00 15.00
16 Terry Rozier 8.00 20.00
17 Rashad Vaughn 2.00 5.00
18 Sam Dekker 2.00 5.00
19 Jerian Grant 2.00 5.00
21 Justin Anderson 2.00 5.00
22 Bobby Portis 5.00 12.00
23 Rondae Hollis-Jefferson 2.50 6.00
24 Tyus Jones 2.50 6.00
25 Jarell Martin 2.00 5.00
26 Kevon Looney 6.00 15.00
27 R.J. Hunter 2.00 5.00
28 Chris McCullough 2.00 5.00
29 Montrezl Harrell 6.00 15.00
30 Jordan Mickey 2.00 5.00
32 Rakeem Christmas 2.00 5.00
33 Walter Tavares 2.00 5.00

2015-16 Absolute Memorabilia Tools of the Trade Rookie Materials Jumbo

STATED PRINT RUN 149 SER.#'d SETS
*PRIME/49: .75X TO 2X BASIC
*PATCH/25: 1.2X TO 3X BASIC
1 Karl-Anthony Towns 10.00 25.00
2 D'Angelo Russell 5.00 12.00
3 Jahlil Okafor 5.00 12.00
4 Kristaps Porzingis 8.00 20.00
5 Mario Hezonja 2.50 6.00
6 Willie Cauley-Stein 2.50 6.00
7 Emmanuel Mudiay 4.00 10.00
8 Stanley Johnson 2.50 6.00
9 Frank Kaminsky 2.50 6.00
10 Justise Winslow 3.00 8.00
11 Myles Turner 8.00 20.00
12 Trey Lyles 2.50 6.00
13 Devin Booker 25.00 60.00
14 Cameron Payne 3.00 8.00
15 Kelly Oubre Jr. 6.00 15.00
16 Terry Rozier 8.00 20.00
17 Rashad Vaughn 2.00 5.00
18 Sam Dekker 2.00 5.00
19 Jerian Grant 2.00 5.00
20 Delon Wright 2.50 6.00
21 Justin Anderson 2.00 5.00
22 Bobby Portis 5.00 12.00
23 Rondae Hollis-Jefferson 2.50 6.00
24 Tyus Jones 2.50 6.00
25 Jarell Martin 2.00 5.00
26 Kevon Looney 6.00 15.00
27 R.J. Hunter 2.00 5.00
28 Chris McCullough 2.00 5.00
29 Montrezl Harrell 6.00 15.00
30 Jordan Mickey 2.00 5.00
31 Anthony Brown 2.00 5.00
32 Rakeem Christmas 2.00 5.00
33 Walter Tavares 2.00 5.00

2015-16 Absolute Memorabilia Tools of the Trade Rookie Materials Quad

STATED PRINT RUN 75 SER.#'d SETS
*PRIME/49: .75X TO 2X BASIC
*PATCH/25: 1.2X TO 3X BASIC
TTMAB Anthony Brown 2.00 5.00
TTMBP Bobby Portis 5.00 12.00
TTMCM Chris McCullough 2.00 5.00
TTMCP Cameron Payne 3.00 8.00
TTMDB Devin Booker AU/99 200.00 500.00
TTMDR D'Angelo Russell 6.00 15.00
TTMDW Delon Wright 2.50 6.00
TTMEM Emmanuel Mudiay 4.00 10.00
TTMFK Frank Kaminsky 2.50 6.00
TTMJA Justin Anderson 2.00 5.00
TTMJG Jerian Grant 2.00 5.00
TTMJM Jarell Martin 2.00 5.00
TTMJM Jordan Mickey 2.00 5.00
TTMJO Jahlil Okafor 5.00 12.00
TTMJW Justise Winslow 3.00 8.00
TTMKL Kevon Looney 6.00 15.00
TTMKO Kelly Oubre Jr. 6.00 15.00
TTMKP Kristaps Porzingis 12.00 30.00
TTMKT Karl-Anthony Towns 12.00 30.00
TTMMH Montrezl Harrell 6.00 15.00
TTMMH Mario Hezonja 2.50 6.00
TTMMT Myles Turner 8.00 20.00
TTMRC Rakeem Christmas 2.00 5.00
TTMRH Rondae Hollis-Jefferson 2.50 6.00
TTMRH R.J. Hunter 2.00 5.00
TTMRV Rashad Vaughn 2.00 5.00
TTMSD Sam Dekker 2.00 5.00
TTMSJ Stanley Johnson 2.50 6.00
TTMTJ Tyus Jones 2.50 6.00
TTMTL Trey Lyles 2.50 6.00
TTMTR Terry Rozier 8.00 20.00
TTMWC Willie Cauley-Stein 2.50 6.00
TTMWT Walter Tavares 2.00 5.00

2015-16 Absolute Memorabilia Tools of the Trade Rookie Materials Six

STATED PRINT RUN 60 SER.#'d SETS
*PRIME/49: .6X TO 1.5X BASIC
*PATCH/25: .75X TO 2X BASIC
1 Karl-Anthony Towns 20.00 50.00
2 D'Angelo Russell 10.00 25.00
3 Jahlil Okafor 3.00 8.00
4 Kristaps Porzingis 25.00 60.00
5 Mario Hezonja 3.00 8.00
6 Willie Cauley-Stein 3.00 8.00
7 Emmanuel Mudiay 3.00 8.00
8 Stanley Johnson 3.00 8.00
9 Frank Kaminsky 3.00 8.00
10 Justise Winslow 4.00 10.00
11 Myles Turner 6.00 15.00
12 Trey Lyles 3.00 8.00
13 Devin Booker 10.00 25.00
14 Cameron Payne 4.00 10.00
15 Kelly Oubre Jr. 8.00 20.00
16 Terry Rozier 10.00 25.00
17 Rashad Vaughn 2.50 6.00
18 Sam Dekker 2.50 6.00
19 Jerian Grant 2.50 6.00
20 Delon Wright 3.00 8.00
21 Justin Anderson 2.50 6.00
22 Bobby Portis 6.00 15.00
23 Rondae Hollis-Jefferson 3.00 8.00
24 Tyus Jones 3.00 8.00
25 Jarell Martin 2.50 6.00
26 Kevon Looney 8.00 20.00
27 R.J. Hunter 2.50 6.00
28 Chris McCullough 2.50 6.00
29 Montrezl Harrell 8.00 20.00
30 Jordan Mickey 2.50 6.00
31 Anthony Brown 2.50 6.00
32 Rakeem Christmas 2.50 6.00
33 Walter Tavares 2.50 6.00

2015-16 Absolute Memorabilia Tools of the Trade Rookie Materials Trio

STATED PRINT RUN 99 SER.#'d SETS
*PRIME/49: .75X TO 2X BASIC
*PATCH/25: 1.2X TO 3X BASIC
1 Karl-Anthony Towns 12.00 30.00
2 D'Angelo Russell 5.00 12.00
3 Jahlil Okafor 5.00 12.00
4 Kristaps Porzingis 6.00 15.00
5 Mario Hezonja 2.50 6.00
6 Willie Cauley-Stein 2.50 6.00
7 Emmanuel Mudiay 4.00 10.00
8 Stanley Johnson 2.50 6.00
9 Frank Kaminsky 2.50 6.00
10 Justise Winslow 3.00 8.00
11 Myles Turner 8.00 20.00
12 Trey Lyles 2.50 6.00
13 Devin Booker 4.00 10.00
14 Cameron Payne 3.00 8.00
15 Kelly Oubre Jr. 6.00 15.00
16 Terry Rozier 8.00 20.00
17 Rashad Vaughn 2.00 5.00
18 Sam Dekker 2.00 5.00
19 Jerian Grant 2.00 5.00
20 Delon Wright 2.50 6.00
21 Justin Anderson 2.00 5.00
22 Bobby Portis 5.00 12.00
23 Rondae Hollis-Jefferson 2.50 6.00
24 Tyus Jones 2.50 6.00
25 Jarell Martin 2.00 5.00
26 Kevon Looney 6.00 15.00
27 R.J. Hunter 2.00 5.00
28 Chris McCullough 2.00 5.00
29 Montrezl Harrell 6.00 15.00
30 Jordan Mickey 2.00 5.00
31 Anthony Brown 2.00 5.00
32 Rakeem Christmas 2.00 5.00
33 Walter Tavares 2.00 5.00

2016-17 Absolute Memorabilia Draft Day Ink

STATED PRINT RUN 25 SER.#'d SETS
EXCHANGE DEADLINE 8/21/2018
1 Brandon Ingram 100.00 250.00
2 Jaylen Brown 150.00 400.00
3 Dragan Bender 5.00 12.00
4 Kris Dunn 10.00 25.00
5 Buddy Hield 25.00 60.00
6 Jamal Murray 100.00 250.00
7 Marquese Chriss 6.00 15.00
8 Jakob Poeltl 15.00 40.00
9 Domantas Sabonis 75.00 200.00
10 Thon Maker 6.00 15.00
11 Taurean Prince 10.00 25.00
12 Denzel Valentine 8.00 20.00
13 Wade Baldwin IV 5.00 12.00
14 Brice Johnson 5.00 12.00
15 Skal Labissiere 5.00 12.00

2016-17 Absolute Memorabilia Frequent Flyer Material Autographs

STATED PRINT RUN 75 SER.#'d SETS
EXCHANGE DEADLINE 8/21/2018
1 Bobby Portis 5.00 12.00
2 Tristan Thompson 4.00 10.00
3 Dirk Nowitzki 50.00 120.00
4 Devin Harris 3.00 8.00
5 Reggie Jackson 4.00 10.00
6 Justise Winslow 4.00 10.00
7 Zach LaVine 12.00 30.00
8 Carmelo Anthony 12.00 30.00
9 Jordan Clarkson 8.00 20.00
10 Tyler Ennis 3.00 8.00
12 Karl-Anthony Towns 30.00 80.00
13 Aaron Gordon 5.00 12.00
14 Alex Len 3.00 8.00
15 Archie Goodwin 3.00 8.00
16 C.J. McCollum 5.00 12.00
17 Jonathon Simmons 3.00 8.00
18 Kent Bazemore 3.00 8.00
20 Andrew Wiggins 8.00 20.00

2016-17 Absolute Memorabilia Frequent Flyer Materials

STATED PRINT RUN 149 SER.#'d SETS
1 Karl-Anthony Towns 5.00 12.00
2 Stanley Johnson 2.00 5.00
3 DeMar DeRozan 4.00 10.00
4 LeBron James 25.00 60.00
5 James Harden 6.00 15.00
6 Giannis Antetokounmpo 5.00 12.00
7 Kenneth Faried 2.50 6.00
8 Shabazz Muhammad 2.00 5.00
9 Aaron Gordon 3.00 8.00
10 Bobby Portis 3.00 8.00
11 Jusuf Nurkic 2.50 6.00
12 Marcus Morris 2.00 5.00
13 Russell Westbrook 5.00 12.00
14 Enes Kanter 2.00 5.00
15 Kevin Durant 6.00 15.00
16 Tyler Ennis 2.00 5.00
17 Alex Len 2.00 5.00
18 Tristan Thompson 2.50 6.00
19 Emmanuel Mudiay 2.50 6.00
20 J.R. Smith 3.00 8.00
21 Dwyane Wade 5.00 12.00
22 Dwight Powell 2.00 5.00
23 Jimmy Butler 6.00 15.00
24 Jordan Clarkson 3.00 8.00
25 Archie Goodwin 2.00 5.00
26 Dirk Nowitzki 8.00 20.00
27 Anthony Davis 5.00 12.00
28 Michael Beasley 2.00 5.00
29 John Henson 2.00 5.00
30 Reggie Jackson 2.50 6.00
31 Zach LaVine 6.00 15.00
32 Justise Winslow 2.50 6.00
33 Andrew Wiggins 4.00 10.00
34 Carmelo Anthony 5.00 12.00
35 Jonathon Simmons 2.00 5.00
36 Kent Bazemore 2.00 5.00
37 C.J. McCollum 3.00 8.00
39 Devin Harris 2.00 5.00
40 Kawhi Leonard 8.00 20.00
41 LaMarcus Aldridge 3.00 8.00
42 Trevor Ariza 2.00 5.00
43 Nicolas Batum 2.50 6.00
44 Khris Middleton 3.00 8.00
45 Kyle Lowry 3.00 8.00
46 Kobe Bryant 8.00 20.00
47 Larry Nance 2.50 6.00
48 Clyde Drexler 5.00 12.00
49 Steve Francis 2.50 6.00
50 Bernard King 4.00 10.00
51 Julius Erving 8.00 20.00
52 Dan Majerle 2.50 6.00
53 Tom Chambers 2.50 6.00
54 Shaquille O'Neal 5.00 12.00
55 Shawn Marion 2.50 6.00
56 Kenny Smith 2.50 6.00
57 Larry Johnson 4.00 10.00
58 Manu Ginobili 6.00 15.00
59 Rashard Lewis 2.50 6.00
60 Ray Allen 5.00 12.00

2016-17 Absolute Memorabilia Freshman Flyer Jersey Autographs

STATED PRINT RUN 75 SER.#'d SETS
EXCHANGE DEADLINE 8/21/2018
1 Brandon Ingram 30.00 80.00
2 Wade Baldwin IV 3.00 8.00
3 Cheick Diallo 3.00 8.00
4 Tyler Ulis 4.00 10.00
5 Jaylen Brown 75.00 200.00
6 Henry Ellenson 3.00 8.00
7 Patrick McCaw 3.00 8.00
8 Dragan Bender 6.00 15.00
9 Malik Beasley 6.00 15.00
10 Kris Dunn 5.00 12.00
11 DeAndre' Bembry 5.00 12.00
12 Isaiah Whitehead 3.00 8.00
13 Demetrius Jackson 3.00 8.00
14 Buddy Hield 10.00 25.00
15 Malachi Richardson 3.00 8.00
16 Kay Felder 3.00 8.00
17 Jamal Murray 75.00 200.00
18 Timothe Luwawu-Cabarrot 5.00 12.00
19 Marquese Chriss 4.00 10.00
20 Brice Johnson 3.00 8.00
21 Ivica Zubac 8.00 20.00
22 Malcolm Brogdon 10.00 25.00
23 Jakob Poeltl 6.00 15.00
24 Pascal Siakam 20.00 50.00
25 Diamond Stone 3.00 8.00
26 Thon Maker 4.00 10.00
27 Skal Labissiere 6.00 15.00
28 Taurean Prince 4.00 10.00
29 Dejounte Murray 100.00 250.00
30 Damian Jones 3.00 8.00
31 Gary Payton II 8.00 20.00
32 Caris LeVert 8.00 20.00
33 Denzel Valentine 3.00 8.00
34 Deyonta Davis 3.00 8.00
35 Chinanu Onuaku 3.00 8.00
36 Juan Hernangomez 12.00 30.00
37 Georgios Papagiannis 3.00 8.00
38 Stephen Zimmerman 3.00 8.00

2016-17 Absolute Memorabilia Freshman Flyer Jumbo Jerseys

STATED PRINT RUN 75 SER.#'d SETS
1 Brandon Ingram 6.00 15.00
2 Jaylen Brown 6.00 15.00
3 Dragan Bender 2.00 5.00
4 Kris Dunn 3.00 8.00
5 Buddy Hield 5.00 12.00
6 Jamal Murray 12.00 30.00
7 Marquese Chriss 2.50 6.00
8 Jakob Poeltl 4.00 10.00
9 Thon Maker 2.50 6.00
11 Taurean Prince 2.50 6.00
12 Denzel Valentine 2.00 5.00
13 Wade Baldwin IV 2.00 5.00
14 Henry Ellenson 2.00 5.00
15 Malik Beasley 4.00 10.00
16 DeAndre' Bembry 3.00 8.00
17 Malachi Richardson 2.00 5.00
18 Timothe Luwawu-Cabarrot 3.00 8.00
19 Brice Johnson 2.00 5.00
20 Pascal Siakam 12.00 30.00
21 Skal Labissiere 2.00 5.00
22 Damian Jones 2.00 5.00
23 Deyonta Davis 2.00 5.00
24 Cheick Diallo 2.00 5.00
25 Tyler Ulis 2.50 6.00
26 Patrick McCaw 2.00 5.00
27 Isaiah Whitehead 2.00 5.00
28 Demetrius Jackson 2.00 5.00
29 Kay Felder 2.00 5.00
30 Ivica Zubac 5.00 12.00
31 Malcolm Brogdon 6.00 15.00
32 A.J. Hammons 2.00 5.00
33 Diamond Stone 2.00 5.00
34 Gary Payton II 5.00 12.00
35 Caris LeVert 5.00 12.00
36 Chinanu Onuaku 2.00 5.00
37 Juan Hernangomez 4.00 10.00
38 Georgios Papagiannis 2.00 5.00
39 Dejounte Murray 10.00 25.00
40 Stephen Zimmerman 2.00 5.00

2016-17 Absolute Memorabilia Glass

EXCHANGE DEADLINE 8/21/2018
1 Ben Simmons 25.00 60.00
2 Brandon Ingram 60.00 150.00
3 Kris Dunn 12.00 30.00
4 Jaylen Brown 60.00 150.00
5 Buddy Hield 25.00 60.00
6 Jamal Murray 60.00 150.00
7 Anthony Davis 40.00 100.00
8 Kyrie Irving 25.00 60.00
9 Kevin Durant 50.00 120.00
10 Chris Paul 20.00 50.00
11 Karl-Anthony Towns 25.00 60.00
12 Russell Westbrook 20.00 50.00
13 Andrew Wiggins 15.00 40.00
14 Stephen Curry 100.00 250.00
15 LeBron James 100.00 250.00
16 Kawhi Leonard 30.00 80.00
17 Dirk Nowitzki 30.00 80.00
18 Jimmy Butler 30.00 80.00
19 James Harden 25.00 60.00
20 Karl Malone 25.00 60.00
21 Kobe Bryant 100.00 250.00
22 Steve Nash 20.00 50.00
23 Patrick Ewing 20.00 50.00
24 Scottie Pippen 25.00 60.00
25 Allen Iverson 25.00 60.00

2016-17 Absolute Memorabilia Heroes Autographs

PRINT RUN B/WN 60-75 COPIES PER
EXCHANGE DEADLINE 8/21/2018
3 Kevin Durant/60 125.00 300.00
4 Blake Griffin/60 8.00 20.00
5 Elfrid Payton/75 4.00 10.00
6 Kevin Love/60 12.00 30.00
7 D'Angelo Russell/60 12.00 30.00
8 Chris Paul/60 75.00 200.00
9 Devin Booker/75 125.00 300.00
10 Bobby Portis/75 5.00 12.00
11 Jabari Parker/60 3.00 8.00
12 Myles Turner/75 8.00 20.00
13 Anthony Davis/60 60.00 150.00
14 Victor Oladipo/75 4.00 10.00
15 Reggie Jackson/75 4.00 10.00
16 Andrew Wiggins/60 20.00 50.00
17 Julius Randle/75 20.00 50.00
18 Tony Parker/60 20.00 50.00
19 Paul Millsap/75 4.00 10.00
21 Eric Bledsoe/75 4.00 10.00
22 LaMarcus Aldridge/75 15.00 40.00
23 Chris Bosh/60 12.00 30.00
24 Karl-Anthony Towns/60 25.00 60.00
25 Kristaps Porzingis/75 12.00 30.00
26 Jahlil Okafor/60 3.00 8.00
27 Draymond Green/75 25.00 60.00
28 Dwyane Wade/60 75.00 200.00
29 Emmanuel Mudiay/75 3.00 8.00
30 Carmelo Anthony/60 40.00 100.00

2016-17 Absolute Memorabilia Heroes Materials

PRINT RUNS B/WN 49-149 COPIES PER
1 Alvan Adams/99 2.50 6.00
2 Allen Iverson/99 5.00 12.00
3 Manute Bol/99 3.00 8.00
4 Kevin McHale/99 5.00 12.00
5 Danny Ainge/99 3.00 8.00
6 Yao Ming/99 5.00 12.00
7 Kobe Bryant/149 8.00 20.00
8 Shaquille O'Neal/149 5.00 12.00
9 Christian Laettner/149 3.00 8.00
10 Tim Duncan/149 4.00 10.00
11 Stephen Curry/149 25.00 60.00
12 LeBron James/149 25.00 60.00
14 Chris Paul/149 5.00 12.00
16 Steve Nash/90 5.00 12.00
17 Xavier McDaniel/149 2.00 5.00
18 Detlef Schrempf/149 3.00 8.00
19 James Harden/149 6.00 15.00
20 Joe Johnson/149 3.00 8.00
21 Andrei Kirilenko/99 3.00 8.00
22 Manu Ginobili/149 6.00 15.00
23 Walter Davis/149 3.00 8.00
24 Bill Walton/49 5.00 12.00
25 Nate Thurmond/49 2.50 6.00
26 Paul Pierce/149 5.00 12.00
27 Rashard Lewis/149 2.50 6.00
28 Rik Smits/149 2.50 6.00
29 Robert Parish/149 4.00 10.00
30 Reggie Lewis/149 3.00 8.00
31 Mitch Richmond/149 3.00 8.00
32 Kevin Duckworth/149 2.00 5.00
33 Glen Rice/149 3.00 8.00
34 George Mikan/49 8.00 20.00
35 Elgin Baylor/49 6.00 15.00
36 Dwyane Wade/149 5.00 12.00
37 Derrick Rose/149 5.00 12.00
38 Chris Bosh/149 4.00 10.00
39 Walter Berry/149 2.00 5.00
40 Clifford Robinson/149 8.00 20.00

2016-17 Absolute Memorabilia Iconic Autographs

PRINT RUN B/WN 60-75 COPIES PER
EXCHANGE DEADLINE 8/21/2018
1 Jason Kidd/60 10.00 25.00
2 Danny Manning/75 4.00 10.00
3 Isiah Thomas/75 8.00 20.00
4 Ray Allen/60 15.00 40.00
5 Robert Parish/75 6.00 15.00
6 Gary Payton/60 10.00 25.00
7 Jalen Rose/75 4.00 10.00
8 Walt Frazier/75 5.00 12.00
9 A.C. Green/75 5.00 12.00
11 Hersey Hawkins/75 3.00 8.00
12 Glen Rice/75 5.00 12.00
13 Bob McAdoo/75 8.00 20.00
14 Clyde Drexler/60 12.00 30.00
15 Michael Finley/75 5.00 12.00
16 Mitch Richmond/75 8.00 20.00
17 Joe Dumars/75 5.00 12.00
18 Anfernee Hardaway/60 20.00 50.00
19 Bill Walton/75 25.00 60.00
20 Dominique Wilkins/60 8.00 20.00
21 Tracy McGrady/60 125.00 300.00
22 Grant Hill/60 12.00 30.00
25 Dikembe Mutombo/75 8.00 20.00
26 Dan Majerle/75 5.00 12.00
27 Damon Stoudamire/75 5.00 12.00
28 Steve Smith/75 4.00 10.00
29 Antonio McDyess/75 4.00 10.00
30 Ralph Sampson/75 4.00 10.00
31 Jo Jo White/75 4.00 10.00
32 Robert Horry/75 6.00 15.00
33 Mark Jackson/75 4.00 10.00
34 John Starks/75 5.00 12.00
35 Horace Grant/75 5.00 12.00
36 Jeff Hornacek/75 4.00 10.00
37 Bob Dandridge/75 5.00 12.00
38 Magic Johnson/60 25.00 60.00
39 Mark Aguirre/75 4.00 10.00
40 Cedric Maxwell/75 4.00 10.00

2016-17 Absolute Memorabilia Iconic Materials

PRINT RUNS B/WN 49-149 COPIES PER
1 Kobe Bryant/149 8.00 20.00
2 Clyde Drexler/149 5.00 12.00
3 Hakeem Olajuwon/149 6.00 15.00
4 Patrick Ewing/149 4.00 10.00
5 Shaquille O'Neal/149 5.00 12.00
6 Chauncey Billups/149 4.00 10.00
7 Chris Mullin/149 3.00 8.00
8 Dennis Johnson/149 2.50 6.00
9 Larry Bird/49 6.00 15.00
10 Dikembe Mutombo/149 5.00 12.00
11 Lucius Allen/149 3.00 8.00
12 Wilt Chamberlain/49 30.00 80.00
13 Karl Malone/149 5.00 12.00
14 John Stockton/149 5.00 12.00
15 Tom Chambers/149 2.50 6.00
16 Michael Redd/149 2.50 6.00
17 Jason Kidd/49 5.00 12.00
18 Magic Johnson/149 12.00 30.00
19 Bernard King/149 4.00 10.00
20 Earl Monroe/99 5.00 12.00
21 John Starks/149 3.00 8.00
22 Kelly Tripucka/149 2.00 5.00
23 Jamaal Wilkes/149 3.00 8.00
24 James Worthy/149 4.00 10.00
25 LeBron James/149 10.00 25.00
26 Kevin Garnett/149 8.00 20.00
27 Dirk Nowitzki/149 8.00 20.00
28 Tim Duncan/149 4.00 10.00
29 DeMar DeRozan/149 4.00 10.00
30 Carmelo Anthony/149 5.00 12.00

2016-17 Absolute Memorabilia Marks of Fame

PRINT RUN B/WN 60-75 COPIES PER
EXCHANGE DEADLINE 8/21/2018
1 Kobe Bryant/75 500.00 1,000.00
2 Kevin Durant/60 60.00 150.00
3 Kyrie Irving/60 25.00 60.00
4 Paul Westphal/75 5.00 12.00
5 Jeff Hornacek/75 4.00 10.00
6 Sean Elliott/75 4.00 10.00
7 Tony Parker/60 12.00 30.00
8 Chris Bosh/60 6.00 15.00
9 Dan Issel/75 6.00 15.00
10 Jamaal Wilkes/75 5.00 12.00
11 Bernard King/60 6.00 15.00
12 Adrian Dantley/75 5.00 12.00
13 Toni Kukoc/75 6.00 15.00
14 Andrew Wiggins/60 15.00 40.00
15 Isiah Thomas/60 8.00 20.00
16 Robert Horry/60 6.00 15.00
17 Zach LaVine/75 10.00 25.00
18 Robert Parish/60 6.00 15.00
19 Dennis Schroder/75 5.00 12.00
20 Giannis Antetokounmpo/75 60.00 150.00
21 Nick Van Exel/60 8.00 20.00
22 Bill Laimbeer/75 5.00 12.00
23 Bill Russell/60 600.00 1,200.00
24 Jim Jackson/75 4.00 10.00
25 Mark Price/75 5.00 12.00
26 Evan Turner/75 3.00 8.00
27 Kiki Vandeweghe/75 4.00 10.00
28 David Robinson/60 20.00 50.00
29 Tim Hardaway/75 10.00 25.00
30 Kurt Rambis/75 5.00 12.00

2016-17 Absolute Memorabilia NBA Stars Materials

STATED PRINT RUN 149 SER.#'d SETS
1 Dirk Nowitzki 8.00 20.00
2 Kyrie Irving 5.00 12.00
3 Eric Bledsoe 2.50 6.00
4 LeBron James 25.00 60.00
5 Karl-Anthony Towns 5.00 12.00
6 Stephen Curry 25.00 60.00
7 DeMar DeRozan 4.00 10.00
8 Isaiah Thomas 2.50 6.00
9 Deron Williams 2.50 6.00
10 James Harden 6.00 15.00
11 Russell Westbrook 5.00 12.00
12 Andrew Wiggins 4.00 10.00
13 Carmelo Anthony 5.00 12.00
14 Damian Lillard 5.00 12.00
15 John Wall 4.00 10.00
16 Anthony Davis 5.00 12.00
17 Blake Griffin 3.00 8.00
18 Kevin Garnett 8.00 20.00
19 Jabari Parker 2.00 5.00
20 Jimmy Butler 6.00 15.00
21 Paul George 5.00 12.00
22 Gordon Hayward 3.00 8.00
23 DeMarcus Cousins 2.50 6.00
24 Draymond Green 4.00 10.00
25 Brandon Knight 2.50 6.00
26 Kenneth Faried 2.50 6.00
27 Myles Turner 3.00 8.00
28 Dwight Howard 4.00 10.00
29 Giannis Antetokounmpo 5.00 12.00
30 Nerlens Noel 2.00 5.00

2016-17 Absolute Memorabilia Rookie Autographs

STATED PRINT RUN 99 SER.#'d SETS
EXCHANGE DEADLINE 8/21/2018
1 Brandon Ingram 25.00 60.00
2 Jaylen Brown 125.00 300.00
3 Dragan Bender 6.00 15.00
4 Kris Dunn 5.00 12.00
5 Buddy Hield 10.00 25.00
6 Jamal Murray 30.00 80.00
7 Marquese Chriss 4.00 10.00
8 Jakob Poeltl 6.00 15.00
9 Thon Maker 10.00 25.00
10 Domantas Sabonis 20.00 50.00
11 Taurean Prince 4.00 10.00
12 Denzel Valentine 3.00 8.00
13 Wade Baldwin IV 3.00 8.00
14 Henry Ellenson 3.00 8.00
15 Malik Beasley 6.00 15.00
16 DeAndre' Bembry 5.00 12.00
17 Malachi Richardson 3.00 8.00
18 Timothe Luwawu-Cabarrot 5.00 12.00
19 Brice Johnson 3.00 8.00
20 Pascal Siakam 20.00 50.00
21 Skal Labissiere 3.00 8.00
22 Damian Jones 3.00 8.00
23 Deyonta Davis 3.00 8.00
24 Cheick Diallo 3.00 8.00
25 Tyler Ulis 4.00 10.00
26 Patrick McCaw 3.00 8.00
27 Isaiah Whitehead 3.00 8.00
28 Demetrius Jackson 3.00 8.00
29 Kay Felder 3.00 8.00
30 Ivica Zubac 8.00 20.00
31 Malcolm Brogdon 10.00 25.00
32 A.J. Hammons 3.00 8.00
33 Diamond Stone 3.00 8.00
34 Gary Payton II 8.00 20.00
35 Caris LeVert 8.00 20.00

2016-17 Absolute Memorabilia Team Quads Materials

STATED PRINT RUN 25 SER.#'d SETS
1 Wiggins/Towns/Garnett/LaVine 10.00 25.00
2 Love/Irving/James/Thompson 25.00 60.00
3 Mudiay/Nurkic/Faried/Jokic 20.00 50.00
4 Williams/Nowitzki/Anderson/Matthews 10.00 25.00
5 Bradley/Thomas/Crowder/Smart 5.00 12.00

2016-17 Absolute Memorabilia Team Tandems Materials

STATED PRINT RUN 149 SER.#'d SETS
*PRIME/25: .75X TO 2X BASIC
1 K.Thompson/S.Curry 10.00 25.00
2 D.Schroder/P.Millsap 3.00 8.00
3 C.Anthony/K.Porzingis 5.00 12.00
4 A.Davis/T.Evans 5.00 12.00
5 E.Kanter/S.Adams 2.50 6.00
6 A.Gordon/E.Payton 3.00 8.00
7 B.Griffin/D.Jordan 3.00 8.00
8 D.Russell/J.Randle 4.00 10.00
9 M.Conley/Z.Randolph 3.00 8.00
10 A.Wiggins/Z.LaVine 6.00 15.00
11 D.DeRozan/K.Lowry 4.00 10.00
12 B.Bogdanovic/B.Lopez 2.50 6.00
13 J.Wall/M.Gortat 4.00 10.00
14 C.Drexler/H.Olajuwon 6.00 15.00
15 K.Bryant/S.O'Neal 12.00 30.00
16 I.Thomas/J.Dumars 5.00 12.00
17 R.Parish/S.Pippen 5.00 12.00
18 A.Mourning/L.Johnson 5.00 12.00
19 J.Kidd/J.Jackson 5.00 12.00

2016-17 Absolute Memorabilia Team Trios Materials

STATED PRINT RUN 49 SER.#'d SETS
1 Wiggins/Towns/LaVine 6.00 15.00
2 Love/Irving/James 30.00 80.00
3 Mudiay/Faried/Jokic 20.00 50.00
4 Williams/Nowitzki/Anderson 10.00 25.00
5 Bradley/Thomas/Crowder 8.00 20.00
6 Capela/Brewer/Harden 5.00 12.00
7 Ellis/Turner/George 6.00 15.00
8 Griffin/Paul/Jordan 6.00 15.00
9 Drummond/Caldwell-Pope/Jackson 4.00 10.00
10 Antetokounmpo/Monroe
Carter-Williams 5.00 12.00

2016-17 Absolute Memorabilia Tools of the Trade Jumbo Rookie Material Signatures

STATED PRINT RUN 49 SER.#'d SETS
EXCHANGE DEADLINE 8/21/2018
1 Brandon Ingram 30.00 80.00
2 Isaiah Whitehead 3.00 8.00
3 DeAndre' Bembry 5.00 12.00
4 Marquese Chriss 4.00 10.00
5 Wade Baldwin IV 3.00 8.00
6 Denzel Valentine 8.00 20.00
7 Dragan Bender 10.00 25.00
8 Deyonta Davis 3.00 8.00
9 Georgios Papagiannis 3.00 8.00
10 Jamal Murray 125.00 300.00
11 Demetrius Jackson 3.00 8.00
12 Kris Dunn 5.00 12.00
13 Brice Johnson 3.00 8.00
14 Tyler Ulis 4.00 10.00
15 Jaylen Brown 125.00 300.00
16 Jakob Poeltl 6.00 15.00
17 Timothe Luwawu-Cabarrot 5.00 12.00
18 Buddy Hield 12.00 30.00
19 Malik Beasley 6.00 15.00
20 Pascal Siakam 20.00 50.00
21 Ivica Zubac 8.00 20.00
22 Henry Ellenson 3.00 8.00
23 Diamond Stone 3.00 8.00
24 Thon Maker 4.00 10.00
25 Skal Labissiere 5.00 12.00
26 Taurean Prince 4.00 10.00
27 Juan Hernangomez 6.00 15.00
29 Stephen Zimmerman 3.00 8.00
30 Damian Jones 3.00 8.00
31 Chinanu Onuaku 3.00 8.00
32 Caris LeVert 8.00 20.00
33 Malachi Richardson 3.00 8.00

2016-17 Absolute Memorabilia Tools of the Trade Rookie Autograph Materials

STATED PRINT RUN 75 SER. #'d SETS
EXCHANGE DEADLINE 8/21/2018
1 Brandon Ingram 15.00 40.00
2 Isaiah Whitehead 4.00 10.00
3 DeAndre' Bembry 6.00 15.00
4 Marquese Chriss 5.00 12.00
5 Wade Baldwin IV 4.00 10.00
6 Denzel Valentine 4.00 10.00
7 Dragan Bender 4.00 10.00
8 Deyonta Davis 4.00 10.00
9 Georgios Papagiannis 4.00 10.00
10 Jamal Murray 125.00 300.00
11 Demetrius Jackson 4.00 10.00
12 Kris Dunn 6.00 15.00
13 Brice Johnson 4.00 10.00
14 Tyler Ulis 5.00 12.00
15 Jaylen Brown 125.00 300.00
16 Jakob Poeltl 8.00 20.00
17 Timothe Luwawu-Cabarrot 6.00 15.00
18 Buddy Hield 15.00 40.00
19 Malik Beasley 6.00 15.00
20 Pascal Siakam 20.00 50.00
21 Ivica Zubac 10.00 25.00
22 Henry Ellenson 4.00 10.00
23 Diamond Stone 4.00 10.00
24 Thon Maker 5.00 12.00
25 Skal Labissiere 4.00 10.00
26 Taurean Prince 5.00 12.00
27 Juan Hernangomez 8.00 20.00
29 Stephen Zimmerman 4.00 10.00
30 Damian Jones 4.00 10.00
31 Chinanu Onuaku 4.00 10.00
32 Caris LeVert 10.00 25.00
33 Malachi Richardson 4.00 10.00

2016-17 Absolute Memorabilia Tools of the Trade Rookie Materials Dual

STATED PRINT RUN 149 SER. #'d SETS
*PRIME/49: .5X TO 1.2X BASIC
*PATCH/25: .6X TO 1.5X BASIC
1 Brandon Ingram 6.00 15.00
2 Isaiah Whitehead 2.50 6.00
3 DeAndre' Bembry 4.00 10.00
4 Marquese Chriss 3.00 8.00
5 Wade Baldwin IV 2.50 6.00
6 Denzel Valentine 2.50 6.00
7 Dragan Bender 2.50 6.00
8 Deyonta Davis 2.50 6.00
9 Georgios Papagiannis 2.50 6.00
10 Jamal Murray 12.00 30.00
11 Demetrius Jackson 2.50 6.00
12 Kris Dunn 4.00 10.00
13 Brice Johnson 2.50 6.00
14 Tyler Ulis 3.00 8.00
15 Jaylen Brown 6.00 15.00
16 Jakob Poeltl 5.00 12.00
17 Timothe Luwawu-Cabarrot 4.00 10.00
18 Buddy Hield 8.00 20.00
19 Malik Beasley 5.00 12.00
20 Pascal Siakam 15.00 40.00
21 Ivica Zubac 6.00 15.00
22 Henry Ellenson 2.50 6.00
23 Diamond Stone 2.50 6.00
24 Thon Maker 3.00 8.00
25 Skal Labissiere 2.50 6.00
26 Taurean Prince 3.00 8.00
27 Juan Hernangomez 5.00 12.00
28 Dejounte Murray 12.00 30.00
29 Stephen Zimmerman 2.50 6.00
30 Damian Jones 2.50 6.00
31 Chinanu Onuaku 2.50 6.00
32 Caris LeVert 6.00 15.00
33 Malachi Richardson 2.50 6.00

2016-17 Absolute Memorabilia Tools of the Trade Rookie Materials Jumbo

STATED PRINT RUN 149 SER. #'d SETS
*PRIME/25: .75X TO 2X BASIC
1 Brandon Ingram 6.00 15.00
2 Isaiah Whitehead 2.50 6.00
3 DeAndre' Bembry 4.00 10.00
4 Marquese Chriss 3.00 8.00
5 Wade Baldwin IV 2.50 6.00
6 Denzel Valentine 2.50 6.00
7 Dragan Bender 2.50 6.00
8 Deyonta Davis 2.50 6.00
9 Georgios Papagiannis 2.50 6.00
10 Jamal Murray 12.00 30.00
11 Demetrius Jackson 2.50 6.00
12 Kris Dunn 4.00 10.00
13 Brice Johnson 2.50 6.00
14 Tyler Ulis 3.00 8.00
15 Jaylen Brown 6.00 15.00
16 Jakob Poeltl 5.00 12.00
17 Timothe Luwawu-Cabarrot 4.00 10.00
18 Buddy Hield 8.00 20.00
19 Malik Beasley 5.00 12.00
20 Pascal Siakam 15.00 40.00
21 Ivica Zubac 6.00 15.00
22 Henry Ellenson 2.50 6.00
23 Diamond Stone 2.50 6.00
24 Thon Maker 3.00 8.00
25 Skal Labissiere 2.50 6.00
26 Taurean Prince 3.00 8.00
27 Juan Hernangomez 5.00 12.00
28 Dejounte Murray 12.00 30.00
29 Stephen Zimmerman 2.50 6.00
30 Damian Jones 2.50 6.00
31 Chinanu Onuaku 2.50 6.00
32 Caris LeVert 6.00 15.00
33 Malachi Richardson 2.50 6.00

2016-17 Absolute Memorabilia Tools of the Trade Rookie Materials Quad

STATED PRINT RUN 125 SER. #'d SETS
*PRIME: .6X TO 1.5X BASIC
1 Brandon Ingram 8.00 20.00
2 Isaiah Whitehead 3.00 8.00
3 DeAndre' Bembry 5.00 12.00
4 Marquese Chriss 4.00 10.00
5 Wade Baldwin IV 3.00 8.00
6 Denzel Valentine 3.00 8.00
7 Dragan Bender 3.00 8.00
8 Deyonta Davis 3.00 8.00
9 Georgios Papagiannis 3.00 8.00
10 Jamal Murray 15.00 40.00
11 Demetrius Jackson 3.00 8.00
12 Kris Dunn 5.00 12.00
13 Brice Johnson 3.00 8.00
14 Tyler Ulis 4.00 10.00
15 Jaylen Brown 6.00 15.00
16 Jakob Poeltl 6.00 15.00
17 Timothe Luwawu-Cabarrot 5.00 12.00
18 Buddy Hield 10.00 25.00
19 Malik Beasley 6.00 15.00
20 Pascal Siakam 20.00 50.00
21 Ivica Zubac 8.00 20.00
22 Henry Ellenson 3.00 8.00
23 Diamond Stone 3.00 8.00
24 Thon Maker 4.00 10.00
25 Skal Labissiere 3.00 8.00
26 Taurean Prince 4.00 10.00
27 Juan Hernangomez 6.00 15.00
28 Dejounte Murray 15.00 40.00
29 Stephen Zimmerman 3.00 8.00
30 Damian Jones 3.00 8.00
31 Chinanu Onuaku 3.00 8.00
32 Caris LeVert 8.00 20.00
33 Malachi Richardson 3.00 8.00

2016-17 Absolute Memorabilia Tools of the Trade Rookie Materials Six

STATED PRINT RUN 75 SER. #'d SETS
*PRIME/25: .6X TO 1.5X BASIC
1 Brandon Ingram 8.00 20.00
2 Isaiah Whitehead 3.00 8.00
3 DeAndre' Bembry 5.00 12.00
4 Marquese Chriss 4.00 10.00
5 Wade Baldwin IV 3.00 8.00
6 Denzel Valentine 3.00 8.00
7 Dragan Bender 3.00 8.00
8 Deyonta Davis 3.00 8.00
9 Georgios Papagiannis 3.00 8.00
10 Jamal Murray 15.00 40.00
11 Demetrius Jackson 3.00 8.00
12 Kris Dunn 5.00 12.00
13 Brice Johnson 3.00 8.00
14 Tyler Ulis 4.00 10.00
15 Jaylen Brown 8.00 20.00
16 Jakob Poeltl 6.00 15.00
17 Timothe Luwawu-Cabarrot 6.00 15.00
18 Buddy Hield 10.00 25.00
19 Malik Beasley 6.00 15.00
20 Pascal Siakam 20.00 50.00
21 Ivica Zubac 10.00 25.00
22 Henry Ellenson 3.00 8.00
23 Diamond Stone 3.00 8.00
24 Thon Maker 4.00 10.00
25 Skal Labissiere 3.00 8.00
26 Taurean Prince 4.00 10.00
27 Juan Hernangomez 6.00 15.00
28 Dejounte Murray 15.00 40.00
29 Stephen Zimmerman 3.00 8.00
30 Damian Jones 3.00 8.00
31 Chinanu Onuaku 3.00 8.00
32 Caris LeVert 8.00 20.00
33 Malachi Richardson 3.00 8.00

2016-17 Absolute Memorabilia Tools of the Trade Rookie Materials Trio

STATED PRINT RUN 149 SER. #'d SETS
*PRIME/25: .6X TO 1.5X BASIC
1 Brandon Ingram 6.00 15.00
2 Isaiah Whitehead 2.50 6.00
3 DeAndre' Bembry 4.00 10.00
4 Marquese Chriss 3.00 8.00
5 Wade Baldwin IV 2.50 6.00
6 Denzel Valentine 2.50 6.00
7 Dragan Bender 2.50 6.00
8 Deyonta Davis 2.50 6.00
9 Georgios Papagiannis 2.50 6.00
10 Jamal Murray 12.00 30.00
11 Demetrius Jackson 2.50 6.00
12 Kris Dunn 4.00 10.00
13 Brice Johnson 2.50 6.00
14 Tyler Ulis 2.50 6.00
15 Jaylen Brown 6.00 15.00
16 Jakob Poeltl 5.00 12.00
17 Timothe Luwawu-Cabarrot 4.00 10.00
18 Buddy Hield 8.00 20.00
19 Malik Beasley 5.00 12.00
20 Pascal Siakam 15.00 40.00
21 Ivica Zubac 6.00 15.00
22 Henry Ellenson 2.50 6.00
23 Diamond Stone 2.50 6.00
24 Thon Maker 3.00 8.00
25 Skal Labissiere 2.50 6.00
26 Taurean Prince 2.50 6.00
27 Juan Hernangomez 5.00 12.00
28 Dejounte Murray 12.00 30.00
29 Stephen Zimmerman 2.50 6.00
30 Damian Jones 2.50 6.00
31 Chinanu Onuaku 2.50 6.00
32 Caris LeVert 6.00 15.00
33 Malachi Richardson 2.50 6.00

2017-18 Absolute Memorabilia

1 Kyrie Irving 3.00 8.00
2 Kevin Durant 6.00 15.00
3 Giannis Antetokounmpo 8.00 20.00
4 Carmelo Anthony 2.50 6.00
5 Russell Westbrook 2.50 6.00
6 Jimmy Butler 2.50 6.00
7 Damian Lillard 4.00 10.00
8 Dwyane Wade 3.00 8.00
9 Kawhi Leonard 4.00 10.00
10 Devin Booker 4.00 10.00
11 Rudy Gobert 2.00 5.00
12 Marc Gasol 1.50 4.00
13 LeBron James 10.00 25.00
14 Zach Randolph 1.50 4.00
15 Brandon Ingram 2.00 5.00
16 Blake Griffin 1.50 4.00
17 Tony Parker 2.50 6.00
18 Dennis Schroder 1.25 3.00
19 Ben Simmons 1.50 4.00
20 Andre Drummond 1.25 3.00
21 DeMar DeRozan 2.00 5.00
22 Jeremy Lin 2.50 6.00
23 Goran Dragic 1.25 3.00
24 Buddy Hield 1.50 4.00
25 Harrison Barnes 1.25 3.00
26 Pau Gasol 2.50 6.00
27 Eric Bledsoe 1.25 3.00
28 Kyle Lowry 1.50 4.00
29 Gordon Hayward 1.25 3.00
30 James Harden 3.00 8.00
31 Steven Adams 1.25 3.00
32 Nikola Jokic 10.00 25.00
33 Evan Fournier 1.25 3.00
34 Stephen Curry 12.00 30.00
35 Kemba Walker 1.25 3.00
36 Joel Embiid 3.00 8.00
37 C.J. McCollum 1.50 4.00
38 Derrick Rose 2.50 6.00
39 Willie Cauley-Stein 1.00 2.50
40 Kentavious Caldwell-Pope 1.25 3.00
41 Anthony Davis 4.00 10.00
42 Mike Conley 1.25 3.00
43 Nerlens Noel 1.00 2.50
44 DeAndre Jordan 1.25 3.00
45 Karl-Anthony Towns 2.50 6.00
46 Tobias Harris 1.25 3.00
47 Chris Paul 2.50 6.00
48 D'Angelo Russell 1.25 3.00
49 Elfrid Payton 1.00 2.50
50 Paul Millsap 1.25 3.00
51 Paul George 2.50 6.00
52 Draymond Green 2.00 5.00
53 Zach LaVine 2.50 6.00
54 Kristaps Porzingis 2.00 5.00
55 Dwight Howard 2.00 5.00
56 Brook Lopez 1.25 3.00
57 DeMarcus Cousins 1.25 3.00
58 Malcolm Brogdon 1.25 3.00
59 Dirk Nowitzki 4.00 10.00
60 Aaron Gordon 1.50 4.00
61 Isaiah Thomas 1.25 3.00
62 Myles Turner 1.50 4.00
63 Vince Carter 3.00 8.00
64 Jabari Parker 1.00 2.50
65 Trevor Ariza 1.00 2.50
66 Markelle Fultz RC 5.00 12.00
67 Lonzo Ball RC 8.00 20.00
68 Jayson Tatum RC 30.00 80.00
69 Josh Jackson RC 2.50 6.00
70 De'Aaron Fox RC 15.00 40.00
71 Jonathan Isaac RC 5.00 12.00
72 Lauri Markkanen RC 12.00 30.00
73 Frank Ntilikina RC 2.50 6.00
74 Dennis Smith Jr. RC 2.50 6.00
75 Zach Collins RC 3.00 8.00
76 Malik Monk RC 8.00 20.00
77 Luke Kennard RC 4.00 10.00
78 Donovan Mitchell RC 30.00 80.00
79 Bam Adebayo RC 30.00 80.00
80 Justin Jackson RC 2.00 5.00
81 Justin Patton RC 2.00 5.00
82 D.J. Wilson RC 2.00 5.00
83 T.J. Leaf RC 2.00 5.00
84 John Collins RC 5.00 12.00
85 Harry Giles RC 2.00 5.00
86 Jarrett Allen RC 5.00 12.00
87 OG Anunoby RC 10.00 25.00
88 Tyler Lydon RC 2.00 5.00
89 Kyle Kuzma RC 8.00 20.00
90 Tony Bradley RC 2.00 5.00
91 Caleb Swanigan RC 2.00 5.00
92 Derrick White RC 8.00 20.00
93 Frank Jackson RC 5.00 12.00
94 Josh Hart RC 5.00 12.00
95 Jordan Bell RC 2.00 5.00
96 Jawun Evans RC 2.00 5.00
97 Dwayne Bacon RC 2.00 5.00
98 Wesley Iwundu RC 2.00 5.00
99 Ivan Rabb RC 2.00 5.00
100 Semi Ojeleye RC 2.50 6.00

2017-18 Absolute Memorabilia Determination Autographs

PRINT RUNS B/WN 15-49 COPIES PER
NO PRICING ON QTY 15
EXCHANGE DEADLINE 6/29/2019
*ORANGE/25: .5X TO 1.2X p/r 49-99
1 Walt Frazier/49 8.00 20.00
2 Chauncey Billups/49 6.00 15.00
3 John Starks/99 4.00 10.00
4 Shawn Marion/49 4.00 10.00
5 Kobe Bryant/25 500.00 1,000.00
6 Richard Jefferson/99 4.00 10.00
7 Andrew Wiggins/25 15.00 40.00
8 Evan Turner/99 3.00 8.00
9 Mike Muscala/99 3.00 8.00
11 Justise Winslow/49 3.00 8.00
12 Cedric Maxwell/99 4.00 10.00
13 Dave Cowens/49 8.00 20.00
14 Ralph Sampson/49 5.00 12.00
15 Magic Johnson/25 25.00 60.00
16 Kyle Korver/99 5.00 12.00
17 Karl-Anthony Towns/25 20.00 50.00
18 Juwan Howard/99 4.00 10.00
19 Malcolm Brogdon/99 4.00 10.00
20 Mark Aguirre/99 4.00 10.00
21 Robert Horry/49 5.00 12.00
22 Yogi Ferrell/99 3.00 8.00
23 Bill Walton/49 8.00 20.00
24 Robert Parish/49 6.00 15.00
26 DeMarre Carroll/99 3.00 8.00
27 Ron Baker/99 3.00 8.00
28 Seth Curry/99 5.00 12.00
29 Justin Anderson/99 3.00 8.00
30 Udonis Haslem/99 3.00 8.00
31 Latrell Sprewell/49 6.00 15.00
32 Mason Plumlee/99 3.00 8.00
33 Danny Manning/49 4.00 10.00
34 Ben Wallace/49 8.00 20.00

2017-18 Absolute Memorabilia Draft Day Ink

EXCHANGE DEADLINE 6/29/2019
1 Markelle Fultz 75.00 200.00
2 Lonzo Ball 125.00 300.00
3 Jayson Tatum 400.00 800.00
4 Josh Jackson 10.00 25.00
5 De'Aaron Fox 40.00 100.00
6 Jonathan Isaac 25.00 60.00
7 Lauri Markkanen 125.00 300.00
8 Frank Ntilikina 30.00 80.00
9 Dennis Smith Jr. 10.00 25.00
10 Zach Collins 12.00 30.00
11 Malik Monk 25.00 60.00
12 Luke Kennard 30.00 80.00
13 Bam Adebayo 25.00 60.00
14 OG Anunoby 20.00 50.00
15 Frank Jackson 8.00 20.00

2017-18 Absolute Memorabilia Established Threads

PRINT RUNS B/WN 49-199 COPIES PER
1 Taj Gibson/199 1.50 4.00
2 Hakeem Olajuwon/49 5.00 12.00
3 Kobe Bryant/49 20.00 50.00
4 Aaron Gordon/99 2.50 6.00
5 Kawhi Leonard/199 6.00 15.00
6 Buddy Hield/199 2.50 6.00
7 Nik Stauskas/199 1.50 4.00
8 Danny Green/199 2.00 5.00
9 Marcus Smart/199 2.50 6.00
10 Derrick Favors/199 1.50 4.00
11 Terrence Ross/99 2.00 5.00
12 Harrison Barnes/199 2.00 5.00
13 Jaylen Brown/199 6.00 15.00
14 Al-Farouq Aminu/199 1.50 4.00
15 Kelly Oubre Jr./199 2.50 6.00
16 C.J. McCollum/99 2.50 6.00
17 Patrick Ewing/49 5.00 12.00
18 Dante Exum/199 1.50 4.00
19 Reggie Miller/49 6.00 15.00
20 Dion Waiters/99 1.50 4.00
21 Trevor Ariza/199 1.50 4.00
22 Hassan Whiteside/99 2.00 5.00
23 John Stockton/49 5.00 12.00
24 Andrew Wiggins/99 3.00 8.00
25 Kemba Walker/99 2.00 5.00
26 Caris LeVert/199 2.50 6.00
27 Paul George/99 4.00 10.00
28 Dario Saric/99 2.00 5.00
29 Robert Parish/49 3.00 8.00
30 Dirk Nowitzki/99 6.00 15.00
31 Trevor Booker/199 1.50 4.00
32 Isaiah Thomas/99 2.00 5.00
33 John Wall/99 3.00 8.00
34 Blake Griffin/99 2.50 6.00
35 LaMarcus Aldridge/199 2.50 6.00
36 Carmelo Anthony/99 4.00 10.00
37 Gordon Hayward/199 2.00 5.00
38 DeAndre' Bembry/199 1.50 4.00
39 Rudy Gobert/199 3.00 8.00
40 Evan Turner/199 1.50 4.00
41 Wade Baldwin IV/199 1.50 4.00
42 Ivica Zubac/199 2.00 5.00
43 Karl Malone/99 5.00 12.00
44 Bobby Portis/99 1.50 4.00
45 LeBron James/49 20.00 50.00
46 Chris Paul/99 4.00 10.00
47 Kyle Korver/199 2.00 5.00
48 Dejounte Murray/199 2.50 6.00
49 Jusuf Nurkic/199 2.00 5.00
50 Frank Kaminsky/199 1.50 4.00
51 Jamal Crawford/199 2.50 6.00
52 Wesley Matthews/99 1.50 4.00
53 Karl-Anthony Towns/99 4.00 10.00
54 Wilson Chandler/199 2.00 5.00
55 Kris Dunn/99 1.50 4.00
56 Damian Lillard/99 4.00 10.00
57 Kevin Love/99 2.50 6.00
58 Denzel Valentine/199 1.50 4.00
59 Goran Dragic/99 2.00 5.00
60 Scottie Pippen/49 6.00 15.00

2017-18 Absolute Memorabilia Glass

EXCHANGE DEADLINE 6/29/2019
1 Kobe Bryant 50.00 120.00
2 Magic Johnson 20.00 50.00
3 Larry Bird 20.00 50.00
4 Scottie Pippen 15.00 40.00
5 Shaquille O'Neal 20.00 50.00
6 Stephen Curry 40.00 100.00
7 Kevin Durant 30.00 80.00
8 LeBron James 50.00 120.00
9 Kyrie Irving 20.00 50.00
10 Isaiah Thomas 8.00 20.00
11 Russell Westbrook 20.00 50.00
12 James Harden 15.00 40.00
13 Kawhi Leonard 15.00 40.00
14 Giannis Antetokounmpo 40.00 100.00
15 Anthony Davis 15.00 40.00
16 Jimmy Butler 15.00 40.00
17 John Wall 12.00 30.00
18 Chris Paul 15.00 40.00
19 Paul George 20.00 50.00
20 Damian Lillard 15.00 40.00
21 Markelle Fultz 30.00 80.00
22 Lonzo Ball 60.00 150.00
23 Dennis Smith Jr. 5.00 12.00
24 Jayson Tatum 60.00 150.00
25 De'Aaron Fox 30.00 80.00

2017-18 Absolute Memorabilia Ink and Leather

PRINT RUNS B/WN 25-99 COPIES PER
EXCHANGE DEADLINE 6/29/2019
1 Kristaps Porzingis/25 20.00 50.00
2 Kobe Bryant/25 500.00 1,000.00
3 Karl-Anthony Towns/25 20.00 50.00
4 Gordon Hayward/99 12.00 30.00
6 Markelle Fultz/99 15.00 40.00
7 Lonzo Ball/99 25.00 60.00
8 Jayson Tatum/99 50.00 120.00
10 De'Aaron Fox/99 30.00 80.00
11 Jonathan Isaac/99 8.00 20.00
12 Frank Ntilikina/99 4.00 10.00
13 Dennis Smith Jr./99 4.00 10.00
14 Zach Collins/99 5.00 12.00
15 Malik Monk/99 12.00 30.00
16 Luke Kennard/99 6.00 15.00
17 Donovan Mitchell/99 50.00 120.00
18 Bam Adebayo/99 20.00 50.00
19 D.J. Wilson/99 3.00 8.00
20 T.J. Leaf/99 3.00 8.00
21 John Collins/99 8.00 20.00
23 Terrance Ferguson/99 3.00 8.00
24 Jarrett Allen/99 8.00 20.00
25 OG Anunoby/99 15.00 40.00

2017-18 Absolute Memorabilia Pass the Rock

PRINT RUNS B/WN 99-199 COPIES PER
1 Kyle Kuzma/199 6.00 15.00
2 Jayson Tatum/149 8.00 20.00
3 Frank Jackson/99 1.50 4.00
4 Frank Ntilikina/179 2.00 5.00
5 Luke Kennard/149 3.00 8.00
6 Aaron Gordon/99 2.50 6.00
7 T.J. Leaf/99 1.50 4.00
8 Gordon Hayward/109 2.00 5.00
9 Jarrett Allen/179 4.00 10.00
10 Rudy Gobert/99 3.00 8.00
11 Tony Bradley/99 1.50 4.00
12 Josh Jackson/199 2.00 5.00
13 Wesley Iwundu/99 1.50 4.00
14 Dennis Smith Jr./165 2.00 5.00
15 Donovan Mitchell/199 8.00 20.00
16 Carmelo Anthony/99 4.00 10.00
17 John Collins/99 4.00 10.00
18 Karl-Anthony Towns/169 4.00 10.00
19 OG Anunoby/99 8.00 20.00
20 Russell Westbrook/109 5.00 12.00
21 Derrick White/199 6.00 15.00
22 De'Aaron Fox/169 12.00 30.00
23 Frank Mason III/199 1.50 4.00
24 Zach Collins/169 2.50 6.00
25 Bam Adebayo/199 10.00 25.00
26 Trey Lyles/99 1.50 4.00
27 Harry Giles/199 1.50 4.00
28 Kawhi Leonard/104 6.00 15.00
29 Tyler Lydon/99 1.50 4.00
30 Markelle Fultz/199 5.00 12.00
31 Josh Hart/199 4.00 10.00
32 Jonathan Isaac/189 4.00 10.00
33 Ivan Rabb/199 1.50 4.00
34 Malik Monk/165 6.00 15.00
35 D.J. Wilson/125 1.50 4.00
36 Elfrid Payton/99 1.50 4.00
37 Terrance Ferguson/199 1.50 4.00
38 Kristaps Porzingis/102 3.00 8.00
39 Caleb Swanigan/199 1.50 4.00
40 Lonzo Ball/165 6.00 15.00

2017-18 Absolute Memorabilia Precision Signatures

PRINT RUNS B/WN 15-49 COPIES PER
NO PRICING ON QTY 15
EXCHANGE DEADLINE 6/29/2019
*ORANGE/25: .5X TO 1.2X p/r 49-99
2 Kyle Korver/99 5.00 12.00
3 Jason Kidd/25 12.00 30.00
4 Jerry Stackhouse/99 4.00 10.00
5 Ron Baker/99 3.00 8.00
6 Andrei Kirilenko/99 4.00 10.00
7 Mahmoud Abdul-Rauf/99 3.00 8.00
8 Frank Kaminsky/99 3.00 8.00
9 Kobe Bryant/25 500.00 1,000.00
10 Jason Terry/49 4.00 10.00
11 Jerry West/25 20.00 50.00
12 Glen Rice/99 4.00 10.00
13 Anfernee Hardaway/25 15.00 40.00
14 John Starks/99 4.00 10.00
15 Mike Muscala/99 3.00 8.00
16 Bob Dandridge/99 5.00 12.00
17 Ricky Pierce/99 4.00 10.00
18 Chauncey Billups/49 6.00 15.00
20 Rick Fox/49 4.00 10.00
21 Earl Monroe/25 8.00 20.00
22 Michael Cooper/99 4.00 10.00
24 Tom Gugliotta/99 3.00 8.00
25 Malcolm Brogdon/99 4.00 10.00
26 Sidney Moncrief/99 4.00 10.00
27 Keith Van Horn/99 4.00 10.00
28 Victor Oladipo/49 12.00 30.00
30 George Gervin/49 8.00 20.00
31 Ray Allen/25 10.00 25.00
32 Adrian Dantley/99 5.00 12.00
33 Grant Hill/25 12.00 30.00
34 Eddie Jones/99 5.00 12.00
35 Justin Anderson/99 3.00 8.00

2017-18 Absolute Memorabilia PreGame Materials

STATED PRINT RUN 199 SER.#'d SETS
1 Aaron Gordon 2.50 6.00
2 Alec Burks 1.50 4.00
3 Andrew Wiggins 3.00 8.00
4 Blake Griffin 2.50 6.00
5 C.J. McCollum 2.50 6.00
6 Damian Lillard 4.00 10.00
7 DeAndre Jordan 2.00 5.00
8 Derrick Favors 1.50 4.00
9 Emmanuel Mudiay 1.50 4.00
10 Gary Harris 2.00 5.00
11 Gordon Hayward 2.00 5.00
12 Gorgui Dieng 1.50 4.00
13 Jamal Crawford 2.50 6.00
14 Jamal Murray 4.00 10.00
15 Jameer Nelson 1.50 4.00
16 JJ Redick 2.50 6.00
17 Juan Hernangomez 2.50 6.00
18 Jusuf Nurkic 2.00 5.00
19 Karl-Anthony Towns 4.00 10.00
20 Kenneth Faried 2.00 5.00
21 Kevin Garnett 6.00 15.00
22 Kevin Love 2.50 6.00
23 LeBron James 20.00 50.00
24 Nikola Jokic 15.00 40.00
25 Noah Vonleh 1.50 4.00
26 Pau Gasol 4.00 10.00
27 Ricky Rubio 2.00 5.00
28 Rodney Hood 1.50 4.00
29 Rudy Gobert 3.00 8.00
30 Scottie Pippen 3.00 8.00
31 Trevor Booker 1.50 4.00
32 Tyus Jones 1.50 4.00
33 Wilson Chandler 2.00 5.00
34 Zach LaVine 4.00 10.00
35 Tyson Chandler 2.00 5.00

2017-18 Absolute Memorabilia Rookie Autographs

STATED PRINT RUN 99 SER.#'d SETS
EXCHANGE DEADLINE 6/29/2019
1 Markelle Fultz 20.00 50.00
2 Lonzo Ball 40.00 100.00
3 Jayson Tatum 150.00 400.00
4 Josh Jackson 4.00 10.00
5 De'Aaron Fox 50.00 120.00
6 Jonathan Isaac 8.00 20.00
7 Lauri Markkanen 12.00 30.00
8 Frank Ntilikina 4.00 10.00
9 Dennis Smith Jr. 4.00 10.00
10 Malik Monk 12.00 30.00
11 Luke Kennard 6.00 15.00
12 Donovan Mitchell 100.00 250.00
AR-BA Bam Adebayo 20.00 50.00
14 Justin Jackson 3.00 8.00
15 Justin Patton 3.00 8.00
16 D.J. Wilson 3.00 8.00
17 T.J. Leaf 3.00 8.00
18 John Collins 12.00 30.00
19 Harry Giles 3.00 8.00
20 Jarrett Allen 8.00 20.00
21 OG Anunoby 15.00 40.00
22 Tyler Lydon 3.00 8.00
23 Kyle Kuzma 12.00 30.00
24 Tony Bradley 3.00 8.00
25 Derrick White 6.00 15.00
26 Josh Hart 20.00 50.00
27 Frank Jackson 3.00 8.00
28 Frank Mason III 3.00 8.00
29 Jordan Bell 3.00 8.00
30 Jawun Evans 3.00 8.00
31 Dwayne Bacon 3.00 8.00
32 Ike Anigbogu 3.00 8.00
33 Milos Teodosic 4.00 10.00
34 Wesley Iwundu 3.00 8.00
35 Edmond Sumner 5.00 12.00

2017-18 Absolute Memorabilia Rookie Materials

PRINT RUNS B/WN 25-199 COPIES PER
*PRIME/25: 1X TO 2.5X BASIC
1 Markelle Fultz/199 5.00 12.00
2 Lonzo Ball/199 6.00 15.00
3 Jayson Tatum/199 15.00 40.00
4 Josh Jackson/199 2.00 5.00
5 De'Aaron Fox/199 12.00 30.00
6 Jonathan Isaac/199 4.00 10.00
7 Frank Mason III/199 1.50 4.00
8 Frank Ntilikina/199 2.00 5.00
9 Dennis Smith Jr./199 2.00 5.00
10 Malik Monk/199 6.00 15.00
11 Luke Kennard/199 3.00 8.00
12 Donovan Mitchell/199 8.00 20.00
13 Bam Adebayo/199 10.00 25.00
15 Justin Patton/199 1.50 4.00
16 D.J. Wilson/199 1.50 4.00
17 T.J. Leaf/199 1.50 4.00
18 John Collins/199 4.00 10.00
19 Harry Giles/199 1.50 4.00
20 Jarrett Allen/199 4.00 10.00
21 OG Anunoby/199 8.00 20.00
22 Tyler Lydon/199 1.50 4.00
23 Kyle Kuzma/25 6.00 15.00
24 Tony Bradley/199 1.50 4.00
25 Derrick White/199 6.00 15.00
26 Josh Hart/25 4.00 10.00
27 Frank Jackson/199 1.50 4.00
28 Jordan Bell/199 1.50 4.00
29 Jawun Evans/199 1.50 4.00
30 Dwayne Bacon/199 1.50 4.00
31 Wesley Iwundu/199 1.50 4.00
32 Caleb Swanigan/199 1.50 4.00
33 Zach Collins/199 2.50 6.00
34 Semi Ojeleye/199 2.00 5.00
35 Sterling Brown/199 1.50 4.00
36 Ante Zizic/199 2.00 5.00
37 Sindarius Thornwell/199 1.50 4.00
38 Tyler Dorsey/199 1.50 4.00
39 Davon Reed/199 1.50 4.00
40 Ivan Rabb/199 1.50 4.00

2017-18 Absolute Memorabilia Signature Standouts

PRINT RUNS B/WN 10-49 COPIES PER
NO PRICING ON QTY 15 OR LESS
EXCHANGE DEADLINE 6/29/2019
2 Marcus Smart/49 5.00 12.00
3 Bob Lanier/49 6.00 15.00
5 Andre Drummond/49 4.00 10.00
7 Joe Dumars/49 6.00 15.00
8 Hakeem Olajuwon/25 20.00 50.00
9 Cliff Hagan/49 6.00 15.00
10 Dennis Rodman/25 15.00 40.00
11 Willis Reed/49 40.00 100.00
13 Zach Randolph/49 5.00 12.00
14 Magic Johnson/25 25.00 60.00
15 LaMarcus Aldridge/49 8.00 20.00
16 Alonzo Mourning/25 15.00 40.00
17 Connie Hawkins/34 5.00 12.00
18 Earl Monroe/25 8.00 20.00
19 Nikola Vucevic/49 4.00 10.00
20 Vince Carter/25 20.00 50.00
21 Julius Randle/49 5.00 12.00
24 Kareem Abdul-Jabbar/25 20.00 50.00
25 Lenny Wilkens/49 6.00 15.00
26 Karl-Anthony Towns/25 20.00 50.00
27 Frank Ramsey/49 6.00 15.00
28 Jason Kidd/25 12.00 30.00
29 Tom Heinsohn/49 12.00 30.00
30 Grant Hill/49 10.00 25.00

2017-18 Absolute Memorabilia Signature Standouts Orange

*ORANGE/25: .5X TO 1.2X p/r 34-99
PRINT RUNS B/WN 15-25 COPIES PER
NO PRICING ON QTY 15
EXCHANGE DEADLINE 6/29/2019
23 C.J. McCollum/25 6.00 15.00

2017-18 Absolute Memorabilia Tools of the Trade Four Swatch Signatures

STATED PRINT RUN 99 SER.#'d SETS
EXCHANGE DEADLINE 6/29/2019
*ORANGE/25: .75X TO 2X BASIC
1 Markelle Fultz 25.00 60.00
2 Lonzo Ball 30.00 80.00
3 Jayson Tatum 50.00 120.00
5 De'Aaron Fox 30.00 80.00
6 Jonathan Isaac 8.00 20.00
7 Zach Collins 5.00 12.00
8 Frank Ntilikina 10.00 25.00
9 Dennis Smith Jr. 4.00 10.00
11 Luke Kennard 6.00 15.00
12 Donovan Mitchell 60.00 150.00
13 Bam Adebayo 10.00 25.00
14 Justin Patton 3.00 8.00
15 Tyler Lydon 3.00 8.00
16 D.J. Wilson 3.00 8.00
17 T.J. Leaf 3.00 8.00
18 John Collins 10.00 25.00
20 Jarrett Allen 8.00 20.00
21 OG Anunoby 15.00 40.00
22 Jordan Bell 3.00 8.00
23 Jawun Evans 3.00 8.00
24 Tony Bradley 3.00 8.00
25 Derrick White 12.00 30.00
26 Frank Mason III 3.00 8.00
27 Frank Jackson 3.00 8.00
28 Wesley Iwundu 3.00 8.00
29 Dwayne Bacon 3.00 8.00
30 Semi Ojeleye 4.00 10.00
31 Sterling Brown 3.00 8.00
32 Caleb Swanigan 3.00 8.00

2017-18 Absolute Memorabilia Tools of the Trade Six Swatch Signatures

STATED PRINT RUN 75 SER.#'d SETS
EXCHANGE DEADLINE 6/29/2019
*ORANGE/25: .75X TO 2X BASIC
1 Markelle Fultz 30.00 80.00
2 Lonzo Ball 40.00 100.00
3 Jayson Tatum 60.00 150.00
5 De'Aaron Fox 40.00 100.00
6 Jonathan Isaac 10.00 25.00
7 Zach Collins 6.00 15.00
8 Frank Ntilikina 12.00 30.00
9 Dennis Smith Jr. 5.00 12.00
11 Luke Kennard 8.00 20.00
12 Donovan Mitchell 75.00 200.00
13 Bam Adebayo 12.00 30.00
14 Justin Patton 4.00 10.00
15 Tyler Lydon 4.00 10.00
16 D.J. Wilson 4.00 10.00
17 T.J. Leaf 4.00 10.00
18 John Collins 12.00 30.00
20 Jarrett Allen 10.00 25.00
21 OG Anunoby 20.00 50.00
22 Jordan Bell 4.00 10.00
23 Jawun Evans 4.00 10.00
24 Tony Bradley 4.00 10.00
25 Derrick White 15.00 40.00
26 Frank Mason III 4.00 10.00
27 Frank Jackson 4.00 10.00
28 Wesley Iwundu 4.00 10.00
29 Dwayne Bacon 4.00 10.00
30 Semi Ojeleye 5.00 12.00
31 Sterling Brown 4.00 10.00
32 Caleb Swanigan 4.00 10.00

2017-18 Absolute Memorabilia Tools of the Trade Three Swatch Signatures

PRINT RUNS B/WN 149-199 COPIES PER
EXCHANGE DEADLINE 6/29/2019
*ORANGE/25: .75X TO 2X BASIC
1 Markelle Fultz/149 25.00 60.00
2 Lonzo Ball/149 30.00 80.00
3 Jayson Tatum/199 50.00 120.00
5 De'Aaron Fox/199 30.00 80.00
6 Jonathan Isaac/199 8.00 20.00
7 Zach Collins/199 5.00 12.00
8 Frank Ntilikina/149 10.00 25.00
9 Dennis Smith Jr./149 4.00 10.00
11 Luke Kennard/149 6.00 15.00
12 Donovan Mitchell/149 60.00 150.00
13 Bam Adebayo/149 10.00 25.00
14 Justin Patton/149 3.00 8.00
15 Tyler Lydon/149 3.00 8.00
16 D.J. Wilson/149 3.00 8.00
17 T.J. Leaf/199 3.00 8.00
18 John Collins/149 10.00 25.00
20 Jarrett Allen/199 8.00 20.00
21 OG Anunoby/149 15.00 40.00
22 Jordan Bell/149 3.00 8.00
23 Jawun Evans/149 3.00 8.00
24 Tony Bradley/149 3.00 8.00
25 Derrick White/199 12.00 30.00
26 Frank Mason III/149 6.00 15.00
27 Frank Jackson/149 3.00 8.00
28 Wesley Iwundu/149 3.00 8.00
29 Dwayne Bacon/199 3.00 8.00
30 Semi Ojeleye/149 4.00 10.00
31 Sterling Brown/149 3.00 8.00
32 Caleb Swanigan/199 3.00 8.00

2018-19 Absolute Memorabilia

1 Stephen Curry 10.00 25.00
2 Kyle Lowry 1.25 3.00
3 Tyreke Evans .75 2.00
4 Lonzo Ball 1.25 3.00
5 Jeremy Lin 2.00 5.00
6 Tim Hardaway Jr. .75 2.00
7 Lauri Markkanen 2.00 5.00
8 Ben Simmons 1.25 3.00
9 Dennis Smith Jr. .75 2.00
10 CJ McCollum 1.25 3.00
11 Kevin Durant 5.00 12.00
12 Donovan Mitchell 4.00 10.00
13 Lou Williams 1.00 2.50
14 Giannis Antetokounmpo 6.00 15.00
15 Kyrie Irving 3.00 8.00
16 Russell Westbrook 2.00 5.00
17 Zach LaVine 2.00 5.00
18 Joel Embiid 3.00 8.00
19 Nikola Jokic 6.00 15.00
20 De'Aaron Fox 2.50 6.00
21 Chris Paul 2.50 6.00
22 Rudy Gobert 1.50 4.00
23 LeBron James 20.00 50.00
24 Jimmy Butler 2.00 5.00
25 Jayson Tatum 5.00 12.00
26 Paul George 2.00 5.00
27 Kevin Love 1.00 2.50
28 Devin Booker 3.00 8.00
29 Isaiah Thomas 1.00 2.50
30 DeMar DeRozan 1.50 4.00
31 James Harden 2.50 6.00
32 John Wall 1.50 4.00
33 Kyle Kuzma 1.25 3.00
34 Karl-Anthony Towns 2.00 5.00
35 D'Angelo Russell 1.25 3.00
36 Aaron Gordon 1.50 4.00
37 JR Smith 1.25 3.00
38 TJ Warren .75 2.00
39 Blake Griffin 1.25 3.00
40 LaMarcus Aldridge 1.25 3.00

41 Victor Oladipo 1.00 2.50
42 Bradley Beal 1.50 4.00
43 Marc Gasol 1.25 3.00
44 Anthony Davis 3.00 8.00
45 Kemba Walker 1.00 2.50
46 Nikola Vucevic 1.00 2.50
47 Dirk Nowitzki 3.00 8.00
48 Damian Lillard 3.00 8.00
49 Andre Drummond 1.00 2.50
50 Kawhi Leonard 3.00 8.00
51 Mike Conley 1.00 2.50
52 DeMarcus Cousins 1.00 2.50
53 Goran Dragic 1.00 2.50
54 Kristaps Porzingis 1.50 4.00
55 Tony Parker 2.00 5.00
56 Deandre Ayton RC 3.00 8.00
57 Marvin Bagley III RC 1.50 4.00
58 Luka Doncic RC 150.00 400.00
59 Jaren Jackson Jr. RC 8.00 20.00
60 Trae Young RC 15.00 40.00
61 Mo Bamba RC 1.50 4.00
62 Wendell Carter Jr. RC 2.50 6.00
63 Collin Sexton RC 3.00 8.00
64 Kevin Knox RC 1.25 3.00
65 Mikal Bridges RC 5.00 12.00
66 Shai Gilgeous-Alexander RC 75.00 200.00
67 Miles Bridges RC 2.50 6.00
68 Jerome Robinson RC 1.00 2.50
69 Michael Porter Jr. RC 4.00 10.00
70 Troy Brown Jr. RC 1.25 3.00
71 Zhaire Smith RC 1.00 2.50
72 Donte DiVincenzo RC 2.50 6.00
73 Lonnie Walker IV RC 2.00 5.00
74 Kevin Huerter RC 2.00 5.00
75 Josh Okogie RC 1.50 4.00
76 Grayson Allen RC 2.00 5.00
77 Chandler Hutchison RC 1.25 3.00
78 Aaron Holiday RC 1.50 4.00
79 Alize Johnson RC 1.50 4.00
80 Anfernee Simons RC 5.00 12.00
81 Moritz Wagner RC 2.00 5.00
82 Landry Shamet RC 2.00 5.00
83 Robert Williams III RC 2.00 5.00
84 Jacob Evans III RC 1.00 2.50
85 Dzanan Musa RC 1.00 2.50
86 Omari Spellman RC 1.00 2.50
87 Elie Okobo RC 1.00 2.50
88 Jevon Carter RC 1.50 4.00
89 Jalen Brunson RC 8.00 20.00
90 Devonte' Graham RC 1.50 4.00
91 Gary Trent Jr. RC 2.00 5.00
92 Jarred Vanderbilt RC 2.00 5.00
93 Keita Bates-Diop RC 1.25 3.00
94 Bruce Brown RC 2.00 5.00
95 De'Anthony Melton RC 2.00 5.00
96 Hamidou Diallo RC 1.50 4.00
97 Vincent Edwards RC 1.00 2.50
98 Svi Mykhailiuk RC 1.25 3.00
99 Kostas Antetokounmpo RC 1.25 3.00
100 Mitchell Robinson RC 2.50 6.00

2018-19 Absolute Memorabilia 10th Anniversary Autographs

STATED PRINT RUN 20 SER.#'d SETS
EXCHANGE DEADLINE 5/28/2020
*LEVEL 2/15: .4X TO 1X BASIC
1 Kobe Bryant EXCH 1,250.00 2,500.00
AASC Stephen Curry 800.00 1,500.00
AALB Larry Bird 100.00 250.00
AAMJ Magic Johnson 100.00 250.00
AAKI Kyrie Irving 75.00 200.00
AAKD Kevin Durant 100.00 250.00
AASQ Shaquille O'Neal 125.00 300.00
AADK Dirk Nowitzki 125.00 300.00
9 Donovan Mitchell 75.00 200.00
10 Jayson Tatum EXCH 150.00 400.00

2018-19 Absolute Memorabilia Draft Day Ink

STATED PRINT RUN 125 SER.#'d SETS
EXCHANGE DEADLINE 5/28/2020
*LEVEL 2/25: .75X TO 2X BASIC
1 Deandre Ayton 10.00 25.00
2 Marvin Bagley III 5.00 12.00
3 Luka Doncic 800.00 1,500.00
4 Jaren Jackson Jr. 200.00 500.00
5 Trae Young 150.00 400.00
6 Mo Bamba 5.00 12.00
7 Wendell Carter Jr. 8.00 20.00
8 Collin Sexton 10.00 25.00
9 Kevin Knox 4.00 10.00
10 Mikal Bridges 15.00 40.00
11 Shai Gilgeous-Alexander 600.00 1,200.00
12 Jevon Carter 5.00 12.00
13 Jerome Robinson 3.00 8.00
14 Michael Porter Jr. 20.00 50.00
15 Troy Brown Jr. 4.00 10.00
16 Zhaire Smith 3.00 8.00
17 Donte DiVincenzo 8.00 20.00
18 Lonnie Walker IV 6.00 15.00
19 Kevin Huerter 6.00 15.00
20 Josh Okogie 5.00 12.00
21 Grayson Allen 6.00 15.00
22 Chandler Hutchison 4.00 10.00
23 Aaron Holiday 5.00 12.00
24 Anfernee Simons 15.00 40.00
25 Moritz Wagner 6.00 15.00
26 Landry Shamet 5.00 12.00
27 Jalen Brunson 100.00 250.00
28 Jacob Evans III 3.00 8.00
29 Dzanan Musa 3.00 8.00
30 Omari Spellman 3.00 8.00

2018-19 Absolute Memorabilia Established Threads

PRINT RUNS B/WN 99-199 COPIES PER
*LEVEL 2/75-149: .4X TO 1X BASIC
*LEVEL 3/49-75: .4X TO 1X BASIC
1 Dirk Nowitzki/199 6.00 15.00
2 Karl-Anthony Towns/199 4.00 10.00
3 Andrew Wiggins/199 3.00 8.00
4 Vince Carter/99 5.00 12.00
5 Carmelo Anthony/199 4.00 10.00
6 Kevin Love/199 2.00 5.00
7 Shaquille O'Neal/199 8.00 20.00
8 Enes Kanter/199 2.00 5.00
9 Rondae Hollis-Jefferson/199 1.50 4.00
10 Kobe Bryant/199 40.00 100.00
11 Pau Gasol/99 4.00 10.00
12 Dwight Powell/199 1.50 4.00
13 Gorgui Dieng/199 1.50 4.00
14 Harrison Barnes/199 2.00 5.00
15 Kevin Garnett/99 6.00 15.00
16 Jimmy Butler/199 4.00 10.00
17 John Wall/99 3.00 8.00
18 J.J. Barea/199 2.50 6.00
19 Bradley Beal/99 3.00 8.00
20 Rudy Gobert/199 3.00 8.00
21 Eric Gordon/99 2.00 5.00
22 Kristaps Porzingis/199 3.00 8.00
23 Wesley Matthews/199 1.50 4.00
24 Larry Bird/99 10.00 25.00
25 DeAndre Jordan/199 2.00 5.00
26 Jarrett Allen/199 2.50 6.00
27 Nicolas Batum/99 1.50 4.00
28 Serge Ibaka/199 2.00 5.00
29 Trevor Ariza/99 1.50 4.00
30 Marcin Gortat/99 1.50 4.00
31 Grant Hill/199 4.00 10.00
32 Nerlens Noel/199 1.50 4.00
33 Danny Granger/199 1.50 4.00
34 Shawn Marion/199 2.00 5.00
35 Karl Malone/99 5.00 12.00
36 Derrick Favors/199 1.50 4.00
37 Anthony Davis/99 6.00 15.00
38 Nikola Vucevic/199 2.00 5.00
39 Jonas Valanciunas/99 2.50 6.00
40 Ryan Anderson/99 1.50 4.00
41 Maxi Kleber/199 2.00 5.00
42 Dwyane Wade/199 5.00 12.00
43 Dennis Smith Jr./99 1.50 4.00
44 Hakeem Olajuwon/199 3.00 8.00
45 Andre Iguodala/199 2.00 5.00
46 Scottie Pippen/99 6.00 15.00
47 Klay Thompson/199 6.00 15.00
48 Otto Porter Jr./199 2.00 5.00
49 LeBron James/99 40.00 100.00
50 Danilo Gallinari/99 2.00 5.00
51 Draymond Green/199 3.00 8.00
52 David Robinson/199 5.00 12.00
53 Blake Griffin/199 2.50 6.00
54 Allen Iverson/199 6.00 15.00
55 Andre Drummond/99 2.00 5.00
56 Markieff Morris/99 1.50 4.00
57 Tim Hardaway Jr./99 1.50 4.00
58 DeMar DeRozan/199 3.00 8.00
59 Dennis Schroder/199 2.00 5.00
60 Yao Ming/99 6.00 15.00

2018-19 Absolute Memorabilia Glass

EXCHANGE DEADLINE 5/28/2020
1 Anthony Davis 40.00 100.00
2 LeBron James 125.00 300.00
3 DeMar DeRozan 12.00 30.00
4 Kevin Durant 60.00 150.00
5 Chris Paul 40.00 100.00
6 Kyrie Irving 40.00 100.00
7 Devin Booker 40.00 100.00
8 Donovan Mitchell 30.00 80.00
9 Jimmy Butler 25.00 60.00
10 Lonzo Ball 15.00 40.00
11 Blake Griffin 8.00 20.00
12 Stephen Curry 125.00 300.00
13 James Harden 40.00 100.00
14 Giannis Antetokounmpo 60.00 150.00
15 Kawhi Leonard 40.00 100.00
16 Marvin Bagley III 8.00 20.00
17 Russell Westbrook 30.00 80.00
18 Kristaps Porzingis 30.00 80.00
19 Damian Lillard 40.00 100.00
20 Dirk Nowitzki 40.00 100.00
21 Deandre Ayton 15.00 40.00
22 Luka Doncic 500.00 1,000.00
23 Trae Young 125.00 300.00
24 Mo Bamba 8.00 20.00
25 Jaren Jackson Jr. 75.00 200.00

2018-19 Absolute Memorabilia Hoopla Signatures

PRINT RUNS B/WN 20-125 COPIES PER
EXCHANGE DEADLINE 5/28/2020
1 Gerald Green/125 5.00 12.00
2 Bruce Brown/125 8.00 20.00
3 Svi Mykhailiuk/125 5.00 12.00
5 Keita Bates-Diop/125 5.00 12.00
6 De'Anthony Melton/125 8.00 20.00
8 Devonte' Graham/125 6.00 15.00
9 Melvin Frazier Jr./125 4.00 10.00
10 Giannis Antetokounmpo/20 125.00 300.00
11 Damian Lillard/20 75.00 200.00
12 Kiki Vandeweghe/125 5.00 12.00
14 Bruce Bowen/125 5.00 12.00
16 Mike Bibby/125 6.00 15.00
17 Felipe Lopez/125 4.00 10.00
18 Vlade Divac/125 6.00 15.00
19 Charles Barkley/20 125.00 300.00
20 Arvydas Sabonis/125 6.00 15.00
21 David Robinson/20 50.00 120.00
22 Damon Stoudamire/125 6.00 15.00
23 Jerry Stackhouse/125 8.00 20.00
24 David Thompson/125 8.00 20.00
25 Toni Kukoc/125 8.00 20.00

2018-19 Absolute Memorabilia Hoopla Signatures Level 2

*LEVEL 2/25: .5X TO 2X BASIC
PRINT RUNS B/WN 15-25 COPIES PER
10 Giannis Antetokounmpo/15 125.00 300.00
11 Damian Lillard/15 75.00 200.00
19 Charles Barkley/15 125.00 300.00
21 David Robinson/15 50.00 120.00

2018-19 Absolute Memorabilia Ink and Leather

STATED PRINT RUN 25 SER.#'d SETS
EXCHANGE DEADLINE 5/28/2020
2 Marvin Bagley III 5.00 12.00
3 Luka Doncic 1,000.00 2,000.00
4 Jaren Jackson Jr. 75.00 200.00
5 Trae Young 400.00 800.00
6 Mo Bamba 5.00 12.00
7 Wendell Carter Jr. 8.00 20.00
9 Kevin Knox 4.00 10.00

2018-19 Absolute Memorabilia Limitless Signatures

PRINT RUNS B/WN 49-99 COPIES PER
EXCHANGE DEADLINE 5/28/2020
*LEVEL 2/25: .5X TO 1.2X BASIC
1 Trae Young/49 75.00 200.00
2 Luka Doncic/49 500.00 1,000.00
3 Mo Bamba/99 5.00 12.00
4 Michael Porter Jr./99 12.00 30.00
5 Troy Brown Jr./99 4.00 10.00
6 Anfernee Simons/99 15.00 40.00
7 Kevin Knox/99 4.00 10.00
8 Shai Gilgeous-Alexander/99 300.00 600.00
9 Donte DiVincenzo/99 8.00 20.00
10 Zhaire Smith/99 3.00 8.00
11 Lonnie Walker IV/99 6.00 15.00
12 Moritz Wagner/99 6.00 15.00
13 Jacob Evans III/99 3.00 8.00
14 Deandre Ayton/49 10.00 25.00
15 Marvin Bagley III/49 5.00 12.00
16 Mikal Bridges/99 15.00 40.00
17 Aaron Holiday/99 5.00 12.00
18 Dzanan Musa/99 3.00 8.00
20 Kevin Huerter/99 6.00 15.00
21 Chandler Hutchison/99 4.00 10.00
23 Jevon Carter/99 5.00 12.00
24 Jaren Jackson Jr./49 100.00 250.00
25 Collin Sexton/99 10.00 25.00
26 Jalen Brunson/99 60.00 150.00
27 Grayson Allen/99 6.00 15.00
28 Robert Williams III/99 6.00 15.00
29 Wendell Carter Jr./99 8.00 20.00
31 Josh Okogie/99 5.00 12.00
32 Omari Spellman/99 3.00 8.00
33 Elie Okobo/99 3.00 8.00
34 Jarred Vanderbilt/99 6.00 15.00
35 Svi Mykhailiuk/99 4.00 10.00

2018-19 Absolute Memorabilia Past Autographs

STATED PRINT RUN 125 SER.#'d SETS
EXCHANGE DEADLINE 5/28/2020
*LEVEL 2/25: .6X TO 1.5X BASIC
1 Dave Cowens 6.00 15.00
2 Louie Dampier 5.00 12.00
3 Robert Parish 8.00 20.00
4 Avery Johnson 4.00 10.00
5 Jalen Rose 4.00 10.00
6 Rick Fox 4.00 10.00
7 Bill Walton 15.00 40.00
8 Ralph Sampson 4.00 10.00
9 Chauncey Billups 6.00 15.00
10 Jermaine O'Neal 4.00 10.00
12 Allan Houston 5.00 12.00
13 B.J. Armstrong 5.00 12.00
14 Toni Kukoc 6.00 15.00
15 A.C. Green 5.00 12.00
16 Alvan Adams 4.00 10.00
17 Mitch Richmond 6.00 15.00
18 Alex English 5.00 12.00
19 Kenny "Sky" Walker 3.00 8.00
20 Tom Chambers 4.00 10.00
21 Damon Stoudamire 5.00 12.00
22 Tom Gugliotta 3.00 8.00
23 Charlie Scott 5.00 12.00
24 Rolando Blackman 4.00 10.00
25 Dan Issel 6.00 15.00
26 Rafer Alston 4.00 10.00
27 Arvydas Sabonis 5.00 12.00
28 Paul Silas 5.00 12.00
29 Kevin Johnson 5.00 12.00
30 Mark Eaton 5.00 12.00

2018-19 Absolute Memorabilia Present Autographs

PRINT RUNS B/WN 49-75 COPIES PER
EXCHANGE DEADLINE 5/28/2020
*LEVEL 2/25: .5X TO 1.2X BASIC
1 Dion Waiters/49 3.00 8.00
2 Rodney Hood/49 4.00 10.00
3 Al Horford/49 5.00 12.00
4 Kentavious Caldwell-Pope/49 3.00 8.00
5 Eric Bledsoe/49 4.00 10.00
6 Nikola Mirotic/49 3.00 8.00
7 Tyson Chandler/49 4.00 10.00
8 Avery Bradley/49 3.00 8.00
9 Derrick Favors/49 3.00 8.00
10 Terry Rozier/75 4.00 10.00
11 Michael Kidd-Gilchrist/75 3.00 8.00
12 Reggie Jackson/75 4.00 10.00
13 Clint Capela/75 4.00 10.00
14 Trevor Ariza/75 3.00 8.00
15 Myles Turner/75 5.00 12.00
16 Kyle Korver/75 4.00 10.00
17 Jrue Holiday/75 12.00 30.00
18 Nerlens Noel/75 3.00 8.00
19 Elfrid Payton/75 4.00 10.00
20 Channing Frye/75 3.00 8.00
21 Jonathan Isaac/75 5.00 12.00
22 Cody Zeller/75 3.00 8.00
23 Enes Kanter/75 4.00 10.00
24 Iman Shumpert/75 3.00 8.00
25 John Collins/75 5.00 12.00
26 Nene/75 4.00 10.00
27 Malcolm Brogdon/75 5.00 12.00
28 Frank Ntilikina/75 3.00 8.00
29 Terrence Ross/75 4.00 10.00
30 Danny Green/75 4.00 10.00
31 Thaddeus Young/75 3.00 8.00
32 Willie Cauley-Stein/75 3.00 8.00
33 Matthew Dellavedova/75 4.00 10.00
34 J.J. Barea/75 4.00 10.00
35 Lou Williams/75 4.00 10.00

2018-19 Absolute Memorabilia Rookie Autographs

STATED PRINT RUN 125 SER.#'d SETS
EXCHANGE DEADLINE 5/28/2020
*LEVEL 2/25: .75X TO 2X BASIC
1 Deandre Ayton 10.00 25.00
2 Marvin Bagley III 5.00 12.00
3 Luka Doncic 800.00 1,500.00
4 Jaren Jackson Jr. 125.00 300.00
5 Trae Young 75.00 200.00
6 Mo Bamba 5.00 12.00
7 Wendell Carter Jr. 8.00 20.00
8 Collin Sexton 10.00 25.00
9 Kevin Knox 4.00 10.00
10 Mikal Bridges 15.00 40.00
11 Shai Gilgeous-Alexander 600.00 1,200.00
12 Keita Bates-Diop 4.00 10.00
13 Jerome Robinson 3.00 8.00
14 Michael Porter Jr. 20.00 50.00
15 Troy Brown Jr. 4.00 10.00
16 Zhaire Smith 3.00 8.00
17 Donte DiVincenzo 8.00 20.00
18 Lonnie Walker IV 6.00 15.00
19 Kevin Huerter 6.00 15.00
20 Josh Okogie 5.00 12.00
21 Grayson Allen 6.00 15.00
22 Chandler Hutchison 4.00 10.00
23 Aaron Holiday 5.00 12.00
24 Anfernee Simons 20.00 50.00
25 Moritz Wagner 6.00 15.00
26 Landry Shamet 5.00 12.00
27 Robert Williams III 6.00 15.00
28 Jacob Evans III 3.00 8.00
29 Dzanan Musa 3.00 8.00
30 Omari Spellman 3.00 8.00
31 Elie Okobo 3.00 8.00
32 Jevon Carter 5.00 12.00
33 Jalen Brunson 100.00 250.00
34 Devonte' Graham 5.00 12.00
35 Gary Trent Jr. 6.00 15.00

2018-19 Absolute Memorabilia Rookie Threads

STATED PRINT RUN 199 SER.#'d SETS
*LEVEL 2/149: .4X TO 1X BASIC
*LEVEL 3/75: .5X TO 1.2X BASIC
1 Deandre Ayton 5.00 12.00
2 Marvin Bagley III 2.50 6.00
3 Luka Doncic 75.00 200.00
4 Jaren Jackson Jr. 12.00 30.00
5 Trae Young 12.00 30.00
6 Mo Bamba 2.50 6.00
7 Wendell Carter Jr. 4.00 10.00
8 Collin Sexton 5.00 12.00
9 Kevin Knox 2.00 5.00
10 Mikal Bridges 8.00 20.00
11 Shai Gilgeous-Alexander 30.00 80.00
12 Svi Mykhailiuk 2.00 5.00
13 Jerome Robinson 1.50 4.00
14 Michael Porter Jr. 6.00 15.00
15 Troy Brown Jr. 2.00 5.00
16 Zhaire Smith 1.50 4.00
17 Donte DiVincenzo 4.00 10.00
18 Lonnie Walker IV 3.00 8.00
19 Kevin Huerter 3.00 8.00
20 Josh Okogie 2.50 6.00
21 Grayson Allen 3.00 8.00
22 Chandler Hutchison 2.00 5.00
23 Aaron Holiday 2.50 6.00
24 Anfernee Simons 8.00 20.00
25 Moritz Wagner 3.00 8.00
26 Landry Shamet 2.50 6.00
27 Robert Williams III 3.00 8.00
28 Jacob Evans III 1.50 4.00
29 Dzanan Musa 1.50 4.00
30 Jalen Brunson 12.00 30.00
31 Omari Spellman 1.50 4.00
32 Elie Okobo 1.50 4.00
33 Jevon Carter 2.50 6.00
34 Devonte' Graham 2.50 6.00
35 Gary Trent Jr. 3.00 8.00
36 Jarred Vanderbilt 3.00 8.00
37 Keita Bates-Diop 2.00 5.00
38 Bruce Brown 3.00 8.00
39 De'Anthony Melton 3.00 8.00
40 Hamidou Diallo 2.50 6.00

2018-19 Absolute Memorabilia Tools of the Trade Four Swatch Signatures

STATED PRINT RUN 99 SER.#'d SETS
EXCHANGE DEADLINE 5/28/2020
1 Deandre Ayton 10.00 25.00
2 Marvin Bagley III 5.00 12.00
3 Luka Doncic 500.00 1,000.00
4 Jaren Jackson Jr. 75.00 200.00
5 Trae Young 150.00 400.00
6 Mo Bamba 10.00 25.00
7 Wendell Carter Jr. 8.00 20.00
8 Collin Sexton 10.00 25.00
9 Kevin Knox 4.00 10.00
10 Mikal Bridges 15.00 40.00
11 Shai Gilgeous-Alexander 300.00 600.00
12 Gary Trent Jr. 6.00 15.00
14 Michael Porter Jr. 12.00 30.00
15 Troy Brown Jr. 4.00 10.00
16 Zhaire Smith 3.00 8.00
17 Donte DiVincenzo 8.00 20.00
18 Lonnie Walker IV 6.00 15.00
19 Kevin Huerter 6.00 15.00
20 Josh Okogie 5.00 12.00
21 Grayson Allen 6.00 15.00
22 Chandler Hutchison 4.00 10.00
23 Aaron Holiday 5.00 12.00
24 Anfernee Simons 20.00 50.00
25 Moritz Wagner 6.00 15.00
26 Landry Shamet 5.00 12.00
27 Robert Williams III 6.00 15.00
28 Jacob Evans III 3.00 8.00
29 Dzanan Musa 3.00 8.00
30 Jalen Brunson 25.00 60.00

2018-19 Absolute Memorabilia Tools of the Trade Four Swatch Signatures Level 2

*LEVEL 2: .75X TO 2X BASIC
STATED PRINT RUN 25 SER.#'d SETS
EXCHANGE DEADLINE 5/28/2020
13 Jerome Robinson 6.00 15.00

2018-19 Absolute Memorabilia Tools of the Trade Six Swatch Signatures

STATED PRINT RUN 49 SER.#'d SETS
EXCHANGE DEADLINE 5/28/2020
*LEVEL 2/25: .5X TO 1.2X BASIC
1 Deandre Ayton 10.00 25.00
2 Marvin Bagley III 5.00 12.00
3 Luka Doncic 500.00 1,000.00
4 Jaren Jackson Jr. 75.00 200.00
5 Trae Young 200.00 500.00
6 Mo Bamba 10.00 25.00
7 Wendell Carter Jr. 8.00 20.00
8 Collin Sexton 10.00 25.00
9 Kevin Knox 4.00 10.00
10 Mikal Bridges 15.00 40.00
11 Shai Gilgeous-Alexander 300.00 600.00
12 Gary Trent Jr. 6.00 15.00
14 Michael Porter Jr. 12.00 30.00
15 Troy Brown Jr. 4.00 10.00
16 Zhaire Smith 3.00 8.00
17 Donte DiVincenzo 8.00 20.00
18 Lonnie Walker IV 6.00 15.00
19 Kevin Huerter 6.00 15.00
20 Josh Okogie 5.00 12.00
21 Grayson Allen 6.00 15.00
22 Chandler Hutchison 4.00 10.00
23 Aaron Holiday 5.00 12.00
24 Anfernee Simons 30.00 80.00
25 Moritz Wagner 6.00 15.00
26 Landry Shamet 5.00 12.00
27 Robert Williams III 6.00 15.00
28 Jacob Evans III 3.00 8.00
29 Dzanan Musa 3.00 8.00
30 Jalen Brunson 25.00 60.00

2018-19 Absolute Memorabilia Tools of the Trade Three Swatch Signatures

STATED PRINT RUN 149 SER.#'d SETS
EXCHANGE DEADLINE 5/28/2020
1 Deandre Ayton 10.00 25.00
2 Marvin Bagley III 5.00 12.00
3 Luka Doncic 500.00 1,000.00
4 Jaren Jackson Jr. 75.00 200.00
5 Trae Young 150.00 400.00
6 Mo Bamba 10.00 25.00
7 Wendell Carter Jr. 8.00 20.00
8 Collin Sexton 10.00 25.00
9 Kevin Knox 4.00 10.00
10 Mikal Bridges 15.00 40.00
11 Shai Gilgeous-Alexander 300.00 600.00
12 Gary Trent Jr. 6.00 15.00
14 Michael Porter Jr. 12.00 30.00
15 Troy Brown Jr. 4.00 10.00
16 Zhaire Smith 3.00 8.00
17 Donte DiVincenzo 8.00 20.00
18 Lonnie Walker IV 6.00 15.00
19 Kevin Huerter 6.00 15.00
20 Josh Okogie 5.00 12.00
21 Grayson Allen 6.00 15.00
22 Chandler Hutchison 4.00 10.00
23 Aaron Holiday 5.00 12.00
24 Anfernee Simons 15.00 40.00
25 Moritz Wagner 6.00 15.00
26 Landry Shamet 5.00 12.00
27 Robert Williams III 6.00 15.00
28 Jacob Evans III 3.00 8.00
29 Dzanan Musa 3.00 8.00
30 Jalen Brunson 25.00 60.00

2018-19 Absolute Memorabilia Tools of the Trade Three Swatch Signatures Level 2

*LEVEL 2: .75X TO 2X BASIC
STATED PRINT RUN 25 SER.#'d SETS
EXCHANGE DEADLINE 5/28/2020

2019-20 Absolute Memorabilia

1 Derrick Rose 1.25 3.00
2 Bol Bol RC 1.50 4.00
3 Keldon Johnson RC 2.00 5.00
4 Kevin Durant 2.00 5.00
5 Kawhi Leonard 1.50 4.00
6 Julius Randle .75 2.00
7 James Harden 1.25 3.00
8 De'Aaron Fox 1.00 2.50
9 Grant Williams RC 1.00 2.50
10 Kemba Walker .50 1.25
11 Klay Thompson 1.50 4.00
12 Brandon Clarke RC 1.25 3.00
13 Eric Paschall RC .75 2.00
14 Kyle Lowry .60 1.50
15 Collin Sexton .75 2.00
16 Zion Williamson RC 15.00 40.00
17 RJ Barrett RC 2.50 6.00
18 Kevin Porter Jr. RC 1.25 3.00
19 Donovan Mitchell 1.25 3.00
20 John Collins .60 1.50
21 Rudy Gobert .75 2.00
22 Karl-Anthony Towns 1.00 2.50
23 Trae Young 1.50 4.00
24 Darius Bazley RC .60 1.50
25 DeMar DeRozan .75 2.00
26 Paul George 1.00 2.50
27 Khris Middleton .60 1.50
28 Quinndary Weatherspoon RC .60 1.50
29 Talen Horton-Tucker RC 1.00 2.50
30 Anthony Davis 1.50 4.00
31 Brandon Ingram .60 1.50
32 Zach LaVine 1.00 2.50
33 Luka Doncic 4.00 10.00
34 Bruno Fernando RC .75 2.00
35 Joel Embiid 1.25 3.00
36 Damian Lillard 1.50 4.00
37 PJ Washington Jr. RC 2.00 5.00
38 Kevin Love .60 1.50
39 CJ McCollum .60 1.50
40 Rui Hachimura RC 2.50 6.00
41 Kristaps Porzingis .75 2.00
42 Blake Griffin .60 1.50
43 Cody Martin RC 1.00 2.50
44 Victor Oladipo .50 1.25
45 Tremont Waters RC .75 2.00
46 Ignas Brazdeikis RC .75 2.00
47 Cameron Johnson RC 1.50 4.00
48 Romeo Langford RC .60 1.50
49 KZ Okpala RC .75 2.00
50 Jimmy Butler 1.25 3.00
51 Mike Conley .50 1.25
52 Russell Westbrook 1.00 2.50
53 DeMarcus Cousins .50 1.25
54 Jamal Murray 1.00 2.50
55 Lonzo Ball .60 1.50
56 Kyle Guy RC .75 2.00
57 Deandre Ayton .60 1.50
58 Lauri Markkanen .75 2.00
59 Pascal Siakam 1.00 2.50
60 Ty Jerome RC 1.25 3.00
61 Dennis Smith Jr. .40 1.00
62 Jarrett Culver RC .60 1.50
63 Sekou Doumbouya RC .60 1.50
64 Jaxson Hayes RC 1.00 2.50
65 Stephen Curry 5.00 12.00
66 LeBron James 5.00 12.00
67 Jonas Valanciunas .50 1.25
68 Kyrie Irving 1.25 3.00
69 Cam Reddish RC 1.00 2.50
70 Jaren Jackson Jr. 1.00 2.50
71 Terry Rozier .50 1.25
72 Ja Morant RC 10.00 25.00
73 Jordan Poole RC 2.50 6.00
74 Matisse Thybulle RC 1.25 3.00
75 Giannis Antetokounmpo 3.00 8.00
76 Nickeil Alexander-Walker RC 1.00 2.50
77 Nikola Jokic 3.00 8.00
78 Ben Simmons .60 1.50
79 Dylan Windler RC .75 2.00
80 Jaylen Nowell RC .75 2.00
81 Carsen Edwards RC .75 2.00
82 Darius Garland RC 2.50 6.00
83 John Wall .75 2.00
84 Nikola Vucevic .50 1.25
85 De'Andre Hunter RC 2.50 6.00
86 Coby White RC 2.00 5.00
87 Chris Paul 1.25 3.00
88 Goga Bitadze RC 1.00 2.50
89 Tyler Herro RC 3.00 8.00
90 Mfiondu Kabengele RC .75 2.00
91 Jayson Tatum 2.50 6.00
92 Isaiah Roby RC .75 2.00
93 Admiral Schofield RC .75 2.00
94 Miles Bridges .60 1.50
95 Luka Samanic RC .75 2.00
96 Bradley Beal .75 2.00
97 D'Angelo Russell .50 1.25
98 Nicolas Claxton RC 1.25 3.00
99 Nassir Little RC 1.00 2.50
100 Devin Booker .15 .40

2019-20 Absolute Memorabilia Blue

16 Zion Williamson 75.00 200.00
40 Rui Hachimura 8.00 20.00
66 LeBron James 15.00 60.00
72 Ja Morant 20.00 50.00

2019-20 Absolute Memorabilia Orange

16 Zion Williamson 75.00 200.00
40 Rui Hachimura 8.00 20.00
66 LeBron James 40.00 100.00
72 Ja Morant 20.00 50.00

2019-20 Absolute Memorabilia Purple

2 Bol Bol 25.00 60.00
12 Brandon Clarke 10.00 25.00
16 Zion Williamson 125.00 300.00
17 RJ Barrett 15.00 40.00
33 Luka Doncic 25.00 60.00
40 Rui Hachimura 25.00 60.00
62 Jarrett Culver 1.50 4.00
66 LeBron James 150.00 400.00
72 Ja Morant 40.00 100.00

2019-20 Absolute Memorabilia Red

16 Zion Williamson 60.00 150.00
40 Rui Hachimura 6.00 15.00
66 LeBron James 40.00 100.00
72 Ja Morant 30.00 80.00

2019-20 Absolute Memorabilia Established Threads Level 1

EXCHANGE DEADLINE 5/27/2021
*LEVEL 2: .6X TO 1.5X BASIC
1 Bradley Beal 3.00 8.00
2 Larry Bird 10.00 25.00
3 Dennis Smith Jr. 1.50 4.00
4 Otto Porter Jr. 1.50 4.00
5 Dwyane Wade 5.00 12.00
6 Stephen Curry 4.00 10.00
7 Harrison Barnes 2.00 5.00
8 John Wall 3.00 8.00
9 Aaron Gordon 2.50 6.00
10 Kevin Love 2.50 6.00
11 Chris Paul 5.00 12.00
12 Marc Gasol 2.50 6.00
13 Dirk Nowitzki 6.00 15.00
14 Rondae Hollis-Jefferson 1.50 4.00
15 Eric Gordon 2.00 5.00
16 Thaddeus Young 1.50 4.00
17 Jarrett Allen 2.50 6.00
18 Karl-Anthony Towns 4.00 10.00
19 Andre Drummond 2.00 5.00
20 Kobe Bryant 20.00 50.00
21 DeMarcus Cousins 2.00 5.00
22 Nikola Jokic 12.00 30.00
23 Draymond Green 3.00 8.00
24 Rudy Gobert 3.00 8.00
25 Goran Dragic 2.00 5.00
26 Victor Oladipo 2.00 5.00
27 Jimmy Butler 5.00 12.00
28 Kevin Garnett 6.00 15.00
29 Anthony Davis 6.00 15.00
30 Kyle Lowry 2.50 6.00

2019-20 Absolute Memorabilia Future Signatures Level 1

STATED PRINT RUN 49 SER.#'d SETS
EXCHANGE DEADLINE 5/27/2021
*LEVEL 2: .5X TO 1.2X BASIC
1 Jaylen Hoard 3.00 8.00
2 Luguentz Dort 12.00 30.00
3 Ignas Brazdeikis 4.00 10.00
4 Terance Mann 6.00 15.00
5 Quinndary Weatherspoon 3.00 8.00
6 Jarrell Brantley 3.00 8.00
7 Tremont Waters 4.00 10.00
8 Brian Bowen II 3.00 8.00
9 Justin Wright-Foreman 3.00 8.00
10 Marial Shayok 3.00 8.00
11 Kyle Guy 20.00 50.00
12 Amir Coffey 5.00 12.00
13 Jordan Bone 3.00 8.00
14 Miye Oni 3.00 8.00
15 Ty Jerome 6.00 15.00
16 Nassir Little 5.00 12.00
17 Dylan Windler 4.00 10.00
18 Mfiondu Kabengele 4.00 10.00
19 Jordan Poole 12.00 30.00
20 Keldon Johnson 10.00 25.00
21 Kevin Porter Jr. 6.00 15.00
22 Nicolas Claxton 6.00 15.00
23 KZ Okpala 4.00 10.00
24 Carsen Edwards 4.00 10.00
25 Bruno Fernando 8.00 20.00
26 Jalen Lecque 6.00 15.00
27 Cody Martin 5.00 12.00
28 Justin Robinson 3.00 8.00
29 Daniel Gafford 6.00 15.00
30 Alen Smailagic 3.00 8.00
31 Justin James 3.00 8.00
32 Eric Paschall 4.00 10.00
33 Admiral Schofield 4.00 10.00
34 Jaylen Nowell 4.00 10.00
35 Matisse Thybulle 8.00 20.00
36 Isaiah Roby 4.00 10.00
37 Zach Norvell Jr. 4.00 10.00
38 Robert Franks 3.00 8.00

2019-20 Absolute Memorabilia Future Signatures Level 2

*LEVEL 2: .5X TO 1.2X BASIC
STATED PRINT RUN 25 SER.#'d SETS
EXCHANGE DEADLINE 5/27/2021
32 Eric Paschall 5.00 12.00

2019-20 Absolute Memorabilia Glass

EXCHANGE DEADLINE 5/27/2021
1 LeBron James 500.00 1,000.00
2 Kobe Bryant 500.00 1,000.00
3 Giannis Antetokounmpo 100.00 250.00
4 Anthony Davis 75.00 200.00
5 Kevin Durant 125.00 300.00
6 Stephen Curry 200.00 500.00
7 James Harden 75.00 200.00
8 Joel Embiid 75.00 200.00
9 Russell Westbrook 40.00 100.00
10 Paul George 40.00 100.00
11 Kawhi Leonard 75.00 200.00
12 Damian Lillard 125.00 300.00
13 Ben Simmons 40.00 100.00
14 Karl-Anthony Towns 40.00 100.00
15 Trae Young 100.00 250.00
16 Luka Doncic 300.00 600.00
17 Jayson Tatum 75.00 200.00
18 Donovan Mitchell 40.00 100.00
19 Kyrie Irving 40.00 100.00
20 Charles Barkley 100.00 250.00
21 Zion Williamson 800.00 1,500.00
22 Ja Morant 400.00 800.00
23 RJ Barrett 125.00 300.00
24 Rui Hachimura 125.00 300.00
25 Darius Garland 75.00 200.00

2019-20 Absolute Memorabilia Jumbo Basketball Spalding Name

PRINT RUNS B/WN 20-24 COPIES PER
1 Matisse Thybulle/20 10.00 25.00
2 Bruno Fernando/20 6.00 15.00
3 KZ Okpala/20 6.00 15.00
4 Tremont Waters/20 6.00 15.00
5 Ignas Brazdeikis/20 6.00 15.00
6 Kevin Porter Jr./20 10.00 25.00
7 Jordan Poole/20 20.00 50.00
8 Jaylen Nowell/20 6.00 15.00
9 Eric Paschall/20 6.00 15.00
10 Nassir Little/20 8.00 20.00
11 RJ Barrett/24 20.00 50.00
12 De'Andre Hunter/24 20.00 50.00
13 Zion Williamson/24 75.00 200.00
14 Sekou Doumbouya/20 5.00 12.00
15 Tyler Herro/24 25.00 60.00
16 PJ Washington Jr./24 15.00 40.00
17 Brandon Clarke/20 10.00 25.00
18 Rui Hachimura/20 50.00 120.00
19 Coby White/24 15.00 40.00
20 Jarrett Culver/24 5.00 12.00
21 Mfiondu Kabengele/20 5.00 12.00
22 Bol Bol/20 12.00 30.00
23 Admiral Schofield/20 10.00 25.00
24 Dylan Windler/20 6.00 15.00
25 Ty Jerome/20 10.00 25.00
26 Cody Martin/20 8.00 20.00
27 Carsen Edwards/20 6.00 15.00
28 Quinndary Weatherspoon/20 5.00 12.00
29 Isaiah Roby/20 6.00 15.00
30 Keldon Johnson/20 15.00 40.00
31 Jaxson Hayes/20 8.00 20.00
32 Grant Williams/20 12.00 30.00
33 Luka Samanic/20 6.00 15.00
34 Goga Bitadze/20 10.00 25.00
35 Chuma Okeke/20 8.00 20.00
36 Nickeil Alexander-Walker/20 10.00 25.00
37 Romeo Langford/24 5.00 12.00
38 Ja Morant/24 30.00 80.00
39 Cameron Johnson/20 12.00 30.00
40 Cam Reddish/24 8.00 20.00

2019-20 Absolute Memorabilia Jumbo Hat Team Logo

STATED PRINT RUN 20 SER.#'d SETS
1 Eric Paschall 50.00 120.00
2 Nassir Little 30.00 80.00
3 Matisse Thybulle 50.00 120.00
4 Bruno Fernando 20.00 50.00
5 KZ Okpala 6.00 15.00
6 Tremont Waters 15.00 40.00
7 Ignas Brazdeikis 6.00 15.00
8 Kevin Porter Jr. 10.00 25.00
9 Jordan Poole 25.00 60.00
10 Jaylen Nowell 60.00 150.00
11 Coby White 75.00 200.00
13 RJ Barrett 100.00 250.00
14 De'Andre Hunter 30.00 80.00
17 Tyler Herro 60.00 150.00
18 PJ Washington Jr. 25.00 60.00
19 Brandon Clarke 40.00 100.00
20 Rui Hachimura 125.00 300.00
21 Isaiah Roby 25.00 60.00
22 Keldon Johnson 20.00 50.00
23 Mfiondu Kabengele 10.00 25.00
25 Admiral Schofield 25.00 60.00
26 Dylan Windler 20.00 50.00
27 Ty Jerome 12.00 30.00
28 Cody Martin 30.00 80.00
29 Carsen Edwards 6.00 15.00
30 Quinndary Weatherspoon 5.00 12.00
31 Cameron Johnson 30.00 80.00
32 Cam Reddish 8.00 20.00
33 Jaxson Hayes 30.00 80.00
35 Luka Samanic 6.00 15.00
36 Goga Bitadze 12.00 30.00
37 Chuma Okeke 25.00 60.00
39 Romeo Langford 75.00 200.00
40 Ja Morant 150.00 400.00

2019-20 Absolute Memorabilia Limitless Signatures Level 1
STATED PRINT RUN 25 SER.#'d SETS
EXCHANGE DEADLINE 5/27/2021
1 Kobe Bryant 800.00 1,500.00
2 Allen Iverson 40.00 100.00
3 Karl-Anthony Towns 12.00 30.00
4 Donovan Mitchell EXCH 20.00 50.00
5 Magic Johnson 20.00 60.00
6 Kristaps Porzingis 8.00 20.00
7 Damian Lillard 15.00 40.00
8 Zach LaVine 10.00 25.00
9 Karl Malone 15.00 40.00
10 De'Aaron Fox 15.00 40.00
11 Dwyane Wade 25.00 60.00
12 Lauri Markkanen 10.00 25.00
13 Kyle Kuzma 15.00 40.00
14 Charles Barkley 75.00 200.00
15 Pascal Siakam 12.00 30.00
16 Caris LeVert 5.00 12.00
17 Wendell Carter Jr. 6.00 15.00
18 Grant Hill 15.00 40.00
19 Robert Horry 5.00 12.00
20 Nikola Jokic 125.00 300.00

2019-20 Absolute Memorabilia Retired Autographs Level 1
STATED PRINT RUN 49 SER.#'d SETS
EXCHANGE DEADLINE 5/27/2021
*LEVEL 2: .5X TO 1.2X BASIC
1 Kenny Sky Walker 4.00 10.00
2 Sam Cassell 6.00 15.00
3 Alvan Adams 3.00 8.00
4 Raja Bell 4.00 10.00
5 Caron Butler 4.00 10.00
6 Maurice Cheeks 4.00 10.00
7 Ricky Davis 4.00 10.00
8 Antoine Walker 4.00 10.00
9 Cedric Maxwell 4.00 10.00
10 Kelly Tripucka 4.00 10.00
11 Stromile Swift 3.00 8.00
12 Fat Lever 4.00 10.00
13 Devean George 4.00 10.00
14 Don Chaney 5.00 12.00
15 Lionel Hollins 3.00 8.00
16 Quinn Buckner 8.00 20.00
17 Mark Price 5.00 12.00
18 Bob McAdoo 6.00 15.00
19 Tyronn Lue 3.00 8.00
20 Shane Battier 4.00 10.00
21 Dino Radja 3.00 8.00
22 Bill Cartwright 4.00 10.00
23 John Starks 5.00 12.00
24 Eddie Jones 4.00 10.00
25 Arvydas Sabonis 5.00 12.00
26 Wally Szczerbiak 4.00 10.00
27 Adrian Dantley 5.00 12.00
28 Cherokee Parks 3.00 8.00
29 Rik Smits 4.00 10.00
30 David Thompson 5.00 12.00

2019-20 Absolute Memorabilia Rookie Autographs Level 1
EXCHANGE DEADLINE 5/27/2021
*LEVEL 2/49: .5X TO 1.2X BASIC
*LEVEL 2/25: .6X TO 1.5X BASIC
1 Zion Williamson 300.00 600.00
2 Ja Morant 75.00 200.00
3 RJ Barrett 20.00 50.00
4 De'Andre Hunter 12.00 30.00
5 Jarrett Culver 2.50 6.00
6 Coby White 15.00 40.00
7 Jaxson Hayes 10.00 25.00
8 Rui Hachimura 60.00 150.00
9 Cam Reddish 4.00 10.00
10 Cameron Johnson 6.00 15.00
11 PJ Washington Jr. 8.00 20.00
12 Tyler Herro 30.00 80.00
13 Romeo Langford 2.50 6.00
14 Sekou Doumbouya 2.50 6.00
15 Chuma Okeke 5.00 12.00
16 Nickeil Alexander-Walker 4.00 10.00
17 Goga Bitadze 4.00 10.00
18 Luka Samanic 3.00 8.00
19 Brandon Clarke 12.00 30.00
20 Grant Williams 6.00 15.00
21 Ty Jerome 5.00 12.00
22 Nassir Little 4.00 10.00
23 Dylan Windler 3.00 8.00
24 Mfiondu Kabengele 3.00 8.00
25 Jordan Poole 10.00 25.00
26 Keldon Johnson 8.00 20.00
27 Kevin Porter Jr. 8.00 20.00
28 KZ Okpala 3.00 8.00
29 Carsen Edwards 3.00 8.00
30 Bol Bol 10.00 25.00
31 Admiral Schofield 3.00 8.00
32 Tremont Waters 3.00 8.00
33 Isaiah Roby 3.00 8.00
34 Bruno Fernando 3.00 8.00
35 Cody Martin 4.00 10.00
37 Jaylen Nowell 3.00 8.00
38 Ignas Brazdeikis 5.00 12.00
39 Quinndary Weatherspoon 2.50 6.00
40 Matisse Thybulle 20.00 50.00

2019-20 Absolute Memorabilia Rookie Autographs Level 2
*LEVEL 2/49: .5X TO 1.2X BASIC
*LEVEL 2/25: .6X TO 1.5X BASIC
PRINT RUNS B/WN 25-49 COPIES PER
EXCHANGE DEADLINE 5/27/2021
3 RJ Barrett/49 40.00 100.00
10 Cameron Johnson/49 10.00 25.00
12 Tyler Herro/49 40.00 100.00

2019-20 Absolute Memorabilia Rookie Autographs Variation Level 1
EXCHANGE DEADLINE 5/27/2021
*LEVEL 2: .5X TO 1.2X BASIC
1 Zion Williamson 300.00 600.00
2 Ja Morant 75.00 200.00
3 RJ Barrett 20.00 50.00
4 De'Andre Hunter 12.00 30.00
5 Jarrett Culver 2.50 6.00
6 Coby White 15.00 40.00
7 Jaxson Hayes 10.00 25.00
8 Rui Hachimura 60.00 150.00
9 Cam Reddish 8.00 20.00
10 Cameron Johnson 6.00 15.00
11 PJ Washington Jr. 8.00 20.00
12 Tyler Herro 30.00 80.00
13 Romeo Langford 2.50 6.00
14 Sekou Doumbouya 2.50 6.00
15 Chuma Okeke 5.00 12.00
16 Nickeil Alexander-Walker 4.00 10.00
17 Goga Bitadze 4.00 10.00
18 Luka Samanic 3.00 8.00
19 Brandon Clarke 15.00 40.00
20 Grant Williams 6.00 15.00
21 Ty Jerome 5.00 12.00
22 Nassir Little 4.00 10.00
23 Dylan Windler 3.00 8.00
24 Mfiondu Kabengele 3.00 8.00
25 Jordan Poole 10.00 25.00
26 Keldon Johnson 8.00 20.00
27 Kevin Porter Jr. 8.00 20.00
28 KZ Okpala 3.00 8.00
29 Carsen Edwards 3.00 8.00
30 Bol Bol 10.00 25.00
31 Admiral Schofield 3.00 8.00
32 Tremont Waters 3.00 8.00
33 Isaiah Roby 3.00 8.00
34 Bruno Fernando 3.00 8.00
35 Cody Martin 4.00 10.00
37 Jaylen Nowell 3.00 8.00
38 Ignas Brazdeikis 5.00 12.00
39 Quinndary Weatherspoon 2.50 6.00
40 Matisse Thybulle 20.00 50.00

2019-20 Absolute Memorabilia Rookie Autographs Variation Level 2
*LEVEL 2: .5X TO 1.2X BASIC
STATED PRINT RUN 49 SER.#'d SETS
EXCHANGE DEADLINE 5/27/2021
3 RJ Barrett 40.00 100.00
10 Cameron Johnson 10.00 25.00
12 Tyler Herro 30.00 80.00

2019-20 Absolute Memorabilia Rookie Threads Level 1
*LEVEL 2: .6X TO 1.5X BASIC
1 Eric Paschall 2.00 5.00
2 Coby White 5.00 12.00
3 Isaiah Roby 2.00 5.00
4 Cameron Johnson 4.00 10.00
5 Matisse Thybulle 3.00 8.00
6 RJ Barrett 6.00 15.00
7 Mfiondu Kabengele 2.00 5.00
8 Jaxson Hayes 2.50 6.00
9 KZ Okpala 2.00 5.00
10 Zion Williamson 30.00 80.00
11 Admiral Schofield 2.00 5.00
12 Luka Samanic 2.00 5.00
13 Ignas Brazdeikis 2.00 5.00
14 Tyler Herro 8.00 20.00
15 Ty Jerome 3.00 8.00
16 Chuma Okeke 2.50 6.00
17 Jordan Poole 6.00 15.00
18 Brandon Clarke 3.00 8.00
19 Carsen Edwards 2.00 5.00
20 Romeo Langford 1.50 4.00
21 Jaylen Nowell 2.00 5.00
22 Rui Hachimura 6.00 15.00
23 Quinndary Weatherspoon 1.50 4.00
24 Ja Morant 12.00 30.00
25 Nassir Little 2.50 6.00
26 Jarrett Culver 1.50 4.00
27 Keldon Johnson 5.00 12.00
28 Cam Reddish 2.50 6.00
29 Bruno Fernando 2.00 5.00
30 De'Andre Hunter 6.00 15.00
31 Bol Bol 4.00 10.00
32 Grant Williams 2.50 6.00
33 Tremont Waters 2.00 5.00
34 Sekou Doumbouya 1.50 4.00
35 Dylan Windler 2.00 5.00
36 Goga Bitadze 2.50 6.00
37 Kevin Porter Jr. 3.00 8.00
38 PJ Washington Jr. 5.00 12.00
39 Cody Martin 2.50 6.00
40 Nickeil Alexander-Walker 2.50 6.00

2019-20 Absolute Memorabilia Rookie Threads Level 2
*LEVEL 2: .6X TO 1.5X BASIC
STATED PRINT RUN 25 SER.#'d SETS
EXCHANGE DEADLINE 5/27/2021
8 Jaxson Hayes 8.00 20.00
10 Zion Williamson 100.00 250.00
18 Brandon Clarke 8.00 20.00
24 Ja Morant 25.00 60.00

2019-20 Absolute Memorabilia Rookies Yellow
1 Zion Williamson 12.00 30.00
2 Ja Morant 8.00 20.00
3 RJ Barrett 2.00 5.00
4 De'Andre Hunter 2.00 5.00
5 Jarrett Culver .50 1.25
6 Coby White 1.50 4.00
7 Jaxson Hayes .75 2.00
8 Rui Hachimura 2.00 5.00
9 Cam Reddish .75 2.00
10 Cameron Johnson 1.25 3.00
11 PJ Washington Jr. 1.50 4.00
12 Tyler Herro 2.50 6.00
13 Romeo Langford .50 1.25
14 Sekou Doumbouya .50 1.25
15 Darius Bazley .50 1.25
19 Brandon Clarke 1.00 2.50
21 Darius Garland 2.00 5.00
22 Matisse Thybulle 1.00 2.50
23 Bol Bol 1.25 3.00

2019-20 Absolute Memorabilia Tools of the Trade Four Swatch Signatures Level 1
PRINT RUNS B/WN 25-175 COPIES PER
EXCHANGE DEADLINE 5/27/2021
1 Zion Williamson/25 400.00 800.00
TT4-JMT Ja Morant/175 60.00 150.00
3 RJ Barrett/175 30.00 80.00
4 De'Andre Hunter/175 10.00 25.00
5 Jarrett Culver/175 3.00 8.00
6 Coby White/175 10.00 25.00
7 Jaxson Hayes/175 10.00 25.00
8 Rui Hachimura/175 50.00 120.00
9 Cam Reddish/175 5.00 12.00
10 Cameron Johnson/175 8.00 20.00
11 PJ Washington Jr./175 10.00 25.00
12 Tyler Herro/175 20.00 50.00
13 Romeo Langford/175 3.00 8.00
14 Sekou Doumbouya/175 3.00 8.00
15 Chuma Okeke/175 6.00 15.00
16 Nickeil Alexander-Walker/175 5.00 12.00
17 Goga Bitadze/175 6.00 15.00
18 Luka Samanic/175 4.00 10.00
19 Brandon Clarke/175 6.00 15.00
20 Grant Williams/175 8.00 20.00
21 Ty Jerome/175 6.00 15.00
22 Nassir Little/175 5.00 12.00
23 Dylan Windler/175 4.00 10.00
24 Mfiondu Kabengele/175 4.00 10.00
25 Jordan Poole/175 12.00 30.00
26 Keldon Johnson/175 10.00 25.00
27 Kevin Porter Jr./175 6.00 15.00
28 KZ Okpala/175 4.00 10.00
29 Carsen Edwards/175 4.00 10.00
30 Bol Bol/175 8.00 20.00
31 Admiral Schofield/175 8.00 20.00
32 Tremont Waters/175 4.00 10.00
33 Cody Martin/175 5.00 12.00

2019-20 Absolute Memorabilia Tools of the Trade Four Swatch Signatures Level 2
*LEVEL 2: .8X TO 2X BASIC
PRINT RUNS B/WN 10-25 COPIES PER
NO PRICING QTY 15 OR LESS
EXCHANGE DEADLINE 5/27/2021
4 De'Andre Hunter/25 30.00 80.00
9 Cam Reddish/25 10.00 25.00
12 Tyler Herro/25 50.00 120.00
29 Carsen Edwards/25 8.00 20.00

2019-20 Absolute Memorabilia Tools of the Trade Six Swatch Signatures Level 1
PRINT RUNS B/WN 25-199 COPIES PER
EXCHANGE DEADLINE 5/27/2021
1 Zion Williamson/25 400.00 800.00
TT4-JMT Ja Morant/149 60.00 150.00
3 RJ Barrett/149 30.00 80.00
4 De'Andre Hunter/149 10.00 25.00
5 Jarrett Culver/149 3.00 8.00
6 Coby White/149 10.00 25.00
7 Jaxson Hayes/149 10.00 25.00
8 Rui Hachimura/149 50.00 120.00
9 Cam Reddish/149 5.00 12.00
10 Cameron Johnson/149 8.00 20.00
11 PJ Washington Jr./149 10.00 25.00
12 Tyler Herro/149 20.00 50.00
13 Romeo Langford/149 3.00 8.00
14 Sekou Doumbouya/149 3.00 8.00
15 Chuma Okeke/149 6.00 15.00
16 Nickeil Alexander-Walker/149 5.00 12.00
17 Goga Bitadze/149 6.00 15.00
18 Luka Samanic/149 4.00 10.00
19 Brandon Clarke/149 6.00 15.00
20 Grant Williams/149 8.00 20.00
21 Ty Jerome/149 6.00 15.00
22 Nassir Little/149 5.00 12.00
23 Dylan Windler/149 4.00 10.00
24 Mfiondu Kabengele/149 4.00 10.00
25 Jordan Poole/149 12.00 30.00
26 Keldon Johnson/149 10.00 25.00
27 Kevin Porter Jr./149 6.00 15.00
28 KZ Okpala/149 4.00 10.00
29 Carsen Edwards/149 4.00 10.00
30 Bol Bol/149 8.00 20.00
31 Admiral Schofield/149 8.00 20.00
32 Tremont Waters/149 4.00 10.00
33 Cody Martin/149 5.00 12.00

2019-20 Absolute Memorabilia Tools of the Trade Six Swatch Signatures Level 2
*LEVEL 2: .8X TO 2X BASIC
PRINT RUNS B/WN 10-25 COPIES PER
NO PRICING QTY 15 OR LESS
EXCHANGE DEADLINE 5/27/2021
4 De'Andre Hunter/25 30.00 80.00
9 Cam Reddish/25 10.00 25.00
12 Tyler Herro/25 50.00 120.00
29 Carsen Edwards/25 8.00 20.00

2019-20 Absolute Memorabilia Tools of the Trade Three Swatch Signatures Level 1
PRINT RUNS B/WN 25-199 COPIES PER
EXCHANGE DEADLINE 5/27/2021
1 Zion Williamson/25 400.00 800.00
2 Ja Morant/199 60.00 150.00
3 RJ Barrett/199 30.00 80.00
4 De'Andre Hunter/199 10.00 25.00
5 Jarrett Culver/199 3.00 8.00
6 Coby White/199 10.00 25.00
7 Jaxson Hayes/199 10.00 25.00
8 Rui Hachimura/199 50.00 120.00
9 Cam Reddish/199 5.00 12.00
10 Cameron Johnson/199 8.00 20.00
11 PJ Washington Jr./199 10.00 25.00
12 Tyler Herro/199 20.00 50.00
13 Romeo Langford/199 3.00 8.00
14 Sekou Doumbouya/199 3.00 8.00
15 Chuma Okeke/199 6.00 15.00
16 Nickeil Alexander-Walker/199 5.00 12.00
17 Goga Bitadze/199 6.00 15.00
18 Luka Samanic/199 4.00 10.00
19 Brandon Clarke/199 6.00 15.00
20 Grant Williams/199 8.00 20.00
21 Ty Jerome/199 6.00 15.00
22 Nassir Little/199 5.00 12.00
23 Dylan Windler/199 4.00 10.00
24 Mfiondu Kabengele/199 4.00 10.00
25 Jordan Poole/199 12.00 30.00
26 Keldon Johnson/199 10.00 25.00
27 Kevin Porter Jr./199 6.00 15.00
28 KZ Okpala/199 4.00 10.00
29 Carsen Edwards/199 4.00 10.00
30 Bol Bol/199 8.00 20.00
31 Admiral Schofield/199 8.00 20.00
32 Tremont Waters/199 4.00 10.00
33 Cody Martin/199 5.00 12.00

2019-20 Absolute Memorabilia Tools of the Trade Three Swatch Signatures Level 2
*LEVEL 2: .8X TO 2X BASIC
PRINT RUNS B/WN 10-25 COPIES PER
NO PRICING QTY 15 OR LESS
EXCHANGE DEADLINE 5/27/2021
4 De'Andre Hunter/25 30.00 80.00
9 Cam Reddish/25 10.00 25.00
12 Tyler Herro/25 50.00 120.00
29 Carsen Edwards/25 8.00 20.00

2019-20 Absolute Memorabilia Veteran Autographs Level 1
STATED PRINT RUN 49 SER.#'d SETS
EXCHANGE DEADLINE 5/27/2021
*LEVEL 2: .5X TO 1.2X BASIC
1 Cedi Osman 4.00 10.00
2 Montrezl Harrell 4.00 10.00
3 Robert Covington 3.00 8.00
4 Malcolm Brogdon 4.00 10.00
5 Thon Maker 3.00 8.00
6 Quinn Cook 4.00 10.00
7 Willie Cauley-Stein 3.00 8.00
8 TJ Leaf 3.00 8.00
9 Pascal Siakam 10.00 25.00
10 Yuta Watanabe 10.00 25.00
11 Josh Hart 4.00 10.00
12 Julius Randle 6.00 15.00
13 Cody Zeller 3.00 8.00
14 Cam Reynolds 3.00 8.00
15 Danilo Gallinari 4.00 10.00
16 Nemanja Bjelica 3.00 8.00
17 Wesley Matthews 3.00 8.00
19 Myles Turner 5.00 12.00
20 Caris LeVert 4.00 10.00
21 P.J. Tucker 4.00 10.00
22 Justin Jackson 3.00 8.00
23 DeAndre' Bembry 3.00 8.00
24 Troy Brown Jr. 3.00 8.00
25 Hamidou Diallo 4.00 10.00
26 Kelly Olynyk 3.00 8.00
27 Rodions Kurucs 5.00 12.00
28 Kevin Knox II 3.00 8.00
29 Frank Mason III 3.00 8.00
30 Gary Harris 4.00 10.00

2019-20 Absolute Memorabilia Veteran Autographs Level 2
*LEVEL 2: .5X TO 1.2X BASIC
STATED PRINT RUN 25 SER.#'d SETS
EXCHANGE DEADLINE 5/27/2021
27 Rodions Kurucs 10.00 25.00

2019-20 Absolute Memorabilia Veteran Tools of the Trade Level 1
*LEVEL 2: 1.25X TO 3X BASIC
1 Steven Adams 2.00 5.00
2 J.J. Barea 2.00 5.00
3 Karl Malone 5.00 12.00
4 Allen Crabbe 1.50 4.00
5 Klay Thompson 6.00 15.00
6 Caris LeVert 2.00 5.00
7 LeBron James 40.00 100.00
8 Derrick Rose 5.00 12.00
9 Paul Millsap 2.00 5.00
10 Enes Kanter 1.50 4.00
11 Tyus Jones 1.50 4.00
12 Jeff Teague 1.50 4.00
13 Kevin Durant 8.00 20.00
14 Andrew Wiggins 3.00 8.00
15 Kristaps Porzingis 3.00 8.00
16 CJ McCollum 2.50 6.00
17 Myles Turner 2.50 6.00
18 Domantas Sabonis 3.00 8.00
19 Roy Hibbert 2.00 5.00
20 Evan Turner 1.50 4.00
21 Wesley Matthews 1.50 4.00
22 Joe Harris 2.00 5.00
23 Kevin Knox II 1.50 4.00
24 Blake Griffin 2.50 6.00
25 LaMarcus Aldridge 2.50 6.00
26 DeMarre Carroll 1.50 4.00
27 Nikola Vucevic 2.00 5.00
28 Dwight Powell 1.50 4.00
29 Shaquille O'Neal 10.00 25.00
30 Grant Hill 4.00 10.00

2020-21 Absolute Memorabilia
*DOLLAR TREE: .5X TO 1.2X BASIC
1 Trae Young 1.50 4.00
2 Onyeka Okongwu 1.50 4.00
3 Cam Reddish .75 2.00
4 Jayson Tatum 2.50 6.00
5 Aaron Nesmith 1.50 4.00
6 Kemba Walker .60 1.50
7 Payton Pritchard 2.50 6.00
8 Kyrie Irving 1.25 3.00
9 Kevin Durant 2.50 6.00
10 Jarrett Allen .60 1.50
11 PJ Washington Jr. .60 1.50
12 LaMelo Ball 6.00 15.00
13 Vernon Carey Jr. .75 2.00
14 Coby White .75 2.00
15 Patrick Williams 2.00 5.00
16 Zach LaVine 1.00 2.50
17 Darius Garland 1.00 2.50
18 Isaac Okoro 1.25 3.00
19 Kevin Love .60 1.50
20 Luka Doncic 4.00 10.00
21 Kristaps Porzingis .75 2.00
22 Josh Green 1.50 4.00
23 Tyrell Terry .60 1.50
24 Jamal Murray 1.00 2.50
25 Zeke Nnaji 1.00 2.50
26 Nikola Jokic 3.00 8.00
27 RJ Hampton .75 2.00
28 Blake Griffin .60 1.50
29 Killian Hayes .75 2.00
30 Derrick Rose 1.00 2.50
31 Isaiah Stewart 1.50 4.00
32 Stephen Curry 5.00 12.00
33 James Wiseman 1.00 2.50
34 Draymond Green .75 2.00
35 Andrew Wiggins .75 2.00
36 James Harden 1.25 3.00
37 Russell Westbrook 1.25 3.00
38 Eric Gordon .50 1.25
39 Malcolm Brogdon .60 1.50
40 Cassius Stanley .75 2.00
41 Myles Turner .60 1.50
42 Kawhi Leonard 1.50 4.00
43 Paul George 1.00 2.50
44 Patrick Beverley .40 1.00
45 LeBron James 5.00 12.00
46 Anthony Davis 1.50 4.00
47 Kentavious Caldwell-Pope .50 1.25
48 Ja Morant 2.00 5.00
49 Desmond Bane 2.50 6.00
50 Xavier Tillman 1.00 2.50
51 Jaren Jackson Jr. 1.00 2.50
52 Jimmy Butler 1.25 3.00
53 Precious Achiuwa 1.50 4.00
54 Tyler Herro 1.25 3.00
55 Giannis Antetokounmpo 3.00 8.00
56 Khris Middleton .75 2.00
57 Jrue Holiday .60 1.50
58 Karl-Anthony Towns 1.00 2.50
59 Anthony Edwards RC 8.00 20.00
60 Jordan Nwora 1.00 2.50
61 Jaden McDaniels 2.50 6.00
62 Zion Williamson 2.00 5.00
63 Lonzo Ball .75 2.00
64 Kira Lewis Jr. .75 2.00
65 Brandon Ingram .75 2.00
66 RJ Barrett 1.00 2.50
67 Obi Toppin 1.50 4.00
68 Immanuel Quickley 2.00 5.00
69 Shai Gilgeous-Alexander 3.00 8.00
70 Aleksej Pokusevski 1.00 2.50
71 Theo Maledon .75 2.00
72 Darius Bazley .40 1.00
73 Cole Anthony 2.00 5.00
74 Aaron Gordon .60 1.50
75 Nikola Vucevic .60 1.50
76 Ben Simmons .60 1.50
77 Joel Embiid 1.50 4.00
78 Tyrese Maxey 6.00 15.00
79 Devin Booker 1.50 4.00
80 Jalen Smith 1.50 4.00
81 Deandre Ayton .60 1.50
82 Damian Lillard 1.50 4.00
83 CJ McCollum .60 1.50
84 CJ Elleby .75 2.00
85 De'Aaron Fox 1.00 2.50
86 Tyrese Haliburton 6.00 15.00
87 Robert Woodard II .75 2.00
88 DeMar DeRozan .75 2.00
89 LaMarcus Aldridge .60 1.50
90 Devin Vassell 2.50 6.00
91 Kyle Lowry .75 2.00
92 Fred VanVleet 1.00 2.50
93 Pascal Siakam 1.00 2.50
94 Malachi Flynn 1.50 4.00
95 Donovan Mitchell 1.25 3.00
96 Elijah Hughes .75 2.00
97 Udoka Azubuike 1.00 2.50
98 Bradley Beal .75 2.00
99 Deni Avdija 2.00 5.00
100 Rui Hachimura .75 2.00

2020-21 Absolute Memorabilia Blue
*BLUE: 1.25X TO 3X BASIC
STATED PRINT RUN 99 SER.#'d SETS
59 Anthony Edwards 60.00 150.00

2020-21 Absolute Memorabilia Orange
*ORANGE: 1.25X TO 3X BASIC
STATED PRINT RUN 75 SER.#'d SETS
59 Anthony Edwards 75.00 200.00

2020-21 Absolute Memorabilia Purple
*PURPLE: 2.5X TO 6X BASIC
STATED PRINT RUN 25 SER.#'d SETS
59 Anthony Edwards 150.00 400.00

2020-21 Absolute Memorabilia Red
*RED: .75X TO 2X BASIC
STATED PRINT RUN 199 SER.#'d SETS
59 Anthony Edwards 40.00 100.00

2020-21 Absolute Memorabilia Teal
*TEAL: 1.5X TO 4X BASIC
STATED PRINT RUN 49 SER.#'d SETS
59 Anthony Edwards 100.00 250.00

2020-21 Absolute Memorabilia Established Threads Level 1
COMMON CARD 1.50 4.00
SEMISTARS 2.00 5.00
UNLISTED STARS 2.50 6.00
*LEVEL 2/25: 1.25X TO 3X BASIC
1 Aaron Gordon 2.50 6.00
2 Trae Young 6.00 15.00
3 Danny Ainge 2.50 6.00
4 Jarrett Allen 2.50 6.00
5 PJ Washington Jr. 2.50 6.00
6 Wendell Carter Jr. 2.00 5.00
7 Darius Garland 4.00 10.00
8 Dirk Nowitzki 6.00 15.00
9 Jamal Murray 4.00 10.00
10 Joe Dumars 3.00 8.00
11 Chris Mullin 3.00 8.00
12 Hakeem Olajuwon 5.00 12.00
13 Doug McDermott 2.00 5.00
14 Danny Manning 2.00 5.00
15 Anthony Davis 6.00 15.00
16 Dillon Brooks 2.00 5.00
17 Bam Adebayo 4.00 10.00
18 Khris Middleton 3.00 8.00
19 Josh Okogie 2.00 5.00
20 Brandon Ingram 3.00 8.00
21 Kevin Knox II 1.50 4.00
22 Darius Bazley 1.50 4.00
23 Joel Embiid 6.00 15.00
24 Deandre Ayton 2.50 6.00
25 Damian Lillard 6.00 15.00
26 Marvin Bagley III 2.00 5.00
27 David Robinson 5.00 12.00
28 Fred VanVleet 4.00 10.00
29 John Stockton 5.00 12.00
30 Bradley Beal 3.00 8.00

2020-21 Absolute Memorabilia Established Threads Level 2
*LEVEL 2: .75X TO 2X BASIC
STATED PRINT RUN 25 SER.#'d SETS

2020-21 Absolute Memorabilia Future Signatures Level 1
COMMON CARD 4.00 10.00
SEMISTARS 5.00 12.00
UNLISTED STARS 6.00 15.00
STATED PRINT RUN 49 SER.#'d SETS
EXCHANGE DEADLINE 9/24/2022
*LEVEL 2: .5X TO 1.2X BASIC
1 Anthony Edwards 300.00 600.00
2 LaMelo Ball 50.00 120.00
3 Isaac Okoro 8.00 20.00
4 Killian Hayes 5.00 12.00
5 Deni Avdija 12.00 30.00
6 Devin Vassell 15.00 40.00
7 Kira Lewis Jr. 5.00 12.00
8 Cole Anthony 12.00 30.00
9 Aleksej Pokusevski 6.00 15.00
10 Saddiq Bey 10.00 25.00
11 Tyrese Maxey 40.00 100.00
12 Caleb Martin 10.00 25.00
13 Immanuel Quickley 12.00 30.00
14 Udoka Azubuike 6.00 15.00
15 Malachi Flynn 5.00 12.00
16 Tyrell Terry 4.00 10.00
17 Daniel Oturu 5.00 12.00
18 Xavier Tillman 6.00 15.00
19 Robert Woodard II 5.00 12.00
20 Jordan Nwora 6.00 15.00
21 James Wiseman 6.00 15.00
22 Patrick Williams 12.00 30.00
23 Onyeka Okongwu 10.00 25.00
24 Obi Toppin 10.00 25.00
26 Tyrese Haliburton 40.00 100.00
27 Aaron Nesmith 10.00 25.00
28 Isaiah Stewart 10.00 25.00
29 Josh Green 10.00 25.00
30 Precious Achiuwa 10.00 25.00
31 Zeke Nnaji 6.00 15.00
32 RJ Hampton 5.00 12.00
33 Payton Pritchard 15.00 40.00
34 Jaden McDaniels 15.00 40.00
35 Desmond Bane 15.00 40.00
36 Vernon Carey Jr. 5.00 12.00
37 Theo Maledon 5.00 12.00
38 Tyler Bey 5.00 12.00
39 Tre Jones 8.00 20.00
40 Nico Mannion 5.00 12.00

2020-21 Absolute Memorabilia Glass
COMMON CARD 6.00 15.00
SEMISTARS 8.00 20.00
UNLISTED STARS 10.00 25.00
EXCHANGE DEADLINE 9/24/2022
1 Luka Doncic 100.00 250.00
2 LeBron James 125.00 300.00
3 Stephen Curry 100.00 250.00
4 Trae Young 60.00 150.00
5 Giannis Antetokounmpo 75.00 200.00
6 Anthony Davis 60.00 150.00
7 Damian Lillard 60.00 150.00
8 Zion Williamson 100.00 250.00
9 Kawhi Leonard 60.00 150.00
10 Ja Morant 125.00 300.00
11 Jayson Tatum 75.00 200.00
12 Kevin Durant 60.00 150.00
13 James Harden 40.00 100.00
14 Jimmy Butler 30.00 80.00
15 Chris Paul 40.00 100.00
16 Joel Embiid 40.00 100.00
17 Donovan Mitchell 40.00 100.00
18 Jamal Murray 40.00 100.00
19 Devin Booker 50.00 120.00
20 Ben Simmons 30.00 80.00
21 Russell Westbrook 40.00 100.00
22 Anthony Edwards 200.00 500.00
23 LaMelo Ball 100.00 250.00
24 James Wiseman 10.00 25.00
25 Deni Avdija 40.00 100.00

2020-21 Absolute Memorabilia Retired Autographs Level 1
COMMON CARD 3.00 8.00
SEMISTARS 4.00 10.00
UNLISTED STARS 5.00 12.00
STATED PRINT RUN 10-49 SER.#'d SETS
NO PRICING ON QTY 10
EXCHANGE DEADLINE 9/24/2022
*LEVEL 2: .5X TO 1.2X BASIC
1 Eddie Jones/49 5.00 12.00
2 Cherokee Parks/49 3.00 8.00
3 Kareem Abdul-Jabbar/25 100.00 250.00
4 Jamaal Wilkes/49 5.00 12.00
5 Sam Perkins/49 4.00 10.00
6 Oscar Robertson/25 40.00 100.00
7 Latrell Sprewell/49 20.00 50.00
8 Ernie DiGregorio/49 4.00 10.00
9 Richard Jefferson/49 3.00 8.00
10 Raef LaFrentz/49 4.00 10.00
11 Rik Smits/49 4.00 10.00
12 John Stockton/25 40.00 100.00
13 Mark Jackson/49 4.00 10.00
14 Nick Van Exel/49 20.00 50.00
15 Dan Majerle/49 5.00 12.00
16 Mark Aguirre/49 4.00 10.00
17 Spud Webb/49 5.00 12.00
18 Walt Frazier/49 12.00 30.00
19 Shane Battier/49 4.00 10.00
20 Dirk Nowitzki/25 100.00 250.00
22 Dennis Rodman/49 25.00 60.00
23 Jerry West/25 30.00 80.00
24 Larry Bird/25 75.00 200.00
25 Vlade Divac/49 4.00 10.00
26 Juwan Howard/49 4.00 10.00
27 Bob Dandridge/49 4.00 10.00
28 George Gervin/49 12.00 30.00
29 Karl Malone/25 40.00 100.00
30 Shawn Kemp/49 30.00 80.00

2020-21 Absolute Memorabilia Rookie Autographs Level 1
COMMON CARD 3.00 8.00
SEMISTARS 4.00 10.00
UNLISTED STARS 5.00 12.00
EXCHANGE DEADLINE 9/24/2022
*LEVEL 2/49: .6X TO 1.5X BASIC
*LEVEL 1 VARIATION: .5X TO 1.2X BASIC
*LEVEL 2 VARIATION: .75X TO 2X BASIC
1 Anthony Edwards 100.00 250.00
2 James Wiseman 5.00 12.00
3 LaMelo Ball 300.00 600.00
4 Patrick Williams 10.00 25.00
5 Isaac Okoro 6.00 15.00
6 Onyeka Okongwu 8.00 20.00
7 Killian Hayes 4.00 10.00
8 Obi Toppin 8.00 20.00
9 Deni Avdija 10.00 25.00
11 Devin Vassell 12.00 30.00
12 Tyrese Haliburton 50.00 120.00
13 Kira Lewis Jr. 4.00 10.00
14 Aaron Nesmith 8.00 20.00
15 Cole Anthony 30.00 80.00
16 Isaiah Stewart 8.00 20.00
17 Aleksej Pokusevski 5.00 12.00
18 Josh Green 8.00 20.00
19 Saddiq Bey 20.00 50.00
20 Precious Achiuwa 8.00 20.00
21 Tyrese Maxey 30.00 80.00
22 Zeke Nnaji 5.00 12.00
23 Caleb Martin 8.00 20.00
24 RJ Hampton 4.00 10.00
25 Immanuel Quickley 10.00 25.00
26 Payton Pritchard 12.00 30.00
27 Udoka Azubuike 5.00 12.00
28 Jaden McDaniels 20.00 50.00
29 Malachi Flynn 4.00 10.00
30 Desmond Bane 20.00 50.00
31 Tyrell Terry 3.00 8.00
32 Vernon Carey Jr. 4.00 10.00
33 Daniel Oturu 4.00 10.00
34 Theo Maledon 4.00 10.00
35 Xavier Tillman 5.00 12.00
36 Tyler Bey 4.00 10.00
37 Robert Woodard II 4.00 10.00
38 Tre Jones 6.00 15.00
39 Jordan Nwora 5.00 12.00
40 Nico Mannion 12.00 30.00
41 Saben Lee 4.00 10.00
42 Elijah Hughes 4.00 10.00
43 Nick Richards 5.00 12.00
44 Jahmi'us Ramsey 4.00 10.00
45 CJ Elleby 4.00 10.00
46 Skylar Mays 4.00 10.00
48 Cassius Winston 4.00 10.00
49 Cassius Stanley 4.00 10.00
50 Grant Riller 4.00 10.00

2020-21 Absolute Memorabilia Rookie Threads Level 1
COMMON CARD 1.50 4.00
SEMISTARS 2.00 5.00
UNLISTED STARS 2.50 6.00
*LEVEL 2/25: .75X TO 2X BASIC
1 Anthony Edwards 20.00 50.00
2 Killian Hayes 2.00 5.00
3 Kira Lewis Jr. 2.00 5.00
4 Saddiq Bey 4.00 10.00
5 Immanuel Quickley 5.00 12.00
6 Tyrell Terry 1.50 4.00
7 Robert Woodard II 2.00 5.00
8 Patrick Williams 5.00 12.00
9 Jalen Smith 4.00 10.00
10 Isaiah Stewart 4.00 10.00
11 Zeke Nnaji 2.50 6.00
12 Jaden McDaniels 6.00 15.00
13 Theo Maledon 2.00 5.00
14 Nico Mannion 2.00 5.00
15 LaMelo Ball 15.00 40.00
16 Deni Avdija 5.00 12.00
17 Cole Anthony 5.00 12.00
18 Tyrese Maxey 15.00 40.00
19 Udoka Azubuike 2.50 6.00
20 Daniel Oturu 2.00 5.00
21 Jordan Nwora 2.50 6.00
22 Onyeka Okongwu 4.00 10.00
23 Tyrese Haliburton 15.00 40.00
24 Josh Green 4.00 10.00
25 RJ Hampton 2.00 5.00
26 Desmond Bane 6.00 15.00
27 CJ Elleby 2.00 5.00
28 Isaac Okoro 3.00 8.00
29 Devin Vassell 6.00 15.00
30 Aleksej Pokusevski 2.50 6.00
31 Caleb Martin 4.00 10.00
32 Malachi Flynn 2.00 5.00
33 Xavier Tillman 2.50 6.00
34 James Wiseman 2.50 6.00
35 Obi Toppin 4.00 10.00
36 Aaron Nesmith 4.00 10.00
37 Precious Achiuwa 4.00 10.00
38 Vernon Carey Jr. 2.00 5.00
39 Tre Jones 3.00 8.00
40 Payton Pritchard 6.00 15.00

2020-21 Absolute Memorabilia Rookies Yellow
1 Anthony Edwards 8.00 20.00
2 James Wiseman 1.00 2.50
3 LaMelo Ball 6.00 15.00
4 Patrick Williams 2.00 5.00
5 Isaac Okoro 1.25 3.00
6 Onyeka Okongwu 1.50 4.00
7 Killian Hayes .75 2.00
8 Obi Toppin 1.50 4.00
9 Deni Avdija 2.00 5.00
10 Jalen Smith 1.50 4.00
11 Devin Vassell 2.50 6.00
12 Tyrese Haliburton 6.00 15.00
13 Kira Lewis Jr. .75 2.00
14 Aaron Nesmith 1.50 4.00
15 Cole Anthony 2.00 5.00
16 Isaiah Stewart 1.50 4.00
17 Aleksej Pokusevski 1.00 2.50
18 Josh Green 1.50 4.00
19 Saddiq Bey 1.50 4.00
20 Precious Achiuwa 1.50 4.00
21 Tyrese Maxey 6.00 15.00
22 Zeke Nnaji 1.00 2.50
23 Jordan Nwora 1.00 2.50
24 RJ Hampton .75 2.00
25 Immanuel Quickley 2.00 5.00

2020-21 Absolute Memorabilia Tools of the Trade Four Swatch Signatures Level 1
COMMON CARD 3.00 8.00
SEMISTARS 4.00 10.00

UNLISTED STARS 5.00 12.00
PRINT RUNS B/WN 99-199 COPIES PER
EXCHANGE DEADLINE 9/24/2022
*LEVEL 2: .75X TO 2X BASIC
1 Anthony Edwards/99 200.00 500.00
2 LaMelo Ball/99 75.00 200.00
3 Isaac Okoro/199 6.00 15.00
4 Killian Hayes/199 4.00 10.00
5 Deni Avdija/199 10.00 25.00
6 Devin Vassell/199 12.00 30.00
7 Kira Lewis Jr./199 4.00 10.00
8 Cole Anthony/199 10.00 25.00
9 Aleksej Pokusevski/199 5.00 12.00
10 Saddiq Bey/199 8.00 20.00
11 Tyrese Maxey/199 30.00 80.00
12 Theo Maledon/199 4.00 10.00
13 Immanuel Quickley/199 10.00 25.00
14 Udoka Azubuike/199 5.00 12.00
15 Malachi Flynn/199 4.00 10.00
16 Tyrell Terry/199 3.00 8.00
17 Daniel Oturu/199 4.00 10.00
18 James Wiseman/99 5.00 12.00
19 Patrick Williams/199 10.00 25.00
20 Onyeka Okongwu/199 8.00 20.00
21 Obi Toppin/199 8.00 20.00
23 Tyrese Haliburton/199 60.00 150.00
24 Aaron Nesmith/199 8.00 20.00
25 Isaiah Stewart/199 8.00 20.00
26 Josh Green/199 8.00 20.00
27 Precious Achiuwa/199 8.00 20.00
28 Zeke Nnaji/199 5.00 12.00
29 RJ Hampton/199 4.00 10.00
30 Payton Pritchard/199 12.00 30.00
31 Jaden McDaniels/199 12.00 30.00
32 Desmond Bane/199 12.00 30.00
33 Vernon Carey Jr./199 4.00 10.00

2020-21 Absolute Memorabilia Tools of the Trade Six Swatch Signatures Level 1

COMMON CARD 4.00 10.00
SEMISTARS 5.00 12.00
UNLISTED STARS 6.00 15.00
PRINT RUNS B/WN 99-199 COPIES PER
EXCHANGE DEADLINE 9/24/2022
*LEVEL 2: .75X TO 2X BASIC
1 Anthony Edwards/99 300.00 600.00
2 LaMelo Ball/99 100.00 250.00
3 Isaac Okoro/199 8.00 20.00
4 Killian Hayes/199 5.00 12.00
5 Deni Avdija/199 12.00 30.00
6 Devin Vassell/199 15.00 40.00
7 Kira Lewis Jr./199 5.00 12.00
8 Cole Anthony/199 12.00 30.00
9 Aleksej Pokusevski/199 6.00 15.00
10 Saddiq Bey/199 10.00 25.00
11 Tyrese Maxey/199 40.00 100.00
12 Theo Maledon/199 5.00 12.00
13 Immanuel Quickley/199 12.00 30.00
14 Udoka Azubuike/199 6.00 15.00
15 Malachi Flynn/199 5.00 12.00
16 Tyrell Terry/199 4.00 10.00
17 Daniel Oturu/199 5.00 12.00
18 James Wiseman/99 6.00 15.00
19 Patrick Williams/199 12.00 30.00
20 Onyeka Okongwu/199 10.00 25.00
21 Obi Toppin/199 10.00 25.00
23 Tyrese Haliburton/199 75.00 200.00
24 Aaron Nesmith/199 10.00 25.00
25 Isaiah Stewart/199 10.00 25.00
26 Josh Green/199 10.00 25.00
27 Precious Achiuwa/199 10.00 25.00
28 Zeke Nnaji/199 6.00 15.00
29 RJ Hampton/199 5.00 12.00
30 Payton Pritchard/199 15.00 40.00
31 Jaden McDaniels/199 15.00 40.00
32 Desmond Bane/199 15.00 40.00
33 Vernon Carey Jr./199 5.00 12.00

2020-21 Absolute Memorabilia Tools of the Trade Three Swatch Signatures Level 1

COMMON CARD 3.00 8.00
SEMISTARS 4.00 10.00
UNLISTED STARS 5.00 12.00
PRINT RUNS B/WN 99-199 COPIES PER
EXCHANGE DEADLINE 9/24/2022
*LEVEL 2: .75X TO 2X BASIC
1 Anthony Edwards/99 200.00 500.00
2 LaMelo Ball/99 75.00 200.00
3 Isaac Okoro/199 6.00 15.00
4 Killian Hayes/199 4.00 10.00
5 Deni Avdija/199 10.00 25.00
6 Devin Vassell/199 12.00 30.00
7 Kira Lewis Jr./199 4.00 10.00
8 Cole Anthony/199 10.00 25.00
9 Aleksej Pokusevski/199 5.00 12.00
10 Saddiq Bey/199 8.00 20.00
11 Tyrese Maxey/199 30.00 80.00
12 Theo Maledon/199 4.00 10.00
13 Immanuel Quickley/199 10.00 25.00
14 Udoka Azubuike/199 5.00 12.00
15 Malachi Flynn/199 4.00 10.00
16 Tyrell Terry/199 3.00 8.00
17 Daniel Oturu/199 4.00 10.00
18 James Wiseman/99 5.00 12.00
19 Patrick Williams/199 10.00 25.00
20 Onyeka Okongwu/199 8.00 20.00
21 Obi Toppin/199 8.00 20.00
23 Tyrese Haliburton/199 60.00 150.00
24 Aaron Nesmith/199 8.00 20.00
25 Isaiah Stewart/199 8.00 20.00
26 Josh Green/199 8.00 20.00
27 Precious Achiuwa/199 8.00 20.00
28 Zeke Nnaji/199 5.00 12.00
29 RJ Hampton/199 4.00 10.00
30 Payton Pritchard/199 12.00 30.00
31 Jaden McDaniels/199 12.00 30.00
32 Desmond Bane/199 12.00 30.00
33 Vernon Carey Jr./199 4.00 10.00

2020-21 Absolute Memorabilia Veteran Autographs Level 1

COMMON CARD/49 3.00 8.00
SEMISTARS/49 4.00 10.00
UNLISTED STARS/49 5.00 12.00
COMMON CARD/25 4.00 10.00
SEMISTARS/25 5.00 12.00
UNLISTED STARS/25 6.00 15.00
STATED PRINT RUN 10-49 SER.#'d SETS
NO PRICING ON QTY 15 & UNDER
EXCHANGE DEADLINE 9/24/2022
*LEVEL 2: .5X TO 1.2X BASIC
1 Kristaps Porzingis/25 15.00 40.00
2 Lonzo Ball/25 20.00 50.00
3 Doug McDermott/49 4.00 10.00
4 Jaxson Hayes/49 8.00 20.00
5 Darius Bazley/49 12.00 30.00
6 Kevin Porter Jr./49 4.00 10.00
7 Elfrid Payton/49 4.00 10.00
8 Derrick White/49 5.00 12.00
9 Eric Gordon/49 4.00 10.00
10 Josh Okogie/49 4.00 10.00
11 Trae Young/25 60.00 150.00
12 Kevin Knox II/49 3.00 8.00
13 Ja Morant/25 100.00 250.00
14 Kendrick Nunn/49 4.00 10.00
15 Myles Turner/49 5.00 12.00
16 Daniel Theis/49 4.00 10.00
17 Coby White/49 12.00 30.00
18 Lou Williams/49 5.00 12.00
19 Cody Zeller/49 3.00 8.00
21 Wendell Carter Jr./49 4.00 10.00
23 Jarrett Culver/49 3.00 8.00
24 Al Horford/49 5.00 12.00
25 Donovan Mitchell/25 20.00 50.00
26 Larry Nance Jr./49 4.00 10.00
27 RJ Barrett/25 30.00 80.00
28 Danny Green/49 4.00 10.00
29 Montrezl Harrell/49 5.00 12.00
30 Luke Kennard/49 4.00 10.00

1990 Action Packed Promos Gold

COMPLETE SET (4) 100.00 200.00
*SILVER: .4X TO 1X GOLD
1 Patrick Ewing 10.00 25.00
2 Magic Johnson 15.00 40.00
3 Michael Jordan 100.00 250.00

1993 Action Packed Hall of Fame

COMPLETE SET (84) 10.00 25.00
COMPLETE SERIES 1 (42) 5.00 12.00
COMPLETE SERIES 2 (42) 5.00 12.00
1 Walt Frazier .20 .50
2 Jerry West .40 1.00
3 Dave Bing .15 .40
4 Earl Monroe .25 .60
5 Willis Reed .20 .50
6 Dave Cowens .20 .50
7 Bill Bradley .20 .50
8 Elgin Baylor .25 .60
9 Elvin Hayes .20 .50
10 Nate Thurmond .20 .50
11 Red Auerbach CO .25 .60
12 John Wooden CO .25 .60
13 Red Holzman CO .20 .50
14 Lou Carnesecca CO .15 .40
15 Bob Knight CO 1.25 3.00
16 Dean Smith CO .20 .50
17 Larry Bird .50 1.25
18 Larry Bird .50 1.25
19 Larry Bird .50 1.25
20 Larry Bird .50 1.25
21 Larry Bird .50 1.25
22 K.C. Jones .15 .40
23 Slater Martin .15 .40
24 Bob Wanzer .15 .40
25 Bob Davies .15 .40
26 Nate Archibald .20 .50
27 Bill Sharman .20 .50
28 Tom Gola .15 .40
29 Tom Heinsohn .20 .50
30 Clyde Lovellette .20 .50
31 Bob Pettit .25 .60
32 Dolph Schayes .20 .50
33 Jack Twyman .20 .50
34 Hal Greer .20 .50
35 Sam Jones .20 .50
36 Dave DeBusschere .20 .50
37 Connie Hawkins .20 .50
38 Jerry Lucas .20 .50
39 Pete Maravich .40 1.00
40 Oscar Robertson .30 .75
41 Lenny Wilkens .20 .50
42 Bob Lanier .20 .50
43 Paul Arizin .20 .50
44 Harry Gallatin .20 .50
45 Frank Ramsey .25 .60
46 Ed Macauley .15 .40
47 Bob Kurland .15 .40
48 Rick Barry .20 .50
49 John Havlicek .25 .60
50 Hank Luisetti .15 .40
51 Wes Unseld .20 .50
52 Al McGuire .20 .50
53 Frank McGuire .15 .40
54 Ray Meyer .15 .40
55 Pete Newell .15 .40
56 Jack Ramsay .20 .50
57 Adolph Rupp .20 .50
58 Clarence Gaines .15 .40
59 Henry Iba .20 .50
60 Dan Issel .20 .50
61 Walt Bellamy .20 .50
62 Dick McGuire .15 .40
63 Calvin Murphy .20 .50
64 Uljana Semjonova .15 .40
65 Bill Walton .25 .60
66 Ann Meyers .15 .40
67 Julius Erving .30 .75
68 Julius Erving .30 .75
69 Julius Erving .30 .75
70 Julius Erving .30 .75
71 Julius Erving .30 .75
72 Julius Erving .30 .75
73 Larry O'Brien .15 .40
74 Bill Bradley .20 .50
75 Pete Maravich .40 1.00
76 Elvin Hayes .20 .50
77 Jerry West .40 1.00
78 Oscar Robertson .30 .75
79 K.C. Jones .15 .40
80 Tom Heinsohn .20 .50
81 Billy Cunningham .20 .50
82 Red Holzman .20 .50
83 Lenny Wilkens .20 .50
84 Bill Sharman .20 .50
XX Oscar Robertson PROMO 1.25 3.00

1993 Action Packed Hall of Fame 24K Gold

*GOLD: 5X TO 12X VALUE
56G Julius Erving/2500 4.00 10.00
72G Julius Erving AU/2500 100.00 250.00

1995 Action Packed Hall of Fame

COMPLETE SET (38) 5.00 12.00
COMPLETE SERIES 1 (20) 2.50 6.00
COMPLETE SERIES 2 (18) 2.50 6.00
1 Nate Archibald .20 .50
2 Dick McGuire .25 .60
3 Lou Carnesecca .25 .60
4 Red Holzman .25 .60
5 Rick Barry .20 .50
6 Billy Cunningham .25 .60
7 Connie Hawkins .25 .60
8 Dan Issel .20 .50
9 Walt Bellamy .20 .50
10 Elvin Hayes .25 .60
11 Calvin Murphy .20 .50
12 Bob Knight 1.25 3.00
13 Al McGuire .25 .60
14 K.C. Jones .25 .60
15 Jack Ramsay .25 .60
16 John Wooden .30 .75
17 Ray Meyer .25 .60
18 Lenny Wilkens .25 .60
19 Dean Smith .30 .75
20 Ed Macauley .25 .60
21 Nate Thurmond .20 .50
22 Dolph Schayes .25 .60
23 Bill Sharman .25 .60
24 Jerry Lucas .25 .60
25 Frank Ramsey .25 .60
26 Pete Maravich .40 1.00
27 Bob Pettit .25 .60
28 Hal Greer .20 .50
29 Bill Walton .25 .60
30 Bill Bradley .30 .75
31 Tom Gola .25 .60
32 Carol Blazejowski .25 .60
33 Denny Crum .25 .60
34 Chuck Daly .25 .60
35 Buddy Jeanette .25 .60
36 Cesare Rubini .25 .60
37 Bill Bradley .30 .75
38 Bill Walton .25 .60

1995 Action Packed Hall of Fame 24K Gold

*GOLD: 6X TO 15X VALUE

1995 Action Packed Hall of Fame Autographs

COMPLETE SET (40) 400.00 700.00
1 Nate Archibald 6.00 15.00
2 Dick McGuire 8.00 20.00
3 Lou Carnesecca 8.00 20.00
4 Red Holzman 8.00 20.00
5 Rick Barry 6.00 15.00
6 Billy Cunningham 8.00 20.00
7 Connie Hawkins 8.00 20.00
8 Dan Issel 6.00 15.00
9 Walt Bellamy 6.00 15.00
10 Elvin Hayes 8.00 20.00
11 Calvin Murphy 6.00 15.00
12 Bob Knight 100.00 250.00
13 Al McGuire 8.00 20.00
14 K.C. Jones 8.00 20.00
15 Jack Ramsay 8.00 20.00
16 John Wooden 10.00 25.00
17 Ray Meyer 8.00 20.00
18 Lenny Wilkens 8.00 20.00
19 Dean Smith 20.00 50.00
20 Ed Macauley 10.00 25.00
21 Nate Thurmond 6.00 15.00
22 Dolph Schayes 8.00 20.00
23 Bill Sharman 8.00 20.00
24 Jerry Lucas 8.00 20.00
25 Frank Ramsey 8.00 20.00
26 Pete Maravich 12.00 30.00
27 Bob Pettit 8.00 20.00
28 Hal Greer 6.00 15.00
29 Bill Walton 8.00 20.00
30 Bill Bradley 10.00 25.00
31 Tom Gola 8.00 20.00
32 Carol Blazejowski 8.00 20.00
33 Denny Crum 8.00 20.00
34 Chuck Daly 8.00 20.00
35 Buddy Jeanette 8.00 20.00
36 Cesare Rubini 8.00 20.00
37 Bill Bradley 10.00 25.00
38 Bill Walton 8.00 20.00
39 Bob Cousy 20.00 50.00
40 Bill Russell 125.00 300.00

2009-10 Adrenalyn XL

COMPLETE SET (300) 30.00 80.00
1 Arron Afflalo .12 .30
2 Alexis Ajinca .12 .30
3 LaMarcus Aldridge .20 .50
4 Joe Alexander .12 .30
5 Ray Allen .30 .75
6 Rafer Alston .12 .30
7 Chris Andersen .20 .50
8 David Andersen RC .30 .75
9 Ryan Anderson .12 .30
10 Carmelo Anthony .30 .75
11 Joel Anthony RC .50 1.25
12 Gilbert Arenas .15 .40
13 Trevor Ariza .12 .30
14 Hilton Armstrong .12 .30
15 Ron Artest .20 .50
16 Darrell Arthur .12 .30
17 D.J. Augustin .12 .30
18 Kelenna Azubuike .12 .30
19 Renaldo Balkman .12 .30
20 Leandro Barbosa .15 .40
21 J.J. Barea .20 .50
22 Andrea Bargnani .12 .30
23 Matt Barnes .12 .30
24 Brandon Bass .12 .30
25 Tony Battie .12 .30
26 Shane Battier .20 .50
27 Nicolas Batum .15 .40
28 Michael Beasley .12 .30
29 Rodrigue Beaubois RC .30 .75
30 Raja Bell .15 .40
31 Charlie Bell .12 .30
32 Mike Bibby .20 .50
33 Andris Biedrins .12 .30
34 Chauncey Billups .25 .60
35 DeJuan Blair RC .40 1.00
36 Steve Blake .12 .30
37 Andray Blatche .12 .30
38 Andrew Bogut .15 .40
39 Matt Bonner .12 .30
40 Carlos Boozer .15 .40
41 Chris Bosh .25 .60
42 Elton Brand .15 .40
43 Corey Brewer .12 .30
44 Ronnie Brewer .12 .30
45 Primoz Brezec .12 .30
46 Aaron Brooks .12 .30
47 Derrick Brown .12 .30
48 Devin Brown .12 .30
49 Kobe Bryant 1.50 4.00
50 Rasual Butler .12 .30
51 Caron Butler .15 .40
52 Will Bynum .12 .30
53 Andrew Bynum .15 .40
54 Jose Calderon .12 .30
55 Marcus Camby .15 .40
56 Brian Cardinal .12 .30
57 DeMarre Carroll RC .40 1.00
58 Vince Carter .40 1.00
59 Omri Casspi RC .30 .75
60 Mario Chalmers .15 .40
61 Tyson Chandler .15 .40
62 Darren Collison RC .50 1.25
63 Mike Conley Jr. .15 .40
64 Daequan Cook .12 .30
65 Jamal Crawford .20 .50
66 Joe Crawford .12 .30
67 Stephen Curry RC 75.00 200.00
68 Samuel Dalembert .12 .30
69 Erick Dampier .12 .30
70 Glen Davis .12 .30
71 Baron Davis .15 .40
72 Austin Daye RC .30 .75
73 Luol Deng .15 .40
74 DeMar DeRozan RC 2.00 5.00
75 Boris Diaw .15 .40
76 Dan Dickau .12 .30
77 Travis Diener .12 .30
78 Toney Douglas RC .30 .75
79 Jared Dudley .12 .30
80 Chris Duhon .12 .30
81 Tim Duncan .50 1.25
82 Mike Dunleavy .12 .30
83 Kevin Durant .75 2.00
84 Wayne Ellington RC .40 1.00
85 Monta Ellis .15 .40
86 Melvin Ely .12 .30
87 Maurice Evans .12 .30
88 Tyreke Evans RC .40 1.00
89 Reggie Evans .12 .30
90 Jordan Farmar .12 .30
91 Raymond Felton .12 .30
92 Rudy Fernandez .12 .30
93 Michael Finley .20 .50
94 Derek Fisher .20 .50
95 Jonny Flynn RC .30 .75
96 T.J. Ford .12 .30
97 Jeff Foster .12 .30
98 Randy Foye .12 .30
99 Adonal Foyle .12 .30
100 Channing Frye .12 .30
101 Francisco Garcia .12 .30
102 Kevin Garnett .50 1.25
103 Pau Gasol .30 .75
104 Marc Gasol .20 .50
105 Rudy Gay .20 .50
106 Devean George .12 .30
107 Taj Gibson RC .40 1.00
108 Daniel Gibson .12 .30
109 Manu Ginobili .40 1.00
110 Ryan Gomes .12 .30
111 Ben Gordon .15 .40
112 Eric Gordon .15 .40
113 Danny Granger .12 .30
114 Jeff Green .15 .40
115 Blake Griffin RC 2.00 5.00
116 Taylor Griffin RC .30 .75
117 Richard Hamilton .12 .30
118 Tyler Hansbrough RC .40 1.00
119 James Harden RC 6.00 15.00
120 Matt Harpring .12 .30
121 Al Harrington .12 .30
122 Devin Harris .15 .40
123 Udonis Haslem .12 .30
124 Trenton Hassell .12 .30
125 Spencer Hawes .12 .30
126 Jarvis Hayes .12 .30
127 Brendan Haywood .12 .30
128 Gerald Henderson RC .30 .75
129 Roy Hibbert .15 .40
130 Jordan Hill RC .30 .75
131 Grant Hill .30 .75
132 Kirk Hinrich .15 .40
133 Jrue Holiday RC 1.50 4.00
134 Ryan Hollins .12 .30
135 Al Horford .20 .50
136 Eddie House .12 .30
137 Josh Howard .15 .40
138 Dwight Howard .25 .60
139 Lester Hudson RC .30 .75
140 Larry Hughes .15 .40
141 Othello Hunter .12 .30
142 Lindsey Hunter .12 .30
143 Andre Iguodala .12 .30
144 Zydrunas Ilgauskas .15 .40
145 Didier Ilunga-Mbenga .12 .30
146 Ersan Ilyasova .12 .30
147 Allen Iverson .40 1.00
148 Jarrett Jack .15 .40
149 Stephen Jackson .15 .40
150 LeBron James 1.50 4.00
151 Antawn Jamison .15 .40
152 Marko Jaric .12 .30
153 Al Jefferson .12 .30
154 Richard Jefferson .15 .40
155 Jared Jeffries .12 .30
156 Brandon Jennings RC .50 1.25
157 Yi Jianlian .25 .60
158 Joe Johnson .20 .50
159 Amir Johnson .12 .30
160 Dahntay Jones .12 .30
161 James Jones .20 .50
162 Chris Kaman .15 .40
163 Jason Kapono .12 .30
164 Jason Kidd .30 .75
165 Andrei Kirilenko .15 .40
166 Kyle Korver .15 .40
167 Kosta Koufos .12 .30
168 Nenad Krstic .12 .30
169 Carl Landry .12 .30
170 Acie Law .12 .30
171 Ty Lawson RC .40 1.00
172 Courtney Lee .12 .30
173 David Lee .12 .30
174 Rashard Lewis .15 .40
175 Shaun Livingston .12 .30
176 Brook Lopez .20 .50
177 Robin Lopez .12 .30
178 Kevin Love .20 .50
179 Kyle Lowry .20 .50
180 Corey Maggette .15 .40
181 Shawn Marion .20 .50
182 Kenyon Martin .15 .40
183 Kevin Martin .15 .40
184 Roger Mason .12 .30
185 Jason Maxiell .12 .30
186 Eric Maynor RC .30 .75
187 O.J. Mayo .12 .30
188 Luc Mbah a Moute .12 .30
189 JaVale McGee .15 .40
190 Tracy McGrady .40 1.00
191 Dominic McGuire .12 .30
192 Darko Milicic .12 .30
193 Brad Miller .15 .40
194 Andre Miller .20 .50
195 Mike Miller .15 .40
196 Paul Millsap .15 .40
197 Yao Ming .50 1.25
198 Jamario Moon .12 .30
199 Anthony Morrow .12 .30
200 B.J. Mullens RC .30 .75
201 Troy Murphy .12 .30
202 Steve Nash .40 1.00
203 Jameer Nelson .12 .30
204 Nene .15 .40
205 Joakim Noah .12 .30
206 Andres Nocioni .12 .30
207 Steve Novak .12 .30
208 Dirk Nowitzki .50 1.25
209 Patrick O'Bryant .12 .30
210 Greg Oden .12 .30
211 Lamar Odom .15 .40
212 Emeka Okafor .15 .40
213 Mehmet Okur .12 .30
214 Shaquille O'Neal .60 1.50
215 Jermaine O'Neal .20 .50
216 Travis Outlaw .12 .30
217 Zaza Pachulia .12 .30
218 Jannero Pargo .12 .30
219 Anthony Parker .12 .30
220 Tony Parker .30 .75
221 Chris Paul .40 1.00
222 Sasha Pavlovic .12 .30
223 Jeff Pendergraph .12 .30
224 Kendrick Perkins .12 .30
225 Johan Petro .12 .30
226 Paul Pierce .30 .75
227 Mickael Pietrus .12 .30
228 James Posey .12 .30
229 Leon Powe .12 .30
230 Tayshaun Prince .20 .50
231 Joel Przybilla .12 .30
232 Chris Quinn .12 .30
233 Vladimir Radmanovic .12 .30
234 Zach Randolph .20 .50
235 Theo Ratliff .12 .30
236 Michael Redd .15 .40
237 J.J. Redick .20 .50
238 Quentin Richardson .12 .30
239 Jason Richardson .20 .50
240 Luke Ridnour .15 .40
241 Nate Robinson .15 .40
242 Rajon Rondo .25 .60
243 Derrick Rose .30 .75
244 Brandon Roy .25 .60
245 Brandon Rush .12 .30
246 John Salmons .15 .40
247 Luis Scola .15 .40
248 Thabo Sefolosha .12 .30
249 Ramon Sessions .12 .30
250 Bobby Simmons .12 .30
251 Josh Smith .12 .30
252 J.R. Smith .20 .50
253 Craig Smith .12 .30
254 Jason Smith .12 .30
255 Marreese Speights .15 .40
256 Peja Stojakovic .15 .40
257 Amare Stoudemire .15 .40
258 Rodney Stuckey .12 .30
259 Jermaine Taylor RC .30 .75
260 Jeff Teague RC .40 1.00
261 Sebastian Telfair .12 .30
262 Jason Terry .15 .40
263 Hasheem Thabeet RC .30 .75
264 Tyrus Thomas .12 .30
265 Kurt Thomas .12 .30
266 Kenny Thomas .12 .30
267 Jason Thompson .12 .30
268 Al Thornton .12 .30
269 Marcus Thornton .15 .40
270 Ronny Turiaf .12 .30
271 Hedo Turkoglu .15 .40
272 Beno Udrih .12 .30
273 Anderson Varejao .12 .30
274 Charlie Villanueva .12 .30
275 Jake Voskuhl .12 .30
276 Sasha Vujacic .12 .30
277 Dwyane Wade .40 1.00
278 Rasheed Wallace .25 .60
279 Gerald Wallace .15 .40
280 Ben Wallace .25 .60
281 Luke Walton .15 .40
282 Hakim Warrick .12 .30
283 Kyle Weaver .12 .30
284 Delonte West .12 .30
285 David West .15 .40
286 Russell Westbrook .40 1.00
287 D.J. White .12 .30
288 Chris Wilcox .12 .30
289 Marvin Williams .12 .30
290 Shelden Williams .12 .30
291 Mo Williams .15 .40
292 Shawne Williams .12 .30
293 Terrence Williams RC .30 .75
294 Louis Williams .20 .50
295 Marcus Williams .12 .30
296 Deron Williams .15 .40
297 Julian Wright .12 .30
298 Antoine Wright .12 .30
299 Thaddeus Young .12 .30
300 Nick Young .12 .30

2009-10 Adrenalyn XL Extra

COMPLETE SET (30) 30.00 60.00
STATED ODDS 1:8 PACKS
1 Ron Artest 2.00 5.00
2 Michael Beasley 1.25 3.00
3 Chauncey Billups 2.50 6.00
4 Elton Brand 1.50 4.00
5 Jose Calderon 1.25 3.00
6 Vince Carter 4.00 10.00
7 Jamal Crawford 2.00 5.00
8 Boris Diaw 1.50 4.00
9 Mike Dunleavy 1.25 3.00
10 Monta Ellis 1.50 4.00
11 Kevin Garnett 5.00 12.00
12 Ryan Gomes 1.25 3.00
13 Ben Gordon 1.50 4.00
14 Eric Gordon 1.50 4.00
15 Antawn Jamison 1.50 4.00
16 David Lee 1.25 3.00
17 Brook Lopez 2.00 5.00
18 Andre Miller 2.00 5.00
19 Yao Ming 5.00 12.00
20 Steve Nash 4.00 10.00
21 Andres Nocioni 1.25 3.00
22 Mehmet Okur 1.25 3.00
23 Shaquille O'Neal 6.00 15.00
24 Tony Parker 3.00 8.00
25 Zach Randolph 2.00 5.00
26 John Salmons 1.50 4.00
27 Jason Terry 1.50 4.00
28 Hakim Warrick 1.25 3.00
29 David West 1.50 4.00
30 Russell Westbrook 12.00 30.00

2009-10 Adrenalyn XL Extra Signature

COMPLETE SET (30) 50.00 120.00
STATED ODDS 1:8 PACKS
1 Carmelo Anthony 5.00 12.00
2 Gilbert Arenas 2.50 6.00
3 Chris Bosh 4.00 10.00
4 Kobe Bryant 10.00 25.00
5 Tim Duncan 8.00 20.00
6 Kevin Durant 12.00 30.00
7 Rudy Gay 3.00 8.00
8 Danny Granger 2.00 5.00
9 Blake Griffin 12.00 30.00
10 Richard Hamilton 3.00 8.00
11 Devin Harris 2.00 5.00
12 Dwight Howard 4.00 10.00
13 Andre Iguodala 3.00 8.00
14 Stephen Jackson 2.50 6.00
15 LeBron James 10.00 25.00
16 Al Jefferson 2.00 5.00
17 Joe Johnson 3.00 8.00
18 Kevin Martin 2.50 6.00
19 Tracy McGrady 6.00 15.00
20 Dirk Nowitzki 8.00 20.00
21 Chris Paul 6.00 15.00
22 Paul Pierce 5.00 12.00
23 Michael Redd 2.50 6.00
24 Nate Robinson 2.50 6.00
25 Derrick Rose 5.00 12.00
26 Brandon Roy 4.00 10.00
27 Amare Stoudemire 2.50 6.00
28 Dwyane Wade 6.00 15.00
29 Gerald Wallace 2.50 6.00
30 Deron Williams 2.50 6.00

2009-10 Adrenalyn XL Special

COMPLETE SET (60) 15.00 30.00
STATED ODDS 1:2 PACKS
1 LaMarcus Aldridge .60 1.50
2 Ray Allen 1.00 2.50
3 Rafer Alston .40 1.00
4 Kelenna Azubuike .40 1.00
5 Andrea Bargnani .40 1.00
6 Shane Battier .60 1.50
7 Raja Bell .50 1.25
8 Mike Bibby .60 1.50
9 Andrew Bogut .50 1.25
10 Carlos Boozer .50 1.25
11 Caron Butler .50 1.25
12 Baron Davis .50 1.25
13 Raymond Felton .40 1.00
14 T.J. Ford .40 1.00
15 Randy Foye .40 1.00
16 Francisco Garcia .40 1.00
17 Marc Gasol .60 1.50
18 Pau Gasol 1.00 2.50
19 Manu Ginobili 1.25 3.00
20 Jeff Green .50 1.25
21 Al Harrington .50 1.25
22 Udonis Haslem .40 1.00
23 Spencer Hawes .40 1.00
24 Grant Hill 1.00 2.50
25 Larry Hughes .50 1.25
26 Zydrunas Ilgauskas .50 1.25
27 Richard Jefferson .50 1.25
28 Yi Jianlian .75 2.00
29 Jason Kidd 1.00 2.50
30 Andrei Kirilenko .50 1.25
31 Nenad Krstic .40 1.00
32 Rashard Lewis .50 1.25
33 Kevin Love .60 1.50
34 Corey Maggette .50 1.25
35 Shawn Marion .60 1.50
36 Kenyon Martin .50 1.25
37 O.J. Mayo .40 1.00
38 Troy Murphy .40 1.00
39 Jameer Nelson .40 1.00
40 Nene .50 1.25
41 Joakim Noah .40 1.00
42 Greg Oden .40 1.00
43 Lamar Odom .50 1.25
44 Emeka Okafor .50 1.25
45 Jermaine O'Neal .60 1.50
46 Tayshaun Prince .60 1.50
47 Jason Richardson .60 1.50
48 Luke Ridnour .50 1.25
49 Rajon Rondo .75 2.00
50 Luis Scola .50 1.25
51 Ramon Sessions .40 1.00
52 Josh Smith .40 1.00
53 Peja Stojakovic .50 1.25
54 Tyrus Thomas .40 1.00
55 Al Thornton .40 1.00
56 Hedo Turkoglu .50 1.25
57 Charlie Villanueva .40 1.00
58 Mo Williams .50 1.25
59 Louis Williams .60 1.50
60 Thaddeus Young .40 1.00

2009-10 Adrenalyn XL Ultimate Signature

COMPLETE SET (30) 60.00 120.00
STATED ODDS 1:23 PACKS
1 Carmelo Anthony 6.00 15.00
2 Gilbert Arenas 3.00 8.00
3 Chris Bosh 5.00 12.00
4 Kobe Bryant 15.00 40.00
5 Tim Duncan 10.00 25.00
6 Kevin Durant 15.00 40.00
7 Rudy Gay 4.00 10.00
8 Danny Granger 2.50 6.00
9 Blake Griffin 8.00 20.00
10 Richard Hamilton 4.00 10.00
11 Devin Harris 2.50 6.00
12 Dwight Howard 5.00 12.00
13 Andre Iguodala 4.00 10.00
14 Stephen Jackson 3.00 8.00
15 LeBron James 15.00 40.00
16 Al Jefferson 2.50 6.00
17 Joe Johnson 4.00 10.00
18 Kevin Martin 3.00 8.00
19 Tracy McGrady 8.00 20.00
20 Dirk Nowitzki 10.00 25.00
21 Chris Paul 8.00 20.00
22 Paul Pierce 6.00 15.00
23 Michael Redd 3.00 8.00
24 Nate Robinson 3.00 8.00
25 Derrick Rose 6.00 15.00
26 Brandon Roy 5.00 12.00
27 Amare Stoudemire 3.00 8.00
28 Dwyane Wade 8.00 20.00
29 Gerald Wallace 3.00 8.00
30 Deron Williams 3.00 8.00

2010-11 Adrenalyn XL

COMPLETE SET (300) 25.00 60.00
1 Brendan Haywood .12 .30
2 Caron Butler .15 .40
3 Dirk Nowitzki .50 1.25
4 Dominique Jones RC .30 .75
5 J.J. Barea .15 .40
6 Jason Kidd .30 .75
7 Jason Terry .15 .40
8 Rodrigue Beaubois .12 .30
9 Shawn Marion .20 .50
10 Tyson Chandler .15 .40
11 Aaron Brooks .12 .30
12 Brad Miller .15 .40
13 Chase Budinger .12 .30
14 Courtney Lee .12 .30
15 Jordan Hill .12 .30
16 Kevin Martin .15 .40
17 Luis Scola .15 .40
18 Patrick Patterson RC .40 1.00
19 Shane Battier .15 .40
20 Yao Ming .40 1.00
21 Acie Law .12 .30
22 Darrell Arthur .12 .30
23 DeMarre Carroll .12 .30
24 Hasheem Thabeet .12 .30
25 Marc Gasol .20 .50
26 Mike Conley Jr. .15 .40
27 O.J. Mayo .12 .30
28 Rudy Gay .20 .50
29 Xavier Henry RC .30 .75
30 Zach Randolph .20 .50
31 Chris Paul .40 1.00
32 David West .15 .40
33 Emeka Okafor .15 .40
34 Marco Belinelli .12 .30
35 Marcus Thornton .15 .40
36 Peja Stojakovic .15 .40
37 Pops Mensah-Bonsu .12 .30
38 Quincy Pondexter RC .30 .75
39 Trevor Ariza .12 .30
40 Willie Green .12 .30
41 Antonio McDyess .15 .40
42 DeJuan Blair .12 .30
43 Garrett Temple .12 .30
44 George Hill .15 .40
45 James Anderson RC .30 .75
46 Manu Ginobili .40 1.00
47 Matt Bonner .12 .30
48 Richard Jefferson .15 .40
49 Tim Duncan .50 1.25
50 Tony Parker .30 .75
51 Al Harrington .15 .40
52 Arron Afflalo .12 .30
53 Carmelo Anthony .30 .75
54 Chauncey Billups .25 .60
55 Chris Andersen .20 .50
56 J.R. Smith .20 .50
57 Kenyon Martin .20 .50
58 Nene .15 .40
59 Renaldo Balkman .12 .30
60 Ty Lawson .12 .30
61 Corey Brewer .12 .30
62 Darko Milicic .12 .30
63 Jonny Flynn .12 .30

64 Kevin Love .20 .50
65 Luke Ridnour .12 .30
66 Martell Webster .15 .40
67 Michael Beasley .12 .30
68 Sebastian Telfair .12 .30
69 Wayne Ellington .12 .30
70 Wesley Johnson RC .30 .75
71 Andre Miller .15 .40
72 Brandon Roy .25 .60
73 Dante Cunningham .12 .30
74 Elliot Williams RC .30 .75
75 Greg Oden .12 .30
76 LaMarcus Aldridge .20 .50
77 Luke Babbitt RC .30 .75
78 Marcus Camby .15 .40
79 Patrick Mills .20 .50
80 Rudy Fernandez .12 .30
81 Cole Aldrich RC .30 .75
82 Daequan Cook .12 .30
83 Eric Maynor .12 .30
84 James Harden .50 1.25
85 Jeff Green .15 .40
86 Kevin Durant .75 2.00
87 Nenad Krstic .12 .30
88 Royal Ivey .12 .30
89 Russell Westbrook .30 .75
90 Serge Ibaka .15 .40
91 Al Jefferson .12 .30
92 Andrei Kirilenko .15 .40
93 C.J. Miles .12 .30
94 Deron Williams .15 .40
95 Gordon Hayward RC 1.25 3.00
96 Kyrylo Fesenko .12 .30
97 Mehmet Okur .15 .40
98 Paul Millsap .15 .40
99 Raja Bell .15 .40
100 Ronnie Price .12 .30
101 Andris Biedrins .12 .30
102 Brandan Wright .12 .30
103 Charlie Bell .12 .30
104 Dan Gadzuric .12 .30
105 David Lee .12 .30
106 Ekpe Udoh RC .30 .75
107 Monta Ellis .15 .40
108 Reggie Williams RC .15 .40
109 Stephen Curry 1.50 4.00
110 Vladimir Radmanovic .12 .30
111 Al-Farouq Aminu RC .40 1.00
112 Baron Davis .20 .50
113 Blake Griffin .20 .50
114 Chris Kaman .12 .30
115 Craig Smith .12 .30
116 Eric Bledsoe RC .60 1.50
117 Eric Gordon .15 .40
118 Randy Foye .12 .30
119 Rasual Butler .12 .30
120 Ryan Gomes .12 .30
121 Andrew Bynum .12 .30
122 Derek Fisher .20 .50
123 Devin Ebanks RC .30 .75
124 Kobe Bryant 1.50 4.00
125 Lamar Odom .15 .40
126 Luke Walton .12 .30
127 Pau Gasol .30 .75
128 Ron Artest .20 .50
129 Sasha Vujacic .12 .30
130 Theo Ratliff .12 .30
131 Channing Frye .12 .30
132 Earl Clark .12 .30
133 Goran Dragic .25 .60
134 Grant Hill .30 .75
135 Hakim Warrick .12 .30
136 Hedo Turkoglu .15 .40
137 Jared Dudley .12 .30
138 Jason Richardson .20 .50
139 Robin Lopez .12 .30
140 Steve Nash .40 1.00
141 Beno Udrih .12 .30
142 Carl Landry .12 .30
143 DeMarcus Cousins RC 1.00 2.50
144 Donte Greene .12 .30
145 Francisco Garcia .12 .30
146 Hassan Whiteside RC .60 1.50
147 Jason Thompson .12 .30
148 Omri Casspi .12 .30
149 Samuel Dalembert .12 .30
150 Tyreke Evans .15 .40
151 Avery Bradley RC .50 1.25
152 Glen Davis .12 .30
153 Jermaine O'Neal .20 .50
154 Kendrick Perkins .12 .30
155 Kevin Garnett .50 1.25
156 Nate Robinson .15 .40
157 Paul Pierce .30 .75
158 Rajon Rondo .25 .60
159 Ray Allen .30 .75
160 Shaquille O'Neal .75 2.00
161 Anthony Morrow .12 .30
162 Brook Lopez .15 .40
163 Damion James RC .30 .75
164 Derrick Favors RC .50 1.25
165 Devin Harris .12 .30
166 Jordan Farmar .12 .30
167 Quinton Ross .12 .30
168 Terrence Williams .12 .30
169 Travis Outlaw .15 .40
170 Troy Murphy .12 .30
171 Amare Stoudemire .20 .50
172 Andy Rautins RC .30 .75
173 Anthony Randolph .12 .30
174 Danilo Gallinari .15 .40
175 Kelenna Azubuike .12 .30
176 Raymond Felton .12 .30
177 Ronny Turiaf .12 .30
178 Timofey Mozgov RC .40 1.00
179 Toney Douglas .12 .30
180 Wilson Chandler .15 .40
181 Andre Iguodala .20 .50
182 Andres Nocioni .12 .30
183 Elton Brand .15 .40
184 Evan Turner RC .40 1.00
185 Jason Kapono .12 .30
186 Jodie Meeks .12 .30
187 Jrue Holiday .25 .60
188 Louis Williams .15 .40
189 Spencer Hawes .12 .30
190 Thaddeus Young .12 .30
191 Andrea Bargnani .12 .30
192 David Andersen .12 .30
193 DeMar DeRozan .30 .75
194 Ed Davis RC .40 1.00
195 Jarrett Jack .15 .40
196 Jose Calderon .12 .30
197 Julian Wright .12 .30
198 Leandro Barbosa .15 .40
199 Linas Kleiza .12 .30
200 Reggie Evans .12 .30
201 C.J. Watson .12 .30
202 Carlos Boozer .15 .40
203 Derrick Rose .40 1.00
204 James Johnson .12 .30
205 Joakim Noah .20 .50
206 Keith Bogans .12 .30
207 Kyle Korver .15 .40
208 Luol Deng .15 .40
209 Ronnie Brewer .12 .30
210 Taj Gibson .12 .30
211 Anderson Varejao .12 .30
212 Antawn Jamison .15 .40
213 Anthony Parker .12 .30
214 Daniel Gibson .12 .30
215 J.J. Hickson .12 .30
216 Jamario Moon .12 .30
217 Leon Powe .12 .30
218 Mo Williams .15 .40
219 Ramon Sessions .12 .30
220 Ryan Hollins .12 .30
221 Austin Daye .12 .30
222 Ben Gordon .15 .40
223 Ben Wallace .25 .60
224 Charlie Villanueva .12 .30
225 Greg Monroe RC .40 1.00
226 Jason Maxiell .12 .30
227 Richard Hamilton .25 .60
228 Rodney Stuckey .12 .30
229 Tayshaun Prince .20 .50
230 Tracy McGrady .30 .75
231 Brandon Rush .12 .30
232 Dahntay Jones .12 .30
233 Danny Granger .12 .30
234 Darren Collison .12 .30
235 Jeff Foster .12 .30
236 Mike Dunleavy .12 .30
237 Paul George RC 2.50 6.00
238 Roy Hibbert .15 .40
239 T.J. Ford .12 .30
240 Tyler Hansbrough .12 .30
241 Andrew Bogut .15 .40
242 Brandon Jennings .12 .30
243 Carlos Delfino .12 .30
244 Chris Douglas-Roberts .12 .30
245 Drew Gooden .15 .40
246 Ersan Ilyasova .15 .40
247 John Salmons .12 .30
248 Larry Sanders RC .30 .75
249 Luc Mbah a Moute .12 .30
250 Michael Redd .15 .40
251 Al Horford .20 .50
252 Jamal Crawford .20 .50
253 Jeff Teague .12 .30
254 Joe Johnson .20 .50
255 Jordan Crawford RC .30 .75
256 Josh Smith .12 .30
257 Marvin Williams .12 .30
258 Maurice Evans .12 .30
259 Mike Bibby .20 .50
260 Zaza Pachulia .12 .30
261 Boris Diaw .15 .40
262 D.J. Augustin .12 .30
263 Derrick Brown .12 .30
264 Eduardo Najera .12 .30
265 Gerald Wallace .15 .40
266 Kwame Brown .12 .30
267 Matt Carroll .12 .30
268 Nazr Mohammed .12 .30
269 Stephen Jackson .15 .40
270 Tyrus Thomas .12 .30
271 Chris Bosh .25 .60
272 Dwyane Wade .40 1.00
273 Eddie House .12 .30
274 Joel Anthony .12 .30
275 Juwan Howard .15 .40
276 LeBron James 1.50 4.00
277 Mario Chalmers .15 .40
278 Mike Miller .15 .40
279 Udonis Haslem .12 .30
280 Zydrunas Ilgauskas .15 .40
281 Daniel Orton RC .30 .75
282 Dwight Howard .25 .60
283 J.J. Redick .20 .50
284 Jameer Nelson .12 .30
285 Marcin Gortat .15 .40
286 Mickael Pietrus .12 .30
287 Quentin Richardson .12 .30
288 Rashard Lewis .15 .40
289 Ryan Anderson .15 .40
290 Vince Carter .40 1.00
291 Al Thornton .12 .30
292 Andray Blatche .12 .30
293 Gilbert Arenas .15 .40
294 Hamady N'Diaye RC .50 1.25
295 JaVale McGee .15 .40
296 John Wall RC 1.50 4.00
297 Josh Howard .15 .40
298 Kevin Seraphin RC .30 .75
299 Kirk Hinrich .15 .40
300 Yi Jianlian .20 .50

2010-11 Adrenalyn XL Extra

COMPLETE SET (30) 30.00 60.00
STATED ODDS 1:8 PACKS
1 Dirk Nowitzki 5.00 12.00
2 Luis Scola 1.50 4.00
3 Rudy Gay 2.00 5.00
4 Peja Stojakovic 1.50 4.00
5 Manu Ginobili 4.00 10.00
6 Nene 1.50 4.00
7 Martell Webster 1.50 4.00
8 Greg Oden 1.25 3.00
9 Jeff Green 1.50 4.00
10 Andrei Kirilenko 1.50 4.00
11 David Lee 1.25 3.00
12 Baron Davis 2.00 5.00
13 Ron Artest 2.00 5.00
14 Hedo Turkoglu 1.50 4.00
15 Omri Casspi 1.25 3.00
16 Jermaine O'Neal 2.00 5.00
17 Derrick Favors 2.00 5.00
18 Anthony Randolph 1.25 3.00
19 Elton Brand 1.50 4.00
20 DeMar DeRozan 3.00 8.00
21 Derrick Rose 4.00 10.00
22 Ramon Sessions 1.25 3.00
23 Richard Hamilton 2.50 6.00
24 T.J. Ford 1.25 3.00
25 John Salmons 1.25 3.00
26 Joe Johnson 2.00 5.00
27 Boris Diaw 1.50 4.00
28 Chris Bosh 2.50 6.00
29 Rashard Lewis 1.50 4.00
30 Gilbert Arenas 1.50 4.00

2010-11 Adrenalyn XL Extra Signature

COMPLETE SET (30) 60.00 120.00
STATED ODDS 1:8 PACKS
1 Jason Terry 2.50 6.00
2 Kevin Martin 2.50 6.00
3 Zach Randolph 3.00 8.00
4 David West 2.50 6.00
5 Tim Duncan 8.00 20.00
6 Chauncey Billups 4.00 10.00
7 Michael Beasley 2.00 5.00
8 Brandon Roy 4.00 10.00
9 Russell Westbrook 5.00 12.00
10 Al Jefferson 2.00 5.00
11 Monta Ellis 2.50 6.00
12 Blake Griffin 3.00 8.00
13 Pau Gasol 5.00 12.00
14 Jason Richardson 3.00 8.00
15 Carl Landry 2.00 5.00
16 Ray Allen 5.00 12.00
17 Devin Harris 2.00 5.00
18 Danilo Gallinari 2.50 6.00
19 Evan Turner 2.50 6.00
20 Leandro Barbosa 2.50 6.00
21 Joakim Noah 3.00 8.00
22 Antawn Jamison 2.50 6.00
23 Ben Gordon 2.50 6.00
24 Mike Dunleavy 2.00 5.00
25 Andrew Bogut 2.50 6.00
26 Mike Bibby 3.00 8.00
27 Gerald Wallace 2.50 6.00
28 Dwyane Wade 6.00 15.00
29 Vince Carter 6.00 15.00
30 Al Thornton 2.00 5.00

2010-11 Adrenalyn XL Special

COMPLETE SET (60) 20.00 40.00
STATED ODDS 1:2 PACKS
1 Caron Butler .50 1.25
2 Tyson Chandler .50 1.25
3 Aaron Brooks .40 1.00
4 Courtney Lee .40 1.00
5 Marc Gasol .60 1.50
6 Mike Conley Jr. .50 1.25
7 Emeka Okafor .50 1.25
8 Marcus Thornton .40 1.00
9 George Hill .50 1.25
10 Richard Jefferson .50 1.25
11 Chris Andersen .60 1.50
12 Kenyon Martin .60 1.50
13 Darko Milicic .40 1.00
14 Wesley Johnson .40 1.00
15 Andre Miller .50 1.25
16 Rudy Fernandez .40 1.00
17 Cole Aldrich .40 1.00
18 James Harden 1.50 4.00
19 Mehmet Okur .40 1.00
20 Raja Bell .50 1.25
21 Charlie Bell .40 1.00
22 Reggie Williams .50 1.25
23 Eric Gordon .50 1.25
24 Randy Foye .40 1.00
25 Derek Fisher .60 1.50
26 Lamar Odom .50 1.25
27 Channing Frye .40 1.00
28 Robin Lopez .40 1.00
29 DeMarcus Cousins 1.25 3.00
30 Francisco Garcia .40 1.00
31 Kevin Garnett 1.50 4.00
32 Paul Pierce 1.00 2.50
33 Terrence Williams .40 1.00
34 Troy Murphy .40 1.00
35 Raymond Felton .40 1.00
36 Wilson Chandler .50 1.25
37 Andres Nocioni .40 1.00
38 Louis Williams .50 1.25
39 Ed Davis .50 1.25
40 Jose Calderon .40 1.00
41 Kyle Korver .50 1.25
42 Luol Deng .50 1.25
43 Anderson Varejao .40 1.00
44 Anthony Parker .40 1.00
45 Rodney Stuckey .40 1.00
46 Tracy McGrady 1.00 2.50
47 Darren Collison .40 1.00
48 Tyler Hansbrough .40 1.00
49 Chris Douglas-Roberts .40 1.00
50 Michael Redd .50 1.25
51 Jamal Crawford .60 1.50
52 Jeff Teague .40 1.00
53 D.J. Augustin .40 1.00
54 Nazr Mohammed .40 1.00
55 Mario Chalmers .50 1.25
56 Udonis Haslem .40 1.00
57 J.J. Redick .60 1.50
58 Jameer Nelson .40 1.00
59 JaVale McGee .50 1.25
60 Kirk Hinrich .50 1.25

2010-11 Adrenalyn XL Ultimate Signature

COMPLETE SET (30) 125.00 250.00
STATED ODDS 1:23 PACKS
1 Jason Kidd 6.00 15.00
2 Yao Ming 8.00 20.00
3 O.J. Mayo 2.50 6.00
4 Chris Paul 8.00 20.00
5 Tony Parker 6.00 15.00
6 Carmelo Anthony 6.00 15.00
7 Kevin Love 4.00 10.00
8 LaMarcus Aldridge 4.00 10.00
9 Kevin Durant 15.00 40.00
10 Deron Williams 3.00 8.00
11 Stephen Curry 30.00 80.00
12 Chris Kaman 2.50 6.00
13 Kobe Bryant 30.00 80.00
14 Steve Nash 8.00 20.00
15 Tyreke Evans 3.00 8.00
16 Rajon Rondo 5.00 12.00
17 Brook Lopez 3.00 8.00
18 Amare Stoudemire 4.00 10.00
19 Andre Iguodala 4.00 10.00
20 Andrea Bargnani 2.50 6.00
21 Carlos Boozer 3.00 8.00
22 Mo Williams 3.00 8.00
23 Tayshaun Prince 4.00 10.00
24 Danny Granger 2.50 6.00
25 Brandon Jennings 2.50 6.00
26 Josh Smith 2.50 6.00
27 Stephen Jackson 3.00 8.00
28 LeBron James 15.00 40.00
29 Dwight Howard 5.00 12.00
30 John Wall 12.00 30.00

2010 Adrenalyn XL All-Star Game

COMPLETE SET (10) 6.00 15.00
1 Carmelo Anthony .60 1.50
2 Kobe Bryant 2.50 6.00
3 Tim Duncan .75 2.00
4 Kevin Garnett 1.00 2.50
5 Dwight Howard .75 2.00
6 Allen Iverson .60 1.50
7 LeBron James 2.50 6.00
8 Steve Nash .50 1.25
9 Amare Stoudemire .60 1.50
10 Dwyane Wade 1.00 2.50

2011 Adrenalyn XL All-Star Game

COMPLETE SET (6) 10.00 20.00
AS3 John Wall 6.00 15.00
AS4 Tony Parker .60 1.50
AS5 Stephen Curry .75 2.00
AS6 Blake Griffin 4.00 10.00
AS7 Ron Artest .60 1.50
AS8 Kobe Bryant 3.00 8.00

2009-10 Adrenalyn XL Italian

COMPLETE SET (302) 75.00 150.00
1 Arron Afflalo .15 .40
2 Alexis Ajinca .15 .40
3 LaMarcus Aldridge .25 .60
4 Joe Alexander .15 .40
5 Ray Allen .40 1.00
6 Rafer Alston .15 .40
7 Chris Andersen .25 .60
8 David Andersen .40 1.00
9 Ryan Anderson .15 .40
10 Carmelo Anthony .40 1.00
11 Joel Anthony .60 1.50
12 Gilbert Arenas .20 .50
13 Trevor Ariza .15 .40
14 Hilton Armstrong .15 .40
15 Ron Artest .25 .60
16 Darrell Arthur .15 .40
17 D.J. Augustin .15 .40
18 Kelenna Azubuike .15 .40
19 Renaldo Balkman .15 .40
20 Leandro Barbosa .20 .50
21 J.J. Barea .25 .60
22 Andrea Bargnani .15 .40
23 Matt Barnes .15 .40
24 Brandon Bass .15 .40
25 Tony Battie .15 .40
26 Shane Battier .25 .60
27 Nicolas Batum .20 .50
28 Michael Beasley .15 .40
29 Rodrigue Beaubois .40 1.00
30 Raja Bell .20 .50
31 Charlie Bell .15 .40
32 Mike Bibby .25 .60
33 Andris Biedrins .15 .40
34 Chauncey Billups .30 .75
35 DeJuan Blair .50 1.25
36 Steve Blake .15 .40
37 Andray Blatche .15 .40
38 Andrew Bogut .20 .50
39 Matt Bonner .15 .40
40 Carlos Boozer .20 .50
41 Chris Bosh .30 .75
42 Elton Brand .20 .50
43 Corey Brewer .15 .40
44 Ronnie Brewer .15 .40
45 Primoz Brezec .15 .40
46 Aaron Brooks .15 .40
47 Derrick Brown .15 .40
48 Devin Brown .15 .40
49 Kobe Bryant 2.00 5.00
50 Rasual Butler .15 .40
51 Caron Butler .20 .50
52 Will Bynum .15 .40
53 Andrew Bynum .15 .40
54 Jose Calderon .15 .40
55 Marcus Camby .20 .50
56 Brian Cardinal .15 .40
57 DeMarre Carroll .50 1.25
58 Vince Carter .50 1.25
59 Omri Casspi .40 1.00
60 Mario Chalmers .20 .50
61 Tyson Chandler .20 .50
62 Darren Collison .60 1.50
63 Mike Conley Jr. .20 .50
64 Daequan Cook .15 .40
65 Jamal Crawford .25 .60
66 Joe Crawford .15 .40
67 Stephen Curry 50.00 120.00
68 Samuel Dalembert .15 .40
69 Erick Dampier .15 .40
70 Glen Davis .15 .40
71 Baron Davis .20 .50
72 Austin Daye .40 1.00
73 Luol Deng .20 .50
74 DeMar DeRozan 2.50 6.00
75 Boris Diaw .20 .50
76 Dan Dickau .15 .40
77 Travis Diener .15 .40
78 Toney Douglas .40 1.00
79 Jared Dudley .15 .40
80 Chris Duhon .15 .40
81 Tim Duncan .60 1.50
82 Mike Dunleavy .15 .40
83 Kevin Durant 1.00 2.50
84 Wayne Ellington .50 1.25
85 Monta Ellis .20 .50
86 Melvin Ely .15 .40
87 Maurice Evans .15 .40
88 Tyreke Evans .50 1.25
89 Reggie Evans .15 .40
90 Jordan Farmar .15 .40
91 Raymond Felton .15 .40
92 Rudy Fernandez .15 .40
93 Michael Finley .25 .60
94 Derek Fisher .25 .60
95 Jonny Flynn .40 1.00
96 T.J. Ford .15 .40
97 Jeff Foster .15 .40
98 Randy Foye .15 .40
99 Adonal Foyle .15 .40
100 Channing Frye .15 .40
101 Francisco Garcia .15 .40
102 Kevin Garnett .60 1.50
103 Pau Gasol .40 1.00
104 Marc Gasol .25 .60
105 Rudy Gay .25 .60
106 Devean George .15 .40
107 Taj Gibson .50 1.25
108 Daniel Gibson .15 .40
109 Manu Ginobili .50 1.25
110 Ryan Gomes .15 .40
111 Ben Gordon .20 .50
112 Eric Gordon .20 .50
113 Danny Granger .15 .40
114 Jeff Green .20 .50
115 Blake Griffin 8.00 20.00
116 Taylor Griffin .40 1.00
117 Richard Hamilton .25 .60
118 Tyler Hansbrough .50 1.25
119 James Harden 4.00 10.00
120 Matt Harpring .15 .40
121 Al Harrington .20 .50
122 Devin Harris .15 .40
123 Udonis Haslem .15 .40
124 Trenton Hassell .15 .40
125 Spencer Hawes .15 .40
126 Jarvis Hayes .15 .40
127 Brendan Haywood .15 .40
128 Gerald Henderson .40 1.00
129 Roy Hibbert .20 .50
130 Jordan Hill .40 1.00
131 Grant Hill .40 1.00
132 Kirk Hinrich .20 .50
133 Jrue Holiday 2.00 5.00
134 Ryan Hollins .15 .40
135 Al Horford .25 .60
136 Eddie House .15 .40
137 Josh Howard .20 .50
138 Dwight Howard .30 .75
139 Lester Hudson .40 1.00
140 Larry Hughes .20 .50
141 Othello Hunter .15 .40
142 Lindsey Hunter .15 .40
143 Andre Iguodala .25 .60
144 Zydrunas Ilgauskas .20 .50
145 Didier Ilunga-Mbenga .15 .40
146 Ersan Ilyasova .15 .40
147 Allen Iverson .50 1.25
148 Jarrett Jack .20 .50
149 Stephen Jackson .20 .50
150 LeBron James 2.00 5.00
151 Antawn Jamison .20 .50
152 Marko Jaric .15 .40
153 Al Jefferson .15 .40
154 Richard Jefferson .20 .50
155 Jared Jeffries .15 .40
156 Brandon Jennings .60 1.50
157 Yi Jianlian .30 .75
158 Joe Johnson .25 .60
159 Amir Johnson .15 .40
160 Dahntay Jones .15 .40
161 James Jones .25 .60
162 Chris Kaman .20 .50
163 Jason Kapono .15 .40
164 Jason Kidd .40 1.00
165 Andrei Kirilenko .20 .50
166 Kyle Korver .20 .50
167 Kosta Koufos .15 .40
168 Nenad Krstic .15 .40
169 Carl Landry .15 .40
170 Acie Law .15 .40
171 Ty Lawson .50 1.25
172 Courtney Lee .15 .40
173 David Lee .15 .40
174 Rashard Lewis .20 .50
175 Shaun Livingston .15 .40
176 Brook Lopez .25 .60
177 Robin Lopez .15 .40
178 Kevin Love .25 .60
179 Kyle Lowry .25 .60
180 Corey Maggette .20 .50
181 Shawn Marion .25 .60
182 Kenyon Martin .20 .50
183 Kevin Martin .20 .50
184 Roger Mason .15 .40
185 Jason Maxiell .15 .40
186 Eric Maynor .40 1.00
187 O.J. Mayo .15 .40
188 Luc Mbah a Moute .15 .40
189 JaVale McGee .20 .50
190 Tracy McGrady .50 1.25
191 Dominic McGuire .15 .40
192 Darko Milicic .15 .40
193 Brad Miller .20 .50
194 Andre Miller .25 .60
195 Mike Miller .20 .50
196 Paul Millsap .20 .50
197 Yao Ming .60 1.50
198 Jamario Moon .15 .40
199 Anthony Morrow .15 .40
200 B.J. Mullens .40 1.00
201 Troy Murphy .15 .40
202 Steve Nash .50 1.25
203 Jameer Nelson .15 .40
204 Nene .20 .50
205 Joakim Noah .15 .40
206 Andres Nocioni .15 .40
207 Steve Novak .15 .40
208 Dirk Nowitzki .60 1.50
209 Patrick O'Bryant .15 .40
210 Greg Oden .15 .40
211 Lamar Odom .20 .50
212 Emeka Okafor .20 .50
213 Mehmet Okur .15 .40
214 Shaquille O'Neal .75 2.00
215 Jermaine O'Neal .25 .60
216 Travis Outlaw .15 .40
217 Zaza Pachulia .15 .40
218 Jannero Pargo .15 .40
219 Anthony Parker .15 .40
220 Tony Parker .40 1.00
221 Chris Paul .50 1.25
222 Sasha Pavlovic .15 .40
223 Jeff Pendergraph .15 .40
224 Kendrick Perkins .15 .40
225 Johan Petro .15 .40
226 Paul Pierce .40 1.00
227 Mickael Pietrus .15 .40
228 James Posey .15 .40
229 Leon Powe .15 .40
230 Tayshaun Prince .25 .60
231 Joel Przybilla .15 .40
232 Chris Quinn .15 .40
233 Vladimir Radmanovic .15 .40
234 Zach Randolph .25 .60
235 Theo Ratliff .15 .40
236 Michael Redd .20 .50
237 J.J. Redick .25 .60
238 Quentin Richardson .15 .40
239 Jason Richardson .25 .60
240 Luke Ridnour .20 .50
241 Nate Robinson .20 .50
242 Rajon Rondo .30 .75
243 Derrick Rose .40 1.00
244 Brandon Roy .30 .75
245 Brandon Rush .15 .40
246 John Salmons .20 .50
247 Luis Scola .20 .50
248 Thabo Sefolosha .15 .40
249 Ramon Sessions .15 .40
250 Bobby Simmons .15 .40
251 Josh Smith .15 .40
252 J.R. Smith .25 .60
253 Craig Smith .15 .40
254 Jason Smith .15 .40
255 Marreese Speights .20 .50
256 Peja Stojakovic .20 .50
257 Amare Stoudemire .20 .50
258 Rodney Stuckey .15 .40
259 Jermaine Taylor .40 1.00
260 Jeff Teague .50 1.25
261 Sebastian Telfair .15 .40
262 Jason Terry .20 .50
263 Hasheem Thabeet .40 1.00
264 Tyrus Thomas .15 .40
265 Kurt Thomas .15 .40
266 Kenny Thomas .15 .40
267 Jason Thompson .15 .40
268 Al Thornton .15 .40
269 Marcus Thornton .20 .50
270 Ronny Turiaf .15 .40
271 Hedo Turkoglu .20 .50
272 Beno Udrih .15 .40
273 Anderson Varejao .15 .40
274 Charlie Villanueva .15 .40
275 Jake Voskuhl .15 .40
276 Sasha Vujacic .15 .40
277 Dwyane Wade .50 1.25
278 Rasheed Wallace .30 .75
279 Gerald Wallace .20 .50
280 Ben Wallace .30 .75
281 Luke Walton .20 .50
282 Hakim Warrick .15 .40
283 Kyle Weaver .15 .40
284 Delonte West .15 .40
285 David West .20 .50
286 Russell Westbrook .50 1.25
287 D.J. White .15 .40
288 Chris Wilcox .15 .40
289 Marvin Williams .15 .40
290 Shelden Williams .15 .40
291 Mo Williams .20 .50
292 Shawne Williams .15 .40
293 Terrence Williams .40 1.00
294 Louis Williams .25 .60
295 Marcus Williams .15 .40
296 Deron Williams .20 .50
297 Julian Wright .15 .40
298 Antoine Wright .15 .40
299 Thaddeus Young .15 .40
300 Nick Young .15 .40
301 Marco Belinelli 1.25 3.00
302 Danilo Gallinari 1.25 3.00

2006-07 Albany Patroons CBA

COMPLETE SET (16) 2.50 6.00
1 Jamario Moon 2.00 5.00
2 Carl Mitchell .15 .40
3 Felipe Lopez .30 .75
4 Chris Sockwell .15 .40
5 T.J. Thompson .15 .40
6 Kwan Johnson .15 .40
7 Eric Williams .30 .75
8 Reggie Jessie .15 .40
9 Jordan Klaiber .15 .40
10 Kareem Reid .15 .40
11 Marvin Phillips .15 .40
12 Lucious Jordan .15 .40
13 John Strickland .15 .40
14 Michael Ray Richardson CO .40 1.00
15 Derrick Rowland ACO .15 .40
16 Lito The Panda Mascot .15 .40

1995-96 All-Star Jam Session David Robinson

COMPLETE SET (4) 4.00 10.00
1 David Robinson Upper Deck 1.25 3.00
2 David Robinson Stadium Club 1.25 3.00
3 David Robinson Fleer 1.25 3.00
4 David Robinson SkyBox 1.25 3.00

1996-97 All-Star Jam Session Terrell Brandon

COMPLETE SET (3) 2.00 4.00
1 Terrell Brandon Ultra .60 1.50
2 Terrell Brandon SkyBox .60 1.50
3 Terrell Brandon Stadium Club .60 1.50

1996-97 All-Star Jam Session Terrell Brandon Ticket

NNO Terrell Brandon .40 1.00

1997-98 All-Star Jam Session Knicks Sheet A

1 Knicks All-Star Sheet
Patrick Ewing
Larry Johnson
John Starks
Chris Dudley
Charlie Ward
Chris Mills 2.00 5.00

1997-98 All-Star Jam Session Knicks Sheet B

1 Knicks All-Star Sheet
Patrick Ewing
Larry Johnson
John Starks
Buck Williams
Chris Childs
Allan Houston 2.50 6.00

2007 Americana Sports Legends

STATED PRINT RUN 500 SERIAL #'d SETS
3 Walt Frazier 1.50 4.00
10 Larry Bird 4.00 10.00

2007 Americana Sports Legends Material

PRINT RUNS B/WN 25-500 COPIES PER
3 Walt Frazier Jsy/500 4.00 10.00

2007 Americana Sports Legends Signature

PRINT RUNS B/WN 25-50 COPIES PER
3 Walt Frazier/25 15.00 40.00
10 Larry Bird/25 70.00 120.00

2007 Americana Sports Legends Signature Material

*MTL: .5X TO 1.2X BASIC SIG
PRINT RUNS B/WN 25-50 COPIES PER

2008 Americana II Sports Legends

STATED PRINT RUN 500 SERIAL #'d SETS
13 Dick Vitale 1.25 3.00
14 John Wooden 1.50 4.00

2008 Americana II Sports Legends Signature

PRINT RUNS B/WN 50-100 COPIES PER
13 Dick Vitale/100 15.00 40.00
14 John Wooden/100 50.00 100.00

2000 American Express Postcards

COMPLETE SET (4) 2.50 6.00
1 Marcus Camby .40 1.00
2 M.Camby/A.Houston .80 2.00
3 Walt Frazier .40 1.00
4 Shaquille O'Neal 2.00 5.00

1979 Arizona Sports Collectors Show

COMPLETE SET (10) 7.50 15.00
8 Dick Van Arsdale 2.00 5.00
9 Tom Van Arsdale 2.00 5.00

2007-08 Artifacts

COMP.SET w/o SP's (100) 15.00 40.00
101-110 PRINT RUN 699 SER.#'d SETS
111-150 PRINT RUN 1299 SER.#'d SETS
151-200 PRINT RUN 999 SER.#'d SETS
FOUR CARDS AS BOX TOPPER
1 Joe Johnson .30 .75
2 Josh Smith .25 .60
3 Marvin Williams .25 .60
4 Josh Childress .25 .60
5 Al Jefferson .25 .60
6 Paul Pierce .60 1.50
7 Gerald Green .30 .75
8 Adam Morrison .25 .60
9 Gerald Wallace .30 .75
10 Emeka Okafor .30 .75
11 Raymond Felton .30 .75
12 Ben Gordon .30 .75
13 Luol Deng .30 .75
14 Kirk Hinrich .40 1.00
15 Andres Nocioni .25 .60
16 LeBron James 3.00 8.00
17 Larry Hughes .30 .75
18 Zydrunas Ilgauskas .30 .75
19 Dirk Nowitzki 1.00 2.50
20 Josh Howard .30 .75
21 Jason Terry .30 .75
22 Carmelo Anthony .60 1.50
23 Allen Iverson 1.00 2.50
24 J.R. Smith .40 1.00
25 Richard Hamilton .50 1.25
26 Tayshaun Prince .40 1.00
27 Chauncey Billups .50 1.25
28 Baron Davis .30 .75
29 Monta Ellis .30 .75
30 Jason Richardson .40 1.00
31 Yao Ming 1.00 2.50
32 Tracy McGrady .60 1.50
33 Rafer Alston .40 1.00
34 Jermaine O'Neal .40 1.00
35 Jamaal Tinsley .25 .60
36 Mike Dunleavy .25 .60
37 Elton Brand .30 .75
38 Cuttino Mobley .30 .75
39 Corey Maggette .30 .75
40 Kobe Bryant 3.00 8.00
41 Lamar Odom .30 .75
42 Jordan Farmar .25 .60
43 Pau Gasol .60 1.50
44 Rudy Gay .30 .75
45 Mike Miller .30 .75
46 Shaquille O'Neal 1.50 4.00
47 Dwyane Wade .75 2.00
48 Jason Kapono .25 .60
49 Alonzo Mourning .60 1.50
50 Andrew Bogut .30 .75
51 Michael Redd .30 .75
52 Maurice Williams .30 .75
53 Kevin Garnett 1.00 2.50
54 Ricky Davis .30 .75
55 Randy Foye .30 .75
56 Rashad McCants .25 .60
57 Jason Kidd .60 1.50

58 Vince Carter .75 2.00
59 Richard Jefferson .30 .75
60 Peja Stojakovic .30 .75
61 Chris Paul .75 2.00
62 David West .30 .75
63 David Lee .25 .60
64 Stephon Marbury .50 1.25
65 Eddy Curry .25 .60
66 Jamal Crawford .40 1.00
67 Dwight Howard .50 1.25
68 Grant Hill .60 1.50
69 Jameer Nelson .25 .60
70 J.J. Redick .40 1.00
71 Andre Iguodala .40 1.00
72 Andre Miller .30 .75
73 Samuel Dalembert .25 .60
74 Steve Nash .75 2.00
75 Amare Stoudemire .40 1.00
76 Shawn Marion .40 1.00
77 Leandro Barbosa .30 .75
78 Zach Randolph .40 1.00
79 Brandon Roy .50 1.25
80 LaMarcus Aldridge .40 1.00
81 Jarrett Jack .30 .75
82 Mike Bibby .40 1.00
83 Kevin Martin .30 .75
84 Brad Miller .30 .75
85 Tim Duncan 1.00 2.50
86 Manu Ginobili .75 2.00
87 Tony Parker .60 1.50
88 Rashard Lewis .30 .75
89 Ray Allen .60 1.50
90 Chris Wilcox .25 .60
91 Chris Bosh .50 1.25
92 Andrea Bargnani .25 .60
93 T.J. Ford .25 .60
94 Anthony Parker .25 .60
95 Deron Williams .30 .75
96 Carlos Boozer .30 .75
97 Mehmet Okur .25 .60
98 Gilbert Arenas .40 1.00
99 Caron Butler .30 .75
100 Antawn Jamison .30 .75
101 Greg Oden RC 1.50 4.00
102 Kevin Durant RC 40.00 100.00
103 Al Horford RC 4.00 10.00
104 Mike Conley Jr. RC 4.00 10.00
105 Jeff Green RC 1.25 3.00
106 Sun Yue RC 1.50 4.00
107 Corey Brewer RC 1.25 3.00
108 Brandan Wright RC 1.25 3.00
109 Joakim Noah RC 1.50 4.00
110 Spencer Hawes RC 1.00 2.50
111 Acie Law RC 1.00 2.50
112 Thaddeus Young RC 1.50 4.00
113 Julian Wright RC 1.00 2.50
114 Al Thornton RC 1.00 2.50
115 Rodney Stuckey RC 1.00 2.50
116 Nick Young RC 1.50 4.00
117 Sean Williams RC 1.00 2.50
118 Marco Belinelli RC 1.25 3.00
119 Javaris Crittenton RC 1.00 2.50
120 Jason Smith RC 1.00 2.50
121 Daequan Cook RC 1.25 3.00
122 Jared Dudley RC 1.25 3.00
123 Wilson Chandler RC 1.25 3.00
124 Morris Almond RC 1.00 2.50
125 Aaron Brooks RC 1.25 3.00
126 Arron Afflalo RC 1.25 3.00
127 Alando Tucker RC 1.00 2.50
128 Petteri Koponen RC 1.25 3.00
129 Carl Landry RC 1.00 2.50
130 Gabe Pruitt RC 1.00 2.50
131 Marcus Williams RC 1.00 2.50
132 Nick Fazekas RC 1.00 2.50
133 Glen Davis RC 1.25 3.00
134 Jermareo Davidson RC 1.00 2.50
135 Josh McRoberts RC 1.00 2.50
136 Chris Richard RC 1.00 2.50
137 Derrick Byars RC 1.00 2.50
138 Adam Haluska RC 1.00 2.50
139 Reyshawn Terry RC 1.00 2.50
140 Jared Jordan RC 1.00 2.50
141 Stephane Lasme RC 1.00 2.50
142 Dominic McGuire RC 1.00 2.50
143 Aaron Gray RC 1.00 2.50
144 JamesOn Curry RC 1.00 2.50
145 Taurean Green RC 1.00 2.50
146 Demetris Nichols RC 1.00 2.50
147 Herbert Hill RC 1.00 2.50
148 Ramon Sessions RC 1.25 3.00
149 Sammy Mejia RC 1.00 2.50
150 D.J. Strawberry RC 1.00 2.50
151 Bernard King 1.00 2.50
152 Bill Laimbeer 1.00 2.50
153 Bill Russell 4.00 10.00
154 Bill Sharman 1.25 3.00
155 Bill Walton 1.50 4.00
156 Billy Cunningham 1.25 3.00
157 Bob Cousy 2.00 5.00
158 Bob McAdoo 1.00 2.50
159 Bob Pettit 1.25 3.00
160 Chris Mullin 1.50 4.00
161 Clyde Drexler 2.00 5.00
162 Dave Bing 1.25 3.00
163 Dave Cowens 1.00 2.50
164 David Robinson 2.50 6.00
165 David Thompson 1.00 2.50
166 Dennis Rodman 3.00 8.00
167 Dolph Schayes 1.25 3.00
168 Earl Monroe 1.25 3.00
169 Elgin Baylor 1.25 3.00
170 Elvin Hayes 1.25 3.00
171 George Gervin 1.50 4.00
172 George Mikan 2.50 6.00
173 Hakeem Olajuwon 2.50 6.00
174 Hal Greer 1.50 4.00
175 Isiah Thomas 1.25 3.00
176 James Worthy 2.00 5.00
177 Jerry West 3.00 8.00
178 John Havlicek 2.50 6.00
179 John Stockton 2.50 6.00
180 Julius Erving 3.00 8.00
181 Karl Malone 1.50 4.00
182 Kevin McHale 1.50 4.00
183 Larry Bird 5.00 12.00
184 Lenny Wilkens 1.25 3.00
185 Magic Johnson 5.00 12.00
186 Michael Jordan 12.00 30.00
187 Moses Malone 2.00 5.00
188 Nate Archibald 1.00 2.50
189 Nate Thurmond 1.00 2.50
190 Oscar Robertson 1.25 3.00
191 Paul Arizin 1.25 3.00
192 Paul Westphal 1.50 4.00
193 Pete Maravich 3.00 8.00
194 Rick Barry 1.00 2.50
195 Robert Parish 1.25 3.00
196 Sam Jones 1.50 4.00
197 Walt Frazier 2.00 5.00
198 Wes Unseld 1.50 4.00
199 Willis Reed 2.00 5.00
200 Wilt Chamberlain 4.00 10.00
201 Yao Ming EX 1.25 3.00
202 Steve Nash EX 1.00 2.50
203 Chris Paul EX 1.00 2.50
204 Brandon Roy EX .60 1.50
205 Rudy Gay EX .40 1.00
206 Al Horford Uni EX 1.25 3.00
207 LaMarcus Aldridge EX .50 1.25
208 Tyrus Thomas EX .30 .75
209 Julian Wright EX .30 .75
210 Al Horford Suit EX 1.25 3.00
211 Corey Brewer EX .40 1.00
212 Joakim Noah EX .50 1.25
213 Mike Conley Jr. EX 1.25 3.00
214 Jeff Green EX .40 1.00
215 Kevin Durant Suit EX 5.00 12.00
216 Michael Jordan Red EX 5.00 12.00
217 Kobe Bryant Prpl EX 4.00 10.00
218 LeBron James Red EX 4.00 10.00
219 Kevin Durant Ball EX 5.00 12.00
220 Michael Jordan White EX 5.00 12.00
221 Kobe Bryant Yllw EX 4.00 10.00
222 LeBron James Blue EX 4.00 10.00
223 Kevin Durant Uni EX 5.00 12.00
224 Michael Jordan Red EX 5.00 12.00
225 Kobe Bryant Yllw EX 4.00 10.00
226 LeBron James White EX 4.00 10.00
227 Kevin Durant Back EX 5.00 12.00
228 Michael Jordan Black EX 5.00 12.00
229 Kobe Bryant White EX 4.00 10.00
230 LeBron James Orange EX 4.00 10.00

2007-08 Artifacts Blue

*BLUE 1-100: 4X TO 10X BASE HI
*BLUE 101-150: 1.25X TO 3X
*BLUE 151-200: 2X TO 5X BASE HI
BLUE PRINT RUN 10 TO 25 SER.#'d SETS

2007-08 Artifacts Gold

*GOLD 1-100: 1.5X TO 4X BASE HI
*GOLD 101-150: .75X TO 2X BASE HI
*GOLD 151-200: .75X TO 2X BASE HI
GOLD PRINT RUN 100 SER.#'d SETS

2007-08 Artifacts Red

*RED 1-100: 2X TO 5X BASE HI
*RED 101-150: 1X TO 2.5X BASE HI
*RED 151-200: 1.25X TO 3X BASE HI
RED PRINT RUN 50 SER.#'d SETS

2007-08 Artifacts Autofacts

APPROXIMATELY ONE PER BOX
AFAB Andrea Bargnani 3.00 8.00
AFAG Maurice Ager 3.00 8.00
AFAH Al Horford 12.00 30.00
AFAJ Antawn Jamison 4.00 10.00
AFAR Allan Ray 3.00 8.00
AFBA B.J. Armstrong 8.00 20.00
AFBB Bruce Bowen 3.00 8.00
AFBD Brad Daugherty 4.00 10.00
AFBG Ben Gordon 4.00 10.00
AFBJ Bobby Jones 4.00 10.00
AFBL Bill Laimbeer 5.00 12.00
AFBM Brad Miller 4.00 10.00
AFBR Brandon Roy 6.00 15.00
AFBW Bill Walton 8.00 20.00
AFCD Chris Duhon 3.00 8.00
AFCF Channing Frye 3.00 8.00
AFCH Connie Hawkins 8.00 20.00
AFCM Cedric Maxwell 4.00 10.00
AFCO Michael Cooper 5.00 12.00
AFCS Cedric Simmons 3.00 8.00
AFDB Dee Brown 3.00 8.00
AFDG Daniel Gibson 3.00 8.00
AFDL David Lee 3.00 8.00
AFDM Donyell Marshall 3.00 8.00
AFDN David Noel 3.00 8.00
AFDR David Robinson 25.00 60.00
AFDU Kevin Durant 300.00 600.00
AFEC Eddy Curry 3.00 8.00
AFEO Emeka Okafor 4.00 10.00
AFEV Maurice Evans 3.00 8.00
AFFE Raymond Felton 4.00 10.00
AFFG Francisco Garcia 3.00 8.00
AFGG George Gervin 6.00 15.00
AFGR Aaron Gray 3.00 8.00
AFJA James Augustine 3.00 8.00
AFJB Josh Boone 3.00 8.00
AFJE Julius Erving 30.00 60.00
AFJG Joey Graham 3.00 8.00
AFJK Jason Kapono 3.00 8.00
AFJM Jamaal Magloire 3.00 8.00
AFJR Jalen Rose 4.00 10.00
AFJS J.R. Smith 5.00 12.00
AFJW Julian Wright 3.00 8.00
AFKB Kobe Bryant 125.00 300.00
AFKI Jason Kidd 20.00 50.00
AFKL Kyle Lowry 5.00 12.00
AFLA LaMarcus Aldridge 5.00 12.00
AFLH Larry Hughes 4.00 10.00
AFLJ LeBron James 1,000.00 2,000.00
AFMA Corey Maggette 4.00 10.00
AFMB Mike Bibby 5.00 12.00
AFMC Mardy Collins 3.00 8.00
AFME Mark Eaton 3.00 8.00
AFMI Mike James 3.00 8.00
AFMJ Michael Jordan 400.00 800.00
AFMP Pops Mensah-Bonsu 3.00 8.00
AFMW Marcus Williams 3.00 8.00
AFNO Steve Novak 3.00 8.00
AFPD Paul Davis 3.00 8.00
AFPM Paul Millsap 4.00 10.00
AFPO Patrick O'Bryant 3.00 8.00
AFPP Paul Pierce 15.00 40.00
AFQR Quentin Richardson 3.00 8.00
AFRE Renaldo Balkman 3.00 8.00
AFRF Randy Foye 4.00 10.00
AFRG Rudy Gay 4.00 10.00
AFRH Ryan Hollins 3.00 8.00
AFRP Robert Parish 6.00 15.00
AFRR Rajon Rondo 15.00 40.00
AFSB Shannon Brown 3.00 8.00
AFSJ Solomon Jones 3.00 8.00
AFSL Shaun Livingston 4.00 10.00
AFSM Sean May 3.00 8.00
AFSN Steve Nash 30.00 80.00
AFSR Sergio Rodriguez 3.00 8.00
AFSS Saer Sene 3.00 8.00
AFST John Stockton 40.00 80.00
AFSW Shawne Williams 3.00 8.00
AFTC Tyson Chandler 5.00 12.00
AFTF T.J. Ford 3.00 8.00
AFTM Tracy McGrady 20.00 50.00
AFTP Tayshaun Prince 5.00 12.00
AFTS Thabo Sefolosha 3.00 8.00
AFTT Tyrus Thomas 3.00 8.00
AFWE Martell Webster 4.00 10.00
AFWF Walt Frazier 8.00 20.00
AFWI Shelden Williams 3.00 8.00
AFYM Yao Ming 15.00 40.00

2007-08 Artifacts Conference Pairings

PRINT RUN 150 SER.#'d SETS
CPAH C.Anthony/A.Harrington 4.00 10.00
CPAJ G.Arenas/J.Johnson 3.00 8.00
CPAK N.Krstic/T.Ariza 3.00 8.00
CPAM A.Kirilenko/B.Miller 3.00 8.00
CPAN R.Allen/J.Nelson 3.00 8.00
CPAO L.Aldridge/M.Okur 3.00 8.00
CPAS T.Allen/J.Starks 3.00 8.00
CPBA S.Battier/M.Ager 3.00 8.00
CPBB C.Boozer/S.Battier 3.00 8.00
CPBC C.Bosh/V.Carter 6.00 15.00
CPBE L.Bird/J.Erving 12.00 30.00
CPBG F.Garcia/A.Bynum 3.00 8.00
CPBH C.Billups/L.Hughes 3.00 8.00
CPBI K.Bryant/A.Iverson 40.00 100.00
CPBN A.Bargnani/A.Nocioni 3.00 8.00
CPBR J.Farmar/B.Roy 3.00 8.00
CPCB C.Maggette/C.Boozer 3.00 8.00
CPCC J.Childress/J.Collins 3.00 8.00
CPCD S.Cassell/B.Davis 3.00 8.00
CPCO M.Camby/M.Okur 3.00 8.00
CPCS A.Bargnani/A.Bogut 3.00 8.00
CPDC M.Collins/I.Diogu 3.00 8.00
CPDF B.Davis/J.Farmar 3.00 8.00
CPDM M.Jordan/D.Rodman 25.00 60.00
CPDN A.Nocioni/R.Dupree 3.00 8.00
CPDO C.Drexler/H.Olajuwon 8.00 20.00
CPDP S.Dalembert/R.Parish 3.00 8.00
CPDR M.Dunleavy/J.Redick 3.00 8.00
CPDT L.Deng/J.Tinsley 3.00 8.00
CPED M.Ellis/R.Davis 3.00 8.00
CPEJ M.Ellis/J.Jack 3.00 8.00
CPES E.Brand/S.Battier 3.00 8.00
CPFG R.Foye/R.Gay 3.00 8.00
CPFH M.Finley/J.Howard 3.00 8.00
CPFR R.Felton/M.Redd 3.00 8.00
CPGB D.Gooden/C.Butler 3.00 8.00
CPGH M.Ginobili/L.Head 4.00 10.00
CPGK J.Kapono/D.Gibson 3.00 8.00
CPGM M.Ginobili/S.Marion 4.00 10.00
CPGR D.Gibson/N.Robinson 3.00 8.00
CPGS P.Gasol/A.Stoudemire 4.00 10.00
CPGW D.West/R.Gay 3.00 8.00
CPHF J.Howard/M.Finley 3.00 8.00
CPHG B.Gordon/R.Hamilton 3.00 8.00
CPHH K.Hinrich/R.Hamilton 3.00 8.00
CPHM B.Haywood/S.May 3.00 8.00
CPHR J.Howard/J.Rose 3.00 8.00
CPIJ A.Iguodala/R.Jefferson 3.00 8.00
CPJA F.Jones/T.Ariza 3.00 8.00
CPJF J.Johnson/R.Felton 3.00 8.00
CPJJ L.James/M.Jordan 40.00 100.00
CPJL D.Lee/A.Jamison 3.00 8.00
CPJM M.Johnson/P.Maravich 20.00 50.00
CPJN B.Jones/D.Noel 3.00 8.00
CPJP L.James/T.Prince 8.00 20.00
CPJR J.Jack/J.Rose 3.00 8.00
CPJS L.James/J.Smith 8.00 20.00
CPJV L.Jackson/C.Villanueva 3.00 8.00
CPJW A.Jamison/M.Williams 3.00 8.00
CPKA K.Martin/A.Kirilenko 3.00 8.00
CPKM J.Kidd/S.Marbury 6.00 15.00
CPMB T.McGrady/K.Bryant 40.00 100.00
CPMC A.Miller/J.Crawford 3.00 8.00
CPMD M.Bibby/D.Stoudamire 3.00 8.00
CPMG D.Gooden/D.Mason 3.00 8.00
CPMH K.Martin/D.Harris 3.00 8.00
CPMK C.Kaman/B.Miller 3.00 8.00
CPMP M.Pietrus/T.Parker 5.00 12.00
CPMW S.May/M.Williams 3.00 8.00
CPNA Nene/H.Armstrong 3.00 8.00
CPNS D.Nowitzki/P.Stojakovic 5.00 12.00
CPOB L.Odom/E.Brand 3.00 8.00
CPOH E.Okafor/D.Howard 3.00 8.00
CPOO S.O'Neal/L.Odom 5.00 12.00
CPPD M.Pietrus/B.Diaw 3.00 8.00
CPPH P.Pierce/K.Hinrich 4.00 10.00
CPPL J.Petro/S.Livingston 3.00 8.00
CPPM T.Parker/M.Miller 4.00 10.00
CPPW D.Williams/C.Paul 4.00 10.00
CPRA Q.Richardson/G.Arenas 3.00 8.00
CPRF B.Roy/R.Foye 3.00 8.00
CPRH Q.Richardson/U.Haslem 3.00 8.00
CPRL R.Artest/L.Odom 3.00 8.00
CPRO D.Robinson/H.Olajuwon 6.00 15.00
CPRR Z.Randolph/J.Richardson 3.00 8.00
CPRW R.Rondo/M.Williams 3.00 8.00
CPSH J.Smith/D.Harris 3.00 8.00
CPSJ J.Calderon/S.Brown 3.00 8.00
CPSN S.Nash/J.Stockton 8.00 20.00
CPSS C.Simmons/S.Swift 3.00 8.00
CPTW J.Terry/L.Walton 3.00 8.00
CPWD C.Wilcox/B.Diaw 3.00 8.00
CPWG G.Wallace/D.Gibson 3.00 8.00
CPWK J.Williams/K.Korver 5.00 12.00
CPWM C.Webber/A.Mourning 8.00 20.00
CPWO B.Wallace/S.O'Neal 6.00 15.00
CPWP A.Walker/T.Prince 3.00 8.00
CPWR M.Webster/L.Ridnour 3.00 8.00
CPWW B.Wallace/R.Wallace 4.00 10.00
CPYD Y.Ming/T.Duncan 8.00 20.00

2007-08 Artifacts Divisional Artifacts

PRINT RUN 250 SER.#'d SETS
*BLUE: .6X TO 1.5X BASE HI
BLUE PRINT RUN 50 SER.#'d SETS
*COPPER: 1.25X TO 3X BASE HI
COPPER PRINT RUN 25 SER.#'d SETS
*RED: .5X TO 1.25X BASE HI
RED PRINT RUN 100 SER.#'d SETS
*PATCH RED: 1.5X TO 4X BASE HI
PATCH RED PRINT RUN 29 SER.#'d SETS
DAAB Andrew Bogut 3.00 8.00
DAAI Andre Iguodala 4.00 10.00
DAAJ Antawn Jamison 3.00 8.00
DAAK Andrei Kirilenko 3.00 8.00
DAAL Al Harrington 3.00 8.00
DAAM Alonzo Mourning 6.00 15.00
DAAR Allan Ray 2.50 6.00
DAAS Amare Stoudemire 4.00 10.00
DABC Brian Cardinal 2.50 6.00
DABD Boris Diaw 3.00 8.00
DABG Ben Gordon 3.00 8.00
DABI Chauncey Billups 5.00 12.00
DABJ Bobby Jones 4.00 10.00
DABR Brandon Roy 5.00 12.00
DABU Caron Butler 3.00 8.00
DACA Carmelo Anthony 6.00 15.00
DACB Chris Bosh 5.00 12.00
DACF Channing Frye 2.50 6.00
DACH Josh Childress 2.50 6.00
DACM Corey Maggette 3.00 8.00
DACP Chris Paul 8.00 20.00
DACS Cedric Simmons 2.50 6.00
DACW Chris Wilcox 2.50 6.00
DADA Baron Davis 3.00 8.00
DADH Dwight Howard 5.00 12.00
DADN David Noel 2.50 6.00
DADR David Robinson 8.00 20.00
DADS DeShawn Stevenson 2.50 6.00
DADW Deron Williams 3.00 8.00
DAEB Elton Brand 3.00 8.00
DAEO Emeka Okafor 3.00 8.00
DAGH Grant Hill 6.00 15.00
DAGW Gerald Wallace 3.00 8.00
DAHA Devin Harris 2.50 6.00
DAHO Josh Howard 3.00 8.00
DAIV Allen Iverson 10.00 25.00
DAJC Jose Calderon 2.50 6.00
DAJE Julius Erving 10.00 25.00
DAJH Juwan Howard 4.00 10.00
DAJK Jason Kidd 6.00 15.00
DAJM Jamaal Magloire 2.50 6.00
DAJO Jermaine O'Neal 4.00 10.00
DAJR J.J. Redick 4.00 10.00
DAJS Josh Smith 2.50 6.00
DAJT Jamaal Tinsley 2.50 6.00
DAKB Kobe Bryant 40.00 100.00
DAKE Kenyon Martin 3.00 8.00
DAKG Kevin Garnett 10.00 25.00
DAKT Kenny Thomas 2.50 6.00
DALA LaMarcus Aldridge 4.00 10.00
DALB Larry Bird 15.00 40.00
DALD Luol Deng 3.00 8.00
DALH Larry Hughes 3.00 8.00
DALJ LeBron James 40.00 100.00
DALO Lamar Odom 3.00 8.00
DALR Luke Ridnour 3.00 8.00
DALW Luke Walton 3.00 8.00
DAMA Sean May 2.50 6.00
DAMB Mike Bibby 4.00 10.00
DAMD Mike Dunleavy 2.50 6.00
DAMG Manu Ginobili 8.00 20.00
DAMJ Michael Jordan 75.00 200.00
DAMM Mike Miller 3.00 8.00
DAMO Mehmet Okur 2.50 6.00
DAMP Morris Peterson 2.50 6.00
DAMR Michael Redd 3.00 8.00
DAMW Marvin Williams 2.50 6.00
DANO Dirk Nowitzki 10.00 25.00
DANR Nate Robinson 4.00 10.00
DAPG Pau Gasol 6.00 15.00
DAPI Mickael Pietrus 2.50 6.00
DAPO Patrick O'Bryant 2.50 6.00
DAPP Paul Pierce 6.00 15.00
DAPS Peja Stojakovic 3.00 8.00
DARA Ray Allen 6.00 15.00
DARI Jason Richardson 4.00 10.00
DARJ Richard Jefferson 3.00 8.00
DARL Rashard Lewis 3.00 8.00
DARW Rasheed Wallace 5.00 12.00
DASC Sam Cassell 3.00 8.00
DASD Samuel Dalembert 2.50 6.00
DASH Shawn Marion 4.00 10.00
DASM Stephon Marbury 5.00 12.00
DASN Steve Nash 8.00 20.00
DASO Shaquille O'Neal 15.00 40.00
DAST John Stockton 8.00 20.00
DATD Tim Duncan 10.00 25.00
DATE Jason Terry 3.00 8.00
DATH J.R. Smith 4.00 10.00
DATM Tracy McGrady 6.00 15.00
DATP Tayshaun Prince 4.00 10.00
DAUD Beno Udrih 2.50 6.00
DAUH Udonis Haslem 2.50 6.00
DAVC Vince Carter 8.00 20.00
DAWA Ben Wallace 5.00 12.00
DAWF Walt Frazier 6.00 15.00
DAWR Bracey Wright 2.50 6.00
DAYM Yao Ming 10.00 25.00
DAZI Zydrunas Ilgauskas 3.00 8.00
DAZR Zach Randolph 4.00 10.00

2007-08 Artifacts Triple Jerseys

PRINT RUN 50 SER.#'d SETS
BA Andrea Bargnani 3.00 8.00
AB Andrew Bogut 4.00 10.00
AI Allen Iverson 10.00 25.00
AJ Antawn Jamison 4.00 10.00
AK Andrei Kirilenko 4.00 10.00
AM Alonzo Mourning 12.00 30.00
AW Antoine Walker 5.00 12.00
BR Brandon Roy 6.00 15.00
CB Chauncey Billups 6.00 15.00
CD Clyde Drexler 15.00 40.00
DR David Robinson 15.00 40.00
DW Deron Williams 4.00 10.00
GG Gerald Green 4.00 10.00
HO Hakeem Olajuwon 10.00 25.00
JC Josh Childress 3.00 8.00
JE Julius Erving 12.00 30.00
JF Jordan Farmar 3.00 8.00
JK Jason Kidd 8.00 20.00
JO Jermaine O'Neal 5.00 12.00
JS John Stockton 10.00 25.00
JW Jason Williams 8.00 20.00
KB Kobe Bryant 100.00 250.00
KG Kevin Garnett 10.00 25.00
LA LaMarcus Aldridge 5.00 12.00
LB Larry Bird 20.00 50.00
LJ LeBron James 50.00 120.00
MG Manu Ginobili 10.00 25.00
MA Magic Johnson 20.00 50.00
MJ Michael Jordan 60.00 150.00
MR Michael Redd 4.00 10.00
PA Tony Parker 8.00 20.00
PM Pete Maravich 50.00 120.00
RH Richard Hamilton 6.00 15.00
RJ Richard Jefferson 4.00 10.00
RW Rasheed Wallace 6.00 15.00
SB Shane Battier 4.00 10.00
SM Josh Smith 3.00 8.00
TD Tim Duncan 20.00 50.00
TM Tracy McGrady 8.00 20.00
VC Vince Carter 10.00 25.00
YM Yao Ming 10.00 25.00
ZR Zach Randolph 5.00 12.00

1955 Ashland/Aetna Oil

COMPLETE SET (96) 5,000.00 9,000.00
COMMON CARD (1-36/73-84) 30.00 80.00
COMMON CARD (37-60) 30.00 80.00
COMMON CARD (61-72) 40.00 100.00
COMMON CARD (85-96) 50.00 120.00
1 Jack Adams 30.00 80.00
2 William Baxter 30.00 80.00
3 Jeffrey Brock 30.00 80.00
4 Paul Collins 30.00 80.00
5 Richard Culberson 30.00 80.00
6 James Floyd 30.00 80.00
7 Harold Fraler 30.00 80.00
8 George Francis Jr. 30.00 80.00
9 Paul McBrayer CO 50.00 120.00
10 James Mitchell 30.00 80.00
11 Ronald Pellegrinon 30.00 80.00
12 Guy Strong 30.00 80.00
13 Earl Adkins 30.00 80.00
14 William Bibb 30.00 80.00
15 Jerry Bird 30.00 80.00
16 John Brewer 30.00 80.00
17 Robert Burrow 30.00 80.00
18 Gerry Calvert 30.00 80.00
19 William Evans 40.00 100.00
20 Phillip Grawemeyer 30.00 80.00
21 Ray Mills 30.00 80.00
22 Linville Puckett 30.00 80.00
23 Gayle Rose 40.00 100.00
24 Adolph Rupp CO 300.00 600.00
25 William Darragh 30.00 80.00
26 Vladimir Gastevich 30.00 80.00
27 Allan Glaza 30.00 80.00
28 Herbert Harrah 30.00 80.00
29 Bernard Peck Hickman CO 50.00 120.00
30 Richard Keffer 30.00 80.00
31 Gerald Moreman 30.00 80.00
32 James Morgan 30.00 80.00
33 John Prudhoe 30.00 80.00
34 Phillip Rollins 30.00 80.00
35 Roscoe Shackelford 30.00 80.00
36 Charles Tyra 50.00 120.00
37 Robert Ashley 30.00 80.00
38 Lewis Burns 30.00 80.00
39 Francis Crum 30.00 80.00
40 Raymond Frazier 30.00 80.00
41 Cam Henderson CO 40.00 100.00
42 Joseph Hunnicutt 30.00 80.00
43 Clarence Parkins 30.00 80.00
44 Jerry Pierson 30.00 80.00
45 David Robinson 30.00 80.00
46 Paul Underwood 30.00 80.00
47 Cebert Price 30.00 80.00
48 Charles Slack 30.00 80.00
49 David Breeze 30.00 80.00
50 Leonard Carpenter 30.00 80.00
51 Omar Fannin 30.00 80.00
52 Donnie Gaunce 30.00 80.00
53 Steve Hamilton 60.00 150.00
54 Bobby Laughlin CO 30.00 80.00
55 Jesse Mayabb 30.00 80.00
56 Jerry Riddle 30.00 80.00
57 Howard Shumate 30.00 80.00
58 Dan Swartz 30.00 80.00
59 Harlan Tolle 30.00 80.00
60 Donald Whitehouse 30.00 80.00
61 Rex Alexander CO 40.00 100.00
62 Jorgen Anderson 40.00 100.00
63 Jack Clutter 40.00 100.00
64 Howard Crittenden 40.00 100.00
65 James Gainey 40.00 100.00
66 Richard Kinder 40.00 100.00
67 Theo. Koenigsmark 40.00 100.00
68 Joseph Mikez 40.00 100.00
69 John Powless 50.00 120.00
70 Dolph Regelsky 40.00 100.00
71 Reinhard Tauck 40.00 100.00
72 Francis Watrous 40.00 100.00
73 Forrest Able 30.00 80.00
74 Tom Benbrook 30.00 80.00
75 Ronald Clark 30.00 80.00
76 Lynn Cole 30.00 80.00
77 Robert Daniels 30.00 80.00
78 Ed Diddle CO 125.00 300.00
79 Victor Harned 30.00 80.00
80 Dencil Miller 30.00 80.00
81 Ferel Miller 30.00 80.00
82 George Orr 30.00 80.00
83 Jerry Weber 30.00 80.00
84 Jerry Whitsell 30.00 80.00
85 William Bergines 50.00 120.00
86 James Brennan 50.00 120.00
87 Marc Constantine 50.00 120.00
88 Michael Holt 50.00 120.00
89 Hot Rod Hundley 300.00 600.00
90 Clayce Kishbaugh 50.00 120.00
91 Ronald LaNeve 50.00 120.00
92 Gary Mullins 50.00 120.00
93 Fred Schaus CO 125.00 300.00
94 Frank Spadafore 50.00 120.00
95 Peter White 50.00 120.00
96 Paul Witting 50.00 120.00

1997 AT and T NBA PrePaid Phone Cards

COMPLETE SET (28) 120.00 300.00
COMP.15 MINUTE SET (12) 20.00 50.00
COMP.30 MINUTE SET (8) 30.00 80.00
COMP.60 MINUTE SET (8) 80.00 200.00
1 Vin Baker 15 MIN 2.00 5.00
2 Shawn Bradley 15 MIN 2.00 5.00
3 Dale Ellis 15 MIN 2.00 5.00
4 Tom Gugliotta 15 MIN 2.00 5.00
5 Juwan Howard 15 MIN 2.00 5.00
6 Jim Jackson 15 MIN 2.00 5.00
7 Dikembe Mutombo 15 MIN 2.50 6.00
8 Bobby Phills 15 MIN 2.00 5.00
9 Dino Radja 15 MIN 2.00 5.00
10 Clifford Robinson 15 MIN 2.00 5.00
11 David Robinson 15 MIN 3.00 8.00
12 Latrell Sprewell 15 MIN 2.50 6.00
13 Greg Anthony 30 MIN 4.00 10.00
14 Brent Barry 30 MIN 4.00 10.00
15 Anfernee Hardaway 30 MIN 8.00 20.00
16 Kevin Johnson 30 MIN 5.00 12.00
17 Shawn Kemp 30 MIN 5.00 12.00
18 Karl Malone 30 MIN 8.00 20.00
19 Alonzo Mourning 30 MIN 6.00 15.00
20 Mitch Richmond 30 MIN 5.00 12.00
22 Clyde Drexler 60 MIN 12.00 30.00
23 Grant Hill 60 MIN 12.00 30.00
24 Eddie Jones 60 MIN 10.00 25.00
25 Toni Kukoc 60 MIN 10.00 25.00
26 Reggie Miller 60 MIN 12.00 30.00
27 Charles Oakley 60 MIN 8.00 20.00
28 Glen Rice 60 MIN 8.00 20.00
29 Damon Stoudamire 60 MIN 8.00 20.00

1992 Australian Futera NBL

COMPLETE SET (96) 20.00 50.00
1 Mark Bradtke .60 1.50
2 Mike Corkeron .20 .50
3 Mark Davis .40 1.00
4 Jerry Dennard .20 .50
5 Butch Hays .60 1.50
6 Graham Kubank .20 .50
7 Albert Leslie ACO .20 .50
8 Brett Maher .20 .50
9 Michael McKay .20 .50
10 Don Shipway CO .20 .50
11 Kym Taylor .20 .50
12 Brett Wheeler .20 .50
13 Adrian Branch 1.00 2.50
14 Lyndon Brieffies .20 .50
15 Greg Fox .20 .50
16 Luke Gribble .20 .50
17 Shane Heal .75 2.00
18 Brian Kerle CO .20 .50
19 Simon Kerle .20 .50
20 Leroy Loggins .75 2.00
21 Gordie McLeod ACO .20 .50
22 Andre Moore .40 1.00
23 Paul Rees .20 .50
24 Blair Smith .20 .50
25 Lachlan Armfield .20 .50
26 Barry Barnes CO .20 .50
27 Simon Cottrell .20 .50
28 Ian Ellis ACO .20 .50
29 Steve Hood .40 1.00
30 Jamie Kennedy .20 .50
31 Herb McEachin .20 .50
32 Jason Reese .20 .50
33 Phil Smyth .20 .50
34 John Stelzer .20 .50
35 Matt Witkowski .20 .50
36 Mat Zauner .20 .50
37 Lanard Copeland .60 1.50
38 Andrew Gaze 1.25 3.00
39 Lindsay Gaze CO .20 .50
40 Warrick Giddey .20 .50
41 Ray Gordon .20 .50
42 Steven Lunardon .20 .50
43 Nigel Purchase .20 .50
44 Robert Sibley .20 .50
45 David Simmons .40 1.00
46 Dean Vickerman .20 .50
47 Alan Westover ACO .20 .50
48 Steven Whitehead .30 .75
49 Glenn Binnes ACO .20 .50
50 Ray Borner .20 .50
51 Martin Clarke .20 .50
52 Scott Fisher .40 1.00
53 David Graham .20 .50
54 Rod Johnson .20 .50
55 Mark Leader .20 .50
56 Paul Maley .30 .75
57 Bruce Palmer CO .20 .50
58 Darryl Pearce .20 .50
59 Pat Reidy .20 .50
60 Andrew Simons .20 .50
61 Murray Arnold CO .20 .50
62 James Crawford .30 .75
63 Michael Ellis .20 .50
64 Ricky Grace .60 1.50
65 Dave Hancock ACO .20 .50
66 Peter Hansen .20 .50
67 Vince Hinchen .20 .50
68 Griffin Longley .20 .50
69 Tiny Pinder 1.25 3.00
70 Trevor Torrance .20 .50
71 Andrew Vlahov .60 1.50
72 Eric Watterson .20 .50
73 Lucas Agrums .20 .50
74 Bruce Bolden .50 1.25
75 John Dorge .30 .75
76 Brian Goorjian CO .20 .50
77 Andrew Howey .20 .50
78 Darren Lucas .20 .50
79 Milt Newton .75 2.00
80 Scott Ninnis .20 .50
81 Andrew Parkinson .20 .50
82 Darren Perry .30 .75
83 Tony Ronaldson .20 .50
84 Ian Stacker .20 .50
85 Jody Austin .20 .50
86 Brad Dalton .20 .50
87 Mark Dalton .20 .50
88 Tony De Ambrosis .20 .50
89 Peter Hill .20 .50
90 Damian Keogh .20 .50
91 Dwayne McClain .75 2.00
92 Ken McClary .20 .50
93 Tim Morrissey .20 .50
94 Cory Reader .20 .50
95 Bob Turner CO .20 .50
96 Dean Uthoff .75 2.00

1992 Australian Stops NBL

COMPLETE SET (92) 35.00 70.00
1 Ken Watson CO .40 1.00
2 Mark Bradtke .75 2.00
3 Mark Davis .50 1.25
4 Butch Hays .75 2.00
5 Michael McKay .20 .50
6 Graham Kubank .20 .50
7 Leroy Loggins .75 2.00
8 Andre Moore .75 2.00
9 Shane Heal 1.25 3.00
10 Simon Kerle .20 .50
11 Greg Fox .20 .50
12 Adrian Branch 1.50 4.00
13 Jamie Kennedy .20 .50
14 Herb McEachin .20 .50
15 Phil Smyth .20 .50
16 Simon Cottrell .20 .50
17 Jason Reese UER (Card front says Canberra Cannons) .40 1.00
18 Steve Hood .60 1.50
19 Robert Locke .40 1.00
20 Cecil Exum .50 1.25
21 Matthew Alexander .40 1.00
22 Wayne Larkins .20 .50
23 Mike Mitchell .75 2.00
24 Larry Sengstock .20 .50
25 Andre LaFleur .60 1.50
26 Matthew Reece UER (Card front says Gold Coast Rollers) .20 .50
27 Ron Radliff .20 .50
28 Rodger Smith .20 .50
29 Cal Bruton CO .20 .50
30 Wayne McDaniel .40 1.00
31 Justin Cass .20 .50
32 Shane Froling .20 .50
33 David Stiff .20 .50
34 Lindsay Gaze CO .40 1.00
35 Andrew Gaze 2.00 5.00
36 David Simmons .50 1.25
37 Stephen Whitehead .50 1.25
38 Warrick Giddey .20 .50
39 Lanard Copeland 1.25 3.00
40 Robert Sibley .20 .50
41 Terry Dozier .75 2.00
42 Michael Johnson .20 .50
43 Al Green .20 .50
44 Paul Kuiper .20 .50
45 Bruce Palmer CO .20 .50
46 Scott Fisher .40 1.00
47 Ray Borner .20 .50
48 Paul Maley .40 1.00
49 Pat Reidy .40 1.00
50 Mark Leader .20 .50
51 Darryl Pearce UER (Card front says North Melbourne Giants) .20 .50
52 Murray Arnold CO .20 .50
53 Ricky Grace .75 2.00
54 Andrew Vlahov .75 2.00
55 Tiny Pinder .75 2.00
56 James Crawford .60 1.50
57 Mike Ellis .20 .50
58 Vince Hinchen UER (Card front says Perth Wildcats) .40 1.00
59 Perth Team Photo .40 1.00
60 Justin Withers .40 1.00
61 Greg Hubbard .40 1.00
62 Chuck Harmison .75 2.00
63 Melvin Thomas .60 1.50
64 Doug Overton 1.50 4.00
65 Brian Goorjian CO .20 .50
66 Bruce Bolden .60 1.50
67 Darren Lucas .20 .50
68 Darren Perry .40 1.00
69 John Dorge .20 .50
70 Andrew Parkinson .40 1.00
71 Scott Ninnis .40 1.00
72 Bob Turner CO .20 .50
73 Dean Uthoff .75 2.00
74 Damian Keogh .40 1.00
75 Dwayne McClain 1.50 4.00
76 Ken McClary .40 1.00
77 Tim Morrissey .20 .50
78 Mark Dalton .20 .50
79 The Jester (Sydney Kings mascot) .40 1.00
80 Balmy Melbourne Tigers mascot) .40 1.00
81 Eddie Crouch REF .20 .50
82 Jim Pappas CO .20 .50
83 Debbie Black .20 .50
84 Joanne Moyle .20 .50
85 Australian Women's Team .40 1.00
86 Annie Burgess .20 .50
87 Dandenong Rangers Team Photo .40 1.00
88 Eric Cooks Ballarat Miners .20 .50
89 Knox Raiders Team Photo .40 1.00
90 Checklist .20 .50
91 Ricky Grace SP James Crawford (Back to Back Champions) 1.25 3.00
92 Logo Card SP .75 2.00

1993 Australian Futera NBL
COMPLETE SET (110) 20.00 50.00
1 Chris Blakemore .30 .75
2 Brett Maher .20 .50
3 Phil Smyth .20 .50
4 Scott Ninnis .20 .50
5 Mark Davis .40 1.00
6 Mike McKay .20 .50
7 Jerry Dennard .20 .50
8 Nigel Purchase .20 .50
9 Shane Heal .75 2.00
10 Leroy Loggins .40 1.00
11 Dave Colbert .20 .50
12 Andre Moore .40 1.00
13 Rodger Smith .20 .50
14 Luke Gribble .20 .50
15 Shane Froling .20 .50
16 Lachlan Armfield .20 .50
17 John Stelzer .20 .50
18 Simon Cottrell .20 .50
19 Rodney Monroe .75 2.00
20 Fred Herzog .20 .50
21 Matt Witkowski .20 .50
22 Adam Kendrick .20 .50
23 Justin Withers .20 .50
24 Michael Morrison .20 .50
25 Cecil Exum .40 1.00
26 Ray Borner .20 .50
27 Adrian Branch 1.00 2.50
28 Wayne Larkins .20 .50
29 Alex Hetenyi .20 .50
30 Vince Hinchen .20 .50
31 Mike Mitchell .40 1.00
32 Andre LaFleur .40 1.00
33 Andrew Goodwin .20 .50
34 Greg Fox .20 .50
35 Matthew Reece .20 .50
36 Peter Hill .20 .50
37 Chuck Harmison .50 1.25
38 Bruce Hays .40 1.00
39 Melvin Thomas .40 1.00
40 Chris Steele .20 .50
41 Dene MacDonald .20 .50
42 Mike Corkeron .20 .50
43 Wayne McDaniel .30 .75
44 Jim Havrilla .20 .50
45 Donald Whiteside .20 .50
46 David Close .20 .50
47 Neil Turner .20 .50
48 Anthony Stewart .20 .50
49 Justin Cass .20 .50
50 Andrew Svaldenis .20 .50
51 Warrick Giddey .20 .50
52 Andrew Gaze 1.00 2.50
53 Mark Bradtke .50 1.25
54 Lanard Copeland .50 1.25
55 Ray Gordon .20 .50
56 Stephen Whitehead .20 .50
57 Robert Sibley .20 .50
58 David Simmons .30 .75
59 Shawn Dennis .20 .50
60 Michael Johnson .20 .50
61 Everette Stephens .75 2.00
62 Al Green .20 .50
63 Grant Kruger .20 .50
64 Jason Joynes .20 .50
65 Terry Dozier .60 1.50
66 Peter Harvey .20 .50
67 Paul Kuiper .20 .50
68 Terry Johnson .20 .50
69 Darryl Pearce .20 .50
70 Mark Leader .20 .50
71 Larry Sengstock .20 .50
72 Pat Reidy .20 .50
73 Jason Reese .30 .75
74 Rod Johnson .20 .50
75 Paul Rees .20 .50
76 Paul Maley .20 .50
77 Scott Fisher .30 .75
78 James Crawford .20 .50
79 Andrew Vlahov .50 1.25
80 Eric Watterson .20 .50
81 Ricky Grace .40 1.00
82 Chris Carroll .20 .50
83 Trevor Torrance .20 .50
84 Steve Davis .20 .50
85 David Blades .20 .50
86 Rimas Kurtinaitis .30 .75
87 Ricky Jones .40 1.00
88 Lucas Agrums .20 .50
89 Graham Kubank .20 .50
90 Tonny Jensen .20 .50
91 Paul Simpson .20 .50
92 Darren Perry .20 .50
93 Bruce Bolden .40 1.00
94 Robert Rose .40 1.00
95 Darren Lucas .20 .50
96 Andrew Parkinson .20 .50
97 Tony Ronaldson .20 .50
98 Shane Bright .20 .50
99 David Graham .20 .50
100 Simon Kerle .20 .50
101 Andre Lemanis UER
(Misspelled Andrej on back) .20 .50
102 John Dorge .20 .50
103 Dwayne McClain .50 1.25
104 Damian Keogh .20 .50
105 Ken McClary .20 .50
106 Tony De Ambrosis .20 .50
107 Greg Hubbard .20 .50
108 Tim Morrissey .20 .50
109 Dean Uthoff .50 1.25
110 Mark Dalton .20 .50
NNO Melbourne Magic 8.00 20.00
NNO Herb McEachin
Legends Card 12.50 30.00

1993 Australian Futera Best of Both Worlds
COMPLETE SET (4) 60.00 150.00
1 Terry Dozier 15.00 40.00
2 Dwayne McClain 15.00 40.00
3 Adrian Branch 15.00 40.00
4 Doug Overton 15.00 40.00

1993 Australian Futera Honours Awards
COMPLETE SET (11) 80.00 200.00
1 Scott Fisher MVP 6.00 15.00
2 Andrew Gaze MVP 10.00 25.00
3 Andrew Svaldenis MIP 3.00 8.00
4 Terry Dozier D-POY 6.00 15.00
5 Lachlan Armfield ROY 3.00 8.00
6 Brian Goorjian COY 3.00 8.00
7 Doug Overton 1st 8.00 20.00
8 Andrew Gaze 1st 10.00 25.00
9 Dwayne McClain 1st 6.00 15.00
10 Andrew Vlahov 1st 8.00 20.00
11 Scott Fisher 1st 6.00 15.00

1993 Australian Futera Super Gold
COMPLETE SET (14) 50.00 125.00
1 John Dorge 3.00 8.00
2 Lanard Copeland 8.00 20.00
3 Pat Reidy 3.00 8.00
4 Cecil Exum 3.00 8.00
5 Melvin Thomas 6.00 15.00
6 Dean Uthoff 4.00 10.00
7 Terry Dozier 8.00 20.00
8 Mark Davis 8.00 20.00
9 Rimas Kurtinaitias 6.00 15.00
10 Shane Heal 10.00 25.00
11 Mike Mitchell 6.00 15.00
12 Justin Withers 3.00 8.00
13 Ricky Grace 10.00 25.00
14 Donald Whiteside 3.00 8.00

1993 Australian Stops NBL
COMPLETE SET (92) 20.00 50.00
1 Terry Dozier .50 1.25
2 Steve Hood SD .40 1.00
3 Shane Heal 1.25 3.00
4 Tim Morrissey .20 .50
5 Cecil Exum .30 .75
6 Andrew Svaldenis .20 .50
7 Andrew Goodwin .20 .50
8 Al Green .20 .50
9 Wayne McDaniel .30 .75
10 Couch REF
Mildenhall REF .20 .50
11 Cal Bruton CO .20 .50
12 American All-Stars .40 1.00
13 Craig Adams .20 .50
14 Stephen Whitehead .20 .50
15 Michael Johnson .20 .50
16 Everette Stephens .75 2.00
17 Donald Whiteside .20 .50
18 Michael McKay .20 .50
19 Grant Kruger .20 .50
20 James Crawford .30 .75
21 Paul Maley .20 .50
22 Pat Reidy .20 .50
23 Australian Boomers .20 .50
24 Trevor Torrance .20 .50
25 Luc Longley 2.00 5.00
26 Chuck Harmison .60 1.50
27 Tony Ronaldson .20 .50
28 Tony De Ambrosis .20 .50
29 Mark Davis .40 1.00
30 Lanard Copeland SD .50 1.25
31 Darren Perry .40 1.00
32 Everette Stephens SD .50 1.25
33 Checklist .30 .75
34 Andrew Parkinson .20 .50
35 David Simmons .30 .75
36 Warrick Giddey .20 .50
37 Phil Smyth .20 .50
38 Scott Ninnis .20 .50
39 Leroy Loggins .60 1.50
40 Rodney Monroe .75 2.00
41 Lachlan Armfield .30 .75
42 Michael Morrison .30 .75
43 Ray Borner .20 .50
44 Mike Mitchell .60 1.50
45 Andre La Fleur .40 1.00
46 Andrew Vlahov .40 1.00
47 Scott Fisher .40 1.00
48 Dean Uthoff .50 1.25
49 Bruce Bolden .40 1.00
50 Greg Hubbard .30 .75
51 Damian Keogh .30 .75
52 Rimas Kurtinaitas .40 1.00
53 Adrian Branch 1.00 2.50
54 Vince Hinchen .20 .50
55 Ricky Jones .30 .75
56 Paris McCurdy .40 1.00
57 Brett Maher .20 .50
58 Shane Froling .20 .50
59 1992 Magic Champs .40 1.00
60 Andre Moore .40 1.00
61 Fred Herzog .20 .50
62 Justin Withers .20 .50
63 Graham Kubank .20 .50
64 Wayne Larkins .20 .50
65 Lucas Agrums .20 .50
66 Matthew Reese .20 .50
67 Jim Havrilla .30 .75
68 Chris Steele .20 .50
69 Ray Gordan .20 .50
70 Mark Bradtke .50 1.25
71 Larry Sengstock .20 .50
72 Darryl Pearce .20 .50
73 Rod Johnson .20 .50
74 Brett Brown CO .20 .50
75 Jason Reese .20 .50
76 Ricky Grace .60 1.50
77 Darren Lucas .20 .50
78 Bruce Palmer CO .20 .50
79 Tigerman .30 .75
80 Robert Sibley .20 .50
81 Robert Rose .40 1.00
82 David Graham .20 .50
83 Ken McClary .20 .50
84 Dwayne McClain .75 2.00
85 Brian Goorjian CO .20 .50
86 Peter Hill .20 .50
87 Butch Hays .40 1.00
88 Andrew Gaze 1.25 3.00
89 Tonny Jensen .20 .50
90 Melvin Thomas .30 .75
91 Lanard Copeland .75 2.00
92 Checklist .40 1.00

1994 Australian Futera NBL Promos
COMPLETE SET (5) 2.50 6.00
RC5 Andrew Gaze BK 1.00 2.50

1994 Australian Futera NBL
COMPLETE SET (220) 30.00 60.00
COMPLETE SERIES 1 (110) 15.00 30.00
COMPLETE SERIES 2 (110) 15.00 30.00
1 Phil Smyth .20 .50
2 Scott Ninnis .20 .50
3 Brett Maher .20 .50
4 Michael McKay .20 .50
5 Mark Davis .40 1.00
6 David Robinson .40 1.00
7 Dave Colbert .20 .50
8 Shane Froling .20 .50
9 Rodger Smith .20 .50
10 Leroy Loggins .40 1.00
11 Andre Moore .30 .75
12 Shane Heal .60 1.50
13 Luke Gribble .20 .50
14 Rodney Monroe .40 1.00
15 Justin Withers .20 .50
16 Matt Witkowski .20 .50
17 Fred Herzog .20 .50
18 Lachlan Armfield .20 .50
19 John Stelzer .20 .50
20 Wayne Larkins .20 .50
21 Adrian Branch .75 2.00
22 Cecil Exum .30 .75
23 Ray Borner .20 .50
24 Michael Morrison .30 .75
25 Vince Hinchen .20 .50
26 Andrew Goodwin .20 .50
27 Andre LaFleur .20 .50
28 John Szigeti .20 .50
29 Matthew Reece .20 .50
30 Mike Mitchell .30 .75
31 Greg Fox .20 .50
32 Justin Cass .20 .50
33 David Close .20 .50
34 Andrew Svaldenis .20 .50
35 Donald Whiteside .30 .75
36 Wayne McDaniel .30 .75
37 Anthony Stewart .20 .50
38 Butch Hays .40 1.00
39 Chris Steele .20 .50
40 Melvin Thomas .30 .75
41 Dene MacDonald .20 .50
42 Chuck Harmison .50 1.25
43 Mike Corkeron .20 .50
44 Lanard Copeland .40 1.00
45 Stephen Whitehead .20 .50
46 Robert Sibley .20 .50
47 Mark Bradtke .50 1.25
48 Andrew Gaze .50 1.25
49 David Simmons .20 .50
50 Warrick Giddey .20 .50
51 Michael Johnson .20 .50
52 Al Green .20 .50
53 Peter Harvey .20 .50
54 Everette Stephens .30 .75
55 Grant Kruger .20 .50
56 Terry Dozier .40 1.00
57 Simon O'Donnell .20 .50
58 Paul Maley .20 .50
59 Darryl Pearce .20 .50
60 Mark Leader .20 .50
61 Jason Reese .20 .50
62 Rod Johnson .20 .50
63 Pat Reidy .20 .50
64 Paul Rees .20 .50
65 Larry Sengstock .20 .50
66 Trevor Torrance .20 .50
67 Andrew Vlahov .30 .75
68 James Crawford .20 .50
69 Ricky Grace .40 1.00
70 Scott Fisher .20 .50
71 Eric Watterson .20 .50
72 Chris Carroll .20 .50
73 Darren Lucas .20 .50
74 Bruce Bolden .30 .75
75 Robert Rose .40 1.00
76 John Dorge .20 .50
77 Andrew Parkinson .20 .50
78 David Graham .20 .50
79 Darren Perry .20 .50
80 Tony Ronaldson .20 .50
81 Greg Hubbard .20 .50
82 Dwayne McClain .40 1.00
83 Ken McClary .20 .50
84 Tim Morrissey .20 .50
85 Damian Keogh .20 .50
86 Tony De Ambrosis .20 .50
87 Dean Uthoff .50 1.25
88 Wayne Womack .20 .50
89 David Blades .20 .50
90 Ricky Jones .40 1.00
91 Rimas Kurtinaitas .20 .50
92 Brian Andrews .20 .50
93 Lucas Agrums .20 .50
94 Tonny Jensen .20 .50
95 Paul Simpson .20 .50
96 Darren Smith .20 .50
97 Robert Rose
MVP Award .30 .75
98 Andrew Gaze
Most Efficient Player .40 1.00
99 Andrew Gaze
Top Point Scorer .40 1.00
100 Terry Dozier
Best Defensive Player .40 1.00
101 Andre LaFleur
Good Hands Award .30 .75
102 Bruce Bolden
Top Rebounder .20 .50
103 Chris Blakemore
Rookie of the Year .20 .50
104 Scott Ninnis
Most Improved Player .20 .50
105 Andrew Vlahov
Int'l. POY .20 .50
106 Alan Black
Coach of the Year .20 .50
107 Checklist 1-37 .20 .50
108 Checklist 38-80 .20 .50
109 Checklist 81-110 .20 .50
110 Checklist Specials .20 .50
111 Robert Rose .40 1.00
112 Mark Davis .30 .75
113 Chris Blakemore .20 .50
114 Phil Smyth .20 .50
115 Brett Maher .20 .50
116 Mike McKay .20 .50
117 Dave Colbert .20 .50
118 Shane Heal .40 1.00
119 Leroy Loggins .40 1.00
120 Andre Moore .30 .75
121 Robert Sibley .20 .50
122 Jason Reese .20 .50
123 Lachlan Armfield .20 .50
124 Fred Herzog .20 .50
125 Justin Withers .20 .50
126 Adam Kendrick .20 .50
127 Everette Stephens .30 .75
128 Ray Borner .20 .50
129 Cecil Exum .30 .75
130 Simon Kerle .20 .50
131 Mike Mitchell .30 .75
132 Matthew Reece .20 .50
133 Tony De Ambrosis .20 .50
134 Andre LaFleur .30 .75
135 Peter Hill .20 .50
136 Calvin Talford .50 1.25
137 Darren Perry .20 .50
138 Wayne McDaniel .30 .75
139 Anthony Stewart .20 .50
140 Keith Nelson .20 .50
141 Butch Hays .30 .75
142 Melvin Thomas .30 .75
143 Chuck Harmison .50 1.25
144 Chris Steele .20 .50
145 Dene MacDonald .20 .50
146 Lanard Copeland .40 1.00
147 David Simmons .20 .50
148 Mark Bradtke .40 1.00
149 Andrew Gaze .50 1.25
150 Warrick Giddey .20 .50
151 Ray Gordon .20 .50
152 Derek Rucker .30 .75
153 Terry Dozier .40 1.00
154 Tonny Jensen .20 .50
155 Grant Kruger .20 .50
156 Paul Kuiper .20 .50
157 Darryl McDonald .60 1.50
158 Paul Maley .20 .50
159 Mark Leader .20 .50
160 Larry Sengstock .20 .50
161 Pat Reidy .20 .50
162 Paul Rees .20 .50
163 Ricky Grace .40 1.00
164 James Crawford .20 .50
165 Andrew Vlahov .30 .75
166 Scott Fisher .20 .50
167 Martin Cattalini .20 .50
168 Adonis Jordan .75 2.00
169 Darren Lucas .20 .50
171 Andrew Parkinson .20 .50
172 Tony Ronaldson .20 .50
173 David Graham .20 .50
174 Mario Donaldson .20 .50
175 Leon Trimmingham .60 1.50
176 Tim Morrissey .20 .50
177 Greg Hubbard .20 .50
178 Dean Uthoff .50 1.25
179 Damian Keogh .20 .50
180 Brendan LeGassick .20 .50
181 Ricky Jones .40 1.00
182 Lucas Agrums .20 .50
183 Graham Kubank .20 .50
184 1993 Finals Series
Perth Defeats Brisbane .20 .50
185 1993 Finals Series
Melbourne Defeats SE Melbourne .20 .50
186 1993 Finals Series
Melbourne Leads Perth .20 .50
187 1993 Finals Series
Perth Squares the Series .20 .50
188 1993 Finals Series
Melbourne Defeats Perth .20 .50
189 1993 Finals Series
Grand Final MVP .20 .50
190 1993 Finals Series
Victory At Last .20 .50
191 Lanard Copeland
Andrew Gaze .40 1.00
192 Ricky Grace
James Crawford .30 .75
193 Andre LaFleur
Mike Mitchell .30 .75
194 Shane Heal
Leroy Loggins .30 .75
195 Melvin Thomas
Butch Hays .40 1.00
196 Leon Trimmingham
Mario Donaldson .30 .75
197 Patrick Reidy
Darryl McDonald .30 .75
198 Sam MacKinnon .60 1.50
199 C.J. Bruton .20 .50
200 Aaron Trahair .40 1.00
201 Brad Williams .20 .50
202 Ryan Knights .20 .50
203 Darren Smith .20 .50
204 Opals Header .20 .50
204A Jenny Whittel .20 .50
205 Annie Burgess .20 .50
206 Sandy Brondello .20 .50
207 Allison Cook .20 .50
208 Michele Timms 1.00 2.50
209 Shelley Gorman .20 .50
210 Robyn Maher .20 .50
211 Trish Fallon .20 .50
212 Rachael Sporn .20 .50
213 Karen Dalton .20 .50
214 Michelle Brogan .20 .50
215 Samantha Thornton .20 .50
216 Tom Maher .20 .50
217 Checklist 111-151 .20 .50
218 Checklist 152-183 .20 .50
219 Checklist 184-220 .20 .50
220 Checklist Specials .20 .50

1994 Australian Futera Best of Both Worlds
COMPLETE SET (12) 125.00 250.00
BW1 Ricky Grace
Picture Card 12.50 30.00
BW2 Lanard Copeland
Picture Card 12.50 30.00
BW3 Andrew Gaze
Picture Card 15.00 40.00
BW4 Adonis Jordan
Picture Card 15.00 50.00
CC3 Andrew Gaze
Certification Card 10.00 20.00
CC4 Adonis Jordan
Certification Card 10.00 20.00
CD1 Ricky Grace
Certification Card 6.00 15.00
CD2 Lanard Copeland
Certification Card 8.00 20.00
RC3 Andrew Gaze
Redemption Card 10.00 25.00
RC4 Adonis Jordan
Redemption Card 8.00 20.00
RD1 Ricky Grace
Redemption Card 8.00 20.00
RD2 Lanard Copeland
Redemption Card 8.00 20.00

1994 Australian Futera Defensive Giants
COMPLETE SET (7) 20.00 50.00
DG1 Terry Dozier 3.00 8.00
DG2 Robert Rose 5.00 12.00
DG3 Darren Lucas 2.00 5.00
DG4 Melvin Thomas 5.00 12.00
DG5 Derek Rucker 5.00 12.00
DG6 Mark Davis 5.00 12.00
DG7 Mark Bradtke 6.00 15.00

1994 Australian Futera Lords of the Ring
COMPLETE SET (12) 25.00 60.00
LR1 Robert Rose 3.00 8.00
LR2 Lanard Copeland 3.00 8.00
LR3 Ricky Jones 1.50 4.00
LR4 Mark Bradtke 3.00 8.00
LR5 David Simmons 2.00 5.00
LR6 Andrew Vlahov 3.00 8.00
LR7 James Crawford 3.00 8.00
LR8 Bruce Bolden 3.00 8.00
LR9 Mike Mitchell 3.00 8.00
LR10 Darryl McDonald 4.00 10.00
LR11 Paul Maley 3.00 8.00
LR12 Leon Trimmingham 4.00 10.00

1994 Australian Futera NBL Heroes
COMPLETE SET (14) 10.00 25.00
NH1 Leroy Loggins
Drawing 1.50 4.00
NH2 Leroy Loggins 1989 1.25 3.00
NH3 Leroy Loggins 1990 1.25 3.00
NH4 Leroy Loggins 1991 1.25 3.00
NH5 Leroy Loggins 1992 1.25 3.00
NH6 Leroy Loggins 1993 1.25 3.00
NH7 Leroy Loggins
Olympic Career 1.25 3.00
NH8 Scott Fisher
Drawing 1.50 4.00
NH9 Scott Fisher 1988 1.00 2.50
NH10 Scott Fisher 1989 1.00 2.50
NH11 Scott Fisher 1990 1.00 2.50
NH12 Scott Fisher 1991 1.00 2.50
NH13 Scott Fisher 1992 1.00 2.50
NH14 Scott Fisher 1993 1.00 2.50

1994 Australian Futera New Horizons
COMPLETE SET (6) 12.00 30.00
HZ1 Calvin Talford 4.00 10.00
HZ2 Darryl McDonald 5.00 12.00
HZ3 Leon Trimmingham 5.00 12.00
HZ4 Mario Donaldson 2.00 5.00
HZ5 Adonis Jordan 4.00 10.00
HZ6 Keith Jordan 2.00 5.00

1994 Australian Futera Offensive Threats
COMPLETE SET (14) 20.00 50.00
OT1 Andrew Gaze 4.00 10.00
OT2 Ricky Jones 1.50 4.00
OT3 Adrian Branch 2.50 6.00
OT4 Jason Reese 1.50 4.00
OT5 Melvin Thomas 1.50 4.00
OT6 Rodney Monroe 2.50 6.00
OT7 Dwayne McClain 2.50 6.00
OT8 Scott Fisher 2.50 6.00
OT9 Leroy Loggins 2.50 6.00
OT10 Mike Mitchell 2.50 6.00
OT11 Mark Davis 1.50 4.00
OT12 Bruce Bolden 2.50 6.00
OT13 Everette Stephens 2.50 6.00
OT14 Wayne McDaniel 1.50 4.00

1994 Australian Futera Signature Series
COMPLETE SET (7) 175.00 350.00
SS1 Checklist 8.00 20.00
SS2 Calvin Talford 24.00 60.00
SS3 Darryl McDonald 40.00 100.00
SS4 Mario Donaldson 20.00 50.00
SS5 Leon Trimmingham 50.00 125.00
SS6 Andrew Vlahov 24.00 60.00
SS7 Bruce Bolden 20.00 50.00

1995 Australian Futera NBL
COMPLETE SET (110) 12.00 30.00
1 Darryl McDonald .40 1.00
2 Ricky Grace .30 .75
3 Fred Cofield .40 1.00
4 Brett Maher .10 .30
5 Lanard Copeland .40 1.00
6 Dean Uthoff .40 1.00
7 Everette Stephens .40 1.00
8 Andre LaFleur .25 .60
9 Graham Kubank .10 .30
10 Luke Gribble .10 .30
11 Darryl Johnson .20 .50
12 Mike Corkeron .10 .30
13 Keith Nelson .10 .30
14 Greg Hubbard .10 .30
15 Robert Rose .30 .75
16 Andrew Vlahov .30 .75
17 Paul Kuiper .10 .30
18 Wayne McDaniel .20 .50
19 Jason Reese .10 .30
20 Justin Cass .10 .30
21 Butch Hays .30 .75
22 Paul Maley .20 .50
23 Dave Simmons .10 .30
24 Mike Mitchell .30 .75
25 Bruce Bolden .30 .75
26 David Colbert .10 .30
27 Pat Reidy .10 .30
28 Mark Dalton .10 .30
29 Chris Blakemore .20 .50
30 Checklist 1-44 .10 .30
31 Simon Kerle .10 .30
32 Chris Steele .10 .30
33 Paul Rees .10 .30
34 Warrick Giddey .10 .30
35 Doug Peacock .10 .30
36 Damian Keogh .10 .30
37 Michael Johnson .10 .30
38 Justin Withers .10 .30
39 Aaron Trahair .20 .50
40 Leroy Loggins .30 .75
41 Mark Leader .10 .30
42 Anthony Stewart .10 .30
43 Adonis Jordan .75 2.00
44 Scott Ninnis .15 .40
45 Leon Trimmingham .50 1.25
46 David Blades .10 .30
47 Grant Kruger .10 .30
48 Robert Sibley .10 .30
49 Vince Hinchen .10 .30
50 Chuck Harmison .40 1.00
51 Matthew Alexander .10 .30
52 Simon Cottrell .10 .30
53 Tony De Ambrosis .10 .30
54 Calvin Talford .40 1.00
55 Sam MacKinnon .30 .75
56 Martin Cattalini .10 .30
57 Mike McKay .10 .30
58 Larry Sengstock .10 .30
59 Andrew Gaze .75 2.00
60 Checklist 45-88 .10 .30
61 Rodger Smith .10 .30
62 Melvin Thomas .20 .50
63 Peter Hill .10 .30
64 Mario Donaldson .10 .30
65 Darren Perry .10 .30
66 Matt Witkowski .10 .30
67 Derek Rucker .30 .75
68 Cecil Exum .30 .75
69 Lucas Agrums .10 .30
70 Darren Lucas .10 .30
71 Mark Bradtke .30 .75
72 Mark Davis .30 .75
73 Peter Harvey .10 .30
74 Ray Borner .10 .30
75 Dene MacDonald .10 .30
76 John Dorge .10 .30
77 Ricky Jones .30 .75
78 Shane Heal .40 1.00
79 Terry Dozier .40 1.00
80 Paul Crombie .10 .30
81 Stephen Whitehead .15 .40
82 Lachlan Armfield .10 .30
83 James Crawford .15 .40
84 Cameron Dickinson .10 .30
85 Tony Ronaldson .10 .30
86 Scott Fisher .15 .40
87 Andrew Parkinson .10 .30
88 Ray Gordon .10 .30
89 Checklist 89-110 .10 .30
90 Giants vs Magic
Semi-Finals .10 .30
91 Sixers vs Tigers
Semi-Finals .10 .30
92 Sixers vs Giants
Semi-Finals .10 .30
93 Giants vs Sixers
Semi-Finals .10 .30
94 N Melbourne Giants
Championship Team .10 .30
95 Paul Rees .10 .30
96 Shane Heal .50 1.25
97 Derek Rucker .20 .50
98 Shane Heal .40 1.00
99 Mark Bradtke .30 .75
100 Keith Nelson .10 .30
101 Andrew Gaze .75 2.00
102 Darryl McDonald .30 .75
103 Sam MacKinnon .20 .50
104 Brett Brown .10 .30
105 Andrew Gaze .75 2.00
106 Darren Lucas .10 .30
107 Chris Blakemore .20 .50
108 Mark Bradtke .30 .75
109 Checklist .10 .30
110 Checklist Specials .10 .30

1995 Australian Futera Airborne
COMPLETE SET (9) 2.00 5.00
NA1 Sam MacKinnon .60 1.50
NA2 Butch Hays .30 .75
NA3 Paul Maley .30 .75
NA4 Calvin Talford .40 1.00
NA5 Mike Mitchell .40 1.00
NA6 Dave Simmons .20 .50
NA7 Ricky Jones .30 .75
NA8 Darryl McDonald .75 2.00
NA9 Checklist .20 .50

1995 Australian Futera Clutchmen
COMPLETE SET (15) 5.00 12.00
CM1 Robert Rose .40 1.00
CM2 Leroy Loggins .75 2.00
CM3 Fred Cofield .40 1.00
CM4 Cecil Exum .30 .75
CM5 Doug Peacock .20 .50
CM6 Darren Perry .20 .50
CM7 Butch Hays .40 1.00
CM8 Andrew Gaze 1.00 2.50
CM9 Derek Rucker .75 2.00
CM10 Darryl McDonald .75 2.00
CM11 Ricky Grace .60 1.50
CM12 Tony Ronaldson .20 .50
CM13 Leon Trimmingham .30 .75
CM14 Cameron Dickinson 1.00 2.50
CM15 Checklist .20 .50

1995 Australian Futera Head To Head
COMPLETE SET (6) 30.00 80.00
H1 Andrew Gaze
Darren Lucas 12.50 30.00
H2 Leroy Loggins
Robert Rose 10.00 25.00
H3 Leon Trimmingham
Ricky Jones 10.00 25.00
H4 Melvin Thomas
Keith Nelson 6.00 15.00
H5 Fred Cofield
Tonny Jensen 5.00 12.00
H6 Peter Hill
Simon Kerle 4.00 10.00

1995 Australian Futera Instant Impact
COMPLETE SET (6) 25.00 60.00
II1 Darryl McDonald 6.00 15.00
II2 Sam MacKinnon 6.00 15.00
II3 Leon Trimmingham 8.00 20.00
II4 Chris Blakemore 4.00 10.00
II5 Derek Rucker 6.00 15.00
II6 Calvin Talford 4.00 10.00

1995 Australian Futera MVP/Rookie Redemption
COMPLETE SET (3) 125.00 250.00
MR1 Redemption Card 10.00 25.00
MR2 Andrew Gaze
Sam MacKinnon 100.00 250.00
MR3 Certification Card 10.00 25.00

1995 Australian Futera Star Challenge
COMPLETE SET (10) 15.00 40.00
NBL1 Tony Ronaldson 1.50 4.00
NBL2 Paul Rees 1.00 2.50
NBL3 Mark Bradtke 1.50 4.00
NBL4 Andrew Gaze 4.00 10.00
NBL5 Shane Heal 3.00 8.00
NBL6 Derek Rucker 2.50 6.00
NBL7 Butch Hays 1.50 4.00
NBL8 Mario Donaldson 1.00 2.50
NBL9 Leon Trimmingham 4.00 10.00
NBL10 Lanard Copeland 2.50 6.00

1995 Australian Futera 300 Club
COMPLETE SET (17) 2.50 6.00
GC1 Larry Sengstock .20 .50
GC2 Leroy Loggins .40 1.00
GC3 Damian Keogh .20 .50
GC4 Herb McEachin .20 .50
GC5 James Crawford .30 .75
GC6 Al Green .20 .50
GC7 Ray Borner .20 .50
GC8 Darryl Pearce .20 .50
GC9 Michael Johnson .20 .50
GC10 Phil Smyth .20 .50
GC11 Chuck Harmison .40 1.00
GC12 Mike Ellis .20 .50
GC13 Tim Morrissey .20 .50
GC14 Simon Cottrell .20 .50
GC15 Eric Waterson .20 .50
GC16 Mike McKay .20 .50
GC17 Checklist .20 .50

1995 Australian Futera Abdul-Jabbar Adidas Promo
COMPLETE SET (4) 15.00 40.00
COMMON CARD (K1-K4) 5.00 12.00

1996 Australian Futera NBL
COMPLETE SET (100) 10.00 25.00
1 Mark Davis .40 1.00
2 Brett Maher .10 .30
3 Chris Blakemore .10 .30
4 Scott Ninnis .10 .30
5 Robert Rose .30 .75
6 Mike McKay .10 .30
7 Leroy Loggins .50 1.25
8 Mike Mitchell .20 .50
9 Robert Sibley .15 .40
10 Andrew Goodwin .10 .30
11 Shane Heal .30 .75
12 John Rillie .10 .30
13 Ray Borner .10 .30
14 Jamie Pearlman .10 .30
15 David Close .10 .30
16 Simon Dwight .10 .30
17 Lachlan Armfield .10 .30
18 Jervaughn Scales .20 .50
19 Andrew Svaldenis .10 .30
20 Cecil Exum .30 .75
21 Joey Wright .10 .30
22 Simon Kerle .10 .30
23 Greg Smith .10 .30
24 Justin Cass .10 .30
25 Trevor Torrance .10 .30
26 John Szigeti .10 .30
27 Peter Harvey .10 .30
28 Doug Peacock .10 .30
29 Tony De Ambrosis .10 .30
30 Steve Woodberry .60 1.50
31 Darren Smith .10 .30
32 Mark Nash .10 .30
33 Darren Perry .10 .30
34 David Stiff .10 .30
35 Andre Moore .30 .75
36 Jerome Scott .10 .30
37 Chuck Harmison .40 1.00
38 Terry Johnson .10 .30
39 Dene MacDonald .10 .30
40 Melvin Thomas .20 .50
41 Andre LaFleur .10 .30
42 Marc Brandon .10 .30
43 Andrew Gaze .75 2.00
44 Mark Bradtke .30 .75
45 Lanard Copeland .40 1.00
46 Blair Smith .10 .30
47 Dave Simmons .10 .30
48 Stephen Whitehead .10 .30
49 Butch Hays .30 .75
50 Michael Johnson .10 .30
51 Tonny Jensen .10 .30
52 Grant Kruger .10 .30
53 Martin McClean .10 .30
54 Matthew Alexander .10 .30
55 Darryl McDonald .10 .30
56 Paul Rees .10 .30
57 Larry Sengstock .10 .30
58 Paul Maley .10 .30
59 Pat Reidy .10 .30
60 Rod Johnson .10 .30
61 Andrew Vlahov .30 .75
62 Aaron Trahair .10 .30

63 Anthony Stewart .10 .30
64 Ricky Grace .40 1.00
65 Scott Fisher .50 1.25
66 James Crawford .30 .75
67 John Dorge .10 .30
68 Darren Lucas .10 .30
69 Tony Ronaldson .10 .30
70 Chris Anstey 1.25 3.00
71 Andrew Parkinson .10 .30
72 Sam MacKinnon .10 .30
73 Bruce Bolden .30 .75
74 Leon Trimmingham .30 .75
75 Justin Withers .10 .30
76 Brad Williams .10 .30
77 Greg Hubbard .10 .30
78 Mark Dalton .10 .30
79 Derek Rucker .10 .30
80 Clarence Tyson .15 .40
81 Shane Froling .10 .30
82 Cameron Dickinson .10 .30
83 David Blades .10 .30
84 Jason Cameron .10 .30
85 Michele Timms .60 1.50
86 Allison Cook .10 .30
87 Trish Fallon .10 .30
88 Sandy Brondello .10 .30
89 Shelley Gorman .10 .30
90 Andrew Gaze MVP .40 1.00
91 John Rillie ROY .20 .50
92 Darren Lucas .10 .30
93 Reggie Smith .20 .50
94 Tonny Jensen .10 .30
95 Darryl McDonald .10 .30
96 Andrew Gaze .40 1.00
97 Alan Black
Tom Wisman CO .10 .30
98 Championship Team
Perth Wildcats .10 .30
99 Checklist 1 .10 .30
100 Checklist 2 .10 .30

1996 Australian Futera NBL All-Stars

COMPLETE SET (10) 25.00 60.00
ASN1 Shane Heal 6.00 15.00
ASN2 Derek Rucker 2.00 5.00
ASN3 Leroy Loggins 6.00 15.00
ASN4 Leon Trimmingham 2.00 5.00
ASN5 Clarence Tyson 2.00 5.00
ASS1 Andrew Gaze 10.00 25.00
ASS2 Darryl McDonald 2.00 5.00
ASS3 Mark Davis 2.00 5.00
ASS4 Andrew Vlahov 2.00 5.00
ASS5 John Dorge 2.00 5.00

1996 Australian Futera NBL Futera Dream Team

COMPLETE SET (5) 8.00 20.00
1 Andrew Gaze
Ray Borner
Peter Harvey
Brett Maher
Paul Rees 5.00 12.00
2 Derek Rucker
Andrew Vlahov
Butch Hays
Mike Mitchell
Blair Smith 1.50 4.00
3 Leon Trimmingham
David Simmons
Andre LaFleur
Leroy Loggins
Simon Dwight 1.50 4.00
4 Melvin Thomas
Bruce Bolden
Ricky Grace
Jamie Pearlman
Clarence Tyson 1.50 4.00
5 Lanard Copeland
Mark Davis
Darryl McDonald
Sam MacKinnon
John Dorge 2.50 6.00

1996 Australian Futera NBL Future Forces

COMPLETE SET (10) 15.00 40.00
FFB1 Chris Blakemore 2.00 5.00
FFB2 David Stiff 2.00 5.00
FFB3 John Rillie 2.00 5.00
FFB4 Jason Smith 2.00 5.00
FFB5 Rupert Sapwell 2.00 5.00
FFC1 Brett Maher 2.00 5.00
FFC2 Chris Anstey 8.00 20.00
FFC3 Terry Johnson 2.00 5.00
FFC4 Brad Williams 2.00 5.00
FFC5 Martin Catalini 2.00 5.00

1996 Australian Futera NBL Outer Limits

COMPLETE SET (8) 8.00 20.00
OL1 Shane Heal 1.50 4.00
OL2 Andrew Gaze 3.00 8.00
OL3 Aaron Trahair 1.25 3.00
OL4 Simon Kerle 1.25 3.00
OL5 Chris Jent 1.50 4.00
OL6 Derek Rucker 1.25 3.00
OL7 Terry Johnson 1.25 3.00
OL8 Andrew Parkinson 1.25 3.00

1996 Australian Futera NBL Ten Thousand Point Card

TTP2 Andrew Gaze
Leroy Loggins 30.00 80.00

1993-94 Avia Clyde Drexler

COMPLETE SET (6) 3.00 8.00
COMMON CARD 1.00 2.50
NNO Redemption Card .40 1.00

1993 Charles Barkley Collector's Edition

COMPLETE SET (14) 2.00 5.00
COMMON CARD (1-14) .20 .50

1994-95 Basketball USA

COMPLETE SET (64) 150.00 300.00
1 Mahmoud Abdul-Rauf 1.50 4.00
2 Danny Ainge 2.50 6.00
3 Kenny Anderson 2.00 5.00
4 Nick Anderson 1.50 4.00
5 B.J. Armstrong 2.50 6.00
6 Stacey Augmon 2.00 5.00
7 Charles Barkley 6.00 15.00
8 Dana Barros 1.50 4.00
9 Muggsy Bogues 2.00 5.00
10 Cedric Ceballos 2.00 5.00
11 Derrick Coleman 2.50 6.00
12 Vlade Divac 2.50 6.00
13 Clyde Drexler 5.00 12.00
14 Joe Dumars 2.50 6.00
15 Sean Elliott 2.00 5.00
16 Patrick Ewing 5.00 12.00
17 Kendall Gill 1.50 4.00
18 Horace Grant 2.50 6.00
19 Anfernee Hardaway 5.00 12.00
20 Tim Hardaway 3.00 8.00
21 Carl Herrera 1.50 4.00
22 Jeff Hornacek 2.00 5.00
23 Robert Horry 2.50 6.00
24 Kevin Johnson 2.50 6.00
25 Larry Johnson 3.00 8.00
26 Michael Jordan 20.00 50.00
27 Shawn Kemp 4.00 10.00
28 Toni Kukoc 3.00 8.00
29 Christian Laettner 2.00 5.00
30 Dan Majerle 2.50 6.00
31 Karl Malone 5.00 12.00
32 Anthony Mason 2.00 5.00
33 Vernon Maxwell 1.50 4.00
34 Derrick McKey 1.50 4.00
35 Nate McMillan 2.00 5.00
36 Reggie Miller 5.00 12.00
37 Alonzo Mourning 5.00 12.00
38 Tracy Murray 1.50 4.00
39 Dikembe Mutombo 4.00 10.00
40 Charles Oakley 2.50 6.00
41 Hakeem Olajuwon 5.00 12.00
42 Shaquille O'Neal 6.00 15.00
43 Shaquille O'Neal 6.00 15.00
44 Billy Owens 1.50 4.00
45 Gary Payton 4.00 10.00
46 Sam Perkins 1.50 4.00
47 Ricky Pierce 1.50 4.00
48 Scottie Pippen 6.00 15.00
49 Mark Price 2.50 6.00
50 Glen Rice 2.50 6.00
51 Mitch Richmond 3.00 8.00
52 David Robinson 5.00 12.00
53 Dennis Rodman 5.00 12.00
54 Detlef Schrempf Dribbling 2.50 6.00
55 Detlef Schrempf Passing 2.50 6.00
56 Charles Smith 1.50 4.00
57 Rik Smits 2.00 5.00
58 Latrell Sprewell 3.00 8.00
59 John Starks 2.50 6.00
60 John Stockton 6.00 15.00
61 Rod Strickland 1.50 4.00
62 Otis Thorpe 1.50 4.00
63 Dominique Wilkins 4.00 10.00
64 Kevin Willis 2.00 5.00

1984-85 Bay State Bombardiers

1 John Ligums
Dave Cowens
Eddie Chavez
Joe Dawson
Pete DeBisschop
Mark Halsel
Kirk Richards
Kevin Springman
Kevin Williams
Leon Wilson 4.00 10.00

2003-04 Bazooka

COMP.SET w/o RC's (220) 15.00 30.00
221-275 RC STATED ODDS: 1:3
276-288 BAZ. JOE STATED ODDS 1:6
SOME CARDS HAVE HOME AND AWAY VERSION
B (AWAY) VERSION SAME VALUE AS A (HOME)
1A Tracy McGrady Home .40 1.00
1B Tracy McGrady Away .40 1.00
2 DaJuan Wagner .15 .40
3A Allen Iverson Home .60 1.50
3B Allen Iverson Away .60 1.50
4 Stromile Swift .15 .40
5 Jalen Rose .20 .50
6 Morris Peterson .15 .40
7 Lamar Odom .20 .50
8 Kobe Bryant 2.00 5.00
9 Chauncey Billups .30 .75
10 Jason Kidd .40 1.00
11 Yao Ming .60 1.50
12 Stephon Marbury .30 .75
13 Ricky Davis .20 .50
14 Andrei Kirilenko .20 .50
15 Courtney Alexander .15 .40
16 Brad Miller .20 .50
17 Bobby Jackson .20 .50
18 Rashard Lewis .20 .50
19 Juwan Howard .20 .50
20 Allan Houston .25 .60
21 Kevin Garnett .60 1.50
22 Jason Terry .20 .50
23A Jason Richardson Home .25 .60
23B Jason Richardson Away .25 .60
24 Jerry Stackhouse .30 .75
25 Tyson Chandler .20 .50
26 Drew Gooden .20 .50
27 Jason Williams .40 1.00
28 Eddie Jones .25 .60
29 Quentin Richardson .15 .40
30 Rasheed Wallace .30 .75
31A Shawn Marion Home .25 .60
31B Shawn Marion Away .25 .60
32 Malik Rose .15 .40
33 Ben Wallace .30 .75
34 Paul Pierce .40 1.00
35 Matt Harpring .15 .40
36 Eddie Griffin .15 .40
37 Toni Kukoc .25 .60
38 Mike Bibby .25 .60
39 Kwame Brown .15 .40
40 Kurt Thomas .15 .40
41 Dirk Nowitzki .60 1.50
42 Theo Ratliff .15 .40
43 Ray Allen .40 1.00
44 Michael Finley .25 .60
45 Lucious Harris .15 .40
46 Anfernee Hardaway .60 1.50
47 Christian Laettner .20 .50
48 Manu Ginobili .50 1.25
49 Tayshaun Prince .25 .60
50 Shaquille O'Neal 1.00 2.50
51 Vladimir Radmanovic .15 .40
52 Calbert Cheaney .15 .40
53 Eric Snow .15 .40
54A Pau Gasol Home .40 1.00
54B Pau Gasol Away .40 1.00
55 Dikembe Mutombo .30 .75
56 Alvin Williams .15 .40
57 Corliss Williamson .15 .40
58 Kedrick Brown .15 .40
59 Jamaal Tinsley .15 .40
60 Chris Webber .30 .75
61 Donyell Marshall .15 .40
62 Darrell Armstrong .15 .40
63 Kenny Thomas .15 .40
64 Mehmet Okur .20 .50
65 Carlos Boozer .20 .50
66A Kenyon Martin Home .25 .60
66B Kenyon Martin Away .25 .60
67 Speedy Claxton .15 .40
68 Brent Barry .15 .40
69 Ron Artest .25 .60
70 Elton Brand .20 .50
71 Troy Hudson .15 .40
72A Steve Nash Home .50 1.25
72B Steve Nash Away .50 1.25
73 Tony Parker .40 1.00
74 Earl Boykins .15 .40
75 Kerry Kittles .20 .50
76 Shawn Bradley .15 .40
77 Tony Delk .20 .50
78 Zydrunas Ilgauskas .20 .50
79 Doug Christie .20 .50
80 Amare Stoudemire .30 .75
81 Rick Fox .20 .50
82 Brian Skinner .15 .40
83 Jamal Mashburn .20 .50
84 Qyntel Woods .15 .40
85 Rafer Alston .20 .50
86 Derek Anderson .20 .50
87 Andre Miller .20 .50
88 Antoine Walker .25 .60
89 Frank Williams .15 .40
90A Vince Carter Home .50 1.25
90B Vince Carter Away .50 1.25
91 Donnell Harvey .15 .40
92 Raef Lafrentz .15 .40
93 Desmond Mason .20 .50
94 Rodney Rogers .15 .40
95 Juan Dixon .15 .40
96 Kareem Rush .15 .40
97 Bryon Russell .15 .40
98 Shandon Anderson .15 .40
99 Gordan Giricek .15 .40
100 Tim Duncan .60 1.50
101 Zach Randolph .20 .50
102 Malik Allen .15 .40
103 Richard Hamilton .30 .75
104 Maurice Taylor .15 .40
105 Marko Jaric .15 .40
106 Joe Smith .20 .50
107 Peja Stojakovic .20 .50
108 Othella Harrington .15 .40
109 Anthony Carter .15 .40
110 Wally Szczerbiak .20 .50
111 Troy Murphy .15 .40
112 Shareef Abdur-Rahim .25 .60
113 Reggie Miller .50 1.25
114 Vin Baker .15 .40
115 Brian Scalabrine .15 .40
116 Eric Piatkowski .15 .40
117 Cuttino Mobley .15 .40
118 Erick Dampier .15 .40
119 Walter Mccarty .15 .40
120 Caron Butler .20 .50
121 Keyon Dooling .15 .40
122 Michael Redd .25 .60
123 Kenny Anderson .20 .50
124 P.J. Brown .15 .40
125 Devean George .15 .40
126 Joe Johnson .20 .50
127 Adrian Griffin .15 .40
128 Bonzi Wells .15 .40
129 Rasual Butler .15 .40
130 Baron Davis .25 .60
131 Wesley Person .15 .40
132 Shammond Williams .15 .40
133 Tyronn Lue .15 .40
134 Brian Grant .15 .40
135 Elden Campbell .15 .40
136 Glen Rice .15 .40
137 Michael Olowokandi .15 .40
138 Anthony Peeler .15 .40
139 Steven Hunter .15 .40
140 Eddy Curry .15 .40
141 Jerome James .15 .40
142 Travis Best .15 .40
143 Nazr Mohammed .15 .40
144 Tony Battie .15 .40
145 Scot Pollard .15 .40
146 Stanislav Medvedenko .15 .40
147 Jim Jackson .15 .40
148 Marcus Camby .20 .50
149 Marcus Haislip .15 .40
150 Glenn Robinson .20 .50
151 Jerome Williams .15 .40
152 Greg Ostertag .15 .40
153 Stephen Jackson .20 .50
154 David Wesley .15 .40
155 Sam Cassell .30 .75
156 Hedo Turkoglu .20 .50
157 Al Harrington .20 .50
158 John Salmons .15 .40
159 Nikoloz Tskitishvili .15 .40
160 Samaki Walker .15 .40
161 Jake Tsakalidis .15 .40
162 Tim Thomas .15 .40
163 Ronald Murray .15 .40
164 Alonzo Mourning .30 .75
165 Chris Jefferies .15 .40
166 Darius Miles .15 .40
167 Kendall Gill .25 .60
168 Lonny Baxter .15 .40
169 Jonathan Bender .15 .40
170 Antawn Jamison .25 .60
171 Keon Clark .15 .40
172 Chris Wilcox .15 .40
173 Brendan Haywood .15 .40
174 Predrag Drobnjak .15 .40
175 Nene .20 .50
176 Casey Jacobsen .15 .40
177 Marcus Fizer .15 .40
178 Howard Eisley .15 .40
179 Damon Stoudamire .20 .50
180 Gary Payton .40 1.00
181 Shane Battier .20 .50
182 Desagana Diop .15 .40
183 Antonio Davis .20 .50
184 Keith Van Horn .20 .50
185 Corey Maggette .20 .50
186 Jarron Collins .15 .40
187 James Posey .15 .40
188 Latrell Sprewell .30 .75
189 Aaron McKie .15 .40
190 Vlade Divac .25 .60
191 Pat Garrity .15 .40
192 Eric Williams .15 .40
193 Radoslav Nesterovic .15 .40
194 Dan Gadzuric .15 .40
195 Moochie Norris .15 .40
196 Clifford Robinson .15 .40
197 Richard Jefferson .20 .50
198 Lorenzen Wright .15 .40
199 Nick Van Exel .25 .60
200 Gilbert Arenas .25 .60
201 Robert Horry .25 .60
202 Scottie Pippen .60 1.50
203 Jon Barry .15 .40
204 Derrick Coleman .25 .60
205 Ron Mercer .15 .40
206 DeShawn Stevenson .15 .40
207 Ruben Patterson .15 .40
208 Rodney White .15 .40
209 Jamal Crawford .25 .60
210 Jermaine O'Neal .25 .60
211 Eduardo Najera .15 .40
212 Dan Dickau .15 .40
213 Antonio McDyess .20 .50
214 J.R. Bremer .15 .40
215 Dion Glover .15 .40
216 Lamond Murray .15 .40
217 Larry Hughes .20 .50
218 Mike Miller .20 .50
219 Mike Dunleavy .20 .50
220 Karl Malone .50 1.25
221 David West RC .75 2.00
222 Steve Blake RC .50 1.25
223A LeBron James Home RC 75.00 200.00
223B LeBron James Away RC 75.00 200.00
224 Keith Bogans RC .40 1.00
225 Josh Howard RC .60 1.50
226A Chris Kaman Home RC .60 1.50
226B Chris Kaman Away RC .60 1.50
227A Marcus Banks Home RC .40 1.00
227B Marcus Banks Away RC .40 1.00
228A Chris Bosh Home RC 2.00 5.00
228B Chris Bosh Away RC 2.00 5.00
229 Troy Bell RC .40 1.00
230 Luke Walton RC .60 1.50
231 Francisco Elson RC .40 1.00
232 Ndudi Ebi RC .40 1.00
233 Maurice Williams RC .60 1.50
234 Kendrick Perkins RC .50 1.25
235 Dahntay Jones RC .50 1.25
236 Jason Kapono RC .40 1.00
237 Kyle Korver RC .75 2.00
238 Josh Moore RC .40 1.00
239 Travis Hansen RC .40 1.00
240A Carmelo Anthony Blue RC 3.00 8.00
240B Carmelo Anthony White RC 3.00 8.00
241 Keith McLeod RC .40 1.00
242 Zoran Planinic RC .40 1.00
243A Jarvis Hayes Home RC .40 1.00
243B Jarvis Hayes Away RC .40 1.00
244A Mickael Pietrus Home RC .50 1.25
244B Mickael Pietrus Away RC .50 1.25
245A Mike Sweetney Home RC .40 1.00
245B Mike Sweetney Away RC .40 1.00
246 Jerome Beasley RC .40 1.00
247 Zaza Pachulia RC .60 1.50
248 Ben Handlogten RC .40 1.00
249 Torraye Braggs RC .40 1.00
250A Nick Collison White RC .50 1.25
250B Nick Collison Green RC .50 1.25
251 Reece Gaines RC .40 1.00
252A Dwyane Wade Dribble RC 8.00 20.00
252B Dwyane Wade Layup RC 8.00 20.00
253 Devin Brown RC .40 1.00
254 Leandro Barbosa RC .60 1.50
255 Boris Diaw RC .60 1.50
256 Aleksandar Pavlovic RC .50 1.25
257 Udonis Haslem RC .75 2.00
258 Brian Cook RC .40 1.00
259 Maciej Lampe RC .40 1.00
260A T.J. Ford Home RC .50 1.25
260B T.J. Ford Away RC .50 1.25
261 Matt Carroll RC .40 1.00
262 James Jones RC .40 1.00
263 Brandon Hunter RC .40 1.00
264 Luke Ridnour RC .60 1.50
265 Theron Smith RC .40 1.00
266 Jon Stefansson RC .40 1.00
267 Zarko Cabarkapa RC .40 1.00
268 Marquis Daniels RC .50 1.25
269 Willie Green RC .60 1.50
270A Kirk Hinrich Left RC .60 1.50
270B Kirk Hinrich Right RC .60 1.50
271 Linton Johnson RC .40 1.00
272 Travis Outlaw RC .50 1.25
273 James Lang RC .40 1.00
274 Slavko Vranes RC .40 1.00
275A Darko Milicic Home RC .50 1.25
275B Darko Milicic Away RC .50 1.25
276 LeBron James BAZ 75.00 200.00
277 Darko Milicic BAZ .40 1.00
278 Carmelo Anthony BAZ 2.50 6.00
279 Chris Bosh BAZ 1.50 4.00
280 Dwyane Wade BAZ 8.00 20.00
281 Chris Kaman BAZ .50 1.25
282 Kirk Hinrich BAZ .50 1.25
283 T.J. Ford BAZ .40 1.00
284 Mike Sweetney BAZ .30 .75
285 Jarvis Hayes BAZ .30 .75
286 Mickael Pietrus BAZ .40 1.00
287 Nick Collison BAZ .40 1.00
288 Marcus Banks BAZ .30 .75

2003-04 Bazooka Parallel

*PARALLEL SINGLES: .5X TO 1.25X BASE HI
*PARALLEL RCs: .6X TO 1.5X BASE HI
*PARALLEL BAZ. JOE: .75X TO 2X BASE HI
STATED ODDS: 1:1

2003-04 Bazooka Mini

*MINI SINGLES: .6X TO 1.5X BASE HI
*MINI RCs: .5X TO 1.25X BASE HI
*MINI BAZ. JOE: .5X TO 1.25X BASE HI
STATED ODDS: 1:3

2003-04 Bazooka Beginnings

STATED ODDS 1:26
*PARALLEL: .75X TO 2X BASE HI
PARALLEL PRINT RUN 25 SER.#'d SETS
BC Brian Cook 1.50 4.00
CA Carmelo Anthony UER 12.00 30.00
CB Chris Bosh 8.00 20.00
CK Chris Kaman 2.50 6.00
DJ Dahntay Jones 2.00 5.00
DW Dwyane Wade 20.00 50.00
DWE David West 3.00 8.00
JH Jarvis Hayes 1.50 4.00
JHO Josh Howard 2.50 6.00
JK Jason Kapono 1.50 4.00
KH Kirk Hinrich 2.50 6.00
KP Kendrick Perkins 2.00 5.00
LB Leandro Barbosa 2.50 6.00
LR Luke Ridnour 2.50 6.00
LW Luke Walton 2.50 6.00
MB Marcus Banks 1.50 4.00
MP Mickael Pietrus 2.00 5.00
MS Mike Sweetney 1.50 4.00
NC Nick Collison 2.00 5.00
NE Ndudi Ebi 1.50 4.00
RG Reece Gaines 1.50 4.00
TB Troy Bell 1.50 4.00
TF T.J. Ford 2.00 5.00
TO Travis Outlaw 2.00 5.00

2003-04 Bazooka Blasts

ODDS: GROUP A 1:850, GROUP B 1:143
*PARALLEL: 1X TO 2.5X BASE HI
PARALLEL PRINT RUN 25 SER.#'d SETS
JK Jason Kidd D 4.00 10.00
AG Adrian Griffin D 2.00 5.00
AHO Allan Houston C 2.50 6.00
AJ Avery Johnson D 2.00 5.00
AW Antoine Walker D 2.50 6.00
BD Baron Davis C 2.50 6.00
CB Caron Butler D 2.00 5.00
CM Cuttino Mobley C 1.50 4.00
CW Chris Wilcox D 2.00 5.00
DF Derek Fisher B 2.50 6.00
DM Dikembe Mutombo D 3.00 8.00
DW DaJuan Wagner D 2.00 5.00
EN Eduardo Najera D 2.00 5.00
FW Frank Williams D 2.00 5.00
GA Gilbert Arenas B 2.50 6.00
GP Gary Payton B 4.00 10.00
GR Glenn Robinson C 2.00 5.00
HT Hedo Turkoglu D 2.00 5.00
JD Juan Dixon B 2.00 5.00
JJ Joe Johnson B 2.00 5.00
JM Jamal Mashburn D 2.00 5.00
JO Jermaine O'Neal C 2.50 6.00
JR Jason Richardson D 2.50 6.00
JT Jamaal Tinsley D 2.00 5.00
KG Kevin Garnett C 6.00 15.00
KM Karl Malone D 5.00 12.00
KMA Kenyon Martin C 2.50 6.00
KR Kareem Rush D 2.00 5.00
LS Latrell Sprewell D 3.00 8.00
MB Mike Bibby D 2.50 6.00
MF Marcus Fizer B 2.00 5.00
MH Marcus Haislip C 2.00 5.00
MJ Marko Jaric/112 A 2.00 5.00
MP Morris Peterson B 1.50 4.00
MR Michael Redd D 2.50 6.00
N Nene D 2.00 5.00
NT Nikoloz Tskitishvili D 2.00 5.00
PP Paul Pierce D 4.00 10.00
PS Peja Stojakovic B 2.00 5.00
QR Quentin Richardson C 1.50 4.00
QW Qyntel Woods D 2.00 5.00
RA Ray Allen B 4.00 10.00
RJ Richard Jefferson D 2.00 5.00
RW Rasheed Wallace D 3.00 8.00
SAR Shareef Abdur-Rahim B 2.50 6.00
SF Steve Francis C 2.50 6.00
SM Stephon Marbury D 3.00 8.00
SMA Shawn Marion C 2.50 6.00
SN Steve Nash C 5.00 12.00
SO Shaquille O'Neal C 10.00 25.00
TAP Tayshaun Prince/182 A 2.50 6.00
TAW Tariq Abdul-Wahad D 2.00 5.00
TP Tony Parker D 4.00 10.00
VD Vlade Divac C 2.50 6.00
VR Vladimir Radmanovic C 2.00 5.00
WS Wally Szczerbiak B 2.00 5.00
YM Yao Ming D 6.00 15.00
ZI Zydrunas Ilgauskas D 2.00 5.00
ZR Zeljko Rebraca D 2.00 5.00

2003-04 Bazooka Boo-Yah

ODDS: GROUP A 1:850, GROUP B 1:143
*PARALLEL: 1X TO 2.5X BASE HI
PARALLEL PRINT RUN 25 SER.#'d SETS
AM Alonzo Mourning D 3.00 8.00
AS Amare Stoudemire D 3.00 8.00
AW Antoine Walker C 2.50 6.00
BD Baron Davis B 2.50 6.00
BW Ben Wallace B 3.00 8.00
CB Caron Butler C 2.00 5.00
CW Chris Webber B 3.00 8.00
DAM Darius Miles D 2.00 5.00
DG Devean George C 2.00 5.00
DM Dikembe Mutombo B 3.00 8.00
DN Dirk Nowitzki D 6.00 15.00
DW DaJuan Wagner B 2.00 5.00
EC Elden Campbell D 2.00 5.00
EG Eddie Griffin D 2.00 5.00
GA Gilbert Arenas D 2.50 6.00
JO Jermaine O'Neal B 2.50 6.00
JR Jason Richardson C 2.50 6.00
JS Jerry Stackhouse D 3.00 8.00
JT Jason Terry B 2.00 5.00
JW Jerome Williams D 2.00 5.00
KG Kevin Garnett C 6.00 15.00
KM Karl Malone B 5.00 12.00
KMA Kenyon Martin C 2.50 6.00
LO Lamar Odom B 2.00 5.00
LS Latrell Sprewell C 3.00 8.00
MF Michael Finley D 2.50 6.00
MFZ Marcus Fizer C 2.00 5.00
MO Michael Olowokandi D 2.00 5.00
N Nene D 2.00 5.00
NVE Nick Van Exel B 2.50 6.00
PG Pau Gasol D 4.00 10.00
PP Paul Pierce C 4.00 10.00
QR Quentin Richardson B 1.50 4.00
RA Ray Allen B 4.00 10.00
RJ Richard Jefferson C 2.00 5.00
RL Rashard Lewis C 2.00 5.00
RLA Raef Lafrentz A 2.00 5.00
RW Rasheed Wallace D 3.00 8.00
SB Shawn Bradley B 2.00 5.00
SF Steve Francis C 2.50 6.00
SM Shawn Marion C 2.50 6.00
SMA Stephon Marbury C 3.00 8.00
SN Steve Nash B 5.00 12.00
SO Shaquille O'Neal B 10.00 25.00
TC Tyson Chandler/164 A 2.00 5.00
TD Tim Duncan D 6.00 15.00
TMG Tracy McGrady B 4.00 10.00
YM Yao Ming D 6.00 15.00

2003-04 Bazooka Comics

COMPLETE SET (24) 200.00 500.00
STATED ODDS: 1:3 .50 1.25
1 Tracy McGrady .75 2.00
2 Paul Pierce .75 2.00
3 Allen Iverson 1.25 3.00
4 Amare Stoudemire .60 1.50
5 Jason Kidd .75 2.00
6 Allan Houston .50 1.25
7 Shaquille O'Neal 2.00 5.00
8 Kobe Bryant 15.00 40.00
9 Yao Ming 1.25 3.00
10 Tim Duncan 1.25 3.00
11 Ben Wallace .60 1.50
12 Karl Malone 1.00 2.50
13 Kevin Garnett 1.25 3.00
14 Jason Richardson .50 1.25
15 LeBron James 25.00 60.00
16 Darko Milicic .40 1.00
17 Carmelo Anthony 8.00 20.00
18 T.J. Ford .40 1.00
19 Kirk Hinrich .50 1.25
20 Nick Collison .40 1.00
21 Chris Bosh 1.50 4.00
22 Mike Sweetney .30 .75
23 Reece Gaines .30 .75
24 Luke Walton .50 1.25

2003-04 Bazooka Four on One Stickers

COMPLETE SET (55) 60.00 150.00
STATED ODDS 1:4
1 Duncan/Yao/Shaq/KG 1.25 3.00
2 T-Mac/Kobe/Vince/AI 1.50 4.00
3 Pierce/Dirk/C-Web/Mash .50 1.25
4 Kidd/J-Will/Marb/Payton .50 1.25
5 Tinsley/Terry/Nash/Andre .50 1.25
6 B.Wall/J.O'Ne/Grant/Murphy .50 1.25
7 Butler/Amare/Wagnr/Goodn .50 1.25
8 Giricek/Nene/Boozer/J.R. .50 1.25
9 J-Rich/Marian/Mason/Jeffer .50 1.25
10 Houston/Allen/Hudson/Reg .50 1.25
11 Redd/Person/Wesley/Wally .50 1.25
12 Artest/Martin/Christie/Pipp .50 1.25
13 Malone/Juwan/Rash/Brand .50 1.25
14 Parker/Baron/Cassel/Vexel .50 1.25
15 Horn/Bradley/Harpr/Laettnr .50 1.25
16 Gasol/Jaric/Peja/Kirilenko .50 1.25
17 Billi/B.Jack/Rogers/Thomas .50 1.25
18 Theo/Bradley/Ilgas/Griffin .50 1.25
19 M.Mill/Dunl/E.Jones/Finley .50 1.25
20 Swift/Rose/Mo/Odom .50 1.25
21 R.Davis/C.Alex/Lewis/Stack .50 1.25
22 Tyson/Kwme/Woods/Rasho .50 1.25
23 QRich/Rose/Kukoc/Bibby .50 1.25
24 Thomas/Harris/Anf/Gino .50 1.25
25 Prince/Rad/Cheaney/Snow .50 1.25
26 Mutom/A.Will/C.Will/Perkins .50 1.25
27 BArmstr/Speed/Barry/D.Stod .50 1.25
28 Alston/F.Willms/Dixon/Delk .50 1.25
29 Donyell/Ke.Thom/Raef/Fox .50 1.25
30 AWalk/Hamilt/Bonzi/G.Rob .50 1.25
31 Alonzo/Hayw/Divac/Olowo .50 1.25
32 Rush/Randl/George/Curry .50 1.25
33 Rice/Peeler/Horry/Spree .50 1.25
34 Coles/Gadzur/Keon/Wilcox .50 1.25
35 C.Jacob/Sketa/Battier/McDy .50 1.25
36 Arenas/Magg/Miles/Crawfrd .50 1.25
37 Najera/Hedo/Nazr/Tsakilid .50 1.25
38 J.Smith/P.Brwn/Rahim/Jwill .50 1.25
39 Jamison/Fizer/Taylor/Hunter .50 1.25
40 J.John/Diop/Pollard/Salmon .50 1.25
41 Norris/R.Pat/L.Hugh/Keyon .50 1.25
42 Mercer/Eric/Derek/Cutt .50 1.25
43 Boyk/Lue/Eis/Best .50 1.25
44 Battie/James/C.Rob/Damp .50 1.25
45 Piatk/McCar/Garr/Harr .50 1.25
46 Haislip/Gill/Murray/Wright .50 1.25
47 DeShawn/Kitt/Posey/McKie .50 1.25
48 Scalb/K.And/Oster/Shandon .50 1.25
49 A.Dav/J.Coll/A.Griff/J.Jones .50 1.25
50 Lebron/Darko/Melo/Bosh 60.00 150.00
51 Wade/Kaman/Hinr/Ford 4.00 10.00
52 Sweet/Hayes/Pietrus/Collisn .50 1.25
53 Banks/Ridnour/Gaines/Bell .50 1.25
54 West/D.Jones/Outlaw/Cook .50 1.25
55 Ebi/Perkins/Barb/Josh .50 1.25

2003-04 Bazooka Piece of Americana

ODDS: GROUP A 1:850, GROUP B 1:143
*PARALLEL: 1X TO 2.5X BASE HI
PARALLEL PRINT RUN 25 SER.#'d SETS
AD Antonio Davis B 2.00 5.00
AH Allan Houston B 2.50 6.00
AM Alonzo Mourning C 3.00 8.00
AS Amare Stoudemire C 3.00 8.00
BH Brendan Haywood D 2.00 5.00
BM Brad Miller D 2.00 5.00
BW Ben Wallace C 3.00 8.00
CB Carlos Boozer D 2.00 5.00
DA Darrell Armstrong C 2.00 5.00
DD Dan Dickau/150 A 2.00 5.00
DM Darius Miles C 2.00 5.00
DW David Wesley D 2.00 5.00
ES Eric Snow B 2.00 5.00
GH Grant Hill D 3.00 8.00
JJ Jared Jeffries B 2.00 5.00
JT Jamaal Tinsley B 2.00 5.00
LO Lamar Odom/150 A 2.00 5.00
MD Mike Dunleavy D 2.00 5.00
MP Morris Peterson/150 A 1.50 4.00
PG Pat Garrity D 2.00 5.00
SB Shane Battier/44 A 2.00 5.00
SC Sam Cassell B 2.00 5.00
SO Shaquille O'Neal D 10.00 25.00
SS Steve Smith D 2.00 5.00
TD Tim Duncan D 6.00 15.00
TM Troy Murphy B 1.50 4.00
WP Wesley Person D 2.00 5.00

2003-04 Bazooka Signs

ODDS: GROUP A 1:5840; B 1:4328, C 1:2000
CA Carmelo Anthony/100 A 50.00 120.00
FW Frank Williams B 5.00 12.00
KH Kirk Hinrich/100 A 20.00 50.00
SO Shaquille O'Neal C 30.00 80.00

2003-04 Bazooka Stand Ups

COMPLETE SET (4) 1.25 3.00
ONE PERFORATED CARD PER HOBBY BOX
PRICES GIVEN FOR SEPARATED CARDS
NNO Nick Collison .25 .60
NNO T.J. Ford .25 .60
NNO Carmelo Anthony 1.50 4.00
NNO Kirk Hinrich .30 .75

2003-04 Bazooka Tattoos

COMPLETE SET (34) 5.00 12.00
STATED ODDS 1:3
1 Bazooka Logo .30 .75
2 Eastern Conference .30 .75
3 Western Conference .30 .75
4 NBA .30 .75
5 Atlanta Hawks .30 .75
6 Boston Celtics .30 .75
7 Charlotte Bobcats .30 .75
8 Chicago Bulls .30 .75
9 Cleveland Cavaliers .30 .75
10 Dallas Mavericks .30 .75
11 Denver Nuggets .30 .75
12 Detroit Pistons .30 .75
13 Golden State Warriors .30 .75
14 Houston Rockets .30 .75
15 Indiana Pacers .30 .75
16 Los Angeles Clippers .30 .75
17 Los Angeles Lakers .30 .75
18 Memphis Grizzlies .30 .75
19 Miami Heat .30 .75
20 Milwaukee Bucks .30 .75
21 Minnesota Timberwolves .30 .75
22 New Jersey Nets .30 .75
23 New Orleans Hornets .30 .75
24 New York Knicks .30 .75
25 Orlando Magic .30 .75
26 Philadelphia 76ers .30 .75
27 Phoenix Suns .30 .75
28 Portland Trailblazers .30 .75
29 Sacramento Kings .30 .75
30 San Antonio Spurs .30 .75
31 Seattle Supersonics .30 .75
32 Toronto Raptors .30 .75
33 Utah Jazz .30 .75
34 Washington Wizards .30 .75

2004-05 Bazooka

COMP.SET w/o RC's (165) 10.00 25.00
2 Marquis Daniels .25 .60
1 Shaquille O'Neal 1.50 4.00
3 Ben Wallace .50 1.25
4 Jarvis Hayes .25 .60
5 Gerald Wallace .30 .75
6 Fred Jones .25 .60
7 Pau Gasol .60 1.50
8 Latrell Sprewell .50 1.25
9 Steve Francis .40 1.00
10 Mike Bibby .40 1.00
11 Chris Bosh .60 1.50
12 Steve Nash .75 2.00
13 Kirk Hinrich .40 1.00
14 Richard Jefferson .30 .75
15 Zach Randolph .40 1.00
16 Willie Green .40 1.00
17 Al Harrington .30 .75
18 Rashard Lewis .30 .75
19 Ricky Davis .30 .75
20 Dwyane Wade 1.50 4.00
21 Tim Duncan 1.00 2.50
22 Eddy Curry .25 .60
23 Andre Miller .30 .75
24 Chris Wilcox .25 .60
25 Bobby Jackson .30 .75
26 Stephen Jackson .30 .75
27 Shane Battier .30 .75
28 Antawn Jamison .30 .75
29 Brent Barry .25 .60
30 Stephon Marbury .50 1.25
31 Gordan Giricek .25 .60
32 Jamal Mashburn .25 .60
33 Allen Iverson 1.00 2.50
34 Paul Pierce .60 1.50
35 Mike Dunleavy .25 .60
36 Gary Payton .60 1.50
37 Brad Miller .30 .75
38 Eric Snow .25 .60
39 Theo Ratliff .25 .60
40 Richard Hamilton .50 1.25
41 Dirk Nowitzki 1.00 2.50
42 Elton Brand .30 .75
43 Reggie Miller .75 2.00
44 Baron Davis .40 1.00
45 Jerome Williams .25 .60

46 Stromile Swift .25 .60
47 Andrei Kirilenko .30 .75
48 Jason Richardson .40 1.00
49 Larry Hughes .30 .75
50 Yao Ming 1.00 2.50
51 Tim Thomas .25 .60
52 Erick Dampier .25 .60
53 Keith Van Horn .30 .75
54 Grant Hill .50 1.25
55 Shareef Abdur-Rahim .40 1.00
56 Amare Stoudemire .40 1.00
57 David Wesley .25 .60
58 Chris Kaman .30 .75
59 Caron Butler .30 .75
60 Kenyon Martin .40 1.00
61 Ray Allen .60 1.50
62 Jerry Stackhouse .40 1.00
63 Jason Kapono .25 .60
64 Mark Blount .25 .60
65 Hedo Turkoglu .30 .75
66 Carlos Boozer .30 .75
67 Kenny Thomas .25 .60
68 Manu Ginobili .75 2.00
69 Kobe Bryant 3.00 8.00
70 Vince Carter .75 2.00
71 Troy Murphy .30 .75
72 Maurice Taylor .25 .60
73 Earl Boykins .25 .60
74 Boris Diaw .30 .75
75 Kerry Kittles .30 .75
76 Jamaal Tinsley .25 .60
77 Lamar Odom .40 1.00
78 Jamaal Magloire .25 .60
79 Wally Szczerbiak .30 .75
80 Tayshaun Prince .40 1.00
81 Mehmet Okur .30 .75
82 Eddie Jones .40 1.00
83 Voshon Lenard .25 .60
84 Jamal Crawford .40 1.00
85 Marko Jaric .25 .60
86 Ron Mercer .25 .60
87 Steve Smith .30 .75
88 Antoine Walker .40 1.00
89 Kurt Thomas .25 .60
90 Primoz Brezec .25 .60
91 Luke Walton .30 .75
92 Dajuan Wagner .25 .60
93 Luke Ridnour .30 .75
94 Nene .30 .75
95 Josh Howard .30 .75
96 Juwan Howard .30 .75
97 David West .30 .75
98 Jonathan Bender .25 .60
99 Tony Parker .60 1.50
100 LeBron James 12.00 30.00
101 Chris Webber .50 1.25
102 Cuttino Mobley .30 .75
103 Rasheed Wallace .50 1.25
104 Marcus Banks .25 .60
105 Ronald Murray .25 .60
106 Quentin Richardson .25 .60
107 Antonio McDyess .30 .75
108 Sam Cassell .30 .75
109 Allan Houston .40 1.00
110 Leandro Barbosa .30 .75
111 Joe Smith .25 .60
112 Jason Kidd .60 1.50
113 Aleksandar Pavlovic .25 .60
114 Bruce Bowen .30 .75
115 Carmelo Anthony .75 2.00
116 Kwame Brown .25 .60
117 Mickael Pietrus .25 .60
118 Tony Battie .25 .60
119 Joe Johnson .30 .75
120 Damon Stoudamire .40 1.00
121 Kevin Garnett 1.00 2.50
122 Michael Redd .30 .75
123 Doug Christie .30 .75
124 Darrell Armstrong .25 .60
125 James Posey .30 .75
126 Jim Jackson .25 .60
127 Udonis Haslem .30 .75
128 Drew Gooden .25 .60
129 Rasho Nesterovic .25 .60
130 Jermaine O'Neal .30 .75
131 Shawn Marion .40 1.00
132 Samuel Dalembert .25 .60
133 Marcus Camby .30 .75
134 Devean George .25 .60
135 Darius Miles .30 .75
136 Michael Olowokandi .25 .60
137 Mike Miller .30 .75
138 Kareem Rush .25 .60
139 Jalen Rose .30 .75
140 Chauncey Billups .50 1.25
141 Jason Williams .30 .75
142 Derek Fisher .30 .75
143 Donyell Marshall .30 .75
144 Alonzo Mourning .50 1.25
145 T.J. Ford .25 .60
146 Tony Delk .25 .60
147 Gilbert Arenas .40 1.00
148 Glenn Robinson .30 .75
149 Peja Stojakovic .30 .75
150 Tracy McGrady .60 1.50
151 Rafer Alston .25 .60
152 Nazr Mohammed .25 .60
153 Corey Maggette .30 .75
154 Michael Doleac .25 .60
155 Zydrunas Ilgauskas .30 .75
156 Troy Hudson .25 .60
157 Vladimir Radmanovic .25 .60
158 Jason Collins .25 .60
159 Dikembe Mutombo .40 1.00
160 Bonzi Wells .25 .60
161 Jason Terry .30 .75
162 Tyson Chandler .30 .75
163 Desmond Mason .30 .75
164 Carlos Arroyo .25 .60
165 Darko Milicic .25 .60
166 Ben Gordon RC .60 1.50
167 Kevin Martin RC .75 2.00
168 Jackson Vroman RC .40 1.00
169 Delonte West RC .50 1.25
170 Dorell Wright RC .50 1.25
171 Erik Daniels RC .50 1.25
172 Josh Childress RC .40 1.00
173 Anderson Varejao RC .50 1.25
174 Andre Emmett RC .40 1.00
175 Chris Duhon RC .50 1.25
176 Bernard Robinson RC .40 1.00
177 D.J. Mbenga RC .40 1.00
178 Kirk Snyder RC .40 1.00
179 Damien Wilkins RC .50 1.25
180 Andre Iguodala RC 1.00 2.50
181 Nenad Krstic RC .50 1.25
182 Pape Sow RC .40 1.00
183 Maurice Evans RC .60 1.50
184 John Edwards RC .40 1.00
185 Andres Nocioni RC .60 1.50
186 Arthur Johnson RC .50 1.25
187 Beno Udrih RC .50 1.25
188 Andris Biedrins RC .40 1.00
189 Kris Humphries RC .50 1.25
190 Trevor Ariza RC .60 1.50
191 Devin Harris RC .50 1.25
192 J.R. Smith RC .60 1.50
193 Romain Sato RC .40 1.00
194 Lionel Chalmers RC .50 1.25
195 Al Jefferson RC .60 1.50
196 Josh Smith RC .60 1.50
197 Antonio Burks RC .40 1.00
198 Matt Freije RC .40 1.00
199 Justin Reed RC .40 1.00
200 Emeka Okafor RC .50 1.25
201 Sebastian Telfair RC .50 1.25
202 Sasha Vujacic RC .50 1.25
203 Royal Ivey RC .40 1.00
204 Rafael Araujo RC .50 1.25
205 Ibrahim Kutluay RC .60 1.50
206 Pavel Podkolzin RC .40 1.00
207 Jared Reiner RC .60 1.50
208 Luis Flores RC .50 1.25
209 Robert Swift RC .40 1.00
210 Shaun Livingston RC .60 1.50
211 Peter John Ramos RC .40 1.00
212 Luke Jackson RC .40 1.00
213 Luol Deng RC .60 1.50
214 Jameer Nelson RC .60 1.50
215 Tony Allen RC .60 1.50
216 Josh Davis RC .60 1.50
217 Yuta Tabuse RC .60 1.50
218 Donta Smith RC .40 1.00
219 David Harrison RC .40 1.00
220 Dwight Howard RC 2.00 5.00

2004-05 Bazooka Gold

*GOLD: .75X TO 2X BASE CARD HI
STATED ODDS ONE PER PACK
69 Kobe Bryant 8.00 20.00

2004-05 Bazooka Mini

*MINI SINGLES: .5X TO 1.25X BASE HI
*MINI RC's: .6X TO 1.5X BASE HI
STATED ODDS ONE PER PACK

2004-05 Bazooka 4-on-1 Stickers

COMPLETE SET (55) 12.50 30.00
1 Shaq/Okafor/Kobe/Iggy .75 2.00
2 B.Wall/Duncan/Yao/Damp .75 2.00
3 Brand/Duhon/Battier/Dunlvy .50 1.25
4 Marbry/Livingstn/Kidd/Bassy .50 1.25
5 Webb/Rose/Howrd/Crawfrd .50 1.25
6 Garnett/T-Mac/Bron/J.O'N 1.50 4.00
7 Vince/Jones/J-Rich/Mason .75 2.00
8 Gasol/Dirk/AK47/Peja .50 1.25
9 Melo/Artest/Dalem/Rip .50 1.25
10 Boozer/Redd/Mobley/Lewis .50 1.25
11 Alston/Arroyo/Williams/Nash .50 1.25
12 RJeff/Waltn/DStoud/Bibby .50 1.25
13 Wilcox/Frncis/Jamisn/Stack .50 1.25
14 Wade/Hinrich/Al/Arenas 1.00 2.50
15 S.Abdur/Nazr/Hedo/Okur .50 1.25
16 Wallace/Martin/Spree/Glove .50 1.25
17 Wright/Daniels/L.Rid/Nelson .50 1.25
18 Howard/Brown/Kandi/Smith .75 2.00
19 Miller/Mash/Cassell/Jackson .50 1.25
20 Amare/Curry/Z.Rand/Prince .50 1.25
21 Magl/Kaman/Chand/Camby .50 1.25
22 Wilkins/Swift/Harrisn/Ramos .50 1.25
23 Parker/Gordon/Miller/Harris .75 2.00
24 Bosh/Odom/Miles/Marion .50 1.25
25 L.Jack/Vrmn/B.Jack/S.Jack .50 1.25
26 Pierce/Davis/Magg/Terry .50 1.25
27 Thomas/Deng/Miller/Walker .60 1.50
28 K.Hum/Murphy/Araujo/Miller .50 1.25
29 Johnsn/Hayes/Green/Butler .50 1.25
30 Thomas/Nene/BigAl/Varejao .60 1.50
31 T-Hud/Flip/Banks/Boykins .50 1.25
32 Blount/Battie/Rasho/Ilgausk .50 1.25
33 Emmett/Allen/Houston/Childr .50 1.25
34 Q-Rich/Hughes/Davis/Wall .50 1.25
35 K.Van-H/Darko/Swift/McDy .50 1.25
36 Hwrd/Al Har/Bender/Pietrus .50 1.25
37 Smith/Allen/Vujacic/Martin .75 2.00
38 Snyder/Smith/Ber.Rob/West .50 1.25
39 Rush/Ariza/Podkolz/ZO .50 1.25
40 Szcz./Barry/Giricek/Kapono .50 1.25
41 Bowen/Snow/Kittles/Tinsley .50 1.25
42 Thmas/Haslm/Goodn/Manu .50 1.25
43 Jaric/Wagner/Sato/Chalmer .50 1.25
44 George/Willims/West/Posey .50 1.25
45 Robnsn/C.Billp/Fish/Donyell .60 1.50
46 Doleac/Theo/Krstic/Mbenga .50 1.25
47 Barbosa/Wsley/Jones/Diaw .50 1.25
48 Biedrins/Johnson/Udrih/Yuta .75 2.00
49 Vu/Christie/Armstrng/Ford .50 1.25
50 Wells/Taylor/Smith/Delk .50 1.25
51 Reiner/Flores/Burks/Freije .50 1.25
52 Zaur/Mercr/Nconi/VladRad .50 1.25
53 Sow/Evans/Edwards/Ivey .50 1.25
54 Hill/Collins/Mutombo/Davis .50 1.25
55 Reed/Kutluay/Daniels/Smith .50 1.25

2004-05 Bazooka Admissions

GROUP A ODDS 1:927
GROUP B ODDS 1:46
AE Andre Emmett B 1.25 3.00
AI Andre Iguodala A 3.00 8.00
AJ Al Jefferson B 2.00 5.00
AV Anderson Varejao B 1.50 4.00
BG Ben Gordon B 2.00 5.00
DH Devin Harris A 1.50 4.00
DW Dorell Wright B 1.50 4.00
EO Emeka Okafor B 1.50 4.00
JC Josh Childress B 1.25 3.00
JN Jameer Nelson B 2.00 5.00
JS Josh Smith B 2.00 5.00
KH Kris Humphries B 1.50 4.00
KM Kevin Martin B 2.50 6.00
KS Kirk Snyder B 1.25 3.00
LD Luol Deng B 2.00 5.00
LJ Luke Jackson B 1.25 3.00
SL Shaun Livingston B 2.00 5.00
ST Sebastian Telfair B 1.50 4.00
TA Tony Allen B 2.00 5.00
DHA David Harrison B 1.25 3.00
DHO Dwight Howard B 6.00 15.00
DWE Delonte West B 1.50 4.00
JRS J.R. Smith B 2.00 5.00

2004-05 Bazooka Adventures

GROUP A ODDS 1:515
GROUP B ODDS 1:52
BD Baron Davis B 2.50 6.00
CA Carmelo Anthony B 5.00 12.00
CB Carlos Boozer A 2.00 5.00
CM Cuttino Mobley B 2.00 5.00
FM Frank Williams B 2.00 5.00
GP Gary Payton B 4.00 10.00
JK Jason Kidd B 4.00 10.00
JM Jamaal Magloire A 2.00 5.00
JM2 Jamal Mashburn B 2.00 5.00
JO Jermaine O'Neal A 2.00 5.00
JS Joe Smith B 2.00 5.00
KH Kirk Hinrich B 2.50 6.00
MB Mike Bibby B 2.50 6.00
MG Manu Ginobili A 5.00 12.00
MP Morris Peterson B 2.00 5.00
PS Peja Stojakovic B 2.00 5.00
RJ Richard Jefferson B 2.00 5.00
SF Steve Francis B 2.50 6.00
SO Shaquille O'Neal B 10.00 25.00
TD Tim Duncan B 6.00 15.00
YM Yao Ming B 6.00 15.00
ZR Zach Randolph B 2.50 6.00

2004-05 Bazooka Back-Up

GROUP A ODDS 1:849
GROUP B ODDS 1:43
N Nene B 2.50 6.00
AM Antonio McDyess B 2.50 6.00
AP Aleksandar Pavlovic B 2.00 5.00
BD Boris Diaw B 2.50 6.00
CK Chris Kaman B 2.50 6.00
DC Derrick Coleman B 2.50 6.00
DF Derek Fisher B 2.50 6.00
DM Dikembe Mutombo B 3.00 8.00
DW David Wesley B 2.00 5.00
GR Glenn Robinson B 2.50 6.00
HG Horace Grant B 2.00 5.00
JC Jason Collins B 2.00 5.00
JJ Jim Jackson B 2.50 6.00
JK Jason Kapono B 2.00 5.00
MJ Marko Jaric B 2.00 5.00
MM Mike Miller B 2.50 6.00
PG Pat Garrity B 2.00 5.00
SP Scot Pollard B 2.00 5.00
TC Tyson Chandler B 2.50 6.00
VL Voshon Lenard B 2.00 5.00
VR Vladimir Radmanovic B 2.00 5.00
DWE David West B 2.50 6.00

2004-05 Bazooka Breakaway

GROUP A ODDS 1:363
GROUP B ODDS 1:18
AF Anfernee Hardaway B 6.00 15.00
AI Allen Iverson B 6.00 15.00
AS Amare Stoudemire A 2.50 6.00
AW Antoine Walker B 2.50 6.00
BD Baron Davis B 2.50 6.00
BW Ben Wallace B 3.00 8.00
CA Chris Andersen B 2.50 6.00
CB Chris Bosh B 4.00 10.00
DM Desmond Mason B 2.00 5.00
DN Dirk Nowitzki B 6.00 15.00
EB Elton Brand A 2.00 5.00
JR Jason Richardson B 2.50 6.00
JS Jerry Stackhouse A 2.50 6.00
KH Kirk Hinrich B 2.50 6.00
LS Latrell Sprewell B 3.00 8.00
MJ Marko Jaric B 2.00 5.00
MR Michael Redd B 2.00 5.00
PG Pau Gasol B 4.00 10.00
PP Paul Pierce B 4.00 10.00
RA Ray Allen B 3.00 8.00
RH Richard Hamilton B 3.00 8.00
RJ Richard Jefferson B 2.00 5.00
SF Steve Francis B 2.50 6.00
SO Shaquille O'Neal B 10.00 25.00
TD Tim Duncan B 6.00 15.00
TM Tracy McGrady A 4.00 10.00
TP Tayshaun Prince B 2.50 6.00
UH Udonis Haslem B 1.50 4.00
YM Yao Ming B 6.00 15.00
SMA Stephon Marbury B 3.00 8.00
TOP Tony Parker B 2.00 5.00

2004-05 Bazooka Comics

COMPLETE SET (24) 40.00 100.00
1 Tracy McGrady 1.00 2.50
2 Peja Stojakovic .50 1.25
3 Kevin Garnett 1.50 4.00
4 Ben Wallace .75 2.00
5 Stephon Marbury .75 2.00
6 Michael Redd .50 1.25
7 Kenyon Martin .60 1.50
8 Carmelo Anthony 8.00 20.00
9 Jermaine O'Neal .50 1.25
10 LeBron James 30.00 80.00
11 Zach Randolph .60 1.50
12 Vince Carter 1.25 3.00
13 Andrei Kirilenko .50 1.25
14 Pau Gasol 1.00 2.50
15 Steve Francis .60 1.50
16 Dwight Howard 2.00 5.00
17 Emeka Okafor .50 1.25
18 Ben Gordon .60 1.50
19 Shaun Livingston .60 1.50
20 Devin Harris .50 1.25
21 Luol Deng .60 1.50
22 Andre Iguodala 1.00 2.50
23 Sebastian Telfair .50 1.25

2004-05 Bazooka Signs

NO ODDS GIVEN
AB Andris Biedrins B 2.50 6.00
AJ Al Jefferson B 4.00 10.00
BG Ben Gordon B 4.00 10.00
DH Devin Harris B 3.00 8.00
EO Emeka Okafor C 3.00 8.00
JC Josh Childress B 2.50 6.00
JS Josh Smith B 4.00 10.00
LD Luol Deng B 4.00 10.00
ST Sebastian Telfair B 3.00 8.00
TD Tim Duncan A 500.00 1,000.00

2005-06 Bazooka

COMPLETE SET (220) 15.00 40.00
1 Gilbert Arenas .25 .60
2 Josh Smith .20 .50
3 Carlos Boozer .20 .50
4 Al Jefferson .15 .40
5 Jalen Rose .20 .50
6 Primoz Brezec .15 .40
7 Rashard Lewis .20 .50
8 Ben Gordon .20 .50
9 Tony Parker .40 1.00
10 Drew Gooden .20 .50
11 Mike Bibby .25 .60
12 Josh Howard .20 .50
13 Sebastian Telfair .20 .50
14 Earl Boykins .15 .40
15 Joe Johnson .20 .50
16 Rasheed Wallace .25 .60
17 Marc Jackson .15 .40
18 Baron Davis .25 .60
19 Dwight Howard .30 .75
20 Tracy McGrady .40 1.00
21 Trevor Ariza .15 .40
22 David Harrison .15 .40
23 J.R. Smith .25 .60
24 Chris Kaman .20 .50
25 Richard Jefferson .20 .50
26 Chris Mihm .15 .40
27 Sam Cassell .20 .50
28 Mike Miller .20 .50
29 Joe Smith .20 .50
30 Dwyane Wade .50 1.25
31 Tony Allen .15 .40
32 Antawn Jamison .20 .50
33 Eddy Curry .15 .40
34 Rafael Araujo .15 .40
35 Jerry Stackhouse .20 .50
36 Manu Ginobili .50 1.25
37 Antonio McDyess .20 .50
38 Zach Randolph .25 .60
39 Mike James .15 .40
40 Chris Webber .30 .75
41 Bobby Simmons .15 .40
42 Jamal Crawford .25 .60
43 Pau Gasol .40 1.00
44 Brian Scalabrine .15 .40
45 Desmond Mason .15 .40
46 Tyronn Lue .15 .40
47 Andrei Kirilenko .20 .50
48 Luke Ridnour .20 .50
49 Gerald Wallace .20 .50
50 LeBron James 2.00 5.00
51 Peja Stojakovic .20 .50
52 Andre Miller .20 .50
53 Quentin Richardson .15 .40
54 Mike Dunleavy .15 .40
55 Steve Francis .25 .60
56 Stephen Jackson .20 .50
57 P.J. Brown .15 .40
58 Caron Butler .20 .50
59 Keith Van Horn .20 .50
60 Shaquille O'Neal .75 2.00
61 Josh Childress .15 .40
62 Michael Doleac .15 .40
63 Lamar Odom .20 .50
64 Stephon Marbury .30 .75
65 Chris Duhon .15 .40
66 Shaun Livingston .20 .50
67 Eric Snow .15 .40
68 Travis Outlaw .20 .50
69 Ron Artest .20 .50
70 Emeka Okafor .20 .50
71 Chauncey Billups .30 .75
72 Jason Williams .40 1.00
73 Jameer Nelson .15 .40
74 Eduardo Najera .15 .40
75 Speedy Claxton .15 .40
76 Kirk Snyder .15 .40
77 Rafer Alston .20 .50
78 Kobe Bryant 2.00 5.00
79 Michael Redd .20 .50
80 Tim Duncan .60 1.50
81 Tayshaun Prince .25 .60
82 Brendan Haywood .15 .40
83 Kyle Korver .20 .50
84 Tony Delk .15 .40
85 Luol Deng .20 .50
86 Elton Brand .20 .50
87 Jason Richardson .25 .60
88 Antoine Walker .20 .50
89 Ray Allen .40 1.00
90 Yao Ming .50 1.25
91 Damon Jones .15 .40
92 Anderson Varejao .15 .40
93 Kurt Thomas .15 .40
94 Latrell Sprewell .25 .60
95 Cuttino Mobley .15 .40
96 Chris Wilcox .15 .40
97 Devin Harris .15 .40
98 Jared Jeffries .15 .40
99 Nenad Krstic .15 .40
100 Steve Nash .50 1.25
101 Reggie Evans .15 .40
102 Ben Wallace .30 .75
103 Allen Iverson .50 1.25
104 Bruce Bowen .20 .50
105 Paul Pierce .40 1.00
106 Shareef Abdur-Rahim .25 .60
107 Vladimir Radmanovic .15 .40
108 Michael Finley .25 .60
109 Brent Barry .20 .50
110 Carmelo Anthony .40 1.00
111 Andre Iguodala .25 .60
112 Shane Battier .20 .50
113 Richard Hamilton .30 .75
114 Kenny Thomas .15 .40
115 Tyson Chandler .20 .50
116 Jim Jackson .15 .40
117 David Wesley .15 .40
118 Grant Hill .40 1.00
119 Wally Szczerbiak .20 .50
120 Dirk Nowitzki .60 1.50
121 Udonis Haslem .15 .40
122 Jason Hart .15 .40
123 Marcus Camby .20 .50
124 Kirk Hinrich .20 .50
125 Jermaine O'Neal .20 .50
126 Derek Fisher .25 .60
127 Donyell Marshall .15 .40
128 Darius Miles .15 .40
129 Kenyon Martin .20 .50
130 Jason Kidd .40 1.00
131 Marquis Daniels .15 .40
132 Kevin Garnett .60 1.50
133 Juwan Howard .20 .50
134 Shawn Marion .20 .50
135 Morris Peterson .15 .40
136 Kevin Martin .20 .50
137 Gary Payton .40 1.00
138 Maurice Williams .20 .50
139 Eddie Jones .20 .50
140 Vince Carter .50 1.25
141 Lorenzen Wright .15 .40
142 Dan Dickau .15 .40
143 Chucky Atkins .15 .40
144 Mike Sweetney .15 .40
145 Corey Maggette .20 .50
146 Hedo Turkoglu .20 .50
147 Jamaal Tinsley .15 .40
148 Samuel Dalembert .15 .40
149 Bob Sura .15 .40
150 Amare Stoudemire .25 .60
151 Troy Murphy .15 .40
152 Joel Przybilla .15 .40
153 Carlos Arroyo .15 .40
154 Brad Miller .20 .50
155 Jason Terry .20 .50
156 Beno Udrih .15 .40
157 Zydrunas Ilgauskas .20 .50
158 Nick Collison .15 .40
159 Andres Nocioni .15 .40
160 Chris Bosh .30 .75
161 Brevin Knight .15 .40
162 Mehmet Okur .15 .40
163 Ricky Davis .20 .50
164 Larry Hughes .20 .50
165 Al Harrington .20 .50
166 Chris Paul RC 3.00 8.00
167 Danny Granger RC .60 1.50
168 Jarrett Jack RC .60 1.50
169 Wayne Simien RC .40 1.00
170 Deron Williams RC 1.00 2.50
171 Ryan Gomes RC .50 1.25
172 Daniel Ewing RC .50 1.25
173 Sean May RC .40 1.00
174 Alan Anderson RC .40 1.00
175 Hakim Warrick RC .50 1.25
176 Francisco Garcia RC .40 1.00
177 Nate Robinson RC .60 1.50
178 Luther Head RC .40 1.00
179 Joey Graham RC .50 1.25
180 Marvin Williams RC .60 1.50
181 Antoine Wright RC .50 1.25
182 Andrew Bynum RC .50 1.25
183 Johan Petro RC .40 1.00
184 Louis Williams RC 1.50 4.00
185 Andray Blatche RC .60 1.50
186 Sarunas Jasikevicius RC .60 1.50
187 Ike Diogu RC .40 1.00
188 Channing Frye RC .50 1.25
189 Julius Hodge RC .40 1.00
190 Rashad McCants RC .40 1.00
191 Yaroslav Korolev RC .40 1.00
192 C.J. Miles RC .50 1.25
193 Brandon Bass RC .50 1.25
194 Travis Diener RC .40 1.00
195 Monta Ellis RC .75 2.00
196 Linas Kleiza RC .50 1.25
197 Gerald Green RC .60 1.50
198 Jason Maxiell RC .50 1.25
199 David Lee RC .60 1.50
200 Andrew Bogut RC .75 2.00
201 Salim Stoudamire RC .50 1.25
202 Raymond Felton RC .50 1.25
203 Martell Webster RC .50 1.25
204 Chris Taft RC .40 1.00
205 Charlie Villanueva RC .50 1.25
206 Lawrence Roberts RC .40 1.00
207 Ersan Ilyasova RC .50 1.25
208 Martynas Andriuskevicius RC .40 1.00
209 Bracey Wright RC .40 1.00
210 Von Wafer RC .40 1.00
211 Eddie Basden RC .40 1.00
212 Dijon Thompson RC .40 1.00
213 Robert Whaley RC .40 1.00
214 Matt Walsh RC .60 1.50
215 Ricky Sanchez RC .60 1.50
216 Jay-Z 1.25 3.00
217 Shannon Elizabeth .75 2.00
218 Christie Brinkley .75 2.00
219 Jenny McCarthy .75 2.00
220 Carmen Electra .75 2.00

2005-06 Bazooka Gold

*1-165 GOLD: .6X TO 1.5X BASE HI
*166-220 GOLD: .75X TO 2X BASE HI
STATED ODDS ONE PER PACK

2005-06 Bazooka 4-on-1 Stickers

STATED ODDS 1:4
1 Nash/Okafor/Gordn/BigBen .50 1.25
2 J.O'Neal/Arena/Smmns/Rndlph .50 1.25
3 JshSmith/J-Rich/B.Barry/Mason .50 1.25
4 Al/Kobe/LeBron/Amare 1.50 4.00
5 Dirk/T-Mac/Pierce/Wade .75 2.00
6 R.Allen/Q-Rich/Redd/D.Jones .50 1.25
7 Shaq/Duncan/KG/Yao 1.25 3.00
8 Parker/Marbury/Hinrich/Telfair .50 1.25
9 Bosh/R.Lewis/Sheed/Jamison .50 1.25
10 May/Felton/Mv.Wllms/McCants .50 1.25
11 Webb/Big Al/D.Howard/Brand .50 1.25
12 R.Davis/Artest/Spree/K-Martin .50 1.25
13 Prince/Marion/Manu/AK-47 .50 1.25
14 Scala/Brezec/Araujo/Kaman .50 1.25
15 Rose/M.Millr/G.Wlice/SJcksn .50 1.25
16 K.Thomas/Reef/Wilcox/Boozer .50 1.25
17 A.Hrrngtn/Magg/Donyell/Kn.Thomas .50 1.25
18 Dunlvy/Varjao/Chldrss/Lvngstn .50 1.25
19 B.Davis/Bibby/A.Millr/Francis .50 1.25
20 Peja/Billups/A.Wlkr/Szcz .50 1.25
21 JayZ/Vince/Kidd/R.Jeffrsn 2.50 6.00
22 Paul/Deron/N.Rbnsn/J.Jack 1.25 3.00
23 Przy/Z.Ilg/Brd.Miller/Krstic .50 1.25
24 Bogut/Frye/Bynum/Blatche .75 2.00
25 Battier/Goodn/Evans/Sweet .50 1.25
26 Wesley/Hughes/Glove/Bowen .50 1.25
27 Marquis/Jeffries/Snydr/Ariza .50 1.25
28 Boykins/Lue/Alston/Arroyo .50 1.25
29 Chandlr/Collison/Okur/L.Wright .50 1.25
30 Haywd/Haslem/Ju.Hwrd/Jjax .50 1.25
31 Hill/Melo/Iggy/Jo.Johnson .50 1.25
32 Camby/Dalemb/Taft/Villnva .50 1.25
33 S.Eliz/C.Brink/J.McCr/Elektra 1.25 3.00
34 Green/Hodge/An.Wright/F.Garcia .50 1.25
35 Crawf/Stack/JDub/Jameer .50 1.25
36 Rip/E.Jones/JR.Smith/T.Allen .50 1.25
37 Eddy/M.Jackson/Mihm/Harrison .50 1.25
38 Odom/McDyess/Pau/Deng .50 1.25
39 Miles/Mobley/Finley/Butler .50 1.25
40 Jo.Smith/Ncni/Jo.Hwrd/Korver .50 1.25
41 Martell/Salim/Head/D.Ewing .50 1.25
42 Ridnour/Cssll/M.Jms/Duhon .50 1.25
43 Lee/Warrick/Grangr/Graham .50 1.25
44 Terry/Beno/Dickau/Atkins .50 1.25
45 Devin/Speed/Kv.Mrtn/Mc.Will .50 1.25
46 A.And/Kleiza/Maxiell/Simien .60 1.50
47 Gomes/Jasik/Korolv/Diener .50 1.25
48 T.Murphy/VanH/Doleac/Hedo .50 1.25
49 Fisher/Snow/Sura/Knight .50 1.25
50 Delk/L.Wllms/C.Miles/Ellis .75 2.00
51 Outlaw/Hart/MoPete/Tinsley .50 1.25
52 P.Brown/Radman/Najera/Krstic .50 1.25
53 May/Petro/Diogu/Bass .40 1.00
54 Bogut/Duncn/Shaq/Mv.Willms .60 1.50
55 Wade/Al/JayZ/Amare 2.50 6.00

2005-06 Bazooka All-Access Relics

STATED ODDS 1:24
AW Antoine Wright 2.00 5.00
CF Channing Frye 2.00 5.00
CP Chris Paul 8.00 20.00
CV Charlie Villanueva 2.00 5.00
DG Danny Granger 2.50 6.00
DL David Lee 2.50 6.00
DW Deron Williams 4.00 10.00
FG Francisco Garcia 1.50 4.00
GG Gerald Green 2.50 6.00
HW Hakim Warrick 2.00 5.00
JG Joey Graham 2.00 5.00
JH Julius Hodge 1.50 4.00
JJ Jarrett Jack 2.50 6.00
JM Jason Maxiell 2.00 5.00
LH Luther Head 1.50 4.00
ME Monta Ellis 3.00 8.00
MW Martell Webster 2.00 5.00
NR Nate Robinson 2.50 6.00
RF Raymond Felton 2.00 5.00
RG Ryan Gomes 2.00 5.00
RM Rashad McCants 1.50 4.00
SJ Sarunas Jasikevicius 2.50 6.00
SM Sean May 1.50 4.00
WS Wayne Simien 1.50 4.00
ABO Andrew Bogut 3.00 8.00

2005-06 Bazooka All-Star Relics

STATED ODDS 1:46
AJ Antawn Jamison Shirt 2.50 6.00
BU Beno Udrih Shirt 2.00 5.00
BW Ben Wallace Warm 4.00 10.00
CA Chris Andersen Shorts 3.00 8.00
DH Dwight Howard Warm 4.00 10.00
EB Earl Boykins Warm 2.00 5.00
EO Emeka Okafor Shorts 2.50 6.00
GH Grant Hill Warm 5.00 12.00
JH Josh Howard Shorts 2.50 6.00
KH Kirk Hinrich Warm 2.50 6.00
KK Kyle Korver Shorts 2.50 6.00
LR Luke Ridnour 2.50 6.00
MG Manu Ginobili Warm 6.00 15.00
RA Ray Allen Shirt 5.00 12.00
RD Ronald Dupree 2.00 5.00
SM Shawn Marion Warm 2.50 6.00
SO Shaquille O'Neal Shorts 10.00 25.00
UH Udonis Haslem Shirt 2.00 5.00
YM Yao Ming Warm 6.00 15.00
AJE Al Jefferson Shorts 2.00 5.00

2005-06 Bazooka Blog Squad Relics

STATED ODDS 1:37
AJ Al Jefferson 2.00 5.00
AN Andres Nocioni 2.00 5.00
AV Anderson Varejao 2.00 5.00
CA Carlos Arroyo 2.00 5.00
CB Caron Butler 2.50 6.00
CW Chris Wilcox 2.00 5.00
DW Dwyane Wade 6.00 15.00
GW Gerald Wallace 2.50 6.00
JC Josh Childress 2.00 5.00
JJ Joe Johnson 2.50 6.00
MD Marquis Daniels 2.00 5.00
NC Nick Collison 2.00 5.00
RA Ray Allen 5.00 12.00
RJ Richard Jefferson 2.50 6.00
SL Shaun Livingston 2.50 6.00
SO Shaquille O'Neal 10.00 25.00
ST Sebastian Telfair 2.50 6.00
UH Udonis Haslem 2.00 5.00
YM Yao Ming 6.00 15.00
DWE Delonte West 2.00 5.00
DWR Dorell Wright 2.00 5.00
MDU Mike Dunleavy 2.00 5.00
RAL Rafer Alston 2.50 6.00
RAR Ron Artest 2.50 6.00
SAR Shareef Abdur-Rahim 3.00 8.00

2005-06 Bazooka Comics

COMPLETE SET (24) 10.00 25.00
STATED ODDS 1:4
1 Dwyane Wade 1.00 2.50
2 Steve Nash 1.00 2.50
3 Josh Smith .40 1.00
4 Emeka Okafor .40 1.00
5 Gilbert Arenas .50 1.25
6 Tim Duncan 1.25 3.00
7 Grant Hill .75 2.00
8 Ben Gordon .40 1.00
9 Dirk Nowitzki 1.25 3.00
10 Shaquille O'Neal 1.50 4.00
11 Ray Allen .75 2.00
12 Chris Bosh .60 1.50
13 Jason Richardson .50 1.25
14 Allen Iverson 1.00 2.50
15 Amare Stoudemire .50 1.25
16 LeBron James 4.00 10.00
17 Carmelo Anthony .75 2.00
18 Manu Ginobili 1.00 2.50
19 Andrew Bogut .60 1.50
20 Marvin Williams .50 1.25
21 Deron Williams .75 2.00
22 Raymond Felton .40 1.00
23 Channing Frye .40 1.00
24 Sean May .30 .75

2005-06 Bazooka Minis

*MINI STARS: .4X TO 1X BASE HI
*MINI RCs: .6X TO 1.5X HI
STATED ODDS ONE PER PACK

2005-06 Bazooka Power Relics

STATED ODDS 1:29
AK Andrei Kirilenko 2.50 6.00
BG Ben Gordon 2.50 6.00
BJ Bobby Jackson 2.50 6.00
BW Bonzi Wells 2.00 5.00
CA Carmelo Anthony 5.00 12.00
CB Carlos Boozer 2.50 6.00
DG Drew Gooden 2.50 6.00
DH Dwight Howard 4.00 10.00
DM Desmond Mason Shirt 2.00 5.00
EB Elton Brand 2.50 6.00
EO Emeka Okafor 2.50 6.00
JK Jason Kidd 5.00 12.00
JM Jamaal Magloire 2.00 5.00
JO Jermaine O'Neal 2.50 6.00
JR Jalen Rose 2.50 6.00
JS Josh Smith 2.50 6.00
LD Luol Deng 2.50 6.00
LH Larry Hughes 2.50 6.00
PG Pau Gasol 5.00 12.00
PS Peja Stojakovic 2.50 6.00
RA Rafael Araujo 2.00 5.00
RL Rashard Lewis 2.50 6.00
RM Ronald Murray 2.00 5.00
SF Steve Francis 3.00 8.00
SO Shaquille O'Neal 10.00 25.00
TD Tim Duncan 8.00 20.00
ZR Zach Randolph 3.00 8.00
CBO Chris Bosh 4.00 10.00
JRS J.R. Smith 3.00 8.00
KBR Kobe Bryant 40.00 100.00

2005-06 Bazooka Signs

STATED ODDS 1:236
AB Andrew Bogut 6.00 15.00
AI Allen Iverson 75.00 150.00
CA Carmelo Anthony 20.00 50.00
CB Christie Brinkley 40.00 80.00
DW Dwyane Wade 30.00 80.00
EO Emeka Okafor 5.00 12.00
GG Gerald Green 6.00 15.00
JM Jenny McCarthy 60.00 120.00
JN Jameer Nelson 5.00 12.00
JZ Jay-Z 500.00 1,000.00
ME Monta Ellis 8.00 20.00
RF Raymond Felton 6.00 15.00
SE Shannon Elizabeth 60.00 120.00
SM Stephon Marbury 8.00 20.00
SO Shaquille O'Neal 40.00 100.00
DWI Deron Williams 12.00 30.00
SMA Sean May 5.00 12.00

2005-06 Bazooka Window Clings

STATED ODDS 1:4
1 Atlanta Hawks .60 1.50
2 Boston Celtics .60 1.50
3 Charlotte Bobcats .60 1.50
4 Chicago Bulls .60 1.50
5 Cleveland Cavaliers .60 1.50
6 Dallas Mavericks .60 1.50
7 Denver Nuggets .60 1.50
8 Detroit Pistons .60 1.50
9 Golden State Warriors .60 1.50
10 Houston Rockets .60 1.50
11 Indiana Pacers .60 1.50
12 Los Angeles Clippers .60 1.50
13 Los Angeles Lakers .60 1.50
14 Memphis Grizzlies .60 1.50
15 Miami Heat .60 1.50
16 Milwaukee Bucks .60 1.50
17 Minnesota Timberwolves .60 1.50
18 New Jersey Nets .60 1.50
19 New Orleans Hornets .60 1.50
20 New York Knicks .60 1.50
21 Orlando Magic .60 1.50
22 Philadelphia 76ers .60 1.50
23 Phoenix Suns .60 1.50
24 Portland Trail Blazers .60 1.50
25 Sacramento Kings .60 1.50
26 San Antonio Spurs .60 1.50
27 Seattle SuperSonics .60 1.50
28 Toronto Raptors .60 1.50
29 Utah Jazz .60 1.50
30 Washington Wizards .60 1.50

1998-99 Black Diamond

COMPLETE SET (120) 40.00 80.00
COMPLETE SET w/o RC (90) 20.00 40.00
RC STATED ODDS 1:4 HOB/RET
1 Michael Jordan 3.00 8.00
2 Michael Jordan 3.00 8.00
3 Michael Jordan 3.00 8.00
4 Michael Jordan 3.00 8.00
5 Michael Jordan 3.00 8.00
6 Michael Jordan 3.00 8.00
7 Michael Jordan 3.00 8.00
8 Michael Jordan 3.00 8.00
9 Michael Jordan 3.00 8.00
10 Michael Jordan 3.00 8.00
11 Michael Jordan 3.00 8.00

12 Michael Jordan 3.00 8.00
13 Michael Jordan 3.00 8.00
14 Dikembe Mutombo .50 1.25
15 Steve Smith .25 .60
16 Mookie Blaylock .25 .60
17 Antoine Walker .30 .75
18 Kenny Anderson .25 .60
19 Ron Mercer .25 .60
20 Glen Rice .30 .75
21 Derrick Coleman .25 .60
22 Michael Jordan 1.50 4.00
23 Toni Kukoc .30 .75
24 Brent Barry .25 .60
25 Brevin Knight .20 .50
26 Derek Anderson .25 .60
27 Shawn Kemp .50 1.25
28 Shawn Bradley .20 .50
29 Michael Finley .30 .75
30 Nick Van Exel .30 .75
31 Chauncey Billups .40 1.00
32 Antonio McDyess .25 .60
33 Grant Hill .50 1.25
34 Jerry Stackhouse .30 .75
35 Bison Dele .20 .50
36 John Starks .30 .75
37 Chris Mills .20 .50
38 Scottie Pippen .75 2.00
39 Hakeem Olajuwon .60 1.50
40 Charles Barkley .75 2.00
41 Antonio Davis .20 .50
42 Reggie Miller .60 1.50
43 Mark Jackson .20 .50
44 Eddie Jones .30 .75
45 Shaquille O'Neal 1.25 3.00
46 Kobe Bryant 2.50 6.00
47 Rodney Rogers .20 .50
48 Maurice Taylor .20 .50
49 Tim Hardaway .40 1.00
50 Jamal Mashburn .30 .75
51 Alonzo Mourning .50 1.25
52 Ray Allen .50 1.25
53 Terrell Brandon .25 .60
54 Glenn Robinson .30 .75
55 Joe Smith .20 .50
56 Stephon Marbury .40 1.00
57 Kevin Garnett .75 2.00
58 Kerry Kittles .25 .60
59 Jayson Williams .20 .50
60 Keith Van Horn .30 .75
61 Patrick Ewing .50 1.25
62 Allan Houston .20 .50
63 Latrell Sprewell .40 1.00
64 Anfernee Hardaway .75 2.00
65 Horace Grant .30 .75
66 Allen Iverson .75 2.00
67 Tim Thomas .25 .60
68 Jason Kidd .50 1.25
69 Danny Manning .25 .60
70 Tom Gugliotta .25 .60
71 Damon Stoudamire .30 .75
72 Rasheed Wallace .40 1.00
73 Isaiah Rider .25 .60
74 Corliss Williamson .20 .50
75 Chris Webber .40 1.00
76 Tim Duncan .75 2.00
77 David Robinson .60 1.50
78 Sean Elliott .30 .75
79 Gary Payton .50 1.25
80 Vin Baker .25 .60
81 John Wallace .20 .50
82 Tracy McGrady .50 1.25
83 Jeff Hornacek .25 .60
84 Karl Malone .60 1.50
85 John Stockton .60 1.50
86 Bryant Reeves .20 .50
87 Shareef Abdur-Rahim .30 .75
88 Rod Strickland .25 .60
89 Juwan Howard .25 .60
90 Mitch Richmond .40 1.00
91 Michael Olowokandi RC 1.00 2.50
92 Dirk Nowitzki RC 6.00 15.00
93 Raef LaFrentz RC 1.00 2.50
94 Mike Bibby RC 1.50 4.00
95 Ricky Davis RC 1.25 3.00
96 Jason Williams RC 2.50 6.00
97 Al Harrington RC 1.00 2.50
98 Bonzi Wells RC .75 2.00
99 Keon Clark RC .75 2.00
100 Rashard Lewis RC 1.25 3.00
101 Paul Pierce RC 3.00 8.00
102 Antawn Jamison RC 1.25 3.00
103 Nazr Mohammed RC .75 2.00
104 Brian Skinner RC .60 1.50
105 Corey Benjamin RC .50 1.25
106 Peja Stojakovic RC 1.50 4.00
107 Bryce Drew RC .50 1.25
108 Matt Harpring RC .75 2.00
109 Toby Bailey RC .60 1.50
110 Tyronn Lue RC 1.00 2.50
111 Michael Dickerson RC .75 2.00
112 Roshown McLeod RC .50 1.25
113 Felipe Lopez RC .50 1.25
114 Michael Doleac RC .60 1.50
115 Ruben Patterson RC .75 2.00
116 Robert Traylor RC .75 2.00
117 Sam Jacobson RC .50 1.25
118 Larry Hughes RC 1.25 3.00
119 Pat Garrity RC .60 1.50
120 Vince Carter RC 4.00 10.00

1998-99 Black Diamond Double Diamond

COMMON MJ (1-13/22) 6.00 15.00
*STARS: 1X TO 2.5X BASE CARD HI
*RCs: .5X TO 1.25X BASE HI
STARS: PRINT RUN 3000 SERIAL #'d SETS
RCs: PRINT RUN 2500 SERIAL #'d SETS

1998-99 Black Diamond Triple Diamond

COMMON MJ (1-13/22) 10.00 25.00
*STARS: 1.5X TO 4X BASE CARD HI
*RCs: 1X TO 2.5X BASE CARD HI
STARS: PRINT RUN 1500 SERIAL #'d SETS
RCs: PRINT RUN 1000 SERIAL #'d SETS
92 Dirk Nowitzki 60.00 150.00

1998-99 Black Diamond Quadruple Diamond

COMMON MJ (1-13/22) 100.00 250.00
*STARS: 15X TO 40X BASE CARD HI
*RCs: 4X TO 10X HI
STARS: PRINT RUN 150 SERIAL #'d SETS
RCs: PRINT RUN 50 SERIAL #'d SETS
46 Kobe Bryant 125.00 300.00
92 Dirk Nowitzki/50 200.00 500.00
96 Jason Williams/50 75.00 200.00
101 Paul Pierce 75.00 200.00
120 Vince Carter 125.00 300.00

1998-99 Black Diamond Diamond Dominance

STATED PRINT RUN 1000 SERIAL #'d SETS
*EMERALD: 5X TO 12X HI COLUMN
EMERALD: PRINT RUN 100 SERIAL #'d SETS
D1 Steve Smith .75 2.00
D2 Paul Pierce 4.00 10.00
D3 Glen Rice 1.00 2.50
D4 Toni Kukoc 1.00 2.50
D5 Shawn Kemp 1.50 4.00
D6 Michael Finley 1.00 2.50
D7 Antonio McDyess .75 2.00
D8 Grant Hill 1.50 4.00
D9 Antawn Jamison 1.50 4.00
D10 Scottie Pippen 2.50 6.00
D11 Reggie Miller 2.00 5.00
D12 Michael Olowokandi 1.25 3.00
D13 Shaquille O'Neal 4.00 10.00
D14 Alonzo Mourning 1.50 4.00
D15 Ray Allen 1.50 4.00
D16 Stephon Marbury 1.25 3.00
D17 Keith Van Horn 1.00 2.50
D18 Allan Houston 1.00 2.50
D19 Anfernee Hardaway 2.50 6.00
D20 Allen Iverson 4.00 10.00
D21 Jason Kidd 1.50 4.00
D22 Damon Stoudamire 1.00 2.50
D23 Chris Webber 1.25 3.00
D24 Tim Duncan 3.00 8.00
D25 Gary Payton 1.50 4.00
D26 Vince Carter 5.00 12.00
D27 Karl Malone 2.00 5.00
D28 Mike Bibby 2.00 5.00
D29 Mitch Richmond 1.25 3.00
D30 Michael Jordan 20.00 50.00

1998-99 Black Diamond MJ Sheer Brilliance

COMMON CARD (B1-B30) 40.00 100.00
STATED PRINT RUN 230 SERIAL #'d SETS

1998-99 Black Diamond MJ Sheer Brilliance Extreme

COMMON CARD (B1-B30) 200.00 500.00
STATED PRINT RUN 23 SERIAL #'d SETS

1998-99 Black Diamond UD Authentics

STATED PRINT RUN 475 SETS
AJ Antawn Jamison 10.00 25.00
BW Bonzi Wells 6.00 15.00
LH Larry Hughes 10.00 25.00
MB Mike Bibby 12.00 30.00
RT Robert Traylor 6.00 15.00

1999-00 Black Diamond

COMPLETE SET (120) 25.00 50.00
COMPLETE SET w/o RC (90) 10.00 25.00
91-120 STATED ODDS 1:3 H/R
MJ FINAL FLOOR LISTED UNDER 99-00 UD
*DIAMOND CUT: 1.5X TO 4X BASE CARD HI
*FINAL CUT/100: 20X TO 50X BASE CARD HI
*FINAL CUT RC/50: 20X TO 50X BASE CARD HI
1 Dikembe Mutombo .60 1.50
2 Alan Henderson .25 .60
3 Roshown McLeod .25 .60
4 Kenny Anderson .30 .75
5 Paul Pierce .75 2.00
6 Antoine Walker .40 1.00
7 Eddie Jones .40 1.00
8 Elden Campbell .25 .60
9 David Wesley .25 .60
10 Toni Kukoc .50 1.25
11 Randy Brown .25 .60
12 Dickey Simpkins .25 .60
13 Shawn Kemp .60 1.50
14 Zydrunas Ilgauskas .30 .75
15 Brevin Knight .25 .60
16 Michael Finley .40 1.00
17 Dirk Nowitzki 1.25 3.00
18 Robert Pack .25 .60
19 Antonio McDyess .30 .75
20 Nick Van Exel .30 .75
21 Ron Mercer .30 .75
22 Grant Hill .60 1.50
23 Lindsey Hunter .25 .60
24 Jerry Stackhouse .40 1.00
25 Antawn Jamison .40 1.00
26 John Starks .40 1.00
27 Donyell Marshall .30 .75
28 Hakeem Olajuwon .75 2.00
29 Charles Barkley 1.00 2.50
30 Cuttino Mobley .25 .60
31 Reggie Miller .75 2.00
32 Rik Smits .30 .75
33 Jalen Rose .30 .75
34 Maurice Taylor .25 .60
35 Tyrone Nesby RC .25 .60
36 Michael Olowokandi .25 .60
37 Shaquille O'Neal 1.50 4.00
38 Kobe Bryant 3.00 8.00
39 Glen Rice .40 1.00
40 P.J. Brown .25 .60
41 Tim Hardaway .50 1.25
42 Alonzo Mourning .60 1.50
43 Jamal Mashburn .30 .75
44 Glenn Robinson .30 .75
45 Ray Allen .60 1.50
46 Tim Thomas .30 .75
47 Kevin Garnett 1.00 2.50
48 Joe Smith .30 .75
49 Terrell Brandon .25 .60
50 Stephon Marbury .50 1.25
51 Jayson Williams .25 .60
52 Keith Van Horn .30 .75
53 Latrell Sprewell .50 1.25
54 Allan Houston .30 .75
55 Patrick Ewing .50 1.25
56 Marcus Camby .30 .75
57 Darrell Armstrong .25 .60
58 Bo Outlaw .25 .60
59 Michael Doleac .25 .60
60 Allen Iverson 1.00 2.50
61 Theo Ratliff .25 .60
62 Larry Hughes .30 .75
63 Anfernee Hardaway 1.00 2.50
64 Jason Kidd .60 1.50
65 Tom Gugliotta .30 .75
66 Brian Grant .25 .60
67 Damon Stoudamire .40 1.00
68 Rasheed Wallace .50 1.25
69 Jason Williams .60 1.50
70 Chris Webber .50 1.25
71 Vlade Divac .40 1.00
72 Tim Duncan 1.00 2.50
73 David Robinson .75 2.00
74 Avery Johnson .30 .75
75 Sean Elliott .30 .75
76 Gary Payton .60 1.50
77 Vin Baker .30 .75
78 Brent Barry .30 .75
79 Vince Carter 1.00 2.50
80 Tracy McGrady .60 1.50
81 Doug Christie .30 .75
82 Karl Malone .75 2.00
83 John Stockton .60 1.50
84 Bryon Russell .25 .60
85 Shareef Abdur-Rahim .40 1.00
86 Mike Bibby .40 1.00
87 Felipe Lopez .25 .60
88 Juwan Howard .30 .75
89 Rod Strickland .25 .60
90 Mitch Richmond .50 1.25
91 Elton Brand RC .75 2.00
92 Steve Francis RC .75 2.00
93 Baron Davis RC 1.00 2.50
94 Lamar Odom RC .75 2.00
95 Jonathan Bender RC .40 1.00
96 Wally Szczerbiak RC .60 1.50
97 Richard Hamilton RC 1.00 2.50
98 Andre Miller RC .75 2.00
99 Shawn Marion RC .75 2.00
100 Jason Terry RC .60 1.50
101 Trajan Langdon RC .30 .75
102 A.Radojevic RC .25 .60
103 Corey Maggette RC .50 1.25
104 William Avery RC .25 .60
105 Ron Artest RC 1.00 2.50
106 Adrian Griffin RC .30 .75
107 James Posey RC .40 1.00
108 Quincy Lewis RC .25 .60
109 Dion Glover RC .25 .60
110 Jeff Foster RC .40 1.00
111 Kenny Thomas RC .40 1.00
112 Devean George RC .30 .75
113 Tim James RC .25 .60
114 Vonteego Cummings RC .25 .60
115 Jumaine Jones RC .25 .60
116 Scott Padgett RC .30 .75
117 Obinna Ekezie RC .25 .60
118 Ryan Robertson RC .25 .60
119 Chucky Atkins RC .30 .75
120 A.J. Bramlett RC .40 1.00

1999-00 Black Diamond A Piece of History

STATED ODDS 1:144 H; 1:336 H/R
*DOUBLE: 1.25X TO 3X BASE HI
DOUBLE STATED ODDS 1:864 H; 1:1008 H/R
*TRIPLE: 3X TO 8X HI
TRIPLE: PRINT RUN 25 SER.#'d SETS
AH Allan Houston H/R 4.00 10.00
AW Antoine Walker H 5.00 12.00
BD Baron Davis H 12.00 30.00
CB Charles Barkley H/R 12.00 30.00
CM Corey Maggette H/R 6.00 15.00
CW Chris Webber H 6.00 15.00
DG Devean George H 4.00 10.00
DR David Robinson H/R 10.00 25.00
GP Gary Payton H 8.00 20.00
HO Hakeem Olajuwon H 10.00 25.00
JB Jonathan Bender H 5.00 12.00
JS John Stockton H/R 8.00 20.00
JT Jason Terry H/R 8.00 20.00
JW Jason Williams H 8.00 20.00
KG Kevin Garnett H 12.00 30.00
KM Karl Malone H 10.00 25.00
KT Kenny Thomas H/R 5.00 12.00
MF Michael Finley H/R 5.00 12.00
PP Paul Pierce H/R 10.00 25.00
RM Reggie Miller H 10.00 25.00
SA Shareef Abdur-Rahim H/R 5.00 12.00
SF Steve Francis H 10.00 25.00
SO Shaquille O'Neal H/R 20.00 50.00
TB Terrell Brandon H 3.00 8.00
WS Wally Szczerbiak H/R 8.00 20.00

1999-00 Black Diamond Diamonation

COMPLETE SET (10) 12.00 30.00
STATED ODDS 1:8 HOB/RET
D1 Vince Carter 2.50 6.00
D2 Tim Duncan 2.50 6.00
D3 Kobe Bryant 8.00 20.00
D4 Stephon Marbury 1.25 3.00
D5 Ron Mercer .75 2.00
D6 Allen Iverson 2.50 6.00
D7 Shareef Abdur-Rahim 1.00 2.50
D8 Kevin Garnett 2.50 6.00
D9 Jason Kidd 1.50 4.00
D10 Allan Houston .75 2.00

1999-00 Black Diamond Jordan Diamond Gallery

COMPLETE SET (10) 75.00 200.00
COMMON CARD (DG1-DG10) 12.00 30.00
STATED ODDS 1:12 HOB/RET

1999-00 Black Diamond Might

COMPLETE SET (20) 6.00 15.00
STATED ODDS 1:3 HOB/RET
DM1 Shaquille O'Neal 2.50 6.00
DM2 Allan Houston .50 1.25
DM3 Keith Van Horn .50 1.25
DM4 Antonie Walker .60 1.50
DM5 Latrell Sprewell .75 2.00
DM6 Hakeem Olajuwon 1.25 3.00
DM7 David Robinson 1.25 3.00
DM8 Antonio McDyess .50 1.25
DM9 Shawn Kemp 1.00 2.50
DM10 Ray Allen 1.00 2.50
DM11 Karl Malone 1.25 3.00
DM12 Tim Hardaway .75 2.00
DM13 Mike Bibby .60 1.50
DM14 Antawn Jamison .60 1.50
DM15 Dikembe Mutombo 1.00 2.50
DM16 Michael Finley .60 1.50
DM17 Juwan Howard .50 1.25
DM18 Maurice Taylor .40 1.00
DM19 Gary Payton 1.00 2.50
DM20 Shareef Abdur-Rahim .60 1.50

1999-00 Black Diamond Myriad

COMPLETE SET (10) 12.00 30.00
STATED ODDS 1:24 HOB/RET
M1 Kobe Bryant 10.00 25.00
M2 Tim Duncan 3.00 8.00
M3 Kevin Garnett 3.00 8.00
M4 Keith Van Horn 1.00 2.50
M5 Vince Carter 3.00 8.00
M6 Grant Hill 2.00 5.00
M7 Anfernee Hardaway 3.00 8.00
M8 Karl Malone 2.50 6.00
M9 Allen Iverson 3.00 8.00
M10 Jason Williams 2.00 5.00

1999-00 Black Diamond Skills

COMPLETE SET (10) 6.00 15.00
STATED ODDS 1:24 HOB/RET
DS1 Stephon Marbury 1.25 3.00
DS2 Grant Hill 1.50 4.00
DS3 Reggie Miller 2.00 5.00
DS4 Jason Kidd 1.50 4.00
DS5 Mike Bibby 1.00 2.50
DS6 John Stockton 1.50 4.00
DS7 Jason Williams 1.50 4.00
DS8 Shaquille O'Neal 4.00 10.00
DS9 Antonio McDyess .75 2.00
DS10 Hakeem Olajuwon 2.00 5.00

2000-01 Black Diamond

COMP.SET w/o SP's (90) 8.00 20.00
91-100 PRINT RUN 2000 SER.#'d SETS
101-110 PRINT RUN 1000 SER.#'d SETS
111-120 PRINT RUN 750 SER.#'d SETS
121-126 PRINT RUN 1750 SER.#'d SETS
127-132 PRINT RUN 900 SER.#'d SETS
1 Dikembe Mutombo .60 1.50
2 Alan Henderson .25 .60
3 Jason Terry .40 1.00
4 Paul Pierce .60 1.50
5 Antoine Walker .40 1.00
6 Kenny Anderson .30 .75
7 Jamal Mashburn .30 .75
8 Derrick Coleman .40 1.00
9 Baron Davis .40 1.00
10 Elton Brand .40 1.00
11 Ron Artest .40 1.00
12 Ron Mercer .30 .75
13 Lamond Murray .25 .60
14 Andre Miller .30 .75
15 Matt Harpring .25 .60
16 Michael Finley .40 1.00
17 Dirk Nowitzki 1.00 2.50
18 Steve Nash .60 1.50
19 Antonio McDyess .30 .75
20 Nick Van Exel .40 1.00
21 Raef LaFrentz .30 .75
22 Jerry Stackhouse .40 1.00
23 Joe Smith .30 .75
24 Chucky Atkins .25 .60
25 Antawn Jamison .40 1.00
26 Larry Hughes .40 1.00
27 Chris Mills .25 .60
28 Steve Francis .40 1.00
29 Hakeem Olajuwon .75 2.00
30 Cuttino Mobley .30 .75
31 Reggie Miller .75 2.00
32 Jalen Rose .30 .75
33 Jermaine O'Neal .30 .75
34 Austin Croshere .25 .60
35 Lamar Odom .40 1.00
36 Corey Maggette .30 .75
37 Jeff McInnis .25 .60
38 Kobe Bryant 3.00 8.00
39 Shaquille O'Neal 1.50 4.00
40 Ron Harper .40 1.00
41 Isaiah Rider .30 .75
42 Eddie Jones .40 1.00
43 Tim Hardaway .50 1.25
44 Brian Grant .30 .75
45 Glenn Robinson .40 1.00
46 Sam Cassell .30 .75
47 Ray Allen .60 1.50
48 Kevin Garnett 1.00 2.50
49 Terrell Brandon .30 .75
50 Wally Szczerbiak .30 .75
51 Stephon Marbury .50 1.25
52 Keith Van Horn .30 .75
53 Kendall Gill .40 1.00
54 Latrell Sprewell .50 1.25
55 Allan Houston .40 1.00
56 Marcus Camby .30 .75
57 Grant Hill .60 1.50
58 Tracy McGrady .75 2.00
59 Darrell Armstrong .25 .60
60 Allen Iverson 1.00 2.50
61 Toni Kukoc .50 1.25
62 Theo Ratliff .25 .60
63 Jason Kidd .60 1.50
64 Shawn Marion .40 1.00
65 Anfernee Hardaway .60 1.50
66 Scottie Pippen 1.00 2.50
67 Rasheed Wallace .50 1.25
68 Damon Stoudamire .40 1.00
69 Steve Smith .40 1.00
70 Chris Webber .50 1.25
71 Jason Williams .60 1.50
72 Peja Stojakovic .30 .75
73 Tim Duncan 1.00 2.50
74 David Robinson .75 2.00
75 Derek Anderson .30 .75
76 Gary Payton .60 1.50
77 Patrick Ewing .60 1.50
78 Rashard Lewis .30 .75
79 Vince Carter .75 2.00
80 Mark Jackson .30 .75
81 Antonio Davis .30 .75
82 Karl Malone .75 2.00
83 John Stockton .75 2.00
84 Bryon Russell .25 .60
85 Shareef Abdur-Rahim .40 1.00
86 Michael Dickerson .25 .60
87 Mike Bibby .40 1.00
88 Mitch Richmond .50 1.25
89 Richard Hamilton .50 1.25
90 Juwan Howard .30 .75
91 Eduardo Najera RC 1.25 3.00
92 Eddie House RC 1.00 2.50
93 Michael Redd RC 3.00 8.00
94 Ruben Wolkowyski RC .75 2.00
95 Dan Langhi RC .75 2.00
96 Mark Madsen RC 1.25 3.00
97 Speedy Claxton RC 1.25 3.00
98 Iakovos Tsakalidis RC .75 2.00
99 Dragan Tarlac RC .75 2.00
100 Donnell Harvey RC 1.00 2.50
101 Etan Thomas RC 1.25 3.00
102 Hedo Turkoglu RC 2.50 6.00
103 Mike Penberthy RC 1.50 4.00
104 Paul McPherson RC 1.00 2.50
105 Jason Collier RC 1.50 4.00
106 Hanno Mottola RC 1.00 2.50
107 A.J. Guyton RC 1.00 2.50
108 Daniel Santiago RC 1.50 4.00
109 Lavor Postell RC 1.00 2.50
110 Erick Barkley RC 1.00 2.50
111 Chris Porter RC 1.00 2.50
112 Mateen Cleaves RC 1.25 3.00
113 Marc Jackson RC 1.25 3.00
114 Joel Przybilla RC 1.25 3.00
115 Courtney Alexander RC 1.00 2.50
116 Khalid El-Amin RC 1.00 2.50
117 Keyon Dooling RC 1.25 3.00
118 Desmond Mason RC 2.00 5.00
119 Stephen Jackson RC 3.00 8.00
120 Morris Peterson RC 1.50 4.00
121 Jerome Moiso JSY RC 2.00 5.00
122 Jamal Crawford JSY RC 8.00 20.00
123 D.Stevenson JSY RC 3.00 8.00
124 Q.Richardson JSY RC 2.50 6.00
125 Marcus Fizer JSY RC 2.50 6.00
126 Mike Miller JSY RC 5.00 12.00
127 Jamaal Magloire JSY RC 4.00 10.00
128 Chris Mihm JSY RC 2.50 6.00
129 DerMarr Johnson JSY RC 2.50 6.00
130 Stromile Swift JSY RC 3.00 8.00
131 Darius Miles JSY RC 4.00 10.00
132 Kenyon Martin JSY RC 8.00 20.00

2000-01 Black Diamond Gold

*STARS 1-90: 2X TO 5X BASE HI
1-90 PRINT RUN 500 SERIAL #'d SETS
*GEMS 91-100: 1.25X TO 3X BASE HI
*GEMS 101-120: 1X TO 2.5X BASE HI
91-120 PRINT RUN 250 SERIAL #'d SETS
*JERSEY 121-126: .75X TO 2X BASE HI
*JERSEY 127-132: .6X TO 1.5X BASE HI
121-132 PRINT RUN 100 SERIAL #'d SETS
38 Kobe Bryant 60.00 150.00

2000-01 Black Diamond Gold Jersey Autographs

STATED ODDS 1:280
121A Jerome Moiso/150 4.00 10.00
122A Jamal Crawford/200 15.00 40.00
123A DeShawn Stevenson/200 6.00 15.00
124A Quentin Richardson/150 5.00 12.00
125A Marcus Fizer/150 5.00 12.00
126A Mike Miller/150 10.00 25.00
130A Stromile Swift/100 5.00 12.00
131A Darius Miles/100 6.00 15.00

2000-01 Black Diamond Diamonation

COMPLETE SET (14) 10.00 25.00
STATED ODDS 1:10
D1 Kobe Bryant 5.00 12.00
D2 Steve Francis .60 1.50
D3 Allen Iverson 1.50 4.00
D4 Kevin Garnett 1.50 4.00
D5 Tracy McGrady 1.25 3.00
D6 Michael Finley .60 1.50
D7 Paul Pierce 1.00 2.50
D8 Shaquille O'Neal 2.50 6.00
D9 Vince Carter 1.25 3.00
D10 Larry Hughes .60 1.50
D11 Grant Hill 1.00 2.50
D12 Latrell Sprewell .75 2.00
D13 Jerry Stackhouse .60 1.50
D14 Tim Duncan 1.50 4.00

2000-01 Black Diamond Gallery

COMPLETE SET (6) 10.00 25.00
STATED ODDS 1:18
DG1 Kobe Bryant 6.00 15.00
DG2 Vince Carter 1.50 4.00
DG3 Kevin Garnett 2.00 5.00
DG4 Shaquille O'Neal 3.00 8.00
DG5 Tim Duncan 2.00 5.00
DG6 Steve Francis .75 2.00

2000-01 Black Diamond Game Gear

STATED ODDS 1:20 HOBBY
AH Anfernee Hardaway 5.00 12.00
AW Antoine Walker 3.00 8.00
BD Baron Davis 3.00 8.00
CP Chris Porter 2.00 5.00
DM Dikembe Mutombo 5.00 12.00
DN Dirk Nowitzki 8.00 20.00
DS DeShawn Stevenson 3.00 8.00
GH Grant Hill 5.00 12.00
GR Glen Rice 3.00 8.00
IR Isaiah Rider 2.50 6.00
JM Jamal Mashburn 2.50 6.00
KB Kobe Bryant 75.00 200.00
KE Khalid El-Amin 2.00 5.00
KG1 Kevin Garnett 8.00 20.00
KG2 Kevin Garnett 8.00 20.00
KM Karl Malone 6.00 15.00
LH Larry Hughes 3.00 8.00
LS Latrell Sprewell 4.00 10.00
MC Marcus Camby 2.50 6.00
MF Michael Finley 3.00 8.00
MM Mike Miller 5.00 12.00
PP Paul Pierce 5.00 12.00
RA Ron Artest 3.00 8.00
SM Stephon Marbury 4.00 10.00
TB Terrell Brandon 2.50 6.00
TG Tom Gugliotta 2.50 6.00
TM Tracy McGrady 6.00 15.00
WS Wally Szczerbiak 2.50 6.00

2000-01 Black Diamond Might

COMPLETE SET (11) 12.00 30.00
STATED ODDS 1:8
DM1 Shaquille O'Neal 3.00 8.00
DM2 Allen Iverson 2.00 5.00
DM3 Vince Carter 1.50 4.00
DM4 Chris Webber 1.00 2.50
DM5 Elton Brand .75 2.00
DM6 Karl Malone 1.50 4.00
DM7 Rasheed Wallace 1.00 2.50
DM8 Antawn Jamison .75 2.00
DM9 Kevin Garnett 2.00 5.00
DM10 Antonio McDyess .60 1.50
DM11 Kobe Bryant 6.00 15.00

2000-01 Black Diamond Skills

COMPLETE SET (11) 10.00 25.00
STATED ODDS 1:8
DS1 Kevin Garnett 2.00 5.00
DS2 Jason Kidd 1.25 3.00
DS3 Allen Iverson 2.00 5.00
DS4 Gary Payton 1.25 3.00
DS5 Tim Duncan 2.00 5.00
DS6 Eddie Jones .75 2.00
DS7 Grant Hill 1.25 3.00
DS8 Andre Miller .60 1.50
DS9 Jason Williams 1.25 3.00
DS10 Kobe Bryant 6.00 15.00
DS11 Ray Allen 1.25 3.00

2003-04 Black Diamond

COMP.SET w/o SP's (84) 6.00 15.00
85-126 STATED ODDS 1:2
127-168 STATED ODDS 1:8
169-198 STATED ODDS 1:48
KORVER AND KITTLES HAVE 2 CARDS
1 Carlos Boozer .25 .60
2 Dajuan Wagner .20 .50
3 Steve Francis .30 .75
4 Michael Finley .30 .75
5 Jalen Rose .25 .60
6 Kenyon Martin .30 .75
7 Quentin Richardson .20 .50
8 Antoine Walker .30 .75
9 Drew Gooden .25 .60
10 Mike Bibby .30 .75
11 Zydrunas Ilgauskas .25 .60
12 Dan Dickau .20 .50
13 Steve Nash .60 1.50
14 Eduardo Najera .20 .50
15 Joe Smith .25 .60
16 Pau Gasol .50 1.25
17 Anthony Mason .20 .50
18 Lamar Odom .25 .60
19 Sam Cassell .25 .60
20 Marko Jaric .20 .50
21 Marcus Fizer .20 .50
22 Jay Williams .20 .50
23 Jason Richardson .30 .75
24 Richard Jefferson .25 .60
25 Gerald Wallace .25 .60
26 Reggie Evans .20 .50
27 Jerome Williams .20 .50
28 Grant Hill .40 1.00
29 Darrell Armstrong .20 .50
30 Rasheed Wallace .40 1.00
31 Shane Battier .25 .60
32 Richard Hamilton .40 1.00
33 Antonio Davis .25 .60
34 Ray Allen .50 1.25
35 Terrell Brandon .20 .50
36 Tim Thomas .20 .50
37 Al Harrington .25 .60
38 Brian Grant .20 .50
39 Zeljko Rebraca .20 .50
40 Kerry Kittles .25 .60
41 Maurice Taylor .20 .50
42 Jerry Stackhouse .40 1.00
43 Nikoloz Tskitishvili .20 .50
44 Derrick Coleman .30 .75
45 Raef LaFrentz .20 .50
46 Dale Davis .20 .50
47 Andrei Kirilenko .25 .60
48 Melvin Ely .20 .50
49 Speedy Claxton .20 .50
50 Mike Miller .25 .60
51 Scot Pollard .20 .50
52 Popeye Jones .20 .50
53 Wesley Person .20 .50
54 Chris Wilcox .20 .50
55 Dikembe Mutombo .40 1.00
56 Toni Kukoc .30 .75
57 Eddie Griffin .20 .50
58 Kedrick Brown .20 .50
59 Eddie Jones .30 .75
60 Jon Barry .20 .50
61 Jonathan Bender .20 .50
62 Larry Hughes .25 .60
63 Rodney White .20 .50
64 Eddy Curry .20 .50
65 Theo Ratliff .20 .50
66 Jamaal Tinsley .20 .50
67 Zach Randolph .30 .75
68 Alvin Williams .20 .50
69 Derek Fisher .30 .75
70 Vin Baker .20 .50
71 Juan Dixon .20 .50
72 Devean George .20 .50
73 Damon Stoudamire .25 .60
74 Joe Johnson .25 .60
75 Jared Jeffries .20 .50
76 Cuttino Mobley .20 .50
77 Vladimir Radmanovic .20 .50
78 Ron Mercer .20 .50
79 Kenny Thomas .20 .50
80 Nazr Mohammed .20 .50
81 Donyell Marshall .20 .50
82 Lorenzen Wright .20 .50
83 Nick Van Exel .30 .75
84 Jason Terry .25 .60
85 Ben Wallace .50 1.25
86 Glenn Robinson .30 .75
87 Gilbert Arenas .40 1.00
88 Caron Butler .30 .75
89 Marcus Camby .30 .75
90 Jason Kidd .60 1.50
91 Antawn Jamison .40 1.00
92 Rashard Lewis .30 .75
93 Juwan Howard .30 .75
94 Andre Miller .30 .75
95 Hedo Turkoglu .30 .75
96 Jason Williams .60 1.50
97 Chauncey Billups .50 1.25
98 P.J. Brown .25 .60
99 Tyson Chandler .30 .75
100 Jamal Mashburn .30 .75
101 Bonzi Wells .25 .60
102 Brad Miller .30 .75
103 Gordan Giricek .25 .60
104 Nene .30 .75
105 Mike Dunleavy .30 .75
106 Kerry Kittles .30 .75
107 Jamaal Magloire .25 .60
108 Desmond Mason .30 .75
109 Corey Maggette .30 .75
110 Michael Olowokandi .25 .60
111 Tayshaun Prince .40 1.00
112 Earl Boykins .25 .60
113 Allan Houston .40 1.00
114 Morris Peterson .25 .60
115 Ricky Davis .30 .75
116 Keith Van Horn .30 .75
117 Shareef Abdur-Rahim .40 1.00
118 Willie Green RC 1.25 3.00
119 Kyle Korver RC 1.50 4.00
120 Brandon Hunter RC .75 2.00
121 Keith Bogans RC .75 2.00
122 Maurice Williams RC 1.25 3.00
123 James Lang RC .75 2.00
124 Zaur Pachulia RC 1.25 3.00
125 Slavko Vranes RC .75 2.00
126 Theron Smith RC .75 2.00
127 Paul Pierce 1.25 3.00
128 Alonzo Mourning 1.00 2.50
129 Elton Brand .60 1.50
130 Manu Ginobili 1.50 4.00
131 Peja Stojakovic .60 1.50
132 Latrell Sprewell 1.00 2.50
133 Baron Davis .75 2.00
134 Stephon Marbury 1.00 2.50
135 Darius Miles .50 1.25
136 Antonio McDyess .60 1.50
137 Jermaine O'Neal .75 2.00
138 Scottie Pippen 2.00 5.00
139 Wally Szczerbiak .60 1.50
140 Chris Webber 1.00 2.50
141 Reggie Miller 1.50 4.00
142 Tony Parker 1.25 3.00
143 Karl Malone 1.50 4.00
144 David Robinson 1.50 4.00
145 Matt Harpring .50 1.25
146 Shawn Marion .75 2.00
147 Tim Duncan 2.00 5.00
148 Dwyane Wade RC 12.00 30.00
149 Chris Kaman RC 1.50 4.00
150 Chris Bosh RC 5.00 12.00
151 Mickael Pietrus RC 1.25 3.00
152 Boris Diaw RC 1.50 4.00
153 Marcus Banks RC 1.00 2.50
154 Troy Bell RC 1.00 2.50
155 Zarko Cabarkapa RC 1.00 2.50
156 David West RC 2.00 5.00
157 Zoran Planinic RC 1.00 2.50
158 Aleksandar Pavlovic RC 1.25 3.00
159 Jerome Beasley RC 1.00 2.50
160 Kyle Korver 2.00 5.00
161 Travis Hansen RC 1.00 2.50
162 Steve Blake RC 1.25 3.00
163 Leandro Barbosa RC 1.50 4.00
164 Kendrick Perkins RC 1.25 3.00
165 Kirk Penney RC 1.25 3.00
166 Maciej Lampe RC 1.00 2.50
167 Jason Kapono RC 1.00 2.50
168 Luke Walton RC 1.50 4.00
169 Gary Payton 2.50 6.00
170 Wilt Chamberlain 3.00 8.00
171 Tracy McGrady 2.50 6.00
172 Amare Stoudemire 2.00 5.00
173 Vince Carter 3.00 8.00
174 Shaquille O'Neal 6.00 15.00
175 Larry Bird 4.00 10.00
176 Julius Erving 2.50 6.00
177 Magic Johnson 4.00 10.00
178 Dirk Nowitzki 4.00 10.00
179 Yao Ming 4.00 10.00
180 Allen Iverson 4.00 10.00
181 Kevin Garnett 4.00 10.00
182 Kobe Bryant 12.00 30.00
183 Michael Jordan 15.00 40.00
184 LeBron James RC 200.00 500.00
185 Darko Milicic RC 2.50 6.00
186 Carmelo Anthony RC 15.00 40.00
187 T.J. Ford RC 2.50 6.00
188 Mike Sweetney RC 2.00 5.00
189 Kirk Hinrich RC 3.00 8.00
190 Nick Collison RC 2.50 6.00
191 Travis Outlaw RC 2.50 6.00
192 Jarvis Hayes RC 2.00 5.00
193 Luke Ridnour RC 3.00 8.00
194 Reece Gaines RC 2.00 5.00
195 Ndudi Ebi RC 2.00 5.00
196 Dahntay Jones RC 2.50 6.00
197 Brian Cook RC 2.00 5.00
198 Josh Howard RC 3.00 8.00
NNO Lebron James PROMO with product information 15.00 40.00

2003-04 Black Diamond Bronze

*1-84 SINGLES: 4X TO 10X BASE HI
*85-117 SINGLES: 3X TO 8X BASE HI
*118-126 RCs: 1.5X TO 4X BASE HI
*127-147 SINGLES: 1.5X TO 4X BASE HI
*148-168 RCs: 1.25X TO 3X BASE HI
*169-183 SINGLES: .75X TO 2X BASE HI
*184-198 RCs: .6X TO 1.5X BASE HI
183 Michael Jordan 125.00 300.00
184 LeBron James 1,500.00 3,000.00

2003-04 Black Diamond Gold
*1-84 SINGLES: 10X TO 25X BASE HI
*85-117 SINGLES: 8X TO 20X BASE HI
*118-126 RCs: 2.5X TO 6X BASE HI
*127-147 SINGLES: 4X TO 10X BASE HI
*148-168 RCs: 2X TO 5X BASE HI
*169-183 SINGLES: 2.5X TO 6X BASE HI
*184-198 RCs: 1X TO 2.5X BASE HI
GOLD PRINT RUN 25 SER.#'d SETS
148 Dwyane Wade 50.00 120.00
183 Michael Jordan 200.00 500.00
184 LeBron James 5,000.00 10,000.00

2003-04 Black Diamond 24 Karat Signatures
STATED ODDS 1:72
AJ Antawn Jamison 4.00 10.00
BA Marcus Banks 2.50 6.00
BE Jerome Beasley 2.50 6.00
BI Chauncey Billups 10.00 25.00
CA Carmelo Anthony/100 60.00 150.00
CB Caron Butler 3.00 8.00
CK Chris Kaman 4.00 10.00
CM Corey Maggette 3.00 8.00
CM Cuttino Mobley 2.50 6.00
DD Dan Dickau 2.50 6.00
DJ DerMarr Johnson 2.50 6.00
DM Darko Milicic/100 3.00 8.00
EB Earl Boykins 2.50 6.00
EG Eddie Griffin 2.50 6.00
GA Gilbert Arenas 4.00 10.00
GI Manu Ginobili 20.00 50.00
GP Gary Payton 12.00 30.00
JH Jarvis Hayes 2.50 6.00
JK Jason Kidd 15.00 40.00
JM Jerome Moiso 2.50 6.00
JR Jason Richardson 4.00 10.00
JS Jerry Stackhouse 6.00 15.00
KA Jason Kapono 2.50 6.00
KB Kobe Bryant/100 1,500.00 3,000.00
KE Keith Bogans 2.50 6.00
LJ LeBron James/100 8,000.00 12,000.00
LW Luke Walton 4.00 10.00
MB Mike Bibby 4.00 10.00
MJ Michael Jordan/23 3,000.00 6,000.00
ML Maciej Lampe 2.50 6.00
MS Mike Sweetney 2.50 6.00
PP Paul Pierce 20.00 50.00
PS Peja Stojakovic 3.00 8.00
RE Reggie Evans 2.50 6.00
RG Reece Gaines 2.50 6.00
RH Richard Hamilton 5.00 12.00
RJ Richard Jefferson 3.00 8.00
SB Shane Battier 3.00 8.00
SM Shawn Marion 4.00 10.00
TM Tracy McGrady/100 75.00 200.00
TP Tony Parker/100 20.00 50.00
YM Yao Ming/100 100.00 250.00

2003-04 Black Diamond Jerseys
STATED ODDS 1:14
*GOLD: .6X TO 1.5X BASE JSY HI
GOLD PRINT RUN 100 SER.#'d SETS
BDAD Antonio Davis 2.00 5.00
BDAH Anfernee Hardaway 6.00 15.00
BDAI Allen Iverson 6.00 15.00
BDAM Aaron McKie 2.00 5.00
BDAW Antoine Walker 2.50 6.00
BDBA Lonny Baxter 2.00 5.00
BDBW Ben Wallace 3.00 8.00
BDCB Caron Butler 2.00 5.00
BDCM Corey Maggette 2.00 5.00
BDCW Charlie Ward 2.00 5.00
BDDF Derek Fisher 2.50 6.00
BDDM Darius Miles 2.00 5.00
BDDN Dirk Nowitzki 6.00 15.00
BDDW David Wesley 2.00 5.00
BDEB Elton Brand 2.00 5.00
BDEC Eddy Curry 1.50 4.00
BDEG Manu Ginobili 5.00 12.00
BDEJ Eddie Jones 2.50 6.00
BDES Eric Snow 2.00 5.00
BDFW Frank Williams 2.00 5.00
BDGH Grant Hill SP 5.00 12.00
BDGR Glenn Robinson 2.00 5.00
BDHO Allan Houston 2.50 6.00
BDHO Robert Horry 2.50 6.00
BDJA Mark Jackson 2.50 6.00
BDJB Jonathan Bender 2.00 5.00
BDJF Joe Forte 2.00 5.00
BDJJ Joe Johnson 2.00 5.00
BDJK Jason Kidd 4.00 10.00
BDJM Jamaal Magloire 2.00 5.00
BDJR Jason Richardson 2.50 6.00
BDKB Kobe Bryant SP 15.00 40.00
BDKG Kevin Garnett 6.00 15.00
BDKM Karl Malone 5.00 12.00
BDKR Kareem Rush 2.00 5.00
BDKV Keith Van Horn 2.00 5.00
BDKY Kenyon Martin 2.50 6.00
BDLH Larry Hughes 2.00 5.00
BDLO Lamar Odom 2.00 5.00
BDLS Latrell Sprewell 3.00 8.00
BDMA Jamal Mashburn 2.00 5.00
BDMB Mike Bibby 2.50 6.00
BDMC Marcus Camby 2.00 5.00
BDMF Marcus Fizer 2.00 5.00
BDMJ Michael Jordan SP 40.00 100.00
BDMM Mike Miller 2.00 5.00
BDMO Alonzo Mourning 4.00 10.00
BDMO Michael Olowokandi 2.00 5.00
BDMU Dikembe Mutombo 3.00 8.00
BDPG Pau Gasol 4.00 10.00
BDPP Paul Pierce 4.00 10.00
BDPS Peja Stojakovic 2.00 5.00
BDQW Qyntel Woods 2.00 5.00
BDRA Ray Allen 4.00 10.00
BDRL Rashard Lewis 2.00 5.00
BDRM Reggie Miller 5.00 12.00
BDRW Rasheed Wallace 3.00 8.00
BDSM Joe Smith 2.00 5.00
BDST Stephon Marbury 3.00 8.00
BDTM Tracy McGrady 4.00 10.00
BDWE Chris Webber 3.00 8.00
BDWI Chris Wilcox 2.00 5.00
BDYM Yao Ming 6.00 15.00

2003-04 Black Diamond Jerseys Double Diamond
PRINT RUN 250 SER.#'d SETS
*GOLD: .6X TO 1.5X JSY HI
GOLD PRINT RUN 75 SER.#'d SETS
BD2AW Antoine Walker 4.00 10.00
BD2CA Carmelo Anthony 20.00 50.00
BD2CB Caron Butler 3.00 8.00
BD2DM Darius Miles 2.50 6.00
BD2EB Elton Brand 3.00 8.00
BD2EG Manu Ginobili 8.00 20.00
BD2GA Gilbert Arenas 4.00 10.00
BD2GH Grant Hill 5.00 12.00
BD2JR Jason Richardson 4.00 10.00
BD2KB Kobe Bryant 30.00 80.00
BD2KM Kenyon Martin 4.00 10.00
BD2LJ LeBron James 300.00 600.00
BD2LS Latrell Sprewell 5.00 12.00
BD2MB Mike Bibby 4.00 10.00
BD2MI Darko Milicic 3.00 8.00
BD2MJ Michael Jordan 60.00 150.00
BD2MM Mike Miller 3.00 8.00
BD2PG Pau Gasol 6.00 15.00
BD2PP Paul Pierce 6.00 15.00
BD2RA Ray Allen 6.00 15.00
BD2RL Rashard Lewis 3.00 8.00
BD2RM Reggie Miller 8.00 20.00
BD2RW Rasheed Wallace 5.00 12.00
BD2SM Stephon Marbury 5.00 12.00
BD2SO Shaquille O'Neal 15.00 40.00
BD2TP Tony Parker 6.00 15.00

2003-04 Black Diamond Jerseys Quadruple Diamond
PRINT RUN 50 SER.#'d SETS
*GOLD: .6X TO 1.5X BASE HI
GOLD PRINT RUN 25 SER.#'d SETS
BD4AI Allen Iverson 20.00 50.00
BD4KB Kobe Bryant 40.00 100.00
BD4LJ LeBron James 500.00 1,000.00
BD4MJ Michael Jordan 100.00 225.00
BD4TM Tracy McGrady 12.00 30.00
BD4YM Yao Ming 20.00 50.00

2003-04 Black Diamond Jerseys Triple Diamond
PRINT RUN 100 SER.#'d SETS
*GOLD: .6X TO 1.5X BASE JSY HI
GOLD PRINT RUN 50 SER.#'d SETS
BD3AS Amare Stoudemire 6.00 15.00
BD3CW Chris Webber 6.00 15.00
BD3DN Dirk Nowitzki 12.00 30.00
BD3JK Jason Kidd 8.00 20.00
BD3KB Kobe Bryant 40.00 100.00
BD3KG Kevin Garnett 12.00 30.00
BD3LJ LeBron James 350.00 700.00
BD3MJ Michael Jordan 60.00 150.00
BD3SN Steve Nash 10.00 25.00
BD3TD Tim Duncan 12.00 30.00

2004-05 Black Diamond
COMP.SET w/o SPs (84) 8.00 20.00
85-126 DOUBLE STATED ODDS 1:2
127-147 TRIPLE STATED ODDS 1:8
148-162 QUAD STATED ODDS 1:30
163-183 TRIPLE RC STATED ODDS 1:8
184-198 QUAD RC STATED ODDS 1:30
1 Tony Delk .20 .50
2 Boris Diaw .25 .60
3 Chris Crawford .20 .50
4 Ricky Davis .25 .60
5 Jiri Welsch .20 .50
6 Raef LaFrentz .20 .50
7 Jason Kapono .20 .50
8 Brevin Knight .20 .50
9 Bernard Robinson RC .75 2.00
10 Jahidi White .20 .50
11 Tyson Chandler .25 .60
12 Antonio Davis .20 .50
13 Andres Nocioni RC 1.25 3.00
14 Dajuan Wagner .25 .60
15 Zydrunas Ilgauskas .25 .60
16 Jeff McInnis .20 .50
17 Josh Howard .25 .60
18 Marquis Daniels .25 .60
19 Jason Terry .25 .60
20 Andre Miller .25 .60
21 Earl Boykins .20 .50
22 Carlos Delfino .20 .50
23 Ben Wallace .40 1.00
24 Tayshaun Prince .30 .75
25 Mickael Pietrus .20 .50
26 Mike Dunleavy .25 .60
27 Speedy Claxton .20 .50
28 Jim Jackson .25 .60
29 Juwan Howard .25 .60
30 Maurice Taylor .20 .50
31 Tyronn Lue .20 .50
32 Jamaal Tinsley .20 .50
33 Stephen Jackson .25 .60
34 Fred Jones .20 .50
35 Kerry Kittles .25 .60
36 Marko Jaric .20 .50
37 Chris Kaman .25 .60
38 Caron Butler .25 .60
39 Kareem Rush .20 .50
40 Mike Miller .25 .60
41 James Posey .25 .60
42 Stromile Swift .20 .50
43 Eddie Jones .30 .75
44 Udonis Haslem .20 .50
45 Matt Freije RC .75 2.00
46 T.J. Ford .20 .50
47 Toni Kukoc .30 .75
48 Joe Smith .20 .50
49 Michael Olowokandi .20 .50
50 Wally Szczerbiak .20 .50
51 Troy Hudson .20 .50
52 Aaron Williams .20 .50
53 Alonzo Mourning .40 1.00
54 Nenad Krstic RC 1.00 2.50
55 Jamal Mashburn .25 .60
56 David Wesley .20 .50
57 Tim Pickett RC 1.00 2.50
58 Trevor Ariza RC 1.25 3.00
59 Tim Thomas .20 .50
60 Grant Hill .40 1.00
61 Hedo Turkoglu .25 .60
62 Kelvin Cato .20 .50
63 Kenny Thomas .20 .50
64 Aaron McKie .20 .50
65 Joe Johnson .25 .60
66 Quentin Richardson .20 .50
67 Damon Stoudamire .30 .75
68 Derek Anderson .25 .60
69 Nick Van Exel .30 .75
70 Doug Christie .25 .60
71 Bobby Jackson .25 .60
72 Malik Rose .20 .50
73 Rasho Nesterovic .20 .50
74 Romain Sato RC .75 2.00
75 Ronald Murray .20 .50
76 Luke Ridnour .25 .60
77 Pape Sow RC .75 2.00
78 Rafer Alston .20 .50
79 Morris Peterson .20 .50
80 Matt Harpring .25 .60
81 Mehmet Okur .25 .60
82 Larry Hughes .25 .60
83 Jarvis Hayes .20 .50
84 Kwame Brown .20 .50
85 Antoine Walker .50 1.25
86 Al Harrington .40 1.00
87 Gary Payton .75 2.00
88 Gerald Wallace .40 1.00
89 Eddy Curry .30 .75
90 Kirk Hinrich .50 1.25
91 Drew Gooden .30 .75
92 Michael Finley .50 1.25
93 Jerry Stackhouse .50 1.25
94 Kenyon Martin .50 1.25
95 Nene .40 1.00
96 Chauncey Billups .60 1.50
97 Richard Hamilton .60 1.50
98 Derek Fisher .40 1.00
99 Reggie Miller 1.00 2.50
100 Ron Artest .50 1.25
101 Corey Maggette .40 1.00
102 Lamar Odom .50 1.25
103 Karl Malone 1.00 2.50
104 Jason Williams .40 1.00
105 Bonzi Wells .30 .75
106 Desmond Mason .40 1.00
107 Sam Cassell .40 1.00
108 Jamaal Magloire .30 .75
109 Jamal Crawford .50 1.25
110 Allan Houston .50 1.25
111 Cuttino Mobley .40 1.00
112 Glenn Robinson .40 1.00
113 Shawn Marion .50 1.25
114 Darius Miles .30 .75
115 Zach Randolph .50 1.25
116 Chris Webber .60 1.50
117 Mike Bibby .50 1.25
118 Brad Miller .40 1.00
119 Manu Ginobili 1.00 2.50
120 Rashard Lewis .40 1.00
121 Jalen Rose .40 1.00
122 Chris Bosh .75 2.00
123 Carlos Boozer .40 1.00
124 Carlos Arroyo .30 .75
125 Gilbert Arenas .50 1.25
126 Antawn Jamison .40 1.00
127 Paul Pierce 1.50 4.00
128 Dirk Nowitzki 2.50 6.00
129 Rasheed Wallace 1.25 3.00
130 Jason Richardson 1.00 2.50
131 Jermaine O'Neal .75 2.00
132 Elton Brand .75 2.00
133 Pau Gasol 1.50 4.00
134 Dwyane Wade 4.00 10.00
135 Michael Redd .75 2.00
136 Latrell Sprewell 1.25 3.00
137 Richard Jefferson .75 2.00
138 Baron Davis 1.00 2.50
139 Stephon Marbury 1.25 3.00
140 Steve Francis 1.00 2.50
141 Steve Nash 2.00 5.00
142 Shareef Abdur-Rahim 1.00 2.50
143 Peja Stojakovic .75 2.00
144 Tony Parker 1.50 4.00
145 Ray Allen 1.50 4.00
146 Vince Carter 2.00 5.00
147 Andrei Kirilenko .75 2.00
148 Larry Bird 5.00 12.00
149 Michael Jordan 10.00 25.00
150 LeBron James 10.00 25.00
151 Carmelo Anthony 2.50 6.00
152 Tracy McGrady 2.50 6.00
153 Yao Ming 3.00 8.00
154 Kobe Bryant 10.00 25.00
155 Magic Johnson 5.00 12.00
156 Shaquille O'Neal 5.00 12.00
157 Kevin Garnett 3.00 8.00
158 Jason Kidd 2.00 5.00
159 Allen Iverson 3.00 8.00
160 Julius Erving 3.00 8.00
161 Amare Stoudemire 1.25 3.00
162 Tim Duncan 3.00 8.00
163 Andris Biedrins RC 1.50 4.00
164 Robert Swift RC 1.50 4.00
165 Al Jefferson RC 2.50 6.00
166 Kirk Snyder RC 1.50 4.00
167 Dorell Wright RC 2.00 5.00
168 Pavel Podkolzin RC 1.50 4.00
169 Viktor Khryapa RC 1.50 4.00
170 Delonte West RC 2.00 5.00
171 Tony Allen RC 2.00 5.00
172 Kevin Martin RC 3.00 8.00
173 Sasha Vujacic RC 2.00 5.00
174 Beno Udrih RC 2.00 5.00
175 David Harrison RC 1.50 4.00
176 Anderson Varejao RC 2.00 5.00
177 Jackson Vroman RC 1.50 4.00
178 Peter John Ramos RC 1.50 4.00
179 Lionel Chalmers RC 2.00 5.00
180 Andre Emmett RC 1.50 4.00
181 Yuta Tabuse RC 2.50 6.00
182 Trevor Ariza RC 2.50 6.00
183 Chris Duhon RC 2.00 5.00
184 Dwight Howard RC 10.00 25.00
185 Emeka Okafor RC 2.50 6.00
186 Ben Gordon RC 3.00 8.00
187 Shaun Livingston RC 3.00 8.00
188 Devin Harris RC 2.50 6.00
189 Josh Childress RC 2.00 5.00
190 Luol Deng RC 3.00 8.00
191 Andre Iguodala RC 5.00 12.00
192 Luke Jackson RC 2.00 5.00
193 Sebastian Telfair RC 2.50 6.00
194 Kris Humphries RC 2.50 6.00
195 Josh Smith RC 3.00 8.00
196 J.R. Smith RC 3.00 8.00
197 Jameer Nelson RC 3.00 8.00
198 Rafael Araujo RC 2.00 5.00

2004-05 Black Diamond Green
*1-84 SINGLE: 6X TO 15X BASE HI
*1-84 SINGLE RC: 2.5X TO 6X BASE HI
*85-126 DOUBLE: 4X TO 10X BASE HI
*127-147 TRIPLE: 2X TO 5X BASE HI
*148-162 QUAD: 1.5X TO 4X BASE HI
*163-183 RC TRIPLE: .75X TO 2X BASE HI
*184-198 RC QUAD: .6X TO 1.5X BASE HI
PRINT RUN 25 SER.#'d SETS
134 Dwyane Wade 20.00 50.00
149 Michael Jordan 75.00 200.00
150 LeBron James 75.00 200.00

2004-05 Black Diamond Red
*1-84 SINGLE: 3X TO 8X BASE HI
*1-84 SINGLE RC: 1X TO 2.5X BASE HI
*85-126 DOUBLE: 2X TO 5X BASE HI
*127-147 TRIPLE: 1X TO 2.5X BASE HI
*148-162 QUAD: .75X TO 2X BASE HI
*163-183 RC TRIPLE: .5X TO 1.25X BASE HI
*184-198 RC QUAD: .4X TO 1X BASE HI
PRINT RUN 100 SER.#'d SETS
149 Michael Jordan 50.00 120.00

2004-05 Black Diamond UD Promos
*PROMOS: .75X TO 2X BASIC

2004-05 Black Diamond Die Cuts
STATED ODDS 1:10
*DC DOUBLE: .5X TO 1.25X BASE HI
DC DOUBLE STATED ODDS 1:20
*DC TRIPLE: .6X TO 1.5X BASE HI
DC TRIPLE STATED ODDS 1:100
*DC QUAD: 2X TO 5X BASE HI
DC QUAD STATED ODDS 1:400
DC1 LeBron James 10.00 25.00
DC2 Michael Jordan 10.00 25.00
DC3 Kobe Bryant 10.00 25.00
DC4 Dwight Howard 4.00 10.00
DC5 Tracy McGrady 2.00 5.00
DC6 Kevin Garnett 3.00 8.00
DC7 Emeka Okafor 1.00 2.50
DC8 Ben Gordon 1.25 3.00
DC9 Shaun Livingston 1.25 3.00
DC10 Devin Harris 1.00 2.50
DC11 Josh Childress .75 2.00
DC12 Luol Deng 1.25 3.00
DC13 Andre Iguodala 2.00 5.00
DC14 Sebastian Telfair 1.00 2.50
DC15 Josh Smith 1.25 3.00
DC16 J.R. Smith 1.25 3.00
DC17 Jameer Nelson 1.25 3.00
DC18 Larry Bird 5.00 12.00
DC19 Carmelo Anthony 2.50 6.00
DC20 Yao Ming 3.00 8.00
DC21 Magic Johnson 5.00 12.00
DC22 Shaquille O'Neal 5.00 12.00
DC23 Jason Kidd 2.00 5.00
DC24 Allen Iverson 3.00 8.00
DC25 Julius Erving 3.00 8.00
DC26 Amare Stoudemire 1.25 3.00
DC27 Tim Duncan 3.00 8.00
DC28 Paul Pierce 2.00 5.00
DC29 Dirk Nowitzki 3.00 8.00
DC30 Dwyane Wade 5.00 12.00
DC31 Baron Davis 1.25 3.00
DC32 Stephon Marbury 1.50 4.00
DC33 Steve Francis 1.25 3.00
DC34 Steve Nash 2.50 6.00
DC35 Peja Stojakovic 1.00 2.50
DC36 Tony Parker 2.00 5.00
DC37 Ray Allen 2.00 5.00
DC38 Vince Carter 2.50 6.00
DC39 Andrei Kirilenko 1.00 2.50
DC40 Mike Bibby 1.25 3.00
DC41 Ben Wallace 1.50 4.00
DC42 Manu Ginobili 2.50 6.00

2004-05 Black Diamond GemoGRAPHy
STATED ODDS 1:20
AH Al Harrington 3.00 8.00
AI Andre Iguodala 6.00 15.00
AK Andrei Kirilenko 3.00 8.00
AS Amare Stoudemire SP 12.00 30.00
BG Ben Gordon 4.00 10.00
BR Bernard Robinson 2.50 6.00
CA Carmelo Anthony SP 20.00 50.00
CB Carlos Boozer 3.00 8.00
DE Devin Harris 3.00 8.00
DH Dwight Howard 12.00 30.00
CJ Josh Childress 2.50 6.00
JN Jameer Nelson 4.00 10.00
JR J.R. Smith 4.00 10.00
JS Josh Smith 4.00 10.00
KB Kobe Bryant SP 150.00 400.00
KG Kevin Garnett SP 20.00 50.00
KH Kris Humphries 3.00 8.00
LD Luol Deng 4.00 10.00
LJ LeBron James SP 1,000.00 2,000.00
LU Luke Jackson 2.50 6.00
MB Mike Bibby 4.00 10.00
MF Matt Freije 2.50 6.00
MJ Michael Jordan SP 1,500.00 3,000.00
PG Pau Gasol 6.00 15.00
PS Pape Sow 2.50 6.00
RA Rafael Araujo 2.50 6.00
RJ Richard Jefferson 3.00 8.00
RM Reggie Miller 75.00 200.00
RO Romain Sato 2.50 6.00
RS Robert Swift 2.50 6.00
SE Sebastian Telfair 3.00 8.00
SL Shaun Livingston 4.00 10.00
ST Stephon Marbury 6.00 15.00
TA Trevor Ariza 4.00 10.00
TM Tracy McGrady SP 20.00 50.00
ZR Zach Randolph 4.00 10.00

2004-05 Black Diamond Jerseys
STATED ODDS 1:13
*DOUBLE: .5X TO 1.25X BASE HI
DOUBLE PRINT RUN 250 SER.#'d SETS
*TRIPLE: .6X TO 1.5X BASE HI
TRIPLE PRINT RUN 100 SER.#'d SETS
AI Allen Iverson 6.00 15.00
AN Andre Iguodala 4.00 10.00
AS Amare Stoudemire 2.50 6.00
AV Anderson Varejao 2.00 5.00
BD Baron Davis 2.50 6.00
BG Ben Gordon 2.50 6.00
CA Carmelo Anthony 5.00 12.00
CB Chauncey Billups 3.00 8.00
CD Chris Duhon 2.00 5.00
DA David Harrison 1.50 4.00
DB Elton Brand 2.00 5.00
DE Devin Harris 2.00 5.00
DH Dwight Howard 8.00 20.00
DN Dirk Nowitzki 6.00 15.00
DW Dajuan Wagner 2.00 5.00
EG Manu Ginobili 5.00 12.00
JC Jamal Crawford 2.50 6.00
JK Jason Kidd 4.00 10.00
JO Josh Childress 1.50 4.00
JR J.R. Smith 2.50 6.00
JS Josh Smith 2.50 6.00
JV Jackson Vroman 1.50 4.00
KB Kobe Bryant SP 75.00 200.00
KG Kevin Garnett 6.00 15.00
KM Kevin Martin 3.00 8.00
LC Lionel Chalmers 2.00 5.00
LD Luol Deng 2.50 6.00
LJ LeBron James SP 20.00 50.00
LU Luke Jackson 1.50 4.00
MJ Michael Jordan SP 30.00 80.00
RJ Richard Jefferson 2.00 5.00
RW Rasheed Wallace 3.00 8.00
SE Sebastian Telfair 2.00 5.00
SF Steve Francis 2.50 6.00
SL Shaun Livingston 2.50 6.00
SO Shaquille O'Neal 10.00 25.00
TA Tony Allen 2.50 6.00
TD Tim Duncan 6.00 15.00
TM Tracy McGrady 4.00 10.00
WE Delonte West 2.00 5.00
YT Yuta Tabuse 2.50 6.00
AU Andre Emmett 1.50 4.00

1994 Bleachers 23 Karat Promos
COMPLETE SET (7) 1.00 2.50
1 Alonzo Mourning .08 .25
2 Shaquille O'Neal .20 .50
3 Shaquille O'Neal .20 .50
4 Shaquille O'Neal .20 .50
5 Shaquille O'Neal .20 .50
6 Chris Webber .08 .25
7 Class of '93 .20 .50

1997 Bleachers/Fleer Gold Promos
COMPLETE SET (2) 2.00 5.00
1 Anfernee Hardaway 2.00 5.00
2 Grant Hill 1.25 3.00

1997 Bleachers/Fleer Gold
COMPLETE SET (12) 40.00 100.00
1 Charles Barkley 1986-87 8.00 20.00
2 Clyde Drexler 1986-87 4.00 10.00
3 Patrick Ewing 1986-87 5.00 12.00
4 Anfernee Hardaway 1993-94 8.00 20.00
5 Grant Hill 1994-95 5.00 12.00
6 Michael Jordan 1986-87 12.00 30.00
7 Shawn Kemp 1990-91 4.00 10.00
8 Karl Malone 1986-87 6.00 15.00
9 Hakeem Olajuwon 1986-87 6.00 15.00
10 Shaquille O'Neal 1992-93 10.00 25.00
11 Scottie Pippen 1988-89 6.00 15.00
12 Dennis Rodman 1988-89 8.00 20.00

1997 Bleachers/Fleer Gold Black Foil
COMPLETE SET (12) 60.00 150.00
1 Charles Barkley 1986-87 12.00 30.00
2 Clyde Drexler 1986-87 6.00 15.00
3 Patrick Ewing 1986-87 8.00 20.00
4 Anfernee Hardaway 1993-94 12.00 30.00
5 Grant Hill 1994-95 8.00 20.00
6 Michael Jordan 1986-87 20.00 50.00
7 Shawn Kemp 1990-91 6.00 15.00
8 Karl Malone 1986-87 10.00 25.00
9 Hakeem Olajuwon 1986-87 10.00 25.00
10 Shaquille O'Neal 1992-93 15.00 40.00
11 Scottie Pippen 1988-89 10.00 25.00
12 Dennis Rodman 1988-89 12.00 30.00

1997 Bleachers/Fleer Gold Holographic Foil
COMPLETE SET (12) 150.00 300.00
1 Charles Barkley 1986-87 20.00 50.00
2 Clyde Drexler 1986-87 10.00 25.00
3 Patrick Ewing 1986-87 12.00 30.00
4 Anfernee Hardaway 1993-94 20.00 50.00
5 Grant Hill 1994-95 12.00 30.00
6 Michael Jordan 1986-87 30.00 80.00
7 Shawn Kemp 1990-91 10.00 25.00
8 Karl Malone 1986-87 15.00 40.00
9 Hakeem Olajuwon 1986-87 15.00 40.00
10 Shaquille O'Neal 1992-93 25.00 60.00
11 Scottie Pippen 1988-89 15.00 40.00
12 Dennis Rodman 1988-89 20.00 50.00

1996-97 Blockbuster NBA at 50 Postcards
COMPLETE SET (5) 4.00 10.00
1 Shareef Abdur-Rahim 1.50 4.00
2 Grant Hill 1.50 4.00
3 Hakeem Olajuwon 2.00 5.00
4 Scottie Pippen 2.50 6.00
5 Damon Stoudamire 1.00 2.50

1948 Bowman
COMPLETE SET (72) 20,000.00 30,000.00
CARDS PRICED IN EX-MT CONDITION
1 Ernie Calverley RC 75.00 200.00
2 Ralph Hamilton 40.00 100.00
3 Gale Bishop 25.00 60.00
4 Fred Lewis RC 40.00 100.00
5 Basketball Play
Single cut off post 30.00 80.00
6 Bob Feerick RC 30.00 80.00
7 John Logan 30.00 80.00
8 Mel Riebe 60.00 150.00
9 Andy Phillip RC 60.00 150.00
10 Bob Davies RC 60.00 150.00
11 Basketball Play
Single cut with return pass to post 30.00 80.00
12 Kenny Sailors RC 100.00 250.00
13 Paul Armstrong 30.00 80.00
14 Howard Dallmar RC 30.00 80.00
15 Bruce Hale RC 30.00 80.00
16 Sid Hertzberg 40.00 100.00
17 Basketball Play
Single cut 25.00 60.00
18 Red Rocha 30.00 80.00
19 Eddie Ehlers 40.00 100.00
20 Ellis(Gene) Vance 40.00 100.00
21 Fuzzy Levane RC 30.00 80.00
22 Earl Shannon 30.00 80.00
23 Basketball Play
Double cut off post 20.00 50.00
24 Leo (Crystal) Klier 40.00 100.00
25 George Senesky 50.00 120.00
26 Price Brookfield 25.00 60.00
27 John Norlander 30.00 80.00
28 Don Putman 25.00 60.00
29 Basketball Play
Double post 30.00 50.00
30 Jack Garfinkel 60.00 150.00
31 Chuck Gilmur 30.00 80.00
32 Red Holzman RC 150.00 400.00
33 Jack Smiley 50.00 120.00
34 Joe Fulks RC 100.00 250.00
35 Basketball Play
Screen play 60.00 150.00
36 Hal Tidrick 40.00 100.00
37 Don (Swede) Carlson 75.00 200.00
38 Buddy Jeanette CO RC 125.00 300.00
39 Ray Kuka 75.00 200.00
40 Stan Miasek 30.00 80.00
41 Basketball Play
Double screen 40.00 100.00
42 George Nostrand 30.00 80.00
43 Chuck Halbert RC 100.00 250.00
44 Arnie Johnson 75.00 200.00
45 Bob Doll 125.00 300.00
46 Bones McKinney RC 75.00 200.00
47 Basketball Play
Out of bounds 50.00 120.00
48 Ed Sadowski 50.00 120.00
49 Bob Kinney 30.00 80.00
50 Charles (Hawk) Black 75.00 200.00
51 Jack Dwan 100.00 250.00
52 Connie Simmons RC 75.00 200.00
53 Basketball Play
Out of bounds 40.00 100.00
54 Bud Palmer RC 100.00 250.00
55 Max Zaslofsky RC 150.00 400.00
56 Lee Roy Robbins 75.00 200.00
57 Arthur Spector 125.00 300.00
58 Arnie Risen RC 75.00 200.00
59 Basketball Play
Out of bounds play 50.00 120.00
60 Ariel Maughan 75.00 200.00
61 Dick O'Keefe 50.00 120.00
62 Herman Schaefer 50.00 120.00
63 John Mahnken 50.00 120.00
64 Tommy Byrnes 60.00 150.00
65 Basketball Play
Held ball 75.00 200.00
66 Jim Pollard RC 300.00 600.00
67 Lee Mogus 125.00 300.00
68 Lee Knorek 75.00 200.00
69 George Mikan RC 8,000.00 15,000.00
70 Walter Budko 50.00 120.00
71 Basketball Play
Guards Play 40.00 100.00
72 Carl Braun RC 300.00 600.00

2003-04 Bowman
COMP.SET w/o RC's (110) 15.00 40.00
1 Yao Ming .75 2.00
2 Glenn Robinson .25 .60
3 Antoine Walker .30 .75
4 Jalen Rose .25 .60
5 Ricky Davis .25 .60
6 Juwan Howard .25 .60
7 Kwame Brown .20 .50
8 Mike Bibby .30 .75
9 Wally Szczerbiak .25 .60
10 Allen Iverson .75 2.00
11 Shareef Abdur-Rahim .30 .75
12 Jamal Mashburn .25 .60
13 Stephon Marbury .40 1.00
14 Desmond Mason .25 .60
15 Gordan Giricek .25 .60
16 Caron Butler .25 .60
17 Jermaine O'Neal .30 .75
18 Kenyon Martin .30 .75
19 Andrei Kirilenko .30 .75
20 Dirk Nowitzki .75 2.00
21 Richard Hamilton .40 1.00
22 Troy Murphy .20 .50
23 Shawn Marion .30 .75
24 Allan Houston .30 .75
25 Keith Van Horn .25 .60
26 Brian Grant .25 .60
27 Mike Miller .25 .60
28 Chris Webber .40 1.00
29 Brent Barry .25 .60
30 Elton Brand .25 .60
31 Juan Dixon .20 .50
32 Karl Malone .60 1.50
33 Darrell Armstrong .20 .50
34 Rasheed Wallace .40 1.00
35 Michael Redd .30 .75
36 Rashard Lewis .25 .60
37 Ron Artest .30 .75
38 P.J. Brown .20 .50
39 Eddie Griffin .20 .50
40 Tim Duncan .75 2.00
41 Kurt Thomas .20 .50
42 Raef Lafrentz .20 .50
43 Ben Wallace .40 1.00
44 Lamar Odom .25 .60
45 Vince Carter .60 1.50
46 Derek Anderson .25 .60
47 Stromile Swift .20 .50
48 Bobby Jackson .25 .60
49 Richard Jefferson .25 .60
50 Shaquille O'Neal 1.25 3.00
51 Calbert Cheaney .20 .50
52 Troy Hudson .20 .50
53 Ray Allen .50 1.25
54 Howard Eisley .20 .50
55 Alonzo Mourning .40 1.00
56 Sam Cassell .25 .60
57 Derrick Coleman .30 .75
58 Andre Miller .25 .60
59 Antawn Jamison .30 .75
60 Kevin Garnett .75 2.00
61 Steve Francis .30 .75
62 Tyson Chandler .25 .60
63 Drew Gooden .25 .60
64 Scottie Pippen .75 2.00
65 Pau Gasol .50 1.25
66 Steve Nash .60 1.50
67 DaJuan Wagner .20 .50
68 Jason Terry .25 .60
69 Reggie Miller .60 1.50
70 Tracy McGrady .50 1.25
71 Nene Hilario .25 .60
72 Morris Peterson .20 .50
73 Peja Stojakovic .25 .60
74 Eddie Jones .30 .75
75 Tony Parker .50 1.25
76 Corliss Williamson .20 .50
77 Vladimir Radmanovic .20 .50
78 Amare Stoudemire .40 1.00
79 Tony Delk .25 .60
80 Jason Kidd .50 1.25
81 Gary Payton .50 1.25
82 Corey Maggette .25 .60
83 Darius Miles .20 .50
84 Cuttino Mobley .20 .50
85 Eric Snow .20 .50
86 Matt Harpring .20 .50
87 Manu Ginobili .60 1.50
88 Latrell Sprewell .40 1.00
89 Alvin Williams .20 .50
90 Paul Pierce .50 1.25
91 Anfernee Hardaway .75 2.00
92 Gilbert Arenas .30 .75
93 Jerry Stackhouse .40 1.00
94 Tim Thomas .20 .50
95 Nikoloz Tskitishvili .20 .50
96 Doug Christie .25 .60
97 Zydrunas Ilgauskas .25 .60
98 Jamaal Tinsley .25 .60
99 Theo Ratliff .20 .50
100 Kobe Bryant 2.50 6.00
101 Chauncey Billups .40 1.00
102 Michael Finley .30 .75
103 Jason Williams .50 1.25
104 Bonzi Wells .20 .50
105 Voshon Lenard .20 .50
106 Jason Richardson .30 .75
107 Baron Davis .30 .75
108 Radoslav Nesterovic .20 .50
109 Eddy Curry .20 .50
110 Michael Olowokandi .20 .50
111 Josh Howard RC 1.50 4.00
112 Mario Austin RC 1.00 2.50
113 Rick Rickert RC 1.00 2.50
114 Tommy Smith RC 1.50 4.00
115 Dahntay Jones RC 1.25 3.00
116 Ndudi Ebi RC 1.00 2.50
117 Maurice Williams RC 1.50 4.00
118 Kendrick Perkins RC 1.25 3.00
119 Steve Blake RC 1.25 3.00
120 David West RC 2.00 5.00
121 Chris Kaman RC 1.50 4.00
122 Keith Bogans RC 1.00 2.50
123 LeBron James RC 150.00 400.00
124 Devin Brown RC 1.00 2.50
125 Jason Kapono RC 1.00 2.50
126 Zoran Planinic RC 1.00 2.50
127 Zaur Pachulia RC 1.50 4.00
128 Malick Badiane RC 1.50 4.00
129 Kyle Korver RC 2.00 5.00
130 Darko Milicic RC 1.25 3.00
131 Troy Bell RC 1.00 2.50
132 Luke Walton RC 1.50 4.00
133 Mike Sweetney RC 1.00 2.50
134 Jarvis Hayes RC 1.00 2.50
135 Leandro Barbosa RC 1.50 4.00
136 Carlos Delfino RC 1.25 3.00
137 Sofoklis Schortsanitis RC 1.00 2.50
138 Slavko Vranes RC 1.00 2.50
139 Travis Hansen RC 1.00 2.50
140 Carmelo Anthony RC 8.00 20.00
141 Reece Gaines RC 1.00 2.50
142 Maciej Lampe RC 1.00 2.50
143 Travis Outlaw RC 1.25 3.00
144 Jerome Beasley RC 1.25 3.00
145 Michael Pietrus RC 1.25 3.00
146 Brian Cook RC 1.00 2.50
148 Kirk Hinrich AU RC 6.00 15.00
149 Dwyane Wade AU RC 75.00 200.00
150 Marcus Banks AU RC 4.00 10.00
151 Nick Collison AU RC 5.00 12.00
152 Boris Diaw AU RC 6.00 15.00
153 Chris Bosh AU RC 20.00 50.00
154 T.J. Ford AU RC 5.00 12.00
155 Luke Ridnour AU RC 6.00 15.00
156 A.Pavlovic AU RC 5.00 12.00
157 Z.Cabarkapa AU RC 4.00 10.00

2003-04 Bowman Gold
*1-110 GOLD: 1.25X TO 3X BASE HI
*111-146 GOLD RCs: .5X TO 1.25X BASE HI
*148-157 GOLD RCs: .1X TO .3X BASE HI
148-157 GOLD NOT AUTOGRAPHED
CARD 147 NOT RELEASED
123 LeBron James 800.00 1,500.00
149 Dwyane Wade 4.00 10.00

2003-04 Bowman Fabric of the Future
STATED ODDS 1:37
BC Brian Cook 1.50 4.00
CA Carmelo Anthony 12.00 30.00
CB Chris Bosh 8.00 20.00
CK Chris Kaman 2.50 6.00
DJ Dahntay Jones 2.00 5.00
DW Dwyane Wade 20.00 50.00
JH Jarvis Hayes 1.50 4.00
KB Keith Bogans 1.50 4.00

KH Kirk Hinrich 2.50 6.00
KP Kendrick Perkins 2.00 5.00
LB Leandro Barbosa 2.50 6.00
LR Luke Ridnour 2.50 6.00
LW Luke Walton 2.50 6.00
MB Marcus Banks 1.50 4.00
MP Mickael Pietrus 2.00 5.00
MS Mike Sweetney 1.50 4.00
NC Nick Collison 2.00 5.00
RG Reece Gaines 1.50 4.00
SB Steve Blake 2.00 5.00
SV Slavko Vranes 1.50 4.00
TB Troy Bell 1.50 4.00
TF T.J. Ford 2.00 5.00
TO Travis Outlaw 2.00 5.00
DWE David West 3.00 8.00
JHO Josh Howard 2.50 6.00

2003-04 Bowman Remembering Rookies
STATED ODDS 1:1282
RREB Elton Brand 6.00 15.00
RRSO Shaquille O'Neal 50.00 120.00

2003-04 Bowman Rookie Recalls
STATED ODDS 1:46
RREAM Andre Miller 2.00 5.00
RREDM Darius Miles 2.00 5.00
RREEB Elton Brand 2.00 5.00
RREGH Grant Hill 3.00 8.00
RREGP Gary Payton 4.00 10.00
RREGR Glenn Robinson 2.00 5.00
RREKG Kevin Garnett 6.00 15.00
RREKM Karl Malone 5.00 12.00
RRELH Larry Hughes 2.00 5.00
RRERH Richard Hamilton 3.00 8.00
RRESF Steve Francis 2.50 6.00
RRETD Tim Duncan 6.00 15.00
RRETM Tracy McGrady 4.00 10.00

2003-04 Bowman Signs of the Future
STATED ODDS: A 1:171 B 1:43
AP Aleksandar Pavlovic 3.00 8.00
BC Brian Cook 2.50 6.00
CA Carmelo Anthony 15.00 40.00
CB Chris Bosh 6.00 15.00
CD Carlos Delfino 3.00 8.00
DJ Dahntay Jones 3.00 8.00
DW Dwyane Wade 40.00 100.00
JB Jerome Beasley 2.50 6.00
JH Josh Howard 4.00 10.00
JK Jason Kapono 2.50 6.00
KB Keith Bogans 2.50 6.00
KH Kirk Hinrich 6.00 15.00
KP Kendrick Perkins 3.00 8.00
LB Leandro Barbosa 2.50 6.00
LR Luke Ridnour 4.00 10.00
LW Luke Walton 4.00 10.00
MA Mario Austin 2.50 6.00
MB Marcus Banks 2.50 6.00
ML Maciej Lampe 2.50 6.00
MP Mickael Pietrus 3.00 8.00
MS Mike Sweetney 2.50 6.00
NE Ndudi Ebi 2.50 6.00
NV Nick Collison 3.00 8.00
RG Reece Gaines 2.50 6.00
SB Steve Blake 3.00 8.00
SS Sofoklis Schortsanitis 2.50 6.00
SV Slavko Vranes 2.50 6.00
TB Troy Bell 2.50 6.00
TH Travis Hansen 2.50 6.00
TJ T.J. Ford 3.00 8.00
TO Travis Outlaw 3.00 8.00
TS Tommy Smith 4.00 10.00
ZP Zaur Pachulia 4.00 10.00
DWE David West 5.00 12.00
JHA Jarvis Hayes 2.50 6.00
MBA Malick Badiane 4.00 10.00
ZOP Zoran Planinic 2.50 6.00

2003-04 Bowman Sophomore Strands
STATED ODDS 1:46
AS Amare Stoudemire 3.00 8.00
CB Carlos Boozer 2.00 5.00
DG Drew Gooden 2.00 5.00
DW DaJuan Wagner 2.00 5.00
EG Manu Ginobili 5.00 12.00
JD Juan Dixon 2.00 5.00
MD Mike Dunleavy Jr. 2.00 5.00
MH Marcus Haislip 2.00 5.00
NH Nene Hilario 2.00 5.00
RH Ryan Humphrey 2.00 5.00
TP Tayshaun Prince 2.50 6.00
YM Yao Ming 6.00 15.00
CBU Caron Butler 2.00 5.00
JRB J.R. Bremer 2.00 5.00

2004-05 Bowman
COMP.SET w/o RC's (110) 20.00 50.00
147-156 RC STATED ODDS 1:105
1 Yao Ming .75 2.00
2 Eddy Curry .20 .50
3 Stephon Marbury .40 1.00
4 Chris Webber .40 1.00
5 Jason Kidd .50 1.25
6 Cuttino Mobley .25 .60
7 Jermaine O'Neal .25 .60
8 Kobe Bryant 2.50 6.00
9 Tony Parker .50 1.25
10 Gary Payton .50 1.25
11 T.J. Ford .20 .50
12 Tim Duncan .75 2.00
13 Glenn Robinson .25 .60
14 Jason Richardson .25 .60
15 Carmelo Anthony .60 1.50
16 Pau Gasol .50 1.25
17 Kirk Hinrich .50 1.25
18 Kenyon Martin .30 .75
19 Jamal Crawford .30 .75
20 Elton Brand .25 .60
21 Kevin Garnett .75 2.00
22 Michael Redd .25 .60
23 LeBron James 15.00 40.00
24 Andre Miller .25 .60
25 Peja Stojakovic .25 .60
26 Jarvis Hayes .20 .50
27 David Wesley .20 .50
28 Jason Kapono .20 .50
29 Corey Maggette .25 .60
30 Rasheed Wallace .40 1.00
31 Nene .25 .60
32 Amare Stoudemire .30 .75
33 Allen Iverson .75 2.00
34 Shaquille O'Neal 1.25 3.00
35 Mike Dunleavy .20 .50
36 Steve Nash .60 1.50
37 Brad Miller .25 .60
38 Chris Bosh .50 1.25
39 Boris Diaw .25 .60
40 Steve Francis .30 .75
41 Dirk Nowitzki .75 2.00
42 Jason Williams .25 .60
43 Gilbert Arenas .30 .75
44 Keith Van Horn .25 .60
45 Jamal Mashburn .25 .60
46 Derek Fisher .25 .60
47 Andrei Kirilenko .25 .60
48 Ricky Davis .25 .60
49 Gerald Wallace .25 .60
50 Tracy McGrady .50 1.25
51 Zach Randolph .30 .75
52 Rafer Alston .20 .50
53 Bobby Jackson .25 .60
54 Desmond Mason .25 .60
55 Tim Thomas .20 .50
56 Jamaal Tinsley .20 .50
57 Kwame Brown .25 .60
58 Chauncey Billups .40 1.00
59 Brandon Hunter .20 .50
60 Reggie Miller .60 1.50
61 Samuel Dalembert .20 .50
62 James Posey .25 .60
63 Erick Dampier .20 .50
64 Carlos Arroyo .20 .50
65 Reece Gaines .20 .50
66 Darko Milicic .25 .60
67 Sam Cassell .25 .60
68 Dwyane Wade 1.25 3.00
69 Allan Houston .30 .75
70 Ray Allen .50 1.25
71 Tyson Chandler .25 .60
72 Bonzi Wells .25 .60
73 Jalen Rose .25 .60
74 Marquis Daniels .20 .50
75 Zydrunas Ilgauskas .25 .60
76 Tayshaun Prince .30 .75
77 Lamar Odom .30 .75
78 Luke Ridnour .25 .60
79 Joe Johnson .25 .60
80 Vince Carter .60 1.50
81 Antoine Walker .30 .75
82 Shareef Abdur-Rahim .30 .75
83 Richard Jefferson .25 .60
84 Maurice Taylor .20 .50
85 Chris Kaman .25 .60
86 Marcus Banks .20 .50
87 Mike Bibby .30 .75
88 Latrell Sprewell .40 1.00
89 Rashard Lewis .25 .60
90 Baron Davis .30 .75
91 Caron Butler .25 .60
92 Michael Finley .30 .75
93 Mike Miller .25 .60
94 Al Harrington .25 .60
95 Quentin Richardson .20 .50
96 Jamaal Magloire .20 .50
97 Darius Miles .20 .50
98 Jeff Foster .20 .50
99 Karl Malone .60 1.50
100 Shawn Marion .30 .75
101 Antawn Jamison .25 .60
102 Manu Ginobili .60 1.50
103 Ben Wallace .40 1.00
104 Paul Pierce .50 1.25
105 Mike Sweetney .20 .50
106 Ron Artest .30 .75
107 Michael Olowokandi .20 .50
108 Jason Terry .25 .60
109 Gordan Giricek .20 .50
110 Carlos Boozer .25 .60
111 Romain Sato RC .60 1.50
112 Chris Duhon RC .75 2.00
113 Ben Gordon RC 1.00 2.50
114 Matt Freije RC .60 1.50
115 Al Jefferson RC 1.00 2.50
116 Beno Udrih RC .75 2.00
117 Kirk Snyder RC .60 1.50
118 Anderson Varejao RC .75 2.00
119 Devin Harris RC .75 2.00
120 Tony Allen RC 1.00 2.50
121 Ha Seung-Jin RC .60 1.50
122 J.R. Smith RC 1.00 2.50
123 Blake Stepp RC 1.00 2.50
124 Jameer Nelson RC 1.00 2.50
125 Kris Humphries RC .75 2.00
126 Josh Childress RC .60 1.50
127 Tim Pickett RC .75 2.00
128 Delonte West RC .75 2.00
129 Dwight Howard RC 3.00 8.00
130 Luke Jackson RC .60 1.50
131 Rickey Paulding RC .60 1.50
132 Andre Emmett RC .60 1.50
133 Josh Smith RC 1.00 2.50
134 Antonio Burks RC .60 1.50
135 Ricky Minard RC .75 2.00
136 Lionel Chalmers RC .75 2.00
137 Shaun Livingston RC 1.00 2.50
138 Trevor Ariza RC 1.00 2.50
139 Sergei Lishouk RC .75 2.00
140 Pape Sow RC .60 1.50
141 Rashad Wright RC .60 1.50
142 Jackson Vroman RC .60 1.50
143 Luis Flores RC .75 2.00
144 Royal Ivey RC .60 1.50
145 Kevin Martin RC 1.25 3.00
146 Andre Iguodala RC 1.50 4.00
147 Andris Biedrins AU RC 3.00 8.00
148 Pavel Podkolzin AU RC 3.00 8.00
149 Luol Deng AU RC 5.00 12.00
150 Robert Swift AU RC 3.00 8.00
151 Sebastian Telfair AU RC 4.00 10.00
152 Emeka Okafor AU RC 4.00 10.00
153 Dorell Wright AU RC 4.00 10.00
154 Sasha Vujacic AU RC 4.00 10.00
155 Rafael Araujo AU RC 3.00 8.00
156 David Harrison AU RC 3.00 8.00

2004-05 Bowman Gold
*1-110 GOLD: 1.25 X TO 3X BASE HI
*111-146 GOLD: .6X TO 1.5X BASE HI
STATED ODDS ONE PER PACK
147 Andris Biedrins 1.00 2.50
148 Pavel Podkolzin 1.00 2.50
149 Luol Deng 1.50 4.00
150 Robert Swift 1.00 2.50
151 Sebastian Telfair 1.25 3.00
152 Emeka Okafor 1.25 3.00
153 Dorell Wright 1.25 3.00
154 Sasha Vujacic 1.25 3.00
155 Rafael Araujo 1.00 2.50
156 David Harrison 1.00 2.50

2004-05 Bowman Cityscape Relics
STATED ODDS 1:150
AH G.Arenas/J.Hayes 3.00 8.00
AR R.Allen/L.Ridnour 3.00 8.00
BK E.Brand/C.Kaman 3.00 8.00
CH E.Curry/K.Hinrich 3.00 8.00
DG T.Duncan/M.Ginobili 12.00 30.00
FG S.Francis/D.Gooden 3.00 8.00
GJ P.Gasol/D.Jones 3.00 8.00
GO K.Garnett/M.Olowokandi 6.00 15.00
IB Z.Ilgauskas/C.Boozer 3.00 8.00
IG A.Iverson/W.Green 6.00 15.00
KJ J.Kidd/R.Jefferson 5.00 12.00
MA A.Miller/C.Anthony 5.00 12.00
MF D.Mason/T.Ford 3.00 8.00
MM T.McGrady/Y.Ming 8.00 20.00
MO R.Miller/J.O'Neal 6.00 15.00
MS S.Marbury/M.Sweetney 3.00 8.00
MW J.Mashburn/D.West 3.00 8.00
NH D.Nowitzki/J.Howard 3.00 8.00
OW L.Odom/D.Wade 6.00 15.00
PB P.Pierce/M.Banks 3.00 8.00
PR G.Payton/K.Rush 3.00 8.00
RP J.Richardson/M.Pietrus 3.00 8.00
TD J.Terry/B.Diaw 3.00 8.00
WP B.Wallace/T.Prince 3.00 8.00
WS C.Webber/P.Stojakovic 4.00 10.00
ARR S.Abdur-Rahim/Z.Randolph 3.00 8.00
MAS S.Marion/A.Stoudemire 5.00 12.00
OWA S.O'Neal/L.Walton 8.00 20.00
PEB M.Peterson/C.Bosh 3.00 8.00

2004-05 Bowman Instant Impact Relics
STATED ODDS 1:120
AI Allen Iverson 6.00 15.00
AK Andrei Kirilenko 2.00 5.00
AS Amare Stoudemire 2.50 6.00
AW Antoine Walker 2.50 6.00
CA Carmelo Anthony 5.00 12.00
EB Elton Brand 2.00 5.00
JK Jason Kidd 4.00 10.00
JR Jason Richardson 2.50 6.00
PG Pau Gasol 4.00 10.00
SF Steve Francis 2.50 6.00
SM Stephon Marbury 3.00 8.00
SO Shaquille O'Neal 10.00 25.00
TD Tim Duncan 6.00 15.00
TP Tony Parker 4.00 10.00
YM Yao Ming 6.00 15.00

2004-05 Bowman Original Rookies
COMPLETE SET (8) 50.00 100.00
PRINT RUN 50 TO 100 SER.#'d SETS
115 T.Duncan 97-98T 5.00 12.00
138 K.Bryant 96-97T 60.00 150.00
171 A.Iverson 96-97T 6.00 15.00
185 Y.Ming 02-03T 6.00 15.00
199 V.Carter 98-99T 5.00 12.00
221 L.James 03-04T/50 200.00 500.00
225 D.Wade 03-04T 8.00 20.00
237 K.Garnett 95-96T 5.00 12.00
362 S.O'Neal 92-93T 15.00 40.00

2004-05 Bowman Remembering Rookies Autographs
STATED ODDS: GROUP A 1:658, B 1:1579
AS Amare Stoudemire A 6.00 15.00
BD Baron Davis B 6.00 15.00
CA Carmelo Anthony A 12.00 30.00
JK Jason Kidd A 15.00 40.00
JO Jermaine O'Neal A 6.00 15.00
LO Lamar Odom A 6.00 15.00
PS Peja Stojakovic A 6.00 15.00
RH Richard Hamilton A 8.00 20.00
SM Shawn Marion A 6.00 15.00
SO Shaquille O'Neal A 40.00 80.00
TD Tim Duncan A 200.00 500.00
TM Tracy McGrady A 20.00 50.00
SMA Stephon Marbury B 12.00 30.00

2004-05 Bowman Rookie Registration Relics
STATED ODDS 1:44
AE Andre Emmett 1.50 4.00
AI Andre Iguodala 4.00 10.00
AJ Al Jefferson 2.50 6.00
AV Anderson Varejao 2.00 5.00
BG Ben Gordon 2.50 6.00
CD Chris Duhon 2.50 6.00
DH Dwight Howard 8.00 20.00
DW Dorell Wright 2.00 5.00
EO Emeka Okafor 2.50 6.00
JC Josh Childress 1.50 4.00
JN Jameer Nelson 2.00 5.00
JS Josh Smith 2.50 6.00
KH Kris Humphries 2.00 5.00
KM Kevin Martin 3.00 8.00
KS Kirk Snyder 1.50 4.00
LD Luol Deng 2.50 6.00
LJ Luke Jackson 1.50 4.00
RA Rafael Araujo 1.50 4.00
SL Shaun Livingston 2.50 6.00
ST Sebastian Telfair 2.00 5.00
TA Tony Allen 2.50 6.00
DEH Devin Harris 2.00 5.00
DHA David Harrison 1.50 4.00
DWE Delonte West 2.00 5.00
JRS J.R. Smith 2.50 6.00

2004-05 Bowman Signs of the Future
STATED ODDS 1:38
DREJER AND MONIA NEVER ISSUED
AB Antonio Burks 2.00 5.00
AE Andre Emmett 2.00 5.00
AJ Al Jefferson 3.00 8.00
AV Anderson Varejao 2.50 6.00
BG Ben Gordon 3.00 8.00
BR Bernard Robinson 2.00 5.00
BS Blake Stepp 3.00 8.00
BU Beno Udrih 2.50 6.00
CD Chris Duhon 2.50 6.00
DH Devin Harris 2.50 6.00
DW Delonte West 2.50 6.00
EO Emeka Okafor 2.50 6.00
JN Jameer Nelson 3.00 8.00
JO Josh Childress 2.00 5.00
JR Justin Reed 2.00 5.00
JS Josh Smith 3.00 8.00
JV Jackson Vroman 2.00 5.00
KM Kevin Martin 4.00 10.00
KS Kirk Snyder 2.00 5.00
KY Kris Humphries 2.50 6.00
LJ Luke Jackson 2.00 5.00
MF Matt Freije 2.00 5.00
PS Pape Sow 2.00 5.00
RM Ricky Minard 2.50 6.00
RP Rickey Paulding 2.00 5.00
RS Romain Sato 2.00 5.00
RW Rashad Wright 2.00 5.00
SL Sergei Lishouk 2.50 6.00
TA Trevor Ariza 3.00 8.00
TP Tim Pickett 2.50 6.00
HSJ Ha Seung-Jin 2.50 6.00
JRS J.R. Smith 3.00 8.00
SLI Shaun Livingston 3.00 8.00
TAI Tony Allen 3.00 8.00

2004-05 Bowman Twice As Nice Relics
STATED ODDS 1:207
CB Carlos Boozer 2.50 6.00
CM Cuttino Mobley 2.50 6.00
EN Eduardo Najera 2.00 5.00
GA Gilbert Arenas 3.00 8.00
MG Manu Ginobili 6.00 15.00
MJ Marko Jaric 2.00 5.00
MR Michael Redd 2.50 6.00
RL Rashard Lewis 2.50 6.00
RM Ronald Murray 2.00 5.00

2005-06 Bowman
COMP.SET w/o RC's (110) 20.00 50.00
AU RC STATED ODDS 1:63
1 Steve Nash 1.00 2.50
2 Primoz Brezec .30 .75
3 Baron Davis .50 1.25
4 Al Harrington .40 1.00
5 Caron Butler .40 1.00
6 Marcus Camby .40 1.00
7 Carlos Boozer .40 1.00
8 Ben Gordon .40 1.00
9 Stephen Jackson .40 1.00
10 Dirk Nowitzki 1.25 3.00
11 Nenad Krstic .30 .75
12 Jason Richardson .50 1.25
13 Brendan Haywood .30 .75
14 Chauncey Billups .60 1.50
15 Corey Maggette .40 1.00
16 Peja Stojakovic .60 1.50
17 Grant Hill .75 2.00
18 Pau Gasol .75 2.00
19 Vladimir Radmanovic .30 .75
20 Jason Kidd .75 2.00
21 Tim Duncan 1.25 3.00
22 David Harrison .30 .75
23 LeBron James 4.00 10.00
24 Udonis Haslem .30 .75
25 Dan Dickau .30 .75
26 Cuttino Mobley .30 .75
27 Chris Bosh .60 1.50
28 Sebastian Telfair .40 1.00
29 Latrell Sprewell .50 1.25
30 Emeka Okafor .40 1.00
31 Mike James .30 .75
32 Trevor Ariza .30 .75
33 Larry Hughes .40 1.00
34 Desmond Mason .30 .75
35 Tayshaun Prince .50 1.25
36 Manu Ginobili 1.00 2.50
37 Mike Bibby .50 1.25
38 Andre Iguodala .50 1.25
39 Jamaal Magloire .30 .75
40 Amare Stoudemire .50 1.25
41 Rafer Alston .30 .75
42 Elton Brand .50 1.25
43 Steve Francis .50 1.25
44 Rashard Lewis .40 1.00
45 Lorenzen Wright .30 .75
46 Kirk Hinrich .40 1.00
47 Andrei Kirilenko .40 1.00
48 Brad Miller .40 1.00
49 Jamal Crawford .50 1.25
50 Shaquille O'Neal 1.50 4.00
51 Shaun Livingston .40 1.00
52 Troy Murphy .40 1.00
53 Drew Gooden .40 1.00
54 Paul Pierce .75 2.00
55 Vince Carter .40 1.00
56 Wally Szczerbiak .40 1.00
57 Antawn Jamison .40 1.00
58 Marquis Daniels .30 .75
59 Gerald Wallace .40 1.00
60 Ray Allen .75 2.00
61 Jamaal Tinsley .30 .75
62 Shane Battier .40 1.00
63 Zydrunas Ilgauskas .40 1.00
64 Mehmet Okur .30 .75
65 Rasheed Wallace .50 1.25
66 Maurice Williams .40 1.00
67 Josh Howard .40 1.00
68 Zach Randolph .50 1.25
69 Kobe Bryant 4.00 10.00
70 Tracy McGrady .75 2.00
71 Luke Ridnour .40 1.00
72 Damon Jones .30 .75
73 Tony Allen .30 .75
74 Mike Miller .40 1.00
75 Sam Cassell .40 1.00
76 Ben Wallace .60 1.50
77 Mike Sweetney .30 .75
78 Eddy Curry .30 .75
79 Michael Redd .40 1.00
80 Carmelo Anthony .75 2.00
81 Dwight Howard .60 1.50
82 Josh Smith .40 1.00
83 Richard Jefferson .40 1.00
84 Richard Hamilton .60 1.50
85 Chris Webber .60 1.50
86 Shawn Marion .40 1.00
87 Jalen Rose .40 1.00
88 Bob Sura .30 .75
89 Mike Dunleavy .30 .75
90 Dwyane Wade 1.00 2.50
91 Gary Payton .75 2.00
92 Luol Deng .40 1.00
93 Kenyon Martin .40 1.00
94 Beno Udrih .30 .75
95 J.R. Smith .50 1.25
96 Lamar Odom .40 1.00
97 Andre Miller .40 1.00
98 Jermaine O'Neal .40 1.00
99 Yao Ming 1.00 2.50
100 Allen Iverson 1.00 2.50
101 Quentin Richardson .30 .75
102 Gilbert Arenas .50 1.25
103 Stephon Marbury .60 1.50
104 Antoine Walker .40 1.00
105 Jameer Nelson .30 .75
106 Joel Przybilla .30 .75
107 Devin Harris .30 .75
108 Tony Parker .75 2.00
109 Josh Childress .30 .75
110 Kevin Garnett 1.25 3.00
111 Chris Paul RC 5.00 12.00
112 Danny Granger RC 1.00 2.50
113 Antoine Wright RC .75 2.00
114 Joey Graham RC .75 2.00
115 Wayne Simien RC .60 1.50
116 Channing Frye RC .75 2.00
117 Charlie Villanueva RC .75 2.00
118 Francisco Garcia RC .60 1.50
119 Ike Diogu RC .60 1.50
120 Jarrett Jack RC 1.00 2.50
121 Robert Whaley RC .60 1.50
122 C.J. Miles RC .75 2.00
123 Ryan Gomes RC .75 2.00
124 Nate Robinson RC 1.00 2.50
125 Daniel Ewing RC .75 2.00
126 Andray Blatche RC .75 2.00
127 Luther Head RC .60 1.50
128 Julius Hodge RC .60 1.50
129 Lawrence Roberts RC .60 1.50
130 Jason Maxiell RC .60 1.50
131 Martynas Andriuskevicius RC .75 2.00
132 Ersan Ilyasova RC .75 2.00
133 Martell Webster RC .75 2.00
134 Andrew Bynum RC .75 2.00
135 Louis Williams RC 2.50 6.00
136 Johan Petro RC .60 1.50
137 Brandon Bass RC .75 2.00
138 Travis Diener RC .60 1.50
139 Bracey Wright RC .60 1.50
140 Marvin Williams RC 1.00 2.50
141 Eddie Basden RC .60 1.50
142 Von Wafer RC .60 1.50
143 David Lee RC 1.00 2.50
144 Linas Kleiza RC .75 2.00
145 Luke Schenscher RC .60 1.50
146 Yaroslav Korolev RC .60 1.50
147 Carmen Electra 2.50 6.00
148 Christie Brinkley 2.50 6.00
149 Shannon Elizabeth 2.50 6.00
150 Jenny McCarthy 2.50 6.00
151 Jay-Z 1.25 3.00
152 Raymond Felton AU RC 3.00 8.00
153 Gerald Green AU RC 4.00 10.00
154 Rashad McCants AU RC 2.50 6.00
155 Andrew Bogut AU RC 5.00 12.00
156 Chris Taft AU RC 2.50 6.00
157 Sarunas Jasikevicius AU RC 4.00 10.00
158 Hakim Warrick AU RC 3.00 8.00
159 Deron Williams AU RC 6.00 15.00
160 Sean May AU RC 2.50 6.00
161 Monta Ellis AU RC 5.00 12.00
DSBS A.Bogut/A.Smith AU/100 50.00 120.00

2005-06 Bowman Gold
*1-110 GOLD: .75X TO 2X BASE HI
*111-151 GOLD: .6X TO 1.5X BASE HI
152-161 CARDS ARE NOT AUTOGRAPHED
STATED ODDS ONE PER PACK

2005-06 Bowman Back to the Future Autographs
GROUP A ODDS 1:511, GROUP B 1:8263
AI Allen Iverson B 75.00 200.00
BD Baron Davis B 10.00 25.00
BW Ben Wallace A 15.00 40.00
JK Jason Kidd B 30.00 80.00
LO Lamar Odom A 12.00 30.00
RH Richard Hamilton B 12.00 30.00
SM Stephon Marbury B 12.00 30.00
SO Shaquille O'Neal B ERR 75.00 200.00
TD Tim Duncan A 500.00 1,000.00

2005-06 Bowman Beginnings Relics
STATED ODDS 1:324
AA C.Anthony/R.Artest 5.00 12.00
AI G.Arenas Warm/A.Iguodala 5.00 12.00
BM C.Bosh/S.Marbury 5.00 12.00
DH Luol Deng/Grant Hill Warm 6.00 15.00
GH B.Gordon/R.Hamilton Warm 5.00 12.00
HF D.Harris Shirt/M.Finley 5.00 12.00
JW A.Jamison/R.Wallace 5.00 12.00
OA E.Okafor/R.Allen 5.00 12.00
PH P.Pierce/K.Hinrich Shirt 6.00 15.00
DHO Duncan Shirt/Howard Shorts 6.00 15.00

2005-06 Bowman Bravo Relics
STATED ODDS 1:60
AI Andre Iguodala 3.00 8.00
AK Andrei Kirilenko 2.50 6.00
AS Amare Stoudemire Shirt 3.00 8.00
AV Anderson Varejao 2.00 5.00
BG Ben Gordon 2.50 6.00
CA Carmelo Anthony 5.00 12.00
CB Christie Brinkley Jeans 8.00 20.00
CE Carmen Electra Jeans 10.00 25.00
DH Dwight Howard 4.00 10.00
DW Dwyane Wade 6.00 15.00
EO Emeka Okafor 2.50 6.00
GA Gilbert Arenas Shirt 3.00 8.00
JM Jenny McCarthy Jeans 8.00 20.00
JS Josh Smith 2.50 6.00
JZ Jay-Z Jeans 40.00 100.00
KB Kobe Bryant 40.00 100.00
KH Kirk Hinrich Shorts 2.50 6.00
LD Luol Deng 2.50 6.00
PG Pau Gasol 5.00 12.00
RL Rashard Lewis 2.50 6.00
RW Rasheed Wallace 3.00 8.00
SE Shannon Elizabeth Jeans 8.00 20.00
SO Shaquille O'Neal 10.00 25.00
TD Tim Duncan Warm 8.00 20.00
YM Yao Ming 6.00 15.00
ZR Zach Randolph 3.00 8.00
DHA Devin Harris 2.00 5.00

2005-06 Bowman Signs of the Future
STATED ODDS 1:41
AB Andrew Bynum 3.00 8.00
AW Antoine Wright 3.00 8.00
BB Brandon Bass 3.00 8.00
CV Charlie Villanueva 3.00 8.00
DE Daniel Ewing 3.00 8.00
DG Danny Granger 4.00 10.00
DL David Lee 4.00 10.00
FG Francisco Garcia 2.50 6.00
ID Ike Diogu 2.50 6.00
JG Joey Graham 3.00 8.00
JH Julius Hodge 2.50 6.00
JJ Jarrett Jack 4.00 10.00
JM Jason Maxiell 3.00 8.00
JP Johan Petro 2.50 6.00
LH Luther Head 2.50 6.00
MW Martell Webster 3.00 8.00
RU Roko Ukic 4.00 10.00
SJ Sarunas Jasikevicius 4.00 10.00
TD Travis Diener 2.50 6.00
VW Von Wafer 2.50 6.00
WS Wayne Simien 2.50 6.00

2005-06 Bowman Skills Nation Relics
STATED ODDS 1:81
AI Allen Iverson 6.00 15.00
AM Andre Miller 2.50 6.00
BW Ben Wallace Warm 4.00 10.00
DM Desmond Mason 2.00 5.00
DW Dwyane Wade 6.00 15.00
FJ Fred Jones 2.00 5.00
JK Jason Kidd 5.00 12.00
JR Jason Richardson 3.00 8.00
JS Josh Smith 2.50 6.00
MB Mike Bibby 3.00 8.00
MC Marcus Camby 2.50 6.00
MR Michael Redd 2.50 6.00
PS Peja Stojakovic 2.50 6.00
QR Quentin Richardson 2.00 5.00
RA Ray Allen 5.00 12.00
SM Stephon Marbury 4.00 10.00
SN Steve Nash 6.00 15.00
SO Shaquille O'Neal 10.00 25.00
VL Voshon Lenard 2.00 5.00
DMU Dikembe Mutombo 4.00 10.00

2005-06 Bowman Welcome to the Show Relics
STATED ODDS 1:41
AW Antoine Wright 2.50 6.00
BB Brandon Bass 2.50 6.00
CF Channing Frye 2.50 6.00
CP Chris Paul 15.00 40.00
CV Charlie Villanueva 2.50 6.00
DE Daniel Ewing 2.50 6.00
DG Danny Granger 3.00 8.00
DL David Lee 3.00 8.00
DW Deron Williams 5.00 12.00
EI Ersan Ilyasova 2.50 6.00
FG Francisco Garcia 2.00 5.00
GG Gerald Green 3.00 8.00
HW Hakim Warrick 2.50 6.00
JG Joey Graham 2.50 6.00
JH Julius Hodge 2.00 5.00
JJ Jarrett Jack 3.00 8.00
JM Jason Maxiell 2.00 5.00
LH Luther Head 2.00 5.00
MW Martell Webster 2.50 6.00
NR Nate Robinson 3.00 8.00
RF Raymond Felton 2.50 6.00
RM Rashad McCants 2.00 5.00
SJ Sarunas Jasikevicius 3.00 8.00
SM Sean May 2.00 5.00
WS Wayne Simien 2.00 5.00
ABO Andrew Bogut 4.00 10.00
CJM C.J. Miles 2.50 6.00

2006-07 Bowman
COMPLETE SET (165) 25.00 60.00
COMP.SET w/o RC'S (115) 10.00 25.00
1 Gilbert Arenas .50 1.25
2 Delonte West .30 .75
3 Gerald Wallace .40 1.00
4 Ike Diogu .30 .75
5 Mike Miller .40 1.00
6 Kobe Bryant 4.00 10.00
7 Richard Hamilton .50 1.25
8 Vince Carter 1.00 2.50
9 Elton Brand .40 1.00
10 Boris Diaw .40 1.00
11 Carmelo Anthony .75 2.00
12 Jermaine O'Neal .50 1.25
13 Al Harrington .40 1.00
14 Dwight Howard .60 1.50
15 Chris Bosh .60 1.50
16 Ben Gordon .60 1.50
17 Josh Howard .40 1.00
18 Yao Ming 1.25 3.00
19 David West .40 1.00
20 Tim Duncan 1.25 3.00
21 Andre Iguodala .50 1.25
22 LeBron James 4.00 10.00
23 Channing Frye .30 .75
24 Antoine Walker .50 1.25
25 Ricky Davis .40 1.00
26 Lamar Odom .40 1.00
27 Amare Stoudemire .50 1.25
28 Mike Bibby .50 1.25
29 Allen Iverson 1.25 3.00
30 Marvin Williams .30 .75
31 Wally Szczerbiak .40 1.00
32 Ben Wallace .60 1.50
33 Nenad Krstic .30 .75
34 Deron Williams .40 1.00
35 Troy Murphy .30 .75
36 Raymond Felton .30 .75
37 Jason Terry .40 1.00
38 Zach Randolph .50 1.25
39 Pau Gasol .75 2.00
40 Larry Hughes .40 1.00
41 Luol Deng .40 1.00
42 Steve Francis .50 1.25
43 Chauncey Billups .60 1.50
44 Smush Parker .30 .75
45 Shareef Abdur-Rahim .50 1.25
46 Andrei Kirilenko .40 1.00
47 Shawn Marion .50 1.25
48 Darko Milicic .30 .75
49 Shaquille O'Neal 2.00 5.00
50 Kevin Garnett 1.25 3.00
51 Michael Finley .50 1.25
52 Peja Stojakovic .40 1.00
53 Michael Redd .40 1.00
54 Desmond Mason .30 .75
55 Luke Ridnour .40 1.00
56 Kenyon Martin .40 1.00
57 Morris Peterson .30 .75
58 Chris Kaman .30 .75
59 Jason Richardson .50 1.25
60 Jason Kidd .75 2.00
61 Carlos Boozer .40 1.00
62 Rashad McCants .30 .75
63 Nate Robinson .40 1.00
64 Devin Harris .30 .75
65 Andrew Bogut .40 1.00
66 Chris Duhon .30 .75
67 Drew Gooden .40 1.00
68 Manu Ginobili 1.00 2.50
69 Jameer Nelson .30 .75
70 Corey Maggette .40 1.00
71 Charlie Villanueva .30 .75
72 Shane Battier .40 1.00
73 Udonis Haslem .30 .75
74 Tracy McGrady .75 2.00
75 Bobby Simmons .30 .75
76 Baron Davis .50 1.25
77 Zydrunas Ilgauskas .40 1.00
78 Danny Granger .30 .75
79 Hakim Warrick .30 .75
80 Josh Smith .30 .75
81 Tayshaun Prince .50 1.25
82 Rashard Lewis .40 1.00
83 Luther Head .30 .75
84 Andre Miller .40 1.00
85 T.J. Ford .30 .75
86 Sebastian Telfair .30 .75
87 Dirk Nowitzki 1.25 3.00
88 Kwame Brown .30 .75
89 Antawn Jamison .40 1.00
90 Ron Artest .50 1.25
91 Mehmet Okur .30 .75
92 Emeka Okafor .40 1.00
93 Sam Cassell .40 1.00
94 Chris Paul 1.00 2.50
95 Chris Webber .60 1.50
96 Richard Jefferson .40 1.00
97 Dwyane Wade 1.00 2.50
98 Tony Parker .75 2.00
99 Paul Pierce .75 2.00
100 Marcus Camby .40 1.00
101 Ray Allen .75 2.00
102 Stephon Marbury .60 1.50
103 Rasheed Wallace .60 1.50
104 Brad Miller .40 1.00
105 Kirk Hinrich .40 1.00
106 Steve Nash 1.00 2.50
107 Sarunas Jasikevicius .40 1.00
108 Darius Miles .30 .75
109 Joe Johnson .50 1.25
110 Caron Butler .40 1.00
111 John Wooden CO 1.25 3.00
112 Ben Howland CO 1.00 2.50
113 Jim Calhoun CO 1.00 2.50
114 Jim Boeheim CO 1.00 2.50
115 Roy Williams CO 1.00 2.50
116 LaMarcus Aldridge RC 2.50 6.00
117 Marcus Vinicius RC .60 1.50
118 Sergio Rodriguez RC .75 2.00
119 Will Blalock RC .60 1.50
120 Paul Millsap RC 1.25 3.00
121 Leon Powe RC .60 1.50
122 Rudy Gay RC 1.25 3.00
123 Tyrus Thomas RC .75 2.00
124 Brandon Roy RC 2.00 5.00
125 J.R. Pinnock RC .60 1.50
126 Kevin Pittsnogle RC .75 2.00
127 Mile Ilic RC .60 1.50
128 Mardy Collins RC .60 1.50
129 Craig Smith RC .75 2.00
130 Jordan Farmar RC .75 2.00
131 Quincy Douby RC .60 1.50
132 James Augustine RC .60 1.50
133 Josh Boone RC .60 1.50
134 Shannon Brown RC .60 1.50
135 David Noel RC .60 1.50
136 Kyle Lowry RC 3.00 8.00
137 Ryan Hollins RC .60 1.50
138 Renaldo Balkman RC .75 2.00
139 James White RC .60 1.50
140 Damir Markota RC .60 1.50
141 Paul Davis RC .60 1.50
142 Alexander Johnson RC .60 1.50
143 Steve Novak RC .75 2.00
144 P.J. Tucker RC 1.00 2.50
145 Saer Sene RC .60 1.50
146 Bobby Jones RC .60 1.50
147 Cedric Simmons RC .60 1.50
148 Allan Ray RC .60 1.50
149 Solomon Jones RC .60 1.50
150 Ronnie Brewer RC 1.00 2.50
151 Thabo Sefolosha RC .75 2.00
152 Maurice Ager RC .60 1.50
153 Daniel Gibson RC .75 2.00
154 Shawne Williams RC .60 1.50
155 Dee Brown RC .60 1.50
156 Andrea Bargnani RC .75 2.00

157 Patrick O'Bryant RC .60 1.50
158 Shelden Williams RC .60 1.50
159 Hilton Armstrong RC .60 1.50
160 Adam Morrison RC .75 2.00
161 Rodney Carney RC .60 1.50
162 Randy Foye RC .75 2.00
163 Rajon Rondo RC 3.00 8.00
164 Marcus Williams RC .60 1.50
165 J.J. Redick RC 2.00 5.00

2006-07 Bowman Bronze

*BRONZE 1-115: 3X TO 8X BASE HI
*BRONZE 116-165: 1.5X TO 4X BASE HI
STATED PRINT RUN 50 SER.#'d SETS
6 Kobe Bryant 60.00 150.00
20 Tim Duncan 8.00 20.00
22 LeBron James 75.00 200.00

2006-07 Bowman Silver

*SILVER 1-115: 1.25X TO 3X BASE HI
*SILVER 116-165: .75X TO 2X BASE HI
STATED PRINT RUN 379 SER.#'d SETS

2006-07 Bowman McDonald's All-American Rookie Relics

STATED ODDS 1:60
1 Jordan Farmar 2.00 5.00
2 Rajon Rondo 8.00 20.00
3 Shannon Brown 1.50 4.00
4 Dee Brown 1.50 4.00
5 Paul Davis 1.50 4.00
6 J.J. Redick 5.00 12.00

2006-07 Bowman McDonald's All-American Rookie Relics Autographs

PRINT RUN 50 SER.#'d SETS
1 Jordan Farmar 5.00 12.00
2 Rajon Rondo 30.00 80.00
3 Shannon Brown 4.00 10.00
4 Dee Brown 4.00 10.00
5 Paul Davis 4.00 10.00
6 J.J. Redick 12.00 30.00

2006-07 Bowman Power of 2 Autographs

PRINT RUN 10 TO 25 SER.#'d SETS
MW A.Morrison/D.Wade B 50.00 125.00

2006-07 Bowman Relics

GROUP A STATED ODDS 1:107
GROUP B STATED ODDS 1:19
*DUAL: .5X TO 1.25X BASE HI
DUAL PRINT RUN 249 SER.#'d SETS
*TRIPLE: .6X TO 1.5X BASE HI
TRIPLE PRINT RUN 50 SER.#'d SETS
AB Andrew Bogut B 2.00 5.00
AI Allen Iverson A 6.00 15.00
AJ Antawn Jamison A 2.00 5.00
AM Adam Morrison B 2.00 5.00
BJ Bobby Jones B 1.50 4.00
BW Ben Wallace A Shorts 3.00 8.00
CA Carmelo Anthony B 4.00 10.00
CB Chris Bosh B Shirt 3.00 8.00
CP Chris Paul B Shorts 5.00 12.00
CS Cedric Simmons B 1.50 4.00
CW Chris Webber A 3.00 8.00
DH Dwight Howard A 3.00 8.00
DN Dirk Nowitzki A Shorts 6.00 15.00
DW Dwyane Wade B 5.00 12.00
GA Gilbert Arenas B Shirt 2.50 6.00
HA Hilton Armstrong B 1.50 4.00
JB Josh Boone B 1.50 4.00
JF Jordan Farmar B 2.00 5.00
JS Josh Smith A 1.50 4.00
KB Kobe Bryant B 40.00 100.00
KG Kevin Garnett A Warm 6.00 15.00
LA LaMarcus Aldridge B 6.00 15.00
MB Mike Bibby B 2.50 6.00
MC Mardy Collins B 1.50 4.00
MW Marcus Williams B 1.50 4.00
PD Paul Davis B 1.50 4.00
PO Patrick O'Bryant B 1.50 4.00
PP Paul Pierce A Warm 4.00 10.00
QD Quincy Douby B 1.50 4.00
RA Ray Allen B 4.00 10.00
RB Renaldo Balkman B 2.00 5.00
RC Rodney Carney B 1.50 4.00
RF Randy Foye B 2.00 5.00
RG Rudy Gay B 3.00 8.00
RR Rajon Rondo B 6.00 15.00
RW Rasheed Wallace B 3.00 8.00
SJ Solomon Jones B 1.50 4.00
SM Shawn Marion A 2.50 6.00
SN Steve Nash A Warm 5.00 12.00
SO Shaquille O'Neal B 10.00 25.00
SW Shelden Williams B 1.50 4.00
TD Tim Duncan B 6.00 15.00
YM Yao Ming B 6.00 15.00
CSM Craig Smith B 2.00 5.00
DNO David Noel B 1.50 4.00
JJR J.J. Redick B 5.00 12.00
PJT P.J. Tucker B 2.50 6.00
RAR Ron Artest A 2.50 6.00
RBR Ronnie Brewer B 2.50 6.00
SNO Steve Novak B 2.00 5.00

2006-07 Bowman Rookie Snapshots Relics

PRINT RUN 199 SER.#'d SETS
AM Adam Morrison 2.50 6.00
CS Cedric Simmons 2.00 5.00
DB Dee Brown 2.00 5.00
HA Hilton Armstrong 2.00 5.00
JB Josh Boone 2.00 5.00
JF Jordan Farmar 2.50 6.00
JW James White 2.00 5.00
KL Kyle Lowry 10.00 25.00
KP Kevin Pittsnogle 2.50 6.00
LA LaMarcus Aldridge 8.00 20.00
MA Maurice Ager 2.00 5.00
MW Marcus Williams 2.00 5.00
PO Patrick O'Bryant 2.00 5.00
QD Quincy Douby 2.00 5.00
RB Renaldo Balkman 2.50 6.00
RC Rodney Carney 2.00 5.00
RF Randy Foye 2.50 6.00
RG Rudy Gay 4.00 10.00
RR Rajon Rondo 8.00 20.00
SB Shannon Brown 2.00 5.00
SW Shelden Williams 2.00 5.00
CSM Craig Smith 2.50 6.00
JJR J.J. Redick 6.00 15.00
RBR Ronnie Brewer 3.00 8.00
SWI Shawne Williams 2.00 5.00

2007-08 Bowman

COMPLETE SET (160) 30.00 80.00
COMP.SET w/o SP's (110) 15.00 40.00
RC PRINT RUN 2999 SER.#'d SETS
1 Gilbert Arenas .50 1.25
2 Dwight Howard .60 1.50
3 Dwyane Wade 1.00 2.50
4 Chris Bosh .60 1.50
5 Josh Smith .30 .75
6 Andrew Bogut .40 1.00
7 Ben Gordon .40 1.00
8 Deron Williams .40 1.00
9 Tony Parker .75 2.00
10 Mike Bibby .50 1.25
11 Yao Ming 1.25 3.00
12 Raymond Felton .40 1.00
13 Steve Nash 1.00 2.50
14 Jameer Nelson .30 .75
15 Carmelo Anthony .75 2.00
16 Pau Gasol .75 2.00
17 Rashard Lewis .40 1.00
18 Eddy Curry .30 .75
19 Luol Deng .40 1.00
20 Kevin Garnett 1.25 3.00
21 Tim Duncan 1.25 3.00
22 Michael Redd .40 1.00
23 LeBron James 4.00 10.00
24 Kobe Bryant 4.00 10.00
25 Al Jefferson .30 .75
26 Mike Dunleavy .30 .75
27 Tyson Chandler .50 1.25
28 Zach Randolph .50 1.25
29 Jason Richardson .50 1.25
30 Rasheed Wallace .60 1.50
31 Shawn Marion .50 1.25
32 Shaquille O'Neal 2.00 5.00
33 Allen Iverson 1.25 3.00
34 Paul Pierce .75 2.00
35 Adam Morrison .30 .75
36 Mike Miller .40 1.00
37 Larry Hughes .40 1.00
38 Kevin Martin .40 1.00
39 Charlie Villanueva .30 .75
40 Vince Carter 1.00 2.50
41 Dirk Nowitzki 1.25 3.00
42 Elton Brand .40 1.00
43 Ray Allen .75 2.00
44 Luke Walton .40 1.00
45 Chris Paul 1.00 2.50
46 Marcus Camby .40 1.00
47 Andrei Kirilenko .40 1.00
48 J.J. Redick .50 1.25
49 Richard Hamilton .60 1.50
50 Emeka Okafor .40 1.00
51 Manu Ginobili 1.00 2.50
52 Monta Ellis .40 1.00
53 Jorge Garbajosa .40 1.00
54 Kyle Korver .50 1.25
55 Jason Kidd .75 2.00
56 Randy Foye .40 1.00
57 Shane Battier .40 1.00
58 Shaun Livingston .40 1.00
59 Jason Terry .40 1.00
60 Joe Johnson .40 1.00
61 Lamar Odom .40 1.00
62 Tayshaun Prince .50 1.25
63 Chris Wilcox .30 .75
64 Leandro Barbosa .40 1.00
65 Al Harrington .40 1.00
66 Jamal Crawford .50 1.25
67 Caron Butler .40 1.00
68 Chauncey Billups .60 1.50
69 Ricky Davis .40 1.00
70 Andrea Bargnani .30 .75
71 Samuel Dalembert .30 .75
72 LaMarcus Aldridge .50 1.25
73 Mehmet Okur .30 .75
74 Marcus Williams .30 .75
75 Andre Miller .40 1.00
76 Rudy Gay .40 1.00
77 Jermaine O'Neal .50 1.25
78 Boris Diaw .40 1.00
79 Ryan Gomes .30 .75
80 Gerald Wallace .40 1.00
81 Udonis Haslem .30 .75
82 Mo Williams .40 1.00
83 Jarrett Jack .40 1.00
84 Chris Webber .60 1.50
85 Trevor Ariza .30 .75
86 Kirk Hinrich .50 1.25
87 Rafer Alston .50 1.25
88 Danny Granger .40 1.00
89 David West .40 1.00
90 Drew Gooden .40 1.00
91 Stephon Marbury .60 1.50
92 Antawn Jamison .40 1.00
93 Ron Artest .50 1.25
94 Richard Jefferson .40 1.00
95 Carlos Boozer .40 1.00
96 Hakim Warrick .30 .75
97 T.J. Ford .30 .75
98 Desmond Mason .30 .75
99 Andre Iguodala .50 1.25
100 Amare Stoudemire 1.00 2.50
101 Tracy McGrady .75 2.00
102 Jason Kapono .30 .75
103 Ben Wallace .60 1.50
104 Marvin Williams .30 .75
105 Baron Davis .40 1.00
106 Andrew Bynum .30 .75
107 Brandon Roy .60 1.50
108 David Lee .30 .75
109 Corey Maggette .40 1.00
110 Josh Howard .40 1.00
111 Kevin Durant RC 125.00 300.00
112 Al Horford RC 4.00 10.00
113 Mike Conley Jr. RC 4.00 10.00
114 Jeff Green RC 1.25 3.00
115 Corey Brewer RC 1.25 3.00
116 Joakim Noah RC 1.50 4.00
117 Julian Wright RC 1.00 2.50
118 Ramon Sessions RC 1.25 3.00
119 Sammy Mejia RC 1.00 2.50
120 Luis Scola RC 1.50 4.00
121 Yi Jianlian RC 2.00 5.00
122 Aaron Afflalo RC 1.25 3.00
123 Carl Landry RC 1.00 2.50
124 Alando Tucker RC 1.00 2.50
125 Gabe Pruitt RC 1.00 2.50
126 Marcus Williams RC 1.00 2.50
127 Spencer Hawes RC 1.00 2.50
128 Acie Law RC 1.00 2.50
129 Thaddeus Young RC 1.50 4.00
130 Nick Fazekas RC 1.00 2.50
131 Al Thornton RC 1.00 2.50
132 Rodney Stuckey RC 1.00 2.50
133 Nick Young RC 1.50 4.00
134 Glen Davis RC 1.25 3.00
135 Jermareo Davidson RC 1.00 2.50
136 JamesOn Curry RC 1.00 2.50
137 Jason Smith RC 1.00 2.50
138 Daequan Cook RC 1.25 3.00
139 Jared Dudley RC 1.00 2.50
140 Derrick Byars RC 1.00 2.50
141 Josh McRoberts RC 1.00 2.50
142 Adam Haluska RC 1.00 2.50
143 Reyshawn Terry RC 1.00 2.50
144 Aaron Gray RC 1.00 2.50
145 Herbert Hill RC 1.00 2.50
146 Jared Jordan RC 1.00 2.50
147 Wilson Chandler RC 1.25 3.00
148 Morris Almond RC 1.00 2.50
149 Aaron Brooks RC 1.25 3.00
150 Petteri Koponen RC 1.25 3.00
151 Dominic McGuire RC 1.00 2.50
152 Greg Oden RC 1.50 4.00
153 Stephane Lasme RC 1.00 2.50
154 D.J. Strawberry RC 1.00 2.50
155 Sean Williams RC 1.00 2.50
156 Marco Belinelli RC 1.25 3.00
157 Javaris Crittenton RC 1.00 2.50
158 Demetris Nichols RC 1.00 2.50
159 Taurean Green RC 1.00 2.50
160 Brandan Wright RC 1.25 3.00

2007-08 Bowman Copper

*COPPER: .5X TO 1.25X BASE HI
COPPER PRINT RUN 399 SER.#'d SETS
23 LeBron James 12.00 30.00
24 Kobe Bryant 12.00 30.00
111 Kevin Durant 300.00 600.00

2007-08 Bowman Gold

*GOLD 1-110: 1.25X TO 3X BASE HI
*GOLD 111-160: 1.5X TO 4X BASE HI
GOLD PRINT RUN 99 SER.#'d SETS
111 Kevin Durant 600.00 1,200.00

2007-08 Bowman Silver

*SILVER: .75X TO 2X BASE HI
SILVER PRINT RUN 199 SER.#'d SETS
111 Kevin Durant 500.00 1,000.00

2007-08 Bowman Relics

*BRONZE: .6X TO 1.25X BASE HI
BRONZE PRINT RUN 50 SER.#'d SETS
*SILVER: .6X TO 1.5X BASE HI
SILVER PRINT RUN 25 SER.#'d SETS
*DUAL: .5X TO 1.25X BASE HI
DUAL PRINT RUN 199 SER.#'d SETS
*DUAL BRONZE: .6X TO 1.5X HI
DUAL BRONZE PRINT RUN 50 SETS
*DUAL SILVER: .75X TO 2X BASE HI
DUAL SILVER PRINT RUN 25 SETS
*TRIPLE: .6X TO 1.5X BASE HI
TRIPLE PRINT RUN 99 SER.#'d SETS
TRIPLE BRONZE: .75X TO 2X BASE HI
TRIPLE BRONZE PRINT RUN 50 SETS
*TRIPLE SILVER: 1X TO 2.5X BASE HI
TRIPLE SILVER PRINT RUN 25 SETS
AH Al Horford 6.00 15.00
AIG Andre Iguodala 2.50 6.00
AL Acie Law 1.50 4.00
AM Adam Morrison 1.50 4.00
AS Amare Stoudemire 2.50 6.00
AT Al Thornton 1.50 4.00
BG Ben Gordon 2.00 5.00
BR Brandon Roy 3.00 8.00
BWR Brandan Wright 2.00 5.00
C Corey Brewer 2.00 5.00
CA Carmelo Anthony 4.00 10.00
CB Chris Bosh 3.00 8.00
DH Dwight Howard 3.00 8.00
DN Dirk Nowitzki 6.00 15.00
DW Dwyane Wade 5.00 12.00
DWI Deron Williams 2.00 5.00
EB Elton Brand 2.00 5.00
GO Greg Oden 2.50 6.00
GW Gerald Wallace 2.00 5.00
JC Javaris Crittenton 1.50 4.00
JG Jeff Green 2.00 5.00
JK Jason Kidd 4.00 10.00
JN Joakim Noah 2.50 6.00
JR Jason Richardson 2.50 6.00
JS Josh Smith 1.50 4.00
JSM Jason Smith 1.50 4.00
JW Julian Wright 1.50 4.00
KB Kobe Bryant 50.00 120.00
KG Kevin Garnett 6.00 15.00
LB Larry Bird 10.00 25.00
LD Luol Deng 2.00 5.00
MB Mike Bibby 2.50 6.00
MC Mike Conley Jr. 6.00 15.00
MJ Magic Johnson 10.00 25.00
NY Nick Young 2.50 6.00
PG Pau Gasol 4.00 10.00
RA Ray Allen 4.00 10.00
RH Richard Hamilton 3.00 8.00
RS Rodney Stuckey 1.50 4.00
SH Spencer Hawes 1.50 4.00
SM Shawn Marion 2.50 6.00
SN Steve Nash 5.00 12.00
SO Shaquille O'Neal 10.00 25.00
SW Sean Williams 1.50 4.00
TD Tim Duncan 6.00 15.00
TM Tracy McGrady 4.00 10.00
TP Tony Parker 4.00 10.00
TY Thaddeus Young 2.50 6.00
VC Vince Carter 5.00 12.00
YM Yao Ming 6.00 15.00

2008-09 Bowman

COMPLETE SET (150) 60.00 150.00
1 Tracy McGrady .60 1.50
2 Jason Kidd .60 1.50
3 LeBron James 3.00 8.00
4 Chris Bosh .50 1.25
5 Kevin Garnett 1.00 2.50
6 Josh Smith .25 .60
7 Richard Hamilton .40 1.00
8 Monta Ellis .30 .75
9 Yi Jianlian .50 1.25
10 Danny Granger .30 .75
11 Richard Jefferson .30 .75
12 Elton Brand .30 .75
13 Rudy Gay .40 1.00
14 Andres Nocioni .25 .60
15 Carmelo Anthony .50 1.25
16 Pau Gasol .50 1.25
17 Corey Brewer .30 .75
18 Hedo Turkoglu .30 .75
19 Andre Iguodala .30 .75
20 Raymond Felton .25 .60
21 Tim Duncan 1.00 2.50
22 Michael Redd .30 .75
23 Chris Paul .75 2.00
24 Kobe Bryant 3.00 8.00
25 Brandon Roy .30 .75
26 Carlos Boozer .30 .75
27 Jeff Green .30 .75
28 Luis Scola .30 .75
29 Al Thornton .25 .60
30 Gilbert Arenas .40 1.00
31 Brandan Wright .25 .60
32 Shaquille O'Neal 1.25 3.00
33 Allen Iverson .75 2.00
34 Paul Pierce .60 1.50
35 Ben Gordon .30 .75
36 Jamal Crawford .40 1.00
37 Andrew Bynum .25 .60
38 Gerald Wallace .30 .75
39 Mike Conley Jr. .30 .75
40 Ben Wallace .50 1.25
41 Dirk Nowitzki 1.00 2.50
42 David Lee .25 .60
43 Mo Williams .30 .75
44 Al Jefferson .25 .60
45 Tayshaun Prince .40 1.00
46 Jameer Nelson .25 .60
47 Andrei Kirilenko .30 .75
48 David West .30 .75
49 Al Horford .40 1.00
50 Steve Nash .75 2.00
51 Ron Artest .40 1.00
52 Greg Oden .25 .60
53 Sean Williams .25 .60
54 Jamario Moon .25 .60
55 Baron Davis .40 1.00
56 Udonis Haslem .25 .60
57 Mike Dunleavy .25 .60
58 Shane Battier .30 .75
59 Andrew Bogut .30 .75
60 Ray Allen .60 1.50
61 Nick Young .25 .60
62 Manu Ginobili .75 2.00
63 Jason Richardson .40 1.00
64 Mike Miller .30 .75
65 Leandro Barbosa .30 .75
66 Luol Deng .30 .75
67 Shawn Marion .40 1.00
68 Peja Stojakovic .30 .75
69 Kevin Durant 1.50 4.00
70 Corey Maggette .30 .75
71 Chauncey Billups .50 1.25
72 Josh Howard .30 .75
73 Kevin Martin .30 .75
74 Anderson Varejao .25 .60
75 Craig Smith .25 .60
76 Antawn Jamison .30 .75
77 Marcus Camby .30 .75
78 Andre Miller .30 .75
79 Zach Randolph .40 1.00
80 Deron Williams .30 .75
81 Devin Harris .25 .60
82 Rashard Lewis .30 .75
83 Damien Wilkins .25 .60
84 LaMarcus Aldridge .40 1.00
85 Larry Hughes .30 .75
86 Brad Miller .30 .75
87 Jermaine O'Neal .40 1.00
88 Caron Butler .30 .75
89 Tyson Chandler .30 .75
90 Joe Johnson .40 1.00
91 Amare Stoudemire .50 1.25
92 Dwight Howard .50 1.25
93 Rajon Rondo .40 1.00
94 T.J. Ford .25 .60
95 Rodney Stuckey .25 .60
96 Samuel Dalembert .25 .60
97 Tony Parker .50 1.25
98 Vince Carter .75 2.00
99 Yao Ming 1.00 2.50
100 Dwyane Wade .75 2.00
101 Dominique Wilkins .60 1.50
102 Rick Barry .50 1.25
103 John Stockton .75 2.00
104 Magic Johnson 1.25 3.00
105 George Gervin .60 1.50
106 Bill Russell 1.25 3.00
107 David Robinson .75 2.00
108 Dennis Rodman .75 2.00
109 Larry Bird 1.25 3.00
110 Jerry West .75 2.00
111 Derrick Rose RC 8.00 20.00
112 Michael Beasley RC .75 2.00
113 O.J. Mayo RC .60 1.50
114 Russell Westbrook RC 12.00 30.00
115 Kevin Love RC 1.50 4.00
116 Danilo Gallinari RC 1.25 3.00
117 Eric Gordon RC 1.25 3.00
118 Joe Alexander RC .50 1.25
119 D.J. Augustin RC .75 2.00
120 Brook Lopez RC 1.00 2.50
121 Jerryd Bayless RC .60 1.50
122 Jason Thompson RC .50 1.25
123 Anthony Randolph RC .50 1.25
124 Robin Lopez RC .60 1.50
125 Marreese Speights RC .60 1.50
126 Roy Hibbert RC .60 1.50
127 JaVale McGee RC .75 2.00
128 J.J. Hickson RC .50 1.25
129 Alexis Ajinca RC .50 1.25
130 Ryan Anderson RC .60 1.50
131 Courtney Lee RC .60 1.50
132 Kosta Koufos RC .50 1.25
133 Donte Greene RC .50 1.25
134 George Hill RC .75 2.00
135 D.J. White RC .50 1.25
136 J.R. Giddens RC .50 1.25
137 Joey Dorsey RC .50 1.25
138 Mario Chalmers RC .75 2.00
139 DeAndre Jordan RC 1.00 2.50
140 Chris Douglas-Roberts RC .50 1.25
141 Malik Hairston RC .50 1.25
142 Sean Singletary RC .50 1.25
143 Kyle Weaver RC .50 1.25
144 Patrick Ewing Jr. RC .50 1.25
145 Walter Sharpe RC .50 1.25
146 Sonny Weems RC .50 1.25
147 Shan Foster RC .50 1.25
148 Nicolas Batum RC 1.00 2.50
149 Brandon Rush RC .50 1.25
150 Darrell Arthur RC .60 1.50

2008-09 Bowman Blue

*BLUE 1-110: .75X TO 2X BASE HI
*BLUE 111-150: 1X TO 2.5X BASE HI
BLUE PRINT RUN 499 SER.#'d SETS
3 LeBron James 20.00 50.00
114 Russell Westbrook 75.00 200.00

2008-09 Bowman Gold

*1-110 GOLD: 3X TO 8X BASE
*111-150 GOLD RC: 2X TO 5X BASE
GOLD PRINT RUN 50 SER.#'d SETS
3 LeBron James 75.00 200.00
111 Derrick Rose 75.00 200.00
114 Russell Westbrook 150.00 400.00

2008-09 Bowman Orange

*1-110 ORANGE: 1.25X TO 3X BASE
*111-150 ORANGE: 1.25X TO 3X BASE
ORANGE PRINT RUN 299 SETS
3 LeBron James 30.00 80.00
114 Russell Westbrook 100.00 250.00

2008-09 Bowman Draft Day Issue Relics

PRINT RUN 399 SER.#'d SETS
*BLUE: .5X TO 1.25X BASE HI
BLUE PRINT RUN 50 SER.#'d SETS
*ORANGE: .6X TO 1.5X BASE HI
ORANGE PRINT RUN 25 SETS
DDIRAR Anthony Randolph 1.50 4.00
DDIRBL Brook Lopez 3.00 8.00
DDIRBR Brandon Rush 1.50 4.00
DDIRDG Danilo Gallinari 4.00 10.00
DDIRDJA D.J. Augustin 2.50 6.00
DDIRDR Derrick Rose 12.00 30.00
DDIREG Eric Gordon 4.00 10.00
DDIRJA Joe Alexander 1.50 4.00
DDIRJB Jerryd Bayless 2.00 5.00
DDIRJD Joey Dorsey 1.50 4.00
DDIRKL Kevin Love 15.00 40.00
DDIRMB Michael Beasley 2.50 6.00
DDIROJM O.J. Mayo 2.00 5.00
DDIRRL Robin Lopez 2.00 5.00
DDIRRW Russell Westbrook 12.00 30.00

2008-09 Bowman Draft Day Issue Relics Autographs

PRINT RUN 75 SER.#'d SETS
*BLUE: .5X TO 1.25X BASE HI
BLUE PRINT RUN 50 SER.#'d SETS
*ORANGE: .6X TO 1.5X BASE HI
ORANGE PRINT RUN 25 SER.#'d SETS
DDIABL Brook Lopez 12.00 30.00
DDIADJA D.J. Augustin 10.00 25.00
DDIADR Derrick Rose 40.00 100.00
DDIAEG Eric Gordon 15.00 40.00
DDIAJA Joe Alexander 6.00 15.00
DDIAJB Jerryd Bayless 8.00 20.00
DDIAKL Kevin Love 20.00 50.00
DDIAMB Michael Beasley 10.00 25.00
DDIAOJM O.J. Mayo 8.00 20.00
DDIARW Russell Westbrook 150.00 400.00

2008-09 Bowman Draft Day Issue Relics Combos

PRINT RUN 99 SER.#'d SET
*BLUE: .5X TO 1.25X BASE HI
BLUE PRINT RUN 50 SER.#'d SETS
*ORANGE: .6X TO 1.5X BASE HI
ORANGE PRINT RUN 25 SETS
DDICAR Anthony Randolph 2.50 6.00
DDICBR Brandon Rush 2.50 6.00
DDICDG Danilo Gallinari 6.00 15.00
DDICJD Joey Dorsey 2.50 6.00
DDICRL Robin Lopez 3.00 8.00

2008-09 Bowman Draft Day Issue Relics Combos Autographs

PRINT RUN 75 SER.#'d SETS
*BLUE: .5X TO 1.25X BASE HI
BLUE PRINT RUN 50 SER.#'d SETS
*ORANGE: .6X TO 1.5X BASE HI
ORANGE PRINT RUN 25 SER.#'d SETS
DDICABL Brook Lopez 12.00 30.00
DDICADJA D.J. Augustin 10.00 25.00
DDICADR Derrick Rose 125.00 300.00
DDICAEG Eric Gordon 15.00 40.00
DDICAJA Joe Alexander 6.00 15.00
DDICAJB Jerryd Bayless 8.00 20.00
DDICAKL Kevin Love 20.00 50.00
DDICAMB Michael Beasley 10.00 25.00
DDICAOJM O.J. Mayo 8.00 20.00
DDICARW Russell Westbrook 50.00 125.00

2008-09 Bowman Relics

STATED ODDS 1:13
*BLUE: .75X TO 2X BASE HI
BLUE PRINT RUN 50 SER.#'d SETS
*ORANGE: 1X TO 2.5X BASE HI
ORANGE PRINT RUN 25 SETS
BRAH Al Horford 2.50 6.00
BRAI Allen Iverson 5.00 12.00
BRAJ Al Jefferson 1.50 4.00
BRAJA Antawn Jamison 2.00 5.00
BRAT Al Thornton 1.50 4.00
BRBR Brandon Roy 2.00 5.00
BRBW Ben Wallace 3.00 8.00
BRCA Carmelo Anthony 3.00 8.00
BRCB Chris Bosh 3.00 8.00
BRCBO Carlos Boozer 2.00 5.00
BRCBU Caron Butler 2.00 5.00
BRCM Corey Maggette 2.00 5.00
BRCP Chris Paul 5.00 12.00
BRDH Devin Harris 1.50 4.00
BRDHO Dwight Howard 3.00 8.00
BRDN Dirk Nowitzki 6.00 15.00
BRDW Dwyane Wade 5.00 12.00
BRDWI Deron Williams 2.00 5.00
BRJJ Joe Johnson 2.50 6.00
BRJO Jermaine O'Neal 2.50 6.00
BRJR Jason Richardson 2.50 6.00
BRKB Kobe Bryant 40.00 100.00
BRKG Kevin Garnett 6.00 15.00
BRLO Lamar Odom 2.00 5.00
BRMB Mike Bibby 2.50 6.00
BRMC Mike Conley Jr. 2.00 5.00
BRMG Manu Ginobili 5.00 12.00
BRMR Michael Redd 2.00 5.00
BRPG Pau Gasol 3.00 8.00
BRPP Paul Pierce 4.00 10.00
BRPS Peja Stojakovic 2.00 5.00
BRRA Ray Allen 4.00 10.00
BRRH Richard Hamilton 2.50 6.00
BRRL Rashard Lewis 2.00 5.00
BRRW Rasheed Wallace 3.00 8.00
BRSN Steve Nash 5.00 12.00
BRSO Shaquille O'Neal 8.00 20.00
BRTD Tim Duncan 6.00 15.00
BRTM Tracy McGrady 4.00 10.00
BRYM Yao Ming 6.00 15.00

2009-10 Bowman 48

COMPLETE SET (121) 800.00 1,500.00
COMP.SET w/o SP's (100) 12.00 30.00
101-114 RC PRINT RUN 2009 SER.#'d SETS
115-121 PRINT RUN 1948 SER.#'d SETS
1 Al Horford .40 1.00
2 Joe Johnson .40 1.00
3 Josh Smith .25 .60
4 Paul Pierce .60 1.50
5 Kevin Garnett 1.00 2.50
6 Ray Allen .60 1.50
7 Rajon Rondo .50 1.25
8 Gerald Wallace .30 .75
9 Emeka Okafor .30 .75
10 Ben Gordon .30 .75
11 Derrick Rose .60 1.50
12 John Salmons .30 .75
13 Mo Williams .30 .75
14 LeBron James 3.00 8.00
15 Anderson Varejao .25 .60
16 Dirk Nowitzki 1.00 2.50
17 Jason Kidd .60 1.50
18 Jason Terry .30 .75
19 Chauncey Billups .50 1.25
20 Carmelo Anthony .60 1.50
21 Richard Hamilton .40 1.00
22 Allen Iverson .75 2.00
23 Rasheed Wallace .50 1.25
24 Monta Ellis .30 .75
25 Corey Maggette .30 .75
26 Anthony Randolph .25 .60
27 Tracy McGrady .75 2.00
28 Yao Ming 1.00 2.50
29 Ron Artest .40 1.00
30 Danny Granger .25 .60
31 T.J. Ford .25 .60
32 Eric Gordon .30 .75
33 Baron Davis .30 .75
34 Marcus Camby .30 .75
35 Pau Gasol .60 1.50
36 Kobe Bryant 3.00 8.00
37 Andrew Bynum .25 .60
38 Rudy Gay .40 1.00
39 O.J. Mayo .25 .60
40 Michael Beasley .25 .60
41 Dwyane Wade .75 2.00
42 Jermaine O'Neal .40 1.00
43 Michael Redd .30 .75
44 Richard Jefferson .30 .75
45 Al Jefferson .25 .60
46 Kevin Love .40 1.00
47 Mike Miller .30 .75
48 Vince Carter .75 2.00
49 Devin Harris .25 .60
50 David West .30 .75
51 Chris Paul .75 2.00
52 Nate Robinson .30 .75
53 David Lee .25 .60
54 Kevin Durant 1.50 4.00
55 Russell Westbrook .75 2.00
56 Dwight Howard .50 1.25
57 Jameer Nelson .25 .60
58 Hedo Turkoglu .30 .75
59 Andre Iguodala .40 1.00
60 Elton Brand .30 .75
61 Andre Miller .40 1.00
62 Shaquille O'Neal 1.25 3.00
63 Amare Stoudemire .30 .75
64 Steve Nash .75 2.00
65 Rudy Fernandez .25 .60
66 Brandon Roy .50 1.25
67 LaMarcus Aldridge .40 1.00
68 Spencer Hawes .25 .60
69 Kevin Martin .30 .75
70 Tony Parker .60 1.50
71 Tim Duncan 1.00 2.50
72 Manu Ginobili .75 2.00
73 Jose Calderon .25 .60
74 Chris Bosh .50 1.25
75 Shawn Marion .40 1.00
76 Carlos Boozer .30 .75
77 Deron Williams .30 .75
78 Caron Butler .30 .75
79 Antawn Jamison .30 .75
80 Gilbert Arenas .30 .75
81 Dominique Wilkins .60 1.50
82 Bill Russell 1.25 3.00
83 Bob Cousy 1.00 2.50
84 Larry Bird 1.50 4.00
85 Rick Barry .30 .75
86 Elgin Baylor 1.00 2.50
87 Jerry West .60 1.50
88 Magic Johnson 1.50 4.00
89 Oscar Robertson .50 1.25
90 George Mikan 1.25 3.00
91 Pete Maravich 1.25 3.00
92 Patrick Ewing .60 1.50
93 Willis Reed .60 1.50
94 Julius Erving 1.00 2.50
95 Moses Malone .60 1.50
96 Wilt Chamberlain 1.50 4.00
97 Bill Walton .60 1.50
98 Clyde Drexler .60 1.50
99 Bob Pettit .50 1.25
100 Karl Malone .50 1.25
101 Blake Griffin RC 15.00 40.00
102 Jonny Flynn RC .75 2.00
103 Hasheem Thabeet RC .75 2.00
104 James Harden RC 200.00 500.00
105 DeMar DeRozan RC 40.00 100.00
106 Stephen Curry RC 1,250.00 2,500.00
107 Brandon Jennings RC 1.25 3.00
108 Jordan Hill RC .75 2.00
109 Earl Clark RC .75 2.00
110 Gerald Henderson RC .75 2.00
111 Tyreke Evans RC 1.00 2.50
112 Jrue Holiday RC 6.00 15.00
113 Tyler Hansbrough RC 1.00 2.50
114 Terrence Williams RC .75 2.00
115 Play Card 1.25 3.00
116 Play Card 1.25 3.00
117 Play Card 1.25 3.00
118 Play Card 1.25 3.00
119 Play Card 1.25 3.00
120 Play Card 1.25 3.00
121 Play Card 1.25 3.00

2009-10 Bowman 48 Black

*1-100 BLACK: 6X TO 15X BASE HI
*101-114 RC BLACK: 2.5X TO 6X BASE
*115-121 BLACK: 1X TO 2.5X BASE HI
BLACK PRINT RUN 48 SER.#'d SETS
14 LeBron James 200.00 500.00
36 Kobe Bryant 200.00 500.00
104 James Harden 2,000.00 4,000.00
105 DeMar DeRozan 500.00 1,000.00
106 Stephen Curry 20,000.00 40,000.00
112 Jrue Holiday 125.00 300.00

2009-10 Bowman 48 Blue

*1-100 BLUE: 1.5X TO 4X BASE HI
*101-114 RC BLUE: .4X TO 1X BASE HI
*PLAY CARDS SAME VALUE AS BASE
BLUE PRINT RUN 1948 SER.#'d SETS
14 LeBron James 25.00 60.00
36 Kobe Bryant 20.00 50.00
105 DeMar DeRozan 50.00 120.00
106 Stephen Curry 2,000.00 4,000.00
112 Jrue Holiday 8.00 20.00

2009-10 Bowman 48 Autographs

STATED ODDS 1:9
*BLACK: .5X TO 1.25X BASE HI
BLACK PRINT RUN 48 SER.#'d SETS
48AAB Andrew Bynum 4.00 10.00
48AAJ Antawn Jamison 4.00 10.00
48ABG Ben Gordon 4.00 10.00
48ABR Bill Russell 600.00 1,200.00
48ABW Bill Walton SP 60.00 150.00
48ACA Carmelo Anthony 75.00 200.00
48ACM Corey Maggette 4.00 10.00
48ACP Chris Paul 75.00 200.00
48ADG Danny Granger 4.00 10.00
48ADH Dwight Howard 10.00 25.00
48ADL David Lee 4.00 10.00
48ADR Derrick Rose 75.00 200.00
48ADW Dwyane Wade 75.00 200.00
48AGO Greg Oden 4.00 10.00
48AJJ Jarrett Jack 4.00 10.00
48AJS Josh Smith 4.00 10.00
48AJW Jerry West 30.00 80.00
48AKH Kirk Hinrich 4.00 10.00
48AKL Kevin Love 20.00 50.00
48ALB Larry Bird SP 125.00 300.00
48ALD Luol Deng 4.00 10.00
48AMJ Magic Johnson 75.00 200.00
48AMW Mo Williams 4.00 10.00
48ARB Rick Barry 6.00 15.00
48AABA Andrea Bargnani 4.00 10.00
48AAIG Andre Iguodala 4.00 10.00
48ABRO Brandon Roy 4.00 10.00
48ADWI Dominique Wilkins 20.00 50.00
48AOJM O.J. Mayo 4.00 10.00
48ATJF T.J. Ford 4.00 10.00

2009-10 Bowman 48 Locker Room Collection Autograph Relics

PRINT RUN 41 SER.#'d SETS
*PATCHES: .75X TO 2X BASE HI
PATCH PRINT RUN 24 SER.#'d SETS
DRCARJW Jerry West 30.00 80.00
LRCARBR Bill Russell 1,000.00 2,000.00
LRCARCA Carmelo Anthony 25.00 50.00
LRCARCP Chris Paul 150.00 400.00
LRCARDG Danny Granger 10.00 25.00
LRCARDH Dwight Howard 15.00 40.00
LRCARDR Derrick Rose 100.00 250.00
LRCARDW Dwyane Wade 25.00 60.00
LRCARJS Josh Smith 10.00 25.00
LRCARLB Larry Bird 40.00 100.00
LRCARMJ Magic Johnson 40.00 100.00
LRCARAIG Andre Iguodala 10.00 25.00
LRCARBRO Brandon Roy 20.00 40.00
LRCARDWI Dominique Wilkins 20.00 50.00
LRCAROJM O.J. Mayo 20.00 40.00

2003-04 Bowman Chrome

COMP.SET w/o RC's (110) 30.00 80.00
148-157 AU RC STATED ODDS 1:385
148-157 AU PRINT RUN 250 SER.#'d SETS
1 Yao Ming 1.25 3.00
2 Glenn Robinson .40 1.00
3 Antoine Walker .50 1.25
4 Jalen Rose .40 1.00
5 Ricky Davis .40 1.00
6 Juwan Howard .40 1.00
7 Kwame Brown .30 .75
8 Mike Bibby .50 1.25
9 Wally Szczerbiak .40 1.00
10 Allen Iverson 1.25 3.00

11 Shareef Abdur-Rahim .50 1.25
12 Jamal Mashburn .40 1.00
13 Stephon Marbury .60 1.50
14 Desmond Mason .40 1.00
15 Gordan Giricek .30 .75
16 Caron Butler .40 1.00
17 Jermaine O'Neal .50 1.25
18 Kenyon Martin .50 1.25
19 Andrei Kirilenko .40 1.00
20 Dirk Nowitzki 1.25 3.00
21 Richard Hamilton .60 1.50
22 Troy Murphy .30 .75
23 Shawn Marion .50 1.25
24 Allan Houston .50 1.25
25 Keith Van Horn .40 1.00
26 Brian Grant .30 .75
27 Mike Miller .40 1.00
28 Chris Webber .60 1.50
29 Brent Barry .30 .75
30 Elton Brand .40 1.00
31 Juan Dixon .30 .75
32 Karl Malone 1.00 2.50
33 Darrell Armstrong .30 .75
34 Rasheed Wallace .60 1.50
35 Michael Redd .50 1.25
36 Rashard Lewis .50 1.25
37 Ron Artest .40 1.00
38 P.J. Brown .30 .75
39 Eddie Griffin .30 .75
40 Tim Duncan 1.25 3.00
41 Kurt Thomas .30 .75
42 Raef LaFrentz .30 .75
43 Ben Wallace .60 1.50
44 Lamar Odom .40 1.00
45 Vince Carter 1.00 2.50
46 Derek Anderson .40 1.00
47 Stromile Swift .30 .75
48 Bobby Jackson .40 1.00
49 Richard Jefferson .40 1.00
50 Shaquille O'Neal 2.00 5.00
51 Calbert Cheaney .30 .75
52 Troy Hudson .30 .75
53 Ray Allen .75 2.00
54 Howard Eisley .30 .75
55 Alonzo Mourning .60 1.50
56 Sam Cassell .40 1.00
57 Derrick Coleman .50 1.25
58 Andre Miller .40 1.00
59 Antawn Jamison .40 1.00
60 Kevin Garnett 1.25 3.00
61 Steve Francis .50 1.25
62 Tyson Chandler .40 1.00
63 Drew Gooden .40 1.00
64 Scottie Pippen 1.25 3.00
65 Pau Gasol .75 2.00
66 Steve Nash 1.00 2.50
67 DaJuan Wagner .30 .75
68 Jason Terry .40 1.00
69 Reggie Miller 1.00 2.50
70 Tracy McGrady .75 2.00
71 Nene Hilario .40 1.00
72 Morris Peterson .30 .75
73 Peja Stojakovic .40 1.00
74 Eddie Jones .50 1.25
75 Tony Parker .75 2.00
76 Corliss Williamson .30 .75
77 Vladimir Radmanovic .30 .75
78 Amare Stoudemire .60 1.50
79 Tony Delk .40 1.00
80 Jason Kidd .75 2.00
81 Gary Payton .75 2.00
82 Corey Maggette .40 1.00
83 Darius Miles .30 .75
84 Cuttino Mobley .30 .75
85 Eric Snow .30 .75
86 Matt Harpring .30 .75
87 Manu Ginobili 1.00 2.50
88 Latrell Sprewell .60 1.50
89 Alvin Williams .30 .75
90 Paul Pierce .75 2.00
91 Anfernee Hardaway 1.25 3.00
92 Gilbert Arenas .50 1.25
93 Jerry Stackhouse .60 1.50
94 Tim Thomas .30 .75
95 Nikoloz Tskitishvili .30 .75
96 Doug Christie .40 1.00
97 Zydrunas Ilgauskas .40 1.00
98 Jamaal Tinsley .30 .75
99 Theo Ratliff .30 .75
100 Kobe Bryant 4.00 10.00
101 Chauncey Billups .60 1.50
102 Michael Finley .50 1.25
103 Jason Williams .75 2.00
104 Bonzi Wells .30 .75
105 Voshon Lenard .30 .75
106 Jason Richardson .50 1.25
107 Baron Davis .50 1.25
108 Radoslav Nesterovic .30 .75
109 Eddy Curry .30 .75
110 Michael Olowokandi .30 .75
111 Josh Howard RC 3.00 8.00
112 Mario Austin RC 2.00 5.00
113 Rick Rickert RC 2.00 5.00
114 Tommy Smith RC 3.00 8.00
115 Dahntay Jones RC 2.50 6.00
116 Ndudi Ebi RC 2.00 5.00
117 Maurice Williams RC 3.00 8.00
118 Kendrick Perkins RC 2.50 6.00
119 Steve Blake RC 2.50 6.00
120 David West RC 4.00 10.00
121 Chris Kaman RC 3.00 8.00
122 Keith Bogans RC 2.00 5.00
123 LeBron James RC 150.00 400.00
124 Devin Brown RC 2.00 5.00
125 Jason Kapono RC 2.00 5.00
126 Zoran Planinic RC 2.00 5.00
127 Zaur Pachulia RC 3.00 8.00
128 Malick Badiane RC 3.00 8.00
129 Kyle Korver RC 4.00 10.00
130 Darko Milicic RC 2.50 6.00
131 Troy Bell RC 2.00 5.00
132 Luke Walton RC 3.00 8.00
133 Mike Sweetney RC 2.00 5.00
134 Jarvis Hayes RC 2.00 5.00
135 Leandro Barbosa RC 3.00 8.00
136 Carlos Delfino RC 2.50 6.00
137 Sofoklis Schortsanitis RC 2.00 5.00
138 Slavko Vranes RC 2.00 5.00
139 Travis Hansen RC 2.00 5.00
140 Carmelo Anthony RC 15.00 40.00
141 Reece Gaines RC 2.00 5.00
142 Maciej Lampe RC 2.00 5.00
143 Travis Outlaw RC 2.50 6.00
144 Jerome Beasley RC 2.00 5.00
145 Mickael Pietrus RC 2.50 6.00
146 Brian Cook RC 2.00 5.00
148 Kirk Hinrich AU RC 6.00 15.00
149 Dwyane Wade AU RC 125.00 300.00
150 Marcus Banks AU RC 5.00 12.00
151 Nick Collison AU RC 6.00 15.00
152 Boris Diaw AU RC 8.00 20.00
153 Chris Bosh AU RC 75.00 200.00
154 T.J. Ford AU RC 5.00 12.00
155 Luke Ridnour AU RC 8.00 20.00
156 A.Pavlovic AU RC 6.00 15.00
157 Zarko Cabarkapa AU RC 5.00 12.00

2003-04 Bowman Chrome Refractors

*1-110: 1.5X TO 4X BASE CARD HI
*111-146: 1.25X TO 3X BASE HI
*148-157 AU RC REF: .75X TO 2X BASE HI
148-157 AU RC REF PRINT RUN 50 SETS
CARD 147 NOT RELEASED
10 Allen Iverson 8.00 20.00
69 Reggie Miller 8.00 20.00
100 Kobe Bryant 100.00 250.00
123 LeBron James 6,000.00 12,000.00

2003-04 Bowman Chrome Refractors Gold

*1-110: 8X TO 20X BASE HI
*111-146 RC: 2X TO 5X BASE HI
1-146 REF.GOLD PRINT RUN 50 SETS
CARD 147 NOT RELEASED
10 Allen Iverson 50.00 120.00
64 Scottie Pippen 20.00 50.00
69 Reggie Miller 20.00 50.00
75 Tony Parker 30.00 80.00
87 Manu Ginobili 30.00 80.00
100 Kobe Bryant 60.00 150.00
123 LeBron James 30,000.00 60,000.00
140 Carmelo Anthony 150.00 300.00

2003-04 Bowman Chrome X-fractors

*1-110: 4X TO 10X BASE CARD HI
*111-146 RCs: 2X TO 5X BASE HI
1-146 X-FRACTOR PRINT RUN 150 SETS
*148-157 RCs: 1.25X TO 3X BASE HI
CARD 147 NOT RELEASED
10 Allen Iverson 10.00 25.00
69 Reggie Miller 10.00 25.00
100 Kobe Bryant 30.00 80.00
123 LeBron James 15,000.00 30,000.00

2004-05 Bowman Chrome

COMP.SET w/o RCs (110) 25.00 60.00
147-156 PRINT RUN 250 SER.#'d SETS
1 Yao Ming 1.25 3.00
2 Eddy Curry .30 .75
3 Stephon Marbury .60 1.50
4 Chris Webber .60 1.50
5 Jason Kidd .75 2.00
6 Cuttino Mobley .40 1.00
7 Jermaine O'Neal .50 1.25
8 Kobe Bryant 4.00 10.00
9 Tony Parker .75 2.00
10 Gary Payton .75 2.00
11 T.J. Ford .30 .75
12 Tim Duncan 1.25 3.00
13 Glenn Robinson .40 1.00
14 Jason Richardson .50 1.25
15 Carmelo Anthony 1.00 2.50
16 Pau Gasol .50 1.25
17 Kirk Hinrich .50 1.25
18 Kenyon Martin .50 1.25
19 Jamal Crawford .50 1.25
20 Elton Brand .40 1.00
21 Kevin Garnett 1.25 3.00
22 Michael Redd .40 1.00
23 LeBron James 20.00 50.00
24 Andre Miller .40 1.00
25 Peja Stojakovic .40 1.00
26 Jarvis Hayes .30 .75
27 David Wesley .30 .75
28 Jason Kapono .30 .75
29 Corey Maggette .40 1.00
30 Rasheed Wallace .60 1.50
31 Nene .40 1.00
32 Amare Stoudemire .50 1.25
33 Allen Iverson 1.25 3.00
34 Shaquille O'Neal 2.00 5.00
35 Mike Dunleavy .30 .75
36 Steve Nash 1.00 2.50
37 Brad Miller .30 .75
38 Chris Bosh .75 2.00
39 Boris Diaw .40 1.00
40 Steve Francis .50 1.25
41 Dirk Nowitzki 1.25 3.00
42 Jason Williams .40 1.00
43 Gilbert Arenas .50 1.25
44 Keith Van Horn .40 1.00
45 Jamal Mashburn .40 1.00
46 Derek Fisher .40 1.00
47 Andrei Kirilenko .40 1.00
48 Ricky Davis .40 1.00
49 Gerald Wallace .40 1.00
50 Tracy McGrady .75 2.00
51 Zach Randolph .50 1.25
52 Rafer Alston .30 .75
53 Bobby Jackson .30 .75
54 Desmond Mason .30 .75
55 Tim Thomas .30 .75
56 Jamaal Tinsley .30 .75
57 Kwame Brown .30 .75
58 Chauncey Billups .60 1.50
59 Brandon Hunter .30 .75
60 Reggie Miller 1.00 2.50
61 Samuel Dalembert .30 .75
62 James Posey .40 1.00
63 Erick Dampier .30 .75
64 Carlos Arroyo .30 .75
65 Reece Gaines .30 .75
66 Darko Milicic .40 1.00
67 Sam Cassell .40 1.00
68 Dwyane Wade 2.00 5.00
69 Allan Houston .50 1.25
70 Ray Allen .75 2.00
71 Tyson Chandler .40 1.00
72 Mike Bibby .30 .75
73 Jalen Rose .40 1.00
74 Marquis Daniels .30 .75
75 Zydrunas Ilgauskas .40 1.00
76 Tayshaun Prince .50 1.25
77 Lamar Odom .50 1.25
78 Luke Ridnour .40 1.00
79 Joe Johnson .40 1.00
80 Vince Carter 1.00 2.50
81 Antoine Walker .50 1.25
82 Shareef Abdur-Rahim .50 1.25
83 Richard Jefferson .40 1.00
84 Maurice Taylor .30 .75
85 Chris Kaman .40 1.00
86 Marcus Banks .30 .75
87 Mike Bibby .50 1.25
88 Latrell Sprewell .60 1.50
89 Rashard Lewis .50 1.25
90 Baron Davis .50 1.25
91 Caron Butler .40 1.00
92 Michael Finley .50 1.25
93 Mike Miller .40 1.00
94 Al Harrington .40 1.00
95 Quentin Richardson .30 .75
96 Jamaal Magloire .30 .75
97 Darius Miles .30 .75
98 Jeff Foster .30 .75
99 Karl Malone 1.00 2.50
100 Shawn Marion .50 1.25
101 Antawn Jamison .40 1.00
102 Manu Ginobili 1.00 2.50
103 Ben Wallace .60 1.50
104 Paul Pierce .75 2.00
105 Mike Sweetney .30 .75
106 Ron Artest .50 1.25
107 Michael Olowokandi .30 .75
108 Jason Terry .40 1.00
109 Gordan Giricek .30 .75
110 Carlos Boozer .40 1.00
111 Romain Sato RC 1.25 3.00
112 Chris Duhon RC 1.50 4.00
113 Ben Gordon RC 2.00 5.00
114 Matt Freije RC 1.25 3.00
115 Al Jefferson RC 2.00 5.00
116 Beno Udrih RC 1.50 4.00
117 Kirk Snyder RC 1.25 3.00
118 Anderson Varejao RC 1.50 4.00
119 Devin Harris RC 1.50 4.00
120 Tony Allen RC 2.00 5.00
121 Ha Seung-Jin RC 2.00 5.00
122 J.R. Smith RC 2.00 5.00
123 Blake Stepp RC 2.00 5.00
124 Jameer Nelson RC 2.00 5.00
125 Kris Humphries RC 1.50 4.00
126 Josh Childress RC 1.25 3.00
127 Tim Pickett RC 1.50 4.00
128 Delonte West RC 1.50 4.00
129 Dwight Howard RC 6.00 15.00
130 Luke Jackson RC 1.25 3.00
131 Rickey Paulding RC 1.25 3.00
132 Andre Emmett RC 1.25 3.00
133 Josh Smith RC 2.00 5.00
134 Antonio Burks RC 1.25 3.00
135 Ricky Minard RC 1.50 4.00
136 Lionel Chalmers RC 1.50 4.00
137 Shaun Livingston RC 2.00 5.00
138 Trevor Ariza RC 2.00 5.00
139 Sergei Lishouk RC 1.50 4.00
140 Pape Sow RC 1.25 3.00
141 Rashad Wright RC 1.25 3.00
142 Jackson Vroman RC 1.25 3.00
143 Luis Flores RC 1.50 4.00
144 Royal Ivey RC 1.25 3.00
145 Kevin Martin RC 2.50 6.00
146 Andre Iguodala RC 3.00 8.00
147 Andris Biedrins AU RC 5.00 12.00
148 Pavel Podkolzin AU RC 5.00 12.00
149 Luol Deng AU RC 5.00 12.00
150 Robert Swift AU RC 5.00 12.00
151 Sebastian Telfair AU RC 6.00 15.00
152 Emeka Okafor AU RC 6.00 15.00
153 Dorell Wright AU RC 6.00 15.00
154 Sasha Vujacic AU RC 6.00 15.00
155 Rafael Araujo AU RC 5.00 12.00
156 David Harrison AU RC 5.00 12.00

2004-05 Bowman Chrome Refractors

*1-110 REFRACTORS: 1.5X TO 4X BASE HI
*111-146 REFRACTORS: 1.25X TO 3X BASE HI
STATED PRINT RUN 300 SER.#'d SETS
*147-156 REFRACTOR AU: 1X TO 2.5X BASE HI
STATED PRINT RUN 50 SER.#'d SETS
8 Kobe Bryant 75.00 200.00
23 LeBron James 125.00 300.00

2004-05 Bowman Chrome Refractors Gold

*1-110 GOLD: 6X TO 15X BASE HI
*111-146 GOLD: 3X TO 8X BASE HI
STATED PRINT RUN 50 SER.#'d SETS
1 Yao Ming 150.00 400.00
8 Kobe Bryant 500.00 1,000.00
12 Tim Duncan 20.00 50.00
23 LeBron James 3,000.00 6,000.00
36 Steve Nash 25.00 60.00
68 Dwyane Wade 20.00 50.00
129 Dwight Howard 60.00 150.00

2004-05 Bowman Chrome X-Fractors

*1-110 X-FRACTORS: 4X TO 10X BASE HI
*111-146 X-FRACTORS: 2X TO 5X BASE HI
STATED PRINT RUN 150 SER.#'d SETS
*147-156 X-FRACTORS AU: 1.5X TO 4X BASE HI
147-156 PRINT RUN 25 SER.#'d SETS
8 Kobe Bryant 125.00 300.00
23 LeBron James 300.00 600.00

2005-06 Bowman Chrome

COMP.SET w/o RC's (110) 25.00 60.00
AU RC PRINT RUN 250 SER.#'d SETS
1 Steve Nash 1.25 3.00
2 Primoz Brezec .40 1.00
3 Baron Davis .60 1.50
4 Al Harrington .50 1.25
5 Caron Butler .50 1.25
6 Marcus Camby .50 1.25
7 Carlos Boozer .50 1.25
8 Ben Gordon .50 1.25
9 Stephen Jackson .50 1.25
10 Dirk Nowitzki 1.50 4.00
11 Nenad Krstic .40 1.00
12 Jason Richardson .60 1.50
13 Brendan Haywood .40 1.00
14 Chauncey Billups .75 2.00
15 Corey Maggette .50 1.25
16 Peja Stojakovic .50 1.25
17 Grant Hill 1.00 2.50
18 Pau Gasol 1.00 2.50
19 Vladimir Radmanovic .40 1.00
20 Jason Kidd 1.00 2.50
21 Tim Duncan 1.50 4.00
22 David Harrison .40 1.00
23 LeBron James 5.00 12.00
24 Udonis Haslem .40 1.00
25 Dan Dickau .40 1.00
26 Cuttino Mobley .40 1.00
27 Chris Bosh .75 2.00
28 Sebastian Telfair .50 1.25
29 Latrell Sprewell .60 1.50
30 Emeka Okafor .60 1.50
31 Mike James .40 1.00
32 Trevor Ariza .40 1.00
33 Larry Hughes .50 1.25
34 Desmond Mason .40 1.00
35 Tayshaun Prince .60 1.50
36 Manu Ginobili 1.25 3.00
37 Mike Bibby .60 1.50
38 Andre Iguodala .60 1.50
39 Jamaal Magloire .40 1.00
40 Amare Stoudemire .60 1.50
41 Rafer Alston .50 1.25
42 Elton Brand .50 1.25
43 Steve Francis .60 1.50
44 Rashard Lewis .50 1.25
45 Lorenzen Wright .40 1.00
46 Kirk Hinrich .50 1.25
47 Andrei Kirilenko .50 1.25
48 Brad Miller .50 1.25
49 Jamal Crawford .60 1.50
50 Shaquille O'Neal 2.00 5.00
51 Shaun Livingston .50 1.25
52 Troy Murphy .40 1.00
53 Drew Gooden .40 1.00
54 Paul Pierce 1.00 2.50
55 Vince Carter 1.25 3.00
56 Wally Szczerbiak .50 1.25
57 Antawn Jamison .50 1.25
58 Marquis Daniels .40 1.00
59 Gerald Wallace .50 1.25
60 Ray Allen 1.00 2.50
61 Jamaal Tinsley .40 1.00
62 Shane Battier .60 1.50
63 Zydrunas Ilgauskas .50 1.25
64 Mehmet Okur .50 1.25
65 Rasheed Wallace .60 1.50
66 Maurice Williams .40 1.00
67 Josh Howard .50 1.25
68 Zach Randolph .50 1.25
69 Kobe Bryant 5.00 12.00
70 Tracy McGrady 1.00 2.50
71 Luke Ridnour .50 1.25
72 Damon Jones .40 1.00
73 Tony Allen .40 1.00
74 Mike Miller .50 1.25
75 Sam Cassell .50 1.25
76 Ben Wallace .75 2.00
77 Mike Sweetney .40 1.00
78 Eddy Curry .40 1.00
79 Michael Redd .40 1.00
80 Carmelo Anthony 1.00 2.50
81 Dwight Howard .75 2.00
82 Josh Smith .50 1.25
83 Richard Jefferson .50 1.25
84 Richard Hamilton .75 2.00
85 Chris Webber .75 2.00
86 Shawn Marion .50 1.25
87 Jalen Rose .50 1.25
88 Bob Sura .40 1.00
89 Mike Dunleavy .40 1.00
90 Dwyane Wade 1.25 3.00
91 Gary Payton 1.00 2.50
92 Luol Deng .50 1.25
93 Kenyon Martin .50 1.25
94 Beno Udrih .50 1.25
95 J.R. Smith .60 1.50
96 Lamar Odom .50 1.25
97 Andre Miller .50 1.25
98 Jermaine O'Neal .50 1.25
99 Yao Ming 1.25 3.00
100 Allen Iverson 1.25 3.00
101 Quentin Richardson .40 1.00
102 Gilbert Arenas .60 1.50
103 Stephon Marbury .75 2.00
104 Antoine Walker .60 1.50
105 Jameer Nelson .40 1.00
106 Joel Przybilla .40 1.00
107 Devin Harris .40 1.00
108 Tony Parker 1.00 2.50
109 Josh Childress .50 1.25
110 Kevin Garnett 1.50 4.00
111 Chris Paul RC 6.00 15.00
112 Danny Granger RC 1.00 2.50
113 Antoine Wright RC 1.00 2.50
114 Joey Graham RC 1.00 2.50
115 Wayne Simien RC .75 2.00
116 Channing Frye RC 1.00 2.50
117 Charlie Villanueva RC 1.00 2.50
118 Francisco Garcia RC .75 2.00
119 Ike Diogu RC .75 2.00
120 Jarrett Jack RC 1.25 3.00
121 Robert Whaley RC .75 2.00
122 C.J. Miles RC 1.00 2.50
123 Ryan Gomes RC 1.00 2.50
124 Nate Robinson RC 1.25 3.00
125 Daniel Ewing RC 1.00 2.50
126 Andray Blatche RC 1.25 3.00
127 Luther Head RC .75 2.00
128 Julius Hodge RC .75 2.00
129 Lawrence Roberts RC .75 2.00
130 Jason Maxiell RC .75 2.00
131 Martynas Andriuskevicius RC .75 2.00
132 Ersan Ilyasova RC 1.00 2.50
133 Martell Webster RC 1.00 2.50
134 Andrew Bynum RC 1.00 2.50
135 Louis Williams RC 3.00 8.00
136 Johan Petro RC .75 2.00
137 Brandon Bass RC 1.00 2.50
138 Travis Diener RC .75 2.00
139 Bracey Wright RC .75 2.00
140 Marvin Williams RC 1.25 3.00
141 Eddie Basden RC .75 2.00
142 Von Wafer RC .75 2.00
143 David Lee RC 1.25 3.00
144 Linas Kleiza RC 1.00 2.50
145 Luke Schenscher RC .75 2.00
146 Yaroslav Korolev RC .75 2.00
147 Carmen Electra 4.00 10.00
148 Christie Brinkley 4.00 10.00
149 Shannon Elizabeth 4.00 10.00
150 Jenny McCarthy 4.00 10.00
151 Jay-Z 1.50 4.00
152 Raymond Felton AU RC 5.00 12.00
153 Gerald Green AU RC 6.00 15.00
154 Rashad McCants AU RC 4.00 10.00
155 Andrew Bogut AU RC 8.00 20.00
156 Chris Taft AU RC 4.00 10.00
157 S.Jasikevicius AU RC 6.00 15.00
158 Hakim Warrick AU RC 5.00 12.00
159 Deron Williams AU RC 10.00 25.00
160 Sean May AU RC 4.00 10.00
161 Monta Ellis AU RC 8.00 20.00

2005-06 Bowman Chrome Refractors

*1-110: 1.5X TO 4X BASE HI
*111-151: 1X TO 2.5X BASE HI
*152-161: 1X TO 2.5X BASE HI
152-161 AU PRINT RUN 50 SER.#'d SETS
23 LeBron James 75.00 200.00
69 Kobe Bryant 75.00 200.00
111 Chris Paul 75.00 200.00
151 Jay-Z 40.00 100.00

2005-06 Bowman Chrome Refractors Gold

*1-110 GOLD: 3X TO 8X BASE HI
*111-146 GOLD: 2X TO 5X BASE HI
152-161 AU PRINT RUN FIVE SETS
1 Steve Nash 12.00 30.00
21 Tim Duncan 75.00 200.00
23 LeBron James 200.00 500.00
69 Kobe Bryant 40.00 100.00
90 Dwyane Wade 20.00 50.00
100 Allen Iverson 25.00 60.00
108 Tony Parker 12.00 30.00
110 Kevin Garnett 20.00 50.00
111 Chris Paul 400.00 800.00
151 Jay-Z 125.00 300.00

2005-06 Bowman Chrome X-Fractors

*1-110: 2X TO 5X BASE HI
*111-146: 1.25X TO 3X BASE HI
*152-161 AU: 1.5X TO 4X BASE HI
152-161 AU PRINT RUN 25 SER.#'d SETS
23 LeBron James 100.00 250.00
69 Kobe Bryant 20.00 50.00
111 Chris Paul 200.00 500.00
151 Jay-Z 75.00 200.00

2006-07 Bowman Chrome

COMP.SET w/o SP's (115) 30.00 60.00
116-125 RC APPROXIMATE ODDS 1:9
126-165 AU RC GROUP A ODDS 1:140
126-165 AU RC GROUP B ODDS 1:34
126-165 AU RC GROUP C ODDS 1:63
1 Gilbert Arenas .60 1.50
2 Delonte West .40 1.00
3 Gerald Wallace .50 1.25
4 Ike Diogu .40 1.00
5 Mike Miller .50 1.25
6 Kobe Bryant 5.00 12.00
7 Richard Hamilton .60 1.50
8 Vince Carter 1.25 3.00
9 Elton Brand .50 1.25
10 Boris Diaw .50 1.25
11 Carmelo Anthony 1.00 2.50
12 Jermaine O'Neal .60 1.50
13 Al Harrington .50 1.25
14 Dwight Howard .75 2.00
15 Chris Bosh .75 2.00
16 Ben Gordon .50 1.25
17 Josh Howard .50 1.25
18 Yao Ming 1.50 4.00
19 David West .50 1.25
20 Tim Duncan 1.50 4.00
21 Andre Iguodala .60 1.50
22 LeBron James 5.00 12.00
23 Channing Frye .40 1.00
24 Antoine Walker .60 1.50
25 Ricky Davis .50 1.25
26 Lamar Odom .60 1.50
27 Amare Stoudemire .60 1.50
28 Mike Bibby .60 1.50
29 Allen Iverson 1.50 4.00
30 Marvin Williams .40 1.00
31 Wally Szczerbiak .50 1.25
32 Ben Wallace .75 2.00
33 Nenad Krstic .40 1.00
34 Deron Williams .50 1.25
35 Troy Murphy .40 1.00
36 Raymond Felton .40 1.00
37 Jason Terry .50 1.25
38 Zach Randolph .50 1.25
39 Pau Gasol 1.00 2.50
40 Larry Hughes .50 1.25
41 Luol Deng .50 1.25
42 Steve Francis .60 1.50
43 Chauncey Billups .75 2.00
44 Smush Parker .40 1.00
45 Shareef Abdur-Rahim .60 1.50
46 Andrei Kirilenko .60 1.50
47 Shawn Marion .60 1.50
48 Darko Milicic .40 1.00
49 Shaquille O'Neal 2.50 6.00
50 Kevin Garnett 1.50 4.00
51 Michael Finley .60 1.50
52 Peja Stojakovic .50 1.25
53 Michael Redd .50 1.25
54 Desmond Mason .40 1.00
55 Luke Ridnour .40 1.00
56 Kenyon Martin .50 1.25
57 Morris Peterson .40 1.00
58 Chris Kaman .40 1.00
59 Jason Richardson .60 1.50
60 Jason Kidd 1.00 2.50
61 Carlos Boozer .50 1.25
62 Rashad McCants .40 1.00
63 Nate Robinson .50 1.25
64 Devin Harris .50 1.25
65 Andrew Bogut .50 1.25
66 Chris Duhon .40 1.00
67 Drew Gooden .50 1.25
68 Manu Ginobili 1.25 3.00
69 Jameer Nelson .40 1.00
70 Corey Maggette .50 1.25
71 Charlie Villanueva .40 1.00
72 Shane Battier .50 1.25
73 Udonis Haslem .40 1.00
74 Tracy McGrady 1.00 2.50
75 Bobby Simmons .40 1.00
76 Baron Davis .60 1.50
77 Zydrunas Ilgauskas .50 1.25
78 Danny Granger .40 1.00
79 Hakim Warrick .40 1.00
80 Josh Smith .40 1.00
81 Tayshaun Prince .60 1.50
82 Rashard Lewis .50 1.25
83 Luther Head .40 1.00
84 Andre Miller .50 1.25
85 T.J. Ford .40 1.00
86 Sebastian Telfair .40 1.00
87 Dirk Nowitzki 1.50 4.00
88 Kwame Brown .40 1.00
89 Antawn Jamison .50 1.25
90 Ron Artest .60 1.50
91 Mehmet Okur .40 1.00
92 Emeka Okafor .50 1.25
93 Sam Cassell .50 1.25
94 Chris Paul 1.25 3.00
95 Chris Webber .75 2.00
96 Richard Jefferson .50 1.25
97 Dwyane Wade 1.25 3.00
98 Tony Parker 1.00 2.50
99 Paul Pierce 1.00 2.50
100 Marcus Camby .50 1.25
101 Ray Allen 1.00 2.50
102 Stephon Marbury .75 2.00
103 Rasheed Wallace .75 2.00
104 Brad Miller .50 1.25
105 Kirk Hinrich .50 1.25
106 Steve Nash 1.25 3.00
107 Sarunas Jasikevicius .50 1.25
108 Darius Miles .40 1.00
109 Joe Johnson .60 1.50
110 Caron Butler .60 1.50
111 John Wooden CO 2.50 6.00
112 Ben Howland CO 2.00 5.00
113 Jim Calhoun CO 2.00 5.00
114 Jim Boeheim CO 2.00 5.00
115 Roy Williams CO 2.00 5.00
116 LaMarcus Aldridge RC 5.00 12.00
117 Marcus Vinicius RC 1.25 3.00
118 Sergio Rodriguez RC 1.50 4.00
119 Will Blalock RC 1.25 3.00
120 Paul Millsap RC 2.50 6.00
121 Leon Powe RC 1.25 3.00
122 Rudy Gay RC 2.50 6.00
123 Tyrus Thomas RC 1.50 4.00
124 Brandon Roy RC 4.00 10.00
125 J.R. Pinnock RC 1.25 3.00
126 Kevin Pittsnogle B AU RC 4.00 10.00
127 Mile Ilic C AU RC 3.00 8.00
128 Mardy Collins B AU RC 3.00 8.00
129 Craig Smith C AU RC 4.00 10.00
130 Jordan Farmar B AU RC 4.00 10.00
131 Quincy Douby B AU RC 3.00 8.00
132 James Augustine B AU RC 3.00 8.00
133 Josh Boone B AU RC 3.00 8.00
134 Shannon Brown B AU RC 3.00 8.00
135 David Noel B AU RC 3.00 8.00
136 Kyle Lowry B AU RC 40.00 100.00
137 Ryan Hollins C AU RC 3.00 8.00
138 Renaldo Balkman B AU RC 4.00 10.00
139 James White C AU RC 3.00 8.00
140 Damir Markota C AU RC 3.00 8.00
141 Paul Davis B AU RC 3.00 8.00
142 Alexander Johnson C AU RC 3.00 8.00
143 Steve Novak B AU RC 4.00 10.00
144 P.J. Tucker B AU RC 5.00 12.00
145 Saer Sene B AU RC 3.00 8.00
146 Bobby Jones B AU RC 3.00 8.00
147 Cedric Simmons B AU RC 3.00 8.00
148 Allan Ray C AU RC 3.00 8.00
149 Solomon Jones B AU RC 3.00 8.00
150 Ronnie Brewer A AU RC 5.00 12.00
151 Thabo Sefolosha B AU RC 4.00 10.00
152 Maurice Ager B AU RC 3.00 8.00
153 Daniel Gibson C AU RC 4.00 10.00
154 Shawne Williams B AU RC 3.00 8.00
155 Dee Brown B AU RC 3.00 8.00
156 Andrea Bargnani A AU RC 4.00 10.00
157 Patrick O'Bryant A AU RC 3.00 8.00
158 Shelden Williams A AU RC 3.00 8.00
159 Hilton Armstrong A AU RC 3.00 8.00
160 Adam Morrison A AU RC 3.00 8.00
161 Rodney Carney B AU RC 3.00 8.00
162 Randy Foye A AU RC 4.00 10.00
163 Rajon Rondo B AU RC 10.00 25.00
164 Marcus Williams A AU RC 3.00 8.00
165 J.J. Redick A AU RC 40.00 100.00

2006-07 Bowman Chrome Refractors

*1-115 REFRACTORS: 1X TO 2.5X BASE HI
*116-125 RC's: .75X TO 2X BASE HI
*126-165 RC's: .4X TO .8X BASE HI
REF.PRINT RUN 249 SER.#'d SETS
126-165 REF.RC's NOT AUTOGRAPHED
22 LeBron James 125.00 300.00
136 Kyle Lowry 30.00 80.00

2006-07 Bowman Chrome Refractors Gold

*1-110 GOLD: 4X TO 10X BASE HI
*111-125 GOLD: 2.5X TO 6X BASE HI
*125-165 GOLD: 1.25X TO 3X BASE HI
REF.GOLD PRINT RUN 50 SER.#'d SETS
18 Yao Ming 25.00 60.00
22 LeBron James 2,000.00 4,000.00
29 Allen Iverson 40.00 100.00
94 Chris Paul 20.00 50.00
99 Paul Pierce 15.00 40.00
136 Kyle Lowry AU 150.00 400.00
163 Rajon Rondo AU 75.00 200.00
165 J.J. Redick AU 150.00 400.00

2006-07 Bowman Chrome X-Fractors

*1-110 X-FRACTORS: 2X TO 5X BASE HI
*111-125: 1.25X TO 3X BASE HI
*126-165: .5X TO 1.25X BASE HI
X-FRAC PRINT RUN 150 SER.#'d SETS
126-165 RC's NOT AUTOGRAPHED
6 Kobe Bryant 20.00 50.00
22 LeBron James 300.00 600.00

2007-08 Bowman Chrome

COMPLETE SET (160) 50.00 100.00
COMP.SET w/o SP's (110) 20.00 50.00
1 Gilbert Arenas .60 1.50
2 Dwight Howard .75 2.00
3 Dwyane Wade 1.25 3.00
4 Chris Bosh .75 2.00
5 Josh Smith .40 1.00
6 Andrew Bogut .50 1.25
7 Ben Gordon .50 1.25
8 Deron Williams .50 1.25
9 Tony Parker 1.00 2.50
10 Mike Bibby .60 1.50
11 Yao Ming 1.50 4.00
12 Raymond Felton .50 1.25
13 Steve Nash 1.25 3.00
14 Jameer Nelson .40 1.00
15 Carmelo Anthony 1.00 2.50
16 Pau Gasol 1.00 2.50
17 Rashard Lewis .50 1.25
18 Eddy Curry .40 1.00
19 Luol Deng .50 1.25
20 Kevin Garnett 1.50 4.00
21 Tim Duncan 1.50 4.00
22 Michael Redd .50 1.25
23 LeBron James 12.00 30.00
24 Kobe Bryant 8.00 20.00
25 Al Jefferson .40 1.00
26 Mike Dunleavy .40 1.00
27 Tyson Chandler .60 1.50
28 Zach Randolph .60 1.50
29 Jason Richardson .60 1.50
30 Rasheed Wallace .75 2.00
31 Shawn Marion .60 1.50
32 Shaquille O'Neal 2.50 6.00
33 Allen Iverson 1.50 4.00
34 Paul Pierce 1.00 2.50
35 Adam Morrison .40 1.00
36 Mike Miller .50 1.25
37 Larry Hughes .50 1.25
38 Kevin Martin .50 1.25
39 Charlie Villanueva .40 1.00
40 Vince Carter 1.25 3.00
41 Dirk Nowitzki 1.50 4.00
42 Elton Brand .50 1.25
43 Ray Allen 1.00 2.50
44 Luke Walton .50 1.25
45 Chris Paul 1.25 3.00
46 Marcus Camby .50 1.25
47 Andrei Kirilenko .50 1.25
48 J.J. Redick .60 1.50
49 Richard Hamilton .75 2.00
50 Emeka Okafor .50 1.25
51 Manu Ginobili 1.25 3.00
52 Monta Ellis .50 1.25
53 Jorge Garbajosa .50 1.25
54 Kyle Korver .50 1.25
55 Jason Kidd 1.00 2.50
56 Randy Foye .50 1.25
57 Shane Battier .50 1.25
58 Shaun Livingston .50 1.25
59 Jason Terry .50 1.25
60 Joe Johnson .50 1.25
61 Lamar Odom .50 1.25
62 Tayshaun Prince .60 1.50
63 Chris Wilcox .40 1.00
64 Leandro Barbosa .50 1.25
65 Al Harrington .50 1.25
66 Jamal Crawford .50 1.25
67 Caron Butler .60 1.50
68 Chauncey Billups .75 2.00
69 Ricky Davis .50 1.25
70 Andrea Bargnani .40 1.00
71 Samuel Dalembert .40 1.00
72 LaMarcus Aldridge .60 1.50
73 Mehmet Okur .40 1.00
74 Marcus Williams .40 1.00
75 Andre Miller .50 1.25
76 Rudy Gay .50 1.25
77 Jermaine O'Neal .60 1.50
78 Boris Diaw .50 1.25
79 Ryan Gomes .40 1.00
80 Gerald Wallace .50 1.25
81 Udonis Haslem .40 1.00
82 Mo Williams .50 1.25
83 Jarrett Jack .50 1.25
84 Chris Webber .75 2.00
85 Trevor Ariza .40 1.00
86 Kirk Hinrich .60 1.50
87 Rafer Alston .60 1.50
88 Danny Granger .40 1.00
89 David West .50 1.25
90 Drew Gooden .40 1.00
91 Stephon Marbury .75 2.00
92 Antawn Jamison .50 1.25
93 Ron Artest .60 1.50
94 Richard Jefferson .50 1.25
95 Carlos Boozer .50 1.25
96 Hakim Warrick .40 1.00
97 T.J. Ford .40 1.00
98 Desmond Mason .40 1.00
99 Andre Iguodala .60 1.50
100 Amare Stoudemire .60 1.50
101 Tracy McGrady 1.00 2.50
102 Jason Kapono .40 1.00
103 Ben Wallace .75 2.00
104 Marvin Williams .40 1.00
105 Baron Davis .50 1.25
106 Andrew Bynum .40 1.00
107 Brandon Roy .75 2.00
108 David Lee .40 1.00
109 Corey Maggette .50 1.25

2003-04 Bowman Chrome Refractors

110 Josh Howard .50 1.25
111 Kevin Durant RC 60.00 150.00
112 Al Horford RC 6.00 15.00
113 Mike Conley Jr. RC 6.00 15.00
114 Jeff Green RC 2.00 5.00
115 Corey Brewer RC 2.00 5.00
116 Joakim Noah RC 2.50 6.00
117 Julian Wright RC 1.50 4.00
118 Ramon Sessions RC 2.00 5.00
119 Sammy Mejia RC 1.50 4.00
120 Luis Scola RC 2.50 6.00
121 Yi Jianlian RC 3.00 8.00
122 Arron Afflalo RC 2.00 5.00
123 Carl Landry RC 1.50 4.00
124 Alando Tucker RC 1.50 4.00
125 Gabe Pruitt RC 1.50 4.00
126 Marcus Williams RC 1.50 4.00
127 Spencer Hawes RC 1.50 4.00
128 Acie Law RC 1.50 4.00
129 Thaddeus Young RC 2.50 6.00
130 Nick Fazekas RC 1.50 4.00
131 Al Thornton RC 1.50 4.00
132 Rodney Stuckey RC 1.50 4.00
133 Nick Young RC 2.50 6.00
134 Glen Davis RC 2.00 5.00
135 Jermareo Davidson RC 1.50 4.00
136 JamesOn Curry RC 1.50 4.00
137 Jason Smith RC 1.50 4.00
138 Daequan Cook RC 2.00 5.00
139 Jared Dudley RC 2.00 5.00
140 Derrick Byars RC 1.50 4.00
141 Josh McRoberts RC 1.50 4.00
142 Adam Haluska RC 1.50 4.00
143 Reyshawn Terry RC 1.50 4.00
144 Aaron Gray AU RC 1.50 4.00
145 Herbert Hill RC 1.50 4.00
146 Jared Jordan RC 1.50 4.00
147 Wilson Chandler RC 2.00 5.00
148 Morris Almond RC 1.50 4.00
149 Aaron Brooks RC 2.00 5.00
150 Petteri Koponen RC 2.00 5.00
151 Dominic McGuire RC 1.50 4.00
152 Greg Oden RC 2.50 6.00
153 Stephane Lasme RC 1.50 4.00
154 D.J. Strawberry RC 1.50 4.00
155 Sean Williams RC 1.50 4.00
156 Marco Belinelli RC 2.00 5.00
157 Javaris Crittenton RC 1.50 4.00
158 Demetris Nichols RC 1.50 4.00
159 Taurean Green RC 1.50 4.00
160 Brandan Wright RC 2.00 5.00

2007-08 Bowman Chrome Refractors

*REF 1-110: 2.5X TO 6X BASE HI
PRINT RUN 299 SER.#'d SETS
*REF 111-160: .75X TO 2X BASE HI
PRINT RUN 299 SER.#'d SETS
3 Dwyane Wade 8.00 20.00
20 Kevin Garnett 8.00 20.00
23 LeBron James 400.00 800.00
24 Kobe Bryant 200.00 500.00
32 Shaquille O'Neal 8.00 20.00
111 Kevin Durant 300.00 600.00

2007-08 Bowman Chrome Refractors Black

*BLACK 1-110: 4X TO 10X BASE HI
*BLACK 111-160: 1X TO 2.5X BASE HI
BLACK PRINT RUN 199 SER.#'d SETS
3 Dwyane Wade 12.00 30.00
20 Kevin Garnett 12.00 30.00
23 LeBron James 500.00 1,000.00
24 Kobe Bryant 300.00 600.00
111 Kevin Durant 3,000.00 6,000.00

2007-08 Bowman Chrome Refractors Gold

*GOLD 1-110: 6X TO 15X BASE HI
*GOLD 111-160: 1.5X TO 3X BASE HI
GOLD PRINT RUN 99 SER.#'d SETS
3 Dwyane Wade 150.00 400.00
4 Chris Bosh 20.00 50.00
11 Yao Ming 150.00 400.00
13 Steve Nash 75.00 200.00
15 Carmelo Anthony 125.00 300.00
20 Kevin Garnett 150.00 400.00
21 Tim Duncan 150.00 400.00
23 LeBron James 1,500.00 3,000.00
24 Kobe Bryant 1,000.00 2,000.00
30 Rasheed Wallace 20.00 50.00
32 Shaquille O'Neal 150.00 400.00
33 Allen Iverson 125.00 300.00
34 Paul Pierce 75.00 200.00
40 Vince Carter 75.00 200.00
41 Dirk Nowitzki 150.00 400.00
51 Manu Ginobili 75.00 200.00
55 Jason Kidd 12.00 30.00
101 Tracy McGrady 25.00 60.00
111 Kevin Durant 4,000.00 8,000.00
121 Yi Jianlian 25.00 60.00

2007-08 Bowman Chrome X-Fractors

*X-FRAC 1-110: 5X TO 12X BASE HI
*X-FRAC 111-160: 1.5X TO 4X BASE HI
X-FRAC PRINT RUN 50 SER.#'d SETS
3 Dwyane Wade 75.00 200.00
11 Yao Ming 100.00 250.00
13 Steve Nash 60.00 150.00
15 Carmelo Anthony 60.00 150.00
20 Kevin Garnett 100.00 250.00
21 Tim Duncan 100.00 250.00
23 LeBron James 1,000.00 2,000.00
24 Kobe Bryant 800.00 1,500.00
32 Shaquille O'Neal 100.00 250.00
33 Allen Iverson 75.00 200.00
34 Paul Pierce 60.00 150.00
40 Vince Carter 60.00 150.00
41 Dirk Nowitzki 100.00 250.00
111 Kevin Durant 4,000.00 8,000.00

2007-08 Bowman Chrome Refractors Rookie Autographs

PRINT RUN 599 SER.#'d SETS
*BLACK: .5X TO 1.25X BASE HI
BLACK PRINT RUN 99 SER.#'d SETS
*GOLD: .75X TO 2X BASE HI
GOLD PRINT RUN 50 SER.#'d SETS
EXCH EXPIRATION 10/31/09
121 Yi Jianlian AU 8.00 20.00
122 Arron Afflalo AU 4.00 10.00
123 Carl Landry AU 3.00 8.00
124 Alando Tucker AU/479 3.00 8.00
125 Gabe Pruitt AU 3.00 8.00
126 Marcus Williams AU/479 3.00 8.00
127 Spencer Hawes AU/479 3.00 8.00
128 Acie Law AU/479 3.00 8.00
129 Thaddeus Young AU 5.00 12.00
130 Nick Fazekas AU 3.00 8.00
131 Al Thornton AU/479 3.00 8.00
132 Rodney Stuckey AU 3.00 8.00
133 Nick Young AU/479 5.00 12.00
134 Glen Davis AU 4.00 10.00
135 Jermareo Davidson AU 3.00 8.00
136 JamesOn Curry AU 3.00 8.00
137 Jason Smith AU 3.00 8.00
138 Daequan Cook AU 4.00 10.00
139 Jared Dudley AU 4.00 10.00
140 Derrick Byars AU 3.00 8.00
141 Josh McRoberts AU 3.00 8.00
142 Adam Haluska AU 3.00 8.00
143 Reyshawn Terry AU 3.00 8.00
144 Aaron Gray AU 3.00 8.00
145 Herbert Hill AU 3.00 8.00
146 Jared Jordan AU 3.00 8.00
147 Wilson Chandler AU 4.00 10.00
148 Morris Almond AU 3.00 8.00
149 Aaron Brooks AU 4.00 10.00
150 Petteri Koponen AU 4.00 10.00
151 Dominic McGuire AU 3.00 8.00
152 Greg Oden AU/479 5.00 12.00
153 Stephane Lasme AU 3.00 8.00
154 D.J. Strawberry AU 3.00 8.00
155 Sean Williams AU 3.00 8.00
156 Marco Belinelli AU 4.00 10.00
157 Javaris Crittenton AU/479 3.00 8.00
158 Demetris Nichols AU 3.00 8.00
159 Taurean Green AU 3.00 8.00
160 Brandan Wright AU/479 4.00 10.00

2008-09 Bowman Chrome

COMP.SET w/o RC (110) 20.00 50.00
1 Tracy McGrady 1.00 2.50
2 Jason Kidd 1.00 2.50
3 LeBron James 10.00 25.00
4 Chris Bosh .75 2.00
5 Kevin Garnett 1.50 4.00
6 Josh Smith .40 1.00
7 Richard Hamilton .60 1.50
8 Monta Ellis .50 1.25
9 Yi Jianlian .75 2.00
10 Danny Granger .50 1.25
11 Richard Jefferson .50 1.25
12 Elton Brand .50 1.25
13 Rudy Gay .60 1.50
14 Andres Nocioni .40 1.00
15 Carmelo Anthony .75 2.00
16 Pau Gasol .75 2.00
17 Corey Brewer .50 1.25
18 Hedo Turkoglu .50 1.25
19 Andre Iguodala .50 1.25
20 Raymond Felton .40 1.00
21 Tim Duncan 1.50 4.00
22 Michael Redd .50 1.25
23 Chris Paul 1.25 3.00
24 Kobe Bryant 10.00 25.00
25 Brandon Roy .50 1.25
26 Carlos Boozer .50 1.25
27 Jeff Green .50 1.25
28 Luis Scola .50 1.25
29 Al Thornton .40 1.00
30 Gilbert Arenas .60 1.50
31 Brandan Wright .40 1.00
32 Shaquille O'Neal 2.00 5.00
33 Allen Iverson 1.25 3.00
34 Paul Pierce 1.00 2.50
35 Ben Gordon .50 1.25
36 Jamal Crawford .60 1.50
37 Andrew Bynum .40 1.00
38 Gerald Wallace .50 1.25
39 Mike Conley Jr. .50 1.25
40 Ben Wallace .75 2.00
41 Dirk Nowitzki 1.50 4.00
42 David Lee .40 1.00
43 Mo Williams .50 1.25
44 Al Jefferson .40 1.00
45 Tayshaun Prince .60 1.50
46 Jameer Nelson .40 1.00
47 Andrei Kirilenko .50 1.25
48 David West .50 1.25
49 Al Horford .60 1.50
50 Steve Nash 1.25 3.00
51 Ron Artest .60 1.50
52 Greg Oden .40 1.00
53 Sean Williams .40 1.00
54 Jamario Moon .40 1.00
55 Baron Davis .60 1.50
56 Udonis Haslem .40 1.00
57 Mike Dunleavy .40 1.00
58 Shane Battier .50 1.25
59 Andrew Bogut .50 1.25
60 Ray Allen 1.00 2.50
61 Nick Young .40 1.00
62 Manu Ginobili 1.25 3.00
63 Jason Richardson .60 1.50
64 Mike Miller .50 1.25
65 Leandro Barbosa .50 1.25
66 Luol Deng .50 1.25
67 Shawn Marion .60 1.50
68 Peja Stojakovic .60 1.50
69 Kevin Durant 10.00 25.00
70 Corey Maggette .50 1.25
71 Chauncey Billups .75 2.00
72 Josh Howard .50 1.25
73 Kevin Martin .50 1.25
74 Anderson Varejao .40 1.00
75 Craig Smith .40 1.00
76 Antawn Jamison .50 1.25
77 Marcus Camby .50 1.25
78 Andre Miller .50 1.25
79 Zach Randolph .60 1.50
80 Deron Williams .50 1.25
81 Devin Harris .50 1.25
82 Rashard Lewis .50 1.25
83 Damien Wilkins .40 1.00
84 LaMarcus Aldridge .60 1.50
85 Larry Hughes .50 1.25
86 Brad Miller .50 1.25
87 Jermaine O'Neal .60 1.50
88 Caron Butler .50 1.25
89 Tyson Chandler .50 1.25
90 Joe Johnson .60 1.50
91 Amare Stoudemire .60 1.50
92 Dwight Howard .75 2.00
93 Rajon Rondo .75 2.00
94 T.J. Ford .40 1.00
95 Rodney Stuckey .40 1.00
96 Samuel Dalembert .40 1.00
97 Tony Parker .75 2.00
98 Vince Carter 1.25 3.00
99 Yao Ming 1.50 4.00
100 Dwyane Wade 1.25 3.00
101 Dominique Wilkins 1.00 2.50
102 Rick Barry .75 2.00
103 John Stockton 1.25 3.00
104 Magic Johnson 2.00 5.00
105 George Gervin 1.00 2.50
106 Bill Russell 2.00 5.00
107 David Robinson 1.25 3.00
108 Dennis Rodman 1.25 3.00
109 Larry Bird 2.00 5.00
110 Jerry West 1.25 3.00
111 Derrick Rose RC 25.00 60.00
112 Michael Beasley RC 1.50 4.00
113 O.J. Mayo RC 1.25 3.00
114 Russell Westbrook RC 75.00 200.00
115 Kevin Love RC 3.00 8.00
116 Danilo Gallinari RC 2.50 6.00
117 Eric Gordon RC 2.50 6.00
118 Joe Alexander RC 1.00 2.50
119 D.J. Augustin RC 1.50 4.00
120 Brook Lopez RC 2.00 5.00
121 Jerryd Bayless RC 1.25 3.00
122 Jason Thompson RC 1.00 2.50
123 Anthony Randolph RC 1.00 2.50
124 Robin Lopez RC 1.25 3.00
125 Marreese Speights RC 1.25 3.00
126 Roy Hibbert RC 1.25 3.00
127 JaVale McGee RC 1.50 4.00
128 J.J. Hickson RC 1.00 2.50
129 Alexis Ajinca RC 1.00 2.50
130 Ryan Anderson RC 1.25 3.00
131 Courtney Lee RC 1.25 3.00
132 Kosta Koufos RC 1.00 2.50
133 Donte Greene RC 1.00 2.50
134 George Hill RC 1.50 4.00
135 D.J. White RC 1.00 2.50
136 J.R. Giddens RC 1.00 2.50
137 Joey Dorsey RC 1.00 2.50
138 Mario Chalmers RC 1.50 4.00
139 DeAndre Jordan RC 2.00 5.00
140 Chris Douglas-Roberts RC 1.00 2.50
141 Malik Hairston RC 1.00 2.50
142 Sean Singletary RC 1.00 2.50
143 Kyle Weaver RC 1.00 2.50
144 Patrick Ewing Jr. RC 1.00 2.50
145 Walter Sharpe RC 1.00 2.50
146 Sonny Weems RC 1.00 2.50
147 Shan Foster RC 1.00 2.50
148 Nicolas Batum RC 2.00 5.00
149 Brandon Rush RC 1.00 2.50
150 Darrell Arthur RC 1.25 3.00
151 Derrick Rose AU A 125.00 300.00
152 Michael Beasley AU A 5.00 12.00
153 O.J. Mayo AU A 4.00 10.00
154 Russell Westbrook AU A 300.00 600.00
155 Kevin Love AU A 40.00 100.00
156 Danilo Gallinari AU A 10.00 25.00
157 Eric Gordon AU A 12.00 30.00
158 Joe Alexander AU A 3.00 8.00
159 D.J. Augustin AU B 5.00 12.00
160 Brook Lopez AU A 6.00 15.00
161 Jerryd Bayless AU A 4.00 10.00
162 Jason Thompson AU B 3.00 8.00
163 Anthony Randolph AU B 3.00 8.00
164 Robin Lopez AU B 3.00 8.00
165 Marreese Speights AU B 4.00 10.00
166 Roy Hibbert AU B 3.00 8.00
167 J.J. Hickson AU B 3.00 8.00
168 Ryan Anderson AU B 4.00 10.00
169 Alexis Ajinca AU B 3.00 8.00
170 Kosta Koufos AU B 3.00 8.00
171 George Hill AU B 5.00 12.00
172 D.J. White AU B 3.00 8.00
173 J.R. Giddens AU B 3.00 8.00
174 Joey Dorsey AU B 3.00 8.00
175 Mario Chalmers AU B 4.00 10.00
176 DeAndre Jordan AU B 10.00 25.00
177 Chris Douglas-Roberts AU B 3.00 8.00
178 JaVale McGee AU B 5.00 12.00
179 Kyle Weaver AU B 3.00 8.00
180 Patrick Ewing Jr. AU B 3.00 8.00
181 Sonny Weems AU B 3.00 8.00
182 Brandon Rush AU B 3.00 8.00
183 Darrell Arthur AU B 4.00 10.00

2008-09 Bowman Chrome Refractors

*1-110 REF: .75X TO 2X BASE HI
*101-150 REF: .75X TO 2X BASE HI
1-150 PRINT RUN 499 SER.#'d SETS
*151-183 AU REF.: .75X TO 2X BASE HI
151-183 AU PRINT RUN 50 SETS
3 LeBron James 300.00 600.00
23 Chris Paul 15.00 40.00
24 Kobe Bryant 300.00 600.00
41 Dirk Nowitzki 15.00 40.00
69 Kevin Durant 125.00 300.00
111 Derrick Rose 50.00 120.00
114 Russell Westbrook 125.00 300.00
154 Russell Westbrook AU 600.00 1,200.00

2008-09 Bowman Chrome Refractors Blue

*1-110 REF.BLUE: 2.5X TO 6X BASE HI
*111-150 REF.BLUE: 2X TO 5X BASE
PRINT RUN 99 SER.#'d SETS
3 LeBron James 1,000.00 2,000.00
23 Chris Paul 75.00 200.00
24 Kobe Bryant 1,000.00 2,000.00
41 Dirk Nowitzki 30.00 80.00
69 Kevin Durant 400.00 800.00
100 Dwyane Wade 10.00 25.00
111 Derrick Rose 200.00 500.00
114 Russell Westbrook 400.00 800.00

2008-09 Bowman Chrome Refractors Gold

*1-110 REF.GOLD: 5X TO 12X BASE
*111-150 REF.GOLD: 2.5X TO 6X BASE
1-150 PRINT RUN 50 SER.#'d SETS
*151-183 REF.GOLD: 1.5X TO 4X BASE
151-183 PRINT RUN 25 SER.#'d SETS
3 LeBron James 2,000.00 4,000.00
9 Yi Jianlian 40.00 100.00
15 Carmelo Anthony 10.00 25.00
23 Chris Paul 150.00 400.00
24 Kobe Bryant 2,000.00 4,000.00
34 Paul Pierce 15.00 40.00
41 Dirk Nowitzki 60.00 150.00
69 Kevin Durant 1,000.00 2,000.00
114 Russell Westbrook 500.00 1,000.00
154 Russell Westbrook AU 1,500.00 3,000.00
157 Eric Gordon AU 150.00 300.00

2008-09 Bowman Chrome X-Fractors

*X-FRACTORS 1-110: 1X TO 2.5X BASE HI
*X-FRACTORS 111-150: 1.25X TO 3X BASE HI
STATED PRINT RUN 299 SER.#'d SETS
3 LeBron James 400.00 800.00
21 Tim Duncan 15.00 40.00
23 Chris Paul 25.00 60.00
24 Kobe Bryant 400.00 800.00
41 Dirk Nowitzki 20.00 50.00
69 Kevin Durant 150.00 400.00
111 Derrick Rose 75.00 200.00
114 Russell Westbrook 150.00 400.00

2024-25 Bowman Chrome Sapphire University

*PURPLE REF/100: 1.5X TO 4X BASIC
*YELLOW REF/75: 2X TO 5X BASIC
*GREEN REF/65: 2.5X TO 6X BASIC
*GOLD REF/50: 2.5X TO 6X BASIC
*ORANGE REF/25: 3X TO 8X BASIC
1 Ace Bailey 2.50 6.00
2 Ahmad Nowell 1.00 2.50
3 Aiden Sherrell 1.00 2.50
4 AJ Storr 1.00 2.50
5 Allie Ziebell 1.00 2.50
6 Aneesah Morrow 1.25 3.00
7 Annor Boateng 1.00 2.50
8 Asa Newell 1.50 4.00
9 Audi Crooks 1.50 4.00
10 Billy Richmond III 1.25 3.00
11 Boogie Fland 1.25 3.00
12 Braden Smith 1.50 4.00
13 Cam Scott 1.00 2.50
14 Clifford Omoruyi 1.00 2.50
15 Robert Wright III 1.00 2.50
16 Cooper Flagg 40.00 100.00
17 Dame Sarr 2.50 6.00
18 Darren Harris 1.00 2.50
19 Derik Queen 2.00 5.00
20 Derrion Reid 1.00 2.50
21 Donavan Freeman 1.00 2.50
22 Dylan Harper 2.50 6.00
23 Emanuel Sharp 1.00 2.50
24 Flory Bidunga 1.00 2.50
25 Grant Nelson 1.00 2.50
26 Hannah Hidalgo 2.50 6.00
27 Isaiah Evans 1.25 3.00
28 Jalil Bethea 1.00 2.50
29 Jaloni Cambridge 1.25 3.00
30 Jayden Nunn 1.00 2.50
31 John Bol 1.00 2.50
32 Jonas Aidoo 1.00 2.50
33 Jordan Gainey 1.00 2.50
34 Jordan Lee 1.00 2.50
35 Josh Hubbard 1.00 2.50
36 Joyce Edwards 1.50 4.00
37 Juju Watkins 4.00 10.00
38 Justice Carlton 1.00 2.50
39 Kam Jones 1.00 2.50
40 Kanon Catchings 1.00 2.50
41 Karter Knox 1.25 3.00
42 Kate Koval 1.00 2.50
43 Kayleigh Heckel 1.00 2.50
44 Kennedy Smith 1.00 2.50
45 Keshon Gilbert 1.00 2.50
46 Khaman Maluach 1.50 4.00
47 Kiki Iriafen 2.00 5.00
48 Kon Knueppel 2.50 6.00
49 Labaron Philon 1.00 2.50
50 Langston Love 1.00 2.50
51 Latrell Wrightsell 1.00 2.50
52 Liam McNeeley 1.50 4.00
53 Mackenly Randolph 1.00 2.50
54 Meechie Johnson 1.00 2.50
55 Mikayla Blakes 2.00 5.00
56 Nolan Traore 1.50 4.00
57 Aden Holloway 1.00 2.50
58 Patrick Ngongba 1.00 2.50
59 PJ Haggerty 1.00 2.50
60 Raven Johnson 1.00 2.50
61 Robbie Avila 1.00 2.50
62 Sarah Strong 2.50 6.00
63 Sion James 1.00 2.50
64 Sonia Citron 2.50 6.00
65 Syla Swords 2.00 5.00
66 Tamin Lipsey 1.00 2.50
67 Trent Perry 1.00 2.50
68 Tyler Hendricks 1.00 2.50
69 Drake Powell 1.25 3.00
70 Riley Kugel 1.00 2.50
71 Simeon Wilcher 1.00 2.50
72 Ryan Nembhard 1.00 2.50
73 Nick Boyd 1.00 2.50
74 TJ Bamba 1.00 2.50
75 Jeremy Fears 1.00 2.50
76 Miles Kelly 1.00 2.50
77 Jackson Shelstad 1.00 2.50
78 Kylan Boswell .75 2.00
79 Miro Little 1.00 2.50
80 Jaden Akins 1.00 2.50
81 Jamari McDowell 1.00 2.50
82 Prince Aligbe 1.00 2.50
83 Xavier Booker 1.00 2.50
84 RJ Jones 1.00 2.50
85 DeShawn Harris-Smith 1.00 2.50
86 Diamond Johnson 1.00 2.50
87 Solomon Ball 1.25 3.00
88 Tre Norman 1.00 2.50
89 Dennis Evans 1.00 2.50
90 Zaide Lowery 1.00 2.50
91 Isaac McKneely 1.00 2.50
92 Steele Venters 1.00 2.50
93 Ashton Hardaway 1.00 2.50
94 Scotty Middleton 1.00 2.50
95 Layden Blocker 1.00 2.50
96 Freddie Dilione V 1.00 2.50
97 Fletcher Loyer 1.00 2.50
98 Johni Broome 1.00 2.50
99 Mark Sears 1.00 2.50
100 Alex Karaban 1.25 3.00

2024-25 Bowman Chrome Sapphire University Prospect Autographs

*ORANGE REF/25: .75X TO 2X BASIC
1 Ace Bailey 40.00 100.00
2 Ahmad Nowell 6.00 15.00
3 Aiden Sherrell 6.00 15.00
4 AJ Storr 6.00 15.00
5 Allie Ziebell 6.00 15.00
6 Aneesah Morrow 8.00 20.00
7 Annor Boateng 6.00 15.00
8 Asa Newell 10.00 25.00
9 Audi Crooks 10.00 25.00
10 Billy Richmond III 8.00 20.00
11 Boogie Fland 8.00 20.00
12 Braden Smith 10.00 25.00
13 Cam Scott 6.00 15.00
14 Clifford Omoruyi 6.00 15.00
15 Robert Wright III 6.00 15.00
16 Cooper Flagg 800.00 1,500.00
17 Dame Sarr 15.00 40.00
18 Darren Harris 6.00 15.00
19 Derik Queen 12.00 30.00
20 Derrion Reid 6.00 15.00
21 Donavan Freeman 6.00 15.00
22 Dylan Harper 60.00 150.00
23 Emanuel Sharp 6.00 15.00
24 Flory Bidunga 6.00 15.00
25 Grant Nelson 6.00 15.00
26 Hannah Hidalgo 40.00 100.00
27 Isaiah Evans 8.00 20.00
28 Jalil Bethea 6.00 15.00
29 Jaloni Cambridge 8.00 20.00
30 Jayden Nunn 6.00 15.00
31 John Bol 6.00 15.00
32 Jonas Aidoo 6.00 15.00
33 Jordan Gainey 6.00 15.00
34 Jordan Lee 6.00 15.00
35 Josh Hubbard 6.00 15.00
36 Joyce Edwards 10.00 25.00
37 Juju Watkins 125.00 300.00
38 Justice Carlton 6.00 15.00
39 Kam Jones 6.00 15.00
40 Kanon Catchings 6.00 15.00
41 Karter Knox 8.00 20.00
42 Kate Koval 6.00 15.00
43 Kayleigh Heckel 6.00 15.00
44 Kennedy Smith 6.00 15.00
45 Keshon Gilbert 6.00 15.00
46 Khaman Maluach 10.00 25.00
47 Kiki Iriafen 12.00 30.00
48 Kon Knueppel 40.00 100.00
49 Labaron Philon 6.00 15.00
50 Langston Love 6.00 15.00
51 Latrell Wrightsell 6.00 15.00
52 Liam McNeeley 10.00 25.00
53 Mackenly Randolph 6.00 15.00
54 Meechie Johnson 6.00 15.00
55 Mikayla Blakes 25.00 60.00
56 Nolan Traore 10.00 25.00
57 Aden Holloway 6.00 15.00
58 Patrick Ngongba 6.00 15.00
59 PJ Haggerty 6.00 15.00
60 Raven Johnson 6.00 15.00
61 Robbie Avila 6.00 15.00
62 Sarah Strong 100.00 250.00
63 Sion James 6.00 15.00
64 Sonia Citron 40.00 100.00
65 Syla Swords 12.00 30.00
66 Tamin Lipsey 6.00 15.00
67 Trent Perry 6.00 15.00
68 Tyler Hendricks 6.00 15.00
69 Drake Powell 8.00 20.00
70 Riley Kugel 6.00 15.00
71 Simeon Wilcher 6.00 15.00
72 Ryan Nembhard 6.00 15.00
73 Nick Boyd 6.00 15.00
74 TJ Bamba 6.00 15.00
75 Jeremy Fears 6.00 15.00
76 Miles Kelly 6.00 15.00
77 Jackson Shelstad 6.00 15.00
78 Kylan Boswell 5.00 12.00
79 Miro Little 6.00 15.00
80 Jaden Akins 6.00 15.00
81 Jamari McDowell 6.00 15.00
82 Prince Aligbe 6.00 15.00
83 Xavier Booker 6.00 15.00
84 RJ Jones 6.00 15.00
85 DeShawn Harris-Smith 6.00 15.00
86 Diamond Johnson 8.00 20.00
87 Solomon Ball 8.00 20.00
88 Tre Norman 6.00 15.00
89 Dennis Evans 6.00 15.00
90 Zaide Lowery 6.00 15.00
91 Isaac McKneely 6.00 15.00
92 Steele Venters 6.00 15.00
93 Ashton Hardaway 6.00 15.00
94 Scotty Middleton 6.00 15.00
95 Layden Blocker 6.00 15.00
96 Freddie Dilione V 6.00 15.00
97 Fletcher Loyer 6.00 15.00
98 Johni Broome 6.00 15.00
99 Mark Sears 6.00 15.00
100 Alex Karaban 8.00 20.00

2024-25 Bowman Chrome Sapphire University Sapphire Selections Autographs

*ORANGE REF/25: .75X TO 2X BASIC
SSAAB Ace Bailey 40.00 100.00
SSAAM Aneesah Morrow 8.00 20.00
SSAAN Asa Newell 10.00 25.00
SSABF Boogie Fland 8.00 20.00
SSABR Billy Richmond III 8.00 20.00
SSABS Braden Smith 10.00 25.00
SSACF Cooper Flagg 800.00 1,500.00
SSADF Donavan Freeman 6.00 15.00
SSADH Dylan Harper 60.00 150.00
SSAFB Flory Bidunga 6.00 15.00
SSAHH Hannah Hidalgo 40.00 100.00
SSAIE Isaiah Evans 8.00 20.00
SSAJB Jalil Bethea 6.00 15.00
SSAJC Jaloni Cambridge 8.00 20.00
SSAJE Joyce Edwards 10.00 25.00
SSAJW Juju Watkins 125.00 300.00
SSAKK Kon Knueppel 40.00 100.00
SSALL Langston Love 6.00 15.00
SSAMJ Meechie Johnson 6.00 15.00
SSARA Robbie Avila 6.00 15.00
SSASS Sarah Strong 100.00 250.00
SSATL Tamin Lipsey 6.00 15.00
SSAAST AJ Storr 6.00 15.00
SSAKKN Karter Knox 8.00 20.00

2024-25 Bowman Chrome Sapphire University Treasured Talents

TT1 Ace Bailey 25.00 60.00
TT2 Cooper Flagg 150.00 400.00
TT3 Dylan Harper 40.00 100.00
TT4 Khaman Maluach 15.00 40.00
TT5 Robbie Avila 10.00 25.00
TT6 Derrion Reid 10.00 25.00
TT7 Boogie Fland 12.00 30.00
TT8 Sarah Strong 75.00 200.00
TT9 Sonia Citron 25.00 60.00
TT10 Joyce Edwards 15.00 40.00

2022-23 Bowman Chrome University

COMMON CARD .30 .75
SEMISTARS .40 1.00
UNLISTED STARS .50 1.25
*PINK REFRACTORS: 1.25X TO 3X BASIC
*REFRACTORS: 1.25X TO 3X BASIC
*SHIMMER REF: 1.5X TO 4X BASIC
1 Nick Smith Jr. .60 1.50
2 Collin Chandler .60 1.50
3 Mikey Williams .50 1.25
4 Ayanna Patterson .30 .75
5 Aliyah Boston 1.25 3.00
6 Devin Carter .40 1.00
7 Caroline Ducharme .60 1.50
8 Roddy Gayle Jr. .50 1.25
9 Tyger Campbell .40 1.00
10 RJ Davis .60 1.50
11 Brice Sensabaugh .40 1.00
12 Rasir Bolton .40 1.00
13 Chris Livingston .75 2.00
14 Jarace Walker 1.25 3.00
15 Tyrese Hunter .50 1.25
16 Adam Flagler .50 1.25
17 Keeshawn Barthelemy .40 1.00
18 Kyle Lofton .30 .75
19 PJ Hall .40 1.00
20 Femi Odukale .30 .75
21 Makai Ashton-Langford .40 1.00
22 Cam Whitmore 1.25 3.00
23 Jared Bynum .50 1.25
24 Kiki Rice .75 2.00
25 Jalen Cook .30 .75
26 Timmy Allen .40 1.00
27 Jared McCain 2.00 5.00
28 Tyrese Proctor 1.25 3.00
29 KD Johnson .40 1.00
30 Brandon Slater .40 1.00
31 Will Richardson .40 1.00
32 Tre White .40 1.00
33 Judah Mintz .40 1.00
34 G.G. Jackson 1.00 2.50
35 Jaeden Zackery .30 .75
36 Hunter Dickinson .75 2.00
37 JJ Starling .50 1.25
38 Seth Trimble .50 1.25
39 Jett Howard .75 2.00
40 Brandon Murray .30 .75
41 Gradey Dick 1.25 3.00
42 Trayce Jackson-Davis .75 2.00
43 JuJu Watkins 8.00 20.00
44 Armando Bacot .50 1.25
45 Arterio Morris .30 .75
46 Julian Phillips .60 1.50
47 Kyle Filipowski .60 1.50
48 Mark Mitchell .50 1.25
49 Lauren Betts 1.25 3.00
50 Caitlin Clark 12.00 30.00
51 Kijani Wright .40 1.00
52 Hansel Enmanuel 1.00 2.50
53 Demarr Langford .40 1.00
54 DJ Horne .30 .75
55 Skyy Clark .50 1.25
56 MJ Rice .60 1.50
57 Jalen Hood-Schifino .60 1.50
58 Anthony Black .75 2.00
59 Kendric Davis .50 1.25
60 Avery Anderson .50 1.25
61 Drew Timme .50 1.25
62 Ernest Udeh Jr. .60 1.50
63 Al-Amir Dawes .30 .75
64 Posh Alexander .50 1.25
65 Race Thompson .50 1.25
66 Khalif Battle .50 1.25
67 Jalen Wilson 1.25 3.00
68 Kel'el Ware .75 2.00
69 Amari Bailey .60 1.50
70 Bruce Thornton .30 .75
71 Kris Murray 1.25 3.00
72 Kamari Lands .50 1.25
73 Ashlyn Watkins .30 .75
74 Oscar Tshiebwe .75 2.00
75 Jaden Schutt .75 2.00
76 Jeremy Roach .60 1.50
77 Otega Oweh .50 1.25
78 Jalen Washington .50 1.25
79 Zach Edey 1.25 3.00
80 Brandon Miller 2.00 5.00
81 Jordan Walsh .60 1.50
82 Malik Reneau .50 1.25
83 Daron Holmes .50 1.25
84 Matas Buzelis 1.50 4.00
85 Jordan Hawkins 1.25 3.00
86 Chance Westry .50 1.25
87 LJ Cryer .60 1.50
88 Mike Miles .40 1.00
89 Caleb Love 1.25 3.00
90 Dajuan Harris Jr. .50 1.25
91 Zion Cruz .50 1.25
92 Vincent Iwuchukwu .50 1.25
93 Marcus Sasser .75 2.00
94 Felix Okpara .30 .75
95 Mark Armstrong .30 .75
96 Ryan Nembhard .50 1.25
97 Frankie Collins .30 .75
98 Jaxon Kohler .50 1.25
99 Jalen Bridges .50 1.25
100 Dereck Lively II 1.25 3.00
101 Victor Wembanyama SP 100.00 250.00

2022-23 Bowman Chrome University Aqua Refractors

*AQUA REF: 2X TO 5X BASIC
STATED PRINT RUN 299 SER. #'D SETS
43 JuJu Watkins 60.00 150.00
50 Caitlin Clark 150.00 400.00

2022-23 Bowman Chrome University Aqua Wave Refractors

*AQUA WAVE REF: 2X TO 5X BASIC
STATED PRINT RUN 299 SER. #'D SETS
43 JuJu Watkins 60.00 150.00
50 Caitlin Clark 150.00 400.00

2022-23 Bowman Chrome University Blue RayWave Refractors

*BLUE RAYWAVE REF: 2.5X TO 6X BASIC
STATED PRINT RUN 199 SER. #'D SETS
43 JuJu Watkins 75.00 200.00
50 Caitlin Clark 200.00 500.00

2022-23 Bowman Chrome University Blue Refractors

*BLUE REF: 2.5X TO 6X BASIC
STATED PRINT RUN 199 SER. #'D SETS
43 JuJu Watkins 75.00 200.00
50 Caitlin Clark 200.00 500.00

2022-23 Bowman Chrome University Fuchsia Mini-Diamond Refractors

*FUCHSIA MINI-DMND REF: 2.5X TO 6X BASIC
STATED PRINT RUN 150 SER. #'D SETS
43 JuJu Watkins 75.00 200.00
50 Caitlin Clark 200.00 500.00

2022-23 Bowman Chrome University Gold Refractors

*GOLD REF: 4X TO 10X BASIC
STATED PRINT RUN 50 SER. #'D SETS
43 JuJu Watkins 125.00 300.00
50 Caitlin Clark 400.00 800.00

2022-23 Bowman Chrome University Gold Shimmer Refractors

43 JuJu Watkins 125.00 300.00
50 Caitlin Clark 400.00 800.00

2022-23 Bowman Chrome University Green Lava Refractors

*GREEN LAVA REF: 3X TO 8X BASIC
STATED PRINT RUN 99 SER. #'D SETS
43 JuJu Watkins 100.00 250.00
50 Caitlin Clark 300.00 600.00

2022-23 Bowman Chrome University Green Refractors

*GREEN REF: 3X TO 8X BASIC
STATED PRINT RUN 99 SER. #'D SETS
43 JuJu Watkins 100.00 250.00
50 Caitlin Clark 300.00 600.00

2022-23 Bowman Chrome University Green Shimmer Refractors

*GREEN SHIMMER REF: 3X TO 8X BASIC
STATED PRINT RUN 99 SER. #'D SETS
43 JuJu Watkins 100.00 250.00
50 Caitlin Clark 300.00 600.00

2022-23 Bowman Chrome University Orange Refractors

*ORANGE REF: 6X TO 15X BASIC
STATED PRINT RUN 25 SER. #'D SETS
43 JuJu Watkins 200.00 500.00
50 Caitlin Clark 600.00 1,200.00

2022-23 Bowman Chrome University Orange Shimmer Refractors

*ORANGE SHIMMER REF: 6X TO 15X BASIC
STATED PRINT RUN 25 SER. #'D SETS
43 JuJu Watkins 200.00 500.00
50 Caitlin Clark 600.00 1,200.00

2022-23 Bowman Chrome University Pink Wave Refractors

*PINK WAVE REF: 3X TO 8X BASIC
STATED PRINT RUN 125 SER. #'D SETS
43 JuJu Watkins 100.00 250.00
50 Caitlin Clark 300.00 600.00

2022-23 Bowman Chrome University Purple Mini-Diamond Refractors

*PURPLE MINI DMND REF: 2X TO 5X BASIC
STATED PRINT RUN 399 SER. #'D SETS
43 JuJu Watkins 60.00 150.00
50 Caitlin Clark 150.00 400.00

2022-23 Bowman Chrome University Purple Refractors

*PURPLE REF: 2X TO 5X BASIC
STATED PRINT RUN 399 SER. #'D SETS
43 JuJu Watkins 60.00 150.00
50 Caitlin Clark 150.00 400.00

2022-23 Bowman Chrome University Purple Shimmer Refractors

*PURPLE SHMR REF: 2X TO 5X BASIC
43 JuJu Watkins 60.00 150.00
50 Caitlin Clark 150.00 400.00

2022-23 Bowman Chrome University RayWave Refractors

*RAYWAVE REF: 3X TO 8X BASIC
STATED PRINT RUN 100 SER. #'D SETS
43 JuJu Watkins 100.00 250.00
50 Caitlin Clark 300.00 600.00

2022-23 Bowman Chrome University Yellow Refractors

*YELLOW REF: 3X TO 8X BASIC
STATED PRINT RUN 75 SER. #'D SETS
43 JuJu Watkins 100.00 250.00
50 Caitlin Clark 300.00 600.00

2022-23 Bowman Chrome University '09 Bowman

COMMON CARD .50 1.25
SEMISTARS .60 1.50
UNLISTED STARS .75 2.00
09B1 Brandon Miller 3.00 8.00
09B2 Nick Smith Jr. 1.00 2.50
09B3 Anthony Black 1.25 3.00
09B4 Jordan Walsh 1.00 2.50
09B5 Chance Westry .75 2.00
09B6 Mark Mitchell .75 2.00
09B7 Dereck Lively II 2.00 5.00
09B8 Kyle Filipowski 1.00 2.50
09B9 Amari Bailey 1.00 2.50
09B10 Caleb Love 2.00 5.00
09B11 Mikey Williams .75 2.00
09B12 Jarace Walker 2.00 5.00
09B13 Gradey Dick 2.00 5.00
09B14 MJ Rice 1.00 2.50
09B15 Chris Livingston 1.25 3.00
09B16 Oscar Tshiebwe 1.25 3.00
09B17 JJ Starling .75 2.00
09B18 Aliyah Boston 2.00 5.00
09B19 Judah Mintz .60 1.50
09B20 Arterio Morris .50 1.25
09B21 Armando Bacot .75 2.00
09B22 Cam Whitmore 2.00 5.00
09B23 Lauren Betts 2.00 5.00
09B24 KD Johnson .60 1.50
09B25 Adam Flagler .75 2.00
09B26 Kel'el Ware 1.25 3.00
09B27 Drew Timme .75 2.00
09B28 Julian Phillips 1.00 2.50
09B29 Marcus Sasser 1.25 3.00
09B30 Caitlin Clark 12.00 30.00

2022-23 Bowman Chrome University '09 Bowman Aqua Refractors

*AQUA REF: 1.5X TO 4X BASIC
STATED PRINT RUN 150 SER. #'D SETS
09B30 Caitlin Clark 50.00 120.00

2022-23 Bowman Chrome University '09 Bowman Orange Refractors

*ORANGE REF: 5X TO 12X BASIC
STATED PRINT RUN 25 SER. #'D SETS
09B30 Caitlin Clark 200.00 500.00

2022-23 Bowman Chrome University '09 Bowman Autographs

COMMON CARD 4.00 10.00
SEMISTARS 5.00 12.00
UNLISTED STARS 6.00 15.00
STATED PRINT RUN 99 SER.#'d SETS
*ORANGE REF/25: .75X TO 2X BASIC
09B1 Brandon Miller 40.00 100.00
09B2 Nick Smith Jr. 8.00 20.00
09B3 Anthony Black 10.00 25.00
09B4 Jordan Walsh 8.00 20.00
09B5 Chance Westry 6.00 15.00
09B7 Dereck Lively II 15.00 40.00
09B8 Kyle Filipowski 8.00 20.00
09B11 Mikey Williams 6.00 15.00
09B12 Jarace Walker 15.00 40.00
09B15 Chris Livingston 10.00 25.00
09B16 Oscar Tshiebwe 10.00 25.00
09B22 Cam Whitmore 15.00 40.00
09B27 Drew Timme 6.00 15.00
09B28 Julian Phillips 8.00 20.00
09B30 Caitlin Clark 300.00 600.00

2022-23 Bowman Chrome University Bowman Invicta

COMMON CARD .60 1.50
SEMISTARS .75 2.00
UNLISTED STARS 1.00 2.50
BI1 Dereck Lively II 2.50 6.00
BI2 Nick Smith Jr. 1.25 3.00
BI3 Kyle Filipowski 1.25 3.00
BI4 Amari Bailey 1.25 3.00
BI5 Tyrese Proctor 2.50 6.00
BI6 Drew Timme 1.00 2.50
BI7 Jarace Walker 2.50 6.00
BI8 Oscar Tshiebwe 1.50 4.00
BI9 Chris Livingston 1.50 4.00
BI10 Arterio Morris .60 1.50
BI11 JJ Starling 1.00 2.50
BI12 Kel'el Ware 1.50 4.00
BI13 Julian Phillips 1.25 3.00
BI14 Brandon Miller 4.00 10.00
BI15 Caitlin Clark 25.00 60.00
BI16 Anthony Black 1.50 4.00
BI17 Ernest Udeh Jr. 1.25 3.00
BI18 Marcus Sasser 1.50 4.00
BI19 Jordan Walsh 1.25 3.00
BI20 Cam Whitmore 2.50 6.00

2022-23 Bowman Chrome University Bowman Invicta Lava Refractors

*LAVE REF: 1.5X TO 4X BASIC
STATED PRINT RUN 150 SER. #'D SETS
BI15 Caitlin Clark 125.00 300.00

2022-23 Bowman Chrome University Bowman Invicta Orange Refractors

*ORANGE REF: 3X TO 8X BASIC
STATED PRINT RUN 25 SER. #'D SETS
BI15 Caitlin Clark 400.00 800.00

2022-23 Bowman Chrome University Bowman Invicta Autographs

COMMON CARD 4.00 10.00
SEMISTARS 5.00 12.00
UNLISTED STARS 6.00 15.00
STATED PRINT RUN 99 SER.#'d SETS
*ORANGE REF/25: .75X TO 2X BASIC
BI1 Dereck Lively II 15.00 40.00
BI2 Nick Smith Jr. 8.00 20.00
BI3 Kyle Filipowski 8.00 20.00
BI4 Amari Bailey 8.00 20.00
BI5 Tyrese Proctor 15.00 40.00
BI7 Jarace Walker 15.00 40.00
BI8 Oscar Tshiebwe 10.00 25.00
BI9 Chris Livingston 10.00 25.00
BI10 Arterio Morris 4.00 10.00
BI20 Cam Whitmore 15.00 40.00

2022-23 Bowman Chrome University Image Variations

*IMAGE VAR: 4X TO 10X BASIC
50 Caitlin Clark 300.00 600.00

2022-23 Bowman Chrome University Prime Choice Signatures

COMMON CARD 6.00 15.00
SEMISTARS 8.00 20.00
UNLISTED STARS 10.00 25.00
STATED PRINT RUN 50 SER.#'d SETS
*ORANGE REF/25: .6X TO 1.5X BASIC
PCSAB Amari Bailey 12.00 30.00
PCSAF Adam Flagler 10.00 25.00
PCSAM Arterio Morris 6.00 15.00
PCSBM Brandon Miller 40.00 100.00
PCSCC Caitlin Clark 500.00 1,000.00
PCSCL Chris Livingston 15.00 40.00
PCSCW Cam Whitmore 25.00 60.00
PCSDL Dereck Lively II 25.00 60.00
PCSDT Drew Timme 10.00 25.00
PCSEU Ernest Udeh Jr. 12.00 30.00
PCSGD Gradey Dick 25.00 60.00
PCSJM Judah Mintz 8.00 20.00
PCSJP Julian Phillips 12.00 30.00
PCSJS JJ Starling 10.00 25.00
PCSJW Jarace Walker 25.00 60.00
PCSKF Kyle Filipowski 12.00 30.00
PCSKW Kel'el Ware 15.00 40.00
PCSMM Mark Mitchell 10.00 25.00
PCSMR Malik Reneau 10.00 25.00
PCSMS Marcus Sasser 15.00 40.00
PCSMW Mikey Williams 10.00 25.00
PCSNS Nick Smith Jr. 12.00 30.00
PCSOT Oscar Tshiebwe 15.00 40.00
PCSSC Skyy Clark 10.00 25.00
PCSTP Tyrese Proctor 25.00 60.00
PCSABA Armando Bacot 10.00 25.00
PCSABL Anthony Black 15.00 40.00
PCSABO Aliyah Boston 25.00 60.00
PCSCLO Caleb Love 25.00 60.00
PCSJWA Jordan Walsh 12.00 30.00

2022-23 Bowman Chrome University Prospect Autographs

COMMON CARD 3.00 8.00
SEMISTARS 4.00 10.00
UNLISTED STARS 5.00 12.00
1 Nick Smith Jr. 6.00 15.00
2 Collin Chandler 6.00 15.00
3 Mikey Williams 5.00 12.00
4 Ayanna Patterson 3.00 8.00
5 Aliyah Boston 12.00 30.00
6 Devin Carter 4.00 10.00
7 Caroline Ducharme 6.00 15.00
8 Roddy Gayle Jr. 5.00 12.00
9 Tyger Campbell 4.00 10.00
10 RJ Davis 6.00 15.00
11 Brice Sensabaugh 4.00 10.00
12 Rasir Bolton 4.00 10.00
13 Chris Livingston 8.00 20.00
14 Jarace Walker 12.00 30.00
15 Tyrese Hunter 5.00 12.00
16 Adam Flagler 5.00 12.00
17 Keeshawn Barthelemy 4.00 10.00
18 Kyle Lofton 3.00 8.00
19 PJ Hall 4.00 10.00
20 Femi Odukale 3.00 8.00
21 Makai Ashton-Langford 4.00 10.00
22 Cam Whitmore 12.00 30.00
23 Jared Bynum 5.00 12.00
24 Kiki Rice 8.00 20.00
25 Jalen Cook 3.00 8.00
26 Timmy Allen 4.00 10.00
27 Jared McCain 20.00 50.00
28 Tyrese Proctor 12.00 30.00
29 KD Johnson 4.00 10.00
30 Brandon Slater 4.00 10.00
31 Will Richardson 4.00 10.00
32 Tre White 4.00 10.00
33 Judah Mintz 4.00 10.00
34 G.G. Jackson 10.00 25.00
35 Jaeden Zackery 3.00 8.00
36 Hunter Dickinson 8.00 20.00
37 JJ Starling 5.00 12.00
38 Seth Trimble 5.00 12.00
39 Jett Howard 8.00 20.00
40 Brandon Murray 3.00 8.00
41 Gradey Dick 12.00 30.00
42 Trayce Jackson-Davis 8.00 20.00
43 JuJu Watkins 150.00 400.00
44 Armando Bacot 5.00 12.00
45 Arterio Morris 3.00 8.00
46 Julian Phillips 6.00 15.00
47 Kyle Filipowski 6.00 15.00
48 Mark Mitchell 5.00 12.00
49 Lauren Betts 40.00 100.00
50 Caitlin Clark 800.00 1,500.00
51 Kijani Wright 4.00 10.00
52 Hansel Enmanuel 10.00 25.00
53 Demarr Langford 4.00 10.00
54 DJ Horne 3.00 8.00
55 Skyy Clark 5.00 12.00
56 MJ Rice 6.00 15.00
57 Jalen Hood-Schifino 6.00 15.00
58 Anthony Black 8.00 20.00
59 Kendric Davis 5.00 12.00
60 Avery Anderson 5.00 12.00
61 Drew Timme 5.00 12.00
62 Ernest Udeh Jr. 6.00 15.00
63 Al-Amir Dawes 3.00 8.00
64 Posh Alexander 5.00 12.00
65 Race Thompson 5.00 12.00
66 Khalif Battle 5.00 12.00
67 Jalen Wilson 12.00 30.00
68 Kel'el Ware 8.00 20.00
69 Amari Bailey 6.00 15.00
70 Bruce Thornton 3.00 8.00
71 Kris Murray 12.00 30.00
72 Kamari Lands 5.00 12.00
73 Ashlyn Watkins 3.00 8.00
74 Oscar Tshiebwe 8.00 20.00
75 Jaden Schutt 8.00 20.00
76 Jeremy Roach 6.00 15.00
77 Olega Oweh 5.00 12.00
78 Jalen Washington 5.00 12.00
79 Zach Edey 12.00 30.00
80 Brandon Miller 50.00 120.00
81 Jordan Walsh 6.00 15.00
82 Malik Reneau 5.00 12.00
83 Daron Holmes 5.00 12.00
84 Matas Buzelis 15.00 40.00
85 Jordan Hawkins 12.00 30.00
86 Chance Westry 5.00 12.00
87 LJ Cryer 6.00 15.00
88 Mike Miles 4.00 10.00
89 Caleb Love 12.00 30.00
90 Dajuan Harris Jr. 5.00 12.00
91 Zion Cruz 5.00 12.00
92 Vincent Iwuchukwu 5.00 12.00
93 Marcus Sasser 8.00 20.00
94 Felix Okpara 3.00 8.00
95 Mark Armstrong 3.00 8.00
96 Ryan Nembhard 5.00 12.00
97 Frankie Collins 3.00 8.00
98 Jaxon Kohler 5.00 12.00
99 Jalen Bridges 5.00 12.00
100 Dereck Lively II 12.00 30.00
101 Victor Wembanyama 1,500.00 3,000.00
102 Scoot Henderson 20.00 50.00

2022-23 Bowman Chrome University Prospect Autographs Gold Lava Refractors

*GOLD LAVA REF: 1X TO 2.5X BASIC
STATED PRINT RUN 50 SER.#'d SETS
50 Caitlin Clark 2,500.00 5,000.00
101 Victor Wembanyama 4,000.00 8,000.00

2022-23 Bowman Chrome University Prospect Autographs Gold Refractors

*GOLD REF: 1X TO 2.5X BASIC
STATED PRINT RUN 50 SER.#'d SETS
50 Caitlin Clark 2,500.00 5,000.00
101 Victor Wembanyama 4,000.00 8,000.00

2022-23 Bowman Chrome University Prospect Autographs Green Refractors

*GREEN REF: .6X TO 1.5X BASIC
STATED PRINT RUN 99 SER.#'d SETS
50 Caitlin Clark 1,500.00 3,000.00
101 Victor Wembanyama 2,500.00 5,000.00

2022-23 Bowman Chrome University Prospect Autographs Orange Refractors

*ORANGE REF: 1.5X TO 4X BASIC
STATED PRINT RUN 25 SER.#'d SETS
50 Caitlin Clark 4,000.00 8,000.00
101 Victor Wembanyama 6,000.00 12,000.00

2022-23 Bowman Chrome University Prospect Autographs Orange Shimmer Refractors

*ORANGE SHIMMER REF: 1.5X TO 4X BASIC
STATED PRINT RUN 25 SER.#'d SETS
50 Caitlin Clark 4,000.00 8,000.00
101 Victor Wembanyama 6,000.00 12,000.00

2022-23 Bowman Chrome University Prospect Autographs RayWave Refractors

*RAYWAVE REF: .6X TO 1.5X BASIC
STATED PRINT RUN 199 SER.#'d SETS
101 Victor Wembanyama 2,000.00 4,000.00

2022-23 Bowman Chrome University Prospect Autographs Refractors

*REF: .5X TO 1.2X BASIC
STATED PRINT RUN 499 SER.#'d SETS
101 Victor Wembanyama 1,500.00 3,000.00

2022-23 Bowman Chrome University Prospect Autographs Yellow Refractors

*YELLOW REF: .75X TO 2X BASIC
STATED PRINT RUN 75 SER.#'d SETS
50 Caitlin Clark 2,000.00 4,000.00
101 Victor Wembanyama 3,000.00 6,000.00

2022-23 Bowman Chrome University Skyscraping

COMMON CARD .40 1.00
SEMISTARS .50 1.25
UNLISTED STARS .60 1.50
*AQUA REF/150: 2X TO 5X BASIC
*ORANGE REF/25: 5X TO 12X BASIC
S1 Chris Livingston 1.00 2.50
S2 Nick Smith Jr. .75 2.00
S3 Jordan Walsh .75 2.00
S4 Brandon Miller 2.50 6.00
S5 Dereck Lively II 1.50 4.00
S6 Mark Mitchell .60 1.50
S7 MJ Rice .75 2.00
S8 Arterio Morris .40 1.00
S9 Amari Bailey .75 2.00
S10 Jarace Walker 1.50 4.00
S11 Armando Bacot .60 1.50
S12 Cam Whitmore 1.50 4.00
S13 Kijani Wright .50 1.25
S14 Skyy Clark .60 1.50
S15 Judah Mintz .50 1.25

2022-23 Bowman Chrome University Skyscraping Autographs

COMMON CARD 5.00 10.00
SEMISTARS 6.00 15.00
UNLISTED STARS 8.00 20.00
STATED PRINT RUN 99 SER.#'d SETS
*ORANGE REF/25: .75X TO 2X BASIC
S1 Chris Livingston 12.00 30.00
S2 Nick Smith Jr. 10.00 25.00
S3 Jordan Walsh 10.00 25.00
S4 Brandon Miller 30.00 80.00
S5 Dereck Lively II 20.00 50.00
S6 Mark Mitchell 8.00 20.00
S8 Arterio Morris 5.00 12.00
S9 Amari Bailey 10.00 25.00
S10 Jarace Walker 20.00 50.00
S12 Cam Whitmore 20.00 50.00

2022-23 Bowman Chrome University The Big Kahuna

COMMON CARD 2.00 5.00
SEMISTARS 2.50 6.00
UNLISTED STARS 3.00 8.00
*ORANGE REF/25: 1.5X TO 4X BASIC
TBK1 Brandon Miller 12.00 30.00
TBK2 Nick Smith Jr. 4.00 10.00
TBK3 Anthony Black 5.00 12.00
TBK4 Jordan Walsh 4.00 10.00
TBK5 Mark Mitchell 3.00 8.00
TBK6 Dereck Lively II 8.00 20.00
TBK7 Kyle Filipowski 4.00 10.00
TBK8 Judah Mintz 2.50 6.00
TBK9 Julian Phillips 4.00 10.00
TBK10 Drew Timme 3.00 8.00
TBK11 Jarace Walker 8.00 20.00
TBK12 Marcus Sasser 5.00 12.00
TBK13 Malik Reneau 3.00 8.00
TBK14 Ernest Udeh Jr. 4.00 10.00
TBK15 Caitlin Clark 150.00 400.00
TBK16 G.G. Jackson 6.00 15.00
TBK17 Chris Livingston 5.00 12.00
TBK18 Oscar Tshiebwe 5.00 12.00
TBK19 JJ Starling 3.00 8.00
TBK20 Aliyah Boston 8.00 20.00
TBK21 Arterio Morris 2.00 5.00
TBK22 Amari Bailey 4.00 10.00
TBK23 MJ Rice 4.00 10.00
TBK24 Cam Whitmore 8.00 20.00
TBK25 Tyrese Proctor 8.00 20.00

2022-23 Bowman Chrome University The Big Kahuna Autographs

COMMON CARD 6.00 15.00
SEMISTARS 8.00 20.00
UNLISTED STARS 10.00 25.00
STATED PRINT RUN 150 SER.#'d SETS
*ORANGE REF/25: 1X TO 2.5X BASIC
TBK1 Brandon Miller 75.00 200.00
TBK2 Nick Smith Jr. 12.00 30.00
TBK3 Anthony Black 15.00 40.00
TBK4 Jordan Walsh 12.00 30.00
TBK6 Dereck Lively II 25.00 60.00
TBK9 Julian Phillips 12.00 30.00
TBK11 Jarace Walker 25.00 60.00
TBK13 Malik Reneau 10.00 25.00
TBK14 Ernest Udeh Jr. 12.00 30.00
TBK15 Caitlin Clark 1,500.00 3,000.00
TBK17 Chris Livingston 15.00 40.00
TBK18 Oscar Tshiebwe 15.00 40.00
TBK22 Amari Bailey 12.00 30.00
TBK24 Cam Whitmore 25.00 60.00
TBK25 Tyrese Proctor 25.00 60.00

2023-24 Bowman Chrome University

*PINK REF: 1X TO 2.5X BASIC
*REFRACTORS: 1X TO 2.5X BASIC
*PRPL SHMR REF: 1.5X TO 4X BASIC
*X-FRACTOR: 1.5X TO 4X BASIC
*PURPLE REF/399: 2X TO 5X BASIC
*PRPL MINI DMD REF/399: 2X TO 5X BASIC
*AQUA REF/299: 2.5X TO 6X BASIC
*AQUA WAVE REF/299: 2.5X TO 6X BASIC
*BLUE REF/199: 2.5X TO 6X BASIC
*BLUE RAYWAVE REF/199: 2.5X TO 6X BASIC
*FUCHSIA MINI DMD REF/150: 2.5X TO 6X BASIC
*PINK WAVE REF/125: 3X TO 8X BASIC
*RAYWAVE REF/100: 3X TO 8X BASIC
*GREEN REF/99: 3X TO 8X BASIC
*GREEN LAVA REF/99: 3X TO 8X BASIC
*GREEN SHMR REF/99: 3X TO 8X BASIC
*YELLOW REF/75: 4X TO 10X BASIC
*GOLD REF/50: 6X TO 15X BASIC
*GOLD SHMR REF/50: 6X TO 15X BASIC
*ORANGE REF/25: 8X TO 20X BASIC
*ORANGE SHMR REF/25: 8X TO 20X BASIC
1 Dillon Jones .50 1.25
2 Georgia Amoore .75 2.00
3 Kylan Boswell .40 1.00
4 Mikaylah Williams .75 2.00
5 AJ Hoggard .40 1.00
6 Johni Broome .60 1.50
7 Layden Blocker .50 1.25
8 Trevon Brazile .60 1.50
9 Zaccharie Risacher 1.50 4.00
10 Aden Holloway .50 1.25
11 Cormac Ryan .40 1.00
12 Miro Little .50 1.25
13 Prince Aligbe .40 1.00
14 Quinten Post 1.00 2.50
15 Simeon Wilcher .60 1.50
16 Cody Williams .75 2.00
17 Ryan Kalkbrenner .60 1.50
18 Jared McCain 1.50 4.00
19 Aaliyah Edwards .60 1.50
20 Tyrese Proctor 1.00 2.50
21 Sean Stewart .50 1.25
22 Diamond Johnson .50 1.25
23 Kyle Filipowski .75 2.00
24 Darin Green Jr. .40 1.00
25 Hailey van Lith 1.25 3.00
26 Hannah Hidalgo 2.00 5.00
27 Isaac McKneely .40 1.00
28 Dusty Stromer .40 1.00
29 Rejean Ellis .50 1.25
30 Jamal Shead .50 1.25
31 J'Wan Roberts .50 1.25
32 Omaha Biliew .50 1.25
33 Milan Momcilovic .50 1.25
34 Caitlin Clark 10.00 25.00
35 Jordan Dingle .50 1.25
36 Jaden Akins .50 1.25
37 RJ Jones .40 1.00
38 Riley Kugel .40 1.00
39 Chris Johnson .50 1.25
40 Jamari McDowell .40 1.00
41 Elmarko Jackson .40 1.00
42 Aaron Bradshaw .60 1.50
43 DJ Wagner .75 2.00
44 Rob Dillingham 1.25 3.00
45 Reed Sheppard 1.50 4.00
46 Justin Edwards .75 2.00
47 Dennis Evans .40 1.00
48 Dalton Knecht 1.50 4.00
49 Angel Reese 1.50 4.00
50 Tyler Kolek .60 1.50
51 Jahmir Young .40 1.00
52 DeShawn Harris-Smith .50 1.25
53 Javonte Taylor .40 1.00
54 Ashton Hardaway .50 1.25
55 Malik Hall .40 1.00
56 Jeremy Fears .60 1.50
57 Xavier Booker .60 1.50
58 Caleb Love .50 1.25
59 Alijah Martin .40 1.00
60 Kevin McCullar .40 1.00
61 Scotty Middleton .40 1.00
62 Taison Chatman .40 1.00
63 Devin Royal .50 1.25
64 Brandon Garrison .50 1.25
65 Jackson Shelstad .50 1.25
66 Kwame Evans .50 1.25
67 Mookie Cook .50 1.25
68 Blake Hinson .50 1.25
69 Garwey Dual .50 1.25
70 Bryce Hopkins .60 1.50
71 Zach Edey 1.25 3.00
72 Mark Sears .60 1.50
73 Andrej Stojakovic .60 1.50
74 Spencer Jones .50 1.25
75 Cameron Brink 2.50 6.00
76 Freddie Dilione .50 1.25
77 Rickea Jackson 1.25 3.00
78 Santiago Vescovi .50 1.25
79 Terrance Shannon Jr. 1.25 3.00
80 Dylan Disu .50 1.25
81 Max Abmas .50 1.25
82 El Ellis .50 1.25
83 Steele Venters .50 1.25
84 Tyler Burton .50 1.25
85 Wooga Poplar .50 1.25
86 Devin Williams .50 1.25
87 Tre Norman .50 1.25
88 Stephon Castle 2.50 6.00
89 Solomon Ball .60 1.50
90 Paige Bueckers 8.00 20.00
91 Nimari Burnett .50 1.25
92 Mackenzie Mgbako .60 1.50
93 Zayden High .50 1.25
94 Armando Bacot .60 1.50
95 Bronny James 2.00 5.00
96 Isaiah Collier 1.00 2.50
97 Coleman Hawkins .50 1.25
98 Eric Dixon .50 1.25
99 Zaide Lowery .50 1.25
100 Baba Miller .50 1.25

2023-24 Bowman Chrome University '07-08 Bowman

*X-FRACTOR: 1.25X TO 3X BASIC
*AQUA REF/150: 1.5X TO 4X BASIC
*GOLD REF/50: 4X TO 10X BASIC
*ORNG REF/25: 5X TO 12X BASIC
07B1 Bronny James 3.00 8.00
07B2 Aaron Bradshaw 1.00 2.50
07B3 DJ Wagner 1.25 3.00
07B4 Kyle Filipowski 1.25 3.00
07B5 Mackenzie Mgbako 1.00 2.50
07B6 Simeon Wilcher 1.00 2.50
07B7 Dusty Stromer .60 1.50
07B8 Elmarko Jackson .60 1.50
07B9 Omaha Biliew .75 2.00
07B10 Justin Edwards 1.25 3.00
07B11 Angel Reese 2.50 6.00
07B12 Rob Dillingham 2.00 5.00
07B13 Isaiah Collier 1.50 4.00
07B14 Stephon Castle 4.00 10.00
07B15 Jared McCain 2.50 6.00
07B16 Kwame Evans .75 2.00
07B17 Xavier Booker 1.00 2.50
07B18 Armando Bacot 1.00 2.50
07B19 Cody Williams 1.25 3.00
07B20 Trevon Brazile 1.00 2.50
07B21 Mookie Cook .75 2.00
07B22 Caitlin Clark 15.00 40.00
07B23 Paige Bueckers 12.00 30.00
07B24 Riley Kugel .60 1.50
07B25 Zaccharie Risacher 2.50 6.00
07B26 Hailey van Lith 2.00 5.00
07B27 Chris Johnson .75 2.00
07B28 Zach Edey 2.00 5.00
07B29 Matas Buzelis 2.00 5.00
07B30 Tyrese Proctor 1.50 4.00

2023-24 Bowman Chrome University '07-08 Bowman Autographs

STATED PRINT RUN 99 SER.#'d SETS
*ORANGE REF/25: .75X TO 2X BASIC
07BAAB Aaron Bradshaw 8.00 20.00
07BAAR Angel Reese 60.00 150.00
07BABJ Bronny James 100.00 250.00
07BACC Caitlin Clark 300.00 600.00
07BACW Cody Williams 10.00 25.00
07BADS Dusty Stromer 5.00 12.00
07BADW DJ Wagner 10.00 25.00
07BAEJ Elmarko Jackson 5.00 12.00
07BAIC Isaiah Collier 12.00 30.00
07BAJE Justin Edwards 10.00 25.00
07BAJM Jared McCain 20.00 50.00
07BAKE Kwame Evans 6.00 15.00
07BAKF Kyle Filipowski 10.00 25.00
07BAMC Mookie Cook 6.00 15.00
07BAMM Mackenzie Mgbako 8.00 20.00
07BAOB Omaha Biliew 6.00 15.00
07BAPB Paige Bueckers 200.00 500.00
07BARD Rob Dillingham 30.00 80.00
07BASC Stephon Castle 30.00 80.00
07BASW Simeon Wilcher 8.00 20.00
07BATB Trevon Brazile 8.00 20.00
07BATP Tyrese Proctor 12.00 30.00
07BAXB Xavier Booker 8.00 20.00
07BAZE Zach Edey 40.00 100.00
07BAZR Zaccharie Risacher 40.00 100.00
07BAABA Armando Bacot 8.00 20.00
07BAHVL Hailey van Lith 30.00 80.00

2023-24 Bowman Chrome University Big Kahuna

*ORANGE REF/25: 1.25X TO 3X BASIC
BK1 Bronny James 25.00 60.00
BK2 Aaron Bradshaw 4.00 10.00
BK3 DJ Wagner 5.00 12.00
BK4 Tyrese Proctor 6.00 15.00
BK5 Omaha Biliew 3.00 8.00
BK6 Justin Edwards 5.00 12.00
BK7 Angel Reese 10.00 25.00
BK8 Simeon Wilcher 4.00 10.00
BK9 Isaiah Collier 6.00 15.00
BK10 Stephon Castle 15.00 40.00
BK11 Jared McCain 10.00 25.00
BK12 Cody Williams 5.00 12.00
BK13 Caleb Love 3.00 8.00
BK14 Riley Kugel 2.50 6.00
BK15 Caitlin Clark 100.00 250.00
BK16 Paige Bueckers 60.00 150.00
BK17 Zaccharie Risacher 10.00 25.00
BK18 Hailey van Lith 12.00 30.00
BK19 Chris Johnson 3.00 8.00
BK20 Zach Edey 20.00 50.00
BK21 Elmarko Jackson 2.50 6.00
BK22 Kyle Filipowski 5.00 12.00
BK23 Andrej Stojakovic 4.00 10.00
BK24 Matas Buzelis 8.00 20.00
BK25 Mackenzie Mgbako 4.00 10.00

2023-24 Bowman Chrome University Big Kahuna Autographs

STATED PRINT RUN 150 SER.#'d SETS
BKAAB Aaron Bradshaw 12.00 30.00
BKAAR Angel Reese 75.00 200.00
BKAAS Andrej Stojakovic 12.00 30.00
BKABJ Bronny James 100.00 250.00
BKACC Caitlin Clark 500.00 1,000.00
BKACJ Chris Johnson 10.00 25.00
BKACL Caleb Love 10.00 25.00
BKACW Cody Williams 15.00 40.00
BKADW DJ Wagner 15.00 40.00
BKAEJ Elmarko Jackson 8.00 20.00
BKAIC Isaiah Collier 20.00 50.00
BKAJE Justin Edwards 15.00 40.00
BKAJM Jared McCain 30.00 80.00
BKAKF Kyle Filipowski 15.00 40.00
BKAMM Mackenzie Mgbako 12.00 30.00
BKAOB Omaha Biliew 10.00 25.00
BKAPB Paige Bueckers 200.00 500.00
BKASC Stephon Castle 60.00 150.00
BKATP Tyrese Proctor 20.00 50.00
BKAZE Zach Edey 100.00 250.00
BKAZR Zaccharie Risacher 40.00 100.00
BKAHVL Hailey van Lith 60.00 150.00

2023-24 Bowman Chrome University Image Variation Autographs

16 Cody Williams 40.00 100.00
34 Caitlin Clark 800.00 1,500.00
43 DJ Wagner 20.00 50.00
46 Justin Edwards 20.00 50.00
49 Angel Reese 150.00 400.00
88 Stephon Castle 75.00 200.00
90 Paige Bueckers 500.00 1,000.00
92 Mackenzie Mgbako 15.00 40.00
95 Bronny James 300.00 600.00
96 Isaiah Collier 25.00 60.00

2023-24 Bowman Chrome University Image Variations

16 Cody Williams 3.00 8.00
34 Caitlin Clark 50.00 120.00
43 DJ Wagner 3.00 8.00
46 Justin Edwards 3.00 8.00
49 Angel Reese 6.00 15.00
88 Stephon Castle 10.00 25.00
90 Paige Bueckers 125.00 300.00
92 Mackenzie Mgbako 2.50 6.00
95 Bronny James 8.00 20.00
96 Isaiah Collier 4.00 10.00

2023-24 Bowman Chrome University Let's Go

LG1 Bronny James 20.00 50.00
LG2 Justin Edwards 8.00 20.00
LG3 DJ Wagner 8.00 20.00
LG4 Angel Reese 15.00 40.00
LG5 Ron Holland II 12.00 30.00

2023-24 Bowman Chrome University Prime Choice Signatures

STATED PRINT RUN 50 SER.#'d SETS
*ORANGE REF/25: .6X TO 1.5X BASIC
PCSAB Aaron Bradshaw 12.00 30.00
PCSAH Aden Holloway 10.00 25.00
PCSAR Angel Reese 75.00 200.00
PCSAS Andrej Stojakovic 12.00 30.00
PCSBG Brandon Garrison 10.00 25.00
PCSCC Caitlin Clark 600.00 1,200.00
PCSCW Cody Williams 15.00 40.00
PCSDW DJ Wagner 15.00 40.00
PCSEJ Elmarko Jackson 8.00 20.00
PCSFD Freddie Dilione 10.00 25.00
PCSGD Garwey Dual 10.00 25.00
PCSIC Isaiah Collier 20.00 50.00
PCSJE Justin Edwards 15.00 40.00
PCSJF Jeremy Fears 12.00 30.00
PCSJS Jackson Shelstad 10.00 25.00
PCSKB Kylan Boswell 8.00 20.00
PCSLB Layden Blocker 10.00 25.00
PCSMC Mookie Cook 10.00 25.00
PCSML Miro Little 10.00 25.00
PCSMM Mackenzie Mgbako 12.00 30.00
PCSPB Paige Bueckers 400.00 800.00
PCSRD Rob Dillingham 75.00 200.00
PCSRS Reed Sheppard 125.00 300.00
PCSSC Stephon Castle 60.00 150.00
PCSSM Scotty Middleton 8.00 20.00
PCSSS Sean Stewart 10.00 25.00
PCSTC Taison Chatman 8.00 20.00
PCSXB Xavier Booker 12.00 30.00
PCSZH Zayden High 10.00 25.00
PCSABO Armando Bacot 12.00 30.00
PCSDWI Devin Williams 10.00 25.00
PCSLBJ Bronny James 125.00 300.00
PCSTPR Tyrese Proctor 20.00 50.00

2023-24 Bowman Chrome University Prodigal Playmakers

*AQUA REF/150: 1.5X TO 4X BASIC
*ORNG REF/25: 4X TO 10X BASIC
PP1 Bronny James 2.50 6.00
PP2 DJ Wagner 1.00 2.50
PP3 Rob Dillingham 1.50 4.00
PP4 Mackenzie Mgbako .75 2.00
PP5 Ron Holland II 1.50 4.00
PP6 Tyrese Proctor 1.25 3.00
PP7 Isaiah Collier 1.25 3.00
PP8 Stephon Castle 3.00 8.00
PP9 Jared McCain 2.00 5.00
PP10 Cody Williams 1.00 2.50
PP11 Caleb Love .60 1.50
PP12 Santiago Vescovi .60 1.50
PP13 Zaccharie Risacher 2.00 5.00
PP14 Riley Kugel .50 1.25
PP15 Justin Edwards 1.00 2.50

2023-24 Bowman Chrome University Prodigal Playmakers Autographs

*ORANGE REF/25: .6X TO 1.5X BASIC
PPAAH Aden Holloway 8.00 20.00
PPAAS Andrej Stojakovic 10.00 25.00
PPACC Caitlin Clark 400.00 800.00
PPADW DJ Wagner 12.00 30.00
PPAFD Freddie Dilione 8.00 20.00
PPAIC Isaiah Collier 15.00 40.00
PPAJE Justin Edwards 12.00 30.00
PPAKB Kylan Boswell 6.00 15.00
PPALB Layden Blocker 8.00 20.00
PPAMM Mackenzie Mgbako 10.00 25.00
PPARD Rob Dillingham 40.00 100.00
PPASC Stephon Castle 30.00 80.00
PPASM Scotty Middleton 6.00 15.00
PPATP Tyrese Proctor 15.00 40.00
PPALBJ Bronny James 100.00 250.00

2023-24 Bowman Chrome University Prospect Autographs

*REFRACTORS/250: .5X TO 1.25X BASIC
*LAVA REFRACTORS/199: .5X TO 1.25X BASIC
*GREEN REFRACTORS/99: .5X TO 1.25X BASIC
*YELLOW REFRACTORS/75: .6X TO 1.5X BASIC
*GOLD REFRACTORS/50: .75X TO 2X BASIC
*GOLD LAVA REFRACTORS/50: .75X TO 2X BASIC
*ORANGE REFRACTORS/25: 1X TO 2.5X BASIC
*ORANGE SHMR REF/25: 1X TO 2.5X BASIC
BCPAAB Aaron Bradshaw 6.00 15.00
BCPAAE Aaliyah Edwards 6.00 15.00
BCPAAH Aden Holloway 5.00 12.00
BCPAAR Angel Reese 75.00 200.00
BCPAAS Andrej Stojakovic 6.00 15.00
BCPABG Brandon Garrison 5.00 12.00
BCPABH Blake Hinson 5.00 12.00
BCPABJ Bronny James 100.00 250.00
BCPABM Baba Miller 5.00 12.00
BCPACH Coleman Hawkins 5.00 12.00
BCPACJ Chris Johnson 5.00 12.00
BCPACR Cormac Ryan 4.00 10.00
BCPACW Cody Williams 8.00 20.00
BCPADE Dennis Evans 4.00 10.00
BCPADG Darin Green Jr. 4.00 10.00
BCPADH DeShawn Harris-Smith 5.00 12.00
BCPADJ Diamond Johnson 5.00 12.00
BCPADK Dalton Knecht 60.00 150.00
BCPADR Devin Royal 5.00 12.00
BCPADS Dusty Stromer 4.00 10.00
BCPADW DJ Wagner 8.00 20.00
BCPAED Eric Dixon 5.00 12.00
BCPAEE El Ellis 5.00 12.00
BCPAEJ Elmarko Jackson 4.00 10.00
BCPAFD Freddie Dilione 5.00 12.00
BCPAGA Georgia Amoore 15.00 40.00
BCPAGD Garwey Dual 5.00 12.00
BCPAHH Hannah Hidalgo 20.00 50.00
BCPAIC Isaiah Collier 10.00 25.00
BCPAIM Isaac McKneely 4.00 10.00
BCPAJA Jaden Akins 5.00 12.00
BCPAJB Johni Broome 40.00 100.00
BCPAJD Jordan Dingle 5.00 12.00
BCPAJE Justin Edwards 8.00 20.00
BCPAJF Jeremy Fears 6.00 15.00
BCPAJM Jared McCain 15.00 40.00
BCPAJR J'Wan Roberts 5.00 12.00
BCPAJS Jamal Shead 5.00 12.00
BCPAJT Javonte Taylor 4.00 10.00
BCPAJY Jahmir Young 4.00 10.00
BCPAKB Kylan Boswell 4.00 10.00
BCPAKE Kwame Evans 5.00 12.00
BCPAKF Kyle Filipowski 8.00 20.00
BCPAKM Kevin McCullar 4.00 10.00
BCPALB Layden Blocker 5.00 12.00
BCPAMA Max Abmas 5.00 12.00
BCPAMC Mookie Cook 5.00 12.00
BCPAMH Malik Hall 4.00 10.00
BCPAML Miro Little 5.00 12.00
BCPAMM Milan Momcilovic 5.00 12.00
BCPAMS Mark Sears 12.00 30.00
BCPANB Nimari Burnett 5.00 12.00
BCPAPA Prince Aligbe 4.00 10.00
BCPAPB Paige Bueckers 150.00 400.00
BCPAQP Quinten Post 10.00 25.00
BCPARD Rob Dillingham 40.00 100.00
BCPARE Rejean Ellis 5.00 12.00
BCPARJ RJ Jones 4.00 10.00
BCPARK Ryan Kalkbrenner 6.00 15.00
BCPARS Reed Sheppard 60.00 150.00
BCPASB Solomon Ball 6.00 15.00
BCPASC Stephon Castle 25.00 60.00
BCPASJ Spencer Jones 5.00 12.00
BCPASM Scotty Middleton 4.00 10.00
BCPASS Sean Stewart 5.00 12.00
BCPASV Santiago Vescovi 5.00 12.00
BCPATB Trevon Brazile 6.00 15.00
BCPATC Taison Chatman 4.00 10.00
BCPATK Tyler Kolek 6.00 15.00
BCPATN Tre Norman 5.00 12.00
BCPATS Terrance Shannon Jr. 12.00 30.00
BCPAWP Wooga Poplar 5.00 12.00
BCPAXB Xavier Booker 6.00 15.00
BCPAZE Zach Edey 40.00 100.00
BCPAZH Zayden High 5.00 12.00
BCPAZL Zaide Lowery 5.00 12.00
BCPAZR Zaccharie Risacher 40.00 100.00
BCPAABA Armando Bacot 6.00 15.00
BCPAAHA Ashton Hardaway 5.00 12.00
BCPAAJH AJ Hoggard 4.00 10.00
BCPAAMA Alijah Martin 4.00 10.00
BCPABHO Bryce Hopkins 6.00 15.00
BCPACBR Cameron Brink 50.00 120.00
BCPACCL Caitlin Clark 400.00 800.00
BCPACLO Caleb Love 5.00 12.00
BCPADDI Dylan Disu 5.00 12.00
BCPADJJ Dillon Jones 5.00 12.00
BCPADWI Devin Williams 5.00 12.00
BCPAHVL Hailey Van Lith 25.00 60.00
BCPAJMC Jamari McDowell 4.00 10.00
BCPAJSH Jackson Shelstad 5.00 12.00
BCPAMAC Mackenzie Mgbako 6.00 15.00
BCPAMIW Mikaylah Williams 8.00 20.00
BCPAOBI Omaha Biliew 5.00 12.00
BCPARIK Riley Kugel 4.00 10.00
BCPARJA Rickea Jackson 20.00 50.00
BCPASVE Steele Venters 5.00 12.00
BCPASWI Simeon Wilcher 6.00 15.00
BCPATPR Tyrese Proctor 10.00 25.00
BCPATYB Tyler Burton 5.00 12.00

2023-24 Bowman Chrome University Sharp Shooters
*RAYWAVE REF/150: 1.5X TO 4X BASIC
*RAYWAVE REF/25: 5X TO 12X BASIC
SS1 Bronny James 3.00 8.00
SS2 DJ Wagner 1.25 3.00
SS3 Mackenzie Mgbako 1.00 2.50
SS4 Zaccharie Risacher 2.50 6.00
SS5 Justin Edwards 1.25 3.00
SS6 Ron Holland II 2.00 5.00
SS7 Isaiah Collier 1.50 4.00
SS8 Stephon Castle 4.00 10.00
SS9 Jared McCain 2.50 6.00
SS10 Cody Williams 1.25 3.00
SS11 Caleb Love .75 2.00
SS12 Riley Kugel .60 1.50
SS13 Mookie Cook .75 2.00
SS14 Tyrese Proctor 1.50 4.00
SS15 Caitlin Clark 25.00 60.00
SS16 Paige Bueckers 15.00 40.00
SS17 Cameron Brink 8.00 20.00
SS18 Sean Stewart .75 2.00
SS19 Elmarko Jackson .60 1.50
SS20 Simeon Wilcher 1.00 2.50

2023-24 Bowman Chrome University Sharp Shooters Autographs
*ORANGE REF/25: .6X TO 1.5X BASIC
SSAAH Aden Holloway 10.00 25.00
SSAAS Andrej Stojakovic 12.00 30.00
SSACC Caitlin Clark 600.00 1,200.00
SSACW Cody Williams 15.00 40.00
SSADW DJ Wagner 15.00 40.00
SSAFD Freddie Dilione 10.00 25.00
SSAIC Isaiah Collier 20.00 50.00
SSAJE Justin Edwards 15.00 40.00
SSAKB Kylan Boswell 8.00 20.00
SSALB Layden Blocker 10.00 25.00
SSAML Miro Little 10.00 25.00
SSAMM Mackenzie Mgbako 12.00 30.00
SSARD Rob Dillingham 75.00 200.00
SSARS Reed Sheppard 125.00 300.00
SSASC Stephon Castle 60.00 150.00
SSASM Scotty Middleton 8.00 20.00
SSATP Tyrese Proctor 20.00 50.00
SSALBJ Bronny James 100.00 250.00

2024-25 Bowman Chrome University
1 Ace Bailey 1.25 3.00
2 Ahmad Nowell .50 1.25
3 Aiden Sherrell .50 1.25
4 AJ Storr .50 1.25
5 Allie Ziebell .50 1.25
6 Aneesah Morrow .60 1.50
7 Annor Boateng .50 1.25
8 Asa Newell .75 2.00
9 Audi Crooks .75 2.00
10 Billy Richmond III .60 1.50
11 Boogie Fland .60 1.50
12 Braden Smith .75 2.00
13 Cam Scott .50 1.25
14 Clifford Omoruyi .50 1.25
15 Robert Wright III .50 1.25
16 Cooper Flagg 4.00 10.00
17 Dame Sarr 1.25 3.00
18 Darren Harris .50 1.25
19 Derik Queen 1.00 2.50
20 Derrion Reid .50 1.25
21 Donavan Freeman .50 1.25
22 Dylan Harper 1.25 3.00
23 Emanuel Sharp .50 1.25
24 Flory Bidunga .50 1.25
25 Grant Nelson .50 1.25
26 Hannah Hidalgo 1.25 3.00
27 Isaiah Evans .60 1.50
28 Jalil Bethea .60 1.50
29 Jaloni Cambridge .60 1.50
30 Jayden Nunn .50 1.25
31 John Bol .50 1.25
32 Jonas Aidoo .50 1.25
33 Jordan Gainey .50 1.25
34 Jordan Lee .50 1.25
35 Josh Hubbard .50 1.25
36 Joyce Edwards .75 2.00
37 Juju Watkins 2.00 5.00
38 Justice Carlton .50 1.25
39 Kam Jones .50 1.25
40 Kanon Catchings .50 1.25
41 Karter Knox .60 1.50
42 Kate Koval .50 1.25
43 Kayleigh Heckel .50 1.25
44 Kennedy Smith .50 1.25
45 Keshon Gilbert .50 1.25
46 Khaman Maluach .75 2.00
47 Kiki Iriafen 1.00 2.50
48 Kon Knueppel 1.25 3.00
49 Labaron Philon .50 1.25
50 Langston Love .50 1.25
51 Latrell Wrightsell .50 1.25
52 Liam McNeeley .75 2.00
53 Mackenly Randolph .50 1.25
54 Meechie Johnson .50 1.25
55 Mikayla Blakes 1.00 2.50
56 Nolan Traore .75 2.00
57 Aden Holloway .50 1.25
58 Patrick Ngongba .50 1.25
59 PJ Haggerty .50 1.25
60 Raven Johnson .50 1.25
61 Robbie Avila .50 1.25
62 Sarah Strong 1.25 3.00
63 Sion James .50 1.25
64 Sonia Citron 1.25 3.00
65 Syla Swords 1.00 2.50
66 Tamin Lipsey .50 1.25
67 Trent Perry .50 1.25
68 Tyler Hendricks .50 1.25
69 Drake Powell .60 1.50
70 Riley Kugel .50 1.25
71 Simeon Wilcher .50 1.25
72 Ryan Nembhard .50 1.25
73 Nick Boyd .50 1.25
74 TJ Bamba .50 1.25
75 Jeremy Fears .50 1.25
76 Miles Kelly .50 1.25
77 Jackson Shelstad .50 1.25
78 Kylan Boswell .40 1.00
79 Miro Little .50 1.25
80 Jaden Akins .50 1.25
81 Jamari McDowell .50 1.25
82 Prince Aligbe .50 1.25
83 Xavier Booker .50 1.25
84 RJ Jones .50 1.25
85 DeShawn Harris-Smith .50 1.25
86 Diamond Johnson .50 1.25
87 Solomon Ball .60 1.50
88 Tre Norman .50 1.25
89 Dennis Evans .50 1.25
90 Zaide Lowery .50 1.25
91 Isaac McKneely .50 1.25
92 Steele Venters .50 1.25
93 Ashton Hardaway .50 1.25
94 Scotty Middleton .50 1.25
95 Layden Blocker .50 1.25
96 Freddie Dilione V .50 1.25
97 Fletcher Loyer .50 1.25
98 Johni Broome .50 1.25
99 Mark Sears .50 1.25
100 Alex Karaban .60 1.50

2024-25 Bowman Chrome University Aqua Wave Refractors
*AQUA WAVE REF: 2X TO 5X BASIC
STATED PRINT RUN 299 SER. #'D SETS
16 Cooper Flagg 100.00 250.00

2024-25 Bowman Chrome University Black and Gold Stealth Refractors
*B&G STEALTH REF: 6X TO 15X BASIC
STATED PRINT RUN 24 SER. #'D SETS
16 Cooper Flagg 400.00 800.00

2024-25 Bowman Chrome University Black and White Stealth Refractors
*B&W STEALTH REF: 5X TO 12X BASIC
STATED PRINT RUN 48 SER. #'D SETS
16 Cooper Flagg 300.00 600.00

2024-25 Bowman Chrome University Black Wave Refractors
*BLACK WAVE REF: 1X TO 2.5X BASIC
16 Cooper Flagg 40.00 100.00

2024-25 Bowman Chrome University Blue Refractors
*BLUE REF: 2.5X TO 6X BASIC
STATED PRINT RUN 199 SER. #'D SETS
16 Cooper Flagg 125.00 300.00

2024-25 Bowman Chrome University Blue Shimmer Refractors
*BLUE SHM REF: 6X TO 15X BASIC
STATED PRINT RUN 35 SER. #'D SETS
16 Cooper Flagg 400.00 800.00

2024-25 Bowman Chrome University Acropolis
*REFRACTOR: 1X TO 2.5X BASIC
*STEALTH REF: 1X TO 2.5X BASIC
*X-FRACTOR: 1X TO 2.5X BASIC
A1 Cooper Flagg 4.00 10.00
A2 Ace Bailey 1.25 3.00
A3 Dylan Harper 1.25 3.00
A4 Jalil Bethea .50 1.25
A5 Kon Knueppel 1.25 3.00
A6 Boogie Fland .60 1.50
A7 Nolan Traore .75 2.00
A8 Juju Watkins 2.00 5.00
A9 Aneesah Morrow .60 1.50
A10 Sarah Strong 1.25 3.00

2024-25 Bowman Chrome University Acropolis Black Gold Stealth Refractors
*BG STEALTH REF: 6X TO 15X BASIC
STATED PRINT RUN 24 SER. #'D SETS
A1 Cooper Flagg 150.00 400.00

2024-25 Bowman Chrome University Acropolis Black White Stealth Refractors
*BW STEALTH REF: 5X TO 12X BASIC
STATED PRINT RUN 48 SER. #'D SETS
A1 Cooper Flagg 125.00 300.00

2024-25 Bowman Chrome University Acropolis Gold Refractors
*GOLD REF: 6X TO 15X BASIC
STATED PRINT RUN 50 SER. #'D SETS
A1 Cooper Flagg 150.00 400.00

2024-25 Bowman Chrome University After School Special
AS1 Ace Bailey 25.00 60.00
AS2 Cooper Flagg 150.00 400.00
AS3 Dylan Harper 25.00 60.00
AS4 Derrion Reid 10.00 25.00
AS5 Donavan Freeman 10.00 25.00
AS6 Derik Queen 20.00 50.00
AS7 Isaiah Evans 12.00 30.00
AS8 Jalil Bethea 10.00 25.00
AS9 Juju Watkins 75.00 200.00
AS10 Sarah Strong 60.00 150.00

2024-25 Bowman Chrome University Boundless Potential
*REFRACTOR: 1X TO 2.5X BASIC
*X-FRACTOR: 1X TO 2.5X BASIC
BP1 Ace Bailey 1.25 3.00
BP2 Ahmad Nowell .50 1.25
BP3 Cooper Flagg 4.00 10.00
BP4 Dame Sarr 1.25 3.00
BP5 Derrion Reid .50 1.25
BP6 Dylan Harper 1.25 3.00
BP7 Derik Queen 1.00 2.50
BP8 Flory Bidunga .50 1.25
BP9 Isaiah Evans .60 1.50
BP10 Jalil Bethea .50 1.25
BP11 Karter Knox .60 1.50
BP12 Aiden Sherrell .50 1.25
BP13 Asa Newell .75 2.00
BP14 Boogie Fland .60 1.50
BP15 Donavan Freeman .50 1.25
BP16 Sarah Strong 1.25 3.00
BP17 Jaloni Cambridge .60 1.50
BP18 Joyce Edwards .75 2.00
BP19 Syla Swords 1.00 2.50
BP20 Kate Koval .50 1.25
BP21 Kennedy Smith .50 1.25
BP22 Allie Ziebell .50 1.25
BP23 Mikayla Blakes 1.00 2.50
BP24 Jordan Lee .50 1.25
BP25 Kayleigh Heckel .50 1.25

2024-25 Bowman Chrome University Boundless Potential Blue Refractors
*BLUE REF: 2.5X TO 6X BASIC
STATED PRINT RUN 150 SER. #'D SETS
BP3 Cooper Flagg 60.00 150.00

2024-25 Bowman Chrome University Boundless Potential Gold Refractors
*GOLD REF: 6X TO 15X BASIC
STATED PRINT RUN 50 SER. #'D SETS
BP3 Cooper Flagg 150.00 400.00

2024-25 Bowman Chrome University Boundless Potential Orange Refractors
*ORANGE REF: 6X TO 15X BASIC
STATED PRINT RUN 25 SER. #'D SETS
BP3 Cooper Flagg 150.00 400.00

2024-25 Bowman Chrome University Campus Dorms Signatures
CDSAB Ace Bailey 20.00 50.00
CDSAC Audi Crooks 12.00 30.00
CDSAH Ahmad Nowell 8.00 20.00
CDSAM Aneesah Morrow 8.00 20.00
CDSAN Asa Newell 12.00 30.00
CDSAS AJ Storr 8.00 20.00
CDSBF Boogie Fland 10.00 25.00
CDSBR Billy Richmond III 10.00 25.00
CDSBS Braden Smith 12.00 30.00
CDSCF Cooper Flagg 500.00 1,000.00
CDSDF Donavan Freeman 8.00 20.00
CDSDH Dylan Harper 40.00 100.00
CDSDQ Derik Queen 15.00 40.00
CDSDR Derrion Reid 8.00 20.00
CDSES Emanuel Sharp 8.00 20.00
CDSHH Hannah Hidalgo 30.00 80.00
CDSIE Isaiah Evans 10.00 25.00
CDSJB Jalil Bethea 8.00 20.00
CDSJG Jordan Gainey 8.00 20.00
CDSJH Josh Hubbard 8.00 20.00
CDSJN Jayden Nunn 8.00 20.00
CDSKG Keshon Gilbert 8.00 20.00
CDSKI Kiki Iriafen 15.00 40.00
CDSKJ Kam Jones 8.00 20.00
CDSKK Kon Knueppel 30.00 80.00
CDSLL Langston Love 8.00 20.00
CDSMJ Meechie Johnson 8.00 20.00
CDSPH PJ Haggerty 8.00 20.00
CDSSC Sonia Citron 30.00 80.00
CDSTL Tamin Lipsey 8.00 20.00

2024-25 Bowman Chrome University Campus Icons
*REFRACTOR: 1X TO 2.5X BASIC
*STEALTH REF: 1X TO 2.5X BASIC
*X-FRACTOR: 1X TO 2.5X BASIC
CI1 Cooper Flagg 4.00 10.00
CI2 Ace Bailey 1.25 3.00
CI3 Dylan Harper 1.25 3.00
CI4 Jalil Bethea .50 1.25
CI5 Kon Knueppel 1.25 3.00
CI6 Boogie Fland .60 1.50
CI7 Donavan Freeman .50 1.25
CI8 Asa Newell .75 2.00
CI9 Isaiah Evans .60 1.50
CI10 Derrion Reid .50 1.25
CI11 Liam McNeeley .75 2.00
CI12 Derik Queen 1.00 2.50
CI13 Flory Bidunga .50 1.25
CI14 Karter Knox .60 1.50
CI15 Nolan Traore .75 2.00
CI16 Juju Watkins 2.00 5.00
CI17 Audi Crooks .75 2.00
CI18 Labaron Philon .50 1.25
CI19 Sonia Citron 1.25 3.00
CI20 Aneesah Morrow .60 1.50

2024-25 Bowman Chrome University Campus Icons Black Gold Stealth Refractors
*BLK GOLD STEALTH REF: 6X TO 15X BASIC
STATED PRINT RUN 24 SER. #'D SETS
CI1 Cooper Flagg 150.00 400.00

2024-25 Bowman Chrome University Campus Icons Black White Stealth Refractors
*BLK WHITE STEALTH REF: 5X TO 12X BASIC
STATED PRINT RUN 48 SER. #'D SETS
CI1 Cooper Flagg 125.00 300.00

2024-25 Bowman Chrome University Campus Icons Blue Refractors
*BLUE REF: 2.5X TO 6X BASIC
STATED PRINT RUN 150 SER. #'D SETS
CI1 Cooper Flagg 60.00 150.00

2024-25 Bowman Chrome University Campus Icons Gold Refractors
*GOLD REF: 5X TO 12X BASIC
STATED PRINT RUN 50 SER. #'D SETS
CI1 Cooper Flagg 125.00 300.00

2024-25 Bowman Chrome University Campus Visit Autographs
CVAAB Ace Bailey 20.00 50.00
CVAAN Asa Newell 12.00 30.00
CVAAS AJ Storr 8.00 20.00
CVABF Boogie Fland 10.00 25.00
CVACF Cooper Flagg 500.00 1,000.00
CVADF Donavan Freeman 8.00 20.00
CVADH Dylan Harper 40.00 100.00
CVADQ Derik Queen 15.00 40.00
CVADR Derrion Reid 8.00 20.00
CVAFB Flory Bidunga 8.00 20.00
CVAIE Isaiah Evans 10.00 25.00
CVAJB Jalil Bethea 8.00 20.00
CVAJC Jaloni Cambridge 10.00 25.00
CVAJE Joyce Edwards 20.00 50.00
CVAJG Jordan Gainey 8.00 20.00
CVAJJ Juju Watkins 150.00 400.00
CVAKJ Kam Jones 8.00 20.00
CVAKK Kon Knueppel 30.00 80.00
CVALL Langston Love 8.00 20.00
CVAMJ Meechie Johnson 8.00 20.00
CVAPH PJ Haggerty 8.00 20.00
CVARA Robbie Avila 8.00 20.00
CVASC Sonia Citron 30.00 80.00
CAASS Sarah Strong 75.00 200.00
CAAASH Aiden Sherrell 8.00 20.00

2024-25 Bowman Chrome University College Application Autographs
CAAAB Ace Bailey 20.00 50.00
CAAAC Audi Crooks 12.00 30.00
CAAAN Asa Newell 12.00 30.00
CAAAS Aiden Sherrell 8.00 20.00
CAABF Boogie Fland 10.00 25.00
CAABR Billy Richmond III 10.00 25.00
CAABS Braden Smith 12.00 30.00
CAACF Cooper Flagg 500.00 1,000.00
CAADF Donavan Freeman 8.00 20.00
CAADH Dylan Harper 40.00 100.00
CAAES Emanuel Sharp 8.00 20.00
CAAFB Flory Bidunga 8.00 20.00
CAAHH Hannah Hidalgo 30.00 80.00
CAAIE Isaiah Evans 10.00 25.00
CAAJB Jalil Bethea 8.00 20.00
CAAJC Jaloni Cambridge 10.00 25.00
CAAJE Joyce Edwards 20.00 50.00
CAAJG Jordan Gainey 8.00 20.00
CAAJN Jayden Nunn 8.00 20.00
CAAJW Juju Watkins 150.00 400.00
CAAKG Keshon Gilbert 8.00 20.00
CAAKI Kiki Iriafen 15.00 40.00
CAAKK Kon Knueppel 30.00 80.00
CAALL Langston Love 8.00 20.00
CAARA Robbie Avila 8.00 20.00
CAASS Sarah Strong 75.00 200.00
CAATL Tamin Lipsey 8.00 20.00
CAAANO Ahmad Nowell 8.00 20.00
CAAAST AJ Storr 8.00 20.00
CAAKKN Karter Knox 10.00 25.00

2024-25 Bowman Chrome University College Rule Playbook
*REFRACTOR: 1X TO 2.5X BASIC
*X-FRACTOR: 1X TO 2.5X BASIC
CRP1 Ace Bailey 1.25 3.00
CRP2 Ahmad Nowell .50 1.25
CRP3 Asa Newell .75 2.00
CRP4 Boogie Fland .60 1.50
CRP5 Cooper Flagg 4.00 10.00
CRP6 Derik Queen 1.00 2.50
CRP7 Derrion Reid .50 1.25
CRP8 Donavan Freeman .50 1.25
CRP9 Dylan Harper 1.25 3.00
CRP10 Flory Bidunga .50 1.25
CRP11 Jalil Bethea .50 1.25
CRP12 Karter Knox .60 1.50
CRP13 Kon Knueppel 1.25 3.00
CRP14 Liam McNeeley .75 2.00
CRP15 Robbie Avila .50 1.25
CRP16 Khaman Maluach .75 2.00
CRP17 Nolan Traore .75 2.00
CRP18 Dame Sarr 1.25 3.00
CRP19 Kanon Catchings .50 1.25
CRP20 Audi Crooks .75 2.00
CRP21 Hannah Hidalgo 1.25 3.00
CRP22 Joyce Edwards .75 2.00
CRP23 Juju Watkins 2.00 5.00
CRP24 Labaron Philon .50 1.25
CRP25 Aneesah Morrow .60 1.50

2024-25 Bowman Chrome University College Rule Playbook Blue Refractors
*BLUE REF: 2.5X TO 6X BASIC
STATED PRINT RUN 150 SER. #'D SETS
CRP5 Cooper Flagg 60.00 150.00

2024-25 Bowman Chrome University College Rule Playbook Gold Refractors
*GOLD REF: 5X TO 12X BASIC
STATED PRINT RUN 50 SER. #'D SETS
CRP5 Cooper Flagg 150.00 400.00

2024-25 Bowman Chrome University College Rule Playbook Orange Refractors
*ORANGE REF: 6X TO 15X BASIC
STATED PRINT RUN 25 SER. #'D SETS
CRP5 Cooper Flagg 150.00 400.00

2024-25 Bowman Chrome University Course Load Autographs
CLAAB Ace Bailey 20.00 50.00
CLAAC Audi Crooks 12.00 30.00
CLAAM Aneesah Morrow 10.00 25.00
CLAAN Asa Newell 12.00 30.00
CLABF Boogie Fland 10.00 25.00
CLABS Braden Smith 12.00 30.00
CLACF Cooper Flagg 500.00 1,000.00
CLADF Donavan Freeman 8.00 20.00
CLADH Dylan Harper 40.00 100.00
CLADQ Derik Queen 15.00 40.00
CLADR Derrion Reid 8.00 20.00
CLAES Emanuel Sharp 8.00 20.00
CLAHH Hannah Hidalgo 30.00 80.00
CLAIE Isaiah Evans 10.00 25.00
CLAJB Jalil Bethea 8.00 20.00
CLAJG Jordan Gainey 8.00 20.00
CLAJH Josh Hubbard 8.00 20.00
CLAJN Jayden Nunn 8.00 20.00
CLAJW Juju Watkins 30.00 80.00
CLAKG Keshon Gilbert 8.00 20.00
CLAKJ Kam Jones 8.00 20.00
CLAKK Kon Knueppel 30.00 80.00
CLAKR Karter Knox 10.00 25.00
CLAMJ Meechie Johnson 8.00 20.00
CLAPH PJ Haggerty 8.00 20.00
CLARA Robbie Avila 8.00 20.00
CLASC Sonia Citron 30.00 80.00
CLATL Tamin Lipsey 8.00 20.00
CLAANO Ahmad Nowell 8.00 20.00
CLAKIR Kiki Iriafen 15.00 40.00

2024-25 Bowman Chrome University Eye Test Autographs
ETAAB Ace Bailey 20.00 50.00
ETAAN Asa Newell 12.00 30.00
ETAAS Aiden Sherrell 8.00 20.00
ETABF Boogie Fland 10.00 25.00
ETABR Billy Richmond III 10.00 25.00
ETABS Braden Smith 12.00 30.00
ETACF Cooper Flagg 500.00 1,000.00
ETADF Donavan Freeman 8.00 20.00
ETADH Dylan Harper 40.00 100.00
ETAES Emanuel Sharp 8.00 20.00
ETAFB Flory Bidunga 8.00 20.00
ETAIE Isaiah Evans 10.00 25.00
ETAJB Jalil Bethea 8.00 20.00
ETAJC Jaloni Cambridge 10.00 25.00
ETAJE Joyce Edwards 20.00 50.00
ETAJG Jordan Gainey 8.00 20.00
ETAJW Juju Watkins 150.00 400.00
ETAKK Kon Knueppel 30.00 80.00
ETALL Langston Love 8.00 20.00
ETARA Robbie Avila 8.00 20.00
ETASS Sarah Strong 75.00 200.00
ETATL Tamin Lipsey 8.00 20.00
ETAANO Ahmad Nowell 8.00 20.00
ETAAST AJ Storr 8.00 20.00
ETAKKN Karter Knox 10.00 25.00

2024-25 Bowman Chrome University Facilitators
*REFRACTOR: 1X TO 2.5X BASIC
*STEALTH REF: 1X TO 2.5X BASIC
*X-FRACTOR: 1X TO 2.5X BASIC
F1 Boogie Fland .60 1.50
F2 Dylan Harper 1.25 3.00
F3 Robert Wright III .50 1.25
F4 Trent Perry .50 1.25
F5 Labaron Philon .50 1.25
F6 Ahmad Nowell .50 1.25
F7 Jalil Bethea .50 1.25
F8 Kon Knueppel 1.25 3.00
F9 Karter Knox .60 1.50
F10 Cooper Flagg 4.00 10.00
F11 Ace Bailey 1.25 3.00
F12 Liam McNeeley .75 2.00
F13 Isaiah Evans .60 1.50
F14 Kanon Catchings .50 1.25
F15 Nolan Traore .75 2.00
F16 Sonia Citron 1.25 3.00
F17 Mark Sears .50 1.25
F18 Juju Watkins 2.00 5.00
F19 Hannah Hidalgo 1.25 3.00
F20 Kiki Iriafen 1.00 2.50

2024-25 Bowman Chrome University Facilitators Black Gold Stealth Refractors
*BLK GOLD STEALTH REF: 6X TO 15X BASIC
STATED PRINT RUN 24 SER. #'D SETS
F10 Cooper Flagg 150.00 400.00

2024-25 Bowman Chrome University Facilitators Black White Stealth Refractors
*BLK WHITE STEALTH REF: 5X TO 12X BASIC
STATED PRINT RUN 48 SER. #'D SETS
F10 Cooper Flagg 125.00 300.00

2024-25 Bowman Chrome University Facilitators Blue Refractors
*BLUE REF: 2.5X TO 6X BASIC
STATED PRINT RUN 150 SER. #'D SETS
F10 Cooper Flagg 60.00 150.00

2024-25 Bowman Chrome University Facilitators Gold Refractors
*GOLD REF: 5X TO 12X BASIC
STATED PRINT RUN 50 SER. #'D SETS
F10 Cooper Flagg 125.00 300.00

2024-25 Bowman Chrome University Fanatics Fraternity Autographs
FFAAB Ace Bailey 20.00 50.00
FFAAN Ahmad Nowell 8.00 20.00
FFACF Cooper Flagg 500.00 1,000.00
FFADH Dylan Harper 40.00 100.00
FFADR Derrion Reid 8.00 20.00
FFAFB Flory Bidunga 8.00 20.00
FFAIE Isaiah Evans 10.00 25.00
FFAJB Jalil Bethea 8.00 20.00
FFAJW Juju Watkins 150.00 400.00
FFAKK Karter Knox 10.00 25.00

2024-25 Bowman Chrome University Final Exam Autographs
FEAAB Ace Bailey 20.00 50.00
FEAAC Audi Crooks 12.00 30.00
FEAAM Aneesah Morrow 10.00 25.00
FEAAN Asa Newell 12.00 30.00
FEABF Boogie Fland 10.00 25.00
FEACF Cooper Flagg 500.00 1,000.00
FEADF Donavan Freeman 8.00 20.00
FEADH Dylan Harper 40.00 100.00
FEADQ Derik Queen 15.00 40.00
FEADR Derrion Reid 8.00 20.00
FEAHH Hannah Hidalgo 30.00 80.00
FEAIE Isaiah Evans 10.00 25.00
FEAJB Jalil Bethea 8.00 20.00
FEAJH Josh Hubbard 8.00 20.00
FEAJJ Juju Watkins 150.00 400.00
FEAJN Jayden Nunn 8.00 20.00
FEAKG Keshon Gilbert 8.00 20.00
FEAKI Kiki Iriafen 15.00 40.00
FEAKJ Kam Jones 8.00 20.00
FEAKK Kon Knueppel 30.00 80.00
FEAMJ Meechie Johnson 8.00 20.00
FEAPB Sarah Strong 75.00 200.00
FEAPH PJ Haggerty 8.00 20.00
FEASC Sonia Citron 30.00 80.00
FEAANO Ahmad Nowell 8.00 20.00

2024-25 Bowman Chrome University Flash
*REFRACTOR: 1X TO 2.5X BASIC
*STEALTH REF: 1X TO 2.5X BASIC
*X-FRACTOR: 1X TO 2.5X BASIC
FL1 Cooper Flagg 4.00 10.00
FL2 Ace Bailey 1.25 3.00
FL3 Dylan Harper 1.25 3.00
FL4 Derrion Reid .50 1.25
FL5 Boogie Fland .60 1.50
FL6 Kon Knueppel 1.25 3.00
FL7 Flory Bidunga .50 1.25
FL8 Jalil Bethea .50 1.25
FL9 Ahmad Nowell .50 1.25
FL10 Liam McNeeley .75 2.00
FL11 Dame Sarr 1.25 3.00
FL12 Nolan Traore .75 2.00
FL13 Karter Knox .60 1.50
FL14 Khaman Maluach .75 2.00
FL15 Kanon Catchings .50 1.25
FL16 Donavan Freeman .50 1.25
FL17 Trent Perry .50 1.25
FL18 RJ Jones .50 1.25
FL19 AJ Storr .50 1.25
FL20 Grant Nelson .50 1.25
FL21 Syla Swords 1.00 2.50
FL22 Hannah Hidalgo 1.25 3.00
FL23 Raven Johnson .50 1.25
FL24 Sarah Strong 1.25 3.00
FL25 Kennedy Smith .50 1.25

2024-25 Bowman Chrome University Flash Black Gold Stealth Refractors
*BLK GOLD STEALTH REF: 6X TO 15X BASIC
STATED PRINT RUN 24 SER. #'D SETS
FL1 Cooper Flagg 150.00 400.00

2024-25 Bowman Chrome University Flash Black White Stealth Refractors
*BLK WHITE STEALTH REF: 5X TO 12X BASIC
STATED PRINT RUN 48 SER. #'D SETS
FL1 Cooper Flagg 125.00 300.00

2024-25 Bowman Chrome University Flash Blue Refractors
*BLUE REF: 2.5X TO 6X BASIC
STATED PRINT RUN 150 SER. #'D SETS
FL1 Cooper Flagg 60.00 150.00

2024-25 Bowman Chrome University Flash Gold Refractors
*GOLD REF: 5X TO 12X BASIC
STATED PRINT RUN 50 SER. #'D SETS
FL1 Cooper Flagg 125.00 300.00

2024-25 Bowman Chrome University Pep Rally
*REFRACTOR: 1X TO 2.5X BASIC
*X-FRACTOR: 1X TO 2.5X BASIC
PR1 Ace Bailey 1.25 3.00
PR2 Ahmad Nowell .50 1.25
PR3 Asa Newell .75 2.00
PR4 Boogie Fland .60 1.50
PR5 Clifford Omoruyi .50 1.25
PR6 Cooper Flagg 4.00 10.00
PR7 Derrion Reid .50 1.25
PR8 Dylan Harper 1.25 3.00
PR9 Flory Bidunga .50 1.25
PR10 Jalil Bethea .50 1.25
PR11 John Bol .50 1.25
PR12 Khaman Maluach .75 2.00
PR13 Liam McNeeley .75 2.00
PR14 Derik Queen 1.00 2.50
PR15 Alex Karaban .60 1.50
PR16 Isaiah Evans .60 1.50
PR17 Robert Wright III .50 1.25
PR18 Kanon Catchings .50 1.25
PR19 Donavan Freeman .50 1.25
PR20 Sarah Strong 1.25 3.00
PR21 Labaron Philon .50 1.25
PR22 Juju Watkins 2.00 5.00
PR23 Joyce Edwards .75 2.00
PR24 Aneesah Morrow .60 1.50
PR25 Sonia Citron 1.25 3.00

2024-25 Bowman Chrome University Pep Rally Blue Refractors
*BLUE REF: 2.5X TO 6X BASIC
STATED PRINT RUN 150 SER. #'D SETS
PR6 Cooper Flagg 60.00 150.00

2024-25 Bowman Chrome University Pep Rally Gold Refractors
*GOLD REF: 5X TO 12X BASIC
STATED PRINT RUN 50 SER. #'D SETS
PR6 Cooper Flagg 125.00 300.00

2024-25 Bowman Chrome University Pep Rally Orange Refractors
*ORANGE REF: 6X TO 15X BASIC
STATED PRINT RUN 25 SER. #'D SETS
PR6 Cooper Flagg 150.00 400.00

2024-25 Bowman Chrome University Physical Education
PE1 Ace Bailey 12.00 30.00
PE2 Cooper Flagg 40.00 100.00
PE3 Dylan Harper 12.00 30.00
PE4 Kon Knueppel 12.00 30.00
PE5 Labaron Philon 5.00 12.00
PE6 Kanon Catchings 5.00 12.00
PE7 Karter Knox 6.00 15.00
PE8 Nolan Traore 8.00 20.00
PE9 Kiki Iriafen 10.00 25.00
PE10 Audi Crooks 8.00 20.00

2024-25 Bowman Chrome University Prospect Autographs
*REFRACTOR: .5X TO 1.2X BASIC
*BLACK WAVE REF: .5X TO 1.2X BASIC
*GRN SHMR REF: .5X TO 1.2X BASIC
*REPTILIAN BLUE REF/150: .5X TO 1.2X BASIC
*BLACK BLUE STEALTH REF/100: .6X TO 1.5X BASIC
*GREEN REF/99: .6X TO 1.5X BASIC
*GREEN WAVE REF/85: .6X TO 1.5X BASIC
*REPTILIAN GRN REF/75: .6X TO 1.5X BASIC
*ORNG SHMR REF/65: .75X TO 2X BASIC
*BLACK WHITE STEALTH REF/48: .75X TO 2X BASIC
*GOLD REF/50: 1X TO 2.5X BASIC
*BLUE SHMR REF/35: 1X TO 2.5X BASIC
*REPTILIAN ORNG REF/25: 1X TO 2.5X BASIC
*BLACK GOLD STEALTH REF/24: 1X TO 2.5X BASIC
1 Ace Bailey 15.00 40.00
2 Ahmad Nowell 6.00 15.00
3 Aiden Sherrell 6.00 15.00
4 AJ Storr 6.00 15.00
5 Allie Ziebell 6.00 15.00
6 Aneesah Morrow 8.00 20.00
7 Annor Boateng 6.00 15.00
8 Asa Newell 10.00 25.00
9 Audi Crooks 10.00 25.00
10 Billy Richmond III 8.00 20.00
11 Boogie Fland 8.00 20.00
12 Braden Smith 10.00 25.00
13 Cam Scott 6.00 15.00
14 Clifford Omoruyi 6.00 15.00
15 Robert Wright III 6.00 15.00
16 Cooper Flagg 500.00 1,000.00
17 Dame Sarr 15.00 40.00
18 Darren Harris 6.00 15.00
19 Derik Queen 12.00 30.00
20 Derrion Reid 6.00 15.00
21 Donavan Freeman 6.00 15.00
22 Dylan Harper 40.00 100.00
23 Emanuel Sharp 6.00 15.00
24 Flory Bidunga 6.00 15.00
25 Grant Nelson 6.00 15.00
26 Hannah Hidalgo 25.00 60.00
27 Isaiah Evans 8.00 20.00
28 Jalil Bethea 6.00 15.00
29 Jaloni Cambridge 8.00 20.00
30 Jayden Nunn 6.00 15.00
31 John Bol 6.00 15.00
32 Jonas Aidoo 6.00 15.00
33 Jordan Gainey 6.00 15.00
34 Jordan Lee 6.00 15.00
35 Josh Hubbard 6.00 15.00
36 Joyce Edwards 10.00 25.00
37 Juju Watkins 100.00 250.00
38 Justice Carlton 6.00 15.00
39 Kam Jones 6.00 15.00
40 Kanon Catchings 6.00 15.00
41 Karter Knox 8.00 20.00
42 Kate Koval 6.00 15.00
43 Kayleigh Heckel 6.00 15.00
44 Kennedy Smith 6.00 15.00
45 Keshon Gilbert 6.00 15.00
46 Khaman Maluach 10.00 25.00
47 Kiki Iriafen 12.00 30.00
48 Kon Knueppel 30.00 80.00
49 Labaron Philon 6.00 15.00
50 Langston Love 6.00 15.00
51 Latrell Wrightsell 6.00 15.00
52 Liam McNeeley 10.00 25.00
53 Mackenly Randolph 6.00 15.00
54 Meechie Johnson 6.00 15.00
55 Mikayla Blakes 20.00 50.00
56 Nolan Traore 10.00 25.00
57 Aden Holloway 6.00 15.00
58 Patrick Ngongba 6.00 15.00
59 PJ Haggerty 6.00 15.00
60 Raven Johnson 6.00 15.00
61 Robbie Avila 6.00 15.00
62 Sarah Strong 75.00 200.00
63 Sion James 6.00 15.00
64 Sonia Citron 30.00 80.00
65 Syla Swords 12.00 30.00
66 Tamin Lipsey 6.00 15.00
67 Trent Perry 6.00 15.00
68 Tyler Hendricks 6.00 15.00
69 Drake Powell 8.00 20.00
70 Riley Kugel 6.00 15.00
71 Simeon Wilcher 6.00 15.00
72 Ryan Nembhard 6.00 15.00
73 Nick Boyd 6.00 15.00
74 TJ Bamba 6.00 15.00
75 Jeremy Fears 6.00 15.00
76 Miles Kelly 6.00 15.00
77 Jackson Shelstad 6.00 15.00
78 Kylan Boswell 5.00 12.00
79 Miro Little 6.00 15.00
80 Jaden Akins 6.00 15.00
81 Jamari McDowell 6.00 15.00
82 Prince Aligbe 6.00 15.00
83 Xavier Booker 6.00 15.00
84 RJ Jones 6.00 15.00
85 DeShawn Harris-Smith 6.00 15.00
86 Diamond Johnson 6.00 15.00
87 Solomon Ball 8.00 20.00
88 Tre Norman 6.00 15.00
89 Dennis Evans 6.00 15.00
90 Zaide Lowery 6.00 15.00
91 Isaac McKneely 6.00 15.00
92 Steele Venters 6.00 15.00
93 Ashton Hardaway 6.00 15.00
94 Scotty Middleton 6.00 15.00
95 Layden Blocker 6.00 15.00
96 Freddie Dilione V 6.00 15.00
97 Fletcher Loyer 6.00 15.00
98 Johni Broome 6.00 15.00
99 Mark Sears 6.00 15.00
100 Alex Karaban 8.00 20.00

2024-25 Bowman Chrome University Social Studies
*REFRACTOR: 1X TO 2.5X BASIC
*STEALTH REF: 1X TO 2.5X BASIC
*X-FRACTOR: 1X TO 2.5X BASIC
SS1 Cooper Flagg 4.00 10.00
SS2 Ace Bailey 1.25 3.00
SS3 Dylan Harper 1.25 3.00
SS4 Derrion Reid .50 1.25
SS5 Aiden Sherrell .50 1.25
SS6 Boogie Fland .60 1.50
SS7 Karter Knox .60 1.50
SS8 Khaman Maluach .75 2.00
SS9 Kon Knueppel 1.25 3.00
SS10 Nolan Traore .75 2.00
SS11 Liam McNeeley .75 2.00
SS12 Alex Karaban .60 1.50
SS13 Donavan Freeman .50 1.25
SS14 Robbie Avila .50 1.25
SS15 Jalil Bethea .50 1.25
SS16 Dame Sarr 1.25 3.00
SS17 Derik Queen 1.00 2.50
SS18 Asa Newell .75 2.00
SS19 Drake Powell .60 1.50
SS20 Jaloni Cambridge .60 1.50
SS21 Joyce Edwards .75 2.00
SS22 Syla Swords 1.00 2.50
SS23 Kennedy Smith .50 1.25
SS24 Kate Koval .50 1.25
SS25 Sarah Strong 1.25 3.00

2024-25 Bowman Chrome University Social Studies Black Gold Stealth Refractors
*BLK GOLD STEALTH REF: 6X TO 15X BASIC
STATED PRINT RUN 24 SER. #'D SETS
SS1 Cooper Flagg 150.00 400.00

2024-25 Bowman Chrome University Social Studies Black White Stealth Refractors
*BLK WHITE STEALTH REF: 5X TO 12X BASIC
STATED PRINT RUN 48 SER. #'D SETS
SS1 Cooper Flagg 125.00 300.00

2024-25 Bowman Chrome University Social Studies Blue Refractors
*BLUE REF: 2.5X TO 6X BASIC
STATED PRINT RUN 150 SER. #'D SETS
SS1 Cooper Flagg 60.00 150.00

2024-25 Bowman Chrome University The Big Kahuna Autographs

BKAAB Ace Bailey 75.00 200.00
BKAAN Asa Newell 15.00 40.00
BKAAS Aiden Sherrell 10.00 25.00
BKABF Boogie Fland 12.00 30.00
BKABR Billy Richmond III 12.00 30.00
BKABS Braden Smith 15.00 40.00
BKACF Cooper Flagg 800.00 1,500.00
BKADF Donavan Freeman 10.00 25.00
BKADH Dylan Harper 125.00 300.00
BKAFB Flory Bidunga 10.00 25.00
BKAIE Isaiah Evans 12.00 30.00
BKAJB Jalil Bethea 10.00 25.00
BKAJC Jaloni Cambridge 12.00 30.00
BKAJE Joyce Edwards 25.00 60.00
BKAJH Josh Hubbard 10.00 25.00
BKAJW Juju Watkins 300.00 600.00
BKAKK Kon Knueppel 125.00 300.00
BKALL Langston Love 10.00 25.00
BKAPB Hannah Hidalgo 75.00 200.00
BKAPJ PJ Haggerty 10.00 25.00
BKARA Robbie Avila 10.00 25.00
BKASS Sarah Strong 150.00 400.00
BKATL Tamin Lipsey 10.00 25.00
BKAAST AJ Storr 10.00 25.00
BKAKKN Karter Knox 12.00 30.00

2024-25 Bowman Chrome University Warriors of the Paint

*REFRACTOR: 1X TO 2.5X BASIC
*X-FRACTOR: 1X TO 2.5X BASIC
WP1 Donavan Freeman .50 1.25
WP2 Derik Queen 1.00 2.50
WP3 Asa Newell .75 2.00
WP4 Flory Bidunga .50 1.25
WP5 Aiden Sherrell .50 1.25
WP6 Patrick Ngongba .50 1.25
WP7 Cooper Flagg 4.00 10.00
WP8 Ace Bailey 1.25 3.00
WP9 Dylan Harper 1.25 3.00
WP10 Liam McNeeley .75 2.00
WP11 Robbie Avila .50 1.25
WP12 Khaman Maluach .75 2.00
WP13 Kon Knueppel 1.25 3.00
WP14 Boogie Fland .60 1.50
WP15 Drake Powell .60 1.50
WP16 Aneesah Morrow .60 1.50
WP17 Audi Crooks .75 2.00
WP18 Juju Watkins 2.00 5.00
WP19 Labaron Philon .50 1.25
WP20 Sonia Citron 1.25 3.00
WP21 Dame Sarr 1.25 3.00
WP22 Nolan Traore .75 2.00
WP23 Billy Richmond III .60 1.50
WP24 John Bol .50 1.25
WP25 Sarah Strong 1.25 3.00

2024-25 Bowman Chrome University Warriors of the Paint Blue Refractors

*BLUE REF: 2.5X TO 6X BASIC
STATED PRINT RUN 150 SER. #'D SETS
WP7 Cooper Flagg 60.00 150.00

2024-25 Bowman Chrome University Warriors of the Paint Gold Refractors

*GOLD REF: 5X TO 12X BASIC
STATED PRINT RUN 50 SER. #'D SETS
WP7 Cooper Flagg 125.00 300.00

2024-25 Bowman Chrome University Warriors of the Paint Orange Refractors

*ORANGE REF: 6X TO 15X BASIC
STATED PRINT RUN 25 SER. #'D SETS
WP7 Cooper Flagg 150.00 400.00

2023-24 Bowman Chrome University Sapphire

*GREEN REF/99: 1.5X TO 4X BASIC
*YELLOW REF/75: 2X TO 5X BASIC
*GOLD REF/50: 2.5X TO 6X BASIC
*ORANGE REF/25: 3X TO 8X BASIC
1 Dillon Jones 1.00 2.50
2 Georgia Amoore 1.50 4.00
3 Kylan Boswell .75 2.00
4 Mikaylah Williams 1.50 4.00
5 AJ Hoggard .75 2.00
6 Johni Broome 1.25 3.00
7 Layden Blocker 1.00 2.50
8 Trevon Brazile 1.25 3.00
9 Zaccharie Risacher 3.00 8.00
10 Aden Holloway 1.00 2.50
11 Cormac Ryan .75 2.00
12 Miro Little 1.00 2.50
13 Prince Aligbe .75 2.00
14 Quinten Post 2.00 5.00
15 Simeon Wilcher 1.25 3.00
16 Cody Williams 1.50 4.00
17 Ryan Kalkbrenner 1.25 3.00
18 Jared McCain 3.00 8.00
19 Aaliyah Edwards 1.25 3.00
20 Tyrese Proctor 2.00 5.00
21 Sean Stewart 1.00 2.50
22 Diamond Johnson 1.00 2.50
23 Kyle Filipowski 1.50 4.00
24 Darin Green Jr. .75 2.00
25 Hailey van Lith 2.50 6.00
26 Hannah Hidalgo 8.00 20.00
27 Isaac McKneely .75 2.00
28 Dusty Stromer .75 2.00
29 Re;ean Ellis 1.00 2.50
30 Jamal Shead 1.00 2.50
31 J'Wan Roberts 1.00 2.50
32 Omaha Biliew 1.00 2.50
33 Mi an Momcilovic 1.00 2.50
34 Caitlin Clark 30.00 80.00
35 Jordan Dingle 1.00 2.50
36 Jacen Akins 1.00 2.50
37 RJ Jones .75 2.00
38 Riley Kugel .75 2.00
39 Chris Johnson 1.00 2.50
40 Jamari McDowell .75 2.00
41 Elmarko Jackson .75 2.00
42 Aaron Bradshaw 1.25 3.00
43 DJ Wagner 1.50 4.00
44 Rob Dillingham 2.50 6.00
45 Reed Sheppard 8.00 20.00
46 Justin Edwards 1.50 4.00
47 Dennis Evans .75 2.00
48 Dalton Knecht 6.00 15.00
49 Angel Reese 3.00 8.00
50 Tyler Kolek 1.25 3.00
51 Jahmir Young .75 2.00
52 DeShawn Harris-Smith 1.00 2.50
53 Javonte Taylor .75 2.00
54 Ashton Hardaway 1.00 2.50
55 Malik Hall .75 2.00
56 Jeremy Fears 1.25 3.00
57 Xavier Booker 1.25 3.00
58 Caleb Love 1.00 2.50
59 Alijah Martin .75 2.00
60 Kevin McCullar .75 2.00
61 Scotty Middleton .75 2.00
62 Taison Chatman .75 2.00
63 Devin Royal 1.00 2.50
64 Brandon Garrison 1.00 2.50
65 Jackson Shelstad 1.00 2.50
66 Kwame Evans 1.00 2.50
67 Mookie Cook 1.00 2.50
68 Blake Hinson 1.00 2.50
69 Garwey Dual 1.00 2.50
70 Bryce Hopkins 1.25 3.00
71 Zach Edey 2.50 6.00
72 Mark Sears 1.25 3.00
73 Andrej Stojakovic 1.25 3.00
74 Spencer Jones 1.00 2.50
75 Cameron Brink 5.00 12.00
76 Freddie Dilione 1.00 2.50
77 Rickea Jackson 2.50 6.00
78 Santiago Vescovi 1.00 2.50
79 Terrance Shannon Jr. 2.50 6.00
80 Dylan Disu 1.00 2.50
81 Max Abmas 1.00 2.50
82 El Ellis 1.00 2.50
83 Steele Venters 1.00 2.50
84 Tyler Burton 1.00 2.50
85 Wooga Poplar 1.00 2.50
86 Devin Williams 1.00 2.50
87 Tre Norman 1.00 2.50
88 Stephon Castle 5.00 12.00
89 Solomon Ball 1.25 3.00
90 Paige Bueckers 20.00 50.00
91 Nimari Burnett 1.00 2.50
92 Mackenzie Mgbako 1.25 3.00
93 Zayden High 1.00 2.50
94 Armando Bacot 1.25 3.00
95 Bronny James 4.00 10.00
96 Isaiah Collier 2.00 5.00
97 Coleman Hawkins 1.00 2.50
98 Eric Dixon 1.00 2.50
99 Zaide Lowery 1.00 2.50
100 Baba Miller 1.00 2.50

2023-24 Bowman Chrome University Sapphire Selections

*ORANGE REF/25: .75X TO 2X BASIC
SAS1 Bronny James 20.00 50.00
SAS2 Aaron Bradshaw 6.00 15.00
SAS3 DJ Wagner 8.00 20.00
SAS4 Simeon Wilcher 6.00 15.00
SAS5 Cody Williams 8.00 20.00
SAS6 Caitlin Clark 100.00 250.00
SAS7 Paige Bueckers 75.00 200.00
SAS8 Hailey van Lith 12.00 30.00
SAS9 Isaiah Collier 10.00 25.00
SAS10 Mackenzie Mgbako 6.00 15.00
SAS11 Tyrese Proctor 10.00 25.00
SAS12 Xavier Booker 6.00 15.00

2023-24 Bowman Chrome University Sapphire Selections Autographs

STATED PRINT RUN 50 SER.#'d SETS
SAAB Aaron Bradshaw 12.00 30.00
SABJ Bronny James 125.00 300.00
SACC Caitlin Clark 500.00 1,000.00
SACW Cody Williams 15.00 40.00
SADW DJ Wagner 15.00 40.00
SAIC Isaiah Collier 20.00 50.00
SAMM Mackenzie Mgbako 12.00 30.00
SAPB Paige Bueckers 400.00 800.00
SASW Simeon Wilcher 12.00 30.00
SATP Tyrese Proctor 20.00 50.00
SAXB Xavier Booker 12.00 30.00
SAHVL Hailey van Lith 75.00 200.00

2023-24 Bowman Chrome University Sapphire Treasured Talent

TT1 Bronny James 20.00 50.00
TT2 DJ Wagner 8.00 20.00
TT3 Caitlin Clark 150.00 400.00
TT4 Justin Edwards 8.00 20.00
TT5 Zaccharie Risacher 15.00 40.00
TT6 Xavier Booker 6.00 15.00
TT7 Angel Reese 15.00 40.00
TT8 El Ellis 5.00 12.00
TT9 Stephon Castle 25.00 60.00
TT10 Kwame Evans 5.00 12.00

2006-07 Bowman Elevation

COMP.SET w/o SP's (90) 25.00 60.00
ROOKIE PRINT RUN 999 SER.#'d SETS
1 Dwyane Wade 1.25 3.00
2 Elton Brand .50 1.25
3 Dwight Howard .75 2.00
4 Chris Bosh .75 2.00
5 Baron Davis .60 1.50
6 Marcus Camby .50 1.25
7 Rashard Lewis .50 1.25
8 Paul Pierce 1.00 2.50
9 Jermaine O'Neal .60 1.50
10 Gilbert Arenas .60 1.50
11 Larry Hughes .50 1.25
12 Manu Ginobili 1.25 3.00
13 Lamar Odom .60 1.50
14 Ron Artest .60 1.50
15 Carmelo Anthony 1.00 2.50
16 Deron Williams .50 1.25
17 Gerald Wallace .50 1.25
18 Peja Stojakovic .50 1.25
19 Vince Carter 1.25 3.00
20 Kevin Garnett 1.50 4.00
21 Yao Ming 1.50 4.00
22 Josh Howard .50 1.25
23 Michael Redd .50 1.25
24 Eddy Curry .50 1.25
25 Shawn Marion .60 1.50
26 Luol Deng .50 1.25
27 Ben Wallace .75 2.00
28 Sam Cassell .50 1.25
29 Steve Francis .60 1.50
30 Ray Allen 1.00 2.50
31 Andre Iguodala .60 1.50
32 Shaquille O'Neal 2.50 6.00
33 Pau Gasol 1.00 2.50
34 Jason Richardson .60 1.50
35 Ricky Davis .50 1.25
36 Joe Johnson .60 1.50
37 Dirk Nowitzki 1.50 4.00
38 Richard Hamilton .60 1.50
39 Troy Murphy .40 1.00
40 Charlie Villanueva .40 1.00
41 T.J. Ford .40 1.00
42 Zydrunas Ilgauskas .50 1.25
43 Andrei Kirilenko .50 1.25
44 Chris Paul 1.25 3.00
45 Grant Hill 1.00 2.50
46 Kobe Bryant 5.00 12.00
47 Tim Duncan 1.50 4.00
48 Raymond Felton .40 1.00
49 Antawn Jamison .50 1.25
50 Jason Kidd 1.00 2.50
51 Shareef Abdur-Rahim .60 1.50
52 Shane Battier .50 1.25
53 Kirk Hinrich .50 1.25
54 Jason Terry .50 1.25
55 Mehmet Okur .40 1.00
56 Stephon Marbury .75 2.00
57 Steve Nash 1.25 3.00
58 Mike Bibby .60 1.50
59 Sebastian Telfair .40 1.00
60 Richard Jefferson .50 1.25
61 Andre Miller .50 1.25
62 Delonte West .50 1.25
63 Tracy McGrady 1.00 2.50
64 Rasheed Wallace .75 2.00
65 Al Harrington .50 1.25
66 Emeka Okafor .50 1.25
67 Caron Butler .50 1.25
68 Andrew Bogut .50 1.25
69 Tony Parker 1.00 2.50
70 Zach Randolph .60 1.50
71 Allen Iverson 1.50 4.00
72 David West .50 1.25
73 Chris Webber .75 2.00
74 Ben Gordon .50 1.25
75 Corey Maggette .50 1.25
76 Sarunas Jasikevicius .50 1.25
77 Chauncey Billups .75 2.00
78 Amare Stoudemire .60 1.50
79 Luke Ridnour .50 1.25
80 LeBron James 5.00 12.00
81 Kenyon Martin .50 1.25
82 Marko Jaric .40 1.00
83 Antoine Walker .60 1.50
84 J.R. Smith .60 1.50
85 Mike Miller .50 1.25
86 Channing Frye .40 1.00
87 Smush Parker .40 1.00
88 Wally Szczerbiak .50 1.25
89 Morris Peterson .40 1.00
90 Luther Head .40 1.00
91 Randy Foye RC 1.50 4.00
92 Daniel Gibson RC 1.50 4.00
93 Hassan Adams RC 1.25 3.00
94 Hilton Armstrong RC 1.25 3.00
95 Marcus Williams RC 1.25 3.00
96 Paul Davis RC 1.25 3.00
97 Quincy Douby RC 1.25 3.00
98 Ronnie Brewer RC 2.00 5.00
99 Rodney Carney RC 1.25 3.00
100 Rudy Gay RC 2.50 6.00
101 Adam Morrison RC 1.50 4.00
102 Rajon Rondo RC 6.00 15.00
103 Steve Novak RC 1.50 4.00
104 Craig Smith RC 1.50 4.00
105 Leon Powe RC 1.25 3.00
106 James White RC 1.25 3.00
107 Josh Boone RC 1.25 3.00
108 J.J. Redick RC 4.00 10.00
109 Shelden Williams RC 1.25 3.00
110 Alexander Johnson RC 1.25 3.00
111 Guillermo Diaz RC 1.25 3.00
112 Maurice Ager RC 1.25 3.00
113 Jordan Farmar RC 1.50 4.00
114 Mardy Collins RC 1.25 3.00
115 Ryan Hollins RC 1.25 3.00
116 Kyle Lowry RC 6.00 15.00
117 James Augustine RC 1.25 3.00
118 Shawne Williams RC 1.25 3.00
119 LaMarcus Aldridge RC 5.00 12.00
120 Patrick O'Bryant RC 1.25 3.00
121 Cedric Simmons RC 1.25 3.00
122 P.J. Tucker RC 2.00 5.00
123 Brandon Roy RC 4.00 10.00
124 Tyrus Thomas RC 1.50 4.00
125 Andrea Bargnani RC 1.50 4.00
126 Dee Brown RC 1.25 3.00
127 Denham Brown RC 1.25 3.00
128 Saer Sene RC 1.25 3.00
129 Thabo Sefolosha RC 1.50 4.00
130 Shannon Brown RC 1.25 3.00

2006-07 Bowman Elevation Blue

*1-90 BLUE: .6X TO 1.5X BASE HI
*91-130 BLUE RC's SAME VALUE AS BASE
BLUE PRINT RUN 399 SER.#'d SETS
37 Dirk Nowitzki 4.00 10.00
80 LeBron James 15.00 40.00

2006-07 Bowman Elevation Gold

*1-90 GOLD: 1X TO 2.5X BASE HI
*91-130 GOLD RC's: .6X TO 1.5X BASE HI
GOLD PRINT RUN 99 SER.#'d SETS
37 Dirk Nowitzki 6.00 15.00
80 LeBron James 50.00 120.00

2006-07 Bowman Elevation Red

*1-90 RED: .75X TO 2X BASE HI
*91-130 RED RC's: .5X TO 1.25X BASE HI
PRINT RUN 299 SER.#'d SETS
37 Dirk Nowitzki 5.00 12.00
80 LeBron James 20.00 50.00

2006-07 Bowman Elevation Board of Directors Relics

PRINT RUN 99 SER.#'d SETS
*RELICS BLUE SAME VALUE AS BASE
BLUE PRINT RUN 79 SER.#'d SETS
*RELICS GOLD: .75X TO 2X RELIC HI
GOLD PRINT RUN 25 SER.#'d SETS
*RELICS RED: .5X TO 1.25X RELIC HI
RED PRINT RUN 49 SER.#'d SETS
*RELICS DUAL: .5X TO 1.25 RELIC HI
DUAL PRINT RUN 99 SER.#'d SETS
*REL.DUAL BLUE: .5X TO 1.25X RELIC HI
DUAL BLUE PRINT RUN 79 SER.#'d SETS
*REL.DUAL GOLD: .75X TO 2X RELIC HI
DUAL GOLD PRINT RUN 25 SER.#'d SETS
*REL.DUAL RED: .6X TO 1.5X BASE HI
DUAL RED PRINT RUN 49 SER.#'d SETS
ONE OF ONES EXIST FOR RELICS AND DUAL
*PATCHES: 1.25X TO 3X RELIC HI
PATCH PRINT RUN 10 SER.#'d SETS
PATCH DUAL ONE OF ONE'S EXIST
PATCH TRIPLE ONE OF ONE'S EXIST
RAI Allen Iverson 8.00 20.00
RAM Andre Miller 2.50 6.00
RBB Brent Barry 2.00 5.00
RBM Brad Miller 2.50 6.00
RCB Chauncey Billups 4.00 10.00
RCM Corey Maggette 2.50 6.00
RDW David West 2.50 6.00
RGA Gilbert Arenas 3.00 8.00
RJK Jason Kidd 5.00 12.00
RJR Jason Richardson 3.00 8.00
RJS Josh Smith 2.00 5.00
RJT Jamaal Tinsley 2.00 5.00
RJW Jason Williams 4.00 10.00
RKH Kirk Hinrich 2.50 6.00
RLO Lamar Odom 2.50 6.00
RLR Luke Ridnour 2.50 6.00
RMG Manu Ginobili 6.00 15.00
RPG Pau Gasol 5.00 12.00
RPP Paul Pierce 5.00 12.00
RSM Sean May 2.00 5.00
RSO Shaquille O'Neal 12.00 30.00
RTM Tracy McGrady 5.00 12.00
RTP Tony Parker 5.00 12.00
RDWA Dwyane Wade 6.00 15.00
RDWE Delonte West 2.00 5.00
RSMA Stephon Marbury 4.00 10.00
RTJF T.J. Ford 2.00 5.00
RTPR Tayshaun Prince 3.00 8.00

2006-07 Bowman Elevation Board of Directors Relics Autographs

PRINT RUN 25 SER.#'d SETS
RSO Shaquille O'Neal 40.00 100.00
RTP Tony Parker 20.00 50.00
RDWA Dwyane Wade 75.00 150.00
RDWE Delonte West 12.50 30.00

2006-07 Bowman Elevation Board of Directors Relics Autographs Blue

PRINT RUN 19 SER.#'d SETS
ONE OF ONE'S EXIST
RLR Luke Ridnour 10.00 25.00
RSO Shaquille O'Neal 60.00 120.00
RTP Tony Parker 12.00 30.00
RDWE Delonte West 12.50 30.00

2006-07 Bowman Elevation Board of Directors Relics Dual Autographs

PRINT RUN 15 SER.#'d SETS
ONE OF ONE'S EXIST
RAI Allen Iverson 75.00 150.00
RLR Luke Ridnour 10.00 25.00
RDWA Dwyane Wade 75.00 200.00
RDWE Delonte West 15.00 40.00
RTJF T.J. Ford 10.00 25.00

2006-07 Bowman Elevation Executive Level Relics

PRINT RUN 99 SER.#'d SETS
*RELICS BLUE SAME VALUE AS BASE
BLUE PRINT RUN 79 SER.#'d SETS
*RELICS GOLD: .75X TO 2X RELIC HI
GOLD PRINT RUN 25 SER.#'d SETS
*RELICS RED: .5X TO 1.25X RELIC HI
RED PRINT RUN 49 SER.#'d SETS
*RELICS DUAL: .5X TO 1.25 RELIC HI
DUAL PRINT RUN 99 SER.#'d SETS
*REL.DUAL BLUE: .5X TO 1.25X RELIC HI
DUAL BLUE PRINT RUN 79 SER.#'d SETS
*REL.DUAL GOLD: .75X TO 2X RELIC HI
DUAL GOLD PRINT RUN 25 SER.#'d SETS
*REL.DUAL RED: .6X TO 1.5X BASE HI
DUAL RED PRINT RUN 49 SER.#'d SETS
ONE OF ONES EXIST FOR RELICS AND DUAL
*PATCHES: 1.25X TO 3X RELIC HI
PATCH PRINT RUN 10 SER.#'d SETS
PATCH DUAL ONE OF ONE's EXIST
PAT.TRIPLE ONE OF ONE'S EXIST
RAB Andrew Bogut 2.50 6.00
RAI Allen Iverson 8.00 20.00
RAK Andrei Kirilenko 2.50 6.00
RBD Baron Davis 3.00 8.00
RBG Ben Gordon 2.50 6.00
RCA Carmelo Anthony 5.00 12.00
RCB Chris Bosh 4.00 10.00
RCP Chris Paul 6.00 15.00
RCV Charlie Villanueva 2.00 5.00
RDN Dirk Nowitzki 8.00 20.00
RDW Dwyane Wade 6.00 15.00
REB Elton Brand 2.50 6.00
REO Emeka Okafor 2.50 6.00
RJO Jermaine O'Neal 3.00 8.00
RKB Kobe Bryant 50.00 120.00
RKG Kevin Garnett 8.00 20.00
RLO Lamar Odom 2.50 6.00
RMB Mike Bibby 3.00 8.00
RNR Nate Robinson 2.50 6.00
RPG Pau Gasol 5.00 12.00
RPP Paul Pierce 5.00 12.00
RRA Ray Allen 5.00 12.00
RRH Richard Hamilton 3.00 8.00
RSB Shane Battier 2.50 6.00
RSM Sean May 2.00 5.00
RSN Steve Nash 6.00 15.00
RSO Shaquille O'Neal 12.00 30.00
RST Sebastian Telfair 2.00 5.00
RTD Tim Duncan 8.00 20.00
RVC Vince Carter 6.00 15.00
RYM Yao Ming 8.00 20.00
RRHO Robert Horry 3.00 8.00

2006-07 Bowman Elevation Executive Level Relics Autographs

PRINT RUN 25 SER.#'d SETS
RCV Charlie Villanueva 10.00 25.00
RDW Dwyane Wade 25.00 50.00
REO Emeka Okafor 10.00 25.00
RJO Jermaine O'Neal 10.00 25.00
RRH Richard Hamilton 10.00 25.00

2006-07 Bowman Elevation Executive Level Relics Autographs Blue

PRINT RUN 19 SER.#'d SETS
ONE OF ONE'S EXIST
RCV Charlie Villanueva 10.00 25.00
RDW Dwyane Wade 60.00 150.00
REO Emeka Okafor 10.00 25.00
RJO Jermaine O'Neal 10.00 25.00
RRH Richard Hamilton 10.00 25.00
RVC Vince Carter 25.00 50.00

2006-07 Bowman Elevation Executive Level Relics Dual Autographs

PRINT RUN 15 SER.#'d SETS
ONE OF ONE'S EXIST
RDW Dwyane Wade 100.00 200.00
RVC Vince Carter 30.00 60.00

2006-07 Bowman Elevation Power Brokers Relics

PRINT RUN 99 SER.#'d SETS
*RELICS BLUE SAME VALUE AS BASE
BLUE PRINT RUN 79 SER.#'d SETS
*RELICS GOLD: .75X TO 2X RELIC HI
GOLD PRINT RUN 25 SER.#'d SETS
*RELICS RED: .5X TO 1.25X RELIC HI
RED PRINT RUN 49 SER.#'d SETS
*RELICS DUAL: .5X TO 1.25 RELIC HI
DUAL PRINT RUN 99 SER.#'d SETS
*REL.DUAL BLUE: .5X TO 1.25X RELIC HI
DUAL BLUE PRINT RUN 79 SER.#'d SETS
*REL.DUAL GOLD: .75X TO 2X RELIC HI
DUAL GOLD PRINT RUN 25 SER.#'d SETS
*REL.DUAL RED: .6X TO 1.5X BASE HI
DUAL RED PRINT RUN 49 SER.#'d SETS
ONE OF ONES EXIST FOR RELICS AND DUAL
*PATCHES: 1.25X TO 3X RELIC HI
PATCH PRINT RUN 10 SER.#'d SETS
PATCH DUAL ONE OF ONE's EXIST
PAT.TRIPLE ONE OF ONE'S EXIST
RAB Andrew Bogut 2.50 6.00
RAI Allen Iverson 8.00 20.00
RAJ Antawn Jamison 2.50 6.00
RBB Bruce Bowen 2.50 6.00
RBW Ben Wallace 4.00 10.00
RCB Chris Bosh 4.00 10.00
RCF Channing Frye 2.00 5.00
RCK Chris Kaman 2.00 5.00
RCV Charlie Villanueva 2.00 5.00
RCW Chris Webber 4.00 10.00
RDH Dwight Howard 4.00 10.00
RDW Dwyane Wade 6.00 15.00
REB Elton Brand 2.50 6.00
REO Emeka Okafor 2.50 6.00
RHW Hakim Warrick 2.50 6.00
RID Ike Diogu 2.00 5.00
RJO Jermaine O'Neal 3.00 8.00
RKB Kobe Bryant 50.00 120.00
RKG Kevin Garnett 8.00 20.00
RKM Kenyon Martin 2.50 6.00
RLD Luol Deng 2.50 6.00
RMC Marcus Camby 2.50 6.00
RRJ Richard Jefferson 2.50 6.00
RRL Rashard Lewis 2.50 6.00
RRW Rasheed Wallace 4.00 10.00
RSD Samuel Dalembert 2.00 5.00
RSM Shawn Marion 3.00 8.00
RSO Shaquille O'Neal 12.00 30.00
RTC Tyson Chandler 2.50 6.00
RTD Tim Duncan 8.00 20.00
RTP Tayshaun Prince 3.00 8.00
RYM Yao Ming 8.00 20.00
RAIG Andre Iguodala 3.00 8.00
RSAR Shareef Abdur-Rahim 3.00 8.00

2006-07 Bowman Elevation Power Brokers Relics Autographs

PRINT RUN 25 SER.#'d SETS
*BLUE: 4X TO 1X BASE HI
BLUE PRINT RUN 19 SER.#'d SETS
RAI Allen Iverson 75.00 150.00
RCB Chris Bosh 20.00 50.00
RCV Charlie Villanueva 10.00 25.00
RDW Dwyane Wade 40.00 80.00
REO Emeka Okafor 10.00 25.00
RHW Hakim Warrick 10.00 25.00
RLD Luol Deng 10.00 25.00

2006-07 Bowman Elevation Power Brokers Relics Dual Autographs

STATED PRINT RUN 15 SER.#'d SETS
ONE OF ONE'S EXIST
RAI Allen Iverson 75.00 150.00
RCB Chris Bosh 20.00 50.00
RCV Charlie Villanueva 10.00 25.00
RDW Dwyane Wade 75.00 150.00
RHW Hakim Warrick 10.00 25.00
RSO Shaquille O'Neal 75.00 150.00

2006-07 Bowman Elevation Rookie Writing Autographs

APPROXIMATE ODDS ONE PER BOX
AJ Alexander Johnson 2.00 5.00
AM Adam Morrison 2.50 6.00
AR Allan Ray 2.00 5.00
BJ Bobby Jones 2.00 5.00
CS Craig Smith 2.50 6.00
DB Denham Brown 2.00 5.00
DG Daniel Gibson 2.50 6.00
DN David Noel 2.00 5.00
GD Guillermo Diaz 2.00 5.00
HA Hassan Adams 2.00 5.00
JA James Augustine 2.00 5.00
JB Josh Boone 2.00 5.00
JF Jordan Farmar 2.50 6.00
KL Kyle Lowry 10.00 25.00
MA Maurice Ager 2.00 5.00
MC Mardy Collins 2.00 5.00
MW Marcus Williams 2.00 5.00
PD Paul Davis 2.00 5.00
QD Quincy Douby 2.00 5.00
RB Ronnie Brewer 3.00 8.00
RC Rodney Carney 2.00 5.00
RF Randy Foye 2.50 6.00
RH Ryan Hollins 2.00 5.00
RR Rajon Rondo 8.00 20.00
SJ Solomon Jones 2.00 5.00
SN Steve Novak 2.50 6.00
SW Shelden Williams 2.00 5.00
ABA Andrea Bargnani 2.50 6.00
CSI Cedric Simmons 2.00 5.00
DBR Dee Brown 2.00 5.00
HAR Hilton Armstrong 2.00 5.00
JJR J.J. Redick 6.00 15.00
PJT P.J. Tucker 3.00 8.00
POB Patrick O'Bryant 2.00 5.00
RBA Renaldo Balkman 2.50 6.00

2006-07 Bowman Elevation Rookie Writing Autographs Blue

*BLUE: .5X TO 1.25X HI COLUMN
STATED PRINT RUN 79 TO 139 SETS

2006-07 Bowman Elevation Rookie Writing Autographs Red

*RED: .6X TO 1.5X HI COLUMN
STATED PRINT RUN 59 TO 99 SETS

2006-07 Bowman Elevation Rookie Writing Autographs Gold

*GOLD: .75X TO 2X HI COLUMN
STATED PRINT RUN 29 TO 79 SETS
RR Rajon Rondo/39 30.00 80.00
JJR J.J. Redick/29 20.00 60.00

2007-08 Bowman Elevation

COMPLETE SET (100) 25.00 50.00
51-100 RC PRINT RUN 999 SER.#'d SETS
1 Tracy McGrady .60 1.50
2 Shaquille O'Neal 1.50 4.00
3 Allen Iverson 1.00 2.50
4 Chris Bosh .50 1.25
5 Jason Kidd .60 1.50
6 Elton Brand .30 .75
7 Brandon Roy .50 1.25
8 Tony Parker .60 1.50
9 Luol Deng .30 .75
10 Gilbert Arenas .40 1.00
11 Amare Stoudemire .40 1.00
12 Dwight Howard .50 1.25
13 Deron Williams .30 .75
14 Dirk Nowitzki 1.00 2.50
15 Vince Carter .75 2.00
16 Richard Hamilton .50 1.25
17 Baron Davis .30 .75
18 Pau Gasol .60 1.50
19 Kevin Garnett 1.00 2.50
20 LeBron James 3.00 8.00
21 Tim Duncan 1.00 2.50
22 Steve Nash .75 2.00
23 Jason Richardson .40 1.00
24 Kobe Bryant 3.00 8.00
25 Josh Smith .25 .60
26 Eddy Curry .25 .60
27 Mike Bibby .40 1.00
28 Ray Allen .60 1.50
29 Andre Iguodala .40 1.00
30 Chris Paul .75 2.00
31 Yao Ming 1.00 2.50
32 Shawn Marion .40 1.00
33 Dwyane Wade .75 2.00
34 Paul Pierce .60 1.50
35 Carmelo Anthony .60 1.50
36 Jermaine O'Neal .40 1.00
37 Michael Redd .30 .75
38 Gerald Wallace .30 .75
39 Ben Gordon .30 .75
40 Carlos Boozer .30 .75
41 Larry Bird 2.50 6.00
42 Bill Walton .75 2.00
43 Moses Malone 1.00 2.50
44 John Havlicek 1.25 3.00
45 David Robinson 1.25 3.00
46 Bill Russell 2.00 5.00
47 Isiah Thomas .60 1.50
48 John Stockton 1.25 3.00
49 Dominique Wilkins 1.00 2.50
50 Magic Johnson 2.50 6.00
51 Nick Young RC 1.50 4.00
52 Greg Oden RC 1.50 4.00
53 Julian Wright RC 1.00 2.50
54 Dominic Mcguire RC 1.00 2.50
55 Acie Law RC 1.00 2.50
56 Luis Scola RC 1.50 4.00
57 Thaddeus Young RC 1.50 4.00
58 Rodney Stuckey RC 1.00 2.50
59 Jermareo Davidson RC 1.00 2.50
60 Daequan Cook RC 1.25 3.00
61 Josh McRoberts RC 1.00 2.50
62 Aaron Gray RC 1.00 2.50
63 Wilson Chandler RC 1.25 3.00
64 Chris Richard RC 1.00 2.50
65 Stephane Lasme RC 1.00 2.50
66 Kyrylo Fesenko RC 1.00 2.50
67 Taurean Green RC 1.00 2.50
68 Al Thornton RC 1.00 2.50
69 Corey Brewer RC 1.25 3.00
70 Ramon Sessions RC 1.25 3.00
71 Kevin Durant RC 30.00 80.00
72 Alando Tucker RC 1.00 2.50
73 Spencer Hawes RC 1.00 2.50
74 Nick Fazekas RC 1.00 2.50
75 Yi Jianlian RC 2.00 5.00
76 Juan Carlos Navarro RC 1.25 3.00
77 Jared Dudley RC 1.25 3.00
78 Adam Haluska RC 1.00 2.50
79 Herbert Hill RC 1.00 2.50
80 Kosta Perovic RC 1.00 2.50
81 JamesOn Curry RC 1.00 2.50
82 D.J. Strawberry RC 1.00 2.50
83 Javaris Crittenton RC 1.00 2.50
84 Al Horford RC 4.00 10.00
85 Mike Conley Jr. RC 4.00 10.00
86 Joakim Noah RC 1.50 4.00
87 Marco Belinelli RC 1.25 3.00
88 Arron Afflalo RC 1.25 3.00
89 Gabe Pruitt RC 1.00 2.50
90 Carl Landry RC 1.00 2.50
91 Jeff Green RC 1.25 3.00
92 Glen Davis RC 1.25 3.00
93 Jason Smith RC 1.00 2.50
94 Morris Almond RC 1.00 2.50
95 Cheik Samb RC 1.00 2.50
96 Brandon Wallace RC 1.00 2.50
97 Aaron Brooks RC 1.25 3.00
98 Brandan Wright RC 1.25 3.00
99 Sean Williams RC 1.00 2.50
100 Coby Karl RC 1.00 2.50

2007-08 Bowman Elevation Blue

*1-50 BLUE: 1X TO 2.5X BASE HI
*51-100 BLUE RCs: .5X TO 1.25X BASE HI
PRINT RUN 99 SER.#'d SETS
20 LeBron James 10.00 25.00
71 Kevin Durant 400.00 800.00

2007-08 Bowman Elevation Green

*1-40 GREEN: 4X TO 10X BASE HI
*41-50 GREEN: 3X TO 8X BASE HI
*51-100 GREEN RCs: 1X TO 2.5X BASE HI
GREEN PRINT RUN 19 SER.#'d SETS
20 LeBron James 40.00 100.00
71 Kevin Durant 1,000.00 2,000.00

2007-08 Bowman Elevation Red

*1-50 RED: 1.25X TO 3X BASE HI
*51-100 RED RCs: .6X TO 1.5X BASE HI
PRINT RUN 49 SER.#'d SETS
20 LeBron James 12.00 30.00
71 Kevin Durant 500.00 1,000.00

2007-08 Bowman Elevation Autographs Patches

PRINT RUN 15 SER.#'d SETS
AI Andre Iguodala 15.00 30.00
BD Baron Davis 15.00 30.00
BG Ben Gordon 8.00 20.00
BR Bill Russell 800.00 1,500.00
CA Carmelo Anthony 25.00 60.00
CB Carlos Boozer 8.00 20.00
CBO Chris Bosh 20.00 40.00
CM Corey Maggette 8.00 20.00
DL David Lee 8.00 20.00
DR David Robinson 50.00 100.00
DW Dwyane Wade 50.00 120.00
DWI Deron Williams 20.00 40.00
DWK Dominique Wilkins 25.00 50.00
GW Gerald Wallace 15.00 30.00
IT Isiah Thomas 15.00 30.00
JH Josh Howard 8.00 20.00
JST John Stockton 60.00 150.00
PP Paul Pierce 15.00 30.00
RB Rick Barry 20.00 40.00
SO Shaquille O'Neal 50.00 100.00

2007-08 Bowman Elevation Relics

PRINT RUN 179 SER.#'d SETS
*BLUE: .5X TO 1.25X BASE HI
BLUE PRINT RUN 79 SER.#'d SETS
*GOLD: .75X TO 2X BASE HI
GOLD PRINT RUN 19 SER.#'d SETS
*GREEN: .6X TO 1.5X BASE HI
GREEN PRINT RUN 29 SER.#'d SETS
*RED: .5X TO 1.25X BASE HI
RED PRINT RUN 49 SER.#'d SETS
*DUAL: .5X TO 1.25X BASE HI
DUAL PRINT RUN 79 SER.#'d SETS
*DUAL BLUE: .5X TO 1.25X BASE HI
DUAL BLUE PRINT RUN 49 SER.#'d SETS
*DUAL GREEN: .75X TO 2X BASE HI
DUAL GREEN PRINT RUN 19 SER.#'d SETS
*DUAL RED: .6X TO 1.5X BASE HI
DUAL RED PRINT RUN 29 SER.#'d SETS
*TRIPLE: .6X TO 1.5X BASE HI
TRIPLE PRINT RUN 39 SER.#'d SETS
*TRIP.BLUE: .6X TO 1.5X BASE HI
TRIP.BLUE PRINT RUN 29 SER.#'d SETS
*TRIP.RED: .75X TO 2X BASE HI
TRIP.RED PRINT RUN 19 SER.#'d SETS
*PATCHES: 1.25X TO 3X BASE HI
PATCH PRINT RUN 29 SER.#'d SETS
*PAT.BLUE: 1.5X TO 4X BASE HI
PAT.BLUE PRINT RUN 19 SER.#'d SETS
AB Andrea Bargnani 2.00 5.00
AI Andre Iguodala 3.00 8.00
AJ Al Jefferson 2.00 5.00
AJA Antawn Jamison 2.50 6.00
AS Amare Stoudemire 3.00 8.00
BD Baron Davis 2.50 6.00
BRO Brandon Roy 4.00 10.00
BW Ben Wallace 4.00 10.00
CBI Chauncey Billups 4.00 10.00
CBO Chris Bosh 4.00 10.00
CM Corey Maggette 2.50 6.00
CP Chris Paul 6.00 15.00
DH Dwight Howard 4.00 10.00
DL David Lee 2.00 5.00
DN Dirk Nowitzki 8.00 20.00
DR David Robinson 6.00 15.00
DW Dwyane Wade 6.00 15.00
DWI Deron Williams 2.50 6.00
DWK Dominique Wilkins 5.00 12.00
EB Elton Brand 2.50 6.00
GA Gilbert Arenas 3.00 8.00
IT Isiah Thomas 3.00 8.00
JO Jermaine O'Neal 3.00 8.00
JR Jason Richardson 3.00 8.00
JS Josh Smith 2.00 5.00
JST John Stockton 6.00 15.00
KB Kobe Bryant 40.00 100.00
KG Kevin Garnett 5.00 12.00
LB Larry Bird 8.00 20.00
LD Luol Deng 2.50 6.00
LO Lamar Odom 2.50 6.00
MJ Magic Johnson 6.00 15.00
MR Michael Redd 2.50 6.00
PM Pete Maravich 15.00 30.00
PP Paul Pierce 5.00 12.00
RA Ray Allen 5.00 12.00
RH Richard Hamilton 4.00 10.00
RL Rashard Lewis 2.50 6.00
SM Stephon Marbury 4.00 10.00
SN Steve Nash 6.00 15.00
SO Shaquille O'Neal 8.00 20.00
TD Tim Duncan 8.00 20.00
TM Tracy McGrady 5.00 12.00
TT Tyrus Thomas 2.00 5.00
YM Yao Ming 8.00 20.00

2007-08 Bowman Elevation Rookie Relics

PRINT RUN 199 SER.#'d SETS
*RELICS 99: SAME VALUE AS BASE
*RELICS 69: .5X TO 1.25X BASE
*RELICS 49: .5X TO 1.25X BASE
*RELICS 29: .6X TO 1.5X BASE
*DUAL 99: .5X TO 1.25X BASE
*DUAL 79: .5X TO 1.25X BASE
*DUAL 29: .6X TO 1.5X BASE
*DUAL 19: .75X TO 2X BASE
*TRIPLE 49: .6X TO 1.5X BASE
*TRIPLE 39: .6X TO 1.5X BASE
*TRIPLE 29: .75X TO 2X BASE
*TRIPLE 19: 1X TO 2.5X BASE
AA Arron Afflalo 2.00 5.00
AB Aaron Brooks 2.00 5.00
AH Al Horford 6.00 15.00
AHA Adam Haluska 1.50 4.00
AL4 Acie Law 1.50 4.00
AT Al Thornton 1.50 4.00
ATU Alando Tucker 1.50 4.00
BW Brandan Wright 2.00 5.00
CB Corey Brewer 2.00 5.00
CL Carl Landry 1.50 4.00
CR Chris Richard 1.50 4.00
DC Daequan Cook 2.00 5.00
DJS D.J. Strawberry 1.50 4.00
DM Dominic McGuire 1.50 4.00
GD Glen Davis 2.00 5.00
GO Greg Oden 2.50 6.00
GP Gabe Pruitt 1.50 4.00
HH Herbert Hill 1.50 4.00
JC Javaris Crittenton 1.50 4.00
JD Jared Dudley 2.00 5.00
JDA Jermareo Davidson 1.50 4.00
JG Jeff Green 2.00 5.00
JN Joakim Noah 2.50 6.00
JS Jason Smith 1.50 4.00
JW Julian Wright 1.50 4.00
MA Morris Almond 1.50 4.00
MC Mike Conley Jr. 6.00 15.00
NF Nick Fazekas 1.50 4.00
NY Nick Young 2.50 6.00
RS Rodney Stuckey 1.50 4.00
SH Spencer Hawes 1.50 4.00
SW Sean Williams 1.50 4.00
TG Taurean Green 1.50 4.00
TY Thaddeus Young 2.50 6.00
WC Wilson Chandler 2.00 5.00

2007-08 Bowman Elevation Rookie Writings

STATED PRINT RUN 49 TO 299 SER.#'d SETS
*BLUE: .5X TO 1.25X BASE
BLUE PRINT RUN 29 SER.#'d SETS
*GREEN: .6X TO 1.5X BASE
GREEN PRINT RUN 15 SER.#'d SETS
*RED: .6X TO 1.5X BASE
RED PRINT RUN 19 SER.#'d SETS
RWAA Arron Afflalo/299 3.00 8.00
RWAB Aaron Brooks/299 3.00 8.00
RWAG Aaron Gray/299 2.50 6.00
RWAH Adam Haluska/299 2.50 6.00
RWAL4 Acie Law/199 2.50 6.00
RWAT Al Thornton/199 2.50 6.00
RWCL Carl Landry/299 2.50 6.00
RWDJS D.J. Strawberry/299 2.50 6.00
RWGO Greg Oden/49 4.00 10.00
RWHH Herbert Hill/299 2.50 6.00
RWJC Javaris Crittenton/299 2.50 6.00
RWJD Jermareo Davidson/299 2.50 6.00
RWJS Jason Smith/199 2.50 6.00
RWMA Morris Almond/299 2.50 6.00
RWMB Marco Belinelli/299 3.00 8.00
RWNF Nick Fazekas/299 2.50 6.00
RWNY Nick Young/49 4.00 10.00
RWRS Rodney Stuckey/299 2.50 6.00
RWSW Sean Williams/299 2.50 6.00
RWTY Thaddeus Young/49 12.00 30.00
RWWC Wilson Chandler/199 3.00 8.00
RWYJ Yi Jianlian/49 12.00 30.00

2007-08 Bowman Elevation Rookie Writings Relics

STATED PRINT RUN 29 TO 169 SER.#'d SETS
*BLUE: .5X TO 1.25X BASE HI
BLUE PRINT RUN 19 SER.#'d SETS
*RED: .6X TO 1.5X BASE HI
RED PRINT RUN 15 SER.#'d SETS
RWAA Arron Afflalo/169 4.00 10.00
RWAB Aaron Brooks/169 4.00 10.00
RWAG Aaron Gray/169 3.00 8.00
RWAH Adam Haluska/169 3.00 8.00
RWAL4 Acie Law/79 3.00 8.00
RWAT Al Thornton/79 3.00 8.00
RWCL Carl Landry/169 3.00 8.00
RWDJS D.J. Strawberry/169 3.00 8.00
RWGO Greg Oden/29 5.00 12.00
RWHH Herbert Hill/169 3.00 8.00
RWJC Javaris Crittenton/169 3.00 8.00
RWJD Jermareo Davidson/169 3.00 8.00
RWJS Jason Smith/79 3.00 8.00
RWMA Morris Almond/169 3.00 8.00
RWMB Marco Belinelli/169 4.00 10.00
RWNF Nick Fazekas/169 3.00 8.00
RWNY Nick Young/29 5.00 12.00
RWRS Rodney Stuckey/169 3.00 8.00
RWSW Sean Williams/169 3.00 8.00
RWTY Thaddeus Young/29 15.00 40.00
RWWC Wilson Chandler/79 4.00 10.00
RWYJ Yi Jianlian/29 15.00 40.00

2007-08 Bowman Elevation Rookie Writings Patches

PRINT RUN 15 SER.#'d SETS
RWAA Arron Afflalo 6.00 15.00
RWAB Aaron Brooks 6.00 15.00
RWAG Aaron Gray 5.00 12.00
RWAH Adam Haluska 5.00 12.00
RWAL4 Acie Law 5.00 12.00
RWAT Al Thornton 5.00 12.00
RWCL Carl Landry 5.00 12.00
RWDJS D.J. Strawberry 5.00 12.00
RWGO Greg Oden 60.00 150.00
RWHH Herbert Hill 5.00 12.00
RWJC Javaris Crittenton 5.00 12.00
RWJD Jermareo Davidson 5.00 12.00
RWJS Jason Smith 5.00 12.00
RWMA Morris Almond 5.00 12.00
RWMB Marco Belinelli 6.00 15.00
RWNF Nick Fazekas 5.00 12.00
RWRS Rodney Stuckey 5.00 12.00
RWSW Sean Williams 5.00 12.00
RWTY Thaddeus Young 10.00 25.00
RWWC Wilson Chandler 6.00 15.00
RWYJ Yi Jianlian 30.00 80.00

2008-09 Bowman Retail Relics

BSRAA Arron Afflalo 1.50 4.00
BSRAB Aaron Brooks 1.50 4.00
BSRAL4 Acie Law IV 2.00 5.00
BSRAT Alando Tucker 1.50 4.00
BSRATH Al Thornton 1.50 4.00
BSRBW Brandan Wright 1.50 4.00
BSRDC Daequan Cook 1.50 4.00
BSRGD Glen Davis 1.50 4.00
BSRGO Greg Oden 1.50 4.00
BSRJC Javaris Crittenton 1.50 4.00
BSRJD Jared Dudley 2.00 5.00
BSRJS Jason Smith 1.50 4.00
BSRMA Morris Almond 1.50 4.00
BSRNY Nick Young 1.50 4.00
BSRRS Rodney Stuckey 1.50 4.00
BSRSW Sean Williams 1.50 4.00
BSRTY Thaddeus Young 2.00 5.00
BSRWC Wilson Chandler 2.00 5.00

2002-03 Bowman Signature Edition

RC PRINT RUN 999 SER.#'d SETS
SEAI Allen Iverson 2.00 5.00
SEAJ Antawn Jamison .60 1.50
SEAK Andrei Kirilenko .60 1.50
SEAM Alonzo Mourning 1.25 3.00
SEAS Stoudemire JSY AU RC 10.00 25.00
SEAW Antoine Walker .60 1.50
SEAKM Antonio McDyess .60 1.50
SEALM Andre Miller .60 1.50
SEBD Baron Davis .75 2.00
SEBN Bostjan Nachbar AU RC 3.00 8.00
SEBW Ben Wallace 1.00 2.50
SECB Curtis Borchardt AU RC 2.50 6.00
SECM Cuttino Mobley .50 1.25
SECO Chris Owens AU RC 2.50 6.00
SECT Cezary Trybanski AU RC 4.00 10.00
SECW Chris Wilcox JSY AU RC 3.00 8.00
SECBO C.Boozer JSY AU RC 4.00 10.00
SECBU Caron Butler JSY AU RC 4.00 10.00
SECJA C.Jacobsen JSY AU RC 3.00 8.00
SECJE C.Jefferies JSY AU RC 3.00 8.00
SEDD Dan Dickau AU RC 2.50 6.00
SEDN Dirk Nowitzki 2.00 5.00
SEDW D.Wagner JSY AU RC 3.00 8.00
SEDGA D.Gadzuric JSY AU RC 3.00 8.00
SEDGO D.Gooden JSY AU RC 4.00 10.00
SEDLM Darius Miles .50 1.25
SEEB Elton Brand .60 1.50
SEEC Eddy Curry .50 1.25
SEEG Manu Ginobili AU RC 150.00 400.00
SEEJ Eddie Jones .75 2.00
SEER E.Rentzias AU RC 2.50 6.00
SEFJ Fred Jones JSY AU RC 3.00 8.00
SEFR Frank Williams AU RC 2.50 6.00
SEGG Gordan Giricek AU RC 4.00 10.00
SEGP Gary Payton 1.25 3.00
SEGR Glenn Robinson .75 2.00
SEJB J.R. Bremer AU RC 2.50 6.00
SEJD Juan Dixon JSY AU RC 3.00 8.00
SEJJ J.Jeffries JSY AU RC 3.00 8.00
SEJK Jason Kidd 1.25 3.00
SEJM Jamal Mashburn .60 1.50
SEJO Jermaine O'Neal .60 1.50
SEJP Jannero Pargo AU RC 2.50 6.00
SEJS John Salmons JSY AU RC 4.00 10.00
SEJT Jamaal Tinsley .50 1.25
SEJAW Jay Williams/1249 RC 2.50 6.00
SEJDS Jerry Stackhouse .75 2.00
SEJOS John Stockton 1.50 4.00
SEJWE Jiri Welsch AU RC 3.00 8.00
SEJWI Jerome Williams .50 1.25
SEKB Kobe Bryant 6.00 15.00
SEKG Kevin Garnett 2.00 5.00
SEKM Karl Malone 1.50 4.00
SEKR K.Rush JSY AU RC 3.00 8.00
SEKS Kenny Satterfield .50 1.25
SEKLM Kenyon Martin .75 2.00
SELS Latrell Sprewell .75 2.00
SEMB Mike Bibby .75 2.00
SEMD M.Dunleavy JSY AU RC 4.00 10.00
SEME Melvin Ely JSY AU RC 3.00 8.00
SEMH M.Haislip JSY AU RC 2.50 6.00
SEMO Mehmet Okur AU RC 4.00 10.00
SEMCW Chris Webber 1.00 2.50
SEMJA Marko Jaric AU 3.00 8.00
SEMJJ Michael Jordan 8.00 20.00
SENH N.Hilario JSY AU RC 4.00 10.00
SENT N.Tskitishvili JSY AU RC 2.50 6.00
SEPG Pau Gasol 1.25 3.00
SEPP Paul Pierce 1.25 3.00
SEPS Peja Stojakovic .60 1.50
SEPSA P.Savovic JSY AU RC 3.00 8.00
SEQR Quentin Richardson .50 1.25
SERA R.Archibald JSY AU RC 2.50 6.00
SERA Ray Allen 1.25 3.00
SERB Rasual Butler AU RC 3.00 8.00
SERJ Richard Jefferson .60 1.50
SERL Rashard Lewis .60 1.50
SERW Rasheed Wallace 1.00 2.50
SERCH Richard Hamilton 1.00 2.50
SERHU R.Humphrey JSY AU RC 3.00 8.00
SERMA Roger Mason JSY AU RC 3.00 8.00
SERMU R.Murray JSY AU RC 4.00 10.00
SESA Shareef Abdur-Rahim .75 2.00
SESC Sam Clancy JSY AU RC 3.00 8.00
SESF Steve Francis .75 2.00
SESM Stephon Marbury 1.00 2.50
SESN Steve Nash 1.50 4.00
SESO Shaquille O'Neal 3.00 8.00
SESCB Shane Battier .75 2.00
SESDM Shawn Marion .75 2.00
SETC Tyson Chandler .75 2.00
SETD Tim Duncan 2.00 5.00
SETP T.Prince JSY AU RC 6.00 15.00
SETP Tony Parker 1.25 3.00
SETS Tamar Slay AU RC 2.50 6.00
SETLM Tracy McGrady 1.25 3.00
SEVC Vince Carter 1.50 4.00
SEVY V.Yarbrough JSY AU RC 2.50 6.00
SEWS Wally Szczerbiak .60 1.50
SEYM Yao Ming AU RC 400.00 800.00

2002-03 Bowman Signature Edition Parallel

*STARS: 1X TO 2.5X BASE CARD HI
*RCs: .6X TO 1.5X BASE HI
RC PRINT RUN 99 SER.#'d SETS
SEEG Manu Ginobili AU 100.00 250.00
SEJAW Jay Williams/249 6.00 15.00
SEMJJ Michael Jordan 20.00 50.00
SEYM Yao Ming AU 100.00 250.00

2003-04 Bowman Signature Edition

COMP.SET w/o SP's (55) 15.00 40.00
56-60 RC PRINT RUN 1250 SER.#'d SETS
1 Tracy McGrady 1.25 3.00
2 Baron Davis .75 2.00
3 Allen Iverson 2.00 5.00
4 Bonzi Wells .50 1.25
5 Tony Parker 1.25 3.00
6 Morris Peterson .50 1.25
7 Jerry Stackhouse 1.00 2.50
8 Jason Terry .60 1.50
9 Tyson Chandler .60 1.50
10 Dirk Nowitzki 2.00 5.00
11 Nene .60 1.50
12 Antawn Jamison .60 1.50
13 Richard Hamilton 1.00 2.50
14 Steve Francis .75 2.00
15 Jermaine O'Neal .75 2.00
16 Elton Brand .60 1.50
17 Mike Miller .60 1.50
18 Caron Butler .60 1.50
19 Gary Payton 1.25 3.00
20 Shaquille O'Neal 3.00 8.00
21 Kevin Garnett 2.00 5.00
22 Desmond Mason .60 1.50
23 Jamal Mashburn .60 1.50
24 Drew Gooden .60 1.50
25 Eric Snow .50 1.25
26 Shawn Marion .75 2.00
27 Peja Stojakovic .60 1.50
28 Karl Malone 1.50 4.00
29 Shareef Abdur-Rahim .75 2.00
30 Paul Pierce 1.25 3.00
31 Dajuan Wagner .60 1.50
32 Steve Nash 1.50 4.00
33 Ben Wallace 1.00 2.50
34 Jason Richardson .75 2.00
35 Yao Ming 2.00 5.00
36 Ron Artest .75 2.00
37 Andre Miller .60 1.50
38 Kobe Bryant 6.00 15.00
39 Pau Gasol 1.25 3.00
40 Tim Duncan 2.00 5.00
41 Ray Allen 1.25 3.00
42 Vince Carter 1.50 4.00
43 Andrei Kirilenko .60 1.50
44 Chris Webber 1.00 2.50
45 Rasheed Wallace 1.00 2.50
46 Amare Stoudemire 1.00 2.50
47 Latrell Sprewell 1.00 2.50
48 Kenyon Martin .75 2.00
49 Wally Szczerbiak .60 1.50
50 Jason Kidd 1.25 3.00
51 Eddie Jones .75 2.00
52 Jalen Rose .60 1.50
53 Ricky Davis .60 1.50
54 Antoine Walker .75 2.00
55 Allan Houston .75 2.00
56 LeBron James RC 500.00 1,000.00
57 Darko Milicic RC 2.00 5.00
58 Chris Kaman RC 2.50 6.00
59 Kyle Korver RC 3.00 8.00
60 Willie Green RC 2.50 6.00
61 James Lang AU RC 2.00 5.00
62 Carl English AU RC 2.00 5.00
63 Devin Brown AU RC 2.00 5.00
64 Theron Smith AU RC 2.00 5.00
65 Rick Rickert AU RC 2.00 5.00
66 Z.Cabarkapa AU RC 2.00 5.00
67 D.Zimmerman AU RC 3.00 8.00
68 A.Pavlovic AU RC 2.50 6.00
69 Malick Badiane AU RC 3.00 8.00
70 Boris Diaw AU RC 3.00 8.00
71 Zaur Pachulia AU RC 3.00 8.00
72 Zoran Planinic AU RC 2.00 5.00
73 Carlos Delfino AU RC 2.50 6.00
74 Maciej Lampe AU RC 3.00 8.00
75 S.Schortsanitis AU RC 2.00 5.00
76 Mario Austin AU RC 2.00 5.00
77 C.Anthony/1170 JSY AU RC 20.00 50.00
78 Chris Bosh JSY AU RC 6.00 15.00
79 D.Wade JSY AU RC 30.00 80.00
80 Kirk Hinrich JSY AU RC 5.00 12.00
81 T.J. Ford JSY AU RC 4.00 10.00
82 D.West/1245 JSY AU RC 6.00 15.00
83 Marcus Banks JSY AU RC 3.00 8.00
84 Dahntay Jones JSY AU RC 4.00 10.00
85 Luke Ridnour JSY AU RC 5.00 12.00
86 Reece Gaines JSY AU RC 3.00 8.00
87 T.Outlaw/1075 JSY AU RC 3.00 8.00
88 B.Cook/1063 JSY AU RC 3.00 8.00
89 Troy Bell JSY AU RC 3.00 8.00
90 Ndudi Ebi JSY AU RC 3.00 8.00
91 K.Perkins/1238 JSY AU RC 4.00 10.00
92 L.Barbosa JSY AU RC 5.00 12.00
93 J.Howard/1111 JSY AU RC 5.00 12.00
94 Slavko Vranes JSY AU RC 3.00 8.00
95 Jason Kapono JSY AU RC 3.00 8.00
96 Luke Walton JSY AU RC 5.00 12.00
97 M.Williams/1172 JSY AU RC 5.00 12.00
98 M.Bonner/960 JSY AU RC 5.00 12.00
99 Travis Hansen JSY AU RC 3.00 8.00
100 Steve Blake JSY AU RC 3.00 8.00
101 Keith Bogans JSY AU RC 3.00 8.00
102 Mike Sweetney JSY AU RC 4.00 10.00
103 Jarvis Hayes JSY AU RC 3.00 8.00
104 Mickael Pietrus JSY AU RC 4.00 10.00
105 Nick Collison JSY AU RC 4.00 10.00
107 James Jones AU RC 2.00 5.00
108 Brandon Hunter AU RC 2.00 5.00
109 Tommy Smith AU RC 3.00 8.00
110 Marcus Hatten AU RC 2.50 6.00
111 Koko Archibong AU RC 3.00 8.00
112 Ime Udoka AU RC 30.00 80.00
113 Eric Chenowith AU RC 3.00 8.00
114 Stephane Pelle AU RC 3.00 8.00
115 Marquis Daniels AU RC 2.50 6.00
116 Paccelis Morlende AU RC 3.00 8.00
117 George Williams AU RC 3.00 8.00
118 Udonis Haslem AU RC 4.00 10.00

2003-04 Bowman Signature Edition Foil

*FOIL 1-55 SINGLES: 1.25X TO 3X BASE HI
*FOIL 56-60 SINGLES: 1X TO 2.5X BASE HI
*FOIL 61-76 SINGLES: .75X TO 2X BASE HI
*FOIL 77-105 SINGLES: .5X TO 1.25X BASE HI
*FOIL 106-118 SINGLES: .75X TO 2X BASE HI
FOIL PRINT RUN 125 SER.#'d SETS
FOIL RC PLAYERS NO JSY OR AUTO
56 LeBron James 2,500.00 5,000.00
77 Carmelo Anthony 30.00 80.00
79 Dwyane Wade 50.00 125.00

2003-04 Bowman Signature Edition Gold

*GOLD 1-55 SINGLES: 1.5X TO 4X BASE HI
*GOLD 56-60 SINGLES: 1.25X TO 3X BASE HI
*GOLD 61-76 SINGLES: 1X TO 2.5X BASE HI
*GOLD 77-105 SINGLES: .75X TO 2X BASE HI
*GOLD 106-118 SINGLES: 1X TO 2.5X BASE HI
GOLD PRINT RUN 99 SER.#'d SETS
56 LeBron James 3,000.00 6,000.00
79 Dwyane Wade 75.00 150.00

2003-04 Bowman Signature Edition Silver

*SLVR 1-55 SINGLES: 1X TO 2.5X BASE HI
*SLVR 56-60 SINGLES: .75X TO 2X BASE HI
*SLVR 61-76 SINGLES: .6X TO 1.5X BASE HI
*SLVR 77-105 SINGLES: .5X TO 1.25X BASE HI
*SLVR 106-118 SINGLES: .6X TO 1.5X BASE HI
SILVER PRINT RUN 249 SER.#'d SETS
56 LeBron James 2,000.00 4,000.00

2004-05 Bowman Signature Edition

COMP.SET w/o SP's (55) 20.00 50.00
56-57 RC JSY PRINT RUN 100 SER.#'d SETS
58-103 PRINT RUN 399 SER.#'d SETS
1 Kevin Garnett 2.00 5.00
2 Eddy Curry .50 1.25
3 Ben Wallace 1.00 2.50
4 Cuttino Mobley .60 1.50
5 Vince Carter 1.50 4.00
6 Bonzi Wells .50 1.25
7 Jermaine O'Neal .60 1.50
8 Kobe Bryant 6.00 15.00
9 Stephon Marbury 1.00 2.50
10 Mike Bibby .75 2.00
11 Yao Ming 2.00 5.00
12 Richard Jefferson .60 1.50
13 Steve Nash 1.50 4.00
14 Luke Ridnour .60 1.50
15 Carmelo Anthony 1.50 4.00
16 Pau Gasol 1.25 3.00
17 Amare Stoudemire .75 2.00
18 Chris Webber 1.00 2.50
19 Sam Cassell .60 1.50
20 Tracy McGrady 1.25 3.00
21 Tim Duncan 2.00 5.00
22 Michael Redd .60 1.50
23 LeBron James 6.00 15.00
24 Baron Davis .75 2.00
25 Zach Randolph .75 2.00
26 Peja Stojakovic .60 1.50
27 Lamar Odom .75 2.00
28 Michael Finley .75 2.00
29 Zydrunas Ilgauskas .60 1.50
30 Rasheed Wallace 1.00 2.50
31 Mike Sweetney .60 1.50
32 Elton Brand .60 1.50
33 Steve Francis .75 2.00
34 Paul Pierce 1.25 3.00
35 Ray Allen 1.25 3.00
36 Tony Parker 1.25 3.00
37 Gerald Wallace .60 1.50
38 Chris Bosh 1.25 3.00
39 Desmond Mason .60 1.50
40 Allen Iverson 2.00 5.00
41 Dirk Nowitzki 2.00 5.00
42 Antoine Walker .75 2.00
43 Ron Artest .75 2.00
44 Jamaal Magloire .50 1.25
45 Kirk Hinrich .75 2.00
46 Jason Richardson .75 2.00
47 Andrei Kirilenko .60 1.50
48 Kenyon Martin .75 2.00
49 Carlos Boozer .60 1.50
50 Shaquille O'Neal 3.00 8.00
51 Shawn Marion .75 2.00
52 Kwame Brown .50 1.25
53 Corey Maggette .60 1.50
54 Dwyane Wade 3.00 8.00
55 Jason Kidd 1.25 3.00
56 Dwight Howard JSY RC 6.00 15.00
57 Andre Iguodala JSY RC 5.00 12.00
58 Andre Emmett JSY AU RC 3.00 8.00
59 Al Jefferson JSY AU RC 5.00 12.00
60 A.Varejao JSY AU RC 4.00 10.00
61 Ben Gordon JSY AU RC 5.00 12.00
62 David Harrison JSY AU RC 3.00 8.00
63 Delonte West JSY AU RC 4.00 10.00
64 Devin Harris JSY AU RC 4.00 10.00
65 Dorell Wright JSY AU RC 4.00 10.00
66 Ha Seung-Jin JSY AU RC 5.00 12.00
67 J.R. Smith JSY AU RC 5.00 12.00
68 Jackson Vroman JSY AU RC 3.00 8.00
69 Jameer Nelson JSY AU RC 5.00 12.00
70 Kris Humphries JSY AU RC 4.00 10.00
71 Josh Smith JSY AU RC 5.00 12.00
72 Kevin Martin JSY AU RC 6.00 15.00
73 Kirk Snyder JSY AU RC 3.00 8.00
74 Trevor Ariza JSY AU RC 5.00 12.00
75 Lionel Chalmers JSY AU RC 4.00 10.00
76 Luke Jackson JSY AU RC 3.00 8.00
77 Luol Deng JSY AU RC 5.00 12.00
78 Rafael Araujo JSY AU RC 3.00 8.00
79 Rickey Paulding JSY AU RC 3.00 8.00
80 Sebastian Telfair JSY AU RC 4.00 10.00
81 S.Livingston JSY AU RC 5.00 12.00
82 Tony Allen JSY AU RC 5.00 12.00
83 Josh Childress JSY AU RC 3.00 8.00
84 Emeka Okafor JSY AU RC 4.00 10.00
85 Ber.Robinson JSY AU RC 3.00 8.00
86 Chris Duhon JSY AU RC 4.00 10.00
87 Blake Stepp AU RC 3.00 8.00
88 Andris Biedrins AU RC 2.00 5.00
89 Donta Smith AU RC 2.00 5.00
90 Beno Udrih AU RC 2.50 6.00
91 Justin Reed AU RC 2.00 5.00
92 Pavel Podkolzin AU RC 2.00 5.00
93 Matt Freije AU RC 2.00 5.00
94 Pape Sow AU RC 2.00 5.00
95 Antonio Burks AU RC 2.00 5.00
96 Rashad Wright AU RC 2.00 5.00
97 Ricky Minard AU RC 2.50 6.00
98 Robert Swift AU RC 2.00 5.00
99 Romain Sato AU RC 2.00 5.00
100 Sasha Vujacic AU RC 2.50 6.00
102 Tim Pickett AU RC 2.50 6.00
103 Yuta Tabuse AU RC 3.00 8.00

2004-05 Bowman Signature Edition 169

*1-55 169 SINGLES: 1.25X TO 3X BASE HI
*56-57 JSY 169: .4X TO 1X BASE HI
*58-86 JSY AU 169: .5X TO 1.25X BASE HI
*87-103 AU 169: .5X TO 1.25X BASE HI

2004-05 Bowman Signature Edition 50

*1-55 50 SINGLES: 1.5X TO 4X BASE HI
*56-57 JSY 50 SINGLES: .6X TO 1.5X BASE HI
*58-86 JSY AU 50: .75X TO 2X BASE HI
*87-103 AU 50: .6X TO 1.5X BASE HI
23 LeBron James 30.00 80.00
103 Yuta Tabuse AU 5.00 12.00

2004-05 Bowman Signature Edition Foil

FOIL PRINT RUN 50 SER.#'d SETS
ONE PER BOX AS TOPPER
56 Dwight Howard 12.00 30.00
57 Andre Iguodala 6.00 15.00
58 Andre Emmett 2.50 6.00
59 Al Jefferson 4.00 10.00
60 Anderson Varejao 3.00 8.00
61 Ben Gordon 4.00 10.00
62 David Harrison 2.50 6.00
63 Delonte West 3.00 8.00
64 Devin Harris 3.00 8.00
65 Dorell Wright 3.00 8.00
66 Ha Seung-Jin 4.00 10.00
67 J.R. Smith 4.00 10.00
68 Jackson Vroman 2.50 6.00
69 Jameer Nelson 4.00 10.00
70 Kris Humphries 3.00 8.00
71 Josh Smith 4.00 10.00
72 Kevin Martin 5.00 12.00
73 Kirk Snyder 2.50 6.00
74 Trevor Ariza 4.00 10.00
75 Lionel Chalmers 2.50 6.00
76 Luke Jackson 2.50 6.00
77 Luol Deng 4.00 10.00
78 Rafael Araujo 2.50 6.00
79 Rickey Paulding 2.50 6.00
80 Sebastian Telfair 3.00 8.00
81 Shaun Livingston 4.00 10.00
82 Tony Allen 4.00 10.00
83 Josh Childress 2.50 6.00
84 Emeka Okafor 5.00 12.00
85 Bernard Robinson 2.50 6.00
86 Chris Duhon 3.00 8.00
87 Blake Stepp 4.00 10.00
88 Andris Biedrins 2.50 6.00
89 Donta Smith 3.00 8.00
90 Beno Udrih 3.00 8.00
91 Justin Reed 2.50 6.00
92 Pavel Podkolzin 2.50 6.00
93 Matt Freije 2.50 6.00
94 Pape Sow 2.50 6.00
95 Antonio Burks 2.50 6.00
96 Rashad Wright 2.50 6.00
97 Ricky Minard 3.00 8.00
98 Robert Swift 2.50 6.00
99 Romain Sato 2.50 6.00
100 Sasha Vujacic 3.00 8.00
102 Tim Pickett 3.00 8.00
103 Yuta Tabuse 4.00 10.00

2004-05 Bowman Signature Edition Flashback Autographs

PRINT RUN 60 SER.#'d SETS
AS Amare Stoudemire 10.00 25.00
BD Baron Davis 12.00 30.00
CA Carmelo Anthony 20.00 50.00
FJ Fred Jones 10.00 25.00
JK Jason Kidd 25.00 60.00
JO Jermaine O'Neal 10.00 25.00
LO Lamar Odom 10.00 25.00
PS Peja Stojakovic 10.00 25.00
RH Richard Hamilton 15.00 40.00
SM Stephon Marbury 15.00 40.00
SO Shaquille O'Neal 40.00 100.00
TD Tim Duncan 200.00 500.00
TM Tracy McGrady 25.00 60.00
SMA Shawn Marion 10.00 25.00

2006-07 Bowman Sterling

1 Ben Wallace JSY 4.00 10.00
2 Jason Richardson JSY 3.00 8.00
3 Steve Nash JSY 2.00 5.00
4 Pau Gasol JSY 5.00 12.00
5 Carmelo Anthony JSY 5.00 12.00
6 Kevin Garnett JSY 5.00 12.00
7 Tim Duncan JSY 8.00 20.00
8 Chauncey Billups JSY 4.00 10.00
9 Chris Paul JSY 6.00 15.00
10 Kobe Bryant JSY 40.00 100.00
11 Tony Parker JSY 5.00 12.00
12 Shaquille O'Neal JSY 12.00 30.00
13 Allen Iverson JSY 8.00 20.00
14 Dirk Nowitzki JSY 8.00 20.00
15 Paul Pierce JSY 5.00 12.00
16 Tracy McGrady JSY 5.00 12.00
17 Channing Frye JSY 3.00 8.00
18 Amare Stoudemire JSY 5.00 12.00
19 Dwight Howard JSY 5.00 12.00
20 Dwyane Wade JSY 5.00 12.00
21 Yao Ming JSY 2.00 5.00
22 Andrei Kirilenko JSY 3.00 8.00
23 Gilbert Arenas JSY 3.00 8.00
24 Shawn Marion JSY 3.00 8.00
25 Bob Lanier JSY 2.50 6.00
26 Pete Maravich JSY 15.00 40.00
27 Bill Walton JSY 4.00 10.00
28 Dennis Rodman JSY 6.00 15.00
29 Magic Johnson JSY 10.00 25.00
30 John Stockton JSY 3.00 8.00
31 Larry Bird JSY AU 30.00 80.00
32 Rick Barry JSY AU 8.00 20.00
33 Isiah Thomas JSY AU 10.00 25.00
34 Dominique Wilkins JSY AU 10.00 25.00
35 Ben Gordon JSY AU 8.00 20.00
36 Raymond Felton JSY AU 4.00 10.00
37 T.J. Ford JSY AU 4.00 10.00
38 Josh Howard JSY AU 5.00 12.00
39 Dwyane Wade JSY AU 30.00 60.00
40 Andre Iguodala JSY AU 4.00 10.00
41 Tarence Kinsey RC 1.25 3.00
42 Mickael Gelabale RC 1.25 3.00
43 Kelenna Azubuike RC 2.50 6.00
44 Pops Mensah-Bonsu RC 1.25 3.00
45 Walter Herrmann RC 1.25 3.00
46 Tyrus Thomas RC 1.50 4.00
47 Lynn Greer RC 1.25 3.00
48 Leon Powe RC 1.25 3.00
49 Yakhouba Diawara RC 1.25 3.00
50 Jose Barea RC 6.00 15.00
51 Saer Sene JSY RC 1.50 4.00
52 Steve Novak JSY RC 2.00 5.00
53 Josh Boone JSY RC 1.50 4.00
54 James White JSY RC 1.50 4.00
55 Rudy Gay JSY RC 3.00 8.00
56 David Noel JSY RC 1.50 4.00
57 Allan Ray JSY RC 1.50 4.00
58 Paul Davis JSY RC 1.50 4.00
59 Shawne Williams JSY RC 1.50 4.00
60 LaMarcus Aldridge JSY RC 6.00 15.00
61 Mardy Collins JSY RC 1.50 4.00
62 Solomon Jones JSY RC 1.50 4.00
63 Craig Smith JSY RC 2.00 5.00
64 Rajon Rondo JSY RC 8.00 20.00
65 Jorge Garbajosa JSY RC 2.00 5.00
66 Patrick O'Bryant JSY RC 1.50 4.00
67 Dee Brown JSY RC 1.50 4.00
68 Brandon Roy JSY RC 5.00 12.00
69 Bobby Jones JSY RC 1.50 4.00
70 Kyle Lowry JSY RC 8.00 20.00
71 Paul Millsap AU RC 5.00 12.00
72 Vassilis Spanoulis AU RC 2.50 6.00
73 Daniel Gibson AU RC 3.00 8.00
74 Marcus Vinicius AU RC 2.50 6.00
75 Ronnie Brewer AU RC 4.00 10.00
76 Damir Markota AU RC 2.50 6.00
77 Hilton Armstrong AU RC 2.50 6.00
78 Shannon Brown AU RC 2.50 6.00
79 Mile Ilic AU RC 2.50 6.00
80 Alexander Johnson AU RC 2.50 6.00
81 Will Blalock AU RC 2.50 6.00
82 P.J. Tucker AU RC 4.00 10.00
83 Sergio Rodriguez AU RC 3.00 8.00
84 Jordan Farmar AU RC 3.00 8.00
85 Renaldo Balkman AU RC 3.00 8.00
86 Quincy Douby AU RC 2.50 6.00
87 Hassan Adams AU RC 2.50 6.00
88 Chris Quinn AU RC 2.50 6.00
89 James Augustine AU RC 2.50 6.00
90 Ryan Hollins AU RC 2.50 6.00
91 J.J. Redick JSY AU RC 25.00 60.00
92 Adam Morrison JSY AU RC 4.00 10.00
93 Maurice Ager JSY AU RC 3.00 8.00
94 Shelden Williams JSY AU RC 3.00 8.00
95 Marcus Williams JSY AU RC 3.00 8.00
96 Andrea Bargnani JSY AU RC 4.00 10.00
97 Thabo Sefolosha JSY AU RC 4.00 10.00
98 Randy Foye JSY AU RC 4.00 10.00
99 Cedric Simmons JSY AU RC 3.00 8.00
100 Rodney Carney JSY AU RC 3.00 8.00

2006-07 Bowman Sterling Refractors

*1-30 REF: .5X TO 1.25X BASE HI
*31-40 AU REF SAME VALUE AS BASE
*41-100 RC REF: .5X TO 1.25X BASE HI
PRINT RUN 199 SER.#'d SETS
50 Jose Barea 12.00 30.00
91 J.J. Redick JSY AU 40.00 100.00

2006-07 Bowman Sterling Refractors Black

*1-30 JSY REF.BLK: .75X TO 2X BASE HI
*31-40 JSY AU REF.BLK: .5X TO 1.25X HI
*42-100 RC REF.BLK: .75X TO 2X HI
PRINT RUN 25 SER.#'d SETS
26 Pete Maravich JSY 40.00 100.00
50 Jose Barea 60.00 150.00
91 J.J. Redick JSY AU 125.00 300.00

2006-07 Bowman Sterling Refractors Gold

*31-40 REF.GOLD: .5X TO 1.25X BASE HI
31-40 PRINT RUN 25 SER.#'d SETS
*71-90 REF.GOLD: .6X TO 1.5X BASE HI
71-90 PRINT RUN 219 TO 599 SETS
*91-100 REF.GOLD: .6X TO 1.5X BASE HI
91-100 PRINT RUN 25 SER.#'d SETS
91 J.J. Redick JSY AU 125.00 300.00

2007-08 Bowman Sterling

AA Arron Afflalo JSY AU/218 RC 4.00 10.00
AB Andrea Bargnani JSY/385 2.50 6.00
ABR Aaron Brooks JSY AU/218 5.00 12.00
ABY Andrew Bynum JSY/385 2.50 6.00
AG Aaron Gray AU/412 RC 3.00 8.00
AH1 Al Horford RC 8.00 20.00
AH2 Al Horford JSY/975 4.00 10.00
AHA Al Harrington JSY/385 2.50 6.00
AHK Adam Haluska JSY AU/218 RC 5.00 12.00
AI Allen Iverson JSY/385 12.00 30.00
AIG Andre Iguodala JSY AU/190 6.00 15.00
AJ Al Jefferson JSY/385 2.50 6.00
AJA Antawn Jamison JSY/385 2.50 6.00
AL1 Acie Law JSY AU/113 5.00 12.00
AL2 Acie Law AU/412 RC 5.00 12.00
AS Amare Stoudemire JSY/385 4.00 10.00
AT1 Alando Tucker JSY AU/218 3.00 8.00
AT2 Alando Tucker AU/829 RC 2.50 6.00
ATH2 Al Thornton AU/412 RC 2.50 6.00
BD Baron Davis JSY AU/275 6.00 15.00
BG Ben Gordon JSY/385 2.50 6.00
BK Bernard King JSY/385 3.00 8.00
BL Bill Laimbeer JSY/385 3.00 8.00
BR Brandon Roy JSY/385 3.00 8.00
BRU Bill Russell JSY AU/15 1,000.00 2,000.00
BWR1 B. Wright JSY AU/21 10.00 25.00
BWR2 Brandan Wright JSY/975 RC 2.50 6.00
CA C. Anthony JSY AU/15 75.00 200.00
CB1 Corey Brewer RC 1.25 3.00
CB2 Corey Brewer JSY/975 3.00 8.00
CBO Chris Bosh JSY AU/89 10.00 25.00
CBZ Carlos Boozer JSY AU/340 6.00 15.00
CD Clyde Drexler JSY/385 6.00 15.00
CK Coby Karl AU/829 RC 2.50 6.00
CL Carl Landry JSY AU/218 RC 3.00 8.00
CM Corey Maggette JSY/385 2.50 6.00
CP Chris Paul JSY/385 8.00 20.00
CR Chris Richard RC 1.00 2.50
CR2 Chris Richard JSY/975 2.50 6.00
DC Daequan Cook JSY AU/113 RC 5.00 12.00
DH Dwight Howard JSY AU/89 20.00 50.00
DJS1 D.J. Strawberry JSY AU/218 3.00 8.00
DJS2 D.J. Strawberry AU/829 RC 2.50 6.00
DM D.McGuire JSY AU/113 RC 5.00 12.00
DN Dirk Nowitzki JSY/385 12.00 30.00
DNI D.Nichols JSY AU/218 RC 5.00 12.00
DR David Robinson JSY AU/15 60.00 150.00
DRO D. Rodman JSY AU/89 40.00 100.00
DW Dwyane Wade JSY AU/15 75.00 200.00
DWI D.Wilkins JSY AU/275 20.00 50.00
EM Earl Monroe JSY/385 3.00 8.00
GA1 Gilbert Arenas JSY/385 2.50 6.00
GD1 Glen Davis JSY AU/218 4.00 10.00
GD2 Glen Davis AU/829 RC 3.00 8.00
GG George Gervin JSY/385 4.00 10.00
GO1 Greg Oden JSY AU/21 5.00 12.00
GO2 Greg Oden JSY/975 RC 4.00 10.00
GP1 Gabe Pruitt JSY AU/218 5.00 12.00
GP2 Gabe Pruitt AU/829 RC 2.50 6.00
HH1 Herbert Hill JSY AU/218 3.00 8.00
HH2 Herbert Hill AU/829 RC 1.00 2.50
IT Isiah Thomas JSY AU/89 15.00 30.00
JC1 J.Crittenton JSY/218 AU 5.00 12.00
JC2 Javaris Crittenton AU/412 RC 5.00 12.00
JCN Juan Navarro AU/129 RC 5.00 12.00
JD Jared Dudley JSY AU/218 RC 5.00 12.00
JDA J.Davidson JSY AU/218 RC 5.00 12.00
JG1 Jeff Green RC 1.25 3.00
JG2 Jeff Green JSY/975 2.50 6.00
JJ Joe Johnson JSY/385 2.50 6.00
JK Jason Kidd JSY/385 6.00 15.00
JMC J.McRoberts JSY AU/218 RC 5.00 12.00
JN1 Joakim Noah RC 1.50 4.00
JN2 Joakim Noah JSY/975 2.50 6.00
JO Jermaine O'Neal JSY/385 2.50 6.00
JOC J.Curry AU/412 RC 5.00 12.00
JR Jason Richardson JSY/385 2.50 6.00
JS Jason Smith JSY AU/113 RC 5.00 12.00
JW1 Julian Wright RC 1.00 2.50
JW2 Julian Wright JSY/975 2.50 6.00
KB Kobe Bryant JSY/385 75.00 200.00
KD Kevin Durant RC 20.00 50.00
KG Kevin Garnett JSY/385 5.00 12.00
KMA Karl Malone JSY/385 5.00 12.00
LB Larry Bird JSY AU/15 60.00 120.00
LD Luol Deng JSY/385 2.50 6.00
LS Luis Scola RC 1.50 4.00
MA Morris Almond JSY AU/113 RC 5.00 12.00
MB Mike Bibby JSY/385 2.50 6.00
MBE Marco Belinelli AU/129 RC 5.00 12.00
MC1 Mike Conley Jr. RC 4.00 10.00
MC2 Mike Conley Jr. JSY/975 10.00 25.00
MCO Michael Cooper JSY/385 3.00 8.00
MG Marcin Gortat AU/829 RC 5.00 12.00
MG Manu Ginobili JSY/385 10.00 25.00
MJ Magic Johnson JSY AU/15 125.00 300.00
MM Mike Miller JSY/385 2.50 6.00
MR Michael Redd JSY/385 2.50 6.00
NF Nick Fazekas JSY AU/218 RC 5.00 12.00
NTA Nate Archibald JSY/385 3.00 8.00
NY2 Nick Young JSY RC 3.00 8.00
PG Pau Gasol JSY/385 2.50 6.00
PP Paul Pierce JSY AU/190 60.00 150.00
RA Ray Allen JSY AU/190 60.00 150.00
RB Rick Barry JSY AU/340 20.00 50.00
RH Richard Hamilton JSY/385 2.50 6.00
RS R.Stuckey JSY AU/218 RC 5.00 12.00
RS Ramon Sessions RC 1.25 3.00
SH Spencer Hawes JSY AU/113 RC 3.00 8.00
SM Stephon Marbury JSY/385 6.00 15.00
SMA Shawn Marion JSY/385 2.50 6.00
SN Steve Nash JSY/385 10.00 25.00
SO Shaquille O'Neal JSY AU/15 60.00 150.00
SW Sean Williams JSY AU/218 RC 5.00 12.00
TD Tim Duncan JSY/385 12.00 30.00
TG T.Green JSY AU/218 RC 3.00 8.00
TM Tracy McGrady JSY/385 12.00 30.00
TY T.Young JSY AU/21 RC 20.00 50.00
VC Vince Carter JSY AU/89 100.00 250.00
WC W.Chandler JSY AU/218 RC 6.00 15.00
YJ Yi Jianlian AU/129 RC 75.00 200.00
YM Yao Ming JSY/385 12.00 30.00

2007-08 Bowman Sterling Refractors

*RC REFRACTORS: .6X TO 1.5X BASE
*AU REFRACTOR: .5X TO 1.25X BASE
AUTO PRINT RUN 99 SER.#'d SETS
*JSY REFRACTOR: .5X TO 1.25X BASE
JSY.REF.PRINT RUN 199 SER.#'d SETS
JSY AU REF.PRINT RUN 10 SETS
JW1 Julian Wright 1.50 4.00
KD Kevin Durant/399 100.00 250.00
NY1 Nick Young JSY AU/19 15.00 40.00
RS Ramon Sessions RC 2.00 5.00
TY T.Young JSY AU/19 20.00 50.00

2007-08 Bowman Sterling Refractors Black

*RC REF.: .75X TO 2X BASE
*AU REF.: .6X TO 1.5X BASE
AUTO PRINT RUN 25 SER.#'d SETS
*JSY REF.: .6X TO 1.5X BASE
JSY.REF.PRINT RUN 199 SER.#'d SETS
JSY AU REF.PRINT RUN 5 SETS
KD Kevin Durant 150.00 400.00

2007-08 Bowman Sterling Refractors Gold
*RC REF.: 1.25X TO 3X BASE
*JSY REF.: 1X TO 2.5X BASE
JSY REF.PRINT RUN 25 SETS
JSY AU REF.PRINT RUN ONE SET
DN Dirk Nowitzki JSY 12.00 30.00
KB Kobe Bryant JSY 200.00 500.00
KD Kevin Durant 300.00 600.00

2007-08 Bowman Sterling Refractors Red
*RC REF.: 1.25X TO 3X BASE
REF.AU/JSY PRINT RUN ONE SET
KD Kevin Durant 400.00 800.00

2007-08 Bowman Sterling X-Fractors
*RC X-FRAC: 1.5X TO 4X BASE
PRINT RUN 25 SER.#'d SETS
KD Kevin Durant 2,000.00 4,000.00

2007-08 Bowman Sterling Box Loaders
*REFRACTORS: .75X TO 2X BASE
REF.PRINT RUN 50 SER.#'d SETS
*REF.BLACK: 1.5X TO 4X BASE
REF.BLACK PRINT RUN 25 SER.#'d SETS
*REF.GOLD: 2X TO 5X BASE
REF.GOLD PRINT RUN 15 SER.#'d SETS
BL1 Acie Law/199 1.00 2.50
BL2 Yi Jianlian/199 2.00 5.00
BL3 Brandan Wright/99 1.25 3.00
BL4 Corey Brewer/99 1.25 3.00
BL5 Greg Oden/199 1.50 4.00
BL6 Javaris Crittenton/99 1.00 2.50
BL7 Nick Young/199 1.50 4.00
BL8 Julian Wright/99 1.00 2.50
BL9 Thaddeus Young/199 1.50 4.00
BL10 Kevin Durant/199 125.00 300.00
BL11 Al Horford/199 4.00 10.00
BL12 Mike Conley Jr./199 4.00 10.00
BL13 Joakim Noah/99 1.50 4.00
BL14 Jeff Green/199 1.25 3.00

2007-08 Bowman Sterling Relics Autographs Dual
REFRACTOR PRINT RUN FIVE SETS
REF.BLACK PRINT RUN FIVE SETS
REF.GOLD PRINT RUN ONE SET
REF.RED PRINT RUN FIVE SETS
BC C.Bosh/V.Carter/25 30.00 80.00
BJ Billups/Johnson/85 12.50 30.00
BW C.Boozer/D.Williams/85 20.00 50.00
CJ V.Carter/A.Jamison/85 15.00 40.00
HB J.Havlicek/E.Baylor/15 50.00 100.00
HM D.Howard/M.Malone/85 30.00 60.00
IW A.Iguodala/L.Walton/85 12.50 30.00
JO Y.Jianlian/G.Oden 30.00 80.00
LM D.Lee/M.Miller/85 12.50 30.00
PA P.Pierce/R.Allen/25 40.00 80.00
RR D.Robinson/D.Rodman/15 100.00 200.00
WB J.West/E.Baylor/15 100.00 200.00
WW S.Webb/D.Wilkins/85 25.00 60.00

1996-97 Bowman's Best
COMPLETE SET (125) 75.00 200.00
1 Scottie Pippen 1.25 3.00
2 Glen Rice .50 1.25
3 Bryant Stith .30 .75
4 Dino Radja .30 .75
5 Horace Grant .50 1.25
6 Mahmoud Abdul-Rauf .40 1.00
7 Mookie Blaylock .50 1.25
8 Clifford Robinson .50 1.25
9 Vin Baker .40 1.00
10 Grant Hill .75 2.00
11 Terrell Brandon .40 1.00
12 P.J. Brown .30 .75
13 Kendall Gill .50 1.25
14 Brent Barry .40 1.00
15 Hakeem Olajuwon 1.00 2.50
16 Allan Houston .50 1.25
17 Elden Campbell .30 .75
18 Latrell Sprewell .50 1.25
19 Jerry Stackhouse .60 1.50
20 Robert Horry .50 1.25
21 Mitch Richmond .60 1.50
22 Gary Payton .75 2.00
23 Rik Smits .40 1.00
24 Jim Jackson .30 .75
25 Damon Stoudamire .50 1.25
26 Bobby Phills .30 .75
27 Chris Webber .60 1.50
28 Shawn Bradley .30 .75
29 Arvydas Sabonis .50 1.25
30 John Stockton 1.00 2.50
31 Anfernee Hardaway 1.25 3.00
32 Christian Laettner .50 1.25
33 Juwan Howard .50 1.25
34 Anthony Mason .40 1.00
35 Tom Gugliotta .30 .75
36 Avery Johnson .40 1.00
37 Cedric Ceballos .40 1.00
38 Patrick Ewing .50 1.25
39 Joe Smith .40 1.00
40 Dennis Rodman 1.25 3.00
41 Alonzo Mourning .75 2.00
42 Kevin Garnett 1.50 4.00
43 Antonio McDyess .50 1.25
44 Detlef Schrempf .40 1.00
45 Reggie Miller 1.00 2.50
46 Charles Barkley 1.25 3.00
47 Derrick Coleman .40 1.00
48 Brian Grant .40 1.00
49 Kenny Anderson .40 1.00
50 Otis Thorpe .40 1.00
51 Rod Strickland .50 1.25
52 Eric Williams .30 .75
53 Rony Seikaly .40 1.00
54 Danny Manning .40 1.00
55 Karl Malone 1.00 2.50
56 B.J. Armstrong .40 1.00
57 Greg Anthony .30 .75
58 Larry Johnson .60 1.50
59 Loy Vaught .30 .75
60 Sean Elliott .50 1.25
61 Dikembe Mutombo .75 2.00
62 Clarence Weatherspoon .30 .75
63 Jamal Mashburn .50 1.25
64 Bryant Reeves .30 .75
65 Vlade Divac .50 1.25
66 Shawn Kemp .75 2.00
67 LaPhonso Ellis .30 .75
68 Tyrone Hill .30 .75
69 David Robinson 1.00 2.50
70 Shaquille O'Neal 2.00 5.00
71 Doug Christie .30 .75
72 Jayson Williams .30 .75
73 Michael Finley .50 1.25
74 Tim Hardaway .60 1.50
75 Clyde Drexler .75 2.00
76 Joe Dumars .60 1.50
77 Glenn Robinson .50 1.25
78 Dana Barros .30 .75
79 Jason Kidd .75 2.00
80 Michael Jordan 12.00 30.00
R1 Allen Iverson RC 8.00 20.00
R2 Stephon Marbury RC 3.00 8.00
R3 Shareef Abdur-Rahim RC 1.50 4.00
R4 Marcus Camby RC 1.50 4.00
R5 Ray Allen RC 5.00 12.00
R6 Antoine Walker RC 1.50 4.00
R7 Lorenzen Wright RC .75 2.00
R8 Kerry Kittles RC 1.00 2.50
R9 Samaki Walker RC .75 2.00
R10 Tony Delk RC 1.00 2.50
R11 Vitaly Potapenko RC .75 2.00
R12 Jerome Williams RC .75 2.00
R13 Todd Fuller RC .60 1.50
R14 Erick Dampier RC 1.00 2.50
R15 Derek Fisher RC 1.25 3.00
R16 Donald Whiteside RC 1.00 2.50
R17 John Wallace RC .75 2.00
R18 Steve Nash RC 6.00 15.00
R19 Brian Evans RC .60 1.50
R20 Jermaine O'Neal RC 1.50 4.00
R21 Roy Rogers RC .75 2.00
R22 Priest Lauderdale RC .60 1.50
R23 Kobe Bryant RC 60.00 150.00
R24 Martin Muursepp RC .60 1.50
R25 Zydrunas Ilgauskas RC 1.50 4.00
TB1 Avery Johnson RET .40 1.00
TB2 Chris Webber RET .60 1.50
TB3 Sean Elliott RET .50 1.25
TB4 Joe Dumars RET .60 1.50
TB5 Grant Hill RET .75 2.00
TB6 Gary Payton RET .75 2.00
TB7 Shawn Kemp RET .75 2.00
TB8 Shaquille O'Neal RET 2.00 5.00
TB9 Eddie Jones RET .50 1.25
TB10 John Wallace RET .75 2.00
TB11 Patrick Ewing RET .75 2.00
TB12 Jerry Stackhouse RET .60 1.50
TB13 Allen Iverson RET 8.00 20.00
TB14 Latrell Sprewell RET .50 1.25
TB15 Dino Radja RET .30 .75
TB16 David Wesley RET .30 .75
TB17 Joe Smith RET .40 1.00
TB18 Damon Stoudamire RET .50 1.25
TB19 Marcus Camby RET 1.50 4.00
TB20 Juwan Howard RET .50 1.25

1996-97 Bowman's Best Refractors
*REFRACTOR: 4X TO 10X BASE CARD HI
STATED ODDS 1:12 HOBBY, 1:20 RETAIL
80 Michael Jordan 300.00 600.00
R1 Allen Iverson 100.00 250.00
R23 Kobe Bryant 800.00 1,500.00

1996-97 Bowman's Best Atomic Refractors
*STARS: 8X TO 20X HI COLUMN
*RCs/RET RCs: 4X TO 10X HI
*RETRO STARS: 15X TO 40X HI
STATED ODDS 1:24 HOBBY, 1:40 RETAIL
80 Michael Jordan 600.00 1,200.00
R1 Allen Iverson 200.00 500.00
R23 Kobe Bryant 3,000.00 6,000.00

1996-97 Bowman's Best Cuts
COMPLETE SET (20) 40.00 100.00
STATED ODDS 1:24 HOBBY, 1:40 RETAIL
*ATOMIC REFRACTORS: 2X TO 5X HI
ATO: STATED ODDS 1:192 HOB, 1:320 RET
*REFRACTORS: 1.5X TO 4X HI COLUMN
REF: STATED ODDS 1:96 HOB, 1:160 RET
BC1 Karl Malone 3.00 8.00
BC2 Michael Jordan 40.00 100.00
BC3 Juwan Howard 1.50 4.00
BC4 Charles Barkley 4.00 10.00
BC5 Jerry Stackhouse 2.00 5.00
BC6 Anfernee Hardaway 4.00 10.00
BC7 Shaquille O'Neal 6.00 15.00
BC8 Alonzo Mourning 2.50 6.00
BC9 Shawn Kemp 2.50 6.00
BC10 Scottie Pippen 4.00 10.00
BC11 David Robinson 3.00 8.00
BC12 Kevin Garnett 5.00 12.00
BC13 Patrick Ewing 2.50 6.00
BC14 Hakeem Olajuwon 3.00 8.00
BC15 Damon Stoudamire 1.50 4.00
BC16 Grant Hill 2.50 6.00
BC17 Dennis Rodman 4.00 10.00
BC18 Chris Webber 2.00 5.00
BC19 Gary Payton 2.50 6.00
BC20 John Stockton 3.00 8.00

1996-97 Bowman's Best Honor Roll
COMPLETE SET (10) 40.00 100.00
STATED ODDS 1:48 HOBBY, 1:80 RETAIL
*REFRACTORS: 4X TO 10X HI COLUMN
REF: STATED ODDS 1:192 HOB, 1:320 RET
*ATOMIC REF: 8X TO 20X VALUE
STATED ODDS 1:384
HR1 C.Barkley/J.Stockton 2.50 6.00
HR2 M.Jordan/H.Olajuwon 50.00 120.00
HR3 P.Ewing/K.Malone 2.00 5.00
HR4 D.Rodman/A.Sabonis 2.50 6.00
HR5 S.Pippen/D.Robinson 2.50 6.00
HR6 G.Rice/S.Kemp 1.50 4.00
HR7 S.O'Neal/A.Mourning 4.00 10.00
HR8 A.Hardaway/C.Webber 2.50 6.00
HR9 G.Hill/J.Howard 1.50 4.00
HR10 K.Garnett/J.Stackhouse 3.00 8.00

1996-97 Bowman's Best Picks
COMPLETE SET (10) 100.00 250.00
STATED ODDS 1:24 HOBBY, 1:40 RETAIL
*REFRACTORS: 2X TO 5X HI COLUMN
REF: STATED ODDS 1:96 HOB, 1:160 RET
*ATOMIC REF: 4X TO 10X VALUE
BP1 Stephon Marbury 3.00 8.00
BP2 Marcus Camby 1.50 4.00
BP3 Lorenzen Wright .75 2.00
BP4 John Wallace .75 2.00
BP5 Ray Allen 5.00 12.00
BP6 Kerry Kittles 1.00 2.50
BP7 Shareef Abdur-Rahim 1.50 4.00
BP8 Todd Fuller .60 1.50
BP9 Allen Iverson 12.00 30.00
BP10 Kobe Bryant 75.00 200.00

1996-97 Bowman's Best Shots
COMPLETE SET (10) 30.00 80.00
STATED ODDS 1:12 HOBBY, 1:20 RETAIL
*ATOMIC REFRACTORS: 4X TO 10X HI
ATO: STATED ODDS 1:96 HOB, 1:160 RET
*REFRACTORS: 2X TO 5X HI COLUMN
REF: STATED ODDS 1:48 HOB, 1:80 RET
BS1 Scottie Pippen 2.50 6.00
BS2 Gary Payton 1.50 4.00
BS3 Shaquille O'Neal 4.00 10.00
BS4 Hakeem Olajuwon 2.00 5.00
BS5 Kevin Garnett 3.00 8.00
BS6 Michael Jordan 30.00 80.00
BS7 Anfernee Hardaway 2.50 6.00
BS8 Grant Hill 1.50 4.00
BS9 Shawn Kemp 1.50 4.00
BS10 Dennis Rodman 2.50 6.00

1997-98 Bowman's Best
COMPLETE SET (125) 15.00 40.00
BP SUBSET CARDS HALF VALUE
1 Scottie Pippen 1.25 3.00
2 Michael Finley .50 1.25
3 David Wesley .40 1.00
4 Brent Barry .40 1.00
5 Gary Payton .75 2.00
6 Christian Laettner .50 1.25
7 Grant Hill .75 2.00
8 Glenn Robinson .50 1.25
9 Reggie Miller 1.00 2.50
10 Tyus Edney .30 .75
11 Jim Jackson .40 1.00
12 John Stockton 1.00 2.50
13 Karl Malone 1.00 2.50
14 Samaki Walker .30 .75
15 Bryant Stith .30 .75
16 Clyde Drexler .75 2.00
17 Danny Ferry .30 .75
18 Shawn Bradley .30 .75
19 Bryant Reeves .30 .75
20 John Starks .50 1.25
21 Joe Dumars .60 1.50
22 Checklist .20 .50
23 Antonio McDyess .50 1.25
24 Jeff Hornacek .50 1.25
25 Terrell Brandon .40 1.00
26 Kendall Gill .40 1.00
27 LaPhonso Ellis .40 1.00
28 Shaquille O'Neal 1.50 4.00
29 Mahmoud Abdul-Rauf .30 .75
30 Eric Williams .30 .75
31 Lorenzen Wright .30 .75
32 Shareef Abdur-Rahim .50 1.25
33 Avery Johnson .40 1.00
34 Juwan Howard .40 1.00
35 Vin Baker .40 1.00
36 Dikembe Mutombo .75 2.00
37 Patrick Ewing .50 1.25
38 Allen Iverson 1.50 4.00
39 Alonzo Mourning .75 2.00
40 Travis Knight .30 .75
41 Ray Allen 1.00 2.50
42 Detlef Schrempf .50 1.25
43 Kevin Johnson .50 1.25
44 David Robinson 1.00 2.50
45 Tim Hardaway .60 1.50
46 Shawn Kemp .75 2.00
47 Marcus Camby .50 1.25
48 Rony Seikaly .40 1.00
49 Eddie Jones .50 1.25
50 Rik Smits .40 1.00
51 Jayson Williams .30 .75
52 Malik Sealy .40 1.00
53 Chris Mullin .60 1.50
54 Larry Johnson .60 1.50
55 Isaiah Rider .40 1.00
56 Dennis Rodman 1.25 3.00
57 Bob Sura .30 .75
58 Hakeem Olajuwon 1.00 2.50
59 Steve Smith .50 1.25
60 Michael Jordan 4.00 10.00
61 Jerry Stackhouse .50 1.25
62 Joe Smith .40 1.00
63 Walt Williams .40 1.00
64 Anthony Peeler .30 .75
65 Charles Barkley 1.25 3.00
66 Erick Dampier .40 1.00
67 Horace Grant .50 1.25
68 Anthony Mason .40 1.00
69 Anfernee Hardaway 1.25 3.00
70 Elden Campbell .30 .75
71 Cedric Ceballos .40 1.00
72 Allan Houston .50 1.25
73 Kerry Kittles .40 1.00
74 Antoine Walker .50 1.25
75 Sean Elliott .40 1.00
76 Jamal Mashburn .40 1.00
77 Mitch Richmond .60 1.50
78 Damon Stoudamire .50 1.25
79 Tom Gugliotta .40 1.00
80 Jason Kidd .75 2.00
81 Chris Webber .60 1.50
82 Glen Rice .50 1.25
83 Loy Vaught .30 .75
84 Olden Polynice .30 .75
85 Kenny Anderson .40 1.00
86 Stephon Marbury .60 1.50
87 Calbert Cheaney .40 1.00
88 Kobe Bryant 5.00 12.00
89 Arvydas Sabonis .60 1.50
90 Kevin Garnett 1.25 3.00
91 Grant Hill BP .75 2.00
92 Clyde Drexler BP .75 2.00
93 Patrick Ewing BP .75 2.00
94 Shawn Kemp BP .75 2.00
95 Shaquille O'Neal BP 1.50 4.00
96 Michael Jordan BP UER 12.00 30.00
97 Karl Malone BP 1.00 2.50
98 Allen Iverson BP 1.50 4.00
99 Shareef Abdur-Rahim BP .50 1.25
100 Dikembe Mutombo BP .75 2.00
101 Bobby Jackson RC 1.25 3.00
102 Tony Battie RC 1.00 2.50
103 Keith Booth RC .75 2.00
104 Keith Van Horn RC 1.50 4.00
105 Paul Grant RC .60 1.50
106 Tim Duncan RC 6.00 15.00
107 Scot Pollard RC .75 2.00
108 Maurice Taylor RC .75 2.00
109 Antonio Daniels RC 1.00 2.50
110 Austin Croshere RC .75 2.00
111 Tracy McGrady RC 5.00 12.00
112 Charles O'Bannon RC .75 2.00
113 Rodrick Rhodes RC .75 2.00
114 Johnny Taylor RC .60 1.50
115 Danny Fortson RC 1.00 2.50
116 Chauncey Billups RC 3.00 8.00
117 Tim Thomas RC 1.25 3.00
118 Derek Anderson RC 1.00 2.50
119 Ed Gray RC 1.00 2.50
120 Jacque Vaughn RC 1.00 2.50
121 Kelvin Cato RC .75 2.00
122 Tariq Abdul-Wahad RC .75 2.00
123 Ron Mercer RC 1.25 3.00
124 Brevin Knight RC 1.00 2.50
125 Adonal Foyle RC .75 2.00

1997-98 Bowman's Best Refractors
*REF: 2.5X TO 6X BASE CARD HI
STATED ODDS 1:12 HOB, 1:20 RET
STATED ODDS 1:12 HOB, 1:20 RET
60 Michael Jordan 125.00 300.00
88 Kobe Bryant 75.00 200.00
96 Michael Jordan BP UER
Stoudamire date on back
should be '96 125.00 300.00
106 Tim Duncan 100.00 250.00

1997-98 Bowman's Best Atomic Refractors
*ATOMIC REF: 5X TO 12X BASE CARD HI
STATED ODDS 1:24 HOB, 1:40 RET
STATED ODDS 1:24 HOB, 1:40 RET
60 Michael Jordan 500.00 1,000.00
88 Kobe Bryant 150.00 400.00
96 Michael Jordan BP UER
Stoudamire date on back
should be '96 500.00 1,000.00
106 Tim Duncan 200.00 500.00

1997-98 Bowman's Best Autographs
STATED ODDS 1:373 HOB, 1:745 RET
*REFRACTORS: .75X TO 2X HI COLUMN
REF: STATED ODDS 1:1,987 H, 1:3,974 R
*ATOMIC REFRACTORS: 2.5X TO 6X HI
ATO: STATED ODDS 1:5,961 H, 1:11,922 R
8 Glenn Robinson 12.00 30.00
13 Karl Malone 25.00 60.00
36 Dikembe Mutombo 12.00 30.00
59 Steve Smith 6.00 15.00
77 Mitch Richmond 12.50 25.00
102 Tony Battie 6.00 15.00
104 Keith Van Horn 10.00 25.00
116 Chauncey Billups 8.00 20.00
123 Ron Mercer 8.00 20.00
125 Adonal Foyle 6.00 20.00
KM Karl Malone MVP 25.00 60.00

1997-98 Bowman's Best Cuts
COMPLETE SET (10) 20.00 50.00
STATED ODDS 1:24 HOB, 1:40 RET
*ATOMIC REFRACTORS: 1.25X TO 3X HI
ATO: STATED ODDS 1:96 HOB, 1:160 RET
*REFRACTORS: .6X TO 1.5X HI COLUMN
REF: STATED ODDS 1:48 HOB, 1:80 RET
BC1 Vin Baker 1.50 4.00
BC2 Patrick Ewing 3.00 8.00
BC3 Scottie Pippen 5.00 12.00
BC4 Karl Malone 4.00 10.00
BC5 Kevin Garnett 5.00 12.00
BC6 Anfernee Hardaway 5.00 12.00
BC7 Shawn Kemp 3.00 8.00
BC8 Charles Barkley 5.00 12.00
BC9 Stephon Marbury 2.50 6.00
BC10 Shaquille O'Neal 6.00 15.00

1997-98 Bowman's Best Mirror Image
COMPLETE SET (10) 30.00 80.00
STATED ODDS 1:48 HOB, 1:80 RET
*ATOMIC REFRACTORS: 1.25X TO 3X HI
ATO: STATED ODDS 1:192 HOB, 1:320 RET
*REFRACTORS: .6X TO 1.5X HI COLUMN
REF: STATED ODDS 1:96 HOB, 1:160 RET
MI1 MJ/Mercer/Marbry/Pay 8.00 20.00
MI2 Thom/Web/O'Neal/Foyle 2.50 6.00
MI3 THard/Ivrsn/BJack/Kidd 2.50 6.00
MI4 Pip/VnHorn/Kobe/Ceblls 8.00 20.00
MI5 Hill/McGrady/Rahim/KG 4.00 10.00
MI6 Kemp/Cmby/Dncn/Rob 5.00 12.00
MI7 Allen/Smith/Andrsn/Elliott 1.50 4.00
MI8 Billups/Brndn/Daniels/KJ 2.50 6.00
MI9 Kittles/Miller/Battie/Olaj 1.50 4.00
MI10 LJ/Walker/Taylor/Baker 1.00 2.50

1997-98 Bowman's Best Picks
COMPLETE SET (10) 8.00 20.00
STATED ODDS 1:24 HOB, 1:40 RET
*ATOMIC REFRACTORS: 1.5X TO 4X HI
ATO: STATED ODDS 1:96 HOB, 1:160 RET
*REFRACTORS: .75X TO 2X HI COLUMN
REF: STATED ODDS 1:48 HOB, 1:80 RET
BP1 Adonal Foyle .40 1.00
BP2 Maurice Taylor .40 1.00
BP3 Austin Croshere .40 1.00
BP4 Tracy McGrady 2.50 6.00
BP5 Antonio Daniels .50 1.25
BP6 Tony Battie .50 1.25
BP7 Chauncey Billups 1.50 4.00
BP8 Tim Duncan 4.00 10.00
BP9 Ron Mercer .60 1.50
BP10 Keith Van Horn .75 2.00

1997-98 Bowman's Best Techniques
COMPLETE SET (10) 12.50 30.00
SEMISTARS .50 1.25
UNLISTED STARS .60 1.50
STATED ODDS 1:12 HOB, 1:20 RET
*ATOMIC REFRACTORS: 2.5X TO 6X HI
ATO: STATED ODDS 1:96 HOB, 1:160 RET
*REFRACTORS: 1.2X TO 3X HI COLUMN
REF: STATED ODDS 1:48 HOB, 1:80 RET
T1 Dikembe Mutombo 1.00 2.50
T2 Michael Jordan 12.00 30.00
T3 Grant Hill 1.00 2.50
T4 Kobe Bryant 6.00 15.00
T5 Gary Payton 1.00 2.50
T6 Glen Rice .60 1.50
T7 Dennis Rodman 1.50 4.00
T8 Hakeem Olajuwon 1.25 3.00
T9 Allen Iverson 2.00 5.00
T10 John Stockton 1.25 3.00

1998-99 Bowman's Best
COMPLETE SET (125) 50.00 100.00
COMPLETE SET w/o SP (100) 10.00 20.00
ROOKIES STATED ODDS 1:4
1 Jason Kidd .75 2.00
2 Dikembe Mutombo .75 2.00
3 Chris Mullin .60 1.50
4 Terrell Brandon .40 1.00
5 Cedric Ceballos .40 1.00
6 Rod Strickland .40 1.00
7 Darrell Armstrong .30 .75
8 Anfernee Hardaway 1.25 3.00
9 Eddie Jones .50 1.25
10 Allen Iverson 1.25 3.00
11 Kenny Anderson .40 1.00
12 Toni Kukoc .50 1.25
13 Lawrence Funderburke .30 .75
14 P.J. Brown .30 .75
15 Jeff Hornacek .40 1.00
16 Mookie Blaylock .40 1.00
17 Avery Johnson .40 1.00
18 Donyell Marshall .40 1.00
19 Detlef Schrempf .50 1.25
20 Joe Dumars .50 1.25
21 Charles Barkley 1.25 3.00
22 Maurice Taylor .40 1.00
23 Chauncey Billups .60 1.50
24 Lee Mayberry .30 .75
25 Glen Rice .50 1.25
26 John Stockton 1.00 2.50
27 Rik Smits .40 1.00
28 LaPhonso Ellis .30 .75
29 Kerry Kittles .40 1.00
30 Damon Stoudamire .50 1.25
31 Kevin Garnett 1.25 3.00
32 Chris Mills .30 .75
33 Kendall Gill .40 1.00
34 Tim Thomas .40 1.00
35 Derek Anderson .40 1.00
36 Billy Owens .40 1.00
37 Bobby Jackson .40 1.00
38 Allan Houston .50 1.25
39 Horace Grant .50 1.25
40 Ray Allen .75 2.00
41 Shawn Bradley .30 .75
42 Arvydas Sabonis .50 1.25
43 Rex Chapman .40 1.00
44 Larry Johnson .50 1.25
45 Jayson Williams .30 .75
46 Joe Smith .40 1.00
47 Ron Mercer .40 1.00
48 Rodney Rogers .30 .75
49 Corliss Williamson .30 .75
50 Tim Duncan 1.25 3.00
51 Rasheed Wallace .60 1.50
52 Vin Baker .40 1.00
53 Reggie Miller 1.00 2.50
54 Patrick Ewing .75 2.00
55 Michael Finley .50 1.25
56 Bryant Reeves .30 .75
57 Glenn Robinson .50 1.25
58 Walter McCarty .30 .75
59 Brent Barry .40 1.00
60 John Starks .50 1.25
61 Clarence Weatherspoon .30 .75
62 Calbert Cheaney .30 .75
63 Lamond Murray .30 .75
64 Zydrunas Ilgauskas .50 1.25
65 Anthony Mason .40 1.00
66 Bryon Russell .30 .75
67 Dean Garrett .30 .75
68 Tom Gugliotta .40 1.00
69 Dennis Rodman 1.25 3.00
70 Keith Van Horn .50 1.25
71 Jamal Mashburn .50 1.25
72 Steve Smith .50 1.25
73 David Wesley .30 .75
74 Chris Webber .60 1.50
75 Isaiah Rider .40 1.00
76 Stephon Marbury .60 1.50
77 Tim Hardaway .60 1.50
78 Jerry Stackhouse .50 1.25
79 John Wallace .30 .75
80 Karl Malone 1.00 2.50
81 Juwan Howard .40 1.00
82 Antonio McDyess .50 1.25
83 David Robinson 1.00 2.50
84 Bobby Phills .30 .75
85 Scottie Pippen 1.25 3.00
86 Brevin Knight .30 .75
87 Alan Henderson .30 .75
88 Kobe Bryant 4.00 10.00
89 Shawn Kemp .75 2.00
90 Antoine Walker .50 1.25
91 Tracy McGrady .75 2.00
92 Hakeem Olajuwon 1.00 2.50
93 Mark Jackson .40 1.00
94 Bison Dele .30 .75
95 Gary Payton .75 2.00
96 Ron Harper .50 1.25
97 Shareef Abdur-Rahim .50 1.25
98 Alonzo Mourning .75 2.00
99 Grant Hill .75 2.00
100 Shaquille O'Neal 2.00 5.00
101 Michael Olowokandi RC 1.25 3.00
102 Mike Bibby RC 2.00 5.00
103 Raef LaFrentz RC 1.25 3.00
104 Antawn Jamison RC 1.50 4.00
105 Vince Carter RC 5.00 12.00
106 Robert Traylor RC 1.00 2.50
107 Jason Williams RC 3.00 8.00
108 Larry Hughes RC 1.50 4.00
109 Dirk Nowitzki RC 6.00 15.00
110 Paul Pierce RC 4.00 10.00
111 Bonzi Wells RC 1.00 2.50
112 Michael Doleac RC .75 2.00
113 Keon Clark RC 1.00 2.50
114 Michael Dickerson RC 1.00 2.50
115 Matt Harpring RC 1.00 2.50
116 Bryce Drew RC .60 1.50
117 Pat Garrity RC .75 2.00
118 Roshown McLeod RC .60 1.50
119 Ricky Davis RC 1.50 4.00
120 Brian Skinner RC .75 2.00
121 Tyronn Lue RC 1.25 3.00
122 Felipe Lopez RC .60 1.50
123 Al Harrington RC 1.25 3.00
124 Corey Benjamin RC .60 1.50
125 Nazr Mohammed RC 1.00 2.50

1998-99 Bowman's Best Refractors
*STARS: 5X TO 12X BASE CARD HI
*RCs: 1.25X TO 3X BASE HI
STATED PRINT RUN 400 SERIAL #'d SETS
STATED ODDS 1:25
69 Dennis Rodman 12.00 30.00
105 Vince Carter 125.00 300.00
107 Jason Williams 15.00 40.00
109 Dirk Nowitzki 150.00 400.00
110 Paul Pierce 100.00 250.00

1998-99 Bowman's Best Atomic Refractors
*STARS: 20X TO 50X BASE CARD HI
*RCs: 3X TO 8X BASE HI
STATED PRINT RUN 100 SERIAL #'d SETS
STATED ODDS 1:100
8 Anfernee Hardaway 100.00 250.00
10 Allen Iverson 150.00 400.00
31 Kevin Garnett 75.00 200.00
40 Ray Allen 25.00 60.00
44 Larry Johnson 25.00 60.00
53 Reggie Miller 100.00 250.00
69 Dennis Rodman 75.00 200.00
74 Chris Webber 30.00 80.00
85 Scottie Pippen 25.00 60.00
88 Kobe Bryant 800.00 1,500.00
89 Shawn Kemp 25.00 60.00
91 Tracy McGrady 75.00 200.00
95 Gary Payton 15.00 40.00
99 Grant Hill 60.00 150.00
100 Shaquille O'Neal 60.00 150.00
105 Vince Carter 125.00 300.00
107 Jason Williams 200.00 500.00
109 Dirk Nowitzki 300.00 600.00
110 Paul Pierce 100.00 250.00
121 Tyronn Lue 60.00 150.00

1998-99 Bowman's Best Autographs
STATED ODDS VET 1:628; RC 1:598
A1 Kobe Bryant 3,000.00 6,000.00
A2 Tim Duncan 500.00 1,000.00
A3 Eddie Jones 12.00 30.00
A4 Gary Payton 20.00 50.00
A5 Antoine Walker 6.00 15.00
A6 Antawn Jamison 10.00 25.00
A8 Mike Bibby 12.00 30.00
A9 Vince Carter 75.00 200.00
A10 Michael Doleac 5.00 12.00

1998-99 Bowman's Best Autographs Atomic Refractors
*ATO.REF: 2X TO 5X VALUE
VETERAN STATED ODDS 1:10073
RC STATED ODDS 1:12515
A9 Vince Carter 1,500.00 3,000.00

1998-99 Bowman's Best Autographs Refractors
*REF: .75X TO 2X VALUE
VETERAN STATED ODDS 1:3358
RC STATED ODDS 1:4172
A1 Kobe Bryant 8,000.00 15,000.00
A9 Vince Carter 400.00 800.00

1998-99 Bowman's Best Franchise Best
COMPLETE SET (10) 10.00 25.00
STATED ODDS 1:23
FB1 Michael Jordan 10.00 25.00
FB2 Karl Malone 1.50 4.00
FB3 Antoine Walker .75 2.00
FB4 Grant Hill 1.25 3.00
FB5 Kevin Garnett 2.00 5.00
FB6 Shaquille O'Neal 3.00 8.00
FB7 Gary Payton 1.25 3.00
FB8 Keith Van Horn .75 2.00
FB9 Tim Duncan 2.00 5.00
FB10 Allen Iverson 2.00 5.00

1998-99 Bowman's Best Mirror Image
COMPLETE SET (20) 20.00 40.00
STATED ODDS 1:12
*REF: 6X TO 15X HI COLUMN
REF: PRINT RUN 100 SERIAL #'d SETS
*ATO.REF: 25X TO 60X HI
ATO.REF: PRINT RUN 25 SERIAL #'d SETS
ATO.REF: STATED ODDS 1:2504
MI1 T.Hardaway/B.Knight 1.00 2.50
MI2 G.Payton/D.Stoudamire 1.25 3.00
MI3 A.Hardaway/A.Iverson 2.00 5.00
MI4 J.Stockton/S.Marbury 1.50 4.00
MI5 R.Allen/K.Kittles 1.25 3.00
MI6 E.Jones/K.Bryant 6.00 15.00
MI7 S.Smith/R.Mercer .60 1.50
MI8 I.Rider/M.Finley .75 2.00
MI9 L.Sprewell/A.Walker 1.00 2.50
MI10 D.Schrempf/S.A-Rahim .75 2.00
MI11 G.Hill/T.Thomas 1.25 3.00
MI12 S.Pippen/K.Garnett 2.00 5.00
MI13 J.Williams/J.Howard .60 1.50
MI14 V.Baker/A.McDyess .60 1.50
MI15 S.Kemp/K.Van Horn 1.25 3.00
MI16 K.Malone/T.Duncan 2.00 5.00
MI17 A.Mourning/Z.Ilgauskas 1.25 3.00
MI18 S.O'Neal/B.Reeves 3.00 8.00
MI19 D.Mutombo/T.Ratliff 1.25 3.00
MI20 D.Robinson/G.Ostertag 1.50 4.00

1998-99 Bowman's Best Performers
COMPLETE SET (10) 10.00 20.00
STATED ODDS 1:12
*REF: 4X TO 10X HI COLUMN
REF: PRINT RUN 200 SERIAL #'d SETS
*ATO.REF: 12X TO 30X HI
ATO.REF: PRINT RUN 50 SERIAL #'d SETS
ATO.REF: STATED ODDS 1:2504
BP1 Shaquille O'Neal 3.00 8.00
BP2 Kevin Garnett 2.00 5.00
BP3 Dikembe Mutombo 1.25 3.00
BP4 Grant Hill 1.25 3.00
BP5 Tim Duncan 2.00 5.00
BP6 Antawn Jamison .60 1.50
BP7 Raef LaFrentz .50 1.25
BP8 Mike Bibby .75 2.00
BP9 Paul Pierce 1.50 4.00
BP10 Jason Williams 1.25 3.00

1998-99 Bowman's Best Performers Refractors
*REFRACTORS: 4X TO 10X BASE CARD HI
BP9 Paul Pierce 25.00 60.00
BP10 Jason Williams 20.00 50.00

1999-00 Bowman's Best
COMPLETE SET (133) 30.00 60.00
1 Vince Carter 1.25 3.00
2 Dikembe Mutombo .75 2.00
3 Steve Nash 1.00 2.50
4 Matt Harpring .30 .75
5 Stephon Marbury .60 1.50
6 Chris Webber .60 1.50
7 Jason Kidd .75 2.00
8 Theo Ratliff .40 1.00
9 Damon Stoudamire .50 1.25
10 Shareef Abdur-Rahim .50 1.25
11 Rod Strickland .40 1.00
12 Jeff Hornacek .40 1.00
13 Vin Baker .40 1.00
14 Joe Smith .40 1.00
15 Alonzo Mourning .75 2.00
16 Isaiah Rider .40 1.00
17 Shaquille O'Neal 2.00 5.00
18 Chris Mullin .50 1.25
19 Charles Barkley 1.25 3.00
20 Grant Hill .75 2.00
21 Chris Mills .30 .75
22 Antonio McDyess .40 1.00
23 Brevin Knight .30 .75
24 Toni Kukoc .60 1.50
25 Antoine Walker .50 1.25
26 Eddie Jones .50 1.25
27 Tim Thomas .40 1.00
28 Latrell Sprewell .60 1.50
29 Larry Hughes .40 1.00
30 Tim Duncan 1.25 3.00
31 Horace Grant .40 1.00
32 John Stockton .75 2.00
33 Mike Bibby .50 1.25
34 Mitch Richmond .60 1.50
35 Allan Houston .40 1.00
36 Terrell Brandon .30 .75
37 Glenn Robinson .40 1.00
38 Tyrone Nesby RC .30 .75
39 Glen Rice .50 1.25
40 Hakeem Olajuwon 1.00 2.50
41 Jerry Stackhouse .50 1.25
42 Elden Campbell .30 .75
43 Ron Harper .40 1.00
44 Kenny Anderson .40 1.00
45 Michael Finley .50 1.25
46 Scottie Pippen 1.25 3.00
47 Lindsey Hunter .30 .75
48 Michael Olowokandi .30 .75
49 P.J. Brown .30 .75
50 Keith Van Horn .40 1.00
51 Michael Doleac .30 .75
52 Anfernee Hardaway 1.25 3.00
53 Rasheed Wallace .60 1.50
54 Nick Anderson .30 .75
55 Gary Payton .75 2.00
56 Tracy McGrady .75 2.00
57 Ray Allen .75 2.00
58 Kobe Bryant 4.00 10.00
59 Ron Mercer .40 1.00
60 Shawn Kemp .75 2.00
61 Anthony Mason .50 1.25
62 Tim Hardaway .60 1.50
63 Antawn Jamison .50 1.25
64 Mark Jackson .40 1.00
65 Tom Gugliotta .40 1.00
66 Marcus Camby .40 1.00
67 Kerry Kittles .40 1.00
68 Vlade Divac .50 1.25
69 Avery Johnson .40 1.00
70 Karl Malone 1.00 2.50
71 Juwan Howard .40 1.00
72 Alan Henderson .30 .75
73 Hersey Hawkins .30 .75
74 Darrell Armstrong .30 .75
75 Allen Iverson 1.25 3.00
76 Maurice Taylor .30 .75
77 Gary Trent .30 .75
78 John Starks .50 1.25
79 Paul Pierce 1.00 2.50
80 Kevin Garnett 1.25 3.00
81 Patrick Ewing .60 1.50
82 Steve Smith .40 1.00
83 Jason Williams .75 2.00
84 David Robinson 1.00 2.50
85 Charles Oakley .50 1.25
86 Bryant Reeves .30 .75
87 Nick Van Exel .40 1.00
88 Reggie Miller 1.00 2.50
89 Chris Gatling .30 .75
90 Brian Grant .30 .75
91 Allen Iverson BP 1.25 3.00
92 Tim Duncan BP 1.25 3.00
93 Keith Van Horn BP .40 1.00
94 Kevin Garnett BP 1.25 3.00
95 Kobe Bryant BP 4.00 10.00
96 Elton Brand BP 1.00 2.50
97 Baron Davis BP 1.25 3.00
98 Lamar Odom BP 1.00 2.50
99 Wally Szczerbiak BP .75 2.00
100 Jason Terry BP .75 2.00
101 Elton Brand RC 2.00 5.00
102 Steve Francis RC 2.00 5.00
103 Baron Davis RC 2.50 6.00

104 Lamar Odom RC 2.00 5.00
105 Jonathan Bender RC 1.00 2.50
106 Wally Szczerbiak RC 1.50 4.00
107 Richard Hamilton RC 2.50 6.00
108 Andre Miller RC 2.00 5.00
109 Shawn Marion RC 2.00 5.00
110 Jason Terry RC 1.50 4.00
111 Trajan Langdon RC .75 2.00
112 A.Radojevic RC .60 1.50
113 Corey Maggette RC 1.25 3.00
114 William Avery RC .60 1.50
115 DeMarco Johnson RC 1.00 2.50
116 Ron Artest RC 2.50 6.00
117 Cal Bowdler RC .60 1.50
118 James Posey RC 1.00 2.50
119 Quincy Lewis RC .60 1.50
120 Dion Glover RC .60 1.50
121 Jeff Foster RC 1.00 2.50
122 Kenny Thomas RC 1.00 2.50
123 Devean George RC .75 2.00
124 Tim James RC .60 1.50
125 Vonteego Cummings RC .60 1.50
126 Jumaine Jones RC .60 1.50
127 Scott Padgett RC .75 2.00
128 Anthony Carter RC .75 2.00
129 Chris Herren RC .75 2.00
130 Todd MacCulloch RC .75 2.00
131 John Celestand RC .60 1.50
132 Adrian Griffin RC .75 2.00
133 Mirsad Turkcan RC 1.00 2.50

1999-00 Bowman's Best Atomic Refractors

*STARS: 10X TO 25X BASE CARD HI
*RCs: 5X TO 12X BASE HI
STATED PRINT RUN 100 SERIAL #'d SETS
1 Vince Carter 20.00 50.00
20 Grant Hill 30.00 80.00
32 John Stockton 15.00 40.00
58 Kobe Bryant 75.00 200.00
75 Allen Iverson 50.00 120.00
83 Jason Williams 60.00 150.00
91 Allen Iverson BP 50.00 120.00

1999-00 Bowman's Best Refractors

*STARS: 3X TO 8X BASE CARD HI
*RCs: 2X TO 5X BASE HI
STATED PRINT RUN 400 SERIAL #'d SETS
58 Kobe Bryant 25.00 60.00
95 Kobe Bryant BP 20.00 50.00

1999-00 Bowman's Best Autographs

STATED ODDS 1:79
BBA1 Mitch Richmond 8.00 20.00
BBA2 Damon Stoudamire 6.00 15.00
BBA3 Antoine Walker 6.00 15.00
BBA4 Antonio McDyess 5.00 12.00
BBA5 Trajan Langdon 5.00 12.00
BBA6 Jumaine Jones 4.00 10.00
BBA7 Andre Miller 12.00 30.00
BBA8 Richard Hamilton 15.00 40.00
BBA9 Jonathan Bender 6.00 15.00
BBA10 William Avery 4.00 10.00
BBA11 Shawn Marion 12.00 30.00

1999-00 Bowman's Best Class Photo

STATED ODDS 1:100
REF: STATED ODDS 1:3478
REF: PRINT RUN 125 SERIAL #'d SETS
AR: STATED ODDS 1:12420
AR: PRINT RUN 35 SERIAL #'d SETS
CS1 Draft Picks 3.00 8.00
CS1 Draft Picks REF 25.00 60.00
CS1 Draft Picks AR 100.00 200.00

1999-00 Bowman's Best Franchise Favorites

COMPLETE SET (3) 1.50 4.00
STATED ODDS 1:14
DUNCAN AU: STATED ODDS 1:2174
GERVIN AU: STATED ODDS 1:966
COMBO AU: STATED ODDS 1:8694
FR1A Tim Duncan 1.00 2.50
FR1B George Gervin .40 1.00
FR1C T.Duncan/G.Gervin 1.25 3.00
FRA1A Tim Duncan AU 125.00 250.00
FRA1B George Gervin AU 8.00 20.00
FRA1C T.Duncan/G.Gervin AU 200.00 400.00

1999-00 Bowman's Best Franchise Foundations

COMPLETE SET (13) 12.50 30.00
STATED ODDS 1:21
FF1 Allen Iverson 2.50 6.00
FF2 Tim Duncan 2.50 6.00
FF3 Kevin Garnett 2.50 6.00
FF4 Shareef Abdur-Rahim 1.00 2.50
FF5 Kobe Bryant 8.00 20.00
FF6 Grant Hill 1.50 4.00
FF7 Keith Van Horn .75 2.00
FF8 Vince Carter 2.50 6.00
FF9 Antoine Walker 1.00 2.50
FF10 Shaquille O'Neal 4.00 10.00
FF11 Jason Williams 1.50 4.00
FF12 Stephon Marbury 1.25 3.00
FF13 Antonio McDyess .75 2.00

1999-00 Bowman's Best Franchise Futures

COMPLETE SET (10) 6.00 15.00
STATED ODDS 1:27
FFT1 Elton Brand 1.00 2.50
FFT2 Steve Francis 1.00 2.50
FFT3 Baron Davis 1.25 3.00
FFT4 Lamar Odom 1.00 2.50
FFT5 Jonathan Bender .50 1.25
FFT6 Wally Szczerbiak .75 2.00
FFT7 Richard Hamilton 1.25 3.00
FFT8 Andre Miller 1.00 2.50
FFT9 Shawn Marion 1.00 2.50
FFT10 Jason Terry .75 2.00

1999-00 Bowman's Best Rookie Locker Room Collection

AU STATED ODDS 1:174
JERSEY STATED ODDS 1:197
LRCA1 Elton Brand AU 6.00 15.00
LRCA2 Steve Francis AU 6.00 15.00
LRCA3 Wally Szczerbiak AU 5.00 12.00
LRCA4 Baron Davis AU 6.00 15.00
LRCA5 Corey Maggette AU 4.00 10.00
LRCJ1 Elton Brand 4.00 10.00
LRCJ2 Steve Francis 4.00 10.00
LRCJ3 Wally Szczerbiak 3.00 8.00
LRCJ4 Baron Davis 5.00 12.00

1999-00 Bowman's Best Techniques

COMPLETE SET (13) 8.00 20.00
STATED ODDS 1:21
BT1 Tim Duncan 2.50 6.00
BT2 Tim Hardaway 1.25 3.00
BT3 Shaquille O'Neal 4.00 10.00
BT4 Vince Carter 2.50 6.00
BT5 Dikembe Mutombo 1.50 4.00
BT6 Grant Hill 1.50 4.00
BT7 Gary Payton 1.50 4.00
BT8 Jason Williams 1.50 4.00
BT9 Stephon Marbury 1.25 3.00
BT10 Reggie Miller 2.00 5.00
BT11 Scottie Pippen 2.50 6.00
BT12 John Stockton 1.50 4.00
BT13 Karl Malone 2.00 5.00

1999-00 Bowman's Best World's Best

COMPLETE SET (9) 6.00 15.00
STATED ODDS 1:30
WB1 Allan Houston 1.00 2.50
WB2 Kevin Garnett 3.00 8.00
WB3 Gary Payton 2.00 5.00
WB4 Steve Smith 1.00 2.50
WB5 Tim Hardaway 1.50 4.00
WB6 Tim Duncan 3.00 8.00
WB7 Jason Kidd 2.00 5.00
WB8 Tom Gugliotta 1.00 2.50
WB9 Vin Baker 1.00 2.50

2000-01 Bowman's Best Promos

COMPLETE SET (6) 2.50 6.00
PP1 Jason Kidd .75 2.00
PP2 Alonzo Mourning .75 2.00
PP3 John Stockton 1.00 2.50
PP4 Antoine Walker .50 1.25
PP5 Scottie Pippen 1.25 3.00
PP6 Allan Houston .50 1.25

2000-01 Bowman's Best

COMPLETE SET w/o RC (100) 25.00 60.00
ROOKIE STATED ODDS 1:23
ROOKIE PRINT RUN 499 SERIAL #'d SETS
THREE VERSIONS OF EACH RC SAME VALUE
LCP1: STATED ODDS 1:767
LCP1: PRINT RUN 499 SERIAL #'d SETS
1 Allen Iverson 1.00 2.50
2 Darrell Armstrong .25 .60
3 Kendall Gill .40 1.00
4 Marcus Camby .30 .75
5 Glen Rice .40 1.00
6 Eddie Jones .40 1.00
7 Wally Szczerbiak .30 .75
8 Antawn Jamison .40 1.00
9 Raef LaFrentz .30 .75
10 Steve Francis .40 1.00
11 Tracy McGrady .75 2.00
12 Brian Grant .30 .75
13 Vlade Divac .40 1.00
14 Gary Payton .60 1.50
15 Vince Carter .75 2.00
16 John Stockton .75 2.00
17 Mike Bibby .40 1.00
18 Derek Anderson .30 .75
19 Juwan Howard .30 .75
20 Allan Houston .40 1.00
21 Kevin Garnett 1.00 2.50
22 Michael Olowokandi .25 .60
23 Maurice Taylor .25 .60
24 Jerry Stackhouse .40 1.00
25 Nick Van Exel .40 1.00
26 Andre Miller .30 .75
27 Michael Finley .40 1.00
28 Jamal Mashburn .30 .75
29 Ron Mercer .30 .75
30 Jim Jackson .30 .75
31 Kenny Anderson .30 .75
32 Karl Malone .75 2.00
33 Rod Strickland .25 .60
34 Shaquille O'Neal 1.50 4.00
35 Glenn Robinson .40 1.00
36 Keith Van Horn .30 .75
37 Grant Hill .60 1.50
38 Eric Snow .30 .75
39 Anfernee Hardaway .60 1.50
40 Scottie Pippen 1.00 2.50
41 Jason Williams .60 1.50
42 Elton Brand .40 1.00
43 Stephon Marbury .50 1.25
44 David Robinson .75 2.00
45 Antonio Davis .25 .60
46 Michael Dickerson .25 .60
47 Mitch Richmond .50 1.25
48 Rashard Lewis .30 .75
49 Jermaine O'Neal .30 .75
50 Tim Duncan 1.00 2.50
51 Tom Gugliotta .30 .75
52 Theo Ratliff .25 .60
53 Joe Smith .30 .75
54 Tim Thomas .30 .75
55 Brevin Knight .25 .60
56 Dale Davis .30 .75
57 Cuttino Mobley .30 .75
58 Cedric Ceballos .30 .75
59 Christian Laettner .40 1.00
60 Dirk Nowitzki 1.00 2.50
61 Paul Pierce .60 1.50
62 Derrick Coleman .40 1.00
63 Dikembe Mutombo .60 1.50
64 Lamond Murray .25 .60
65 Antonio McDyess .30 .75
66 Reggie Miller .60 1.50
67 Hakeem Olajuwon .75 2.00
68 Corey Maggette .30 .75
69 Lamar Odom .40 1.00
70 Larry Hughes .40 1.00
71 Anthony Mason .40 1.00
72 Sam Cassell .30 .75
73 Terrell Brandon .30 .75
74 Latrell Sprewell .50 1.25
75 Kobe Bryant 20.00 50.00
76 Tim Hardaway .50 1.25
77 Mark Jackson .30 .75
78 Vin Baker .30 .75
79 Jonathan Bender .25 .60
80 Chris Webber .50 1.25
81 Rasheed Wallace .50 1.25
82 Shawn Marion .40 1.00
83 Toni Kukoc .50 1.25
84 Patrick Ewing .60 1.50
85 Ray Allen .60 1.50
86 Isaiah Rider .30 .75
87 Danny Fortson .30 .75
88 Jerome Williams .25 .60
89 Shawn Kemp .60 1.50
90 Ron Artest .40 1.00
91 P.J. Brown .25 .60
92 Baron Davis .40 1.00
93 Antoine Walker .40 1.00
94 Jason Terry .40 1.00
95 Jalen Rose .30 .75
96 Avery Johnson .30 .75
97 Shareef Abdur-Rahim .40 1.00
98 Bryon Russell .25 .60
99 Richard Hamilton .50 1.25
100 Jason Kidd .60 1.50
101A Kenyon Martin RC 2.00 5.00
101B Kenyon Martin RC 2.00 5.00
101C Kenyon Martin RC 2.00 5.00
102A Stromile Swift RC .75 2.00
102B Stromile Swift RC .75 2.00
102C Stromile Swift RC .75 2.00
103A Darius Miles RC 1.00 2.50
103B Darius Miles RC 1.00 2.50
103C Darius Miles RC 1.00 2.50
104A Marcus Fizer RC .75 2.00
104B Marcus Fizer RC .75 2.00
104C Marcus Fizer RC .75 2.00
105A Mike Miller RC 1.50 4.00
105B Mike Miller RC 1.50 4.00
105C Mike Miller RC 1.50 4.00
106A DerMarr Johnson RC .60 1.50
106B DerMarr Johnson RC .60 1.50
106C DerMarr Johnson RC .60 1.50
107A Chris Mihm RC .60 1.50
107B Chris Mihm RC .60 1.50
107C Chris Mihm RC .60 1.50
108A Jamal Crawford RC 2.50 6.00
108B Jamal Crawford RC 2.50 6.00
108C Jamal Crawford RC 2.50 6.00
109A Joel Przybilla RC .75 2.00
109B Joel Przybilla RC .75 2.00
109C Joel Przybilla RC .75 2.00
110A Keyon Dooling RC .75 2.00
110B Keyon Dooling RC .75 2.00
110C Keyon Dooling RC .75 2.00
111A Jerome Moiso RC .60 1.50
111B Jerome Moiso RC .60 1.50
111C Jerome Moiso RC .60 1.50
112A Etan Thomas RC .75 2.00
112B Etan Thomas RC .75 2.00
112C Etan Thomas RC .75 2.00
113A Courtney Alexander RC .60 1.50
113B Courtney Alexander RC .60 1.50
113C Courtney Alexander RC .60 1.50
114A Mateen Cleaves RC .75 2.00
114B Mateen Cleaves RC .75 2.00
114C Mateen Cleaves RC .75 2.00
115A Jason Collier RC 1.00 2.50
115B Jason Collier RC 1.00 2.50
115C Jason Collier RC 1.00 2.50
116A Hedo Turkoglu RC 1.50 4.00
116B Hedo Turkoglu RC 1.50 4.00
116C Hedo Turkoglu RC 1.50 4.00
117A Desmond Mason RC 1.25 3.00
117B Desmond Mason RC 1.25 3.00
117C Desmond Mason RC 1.25 3.00
118A Quentin Richardson RC .75 2.00
118B Quentin Richardson RC .75 2.00
118C Quentin Richardson RC .75 2.00
119A Jamaal Magloire RC 1.00 2.50
119B Jamaal Magloire RC 1.00 2.50
119C Jamaal Magloire RC 1.00 2.50
120A Speedy Claxton RC 1.00 2.50
120B Speedy Claxton RC 1.00 2.50
120C Speedy Claxton RC 1.00 2.50
121A Morris Peterson RC 1.00 2.50
121B Morris Peterson RC 1.00 2.50
121C Morris Peterson RC 1.00 2.50
122A Donnell Harvey RC .75 2.00
122B Donnell Harvey RC .75 2.00
122C Donnell Harvey RC .75 2.00
123A D.Stevenson RC 1.00 2.50
123B D.Stevenson RC 1.00 2.50
123C D.Stevenson RC 1.00 2.50
124A Dalibor Bagaric RC .75 2.00
124B Dalibor Bagaric RC .75 2.00
124C Dalibor Bagaric RC .75 2.00
125A Iakovos Tsakalidis RC .60 1.50
125B Iakovos Tsakalidis RC .60 1.50
125C Iakovos Tsakalidis RC .60 1.50
126A Mamadou N'Diaye RC .60 1.50
126B Mamadou N'Diaye RC .60 1.50
126C Mamadou N'Diaye RC .60 1.50
127A Lavor Postell RC .60 1.50
127B Lavor Postell RC .60 1.50
127C Lavor Postell RC .60 1.50
128A Erick Barkley RC .60 1.50
128B Erick Barkley RC .60 1.50
128C Erick Barkley RC .60 1.50
129A Mark Madsen RC 1.00 2.50
129B Mark Madsen RC 1.00 2.50
129C Mark Madsen RC 1.00 2.50
130A Khalid El-Amin RC .60 1.50
130B Khalid El-Amin RC .60 1.50
130C Khalid El-Amin RC .60 1.50
131A A.J. Guyton RC .60 1.50
131B A.J. Guyton RC .60 1.50
131C A.J. Guyton RC .60 1.50
132A Stephen Jackson RC 2.00 5.00
132B Stephen Jackson RC 2.00 5.00
132C Stephen Jackson RC 2.00 5.00
133A Michael Redd RC 2.50 6.00
133B Michael Redd RC 2.50 6.00
133C Michael Redd RC 2.50 6.00
LCP1 Draft Picks 4.00 10.00

2000-01 Bowman's Best Elements of the Game

COMPLETE SET (13) 40.00 100.00
STATED ODDS 1:12
EG1 Shaquille O'Neal 10.00 25.00
EG2 Allen Iverson 6.00 15.00
EG3 Vince Carter 5.00 12.00
EG4 Jason Kidd 4.00 10.00
EG5 Kevin Garnett 6.00 15.00
EG6 Tracy McGrady 5.00 12.00
EG7 Tim Duncan 6.00 15.00
EG8 Gary Payton 4.00 10.00
EG9 Larry Hughes 2.50 6.00
EG10 Lamar Odom 2.50 6.00
EG11 Jason Williams 4.00 10.00
EG12 Kobe Bryant 40.00 100.00
EG13 Karl Malone 5.00 12.00

2000-01 Bowman's Best Expressions

COMPLETE SET (20) 15.00 40.00
STATED ODDS 1:8
E1 Shaquille O'Neal 10.00 25.00
E2 Kevin Garnett 6.00 15.00
E3 Allen Iverson 6.00 15.00
E4 Antonio McDyess 2.00 5.00
E5 Rasheed Wallace 3.00 8.00
E6 Steve Francis 2.50 6.00
E7 Kobe Bryant 20.00 50.00
E8 Vince Carter 5.00 12.00
E9 Chris Webber 3.00 8.00
E10 Gary Payton 4.00 10.00
E11 Latrell Sprewell 3.00 8.00
E12 Tracy McGrady 5.00 12.00
E13 Reggie Miller 5.00 12.00
E14 Antoine Walker 2.50 6.00
E15 Jason Williams 4.00 10.00
E16 Michael Finley 2.50 6.00
E17 Patrick Ewing 4.00 10.00
E18 Karl Malone 5.00 12.00
E19 Elton Brand 2.50 6.00
E20 Lamar Odom 2.50 6.00

2000-01 Bowman's Best Franchise Favorites

SHAQ AU: STATED ODDS 1:1926
MAGIC AU: STATED ODDS 1:852
COMBO AU: STATED ODDS 1:5488
OVERALL AU: STATED ODDS 1:320
GJ: STATED ODDS 1:637
GJ: PRINT RUN 100 SERIAL #'d SETS
FFA1 Shaquille O'Neal AU 125.00 300.00
FFA2 Magic Johnson AU 75.00 200.00
FFA3 S.O'Neal/Magic AU 150.00 400.00
FFJ1 T.McGrady/G.Hill JSY 15.00 40.00
FFJ2 A.Walker/P.Pierce JSY 12.00 30.00
FFJ3 D.Miles/K.Dooling JSY 8.00 20.00
FFJ4 S.Marbury/K.Martin JSY 10.00 25.00
FFJ5 J.Kidd/A.Hardaway JSY 25.00 60.00
FFJ6 S.A-Rahim/S.Swift JSY 8.00 20.00
FFJ7 J.Howard/Strickland JSY 8.00 20.00

2000-01 Bowman's Best Rookie Locker Room Collection

INSERTS: STATED ODDS 1:4
AU: OVERALL STATED ODDS 1:32
FB AU: OVERALL STATED ODDS 1:274
JSY: OVERALL STATED ODDS 1:41
LRC1 Kenyon Martin .75 2.00
LRC2 Stromile Swift .30 .75
LRC3 Darius Miles .40 1.00
LRC4 Marcus Fizer .30 .75
LRC5 Mike Miller .60 1.50
LRC6 DerMarr Johnson .25 .60
LRC7 Chris Mihm .25 .60
LRC8 Jamal Crawford 1.00 2.50
LRC9 Joel Przybilla .30 .75
LRC10 Keyon Dooling .30 .75
LRC11 Jerome Moiso .25 .60
LRC12 Courtney Alexander .25 .60
LRC13 Mateen Cleaves .30 .75
LRC14 Speedy Claxton .40 1.00
LRC15 DeShawn Stevenson .40 1.00
LRCA1 Jamal Crawford AU 12.00 30.00
LRCA2 Courtney Alexander AU 4.00 10.00
LRCA3 Keyon Dooling AU 5.00 12.00
LRCA4 Mateen Cleaves AU 5.00 12.00
LRCA5 A.J. Guyton AU 4.00 10.00
LRCA6 Khalid El-Amin AU 4.00 10.00
LRCA7 Mike Bibby AU 6.00 15.00
LRCA8 Raef LaFrentz AU 5.00 12.00
LRCA9 Larry Hughes AU 6.00 15.00
LRCA10 Maurice Taylor AU 4.00 10.00
LRCA11 Tim Thomas AU 4.00 10.00
LRCA12 Antawn Jamison AU 6.00 15.00
LRCA13 Jonathan Bender AU 4.00 10.00
LRCA14 Baron Davis AU 6.00 15.00
LRCF1 Steve Francis AU 6.00 15.00
LRCF2 Elton Brand AU 5.00 12.00
LRCF3 S.Francis/Brand AU 12.00 30.00
LRCR1 Kenyon Martin JSY 5.00 12.00
LRCR2 Stromile Swift JSY 2.00 5.00
LRCR3 Darius Miles JSY 2.50 6.00
LRCR4 Marcus Fizer JSY 2.00 5.00
LRCR5 Mike Miller JSY 4.00 10.00
LRCR6 DerMarr Johnson JSY 1.50 4.00
LRCR7 Chris Mihm JSY 1.50 4.00
LRCR8 Mark Madsen JSY 2.50 6.00
LRCR9 Joel Przybilla JSY 2.00 5.00
LRCR10 Keyon Dooling JSY 2.00 5.00
LRCR11 Jerome Moiso JSY 1.50 4.00
LRCR12 Etan Thomas JSY 2.00 5.00
LRCR13 Courtney Alexander JSY 1.50 4.00
LRCR14 Mateen Cleaves JSY 2.00 5.00
LRCR15 Jason Collier JSY 2.50 6.00
LRCR16 Desmond Mason JSY 3.00 8.00
LRCR17 Quentin Richardson JSY 2.00 5.00
LRCR18 Jamaal Magloire JSY 2.50 6.00
LRCR19 Speedy Claxton JSY 2.50 6.00
LRCR20 Morris Peterson JSY 2.50 6.00
LRCR21 Donnell Harvey JSY 2.00 5.00
LRCR22 DeShawn Stevenson JSY 2.50 6.00
LRCR23 Mamadou N'Diaye JSY 1.50 4.00
LRCR24 Erick Barkley JSY 1.50 4.00
LRCR25 Hedo Turkoglu JSY 4.00 10.00

2022-23 Bowman's Best University

COMMON CARD .30 .75
SEMISTARS .40 1.00
UNLISTED STARS .50 1.25
*REFRACTORS: .75X TO 2X BASIC
*SPECKLE REF: 1.25X TO 3X BASIC
*MINI DMD REF/299: 1.5X TO 4X BASIC
*PURPLE REF/250: 1.5X TO 4X BASIC
*AQUA LAVA REF/199: 2X TO 5X BASIC
*BLUE REF/150: 2.5X TO 6X BASIC
*PINK LAVA REF/150: 2.5X TO 6X BASIC
*GREEN REF/99: 3X TO 8X BASIC
*GRN MINI DMD REF/99: 3X TO 8X BASIC
*GOLD LAVA REF/75: 4X TO 10X BASIC
*GOLD REF/50: 5X TO 12X BASIC
*ORNG REF/25: 6X TO 15X BASIC
1 Dereck Lively II 1.25 3.00
2 Race Thompson .50 1.25
3 Jett Howard .75 2.00
4 Arthur Kaluma .40 1.00
5 Armando Bacot .50 1.25
6 Jordan Walsh .60 1.50
7 Khalif Battle .50 1.25
8 Malik Reneau .50 1.25
9 Ernest Udeh Jr. .60 1.50
10 Brandon Miller 2.00 5.00
11 Caleb Love 1.25 3.00
12 Bruce Thornton .30 .75
13 Haley Cavinder .60 1.50
14 Kyle Filipowski .60 1.50
15 Roddy Gayle Jr. .50 1.25
16 Demarr Langford .40 1.00
17 Jalen Hood-Schifino .60 1.50
18 Kiki Rice .75 2.00
19 Donovan Clingan 1.50 4.00
20 Otega Oweh .50 1.25
21 Jaden Schutt .75 2.00
22 Kel'el Ware .75 2.00
23 Tre White .40 1.00
24 PJ Hall .40 1.00
25 Chris Livingston .75 2.00
26 Cam Whitmore 1.25 3.00
27 DJ Horne .30 .75
28 Daron Holmes .50 1.25
29 Jalen Cook .30 .75
30 Kijani Wright .40 1.00
31 Julian Phillips .60 1.50
32 Jared McCain 2.00 5.00
33 Dajuan Harris Jr. .50 1.25
34 Tyrese Hunter .50 1.25
35 Jaeden Zackery .30 .75
36 Jaxon Kohler .50 1.25
37 Aliyah Boston 1.25 3.00
38 Avery Anderson .50 1.25
39 Mark Armstrong .30 .75
40 Tyger Campbell .40 1.00
41 Leaky Black .50 1.25
42 Trey Alexander .30 .75
43 Devin Carter .40 1.00
44 RJ Davis .60 1.50
45 Al-Amir Dawes .30 .75
46 Mark Mitchell .50 1.25
47 Will Richardson .40 1.00
48 MJ Rice .60 1.50
49 Seth Trimble .50 1.25
50 Caitlin Clark 10.00 25.00
51 Victor Wembanyama 8.00 20.00
52 Jalen Bridges .50 1.25
53 Tyrese Proctor 1.25 3.00
54 Marcus Sasser .75 2.00
55 LJ Cryer .60 1.50
56 Caroline Ducharme .60 1.50
57 Adam Flagler .50 1.25
58 Brandon Slater .40 1.00
59 Jalen Washington .50 1.25
60 JJ Starling .50 1.25
61 Felix Okpara .30 .75
62 Keeshawn Barthelemy .40 1.00
63 Brice Sensabaugh .40 1.00
64 Hansel Enmanuel 1.00 2.50
65 Kris Murray 1.25 3.00
66 Hanna Cavinder .60 1.50
67 Lauren Betts 1.25 3.00
68 Chance Westry .50 1.25
69 Matas Buzelis 1.50 4.00
70 Ashlyn Watkins .30 .75
71 Mikey Williams .50 1.25
72 Gradey Dick 1.25 3.00
73 Amari Bailey .60 1.50
74 Zach Edey 1.25 3.00
75 Judah Mintz .40 1.00
76 Jordan Hawkins 1.25 3.00
77 Kamari Lands .50 1.25
78 KD Johnson .40 1.00
79 Anthony Black .75 2.00
80 Jalen Wilson 1.25 3.00
81 Oscar Tshiebwe .75 2.00
82 Jared Bynum .50 1.25
83 GG Jackson 1.00 2.50
84 Mike Miles .40 1.00
85 Nick Smith Jr. .60 1.50
86 Makai Ashton-Langford .40 1.00
87 Brandon Murray .30 .75
88 Arterio Morris .30 .75
89 Kyle Lofton .30 .75
90 Kendric Davis .50 1.25
91 Hunter Dickinson .75 2.00
92 Jeremy Roach .60 1.50
93 Vincent Iwuchukwu .50 1.25
94 Hunter Cattoor .50 1.25
95 Rasir Bolton .40 1.00
96 Jarace Walker 1.25 3.00
97 Timmy Allen .40 1.00
98 Frankie Collins .30 .75
99 Trayce Jackson-Davis .75 2.00
100 Drew Timme .50 1.25

2022-23 Bowman's Best University Best of '22 Autographs

*REFRACTOR: .5X TO 1.2X BASIC
*BLUE REF/150: .6X TO 1.5X BASIC
*GREEN REF/99: .75X TO 2X BASIC
*GOLD LAVA REF/75: .75X TO 2X BASIC
*GOLD REF/50: 1X TO 2.5X BASIC
*SPECKLE REF/25: 1.5X TO 4X BASIC
BOAAB Armando Bacot 5.00 12.00
BOAAD Al-Amir Dawes 3.00 8.00
BOAAF Adam Flagler 5.00 12.00
BOAAK Arthur Kaluma 4.00 10.00
BOAAM Arterio Morris 3.00 8.00
BOAAW Ashlyn Watkins 3.00 8.00
BOABM Brandon Miller 20.00 50.00
BOABS Brice Sensabaugh 4.00 10.00
BOABT Bruce Thornton 3.00 8.00
BOACC Caitlin Clark 500.00 1,000.00
BOACD Caroline Ducharme 6.00 15.00
BOACL Chris Livingston 8.00 20.00
BOACW Cam Whitmore 12.00 30.00
BOADC Donovan Clingan 15.00 40.00
BOADH Daron Holmes 5.00 12.00
BOADL Dereck Lively II 12.00 30.00
BOADT Drew Timme 5.00 12.00
BOAEU Ernest Udeh Jr. 6.00 15.00
BOAFC Frankie Collins 3.00 8.00
BOAFO Felix Okpara 3.00 8.00
BOAGJ GG Jackson 10.00 25.00
BOAHC Hunter Cattoor 5.00 12.00
BOAHD Hunter Dickinson 8.00 20.00
BOAHE Hansel Enmanuel 10.00 25.00
BOAJB Jalen Bridges 5.00 12.00
BOAJH Jett Howard 8.00 20.00
BOAJK Jaxon Kohler 5.00 12.00
BOAJM Jared McCain 20.00 50.00
BOAJP Julian Phillips 6.00 15.00
BOAJR Jeremy Roach 6.00 15.00
BOAJS Jaden Schutt 8.00 20.00
BOAJT Jacob Toppin 3.00 8.00
BOAJW Jordan Walsh 6.00 15.00
BOAJZ Jaeden Zackery 3.00 8.00
BOAKB Keeshawn Barthelemy 4.00 10.00
BOAKD Kendric Davis 5.00 12.00
BOAKF Kyle Filipowski 6.00 15.00
BOAKJ KD Johnson 4.00 10.00
BOAKL Kyle Lofton 3.00 8.00
BOAKM Kris Murray 12.00 30.00
BOAKR Kiki Rice 8.00 20.00
BOAKW Kel'el Ware 8.00 20.00
BOALB Leaky Black 5.00 12.00
BOALC LJ Cryer 6.00 15.00
BOAMB Matas Buzelis 15.00 40.00
BOAMR Malik Reneau 5.00 12.00
BOAMS Marcus Sasser 8.00 20.00
BOANS Nick Smith Jr. 6.00 15.00
BOAPA Posh Alexander 5.00 12.00
BOAPH PJ Hall 4.00 10.00
BOARB Rasir Bolton 4.00 10.00
BOARD RJ Davis 6.00 15.00
BOARN Ryan Nembhard 5.00 12.00
BOASC Skyy Clark 5.00 12.00
BOASH Scoot Henderson 20.00 50.00
BOAST Seth Trimble 5.00 12.00
BOATA Trey Alexander 3.00 8.00
BOATJ Trayce Jackson-Davis 8.00 20.00
BOATW Tre White 4.00 10.00
BOAVI Vincent Iwuchukwu 5.00 12.00
BOAVW Victor Wembanyama 800.00 1,500.00
BOAWR Will Richardson 4.00 10.00
BOAZE Zach Edey 12.00 30.00
BOAABA Amari Bailey 6.00 15.00
BOAABO Aliyah Boston 12.00 30.00
BOABMU Brandon Murray 3.00 8.00
BOACLO Caleb Love 12.00 30.00
BOACWE Chance Westry 5.00 12.00
BOADHJ Dajuan Harris Jr. 5.00 12.00
BOADJH DJ Horne 3.00 8.00
BOADLA Demarr Langford 4.00 10.00
BOAHAC Hanna Cavinder 15.00 40.00
BOAHYC Haley Cavinder 15.00 40.00
BOAJBY Jared Bynum 5.00 12.00
BOAJHS Jalen Hood-Schifino 6.00 15.00
BOAJMZ Judah Mintz 4.00 10.00
BOAJWA Jalen Washington 5.00 12.00
BOAJWR Jarace Walker 12.00 30.00
BOAKBA Khalif Battle 5.00 12.00
BOAKWR Kijani Wright 4.00 10.00
BOAMAL Makai Ashton-Langford 4.00 10.00

2022-23 Bowman's Best University Bowman Masterpieces Autographs

*SPECKLE REF/25: .6X TO 1.5X BASIC
BMAAB Amari Bailey 8.00 20.00
BMACL Chris Livingston 10.00 25.00
BMADL Dereck Lively II 15.00 40.00
BMADT Drew Timme 6.00 15.00
BMANS Nick Smith Jr. 8.00 20.00
BMAOT Oscar Tshiebwe 10.00 25.00

2022-23 Bowman's Best University Bowman U Buckets Die Cut

*SPECKLE REF: 1.25X TO 3X BASIC
*LAVA REF/50: 2X TO 5X BASIC
BB1 Cam Whitmore 3.00 8.00
BB2 Dereck Lively II 3.00 8.00
BB3 Anthony Black 2.00 5.00
BB4 Chris Livingston 2.00 5.00
BB5 Jarace Walker 3.00 8.00
BB6 Nick Smith Jr. 1.50 4.00
BB7 Tyrese Proctor 3.00 8.00
BB8 MJ Rice 1.50 4.00
BB9 Oscar Tshiebwe 2.00 5.00
BB10 Arterio Morris .75 2.00
BB11 Drew Timme 1.25 3.00
BB12 Skyy Clark 1.25 3.00
BB13 Marcus Sasser 2.00 5.00
BB14 JJ Starling 1.25 3.00
BB15 Julian Phillips 1.50 4.00
BB16 Caleb Love 3.00 8.00
BB17 Judah Mintz 1.00 2.50
BB18 Caitlin Clark 40.00 100.00
BB19 Aliyah Boston 3.00 8.00
BB20 Amari Bailey 1.50 4.00

2022-23 Bowman's Best University Bowman U Buckets Die Cut Autographs

STATED PRINT RUN 99 SER.#'d SETS
*LAVA REF/50: .5X TO 1.25X BASIC
*SPECKLE REF/25: .75X TO 2X BASIC
BBAAB Anthony Black 10.00 25.00
BBAAM Arterio Morris 4.00 10.00
BBACC Caitlin Clark 1,000.00 2,000.00
BBACL Chris Livingston 10.00 25.00
BBACW Cam Whitmore 15.00 40.00
BBADL Dereck Lively II 15.00 40.00
BBAJW Jarace Walker 15.00 40.00
BBANS Nick Smith Jr. 8.00 20.00
BBAOT Oscar Tshiebwe 10.00 25.00
BBATP Tyrese Proctor 15.00 40.00

2022-23 Bowman's Best University Constellations of Greatness

COG1 Nick Smith Jr. 2.50 6.00
COG2 Dereck Lively II 5.00 12.00
COG3 Chris Livingston 3.00 8.00
COG4 Oscar Tshiebwe 3.00 8.00
COG5 Drew Timme 2.00 5.00
COG6 Amari Bailey 2.50 6.00
COG7 Julian Phillips 2.50 6.00
COG8 Cam Whitmore 5.00 12.00
COG9 Arterio Morris 1.25 3.00
COG10 Jordan Walsh 2.50 6.00
COG11 Jarace Walker 5.00 12.00
COG12 Tyrese Proctor 5.00 12.00
COG13 Ernest Udeh Jr. 2.50 6.00
COG14 Anthony Black 3.00 8.00
COG15 Kel'el Ware 3.00 8.00
COG16 Kyle Filipowski 2.50 6.00
COG17 Gradey Dick 5.00 12.00
COG18 Mark Mitchell 2.00 5.00
COG19 Caitlin Clark 400.00 800.00
COG20 Aliyah Boston 5.00 12.00
COG21 Caleb Love 5.00 12.00
COG22 Armando Bacot 2.00 5.00
COG23 Malik Reneau 2.00 5.00
COG24 Brandon Miller 8.00 20.00
COG25 GG Jackson 4.00 10.00

2022-23 Bowman's Best University Dual Autographs

STATED PRINT RUN 25 SER.#'d SETS
DABC Amari Bailey
Tyger Campbell 15.00 40.00
DACB Aliyah Boston
Caitlin Clark 2,000.00 4,000.00
DALB Armando Bacot
Caleb Love 20.00 50.00
DATL Oscar Tshiebwe
Chris Livingston 25.00 60.00
DAWS Marcus Sasser
Jarace Walker 40.00 100.00

2022-23 Bowman's Best University Flashing Lights

*SPECKLE REF: 1.25X TO 3X BASIC
*LAVA REF/50: 2X TO 5X BASIC
FL1 Cam Whitmore 2.50 6.00
FL2 Dereck Lively II 2.50 6.00
FL3 Amari Bailey 1.25 3.00
FL4 Chris Livingston 1.50 4.00
FL5 Jarace Walker 2.50 6.00
FL6 Nick Smith Jr. 1.25 3.00
FL7 Tyrese Proctor 2.50 6.00
FL8 Chance Westry 1.00 2.50
FL9 Oscar Tshiebwe 1.50 4.00
FL10 Arterio Morris .60 1.50
FL11 Kyle Filipowski 1.25 3.00
FL12 Drew Timme 1.00 2.50
FL13 Malik Reneau 1.00 2.50
FL14 Caleb Love 2.50 6.00
FL15 Kel'el Ware 1.50 4.00
FL16 Julian Phillips 1.25 3.00
FL17 Ernest Udeh Jr. 1.25 3.00
FL18 Brandon Miller 4.00 10.00
FL19 Anthony Black 1.50 4.00
FL20 JJ Starling 1.00 2.50

2022-23 Bowman's Best University Flashing Lights Autographs

STATED PRINT RUN 99 SER.#'d SETS
*SPECKLE REF/25: .6X TO 1.5X BASIC
FLAAB Amari Bailey 8.00 20.00
FLAAM Arterio Morris 4.00 10.00
FLACL Chris Livingston 10.00 25.00
FLACW Cam Whitmore 15.00 40.00
FLADL Dereck Lively II 15.00 40.00
FLAJW Jarace Walker 15.00 40.00
FLANS Nick Smith Jr. 8.00 20.00
FLATP Tyrese Proctor 15.00 40.00
FLACWE Chance Westry 6.00 15.00

2022-23 Bowman's Best University Hardwood Warriors

*SPECKLE REF: 1.25X TO 3X BASIC
*LAVA REF/50: 2X TO 5X BASIC
HW1 Cam Whitmore 2.00 5.00
HW2 Dereck Lively II 2.00 5.00
HW3 Amari Bailey 1.00 2.50
HW4 Chris Livingston 1.25 3.00
HW5 Jarace Walker 2.00 5.00
HW6 Nick Smith Jr. 1.00 2.50
HW7 Tyger Campbell .60 1.50
HW8 Tyrese Proctor 2.00 5.00
HW9 Oscar Tshiebwe 1.25 3.00
HW10 Arterio Morris .50 1.25
HW11 Kyle Filipowski 1.00 2.50
HW12 Drew Timme .75 2.00
HW13 Malik Reneau .75 2.00
HW14 Caleb Love 2.00 5.00
HW15 Kel'el Ware 1.25 3.00
HW16 Julian Phillips 1.00 2.50
HW17 Ernest Udeh Jr. 1.00 2.50
HW18 Brandon Miller 3.00 8.00
HW19 Anthony Black 1.25 3.00
HW20 JJ Starling .75 2.00
HW21 Caitlin Clark 25.00 60.00
HW22 Aliyah Boston 2.00 5.00
HW23 Judah Mintz .60 1.50
HW24 Armando Bacot .75 2.00
HW25 Jordan Walsh .75 2.00
HW26 Gradey Dick 2.00 5.00
HW27 Adam Flagler .75 2.00
HW28 GG Jackson 1.50 4.00
HW29 Mikey Williams .75 2.00
HW30 Marcus Sasser 1.25 3.00

2022-23 Bowman's Best University Masterpieces

*SPECKLE REF: 1.25X TO 3X BASIC
*LAVA REF/50: 2X TO 5X BASIC
BM1 Nick Smith Jr. 1.25 3.00
BM2 Dereck Lively II 2.50 6.00
BM3 Chris Livingston 1.50 4.00
BM4 Oscar Tshiebwe 1.50 4.00
BM5 Drew Timme 1.00 2.50
BM6 Amari Bailey 1.25 3.00
BM7 Julian Phillips 1.25 3.00
BM8 Cam Whitmore 2.50 6.00
BM9 Arterio Morris .60 1.50
BM10 Jordan Walsh 1.25 3.00
BM11 Jarace Walker 2.50 6.00
BM12 JJ Starling 1.00 2.50

2022-23 Bowman's Best University Neon Neophytes

*SPECKLE REF: 1.25X TO 3X BASIC

*LAVA REF/50: 2X TO 5X BASIC
NN1 Arterio Morris .60 1.50
NN2 Anthony Black 1.50 4.00
NN3 Caitlin Clark 30.00 80.00
NN4 Skyy Clark 1.00 2.50
NN5 Amari Bailey 1.25 3.00
NN6 Judah Mintz .75 2.00
NN7 Nick Smith Jr. 1.25 3.00
NN8 JJ Starling 1.00 2.50
NN9 Marcus Sasser 1.50 4.00
NN10 Cam Whitmore 2.50 6.00
NN11 Chris Livingston 1.50 4.00
NN12 Julian Phillips 1.25 3.00
NN13 Jarace Walker 2.50 6.00
NN14 Drew Timme 1.00 2.50
NN15 Dereck Lively II 2.50 6.00
NN16 Kel'el Ware 1.50 4.00
NN17 Oscar Tshiebwe 1.50 4.00
NN18 Armando Bacot 1.00 2.50

2022-23 Bowman's Best University Neon Neophytes Autographs

STATED PRINT RUN 99 SER.#'d SETS
*LAVA REF/50: .5X TO 1.25X BASIC
*SPECKLE REF/25: .75X TO 2X BASIC
NNAAB Anthony Black 10.00 25.00
NNAAM Arterio Morris 4.00 10.00
NNACC Caitlin Clark 500.00 1,000.00
NNACL Chris Livingston 10.00 25.00
NNACW Cam Whitmore 15.00 40.00
NNADL Dereck Lively II 15.00 40.00
NNADT Drew Timme 6.00 15.00
NNAJM Judah Mintz 5.00 12.00
NNAJP Julian Phillips 8.00 20.00
NNAJS JJ Starling 6.00 15.00
NNAJW Jarace Walker 15.00 40.00
NNAKW Kel'el Ware 10.00 25.00
NNAMS Marcus Sasser 10.00 25.00
NNANS Nick Smith Jr. 8.00 20.00
NNAOT Oscar Tshiebwe 10.00 25.00
NNASC Skyy Clark 6.00 15.00
NNAABA Armando Bacot 6.00 15.00
NNAABI Amari Bailey 8.00 20.00

2023-24 Bowman's Best University

*REFRACTORS: 1.25X TO 3X BASIC
*SPECKLE REF: 1.5X TO 4X BASIC
*BLUE REF/150: 2.5X TO 6X BASIC
*PINK LAVA REF/100: 3X TO 8X BASIC
*GRN MINI DMD REF/99: 3X TO 8X BASIC
*YELLOW REF/75: 4X TO 10X BASIC
*GOLD GEO REF/50: 6X TO 15X BASIC
*GOLD REF/50: 6X TO 15X BASIC
*ORNG GEO REF/25: 2.5X TO 6X BASIC
*ORNG REF/25: 6X TO 15X BASIC
1 Enrique Freeman .50 1.25
2 Caleb Love .50 1.25
3 Kylan Boswell .40 1.00
4 Layden Blocker .50 1.25
5 Trevon Brazile .60 1.50
6 El Ellis .50 1.25
7 Aden Holloway .50 1.25
8 Miro Little .50 1.25
9 Prince Aligbe .40 1.00
10 Cody Williams .75 2.00
11 Ryan Kalkbrenner .60 1.50
12 Tyrese Proctor 1.00 2.50
13 Jared McCain 1.50 4.00
14 Sean Stewart .50 1.25
15 Johnell Davis .50 1.25
16 Nicholas Boyd .50 1.25
17 Alijah Martin .40 1.00
18 Riley Kugel .40 1.00
19 Baba Miller .50 1.25
20 Miles Kelly .40 1.00
21 Dusty Stromer .40 1.00
22 Cormac Ryan .40 1.00
23 Steele Venters .50 1.25
24 Ryan Nembhard .50 1.25
25 Jamal Shead .50 1.25
26 J'Wan Roberts .50 1.25
27 Cam Spencer .60 1.50
28 Mackenzie Mgbako .60 1.50
29 Zaccharie Risacher 1.50 4.00
30 Caitlin Clark 10.00 25.00
31 Omaha Biliew .50 1.25
32 Milan Momcilovic .50 1.25
33 Elmarko Jackson .40 1.00
34 Chris Johnson .50 1.25
35 Kevin McCullar Jr. .40 1.00
36 Jamarl McDowell .40 1.00
37 RJ Jones .40 1.00
38 DJ Wagner .75 2.00
39 Justin Edwards .75 2.00
40 Rob Dillingham 1.25 3.00
41 Aaron Bradshaw .60 1.50
42 Reed Sheppard 1.50 4.00
43 Dalton Knecht 1.50 4.00
44 Angel Reese 1.50 4.00
45 Hailey Van Lith 1.25 3.00
46 Mikaylah Williams .75 2.00
47 Tre Norman .50 1.25
48 Zaide Lowery .50 1.25
49 Tyler Kolek .60 1.50
50 DeShawn Harris-Smith .50 1.25
51 Javonte Taylor .40 1.00
52 Ashton Hardaway .50 1.25
53 Wooga Poplar .50 1.25
54 Nimari Burnett .50 1.25
55 Xavier Booker .60 1.50
56 Jeremy Fears .60 1.50
57 Malik Hall .40 1.00
58 Jaden Akins .50 1.25
59 AJ Hoggard .40 1.00
60 Dennis Evans .40 1.00
61 Will Baker .40 1.00
62 Diamond Johnson .50 1.25
63 Hannah Hidalgo 2.00 5.00
64 Scotty Middleton .40 1.00
65 Taison Chatman .40 1.00
66 Devin Royal .50 1.25
67 Brandon Garrison .50 1.25
68 Kwame Evans .50 1.25
69 Mookie Cook .50 1.25
70 Jackson Shelstad .50 1.25
71 Blake Hinson .50 1.25
72 Bryce Hopkins .60 1.50
73 Garwey Dual .50 1.25
74 Zach Edey 1.25 3.00
75 Fletcher Loyer .50 1.25
76 Simeon Wilcher .60 1.50
77 Jordan Dingle .50 1.25
78 Cameron Brink 2.50 6.00
79 Andrej Stojakovic .60 1.50
80 Rickea Jackson 1.25 3.00
81 Freddie Dilione .50 1.25
82 Santiago Vescovi .50 1.25
83 Zakai Zeigler .75 2.00
84 Max Abmas .50 1.25
85 Devin Williams .50 1.25
86 Aaliyah Edwards .60 1.50
87 Paige Bueckers 8.00 20.00
88 Stephon Castle 2.50 6.00
89 Solomon Ball .60 1.50
90 Armando Bacot .60 1.50
91 Zayden High .50 1.25
92 Bronny James 2.00 5.00
93 Isaiah Collier 1.00 2.50
94 Branden Carlson .40 1.00
95 Tyrin Lawrence .40 1.00
96 Eric Dixon .50 1.25
97 TJ Bamba .40 1.00
98 Isaac McKneely .40 1.00
99 Georgia Amoore .75 2.00
100 Dillon Jones .50 1.25

2023-24 Bowman's Best University Best of '23 Autographs

*REFRACTOR/150: .5X TO 1.25X BASIC
*GOLD GEO REF/50: .75X TO 2X BASIC
*ORNG GEO REF/25: 1X TO 2.5X BASIC
B23AB Aaron Bradshaw 6.00 15.00
B23AE Aaliyah Edwards 6.00 15.00
B23AM Alijah Martin 4.00 10.00
B23AR Angel Reese 60.00 150.00
B23AS Andrej Stojakovic 6.00 15.00
B23AW Anton Watson 5.00 12.00
B23BC Branden Carlson 4.00 10.00
B23BG Brandon Garrison 5.00 12.00
B23BH Bryce Hopkins 6.00 15.00
B23BM Baba Miller 5.00 12.00
B23CC Caitlin Clark 400.00 800.00
B23CJ Chris Johnson 5.00 12.00
B23CR Cormac Ryan 4.00 10.00
B23CS Cam Spencer 6.00 15.00
B23CW Cody Williams 8.00 20.00
B23DD Dylan Disu 5.00 12.00
B23DE Dennis Evans 4.00 10.00
B23DJ Dillon Jones 5.00 12.00
B23DK Dalton Knecht 40.00 100.00
B23DR Devin Royal 5.00 12.00
B23DS Dusty Stromer 4.00 10.00
B23DW DJ Wagner 8.00 20.00
B23ED Eric Dixon 5.00 12.00
B23EE El Ellis 5.00 12.00
B23EF Enrique Freeman 5.00 12.00
B23EJ Elmarko Jackson 4.00 10.00
B23FD Freddie Dilione 5.00 12.00
B23FL Fletcher Loyer 5.00 12.00
B23GA Georgia Amoore 8.00 20.00
B23GD Garwey Dual 5.00 12.00
B23HH Hannah Hidalgo 30.00 80.00
B23IC Isaiah Collier 10.00 25.00
B23IM Isaac McKneely 4.00 10.00
B23JA Jaden Akins 5.00 12.00
B23JD Johnell Davis 5.00 12.00
B23JE Justin Edwards 8.00 20.00
B23JF Jeremy Fears 6.00 15.00
B23JR J'Wan Roberts 5.00 12.00
B23JS Jackson Shelstad 5.00 12.00
B23JT Javonte Taylor 4.00 10.00
B23JY Jahmir Young 4.00 10.00
B23KB Kylan Boswell 4.00 10.00
B23KE Kwame Evans 5.00 12.00
B23KM Kevin McCullar Jr. 4.00 10.00
B23LB Layden Blocker 5.00 12.00
B23MA Max Abmas 5.00 12.00
B23MC Mookie Cook 5.00 12.00
B23MH Malik Hall 4.00 10.00
B23MK Miles Kelly 4.00 10.00
B23ML Miro Little 5.00 12.00
B23MM Mackenzie Mgbako 6.00 15.00
B23MW Mikaylah Williams 8.00 20.00
B23NB Nicholas Boyd 5.00 12.00
B23OB Omaha Biliew 5.00 12.00
B23PA Prince Aligbe 4.00 10.00
B23PB Paige Bueckers 125.00 300.00
B23RD Rob Dillingham 20.00 50.00
B23RJ Rickea Jackson 20.00 50.00
B23RK Riley Kugel 4.00 10.00
B23RN Ryan Nembhard 5.00 12.00
B23RS Reed Sheppard 60.00 150.00
B23SB Solomon Ball 6.00 15.00
B23SC Stephon Castle 25.00 60.00
B23SJ Spencer Jones 5.00 12.00
B23SM Scotty Middleton 4.00 10.00
B23SS Sean Stewart 5.00 12.00
B23SV Santiago Vescovi 5.00 12.00
B23SW Simeon Wilcher 6.00 15.00
B23TB Trevon Brazile 6.00 15.00
B23TC Taison Chatman 4.00 10.00
B23TK Tyler Kolek 6.00 15.00
B23TL Tyrin Lawrence 4.00 10.00
B23TN Tre Norman 5.00 12.00
B23TP Tyrese Proctor 10.00 25.00
B23WB Will Baker 4.00 10.00
B23WP Wooga Poplar 5.00 12.00
B23XB Xavier Booker 6.00 15.00
B23ZH Zayden High 5.00 12.00
B23ZL Zaide Lowery 5.00 12.00
B23ZR Zaccharie Risacher 40.00 100.00
B23ZZ Zakai Zeigler 8.00 20.00
B23AHA Ashton Hardaway 5.00 12.00
B23DGJ Darin Green Jr. 4.00 10.00
B23DHS DeShawn HarrisSmith 4.00 10.00
B23DJO Diamond Johnson 5.00 12.00
B23DWI Devin Williams 5.00 12.00
B23HVL Hailey Van Lith 30.00 80.00
B23JDI Jordan Dingle 5.00 12.00
B23JMC Jamari McDowell 4.00 10.00
B23JSH Jamal Shead 5.00 12.00
B23LBJ Bronny James 60.00 150.00
B23MMO Milan Momcilovic 5.00 12.00
B23RBE Rejean Boogie Ellis 5.00 12.00
B23RJJ RJ Jones 4.00 10.00
B23SVE Steele Venters 5.00 12.00
B23TBU Tyler Burton 5.00 12.00
B23TJB TJ Bamba 4.00 10.00
B23TNW Tristen Newton 10.00 25.00

2023-24 Bowman's Best University Buckets Die Cuts

*SPECKLE REF: .75X TO 2X BASIC
*SHIMMER REF/50: 2X TO 5X BASIC
BUB1 Aaron Bradshaw 1.50 4.00
BUB2 DJ Wagner 2.00 5.00
BUB3 Rob Dillingham 3.00 8.00
BUB4 Mackenzie Mgbako 1.50 4.00
BUB5 Paige Bueckers 25.00 60.00
BUB6 Omaha Biliew 1.25 3.00
BUB7 Justin Edwards 2.00 5.00
BUB8 Angel Reese 4.00 10.00
BUB9 Bronny James 5.00 12.00
BUB10 Simeon Wilcher 1.50 4.00
BUB11 Isaiah Collier 2.50 6.00
BUB12 Stephon Castle 6.00 15.00
BUB13 Jared McCain 4.00 10.00
BUB14 Kwame Evans 1.25 3.00
BUB15 Xavier Booker 1.50 4.00
BUB16 Cody Williams 2.00 5.00
BUB17 Caleb Love 1.25 3.00
BUB18 Trevon Brazile 1.50 4.00
BUB19 Tyrese Proctor 2.50 6.00
BUB20 Caitlin Clark 50.00 120.00

2023-24 Bowman's Best University Buckets Die Cuts Autographs

STATED PRINT RUN 75 SER.#'d SETS
*GOLD GEO REF/50: .5X TO 1.25X BASIC
*ORNG GEO REF/25: .6X TO 1.5X BASIC
BDAAB Aaron Bradshaw 10.00 25.00
BDAAB Armando Bacot 10.00 25.00
BDAAR Angel Reese 100.00 250.00
BDACB Cameron Brink 75.00 200.00
BDACC Caitlin Clark 600.00 1,200.00
BDACJ Chris Johnson 8.00 20.00
BDACW Cody Williams 12.00 30.00
BDADJ Dillon Jones 8.00 20.00
BDAEJ Elmarko Jackson 6.00 15.00
BDAIC Isaiah Collier 15.00 40.00
BDAJE Justin Edwards 12.00 30.00
BDAJM Jared McCain 25.00 60.00
BDAKE Kwame Evans 8.00 20.00
BDAKF Kyle Filipowski 12.00 30.00
BDAMM Mackenzie Mgbako 10.00 25.00
BDAPB Paige Bueckers 300.00 600.00
BDARD Rob Dillingham 40.00 100.00
BDARK Riley Kugel 6.00 15.00
BDASC Stephon Castle 40.00 100.00
BDASS Sean Stewart 8.00 20.00
BDATB Trevon Brazile 10.00 25.00
BDATP Tyrese Proctor 15.00 40.00
BDAXB Xavier Booker 10.00 25.00
BDADJW DJ Wagner 12.00 30.00
BDALJJ Bronny James 75.00 200.00

2023-24 Bowman's Best University Dual Autographs

STATED PRINT RUN 75 SER.#'d SETS
DABR Riley Kugel
Baba Miller 10.00 25.00
DACA Caitlin Clark
Angel Reese 1,500.00 3,000.00
DACK Kylan Boswell
Caleb Love 20.00 50.00
DADA Aaron Bradshaw
DJ Wagner 30.00 80.00
DAEZ Elmarko Jackson
Zaccharie Risacher 60.00 150.00
DAJA Javonte Taylor
Ashton Hardaway 10.00 25.00
DAJJ Jamal Shead
J'Wan Roberts 30.00 80.00
DAJR Justin Edwards
Rob Dillingham 60.00 150.00
DALI Isaiah Collier
Bronny James 125.00 300.00
DAMH Hailey Van Lith
Mikaylah Williams 60.00 150.00
DAPS Stephon Castle
Paige Bueckers 400.00 800.00
DATE Trevon Brazile
El Ellis 12.00 30.00
DATJ Tyrese Proctor
Jared McCain 50.00 120.00
DAXJ Jeremy Fears
Xavier Booker 20.00 50.00

2023-24 Bowman's Best University Elements of the Game

*SPECKLE REF: .75X TO 2X BASIC
*GOLD REF/50: 2X TO 5X BASIC
*ORNG REF/25: 2.5X TO 6X BASIC
EG1 Bronny James 5.00 12.00
EG2 DJ Wagner 2.00 5.00
EG3 Caitlin Clark 30.00 80.00
EG4 Isaiah Collier 2.50 6.00
EG5 Mackenzie Mgbako 1.50 4.00
EG6 Paige Bueckers 20.00 50.00
EG7 Justin Edwards 2.00 5.00
EG8 Simeon Wilcher 1.50 4.00
EG9 Zaccharie Risacher 4.00 10.00
EG10 Tyrese Proctor 2.50 6.00
EG11 Jared McCain 4.00 10.00
EG12 Cody Williams 2.00 5.00
EG13 Aaron Bradshaw 1.50 4.00
EG14 Angel Reese 4.00 10.00
EG15 Kylan Boswell 1.00 2.50
EG16 Elmarko Jackson 1.00 2.50
EG17 Hailey Van Lith 2.00 5.00
EG18 Stephon Castle 6.00 15.00
EG19 Baba Miller 1.25 3.00
EG20 Trevon Brazile 1.25 3.00

2023-24 Bowman's Best University Flight Club

FC1 DJ Wagner 15.00 40.00
FC2 Justin Edwards 15.00 40.00
FC3 Elmarko Jackson 8.00 20.00
FC4 Isaiah Collier 20.00 50.00
FC5 Stephon Castle 50.00 120.00
FC6 Tyrese Proctor 20.00 50.00
FC7 Zaccharie Risacher 30.00 80.00
FC8 Jared McCain 30.00 80.00
FC9 Trevon Brazile 12.00 30.00
FC10 Javonte Taylor 8.00 20.00
FC11 Kwame Evans 10.00 25.00
FC12 Simeon Wilcher 12.00 30.00
FC13 Mackenzie Mgbako 12.00 30.00
FC14 Bronny James 40.00 100.00
FC15 Omaha Biliew 10.00 25.00
FC16 Dillon Jones 10.00 25.00
FC17 Riley Kugel 8.00 20.00
FC18 Caitlin Clark 800.00 1,500.00
FC19 Angel Reese 30.00 80.00
FC20 Paige Bueckers 400.00 800.00

2023-24 Bowman's Best University Greatness Awaits

*SPECKLE REF: .75X TO 2X BASIC
*GOLD REF/50: 2X TO 5X BASIC
*ORNG REF/25: 2.5X TO 6X BASIC
GA1 Aaron Bradshaw .75 2.00
GA2 Trevon Brazile .75 2.00
GA3 Baba Miller .60 1.50
GA4 Cody Williams 1.00 2.50
GA5 Xavier Booker .75 2.00
GA6 DJ Wagner 1.00 2.50
GA7 Elmarko Jackson .50 1.25
GA8 Isaiah Collier 1.25 3.00
GA9 Jared McCain 2.00 5.00
GA10 Dillon Jones .60 1.50
GA11 Justin Edwards 1.00 2.50
GA12 Bronny James 2.50 6.00
GA13 Mackenzie Mgbako .75 2.00
GA14 Riley Kugel .50 1.25
GA15 Omaha Biliew .60 1.50
GA16 Tyrese Proctor 1.25 3.00
GA17 Rob Dillingham 1.50 4.00
GA18 Simeon Wilcher .75 2.00
GA19 Sean Stewart .60 1.50
GA20 Stephon Castle 3.00 8.00

2023-24 Bowman's Best University Greatness Awaits Autographs

STATED PRINT RUN 75 SER.#'d SETS
*GOLD REF/50: .5X TO 1.25X BASIC
*ORNG REF/25: .6X TO 1.5X BASIC
GAAAB Aaron Bradshaw 10.00 25.00
GAAAR Angel Reese 100.00 250.00
GAACC Caitlin Clark 600.00 1,200.00
GAACW Cody Williams 12.00 30.00
GAADJ Dillon Jones 8.00 20.00
GAAEE El Ellis 8.00 20.00
GAAEJ Elmarko Jackson 6.00 15.00
GAAIC Isaiah Collier 15.00 40.00
GAAJE Justin Edwards 12.00 30.00
GAAJM Jared McCain 25.00 60.00
GAAKM Kevin McCullar Jr. 6.00 15.00
GAAMM Mackenzie Mgbako 10.00 25.00
GAAMW Mikaylah Williams 12.00 30.00
GAAPB Paige Bueckers 300.00 600.00
GAARD Rob Dillingham 40.00 100.00
GAARK Riley Kugel 6.00 15.00
GAASB Solomon Ball 10.00 25.00
GAASC Stephon Castle 40.00 100.00
GAASJ Spencer Jones 8.00 20.00
GAASS Sean Stewart 8.00 20.00
GAATB Trevon Brazile 8.00 20.00
GAATP Tyrese Proctor 15.00 40.00
GAAXB Xavier Booker 10.00 25.00
GAADJW DJ Wagner 12.00 30.00
GAALJJ Bronny James 100.00 250.00

2023-24 Bowman's Best University Masterpieces

*SPECKLE REF: .75X TO 2X BASIC
*GOLD REF/50: 2X TO 5X BASIC
*ORNG REF/25: 2.5X TO 6X BASIC
BM1 DJ Wagner 2.00 5.00
BM2 Justin Edwards 2.00 5.00
BM3 Elmarko Jackson 1.00 2.50
BM4 Isaiah Collier 2.50 6.00
BM5 Stephon Castle 6.00 15.00
BM6 Aaron Bradshaw 1.50 4.00
BM7 Kyle Filipowski 2.00 5.00
BM8 Cody Williams 2.00 5.00
BM9 Mackenzie Mgbako 1.50 4.00
BM10 Bronny James 5.00 12.00
BM11 Zaccharie Risacher 4.00 10.00
BM12 Trevon Brazile 1.50 4.00
BM13 Baba Miller 1.25 3.00
BM14 Omaha Biliew 1.25 3.00
BM15 Riley Kugel 1.00 2.50
BM16 Kylan Boswell 1.00 2.50
BM17 Kwame Evans 1.25 3.00
BM18 Xavier Booker 1.50 4.00
BM19 Caitlin Clark 30.00 80.00
BM20 Angel Reese 4.00 10.00

2023-24 Bowman's Best University Masterpieces Autographs

STATED PRINT RUN 75 SER.#'d SETS
*GOLD GEO REF/50: .5X TO 1.25X BASIC
*ORNG GEO REF/25: .6X TO 1.5X BASIC
BMAAB Aaron Bradshaw 10.00 25.00
BMABM Baba Miller 8.00 20.00
BMACC Caitlin Clark 600.00 1,200.00
BMACW Cody Williams 12.00 30.00
BMADJ Dillon Jones 8.00 20.00
BMADW DJ Wagner 12.00 30.00
BMAEJ Elmarko Jackson 6.00 15.00
BMAIC Isaiah Collier 15.00 40.00
BMAJB Johni Broome 60.00 150.00
BMAJE Justin Edwards 12.00 30.00
BMAJM Jared McCain 25.00 60.00
BMAKB Kylan Boswell 6.00 15.00
BMAMC Mookie Cook 8.00 20.00
BMAMM Mackenzie Mgbako 10.00 25.00
BMAPB Paige Bueckers 300.00 600.00
BMARK Riley Kugel 6.00 15.00
BMASC Stephon Castle 40.00 100.00
BMASM Scotty Middleton 6.00 15.00
BMASW Simeon Wilcher 10.00 25.00
BMATB Trevon Brazile 10.00 25.00
BMATP Tyrese Proctor 15.00 40.00
BMAXB Xavier Booker 10.00 25.00
BMAZR Zaccharie Risacher 40.00 100.00
BMAHVL Hailey Van Lith 30.00 80.00
BMALBJ Bronny James 75.00 200.00

2023-24 Bowman's Best University Mirror Image Fusion

MIF1 Justin Edwards
DJ Wagner 3.00 8.00
MIF2 Rob Dillingham
Aaron Bradshaw 5.00 12.00
MIF3 Kevin McCullar Jr.
Elmarko Jackson 1.50 4.00
MIF4 Kylan Boswell
Caleb Love 2.00 5.00
MIF5 Layden Blocker
Trevon Brazile 2.00 5.00
MIF6 Jared McCain
Tyrese Proctor 6.00 15.00
MIF7 Stephon Castle
Cam Spencer 10.00 25.00
MIF8 Omaha Biliew
Milan Momcilovic 2.00 5.00
MIF9 Angel Reese
Hailey Van Lith 6.00 15.00
MIF10 Caitlin Clark
Paige Bueckers 125.00 300.00
MIF11 Jordan Dingle
Simeon Wilcher 2.00 5.00
MIF12 Zach Edey
Fletcher Loyer 5.00 12.00
MIF13 Jackson Shelstad
Mookie Cook 2.00 5.00
MIF14 Taison Chatman
Devin Royal 2.00 5.00
MIF15 Armando Bacot
Zayden High 2.50 6.00
MIF16 Isaiah Collier
Bronny James 8.00 20.00
MIF17 Johni Broome
Aden Holloway 2.50 6.00
MIF18 Baba Miller
Darin Green Jr. 2.00 5.00
MIF19 Ryan Nembhard
Dusty Stromer 2.00 5.00
MIF20 Javonte Taylor
Ashton Hardaway 2.00 5.00

2023-24 Bowman's Best University Prospect Jumbo Relic Autographs

*HONOR ROLL/49: .75X TO 2X BASIC
PJRAB Aaron Bradshaw 10.00 25.00
PJRAB Armando Bacot 10.00 25.00
PJRAH Aden Holloway 8.00 20.00
PJRAR Angel Reese 125.00 300.00
PJRAS Andrej Stojakovic 10.00 25.00
PJRBJ Bronny James 100.00 250.00
PJRCC Caitlin Clark 500.00 1,000.00
PJRCW Cody Williams 12.00 30.00
PJRDJ DJ Wagner 12.00 30.00
PJREL El Ellis 8.00 20.00
PJRFD Freddie Dilione 8.00 20.00
PJRIC Isaiah Collier 15.00 40.00
PJRJE Justin Edwards 12.00 30.00
PJRKB Kylan Boswell 6.00 15.00
PJRMA Max Abmas 8.00 20.00
PJRMM Mackenzie Mgbako 10.00 25.00
PJRPB Paige Bueckers 300.00 600.00
PJRRD Rob Dillingham 40.00 100.00
PJRRK Riley Kugel 6.00 15.00
PJRSC Stephon Castle 40.00 100.00
PJRSM Scotty Middleton 6.00 15.00
PJRSS Sean Stewart 8.00 20.00
PJRZE Zach Edey 50.00 120.00
PJRMMO Milan Momcilovic 8.00 20.00

2023-24 Bowman's Best University Triple Autographs

TACAP Paige Bueckers
Angel Reese
Caitlin Clark 1,500.00 3,000.00
TACOD Cody Williams
Dillon Jones
Omaha Biliew 20.00 50.00
TADJA Justin Edwards
Aaron Bradshaw
DJ Wagner 20.00 50.00
TAEIS Elmarko Jackson
Stephon Castle
Isaiah Collier 60.00 150.00
TAKMJ Mookie Cook
Kwame Evans
Jackson Shelstad 12.00 30.00
TALAA Andrej Stojakovic
Ashton Hardaway
Bronny James 125.00 300.00
TARRK Rob Dillingham
Riley Kugel
Kylan Boswell 30.00 80.00
TAXMS Sean Stewart
Xavier Booker
Mackenzie Mgbako 15.00 40.00
TAZTB Baba Miller
Trevon Brazile
Zaccharie Risacher 60.00 150.00

2023-24 Bowman's Best University Victory Vibes

*SPECKLE REF: .75X TO 2X BASIC
*GOLD REF/50: 2X TO 5X BASIC
*ORNG REF/25: 2.5X TO 6X BASIC
VV1 Tyrese Proctor 2.50 6.00
VV2 Zaccharie Risacher 4.00 10.00
VV3 Trevon Brazile 1.25 3.00
VV4 Baba Miller 1.25 3.00
VV5 Dillon Jones 1.25 3.00
VV6 Riley Kugel 1.00 2.50
VV7 Kylan Boswell 1.00 2.50
VV8 El Ellis 1.25 3.00
VV9 Johni Broome 1.50 4.00
VV10 Caitlin Clark 40.00 100.00
VV11 Angel Reese 4.00 10.00
VV12 Paige Bueckers 25.00 60.00
VV13 Kyle Filipowski 2.00 5.00
VV14 Ryan Kalkbrenner 1.25 3.00
VV15 Johnell Davis 1.25 3.00
VV16 Zach Edey 3.00 8.00
VV17 Armando Bacot 1.50 4.00
VV18 Anton Watson 1.25 3.00
VV19 Quinten Post 1.25 3.00
VV20 Dylan Disu 1.25 3.00

1974-75 Braves Buffalo Linnett

COMPLETE SET (3) 10.00 20.00
1 Ernie DiGregorio 5.00 10.00
2 Garfield Heard 2.50 6.00
3 Jim McMillian 2.50 6.00

1976-77 Braves Team Issue

COMPLETE SET (14) 15.00 30.00
1 Don Adams .75 2.00
2 Bird Averitt .75 2.00
3 Gary Brewster .75 2.00
4 Fred Foster .75 2.00
5 George Jackson .75 2.00
6 Greg Jackson .75 2.00
7 Bob McAdoo 5.00 12.00
8 John Neumann .75 2.00
9 Dale Schlueter .75 2.00
10 Randy Smith 2.50 6.00
11 John Shumate 1.00 2.50
12 Claude Terry .75 2.00
13 Bob MacKinnon GM
Tates Locke CO .75 2.00
14 Charlie Harrison ACO
Ray Melchiorre TR .75 2.00

1950-51 Bread for Health

COMPLETE SET (32) 18,000.00 22,000.00
1 Paul Armstrong 200.00 500.00
2 Ralph Beard 400.00 800.00
3 Vince Boryla 300.00 600.00
4 Walter Budko 200.00 500.00
5 Al Cervi 200.00 500.00
6 Bob Davies 600.00 1,200.00
7 Dwight Eddleman 300.00 600.00
8 Arnold Ferrin 300.00 600.00
9 Joe Fulks 800.00 1,200.00
10 Harry Gallatin 400.00 800.00
11 Chuck Gilmur 200.00 500.00
12 Alex Groza 400.00 800.00
13 Bruce Hale 300.00 600.00
14 Paul Hoffman 200.00 500.00
15 Buddy Jeanette 400.00 800.00
16 Bob Kinney 200.00 500.00
17 Tony Lavelli 200.00 500.00
18 Ron Livingstone 200.00 500.00
19 Horace McKinney 600.00 1,200.00
20 Stan Miasek 200.00 500.00
21 George Mikan 2,500.00 5,000.00
22 Andy Phillip 300.00 600.00
23 Arnie Risen 400.00 800.00
24 Fred Schaus 400.00 800.00
25 Dolph Schayes 800.00 1,500.00
26 Fred Scolari 200.00 500.00
27 George Senesky 200.00 500.00
28 Paul Seymour 300.00 600.00
29 Cornelius Simmons 300.00 600.00
30 Gene Vance 200.00 500.00
31 Brady Walker 200.00 500.00
32 Max Zaslofsky 400.00 800.00

1976 Buckmans Discs

COMPLETE SET (20) 25.00 60.00
1 Kareem Abdul-Jabbar 4.00 10.00
2 Nate Archibald 2.00 5.00
3 Rick Barry 2.00 5.00
4 Tom Boerwinkle .75 2.00
5 Bill Bradley 2.00 5.00
6 Dave Cowens 2.50 6.00
7 Bob Dandridge 1.00 2.50
8 Walt Frazier 2.50 6.00
9 Gail Goodrich 2.50 6.00
10 John Havlicek 3.00 8.00
11 Connie Hawkins 2.50 6.00
12 Lou Hudson 1.25 3.00
13 Sam Lacey .75 2.00
14 Bob Lanier 2.00 5.00
15 Bob Love 1.50 4.00
16 Bob McAdoo 2.00 5.00
17 Earl Monroe 2.00 5.00
18 Jerry Sloan 2.00 5.00
19 Norm Van Lier 1.25 3.00
20 Jo Jo White 1.25 3.00

1977-78 Bucks Action Photos

COMPLETE SET (10) 6.00 15.00
1 Kent Benson .75 2.00
2 Junior Bridgeman .75 2.00
3 Quinn Buckner 1.00 2.50
4 Alex English 3.00 8.00
5 John Gianelli .60 1.50
6 Ernie Grunfeld 1.00 2.50
7 Marques Johnson 2.00 5.00
8 Dave Meyers .75 2.00
9 Lloyd Walton .60 1.50
10 Brian Winters 1.00 2.50

1985 Bucks Card Night/Star

COMPLETE SET (13) 25.00 60.00
1 Don Nelson CO 1.50 4.00
2 Randy Breuer .75 2.00
3 Terry Cummings 2.00 5.00
4 Charlie Davis .75 2.00
5 Mike Dunleavy 1.50 4.00
6 Kenny Fields .75 2.00
7 Kevin Grevey .75 2.00
8 Craig Hodges 1.25 3.00
9 Alton Lister .75 2.00
10 Larry Micheaux SP 10.00 25.00
11 Paul Mokeski 1.25 3.00
12 Sidney Moncrief 2.50 6.00
13 Paul Pressey 1.25 3.00

1988-89 Bucks Green Border

COMPLETE SET (16) 12.50 30.00
1 Kareem Abdul-Jabbar 5.00 12.00
2 Randy Breuer .75 2.00
3 Terry Cummings 1.50 4.00
4 Jeff Grayer .75 2.00
5 Del Harris CO 1.25 3.00
6 Tito Horford .75 2.00
7 Jay Humphries 1.25 3.00
8 Larry Krystkowiak .75 2.00
9 Paul Mokeski .75 2.00
10 Sidney Moncrief 2.00 5.00
11 Ricky Pierce 1.25 3.00
12 Paul Pressey .75 2.00
13 Fred Roberts .75 2.00
14 Jack Sikma 1.50 4.00
15 The Bradley Center .75 2.00
16 Del Harris CO
Frank Hamblen ACO
Mack Calvin ACO
Mike Dunleavy ACO
Jeff Snedeker TR 1.00 2.50

1986 Bucks Lifebuoy/Star

COMPLETE SET (13) 6.00 15.00
1 Don Nelson CO 1.25 3.00
2 Randy Breuer .60 1.50
3 Terry Cummings 1.25 3.00
4 Charlie Davis .60 1.50
5 Kenny Fields .60 1.50
6 Craig Hodges .75 2.00
7 Jeff Lamp .75 2.00
8 Alton Lister .60 1.50
9 Paul Mokeski .75 2.00
10 Sidney Moncrief 1.50 4.00
11 Ricky Pierce .75 2.00
12 Paul Pressey .75 2.00
13 Jerry Reynolds .60 1.50

1973-74 Bucks Linnett

COMPLETE SET (6) 20.00 40.00
1 Kareem Abdul-Jabbar 12.50 25.00
2 Lucius Allen 1.50 4.00
3 Terry Driscoll 1.25 3.00
4 Russell Lee 1.25 3.00
5 Curtis Perry 1.25 3.00
6 Oscar Robertson 10.00 20.00

1974-75 Bucks Linnett

COMPLETE SET (10) 25.00 50.00
1 Kareem Abdul-Jabbar 12.50 25.00
2 Gary Brokaw 1.25 3.00
3 Bob Dandridge 1.50 4.00
4 Mickey Davis 1.00 2.50
5 Steve Kuberski 1.00 2.50
6 Jon McGlocklin 1.50 4.00
7 Jim Price 1.00 2.50
8 Kevin Restani 1.00 2.50
9 George Thompson 1.00 2.50
10 Cornell Warner 1.00 2.50

1976-77 Bucks Playing Cards

COMP.FACT SET (55) 30.00 80.00
C1 Bucks Logo .30 .75
C2 Brian Winters 1.25 3.00
C3 Lloyd Walton .30 .75
C4 Junior Bridgeman .75 2.00
C5 Alex English 5.00 12.00
C6 Quinn Buckner 1.25 3.00
C7 David Meyers .75 2.00
C8 Swen Nater .75 2.00
C9 Scott Lloyd .30 .75
C10 Bob Dandridge 1.00 2.50
C11 Kevin Restani .40 1.00
C12 Rowland Garrett .30 .75
C13 Fred Carter 1.25 3.00
D1 Bucks Logo .30 .75
D2 Fred Carter .75 2.00
D3 Rowland Garrett .30 .75
D4 Kevin Restani .40 1.00
D5 Bob Dandridge 1.00 2.50
D6 Scott Lloyd .30 .75
D7 Swen Nater .75 2.00
D8 David Meyers .75 2.00
D9 Quinn Buckner 1.25 3.00
D10 Alex English 5.00 12.00
D11 Junior Bridgeman 1.00 2.50
D12 Lloyd Walton .30 .75
D13 Brian Winters 1.00 2.50
H1 Bucks Logo .30 .75
H2 Fred Carter .60 1.50
H3 Rowland Garrett .30 .75
H4 Kevin Restani .40 1.00
H5 Bob Dandridge 1.00 2.50
H6 Scott Lloyd .30 .75
H7 Swen Nater .75 2.00
H8 David Meyers .75 2.00
H9 Quinn Buckner 1.25 3.00
H10 Alex English 5.00 12.00
H11 Junior Bridgeman 1.00 2.50
H12 Lloyd Walton .30 .75
H13 Brian Winters 1.25 3.00
S1 Bucks Logo .30 .75
S2 Brian Winters 1.25 3.00
S3 Lloyd Walton .30 .75
S4 Junior Bridgeman 1.00 2.50
S5 Alex English 5.00 12.00
S6 Quinn Buckner 1.25 3.00
S7 David Meyers .75 2.00
S8 Swen Nater .75 2.00
S9 Scott Lloyd .30 .75
S10 Bob Dandridge 1.00 2.50
S11 Kevin Restani .40 1.00
S12 Rowland Garrett .30 .75
S13 Fred Carter .75 2.00
NNO Bucks Logo
White Hen Pantry Ad .30 .75
NNO Don Nelson CO 2.50 6.00
NNO K.C. Jones ACO 2.00 5.00

1987-88 Bucks Polaroid

COMPLETE SET (16) 12.00 30.00
2 Junior Bridgeman 1.25 3.00
3 Pace Mannion .75 2.00
4 Sidney Moncrief 2.50 6.00
10 John Lucas 2.00 5.00
15 Craig Hodges 1.25 3.00
21 Conner Henry 1.00 2.50
25 Paul Pressey 1.25 3.00
34 Terry Cummings 2.00 5.00
35 Jerry Reynolds .75 2.00
42 Larry Krystkowiak 1.25 3.00
43 Jack Sikma 2.00 5.00
44 Paul Mokeski .75 2.00
45 Randy Breuer .75 2.00
54 John Stroeder .75 2.00
NNO Del Harris CO
Frank Hamblen ACO
Mack Calvin ACO
Mike Dunleavy ACO
Jeff Snedeker TR 1.25 3.00
NNO Title Card
(discount offer
detailed on back) 1.00 2.50

1979-80 Bucks Police/Spic'n'Span

COMPLETE SET (13) 40.00 100.00
2 Junior Bridgeman 3.00 8.00
4 Sidney Moncrief 15.00 40.00
6 Pat Cummings 2.00 5.00

7 Dave Meyers 3.00 8.00
8 Marques Johnson 8.00 20.00
11 Lloyd Walton 1.50 4.00
21 Quinn Buckner 2.50 6.00
31 Richard Washington 2.50 6.00
32 Brian Winters 3.00 8.00
42 Harvey Catchings 2.00 5.00
54 Kent Benson 2.50 6.00
NNO Don Nelson CO and
John Killilea ACO 5.00 12.00
NNO Coupon Card 10.00 25.00

1972-73 Bucks Ruler
1 Kareem Abdul-Jabbar
Jon McGlocklin
Curtis Perry
Dick Cunningham
Russell Lee
Oscar Robertson
Mickey Davis
Lucius Allen
Terry Driscoll
Bob Dandridge
Bill Bates TR
Hubie Brown ACO
Larry Costello CO 6.00 15.00

1970-71 Bucks Team Issue
COMPLETE SET (10) 25.00 60.00
1 Lew Alcindor 12.00 30.00
2 Lucius Allen 2.00 5.00
3 Bob Boozer 1.50 4.00
4 Larry Costello CO 1.25 3.00
5 Dick Cunningham .75 2.00
6 Bob Dandridge 2.00 5.00
7 Bob Greacen .75 2.00
8 Jon McGlocklin 1.50 4.00
9 Oscar Robertson 10.00 25.00
10 Greg Smith .75 2.00

1971-72 Bucks Team Issue
COMPLETE SET (12) 20.00 50.00
1 Kareem Abdul-Jabbar 10.00 25.00
2 Lucius Allen 1.50 4.00
3 John Block .75 2.00
4 Larry Costello CO 1.00 2.50
5 Bob Dandridge 1.50 4.00
6 Toby Kimball .75 2.00
7 Jon McGlocklin 1.25 3.00
8 McCoy McLemore .75 2.00
9 Barry Nelson .75 2.00
10 Oscar Robertson 8.00 20.00
11 Greg Smith .75 2.00
12 Jeff Webb .75 2.00

1992-93 Bullets Crown/Topps
COMPLETE SET (12) 2.50 6.00
WB1 Tom Gugliotta .75 2.00
WB2 Rex Chapman .30 .75
WB3 Phil Chenier .20 .50
WB4 Pervis Ellison .20 .50
WB5 Brent Price .20 .50
WB6 Wes Unseld .60 1.50
WB7 Michael Adams .20 .50
WB8 Harvey Grant .20 .50
WB9 Elvin Hayes 1.00 2.50
NNO Crown Gasoline Coupon 1 .08 .25
NNO Crown Gasoline Coupon 2 .08 .25
NNO Crown Gasoline Coupon 3 .08 .25

1954-55 Bullets Gunther Beer
COMPLETE SET (11) 2,000.00 3,500.00
1 Leo Barnhorst 150.00 300.00
2 Clair Bee CO 400.00 800.00
3 Bill Bolger 150.00 300.00
4 Ray Felix 250.00 500.00
5 Jim Fritsche 150.00 300.00
6 Rollen Hans 150.00 300.00
7 Paul Hoffman 200.00 400.00
8 Bob Houbregs 250.00 500.00
9 Ed Miller 150.00 300.00
10 Al Roges 150.00 300.00
11 Harold Uplinger 150.00 300.00

1995-96 Bullets Police
COMPLETE SET (6) 4.00 10.00
1 Calbert Cheaney .40 1.00
2 Juwan Howard .75 2.00
3 Gheorghe Muresan .40 1.00
4 Robert Pack .40 1.00
5 Rasheed Wallace 1.50 4.00
6 Chris Webber 2.50 6.00
NNO Hoops Mascot Card .40 1.00

1973-74 Bullets Standups
COMPLETE SET (12) 25.00 50.00
1 Phil Chenier 2.00 5.00
2 Archie Clark 2.00 5.00
3 Elvin Hayes 8.00 20.00
4 Tom Kozelko 1.25 3.00
5 Manny Leaks 1.25 3.00
6 Louie Nelson 1.25 3.00
7 Kevin Porter 1.50 4.00
8 Mike Riordan 1.50 4.00
9 Dave Stallworth 1.50 4.00
10 Wes Unseld 6.00 15.00
11 Nick Weatherspoon 1.25 3.00
12 Walt Wesley 1.25 3.00

1977-78 Bullets Standups
COMPLETE SET (11) 12.00 30.00
1 Greg Ballard .75 2.00
2 Phil Chenier 1.50 4.00
3 Bob Dandridge 1.25 3.00
4 Kevin Grevey 1.25 3.00
5 Elvin Hayes 6.00 15.00
6 Tom Henderson .75 2.00
7 Mitch Kupchak 1.50 4.00
8 Joe Pace .75 2.00
9 Wes Unseld 4.00 10.00
10 Phil Walker .75 2.00
11 Larry Wright .75 2.00

1964-65 Bullets Team Issue
COMPLETE SET (7) 60.00 150.00
1 Gary Bradds 8.00 20.00
2 Bob Ferry 10.00 25.00
3 Si Green 8.00 20.00
4 Les Hunter 8.00 20.00
5 Wally Jones 10.00 25.00
6 Kevin Loughery 12.00 30.00
7 Don Ohl 8.00 20.00

1968-69 Bullets Team Issue
COMPLETE SET (12) 125.00 300.00
1 Leroy Ellis 12.00 30.00
2 Bob Ferry 12.00 30.00
3 Gus Johnson 12.00 30.00
4 Kevin Loughery 12.00 30.00
5 Jack Marin 12.00 30.00
6 Earl Monroe 20.00 50.00
7 Barry Orms 12.00 30.00
8 Bob Quick 12.00 30.00
9 Ray Scott 12.00 30.00
10 Gene Shue 12.00 30.00
11 Wes Unseld 20.00 50.00
12 Tom Workman 12.00 30.00

1969-70 Bullets Team Issue
COMPLETE SET (12) 20.00 50.00
1 Mike Davis .75 2.00
2 Fred Carter 2.00 5.00
3 Leroy Ellis 1.25 3.00
4 Gus Johnson 2.00 5.00
5 Kevin Loughery 2.00 5.00
6 Ed Manning 1.25 3.00
7 Jack Marin .75 2.00
8 Earl Monroe 6.00 15.00
9 Bob Quick .75 2.00
10 Ray Scott .75 2.00
11 Gene Shue CO 2.00 5.00
12 Wes Unseld 5.00 12.00

1975-76 Bullets Team Issue
COMPLETE SET (11) 15.00 40.00
1 Dave Bing 2.50 6.00
2 Bernie Bickerstaff ACO 2.00 5.00
3 Clem Haskins 1.25 3.00
4 Elvin Hayes 6.00 15.00
5 Jimmy Jones .75 2.00
6 K.C. Jones CO 1.25 3.00
7 Tom Kozelko .75 2.00
8 Mike Riordan 1.00 2.50
9 Leonard Robinson 1.25 3.00
10 Nick Weatherspoon .75 2.00
11 Wes Unseld 2.50 6.00

1976-77 Bullets Team Issue
COMPLETE SET (15) 15.00 40.00
1 Bernie Bickerstaff ACO .75 2.00
2 Dave Bing 1.50 4.00
3 Phil Chenier 1.25 3.00
4 Leonard Gray .60 1.50
5 Kevin Grevey 1.25 3.00
6 Elvin Hayes 5.00 12.00
7 Jimmy Jones .60 1.50
8 Mitch Kupchak 1.50 4.00
9 Dick Motta CO .75 2.00
10 Joe Pace .60 1.50
11 Mike Riordan .75 2.00
12 Len Robinson .75 2.00
13 Wes Unseld 2.00 5.00
14 Bob Weiss .75 2.00
15 Larry Wright .60 1.50

1977-78 Bullets Team Issue 5x7
COMPLETE SET (12) 15.00 40.00
1 Greg Ballard 1.25 3.00
2 Bernie Bickerstaff ACO 1.25 3.00
3 Phil Chenier 1.50 4.00
4 Bob Dandridge 2.00 5.00
5 Elvin Hayes 2.50 6.00
6 Tom Henderson 1.25 3.00
7 Mitch Kupchak 1.25 3.00
8 Dick Motta CO 1.50 4.00
9 Joe Pace 1.25 3.00
10 Wes Unseld 2.00 5.00
11 Phil Walker 1.25 3.00
12 Larry Wright 1.25 3.00

1977-78 Bullets Team Issue
COMPLETE SET (13) 12.00 30.00
1 Greg Ballard .75 2.00
2 Dave Corzine .75 2.00
3 Bob Dandridge 1.00 2.50
4 Kevin Grevey 1.00 2.50
5 Elvin Hayes 2.50 6.00
6 Tom Henderson .75 2.00
7 Charles Johnson .75 2.00
8 Mitch Kupchak 1.00 2.50
9 Dick Motta CO 1.00 2.50
10 Roger Phegley .75 2.00
11 Wes Unseld 2.00 5.00
12 Larry Wright .75 2.00
13 Bernie Bickerstaff ACO
John Lally TR 1.00 2.50

1989-90 Bulls Dairy Council
COMPLETE SET (6) 75.00 150.00
1 Bill Cartwright
(Milk is Good for Snacks) 2.50 6.00
2 Horace Grant
(Milk is Good for Teeth) 3.00 8.00
3 Michael Jordan
(Milk is Good for Breakfast) 50.00 120.00
4 Stacey King
(Milk is Good for Skin) 1.50 4.00
5 John Paxson
(Milk is Good for Bones) 3.00 8.00
6 Scottie Pippen
(Milk is Good for Eyes) 12.00 30.00

1987-88 Bulls Entenmann's
COMPLETE SET (12) 300.00 600.00
2 Rory Sparrow .75 2.00
3 Sedale Threatt 1.25 2.50
5 John Paxson 2.00 5.00
6 Brad Sellers .75 2.00
17 Mike Brown 1.50 4.00
23 Michael Jordan 150.00 400.00
31 Granville Waiters 1.25 3.00
33 Scottie Pippen 75.00 200.00
34 Charles Oakley 1.50 4.00
40 Dave Corzine .75 2.00
54 Horace Grant 4.00 10.00
NNO Doug Collins CO 3.00 8.00

1988-89 Bulls Entenmann's
COMPLETE SET (12) 125.00 300.00
2 Brad Sellers .75 2.00
5 John Paxson 1.50 4.00
11 Sam Vincent .75 2.00
14 Craig Hodges .75 2.00
15 Jack Haley .75 2.00
22 Charles Davis .75 2.00
23 Michael Jordan 100.00 250.00
24 Bill Cartwright 1.50 4.00
32 Will Perdue .75 2.00
33 Scottie Pippen 20.00 50.00
40 Dave Corzine .75 2.00
54 Horace Grant 2.00 5.00

1989-90 Bulls Equal
COMPLETE SET (12) 6.00 15.00
1 B.J. Armstrong .75 2.00
2 Bill Cartwright .60 1.50
3 Charles Davis .30 .75
4 Horace Grant 1.00 2.50
5 Craig Hodges .40 1.00
6 Michael Jordan 3.00 8.00
7 Stacey King .60 1.50
8 Ed Nealy .30 .75
9 John Paxson .75 2.00
10 Will Perdue .40 1.00
11 Scottie Pippen 1.50 4.00
12 Jeff Sanders .30 .75

1990-91 Bulls Equal/Star
COMPLETE SET (16) 5.00 12.00
2 Tom Boerwinkle .20 .50
3 Bob Boozer .20 .50
4 Bill Cartwright .30 .75
5 Artis Gilmore .40 1.00
6 Horace Grant .40 1.00
7 Phil Jackson CO .40 1.00
8 Johnny Kerr .40 1.00
9 Bob Love .40 1.00
10 Dick Motta CO .20 .50
11 John Paxson .40 1.00
12 Scottie Pippen .75 2.00
13 Guy Rodgers .20 .50
14 Jerry Sloan .60 1.50
15 Norm Van Lier .20 .50
16 Chet Walker .40 1.00
1 Michael Jordan 1.50 4.00

1970-71 Bulls Hawthorne Milk
COMPLETE SET (6) 1,000.00 2,000.00
1 Bob Love 200.00 500.00
2 Jerry Sloan 200.00 500.00
3 Jerry Sloan 200.00 500.00
4 Chet Walker 125.00 300.00
5 Bob Weiss 100.00 250.00
6 Bob Weiss 100.00 250.00

1985 Bulls Interlake
COMPLETE SET (2) 500.00 1,000.00
1 Michael Jordan 1,500.00 3,000.00
2 Orlando Woolridge 10.00 25.00

1969-70 Bulls Pepsi
COMPLETE SET (13) 60.00 150.00
1 Tom Boerwinkle 5.00 12.00
2 Shaler Halimon 2.50 6.00
3 Clem Haskins 4.00 10.00
4 Bob Kauffman 2.50 6.00
5 Bob Love 15.00 40.00
6 Ed Manning 3.00 8.00
7 Dick Motta CO 4.00 10.00
8 Loy Petersen 2.50 6.00
9 Jerry Sloan 15.00 40.00
10 Al Tucker 2.50 6.00
11 Chet Walker 10.00 25.00
12 Bob Weiss 5.00 12.00
13 Walt Wesley 3.00 8.00

1979-80 Bulls Police
COMPLETE SET (16) 30.00 80.00
1 Delmer Beshore .75 2.00
13 Dwight Jones .75 2.00
15 John Mengelt .75 2.00
17 Scott May 1.25 3.00
20 Dennis Awtrey 1.00 2.50
24 Reggie Theus SP 15.00 40.00
26 Coby Dietrick SP 6.00 15.00
27 Ollie Johnson .75 2.00
28 Sam Smith .75 2.00
34 David Greenwood 2.00 5.00
40 Ricky Sobers 1.25 3.00
53 Artis Gilmore 2.50 6.00
54 Mark Landsberger 1.25 3.00
NNO Jerry Sloan CO 2.50 6.00
NNO Phil Johnson ACO 1.25 3.00
NNO Luv-A-Bull .75 2.00

1976-77 Bulls Team Issue
COMPLETE SET (17) 12.00 30.00
1 Ed Badger CO 1.00 2.50
2 Leon Benbow .75 2.00
3 Tom Boerwinkle .75 2.00
4 Eric Fernsten .75 2.00
5 Mickey Johnson .75 2.00
6 Tom Kropp .75 2.00
7 John Laskowski .75 2.00
8 Bob Love 1.25 3.00
9 Jack Marin 1.00 2.50
10 Scott May 1.00 2.50
11 Cliff Pondexter .75 2.00
12 Jerry Sloan 1.25 3.00
13 Willie Smith .75 2.00
14 Keith Starr .75 2.00
15 Norm Van Lier 1.00 2.50
16 Bob Wilson .75 2.00
17 Doug Atkinson TR
Gene Tormohlen ACO .75 2.00

1985-86 Bulls Team Issue
COMPLETE SET (2)
2 Stan Albeck CO
Murray Arnold ACO
Gene Banks
Dave Corzine
George Gervin
Jerry Krause GM
Mike Thibault ACO
Tex Winter ACO 4.00 10.00

2008-09 Bulls Upper Deck
COMPLETE SET (14) 8.00 20.00
1 Luol Deng .25 .60
2 Ben Gordon .25 .60
3 Kirk Hinrich .25 .60
4 Drew Gooden .25 .60
5 Larry Hughes .25 .60
6 Andres Nocioni .20 .50
7 Thabo Sefolosha .20 .50
8 Joakim Noah .20 .50
9 Tyrus Thomas .20 .50
10 Aaron Gray .20 .50
11 Cedric Simmons .20 .50
12 Derrick Rose 6.00 15.00
13 Vinny Del Negro CO .20 .50
14 Michael Jordan 2.50 6.00

1977-78 Bulls White Hen Pantry
COMPLETE SET (7) 5.00 12.00
1 Tom Boerwinkle .75 2.00
2 Artis Gilmore 2.00 5.00
3 Wilbur Holland .60 1.50
4 Mickey Johnson .75 2.00
5 Scott May 1.00 2.50
6 John Mengelt .60 1.50
7 Norm Van Lier 1.00 2.50

1992 Canadian Kraft Olympic 3D
COMPLETE SET (10) 2.00 5.00
1 Basketball .40 1.00

1989 CAO Muflon Yugoslavian
COMPLETE SET (73) 4,000.00 5,200.00
1 Magic Johnson
Pat Riley 12.00 30.00
2 Mitch Richmond 6.00 15.00
3 Mark Jackson 3.00 8.00
4 Moses Malone 3.00 8.00
5 Mark Price 2.00 5.00
6 Vern Fleming 1.25 3.00
7 Spud Webb 2.50 6.00
8 Rumeal Robinson 1.25 3.00
9 Lionel Simmons 1.25 3.00
10 John Stockton 15.00 40.00
11 Michael Adams 1.25 3.00
12 Fat Lever 1.25 3.00
13 Muggsy Bogues 3.00 8.00
14 Maurice Cheeks 2.50 6.00
15 Kenny Smith
Jordan in background 25.00 60.00
16 Larry Bird
James Worthy 15.00 40.00
17 Gerald Wilkins 1.25 3.00
18 Rolando Blackman 1.25 3.00
19 Arijan Komazec 1.25 3.00
20 Kevin Johnson 2.00 5.00
21 Zoran Radovic 1.25 3.00
22 Sarunas Marcillonis 2.50 6.00
23 Mario Primorac 1.25 3.00
24 Clyde Drexler 15.00 40.00
25 Jure Zdovc 1.25 3.00
26 Drazen Petrovic 15.00 40.00
27 Predrag Danilovic 1.50 4.00
28 Dale Ellis 1.50 4.00
29 John Battle 1.25 3.00
30 Nikos Galis 2.50 6.00
31 Antdanelo Riva 1.50 4.00
32 Toni Kukoc 6.00 15.00
33 Zoran Cutura 1.25 3.00
34 Kevin McHale 6.00 15.00
35 Valdemar Homicus 1.25 3.00
36 Charles Barkley 15.00 40.00
37 Detlef Schrempf 2.00 5.00
38 Larry Nance 2.50 6.00
39 Danny Manning 3.00 8.00
40 Mark Aguirre
Magic Johnson 8.00 20.00
41 Chris Mullin
Kevin McHale 6.00 15.00
42 Chuck Person 1.25 3.00
43 A.C. Green
Bill Laimbeer 3.00 8.00
44 Dominique Wilkins 10.00 25.00
45 Jack Sikma 1.25 3.00
46 James Worthy
Larry Bird 15.00 40.00
47 Otis Thorpe 1.25 3.00
48 Adrian Dantley
Larry Bird 15.00 40.00
49 Karl Malone 10.00 25.00
50 Alex English 2.50 6.00
51 Terry Cummings 1.25 3.00
52 Willie Anderson 1.25 3.00
53 Zarko Paspalj 2.00 5.00
54 Robert Parish 3.00 8.00
55 Patrick Ewing 6.00 15.00
56 Dusko Ivanovic 1.25 3.00
57 Pat Cummings 1.25 3.00
58 Bill Laimbeer 3.00 8.00
59 Craig Hodges 1.25 3.00
60 Moses Malone 3.00 8.00
61 Hakeem Olajuwon
Karl Malone 10.00 25.00
62 Julius Erving 20.00 50.00
63 Kareem Abdul-Jabbar 8.00 20.00
64 Manute Bol 3.00 8.00
65 Stefan Ostrowski 1.25 3.00
66 San Epifanio 1.25 3.00
67 Arvydas Sabonis 8.00 20.00
68 Dino Radja 2.50 6.00
69 Isiah Thomas 6.00 15.00
70 Vlade Divac 4.00 10.00
72 Michael Jordan 3,000.00 5,000.00
73 Magic Johnson 20.00 50.00

1975 Carvel Discs Blue
COMPLETE SET (36) 40.00 80.00
NNO Kareem Abdul-Jabbar 4.00 10.00
NNO Nate Archibald 2.00 5.00
NNO Bill Bradley 2.00 5.00
NNO Don Chaney 1.25 3.00
NNO Dave Cowens 2.00 5.00
NNO Bob Dandridge 1.00 2.50
NNO Ernie DiGregorio 1.25 3.00
NNO Walt Frazier 2.00 5.00
NNO John Gianelli .75 2.00
NNO Gail Goodrich 2.00 5.00
NNO Happy Hairston 1.25 3.00
NNO John Havlicek 3.00 8.00
NNO Spencer Haywood 1.25 3.00
NNO Garfield Heard .75 2.00
NNO Lou Hudson 1.00 2.50
NNO Phil Jackson 2.00 5.00
NNO Sam Lacey .75 2.00
NNO Bob Lanier 2.00 5.00
NNO Bob Love 1.50 4.00
NNO Bob McAdoo 2.00 5.00
NNO Jim McMillian 1.25 3.00
NNO Dean Meminger .75 2.00
NNO Earl Monroe 2.00 5.00
NNO Don Nelson 1.50 4.00
NNO Jim Price .75 2.00
NNO Clifford Ray .75 2.00
NNO Charlie Scott 1.00 2.50
NNO Paul Silas 1.50 4.00
NNO Jerry Sloan 2.00 5.00
NNO Randy Smith 1.25 3.00
NNO Dick Van Arsdale 1.25 3.00
NNO Norm Van Lier 1.25 3.00
NNO Chet Walker 1.25 3.00
NNO Paul Westphal 2.00 5.00
NNO Jo Jo White 1.25 3.00
NNO Hawthorne Wingo .75 2.00

1993-94 Cavaliers Nickles Bread
COMPLETE SET (13) 6.00 15.00
1 John Battle .40 1.00
2 Terrell Brandon .75 2.00
3 Brad Daugherty .40 1.00
4 Danny Ferry .40 1.00
5 Jay Guidinger .40 1.00
6 Tyrone Hill .40 1.00
7 Gerald Madkins .40 1.00
8 Chris Mills .60 1.50
9 Larry Nance .75 2.00
10 Bobby Phills .40 1.00
11 Mark Price .75 2.00
12 Gerald Wilkins .50 1.25
13 John Williams .40 1.00

1973-74 Cavaliers Postcards
COMPLETE SET (8) 15.00 40.00
1 Lenny Wilkens CO 2.50 6.00
2 Austin Carr 1.50 4.00
3 Barry Clemens 1.25 3.00
4 Bobby Smith 1.25 3.00
5 Jim Brewer 1.25 3.00
6 Dwight Davis 1.25 3.00
7 Steve Patterson 1.25 3.00
8 Fred Foster 1.25 3.00
9 Jim Cleamons 1.50 4.00
10 Luke Witte 1.25 3.00
11 Bob Rule 1.25 3.00
12 John Warren 1.25 3.00

1976 Cavaliers Royal Crown Cola Cans
COMPLETE SET (7) 15.00 40.00
1 Jim Brewer 2.00 5.00
2 Austin Carr 3.00 8.00
3 Bill Fitch CO 2.50 6.00
4 Jim Chones 2.50 6.00
5 Jim Cleamons 2.50 6.00
6 Dick Snyder
with autograph 2.00 5.00
6A Dick Snyder
without autograph 2.00 5.00
7 Bingo Smith 2.50 6.00

1980-81 Cavaliers Team Issue
COMPLETE SET (10) 15.00 30.00
1 Kenny Carr 1.25 3.00
2 Mack Calvin 1.50 4.00
3 Mike Bratz 1.25 3.00
4 Geoff Huston 1.25 3.00
5 Walter Jordan 1.25 3.00
6 Bill Laimbeer 2.50 6.00
7 Don Ford 1.25 3.00
8 Mike Mitchell 1.50 4.00
9 Roger Phegley 1.25 3.00
10 Randy Smith 1.50 4.00

2008-09 Cavaliers Upper Deck
COMPLETE SET (14) 2.50 6.00
1 LeBron James 2.50 6.00
2 Delonte West .20 .50
3 Daniel Gibson .20 .50
4 Zydrunas Ilgauskas .25 .60
5 Anderson Varejao .20 .50
6 Ben Wallace .40 1.00
7 Aleksandar Pavlovic .20 .50
8 Lorenzen Wright .20 .50
9 Wally Szczerbiak .25 .60
10 Eric Snow .20 .50
11 Mo Williams .25 .60
12 J.J. Hickson .20 .50
13 Mike Brown CO .20 .50
14 Mark Price .50 1.25

2008-09 Cavaliers Upper Deck LeBron James
COMPLETE SET (10) 8.00 20.00
COMMON CARD 1.25 3.00

2007 Cavaliers Upper Deck Rite Aid
COMPLETE SET (16) 5.00 12.00
1 Shannon Brown .60 1.50
2 Daniel Gibson .40 1.00
3 Drew Gooden .40 1.00
4 Larry Hughes .60 1.50
5 Zydrunas Ilgauskas .60 1.50
6 LeBron James 3.00 8.00
7 Damon Jones .40 1.00
8 Dwayne Jones .40 1.00
9 Donyell Marshall .40 1.00
10 Ira Newble .40 1.00
11 Aleksandar Pavlovic .40 1.00
12 Scot Pollard .40 1.00
13 Eric Snow .40 1.00
14 Anderson Varejao .60 1.50
15 David Wesley .40 1.00
16 Mike Brown .40 1.00

1977-78 Celtics Citgo
COMPLETE SET (17) 40.00 75.00
1 Dave Bing 2.50 6.00
2 Tommy Boswell 1.25 3.00
3 Don Chaney 2.00 5.00
4 Dave Cowens 3.00 8.00
5 Dave Cowens 3.00 8.00
6 Dave Cowens 3.00 8.00
7 John Havlicek 7.50 15.00
8 Sam Jones 2.50 6.00
9 Cedric Maxwell 1.50 4.00
10 Curtis Rowe 1.25 3.00
11 Tom Sanders CO 1.50 4.00
12 Fred Saunders 1.25 3.00
13 Kevin Stacom 1.25 3.00
14 Kermit Washington 1.25 3.00
15 Jo Jo White 2.50 6.00
16 Sidney Wicks 2.50 6.00
17 Ballboy Contest 1.25 3.00

1988-89 Celtics Citgo
COMPLETE SET (7) 20.00 50.00
1 Danny Ainge 3.00 8.00
2 Larry Bird 8.00 20.00
3 Dennis Johnson 3.00 8.00
4 Reggie Lewis 2.00 5.00
5 Kevin McHale 4.00 10.00
6 Robert Parish 2.50 6.00
7 Team Picture 3.00 8.00

1989-90 Celtics Citgo Posters
COMPLETE SET (6) 10.00 25.00
1 Bob Cousy 3.00 8.00
1 Dave Cowens 2.50 6.00
2 Tom Heinsohn 2.50 6.00
3 Sam Jones 2.50 6.00
4 Tom Sanders 1.25 3.00
5 Paul Silas 1.50 4.00

1986 Celtics Cups
COMPLETE SET (4) 8.00 20.00
1 Dennis Johnson
Greg Kite 1.25 3.00
2 Bill Walton
Jerry Sichting 2.00 5.00
3 Larry Bird
Danny Ainge 4.00 10.00
4 Robert Parish
Kevin McHale 2.50 6.00

1974-75 Celtics Linnett
COMPLETE SET (9) 30.00 60.00
1 Don Chaney 2.50 6.00
2 Dave Cowens 7.50 15.00
3 Steve Downing 2.00 5.00
4 Henry Finkel 2.50 6.00
5 Phil Hankinson 2.00 5.00
6 John Havlicek 10.00 20.00
7 Don Nelson 5.00 10.00
8 Paul Silas 3.00 8.00
9 Jo Jo White 3.00 8.00

1975-76 Celtics Linnett Green Borders
COMPLETE SET (3) 8.00 20.00
1 Dave Cowens 3.00 8.00
2 John Havlicek 4.00 10.00
3 Jo Jo White 2.50 6.00

1956-57 Celtics Photos
COMPLETE SET (10) 1,000.00 2,000.00
1 Bob Cousy 250.00 500.00
2 Tom Heinsohn 200.00 400.00
3 Dick Hemric 75.00 150.00
4 Jim Loscutoff 100.00 200.00
5 Jack Nichols 75.00 150.00
6 Togo Palazzi 75.00 150.00
7 Andy Phillip 100.00 200.00
8 Arnie Risen 100.00 200.00
9 Bill Sharman 150.00 300.00
10 Lou Tsioropoulos 75.00 150.00

1976-77 Celtics Team Issue
COMPLETE SET (12) 15.00 30.00
1 Jerome Anderson .75 2.00
2 Jim Ard .75 2.00
3 Tom Boswell .75 2.00
4 Norm Cook .75 2.00
5 John Havlicek 3.00 8.00
6 Steve Kuberski .75 2.00
7 Glenn McDonald .75 2.00
8 Curtis Rowe 1.00 2.50
9 Fred Saunders .75 2.00
10 Paul Silas 1.50 4.00
11 Kevin Stacom .75 2.00
12 Sidney Wicks 1.00 2.50

2001-02 Celtics Topps
COMPLETE SET (10) 2.50 6.00
BC1 Antoine Walker .50 1.25
BC2 Paul Pierce 1.00 2.50
BC3 Kenny Anderson .50 1.25
BC4 Bryant Stith .40 1.00
BC5 Vitaly Potapenko .40 1.00
BC6 Eric Williams .40 1.00
BC7 Mark Blount .40 1.00
BC8 Tony Battie .40 1.00
BC9 Jerome Moiso .40 1.00
BC10 Randy Brown .40 1.00

1994-95 Celtics Tribute
COMPLETE SET (8) 8.00 20.00
1 Red Auerbach CO 2.00 5.00
2 Larry Bird 3.00 8.00
3 Bob Cousy 1.50 4.00
4 Dave Cowens 1.25 3.00
5 John Havlicek 1.50 4.00
6 Tom Heinsohn 1.25 3.00
7 K.C. Jones 1.25 3.00
8 Kevin McHale 1.50 4.00

2008-09 Celtics Upper Deck
COMPLETE SET (14) 2.50 6.00
1 Paul Pierce .50 1.25
2 Kevin Garnett .75 2.00
3 Ray Allen .50 1.25
4 Rajon Rondo .40 1.00
5 Kendrick Perkins .20 .50
6 Leon Powe .20 .50
7 Glen Davis .20 .50
8 Sam Cassell .25 .60
9 Patrick O'Bryant .20 .50
10 Eddie House .20 .50
11 Gabe Pruitt .20 .50
12 J.R. Giddens .20 .50
13 Doc Rivers CO .30 .75
14 Larry Bird 1.00 2.50

1992-93 Center Court
COMPLETE SET (53) 12.00 30.00
COMPLETE SERIES 1 (26) 6.00 15.00
COMPLETE SERIES 2 (27) 6.00 15.00
1 George Mikan 1.50 4.00
2 Bill Bradley .75 2.00
3 Bobby Wanzer .60 1.50
4 Ed Macauley .75 2.00
5 Harry Gallatin .75 2.00
6 William (Pop) Gates .75 2.00
7 Bobby Knight CO 5.00 12.00
8 Dolph Schayes .75 2.00
9 Bob Pettit 1.25 3.00
10 Walt Frazier .75 2.00
11 Elvin Hayes .75 2.00
12 Paul Arizin .75 2.00
13 Forrest (Phog) Allen CO .75 2.00
14 Oscar Robertson 1.25 3.00
15 John Wooden CO 1.25 3.00
16 Red Holzman CO 1.25 3.00
17 Jack Twyman .75 2.00
18 Dean Smith CO 1.25 3.00
19 John Nucatola .60 1.50
20 Elgin Baylor 1.00 2.50
21 Dave Bing .60 1.50
22 Lester Harrison .60 1.50
23 Joe Lapchick .60 1.50
24 Rick Barry .75 2.00
25 Lou Carnesecca CO .75 2.00
26 Checklist Card .75 2.00
27 Red Auerbach 1.25 3.00
28 Dave DeBusschere .75 2.00
29 Clarence Gaines .60 1.50
30 Tom Gola .75 2.00
31 Hal Greer .75 2.00
32 Lusia Harris-Stewart .75 2.00
33 K.C. Jones .75 2.00
34 Sam Jones 1.00 2.50
35 Robert Davies .60 1.50
36 Harry Litwack .60 1.50
37 Clyde Lovellette .75 2.00
38 Slater Martin .75 2.00
39 Al McGuire .75 2.00
40 Ray Meyer .75 2.00
41 Earl Monroe .75 2.00
42 Andy Phillip .75 2.00
43 Jim Pollard .75 2.00
44 Bill Sharman 1.25 3.00
45 J.Dallas Shirley .60 1.50
46 Nate Thurmond .75 2.00
47 Stan Walts .60 1.50
48 Bobby McDermott .60 1.50
49 Clair Bee .60 1.50
50 Willis Reed .75 2.00
51 Larry O'Brien .60 1.50
52 Checklist Card .60 1.50
PD1 George Mikan 1.50 4.00
NNO Elgin Baylor PROMO .60 1.50

2009-10 Certified
COMP.SET w/o SPs (150) 50.00 100.00
151-170 PRINT RUN 500 SER.#'d SETS
171-200 RC PRINT RUN 399 SER.#'d SETS
1 Dirk Nowitzki 2.00 5.00
2 Jason Kidd 1.25 3.00
3 Jason Terry .60 1.50
4 J.J. Barea .75 2.00
5 Josh Howard .60 1.50
6 Shawn Marion .75 2.00
7 Luis Scola .60 1.50
8 Shane Battier .75 2.00
9 Tracy McGrady 1.50 4.00
10 Trevor Ariza .50 1.25
11 Yao Ming 2.00 5.00
12 Allen Iverson 1.50 4.00
13 Marc Gasol .75 2.00
14 O.J. Mayo .50 1.25
15 Rudy Gay .75 2.00
16 Zach Randolph .75 2.00
17 Chris Paul 1.50 4.00
18 David West .60 1.50
19 Emeka Okafor .60 1.50
20 James Posey .50 1.25
21 Peja Stojakovic .60 1.50
22 Manu Ginobili 1.50 4.00
23 Michael Finley .75 2.00
24 Richard Jefferson .60 1.50
25 Tim Duncan 2.00 5.00
26 Tony Parker 1.25 3.00
27 Carmelo Anthony 1.25 3.00
28 Chauncey Billups 1.00 2.50
29 Chris Andersen .75 2.00
30 J.R. Smith .75 2.00
31 Kenyon Martin .60 1.50
32 Nene .60 1.50
33 Al Jefferson .50 1.25
34 Kevin Love .75 2.00
35 Ramon Sessions .50 1.25
36 Ryan Gomes .50 1.25
37 Andre Miller .75 2.00
38 Brandon Roy 1.00 2.50
39 Greg Oden .60 1.50
40 LaMarcus Aldridge .75 2.00
41 Rudy Fernandez .50 1.25
42 Jeff Green .60 1.50
43 Kevin Durant 3.00 8.00
44 Nick Collison .50 1.25
45 Russell Westbrook 1.50 4.00
46 Andrei Kirilenko .60 1.50
47 Carlos Boozer .60 1.50
48 Deron Williams .60 1.50
49 Mehmet Okur .50 1.25
50 Paul Millsap .60 1.50
51 Andris Biedrins .50 1.25
52 Anthony Randolph .50 1.25
53 Corey Maggette .50 1.25
54 Devean George .50 1.25
55 Kelenna Azubuike .50 1.25
56 Stephen Jackson .60 1.50
57 Al Thornton .50 1.25
58 Baron Davis .60 1.50
59 Chris Kaman .60 1.50
60 Eric Gordon .60 1.50
61 Marcus Camby .60 1.50
62 Andrew Bynum .50 1.25
63 Derek Fisher .75 2.00
64 Kobe Bryant 6.00 15.00
65 Lamar Odom .60 1.50
66 Luke Walton .60 1.50
67 Pau Gasol 1.25 3.00
68 Ron Artest .75 2.00
69 Amare Stoudemire .60 1.50
70 Grant Hill 1.25 3.00
71 Jason Richardson .75 2.00
72 Leandro Barbosa .60 1.50
73 Steve Nash 1.50 4.00
74 Andres Nocioni .50 1.25
75 Francisco Garcia .50 1.25
76 Kevin Martin .60 1.50
77 Sean May .50 1.25
78 Kevin Garnett 2.00 5.00
79 Paul Pierce 1.25 3.00
80 Rajon Rondo 1.00 2.50

81 Fasheed Wallace 1.00 2.50
82 Ray Allen 1.25 3.00
83 Brook Lopez .75 2.00
84 Courtney Lee .50 1.25
85 Devin Harris .50 1.25
86 Yi Jianlian 1.00 2.50
87 Al Harrington .60 1.50
88 Chris Duhon .50 1.25
89 Danilo Gallinari .60 1.50
90 Darko Milicic .50 1.25
91 David Lee .50 1.25
92 Nate Robinson .60 1.50
93 Andre Iguodala .75 2.00
94 Elton Brand .60 1.50
95 Samuel Dalembert .50 1.25
96 Thaddeus Young .50 1.25
97 Andrea Bargnani .50 1.25
98 Chris Bosh 1.00 2.50
99 Hedo Turkoglu .60 1.50
100 Jarrett Jack .60 1.50
101 Jose Calderon .50 1.25
102 Derrick Rose 1.25 3.00
103 Joakim Noah .50 1.25
104 Luol Deng .60 1.50
105 Tyrus Thomas .50 1.25
106 Anderson Varejao .50 1.25
107 LeBron James 6.00 15.00
108 Mo Williams .60 1.50
109 Shaquille O'Neal 2.50 6.00
110 Zydrunas Ilgauskas .60 1.50
111 Ben Gordon .60 1.50
112 Ben Wallace 1.00 2.50
113 Charlie Villanueva .50 1.25
114 Richard Hamilton .75 2.00
115 Rodney Stuckey .50 1.25
116 Tayshaun Prince .75 2.00
117 Danny Granger .50 1.25
118 Jeff Foster .50 1.25
119 T.J. Ford .50 1.25
120 Troy Murphy .50 1.25
121 Andrew Bogut .60 1.50
122 Hakim Warrick .50 1.25
123 Luke Ridnour .60 1.50
124 Michael Redd .60 1.50
125 Al Horford .75 2.00
126 Jamal Crawford .75 2.00
127 Joe Johnson .75 2.00
128 Josh Smith .50 1.25
129 Mike Bibby .75 2.00
130 Boris Diaw .60 1.50
131 D.J. Augustin .50 1.25
132 Gerald Wallace .60 1.50
133 Raja Bell .60 1.50
134 Raymond Felton .50 1.25
135 Tyson Chandler .60 1.50
136 Dwyane Wade 1.50 4.00
137 Jermaine O'Neal .75 2.00
138 Mario Chalmers .60 1.50
139 Michael Beasley .50 1.25
140 Quentin Richardson .50 1.25
141 Udonis Haslem .50 1.25
142 Dwight Howard 1.00 2.50
143 J.J. Redick .75 2.00
144 Jameer Nelson .50 1.25
145 Mickael Pietrus .50 1.25
146 Rashard Lewis .60 1.50
147 Antawn Jamison .60 1.50
148 Caron Butler .60 1.50
149 Gilbert Arenas .60 1.50
150 Randy Foye .50 1.25
151 Isiah Thomas 1.50 4.00
152 Byron Scott 1.25 3.00
153 Frank Ramsey 1.50 4.00
154 Dikembe Mutombo 2.50 6.00
155 Alonzo Mourning 2.50 6.00
156 John Starks 1.25 3.00
157 Adrian Dantley 1.25 3.00
158 Bailey Howell 1.50 4.00
159 Al Attles 1.25 3.00
160 Walt Frazier 2.50 6.00
161 Tim Hardaway 1.50 4.00
162 Pat Riley 1.50 4.00
163 Paul Westphal 1.50 4.00
164 Bill Walton 2.50 6.00
165 Jack Sikma 1.25 3.00
166 Magic Johnson 6.00 15.00
167 Spud Webb 1.25 3.00
168 Wilt Chamberlain 6.00 15.00
169 Wes Unseld 1.50 4.00
170 James Worthy 2.00 5.00
171 Blake Griffin JSY AU RC 40.00 100.00
172 Hasheem Thabeet JSY AU RC 3.00 8.00
173 James Harden JSY AU RC 200.00 500.00
174 Tyreke Evans JSY AU RC 4.00 10.00
175 Jonny Flynn JSY AU RC 3.00 8.00
176 Stephen Curry JSY AU RC 1,500.00 3,000.00
177 Jordan Hill JSY AU RC 3.00 8.00
178 Brandon Jennings JSY AU RC 5.00 12.00
179 T.Williams JSY AU RC 3.00 8.00
180 Henderson JSY AU RC 3.00 8.00
181 Tyler Hansbrough JSY AU RC 4.00 10.00
182 Earl Clark JSY AU RC 3.00 8.00
183 Austin Daye JSY AU RC 3.00 8.00
184 James Johnson JSY AU RC 4.00 10.00
185 Jrue Holiday JSY AU RC 15.00 40.00
186 Ty Lawson JSY AU RC 4.00 10.00
187 Jeff Teague JSY AU RC 4.00 10.00
188 Eric Maynor JSY AU RC 3.00 8.00
189 Darren Collison JSY AU RC 5.00 12.00
190 Omri Casspi JSY AU RC 3.00 8.00
191 B.J. Mullens JSY AU RC 3.00 8.00
192 Rodrigue Beaubois JSY AU RC 3.00 8.00
193 Taj Gibson JSY AU RC 4.00 10.00
194 DeMarre Carroll JSY AU RC 4.00 10.00
195 Wayne Ellington JSY AU RC 4.00 10.00
196 Toney Douglas JSY AU RC 3.00 8.00
197 Jeff Pendergraph JSY AU RC 3.00 8.00
198 Jermaine Taylor JSY AU RC 3.00 8.00
199 DeJuan Blair JSY AU RC 4.00 10.00
200 Jodie Meeks JSY AU RC 3.00 8.00

2009-10 Certified Mirror Blue

*BLUE 1-150: 1X TO 2.5X BASE HI
*BLUE 151-170: .6X TO 1.5X BASE HI
BLUE 1-170 PRINT RUN 100 SER.#'d SETS
*BLUE RC 171-200: .6X TO 1.5X BASE HI
BLUE RC PRINT RUN 50 SER.#'d SETS
107 LeBron James 25.00 60.00
171 Blake Griffin JSY AU 75.00 200.00
173 James Harden JSY AU 600.00 1,200.00
176 Stephen Curry JSY AU 2,500.00 5,000.00

2009-10 Certified Mirror Blue Materials

STATED PRINT RUN 10 TO 50 SER.#'d SETS
1 Dirk Nowitzki/50 10.00 25.00
2 Jason Kidd/50 6.00 15.00
3 Jason Terry/50 3.00 8.00
4 J.J. Barea/50 10.00 25.00
5 Josh Howard/50 3.00 8.00
6 Shawn Marion/50 4.00 10.00
7 Luis Scola/50 3.00 8.00
8 Shane Battier/50 4.00 10.00
9 Tracy McGrady/50 8.00 20.00
11 Yao Ming/25 10.00 25.00
14 O.J. Mayo/25 2.50 6.00
17 Chris Paul/50 8.00 20.00
18 David West/50 3.00 8.00
25 Tim Duncan/50 10.00 25.00
27 Carmelo Anthony/50 6.00 15.00
28 Chauncey Billups/25 5.00 12.00
29 Chris Andersen/25 4.00 10.00
31 Kenyon Martin/50 3.00 8.00
32 Nene/25 3.00 8.00
33 Al Jefferson/50 2.50 6.00
34 Kevin Love/50 4.00 10.00
36 Ryan Gomes/25 2.50 6.00
38 Brandon Roy/50 5.00 12.00
39 Greg Oden/50 2.50 6.00
40 LaMarcus Aldridge/25 4.00 10.00
46 Andrei Kirilenko/50 3.00 8.00
47 Carlos Boozer/50 3.00 8.00
48 Deron Williams/50 3.00 8.00
49 Mehmet Okur/50 2.50 6.00
50 Paul Millsap/25 3.00 8.00
59 Chris Kaman/25 3.00 8.00
62 Andrew Bynum/50 2.50 6.00
64 Kobe Bryant/50 15.00 40.00
67 Pau Gasol/50 3.00 8.00
74 Andres Nocioni/25 2.50 6.00
78 Kevin Garnett/25 10.00 25.00
79 Paul Pierce/25 6.00 15.00
82 Ray Allen/25 6.00 15.00
87 Al Harrington/25 3.00 8.00
89 Danilo Gallinari/50 3.00 8.00
91 David Lee/50 2.50 6.00
92 Nate Robinson/25 3.00 8.00
93 Andre Iguodala/50 4.00 10.00
94 Elton Brand/25 3.00 8.00
95 Samuel Dalembert/50 2.50 6.00
96 Thaddeus Young/50 2.50 6.00
97 Andrea Bargnani/50 2.50 6.00
98 Chris Bosh/50 5.00 12.00
101 Jose Calderon/50 2.50 6.00
102 Derrick Rose/50 6.00 15.00
107 LeBron James/25 15.00 40.00
108 Mo Williams/25 3.00 8.00
109 Shaquille O'Neal/50 12.00 30.00
110 Zydrunas Ilgauskas/50 3.00 8.00
111 Ben Gordon/50 3.00 8.00
113 Charlie Villanueva/50 2.50 6.00
114 Richard Hamilton/50 4.00 10.00
116 Tayshaun Prince/50 4.00 10.00
118 Jeff Foster/50 2.50 6.00
125 Al Horford/50 4.00 10.00
127 Joe Johnson/25 4.00 10.00
128 Josh Smith/25 2.50 6.00
130 Boris Diaw/25 3.00 8.00
131 D.J. Augustin/50 2.50 6.00
132 Gerald Wallace/50 3.00 8.00
134 Raymond Felton/25 2.50 6.00
136 Dwyane Wade/50 8.00 20.00
137 Jermaine O'Neal/25 4.00 10.00
139 Michael Beasley/25 2.50 6.00
141 Udonis Haslem/25 2.50 6.00
142 Dwight Howard/50 5.00 12.00
146 Rashard Lewis/25 3.00 8.00
147 Antawn Jamison/50 3.00 8.00
149 Gilbert Arenas/50 3.00 8.00
151 Isiah Thomas/50 4.00 10.00
154 Dikembe Mutombo/50 4.00 10.00
157 Adrian Dantley/50 3.00 8.00
166 Magic Johnson/50 15.00 40.00

2009-10 Certified Mirror Gold

*1-150: 2.5X TO 6X BASE HI
*151-170: 1.5X TO 4X BASE HI
*171-200 RC: 1X TO 2.5X BASE HI
STATED PRINT RUN 25 SER.#'d SETS
107 LeBron James 60.00 150.00
176 Stephen Curry JSY AU 4,000.00 8,000.00

2009-10 Certified Mirror Gold Materials Prime

STATED PRINT RUN 5 TO 25 SER.#'d SETS
1 Dirk Nowitzki/25 20.00 50.00
2 Jason Kidd/25 12.00 30.00
3 Jason Terry/25 6.00 15.00
4 J.J. Barea/25 12.00 30.00
6 Shawn Marion/25 8.00 20.00
8 Shane Battier/25 8.00 20.00
25 Tim Duncan/25 20.00 50.00
33 Al Jefferson/25 5.00 12.00
34 Kevin Love/25 8.00 20.00
46 Andrei Kirilenko/25 6.00 15.00
59 Chris Kaman/25 6.00 15.00
64 Kobe Bryant/25 30.00 80.00
87 Al Harrington/15 6.00 15.00
89 Danilo Gallinari/25 6.00 15.00
91 David Lee/25 5.00 12.00
93 Andre Iguodala/25 8.00 20.00
95 Samuel Dalembert/25 5.00 12.00
96 Thaddeus Young/25 5.00 12.00
109 Shaquille O'Neal/25 20.00 50.00
110 Zydrunas Ilgauskas/25 6.00 15.00
118 Jeff Foster/25 5.00 12.00
125 Al Horford/25 8.00 20.00
131 D.J. Augustin/25 5.00 12.00
151 Isiah Thomas/25 8.00 20.00
154 Dikembe Mutombo/25 10.00 25.00
157 Adrian Dantley/25 6.00 15.00
166 Magic Johnson/25 12.00 30.00

2009-10 Certified Mirror Gold Signatures

STATED PRINT RUN 10 TO 25 SER.#'d SETS
5 Josh Howard/25 6.00 15.00
19 Emeka Okafor/25 6.00 15.00
26 Tony Parker/25 15.00 30.00
34 Kevin Love/25 25.00 60.00
36 Ryan Gomes/25 6.00 15.00
45 Russell Westbrook/25 50.00 120.00
47 Carlos Boozer/25 8.00 20.00
48 Deron Williams/25 8.00 20.00
59 Chris Kaman/25 6.00 15.00
60 Eric Gordon/25 10.00 25.00
64 Kobe Bryant/25 800.00 1,500.00
80 Rajon Rondo/25 20.00 50.00
82 Ray Allen/25 15.00 40.00
85 Devin Harris/25 10.00 25.00
91 David Lee/15 10.00 25.00
93 Andre Iguodala/25 8.00 20.00
94 Elton Brand/25 8.00 20.00
113 Charlie Villanueva/25 6.00 15.00
117 Danny Granger/25 8.00 20.00
137 Jermaine O'Neal/25 8.00 20.00
150 Randy Foye/25 6.00 15.00
152 Byron Scott/25 8.00 20.00
153 Frank Ramsey/25 6.00 15.00
157 Adrian Dantley/25 6.00 15.00
158 Bailey Howell/25 8.00 20.00
164 Bill Walton/25 12.00 30.00
170 James Worthy/25 20.00 40.00

2009-10 Certified Mirror Red

*1-170: .5X TO 1.25X BASE HI
PRINT RUN 250 SER.#'d SETS
*171-200 RC: .5X TO 1.25X BASE HI
171-200 RC PRINT RUN 100 SER.#'d SETS
107 LeBron James 12.00 30.00
171 Blake Griffin JSY AU 60.00 150.00
176 Stephen Curry JSY AU 2,000.00 4,000.00

2009-10 Certified Champions

COMPLETE SET (25) 20.00 40.00
PRINT RUN 500 SER.#'d SETS
*BLUE: .6X TO 1.5X BASE HI
BLUE PRINT RUN 100 SER.#'d SETS
*GOLD: 1.25X TO 3X BASE HI
GOLD PRINT RUN 25 SER.#'d SETS
*RED: .5X TO 1.25X BASE HI
RED PRINT RUN 250 SER.#'d SETS
1 Kobe Bryant 8.00 20.00
2 Bill Laimbeer 1.00 2.50
3 Bill Russell 3.00 8.00
4 Bill Walton 1.50 4.00
5 Dwyane Wade 2.00 5.00
6 Hakeem Olajuwon 1.25 3.00
7 Isiah Thomas 1.00 2.50
8 Jerry West 1.50 4.00
9 John Havlicek 2.50 6.00
10 Kevin Garnett 2.50 6.00
11 Magic Johnson 4.00 10.00
12 Oscar Robertson 1.25 3.00
13 Rick Barry .75 2.00
14 Shaquille O'Neal 3.00 8.00
15 Tim Duncan 2.50 6.00
16 Walt Frazier 1.50 4.00
17 Chauncey Billups 1.25 3.00
18 Tony Parker 1.50 4.00
19 Wes Unseld 1.00 2.50
20 Willis Reed 1.50 4.00
21 Kareem Abdul-Jabbar 3.00 8.00
22 Joe Dumars 1.25 3.00
23 Paul Pierce 1.50 4.00
24 Dolph Schayes 1.00 2.50
25 Arnie Risen 1.00 2.50

2009-10 Certified Champions Materials

STATED PRINT RUN 10 TO 99 SER.#'d SETS
*PRIME: .6X TO 1.5X HI COLUMN
PRIME PRINT RUN ONE TO 25 SETS
1 Kobe Bryant/99 10.00 25.00
5 Dwyane Wade/99 6.00 15.00
6 Hakeem Olajuwon/99 5.00 12.00
7 Isiah Thomas/99 4.00 10.00
8 Jerry West/99 6.00 15.00
9 John Havlicek/50 6.00 15.00
10 Kevin Garnett/50 8.00 20.00
11 Magic Johnson/99 8.00 20.00
15 Tim Duncan/99 8.00 20.00
22 Joe Dumars/99 5.00 12.00
23 Paul Pierce/99 5.00 12.00

2009-10 Certified Champions Signatures

STATED PRINT RUN 10 TO 50 SER.#'d SETS
1 Kobe Bryant/50 800.00 1,500.00
2 Bill Laimbeer/50 10.00 25.00
3 Bill Russell/50 400.00 800.00
4 Bill Walton/50 10.00 25.00
7 Isiah Thomas/50 10.00 25.00
8 Jerry West/35 30.00 80.00
9 John Havlicek/50 75.00 200.00
12 Oscar Robertson/50 40.00 100.00
13 Rick Barry/50 10.00 25.00
18 Tony Parker/50 15.00 40.00
19 Wes Unseld/25 10.00 25.00
20 Willis Reed/50 30.00 80.00
21 Kareem Abdul-Jabbar/50 75.00 200.00
24 Dolph Schayes/50 10.00 25.00
25 Arnie Risen/50 10.00 25.00

2009-10 Certified Fabric of the Game

STATED PRINT RUN 10 TO 250 SETS
*JSY NUMBER: .5X TO 1.25X BASE HI
JSY NUMBER PRINT RUN 10 TO 99 SETS
*JSY NUM.PRIME: .75X TO 2X BASE HI
JSY NUM.PRIME PRINT RUN ONE TO 25 SETS
*NBA DC: .6X TO 1.5X BASE HI
NBA DC STATED PRINT RUN 5 TO 50 SETS
*NBA DC PRIME: 1.5X TO 4X BASE HI
NBA DC PRIME PRINT RUN ONE TO 25 SETS
*PRIME: .75X TO 2X BASE HI
PRIME STATED PRINT RUN ONE TO 25 SETS
*TEAM DC: 1X TO 2.5X BASE HI
TEAM DC STATED PRINT RUN ONE TO 25 SETS
1 Dirk Nowitzki/250 8.00 20.00
2 Jason Kidd/250 5.00 12.00
3 Jason Terry/250 2.50 6.00
4 J.J. Barea/250 3.00 8.00
5 Josh Howard/250 2.50 6.00
6 Shawn Marion/250 3.00 8.00
7 Luis Scola/250 2.50 6.00
8 Shane Battier/250 3.00 8.00
9 Tracy McGrady/250 6.00 15.00
11 Yao Ming/250 8.00 20.00
14 O.J. Mayo/100 2.00 5.00
17 Chris Paul/250 6.00 15.00
18 David West/250 2.50 6.00
21 Peja Stojakovic/100 2.50 6.00
25 Tim Duncan/250 8.00 20.00
27 Carmelo Anthony/250 5.00 12.00
28 Chauncey Billups/250 4.00 10.00
29 Chris Andersen/250 2.50 6.00
31 Kenyon Martin/250 2.50 6.00
32 Nene/250 2.50 6.00
33 Al Jefferson/250 2.50 6.00
34 Kevin Love/250 3.00 8.00
36 Ryan Gomes/250 3.00 8.00
38 Brandon Roy/50 4.00 10.00
39 Greg Oden/250 2.00 5.00
40 LaMarcus Aldridge/250 3.00 8.00
46 Andrei Kirilenko/250 2.50 6.00
47 Carlos Boozer/250 2.50 6.00
48 Deron Williams/250 2.50 6.00
49 Mehmet Okur/250 2.00 5.00
50 Paul Millsap/250 2.50 6.00
59 Chris Kaman/250 2.50 6.00
62 Andrew Bynum/100 2.50 6.00
64 Kobe Bryant/250 12.00 30.00
67 Pau Gasol/250 5.00 12.00
74 Andres Nocioni/250 2.00 5.00
78 Kevin Garnett/250 8.00 20.00
79 Paul Pierce/250 5.00 12.00
80 Rajon Rondo/100 4.00 10.00
82 Ray Allen/100 5.00 12.00
87 Al Harrington/250 2.50 6.00
89 Danilo Gallinari/250 2.50 6.00
91 David Lee/250 2.00 5.00
92 Nate Robinson/250 2.50 6.00
93 Andre Iguodala/250 3.00 8.00
94 Elton Brand/250 2.50 6.00
95 Samuel Dalembert/250 2.00 5.00
96 Thaddeus Young/250 2.00 5.00
97 Andrea Bargnani/250 2.00 5.00
98 Chris Bosh/250 4.00 10.00
101 Jose Calderon/250 2.00 5.00
102 Derrick Rose/100 5.00 12.00
107 LeBron James/250 10.00 25.00
108 Mo Williams/250 2.00 5.00
109 Shaquille O'Neal/250 8.00 20.00
110 Zydrunas Ilgauskas/250 2.50 6.00
111 Ben Gordon/250 2.50 6.00
113 Charlie Villanueva/250 2.00 5.00
114 Richard Hamilton/250 3.00 8.00
116 Tayshaun Prince/250 3.00 8.00
118 Jeff Foster/250 2.00 5.00
124 Michael Redd/100 2.50 6.00
125 Al Horford/250 3.00 8.00
127 Joe Johnson/100 3.00 8.00
128 Josh Smith/250 2.00 5.00
129 Mike Bibby/100 3.00 8.00
130 Boris Diaw/250 2.50 6.00
131 D.J. Augustin/250 2.00 5.00
132 Gerald Wallace/250 2.50 6.00
134 Raymond Felton/250 2.00 5.00
136 Dwyane Wade/250 6.00 15.00
137 Jermaine O'Neal/25 3.00 8.00
139 Michael Beasley/250 2.00 5.00
141 Udonis Haslem/250 2.00 5.00
142 Dwight Howard/250 4.00 10.00
146 Rashard Lewis/250 2.50 6.00
147 Antawn Jamison/100 2.50 6.00
149 Gilbert Arenas/250 2.50 6.00
151 Isiah Thomas/250 3.00 8.00
154 Dikembe Mutombo/250 5.00 12.00
157 Adrian Dantley/50 2.50 6.00
160 Walt Frazier/50 5.00 12.00
166 Magic Johnson/250 12.00 30.00
171 Blake Griffin/250 6.00 15.00
172 Hasheem Thabeet/250 1.25 3.00
173 James Harden/250 12.00 30.00
174 Tyreke Evans/250 1.50 4.00
175 Jonny Flynn/250 1.25 3.00
176 Stephen Curry/250 150.00 400.00
177 Jordan Hill/250 1.25 3.00
178 Brandon Jennings/250 2.00 5.00
179 Terrence Williams/250 1.25 3.00
180 Gerald Henderson/250 1.25 3.00
181 Tyler Hansbrough/250 1.50 4.00
182 Earl Clark/250 1.25 3.00
183 Austin Daye/250 1.25 3.00
184 James Johnson/250 1.50 4.00
185 Jrue Holiday/250 6.00 15.00
186 Ty Lawson/250 1.50 4.00
187 Jeff Teague/250 1.50 4.00
188 Eric Maynor/250 1.25 3.00
189 Darren Collison/250 2.00 5.00
190 Omri Casspi/250 1.25 3.00
191 B.J. Mullens/250 1.25 3.00
192 Rodrigue Beaubois/250 1.25 3.00
193 Taj Gibson/250 1.50 4.00
194 DeMarre Carroll/250 1.50 4.00
195 Wayne Ellington/250 1.50 4.00
196 Toney Douglas/250 1.50 4.00
197 Jeff Pendergraph/250 1.25 3.00
198 Jermaine Taylor/250 1.25 3.00
199 DeJuan Blair/250 1.50 4.00
200 Jodie Meeks/250 1.25 3.00

2009-10 Certified Fabric of the Game Jersey Number Signatures

STATED PRINT RUN ONE TO 25 SER.#'d SETS
2 Jason Kidd/25 20.00 50.00
5 Josh Howard/25 8.00 20.00
34 Kevin Love/25 12.00 30.00
36 Ryan Gomes/25 8.00 20.00
48 Deron Williams/25 8.00 20.00
59 Chris Kaman/25 8.00 20.00
64 Kobe Bryant/25 800.00 1,500.00
67 Pau Gasol/25 25.00 60.00
91 David Lee/25 8.00 20.00
93 Andre Iguodala/25 8.00 20.00
98 Chris Bosh/25 8.00 20.00
113 Charlie Villanueva/25 8.00 20.00
137 Jermaine O'Neal/25 8.00 20.00
139 Michael Beasley/25 8.00 20.00
151 Isiah Thomas/25 12.00 30.00
154 Dikembe Mutombo/25 15.00 40.00
157 Adrian Dantley/25 8.00 20.00
171 Blake Griffin/25 50.00 120.00
172 Hasheem Thabeet/25 5.00 12.00
173 James Harden/25 60.00 150.00
174 Tyreke Evans/25 8.00 20.00
175 Jonny Flynn/25 5.00 12.00
176 Stephen Curry/25 2,000.00 4,000.00
177 Jordan Hill/25 5.00 12.00
178 Brandon Jennings/25 8.00 20.00
179 Terrence Williams/25 5.00 12.00
180 Gerald Henderson/25 5.00 12.00
181 Tyler Hansbrough/25 6.00 15.00
182 Earl Clark/25 5.00 12.00
183 Austin Daye/25 5.00 12.00
184 James Johnson/25 6.00 15.00
185 Jrue Holiday/25 25.00 60.00
186 Ty Lawson/25 6.00 15.00
187 Jeff Teague/25 6.00 15.00
188 Eric Maynor/25 5.00 12.00
189 Darren Collison/25 8.00 20.00
190 Omri Casspi/25 5.00 12.00
191 B.J. Mullens/25 5.00 12.00
192 Rodrigue Beaubois/25 5.00 12.00
193 Taj Gibson/25 6.00 15.00
194 DeMarre Carroll/25 6.00 15.00
195 Wayne Ellington/25 6.00 15.00
196 Toney Douglas/25 5.00 12.00
197 Jeff Pendergraph/25 5.00 12.00
198 Jermaine Taylor/25 5.00 12.00
199 DeJuan Blair/25 6.00 15.00
200 Jodie Meeks/25 6.00 15.00

2009-10 Certified Gold Team

COMPLETE SET (25) 10.00 25.00
PRINT RUN 500 SER.#'d SETS
*BLUE: .6X TO 1.5X BASE HI
BLUE PRINT RUN 100 SER.#'d SETS
*GOLD: 1.25X TO 3X BASE HI
GOLD PRINT RUN 25 SER.#'d SETS
*RED: .5X TO 1.25X BASE HI
RED PRINT RUN 250 SER.#'d SETS
1 Kobe Bryant 8.00 20.00
2 Dwyane Wade 2.00 5.00
3 Chris Paul 2.00 5.00
4 Dwight Howard 1.25 3.00
5 Danny Granger .60 1.50
6 Deron Williams .75 2.00
7 Carmelo Anthony 1.50 4.00
8 Kevin Durant 4.00 10.00
9 Paul Pierce 1.50 4.00
10 LeBron James 8.00 20.00

2009-10 Certified Gold Team Materials

STATED PRINT RUN 99 SER.#'d SETS
*PRIME: 1X TO 2.5X HI COLUMN
PRIME PRINT RUN ONE TO 25 SETS
1 Kobe Bryant 12.00 30.00
2 Dwyane Wade 6.00 15.00
3 Chris Paul 6.00 15.00
4 Dwight Howard 4.00 10.00
6 Deron Williams 2.50 6.00
7 Carmelo Anthony 5.00 12.00
9 Paul Pierce 5.00 12.00
10 LeBron James 25.00 60.00

2009-10 Certified Gold Team Signatures

STATED PRINT RUN 25 TO 50 SER.#'d SETS
1 Kobe Bryant/50 800.00 1,500.00
5 Danny Granger/25 8.00 20.00
6 Deron Williams/50 10.00 25.00

2009-10 Certified Imports

COMPLETE SET (15) 7.50 15.00
STATED PRINT RUN 500 SER.#'d SETS
*BLUE: .6X TO 1.5X BASE HI
BLUE PRINT RUN 100 SER.#'d SETS
*GOLD: 1.25X TO 3X BASE HI
GOLD PRINT RUN 25 SER.#'d SETS
*RED: .5X TO 1.25X BASE HI
RED PRINT RUN 250 SER.#'d SETS
1 Andrea Bargnani .60 1.50
2 Andrew Bogut .75 2.00
3 Boris Diaw .75 2.00
4 Dirk Nowitzki 2.50 6.00
5 Hasheem Thabeet .60 1.50
6 Hedo Turkoglu .75 2.00
7 Kelenna Azubuike .60 1.50
8 Manu Ginobili 2.00 5.00
9 Nene .75 2.00
10 Omri Casspi .60 1.50
11 Pau Gasol 1.50 4.00
12 Steve Nash 2.00 5.00
13 Yao Ming 2.50 6.00
14 Zydrunas Ilgauskas .75 2.00
15 Andrei Kirilenko .75 2.00

2009-10 Certified Imports Materials

STATED PRINT RUN 25 TO 99 SER.#'d SETS
*PRIME: .75X TO 2X BASE HI
PRIME PRINT RUN 5 TO 25 SER.#'d SETS
1 Andrea Bargnani/25 2.00 5.00
3 Boris Diaw/50 2.50 6.00
4 Dirk Nowitzki/99 8.00 20.00
5 Hasheem Thabeet/99 2.00 5.00
8 Manu Ginobili/25 6.00 15.00
9 Nene/99 2.50 6.00
10 Omri Casspi/99 2.00 5.00
11 Pau Gasol/99 5.00 12.00
13 Yao Ming/99 8.00 20.00
14 Zydrunas Ilgauskas/99 2.50 6.00
15 Andrei Kirilenko/99 2.50 6.00

2009-10 Certified Imports Signatures

STATED PRINT RUN 10 TO 50 SER.#'d SETS
5 Hasheem Thabeet/50 8.00 20.00
10 Omri Casspi/50 8.00 20.00
11 Pau Gasol/25 25.00 50.00

2009-10 Certified Potential

COMPLETE SET (35)
STATED PRINT RUN 500 SER.#'d SETS
*BLUE STARS: .75X TO 2X BASE HI
*BLUE RCs: 1X TO 2.5X BASE HI
BLUE PRINT RUN 50 SER.#'d SETS
*RED STARS: .6X TO 1.5X BASE HI
*RED RCs: .75X TO 2X BASE HI
RED PRINT RUN 100 SER.#'d SETS
1 Anthony Morrow .60 1.50
2 Anthony Randolph .60 1.50
3 Brook Lopez 1.00 2.50
4 D.J. Augustin .60 1.50
5 Derrick Rose 1.50 4.00
6 Eric Gordon .75 2.00
7 Greg Oden .60 1.50
8 Jason Thompson .60 1.50
9 Kevin Love 1.00 2.50
10 Marc Gasol 1.00 2.50
11 Mario Chalmers .75 2.00
12 Michael Beasley .60 1.50
13 O.J. Mayo .60 1.50
14 Rudy Fernandez .60 1.50
15 Russell Westbrook 2.00 5.00
16 Brandon Rush .60 1.50
17 Courtney Lee .60 1.50
18 Luc Mbah a Moute .60 1.50
19 Ryan Anderson .60 1.50
20 Blake Griffin 4.00 10.00
21 Brandon Jennings 1.00 2.50
22 DeMar DeRozan 8.00 20.00
23 Earl Clark .60 1.50
24 Gerald Henderson .60 1.50
25 James Harden 20.00 50.00
26 Jordan Hill .60 1.50
27 Stephen Curry 100.00 250.00
28 Tyreke Evans .75 2.00
29 DeJuan Blair .75 2.00
30 Jeff Teague .75 2.00
31 Sam Young .60 1.50
32 Taj Gibson .75 2.00
33 Chase Budinger .60 1.50
34 Hasheem Thabeet .60 1.50
35 Jonny Flynn .60 1.50

2009-10 Certified Potential Gold

*GOLD STARS: 1.25X TO 3X BASE HI
*GOLD RCs: 1.5X TO 4X BASE HI
STATED PRINT RUN 25 SER.#'d SETS

2009-10 Certified Potential Materials

STATED PRINT RUN 100 TO 599 SETS
*PRIME STARS: .75X TO 2X BASE HI
*PRIME RCs: 1X TO 4X BASE HI
PRIME PRINT RUN 5 TO 25 SER.#'d SETS
4 D.J. Augustin/100 2.00 5.00
5 Derrick Rose/100 5.00 12.00
7 Greg Oden/100 2.00 5.00
9 Kevin Love/599 3.00 8.00
12 Michael Beasley/250 2.00 5.00
20 Blake Griffin/599 6.00 15.00
21 Brandon Jennings/599 2.00 5.00
22 DeMar DeRozan/599 15.00 40.00
23 Earl Clark/599 1.25 3.00
24 Gerald Henderson/599 1.25 3.00
25 James Harden/599 40.00 100.00
26 Jordan Hill/599 1.25 3.00
27 Stephen Curry/599 100.00 250.00
28 Tyreke Evans/599 1.50 4.00
29 DeJuan Blair/599 1.50 4.00
30 Jeff Teague/599 1.50 4.00
31 Sam Young/599 1.25 3.00
32 Taj Gibson/599 1.50 4.00
33 Chase Budinger/599 1.25 3.00
34 Hasheem Thabeet/599 1.25 3.00
35 Jonny Flynn/599 1.25 3.00

2009-10 Certified Potential Signatures

STATED PRINT RUN 25 SER.#'d SETS
6 Eric Gordon 8.00 20.00
9 Kevin Love 15.00 40.00
12 Michael Beasley 15.00 30.00
15 Russell Westbrook 30.00 80.00
20 Blake Griffin 40.00 100.00
21 Brandon Jennings 8.00 20.00
23 Earl Clark 5.00 12.00
24 Gerald Henderson 5.00 12.00
25 James Harden 60.00 150.00
26 Jordan Hill 5.00 12.00
27 Stephen Curry 2,000.00 4,000.00
28 Tyreke Evans 6.00 15.00
29 DeJuan Blair 6.00 15.00
30 Jeff Teague 6.00 15.00
31 Sam Young 5.00 12.00
32 Taj Gibson 6.00 15.00
34 Hasheem Thabeet 5.00 12.00
35 Jonny Flynn 5.00 12.00

2009-10 Certified Shirt Off My Back Combos

STATED PRINT RUN 25 TO 99 SER.#'d SETS
1 R.Rondo/R.Allen/99 8.00 20.00
2 J.Kidd/J.Howard/99 5.00 12.00
3 S.Battier/McGrady/99 4.00 10.00
7 J.O'Neal/Beasley/49 4.00 10.00
8 A.Jefferson/Gomes/99 4.00 10.00
9 Iguodala/E.Brand/99 4.00 10.00
10 Bargnani/C.Bosh/99 5.00 12.00
12 McHale/R.Parish/99 8.00 20.00
13 A.Gilmore/Gervin/99 6.00 15.00
14 Drexler/S.Pippen/99 15.00 30.00
15 P.Ewing/Frazier/25 25.00 60.00

2009-10 Certified Shirt Off My Back Combos Prime

*PRIME: .75X TO 2X BASE HI
STATED PRINT RUN 10 TO 25 SER.#'d SETS
14 C.Drexler/S.Pippen/25 30.00 80.00

2010 Certified National Convention

COMPLETE SET (4) 6.00 15.00
ET Evan Turner 1.00 2.50
KB Kobe Bryant 5.00 12.00
LB Larry Bird 3.00 8.00
RR Rajon Rondo 1.00 2.50

2010 Certified National Convention Blue

COMPLETE SET (5) 40.00 80.00
ANNOUNCED PRINT RUN 25 SETS
ET Evan Turner 3.00 8.00
JW John Wall 15.00 40.00
KB Kobe Bryant 10.00 25.00
LB Larry Bird 6.00 15.00
RR Rajon Rondo 2.00 5.00

2010 Certified National Convention Green

COMPLETE SET (5) 15.00 30.00
ANNOUNCED PRINT RUN 50 SETS
ET Evan Turner 1.25 3.00
JW John Wall 6.00 15.00
KB Kobe Bryant 6.00 15.00
LB Larry Bird 4.00 10.00
RR Rajon Rondo 1.25 3.00

1992 Champion HOF Inductees

COMPLETE SET (10) 25.00 60.00
1 Bob Lanier 5.00 12.00
2 Sergei Belov 3.00 8.00
3 Lou Carnesecca CO 3.00 8.00
4 Connie Hawkins 6.00 15.00
5 Al McGuire CO 3.00 8.00
6 Jack Ramsay CO 2.50 6.00
7 Nera White 2.00 5.00
8 Phil Woolpert CO 2.00 5.00
9 Lusia Harris-Stewart 2.50 6.00
10 Title card 3.00 8.00

1989-90 Chicle Metalicas Spanish Stickers

JW James Worthy 20.00 40.00
MJ1 Michael Jordan 150.00 300.00
MJ2 Michael Jordan IA 125.00 250.00

1993 Chicle Metalicas Spanish Wrappers

BW Buck Williams with Michael Jordan 100.00 200.00
MJ Michael Jordan guarded by #20 100.00 200.00
MJP Michael Jordan Portrait 100.00 200.00

2018-19 Certified

COMPLETE SET (200)
1 Ben Simmons .40 1.00
2 Markelle Fultz .30 .75
3 Joel Embiid 1.00 2.50
4 Dario Saric .30 .75
5 JJ Redick .40 1.00
6 Giannis Antetokounmpo 2.00 5.00
7 Khris Middleton .40 1.00
8 Malcolm Brogdon .40 1.00
9 Thon Maker .25 .60
10 Eric Bledsoe .30 .75
11 Zach LaVine .60 1.50
12 Lauri Markkanen .60 1.50
13 Kris Dunn .25 .60
14 Antonio Blakeney .40 1.00
15 Jabari Parker .25 .60
16 Kevin Love .30 .75
17 JR Smith .40 1.00
18 Tristan Thompson .25 .60
19 Jordan Clarkson .40 1.00
20 Larry Nance Jr. .25 .60
21 Kyrie Irving 1.00 2.50
22 Jayson Tatum 1.50 4.00
23 Gordon Hayward .40 1.00
24 Jaylen Brown .60 1.50
25 Al Horford .40 1.00
26 Lou Williams .30 .75
27 Tobias Harris .30 .75
28 Avery Bradley .25 .60
29 Patrick Beverley .25 .60
30 Danilo Gallinari .30 .75
31 Mike Conley .30 .75
32 Marc Gasol .40 1.00
33 Dillon Brooks .40 1.00
34 Wayne Selden .30 .75
35 MarShon Brooks .25 .60
36 John Collins .40 1.00
37 Jeremy Lin .60 1.50
38 Kent Bazemore .25 .60
39 Taurean Prince .25 .60
40 Tyler Dorsey .25 .60
41 Tyler Johnson .25 .60
42 Goran Dragic .30 .75
43 Dwyane Wade .75 2.00
44 Dion Waiters .25 .60
45 Bam Adebayo .60 1.50
46 Kemba Walker .30 .75
47 Tony Parker .60 1.50
48 Nicolas Batum .25 .60
49 Malik Monk .40 1.00
50 Michael Kidd-Gilchrist .25 .60
51 Donovan Mitchell 1.25 3.00
52 Rudy Gobert .50 1.25
53 Ricky Rubio .30 .75
54 Joe Ingles .30 .75
55 Jae Crowder .25 .60
56 Buddy Hield .40 1.00
57 De'Aaron Fox .75 2.00
58 Harry Giles .25 .60
59 Bogdan Bogdanovic .40 1.00
60 Justin Jackson .25 .60
61 Kristaps Porzingis .50 1.25
62 Frank Ntilikina .25 .60
63 Enes Kanter .25 .60
64 Tim Hardaway Jr. .25 .60
65 Courtney Lee .25 .60
66 LeBron James 3.00 8.00
67 Lonzo Ball .40 1.00
68 Kyle Kuzma .40 1.00
69 Brandon Ingram .40 1.00
70 Rajon Rondo .50 1.25
71 Aaron Gordon .40 1.00
72 Jonathan Isaac .40 1.00
73 Evan Fournier .30 .75
74 Jonathon Simmons .25 .60
75 Nikola Vucevic .30 .75
76 Dirk Nowitzki 1.00 2.50
77 DeAndre Jordan .30 .75
78 Harrison Barnes .30 .75
79 Dennis Smith Jr. .25 .60
80 J.J. Barea .40 1.00
81 D'Angelo Russell .40 1.00
82 Jarrett Allen .40 1.00
83 Joe Harris .30 .75
84 Rondae Hollis-Jefferson .25 .60
85 Caris LeVert .40 1.00
86 Nikola Jokic 2.00 5.00
87 Jamal Murray .75 2.00
88 Paul Millsap .30 .75
89 Will Barton .25 .60
90 Victor Oladipo .30 .75
91 Tyreke Evans .25 .60
92 Myles Turner .40 1.00
93 Bojan Bogdanovic .30 .75
94 Thaddeus Young .25 .60
95 Anthony Davis 1.00 2.50
96 Julius Randle .40 1.00

97 Jrue Holiday .50 1.25
98 Nikola Mirotic .25 .60
99 Elfrid Payton .30 .75
100 Blake Griffin .40 1.00
101 Andre Drummond .30 .75
102 Reggie Jackson .30 .75
103 Isaiah Thomas .30 .75
104 Stanley Johnson .25 .60
105 Luke Kennard .30 .75
106 DeMar DeRozan .50 1.25
107 Kyle Lowry .40 1.00
108 Fred VanVleet .50 1.25
109 OG Anunoby .40 1.00
110 Jonas Valanciunas .40 1.00
111 James Harden .75 2.00
112 Clint Capela .30 .75
113 Chris Paul .75 2.00
114 Eric Gordon .30 .75
115 P.J. Tucker .25 .60
116 LaMarcus Aldridge .40 1.00
117 Pau Gasol .60 1.50
118 Rudy Gay .40 1.00
119 Patty Mills .40 1.00
120 Dejounte Murray .50 1.25
121 Devin Booker 1.00 2.50
122 Tyson Chandler .30 .75
123 Josh Jackson .25 .60
124 TJ Warren .25 .60
125 Davon Reed .25 .60
126 Steven Adams .30 .75
127 Terrance Ferguson .25 .60
128 Paul George .60 1.50
129 Russell Westbrook .60 1.50
130 Andre Roberson .25 .60
131 Jimmy Butler .60 1.50
132 Taj Gibson .25 .60
133 Derrick Rose .75 2.00
134 Karl-Anthony Towns .60 1.50
135 Andrew Wiggins .50 1.25
136 Al-Farouq Aminu .25 .60
137 Damian Lillard 1.00 2.50
138 CJ McCollum .40 1.00
139 Jusuf Nurkic .30 .75
140 Evan Turner .25 .60
141 Stephen Curry 3.00 8.00
142 Kevin Durant 1.50 4.00
143 Klay Thompson 1.00 2.50
144 Draymond Green .50 1.25
145 Jordan Bell .25 .60
146 Bradley Beal .50 1.25
147 John Wall .50 1.25
148 Jeff Green .25 .60
149 Dwight Howard .50 1.25
150 Markieff Morris .25 .60
151 Deandre Ayton RC 1.50 4.00
152 Marvin Bagley III RC .75 2.00
153 Luka Doncic RC 15.00 40.00
154 Jaren Jackson Jr. RC 4.00 10.00
155 Trae Young RC 4.00 10.00
156 Mo Bamba RC .75 2.00
157 Wendell Carter Jr. RC 1.25 3.00
158 Collin Sexton RC 1.50 4.00
159 Kevin Knox RC .60 1.50
160 Mikal Bridges RC 2.50 6.00
161 Shai Gilgeous-Alexander RC 10.00 25.00
162 Miles Bridges RC 1.25 3.00
163 Jerome Robinson RC .50 1.25
164 Michael Porter Jr. RC 2.00 5.00
165 Troy Brown Jr. RC .60 1.50
166 Zhaire Smith RC .60 1.50
167 Donte DiVincenzo RC 1.25 3.00
168 Lonnie Walker IV RC 1.00 2.50
169 Kevin Huerter RC 1.00 2.50
170 Josh Okogie RC .75 2.00
171 Grayson Allen RC 1.00 2.50
172 Chandler Hutchison RC .60 1.50
173 Aaron Holiday RC .75 2.00
174 Anfernee Simons RC 2.50 6.00
175 Moritz Wagner RC 1.00 2.50
176 Landry Shamet RC .75 2.00
177 Robert Williams III RC 1.00 2.50
178 Jacob Evans III RC .50 1.25
179 Dzanan Musa RC .50 1.25
180 Omari Spellman RC .50 1.25
181 Elie Okobo RC .50 1.25
182 Jevon Carter RC .75 2.00
183 Jalen Brunson RC 4.00 10.00
184 Devonte' Graham RC .75 2.00
185 Melvin Frazier Jr. RC .50 1.25
186 Mitchell Robinson RC 1.25 3.00
187 Gary Trent Jr. RC 1.00 2.50
188 Khyri Thomas RC .50 1.25
189 Rodions Kurucs RC .60 1.50
190 Bruce Brown RC 1.00 2.50
191 Kevin Hervey RC .50 1.25
192 Hamidou Diallo RC .75 2.00
193 De'Anthony Melton RC 1.00 2.50
194 Svi Mykhailiuk RC .60 1.50
195 Keita Bates-Diop RC .60 1.50
196 Chimezie Metu RC .60 1.50
197 Alize Johnson RC .75 2.00
198 Allonzo Trier RC .50 1.25
199 Vincent Edwards RC .50 1.25
200 Kostas Antetokounmpo RC .60 1.50

2018-19 Certified Mirror

*MIRROR VET: .5X TO 1.2X BASIC VET
*MIRROR RC: .5X TO 1.2X BASIC RC

2018-19 Certified Mirror Blue

*MIRROR BLUE VET: .75X TO 2X BASIC VET
*MIRROR BLUE RC: .75X TO 2X BASIC RC
STATED PRINT 199 SER. #'d SETS
153 Luka Doncic 100.00 250.00
155 Trae Young 15.00 40.00
161 Shai Gilgeous-Alexander 30.00 80.00

2018-19 Certified Mirror Orange

*MIRROR ORNG VET: 1X TO 2.5X BASIC VET
*MIRROR ORNG RC: 1X TO 2.5X BASIC RC
STATED PRINT 99 SER. #'d SETS
153 Luka Doncic 125.00 300.00
155 Trae Young 20.00 50.00
161 Shai Gilgeous-Alexander 40.00 100.00

2018-19 Certified Mirror Purple

*MIRROR PURP VET: 1.25X TO 3X BASIC VET
*MIRROR PURP RC: 1.25X TO 3X BASIC RC
STATED PRINT 49 SER. #'d SETS
153 Luka Doncic 150.00 400.00
155 Trae Young 25.00 60.00
161 Shai Gilgeous-Alexander 50.00 120.00

2018-19 Certified Mirror Red

*MIRROR RED VET: .6X TO 1.5X BASIC VET
*MIRROR RED RC: .6X TO 1.5X BASIC RC
STATED PRINT 299 SER. #'d SETS
153 Luka Doncic 75.00 200.00
155 Trae Young 12.00 30.00
161 Shai Gilgeous-Alexander 25.00 60.00

2018-19 Certified 2018

1 Jalen Brunson 3.00 8.00
2 Jerome Robinson .40 1.00
3 Bruce Brown .75 2.00
4 Donte DiVincenzo 1.00 2.50
5 Grayson Allen .75 2.00
6 Deandre Ayton 1.25 3.00
7 Moritz Wagner .75 2.00
8 Trae Young 3.00 8.00
9 Dzanan Musa .40 1.00
10 Kevin Knox .50 1.25
11 Devonte' Graham .60 1.50
12 Michael Porter Jr. 1.50 4.00
13 De'Anthony Melton .75 2.00
14 Lonnie Walker IV .75 2.00
15 Chandler Hutchison .50 1.25
16 Marvin Bagley III .60 1.50
17 Landry Shamet .60 1.50
18 Mo Bamba .60 1.50
19 Omari Spellman .40 1.00
20 Mikal Bridges 2.00 5.00
21 Gary Trent Jr. .75 2.00
22 Troy Brown Jr. .50 1.25
23 Hamidou Diallo .60 1.50
24 Kevin Huerter .75 2.00
25 Aaron Holiday .60 1.50
26 Luka Doncic 15.00 40.00
27 Robert Williams III .75 2.00
28 Wendell Carter Jr. 1.00 2.50
29 Elie Okobo .40 1.00
30 Shai Gilgeous-Alexander 4.00 10.00
31 Keita Bates-Diop .50 1.25
32 Zhaire Smith .40 1.00
33 Miles Bridges 1.00 2.50
34 Josh Okogie .60 1.50
35 Anfernee Simons 2.00 5.00
36 Jaren Jackson Jr. 3.00 8.00
37 Jacob Evans III .40 1.00
38 Collin Sexton 1.25 3.00
39 Jevon Carter .60 1.50
40 Svi Mykhailiuk .50 1.25

2018-19 Certified Certified Future

CF1 Deandre Ayton 1.25 3.00
CF2 Marvin Bagley III .60 1.50
CF3 Luka Doncic 6.00 15.00
CF4 Jaren Jackson Jr. 3.00 8.00
CF5 Trae Young 15.00 40.00
CF6 Mo Bamba .60 1.50
CF7 Wendell Carter Jr. 1.00 2.50
CF8 Collin Sexton 1.25 3.00
CF9 Kevin Knox .50 1.25
CF10 Mikal Bridges 2.00 5.00
CF11 Shai Gilgeous-Alexander 4.00 10.00
CF12 Miles Bridges 1.00 2.50
CF13 Jerome Robinson .40 1.00
CF14 Michael Porter Jr. 1.50 4.00
CF15 Troy Brown Jr. .50 1.25
CF16 Zhaire Smith .40 1.00
CF17 Donte DiVincenzo 1.00 2.50
CF18 Lonnie Walker IV .75 2.00
CF19 Kevin Huerter .75 2.00
CF20 Grayson Allen .75 2.00

2018-19 Certified Certified Potential Autographs

EXCHANGE DEADLINE 5/14/2020
1 Deandre Ayton 10.00 25.00
2 Marvin Bagley III 5.00 12.00
3 Luka Doncic 800.00 1,500.00
4 Jaren Jackson Jr. 200.00 500.00
5 Trae Young 200.00 500.00
6 Mo Bamba 5.00 12.00
7 Wendell Carter Jr. 8.00 20.00
8 Collin Sexton 10.00 25.00
9 Kevin Knox 4.00 10.00
10 Mikal Bridges 15.00 40.00
11 Shai Gilgeous-Alexander 400.00 800.00
12 Vincent Edwards 3.00 8.00
13 Jerome Robinson 3.00 8.00
14 Michael Porter Jr. 12.00 30.00
15 Troy Brown Jr. 4.00 10.00
16 Zhaire Smith 3.00 8.00
17 Donte DiVincenzo 8.00 20.00
18 Lonnie Walker IV 6.00 15.00
19 Kevin Huerter 6.00 15.00
20 Josh Okogie 5.00 12.00
21 Grayson Allen 6.00 15.00
22 Chandler Hutchison 4.00 10.00
23 Aaron Holiday 6.00 15.00
24 Anfernee Simons 15.00 40.00
25 Moritz Wagner 6.00 15.00
26 Landry Shamet 6.00 15.00
27 Robert Williams III 6.00 15.00
28 Jacob Evans III 3.00 8.00
29 Dzanan Musa 3.00 8.00
30 Omari Spellman 3.00 8.00
31 Elie Okobo 3.00 8.00
32 Jevon Carter 5.00 12.00
33 Jalen Brunson 75.00 200.00
34 Devonte' Graham 5.00 12.00
35 Gary Trent Jr. 6.00 15.00
36 Svi Mykhailiuk 4.00 10.00
37 Keita Bates-Diop 4.00 10.00
38 Bruce Brown 6.00 15.00
39 De'Anthony Melton 6.00 15.00
40 Hamidou Diallo 5.00 12.00

2018-19 Certified Certified Stars

1 Ben Simmons .60 1.50
2 Dwight Howard .75 2.00
3 Damian Lillard 1.50 4.00
4 Anthony Davis 1.50 4.00
5 Karl-Anthony Towns 1.00 2.50
6 Kevin Love .50 1.25
7 Giannis Antetokounmpo 3.00 8.00
8 Kevin Durant 2.50 6.00
9 DeMar DeRozan .75 2.00
10 Kyle Kuzma .60 1.50
11 Joel Embiid 1.50 4.00
12 James Harden 1.25 3.00
13 Russell Westbrook 1.00 2.50
14 Dirk Nowitzki 1.50 4.00
15 Andrew Wiggins .75 2.00
16 Victor Oladipo .50 1.25
17 Blake Griffin .60 1.50
18 Devin Booker 1.50 4.00
19 Kyrie Irving 1.50 4.00
20 Goran Dragic .50 1.25
21 Kristaps Porzingis .75 2.00
22 Chris Paul 1.25 3.00
23 Donovan Mitchell 2.00 5.00
24 Dennis Smith Jr. .40 1.00
25 LeBron James 5.00 12.00
26 Paul George 1.00 2.50
27 Stephen Curry 5.00 12.00
28 Lonzo Ball .60 1.50
29 Jayson Tatum 2.50 6.00
30 John Wall .75 2.00

2018-19 Certified Choice Signatures

STATED PRINT RUNS B/WN 15-199 COPIES PER
EXCHANGE DEADLINE 5/14/2020
1 Jason Kidd/25 12.00 30.00
2 Gerald Henderson Sr./199 2.50 6.00
3 Antoine Walker/199 3.00 8.00
4 Jacque Vaughn/199 2.50 6.00
5 Brad Daugherty/199 3.00 8.00
6 Jerami Grant/99 5.00 12.00
7 Damon Stoudamire/99 5.00 12.00
8 Domantas Sabonis/99 6.00 15.00
10 Erick Dampier/199 2.50 6.00
11 Tony Parker/25 12.00 30.00
12 Hersey Hawkins/199 2.50 6.00
13 Arvydas Sabonis/199 4.00 10.00
14 Jamal Mashburn/199 3.00 8.00
15 Bryant Reeves/199 2.50 6.00
16 Jerian Grant/99 3.00 8.00
17 Dan Issel/99 6.00 15.00
18 Doug Collins/199 4.00 10.00
20 Ernie DiGregorio/199 3.00 8.00
21 A.C. Green/99 5.00 12.00
22 Isaiah Rider/199 3.00 8.00
23 Avery Johnson/49 5.00 12.00
24 James Johnson/199 2.50 6.00
25 Caris LeVert/99 5.00 12.00
26 Joe Smith/199 3.00 8.00
27 Daniel Theis/199 4.00 10.00
28 Ed Pinckney/199 2.50 6.00
29 Alonzo Mourning/25 12.00 30.00
30 Felipe Lopez/199 2.50 6.00
31 Alvan Adams/99 4.00 10.00
32 Ivica Zubac/99 4.00 10.00
33 B.J. Armstrong/49 6.00 15.00
34 Joe Dumars/49 8.00 20.00
35 Channing Frye/49 4.00 10.00
36 Jose Calderon/99 3.00 8.00
37 Detlef Schrempf/199 4.00 10.00
38 Derek Harper/199 3.00 8.00
39 Hakeem Olajuwon/25 10.00 25.00
40 Frank Ntilikina/49 4.00 10.00
41 Andrei Kirilenko/199 3.00 8.00
42 Jack Sikma/199 3.00 8.00
43 Bam Adebayo/199 6.00 15.00
44 Jeff Hornacek/199 3.00 8.00
45 Craig Hodges/199 3.00 8.00
46 JR Smith/49 6.00 15.00
47 Dino Radja/199 2.50 6.00
48 Elden Campbell/199 2.50 6.00
49 Clyde Drexler/25 12.00 30.00
50 Gerald Green/99 4.00 10.00

2018-19 Certified Energizers

1 Stephen Curry 5.00 12.00
2 James Harden 1.25 3.00
3 Ben Simmons .60 1.50
4 Russell Westbrook 1.00 2.50
5 Victor Oladipo .50 1.25
6 DeMar DeRozan .75 2.00
7 Donovan Mitchell 2.00 5.00
8 Kyle Lowry .60 1.50
9 Jayson Tatum 2.50 6.00
10 Klay Thompson 1.50 4.00
11 Goran Dragic .50 1.25
12 Chris Paul 1.25 3.00
13 Damian Lillard 1.50 4.00
14 Bradley Beal .75 2.00
15 CJ McCollum .60 1.50
16 Kemba Walker .50 1.25
17 Lonzo Ball .60 1.50
18 Kyrie Irving 1.50 4.00
19 Dennis Smith Jr. .40 1.00
20 Devin Booker 1.50 4.00

2018-19 Certified Fabric of the Game Relics

STATED PRINT RUN 149 SER.#'d SETS
1 Kenny Anderson 2.00 5.00
2 Aaron Gordon 2.50 6.00
3 Larry Johnson 3.00 8.00
4 Carmelo Anthony 4.00 0.00
5 Nikola Vucevic 2.00 5.00
6 DeAndre Jordan 2.00 5.00
7 Rudy Gay 2.50 6.00
8 Elfrid Payton 2.00 5.00
9 Tim Duncan 6.00 5.00
10 James Harden 5.00 2.00
11 Kevin Garnett 6.00 5.00
12 Amar'e Stoudemire 2.50 6.00
13 Marcin Gortat 1.50 4.00
14 CJ McCollum 2.50 6.00
15 Patrick Ewing 4.00 0.00
16 DeMarcus Cousins 2.00 5.00
17 Scottie Pippen 6.00 5.00
18 Eric Bledsoe 2.00 5.00
19 Trevor Ariza 1.50 4.00
20 Jeff Teague 1.50 4.00
21 Kobe Bryant 20.00 0.00
22 Andre Iguodala 2.00 5.00
23 Maxi Kleber 2.00 5.00
24 Damian Lillard 6.00 5.00
25 Paul Pierce 4.00 0.00
26 Dennis Smith Jr. 1.50 4.00
27 Shaquille O'Neal 8.00 0.00
28 George Hill 2.00 5.00
29 Victor Oladipo 2.00 5.00
30 Joel Embiid 6.00 15.00
31 Kyle Lowry 2.50 6.00
32 Anthony Davis 6.00 15.00
33 Myles Turner 2.50 6.00
34 Danny Granger 1.50 4.00
35 Rajon Rondo 3.00 8.00
36 Derrick Rose 5.00 12.00
37 Shawn Marion 2.00 5.00
38 Gorgui Dieng 1.50 4.00
39 Willie Cauley-Stein 1.50 4.00
40 Julius Randle 2.50 6.00
41 LaMarcus Aldridge 2.50 6.00
42 Bradley Beal 3.00 8.00
43 Nerlens Noel 1.50 4.00
44 David Robinson 5.00 12.00
45 Rodney Hood 2.00 5.00
46 Dirk Nowitzki 6.00 15.00
47 Steven Adams 2.00 5.00
48 Hakeem Olajuwon 3.00 8.00
49 Yao Ming 6.00 15.00
50 Karl Malone 5.00 12.00

2018-19 Certified Fabric of the Game Rookie Relics

STATED PRINT RUN 149 SER.#'d SETS
1 Deandre Ayton 5.00 12.00
2 Marvin Bagley III 2.50 6.00
3 Luka Doncic 75.00 200.00
4 Jaren Jackson Jr. 12.00 30.00
FG-TY Trae Young 12.00 30.00
6 Mo Bamba 2.50 6.00
7 Wendell Carter Jr. 4.00 10.00
8 Collin Sexton 5.00 12.00
9 Kevin Knox 2.00 5.00
10 Mikal Bridges 8.00 20.00
11 Shai Gilgeous-Alexander 15.00 40.00
12 Svi Mykhailiuk 2.00 5.00
13 Jerome Robinson 1.50 4.00
14 Michael Porter Jr. 6.00 15.00
15 Troy Brown Jr. 2.00 5.00
16 Jalen Brunson 12.00 30.00
17 Donte DiVincenzo 4.00 10.00
18 Lonnie Walker IV 3.00 8.00
19 Kevin Huerter 3.00 8.00
20 Josh Okogie 2.50 6.00
21 Grayson Allen 3.00 8.00
22 Chandler Hutchison 2.00 5.00
23 Aaron Holiday 2.50 6.00
24 Anfernee Simons 8.00 20.00
25 Devonte' Graham 2.50 6.00
26 Landry Shamet 2.50 6.00
27 Robert Williams III 3.00 8.00
28 Jacob Evans III 1.50 4.00
29 Dzanan Musa 1.50 4.00
30 Omari Spellman 1.50 4.00

2018-19 Certified Freshman Fabric Signatures

PRINT RUNS B/WN 99-149 COPIES PER
EXCHANGE DEADLINE 5/14/2020
1 Deandre Ayton/99 15.00 40.00
2 Marvin Bagley III/99 8.00 20.00
3 Luka Doncic/99 500.00 1,000.00
4 Jaren Jackson Jr./99 40.00 100.00
5 Trae Young/99 150.00 400.00
6 Mo Bamba/99 8.00 20.00
7 Wendell Carter Jr./99 12.00 30.00
8 Collin Sexton/99 15.00 40.00
9 Kevin Knox/99 6.00 15.00
10 Mikal Bridges/99 25.00 60.00
11 Shai Gilgeous-Alexander/99 400.00 800.00
12 Svi Mykhailiuk/149 5.00 12.00
13 Jerome Robinson/99 5.00 12.00
14 Michael Porter Jr./99 20.00 50.00
15 Troy Brown Jr./149 5.00 12.00
16 Zhaire Smith/149 4.00 10.00
17 Donte DiVincenzo/149 10.00 25.00
18 Lonnie Walker IV/149 8.00 20.00
19 Kevin Huerter/149 8.00 20.00
20 Josh Okogie/149 6.00 15.00
21 Grayson Allen/149 8.00 20.00
22 Chandler Hutchison/149 5.00 12.00
23 Aaron Holiday/149 6.00 15.00
24 Anfernee Simons/149 20.00 50.00
25 Moritz Wagner/149 8.00 20.00
26 Landry Shamet/149 6.00 15.00
27 Robert Williams III/149 8.00 20.00
28 Jacob Evans III/149 4.00 10.00
29 Dzanan Musa/149 4.00 10.00
30 Omari Spellman/149 4.00 10.00
31 Elie Okobo/149 4.00 10.00
33 Jalen Brunson/149 30.00 80.00
34 Devonte' Graham/149 6.00 15.00
35 Gary Trent Jr./149 8.00 20.00
36 Jarred Vanderbilt/149 8.00 20.00
37 Keita Bates-Diop/149 5.00 12.00
38 Bruce Brown/149 8.00 20.00
39 De'Anthony Melton/149 8.00 20.00
40 Hamidou Diallo/149 6.00 15.00

2018-19 Certified Gold Team

1 LaMarcus Aldridge .60 1.50
2 Giannis Antetokounmpo 3.00 8.00
3 Stephen Curry 3.00 8.00
4 DeMar DeRozan .75 2.00
5 De'Aaron Fox 1.25 3.00
6 Kristaps Porzingis .75 2.00
7 John Wall .75 2.00
8 Russell Westbrook 1.00 2.50
9 Dennis Schroder .50 1.25
10 Karl-Anthony Towns 1.00 2.50
11 Dennis Smith Jr. .40 1.00
12 Blake Griffin .60 1.50
13 Lou Williams .50 1.25
14 Kyrie Irving 1.50 4.00
15 Devin Booker 1.50 4.00
16 D'Angelo Russell .60 1.50
17 Dwight Howard .60 1.50
18 Donovan Mitchell 2.00 5.00
19 James Harden 1.25 3.00
20 LeBron James 5.00 12.00
21 Marc Gasol .60 1.50
22 Lauri Markkanen 1.00 2.50
23 Lonzo Ball .60 1.50
24 Ben Simmons .60 1.50
25 Goran Dragic .50 1.25
26 Damian Lillard 1.50 4.00
27 Aaron Gordon .60 1.50
28 Nikola Jokic 3.00 8.00
29 Anthony Davis 1.50 4.00
30 Victor Oladipo .50 1.25

2018-19 Certified Lasting Impressions

1 Shaquille O'Neal 2.00 5.00
2 Hakeem Olajuwon .75 2.00
3 Tim Duncan 1.50 4.00
4 Julius Erving 1.50 4.00
5 Kevin Garnett 1.50 4.00
6 Allen Iverson 1.50 4.00
7 Magic Johnson 2.50 6.00
8 Charles Barkley 1.25 3.00
9 Pete Maravich 1.50 4.00
10 Wilt Chamberlain 2.00 5.00
11 Stephon Marbury .75 2.00
12 Jerry West 1.25 3.00
13 David Robinson 1.25 3.00
14 Oscar Robertson 1.25 3.00
15 Kobe Bryant 5.00 12.00
16 Alonzo Mourning 1.00 2.50
17 Kareem Abdul-Jabbar 2.00 5.00
18 Chris Webber .75 2.00
19 Reggie Miller 1.25 3.00
20 Dennis Johnson .60 1.50
21 Steve Nash 1.25 3.00
22 John Stockton 1.25 3.00
23 Yao Ming 1.50 4.00
24 Karl Malone 1.25 3.00
25 Larry Bird 2.50 6.00
26 Patrick Ewing 1.00 2.50
27 Bill Russell 2.00 5.00
28 Clyde Drexler 1.00 2.50
29 Scottie Pippen 1.50 4.00
30 Drazen Petrovic .75 2.00

2018-19 Certified Materials

STATED PRINT RUN 149 SER.#'d SETS
1 Otto Porter Jr. 2.00 5.00
2 DeMar DeRozan 3.00 8.00
3 Enes Kanter 2.00 5.00
4 Rudy Gobert 3.00 8.00
5 Tim Hardaway Jr. 1.50 4.00
6 Kevin Durant 10.00 25.00
7 Jason Kidd 4.00 10.00
8 Allen Iverson 6.00 15.00
9 LeBron James 20.00 50.00
10 Chris Paul 5.00 12.00
11 Paul George 4.00 10.00
12 Dennis Schroder 2.00 5.00
13 Seth Curry 2.00 5.00
14 Evan Turner 1.50 4.00
15 Tristan Thompson 1.50 4.00
16 Jimmy Butler 4.00 10.00
17 Kevin Love 2.00 5.00
18 Andre Drummond 2.00 5.00
19 Mario Hezonja 1.50 4.00
20 Clyde Drexler 4.00 10.00
21 Rafer Alston 2.00 5.00
22 Derrick Favors 1.50 4.00
23 Shawn Bradley 1.50 4.00
24 Goran Dragic 2.00 5.00
25 Walter Davis 2.50 6.00
26 Julius Erving 6.00 15.00
27 Kristaps Porzingis 3.00 8.00
28 Andrew Wiggins 3.00 8.00
29 Michael Redd 2.00 5.00
30 D'Angelo Russell 2.50 6.00
31 Ray Allen 3.00 8.00
32 Dion Waiters 1.50 4.00
33 Stephen Curry 20.00 50.00
34 Grant Hill 4.00 10.00
35 Xavier McDaniel 2.00 5.00
36 Jusuf Nurkic 2.00 5.00
37 Kyrie Irving 6.00 15.00
38 Blake Griffin 2.50 6.00
39 Nene 2.00 5.00
40 Dario Saric 2.00 5.00
41 Rondae Hollis-Jefferson 1.50 4.00
42 Dwyane Wade 5.00 12.00
43 Taj Gibson 1.50 4.00
44 Harrison Barnes 2.00 5.00
45 Zach LaVine 4.00 10.00
46 Karl-Anthony Towns 4.00 10.00
47 Larry Bird 10.00 25.00
48 Brandon Knight 1.50 4.00
49 Nicolas Batum 1.50 4.00
50 DeAndre' Bembry 1.50 4.00

2018-19 Certified New Generation Jerseys

STATED PRINT RUN 149 SER.#'d SETS
1 Deandre Ayton 5.00 12.00
2 Marvin Bagley III 2.50 6.00
3 Luka Doncic 75.00 200.00
4 Jaren Jackson Jr. 12.00 30.00
5 Trae Young 12.00 30.00
6 Mo Bamba 2.50 6.00
7 Wendell Carter Jr. 4.00 10.00
8 Collin Sexton 5.00 12.00
9 Kevin Knox 2.00 5.00
10 Mikal Bridges 8.00 20.00
11 Shai Gilgeous-Alexander 15.00 40.00
12 Svi Mykhailiuk 2.00 5.00
13 Jerome Robinson 1.50 4.00
14 Michael Porter Jr. 6.00 15.00
15 Troy Brown Jr. 2.00 5.00
16 Jalen Brunson 12.00 30.00
17 Donte DiVincenzo 4.00 10.00
18 Lonnie Walker IV 3.00 8.00
19 Kevin Huerter 3.00 8.00
20 Josh Okogie 2.50 6.00
21 Grayson Allen 3.00 8.00
22 Chandler Hutchison 2.00 5.00
23 Aaron Holiday 2.50 6.00
24 Anfernee Simons 8.00 20.00
25 Devonte' Graham 2.50 6.00
26 Landry Shamet 2.50 6.00
27 Robert Williams III 3.00 8.00
28 Jacob Evans III 1.50 4.00
29 Dzanan Musa 1.50 4.00
30 Omari Spellman 1.50 4.00

2018-19 Certified Priority Mail

1 Anthony Davis 1.50 4.00
2 Giannis Antetokounmpo 3.00 8.00
3 Stephen Curry 5.00 12.00
4 James Harden 1.25 3.00
5 Kyrie Irving 1.50 4.00
6 Ben Simmons .60 1.50
7 LeBron James 5.00 12.00
8 Kevin Durant 2.50 6.00
9 Russell Westbrook 1.00 2.50
10 Damian Lillard 1.50 4.00

2018-19 Certified Rookie Roll Call Autographs

1 Grayson Allen 8.00 20.00
2 Deandre Ayton 12.00 30.00
3 Marvin Bagley III 6.00 15.00
4 Mo Bamba 6.00 15.00
5 Keita Bates-Diop 5.00 12.00
6 Mikal Bridges 20.00 50.00
7 Shake Milton 6.00 15.00
8 Bruce Brown 8.00 20.00
9 Troy Brown Jr. 5.00 12.00
10 Jalen Brunson 75.00 200.00
11 Jevon Carter 6.00 15.00
12 Wendell Carter Jr. 10.00 25.00
13 Hamidou Diallo 6.00 15.00
14 Donte DiVincenzo 10.00 25.00
15 Luka Doncic 800.00 1,500.00
16 Jacob Evans III 4.00 10.00
17 Shai Gilgeous-Alexander 400.00 800.00
18 Devonte' Graham 6.00 15.00
19 Aaron Holiday 6.00 15.00
20 Kevin Huerter 8.00 20.00
21 Chandler Hutchison 5.00 12.00
22 Jaren Jackson Jr. 200.00 500.00
23 Kevin Knox 5.00 12.00
24 De'Anthony Melton 8.00 20.00
25 Dzanan Musa 4.00 10.00
26 Elie Okobo 4.00 10.00
27 Josh Okogie 6.00 15.00
28 Michael Porter Jr. 15.00 40.00
29 Jerome Robinson 4.00 10.00
30 Collin Sexton 12.00 30.00
31 Landry Shamet 6.00 15.00
32 Anfernee Simons 20.00 50.00
33 Zhaire Smith 4.00 10.00
34 Omari Spellman 4.00 10.00
35 Gary Trent Jr. 8.00 20.00
36 Ray Spalding 4.00 10.00
37 Moritz Wagner 8.00 20.00
38 Lonnie Walker IV 8.00 20.00
39 Robert Williams III 8.00 20.00
RRC-TY Trae Young 200.00 500.00
41 Vincent Edwards 4.00 10.00
42 Tony Carr 4.00 10.00
43 Kostas Antetokounmpo 5.00 12.00
44 Chimezie Metu 5.00 12.00
45 Svi Mykhailiuk 5.00 12.00
46 Melvin Frazier Jr. 4.00 10.00
47 Kevin Hervey 4.00 10.00
48 Khyri Thomas 4.00 10.00
49 Justin Jackson 4.00 10.00
50 Devon Hall 4.00 10.00

2018-19 Certified Signed Sealed Delivered Autographs

STATED PRINT RUNS B/WN 15-199 COPIES PER
EXCHANGE DEADLINE 5/14/2020
1 Sam Perkins/199 3.00 8.00
2 Kerry Kittles/199 2.50 6.00
3 Stacey Augmon/199 2.50 6.00
4 MarShon Brooks/199 2.50 6.00
5 Toni Kukoc/99 6.00 15.00
6 Cedric Ceballos/199 2.50 6.00
7 Patrick Patterson/49 4.00 10.00
9 Rolando Blackman/99 4.00 10.00
10 Anfernee Hardaway/25 30.00 80.00
11 Antonio McDyess/199 3.00 8.00
12 Kevin Johnson/199 4.00 10.00
13 Stephen Jackson/99 4.00 10.00
14 Matthew Dellavedova/99 4.00 10.00
15 Tyus Jones/99 3.00 8.00
16 Nerlens Noel/49 4.00 10.00
17 Paul Silas/199 4.00 10.00
19 Ron Mercer/199 2.50 6.00
20 Kristaps Porzingis/25 10.00 25.00
21 Shareef Abdur-Rahim/199 3.00 8.00
22 Malcolm Brogdon/49 6.00 15.00
23 Tariq Abdul-Wahad/199 2.50 6.00
24 Maurice Harkless/99 3.00 8.00
25 Mark Aguirre/99 4.00 10.00
26 Omri Casspi/99 3.00 8.00
27 Rick Fox/49 5.00 12.00
28 Karl-Anthony Towns/25 12.00 30.00
29 Rony Seikaly/199 2.50 6.00
30 Jrue Holiday/49 8.00 20.00
31 Spencer Dinwiddie/199 3.00 8.00
32 Mark Price/199 4.00 10.00
33 James Silas/199 4.00 10.00
34 Mitch Richmond/99 6.00 15.00
35 World B. Free/49 5.00 12.00
36 Otis Birdsong/199 3.00 8.00
37 Rik Smits/99 4.00 10.00
38 Marc Gasol/25 8.00 20.00
39 Sam Bowie/199 2.50 6.00
40 Kelly Oubre Jr./99 5.00 12.00
41 Spencer Haywood/199 4.00 10.00
42 Marques Johnson/99 4.00 10.00
43 Tom Gugliotta/99 3.00 8.00
44 Myles Turner/49 6.00 15.00
45 Zydrunas Ilgauskas/199 3.00 8.00
46 Patrick Beverley/99 3.00 8.00
47 Robert Parish/49 10.00 25.00
48 Paul Pierce/25 12.00 30.00
49 Sam Cassell/99 4.00 10.00
50 Kenny "Sky" Walker/99 3.00 8.00

2018-19 Certified The Mighty

1 Anthony Davis 2.50 6.00
2 Dennis Smith Jr. .60 1.50
3 Giannis Antetokounmpo 5.00 12.00
4 Stephen Curry 8.00 20.00
5 DeMar DeRozan 1.25 3.00
6 Jayson Tatum 4.00 10.00
7 James Harden 2.00 5.00
8 Kyrie Irving 2.50 6.00
9 Ben Simmons 1.00 2.50
10 Chris Paul 2.00 5.00
11 Karl-Anthony Towns 1.50 4.00
12 LeBron James 8.00 20.00
13 Kevin Durant 4.00 10.00
14 Lonzo Ball 1.00 2.50
15 Joel Embiid 2.50 6.00
16 John Wall 1.25 3.00
17 Russell Westbrook 1.50 4.00
18 Kristaps Porzingis 1.25 3.00
19 Damian Lillard 2.50 6.00
20 Donovan Mitchell 3.00 8.00

2019-20 Certified

1 Trae Young 1.00 2.50
2 John Collins .40 1.00
3 Kevin Huerter .40 1.00
4 Miles Bridges .40 1.00
5 Malik Monk .40 1.00
6 Nicolas Batum .25 .60
7 Dwayne Bacon .25 .60
8 Bam Adebayo .60 1.50
9 Goran Dragic .30 .75
10 Justise Winslow .25 .60
11 Dion Waiters .25 .60
12 Mo Bamba .30 .75
13 Nikola Vucevic .30 .75
14 Aaron Gordon .40 1.00
15 Markelle Fultz .30 .75
16 Jonathan Isaac .40 1.00
17 Bradley Beal .50 1.25
18 Thomas Bryant .30 .75
19 John Wall .50 1.25
20 Jabari Parker .25 .60
21 Luka Doncic 2.50 6.00
22 Tim Hardaway Jr. .25 .60
23 Kristaps Porzingis .50 1.25
24 Dwight Powell .25 .60
25 Clint Capela .30 .75
26 James Harden .75 2.00
27 Chris Paul .75 2.00
28 Iman Shumpert .25 .60
29 Eric Gordon .30 .75
30 Jaren Jackson Jr. .60 1.50
31 Jonas Valanciunas .30 .75
32 Chandler Parsons .25 .60
33 Jahlil Okafor .25 .60
34 LaMarcus Aldridge .40 1.00
35 DeMar DeRozan .50 1.25
36 Lonnie Walker IV .30 .75
37 Derrick White .40 1.00
38 Dejounte Murray .40 1.00
39 Zach LaVine .60 1.50
40 Lauri Markkanen .50 1.25
41 Otto Porter Jr. .25 .60
42 Kris Dunn .25 .60
43 Wendell Carter Jr. .40 1.00
44 Jordan Clarkson .40 1.00
45 Matthew Dellavedova .30 .75
46 Kevin Love .40 1.00
47 Tristan Thompson .25 .60
48 Collin Sexton .50 1.25
49 Andre Drummond .30 .75
50 Blake Griffin .40 1.00
51 Luke Kennard .30 .75
52 Reggie Jackson .30 .75
53 Aaron Holiday .30 .75
54 Myles Turner .40 1.00
55 Victor Oladipo .30 .75
56 Giannis Antetokounmpo 2.00 5.00
57 Khris Middleton .40 1.00
58 Eric Bledsoe .30 .75
59 Brook Lopez .30 .75
60 Pau Gasol .60 1.50
61 Stephen Curry 3.00 8.00
62 Draymond Green .50 1.25
63 DeMarcus Cousins .30 .75
64 Klay Thompson 1.00 2.50
65 Patrick Beverley .30 .75
66 Lou Williams .40 1.00
67 Montrezl Harrell .30 .75
68 Danilo Gallinari .30 .75
69 Shai Gilgeous-Alexander 2.00 5.00
70 LeBron James 3.00 8.00
71 Kyle Kuzma .50 1.25
72 Rajon Rondo .50 1.25
73 Talen Horton-Tucker RC .75 2.00
74 Deandre Ayton .40 1.00
75 Devin Booker .10 .25
76 Marvin Bagley III .30 .75
77 De'Aaron Fox .60 1.50
78 Harrison Barnes .30 .75
79 Bogdan Bogdanovic .40 1.00
80 Willie Cauley-Stein .25 .60
81 Jaylen Brown .60 1.50
82 Jayson Tatum 1.50 4.00
83 Marcus Smart .30 .75
84 Gordon Hayward .30 .75
85 Jarrett Allen .40 1.00
86 Caris LeVert .30 .75
87 Kevin Knox II .25 .60
88 Frank Ntilikina .25 .60
89 Dennis Smith Jr. .25 .60
90 Mitchell Robinson .40 1.00
91 Joel Embiid .75 2.00
92 Ben Simmons .40 1.00
93 Tobias Harris .30 .75
94 Pascal Siakam .60 1.50
95 Kawhi Leonard 1.00 2.50
96 Kyle Lowry .40 1.00
97 Marc Gasol .40 1.00
98 Fred VanVleet .50 1.25
99 Jamal Murray .60 1.50
100 Nikola Jokic 2.00 5.00
101 Michael Porter Jr. .60 1.50
102 Paul Millsap .30 .75
103 Will Barton .25 .60
104 Karl-Anthony Towns .60 1.50
105 Andrew Wiggins .50 1.25
106 Jeff Teague .25 .60
107 Gorgui Dieng .25 .60
108 Steven Adams .30 .75
109 Paul George .60 1.50
110 Russell Westbrook .60 1.50
111 Hamidou Diallo .30 .75
112 Terrance Ferguson .25 .60
113 Damian Lillard 1.00 2.50
114 CJ McCollum .40 1.00
115 Jusuf Nurkic .30 .75
116 Rudy Gobert .50 1.25
117 Donovan Mitchell .75 2.00
118 Derrick Favors .25 .60
119 Dante Exum .25 .60

120 Allen Crabbe .25 .60
121 Evan Turner .25 .60
122 Terry Rozier .30 .75
123 Jimmy Butler .75 2.00
124 Moritz Wagner .25 .60
125 Seth Curry .30 .75
126 Andre Iguodala .30 .75
127 Jae Crowder .25 .60
128 Lonzo Ball .40 1.00
129 Jrue Holiday .50 1.25
130 Brandon Ingram .40 1.00
131 JJ Redick .40 1.00
132 Derrick Rose .75 2.00
133 Malcolm Brogdon .30 .75
134 T.J. Warren .30 .75
135 D'Angelo Russell .30 .75
136 Anthony Davis 1.00 2.50
137 Ricky Rubio .30 .75
138 Dario Saric .30 .75
139 Tyler Johnson .25 .60
140 Kemba Walker .30 .75
141 Kevin Durant 1.25 3.00
142 Kyrie Irving .75 2.00
143 DeAndre Jordan .30 .75
144 Julius Randle .50 1.25
145 Al Horford .40 1.00
146 Josh Richardson .25 .60
147 Jordan Bell .25 .60
148 Hassan Whiteside .25 .60
149 Kent Bazemore .25 .60
150 Mike Conley .30 .75
151 Zion Williamson RC 8.00 20.00
152 Ja Morant RC 8.00 20.00
153 RJ Barrett RC 2.00 5.00
154 De'Andre Hunter RC 2.00 5.00
155 Jarrett Culver RC .50 1.25
156 Coby White RC 1.50 4.00
157 Jaxson Hayes RC .75 2.00
158 Rui Hachimura RC 2.00 5.00
159 Cam Reddish RC .75 2.00
160 Cameron Johnson RC 1.25 3.00
161 PJ Washington Jr. RC 1.50 4.00
162 Tyler Herro RC 2.50 6.00
163 Romeo Langford RC .50 1.25
164 Sekou Doumbouya RC .50 1.25
165 Chuma Okeke RC .75 2.00
166 Nickeil Alexander-Walker RC .75 2.00
167 Goga Bitadze RC .75 2.00
168 Luka Samanic RC .60 1.50
169 Brandon Clarke RC 1.00 2.50
170 Grant Williams RC .75 2.00
171 Ty Jerome RC 1.00 2.50
172 Nassir Little RC .75 2.00
173 Dylan Windler RC .60 1.50
174 Mfiondu Kabengele RC .60 1.50
175 Jordan Poole RC 2.00 5.00
176 Keldon Johnson RC 1.50 4.00
177 Kevin Porter Jr. RC 1.00 2.50
178 KZ Okpala RC .60 1.50
179 Carsen Edwards RC .60 1.50
180 Bruno Fernando RC .60 1.50
181 Cody Martin RC .75 2.00
182 Eric Paschall RC .60 1.50
183 Admiral Schofield RC .60 1.50
184 Jaylen Nowell RC .60 1.50
185 Bol Bol RC 1.25 3.00
186 Isaiah Roby RC .60 1.50
187 Ignas Brazdeikis RC .60 1.50
188 Quinndary Weatherspoon RC .50 1.25
189 Tremont Waters RC .50 1.25
190 Kyle Guy RC .60 1.50
191 Darius Garland RC 2.00 5.00
192 Darius Bazley RC .50 1.25
193 Matisse Thybulle RC 1.00 2.50
194 Jordan Bone RC .50 1.25
195 Nicolas Claxton RC 1.00 2.50
196 Dewan Hernandez RC .50 1.25
197 Daniel Gafford RC 1.00 2.50
198 Justin James RC .50 1.25
199 Terance Mann RC 1.00 2.50
200 Alen Smailagic RC .50 1.25

2019-20 Certified Mirror Camo
*MIR.CAMO VET: 4X TO 10X BASIC VET
*MIR.CAMO RC: 4X TO 10X BASIC RC
STATED PRINT 25 SER. #'d SETS
151 Zion Williamson 100.00 250.00
152 Ja Morant 100.00 250.00

2019-20 Certified 2019
1 Darius Garland 3.00 8.00
2 Keldon Johnson 2.50 6.00
3 Rui Hachimura 3.00 8.00
4 Tyler Herro 4.00 10.00
5 Nickeil Alexander-Walker 1.25 3.00
6 Brandon Clarke 1.50 4.00
7 Zion Williamson 15.00 40.00
8 Nassir Little 1.25 3.00
9 Jarrett Culver .75 2.00
10 Cam Reddish 1.25 3.00
11 Romeo Langford .75 2.00
12 Goga Bitadze 1.25 3.00
13 Grant Williams 1.25 3.00
14 Ja Morant 15.00 40.00
15 Dylan Windler 1.00 2.50
16 Coby White 2.50 6.00
17 Kevin Porter Jr. 1.50 4.00
18 Cameron Johnson 2.00 5.00
19 Sekou Doumbouya .75 2.00
20 Luka Samanic 1.00 2.50
21 Darius Bazley .75 2.00
22 RJ Barrett 3.00 8.00
23 Mfiondu Kabengele 1.00 2.50
24 Jaxson Hayes 1.25 3.00
25 PJ Washington Jr. 2.50 6.00
26 Chuma Okeke 1.25 3.00
27 Matisse Thybulle 1.50 4.00
28 Ty Jerome 1.50 4.00
29 De'Andre Hunter 3.00 8.00
30 Jordan Poole 3.00 8.00

2019-20 Certified Ballot Busters Autographs
EXCHANGE DEADLINE 5/13/2021
*CAMO/25: .6X TO 1.5X BASIC
1 David Robinson 25.00 60.00
2 Gail Goodrich 6.00 15.00
3 Larry Bird 75.00 200.00
4 Magic Johnson 75.00 200.00
5 Dave Cowens 8.00 20.00
6 Adrian Dantley 6.00 15.00
8 Alex English 8.00 20.00
9 George Gervin 12.00 30.00
10 Dan Issel 8.00 20.00
11 Charles Barkley 50.00 120.00
12 Jerry Lucas 8.00 20.00
13 Karl Malone 40.00 100.00
14 Bob McAdoo 8.00 20.00
15 Chris Mullin 8.00 20.00
16 Reggie Miller 125.00 300.00
17 Rick Barry 8.00 20.00
18 Bill Walton 15.00 40.00
19 James Worthy 10.00 25.00
20 Shaquille O'Neal 125.00 300.00

2019-20 Certified Established Autographs
EXCHANGE DEADLINE 5/13/2021
*CAMO/25: .6X TO 1.5X BASIC
1 Sam Cassell 5.00 12.00
2 Jamaal Wilkes 6.00 15.00
4 Doc Rivers 6.00 15.00
5 Emmanuel Mudiay 4.00 10.00
6 David Thompson 6.00 15.00
7 Juwan Howard 5.00 12.00
8 Donovan Mitchell EXCH 30.00 80.00
9 Patrick Beverley 5.00 12.00
10 Jerry Stackhouse 6.00 15.00
11 Mark Aguirre 5.00 12.00
12 Buddy Hield/49
inserted in 20/21 Chronicles 5.00 12.00
13 Jarrett Allen 6.00 15.00
14 Bam Adebayo 10.00 25.00
15 Shaun Livingston 6.00 15.00
16 Robert Covington 4.00 10.00
17 Fred VanVleet EXCH 30.00 80.00
18 Damian Lillard 60.00 150.00
19 Rondae Hollis-Jefferson 4.00 10.00
20 Pascal Siakam 10.00 25.00

2019-20 Certified Fabric of the Game Signatures
PRINT RUNS B/WN 15-99 COPIES PER
NO PRICING ON QTY 15 OR LESS
EXCHANGE DEADLINE 5/13/2021
*CAMO/25: .5X TO 1.2X p/r 49-99
1 Wesley Matthews/25 5.00 12.00
2 Goran Dragic/25 6.00 15.00
3 Aaron Holiday/99 5.00 12.00
4 Danny Green/99 5.00 12.00
5 Lauri Markkanen/25 20.00 50.00
6 Lou Williams/99 6.00 15.00
7 Malcolm Brogdon/49 5.00 12.00
8 Mike Bibby/99 6.00 15.00
9 Myles Turner/99 6.00 15.00
10 Nikola Jokic/25 150.00 400.00
11 Nikola Vucevic/25 6.00 15.00
12 Caron Butler/25 6.00 15.00
15 Collin Sexton/99 8.00 20.00
16 Wendell Carter Jr./99 6.00 15.00
17 Shai Gilgeous-Alexander/99 300.00 600.00
18 Mo Bamba/99 5.00 12.00
19 Lonnie Walker IV/99 5.00 12.00

2019-20 Certified Fresh Faces Signatures
EXCHANGE DEADLINE 5/13/2021
*CAMO/25: .6X TO 1.5X BASIC
1 Justin Jackson 3.00 8.00
2 De'Anthony Melton 3.00 8.00
3 Chandler Hutchison 3.00 8.00
4 Lauri Markkanen 6.00 15.00
5 Devonte' Graham 4.00 10.00
6 Allonzo Trier 3.00 8.00
7 Jarrett Allen 5.00 12.00
8 Josh Okogie 4.00 10.00
9 Larry Nance Jr. 4.00 10.00
10 Hamidou Diallo 4.00 10.00
11 Rodions Kurucs 5.00 12.00
12 Mo Bamba 4.00 10.00
13 Maxi Kleber 3.00 8.00
14 Spencer Dinwiddie 4.00 10.00
15 Svi Mykhailiuk 4.00 10.00
16 Dwayne Bacon 3.00 8.00
17 Zhaire Smith 3.00 8.00
18 Troy Brown Jr. 3.00 8.00
19 Jevon Carter 3.00 8.00
20 Jalen Brunson 12.00 30.00
21 Zion Williamson 125.00 300.00
22 Ja Morant 125.00 300.00
23 RJ Barrett 12.00 30.00
24 De'Andre Hunter 12.00 30.00
25 Jarrett Culver 3.00 8.00
26 Coby White 10.00 25.00
27 Jaxson Hayes 5.00 12.00
28 Rui Hachimura 12.00 30.00
29 Cam Reddish 5.00 12.00
30 Kevin Porter Jr. 5.00 12.00
31 Goga Bitadze 5.00 12.00
32 Ty Jerome 6.00 15.00
33 Nicolas Claxton 6.00 15.00
34 Grant Williams 5.00 12.00
35 Bruno Fernando 4.00 10.00
36 Isaiah Roby 4.00 10.00
37 Terance Mann 6.00 15.00
38 Tremont Waters 4.00 10.00
39 Kyle Guy 4.00 10.00
40 Jaylen Nowell 4.00 10.00

2019-20 Certified Freshman Fabric Signatures
EXCHANGE DEADLINE 5/13/2021
*RED/99: .5X TO 1.2X BASIC
*RED/49: .6X TO 1.5X BASIC
*RED/25: .8X TO 2X BASIC
*BLUE/49: .6X TO 1.5X BASIC
*CAMO/25: .75X TO 2X BASIC
FF-ZW Zion Williamson 150.00 400.00
FF-RJ RJ Barrett 15.00 40.00
3 Jarrett Culver 4.00 10.00
4 Jaxson Hayes 6.00 15.00
5 Cam Reddish 6.00 15.00
6 PJ Washington Jr. 12.00 30.00
7 Romeo Langford 4.00 10.00
8 Chuma Okeke 6.00 15.00
9 Goga Bitadze 6.00 15.00
10 Brandon Clarke 8.00 20.00
11 Ty Jerome 8.00 20.00
12 Dylan Windler 5.00 12.00
13 Jordan Poole 40.00 100.00
14 Kevin Porter Jr. 8.00 20.00
15 Carsen Edwards 5.00 12.00
16 Cody Martin 6.00 15.00
17 Admiral Schofield 5.00 12.00
18 Bol Bol 10.00 25.00
19 Ignas Brazdeikis 5.00 12.00
20 Tremont Waters 5.00 12.00
21 Matisse Thybulle 8.00 20.00
22 Quinndary Weatherspoon 4.00 10.00
23 Isaiah Roby 5.00 12.00
24 Jaylen Nowell 5.00 12.00
25 Eric Paschall 5.00 12.00
26 Bruno Fernando 5.00 12.00
27 KZ Okpala 5.00 12.00
28 Keldon Johnson 12.00 30.00
29 Mfiondu Kabengele 5.00 12.00
30 Nassir Little 6.00 15.00
31 Grant Williams 6.00 15.00
32 Luka Samanic 5.00 12.00
33 Nickeil Alexander-Walker 6.00 15.00
34 Sekou Doumbouya 4.00 10.00
35 Tyler Herro 20.00 50.00
36 Cameron Johnson 10.00 25.00
37 Rui Hachimura 15.00 40.00
38 Coby White 12.00 30.00
39 De'Andre Hunter 15.00 40.00
40 Ja Morant 150.00 400.00

2019-20 Certified Gold Team
*MIR.CAMO: 3X TO 8X BASIC
1 Damian Lillard 2.00 5.00
2 Kawhi Leonard 2.00 5.00
3 Kemba Walker .60 1.50
4 Luka Doncic 5.00 12.00
5 James Harden 1.50 4.00
6 Giannis Antetokounmpo 4.00 10.00
7 D'Angelo Russell .60 1.50
8 Kyle Lowry .75 2.00
9 Anthony Davis 2.00 5.00
10 Joel Embiid 1.50 4.00
11 Trae Young 2.00 5.00
12 Nikola Vucevic .60 1.50
13 Ben Simmons .75 2.00
14 Donovan Mitchell 1.50 4.00
15 Victor Oladipo .60 1.50
16 Kevin Durant 2.50 6.00
17 LeBron James 6.00 15.00
18 Blake Griffin .75 2.00
19 Stephen Curry 6.00 15.00
20 Kyrie Irving 1.50 4.00
21 Bradley Beal 1.00 2.50
22 Khris Middleton .75 2.00
23 Nikola Jokic 4.00 10.00
24 Pascal Siakam 1.25 3.00
25 Russell Westbrook 1.25 3.00
26 Klay Thompson 2.00 5.00
27 Karl-Anthony Towns 1.25 3.00
28 LaMarcus Aldridge .75 2.00
29 Jayson Tatum 3.00 8.00
30 Paul George 1.25 3.00

2019-20 Certified Legendary Signatures
EXCHANGE DEADLINE 5/13/2021
*CAMO/25: .6X TO 1.5X BASIC
1 Dennis Rodman 40.00 100.00
2 Toni Kukoc 6.00 15.00
3 Robert Parish 6.00 15.00
4 Kiki Vandeweghe 4.00 10.00
5 Kelly Tripucka 4.00 10.00
6 Mark Price 5.00 12.00
7 Larry Nance 4.00 10.00
8 John Starks 12.00 30.00
9 Fat Lever 4.00 10.00
10 Cedric Maxwell 4.00 10.00
11 Larry Bird 30.00 80.00
12 Magic Johnson 30.00 80.00
13 Maurice Cheeks 4.00 10.00
14 Tom Chambers 5.00 12.00
15 Kenny Sky Walker 4.00 10.00
16 Nate McMillan 4.00 10.00
17 Sidney Moncrief 5.00 12.00
18 Larry Johnson 12.00 30.00
19 Rolando Blackman 4.00 10.00
20 Julius Erving 25.00 60.00

2019-20 Certified Raise the Banner
*MIR.CAMO/25: 2.5X TO 6X BASIC
1 Kawhi Leonard 2.00 5.00
2 Klay Thompson 2.00 5.00
3 Toni Kukoc 1.00 2.50
4 John Salley .50 1.25
5 Andre Iguodala .60 1.50
6 Robert Horry .60 1.50
7 Byron Scott .60 1.50
8 Ron Harper .75 2.00
9 Jerry West 1.25 3.00
10 Stephen Curry 6.00 15.00
11 Kareem Abdul-Jabbar 2.50 6.00
12 Tom Satch Sanders .75 2.00
13 Steve Kerr 1.00 2.50
14 LeBron James 6.00 15.00
15 Bob Cousy 1.25 3.00
16 Scottie Pippen 2.00 5.00
17 Kyle Lowry .75 2.00
18 Kobe Bryant 6.00 15.00
19 Derek Fisher .75 2.00
20 Shaquille O'Neal 3.00 8.00
21 Magic Johnson 2.50 6.00
22 Tim Duncan 2.00 5.00
23 Dennis Rodman 2.00 5.00
24 Kevin Durant 2.50 6.00
25 Pascal Siakam 1.25 3.00
26 David Robinson 1.50 4.00
27 Draymond Green 1.00 2.50
28 Bill Russell 2.50 6.00
29 Robert Parish 1.00 2.50
30 Larry Bird 3.00 8.00

2019-20 Certified Record Breakers
1 Dirk Nowitzki 2.00 5.00
2 Klay Thompson 2.00 5.00
3 Vince Carter 1.50 4.00
4 Russell Westbrook 1.25 3.00
5 Lou Williams .75 2.00
6 James Harden 1.50 4.00
7 Rudy Gobert 1.00 2.50
8 Luka Doncic 5.00 12.00
9 Buddy Hield .60 1.50
10 Jamal Crawford .75 2.00

2019-20 Certified Record Breakers Mirror Camo
*MIR.CAMO: 1.2X TO 3X BASIC
STATED PRINT RUN 25 SER. #'d SETS

2019-20 Certified Rookie Roll Call Autographs
EXCHANGE DEADLINE 5/13/2021
*CAMO/25: .6X TO 1.5X BASIC
1 Zion Williamson 150.00 400.00
2 Coby White 12.00 30.00
3 PJ Washington Jr. 12.00 30.00
4 Chuma Okeke 6.00 15.00
5 Luka Samanic 5.00 12.00
6 Nassir Little 6.00 15.00
7 Keldon Johnson 12.00 30.00
8 Cody Martin 6.00 15.00
9 Bol Bol 10.00 25.00
10 Kyle Guy 5.00 12.00
11 Tremont Waters 5.00 12.00
12 Daniel Gafford 8.00 20.00
13 Terance Mann 8.00 20.00
14 Jordan Bone 4.00 10.00
15 Isaiah Roby 5.00 12.00
16 Admiral Schofield 5.00 12.00
17 Carsen Edwards 5.00 12.00
18 Mfiondu Kabengele 5.00 12.00
19 Grant Williams 6.00 15.00
20 Rui Hachimura 15.00 40.00
21 RJ Barrett 15.00 40.00
22 De'Andre Hunter 15.00 40.00
23 Jaxson Hayes 6.00 15.00
24 Tyler Herro 20.00 50.00
25 Nickeil Alexander-Walker 6.00 15.00
26 Brandon Clarke 8.00 20.00
27 Dylan Windler 5.00 12.00
28 KZ Okpala 5.00 12.00
29 Eric Paschall 5.00 12.00
30 Jaylen Nowell 5.00 12.00
31 Quinndary Weatherspoon 4.00 10.00
32 Justin James 4.00 10.00
33 Alen Smailagic 4.00 10.00
35 Nicolas Claxton 8.00 20.00
36 Ja Morant 150.00 400.00
37 Jarrett Culver 4.00 10.00
38 Cam Reddish 6.00 15.00
39 Romeo Langford 4.00 10.00
40 Goga Bitadze 6.00 15.00
41 Ty Jerome 8.00 20.00
42 Jordan Poole 40.00 100.00
43 Kevin Porter Jr. 8.00 20.00
44 Bruno Fernando 5.00 12.00
45 Ignas Brazdeikis 5.00 12.00
46 Matisse Thybulle 8.00 20.00
49 Cameron Johnson 10.00 25.00
50 Sekou Doumbouya 4.00 10.00

2019-20 Certified Signatures
EXCHANGE DEADLINE 5/13/2021
*CAMO/25: .6X TO 1.5X BASIC
1 Kobe Bryant 600.00 1,200.00
2 Montrezl Harrell 4.00 10.00
3 Bruce Bowen 5.00 12.00
4 Chandler Hutchison 3.00 8.00
5 Willie Cauley-Stein 3.00 8.00
6 John Salley 3.00 8.00
7 Meyers Leonard 3.00 8.00
8 David Thompson 5.00 12.00
9 Josh Hart 4.00 10.00
10 Kurt Rambis 4.00 10.00
11 Jalen Brunson 12.00 30.00
12 Mike Bibby 5.00 12.00
13 Allonzo Trier 3.00 8.00
14 Sean Elliott 4.00 10.00
15 Kelly Olynyk 3.00 8.00
16 Hamidou Diallo 4.00 10.00
17 Muggsy Bogues 10.00 25.00
19 Anthony Davis EXCH 40.00 100.00
20 Brad Davis 3.00 8.00
21 Zydrunas Ilgauskas 5.00 12.00
22 E'Twaun Moore 3.00 8.00
23 Corey Maggette 4.00 10.00
24 Kevin Knox II 3.00 8.00
25 Kevin Johnson 5.00 12.00
26 Luka Doncic 400.00 800.00
27 Brian Scalabrine 3.00 8.00
28 Rik Smits 4.00 10.00
29 Caris LeVert 4.00 10.00
30 Rafer Alston 3.00 8.00
31 Jose Calderon 3.00 8.00
32 Kevin Durant EXCH 60.00 150.00
33 Grayson Allen 5.00 12.00
34 P.J. Tucker 4.00 10.00
35 Larry Hughes 4.00 10.00
36 Vlade Divac 5.00 12.00
37 Gary Trent Jr. 3.00 8.00
38 Cuttino Mobley EXCH 3.00 8.00
39 Kyrie Irving 20.00 50.00
40 Doug Collins 5.00 12.00

2020-21 Certified
*ASIA: .75X TO 2X BASIC
*ASIA RED: .75X TO 2X BASIC
*MIR.RED: .75X TO 2X BASIC
*MIR ORANGE/99: 2X TO 5X BASIC
*MIR.CAMO/25: 4X TO 10X BASIC
1 Spencer Dinwiddie .30 .75
2 Andrew Wiggins .50 1.25
3 Bryn Forbes .25 .60
4 JJ Redick .40 1.00
5 Draymond Green .50 1.25
6 Tobias Harris .40 1.00
7 Will Barton .25 .60
8 Hassan Whiteside .30 .75
9 Patrick Beverley .25 .60
10 Ja Morant 1.25 3.00
11 Tim Hardaway Jr. .25 .60
12 Dwight Powell .25 .60
13 Marcus Smart .40 1.00
14 Kelly Oubre Jr. .40 1.00
15 Brandon Ingram .50 1.25
16 Trae Young 1.00 2.50
17 Russell Westbrook .75 2.00
18 Gordon Hayward .40 1.00
19 Joe Harris .30 .75
20 Caris LeVert .40 1.00
21 Malcolm Brogdon .40 1.00
22 Terry Rozier .40 1.00
23 Kyle Lowry .50 1.25
24 Darius Garland .60 1.50
25 Josh Richardson .30 .75
26 CJ McCollum .40 1.00
27 Eric Paschall .30 .75
28 Markelle Fultz .30 .75
29 James Harden .75 2.00
30 PJ Washington Jr. .40 1.00
31 Domantas Sabonis .50 1.25
32 Tyler Herro .75 2.00
33 Kyrie Irving .75 2.00
34 Anthony Davis 1.00 2.50
35 Aaron Gordon .40 1.00
36 Fred VanVleet .60 1.50
37 RJ Barrett .60 1.50
38 Jamal Murray .60 1.50
39 Devin Booker 1.00 2.50
40 Kyle Kuzma .50 1.25
41 Jonas Valanciunas .30 .75
42 Montrezl Harrell .40 1.00
43 Cody Zeller .25 .60
44 Derrick Rose .60 1.50
45 Christian Wood .40 1.00
46 Carmelo Anthony .60 1.50
47 Robert Covington .30 .75
48 Lonnie Walker IV .30 .75
49 Eric Gordon .30 .75
50 Buddy Hield .40 1.00
51 Cam Reddish .50 1.25
52 Zach LaVine .60 1.50
53 Danilo Gallinari .30 .75
54 Jonathan Isaac .40 1.00
55 LeBron James 3.00 8.00
56 Jrue Holiday .40 1.00
57 Otto Porter Jr. .25 .60
58 Chris Paul .75 2.00
59 Kevin Durant 1.50 4.00
60 LaMarcus Aldridge .40 1.00
61 Myles Turner .40 1.00
62 Pascal Siakam .60 1.50
63 Luka Doncic 2.50 6.00
64 Dennis Schroder .40 1.00
65 Marvin Bagley III .30 .75
66 Danny Green .30 .75
67 Jaylen Brown .60 1.50
68 John Wall .50 1.25
69 Kevin Huerter .30 .75
70 Deandre Ayton .40 1.00
71 Rui Hachimura .50 1.25
72 Harrison Barnes .30 .75
73 Klay Thompson 1.00 2.50
74 John Collins .40 1.00
75 Joe Ingles .30 .75
76 Patty Mills .40 1.00
77 DeMar DeRozan .50 1.25
78 Thomas Bryant .30 .75
79 Paul Millsap .30 .75
80 Zion Williamson 1.25 3.00
81 Luke Kennard .30 .75
82 Wendell Carter Jr. .30 .75
83 Marc Gasol .40 1.00
84 Bam Adebayo .60 1.50
85 Ben Simmons .40 1.00
86 Steven Adams .40 1.00
87 Khris Middleton .50 1.25
88 Jarrett Culver .25 .60
89 Bogdan Bogdanovic .40 1.00
90 Rudy Gobert .50 1.25
91 Joel Embiid 1.00 2.50
92 Karl-Anthony Towns .60 1.50
93 Norman Powell .40 1.00
94 Bradley Beal .50 1.25
95 Damian Lillard 1.00 2.50
96 Juancho Hernangomez .40 1.00
97 Stephen Curry 3.00 8.00
98 Lou Williams .40 1.00
99 Davis Bertans .30 .75
100 Donovan Mitchell .75 2.00
101 Goran Dragic .40 1.00
102 Devonte' Graham .30 .75
103 Evan Fournier .30 .75
104 Kendrick Nunn .30 .75
105 Jayson Tatum 1.50 4.00
106 Lonzo Ball .50 1.25
107 Jerami Grant .40 1.00
108 De'Andre Hunter .40 1.00
109 Elfrid Payton .30 .75
110 Paul George .60 1.50
111 D'Angelo Russell .40 1.00
112 Bojan Bogdanovic .30 .75
113 Jimmy Butler .75 2.00
114 Jeff Green .25 .60
115 Mitchell Robinson .40 1.00
116 Miles Bridges .40 1.00
117 Kawhi Leonard 1.00 2.50
118 Nikola Vucevic .40 1.00
119 Shai Gilgeous-Alexander 2.00 5.00
120 Jaren Jackson Jr. .60 1.50
121 Kevin Love .40 1.00
122 Anfernee Simons .50 1.25
123 Eric Bledsoe .30 .75
124 Mike Conley .30 .75
125 Collin Sexton .40 1.00
126 Kevin Porter Jr. .40 1.00
127 Giannis Antetokounmpo 2.00 5.00
128 Kristaps Porzingis .50 1.25
129 Aron Baynes .25 .60
130 Victor Oladipo .30 .75
131 Dejounte Murray .40 1.00
132 Nikola Jokic 2.00 5.00
133 Julius Randle .40 1.00
134 Ricky Rubio .40 1.00
135 Seth Curry .40 1.00
136 De'Aaron Fox .60 1.50
137 Brook Lopez .30 .75
138 Bobby Portis .40 1.00
139 Blake Griffin .40 1.00
140 Kentavious Caldwell-Pope .40 1.00
141 Coby White .50 1.25
142 Kemba Walker .40 1.00
143 T.J. Warren .30 .75
144 Sekou Doumbouya .25 .60
145 Lauri Markkanen .50 1.25
146 Brandon Clarke .40 1.00
147 Al Horford .40 1.00
148 George Hill .30 .75
149 Josh Jackson .25 .60
150 Andre Drummond .40 1.00
151 Grant Riller RC .60 1.50
152 Cassius Stanley RC .60 1.50
153 Cassius Winston RC .60 1.50
154 Kenyon Martin Jr. RC 1.00 2.50
155 Skylar Mays RC .60 1.50
156 CJ Elleby RC .60 1.50
157 Jahmi'us Ramsey RC .60 1.50
158 Nick Richards RC .75 2.00
159 Elijah Hughes RC .60 1.50
160 Saben Lee RC .60 1.50
161 Nico Mannion RC .60 1.50
162 Jordan Nwora RC .75 2.00
163 Tre Jones RC 1.00 2.50
164 Robert Woodard II RC .60 1.50
165 Tyler Bey RC .60 1.50
166 Xavier Tillman RC .75 2.00
167 Theo Maledon RC .60 1.50
168 Daniel Oturu RC .60 1.50
169 Vernon Carey Jr. RC .60 1.50
170 Tyrell Terry RC .50 1.25
171 Desmond Bane RC 2.00 5.00
172 Malachi Flynn RC .60 1.50
173 Jaden McDaniels RC 2.00 5.00
174 Udoka Azubuike RC .75 2.00
175 Payton Pritchard RC 2.00 5.00
176 Immanuel Quickley RC 1.50 4.00
177 RJ Hampton RC .60 1.50
178 Cole Anthony RC 1.25 3.00
179 Zeke Nnaji RC .75 2.00
180 Tyrese Maxey RC 5.00 12.00
181 Precious Achiuwa RC 1.25 3.00
182 Saddiq Bey RC 1.25 3.00
183 Josh Green RC 1.25 3.00
184 Aleksej Pokusevski RC .75 2.00
185 Isaiah Stewart RC 1.25 3.00
186 Cole Anthony RC 1.50 4.00
187 Aaron Nesmith RC 1.25 3.00
188 Kira Lewis Jr. RC .60 1.50
189 Tyrese Haliburton RC 5.00 12.00
190 Devin Vassell RC 2.00 5.00
191 Jalen Smith RC 1.25 3.00
192 Deni Avdija RC 1.50 4.00
193 Obi Toppin RC 1.25 3.00
194 Killian Hayes RC .60 1.50
195 Onyeka Okongwu RC 1.25 3.00
196 Isaac Okoro RC 1.00 2.50
197 Patrick Williams RC 1.50 4.00
198 LaMelo Ball RC 5.00 12.00
199 James Wiseman RC .75 2.00
200 Anthony Edwards RC 6.00 15.00

2020-21 Certified Mirror Blue
COMPLETE SET (200)
*MIR.BLUE: .75X TO 2X BASIC
200 Anthony Edwards 40.00 100.00

2020-21 Certified 2020
*MIR.CAMO/25: 2X TO 5X BASIC
1 Kenyon Martin Jr. 1.25 3.00
2 Nico Mannion .75 2.00
3 Tre Jones 1.25 3.00
4 Tyrell Terry .60 1.50
5 Malachi Flynn .75 2.00
6 Payton Pritchard 2.50 6.00
7 RJ Hampton .75 2.00
8 Jordan Nwora 1.00 2.50
9 Zeke Nnaji 1.00 2.50
10 Tyrese Maxey 6.00 15.00
11 Precious Achiuwa 1.50 4.00
12 Saddiq Bey 1.50 4.00
13 Josh Green 1.50 4.00
14 Aleksej Pokusevski 1.00 2.50
15 Isaiah Stewart 1.50 4.00
16 Cole Anthony 2.00 5.00
17 Aaron Nesmith 1.50 4.00
18 Kira Lewis Jr. .75 2.00
19 Tyrese Haliburton 6.00 15.00
20 Devin Vassell 2.50 6.00
21 Jalen Smith 1.50 4.00
22 Deni Avdija 2.00 5.00
23 Obi Toppin 1.50 4.00
24 Killian Hayes .75 2.00
25 Onyeka Okongwu 1.50 4.00
26 Isaac Okoro 1.25 3.00
27 Patrick Williams 2.00 5.00
28 LaMelo Ball 12.00 30.00
29 James Wiseman 1.00 2.50
30 Anthony Edwards 15.00 40.00

2020-21 Certified Fabric of the Game Signatures Camo
COMMON CARD 5.00 12.00
SEMISTARS 6.00 15.00
UNLISTED STARS 8.00 20.00
PRINT RUNS B/WN 18-25 COPIES PER
EXCHANGE DEADLINE 8/17/2022
1 Jayson Tatum/25* 150.00 400.00
2 Sam Cassell/25* 6.00 15.00
3 David Robinson/25* 50.00 120.00
4 Luc Longley/25* 10.00 25.00
5 Toni Kukoc/25* 20.00 50.00
6 Ray Allen/25* 60.00 150.00
7 Shawn Kemp/25* 50.00 120.00
8 Kevin Johnson/22* 20.00 50.00
9 Thomas Bryant/25* 20.00 50.00
10 Grant Williams/25* 10.00 25.00
11 Daniel Theis/25* 20.00 50.00
12 Taj Gibson/25* 5.00 12.00
13 Brook Lopez/25* 12.00 30.00
14 Rick Fox/25* 10.00 25.00
15 Ricky Rubio/25* 20.00 50.00
16 Terry Cummings/25* 12.00 30.00
17 Boban Marjanovic/25* 15.00 40.00
19 De'Aaron Fox/18* 75.00 200.00

2020-21 Certified Fabric of the Game Signatures Jersey Number
PRINT RUNS B/WN 1-67 COPIES PER
NO PRICING ON QTY 15 OR LESS
EXCHANGE DEADLINE 8/17/2022
3 David Robinson/50* 40.00 100.00
6 Ray Allen/34* 60.00 150.00
7 Shawn Kemp/40* 50.00 120.00
11 Daniel Theis/27* 20.00 50.00
12 Taj Gibson/67* 5.00 12.00
16 Terry Cummings/34* 10.00 25.00
17 Boban Marjanovic/51* 12.00 30.00
18 Harry Giles III/20* 10.00 25.00

2020-21 Certified Fresh Faces Signatures
EXCHANGE DEADLINE 8/17/2022
1 Anthony Edwards 125.00 300.00
2 James Wiseman 5.00 12.00
3 LaMelo Ball 125.00 300.00
4 Patrick Williams 10.00 25.00
5 Isaac Okoro 6.00 15.00
6 Onyeka Okongwu 8.00 20.00
7 Killian Hayes 4.00 10.00
8 Obi Toppin 8.00 20.00
9 Deni Avdija 10.00 25.00
10 Jalen Smith 4.00 10.00
11 Devin Vassell 12.00 30.00
12 Tyrese Haliburton 60.00 150.00
13 Kira Lewis Jr. 4.00 10.00
14 Aaron Nesmith 8.00 20.00
15 Cole Anthony 10.00 25.00
16 Isaiah Stewart 8.00 20.00
17 Aleksej Pokusevski 5.00 12.00
18 Josh Green 8.00 20.00
19 Saddiq Bey 8.00 20.00
20 Precious Achiuwa 8.00 20.00
21 Tyrese Maxey 30.00 80.00
22 Zeke Nnaji 5.00 12.00
23 Caleb Martin 8.00 20.00
24 RJ Hampton 4.00 10.00
25 Immanuel Quickley 10.00 25.00
26 Payton Pritchard 12.00 30.00
27 Udoka Azubuike 5.00 12.00
28 Jaden McDaniels 12.00 30.00
29 Malachi Flynn 4.00 10.00
30 Desmond Bane 12.00 30.00
31 Tyrell Terry 3.00 8.00
32 Vernon Carey Jr. 4.00 10.00
33 Daniel Oturu 4.00 10.00
34 Theo Maledon 4.00 10.00
35 Xavier Tillman 5.00 12.00
36 Tyler Bey 4.00 10.00
37 Robert Woodard II 4.00 10.00
38 Tre Jones 6.00 15.00
39 Jordan Nwora 5.00 12.00
40 Nico Mannion 4.00 10.00

2020-21 Certified Fresh Faces Signatures Camo
STATED PRINT RUN 25 SER. #'d SETS
EXCHANGE DEADLINE 8/17/2022
7 Killian Hayes 8.00 20.00
17 Aleksej Pokusevski 10.00 25.00

2020-21 Certified Freshman Fabric Signatures
EXCHANGE DEADLINE 8/17/2022
1 Nico Mannion 5.00 12.00
2 Jordan Nwora 6.00 15.00
3 Tre Jones 8.00 20.00
4 Robert Woodard II 5.00 12.00
5 Tyler Bey 5.00 12.00
6 Xavier Tillman 6.00 15.00
7 Theo Maledon 5.00 12.00
8 Daniel Oturu 5.00 12.00
9 Vernon Carey Jr. 5.00 12.00
10 Tyrell Terry 4.00 10.00
11 Desmond Bane 40.00 100.00
12 Malachi Flynn 5.00 12.00
13 Jaden McDaniels 15.00 40.00
14 Udoka Azubuike 6.00 15.00
15 Payton Pritchard 15.00 40.00
16 Immanuel Quickley 12.00 30.00
17 RJ Hampton 5.00 12.00
18 Jahmi'us Ramsey 5.00 12.00
19 Zeke Nnaji 6.00 15.00
20 Tyrese Maxey 40.00 100.00
21 Precious Achiuwa 10.00 25.00
22 Saddiq Bey 10.00 25.00
23 Josh Green 10.00 25.00
24 Aleksej Pokusevski 6.00 15.00
25 Isaiah Stewart 10.00 25.00
26 Cole Anthony 12.00 30.00
27 Aaron Nesmith 10.00 25.00
28 Kira Lewis Jr. 5.00 12.00
29 Tyrese Haliburton 75.00 200.00
30 Devin Vassell 15.00 40.00
31 Jalen Smith 10.00 25.00
32 Deni Avdija 12.00 30.00
33 Obi Toppin 10.00 25.00
34 Killian Hayes 5.00 12.00
35 Onyeka Okongwu 10.00 25.00
36 Isaac Okoro 8.00 20.00
37 Patrick Williams 12.00 30.00
38 LaMelo Ball 125.00 300.00
39 James Wiseman 6.00 15.00
40 Anthony Edwards 125.00 300.00

2020-21 Certified Gold Team
*MIR.CAMO/25: 1.2X TO 3X BASIC
1 Nikola Jokic 5.00 12.00
2 Anthony Davis 2.50 6.00
3 Damian Lillard 2.50 6.00
4 Paul George 1.50 4.00
5 Chris Paul 2.00 5.00
6 Jimmy Butler 2.00 5.00
7 Luka Doncic 6.00 15.00
8 Kawhi Leonard 2.50 6.00
9 Donovan Mitchell 2.00 5.00
10 Bam Adebayo 1.50 4.00
11 Brandon Ingram 1.25 3.00
12 Ja Morant 3.00 8.00
13 Russell Westbrook 2.00 5.00
14 Kyrie Irving 2.00 5.00
15 Karl-Anthony Towns 1.50 4.00
16 RJ Barrett 1.50 4.00
17 Zion Williamson 3.00 8.00
18 D'Angelo Russell 1.00 2.50
19 Jaylen Brown 1.50 4.00
20 James Harden 2.00 5.00
21 Kyle Lowry 1.25 3.00
22 Stephen Curry 8.00 20.00
23 Devin Booker 2.50 6.00
24 Giannis Antetokounmpo 5.00 12.00
25 Joel Embiid 2.50 6.00
26 Ben Simmons 1.00 2.50

27 Jamal Murray 1.50 4.00
28 Pascal Siakam 1.50 4.00
29 LeBron James 8.00 20.00
30 Jayson Tatum 4.00 10.00

2020-21 Certified Gold Team Rookies

*MIR.CAMO/25: 2X TO 5X BASIC
1 Anthony Edwards 12.00 30.00
2 James Wiseman 1.00 2.50
3 LaMelo Ball 12.00 30.00
4 Patrick Williams 2.00 5.00
5 Isaac Okoro 1.25 3.00
6 Onyeka Okongwu 1.50 4.00
7 Killian Hayes .75 2.00
8 Obi Toppin 1.50 4.00
9 Deni Avdija 2.00 5.00
10 Jalen Smith 1.50 4.00

2020-21 Certified Legendary Signatures

EXCHANGE DEADLINE 8/17/2022
1 Shaquille O'Neal 100.00 250.00
2 Mehmet Okur 3.00 8.00
3 Larry Bird 60.00 150.00
4 Spud Webb 8.00 20.00
5 Shawn Kemp 12.00 30.00
6 Kevin Willis 4.00 10.00
7 Ron Harper 5.00 12.00
8 Slick Watts 4.00 10.00
9 Dirk Nowitzki 75.00 200.00
10 Bob Love 5.00 12.00
11 Magic Johnson 60.00 150.00
12 Hedo Turkoglu 4.00 10.00
13 Dave Bing 6.00 15.00
14 Desmond Mason 4.00 10.00
15 Jason Williams 20.00 50.00
16 Dick Barnett 4.00 10.00
17 Harold Miner 4.00 10.00
18 Alvin Robertson 4.00 10.00
19 Charles Barkley 60.00 150.00
20 Greg Ostertag 3.00 8.00

2020-21 Certified Rookie Roll Call

EXCHANGE DEADLINE 8/17/2022
*CAMO/25: .75X TO 2X BASIC
1 Grant Riller 4.00 10.00
2 Cassius Winston 4.00 10.00
3 Skylar Mays 4.00 10.00
4 Isaiah Joe 5.00 12.00
5 Elijah Hughes 4.00 10.00
6 Nico Mannion 4.00 10.00
7 Tre Jones 6.00 15.00
8 Tyler Bey 4.00 10.00
9 Theo Maledon 4.00 10.00
10 Vernon Carey Jr. 4.00 10.00
11 Desmond Bane 12.00 30.00
12 Jaden McDaniels 12.00 30.00
13 Payton Pritchard 12.00 30.00
14 RJ Hampton 4.00 10.00
15 Zeke Nnaji 5.00 12.00
16 Precious Achiuwa 8.00 20.00
17 Josh Green 8.00 20.00
18 Isaiah Stewart 8.00 20.00
19 Aaron Nesmith 8.00 20.00
20 Tyrese Haliburton 60.00 150.00
21 Jalen Smith 8.00 20.00
22 Obi Toppin 8.00 20.00
23 Onyeka Okongwu 8.00 20.00
24 Patrick Williams 10.00 25.00
25 James Wiseman 5.00 12.00
26 Anthony Edwards 125.00 300.00
27 LaMelo Ball 125.00 300.00
28 Isaac Okoro 6.00 15.00
29 Killian Hayes 4.00 10.00
30 Deni Avdija 10.00 25.00
31 Devin Vassell 12.00 30.00
32 Kira Lewis Jr. 4.00 10.00
33 Cole Anthony 10.00 25.00
34 Aleksej Pokusevski 5.00 12.00
35 Saddiq Bey 8.00 20.00
36 Tyrese Maxey 30.00 80.00
37 Caleb Martin 8.00 20.00
38 Immanuel Quickley 10.00 25.00
39 Udoka Azubuike 5.00 12.00
40 Malachi Flynn 4.00 10.00
41 Tyrell Terry 3.00 8.00
42 Daniel Oturu 4.00 10.00
43 Xavier Tillman 5.00 12.00
44 Robert Woodard II 4.00 10.00
45 Jordan Nwora 5.00 12.00
46 Saben Lee 4.00 10.00
47 Nick Richards 5.00 12.00
48 CJ Elleby 4.00 10.00
49 Kenyon Martin Jr. 6.00 15.00
50 Cassius Stanley 4.00 10.00

2020-21 Certified Signatures

EXCHANGE DEADLINE 8/17/2022
*CAMO/25: .75X TO 2X BASIC
1 Larry Nance Jr. 4.00 10.00
2 Donovan Mitchell 30.00 80.00
3 Alec Burks 3.00 8.00
4 Dave Bing 6.00 15.00
5 Sterling Brown 3.00 8.00
6 DeAndre Bembry 3.00 8.00
7 Isaac Bonga 3.00 8.00
8 Michael Kidd-Gilchrist 3.00 8.00
9 Thomas Bryant 4.00 10.00
10 Zach Collins 4.00 10.00
11 Ron Harper 5.00 12.00
12 Stephon Marbury 6.00 15.00
13 Boban Marjanovic 4.00 10.00
14 Tobias Harris 5.00 12.00
15 Kent Benson 3.00 8.00
16 Shawn Kemp 12.00 30.00
17 E'Twaun Moore 3.00 8.00
18 Jonas Valanciunas 4.00 10.00
19 James Johnson 3.00 8.00
20 Gerald Green 3.00 8.00
21 Derrick Coleman 5.00 12.00
22 Eric Bledsoe 4.00 10.00
23 Kelly Olynyk 3.00 8.00
24 Spencer Dinwiddie 4.00 10.00
25 Ben McLemore 3.00 8.00
26 Devonte' Graham 4.00 10.00
27 Jevon Carter 4.00 10.00
28 Kevin Huerter 4.00 10.00
29 Monte Morris 3.00 8.00
30 Austin Rivers 4.00 10.00
31 Kevin Willis 4.00 10.00
32 Dorian Finney-Smith 4.00 10.00
33 Robin Lopez 3.00 8.00
34 Nerlens Noel 3.00 8.00
35 Mike Scott 3.00 8.00
36 Kelly Oubre Jr. 5.00 12.00
37 Torrey Craig 4.00 10.00
38 Anfernee Simons 15.00 40.00
39 Dewayne Dedmon 3.00 8.00
40 Mikal Bridges 12.00 30.00

2020-21 Certified Signed Sealed and Delivered

EXCHANGE DEADLINE 8/17/2022
*CAMO/25: .75X TO 2X BASIC
1 Austin Rivers 4.00 10.00
2 John Collins 5.00 12.00
3 Thomas Bryant 4.00 10.00
4 Kyle Kuzma 6.00 15.00
5 Jarrett Culver 3.00 8.00
6 Tobias Harris 5.00 12.00
7 Devonte' Graham 4.00 10.00
8 Stephen Curry 300.00 600.00
9 Kelly Oubre Jr. 5.00 12.00
10 Anthony Davis 40.00 100.00
11 Boban Marjanovic 4.00 10.00
12 Al Horford 5.00 12.00
13 Larry Nance Jr. 4.00 10.00
14 Eric Bledsoe 4.00 10.00
15 Duncan Robinson 5.00 12.00
16 Spencer Dinwiddie 4.00 10.00
17 Jarrett Allen 8.00 20.00
18 Kevin Durant 75.00 200.00
19 Anfernee Simons 15.00 40.00
20 Donovan Mitchell 30.00 80.00

2020-21 Certified Sophomore Sensations Autographs

EXCHANGE DEADLINE 8/17/2022
*CAMO/25: .75X TO 2X BASIC
1 Alen Smailagic 3.00 8.00
2 Jordan Poole 25.00 60.00
3 Ky Bowman 3.00 8.00
4 Zion Williamson 125.00 300.00
5 Keldon Johnson 8.00 20.00
6 RJ Barrett 8.00 20.00
7 Naz Reid 6.00 15.00
8 Kendrick Nunn 4.00 10.00
9 Daniel Gafford 4.00 10.00
10 Nickeil Alexander-Walker 5.00 12.00
11 Nicolo Melli 3.00 8.00
12 Chuma Okeke 5.00 12.00
13 Terence Davis II 5.00 12.00
14 Ja Morant 125.00 300.00
15 De'Andre Hunter 5.00 12.00
16 Coby White 6.00 15.00
17 DaQuan Jeffries 3.00 8.00
18 Eric Paschall 4.00 10.00
19 Nicolas Claxton 5.00 12.00
20 Brandon Clarke 5.00 12.00

2020-21 Certified The Mighty

1 Trae Young 2.50 6.00
2 Joel Embiid 2.50 6.00
3 Jimmy Butler 2.00 5.00
4 Domantas Sabonis 1.25 3.00
5 LeBron James 8.00 20.00
6 Anthony Davis 2.50 6.00
7 Damian Lillard 2.50 6.00
8 Devin Booker 2.50 6.00
9 Stephen Curry 8.00 20.00
10 James Harden 2.00 5.00
11 Kevin Durant 4.00 10.00
12 John Wall 1.25 3.00
13 Zion Williamson 3.00 8.00
14 Donovan Mitchell 2.00 5.00
15 Giannis Antetokounmpo 5.00 12.00
16 Kyle Lowry 1.25 3.00
17 Bam Adebayo 1.50 4.00
18 Chris Paul 2.00 5.00
19 Brandon Ingram 1.25 3.00
20 Ja Morant 3.00 8.00
21 Kyrie Irving 2.00 5.00
22 Bradley Beal 1.25 3.00
23 Nikola Jokic 5.00 12.00
24 Russell Westbrook 2.00 5.00
25 Kawhi Leonard 2.50 6.00
26 Luka Doncic 6.00 15.00
27 Ben Simmons 1.00 2.50
28 Pascal Siakam 1.50 4.00
29 Jayson Tatum 4.00 10.00
30 Kemba Walker 1.00 2.50

2020-21 Certified The Mighty Mirror Camo

STATED PRINT RUN 25 SER.#'d SETS

2006-07 Chronology

1-100 PRINT RUN 199 SER.#'d SETS
101-142 PRINT RUN 99 SER.#'d SETS
143-148 NOT ISSUED IN PACKS
149-184 PRINT RUN 99 SER.#'d SETS
185-226 PRINT RUN 40 SER.#'d SETS
227-246 PRINT RUN 50 SER.#'d SETS
247-276 PRINT RUN 250 SER.#'d SETS
1 Slick Watts 1.50 4.00
2 Louie Dampier 1.50 4.00
3 Al Attles 2.00 5.00
4 Alvin Robertson 1.50 4.00
5 Detlef Schrempf 2.50 6.00
6 Artis Gilmore 2.00 5.00
7 Austin Carr 2.50 6.00
8 Avery Johnson 2.00 5.00
9 B.J. Armstrong 2.00 5.00
10 Dave Bing 2.50 6.00
11 Bingo Smith 2.50 6.00
12 Bob Dandridge 1.50 4.00
13 Bill Bradley 3.00 8.00
14 Bobby Jones 2.00 5.00
15 Brad Daugherty 2.00 5.00
16 Byron Scott 2.00 5.00
17 Cazzie Russell 2.00 5.00
18 Cedric Maxwell 1.50 4.00
19 Charles Oakley 2.50 6.00
20 Chet Walker 2.00 5.00
21 Chuck Share 2.50 6.00
22 Dan Majerle 2.00 5.00
23 Danny Ainge 2.50 6.00
24 Danny Manning 2.00 5.00
25 Darrell Griffith 1.50 4.00
26 Darryl Dawkins 1.50 4.00
27 Dennis Johnson 2.00 5.00
28 Gheorghe Muresan 1.50 4.00
29 Dick Barnett 2.00 5.00
30 Dick Van Arsdale 2.00 5.00
31 Dominique Wilkins 4.00 10.00
32 Don Buse 2.50 6.00
33 Don Ohl 2.50 6.00
34 Ernie DiGregorio 2.50 6.00
35 Fred Brown 1.50 4.00
36 Julius Erving 5.00 12.00
37 George McGinnis 1.50 4.00
38 Calvin Natt 1.50 4.00
39 Rick Mahorn 1.50 4.00
40 Gus Williams 1.50 4.00
41 Jack Sikma 2.00 5.00
42 Jamaal Wilkes 2.00 5.00
43 James Edwards 2.50 6.00
44 Jerry Sloan 2.50 6.00
45 Jim Loscutoff 3.00 8.00
46 Jo Jo White 2.00 5.00
47 John Johnson 2.50 6.00
48 Johnny Kerr 3.00 8.00
49 Karl Malone 3.00 8.00
50 Junior Bridgeman 1.50 4.00
51 Kiki Vandeweghe 2.00 5.00
52 Kurt Rambis 1.50 4.00
53 Larry Nance 2.00 5.00
54 Lonnie Shelton 1.50 4.00
55 Lou Hudson 1.50 4.00
56 Kevin McHale 3.00 8.00
57 Tree Rollins 1.50 4.00
58 George Karl 3.00 8.00
59 Maurice Lucas 2.50 6.00
60 Mel Daniels 2.50 6.00
61 Michael Cooper 2.00 5.00
62 Mitch Richmond 2.50 6.00
63 Joe Dumars 2.50 6.00
64 Mike Dunleavy Sr. 2.50 6.00
65 Moses Malone 4.00 10.00
66 Muggsy Bogues 2.00 5.00
67 Norm Nixon 1.50 4.00
68 Norm Van Lier 3.00 8.00
69 Oscar Robertson 6.00 15.00
70 Paul Arizin 2.50 6.00
71 Paul Westphal 2.50 6.00
72 Phil Chenier 1.50 4.00
73 Phil Ford 2.50 6.00
74 John Starks 2.00 5.00
75 Richie Guerin 2.50 6.00
76 Rolando Blackman 2.00 5.00
77 World B. Free 2.00 5.00
78 Rudy Tomjanovich 2.00 5.00
79 Sam Perkins 1.50 4.00
80 Sean Elliott 2.00 5.00
81 Ricky Pierce 1.50 4.00
82 Sidney Moncrief 1.50 4.00
83 Horace Grant 2.50 6.00
84 Spencer Haywood 1.50 4.00
85 Steve Kerr 2.50 6.00
86 Terry Dischinger 2.50 6.00
87 Mitch Kupchak 2.50 6.00
88 Tom Chambers 2.00 5.00
89 Tom Sanders 2.50 6.00
90 Michael Ray Richardson 2.00 5.00
91 Terry Cummings 2.00 5.00
92 Spud Webb 2.00 5.00
93 Walter Davis 2.50 6.00
94 Wayman Tisdale 2.50 6.00
95 Wayne Embry 1.50 4.00
96 Wilt Chamberlain 8.00 20.00
97 Jeff Hornacek 2.00 5.00
98 Eddie Johnson 1.50 4.00
99 Xavier McDaniel 1.50 4.00
100 Zelmo Beaty 2.50 6.00
101 Allan Ray JSY AU RC 4.00 10.00
102 A.Bargnani JSY AU RC 5.00 12.00
103 Bobby Jones JSY AU RC 4.00 10.00
104 Brandon Roy JSY AU RC 12.00 30.00
105 Cedric Simmons JSY AU RC 4.00 10.00
106 Craig Smith JSY AU RC 5.00 12.00
107 Daniel Gibson JSY AU RC 5.00 12.00
108 Dee Brown JSY AU RC 4.00 10.00
109 D.Markota JSY AU RC 4.00 10.00
110 Hilton Armstrong JSY AU RC 4.00 10.00
111 James Augustine JSY AU RC 4.00 10.00
112 James White JSY AU RC 4.00 10.00
113 H.Adams JSY AU RC 4.00 10.00
114 J.Garbajosa JSY AU RC 5.00 12.00
115 Josh Boone JSY AU RC 4.00 10.00
116 Kyle Lowry JSY AU RC 20.00 50.00
117 L.Aldridge JSY AU RC 20.00 50.00
118 David Noel JSY AU RC 4.00 10.00
119 M.Williams JSY AU RC 4.00 10.00
120 Mardy Collins JSY AU RC 4.00 10.00
121 Maurice Ager JSY AU RC 4.00 10.00
122 P.J. Tucker JSY AU RC 6.00 15.00
123 P.O'Bryant JSY AU RC 4.00 10.00
124 Paul Davis JSY AU RC 4.00 10.00
125 Paul Millsap JSY AU RC 8.00 20.00
126 Q.Douby JSY AU RC 4.00 10.00
127 Rajon Rondo JSY AU RC 20.00 50.00
128 Randy Foye JSY AU RC 5.00 12.00
129 R.Balkman JSY AU RC 4.00 10.00
130 Y.Diawara JSY AU RC 4.00 10.00
131 Rodney Carney JSY AU RC 4.00 10.00
132 Ronnie Brewer JSY AU RC 6.00 15.00
133 Rudy Gay JSY AU RC 8.00 20.00
134 Saer Sene JSY AU RC 4.00 10.00
135 S.Rodriguez JSY AU RC 5.00 12.00
136 Sh.Brown JSY AU RC 4.00 10.00
137 Sha.Williams JSY AU RC 4.00 10.00
138 She.Williams JSY AU RC 4.00 10.00
139 Solomon Jones JSY AU RC 4.00 10.00
140 T.Sefolosha JSY AU RC 5.00 12.00
141 Tyrus Thomas JSY AU RC 5.00 12.00
142 Steve Novak JSY AU RC 5.00 12.00
149 Al Cervi JSY AU 10.00 25.00
150 Alex English JSY AU 10.00 25.00
151 Arnie Risen JSY AU 10.00 25.00
152 Bailey Howell JSY AU 10.00 25.00
153 Bill Sharman JSY AU 10.00 25.00
154 Don Nelson JSY AU 20.00 50.00
155 Bob Lanier JSY AU 15.00 30.00
156 Bob McAdoo JSY AU 25.00 50.00
157 Bob Pettit JSY AU 15.00 40.00
158 Bobby Wanzer JSY AU 10.00 25.00
159 Calvin Murphy JSY AU 10.00 25.00
160 Clyde Lovellette JSY AU 15.00 40.00
161 Bill Laimbeer JSY AU 25.00 50.00
162 Dave Cowens JSY AU 12.00 30.00
163 David Thompson JSY AU 12.00 30.00
164 Dick McGuire JSY AU 10.00 25.00
165 John Wooden JSY AU 125.00 250.00
166 Ed Macauley JSY AU 20.00 50.00
167 Elgin Baylor JSY AU 25.00 60.00
168 Elvin Hayes JSY AU 15.00 30.00
169 Frank Ramsey JSY AU 25.00 60.00
170 Gail Goodrich JSY AU 15.00 40.00
171 Hal Greer JSY AU 10.00 25.00
172 Adrian Dantley JSY AU 10.00 25.00
173 Jerry Lucas JSY AU 15.00 40.00
174 Reggie Theus JSY AU 10.00 25.00
175 Charlie Scott JSY AU 12.00 30.00
176 Nate Archibald JSY AU 12.00 30.00
177 Nate Thurmond JSY AU 10.00 25.00
178 Rick Barry JSY AU 10.00 25.00
179 Slater Martin JSY AU 25.00 50.00
180 Tom Heinsohn JSY AU 12.00 30.00
181 Vern Mikkelsen JSY AU 25.00 50.00
182 Walt Bellamy JSY AU 10.00 25.00
183 Walt Frazier JSY AU 20.00 50.00
184 Rod Hundley JSY AU 15.00 40.00
185 Ralph Sampson JSY AU 12.00 30.00
186 Bill Russell JSY AU 1,500.00 3,000.00
187 Julius Erving JSY AU 80.00 200.00
188 Larry Bird JSY AU 100.00 200.00
189 James Worthy JSY AU 50.00 120.00
190 K.Abdul-Jabbar JSY AU 50.00 100.00
191 Clyde Drexler JSY AU 40.00 80.00
192 Magic Johnson JSY AU 80.00 160.00
193 Wes Unseld JSY AU 12.00 30.00
194 John Stockton JSY AU 100.00 200.00
195 George Gervin JSY AU 15.00 40.00
197 David Robinson JSY AU 50.00 100.00
198 Sam Jones JSY AU 50.00 100.00
199 Bill Walton JSY AU 12.00 30.00
200 Earl Lloyd JSY AU 12.00 30.00
201 Mark Price JSY AU 40.00 80.00
202 John Havlicek JSY AU 50.00 100.00
203 Cliff Hagan JSY AU 12.00 30.00
204 Dolph Schayes JSY AU 12.00 30.00
205 Harry Gallatin JSY AU 12.00 30.00
206 Jerry West JSY AU 50.00 120.00
207 Connie Hawkins JSY AU 12.00 30.00
208 Lenny Wilkens JSY AU 12.00 30.00
209 Michael Jordan JSY AU 500.00 1,000.00
210 Hakeem Olajuwon JSY AU 50.00 100.00
211 Dan Issel JSY AU 12.00 30.00
212 Robert Parish JSY AU 20.00 50.00
213 Dennis Rodman JSY AU 75.00 150.00
214 Pat Riley JSY AU 30.00 80.00
215 Maurice Cheeks JSY AU 12.00 30.00
216 Bob Houbregs JSY AU 10.00 25.00
217 Tracy McGrady JSY AU 20.00 50.00
218 Yao Ming JSY AU 30.00 80.00
219 Paul Pierce JSY AU 25.00 60.00
220 Ben Gordon JSY AU 30.00 80.00
221 Kobe Bryant JSY AU 1,500.00 3,000.00
222 Steve Nash JSY AU 100.00 250.00
223 LeBron James JSY AU 2,000.00 4,000.00
224 Carmelo Anthony JSY AU 25.00 60.00
225 Jason Kidd JSY AU 40.00 100.00
226 Chris Paul JSY AU 30.00 80.00
227 Bill Fitch AU 10.00 25.00
228 Jack Ramsay AU 15.00 40.00
229 John Kundla AU 50.00 120.00
230 Dean Smith AU 25.00 60.00
231 Pat Riley AU 15.00 30.00
232 Jerry Sloan AU 75.00 200.00
233 Don Haskins AU 30.00 80.00
234 Rick Pitino AU 20.00 50.00
235 John Chaney AU 15.00 40.00
238 Lenny Wilkens AU 10.00 25.00
239 Chuck Daly AU 25.00 50.00
240 George Karl AU 20.00 50.00
241 John Wooden AU 100.00 200.00
242 Digger Phelps AU 10.00 25.00
243 Jud Heathcote AU 20.00 40.00
244 Dick Motta AU 10.00 25.00
245 Gene Shue AU 30.00 80.00
246 Jim Calhoun AU 12.00 30.00
247 Greg Oden XRC 6.00 15.00
248 Kevin Durant AU XRC 500.00 1,000.00
249 Al Horford XRC 8.00 20.00
250 Mike Conley Jr. XRC 8.00 20.00
251 Jeff Green XRC 6.00 15.00
252 Yi Jianlian XRC 10.00 25.00
253 Corey Brewer XRC 5.00 12.00
254 Brandan Wright XRC 5.00 12.00
255 Joakim Noah XRC 6.00 15.00
256 Spencer Hawes XRC 6.00 15.00
257 Acie Law XRC 4.00 10.00
258 Thaddeus Young XRC 8.00 20.00
259 Julian Wright XRC 4.00 10.00
260 Al Thornton XRC 5.00 12.00
261 Rodney Stuckey XRC 6.00 15.00
262 Nick Young XRC 8.00 20.00
263 Sean Williams XRC 5.00 12.00
264 Marco Belinelli XRC 6.00 15.00
265 Javaris Crittenton XRC 5.00 12.00
266 Jason Smith XRC 6.00 15.00
267 Daequan Cook XRC 6.00 15.00
268 Jared Dudley XRC 8.00 20.00
269 Wilson Chandler XRC 6.00 15.00
270 Morris Almond XRC 4.00 10.00
271 Arron Afflalo XRC 8.00 20.00
272 Aaron Brooks XRC 6.00 15.00
273 Alando Tucker XRC 4.00 10.00
274 Marcus Williams XRC 4.00 10.00
275 Carl Landry XRC 6.00 15.00
276 Gabe Pruitt XRC 4.00 10.00

2006-07 Chronology 2007-08 Rookie Draft Redemptions Silver

*SILVER: .6X TO 1.5X BASE HI
SILVER PRINT RUN 50 SER.#'d SETS

2006-07 Chronology 20,000 Point Club

PRINT RUN 25 SER.#'d SETS
20KAD Adrian Dantley 12.00 30.00
20KAE Alex English 12.00 30.00
20KBP Bob Pettit 40.00 100.00
20KCD Clyde Drexler 40.00 100.00
20KDR David Robinson 75.00 200.00
20KEB Elgin Baylor 60.00 150.00
20KEH Elvin Hayes 20.00 50.00
20KGG George Gervin 25.00 60.00
20KHG Hal Greer 25.00 60.00
20KHO Hakeem Olajuwon 75.00 200.00
20KJH John Havlicek 125.00 300.00
20KJW Jerry West 75.00 200.00
20KKA Kareem Abdul-Jabbar 150.00 400.00
20KLB Larry Bird 125.00 300.00
20KMJ Michael Jordan 2,000.00 4,000.00
20KMR Mitch Richmond 30.00 80.00
20KRP Robert Parish 30.00 80.00
20KTC Tom Chambers 12.00 30.00
20KWB Walt Bellamy 15.00 40.00

2006-07 Chronology Autographs

APPROXIMATELY ONE PER PACK
1 Slick Watts 6.00 15.00
1a Slick Watts Slick only 10.00 25.00
2 Louie Dampier 15.00 40.00
3 Al Attles 6.00 15.00
4 Alvin Robertson 6.00 15.00
6 Artis Gilmore 6.00 15.00
7 Austin Carr 8.00 20.00
8 Avery Johnson 6.00 15.00
9 B.J. Armstrong 10.00 25.00
12 Bob Dandridge 8.00 20.00
14 Bobby Jones 12.00 30.00
15 Brad Daugherty 6.00 15.00
16 Byron Scott 12.00 30.00
16a B.Scott 3 Time Champs 30.00 80.00
17 Cazzie Russell 6.00 15.00
18 Cedric Maxwell 6.00 15.00
20 Chet Walker 8.00 20.00
21 Chuck Share 6.00 15.00
24 Danny Manning 8.00 20.00
25 Darrell Griffith 6.00 15.00
26 Darryl Dawkins Silver 8.00 20.00
29 Dick Barnett 10.00 25.00
30 Dick Van Arsdale 15.00 30.00
30a D.Van Arsdale Orig.Sun 25.00 50.00
32 Don Buse 12.00 30.00
33 Don Ohl 10.00 25.00
34 Ernie DeGregorio 15.00 40.00
35 Fred Brown 6.00 15.00
37 George McGinnis 6.00 15.00
39 Rick Mahorn 8.00 20.00
40 Gus Williams 8.00 20.00
41 Jack Sikma 6.00 15.00
42 Jamaal Wilkes 6.00 15.00
44 Jerry Sloan 75.00 200.00
44a Jerry Sloan Spider 150.00 400.00
45 Jim Loscutoff 125.00 300.00
46 Jo Jo White 8.00 20.00
47 John Johnson 6.00 15.00
48 Johnny Kerr 20.00 50.00
50 Junior Bridgeman 8.00 20.00
51 Kiki Vandeweghe 6.00 15.00
53 Larry Nance 6.00 15.00
54 Lonnie Shelton 8.00 20.00
55 Lou Hudson 6.00 15.00
57 Tree Rollins 6.00 15.00
58 George Karl 20.00 35.00
59 Maurice Lucas 6.00 15.00
60 Mel Daniels 12.00 30.00
61 Michael Cooper 8.00 20.00
61a Michael Cooper Gold 10.00 25.00
66 Muggsy Bogues 8.00 20.00
67 Norm Nixon 6.00 15.00
68 Norm Van Lier 60.00 150.00
71 Paul Westphal 6.00 15.00
72 Phil Chenier 6.00 15.00
73 Phil Ford 8.00 20.00
73a Phil Ford UNC 10.00 25.00
75 Richie Guerin 20.00 50.00
76 Rolando Blackman 8.00 20.00
78 R.Tomjanovich Rudy T. 10.00 25.00
78a R.Tomjanovich signed twice 12.00 30.00
79 Sam Perkins 6.00 15.00
80 Sean Elliott 6.00 15.00
82 Sidney Moncrief 6.00 15.00
83 Horace Grant 25.00 60.00
84 Spencer Haywood 6.00 15.00
85 Steve Kerr 20.00 50.00
85a Steve Kerr 30.00 80.00
86 Terry Dischinger 8.00 20.00
88 Tom Chambers 6.00 15.00
89 Tom Sanders 40.00 100.00
90 Michael Ray Richardson 6.00 15.00
91 Terry Cummings 6.00 15.00
93 Walter Davis 6.00 15.00
94 Wayman Tisdale 8.00 20.00
97 Jeff Hornacek 10.00 25.00
98 Eddie Johnson 6.00 15.00
99 Xavier McDaniel 6.00 15.00
100 Zelmo Beaty 60.00 150.00
100a Zelmo Beaty Big E only 60.00 150.00

2006-07 Chronology Contemporaries

PRINT RUN 25 SER.#'d SETS
COBW R.Barry/J.Wilkes 25.00 60.00
COCE M.Cheeks/J.Erving 100.00 250.00
CODH D.Cowens/J.Havlicek 125.00 300.00
CODO C.Drexler/H.Olajuwon 125.00 300.00
COFA W.Frazier/N.Archibald 40.00 100.00
COFB B.Fitch/L.Bird 125.00 300.00
COGB H.Grant/K.Bryant 1,000.00 2,000.00
COGC H.Greer/E.Baylor 75.00 200.00
COGD D.Griffith/D.Dawkins 30.00 80.00
COGT G.Gervin/D.Thompson 25.00 60.00
COGW G.Goodrich/J.West 75.00 200.00
COHL C.Hawkins/B.Lanier 30.00 80.00
COHS T.Heinsohn/B.Sharman 40.00 100.00
COHU E.Hayes/W.Unseld 30.00 80.00
COHW L.Hudson/L.Wilkens 20.00 50.00
COJH M.Johnson/J.Heathcote 125.00 300.00
COKM J.Kerr/V.Mikkelsen 40.00 100.00
COKS J.Kundla/D.Schayes 40.00 100.00
COLW M.Lucas/B.Walton 25.00 60.00
COMM S.Martin/V.Mikkelsen 40.00 100.00
CORE D.Robinson/S.Elliott 60.00 150.00
CORL D.Rodman/B.Laimbeer 50.00 120.00
CORS P.Riley/B.Sharman 75.00 200.00
COSA D.Scott/K.Anderson 20.00 50.00
COSJ D.Smith/M.Jordan 5,000.00 10,000.00
COSO R.Sampson/H.Olajuwon 60.00 150.00
COWA J.Wooden/K.Abdul-Jabbar 200.00 500.00

2006-07 Chronology Cut Signatures

STATED PRINT RUN 6 TO 17 SER.#'d SETS
CSDD Dave DeBusschere/17 150.00 400.00

2006-07 Chronology HOF Inscriptions

PRINT RUN 50 SER.#'d SETS
HOFAE Alex English 10.00 25.00
HOFBH Bailey Howell 10.00 25.00
HOFBW Bobby Wanzer 20.00 50.00
HOFCD Clyde Drexler 30.00 80.00
HOFCH Cliff Hagan 12.00 30.00
HOFCL Clyde Lovellette 25.00 60.00
HOFCM Calvin Murphy 6.00 15.00
HOFDI Dan Issel 12.00 30.00
HOFDM Dick McGuire 10.00 25.00
HOFFR Frank Ramsey 25.00 60.00
HOFHG Hal Greer 20.00 50.00
HOFJE Julius Erving 100.00 250.00
HOFJS Jack Sikma 8.00 20.00
HOFKA Kareem Abdul-Jabbar 150.00 400.00
HOFLB Larry Bird 125.00 300.00
HOFMJ Magic Johnson 125.00 300.00
HOFNT Nate Thurmond 25.00 60.00

2006-07 Chronology MVP Winners

PRINT RUN 50 SER.#'d SETS
MVPAG Artis Gilmore 20.00 50.00
MVPBL Bob Lanier 20.00 50.00
MVPBM Bob McAdoo 30.00 80.00
MVPBP Bob Pettit 30.00 80.00
MVPBR Bill Russell 1,250.00 2,500.00
MVPBS Bill Sharman 20.00 50.00
MVPBW Bill Walton 20.00 50.00
MVPCM Cedric Maxwell 10.00 25.00
MVPDC Dave Cowens 15.00 40.00
MVPDT David Thompson 15.00 40.00
MVPEB Elgin Baylor 40.00 100.00
MVPEM Ed Macauley 40.00 100.00
MVPGG George Gervin 25.00 60.00
MVPHG Hal Greer 25.00 60.00
MVPHO Hakeem Olajuwon 75.00 200.00
MVPJL Jerry Lucas 40.00 100.00
MVPJS John Stockton 75.00 200.00
MVPJW James Worthy 40.00 100.00
MVPLJ LeBron James 2,500.00 5,000.00
MVPLW Lenny Wilkens 10.00 25.00
MVPMJ Michael Jordan 3,000.00 6,000.00
MVPNA Nate Archibald 12.00 30.00
MVPRB Rick Barry 10.00 25.00
MVPRS Ralph Sampson 10.00 25.00
MVPSH Spencer Haywood 10.00 25.00
MVPTC Tom Chambers 10.00 25.00
MVPWE Jerry West 40.00 100.00
MVPWF Walt Frazier 25.00 60.00
MVPWH Jo Jo White 15.00 40.00
MVPWU Wes Unseld 15.00 40.00

2006-07 Chronology Retired Numbers

STATED PRINT RUN ONE TO 44 SER.#'d SETS
RNBL Bill Laimbeer/40 25.00 60.00
RNDG Darrell Griffith/35 10.00 25.00
RNGG Gail Goodrich/25 20.00 50.00
RNGM George McGinnis/30 20.00 50.00
RNHG Hal Greer/32 30.00 80.00
RNLB Larry Bird/33 125.00 300.00
RNLN Larry Nance/22 15.00 40.00
RNMP Mark Price/25 25.00 60.00
RNPW Paul Westphal/44 12.00 30.00
RNRB Rolando Blackman/22 8.00 20.00
RNTH Tom Heinsohn/15 40.00 100.00
RNTS Tom Sanders/25 25.00 60.00

2006-07 Chronology Signature Decades

STATED PRINT RUN 50 TO 90 SER.#'d SETS
DAC Al Cervi/50 25.00 60.00
DAE Alex English/80 8.00 20.00
DAM Alonzo Mourning/90 20.00 50.00
DAR Arnie Risen/50 40.00 100.00
DBH Bob Houbregs/50 10.00 25.00
DBL Bob Lanier/70 15.00 40.00
DBM Bob McAdoo/70 25.00 60.00
DBP Bob Pettit/60 20.00 50.00
DBS Bill Sharman/50 12.00 30.00
DBW Bill Walton/80 15.00 40.00
DCD Clyde Drexler/90 20.00 50.00
DCH Cliff Hagan/60 15.00 40.00
DCL Clyde Lovellette/50 25.00 60.00
DCM Calvin Murphy/70 8.00 20.00
DDC Dave Cowens/70 10.00 25.00
DDD Darryl Dawkins/80 12.00 30.00
DDM Dick McGuire/50 10.00 25.00
DDR David Robinson/90 50.00 120.00
DDS Dolph Schayes/50 8.00 20.00
DDT David Thompson/70 10.00 25.00
DEB Elgin Baylor/60 25.00 60.00
DEH Elvin Hayes/70 15.00 40.00
DFR Frank Ramsey/50 20.00 50.00
DGG George Gervin/70 20.00 50.00
DGR Hal Greer/60 20.00 50.00
DHG Harry Gallatin/50 15.00 40.00
DHO Bailey Howell/60 15.00 40.00
DJH John Havlicek/70 75.00 200.00
DJK Jason Kidd/90 30.00 80.00
DJL Jerry Lucas/70 15.00 40.00
DJO Mark Price/90 25.00 60.00
DJW James Worthy/80 25.00 60.00
DKM Kevin McHale/80 15.00 40.00
DLA Bill Laimbeer/80 15.00 40.00
DMA Dan Majerle/90 20.00 50.00
DMC Maurice Cheeks/80 8.00 20.00
DMR Mitch Richmond/90 15.00 40.00
DNA Nate Archibald/70 10.00 25.00
DNT Nate Thurmond/60 12.00 30.00
DOL Hakeem Olajuwon/90 50.00 120.00
DRO Dennis Rodman/90 100.00 250.00
DRP Robert Parish/80 15.00 40.00
DSE Sean Elliott/90 12.00 30.00
DSJ Sam Jones/60 15.00 40.00
DSM Slater Martin/50 125.00 300.00
DTH Tom Heinsohn/60 15.00 40.00
DWB Walt Bellamy/60 8.00 20.00
DWD Walter Davis/80 10.00 25.00
DWF Walt Frazier/70 15.00 40.00

2006-07 Chronology Stitches in Time

PRINT RUN 199 SER.#'d SETS
*GOLD: .5X TO 1.25X BASE HI
GOLD PRINT RUN 75 SER.#'d SETS
SITAB Andrea Bargnani 2.50 6.00
SITAI Allen Iverson 8.00 20.00
SITBR Brandon Roy 6.00 15.00
SITCA Carmelo Anthony 5.00 12.00
SITDR Dennis Rodman 6.00 15.00
SITHO Hakeem Olajuwon 6.00 15.00
SITJE Julius Erving 6.00 15.00
SITJO Magic Johnson 10.00 25.00
SITJR J.J. Redick 6.00 15.00
SITJS John Stockton 5.00 12.00
SITJW Jerry West 8.00 20.00
SITKB Kobe Bryant 75.00 200.00
SITKG Kevin Garnett 8.00 20.00
SITKM Kevin McHale 4.00 10.00
SITLA LaMarcus Aldridge 6.00 15.00
SITLB Larry Bird 10.00 25.00
SITLJ LeBron James 25.00 60.00
SITMJ Michael Jordan 75.00 200.00
SITPM Pete Maravich 25.00 60.00
SITRB Ronnie Brewer 3.00 8.00
SITRF Randy Foye 2.50 6.00
SITRG Rudy Gay 4.00 10.00
SITSO Shaquille O'Neal 12.00 30.00
SITSW Shelden Williams 2.00 5.00
SITTD Tim Duncan 8.00 20.00
SITTM Tracy McGrady 5.00 12.00
SITTS Thabo Sefolosha 2.50 6.00
SITTT Tyrus Thomas 2.50 6.00
SITVC Vince Carter 6.00 15.00
SITYM Yao Ming 8.00 20.00

2006-07 Chronology Stitches in Time Autographs

PRINT RUN 25 SER.#'d SETS
SITSAB Andrea Bargnani 15.00 40.00
SITSBR Brandon Roy 15.00 40.00
SITSCA Carmelo Anthony 30.00 80.00
SITSDR Dennis Rodman 40.00 80.00
SITSHO Hakeem Olajuwon 25.00 50.00
SITSJE Julius Erving 75.00 150.00
SITSJO Michael Jordan 500.00 1,000.00
SITSJS John Stockton 50.00 100.00
SITSKB Kobe Bryant 1,500.00 3,000.00
SITSLA LaMarcus Aldridge 25.00 60.00
SITSLB Larry Bird 75.00 200.00
SITSLJ LeBron James 2,000.00 4,000.00
SITSMJ Magic Johnson 60.00 120.00
SITSRF Randy Foye 15.00 40.00
SITSRG Rudy Gay 15.00 40.00
SITSTM Tracy McGrady 25.00 50.00
SITSTT Tyrus Thomas 15.00 40.00
SITSVC Vince Carter 30.00 80.00
SITSYM Yao Ming 30.00 80.00

2006-07 Chronology Stitches in Time Dual

PRINT RUN 25 SER.#'d SETS
SITDAR L.Aldridge/B.Roy 10.00 25.00
SITDBJ L.Bird/M.Johnson 20.00 50.00
SITDIA A.Iverson/C.Anthony 10.00 25.00
SITDJB M.Johnson/K.Bryant 75.00 200.00
SITDJE M.Jordan/J.Erving 60.00 150.00
SITDJJ L.James/M.Jordan 75.00 200.00
SITDMM T.McGrady/Y.Ming 10.00 25.00
SITDOD S.O'Neal/T.Duncan 12.00 30.00
SITDTS T.Thomas/T.Sefolosha 6.00 15.00
SITDWS J.West/J.Stockton 15.00 40.00

2007-08 Chronology

1-100 PRINT RUN 250 SER.#'d SETS
101-130 AU PRINT RUN 25 SER.#'d SETS
131-214 AU PRINT RUN 99 SER.#'d SETS
215-244 AU RC PRINT RUN 99 SER.#'d SETS
245-250 RC PRINT RUN 99 SER.#'d SETS
251-283 XRC PRINT RUN 250 SER.#'d SETS
1 Andrew Toney 2.50 6.00
2 Artis Gilmore 2.50 6.00
3 B.J. Armstrong 2.50 6.00
4 Bernard King 2.00 5.00
5 Bill Cartwright 2.00 5.00
6 Bill Laimbeer 2.00 5.00
7 Bill Russell 8.00 20.00
8 Bill Walton 3.00 8.00
9 Bill Wennington 2.50 6.00
10 Billy Cunningham 2.50 6.00
11 Bob Cousy 4.00 10.00
12 Bob McAdoo 2.00 5.00
13 Brad Davis 2.50 6.00
14 Byron Scott 2.00 5.00
15 Cedric Maxwell 2.50 6.00
16 Charles Oakley 2.50 6.00
17 Clyde Drexler 4.00 10.00
18 Clyde Lovellette 2.50 6.00
19 Dan Issel 2.00 5.00
20 Danny Ainge 2.50 6.00
21 Darrell Walker 2.50 6.00
22 Dave Bing 2.50 6.00
23 Dave Cowens 2.00 5.00
24 Dave DeBusschere 2.00 5.00
25 David Robinson 5.00 12.00
26 Dennis Rodman 6.00 15.00
27 Derrick Coleman 2.50 6.00
28 Dino Radja 1.50 4.00
29 Doc Rivers 2.00 5.00
30 Dominique Wilkins 4.00 10.00
31 Earl Monroe 2.50 6.00
32 Elgin Baylor 2.50 6.00
33 Freddie Lewis 1.50 4.00
34 George Gervin 3.00 8.00
35 George Mikan 5.00 12.00
36 Gheorghe Muresan 2.50 6.00
37 Gus Williams 1.50 4.00
38 Hakeem Olajuwon 5.00 12.00
39 Hal Greer 3.00 8.00
40 Harry Gallatin 2.50 6.00
41 Horace Grant 2.50 6.00
42 Isiah Thomas 2.50 6.00
43 Jack Sikma 2.50 6.00
44 James Worthy 4.00 10.00
45 Jay Vincent 2.50 6.00
46 Jerry Lucas 2.50 6.00
47 Jerry West 6.00 15.00
48 Jim Paxson 2.50 6.00
49 Jim Price 2.50 6.00

50 Joe Dumars 2.50 6.00
51 John Havlicek 5.00 12.00
52 John Paxson 2.50 6.00
53 John Salley 1.50 4.00
54 Julius Erving 6.00 15.00
55 Kareem Abdul-Jabbar 8.00 20.00
56 Karl Malone 3.00 8.00
57 Kenny Smith 2.00 5.00
58 Kermit Washington 2.50 6.00
59 Kevin McHale 3.00 8.00
60 Kurt Rambis 1.50 4.00
61 Larry Bird 10.00 25.00
62 Lenny Wilkens 2.50 6.00
63 Lionel Hollins 1.50 4.00
64 Luc Longley 1.50 4.00
65 Magic Johnson 10.00 25.00
66 Manute Bol 2.50 6.00
67 Mark Aguirre 2.00 5.00
68 Marques Johnson 2.00 5.00
69 Michael Jordan 40.00 100.00
70 Michael Ray Richardson 2.00 5.00
71 Moses Malone 4.00 10.00
72 Nate Archibald 2.00 5.00
73 Oscar Robertson 2.50 6.00
74 Paul Arizin 2.50 6.00
75 Paul Silas 2.50 6.00
76 Paul Westphal 3.00 8.00
77 Pete Maravich 6.00 15.00
78 Phil Jackson 3.00 8.00
79 Pooh Richardson 1.50 4.00
80 Reggie Miller 4.00 10.00
81 Rick Barry 2.00 5.00
82 Ron Harper 2.50 6.00
83 Joe Barry Carroll 2.50 6.00
84 Spencer Haywood 1.50 4.00
85 Stacey Augmon 1.50 4.00
86 Steve Kerr 3.00 8.00
87 Swen Nater 2.50 6.00
88 Lonnie Shelton 2.50 6.00
89 Thurl Bailey 2.50 6.00
90 Tom Chambers 2.50 6.00
91 Tom Sanders 2.50 6.00
92 Toni Kukoc 2.50 6.00
93 Vernon Maxwell 1.50 4.00
94 Vlade Divac 2.50 6.00
95 Walt Bellamy 2.00 5.00
96 Will Perdue 1.50 4.00
97 Reggie Theus 2.00 5.00
98 Willis Reed 4.00 10.00
99 Wilt Chamberlain 8.00 20.00
100 Xavier McDaniel 1.50 4.00
101 James Silas AU 15.00 40.00
102 Steve Nash AU 100.00 250.00
103 Yao Ming AU 500.00 1,000.00
104 Kevin Durant AU 8,000.00 12,000.00
106 Carmelo Anthony AU 75.00 200.00
108 Chris Paul AU 500.00 1,000.00
109 Dwight Howard AU 40.00 100.00
110 Vince Carter AU 100.00 250.00
111 Bill Laimbeer AU 20.00 50.00
112 Rick Barry AU 20.00 50.00
113 Spencer Haywood AU 12.00 30.00
114 Paul Pierce AU 40.00 100.00
115 Jason Kidd AU 30.00 80.00
116 Wes Unseld AU 12.00 30.00
117 Artis Gilmore AU 30.00 80.00
118 Tracy McGrady AU 100.00 250.00
119 David Robinson AU 75.00 200.00
120 Moses Malone AU 100.00 250.00
121 Dennis Rodman AU 100.00 250.00
122 Pat Riley AU 15.00 40.00
123 Michael Jordan AU 15,000.00 30,000.00
124 LaMarcus Aldridge AU 15.00 40.00
125 Randy Foye AU 12.00 30.00
126 Jermaine O'Neal AU 12.00 30.00
127 Brad Daugherty AU 40.00 100.00
128 Muggsy Bogues AU 20.00 50.00
129 Kiki Vandeweghe AU 12.00 30.00
130 Micheal Ray Richardson AU 12.00 30.00
131 David Robinson AU 75.00 200.00
132 Kobe Bryant AU 5,000.00 10,000.00
133 Vince Carter AU 75.00 200.00
134 Kobe Bryant AU 5,000.00 10,000.00
135 Kevin Durant AU RC 3,000.00 6,000.00
136 Michael Jordan AU Blue 8,000.00 15,000.00
137 Magic Johnson AU 200.00 500.00
138 Michael Jordan AU 8,000.00 15,000.00
139 Jerry West AU 300.00 60.00
140 Tom Chambers AU 25.00 60.00
141 Bill Laimbeer AU 75.00 200.00
142 Julius Erving AU 400.00 800.00
143 Spud Webb AU 50.00 120.00
144 Clyde Drexler AU 125.00 300.00
145 Sean Elliott AU 10.00 25.00
146 Dominique Wilkins AU 60.00 150.00
147 Magic Johnson AU 500.00 1,000.00
148 John Wooden AU 125.00 300.00
149 Kareem Abdul-Jabbar AU 400.00 800.00
150 L.Bird/Magic Johnson AU 400.00 800.00
151 Steve Kerr AU 75.00 200.00
152 Rick Barry AU 50.00 120.00
153 James Worthy AU 75.00 200.00
154 John Paxson AU 75.00 200.00
155 Baron Davis AU 40.00 100.00
156 Chris Paul AU 400.00 800.00
157 LeBron James AU 2,000.00 4,000.00
158 Kobe Bryant AU 2,000.00 4,000.00
159 Kevin Durant AU RC 4,000.00 8,000.00
160 Kevin Garnett AU 500.00 1,000.00
161 Bailey Howell AU 50.00 120.00
162 Bob Love AU 25.00 60.00
162a Bob Love #10 25.00 60.00
163 Norm Nixon AU 12.00 30.00
164 Horace Grant AU 50.00 120.00
165 Darrell Griffith AU 15.00 40.00
165a D.Griffith AU Dr. Dunk 25.00 60.00
166 Dick McGuire AU 25.00 60.00
167 Chet Walker AU 10.00 25.00
168 Clyde Drexler AU 75.00 200.00
169 Gail Goodrich AU 20.00 50.00
170 Walt Frazier AU 75.00 200.00
171 George Gervin AU 40.00 100.00
172 Hal Greer AU 25.00 60.00
173 Sam Jones AU 20.00 50.00
174 Jerry Lucas AU 30.00 80.00
175 Hakeem Olajuwon AU 125.00 300.00
175a H.Olajuwon AU 94 MVP 600.00 1,200.00
176 Robert Parish AU 40.00 100.00
177 Bob Pettit AU 30.00 80.00
178 Spud Webb AU 50.00 120.00
179 Pat Riley AU 60.00 150.00
180 Bill Sharman AU 125.00 300.00
181 John Stockton AU 400.00 800.00
182 Nate Thurmond AU 15.00 40.00
183 Wes Unseld AU 15.00 40.00
184 Bill Walton AU 15.00 40.00
185 Sam Perkins AU 10.00 25.00
186 Lenny Wilkens AU 15.00 40.00
187 Rudy Tomjanovich AU 40.00 100.00
188 Artis Gilmore AU 30.00 80.00
189 Adrian Dantley AU 12.00 30.00
190 David Thompson AU 20.00 50.00
190a D.Thompson AU Skywalker 25.00 60.00
190b D.Thompson AU Wolfpack 25.00 60.00
191 Dominique Wilkins AU 30.00 80.00
192 Dennis Rodman AU 30.00 80.00
193 Kiki Vandeweghe AU 10.00 25.00
194 Bob McAdoo AU 40.00 100.00
195 Alex English AU 30.00 80.00
196 George McGinnis AU 10.00 25.00
196a G.McGinnis AU 75 ABA MVP 15.00 40.00
197 Vern Mikkelsen AU 10.00 25.00
198 Walt Bellamy AU 10.00 25.00
199 Bob Lanier AU 12.00 30.00
199a Bob Lanier AU MVP 60.00 150.00
200 Connie Hawkins AU 10.00 25.00
201 Bobby Wanzer AU 25.00 60.00
202 Tom Heinsohn AU 20.00 50.00
202a Tom Heinsohn AU Blue ROY 50.00 120.00
203 Slater Martin AU 75.00 200.00
204 Michael Cooper AU 10.00 25.00
205 Darryl Dawkins AU 40.00 100.00
206 Bobby Jones AU 40.00 100.00
207 Dolph Schayes AU 40.00 100.00
208 Louie Dampier AU 12.00 30.00
209 Don Nelson AU 20.00 50.00
210 Marques Johnson AU 30.00 80.00
211 Moses Malone AU 125.00 300.00
212 Dick Barnett AU 50.00 120.00
213 Cliff Hagan AU 75.00 200.00
213a Cliff Hagan AU 78 HOF 150.00 400.00
214 Meadowlark Lemon AU 150.00 400.00
215 Kevin Durant AU RC 3,000.00 6,000.00
216 Al Horford AU RC 15.00 40.00
217 Corey Brewer AU RC 5.00 12.00
218 Mike Conley Jr. AU RC 12.00 30.00
218a M.Conley Jr. AU Go Buckeyes 25.00 50.00
219 Joakim Noah AU RC 12.00 30.00
220 Julian Wright AU RC 4.00 10.00
220a J.Wright AU Go Jayhawks 20.00 40.00
221 Jeff Green AU RC 5.00 12.00
222 Spencer Hawes AU RC 4.00 10.00
222a S.Hawes AU Go Huskies 15.00 30.00
223 Acie Law AU RC 4.00 10.00
224 Al Thornton AU RC 4.00 10.00
225 Rodney Stuckey AU RC 4.00 10.00
226 Sean Williams AU RC 4.00 10.00
226a Sean Williams AU Area 51 4.00 10.00
227 Marco Belinelli AU RC 5.00 12.00
228 Javaris Crittenton AU RC 5.00 12.00
229 Jason Smith AU RC 4.00 10.00
230 Daequan Cook AU RC 10.00 25.00
231 Jared Dudley AU RC 5.00 12.00
231a Jared Dudley AU Junkyard Dog 5.00 12.00
232 Wilson Chandler AU RC 5.00 12.00
233 Morris Almond AU RC 4.00 10.00
234 Aaron Brooks AU RC 5.00 12.00
235 Arron Afflalo AU RC 5.00 12.00
235a A.Afflalo AU Go Bruins 5.00 12.00
236 Alando Tucker AU RC 4.00 10.00
237 Jermareo Davidson AU RC 4.00 10.00
238 Carl Landry AU RC 4.00 10.00
239 Gabe Pruitt AU RC 4.00 10.00
240 Dominic McGuire AU RC 4.00 10.00
241 Glen Davis AU RC 5.00 12.00
241a Glen Davis AU Big Baby 5.00 12.00
242 Josh McRoberts AU RC 4.00 10.00
243 Luis Scola AU RC 6.00 15.00
244 Juan Navarro AU RC 5.00 12.00
245 Greg Oden RC 4.00 10.00
246 Yi Jianlian RC 5.00 12.00
247 Brandan Wright RC 3.00 8.00
248 Nick Young RC 4.00 10.00
249 Thaddeus Young RC 4.00 10.00
250 Kyrylo Fesenko RC 2.50 6.00
251 Derrick Rose XRC 8.00 20.00
252 Michael Beasley XRC 4.00 10.00
253 O.J. Mayo XRC 4.00 10.00
254 Russell Westbrook XRC 40.00 100.00
255 Kevin Love XRC 6.00 15.00
256 Danilo Gallinari XRC 6.00 15.00
257 Eric Gordon XRC 8.00 20.00
258 Joe Alexander XRC 2.50 6.00
259 D.J. Augustin XRC 4.00 10.00
260 Brook Lopez XRC 5.00 12.00
261 Jerryd Bayless XRC 3.00 8.00
262 Jason Thompson XRC 3.00 8.00
263 Brandon Rush XRC 3.00 8.00
264 Anthony Randolph XRC 3.00 8.00
265 Robin Lopez XRC 4.00 10.00
266 Marreese Speights XRC 3.00 8.00
267 Roy Hibbert XRC 4.00 10.00
268 JaVale McGee XRC 4.00 10.00
269 J.J. Hickson XRC 3.00 8.00
270 Alexis Ajinca XRC 2.50 6.00
271 Ryan Anderson XRC 4.00 10.00
272 Courtney Lee XRC 4.00 10.00
273 Kosta Koufos XRC 3.00 8.00
274 Kyle Weaver XRC 4.00 10.00
275 Nicolas Batum XRC 5.00 12.00
276 George Hill XRC 5.00 12.00
277 Darrell Arthur XRC 4.00 10.00
278 Donte Greene XRC 2.50 6.00
279 D.J. White XRC 2.50 6.00
280 J.R. Giddens XRC 2.50 6.00
281 Mario Chalmers XRC 5.00 12.00
282 Walter Sharpe XRC 3.00 8.00
283 DeAndre Jordan XRC 8.00 20.00

2007-08 Chronology Rookie Redemptions Gold

GOLD: .75X TO 2X BASE HI
STATED PRINT RUN 25 SER.#'d SETS

2007-08 Chronology Rookie Redemptions Silver

*SILVER: .5X TO 1.25X BASE
STATED PRINT RUN 99 SER.#'d SETS
251 Derrick Rose 30.00 80.00

2007-08 Chronology Autographs

2 Artis Gilmore 12.00 30.00
3 B.J. Armstrong 12.00 30.00
4 Bernard King 10.00 25.00
5 Bill Cartwright 10.00 25.00
6 Bill Laimbeer 10.00 25.00
8a Bill Walton Grateful Red 30.00 80.00
9 Bill Wennington 8.00 20.00
12 Bob McAdoo 10.00 25.00
13 Brad Davis 6.00 15.00
14 Byron Scott 8.00 20.00
15 Cedric Maxwell 8.00 20.00
17 Clyde Drexler 15.00 40.00
18 Clyde Lovellette 12.00 30.00
19 Dan Issel 8.00 20.00
21 Darrell Walker 6.00 15.00
23 Dave Cowens 10.00 25.00
25 David Robinson 30.00 60.00
28 Dino Radja 12.00 30.00
28a Dino Radja All Rookie 12.00 30.00
32 Elgin Baylor 20.00 50.00
32a Elgin Baylor 77 HOF 30.00 80.00
32b E.Baylor Kappa Alpha Psi 30.00 80.00
33 Freddie Lewis 6.00 15.00
34 George Gervin 10.00 25.00
36 Gheorghe Muresan 6.00 15.00
37 Gus Williams 6.00 15.00
38 Hakeem Olajuwon 30.00 80.00
39 Hal Greer 8.00 20.00
40 Harry Gallatin 12.00 30.00
41 Horace Grant 12.00 30.00
43 Jack Sikma 6.00 15.00
44 James Worthy 15.00 40.00
45 Jay Vincent 6.00 15.00
46 Jerry Lucas 15.00 40.00
47 Jerry West 40.00 100.00
48 Jim Paxson 12.00 30.00
49 Jim Price 6.00 15.00
50 Joe Dumars 15.00 30.00
52 John Paxson 10.00 25.00
53 John Salley 6.00 15.00
54 Julius Erving 30.00 60.00
55 Kareem Abdul-Jabbar 125.00 300.00
57 Kenny Smith 8.00 20.00
58 Kermit Washington 6.00 20.00
61 Larry Bird 125.00 300.00
62 Lenny Wilkens 10.00 25.00
63 Lionel Hollins 8.00 20.00
65 Magic Johnson 125.00 300.00
68 Marques Johnson 6.00 15.00
69 Michael Jordan 3,000.00 6,000.00
70 Michael Ray Richardson 6.00 15.00
71 Moses Malone 30.00 80.00
72 Nate Archibald 8.00 20.00
76 Paul Westphal 6.00 15.00
79 Pooh Richardson 6.00 15.00
81 Rick Barry 12.00 30.00
82 Ron Harper 30.00 60.00
84 Spencer Haywood 6.00 15.00
85 Stacey Augmon 6.00 15.00
86 Steve Kerr 12.00 30.00
87 Swen Nater 6.00 15.00
88 Lonnie Shelton 6.00 15.00
89 Thurl Bailey 6.00 15.00
90 Tom Chambers 6.00 15.00
91 Tom Sanders 6.00 15.00
92 Toni Kukoc 8.00 20.00
94 Vlade Divac 12.00 30.00
95 Walt Bellamy 6.00 15.00
96 Will Perdue 8.00 20.00
97 Reggie Theus 6.00 15.00
100 Xavier McDaniel 6.00 15.00

2007-08 Chronology Dedications

PRINT RUN 50 SER.#'d SETS
DAC Al Cervi 6.00 15.00
DAD Adrian Dantley 6.00 15.00
DAE Alex English 10.00 25.00
DAG Artis Gilmore 10.00 25.00
DBL Bob Lanier 12.00 30.00
DBM Bob McAdoo 15.00 30.00
DBP Bob Pettit 15.00 30.00
DBS Bill Sharman 15.00 40.00
DBW Bill Walton 12.00 30.00
DCD Clyde Drexler 30.00 80.00
DCW Chet Walker 6.00 15.00
DDC Dave Cowens 20.00 50.00
DDG Darrell Griffith 6.00 15.00
DDT David Thompson 12.00 30.00
DGE George Gervin 12.00 30.00
DGG Gail Goodrich 8.00 20.00
DHG Hal Greer 12.00 30.00
DJR Jack Ramsay 12.00 30.00
DLA Bill Laimbeer 10.00 25.00
DLW Lenny Wilkens 6.00 15.00
DMC Maurice Cheeks 6.00 15.00
DNN Norm Nixon 6.00 15.00
DRB Rick Barry 12.00 30.00
DRO Rolando Blackman 6.00 15.00
DRP Robert Parish 12.00 30.00
DSM Sidney Moncrief 6.00 15.00
DTH Tom Heinsohn 15.00 40.00
DWU Wes Unseld 20.00 50.00

2007-08 Chronology Era Associates

PRINT RUN 15 SER.#'d SETS
BLGW Lucas/Greer/Wlkns/Gdrch 40.00 100.00
EJBJ Bird/Dr.J/Magic/MJ 3,000.00 6,000.00
GDDE Artis/Glide/Dant/Eng 80.00 200.00
JCHP Jamisn/Vince/Hughs/Pierc 100.00 250.00
MHSD Amare/Durant/Howard/Yao 300.00 600.00
MLAW Kareem/McAd/Wltn/Lanier 200.00 500.00
ORMP Malone/Parish/Olaj/DRob 200.00 500.00
PSHS Pettit/Heinshn/Shrmn/Dolph 75.00 200.00

2007-08 Chronology Freshman Registry

PRINT RUN 25 SER.#'d SETS
BCB Williams/Chambers/Blackman 25.00 60.00
DGC Durant/Green/Conley 200.00 500.00
DHP Daugherty/Harper/Price 40.00 100.00
HBN Horford/Brewer/Noah 25.00 60.00
HWN Havlicek/Walker/Nelson 100.00 250.00
JMB Magic/Bird/Moncrief 150.00 400.00
LTC Lanier/Tomjanovich/Cowens 40.00 100.00
MKS King/Sikma/Maxwell 20.00 50.00
PKG Pettit/Kerr/Guerin 30.00 80.00
RHJ Heinsohn/Russell/Jones 1,000.00 2,000.00
SSD Sampson/Scott/Drexler 60.00 150.00
WCW Worthy/Cummings/Wilkins 75.00 200.00
WSW West/Wilkens/Sanders 50.00 120.00
WWW Walton/Winters/Wilkes 25.00 60.00

2007-08 Chronology Historically Accurate

PRINT RUN 50 SER.#'d SETS
HAAD Adrian Dantley 6.00 15.00
HAAG Artis Gilmore 6.00 15.00
HABA B.J. Armstrong 10.00 25.00
HACM Cedric Maxwell 10.00 25.00
HADI Dan Issel 6.00 15.00
HAJR Jeff Ruland 6.00 15.00
HAKV Kiki Vandeweghe 6.00 15.00
HAMP Mark Price 25.00 60.00
HASK Steve Kerr 12.00 30.00

2007-08 Chronology My Generation

STATED PRINT RUN 62 TO 75 SER.#'d SETS
MGAG Artis Gilmore/71 12.00 30.00
MGBL Bob Love/67 12.00 30.00
MGBM Bob McAdoo/72 20.00 50.00
MGBW Bill Walton/74 15.00 40.00
MGCW Chet Walker/62 8.00 20.00
MGDI Dan Issel/70 8.00 20.00
MGDT David Thompson/75 12.00 30.00
MGGG George Gervin/72 20.00 50.00
MGGM George McGinnis/71 10.00 25.00
MGJL Jerry Lucas/71 12.00 30.00
MGJS James Silas/72 8.00 20.00
MGJW Jamaal Wilkes/74 10.00 25.00
MGLD Louie Dampier/69 8.00 20.00
MGMD Mel Daniels/67 8.00 20.00
MGMM Moses Malone/74 40.00 100.00
MGRB Rick Barry/65 25.00 60.00
MGSH Spencer Haywood/69 12.00 30.00
MGSN Swen Nater/73 8.00 20.00
MGWF Walt Frazier/67 20.00 50.00

2007-08 Chronology Seriatim

STATED PRINT RUN 8 TO 90 SER.#'d SETS
AM N.Archibald/C.Maxwell/80 8.00 20.00
BH B.Hodges/L.Bird/70 100.00 250.00
BT N.Thurmond/R.Barry/70 12.00 30.00
CA D.Cowens/N.Archibald/70 15.00 40.00
CC M.Conley Sr./M.Conley/80 10.00 25.00
CL Bob Lanier/ML Carr/70 8.00 20.00
DD A.Dantley/W.Davis/80 8.00 20.00
DF W.Davis/P.Ford/80 8.00 20.00
DS D.Wilkins/S.Webb/80 20.00 50.00
FR W.Frazier/C.Russell/60 15.00 40.00
FW Walt Frazier/B.Wanzer/60 15.00 40.00
GA G.Gervin/N.Archibald/80 12.00 30.00
GC H.Grant/B.Cartwright/90 15.00 40.00
GG A.Gilmore/G.Gervin/80 15.00 40.00
GW D.Griffith/D.Williams/80 12.00 30.00
HB S.Haywood/F.Brown/70 15.00 40.00
HH A.Horford/A.Horford/80 8.00 20.00
HK T.Kukoc/R.Harper/90 40.00 100.00
HR R.Guerin/H.Gallatin/50 8.00 20.00
IN G.McGinnis/M.Daniels/80 15.00 40.00
IW B.Walton/D.Issel/70 12.00 30.00
KA S.Kerr/B.Armstrong/90 15.00 40.00
KG K.Garnett/J.Kidd/90 75.00 200.00
KP S.Kerr/J.Paxson/90 20.00 50.00
LC D.Cowens/B.Laimbeer/70 15.00 40.00
LD B.Laimbeer/A.Dantley/80 12.00 30.00
LH H.Greer/C.Walker/70 20.00 50.00
MK B.McAdoo/K.Karl/70 20.00 50.00
MM V.Mikkelsen/S.Martin/50 15.00 40.00
NN Vandeweghe/Vandeweghe/50 25.00 60.00
OD C.Drexler/Olajuwon/80 75.00 200.00
OR D.Robinson/Olajuwon/90 125.00 300.00
PW Perdue/Wennington/90 15.00 40.00
RB R.Parish/B.Walton/80 25.00 60.00
RG G.Goodrich/C.Russell/70 12.00 30.00
RJ S.Jones/B.Russell/50 500.00 1,000.00
RL D.Rodman/Laimbeer/80 40.00 100.00
RS B.Sharman/A.Risen/50 40.00 100.00
SH T.Sanders/T.Heinsohn/60 40.00 100.00
SK D.Schayes/J.Kerr/60 12.00 30.00
TE English/D.Thompson/80 15.00 40.00
TG Gervin/D.Thompson/80 15.00 40.00
WC J.Worthy/M.Cooper/80 25.00 50.00
WL J.Lucas/J.West/60 30.00 80.00
WP R.Parish/J.Worthy/80 30.00 80.00
WR L.Wilkens/J.Ramsay/70 12.00 30.00
WS J.Wilkes/B.Scott/80 12.00 30.00

2007-08 Chronology Stitches in Time

PRINT RUN 99 SER.#'d SETS
*STITCH 50: .5X TO 1.25X BASE HI
STITCH 50 PRINT RUN 50 SETS
*STITCH 15: .75X TO 2X BASE HI
STITCH 15 PRINT RUN 15 SETS
AB Aaron Brooks R 3.00 8.00
AD Adrian Dantley L 3.00 8.00
AH Al Horford R 10.00 25.00
AI Allen Iverson V 12.00 30.00
AL Acie Law R 2.50 6.00
AT Al Thornton R 2.50 6.00
BG Ben Gordon V 3.00 8.00
BI Bill Russell L 75.00 200.00
BR Brandon Roy V 5.00 12.00
BW Bill Walton L 5.00 12.00
CA Carmelo Anthony V 8.00 20.00
CB Corey Brewer R 3.00 8.00
CD Clyde Drexler L 6.00 15.00
CK Maurice Cheeks L 3.00 8.00
CM Chris Mullin L 5.00 12.00
CP Chris Paul V 12.00 30.00
DC Daequan Cook R 3.00 8.00
DE Deron Williams V 3.00 8.00
DH Dwight Howard V 5.00 12.00
DR Dennis Rodman L 12.00 30.00
DW Dominique Wilkins L 6.00 15.00
GD Glen Davis R 3.00 8.00
GG George Gervin L 5.00 12.00
HO Hakeem Olajuwon L 12.00 30.00
JA Jason Smith R 2.50 6.00
JC Javaris Crittenton R 2.50 6.00
JD Jared Dudley R 3.00 8.00
JE Julius Erving L 15.00 40.00
JG Jeff Green R 3.00 8.00
JK Jason Kidd V 6.00 15.00
JN Joakim Noah R 4.00 10.00
JO Michael Jordan L 200.00 500.00
JS John Stockton L 8.00 20.00
JW Julian Wright R 2.50 6.00
KA Kareem Abdul-Jabbar L 15.00 40.00
KB Kobe Bryant V 100.00 250.00
KD Kevin Durant R 100.00 250.00
KG Kevin Garnett V 12.00 30.00
KH Kirk Hinrich V 4.00 10.00
LB Larry Bird L 15.00 40.00
LJ LeBron James V 100.00 250.00
MA Morris Almond R 2.50 6.00
MC Mike Conley Jr. R 10.00 25.00
MI Michael Cooper L 4.00 10.00
MJ Magic Johnson L 15.00 40.00
MM Moses Malone L 8.00 20.00
PP Paul Pierce V 8.00 20.00
RO David Robinson L 10.00 25.00
RS Rodney Stuckey R 2.50 6.00
SH Spencer Hawes R 2.50 6.00
SN Steve Nash V 12.00 30.00
SO Shaquille O'Neal V 15.00 40.00
SW Sean Williams R 2.50 6.00
TM Tracy McGrady V 10.00 25.00
TP Tony Parker V 6.00 15.00
VC Vince Carter V 10.00 25.00
WA Dwyane Wade V 12.00 30.00
WC Wilson Chandler R 3.00 8.00
WF Walt Frazier L 6.00 15.00
YM Yao Ming V 12.00 30.00

2007-08 Chronology Stitches in Time Patches Autographs

PRINT RUN 35 SER.#'d SETS
*STITCH AUTO 25: .5X TO 1.25X HI
STITCH AUTO 25 PRINT RUN 25 SER.#'d SETS
*STITCH AUTO 15: .6X TO 1.5X HI
STITCH AUTO 15 PRINT RUN 15 SER.#'d SETS
AB Aaron Brooks 6.00 15.00
AD Adrian Dantley 20.00 50.00
AH Al Horford 20.00 50.00
AL Acie Law 5.00 12.00
CB Corey Brewer 6.00 15.00
CM Chris Mullin 30.00 80.00
DC Daequan Cook 6.00 15.00
DE Deron Williams 6.00 15.00
GD Glen Davis 6.00 15.00
JA Jason Smith 5.00 12.00
JC Javaris Crittenton 5.00 12.00
JD Jared Dudley 6.00 15.00
JG Jeff Green 6.00 15.00
JN Joakim Noah 8.00 20.00
JW Julian Wright 5.00 12.00
KB Kobe Bryant 2,000.00 4,000.00
KD Kevin Durant 4,000.00 8,000.00
KG Kevin Garnett 500.00 1,000.00
KH Kirk Hinrich 25.00 60.00
LJ LeBron James 4,000.00 8,000.00
MA Morris Almond 5.00 12.00
MC Mike Conley Jr. 12.00 30.00
MM Moses Malone 200.00 500.00
RS Rodney Stuckey 5.00 12.00
SH Spencer Hawes 5.00 12.00
SW Sean Williams 5.00 12.00
WC Wilson Chandler 6.00 15.00
WF Walt Frazier 40.00 100.00

2007-08 Chronology Stitches in Time Patches Autographs 25

*PATCH AU 25: .5X TO 1.25X BASE HI
PRINT RUN 25 SER.#'d SETS
JO Michael Jordan 10,000.00 15,000.00
SN Steve Nash 800.00 1,500.00
TM Tracy McGrady 400.00 800.00
YM Yao Ming 800.00 1,500.00

2007-08 Chronology The LeBrons

LJ LeBron James Red 12.00 30.00
LJ LeBron James Blue 12.00 30.00

2007-08 Chronology Through the Years

PRINT RUN 50 SER.#'d SETS
TEAD Adrian Dantley 10.00 25.00
TEAG Artis Gilmore 12.00 30.00
TEBC Bill Cartwright 15.00 40.00
TEBL Bill Laimbeer 12.00 30.00
TEBM Bob McAdoo 15.00 40.00
TEBO Bob Lanier 10.00 25.00
TECD Clyde Drexler 40.00 100.00
TEDR Dennis Rodman 60.00 150.00
TEDT David Thompson 15.00 40.00
TEDW Dominique Wilkins 40.00 100.00
TEHG Horace Grant 15.00 40.00
TEJE Julius Erving 100.00 250.00
TEJP John Paxson 10.00 25.00
TEJS Jack Sikma 10.00 25.00
TERB Rick Barry 12.00 30.00
TERP Robert Parish 15.00 40.00
TESP Sam Perkins 12.00 30.00
TEVD Vlade Divac 25.00 60.00

2007-08 Chronology Uniformity

STATED PRINT RUN 2 TO 44 SER.#'d SETS
UNBA Abdul-Jabbar/Bird/33 200.00 500.00
UNBJ S.Jones/R.Barry/24 30.00 80.00
UNDS Daugherty/Sikma/43 15.00 40.00
UNFW F.Brown/B.Walton/32 20.00 50.00
UNGH Greer/Heinsohn/15 40.00 100.00
UNGW G.Gervin/J.West/44 60.00 150.00
UNIW D.Issel/Westphal/44 20.00 50.00
UNJB K.Bryant/S.Jones/24 1,000.00 2,000.00
UNKM B.King/McGinnis/30 20.00 50.00
UNTW Worthy/Thurmond/42 25.00 60.00
UNWN Nelson/L.Wilkens/19 25.00 60.00

1996 Classic Legends of the Final Four

COMPLETE SET (32) 12.00 30.00
1 Sheryl Swoopes 3.00 8.00
2 Cheryl Miller 3.00 8.00
3 Rebecca Lobo 2.00 5.00
4 Jennifer Azzi 1.50 4.00
5 Dawn Staley 2.00 5.00
6 Charlotte Smith 1.00 2.50
7 Bridgette Gordon .40 1.00
8 Erica Westbrooks .20 .50
9 Tracy Claxton .20 .50
10 Clarissa Davis .20 .50
11 Kareem Abdul-Jabbar .40 1.00
12 Hakeem Olajuwon .40 1.00
13 Bill Walton .40 1.00
14 James Worthy .40 1.00
15 Isiah Thomas .40 1.00
16 Darrell Griffith .20 .50
17 Bobby Hurley .20 .50
18 Glen Rice .20 .50
19 Ed Pinckney .20 .50
20 Danny Manning .20 .50
MC1 John Wooden 1.00 2.50
MC2 Dean Smith .60 1.50
MC3 Nolan Richardson .40 1.00
MC4 Mike Krzyzewski .60 1.50
MC5 John Thompson .40 1.00
WC1 Tara Vanderveer .40 1.00
WC2 Pat Summitt 3.00 8.00
WC3 Marianne Stanley .40 1.00
WC4 Sylvia Hatchell .40 1.00
WC5 Geno Auriemma .40 1.00
NNO Checklist
(Sears Trophy) .20 .50
NNO Coaches vs. Cancer DP .20 .50

2002 Classic Signature Series Shaquille O'Neal

SS1 Shaquille O'Neal 6.00 15.00

2009-10 Classics

COMP.SET w/o SP's (100) 15.00 30.00
101-160 PRINT RUN 999 SER.#'d SETS
161-200 PRINT RUNS LISTED IN CHECKLIST
1 Kevin Garnett 1.25 3.00
2 Rasheed Wallace .60 1.50
3 Paul Pierce .75 2.00
4 Kendrick Perkins .30 .75
5 Brook Lopez .50 1.25
6 Devin Harris .30 .75
7 Chris Douglas-Roberts .30 .75
8 Al Harrington .40 1.00
9 David Lee .30 .75
10 Danilo Gallinari .40 1.00
11 Andre Iguodala .50 1.25
12 Louis Williams .50 1.25
13 Elton Brand .40 1.00
14 Chris Bosh .60 1.50
15 Andrea Bargnani .30 .75
16 Hedo Turkoglu .40 1.00
17 Jose Calderon .30 .75
18 Dirk Nowitzki 1.25 3.00
19 Shawn Marion .50 1.25
20 Drew Gooden .40 1.00
21 J.J. Barea .50 1.25
22 Shane Battier .50 1.25
23 Aaron Brooks .30 .75
24 Trevor Ariza .30 .75
25 Rudy Gay .50 1.25
26 Zach Randolph .50 1.25
27 O.J. Mayo .50 1.25
28 Chris Paul 1.00 2.50
29 David West .40 1.00
30 Emeka Okafor .40 1.00
31 Tim Duncan 1.25 3.00
32 Tony Parker .75 2.00
33 Richard Jefferson .40 1.00
34 Manu Ginobili 1.00 2.50
35 Luol Deng .40 1.00
36 Derrick Rose .75 2.00
37 John Salmons .40 1.00
38 LeBron James 4.00 10.00
39 Mo Williams .40 1.00
40 Shaquille O'Neal 1.50 4.00
41 Anderson Varejao .30 .75
42 Ben Gordon .40 1.00
43 Rodney Stuckey .30 .75
44 Charlie Villanueva .30 .75
45 Danny Granger .30 .75
46 Mike Dunleavy .30 .75
47 Dahntay Jones .30 .75
48 Andrew Bogut .40 1.00
49 Michael Redd .40 1.00
50 Hakim Warrick .30 .75
51 Carmelo Anthony .75 2.00
52 Chauncey Billups .60 1.50
53 Nene .40 1.00
54 Chris Andersen .50 1.25
55 Al Jefferson .30 .75
56 Corey Brewer .30 .75
57 Ryan Gomes .30 .75
58 Brandon Roy .60 1.50
59 LaMarcus Aldridge .50 1.25
60 Andre Miller .50 1.25
61 Kevin Durant 2.00 5.00
62 Russell Westbrook 1.00 2.50
63 Jeff Green .40 1.00
64 Carlos Boozer .40 1.00
65 Deron Williams .40 1.00
66 Andrei Kirilenko .40 1.00
67 Joe Johnson .50 1.25
68 Josh Smith .40 1.00
69 Jamal Crawford .50 1.25
70 Stephen Jackson .40 1.00
71 Raymond Felton .30 .75
72 Gerald Wallace .40 1.00
73 Dwyane Wade 1.00 2.50
74 Jermaine O'Neal .50 1.25
75 Michael Beasley .30 .75
76 Udonis Haslem .30 .75
77 Vince Carter 1.00 2.50
78 Dwight Howard .60 1.50
79 Rashard Lewis .40 1.00
80 J.J. Redick .50 1.25
81 Antawn Jamison .40 1.00
82 Caron Butler .40 1.00
83 Randy Foye .30 .75
84 Monta Ellis .40 1.00
85 Corey Maggette .40 1.00
86 Anthony Randolph .30 .75
87 Chris Kaman .40 1.00
88 Eric Gordon .40 1.00
89 Baron Davis .40 1.00
90 Kobe Bryant 4.00 10.00
91 Andrew Bynum .30 .75
92 Lamar Odom .40 1.00
93 Ron Artest .50 1.25
94 Amare Stoudemire .40 1.00
95 Jason Richardson .50 1.25
96 Steve Nash 1.00 2.50
97 Grant Hill .75 2.00
98 Kevin Martin .40 1.00
99 Beno Udrih .30 .75
100 Jason Thompson .30 .75
101 Larry Bird 5.00 12.00
102 Gail Goodrich 1.25 3.00
103 Harry Gallatin 1.25 3.00
104 Chris Webber 1.50 4.00
105 Nate McMillan .75 2.00
106 George Mikan 4.00 10.00
107 Drazen Petrovic 2.50 6.00
108 Jalen Rose 1.00 2.50
109 Mitch Richmond 1.25 3.00
110 Mark Price 1.25 3.00
111 David Robinson 2.50 6.00
112 Rick Barry 1.00 2.50
113 Lenny Wilkens 1.25 3.00
114 Robert Horry 1.00 2.50
115 Walt Frazier 2.00 5.00
116 Buck Williams .75 2.00
117 Patrick Ewing 2.00 5.00
118 Danny Manning 1.00 2.50
119 Dennis Johnson 1.00 2.50
120 Rony Seikaly .75 2.00
121 Chris Mullin 1.50 4.00
122 Hakeem Olajuwon 1.50 4.00
123 George Gervin 1.50 4.00
124 Rex Chapman 1.25 3.00
125 Bob McAdoo 1.50 4.00
126 Dana Barros .75 2.00
127 B.J. Armstrong 1.25 3.00
128 Danny Roundfield 1.25 3.00
129 Oscar Robertson 1.50 4.00
130 Bill Russell 4.00 10.00
131 Doc Rivers 1.25 3.00
132 Clyde Drexler 2.00 5.00
133 Kareem Abdul-Jabbar 4.00 10.00
134 Bernard King 1.50 4.00
135 Don Nelson 1.25 3.00
136 John Salley 1.00 2.50
137 Jerry Sloan 1.50 4.00
138 Joe Dumars 1.50 4.00
139 Karl Malone 1.50 4.00
140 Magic Johnson 5.00 12.00
141 Dominique Wilkins 2.00 5.00
142 Jack Sikma 1.00 2.50
143 Wes Unseld 1.25 3.00
144 Sidney Moncrief 1.00 2.50
145 Sleepy Floyd 1.00 2.50
146 Spencer Haywood .75 2.00
147 Kevin McHale 2.00 5.00
148 Glen Rice 1.00 2.50
149 Isiah Thomas 1.25 3.00
150 Jerry West 2.00 5.00
151 Willis Reed 2.00 5.00
152 Bob Lanier 1.50 4.00
153 Elgin Baylor 3.00 8.00
154 Scottie Pippen 3.00 8.00
155 Elvin Hayes 2.00 5.00
156 Scott Skiles 1.00 2.50
157 Ed Macauley 1.25 3.00
158 Pete Maravich 4.00 10.00
159 Bob Cousy 3.00 8.00
160 Wilt Chamberlain 5.00 12.00
161 Blake Griffin AU/499 RC 60.00 150.00
162 Hasheem Thabeet AU/499 RC 3.00 8.00
163 James Harden AU/499 RC 500.00 1,000.00
164 Tyreke Evans AU/499 RC 4.00 10.00
165 Jonny Flynn AU/499 RC 3.00 8.00
166 Stephen Curry AU/499 RC 1,500.00 3,000.00
167 Jordan Hill AU/469 RC 3.00 8.00
168 B.Jennings AU/499 RC 5.00 12.00
169 Terrence Williams AU/499 RC 3.00 8.00
170 Gerald Henderson AU/499 RC 3.00 8.00
171 Tyler Hansbrough AU/499 RC 4.00 10.00
172 Earl Clark AU/571 RC 3.00 8.00
173 Austin Daye AU/598 RC 3.00 8.00
174 James Johnson AU/199 RC 4.00 10.00
175 Jrue Holiday AU/499 RC 15.00 40.00
176 Ty Lawson AU/599 RC 4.00 10.00
177 Jeff Teague AU/553 RC 4.00 10.00
178 Eric Maynor AU/599 RC 3.00 8.00
179 D.Collison AU/799 RC 5.00 12.00
180 Omri Casspi AU/862 RC 3.00 8.00
181 B.J. Mullens AU/872 RC 3.00 8.00
182 R.Beaubois AU/199 RC 3.00 8.00
183 Taj Gibson AU/823 RC 4.00 10.00
184 DeMarre Carroll AU/864 RC 4.00 10.00
185 Wayne Ellington AU/575 RC 4.00 10.00
186 Toney Douglas AU/933 RC 3.00 8.00
187 DeJuan Blair AU/999 RC 4.00 10.00
188 Sam Young AU/249 RC 3.00 8.00
189 A.J. Price AU/999 RC 3.00 8.00
190 Chase Budinger AU/999 RC 3.00 8.00
191 David Andersen AU/99 RC 3.00 8.00
192 Jonas Jerebko AU/999 RC 4.00 10.00
193 Marcus Landry AU/999 RC 3.00 8.00
194 Serge Ibaka AU/99 RC 15.00 40.00
195 Patrick Mills AU/99 RC 40.00 100.00
196 Wesley Matthews AU/99 RC 30.00 80.00
197 Taylor Griffin AU/999 RC 3.00 8.00
198 Jermaine Taylor AU/999 RC 3.00 8.00
199 Jodie Meeks AU/249 RC 3.00 8.00
200 DaJuan Summers AU/999 RC 3.00 8.00

2009-10 Classics Timeless Tributes Gold

*1-100 GOLD: 2X TO 5X BASE HI
*101-160 GOLD: .75X TO 2X BASE HI
*161-200 GOLD: .6X TO 1.5X SILVER HI
GOLD PRINT RUN 25 SER.#'d SETS
161 Blake Griffin 30.00 80.00
166 Stephen Curry 1,000.00 2,000.00

2009-10 Classics Timeless Tributes Platinum

*1-100 PLATINUM: 3X TO 8X BASE HI
*101-160 PLATINUM: 1.25X TO 3X BASE HI
*161-200 PLAT: .75X TO 2X SILVER HI
PLATINUM PRINT RUN 25 SER.#'d SETS
166 Stephen Curry 1,500.00 3,000.00

2009-10 Classics Timeless Tributes Silver

*1-100 SILVER: 1.25X TO 3X BASE HI
*101-160 SILVER: .5X TO 1.25X BASE HI

SILVER PRINT RUN 100 SER.#'d SETS
161 Blake Griffin 10.00 25.00
162 Hasheem Thabeet 1.50 4.00
163 James Harden 15.00 40.00
164 Tyreke Evans 2.00 5.00
165 Jonny Flynn 1.50 4.00
166 Stephen Curry 600.00 1,200.00
167 Jordan Hill 1.50 4.00
168 Brandon Jennings 2.50 6.00
169 Terrence Williams 1.50 4.00
170 Gerald Henderson 1.50 4.00
171 Tyler Hansbrough 2.00 5.00
172 Earl Clark 1.50 4.00
173 Austin Daye 1.50 4.00
174 James Johnson 2.00 5.00
175 Jrue Holiday 8.00 20.00
176 Ty Lawson 2.00 5.00
177 Jeff Teague 2.00 5.00
178 Eric Maynor 1.50 4.00
179 Darren Collison 2.50 6.00
180 Omri Casspi 1.50 4.00
181 B.J. Mullens 1.50 4.00
182 Rodrigue Beaubois 1.50 4.00
183 Taj Gibson 2.00 5.00
184 DeMarre Carroll 2.00 5.00
185 Wayne Ellington 2.00 5.00
186 Toney Douglas 1.50 4.00
187 DeJuan Blair 2.00 5.00
188 Sam Young 1.50 4.00
189 A.J. Price 1.50 4.00
190 Chase Budinger 1.50 4.00
191 David Andersen 1.50 4.00
192 Jonas Jerebko 2.00 5.00
193 Marcus Landry 1.50 4.00
194 Serge Ibaka 2.50 6.00
195 Patrick Mills 4.00 10.00
196 Wesley Matthews 2.50 6.00
197 Taylor Griffin 1.50 4.00
198 Jermaine Taylor 1.50 4.00
199 Jodie Meeks 1.50 4.00
200 DaJuan Summers 1.50 4.00

2009-10 Classics Blast From The Past Jerseys
STATED PRINT RUN 25 TO 199 SETS
1 Dan Issel/99 3.00 8.00
2 Adrian Dantley/99 3.00 8.00
3 Anfernee Hardaway/199 10.00 25.00
4 Bernard King/199 5.00 12.00
5 Clyde Drexler/199 6.00 15.00
6 Glen Rice/199 3.00 8.00
7 John Stockton/25 8.00 20.00
8 Robert Horry/199 3.00 8.00
9 Karl Malone/199 5.00 12.00
10 Larry Johnson/199 10.00 25.00
11 Danny Manning/199 3.00 8.00
12 Reggie Lewis/199 10.00 25.00
13 Kevin Johnson/199 4.00 10.00
14 Sleepy Floyd/199 3.00 8.00
15 Tom Heinsohn/99 4.00 10.00
16 Xavier McDaniel/199 2.50 6.00
17 Artis Gilmore/199 5.00 12.00
18 Toni Kukoc/199 4.00 10.00
19 Chuck Person/199 3.00 8.00
20 Bob Lanier/199 5.00 12.00
21 Dominique Wilkins/199 6.00 15.00
22 Hakeem Olajuwon/199 5.00 12.00
23 Sam Perkins/199 2.50 6.00
24 Chris Mullin/199 5.00 12.00
25 Michael Cage/199 2.50 6.00

2009-10 Classics Blast From The Past Jerseys Prime
*PRIME: .6X TO 1.5X HI COLUMN
STATED PRINT RUN 10 TO 30 SER.#'d SETS
5 Clyde Drexler/30 12.00 30.00
6 Glen Rice/30 15.00 30.00
9 Karl Malone/30 15.00 30.00
10 Larry Johnson/30 25.00 60.00
11 Danny Manning/30 15.00 30.00
12 Reggie Lewis/30 30.00 60.00
13 Kevin Johnson/30 8.00 20.00
21 Dominique Wilkins/30 10.00 25.00
22 Hakeem Olajuwon/30 10.00 25.00

2009-10 Classics Blast From The Past Jerseys Signatures
PRINT RUN 25 SER.#'d SETS
1 Dan Issel 8.00 20.00
2 Adrian Dantley 8.00 20.00
3 Anfernee Hardaway 50.00 100.00
4 Bernard King 8.00 20.00
5 Clyde Drexler 20.00 50.00
6 Glen Rice 20.00 50.00
10 Larry Johnson 25.00 60.00
11 Danny Manning 15.00 30.00
13 Kevin Johnson 30.00 80.00
14 Sleepy Floyd 8.00 20.00
16 Xavier McDaniel 8.00 20.00
17 Artis Gilmore 8.00 20.00
18 Toni Kukoc 25.00 60.00
23 Sam Perkins 8.00 20.00

2009-10 Classics Blast From The Past Jerseys Prime Signatures
PRINT RUNS LISTED IN CHECKLIST
2 Adrian Dantley/25 12.50 30.00
3 Anfernee Hardaway/25 75.00 150.00
6 Glen Rice/25 25.00 60.00
10 Larry Johnson/25 50.00 120.00
11 Danny Manning/25 20.00 40.00
13 Kevin Johnson/25 50.00 100.00
14 Sleepy Floyd/25 15.00 40.00
16 Xavier McDaniel/25 12.50 30.00
18 Toni Kukoc/25 30.00 80.00
23 Sam Perkins/25 12.50 30.00

2009-10 Classics Classic Combos
COMPLETE SET (10) 10.00 25.00
*GOLD: .75X TO 2X BASE HI
GOLD PRINT RUN 100 SER.#'d SETS
*PLATINUM: 1.5X TO 4X BASE HI
PLATINUM PRINT RUN 25 SER.#'d SETS
*SILVER: .5X TO 1.25X BASE HI
SILVER PRINT RUN 250 SER.#'d SETS
1 K.Bryant/L.Odom 6.00 15.00
2 L.James/S.O'Neal 6.00 15.00
3 P.Pierce/K.Garnett 2.00 5.00
4 D.Nowitzki/S.Marion 2.00 5.00
5 D.Wade/J.O'Neal 1.50 4.00
6 B.Russell/B.Sharman 2.50 6.00
7 A.Mourning/T.Hardaway 1.25 3.00
8 H.Olajuwon/C.Drexler 1.25 3.00
9 I.Thomas/J.Dumars 1.00 2.50
10 J.Stockton/K.Malone 1.25 3.00

2009-10 Classics Classic Combos Jerseys
STATED PRINT RUN ONE TO 99 SER.#'d SETS
2 L.James/S.O'Neal/99 10.00 25.00
3 P.Pierce/K.Garnett/99 6.00 15.00
4 D.Nowitzki/S.Marion/99 6.00 15.00
8 H.Olajuwon/C.Drexler/99 6.00 15.00
9 I.Thomas/J.Dumars/99 8.00 20.00
10 J.Stockton/K.Malone/99 6.00 15.00

2009-10 Classics Classic Combos Jerseys Prime
*PRIME: 1X TO 2.5X BASE HI
PRINT RUN 25 SER.#'d SETS
2 L.James/S.O'Neal 75.00 200.00
3 P.Pierce/K.Garnett 12.00 30.00
9 I.Thomas/J.Dumars 10.00 25.00

2009-10 Classics Classic Confrontations
COMPLETE SET (10) 10.00 25.00
*GOLD: .75X TO 2X BASE HI
GOLD PRINT RUN 50 SER.#'d SETS
*PLATINUM: 1.5X TO 4X BASE HI
PLATINUM PRINT RUN 25 SER.#'d SETS
*SILVER: .5X TO 1.25X BASE HI
SILVER PRINT RUN 250 SER.#'d SETS
1 L.Bird/M.Johnson 3.00 8.00
2 E.Monroe/W.Frazier 1.25 3.00
3 W.Reed/K.Abdul-Jabbar 2.50 6.00
4 J.Worthy/R.Parish 1.00 2.50
5 K.Bryant/L.James 6.00 15.00
6 D.Nowitzki/T.Duncan 2.00 5.00
7 C.Paul/D.Wade 1.50 4.00
8 K.Garnett/S.O'Neal 2.50 6.00
9 J.Kidd/S.Nash 1.50 4.00
10 J.West/O.Robertson 1.25 3.00

2009-10 Classics Classic Confrontations Jerseys
STATED PRINT RUN 199 SER.#'d SETS
*PRIME: 1X TO 2.5X BASE HI
PRIME PRINT RUN 25 SER.#'d SETS
1 L.Bird/M.Johnson 12.00 30.00
5 K.Bryant/L.James 30.00 80.00
6 D.Nowitzki/T.Duncan 5.00 12.00
7 C.Paul/D.Wade 5.00 12.00
8 K.Garnett/S.O'Neal 10.00 25.00

2009-10 Classics Classic Confrontations Jerseys Signatures
STATED PRINT RUN 25 SER.#'d SETS
*PRIME: .5X TO 1.25X BASE HI
PRIME PRINT RUN 25 SER.#'d SETS
1 L.Bird/M.Johnson 100.00 200.00

2009-10 Classics Classic Greats
COMPLETE SET (30) 25.00 50.00
*GOLD: .6X TO 1.5X BASE HI
GOLD PRINT RUN 100 SER.#'d SETS
*PLATINUM: 1X TO 2.5X BASE HI
PLATINUM PRINT RUN 25 SER.#'d SETS
*SILVER: .5X TO 1.25X BASE HI
SILVER PRINT RUN 250 SER.#'d SETS
1 Bill Russell 4.00 10.00
2 Bill Sharman 1.50 4.00
3 Bill Walton 2.00 5.00
4 Bob Cousy 3.00 8.00
5 Clyde Drexler 2.00 5.00
6 Dave Cowens 1.50 4.00
7 Earl Monroe 1.50 4.00
8 Elvin Hayes 2.00 5.00
9 George Gervin 1.50 4.00
10 Hakeem Olajuwon 1.50 4.00
11 Hal Greer 1.50 4.00
12 Isiah Thomas 1.25 3.00
13 James Worthy 1.50 4.00
14 Jerry West 2.00 5.00
15 John Havlicek 1.50 4.00
16 Kareem Abdul-Jabbar 4.00 10.00
17 Karl Malone 1.50 4.00
18 Kevin McHale 2.00 5.00
19 Larry Bird 5.00 12.00
20 Lenny Wilkens 1.25 3.00
21 Magic Johnson 5.00 12.00
22 Moses Malone 2.00 5.00
23 Nate Archibald 1.50 4.00
24 Nate Thurmond 1.00 2.50
25 Oscar Robertson 1.50 4.00
26 Rick Barry 1.00 2.50
27 Robert Parish 1.50 4.00
28 Walt Frazier 2.00 5.00
29 Wes Unseld 1.25 3.00
30 Willis Reed 2.00 5.00

2009-10 Classics Classic Greats Jerseys
STATED PRINT RUN 10 TO 99 SER.#'d SETS
5 Clyde Drexler/99 6.00 15.00
6 Dave Cowens/99 5.00 12.00
7 Earl Monroe/99 5.00 12.00
10 Hakeem Olajuwon/99 5.00 12.00
12 Isiah Thomas/99 4.00 10.00
14 Jerry West/49 6.00 15.00
15 John Havlicek/49 10.00 25.00
16 Kareem Abdul-Jabbar/99 8.00 20.00
17 Karl Malone/99 5.00 12.00
18 Kevin McHale/99 6.00 15.00
19 Larry Bird/99 8.00 20.00
21 Magic Johnson/99 6.00 15.00
22 Moses Malone/25 6.00 15.00
26 Rick Barry/99 3.00 8.00
27 Robert Parish/99 5.00 12.00

2009-10 Classics Classic Greats Jerseys Prime
*PRIME: .6X TO 1.5X HI COLUMN
STATED PRINT RUN 10 TO 25 SER.#'d SETS
6 Dave Cowens/25 8.00 20.00
15 John Havlicek/25 8.00 20.00
19 Larry Bird/25 15.00 40.00
21 Magic Johnson/25 12.50 30.00
26 Rick Barry/25 5.00 12.00

2009-10 Classics Classic Greats Jerseys Signatures
STATED PRINT RUN 5 TO 25 SER.#'d SETS
5 Clyde Drexler/25 25.00 60.00
6 Dave Cowens/25 10.00 25.00
7 Earl Monroe/25 15.00 40.00
12 Isiah Thomas/25 12.50 30.00
16 Kareem Abdul-Jabbar/25 30.00 80.00
18 Kevin McHale/25 40.00 100.00
19 Larry Bird/25 40.00 100.00
21 Magic Johnson/25 40.00 100.00
26 Rick Barry/25 12.50 30.00
27 Robert Parish/25 10.00 25.00

2009-10 Classics Classic Greats Jerseys Prime Signatures
STATED PRINT RUN 5 TO 25 SER.#'d SETS
6 Dave Cowens/25 12.50 30.00
7 Earl Monroe/25 15.00 40.00
12 Isiah Thomas/25 15.00 40.00
16 Kareem Abdul-Jabbar/25 50.00 120.00
18 Kevin McHale/25 50.00 120.00
19 Larry Bird/25 50.00 120.00
21 Magic Johnson/25 40.00 100.00
26 Rick Barry/25 12.50 30.00
27 Robert Parish/25 12.50 30.00

2009-10 Classics Dress Code
COMPLETE SET (25) 20.00 40.00
*GOLD: .6X TO 1.5X BASE HI
GOLD PRINT RUN 100 SER.#'d SETS
*PLATINUM: 1.25X TO 3X BASE HI
PLATINUM PRINT RUN 25 SER.#'d SETS
*SILVER: .5X TO 1.25X BASE HI
SILVER PRINT RUN 250 SER.#'d SETS
1 Al Horford .75 2.00
2 Alex English 1.00 2.50
3 Andre Iguodala .75 2.00
4 Yao Ming 2.00 5.00
5 Tracy McGrady 1.50 4.00
6 Tim Duncan 2.00 5.00
7 Thaddeus Young .50 1.25
8 Shawn Marion .75 2.00
9 Samuel Dalembert .50 1.25
10 Sam Perkins .50 1.25
11 David Lee .50 1.25
12 Dwight Howard 1.00 2.50
13 Erick Dampier .50 1.25
14 Randy Foye .50 1.25
15 Jeff Hornacek .60 1.50
16 Kevin Garnett 2.00 5.00
17 Kobe Bryant 6.00 15.00
18 LeBron James 6.00 15.00
19 Mark Price .75 2.00
20 Mehmet Okur .50 1.25
21 Mitch Richmond .75 2.00
22 Nene .60 1.50
23 Patrick Ewing 1.25 3.00
24 Carlos Boozer .60 1.50
25 Chauncey Billups 1.00 2.50

2009-10 Classics Dress Code Jerseys
STATED PRINT RUN 49 TO 199 SER.#'d SETS
1 Al Horford/199 3.00 8.00
2 Alex English/199 4.00 10.00
3 Andre Iguodala/199 3.00 8.00
4 Yao Ming/99 8.00 20.00
5 Tracy McGrady/199 6.00 15.00
6 Tim Duncan/199 8.00 20.00
7 Thaddeus Young/199 2.00 5.00
8 Shawn Marion/199 3.00 8.00
9 Samuel Dalembert/199 2.00 5.00
10 Sam Perkins/199 2.00 5.00
11 David Lee/49 2.00 5.00
12 Dwight Howard/199 4.00 10.00
13 Erick Dampier/199 2.00 5.00
14 Randy Foye/199 2.00 5.00
15 Jeff Hornacek/199 2.50 6.00
16 Kevin Garnett/199 8.00 20.00
17 Kobe Bryant/99 12.00 30.00
18 LeBron James/199 8.00 20.00
19 Mark Price/199 6.00 15.00
21 Mitch Richmond/199 3.00 8.00
22 Nene/199 2.50 6.00
23 Patrick Ewing/199 5.00 12.00
24 Carlos Boozer/199 2.50 6.00
25 Chauncey Billups/199 4.00 10.00

2009-10 Classics Dress Code Jerseys Prime
*PRIME: .75X TO 2X BASE HI
STATED PRINT RUN 5 TO 25 SER.#'d SETS

2009-10 Classics Dress Code Jerseys Signatures
STATED PRINT RUN 10 TO 25 SER.#'d SETS
2 Alex English/25 8.00 20.00
3 Andre Iguodala/25 6.00 15.00
10 Sam Perkins/25 6.00 15.00
15 Jeff Hornacek/25 8.00 20.00
17 Kobe Bryant/25 800.00 1,500.00
24 Carlos Boozer/25 6.00 15.00
25 Chauncey Billups/25 12.50 30.00

2009-10 Classics Dress Code Jerseys Prime Signatures
STATED PRINT RUN 10 TO 25 SER.#'d SETS
2 Alex English/25 10.00 25.00
3 Andre Iguodala/25 8.00 20.00
10 Sam Perkins/25 12.50 30.00
11 David Lee/25 10.00 25.00
15 Jeff Hornacek/25 10.00 25.00
24 Carlos Boozer/25 8.00 20.00
25 Chauncey Billups/25 10.00 25.00

2009-10 Classics Significant Signatures Gold
STATED PRINT RUN 13 TO 50 SER.#'d SETS
6 Devin Harris/50 5.00 12.00
22 Shane Battier/50 5.00 12.00
23 Aaron Brooks/50 5.00 12.00
24 Trevor Ariza/27 5.00 12.00
30 Emeka Okafor/50 6.00 15.00
32 Tony Parker/50 10.00 25.00
44 Charlie Villanueva/50 5.00 12.00
45 Danny Granger/39 10.00 25.00
57 Ryan Gomes/50 5.00 12.00
74 Jermaine O'Neal/13 10.00 25.00
88 Eric Gordon/50 8.00 20.00
90 Kobe Bryant/50 500.00 1,000.00
101 Larry Bird/50 40.00 100.00
102 Gail Goodrich/50 10.00 25.00
103 Harry Gallatin/50 6.00 15.00
108 Jalen Rose/50 8.00 20.00
112 Rick Barry/50 8.00 20.00
113 Lenny Wilkens/50 8.00 20.00
114 Robert Horry/50 8.00 20.00
115 Walt Frazier/50 10.00 25.00
118 Danny Manning/50 10.00 20.00
121 Chris Mullin/50 25.00 50.00
123 George Gervin/50 10.00 25.00
125 Bob McAdoo/50 15.00 30.00
129 Oscar Robertson/50 60.00 120.00
130 Bill Russell/50 500.00 1,000.00
131 Doc Rivers/50 10.00 25.00
132 Clyde Drexler/50 30.00 80.00
133 Kareem Abdul-Jabbar/50 50.00 120.00
134 Bernard King/50 8.00 20.00
138 Joe Dumars/50 15.00 40.00
140 Magic Johnson/49 50.00 120.00
141 Dominique Wilkins/50 15.00 40.00
143 Wes Unseld/45 10.00 25.00
144 Sidney Moncrief/50 8.00 20.00
145 Sleepy Floyd/48 8.00 20.00
146 Spencer Haywood/50 6.00 15.00
147 Kevin McHale/50 30.00 60.00
148 Glen Rice/50 12.50 30.00
149 Isiah Thomas/50 12.50 30.00
150 Jerry West/50 30.00 80.00
151 Willis Reed/50 40.00 100.00
153 Elgin Baylor/50 15.00 40.00
154 Scottie Pippen/50 125.00 250.00
155 Elvin Hayes/50 10.00 25.00
159 Bob Cousy/50 20.00 50.00

2009-10 Classics Significant Signatures Platinum
*PLATINUM: .5X TO 1.25X HI COLUMN
STATED PRINT RUN ONE TO 25 SER.#'d SETS
74 Jermaine O'Neal/25 8.00 20.00
90 Kobe Bryant/25 800.00 1,500.00
110 Mark Price/25 30.00 80.00
122 Hakeem Olajuwon/25 30.00 80.00
131 Doc Rivers/25 15.00 40.00
141 Dominique Wilkins/25 20.00 50.00

2009-10 Classics Timeless Threads
STATED PRINT RUN ONE TO 265 SETS
1 Kevin Garnett/199 8.00 20.00
3 Paul Pierce/199 5.00 12.00
9 David Lee/49 2.00 5.00
10 Danilo Gallinari/25 2.50 6.00
11 Andre Iguodala/199 3.00 8.00
13 Elton Brand/199 2.50 6.00
14 Chris Bosh/199 4.00 10.00
15 Andrea Bargnani/25 2.00 5.00
17 Jose Calderon/299 2.00 5.00
18 Dirk Nowitzki/199 8.00 20.00
19 Shawn Marion/199 3.00 8.00
21 J.J. Barea/199 5.00 12.00
22 Shane Battier/199 3.00 8.00
23 Aaron Brooks/199 2.00 5.00
27 O.J. Mayo/199 2.00 5.00
28 Chris Paul/199 6.00 15.00
29 David West/199 2.50 6.00
31 Tim Duncan/199 8.00 20.00
32 Tony Parker/25 6.00 15.00
38 LeBron James/199 10.00 25.00
39 Mo Williams/99 2.50 6.00
40 Shaquille O'Neal/199 10.00 25.00
44 Charlie Villanueva/199 2.00 5.00
51 Carmelo Anthony/199 5.00 12.00
52 Chauncey Billups/199 4.00 10.00
53 Nene/299 2.50 6.00
55 Al Jefferson/199 2.00 5.00
57 Ryan Gomes/299 2.00 5.00
58 Brandon Roy/199 4.00 10.00
59 LaMarcus Aldridge/199 3.00 8.00
61 Kevin Durant/199 8.00 20.00
64 Carlos Boozer/199 2.50 6.00
65 Deron Williams/199 2.50 6.00
66 Andrei Kirilenko/199 2.50 6.00
68 Josh Smith/199 2.00 5.00
72 Gerald Wallace/199 2.50 6.00
73 Dwyane Wade/199 6.00 15.00
75 Michael Beasley/99 2.00 5.00
76 Udonis Haslem/199 2.00 5.00
78 Dwight Howard/199 4.00 10.00
79 Rashard Lewis/199 2.50 6.00
81 Antawn Jamison/199 2.50 6.00
83 Randy Foye/199 2.00 5.00
87 Chris Kaman/199 2.00 5.00
90 Kobe Bryant/99 8.00 20.00
109 Mitch Richmond/99 4.00 10.00
110 Mark Price/99 3.00 8.00
112 Rick Barry/99 6.00 15.00
117 Patrick Ewing/99 12.50 30.00
119 Dennis Johnson/99 10.00 25.00
121 Chris Mullin/99 6.00 15.00
122 Hakeem Olajuwon/99 6.00 15.00
132 Clyde Drexler/99 8.00 20.00
133 Kareem Abdul-Jabbar/99 8.00 20.00
138 Joe Dumars/99 4.00 10.00
139 Karl Malone/99 8.00 20.00
140 Magic Johnson/99 6.00 15.00
141 Dominique Wilkins/49 6.00 15.00
147 Kevin McHale/99 6.00 15.00
149 Isiah Thomas/99 6.00 15.00
150 Jerry West/49 6.00 15.00
161 Blake Griffin/265 8.00 20.00
162 Hasheem Thabeet/265 1.25 3.00
163 James Harden/265 12.00 30.00
164 Tyreke Evans/265 1.50 4.00
165 Jonny Flynn/265 1.25 3.00
166 Stephen Curry/265 200.00 500.00
167 Jordan Hill/265 1.25 3.00
168 Brandon Jennings/265 2.00 5.00
169 Terrence Williams/265 1.25 3.00
170 Gerald Henderson/265 1.25 3.00
171 Tyler Hansbrough/265 1.50 4.00
172 Earl Clark/265 1.25 3.00
173 Austin Daye/265 1.25 3.00
174 James Johnson/265 1.50 4.00
175 Jrue Holiday/265 6.00 15.00
176 Ty Lawson/265 1.50 4.00
177 Jeff Teague/265 1.50 4.00
178 Eric Maynor/265 1.25 3.00
179 Darren Collison/265 2.00 5.00
180 Omri Casspi/265 1.25 3.00
181 B.J. Mullens/265 1.25 3.00
182 Rodrigue Beaubois/265 1.25 3.00
183 Taj Gibson/265 1.50 4.00
184 DeMarre Carroll/265 1.50 4.00
185 Wayne Ellington/265 1.50 4.00
186 Toney Douglas/265 1.25 3.00
187 DeJuan Blair/265 1.50 4.00
188 Sam Young/265 1.25 3.00
190 Chase Budinger/265 1.25 3.00
197 Taylor Griffin/265 1.25 3.00
198 Jermaine Taylor/265 1.25 3.00
199 Jodie Meeks/265 1.25 3.00
200 DaJuan Summers/265 1.25 3.00

2009-10 Classics Timeless Threads Prime
*PRIME: .75X TO 2X HI COLUMN
*PRIME RCs: 1X TO 2.5X HI COLUMN
STATED PRINT RUN ONE TO 25 SER.#'d SETS
21 J.J. Barea/25 12.50 30.00
40 Shaquille O'Neal/25 20.00 50.00
73 Dwyane Wade/25 15.00 40.00

2010-11 Classics
COMP.SET w/o SPs (100) 15.00 30.00
RETIRED PRINT RUN 999 SER.#'d SETS
AU RC PRINT RUN 199 TO 699 SER.#'d SETS
EXCH.EXPIRATION 10/13/2012
1 Dirk Nowitzki 1.25 3.00
2 Caron Butler .40 1.00
3 Tyson Chandler .40 1.00
4 Ian Mahinmi RC .50 1.25
5 George Hill .40 1.00
6 Tim Duncan 1.25 3.00
7 Manu Ginobili 1.00 2.50
8 Chris Paul 1.00 2.50
9 Marco Belinelli .30 .75
10 David West .40 1.00
11 Marc Gasol .50 1.25
12 Zach Randolph .50 1.25
13 Mike Conley Jr. .40 1.00
14 Aaron Brooks .30 .75
15 Kevin Martin .40 1.00
16 Luis Scola .40 1.00
17 Kobe Bryant 4.00 10.00
18 Derek Fisher .50 1.25
19 Pau Gasol .75 2.00
20 Lamar Odom .40 1.00
21 Eric Gordon .40 1.00
22 Blake Griffin .50 1.25
23 Chris Kaman .30 .75
24 Steve Nash 1.00 2.50
25 Vince Carter 1.00 2.50
26 Channing Frye .30 .75
27 Stephen Curry 4.00 10.00
28 Monta Ellis .40 1.00
29 David Lee .30 .75
30 Tyreke Evans .40 1.00
31 Beno Udrih .30 .75
32 Carl Landry .30 .75
33 Kevin Durant 2.00 5.00
34 Jeff Green .40 1.00
35 Russell Westbrook .75 2.00
36 Michael Beasley .30 .75
37 Kevin Love .50 1.25
38 Corey Brewer .30 .75
39 Carmelo Anthony .75 2.00
40 Nene .40 1.00
41 Chauncey Billups .60 1.50
42 Arron Afflalo .30 .75
43 Brandon Roy .60 1.50
44 Wesley Matthews .30 .75
45 LaMarcus Aldridge .50 1.25
46 Rudy Fernandez .30 .75
47 Al Jefferson .30 .75
48 Deron Williams .40 1.00
49 Andrei Kirilenko .40 1.00
50 Rajon Rondo .60 1.50
51 Paul Pierce .75 2.00
52 Kevin Garnett 1.25 3.00
53 Ray Allen .75 2.00
54 Amare Stoudemire .50 1.25
55 Raymond Felton .30 .75
56 Toney Douglas .30 .75
57 Danilo Gallinari .40 1.00
58 Bill Walker .30 .75
59 Andrea Bargnani .30 .75
60 Sonny Weems .30 .75
61 DeMar DeRozan .75 2.00
62 Jrue Holiday .60 1.50
63 Elton Brand .40 1.00
64 Andre Iguodala .50 1.25
65 Brook Lopez .40 1.00
66 Anthony Morrow .30 .75
67 Devin Harris .30 .75
68 Derrick Rose 1.00 2.50
69 Luol Deng .40 1.00
70 Carlos Boozer .40 1.00
71 Joakim Noah .50 1.25
72 Danny Granger .30 .75
73 Darren Collison .30 .75
74 Roy Hibbert .40 1.00
75 J.J. Hickson .30 .75
76 Antawn Jamison .40 1.00
77 Mo Williams .40 1.00
78 Andrew Bogut .40 1.00
79 Brandon Jennings .30 .75
80 John Salmons .30 .75
81 Tayshaun Prince .50 1.25
82 Rodney Stuckey .30 .75
83 Charlie Villanueva .30 .75
84 Dwight Howard .60 1.50
85 Jameer Nelson .30 .75
86 Hedo Turkoglu .40 1.00
87 Jason Richardson .50 1.25
88 Stephen Jackson .40 1.00
89 Boris Diaw .40 1.00
90 Gerald Wallace .40 1.00
91 Jamal Crawford .50 1.25
92 Josh Smith .30 .75
93 Joe Johnson .50 1.25
94 Dwyane Wade 1.00 2.50
95 LeBron James 4.00 10.00
96 Chris Bosh .60 1.50
97 Erick Dampier .30 .75
98 Nick Young .30 .75
99 Andray Blatche .30 .75
100 Kirk Hinrich .40 1.00
101 Bill Walton 1.50 4.00
102 Byron Scott 1.00 2.50
103 Mark Aguirre .75 2.00
104 Michael Finley 1.00 2.50
105 Nate McMillan .60 1.50
106 Nick Anderson .75 2.00
107 Artis Gilmore 1.25 3.00
108 Jamal Mashburn .75 2.00
109 Larry Bird 4.00 10.00
110 Julius Erving 2.00 5.00
111 Sidney Moncrief .60 1.50
112 Rony Seikaly .60 1.50
113 Jalen Rose .75 2.00
114 Rickey Green 1.00 2.50
115 Robert Horry 1.00 2.50
116 Rex Chapman 1.00 2.50
117 Jack Sikma .75 2.00
118 Nate Thurmond 1.25 3.00
119 Glenn Robinson 1.00 2.50
120 Doc Rivers 1.00 2.50
121 David Robinson 2.00 5.00
122 Michael Cooper 1.00 2.50
123 Al Attles 1.00 2.50
124 Alonzo Mourning 1.50 4.00
125 Dave Bing 1.25 3.00
126 Bobby Jones .75 2.00
127 Moses Malone 1.50 4.00
128 Tim Hardaway 1.25 3.00
129 Tom Heinsohn 1.00 2.50
130 Chris Webber 1.25 3.00
131 Gus Williams .60 1.50
132 Campy Russell .60 1.50
133 Charles D. Smith 1.00 2.50
134 Magic Johnson 4.00 10.00
135 Spud Webb .75 2.00
136 Charles Oakley 1.00 2.50
137 Pete Maravich 2.50 6.00
138 Jerry West 2.00 5.00
139 Derek Harper .75 2.00
140 Hakeem Olajuwon 2.00 5.00
141 Luke Babbitt/699 AU RC 3.00 8.00
142 Kevin Seraphin/699 AU RC 3.00 8.00
143 Eric Bledsoe/699 AU RC 5.00 12.00
144 Avery Bradley/699 AU RC 5.00 12.00
145 James Anderson/699 AU RC 3.00 8.00
146 Elliot Williams/699 AU RC 3.00 8.00
147 Trevor Booker/699 AU RC 3.00 8.00
148 Damion James/699 AU RC 3.00 8.00
149 Dominique Jones/689 AU RC 3.00 8.00
150 Quincy Pondexter/699 AU RC 3.00 8.00
151 Jordan Crawford/699 AU RC 3.00 8.00
152 Greivis Vasquez/699 AU RC 3.00 8.00
153 Daniel Orton/699 AU RC 3.00 8.00
154 Lazar Hayward/699 AU RC 3.00 8.00
155 John Wall/199 AU RC 25.00 60.00
156 Evan Turner/299 AU RC 4.00 10.00
157 Derrick Favors/299 AU RC 4.00 10.00
158 Wesley Johnson/299 AU RC 3.00 8.00
159 D.Cousins/349 AU RC 20.00 50.00
160 Ekpe Udoh/399 AU RC 3.00 8.00
161 Greg Monroe/399 AU RC 4.00 10.00
162 Al-Farouq Aminu/699 AU RC 4.00 10.00
163 Gordon Hayward/449 AU RC 12.00 30.00
164 Paul George/449 AU RC 75.00 200.00
165 Cole Aldrich/449 AU RC 3.00 8.00
166 Xavier Henry/449 AU RC 3.00 8.00
167 Ed Davis/449 AU RC 4.00 10.00
168 Patrick Patterson/449 AU RC 4.00 10.00
169 Larry Sanders/699 AU RC 3.00 8.00
170 Luke Harangody/699 AU RC 3.00 8.00
171 Dexter Pittman/699 AU RC 3.00 8.00
172 Hassan Whiteside/699 AU RC 6.00 15.00
173 Andy Rautins/699 AU RC 3.00 8.00
174 L.Stephenson/699 AU RC 5.00 12.00
175 Armon Johnson/699 AU RC 3.00 8.00
176 Terrico White/699 AU RC 3.00 8.00
177 S.Collins/699 AU RC EXCH 3.00 8.00
178 Landry Fields/699 AU RC 3.00 8.00
179 Jeremy Lin/699 AU RC 30.00 80.00
180 Timofey Mozgov/699 AU RC 3.00 8.00

2010-11 Classics Timeless Tributes Platinum
*STARS: 3X TO 8X BASE HI
*RETIRED: 1.5X TO 4X BASE HI
124 Alonzo Mourning 10.00 25.00

2010-11 Classics Timeless Tributes Silver
*SILVER: 1X TO 2.5X BASE HI
*GOLD: 1.5X TO 4X BASE HI

2010-11 Classics Blast From The Past
COMPLETE SET (25) 10.00 25.00
1 Amare Stoudemire .75 2.00
2 Al Jefferson .50 1.25
3 LeBron James 6.00 15.00
4 David Lee .50 1.25
5 Carlos Boozer .60 1.50
6 Troy Murphy .60 1.50
7 Kirk Hinrich .60 1.50
8 Kevin Martin .60 1.50
9 Kevin Durant 3.00 8.00
10 Josh Howard .60 1.50
11 Hedo Turkoglu .60 1.50
12 Caron Butler .60 1.50
13 Jason Kidd 1.25 3.00
14 Michael Beasley .50 1.25
15 John Salmons .50 1.25
16 Vince Carter 1.50 4.00
17 Yi Jianlian .75 2.00
18 Al Harrington .60 1.50
19 Andres Nocioni .50 1.25
20 Antawn Jamison .60 1.50
21 Anthony Randolph .50 1.25
22 Chris Bosh 1.00 2.50
23 Quentin Richardson .50 1.25
24 Nate Robinson .60 1.50
25 Kareem Abdul-Jabbar 2.50 6.00

2010-11 Classics Blast From The Past Jerseys
STATED PRINT RUN 99 TO 199 SER.#'d SETS
1 Amare Stoudemire/199 2.50 6.00
2 Al Jefferson/199 1.50 4.00
3 LeBron James/199 40.00 100.00
4 David Lee/199 1.50 4.00
5 Carlos Boozer/199 2.00 5.00
6 Troy Murphy/99 1.50 4.00
7 Kirk Hinrich/199 2.00 5.00
8 Kevin Martin/199 2.00 5.00
9 Kevin Durant/199 15.00 40.00
10 Josh Howard/199 2.00 5.00
11 Hedo Turkoglu/199 2.00 5.00
12 Caron Butler/199 2.00 5.00
13 Jason Kidd/199 6.00 15.00
14 Michael Beasley/199 1.50 4.00
15 John Salmons/199 1.50 4.00
16 Vince Carter/199 6.00 15.00
17 Yi Jianlian/199 2.50 6.00
18 Al Harrington/199 2.00 5.00
19 Andres Nocioni/199 1.50 4.00
20 Antawn Jamison/199 2.00 5.00
21 Anthony Randolph/199 1.50 4.00
22 Chris Bosh/199 3.00 8.00
23 Quentin Richardson/199 1.50 4.00
24 Nate Robinson/199 2.00 5.00
25 Kareem Abdul-Jabbar/99 12.00 30.00

2010-11 Classics Blast From The Past Jerseys Signatures
STATED PRINT RUN 5 TO 25 SER.#'d SETS
1 Amare Stoudemire/25 15.00 40.00
2 Al Jefferson/25 6.00 15.00
4 David Lee/25 6.00 15.00
9 Kevin Durant/25 125.00 300.00
12 Caron Butler/25 8.00 20.00
13 Jason Kidd/25 40.00 100.00
21 Anthony Randolph/25 6.00 15.00

2010-11 Classics Blast From The Past Jerseys Prime Signatures
STATED PRINT RUN 5 TO 25 SER.#'d SETS
2 Al Jefferson/25 8.00 20.00
4 David Lee/25 8.00 20.00
9 Kevin Durant/15 200.00 500.00
12 Caron Butler/25 10.00 25.00
13 Jason Kidd/25 60.00 150.00
21 Anthony Randolph/25 8.00 20.00

2010-11 Classics Classic Combos
COMPLETE SET (10) 6.00 15.00
*GOLD: 1X TO 2.5X BASE HI
GOLD PRINT RUN 100 SER.#'d SETS
*PLATINUM: 1.25X TO 3X BASE HI
PLATINUM PRINT RUN 25 SER.#'d SETS
*SILVER: .5X TO 1.25X BASE HI
SILVER PRINT RUN 250 SER.#'d SETS
1 L.Bird/R.Parish 3.00 8.00
2 J.Worthy/M.Johnson 3.00 8.00
3 J.Stockton/K.Malone 1.50 4.00
4 K.Abdul-Jabbar/O.Robertson 2.50 6.00
5 G.Goodrich/J.West 1.50 4.00
6 W.Frazier/W.Reed 1.25 3.00
7 I.Thomas/J.Dumars 1.25 3.00
8 N.Thurmond/R.Barry 1.00 2.50
9 D.Rodman/S.Pippen 2.00 5.00
10 D.Issel/D.Thompson 1.00 2.50

2010-11 Classics Classic Combos Platinum
9 D.Rodman/S.Pippen 8.00 20.00

2010-11 Classics Classic Combos Jerseys
STATED PRINT RUN 99 SER.#'d SETS
*PRIME: 1X TO 2.5X BASE HI
PRIME PRINT RUN 25 SER.#'d SETS
1 L.Bird/R.Parish 15.00 40.00
2 J.Worthy/M.Johnson 15.00 40.00
3 J.Stockton/K.Malone 15.00 40.00
7 I.Thomas/J.Dumars 10.00 25.00
9 D.Rodman/S.Pippen 15.00 40.00

2010-11 Classics Classic Greats
COMPLETE SET (30) 15.00 40.00
*SILVER: .6X TO 1.5X BASE HI
SILVER PRINT RUN 250 SER.#'d SETS
1 Bill Russell 3.00 8.00
2 Adrian Dantley 1.00 2.50
3 Nate Archibald 1.00 2.50
4 Patrick Ewing 1.50 4.00
5 Kevin McHale 1.50 4.00
6 Magic Johnson 4.00 10.00
7 Sam Jones 1.25 3.00
8 Walter Berry .60 1.50
9 Spencer Haywood 1.00 2.50
10 Alonzo Mourning 1.50 4.00
11 Artis Gilmore 1.25 3.00
12 James Worthy 1.25 3.00
13 Paul Westphal 1.00 2.50
14 Scottie Pippen 2.50 6.00
15 Shawn Kemp 1.50 4.00
16 Larry Bird 4.00 10.00
17 Lenny Wilkens 1.00 2.50
18 Mark Jackson .75 2.00
19 Toni Kukoc 1.00 2.50
20 Dennis Rodman 2.00 5.00
21 Chris Mullin 1.25 3.00
22 Dominique Wilkins 1.50 4.00
23 Rolando Blackman .75 2.00
24 Walt Frazier 1.50 4.00
25 Cliff Hagan 1.00 2.50
26 Connie Hawkins 1.25 3.00
27 Gary Payton 1.50 4.00
28 George Gervin 1.50 4.00
29 Maurice Cheeks .75 2.00
30 Moses Malone 1.50 4.00

2010-11 Classics Classic Greats Gold
*GOLD: 1X TO 2.5X BASE HI
STATED PRINT RUN 100 SER.#'d SETS

2010-11 Classics Classic Greats Platinum
*PLATINUM: 1.5X TO 4X BASE HI
STATED PRINT RUN 25 SER.#'d SETS
4 Patrick Ewing 10.00 25.00
10 Alonzo Mourning 10.00 25.00
15 Shawn Kemp 40.00 100.00

2010-11 Classics Classic Greats Signatures
STATED PRINT RUN 5 TO 99 SER.#'d SETS
2 Adrian Dantley/49 12.00 30.00
3 Nate Archibald/49 8.00 20.00
7 Sam Jones/25 25.00 60.00
8 Walter Berry/99 6.00 15.00
12 James Worthy/25 20.00 50.00

13 Paul Westphal/49 8.00 20.00
17 Lenny Wilkens/49 8.00 20.00
19 Toni Kukoc/25 25.00 60.00
23 Rolando Blackman/25 8.00 20.00
26 Connie Hawkins/99 15.00 40.00
28 George Gervin/25 12.00 30.00
29 Maurice Cheeks/49 6.00 15.00

2010-11 Classics Classic Moments

COMPLETE SET (10) 10.00 25.00
*GOLD: .75X TO 2X BASE HI
GOLD PRINT RUN 100 SER.#'d SETS
*PLATINUM: 1.25X TO 3X BASE HI
PLATINUM PRINT RUN 25 SER.#'d SETS
*SILVER: .5X TO 1.25X BASE HI
SILVER PRINT RUN 250 SER.#'d SETS
1 Wilt Chamberlain 2.50 6.00
2 Magic Johnson 3.00 8.00
3 Brandon Jennings .50 1.25
4 LeBron James 10.00 25.00
5 Rajon Rondo 1.00 2.50
6 Kevin Durant 3.00 8.00
7 Kareem Abdul-Jabbar 2.50 6.00
8 John Havlicek 1.50 4.00
9 Kobe Bryant 15.00 40.00
10 Blake Griffin .75 2.00

2010-11 Classics Classic Moments Signatures

STATED PRINT RUN 5 TO 99 SER.#'d SETS
5 Rajon Rondo/25 25.00 60.00
6 Kevin Durant/25 125.00 300.00
9 Kobe Bryant/99 1,000.00 2,000.00
10 Blake Griffin/25 15.00 40.00

2010-11 Classics Dress Code

COMPLETE SET (25) 12.00 30.00
*GOLD: .75X TO 2X BASE HI
GOLD PRINT RUN 100 SER.#'d SETS
*PLATINUM: 1.25X TO 3X BASE HI
PLATINUM PRINT RUN 25 SER.#'d SETS
*SILVER: .5X TO 1.25X BASE HI
SILVER PRINT RUN 250 SER.#'d SETS
1 Kobe Bryant 6.00 15.00
2 Andre Iguodala .75 2.00
3 Nene .60 1.50
4 Mo Williams .60 1.50
5 Tim Duncan 2.00 5.00
6 Jason Kidd 1.25 3.00
7 Gerald Wallace .60 1.50
8 Dwight Howard 1.00 2.50
9 David Lee .50 1.25
10 Brandon Jennings .50 1.25
11 Brook Lopez .60 1.50
12 Toney Douglas .50 1.25
13 Shawn Marion .75 2.00
14 Marc Gasol .75 2.00
15 Luol Deng .60 1.50
16 Kevin Love .75 2.00
17 Jrue Holiday 1.00 2.50
18 Dirk Nowitzki 2.00 5.00
19 Stephen Curry 6.00 15.00
20 Dwyane Wade 1.50 4.00
21 Blake Griffin .75 2.00
22 Amare Stoudemire .75 2.00
23 Joe Johnson .75 2.00
24 Andrea Bargnani .50 1.25
25 Andrew Bogut .60 1.50

2010-11 Classics Dress Code Jerseys

STATED PRINT RUN 25 TO 199 SER.#'d SETS
*PRIME: 1X TO 2.5X BASE HI
PRIME PRINT RUN 5 TO 25 SETS
1 Kobe Bryant/199 40.00 100.00
2 Andre Iguodala/199 3.00 8.00
3 Nene/199 2.50 6.00
5 Tim Duncan/199 8.00 20.00
6 Jason Kidd/199 5.00 12.00
7 Gerald Wallace/199 2.50 6.00
8 Dwight Howard/199 4.00 10.00
9 David Lee/199 2.00 5.00
10 Brandon Jennings/199 2.00 5.00
11 Brook Lopez/199 2.50 6.00
12 Toney Douglas/199 2.00 5.00
13 Shawn Marion/199 3.00 8.00
14 Marc Gasol/199 3.00 8.00
15 Luol Deng /199 2.50 6.00
16 Kevin Love/199 3.00 8.00
17 Jrue Holiday/199 4.00 10.00
18 Dirk Nowitzki/199 8.00 20.00
19 Stephen Curry/25 75.00 200.00
20 Dwyane Wade/199 6.00 15.00
21 Blake Griffin/199 3.00 8.00
22 Amare Stoudemire/199 3.00 8.00
23 Joe Johnson/199 3.00 8.00
24 Andrea Bargnani/199 2.00 5.00
25 Andrew Bogut/199 2.50 6.00

2010-11 Classics Dress Code Jerseys Signatures

STATED PRINT RUN 10 TO 25 SER.#'d SETS
1 Kobe Bryant/25 1,500.00 3,000.00
2 Andre Iguodala/25 8.00 20.00
6 Jason Kidd/25 25.00 60.00
7 Gerald Wallace/25 6.00 15.00
9 David Lee/25 6.00 15.00
10 Brandon Jennings/25 6.00 15.00
12 Toney Douglas/25 6.00 15.00
14 Marc Gasol/25 EXCH 15.00 40.00
16 Kevin Love/25 15.00 40.00
17 Jrue Holiday/25 12.00 30.00
19 Stephen Curry/25 1,000.00 2,000.00
21 Blake Griffin/25 12.00 30.00
22 Amare Stoudemire/25 8.00 20.00
24 Andrea Bargnani/25 6.00 15.00
25 Andrew Bogut/25 8.00 20.00

2010-11 Classics Dress Code Jerseys Prime Signatures

STATED PRINT RUN 10 TO 25 SER.#'d SETS
1 Kobe Bryant/25 2,000.00 4,000.00
2 Andre Iguodala/25 10.00 25.00
7 Gerald Wallace/25 8.00 20.00
9 David Lee/25 8.00 20.00
11 Brook Lopez/25 8.00 20.00
12 Toney Douglas/25 8.00 20.00
16 Kevin Love/25 15.00 40.00
17 Jrue Holiday/25 8.00 20.00
19 Stephen Curry/25 600.00 1,200.00
21 Blake Griffin/20 15.00 40.00
23 Joe Johnson/25 8.00 20.00
24 Andrea Bargnani/25 8.00 20.00
25 Andrew Bogut/25 8.00 20.00

2010-11 Classics Hoops Previews

COMPLETE SET (20) 20.00 50.00
1 Amare Stoudemire 1.00 2.50
2 Blake Griffin 1.00 2.50
3 Carmelo Anthony 1.50 4.00
4 Dirk Nowitzki 2.50 6.00
5 Dwight Howard 1.25 3.00
6 Dwyane Wade 2.00 5.00
7 John Wall 3.00 8.00
8 Kevin Durant 4.00 10.00
9 Kobe Bryant 8.00 20.00
10 LeBron James 8.00 20.00
11 Monta Ellis .75 2.00
12 Derrick Rose 2.00 5.00
13 Eric Gordon .75 2.00
14 Russell Westbrook 1.50 4.00
15 Kevin Love 1.00 2.50
16 Chris Paul 2.00 5.00
17 LaMarcus Aldridge 1.00 2.50
18 Paul Pierce 1.50 4.00
19 Steve Nash 2.00 5.00
20 Stephen Curry 8.00 20.00

2010-11 Classics Membership Materials

STATED PRINT RUN 100 TO 499 SER.#'d SETS
1 Mike Bibby/499 3.00 8.00
2 Paul Pierce/499 5.00 12.00
3 Larry Johnson/499 4.00 10.00
4 Scottie Pippen/499 8.00 20.00
5 Dirk Nowitzki/499 8.00 20.00
6 Nene/499 2.50 6.00
7 Tayshaun Prince/499 3.00 8.00
8 Chris Mullin/250 4.00 10.00
9 Yao Ming/499 6.00 15.00
10 Chuck Person/499 2.50 6.00
11 Blake Griffin/499 3.00 8.00
12 Kobe Bryant/499 40.00 100.00
13 O.J. Mayo/499 2.00 5.00
14 Dwyane Wade/499 6.00 15.00
15 Andrew Bogut/499 2.50 6.00
16 Kevin Love/499 3.00 8.00
17 Derrick Coleman/499 3.00 8.00
18 Chris Paul/499 6.00 15.00
19 Charles Oakley/250 3.00 8.00
20 Jameer Nelson/499 2.00 5.00
21 Andre Iguodala/499 3.00 8.00
22 Anfernee Hardaway/499 8.00 20.00
23 LaMarcus Aldridge/499 3.00 8.00
24 Tyreke Evans/499 2.50 6.00
25 Tim Duncan/499 8.00 20.00
26 Karl Malone/499 6.00 15.00
27 Alex English/499 2.50 6.00
28 Kevin Johnson/499 3.00 8.00
29 Clyde Drexler/499 5.00 12.00
30 John Stockton/250 5.00 12.00
31 Kevin McHale/250 5.00 12.00
32 David West/499 2.50 6.00
33 Dwight Howard/250 4.00 10.00
34 Deron Williams/499 2.50 6.00
35 Pau Gasol/499 5.00 12.00
36 Dominique Wilkins/250 5.00 12.00
37 Robert Parish/499 5.00 12.00
38 Dennis Rodman/100 10.00 25.00
39 Shawn Marion/499 3.00 8.00
40 Carmelo Anthony/250 5.00 12.00
41 Dikembe Mutombo/250 5.00 12.00
42 Richard Hamilton/499 4.00 10.00
43 Magic Johnson/100 12.00 30.00
44 Tim Hardaway/499 4.00 10.00
45 Patrick Ewing/499 5.00 12.00
46 Brandon Roy/100 4.00 10.00
47 Chris Webber/499 4.00 10.00
48 David Robinson/100 6.00 15.00
49 Gary Payton/250 5.00 12.00
50 Kevin Durant/499 12.00 30.00

2010-11 Classics Membership Materials Prime

*PRIME: 1.2X TO 3X BASE HI
STATED PRINT RUN 2 TO 49 SER.#'d SETS

2010-11 Classics Significant Signatures

STATED PRINT RUN 10 TO 99 SER.#'d SETS
1 A.C. Green/99 6.00 15.00
2 Adrian Dantley/99 6.00 15.00
3 Al Jefferson/49 6.00 15.00
4 Alonzo Mourning/49 20.00 50.00
5 Amare Stoudemire/49 20.00 50.00
6 Andre Iguodala/99 8.00 20.00
7 Andre Miller/99 6.00 15.00
8 Andrea Bargnani/99 6.00 15.00
9 Artis Gilmore/99 12.00 30.00
10 Bailey Howell/99 10.00 25.00
11 Bill Cartwright/49 15.00 40.00
12 Bob Lanier/99 12.00 30.00
13 Brandon Jennings/99 6.00 15.00
14 David Lee/99 6.00 15.00
15 Dennis Rodman/49 40.00 100.00
16 Dolph Schayes/99 8.00 20.00
17 Dominique Wilkins/49 20.00 50.00
18 Elvin Hayes/49 10.00 25.00
19 Joakim Noah/99 6.00 15.00
20 Kevin Durant/49 200.00 500.00
21 Kobe Bryant/99 1,000.00 2,000.00
22 Larry Johnson/99 20.00 50.00
23 Lenny Wilkens/99 6.00 15.00
24 Marc Gasol/99 12.00 30.00
25 Paul Westphal/99 8.00 20.00
26 Rick Barry/49 12.00 30.00
27 Robert Horry/99 8.00 20.00
28 Rolando Blackman/99 6.00 15.00
29 Sam Perkins/49 8.00 20.00
30 Oscar Robertson/49 50.00 120.00
31 Sean Elliott/99 8.00 20.00
32 Shane Battier/49 6.00 15.00
34 Larry Bird/33 125.00 300.00
35 Sam Jones/49 12.00 30.00
36 Spud Webb/99 8.00 20.00
37 Stephen Curry/49 1,000.00 2,000.00
38 Toni Kukoc/49 8.00 20.00
39 Tyreke Evans/49 6.00 15.00
40 Jason Kidd/49 20.00 50.00
41 Andrew Bynum/49 6.00 15.00
42 Andrew Bogut/49 6.00 15.00
43 Blake Griffin/99 20.00 50.00
44 Magic Johnson/32 125.00 300.00
45 Gary Payton/49 20.00 50.00
46 Jerry West/35 40.00 100.00
47 Chris Bosh/99 12.00 30.00
49 Devin Harris/99 6.00 15.00
50 Rajon Rondo/49 15.00 40.00
51 Kareem Abdul-Jabbar/25 125.00 300.00
52 Pau Gasol/99 20.00 50.00
53 Bill Walton/49 20.00 50.00
54 Carmelo Anthony/20 40.00 100.00
55 Derrick Rose/25 75.00 200.00
57 Deron Williams/99 6.00 15.00
58 Darren Collison/99 6.00 15.00
59 Steve Nash/25 75.00 200.00
60 Elgin Baylor/25 40.00 100.00

2019-20 Clearly Donruss

*GOLD: .5X TO 1.25X BASIC
*PURPLE: .5X TO 1.25X BASIC
*BLUE/99: 1.25X TO 3X BASIC
*RED/49: 1.5X TO 4X BASIC
*GREEN/25: 2.5X TO 6X BASIC
1 Trae Young 1.25 3.00
2 Jayson Tatum 2.00 5.00
3 Kemba Walker .40 1.00
4 Kyrie Irving 1.00 2.50
5 Kevin Durant 1.50 4.00
6 Devonte' Graham .40 1.00
7 Zach LaVine .75 2.00
8 Collin Sexton .60 1.50
9 Luka Doncic 3.00 8.00
10 Kristaps Porzingis .60 1.50
11 Nikola Jokic 2.50 6.00
12 Derrick Rose 1.00 2.50
13 Stephen Curry 4.00 10.00
14 Klay Thompson 1.25 3.00
15 James Harden 1.00 2.50
16 Russell Westbrook .75 2.00
17 Domantas Sabonis .60 1.50
18 Kawhi Leonard 1.25 3.00
19 Paul George .75 2.00
20 LeBron James 4.00 10.00
21 Anthony Davis 1.25 3.00
22 Jaren Jackson Jr. .75 2.00
23 Bam Adebayo .75 2.00
24 Jimmy Butler 1.00 2.50
25 Giannis Antetokounmpo 2.50 6.00
26 Karl-Anthony Towns .75 2.00
27 D'Angelo Russell .40 1.00
28 Brandon Ingram .50 1.25
29 Julius Randle .60 1.50
30 Shai Gilgeous-Alexander 2.50 6.00
31 Chris Paul 1.00 2.50
32 Nikola Vucevic .40 1.00
33 Ben Simmons .50 1.25
34 Joel Embiid 1.00 2.50
35 Deandre Ayton .50 1.25
36 Devin Booker .12 .30
37 Damian Lillard 1.25 3.00
38 De'Aaron Fox .75 2.00
39 DeMar DeRozan .60 1.50
40 Pascal Siakam .75 2.00
41 Kyle Lowry .50 1.25
42 Donovan Mitchell 1.00 2.50
43 Rudy Gobert .60 1.50
44 John Wall .60 1.50
45 Bradley Beal .60 1.50
46 Victor Oladipo .40 1.00
47 CJ McCollum .50 1.25
48 Blake Griffin .50 1.25
49 Khris Middleton .50 1.25
50 Jamal Murray .75 2.00
51 Zion Williamson RR RC 5.00 12.00
52 Ja Morant RR RC 8.00 20.00
53 RJ Barrett RR RC 2.50 6.00
54 De'Andre Hunter RR RC 2.50 6.00
55 Jarrett Culver RR RC .60 1.50
56 Coby White RR RC 2.00 5.00
57 Jaxson Hayes RR RC 1.00 2.50
58 Rui Hachimura RR RC 2.00 5.00
59 Cam Reddish RR RC 2.00 5.00
60 Cameron Johnson RR RC 1.50 4.00
61 PJ Washington Jr. RR RC 1.25 3.00
62 Romeo Langford RR RC .60 1.50
63 Tyler Herro RR RC 3.00 8.00
64 Sekou Doumbouya RR RC .60 1.50
65 Tacko Fall RR RC .75 2.00
66 Nickeil Alexander-Walker RR RC 1.00 2.50
67 Goga Bitadze RR RC 1.00 2.50
68 Luka Samanic RR RC .75 2.00
69 Matisse Thybulle RR RC 1.25 3.00
70 Brandon Clarke RR RC 1.25 3.00
71 Grant Williams RR RC 1.00 2.50
72 Ty Jerome RR RC 1.25 3.00
73 Nassir Little RR RC 1.00 2.50
74 Dylan Windler RR RC .75 2.00
75 Mfiondu Kabengele RR RC .75 2.00
76 Jordan Poole RR RC 2.50 6.00
77 Keldon Johnson RR RC 2.00 5.00
78 Kevin Porter Jr. RR RC 1.25 3.00
79 Nicolas Claxton RR RC 1.25 3.00
80 KZ Okpala RR RC .75 2.00
81 Carsen Edwards RR RC .75 2.00
82 Bruno Fernando RR RC .75 2.00
83 Cody Martin RR RC .75 2.00
84 Bol Bol RR RC 1.50 4.00
85 Isaiah Roby RR RC .75 2.00
86 Daniel Gafford RR RC 1.25 3.00
87 Alen Smailagic RR RC .60 1.50
88 Eric Paschall RR RC .75 2.00
89 Admiral Schofield RR RC .75 2.00
90 Jaylen Nowell RR RC .75 2.00
91 Ignas Brazdeikis RR RC .75 2.00
92 Terence Davis II RR RC .75 2.00
93 Quinndary Weatherspoon RR RC .60 1.50
94 Tremont Waters RR RC .75 2.00
95 Kyle Guy RR RC .75 2.00
96 Kendrick Nunn RR RC 1.00 2.50
97 Nicolo Melli RR RC .75 2.00
98 Talen Horton-Tucker RR RC 1.00 2.50
99 Darius Bazley RR RC .60 1.50
100 Darius Garland RR RC 2.50 6.00

2019-20 Clearly Donruss Purple

*PURPLE: .5X TO 1.25X BASIC

2019-20 Clearly Donruss All Clear For Takeoff

*RED MOSAIC/49: 3X TO 8X BASIC
*GREEN/25: 5X TO 12X BASIC
1 Donovan Mitchell 1.00 2.50
2 LeBron James 4.00 10.00
3 Russell Westbrook .75 2.00
4 Giannis Antetokounmpo 2.50 6.00
5 Ben Simmons .50 1.25
6 Aaron Gordon .50 1.25
7 Paul George .75 2.00
8 Blake Griffin .50 1.25
9 Zion Williamson 2.50 6.00
10 Ja Morant 3.00 8.00

2019-20 Clearly Donruss Defying Gravity

1 Zion Williamson 30.00 80.00
2 LeBron James 30.00 80.00
3 Karl-Anthony Towns 1.50 4.00
4 Russell Westbrook 1.50 4.00
5 Blake Griffin 1.00 2.50
6 Giannis Antetokounmpo 12.00 30.00
7 DeMar DeRozan 1.25 3.00
8 Zach LaVine 1.50 4.00
9 Ben Simmons 6.00 15.00
10 Donovan Mitchell 2.00 5.00

2019-20 Clearly Donruss Defying Gravity Green

*GREEN: 1.5X TO 4X BASIC
STATED PRINT RUN 25 SER. #'D SETS
2 LeBron James 150.00 400.00
3 Karl-Anthony Towns 15.00 40.00

2019-20 Clearly Donruss Defying Gravity Red Mosaic

*RED: 1.25X TO 3X BASIC
STATED PRINT RUN 49 SER. #'D SETS
2 LeBron James 125.00 300.00
3 Karl-Anthony Towns 12.00 30.00
10 Donovan Mitchell 12.00 30.00

2019-20 Clearly Donruss My House

*RED MOSAIC/49: 3X TO 8X BASIC
*GREEN/25: 5X TO 12X BASIC
1 Luka Doncic 3.00 8.00
2 Giannis Antetokounmpo 2.50 6.00
3 Ja Morant 8.00 20.00
4 Coby White 1.00 2.50
5 Jayson Tatum 2.00 5.00
6 LeBron James 4.00 10.00
7 Zion Williamson 2.50 6.00
8 Donovan Mitchell 1.00 2.50
9 RJ Barrett 1.25 3.00
10 Trae Young 1.25 3.00

2019-20 Clearly Donruss My House Red Mosaic

*RED: 1.25X TO 3X BASIC
STATED PRINT RUN 49 SER. #'D SETS
1 Luka Doncic 25.00 60.00
2 Giannis Antetokounmpo 20.00 50.00
3 Ja Morant 60.00 150.00
4 Coby White 8.00 20.00
5 Jayson Tatum 15.00 40.00
6 LeBron James 30.00 80.00
7 Zion Williamson 20.00 50.00
8 Donovan Mitchell 8.00 20.00
9 RJ Barrett 10.00 25.00
10 Trae Young 10.00 25.00

2019-20 Clearly Donruss Rated Rookie Autographs

EXCHANGE DEADLINE 4/28/2022
1 Zion Williamson 125.00 300.00
2 De'Andre Hunter 12.00 30.00
3 Jarrett Culver 3.00 8.00
4 Coby White 10.00 25.00
5 Cam Reddish 5.00 12.00
6 Rui Hachimura 12.00 30.00
7 Brandon Clarke 6.00 15.00
8 Matisse Thybulle 6.00 15.00
9 Nicolas Claxton 6.00 15.00
10 Isaiah Roby 4.00 10.00
11 Bol Bol 8.00 20.00
12 Daniel Gafford 6.00 15.00
13 Eric Paschall 4.00 10.00
14 Terance Mann 6.00 15.00
15 Tremont Waters 4.00 10.00
16 Kyle Guy 4.00 10.00
17 Tacko Fall 4.00 10.00
18 Kendrick Nunn 5.00 12.00
19 Naz Reid 12.00 30.00
20 Sekou Doumbouya 3.00 8.00
21 RJ Barrett 25.00 60.00
22 Cameron Johnson 8.00 20.00
23 PJ Washington Jr. 10.00 25.00
24 Tyler Herro 15.00 40.00
25 Carsen Edwards 4.00 10.00
26 Ky Bowman 4.00 10.00
27 Chris Clemons 3.00 8.00
28 Jaylen Hoard 3.00 8.00
29 Terence Davis II 5.00 12.00
30 Talen Horton-Tucker 5.00 12.00
31 Darius Bazley 3.00 8.00
32 Jalen Lecque 3.00 8.00
33 Jalen McDaniels 8.00 20.00
34 Jordan Bone 3.00 8.00
35 Alen Smailagic 3.00 8.00
36 Kevin Porter Jr. 6.00 15.00
37 Keldon Johnson 10.00 25.00
38 Jordan Poole 25.00 60.00
39 Nickeil Alexander-Walker 5.00 12.00
40 Ja Morant 150.00 400.00

2019-20 Clearly Donruss Rated Rookie Variation

1 Zion Williamson 6.00 15.00
2 Ja Morant 8.00 20.00
3 RJ Barrett 3.00 8.00
4 Rui Hachimura 3.00 8.00
5 Coby White 2.50 6.00
6 Tyler Herro 4.00 10.00
7 Cam Reddish 1.25 3.00
8 Sekou Doumbouya .75 2.00
9 Kendrick Nunn 1.25 3.00

2019-20 Clearly Donruss Rookie Special

1 Zion Williamson 12.00 30.00

2019-20 Clearly Donruss Star Gazing

*RED MOSAIC/49: 3X TO 8X BASIC
*GREEN/25: 5X TO 12X BASIC
1 Stephen Curry 4.00 10.00
2 Anthony Davis 1.25 3.00
3 Ben Simmons .50 1.25
4 Damian Lillard 1.25 3.00
5 LeBron James 4.00 10.00
6 Kawhi Leonard 1.25 3.00
7 Nikola Jokic 2.50 6.00
8 Russell Westbrook .75 2.00
9 Giannis Antetokounmpo 2.50 6.00
10 James Harden 1.00 2.50

2019-20 Clearly Donruss The Rookies

*RED MOSAIC/49: 1.5X TO 4X BASIC
*GREEN/25: 2.5X TO 6X BASIC
1 Zion Williamson 5.00 12.00
2 Ja Morant 6.00 15.00
3 RJ Barrett 2.50 6.00
4 De'Andre Hunter 2.50 6.00
5 Rui Hachimura 2.50 6.00
6 Sekou Doumbouya .60 1.50
7 Tyler Herro 3.00 8.00
8 Kendrick Nunn 1.00 2.50
9 PJ Washington Jr. 2.00 5.00
10 Coby White 2.00 5.00

2020-21 Clearly Donruss

*GOLD: .5X TO 1.25X BASIC
*PURPLE: .5X TO 1.25X BASIC
*BLUE/99: 1.25X TO 3X BASIC
*RED/49: 1.5X TO 4X BASIC
*GREEN/25: 2.5X TO 6X BASIC
1 Tobias Harris .50 1.25
2 Jimmy Butler 1.00 2.50
3 Ben Simmons .50 1.25
4 Jamal Murray .75 2.00
5 Brandon Ingram .60 1.50
6 Domantas Sabonis .60 1.50
7 Zion Williamson 1.50 4.00
8 James Harden 1.00 2.50
9 Kristaps Porzingis .60 1.50
10 De'Aaron Fox .75 2.00
11 Gordon Hayward .50 1.25
12 Khris Middleton .60 1.50
13 Pascal Siakam .75 2.00
14 Jaylen Brown .75 2.00
15 Trae Young 1.25 3.00
16 Bradley Beal .60 1.50
17 Nikola Vucevic .50 1.25
18 Ja Morant 1.50 4.00
19 Stephen Curry 4.00 10.00
20 Damian Lillard 1.25 3.00
21 Giannis Antetokounmpo 2.50 6.00
22 John Wall .60 1.50
23 John Collins .50 1.25
24 Chris Paul 1.00 2.50
25 DeMar DeRozan .60 1.50
26 Joel Embiid 1.25 3.00
27 RJ Barrett .75 2.00
28 Kawhi Leonard 1.25 3.00
29 Devin Booker 1.25 3.00
30 Bam Adebayo .75 2.00
31 Jayson Tatum 2.00 5.00
32 Nikola Jokic 2.50 6.00
33 Collin Sexton .50 1.25
34 Zach LaVine .75 2.00
35 Kevin Durant 2.00 5.00
36 CJ McCollum .50 1.25
37 Tyler Herro 1.00 2.50
38 Anthony Davis 1.25 3.00
39 Kyle Lowry .60 1.50
40 Luka Doncic 3.00 8.00
41 Donovan Mitchell 1.00 2.50
42 Julius Randle .50 1.25
43 Shai Gilgeous-Alexander 2.50 6.00
44 Rudy Gobert .60 1.50
45 Russell Westbrook 1.00 2.50
46 Kyrie Irving 1.00 2.50
47 Jerami Grant .50 1.25
48 Karl-Anthony Towns .75 2.00
49 LeBron James 4.00 10.00
50 Paul George .75 2.00
51 Patrick Williams RR RC 2.00 5.00
52 Cole Anthony RR RC 2.00 5.00
53 Skylar Mays RR RC .75 2.00
54 Moses Brown RR RC .60 1.50
55 Lamar Stevens RR RC 1.00 2.50
56 Kenyon Martin Jr. RR RC 1.25 3.00
57 Tyrell Terry RR RC .60 1.50
58 Malachi Flynn RR RC .75 2.00
59 Paul Reed RR RC 1.00 2.50
60 Theo Maledon RR RC .75 2.00
61 James Wiseman RR RC 1.00 2.50
62 Isaiah Stewart RR RC 1.50 4.00
63 Sam Merrill RR RC 1.25 3.00
64 Josh Green RR RC 1.50 4.00
65 Aaron Nesmith RR RC 1.50 4.00
66 Mason Jones RR RC .60 1.50
67 Payton Pritchard RR RC 2.50 6.00
68 Nico Mannion RR RC .75 2.00
69 Udoka Azubuike RR RC 1.00 2.50
70 Tre Jones RR RC 1.25 3.00
71 Xavier Tillman RR RC 1.00 2.50
72 Isaiah Joe RR RC 1.00 2.50
73 Saben Lee RR RC .75 2.00
74 Tyrese Maxey RR RC 6.00 15.00
75 Tyrese Haliburton RR RC 6.00 15.00
76 Desmond Bane RR RC 2.50 6.00
77 Immanuel Quickley RR RC 2.00 5.00
78 Onyeka Okongwu RR RC 1.50 4.00
79 Zeke Nnaji RR RC 1.00 2.50
80 Obi Toppin RR RC 1.50 4.00
81 Jae'Sean Tate RR RC 1.00 2.50
82 Cassius Winston RR RC .75 2.00
83 CJ Elleby RR RC .75 2.00
84 RJ Hampton RR RC .75 2.00
85 Jalen Smith RR RC 1.50 4.00
86 Aleksej Pokusevski RR RC 1.50 4.00
87 LaMelo Ball RR RC 6.00 15.00
88 Kira Lewis Jr. RR RC .75 2.00
89 Deni Avdija RR RC 2.00 5.00
90 Saddiq Bey RR RC 1.50 4.00
91 Nathan Knight RR RC .75 2.00
92 Jordan Nwora RR RC 1.00 2.50
93 Jaden McDaniels RR RC 2.50 6.00
94 Isaac Okoro RR RC 1.25 3.00
95 Precious Achiuwa RR RC 1.50 4.00
96 Anthony Edwards RR RC 15.00 40.00
97 Killian Hayes RR RC .75 2.00
98 Cassius Stanley RR RC .75 2.00
99 Facundo Campazzo RR RC 1.00 2.50
100 Devin Vassell RR RC 2.50 6.00

2020-21 Clearly Donruss Dominant

*RED/49: 3X TO 8X BASIC
*GREEN/25: 5X TO 12X BASIC
1 LeBron James 4.00 10.00
2 Luka Doncic 3.00 8.00
3 Kevin Durant 2.00 5.00
4 Stephen Curry 4.00 10.00
5 Damian Lillard 1.25 3.00
6 Giannis Antetokounmpo 2.50 6.00
7 Bradley Beal .60 1.50
8 Nikola Jokic 2.50 6.00
9 Kawhi Leonard 1.25 3.00
10 Zion Williamson 1.50 4.00

2020-21 Clearly Donruss My House

*RED/49: 3X TO 8X BASIC
*GREEN/25: 5X TO 12X BASIC
1 Giannis Antetokounmpo 2.50 6.00
2 LeBron James 4.00 10.00
3 Stephen Curry 4.00 10.00
4 Damian Lillard 1.25 3.00
5 Donovan Mitchell 1.00 2.50
6 James Harden 1.00 2.50
7 Luka Doncic 3.00 8.00
8 Devin Booker 1.25 3.00
9 Zion Williamson 1.50 4.00
10 Anthony Davis 1.25 3.00

2020-21 Clearly Donruss Rated Rookie Autographs Holo Mosaic

*GREEN: .75X TO 2X BASIC
1 Deni Avdija 15.00 40.00
2 Jaden McDaniels 20.00 50.00
3 Aleksej Pokusevski 8.00 20.00
4 Nico Mannion 6.00 15.00
5 Tyrese Haliburton 75.00 200.00
6 Tyrese Maxey 60.00 150.00
7 Cassius Winston 6.00 15.00
8 Desmond Bane 20.00 50.00
9 Payton Pritchard 20.00 50.00
10 LaMelo Ball 75.00 200.00
11 Onyeka Okongwu 12.00 30.00
12 Sam Merrill 10.00 25.00
13 Kenyon Martin Jr. 10.00 25.00
14 Josh Green 12.00 30.00
15 Obi Toppin 12.00 30.00
16 Cole Anthony 15.00 40.00
17 Devin Vassell 20.00 50.00
18 Moses Brown 5.00 12.00
19 Jahmi'us Ramsey 6.00 15.00
20 Devon Dotson 6.00 15.00
21 Reggie Perry 6.00 15.00
22 Isaac Okoro 10.00 25.00
23 Saddiq Bey 12.00 30.00
24 Patrick Williams 15.00 40.00
25 Facundo Campazzo 8.00 20.00
26 Killian Hayes 6.00 15.00
27 Paul Reed 8.00 20.00
28 Isaiah Stewart 12.00 30.00
29 Immanuel Quickley 15.00 40.00
30 Anthony Edwards 300.00 600.00
31 Zeke Nnaji 8.00 20.00
32 Jalen Harris 5.00 12.00
33 Mason Jones 5.00 12.00
34 Saben Lee 6.00 15.00
35 Jae'Sean Tate 8.00 20.00
36 Theo Maledon 6.00 15.00
37 Tre Jones 10.00 25.00
38 Ty-Shon Alexander 6.00 15.00
39 Xavier Tillman 8.00 20.00
40 James Wiseman 8.00 20.00

2020-21 Clearly Donruss Retro Rated Rookie '10-11

1 Paul George 4.00 10.00

2020-21 Clearly Donruss Retro Rated Rookie '14-15

2 Joel Embiid 10.00 25.00

2020-21 Clearly Donruss Retro Rated Rookie '15-16

3 Nikola Jokic 15.00 40.00
4 Devin Booker 15.00 40.00

2020-21 Clearly Donruss Retro Rated Rookie '16-17

5 Ben Simmons 3.00 8.00

2020-21 Clearly Donruss Retro Rated Rookie '17-18

6 Donovan Mitchell 6.00 15.00
7 Jayson Tatum 15.00 40.00

2020-21 Clearly Donruss Retro Rated Rookie '18-19

8 Trae Young 8.00 20.00
9 Luka Doncic 40.00 100.00

2020-21 Clearly Donruss Rookie Special

1 LaMelo Ball
Luka Doncic
Zion Williamson 40.00 100.00

2020-21 Clearly Donruss Star Gazing

*RED/49: 3X TO 8X BASIC
*GREEN/25: 5X TO 12X BASIC
1 Ben Simmons .50 1.25
2 Zion Williamson 1.50 4.00
3 LeBron James 4.00 10.00
4 Luka Doncic 3.00 8.00
5 Giannis Antetokounmpo 2.50 6.00
6 Kevin Durant 2.00 5.00
7 Damian Lillard 1.25 3.00
8 Stephen Curry 4.00 10.00
9 James Harden 1.00 2.50
10 Donovan Mitchell 1.00 2.50

2020-21 Clearly Donruss The Rookies

*RED/49: 1.5X TO 4X BASIC
*GREEN/25: 2.5X TO 6X BASIC
1 LaMelo Ball 6.00 15.00
2 Anthony Edwards 12.00 30.00
3 James Wiseman 1.00 2.50
4 Obi Toppin 1.50 4.00
5 Tyrese Haliburton 6.00 15.00
6 Immanuel Quickley 2.00 5.00
7 Patrick Williams 2.00 5.00
8 Saddiq Bey 1.50 4.00
9 Deni Avdija 2.00 5.00
10 Tyrese Maxey 6.00 15.00

2020-21 Clearly Donruss Zero Gravity

*RED/49: 2X TO 5X BASIC
*GREEN/25: 3X TO 8X BASIC
1 Dominique Wilkins 1.50 4.00
2 LeBron James 8.00 20.00
3 Shawn Kemp 1.50 4.00
4 Donovan Mitchell 2.00 5.00
5 Zion Williamson 3.00 8.00
6 Zach LaVine 1.50 4.00
7 Anthony Davis 2.50 6.00
8 Giannis Antetokounmpo 5.00 12.00
9 Anthony Edwards 12.00 30.00
10 LaMelo Ball 6.00 15.00

1989 Cleo Michael Jordan Valentines

COMMON CARD .40 1.00

1991 Cleo Michael Jordan Valentines

COMPLETE SET (11) 3.00 8.00
COMMON CARD (1-11) .50 1.20

1978-79 Clippers Handyman

COMPLETE SET (9) 25.00 50.00
1 Randy Smith 9 2.50 6.00
2 Nick Weatherspoon 12 2.00 5.00
3 Freeman Williams 20 1.50 4.00
4 Sidney Wicks 21 3.00 8.00
5A Lloyd Free 24 2.50 6.00
5B Lloyd Free 24
(Signature variation) 10.00 20.00
6 Swen Nater 31 2.00 5.00
7 Jerome Whitehead 33 1.25 3.00
8 Kermit Washington 42 1.50 4.00
9 Kevin Kunnert 44 10.00 20.00
NNO Gene Shue CO SP 750.00 1,200.00

1990-91 Clippers Star

COMPLETE SET (12) 1.50 4.00
1 Ken Bannister .08 .25
2 Winston Garland .08 .25
3 Tom Garrick .08 .25
4 Gary Grant .08 .25
5 Ron Harper .40 1.00
6 Bo Kimble .08 .25
7 Danny Manning .40 1.00
8 Jeff Martin .08 .25
9 Ken Norman .08 .25
10 Mike Schuler CO .08 .25
11 Charles Smith .08 .25
12 Loy Vaught .40 1.00

2000-01 Clippers Topps

COMPLETE SET (10) 3.00 8.00
NNO AT&T Wireless Sponsor Card .20 .50
LC1 Lamar Odom .50 1.25
LC10 Quentin Richardson .40 1.00
LC2 Michael Olowokandi .30 .75
LC3 Corey Maggette .40 1.00
LC4 Alvin Gentry CO .30 .75
LC6 Eric Piatkowski .30 .75
LC7 Brian Skinner .30 .75
LC8 Darius Miles .50 1.25
LC9 Keyon Dooling .40 1.00

2001-02 Clippers Topps

COMPLETE SET (6) 2.50 6.00
LC2 Michael Olowokandi .40 1.00
LC3 Corey Maggette .50 1.25
LC4 Alvin Gentry CO .40 1.00
LC6 Eric Piatkowski .40 1.00
LC7 Brian Skinner .40 1.00
LC8 Darius Miles .40 1.00

2005-06 Clippers Topps

COMPLETE SET (15) 5.00 12.00
NNO Jet Blue Airways Sponsor Card .40 1.00
LAC1 Elton Brand .50 1.25
LAC10 Vladimir Radmanovic .40 1.00
LAC11 Zeljko Rebraca .40 1.00
LAC12 Quinton Ross .40 1.00
LAC13 James Singleton .40 1.00
LAC14 Mike Dunleavy, Sr. CO .60 1.50
LAC2 Sam Cassell .50 1.25
LAC3 Daniel Ewing .50 1.25
LAC4 Chris Kaman .50 1.25
LAC5 Yaroslav Korolev .40 1.00
LAC6 Corey Maggette .50 1.25
LAC7 Walter McCarty .40 1.00
LAC8 Cuttino Mobley .40 1.00
LAC9 Shaun Livingston .50 1.25

2001-02 Clippers Upper Deck

COMPLETE SET (10) 3.00 8.00
NNO AT&T Wireless Sponsor Card .25 .60
LAC1 Elton Brand .50 1.25
LAC2 Darius Miles .40 1.00
LAC3 Lamar Odom .50 1.25
LAC4 Corey Maggette .50 1.25
LAC5 Quentin Richardson .40 1.00
LAC6 Keyon Dooling .40 1.00
LAC7 Jeff McInnis .40 1.00
LAC8 Eric Piatkowski .40 1.00
LAC9 Michael Olowokandi .40 1.00

2006-07 Clippers Upper Deck JetBlue

COMPLETE SET (14) 3.00 8.00
1 Elton Brand .50 1.25
2 Sam Cassell .50 1.25
3 Paul Davis .40 1.00
4 Daniel Ewing .40 1.00
5 Chris Kaman .40 1.00
6 Shaun Livingston .50 1.25
7 Corey Maggette .50 1.25
8 Cuttino Mobley .50 1.25
9 Quinton Ross .40 1.00
10 James Singleton .40 1.00
11 Tim Thomas .40 1.00
12 Aaron Williams .40 1.00
13 Mike Dunleavy Coach .40 1.00
14 Clipper Nation .20 .50

1994-95 Collector's Choice

COMPLETE SET (420) 20.00 50.00
COMPLETE SERIES 1 (210) 10.00 25.00
COMPLETE SERIES 2 (210) 10.00 25.00
1 Anfernee Hardaway .60 1.50
2 Mark Macon .20 .50

3 Steve Smith .25 .60
4 Chris Webber .60 1.50
5 Donald Royal .20 .50
6 Avery Johnson .25 .60
7 Kevin Johnson .30 .75
8 Doug Christie .25 .60
9 Derrick McKey .20 .50
10 Dennis Rodman .75 2.00
11 Scott Skiles UER .20 .50
12 Johnny Dawkins .20 .50
13 Kendall Gill .20 .50
14 Jeff Hornacek .25 .60
15 Latrell Sprewell .40 1.00
16 Lucious Harris .20 .50
17 Chris Mullin .40 1.00
18 John Williams .20 .50
19 Tony Campbell .20 .50
20 LaPhonso Ellis .20 .50
21 Gerald Wilkins .25 .60
22 Clyde Drexler .50 1.25
23 Michael Jordan BB 5.00 12.00
24 George Lynch .20 .50
25 Mark Price .30 .75
26 James Robinson .20 .50
27 Elmore Spencer .20 .50
28 Stacey King .20 .50
29 Corie Blount .20 .50
30 Dell Curry .20 .50
31 Reggie Miller .60 1.50
32 Karl Malone .60 1.50
33 Scottie Pippen .75 2.00
34 Hakeem Olajuwon .60 1.50
35 Clarence Weatherspoon .20 .50
36 Kevin Edwards .20 .50
37 Pete Myers .20 .50
38 Jeff Turner .20 .50
39 Ennis Whatley .20 .50
40 Calbert Cheaney .25 .60
41 Glen Rice .30 .75
42 Vin Baker .30 .75
43 Grant Long .20 .50
44 Derrick Coleman .30 .75
45 Rik Smits .25 .60
46 Chris Smith .20 .50
47 Carl Herrera .20 .50
48 Bob Martin .20 .50
49 Terrell Brandon .20 .50
50 David Robinson .60 1.50
51 Danny Ferry .20 .50
52 Buck Williams .20 .50
53 Josh Grant .20 .50
54 Ed Pinckney .20 .50
55 Dikembe Mutombo .50 1.25
56 Clifford Robinson .25 .60
57 Luther Wright .20 .50
58 Scott Burrell .20 .50
59 Stacey Augmon .25 .60
60 Jeff Malone .20 .50
61 Byron Houston .20 .50
62 Anthony Peeler .20 .50
63 Michael Adams .20 .50
64 Negele Knight .20 .50
65 Terry Cummings .25 .60
66 Christian Laettner .25 .60
67 Tracy Murray .20 .50
68 Sedale Threatt .20 .50
69 Dan Majerle .30 .75
70 Frank Brickowski .20 .50
71 Ken Norman .20 .50
72 Charles Smith .20 .50
73 Adam Keefe .20 .50
74 P.J. Brown .20 .50
75 Kevin Duckworth .20 .50
76 Shawn Bradley UER .20 .50
77 Darnell Mee .20 .50
78 Nick Anderson .20 .50
79 Mark West .20 .50
80 B.J. Armstrong .30 .75
81 Dennis Scott .25 .60
82 Lindsey Hunter .20 .50
83 Derek Strong .20 .50
84 Mike Brown .20 .50
85 Antonio Harvey .20 .50
86 Anthony Bonner .20 .50
87 Sam Cassell .30 .75
88 Harold Miner .20 .50
89 Spud Webb .25 .60
90 Mookie Blaylock .30 .75
91 Greg Anthony .20 .50
92 Richard Petruska .20 .50
93 Sean Rooks .20 .50
94 Ervin Johnson .20 .50
95 Randy Brown .20 .50
96 Orlando Woolridge .20 .50
97 Charles Oakley .30 .75
98 Craig Ehlo .20 .50
99 Derek Harper .25 .60
100 Doug Edwards .20 .50
101 Muggsy Bogues .25 .60
102 Mitch Richmond .40 1.00
103 Mahmoud Abdul-Rauf .20 .50
104 Joe Dumars .30 .75
105 Eric Riley .20 .50
106 Terry Mills .20 .50
107 Toni Kukoc .40 1.00
108 Jon Koncak .20 .50
109 Haywoode Workman .20 .50
110 Todd Day .20 .50
111 Detlef Schrempf .30 .75
112 David Wesley .20 .50
113 Mark Jackson .25 .60
114 Doug Overton .20 .50
115 Vinny Del Negro .20 .50
116 Loy Vaught .20 .50
117 Mike Peplowski .20 .50
118 Bimbo Coles .20 .50
119 Rex Walters .20 .50
120 Sherman Douglas .20 .50
121 David Benoit .20 .50
122 John Salley .20 .50
123 Cedric Ceballos .25 .60
124 Chris Mills .25 .60
125 Robert Horry .30 .75
126 Johnny Newman .20 .50
127 Malcolm Mackey .20 .50
128 Terry Dehere .20 .50
129 Dino Radja .20 .50
130 Reggie Williams .20 .50
131 Xavier McDaniel .20 .50
132 Bobby Hurley .20 .50
133 Alonzo Mourning .50 1.25
134 Isaiah Rider .20 .50
135 Antoine Carr .20 .50
136 Robert Pack .25 .60
137 Walt Williams .20 .50
138 Tyrone Corbin .20 .50
139 Popeye Jones .20 .50
140 Shawn Kemp .50 1.25
141 Thurl Bailey .20 .50
142 James Worthy .40 1.00
143 Scott Haskin .20 .50
144 Hubert Davis .20 .50
145 A.C. Green .25 .60
146 Dale Davis .20 .50
147 Nate McMillan .25 .60
148 Chris Morris .20 .50
149 Will Perdue .20 .50
150 Felton Spencer .20 .50
151 Rod Strickland .20 .50
152 Blue Edwards .20 .50
153 John Williams .20 .50
154 Rodney Rogers .20 .50
155 Acie Earl .20 .50
156 Hersey Hawkins .20 .50
157 Jamal Mashburn .30 .75
158 Don MacLean .20 .50
159 Micheal Williams .20 .50
160 Kenny Gattison .20 .50
161 Rich King .20 .50
162 Allan Houston .30 .75
163 Hoop-it up .07 .20
164 Hoop-it up .07 .20
165 Hoop-it up .07 .20
166 Danny Manning TO .25 .60
167 Dee Brown TO .25 .60
168 Alonzo Mourning TO .50 1.25
169 Scottie Pippen TO .75 2.00
170 Mark Price TO .30 .75
171 Jamal Mashburn TO .30 .75
172 Dikembe Mutombo TO .50 1.25
173 Joe Dumars TO .30 .75
174 Chris Webber TO .60 1.50
175 Hakeem Olajuwon TO .60 1.50
176 Reggie Miller TO .60 1.50
177 Ron Harper TO .25 .60
178 Nick Van Exel TO .30 .75
179 Steve Smith TO .25 .60
180 Vin Baker TO .30 .75
181 Isaiah Rider TO .30 .75
182 Derrick Coleman TO .30 .75
183 Patrick Ewing TO .50 1.25
184 Shaquille O'Neal TO 1.25 3.00
185 Clarence Weatherspoon TO .20 .50
186 Charles Barkley TO .75 2.00
187 Clyde Drexler TO .50 1.25
188 Mitch Richmond TO .40 1.00
189 David Robinson TO .60 1.50
190 Shawn Kemp TO .50 1.25
191 Karl Malone TO .60 1.50
192 Tom Gugliotta TO .20 .50
193 Kenny Anderson ASA .25 .60
194 Alonzo Mourning ASA .50 1.25
195 Mark Price ASA .30 .75
196 John Stockton ASA .60 1.50
197 Shaquille O'Neal ASA 1.25 3.00
198 Latrell Sprewell ASA .40 1.00
199 Charles Barkley PRO .75 2.00
200 Chris Webber PRO .60 1.50
201 Patrick Ewing PRO .50 1.25
202 Dennis Rodman PRO .75 2.00
203 Shawn Kemp PRO .50 1.25
204 Michael Jordan PRO 2.50 6.00
205 Shaquille O'Neal PRO 1.25 3.00
206 Larry Johnson PRO .40 1.00
207 Tim Hardaway CL .40 1.00
208 John Stockton CL .60 1.50
209 Harold Miner CL .20 .50
210 B.J. Armstrong CL .30 .75
211 Vernon Maxwell .20 .50
212 John Stockton .60 1.50
213 Luc Longley .25 .60
214 Sam Perkins .20 .50
215 Pooh Richardson .20 .50
216 Tyrone Corbin .20 .50
217 Mario Elie .20 .50
218 Bobby Phills .20 .50
219 Grant Hill RC 1.50 4.00
220 Gary Payton .50 1.25
221 Tom Hammonds .20 .50
222 Danny Ainge .30 .75
223 Gary Grant .20 .50
224 Jim Jackson .25 .60
225 Chris Gatling .20 .50
226 Sergei Bazarevich RC .30 .75
227 Tony Dumas RC .25 .60
228 Andrew Lang .20 .50
229 Wesley Person RC .30 .75
230 Terry Porter .20 .50
231 Duane Causwell .20 .50
232 Shaquille O'Neal 1.25 3.00
233 Antonio Davis .25 .60
234 Charles Barkley .75 2.00
235 Tony Massenburg .20 .50
236 Ricky Pierce .20 .50
237 Scott Skiles .20 .50
238 Jalen Rose RC .75 2.00
239 Charlie Ward RC .30 .75
240 Michael Jordan COMM 2.50 6.00
241 Elden Campbell .20 .50
242 Bill Cartwright .25 .60
243 Armon Gilliam UER .20 .50
244 Rick Fox .20 .50
245 Tim Breaux .20 .50
246 Monty Williams RC .40 1.00
247 Dominique Wilkins .50 1.25
248 Robert Parish .30 .75
249 Mark Jackson .25 .60
250 Jason Kidd RC 1.50 4.00
251 Andres Guibert .20 .50
252 Matt Geiger .20 .50
253 Stanley Roberts .20 .50
254 Jack Haley .20 .50
255 David Wingate .20 .50
256 John Crotty .20 .50
257 Brian Grant RC .50 1.25
258 Otis Thorpe .20 .50
259 Clifford Rozier RC .20 .50
260 Grant Long .20 .50
261 Eric Mobley RC .20 .50
262 Dickey Simpkins RC .25 .60
263 J.R. Reid .20 .50
264 Kevin Willis .25 .60
265 Scott Brooks .20 .50
266 Glenn Robinson RC .60 1.50
267 Dana Barros .20 .50
268 Ken Norman .20 .50
269 Herb Williams .20 .50
270 Dee Brown .25 .60
271 Steve Kerr .25 .60
272 Jon Barry .20 .50
273 Sean Elliott .25 .60
274 Elliot Perry .20 .50
275 Kenny Smith .25 .60
276 Sean Rooks .20 .50
277 Gheorghe Muresan .20 .50
278 Juwan Howard RC .50 1.25
279 Steve Smith .25 .60
280 Anthony Bowie .20 .50
281 Moses Malone .30 .75
282 Olden Polynice .20 .50
283 Jo Jo English .20 .50
284 Marty Conlon .20 .50
285 Sam Mitchell .20 .50
286 Doug West .20 .50
287 Cedric Ceballos .25 .60
288 Lorenzo Williams .20 .50
289 Harold Ellis .20 .50
290 Doc Rivers .25 .60
291 Keith Tower .20 .50
292 Mark Bryant .20 .50
293 Oliver Miller .20 .50
294 Michael Adams .20 .50
295 Tree Rollins .20 .50
296 Eddie Jones RC 1.00 2.50
297 Malik Sealy .20 .50
298 Blue Edwards .20 .50
299 Brooks Thompson RC .25 .60
300 Benoit Benjamin .20 .50
301 Avery Johnson .25 .60
302 Larry Johnson .40 1.00
303 John Starks .30 .75
304 Byron Scott .30 .75
305 Eric Murdock .20 .50
306 Jay Humphries .20 .50
307 Kenny Anderson .25 .60
308 Brian Williams .20 .50
309 Nick Van Exel .30 .75
310 Tim Hardaway .40 1.00
311 Lee Mayberry .20 .50
312 Vlade Divac .30 .75
313 Donyell Marshall RC .30 .75
314 Anthony Mason .25 .60
315 Danny Manning .25 .60
316 Tyrone Hill .20 .50
317 Vincent Askew .20 .50
318 Khalid Reeves RC .25 .60
319 Ron Harper .25 .60
320 Brent Price .20 .50
321 Byron Houston .20 .50
322 Lamond Murray RC .30 .75
323 Bryant Stith .20 .50
324 Tom Gugliotta .20 .50
325 Jerome Kersey .20 .50
326 B.J.Tyler RC .20 .50
327 Antonio Lang RC .30 .75
328 Carlos Rogers RC .25 .60
329 Wayman Tisdale .20 .50
330 Kevin Gamble .20 .50
331 Eric Piatkowski RC .30 .75
332 Mitchell Butler .20 .50
333 Patrick Ewing .50 1.25
334 Doug Smith .20 .50
335 Joe Kleine .20 .50
336 Keith Jennings .20 .50
337 Bill Curley RC .20 .50
338 Johnny Newman .20 .50
339 Howard Eisley RC .30 .75
340 Willie Anderson .20 .50
341 Aaron McKie RC .30 .75
342 Tom Chambers .25 .60
343 Scott Williams .20 .50
344 Harvey Grant .20 .50
345 Billy Owens .20 .50
346 Sharone Wright RC .20 .50
347 Michael Cage .20 .50
348 Vern Fleming .20 .50
349 Darrin Hancock RC .25 .60
350 Matt Fish .20 .50
351 Rony Seikaly .20 .50
352 Victor Alexander .20 .50
353 Anthony Miller RC .30 .75
354 Horace Grant .30 .75
355 Jayson Williams .30 .75
356 Dale Ellis .20 .50
357 Sarunas Marciulionis .20 .50
358 Anthony Avent .20 .50
359 Rex Chapman .20 .50
360 Askia Jones RC .30 .75
361 Bo Outlaw RC .30 .75
362 Chuck Person .25 .60
363 Danny Schayes .20 .50
364 Morlon Wiley .20 .50
365 Donlonio Wingfield RC .30 .75
366 Tony Smith .20 .50
367 Bill Wennington .20 .50
368 Bryon Russell .20 .50
369 Geert Hammink .20 .50
370 Eric Montross RC .25 .60
371 Clift Levingston .20 .50
372 Stacey Augmon BP .25 .60
373 Eric Montross BP .25 .60
374 Alonzo Mourning BP .50 1.25
375 Scottie Pippen BP .75 2.00
376 Mark Price BP .30 .75
377 Jason Kidd BP 1.50 4.00
378 Jalen Rose BP .75 2.00
379 Grant Hill BP 1.50 4.00
380 Latrell Sprewell BP .40 1.00
381 Hakeem Olajuwon BP .60 1.50
382 Reggie Miller BP .60 1.50
383 Lamond Murray BP .30 .75
384 Eddie Jones BP 1.00 2.50
385 Khalid Reeves BP .25 .60
386 Glenn Robinson BP .60 1.50
387 Donyell Marshall BP .30 .75
388 Derrick Coleman BP .30 .75
389 Patrick Ewing BP .50 1.25
390 Shaquille O'Neal BP 1.25 3.00
391 Sharone Wright BP .25 .60
392 Charles Barkley BP .75 2.00
393 Aaron McKie BP .30 .75
394 Brian Grant BP .50 1.25
395 David Robinson BP .60 1.50
396 Shawn Kemp BP .50 1.25
397 Karl Malone BP .60 1.50
398 Tom Gugliotta BP .20 .50
399 Hakeem Olajuwon TRIV .60 1.50
400 Shaquille O'Neal TRIV 1.25 3.00
401 Chris Webber TRIV .60 1.50
402 Michael Jordan TRIV 2.50 6.00
403 David Robinson TRIV .60 1.50
404 Shawn Kemp TRIV .50 1.25
405 Patrick Ewing TRIV .50 1.25
406 Charles Barkley TRIV .75 2.00
407 Glenn Robinson DC .60 1.50
408 Jason Kidd DC 1.50 4.00
409 Grant Hill DC 1.50 4.00
410 Donyell Marshall DC .30 .75
411 Sharone Wright DC .25 .60
412 Lamond Murray DC .30 .75
413 Brian Grant DC .50 1.25
414 Eric Montross DC .25 .60
415 Eddie Jones DC 1.00 2.50
416 Carlos Rogers DC .25 .60
417 Shawn Kemp CL .50 1.25
418 Bobby Hurley CL .20 .50
419 Shawn Bradley CL .20 .50
420 Michael Jordan CL 2.50 6.00

1994-95 Collector's Choice Silver Signature

COMPLETE SET (420) 50.00 120.00
COMPLETE SERIES 1 (210) 20.00 50.00
COMPLETE SERIES 2 (210) 30.00 60.00
*SILVER: .6X TO 1.5X BASE HI

1994-95 Collector's Choice Gold Signature

*GOLD: 5X TO 12X BASE CARD HI
SER.1/2 STATED ODDS 1:35 HOB/RET
1 Anfernee Hardaway 25.00 60.00
4 Chris Webber 8.00 20.00
23 Michael Jordan BB 200.00 500.00
140 Shawn Kemp 6.00 15.00
204 Michael Jordan PRO 60.00 150.00
240 Michael Jordan COMM 500.00 1,000.00
402 Michael Jordan TRIV 25.00 60.00
420 Michael Jordan CL 75.00 200.00

1994-95 Collector's Choice Blow-Ups

COMPLETE SET (5) 5.00 10.00
23 Michael Jordan BB 3.00 8.00
40 Calbert Cheaney .30 .75
76 Shawn Bradley .25 .60
132 Bobby Hurley .25 .60
140 Shawn Kemp .60 1.50
A23 Michael Jordan AU 3,000.00 6,000.00
A40 Calbert Cheaney AU 15.00 30.00
A76 Shawn Bradley AU 15.00 30.00
A132 Bobby Hurley AU 15.00 30.00
A140 Shawn Kemp AU 20.00 50.00

1994-95 Collector's Choice Crash the Game Assists

COMPLETE SET (15) 4.00 10.00
SER.1 STATED ODDS 1:20 RETAIL
*RED.CARDS: .2X TO .5X HI COLUMN
A1 Michael Adams .40 1.00
A2 Kenny Anderson .50 1.25
A3 Mookie Blaylock .60 1.50
A4 Muggsy Bogues .50 1.25
A5 Sherman Douglas .40 1.00
A6 Anfernee Hardaway 1.25 3.00
A7 Tim Hardaway .75 2.00
A8 Lindsey Hunter .40 1.00
A9 Mark Jackson .50 1.25
A10 Kevin Johnson .60 1.50
A11 Aaron McKie .40 1.00
A12 Mark Price .60 1.50
A13 John Stockton 1.25 3.00
A14 Rod Strickland .40 1.00
A15 Micheal Williams .40 1.00

1994-95 Collector's Choice Crash the Game Rebounds

COMPLETE SET (15) 6.00 15.00
SER.2 STATED ODDS 1:20 RETAIL
*RED.CARDS: .2X TO .5X HI COLUMN
R1 Derrick Coleman .60 1.50
R2 Patrick Ewing 1.00 2.50
R3 Horace Grant .60 1.50
R4 Shawn Kemp 1.00 2.50
R5 Karl Malone 1.25 3.00
R6 Alonzo Mourning 1.00 2.50
R7 Dikembe Mutombo 1.00 2.50
R8 Charles Oakley .60 1.50
R9 Hakeem Olajuwon 1.25 3.00
R10 Shaquille O'Neal 2.50 6.00
R11 Olden Polynice .40 1.00
R12 David Robinson 1.25 3.00
R13 Dennis Rodman 1.50 4.00
R14 Otis Thorpe .40 1.00
R15 Kevin Willis .50 1.25

1994-95 Collector's Choice Crash the Game Rookie Scoring

COMPLETE SET (15) 4.00 10.00
SER.2 STATED ODDS 1:20 HOBBY
*RED.CARDS: .2X TO .5X HI COLUMN
S1 Tony Dumas .20 .50
S2 Brian Grant .40 1.00
S3 Grant Hill 1.25 3.00
S4 Juwan Howard .40 1.00
S5 Eddie Jones .75 2.00
S6 Jason Kidd 1.25 3.00
S7 Donyell Marshall .25 .60
S8 Eric Montross .20 .50
S9 Lamond Murray .25 .60
S10 Khalid Reeves .20 .50
S11 Glenn Robinson .50 1.25
S12 Jalen Rose .60 1.50
S13 Dickey Simpkins .20 .50
S14 Charlie Ward .25 .60
S15 Sharone Wright .20 .50

1994-95 Collector's Choice Crash the Game Scoring

COMPLETE SET (15) 6.00 15.00
SER.1 STATED ODDS 1:20 HOBBY
*RED.CARDS: 2X TO .5X HI COLUMN
S1 Charles Barkley 1.50 4.00
S2 Derrick Coleman .60 1.50
S3 Joe Dumars .60 1.50
S4 Patrick Ewing 1.00 2.50
S5 Karl Malone 1.25 3.00
S6 Reggie Miller 1.25 3.00
S7 Shaquille O'Neal 2.50 6.00
S8 Hakeem Olajuwon 1.25 3.00
S9 Scottie Pippen 1.50 4.00
S10 Glen Rice .60 1.50
S11 Mitch Richmond .75 2.00
S12 David Robinson 1.25 3.00
S13 Latrell Sprewell .75 2.00
S14 Chris Webber 1.25 3.00
S15 Dominique Wilkins 1.00 2.50

1994-95 Collector's Choice Draft Trade

COMPLETE SET (10) 2.50 6.00
DT CARD: SER.1 STATED ODDS 1:36
1 Glenn Robinson .40 1.00
2 Jason Kidd 1.00 2.50
3 Grant Hill 1.00 2.50
4 Donyell Marshall .20 .50
5 Juwan Howard .30 .75
6 Sharone Wright .15 .40
7 Lamond Murray .20 .50
8 Brian Grant .30 .75
9 Eric Montross .15 .40
10 Eddie Jones .60 1.50

1995-96 Collector's Choice

COMPLETE SET (410) 20.00 50.00
COMP.FACTORY SET (419) 20.00 50.00
COMPLETE SERIES 1 (210) 10.00 25.00
COMPLETE SERIES 2 (200) 10.00 25.00
SUBSET CARDS SAME VALUE AS BASE CARDS
1 Rod Strickland .20 .50
2 Larry Johnson .40 1.00
3 Mahmoud Abdul-Rauf .25 .60
4 Joe Dumars .30 .75
5 Jason Kidd .50 1.25
6 Avery Johnson .25 .60
7 Dee Brown .25 .60
8 Brian Williams .20 .50
9 Nick Van Exel .30 .75
10 Dennis Rodman .60 1.50
11 Rony Seikaly .20 .50
12 Harvey Grant .20 .50
13 Craig Ehlo .20 .50
14 Derek Harper .25 .60
15 Oliver Miller .20 .50
16 Dennis Scott .20 .50
17 Ed Pinckney .20 .50
18 Eric Platkowski .20 .50
19 B.J. Armstrong .30 .75
20 Tyrone Hill .20 .50
21 Malik Sealy .20 .50
22 Clyde Drexler .50 1.25
23 Aaron McKie .20 .50
24 Harold Miner .20 .50
25 Bobby Hurley .20 .50
26 Dell Curry .30 .75
27 Micheal Williams .20 .50
28 Adam Keefe .20 .50
29 Antonio Harvey .20 .50
30 Billy Owens .20 .50
31 Nate McMillan .20 .50
32 J.R. Reid .20 .50
33 Grant Hill .50 1.25
34 Charles Barkley .75 2.00
35 Tyrone Corbin .20 .50
36 Don MacLean .20 .50
37 Kenny Smith .20 .50
38 Juwan Howard .30 .75
39 Charles Smith .20 .50
40 Shawn Kemp .50 1.25
41 Dana Barros .25 .60
42 Vin Baker .25 .60
43 Armon Gilliam .20 .50
44 Spud Webb .20 .50
45 Michael Jordan 3.00 8.00
46 Scott Williams .20 .50
47 Vlade Divac .25 .60
48 Roy Tarpley .25 .60
49 Bimbo Coles .20 .50
50 David Robinson .60 1.50
51 Terry Dehere .25 .60
52 Bobby Phills .25 .60
53 Sherman Douglas .20 .50
54 Rodney Rogers .20 .50
55 Detlef Schrempf .30 .75
56 Calbert Cheaney .20 .50
57 Tom Gugliotta .20 .50
58 Jeff Turner .20 .50
59 Mookie Blaylock .30 .75
60 Bill Curley .20 .50
61 Chris Dudley .20 .50
62 Popeye Jones .20 .50
63 Scott Burrell .20 .50
64 Dale Davis .20 .50
65 Mitchell Butler .20 .50
66 Pervis Ellison .20 .50
67 Todd Day .20 .50
68 Carl Herrera .20 .50
69 Jeff Hornacek .25 .60
70 Vincent Askew .20 .50
71 A.C. Green .25 .60
72 Kevin Gamble .20 .50
73 Chris Gatling .20 .50
74 Otis Thorpe .20 .50
75 Michael Cage .20 .50
76 Carlos Rogers .20 .50
77 Gheorghe Muresan .20 .50
78 Olden Polynice .20 .50
79 Grant Long .20 .50
80 Allan Houston .25 .60
81 Bo Outlaw .20 .50
82 Clarence Weatherspoon .20 .50
83 Tony Dumas .20 .50
84 Herb Williams .20 .50
85 P.J. Brown .20 .50
86 Robert Horry .30 .75
87 Byron Scott .30 .75
88 Horace Grant .25 .60
89 Dominique Wilkins .50 1.25
90 Doug West .20 .50
91 Antoine Carr .20 .50
92 Dickey Simpkins .20 .50
93 Elden Campbell .20 .50
94 Kevin Johnson .30 .75
95 Rex Chapman .20 .50
96 John Williams .20 .50
97 Tim Hardaway .40 1.00
98 Rik Smits .25 .60
99 Rex Walters .20 .50
100 Robert Parish .40 1.00
101 Isaiah Rider .30 .75
102 Sarunas Marciulionis .20 .50
103 Andrew Lang .20 .50
104 Eric Mobley .20 .50
105 Randy Brown .20 .50
106 John Stockton .60 1.50
107 Lamond Murray .20 .50
108 Will Perdue .25 .60
109 Wayman Tisdale .20 .50
110 John Starks .30 .75
111 John Salley .20 .50
112 Lucious Harris .20 .50
113 Jeff Malone .20 .50
114 Anthony Bowie .20 .50
115 Vinny Del Negro .20 .50
116 Michael Adams .20 .50
117 Chris Mullin .30 .75
118 Benoit Benjamin .20 .50
119 Byron Houston .20 .50
120 LaPhonso Ellis .25 .60
121 Doug Overton .20 .50
122 Jerome Kersey .20 .50
123 Greg Minor .20 .50
124 Christian Laettner .25 .60
125 Mark Price .30 .75
126 Kevin Willis .25 .60
127 Kenny Anderson .25 .60
128 Marty Conlon .20 .50
129 Blue Edwards .20 .50
130 Danny Schayes .20 .50
131 Duane Ferrell .20 .50
132 Charles Oakley .25 .60
133 Brian Grant .25 .60
134 Reggie Williams .20 .50
135 Steve Kerr .30 .75
136 Khalid Reeves .20 .50
137 David Benoit .20 .50
138 Derrick Coleman .25 .60
139 Anthony Peeler .20 .50
140 Jim Jackson .25 .60
141 Stacey Augmon .25 .60
142 Sam Cassell .30 .75
143 Derrick McKey .20 .50
144 Danny Ferry .20 .50
145 Anfernee Hardaway .75 2.00
146 Clifford Robinson .30 .75
147 B.J. Tyler .20 .50
148 Mark West .20 .50
149 David Wingate .20 .50
150 Willie Anderson .20 .50
151 Hersey Hawkins .25 .60
152 Bryant Stith .20 .50
153 Dan Majerle .30 .75
154 Chris Smith .20 .50
155 Donyell Marshall .20 .50
156 Loy Vaught .20 .50
157 Reggie Miller .60 1.50
158 Hubert Davis .20 .50
159 Ron Harper .25 .60
160 Lee Mayberry .20 .50
161 Eddie Jones .30 .75
162 Shawn Bradley .20 .50
163 Nick Anderson .25 .60
164 Ervin Johnson .20 .50
165 Walt Williams .20 .50
166 Steve Smith FF .25 .60
167 Dino Radja FF .20 .50
168 Alonzo Mourning FF .50 1.25
169 Michael Jordan FF 3.00 8.00
170 Tyrone Hill FF .20 .50
171 Jamal Mashburn FF .30 .75
172 Dikembe Mutombo FF .50 1.25
173 Grant Hill FF w/Jordan .20 .50
174 Latrell Sprewell FF .30 .75
175 Hakeem Olajuwon FF .60 1.50
176 Reggie Miller FF .60 1.50
177 Pooh Richardson FF .20 .50
178 Cedric Ceballos FF .25 .60
179 Glen Rice FF .30 .75
180 Glenn Robinson FF .30 .75
181 Isaiah Rider FF .30 .75
182 Derrick Coleman FF .25 .60
183 Patrick Ewing FF .50 1.25
184 Shaquille O'Neal FF 1.25 3.00
185 Dana Barros FF .25 .60
186 Dan Majerle FF .30 .75
187 Clifford Robinson FF .30 .75
188 Mitch Richmond FF .40 1.00
189 David Robinson FF .60 1.50
190 Gary Payton FF .50 1.25
191 Oliver Miller FF .20 .50
192 Karl Malone FF .60 1.50
193 Kevin Pritchard FF .20 .50
194 Chris Webber FF .40 1.00
195 Michael Jordan PD 3.00 8.00
196 Hakeem Olajuwon PD .60 1.50
197 Vin Baker PD .25 .60
198 Grant Hill PD .50 1.25
199 Clyde Drexler PD .50 1.25
200 Chris Webber PD .40 1.00
201 Shawn Kemp PD .50 1.25
202 Shaquille O'Neal PD 1.25 3.00
203 Stacey Augmon PD .25 .60
204 David Benoit PD .20 .50
205 Rodney Rogers PD .25 .60
206 Latrell Sprewell PD .30 .75
207 Brian Grant PD .25 .60
208 Lamond Murray PD .20 .50
209 Shawn Kemp CL .10 .25
210 Michael Jordan CL .40 1.00
211 Cory Alexander RC .30 .75
212 Vernon Maxwell .20 .50
213 George Lynch .20 .50
214 Terry Mills .20 .50
215 Scottie Pippen .75 2.00
216 Donald Royal .20 .50
217 Wesley Person .20 .50
218 Antonio Davis .20 .50
219 Glenn Robinson .30 .75
220 Jerry Stackhouse RC 1.00 2.50
221 James Robinson .20 .50
222 Chris Mills .20 .50
223 Chuck Person .25 .60
224 Duane Causwell .20 .50
225 Gary Payton .50 1.25
226 Eric Montross .20 .50
227 Felton Spencer .20 .50
228 Scott Skiles .20 .50
229 Latrell Sprewell .30 .75
230 Sedale Threatt .20 .50
231 Mark Bryant .20 .50
232 Buck Williams .20 .50
233 Brian Williams .20 .50
234 Sharone Wright .20 .50
235 Karl Malone .60 1.50
236 Kevin Edwards .20 .50
237 Muggsy Bogues .30 .75
238 Mario Elie .20 .50
239 Rasheed Wallace RC 1.00 2.50
240 George Zidek RC .25 .60
241 Cedric Ceballos .25 .60
242 Alan Henderson RC .30 .75
243 Joe Kleine .20 .50
244 Patrick Ewing .50 1.25
245 Sasha Danilovic RC .30 .75
246 Bill Wennington .20 .50
247 Steve Smith .25 .60
248 Bryant Stith .20 .50
249 Dino Radja .20 .50
250 Monty Williams .20 .50
251 Andrew DeClercq RC .30 .75
252 Sean Elliott .25 .60
253 Rick Fox .25 .60
254 Lionel Simmons .20 .50
255 Dikembe Mutombo .50 1.25
256 Lindsey Hunter .20 .50
257 Terrell Brandon .25 .60
258 Shawn Respert RC .25 .60
259 Rodney Rogers .25 .60
260 Bryon Russell .25 .60
261 David Wesley .20 .50
262 Ken Norman .20 .50
263 Mitch Richmond .40 1.00
264 Sam Perkins .25 .60
265 Hakeem Olajuwon .60 1.50
266 Brian Shaw .20 .50
267 B.J. Armstrong .30 .75
268 Jalen Rose .40 1.00
269 Bryant Reeves RC .25 .60
270 Cherokee Parks RC .25 .60
271 Dennis Rodman .60 1.50
272 Kendall Gill .20 .50
273 Elliot Perry .20 .50
274 Anthony Mason .20 .50
275 Kevin Garnett RC 2.50 6.00
276 Damon Stoudamire RC .75 2.00
277 Lawrence Moten RC .30 .75
278 Ed O'Bannon RC .25 .60
279 Toni Kukoc .40 1.00
280 Greg Ostertag RC .30 .75
281 Tom Hammonds .20 .50
282 Yinka Dare .20 .50
283 Michael Smith .20 .50
284 Clifford Rozier .20 .50
285 Gary Trent RC .25 .60
286 Shaquille O'Neal 1.25 3.00
287 Luc Longley .25 .60
288 Bob Sura RC .25 .60
289 Dana Barros .25 .60
290 Lorenzo Williams .20 .50
291 Haywoode Workman .20 .50
292 Randolph Childress RC .25 .60
293 Doc Rivers .25 .60
294 Chris Webber .40 1.00
295 Kurt Thomas RC .30 .75
296 Greg Anthony .20 .50
297 Tyus Edney RC .30 .75
298 Danny Manning .25 .60
299 Brent Barry RC .50 1.25
300 Joe Smith RC .40 1.00
301 Pooh Richardson .20 .50
302 Mark Jackson .25 .60
303 Richard Dumas .20 .50
304 Michael Finley RC .75 2.00
305 Theo Ratliff RC .50 1.25
306 Gary Grant .20 .50
307 Jamal Mashburn .30 .75
308 Corliss Williamson RC .30 .75
309 Eric Williams RC .30 .75
310 Zan Tabak .20 .50
311 Eric Murdock .20 .50
312 Sherrell Ford RC .25 .60
313 Terry Davis .20 .50
314 Vern Fleming .20 .50
315 Jason Caffey RC .30 .75
316 Mario Bennett RC .25 .60
317 David Vaughn RC .30 .75
318 Loren Meyer RC .20 .50
319 Travis Best RC .30 .75
320 Byron Scott .30 .75
321 Mookie Blaylock SR .30 .75
322 Dee Brown SR .20 .50
323 Alonzo Mourning SR .50 1.25
324 Michael Jordan SR 3.00 8.00
325 Terrell Brandon SR .25 .60
326 Jim Jackson SR .25 .60
327 Dikembe Mutombo SR .50 1.25
328 Grant Hill SR .50 1.25
329 Joe Smith SR UER .40 1.00
330 Clyde Drexler SR .50 1.25
331 Reggie Miller SR .60 1.50

332 Lamond Murray SR .20 .50
333 Nick Van Exel SR .30 .75
334 Glen Rice SR .30 .75
335 Glenn Robinson SR .30 .75
336 Christian Laettner SR .25 .60
337 Kenny Anderson SR .25 .60
338 Patrick Ewing SR .50 1.25
339 Shaquille O'Neal SR 1.25 3.00
340 Jerry Stackhouse SR 1.00 2.50
341 Charles Barkley SR .75 2.00
342 Clifford Robinson SR .30 .75
343 Brian Grant SR .25 .60
344 David Robinson SR .60 1.50
345 Shawn Kemp SR .50 1.25
346 Damon Stoudamire SR .75 2.00
347 Karl Malone SR .60 1.50
348 Bryant Reeves SR .25 .60
349 Juwan Howard SR .30 .75
350 N.Anderson/D.Brown PT .25 .60
351 Rik Smits PT .25 .60
352 H.Williams/T.Tolbert PT .20 .50
353 Michael Jordan PT 3.00 8.00
354 David Robinson PT .60 1.50
355 T.Porter/K.Johnson PT .30 .75
356 Clyde Drexler PT .50 1.25
357 Cedric Ceballos PT .25 .60
358 Horace Grant Group PT .25 .60
359 Reggie Miller PT .60 1.50
360 A.Johnson/N.Van Exel PT .30 .75
361 H.Olajuwon/R.Horry PT .60 1.50
362 Rik Smits PT .25 .60
363 D.Rob/H.Olajuwon PT .60 1.50
364 Robert Horry PT .30 .75
365 Kenny Smith PT .25 .60
366 Stacey Augmon LOVE .25 .60
367 Sherman Douglas LOVE .20 .50
368 Larry Johnson LOVE .40 1.00
369 Scottie Pippen LOVE .75 2.00
370 Tyrone Hill LOVE .20 .50
371 Jamal Mashburn LOVE .30 .75
372 Mahmoud Abdul-Rauf LOVE .25 .60
373 Grant Hill LOVE .50 1.25
374 Latrell Sprewell LOVE .30 .75
375 Sam Cassell LOVE .30 .75
376 Rik Smits LOVE .25 .60
377 Terry Dehere LOVE .20 .50
378 Eddie Jones LOVE .30 .75
379 Billy Owens LOVE .20 .50
380 Vin Baker LOVE .25 .60
381 Isaiah Rider LOVE .30 .75
382 Kenny Anderson LOVE .25 .60
383 John Starks LOVE .30 .75
384 Anfernee Hardaway LOVE .75 2.00
385 Sharone Wright LOVE .20 .50
386 Charles Barkley LOVE .75 2.00
387 Clifford Robinson LOVE .30 .75
388 Walt Williams LOVE .20 .50
389 Sean Elliott LOVE .25 .60
390 Gary Payton LOVE .50 1.25
391 Carlos Rogers LOVE .20 .50
392 John Stockton LOVE .60 1.50
393 Greg Anthony LOVE .20 .50
394 Chris Webber LOVE .40 1.00
395 Gary Payton PG .50 1.25
396 Mookie Blaylock PG .30 .75
397 Charles Barkley PG .75 2.00
398 Grant Hill PG .50 1.25
399 Anfernee Hardaway PG .75 2.00
400 Kenny Anderson PG .25 .60
401 Mark Jackson PG .25 .60
402 Karl Malone PG .60 1.50
403 Avery Johnson PG .25 .60
404 Larry Johnson 40 .40 1.00
405 Nick Van Exel 40 .30 .75
406 Vin Baker 40 .25 .60
407 Jason Kidd 40 .50 1.25
408 David Robinson 40 .60 1.50
409 Shawn Kemp CL .08 .25
410 Michael Jordan CL 3.00 8.00
NNO Bulls Fact.Set Comm. 2.50 6.00

1995-96 Collector's Choice Player's Club

COMPLETE SET (410) 35.00 70.00
COMPLETE SERIES 1 (210) 15.00 30.00
COMPLETE SERIES 2 (200) 20.00 40.00
*STARS: 1.25X TO 3X BASE CARD HI
*RCs: 1X TO 2.5X BASE HI
*SUBSETS: .75X TO 2X BASE HI
ONE PER PACK

1995-96 Collector's Choice Player's Club Platinum

*STARS: 10X TO 25X BASE CARD HI
*RCs: 6X TO 15X BASE HI
*SUBSETS: 6X TO 15X BASE HI
SER.1/2 STATED ODDS 1:35
173 Grant Hill FF w/Jordan 8.00 20.00

1995-96 Collector's Choice Crash the Game Assists/Rebounds

SER.2 STATED ODDS 1:5
*GOLD CARDS: 1.25X TO 3X HI COLUMN
GOLD: SER.2 STATED ODDS 1:49
*SILVER RED.CARDS: .2X TO .5X HI COLUMN
*GOLD RED.CARDS: 1.5X TO 4X SILVER RED.
ONE RED.SET PER WINNER BY MAIL
C1 Michael Jordan 5.00 12.00
C1B Michael Jordan 5.00 12.00
C1C Michael Jordan 5.00 12.00
C2 Tim Hardaway .60 1.50
C2B Tim Hardaway .60 1.50
C2C Tim Hardaway .60 1.50
C3 Juwan Howard .50 1.25
C3B Juwan Howard .50 1.25
C3C Juwan Howard .50 1.25
C4 Shawn Kemp .75 2.00
C4B Shawn Kemp .75 2.00
C4C Shawn Kemp .75 2.00
C5 Nick Van Exel .50 1.25
C5B Nick Van Exel .50 1.25
C5C Nick Van Exel .50 1.25
C6 Mookie Blaylock .50 1.25
C6B Mookie Blaylock .50 1.25
C6C Mookie Blaylock .50 1.25
C7 John Stockton 1.00 2.50
C7B John Stockton 1.00 2.50
C7C John Stockton 1.00 2.50
C8 Scottie Pippen 1.25 3.00
C8B Scottie Pippen 1.25 3.00
C8C Scottie Pippen 1.25 3.00
C9 Vin Baker .40 1.00
C9B Vin Baker .40 1.00
C9C Vin Baker .40 1.00
C10 Lamond Murray .30 .75
C10B Lamond Murray .30 .75
C10C Lamond Murray .30 .75
C11 David Robinson 1.00 2.50
C11B David Robinson 1.00 2.50
C11C David Robinson 1.00 2.50
C12 Jason Kidd .75 2.00
C12B Jason Kidd .75 2.00
C12C Jason Kidd .75 2.00
C13 Rod Strickland .30 .75
C13B Rod Strickland .30 .75
C13C Rod Strickland .30 .75
C14 Glen Rice .50 1.25
C14B Glen Rice .50 1.25
C14C Glen Rice .50 1.25
C15 Anfernee Hardaway 1.25 3.00
C15B Anfernee Hardaway 1.25 3.00
C15C Anfernee Hardaway 1.25 3.00
C16 Hakeem Olajuwon 1.00 2.50
C16B Hakeem Olajuwon 1.00 2.50
C16C Hakeem Olajuwon 1.00 2.50
C17 Kenny Anderson .40 1.00
C17B Kenny Anderson .40 1.00
C17C Kenny Anderson .40 1.00
C18 Sharone Wright .30 .75
C18B Sharone Wright .30 .75
C18C Sharone Wright .30 .75
C19 Dikembe Mutombo .75 2.00
C19B Dikembe Mutombo .75 2.00
C19C Dikembe Mutombo .75 2.00
C20 Muggsy Bogues .50 1.25
C20B Muggsy Bogues .50 1.25
C20C Muggsy Bogues .50 1.25
C21 Reggie Miller 1.00 2.50
C21B Reggie Miller 1.00 2.50
C21C Reggie Miller 1.00 2.50
C22 Danny Manning .40 1.00
C22B Danny Manning .40 1.00
C22C Danny Manning .40 1.00
C23 Christian Laettner .40 1.00
C23B Christian Laettner .40 1.00
C23C Christian Laettner .40 1.00
C24 Eric Montross .30 .75
C24B Eric Montross .30 .75
C24C Eric Montross .30 .75
C25 Patrick Ewing .75 2.00
C25B Patrick Ewing .75 2.00
C25C Patrick Ewing .75 2.00
C26 Damon Stoudamire 1.25 3.00
C26B Damon Stoudamire 1.25 3.00
C26C Damon Stoudamire 1.25 3.00
C27 Bryant Reeves .40 1.00
C27B Bryant Reeves .40 1.00
C27C Bryant Reeves .40 1.00
C28 Joe Dumars .50 1.25
C28B Joe Dumars .50 1.25
C28C Joe Dumars .50 1.25
C29 Tyrone Hill .30 .75
C29B Tyrone Hill .30 .75
C29C Tyrone Hill .30 .75
C30 Brian Grant .40 1.00
C30B Brian Grant .40 1.00
C30C Brian Grant .40 1.00

1995-96 Collector's Choice Crash the Game Scoring

SER.1 STATED ODDS 1:5
*GOLD CARDS: 1.5X TO 4X HI COLUMN
GOLD: SER.1 STATED ODDS 1:50
*SILVER RED.CARDS: .2X TO .5X HI COLUMN
*GOLD RED.CARDS: 1.5X TO 4X SILVER RED.
ONE RED.SET PER WINNER BY MAIL
C1 Michael Jordan 5.00 12.00
C1B Michael Jordan 5.00 12.00
C1C Michael Jordan 5.00 12.00
C2 Kenny Anderson .40 1.00
C2B Kenny Anderson .40 1.00
C2C Kenny Anderson .40 1.00
C3 Charles Barkley 1.25 3.00
C3B Charles Barkley 1.25 3.00
C3C Charles Barkley 1.25 3.00
C4 Dana Barros .40 1.00
C4B Dana Barros .40 1.00
C4C Dana Barros .40 1.00
C5 Anfernee Hardaway 1.25 3.00
C5B Anfernee Hardaway 1.25 3.00
C5C Anfernee Hardaway 1.25 3.00
C6 Mookie Blaylock .50 1.25
C6B Mookie Blaylock .50 1.25
C6C Mookie Blaylock .50 1.25
C7 Lamond Murray .30 .75
C7B Lamond Murray .30 .75
C7C Lamond Murray .30 .75
C8 Karl Malone 1.00 2.50
C8B Karl Malone 1.00 2.50
C8C Karl Malone 1.00 2.50
C9 Alonzo Mourning .75 2.00
C9B Alonzo Mourning .75 2.00
C9C Alonzo Mourning .75 2.00
C10 Hakeem Olajuwon 1.00 2.50
C10B Hakeem Olajuwon 1.00 2.50
C10C Hakeem Olajuwon 1.00 2.50
C11 Mark Price .50 1.25
C11B Mark Price .50 1.25
C11C Mark Price .50 1.25
C12 Isiah Rider .50 1.25
C12B Isaiah Rider .50 1.25
C12C Isaiah Rider .50 1.25
C13 Glen Rice .50 1.25
C13B Glen Rice .50 1.25
C13C Glen Rice .50 1.25
C14 Mitch Richmond .60 1.50
C14B Mitch Richmond .60 1.50
C14C Mitch Richmond .60 1.50
C15 Chris Webber .60 1.50
C15B Chris Webber .60 1.50
C15C Chris Webber .60 1.50
C16 Nick Van Exel .50 1.25
C16B Nick Van Exel .50 1.25
C16C Nick Van Exel .50 1.25
C17 Mahmoud Abdul-Rauf .40 1.00
C17B Mahmoud Abdul-Rauf .40 1.00
C17C Mahmoud Abdul-Rauf .40 1.00
C18 Dominique Wilkins .75 2.00
C18B Dominique Wilkins .75 2.00
C18C Dominique Wilkins .75 2.00
C19 Patrick Ewing .75 2.00
C19B Patrick Ewing .75 2.00
C19C Patrick Ewing .75 2.00
C20 David Robinson 1.00 2.50
C20B David Robinson 1.00 2.50
C20C David Robinson 1.00 2.50
C21 Shawn Kemp .75 2.00
C21B Shawn Kemp .75 2.00
C21C Shawn Kemp .75 2.00
C22 Jason Kidd .75 2.00
C22B Jason Kidd .75 2.00
C22C Jason Kidd .75 2.00
C23 Glenn Robinson .50 1.25
C23B Glenn Robinson .50 1.25
C23C Glenn Robinson .50 1.25
C24 Reggie Miller 1.00 2.50
C24B Reggie Miller 1.00 2.50
C24C Reggie Miller 1.00 2.50
C25 Joe Dumars .50 1.25
C25B Joe Dumars .50 1.25
C25C Joe Dumars .50 1.25
C26 Latrell Sprewell .50 1.25
C26B Latrell Sprewell .50 1.25
C26C Latrell Sprewell .50 1.25
C27 Clifford Robinson .50 1.25
C27B Clifford Robinson .50 1.25
C27C Clifford Robinson .50 1.25
XC28 Damon Stoudamire 1.25 3.00
XC29 Bryant Reeves .40 1.00
XC30 Michael Jordan 5.00 12.00

1995-96 Collector's Choice Debut Trade

TRADE: SER.2 STATED ODDS 1:30
*PLAYER'S CLUB: .75X TO 2X HI COLUM
PC TRADE: SER.2 STATED ODDS 1:144
*PC PLATINUM STARS: 8X TO 20X HI COLUMN
*PC PLATINUM RCs: 6X TO 15X HI
PCP TRADE: SER.2 STATED ODDS 1:720
T1 Magic Johnson .50 1.25
T2 Arvydas Sabonis .30 .75
T3 Kenny Anderson .12 .30
T4 Antonio McDyess .20 .50
T5 Sherman Douglas .10 .25
T6 Spud Webb .15 .40
T7 Glen Rice .15 .40
T8 Todd Day .10 .25
T9 John Williams .10 .25
T10 Chris Morris .10 .25
T11 Shawn Bradley .10 .25
T12 Dan Majerle .15 .40
T13 George McCloud .10 .25
T14 Derrick Coleman .12 .30
T15 Kendall Gill .10 .25
T16 Ricky Pierce .10 .25
T17 Robert Pack .10 .25
T18 Alonzo Mourning .25 .60
T19 Matt Geiger .10 .25
T20 Don MacLean .10 .25
T21 Willie Anderson .10 .25
T22 Oliver Miller .10 .25
T23 Tracy Murray .10 .25
T24 Ed Pinckney .10 .25
T25 Alvin Robertson .10 .25
T26 Anthony Avent .10 .25
T27 Blue Edwards .10 .25
T28 Kenny Gattison .10 .25
T29 Chris King .10 .25
T30 Eric Murdock .10 .25

1995-96 Collector's Choice Draft Trade

COMPLETE SET (10) 6.00 15.00
ONE SET PER DRAFT TRADE CARD VIA MAIL
TRADE: SER.1 STATED ODDS 1:144
D1 Joe Smith .60 1.50
D2 Antonio McDyess .60 1.50
D3 Jerry Stackhouse 1.50 4.00
D4 Rasheed Wallace 1.50 4.00
D5 Kevin Garnett 4.00 10.00
D6 Bryant Reeves .40 1.00
D7 Damon Stoudamire 1.25 3.00
D8 Shawn Respert .40 1.00
D9 Ed O'Bannon .40 1.00
D10 Kurt Thomas .50 1.25

1995-96 Collector's Choice Jordan He's Back

COMMON JORDAN (M1-M5) 1.25 3.00

1995-96 Collector's Choice Jordan He's Back Jumbos

COMPLETE SET (3) 10.00 25.00
COMMON CARD 4.00 10.00

1995-96 Collector's Choice Jordan Collection

COMPLETE SET (8) 10.00 25.00
COMPLETE SER.1 SET (4) 5.00 12.00
COMPLETE SER.2 SET (4) 5.00 12.00
COMMON SER.1 (JC1-JC8) 2.00 5.00
COMMON SER.2 (JC9-JC12) 2.00 5.00
STATED ODDS 1:11 PACKS

1996-97 Collector's Choice

COMPLETE SET (400) 12.00 30.00
COMP.FACT.SET (406) 15.00 40.00
COMPLETE SERIES 1 (200) 6.00 15.00
COMPLETE SERIES 2 (200) 6.00 15.00
COMP.UPDATE SET (30) 4.00 10.00
401-430 ONE UP.SET VIA TRADE CARD
401-430 STATED ODDS 1:71
1 Mookie Blaylock .20 .50
2 Grant Long .12 .30
3 Christian Laettner .20 .50
4 Craig Ehlo .12 .30
5 Ken Norman .12 .30
6 Stacey Augmon .15 .40
7 Dana Barros .12 .30
8 Dino Radja .12 .30
9 Rick Fox .12 .30
10 Eric Montross .12 .30
11 David Wesley .12 .30
12 Eric Williams .12 .30
13 Glen Rice .20 .50
14 Dell Curry .20 .50
15 Matt Geiger .12 .30
16 Scott Burrell .12 .30
17 George Zidek .12 .30
18 Muggsy Bogues .20 .50
19 Ron Harper .15 .40
20 Steve Kerr .15 .40
21 Toni Kukoc .20 .50
22 Dennis Rodman .50 1.25
23 Michael Jordan 2.00 5.00
24 Luc Longley .15 .40
25 M.Jordan/V.Divac Bulls VT 2.00 5.00
26 Michael Jordan Bulls VT 2.00 5.00
27 Luc Longley Bulls VT .15 .40
28 Scottie Pippen Bulls VT .50 1.25
29 T.Kukoc/J.Howard Bulls VT .20 .50
30 Terrell Brandon .15 .40
31 Bobby Phills .12 .30
32 Tyrone Hill .12 .30
33 Michael Cage .12 .30
34 Bob Sura .12 .30
35 Tony Dumas .12 .30
36 Jim Jackson .12 .30
37 Loren Meyer .12 .30
38 Cherokee Parks .12 .30
39 Jamal Mashburn .20 .50
40 Popeye Jones .12 .30
41 LaPhonso Ellis .12 .30
42 Jalen Rose .15 .40
43 Antonio McDyess .20 .50
44 Tom Hammonds .12 .30
45 Mahmoud Abdul-Rauf .15 .40
46 Dale Ellis .15 .40
47 Joe Dumars .25 .60
48 Theo Ratliff .12 .30
49 Lindsey Hunter .12 .30
50 Terry Mills .12 .30
51 Don Reid .12 .30
52 B.J. Armstrong .15 .40
53 Bimbo Coles .12 .30
54 Joe Smith .15 .40
55 Chris Mullin .25 .60
56 Rony Seikaly .15 .40
57 Donyell Marshall .12 .30
58 Hakeem Olajuwon .40 1.00
59 Robert Horry .20 .50
60 Mario Elie .12 .30
61 Mark Bryant .12 .30
62 Chucky Brown .12 .30
63 Rik Smits .15 .40
64 Derrick McKey .12 .30
65 Eddie Johnson .12 .30
66 Mark Jackson .15 .40
67 Ricky Pierce .15 .40
68 Travis Best .12 .30
69 Rodney Rogers .12 .30
70 Brent Barry .15 .40
71 Lamond Murray .12 .30
72 Eric Piatkowski .12 .30
73 Pooh Richardson .12 .30
74 Cedric Ceballos .15 .40
75 Eddie Jones .20 .50
76 Anthony Peeler .12 .30
77 George Lynch .12 .30
78 Vlade Divac .20 .50
79 Rex Chapman .12 .30
80 Sasha Danilovic .12 .30
81 Kurt Thomas .12 .30
82 Keith Askins .12 .30
83 Walt Williams .12 .30
84 Vin Baker .15 .40
85 Shawn Respert .12 .30
86 Sherman Douglas .12 .30
87 Marty Conlon .12 .30
88 Johnny Newman .12 .30
89 Kevin Garnett .60 1.50
90 Andrew Lang .12 .30
91 Terry Porter .12 .30
92 Sam Mitchell .12 .30
93 Tom Gugliotta .12 .30
94 Spud Webb .15 .40
95 Kendall Gill .20 .50
96 Vern Fleming .12 .30
97 Shawn Bradley .12 .30
98 Yinka Dare .12 .30
99 Jayson Williams .12 .30
100 Kevin Edwards .12 .30
101 Charles Oakley .20 .50
102 Anthony Mason .15 .40
103 John Starks .20 .50
104 J.R. Reid .12 .30
105 Hubert Davis .12 .30
106 Gary Grant .12 .30
107 Nick Anderson .12 .30
108 Donald Royal .12 .30
109 Brian Shaw .12 .30
110 Brooks Thompson .12 .30
111 Anfernee Hardaway .50 1.25
112 Dennis Scott .15 .40
113 Anfernee Hardaway PEN .50 1.25
114 Anfernee Hardaway PEN .50 1.25
115 Anfernee Hardaway PEN .50 1.25
116 Anfernee Hardaway PEN .50 1.25
117 Anfernee Hardaway PEN .50 1.25
118 Derrick Coleman .15 .40
119 Rex Walters .12 .30
120 Sean Higgins .12 .30
121 Clarence Weatherspoon .12 .30
122 Jerry Stackhouse .25 .60
123 Elliot Perry .12 .30
124 Wayman Tisdale .15 .40
125 Wesley Person .12 .30
126 Charles Barkley .50 1.25
127 A.C. Green .15 .40
128 Harvey Grant .12 .30
129 Arvydas Sabonis .20 .50
130 Aaron McKie .12 .30
131 Gary Trent .12 .30
132 Buck Williams .20 .50
133 Billy Owens .12 .30
134 Brian Grant .15 .40
135 Corliss Williamson .12 .30
136 Tyus Edney .12 .30
137 Olden Polynice .12 .30
138 Avery Johnson .15 .40
139 Vinny Del Negro .12 .30
140 Sean Elliott .20 .50
141 Chuck Person .15 .40
142 Will Perdue .12 .30
143 Nate McMillan .12 .30
144 Vincent Askew .12 .30
145 Detlef Schrempf .20 .50
146 Hersey Hawkins .12 .30
147 Sharone Wright .12 .30
148 Zan Tabak .12 .30
149 Oliver Miller .12 .30
150 Doug Christie .12 .30
151 Damon Stoudamire .20 .50
152 Jeff Hornacek .15 .40
153 Chris Morris .12 .30
154 Antoine Carr .12 .30
155 Karl Malone .40 1.00
156 Adam Keefe .12 .30
157 Greg Anthony .12 .30
158 Blue Edwards .12 .30
159 Bryant Reeves .12 .30
160 Anthony Avent .12 .30
161 Lawrence Moten .12 .30
162 Calbert Cheaney .12 .30
163 Chris Webber .25 .60
164 Tim Legler .12 .30
165 Gheorghe Muresan .12 .30
166 Stacey Augmon FUND .15 .40
167 Dee Brown FUND .12 .30
168 Glen Rice FUND .20 .50
169 Scottie Pippen FUND .50 1.25
170 Danny Ferry FUND .12 .30
171 Jason Kidd FUND .30 .75
172 LaPhonso Ellis FUND .12 .30
173 Grant Hill FUND .30 .75
174 Chris Mullin FUND .25 .60
175 Clyde Drexler FUND .30 .75
176 Rik Smits FUND .15 .40
177 Loy Vaught FUND .12 .30
178 Nick Van Exel FUND .20 .50
179 Alonzo Mourning FUND .30 .75
180 Glenn Robinson FUND .20 .50
181 Isaiah Rider FUND .15 .40
182 Ed O'Bannon FUND .12 .30
183 Patrick Ewing FUND .30 .75
184 Shaquille O'Neal FUND .75 2.00
185 Derrick Coleman FUND .15 .40
186 Danny Manning FUND .15 .40
187 Clifford Robinson FUND .12 .30
188 Mitch Richmond FUND .25 .60
189 David Robinson FUND .40 1.00
190 Shawn Kemp FUND .30 .75
191 Oliver Miller FUND .12 .30
192 John Stockton FUND .40 1.00
193 Greg Anthony FUND .12 .30
194 Rasheed Wallace FUND .25 .60
195 Michael Jordan FUND 2.00 5.00
196 M.Jordan/M.Geiger CL .20 .50
197 E.Jones/A.McDyess CL .07 .20
198 A.Hardaway/K.Garnett CL .20 .50
199 D.Stoudamire/A.Johnson CL .07 .20
200 D.Robinson/C.Mullin CL .12 .30
201 Alan Henderson .12 .30
202 Steve Smith .15 .40
203 Donnie Boyce RC .20 .50
204 Priest Lauderdale RC .12 .30
205 Dikembe Mutombo .30 .75
206 Dee Brown .12 .30
207 Junior Burrough .12 .30
208 Todd Day .12 .30
209 Pervis Ellison .12 .30
210 Greg Minor .12 .30
211 Antoine Walker RC .30 .75
212 Rafael Addison .12 .30
213 Tony Delk RC .20 .50
214 Vlade Divac .20 .50
215 Anthony Goldwire .12 .30
216 Anthony Mason .15 .40
217 Dickey Simpkins .12 .30
218 Randy Brown .12 .30
219 Jud Buechler .12 .30
220 Jason Caffey .12 .30
221 Scottie Pippen .50 1.25
222 Bill Wennington .12 .30
223 Danny Ferry .12 .30
224 Antonio Lang .12 .30
225 Chris Mills .12 .30
226 Vitaly Potapenko RC .15 .40
227 Terry Davis .12 .30
228 Chris Gatling .12 .30
229 Jason Kidd .30 .75
230 George McCloud .12 .30
231 Eric Montross .12 .30
232 Samaki Walker RC .15 .40
233 Mark Jackson .15 .40
234 Ervin Johnson .12 .30
235 Sarunas Marciulionis .12 .30
236 Eric Murdock .12 .30
237 Ricky Pierce .12 .30
238 Bryant Stith .12 .30
239 Stacey Augmon .15 .40
240 Grant Hill .30 .75
241 Otis Thorpe .12 .30
242 Jerome Williams RC .15 .40
243 Andrew DeClercq .12 .30
244 Todd Fuller RC .12 .30
245 Mark Price .20 .50
246 Clifford Rozier .12 .30
247 Latrell Sprewell .20 .50
248 Charles Barkley .50 1.25
249 Clyde Drexler .30 .75
250 Othella Harrington RC .15 .40
251 Sam Mack .12 .30
252 Kevin Willis .15 .40
253 Erick Dampier RC .20 .50
254 Antonio Davis .12 .30
255 Dale Davis .12 .30
256 Duane Ferrell .12 .30
257 Reggie Miller .40 1.00
258 Jalen Rose .15 .40
259 Reggie Williams .12 .30
260 Terry Dehere .12 .30
261 Bo Outlaw .12 .30
262 Stanley Roberts .12 .30
263 Malik Sealy .12 .30
264 Loy Vaught .12 .30
265 Lorenzen Wright RC .15 .40
266 Corie Blount .12 .30
267 Kobe Bryant RC 10.00 25.00
268 Elden Campbell .12 .30
269 Derek Fisher RC .25 .60
270 Shaquille O'Neal .75 2.00
271 Nick Van Exel .20 .50
272 P.J. Brown .12 .30
273 Tim Hardaway .25 .60
274 Voshon Lenard RC .20 .50
275 Dan Majerle .20 .50
276 Alonzo Mourning .30 .75
277 Martin Muursepp RC .12 .30
278 Ray Allen RC 1.00 2.50
279 Elliot Perry .12 .30
280 Glenn Robinson .20 .50
281 Stephon Marbury RC .60 1.50
282 Cherokee Parks .12 .30
283 Doug West .12 .30
284 Micheal Williams .12 .30
285 Kerry Kittles RC .20 .50
286 Ed O'Bannon .12 .30
287 Robert Pack .12 .30
288 Khalid Reeves .12 .30
289 David Benoit .12 .30
290 Patrick Ewing .30 .75
291 Allan Houston .20 .50
292 Larry Johnson .25 .60
293 Dontae' Jones RC .15 .40
294 Walter McCarty RC .12 .30
295 John Wallace RC .15 .40
296 Charlie Ward .12 .30
297 Brian Evans RC .12 .30
298 Horace Grant .20 .50
299 Jon Koncak .12 .30
300 Felton Spencer .12 .30
301 Allen Iverson RC 3.00 8.00
302 Don MacLean .12 .30
303 Scott Williams .12 .30
304 Sam Cassell .15 .40
305 Michael Finley .20 .50
306 Robert Horry .20 .50
307 Kevin Johnson .20 .50
308 Joe Kleine .12 .30
309 Danny Manning .15 .40
310 Steve Nash RC 1.25 3.00
311 John Williams .12 .30
312 Kenny Anderson .15 .40
313 Randolph Childress .12 .30
314 Chris Dudley .12 .30
315 Jermaine O'Neal RC .30 .75
316 Isaiah Rider .15 .40
317 Clifford Robinson .20 .50
318 Rasheed Wallace .25 .60
319 Mahmoud Abdul-Rauf .15 .40
320 Duane Causwell .12 .30
321 Bobby Hurley .12 .30
322 Mitch Richmond .25 .60
323 Lionel Simmons .12 .30
324 Michael Smith .12 .30
325 Dominique Wilkins .30 .75
326 Cory Alexander .12 .30
327 Greg Anderson .12 .30
328 Carl Herrera .12 .30
329 David Robinson .40 1.00
330 Charles Smith .12 .30
331 Craig Ehlo .12 .30
332 Sherrell Ford .12 .30
333 Shawn Kemp .30 .75
334 Jim McIlvaine .12 .30
335 Gary Payton .30 .75
336 Sam Perkins .15 .40
337 Eric Snow RC .20 .50
338 David Wingate .12 .30
339 Marcus Camby RC .30 .75
340 Acie Earl .12 .30
341 Carlos Rogers .12 .30
342 Greg Ostertag .12 .30
343 Bryon Russell .12 .30
344 John Stockton .40 1.00
345 Jamie Watson .12 .30
346 Shareef Abdur-Rahim RC .30 .75
347 Doug Edwards .12 .30
348 George Lynch .12 .30
349 Eric Mobley .12 .30
350 Anthony Peeler .12 .30
351 Roy Rogers RC .15 .40
352 Juwan Howard .20 .50
353 Harvey Grant .12 .30
354 Tracy Murray .12 .30
355 Rod Strickland .20 .50
356 A.Hardaway/M.Jordan ONE .50 1.25
357 H.Olajuwon/S.O'Neal ONE .25 .60
358 J.Smith/S.Kemp ONE .15 .40
359 D.Schrempf/T.Kukoc ONE .08 .25
360 J.Jackson/Stackhouse ONE .15 .40
361 Bryant/Abdur-Rahim ONE 5.00 12.00
362 N.Anderson/M.Jordan AJ .30 .75
363 J.Dumars/M.Jordan AJ .30 .75
364 J.Starks/M.Jordan AJ .30 .75
365 R.Miller/M.Jordan AJ .50 1.25
366 G.Payton/M.Jordan AJ .40 1.00
367 Mookie Blaylock PLAY .20 .50
368 D.Radja/Fox/Wesley PLAY .07 .20
369 Glen Rice PLAY .20 .50
370 M.Jordan/S.Pippen PLAY .50 1.25
371 Terrell Brandon PLAY .15 .40
372 Jason Kidd PLAY .30 .75
373 Antonio McDyess PLAY .20 .50
374 Grant Hill PLAY .30 .75
375 Joe Smith PLAY .15 .40
376 Barkley/Olaj/Drexler PLAY .30 .75
377 Reggie Miller PLAY .40 1.00
378 L.A. Clippers PLAY .07 .20
379 Nick Van Exel PLAY .20 .50
380 Alonzo Mourning PLAY .30 .75
381 Ray Allen PLAY .25 .60
382 Stephon Marbury PLAY .25 .60
383 Shawn Bradley PLAY .12 .30
384 Patrick Ewing PLAY .30 .75
385 Anfernee Hardaway PLAY .50 1.25
386 Jerry Stackhouse PLAY .25 .60
387 Danny Manning PLAY .15 .40
388 Clifford Robinson PLAY .20 .50
389 Tyus Edney PLAY .12 .30
390 San Antonio Spurs PLAY .07 .20
391 Shawn Kemp PLAY .30 .75
392 Toronto Raptors PLAY .07 .20
393 John Stockton PLAY .40 1.00
394 Greg Anthony PLAY .12 .30
395 Gheorghe Muresan PLAY .12 .30
396 Checklist .07 .20
397 Checklist .07 .20
398 Checklist .07 .20
399 Checklist .07 .20
400 Checklist .07 .20
401 Henry James TRADE .20 .50
402 Shawn Bradley TRADE .20 .50
403 Sasha Danilovic TRADE .20 .50
404 Michael Finley TRADE .30 .75
405 A.C. Green TRADE .25 .60
406 Derek Harper TRADE .25 .60
407 Khalid Reeves TRADE .20 .50
408 Aaron McKie TRADE .20 .50
409 Matt Maloney TRADE RC .25 .60
410 Darrick Martin TRADE .20 .50
411 Robert Horry TRADE .30 .75
412 Travis Knight TRADE RC .25 .60
413 Isaac Austin TRADE .20 .50
414 Jamal Mashburn TRADE .30 .75
415 Armon Gilliam TRADE .20 .50
416 Chris Carr TRADE RC .30 .75
417 Dean Garrett TRADE RC .30 .75
418 Shane Heal TRADE RC .30 .75
419 Sam Cassell TRADE .25 .60
420 Chris Gatling TRADE .20 .50
421 Jim Jackson TRADE .20 .50
422 Chris Childs TRADE .20 .50
423 Rony Seikaly TRADE .25 .60
424 Gerald Wilkins TRADE .25 .60
425 Cedric Ceballos TRADE .25 .60
426 Tony Dumas TRADE .20 .50
427 Jason Kidd TRADE .50 1.25
428 Popeye Jones TRADE .20 .50
429 Walt Williams TRADE .20 .50
430 Jaren Jackson TRADE .20 .50
NNO Michael Jordan 5x7 DD 4.00 10.00
NNO Michael Jordan 5x7 MM 4.00 10.00
NNO Update Trade Card 2.00 5.00

1996-97 Collector's Choice Crash the Game Scoring 1

COMPLETE SILVER SET (60) 20.00 50.00
SER.1 STATED ODDS 1:5
*GOLD CARDS: 1.25X TO 3X HI COLUMN
GOLD: SER.1 STATED ODDS 1:49
*SILVER RED.CARDS: .5X TO 1.25X SILVER HI
*GOLD RED.CARDS: 1.5X TO 4X SILVER HI
ONE RED.CARD PER WINNER BY MAIL
C1 Mookie Blaylock .60 1.50
C1B Mookie Blaylock .60 1.50
C2 Dino Radja .40 1.00
C2B Dino Radja .40 1.00
C3 Glen Rice .60 1.50
C3B Glen Rice .60 1.50
C4 Scottie Pippen 1.50 4.00
C4B Scottie Pippen 1.50 4.00
C5 Terrell Brandon .50 1.25
C5B Terrell Brandon .50 1.25
C6 Jason Kidd 1.00 2.50
C6B Jason Kidd 1.00 2.50
C7 Antonio McDyess .60 1.50
C7B Antonio McDyess .60 1.50
C8 Joe Dumars .75 2.00
C8B Joe Dumars .75 2.00
C9 Joe Smith .50 1.25
C9B Joe Smith .50 1.25
C10 Hakeem Olajuwon 1.25 3.00
C10B Hakeem Olajuwon 1.25 3.00
C11 Reggie Miller 1.25 3.00
C11B Reggie Miller 1.25 3.00
C12 Loy Vaught .40 1.00
C12B Loy Vaught .40 1.00
C13 Cedric Ceballos .50 1.25
C13B Cedric Ceballos .50 1.25
C14 Alonzo Mourning 1.00 2.50
C14B Alonzo Mourning 1.00 2.50
C15 Vin Baker .50 1.25
C15B Vin Baker .50 1.25
C16 Kevin Garnett 2.00 5.00
C16B Kevin Garnett 2.00 5.00
C17 Ed O'Bannon .40 1.00
C17B Ed O'Bannon .40 1.00
C18 Patrick Ewing 1.00 2.50
C18B Patrick Ewing 1.00 2.50
C19 Anfernee Hardaway 1.50 4.00
C19B Anfernee Hardaway 1.50 4.00
C20 Clarence Weatherspoon .40 1.00
C20B Clarence Weatherspoon .40 1.00
C21 Kevin Johnson .60 1.50
C21B Kevin Johnson .60 1.50
C22 Clifford Robinson .60 1.50
C22B Clifford Robinson .60 1.50
C23 Mitch Richmond .75 2.00
C23B Mitch Richmond .75 2.00
C24 Sean Elliott .60 1.50
C24B Sean Elliott .60 1.50
C25 Shawn Kemp 1.00 2.50
C25B Shawn Kemp 1.00 2.50
C26 Damon Stoudamire .60 1.50
C26B Damon Stoudamire .60 1.50
C27 John Stockton 1.25 3.00
C27B John Stockton 1.25 3.00
C28 Bryant Reeves .40 1.00
C28B Bryant Reeves .40 1.00
C29 Rasheed Wallace .75 2.00
C29B Rasheed Wallace .75 2.00
C30 Michael Jordan 6.00 15.00
C30B Michael Jordan 6.00 15.00

1996-97 Collector's Choice Crash the Game Scoring 2

SER.2 STATED ODDS 1:5
*GOLD CARDS: 1.25X TO 3X HI COLUMN
GOLD: SER.2 STATED ODDS 1:49
*SILVER RED.CARDS: .5X TO 1.25X SILVER HI
*GOLD RED.CARDS: 1.5X TO 4X SILVER HI
ONE RED.CARD PER WINNER BY MAIL
C1 Steve Smith .50 1.25
C1B Steve Smith .50 1.25
C2 Dana Barros .40 1.00
C2B Dana Barros .40 1.00
C3 Tony Delk .60 1.50

C3B Tony Delk .60 1.50
C4 Toni Kukoc .60 1.50
C4B Toni Kukoc .60 1.50
C5 Bobby Phills .40 1.00
C5B Bobby Phills .40 1.00
C6 Jamal Mashburn .60 1.50
C6B Jamal Mashburn .60 1.50
C7 LaPhonso Ellis .40 1.00
C7B LaPhonso Ellis .40 1.00
C8 Jerome Williams .50 1.25
C8B Jerome Williams .50 1.25
C9 Latrell Sprewell .60 1.50
C9B Latrell Sprewell .60 1.50
C10 Clyde Drexler 1.00 2.50
C10B Clyde Drexler 1.00 2.50
C11 Dale Davis .40 1.00
C11B Dale Davis .40 1.00
C12 Brent Barry .50 1.25
C12B Brent Barry .50 1.25
C13 Nick Van Exel .60 1.50
C13B Nick Van Exel .60 1.50
C14 Sasha Danilovic .40 1.00
C14B Sasha Danilovic .40 1.00
C15 Glenn Robinson .60 1.50
C15B Glenn Robinson .60 1.50
C16 Stephon Marbury 2.00 5.00
C16B Stephon Marbury 2.00 5.00
C17 Shawn Bradley .40 1.00
C17B Shawn Bradley .40 1.00
C18 John Wallace .50 1.25
C18B John Wallace .50 1.25
C19 Anfernee Hardaway 1.50 4.00
C19B Anfernee Hardaway 1.50 4.00
C20 Jerry Stackhouse .75 2.00
C20B Jerry Stackhouse .75 2.00
C21 Danny Manning .50 1.25
C21B Danny Manning .50 1.25
C22 Arvydas Sabonis .60 1.50
C22B Arvydas Sabonis .60 1.50
C23 Brian Grant .50 1.25
C23B Brian Grant .50 1.25
C24 David Robinson 1.25 3.00
C24B David Robinson 1.25 3.00
C25 Gary Payton 1.00 2.50
C25B Gary Payton 1.00 2.50
C26 Marcus Camby 1.00 2.50
C26B Marcus Camby 1.00 2.50
C27 Karl Malone 1.25 3.00
C27B Karl Malone 1.25 3.00
C28 Shareef Abdur-Rahim 1.00 2.50
C28B Shareef Abdur-Rahim 1.00 2.50
C29 Juwan Howard .60 1.50
C29B Juwan Howard .60 1.50
C30 Michael Jordan 6.00 15.00
C30B Michael Jordan 6.00 15.00

1996-97 Collector's Choice Draft Trade

COMPLETE SET (10) 10.00 20.00
TRADE: SER.1 STATED ODDS 1:144
DRAFT TRADE EXPIRATION: 5/9/97
DR1 Allen Iverson 5.00 12.00
DR2 Marcus Camby 1.00 2.50
DR3 Shareef Abdur-Rahim 1.00 2.50
DR4 Stephon Marbury 2.00 5.00
DR5 Ray Allen 3.00 8.00
DR6 Antoine Walker 1.00 2.50
DR7 Lorenzen Wright .50 1.25
DR8 Kerry Kittles .60 1.50
DR9 Samaki Walker .50 1.25
DR10 Erick Dampier .60 1.50
NNO Expired Trade Card .40 1.00

1996-97 Collector's Choice Factory Blow-Ups

COMPLETE SET (4) 2.50 6.00
1 Michael Jordan 2.50 6.00
2 Shawn Kemp .40 1.00
3 Anfernee Hardaway .60 1.50
4 Michael Jordan
Anfernee Hardaway 1.50 4.00

1996-97 Collector's Choice Game Face

COMPLETE SET (10) 4.00 10.00
ONE PER SPECIAL SER.1 RETAIL PACK
GF1 Anfernee Hardaway 1.00 2.50
GF2 Michael Jordan 4.00 10.00
GF3 Shawn Kemp .60 1.50
GF4 Alonzo Mourning .60 1.50
GF5 Cherokee Parks .25 .60
GF6 Avery Johnson .30 .75
GF7 LaPhonso Ellis .25 .60
GF8 Rasheed Wallace .50 1.25
GF9 Jim Jackson .25 .60
GF10 Larry Johnson .50 1.25

1996-97 Collector's Choice Jordan A Cut Above

COMPLETE SET (10) 8.00 20.00
COMMON JORDAN (CA1-CA10) 1.00 2.50

1996-97 Collector's Choice Jordan A Cut Above Jumbos

COMP.FACT SET (10) 8.00 20.00
COMMON CARD (CA1-CA10) 1.00 2.50

1996-97 Collector's Choice Memorable Moments

COMPLETE SET (10) 5.00 12.00
ONE PER SPECIAL SER.2 RETAIL PACK
1 Michael Jordan 4.00 10.00
2 Nick Van Exel .40 1.00
3 Karl Malone .75 2.00
4 Latrell Sprewell .40 1.00
5 Anfernee Hardaway 1.00 2.50
6 Glenn Robinson .40 1.00
7 Shaquille O'Neal 1.50 4.00
8 Damon Stoudamire .40 1.00
9 Clyde Drexler .60 1.50
10 Shawn Kemp .60 1.50

1996-97 Collector's Choice Mini-Cards

COMPLETE SET (60) 8.00 20.00
COMPLETE SERIES 1 (30) 3.00 8.00
COMPLETE SERIES 2 (30) 5.00 12.00
*GOLD: 2.5X TO 6X HI COLUMN
GOLD: SER.1/2 STATED ODDS 1:35
SKIP-NUMBERED SET
M2 Walters/Hornacek/Blaylock .20 .50
M5 Schrempf/Kukoc/Radja .20 .50
M6 Amaya/S.Wright/E.Williams .12 .30
M10 Edney/O'Bannon/Zidek .12 .30
M13 Ratliff/Bradley/Longley .15 .40
M22 Phills/A.Johnson/Abdul-Rauf .15 .40
M23 P.Jones/C.Morris/Hammonds .12 .30
M25 Hurley/Laettner/G.Hill .30 .75
M28 Douglas/Coleman/Seikaly .15 .40
M30 Van Exel/Starks/Cassell .20 .50
M33 Geiger/D.Scott/Best .15 .40
M36 Ceballos/Rider/B.Barry .15 .40
M37 Kidd/K.Johnson/L.Murray .30 .75
M38 Mullin/J.Williams/Dehere .25 .60
M39 Sabonis/Danilovic/Divac .20 .50
M43 T.Hill/B.Grant/K.Thomas .15 .40
M44 McKey/Horry/Askins .20 .50
M46 Childress/D.Rob/Respert .40 1.00
M49 Day/O.Miller/Lang .12 .30
M56 Curry/Coles/Oakley .20 .50
M57 Wallace/Stackhouse/Reid .25 .60
M66 Dumars/Drexler/Green .30 .75
M67 Gill/N.Anderson/McKie .20 .50
M75 Ferry/M.Jackson/Rivers .15 .40
M78 Jordan/Hardaway/Kemp 2.00 5.00
M79 Rose/Webber/J.King .25 .60
M83 Rodman/Barkley/Malone .75 2.00
M85 Augmon/Johnson/Anthony .25 .60
M86 McMillan/Gugliotta/B.Edwards .12 .30
M90 J.Jackson/G.Rob/Cheaney .20 .50
M92 Norman/West/K.Edwards .12 .30
M93 Smith/T.Hard/Armstrong .25 .60
M99 Rice/Manning/Perkins .20 .50
M102 Kerr/R.Miller/Barros .40 1.00
M109 S.Walker/L.Wright/Minor .15 .40
M110 L.Ellis/K.Willis/W'spoon .15 .40
M111 McDyess/Sprewell/Caffey .20 .50
M112A Stith/Del Negro/K.Anderson .15 .40
M112B Sura/R.Rogers/Polynice .12 .30
M113 Hunter/E.Jones/R.Harper .20 .50
M115 Thorpe/Stockton/Carr .40 1.00
M125 Smits/Olajuwon/Muresan .40 1.00
M129 Bryant/J.O'Neal/Garnett 8.00 20.00
M135 Mourning/Mut/Ewing .30 .75
M137 Baker/Mashburn/Pippen .50 1.25
M140 Marbury/Hancock/Person .60 1.50
M146 Houston/Camby/Kittles .30 .75
M148 Wallace/McCarty/Walker .30 .75
M149 H.Grant/Campbell/D.Davis .20 .50
M150 Royal/Legler/Elie .12 .30
M151 Shaw/A.Davis/PJ Brown .12 .30
M152 Iverson/Smith/S.O'Neal 1.50 4.00
M159 Robinson/Burrell/Allen 1.00 2.50
M161 Richmond/Perdue/Hawk .25 .60
M167 Payton/Brandon/Elliott .30 .75
M170 Christie/Newman/T.Dumas .12 .30
M175 Rahim/Mills/K.Reeves .30 .75
M176 Moten/M.Smith/Russell .12 .30
M177 B.Reeves/Finley/Stoudamire .20 .50
M178 Howard/Vaught/T.Mills .20 .50

1996-97 Collector's Choice Stick Ums 1

COMPLETE SET (30) 3.00 8.00
SER.1 STATED ODDS 1:4
S1 Mookie Blaylock .20 .50
S2 Dana Barros .12 .30
S3 Scott Burrell .12 .30
S4 Dennis Rodman .50 1.25
S5 Terrell Brandon .15 .40
S6 Jamal Mashburn .20 .50
S7 LaPhonso Ellis .12 .30
S8 Grant Hill .30 .75
S9 Joe Smith .15 .40
S10 Hakeem Olajuwon .40 1.00
S11 Rik Smits .15 .40
S12 Brent Barry .15 .40
S13 Nick Van Exel .20 .50
S14 Sasha Danilovic .12 .30
S15 Vin Baker .15 .40
S16 Kevin Garnett .60 1.50
S17 Shawn Bradley .12 .30
S18 Patrick Ewing .30 .75
S19 Anfernee Hardaway .50 1.25
S20 Clarence Weatherspoon .12 .30
S21 Charles Barkley .50 1.25
S22 Clifford Robinson .20 .50
S23 Mitch Richmond .25 .60
S24 David Robinson .40 1.00
S25 Shawn Kemp .30 .75
S26 Damon Stoudamire .20 .50
S27 Karl Malone .40 1.00
S28 Bryant Reeves .12 .30
S29 Gheorghe Muresan .12 .30
S30 Michael Jordan 2.00 5.00

1996-97 Collector's Choice Stick Ums 2

COMPLETE SET (30) 3.00 8.00
SER.2 STATED ODDS 1:3
S1 Steve Smith .15 .40
S2 Dino Radja .12 .30
S3 Glen Rice .20 .50
S4 Toni Kukoc .20 .50
S5 Bobby Phills .12 .30
S6 Jason Kidd .30 .75
S7 Antonio McDyess .30 .75
S8 Joe Dumars .25 .60
S9 Latrell Sprewell .20 .50
S10 Clyde Drexler .30 .75
S11 Reggie Miller .40 1.00
S12 Loy Vaught .12 .30
S13 Eddie Jones .20 .50
S14 Alonzo Mourning .30 .75
S15 Glenn Robinson .20 .50
S16 Tom Gugliotta .12 .30
S17 Ed O'Bannon .12 .30
S18 John Starks .20 .50
S19 Anfernee Hardaway .50 1.25
S20 Jerry Stackhouse .25 .60
S21 Kevin Johnson .20 .50
S22 Arvydas Sabonis .20 .50
S23 Bryan Grant .15 .40
S24 Sean Elliott .20 .50
S25 Gary Payton .30 .75
S26 Zan Tabak .12 .30
S27 John Stockton .40 1.00
S28 Greg Anthony .12 .30
S29 Juwan Howard .20 .50
S30 Michael Jordan 2.00 5.00

1996-97 Collector's Choice Chicago Bulls

COMP.FACT SET (11) 3.00 8.00
B1 Ron Harper
Michael Jordan
Steve Kerr 1.50 4.00
B2 Toni Kukoc
Scottie Pippen
Dennis Rodman 1.25 3.00
CH1 Jason Caffey .20 .50
CH2 Ron Harper .25 .60
CH3 Michael Jordan 1.50 4.00
CH4 Steve Kerr .25 .60
CH5 Toni Kukoc .30 .75
CH6 Luc Longley .25 .60
CH7 Scottie Pippen .75 2.00
CH8 Dennis Rodman .75 2.00
CH9 Bill Wennington .20 .50

1996-97 Collector's Choice Houston Rockets

COMP.FACT SET (9) 1.50 4.00
HT1 Charles Barkley .75 2.00
HT2 Matt Bullard .20 .50
HT3 Clyde Drexler .50 1.25
HT4 Mario Elie .20 .50
HT5 Othella Harrington .25 .60
HT6 Sam Mack .20 .50
HT7 Matt Maloney .25 .60
HT8 Hakeem Olajuwon .60 1.50
HT9 Kevin Willis .25 .60
NNO Houston Rockets Blow-Up .75 2.00

1996-97 Collector's Choice Los Angeles Lakers

COMP.FACT SET (11) 8.00 20.00
L1 Kobe Bryant
Elden Campbell
Derek Fisher 8.00 20.00
L2 Eddie Jones
Shaquille O'Neal
Nick Van Exel .75 2.00
LA1 Corie Blount .20 .50
LA2 Kobe Bryant 20.00 50.00
LA3 Elden Campbell .20 .50
LA4 Derek Fisher .40 1.00
LA5 Eddie Jones .30 .75
LA6 Travis Knight .25 .60
LA7 Shaquille O'Neal 1.25 3.00
LA8 Byron Scott .30 .75
LA9 Nick Van Exel .30 .75

1996-97 Collector's Choice Miami Heat Team Set

COMP.FACT SET (9) 1.50 4.00
MI1 Keith Askins .20 .50
MI2 P.J. Brown .20 .50
MI3 Sasha Danilovic .20 .50
MI4 Tim Hardaway .40 1.00
MI5 Voshon Lenard .30 .75
MI6 Dan Majerle .30 .75
MI7 Alonzo Mourning .50 1.25
MI8 Martin Muursepp .20 .50
MI9 Kurt Thomas .20 .50
NNO Miami Heat BW Blow-Up .60 1.50

1996-97 Collector's Choice Orlando Magic Team Set

COMP. FACT SET (11) 1.50 4.00
O1 Nick Anderson
Horace Grant
Anfernee Hardaway .40 1.00
O2 Dennis Scott
Rony Seikaly
Brian Shaw .20 .50
OR1 Nick Anderson .20 .50
OR2 Brian Evans .20 .50
OR3 Horace Grant .30 .75
OR4 Anfernee Hardaway .75 2.00
OR5 Derek Strong .20 .50
OR6 Rony Seikaly .25 .60
OR7 Dennis Scott .25 .60
OR8 Brian Shaw .20 .50
OR9 Gerald Wilkins .25 .60

1996-97 Collector's Choice Penny! Blow Ups

COMPLETE SET (5) 5.00 12.00
COMMON CARD (113-117) 1.25 3.00

1996-97 Collector's Choice San Antoino Spurs

COMP.FACT SET (9) 1.50 4.00
ST1 Cory Alexander .20 .50
ST2 Vinny Del Negro .20 .50
ST3 Sean Elliott .30 .75
ST4 Carl Herrera .20 .50
ST5 Avery Johnson .25 .60
ST6 Will Perdue .20 .50
ST7 David Robinson .60 1.50
ST8 Charles Smith .20 .50
ST9 Dominique Wilkins .50 1.25
NNO San Antonio Spurs Blow-Up .60 1.50

1996-97 Collector's Choice Seattle Supersonics

COMP.FACT SET (11) 1.50 4.00
B1 Hersey Hawkins
Shawn Kemp
Nate McMillan .60 1.50
B2 Gary Payton
Sam Perkins
Detlef Schrempf .40 1.00
ST1 Craig Ehlo .20 .50
ST2 Hersey Hawkins .20 .50
ST3 Shawn Kemp .50 1.25
ST4 Jim McIlvaine .20 .50
ST5 Nate McMillan .20 .50
ST6 Gary Payton .50 1.25
ST7 Sam Perkins .25 .60
ST8 Detlef Schrempf .30 .75
ST9 Eric Snow .30 .75

1997-98 Collector's Choice

COMPLETE SET (400) 12.00 30.00
COMP.FACTORY SET (415) 15.00 40.00
COMPLETE SERIES 1 (200) 6.00 15.00
COMPLETE SERIES 2 (200) 6.00 15.00
1 Mookie Blaylock .12 .30
2 Dikembe Mutombo .20 .50
3 Eldridge Recasner .07 .20
4 Christian Laettner .12 .30
5 Tyrone Corbin .07 .20
6 Antoine Walker .12 .30
7 Eric Williams .07 .20
8 Dana Barros .07 .20
9 David Wesley .10 .25
10 Dino Radja .07 .20
11 Vlade Divac .12 .30
12 Dell Curry .10 .25
13 Muggsy Bogues .10 .25
14 Tony Smith .07 .20
15 Glen Rice .12 .30
16 Anthony Mason .10 .25
17 Dennis Rodman .30 .75
18 Brian Williams .10 .25
19 Toni Kukoc .15 .40
20 Jason Caffey .07 .20
21 Steve Kerr .15 .40
22 Luc Longley .12 .30
23 Michael Jordan 1.25 3.00
24 Chris Mills .07 .20
25 Tyrone Hill .10 .25
26 Vitaly Potapenko .07 .20
27 Bob Sura .07 .20
28 Robert Pack .07 .20
29 Ed O'Bannon .07 .20
30 Michael Finley .12 .30
31 Shawn Bradley .07 .20
32 Khalid Reeves .07 .20
33 Antonio McDyess .12 .30
34 Ervin Johnson .07 .20
35 Dale Ellis .10 .25
36 Bryant Stith .07 .20
37 Tom Hammonds .07 .20
38 Otis Thorpe .10 .25
39 Lindsey Hunter .07 .20
40 Grant Long .07 .20
41 Aaron McKie .07 .20
42 Randolph Childress .07 .20
43 Scott Burrell .07 .20
44 Bimbo Coles .07 .20
45 B.J. Armstrong .07 .20
46 Mark Price .12 .30
47 Latrell Sprewell .15 .40
48 Felton Spencer .07 .20
49 Charles Barkley .30 .75
50 Mario Elie .07 .20
51 Clyde Drexler .20 .50
52 Kevin Willis .10 .25
53 Antonio Davis .10 .25
54 Reggie Miller .25 .60
55 Dale Davis .10 .25
56 Mark Jackson .10 .25
57 Erick Dampier .10 .25
58 Pooh Richardson .07 .20
59 Terry Dehere .07 .20
60 Brent Barry .10 .25
61 Loy Vaught .10 .25
62 Lorenzen Wright .07 .20
63 Eddie Jones .12 .30
64 Kobe Bryant 1.25 3.00
65 Elden Campbell .07 .20
66 Corie Blount .07 .20
67 Shaquille O'Neal .40 1.00
68 Dan Majerle .12 .30
69 P.J. Brown .07 .20
70 Tim Hardaway .15 .40
71 Isaac Austin .07 .20
72 Jamal Mashburn .10 .25
73 Ray Allen .25 .60
74 Glenn Robinson .12 .30
75 Armon Gilliam .07 .20
76 Johnny Newman .07 .20
77 Elliot Perry .07 .20
78 Sherman Douglas .07 .20
79 Doug West .07 .20
80 Kevin Garnett .30 .75
81 Sam Mitchell .07 .20
82 Tom Gugliotta .10 .25
83 Terry Porter .07 .20
84 Chris Carr .07 .20
85 Kevin Edwards .07 .20
86 Jayson Williams .07 .20
87 Kendall Gill .10 .25
88 Kerry Kittles .10 .25
89 Chris Gatling .07 .20
90 John Starks .12 .30
91 Charlie Ward .10 .25
92 Larry Johnson .15 .40
93 Charles Oakley .10 .25
94 Chris Childs .07 .20
95 Allan Houston .12 .30
96 Horace Grant .12 .30
97 Darrell Armstrong .07 .20
98 Rony Seikaly .10 .25
99 Dennis Scott .10 .25
100 Anfernee Hardaway .30 .75
101 Brian Shaw .10 .25
102 Jerry Stackhouse .12 .30
103 Rex Walters .07 .20
104 Don MacLean .07 .20
105 Derrick Coleman .12 .30
106 Lucious Harris .07 .20
107 Clarence Weatherspoon .07 .20
108 Cedric Ceballos .10 .25
109 Danny Manning .10 .25
110 Jason Kidd .20 .50
111 Loren Meyer .07 .20
112 Wesley Person .10 .25
113 Steve Nash .30 .75
114 Isaiah Rider .10 .25
115 Stacey Augmon .10 .25
116 Arvydas Sabonis .15 .40
117 Kenny Anderson .10 .25
118 Jermaine O'Neal .10 .25
119 Gary Trent .07 .20
120 Michael Smith .07 .20
121 Kevin Gamble .07 .20
122 Olden Polynice .07 .20
123 Billy Owens .07 .20
124 Corliss Williamson .07 .20
125 Cory Alexander .07 .20
126 Vinny Del Negro .10 .25
127 Sean Elliott .10 .25
128 Will Perdue .07 .20
129 Carl Herrera .07 .20
130 Shawn Kemp .20 .50
131 Hersey Hawkins .10 .25
132 Nate McMillan .07 .20
133 Craig Ehlo .07 .20
134 Detlef Schrempf .12 .30
135 Sam Perkins .10 .25
136 Sharone Wright .07 .20
137 Doug Christie .07 .20
138 Popeye Jones .07 .20
139 Shawn Respert .07 .20
140 Marcus Camby .12 .30
141 Adam Keefe .07 .20
142 Karl Malone .25 .60
143 John Stockton .25 .60
144 Greg Ostertag .07 .20
145 Chris Morris .07 .20
146 Shareef Abdur-Rahim .12 .30
147 Roy Rogers .07 .20
148 George Lynch .07 .20
149 Anthony Peeler .07 .20
150 Lee Mayberry .07 .20
151 Calbert Cheaney .10 .25
152 Harvey Grant .07 .20
153 Rod Strickland .10 .25
154 Tracy Murray .07 .20
155 Chris Webber .15 .40
156 Mookie Blaylock/Hawks GN .20 .50
157 A.Walker/Celtics GN .12 .30
158 Glen Rice/Hornets GN .12 .30
159 M.Jordan/Bulls GN 1.25 3.00
160 Tyrone Hill/Cavaliers GN .10 .25
161 Shawn Bradley/Mavericks GN .12 .30
162 Antonio McDyess/Nuggets GN .12 .30
163 G.Hill/Pistons GN .20 .50
164 Latrell Sprewell/Warriors GN .15 .40
165 H.Olajuwon/Rockets GN .30 .75
166 Reggie Miller/Pacers GN .25 .60
167 Loy Vaught/Clippers GN .10 .25
168 K.Bryant/Lakers GN 1.25 3.00
169 Mourning/Heat GN .20 .50
170 R.Allen/Bucks GN .25 .60
171 K.Garnett/T'wolves GN .30 .75
172 Kendall Gill/Nets GN .10 .25
173 Patrick Ewing/Knicks GN .20 .50
174 A.Hardaway/Magic GN .30 .75
175 A.Iverson/76ers GN .40 1.00
176 J.Kidd/Suns GN .20 .50
177 Rasheed Wallace/Trail Blazers GN .15 .40
178 Mitch Richmond/Kings GN .15 .40
179 D.Robinson/Spurs GN .25 .60
180 G.Payton/SuperSonics GN .20 .50
181 D.Stoudamire/Raptors GN .12 .30
182 Karl Malone/Jazz GN .25 .60
183 S.Abdur-Rahim/Griz. GN .12 .30
184 C.Webber/Wizards GN .15 .40
185 M.Jordan/97 Finals GN 1.25 3.00
186 Michael Jordan C23 .60 1.50
187 Michael Jordan C23 .60 1.50
188 Michael Jordan C23 .60 1.50
189 Michael Jordan C23 .60 1.50
190 Michael Jordan C23 .60 1.50
191 Michael Jordan C23 .60 1.50
192 Michael Jordan C23 .60 1.50
193 Michael Jordan C23 .60 1.50
194 Michael Jordan C23 .60 1.50
195 Michael Jordan C23 .60 1.50
196 Checklist #1 .07 .20
197 Checklist #2 .07 .20
198 Checklist #3 .07 .20
199 Checklist #4 .07 .20
200 Checklist #5 .07 .20
201 Steve Smith .10 .25
202 Chris Crawford RC .12 .30
203 Ed Gray RC .12 .30
204 Alan Henderson .07 .20
205 Walter McCarty .07 .20
206 Dee Brown .10 .25
207 Chauncey Billups RC .40 1.00
208 Ron Mercer RC .15 .40
209 Travis Knight .07 .20
210 Andrew DeClercq .07 .20
211 Tyus Edney .07 .20
212 Matt Geiger .07 .20
213 Tony Delk .10 .25
214 J.R. Reid .10 .25
215 Bobby Phills .10 .25
216 David Wesley .10 .25
217 Ron Harper .12 .30
218 Scottie Pippen .30 .75
219 Scott Burrell .07 .20
220 Keith Booth RC .10 .25
221 Bill Wennington .07 .20
222 Shawn Kemp .20 .50
223 Zydrunas Ilgauskas .12 .30
224 Brevin Knight RC .12 .30
225 Danny Ferry .07 .20
226 Derek Anderson RC .12 .30
227 Wesley Person .10 .25
228 A.C. Green .10 .25
229 Samaki Walker .07 .20
230 Hubert Davis .07 .20
231 Erick Strickland RC .07 .20
232 Dennis Scott .10 .25
233 Tony Battie RC .12 .30
234 LaPhonso Ellis .10 .25
235 Eric Williams .07 .20
236 Bobby Jackson RC .15 .40
237 Anthony Goldwire .07 .20
238 Danny Fortson RC .12 .30
239 Joe Dumars .15 .40
240 Grant Hill .20 .50
241 Malik Sealy .10 .25
242 Brian Williams .10 .25
243 Theo Ratliff .10 .25
244 Scot Pollard RC .10 .25
245 Erick Dampier .10 .25
246 Duane Ferrell .07 .20
247 Joe Smith .10 .25
248 Todd Fuller .07 .20
249 Adonal Foyle RC .10 .25
250 Othella Harrington .10 .20
251 Matt Maloney .07 .20
252 Hakeem Olajuwon .25 .60
253 Rodrick Rhodes RC .10 .25
254 Eddie Johnson .10 .25
255 Brent Price .07 .20
256 Austin Croshere RC .10 .25
257 Derrick McKey .07 .20
258 Chris Mullin .15 .40
259 Rik Smits .10 .25
260 Jalen Rose .10 .25
261 Darrick Martin .07 .20
262 Lamond Murray .07 .20
263 Maurice Taylor RC .10 .25
264 Rodney Rogers .10 .25
265 James Robinson .07 .20
266 Rick Fox .10 .25
267 Nick Van Exel .12 .30
268 Sean Rooks .07 .20
269 Derek Fisher .12 .30
270 Jon Barry .07 .20
271 Robert Horry .12 .30
272 Terry Mills .07 .20
273 Charles Smith RC .10 .25
274 Alonzo Mourning .20 .50
275 Voshon Lenard .07 .20
276 Todd Day .07 .20
277 Ervin Johnson .07 .20
278 Terrell Brandon .10 .25
279 Michael Curry .07 .20
280 Andrew Lang .07 .20
281 Tyrone Hill .10 .25
282 Stephon Marbury .15 .40
283 Cherokee Parks .07 .20
284 Stanley Roberts .07 .20
285 Paul Grant RC .07 .20
286 David Benoit .07 .20
287 Lucious Harris .07 .20
288 Don MacLean .07 .20
289 Sam Cassell .10 .25
290 Keith Van Horn RC .20 .50
291 Patrick Ewing .20 .50
292 Walter McCarty .07 .20
293 Chris Dudley .07 .20
294 Chris Mills .07 .20
295 Buck Williams .07 .20
296 Nick Anderson .10 .25
297 Derek Strong .07 .20
298 Gerald Wilkins .07 .20
299 Johnny Taylor RC .07 .20
300 Derek Harper .10 .25
301 Anthony Parker RC .12 .30
302 Allen Iverson .40 1.00
303 Jim Jackson .10 .25
304 Eric Montross .07 .20
305 Tim Thomas RC .15 .40
306 Kebu Stewart RC .12 .30
307 Rex Chapman .07 .20
308 Tom Chambers .10 .25
309 Kevin Johnson .12 .30
310 John Williams .07 .20
311 Clifford Robinson .10 .25
312 Antonio McDyess .12 .30
313 Rasheed Wallace .15 .40
314 Brian Grant .10 .25
315 Dontonio Wingfield .07 .20
316 Kelvin Cato RC .10 .25
317 Mahmoud Abdul-Rauf .07 .20
318 Lawrence Funderburke RC .10 .25
319 Mitch Richmond .15 .40
320 Tariq Abdul-Wahad RC .10 .25
321 Terry Dehere .07 .20
322 Michael Stewart RC .12 .30
323 Tim Duncan RC .75 2.00
324 Avery Johnson .10 .25
325 David Robinson .25 .60
326 Charles Smith .07 .20
327 Chuck Person .10 .25
328 Monty Williams .10 .25
329 Jim McIlvaine .07 .20
330 Gary Payton .20 .50
331 Eric Snow .07 .20
332 Dale Ellis .10 .25
333 Vin Baker .10 .25
334 Walt Williams .10 .25
335 Tracy McGrady RC .60 1.50
336 Damon Stoudamire .12 .30
337 Carlos Rogers .07 .20
338 John Wallace .07 .20
339 Shandon Anderson .07 .20
340 Jeff Hornacek .12 .30
341 Howard Eisley .07 .20
342 Jacque Vaughn RC .10 .25
343 Bryon Russell .07 .20
344 Antoine Carr .07 .20
345 Antonio Daniels RC .12 .30
346 Pete Chilcutt .07 .20
347 Blue Edwards .07 .20
348 Bryant Reeves .07 .20
349 Chris Robinson RC .12 .30
350 Otis Thorpe .10 .25
351 Tim Legler .07 .20
352 Juwan Howard .10 .25
353 God Shammgod RC .12 .30
354 Gheorghe Muresan .12 .30
355 Chris Whitney .07 .20
356 Dikembe Mutombo HP .20 .50
357 Antoine Walker HP .12 .30
358 Glen Rice HP .12 .30
359 Scottie Pippen HP .30 .75
360 Derek Anderson HP .12 .30
361 Michael Finley HP .12 .30
362 LaPhonso Ellis HP .10 .25
363 Grant Hill HP .20 .50
364 Joe Smith HP .10 .25
365 Charles Barkley HP .30 .75
366 Reggie Miller HP .25 .60
367 Loy Vaught HP .10 .25
368 Shaquille O'Neal HP .40 1.00
369 Alonzo Mourning HP .20 .50
370 Glenn Robinson HP .12 .30
371 Kevin Garnett HP .30 .75
372 Kendall Gill HP .10 .25
373 Allan Houston HP .12 .30
374 Anfernee Hardaway HP .30 .75
375 Tim Thomas HP .15 .40
376 Jason Kidd HP .20 .50
377 Kenny Anderson HP .10 .25
378 Mitch Richmond HP .15 .40
379 Tim Duncan HP .75 2.00
380 Gary Payton HP .20 .50
381 Marcus Camby HP .12 .30
382 Karl Malone HP .25 .60
383 Shareef Abdur-Rahim HP .12 .30
384 Chris Webber HP .15 .40
385 Michael Jordan HP 1.25 3.00
386 Michael Jordan MM .60 1.50
387 Michael Jordan MM .60 1.50
388 Michael Jordan MM .60 1.50
389 Michael Jordan MM .60 1.50
390 Michael Jordan MM .60 1.50
391 Michael Jordan MM .60 1.50
392 Michael Jordan MM .60 1.50
393 Michael Jordan MM .60 1.50
394 Michael Jordan MM .60 1.50
395 Michael Jordan MM .60 1.50
396 Checklist #1 .07 .20
397 Checklist #2 .07 .20
398 Checklist #3 .07 .20
399 Checklist #4 .07 .20
400 Checklist #5 .07 .20

1997-98 Collector's Choice Crash the Game Scoring

COMPLETE SET (60) 25.00 50.00
SER.1 STATED ODDS 1:5
*RED.CARDS: .25X TO .6X HI COLUMN
ONE RED.SET PER WINNER BY MAIL
ONE RED.SET PER 15 NON-WIN BY MAIL
C1A Dikembe Mutombo .75 2.00
C1B Dikembe Mutombo .75 2.00
C2A Dana Barros .30 .75
C2B Dana Barros .30 .75
C3A Glen Rice .50 1.25
C3B Glen Rice .50 1.25
C4A Scottie Pippen 1.25 3.00
C4B Scottie Pippen 1.25 3.00
C5A Terrell Brandon .40 1.00
C5B Terrell Brandon .40 1.00
C6A Shawn Bradley .30 .75
C6B Shawn Bradley .30 .75
C7A Antonio McDyess .50 1.25
C7B Antonio McDyess .50 1.25
C8A Lindsey Hunter .30 .75
C8B Lindsey Hunter .30 .75
C9A Joe Smith .40 1.00
C9B Joe Smith .40 1.00
C10A Hakeem Olajuwon 1.00 2.50
C10B Hakeem Olajuwon 1.00 2.50
C11A Reggie Miller 1.00 2.50
C11B Reggie Miller 1.00 2.50
C12A Rodney Rogers .40 1.00
C12B Rodney Rogers .40 1.00
C13A Nick Van Exel .50 1.25
C13B Nick Van Exel .50 1.25
C14A Tim Hardaway .60 1.50
C14B Tim Hardaway .60 1.50
C15A Glenn Robinson .50 1.25
C15B Glenn Robinson .50 1.25
C16A Kevin Garnett 1.25 3.00
C16B Kevin Garnett 1.25 3.00
C17A Kerry Kittles .40 1.00
C17B Kerry Kittles .40 1.00
C18A Larry Johnson .60 1.50
C18B Larry Johnson .60 1.50
C19A Anfernee Hardaway 1.25 3.00
C19B Anfernee Hardaway 1.25 3.00
C20A Allen Iverson 1.50 4.00
C20B Allen Iverson 1.50 4.00
C21A Jason Kidd .75 2.00
C21B Jason Kidd .75 2.00
C22A Arvydas Sabonis .60 1.50
C22B Arvydas Sabonis .60 1.50
C23A Mitch Richmond .60 1.50
C23B Mitch Richmond .60 1.50
C24A David Robinson 1.00 2.50
C24B David Robinson 1.00 2.50
C25A Gary Payton .75 2.00
C25B Gary Payton .75 2.00
C26A Marcus Camby .50 1.25
C26B Marcus Camby .50 1.25
C27A Karl Malone 1.00 2.50
C27B Karl Malone 1.00 2.50
C28A Bryant Reeves .30 .75
C28B Bryant Reeves .30 .75
C29A Chris Webber .60 1.50
C29B Chris Webber .60 1.50
C30A Michael Jordan 5.00 12.00
C30B Michael Jordan 5.00 12.00

1997-98 Collector's Choice Draft Trade

COMPLETE SET (10) 25.00 60.00
1 Tim Duncan 20.00 50.00
2 Keith Van Horn 5.00 12.00
3 Chauncey Billups 10.00 25.00
4 Antonio Daniels 3.00 8.00
5 Tony Battie 3.00 8.00
6 Ron Mercer 4.00 10.00
7 Tim Thomas 4.00 10.00
8 Adonal Foyle 2.50 6.00
9 Tracy McGrady 15.00 40.00
10 Danny Fortson 3.00 8.00

1997-98 Collector's Choice Factory All StarQuest

COMPLETE SET (10) 50.00 120.00
AS1 Kobe Bryant 20.00 50.00
AS2 Gary Payton .60 1.50
AS3 Kevin Garnett 1.00 2.50
AS4 Karl Malone .75 2.00
AS5 Shaquille O'Neal 1.25 3.00
AS6 Michael Jordan 40.00 100.00
AS7 Anfernee Hardaway 1.00 2.50
AS8 Grant Hill .60 1.50
AS9 Shawn Kemp .60 1.50
AS10 Dikembe Mutombo .60 1.50

1997-98 Collector's Choice Memorable Moments

COMPLETE SET (10) 6.00 15.00
1 Michael Jordan 4.00 10.00
2 Grant Hill .60 1.50
3 Anfernee Hardaway 1.00 2.50
4 Kobe Bryant 4.00 10.00
5 Kevin Garnett 1.00 2.50
6 Jason Kidd .60 1.50
7 Karl Malone .75 2.00
8 Hakeem Olajuwon .75 2.00

9 Gary Payton .60 1.50
10 Dennis Rodman 1.00 2.50

1997-98 Collector's Choice Miniatures

COMPLETE SET (30) 4.00 10.00
SER.2 STATED ODDS 1:3
M1 Mookie Blaylock .15 .40
M2 Chauncey Billups .50 1.25
M3 Glen Rice .15 .40
M4 Scottie Pippen .40 1.00
M5 Bob Sura .10 .25
M6 Erick Strickland .10 .25
M7 Tony Battie .15 .40
M8 Joe Dumars .20 .50
M9 Adonal Foyle .20 .50
M10 Charles Barkley .40 1.00
M11 Dale Davis .12 .30
M12 Lamond Murray .10 .25
M13 Kobe Bryant 1.50 4.00
M14 Tim Hardaway .20 .50
M15 Glenn Robinson .15 .40
M16 Kevin Garnett .40 1.00
M17 Keith Van Horn .25 .60
M18 Patrick Ewing .25 .60
M19 Anfernee Hardaway .40 1.00
M20 Tim Thomas .20 .50
M21 Jason Kidd .25 .60
M22 Isaiah Rider .12 .30
M23 Mahmoud Abdul-Rauf .10 .25
M24 Tim Duncan 1.00 2.50
M25 Detlef Schrempf .15 .40
M26 Damon Stoudamire .15 .40
M27 John Stockton .30 .75
M28 Bryant Reeves .10 .25
M29 Juwan Howard .12 .30
M30 Michael Jordan 1.50 4.00

1997-98 Collector's Choice MJ Bullseye

COMMON JORDAN (B1-B30) 2.00 5.00
SER.2 STATED ODDS 1:5

1997-98 Collector's Choice MJ Rewind Redemption

COMPLETE SET (13) 30.00 80.00
COMMON CARD (R1-R13) 1.50 4.00

1997-98 Collector's Choice Star Attractions

COMPLETE SET (20) 15.00 40.00
COMPLETE SERIES 1 (10) 10.00 25.00
COMPLETE SERIES 2 (10) 6.00 15.00
*GOLD: 2X TO 5X HI COLUMN
GOLD: SER.1/2 STATED ODDS 1:20 SPEC.
SA1 Michael Jordan 6.00 15.00
SA2 Joe Smith .50 1.25
SA3 Karl Malone 1.25 3.00
SA4 Chauncey Billups 1.00 2.50
SA5 Charles Barkley 1.50 4.00
SA6 Shaquille O'Neal 2.00 5.00
SA7 Jason Kidd 1.00 2.50
SA8 Chris Webber .75 2.00
SA9 Allen Iverson 2.00 5.00
SA10 Patrick Ewing 1.00 2.50
SA11 Tim Duncan 2.00 5.00
SA12 Kevin Garnett 1.50 4.00
SA13 Tony Battie .30 .75
SA14 Gary Payton 1.00 2.50
SA15 Hakeem Olajuwon 1.25 3.00
SA16 Antonio Daniels .30 .75
SA17 Grant Hill 1.00 2.50
SA18 Anfernee Hardaway 1.50 4.00
SA19 Scottie Pippen 1.50 4.00
SA20 Keith Van Horn .50 1.25

1997-98 Collector's Choice StarQuest

1-45/91-135 SER.1/2 STATED ODDS 1:1
46-65/136-155 SER.1/2 STATED ODDS 1:21
66-80/156-170 SER.1/2 STATED ODDS 1:71
81-90/171-180 SER.1/2 STATED ODDS 1:145
1 Dale Davis .20 .50
2 Jamal Mashburn .20 .50
3 Christian Laettner .25 .60
4 Billy Owens .15 .40
5 Vlade Divac .25 .60
6 Sean Elliott .20 .50
7 Marcus Camby .25 .60
8 Dana Barros .15 .40
9 Rod Strickland .20 .50
10 Jim Jackson .20 .50
11 Tyrone Hill .20 .50
12 Ervin Johnson .15 .40
13 Antoine Walker .25 .60
14 Lorenzen Wright .15 .40
15 Shawn Bradley .15 .40
16 John Starks .25 .60
17 Corliss Williamson .15 .40
18 Steve Smith .20 .50
19 Chris Mills .15 .40
20 Vinny Del Negro .20 .50
21 Jayson Williams .15 .40
22 Anthony Mason .20 .50
23 Dennis Scott .20 .50
24 Mark Jackson .20 .50
25 Dino Radja .15 .40
26 Greg Ostertag .15 .40
27 Anthony Peeler .15 .40
28 Toni Kukoc .30 .75
29 Michael Finley .25 .60
30 Brent Barry .20 .50
31 Wesley Person .20 .50
32 Horace Grant .25 .60
33 Walt Williams .20 .50
34 Bryant Stith .20 .50
35 Ray Allen .50 1.25
36 Otis Thorpe .20 .50
37 Rasheed Wallace .30 .75
38 Charles Oakley .20 .50
39 Robert Pack .15 .40
40 Kendall Gill .20 .50
41 Lindsey Hunter .15 .40
42 Cedric Ceballos .20 .50
43 Allan Houston .25 .60
44 Bryant Reeves .15 .40
45 Derrick Coleman .25 .60
46 Isaiah Rider 1.00 2.50
47 Detlef Schrempf 1.25 3.00
48 Antonio McDyess 1.25 3.00
49 Glenn Robinson 1.25 3.00
50 Damon Stoudamire 1.25 3.00
51 Terrell Brandon 1.00 2.50
52 Joe Smith 1.00 2.50
53 Tom Gugliotta 1.00 2.50
54 Loy Vaught 1.00 2.50
55 Kenny Anderson 1.00 2.50
56 Dikembe Mutombo 2.00 5.00
57 Tim Hardaway 1.50 4.00
58 Chris Webber 1.50 4.00
59 Nick Van Exel 1.25 3.00
60 Kerry Kittles 1.00 2.50
61 Chris Mullin 1.50 4.00
62 Stephon Marbury 1.50 4.00
63 Juwan Howard 1.00 2.50
64 Larry Johnson 1.50 4.00
65 Shareef Abdur-Rahim 1.25 3.00
66 Dennis Rodman 5.00 12.00
67 Vin Baker 1.50 4.00
68 Clyde Drexler 3.00 8.00
69 Eddie Jones 2.00 5.00
70 Jerry Stackhouse 2.00 5.00
71 Karl Malone 4.00 10.00
72 Mitch Richmond 2.50 6.00
73 Glen Rice 2.00 5.00
74 Jason Kidd 3.00 8.00
75 Latrell Sprewell 2.50 6.00
76 David Robinson 4.00 10.00
77 Charles Barkley 5.00 12.00
78 Gary Payton 3.00 8.00
79 Scottie Pippen 5.00 12.00
80 Reggie Miller 4.00 10.00
81 Alonzo Mourning 4.00 10.00
82 Allen Iverson 8.00 20.00
83 Michael Jordan 40.00 100.00
84 Shawn Kemp 4.00 10.00
85 Kevin Garnett 6.00 15.00
86 Grant Hill 4.00 10.00
87 Anfernee Hardaway 6.00 15.00
88 Shaquille O'Neal 8.00 20.00
89 John Stockton 5.00 12.00
90 Hakeem Olajuwon 5.00 12.00
91 Billy Owens .15 .40
92 Derek Anderson .25 .60
93 Hersey Hawkins .20 .50
94 Bryon Russell .15 .40
95 Rik Smits .20 .50
96 Tracy McGrady 1.25 3.00
97 Kendall Gill .20 .50
98 Tim Thomas .30 .75
99 Robert Horry .25 .60
100 Marcus Camby .25 .60
101 Rodney Rogers .20 .50
102 Danny Manning .20 .50
103 John Starks .20 .50
104 Mahmoud Abdul-Rauf .15 .40
105 Chris Childs .15 .40
106 Antonio Davis .20 .50
107 Lamond Murray .15 .40
108 Nick Anderson .20 .50
109 Antoine Walker .25 .60
110 Christian Laettner .25 .60
111 Gary Trent .15 .40
112 Tony Battie .15 .40
113 Vlade Divac .25 .60
114 Kevin Johnson .25 .60
115 Erick Strickland .15 .40
116 Ray Allen .50 1.25
117 Antonio Daniels .20 .50
118 Sean Elliott .20 .50
119 Horace Grant .25 .60
120 Walt Williams .15 .40
121 Rony Seikaly .20 .50
122 Allan Houston .25 .60
123 Michael Finley .25 .60
124 Rasheed Wallace .30 .75
125 Doug Christie .15 .40
126 Danny Ferry .15 .40
127 Arvydas Sabonis .30 .75
128 Shandon Anderson .15 .40
129 Otis Thorpe .20 .50
130 Adonal Foyle .20 .50
131 Bryant Reeves .15 .40
132 Theo Ratliff .20 .50
133 Matt Maloney .15 .40
134 Voshon Lenard .15 .40
135 Danny Fortson .25 .60
136 Joe Smith 1.00 2.50
137 Mookie Blaylock 1.00 2.50
138 Loy Vaught 1.00 2.50
139 Tom Gugliotta 1.00 2.50
140 Damon Stoudamire 1.25 3.00
141 Antonio McDyess 1.25 3.00
142 Kobe Bryant 12.00 30.00
143 Juwan Howard 1.00 2.50
144 Tim Hardaway 1.50 4.00
145 Ron Mercer 1.50 4.00
146 Joe Dumars 1.50 4.00
147 Clyde Drexler 2.00 5.00
148 Shareef Abdur-Rahim 1.25 3.00
149 LaPhonso Ellis 1.00 2.50
150 Dikembe Mutombo 2.00 5.00
151 Chauncey Billups 4.00 10.00
152 Chris Webber 1.50 4.00
153 Glenn Robinson 1.25 3.00
154 Patrick Ewing 2.00 5.00
155 Stephon Marbury 1.50 4.00
156 Keith Van Horn 3.00 8.00
157 Karl Malone 4.00 10.00
158 Terrell Brandon 1.50 4.00
159 Sam Cassell 1.50 4.00
160 Jerry Stackhouse 2.00 5.00
161 Vin Baker 1.50 4.00
162 Jason Kidd 3.00 8.00
163 Charles Barkley 5.00 12.00
164 Reggie Miller 4.00 10.00
165 Alonzo Mourning 3.00 8.00
166 Scottie Pippen 5.00 12.00
167 Glen Rice 2.00 5.00
168 Allen Iverson 6.00 15.00
169 David Robinson 4.00 10.00
170 Shawn Kemp 3.00 8.00
171 Michael Jordan 25.00 60.00
172 Tim Duncan 12.00 30.00
173 Anfernee Hardaway 6.00 15.00
174 Shaquille O'Neal 8.00 20.00
175 John Stockton 5.00 12.00
176 Gary Payton 4.00 10.00
177 Mitch Richmond 3.00 8.00
178 Kevin Garnett 6.00 15.00
179 Hakeem Olajuwon 5.00 12.00
180 Grant Hill 4.00 10.00

1997-98 Collector's Choice Stick Ums

COMPLETE SET (30) 3.00 8.00
SER.1 STATED ODDS 1:3
S1 Steve Smith .12 .30
S2 Antoine Walker .15 .40
S3 Anthony Mason .12 .30
S4 Dennis Rodman .40 1.00
S5 Terrell Brandon .12 .30
S6 Michael Finley .15 .40
S7 Antonio McDyess .15 .40
S8 Grant Hill .25 .60
S9 Joe Smith .12 .30
S10 Hakeem Olajuwon .30 .75
S11 Reggie Miller .30 .75
S12 Loy Vaught .12 .30
S13 Shaquille O'Neal .50 1.25
S14 Alonzo Mourning .20 .50
S15 Vin Baker .12 .30
S16 Stephon Marbury .20 .50
S17 Jim Jackson .12 .30
S18 John Starks .15 .40
S19 Anfernee Hardaway .40 1.00
S20 Allen Iverson .50 1.25
S21 Jason Kidd .25 .60
S22 Kenny Anderson .12 .30
S23 Mitch Richmond .20 .50
S24 David Robinson .30 .75
S25 Shawn Kemp .20 .50
S26 Damon Stoudamire .15 .40
S27 Karl Malone .30 .75
S28 Bryant Reeves .12 .30
S29 Juwan Howard .12 .30
S30 Michael Jordan 1.50 4.00

1997-98 Collector's Choice Stick Ums Base Card

COMPLETE SET (30) 3.00 8.00
B1 Steve Smith .12 .30
B2 Antoine Walker .15 .40
B3 Anthony Mason .12 .30
B4 Dennis Rodman .40 1.00
B5 Terrell Brandon .12 .30
B6 Michael Finley .15 .40
B7 Antonio McDyess .15 .40
B8 Grant Hill .25 .60
B9 Joe Smith .12 .30
B10 Hakeem Olajuwon .30 .75
B11 Reggie Miller .30 .75
B12 Loy Vaught .12 .30
B13 Shaquille O'Neal .50 1.25
B14 Alonzo Mourning .25 .60
B15 Vin Baker .12 .30
B16 Stephon Marbury .20 .50
B17 Jim Jackson .12 .30
B18 John Starks .15 .40
B19 Anfernee Hardaway .40 1.00
B20 Allen Iverson .50 1.25
B21 Jason Kidd .25 .60
B22 Kenny Anderson .12 .30
B23 Mitch Richmond .20 .50
B24 David Robinson .30 .75
B25 Gary Payton .25 .60
B26 Damon Stoudamire .15 .40
B27 Karl Malone .30 .75
B28 Bryant Reeves .10 .25
B29 Juwan Howard .12 .30
B30 Michael Jordan 1.50 4.00

1997-98 Collector's Choice The Jordan Dynasty

COMPLETE SET (5) 15.00 40.00
COMMON CARD (1-5) 6.00 15.00
STATED PRINT RUN 23,000 EACH

1997-98 Collector's Choice Catch 23

COMPLETE SET (10) 10.00 25.00
COMMON CARD (C1-C10) 1.25 3.00

1997-98 Collector's Choice Jumbos

COMPLETE SET (15) 15.00 40.00
1 Michael Jordan 2.00 5.00
2 Michael Jordan 2.00 5.00
3 Michael Jordan 2.00 5.00
4 Michael Jordan 2.00 5.00
5 Michael Jordan 2.00 5.00
6 Michael Jordan 2.00 5.00
7 Michael Jordan 2.00 5.00
8 Michael Jordan 2.00 5.00
9 Michael Jordan 2.00 5.00
10 Michael Jordan 2.00 5.00
GN1 Utah Jazz Game Night 1.25 3.00
GN2 Los Angeles Lakers Game Night 1.50 4.00
GN3 Minnesota Timberwolves Game Night 1.25 3.00
GN4 Orlando Magic Game Night 1.25 3.00
GN5 Chicago Bulls Game Night 2.00 5.00

1995-96 Collector's Choice Argentina Stickers

1 Golden State Warriors Logo .10 .25
2 Latrell Sprewell .40 1.00
3 Ricky Pierce .25 .60
4 Tim Hardaway .50 1.25
5 Chris Mullin .40 1.00
6 Donyell Marshall .25 .60
7 Clifford Rozier .25 .60
8 Carlos Rogers .25 .60
9 Rony Seikaly .25 .60
10 Los Angeles Clippers Logo .10 .25
11 Pooh Richardson .25 .60
12 Terry Dehere .25 .60
13 Eric Piatkowski .25 .60
14 Loy Vaught .25 .60
15 Malik Sealy .25 .60
16 Lamond Murray .25 .60
17 Los Angeles Lakers Logo .10 .25
18 Sedale Threatt .25 .60
19 Nick Van Exel .10 .25
20 Cedric Ceballos .30 .75
21 George Lynch .25 .60
22 Eddie Jones .40 1.00
23 Elden Campbell .25 .60
24 Vlade Divac .40 1.00
25 Phoenix Suns Logo .10 .25
26 Kevin Johnson .40 1.00
27 Wesley Person .25 .60
28 Dan Majerle .40 1.00
29 A.C. Green .30 .75
30 Charles Barkley 1.00 2.50
31 Danny Manning .30 .75
32 Wayman Tisdale .25 .60
33 Portland Trail Blazers Logo .10 .25
34 Rod Strickland .25 .60
35 Terry Porter .25 .60
36 Aaron McKie .25 .60
37 Otis Thorpe .30 .75
38 Buck Williams .25 .60
39 Clifford Robinson .40 1.00
40 Harvey Grant .25 .60
41 Sacramento Kings Logo .10 .25
42 Randy Brown .25 .60
43 Mitch Richmond .50 1.25
44 Bobby Hurley .25 .60
45 Walt Williams .25 .60
46 Brian Grant .30 .75
47 Olden Polynice .25 .60
48 Duane Causwell .25 .60
49 Seattle Supersonics Logo .10 .25
50 Kendall Gill .25 .60
51 Gary Payton .60 1.50
52 Sarunas Marciulionis .25 .60
53 Nate McMillan .25 .60
54 Detlef Schrempf .40 1.00
55 Shawn Kemp .60 1.50
56 Sam Perkins .25 .60
57 Dallas Mavericks Logo .10 .25
58 Jim Jackson .30 .75
59 Jason Kidd .60 1.50
60 Tony Dumas .25 .60
61 Jamal Mashburn .40 1.00
62 Doug Smith .25 .60
63 Popeye Jones .25 .60
64 Denver Nuggets Logo .10 .25
65 Robert Pack .25 .60
66 Bryant Stith .25 .60
67 Mahmoud Abdul-Rauf .30 .75
68 Jalen Rose .50 1.25
69 Reggie Williams .25 .60
70 LaPhonso Ellis .30 .75
71 Dikembe Mutombo .60 1.50
72 Houston Rockets Logo .10 .25
73 Sam Cassell .40 1.00
74 Kenny Smith .30 .75
75 Clyde Drexler .60 1.50
76 Carl Herrera .25 .60
77 Robert Horry .40 1.00
78 Otis Thorpe .30 .75
79 Hakeem Olajuwon .75 2.00
80 Minnesota Timberwolves Logo .10 .25
81 Chris Smith .25 .60
82 Micheal Williams .25 .60
83 Doug West .25 .60
84 Isaiah Rider .40 1.00
85 Christian Laettner .30 .75
86 Tom Gugliotta .30 .75
87 San Antonio Spurs Logo .10 .25
88 Avery Johnson .30 .75
89 Vinny Del Negro .25 .60
90 Dennis Rodman .75 2.00
91 Sean Elliott .30 .75
92 Chuck Person .30 .75
93 J.R. Reid .25 .60
94 David Robinson .75 2.00
95 Utah Jazz Logo .10 .25
96 Jeff Hornacek .30 .75
97 John Stockton .75 2.00
98 David Benoit .25 .60
99 Karl Malone .75 2.00
100 Tom Chambers .30 .75
101 Antoine Carr .25 .60
102 Felton Spencer .25 .60
103 Atlanta Hawks Logo .10 .25
104 Mookie Blaylock .40 1.00
105 Craig Ehlo .25 .60
106 Steve Smith .30 .75
107 Stacey Augmon .30 .75
108 Grant Long .25 .60
109 Ken Norman .25 .60
110 Jon Koncak .25 .60
111 Charlotte Hornets Logo .10 .25
112 Hersey Hawkins .30 .75
113 Dell Curry .40 1.00
114 Muggsy Bogues .40 1.00
115 Scott Burrell .25 .60
116 Larry Johnson .50 1.25
117 Robert Parish .50 1.25
118 Alonzo Mourning .60 1.50
119 Chicago Bulls Logo .10 .25
120 Michael Jordan 4.00 10.00
121 Ron Harper .30 .75
122 Toni Kukoc .50 1.25
123 Scottie Pippen 1.00 2.50
124 Dickey Simpkins .25 .60
125 Will Perdue .30 .75
126 Cleveland Cavaliers Logo .10 .25
127 Gerald Wilkins .25 .60
128 Mark Price .40 1.00
129 Terrell Brandon .30 .75
130 Bobby Phills .30 .75
131 Chris Mills .25 .60
132 Tyrone Hill .25 .60
133 John Williams .25 .60
134 Detroit Pistons Logo .10 .25
135 Lindsey Hunter .25 .60
136 Joe Dumars .40 1.00
137 Allan Houston .30 .75
138 Terry Mills .25 .60
139 Grant Hill .60 1.50
140 Mark West .25 .60
141 Indiana Pacers Logo .10 .25
142 Reggie Miller .75 2.00
143 Mark Jackson .30 .75
144 Duane Ferrell .25 .60
145 Derrick McKey .25 .60
146 Dale Davis .25 .60
147 Antonio Davis .25 .60
148 Rik Smits .30 .75
149 Milwaukee Bucks Logo .10 .25
150 Lee Mayberry .25 .60
151 Todd Day .25 .60
152 Vin Baker .30 .75
153 Glenn Robinson .40 1.00
154 Marty Conlon .25 .60
155 Johnny Newman .25 .60
156 Eric Mobley .25 .60
157 Boston Celtics Logo .10 .25
158 Sherman Douglas .25 .60
159 Dee Brown .30 .75
160 Rick Fox .30 .75
161 Dino Radja .25 .60
162 Xavier McDaniel .25 .60
163 Dominique Wilkins .60 1.50
164 Eric Montross .25 .60
165 Miami Heat Logo .10 .25
166 Bimbo Coles .25 .60
167 Khalid Reeves .25 .60
168 Glen Rice .40 1.00
169 Billy Owens .25 .60
170 Kevin Willis .25 .60
171 Matt Geiger .25 .60
172 New Jersey Nets Logo .10 .25
173 Kevin Edwards .25 .60
174 Rex Walters .25 .60
175 Kenny Anderson .30 .75
176 Derrick Coleman .30 .75
177 Chris Morris .25 .60
178 Armon Gilliam .25 .60
179 P.J. Brown .25 .60
180 New York Knicks Logo .10 .25
181 Derek Harper .30 .75
182 Charlie Ward .30 .75
183 John Starks .40 1.00
184 Charles Smith .25 .60
185 Charles Oakley .30 .75
186 Anthony Mason .30 .75
187 Patrick Ewing .60 1.50
188 Orlando Magic Logo .10 .25
189 Anthony Bowie .25 .60
190 Anfernee Hardaway 1.00 2.50
191 Nick Anderson .30 .75
192 Dennis Scott .25 .60
193 Donald Royal .25 .60
194 Horace Grant .30 .75
195 Shaquille O'Neal 1.50 4.00
196 Philadelphia 76ers Logo .10 .25
197 Jeff Malone .25 .60
198 Dana Barros .30 .75
199 Clarence Weatherspoon .25 .60
200 Scott Williams .25 .60
201 Sharone Wright .25 .60
202 Shawn Bradley .25 .60
203 Washington Bullets Logo .10 .25
204 Scott Skiles .25 .60
205 Mitchell Butler .25 .60
206 Calbert Cheaney .25 .60
207 Don MacLean .25 .60
208 Juwan Howard .40 1.00
209 Kevin Duckworth .25 .60
210 Gheorghe Muresan .25 .60
211 Toronto Raptors Logo .10 .25
212 Vancouver Grizzlies Logo .10 .25
213 Michael Jordan 1985 NBA ROY 4.00 10.00
214 Michael Jordan 1986-87 3,000 Points 4.00 10.00
215 Michael Jordan 1988 NBA Defensive POY 4.00 10.00
216 Michael Jordan Jordan Collection 4.00 10.00
217 Michael Jordan He's Back 4.00 10.00
218 Michael Jordan He's Back 4.00 10.00
219 Michael Jordan He's Back 4.00 10.00
220 Michael Jordan He's Back 4.00 10.00
221 Michael Jordan He's Back 4.00 10.00

1995-96 Collector's Choice European Stickers

COMPLETE SET (212) 20.00 50.00
1 Golden State Warriors Logo .10 .25
2 Latrell Sprewell .40 1.00
3 Ricky Pierce .25 .60
4 Tim Hardaway .50 1.25
5 Chris Mullin .40 1.00
6 Donyell Marshall .25 .60
7 Clifford Rozier .25 .60
8 Carlos Rogers .25 .60
9 Rony Seikaly .25 .60
10 Los Angeles Clippers Logo .10 .25
11 Pooh Richardson .25 .60
12 Terry Dehere .25 .60
13 Eric Piatkowski .25 .60
14 Loy Vaught .25 .60
15 Malik Sealy .25 .60
16 Lamond Murray .25 .60
17 Los Angeles Lakers Logo .10 .25
18 Sedale Threatt .25 .60
19 Nick Van Exel .40 1.00
20 Cedric Ceballos .30 .75
21 George Lynch .25 .60
22 Eddie Jones .40 1.00
23 Elden Campbell .25 .60
24 Vlade Divac .40 1.00
25 Phoenix Suns Logo .10 .25
26 Kevin Johnson .40 1.00
27 Wesley Person .25 .60
28 Dan Majerle .40 1.00
29 A.C. Green .30 .75
30 Charles Barkley 1.00 2.50
31 Danny Manning .30 .75
32 Wayman Tisdale .25 .60
33 Portland Trail Blazers Logo .10 .25
34 Rod Strickland .25 .60
35 Terry Porter .25 .60
36 Aaron McKie .25 .60
37 Otis Thorpe .30 .75
38 Buck Williams .25 .60
39 Clifford Robinson .40 1.00
40 Harvey Grant .25 .60
41 Sacramento Kings Logo .10 .25
42 Randy Brown .25 .60
43 Mitch Richmond .50 1.25
44 Bobby Hurley .25 .60
45 Walt Williams .25 .60
46 Brian Grant .30 .75
47 Olden Polynice .25 .60
48 Duane Causwell .25 .60
49 Seattle Supersonics Logo .10 .25
50 Kendall Gill .25 .60
51 Gary Payton .60 1.50
52 Sarunas Marciulionis .40 1.00
53 Nate McMillan .25 .60
54 Detlef Schrempf .40 1.00
55 Shawn Kemp .60 1.50
56 Sam Perkins .25 .60
57 Dallas Mavericks Logo .10 .25
58 Jim Jackson .30 .75
59 Jason Kidd .60 1.50
60 Tony Dumas .25 .60
61 Jamal Mashburn .40 1.00
62 Doug Smith .25 .60
63 Popeye Jones .25 .60
64 Denver Nuggets Logo .10 .25
65 Robert Pack .25 .60
66 Bryant Stith .25 .60
67 Mahmoud Abdul-Rauf .30 .75
68 Jalen Rose .50 1.25
69 Reggie Williams .25 .60
70 LaPhonso Ellis .30 .75
71 Dikembe Mutombo .60 1.50
72 Houston Rockets Logo .10 .25
73 Sam Cassell .40 1.00
74 Kenny Smith .30 .75
75 Clyde Drexler .60 1.50
76 Carl Herrera .25 .60
77 Robert Horry .40 1.00
78 Otis Thorpe .30 .75
79 Hakeem Olajuwon .75 2.00
80 Minnesota Timberwolves Logo .10 .25
81 Chris Smith .25 .60
82 Micheal Williams .25 .60
83 Doug West .25 .60
84 Isaiah Rider .40 1.00
85 Christian Laettner .30 .75
86 Tom Gugliotta .30 .75
87 San Antonio Spurs Logo .10 .25
88 Avery Johnson .30 .75
89 Vinny Del Negro .25 .60
90 Dennis Rodman .75 2.00
91 Sean Elliott .30 .75
92 Chuck Person .30 .75
93 J.R. Reid .25 .60
94 David Robinson .75 2.00
95 Utah Jazz Logo .10 .25
96 Jeff Hornacek .30 .75
97 John Stockton .75 2.00
98 David Benoit .25 .60
99 Karl Malone .75 2.00
100 Tom Chambers .30 .75
101 Antoine Carr .25 .60
102 Felton Spencer .25 .60
103 Atlanta Hawks Logo .10 .25
104 Mookie Blaylock .40 1.00
105 Craig Ehlo .25 .60
106 Steve Smith .30 .75
107 Stacey Augmon .30 .75
108 Grant Long .25 .60
109 Ken Norman .25 .60
110 Jon Koncak .25 .60
111 Charlotte Hornets Logo .10 .25
112 Hersey Hawkins .30 .75
113 Dell Curry .40 1.00
114 Muggsy Bogues .40 1.00
115 Scott Burrell .25 .60
116 Larry Johnson .50 1.25
117 Robert Parish .50 1.25
118 Alonzo Mourning .60 1.50
119 Chicago Bulls Logo .10 .25
120 Michael Jordan 4.00 10.00
121 Ron Harper .30 .75
122 Toni Kukoc .50 1.25
123 Scottie Pippen 1.00 2.50
124 Dickey Simpkins .25 .60
125 Will Perdue .30 .75
126 Cleveland Cavaliers Logo .10 .25
127 Gerald Wilkins .25 .60
128 Mark Price .40 1.00
129 Terrell Brandon .30 .75
130 Bobby Phills .30 .75
131 Chris Mills .25 .60
132 Tyrone Hill .25 .60
133 John Williams .25 .60
134 Detroit Pistons Logo .10 .25
135 Lindsey Hunter .25 .60
136 Joe Dumars .40 1.00
137 Allan Houston .30 .75
138 Terry Mills .25 .60
139 Grant Hill .60 1.50
140 Mark West .25 .60
141 Indiana Pacers Logo .10 .25
142 Reggie Miller .75 2.00
143 Mark Jackson .30 .75
144 Duane Ferrell .25 .60
145 Derrick McKey .25 .60
146 Dale Davis .25 .60
147 Antonio Davis .25 .60
148 Rik Smits .30 .75
149 Milwaukee Bucks Logo .10 .25
150 Lee Mayberry .25 .60
151 Todd Day .25 .60
152 Vin Baker .30 .75
153 Glenn Robinson .40 1.00
154 Marty Conlon .25 .60
155 Johnny Newman .25 .60
156 Eric Mobley .25 .60
157 Boston Celtics Logo .10 .25
158 Sherman Douglas .25 .60
159 Dee Brown .30 .75
160 Rick Fox .30 .75
161 Dino Radja .25 .60
162 Xavier McDaniel .25 .60
163 Dominique Wilkins .60 1.50
164 Eric Montross .25 .60
165 Miami Heat Logo .10 .25
166 Bimbo Coles .25 .60
167 Khalid Reeves .25 .60
168 Glen Rice .40 1.00
169 Billy Owens .25 .60
170 Kevin Willis .25 .60
171 Matt Geiger .25 .60
172 New Jersey Nets Logo .10 .25
173 Kevin Edwards .25 .60
174 Rex Walters .25 .60
175 Kenny Anderson .30 .75
176 Derrick Coleman .30 .75
177 Chris Morris .25 .60
178 Armon Gilliam .25 .60
179 P.J. Brown .25 .60
180 New York Knicks Logo .10 .25
181 Derek Harper .30 .75
182 Charlie Ward .30 .75
183 John Starks .40 1.00
184 Charles Smith .25 .60
185 Charles Oakley .30 .75
186 Anthony Mason .25 .60
187 Patrick Ewing .60 1.50
188 Orlando Magic Logo .10 .25
189 Anthony Bowie .25 .60
190 Anfernee Hardaway 1.00 2.50
191 Nick Anderson .30 .75
192 Dennis Scott .25 .60
193 Donald Royal .25 .60
194 Horace Grant .30 .75
195 Shaquille O'Neal 1.50 4.00
196 Philadelphia 76ers Logo .10 .25
197 Jeff Malone .25 .60
198 Dana Barros .30 .75
199 Clarence Weatherspoon .25 .60
200 Scott Williams .25 .60
201 Sharone Wright .25 .60
202 Shawn Bradley .25 .60
203 Washington Bullets Logo .10 .25
204 Scott Skiles .25 .60
205 Mitchell Butler .25 .60
206 Calbert Cheaney .25 .60
207 Don MacLean .25 .60
208 Juwan Howard .40 1.00
209 Kevin Duckworth .25 .60
210 Gheorghe Muresan .25 .60
211 Toronto Raptors Logo 1.00 .25
212 Vancouver Grizzlies Logo .10 .25

1995-96 Collector's Choice European Stickers Michael Jordan

COMPLETE SET (9) 12.00 30.00
COMMON STICKER (1-9) 1.60 4.00

1996 Collector's Choice Hula Hoops European

COMPLETE SET (40) 125.00 250.00
HH1 Mookie Blaylock 3.00 8.00
HH2 Dana Barros 3.00 8.00
HH3 Toni Kukoc 5.00 12.00
HH4 Terrell Brandon 3.00 8.00
HH5 Jamal Mashburn 4.00 10.00
HH6 Antonio McDyess 5.00 12.00
HH7 Chris Mullin 5.00 12.00
HH8 Hakeem Olajuwon 6.00 15.00
HH9 Brent Barry 4.00 10.00
HH10 Eddie Jones 5.00 12.00
HH11 Kurt Thomas 3.00 8.00
HH12 Kevin Garnett 12.00 30.00
HH13 Kendall Gill 3.00 8.00
HH14 John Starks 4.00 10.00
HH15 Dennis Scott 3.00 8.00
HH16 Jerry Stackhouse 6.00 15.00
HH17 Arvydas Sabonis 4.00 10.00
HH18 Billy Owens 3.00 8.00
HH19 Avery Johnson 4.00 10.00
HH20 Damon Stoudamire 4.00 10.00
HH21 Christian Laettner 4.00 10.00
HH22 Dino Radja 3.00 8.00
HH23 Dennis Rodman 10.00 25.00
HH24 Jim Jackson 3.00 8.00
HH25 LaPhonso Ellis 3.00 8.00
HH26 Joe Dumars 4.00 10.00
HH27 Joe Smith 4.00 10.00
HH28 Rik Smits 4.00 10.00
HH29 Cedric Ceballos 3.00 8.00
HH30 Sasha Danilovic 3.00 8.00
HH31 Vin Baker 4.00 10.00
HH32 Shawn Bradley 3.00 8.00
HH33 Charles Oakley 4.00 10.00
HH34 Anfernee Hardaway 8.00 20.00
HH35 Derrick Coleman 4.00 10.00
HH36 Wesley Person 3.00 8.00
HH37 Brian Grant 4.00 10.00
HH38 Sean Elliott 5.00 12.00
HH39 Detlef Schrempf 5.00 12.00
HH40 Karl Malone 6.00 15.00

1994-95 Collector's Choice International Australian Coke

COMPLETE SET (41)
1 B.J. Armstrong .60 1.50
2 Stacey Augmon .50 1.25
3 Vin Baker .60 1.50
4 Shawn Bradley .40 1.00
5 Derrick Coleman .60 1.50
6 Dell Curry .40 1.00
7 Vinny Del Negro .40 1.00
8 Clyde Drexler 1.00 2.50
9 LaPhonso Ellis .40 1.00
10 Kendall Gill .40 1.00
11 Anfernee Hardaway 1.25 3.00
12 Robert Horry .60 1.50
13 Kevin Johnson .60 1.50
14 Shawn Kemp 1.00 2.50
15 Don MacLean .40 1.00
16 Karl Malone 1.25 3.00
17 Dan Majerle .60 1.50
18 Jamal Mashburn .60 1.50
19 Reggie Miller 1.25 3.00
20 Terry Mills .40 1.00
21 Harold Miner .40 1.00
22 Alonzo Mourning 1.00 2.50
23 Chris Mullin .75 2.00
24 Charles Oakley .60 1.50
25 Hakeem Olajuwon 1.25 3.00
26 Anthony Peeler .40 1.00
27 Scottie Pippen 1.50 4.00
28 Mark Price .60 1.50

29 Dino Radja .40 1.00
30 Mitch Richmond .75 2.00
31 Isaiah Rider .60 1.50
32 David Robinson 1.25 3.00
33 Dennis Rodman 1.50 4.00
34 Detlef Schrempf .60 1.50
35 Charles Smith .40 1.00
36 Steve Smith .50 1.25
37 Latrell Sprewell .75 2.00
38 Loy Vaught .40 1.00
39 Rex Walters .40 1.00
40 Spud Webb .50 1.25
41 Shawn Kemp CL 1.00 2.50

1994-95 Collector's Choice International French

COMPLETE SET (429) 20.00 50.00
COMPLETE SERIES 1 (219) 10.00 25.00
COMPLETE SERIES 2 (210) 10.00 25.00
1 Anfernee Hardaway .60 1.50
2 Mark Macon .20 .50
3 Steve Smith .25 .60
4 Chris Webber .60 1.50
5 Donald Royal .20 .50
6 Avery Johnson .25 .60
7 Kevin Johnson .30 .75
8 Doug Christie .25 .60
9 Derrick McKey .20 .50
10 Dennis Rodman .75 2.00
11 Scott Skiles .20 .50
12 Johnny Dawkins .20 .50
13 Kendall Gill .20 .50
14 Jeff Hornacek .25 .60
15 Latrell Sprewell .40 1.00
16 Lucious Harris .20 .50
17 Chris Mullin .40 1.00
18 Jon Williams .20 .50
19 Tony Campbell .20 .50
20 LaPhonso Ellis .20 .50
21 Gerald Wilkins .25 .60
22 Clyde Drexler .50 1.25
23 Michael Jordan BB 2.50 6.00
24 George Lynch .20 .50
25 Mark Price .30 .75
26 James Robinson .20 .50
27 Elmore Spencer .20 .50
28 Stacey King .20 .50
29 Corie Blount .20 .50
30 Dell Curry .20 .50
31 Reggie Miller .60 1.50
32 Karl Malone .60 1.50
33 Scottie Pippen .75 2.00
34 Hakeem Olajuwon .60 1.50
35 Clarence Weatherspoon .20 .50
36 Kevin Edwards .20 .50
37 Pete Myers .20 .50
38 Jeff Turner .20 .50
39 Ennis Whatley .20 .50
40 Calbert Cheaney .25 .60
41 Glen Rice .30 .75
42 Vin Baker .30 .75
43 Grant Long .20 .50
44 Derrick Coleman .30 .75
45 Rik Smits .25 .60
46 Chris Smith .20 .50
47 Carl Herrera .20 .50
48 Bob Martin .20 .50
49 Terrell Brandon .20 .50
50 David Robinson .60 1.50
51 Danny Ferry .20 .50
52 Buck Williams .20 .50
53 Josh Grant .20 .50
54 Ed Pinckney .20 .50
55 Dikembe Mutombo .50 1.25
56 Clifford Robinson .25 .60
57 Luther Wright .20 .50
58 Scott Burrell .20 .50
59 Stacey Augmon .25 .60
60 Jeff Malone .20 .50
61 Byron Houston .20 .50
62 Anthony Peeler .20 .50
63 Michael Adams .20 .50
64 Negele Knight .20 .50
65 Terry Cummings .25 .60
66 Christian Laettner .25 .60
67 Tracy Murray .20 .50
68 Sedale Threatt .20 .50
69 Dan Majerle .30 .75
70 Frank Brickowski .20 .50
71 Ken Norman .20 .50
72 Charles Smith .20 .50
73 Adam Keefe .20 .50
74 P.J. Brown .20 .50
75 Kevin Duckworth .20 .50
76 Shawn Bradley .20 .50
77 Darnell Mee .20 .50
78 Nick Anderson .20 .50
79 Mark West .20 .50
80 B.J. Armstrong .30 .75
81 Dennis Scott .20 .50
82 Lindsey Hunter .20 .50
83 Derek Strong .20 .50
84 Mike Brown .20 .50
85 Antonio Harvey .20 .50
86 Anthony Bonner .20 .50
87 Sam Cassell .30 .75
88 Harold Miner .20 .50
89 Spud Webb .25 .60
90 Mookie Blaylock .30 .75
91 Greg Anthony .20 .50
92 Richard Petruska .20 .50
93 Sean Rooks .20 .50
94 Ervin Johnson .20 .50
95 Randy Brown .20 .50
96 Orlando Woolridge .20 .50
97 Charles Oakley .30 .75
98 Craig Ehlo .20 .50
99 Derek Harper .25 .60
100 Doug Edwards .20 .50
101 Muggsy Bogues .25 .60
102 Mitch Richmond .40 1.00
103 Mahmoud Abdul-Rauf .20 .50
104 Joe Dumars .30 .75
105 Eric Riley .20 .50
106 Terry Mills .20 .50
107 Toni Kukoc .40 1.00
108 Jon Koncak .20 .50
109 Haywoode Workman .20 .50
110 Todd Day .20 .50
111 Detlef Schrempf .30 .75
112 David Wesley .20 .50
113 Mark Jackson .25 .60
114 Doug Overton .20 .50
115 Vinny Del Negro .20 .50
116 Loy Vaught .20 .50
117 Mike Peplowski .20 .50
118 Bimbo Coles .20 .50
119 Rex Walters .20 .50
120 Sherman Douglas .20 .50
121 David Benoit .20 .50
122 John Salley .20 .50
123 Cedric Ceballos .25 .60
124 Chris Mills .25 .60
125 Robert Horry .30 .75
126 Johnny Newman .20 .50
127 Malcolm Mackey .20 .50
128 Terry Dehere .20 .50
129 Dino Radja .20 .50
130 Reggie Williams .20 .50
131 Xavier McDaniel .20 .50
132 Bobby Hurley .20 .50
133 Alonzo Mourning .50 1.25
134 Isaiah Rider .30 .75
135 Antoine Carr .20 .50
136 Robert Pack .25 .60
137 Walt Williams .20 .50
138 Tyrone Corbin .20 .50
139 Popeye Jones .20 .50
140 Shawn Kemp .50 1.25
141 Thurl Bailey .20 .50
142 James Worthy .40 1.00
143 Scott Haskin .20 .50
144 Hubert Davis .20 .50
145 A.C. Green .25 .60
146 Dale Davis .20 .50
147 Nate McMillan .25 .60
148 Chris Morris .20 .50
149 Will Perdue .20 .50
150 Felton Spencer .20 .50
151 Rod Strickland .20 .50
152 Blue Edwards .20 .50
153 John S. Williams .20 .50
154 Rodney Rogers .20 .50
155 Acie Earl .20 .50
156 Hersey Hawkins .20 .50
157 Jamal Mashburn .30 .75
158 Don MacLean .20 .50
159 Micheal Williams .20 .50
160 Kenny Gattison .20 .50
161 Rich King .20 .50
162 Allan Houston .30 .75
163 John Stockton .60 1.50
164 Kenny Anderson .25 .60
165 Shaquille O'Neal 1.25 3.00
166 Danny Manning TO .25 .60
167 Dee Brown TO .25 .60
168 Alonzo Mourning TO .50 1.25
169 Scottie Pippen TO .75 2.00
170 Mark Price TO .30 .75
171 Jamal Mashburn TO .30 .75
172 Dikembe Mutombo TO .50 1.25
173 Joe Dumars TO .30 .75
174 Chris Webber TO .60 1.50
175 Hakeem Olajuwon TO .60 1.50
176 Reggie Miller TO .60 1.50
177 Ron Harper TO .25 .60
178 Nick Van Exel TO .30 .75
179 Steve Smith TO .25 .60
180 Vin Baker TO .30 .75
181 Isaiah Rider TO .30 .75
182 Derrick Coleman TO .30 .75
183 Patrick Ewing TO .50 1.25
184 Shaquille O'Neal TO 1.25 3.00
185 Clarence Weatherspoon TO .20 .50
186 Charles Barkley TO .75 2.00
187 Clyde Drexler TO .50 1.25
188 Mitch Richmond TO .40 1.00
189 David Robinson TO .60 1.50
190 Shawn Kemp TO .50 1.25
191 Karl Malone TO .60 1.50
192 Tom Gugliotta TO .20 .50
193 Kenny Anderson ASA .25 .60
194 Alonzo Mourning ASA .50 1.25
195 Mark Price ASA .30 .75
196 John Stockton ASA .60 1.50
197 Shaquille O'Neal ASA 1.25 3.00
198 Latrell Sprewell ASA .40 1.00
199 Charles Barkley PRO .75 2.00
200 Chris Webber PRO .60 1.50
201 Patrick Ewing PRO .50 1.25
202 Dennis Rodman PRO .75 2.00
203 Shawn Kemp PRO .50 1.25
204 Michael Jordan PRO 2.50 6.00
205 Shaquille O'Neal PRO 1.25 3.00
206 Larry Johnson PRO .40 1.00
207 Tim Hardaway CL .40 1.00
208 John Stockton CL .60 1.50
209 Harold Miner CL .20 .50
210 B.J. Armstrong CL .30 .75
211 Michael Jordan ROY 2.50 6.00
212 Michael Jordan 63-Pt. Game 2.50 6.00
213 Michael Jordan Slam-Dunk 2.50 6.00
214 Michael Jordan MVP 2.50 6.00
215 Michael Jordan All-Star 2.50 6.00
216 Michael Jordan 3,000-Points 2.50 6.00
217 Michael Jordan Champ. 2.50 6.00
218 Michael Jordan
1985-94 M.J.'s
Decade of Dominanc 2.50 6.00
219 Michael Jordan CL 2.50 6.00
220 Gary Payton .50 1.25
221 Tom Hammonds .20 .50
222 Danny Ainge .30 .75
223 Gary Grant .20 .50
224 Jim Jackson .25 .60
225 Chris Gatling .20 .50
226 Sergei Bazarevich .30 .75
227 Tony Dumas .25 .60
228 Andrew Lang .20 .50
229 Wesley Person .30 .75
230 Terry Porter .20 .50
231 Duane Causwell .20 .50
232 Shaquille O'Neal 1.25 3.00
233 Antonio Davis .25 .60
234 Charles Barkley .75 2.00
235 Tony Massenburg .20 .50
236 Ricky Pierce .20 .50
237 Scott Skiles .20 .50
238 Jalen Rose .75 2.00
239 Charlie Ward .30 .75
240 Michael Jordan COMM 2.50 6.00
241 Elden Campbell .20 .50
242 Bill Cartwright .25 .60
243 Armon Gilliam UER
Card numbered 372 .20 .50
244 Rick Fox .20 .50
245 Tim Breaux .20 .50
246 Monty Williams .40 1.00
247 Dominique Wilkins .50 1.25
248 Robert Parish .30 .75
249 Mark Jackson .25 .60
250 Jason Kidd 1.50 4.00
251 Andres Guibert .20 .50
252 Matt Geiger .20 .50
253 Stanley Roberts .20 .50
254 Jack Haley .20 .50
255 David Wingate .20 .50
256 John Crotty .20 .50
257 Brian Grant .50 1.25
258 Otis Thorpe .20 .50
259 Clifford Rozier .20 .50
260 Grant Long .20 .50
261 Eric Mobley .20 .50
262 Dickey Simpkins .25 .60
263 J.R. Reid .20 .50
264 Kevin Willis .25 .60
265 Scott Brooks .20 .50
266 Glenn Robinson .60 1.50
267 Dana Barros .20 .50
268 Ken Norman .20 .50
269 Herb Williams .20 .50
270 Dee Brown .25 .60
271 Steve Kerr .25 .60
272 Jon Barry .20 .50
273 Sean Elliott .25 .60
274 Elliot Perry .20 .50
275 Kenny Smith .25 .60
276 Sean Rooks .20 .50
277 Gheorghe Muresan .20 .50
278 Juwan Howard .50 1.25
279 Steve Smith .25 .60
280 Anthony Bowie .20 .50
281 Moses Malone .30 .75
282 Olden Polynice .20 .50
283 Jo Jo English .20 .50
284 Marty Conlon .20 .50
285 Sam Mitchell .20 .50
286 Doug West .20 .50
287 Cedric Ceballos .25 .60
288 Lorenzo Williams .20 .50
289 Harold Ellis .20 .50
290 Doc Rivers .25 .60
291 Keith Tower .20 .50
292 Mark Bryant .20 .50
293 Oliver Miller .20 .50
294 Michael Adams .20 .50
295 Tree Rollins .20 .50
296 Eddie Jones 1.00 2.50
297 Malik Sealy .20 .50
298 Blue Edwards .20 .50
299 Brooks Thompson .25 .60
300 Benoit Benjamin .20 .50
301 Avery Johnson .25 .60
302 Larry Johnson .40 1.00
303 John Starks .30 .75
304 Byron Scott .25 .60
305 Eric Murdock .20 .50
306 Jay Humphries .20 .50
307 Kenny Anderson .25 .60
308 Brian Williams .20 .50
309 Nick Van Exel .30 .75
310 Tim Hardaway .40 1.00
311 Lee Mayberry .20 .50
312 Vlade Divac .30 .75
313 Donyell Marshall .30 .75
314 Anthony Mason .25 .60
315 Danny Manning .25 .60
316 Tyrone Hill .20 .50
317 Vincent Askew .20 .50
318 Khalid Reeves .25 .60
319 Ron Harper .25 .60
320 Brent Price .20 .50
321 Byron Houston .20 .50
322 Lamond Murray .30 .75
323 Bryant Stith .20 .50
324 Tom Gugliotta .20 .50
325 Jerome Kersey .20 .50
326 B.J. Tyler .20 .50
327 Antonio Lang .30 .75
328 Carlos Rogers .25 .60
329 Wayman Tisdale .20 .50
330 Kevin Gamble .20 .50
331 Eric Piatkowski .30 .75
332 Mitchell Butler .20 .50
333 Patrick Ewing .50 1.25
334 Doug Smith .20 .50
335 Joe Kleine .20 .50
336 Keith Jennings .20 .50
337 Bill Curley .20 .50
338 Johnny Newman .20 .50
339 Howard Eisley .30 .75
340 Willie Anderson .20 .50
341 Aaron McKie .30 .75
342 Tom Chambers .25 .60
343 Scott Williams .20 .50
344 Harvey Grant .20 .50
345 Billy Owens .20 .50
346 Sharone Wright .25 .60
347 Michael Cage .20 .50
348 Vern Fleming .20 .50
349 Darrin Hancock .25 .60
350 Matt Fish .20 .50
351 Rony Seikaly .20 .50
352 Victor Alexander .20 .50
353 Anthony Miller .30 .75
354 Horace Grant .30 .75
355 Jayson Williams .20 .50
356 Dale Ellis .20 .50
357 Sarunas Marciulionis .20 .50
358 Anthony Avent .20 .50
359 Rex Chapman .20 .50
360 Askia Jones .30 .75
361 Bo Outlaw .30 .75
362 Chuck Person .25 .60
363 Danny Schayes .20 .50
364 Morlon Wiley .20 .50
365 Dontonio Wingfield .30 .75
366 Tony Smith .20 .50
367 Bill Wennington .20 .50
368 Bryon Russell .20 .50
369 Geert Hammink .20 .50
370 Eric Montross .25 .60
371 Cliff Levingston .20 .50
372 Stacey Augmon BP .25 .60
373 Eric Montross BP .15 .40
374 Alonzo Mourning BP .50 1.25
375 Scottie Pippen BP .75 2.00
376 Mark Price BP .30 .75
377 Jason Kidd BP 1.00 2.50
378 Jalen Rose BP .50 1.25
379 Grant Hill BP 1.00 2.50
380 Latrell Sprewell BP .40 1.00
381 Hakeem Olajuwon BP .60 1.50
382 Reggie Miller BP .60 1.50
383 Lamond Murray BP .20 .50
384 Eddie Jones BP .60 1.50
385 Khalid Reeves BP .15 .40
386 Glenn Robinson BP .40 1.00
387 Donyell Marshall BP .20 .50
388 Derrick Coleman BP .30 .75
389 Patrick Ewing BP .50 1.25
390 Shaquille O'Neal BP 1.25 3.00
391 Sharone Wright BP .15 .40
392 Charles Barkley BP .75 2.00
393 Aaron McKie BP .20 .50
394 Brian Grant BP .30 .75
395 David Robinson BP .60 1.50
396 Shawn Kemp BP .50 1.25
397 Karl Malone BP .60 1.50
398 Tom Gugliotta BP .20 .50
399 Hakeem Olajuwon TRIV .60 1.50
400 Shaquille O'Neal TRIV 1.25 3.00
401 Chris Webber TRIV .60 1.50
402 Michael Jordan TRIV 2.50 6.00
403 David Robinson TRIV .60 1.50
404 Shawn Kemp TRIV .50 1.25
405 Patrick Ewing TRIV .50 1.25
406 Charles Barkley TRIV .75 2.00
407 Glenn Robinson DC .40 1.00
408 Jason Kidd DC 1.00 2.50
409 Grant Hill DC 1.00 2.50
410 Donyell Marshall DC .20 .50
411 Sharone Wright DC .15 .40
412 Lamond Murray DC .20 .50
413 Brian Grant DC .30 .75
414 Eric Montross DC .15 .40
415 Eddie Jones DC .60 1.50
416 Carlos Rogers DC .15 .40
417 Shawn Kemp CL .50 1.25
418 Bobby Hurley CL .20 .50
419 Shawn Bradley CL .20 .50
420 Michael Jordan CL 2.50 6.00
421 Vernon Maxwell .20 .50
422 John Stockton .60 1.50
423 Luc Longley .25 .60
424 Sam Perkins .20 .50
425 Pooh Richardson .20 .50
426 Tyrone Corbin .20 .50
427 Mario Elie .20 .50
428 Bobby Phills .20 .50
429 Grant Hill 1.50 4.00

1994-95 Collector's Choice International French Gold Signatures

COMPLETE SET (72) 55.00 130.00
COMPLETE SERIES 1 (27) 15.00 30.00
COMPLETE SERIES 2 (45) 40.00 100.00
166 Danny Manning TO 1.00 2.50
167 Dee Brown TO 1.00 2.50
168 Alonzo Mourning TO 2.00 5.00
169 Scottie Pippen TO 3.00 8.00
170 Mark Price TO 1.25 3.00
171 Jamal Mashburn TO 1.25 3.00
172 Dikembe Mutombo TO 2.00 5.00
173 Joe Dumars TO 1.25 3.00
174 Chris Webber TO 2.50 6.00
175 Hakeem Olajuwon TO 2.50 6.00
176 Reggie Miller TO 2.50 6.00
177 Ron Harper TO 1.00 2.50
178 Nick Van Exel TO 1.25 3.00
179 Steve Smith TO 1.00 2.50
180 Vin Baker TO 1.25 3.00
181 Isaiah Rider TO 1.25 3.00
182 Derrick Coleman TO 1.25 3.00
183 Patrick Ewing TO 2.00 5.00
184 Shaquille O'Neal TO 5.00 12.00
185 Clarence Weatherspoon TO .75 2.00
186 Charles Barkley TO 3.00 8.00
187 Clyde Drexler TO 2.00 5.00
188 Mitch Richmond TO 1.50 4.00
189 David Robinson TO 2.50 6.00
190 Shawn Kemp TO 2.00 5.00
191 Karl Malone TO 2.50 6.00
192 Tom Gugliotta TO .75 2.00
372 Stacey Augmon BP 1.00 2.50
373 Eric Montross BP .50 1.25
374 Alonzo Mourning BP 2.00 5.00
375 Scottie Pippen BP 3.00 8.00
376 Mark Price BP 1.25 3.00
377 Jason Kidd BP 3.00 8.00
378 Jalen Rose BP 1.50 4.00
379 Grant Hill BP 3.00 8.00
380 Latrell Sprewell BP 1.50 4.00
381 Hakeem Olajuwon BP 2.50 6.00
382 Reggie Miller BP 2.50 6.00
383 Lamond Murray BP .60 1.50
384 Eddie Jones BP 2.00 5.00
385 Khalid Reeves BP .50 1.25
386 Glenn Robinson BP 1.25 3.00
387 Donyell Marshall BP .60 1.50
388 Derrick Coleman BP 1.25 3.00
389 Patrick Ewing BP 2.00 5.00
390 Shaquille O'Neal BP 5.00 12.00
391 Sharone Wright BP .50 1.25
392 Charles Barkley BP 3.00 8.00
393 Aaron McKie BP .60 1.50
394 Brian Grant BP 1.00 2.50
395 David Robinson BP 2.50 6.00
396 Shawn Kemp BP 2.00 5.00
397 Karl Malone BP 2.50 6.00
398 Tom Gugliotta BP .75 2.00
399 Hakeem Olajuwon TRIV 2.50 6.00
400 Shaquille O'Neal TRIV 5.00 12.00
401 Chris Webber TRIV 2.50 6.00
402 Michael Jordan TRIV 10.00 25.00
403 David Robinson TRIV 2.50 6.00
404 Shawn Kemp TRIV 2.00 5.00
405 Patrick Ewing TRIV 2.00 5.00
406 Charles Barkley TRIV 3.00 8.00
407 Glenn Robinson DC 1.25 3.00
408 Jason Kidd DC 3.00 8.00
409 Grant Hill DC 3.00 8.00
410 Donyell Marshall DC .60 1.50
411 Sharone Wright DC .50 1.25
412 Lamond Murray DC .60 1.50
413 Brian Grant DC 1.00 2.50
414 Eric Montross DC .50 1.25
415 Eddie Jones DC 2.00 5.00
416 Carlos Rogers DC .50 1.25

1994-95 Collector's Choice International French Decade of Dominance

COMPLETE SET (10) 12.00 30.00
J1 Michael Jordan
Career Stats 1.50 4.00
J2 Michael Jordan
'84 NBA ROY 1.50 4.00
J3 Michael Jordan
'87 Slam-Dunk Champion 1.50 4.00
J4 Michael Jordan
NBA All-Star Game Stats 1.50 4.00
J5 Michael Jordan
Efficient Scorer 1.50 4.00
J6 Michael Jordan
'88 NBA Defensive POY 1.50 4.00
J7 Michael Jordan
1991 NBA Title 1.50 4.00
J8 Michael Jordan
Unstoppable 1.50 4.00
J9 Michael Jordan
All-NBA First Team 1.50 4.00
J10 Michael Jordan
Averaging over 30 ppg 1.50 4.00

1994-95 Collector's Choice International German

COMPLETE SET (429) 20.00 50.00
COMPLETE SERIES 1 (219) 10.00 25.00
COMPLETE SERIES 2 (210) 10.00 25.00
*GERMAN: SAME VALUE AS FRENCH

1994-95 Collector's Choice International German Gold Signatures

COMPLETE SET (72) 55.00 130.00
COMPLETE SERIES 1 (27) 15.00 30.00
COMPLETE SERIES 2 (45) 40.00 100.00
*GERMAN: SAME VALUE AS FRENCH

1994-95 Collector's Choice International German Decade of Dominance

COMPLETE SET (10) 12.00 30.00
*GERMAN: SAME VALUE AS FRENCH

1994-95 Collector's Choice International Italian

COMPLETE SET (429) 20.00 50.00
COMPLETE SERIES 1 (219) 10.00 25.00
COMPLETE SERIES 2 (210) 10.00 25.00
*ITALIAN: SAME VALUE AS FRENCH

1994-95 Collector's Choice International Italian Gold Signatures

COMPLETE SET (72) 55.00 130.00
COMPLETE SERIES 1 (27) 15.00 30.00
COMPLETE SERIES 2 (45) 40.00 100.00
*ITALIAN: SAME VALUE AS FRENCH

1994-95 Collector's Choice International Italian Decade of Dominance

COMPLETE SET (10) 12.00 30.00
*ITALIAN: SAME VALUE AS FRENCH

1994-95 Collector's Choice International Japanese I

COMPLETE SET (219) 50.00 100.00
1 Anfernee Hardaway .75 2.00
2 Mark Macon .25 .60
3 Steve Smith .30 .75
4 Chris Webber .75 2.00
5 Donald Royal .25 .60
6 Avery Johnson .30 .75
7 Kevin Johnson .40 1.00
8 Doug Christie .30 .75
9 Derrick McKey .25 .60
10 Dennis Rodman 1.00 2.50
11 Scott Skiles .25 .60
12 Johnny Dawkins .25 .60
13 Kendall Gill .25 .60
14 Jeff Hornacek .30 .75
15 Latrell Sprewell .50 1.25
16 Lucious Harris .25 .60
17 Chris Mullin .50 1.25
18 Jon Williams .25 .60
19 Tony Campbell .25 .60
20 LaPhonso Ellis .25 .60
21 Gerald Wilkins .30 .75
22 Clyde Drexler .60 1.50
23 Michael Jordan BB 3.00 8.00
24 George Lynch .25 .60
25 Mark Price .40 1.00
26 James Robinson .25 .60
27 Elmore Spencer .25 .60
28 Stacey King .25 .60
29 Corie Blount .25 .60
30 Dell Curry .25 .60
31 Reggie Miller .75 2.00
32 Karl Malone .75 2.00
33 Scottie Pippen 1.00 2.50
34 Hakeem Olajuwon .75 2.00
35 Clarence Weatherspoon .25 .60
36 Kevin Edwards .25 .60
37 Pete Myers .25 .60
38 Jeff Turner .25 .60
39 Ennis Whatley .25 .60
40 Calbert Cheaney .30 .75
41 Glen Rice .40 1.00
42 Vin Baker .40 1.00
43 Grant Long .25 .60
44 Derrick Coleman .40 1.00
45 Rik Smits .30 .75
46 Chris Smith .25 .60
47 Carl Herrera .25 .60
48 Bob Martin .25 .60
49 Terrell Brandon .25 .60
50 David Robinson .75 2.00
51 Danny Ferry .25 .60
52 Buck Williams .25 .60
53 Josh Grant .25 .60
54 Ed Pinckney .25 .60
55 Dikembe Mutombo .60 1.50
56 Clifford Robinson .30 .75
57 Luther Wright .25 .60
58 Scott Burrell .25 .60
59 Stacey Augmon .30 .75
60 Jeff Malone .25 .60
61 Byron Houston .25 .60
62 Anthony Peeler .25 .60
63 Michael Adams .25 .60
64 Negele Knight .25 .60
65 Terry Cummings .30 .75
66 Christian Laettner .30 .75
67 Tracy Murray .25 .60
68 Sedale Threatt .25 .60
69 Dan Majerle .40 1.00
70 Frank Brickowski .25 .60
71 Ken Norman .25 .60
72 Charles Smith .25 .60
73 Adam Keefe .25 .60
74 P.J. Brown .25 .60
75 Kevin Duckworth .25 .60
76 Shawn Bradley .25 .60
77 Darnell Mee .25 .60
78 Nick Anderson .25 .60
79 Mark West .25 .60
80 B.J. Armstrong .40 1.00
81 Dennis Scott .30 .75
82 Lindsey Hunter .25 .60
83 Derek Strong .25 .60
84 Mike Brown .25 .60
85 Antonio Harvey .25 .60
86 Anthony Bonner .25 .60
87 Sam Cassell .40 1.00
88 Harold Miner .25 .60
89 Spud Webb .30 .75
90 Mookie Blaylock .40 1.00
91 Greg Anthony .25 .60
92 Richard Petruska .25 .60
93 Sean Rooks .25 .60
94 Ervin Johnson .25 .60
95 Randy Brown .25 .60
96 Orlando Woolridge .25 .60
97 Charles Oakley .40 1.00
98 Craig Ehlo .25 .60
99 Derek Harper .30 .75
100 Doug Edwards .25 .60
101 Muggsy Bogues .30 .75
102 Mitch Richmond .50 1.25
103 Mahmoud Abdul-Rauf .25 .60
104 Joe Dumars .40 1.00
105 Eric Riley .25 .60
106 Terry Mills .25 .60
107 Toni Kukoc .50 1.25
108 Jon Koncak .25 .60
109 Haywoode Workman .25 .60
110 Todd Day .25 .60
111 Detlef Schrempf .40 1.00
112 David Wesley .25 .60
113 Mark Jackson .30 .75
114 Doug Overton .25 .60
115 Vinny Del Negro .25 .60
116 Loy Vaught .25 .60
117 Mike Peplowski .25 .60
118 Bimbo Coles .25 .60
119 Rex Walters .25 .60
120 Sherman Douglas .25 .60
121 David Benoit .25 .60
122 John Salley .25 .60
123 Cedric Ceballos .30 .75
124 Chris Mills .30 .75
125 Robert Horry .40 1.00
126 Johnny Newman .25 .60
127 Malcolm Mackey .25 .60
128 Terry Dehere .25 .60
129 Dino Radja .25 .60
130 Reggie Williams .25 .60
131 Xavier McDaniel .25 .60
132 Bobby Hurley .25 .60
133 Alonzo Mourning .60 1.50
134 Isaiah Rider .40 1.00
135 Antoine Carr .25 .60
136 Robert Pack .30 .75
137 Walt Williams .25 .60
138 Tyrone Corbin .25 .60
139 Popeye Jones .25 .60
140 Shawn Kemp .60 1.50
141 Thurl Bailey .25 .60
142 James Worthy .50 1.25
143 Scott Haskin .25 .60
144 Hubert Davis .25 .60
145 A.C. Green .30 .75
146 Dale Davis .25 .60
147 Nate McMillan .30 .75
148 Chris Morris .25 .60
149 Will Perdue .25 .60
150 Felton Spencer .25 .60
151 Rod Strickland .25 .60
152 Blue Edwards .25 .60
153 John S. Williams .25 .60
154 Rodney Rogers .25 .60
155 Acie Earl .25 .60
156 Hersey Hawkins .25 .60
157 Jamal Mashburn .40 1.00
158 Don MacLean .25 .60
159 Micheal Williams .25 .60
160 Kenny Gattison .25 .60
161 Rich King .25 .60
162 Allan Houston .40 1.00
163 John Stockton .75 2.00
164 Kenny Anderson .30 .75
165 Shaquille O'Neal 1.50 4.00
166 Danny Manning TO .30 .75
167 Dee Brown TO .30 .75
168 Alonzo Mourning TO .60 1.50
169 Scottie Pippen TO 1.00 2.50
170 Mark Price TO .40 1.00
171 Jamal Mashburn TO .40 1.00
172 Dikembe Mutombo TO .60 1.50
173 Joe Dumars TO .40 1.00
174 Chris Webber TO .75 2.00
175 Hakeem Olajuwon TO .75 2.00
176 Reggie Miller TO .75 2.00
177 Ron Harper TO .30 .75
178 Nick Van Exel TO .40 1.00
179 Steve Smith TO .30 .75
180 Vin Baker TO .40 1.00
181 Isaiah Rider TO .40 1.00
182 Derrick Coleman TO .40 1.00
183 Patrick Ewing TO .60 1.50
184 Shaquille O'Neal TO 1.50 4.00
185 Clarence Weatherspoon TO .25 .60
186 Charles Barkley TO 1.00 2.50
187 Clyde Drexler TO .60 1.50
188 Mitch Richmond TO .50 1.25
189 David Robinson TO .75 2.00
190 Shawn Kemp TO .60 1.50
191 Karl Malone TO .75 2.00
192 Tom Gugliotta TO .25 .60
193 Kenny Anderson ASA .30 .75
194 Alonzo Mourning ASA .60 1.50
195 Mark Price ASA .40 1.00
196 John Stockton ASA .75 2.00
197 Shaquille O'Neal ASA 1.50 4.00
198 Latrell Sprewell ASA .50 1.25
199 Charles Barkley PRO 1.00 2.50
200 Chris Webber PRO .75 2.00
201 Patrick Ewing PRO .60 1.50
202 Dennis Rodman PRO 1.00 2.50
203 Shawn Kemp PRO .60 1.50
204 Michael Jordan PRO 3.00 8.00
205 Shaquille O'Neal PRO 1.50 4.00
206 Larry Johnson PRO .50 1.25
207 Tim Hardaway CL .50 1.25
208 John Stockton CL .75 2.00
209 Harold Miner CL .25 .60
210 B.J.Armstrong CL .40 1.00
211 Michael Jordan ROY 3.00 8.00
212 Michael Jordan 63-Pt. Game 3.00 8.00
213 Michael Jordan Slam-Dunk 3.00 8.00
214 Michael Jordan MVP 3.00 8.00
215 Michael Jordan All-Star 3.00 8.00
216 Michael Jordan 3,000-Points 3.00 8.00
217 Michael Jordan Champ. 3.00 8.00
218 Michael Jordan Decade 3.00 8.00
219 Michael Jordan CL 3.00 8.00

1994-95 Collector's Choice International Japanese II

COMPLETE SET (210) 35.00 75.00
220 Gary Payton .60 1.50
221 Tom Hammonds .25 .60
222 Danny Ainge .40 1.00
223 Gary Grant .25 .60
224 Jim Jackson .30 .75
225 Chris Gatling .25 .60
226 Sergei Bazarevich .40 1.00
227 Tony Dumas .30 .75
228 Andrew Lang .25 .60
229 Wesley Person .40 1.00
230 Terry Porter .25 .60
231 Duane Causwell .25 .60
232 Shaquille O'Neal 1.50 4.00
233 Antonio Davis .30 .75
234 Charles Barkley 1.00 2.50
235 Tony Massenburg .25 .60
236 Ricky Pierce .25 .60
237 Scott Skiles .25 .60
238 Jalen Rose 1.00 2.50
239 Charlie Ward .40 1.00
240 Michael Jordan COMM 3.00 8.00
241 Elden Campbell .25 .60
242 Bill Cartwright .30 .75
243 Armon Gilliam UER
Card numbered 372 .25 .60
244 Rick Fox .25 .60
245 Tim Breaux .25 .60
246 Monty Williams .50 1.25
247 Dominique Wilkins .60 1.50
248 Robert Parish .40 1.00
249 Mark Jackson .30 .75
250 Jason Kidd 2.00 5.00
251 Andres Guibert .25 .60
252 Matt Geiger .25 .60
253 Stanley Roberts .25 .60
254 Jack Haley .25 .60
255 David Wingate .25 .60
256 John Crotty .25 .60
257 Brian Grant .60 1.50
258 Otis Thorpe .25 .60
259 Clifford Rozier .25 .60
260 Grant Long .25 .60
261 Eric Mobley .25 .60
262 Dickey Simpkins .30 .75
263 J.R. Reid .25 .60
264 Kevin Willis .30 .75
265 Scott Brooks .25 .60
266 Glenn Robinson .75 2.00
267 Dana Barros .25 .60
268 Ken Norman .25 .60
269 Herb Williams .25 .60
270 Dee Brown .30 .75
271 Steve Kerr .30 .75
272 Jon Barry .25 .60
273 Sean Elliott .30 .75
274 Elliot Perry .25 .60
275 Kenny Smith .30 .75
276 Sean Rooks .25 .60
277 Gheorghe Muresan .25 .60
278 Juwan Howard .60 1.50
279 Steve Smith .30 .75
280 Anthony Bowie .25 .60
281 Moses Malone .40 1.00
282 Olden Polynice .25 .60
283 Jo Jo English .25 .60
284 Marty Conlon .25 .60
285 Sam Mitchell .25 .60
286 Doug West .25 .60
287 Cedric Ceballos .30 .75
288 Lorenzo Williams .25 .60

289 Harold Ellis .25 .60
290 Doc Rivers .30 .75
291 Keith Tower .25 .60
292 Mark Bryant .25 .60
293 Oliver Miller .25 .60
294 Michael Adams .25 .60
295 Tree Rollins .25 .60
296 Eddie Jones 1.25 3.00
297 Malik Sealy .25 .60
298 Blue Edwards .25 .60
299 Brooks Thompson .30 .75
300 Benoit Benjamin .25 .60
301 Avery Johnson .30 .75
302 Larry Johnson .50 1.25
303 John Starks .40 1.00
304 Byron Scott .30 .75
305 Eric Murdock .25 .60
306 Jay Humphries .25 .60
307 Kenny Anderson .30 .75
308 Brian Williams .25 .60
309 Nick Van Exel .40 1.00
310 Tim Hardaway .50 1.25
311 Lee Mayberry .25 .60
312 Vlade Divac .40 1.00
313 Donyell Marshall .40 1.00
314 Anthony Mason .30 .75
315 Danny Manning .30 .75
316 Tyrone Hill .25 .60
317 Vincent Askew .25 .60
318 Khalid Reeves .30 .75
319 Ron Harper .30 .75
320 Brent Price .25 .60
321 Byron Houston .25 .60
322 Lamond Murray .40 1.00
323 Bryant Stith .25 .60
324 Tom Gugliotta .25 .60
325 Jerome Kersey .25 .60
326 B.J. Tyler .25 .60
327 Antonio Lang .40 1.00
328 Carlos Rogers .30 .75
329 Wayman Tisdale .25 .60
330 Kevin Gamble .25 .60
331 Eric Piatkowski .40 1.00
332 Mitchell Butler .25 .60
333 Patrick Ewing .60 1.50
334 Doug Smith .25 .60
335 Joe Kleine .25 .60
336 Keith Jennings .25 .60
337 Bill Curley .25 .60
338 Johnny Newman .25 .60
339 Howard Eisley .40 1.00
340 Willie Anderson .25 .60
341 Aaron McKie .40 1.00
342 Tom Chambers .30 .75
343 Scott Williams .25 .60
344 Harvey Grant .25 .60
345 Billy Owens .25 .60
346 Sharone Wright .30 .75
347 Michael Cage .25 .60
348 Vern Fleming .25 .60
349 Darrin Hancock .30 .75
350 Matt Fish .25 .60
351 Rony Seikaly .25 .60
352 Victor Alexander .25 .60
353 Anthony Miller .40 1.00
354 Horace Grant .40 1.00
355 Jayson Williams .25 .60
356 Dale Ellis .25 .60
357 Sarunas Marciulionis .25 .60
358 Anthony Avent .25 .60
359 Rex Chapman .25 .60
360 Askia Jones .40 1.00
361 Bo Outlaw .40 1.00
362 Chuck Person .30 .75
363 Danny Schayes .25 .60
364 Morlon Wiley .25 .60
365 Dontonio Wingfield .40 1.00
366 Tony Smith .25 .60
367 Bill Wennington .25 .60
368 Bryon Russell .25 .60
369 Geert Hammink .25 .60
370 Eric Montross .30 .75
371 Cliff Levingston .25 .60
372 Stacey Augmon BP .30 .75
373 Eric Montross BP .25 .60
374 Alonzo Mourning BP .60 1.50
375 Scottie Pippen BP 1.00 2.50
376 Mark Price BP .40 1.00
377 Jason Kidd BP 1.50 4.00
378 Jalen Rose BP .75 2.00
379 Grant Hill BP 1.50 4.00
380 Latrell Sprewell BP .50 1.25
381 Hakeem Olajuwon BP .75 2.00
382 Reggie Miller BP .75 2.00
383 Lamond Murray BP .30 .75
384 Eddie Jones BP 1.00 2.50
385 Khalid Reeves BP .25 .60
386 Glenn Robinson BP .60 1.50
387 Donyell Marshall BP .30 .75
388 Derrick Coleman BP .40 1.00
389 Patrick Ewing BP .60 1.50
390 Shaquille O'Neal BP 1.50 4.00
391 Sharone Wright BP .25 .60
392 Charles Barkley BP 1.00 2.50
393 Aaron McKie BP .30 .75
394 Brian Grant BP .50 1.25
395 David Robinson BP .75 2.00
396 Shawn Kemp BP .60 1.50
397 Karl Malone BP .75 2.00
398 Tom Gugliotta BP .25 .60
399 Hakeem Olajuwon TRIV .75 2.00
400 Shaquille O'Neal TRIV 1.50 4.00
401 Chris Webber TRIV .75 2.00
402 Michael Jordan TRIV 3.00 8.00
403 David Robinson TRIV .75 2.00
404 Shawn Kemp TRIV .60 1.50
405 Patrick Ewing TRIV .60 1.50
406 Charles Barkley TRIV 1.00 2.50
407 Glenn Robinson DC .60 1.50
408 Jason Kidd DC 1.50 4.00
409 Grant Hill DC 1.50 4.00
410 Donyell Marshall DC .30 .75
411 Sharone Wright DC .25 .60
412 Lamond Murray DC .30 .75
413 Brian Grant DC .50 1.25
414 Eric Montross DC .25 .60
415 Eddie Jones DC 1.00 2.50
416 Carlos Rogers DC .25 .60
417 Shawn Kemp CL .60 1.50
418 Bobby Hurley CL .25 .60
419 Shawn Bradley CL .25 .60
420 Michael Jordan CL 3.00 8.00
421 Vernon Maxwell .25 .60
422 John Stockton .75 2.00
423 Luc Longley .30 .75
424 Sam Perkins .25 .60
425 Pooh Richardson .25 .60
426 Tyrone Corbin .25 .60
427 Mario Elie .25 .60
428 Bobby Phills .25 .60
429 Grant Hill 2.00 5.00

1994-95 Collector's Choice International Japanese I Gold Signatures

COMPLETE SET (26) 125.00 250.00
166 Danny Manning 3.00 8.00
167 Dee Brown 3.00 8.00
168 Alonzo Mourning 6.00 15.00
169 Scottie Pippen 10.00 25.00
170 Mark Price 4.00 10.00
171 Jamal Mashburn 4.00 10.00
172 Dikembe Mutombo 6.00 15.00
173 Joe Dumars 4.00 10.00
174 Chris Webber 8.00 20.00
175 Hakeem Olajuwon 8.00 20.00
176 Reggie Miller 8.00 20.00
177 Ron Harper 3.00 8.00
178 Nick Van Exel 4.00 10.00
179 Steve Smith 3.00 8.00
180 Vin Baker 4.00 10.00
181 Isaiah Rider 4.00 10.00
182 Derrick Coleman 4.00 10.00
183 Patrick Ewing 6.00 15.00
184 Shaquille O'Neal 15.00 40.00
186 Charles Barkley 10.00 25.00
187 Clyde Drexler 6.00 15.00
188 Mitch Richmond 5.00 12.00
189 David Robinson 8.00 20.00
190 Shawn Kemp 6.00 15.00
191 Karl Malone 8.00 20.00
192 Tom Gugliotta 2.50 6.00

1994-95 Collector's Choice International Japanese II Gold Signatures

COMPLETE SET (44) 200.00 400.00
372 Stacey Augmon BP 3.00 8.00
373 Eric Montross BP 1.50 4.00
374 Alonzo Mourning BP 6.00 15.00
375 Scottie Pippen BP 10.00 25.00
376 Mark Price BP 4.00 10.00
377 Jason Kidd BP 10.00 25.00
378 Jalen Rose BP 5.00 12.00
379 Grant Hill BP 10.00 25.00
380 Latrell Sprewell BP 5.00 12.00
381 Hakeem Olajuwon BP 8.00 20.00
382 Reggie Miller BP 8.00 20.00
383 Lamond Murray BP 2.00 5.00
384 Eddie Jones BP 6.00 15.00
385 Khalid Reeves BP 1.50 4.00
386 Glenn Robinson BP 4.00 10.00
387 Donyell Marshall BP 2.00 5.00
388 Derrick Coleman BP 4.00 10.00
389 Patrick Ewing BP 6.00 15.00
390 Shaquille O'Neal BP 15.00 40.00
391 Sharone Wright BP 1.50 4.00
392 Charles Barkley BP 10.00 25.00
393 Aaron McKie BP 2.00 5.00
394 Brian Grant BP 3.00 8.00
395 David Robinson BP 8.00 20.00
396 Shawn Kemp BP 6.00 15.00
397 Karl Malone BP 8.00 20.00
398 Tom Gugliotta BP 2.50 6.00
400 Shaquille O'Neal TRIV 15.00 40.00
401 Chris Webber TRIV 8.00 20.00
402 Michael Jordan TRIV 30.00 80.00
403 David Robinson TRIV 8.00 20.00
404 Shawn Kemp TRIV 6.00 15.00
405 Patrick Ewing TRIV 6.00 15.00
406 Charles Barkley TRIV 10.00 25.00
407 Glenn Robinson DC 4.00 10.00
408 Jason Kidd DC 10.00 25.00
409 Grant Hill DC 10.00 25.00
410 Donyell Marshall DC 2.00 5.00
411 Sharone Wright DC 1.50 4.00
412 Lamond Murray DC 2.00 5.00
413 Brian Grant DC 3.00 8.00
414 Eric Montross DC 1.50 4.00
415 Eddie Jones DC 6.00 15.00
416 Carlos Rogers DC 1.50 4.00

1994-95 Collector's Choice International Japanese Silver Signatures

COMPLETE SET (25) 6.00 15.00
166 Danny Manning TO .50 1.25
167 Dee Brown TO .50 1.25
168 Alonzo Mourning TO 1.00 2.50
169 Scottie Pippen TO 1.50 4.00
170 Mark Price TO .60 1.50
171 Jamal Mashburn TO .60 1.50
172 Dikembe Mutombo TO 1.00 2.50
173 Joe Dumars TO .60 1.50
174 Chris Webber TO 1.25 3.00
175 Hakeem Olajuwon TO 1.25 3.00
177 Ron Harper TO .50 1.25
178 Nick Van Exel TO .60 1.50
179 Steve Smith TO .50 1.25
180 Vin Baker TO .60 1.50
181 Isaiah Rider TO .60 1.50
182 Derrick Coleman TO .60 1.50
183 Patrick Ewing TO 1.00 2.50
184 Shaquille O'Neal TO 2.50 6.00
185 Clarence Weatherspoon TO .40 1.00
187 Clyde Drexler TO 1.00 2.50
188 Mitch Richmond TO .75 2.00
189 David Robinson TO 1.25 3.00
190 Shawn Kemp TO 1.00 2.50
191 Karl Malone TO 1.25 3.00
192 Tom Gugliotta TO .40 1.00

1994-95 Collector's Choice International Japanese Decade of Dominance

COMPLETE SET (10) 30.00 80.00
COMMON CARD 4.00 10.00

1994-95 Collector's Choice International Spanish I

COMPLETE SET (219) 10.00 25.00
*SPANISH: SAME VALUE AS FRENCH

1994-95 Collector's Choice International Spanish II

COMPLETE SET (210) 10.00 20.00
*SPANISH: SAME VALUE AS FRENCH

1994-95 Collector's Choice International Spanish Gold Signatures

COMPLETE SET (72) 55.00 130.00
COMPLETE SERIES 1 (27) 15.00 30.00
COMPLETE SERIES 2 (45) 40.00 100.00
*SPANISH: SAME VALUE AS FRENCH

1994-95 Collector's Choice International Spanish Decade of Dominance

COMPLETE SET (10) 12.00 30.00
*SPANISH: SAME VALUE AS FRENCH

1995-96 Collector's Choice International French I

COMPLETE SET (210) 8.00 20.00
1 Craig Ehlo .10 .25
2 Tyrone Corbin .10 .25
3 Mookie Blaylock .15 .40
4 Grant Long .10 .25
5 Andrew Lang .10 .25
6 Stacey Augmon .12 .30
7 Dee Brown .12 .30
8 Sherman Douglas .10 .25
9 Pervis Ellison .10 .25
10 Dominique Wilkins .25 .60
11 Greg Minor .10 .25
12 Larry Johnson .20 .50
13 Dell Curry .15 .40
14 Scott Burrell .10 .25
15 Robert Parish .20 .50
16 Michael Adams .10 .25
17 David Wingate .10 .25
18 Hersey Hawkins .12 .30
19 B.J. Armstrong .15 .40
20 Michael Jordan 1.50 4.00
21 Dickey Simpkins .10 .25
22 Will Perdue .12 .30
23 Steve Kerr .15 .40
24 Ron Harper .12 .30
25 Tyrone Hill .10 .25
26 Bobby Phills .12 .30
27 Michael Cage .10 .25
28 John Williams .10 .25
29 Mark Price .15 .40
30 Danny Ferry .10 .25
31 Jason Kidd .60 1.50
32 Roy Tarpley .10 .25
33 Popeye Jones .10 .25
34 Tony Dumas .10 .25
35 Lucious Harris .10 .25
36 Jim Jackson .10 .25
37 Mahmoud Abdul-Rauf .12 .30
38 Brian Williams .10 .25
39 Rodney Rogers .10 .25
40 LaPhonso Ellis .12 .30
41 Reggie Williams .10 .25
42 Bryant Stith .10 .25
43 Joe Dumars .15 .40
44 Oliver Miller .10 .25
45 Grant Hill .25 .60
46 Bill Curley .10 .25
47 Allan Houston .12 .30
48 Mark West .10 .25
49 Rony Seikaly .10 .25
50 Chris Gatling .10 .25
51 Carlos Rogers .10 .25
52 Tim Hardaway .20 .50
53 Chris Mullin .15 .40
54 Donyell Marshall .10 .25
55 Clyde Drexler .25 .60
56 Kenny Smith .12 .30
57 Carl Herrera .10 .25
58 Robert Horry .15 .40
59 Sam Cassell .15 .40
60 Dale Davis .10 .25
61 Byron Scott .15 .40
62 Rik Smits .12 .30
63 Duane Ferrell .10 .25
64 Derrick McKey .10 .25
65 Reggie Miller .30 .75
66 Eric Piatkowski .10 .25
67 Malik Sealy .10 .25
68 Terry Dehere .10 .25
69 Bo Outlaw .10 .25
70 Lamond Murray .10 .25
71 Loy Vaught .10 .25
72 Nick Van Exel .15 .40
73 Antonio Harvey .10 .25
74 Vlade Divac .15 .40
75 Elden Campbell .10 .25
76 Anthony Peeler .10 .25
77 Eddie Jones .15 .40
78 Harold Miner .10 .25
79 Billy Owens .10 .25
80 Bimbo Coles .10 .25
81 Kevin Gamble .10 .25
82 John Salley .10 .25
83 Kevin Willis .10 .25
84 Khalid Reeves .10 .25
85 Ed Pinckney .10 .25
86 Vin Baker .12 .30
87 Todd Day .10 .25
88 Eric Mobley .10 .25
89 Marty Conlon .10 .25
90 Lee Mayberry .10 .25
91 Micheal Williams .10 .25
92 Tom Gugliotta .10 .25
93 Doug West .10 .25
94 Isaiah Rider .15 .40
95 Christian Laettner .12 .30
96 Chris Smith .10 .25
97 Armon Gilliam .10 .25
98 P.J. Brown .10 .25
99 Rex Walters .10 .25
100 Benoit Benjamin .10 .25
101 Kenny Anderson .12 .30
102 Derrick Coleman .12 .30
103 Derek Harper .12 .30
104 Charles Smith .10 .25
105 Herb Williams .10 .25
106 John Starks .15 .40
107 Charles Oakley .12 .30
108 Hubert Davis .10 .25
109 Dennis Scott .10 .25
110 Jeff Turner .10 .25
111 Horace Grant .12 .30
112 Anthony Bowie .10 .25
113 Anfernee Hardaway .40 1.00
114 Nick Anderson .12 .30
115 Dana Barros .12 .30
116 Scott Williams .10 .25
117 Clarence Weatherspoon .10 .25
118 Jeff Malone .10 .25
119 B.J. Tyler .10 .25
120 Shawn Bradley .10 .25
121 Charles Barkley .40 1.00
122 A.C. Green .12 .30
123 Kevin Johnson .15 .40
124 Wayman Tisdale .10 .25
125 Danny Schayes .10 .25
126 Dan Majerle .15 .40
127 Rod Strickland .10 .25
128 Harvey Grant .10 .25
129 Aaron McKie .10 .25
130 Chris Dudley .10 .25
131 Otis Thorpe .12 .30
132 Jerome Kersey .10 .25
133 Clifford Robinson .15 .40
134 Bobby Hurley .10 .25
135 Spud Webb .15 .40
136 Olden Polynice .10 .25
137 Randy Brown .10 .25
138 Brian Grant .12 .30
139 Walt Williams .10 .25
140 Avery Johnson .10 .25
141 Dennis Rodman .30 .75
142 J.R. Reid .10 .25
143 David Robinson .30 .75
144 Vinny Del Negro .10 .25
145 Willie Anderson .10 .25
146 Nate McMillan .10 .25
147 Shawn Kemp .25 .60
148 Detlef Schrempf .15 .40
149 Vincent Askew .10 .25
150 Sarunas Marciulionis .10 .25
151 Byron Houston .10 .25
152 Ervin Johnson .10 .25
153 Adam Keefe .10 .25
154 Jeff Hornacek .12 .30
155 Antoine Carr .10 .25
156 John Stockton .30 .75
157 Blue Edwards .10 .25
158 David Benoit .10 .25
159 Don MacLean .10 .25
160 Juwan Howard .15 .40
161 Calbert Cheaney .10 .25
162 Mitchell Butler .10 .25
163 Gheorghe Muresan .10 .25
164 Rex Chapman .10 .25
165 Doug Overton .10 .25
166 Steve Smith FF .12 .30
167 Dino Radja FF .12 .30
168 Alonzo Mourning FF .25 .60
169 Michael Jordan FF 1.50 4.00
170 Tyrone Hill FF .10 .25
171 Jamal Mashburn FF .15 .40
172 Dikembe Mutombo FF .25 .60
173 Grant Hill FF
with Michael Jordan .40 1.00
174 Latrell Sprewell FF .15 .40
175 Hakeem Olajuwon FF .30 .75
176 Reggie Miller FF .30 .75
177 Pooh Richardson FF .10 .25
178 Cedric Ceballos FF .12 .30
179 Glen Rice FF .15 .40
180 Glenn Robinson FF .15 .40
181 Isaiah Rider FF .15 .40
182 Derrick Coleman FF .12 .30
183 Patrick Ewing FF .25 .60
184 Shaquille O'Neal FF .60 1.50
185 Dana Barros FF .12 .30
186 Dan Majerle FF .15 .40
187 Clifford Robinson FF .12 .30
188 Mitch Richmond FF .20 .50
189 David Robinson FF .30 .75
190 Gary Payton FF .25 .60
191 Oliver Miller FF .10 .25
192 Karl Malone FF .30 .75
193 Kevin Pritchard FF .10 .25
194 Chris Webber FF .20 .50
195 Michael Jordan PD 1.50 4.00
196 Hakeem Olajuwon PD .30 .75
197 Vin Baker PD .12 .30
198 Grant Hill PD .25 .60
199 Clyde Drexler PD .25 .60
200 Chris Webber PD .20 .50
201 Shawn Kemp PD .25 .60
202 Shaquille O'Neal PD .60 1.50
203 Stacey Augmon PD .12 .30
204 David Benoit PD .10 .25
205 Rodney Rogers PD .12 .30
206 Latrell Sprewell PD .15 .40
207 Brian Grant PD .12 .30
208 Lamond Murray PD .10 .25
209 Shawn Kemp CL .25 .60
210 Michael Jordan CL 1.50 4.00

1995-96 Collector's Choice International French II

COMPLETE SET (200) 8.00 20.00
1 Alan Henderson .15 .40
2 Steve Smith .12 .30
3 Ken Norman .10 .25
4 Eric Montross .10 .25
5 Dino Radja .10 .25
6 Rick Fox .10 .25
7 David Wesley .10 .25
8 Dana Barros .12 .30
9 Eric Williams .15 .40
10 George Zidek .12 .30
11 Muggsy Bogues .15 .40
12 Kendall Gill .10 .25
13 Scottie Pippen .40 1.00
14 Bill Wennington .10 .25
15 Dennis Rodman .30 .75
16 Toni Kukoc .20 .50
17 Luc Longley .12 .30
18 Jason Caffey .15 .40
19 Chris Mills .10 .25
20 Terrell Brandon .12 .30
21 Bob Sura .12 .30
22 Cherokee Parks .12 .30
23 Lorenzo Williams .10 .25
24 Jamal Mashburn .15 .40
25 Terry Davis .10 .25
26 Loren Meyer .10 .25
27 Bryant Stith .10 .25
28 Dikembe Mutombo .25 .60
29 Jalen Rose .20 .50
30 Tom Hammonds .10 .25
31 Terry Mills .10 .25
32 Lindsey Hunter .10 .25
33 Theo Ratliff .25 .60
34 Latrell Sprewell .15 .40
35 Andrew DeClercq .15 .40
36 B.J. Armstrong .15 .40
37 Clifford Rozier .10 .25
38 Joe Smith .20 .50
39 Mark Bryant .10 .25
40 Mario Elie .10 .25
41 Hakeem Olajuwon .30 .75
42 Antonio Davis .10 .25
43 Haywoode Workman .10 .25
44 Mark Jackson .12 .30
45 Travis Best .15 .40
46 Brian Williams .15 .40
47 Rodney Rogers .10 .25
48 Brent Barry .25 .60
49 Pooh Richardson .10 .25
50 Gary Grant .10 .25
51 George Lynch .10 .25
52 Sedale Threatt .10 .25
53 Cedric Ceballos .12 .30
54 Sasha Danilovic .15 .40
55 Kurt Thomas .15 .40
56 Glenn Robinson .15 .40
57 Shawn Respert .12 .30
58 Eric Murdock .10 .25
59 Kevin Garnett 1.25 3.00
60 Kevin Edwards .10 .25
61 Ed O'Bannon .12 .30
62 Yinka Dare .10 .25
63 Vern Fleming .10 .25
64 Patrick Ewing .25 .60
65 Monty Williams .10 .25
66 Anthony Mason .10 .25
67 Donald Royal .10 .25
68 Brian Shaw .10 .25
69 Shaquille O'Neal .60 1.50
70 David Vaughn .15 .40
71 Vernon Maxwell .10 .25
72 Jerry Stackhouse .50 1.25
73 Sharone Wright .10 .25
74 Richard Dumas .10 .25
75 Wesley Person .10 .25
76 Joe Kleine .10 .25
77 Elliot Perry .10 .25
78 Danny Manning .12 .30
79 Michael Finley .40 1.00
80 Mario Bennett .12 .30
81 James Robinson .10 .25
82 Buck Williams .10 .25
83 Gary Trent .12 .30
84 Randolph Childress .12 .30
85 Duane Causwell .10 .25
86 Lionel Simmons .10 .25
87 Mitch Richmond .20 .50
88 Michael Smith .10 .25
89 Tyus Edney .15 .40
90 Corliss Williamson .15 .40
91 Cory Alexander .15 .40
92 Chuck Person .12 .30
93 Sean Elliott .12 .30
94 Doc Rivers .12 .30
95 Gary Payton .25 .60
96 Sam Perkins .12 .30
97 Sherrell Ford .12 .30
98 Damon Stoudamire .40 1.00
99 Zan Tabak .10 .25
100 Felton Spencer .10 .25
101 Karl Malone .30 .75
102 Bryon Russell .15 .40
103 Greg Ostertag .15 .40
104 Bryant Reeves .12 .30
105 Lawrence Moten .15 .40
106 Greg Anthony .10 .25
107 Byron Scott .15 .40
108 Scott Skiles .10 .25
109 Rasheed Wallace .50 1.25
110 Chris Webber .20 .50
111 Mookie Blaylock SR .15 .40
112 Dee Brown SR .12 .30
113 Alonzo Mourning SR .25 .60
114 Michael Jordan SR 1.50 4.00
115 Terrell Brandon SR .12 .30
116 Jim Jackson SR .12 .30
117 Dikembe Mutombo SR .25 .60
118 Grant Hill SR .25 .60
119 Joe Smith SR .20 .50
120 Clyde Drexler SR .25 .60
121 Reggie Miller SR .30 .75
122 Lamond Murray SR .10 .25
123 Nick Van Exel SR .15 .40
124 Glen Rice SR .15 .40
125 Glenn Robinson SR .15 .40
126 Christian Laettner SR .12 .30
127 Kenny Anderson SR .12 .30
128 Patrick Ewing SR .25 .60
129 Shaquille O'Neal SR .60 1.50
130 Jerry Stackhouse SR .50 1.25
131 Charles Barkley SR .40 1.00
132 Clifford Robinson SR .15 .40
133 Brian Grant SR .12 .30
134 David Robinson SR .30 .75
135 Shawn Kemp SR .25 .60
136 Damon Stoudamire SR .40 1.00
137 Karl Malone SR .30 .75
138 Bryant Reeves SR .12 .30
139 Juwan Howard SR .15 .40
140 Nick Anderson
Dee Brown PT .12 .30
141 Rik Smits PT .12 .30
142 Herb Williams
Tom Tolbert PT .10 .25
143 Michael Jordan PT 1.50 4.00
144 David Robinson PT .30 .75
145 Terry Porter
Kevin Johnson PT .15 .40
146 Clyde Drexler PT .25 .60
147 Cedric Ceballos PT .12 .30
148 Horace Grant
Group PT .12 .30
149 Reggie Miller PT .30 .75
150 Avery Johnson
Nick Van Exel PT .15 .40
151 Hakeem Olajuwon
Robert Horry PT .30 .75
152 Rik Smits PT .12 .30
153 David Robinson
Hakeem Olajuwon PT .30 .75
154 Robert Horry PT .15 .40
155 Kenny Smith PT .12 .30
156 Stacey Augmon LOVE .12 .30
157 Sherman Douglas LOVE .10 .25
158 Larry Johnson LOVE .20 .50
159 Scottie Pippen LOVE .40 1.00
160 Tyrone Hill LOVE .10 .25
161 Jamal Mashburn LOVE .15 .40
162 Mahmoud Abdul-Rauf LOVE .12 .30
163 Grant Hill LOVE .25 .60
164 Latrell Sprewell LOVE .15 .40
165 Sam Cassell LOVE .15 .40
166 Rik Smits LOVE .12 .30
167 Terry Dehere LOVE .10 .25
168 Eddie Jones LOVE .15 .40
169 Billy Owens LOVE .10 .25
170 Vin Baker LOVE .12 .30
171 Isaiah Rider LOVE .15 .40
172 Kenny Anderson LOVE .12 .30
173 John Starks LOVE .15 .40
174 Anfernee Hardaway LOVE .40 1.00
175 Sharone Wright LOVE .10 .25
176 Charles Barkley LOVE .40 1.00
177 Clifford Robinson LOVE .15 .40
178 Walt Williams LOVE .10 .25
179 Sean Elliott LOVE .12 .30
180 Gary Payton LOVE .25 .60
181 Carlos Rogers LOVE .10 .25
182 John Stockton LOVE .30 .75
183 Greg Anthony LOVE .10 .25
184 Chris Webber LOVE .20 .50
185 Gary Payton PG .25 .60
186 Mookie Blaylock PG .15 .40
187 Charles Barkley PG .40 1.00
188 Grant Hill PG .25 .60
189 Anfernee Hardaway PG .40 1.00
190 Kenny Anderson PG .12 .30
191 Mark Jackson PG .12 .30
192 Karl Malone PG .30 .75
193 Avery Johnson PG .12 .30
194 Larry Johnson 40 .20 .50
195 Nick Van Exel 40 .15 .40
196 Vin Baker 40 .12 .30
197 Jason Kidd 40 .25 .60
198 David Robinson 40 .30 .75
199 Shawn Kemp CL .25 .60
200 Michael Jordan CL 1.50 4.00

1995-96 Collector's Choice International French Crash the Game

COMPLETE SET (30) 20.00 50.00
C1 Michael Jordan 10.00 25.00
C2 Kenny Anderson .75 2.00
C3 Charles Barkley 2.50 6.00
C4 Dana Barros .75 2.00
C5 Anfernee Hardaway 2.50 6.00
C6 Mookie Blaylock 1.00 2.50
C7 Lamond Murray .60 1.50
C8 Karl Malone 2.00 5.00
C9 Alonzo Mourning 1.50 4.00
C10 Hakeem Olajuwon 2.00 5.00
C11 Mark Price 1.00 2.50
C12 Isaiah Rider 1.00 2.50
C13 Glen Rice 1.00 2.50
C14 Mitch Richmond 1.25 3.00
C15 Chris Webber 1.25 3.00
C16 Nick Van Exel 1.00 2.50
C17 Mahmoud Abdul-Rauf .75 2.00
C18 Dominique Wilkins 1.50 4.00
C19 Patrick Ewing 1.50 4.00
C20 David Robinson 2.00 5.00
C21 Shawn Kemp 1.50 4.00
C22 Jason Kidd 1.50 4.00
C23 Glenn Robinson 1.00 2.50
C24 Reggie Miller 2.00 5.00
C25 Joe Dumars 1.00 2.50
C26 Latrell Sprewell 1.00 2.50
C27 Clifford Robinson 1.00 2.50
C28 Damon Stoudamire 2.50 6.00
C29 Bryant Reeves .75 2.00
C30 Michael Jordan 10.00 25.00

1995-96 Collector's Choice International French Jordan Collection

COMPLETE SET (4) 5.00 12.00
COMMON CARD (J1-J4) 1.50 4.00

1995-96 Collector's Choice International French NBA Extremes

COMPLETE SET (9) 1.50 4.00
E1 Muggsy Bogues .50 1.25
E2 Spud Webb .50 1.25
E3 Dana Barros .40 1.00
E4 Avery Johnson .40 1.00
E5 Vlade Divac .50 1.25
E6 Dikembe Mutombo .75 2.00
E7 Rik Smits .40 1.00
E8 Shawn Bradley .30 .75
E9 Gheorghe Muresan .30 .75

1995-96 Collector's Choice International Special Edition Holograms

COMPLETE SET (9) 4.00 10.00
H1 Larry Johnson .75 2.00
H2 Scottie Pippen 1.50 4.00
H3 Grant Hill 1.00 2.50
H4 Reggie Miller 1.25 3.00
H5 Glenn Robinson .60 1.50
H6 Patrick Ewing 1.00 2.50
H7 Shaquille O'Neal 2.50 6.00
H8 John Stockton 1.25 3.00
H9 Chris Webber .75 2.00

1995-96 Collector's Choice International German I

COMPLETE SET (210) 8.00 20.00
*GERMAN: SAME VALUE AS FRENCH

1995-96 Collector's Choice International German II

COMPLETE SET (200) 8.00 20.00
*GERMAN: SAME VALUE AS FRENCH

1995-96 Collector's Choice International German Jordan Collection

COMPLETE SET (4) 5.00 12.00
*GERMAN: SAME VALUE AS FRENCH

1995-96 Collector's Choice International German NBA Extremes

COMPLETE SET (9) 1.50 4.00
*GERMAN: SAME VALUE AS FRENCH

1995-96 Collector's Choice International Italian I

COMPLETE SET (210) 8.00 20.00
*ITALIAN: SAME VALUE AS FRENCH

1995-96 Collector's Choice International Italian II

COMPLETE SET (200) 8.00 20.00
*ITALIAN: SAME VALUE AS FRENCH

1995-96 Collector's Choice International Italian Jordan Collection

COMPLETE SET (4) 5.00 12.00
*ITALIAN: SAME VALUE AS FRENCH

1995-96 Collector's Choice International Italian NBA Extremes

COMPLETE SET (9) 1.50 4.00
*ITALIAN: SAME VALUE AS FRENCH

1995-96 Collector's Choice International Northern European

COMPLETE SET (200)
*NORTHERN EUROPEAN: SAME VALUE AS FRENCH

1995-96 Collector's Choice International Northern European NBA Extremes

COMPLETE SET (9) 1.50 4.00
*NORTHERN EUROPEAN: SAME VALUE AS FRENCH

1995-96 Collector's Choice International Japanese

COMPLETE SET (410) 110.00 220.00
COMPLETE SERIES 1 (210) 50.00 100.00
COMPLETE SERIES 2 (200) 60.00 120.00
1 Craig Ehlo .40 1.00
2 Tyrone Corbin .40 1.00
3 Mookie Blaylock .60 1.50
4 Grant Long .40 1.00
5 Andrew Lang .40 1.00
6 Stacey Augmon .50 1.25
7 Dee Brown .50 1.25
8 Sherman Douglas .40 1.00
9 Pervis Ellison .40 1.00
10 Dominique Wilkins 1.00 2.50
11 Greg Minor .40 1.00
12 Larry Johnson .75 2.00
13 Dell Curry .60 1.50
14 Scott Burrell .40 1.00
15 Robert Parish .75 2.00
16 Michael Adams .40 1.00
17 David Wingate .40 1.00
18 Hersey Hawkins .50 1.25
19 B.J. Armstrong .60 1.50
20 Michael Jordan 6.00 15.00
21 Dickey Simpkins .40 1.00
22 Will Perdue .50 1.25
23 Steve Kerr .60 1.50
24 Ron Harper .50 1.25
25 Tyrone Hill .40 1.00
26 Bobby Phills .50 1.25
27 Michael Cage .40 1.00
28 John Williams .40 1.00
29 Mark Price .60 1.50
30 Danny Ferry .40 1.00
31 Jason Kidd 1.00 2.50
32 Roy Tarpley .50 1.25
33 Popeye Jones .40 1.00
34 Tony Dumas .40 1.00
35 Lucious Harris .40 1.00
36 Jim Jackson .50 1.25
37 Mahmoud Abdul-Rauf .50 1.25
38 Brian Williams .40 1.00
39 Rodney Rogers .50 1.25
40 LaPhonso Ellis .50 1.25
41 Reggie Williams .40 1.00
42 Bryant Stith .40 1.00
43 Joe Dumars .60 1.50
44 Oliver Miller .40 1.00
45 Grant Hill 1.00 2.50
46 Bill Curley .40 1.00
47 Allan Houston .50 1.25
48 Mark West .40 1.00
49 Rony Seikaly .40 1.00
50 Chris Gatling .40 1.00
51 Carlos Rogers .40 1.00
52 Tim Hardaway .75 2.00
53 Chris Mullin .60 1.50
54 Donyell Marshall .40 1.00
55 Clyde Drexler 1.00 2.50
56 Kenny Smith .50 1.25
57 Carl Herrera .40 1.00
58 Robert Horry .60 1.50
59 Sam Cassell .60 1.50
60 Dale Davis .40 1.00
61 Byron Scott .60 1.50
62 Rik Smits .50 1.25
63 Duane Ferrell .40 1.00
64 Derrick McKey .40 1.00
65 Reggie Miller 1.25 3.00
66 Eric Piatkowski .40 1.00
67 Malik Sealy .40 1.00
68 Terry Dehere .40 1.00
69 Bo Outlaw .40 1.00
70 Lamond Murray .40 1.00
71 Loy Vaught .40 1.00

72 Nick Van Exel .60 1.50
73 Antonio Harvey .40 1.00
74 Vlade Divac .60 1.50
75 Elden Campbell .40 1.00
76 Anthony Peeler .40 1.00
77 Eddie Jones .60 1.50
78 Harold Miner .40 1.00
79 Billy Owens .40 1.00
80 Bimbo Coles .40 1.00
81 Kevin Gamble .40 1.00
82 John Salley .40 1.00
83 Kevin Willis .40 1.00
84 Khalid Reeves .40 1.00
85 Ed Pinckney .40 1.00
86 Vin Baker .50 1.25
87 Todd Day .40 1.00
88 Eric Mobley .40 1.00
89 Marty Conlon .40 1.00
90 Lee Mayberry .40 1.00
91 Micheal Williams .40 1.00
92 Tom Gugliotta .40 1.00
93 Doug West .40 1.00
94 Isaiah Rider .60 1.50
95 Christian Laettner .50 1.25
96 Chris Smith .40 1.00
97 Armon Gilliam .40 1.00
98 P.J. Brown .40 1.00
99 Rex Walters .40 1.00
100 Benoit Benjamin .40 1.00
101 Kenny Anderson .50 1.25
102 Derrick Coleman .50 1.25
103 Derek Harper .50 1.25
104 Charles Smith .40 1.00
105 Herb Williams .40 1.00
106 John Starks .60 1.50
107 Charles Oakley .50 1.25
108 Hubert Davis .40 1.00
109 Dennis Scott .40 1.00
110 Jeff Turner .40 1.00
111 Horace Grant .50 1.25
112 Anthony Bowie .40 1.00
113 Anfernee Hardaway 1.50 4.00
114 Nick Anderson .50 1.25
115 Dana Barros .50 1.25
116 Scott Williams .40 1.00
117 Clarence Weatherspoon .40 1.00
118 Jeff Malone .40 1.00
119 B.J. Tyler .40 1.00
120 Shawn Bradley .60 1.50
121 Charles Barkley 1.50 4.00
122 A.C. Green .50 1.25
123 Kevin Johnson .60 1.50
124 Wayman Tisdale .40 1.00
125 Danny Schayes .40 1.00
126 Dan Majerle .60 1.50
127 Rod Strickland .40 1.00
128 Harvey Grant .40 1.00
129 Aaron McKie .40 1.00
130 Chris Dudley .40 1.00
131 Otis Thorpe .50 1.25
132 Jerome Kersey .40 1.00
133 Clifford Robinson .60 1.50
134 Bobby Hurley .40 1.00
135 Spud Webb .60 1.50
136 Olden Polynice .40 1.00
137 Randy Brown .40 1.00
138 Brian Grant .50 1.25
139 Walt Williams .40 1.00
140 Avery Johnson .50 1.25
141 Dennis Rodman 1.25 3.00
142 J.R. Reid .40 1.00
143 David Robinson 1.25 3.00
144 Vinny Del Negro .40 1.00
145 Willie Anderson .40 1.00
146 Nate McMillan .40 1.00
147 Shawn Kemp 1.00 2.50
148 Detlef Schrempf .60 1.50
149 Vincent Askew .40 1.00
150 Sarunas Marciulionis .60 1.50
151 Byron Houston .40 1.00
152 Ervin Johnson .40 1.00
153 Adam Keefe .40 1.00
154 Jeff Hornacek .50 1.25
155 Antoine Carr .40 1.00
156 John Stockton 1.25 3.00
157 Blue Edwards .40 1.00
158 David Benoit .40 1.00
159 Don MacLean .40 1.00
160 Juwan Howard .60 1.50
161 Calbert Cheaney .40 1.00
162 Mitchell Butler .40 1.00
163 Gheorghe Muresan .40 1.00
164 Rex Chapman .40 1.00
165 Doug Overton .40 1.00
166 Steve Smith FF .25 .60
167 Dino Radja FF .20 .50
168 Alonzo Mourning FF .50 1.25
169 Michael Jordan FF 3.00 8.00
170 Tyrone Hill FF .20 .50
171 Jamal Mashburn FF .30 .75
172 Dikembe Mutombo FF .50 1.25
173 Grant Hill FF
w/Michael Jordan 1.00 2.50
174 Latrell Sprewell FF .30 .75
175 Hakeem Olajuwon FF .60 1.50
176 Reggie Miller FF .60 1.50
177 Pooh Richardson FF .20 .50
178 Cedric Ceballos FF .25 .60
179 Glen Rice FF .30 .75
180 Glenn Robinson FF .30 .75
181 Isaiah Rider FF .30 .75
182 Derrick Coleman FF .25 .60
183 Patrick Ewing FF .50 1.25
184 Shaquille O'Neal FF 1.25 3.00
185 Dana Barros FF .25 .60
186 Dan Majerle FF .30 .75
187 Clifford Robinson FF .30 .75
188 Mitch Richmond FF .40 1.00
189 David Robinson FF .60 1.50
190 Gary Payton FF .50 1.25
191 Oliver Miller FF .20 .50
192 Karl Malone FF .60 1.50
193 Kevin Pritchard FF .20 .50
194 Chris Webber FF .40 1.00
195 Michael Jordan PD 3.00 8.00
196 Hakeem Olajuwon PD .60 1.50
197 Vin Baker PD .25 .60
198 Grant Hill PD .50 1.25
199 Clyde Drexler PD .50 1.25
200 Chris Webber PD .40 1.00
201 Shawn Kemp PD .50 1.25
202 Shaquille O'Neal PD 1.25 3.00
203 Stacey Augmon PD .25 .60
204 David Benoit PD .20 .50
205 Rodney Rogers PD .25 .60
206 Latrell Sprewell PD .30 .75
207 Brian Grant PD .25 .60
208 Lamond Murray PD .20 .50
209 Shawn Kemp CL .50 1.25
210 Michael Jordan CL 3.00 8.00
211 Cory Alexander .60 1.50
212 Vernon Maxwell .40 1.00
213 George Lynch .40 1.00
214 Terry Mills .40 1.00
215 Scottie Pippen 1.50 4.00
216 Donald Royal .40 1.00
217 Wesley Person .40 1.00
218 Antonio Davis .40 1.00
219 Glenn Robinson .60 1.50
220 Jerry Stackhouse 2.00 5.00
221 James Robinson .40 1.00
222 Chris Mills .40 1.00
223 Chuck Person .50 1.25
224 Duane Causwell .40 1.00
225 Gary Payton 1.00 2.50
226 Eric Montross .40 1.00
227 Felton Spencer .40 1.00
228 Scott Skiles .40 1.00
229 Latrell Sprewell .60 1.50
230 Sedale Threatt .40 1.00
231 Mark Bryant .40 1.00
232 Buck Williams .40 1.00
233 Brian Williams .40 1.00
234 Sharone Wright .40 1.00
235 Karl Malone 1.25 3.00
236 Kevin Edwards .40 1.00
237 Muggsy Bogues .60 1.50
238 Mario Elie .40 1.00
239 Rasheed Wallace 2.00 5.00
240 George Zidek .50 1.25
241 Cedric Ceballos .50 1.25
242 Alan Henderson .60 1.50
243 Joe Kleine .40 1.00
244 Patrick Ewing 1.00 2.50
245 Sasha Danilovic .60 1.50
246 Bill Wennington .40 1.00
247 Steve Smith .50 1.25
248 Bryant Stith .40 1.00
249 Dino Radja .40 1.00
250 Monty Williams .40 1.00
251 Andrew DeClercq .60 1.50
252 Sean Elliott .50 1.25
253 Rick Fox .40 1.00
254 Lionel Simmons .40 1.00
255 Dikembe Mutombo 1.00 2.50
256 Lindsey Hunter .40 1.00
257 Terrell Brandon .50 1.25
258 Shawn Respert .50 1.25
259 Rodney Rogers .50 1.25
260 Bryon Russell .40 1.00
261 David Wesley .40 1.00
262 Ken Norman .40 1.00
263 Mitch Richmond .75 2.00
264 Sam Perkins .40 1.00
265 Hakeem Olajuwon 1.25 3.00
266 Brian Shaw .40 1.00
267 B.J. Armstrong .60 1.50
268 Jalen Rose .75 2.00
269 Bryant Reeves .50 1.25
270 Cherokee Parks .50 1.25
271 Dennis Rodman 1.25 3.00
272 Kendall Gill .40 1.00
273 Elliot Perry .40 1.00
274 Anthony Mason .40 1.00
275 Kevin Garnett 5.00 12.00
276 Damon Stoudamire 1.50 4.00
277 Lawrence Moten .60 1.50
278 Ed O'Bannon .50 1.25
279 Toni Kukoc .75 2.00
280 Greg Ostertag .60 1.50
281 Tom Hammonds .40 1.00
282 Yinka Dare .40 1.00
283 Michael Smith .40 1.00
284 Clifford Rozier .40 1.00
285 Gary Trent .50 1.25
286 Shaquille O'Neal 2.50 6.00
287 Luc Longley .50 1.25
288 Bob Sura .50 1.25
289 Dana Barros .50 1.25
290 Lorenzo Williams .40 1.00
291 Haywoode Workman .40 1.00
292 Randolph Childress .50 1.25
293 Doc Rivers .50 1.25
294 Chris Webber .75 2.00
295 Kurt Thomas .60 1.50
296 Greg Anthony .40 1.00
297 Tyus Edney .60 1.50
298 Danny Manning .50 1.25
299 Brent Barry 1.00 2.50
300 Joe Smith .75 2.00
301 Pooh Richardson .50 1.25
302 Mark Jackson .50 1.25
303 Richard Dumas .40 1.00
304 Michael Finley 1.50 4.00
305 Theo Ratliff 1.00 2.50
306 Gary Grant .40 1.00
307 Jamal Mashburn .60 1.50
308 Corliss Williamson .60 1.50
309 Eric Williams .60 1.50
310 Zan Tabak .40 1.00
311 Eric Murdock .40 1.00
312 Sherrell Ford .50 1.25
313 Terry Davis .40 1.00
314 Vern Fleming .40 1.00
315 Jason Caffey .60 1.50
316 Mario Bennett .50 1.25
317 David Vaughn .60 1.50
318 Loren Meyer .40 1.00
319 Travis Best .60 1.50
320 Byron Scott .60 1.50
321 Mookie Blaylock SR .30 .75
322 Dee Brown SR .25 .60
323 Alonzo Mourning SR .50 1.25
324 Michael Jordan SR 3.00 8.00
325 Terrell Brandon SR .25 .60
326 Jim Jackson SR .25 .60
327 Dikembe Mutombo SR .50 1.25
328 Grant Hill SR .50 1.25
329 Joe Smith SR .40 1.00
330 Clyde Drexler SR .50 1.25
331 Reggie Miller SR .60 1.50
332 Lamond Murray SR .20 .50
333 Nick Van Exel SR .30 .75
334 Glen Rice SR .30 .75
335 Glenn Robinson SR .30 .75
336 Christian Laettner SR .25 .60
337 Kenny Anderson SR .25 .60
338 Patrick Ewing SR .50 1.25
339 Shaquille O'Neal SR 1.25 3.00
340 Jerry Stackhouse SR 1.00 2.50
341 Charles Barkley SR .75 2.00
342 Clifford Robinson SR .30 .75
343 Brian Grant SR .25 .60
344 David Robinson SR .60 1.50
345 Shawn Kemp SR .50 1.25
346 Damon Stoudamire SR .75 2.00
347 Karl Malone SR .60 1.50
348 Bryant Reeves SR .25 .60
349 Juwan Howard SR .30 .75
350 Nick Anderson
Dee Brown PT .25 .60
351 Rik Smits PT .25 .60
352 Herb Williams
Tom Tolbert PT .20 .50
353 Michael Jordan PT 3.00 8.00
354 David Robinson PT .60 1.50
355 Terry Porter
Kevin Johnson PT .30 .75
356 Clyde Drexler PT .50 1.25
357 Cedric Ceballos PT .25 .60
358 Horace Grant
Group PT .25 .60
359 Reggie Miller PT .60 1.50
360 Avery Johnson
Nick Van Exel PT .30 .75
361 Hakeem Olajuwon
Robert Horry PT .60 1.50
362 Rik Smits PT .25 .60
363 David Robinson
Hakeem Olajuwon PT .60 1.50
364 Robert Horry PT .30 .75
365 Kenny Smith PT .25 .60
366 Stacey Augmon LOVE .25 .60
367 Sherman Douglas LOVE .20 .50
368 Larry Johnson LOVE .40 1.00
369 Scottie Pippen LOVE .75 2.00
370 Tyrone Hill LOVE .20 .50
371 Jamal Mashburn LOVE .30 .75
372 Mahmoud Abdul-Rauf LOVE .25 .60
373 Grant Hill LOVE .50 1.25
374 Latrell Sprewell LOVE .30 .75
375 Sam Cassell LOVE .30 .75
376 Rik Smits LOVE .25 .60
377 Terry Dehere LOVE .20 .50
378 Eddie Jones LOVE .30 .75
379 Billy Owens LOVE .20 .50
380 Vin Baker LOVE .25 .60
381 Isaiah Rider LOVE .30 .75
382 Kenny Anderson LOVE .25 .60
383 John Starks LOVE .30 .75
384 Anfernee Hardaway LOVE .75 2.00
385 Sharone Wright LOVE .20 .50
386 Charles Barkley LOVE .75 2.00
387 Clifford Robinson LOVE .30 .75
388 Walt Williams LOVE .20 .50
389 Sean Elliott LOVE .25 .60
390 Gary Payton LOVE .50 1.25
391 Carlos Rogers LOVE .20 .50
392 John Stockton LOVE .60 1.50
393 Greg Anthony LOVE .20 .50
394 Chris Webber LOVE .40 1.00
395 Gary Payton PG .50 1.25
396 Mookie Blaylock PG .30 .75
397 Charles Barkley PG .75 2.00
398 Grant Hill PG .50 1.25
399 Anfernee Hardaway PG .75 2.00
400 Kenny Anderson PG .25 .60
401 Mark Jackson PG .25 .60
402 Karl Malone PG .60 1.50
403 Avery Johnson PG .25 .60
404 Larry Johnson 40 .40 1.00
405 Nick Van Exel 40 .30 .75
406 Vin Baker 40 .25 .60
407 Jason Kidd 40 .50 1.25
408 David Robinson 40 .60 1.50
409 Shawn Kemp CL .50 1.25
410 Michael Jordan CL 3.00 8.00

1995-96 Collector's Choice International Japanese Jordan Collection

COMPLETE SET (4) 8.00 20.00
COMMON CARD (J1-J4) 2.50 6.00

1995-96 Collector's Choice International Japanese NBA Extremes

COMPLETE SET (9) 2.50 6.00
E1 Muggsy Bogues .75 2.00
E2 Spud Webb .75 2.00
E3 Dana Barros .60 1.50
E4 Avery Johnson .60 1.50
E5 Vlade Divac .75 2.00
E6 Dikembe Mutombo 1.25 3.00
E7 Rik Smits .60 1.50
E8 Shawn Bradley .50 1.25
E9 Gheorghe Muresan .50 1.25

1995-96 Collector's Choice International Portuguese

COMPLETE SET (200) 8.00 20.00
*PORTUGUESE: SAME VALUE AS FRENCH

1995-96 Collector's Choice International Portuguese Jordan Collection

COMPLETE SET (4) 5.00 12.00
*PORTUGUESE: SAME VALUE AS FRENCH

1995-96 Collector's Choice International Portuguese NBA Extremes

COMPLETE SET (9) 1.50 4.00
*PORTUGUESE: SAME VALUE AS FRENCH

1995-96 Collector's Choice International Spanish I

COMPLETE SET (210) 8.00 20.00
*SPANISH: SAME VALUE AS FRENCH

1995-96 Collector's Choice International Spanish II

COMPLETE SET (200) 8.00 20.00
*SPANISH: SAME VALUE AS FRENCH

1995-96 Collector's Choice International Spanish Jordan Collection

COMPLETE SET (4) 5.00 12.00
*SPANISH: SAME VALUE AS FRENCH

1995-96 Collector's Choice International Spanish NBA Extremes

COMPLETE SET (9) 1.50 4.00
*SPANISH: SAME VALUE AS FRENCH

1996-97 Collector's Choice International English Jordan's Journal

COMPLETE SET (6) 8.00 20.00
COMMON CARD (J1-J6) 2.00 5.00

1996-97 Collector's Choice International French

COMPLETE SET (200) 20.00 40.00
1 Mookie Blaylock .25 .60
2 Grant Long .15 .40
3 Christian Laettner .25 .60
4 Craig Ehlo .15 .40
5 Ken Norman .15 .40
6 Stacey Augmon .20 .50
7 Dana Barros .15 .40
8 Dino Radja .15 .40
9 Rick Fox .15 .40
10 Eric Montross .15 .40
11 David Wesley .15 .40
12 Eric Williams .15 .40
13 Glen Rice .25 .60
14 Dell Curry .25 .60
15 Matt Geiger .15 .40
16 Scott Burrell .15 .40
17 George Zidek .15 .40
18 Muggsy Bogues .25 .60
19 Ron Harper .20 .50
20 Steve Kerr .20 .50
21 Toni Kukoc .25 .60
22 Dennis Rodman .60 1.50
23 Michael Jordan 2.50 6.00
24 Luc Longley .20 .50
25 Michael Jordan VT 2.50 6.00
26 Michael Jordan VT 2.50 6.00
27 Luc Longley VT .20 .50
28 Scottie Pippen VT .60 1.50
29 Toni Kukoc VT .25 .60
30 Terrell Brandon .25 .60
31 Bobby Phills .15 .40
32 Tyrone Hill .15 .40
33 Michael Cage .15 .40
34 Bob Sura .15 .40
35 Tony Dumas .15 .40
36 Jim Jackson .15 .40
37 Loren Meyer .15 .40
38 Cherokee Parks .15 .40
39 Jamal Mashburn .25 .60
40 Popeye Jones .15 .40
41 LaPhonso Ellis .15 .40
42 Jalen Rose .20 .50
43 Antonio McDyess .25 .60
44 Tom Hammonds .15 .40
45 Mahmoud Abdul-Rauf .20 .50
46 Dale Ellis .20 .50
47 Joe Dumars .30 .75
48 Theo Ratliff .15 .40
49 Lindsey Hunter .15 .40
50 Terry Mills .15 .40
51 Don Reid .15 .40
52 B.J. Armstrong .20 .50
53 Bimbo Coles .15 .40
54 Joe Smith .20 .50
55 Chris Mullin .30 .75
56 Rony Seikaly .20 .50
57 Donyell Marshall .15 .40
58 Hakeem Olajuwon .50 1.25
59 Robert Horry .20 .50
60 Mario Elie .15 .40
61 Mark Bryant .15 .40
62 Chucky Brown .15 .40
63 Rik Smits .20 .50
64 Derrick McKey .15 .40
65 Eddie Johnson .15 .40
66 Mark Jackson .20 .50
67 Ricky Pierce .20 .50
68 Travis Best .15 .40
69 Rodney Rogers .15 .40
70 Brent Barry .20 .50
71 Lamond Murray .15 .40
72 Eric Piatkowski .15 .40
73 Pooh Richardson .15 .40
74 Cedric Ceballos .20 .50
75 Eddie Jones .25 .60
76 Anthony Peeler .15 .40
77 George Lynch .15 .40
78 Vlade Divac .25 .60
79 Rex Chapman .15 .40
80 Sasha Danilovic .15 .40
81 Kurt Thomas .15 .40
82 Keith Askins .15 .40
83 Walt Williams .15 .40
84 Vin Baker .20 .50
85 Shawn Respert .15 .40
86 Sherman Douglas .15 .40
87 Marty Conlon .15 .40
88 Johnny Newman .15 .40
89 Kevin Garnett .75 2.00
90 Andrew Lang .15 .40
91 Terry Porter .15 .40
92 Sam Mitchell .15 .40
93 Tom Gugliotta .15 .40
94 Spud Webb .20 .50
95 Kendall Gill .25 .60
96 Vern Fleming .15 .40
97 Shawn Bradley .15 .40
98 Yinka Dare .15 .40
99 Jayson Williams .15 .40
100 Kevin Edwards .15 .40
101 Charles Oakley .25 .60
102 Anthony Mason .20 .50
103 John Starks .25 .60
104 J.R. Reid .15 .40
105 Hubert Davis .15 .40
106 Gary Grant .15 .40
107 Nick Anderson .15 .40
108 Donald Royal .15 .40
109 Brian Shaw .15 .40
110 Brooks Thompson .15 .40
111 Anfernee Hardaway .60 1.50
112 Dennis Scott .20 .50
113 Anfernee Hardaway .60 1.50
114 Anfernee Hardaway .60 1.50
115 Anfernee Hardaway .60 1.50
116 Anfernee Hardaway .60 1.50
117 Anfernee Hardaway .60 1.50
118 Derrick Coleman .20 .50
119 Rex Walters .15 .40
120 Sean Higgins .15 .40
121 Clarence Weatherspoon .15 .40
122 Jerry Stackhouse .30 .75
123 Elliot Perry .15 .40
124 Wayman Tisdale .20 .50
125 Wesley Person .15 .40
126 Charles Barkley .60 1.50
127 A.C. Green .20 .50
128 Harvey Grant .15 .40
129 Arvydas Sabonis .25 .60
130 Aaron McKie .15 .40
131 Gary Trent .15 .40
132 Buck Williams .25 .60
133 Billy Owens .15 .40
134 Brian Grant .20 .50
135 Corliss Williamson .15 .40
136 Tyus Edney .15 .40
137 Olden Polynice .15 .40
138 Avery Johnson .20 .50
139 Vinny Del Negro .15 .40
140 Sean Elliott .25 .60
141 Chuck Person .20 .50
142 Will Perdue .15 .40
143 Nate McMillan .15 .40
144 Vincent Askew .15 .40
145 Detlef Schrempf .25 .60
146 Hersey Hawkins .25 .60
147 Sharone Wright .15 .40
148 Zan Tabak .15 .40
149 Oliver Miller .15 .40
150 Doug Christie .15 .40
151 Damon Stoudamire .25 .60
152 Jeff Hornacek .25 .60
153 Chris Morris .15 .40
154 Antoine Carr .15 .40
155 Karl Malone .50 1.25
156 Adam Keefe .15 .40
157 Greg Anthony .15 .40
158 Blue Edwards .15 .40
159 Bryant Reeves .15 .40
160 Anthony Avent .15 .40
161 Lawrence Moten .15 .40
162 Calbert Cheaney .15 .40
163 Chris Webber .30 .75
164 Tim Legler .15 .40
165 Gheorghe Muresan .15 .40
166 Stacey Augmon FUND .20 .50
167 Dee Brown FUND .15 .40
168 Glen Rice FUND .25 .60
169 Scottie Pippen FUND .60 1.50
170 Danny Ferry FUND .15 .40
171 Jason Kidd FUND .40 1.00
172 Tom Hammonds FUND .15 .40
173 Grant Hill FUND .40 1.00
174 Chris Mullin FUND .30 .75
175 Clyde Drexler FUND .40 1.00
176 Rik Smits FUND .20 .50
177 Lamond Murray FUND .15 .40
178 Nick Van Exel FUND .25 .60
179 Alonzo Mourning FUND .40 1.00
180 Glenn Robinson FUND .25 .60
181 Isaiah Rider FUND .20 .50
182 Ed O'Bannon FUND .15 .40
183 Patrick Ewing FUND .40 1.00
184 Shaquille O'Neal FUND 1.00 2.50
185 Derrick Coleman FUND .20 .50
186 Danny Manning FUND .20 .50
187 Clifford Robinson FUND .25 .60
188 Mitch Richmond FUND .30 .75
189 David Robinson FUND .50 1.25
190 Shawn Kemp FUND .40 1.00
191 Oliver Miller FUND .15 .40
192 John Stockton FUND .50 1.25
193 Greg Anthony FUND .15 .40
194 Rasheed Wallace FUND .30 .75
195 Michael Jordan FUND 2.50 6.00
196 Checklist .15 .40
197 Checklist .15 .40
198 Checklist .15 .40
199 Checklist .15 .40
200 Checklist .15 .40

1996-97 Collector's Choice International French Crash the Game Scoring

COMPLETE SET (60) 40.00 80.00
C1A Mookie Blaylock 1.00 2.50
C1B Mookie Blaylock 1.00 2.50
C2A Dino Radja .60 1.50
C2B Dino Radja .60 1.50
C3A Glen Rice 1.00 2.50
C3B Glen Rice 1.00 2.50
C4A Scottie Pippen 2.50 6.00
C4B Scottie Pippen 2.50 6.00
C5A Terrell Brandon .75 2.00
C5B Terrell Brandon .75 2.00
C6A Jason Kidd 1.50 4.00
C6B Jason Kidd 1.50 4.00
C7A Antonio McDyess 1.00 2.50
C7B Antonio McDyess 1.00 2.50
C8A Joe Dumars 1.25 3.00
C8B Joe Dumars 1.25 3.00
C9A Joe Smith .75 2.00
C9B Joe Smith .75 2.00
C10A Hakeem Olajuwon 2.00 5.00
C10B Hakeem Olajuwon 2.00 5.00
C11A Reggie Miller 2.00 5.00
C11B Reggie Miller 2.00 5.00
C12A Loy Vaught .60 1.50
C12B Loy Vaught .60 1.50
C13A Cedric Ceballos .75 2.00
C13B Cedric Ceballos .75 2.00
C14A Alonzo Mourning 1.50 4.00
C14B Alonzo Mourning 1.50 4.00
C15A Vin Baker .75 2.00
C15B Vin Baker .75 2.00
C16A Kevin Garnett 3.00 8.00
C16B Kevin Garnett 3.00 8.00
C17A Ed O'Bannon .60 1.50
C17B Ed O'Bannon .60 1.50
C18A Patrick Ewing 1.50 4.00
C18B Patrick Ewing 1.50 4.00
C19A Anfernee Hardaway 2.50 6.00
C19B Anfernee Hardaway 2.50 6.00
C20A Clarence Weatherspoon .60 1.50
C20B Clarence Weatherspoon .60 1.50
C21A Kevin Johnson 1.00 2.50
C21B Kevin Johnson 1.00 2.50
C22A Clifford Robinson 1.00 2.50
C22B Clifford Robinson 1.00 2.50
C23A Mitch Richmond 1.25 3.00
C23B Mitch Richmond 1.25 3.00
C24A Sean Elliott 1.00 2.50
C24B Sean Elliott 1.00 2.50
C25A Shawn Kemp 1.50 4.00
C25B Shawn Kemp 1.50 4.00
C26A Damon Stoudamire 1.00 2.50
C26B Damon Stoudamire 1.00 2.50
C27A John Stockton 2.00 5.00
C27B John Stockton 2.00 5.00
C28A Bryant Reeves .60 1.50
C28B Bryant Reeves .60 1.50
C29A Rasheed Wallace 1.25 3.00
C29B Rasheed Wallace 1.25 3.00
C30A Michael Jordan 10.00 25.00
C30B Michael Jordan 10.00 25.00

1996-97 Collector's Choice International French Crash the Game Scoring Gold

*GOLD: .5X TO 1.5X

1996-97 Collector's Choice International French Jordan's Journal

COMPLETE SET (6) 8.00 20.00
COMMON CARD 2.00 5.00

1996-97 Collector's Choice International French Mini-Cards

COMPLETE SET (30) 6.00 15.00
M2 Mookie Blaylock/Jeff Hornacek/Rex Walters .40 1.00
M5 Dino Radja/Toni Kukoc Detlef Schrempf .40 1.00
M6 Eric Williams/Sharone Wright/Ashraf Amaya .25 .60
M10 George Zidek/Ed O'Bannon Tyus Edney .25 .60
M13 Luc Longley/Shawn Bradley/Theo Ratliff .30 .75
M22 Mahmoud Abdul-Rauf/Avery Johnson/Bobby Phills .30 .75
M23 Tom Hammonds/Chris Morris/Popeye Jones .25 .60
M25 Grant Hill/Christian Laettner/Bobby Hurley .60 1.50
M28 Rony Seikaly/Derrick Coleman/Sherman Douglas .30 .75
M30 Sam Cassell/John Starks/Nick Van Exel .40 1.00
M33 Travis Best/Dennis Scott/Matt Geiger .30 .75
M36 Brent Barry/Isaiah Rider/Cedric Ceballos .30 .75
M37 Lamond Murray/Kevin Johnson/Jason Kidd .60 1.50
M38 Terry Dehere/Jayson Williams/Chris Mullin .50 1.25
M39 Vlade Divac/Sasha Danilovic/Arvydas Sabonis .40 1.00
M43 Kurt Thomas/Brian Grant/Tyrone Hill .30 .75
M44 Keith Askins/Robert Horry/Derrick McKey .40 1.00
M46 Shawn Respert/David Robinson/Randolph Childress .75 2.00
M49 Andrew Lang/Oliver Miller/Todd Day .25 .60
M56 Charles Oakley/Bimbo Coles/Dell Curry .40 1.00
M57 J.R. Reid/Jerry Stackhouse/Rasheed Wallace .50 1.25
M66 A.C. Green/Clyde Drexler/Joe Dumars .60 1.50
M67 Aaron McKie/Nick Anderson/Kendall Gill .40 1.00
M75 Doc Rivers/Mark Jackson/Danny Ferry .30 .75
M78 Shawn Kemp/Anfernee Hardaway/Michael Jordan 4.00 10.00
M79 Jimmy King/Chris Webber/Jalen Rose .50 1.25
M83 Karl Malone/Charles Barkley/Dennis Rodman 1.00 2.50
M85 Greg Anthony/Larry Johnson/Stacey Augmon .50 1.25
M86 Blue Edwards/Tom Gugliotta/Nate McMillan .25 .60
M90 Calbert Cheaney/Glenn Robinson/Jim Jackson .40 1.00

1996-97 Collector's Choice International French Stick Ums

COMPLETE SET (30) 8.00 20.00
S1 Mookie Blaylock .40 1.00
S2 Dana Barros .25 .60
S3 Scott Burrell .25 .60
S4 Dennis Rodman 1.00 2.50
S5 Terrell Brandon .30 .75
S6 Jamal Mashburn .40 1.00
S7 LaPhonso Ellis .25 .60
S8 Grant Hill .60 1.50
S9 Joe Smith .30 .75
S10 Hakeem Olajuwon .75 2.00
S11 Rik Smits .30 .75
S12 Brent Barry .30 .75
S13 Nick Van Exel .40 1.00
S14 Sasha Danilovic .25 .60
S15 Vin Baker .30 .75
S16 Kevin Garnett 1.25 3.00
S17 Shawn Bradley .25 .60
S18 Patrick Ewing .60 1.50
S19 Anfernee Hardaway 1.00 2.50
S20 Clarence Weatherspoon .25 .60
S21 Charles Barkley 1.00 2.50
S22 Clifford Robinson .40 1.00
S23 Mitch Richmond .50 1.25
S24 David Robinson .75 2.00
S25 Shawn Kemp .60 1.50
S26 Damon Stoudamire .40 1.00
S27 Karl Malone .75 2.00
S28 Bryant Reeves .25 .60
S29 Gheorghe Muresan .25 .60
S30 Michael Jordan 4.00 10.00

1996-97 Collector's Choice International German

COMPLETE SET (200) 20.00 40.00
*GERMAN: SAME VALUE AS FRENCH

1996-97 Collector's Choice International German Jordan's Journal

COMPLETE SET (6) 8.00 20.00
COMMON CARD 2.00 5.00

1996-97 Collector's Choice International German Mini-Cards

COMPLETE SET (30) 6.00 15.00
*GERMAN: SAME VALUE AS FRENCH

1996-97 Collector's Choice International German Stick Ums

COMPLETE SET (30) 8.00 20.00
*GERMAN: SAME VALUE AS FRENCH

1996-97 Collector's Choice International Italian

COMPLETE SET (200) 20.00 40.00
*ITALIAN: SAME VALUE AS FRENCH

1996-97 Collector's Choice International Italian Crash the Game Scoring

COMPLETE SET (60) 40.00 80.00
*ITALIAN: SAME VALUE AS FRENCH

1996-97 Collector's Choice International Italian Crash the Game Scoring Gold

COMPLETE SET (60)
*ITALIAN: SAME VALUE AS FRENCH

1996-97 Collector's Choice International Italian Jordan's Journal

COMPLETE SET (6) 8.00 20.00
COMMON CARD 2.00 5.00

1996-97 Collector's Choice International Italian Mini-Cards

COMPLETE SET (30) 6.00 15.00
*ITALIAN: SAME VALUE AS FRENCH
M2 Mookie Blaylock
Jeff Hornacek
Rex Walters .40 1.00
M5 Dino Radja
Toni Kukoc
Detlef Schrempf .40 1.00
M6 Eric Williams
Sharone Wright
Ashraf Amaya .25 .60
M10 George Zidek
Ed O'Bannon
Tyus Edney .25 .60
M13 Luc Longley
Shawn Bradley
Theo Ratliff .30 .75
M22 Mahmoud Abdul-Rauf
Avery Johnson
Bobby Phills .30 .75
M23 Tom Hammonds
Chris Morris
Popeye Jones .25 .60
M25 Grant Hill
Christian Laettner
Bobby Hurley .60 1.50
M28 Rony Seikaly
Derrick Coleman
Sherman Douglas .30 .75
M30 Sam Cassell
John Starks
Nick Van Exel .40 1.00
M33 Travis Best
Dennis Scott
Matt Geiger .30 .75
M36 Brent Barry
Isaiah Rider
Cedric Ceballos .30 .75
M37 Lamond Murray
Kevin Johnson
Jason Kidd .60 1.50
M38 Terry Dehere
Jayson Williams
Chris Mullin .50 1.25
M39 Vlade Divac
Sasha Danilovic
Arvydas Sabonis .40 1.00
M43 Kurt Thomas
Brian Grant
Tyrone Hill .30 .75
M44 Keith Askins
Robert Horry
Derrick McKey .40 1.00
M46 Shawn Respert
David Robinson
Randolph Childress .75 2.00
M49 Andrew Lang
Oliver Miller
Todd Day .25 .60
M56 Charles Oakley
Bimbo Coles
Dell Curry .40 1.00
M57 J.R. Reid
Jerry Stackhouse
Rasheed Wallace .50 1.25

M66 A.C. Green
Clyde Drexler
Joe Dumars .60 1.50
M67 Aaron McKie
Nick Anderson
Kendall Gill .40 1.00
M75 Doc Rivers
Mark Jackson
Danny Ferry .30 .75
M78 Shawn Kemp
Anfernee Hardaway
Michael Jordan 4.00 10.00
M79 Jimmy King
Chris Webber
Jalen Rose .50 1.25
M83 Karl Malone
Charles Barkley
Dennis Rodman 1.00 2.50
M85 Greg Anthony
Larry Johnson
Stacey Augmon .50 1.25
M86 Blue Edwards
Tom Gugliotta
Nate McMillan .25 .60
M90 Calbert Cheaney
Glenn Robinson
Jim Jackson .40 1.00

1996-97 Collector's Choice International Italian Stick Ums

COMPLETE SET (30) 8.00 20.00
*ITALIAN: SAME VALUE AS FRENCH

1996-97 Collector's Choice International Japanese Crash the Game Scoring 1

COMPLETE SET (60)
*JAPANESE: SAME VALUE AS FRENCH

1996-97 Collector's Choice International Japanese Crash the Game Scoring Gold 1

COMPLETE SET (60)

1996-97 Collector's Choice International Japanese Crash the Game Scoring 2

COMPLETE SET (60)

1996-97 Collector's Choice International Japanese Crash the Game Scoring Gold 2

COMPLETE SET (60)

1996-97 Collector's Choice International Japanese Jordan's Journal

COMPLETE SET (6) 8.00 20.00
COMMON CARD 2.00 5.00

1996-97 Collector's Choice International Spanish

COMPLETE SET (200) 20.00 40.00
*SPANISH: SAME VALUE AS FRENCH

1996-97 Collector's Choice International Spanish Crash the Game Scoring

COMPLETE SET (60) 40.00 80.00
*SPANISH: SAME VALUE AS FRENCH

1996-97 Collector's Choice International Spanish Crash the Game Scoring Gold

COMPLETE SET (60)
*SPANISH: SAME VALUE AS FRENCH

1996-97 Collector's Choice International Spanish Jordan's Journal

COMPLETE SET (6) 8.00 20.00
COMMON CARD 2.00 5.00

1996-97 Collector's Choice International Spanish Mini-Cards

COMPLETE SET (30) 6.00 15.00
*SPANISH: SAME VALUE AS FRENCH

1996-97 Collector's Choice International Spanish Stick Ums

COMPLETE SET (30) 8.00 20.00
*SPANISH: SAME VALUE AS FRENCH

1997-98 Collector's Choice International Japanese Michael Jordan Career

COMPLETE SET (9) 150.00 400.00
COMMON CARD 30.00 80.00

1998 Collector's Edge Air Apparent Jumbos

NNO Kobe Bryant/1998 4.00 10.00

1971-72 Colonels Volpe Marathon Oil

COMPLETE SET (11) 50.00 100.00
1 Darel Carrier 5.00 10.00
2 Bobby Croft 3.00 8.00
3 Louie Dampier 10.00 25.00
4 Les Hunter 3.00 8.00
5 Dan Issel 20.00 40.00
6 Jim Ligon 3.00 8.00
7 Cincy Powell 5.00 12.00
8 Mike Pratt 5.00 10.00
9 Walt Simon 3.00 8.00
10 Sam Smith 3.00 8.00
11 Howard Wright 3.00 8.00

1972-73 Comspec

COMPLETE SET (36) 3,000.00 6,000.00
1 Kareem Abdul-Jabbar 400.00 800.00
2 Rick Adelman 60.00 150.00
3 Nate Archibald 75.00 200.00
4 Rick Barry 75.00 200.00
5 Walt Bellamy 60.00 150.00
6 Dave Bing 60.00 150.00
7 Austin Carr 60.00 150.00
8 Wilt Chamberlain 500.00 1,000.00
9 Dave Cowens 75.00 200.00
10 Walt Frazier 100.00 250.00
11 Gail Goodrich 60.00 150.00
12 John Havlicek 150.00 400.00
13 Connie Hawkins 75.00 200.00
14 Elvin Hayes 75.00 200.00
15 Spencer Haywood 75.00 200.00
16 John Hummer 50.00 120.00
17 Don Kojis 60.00 150.00
18 Bob Lanier 75.00 200.00
19 Kevin Loughery 60.00 150.00
20 Jerry Lucas 75.00 200.00
21 Pete Maravich 500.00 1,000.00
22 Jack Marin 75.00 200.00
23 Calvin Murphy 75.00 200.00
24 Geoff Petrie 60.00 150.00
25 Willis Reed 75.00 200.00
26 Oscar Robertson 300.00 600.00
27 Cazzie Russell 75.00 200.00
28 Elmore Smith 50.00 120.00
29 Dick Snyder 50.00 120.00
30 Wes Unseld 75.00 200.00
31 Dick Van Arsdale 60.00 150.00
32 Tom Van Arsdale 60.00 150.00
33 Norm Van Lier 60.00 150.00
34 Chet Walker 60.00 150.00
35 Jerry West 300.00 600.00
36 Lenny Wilkens 75.00 200.00

1971-72 Condors Pittsburgh Team Issue

COMPLETE SET (11) 35.00 70.00
1 John Brisker 5.00 10.00
2 George Carter 3.00 8.00
3 Mickey Davis 2.50 6.00
4 Stew Johnson 2.50 6.00
5 Arvesta Kelly 2.50 6.00
6 Dave Lattin 5.00 12.00
7 Mike Lewis 2.50 6.00
8 Jimmy O'Brien 4.00 10.00
9 Paul Ruffner 2.50 6.00
10 Skeeter Swift 3.00 8.00
11 George Thompson 5.00 10.00

1971-72 Condors Pittsburgh Team Photo

COMPLETE SET (2) 20.00 40.00
1 John Brisker
George Carter
Mickey Davis
Mike Lewis
Jimmy O'Brien
Paul Ruffner
Skeeter Swift
George Thompson 12.50 25.00
2 Don Bezahler
Mark Binstein
Stew Johnson
Arvesta Kelly
David Lattin
Jack McMahon
Ray Melchiorre
Walt Szczerbiak 10.00 20.00

1969-70 Converse Staff

COMPLETE SET (10) 175.00 350.00
1 Bob Davies 40.00 80.00
2 Joe Dean 12.00 30.00
3 Gib Ford 10.00 25.00
4 Bob Houbregs 15.00 40.00
5 Rod Hundley 40.00 80.00
6 Stu Inman 15.00 40.00
7 Bunny Levitt 15.00 40.00
8 Earl Lloyd 15.00 40.00
9 John Norlander 12.00 30.00
10 Phil Rollins 10.00 25.00

1989 Converse

COMPLETE SET (15) 4.00 10.00
1 Mark Aguirre .20 .50
2 Larry Bird 2.50 5.00
3 Rolando Blackman .30 .75
4 Muggsy Bogues .40 1.00
5 Rex Chapman .40 1.00
6 Magic Johnson 1.25 3.00
7 Bernard King .30 .75
8 Bill Laimbeer .30 .75
9 Karl Malone 1.00 2.50
10 Kevin McHale .50 1.25
11 Mark Price .40 1.00
12 Jack Sikma .20 .50
13 Reggie Theus .30 .75
14 Title Card .20 .50
NNO Free Video Offer .20 .50

1969-70 Cougars Carolina Team Issue

COMPLETE SET (15) 50.00 100.00
1 Carolina Cougars Team Photo 5.00 10.00
2 Bill Bunting 2.50 6.00
3 Cal Fowler 2.50 6.00
4 Steve Kramer 2.50 6.00
5 Gene Littles 3.00 8.00
6 Randy Mahaffey 2.50 6.00
7 Bones McKinney CO 5.00 10.00
8 Larry Miller 3.00 8.00
9 Doug Moe 5.00 10.00
10 Rich Niemann 2.50 6.00
11 George Peeples 2.50 6.00
12 Ron Perry 2.50 6.00
13 George Sutor 2.50 6.00
14 Bob Verga 3.00 8.00
15 Hank Whitney 2.50 6.00

1970-71 Cougars Team Issue

COMPLETE SET 12.50 25.00
1 Gary Bradds 2.00 5.00
2 Jim McDaniels 2.50 6.00
3 Dave Newmark 2.00 5.00
4 George Peeples 2.00 5.00
5 Larry Steele 3.00 8.00

2009-10 Court Kings

COMP.SET w/o RC's (120) 50.00 100.00
1-120 PRINT RUN 450 SER.#'d SETS
ROOKIE PRINT RUN 649 SER.#'d SETS
1 Carmelo Anthony 1.50 4.00
2 Chris Andersen 1.00 2.50
3 J.R. Smith 1.00 2.50
4 Chauncey Billups 1.25 3.00
5 Kevin Love 1.00 2.50
6 Al Jefferson .60 1.50
7 Corey Brewer .60 1.50
8 Kevin Durant 4.00 10.00
9 Russell Westbrook 2.00 5.00
10 Jeff Green .75 2.00
11 Brandon Roy 1.25 3.00
12 LaMarcus Aldridge 1.00 2.50
13 Juwan Howard .75 2.00
14 Deron Williams .75 2.00
15 Carlos Boozer .75 2.00
16 Paul Millsap .75 2.00
17 Dirk Nowitzki 2.50 6.00
18 Jason Kidd 1.50 4.00
19 Drew Gooden .75 2.00
20 J.J. Barea 1.00 2.50
21 Trevor Ariza .60 1.50
22 Aaron Brooks .60 1.50
23 Carl Landry .60 1.50
24 Tony Parker 1.50 4.00
25 Richard Jefferson .75 2.00
26 Tim Duncan 2.50 6.00
27 Marc Gasol 1.00 2.50
28 Rudy Gay 1.00 2.50
29 Zach Randolph 1.00 2.50
30 Emeka Okafor .75 2.00
31 Chris Paul 2.00 5.00
32 David West .75 2.00
33 Jason Thompson .60 1.50
34 Kevin Martin .75 2.00
35 Spencer Hawes .60 1.50
36 Amare Stoudemire .75 2.00
37 Channing Frye .60 1.50
38 Steve Nash 2.00 5.00
39 Pau Gasol 1.50 4.00
40 Kobe Bryant 8.00 20.00
41 Derek Fisher 1.00 2.50
42 Andrew Bynum .60 1.50
43 Monta Ellis .75 2.00
44 Anthony Morrow .60 1.50
45 Corey Maggette .75 2.00
46 Baron Davis .75 2.00
47 Chris Kaman .75 2.00
48 Eric Gordon .75 2.00
49 Kevin Garnett 2.50 6.00
50 Ray Allen 1.50 4.00
51 Paul Pierce 1.50 4.00
52 Kendrick Perkins .60 1.50
53 Nate Robinson .75 2.00
54 Chris Duhon .60 1.50
55 David Lee .60 1.50
56 Danilo Gallinari .75 2.00
57 Allen Iverson 2.00 5.00
58 Andre Iguodala 1.00 2.50
59 Louis Williams 1.00 2.50
60 Elton Brand .75 2.00
61 Andrea Bargnani .60 1.50
62 Chris Bosh 1.25 3.00
63 Hedo Turkoglu .75 2.00
64 Brook Lopez 1.00 2.50
65 Rafer Alston .60 1.50
66 Devin Harris .60 1.50
67 LeBron James 8.00 20.00
68 Anderson Varejao .60 1.50
69 Delonte West .60 1.50
70 Shaquille O'Neal 3.00 8.00
71 Ben Gordon .75 2.00
72 Rodney Stuckey .60 1.50
73 Ben Wallace 1.25 3.00
74 Danny Granger .60 1.50
75 Troy Murphy .60 1.50
76 Dahntay Jones .60 1.50
77 Andrew Bogut .75 2.00
78 Luke Ridnour .75 2.00
79 Hakim Warrick .60 1.50
80 Luol Deng .75 2.00
81 Derrick Rose 1.50 4.00
82 Joakim Noah .60 1.50
83 John Salmons .75 2.00
84 Joe Johnson 1.00 2.50
85 Al Horford 1.00 2.50
86 Jamal Crawford 1.00 2.50
87 Marvin Williams .60 1.50
88 Dwyane Wade 2.00 5.00
89 Jermaine O'Neal 1.00 2.50
90 Michael Beasley .60 1.50
91 Gerald Wallace .75 2.00
92 Stephen Jackson .75 2.00
93 Raymond Felton .60 1.50
94 Dwight Howard 1.25 3.00
95 Vince Carter 2.00 5.00
96 Rashard Lewis .75 2.00
97 Jason Williams .75 2.00
98 Antawn Jamison .75 2.00
99 Mike Miller .75 2.00
100 Caron Butler .75 2.00
101 Harry Gallatin 1.00 2.50
102 Nate Archibald 1.25 3.00
103 Elgin Baylor 2.50 6.00
104 Walt Bellamy .75 2.00
105 Dave Bing 1.25 3.00
106 Louie Dampier .60 1.50
107 Clyde Drexler 1.50 4.00
108 Mark Eaton .60 1.50
109 John Havlicek 2.50 6.00
110 Jerry Lucas 1.00 2.50
111 George McGinnis 1.00 2.50
112 Sidney Moncrief .75 2.00
113 Kurt Rambis .60 1.50
114 Bill Sharman 1.25 3.00
115 Lenny Wilkens 1.00 2.50
116 Elvin Hayes 1.50 4.00
117 Walt Frazier 1.50 4.00
118 Connie Hawkins 1.25 3.00
119 Spencer Haywood .60 1.50
120 Dell Curry 1.00 2.50
121 Jrue Holiday AU RC 12.00 30.00
122 James Johnson AU RC 3.00 8.00
123 Taj Gibson AU RC 3.00 8.00
124 Brandon Jennings AU RC 4.00 10.00
125 Jeff Teague AU RC 3.00 8.00
126 Earl Clark AU RC 2.50 6.00
127 Jordan Hill AU RC 2.50 6.00
128 Toney Douglas AU RC 2.50 6.00
129 Stephen Curry AU RC 1,000.00 2,000.00
130 Austin Daye AU RC 2.50 6.00
131 Jonas Jerebko AU RC 3.00 8.00
132 Jonny Flynn AU RC 2.50 6.00
133 Wayne Ellington AU RC 3.00 8.00
134 Ty Lawson AU RC 3.00 8.00
135 Chase Budinger AU RC 2.50 6.00
136 DeJuan Blair AU RC 3.00 8.00
137 Tyler Hansbrough AU RC 3.00 8.00
138 DeMarre Carroll AU RC 3.00 8.00
139 Hasheem Thabeet AU RC 2.50 6.00
140 Terrence Williams AU RC 2.50 6.00
141 Darren Collison AU RC 4.00 10.00
142 Marcus Thornton AU RC 3.00 8.00
143 Derrick Brown AU RC 2.50 6.00
144 Gerald Henderson AU RC 2.50 6.00
145 James Harden AU RC 300.00 600.00
146 DeMar DeRozan AU RC 125.00 300.00
147 Tyreke Evans AU RC 3.00 8.00
148 Omri Casspi AU RC 2.50 6.00
149 Eric Maynor AU RC 2.50 6.00
150 Blake Griffin AU RC 40.00 100.00

2009-10 Court Kings Bronze

*BRONZE: .5X TO 1.25X BASE HI
STATED PRINT RUN 149 SER.#'d SETS

2009-10 Court Kings Silver

*SILVER: .75X TO 2X BASE HI
STATED PRINT RUN 99 SER.#'d SETS

2009-10 Court Kings Artistry

COMPLETE SET (30) 20.00 40.00
STATED PRINT RUN 249 SER.#'d SETS
*BRONZE: .5X TO 1.25X BASE HI
BRONZE PRINT RUN 199 SER.#'d SETS
*SILVER: .6X TO 1.5X BASE HI
SILVER PRINT RUN 99 SER.#'d SETS
1 Josh Smith .50 1.25
2 Kevin Garnett 2.00 5.00
3 Gerald Wallace .60 1.50
4 Derrick Rose 1.25 3.00
5 LeBron James 6.00 15.00
6 Jason Terry .60 1.50
7 Carmelo Anthony 1.25 3.00
8 Rodney Stuckey .50 1.25
9 Monta Ellis .60 1.50
10 Carl Landry .50 1.25
11 Dahntay Jones .50 1.25
12 Chris Kaman .60 1.50
13 Kobe Bryant 6.00 15.00
14 Rudy Gay .75 2.00
15 Dwyane Wade 1.50 4.00
16 Ersan Ilyasova .50 1.25
17 Al Jefferson .50 1.25
18 Brook Lopez .75 2.00
19 David West .60 1.50
20 Danilo Gallinari .60 1.50
21 Kevin Durant 3.00 8.00
22 Dwight Howard 1.00 2.50
23 Andre Iguodala .75 2.00
24 Jason Richardson .75 2.00
25 Brandon Roy 1.00 2.50
26 Jason Thompson .50 1.25
27 Tim Duncan 2.00 5.00
28 Chris Bosh 1.00 2.50
29 Carlos Boozer .60 1.50
30 Andrew Bogut .60 1.50

2009-10 Court Kings Artistry Materials

PRINT RUN ONE TO 299 SER.#'d SETS
1 Josh Smith/299 1.50 4.00
2 Kevin Garnett/299 6.00 15.00
3 Gerald Wallace/299 2.00 5.00
5 LeBron James/299 8.00 20.00
6 Jason Terry/299 2.00 5.00
7 Carmelo Anthony/299 4.00 10.00
8 Rodney Stuckey/299 1.50 4.00
9 Monta Ellis/299 2.00 5.00
12 Chris Kaman/299 2.00 5.00
13 Kobe Bryant/299 8.00 20.00
14 Rudy Gay/299 2.50 6.00
15 Dwyane Wade/299 5.00 12.00
17 Al Jefferson/299 1.50 4.00
18 Brook Lopez/299 2.50 6.00
19 David West/299 2.00 5.00
20 Danilo Gallinari/49 2.00 5.00
21 Kevin Durant/299 6.00 15.00
22 Dwight Howard/299 3.00 8.00
23 Andre Iguodala/299 2.50 6.00
24 Jason Richardson/299 2.50 6.00
25 Brandon Roy/299 3.00 8.00
27 Tim Duncan/299 6.00 15.00
28 Chris Bosh/299 3.00 8.00
29 Carlos Boozer/299 2.00 5.00
30 Andrew Bogut/299 2.00 5.00

2009-10 Court Kings Artistry Signatures

STATED PRINT RUN 5 TO 99 SER.#'d SETS
13 Kobe Bryant/99 500.00 1,000.00
23 Andre Iguodala/99 5.00 12.00
25 Brandon Roy/49 8.00 20.00

2009-10 Court Kings Dribble Kings

COMPLETE SET (15) 15.00 30.00
STATED PRINT RUN 149 SER.#'d SETS
1 Steve Nash 2.50 6.00
2 Tony Parker 2.00 5.00
3 Chris Paul 2.50 6.00
4 Deron Williams 2.00 5.00
5 Pete Maravich 4.00 10.00
6 John Stockton 2.00 5.00
7 Jerry West 2.00 5.00
8 Carmelo Anthony 2.00 5.00
9 Dwyane Wade 2.50 6.00
10 Bob Cousy 3.00 8.00
11 Rafer Alston .75 2.00
12 Jason Kidd 2.00 5.00
13 Earl Monroe 1.50 4.00
14 Oscar Robertson 1.50 4.00
15 Kobe Bryant 10.00 25.00

2009-10 Court Kings Dribble Kings Materials

STATED PRINT RUN 99 TO 299 SER.#'d SETS
1 Steve Nash/199 5.00 12.00
2 Tony Parker/199 4.00 10.00
3 Chris Paul/299 5.00 12.00
4 Deron Williams/299 2.00 5.00
6 John Stockton/299 4.00 10.00
8 Carmelo Anthony/299 4.00 10.00
9 Dwyane Wade/299 5.00 12.00
11 Rafer Alston/299 2.00 5.00
12 Jason Kidd/299 4.00 10.00
13 Earl Monroe/299 3.00 8.00
15 Kobe Bryant/99 12.00 30.00

2009-10 Court Kings Dribble Kings Signatures

STATED PRINT RUN 5 TO 49 SER.#'d SETS
2 Tony Parker/49 8.00 20.00
12 Jason Kidd/49 12.50 30.00
15 Kobe Bryant/49 500.00 1,000.00

2009-10 Court Kings Gallery of Stars

COMPLETE SET (20) 15.00 30.00
STATED PRINT RUN 249 SER.#'d SETS
*BRONZE: .6X TO 1.5X BASE HI
BRONZE PRINT RUN 149 SER.#'d SETS
*SILVER: .75X TO 2X BASE HI
SILVER PRINT RUN 49 SER.#'d SETS
1 Aaron Brooks .75 2.00
2 Al Jefferson .75 2.00
3 Danny Granger .75 2.00
4 Devin Harris .75 2.00
5 Chauncey Billups 1.50 4.00
6 David Lee .75 2.00
7 Josh Howard 1.00 2.50
8 Luol Deng 1.00 2.50
9 Lamar Odom 1.00 2.50
10 Marc Gasol 1.25 3.00
11 Rajon Rondo 1.50 4.00
12 Ron Artest 1.25 3.00
13 Russell Westbrook 2.50 6.00
14 Shane Battier 1.25 3.00
15 Stephen Jackson 1.00 2.50
16 Tayshaun Prince 1.25 3.00
17 Vince Carter 2.50 6.00
18 Al Harrington 1.00 2.50
19 Joakim Noah .75 2.00
20 Kevin Love 1.25 3.00

2009-10 Court Kings Gallery of Stars Materials

STATED PRINT RUN 25 TO 299 SER.#'d SETS
1 Aaron Brooks/299 1.50 4.00
2 Al Jefferson/299 1.50 4.00
3 Danny Granger/299 1.50 4.00
4 Devin Harris/299 1.50 4.00
5 Chauncey Billups/299 3.00 8.00
6 David Lee/199 1.50 4.00
7 Josh Howard/299 2.00 5.00
8 Luol Deng/299 2.00 5.00
10 Marc Gasol/299 2.50 6.00
11 Rajon Rondo/299 3.00 8.00
12 Ron Artest/299 2.50 6.00
13 Russell Westbrook/299 5.00 12.00
14 Shane Battier/299 2.50 6.00
16 Tayshaun Prince/299 2.50 6.00
17 Vince Carter/299 5.00 12.00
18 Al Harrington/25 3.00 8.00
19 Joakim Noah/299 1.50 4.00
20 Kevin Love/299 2.50 6.00

2009-10 Court Kings Gallery of Stars Signatures

STATED PRINT RUN 49 TO 99 SER.#'d SETS
1 Aaron Brooks/99 4.00 10.00
4 Devin Harris/49 4.00 10.00
5 Chauncey Billups/49 8.00 20.00
7 Josh Howard/49 4.00 10.00
11 Rajon Rondo/49 10.00 25.00
13 Russell Westbrook/49 60.00 150.00
14 Shane Battier/49 5.00 12.00
17 Vince Carter/49 12.00 30.00
20 Kevin Love/49 12.00 30.00

2009-10 Court Kings Hardwood Heroes

COMPLETE SET (20) 20.00 40.00
STATED PRINT RUN 249 SER.#'d SETS
1 LeBron James 8.00 20.00
2 Magic Johnson 4.00 10.00
3 Allen Iverson 2.00 5.00
4 Steve Nash 2.00 5.00
5 Patrick Ewing 1.50 4.00
6 Carmelo Anthony 1.50 4.00
7 Kevin Durant 4.00 10.00
8 Oscar Robertson 1.25 3.00
9 Dirk Nowitzki 2.50 6.00
10 Kobe Bryant 8.00 20.00
11 Scottie Pippen 2.50 6.00
12 Deron Williams .75 2.00
13 Dwyane Wade 2.00 5.00
14 Ty Lawson .75 2.00
15 Bill Russell 3.00 8.00
16 Shaquille O'Neal 3.00 8.00
17 Chris Paul 2.00 5.00
18 Derrick Rose 1.50 4.00
19 Larry Bird 4.00 10.00
20 Blake Griffin 4.00 10.00

2009-10 Court Kings Hardwood Heroes Materials

STATED PRINT RUN ONE TO 299 SER.#'d SETS
1 LeBron James/299 10.00 25.00
2 Magic Johnson/299 12.00 30.00
3 Allen Iverson/99 6.00 15.00
4 Steve Nash/199 6.00 15.00
5 Patrick Ewing/299 5.00 12.00
6 Carmelo Anthony/299 5.00 12.00
7 Kevin Durant/299 6.00 15.00
9 Dirk Nowitzki/299 8.00 20.00
10 Kobe Bryant/299 8.00 20.00
11 Scottie Pippen/299 8.00 20.00
12 Deron Williams/299 2.50 6.00
13 Dwyane Wade/299 5.00 12.00
14 Ty Lawson/299 2.50 6.00
16 Shaquille O'Neal/299 10.00 25.00
17 Chris Paul/299 6.00 15.00
19 Larry Bird/99 12.00 30.00
20 Blake Griffin/299 10.00 25.00

2009-10 Court Kings Hardwood Heroes Signatures

STATED PRINT RUN ONE TO 49 SER.#'d SETS
10 Kobe Bryant/49 500.00 1,000.00
11 Scottie Pippen/49 75.00 150.00

2009-10 Court Kings Jumbo Boxtoppers

COMPLETE SET (50) 100.00 200.00
STATED PRINT RUN 349 SER.#'d SETS
1 Ray Allen 5.00 12.00
2 Tracy McGrady 6.00 15.00
3 Bob Cousy 8.00 20.00
4 Pau Gasol 5.00 12.00
5 Dirk Nowitzki 8.00 20.00
6 Alonzo Mourning 5.00 12.00
7 Bill Walton 5.00 12.00
8 Vince Carter 6.00 15.00
9 Tyreke Evans 2.50 6.00
10 David Lee 2.00 5.00
11 Andrew Bogut 2.50 6.00
12 Pete Maravich 10.00 25.00
13 Cedric Maxwell 3.00 8.00
14 Shaquille O'Neal 10.00 25.00
15 Baron Davis 2.50 6.00
16 Kevin Love 3.00 8.00
17 Artis Gilmore 4.00 10.00
18 Connie Hawkins 4.00 10.00
19 Jermaine O'Neal 3.00 8.00
20 Kevin Durant 12.00 30.00
21 Magic Johnson 12.00 30.00
22 Patrick Ewing 5.00 12.00
23 LeBron James 40.00 100.00
24 Jason Kidd 5.00 12.00
25 Rajon Rondo 4.00 10.00
26 Al Attles 2.50 6.00
27 David Thompson 2.50 6.00
28 Chris Bosh 4.00 10.00
29 Lamar Odom 2.50 6.00
30 Tim Duncan 8.00 20.00
31 Dan Majerle 2.50 6.00
32 Isiah Thomas 3.00 8.00
33 Kareem Abdul-Jabbar 10.00 25.00
34 Stephen Curry 500.00 1,000.00
35 Deron Williams 2.50 6.00
36 Carmelo Anthony 5.00 12.00
37 Darryl Dawkins 3.00 8.00
39 Bob McAdoo 4.00 10.00
40 Brandon Jennings 3.00 8.00
41 Trevor Ariza 2.00 5.00
42 Kevin McHale 5.00 12.00
43 Brandon Roy 4.00 10.00
44 Danny Granger 2.00 5.00
45 Jalen Rose 2.50 6.00
46 Devin Harris 2.00 5.00
47 Elton Brand 2.50 6.00
48 Lenny Wilkens 3.00 8.00
49 Larry Bird 12.00 30.00
50 Kobe Bryant 25.00 60.00

2009-10 Court Kings Jumbo Boxtoppers Autographs

STATED PRINT RUN 10 TO 75 SER.#'d SETS
5 Dirk Nowitzki/20 100.00 250.00
6 Alonzo Mourning/49 40.00 80.00
7 Bill Walton/49 12.00 30.00
8 Vince Carter/49 30.00 60.00
9 Tyreke Evans/75 12.00 30.00
10 David Lee/74 10.00 25.00
11 Andrew Bogut/75 10.00 25.00
13 Cedric Maxwell/75 10.00 25.00
15 Baron Davis/75 10.00 25.00
16 Kevin Love/75 15.00 40.00
17 Artis Gilmore/75 25.00 60.00
18 Connie Hawkins/75 15.00 30.00
19 Jermaine O'Neal/49 10.00 25.00
21 Magic Johnson/15 75.00 200.00
24 Jason Kidd/49 20.00 40.00
25 Rajon Rondo/75 25.00 60.00
26 Al Attles/75 10.00 25.00
27 David Thompson/74 10.00 25.00
28 Chris Bosh/49 15.00 40.00
29 Lamar Odom/75 15.00 30.00
31 Dan Majerle/75 20.00 40.00
32 Isiah Thomas/75 25.00 60.00
34 Stephen Curry/75 2,000.00 4,000.00
35 Deron Williams/49 10.00 25.00
37 Darryl Dawkins/75 10.00 25.00
39 Bob McAdoo/75 12.00 30.00
40 Brandon Jennings/75 12.00 30.00
41 Trevor Ariza/75 10.00 25.00
42 Kevin McHale/20 30.00 80.00
43 Brandon Roy/49 15.00 30.00
44 Danny Granger/75 10.00 25.00
45 Jalen Rose/75 10.00 25.00
46 Devin Harris/75 10.00 25.00
48 Lenny Wilkens/75 10.00 25.00
49 Larry Bird/15 75.00 150.00
50 Kobe Bryant/50 500.00 1,000.00

2009-10 Court Kings Kobe Bryant Lithographs

COMMON EXCH (1-5) 250.00 500.00
STATED PRINT RUN 24 SER.#'d SETS

2009-10 Court Kings Le Cinque Piu Belle

COMPLETE SET (5) 75.00 200.00
COMMON CARD (1-5) 20.00 50.00
STATED PRINT RUN 149 SER.#'d SETS

2009-10 Court Kings Le Cinque Piu Belle Signatures

COMMON CARD (1-5) 1,000.00 3,000.00
STATED PRINT RUN 24 SER.#'d SETS

2009-10 Court Kings Masterpieces

COMPLETE SET (20) 30.00 60.00
STATED PRINT RUN 149 SER.#'d SETS
1 Nate Robinson 1.50 4.00
2 Dwight Howard 2.50 6.00
3 Josh Smith 1.25 3.00
4 Jason Richardson 2.00 5.00
5 Vince Carter 4.00 10.00
6 Kobe Bryant 15.00 40.00
7 Cedric Ceballos 1.25 3.00
8 Dee Brown 1.25 3.00
9 Dominique Wilkins 3.00 8.00
10 Kenny Walker 1.25 3.00
11 Spud Webb 1.50 4.00
12 Larry Nance 1.50 4.00
13 Carmelo Anthony 3.00 8.00
14 Andre Iguodala 2.00 5.00
15 J.R. Smith 2.00 5.00
16 LeBron James 15.00 40.00
17 Larry Johnson 2.00 5.00
18 Kenny Smith 1.50 4.00
19 Clyde Drexler 3.00 8.00
20 Amare Stoudemire 1.50 4.00

2009-10 Court Kings Masterpieces Materials

STATED PRINT RUN 199 TO 299 SER.#'d SETS
2 Dwight Howard/299 3.00 8.00
3 Josh Smith/299 1.50 4.00
4 Jason Richardson/299 2.50 6.00
5 Vince Carter/299 4.00 10.00
6 Kobe Bryant/199 10.00 25.00
9 Dominique Wilkins/299 4.00 10.00
13 Carmelo Anthony/299 4.00 10.00
14 Andre Iguodala/299 2.50 6.00
15 J.R. Smith/299 2.50 6.00
16 LeBron James/299 8.00 20.00
19 Clyde Drexler/299 4.00 10.00
20 Amare Stoudemire/299 2.00 5.00

2009-10 Court Kings Masterpieces Signatures

STATED PRINT RUN 5 TO 49 SER.#'d SETS
5 Vince Carter/49 12.50 30.00
6 Kobe Bryant/49 500.00 1,000.00
10 Kenny Walker/49 8.00 20.00
11 Spud Webb/49 8.00 20.00
14 Andre Iguodala/49 8.00 20.00
17 Larry Johnson/49 20.00 50.00
19 Clyde Drexler/49 20.00 50.00

2009-10 Court Kings Materials

STATED PRINT RUN 25 TO 149 SER.#'d SETS
1 Carmelo Anthony/149 5.00 12.00
2 Chris Andersen/149 3.00 8.00
3 J.R. Smith/149 3.00 8.00
4 Chauncey Billups/149 4.00 10.00
5 Kevin Love/149 3.00 8.00
6 Al Jefferson/149 2.00 5.00
8 Kevin Durant/149 8.00 20.00
9 Russell Westbrook/149 6.00 15.00
10 Jeff Green/149 2.50 6.00
11 Brandon Roy/149 4.00 10.00
12 LaMarcus Aldridge/149 3.00 8.00
13 Juwan Howard/149 2.50 6.00
14 Deron Williams/149 2.50 6.00
15 Carlos Boozer/149 2.50 6.00
16 Paul Millsap/99 2.50 6.00
17 Dirk Nowitzki/149 8.00 20.00
18 Jason Kidd/149 5.00 12.00
20 J.J. Barea/149 5.00 12.00
22 Aaron Brooks/149 2.00 5.00
24 Tony Parker/149 5.00 12.00
25 Richard Jefferson/149 2.50 6.00
26 Tim Duncan/149 8.00 20.00
27 Marc Gasol/149 3.00 8.00
28 Rudy Gay/149 3.00 8.00
30 Emeka Okafor/149 2.50 6.00
31 Chris Paul/149 6.00 15.00
32 David West/149 2.50 6.00
34 Kevin Martin/149 2.50 6.00
36 Amare Stoudemire/149 2.50 6.00
37 Channing Frye/149 2.00 5.00
38 Steve Nash/149 6.00 15.00
39 Pau Gasol/149 5.00 12.00
40 Kobe Bryant/149 12.00 30.00
41 Derek Fisher/149 3.00 8.00
42 Andrew Bynum/149 2.50 6.00
43 Monta Ellis/149 2.50 6.00
45 Corey Maggette/149 2.50 6.00
46 Baron Davis/149 2.50 6.00
47 Chris Kaman/149 2.50 6.00
48 Eric Gordon/149 2.50 6.00
49 Kevin Garnett/149 8.00 20.00
50 Ray Allen/149 5.00 12.00
51 Paul Pierce/149 5.00 12.00
54 Chris Duhon/149 2.00 5.00
55 David Lee/149 2.00 5.00
56 Danilo Gallinari/49 3.00 8.00
57 Allen Iverson/99 6.00 15.00
58 Andre Iguodala/149 3.00 8.00
60 Elton Brand/149 2.50 6.00
61 Andrea Bargnani/149 2.00 5.00
62 Chris Bosh/149 4.00 10.00
63 Hedo Turkoglu/149 2.50 6.00
64 Brook Lopez/149 3.00 8.00
65 Rafer Alston/149 2.00 5.00
66 Devin Harris/149 2.00 5.00
67 LeBron James/149 10.00 25.00
70 Shaquille O'Neal/149 8.00 20.00
71 Ben Gordon/149 2.50 6.00
72 Rodney Stuckey/149 2.00 5.00
74 Danny Granger/149 2.00 5.00
75 Troy Murphy/149 2.00 5.00
77 Andrew Bogut/149 2.50 6.00
80 Luol Deng/149 2.50 6.00
81 Derrick Rose/149 5.00 12.00
82 Joakim Noah/149 2.50 6.00
83 John Salmons/149 2.50 6.00
84 Joe Johnson/149 3.00 8.00
85 Al Horford/149 3.00 8.00
87 Marvin Williams/149 2.00 5.00
88 Dwyane Wade/149 6.00 15.00
89 Jermaine O'Neal/149 3.00 8.00
90 Michael Beasley/149 2.00 5.00
91 Gerald Wallace/149 2.50 6.00
93 Raymond Felton/149 2.00 5.00
94 Dwight Howard/149 4.00 10.00
95 Vince Carter/149 6.00 15.00
96 Rashard Lewis/149 2.50 6.00
97 Jason Williams/149 2.50 6.00
98 Antawn Jamison/149 2.50 6.00
99 Mike Miller/149 2.50 6.00
100 Caron Butler/149 2.50 6.00
107 Clyde Drexler/149 8.00 20.00
108 Mark Eaton/149 3.00 8.00
109 John Havlicek/99 6.00 15.00
117 Walt Frazier/25 8.00 20.00

2009-10 Court Kings Portraits

COMPLETE SET (20) 15.00 30.00
STATED PRINT RUN 149 SER.#'d SETS
1 Chris Andersen 1.00 2.50
2 Ron Artest 1.00 2.50
3 Kobe Bryant 8.00 20.00
4 LeBron James 8.00 20.00
5 Dirk Nowitzki 2.50 6.00
6 Joakim Noah .60 1.50
7 Dwight Howard 1.25 3.00
8 Allen Iverson 2.00 5.00
9 Steve Nash 2.00 5.00
10 Tony Parker 1.50 4.00
11 Shaquille O'Neal 3.00 8.00
12 Chris Bosh 1.25 3.00
13 Rasheed Wallace 1.25 3.00
14 Jason Kidd 1.50 4.00
15 Nene .75 2.00
16 Richard Hamilton 1.00 2.50
17 Zach Randolph 1.00 2.50
18 Chris Paul 2.00 5.00
19 David Lee .60 1.50
20 Vince Carter 2.00 5.00

2009-10 Court Kings Portraits Materials
STATED PRINT RUN 49 TO 299 SER.#'d SETS
1 Chris Andersen/299 3.00 8.00
3 Kobe Bryant/99 10.00 25.00
4 LeBron James/99 10.00 25.00
5 Dirk Nowitzki/299 8.00 20.00
6 Joakim Noah/299 2.00 5.00
7 Dwight Howard/299 4.00 10.00
8 Allen Iverson/99 6.00 15.00
9 Steve Nash/199 6.00 15.00
10 Tony Parker/199 5.00 12.00
11 Shaquille O'Neal/299 10.00 25.00
12 Chris Bosh/299 4.00 10.00
13 Rasheed Wallace/299 4.00 10.00
14 Jason Kidd/299 5.00 12.00
15 Nene/299 2.50 6.00
16 Richard Hamilton/49 3.00 8.00
18 Chris Paul/299 6.00 15.00
19 David Lee/199 2.00 5.00
20 Vince Carter/299 6.00 15.00

2009-10 Court Kings Portraits Signatures
STATED PRINT RUN 49 SER.#'d SETS
1 Chris Andersen 10.00 25.00
3 Kobe Bryant 1,500.00 3,000.00
10 Tony Parker 20.00 50.00
14 Jason Kidd 20.00 50.00
16 Richard Hamilton 12.00 30.00
20 Vince Carter 60.00 150.00

2009-10 Court Kings Signatures
STATED PRINT RUN 5 TO 49 SER.#'d SETS
2 Chris Andersen/49 8.00 20.00
4 Chauncey Billups/49 10.00 25.00
5 Kevin Love/49 8.00 20.00
9 Russell Westbrook/49 75.00 200.00
11 Brandon Roy/49 10.00 25.00
18 Jason Kidd/49 12.00 30.00
20 J.J. Barea/49 8.00 20.00
22 Aaron Brooks/49 5.00 12.00
24 Tony Parker/49 12.00 30.00
30 Emeka Okafor/49 6.00 15.00
40 Kobe Bryant/49 1,500.00 3,000.00
42 Andrew Bynum/49 5.00 12.00
46 Baron Davis/49 6.00 15.00
48 Eric Gordon/49 6.00 15.00
58 Andre Iguodala/49 8.00 20.00
61 Andrea Bargnani/49 5.00 12.00
66 Devin Harris/49 5.00 12.00
89 Jermaine O'Neal/49 8.00 20.00
90 Michael Beasley/49 5.00 12.00
95 Vince Carter/49 60.00 150.00
101 Harry Gallatin/49 8.00 20.00
102 Nate Archibald/49 10.00 25.00
111 George McGinnis/49 8.00 20.00
112 Sidney Moncrief/49 6.00 15.00
114 Bill Sharman/49 10.00 25.00
115 Lenny Wilkens/49 8.00 20.00
116 Elvin Hayes/49 12.00 30.00
117 Walt Frazier/49 12.00 30.00
120 Dell Curry/49 8.00 20.00

2009-10 Court Kings Supreme Court
COMPLETE SET (20) 20.00 40.00
STATED PRINT RUN 149 SER.#'d SETS
1 Vince Carter 2.00 5.00
2 Carmelo Anthony 1.50 4.00
3 Chris Bosh 1.25 3.00
4 David Lee .60 1.50
5 Tyreke Evans .75 2.00
6 Dirk Nowitzki 2.50 6.00
7 Kevin Durant 4.00 10.00
8 Gerald Wallace .75 2.00
9 Kevin Garnett 2.50 6.00
10 Kobe Bryant 8.00 20.00
11 Dwyane Wade 2.00 5.00
12 Dwight Howard 1.25 3.00
13 Shaquille O'Neal 3.00 8.00
14 Danny Granger .60 1.50
15 Tony Parker 1.50 4.00
16 Brandon Jennings 1.00 2.50
17 LeBron James 8.00 20.00
18 Chris Paul 2.00 5.00
19 Ray Allen 1.50 4.00
20 Allen Iverson 2.00 5.00

2009-10 Court Kings Supreme Court Materials
STATED PRINT RUN 99 TO 299 SER.#'d SETS
1 Vince Carter/299 6.00 15.00
2 Carmelo Anthony/299 5.00 12.00
3 Chris Bosh/299 4.00 10.00
4 David Lee/199 2.00 5.00
5 Tyreke Evans/299 2.00 5.00
6 Dirk Nowitzki/299 8.00 20.00
7 Kevin Durant/299 6.00 15.00
8 Gerald Wallace/299 2.50 6.00
9 Kevin Garnett/299 8.00 20.00
10 Kobe Bryant/99 12.00 30.00
11 Dwyane Wade/299 8.00 20.00
12 Dwight Howard/299 4.00 10.00
13 Shaquille O'Neal/99 10.00 25.00
14 Danny Granger/299 2.00 5.00
15 Tony Parker/199 5.00 12.00
16 Brandon Jennings/299 2.50 6.00
17 LeBron James/99 10.00 25.00
18 Chris Paul/299 6.00 15.00
19 Ray Allen/299 5.00 12.00
20 Allen Iverson/99 6.00 15.00

2009-10 Court Kings Supreme Court Signatures
STATED PRINT RUN 10 TO 49 SER.#'d SETS
1 Vince Carter/49 20.00 50.00
4 David Lee/49 8.00 20.00
5 Tyreke Evans/49 20.00 50.00
10 Kobe Bryant/49 500.00 1,000.00
14 Danny Granger/49 8.00 20.00
15 Tony Parker/49 8.00 20.00
16 Brandon Jennings/49 20.00 50.00
19 Ray Allen/49 25.00 60.00

2013-14 Court Kings
126-150 PRINT RUN 225 SER.#'d SETS
176-200 PRINT RUN 49 SER.#'d SETS
126-150 PRINT RUN 125 SER.#'d SETS
1 Anderson Varejao .60 1.50
2 Roy Hibbert .60 1.50
3 Ricky Rubio .75 2.00
4 Jameer Nelson .60 1.50
5 Tony Parker 1.50 4.00
6 Thaddeus Young .60 1.50
7 Tyson Chandler .75 2.00
8 Brandon Knight .75 2.00
9 Blake Griffin 1.00 2.50
10 Steve Nash 2.00 5.00
11 Rodney Stuckey .60 1.50
12 Joakim Noah 1.00 2.50
13 Gerald Wallace .75 2.00
14 Jeff Teague .60 1.50
15 Al Jefferson .60 1.50
16 Vince Carter 2.00 5.00
17 Mike Conley 1.00 2.50
18 Nikola Pekovic .60 1.50
19 Serge Ibaka .75 2.00
20 Eric Bledsoe .75 2.00
21 Isaiah Thomas .75 2.00
22 Gordon Hayward .75 2.00
23 DeMarcus Cousins 1.00 2.50
24 Nikola Vucevic 1.25 3.00
25 Larry Sanders .60 1.50
26 George Hill .75 2.00
27 Shawn Marion .75 2.00
28 Al Horford 1.00 2.50
29 Kevin Garnett 2.50 6.00
30 Kyrie Irving 3.00 8.00
31 Lance Stephenson .75 2.00
32 Kevin Love 1.00 2.50
33 Austin Rivers .75 2.00
34 Glen Davis .60 1.50
35 Greivis Vasquez .60 1.50
36 Gerald Green .75 2.00
37 DeMar DeRozan 1.25 3.00
38 Evan Turner .60 1.50
39 Amar'e Stoudemire 1.00 2.50
40 Dwyane Wade 2.00 5.00
41 Chris Paul 2.00 5.00
42 Andre Drummond 1.00 2.50
43 Luol Deng .75 2.00
44 Paul Millsap .75 2.00
45 Paul Pierce 1.50 4.00
46 Ben Gordon .75 2.00
47 Dirk Nowitzki 2.50 6.00
48 Derrick Rose 1.50 4.00
49 Ty Lawson .60 1.50
50 Andre Iguodala 1.00 2.50
51 Jeremy Lin 1.50 4.00
52 Kobe Bryant 8.00 20.00
53 O.J. Mayo .60 1.50
54 Chris Bosh 1.25 3.00
55 Bradley Beal 1.50 4.00
56 Manu Ginobili 2.00 5.00
57 Damian Lillard 3.00 8.00
58 Kevin Durant 3.00 8.00
59 Marcin Gortat .60 1.50
60 Metta World Peace .75 2.00
61 Tyreke Evans .75 2.00
62 Harrison Barnes 1.00 2.50
63 Dion Waiters .60 1.50
64 Avery Bradley .60 1.50
65 Kemba Walker 1.00 2.50
66 Kenneth Faried .75 2.00
67 James Harden 2.00 5.00
68 Pau Gasol 1.50 4.00
69 Kevin Martin .75 2.00
70 Russell Westbrook 1.50 4.00
71 Goran Dragic .75 2.00
72 Rudy Gay .75 2.00
73 John Wall 1.25 3.00
74 Tim Duncan 2.50 6.00
75 LaMarcus Aldridge 1.00 2.50
76 Zach Randolph .75 2.00
77 Carlos Boozer .75 2.00
78 Brandon Jennings .60 1.50
79 Rajon Rondo 1.25 3.00
80 DeAndre Jordan .75 2.00
81 Jrue Holiday 1.25 3.00
82 Nicolas Batum .75 2.00
83 Derrick Favors .60 1.50
84 Deron Williams .75 2.00
85 Monta Ellis .75 2.00
86 Andre Miller .75 2.00
87 Stephen Curry 8.00 20.00
88 Paul George 1.50 4.00
89 Dwight Howard 1.25 3.00
90 Marc Gasol 1.00 2.50
91 LeBron James 8.00 20.00
92 Ersan Ilyasova .60 1.50
93 Anthony Davis 3.00 8.00
94 Carmelo Anthony 1.50 4.00
95 Jason Richardson 1.00 2.50
96 Kawhi Leonard 3.00 8.00
97 Kyle Lowry 1.00 2.50
98 Brook Lopez 1.00 2.50
99 Klay Thompson 3.00 8.00
100 J.R. Smith 1.00 2.50
101 Anthony Bennett RC .60 1.50
102 Cody Zeller RC .75 2.00
103 Ben McLemore RC .75 2.00
104 C.J. McCollum RC 2.50 6.00
105 Kelly Olynyk RC .75 2.00
106 Dennis Schroder RC 2.00 5.00
107 Sergey Karasev RC .60 1.50
108 Gorgui Dieng RC .75 2.00
109 Solomon Hill RC .75 2.00
110 Isaiah Canaan RC .60 1.50
111 Victor Oladipo RC 1.50 4.00
112 Alex Len RC .75 2.00
113 Kentavious Caldwell-Pope RC 1.00 2.50
114 M.Carter-Williams RC 1.00 2.50
115 Shabazz Muhammad RC .60 1.50
116 Shane Larkin RC .60 1.50
117 Tony Snell RC .60 1.50
118 Mason Plumlee RC .75 2.00
119 Tim Hardaway Jr. RC 1.25 3.00
120 Glen Rice Jr. RC .75 2.00
121 Otto Porter RC 1.00 2.50
122 Nerlens Noel RC .75 2.00
123 Trey Burke RC .75 2.00
124 Steven Adams RC 1.50 4.00
125 G.Antetokounmpo RC 150.00 400.00
126 Anthony Bennett/225 .75 2.00
127 Cody Zeller/225 1.00 2.50
128 Ben McLemore/225 1.00 2.50
129 C.J. McCollum/225 3.00 8.00
130 Kelly Olynyk/225 1.00 2.50
131 Dennis Schroder/225 2.50 6.00
132 Sergey Karasev/225 .75 2.00
133 Gorgui Dieng/225 1.00 2.50
134 Solomon Hill/225 1.00 2.50
135 Isaiah Canaan/225 .75 2.00
136 Victor Oladipo/225 2.00 5.00
137 Alex Len/225 1.00 2.50
138 Kentavious Caldwell-Pope/225 1.25 3.00
139 M.Carter-Williams/225 1.00 2.50
140 Shabazz Muhammad/225 .75 2.00
141 Shane Larkin/225 .75 2.00
142 Tony Snell/225 1.00 2.50
143 Mason Plumlee/225 1.00 2.50
144 Tim Hardaway Jr./225 1.50 4.00
145 Glen Rice Jr./225 .75 2.00
146 Otto Porter/225 1.25 3.00
147 Nerlens Noel/225 1.00 2.50
148 Trey Burke/225 1.00 2.50
149 Steven Adams/225 2.00 5.00
150 G.Antetokounmpo/225 300.00 600.00
151 Anthony Bennett/125 1.00 2.50
152 Cody Zeller/125 1.25 3.00
153 Ben McLemore/125 1.25 3.00
154 C.J. McCollum/125 4.00 10.00
155 Kelly Olynyk/125 1.25 3.00
156 Dennis Schroder/125 3.00 8.00
157 Sergey Karasev/125 1.00 2.50
158 Gorgui Dieng/125 1.25 3.00
159 Solomon Hill/125 1.25 3.00
160 Isaiah Canaan/125 1.00 2.50
161 Victor Oladipo/125 2.50 6.00
162 Alex Len/125 1.25 3.00
163 Kentavious Caldwell-Pope/125 1.50 4.00
164 M.Carter-Williams/125 1.25 3.00
165 Shabazz Muhammad/125 1.00 2.50
166 Shane Larkin/125 1.00 2.50
167 Tony Snell/125 1.25 3.00
168 Mason Plumlee/125 1.25 3.00
169 Tim Hardaway Jr./125 2.00 5.00
170 Glen Rice Jr./125 1.00 2.50
171 Otto Porter/125 1.50 4.00
172 Nerlens Noel/125 1.25 3.00
173 Trey Burke/125 1.25 3.00
174 Steven Adams/125 2.50 6.00
175 G.Antetokounmpo/125 400.00 800.00
176 Anthony Bennett/49 1.50 4.00
177 Cody Zeller/49 2.00 5.00
178 Ben McLemore/49 2.00 5.00
179 C.J. McCollum/49 6.00 15.00
180 Kelly Olynyk/49 2.00 5.00
181 Dennis Schroder/49 5.00 12.00
182 Sergey Karasev/49 1.50 4.00
183 Gorgui Dieng/49 2.00 5.00
184 Solomon Hill/49 2.00 5.00
185 Isaiah Canaan/49 1.50 4.00
186 Victor Oladipo/49 10.00 25.00
187 Alex Len/49 2.00 5.00
188 Kentavious Caldwell-Pope/49 2.50 6.00
189 M.Carter-Williams/49 2.00 5.00
190 Shabazz Muhammad/49 1.50 4.00
191 Shane Larkin/49 1.50 4.00
192 Tony Snell/49 2.00 5.00
193 Mason Plumlee/49 2.00 5.00
194 Tim Hardaway Jr./49 3.00 8.00
195 Glen Rice Jr./49 1.50 4.00
196 Otto Porter/49 2.50 6.00
197 Nerlens Noel/49 2.00 5.00
198 Trey Burke/49 2.00 5.00
199 Steven Adams/49 8.00 20.00
200 G.Antetokounmpo/49 800.00 1,500.00

2013-14 Court Kings Gold
*GOLD: 3X TO 8X BASIC
STATED PRINT RUN 25 SER.#'d SETS

2013-14 Court Kings 2 on 2 Quad Memorabilia
PRINT RUNS B/WN 49-99 COPIES PER
1 Brd/Prsh/Jhnsn/Jbbr/49 25.00 60.00
2 Jms/Wde/Hbbrt/Grge/99 20.00 50.00
3 Englsh/Lvr/Adms/Nnce/99 8.00 20.00
4 Wstbrk/Drnt/Gsl/Rndlph/99 8.00 20.00
5 Mlne/Stcktn/Rbnsn/Ellt/49 12.00 30.00
6 Crry/Thmpsn/Lwsn/Frd/99 15.00 40.00
7 Wllms/Lpz/Anthny/Stdmre/99 10.00 25.00
8 Drxlr/Oljwn/Hrdwy/O'Nl/49 20.00 50.00
9 Brynt/Gsl/Prkr/Dncn/99 20.00 50.00

2013-14 Court Kings 2 on 2 Quad Memorabilia Prime
*PRIME: .75X TO 2X BASIC
PRINT RUNS B/WN 2-25 COPIES PER
NO PRICING ON QTY 3 OR LESS

2013-14 Court Kings 5x7 Box Toppers
1 Magic Johnson 8.00 20.00
2 Grant Hill 3.00 8.00
3 James Harden 4.00 10.00
4 Stephen Curry 15.00 40.00
5 Dikembe Mutombo 3.00 8.00
6 Karl Malone 4.00 10.00
7 Robert Parish 2.50 6.00
8 Clyde Drexler 3.00 8.00
9 Dominique Wilkins 3.00 8.00
10 Adrian Dantley 2.00 5.00
11 Shaquille O'Neal 8.00 20.00
12 Kevin Durant 6.00 15.00
13 Anthony Davis 6.00 15.00
14 Chris Andersen 1.50 4.00
15 Larry Bird 8.00 20.00
16 James Worthy 2.50 6.00
17 Isiah Thomas 2.50 6.00
18 Jason Kidd 3.00 8.00
19 Kyrie Irving 6.00 15.00
20 Dennis Rodman 5.00 12.00
21 Tony Parker 2.50 6.00
22 Anfernee Hardaway 5.00 12.00
23 Kobe Bryant 15.00 40.00
24 Alonzo Mourning 3.00 8.00
25 Blake Griffin 3.00 8.00
26 Bill Russell 6.00 15.00
27 Jeremy Lin 3.00 8.00
28 Russell Westbrook 3.00 8.00
29 John Wall 2.50 6.00
30 Kevin Love 2.00 5.00
31 Vince Carter 4.00 10.00
32 Rajon Rondo 2.50 6.00
33 Dirk Nowitzki 5.00 12.00
34 Steve Nash 4.00 10.00
35 Carmelo Anthony 3.00 8.00
36 Damian Lillard 6.00 15.00
37 Tim Duncan 5.00 12.00
38 Dwyane Wade 4.00 10.00
39 Derrick Rose 3.00 8.00
40 Kevin Garnett 5.00 12.00
41 Dwight Howard 2.50 6.00
42 Ricky Rubio 1.50 4.00
43 Drazen Petrovic 2.50 6.00
44 Deron Williams 1.50 4.00
45 Chris Paul 4.00 10.00
46 Pete Maravich 3.00 8.00
47 Wilt Chamberlain 6.00 15.00
48 LeBron James 15.00 40.00
49 Paul Pierce 3.00 8.00

2013-14 Court Kings 5x7 Box Toppers Autographs
EXCHANGE DEADLINE 9/26/2015
1 Magic Johnson 90.00 150.00
2 Grant Hill 100.00 250.00
4 Stephen Curry 500.00 1,000.00
5 Dikembe Mutombo 20.00 50.00
6 Karl Malone 75.00 150.00
7 Robert Parish 20.00 50.00
8 Clyde Drexler 60.00 120.00
9 Dominique Wilkins EXCH 40.00 80.00
10 Adrian Dantley 15.00 40.00
12 Kevin Durant EXCH 50.00 120.00
13 Anthony Davis 100.00 200.00
14 Chris Andersen EXCH 12.00 30.00
15 Larry Bird 60.00 150.00
17 Isiah Thomas 25.00 60.00
18 Jason Kidd 75.00 150.00
19 Kyrie Irving 150.00 300.00
20 Dennis Rodman 50.00 120.00
21 Tony Parker 50.00 120.00
22 Anfernee Hardaway 60.00 150.00
23 Kobe Bryant EXCH 500.00 1,000.00
24 Alonzo Mourning 100.00 200.00

2013-14 Court Kings Art Nouveau Jerseys
STATED PRINT RUN 325 SER.#'d SETS
1 C.J. McCollum 6.00 15.00
2 Kelly Olynyk 2.00 5.00
3 Mason Plumlee 2.00 5.00
4 Michael Carter-Williams 2.00 5.00
5 Glen Rice Jr. 1.50 4.00
6 Archie Goodwin 1.50 4.00
7 Tony Mitchell 1.50 4.00
8 Victor Oladipo 4.00 10.00
9 Trey Burke 2.00 5.00
10 Cody Zeller 2.00 5.00
11 Nate Wolters 1.50 4.00
12 Tim Hardaway Jr. 3.00 8.00
13 Ricky Ledo 1.50 4.00
14 Nerlens Noel 2.00 5.00
15 Andre Roberson 2.00 5.00
16 Otto Porter 2.50 6.00
17 Solomon Hill 2.00 5.00
18 Ben McLemore 2.00 5.00
19 Allen Crabbe 1.50 4.00
20 Reggie Bullock 2.00 5.00
21 Shane Larkin 1.50 4.00
22 Isaiah Canaan 1.50 4.00
23 Shabazz Muhammad 1.50 4.00
24 Steven Adams 4.00 10.00
25 Kentavious Caldwell-Pope 2.50 6.00
26 Anthony Bennett 1.50 4.00
27 Giannis Antetokounmpo 25.00 60.00
28 Alex Len 2.00 5.00
29 Ryan Kelly 1.50 4.00
30 Tony Snell 2.00 5.00

2013-14 Court Kings Art Nouveau Jerseys Prime
*PRIME: 2X TO 5X BASIC
STATED PRINT RUN 25 SER.#'d SETS

2013-14 Court Kings Autographs
PRINT RUNS B/WN 20-399 COPIES PER
EXCHANGE DEADLINE 9/26/2015
1 Clyde Drexler/20 40.00 100.00
2 Shane Battier/20 4.00 10.00
3 Greg Anthony/399 3.00 8.00
5 Anthony Mason/399 4.00 10.00
6 Andre Iguodala/20 10.00 25.00
7 Tony Parker/20 50.00 100.00
9 Charlie Scott/399 5.00 12.00
10 Tom Gugliotta/399 4.00 10.00
11 Kemba Walker/20 20.00 50.00
12 Kyrie Irving/35 30.00 80.00
13 Raef LaFrentz/399 3.00 8.00
14 Steve Nash/20 40.00 100.00
16 Kevin Love/20 12.00 30.00
17 Dwight Howard/49 30.00 80.00
18 Eddie Jones/299 8.00 20.00
19 Karl Malone/25 25.00 60.00
20 Scottie Pippen/49 60.00 150.00
21 Zaza Pachulia/349 3.00 8.00
23 Raymond Felton/20 3.00 8.00
24 Magic Johnson/25 40.00 100.00
25 Isiah Thomas/20 15.00 40.00
26 Leonard Truck Robinson/399 3.00 8.00
27 Klay Thompson/99 40.00 100.00
28 Keith Van Horn/249 4.00 10.00
29 Earl Monroe/20 20.00 50.00
30 DeMarcus Cousins/20 10.00 25.00
33 Rick Mahorn/349 3.00 8.00
34 Micheal Ray Richardson/349 4.00 10.00
37 Draymond Green/349 12.00 30.00
38 Alexey Shved/349 3.00 8.00
39 Anthony Davis/35 40.00 80.00
40 Kobe Bryant/35 600.00 1,200.00
41 Billy Paultz/399 5.00 12.00
42 Jon McGlocklin/349 4.00 10.00
43 Blake Griffin/20 25.00 60.00
44 Dikembe Mutombo/99 12.00 30.00
45 Jrue Holiday/20 15.00 40.00
46 Corey Brewer/399 3.00 8.00
47 Greg Monroe/299 3.00 8.00
48 Kevin Durant/35 50.00 120.00
49 Byron Scott/20 20.00 50.00

2013-14 Court Kings Blacktop Legends
1 Kareem Abdul-Jabbar 4.00 10.00
2 Connie Hawkins 1.50 4.00
3 Kenny Anderson 1.00 2.50
4 Jason Williams 1.00 2.50
5 Nate Archibald 1.50 4.00
6 Vince Carter 2.50 6.00
7 Wilt Chamberlain 4.00 10.00
8 Kevin Durant 8.00 20.00
9 Julius Erving 3.00 8.00
10 Charlie Scott 1.25 3.00
11 Earl Monroe 2.00 5.00
12 Kobe Bryant 25.00 60.00
13 Chris Mullin 1.50 4.00
14 LeBron James 40.00 100.00
15 Satch Sanders 1.50 4.00

2013-14 Court Kings Coast to Coast
1 Magic Johnson 5.00 12.00
2 John Stockton 2.50 6.00
3 Jason Kidd 2.00 5.00
4 Gary Payton 2.00 5.00
5 Chris Paul 2.50 6.00
6 Derrick Rose 2.00 5.00
7 Rajon Rondo 1.50 4.00
8 Steve Nash 2.50 6.00
9 Tony Parker 2.00 5.00
10 Deron Williams 1.00 2.50
11 Isiah Thomas 2.00 5.00
12 Jerry West 3.00 8.00
13 Walt Frazier 2.00 5.00
14 Bob Cousy 3.00 8.00
15 Kyrie Irving 4.00 10.00

2013-14 Court Kings Expressionists
1 LeBron James 10.00 25.00
2 Russell Westbrook 2.00 5.00
3 Blake Griffin 1.25 3.00
4 Chris Bosh 1.50 4.00
5 DeMarcus Cousins 1.25 3.00
6 Joe Dumars 1.50 4.00
7 Alonzo Mourning 2.00 5.00
8 Larry Johnson 1.50 4.00
9 Hakeem Olajuwon 2.50 6.00
10 Bill Laimbeer 1.25 3.00
11 Anderson Varejao .75 2.00
12 Kevin Garnett 3.00 8.00
13 Anthony Davis 4.00 10.00
14 Metta World Peace 1.00 2.50
15 Zach Randolph 1.00 2.50
16 John Starks 1.25 3.00
17 Rick Mahorn .75 2.00
18 Karl Malone 2.50 6.00
19 Magic Johnson 5.00 12.00
20 Dennis Rodman 3.00 8.00
21 Kenneth Faried 1.00 2.50
22 Kobe Bryant 10.00 25.00
23 Kyrie Irving 4.00 10.00
24 Chris Andersen 1.00 2.50
25 J.R. Smith 1.25 3.00
26 Gary Payton 2.00 5.00
27 Darryl Dawkins 1.00 2.50
28 Shaquille O'Neal 5.00 12.00
29 Larry Bird 5.00 12.00
30 Charles Oakley 1.25 3.00
31 Nate Robinson .75 2.00
32 Joakim Noah 1.25 3.00
33 Dwyane Wade 2.50 6.00
34 Steve Nash 2.50 6.00
35 Udonis Haslem 1.00 2.50
36 Shawn Kemp 2.00 5.00
37 Dikembe Mutombo 2.00 5.00
38 Tim Duncan 3.00 8.00
39 Moses Malone 2.00 5.00
40 Patrick Ewing 2.00 5.00

2013-14 Court Kings Fresh Paint Autographs
PRINT RUNS B/WN 99-499 COPIES PER
EXCHANGE DEADLINE 9/26/2015
1 Kelly Olynyk/499 4.00 10.00
2 M.Carter-Williams/199 4.00 10.00
3 Tony Mitchell 3.00 8.00
4 Cody Zeller/99 4.00 10.00
5 Ricky Ledo/499 3.00 8.00
6 Otto Porter/99 5.00 12.00
8 Isaiah Canaan/499 3.00 8.00
10 Alex Len/99 4.00 10.00
11 C.J. McCollum/149 12.00 30.00
12 Glen Rice Jr./299 3.00 8.00
13 Victor Oladipo/149 8.00 20.00
14 Matthew Dellavedova/499 5.00 12.00
15 Nerlens Noel/99 4.00 10.00
17 Peyton Siva/499 3.00 8.00
18 Shabazz Muhammad/99 3.00 8.00
19 Anthony Bennett/99 3.00 8.00
20 Ryan Kelly/499 3.00 8.00
22 Archie Goodwin/499 3.00 8.00
23 Trey Burke/125 4.00 10.00
24 Tim Hardaway Jr./399 6.00 15.00
26 Ben McLemore/99 4.00 10.00
27 Shane Larkin/499 3.00 8.00
28 G.Antetokounmpo/499 800.00 1,500.00
29 Steven Adams/299 10.00 25.00
30 Nate Wolters/499 3.00 8.00

2013-14 Court Kings Gallery of Stars Jerseys
PRINT RUNS B/WN 10-325 COPIES PER
NO PRICING ON QTY 10
1 Luol Deng/325 3.00 8.00
2 LeBron James/325 10.00 25.00
3 Deron Williams/325 3.00 8.00
4 Manu Ginobili/50 8.00 20.00
5 Kevin Martin/325 3.00 8.00
6 Jose Calderon/325 2.50 6.00
7 Zach Randolph/150 3.00 8.00
8 Dirk Nowitzki/325 10.00 25.00
9 Damian Lillard/325 5.00 12.00
10 Gerald Wallace/325 3.00 8.00
11 Shane Battier/325 3.00 8.00
13 Serge Ibaka/325 3.00 8.00
14 Andre Miller/325 3.00 8.00
15 Raymond Felton/325 2.50 6.00
16 Chris Paul/150 5.00 12.00
17 Joakim Noah/150 4.00 10.00
18 Ray Allen/325 6.00 15.00
20 Anthony Davis/99 12.00 30.00
21 Kevin Durant/325 8.00 20.00
22 Jeremy Lin/325 6.00 15.00
23 Jameer Nelson/99 2.50 6.00
24 Al Horford/325 4.00 10.00
26 Dwyane Wade/325 5.00 12.00
27 Kobe Bryant/150 10.00 25.00
28 Ty Lawson/325 2.50 6.00
29 Russell Westbrook/325 5.00 12.00
30 Andre Iguodala/325 4.00 10.00
31 Tony Parker/99 6.00 15.00
32 Paul Pierce/325 6.00 15.00
33 Carmelo Anthony/325 6.00 15.00
34 Blake Griffin/99 4.00 10.00
35 Tim Duncan/325 5.00 12.00
36 James Harden/325 5.00 12.00
37 Kevin Garnett/325 5.00 12.00
38 Rajon Rondo/325 5.00 12.00
39 Greivis Vasquez/325 2.50 6.00
40 Tyson Chandler/325 3.00 8.00

2013-14 Court Kings Gallery of Stars Jerseys Prime
*PRIME: 1.2X TO 3X BASIC
PRINT RUNS B/WN 1-25 COPIES PER
NO PRICING ON QTY 10 OR LESS

2013-14 Court Kings Impressionist Ink Autographs
PRINT RUNS B/WN 20-399 COPIES PER
EXCHANGE DEADLINE 9/26/2015
1 Stephen Curry/49 500.00 1,000.00
2 Anthony Davis/49 50.00 120.00
3 Bradley Beal/99 8.00 20.00
4 Robert Parish/99 6.00 15.00
5 Glen Rice/249 4.00 10.00
6 Kobe Bryant/49 500.00 1,000.00
7 Artis Gilmore/35 6.00 15.00
8 Tim Hardaway/399 6.00 15.00
9 Steve Blake/399 3.00 8.00
10 Blake Griffin/20 50.00 100.00
12 Adrian Dantley/349 5.00 12.00
13 Kyrie Irving/49 40.00 100.00
14 David Thompson/349 5.00 12.00
15 Kevin Durant/30 60.00 150.00
17 Jeff Hornacek/349 4.00 10.00
19 Magic Johnson/25 30.00 80.00
20 Karl Malone/25 60.00 120.00

2013-14 Court Kings Kings of Springfield
1 Bill Russell 6.00 15.00
3 Larry Bird 30.00 60.00
4 George Mikan 6.00 15.00
5 Dennis Rodman 8.00 20.00
8 John Stockton 10.00 25.00
10 Karl Malone 4.00 10.00
11 Julius Erving 5.00 12.00
13 Dominique Wilkins 3.00 8.00
15 Wilt Chamberlain 6.00 15.00

2013-14 Court Kings Le Cinque Piu Belle
STATED PRINT RUN 35 SER.#'d SETS
1 Kevin Durant 25.00 60.00
2 Kevin Durant 25.00 60.00
3 Kevin Durant 25.00 60.00
4 Kevin Durant 25.00 60.00
5 Kevin Durant 25.00 60.00

2013-14 Court Kings Legacies
1 John Stockton 6.00 15.00
2 Kobe Bryant 25.00 60.00
3 Dirk Nowitzki 8.00 20.00
4 Calvin Murphy 2.50 6.00
5 Dwyane Wade 6.00 15.00
6 Tony Parker 5.00 12.00
7 Larry Bird 12.00 30.00
8 Magic Johnson 12.00 30.00
9 Isiah Thomas 5.00 12.00
10 Alvan Adams 2.00 5.00
11 John Havlicek 8.00 20.00
12 Tim Duncan 8.00 20.00
13 Joe Dumars 4.00 10.00
14 David Robinson 6.00 15.00
15 Wes Unseld 4.00 10.00

2013-14 Court Kings Masterpieces
STATED PRINT RUN 175 SER.#'d SETS
1 Carmelo Anthony 2.00 5.00
2 Dwyane Wade 2.50 6.00
3 Kevin Durant 4.00 10.00
4 Paul George 2.00 5.00
5 Tony Parker 2.00 5.00
6 Kyrie Irving 4.00 10.00
7 Russell Westbrook 2.00 5.00
8 Blake Griffin 1.25 3.00
9 Derrick Rose 2.00 5.00
10 Dirk Nowitzki 3.00 8.00
11 Chris Paul 2.50 6.00
12 Kevin Love 1.25 3.00
13 Rudy Gay 1.00 2.50
14 Tim Duncan 3.00 8.00
15 Andre Iguodala 1.25 3.00
16 LeBron James 10.00 25.00
17 Rajon Rondo 1.50 4.00
18 Damian Lillard 4.00 10.00
19 Stephen Curry 10.00 25.00
20 Manu Ginobili 2.50 6.00
21 Kobe Bryant 10.00 25.00
22 Jrue Holiday 1.50 4.00
23 James Harden 2.50 6.00
24 Deron Williams 1.00 2.50
25 Dwight Howard 1.50 4.00

2013-14 Court Kings Masterpieces Purple
*PURPLE: 2.5X TO 6X BASIC
STATED PRINT RUN 25 SER.#'d SETS

2013-14 Court Kings Next Day Autographs
EXCHANGE DEADLINE 9/26/2015
AB Anthony Bennett 3.00 8.00
AC Allen Crabbe 10.00 25.00
AG Archie Goodwin 10.00 25.00
AL Alex Len 8.00 20.00
AR Andre Roberson 8.00 20.00
BM Ben McLemore 4.00 10.00
CM C.J. McCollum 75.00 200.00
CZ Cody Zeller 4.00 10.00
EM Erik Murphy 3.00 8.00
GA Giannis Antetokounmpo 1,000.00 3,000.00
GD Gorgui Dieng 20.00 50.00
GR Glen Rice Jr. 3.00 8.00
IC Isaiah Canaan 3.00 8.00
JF Jamaal Franklin 3.00 8.00
JW Jeff Withey 3.00 8.00
KC Kentavious Caldwell-Pope 15.00 40.00
KO Kelly Olynyk 8.00 20.00
MC Michael Carter-Williams 6.00 15.00
MP Mason Plumlee 4.00 10.00
NN Nerlens Noel 15.00 40.00
NW Nate Wolters 3.00 8.00
OP Otto Porter 25.00 60.00
PS Peyton Siva 3.00 8.00
RB Reggie Bullock 4.00 10.00
RK Ryan Kelly 3.00 8.00
RL Ricky Ledo 3.00 8.00
SA Steven Adams 25.00 60.00
SH Solomon Hill 4.00 10.00
SL Shane Larkin 3.00 8.00
SM Shabazz Muhammad 8.00 20.00
TB Trey Burke 20.00 50.00
TH Tim Hardaway Jr. 30.00 80.00
TM Tony Mitchell 3.00 8.00
TS Tony Snell 10.00 25.00
VO Victor Oladipo 75.00 200.00

2013-14 Court Kings Performance Art Memorabilia
PRINT RUNS B/WN 49-299 COPIES PER
1 Evan Turner/49 2.50 6.00
2 Kobe Bryant/199 5.00 12.00
3 John Wall/175 5.00 12.00
4 Mario Chalmers/299 3.00 8.00
5 Reggie Evans/299 2.50 6.00
6 LeBron James/299 10.00 25.00
7 Steve Nash/299 8.00 20.00
8 Serge Ibaka/299 3.00 8.00
9 Amar'e Stoudemire/99 4.00 10.00
10 Joe Johnson/150 3.00 8.00
11 Carmelo Anthony/150 6.00 15.00
12 Wesley Matthews/150 2.50 6.00
13 Kevin Durant/299 5.00 12.00
14 Jeremy Lin/299 6.00 15.00
15 J.R. Smith/299 4.00 10.00
16 Andre Miller/299 3.00 8.00
17 Dwyane Wade/150 5.00 12.00
18 Joakim Noah/150 4.00 10.00
19 Ersan Ilyasova/49 5.00 12.00
20 Kobe Bryant/299 4.00 10.00
21 James Harden/299 5.00 12.00
22 Nick Collison/299 2.50 6.00
23 Pau Gasol/299 6.00 15.00
24 Russell Westbrook/299 5.00 12.00
25 Steve Nash/50 5.00 12.00
26 Tim Duncan/99 5.00 12.00
27 Deron Williams/150 3.00 8.00
28 Tony Parker/150 6.00 15.00
29 Matt Barnes/299 2.50 6.00
30 Carmelo Anthony/299 6.00 15.00
31 Rajon Rondo/299 5.00 12.00
32 Chandler Parsons/299 2.50 6.00
33 Chris Paul/299 5.00 12.00
34 Andray Blatche/299 2.50 6.00
35 LeBron James/150 10.00 25.00
36 Luol Deng /150 3.00 8.00
37 David West/150 3.00 8.00
38 Dwyane Wade/150 5.00 12.00
39 Omer Asik/299 2.50 6.00
40 Jamal Crawford/299 4.00 10.00

2013-14 Court Kings Performance Art Memorabilia Prime
*PRIME: 1X TO 2.5X BASIC
PRINT RUNS B/WN 1-25 COPIES PER
NO PRICING ON QTY 25 OR LESS
2 Kobe Bryant/25 40.00 100.00
13 Kevin Durant/18 100.00 200.00
17 Dwyane Wade/25 25.00 60.00
24 Russell Westbrook/15 25.00 60.00
26 Tim Duncan/25 25.00 60.00
35 LeBron James/25 75.00 200.00

2013-14 Court Kings Portraits
1 Klay Thompson 5.00 12.00
2 Jeff Teague 1.00 2.50
3 DeMarcus Cousins 1.50 4.00
4 Kevin Love 1.50 4.00
5 Paul Pierce 2.50 6.00
6 O.J. Mayo 1.00 2.50
7 Avery Bradley 1.00 2.50
8 John Wall 2.00 5.00
9 Deron Williams 1.25 3.00
10 J.R. Smith 1.50 4.00
11 Ricky Rubio 1.25 3.00
12 Al Jefferson 1.00 2.50
13 Nikola Vucevic 2.00 5.00
14 DeMar DeRozan 2.00 5.00
15 Ben Gordon 1.25 3.00
16 Chris Bosh 2.00 5.00
17 Kemba Walker 1.50 4.00
18 Tim Duncan 4.00 10.00
19 Monta Ellis 1.25 3.00
20 Anthony Davis 5.00 12.00
21 Tony Parker 2.50 6.00
22 Vince Carter 3.00 8.00
23 Larry Sanders 1.00 2.50
24 Evan Turner 1.00 2.50
25 Dirk Nowitzki 4.00 10.00
26 Bradley Beal 2.50 6.00
27 Kenneth Faried 1.25 3.00
28 LaMarcus Aldridge 1.50 4.00
29 Stephen Curry 12.00 30.00
30 Carmelo Anthony 2.50 6.00
31 Mike Conley 1.50 4.00
32 Tyson Chandler 1.25 3.00
33 George Hill 1.25 3.00
34 Amar'e Stoudemire 1.50 4.00
35 Derrick Rose 2.50 6.00
36 Manu Ginobili 3.00 8.00
37 James Harden 3.00 8.00
38 Zach Randolph 1.25 3.00
39 Paul George 2.50 6.00
40 Jason Richardson 1.50 4.00
41 Blake Griffin 1.50 4.00
42 Nikola Pekovic 1.00 2.50
43 Shawn Marion 1.25 3.00
44 Dwyane Wade 3.00 8.00
45 Ty Lawson 1.00 2.50

46 Damian Lillard 5.00 12.00
47 Pau Gasol 2.50 6.00
48 Carlos Boozer 1.25 3.00
49 Dwight Howard 2.00 5.00
50 Kawhi Leonard 5.00 12.00
51 Steve Nash 3.00 8.00
52 Serge Ibaka 1.25 3.00
53 Al Horford 1.50 4.00
54 Chris Paul 3.00 8.00
55 Andre Iguodala 1.50 4.00
56 Kevin Durant 5.00 12.00
57 Roy Hibbert 1.00 2.50
58 Brandon Jennings 1.00 2.50
59 Marc Gasol 1.50 4.00
60 Brook Lopez 1.50 4.00
61 Joakim Noah 1.50 4.00
62 Eric Bledsoe 1.25 3.00
63 Kevin Garnett 4.00 10.00
64 Andre Drummond 1.50 4.00
65 Jeremy Lin 2.50 6.00
66 Dion Waiters 1.00 2.50
67 Russell Westbrook 2.50 6.00
68 Rajon Rondo 2.00 5.00
69 LeBron James 40.00 100.00
70 Anderson Varejao 1.00 2.50
71 Gerald Wallace 1.25 3.00
72 Isaiah Thomas 1.25 3.00
73 Kyrie Irving 5.00 12.00
74 Luol Deng 1.25 3.00
75 Kobe Bryant 40.00 100.00

2013-14 Court Kings Portraits Blue Frame
*BLUE FRAME: .5X TO 1.2X BASIC
STATED PRINT RUN 75 SER.#'d SETS

2013-14 Court Kings Portraits Red Frame
*RED FRAME: 1.5X TO 4X BASIC
STATED PRINT RUN 25 SER.#'d SETS

2013-14 Court Kings Renaissance Men
1 James Harden 2.50 6.00
2 Russell Westbrook 2.00 5.00
3 Dwyane Wade 2.50 6.00
4 Josh Smith .75 2.00
5 Anthony Davis 4.00 10.00
6 Tim Duncan 3.00 8.00
7 Tyreke Evans 1.00 2.50
8 Derrick Rose 2.00 5.00
9 Dirk Nowitzki 3.00 8.00
10 Joakim Noah 1.25 3.00
11 LeBron James 15.00 40.00
12 Stephen Curry 10.00 25.00
13 Paul Pierce 2.00 5.00
14 Blake Griffin 1.25 3.00
15 Rajon Rondo 1.50 4.00
16 Ricky Rubio 1.00 2.50
17 Dwight Howard 1.50 4.00
18 Deron Williams 1.00 2.50
19 Damian Lillard 4.00 10.00
20 Kevin Love 1.25 3.00
21 Kevin Durant 4.00 10.00
22 Kobe Bryant 10.00 25.00
23 John Wall 1.50 4.00
24 Kyrie Irving 4.00 10.00
25 Pau Gasol 2.00 5.00
26 Chris Paul 2.50 6.00
27 Steve Nash 2.50 6.00
28 Kevin Garnett 3.00 8.00
29 Tony Parker 2.00 5.00
30 Jeremy Lin 2.00 5.00

2013-14 Court Kings Rookie Portraits
STATED PRINT RUN 125 SER.#'d SETS
1 Anthony Bennett 1.25 3.00
2 Cody Zeller 1.50 4.00
3 Ben McLemore 1.50 4.00
4 C.J. McCollum 5.00 12.00
5 Kelly Olynyk 1.50 4.00
6 Dennis Schroder 4.00 10.00
7 Sergey Karasev 1.25 3.00
8 Gorgui Dieng 1.50 4.00
9 Solomon Hill 1.50 4.00
10 Isaiah Canaan 1.25 3.00
11 Victor Oladipo 3.00 8.00
12 Alex Len 1.50 4.00
13 Kentavious Caldwell-Pope 2.00 5.00
14 Michael Carter-Williams 1.50 4.00
15 Shabazz Muhammad 1.25 3.00
16 Shane Larkin 1.25 3.00
17 Tony Snell 1.50 4.00
18 Mason Plumlee 1.50 4.00
19 Tim Hardaway Jr. 2.50 6.00
20 Glen Rice Jr. 1.25 3.00
22 Nerlens Noel 1.50 4.00
23 Trey Burke 1.50 4.00
24 Steven Adams 3.00 8.00
25 Giannis Antetokounmpo 200.00 500.00

2013-14 Court Kings Rookie Portraits Blue Frame
*BLUE FRAME: .5X TO 1.2X BASIC
STATED PRINT RUN 75 SER.#'d SETS

2013-14 Court Kings Rookie Portraits Red Frame
*RED FRAME: .75X TO 2X BASIC
STATED PRINT RUN 25 SER.#'d SETS
11 Victor Oladipo 12.00 30.00

2013-14 Court Kings Royal Performances
STATED PRINT RUN 175 SER.#'d SETS
1 Kobe Bryant 12.00 30.00
2 Rajon Rondo 2.00 5.00
3 Andrew Bynum 1.00 2.50
4 Joakim Noah 1.50 4.00
5 Elgin Baylor 1.50 4.00
6 Deron Williams 1.25 3.00
7 Steve Nash 3.00 8.00
8 Tim Duncan 4.00 10.00
9 Dwyane Wade 3.00 8.00
10 David Robinson 3.00 8.00
11 Brandon Jennings 1.00 2.50
12 Chris Paul 3.00 8.00
13 John Wall 2.00 5.00
14 Wilt Chamberlain 5.00 12.00
15 Tony Parker 2.50 6.00
16 Kevin Love 1.50 4.00
17 Scott Skiles 1.25 3.00
18 Serge Ibaka 1.25 3.00
19 Dirk Nowitzki 4.00 10.00
20 Manute Bol 1.50 4.00

2013-14 Court Kings Royal Performances Purple
*PURPLE: 1X TO 2.5X BASIC
STATED PRINT RUN 25 SER.#'d SETS

2013-14 Court Kings Sketches and Swatches Autographs
PRINT RUNS B/WN 49-199 COPIES PER
EXCHANGE DEADLINE 9/26/2015
1 Andre Drummond/75 5.00 12.00
2 Jason Terry/75 4.00 10.00
3 Devin Harris/49 3.00 8.00
4 Kawhi Leonard/149 30.00 80.00
5 Luis Scola/149 4.00 10.00
6 Tobias Harris/199 5.00 12.00
7 James Jones/199 3.00 8.00
8 Anthony Davis/49 40.00 100.00
9 Boris Diaw/125 4.00 10.00
10 Tyson Chandler/99 4.00 10.00
11 Enes Kanter/149 4.00 10.00
12 Kevin Durant/49 75.00 200.00
13 Nikola Vucevic/149 6.00 15.00
14 Al Horford/49 5.00 12.00
15 Draymond Green/199 12.00 30.00
16 Tiago Splitter/199 3.00 8.00
17 Iman Shumpert/199 3.00 8.00
18 Udonis Haslem/199 4.00 10.00
19 Danilo Gallinari/99 4.00 10.00
20 Jeff Green/149 3.00 8.00
21 Andrei Kirilenko/99 5.00 12.00
22 Brandon Bass/149 3.00 8.00
23 Kobe Bryant/75 500.00 1,000.00
24 Raymond Felton/99 3.00 8.00
25 Eric Gordon/99 4.00 10.00
26 Andre Miller/199 4.00 10.00
27 Jared Sullinger/99 3.00 8.00
28 Jrue Holiday/75 6.00 15.00
29 Steve Blake/199 3.00 8.00
30 Kyrie Irving/49 30.00 80.00

2013-14 Court Kings Sketches and Swatches Autographs Prime
*PRIME: .75X TO 2X BASIC
PRINT RUNS B/WN 1-25 COPIES PER
NO PRICING ON QTY 10 OR LESS
EXCHANGE DEADLINE 9/26/2015

2013-14 Court Kings Sovereign Signatures
PRINT RUNS B/WN 20-199 COPIES PER
EXCHANGE DEADLINE 9/26/2015
1 Robert Parish/49 6.00 15.00
2 Anfernee Hardaway/49 15.00 40.00
3 Bill Laimbeer/199 5.00 12.00
4 World B. Free/60 4.00 10.00
5 Joe Dumars/60 6.00 15.00
6 Kelly Tripucka/60 4.00 10.00
7 Bob Lanier/20 6.00 15.00
8 Larry Bird/20 50.00 100.00
9 Eddie Johnson/199 3.00 8.00
10 Jalen Rose/160 4.00 10.00
11 Brad Daugherty/199 5.00 12.00
12 Mark Price/199 5.00 12.00
13 Isiah Thomas/49 10.00 25.00
14 Magic Johnson/30 50.00 100.00
15 John Stockton/25 30.00 80.00
16 Scottie Pippen/49 50.00 120.00
17 Shaquille O'Neal/25 75.00 150.00
18 Jayson Williams/199 3.00 8.00
19 David Robinson/35 15.00 40.00
20 Kevin McHale/20 15.00 40.00
21 Larry Johnson/199 6.00 15.00
22 Karl Malone/35 20.00 50.00
23 Kareem Abdul-Jabbar/35 40.00 80.00
24 Jim Jackson/199 3.00 8.00
25 Alex English/199 6.00 15.00
26 Tracy McGrady/49 20.00 50.00
27 Grant Hill/49 15.00 40.00
28 Artis Gilmore/35 6.00 15.00
29 Clyde Drexler/20 12.00 30.00
30 Robert Horry/99 8.00 20.00

2013-14 Court Kings Sovereign Signatures Prime
*PRIME: .75X TO 2X BASIC
PRINT RUNS B/WN 10-25 COPIES PER
NO PRICING ON QTY 10 OR LESS
EXCHANGE DEADLINE 9/26/2015

2013-14 Court Kings Squires
STATED PRINT RUN 175 SER.#'d SETS
1 Tyreke Evans 1.25 3.00
2 Serge Ibaka 1.25 3.00
3 Ricky Rubio 1.25 3.00
4 John Wall 2.00 5.00
5 DeAndre Jordan 1.25 3.00
6 Kenneth Faried 1.25 3.00
7 Eric Bledsoe 1.25 3.00
8 Ty Lawson 1.00 2.50
9 Brandon Jennings 1.00 2.50
10 Nicolas Batum 1.25 3.00
11 Mike Conley 1.50 4.00
12 Danilo Gallinari 1.25 3.00
13 Greg Monroe 1.00 2.50
14 Larry Sanders 1.00 2.50
15 Ed Davis 1.00 2.50
16 DeMarcus Cousins 1.50 4.00
17 JaVale McGee 1.00 2.50
18 Thaddeus Young 1.00 2.50
19 Brook Lopez 1.50 4.00
20 Anthony Davis 5.00 12.00

2013-14 Court Kings Squires Purple
*PURPLE: .75X TO 2X BASIC
STATED PRINT RUN 25 SER.#'d SETS

2013-14 Court Kings Vintage Materials
STATED PRINT RUN 25-299 SER.#'d SETS
2 Kiki VanDeWeghe/299 3.00 8.00
3 Calvin Murphy/35 3.00 8.00
4 Chris Mullin/125 5.00 12.00
5 John Lucas/125 3.00 8.00
6 Joe Dumars/299 5.00 12.00
8 Robert Horry/75 4.00 10.00
9 Bob Lanier/249 5.00 12.00
10 Scottie Pippen/75 6.00 15.00
11 Patrick Ewing/125 6.00 15.00
12 Isiah Thomas/49 6.00 15.00
14 Danny Manning/150 3.00 8.00
15 Bernard King/75 5.00 12.00
16 Moses Malone/35 6.00 15.00
17 Cazzie Russell/35 3.00 8.00
18 Dominique Wilkins/99 6.00 15.00
20 Jim Jackson/299 2.50 6.00

2013-14 Court Kings Vintage Materials Prime
*PRIME: .75X TO 2X BASIC
PRINT RUNS B/WN 1-25 COPIES PER
NO PRICING ON QTY 10 OR LESS

2014-15 Court Kings
134-166 PRINT RUN 225 SER.#'d SETS
167-199 PRINT RUN 149 SER.#'d SETS
200-232 PRINT RUN 49 SER.#'d SETS
1A Jared Sullinger .40 1.00
1B LeBron James VAR 10.00 25.00
2A Monta Ellis .50 1.25
2B Kobe Bryant VAR 10.00 25.00
3A DeAndre Jordan .50 1.25
3B Kyrie Irving VAR 2.50 6.00
4A Kawhi Leonard 1.50 4.00
4B Damian Lillard VAR 3.00 8.00
5A Al Horford .60 1.50
5B Kevin Durant VAR 4.00 10.00
6A Ricky Rubio .50 1.25
6B Chris Paul VAR 2.00 5.00
7A Eric Bledsoe .50 1.25
7B Paul George VAR 2.00 5.00
8A Kyrie Irving 1.25 3.00
8B Anthony Davis VAR 3.00 8.00
9A Brandon Knight .40 1.00
9B Carmelo Anthony VAR 2.00 5.00
10 Tony Parker 1.00 2.50
11 Jeff Green .50 1.25
12 Nerlens Noel .40 1.00
13 DeMar DeRozan .75 2.00
14 Kemba Walker .60 1.50
15 Roy Hibbert .50 1.25
16 Al Jefferson .40 1.00
17 LaMarcus Aldridge .60 1.50
18 Gerald Henderson .40 1.00
19 Carlos Boozer .50 1.25
20 Tony Wroten .40 1.00
21 Jeff Teague .40 1.00
22 Nicolas Batum .50 1.25
23 DeMarcus Cousins .50 1.25
24 Kenneth Faried .40 1.00
25 Andre Drummond .50 1.25
26 Rudy Gay .60 1.50
27 Giannis Antetokounmpo 20.00 50.00
28 Lance Stephenson .50 1.25
29 Carmelo Anthony 1.00 2.50
30 Trevor Ariza .40 1.00
31 Jeremy Lin 1.25 3.00
32 Nikola Vucevic .50 1.25
33 Deron Williams .50 1.25
34 Kevin Durant 2.00 5.00
35 Andre Iguodala .60 1.50
36 Russell Westbrook 1.50 4.00
37 Goran Dragic .60 1.50
38 LeBron James 5.00 12.00
39 Chandler Parsons .40 1.00
40 Trey Burke .40 1.00
41 Joakim Noah .60 1.50
42 O.J. Mayo .40 1.00
43 Derrick Rose 1.25 3.00
44 Kevin Garnett 1.50 4.00
45 Anthony Davis 1.50 4.00
46 Gordon Hayward .50 1.25
47 Ryan Anderson .40 1.00
48 Luol Deng .50 1.25
49 Channing Frye .40 1.00
50 Ty Lawson .40 1.00
51 Joe Johnson .50 1.25
52 Pau Gasol 1.00 2.50
53 Dion Waiters .40 1.00
54 Kevin Love .60 1.50
55 Arron Afflalo .40 1.00
56 Serge Ibaka .50 1.25
57 Greg Monroe .40 1.00
58 Manu Ginobili 1.25 3.00
59 Chris Bosh .75 2.00
60 Tyreke Evans .50 1.25
61 John Wall .75 2.00
62 Paul George 1.00 2.50
63 Dirk Nowitzki 1.50 4.00
64 Kevin Martin .50 1.25
65 Ben McLemore .40 1.00
66 Stephen Curry 5.00 12.00
67 Iman Shumpert .40 1.00
68 Marc Gasol .60 1.50
69 Chris Paul 1.00 2.50
70 Tyson Chandler .60 1.50
71 Jose Calderon .40 1.00
72 Paul Millsap .50 1.25
73 Dwight Howard .75 2.00
74 Klay Thompson 1.50 4.00
75 Blake Griffin .60 1.50
76 Steve Nash 1.25 3.00
77 Isaiah Thomas .50 1.25
78 Marcin Gortat .40 1.00
79 Damian Lillard 1.50 4.00
80 Victor Oladipo .50 1.25
81 Josh Smith .40 1.00
82 Rajon Rondo .75 2.00
83 Dwyane Wade 1.25 3.00
84 Kobe Bryant 5.00 12.00
85 Bradley Beal 1.00 2.50
86 Terrence Ross .50 1.25
87 J.R. Smith .60 1.50
88 Michael Carter-Williams .40 1.00
89 David Lee .40 1.00
90 Vince Carter 1.25 3.00
91 Jrue Holiday .75 2.00
92 Chris Andersen .50 1.25
93 Enes Kanter .50 1.25
94 Kyle Lowry .75 2.00
95 Brandon Jennings .40 1.00
96 Tim Duncan 1.50 4.00
97 James Harden 1.25 3.00
98 Mike Conley .50 1.25
99 David West .50 1.25
100 Zach Randolph .60 1.50
101 Andrew Wiggins RC 3.00 8.00
102 Jabari Parker RC .75 2.00
103 Joel Embiid RC 6.00 15.00
104 Aaron Gordon RC 3.00 8.00
105 Dante Exum RC 1.00 2.50
106 Marcus Smart RC 2.50 6.00
107 Julius Randle RC 3.00 8.00
108 Nik Stauskas RC .60 1.50
109 Noah Vonleh RC .60 1.50
110 Elfrid Payton RC 1.00 2.50
111 Doug McDermott RC 1.00 2.50
112 Zach LaVine RC 4.00 10.00
113 T.J. Warren RC 1.00 2.50
114 Adreian Payne RC .60 1.50
115 James Young RC .60 1.50
116 Tyler Ennis RC .60 1.50
117 Gary Harris RC 1.00 2.50
118 Bruno Caboclo RC .75 2.00
119 Rodney Hood RC .75 2.00
120 Shabazz Napier RC .75 2.00
121 P.J. Hairston RC .60 1.50
122 Kyle Anderson RC 1.00 2.50
123 K.J. McDaniels RC .60 1.50
124 Markel Brown RC .60 1.50
125 Russ Smith RC .60 1.50
126 Cleanthony Early RC .60 1.50
127 Spencer Dinwiddie RC 1.00 2.50
128 Damien Inglis RC .60 1.50
129 James Ennis RC .60 1.50
130 Nick Johnson RC .60 1.50
131 C.J. Wilcox RC .60 1.50
132 Jordan Adams RC .60 1.50
133 Mitch McGary RC .60 1.50
134 Andrew Wiggins/225 4.00 10.00
135 Jabari Parker/225 1.00 2.50
136 Joel Embiid/225 8.00 20.00
137 Aaron Gordon/225 4.00 10.00
138 Dante Exum/225 1.25 3.00
139 Marcus Smart/225 3.00 8.00
140 Julius Randle/225 4.00 10.00
141 Nik Stauskas/225 .75 2.00
142 Noah Vonleh/225 .75 2.00
143 Elfrid Payton/225 1.25 3.00
144 Doug McDermott/225 1.25 3.00
145 Zach LaVine/225 20.00 50.00
146 T.J. Warren/225 1.25 3.00
147 Adreian Payne/225 .75 2.00
148 James Young/225 .75 2.00
149 Tyler Ennis/225 .75 2.00
150 Gary Harris/225 1.25 3.00
151 Bruno Caboclo/225 1.00 2.50
152 Rodney Hood/225 1.00 2.50
153 Shabazz Napier/225 1.00 2.50
154 P.J. Hairston/225 .75 2.00
155 Kyle Anderson/225 1.25 3.00
156 K.J. McDaniels/225 .75 2.00
157 Markel Brown/225 .75 2.00
158 Russ Smith/225 .75 2.00
159 Cleanthony Early/225 .75 2.00
160 Spencer Dinwiddie/225 1.25 3.00
161 Damien Inglis/225 .75 2.00
162 James Ennis/225 .75 2.00
163 Nick Johnson/225 .75 2.00
164 C.J. Wilcox/225 .75 2.00
165 Jordan Adams/225 .75 2.00
166 Mitch McGary/225 .75 2.00
167 Andrew Wiggins/149 12.00 30.00
168 Jabari Parker/149 1.25 3.00
169 Joel Embiid/149 10.00 25.00
170 Aaron Gordon/149 5.00 12.00
171 Dante Exum/149 1.50 4.00
172 Marcus Smart/149 4.00 10.00
173 Julius Randle/149 5.00 12.00
174 Nik Stauskas/149 1.00 2.50
175 Noah Vonleh/149 1.00 2.50
176 Elfrid Payton/149 1.50 4.00
177 Doug McDermott/149 1.50 4.00
178 Zach LaVine/149 25.00 60.00
179 T.J. Warren/149 1.50 4.00
180 Adreian Payne/149 1.00 2.50
181 James Young/149 1.00 2.50
182 Tyler Ennis/149 1.00 2.50
183 Gary Harris/149 1.50 4.00
184 Bruno Caboclo/149 1.25 3.00
185 Rodney Hood/149 1.25 3.00
186 Shabazz Napier/149 1.25 3.00
187 P.J. Hairston/149 1.00 2.50
188 Kyle Anderson/149 1.50 4.00
189 K.J. McDaniels/149 1.00 2.50
190 Markel Brown/149 1.00 2.50
191 Russ Smith/149 1.00 2.50
192 Cleanthony Early/149 1.00 2.50
193 Spencer Dinwiddie/149 1.50 4.00
194 Damien Inglis/149 1.00 2.50
195 James Ennis/149 1.00 2.50
196 Nick Johnson/149 1.00 2.50
197 C.J. Wilcox/149 1.00 2.50
198 Jordan Adams/149 1.00 2.50
199 Mitch McGary/149 1.00 2.50
200 Andrew Wiggins/49 15.00 40.00
201 Jabari Parker/49 4.00 10.00
202 Joel Embiid/49 30.00 80.00
203 Aaron Gordon/49 15.00 40.00
204 Dante Exum/49 5.00 12.00
205 Marcus Smart/49 12.00 30.00
206 Julius Randle/49 15.00 40.00
207 Nik Stauskas/49 3.00 8.00
208 Noah Vonleh/49 3.00 8.00
209 Elfrid Payton/49 5.00 12.00
210 Doug McDermott/49 5.00 12.00
211 Zach LaVine/49 75.00 200.00
212 T.J. Warren/49 5.00 12.00
213 Adreian Payne/49 3.00 8.00
214 James Young/49 3.00 8.00
215 Tyler Ennis/49 3.00 8.00
216 Gary Harris/49 5.00 12.00
217 Bruno Caboclo/49 4.00 10.00
218 Rodney Hood/49 4.00 10.00
219 Shabazz Napier/49 4.00 10.00
220 P.J. Hairston/49 3.00 8.00
221 Kyle Anderson/49 5.00 12.00
222 K.J. McDaniels/49 3.00 8.00
223 Markel Brown/49 3.00 8.00
224 Russ Smith/49 3.00 8.00
225 Cleanthony Early/49 3.00 8.00
226 Spencer Dinwiddie/49 5.00 12.00
227 Damien Inglis/49 3.00 8.00
228 James Ennis/49 3.00 8.00
229 Nick Johnson/49 3.00 8.00
230 C.J. Wilcox/49 3.00 8.00
231 Jordan Adams/49 3.00 8.00
232 Mitch McGary/49 3.00 8.00

2014-15 Court Kings Sapphire
*VETS: 2X TO 5X BASE HI
STATED PRINT RUN 25 SER.#'d SETS
27 Giannis Antetokounmpo 125.00 300.00

2014-15 Court Kings 2 on 2 Quad Memorabilia
STATED PRINT RUN 99 SER.#'d SETS
*PRIME/25: 1X TO 2.5X BASE HI
QBOLA Grntt/Gsl/Brynt/Alln 25.00 60.00
QBOPH McHle/Brd/Ervng/Mloe 12.00 30.00
QBRTO Wllms/Grntt/DRzn/Ross 8.00 20.00
QCLSA Jms/Prkr/Dncn/Ilgsks 25.00 60.00
QDAHR Nwtzki/Hwrd/Hrdn/Ellis 8.00 20.00
QDAMI Wde/Jms/Mrn/Nwtzki 25.00 60.00
QDELA Thms/Dmrs/Wrthy/Jhnsn 12.00 30.00
QDEPO Lmbr/Dmrs/Drxlr/Dckwrth 5.00 12.00
QGOLA Igdla/Paul/Crry/Grffn 25.00 60.00
QLAPH Ivrsn/Brynt/Mtmbo/O'Nl 25.00 60.00
QMIWA Bsh/Wll/Beal/Wade 6.00 15.00
QOKMI Wstbrk/Bsh/Drnt/Jms 25.00 60.00
QOKPO Drnt/Aldrdge/Lllrd/Wstbrk 10.00 25.00
QSACL Lnrd/Wde/Jms/Prker 25.00 60.00

2014-15 Court Kings 5x7 Box Toppers Autographs
BTKI Kyrie Irving 60.00 150.00
BTAW Andrew Wiggins 100.00 200.00
BTJP Jabari Parker 10.00 25.00
BTMS Marcus Smart 40.00 100.00
BTDM Doug McDermott 15.00 40.00
BTSN Shabazz Napier 12.00 30.00
BTLA LaMarcus Aldridge 25.00 60.00
BTSC Stephen Curry 500.00 1,000.00
BTBB Bradley Beal 10.00 25.00
BTEP Elfrid Payton 40.00 100.00
BTJY James Young 10.00 25.00
BTZL Zach LaVine 40.00 100.00
BTJK Jason Kidd 40.00 100.00
BTBW Bill Walton 10.00 25.00
BTJS John Stockton 40.00 100.00
BTWF Walt Frazier 25.00 60.00
BTJR Julius Randle 50.00 120.00
BTJW Jerry West 30.00 80.00

2014-15 Court Kings 5x7 Box Toppers Panoramics
1 Damian Lillard 5.00 12.00
2 Kobe Bryant 6.00 15.00
3 Kevin Durant 6.00 15.00
4 Russell Westbrook 3.00 8.00
5 Kyrie Irving 4.00 10.00
6 James Harden 4.00 10.00
7 Paul George 3.00 8.00
8 LeBron James 6.00 15.00
9 Carmelo Anthony 3.00 8.00
10 Derrick Rose 4.00 10.00
11 Dirk Nowitzki 5.00 12.00
12 Tony Parker 3.00 8.00
13 Rajon Rondo 2.50 6.00
14 Chris Paul 3.00 8.00
15 Blake Griffin 2.00 5.00
16 Ben McLemore 1.25 3.00
17 Michael Carter-Williams 1.25 3.00
18 John Wall 2.50 6.00
19 Bradley Beal 3.00 8.00
20 Terrence Ross 1.50 4.00
21 Ricky Rubio 1.50 4.00
22 Goran Dragic 2.00 5.00
23 Stephen Curry 15.00 40.00
24 Anthony Davis 5.00 12.00
25 Kenneth Faried 1.25 3.00

2014-15 Court Kings 5x7 Box Toppers Rookies
1 Mitch McGary 1.50 4.00
2 Jabari Parker 6.00 15.00
3 Spencer Dinwiddie 2.50 6.00
4 Aaron Gordon 8.00 20.00
5 Cory Jefferson 1.50 4.00
6 Marcus Smart 6.00 15.00
7 Julius Randle 8.00 20.00
8 Nik Stauskas 1.50 4.00
9 Noah Vonleh 1.50 4.00
10 Elfrid Payton 2.50 6.00
11 Doug McDermott 2.50 6.00
12 Zach LaVine 10.00 25.00
13 T.J. Warren 2.50 6.00
14 Adreian Payne 1.50 4.00
15 James Young 1.50 4.00
16 Tyler Ennis 1.50 4.00
17 Gary Harris 2.50 6.00
18 Bruno Caboclo 2.00 5.00
19 Rodney Hood 2.00 5.00
20 Shabazz Napier 2.00 5.00
21 P.J. Hairston 1.50 4.00
22 Kyle Anderson 2.50 6.00
23 K.J. McDaniels 1.50 4.00
24 Russ Smith 1.50 4.00
25 Cleanthony Early 1.50 4.00

2014-15 Court Kings Aficionado
*SAPPHIRE/25: .75X TO 2X BASE HI
1 Kevin Love 1.50 4.00
2 LeBron James 12.00 30.00
3 Joakim Noah 1.50 4.00
4 Russell Westbrook 2.50 6.00
5 DeMarcus Cousins 1.25 3.00
6 Chris Paul 2.50 6.00
7 James Harden 3.00 8.00
8 Kobe Bryant 12.00 30.00
9 Derrick Rose 3.00 8.00
10 Stephen Curry 12.00 30.00
11 LaMarcus Aldridge 1.50 4.00
12 Kevin Durant 5.00 12.00
13 Paul George 2.50 6.00
14 Dwight Howard 2.00 5.00
15 John Wall 2.00 5.00
16 Anthony Davis 4.00 10.00
17 Goran Dragic 1.50 4.00
18 Blake Griffin 1.50 4.00
19 Damian Lillard 4.00 10.00
20 Carmelo Anthony 2.50 6.00

2014-15 Court Kings Also Known As
STATED PRINT RUN 49 SER.#'d SETS
1 Kobe Bryant 30.00 80.00
2 Shawn Marion 5.00 12.00
3 Harrison Barnes 5.00 12.00
4 Paul Pierce 10.00 25.00
5 Chris Andersen 5.00 12.00
6 Danilo Gallinari 8.00 20.00
7 Tim Duncan 20.00 50.00
8 LeBron James 30.00 80.00
9 Marcin Gortat 4.00 10.00
10 Dwight Howard 8.00 20.00
11 Bob Cousy 12.00 30.00
12 Anfernee Hardaway 15.00 40.00
13 Allen Iverson 15.00 40.00
14 Shawn Kemp 10.00 25.00
15 Dennis Rodman 15.00 40.00
16 George Gervin 10.00 25.00
17 Walt Frazier 10.00 25.00
18 Hakeem Olajuwon 20.00 50.00
19 Gary Payton 12.00 30.00
20 Dominique Wilkins 10.00 25.00

2014-15 Court Kings Art Nouveau Jerseys
STATED PRINT RUN 299 SER.#'d SETS
*PRIME/25: 2X TO 5X BASIC
1 Andrew Wiggins 10.00 25.00
2 Jabari Parker 6.00 15.00
3 Joel Embiid 15.00 40.00
4 Aaron Gordon 8.00 20.00
5 Dante Exum 2.50 6.00
6 Marcus Smart 6.00 15.00
7 Julius Randle 8.00 20.00
8 Nik Stauskas 1.50 4.00
9 Noah Vonleh 1.50 4.00
10 Elfrid Payton 2.50 6.00
11 Doug McDermott 2.50 6.00
12 Zach LaVine 10.00 25.00
13 T.J. Warren 2.50 6.00
14 Adreian Payne 1.50 4.00
15 James Young 1.50 4.00
16 Tyler Ennis 1.50 4.00
17 Gary Harris 2.00 5.00
18 Bruno Caboclo 2.00 5.00
19 Mitch McGary 1.50 4.00
20 Jordan Adams 1.50 4.00
21 Rodney Hood 2.00 5.00
22 Shabazz Napier 2.00 5.00
23 P.J. Hairston 1.50 4.00
24 C.J. Wilcox 1.50 4.00
25 Kyle Anderson 2.50 6.00
26 K.J. McDaniels 1.50 4.00
27 Joe Harris 2.50 6.00
28 Cleanthony Early 1.50 4.00
29 Jarnell Stokes 1.50 4.00
30 Spencer Dinwiddie 2.50 6.00
31 Glenn Robinson III 2.00 5.00
32 James Ennis 1.50 4.00
33 Markel Brown 1.50 4.00
34 Cory Jefferson 1.50 4.00
35 Russ Smith 1.50 4.00

2014-15 Court Kings Art Nouveau Jerseys Prime Numbers
*PRIME NUMBERS: 2X TO 5X BASE HI
STATED PRINT RUN 25 SER.#'d SETS

2014-15 Court Kings Artistic Endeavors Jerseys
PRINT RUNS B/WN 99-299 COPIES PER
*PRIME/15-25: 1.5X TO 4X BASE HI
1 LeBron James/299 15.00 40.00
2 Kobe Bryant/299 15.00 40.00
3 Kevin Durant/299 6.00 15.00
4 Dwyane Wade/299 4.00 10.00
5 Russell Westbrook/299 3.00 8.00
6 Blake Griffin/299 2.00 5.00
7 Rajon Rondo/149 2.50 6.00
8 Chris Paul/149 3.00 8.00
9 Kevin Love/299 2.00 5.00
10 Pau Gasol/299 3.00 8.00
11 Damian Lillard/99 5.00 12.00
12 Carmelo Anthony/149 3.00 8.00
13 DeMar DeRozan/149 2.50 6.00
14 John Wall/149 2.50 6.00
15 Kyrie Irving/149 4.00 10.00

2014-15 Court Kings Autographs
STATED PRINT RUN B/WN 35-149 COPIES PER
CKAG Artis Gilmore/50 10.00 25.00
CKBB Bradley Beal/60 10.00 25.00
CKBG Blake Griffin/35 10.00 25.00
CKBW Bill Walton/60 12.00 30.00
CKCC Cedric Ceballos/149 6.00 15.00
CKCL Christian Laettner/50 8.00 20.00
CKCM Chris Mullin/50 10.00 25.00
CKCR Clifford Robinson/149 8.00 20.00
CKDM Dikembe Mutombo/99 12.00 30.00
CKGR Glen Rice/99 8.00 20.00
CKJH Jeff Hornacek/149 6.00 15.00
CKJW John Wall/50 20.00 50.00
CKKB Kobe Bryant/40 600.00 1,200.00
CKKD Kevin Durant/40 75.00 200.00
CKKI Kyrie Irving/40 25.00 60.00
CKMC Maurice Cheeks/99 6.00 15.00
CKMJ Marques Johnson/149 6.00 15.00
CKNA Nick Anderson/99 6.00 15.00
CKNA Nate Archibald/60 10.00 25.00
CKNT Nate Thurmond/60 8.00 20.00
CKSC Stephen Curry/50 600.00 1,200.00
CKSM Sidney Moncrief/149 8.00 20.00
CKTH Tim Hardaway/149 5.00 12.00
CKTP Terry Porter/149 5.00 12.00
CKTP Tony Parker/35 12.00 30.00
CKWF Walt Frazier/60 12.00 30.00
CKAH1 Anfernee Hardaway/50 60.00 150.00
CKAH2 Allan Houston/99 8.00 20.00
CKNVE Nick Van Exel/60 25.00 60.00

2014-15 Court Kings Autographs Sapphire
*SAPPHIRE: .5X TO 1.2X BASE HI
STATED PRINT RUN 25 SER.#'d SETS

2014-15 Court Kings Brush Strokes Autographs
PRINT RUNS B/WN 50-149 COPIES PER
*SAPPHIRE/25: .5X TO 1.2X BASE HI
BRAJ Amir Johnson/99 3.00 8.00
BRIS Iman Shumpert/99 3.00 8.00
BRKI Kyrie Irving/50 60.00 150.00
BRJCA Jose Calderon/60 3.00 8.00
BRKL Kyle Lowry/149 6.00 15.00
BRMC Mike Conley/60 4.00 10.00
BRKO Kelly Olynyk/149 3.00 8.00
BRPM Patty Mills/149 5.00 12.00
BRRJ Reggie Jackson/149 4.00 10.00
BRRL Robin Lopez/149 3.00 8.00
BRSC Stephen Curry/40 600.00 1,200.00
BRTG Taj Gibson/99 3.00 8.00
BRTY Thaddeus Young/149 3.00 8.00
BRJW John Wall/50 20.00 50.00
BRTP Tony Parker/50 15.00 40.00
BRTZ Tyler Zeller/149 3.00 8.00

2014-15 Court Kings Expressionists
*SAPPHIRE/25: 1X TO 2.5X BASE HI
1 Chris Andersen 1.00 2.50
2 Latrell Sprewell 1.50 4.00
3 Kevin Garnett 3.00 8.00
4 Gary Payton 2.00 5.00
5 Patrick Ewing 2.00 5.00
6 Magic Johnson 5.00 12.00
7 Charles Oakley 1.25 3.00
8 Shaquille O'Neal 5.00 12.00
9 DeMarcus Cousins 1.00 2.50
10 David Robinson 2.50 6.00
11 Karl Malone 2.50 6.00
12 Anthony Davis 3.00 8.00
13 Isiah Thomas 2.00 5.00
14 Dwyane Wade 2.50 6.00
15 Bill Laimbeer 1.25 3.00
16 Dwight Howard 1.50 4.00
17 Kevin Durant 4.00 10.00
18 Joe Dumars 1.50 4.00
19 Kyrie Irving 2.50 6.00
20 Dikembe Mutombo 2.00 5.00
21 Blake Griffin 1.25 3.00
22 LeBron James 10.00 25.00
23 Hakeem Olajuwon 2.50 6.00
24 Allen Iverson 3.00 8.00
25 Dennis Rodman 3.00 8.00
26 Larry Johnson 1.50 4.00
27 Chris Bosh 1.50 4.00
28 Kobe Bryant 10.00 25.00
29 Larry Bird 5.00 12.00
30 Chris Webber 1.50 4.00

2014-15 Court Kings Fresh Paint Autographs
PRINT RUNS B/WN 225-260 COPIES PER
FPAG Aaron Gordon/225 12.00 30.00
FPAP Adreian Payne/260 3.00 8.00
FPAW Andrew Wiggins/225 30.00 80.00
FPBC Bruno Caboclo/260 4.00 10.00
FPCE Cleanthony Early/260 3.00 8.00
FPDE Dante Exum/225 5.00 12.00
FPDM Doug McDermott/260 5.00 12.00
FPEP Elfrid Payton/260 5.00 12.00
FPGH Gary Harris/260 5.00 12.00
FPGR Glenn Robinson III/260 4.00 10.00
FPJC Jordan Clarkson/260 12.00 30.00
FPJE Joel Embiid/225 60.00 150.00
FPJG Jerami Grant/260 15.00 40.00
FPJH Joe Harris/260 5.00 12.00
FPJN Jusuf Nurkic/260 10.00 25.00
FPJO Johnny O'Bryant/260 3.00 8.00
FPJP Jabari Parker/225 4.00 10.00
FPJR Julius Randle/225 10.00 25.00
FPJY James Young/260 3.00 8.00
FPKA Kyle Anderson/260 5.00 12.00
FPKM K.J. McDaniels/260 3.00 8.00
FPMB Markel Brown/260 3.00 8.00
FPMS Marcus Smart/225 12.00 30.00
FPNS Nik Stauskas/260 3.00 8.00
FPNV Noah Vonleh/225 3.00 8.00
FPPH P.J. Hairston/260 3.00 8.00
FPRH Rodney Hood/260 4.00 10.00
FPRS Russ Smith/260 3.00 8.00
FPSD Spencer Dinwiddie/260 5.00 12.00
FPSN Shabazz Napier/260 4.00 10.00
FPTA Thanasis Antetokounmpo/260 6.00 15.00
FPTE Tyler Ennis/225 3.00 8.00
FPTW T.J. Warren/260 5.00 12.00
FPZL Zach LaVine/260 15.00 40.00

2014-15 Court Kings Heir Apparent Autographs
STATED PRINT RUN 130 SER.#'d SETS
HAZL Zach LaVine 20.00 50.00
HAEP Elfrid Payton 6.00 15.00
HANS Nik Stauskas 4.00 10.00
HATE Tyler Ennis 4.00 10.00
HANV Noah Vonleh 4.00 10.00
HAJP Jabari Parker 12.00 30.00
HAJE Joel Embiid 75.00 200.00
HAMS Marcus Smart 15.00 40.00
HADM Doug McDermott 6.00 15.00
HAAG Aaron Gordon 20.00 50.00
HADE Dante Exum 6.00 15.00
HAAW Andrew Wiggins 50.00 120.00

2014-15 Court Kings Impressionist Ink Autographs
PRINT RUNS B/WN 35-99 COPIES PER
IIAD Anthony Davis/40 75.00 200.00
IIBM Ben McLemore/49 3.00 8.00
IIDG Danny Green/99 4.00 10.00
IIDG Danilo Gallinari/35 3.00 8.00
IIDS Dennis Schroder/99 5.00 12.00
IIGD Gorgui Dieng/99 3.00 8.00
IIJN Joakim Noah/49 12.00 30.00
IIJT Jason Terry/49 4.00 10.00
IIKB Kobe Bryant/40 400.00 800.00
IIKD Kevin Durant/40 60.00 150.00
IIMC M.Carter-Williams/49 3.00 8.00
IIPA Pero Antic/99 3.00 8.00
IIPP Phil Pressey/99 3.00 8.00
IIRJ Reggie Jackson/99 4.00 10.00
IIRL Robin Lopez/99 3.00 8.00
IIRM Ray McCallum/99 3.00 8.00
IISA Steven Adams/99 6.00 15.00
IISB Steve Blake/99 3.00 8.00

IITB Trey Burke/49 3.00 8.00
IITC Tyson Chandler/35 5.00 12.00
IITH Tim Hardaway Jr./99 4.00 10.00
IITP Tayshaun Prince/35 12.00 30.00
IITP Tony Parker/49 12.00 30.00
IIVO Victor Oladipo/49 10.00 25.00
IIZR Zach Randolph/35 5.00 12.00

2014-15 Court Kings Impressionist Ink Autographs Sapphire

*SAPPHIRE: .6X TO 1.5X BASE HI
STATED PRINT RUN 25 SER.#'d SETS

2014-15 Court Kings Le Cinque Piu Belle

PRINT RUNS B/WN 12-36 COPIES PER
1 Andrew Wiggins/22 150.00 300.00
3 Marcus Smart/36 40.00 100.00
4 Julius Randle/30 50.00 120.00

2014-15 Court Kings New Aesthetic

*SAPPHIRE/25: .75X TO 2X BASE HI
1 Mitch McGary .75 2.00
2 Elfrid Payton 1.25 3.00
3 Andrew Wiggins 10.00 25.00
4 Shabazz Napier 1.00 2.50
5 T.J. Warren 1.25 3.00
6 Aaron Gordon 4.00 10.00
7 Kyle Anderson 1.25 3.00
8 Tyler Ennis .75 2.00
9 Julius Randle 4.00 10.00
10 Glenn Robinson III 1.00 2.50
11 Jordan Adams .75 2.00
12 Doug McDermott 1.25 3.00
13 Jabari Parker 1.00 2.50
14 P.J. Hairston .75 2.00
15 Adreian Payne .75 2.00
16 Dante Exum 1.25 3.00
17 Cleanthony Early .75 2.00
18 Gary Harris 1.25 3.00
19 Nik Stauskas .75 2.00
20 Nick Johnson .75 2.00
21 Rodney Hood 1.00 2.50
22 Zach LaVine 5.00 12.00
23 Joel Embiid 8.00 20.00
24 C.J. Wilcox .75 2.00
25 James Young .75 2.00
26 Spencer Dinwiddie 1.25 3.00
27 Marcus Smart 3.00 8.00
28 Bruno Caboclo 1.00 2.50
29 Noah Vonleh .75 2.00
30 K.J. McDaniels .75 2.00

2014-15 Court Kings Performance Art Jerseys

PRINT RUNS B/WN 49-299 COPIES PER
*PRIME/20-25: 1X TO 2.5X BASE HI
1 Kevin Love/149 3.00 8.00
2 Taj Gibson/99 2.00 5.00
3 Rajon Rondo/110 4.00 10.00
4 Arron Afflalo/199 2.00 5.00
5 George Hill/260 2.50 6.00
6 Eric Bledsoe/299 2.50 6.00
7 Dwight Howard/149 4.00 10.00
8 Mike Conley/249 2.50 6.00
9 Kyle Korver/299 2.50 6.00
10 Tim Duncan/149 8.00 20.00
11 Nene/99 2.50 6.00
12 Blake Griffin/199 3.00 8.00
13 Paul George/49 5.00 12.00
14 Ryan Anderson/199 2.00 5.00
15 Kobe Bryant/299 6.00 15.00
16 Jrue Holiday/99 4.00 10.00
17 Jarrett Jack/99 2.50 6.00
18 Jamal Crawford/99 3.00 8.00
19 David Lee/99 2.00 5.00
20 Kevin Durant/75 6.00 15.00
21 Chris Paul/149 5.00 12.00
22 Jeff Teague/99 2.00 5.00
23 Blake Griffin/149 3.00 8.00
24 Carmelo Anthony/99 5.00 12.00
25 Al Horford/299 3.00 8.00
26 Trey Burke/249 2.00 5.00
27 Brandon Knight/99 2.00 5.00
28 Stephen Curry/149 12.00 30.00
29 Kawhi Leonard/149 8.00 20.00
30 Monta Ellis/149 2.50 6.00
31 James Harden/199 6.00 15.00
32 DeMar DeRozan/99 4.00 10.00
33 Dwight Howard/199 4.00 10.00
34 Dion Waiters/149 2.00 5.00
35 Russell Westbrook/199 5.00 12.00

2014-15 Court Kings Portraits

STATED PRINT RUN 149 SER.#'d SETS
*RUBY/99: .6X TO 1.5X BASE HI
*SAPPHIRE/25: 1.2X TO 3X BASE HI
1 Dwyane Wade 2.50 6.00
2 Carmelo Anthony 2.00 5.00
3 Rajon Rondo 1.50 4.00
4 Nicolas Batum 1.00 2.50
5 Chris Bosh 1.50 4.00
6 Nerlens Noel .75 2.00
7 Kyle Lowry 1.50 4.00
8 Al Horford 1.25 3.00
9 Damian Lillard 3.00 8.00
10 Victor Oladipo 1.00 2.50
11 Zach Randolph 1.25 3.00
12 John Wall 1.50 4.00
13 Ty Lawson .75 2.00
14 Luol Deng 1.00 2.50
15 Chris Paul 2.00 5.00
16 Michael Carter-Williams .75 2.00
17 DeMar DeRozan 1.50 4.00
18 Joakim Noah 1.25 3.00
19 LaMarcus Aldridge 1.25 3.00
20 Tobias Harris 1.00 2.50
21 Anthony Davis 3.00 8.00
22 Bradley Beal 1.00 2.50
23 DeMarcus Cousins 1.00 2.50
24 Pau Gasol 2.00 5.00
25 Blake Griffin 1.25 3.00
26 Dirk Nowitzki 3.00 8.00
27 Serge Ibaka 1.00 2.50
28 Jimmy Butler 2.00 5.00
29 Trey Burke .75 2.00
30 Tim Duncan 3.00 8.00
31 Lance Stephenson 1.00 2.50
32 Marcin Gortat .75 2.00
33 Kyrie Irving 2.50 6.00
34 Chandler Parsons .75 2.00
35 Ben McLemore .75 2.00
36 Steve Nash 2.50 6.00
37 Deron Williams 1.00 2.50
38 Derrick Rose 2.50 6.00
39 Gordon Hayward 1.00 2.50
40 Manu Ginobili 2.50 6.00
41 Paul George 2.00 5.00
42 Goran Dragic 1.25 3.00
43 Kobe Bryant 10.00 25.00
44 Jeremy Lin 2.50 6.00
45 Stephen Curry 10.00 25.00
46 James Harden 2.50 6.00
47 Andrei Kirilenko 1.00 2.50
48 Russell Westbrook 2.00 5.00
49 Roy Hibbert 1.00 2.50
50 Kawhi Leonard 3.00 8.00
51 Kevin Love 1.25 3.00
52 Eric Bledsoe 1.00 2.50
53 LeBron James 10.00 25.00
54 Andre Drummond 1.00 2.50
55 Klay Thompson 3.00 8.00
56 Dwight Howard 1.50 4.00
57 Iman Shumpert .75 2.00
58 Kevin Durant 4.00 10.00
59 Larry Sanders .75 2.00
60 Tony Parker 2.00 5.00
61 Andrew Wiggins 10.00 25.00
62 Jabari Parker 1.00 2.50
63 Joel Embiid 8.00 20.00
64 Aaron Gordon 4.00 10.00
65 Dante Exum 1.25 3.00
66 Marcus Smart 3.00 8.00
67 Julius Randle 4.00 10.00
68 Nik Stauskas .75 2.00
69 Noah Vonleh .75 2.00
70 Elfrid Payton 1.25 3.00
71 Doug McDermott 1.25 3.00
72 Zach LaVine 5.00 12.00
73 T.J. Warren 1.25 3.00
74 Adreian Payne .75 2.00
75 James Young .75 2.00
76 Tyler Ennis .75 2.00
77 Gary Harris 1.25 3.00
78 Bruno Caboclo 1.00 2.50
79 Rodney Hood 1.00 2.50
80 Shabazz Napier 1.00 2.50
81 P.J. Hairston .75 2.00
82 Kyle Anderson 1.25 3.00
83 Markel Brown .75 2.00
84 Russ Smith .75 2.00
85 Cleanthony Early .75 2.00
86 Spencer Dinwiddie 1.25 3.00
87 James Ennis .75 2.00
88 Nick Johnson .75 2.00
89 C.J. Wilcox .75 2.00
90 Jordan Adams .75 2.00
91 Mitch McGary .75 2.00
92 Jusuf Nurkic 2.50 6.00
93 Clint Capela 12.00 30.00
94 Nikola Mirotic 1.25 3.00
95 Johnny O'Bryant .75 2.00
96 Bojan Bogdanovic 1.25 3.00
97 Devyn Marble .75 2.00
98 Joe Harris 1.25 3.00
99 Kostas Papanikolaou .75 2.00
100 Erick Green .75 2.00

2014-15 Court Kings Remarkable Rookies

*SAPPHIRE/499: .6X TO 1.5X BASE
1 Russ Smith .60 1.50
2 Doug McDermott 1.00 2.50
3 Jarnell Stokes .60 1.50
4 Marcus Smart 2.50 6.00
5 C.J. Wilcox .60 1.50
6 Andrew Wiggins 3.00 8.00
7 Damjan Rudez .60 1.50
8 Jordan Adams .60 1.50
9 Cameron Bairstow .60 1.50
10 James Young .60 1.50
11 Cory Jefferson .60 1.50
12 Zach LaVine 4.00 10.00
13 Spencer Dinwiddie 1.00 2.50
14 Julius Randle 3.00 8.00
15 Kyle Anderson 1.00 2.50
16 Jabari Parker .75 2.00
17 Kostas Papanikolaou .60 1.50
18 Rodney Hood 1.00 2.50
19 Damien Inglis .60 1.50
20 Tyler Ennis .60 1.50
21 Johnny O'Bryant .60 1.50
22 T.J. Warren 1.00 2.50
23 Glenn Robinson III .75 2.00
24 Nik Stauskas .60 1.50
25 K.J. McDaniels .60 1.50
26 Joel Embiid 6.00 15.00
27 Bojan Bogdanovic 1.00 2.50
28 Shabazz Napier .75 2.00
29 Devyn Marble .60 1.50
30 Gary Harris 1.00 2.50
31 Tarik Black .60 1.50
32 Adreian Payne .60 1.50
33 Nick Johnson .60 1.50
34 Noah Vonleh .60 1.50
35 Joe Harris 1.00 2.50
36 Aaron Gordon 3.00 8.00
37 Andre Dawkins .60 1.50
38 Clint Capela 5.00 12.00
39 Nikola Mirotic 1.00 2.50
40 Bruno Caboclo .75 2.00
41 Jordan Clarkson 2.50 6.00
42 Jusuf Nurkic 2.00 5.00
43 Markel Brown .60 1.50
44 Elfrid Payton 1.00 2.50
45 Cleanthony Early .60 1.50
46 Dante Exum 1.00 2.50
47 Travis Wear .60 1.50
48 P.J. Hairston .60 1.50
49 James Ennis .60 1.50
50 Mitch McGary .60 1.50

2014-15 Court Kings Remarkable Rookies Memorabilia

1 Aaron Gordon 3.00 8.00
2 Adreian Payne .60 1.50
3 Andrew Wiggins 3.00 8.00
4 Bruno Caboclo .75 2.00
5 C.J. Wilcox .60 1.50
6 Cleanthony Early .60 1.50
7 Cory Jefferson .60 1.50
8 Damien Inglis .60 1.50
9 Dante Exum 1.00 2.50
10 Doug McDermott 1.00 2.50
11 Elfrid Payton 1.00 2.50
12 Gary Harris 1.00 2.50
13 Glenn Robinson III .75 2.00
14 Jabari Parker .75 2.00
15 James Ennis .60 1.50
16 James Young .60 1.50
17 Jarnell Stokes .60 1.50
18 Jerami Grant 3.00 8.00
19 Joe Harris 1.00 2.50
20 Joel Embiid 6.00 15.00
21 Johnny O'Bryant .60 1.50
22 Jordan Adams .60 1.50
23 Julius Randle 3.00 8.00
24 K.J. McDaniels .60 1.50
25 Kyle Anderson 1.00 2.50
26 Marcus Smart 2.50 6.00
27 Markel Brown .60 1.50
28 Mitch McGary .60 1.50
29 Nik Stauskas .60 1.50
30 Noah Vonleh .60 1.50
31 P.J. Hairston .60 1.50
32 Rodney Hood .75 2.00
33 Russ Smith .60 1.50
34 Shabazz Napier .75 2.00
35 Spencer Dinwiddie 1.00 2.50
36 T.J. Warren 1.00 2.50
37 Tyler Ennis .60 1.50
38 Zach LaVine 4.00 10.00

2014-15 Court Kings Remarkable Rookies Signatures

1 Andrew Wiggins 15.00 40.00
2 Jabari Parker 4.00 10.00
3 Joel Embiid 60.00 150.00
4 Aaron Gordon 15.00 40.00
5 Dante Exum 5.00 12.00
6 Marcus Smart 12.00 30.00
7 Julius Randle 12.00 30.00
8 Nik Stauskas 3.00 8.00
9 Noah Vonleh 3.00 8.00
10 Elfrid Payton 5.00 12.00
11 Doug McDermott 5.00 12.00
12 Zach LaVine 20.00 50.00
13 T.J. Warren 5.00 12.00
14 Adreian Payne 3.00 8.00
15 James Young 3.00 8.00
16 Tyler Ennis 3.00 8.00
17 Gary Harris 5.00 12.00
18 Mitch McGary 3.00 8.00
19 Jordan Adams 3.00 8.00
20 Rodney Hood 4.00 10.00
21 Shabazz Napier 4.00 10.00
22 P.J. Hairston 3.00 8.00
23 C.J. Wilcox 3.00 8.00
24 K.J. McDaniels 3.00 8.00
25 Joe Harris 5.00 12.00
26 Jarnell Stokes 3.00 8.00
27 Spencer Dinwiddie 5.00 12.00
28 Glenn Robinson III 4.00 10.00
29 Markel Brown 3.00 8.00
30 Russ Smith 3.00 8.00
31 Cory Jefferson 3.00 8.00
32 Johnny O'Bryant 3.00 8.00
33 Devyn Marble 3.00 8.00
34 Jordan Clarkson 12.00 30.00
35 Cameron Bairstow 3.00 8.00
36 Jusuf Nurkic 8.00 20.00
37 Damjan Rudez 3.00 8.00
38 James Ennis 3.00 8.00
39 Erick Green 3.00 8.00
40 Alex Kirk 3.00 8.00

2014-15 Court Kings Rookie Royalty

1 Anthony Davis 2.50 6.00
2 Blake Griffin 2.00 5.00
3 Carmelo Anthony 2.00 5.00
4 Chris Bosh 1.25 3.00
5 Chris Paul 1.50 4.00
6 Derrick Rose 2.00 5.00
7 Dirk Nowitzki 2.50 6.00
8 Dwight Howard 1.25 3.00
9 Dwyane Wade 2.00 5.00
10 James Harden 2.00 5.00
11 Kevin Durant 3.00 8.00
12 Kevin Garnett 2.50 6.00
13 Kevin Love 1.00 2.50
14 Kobe Bryant 8.00 20.00
15 Kyrie Irving 2.00 5.00
16 LeBron James 8.00 20.00
17 Pau Gasol 1.50 4.00
18 Russell Westbrook 1.50 4.00
19 Steve Nash 2.00 5.00
20 Tim Duncan 2.50 6.00
21 Tony Parker 1.50 4.00
22 Vince Carter 2.00 5.00

2014-15 Court Kings Royal Performances

*SAPPHIRE/25: .6X TO 1.5X BASE HI
1 Tim Duncan 4.00 10.00
2 Shaquille O'Neal 6.00 15.00
3 Jerry West 4.00 10.00
4 Pete Maravich 5.00 12.00
5 Latrell Sprewell 2.00 5.00
6 LeBron James 12.00 30.00
7 Wilt Chamberlain 5.00 12.00
8 Rajon Rondo 2.00 5.00
9 Magic Johnson 6.00 15.00
10 Michael Carter-Williams 1.00 2.50
11 David Thompson 1.50 4.00
12 Clyde Drexler 2.50 6.00
13 Elgin Baylor 2.50 6.00
14 Tracy McGrady 2.50 6.00
15 Carmelo Anthony 2.50 6.00
16 Kevin Durant 5.00 12.00
17 Kobe Bryant 12.00 30.00
18 Timofey Mozgov 1.00 2.50
19 David Robinson 3.00 8.00
20 Anthony Davis 4.00 10.00

2014-15 Court Kings Sketches and Swatches Autographs

PRINT RUNS B/WN 25-149 COPIES PER
*PRIME/25: 1X TO 2.5X BASIC
1 Al Horford/35 4.00 10.00
2 Jeff Teague/99 2.50 6.00
3 Kyle Korver/65 8.00 20.00
4 Antoine Walker/149 3.00 8.00
5 Jeff Green/65 3.00 8.00
6 Mason Plumlee/149 2.50 6.00
7 Ben Gordon/35 3.00 8.00
8 Tony Parker/35 20.00 50.00
9 Dwight Howard/25 8.00 20.00
10 Zydrunas Ilgauskas/149 3.00 8.00
11 Josh Smith/35 2.50 6.00
12 Klay Thompson/99 20.00 50.00
13 George Hill/65 3.00 8.00
14 Luis Scola/65 3.00 8.00
15 Hakeem Olajuwon/35 20.00 50.00
16 Carmelo Anthony/25 40.00 100.00
17 Dominique Wilkins/35 6.00 15.00
18 Tony Allen/35 2.50 6.00
19 Ray Allen/25 25.00 60.00
20 Brandon Knight/35 2.50 6.00
21 Tobias Harris/49 3.00 8.00
22 Eric Gordon/35 3.00 8.00
23 Tim Hardaway Jr./149 3.00 8.00
24 Thabo Sefolosha/99 2.50 6.00
25 Alex Len/35 3.00 8.00
26 Isaiah Thomas/149 10.00 25.00
27 Tiago Splitter/49 2.50 6.00
29 Derrick Favors/35 2.50 6.00
30 Trey Burke/35 2.50 6.00
31 Dennis Schroder/149 4.00 10.00
32 Brandon Bass/49 2.50 6.00
33 Kyle Lowry/149 6.00 15.00
34 Kelly Olynyk/149 2.50 6.00
35 Brook Lopez/35 4.00 10.00
36 Joe Johnson/35 3.00 8.00
37 Michael Kidd-Gilchrist/35 2.50 6.00
38 Raymond Felton/35 2.50 6.00
39 Jared Dudley/49 2.50 6.00
40 Chris Bosh/25 6.00 15.00
41 Tayshaun Prince/35 4.00 10.00
42 John Starks/149 5.00 12.00
43 Danny Manning/35 3.00 8.00
44 Xavier McDaniel/149 3.00 8.00
45 Andre Miller/49 3.00 8.00
46 Cody Zeller/35 2.50 6.00
47 J.J. Redick/65 4.00 10.00
48 Kevin Love/35 5.00 12.00
49 LaMarcus Aldridge/35 15.00 40.00
50 M.Carter-Williams/35 8.00 20.00

2014-15 Court Kings Sovereign Signatures

PRINT RUNS B/WN 20-149 COPIES PER
*PRIME/25: .6X TO 1.5X BASIC
1 Joakim Noah/49 12.00 30.00
2 Michael Finley/65 6.00 15.00
3 John Wall/20 25.00 60.00
5 Joe Dumars/65 8.00 20.00
6 Stephen Curry/49 400.00 800.00
7 Vince Carter/35 20.00 50.00
8 David Robinson/25 20.00 50.00
9 Manu Ginobili/25 20.00 50.00
10 Gary Payton/25 15.00 40.00
11 Chris Mullin/65 10.00 25.00
12 Bradley Beal/65 10.00 25.00
13 Kevin McHale/25 12.00 30.00
14 Toni Kukoc/149 10.00 25.00
15 Dan Majerle/149 5.00 12.00
16 Sam Perkins/149 5.00 12.00
17 Jason Kidd/25 20.00 50.00
18 Jim Jackson/149 5.00 12.00
19 Andre Iguodala/65 20.00 50.00
20 Dwight Howard/20 15.00 40.00
21 Sleepy Floyd/99 5.00 12.00
22 Yao Ming/20 30.00 80.00
23 Dwyane Wade/20 12.00 30.00
24 Chris Bosh/25 8.00 20.00
25 Robert Horry/149 4.00 10.00

2014-15 Court Kings Studio Signatures

STATED PRINT RUN B/WN 40-99 COPIES PER
*SAPPHIRE: .5X TO 1.2X BASE HI
BTAG Archie Goodwin/99 4.00 10.00
BTAN Andrew Nicholson/99 4.00 10.00
BTBL Brook Lopez/40 6.00 15.00
BTDS Dennis Schroder/99 6.00 15.00
BTEJ Eddie Jones/99 6.00 15.00
BTGA G.Antetokounmpo/99 200.00 500.00
BTGH Gordon Hayward/99 8.00 20.00
BTGM George McGinnis/99 4.00 10.00
BTHB Harrison Barnes/40 5.00 12.00
BTHG Horace Grant/99 6.00 15.00
BTJG Jeff Green/99 5.00 12.00
BTJK Jason Kidd/40 20.00 50.00
BTJS John Salley/99 5.00 12.00
BTJS P.J. Tucker/99 5.00 12.00
BTKO Kelly Olynyk/99 5.00 12.00
BTRK Ryan Kelly/99 4.00 10.00
BTSA Steven Adams/99 10.00 25.00
BTSC Stephen Curry/40 500.00 1,000.00

2014-15 Court Kings Vintage Materials

PRINT RUNS B/WN 49-299 COPIES PER
*PRIME/25: .6X TO 1.5X BASE HI
1 Mitch Richmond/49 4.00 10.00
2 Paul Westphal/99 3.00 8.00
3 Walter Davis/299 2.50 6.00
4 Danny Ainge/99 3.00 8.00
5 Doug Collins/199 3.00 8.00
6 Gary Payton/299 5.00 12.00
7 Adrian Dantley/99 3.00 8.00
8 Brad Daugherty/199 2.50 6.00
9 Joe Dumars/199 4.00 10.00
10 Kevin Duckworth/199 2.00 5.00
11 Chris Mullin/99 4.00 10.00
12 Patrick Ewing/299 5.00 12.00
13 Manute Bol/99 3.00 8.00
14 Cedric Maxwell/199 2.50 6.00
15 Scottie Pippen/299 8.00 20.00
16 Glen Rice/199 3.00 8.00
17 Alex English/99 4.00 10.00
18 Kareem Abdul-Jabbar/49 10.00 25.00
19 Kiki Vandeweghe/99 2.50 6.00
20 Byron Scott/199 3.00 8.00
21 Clyde Drexler/299 5.00 12.00
22 Marques Johnson/199 2.50 6.00
23 Moses Malone/49 5.00 12.00
24 Hakeem Olajuwon/199 6.00 15.00
25 Artis Gilmore/49 4.00 10.00

2015-16 Court Kings

167-199 PRINT RUN 299 SER.#'d SETS
200-232 PRINT RUN 149 SER.#'d SETS
233-265 PRINT RUN 75 SER.#'d SETS
266-298 PRINT RUN 10 SER.#'d SETS
NO PRICING AVAILABLE FOR 266-298
1 Al Horford .50 1.25
2 Jimmy Butler 1.00 2.50
3 Brandon Jennings .30 .75
4 DeAndre Jordan .40 1.00
5 Khris Middleton .60 1.50
6 Serge Ibaka .40 1.00
7 DeMarcus Cousins .50 1.25
8 Dennis Schroder .50 1.25
9 Joakim Noah .30 .75
10 Kentavious Caldwell-Pope .40 1.00
11 Lance Stephenson .40 1.00
12 Michael Carter-Williams .30 .75
13 Aaron Gordon .50 1.25
14 Rajon Rondo .60 1.50
15 Jeff Teague .30 .75
16 Nikola Mirotic .30 .75
17 Reggie Jackson .40 1.00
18 Paul Pierce .75 2.00
19 Andrew Wiggins .60 1.50
20 Elfrid Payton .40 1.00
21 Rudy Gay .50 1.25
22 Paul Millsap .40 1.00
23 Pau Gasol .75 2.00
24 Andre Iguodala .50 1.25
25 Jordan Clarkson .50 1.25
26 Kevin Garnett 1.25 3.00
27 Tobias Harris .40 1.00
28 Kawhi Leonard 1.50 4.00
29 Avery Bradley .30 .75
30 Iman Shumpert .30 .75
31 Draymond Green .60 1.50
32 Julius Randle .60 1.50
33 Ricky Rubio .40 1.00
34 Victor Oladipo .40 1.00
35 LaMarcus Aldridge .50 1.25
36 James Young .30 .75
37 Kevin Love .50 1.25
38 Klay Thompson 1.25 3.00
39 Kobe Bryant 4.00 10.00
40 Zach LaVine 1.25 3.00
41 Jerami Grant .50 1.25
42 Tim Duncan 1.25 3.00
43 Jared Sullinger .30 .75
44 Kyrie Irving 1.00 2.50
45 Stephen Curry 4.00 10.00
46 Marc Gasol .50 1.25
47 Anthony Davis 1.25 3.00
48 Nerlens Noel .30 .75
49 Tony Parker .75 2.00
50 Marcus Smart .60 1.50
51 LeBron James 4.00 10.00
52 Dwight Howard .60 1.50
53 Mike Conley .50 1.25
54 Jrue Holiday .60 1.50
55 Brandon Knight .30 .75
56 DeMar DeRozan .60 1.50
57 Brook Lopez .50 1.25
58 Chandler Parsons .30 .75
59 James Harden 1.00 2.50
60 Zach Randolph .50 1.25
61 Arron Afflalo .30 .75
62 Eric Bledsoe .40 1.00
63 Jonas Valanciunas .40 1.00
64 Joe Johnson .40 1.00
65 Deron Williams .40 1.00
66 Patrick Beverley .30 .75
67 Chris Bosh .60 1.50
68 Carmelo Anthony .75 2.00
69 T.J. Warren .50 1.25
70 Kyle Lowry .50 1.25
71 Shane Larkin .30 .75
72 Dirk Nowitzki 1.25 3.00
73 Monta Ellis .40 1.00
74 Dwyane Wade .75 2.00
75 Robin Lopez .30 .75
76 Tyson Chandler .40 1.00
77 Gordon Hayward .50 1.25
78 Al Jefferson .50 1.25
79 Gary Harris .30 .75
80 Paul George .75 2.00
81 Goran Dragic .50 1.25
82 Dion Waiters .30 .75
83 Al-Farouq Aminu .30 .75
84 Rudy Gobert .60 1.50
85 Kemba Walker .50 1.25
86 Jusuf Nurkic .40 1.00
87 Blake Griffin .60 1.50
88 Giannis Antetokounmpo 2.50 6.00
89 Kevin Durant 2.00 5.00
90 C.J. McCollum .50 1.25
91 Bradley Beal .50 1.25
92 Michael Kidd-Gilchrist .30 .75
93 Kenneth Faried .40 1.00
94 Chris Paul 1.00 2.50
95 Jabari Parker .30 .75
96 Russell Westbrook .75 2.00
97 Damian Lillard 1.25 3.00
98 John Wall .60 1.50
99 Derrick Rose .75 2.00
100 Andre Drummond .50 1.25
101 Karl-Anthony Towns RC 3.00 8.00
102 Justise Winslow RC .75 2.00
103 Sam Dekker RC .50 1.25
104 Larry Nance Jr. RC 1.00 2.50
105 D'Angelo Russell RC 2.00 5.00
106 Myles Turner RC 2.00 5.00
107 Jerian Grant RC .50 1.25
108 R.J. Hunter RC .50 1.25
109 Jahlil Okafor RC .60 1.50
110 Trey Lyles RC .60 1.50
111 Delon Wright RC .60 1.50
112 Montrezl Harrell RC 1.50 4.00
113 Kristaps Porzingis RC 3.00 8.00
114 Devin Booker RC 20.00 50.00
115 Justin Anderson RC .50 1.25
116 Jordan Mickey RC .50 1.25
117 Mario Hezonja RC .60 1.50
118 Cameron Payne RC .75 2.00
119 Bobby Portis RC 1.25 3.00
120 Anthony Brown RC .50 1.25
121 Willie Cauley-Stein RC .60 1.50
122 Kelly Oubre Jr. RC 8.00 20.00
123 Rondae Hollis-Jefferson RC .60 1.50
124 Pat Connaughton RC .75 2.00
125 Emmanuel Mudiay RC .60 1.50
126 Terry Rozier RC 2.00 5.00
127 Tyus Jones RC .60 1.50
128 Joe Young RC .50 1.25
129 Stanley Johnson RC .60 1.50
130 Rashad Vaughn RC .50 1.25
131 Jarell Martin RC .50 1.25
132 Branden Dawson RC .50 1.25
133 Frank Kaminsky RC .60 1.50
134 Karl-Anthony Towns 3.00 8.00
135 Justise Winslow .75 2.00
136 Sam Dekker .50 1.25
137 Larry Nance Jr. 1.00 2.50
138 D'Angelo Russell 2.00 5.00
139 Myles Turner 2.00 5.00
140 Jerian Grant .50 1.25
141 R.J. Hunter .50 1.25
142 Jahlil Okafor .60 1.50
143 Trey Lyles .60 1.50
144 Delon Wright .60 1.50
145 Montrezl Harrell 1.50 4.00
146 Kristaps Porzingis 3.00 8.00
147 Devin Booker 20.00 50.00
148 Justin Anderson .50 1.25
149 Jordan Mickey .50 1.25
150 Mario Hezonja .60 1.50
151 Cameron Payne .75 2.00
152 Bobby Portis 1.25 3.00
153 Anthony Brown .50 1.25
154 Willie Cauley-Stein .60 1.50
155 Kelly Oubre Jr. 30.00 80.00
156 Rondae Hollis-Jefferson .60 1.50
157 Pat Connaughton .75 2.00
158 Emmanuel Mudiay .60 1.50
159 Terry Rozier 2.00 5.00
160 Tyus Jones .60 1.50
161 Joe Young .50 1.25
162 Stanley Johnson .60 1.50
163 Rashad Vaughn .50 1.25
164 Jarell Martin .50 1.25
165 Branden Dawson .50 1.25
166 Frank Kaminsky .60 1.50
167 Karl-Anthony Towns/299 6.00 15.00
168 Justise Winslow/299 1.50 4.00
169 Sam Dekker/299 1.00 2.50
170 Larry Nance Jr./299 2.00 5.00
171 D'Angelo Russell/299 4.00 10.00
172 Myles Turner/299 4.00 10.00
173 Jerian Grant/299 1.00 2.50
174 R.J. Hunter/299 1.00 2.50
175 Jahlil Okafor/299 1.25 3.00
176 Trey Lyles/299 1.25 3.00
177 Delon Wright/299 1.25 3.00
178 Montrezl Harrell/299 3.00 8.00
179 Kristaps Porzingis/299 6.00 15.00
180 Devin Booker/299 40.00 100.00
181 Justin Anderson/299 1.00 2.50
182 Jordan Mickey/299 1.00 2.50
183 Mario Hezonja/299 1.25 3.00
184 Cameron Payne/299 1.50 4.00
185 Bobby Portis/299 2.50 6.00
186 Anthony Brown/299 1.00 2.50
187 Willie Cauley-Stein/299 1.25 3.00
188 Kelly Oubre Jr./299 40.00 100.00
189 Rondae Hollis-Jefferson/299 1.25 3.00
190 Pat Connaughton/299 1.50 4.00
191 Emmanuel Mudiay/299 1.25 3.00
192 Terry Rozier/299 4.00 10.00
193 Tyus Jones/299 1.25 3.00
194 Joe Young/299 1.00 2.50
195 Stanley Johnson/299 1.25 3.00
196 Rashad Vaughn/299 1.00 2.50
197 Jarell Martin/299 1.00 2.50
198 Branden Dawson/299 1.00 2.50
199 Frank Kaminsky/299 1.25 3.00
200 Karl-Anthony Towns/175 8.00 20.00
201 Justise Winslow/175 2.00 5.00
202 Sam Dekker/175 1.25 3.00
203 Larry Nance Jr./175 2.50 6.00
204 D'Angelo Russell/175 5.00 12.00
205 Myles Turner/175 5.00 12.00
206 Jerian Grant/175 1.25 3.00
207 R.J. Hunter/175 1.25 3.00
208 Jahlil Okafor/175 1.50 4.00
209 Trey Lyles/175 1.50 4.00
210 Delon Wright/175 1.50 4.00
211 Montrezl Harrell/175 4.00 10.00
212 Kristaps Porzingis/175 8.00 20.00
213 Devin Booker/175 50.00 120.00
214 Justin Anderson/175 1.25 3.00
215 Jordan Mickey/175 1.25 3.00
216 Mario Hezonja/175 1.50 4.00
217 Cameron Payne/175 2.00 5.00
218 Bobby Portis/175 3.00 8.00
219 Anthony Brown/175 1.25 3.00
220 Willie Cauley-Stein/175 1.50 4.00
221 Kelly Oubre Jr./175 50.00 120.00
222 Rondae Hollis-Jefferson/175 1.50 4.00
223 Pat Connaughton/175 2.00 5.00
224 Emmanuel Mudiay/175 1.50 4.00
225 Terry Rozier/175 5.00 12.00
226 Tyus Jones/175 1.50 4.00
227 Joe Young/175 1.25 3.00
228 Stanley Johnson/175 1.50 4.00
229 Rashad Vaughn/175 1.25 3.00
230 Jarell Martin/175 1.25 3.00
231 Branden Dawson/175 1.25 3.00
232 Frank Kaminsky/175 1.50 4.00
233 Karl-Anthony Towns/75 20.00 50.00
234 Justise Winslow/75 2.50 6.00
235 Sam Dekker/75 1.50 4.00
236 Larry Nance Jr./75 3.00 8.00
237 D'Angelo Russell/75 6.00 15.00
238 Myles Turner/75 6.00 15.00
239 Jerian Grant/75 1.50 4.00
240 R.J. Hunter/75 1.50 4.00
241 Jahlil Okafor/75 2.00 5.00
242 Trey Lyles/75 2.00 5.00
243 Delon Wright/75 2.00 5.00
244 Montrezl Harrell/75 5.00 12.00
245 Kristaps Porzingis/75 10.00 25.00
246 Devin Booker/75 60.00 150.00
247 Justin Anderson/75 1.50 4.00
248 Jordan Mickey/75 1.50 4.00
249 Mario Hezonja/75 2.00 5.00
250 Cameron Payne/75 2.50 6.00
251 Bobby Portis/75 4.00 10.00
252 Anthony Brown/75 1.50 4.00
253 Willie Cauley-Stein/75 2.00 5.00
254 Kelly Oubre Jr./75 60.00 150.00
255 Rondae Hollis-Jefferson/75 2.00 5.00
256 Pat Connaughton/75 2.50 6.00
257 Emmanuel Mudiay/75 2.00 5.00
258 Terry Rozier/75 6.00 15.00
259 Tyus Jones/75 2.00 5.00
260 Joe Young/75 1.50 4.00
261 Stanley Johnson/75 2.00 5.00
262 Rashad Vaughn/75 1.50 4.00
263 Jarell Martin/75 1.50 4.00
264 Branden Dawson/75 1.50 4.00
265 Frank Kaminsky/75 2.00 5.00

2015-16 Court Kings Sapphire

*SAPPHIRE: 2X TO 5X BASIC
STATED PRINT RUN 25 SER.#'d SETS

2015-16 Court Kings 2 on 2 Quad Memorabilia

PRINT RUNS B/WN 49-99 COPIES PER
*PRIME/25: 1.2X TO 3X BASE HI
1 Wggns/Pytn/Grdn/LVne 8.00 20.00
2 Thmpsn/Jms/Irvng/Crry 30.00 80.00
3 Paul/Hwrd/Hrdn/Grffn 6.00 15.00
4 Prsns/Nwtzki/Dncn/Lnrd 10.00 25.00
5 Beal/Wall/Mddln/Crtr-Wllms 4.00 10.00
6 Grffn/Jrdn/Gsl/Rndlph 3.00 8.00
7 Grntt/O'Nl/Kobe/Prce 30.00 80.00
8 Stcktn/Kemp/Pytn/Mlne 6.00 15.00
9 Bird/Thms/Dmrs/McHle 12.00 30.00
10 Ervng/Kareem/Magic/Mlne 12.00 30.00
11 Oljwn/Hrdwy/Hrry/O'Nl 10.00 25.00
12 Grtt/Mllsp/Hrfrd 3.00 8.00
13 Hywrd/Knght/Bldse/Brke 3.00 8.00
14 Hrdn/Wstbrk/Drnt/Bvrly 12.00 30.00
15 Wggns/Clrksn/Kobe/Rbo 25.00 60.00
16 Wade/Jhnsn/Deng/Lpz 6.00 15.00

2015-16 Court Kings 5x7 Box Topper Autographs

EXCHANGE DEADLINE 6/9/2017
BTAD Anthony Davis 75.00 200.00
BTDR David Robinson 40.00 100.00
BTDR D'Angelo Russell 40.00 100.00
BTDW Delon Wright 4.00 10.00
BTGP Gary Payton 30.00 80.00
BTJG Jerian Grant 3.00 8.00
BTJO Jahlil Okafor 4.00 10.00
BTKT Karl-Anthony Towns 60.00 150.00
BTRH Robert Horry 12.00 30.00
BTRH R.J. Hunter 3.00 8.00

2015-16 Court Kings 5x7 Box Topper Career Progression

1 Carmelo Anthony 4.00 10.00
2 LeBron James 6.00 15.00
3 Dwight Howard 3.00 8.00
4 Kevin Garnett 6.00 15.00
5 Chris Andersen 2.00 5.00
6 Pau Gasol 4.00 10.00
7 Brandon Knight 1.50 4.00
8 Goran Dragic 2.50 6.00
9 Andre Iguodala 2.50 6.00
10 Kevin Durant 10.00 25.00
11 Chris Paul 5.00 12.00
12 Ray Allen 3.00 8.00
13 Jason Kidd 4.00 10.00
14 Jason Kidd 4.00 10.00
15 Vince Carter 5.00 12.00
16 Vince Carter 5.00 12.00
17 Steve Nash 4.00 10.00
18 Shaquille O'Neal 8.00 20.00
19 Scottie Pippen 6.00 15.00
20 Alonzo Mourning 4.00 10.00
21 Gary Payton 4.00 10.00
22 Anfernee Hardaway 6.00 15.00
23 Dikembe Mutombo 4.00 10.00
24 Dennis Rodman 6.00 15.00
25 Allen Iverson 6.00 15.00

2015-16 Court Kings 5x7 Box Topper Panoramics

1 Kyrie Irving 4.00 10.00
2 Kobe Bryant 25.00 60.00
3 Russell Westbrook 3.00 8.00
4 Blake Griffin 2.00 5.00
5 Dennis Schroder 2.00 5.00
6 LeBron James 25.00 60.00
7 Dwyane Wade 4.00 10.00
8 Damian Lillard 5.00 12.00
9 John Wall 2.50 6.00
10 Jordan Clarkson 2.00 5.00
11 Stephen Curry 25.00 60.00
12 Andrew Wiggins 2.50 6.00
13 Elfrid Payton 1.50 4.00
14 Marcus Smart 2.50 6.00
15 Manu Ginobili 4.00 10.00
16 James Harden 4.00 10.00
17 Anthony Davis 5.00 12.00
18 Kawhi Leonard 6.00 15.00
19 Bradley Beal 2.50 6.00
20 Derrick Rose 3.00 8.00
21 Chris Paul 4.00 10.00
22 Kevin Durant 8.00 20.00
23 DeMar DeRozan 2.50 6.00
24 Dante Exum 1.50 4.00
25 Jimmy Butler 2.00 5.00

2015-16 Court Kings 5x7 Le Cinque Piu Belle Autografo Autographs

PRINT RUNS B/WN 3-35 COPIES PER
NO PRICING ON QTY 3
EXCHANGE DEADLINE 6/9/2017
2 Kobe Bryant/24 1,000.00 2,000.00

3 Kevin Durant/35 200.00 500.00
4 Andrew Wiggins/22 EXCH 100.00 250.00
5 Anthony Davis/23 125.00 300.00

2015-16 Court Kings Art Nouveau Jerseys

STATED PRINT RUN 299 SER.#'d SETS
*PRIME/25: 1.2X TO 3X BASIC
1 Karl-Anthony Towns 10.00 25.00
2 D'Angelo Russell 5.00 12.00
3 Jahlil Okafor 5.00 12.00
4 Kristaps Porzingis 10.00 25.00
5 Mario Hezonja 2.00 5.00
6 Willie Cauley-Stein 2.00 5.00
7 Emmanuel Mudiay 2.00 5.00
8 Stanley Johnson 2.00 5.00
9 Frank Kaminsky 2.00 5.00
10 Justise Winslow 2.50 6.00
11 Myles Turner 6.00 15.00
12 Trey Lyles 2.00 5.00
13 Devin Booker 20.00 50.00
14 Cameron Payne 2.50 6.00
15 Kelly Oubre Jr. 5.00 12.00
16 Terry Rozier 6.00 15.00
18 Sam Dekker 1.50 4.00
19 Jerian Grant 1.50 4.00
20 Delon Wright 2.00 5.00
21 Justin Anderson 1.50 4.00
22 Bobby Portis 4.00 10.00
23 Rondae Hollis-Jefferson 2.00 5.00
24 Tyus Jones 2.00 5.00
25 Jarell Martin 1.50 4.00
26 Kevon Looney 5.00 12.00
27 R.J. Hunter 1.50 4.00
28 Chris McCullough 1.50 4.00
29 Montrezl Harrell 5.00 12.00
30 Jordan Mickey 1.50 4.00
31 Anthony Brown 1.50 4.00
32 Rakeem Christmas 1.50 4.00
33 Richaun Holmes 2.50 6.00
34 Pat Connaughton 2.50 6.00
36 Joe Young 1.50 4.00
37 Walter Tavares 1.50 4.00
38 Josh Richardson 2.50 6.00
39 Josh Huestis 1.50 4.00

2015-16 Court Kings Artistic Endeavors Jerseys

PRINT RUNS B/WN 185-299 COPIES PER
*PRIME/25: 1X TO 2.5X BASIC
1 Khris Middleton/185 3.00 8.00
2 Michael Carter-Williams/299 1.50 4.00
3 Jared Sullinger/299 1.50 4.00
4 Kelly Olynyk/299 1.50 4.00
5 Patrick Beverley/299 1.50 4.00
6 Chris Andersen/299 2.00 5.00
7 Chris Paul/299 5.00 12.00
8 Noah Vonleh/299 1.50 4.00
9 T.J. Warren/299 2.50 6.00
10 Terrence Jones/299 1.50 4.00
11 Damian Lillard/299 6.00 15.00
12 Aaron Gordon/299 2.50 6.00
13 LaMarcus Aldridge/299 2.50 6.00
14 Avery Bradley/299 1.50 4.00
15 Bojan Bogdanovic/299 2.00 5.00
16 Brook Lopez/299 2.50 6.00
17 Chris Bosh/299 3.00 8.00
18 Dwyane Wade/299 5.00 12.00
19 LeBron James/299 8.00 20.00
20 Kyrie Irving/299 5.00 12.00
21 Ricky Rubio/299 2.00 5.00
22 Danny Green/299 2.00 5.00
23 Kawhi Leonard/299 8.00 20.00
24 Andrew Wiggins/299 3.00 8.00
25 Draymond Green/299 8.00 20.00
26 Klay Thompson/299 6.00 15.00
27 Stephen Curry/299 20.00 50.00
28 Dwight Howard/299 3.00 8.00
29 James Harden/299 5.00 12.00
30 Kobe Bryant/299 20.00 50.00
31 Kevin Durant/299 5.00 12.00
32 Russell Westbrook/299 4.00 10.00
33 Jimmy Butler/299 5.00 12.00
34 Derrick Rose/299 4.00 10.00
35 Nikola Vucevic/299 2.00 5.00

2015-16 Court Kings Aurora

1 Derrick Rose 12.00 30.00
2 James Harden 15.00 40.00
3 Zach LaVine 20.00 50.00
4 John Wall 10.00 25.00
5 Bojan Bogdanovic 6.00 15.00
6 Jimmy Butler 15.00 40.00
7 Chris Paul 15.00 40.00
8 Anthony Davis 20.00 50.00
9 Marcus Smart 10.00 25.00
10 Dante Exum 6.00 15.00
11 Kyrie Irving 15.00 40.00
12 Kobe Bryant 150.00 400.00
13 Kevin Durant 30.00 80.00
14 Elfrid Payton 6.00 15.00
15 Dennis Schroder 8.00 20.00
16 LeBron James 150.00 400.00
17 Dwyane Wade 15.00 40.00
18 Russell Westbrook 12.00 30.00
19 Brandon Knight 5.00 12.00
20 Kawhi Leonard 25.00 60.00
21 Stephen Curry 150.00 400.00
22 Andrew Wiggins 10.00 25.00
23 Damian Lillard 20.00 50.00
24 Bradley Beal 10.00 25.00
25 DeMar DeRozan 10.00 25.00

2015-16 Court Kings Autographs

PRINT RUNS B/WN 35-199 COPIES PER
EXCHANGE DEADLINE 6/9/2017
*SAPPHIRE/25: .5X TO 1.2X BASIC
CKAD Anthony Davis/35 40.00 100.00
CKBM Ben McLemore/49 2.50 6.00
CKCM C.J. McCollum/99 8.00 20.00
CKDMJ Dan Majerle/99 4.00 10.00
CKDM Doug McDermott/99 3.00 8.00
CKDN Don Nelson/35 12.00 30.00
CKDR Dennis Rodman/35 30.00 80.00
CKDR David Robinson/35 25.00 60.00
CKEJ Eddie Jones/99 4.00 10.00
CKGG Gail Goodrich/35 4.00 10.00
CKGHR Gary Harris/99 3.00 8.00
CKGH Grant Hill/35 25.00 60.00
CKJHK Jeff Hornacek/99 3.00 8.00
CKJH Jrue Holiday/35 5.00 12.00
CKJI Joe Ingles/199 8.00 20.00
CKJN Jusuf Nurkic/99 6.00 15.00
CKJR Julius Randle/35 8.00 20.00
CKJW John Wall/35 25.00 60.00
CKKB Kobe Bryant/35 500.00 1,000.00
CKKD Kevin Durant/35 125.00 250.00
CKKI Kyrie Irving/35 40.00 100.00
CKKM Khris Middleton/199 5.00 12.00
CKMC Michael Carter-Williams/99 2.50 6.00
CKMD Matthew Dellavedova/199 3.00 8.00
CKMJ Mark Jackson/35 3.00 8.00
CKMP Mason Plumlee/199 2.50 6.00
CKMW Marvin Williams/99 2.50 6.00
CKNC Norris Cole/99 3.00 8.00
CKNM Nikola Mirotic/49 2.50 6.00
CKSS Steve Smith/99 5.00 12.00
CKTM Timofey Mozgov/99 2.50 6.00
CKTP Tony Parker/35 25.00 60.00
CKTP Jordan Clarkson/199 6.00 15.00
CKVD Vlade Divac/99 3.00 8.00
CKZI Zydrunas Ilgauskas/99 3.00 8.00
CKZL Zach LaVine/99 20.00 50.00

2015-16 Court Kings Brush Strokes Autographs

PRINT RUNS B/WN 30-199 COPIES PER
EXCHANGE DEADLINE 6/9/2017
*SAPPHIRE/25: .5X TO 1.2X BASIC
BSAE Alex English/99 5.00 12.00
BSAG A.C. Green/99 6.00 15.00
BSAM Antonio McDyess/199 6.00 15.00
BSAW Antoine Walker/199 3.00 8.00
BSBL Bill Laimbeer/199 4.00 10.00
BSBM Bob McAdoo/99 5.00 12.00
BSBS Byron Scott/30 3.00 8.00
BSDI Dan Issel/199 5.00 12.00
BSDR Dennis Rodman/30 40.00 100.00
BSDR Dino Radja/199 8.00 20.00
BSDS Damon Stoudamire/199 4.00 10.00
BSEJ Eddie Jones/199 4.00 10.00
BSFB Fred Brown/199 2.50 6.00
BSGP Gary Payton/30 6.00 15.00
BSJD Joe Dumars/30 10.00 25.00
BSJS Jerry Stackhouse/99 6.00 15.00
BSJW Jamaal Wilkes/99 4.00 10.00
BSMA Mark Aguirre/99 3.00 8.00
BSNA Nate Archibald/30 5.00 12.00
BSRS Rony Seikaly/199 3.00 8.00
BSRS Rik Smits/199 5.00 12.00
BSSB Sam Bowie/199 2.50 6.00
BSSE Sean Elliott/199 3.00 8.00
BSTD Tony Delk/199 2.50 6.00
BSVN Vinny Del Negro/30 3.00 8.00

2015-16 Court Kings Calligraphy Autographs

PRINT RUNS B/WN 40-199 COPIES PER
EXCHANGE DEADLINE 6/9/2017
*SAPPHIRE/25: .5X TO 1.2X BASIC
CKB Kobe Bryant/40 400.00 800.00
CSM Sidney Moncrief/125 2.50 6.00
CSB Sam Bowie/99 5.00 12.00
CDI Dan Issel/199 5.00 12.00
CDM Dan Majerle/60 4.00 10.00
CJE James Ennis/199 2.50 6.00
CJG Jeff Green/60 2.50 6.00
CKD Kevin Durant/40 60.00 150.00
CWM Wesley Matthews/60 2.50 6.00
CMH Maurice Harkless/199 2.50 6.00
CMP Mason Plumlee/199 2.50 6.00
CJP Jabari Parker/40 15.00 40.00
CJS Jerry Stackhouse/60 12.00 30.00
CSK Steve Kerr/40 8.00 20.00
CRA Rafer Alston/199 2.50 6.00
CTP Tony Parker/40 25.00 40.00
CMC Michael Carter-Williams/40 2.50 6.00
CMA Mark Aguirre/60 3.00 8.00
CAN Andrew Nicholson/199 2.50 6.00
CBM Bob McAdoo/60 10.00 25.00
CDC DeMarre Carroll/199 2.50 6.00
CGP Gary Payton/40 8.00 20.00
CJN Jusuf Nurkic/199 3.00 8.00
CMW Mo Williams/199 3.00 8.00
CLE Len Elmore/199 2.50 6.00
CAA Al-Farouq Aminu/60 2.50 6.00
CBL Bill Laimbeer/199 4.00 10.00
CDS Dennis Schroder/199 6.00 15.00
CEF Evan Fournier/199 3.00 8.00
CJC Jordan Clarkson/199 4.00 10.00
CJR Julius Randle/40 8.00 20.00
CTA Tony Allen/199 2.50 6.00
CNN Nene/60 2.50 6.00
CLG Langston Galloway/199 2.50 6.00
CAE Alex English/60 5.00 12.00
CBML Ben McLemore/40 2.50 6.00
CJI Joe Ingles/199 3.00 8.00
CEK Enes Kanter/60 2.50 6.00
CJH Jrue Holiday/40 5.00 12.00

2015-16 Court Kings Expressionist Memorabilia

STATED PRINT RUN 299 SER.#'d SETS
*PRIME/25: 1X TO 2.5X BASIC
1 Kemba Walker 2.50 6.00
2 Reggie Jackson 2.50 6.00
3 Kobe Bryant 20.00 50.00
4 Russell Westbrook 4.00 10.00
5 Draymond Green 5.00 12.00
6 Derrick Rose 4.00 10.00
7 Stephen Curry 15.00 40.00
8 Dwyane Wade 5.00 12.00
9 Damian Lillard 6.00 15.00
10 DeAndre Jordan 2.00 5.00
11 Jimmy Butler 5.00 12.00
12 Dwight Howard 3.00 8.00
13 Andrew Wiggins 3.00 8.00
14 DeMarcus Cousins 2.50 6.00
15 Mike Conley 2.50 6.00
16 Kyrie Irving 5.00 12.00
17 James Harden 5.00 12.00
18 Zach LaVine 6.00 15.00
19 John Wall 3.00 8.00
20 Chris Bosh 3.00 8.00
21 LeBron James 8.00 20.00
22 Blake Griffin 2.50 6.00
23 Anthony Davis 6.00 15.00
24 Isaiah Thomas 2.00 5.00
25 Giannis Antetokounmpo 12.00 30.00
26 Dirk Nowitzki 6.00 15.00
27 Chris Paul 5.00 12.00
28 Carmelo Anthony 4.00 10.00
29 Joakim Noah 1.50 4.00
30 Eric Bledsoe 2.00 5.00
31 Kenneth Faried 2.00 5.00
32 Jordan Clarkson 2.50 6.00
33 Kevin Durant 5.00 12.00
34 Iman Shumpert 1.50 4.00
35 Jason Terry 2.00 5.00

2015-16 Court Kings Expressionists

*SAPPHIRE/25: 1.5X TO 4X BASIC
1 Kemba Walker .60 1.50
2 Reggie Jackson .50 1.25
3 Kobe Bryant 5.00 12.00
4 Russell Westbrook 1.00 2.50
5 Draymond Green .75 2.00
6 Derrick Rose 1.00 2.50
7 Stephen Curry 5.00 12.00
8 Dwyane Wade 1.25 3.00
9 Damian Lillard 1.50 4.00
10 DeAndre Jordan .50 1.25
11 Jimmy Butler 1.25 3.00
12 Dwight Howard .75 2.00
13 Andrew Wiggins .75 2.00
14 DeMarcus Cousins .60 1.50
15 Mike Conley .60 1.50
16 Kyrie Irving 1.25 3.00
17 James Harden 1.25 3.00
18 Zach LaVine 1.50 4.00
19 John Wall .75 2.00
20 Chris Bosh .75 2.00
21 LeBron James 5.00 12.00
22 Blake Griffin .60 1.50
23 Anthony Davis 1.50 4.00
24 Isaiah Thomas .50 1.25
25 Giannis Antetokounmpo 3.00 8.00
26 Dirk Nowitzki 1.50 4.00
27 Chris Paul 1.25 3.00
28 Carmelo Anthony 1.00 2.50
29 Joakim Noah .40 1.00
30 Eric Bledsoe .50 1.25
31 Kenneth Faried .50 1.25
32 Jordan Clarkson .60 1.50
33 Kevin Durant 2.50 6.00
34 Iman Shumpert .40 1.00
35 Jason Terry .50 1.25

2015-16 Court Kings Fresh Paint Autographs

EXCHANGE DEADLINE 6/9/2017
FPAB Anthony Brown 2.50 6.00
FPAH Andrew Harrison 3.00 8.00
FPBP Bobby Portis 6.00 15.00
FPCM Chris McCullough 2.50 6.00
FPCP Cameron Payne 4.00 10.00
FPDB Devin Booker 300.00 600.00
FPDJ Dakari Johnson 2.50 6.00
FPDR D'Angelo Russell 20.00 50.00
FPDW Delon Wright 3.00 8.00
FPEM Emmanuel Mudiay 3.00 8.00
FPFK Frank Kaminsky 3.00 8.00
FPJA Justin Anderson 2.50 6.00
FPJG Jerian Grant 2.50 6.00
FPJM Jordan Mickey 2.50 6.00
FPJO Jahlil Okafor 3.00 8.00
FPJW Justise Winslow 4.00 10.00
FPJY Joe Young 2.50 6.00
FPKA Karl-Anthony Towns 40.00 100.00
FPKO Kelly Oubre Jr. 30.00 80.00
FPKP Kristaps Porzingis 30.00 80.00
FPLN Larry Nance Jr. 5.00 12.00
FPMH Mario Hezonja 3.00 8.00
FPMT Myles Turner 10.00 25.00
FPPC Pat Connaughton 4.00 10.00
FPRH Richaun Holmes 4.00 10.00
FPRJ R.J. Hunter 2.50 6.00
FPRV Rashad Vaughn 2.50 6.00
FPSD Sam Dekker 2.50 6.00
FPSJ Stanley Johnson 2.50 6.00
FPTH Tyler Harvey 2.50 6.00
FPTJ Tyus Jones 3.00 8.00
FPTL Trey Lyles 3.00 8.00
FPTR Terry Rozier 10.00 25.00
FPJMT Jarell Martin 2.50 6.00
FPMHR Montrezl Harrell 8.00 20.00
FPRHJ Rondae Hollis-Jefferson 3.00 8.00
FPWCS Willie Cauley-Stein 3.00 8.00

2015-16 Court Kings Heir Apparent Autographs

EXCHANGE DEADLINE 6/9/2017
HAKP Kristaps Porzingis 50.00 120.00
HACAP Cameron Payne 5.00 12.00
HADAR D'Angelo Russell 15.00 40.00
HAEMU Emmanuel Mudiay 4.00 10.00
HAFRK Frank Kaminsky 4.00 10.00
HAJAO Jahlil Okafor 4.00 10.00
HAJEG Jerian Grant 3.00 8.00
HAJUW Justise Winslow 12.00 30.00
HAKAT Karl-Anthony Towns 60.00 150.00
HAMAH Mario Hezonja 4.00 10.00
HASDE Sam Dekker 3.00 8.00
HASJO Stanley Johnson 4.00 10.00

2015-16 Court Kings Impressionist Ink

PRINT RUNS B/WN 40-199 COPIES PER
EXCHANGE DEADLINE 6/9/2017
*SAPPHIRE/25: .5X TO 1.2X BASIC
IIAG Aaron Gordon/40 4.00 10.00
IIAL Alex Len/99 2.50 6.00
IIAP Adreian Payne/199 2.50 6.00
IIBB Bojan Bogdanovic/199 3.00 8.00
IIDC DeMarre Carroll/99 2.50 6.00
IIDE Dante Exum/40 10.00 25.00
IIGH Gary Harris/99 3.00 8.00
IIJC Jordan Clarkson/199 8.00 20.00
IIJE James Ennis/199 2.50 6.00
IIJP Jabari Parker/40 15.00 40.00
IIJR Julius Randle/40 12.00 30.00
IIJS J.R. Smith/40 6.00 15.00
IIJW John Wall/40 15.00 40.00
IIKB Kobe Bryant/40 400.00 800.00
IIKD Kevin Durant/40 60.00 150.00
IIKT Klay Thompson/40 25.00 60.00
IILG Langston Galloway/199 2.50 6.00
IIMD Matthew Dellavedova/199 3.00 8.00
IIMS Marcus Smart/40 5.00 12.00
IINC Norris Cole/40 2.50 6.00
IINM Nikola Mirotic/40 8.00 20.00
IITB Tarik Black/199 2.50 6.00
IITE Tyler Ennis/40 2.50 6.00
IITH Tobias Harris/40 3.00 8.00
IITM Timofey Mozgov/99 2.50 6.00
IITT Tristan Thompson/40 2.50 6.00
IITW T.J. Warren/60 5.00 12.00
IIZL Zach LaVine/99 15.00 40.00

2015-16 Court Kings Le Cinque Piu Belle Autographs

PRINT RUNS B/WN 1-32 COPIES PER
NO PRICING ON QTY 8 OR LESS
1 Karl-Anthony Towns/32 60.00 150.00
5 Mario Hezonja/23 5.00 12.00

2015-16 Court Kings Performance Art Jerseys

STATED PRINT RUN 299 SER.#'d SETS
*PRIME/25: 1.2X TO 3X BASIC
1 Damian Lillard 6.00 15.00
2 Rajon Rondo 3.00 8.00
3 Kawhi Leonard 8.00 20.00
4 Tim Duncan 6.00 15.00
5 Iman Shumpert 1.50 4.00
6 Isaiah Thomas 2.00 5.00
7 Goran Dragic 2.50 6.00
8 Chris Bosh 3.00 8.00
9 DeMarre Carroll 1.50 4.00
10 Khris Middleton 3.00 8.00

2015-16 Court Kings Portraits

*RUBY/100: 1X TO 2.5X BASIC
*SAPPHIRE/25: 1.5X TO 4X BASIC
1 Derrick Rose 1.00 2.50
2 Elfrid Payton .50 1.25
3 Jabari Parker .40 1.00
4 Michael Carter-Williams .40 1.00
5 George Hill .50 1.25
6 Jimmy Butler 1.25 3.00
7 Blake Griffin .60 1.50
8 Jamal Crawford .60 1.50
9 Robin Lopez .40 1.00
10 Roy Hibbert .50 1.25
11 Kyrie Irving 1.25 3.00
12 John Wall .75 2.00
13 Tyreke Evans .50 1.25
14 Nerlens Noel .40 1.00
15 Jeff Green .40 1.00
16 LeBron James 5.00 12.00
17 Marcus Smart .75 2.00
18 Brandon Knight .40 1.00
19 T.J. Warren .60 1.50
20 Matt Barnes .40 1.00
21 Stephen Curry 5.00 12.00
22 Bradley Beal .75 2.00
23 Bojan Bogdanovic .50 1.25
24 Rajon Rondo .75 2.00
25 Chris Andersen .50 1.25
26 James Harden 1.25 3.00
27 Dante Exum .50 1.25
28 Dirk Nowitzki 1.50 4.00
29 Tim Duncan 1.50 4.00
30 Shabazz Napier .40 1.00
31 Chris Paul 1.25 3.00
32 Jordan Clarkson .60 1.50
33 Dwight Howard .75 2.00
34 Jonas Valanciunas .50 1.25
35 Greg Monroe .50 1.25
36 Kobe Bryant 5.00 12.00
37 Manu Ginobili 1.25 3.00
38 Isaiah Thomas .50 1.25
39 Gordon Hayward .60 1.50
40 Gorgui Dieng .40 1.00
41 Dwyane Wade 1.25 3.00
42 Zach LaVine 1.50 4.00
43 Joe Johnson .50 1.25
44 Kyle Korver .50 1.25
45 Nikola Vucevic .50 1.25
46 Andrew Wiggins .75 2.00
47 Kemba Walker .60 1.50
48 Pau Gasol 1.00 2.50
49 Thabo Sefolosha .40 1.00
50 Robert Covington .50 1.25
51 Anthony Davis 1.50 4.00
52 Kenneth Faried .50 1.25
53 Kevin Love .60 1.50
54 Nicolas Batum .40 1.00
55 Gerald Henderson .40 1.00
56 Kevin Durant 2.50 6.00
57 Reggie Jackson .50 1.25
58 Brandon Jennings .40 1.00
59 Wesley Matthews .40 1.00
60 Marco Belinelli .40 1.00
61 Russell Westbrook 1.00 2.50
62 Carmelo Anthony 1.00 2.50
63 Klay Thompson 1.50 4.00
64 Joffrey Lauvergne .40 1.00
65 DeMarre Carroll .40 1.00
66 Damian Lillard 1.50 4.00
67 DeMarcus Cousins .60 1.50
68 Paul George 1.00 2.50
69 Harrison Barnes .50 1.25
70 Marcin Gortat .40 1.00

2015-16 Court Kings Rookie Portraits

*RUBY/100: .75X TO 2X BASIC
*SAPPHIRE/25: 1.2X TO 3X BASIC
1 D'Angelo Russell 2.50 6.00
2 Mario Hezonja .75 2.00
3 Karl-Anthony Towns 4.00 10.00
4 Willie Cauley-Stein .75 2.00
5 Devin Booker 8.00 20.00
6 Jerian Grant .60 1.50
7 Cameron Payne 1.00 2.50
8 Delon Wright .60 1.50
9 Anthony Brown .60 1.50
10 Pat Connaughton 1.00 2.50
11 Jahlil Okafor .75 2.00
12 Emmanuel Mudiay .75 2.00
13 Kristaps Porzingis 4.00 10.00
14 Stanley Johnson .75 2.00
15 Kelly Oubre Jr. 2.00 5.00
16 Justin Anderson .60 1.50
17 Terry Rozier 2.50 6.00
18 Bobby Portis 1.50 4.00
19 Joe Young .60 1.50
20 Chris McCullough .60 1.50
21 Myles Turner 2.50 6.00
22 Frank Kaminsky .75 2.00
23 Trey Lyles .75 2.00
24 Justise Winslow 1.00 2.50
25 Rashad Vaughn .60 1.50
26 Tyus Jones .75 2.00
27 Sam Dekker .60 1.50
28 Montrezl Harrell 2.00 5.00
29 Nemanja Bjelica 1.00 2.50
30 Nikola Jokic 100.00 250.00

2015-16 Court Kings Studio Signatures

PRINT RUNS B/WN 40-99 COPIES PER
EXCHANGE DEADLINE 6/9/2017
*SAPPHIRE/25: .5X TO 1.2X BASIC
SSAD Anthony Davis/40 40.00 100.00
SSAL Alex Len/99 2.50 6.00
SSBB Bojan Bogdanovic/99 3.00 8.00
SSCM C.J. McCollum/99 6.00 15.00
SSDC DeMarre Carroll/99 2.50 6.00
SSDR Damjan Rudez/99 2.50 6.00
SSDS Dennis Schroder/99 4.00 10.00
SSGA Giannis Antetokounmpo/75 60.00 150.00
SSGH Grant Hill/40 12.00 30.00
SSGP Gary Payton/40 8.00 20.00
SSJE Julius Erving/40 30.00 80.00
SSJH Jrue Holiday/40 5.00 12.00
SSJW John Wall/40 15.00 40.00
SSKB Kobe Bryant/40 EXCH 400.00 800.00
SSKD Kevin Durant/40 60.00 150.00
SSKI Kyrie Irving/40 25.00 60.00
SSMC Michael Carter-Williams/99 2.50 6.00
SSMG Marcin Gortat/49 2.50 6.00
SSMK Michael Kidd-Gilchrist/40 2.50 6.00
SSNC Norris Cole/99 2.50 6.00
SSNN Nene/49 3.00 8.00
SSNY Nick Young/49 2.50 6.00
SSTH Tim Hardaway Jr./99 3.00 8.00
SSTT Tristan Thompson/40 2.50 6.00
SSWM Wesley Matthews/49 2.50 6.00
SSTBK Tarik Black/99 2.50 6.00

2015-16 Court Kings Swagger

*SAPPHIRE/25: 1X TO 2.5X BASIC
1 Dwyane Wade 2.50 6.00
2 Jonas Valanciunas 1.00 2.50
3 Derrick Rose 2.00 5.00
4 DeMarcus Cousins 1.25 3.00
5 Jusuf Nurkic 1.00 2.50
6 Andrew Wiggins 1.50 4.00
7 DeMar DeRozan 1.50 4.00
8 Jimmy Butler 2.50 6.00
9 DeAndre Jordan 1.00 2.50
10 Zach Randolph 1.25 3.00
11 Ben McLemore .75 2.00
12 Kemba Walker 1.25 3.00
13 Kyrie Irving 2.50 6.00
14 Giannis Antetokounmpo 6.00 15.00
15 Goran Dragic 1.00 2.50
16 Anthony Davis 3.00 8.00
17 Kenneth Faried 1.00 2.50
18 LeBron James 10.00 25.00
19 Eric Bledsoe 1.00 2.50
20 Victor Oladipo 1.00 2.50
21 Kevin Durant 5.00 12.00
22 Reggie Jackson 1.00 2.50
23 Stephen Curry 10.00 25.00
24 Jabari Parker .75 2.00
25 Tony Parker 2.00 5.00
26 Russell Westbrook 2.00 5.00
27 Blake Griffin 1.25 3.00
28 James Harden 2.50 6.00
29 Kobe Bryant 10.00 25.00
30 Rudy Gobert 1.50 4.00
31 Damian Lillard 3.00 8.00
32 Carmelo Anthony 2.00 5.00
33 Chris Paul 2.50 6.00
34 Zach LaVine 3.00 8.00
35 Elfrid Payton 1.00 2.50

2015-16 Court Kings Vintage Materials

STATED PRINT RUN 199 SER.#'d SETS
*PRIME/25: 1X TO 2.5X BASIC
1 Alonzo Mourning 4.00 10.00
2 Clyde Drexler 4.00 10.00
3 Dan Majerle 2.50 6.00
4 Danny Manning 2.00 5.00
5 David Robinson 5.00 12.00
6 Grant Hill 4.00 10.00
7 Herb Williams 1.50 4.00
8 Kareem Abdul-Jabbar 8.00 20.00
9 Reggie Lewis 2.50 6.00
10 Robert Parish 3.00 8.00
11 Ron Harper 2.50 6.00
12 Scottie Pippen 6.00 15.00
13 Shaquille O'Neal 8.00 20.00
14 Vlade Divac 2.50 6.00
15 Walter Davis 1.50 4.00
16 Xavier McDaniel 1.50 4.00
17 Alex English 3.00 8.00
18 Alvan Adams 1.50 4.00
19 Anfernee Hardaway 5.00 12.00
20 Bernard King 3.00 8.00
21 Bill Laimbeer 2.50 6.00
22 Byron Scott 2.00 5.00
23 Charles Oakley 2.00 5.00
24 Dan Issel 3.00 8.00
25 Detlef Schrempf 2.50 6.00

2016-17 Court Kings

1 Anthony Davis 1.50 4.00
2 Kawhi Leonard 1.25 3.00
3 James Harden 1.00 2.50
4 Kyrie Irving 1.00 2.50
5 Vince Carter 1.00 2.50
6 Marc Gasol .50 1.25
7 Eric Bledsoe .40 1.00
8 Damian Lillard 1.25 3.00
9 Emmanuel Mudiay .30 .75
10 Aaron Gordon .50 1.25
11 Trevor Ariza .30 .75
12 Brandon Knight .40 1.00
13 Devin Booker 2.00 5.00
14 Isaiah Thomas .40 1.00
15 Kyle Lowry .50 1.25
16 Avery Bradley .30 .75
17 Marcus Morris .30 .75
18 Ed Davis .30 .75
19 Kristaps Porzingis .75 2.00
20 Bojan Bogdanovic .40 1.00
21 DeMarcus Cousins .40 1.00
22 Myles Turner .50 1.25
23 Kevin Love .50 1.25
24 Doug McDermott .40 1.00
25 Carmelo Anthony .75 2.00
26 Jimmy Butler .75 2.00
27 Gordon Hayward .50 1.25
28 Thaddeus Young .30 .75
29 D'Angelo Russell .60 1.50
30 Rudy Gobert .60 1.50
31 Robin Lopez .30 .75
32 LeBron James 4.00 10.00
33 John Wall .60 1.50
34 Kelly Olynyk .30 .75
35 DeAndre Jordan .40 1.00
36 Marco Belinelli .30 .75
37 Tyreke Evans .40 1.00
38 Chris Paul .75 2.00
39 Nik Stauskas .30 .75
40 DeMar DeRozan .60 1.50
41 Hassan Whiteside .60 1.50
42 Brook Lopez .40 1.00
43 Jrue Holiday .40 1.00
44 Julius Randle .60 1.50
45 Dennis Schroder .50 1.25
46 Bismack Biyombo .30 .75
47 Nikola Vucevic .50 1.25
48 Ian Mahinmi .30 .75
49 Kemba Walker .40 1.00
50 Reggie Jackson .40 1.00
51 Marcin Gortat .30 .75
52 Jordan Clarkson .50 1.25
53 Andre Drummond .50 1.25
54 Alex Len .30 .75
55 Cody Zeller .30 .75
56 Paul George .75 2.00
57 Kevin Durant 2.00 5.00
58 Blake Griffin .50 1.25
59 Steven Adams .40 1.00
60 Rajon Rondo .60 1.50
61 Nicolas Batum .40 1.00
62 Zach Randolph .50 1.25
63 Andrew Wiggins .60 1.50
64 Michael Carter-Williams .30 .75
65 J.R. Smith .30 .75
66 Rodney Hood .40 1.00
67 Stephen Curry 4.00 10.00
68 Giannis Antetokounmpo 2.50 6.00
69 Zach LaVine 1.00 2.50
70 Jabari Parker .30 .75
71 Jahlil Okafor .30 .75
72 Danilo Gallinari .40 1.00
73 Klay Thompson 1.25 3.00
74 Goran Dragic .50 1.25
75 Wesley Matthews .30 .75
76 Will Barton .30 .75
77 Patrick Beverley .30 .75
78 Serge Ibaka .40 1.00
79 Draymond Green .60 1.50
80 Karl-Anthony Towns 1.00 2.50
81 Dwyane Wade 1.00 2.50
82 J.J. Barea .40 1.00
83 C.J. McCollum .50 1.25
84 Justise Winslow .40 1.00
85 Festus Ezeli .30 .75
86 Russell Westbrook .75 2.00
87 Victor Oladipo .50 1.25
88 Jeff Teague .30 .75
89 Nikola Mirotic .30 .75
90 Stanley Johnson .30 .75
91 Tony Parker .75 2.00
92 Elfrid Payton .40 1.00
93 Derrick Rose .75 2.00
94 Bradley Beal .60 1.50
95 DeMarre Carroll .30 .75
96 T.J. McConnell .40 1.00
97 LaMarcus Aldridge .50 1.25
98 Dirk Nowitzki 1.25 3.00
99 Paul Millsap .40 1.00
100 Kenneth Faried .40 1.00
101 Ben Simmons RC 2.00 5.00
102 Brandon Ingram RC 2.00 5.00
103 Jaylen Brown RC 25.00 60.00
104 Dragan Bender RC .50 1.25
105 Kris Dunn RC .75 2.00
106 Buddy Hield RC 1.50 4.00
107 Jamal Murray RC 15.00 40.00
108 Marquese Chriss RC .60 1.50
109 Jakob Poeltl RC 1.00 2.50
110 Thon Maker RC .60 1.50
111 Isaiah Whitehead RC .50 1.25
112 Taurean Prince RC .60 1.50
113 Denzel Valentine RC .50 1.25
114 Wade Baldwin IV RC .50 1.25
115 Henry Ellenson RC .50 1.25
116 Malik Beasley RC 1.00 2.50
117 Caris LeVert RC 1.25 3.00
118 DeAndre' Bembry RC .75 2.00
119 Brice Johnson RC .50 1.25
120 Damian Jones RC .50 1.25
121 Tyler Ulis RC .60 1.50
122 Deyonta Davis RC .50 1.25
123 Skal Labissiere RC .50 1.25
124 Dejounte Murray RC 2.50 6.00
125 Pascal Siakam RC 3.00 8.00
126 Ben Simmons 2.00 5.00
127 Brandon Ingram 2.50 6.00
128 Jaylen Brown 30.00 80.00
129 Dragan Bender .60 1.50
130 Kris Dunn 1.00 2.50
131 Buddy Hield 2.00 5.00
132 Jamal Murray 20.00 50.00
133 Marquese Chriss .75 2.00
134 Jakob Poeltl 1.25 3.00
135 Thon Maker .75 2.00
136 Isaiah Whitehead .60 1.50
137 Taurean Prince .75 2.00
138 Denzel Valentine .60 1.50
139 Wade Baldwin IV .60 1.50
140 Henry Ellenson .60 1.50
141 Malik Beasley 1.25 3.00
142 Caris LeVert 1.50 4.00
143 DeAndre' Bembry 1.00 2.50
144 Brice Johnson .60 1.50
145 Damian Jones .60 1.50
146 Tyler Ulis .75 2.00
147 Deyonta Davis .60 1.50
148 Skal Labissiere .60 1.50
149 Dejounte Murray 3.00 8.00
150 Pascal Siakam 4.00 10.00
151 Ben Simmons 4.00 10.00
152 Brandon Ingram 5.00 12.00
153 Jaylen Brown 60.00 150.00
154 Dragan Bender 1.25 3.00
155 Kris Dunn 2.00 5.00
156 Buddy Hield 4.00 10.00
157 Jamal Murray 40.00 100.00
158 Marquese Chriss 1.50 4.00
159 Jakob Poeltl 2.50 6.00
160 Thon Maker 1.50 4.00
161 Isaiah Whitehead 1.25 3.00
162 Taurean Prince 1.50 4.00
163 Denzel Valentine 1.25 3.00
164 Wade Baldwin IV 1.25 3.00
165 Henry Ellenson 1.25 3.00
166 Malik Beasley 2.50 6.00
167 Caris LeVert 1.50 4.00
168 DeAndre' Bembry 2.00 5.00
169 Brice Johnson 1.25 3.00
170 Damian Jones 1.25 3.00
171 Tyler Ulis 1.50 4.00
172 Deyonta Davis 1.25 3.00
173 Skal Labissiere 1.25 3.00
174 Dejounte Murray 6.00 15.00
175 Pascal Siakam 8.00 20.00
176 Ben Simmons 10.00 25.00
177 Brandon Ingram 12.00 30.00
178 Jaylen Brown 150.00 400.00
179 Dragan Bender 3.00 8.00
180 Kris Dunn 5.00 12.00
181 Buddy Hield 10.00 25.00
182 Jamal Murray 100.00 250.00
183 Marquese Chriss 4.00 10.00
184 Jakob Poeltl 6.00 15.00
185 Thon Maker 4.00 10.00
186 Isaiah Whitehead 3.00 8.00
187 Taurean Prince 4.00 10.00
188 Denzel Valentine 3.00 8.00
189 Wade Baldwin IV 3.00 8.00
190 Henry Ellenson 3.00 8.00
191 Malik Beasley 6.00 15.00
192 Caris LeVert 8.00 20.00
193 DeAndre' Bembry 5.00 12.00
194 Brice Johnson 3.00 8.00
195 Damian Jones 3.00 8.00
196 Tyler Ulis 4.00 10.00
197 Deyonta Davis 3.00 8.00
198 Skal Labissiere 3.00 8.00
199 Dejounte Murray 15.00 40.00
200 Pascal Siakam 20.00 50.00

2016-17 Court Kings Aurora

1 Kyrie Irving 15.00 40.00
2 Stephen Curry 40.00 100.00
3 Damian Lillard 15.00 40.00
4 Jimmy Butler 12.00 30.00
5 Draymond Green 10.00 25.00
6 DeMar DeRozan 8.00 20.00
7 Chris Paul 10.00 25.00
8 Russell Westbrook 10.00 25.00
9 LeBron James 40.00 100.00
10 Kyle Lowry 6.00 15.00
11 Klay Thompson 15.00 40.00
12 James Harden 12.00 30.00
13 Paul George 10.00 25.00
14 Kevin Durant 20.00 50.00
15 Andrew Wiggins 8.00 20.00
16 Reggie Jackson 5.00 12.00
17 Dirk Nowitzki 12.00 30.00
18 Isaiah Thomas 5.00 12.00
19 Kristaps Porzingis 10.00 25.00
20 Karl-Anthony Towns 12.00 30.00

2016-17 Court Kings Sapphire

*SAPPHIRE: 1.5X TO 4X BASIC
RANOM INSERTS IN PACKS
STATED PRINT RUN 25 SER.#'d SETS

2016-17 Court Kings 2 on 2 Quad Memorabilia

PRINT RUNS B/WN 25-99 COPIES PER
1 Mc/Li/Th/Cu/99 15.00 40.00
2 Th/Du/Mc/Bi/25 15.00 40.00
3 Jo/Pa/Wo/Bi/25 15.00 40.00
4 Ja/Cu/Gr/Ir/99 25.00 60.00
5 No/Ba/Du/Pa/99 12.00 30.00
6 Isaiah Thomas
Paul Millsap
Dennis Schroder
Jae Crowder/99 3.00 8.00
7 Pa/Jo/Ha/Ca/99 6.00 15.00
8 Va/El/Lo/Ge/99 5.00 12.00
10 Mu/O'N/Iv/Br/25 20.00 50.00

2016-17 Court Kings 5x7 Box Topper Autographs

EXCHANGE DEADLINE 5/30/2018
2 Anfernee Hardaway 100.00 250.00
3 Jalen Rose 12.00 30.00
4 Damon Stoudamire 12.00 30.00
5 Michael Cooper 15.00 40.00
6 Dell Curry 6.00 15.00
7 Jamal Mashburn 10.00 25.00
8 Nate Archibald 8.00 20.00
9 A.C. Green 8.00 20.00
11 John Starks 12.00 30.00
12 Toni Kukoc 20.00 50.00
13 Rick Barry 30.00 80.00
14 Spud Webb 12.00 30.00
15 Dominique Wilkins 25.00 60.00
16 Gary Payton 40.00 100.00
17 Julius Erving 75.00 200.00
18 Ray Allen 75.00 200.00
19 George Gervin 15.00 40.00
20 Tim Hardaway 12.00 30.00
21 Larry Bird 125.00 300.00
22 James Worthy 20.00 50.00
23 Bill Russell 1,000.00 2,000.00
24 Latrell Sprewell 25.00 60.00

2016-17 Court Kings 5x7 Box Topper Panoramics
1 Carmelo Anthony 3.00 8.00
2 Stephen Curry 25.00 60.00
3 Kyle Lowry 2.00 5.00
4 LeBron James 25.00 60.00
5 Russell Westbrook 3.00 8.00
6 Kyrie Irving 4.00 10.00
7 Andrew Wiggins 2.50 6.00
8 Isaiah Thomas 1.50 4.00
9 Kemba Walker 1.50 4.00
10 Jimmy Butler 4.00 10.00
11 Devin Booker 8.00 20.00
12 Reggie Jackson 1.50 4.00
13 James Harden 4.00 10.00
14 Paul George 3.00 8.00
15 Chris Paul 3.00 8.00
16 D'Angelo Russell 2.50 6.00
17 Karl-Anthony Towns 4.00 10.00
18 Giannis Antetokounmpo 25.00 60.00
19 Anthony Davis 6.00 15.00
20 Kristaps Porzingis 3.00 8.00
21 Blake Griffin 2.00 5.00
22 Klay Thompson 5.00 12.00
23 Damian Lillard 5.00 12.00
24 DeMarcus Cousins 1.50 4.00
25 John Wall 2.50 6.00

2016-17 Court Kings 5x7 Box Topper Rookie Royalty
1 Paul Pierce 4.00 10.00
2 Zach Randolph 2.50 6.00
3 Tyreke Evans 2.00 5.00
4 Derrick Rose 4.00 10.00
5 Kevin Durant 25.00 60.00
6 Stephen Curry 40.00 100.00
7 LeBron James 40.00 100.00
8 Russell Westbrook 4.00 10.00
9 Pau Gasol 4.00 10.00
10 John Wall 3.00 8.00
11 Kevin Love 2.50 6.00
12 Dirk Nowitzki 20.00 50.00
13 Carmelo Anthony 4.00 10.00
14 Chris Bosh 3.00 8.00
15 Blake Griffin 3.00 8.00
16 Vince Carter 15.00 40.00
17 Kevin Garnett 20.00 50.00
18 Scottie Pippen 20.00 50.00
19 Chris Webber 2.50 6.00
20 Shaquille O'Neal 20.00 50.00
21 Allen Iverson 20.00 50.00
22 Jason Kidd 4.00 10.00
23 Yao Ming 20.00 50.00
24 Kobe Bryant 40.00 100.00
25 Shawn Kemp 4.00 10.00

2016-17 Court Kings AKA
1 Anfernee Hardaway 6.00 15.00
2 DeMarcus Cousins 2.00 5.00
3 LeBron James 20.00 50.00
4 Jimmy Butler 5.00 12.00
5 Rudy Gobert 3.00 8.00
6 Bob Cousy 4.00 10.00
7 Allen Iverson 4.00 10.00
8 Kobe Bryant 20.00 50.00
9 Pete Maravich 4.00 10.00

2016-17 Court Kings Arc-eologists
1 Stephen Curry 15.00 40.00
2 James Harden 4.00 10.00
3 Damian Lillard 5.00 12.00
4 J.J. Redick 2.00 5.00
5 J.R. Smith 2.00 5.00
6 Wesley Matthews 1.25 3.00
7 C.J. McCollum 2.00 5.00
8 Evan Fournier 1.50 4.00
9 Kyle Lowry 2.00 5.00
10 Klay Thompson 5.00 12.00

2016-17 Court Kings Art Nouveau Jerseys
*SAPPHIRE/25: 1.2X TO 3X BASIC
1 Brandon Ingram 8.00 20.00
2 Jaylen Brown 15.00 40.00
3 Dragan Bender 2.00 5.00
4 Kris Dunn 3.00 8.00
5 Buddy Hield 6.00 15.00
6 Jamal Murray 15.00 40.00
7 Marquese Chriss 2.50 6.00
8 Jakob Poeltl 4.00 10.00
9 Thon Maker 2.50 6.00
10 Georgios Papagiannis 2.00 5.00
11 T. Luwawu-Cabarrot 3.00 8.00
12 Denzel Valentine 2.00 5.00
13 Wade Baldwin IV 2.00 5.00
14 Henry Ellenson 2.00 5.00
15 Malik Beasley 4.00 10.00
16 Caris LeVert 5.00 12.00
17 Ivica Zubac 5.00 12.00
18 Malachi Richardson 2.00 5.00
19 Brice Johnson 2.00 5.00
20 Pascal Siakam 12.00 30.00
21 Skal Labissiere 2.00 5.00
22 Damian Jones 2.00 5.00
23 Deyonta Davis 2.00 5.00
24 Cheick Diallo 2.00 5.00
25 Tyler Ulis 2.50 6.00
26 Chinanu Onuaku 2.00 5.00
27 Patrick McCaw 2.00 5.00
28 Diamond Stone 2.00 5.00
29 Isaiah Whitehead 2.00 5.00
30 Demetrius Jackson 2.00 5.00
31 A.J. Hammons 2.00 5.00
32 Juan Hernangomez 4.00 10.00
33 Stephen Zimmerman 2.00 5.00

2016-17 Court Kings Art Nouveau Jerseys Jumbo
STATED PRINT RUN 99 SER.#'d SETS
*SAPPHIRE/25: 1.2X TO 3X BASIC
1 Brandon Ingram 10.00 25.00
2 Jaylen Brown 20.00 50.00
3 Dragan Bender 2.50 6.00
4 Kris Dunn 4.00 10.00
5 Buddy Hield 8.00 20.00
6 Jamal Murray 20.00 50.00
7 Marquese Chriss 3.00 8.00
8 Jakob Poeltl 5.00 12.00
9 Thon Maker 3.00 8.00
10 Georgios Papagiannis 2.50 6.00
11 Taurean Prince 3.00 8.00
12 Denzel Valentine 2.50 6.00
13 Wade Baldwin IV 2.50 6.00
14 Henry Ellenson 2.50 6.00
15 Malik Beasley 5.00 12.00
16 Caris LeVert 6.00 15.00
17 DeAndre' Bembry 4.00 10.00
18 Malachi Richardson 2.50 6.00
19 Brice Johnson 2.50 6.00
20 Pascal Siakam 15.00 40.00
21 Skal Labissiere 2.50 6.00
22 Damian Jones 2.50 6.00
23 Deyonta Davis 2.50 6.00
24 Cheick Diallo 2.50 6.00
25 Tyler Ulis 3.00 8.00
26 Chinanu Onuaku 2.50 6.00
27 Patrick McCaw 2.50 6.00
28 Diamond Stone 2.50 6.00
29 Isaiah Whitehead 2.50 6.00
30 Demetrius Jackson 2.50 6.00
31 A.J. Hammons 2.50 6.00
32 Juan Hernangomez 5.00 12.00
33 Kay Felder 2.50 6.00
34 Malcolm Brogdon 8.00 20.00
35 Stephen Zimmerman 2.50 6.00
36 T. Luwawu-Cabarrot 4.00 10.00
37 Gary Payton II 6.00 15.00
38 Ivica Zubac 6.00 15.00

2016-17 Court Kings Artistic Endeavors Jerseys
PRINT RUNS B/WN 49-149 COPIES PER
*PRIME/25: .75X TO 2X BASIC
1 Rudy Gay/149 3.00 8.00
2 Jerian Grant/149 2.00 5.00
3 Danny Green/149 2.50 6.00
4 Karl-Anthony Towns/149 6.00 15.00
5 Kristaps Porzingis/149 5.00 12.00
6 Kemba Walker/149 2.50 6.00
7 Myles Turner/149 3.00 8.00
8 Robert Covington/85 2.50 6.00
9 Carmelo Anthony/149 5.00 12.00
10 Tiago Splitter/149 2.00 5.00
11 Andrew Wiggins/149 4.00 10.00
12 Jonas Valanciunas/149 2.50 6.00
13 Frank Kaminsky/149 2.00 5.00
14 Dwight Howard/149 4.00 10.00
15 Goran Dragic/149 3.00 8.00
16 Gordon Hayward/49 3.00 8.00
17 Klay Thompson/149 8.00 20.00
18 Stephen Curry/149 25.00 60.00
19 LaMarcus Aldridge/149 3.00 8.00
20 Damian Lillard/149 8.00 20.00
21 Tyler Zeller/149 2.00 5.00
22 Bojan Bogdanovic/149 2.50 6.00
23 James Harden/149 6.00 15.00
24 Eric Gordon/149 2.50 6.00
25 Vince Carter/149 6.00 15.00
26 Khris Middleton/149 3.00 8.00
27 Jusuf Nurkic/149 2.50 6.00
28 Kenneth Faried/149 2.50 6.00
29 Dirk Nowitzki/149 8.00 20.00
30 LeBron James/149 25.00 60.00

2016-17 Court Kings Expressionists Memorabilia
STATED PRINT RUN 149 COPIES PER
*SAPPHIRE/25: .75X TO 2X BASIC
1 Karl-Anthony Towns 5.00 12.00
2 Carmelo Anthony 5.00 12.00
3 LeBron James 12.00 30.00
4 Zach LaVine 6.00 15.00
5 Damian Lillard 4.00 10.00
6 DeMar DeRozan 4.00 10.00
7 Jimmy Butler 6.00 15.00
8 Russell Westbrook 5.00 12.00
9 J.R. Smith 3.00 8.00
10 D'Angelo Russell 4.00 10.00
11 Kristaps Porzingis 4.00 10.00
12 Anthony Davis 4.00 10.00
13 Paul George 5.00 12.00
14 Dirk Nowitzki 8.00 20.00

2016-17 Court Kings Fresh Paint Autographs
EXCHANGE DEADLINE 5/30/2018
*VARIATION/200: .5X TO 1.2X BASIC
FPDS Dario Saric EXCH 5.00 12.00
FPMB Malcolm Brogdon 10.00 25.00
FPPM Patrick McCaw 3.00 8.00
FPTC T. Luwawu-Cabarrot 5.00 12.00
FPAJH A.J. Hammons 3.00 8.00
FPBRI Brandon Ingram 12.00 30.00
FPBRJ Brice Johnson 3.00 8.00
FPBUH Buddy Hield 10.00 25.00
FPCHD Cheick Diallo 3.00 8.00
FPCLE Caris LeVert 8.00 20.00
FPCHO Chinanu Onuaku 3.00 8.00
FPDAJ Damian Jones 3.00 8.00
FPDEB DeAndre' Bembry 5.00 12.00
FPDEY Deyonta Davis 3.00 8.00
FPDJA Demetrius Jackson 3.00 8.00
FPDRB Dragan Bender 3.00 8.00
FPDSA Domantas Sabonis 25.00 60.00
FPDST Diamond Stone 3.00 8.00
FPDVA Denzel Valentine 3.00 8.00
FPGP2 Gary Payton II 8.00 20.00
FPGPA Georgios Papagiannis 3.00 8.00
FPHEE Henry Ellenson 3.00 8.00
FPIWH Isaiah Whitehead 3.00 8.00
FPIZU Ivica Zubac 8.00 20.00
FPJAK Jakob Poeltl 6.00 15.00
FPJAM Jamal Murray 60.00 150.00
FPJBR Jaylen Brown 125.00 300.00
FPKFE Kay Felder 3.00 8.00
FPKRD Kris Dunn 5.00 12.00
FPLJC Livio Jean-Charles 3.00 8.00
FPMAC Marquese Chriss 3.00 8.00
FPMAL Malachi Richardson 3.00 8.00
FPMBE Malik Beasley 6.00 15.00
FPPSI Pascal Siakam 20.00 50.00
FPSKL Skal Labissiere 3.00 8.00
FPSZI Stephen Zimmerman 3.00 8.00
FPTMA Thon Maker 4.00 10.00
FPTPR Taurean Prince 4.00 10.00
FPTYU Tyler Ulis 4.00 10.00
FPWB4 Wade Baldwin IV 3.00 8.00

2016-17 Court Kings Fresh Paint Dual Autographs
STATED PRINT RUN 50 SER.#'d SETS
EXCHANGE DEADLINE 5/30/2018
1 Ingram/Dunn 75.00 200.00
2 Hield/Murray 40.00 100.00
3 Brown/Ingram 125.00 250.00
4 Davis/Valentine 12.00 30.00
5 Chriss/Bender 12.00 30.00
6 Jackson/Brown 40.00 100.00
8 Johnson/Stone 10.00 25.00
9 Murray/Ulis 40.00 100.00
10 Saric/Luwawu-Cabarrot 12.00 30.00

2016-17 Court Kings Heir Apparent Autographs
STATED PRINT RUN 150 SER.#'d SETS
EXCHANGE DEADLINE 5/30/2018
1 Brandon Ingram 40.00 100.00
2 Jaylen Brown 75.00 200.00
3 Dragan Bender 3.00 8.00
4 Kris Dunn 5.00 12.00
5 Buddy Hield 12.00 30.00
6 Jamal Murray 40.00 100.00
7 Marquese Chriss 4.00 10.00
8 Domantas Sabonis 10.00 25.00
9 Wade Baldwin IV 3.00 8.00
10 Henry Ellenson 3.00 8.00

2016-17 Court Kings Le Cinque Piu Belle
PRINT RUNS B/WN 2-41 COPIES PER
NO PRICING ON QTY 10 OR LESS
2 Anthony Davis/23 125.00 300.00
5 Dirk Nowitzki/41 125.00 300.00

2016-17 Court Kings Maestros
1 Ish Smith .60 1.50
2 Giannis Antetokounmpo 5.00 12.00
3 Jimmy Butler 2.00 5.00
4 LeBron James 8.00 20.00
5 Marcus Smart 1.25 3.00
6 Blake Griffin 1.00 2.50
7 Marc Gasol 1.00 2.50
8 Paul Millsap .75 2.00
9 Dwyane Wade 2.00 5.00
10 Jeremy Lin 2.00 5.00
11 Gordon Hayward 1.00 2.50
12 DeMarcus Cousins .75 2.00
13 Kristaps Porzingis 1.50 4.00
14 Jordan Clarkson 1.00 2.50
15 Elfrid Payton .75 2.00
16 Dirk Nowitzki 2.50 6.00
17 Brook Lopez .75 2.00
18 Emmanuel Mudiay .60 1.50
19 Paul George 1.50 4.00
20 Anthony Davis 3.00 8.00
21 Andre Drummond 1.00 2.50
22 Kyle Lowry 1.00 2.50
23 James Harden 2.00 5.00
24 Kawhi Leonard 2.50 6.00
25 Devin Booker 4.00 10.00
26 Russell Westbrook 1.50 4.00
27 Karl-Anthony Towns 2.00 5.00
28 Damian Lillard 2.50 6.00
29 Klay Thompson 2.50 6.00
30 John Wall 1.25 3.00
31 Jabari Parker .60 1.50
32 Derrick Rose 1.50 4.00
33 Kyrie Irving 2.00 5.00
34 Isaiah Thomas .75 2.00
35 Chris Paul 1.50 4.00
36 Justise Winslow .75 2.00
37 Kemba Walker .75 2.00
38 Rudy Gay 1.00 2.50
39 Carmelo Anthony 1.50 4.00
40 D'Angelo Russell 1.25 3.00
41 Aaron Gordon 1.00 2.50
42 Myles Turner 1.00 2.50
43 Kentavious Caldwell-Pope .75 2.00
44 Jonas Valanciunas .75 2.00
45 LaMarcus Aldridge 1.00 2.50
46 Eric Bledsoe .75 2.00
47 Steven Adams .75 2.00
48 Andrew Wiggins 1.25 3.00
49 C.J. McCollum 1.00 2.50
50 Stephen Curry 8.00 20.00

2016-17 Court Kings Performance Art Jerseys
STATED PRINT RUN 249 SER.#'d SETS
*SAPPHIRE/25: .75X TO 2X BASIC
1 Jimmy Butler 6.00 15.00
2 Marcus Smart 4.00 10.00
3 Andre Drummond 3.00 8.00
4 Eric Bledsoe 2.50 6.00
5 Al Horford 3.00 8.00
6 Enes Kanter 2.00 5.00
7 Nicolas Batum 2.50 6.00
8 Tristan Thompson 2.50 6.00
9 Marcin Gortat 2.00 5.00
10 Markieff Morris 2.00 5.00
11 Bobby Portis 3.00 8.00
12 Myles Turner 3.00 8.00
13 Langston Galloway 2.00 5.00
14 Kyle Korver 2.50 6.00
15 Reggie Jackson 2.50 6.00

2016-17 Court Kings Portraits
STATED PRINT RUN 175 SER.#'d SETS
*RUBY/75: .75X TO 2X BASIC
*SAPPHIRE/25: 1.2X TO 3X BASIC
1 Stephen Curry 5.00 12.00
2 James Harden 1.50 4.00
3 Russell Westbrook 1.25 3.00
4 Kemba Walker .60 1.50
5 Derrick Rose 1.25 3.00
6 Thaddeus Young .50 1.25
7 Draymond Green 1.00 2.50
8 Clint Capela .60 1.50
9 Kawhi Leonard 2.00 5.00
10 Frank Kaminsky .50 1.25
11 Karl-Anthony Towns 1.50 4.00
12 T.J. McConnell .60 1.50
13 Klay Thompson 2.00 5.00
14 Aaron Gordon .75 2.00
15 Manu Ginobili 1.50 4.00
16 Reggie Jackson .60 1.50
17 Ricky Rubio .60 1.50
18 Robert Covington .60 1.50
19 LeBron James 5.00 12.00
20 Evan Fournier .60 1.50
21 Dirk Nowitzki 2.00 5.00
22 Kentavious Caldwell-Pope .60 1.50
23 Andrew Wiggins 1.00 2.50
24 Vince Carter 1.50 4.00
25 Kevin Love .75 2.00
26 Lou Williams .75 2.00
27 J.J. Barea .60 1.50
28 Khris Middleton .75 2.00
29 Paul Millsap .60 1.50
30 Zach Randolph .75 2.00
31 Kyrie Irving 1.50 4.00
32 D'Angelo Russell 1.00 2.50
33 J.J. Redick .75 2.00
34 Giannis Antetokounmpo 4.00 10.00
35 Dennis Schroder .75 2.00
36 DeMarcus Cousins .60 1.50
37 Rodney Hood .60 1.50
38 Julius Randle 1.00 2.50
39 Chris Paul 1.25 3.00
40 Greg Monroe .50 1.25
41 John Wall 1.00 2.50
42 Kosta Koufos .50 1.25
43 Rudy Gobert 1.00 2.50
44 Kristaps Porzingis 1.25 3.00
45 Paul Pierce 1.25 3.00
46 DeMar DeRozan 1.00 2.50
47 Markieff Morris .50 1.25
48 Al Horford .75 2.00
49 Devin Booker 3.00 8.00
50 Carmelo Anthony 1.25 3.00
51 Damian Lillard 2.00 5.00
52 Kyle Lowry .75 2.00
53 Anthony Davis 2.50 6.00
54 Tyson Chandler .60 1.50
55 Isaiah Thomas .60 1.50
56 Allen Crabbe .50 1.25
57 Cory Joseph .50 1.25
58 Eric Gordon .60 1.50
59 Justise Winslow .60 1.50
60 Hassan Whiteside .60 1.50
61 Jared Sullinger .50 1.25
62 Kenneth Faried .60 1.50
63 Jimmy Butler 1.50 4.00
64 Myles Turner .75 2.00
65 Dwyane Wade 1.50 4.00
66 Enes Kanter .50 1.25
67 Nikola Jokic 4.00 10.00
68 Doug McDermott .60 1.50
69 Paul George 1.25 3.00
70 Bojan Bogdanovic .60 1.50

2016-17 Court Kings Rookie Portraits
STATED PRINT RUN 175 SER.#'d SETS
*RUBY/75: .6X TO 1.5X BASIC
*SAPPHIRE/25: 1.2X TO 3X BASIC
1 Ben Simmons 4.00 10.00
2 Brandon Ingram 5.00 12.00
3 Jaylen Brown 30.00 80.00
4 Dragan Bender 1.25 3.00
5 Kris Dunn 2.00 5.00
6 Buddy Hield 4.00 10.00
7 Jamal Murray 10.00 25.00
8 Marquese Chriss 1.50 4.00
9 Jakob Poeltl 2.50 6.00
10 Thon Maker 1.50 4.00
11 Domantas Sabonis 8.00 20.00
12 Taurean Prince 1.50 4.00
13 Denzel Valentine 1.25 3.00
14 Wade Baldwin IV 1.25 3.00
15 Henry Ellenson 1.25 3.00
16 Malik Beasley 2.50 6.00
17 Isaiah Whitehead 1.25 3.00
18 Demetrius Jackson 1.25 3.00
19 Brice Johnson 1.25 3.00
20 Damian Jones 1.25 3.00
21 Tyler Ulis 1.50 4.00
22 Deyonta Davis 1.25 3.00
23 Skal Labissiere 1.25 3.00
24 Dejounte Murray 6.00 15.00
25 Malachi Richardson 1.25 3.00
26 Ivica Zubac 3.00 8.00
27 A.J. Hammons 1.25 3.00
28 Diamond Stone 1.25 3.00
29 Kay Felder 1.25 3.00
30 Patrick McCaw 1.25 3.00

2016-17 Court Kings Sketches and Swatches
PRINT RUNS B/WN 16-199 COPIES PER
NO PRICING ON QTY 16
EXCHANGE DEADLINE 5/30/2018
*PRIME/25: .6X TO 1.5X BASIC
3 Rod Strickland/199 4.00 10.00
4 Karl-Anthony Towns/60 EXCH 12.00 30.00
5 Kyrie Irving/60 50.00 120.00
8 Cedric Maxwell/199 5.00 12.00
9 Christian Laettner/60 6.00 15.00
10 Alvan Adams/149 5.00 12.00
11 Festus Ezeli/149 4.00 10.00
13 Bill Laimbeer/199 6.00 15.00
15 Andrew Wiggins/60 20.00 50.00
16 Glen Rice/125 6.00 15.00
17 Grant Hill/60 20.00 50.00
18 Shabazz Muhammad/75 4.00 10.00
19 Bernard King/60 8.00 20.00
20 Jusuf Nurkic/65 5.00 12.00
21 Patrick Ewing/60 50.00 120.00
22 Carmelo Anthony/60 30.00 80.00
25 Dirk Nowitzki/60 75.00 200.00
26 Draymond Green/26 25.00 60.00
27 Rodney Stuckey/35 4.00 10.00
28 Robert Covington/199 5.00 12.00
29 Zach LaVine/75 40.00 100.00
30 Larry Bird/60 75.00 200.00
31 Kevin Durant/60 EXCH 100.00 250.00
32 Tom Chambers/125 5.00 12.00
33 Kristaps Porzingis/75 20.00 50.00
34 Mark Price/199 6.00 15.00
35 Robert Parish/55 8.00 20.00
36 Paul Millsap/75 5.00 12.00
37 Jordan Adams/199 4.00 10.00
38 Dwight Powell/199 4.00 10.00
39 Matthew Dellavedova/199 5.00 12.00
40 Kobe Bryant/60 1,000.00 2,000.00

2016-17 Court Kings Vintage Materials
PRINT RUNS B/WN 49-149 COPIES PER
*PRIME/25: .75X TO 2X BASIC
1 Grant Hill/149 4.00 10.00
2 Mark Price/149 3.00 8.00
3 Larry Nance/149 2.00 5.00
4 Danny Manning/75 2.50 6.00
5 Dan Majerle/129 2.50 6.00
6 Rafer Alston/149 2.00 5.00
7 Herb Williams/149 2.00 5.00
8 Kenny Anderson/149 2.50 6.00
9 Tom Chambers/49 2.50 6.00
10 Shane Battier/149 2.50 6.00
11 Kenny Smith/149 2.50 6.00
12 Chauncey Billups/149 3.00 8.00
13 Scottie Pippen/149 5.00 12.00
14 Hakeem Olajuwon/149 6.00 15.00
15 Clyde Drexler/149 5.00 12.00
16 Dan Issel/149 4.00 10.00
17 Chris Mullin/49 3.00 8.00
18 Arvydas Sabonis/149 2.50 6.00
19 Robert Parish/149 4.00 10.00
20 Kobe Bryant/149 8.00 20.00

2017-18 Court Kings
1 Aaron Gordon .50 1.25
2 Al Horford .50 1.25
3 Andre Drummond .40 1.00
4 Andrew Wiggins .60 1.50
5 Anthony Davis 1.25 3.00
6 Avery Bradley .30 .75
7 Ben Simmons .50 1.25
8 Blake Griffin .50 1.25
9 Bradley Beal .60 1.50
10 Brandon Ingram .60 1.50
11 Brook Lopez .40 1.00
12 Buddy Hield .50 1.25
13 C.J. McCollum .50 1.25
14 Carmelo Anthony .75 2.00
15 Chandler Parsons .30 .75
16 Chris Paul .75 2.00
17 Damian Lillard 1.25 3.00
18 D'Angelo Russell .40 1.00
19 Danilo Gallinari .40 1.00
20 Dario Saric .40 1.00
21 DeAndre Bembry .30 .75
22 DeAndre Jordan .40 1.00
23 DeMar DeRozan .60 1.50
24 DeMarcus Cousins .40 1.00
25 Dennis Schroder .40 1.00
26 Derrick Favors .30 .75
27 Derrick Rose .75 2.00
28 Devin Booker 1.25 3.00
29 Dion Waiters .30 .75
30 Dirk Nowitzki 1.25 3.00
31 Draymond Green .60 1.50
32 Dwight Howard .60 1.50
33 Dwyane Wade 1.00 2.50
34 Enes Kanter .40 1.00
35 Eric Bledsoe .40 1.00
36 Eric Gordon .40 1.00
37 Evan Turner .30 .75
38 George Hill .30 .75
39 Giannis Antetokounmpo 2.50 6.00
40 Goran Dragic .40 1.00
41 Gordon Hayward .40 1.00
42 Hassan Whiteside .40 1.00
43 Isaiah Thomas .40 1.00
44 JJ Redick .50 1.25
45 Jabari Parker .30 .75
46 Jamal Murray .75 2.00
47 James Harden 1.00 2.50
48 Jaylen Brown 1.25 3.00
49 Jeff Teague .30 .75
50 Jeremy Lin .75 2.00
51 Jimmy Butler .75 2.00
52 Joakim Noah .30 .75
53 Joel Embiid 1.00 2.50
54 John Wall .60 1.50
55 Jrue Holiday .60 1.50
56 Julius Randle .50 1.25
57 Karl-Anthony Towns .75 2.00
58 Kawhi Leonard 1.25 3.00
59 Kemba Walker .40 1.00
60 Kevin Durant 2.00 5.00
61 Kevin Love .50 1.25
62 Khris Middleton .60 1.50
63 Klay Thompson 1.25 3.00
64 Kris Dunn .30 .75
65 Kristaps Porzingis .60 1.50
66 Kyle Lowry .50 1.25
67 Kyrie Irving 1.00 2.50
68 LaMarcus Aldridge .50 1.25
69 LeBron James 4.00 10.00
70 Malcolm Brogdon .40 1.00
71 Marc Gasol .50 1.25
72 Markieff Morris .30 .75
73 Marquese Chriss .30 .75
74 Mike Conley .40 1.00
75 Myles Turner .50 1.25
76 Nerlens Noel .30 .75
77 Nicolas Batum .30 .75
78 Nikola Jokic 3.00 8.00
79 Nikola Mirotic .30 .75
80 Nikola Vucevic .40 1.00
81 Otto Porter Jr. .40 1.00
82 Pascal Siakam 1.00 2.50
83 Pau Gasol .75 2.00
84 Paul George .75 2.00
85 Paul Millsap .40 1.00
86 Rodney Hood .30 .75
87 Rudy Gay .40 1.00
88 Rudy Gobert .60 1.50
89 Russell Westbrook .75 2.00
90 Serge Ibaka .40 1.00
91 Stephen Curry 4.00 10.00
92 Taurean Prince .30 .75
93 Terrence Ross .30 .75
94 Thaddeus Young .30 .75
95 Tobias Harris .40 1.00
96 Trevor Booker .30 .75
97 Victor Oladipo .40 1.00
98 Vince Carter 1.00 2.50
99 Wesley Matthews .30 .75
100 Zach LaVine .75 2.00
101 Markelle Fultz RC 1.50 4.00
102 Lonzo Ball RC 2.50 6.00
103 Donovan Mitchell RC 20.00 50.00
104 Luke Kennard RC 1.25 3.00
105 Justin Patton RC .60 1.50
106 D.J. Wilson RC .60 1.50
107 T.J. Leaf RC .60 1.50
108 Frank Ntilikina RC .75 2.00
109 Jonathan Isaac RC 1.50 4.00
110 De'Aaron Fox RC 5.00 12.00
111 Dennis Smith Jr. RC .75 2.00
112 Zach Collins RC 1.00 2.50
113 Terrance Ferguson RC .60 1.50
114 Bam Adebayo RC 4.00 10.00
115 Dwayne Bacon RC .60 1.50
116 Frank Mason III RC .60 1.50
117 John Collins RC 1.50 4.00
118 Harry Giles RC .60 1.50
119 Malik Monk RC 2.50 6.00
120 Josh Jackson RC .75 2.00
121 Jayson Tatum RC 40.00 100.00
122 Jarrett Allen RC 1.50 4.00
123 OG Anunoby RC 3.00 8.00
124 Tyler Dorsey RC .60 1.50
125 Frank Jackson RC .60 1.50
126 Tony Bradley RC .60 1.50
127 Kyle Kuzma RC 2.50 6.00
128 Jordan Bell RC .60 1.50
129 Sindarius Thornwell RC .60 1.50
130 Caleb Swanigan RC .60 1.50
131 Tyler Lydon RC .60 1.50
132 Derrick White RC 2.50 6.00
133 Josh Hart RC 1.50 4.00
134 Markelle Fultz 2.50 6.00
135 Lonzo Ball 4.00 10.00
136 Donovan Mitchell 30.00 80.00
137 Luke Kennard 2.00 5.00
138 Justin Patton 1.00 2.50
139 D.J. Wilson 1.00 2.50
140 T.J. Leaf 1.00 2.50
141 Frank Ntilikina 1.25 3.00
142 Jonathan Isaac 2.50 6.00
143 De'Aaron Fox 8.00 20.00
144 Dennis Smith Jr. 1.25 3.00
145 Zach Collins 1.50 4.00
146 Terrance Ferguson 1.00 2.50
147 Bam Adebayo 6.00 15.00
148 Dwayne Bacon 1.00 2.50
149 Frank Mason III 1.00 2.50
150 John Collins 2.50 6.00
151 Harry Giles 1.00 2.50
152 Malik Monk 4.00 10.00
153 Josh Jackson 1.25 3.00
154 Jayson Tatum 60.00 150.00
155 Jarrett Allen 2.50 6.00
156 OG Anunoby 5.00 12.00
157 Tyler Dorsey 1.00 2.50
158 Frank Jackson 1.00 2.50
159 Tony Bradley 1.00 2.50
160 Kyle Kuzma 4.00 10.00
161 Jordan Bell 1.00 2.50
162 Sindarius Thornwell 1.00 2.50
163 Caleb Swanigan 1.00 2.50
164 Tyler Lydon 1.00 2.50
165 Derrick White 4.00 10.00
166 Josh Hart 2.50 6.00
167 Markelle Fultz 4.00 10.00
168 Lonzo Ball 6.00 15.00
169 Donovan Mitchell 50.00 120.00
170 Luke Kennard 3.00 8.00
171 Justin Patton 1.50 4.00
172 D.J. Wilson 1.50 4.00
173 T.J. Leaf 1.50 4.00
174 Frank Ntilikina 2.00 5.00
175 Jonathan Isaac 4.00 10.00
176 De'Aaron Fox 12.00 30.00
177 Dennis Smith Jr. 2.00 5.00
178 Zach Collins 2.50 6.00
179 Terrance Ferguson 1.50 4.00
180 Bam Adebayo 10.00 25.00
181 Dwayne Bacon 1.50 4.00
182 Frank Mason III 1.50 4.00
183 John Collins 4.00 10.00
184 Harry Giles 1.50 4.00
185 Malik Monk 6.00 15.00
186 Josh Jackson 2.00 5.00
187 Jayson Tatum 100.00 250.00
188 Jarrett Allen 4.00 10.00
189 OG Anunoby 8.00 20.00
190 Tyler Dorsey 1.50 4.00
191 Frank Jackson 1.50 4.00
192 Tony Bradley 1.50 4.00
193 Kyle Kuzma 6.00 15.00
194 Jordan Bell 1.50 4.00
195 Sindarius Thornwell 1.50 4.00
196 Caleb Swanigan 1.50 4.00
197 Tyler Lydon 1.50 4.00
198 Derrick White 6.00 15.00
199 Josh Hart 4.00 10.00
200 Markelle Fultz 15.00 40.00
201 Lonzo Ball 25.00 60.00
202 Donovan Mitchell 200.00 500.00
203 Luke Kennard 12.00 30.00
204 Justin Patton 6.00 15.00
205 D.J. Wilson 6.00 15.00
206 T.J. Leaf 6.00 15.00
207 Frank Ntilikina 8.00 20.00
208 Jonathan Isaac 15.00 40.00
209 De'Aaron Fox 50.00 125.00
210 Dennis Smith Jr. 8.00 20.00
211 Zach Collins 10.00 25.00
212 Terrance Ferguson 6.00 15.00
213 Bam Adebayo 40.00 100.00
214 Dwayne Bacon 6.00 15.00
215 Frank Mason III 6.00 15.00
216 John Collins 15.00 40.00
217 Harry Giles 6.00 15.00
218 Malik Monk 25.00 60.00
219 Josh Jackson 8.00 20.00
220 Jayson Tatum 500.00 1,000.00
221 Jarrett Allen 15.00 40.00
222 OG Anunoby 30.00 80.00
223 Tyler Dorsey 6.00 15.00
224 Frank Jackson 6.00 15.00
225 Tony Bradley 6.00 15.00
226 Kyle Kuzma 25.00 60.00
227 Jordan Bell 6.00 15.00
228 Sindarius Thornwell 6.00 15.00
229 Caleb Swanigan 6.00 15.00
230 Tyler Lydon 6.00 15.00
231 Derrick White 25.00 60.00
232 Josh Hart 15.00 40.00

2017-18 Court Kings Aurora
1 Stephen Curry 300.00 600.00
2 Isaiah Thomas 5.00 12.00
3 Kawhi Leonard 60.00 150.00
4 James Harden 25.00 60.00
5 Russell Westbrook 25.00 60.00
6 LeBron James 400.00 800.00
7 Giannis Antetokounmpo 125.00 300.00
8 Kevin Durant 60.00 150.00
9 Damian Lillard 30.00 80.00
10 Anthony Davis 40.00 100.00
11 Kyrie Irving 40.00 100.00
12 Dirk Nowitzki 60.00 150.00
13 John Wall 20.00 50.00
14 DeMar DeRozan 20.00 50.00
15 Kristaps Porzingis 15.00 40.00
16 De'Aaron Fox 60.00 150.00
17 Markelle Fultz 12.00 30.00
18 Lonzo Ball 50.00 120.00
19 Jayson Tatum 400.00 800.00
20 Dennis Smith Jr. 5.00 12.00

2017-18 Court Kings Blank Slate
1 Kevin Durant 300.00 600.00
2 LeBron James 2,000.00 4,000.00
3 James Harden 125.00 300.00
4 Russell Westbrook 125.00 300.00
5 Giannis Antetokounmpo 500.00 1,000.00
6 Kawhi Leonard 150.00 400.00
7 Anthony Davis 200.00 500.00
8 Stephen Curry 1,000.00 2,000.00
9 Kyrie Irving 150.00 400.00
10 Damian Lillard 300.00 600.00
11 Blake Griffin 75.00 200.00
12 Carmelo Anthony 125.00 300.00
13 John Wall 75.00 200.00
14 Dwyane Wade 200.00 500.00
15 Karl-Anthony Towns 75.00 200.00
16 DeMar DeRozan 60.00 150.00
17 Andre Drummond 8.00 20.00
18 DeAndre Jordan 8.00 20.00
19 Kyle Lowry 60.00 150.00
20 Isaiah Thomas 8.00 20.00
21 Marc Gasol 30.00 80.00
22 Andrew Wiggins 60.00 150.00
23 Mike Conley 8.00 20.00
24 Kristaps Porzingis 60.00 150.00
25 Dirk Nowitzki 200.00 500.00
26 Hassan Whiteside 8.00 20.00
27 Klay Thompson 200.00 500.00
28 Rudy Gobert 60.00 150.00
29 Kevin Love 10.00 25.00
30 Kemba Walker 75.00 200.00
31 Pau Gasol 75.00 200.00
32 Devin Booker 200.00 500.00
33 Draymond Green 100.00 250.00
34 DeMarcus Cousins 25.00 60.00
35 LaMarcus Aldridge 25.00 60.00
36 Dennis Schroder 8.00 20.00
37 Bradley Beal 125.00 300.00

2017-18 Court Kings Sapphire
*SAPPHIRE: 1.2X TO 3X BASIC
RANOM INSERTS IN PACKS
STATED PRINT RUN 25 SER.#'d SETS
69 LeBron James 20.00 50.00
91 Stephen Curry 10.00 25.00

2017-18 Court Kings Art Nouveau Jerseys
*SAPPHIRE/25: 1X TO 2.5X BASIC
1 Bam Adebayo 10.00 25.00
2 Lonzo Ball 8.00 20.00
3 Jayson Tatum 8.00 20.00
4 Josh Jackson 2.00 5.00
5 De'Aaron Fox 5.00 12.00
6 Jonathan Isaac 4.00 10.00
7 Frank Ntilikina 2.00 5.00
8 Dennis Smith Jr. 2.00 5.00
9 Zach Collins 2.50 6.00
10 Malik Monk 3.00 8.00
11 Luke Kennard 3.00 8.00
12 Donovan Mitchell 8.00 20.00
13 Markelle Fultz 5.00 12.00
14 Justin Patton 1.50 4.00
15 D.J. Wilson 1.50 4.00
16 T.J. Leaf 1.50 4.00
17 John Collins 4.00 10.00
18 Harry Giles 1.50 4.00
19 Jarrett Allen 1.50 4.00
20 OG Anunoby 8.00 20.00
21 Tyler Lydon 1.50 4.00
22 Caleb Swanigan 1.50 4.00
23 Terrance Ferguson 1.50 4.00
24 Kyle Kuzma 6.00 15.00
25 Tony Bradley 1.50 4.00
26 Derrick White 6.00 15.00
27 Josh Hart 4.00 10.00
28 Frank Jackson 1.50 4.00
29 Tyler Dorsey 1.50 4.00
30 Jordan Bell 1.50 4.00
31 Sindarius Thornwell 1.50 4.00
32 Dwayne Bacon 1.50 4.00
33 Ivan Rabb 1.50 4.00
34 Semi Ojeleye 2.00 5.00
35 Frank Mason III 1.50 4.00

2017-18 Court Kings Art Nouveau Jumbo Jerseys
STATED PRINT RUN 99 SER.#'d SETS
1 Bam Adebayo 12.00 30.00
2 Lonzo Ball 10.00 25.00
3 Jayson Tatum 6.00 15.00
4 Josh Jackson 2.50 6.00
5 De'Aaron Fox 5.00 12.00
6 Jonathan Isaac 5.00 12.00
7 Frank Ntilikina 2.50 6.00
8 Dennis Smith Jr. 2.50 6.00
9 Zach Collins 3.00 8.00
10 Malik Monk 4.00 10.00
11 Luke Kennard 4.00 10.00
12 Donovan Mitchell 8.00 20.00

13 Markelle Fultz 5.00 12.00
14 Justin Patton 2.00 5.00
15 D.J. Wilson 2.00 5.00
16 T.J. Leaf 2.00 5.00
17 John Collins 5.00 12.00
18 Harry Giles 2.00 5.00
19 Jarrett Allen 5.00 12.00
20 OG Anunoby 10.00 25.00
21 Tyler Lydon 2.00 5.00
22 Caleb Swanigan 2.00 5.00
23 Terrance Ferguson 2.00 5.00
24 Kyle Kuzma 8.00 20.00
25 Tony Bradley 2.00 5.00
26 Derrick White 8.00 20.00
28 Frank Jackson 2.00 5.00
29 Tyler Dorsey 2.00 5.00
30 Jordan Bell 2.00 5.00
31 Sindarius Thornwell 2.00 5.00
32 Dwayne Bacon 2.00 5.00
33 Ivan Rabb 2.00 5.00
34 Semi Ojeleye 2.50 6.00
35 Frank Mason III 2.00 5.00

2017-18 Court Kings Artistic Endeavors Jerseys

STATED PRINT RUN 299 SER.#'d SETS
*PRIME/25: .75X TO 2X BASIC
1 Damian Lillard 4.00 10.00
2 Anthony Davis 4.00 10.00
3 C.J. McCollum 2.50 6.00
4 Dwyane Wade 5.00 12.00
5 James Harden 5.00 12.00
6 Aaron Gordon 2.50 6.00
7 DeAndre Jordan 2.00 5.00
8 Jabari Parker 1.50 4.00
9 Ryan Anderson 1.50 4.00
10 DeMarcus Cousins 2.00 5.00
11 Paul George 4.00 10.00
12 Karl-Anthony Towns 4.00 10.00
13 Eric Bledsoe 2.00 5.00
14 Carmelo Anthony 4.00 10.00
15 Bradley Beal 3.00 8.00
16 Harrison Barnes 2.00 5.00
17 Devin Booker 6.00 15.00
18 Malik Beasley 2.00 5.00
19 Trevor Ariza 1.50 4.00
20 DeMar DeRozan 3.00 8.00
21 George Hill 2.00 5.00
22 Andrew Wiggins 3.00 8.00
23 Dirk Nowitzki 6.00 15.00
24 Goran Dragic 2.00 5.00
25 Dario Saric 2.00 5.00
26 Draymond Green 3.00 8.00
27 Taurean Prince 1.50 4.00
28 Kawhi Leonard 6.00 15.00
29 Kemba Walker 2.00 5.00
30 Kyle Lowry 2.50 6.00
31 Willie Cauley-Stein 1.50 4.00
32 Jeremy Lin 4.00 10.00
33 Wesley Matthews 1.50 4.00
34 John Wall 3.00 8.00
35 Al Horford 2.50 6.00
36 Blake Griffin 2.50 6.00
37 Dante Exum 1.50 4.00
38 Patty Mills 2.50 6.00
39 Buddy Hield 2.50 6.00
40 Klay Thompson 6.00 15.00
41 Brook Lopez 2.00 5.00
42 Rodney Hood 1.50 4.00
43 LeBron James 12.00 30.00
44 Giannis Antetokounmpo 12.00 30.00
45 Elfrid Payton 1.50 4.00

2017-18 Court Kings Box Topper Autographs

EXCHANGE DEADLINE 6/6/2019
1 Kyrie Irving 75.00 200.00
2 Karl-Anthony Towns 40.00 100.00
3 Nikola Jokic 200.00 500.00
4 Aaron Gordon 12.00 30.00
5 Harrison Barnes 12.00 30.00
6 D'Angelo Russell 12.00 30.00
7 Eric Gordon 12.00 30.00
8 Joel Embiid 100.00 250.00
9 Tim Hardaway Jr. 5.00 12.00
10 Gordon Hayward 12.00 30.00
11 Kristaps Porzingis 20.00 50.00
12 Pau Gasol 40.00 100.00
13 Kevin Durant 125.00 300.00
15 Shaquille O'Neal 125.00 300.00
16 Damian Lillard 75.00 200.00
17 Ben Wallace 40.00 100.00
18 Malcolm Brogdon 5.00 12.00
19 Dario Saric 5.00 12.00
20 Jeff Teague 4.00 10.00
21 Adrian Dantley 6.00 15.00
22 George Gervin 15.00 40.00
23 Bill Walton 15.00 40.00
24 Kobe Bryant 1,000.00 2,000.00
25 Eddie Jones 12.00 30.00

2017-18 Court Kings Dieci Migliore

1 Russell Westbrook 4.00 10.00
2 James Harden 5.00 12.00
3 Kawhi Leonard 6.00 15.00
4 LeBron James 15.00 40.00
5 Kevin Durant 10.00 25.00
6 Giannis Antetokounmpo 12.00 30.00
7 Isaiah Thomas 2.00 5.00
8 Anthony Davis 6.00 15.00
9 Stephen Curry 20.00 50.00
10 Damian Lillard 6.00 15.00

2017-18 Court Kings Emerging Artists

1 Nerlens Noel .75 2.00
2 Devin Booker 3.00 8.00
3 Marcus Smart 1.25 3.00
4 Mario Hezonja .75 2.00
5 Brandon Ingram 1.50 4.00
6 Dario Saric 1.00 2.50
7 Nikola Jokic 8.00 20.00
8 Jaylen Brown 3.00 8.00
9 Karl-Anthony Towns 2.00 5.00
10 Jamal Murray 2.00 5.00
11 Jabari Parker .75 2.00
12 Julius Randle 1.25 3.00
13 Andrew Wiggins 1.50 4.00
14 Emmanuel Mudiay .75 2.00
15 Malcolm Brogdon 1.00 2.50
16 Buddy Hield 1.25 3.00
17 Ben Simmons 1.25 3.00
18 Yogi Ferrell .75 2.00
19 Taurean Prince .75 2.00
20 Caris LeVert 1.25 3.00
21 Denzel Valentine .75 2.00
22 Kay Felder .75 2.00
23 Patrick McCaw .75 2.00
24 Dejounte Murray 1.25 3.00
25 Pascal Siakam 2.50 6.00
26 Juan Hernangomez 1.25 3.00
27 Kristaps Porzingis 1.50 4.00
28 Marquese Chriss .75 2.00
29 Willy Hernangomez .75 2.00
30 Myles Turner 1.25 3.00
31 Justise Winslow .75 2.00
32 Bobby Portis .75 2.00
33 Joel Embiid 2.50 6.00
34 Aaron Gordon 1.25 3.00

2017-18 Court Kings Fresh Paint Autographs I

EXCHANGE DEADLINE 6/6/2019
*AUTO/200: .5X TO 1.2X BASIC
*AUTO/100: .6X TO 1.5X BASIC
1 Markelle Fultz 15.00 40.00
2 Lonzo Ball 50.00 120.00
3 Jayson Tatum 200.00 500.00
4 Josh Jackson 3.00 8.00
5 De'Aaron Fox 40.00 100.00
6 Jonathan Isaac 6.00 15.00
8 Frank Ntilikina 3.00 8.00
9 Dennis Smith Jr. 3.00 8.00
10 Zach Collins 4.00 10.00
11 Malik Monk 8.00 20.00
12 Luke Kennard 6.00 15.00
13 Donovan Mitchell 75.00 200.00
14 Bam Adebayo 30.00 80.00
15 Justin Jackson 2.50 6.00
16 Justin Patton 2.50 6.00
17 D.J. Wilson 2.50 6.00
18 T.J. Leaf 2.50 6.00
19 John Collins 15.00 40.00
20 Harry Giles 2.50 6.00
21 Jarrett Allen 12.00 30.00
22 OG Anunoby 12.00 30.00
23 Tyler Lydon 2.50 6.00
24 Caleb Swanigan 2.50 6.00
25 Terrance Ferguson 2.50 6.00
26 Kyle Kuzma 10.00 25.00
27 Tony Bradley 2.50 6.00
28 Derrick White 10.00 25.00
29 Josh Hart 12.00 30.00
30 Frank Jackson 2.50 6.00
FP1LAM Lauri Markkanen 25.00 60.00

2017-18 Court Kings Fresh Paint Dual Autographs

STATED PRINT RUN 50 COPIES PER
EXCHANGE DEADLINE 6/6/2019
1 Ball/Fultz 30.00 80.00
2 Tatum/Jackson 150.00 400.00
3 Fox/Monk 60.00 150.00
4 Smith Jr./Ntilikina 10.00 25.00
5 Tatum/Kennard 125.00 300.00

2017-18 Court Kings Heir Apparent Autographs

STATED PRINT RUN 75 COPIES PER
EXCHANGE DEADLINE 6/6/2019
1 Markelle Fultz 100.00 250.00
2 Lonzo Ball 100.00 250.00
3 Jayson Tatum 400.00 800.00
4 De'Aaron Fox 125.00 300.00
5 Frank Ntilikina 50.00 120.00

2017-18 Court Kings Panoramics Box Topper

1 Anthony Davis 5.00 12.00
2 John Wall 2.50 6.00
3 Stephen Curry 60.00 150.00
4 Giannis Antetokounmpo 40.00 100.00
5 Russell Westbrook 3.00 8.00
6 Karl-Anthony Towns 3.00 8.00
7 Kevin Durant 8.00 20.00
8 Blake Griffin 2.00 5.00
9 Dirk Nowitzki 5.00 12.00
10 Devin Booker 5.00 12.00
11 LeBron James 40.00 100.00
12 Dennis Schroder 1.50 4.00
13 DeMar DeRozan 2.50 6.00
14 Damian Lillard 5.00 12.00
15 Jeremy Lin 3.00 8.00
16 James Harden 4.00 10.00
17 Kawhi Leonard 5.00 12.00
18 Goran Dragic 1.50 4.00
19 Joel Embiid 4.00 10.00
20 Rodney Hood 1.25 3.00
21 C.J. McCollum 2.00 5.00
22 Mike Conley 1.50 4.00
23 Malcolm Brogdon 1.50 4.00
24 Kemba Walker 1.50 4.00
25 Bradley Beal 2.50 6.00

2017-18 Court Kings Performance Art Jerseys

PRINT RUNS B/WN 85-299 COPIES PER
*PRIME/25: .75X TO 2X BASIC
1 Blake Griffin/299 2.50 6.00
2 Damian Lillard/299 6.00 15.00
3 Avery Bradley/149 1.50 4.00
4 C.J. McCollum/299 2.50 6.00
5 Jimmy Butler/299 4.00 10.00
6 Klay Thompson/299 6.00 15.00
7 LaMarcus Aldridge/299 2.50 6.00
8 Jamal Crawford/299 2.50 6.00
9 Brook Lopez/299 2.00 5.00
10 Frank Kaminsky/299 1.50 4.00
11 Clint Capela/299 2.00 5.00
12 Courtney Lee/299 1.50 4.00
13 Arron Afflalo/99 1.50 4.00
14 Caris LeVert/299 2.50 6.00
15 Boris Diaw/85 2.00 5.00

2017-18 Court Kings Points in the Paint

1 Andre Drummond .75 2.00
2 DeMarcus Cousins .75 2.00
3 Anthony Davis 2.50 6.00
4 Blake Griffin 1.00 2.50
5 Marquese Chriss .60 1.50
6 Marcin Gortat .60 1.50
7 Karl-Anthony Towns 1.50 4.00
8 Kevin Love 1.00 2.50
9 Giannis Antetokounmpo 5.00 12.00
10 Norman Powell 1.00 2.50
11 Michael Kidd-Gilchrist .60 1.50
12 James Harden 2.00 5.00
13 Aaron Gordon 1.00 2.50
14 Justise Winslow .60 1.50
15 Joel Embiid 2.00 5.00
16 Kevin Durant 4.00 10.00
17 Brandon Ingram 1.25 3.00
18 Dirk Nowitzki 2.50 6.00
19 Kawhi Leonard 2.50 6.00
20 LaMarcus Aldridge 1.00 2.50
21 Russell Westbrook 1.50 4.00
22 Marc Gasol 1.00 2.50
23 Pascal Siakam 2.00 5.00
24 Bobby Portis .60 1.50
25 Draymond Green 1.25 3.00
26 Al Horford 1.00 2.50

2017-18 Court Kings Portraits

STATED PRINT RUN 175 SER.#'d SETS
*RUBY/65: .75X TO 2X BASIC
*SAPPHIRE/25: 1.2X TO 3X BASIC
1 Dennis Schroder .60 1.50
2 Taurean Prince .50 1.25
3 Jeremy Lin 1.25 3.00
4 Trevor Booker .50 1.25
5 Kemba Walker .60 1.50
6 Michael Kidd-Gilchrist .50 1.25
7 Isaiah Thomas .60 1.50
8 Jaylen Brown 2.00 5.00
9 Al Horford .75 2.00
10 Denzel Valentine .50 1.25
11 Dwyane Wade 1.50 4.00
12 Robin Lopez .50 1.25
13 Kevin Love .75 2.00
14 Kyrie Irving 1.50 4.00
15 LeBron James 6.00 15.00
16 Dirk Nowitzki 2.00 5.00
17 Harrison Barnes .60 1.50
18 Juan Hernangomez .75 2.00
19 Nikola Jokic 5.00 12.00
20 Reggie Jackson .60 1.50
21 Tobias Harris .60 1.50
22 Kevin Durant 3.00 8.00
23 Klay Thompson 2.00 5.00
24 Stephen Curry 6.00 15.00
25 James Harden 1.50 4.00
26 Eric Gordon .60 1.50
27 Chris Paul 1.25 3.00
28 Myles Turner .75 2.00
29 Thaddeus Young .50 1.25
30 Austin Rivers .60 1.50
31 Blake Griffin .75 2.00
32 DeAndre Jordan .60 1.50
33 Brandon Ingram 1.00 2.50
34 Jordan Clarkson .75 2.00
35 Julius Randle .75 2.00
36 Marc Gasol .75 2.00
37 Mike Conley .60 1.50
38 Dion Waiters .50 1.25
39 Goran Dragic .60 1.50
40 Giannis Antetokounmpo 4.00 10.00
41 Khris Middleton 1.00 2.50
42 Andrew Wiggins 1.00 2.50
43 Jimmy Butler 1.25 3.00
44 Karl-Anthony Towns 1.25 3.00
45 Anthony Davis 2.00 5.00
46 DeMarcus Cousins .60 1.50
47 Carmelo Anthony 1.25 3.00
48 Kristaps Porzingis 1.00 2.50
49 Willy Hernangomez .50 1.25
50 Paul George 1.25 3.00
51 Russell Westbrook 1.25 3.00
52 Aaron Gordon .75 2.00
53 Elfrid Payton .50 1.25
54 Ben Simmons .75 2.00
55 Joel Embiid 1.50 4.00
56 Devin Booker 2.00 5.00
57 Marquese Chriss .50 1.25
58 C.J. McCollum .75 2.00
59 Damian Lillard 2.00 5.00
60 Buddy Hield .75 2.00
61 Willie Cauley-Stein .50 1.25
62 Kawhi Leonard 2.00 5.00
63 Patty Mills .75 2.00
64 DeMar DeRozan 1.00 2.50
65 Kyle Lowry .75 2.00
66 Rodney Hood .50 1.25
67 Rudy Gobert 1.00 2.50
68 John Wall 1.00 2.50
69 Otto Porter Jr. .60 1.50
70 Bradley Beal 1.00 2.50

2017-18 Court Kings Progressions Box Topper

1 Kevin Durant 4.00 10.00
2 Kemba Walker .75 2.00
3 Dwyane Wade 2.00 5.00
4 Harrison Barnes .75 2.00
5 J.R. Smith .75 2.00
6 James Harden 2.00 5.00
7 DeMarcus Cousins .75 2.00
8 Andre Iguodala 1.00 2.50
9 Pau Gasol 1.50 4.00
10 Kevin Love 1.00 2.50
11 Anthony Davis 2.50 6.00
12 Kyle Lowry 1.00 2.50
13 Markieff Morris .60 1.50
14 Marcin Gortat .60 1.50
15 Eric Bledsoe .75 2.00
16 David West .75 2.00
17 Tracy McGrady 1.50 4.00
18 Ben Wallace .75 2.00
19 Shawn Marion .75 2.00
20 Latrell Sprewell 1.25 3.00
21 Kareem Abdul-Jabbar 3.00 8.00
22 Grant Hill 1.50 4.00
23 Amare Stoudemire 1.00 2.50
24 Damon Stoudamire 1.00 2.50
25 Chris Webber 1.50 4.00

2017-18 Court Kings Renaissance Men

1 Allen Iverson 3.00 8.00
2 Bill Russell 4.00 10.00
3 Bill Walton 2.00 5.00
4 Chauncey Billups 1.50 4.00
5 Clyde Drexler 2.00 5.00
6 Dave Cowens 2.00 5.00
7 David Robinson 2.50 6.00
8 Bob Pettit 1.25 3.00
9 Elgin Baylor 2.00 5.00
10 Elvin Hayes 1.50 4.00
11 George Gervin 2.00 5.00
12 George Mikan 3.00 8.00
13 Hakeem Olajuwon 2.50 6.00
14 Isiah Thomas 2.00 5.00
15 James Worthy 1.50 4.00
16 Jerry West 2.50 6.00
17 John Havlicek 2.50 6.00
18 John Stockton 2.50 6.00
19 Julius Erving 3.00 8.00
20 Kareem Abdul-Jabbar 4.00 10.00
21 Karl Malone 2.50 6.00
22 Kevin McHale 1.50 4.00
23 Kobe Bryant 10.00 25.00
24 Larry Bird 12.00 30.00
25 Lenny Wilkens 1.50 4.00
26 Magic Johnson 5.00 12.00
27 Lou Hudson .75 2.00
28 Nate Archibald 1.50 4.00
29 Oscar Robertson 2.50 6.00
30 Patrick Ewing 2.00 5.00
31 Pete Maravich 3.00 8.00
32 Reggie Miller 2.50 6.00
33 Rick Barry 1.50 4.00
34 Scottie Pippen 3.00 8.00
35 Shaquille O'Neal 4.00 10.00
36 Tim Duncan 3.00 8.00
37 Walt Frazier 2.00 5.00
38 Willis Reed 2.00 5.00
39 Wilt Chamberlain 4.00 10.00
40 Yao Ming 2.50 6.00

2017-18 Court Kings Rookie Portraits

STATED PRINT RUN 175 SER.#'d SETS
*RUBY/65: .6X TO 1.5X BASIC
*SAPPHIRE/25: 1.2X TO 3X BASIC
1 Markelle Fultz 1.50 4.00
2 Lonzo Ball 6.00 15.00
3 Jayson Tatum 50.00 120.00
4 Josh Jackson .75 2.00
5 De'Aaron Fox 5.00 12.00
6 Jonathan Isaac 1.50 4.00
7 Lauri Markkanen 6.00 15.00
8 Frank Ntilikina .75 2.00
9 Dennis Smith Jr. .75 2.00
10 Zach Collins 1.00 2.50
11 Malik Monk 2.50 6.00
12 Luke Kennard 1.25 3.00
13 Donovan Mitchell 12.00 30.00
14 Bam Adebayo 4.00 10.00
15 Justin Jackson .60 1.50
16 D.J. Wilson .60 1.50
17 John Collins 1.50 4.00
18 Harry Giles .60 1.50
19 Jarrett Allen 1.50 4.00
20 OG Anunoby 3.00 8.00
21 Caleb Swanigan .60 1.50
22 Terrance Ferguson .60 1.50
23 Kyle Kuzma 2.50 6.00
24 Frank Jackson .60 1.50
25 Sindarius Thornwell .60 1.50
26 Ivan Rabb .60 1.50
27 Ike Anigbogu .60 1.50
28 Tyler Dorsey .60 1.50
29 Josh Hart 1.50 4.00
30 Jordan Bell .60 1.50

2017-18 Court Kings Sketches and Swatches

PRINT RUNS B/WN 49-399 COPIES PER
EXCHANGE DEADLINE 6/6/2019
1 Isaiah Thomas/60 4.00 10.00
2 Kobe Bryant/99 1,000.00 2,000.00
3 Kyrie Irving/49 75.00 200.00
4 Gordon Hayward/99 15.00 40.00
5 Harrison Barnes/299 4.00 10.00
6 Gorgui Dieng/314 3.00 8.00
7 Jordan Clarkson/363 12.00 30.00
8 Jusuf Nurkic/299 4.00 10.00
9 Karl-Anthony Towns/199 20.00 50.00
11 Andre Drummond/152 4.00 10.00
12 Justin Holiday/399 3.00 8.00
13 Marcus Smart/200 5.00 12.00
14 Tobias Harris/243 4.00 10.00
15 Doug McDermott/299 3.00 8.00
16 Vince Carter/169 40.00 100.00
17 DeMarre Carroll/299 3.00 8.00
18 Caris LeVert/399 5.00 12.00
19 Damian Lillard/49 40.00 100.00
20 C.J. McCollum/192 5.00 12.00
21 Walter Berry/282 3.00 8.00
22 Detlef Schrempf/399 5.00 12.00
23 Danny Manning/299 4.00 10.00
24 Rod Strickland/299 4.00 10.00
25 Anfernee Hardaway/78 40.00 100.00
26 Andrei Kirilenko/344 4.00 10.00
27 Arvydas Sabonis/299 10.00 25.00
28 Sean Kilpatrick/399 3.00 8.00
29 T.J. Warren/299 4.00 10.00
30 Zach LaVine/146 25.00 60.00
31 Thaddeus Young/186 3.00 8.00
32 Tim Hardaway Jr./299 4.00 10.00
33 Markelle Fultz/85 30.00 80.00
34 Lonzo Ball/299 40.00 100.00
35 Jayson Tatum/299 200.00 500.00
36 De'Aaron Fox/399 40.00 100.00
37 Jonathan Isaac/399 8.00 20.00
38 Dennis Smith Jr./299 4.00 10.00
40 Donovan Mitchell/399 100.00 250.00

2018-19 Court Kings

1 Aaron Gordon .50 1.25
2 Russell Westbrook .75 2.00
3 John Collins .50 1.25
4 Rudy Gobert .60 1.50
5 LaMarcus Aldridge .50 1.25
6 Andre Drummond .40 1.00
7 Danilo Gallinari .40 1.00
8 Kawhi Leonard 1.25 3.00
9 Buddy Hield .50 1.25
10 Caris LeVert .50 1.25
11 Evan Fournier .40 1.00
12 Dennis Schroder .40 1.00
13 Jeremy Lin .75 2.00
14 Joe Ingles .40 1.00
15 Rudy Gay .50 1.25
16 Reggie Jackson .40 1.00
17 Lou Williams .40 1.00
18 Serge Ibaka .40 1.00
19 De'Aaron Fox 1.00 2.50
20 D'Angelo Russell .50 1.25
21 Bradley Beal .60 1.50
22 Steven Adams .40 1.00
23 Mike Conley .40 1.00
24 Ricky Rubio .40 1.00
25 Pau Gasol .75 2.00
26 Zach LaVine .75 2.00
27 Kevin Durant 2.00 5.00
28 Kyle Lowry .50 1.25
29 Willie Cauley-Stein .30 .75
30 Joe Harris .30 .75
31 John Wall .60 1.50
32 Damian Lillard 1.25 3.00
33 Marc Gasol .50 1.25
34 Giannis Antetokounmpo 2.50 6.00
35 Anthony Davis 1.25 3.00
36 Kris Dunn .30 .75
37 Stephen Curry 4.00 10.00
38 Joel Embiid 1.25 3.00
39 Devin Booker 1.25 3.00
40 Kristaps Porzingis .60 1.50
41 Dwight Howard .60 1.50
42 CJ McCollum .50 1.25
43 Garrett Temple .30 .75
44 Khris Middleton .50 1.25
45 Jrue Holiday .60 1.50
46 Jabari Parker .30 .75
47 Klay Thompson 1.25 3.00
48 Jimmy Butler .75 2.00
49 T.J. Warren .40 1.00
50 Enes Kanter .40 1.00
51 Otto Porter Jr. .40 1.00
52 Jusuf Nurkic .40 1.00
53 Harrison Barnes .40 1.00
54 Eric Bledsoe .40 1.00
55 Nikola Mirotic .30 .75
56 Lauri Markkanen .75 2.00
57 Draymond Green .60 1.50
58 Ben Simmons .50 1.25
59 Trevor Ariza .30 .75
60 Tim Hardaway Jr. .30 .75
61 Josh Richardson .40 1.00
62 Karl-Anthony Towns .75 2.00
63 Dennis Smith Jr. .30 .75
64 Victor Oladipo .40 1.00
65 James Harden 1.00 2.50
66 Kevin Love .40 1.00
67 LeBron James 4.00 10.00
68 JJ Redick .50 1.25
69 Kemba Walker .50 1.25
70 Jamal Murray 1.00 2.50
71 Goran Dragic .40 1.00
72 Derrick Rose 1.00 2.50
73 DeAndre Jordan .40 1.00
74 Bojan Bogdanovic .40 1.00
75 Chris Paul 1.00 2.50
76 Jordan Clarkson .50 1.25
77 Kyle Kuzma .50 1.25
78 Kyrie Irving 1.25 3.00
79 Jeremy Lamb .30 .75
80 Gary Harris .40 1.00
81 Dwyane Wade 1.00 2.50
82 Andrew Wiggins .60 1.50
83 Dirk Nowitzki 1.25 3.00
84 Domantas Sabonis .60 1.50
85 Clint Capela .40 1.00
86 Rodney Hood .40 1.00
87 Brandon Ingram .50 1.25
88 Jayson Tatum 2.00 5.00
89 Tony Parker .75 2.00
90 Nikola Jokic 2.50 6.00
91 Taurean Prince .30 .75
92 Donovan Mitchell 1.50 4.00
93 DeMar DeRozan .60 1.50
94 Blake Griffin .50 1.25
95 DeMarcus Cousins .50 1.25
96 Tobias Harris .40 1.00
97 Lonzo Ball .50 1.25
98 Jaylen Brown .75 2.00
99 Nikola Vucevic .40 1.00
100 Paul George .75 2.00
101 Aaron Holiday RC 1.00 2.50
102 Landry Shamet RC 1.00 2.50
103 Zhaire Smith RC .60 1.50
104 Mo Bamba RC 1.50 4.00
105 Chandler Hutchison RC .75 2.00
106 Deandre Ayton RC 2.00 5.00
107 Kevin Knox RC .75 2.00
108 Collin Sexton RC 2.00 5.00
109 Elie Okobo RC .60 1.50
110 Allonzo Trier RC .60 1.50
111 Moritz Wagner RC 1.25 3.00
112 Jerome Robinson RC .60 1.50
113 Mikal Bridges RC 3.00 8.00
114 Lonnie Walker IV RC 1.25 3.00
115 Omari Spellman RC .60 1.50
116 Josh Okogie RC 1.00 2.50
117 Luka Doncic RC 150.00 400.00
118 Hamidou Diallo RC 1.00 2.50
119 Wendell Carter Jr. RC 1.50 4.00
120 Grayson Allen RC 1.25 3.00
121 Jaren Jackson Jr. RC 5.00 12.00
122 Michael Porter Jr. RC 6.00 15.00
123 Miles Bridges RC 1.50 4.00
124 Anfernee Simons RC 3.00 8.00
125 Mitchell Robinson RC 1.50 4.00
126 Donte DiVincenzo RC 1.50 4.00
127 Trae Young RC 5.00 12.00
128 Jalen Brunson RC 5.00 12.00
129 Shai Gilgeous-Alexander RC 6.00 15.00
130 Bruce Brown RC 1.25 3.00
131 Marvin Bagley III RC 1.50 4.00
132 Troy Brown Jr. RC .75 2.00
133 Kevin Huerter RC 1.25 3.00
134 Chandler Hutchison 1.25 3.00
135 Deandre Ayton 3.00 8.00
136 Kevin Knox 1.25 3.00
137 Wendell Carter Jr. 2.50 6.00
138 Bruce Brown 2.00 5.00
139 Jaren Jackson Jr. 8.00 20.00
140 Michael Porter Jr. 10.00 25.00
141 Mikal Bridges 5.00 12.00
142 Lonnie Walker IV 2.00 5.00
143 Mo Bamba 1.50 4.00
144 Josh Okogie 1.50 4.00
145 Luka Doncic 150.00 400.00
146 Hamidou Diallo 1.50 4.00
147 Shai Gilgeous-Alexander 10.00 25.00
148 Aaron Holiday 1.50 4.00
149 Marvin Bagley III 1.50 4.00
150 Troy Brown Jr. 1.25 3.00
151 Miles Bridges 2.50 6.00
152 Anfernee Simons 5.00 12.00
153 Omari Spellman 1.00 2.50
154 Donte DiVincenzo 2.50 6.00
155 Trae Young 8.00 20.00
156 Jalen Brunson 8.00 20.00
157 Allonzo Trier 1.00 2.50
158 Jerome Robinson 1.00 2.50
159 Landry Shamet 1.50 4.00
160 Zhaire Smith 1.00 2.50
161 Kevin Huerter 2.00 5.00
162 Moritz Wagner 2.00 5.00
163 Mitchell Robinson 2.50 6.00
164 Grayson Allen 2.00 5.00
165 Collin Sexton 3.00 8.00
166 Elie Okobo 1.00 2.50
167 Deandre Ayton 5.00 12.00
168 Hamidou Diallo 2.50 6.00
169 Wendell Carter Jr. 4.00 10.00
170 Grayson Allen 3.00 8.00
171 Marvin Bagley III 2.50 6.00
172 Jerome Robinson 1.50 4.00
173 Miles Bridges 4.00 10.00
174 Lonnie Walker IV 3.00 8.00
175 Omari Spellman 1.50 4.00
176 Josh Okogie 2.50 6.00
177 Luka Doncic 150.00 400.00
178 Jalen Brunson 12.00 30.00
179 Shai Gilgeous-Alexander 15.00 40.00
180 Bruce Brown 3.00 8.00
181 Landry Shamet 2.50 6.00
182 Michael Porter Jr. 15.00 40.00
183 Kevin Huerter 3.00 8.00
184 Anfernee Simons 8.00 20.00
185 Mitchell Robinson 4.00 10.00
186 Donte DiVincenzo 4.00 10.00
187 Trae Young 12.00 30.00
188 Elie Okobo 1.50 4.00
189 Allonzo Trier 1.50 4.00
190 Aaron Holiday 2.50 6.00
191 Mikal Bridges 8.00 20.00
192 Troy Brown Jr. 2.00 5.00
193 Mo Bamba 2.50 6.00
194 Moritz Wagner 3.00 8.00
195 Chandler Hutchison 2.50 6.00
196 Kevin Knox 2.00 5.00
197 Collin Sexton 5.00 12.00
198 Zhaire Smith 1.50 4.00
199 Jaren Jackson Jr. 12.00 30.00
200 Deandre Ayton 100.00 250.00
201 Luka Doncic 1,000.00 2,000.00
202 Trae Young 200.00 500.00
203 Collin Sexton 50.00 120.00
204 Wendell Carter Jr. 50.00 120.00
205 Shai Gilgeous-Alexander 60.00 150.00
206 Allonzo Trier 6.00 15.00
207 Jaren Jackson Jr. 50.00 120.00
208 Marvin Bagley III 125.00 300.00
209 Landry Shamet 20.00 50.00
210 Mikal Bridges 25.00 60.00
211 Miles Bridges 50.00 120.00
212 Kevin Huerter 50.00 120.00
213 Mo Bamba 30.00 80.00
214 Omari Spellman 6.00 15.00
215 Mitchell Robinson 50.00 120.00
216 Chandler Hutchison 8.00 20.00
217 Josh Okogie 10.00 25.00
218 Donte DiVincenzo 15.00 40.00
219 Kevin Knox 8.00 20.00
220 Hamidou Diallo 20.00 50.00
221 Jalen Brunson 20.00 50.00
222 Elie Okobo 30.00 80.00
223 Grayson Allen 30.00 80.00
224 Bruce Brown 15.00 40.00
225 Aaron Holiday 10.00 25.00
226 Jerome Robinson 12.00 30.00
227 Michael Porter Jr. 150.00 400.00
228 Troy Brown Jr. 30.00 80.00
229 Zhaire Smith 15.00 40.00
230 Lonnie Walker IV 40.00 100.00
231 Anfernee Simons 50.00 120.00
232 Moritz Wagner 12.00 30.00

2018-19 Court Kings Aurora

1 Joel Embiid 50.00 120.00
2 Dirk Nowitzki 20.00 50.00
3 Luka Doncic 2,000.00 4,000.00
4 Donovan Mitchell 30.00 80.00
5 Stephen Curry 60.00 150.00
6 Kemba Walker 8.00 20.00
7 Damian Lillard 30.00 80.00
8 Dwyane Wade 50.00 120.00
9 Mo Bamba 15.00 40.00
10 James Harden 30.00 80.00
11 Ben Simmons 10.00 25.00
12 Klay Thompson 25.00 60.00
13 Marvin Bagley III 10.00 25.00
14 Kevin Durant 40.00 100.00
15 Blake Griffin 10.00 25.00
16 Russell Westbrook 15.00 40.00
17 Kawhi Leonard 50.00 120.00
18 Kyrie Irving 25.00 60.00
19 Dwight Howard 12.00 30.00
20 Anthony Davis 40.00 100.00
21 Deandre Ayton 20.00 50.00
22 Chris Paul 25.00 60.00
23 Kevin Knox 8.00 20.00
24 Jayson Tatum 40.00 100.00
25 Andre Drummond 8.00 20.00
26 Paul George 25.00 60.00
27 DeMar DeRozan 12.00 30.00
28 Karl-Anthony Towns 15.00 40.00
29 Jimmy Butler 25.00 60.00
30 Devin Booker 20.00 50.00
31 Trae Young 300.00 600.00
32 John Wall 12.00 30.00
33 Jaren Jackson Jr. 50.00 120.00
34 Giannis Antetokounmpo 125.00 300.00
35 LeBron James 500.00 1,000.00

2018-19 Court Kings Jade

*JADE: .75X TO 2X BASIC
67 LeBron James 12.00 30.00

2018-19 Court Kings Le Cinque Piu Belle

1 Giannis Antetokounmpo 300.00 600.00
2 Kobe Bryant 300.00 600.00
3 Kevin Durant 150.00 400.00
4 Stephen Curry 300.00 600.00
5 Charles Barkley 75.00 200.00

2018-19 Court Kings Ruby

*RUBY: .6X TO 1.5X BASIC
STATED PRINT RUN 99 SER.#'d SETS
37 Stephen Curry 5.00 12.00
67 LeBron James 8.00 20.00

2018-19 Court Kings Acetate Rookies

COMMON CARD 1.25 3.00
SEMISTARS 1.50 4.00
UNLISTED STARS 2.00 5.00
1 Mo Bamba 2.00 5.00
2 Omari Spellman 1.25 3.00
3 Shai Gilgeous-Alexander 12.00 30.00
4 Donte DiVincenzo 3.00 8.00
5 Jaren Jackson Jr. 10.00 25.00
6 Josh Okogie 2.00 5.00
7 Luka Doncic 75.00 200.00
8 Aaron Holiday 2.00 5.00
9 Wendell Carter Jr. 3.00 8.00
10 Robert Williams III 2.50 6.00
11 Kevin Knox 1.50 4.00
12 Allonzo Trier 1.25 3.00
13 Miles Bridges 3.00 8.00
14 Lonnie Walker IV 2.50 6.00
15 Deandre Ayton 4.00 10.00
16 Grayson Allen 2.50 6.00
17 Trae Young 20.00 50.00
18 Landry Shamet 2.00 5.00
19 Collin Sexton 4.00 10.00
20 Jalen Brunson 10.00 25.00
21 Mikal Bridges 6.00 15.00
22 Mitchell Robinson 3.00 8.00
23 Michael Porter Jr. 5.00 12.00
24 Kevin Huerter 2.50 6.00
25 Marvin Bagley III 2.00 5.00

2018-19 Court Kings Autographs

PRINT RUNS B/WN 25-149 COPIES PER
EXCHANGE DEADLINE 10/03/2020
*RUBY/99: .5X TO 1.2X p/r 149
*RUBY/25: .5X TO 1.2X p/r 49
*SAPPHIRE/25: .6X TO 1.5X p/r 149
1 Dan Issel/149 5.00 12.00
2 Larry Bird/25 40.00 100.00
3 Keyon Dooling/149 2.50 6.00
5 Joel Embiid/49 25.00 60.00
6 Derrick Favors/49 3.00 8.00
7 Shawn Bradley/149 2.50 6.00
8 George McGinnis/149 5.00 12.00
9 Jim Chones/149 2.50 6.00
10 T.J. Warren/149 3.00 8.00
11 Brian Scalabrine/149 5.00 12.00
12 Oscar Robertson/25 25.00 60.00
13 Rudy Tomjanovich/149 3.00 8.00
14 Paul Millsap/49 4.00 10.00
15 Jamal Mashburn/149 3.00 8.00
16 Avery Johnson/49 4.00 10.00
17 Yogi Ferrell/149 2.50 6.00
18 Lauri Markkanen/149 8.00 20.00
19 Nick Anderson/149 3.00 8.00
20 Tom "Satch" Sanders/149 6.00 15.00
21 Henry Ellenson/149 2.50 6.00
22 Jason Kidd/25 20.00 50.00
23 Alonzo Mourning/49 12.00 30.00
24 Kentavious Caldwell-Pope/49 3.00 8.00
25 Marcus Camby/149 5.00 12.00
26 Bill Walton/49 15.00 40.00
27 Derek Harper/149 3.00 8.00
28 Lonzo Ball/49 15.00 40.00
29 Terrell Brandon/149 2.50 6.00
30 Jerian Grant/149 2.50 6.00

2018-19 Court Kings Autographs Sapphire

*SAPPHIRE/25: .6X TO 1.5X p/r 149
PRINT RUNS B/WN 10-25 COPIES PER
NO PRICING QTY 15 OR LESS
EXCHANGE DEADLINE 10/03/2020
13 Rudy Tomjanovich/25 8.00 20.00
25 Marcus Camby/25 8.00 20.00

2018-19 Court Kings Brush Strokes Autographs

PRINT RUNS B/WN 25-149 COPIES PER
EXCHANGE DEADLINE 10/03/2020
*RUBY/99: .5X TO 1.2X p/r 149
*RUBY/25: .5X TO 1.2X p/r 49
*SAPPHIRE/25: .6X TO 1.5X p/r 149
1 Andre Drummond/49 4.00 10.00
2 Jason Williams/149 15.00 40.00
3 Mario Hezonja/49 3.00 8.00
4 Michael Adams/149 2.50 6.00
5 Channing Frye/149 2.50 6.00
6 Spencer Haywood/149 4.00 10.00
7 Jamaal Wilkes/149 4.00 10.00
8 Rolando Blackman/149 3.00 8.00
9 Damian Lillard/25 20.00 50.00
10 Darrell Griffith/149 3.00 8.00
11 Chris Mullin/49 8.00 20.00
12 John Salley/149 3.00 8.00
13 Doc Rivers/49 5.00 12.00
14 Quentin Richardson/149 3.00 8.00
15 Zaza Pachulia/149 2.50 6.00
17 Marvin Williams/149 2.50 6.00
18 Antonio McDyess/149 3.00 8.00
19 Magic Johnson/25 20.00 50.00
20 Dino Radja/149 2.50 6.00
21 Eric Bledsoe/49 4.00 10.00

22 Kenny Anderson/149 3.00 8.00
23 Latrell Sprewell/49 8.00 20.00
24 Rony Seikaly/149 2.50 6.00
25 DeMarre Carroll/149 2.50 6.00
26 Vlade Divac/149 4.00 10.00
27 Thaddeus Young/149 2.50 6.00
28 Brent Barry/149 2.50 6.00
29 Giannis Antetokounmpo/25 75.00 200.00
30 David Robinson/49 12.00 30.00
31 Tyson Chandler/49 4.00 10.00
32 Luc Longley/149 4.00 10.00
33 Nerlens Noel/49 3.00 8.00
34 Sean Elliott/149 3.00 8.00
35 Bill Cartwright/149 3.00 8.00
36 Will Perdue/149 2.50 6.00
37 Udonis Haslem/149 2.50 6.00
38 Clifford Robinson/149 4.00 10.00
39 Kevin Love/49 6.00 15.00
40 Ish Smith/149 2.50 6.00

2018-19 Court Kings Brush Strokes Autographs Ruby

*RUBY/99: .5X TO 1.2X p/r 149
*RUBY/25: .5X TO 1.2X p/r 49
PRINT RUNS B/WN 15-99 COPIES PER
NO PRICING QTY 15 OR LESS
EXCHANGE DEADLINE 10/03/2020
11 Chris Mullin/25 12.00 30.00
20 Dino Radja/99 6.00 15.00
21 Eric Bledsoe/25 6.00 15.00
23 Latrell Sprewell/25 15.00 40.00

2018-19 Court Kings Brush Strokes Autographs Sapphire

*SAPPHIRE/25: .6X TO 1.5X p/r 149
PRINT RUNS B/WN 10-25 COPIES PER
NO PRICING QTY 15 OR LESS
EXCHANGE DEADLINE 10/03/2020
2 Jason Williams/25 30.00 80.00
18 Antonio McDyess/25 8.00 20.00
20 Dino Radja/25 10.00 25.00
32 Luc Longley/25 15.00 40.00
34 Sean Elliott/25 12.00 30.00
36 Will Perdue/25 8.00 20.00

2018-19 Court Kings Emerging Artists

*RUBY/99: .6X TO 1.5X BASIC
*SAPPHIRE/25: 1X TO 2.5X BASIC
1 Troy Brown Jr. .60 1.50
2 Allonzo Trier .50 1.25
3 Donovan Mitchell 2.50 6.00
4 Aaron Holiday .75 2.00
5 Shai Gilgeous-Alexander 5.00 12.00
6 Donte DiVincenzo 1.25 3.00
7 Luka Doncic 75.00 200.00
8 Jaren Jackson Jr. 4.00 10.00
9 Anfernee Simons 2.50 6.00
10 Landry Shamet .75 2.00
11 Lonzo Ball .75 2.00
12 Marvin Bagley III .75 2.00
13 Jayson Tatum 3.00 8.00
14 Collin Sexton 1.50 4.00
15 Michael Porter Jr. 2.00 5.00
16 Deandre Ayton 1.50 4.00
17 Grayson Allen 1.00 2.50
18 Chandler Hutchison .60 1.50
19 Kevin Knox .60 1.50
20 Mikal Bridges 2.50 6.00
21 Kyle Kuzma .75 2.00
22 Trae Young 12.00 30.00
23 Lauri Markkanen 1.25 3.00
24 Robert Williams III 1.00 2.50
25 Lonnie Walker IV 1.00 2.50
26 Kevin Huerter 1.00 2.50
27 Mo Bamba .75 2.00
28 Wendell Carter Jr. 1.25 3.00
29 Miles Bridges 1.25 3.00
30 Jerome Robinson .50 1.25

2018-19 Court Kings Emerging Artists Ruby

*RUBY/99: .6X TO 1.5X BASIC
STATED PRINT RUN 99 SER.#'d SETS
7 Luka Doncic 150.00 400.00
22 Trae Young 30.00 80.00

2018-19 Court Kings Emerging Artists Sapphire

*SAPPHIRE/25: 1X TO 2.5X BASIC
STATED PRINT RUN 25 SER.#'d SETS
7 Luka Doncic 500.00 1,000.00
22 Trae Young 75.00 200.00

2018-19 Court Kings Fresh Paint Autographs

PRINT RUNS B/WN 99-199 COPIES PER
EXCHANGE DEADLINE 10/03/2020
*RUBY/99: .5X TO 1.2X p/r 199
*RUBY/49: .5X TO 1.2X p/r 99
*SAPPHIRE/25: .8X TO 2X p/r 199
*SAPPHIRE/25: .6X TO 1.5X p/r 99
1 Bruce Brown/99 8.00 20.00
2 Kevin Knox/199 4.00 10.00
3 Khyri Thomas/199 3.00 8.00
4 Troy Brown Jr./199 4.00 10.00
5 Grayson Allen/99 8.00 20.00
6 Zhaire Smith/199 3.00 8.00
7 Robert Williams III/199 6.00 15.00
8 Deandre Ayton/199 10.00 25.00
9 Elie Okobo/199 3.00 8.00
10 Trae Young/99 400.00 800.00
11 Hamidou Diallo/199 5.00 12.00
12 Mikal Bridges/199 15.00 40.00
13 Kostas Antetokounmpo/199 15.00 40.00
14 Donte DiVincenzo/199 6.00 15.00
15 Chandler Hutchison/199 4.00 10.00
16 Moritz Wagner/199 6.00 15.00
17 Jacob Evans III/199 3.00 8.00
18 Marvin Bagley III/199 5.00 12.00
19 Jalen Brunson/99 30.00 80.00
20 Mo Bamba/199 8.00 20.00
21 De'Anthony Melton/199 6.00 15.00
22 Shai Gilgeous-Alexander/199 500.00 1,000.00
23 Rodions Kurucs/199 EXCH 8.00 20.00
24 Lonnie Walker IV/199 6.00 15.00
25 Aaron Holiday/199 5.00 12.00
26 Jevon Carter/199 5.00 12.00
27 Dzanan Musa/199 3.00 8.00
28 Luka Doncic/199 500.00 1,000.00
29 Devonte' Graham/199 5.00 12.00
30 Wendell Carter Jr./99 10.00 25.00
31 Svi Mykhailiuk/199 4.00 10.00
32 Jerome Robinson/99 4.00 10.00
33 Mitchell Robinson/199 EXCH 12.00 30.00
34 Kevin Huerter/199 6.00 15.00
35 Anfernee Simons/199 8.00 20.00
36 Jarred Vanderbilt/199 6.00 15.00
37 Omari Spellman/199 3.00 8.00
38 Jaren Jackson Jr./99 125.00 300.00
39 Gary Trent Jr./199 6.00 15.00
40 Collin Sexton/99 20.00 50.00
41 Keita Bates-Diop/199 EXCH 4.00 10.00
42 Michael Porter Jr./199 20.00 50.00
43 Allonzo Trier/199 3.00 8.00
44 Josh Okogie/199 5.00 12.00
45 Landry Shamet/199 EXCH 5.00 12.00

2018-19 Court Kings Fresh Paint Autographs Ruby

*RUBY/99: .5X TO 1.2X p/r 199
*RUBY/49: .5X TO 1.2X p/r 99
PRINT RUNS B/WN 49-99 COPIES PER
EXCHANGE DEADLINE 10/03/2020
19 Jalen Brunson/49 40.00 100.00
28 Luka Doncic/99 800.00 1,500.00

2018-19 Court Kings Fresh Paint Autographs Sapphire

*SAPPHIRE/25: .8X TO 2X p/r 199
*SAPPHIRE/25: .6X TO 1.5X p/r 99
STATED PRINT RUN 25 SER.#'d SETS
EXCHANGE DEADLINE 10/03/2020
5 Grayson Allen 20.00 50.00
7 Robert Williams III 12.00 30.00
12 Mikal Bridges 12.00 30.00
18 Marvin Bagley III 50.00 120.00
19 Jalen Brunson 12.00 30.00
22 Shai Gilgeous-Alexander 1,000.00 2,000.00
26 Jevon Carter 20.00 50.00
28 Luka Doncic 1,500.00 3,000.00
34 Kevin Huerter 20.00 50.00
45 Landry Shamet 30.00 80.00

2018-19 Court Kings Gallery of Stars

1 Karl-Anthony Towns 12.00 30.00
2 Damian Lillard 20.00 50.00
3 Devin Booker 20.00 50.00
4 Jimmy Butler 12.00 30.00
5 Chris Paul 15.00 40.00
6 Kevin Durant 50.00 120.00
7 Kemba Walker 12.00 30.00
8 Stephen Curry 75.00 200.00
9 Dwyane Wade 15.00 40.00
10 Andre Drummond 6.00 15.00
11 James Harden 15.00 40.00
12 Kawhi Leonard 20.00 50.00
13 Dirk Nowitzki 15.00 40.00
14 Joel Embiid 20.00 50.00
15 John Wall 10.00 25.00
16 Jayson Tatum 30.00 80.00
17 Russell Westbrook 12.00 30.00
18 Blake Griffin 8.00 20.00
19 Kyrie Irving 30.00 80.00
20 LeBron James 200.00 500.00
21 Anthony Davis 25.00 60.00
22 DeMar DeRozan 10.00 25.00
23 Klay Thompson 20.00 50.00
24 Ben Simmons 8.00 20.00
25 Donovan Mitchell 40.00 100.00
26 Giannis Antetokounmpo 75.00 200.00
27 Paul George 15.00 40.00

2018-19 Court Kings Heir Apparent Autographs

PRINT RUNS B/WN 99-199 COPIES PER
EXCHANGE DEADLINE 10/03/2020
*RUBY/99: .5X TO 1.2X p/r 199
*RUBY/49: .5X TO 1.2X p/r 99
*SAPPHIRE/25: .8X TO 2X p/r 199
*SAPPHIRE/25: .6X TO 1.5X p/r 99
1 Jarred Vanderbilt/199 6.00 15.00
2 Kostas Antetokounmpo/199 8.00 20.00
3 Collin Sexton/99 12.00 30.00
4 Marvin Bagley III/199 5.00 12.00
5 Rodions Kurucs/199 EXCH 4.00 10.00
6 Bruce Brown/99 8.00 20.00
7 Luka Doncic/199 1,000.00 2,000.00
8 Grayson Allen/99 6.00 15.00
9 Jerome Robinson/99 EXCH 4.00 10.00
10 Elie Okobo/199 3.00 8.00
11 Omari Spellman/199 3.00 8.00
12 Donte DiVincenzo/199 8.00 20.00
13 Keita Bates-Diop/199 EXCH 4.00 10.00
14 Jalen Brunson/99 50.00 120.00
15 Lonnie Walker IV/199 6.00 15.00
16 Kevin Knox/199 4.00 10.00
17 Devonte' Graham/199 5.00 12.00
18 Zhaire Smith/199 3.00 8.00
19 Mitchell Robinson/199 EXCH 8.00 20.00
20 Trae Young/199 400.00 800.00
21 Jaren Jackson Jr./99 150.00 400.00
22 Chandler Hutchison/199 4.00 10.00
23 Michael Porter Jr./199 30.00 80.00
24 Mo Bamba/199 5.00 12.00
25 Aaron Holiday/199 5.00 12.00
26 Khyri Thomas/199 3.00 8.00
27 Wendell Carter Jr./99 10.00 25.00
28 Robert Williams III/199 6.00 15.00
29 Kevin Huerter/199 6.00 15.00
30 Hamidou Diallo/199 5.00 12.00
31 Gary Trent Jr./199 6.00 15.00
32 Moritz Wagner/199 6.00 15.00
33 Allonzo Trier/199 3.00 8.00
34 De'Anthony Melton/199 6.00 15.00
35 Jevon Carter/199 5.00 12.00
36 Troy Brown Jr./199 4.00 10.00
37 Svi Mykhailiuk/199 4.00 10.00
38 Deandre Ayton/199 10.00 25.00
39 Anfernee Simons/199 40.00 100.00
40 Mikal Bridges/199 40.00 100.00
41 Landry Shamet/199 EXCH 5.00 12.00
42 Jacob Evans III/199 3.00 8.00
43 Josh Okogie/199 5.00 12.00
44 Shai Gilgeous-Alexander/199 500.00 1,000.00
45 Dzanan Musa/199 3.00 8.00

2018-19 Court Kings Heir Apparent Autographs Ruby

*RUBY/99: .5X TO 1.2X p/r 199
*RUBY/49: .5X TO 1.2X p/r 99
PRINT RUNS B/WN 49-99 COPIES PER
EXCHANGE DEADLINE 10/03/2020
28 Robert Williams III/99 25.00 60.00

2018-19 Court Kings Heir Apparent Autographs Sapphire

*SAPPHIRE/25: .8X TO 2X p/r 199
*SAPPHIRE/25: .6X TO 1.5X p/r 99
STATED PRINT RUN 25 SER.#'d SETS
EXCHANGE DEADLINE 10/03/2020
23 Michael Porter Jr. 60.00 150.00
28 Robert Williams III 40.00 100.00

2018-19 Court Kings High Court Signatures

PRINT RUNS B/WN 25-149 COPIES PER
EXCHANGE DEADLINE 10/03/2020
*RUBY/99: .5X TO 1.2X p/r 149
*RUBY/25: .5X TO 1.2X p/r 49
*SAPPHIRE/25: .6X TO 1.5X p/r 149
1 Dwyane Wade/25 25.00 60.00
2 Julius Erving/25 20.00 50.00
3 Karl-Anthony Towns/25 15.00 40.00
4 Ray Allen/49 15.00 40.00
5 Sam Jones/49 10.00 25.00
6 Richard Hamilton/49 4.00 10.00
7 Danilo Gallinari/49 4.00 10.00
8 Nick Van Exel/49 8.00 20.00
9 Elvin Hayes/49 6.00 15.00
10 Dave Cowens/49 6.00 15.00
11 Joe Dumars/49 6.00 15.00
12 Myles Turner/49 5.00 12.00
13 Terry Rozier/49 6.00 15.00
14 Kyle Korver/149 6.00 15.00
15 Darren Collison/149 2.50 6.00
16 Al-Farouq Aminu/149 2.50 6.00
18 Mark Aguirre/149 3.00 8.00
19 Stephen Jackson/149 3.00 8.00
20 Maurice Harkless/149 4.00 10.00
21 Omri Casspi/149 2.50 6.00
22 Al Attles/149 3.00 8.00
23 Charlie Ward/149 3.00 8.00
24 Detlef Schrempf/149 4.00 10.00
25 Fat Lever/149 3.00 8.00
26 Isaiah Rider/149 3.00 8.00
27 Jason Smith/149 2.50 6.00
28 Jim Jackson/149 3.00 8.00
29 Kelly Tripucka/149 2.50 6.00
30 Larry Nance/149 3.00 8.00
31 Maxi Kleber/149 3.00 8.00
32 Paul Silas/149 4.00 10.00
33 Rod Strickland/149 2.50 6.00
34 Scott Skiles/149 3.00 8.00
35 Spencer Dinwiddie/149 3.00 8.00
36 Theo Ratliff/149 2.50 6.00
37 Vin Baker/149 2.50 6.00
38 Wayne Ellington/149 2.50 6.00
39 Donovan Mitchell/49 15.00 40.00
40 Jayson Tatum/49 20.00 50.00

2018-19 Court Kings High Court Signatures Ruby

*RUBY/99: .5X TO 1.2X p/r 149
*RUBY/25: .5X TO 1.2X p/r 49
PRINT RUNS B/WN 15-99 COPIES PER
NO PRICING QTY 15 OR LESS
EXCHANGE DEADLINE 10/03/2020
5 Sam Jones/25 15.00 40.00
6 Richard Hamilton/25 8.00 20.00
8 Nick Van Exel/25 20.00 50.00
39 Donovan Mitchell/25 30.00 80.00

2018-19 Court Kings High Court Signatures Sapphire

*SAPPHIRE/25: .6X TO 1.5X p/r 149
PRINT RUNS B/WN 10-25 COPIES PER
NO PRICING QTY 15 OR LESS
EXCHANGE DEADLINE 10/03/2020
14 Kyle Korver/25 15.00 40.00

2018-19 Court Kings Impressionist Ink Autographs

PRINT RUNS B/WN 25-149 COPIES PER
EXCHANGE DEADLINE 10/03/2020
*RUBY/99: .5X TO 1.2X p/r 149
*RUBY/25: .5X TO 1.2X p/r 49
*SAPPHIRE/25: .6X TO 1.5X p/r 149
1 Dwight Powell/149 2.50 6.00
2 Dirk Nowitzki/25 40.00 100.00
3 Mahmoud Abdul-Rauf/149 2.50 6.00
4 Walt Frazier/49 8.00 20.00
5 Dell Curry/149 5.00 12.00
6 Gail Goodrich/49 6.00 15.00
7 Steven Adams/149 3.00 8.00
8 Glen Rice/149 4.00 10.00
9 Kelly Olynyk/149 2.50 6.00
10 D.J. Augustin/149 2.50 6.00
11 Cuttino Mobley/149 2.50 6.00
12 Jerry West/25 15.00 40.00
13 Shareef Abdur-Rahim/149 3.00 8.00
14 Rodney Hood/49 4.00 10.00
15 Jerome Williams/149 2.50 6.00
16 Gary Harris/49 4.00 10.00
17 Brad Davis/149 3.00 8.00
18 Horace Grant/149 4.00 10.00
19 Rick Mahorn/149 2.50 6.00
20 Tracy McGrady/49 15.00 40.00
21 Jae Crowder/149 2.50 6.00
22 Dennis Rodman/49 25.00 60.00
23 Xavier McDaniel/149 3.00 8.00
24 Avery Bradley/49 3.00 8.00
25 Mychal Thompson/149 2.50 6.00
26 Jalen Rose/49 4.00 10.00
27 Ernie DiGregorio/149 3.00 8.00
28 Courtney Lee/149 2.50 6.00
29 Tyler Johnson/149 2.50 6.00
30 J.J. Barea/149 4.00 10.00

2018-19 Court Kings Impressionist Ink Autographs Ruby

*RUBY/99: .5X TO 1.2X p/r 149
*RUBY/25: .5X TO 1.2X p/r 49
PRINT RUNS B/WN 15-99 COPIES PER
NO PRICING QTY 15 OR LESS
EXCHANGE DEADLINE 10/03/2020
7 Steven Adams/99 8.00 20.00
16 Gary Harris/25 8.00 20.00
26 Jalen Rose/25 8.00 20.00

2018-19 Court Kings Impressionist Ink Autographs Sapphire

*SAPPHIRE/25: .6X TO 1.5X p/r 149
PRINT RUNS B/WN 10-25 COPIES PER
NO PRICING QTY 15 OR LESS
EXCHANGE DEADLINE 10/03/2020
3 Mahmoud Abdul-Rauf/25 10.00 25.00
7 Steven Adams/25 10.00 25.00
18 Horace Grant/25 10.00 25.00
27 Ernie DiGregorio/25 10.00 25.00
30 J.J. Barea/25 12.00 30.00

2018-19 Court Kings Legacies Signatures

STATED PRINT RUN 49 SER.#'d SETS
EXCHANGE DEADLINE 10/03/2020
*RUBY/25-35: .5X TO 1.2X BASIC
*SAPPHIRE/25: .5X TO 1.2X BASIC
1 Larry Bird 125.00 300.00
3 Kevin Durant 125.00 300.00
4 Kobe Bryant 1,000.00 2,000.00
5 Magic Johnson 125.00 300.00
6 Bill Russell 800.00 1,500.00
7 Damian Lillard 150.00 400.00
8 Shaquille O'Neal 150.00 400.00
9 Kyrie Irving 75.00 200.00
10 Reggie Miller 125.00 300.00

2018-19 Court Kings Legacies Signatures Sapphire

*SAPPHIRE/25: .5X TO 1.2X BASIC
PRINT RUNS B/WN 10-25 COPIES PER
NO PRICING QTY 15 OR LESS
EXCHANGE DEADLINE 10/03/2020
2 Charles Barkley/25 EXCH 150.00 400.00
3 Kevin Durant/25 100.00 250.00

2018-19 Court Kings Points in the Paint

*RUBY/99: .6X TO 1.5X BASIC
*SAPPHIRE/25: 1X TO 2.5X BASIC
1 Deandre Ayton 1.50 4.00
2 LaMarcus Aldridge .75 2.00
3 Dikembe Mutombo 1.25 3.00
4 Shaquille O'Neal 2.50 6.00
5 David Robinson 1.50 4.00
6 Dwight Howard 1.00 2.50
7 Tim Duncan 2.00 5.00
8 Anthony Davis 2.00 5.00
9 Alonzo Mourning 1.25 3.00
10 Karl-Anthony Towns 1.25 3.00
11 Dave Cowens 1.00 2.50
12 Karl Malone 1.50 4.00
13 Hassan Whiteside .60 1.50
14 Charles Barkley 1.50 4.00
15 Patrick Ewing 1.25 3.00
16 DeAndre Jordan .60 1.50
17 Yao Ming 2.00 5.00
18 Andre Drummond .60 1.50
19 Wendell Carter Jr. 1.25 3.00
20 Joel Embiid 2.00 5.00
21 Bill Walton 1.25 3.00
22 Kareem Abdul-Jabbar 2.50 6.00
23 Al Horford .75 2.00
24 Hakeem Olajuwon 1.00 2.50
25 Chris Webber 1.00 2.50
26 Kevin Love .60 1.50
27 Kevin Garnett 2.00 5.00
28 Rudy Gobert 1.00 2.50
29 Mo Bamba .75 2.00
30 Blake Griffin .75 2.00

2018-19 Court Kings Points in the Paint Sapphire

*SAPPHIRE/25: 1X TO 2.5X BASIC
STATED PRINT RUN 25 SER.#'d SETS
4 Shaquille O'Neal 12.00 30.00

2018-19 Court Kings Portraits

STATED PRINT RUN 199 SER.#'d SETS
*RUBY/99: .6X TO 1.5X BASIC
*SAPPHIRE/25: 1.5X TO 4X BASIC
1 Kevin Durant 3.00 8.00
2 Kyrie Irving 3.00 8.00
3 Anthony Davis 2.00 5.00
4 Giannis Antetokounmpo 4.00 10.00
5 Brandon Ingram .75 2.00
6 Devin Booker 2.00 5.00
7 Chris Paul 1.50 4.00
8 Russell Westbrook 1.25 3.00
9 Tobias Harris .60 1.50
10 Victor Oladipo .60 1.50
11 Taurean Prince .50 1.25
12 Mike Conley .60 1.50
13 Dennis Smith Jr. .50 1.25
14 DeMar DeRozan 1.00 2.50
15 Kristaps Porzingis 1.00 2.50
16 Zach LaVine 1.25 3.00
17 Kemba Walker .60 1.50
18 Andre Drummond .60 1.50
19 Joel Embiid 2.00 5.00
20 D'Angelo Russell .75 2.00
21 Donovan Mitchell 2.50 6.00
22 Dwyane Wade 1.50 4.00
23 Aaron Gordon .75 2.00
24 Lonzo Ball .75 2.00
25 Stephen Curry 6.00 15.00
26 Jordan Clarkson .75 2.00
27 Paul George 1.25 3.00
28 Lauri Markkanen 1.25 3.00
29 Caris LeVert .75 2.00
30 Jimmy Butler 1.25 3.00
31 Nikola Vucevic .60 1.50
32 James Harden 1.50 4.00
33 John Wall 1.00 2.50
34 Goran Dragic .60 1.50
35 Kawhi Leonard 2.00 5.00
36 Andrew Wiggins 1.00 2.50
37 Kevin Love .60 1.50
38 Jayson Tatum 3.00 8.00
39 Jrue Holiday 1.00 2.50
40 Dirk Nowitzki 2.00 5.00
41 Damian Lillard 2.00 5.00
42 Khris Middleton .75 2.00
43 Blake Griffin .75 2.00
44 Klay Thompson 2.00 5.00
45 Myles Turner .75 2.00
46 Ben Simmons .75 2.00
47 LeBron James 8.00 20.00
48 De'Aaron Fox 1.50 4.00
49 Karl-Anthony Towns 1.25 3.00
50 Marc Gasol .75 2.00
51 Kobe Bryant 6.00 15.00
52 Allen Iverson 2.00 5.00
53 Larry Bird 3.00 8.00
54 Magic Johnson 3.00 8.00
55 Shaquille O'Neal 2.50 6.00
56 Charles Barkley 1.50 4.00
57 Kevin Garnett 2.00 5.00
58 Tim Duncan 2.00 5.00
59 Tracy McGrady 1.25 3.00
60 Paul Pierce 1.25 3.00

2018-19 Court Kings Portraits Sapphire

*SAPPHIRE/25: 1.5X TO 4X BASIC
STATED PRINT RUN 25 SER.#'d SETS
2 Kyrie Irving 12.00 30.00
4 Giannis Antetokounmpo 30.00 80.00
8 Russell Westbrook 10.00 25.00
19 Joel Embiid 12.00 30.00
22 Dwyane Wade 12.00 30.00
24 Lonzo Ball 10.00 25.00
25 Stephen Curry 15.00 40.00
32 James Harden 15.00 40.00
40 Dirk Nowitzki 15.00 40.00
44 Klay Thompson 20.00 50.00
47 LeBron James 60.00 150.00
51 Kobe Bryant 25.00 60.00
53 Larry Bird 10.00 25.00
54 Magic Johnson 12.00 30.00
55 Shaquille O'Neal 20.00 50.00
56 Charles Barkley 15.00 40.00
57 Kevin Garnett 15.00 40.00
58 Tim Duncan 15.00 40.00
60 Paul Pierce 12.00 30.00

2018-19 Court Kings Renaissance Men

*RUBY/99: .6X TO 1.5X BASIC
*SAPPHIRE/25: 1X TO 2.5X BASIC
1 Kemba Walker .60 1.50
2 Andrew Wiggins 1.00 2.50
3 Zach LaVine 1.25 3.00
4 Russell Westbrook 1.25 3.00
5 Paul George 1.25 3.00
6 Dwyane Wade 1.50 4.00
7 Kyrie Irving 2.00 5.00
8 Karl-Anthony Towns 1.25 3.00
9 James Harden 1.50 4.00
10 De'Aaron Fox 1.50 4.00
11 Anthony Davis 2.00 5.00
12 DeAndre Jordan .60 1.50
13 Devin Booker 2.00 5.00
14 Dirk Nowitzki 2.00 5.00
15 Tim Hardaway Jr. .50 1.25
16 Chris Paul 1.50 4.00
17 John Wall 1.00 2.50
18 Donovan Mitchell 2.50 6.00
19 Kevin Durant 3.00 8.00
20 Jayson Tatum 3.00 8.00
21 Giannis Antetokounmpo 4.00 10.00
22 Stephen Curry 6.00 15.00
23 Blake Griffin .75 2.00
24 Vince Carter 1.50 4.00
25 Klay Thompson 2.00 5.00
26 Tony Parker 1.25 3.00
27 CJ McCollum .75 2.00
28 Andre Drummond .60 1.50
29 LeBron James 30.00 80.00
30 Kyle Kuzma .75 2.00
31 Damian Lillard 2.00 5.00
32 Kawhi Leonard 2.00 5.00
33 DeMar DeRozan 1.00 2.50
34 Pau Gasol 1.25 3.00
35 Bradley Beal 1.00 2.50
36 Dwight Howard 1.00 2.50
37 Jimmy Butler 1.25 3.00
38 Derrick Rose 1.50 4.00
39 Joel Embiid 2.00 5.00
40 Ben Simmons .75 2.00

2018-19 Court Kings Renaissance Men Ruby

*RUBY/99: .6X TO 1.5X BASIC
STATED PRINT RUN 99 SER.#'d SETS
29 LeBron James 60.00 150.00

2018-19 Court Kings Renaissance Men Sapphire

*SAPPHIRE/25: 1X TO 2.5X BASIC
STATED PRINT RUN 25 SER.#'d SETS
22 Stephen Curry 15.00 40.00
29 LeBron James 300.00 600.00

2018-19 Court Kings Rookie Portraits

STATED PRINT RUN 199 SER.#'d SETS
*RUBY/99: .5X TO 1.2X BASIC
*SAPPHIRE/25: 1.2X TO 3X BASIC
1 Luka Doncic 100.00 250.00
2 Grayson Allen 2.00 5.00
3 Chandler Hutchison 1.25 3.00
4 Kevin Knox 1.25 3.00
5 Deandre Ayton 3.00 8.00
6 Marvin Bagley III 1.50 4.00
7 Trae Young 60.00 150.00
8 Yuta Watanabe 1.50 4.00
9 Jaren Jackson Jr. 8.00 20.00
10 Michael Porter Jr. 4.00 10.00
11 De'Anthony Melton 2.00 5.00
12 Mo Bamba 1.50 4.00
13 Wendell Carter Jr. 2.50 6.00
14 Collin Sexton 3.00 8.00
15 Allonzo Trier 1.00 2.50
16 Landry Shamet 1.50 4.00
17 Shai Gilgeous-Alexander 10.00 25.00
18 Miles Bridges 2.50 6.00
19 Mitchell Robinson 2.50 6.00
20 Donte DiVincenzo 2.50 6.00
21 Elie Okobo 1.00 2.50
22 Josh Okogie 1.50 4.00
23 Mikal Bridges 5.00 12.00
24 Kevin Huerter 2.00 5.00
25 Omari Spellman 1.00 2.50
26 Jerome Robinson 1.00 2.50
27 Jalen Brunson 8.00 20.00
28 Bruce Brown 2.00 5.00
29 Jacob Evans III 1.00 2.50
30 Aaron Holiday 1.50 4.00
31 Robert Williams III 2.00 5.00
32 Gary Trent Jr. 2.00 5.00
33 Anfernee Simons 5.00 12.00
34 Lonnie Walker IV 2.00 5.00
35 Keita Bates-Diop 1.25 3.00
36 Hamidou Diallo 1.50 4.00
37 Rodions Kurucs 1.25 3.00
38 Jared Terrell 1.00 2.50
39 Gary Clark 1.00 2.50
40 Johnathan Williams 1.50 4.00

2018-19 Court Kings Rookie Portraits Sapphire

*SAPPHIRE/25: 1.2X TO 3X BASIC
STATED PRINT RUN 25 SER.#'d SETS
1 Luka Doncic 400.00 800.00
6 Marvin Bagley III 20.00 50.00
14 Collin Sexton 12.00 30.00

2018-19 Court Kings Sovereign Signatures

PRINT RUNS B/WN 25-149 COPIES PER
EXCHANGE DEADLINE 10/03/2020
*RUBY/99: .5X TO 1.2X p/r 149
*RUBY/25: .5X TO 1.2X p/r 49
*SAPPHIRE/25: .6X TO 1.5X p/r 149
1 Kareem Abdul-Jabbar/25 25.00 60.00
2 Raef LaFrentz/149 2.50 6.00
3 Kenny Smith/49 4.00 10.00
4 Herb Williams/149 2.50 6.00
5 Reggie Jackson/49 4.00 10.00
6 Wally Szczerbiak/149 3.00 8.00
7 Enes Kanter/149 3.00 8.00
8 Mark Eaton/149 4.00 10.00
9 Rudy Gobert/149 5.00 12.00
10 Bill Laimbeer/149 3.00 8.00
11 DeMarcus Cousins/25 10.00 25.00
12 Tony Delk/149 2.50 6.00
13 JJ Redick/49 6.00 15.00
14 Langston Galloway/149 2.50 6.00
15 Rick Fox/49 4.00 10.00
16 Darius Miles/149 2.50 6.00
17 Frank Kaminsky/149 2.50 6.00
18 Sidney Moncrief/149 2.50 6.00
19 Sam Cassell/149 3.00 8.00
20 Doug Christie/149 3.00 8.00
21 Isaiah Thomas/49 4.00 10.00
22 Bryon Russell/149 2.50 6.00
23 Calvin Murphy/49 4.00 10.00
24 Sam Perkins/149 3.00 8.00
25 Serge Ibaka/49 4.00 10.00
26 James Silas/149 6.00 15.00
27 Mitch Richmond/149 5.00 12.00
28 Zydrunas Ilgauskas/149 3.00 8.00
29 Marques Johnson/149 3.00 8.00
30 Jonas Jerebko/149 2.50 6.00

2018-19 Court Kings Sovereign Signatures Ruby

*RUBY/99: .5X TO 1.2X p/r 149
*RUBY/25: .5X TO 1.2X p/r 49
PRINT RUNS B/WN 15-99 COPIES PER
NO PRICING QTY 15 OR LESS
EXCHANGE DEADLINE 10/03/2020
15 Rick Fox/25 8.00 20.00
23 Calvin Murphy/25 8.00 20.00

2018-19 Court Kings Sovereign Signatures Sapphire

*SAPPHIRE/25: .6X TO 1.5X p/r 149
PRINT RUNS B/WN 10-25 COPIES PER
NO PRICING QTY 15 OR LESS
EXCHANGE DEADLINE 10/03/2020
27 Mitch Richmond/25 10.00 25.00

2018-19 Court Kings Studio Signatures

PRINT RUNS B/WN 25-149 COPIES PER
EXCHANGE DEADLINE 10/03/2020
*RUBY/99: .5X TO 1.2X p/r 149
*RUBY/25: .5X TO 1.2X p/r 49
*SAPPHIRE/25: .6X TO 1.5X p/r 149
1 Kenny "Sky" Walker/149 2.50 6.00
2 Tyus Jones/149 2.50 6.00
3 John Stockton/25 15.00 40.00
4 Muggsy Bogues/149 4.00 10.00
5 Kyle Kuzma/49 10.00 25.00
6 Elden Campbell/149 2.50 6.00
7 Lenny Wilkens/49 6.00 15.00
8 Tree Rollins/149 2.50 6.00
9 Jonas Valanciunas/149 4.00 10.00
10 Larry Hughes/149 2.50 6.00
11 Kevin Willis/149 3.00 8.00
12 Dee Brown/149 3.00 8.00
13 Andrew Wiggins/25 15.00 40.00
14 Stacey King/149 2.50 6.00
15 George Gervin/49 8.00 20.00
16 Junior Bridgeman/149 2.50 6.00
17 Mark Jackson/49 4.00 10.00
18 Cedric Ceballos/149 2.50 6.00
19 B.J. Armstrong/149 4.00 10.00
20 Sarunas Marciulionis/149 4.00 10.00
21 Jose Calderon/149 2.50 6.00
22 Jeff Hornacek/149 3.00 8.00
23 Josh Jackson/49 3.00 8.00
24 Brad Daugherty/149 3.00 8.00
25 Peja Stojakovic/49 4.00 10.00
26 Rafer Alston/149 3.00 8.00
27 Marquese Chriss/49 3.00 8.00
28 Ian Clark/149 2.50 6.00
29 John Starks/149 3.00 8.00
30 Walter Davis/149 4.00 10.00

2018-19 Court Kings Studio Signatures Ruby

*RUBY/99: .5X TO 1.2X p/r 149
*RUBY/25: .5X TO 1.2X p/r 49
PRINT RUNS B/WN 15-99 COPIES PER
NO PRICING QTY 15 OR LESS
EXCHANGE DEADLINE 10/03/2020
25 Peja Stojakovic/25 8.00 20.00

2018-19 Court Kings Studio Signatures Sapphire

*SAPPHIRE/25: .6X TO 1.5X p/r 149
PRINT RUNS B/WN 10-25 COPIES PER
NO PRICING QTY 15 OR LESS
EXCHANGE DEADLINE 10/03/2020
4 Muggsy Bogues/25 12.00 30.00

2019-20 Court Kings

COMMON CARD (1-67) .30 .75
SEMISTARS .40 1.00
UNLISTED STARS .50 1.20
COMMON RC (68-100) .60 1.50
RC SEMIS .75 2.00
RC UNLISTED 1.00 2.50
COMMON CARD (101-133) 1.00 2.50
SEMISTARS 1.25 3.00
UNLISTED STARS 1.50 4.00
COMMON CARD (134-166) 1.50 4.00
SEMISTARS 2.00 5.00
UNLISTED STARS 2.50 6.00
COMMON CARD (167-199) 6.00 15.00
SEMISTARS 8.00 20.00
UNLISTED STARS 10.00 25.00
1 James Harden 1.00 2.50
2 Lou Williams .50 1.25
3 LeBron James 15.00 40.00
4 Karl-Anthony Towns .75 2.00
5 Trae Young 1.25 3.00
6 Chris Paul 1.00 2.50
7 Lauri Markkanen .60 1.50
8 Damian Lillard 1.25 3.00
9 Jamal Murray .75 2.00
10 Pascal Siakam .75 2.00
11 Russell Westbrook .75 2.00
12 Montrezl Harrell .40 1.00
13 Dillon Brooks .40 1.00
14 Andrew Wiggins .60 1.50
15 John Collins .50 1.25
16 Nikola Vucevic .40 1.00
17 Terry Rozier .40 1.00
18 CJ McCollum .50 1.25
19 Nikola Jokic 2.50 6.00
20 Kyle Lowry .50 1.25
21 Malcolm Brogdon .40 1.00
22 Derrick Rose 1.00 2.50
23 Jaren Jackson Jr. .75 2.00
24 Brandon Ingram .50 1.25
25 Kemba Walker .40 1.00
26 Aaron Gordon .50 1.25
27 Miles Bridges .50 1.25
28 De'Aaron Fox .75 2.00
29 Andre Drummond .40 1.00
30 Donovan Mitchell 1.00 2.50
31 Domantas Sabonis .60 1.50
32 Gordon Hayward .40 1.00
33 Goran Dragic .40 1.00
34 Jrue Holiday .60 1.50
35 Jayson Tatum 2.00 5.00
36 Joel Embiid 1.00 2.50
37 Kevin Love .50 1.25
38 Buddy Hield .40 1.00
39 Blake Griffin .50 1.25
40 Bojan Bogdanovic .40 1.00
41 Kawhi Leonard 1.25 3.00
42 Tobias Harris .40 1.00
43 Jimmy Butler 1.00 2.50
44 Marcus Morris Sr. .30 .75
45 Kyrie Irving 1.00 2.50
46 Ben Simmons .50 1.25
47 Collin Sexton .60 1.50
48 DeMar DeRozan .60 1.50
49 Stephen Curry 4.00 10.00
50 Bradley Beal .60 1.50
51 Paul George .75 2.00
52 Caris LeVert .40 1.00
53 Giannis Antetokounmpo 5.00 12.00
54 Julius Randle .60 1.50
55 Kevin Durant 1.50 4.00
56 Devin Booker .12 .30
57 Luka Doncic 12.00 30.00
58 LaMarcus Aldridge .50 1.25
59 D'Angelo Russell .40 1.00
60 John Wall .60 1.50
61 Anthony Davis 1.25 3.00
62 T.J. Warren .40 1.00
63 Khris Middleton .50 1.25
64 Shai Gilgeous-Alexander 2.50 6.00
65 Zach LaVine .75 2.00
66 Deandre Ayton .50 1.25
67 Kristaps Porzingis .60 1.50
68 Cam Reddish RC 1.00 2.50
69 Keldon Johnson RC 2.00 5.00
70 Romeo Langford RC .60 1.50
71 Luka Samanic RC .75 2.00
72 Zion Williamson RC 75.00 200.00
73 Eric Paschall RC .75 2.00
74 De'Andre Hunter RC 2.50 6.00
75 Jordan Poole RC 2.50 6.00
76 Coby White RC 8.00 20.00
77 Grant Williams RC 1.00 2.50
78 Cameron Johnson RC 1.50 4.00
79 Bruno Fernando RC .75 2.00
80 Sekou Doumbouya RC .60 1.50
81 Matisse Thybulle RC 1.25 3.00
82 Ja Morant RC 40.00 100.00
83 Tacko Fall RC .75 2.00
84 Darius Garland RC 2.50 6.00
85 Darius Bazley RC .60 1.50
86 Jaxson Hayes RC 1.00 2.50
87 Nicolo Melli RC .75 2.00
88 PJ Washington Jr. RC 2.00 5.00
89 Admiral Schofield RC .75 2.00
90 Nickeil Alexander-Walker RC 1.00 2.50
91 Brandon Clarke RC 1.25 3.00
92 RJ Barrett RC 8.00 20.00
93 Kendrick Nunn RC 1.00 2.50
94 Jarrett Culver RC .60 1.50
95 Kevin Porter Jr. RC 1.25 3.00
96 Rui Hachimura RC 8.00 20.00
97 Carsen Edwards RC .75 2.00
98 Tyler Herro RC 8.00 20.00
99 Cody Martin RC 1.00 2.50
100 Goga Bitadze RC 1.00 2.50
101 Cam Reddish 1.50 4.00
102 Keldon Johnson 3.00 8.00
103 Romeo Langford 1.00 2.50
104 Luka Samanic 1.25 3.00
105 Zion Williamson 125.00 300.00
106 Eric Paschall 1.25 3.00
107 De'Andre Hunter 4.00 10.00
108 Jordan Poole 4.00 10.00
109 Coby White 12.00 30.00
110 Grant Williams 1.50 4.00

111 Cameron Johnson 2.50 6.00
112 Bruno Fernando 1.25 3.00
113 Sekou Doumbouya 1.00 2.50
114 Matisse Thybulle 2.00 5.00
115 Ja Morant 60.00 150.00
116 Tacko Fall 1.25 3.00
117 Darius Garland 4.00 10.00
118 Darius Bazley 1.00 2.50
119 Jaxson Hayes 1.50 4.00
120 Nicolo Melli 1.25 3.00
121 PJ Washington Jr. 3.00 8.00
122 Admiral Schofield 1.25 3.00
123 Nickeil Alexander-Walker 1.50 4.00
124 Brandon Clarke 2.00 5.00
125 RJ Barrett 12.00 30.00
126 Kendrick Nunn 1.50 4.00
127 Jarrett Culver 1.00 2.50
128 Kevin Porter Jr. 2.00 5.00
129 Rui Hachimura 12.00 30.00
130 Carsen Edwards 1.25 3.00
131 Tyler Herro 12.00 30.00
132 Cody Martin 1.50 4.00
133 Goga Bitadze 1.50 4.00
134 Cam Reddish 2.50 6.00
135 Keldon Johnson 5.00 12.00
136 Romeo Langford 1.50 4.00
137 Luka Samanic 2.00 5.00
138 Zion Williamson 200.00 500.00
139 Eric Paschall 12.00 30.00
140 De'Andre Hunter 6.00 15.00
141 Jordan Poole 6.00 15.00
142 Coby White 20.00 50.00
143 Grant Williams 2.50 6.00
144 Cameron Johnson 4.00 10.00
145 Bruno Fernando 2.00 5.00
146 Sekou Doumbouya 1.50 4.00
147 Matisse Thybulle 3.00 8.00
148 Ja Morant 100.00 250.00
149 Tacko Fall 2.00 5.00
150 Darius Garland 6.00 15.00
151 Darius Bazley 1.50 4.00
152 Jaxson Hayes 2.50 6.00
153 Nicolo Melli 2.00 5.00
154 PJ Washington Jr. 12.00 30.00
155 Admiral Schofield 2.00 5.00
156 Nickeil Alexander-Walker 2.50 6.00
157 Brandon Clarke 12.00 30.00
158 RJ Barrett 20.00 50.00
159 Kendrick Nunn 2.50 6.00
160 Jarrett Culver 1.50 4.00
161 Kevin Porter Jr. 3.00 8.00
162 Rui Hachimura 20.00 50.00
163 Carsen Edwards 2.00 5.00
164 Tyler Herro 20.00 50.00
165 Cody Martin 2.50 6.00
166 Goga Bitadze 2.50 6.00
167 Cam Reddish 10.00 25.00
168 Keldon Johnson 30.00 80.00
169 Romeo Langford 6.00 15.00
170 Luka Samanic 8.00 20.00
171 Zion Williamson 1,000.00 2,000.00
172 Eric Paschall 40.00 100.00
173 De'Andre Hunter 40.00 100.00
174 Jordan Poole 25.00 60.00
175 Coby White 100.00 250.00
176 Grant Williams 10.00 25.00
177 Cameron Johnson 20.00 50.00
178 Bruno Fernando 8.00 20.00
179 Sekou Doumbouya 6.00 15.00
180 Matisse Thybulle 60.00 150.00
181 Ja Morant 500.00 1,000.00
182 Tacko Fall 8.00 20.00
183 Darius Garland 25.00 60.00
184 Darius Bazley 6.00 15.00
185 Jaxson Hayes 10.00 25.00
186 Nicolo Melli 8.00 20.00
187 PJ Washington Jr. 50.00 120.00
188 Admiral Schofield 8.00 20.00
189 Nickeil Alexander-Walker 10.00 25.00
190 Brandon Clarke 60.00 150.00
191 RJ Barrett 100.00 250.00
192 Kendrick Nunn 10.00 25.00
193 Jarrett Culver 6.00 15.00
194 Kevin Porter Jr. 12.00 30.00
195 Rui Hachimura 100.00 250.00
196 Carsen Edwards 8.00 20.00
197 Tyler Herro 100.00 250.00
198 Cody Martin 10.00 25.00
199 Goga Bitadze 10.00 25.00

2019-20 Court Kings Amethyst

*AMETHYST: .6X TO 1.5X BASIC
STATED PRINT RUN 99 SER.#'d SETS
3 LeBron James 40.00 100.00
35 Jayson Tatum 10.00 25.00
49 Stephen Curry 12.00 30.00
53 Giannis Antetokounmpo 15.00 40.00
57 Luka Doncic 30.00 80.00

2019-20 Court Kings Citrine

*CITRINE: .75X TO 2X BASIC
STATED PRINT RUN 49 SER.#'d SETS
3 LeBron James 100.00 250.00
35 Jayson Tatum 12.00 30.00
49 Stephen Curry 15.00 40.00
53 Giannis Antetokounmpo 20.00 50.00
57 Luka Doncic 75.00 200.00
61 Anthony Davis 8.00 20.00

2019-20 Court Kings Jade

*JADE: 1.2X TO 3X BASIC
STATED PRINT RUN 25 SER.#'d SETS
3 LeBron James 150.00 400.00
35 Jayson Tatum 20.00 50.00
49 Stephen Curry 25.00 60.00
53 Giannis Antetokounmpo 30.00 80.00
57 Luka Doncic 125.00 300.00
61 Anthony Davis 12.00 30.00

2019-20 Court Kings Ruby

*RUBY: .5X TO 1.25X BASIC
STATED PRINT RUN 149 SER.#'d SETS
3 LeBron James 30.00 80.00
35 Jayson Tatum 8.00 20.00
49 Stephen Curry 10.00 25.00
53 Giannis Antetokounmpo 12.00 30.00
57 Luka Doncic 25.00 60.00

2019-20 Court Kings Sapphire

*SAPPHIRE: 1.2X TO 3X BASIC
STATED PRINT RUN 25 SER.#'d SETS
1 James Harden 8.00 20.00
3 LeBron James 150.00 400.00
5 Trae Young 12.00 30.00
8 Damian Lillard 6.00 15.00
30 Donovan Mitchell 8.00 20.00
35 Jayson Tatum 20.00 50.00
49 Stephen Curry 20.00 50.00
53 Giannis Antetokounmpo 30.00 80.00
57 Luka Doncic 125.00 300.00
61 Anthony Davis 12.00 30.00

2019-20 Court Kings Academy of Fine Arts

COMMON CARD .50 1.25
SEMISTARS .60 1.50
UNLISTED STARS .75 2.00
*AMETHYST/99: .6X TO 1.5X BASIC
*JADE/25: 1X TO 2.5X BASIC
1 Julius Erving 2.00 5.00
2 Jason Kidd 1.25 3.00
3 Robert Parish 1.00 2.50
4 Wilt Chamberlain 3.00 8.00
5 Scottie Pippen 2.00 5.00
6 John Stockton 1.50 4.00
7 Kevin McHale 1.25 3.00
8 Charles Barkley 1.50 4.00
9 Kareem Abdul-Jabbar 2.50 6.00
10 Larry Bird 3.00 8.00
11 Pete Maravich 2.00 5.00
12 Moses Malone 1.25 3.00
13 Steve Nash 1.50 4.00
14 Bill Russell 2.50 6.00
15 Dominique Wilkins 1.25 3.00
16 Shaquille O'Neal 3.00 8.00
17 Grant Hill 1.25 3.00
18 Hakeem Olajuwon 1.50 4.00
19 Dennis Rodman 2.00 5.00
20 Gary Payton 1.25 3.00
21 Drazen Petrovic 1.00 2.50
22 Clyde Drexler 1.25 3.00
23 Patrick Ewing 1.25 3.00
24 Karl Malone 1.50 4.00
25 Dikembe Mutombo .75 2.00
26 David Robinson 1.50 4.00
27 Allen Iverson 2.00 5.00
28 Magic Johnson 2.50 6.00
29 Isiah Thomas 1.50 4.00
30 Ray Allen 1.25 3.00

2019-20 Court Kings Academy of Fine Arts Jade

*JADE/25: 1X TO 2.5X BASIC
STATED PRINT RUN 25 SER.#'d SETS
5 Scottie Pippen 12.00 30.00
8 Charles Barkley 12.00 30.00
10 Larry Bird 10.00 25.00
13 Steve Nash 12.00 30.00
16 Shaquille O'Neal 12.00 30.00
18 Hakeem Olajuwon 10.00 25.00
19 Dennis Rodman 12.00 30.00
26 David Robinson 10.00 25.00
27 Allen Iverson 12.00 30.00
28 Magic Johnson 10.00 25.00

2019-20 Court Kings Acetate Rookies

COMMON CARD 1.25 3.00
SEMISTARS 1.50 4.00
UNLISTED STARS 2.00 5.00
1 Romeo Langford 1.25 3.00
2 Kendrick Nunn 2.00 5.00
3 Nassir Little 6.00 15.00
4 Kevin Porter Jr. 2.50 6.00
5 Zion Williamson 100.00 250.00
6 Nickeil Alexander-Walker 2.00 5.00
7 Cam Reddish 2.00 5.00
8 Matisse Thybulle 6.00 15.00
9 De'Andre Hunter 8.00 20.00
10 Admiral Schofield 1.50 4.00
11 Jaxson Hayes 2.00 5.00
12 Darius Garland 8.00 20.00
13 Bol Bol 3.00 8.00
14 Cameron Johnson 3.00 8.00
15 Ja Morant 75.00 200.00
16 Brandon Clarke 8.00 20.00
17 Jarrett Culver 1.25 3.00
18 Grant Williams 2.00 5.00
19 Coby White 15.00 40.00
20 Carsen Edwards 1.50 4.00
21 Rui Hachimura 10.00 25.00
22 Tacko Fall 8.00 20.00
23 PJ Washington Jr. 8.00 20.00
24 Tyler Herro 10.00 25.00
25 RJ Barrett 12.00 30.00

2019-20 Court Kings Apprentice Artists

1 De'Andre Hunter 2.00 5.00
2 Kevin Porter Jr. 1.00 2.50
3 Jaxson Hayes .75 2.00
4 Nicolo Melli .60 1.50
5 Cameron Johnson 1.25 3.00
6 Nickeil Alexander-Walker .75 2.00
7 Romeo Langford .50 1.25
8 Kendrick Nunn .75 2.00
9 Zion Williamson 50.00 120.00
10 Brandon Clarke 1.00 2.50
11 Jarrett Culver .50 1.25
12 Matisse Thybulle 1.00 2.50
13 Rui Hachimura 2.00 5.00
14 Carsen Edwards .60 1.50
15 PJ Washington Jr. 1.50 4.00
16 Admiral Schofield .60 1.50
17 Darius Garland 2.00 5.00
18 Tacko Fall .60 1.50
19 Ja Morant 30.00 80.00
20 Goga Bitadze .75 2.00
21 Coby White 1.50 4.00
22 Grant Williams .75 2.00
23 Cam Reddish .75 2.00
24 Bruno Fernando .60 1.50
25 Tyler Herro 2.50 6.00
26 Cody Martin .75 2.00
27 Eric Paschall .60 1.50
28 Jordan Poole 2.00 5.00
29 RJ Barrett 2.00 5.00
30 Darius Bazley .50 1.25

2019-20 Court Kings Apprentice Artists Citrine

*CITRINE/49: 1X TO 2.5X BASIC
STATED PRINT RUN 49 SER.#'d SETS
8 Kendrick Nunn 2.00 5.00
13 Rui Hachimura 8.00 20.00
21 Coby White 12.00 30.00
23 Cam Reddish 8.00 20.00

2019-20 Court Kings Apprentice Artists Ruby

*RUBY/149: .6X TO 1.5X BASIC
STATED PRINT RUN 149 SER.#'d SETS
21 Coby White 6.00 15.00

2019-20 Court Kings Apprentice Artists Sapphire

*SAPPHIRE/25: 1.25X TO 3X BASIC
STATED PRINT RUN 25 SER.#'d SETS
8 Kendrick Nunn 2.50 6.00
10 Brandon Clarke 12.00 30.00
13 Rui Hachimura 15.00 40.00
21 Coby White 20.00 50.00
23 Cam Reddish 2.50 6.00
29 RJ Barrett 12.00 30.00

2019-20 Court Kings Art Nouveau

COMMON CARD 1.50 4.00
SEMISTARS 2.00 5.00
UNLISTED STARS 2.50 6.00
STATED PRINT RUN 179 SER.#'d SETS
1 Zion Williamson 100.00 250.00
2 PJ Washington Jr. 5.00 12.00
3 Cam Reddish 2.50 6.00
4 Matisse Thybulle 3.00 8.00
5 Goga Bitadze 2.50 6.00
6 Rui Hachimura 6.00 15.00
7 Coby White 5.00 12.00
8 Nickeil Alexander-Walker 2.50 6.00
9 Sekou Doumbouya 1.50 4.00
10 RJ Barrett 6.00 15.00
11 Dylan Windler 2.00 5.00
12 Admiral Schofield 2.00 5.00
13 Cody Martin 2.50 6.00
14 Ty Jerome 3.00 8.00
15 Grant Williams 2.50 6.00
16 Bruno Fernando 2.00 5.00
17 KZ Okpala 2.00 5.00
18 Kyle Guy 2.00 5.00
19 Isaiah Roby 2.00 5.00
20 Jordan Poole 6.00 15.00
21 Jarrett Culver 1.50 4.00
22 Chuma Okeke 2.50 6.00
23 Romeo Langford 1.50 4.00
24 De'Andre Hunter 6.00 15.00
25 Ja Morant 50.00 120.00
26 Tyler Herro 8.00 20.00
27 Cameron Johnson 4.00 10.00
28 Brandon Clarke 3.00 8.00
29 Luka Samanic 2.00 5.00
30 Jaxson Hayes 2.50 6.00
31 Kevin Porter Jr. 3.00 8.00
32 Tremont Waters 2.00 5.00
33 Bol Bol 4.00 10.00
34 Keldon Johnson 5.00 12.00
35 Mfiondu Kabengele 2.00 5.00
36 Jaylen Nowell 2.00 5.00
37 Eric Paschall 2.00 5.00
38 Nassir Little 2.50 6.00
39 Darius Bazley 1.50 4.00
40 Carsen Edwards 2.00 5.00

2019-20 Court Kings Art Nouveau Prime

*PRIME/25: 1X TO 2.5X BASIC
STATED PRINT RUN 25 SER.#'d SETS
1 Zion Williamson 400.00 800.00
3 Cam Reddish 6.00 15.00
4 Matisse Thybulle 15.00 40.00
6 Rui Hachimura 25.00 60.00
10 RJ Barrett 25.00 60.00
25 Ja Morant 200.00 500.00

2019-20 Court Kings Artistic Endeavors

COMMON CARD 1.50 4.00
SEMISTARS 2.00 5.00
UNLISTED STARS 2.50 6.00
STATED PRINT RUN 99-179 SER.#'d SETS
*PRIME/25: 1X TO 2.5X BASIC
1 Joel Embiid/99 5.00 12.00
2 LeBron James/99 75.00 200.00
3 Devin Booker/99 .60 1.50
4 Luka Doncic/99 50.00 120.00
5 Bradley Beal/99 3.00 8.00
6 Derrick Rose/179 5.00 12.00
7 Russell Westbrook/179 4.00 10.00
9 Jimmy Butler/179 5.00 12.00
10 Kawhi Leonard/179 12.00 30.00
11 Ben Simmons/99 2.50 6.00
12 Kemba Walker/179 2.00 5.00
13 Donovan Mitchell/99 5.00 12.00
14 Blake Griffin/99 2.50 6.00
15 Victor Oladipo/99 2.00 5.00
16 James Harden/99 5.00 12.00
17 Paul George/179 4.00 10.00
18 Stephen Curry/179 20.00 50.00
20 Anthony Davis/179 6.00 15.00

2019-20 Court Kings Aurora

COMMON CARD 6.00 15.00
SEMISTARS 8.00 20.00
UNLISTED STARS 10.00 25.00
1 Zion Williamson 1,000.00 2,000.00
2 Kevin Garnett 75.00 200.00
3 RJ Barrett 125.00 300.00
4 Allen Iverson 75.00 200.00
5 Luka Doncic 400.00 800.00
6 Giannis Antetokounmpo 150.00 400.00
7 Kawhi Leonard 125.00 300.00
8 Charles Barkley 75.00 200.00
9 Russell Westbrook 75.00 200.00
10 Rui Hachimura 125.00 300.00
11 Ja Morant 300.00 600.00
12 Shaquille O'Neal 75.00 200.00
13 Stephen Curry 200.00 500.00
14 James Harden 50.00 120.00
15 Trae Young 125.00 300.00
16 LeBron James 500.00 1,000.00
17 Anthony Davis 100.00 250.00

2019-20 Court Kings Blank Slate

COMMON CARD 6.00 15.00
SEMISTARS 8.00 20.00
UNLISTED STARS 10.00 25.00
1 Jarrett Culver 60.00 150.00
2 Donovan Mitchell 150.00 400.00
3 Rui Hachimura 200.00 500.00
4 Derrick Rose 100.00 250.00
5 Eric Paschall 60.00 150.00
6 De'Aaron Fox 100.00 250.00
7 Damian Lillard 125.00 300.00
8 Bradley Beal 100.00 250.00
9 Zion Williamson 1,500.00 3,000.00
10 Devin Booker 200.00 500.00
11 Coby White 300.00 600.00
12 Joel Embiid 125.00 300.00
13 Cam Reddish 125.00 300.00
14 CJ McCollum 75.00 200.00
15 James Harden 100.00 250.00
16 Kristaps Porzingis 100.00 250.00
17 Ben Simmons 125.00 300.00
18 Karl-Anthony Towns 75.00 200.00
19 Ja Morant 1,500.00 3,000.00
20 LeBron James 2,000.00 4,000.00
21 Darius Garland 125.00 300.00
22 Trae Young 300.00 600.00
23 PJ Washington Jr. 100.00 250.00
24 Russell Westbrook 125.00 300.00
25 Kyrie Irving 125.00 300.00
26 Sekou Doumbouya 6.00 15.00
27 Kawhi Leonard 200.00 500.00
28 Luka Doncic 2,000.00 4,000.00
29 RJ Barrett 300.00 600.00
30 Kemba Walker 75.00 200.00
31 Jaxson Hayes 100.00 250.00
32 Shai Gilgeous-Alexander 125.00 300.00
33 Tyler Herro 200.00 500.00
34 Zach LaVine 75.00 200.00
35 Kevin Durant 150.00 400.00
36 Charles Barkley 125.00 300.00
37 Giannis Antetokounmpo 800.00 1,500.00
38 Anthony Davis 300.00 600.00
39 De'Andre Hunter 150.00 400.00
40 Pascal Siakam 100.00 250.00

2019-20 Court Kings Brush Strokes Autographs

COMMON CARD 2.50 6.00
SEMISTARS 3.00 8.00
UNLISTED STARS 4.00 10.00
STATED PRINT RUN 49-179 SER.#'d SETS
EXCHANGE DEADLINE 12/12/2021
1 Danny Green/99 3.00 8.00
2 Magic Johnson/49 25.00 60.00
3 Avery Bradley/149 2.50 6.00
4 Richard Hamilton/149 4.00 10.00
5 Rony Seikaly/149 2.50 6.00
6 Julius Randle/99 5.00 12.00
7 Jason Terry/149 3.00 8.00
8 Bill Walton/149 15.00 40.00
9 Jacque Vaughn/179 2.50 6.00
10 Sam Perkins/149 3.00 8.00
11 Mark Price/99 4.00 10.00
12 Carlos Boozer/149 3.00 8.00
13 Derek Fisher/99 4.00 10.00
14 Cody Zeller/149 2.50 6.00
15 Nate McMillan/125 3.00 8.00
16 Chauncey Billups/149 5.00 12.00
17 Calvin Murphy/179 4.00 10.00
18 Kenyon Martin/179 3.00 8.00
19 Dino Radja/179 2.50 6.00
20 Dave Cowens/99 8.00 20.00
21 Justin Holiday/179 2.50 6.00
22 Malcolm Brogdon/149 3.00 8.00
23 Paul Silas/99 3.00 8.00
24 Erick Dampier/149 2.50 6.00
25 Tom Heinsohn/99 20.00 50.00
26 Terrence Ross/99 4.00 10.00
27 Ersan Ilyasova/179 2.50 6.00
28 Raef LaFrentz/149 2.50 6.00
29 Wally Szczerbiak/99 3.00 8.00
30 Roy Hinson/179 2.50 6.00

2019-20 Court Kings Brush Strokes Autographs Citrine

*CITRINE/49: .6X TO 1.5X BASIC
*CITRINE/25: .75X TO 2X BASIC
STATED PRINT RUN 10-49 SER.#'d SETS
EXCHANGE DEADLINE 12/12/2021

2019-20 Court Kings Brush Strokes Autographs Jade

*JADE/25: .75X TO 2X BASIC
STATED PRINT RUN 5-25 SER.#'d SETS
EXCHANGE DEADLINE 12/12/2021

2019-20 Court Kings Brush Strokes Autographs Ruby

*RUBY/49-99: .5X TO 1.2X BASIC
*RUBY/25: .75X TO 2X BASIC
STATED PRINT RUN 25-99 SER.#'d SETS
EXCHANGE DEADLINE 12/12/2021

2019-20 Court Kings Brush Strokes Autographs Sapphire

*SAPPHIRE/25: .75X TO 2X BASIC
STATED PRINT RUN 5-25 SER.#'d SETS
EXCHANGE DEADLINE 12/12/2021

2019-20 Court Kings Cross-Hatching Handles

COMMON CARD .50 1.25
SEMISTARS .60 1.50
UNLISTED STARS .75 2.00
*AMETHYST/99: .6X TO 1.5X BASIC
*JADE/25: 1X TO 2.5X BASIC
1 Russell Westbrook 1.25 3.00
2 James Harden 1.50 4.00
3 D'Angelo Russell .60 1.50
4 Bradley Beal 1.00 2.50
5 Buddy Hield .60 1.50
6 Kemba Walker .60 1.50
7 Chris Paul 1.50 4.00
8 Kyle Lowry .75 2.00
9 Josh Richardson .50 1.25
10 Lou Williams .75 2.00
11 Zach LaVine 1.25 3.00
12 Kyrie Irving 1.50 4.00
13 Jamal Murray 1.25 3.00
14 Devin Booker .20 .50
15 Collin Sexton 1.00 2.50
16 Donovan Mitchell 1.50 4.00
17 Mike Conley .60 1.50
18 Malcolm Brogdon .60 1.50
19 Jrue Holiday 1.00 2.50
20 Derrick Rose 1.50 4.00
21 Stephen Curry 6.00 15.00
22 Damian Lillard 2.00 5.00
23 De'Aaron Fox 1.25 3.00
24 Ben Simmons .75 2.00
25 Terry Rozier .60 1.50
26 Trae Young 2.00 5.00
27 Ricky Rubio .60 1.50
28 Shai Gilgeous-Alexander 4.00 10.00
29 Lonzo Ball .75 2.00
30 CJ McCollum .75 2.00

2019-20 Court Kings Dressed to Impress

COMMON CARD .50 1.25
SEMISTARS .60 1.50
UNLISTED STARS .75 2.00
*AMETHYST/99: .6X TO 1.5X BASIC
*JADE/25: 1X TO 2.5X BASIC
1 Zion Williamson 125.00 300.00
2 RJ Barrett 2.00 5.00
3 Ja Morant 25.00 60.00
4 Rui Hachimura 2.00 5.00
5 LeBron James 30.00 80.00
6 Russell Westbrook 1.25 3.00
7 Kevin Durant 2.50 6.00
8 Kyrie Irving 1.50 4.00
9 James Harden 1.50 4.00
10 Damian Lillard 2.00 5.00

2019-20 Court Kings Dressed to Impress Jade

*JADE/25: 1X TO 2.5X BASIC
STATED PRINT RUN 25 SER.#'d SETS
3 Ja Morant 125.00 300.00
5 LeBron James 150.00 400.00

2019-20 Court Kings First Steps

COMMON CARD .50 1.25
SEMISTARS .60 1.50
UNLISTED STARS .75 2.00
*RUBY/149: .6X TO 1.5X BASIC
*CITRINE/49: 1X TO 2.5X BASIC
*SAPPHIRE/25: 1.25X TO 3X BASIC
1 Zion Williamson 60.00 150.00
2 Ja Morant 40.00 100.00
3 Cam Reddish .75 2.00
4 Tyler Herro 12.00 30.00
5 Rui Hachimura 10.00 25.00
6 RJ Barrett 12.00 30.00
7 Jarrett Culver .50 1.25
8 PJ Washington Jr. 1.50 4.00
9 Coby White 12.00 30.00
10 Darius Garland 2.00 5.00

2019-20 Court Kings First Steps Citrine

*CITRINE: 1X TO 2.5X BASIC
STATED PRINT RUN 49 SER.#'d SETS
4 Tyler Herro 30.00 80.00
7 Jarrett Culver 1.25 3.00
8 PJ Washington Jr. 12.00 30.00
10 Darius Garland 12.00 30.00

2019-20 Court Kings First Steps Ruby

*RUBY: .6X TO 1.5X BASIC
STATED PRINT RUN 149 SER.#'d SETS
4 Tyler Herro 20.00 50.00
8 PJ Washington Jr. 8.00 20.00
10 Darius Garland 8.00 20.00

2019-20 Court Kings First Steps Sapphire

*SAPPHIRE: 1.2X TO 3X BASIC
STATED PRINT RUN 25 SER.#'d SETS
1 Zion Williamson 400.00 800.00
4 Tyler Herro 40.00 100.00
8 PJ Washington Jr. 15.00 40.00
10 Darius Garland 15.00 40.00

2019-20 Court Kings Fledgling Expressionist Memorabilia

COMMON CARD 1.50 4.00
SEMISTARS 2.00 5.00
UNLISTED STARS 2.50 6.00
STATED PRINT RUN 179 SER.#'d SETS
1 Cam Reddish 2.50 6.00
2 Cody Martin 2.50 6.00
3 Romeo Langford 1.50 4.00
4 Bol Bol 4.00 10.00
5 Goga Bitadze 2.50 6.00
6 Grant Williams 2.50 6.00
7 Zion Williamson 100.00 250.00
8 Dylan Windler 2.00 5.00
9 Jarrett Culver 1.50 4.00
10 Kevin Porter Jr. 3.00 8.00
11 Cameron Johnson 4.00 10.00
12 Eric Paschall 2.00 5.00
13 Sekou Doumbouya 1.50 4.00
14 Isaiah Roby 2.00 5.00
15 Luka Samanic 2.00 5.00
16 Darius Bazley 1.50 4.00
17 Ja Morant 60.00 150.00
18 Mfiondu Kabengele 2.00 5.00
19 Coby White 5.00 12.00
20 KZ Okpala 2.00 5.00
21 PJ Washington Jr. 5.00 12.00
22 Admiral Schofield 2.00 5.00
23 Chuma Okeke 2.50 6.00
24 Ignas Brazdeikis 2.00 5.00
25 Matisse Thybulle 3.00 8.00
26 Ty Jerome 3.00 8.00
27 RJ Barrett 6.00 15.00
28 Jordan Poole 6.00 15.00
29 Jaxson Hayes 2.50 6.00
30 Carsen Edwards 2.00 5.00
31 Tyler Herro 8.00 20.00
32 Jaylen Nowell 2.00 5.00
33 Nickeil Alexander-Walker 2.50 6.00
34 Quinndary Weatherspoon 1.50 4.00
35 Brandon Clarke 3.00 8.00
36 Nassir Little 2.50 6.00
37 De'Andre Hunter 6.00 15.00
38 Keldon Johnson 5.00 12.00
39 Rui Hachimura 6.00 15.00
40 Bruno Fernando 2.00 5.00

2019-20 Court Kings Fledgling Expressionist Memorabilia Prime

*PRIME/25: 1X TO 2.5X BASIC
STATED PRINT RUN 25 SER.#'d SETS
7 Zion Williamson 300.00 600.00

2019-20 Court Kings Fresh Paint Autographs

COMMON CARD 3.00 8.00
SEMISTARS 4.00 10.00
UNLISTED STARS 5.00 12.00
STATED PRINT RUN 75-149 SER.#'d SETS
EXCHANGE DEADLINE 12/12/2021
1 Admiral Schofield/149 4.00 10.00
2 Bol Bol/149 8.00 20.00
FP-BCL Brandon Clarke/149 25.00 60.00
4 Bruno Fernando/149 4.00 10.00
5 Cam Reddish/149 5.00 12.00
6 Cameron Johnson/149 8.00 20.00
7 Carsen Edwards/149 4.00 10.00
8 Chuma Okeke/149 12.00 30.00
9 Coby White/149 75.00 200.00
10 Cody Martin/149 5.00 12.00
11 Darius Bazley/149 3.00 8.00
12 De'Andre Hunter/149 12.00 30.00
13 Dylan Windler/149 4.00 10.00
14 Eric Paschall/149 4.00 10.00
15 Goga Bitadze/149 5.00 12.00
16 Grant Williams/149 5.00 12.00
17 Ignas Brazdeikis/149 4.00 10.00
18 Isaiah Roby/149 4.00 10.00
19 Ja Morant/125 300.00 600.00
20 Jarrett Culver/149 3.00 8.00
21 Jaxson Hayes/149 5.00 12.00
22 Jaylen Nowell/149 4.00 10.00
23 Jordan Poole/149 12.00 30.00
24 Keldon Johnson/149 10.00 25.00
25 Kevin Porter Jr./149 6.00 15.00
26 Kyle Guy/149 12.00 30.00
27 KZ Okpala/149 4.00 10.00
28 Luka Samanic/149 4.00 10.00
29 Matisse Thybulle/149 15.00 40.00
30 Mfiondu Kabengele/149 4.00 10.00
31 Nassir Little/149 5.00 12.00
32 Nickeil Alexander-Walker/149 5.00 12.00
33 PJ Washington Jr./149 10.00 25.00
34 Quinndary Weatherspoon/149 3.00 8.00
35 RJ Barrett/125 75.00 200.00
36 Romeo Langford/149 3.00 8.00
37 Rui Hachimura/149 40.00 100.00
38 Sekou Doumbouya/149 3.00 8.00
39 Talen Horton-Tucker/149 5.00 12.00
40 Tremont Waters/149 4.00 10.00
41 Ty Jerome/149 6.00 15.00
42 Tyler Herro/149 40.00 100.00
43 Zion Williamson/75 800.00 1,500.00
44 Tacko Fall/149 12.00 30.00
45 Justin Robinson/99 3.00 8.00

2019-20 Court Kings Fresh Paint Autographs Citrine

*CITRINE: .6X TO 1.5X BASIC
STATED PRINT RUN 25-49 SER.#'d SETS
EXCHANGE DEADLINE 12/12/2021
19 Ja Morant/49 500.00 1,000.00
43 Zion Williamson/25 2,000.00 3,000.00

2019-20 Court Kings Fresh Paint Autographs Jade

*JADE: .75X TO 2X BASIC
STATED PRINT RUN 25 SER.#'d SETS
EXCHANGE DEADLINE 12/12/2021
19 Ja Morant 600.00 1,200.00
37 Rui Hachimura 60.00 150.00
43 Zion Williamson 2,000.00 3,000.00

2019-20 Court Kings Fresh Paint Autographs Ruby

*RUBY: .5X TO 1.2X BASIC
STATED PRINT RUN 49-99 SER.#'d SETS
EXCHANGE DEADLINE 12/12/2021
19 Ja Morant/99 400.00 800.00
43 Zion Williamson/49 1,000.00 2,000.00

2019-20 Court Kings Fresh Paint Autographs Sapphire

*SAPPHIRE/25: .75X TO 2X BASIC
STATED PRINT RUN 10-25 SER.#'d SETS
EXCHANGE DEADLINE 12/12/2021
2 Bol Bol/25 20.00 50.00
19 Ja Morant/25 600.00 1,200.00
21 Jaxson Hayes/25 20.00 50.00
37 Rui Hachimura/25 60.00 150.00

2019-20 Court Kings Heir Apparent Autographs

COMMON CARD 3.00 8.00
SEMISTARS 4.00 10.00
UNLISTED STARS 5.00 12.00
STATED PRINT RUN 75-149 SER.#'d SETS
EXCHANGE DEADLINE 12/12/2021
1 Quinndary Weatherspoon/149 3.00 8.00
2 Justin Robinson/99 3.00 8.00
3 Grant Williams/149 5.00 12.00
4 Tyler Herro/149 40.00 100.00
5 Jarrett Culver/125 3.00 8.00
6 Zion Williamson/75 800.00 1,500.00
7 Cody Martin/149 5.00 12.00
8 Brandon Clarke/149 25.00 60.00
9 Cameron Johnson/149 8.00 20.00
10 KZ Okpala/149 4.00 10.00
11 Ty Jerome/149 6.00 15.00
12 Alen Smailagic/149 3.00 8.00
HA-KPJ Kevin Porter Jr./149 6.00 15.00
14 Nassir Little/149 5.00 12.00
15 Isaiah Roby/149 4.00 10.00
16 Keldon Johnson/149 10.00 25.00
17 Luka Samanic/149 4.00 10.00
18 Jalen Lecque/149 3.00 8.00
19 Nicolas Claxton/149 6.00 15.00
20 Sekou Doumbouya/149 3.00 8.00
21 Ignas Brazdeikis/149 4.00 10.00
22 Darius Bazley/149 3.00 8.00
23 Goga Bitadze/149 5.00 12.00
24 Coby White/149 75.00 200.00
25 Chuma Okeke/149 12.00 30.00
26 Nickeil Alexander-Walker/149 5.00 12.00
27 Admiral Schofield/149 4.00 10.00
28 Jordan Poole/149 12.00 30.00
29 Cam Reddish/149 5.00 12.00
30 RJ Barrett/125 75.00 200.00
31 Miye Oni/149 3.00 8.00
32 Carsen Edwards/149 4.00 10.00
33 De'Andre Hunter/125 12.00 30.00
34 Luguentz Dort/149 12.00 30.00
35 Jaxson Hayes/149 5.00 12.00
36 Ja Morant/149 300.00 600.00
37 Talen Horton-Tucker/149 5.00 12.00
38 Rui Hachimura/149 40.00 100.00
39 Tacko Fall/149 12.00 30.00
40 Daniel Gafford/149 6.00 15.00
41 PJ Washington Jr./149 10.00 25.00
42 Dylan Windler/149 4.00 10.00
43 Brian Bowen II/149 3.00 8.00
44 Matisse Thybulle/149 15.00 40.00
45 Romeo Langford/149 3.00 8.00

2019-20 Court Kings Heir Apparent Autographs Citrine

*CITRINE: .6X TO 1.5X BASIC
STATED PRINT RUN 25-49 SER.#'d SETS
EXCHANGE DEADLINE 12/12/2021
6 Zion Williamson/25 2,000.00 3,000.00
35 Jaxson Hayes/49 15.00 40.00
36 Ja Morant/49 500.00 1,000.00

2019-20 Court Kings Heir Apparent Autographs Jade

*JADE: .75X TO 2X BASIC
STATED PRINT RUN 25 SER.#'d SETS
EXCHANGE DEADLINE 12/12/2021
6 Zion Williamson 2,000.00 3,000.00
18 Jalen Lecque 25.00 60.00
36 Ja Morant 600.00 1,200.00

2019-20 Court Kings Heir Apparent Autographs Ruby

*RUBY: .5X TO 1.2X BASIC
STATED PRINT RUN 49-99 SER.#'d SETS
EXCHANGE DEADLINE 12/12/2021
6 Zion Williamson/49 1,000.00 2,000.00
36 Ja Morant/99 400.00 800.00

2019-20 Court Kings Heir Apparent Autographs Sapphire

*SAPPHIRE/25: .75X TO 2X BASIC
STATED PRINT RUN 10-25 SER.#'d SETS
EXCHANGE DEADLINE 12/12/2021
18 Jalen Lecque/25 25.00 60.00
36 Ja Morant/25 600.00 1,200.00

2019-20 Court Kings High Court Signatures

COMMON CARD 2.50 6.00
SEMISTARS 3.00 8.00
UNLISTED STARS 4.00 10.00
STATED PRINT RUN 49-179 SER.#'d SETS
EXCHANGE DEADLINE 12/12/2021
1 Cedi Osman/179 3.00 8.00
2 James Ennis/179 2.50 6.00
3 Otis Birdsong/179 4.00 10.00
4 Ralph Sampson/179 3.00 8.00
5 P.J. Tucker /179 3.00 8.00
6 Kerry Kittles/179 2.50 6.00
7 Frank Jackson/179 2.50 6.00
8 Erick Strickland/179 2.50 6.00
9 Fat Lever/179 3.00 8.00
10 Avery Johnson/149 2.50 6.00
11 Dennis Rodman/49 30.00 80.00
12 Chris Mullin/99 5.00 12.00
13 Chandler Hutchison/179 2.50 6.00
14 Alvan Adams/179 2.50 6.00
15 Montrezl Harrell/179 3.00 8.00
16 Kenny ""Sky"" Walker/179 3.00 8.00
17 Bill Cartwright/149 3.00 8.00
18 Eddie Jones/149 3.00 8.00
19 Jamal Mashburn/179 4.00 10.00
20 Thaddeus Young/179 2.50 6.00
21 Micheal Ray Richardson/179 4.00 10.00
22 Arvydas Sabonis/99 4.00 10.00
23 Caron Butler/149 3.00 8.00
24 Nate McMillan/179 3.00 8.00
25 Al-Farouq Aminu/179 2.50 6.00
26 Dee Brown/99 2.50 6.00
27 Robert Covington/179 2.50 6.00
28 Quinn Cook/179 3.00 8.00
29 Jonah Bolden/179 4.00 10.00
30 Aaron Holiday/179 3.00 8.00
31 Ernie DiGregorio/179 3.00 8.00
32 B.J. Armstrong/179 4.00 10.00
33 Damian Jones/179 2.50 6.00
34 Thon Maker/179 2.50 6.00
35 Jalen Brunson/179 10.00 25.00
36 Sidney Moncrief/179 4.00 10.00
37 Wesley Matthews/179 2.50 6.00
38 Bob Dandridge/179 2.50 6.00
39 Tom Chambers/179 4.00 10.00
40 Cherokee Parks/179 2.50 6.00

2019-20 Court Kings High Court Signatures Citrine

*CITRINE/49: .6X TO 1.5X BASIC
*CITRINE/25: .75X TO 2X BASIC
STATED PRINT RUN 10-49 SER.#'d SETS
EXCHANGE DEADLINE 12/12/2021

2019-20 Court Kings High Court Signatures Jade

*JADE/25: .75X TO 2X BASIC
STATED PRINT RUN 10-25 SER.#'d SETS
EXCHANGE DEADLINE 12/12/2021

2019-20 Court Kings High Court Signatures Ruby

*RUBY/49-99: .5X TO 1.2X BASIC
*RUBY/25-35: .75X TO 2X BASIC
STATED PRINT RUN 25-99 SER.#'d SETS
EXCHANGE DEADLINE 12/12/2021

2019-20 Court Kings High Court Signatures Sapphire

*SAPPHIRE/25: .75X TO 2X BASIC
STATED PRINT RUN 5-25 SER.#'d SETS
EXCHANGE DEADLINE 12/12/2021

2019-20 Court Kings Impressionist Ink Autographs

COMMON CARD 2.50 6.00
SEMISTARS 3.00 8.00
UNLISTED STARS 4.00 10.00
STATED PRINT RUN 49-179 SER.#'d SETS
EXCHANGE DEADLINE 12/12/2021
1 Tom Heinsohn/99 4.00 10.00

2 Jack Marin/149 2.50 6.00
3 Alen Smailagic/179 2.50 6.00
4 Nicolas Claxton/179 5.00 12.00
5 Erick Strickland/179 2.50 6.00
6 Quinn Cook/179 3.00 8.00
7 Jalen Brunson/149 10.00 25.00
8 Stephen Jackson/149 2.50 6.00
9 Yuta Watanabe/149 4.00 10.00
10 Dell Curry/99 2.50 6.00
11 Rafer Alston/99 2.50 6.00
12 Brad Daugherty/99 3.00 8.00
13 Rick Fox/179 3.00 8.00
14 Lonzo Ball/49 20.00 50.00
15 Justin James/179 2.50 6.00
16 Cedric Maxwell/149 3.00 8.00
17 James Ennis/179 2.50 6.00
18 Tim Hardaway/99 5.00 12.00
19 Raja Bell/99 3.00 8.00
20 Luguentz Dort/179 10.00 25.00
21 Chandler Hutchison/179 2.50 6.00
22 Noah Vonleh/179 2.50 6.00
23 Frank Jackson/179 2.50 6.00
24 Horace Grant/149 4.00 10.00
25 Glen Rice/99 3.00 8.00
26 Miye Oni/149 2.50 6.00
27 Justin Holiday/179 2.50 6.00
28 Mark Aguirre/149 3.00 8.00
29 Daniel Gafford/179 5.00 12.00
30 Damian Jones/179 2.50 6.00

2019-20 Court Kings Impressionist Ink Autographs Citrine
*CITRINE/49: .6X TO 1.5X BASIC
*CITRINE/25: ..75X TO 2X BASIC
STATED PRINT RUN 10-49 SER.#'d SETS
EXCHANGE DEADLINE 12/12/2021

2019-20 Court Kings Impressionist Ink Autographs Jade
*JADE/25: ..75X TO 2X BASIC
STATED PRINT RUN 10-25 SER.#'d SETS
EXCHANGE DEADLINE 12/12/2021
1 Tom Heinsohn/25 12.00 30.00
20 Luguentz Dort/25 15.00 40.00

2019-20 Court Kings Impressionist Ink Autographs Ruby
*RUBY/49-99: .5X TO 1.2X BASIC
*RUBY/25-35: ..75X TO 2X BASIC
STATED PRINT RUN 25-99 SER.#'d SETS
EXCHANGE DEADLINE 12/12/2021

2019-20 Court Kings Impressionist Ink Autographs Sapphire
*SAPPHIRE/25: .75X TO 2X BASIC
STATED PRINT RUN 5-25 SER.#'d SETS
EXCHANGE DEADLINE 12/12/2021
20 Luguentz Dort/25 15.00 40.00

2019-20 Court Kings Le Cinque Piu Belle
1 Rui Hachimura 80.00 200.00
2 Zion Williamson 1,000.00 2,000.00
3 Stephen Curry 300.00 600.00
4 Ja Morant 500.00 1,000.00
5 RJ Barrett 150.00 400.00
6 Kawhi Leonard 150.00 400.00
7 LeBron James 800.00 1,500.00
8 Charles Barkley 75.00 200.00
9 Giannis Antetokounmpo 200.00 500.00
10 Kevin Garnett 125.00 300.00

2019-20 Court Kings Legacies Signatures
COMMON CARD 4.00 10.00
SEMISTARS 5.00 12.00
UNLISTED STARS 6.00 15.00
STATED PRINT RUN 35-49 SER.#'d SETS
EXCHANGE DEADLINE 12/12/2021
2 Charles Barkley/35 100.00 250.00
3 Kevin Durant/35 150.00 400.00
4 Dennis Rodman/49 100.00 250.00
5 Kevin Garnett/35 100.00 250.00
6 Magic Johnson/49 60.00 150.00
7 Stephen Curry/35 600.00 1,200.00
9 Julius Erving/49 60.00 150.00
10 Hakeem Olajuwon/49 50.00 120.00

2019-20 Court Kings Legacies Signatures Citrine
*CITRINE/25: .5X TO 1.25X BASIC
STATED PRINT RUN 15-25 SER.#'d SETS
EXCHANGE DEADLINE 12/12/2021

2019-20 Court Kings Legacies Signatures Ruby
*RUBY: .5X TO 1.25X BASIC
STATED PRINT RUN 15-35 SER.#'d SETS
EXCHANGE DEADLINE 12/12/2021

2019-20 Court Kings Maestros
COMMON CARD .50 1.25
SEMISTARS .60 1.50
UNLISTED STARS .75 2.00
*RUBY/149: .6X TO 1.5X BASIC
*CITRINE/49: 1X TO 2.5X BASIC
*SAPPHIRE/25: 1.25X TO 3X BASIC
1 RJ Barrett 2.00 5.00
2 Pascal Siakam 1.25 3.00
3 Tyler Herro 2.50 6.00
4 Giannis Antetokounmpo 12.00 30.00
5 Stephen Curry 6.00 15.00
6 Karl-Anthony Towns 1.25 3.00
7 Damian Lillard 2.00 5.00
8 James Harden 1.50 4.00
9 Russell Westbrook 1.25 3.00
10 Luka Doncic 15.00 40.00
11 Eric Paschall .60 1.50
12 Trae Young 2.00 5.00
13 Rui Hachimura 2.00 5.00
14 CJ McCollum .75 2.00
15 Kemba Walker .60 1.50
16 Devin Booker .20 .50
17 Jayson Tatum 3.00 8.00
18 Kawhi Leonard 8.00 20.00
19 Zion Williamson 50.00 120.00
20 LeBron James 20.00 50.00
21 PJ Washington Jr. 1.50 4.00
22 Kyrie Irving 1.50 4.00
23 Coby White 10.00 25.00
24 Anthony Davis 2.00 5.00
25 Donovan Mitchell 1.50 4.00
26 Joel Embiid 1.50 4.00
27 Bradley Beal 1.00 2.50
28 Derrick Rose 1.50 4.00
29 Ja Morant 30.00 80.00
30 De'Aaron Fox 1.25 3.00

2019-20 Court Kings Maestros Citrine
*CITRINE: 1X TO 2.5X BASIC
STATED PRINT RUN 49 SER.#'d SETS
1 RJ Barrett 20.00 50.00
12 Trae Young 12.00 30.00
17 Jayson Tatum 12.00 30.00
20 LeBron James 60.00 150.00

2019-20 Court Kings Maestros Ruby
*RUBY: .6X TO 1.5X BASIC
STATED PRINT RUN 149 SER.#'d SETS
1 RJ Barrett 12.00 30.00
12 Trae Young 8.00 20.00
17 Jayson Tatum 8.00 20.00
20 LeBron James 40.00 100.00

2019-20 Court Kings Maestros Sapphire
*SAPPHIRE: 1.2X TO 3X BASIC
STATED PRINT RUN 25 SER.#'d SETS
1 RJ Barrett 25.00 60.00
3 Tyler Herro 20.00 50.00
4 Giannis Antetokounmpo 60.00 150.00
10 Luka Doncic 75.00 200.00
12 Trae Young 15.00 40.00
13 Rui Hachimura 15.00 40.00
17 Jayson Tatum 40.00 100.00
19 Zion Williamson 300.00 600.00
20 LeBron James 150.00 400.00
24 Anthony Davis 12.00 30.00

2019-20 Court Kings Modern Strokes
COMMON CARD .50 1.25
SEMISTARS .60 1.50
UNLISTED STARS .75 2.00
*AMETHYST/99: .6X TO 1.5X BASIC
*JADE/25: 1.25X TO 3X BASIC
1 Karl-Anthony Towns 1.25 3.00
2 Giannis Antetokounmpo 10.00 25.00
3 Kristaps Porzingis 1.00 2.50
4 Stephen Curry 6.00 15.00
5 James Harden 1.50 4.00
6 Donovan Mitchell 1.50 4.00
7 Derrick Rose 1.50 4.00
8 Jayson Tatum 8.00 20.00
9 LeBron James 25.00 60.00
10 Trae Young 2.00 5.00
11 DeMar DeRozan 1.00 2.50
12 CJ McCollum .75 2.00
13 Brandon Ingram .75 2.00
14 Kemba Walker .60 1.50
15 Shai Gilgeous-Alexander 4.00 10.00
16 Kyle Lowry .75 2.00
17 Luka Doncic 25.00 60.00
18 Bradley Beal 1.00 2.50
19 De'Aaron Fox 1.25 3.00
20 Kyrie Irving 1.50 4.00
21 Devin Booker .20 .50
22 Anthony Davis 2.00 5.00
23 Joel Embiid 1.50 4.00
24 Kevin Love .75 2.00
25 Kawhi Leonard 2.00 5.00
26 Damian Lillard 2.00 5.00
27 Zach LaVine 1.25 3.00
28 Russell Westbrook 1.25 3.00
29 Pascal Siakam 1.25 3.00
30 Andre Drummond .60 1.50

2019-20 Court Kings Modern Strokes Amethyst
*AMETHYST/99: .6X TO 1.5X BASIC
STATED PRINT RUN 99 SER.#'d SETS
9 LeBron James 60.00 150.00

2019-20 Court Kings Modern Strokes Jade
*JADE/25: 1.25X TO 3X BASIC
STATED PRINT RUN 25 SER.#'d SETS
4 Stephen Curry 20.00 50.00
9 LeBron James 125.00 300.00
17 Luka Doncic 100.00 250.00
25 Kawhi Leonard 20.00 50.00

2019-20 Court Kings Mount Zion
1 Zion Williamson 400.00 800.00

2019-20 Court Kings Points in the Paint
COMMON CARD .50 1.25
SEMISTARS .60 1.50
UNLISTED STARS .75 2.00
*RUBY/149: .6X TO 1.5X BASIC
*CITRINE/49: 1X TO 2.5X BASIC
*SAPPHIRE/25: 1.25X TO 3X BASIC
1 Karl-Anthony Towns 1.25 3.00
2 DeMar DeRozan 1.00 2.50
3 Devin Booker .20 .50
4 Kristaps Porzingis 1.00 2.50
5 Brandon Ingram .75 2.00
6 Joel Embiid 1.50 4.00
7 James Harden 1.50 4.00
8 Shai Gilgeous-Alexander 4.00 10.00
9 Kawhi Leonard 6.00 15.00
10 Derrick Rose 1.50 4.00
11 Luka Doncic 25.00 60.00
12 Zach LaVine 1.25 3.00
13 LeBron James 30.00 80.00
14 De'Aaron Fox 1.25 3.00
15 Pascal Siakam 1.25 3.00
16 Trae Young 2.00 5.00
17 Kyrie Irving 1.50 4.00
18 Andre Drummond .60 1.50
19 Giannis Antetokounmpo 8.00 20.00
20 CJ McCollum .75 2.00
21 Anthony Davis 2.00 5.00
22 Stephen Curry 6.00 15.00
23 Kemba Walker .60 1.50
24 Kevin Love .75 2.00
25 Donovan Mitchell 1.50 4.00
26 Kyle Lowry .75 2.00
27 Damian Lillard 2.00 5.00
28 Jayson Tatum 3.00 8.00
29 Bradley Beal 1.00 2.50
30 Russell Westbrook 1.25 3.00

2019-20 Court Kings Points in the Paint Citrine
*CITRINE: 1X TO 2.5X BASIC
STATED PRINT RUN 49 SER.#'d SETS
9 Kawhi Leonard 20.00 50.00
11 Luka Doncic 100.00 250.00
13 LeBron James 125.00 300.00
19 Giannis Antetokounmpo 25.00 60.00
22 Stephen Curry 12.00 30.00
28 Jayson Tatum 25.00 60.00

2019-20 Court Kings Points in the Paint Ruby
*RUBY: .6X TO 1.5X BASIC
STATED PRINT RUN 149 SER.#'d SETS
9 Kawhi Leonard 12.00 30.00
11 Luka Doncic 60.00 150.00
13 LeBron James 75.00 200.00
19 Giannis Antetokounmpo 15.00 40.00
28 Jayson Tatum 15.00 40.00

2019-20 Court Kings Points in the Paint Sapphire
*SAPPHIRE: 1.2X TO 3X BASIC
STATED PRINT RUN 25 SER.#'d SETS
9 Kawhi Leonard 25.00 60.00
11 Luka Doncic 125.00 300.00
13 LeBron James 150.00 400.00
19 Giannis Antetokounmpo 100.00 250.00
22 Stephen Curry 20.00 50.00
28 Jayson Tatum 30.00 80.00

2020-21 Court Kings
*ARTIST PROOF: .6X TO 1.5X BASIC
*RUBY/149: 1.5X TO 4X BASIC
*AMETHYST/99: 2X TO 5X BASIC
*PINK/99: 2X TO 5X BASIC
*VIOLET/49: 2.5X TO 6X BASIC
*JADE/25: 3X TO 8X BASIC
*SAPPHIRE/25: 3X TO 8X BASIC
1 LaMarcus Aldridge .50 1.25
2 Shai Gilgeous-Alexander 2.50 6.00
3 Rudy Gobert .60 1.50
4 CJ McCollum .50 1.25
5 Devin Booker 1.25 3.00
6 Kawhi Leonard 1.25 3.00
7 Kemba Walker .50 1.25
8 Domantas Sabonis .60 1.50
9 Jamal Murray .75 2.00
10 Zach LaVine .75 2.00
11 Nikola Jokic 2.50 6.00
12 Collin Sexton .50 1.25
13 Bradley Beal .60 1.50
14 T.J. Warren .40 1.00
15 Gordon Hayward .50 1.25
16 Devonte' Graham .40 1.00
17 Kristaps Porzingis .60 1.50
18 D'Angelo Russell .50 1.25
19 Jrue Holiday .50 1.25
20 Bam Adebayo .75 2.00
21 Christian Wood .40 1.00
22 Kyle Lowry .60 1.50
23 Andre Drummond .50 1.25
24 Al Horford .50 1.25
25 John Collins .50 1.25
26 Nikola Vucevic .50 1.25
27 Jonas Valanciunas .40 1.00
28 Fred VanVleet .75 2.00
29 Stephen Curry 4.00 10.00
30 Zion Williamson 1.50 4.00
31 Giannis Antetokounmpo 2.50 6.00
32 Kelly Oubre Jr. .50 1.25
33 Khris Middleton .60 1.50
34 Paul George .75 2.00
35 Pascal Siakam .75 2.00
36 Derrick Rose .75 2.00
37 Damian Lillard 1.25 3.00
38 De'Aaron Fox .75 2.00
39 DeMar DeRozan .60 1.50
40 Jayson Tatum 2.00 5.00
41 Karl-Anthony Towns .75 2.00
42 James Harden 1.00 2.50
43 Anthony Davis 1.25 3.00
44 Kevin Durant 2.00 5.00
45 Jaylen Brown .75 2.00
46 Trae Young 1.25 3.00
47 Russell Westbrook 1.00 2.50
48 LeBron James 4.00 10.00
49 Rui Hachimura .60 1.50
50 Donovan Mitchell 1.00 2.50
51 Coby White .60 1.50
52 Mitchell Robinson .50 1.25
53 RJ Barrett .75 2.00
54 Jimmy Butler 1.00 2.50
55 Ja Morant 1.50 4.00
56 Brandon Ingram .60 1.50
57 Tyler Herro 1.00 2.50
58 Kyrie Irving 1.00 2.50
59 Luka Doncic 3.00 8.00
60 Joel Embiid 1.25 3.00
61 Marvin Bagley III .40 1.00
62 Blake Griffin .50 1.25
63 Chris Paul 1.00 2.50
64 Aaron Gordon .50 1.25
65 John Wall .60 1.50
66 Deandre Ayton .50 1.25
67 Ben Simmons .50 1.25
68 Desmond Bane RC 2.50 6.00
69 Vernon Carey Jr. RC .75 2.00
70 Anthony Edwards RC 15.00 40.00
71 Payton Pritchard RC 2.50 6.00
72 Onyeka Okongwu RC 1.50 4.00
73 Saddiq Bey RC 1.50 4.00
74 Cole Anthony RC 2.00 5.00
75 James Wiseman RC 1.00 2.50
76 Jaden McDaniels RC 2.50 6.00
77 RJ Hampton RC .75 2.00
78 Tyrese Maxey RC 6.00 15.00
79 Killian Hayes RC .75 2.00
80 Theo Maledon RC .75 2.00
81 Kira Lewis Jr. RC .75 2.00
82 Zeke Nnaji RC 1.00 2.50
83 Devin Vassell RC 2.50 6.00
84 Immanuel Quickley RC 2.00 5.00
85 Jahmi'us Ramsey RC .75 2.00
86 Jordan Nwora RC 1.00 2.50
87 Patrick Williams RC 2.00 5.00
88 Obi Toppin RC 1.50 4.00
89 Aleksej Pokusevski RC 1.00 2.50
90 Isaac Okoro RC 1.25 3.00
91 Aaron Nesmith RC 1.50 4.00
92 Isaiah Stewart RC 1.50 4.00
93 Precious Achiuwa RC 1.50 4.00
94 Malachi Flynn RC .75 2.00
95 Grant Riller RC .75 2.00
96 Tyrese Haliburton RC 6.00 15.00
97 LaMelo Ball RC 6.00 15.00
98 Jalen Smith RC 1.50 4.00
99 Deni Avdija RC 2.00 5.00
100 Josh Green RC 1.50 4.00
101 Desmond Bane 4.00 10.00
102 Vernon Carey Jr. 1.25 3.00
103 Anthony Edwards 25.00 60.00
104 Payton Pritchard 4.00 10.00
105 Onyeka Okongwu 2.50 6.00
106 Saddiq Bey 2.50 6.00
107 Cole Anthony 3.00 8.00
108 James Wiseman 1.50 4.00
109 Jaden McDaniels 4.00 10.00
110 RJ Hampton 1.25 3.00
111 Tyrese Maxey 10.00 25.00
112 Killian Hayes 1.25 3.00
113 Theo Maledon 1.25 3.00
114 Kira Lewis Jr. 1.25 3.00
115 Zeke Nnaji 1.50 4.00
116 Devin Vassell 4.00 10.00
117 Immanuel Quickley 3.00 8.00
118 Jahmi'us Ramsey 1.25 3.00
119 Jordan Nwora 1.50 4.00
120 Patrick Williams 3.00 8.00
121 Obi Toppin 2.50 6.00
122 Aleksej Pokusevski 1.50 4.00
123 Isaac Okoro 2.00 5.00
124 Aaron Nesmith 2.50 6.00
125 Isaiah Stewart 2.50 6.00
126 Precious Achiuwa 2.50 6.00
127 Malachi Flynn 1.25 3.00
128 Grant Riller 1.25 3.00
129 Tyrese Haliburton 10.00 25.00
130 LaMelo Ball 10.00 25.00
131 Jalen Smith 2.50 6.00
132 Deni Avdija 3.00 8.00
133 Josh Green 2.50 6.00
134 Desmond Bane 6.00 15.00
135 Vernon Carey Jr. 2.00 5.00
136 Anthony Edwards 60.00 150.00
137 Payton Pritchard 6.00 15.00
138 Onyeka Okongwu 4.00 10.00
139 Saddiq Bey 4.00 10.00
140 Cole Anthony 5.00 12.00
141 James Wiseman 2.50 6.00
142 Jaden McDaniels 6.00 15.00
143 RJ Hampton 2.00 5.00
144 Tyrese Maxey 15.00 40.00
145 Killian Hayes 2.00 5.00
146 Theo Maledon 2.00 5.00
147 Kira Lewis Jr. 2.00 5.00
148 Zeke Nnaji 2.50 6.00
149 Devin Vassell 6.00 15.00
150 Immanuel Quickley 5.00 12.00
151 Jahm'us Ramsey 2.00 5.00
152 Jordan Nwora 2.50 6.00
153 Patrick Williams 5.00 12.00
154 Obi Toppin 4.00 10.00
155 Aleksej Pokusevski 2.50 6.00
156 Isaac Okoro 3.00 8.00
157 Aaron Nesmith 4.00 10.00
158 Isaiah Stewart 4.00 10.00
159 Precious Achiuwa 4.00 10.00
160 Malachi Flynn 2.00 5.00
161 Grant Riller 2.00 5.00
162 Tyrese Haliburton 15.00 40.00
163 LaMelo Ball 15.00 40.00
164 Jalen Smith 4.00 10.00
165 Deni Avdija 5.00 12.00
166 Josh Green 4.00 10.00
167 Desmond Bane 25.00 60.00
168 Vernon Carey Jr. 8.00 20.00
169 Anthony Edwards 350.00 700.00
170 Payton Pritchard 25.00 60.00
171 Onyeka Okongwu 15.00 40.00
172 Saddiq Bey 15.00 40.00
173 Cole Anthony 20.00 50.00
174 James Wiseman 10.00 25.00
175 Jaden McDaniels 25.00 60.00
176 RJ Hampton 8.00 20.00
177 Tyrese Maxey 60.00 150.00
178 Killian Hayes 8.00 20.00
179 Theo Maledon 8.00 20.00
180 Kira Lewis Jr. 8.00 20.00
181 Zeke Nnaji 10.00 25.00
182 Devin Vassell 25.00 60.00
183 Immanuel Quickley 20.00 50.00
184 Jahmi'us Ramsey 8.00 20.00
185 Jordan Nwora 10.00 25.00
186 Patrick Williams 20.00 50.00
187 Obi Toppin 15.00 40.00
188 Aleksej Pokusevski 10.00 25.00
189 Isaac Okoro 12.00 30.00
190 Aaron Nesmith 15.00 40.00
191 Isaiah Stewart 15.00 40.00
192 Precious Achiuwa 15.00 40.00
193 Malachi Flynn 8.00 20.00
194 Grant Riller 8.00 20.00
195 Tyrese Haliburton 60.00 150.00
196 LaMelo Ball 60.00 150.00
197 Jalen Smith 15.00 40.00
198 Deni Avdija 20.00 50.00
199 Josh Green 15.00 40.00

2020-21 Court Kings Jade
STATED PRINT RUN 25 SER.#'d SETS

2020-21 Court Kings Acetate Rookies
1 Tyrese Maxey 10.00 25.00
2 RJ Hampton 1.25 3.00
3 Obi Toppin 2.50 6.00
4 Anthony Edwards 20.00 50.00
5 Deni Avdija 3.00 8.00
6 LaMelo Ball 10.00 25.00
7 James Wiseman 1.50 4.00
8 Cole Anthony 3.00 8.00
9 Tyrese Haliburton 10.00 25.00
10 Jalen Smith 2.50 6.00
11 Patrick Williams 3.00 8.00
12 Isaac Okoro 2.00 5.00
13 Kira Lewis Jr. 1.25 3.00
14 Aaron Nesmith 2.50 6.00
15 Killian Hayes 1.25 3.00
16 Onyeka Okongwu 2.50 6.00
17 Josh Green 2.50 6.00
18 Precious Achiuwa 2.50 6.00
19 Saddiq Bey 2.50 6.00
20 Zeke Nnaji 1.50 4.00
21 Aleksej Pokusevski 1.50 4.00
22 Udoka Azubuike 1.50 4.00
23 Isaiah Stewart 2.50 6.00
24 Devin Vassell 4.00 10.00
25 Immanuel Quickley 5.00 12.00

2020-21 Court Kings Art Nouveau Materials
*PRIME/25: 1X TO 2.5X BASIC
1 Anthony Edwards 20.00 50.00
2 James Wiseman 2.50 6.00
3 LaMelo Ball 15.00 40.00
4 Patrick Williams 5.00 12.00
5 Isaac Okoro 3.00 8.00
6 Onyeka Okongwu 4.00 10.00
7 Killian Hayes 2.00 5.00
8 Obi Toppin 4.00 10.00
9 Deni Avdija 5.00 12.00
10 Devin Vassell 6.00 15.00
11 Tyrese Haliburton 15.00 40.00
12 Jalen Smith 4.00 10.00
13 Cole Anthony 5.00 12.00
14 Aaron Nesmith 4.00 10.00
15 Kira Lewis Jr. 2.00 5.00
16 Derrick White 2.50 6.00
17 Victor Oladipo 2.00 5.00
18 Julius Randle 2.50 6.00
19 Ricky Rubio 2.50 6.00
20 Buddy Hield 2.50 6.00
21 Marcus Smart 2.50 6.00
22 Wendell Carter Jr. 2.00 5.00
23 Kyle Kuzma 3.00 8.00
24 Kevin Love 2.50 6.00
25 Spencer Dinwiddie 2.00 5.00
26 Andre Drummond 2.50 6.00
27 Brook Lopez 2.00 5.00
28 Marvin Bagley III 2.00 5.00
29 Dorian Finney-Smith 2.00 5.00
30 Paul Millsap 2.00 5.00
31 Shai Gilgeous-Alexander 12.00 30.00
32 Steven Adams 2.50 6.00
33 John Wall 3.00 8.00
34 Rudy Gobert 3.00 8.00
35 Kyle Lowry 3.00 8.00
36 CJ McCollum 2.50 6.00
37 Kevin Huerter 2.00 5.00
38 Cody Zeller 1.50 4.00
39 Kevon Looney 2.00 5.00
40 Marc Gasol 2.50 6.00

2020-21 Court Kings Artistic Endeavors Materials
STATED PRINT RUN 149 SER.#'d SETS
1 LeBron James 40.00 100.00
2 Stephen Curry 40.00 100.00
3 Kawhi Leonard 6.00 15.00
4 Nikola Jokic 12.00 30.00
5 Deandre Ayton 2.50 6.00
6 Nikola Vucevic 2.50 6.00
7 Trae Young 6.00 15.00
8 Zion Williamson 8.00 20.00
9 Ja Morant 8.00 20.00
10 Luka Doncic 15.00 40.00
11 Anthony Edwards 40.00 100.00
12 LaMelo Ball 30.00 80.00
13 James Wiseman 2.50 6.00
14 Deni Avdija 5.00 12.00
15 Obi Toppin 4.00 10.00
16 James Harden 5.00 12.00
17 Damian Lillard 6.00 15.00
18 Joel Embiid 6.00 15.00
19 Donovan Mitchell 6.00 15.00
20 Bradley Beal 3.00 8.00

2020-21 Court Kings Artistry in Motion
*AMETHYST/99: .75X TO 2X BASIC
*JADE/25: 2X TO 5X BASIC
1 Luka Doncic 8.00 20.00
2 Giannis Antetokounmpo 6.00 15.00
3 Kawhi Leonard 3.00 8.00
4 Anthony Davis 3.00 8.00
5 James Harden 2.50 6.00
6 LeBron James 10.00 25.00
7 Nikola Jokic 6.00 15.00
8 Damian Lillard 3.00 8.00
9 Stephen Curry 10.00 25.00
10 Zion Williamson 4.00 10.00
11 Jayson Tatum 5.00 12.00
12 Donovan Mitchell 2.50 6.00
13 Kevin Durant 5.00 12.00
14 Ja Morant 4.00 10.00
15 Ben Simmons 1.25 3.00
16 Tim Duncan 3.00 8.00
17 Dirk Nowitzki 3.00 8.00
18 Ray Allen 2.00 5.00
19 Anfernee Hardaway 3.00 8.00
20 Allen Iverson 3.00 8.00
21 Dwyane Wade 2.50 6.00
22 Dominique Wilkins 2.00 5.00
23 Chris Webber 1.50 4.00
24 Chauncey Billups 1.50 4.00
25 Dennis Rodman 3.00 8.00
26 Kevin Garnett 3.00 8.00
27 Charles Barkley 3.00 8.00
28 Hakeem Olajuwon 2.50 6.00
29 Paul Pierce 2.00 5.00
30 John Stockton 2.50 6.00

2020-21 Court Kings Aurora
1 LeBron James 150.00 400.00
2 Stephen Curry 150.00 400.00
3 Kevin Durant 80.00 200.00
4 Giannis Antetokounmpo 100.00 250.00
5 Damian Lillard 50.00 125.00
6 Anthony Davis 50.00 120.00
7 James Harden 40.00 100.00
8 Kawhi Leonard 50.00 125.00
9 Zion Williamson 60.00 150.00
10 Luka Doncic 125.00 300.00
11 Ja Morant 60.00 150.00
12 Larry Bird 80.00 200.00
13 Steve Nash 40.00 100.00
14 Obi Toppin 30.00 80.00
15 Tim Duncan 50.00 125.00
16 Anthony Edwards 400.00 800.00
17 LaMelo Ball 200.00 500.00

2020-21 Court Kings Blank Slate
1 Zion Williamson 150.00 400.00
2 Russell Westbrook 125.00 300.00
3 Tyler Herro 125.00 300.00
4 John Wall 60.00 150.00
5 LaMelo Ball 400.00 800.00
6 LeBron James 500.00 1,000.00
7 Luka Doncic 500.00 1,000.00
8 James Harden 150.00 400.00
9 Devin Booker 200.00 500.00
10 Ja Morant 400.00 800.00
11 Donovan Mitchell 150.00 400.00
12 Trae Young 200.00 500.00
13 Ben Simmons 100.00 250.00
14 Obi Toppin 75.00 200.00
15 Stephen Curry 500.00 1,000.00
16 Lauri Markkanen 150.00 400.00
17 James Wiseman 75.00 200.00
18 Kawhi Leonard 200.00 500.00
19 Anthony Edwards 1,500.00 3,000.00
20 Kyrie Irving 150.00 400.00
21 Shai Gilgeous-Alexander 300.00 600.00
22 Giannis Antetokounmpo 300.00 600.00
23 Anthony Davis 200.00 500.00
24 Joel Embiid 200.00 500.00
25 Jamal Murray 125.00 300.00
26 Shaquille O'Neal 200.00 500.00
27 Pascal Siakam 75.00 200.00
28 Kevin Garnett 200.00 500.00
29 Jayson Tatum 300.00 600.00
30 Tyrese Haliburton 400.00 800.00
31 Allen Iverson 200.00 500.00
32 Magic Johnson 200.00 500.00
33 Blake Griffin 75.00 200.00
34 Kemba Walker 20.00 50.00
35 Paul George 150.00 400.00
36 Nikola Jokic 350.00 700.00
37 Jimmy Butler 125.00 300.00
38 Bradley Beal 100.00 250.00
39 Larry Bird 200.00 500.00
40 Karl-Anthony Towns 50.00 120.00

2020-21 Court Kings Brush Strokes Autographs
STATED PRINT RUN 75-99 SER.#'d SETS
EXCHANGE DEADLINE 11/26/2022
*JADE: .4X TO 1X BASIC
*RUBY/49: .5X TO 1.2X BASIC
*VIOLET/35: .5X TO 1.2X BASIC
*SAPPHIRE/25: .6X TO 1.5X BASIC
1 Bradley Beal/75 8.00 20.00
2 T.J. McConnell/99 5.00 12.00
3 John Salmons/99 4.00 10.00
4 Otis Birdsong/99 5.00 12.00
5 Mike Conley/99 5.00 12.00
6 Al Harrington/99 4.00 10.00
7 Lonzo Ball/75 8.00 20.00
8 Myles Turner/99 6.00 15.00
10 Nate Archibald/99 8.00 20.00
11 Jordan Poole/99 10.00 25.00
12 Ty Jerome/99 4.00 10.00
13 Alex English/99 6.00 15.00
14 Rod Strickland/99 5.00 12.00
15 Magic Johnson/75 60.00 150.00
16 De'Andre Hunter/75 6.00 15.00
17 Caron Butler/99 5.00 12.00
18 Tim Hardaway/99 6.00 15.00
19 Isiah Thomas/75 10.00 25.00
20 Torrey Craig/99 5.00 12.00
21 Xavier McDaniel/99 5.00 12.00
22 Roy Hibbert/99 4.00 10.00
23 Harold Miner/99 5.00 12.00
24 Jason Richardson/99 6.00 15.00
25 Aaron Holiday/99 5.00 12.00
26 Jason Williams/99 30.00 80.00
27 Duncan Robinson/99 15.00 40.00
28 B.J. Armstrong/99 5.00 12.00
29 Pat Riley/75 15.00 40.00
30 PJ Washington Jr./99 6.00 15.00

2020-21 Court Kings Contemporaries
*AMETHYST/99: .75X TO 2X BASIC
*JADE/25: 1.5X TO 4X BASIC
1 Gordon Hayward 1.25 3.00
2 Donovan Mitchell 2.50 6.00
3 LeBron James 10.00 25.00
4 John Wall 1.50 4.00
5 RJ Barrett 2.00 5.00
6 Zion Williamson 4.00 10.00
7 Luka Doncic 8.00 20.00
8 CJ McCollum 1.25 3.00
9 Jimmy Butler 2.50 6.00
10 Kevin Durant 5.00 12.00
11 Kemba Walker 1.25 3.00
12 Karl-Anthony Towns 2.00 5.00
13 Ja Morant 4.00 10.00
14 Ben Simmons 1.25 3.00
15 Anthony Davis 3.00 8.00
16 Stephen Curry 10.00 25.00
17 Giannis Antetokounmpo 6.00 15.00
18 Kawhi Leonard 3.00 8.00
19 Devin Booker 3.00 8.00
20 Derrick Rose 2.00 5.00
21 Trae Young 3.00 8.00
22 Pascal Siakam 2.00 5.00
23 De'Aaron Fox 2.00 5.00
24 Paul George 2.00 5.00
25 Jayson Tatum 5.00 12.00
26 Kyrie Irving 2.50 6.00
27 Joel Embiid 3.00 8.00
28 Nikola Jokic 6.00 15.00
29 DeMar DeRozan 1.50 4.00
30 Coby White 1.50 4.00

2020-21 Court Kings Dressed to Impress
*AMETHYST/99: .75X TO 2X BASIC
*JADE/25: 1.5X TO 4X BASIC
1 Giannis Antetokounmpo 5.00 12.00
2 Jamal Murray 1.50 4.00
3 Ben Simmons 1.00 2.50
4 Damian Lillard 2.50 6.00
5 Luka Doncic 6.00 15.00
6 Devin Booker 2.50 6.00
7 Kemba Walker 1.00 2.50
8 Paul George 1.50 4.00
9 Donovan Mitchell 2.00 5.00
10 Stephen Curry 8.00 20.00

2020-21 Court Kings First Steps
*RUBY/149: .75X TO 2X BASIC
*VIOLET/49: 1.5X TO 4X BASIC
*SAPPHIRE/25: 2.5X TO 6X BASIC
1 LaMelo Ball 10.00 25.00
2 Anthony Edwards 12.00 30.00
3 Obi Toppin 2.50 6.00
4 Tyrese Haliburton 10.00 25.00
5 Killian Hayes 1.25 3.00
6 Patrick Williams 3.00 8.00
7 Isaac Okoro 2.00 5.00
8 Cole Anthony 3.00 8.00
9 Tyrese Maxey 10.00 25.00
10 James Wiseman 1.50 4.00

2020-21 Court Kings Fresh Paint Autographs
STATED PRINT RUN 75-149 SER.#'d SETS
EXCHANGE DEADLINE 11/26/2022
*JADE: .4X TO 1X BASIC
*RUBY/49-99: .5X TO 1.2X BASIC
*VIOLET/35: .5X TO 1.2X BASIC
*SAPPHIRE/25: .75X TO 2X BASIC
1 Kenyon Martin Jr./75 8.00 20.00
2 Desmond Bane/99 15.00 40.00
3 Tre Jones/149 8.00 20.00
4 Aaron Nesmith/149 10.00 25.00
5 Xavier Tillman/149 6.00 15.00
6 Josh Green/99 10.00 25.00
7 Elijah Hughes/75 5.00 12.00
8 Saddiq Bey/149 10.00 25.00
9 Tyler Bey/149 5.00 12.00
10 Robert Woodard II/149 5.00 12.00
11 James Wiseman/99 6.00 15.00
12 Cassius Stanley/149 5.00 12.00
13 LaMelo Ball/99 100.00 250.00
14 Theo Maledon/149 5.00 12.00
15 Killian Hayes/149 5.00 12.00
16 Skylar Mays/75 5.00 12.00
17 Deni Avdija/99 12.00 30.00
19 Jordan Nwora/149 6.00 15.00
20 Onyeka Okongwu/149 10.00 25.00
21 Obi Toppin/99 10.00 25.00
22 Cassius Winston/75 5.00 12.00
23 Precious Achiuwa/149 10.00 25.00
24 Vernon Carey Jr./99 5.00 12.00
25 Grant Riller/75 5.00 12.00
26 Saben Lee/75 5.00 12.00
27 Isaiah Stewart/149 10.00 25.00
28 Patrick Williams/149 12.00 30.00
29 Jahmi'us Ramsey/99 5.00 12.00
30 Kira Lewis Jr./75 5.00 12.00
31 Nick Richards/75 6.00 15.00
32 Payton Pritchard/149 15.00 40.00
33 Tyrese Maxey/149 75.00 200.00
34 Devin Vassell/99 15.00 40.00
35 Nico Mannion/149 5.00 12.00
36 Isaac Okoro/149 8.00 20.00
37 Immanuel Quickley/149 12.00 30.00
38 Tyrese Haliburton/149 75.00 200.00
39 Cole Anthony/149 12.00 30.00
40 RJ Hampton/149 5.00 12.00
41 Jaden McDaniels/149 15.00 40.00
42 Anthony Edwards/99 300.00 600.00
43 Malachi Flynn/99 5.00 12.00
45 Jalen Smith/75 10.00 25.00

2020-21 Court Kings Fresh Paint Autographs Violet
*VIOLET: .5X TO 1.2X BASIC
STATED PRINT RUN 35 SER.#'d SETS
EXCHANGE DEADLINE 11/26/2022

2020-21 Court Kings Heir Apparent Autographs
STATED PRINT RUN 99-149 SER.#'d SETS
EXCHANGE DEADLINE 11/26/2022
*JADE: .4X TO 1X BASIC
*RUBY/75-99: .5X TO 1.2X BASIC
*VIOLET/35-49: .5X TO 1.2X BASIC
*SAPPHIRE/25: .75X TO 2X BASIC
1 Daniel Oturu/149 5.00 12.00
3 Jalen Smith/99 10.00 25.00
4 Malachi Flynn/99 5.00 12.00
5 Tyrese Maxey/99 40.00 100.00
6 Elijah Hughes/149 5.00 12.00
7 Kenyon Martin Jr./149 8.00 20.00
8 RJ Hampton/99 5.00 12.00
10 James Wiseman/99 6.00 15.00
11 Precious Achiuwa/99 10.00 25.00
12 Jahmi'us Ramsey/99 5.00 12.00
13 Cole Anthony/99 12.00 30.00
14 Skylar Mays/149 5.00 12.00
15 Isaac Okoro/99 8.00 20.00
16 Saben Lee/149 5.00 12.00
17 Tyler Bey/99 5.00 12.00
18 Grant Riller/99 5.00 12.00
19 Isaiah Stewart/99 10.00 25.00
20 LaMelo Ball/99 100.00 250.00
21 Xavier Tillman/99 5.00 12.00
22 Tyrese Haliburton/99 40.00 100.00
23 Robert Woodard II/99 5.00 12.00
24 Killian Hayes/99 5.00 12.00
25 Onyeka Okongwu/99 10.00 25.00
26 Immanuel Quickley/99 10.00 25.00
27 Saddiq Bey/99 10.00 25.00
28 Aaron Nesmith/99 10.00 25.00
29 Josh Green/99 10.00 25.00
30 Patrick Williams/99 12.00 30.00
31 Devin Vassell/99 15.00 40.00
32 Cassius Winston/99 5.00 12.00
33 Nico Mannion/99 5.00 12.00
34 Jordan Nwora/99 6.00 15.00
35 Payton Pritchard/99 15.00 40.00
36 Zeke Nnaji/99 6.00 15.00
37 Deni Avdija/99 12.00 30.00
38 Vernon Carey Jr./149 5.00 12.00
39 Jaden McDaniels/99 15.00 40.00
40 Udoka Azubuike/149 6.00 15.00
41 Theo Maledon/99 5.00 12.00
42 Kira Lewis Jr./99 5.00 12.00

43 Obi Toppin/99 10.00 25.00
44 Desmond Bane/99 15.00 40.00
45 Anthony Edwards/99 300.00 600.00

2020-21 Court Kings Holding Court Signatures
STATED PRINT RUN 49-99 SER.#'d SETS
EXCHANGE DEADLINE 11/26/2022
*JADE: .4X TO 1X BASIC
*RUBY/49: .5X TO 1.2X BASIC
*VIOLET/35: .5X TO 1.2X BASIC
*SAPPHIRE/25: .6X TO 1.5X BASIC
1 Shawn Kemp/99 25.00 60.00
2 Otto Porter Jr./99 3.00 8.00
4 Dominique Wilkins/75 12.00 30.00
5 Chuma Okeke/99 5.00 12.00
6 Kawhi Leonard/49 75.00 200.00
7 Boban Marjanovic/75 8.00 20.00
8 Nickeil Alexander-Walker/99 5.00 12.00
9 Luke Walton/99 4.00 10.00
10 Mo Bamba/99 5.00 12.00
11 Wally Szczerbiak/99 4.00 10.00
12 Micheal Ray Richardson/99 3.00 8.00
13 Greg Ostertag/99 3.00 8.00
14 Mike Bibby/99 5.00 12.00
15 E'Twaun Moore/99 3.00 8.00
16 Robert Covington/99 4.00 10.00
17 Donte DiVincenzo/99 5.00 12.00
18 Sekou Doumbouya/99 3.00 8.00
19 Kevin Garnett/99 50.00 120.00
20 Danilo Gallinari/99 4.00 10.00
21 Jerry West/75 30.00 80.00
22 Baron Davis/99 5.00 12.00
23 Jarrett Culver/99 3.00 8.00
24 Ricky Rubio/99 5.00 12.00
25 Buddy Hield/99 5.00 12.00
26 Allen Iverson/75 50.00 120.00
27 Malik Beasley/99 4.00 10.00
28 Lou Williams/99 5.00 12.00
29 Vlade Divac/99 4.00 10.00
30 Brian Scalabrine/99 3.00 8.00
31 Cam Reddish/75 6.00 15.00
32 Ricky Pierce/99 3.00 8.00
33 Mitch Richmond/99 10.00 25.00
34 Robert Horry/99 8.00 20.00
35 John Salley/99 4.00 10.00
36 Marcus Camby/99 4.00 10.00
38 Michael Porter Jr./99 6.00 15.00
39 Sterling Brown/99 3.00 8.00
40 Isaac Bonga/99 3.00 8.00

2020-21 Court Kings Impressionist Ink
STATED PRINT RUN 75-99 SER.#'d SETS
EXCHANGE DEADLINE 11/26/2022
*JADE: .4X TO 1X BASIC
*RUBY/49: .5X TO 1.2X BASIC
*VIOLET/35: .5X TO 1.2X BASIC
*SAPPHIRE/25: .6X TO 1.5X BASIC
1 Shawn Bradley/99 5.00 12.00
2 Bam Adebayo/75 10.00 25.00
3 Dino Radja/99 5.00 12.00
4 JJ Redick/99 6.00 15.00
5 Brent Barry/99 5.00 12.00
6 Horace Grant/99 6.00 15.00
7 John Stockton/75 25.00 60.00
8 Collin Sexton/99 6.00 15.00
9 Kelly Oubre Jr./75 6.00 15.00
10 Ja Morant/75 75.00 200.00
11 Trae Young/75 40.00 100.00
12 Clyde Drexler/75 20.00 50.00
13 Avery Johnson/99 5.00 12.00
15 Keith Van Horn/99 5.00 12.00
17 Karl Malone/75 25.00 60.00
18 Daniel Gibson/99 4.00 10.00
19 Tim Legler/99 4.00 10.00
20 Brandon Clarke/99 6.00 15.00
21 Mark Jackson/99 5.00 12.00
22 James Johnson/99 4.00 10.00
23 Kevin Willis/99 5.00 12.00
24 Josh Hart/99 5.00 12.00
25 Doug McDermott/99 5.00 12.00
26 Lenny Wilkens/99 6.00 15.00
27 Lauri Markkanen/75 8.00 20.00
28 Isaiah Rider/99 5.00 12.00
29 Derek Fisher/75 6.00 15.00
30 Larry Bird/75 75.00 200.00

2020-21 Court Kings Le Cinque Piu Belle
1 Zion Williamson 40.00 100.00
2 Stephen Curry 100.00 250.00
3 Giannis Antetokounmpo 60.00 150.00
4 Luka Doncic 80.00 200.00
5 LeBron James 100.00 250.00
6 Kevin Durant 50.00 125.00
7 LaMelo Ball 80.00 200.00
8 Anthony Edwards 300.00 600.00
9 Damian Lillard 30.00 80.00
10 Ja Morant 40.00 100.00

2020-21 Court Kings Legacy Portrait Signatures
STATED PRINT RUN 49 SER.#'d SETS
EXCHANGE DEADLINE 11/26/2022
*JADE: .4X TO 1X BASIC
*RUBY/35: .4X TO 1X BASIC
*VIOLET/25: .5X TO 1.2X BASIC
1 Charles Barkley 100.00 250.00
2 Allen Iverson 100.00 250.00
3 Trae Young 60.00 150.00
4 Kareem Abdul-Jabbar 100.00 250.00
5 Julius Erving 75.00 200.00
6 Stephen Curry 400.00 800.00
7 Dwyane Wade 60.00 150.00
8 Kevin Garnett 50.00 120.00
9 Ja Morant 125.00 300.00
10 Shaquille O'Neal 100.00 250.00

2020-21 Court Kings Maestros
1 Jamal Murray 1.50 4.00
2 Donovan Mitchell 2.00 5.00
3 LeBron James 8.00 20.00
4 James Harden 2.00 5.00
5 Russell Westbrook 2.00 5.00
6 Zion Williamson 3.00 8.00
7 Luka Doncic 6.00 15.00
8 Damian Lillard 2.50 6.00
9 Jimmy Butler 2.00 5.00
10 Kevin Durant 4.00 10.00
11 Kemba Walker 1.00 2.50
12 Karl-Anthony Towns 1.50 4.00
13 Ja Morant 3.00 8.00
14 Ben Simmons 1.00 2.50
15 Anthony Davis 2.50 6.00
16 Stephen Curry 8.00 20.00
17 Giannis Antetokounmpo 5.00 12.00
18 Kawhi Leonard 2.50 6.00
19 Devin Booker 2.50 6.00
20 Blake Griffin 1.00 2.50
21 Trae Young 2.50 6.00
22 Pascal Siakam 1.50 4.00
23 De'Aaron Fox 1.50 4.00
24 Paul George 1.50 4.00
25 Jayson Tatum 4.00 10.00
26 Kyrie Irving 2.00 5.00
27 Joel Embiid 2.50 6.00
28 Nikola Jokic 5.00 12.00
29 Brandon Ingram 1.25 3.00
30 Chris Paul 2.00 5.00

2020-21 Court Kings Modern Strokes
1 Zion Williamson 4.00 10.00
2 Jimmy Butler 2.50 6.00
3 Kawhi Leonard 3.00 8.00
4 Jayson Tatum 5.00 12.00
5 Stephen Curry 10.00 25.00
6 Kemba Walker 1.25 3.00
7 Bradley Beal 1.50 4.00
8 Brandon Ingram 1.50 4.00
9 Luka Doncic 8.00 20.00
10 Donovan Mitchell 2.50 6.00
11 Ja Morant 4.00 10.00
12 James Harden 2.50 6.00
13 LeBron James 10.00 25.00
14 Anthony Davis 3.00 8.00
15 Jamal Murray 2.00 5.00
16 Devin Booker 3.00 8.00
17 Kyrie Irving 2.50 6.00
18 Trae Young 3.00 8.00
19 Khris Middleton 1.50 4.00
20 De'Aaron Fox 2.00 5.00
21 Tyler Herro 2.50 6.00
22 Kristaps Porzingis 1.50 4.00
23 Paul George 2.00 5.00
24 Zach LaVine 2.00 5.00
25 D'Angelo Russell 1.25 3.00
26 Kyle Lowry 1.50 4.00
27 Shai Gilgeous-Alexander 6.00 15.00
28 Joel Embiid 3.00 8.00
29 Damian Lillard 3.00 8.00
30 Kevin Durant 5.00 12.00

2020-21 Court Kings Modern Strokes Amethyst
STATED PRINT RUN 99 SER.#'d SETS

2020-21 Court Kings Modern Strokes Jade
STATED PRINT RUN 25 SER.#'d SETS

2020-21 Court Kings Points in the Paint
1 Bam Adebayo 1.25 3.00
2 Rudy Gobert 1.00 2.50
3 Karl-Anthony Towns 1.25 3.00
4 Joel Embiid 2.00 5.00
5 Nikola Jokic 4.00 10.00
6 Deandre Ayton .75 2.00
7 Kevin Love .75 2.00
8 Ben Simmons .75 2.00
9 Shaquille O'Neal 3.00 8.00
10 Anthony Davis 2.00 5.00
11 Hakeem Olajuwon 1.50 4.00
12 Giannis Antetokounmpo 4.00 10.00
13 Zion Williamson 15.00 40.00
14 LeBron James 20.00 50.00
15 Wilt Chamberlain 2.50 6.00
16 Russell Westbrook 1.50 4.00
17 David Robinson 1.50 4.00
18 Zach LaVine 1.25 3.00
19 Blake Griffin .75 2.00
20 James Harden 1.50 4.00
21 Kawhi Leonard 2.00 5.00
22 Tim Duncan 2.00 5.00
23 Donovan Mitchell 1.50 4.00
24 Patrick Ewing 1.00 2.50
25 Kristaps Porzingis 1.00 2.50
26 Pascal Siakam 1.25 3.00
27 Ja Morant 2.50 6.00
28 Kevin Durant 6.00 15.00
29 Damian Lillard 2.00 5.00
30 John Wall 1.00 2.50

2020-21 Court Kings Rookie Exclusive
1 LaMelo Ball 60.00 150.00

2020-21 Court Kings Rookie Expression Memorabilia
1 Nico Mannion 2.00 5.00
2 Jordan Nwora 2.50 6.00
3 Tre Jones 3.00 8.00
4 Robert Woodard II 2.00 5.00
5 CJ Elleby 2.00 5.00
6 Xavier Tillman 2.50 6.00
7 Theo Maledon 2.00 5.00
8 Daniel Oturu 2.00 5.00
9 Vernon Carey Jr. 2.00 5.00
10 Tyrell Terry 1.50 4.00
11 Desmond Bane 6.00 15.00
12 Malachi Flynn 2.00 5.00
13 Jaden McDaniels 6.00 15.00
14 Udoka Azubuike 2.50 6.00
15 Payton Pritchard 6.00 15.00
16 Immanuel Quickley 5.00 12.00
17 RJ Hampton 2.00 5.00
18 Jahmi'us Ramsey 2.00 5.00
19 Zeke Nnaji 2.50 6.00
20 Tyrese Maxey 15.00 40.00
21 Precious Achiuwa 4.00 10.00
22 Saddiq Bey 4.00 10.00
23 Josh Green 4.00 10.00
24 Aleksej Pokusevski 2.50 6.00
25 Isaiah Stewart 4.00 10.00
26 Cole Anthony 5.00 12.00
27 Aaron Nesmith 4.00 10.00
28 Kira Lewis Jr. 2.00 5.00
29 Tyrese Haliburton 15.00 40.00
30 Devin Vassell 6.00 15.00
31 Jalen Smith 4.00 10.00
32 Deni Avdija 5.00 12.00
33 Obi Toppin 4.00 10.00
34 Killian Hayes 2.00 5.00
35 Onyeka Okongwu 4.00 10.00
36 Isaac Okoro 3.00 8.00
37 Patrick Williams 5.00 12.00
38 LaMelo Ball 15.00 40.00
39 James Wiseman 2.50 6.00
40 Anthony Edwards 20.00 50.00

2020-21 Court Kings Rookie Expression Memorabilia Prime
STATED PRINT RUN 25 SER.#'d SETS

2020-21 Court Kings Works in Progress
*RUBY/149: 1X TO 2.5X BASIC
*VIOLET/49: 2X TO 5X BASIC
*SAPPHIRE/25: 3X TO 8X BASIC
1 Tyrese Haliburton 10.00 25.00
2 Obi Toppin 2.50 6.00
3 LaMelo Ball 50.00 120.00
4 Killian Hayes 1.25 3.00
5 Anthony Edwards 40.00 100.00
6 Patrick Williams 3.00 8.00
7 Aaron Nesmith 2.50 6.00
8 Devin Vassell 4.00 10.00
9 Deni Avdija 3.00 8.00
10 Tyrese Maxey 20.00 50.00
11 James Wiseman 1.50 4.00
12 Onyeka Okongwu 2.50 6.00
13 Cole Anthony 3.00 8.00
14 Isaac Okoro 2.00 5.00
15 Jalen Smith 2.50 6.00
16 Payton Pritchard 4.00 10.00
17 Josh Green 2.50 6.00
18 Jordan Nwora 1.50 4.00
19 Desmond Bane 4.00 10.00
20 Precious Achiuwa 2.50 6.00
21 Kira Lewis Jr. 1.25 3.00
22 Zeke Nnaji 1.50 4.00
23 Immanuel Quickley 3.00 8.00
24 Malachi Flynn 1.25 3.00
25 Saddiq Bey 2.50 6.00
26 Vernon Carey Jr. 1.25 3.00
27 Aleksej Pokusevski 1.50 4.00
28 Jaden McDaniels 4.00 10.00
29 Isaiah Stewart 2.50 6.00
30 RJ Hampton 1.25 3.00

2020-21 Court Kings Works in Progress Sapphire
*SAPPHIRE: 3X TO 8X BASIC
STATED PRINT RUN 25 SER.#'d SETS

2021-22 Court Kings
COMMON CARD (1-67) .30 .75
SEMISTARS .40 1.00
UNLISTED STARS .50 1.25
COMMON RC (68-100) .60 1.50
RC SEMIS .75 2.00
RC UNLISTED 1.00 2.50
COMMON CARD (101-133) 1.00 2.50
SEMISTARS 1.25 3.00
UNLISTED STARS 1.50 4.00
COMMON CARD (134-166) 3.00 8.00
SEMISTARS 4.00 10.00
UNLISTED STARS 5.00 12.00
COMMON CARD (167-199) 10.00 25.00
SEMISTARS 12.00 30.00
UNLISTED STARS 15.00 40.00
*ARTIST PROOF: .5X TO 1.2X BASIC
*RUBY/149: 1.25X TO 3X BASIC
*AMETHYST/99: 1.5X TO 4X BASIC
*PINK/99: 1.5X TO 4X BASIC
*75TH ANN/75: 1.5X TO 4X BASIC
*VIOLET/49: 2X TO 5X BASIC
1 Trae Young 1.25 3.00
2 LaMelo Ball 1.25 3.00
3 DeMar DeRozan .60 1.50
4 Nikola Jokic 2.50 6.00
5 Paul George .75 2.00
6 LeBron James 4.00 10.00
7 Kevin Durant 1.50 4.00
8 Jaylen Brown .75 2.00
9 Luka Doncic 3.00 8.00
10 Anthony Davis 1.25 3.00
11 Julius Randle .60 1.50
12 Ja Morant 1.50 4.00
13 Zach LaVine .75 2.00
14 Cole Anthony .60 1.50
15 Jayson Tatum 2.00 5.00
16 Jerami Grant .50 1.25
17 CJ McCollum .40 1.00
18 Karl-Anthony Towns .75 2.00
19 Bam Adebayo .75 2.00
20 Chris Paul 1.00 2.50
21 RJ Barrett .75 2.00
22 Lonzo Ball .50 1.25
23 James Harden 1.00 2.50
24 Jrue Holiday .60 1.50
25 Kristaps Porzingis .60 1.50
26 Anthony Edwards 2.50 6.00
27 John Collins .50 1.25
28 Klay Thompson 1.25 3.00
29 Tyrese Haliburton 1.00 2.50
30 Stephen Curry 3.00 8.00
31 Fred VanVleet .60 1.50
32 Khris Middleton .60 1.50
33 Jarrett Allen .50 1.25
34 Giannis Antetokounmpo 2.50 6.00
35 Caris LeVert .40 1.00
36 Dejounte Murray .50 1.25
37 Tobias Harris .40 1.00
38 Tyrese Maxey 1.25 3.00
39 Brandon Ingram .60 1.50
40 Devin Booker 1.25 3.00
41 Christian Wood .40 1.00
42 Domantas Sabonis .60 1.50
43 Rudy Gobert .60 1.50
44 Carmelo Anthony .75 2.00
45 Deandre Ayton .50 1.25
46 Pascal Siakam .50 1.25
47 Darius Garland .75 2.00
48 D'Angelo Russell .50 1.25
49 Joel Embiid 1.25 3.00
50 Kyle Lowry .50 1.25
51 De'Aaron Fox .75 2.00
52 Miles Bridges .40 1.00
53 Kawhi Leonard 1.25 3.00
54 Jimmy Butler .75 2.00
55 Jamal Murray .75 2.00
56 Shai Gilgeous-Alexander 2.50 6.00
57 Mike Conley .40 1.00
58 Kyle Kuzma .60 1.50
59 Russell Westbrook .75 2.00
60 Derrick Rose .75 2.00
61 Dennis Schroder .50 1.25
62 Zion Williamson 1.25 3.00
63 Desmond Bane 1.00 2.50
64 Jaren Jackson Jr. .75 2.00
65 Bradley Beal .60 1.50
66 Donovan Mitchell 1.00 2.50
67 Damian Lillard 1.25 3.00
68 Scottie Barnes RC 3.00 8.00
69 Josh Giddey RC 3.00 8.00
70 Joshua Primo RC .75 2.00
71 Jalen Green RC 5.00 12.00
72 James Bouknight RC .75 2.00
73 Bones Hyland RC 1.25 3.00
74 Ziaire Williams RC 1.25 3.00
75 Ayo Dosunmu RC 2.00 5.00
76 Chris Duarte RC .75 2.00
77 Cade Cunningham RC 6.00 15.00
78 Moses Moody RC 2.00 5.00
79 Corey Kispert RC 1.25 3.00
80 Alperen Sengun RC 3.00 8.00
81 Jeremiah Robinson-Earl RC 1.00 2.50
82 Tre Mann RC 1.50 4.00
83 Jalen Suggs RC 2.50 6.00
84 Trey Murphy III RC 3.00 8.00
85 Jalen Johnson RC 3.00 8.00
86 Kai Jones RC .75 2.00
87 Cameron Thomas RC 2.00 5.00
88 Evan Mobley RC 4.00 10.00
89 Josh Christopher RC .75 2.00
90 Keon Johnson RC 1.00 2.50
91 Isaiah Jackson RC 1.00 2.50
92 Franz Wagner RC 3.00 8.00
93 Luka Garza RC 1.00 2.50
94 Quentin Grimes RC 2.00 5.00
95 Brandon Boston Jr. RC 1.00 2.50
96 Davion Mitchell RC 1.00 2.50
97 Usman Garuba RC .75 2.00
98 Santi Aldama RC 1.25 3.00
99 Jared Butler RC 1.00 2.50
100 Jonathan Kuminga RC 3.00 8.00
101 Scottie Barnes 5.00 12.00
102 Josh Giddey 5.00 12.00
103 Joshua Primo 1.25 3.00
104 Jalen Green 8.00 20.00
105 James Bouknight 1.25 3.00
106 Bones Hyland 2.00 5.00
107 Ziaire Williams 2.00 5.00
108 Ayo Dosunmu 3.00 8.00
109 Chris Duarte 1.25 3.00
110 Cade Cunningham 10.00 25.00
111 Moses Moody 3.00 8.00
112 Corey Kispert 2.00 5.00
113 Alperen Sengun 5.00 12.00
114 Jeremiah Robinson-Earl 1.50 4.00
115 Tre Mann 2.50 6.00
116 Jalen Suggs 4.00 10.00
117 Trey Murphy III 5.00 12.00
118 Jalen Johnson 5.00 12.00
119 Kai Jones 1.25 3.00
120 Cameron Thomas 3.00 8.00
121 Evan Mobley 6.00 15.00
122 Josh Christopher 1.25 3.00
123 Keon Johnson 1.50 4.00
124 Isaiah Jackson 1.50 4.00
125 Franz Wagner 5.00 12.00
126 Luka Garza 1.50 4.00
127 Quentin Grimes 3.00 8.00
128 Brandon Boston Jr. 1.50 4.00
129 Davion Mitchell 1.50 4.00
130 Usman Garuba 1.25 3.00
131 Santi Aldama 2.00 5.00
132 Jared Butler 1.50 4.00
133 Jonathan Kuminga 5.00 12.00
134 Scottie Barnes 15.00 40.00
135 Josh Giddey 15.00 40.00
136 Joshua Primo 4.00 10.00
137 Jalen Green 25.00 60.00
138 James Bouknight 4.00 10.00
139 Bones Hyland 6.00 15.00
140 Ziaire Williams 6.00 15.00
141 Ayo Dosunmu 10.00 25.00
142 Chris Duarte 4.00 10.00
143 Cade Cunningham 30.00 80.00
144 Moses Moody 10.00 25.00
145 Corey Kispert 6.00 15.00
146 Alperen Sengun 15.00 40.00
147 Jeremiah Robinson-Earl 5.00 12.00
148 Tre Mann 8.00 20.00
149 Jalen Suggs 12.00 30.00
150 Trey Murphy III 15.00 40.00
151 Jalen Johnson 15.00 40.00
152 Kai Jones 4.00 10.00
153 Cameron Thomas 10.00 25.00
154 Evan Mobley 20.00 50.00
155 Josh Christopher 4.00 10.00
156 Keon Johnson 5.00 12.00
157 Isaiah Jackson 5.00 12.00
158 Franz Wagner 15.00 40.00
159 Luka Garza 5.00 12.00
160 Quentin Grimes 10.00 25.00
161 Brandon Boston Jr. 5.00 12.00
162 Davion Mitchell 5.00 12.00
163 Usman Garuba 4.00 10.00
164 Santi Aldama 6.00 15.00
165 Jared Butler 5.00 12.00
166 Jonathan Kuminga 15.00 40.00
167 Scottie Barnes 50.00 125.00
168 Josh Giddey 50.00 125.00
169 Joshua Primo 12.00 30.00
170 Jalen Green 80.00 200.00
171 James Bouknight 12.00 30.00
172 Bones Hyland 20.00 50.00
173 Ziaire Williams 20.00 50.00
174 Ayo Dosunmu 30.00 80.00
175 Chris Duarte 12.00 30.00
176 Cade Cunningham 150.00 400.00
177 Moses Moody 30.00 80.00
178 Corey Kispert 20.00 50.00
179 Alperen Sengun 50.00 125.00
180 Jeremiah Robinson-Earl 15.00 40.00
181 Tre Mann 25.00 60.00
182 Jalen Suggs 40.00 100.00
183 Trey Murphy III 50.00 125.00
184 Jalen Johnson 50.00 125.00
185 Kai Jones 12.00 30.00
186 Cameron Thomas 30.00 80.00
187 Evan Mobley 60.00 150.00
188 Josh Christopher 12.00 30.00
189 Keon Johnson 15.00 40.00
190 Isaiah Jackson 15.00 40.00
191 Franz Wagner 50.00 125.00
192 Luka Garza 15.00 40.00
193 Quentin Grimes 30.00 80.00
194 Brandon Boston Jr. 15.00 40.00
195 Davion Mitchell 15.00 40.00
196 Usman Garuba 12.00 30.00
197 Santi Aldama 20.00 50.00
198 Jared Butler 15.00 40.00
199 Jonathan Kuminga 50.00 125.00

2021-22 Court Kings Jade
*JADE: 3X TO 8X BASIC
STATED PRINT RUN 25 SER.#'d SETS
6 LeBron James 50.00 120.00
9 Luka Doncic 40.00 100.00
12 Ja Morant 30.00 80.00
30 Stephen Curry 40.00 100.00

2021-22 Court Kings Sapphire
*SAPPHIRE: 3X TO 8X BASIC
STATED PRINT RUN 25 SER.#'d SETS
6 LeBron James 50.00 120.00
9 Luka Doncic 40.00 100.00
12 Ja Morant 30.00 80.00
30 Stephen Curry 40.00 100.00

2021-22 Court Kings Acetate Rookies
COMMON CARD 1.00 2.50
SEMISTARS 1.25 3.00
UNLISTED STARS 1.50 4.00
1 James Bouknight 1.25 3.00
2 Austin Reaves 8.00 20.00
3 Chris Duarte 1.25 3.00
4 Cade Cunningham 10.00 25.00
5 Alperen Sengun 5.00 12.00
6 Jalen Suggs 4.00 10.00
7 Kai Jones 1.25 3.00
8 Franz Wagner 5.00 12.00
9 Herbert Jones 2.00 5.00
10 Josh Giddey 5.00 12.00
11 Bones Hyland 2.00 5.00
12 Ziaire Williams 2.00 5.00
13 Moses Moody 3.00 8.00
14 Jalen Green 8.00 20.00
15 Tre Mann 2.50 6.00
16 Scottie Barnes 5.00 12.00
17 Jalen Johnson 5.00 12.00
18 Jonathan Kuminga 5.00 12.00
19 Cameron Thomas 3.00 8.00
20 Davion Mitchell 1.50 4.00
21 Ayo Dosunmu 3.00 8.00
22 Joshua Primo 1.25 3.00
23 Corey Kispert 2.00 5.00
24 Evan Mobley 6.00 15.00
25 Trey Murphy III 5.00 12.00

2021-22 Court Kings Art Nouveau Materials
COMMON CARD 1.50 4.00
SEMISTARS 2.00 5.00
UNLISTED STARS 2.50 6.00
*PRIME/25: 1X TO 2.5X BASIC
1 Cade Cunningham 15.00 40.00
2 Jalen Green 12.00 30.00
3 Evan Mobley 10.00 25.00
4 Scottie Barnes 8.00 20.00
5 Jalen Suggs 6.00 15.00
6 Josh Giddey 8.00 20.00
7 Jonathan Kuminga 8.00 20.00
8 Franz Wagner 8.00 20.00
9 Davion Mitchell 2.50 6.00
10 Ziaire Williams 3.00 8.00
11 James Bouknight 2.00 5.00
12 Joshua Primo 2.00 5.00
13 Chris Duarte 2.00 5.00
14 Moses Moody 5.00 12.00
15 Corey Kispert 3.00 8.00
16 Kristaps Porzingis 3.00 8.00
17 Aleksej Pokusevski 2.00 5.00
18 Gordon Hayward 2.00 5.00
19 Mike Conley 2.00 5.00
20 Jaylen Brown 4.00 10.00
21 Malcolm Brogdon 2.00 5.00
22 Miles Bridges 2.00 5.00
23 Tyler Herro 4.00 10.00
24 OG Anunoby 2.50 6.00
25 Andrew Wiggins 3.00 8.00
26 Jerami Grant 2.50 6.00
27 Dejounte Murray 2.50 6.00
28 Jaren Jackson Jr. 2.00 5.00
29 Jordan Clarkson 2.50 6.00
30 Collin Sexton 2.50 6.00
31 Christian Wood 2.00 5.00
32 Karl-Anthony Towns 4.00 10.00
33 Julius Randle 3.00 8.00
34 Khris Middleton 2.50 6.00
35 CJ McCollum 2.00 5.00
36 Seth Curry 2.00 5.00
37 De'Aaron Fox 4.00 10.00
38 Cole Anthony 2.00 5.00
39 Bradley Beal 3.00 8.00
40 John Collins 2.50 6.00

2021-22 Court Kings Artistic Endeavors Materials
COMMON CARD 1.50 4.00
SEMISTARS 2.00 5.00
UNLISTED STARS 2.50 6.00
1 Joel Embiid 6.00 15.00
2 LaMelo Ball 6.00 15.00
3 Paul George 4.00 10.00
4 Devin Booker 6.00 15.00
5 Tyrese Maxey 6.00 15.00
6 Jimmy Butler 4.00 10.00
7 Jayson Tatum 10.00 25.00
8 Stephen Curry 40.00 100.00
9 Zach LaVine 4.00 10.00
10 Zion Williamson 6.00 15.00
11 Shai Gilgeous-Alexander 12.00 30.00
12 Donovan Mitchell 5.00 12.00
13 Anthony Davis 6.00 15.00
14 Damian Lillard 6.00 15.00
15 Giannis Antetokounmpo 12.00 30.00
16 Cade Cunningham 15.00 40.00
17 Jalen Green 12.00 30.00
18 Jalen Suggs 6.00 15.00
19 Scottie Barnes 8.00 20.00
20 Evan Mobley 10.00 25.00

2021-22 Court Kings Artistry in Motion
COMMON CARD .60 1.50
SEMISTARS .75 2.00
UNLISTED STARS 1.00 2.50
*AMETHYST/99: 1.5X TO 4X BASIC
*JADE/25: 3X TO 8X BASIC
1 Giannis Antetokounmpo 5.00 12.00
2 Damian Lillard 2.50 6.00
3 Luka Doncic 6.00 15.00
4 Kevin Durant 3.00 8.00
5 LeBron James 8.00 20.00
6 James Harden 2.00 5.00
7 Ja Morant 3.00 8.00
8 Anthony Edwards 5.00 12.00
9 Anthony Davis 2.50 6.00
10 Jayson Tatum 4.00 10.00
11 Donovan Mitchell 2.00 5.00
12 Devin Booker 2.50 6.00
13 Stephen Curry 6.00 15.00
14 Zach LaVine 1.50 4.00
15 Trae Young 2.50 6.00
16 LaMelo Ball 2.50 6.00
17 Paul George 1.50 4.00
18 Tyrese Haliburton 2.00 5.00
19 Jimmy Butler 1.50 4.00
20 Zion Williamson 2.50 6.00
21 Magic Johnson 3.00 8.00
22 Vince Carter 2.00 5.00
23 Manu Ginobili 2.00 5.00
24 Tracy McGrady 1.50 4.00
25 Steve Nash 2.00 5.00
26 Jason Kidd 1.50 4.00
27 Shaquille O'Neal 3.00 8.00
28 Gary Payton 1.50 4.00
29 Isiah Thomas 1.50 4.00
30 Larry Bird 3.00 8.00

2021-22 Court Kings Aurora
1 Luka Doncic 300.00 600.00
2 LeBron James 300.00 600.00
3 Stephen Curry 400.00 800.00
4 Kevin Durant 125.00 300.00
5 Giannis Antetokounmpo 125.00 300.00
6 Trae Young 100.00 250.00
7 Ja Morant 400.00 800.00
8 Damian Lillard 100.00 250.00
9 Donovan Mitchell 60.00 150.00
10 Zion Williamson 125.00 300.00
11 Nikola Jokic 75.00 200.00
12 Josh Giddey 200.00 500.00
13 Jalen Suggs 100.00 250.00
14 Scottie Barnes 300.00 600.00
15 Evan Mobley 200.00 500.00
16 Jalen Green 300.00 600.00
17 Cade Cunningham 300.00 600.00

2021-22 Court Kings Award-Winning Autographs
2 Grant Hill 50.00 120.00
25 Calvin Murphy 12.00 30.00
34 Larry Bird 200.00 500.00
44 Charles Barkley 200.00 500.00
47 Toni Kukoc 40.00 100.00

2021-22 Court Kings Blank Slate
1 Luka Doncic 1,500.00 3,000.00
3 LeBron James 1,500.00 3,000.00
6 Ja Morant 1,000.00 2,000.00
7 Stephen Curry 1,500.00 3,000.00
9 Evan Mobley 1,000.00 2,000.00
10 LaMelo Ball 1,000.00 2,000.00
11 Giannis Antetokounmpo 600.00 1,200.00
14 Devin Booker 400.00 800.00
15 Anthony Edwards 1,000.00 2,000.00
16 Donovan Mitchell 150.00 400.00
17 James Harden 150.00 400.00
18 Scottie Barnes 1,000.00 2,000.00
19 Damian Lillard 200.00 500.00
23 Davion Mitchell 400.00 800.00
25 Zach LaVine 150.00 400.00
26 Vince Carter 400.00 800.00
27 Dwyane Wade 150.00 400.00
28 Tim Duncan 400.00 800.00
29 Dirk Nowitzki 400.00 800.00

2021-22 Court Kings Brush Strokes Autographs
COMMON CARD 4.00 10.00
SEMISTARS 5.00 12.00
UNLISTED STARS 6.00 15.00
STATED PRINT RUN 75 SER.#'d SETS
*RUBY/49: .5X TO 1.25X BASIC
*VIOLET/35: .5X TO 1.25X BASIC
*SAPPHIRE/25: .6X TO 1.5X BASIC
1 Devin Vassell 12.00 30.00
2 Stephen Jackson 6.00 15.00
3 George McGinnis 8.00 20.00
4 Tim Hardaway Jr. 5.00 12.00
6 Kendrick Perkins 6.00 15.00
7 Alex English 10.00 25.00
8 Michael Porter Jr. 10.00 25.00
10 PJ Washington Jr. 8.00 20.00
11 Drew Gooden 6.00 15.00
13 Kyrie Irving 50.00 120.00
14 Tony Allen 5.00 12.00
15 Jason Williams 20.00 50.00
17 B.J. Armstrong 8.00 20.00
18 Montrezl Harrell 6.00 15.00
19 Chris Mullin 10.00 25.00
20 Richard Hamilton 10.00 25.00
22 T.J. Warren 5.00 12.00
23 Jamal Murray 12.00 30.00
24 Wally Szczerbiak 6.00 15.00
25 Joe Harris 6.00 15.00
26 Mark Aguirre 6.00 15.00
27 Bill Walton 20.00 50.00
28 Nate Archibald 8.00 20.00
29 Clint Capela 8.00 20.00

2021-22 Court Kings Brush Strokes Autographs Jade
*JADE: .4X TO 1X BASIC
5 James Worthy 12.00 30.00
30 Ricky Rubio 8.00 20.00

2021-22 Court Kings Contemporaries
COMMON CARD .60 1.50
SEMISTARS .75 2.00
UNLISTED STARS 1.00 2.50
*AMETHYST/99: 1.5X TO 4X BASIC
*JADE/25: 3X TO 8X BASIC
1 LeBron James 8.00 20.00
2 Luka Doncic 6.00 15.00
3 Russell Westbrook 1.50 4.00
4 Carmelo Anthony 1.50 4.00
5 Zion Williamson 2.50 6.00
6 Stephen Curry 6.00 15.00
7 Chris Paul 2.00 5.00
8 Kevin Durant 3.00 8.00
9 Cole Anthony 1.25 3.00
10 Julius Randle 1.25 3.00
11 Karl-Anthony Towns 1.50 4.00
12 Nikola Jokic 5.00 12.00
13 Tyrese Maxey 2.50 6.00
14 Bradley Beal 1.25 3.00
15 Giannis Antetokounmpo 5.00 12.00
16 DeMar DeRozan 1.25 3.00
17 Shai Gilgeous-Alexander 5.00 12.00
18 Tyler Herro 1.50 4.00
19 De'Aaron Fox 1.50 4.00
20 Jaylen Brown 1.50 4.00
21 Dejounte Murray 1.00 2.50
22 Kawhi Leonard 2.50 6.00
23 Joel Embiid 2.50 6.00
24 Jayson Tatum 4.00 10.00
25 Damian Lillard 2.50 6.00
26 LaMelo Ball 2.50 6.00
27 Pascal Siakam 1.50 4.00
28 Khris Middleton 1.00 2.50
29 Anthony Edwards 5.00 12.00
30 Zach LaVine 1.50 4.00

2021-22 Court Kings Dressed to Impress
COMMON CARD .60 1.50
SEMISTARS .75 2.00
UNLISTED STARS 1.00 2.50
*AMETHYST/99: 1.5X TO 4X BASIC
*JADE/25: 3X TO 8X BASIC
1 Luka Doncic 6.00 15.00
2 LaMelo Ball 2.50 6.00
3 Russell Westbrook 1.50 4.00
4 LeBron James 8.00 20.00
5 Kevin Durant 3.00 8.00
6 Jalen Green 5.00 12.00
7 Cade Cunningham 6.00 15.00
8 Scottie Barnes 3.00 8.00
9 Jalen Suggs 2.50 6.00
10 Evan Mobley 4.00 10.00

2021-22 Court Kings First Steps
COMMON CARD 1.25 3.00
SEMISTARS 1.50 4.00
UNLISTED STARS 2.00 5.00
*RUBY/149: .75X TO 2X BASIC
*VIOLET/49: 2X TO 5X BASIC
*SAPPHIRE/25: 3X TO 8X BASIC
1 Cade Cunningham 12.00 30.00
2 Jalen Green 10.00 25.00
3 Evan Mobley 8.00 20.00
4 Jalen Suggs 5.00 12.00
5 Josh Giddey 6.00 15.00
6 Scottie Barnes 6.00 15.00
7 Bones Hyland 2.50 6.00
8 Jonathan Kuminga 6.00 15.00
9 Moses Moody 4.00 10.00
10 Chris Duarte 1.50 4.00

2021-22 Court Kings Fresh Paint Autographs
COMMON CARD 4.00 10.00
SEMISTARS 5.00 12.00
UNLISTED STARS 6.00 15.00
STATED PRINT RUN 125-149 SER.#'d SETS
EXCHANGE DEADLINE 11/04/2023
*JADE: .4X TO 1X BASIC
*RUBY/99: .5X TO 1.25X BASIC
*VIOLET/49: .6X TO 1.5X BASIC
*SAPPHIRE/25: .75X TO 2X BASIC
1 Scottie Barnes/199 20.00 50.00
2 Isaiah Todd/149 5.00 12.00
3 James Bouknight/199 5.00 12.00
4 Alperen Sengun/199 20.00 50.00
5 Jonathan Kuminga/125 20.00 50.00
6 Cameron Thomas/199 12.00 30.00
8 Davion Mitchell/199 6.00 15.00
9 Moses Moody/199 12.00 30.00
10 Greg Brown III/149 5.00 12.00
11 Tre Mann/199 10.00 25.00
12 Jaden Springer/199 6.00 15.00
13 Jared Butler/199 6.00 15.00
14 Ayo Dosunmu/199 12.00 30.00
15 Josh Christopher/199 5.00 12.00
16 Chris Duarte/199 5.00 12.00
17 Keon Johnson/199 6.00 15.00
18 Day'Ron Sharpe/199 6.00 15.00
19 Neemias Queta/149 6.00 15.00
20 Herbert Jones/199 8.00 20.00
22 Jalen Green/125 30.00 80.00
23 Jason Preston/149 5.00 12.00
24 Marko Simonovic/199 5.00 12.00
25 Josh Giddey/199 20.00 50.00
26 Corey Kispert/199 8.00 20.00
27 Kessler Edwards/149 6.00 15.00
28 Evan Mobley/125 25.00 60.00
29 Quentin Grimes/149 12.00 30.00
30 Isaiah Jackson/199 6.00 15.00
31 Usman Garuba/199 5.00 12.00
32 Jalen Johnson/199 20.00 50.00
33 Jeremiah Robinson-Earl/149 6.00 15.00
34 Bones Hyland/149 8.00 20.00
35 Joshua Primo/149 5.00 12.00
36 Dalano Banton/149 8.00 20.00
37 Miles McBride/199 10.00 25.00
38 Franz Wagner/199 20.00 50.00

39 Santi Aldama/149 8.00 20.00
40 Isaiah Livers/149 6.00 15.00
41 Ziaire Williams/199 8.00 20.00
42 Jalen Suggs/125 15.00 40.00
43 Joe Wieskamp/149 5.00 12.00
44 Cade Cunningham/125 60.00 150.00
45 JT Thor/149 6.00 15.00

2021-22 Court Kings Graffiti Greats

COMMON CARD .60 1.50
SEMISTARS .75 2.00
UNLISTED STARS 1.00 2.50
*RUBY/149: 1X TO 2.5X BASIC
*VIOLET/49: 2X TO 5X BASIC
*SAPPHIRE/25: 3X TO 8X BASIC
1 LeBron James 8.00 20.00
2 Ja Morant 3.00 8.00
3 Giannis Antetokounmpo 5.00 12.00
4 Zach LaVine 1.50 4.00
5 Kevin Durant 3.00 8.00
6 Stephen Curry 6.00 15.00
7 Luka Doncic 6.00 15.00
8 James Harden 2.00 5.00
9 Anthony Davis 2.50 6.00
10 Trae Young 2.50 6.00
11 Damian Lillard 2.50 6.00
12 Donovan Mitchell 2.00 5.00
13 Joel Embiid 2.50 6.00
14 Chris Paul 2.00 5.00
15 Nikola Jokic 5.00 12.00
16 Jayson Tatum 4.00 10.00
17 Klay Thompson 2.50 6.00
18 Paul George 1.50 4.00
19 Bradley Beal 1.25 3.00
20 Dennis Rodman 2.50 6.00
21 Dwyane Wade 2.00 5.00
22 Shaquille O'Neal 3.00 8.00
23 Charles Barkley 2.50 6.00
24 Magic Johnson 3.00 8.00
25 Vince Carter 2.00 5.00
26 Kevin Garnett 2.50 6.00
27 Dirk Nowitzki 2.50 6.00
28 Allen Iverson 2.50 6.00
29 Paul Pierce 1.50 4.00
30 Dominique Wilkins 1.50 4.00

2021-22 Court Kings Heir Apparent Autographs

COMMON CARD 4.00 10.00
SEMISTARS 5.00 12.00
UNLISTED STARS 6.00 15.00
STATED PRINT RUN 125-149 SER.#'d SETS
EXCHANGE DEADLINE 11/04/2023
*JADE: .4X TO 1X BASIC
*RUBY/99: .5X TO 1.25X BASIC
*VIOLET/49: .6X TO 1.5X BASIC
*SAPPHIRE/25: .75X TO 2X BASIC
1 Josh Christopher/199 5.00 12.00
2 Corey Kispert/199 8.00 20.00
3 Luka Garza/149 6.00 15.00
4 Austin Reaves/199 30.00 80.00
5 Scottie Barnes/199 20.00 50.00
6 Isaiah Livers/149 6.00 15.00
7 Jalen Johnson/199 20.00 50.00
8 Aaron Wiggins/149 8.00 20.00
9 Jason Preston/149 5.00 12.00
10 Brandon Boston Jr./199 6.00 15.00
11 Josh Giddey/199 20.00 50.00
12 David Johnson/149 5.00 12.00
13 Juan Toscano-Anderson/149 6.00 15.00
14 Franz Wagner/199 20.00 50.00
15 Tre Mann/199 10.00 25.00
16 Isaiah Todd/149 5.00 12.00
17 Jalen Suggs/125 15.00 40.00
18 Alperen Sengun/199 20.00 50.00
19 Jeremiah Robinson-Earl/149 6.00 15.00
20 Cade Cunningham/125 60.00 150.00
22 Davion Mitchell/199 6.00 15.00
23 Miles McBride/199 10.00 25.00
24 Greg Brown III/149 5.00 12.00
26 Jaden Springer/199 6.00 15.00
27 James Bouknight/199 5.00 12.00
28 Ayo Dosunmu/199 12.00 30.00
29 Joe Wieskamp/149 5.00 12.00
30 Cameron Thomas/199 12.00 30.00
31 Keon Johnson/199 6.00 15.00
32 Day'Ron Sharpe/199 6.00 15.00
33 Moses Moody/199 12.00 30.00
34 Herbert Jones/199 8.00 20.00
35 Usman Garuba/199 5.00 12.00
36 Jalen Green/125 30.00 80.00
37 Jared Butler/199 6.00 15.00
38 Bones Hyland/149 8.00 20.00
39 Jonathan Kuminga/125 20.00 50.00
40 Chris Duarte/199 5.00 12.00
41 Kessler Edwards/149 6.00 15.00
42 Evan Mobley/125 25.00 60.00
43 Neemias Queta/149 6.00 15.00
44 Isaiah Jackson/199 6.00 15.00
45 Ziaire Williams/199 8.00 20.00

2021-22 Court Kings Holding Court Signatures

COMMON CARD 5.00 12.00
SEMISTARS 6.00 15.00
UNLISTED STARS 8.00 20.00
STATED PRINT RUN 75 SER.#'d SETS
EXCHANGE DEADLINE 11/04/2023
*JADE: .4X TO 1X BASIC
*RUBY/49: .5X TO 1.25X BASIC
*VIOLET/35: .5X TO 1.25X BASIC
*SAPPHIRE/25: .6X TO 1.5X BASIC
1 Jamal Crawford 8.00 20.00
2 Tony Allen 5.00 12.00
3 Kendrick Perkins 6.00 15.00
4 Magic Johnson 60.00 150.00
5 Anfernee Hardaway 50.00 120.00
6 Maurice Cheeks 6.00 15.00
7 Carlos Boozer 6.00 15.00
8 Ray Allen 40.00 100.00
9 Dominique Wilkins 20.00 50.00
10 Spencer Dinwiddie 6.00 15.00
11 Jason Kidd 20.00 50.00
12 Vince Carter 75.00 200.00
13 Kenny "Sky" Walker 5.00 12.00
14 Mark Aguirre 6.00 15.00
15 Anthony Edwards 125.00 300.00
16 Metta World Peace 8.00 20.00
17 Charles Oakley 6.00 15.00
18 Ron Harper 8.00 20.00
19 Glen Rice 8.00 20.00
20 T.J. McConnell 6.00 15.00
21 Jason Richardson 8.00 20.00
22 Wally Szczerbiak 6.00 15.00
23 Kirk Hinrich 8.00 20.00
24 Marques Johnson 6.00 15.00
25 Arvydas Sabonis 10.00 25.00
26 Mike Bibby 8.00 20.00
27 Clyde Drexler 20.00 50.00
29 Jae'Sean Tate 8.00 20.00
30 Taj Gibson 5.00 12.00
31 Jeff Teague 5.00 12.00
32 Wang Zhi-zhi 75.00 200.00
33 Larry Bird 60.00 150.00
34 Matt Barnes 6.00 15.00
35 Bob Dandridge 8.00 20.00
36 Nikola Jokic 75.00 200.00
37 Dennis Rodman 30.00 80.00
38 Shawn Kemp 30.00 80.00
39 Jalen Rose 6.00 15.00
40 Theo Maledon 6.00 15.00

2021-22 Court Kings Impressionist Ink

COMMON CARD 4.00 10.00
SEMISTARS 5.00 12.00
UNLISTED STARS 6.00 15.00
STATED PRINT RUN 75 SER.#'d SETS
*JADE: .4X TO 1X BASIC
*RUBY/49: .5X TO 1.2X BASIC
*VIOLET/35: .5X TO 1.2X BASIC
*SAPPHIRE/25: .6X TO 1.5X BASIC
1 Julius Randle 8.00 20.00
3 Mark Jackson 5.00 12.00
4 Boban Marjanovic 6.00 15.00
5 Pat Riley 8.00 20.00
6 David Thompson 8.00 20.00
7 Sam Jones 12.00 30.00
8 Gary Payton 20.00 50.00
9 Theo Maledon 5.00 12.00
10 James Wiseman 5.00 12.00
12 Andrea Bargnani 4.00 10.00
13 Mike Conley 5.00 12.00
14 Chauncey Billups 12.00 30.00
15 Ralph Sampson 6.00 15.00
17 Steve Francis 6.00 15.00
18 Glen Rice 6.00 15.00
19 Toni Kukoc 8.00 20.00
20 Jason Richardson 6.00 15.00
21 Kristaps Porzingis 8.00 20.00
22 Ben Wallace 40.00 100.00
23 Myles Turner 6.00 15.00
24 CJ McCollum 5.00 12.00
25 Rick Fox 6.00 15.00
26 Elton Brand 6.00 15.00
27 T.J. McConnell 5.00 12.00
28 Jamal Crawford 6.00 15.00
29 Tyrese Haliburton 40.00 100.00
30 Jerry Lucas 8.00 20.00

2021-22 Court Kings Le Cinque Piu Belle

COMMON CARD 20.00 50.00
SEMISTARS 25.00 60.00
UNLISTED STARS 30.00 80.00
1 Cade Cunningham 400.00 800.00
2 Jalen Green 300.00 600.00
3 LeBron James 300.00 600.00
4 Luka Doncic 300.00 600.00
5 Giannis Antetokounmpo 150.00 400.00
6 Stephen Curry 300.00 600.00
7 Kevin Durant 100.00 250.00
8 Ja Morant 100.00 250.00
9 Trae Young 80.00 200.00
10 Evan Mobley 120.00 300.00

2021-22 Court Kings Legacy Portrait Signatures

COMMON CARD 5.00 12.00
SEMISTARS 6.00 15.00
UNLISTED STARS 8.00 20.00
STATED PRINT RUN 99 SER.#'d SETS
EXCHANGE DEADLINE 11/04/2023
*JADE: .4X TO 1X BASIC
*RUBY/49: .5X TO 1.25X BASIC
*VIOLET/25: .6X TO 1.5X BASIC
2 Karl Malone 40.00 100.00
3 Trae Young 60.00 150.00
4 Anthony Davis 75.00 200.00
5 Dirk Nowitzki 100.00 250.00
6 Charles Barkley 100.00 250.00
7 Allen Iverson 100.00 250.00
8 Luka Doncic 400.00 800.00
9 Ja Morant 200.00 500.00
10 Shaquille O'Neal 100.00 250.00

2021-22 Court Kings Maestros

COMMON CARD .60 1.50
SEMISTARS .75 2.00
UNLISTED STARS 1.00 2.50
*RUBY/149: 1X TO 2.5X BASIC
*VIOLET/49: 2X TO 5X BASIC
*SAPPHIRE/25: 3X TO 8X BASIC
1 LaMelo Ball 2.50 6.00
2 Nikola Jokic 5.00 12.00
3 Shai Gilgeous-Alexander 5.00 12.00
4 Luka Doncic 6.00 15.00
5 Stephen Curry 6.00 15.00
6 Trae Young 2.50 6.00
7 Russell Westbrook 1.50 4.00
8 Cade Cunningham 6.00 15.00
9 LeBron James 8.00 20.00
10 Josh Giddey 3.00 8.00
11 Ja Morant 3.00 8.00
12 Jalen Green 5.00 12.00
13 Donovan Mitchell 2.00 5.00
14 Damian Lillard 2.50 6.00
15 Anthony Edwards 5.00 12.00
16 Tyrese Haliburton 2.00 5.00
17 Jayson Tatum 4.00 10.00
18 Jalen Suggs 2.50 6.00
19 James Harden 2.00 5.00
20 Davion Mitchell 1.00 2.50
21 Chris Paul 2.00 5.00
22 Lonzo Ball 1.00 2.50
23 Tyrese Maxey 2.50 6.00
24 Kyle Lowry 1.00 2.50
25 Paul George 1.50 4.00
26 Giannis Antetokounmpo 5.00 12.00
27 Kevin Durant 3.00 8.00
28 Evan Mobley 4.00 10.00
29 Zach LaVine 1.50 4.00
30 Scottie Barnes 3.00 8.00

2021-22 Court Kings Modern Strokes

COMMON CARD .75 2.00
SEMISTARS 1.00 2.50
UNLISTED STARS 1.25 3.00
*AMETHYST/99: 1.25X TO 3X BASIC
*JADE/25: 3X TO 8X BASIC
1 Stephen Curry 8.00 20.00
2 Trae Young 3.00 8.00
3 Klay Thompson 3.00 8.00
4 Kevin Durant 4.00 10.00
5 Damian Lillard 3.00 8.00
6 Luka Doncic 8.00 20.00
7 James Harden 2.50 6.00
8 Paul George 2.00 5.00
9 DeMar DeRozan 1.50 4.00
10 Bradley Beal 1.50 4.00
11 Jayson Tatum 5.00 12.00
12 Carmelo Anthony 2.00 5.00
13 Khris Middleton 1.25 3.00
14 Devin Booker 3.00 8.00
15 LeBron James 10.00 25.00
16 Donovan Mitchell 2.50 6.00
17 LaMelo Ball 3.00 8.00
18 Anthony Edwards 6.00 15.00
19 Zach LaVine 2.00 5.00
20 Julius Randle 1.50 4.00
21 De'Aaron Fox 2.00 5.00
22 Fred VanVleet 1.50 4.00
23 Tyler Herro 2.00 5.00
24 Jaylen Brown 2.00 5.00
25 Brandon Ingram 1.50 4.00
26 Ja Morant 4.00 10.00
27 Kristaps Porzingis 1.50 4.00
28 Cole Anthony 1.50 4.00
29 Kawhi Leonard 3.00 8.00
30 Tyrese Maxey 3.00 8.00

2021-22 Court Kings Rookie Exclusive

1 Cade Cunningham 75.00 200.00

2021-22 Court Kings Rookie Expression Memorabilia

COMMON CARD 1.50 4.00
SEMISTARS 2.00 5.00
UNLISTED STARS 2.50 6.00
*PRIME/25: 1.2X TO 3X BASIC
1 Cade Cunningham 15.00 40.00
2 Jalen Green 12.00 30.00
3 Evan Mobley 10.00 25.00
4 Scottie Barnes 8.00 20.00
5 Jalen Suggs 6.00 15.00
6 Josh Giddey 8.00 20.00
7 Jonathan Kuminga 8.00 20.00
8 Franz Wagner 8.00 20.00
9 Davion Mitchell 2.50 6.00
10 Ziaire Williams 3.00 8.00
11 James Bouknight 2.00 5.00
12 Joshua Primo 2.00 5.00
13 Chris Duarte 2.00 5.00
14 Moses Moody 5.00 12.00
15 Corey Kispert 3.00 8.00
16 Alperen Sengun 8.00 20.00
17 Trey Murphy III 8.00 20.00
18 Tre Mann 4.00 10.00
19 Kai Jones 2.00 5.00
20 Jalen Johnson 8.00 20.00
21 Keon Johnson 2.50 6.00
22 Isaiah Jackson 2.50 6.00
25 Quentin Grimes 5.00 12.00
26 Bones Hyland 3.00 8.00
27 Cameron Thomas 5.00 12.00
28 Jaden Springer 2.50 6.00
29 Day'Ron Sharpe 2.50 6.00
30 Santi Aldama 3.00 8.00
31 Jeremiah Robinson-Earl 2.50 6.00
32 Miles McBride 4.00 10.00
33 Ayo Dosunmu 5.00 12.00
34 Jared Butler 2.50 6.00
36 Greg Brown III 2.00 5.00
37 Brandon Boston Jr. 2.50 6.00
38 Luka Garza 2.50 6.00
39 Charles Bassey 2.50 6.00
40 Scottie Lewis 2.00 5.00

2021-22 Court Kings State of the Art

COMMON CARD 20.00 50.00
SEMISTARS 25.00 60.00
UNLISTED STARS 30.00 80.00
1 Luka Doncic 400.00 800.00
2 LeBron James 500.00 1,000.00
3 Stephen Curry 300.00 600.00
4 Giannis Antetokounmpo 200.00 500.00
5 LaMelo Ball 200.00 500.00
6 Kevin Durant 100.00 250.00
7 Anthony Edwards 200.00 500.00
8 Evan Mobley 120.00 300.00
9 Cade Cunningham 500.00 1,000.00
10 Jalen Green 300.00 600.00

2021-22 Court Kings Works in Progress

COMMON CARD 1.00 2.50
SEMISTARS 1.25 3.00
UNLISTED STARS 1.50 4.00
*RUBY/149: 1X TO 2.5X BASIC
*VIOLET/49: 2X TO 5X BASIC
*SAPPHIRE/25: 3X TO 8X BASIC
1 Cade Cunningham 10.00 25.00
2 Chris Duarte 1.25 3.00
3 Bones Hyland 2.00 5.00
4 Jalen Green 8.00 20.00
5 Josh Giddey 5.00 12.00
6 Scottie Barnes 5.00 12.00
7 Joshua Primo 1.25 3.00
8 Moses Moody 3.00 8.00
9 Jonathan Kuminga 5.00 12.00
10 Ziaire Williams 2.00 5.00
11 Corey Kispert 2.00 5.00
12 Alperen Sengun 5.00 12.00
13 Ayo Dosunmu 3.00 8.00
14 Herbert Jones 2.00 5.00
15 Franz Wagner 5.00 12.00
16 Trey Murphy III 5.00 12.00
17 Tre Mann 2.50 6.00
18 Jeremiah Robinson-Earl 1.50 4.00
19 Austin Reaves 8.00 20.00
20 Davion Mitchell 1.50 4.00
21 Cameron Thomas 3.00 8.00
22 Kai Jones 1.25 3.00
23 Jalen Johnson 5.00 12.00
24 Jalen Suggs 4.00 10.00
25 Keon Johnson 1.50 4.00
26 Day'Ron Sharpe 1.50 4.00
27 Josh Christopher 1.25 3.00
28 Jared Butler 1.50 4.00
29 James Bouknight 1.25 3.00
30 Evan Mobley 6.00 15.00

2022-23 Court Kings

COMMON CARD (1-67) .30 .75
SEMISTARS .40 1.00
UNLISTED STARS .50 1.25
COMMON RC (68-100) .60 1.50
RC SEMIS .75 2.00
RC UNLISTED 1.00 2.50
COMMON CARD (101-133) 1.25 3.00
SEMISTARS 1.50 4.00
UNLISTED STARS 2.00 5.00
COMMON CARD (134-166) 3.00 8.00
SEMISTARS 4.00 10.00
UNLISTED STARS 5.00 12.00
COMMON CARD (167-199) 15.00 40.00
SEMISTARS 20.00 50.00
UNLISTED STARS 25.00 60.00
*ARTIST PROOF: .6X TO 1.5X BASIC
*STEALTH: .75X TO 2X BASIC
*RUBY/149: 2X TO 5X BASIC
*AMETHYST/99: 2.5X TO 6X BASIC
*PINK/99: 2.5X TO 6X BASIC
*VIOLET/49: 3X TO 8X BASIC
*JADE/25: 5X TO 12X BASIC
*SAPPHIRE/25: 5X TO 12X BASIC
1 RJ Barrett .75 2.00
2 Tyrese Haliburton 1.00 2.50
3 Zach LaVine 1.00 2.50
4 DeMar DeRozan .60 1.50
5 Kyrie Irving 1.00 2.50
6 Julius Randle .60 1.50
7 Jaylen Brown 1.00 2.50
8 Scottie Barnes .75 2.00
9 Jayson Tatum 2.00 5.00
10 Kevin Durant 1.50 4.00
11 Cade Cunningham 1.50 4.00
12 Saddiq Bey .40 1.00
13 Fred VanVleet .60 1.50
14 Evan Mobley 1.25 3.00
15 Donovan Mitchell 1.00 2.50
16 Pascal Siakam .75 2.00
17 Giannis Antetokounmpo 2.50 6.00
18 LaMelo Ball 1.25 3.00
19 Khris Middleton .60 1.50
20 Trae Young 1.25 3.00
21 Dejounte Murray .60 1.50
22 Rudy Gobert .60 1.50
23 Tyler Herro .60 1.50
24 Jimmy Butler 1.00 2.50
25 Franz Wagner 1.25 3.00
26 Nikola Jokic 2.50 6.00
27 Josh Giddey .75 2.00
28 Shai Gilgeous-Alexander 2.50 6.00
29 Jalen Suggs .60 1.50
30 Andrew Wiggins .60 1.50
31 Anthony Edwards 2.50 6.00
32 Bradley Beal .60 1.50
33 Karl-Anthony Towns .75 2.00
34 Jamal Murray .75 2.00
35 LeBron James 4.00 10.00
36 Damian Lillard 1.25 3.00
37 Luka Doncic 3.00 8.00
38 Anthony Davis 1.25 3.00
39 Collin Sexton .60 1.50
40 De'Aaron Fox 1.00 2.50
41 Davion Mitchell .40 1.00
42 Stephen Curry 4.00 10.00
43 Paul George .75 2.00
44 Anfernee Simons .60 1.50
45 Mike Conley .40 1.00
46 Chris Paul 1.00 2.50
47 Jordan Poole .75 2.00
48 Kawhi Leonard 1.25 3.00
49 Devin Booker 1.25 3.00
50 Spencer Dinwiddie .40 1.00
51 Jalen Green 1.50 4.00
52 Kevin Porter Jr. .40 1.00
53 Brandon Ingram .60 1.50
54 Ja Morant 1.50 4.00
55 Joel Embiid .75 2.00
56 Keldon Johnson .60 1.50
57 Devin Vassell .60 1.50
58 Zion Williamson 1.25 3.00
59 Desmond Bane .60 1.50
60 James Harden 1.00 2.50
61 Jalen Brunson 1.00 2.50
62 Klay Thompson 1.25 3.00
63 Bam Adebayo .75 2.00
64 Russell Westbrook .75 2.00
65 Ben Simmons .50 1.25
66 Darius Garland .75 2.00
67 Jonathan Kuminga 1.25 3.00
68 Jeremy Sochan RC 3.00 8.00
69 Blake Wesley RC .60 1.50
70 Ousmane Dieng RC 1.25 3.00
71 Malaki Branham RC 1.00 2.50
72 Patrick Baldwin Jr. RC 1.00 2.50
73 Jake LaRavia RC 1.00 2.50
74 Chet Holmgren RC 5.00 12.00
75 Peyton Watson RC 1.50 4.00
76 Wendell Moore Jr. RC 1.00 2.50
77 Jaden Ivey RC 3.00 8.00
78 Jabari Smith Jr. RC 3.00 8.00
79 Dalen Terry RC 1.00 2.50
80 AJ Griffin RC .75 2.00
81 Shaedon Sharpe RC 4.00 10.00
82 Walker Kessler RC 2.00 5.00
83 Jalen Duren RC 3.00 8.00
84 MarJon Beauchamp RC 1.00 2.50
85 Bennedict Mathurin RC 3.00 8.00
86 Paolo Banchero RC 6.00 15.00
87 Jalen Williams RC 5.00 12.00
88 Dyson Daniels RC 2.50 6.00
89 Jaden Hardy RC 1.50 4.00
90 Ochai Agbaji RC 1.25 3.00
91 Caleb Houstan RC 1.00 2.50
92 Tari Eason RC 2.50 6.00
93 Keegan Murray RC 2.50 6.00
94 Andrew Nembhard RC 2.00 5.00
95 Johnny Davis RC 1.00 2.50
96 TyTy Washington Jr. RC 1.00 2.50
97 Christian Braun RC 2.50 6.00
98 David Roddy RC 1.25 3.00
99 Mark Williams RC 2.00 5.00
100 Nikola Jovic RC 2.00 5.00
101 Jeremy Sochan 6.00 15.00
102 Blake Wesley 2.00 5.00
103 Ousmane Dieng 2.50 6.00
104 Malaki Branham 2.00 5.00
105 Patrick Baldwin Jr. 2.00 5.00
106 Jake LaRavia 2.00 5.00
107 Chet Holmgren 10.00 25.00
108 Peyton Watson 3.00 8.00
109 Wendell Moore Jr. 2.00 5.00
110 Jaden Ivey 6.00 15.00
111 Jabari Smith Jr. 6.00 15.00
112 Dalen Terry 2.00 5.00
113 AJ Griffin 1.50 4.00
114 Shaedon Sharpe 8.00 20.00
115 Walker Kessler 4.00 10.00
116 Jalen Duren 6.00 15.00
117 MarJon Beauchamp 2.00 5.00
118 Bennedict Mathurin 6.00 15.00
119 Paolo Banchero 12.00 30.00
120 Jalen Williams 10.00 25.00
121 Dyson Daniels 5.00 12.00
122 Jaden Hardy 3.00 8.00
123 Ochai Agbaji 2.50 6.00
124 Caleb Houstan 2.00 5.00
125 Tari Eason 5.00 12.00
126 Keegan Murray 5.00 12.00
127 Andrew Nembhard 4.00 10.00
128 Johnny Davis 2.00 5.00
129 TyTy Washington Jr. 2.00 5.00
130 Christian Braun 5.00 12.00
131 David Roddy 2.50 6.00
132 Mark Williams 4.00 10.00
133 Nikola Jovic 4.00 10.00
134 Jeremy Sochan 15.00 40.00
135 Blake Wesley 5.00 12.00
136 Ousmane Dieng 6.00 15.00
137 Malaki Branham 5.00 12.00
138 Patrick Baldwin Jr. 5.00 12.00
139 Jake LaRavia 5.00 12.00
140 Chet Holmgren 25.00 60.00
141 Peyton Watson 8.00 20.00
142 Wendell Moore Jr. 5.00 12.00
143 Jaden Ivey 15.00 40.00
144 Jabari Smith Jr. 15.00 40.00
145 Dalen Terry 5.00 12.00
146 AJ Griffin 4.00 10.00
147 Shaedon Sharpe 20.00 50.00
148 Walker Kessler 10.00 25.00
149 Jalen Duren 15.00 40.00
150 MarJon Beauchamp 5.00 12.00
151 Bennedict Mathurin 15.00 40.00
152 Paolo Banchero 30.00 80.00
153 Jalen Williams 25.00 60.00
154 Dyson Daniels 12.00 30.00
155 Jaden Hardy 8.00 20.00
156 Ochai Agbaji 6.00 15.00
157 Caleb Houstan 5.00 12.00
158 Tari Eason 12.00 30.00
159 Keegan Murray 12.00 30.00
160 Andrew Nembhard 10.00 25.00
161 Johnny Davis 5.00 12.00
162 TyTy Washington Jr. 5.00 12.00
163 Christian Braun 12.00 30.00
164 David Roddy 6.00 15.00
165 Mark Williams 10.00 25.00
166 Nikola Jovic 10.00 25.00
167 Jalen Williams 125.00 300.00
168 TyTy Washington Jr. 25.00 60.00
169 Keegan Murray 60.00 150.00
170 David Roddy 30.00 80.00
171 Andrew Nembhard 50.00 125.00
172 Jalen Duren 80.00 200.00
173 Christian Braun 60.00 150.00
174 Jaden Ivey 80.00 200.00
175 Jabari Smith Jr. 80.00 200.00
176 Nikola Jovic 50.00 125.00
177 Jeremy Sochan 80.00 200.00
178 Dyson Daniels 60.00 150.00
179 Chet Holmgren 120.00 300.00
180 Jaden Hardy 40.00 100.00
181 Peyton Watson 40.00 100.00
182 Johnny Davis 25.00 60.00
183 Blake Wesley 25.00 60.00
184 AJ Griffin 20.00 50.00
185 Shaedon Sharpe 100.00 250.00
186 Ochai Agbaji 30.00 80.00
187 Jake LaRavia 25.00 60.00
188 Walker Kessler 50.00 125.00
189 Tari Eason 60.00 150.00
190 Mark Williams 50.00 125.00
191 Paolo Banchero 150.00 400.00
192 Dalen Terry 25.00 60.00
193 Ousmane Dieng 30.00 80.00
194 Bennedict Mathurin 80.00 200.00
195 Wendell Moore Jr. 25.00 60.00
196 MarJon Beauchamp 25.00 60.00
197 Malaki Branham 25.00 60.00
198 Caleb Houstan 25.00 60.00
199 Patrick Baldwin Jr. 25.00 60.00

2022-23 Court Kings Acetate Rookies

COMMON CARD 1.00 2.50
SEMISTARS 1.25 3.00
UNLISTED STARS 1.50 4.00
1 Dyson Daniels 4.00 10.00
2 Jeremy Sochan 5.00 12.00
3 AJ Griffin 1.25 3.00
4 MarJon Beauchamp 1.50 4.00
5 Patrick Baldwin Jr. 1.50 4.00
6 Ochai Agbaji 2.00 5.00
7 Blake Wesley 1.50 4.00
8 Wendell Moore Jr. 1.50 4.00
9 Paolo Banchero 10.00 25.00
10 Dalen Terry 1.50 4.00
11 Bennedict Mathurin 5.00 12.00
12 Mark Williams 3.00 8.00
13 Jalen Duren 5.00 12.00
14 Jalen Williams 8.00 20.00
15 Jabari Smith Jr. 5.00 12.00
16 Malaki Branham 1.50 4.00
17 Jake LaRavia 1.50 4.00
18 Shaedon Sharpe 6.00 15.00
19 Chet Holmgren 8.00 20.00
20 Jaden Ivey 5.00 12.00
21 Nikola Jovic 3.00 8.00
22 Tari Eason 4.00 10.00
23 Keegan Murray 4.00 10.00
24 Johnny Davis 1.50 4.00
25 Ousmane Dieng 2.00 5.00

2022-23 Court Kings Art Nouveau Jerseys

COMMON CARD 1.50 4.00
SEMISTARS 2.00 5.00
UNLISTED STARS 2.50 6.00
*PRIME/25: 1.25X TO 3X BASIC
1 Ochai Agbaji 3.00 8.00
2 Ousmane Dieng 3.00 8.00
3 Jalen Williams 12.00 30.00
4 Johnny Davis 2.50 6.00
5 Jeremy Sochan 8.00 20.00
6 Jabari Smith Jr. 8.00 20.00
7 Chet Holmgren 12.00 30.00
8 Keegan Murray 6.00 15.00
9 Dyson Daniels 6.00 15.00
10 Paolo Banchero 15.00 40.00
11 Shaedon Sharpe 10.00 25.00
12 Jaden Ivey 8.00 20.00
13 Jalen Duren 8.00 20.00
14 Bennedict Mathurin 8.00 20.00
15 AJ Griffin 2.00 5.00
16 Bradley Beal 3.00 8.00
17 Brandon Ingram 3.00 8.00
18 Darius Garland 4.00 10.00
19 Fred VanVleet 3.00 8.00
20 Jaylen Brown 5.00 12.00
21 Jimmy Butler 5.00 12.00
22 Chris Paul 5.00 12.00
23 Jrue Holiday 3.00 8.00
24 Julius Randle 3.00 8.00
25 Khris Middleton 3.00 8.00
26 Kyrie Irving 5.00 12.00
27 Pascal Siakam 4.00 10.00
28 Paul George 4.00 10.00
29 RJ Barrett 4.00 10.00
30 Tobias Harris 2.00 5.00
31 Klay Thompson 6.00 15.00
32 Karl-Anthony Towns 4.00 10.00
33 John Collins 2.50 6.00
34 Joel Embiid 4.00 10.00
35 James Wiseman 2.00 5.00
36 Michael Porter Jr. 3.00 8.00
37 Deandre Ayton 2.50 6.00
38 De'Aaron Fox 5.00 12.00
39 Bam Adebayo 4.00 10.00
40 Al Horford 2.50 6.00

2022-23 Court Kings Artistic Endeavors Jerseys

COMMON CARD 2.00 5.00
SEMISTARS 2.50 6.00
UNLISTED STARS 3.00 8.00
1 Zion Williamson 8.00 20.00
2 Nikola Jokic 15.00 40.00
3 Luka Doncic 20.00 50.00
4 LeBron James 40.00 100.00
5 LaMelo Ball 8.00 20.00
6 Kevin Durant 10.00 25.00
7 Jayson Tatum 12.00 30.00
8 Devin Booker 8.00 20.00
9 Damian Lillard 8.00 20.00
10 Cade Cunningham 10.00 25.00
11 Anthony Edwards 15.00 40.00
12 Giannis Antetokounmpo 15.00 40.00
13 Ja Morant 10.00 25.00
14 Jalen Green 10.00 25.00
15 Stephen Curry 40.00 100.00
16 Paolo Banchero 20.00 50.00
17 Chet Holmgren 15.00 40.00
18 Jabari Smith Jr. 10.00 25.00
19 Keegan Murray 8.00 20.00
20 Jaden Ivey 10.00 25.00

2022-23 Court Kings Artistry in Motion

COMMON CARD .75 2.00
SEMISTARS 1.00 2.50
UNLISTED STARS 1.25 3.00
*AMETHYST/99: 2X TO 5X BASIC
*JADE/25: 4X TO 10X BASIC
1 Kevin Durant 4.00 10.00
2 Jalen Green 4.00 10.00
3 LaMelo Ball 3.00 8.00
4 Tracy McGrady 2.00 5.00
5 Magic Johnson 5.00 12.00
6 James Harden 2.50 6.00
7 Kawhi Leonard 3.00 8.00
8 Trae Young 3.00 8.00
9 Anfernee Hardaway 3.00 8.00
10 Paul Pierce 2.00 5.00
11 Clyde Drexler 2.00 5.00
12 Donovan Mitchell 2.50 6.00
13 Jayson Tatum 5.00 12.00
14 Isiah Thomas 2.00 5.00
15 Cade Cunningham 4.00 10.00
16 Hakeem Olajuwon 2.50 6.00
17 Devin Booker 3.00 8.00
18 Dominique Wilkins 2.00 5.00
19 Bradley Beal 1.50 4.00
20 Giannis Antetokounmpo 6.00 15.00
21 Dwyane Wade 2.50 6.00
22 Ja Morant 4.00 10.00
23 Damian Lillard 3.00 8.00
24 Anthony Edwards 6.00 15.00
25 Vince Carter 2.50 6.00
26 Luka Doncic 8.00 20.00
27 Zion Williamson 3.00 8.00
28 Scottie Barnes 2.00 5.00
29 LeBron James 10.00 25.00
30 Stephen Curry 10.00 25.00

2022-23 Court Kings Aurora

1 Luka Doncic 150.00 400.00
2 Scottie Barnes 50.00 120.00
3 Giannis Antetokounmpo 125.00 300.00
4 Ja Morant 75.00 200.00
5 LaMelo Ball 75.00 200.00
6 LeBron James 200.00 500.00
7 Cade Cunningham 75.00 200.00
8 Jayson Tatum 125.00 300.00
9 Anthony Edwards 100.00 250.00
10 Stephen Curry 200.00 500.00
11 Zion Williamson 50.00 120.00
12 Bennedict Mathurin 75.00 200.00
13 Jaden Ivey 100.00 250.00
14 Keegan Murray 100.00 250.00
15 Paolo Banchero 150.00 400.00
16 Jabari Smith Jr. 60.00 150.00
17 Chet Holmgren 100.00 250.00

2022-23 Court Kings Blank Slate

1 Anthony Edwards 600.00 1,200.00
2 Ja Morant 300.00 600.00
3 Stephen Curry 1,500.00 3,000.00
4 Jayson Tatum 500.00 1,000.00
5 Luka Doncic 1,000.00 2,000.00
6 Cade Cunningham 400.00 800.00
7 LaMelo Ball 300.00 600.00
8 Kevin Durant 300.00 600.00
9 Giannis Antetokounmpo 500.00 1,000.00
10 Trae Young 300.00 600.00
11 Scottie Barnes 200.00 500.00
12 Kawhi Leonard 200.00 500.00
13 LeBron James 1,500.00 3,000.00
14 Nikola Jokic 400.00 800.00
15 Zion Williamson 300.00 600.00
16 Bennedict Mathurin 400.00 800.00
17 Dyson Daniels 300.00 600.00
18 Chet Holmgren 600.00 1,200.00
19 Shaedon Sharpe 500.00 1,000.00
20 Jaden Ivey 500.00 1,000.00
21 Jabari Smith Jr. 400.00 800.00
22 Johnny Davis 125.00 300.00
23 Keegan Murray 400.00 800.00
24 Jeremy Sochan 500.00 1,000.00
25 Paolo Banchero 2,000.00 4,000.00
26 Charles Barkley 300.00 600.00
27 Shaquille O'Neal 300.00 600.00
28 Steve Nash 200.00 500.00
29 Anfernee Hardaway 300.00 600.00
30 Tracy McGrady 300.00 600.00

2022-23 Court Kings Brush Strokes

COMMON CARD 4.00 10.00
SEMISTARS 5.00 12.00
UNLISTED STARS 6.00 15.00
STATED PRINT RUN 75 SER.#'d SETS
*RUBY/49: .5X TO 1.25X BASIC
*VIOLET/35: .6X TO 1.5X BASIC
*SAPPHIRE/25: .6X TO 1.5X BASIC
1 Aaron Nesmith 6.00 15.00
2 Aleksej Pokusevski 6.00 15.00
3 Anfernee Simons 8.00 20.00
4 Antawn Jamison 6.00 15.00
5 CJ McCollum 6.00 15.00
7 Dale Ellis 6.00 15.00
8 Danny Green 5.00 12.00
9 Derek Fisher 8.00 20.00
10 Elton Brand 6.00 15.00
11 Glen Rice 6.00 15.00
12 Grant Williams 5.00 12.00
13 Jeff Green 4.00 10.00
15 George McGinnis 6.00 15.00
16 Lonnie Walker IV 5.00 12.00
18 Nickeil Alexander-Walker 5.00 12.00
19 Robert Horry 8.00 20.00
20 Spencer Dinwiddie 5.00 12.00
21 Tony Parker 25.00 60.00
22 Vince Carter 75.00 200.00
23 Ayo Dosunmu 8.00 20.00
24 Moses Moody 8.00 20.00
25 Josh Giddey 40.00 100.00
26 Jalen Green 60.00 150.00
27 Jalen Suggs 8.00 20.00
29 Derrick White 8.00 20.00
30 Alex Caruso 8.00 20.00

2022-23 Court Kings Double Exposure

COMMON CARD .60 1.50
SEMISTARS .75 2.00
UNLISTED STARS 1.00 2.50
*AMETHYST/99: 2X TO 5X BASIC
1 Jalen Green 3.00 8.00
2 Giannis Antetokounmpo 5.00 12.00
3 Stephen Curry 8.00 20.00
4 Devin Booker 2.50 6.00
5 Shaquille O'Neal 4.00 10.00
6 Chet Holmgren 5.00 12.00
7 Paolo Banchero 6.00 15.00
8 James Harden 2.00 5.00
9 Jayson Tatum 4.00 10.00
10 Donovan Mitchell 2.00 5.00
11 Kawhi Leonard 2.50 6.00
12 Zion Williamson 2.50 6.00
13 Trae Young 2.50 6.00
14 Ja Morant 3.00 8.00
15 Cade Cunningham 3.00 8.00
16 Damian Lillard 2.50 6.00
17 Luka Doncic 6.00 15.00
18 Keegan Murray 2.50 6.00
19 LaMelo Ball 2.50 6.00
20 Allen Iverson 2.50 6.00
21 Scottie Barnes 1.50 4.00
22 Bradley Beal 1.25 3.00
23 Kevin Durant 3.00 8.00
24 Jaden Ivey 2.50 6.00
25 LeBron James 8.00 20.00
26 Jabari Smith Jr. 3.00 8.00
27 Magic Johnson 4.00 10.00
28 Dirk Nowitzki 2.50 6.00
29 Larry Bird 4.00 10.00
30 Anthony Edwards 5.00 12.00

2022-23 Court Kings Double Exposure Jade

*JADE/25: 4X TO 10X BASIC
7 Paolo Banchero 125.00 300.00

2022-23 Court Kings Dressed to Impress

COMMON CARD .60 1.50
SEMISTARS .75 2.00
UNLISTED STARS 1.00 2.50

*AMETHYST/99: 2X TO 5X BASIC
*JADE/25: 4X TO 10X BASIC
1 Jayson Tatum 4.00 10.00
2 James Harden 2.00 5.00
3 Nikola Jokic 5.00 12.00
4 Chris Paul 2.00 5.00
5 Dejounte Murray 1.25 3.00
6 LaMelo Ball 2.50 6.00
7 Russell Westbrook 1.50 4.00
8 Devin Booker 2.50 6.00
9 Paolo Banchero 6.00 15.00
10 Chet Holmgren 5.00 12.00

2022-23 Court Kings First Steps

COMMON CARD 1.00 2.50
SEMISTARS 1.25 3.00
UNLISTED STARS 1.50 4.00
*RUBY/149: .75X TO 2X BASIC
*VIOLET/49: 1.25X TO 3X BASIC
*SAPPHIRE/25: 2X TO 5X BASIC
1 Paolo Banchero 10.00 25.00
2 Chet Holmgren 8.00 20.00
3 Jabari Smith Jr. 5.00 12.00
4 Keegan Murray 4.00 10.00
5 Jaden Ivey 5.00 12.00
6 Bennedict Mathurin 5.00 12.00
7 Shaedon Sharpe 6.00 15.00
8 Dyson Daniels 4.00 10.00
9 Tari Eason 4.00 10.00
10 Jalen Duren 5.00 12.00

2022-23 Court Kings Fresh Paint

COMMON CARD 3.00 8.00
SEMISTARS 4.00 10.00
UNLISTED STARS 5.00 12.00
STATED PRINT RUN 75-199 SER.#'d SETS
*JADE: .4X TO 1X BASIC
*RUBY/99: .5X TO 1.25X BASIC
*VIOLET/49: .6X TO 1.5X BASIC
*SAPPHIRE/25: .75X TO 2X BASIC
1 Jabari Smith Jr./199 15.00 40.00
2 Jaden Ivey/199 40.00 100.00
3 Paolo Banchero/199 125.00 300.00
4 Jaden Hardy/199 30.00 80.00
5 Jalen Duren/199 15.00 40.00
6 Johnny Davis/199 5.00 12.00
7 Keegan Murray/199 40.00 100.00
8 Shaedon Sharpe/199 50.00 120.00
9 AJ Griffin/199 4.00 10.00
10 Bennedict Mathurin/199 40.00 100.00
11 TyTy Washington Jr./199 5.00 12.00
12 Dyson Daniels/199 12.00 30.00
13 Jeremy Sochan/199 40.00 100.00
14 Ousmane Dieng/199 6.00 15.00
15 Ochai Agbaji/199 6.00 15.00
16 Blake Wesley/199 5.00 12.00
17 Mark Williams/199 10.00 25.00
18 Tari Eason/199 12.00 30.00
19 Jalen Williams/199 25.00 60.00
20 Walker Kessler/199 10.00 25.00
21 Nikola Jovic/199 10.00 25.00
22 Kennedy Chandler/199 5.00 12.00
24 Wendell Moore Jr./199 5.00 12.00
25 E.J. Liddell/199 5.00 12.00
26 Jake LaRavia/199 5.00 12.00
27 Malaki Branham/199 5.00 12.00
28 MarJon Beauchamp/199 5.00 12.00
29 Christian Braun/199 12.00 30.00
30 David Roddy/199 6.00 15.00
31 Max Christie/199 12.00 30.00
32 Andrew Nembhard/199 10.00 25.00
33 Caleb Houstan/199 5.00 12.00
34 Christian Koloko/199 5.00 12.00
35 Trevor Keels/199 4.00 10.00
36 Isaiah Mobley/199 5.00 12.00
37 Moussa Diabate/199 5.00 12.00
38 Jabari Walker/199 4.00 10.00
39 Chet Holmgren/75 100.00 250.00
41 Scotty Pippen Jr./199 6.00 15.00
42 Collin Gillespie/199 5.00 12.00
43 Johnny Juzang/199 6.00 15.00
44 Kenneth Lofton Jr./199 6.00 15.00
45 Michael Foster Jr./199 4.00 10.00

2022-23 Court Kings Heir Apparent

COMMON CARD 3.00 8.00
SEMISTARS 4.00 10.00
UNLISTED STARS 5.00 12.00
STATED PRINT RUN 199 SER.#'d SETS
*JADE: .4X TO 1X BASIC
*RUBY/99: .5X TO 1.25X BASIC
*VIOLET/49: .6X TO 1.5X BASIC
*SAPPHIRE/25: .75X TO 2X BASIC
1 Chet Holmgren 75.00 200.00
2 Nikola Jovic 10.00 25.00
4 Kennedy Chandler 5.00 12.00
5 Wendell Moore Jr. 5.00 12.00
6 E.J. Liddell 5.00 12.00
7 Jake LaRavia 5.00 12.00
8 Malaki Branham 5.00 12.00
9 MarJon Beauchamp 5.00 12.00
10 Christian Braun 12.00 30.00
11 TyTy Washington Jr. 5.00 12.00
12 Dyson Daniels 12.00 30.00
13 Jeremy Sochan 40.00 100.00
14 Ousmane Dieng 6.00 15.00
15 Ochai Agbaji 6.00 15.00
16 Blake Wesley 5.00 12.00
17 Mark Williams 10.00 25.00
18 Andrew Nembhard 10.00 25.00
19 Caleb Houstan 5.00 12.00
20 Christian Koloko 5.00 12.00
21 Trevor Keels 4.00 10.00
22 Isaiah Mobley 5.00 12.00
23 Moussa Diabate 5.00 12.00
24 Scotty Pippen Jr. 6.00 15.00
25 Paolo Banchero 125.00 300.00
26 Jaden Hardy 30.00 80.00
27 Jalen Duren 15.00 40.00
28 Johnny Davis 5.00 12.00
29 Keegan Murray 40.00 100.00
30 Tari Eason 12.00 30.00
31 Jalen Williams 25.00 60.00
32 Walker Kessler 10.00 25.00
33 David Roddy 6.00 15.00
34 Max Christie 12.00 30.00
36 Jabari Smith Jr. 15.00 40.00
37 Jaden Ivey 40.00 100.00
38 Shaedon Sharpe 50.00 120.00
39 AJ Griffin 4.00 10.00
40 Bennedict Mathurin 40.00 100.00
41 Ron Harper Jr. 6.00 15.00
42 Alondes Williams 5.00 12.00
43 Jabari Walker 4.00 10.00
44 Peyton Watson 8.00 20.00
45 Jaylin Williams 6.00 15.00

2022-23 Court Kings Impressionist Ink

COMMON CARD 4.00 10.00
SEMISTARS 5.00 12.00
UNLISTED STARS 6.00 15.00
STATED PRINT RUN 75 SER.#'d SETS
*JADE: .4X TO 1X BASIC
*RUBY/49: .5X TO 1.25X BASIC
*VIOLET/35: .6X TO 1.5X BASIC
*SAPPHIRE/25: .6X TO 1.5X BASIC
1 Antawn Jamison 8.00 20.00
2 Avery Johnson 6.00 15.00
3 B.J. Armstrong 8.00 20.00
4 Brook Lopez 8.00 20.00
5 Cameron Payne 6.00 15.00
6 Carlos Boozer 6.00 15.00
7 Zach Randolph 8.00 20.00
8 De'Aaron Fox 15.00 40.00
9 Dejounte Murray 10.00 25.00
10 Desmond Bane 10.00 25.00
11 Jalen Brunson 40.00 100.00
12 Jason Terry 6.00 15.00
13 Jeff Green 5.00 12.00
14 Jordan Clarkson 8.00 20.00
16 Matt Barnes 6.00 15.00
18 Onyeka Okongwu 8.00 20.00
19 Rick Fox 8.00 20.00
20 Sam Cassell 8.00 20.00
21 Shawn Kemp 12.00 30.00
22 Jonathan Kuminga 20.00 50.00
24 Alperen Sengun 10.00 25.00
25 Cameron Thomas 12.00 30.00
26 Franz Wagner 20.00 50.00
27 Scottie Barnes 12.00 30.00
28 Trey Murphy III 10.00 25.00

2022-23 Court Kings Legacy Portrait Signatures

STATED PRINT RUN 99 SER.#'d SETS
*JADE: .4X TO 1X BASIC
*RUBY/49: .5X TO 1.25X BASIC
*VIOLET/35: .6X TO 1.5X BASIC
1 Jayson Tatum 125.00 300.00
2 Ray Allen 40.00 100.00
3 Paul Pierce 40.00 100.00
5 Anfernee Hardaway 40.00 100.00
6 Dwyane Wade 60.00 150.00
7 Manu Ginobili 40.00 100.00
8 Anthony Edwards 100.00 250.00
9 Ja Morant 100.00 250.00
10 Luka Doncic 300.00 600.00

2022-23 Court Kings Maestros

COMMON CARD .40 1.00
SEMISTARS .50 1.25
UNLISTED STARS .60 1.50
*RUBY/149: 1.25X TO 3X BASIC
*VIOLET/49: 2X TO 5X BASIC
*SAPPHIRE/25: 4X TO 10X BASIC
1 Luka Doncic 4.00 10.00
2 Bradley Beal .75 2.00
3 Josh Giddey 1.00 2.50
4 Paolo Banchero 6.00 15.00
5 Keegan Murray 1.50 4.00
6 Damian Lillard 1.50 4.00
7 Giannis Antetokounmpo 3.00 8.00
8 Kevin Durant 2.00 5.00
9 James Harden 1.25 3.00
10 Jaden Ivey 2.00 5.00
11 Donovan Mitchell 1.25 3.00
12 Collin Sexton .75 2.00
13 Nikola Jokic 3.00 8.00
14 DeMar DeRozan .75 2.00
15 Jimmy Butler 1.25 3.00
16 LeBron James 5.00 12.00
17 Ja Morant 2.00 5.00
18 Jalen Green 2.00 5.00
19 Anthony Edwards 3.00 8.00
20 Scottie Barnes 1.00 2.50
21 Cade Cunningham 2.00 5.00
22 Kawhi Leonard 1.50 4.00
23 Tyrese Haliburton 1.25 3.00
24 Zion Williamson 1.50 4.00
25 Jabari Smith Jr. 2.00 5.00
26 Stephen Curry 5.00 12.00
27 Jayson Tatum 2.50 6.00
28 LaMelo Ball 1.50 4.00
29 Devin Booker 1.50 4.00
30 Trae Young 1.50 4.00

2022-23 Court Kings Masterstrokes

COMMON CARD 4.00 10.00
SEMISTARS 5.00 12.00
UNLISTED STARS 6.00 15.00
STATED PRINT RUN 75 SER.#'d SETS
*JADE: .4X TO 1X BASIC
*RUBY/49: .5X TO 1.25X BASIC
*VIOLET/35: .6X TO 1.5X BASIC
*SAPPHIRE/25: .6X TO 1.5X BASIC
1 Al Horford 6.00 15.00
2 Aleksej Pokusevski 6.00 15.00
3 Amar'e Stoudemire 6.00 15.00
4 Anfernee Simons 8.00 20.00
5 Avery Johnson 5.00 12.00
6 B.J. Armstrong 6.00 15.00
7 Brook Lopez 6.00 15.00
8 Cameron Payne 5.00 12.00
9 Charlie Ward 6.00 15.00
10 Collin Sexton 8.00 20.00
11 Derrick White 12.00 30.00
12 Elton Brand 6.00 15.00
13 Harold Miner 6.00 15.00
14 Jason Williams 25.00 60.00
15 Jerry Stackhouse 8.00 20.00
16 John Lucas 6.00 15.00
17 Karl-Anthony Towns 12.00 30.00
18 Kevin Willis 5.00 12.00
20 Latrell Sprewell 8.00 20.00
21 Luguentz Dort 6.00 15.00
22 Luke Kennard 5.00 12.00
23 Mitch Richmond 8.00 20.00
24 Moses Brown 4.00 10.00
25 Myles Turner 6.00 15.00
26 Nickeil Alexander-Walker 5.00 12.00
27 Pat Connaughton 5.00 12.00
28 Rick Fox 6.00 15.00
29 Robert Williams III 5.00 12.00
30 Robin Lopez 5.00 12.00
31 Sam Cassell 6.00 15.00
32 Wendell Carter Jr. 6.00 15.00
33 Davion Mitchell 5.00 12.00
34 Corey Kispert 6.00 15.00
35 Ziaire Williams 5.00 12.00
36 Keon Johnson 4.00 10.00
37 Jalen Johnson 8.00 20.00
39 Josh Christopher 4.00 10.00
40 Evan Mobley 25.00 60.00

2022-23 Court Kings Modern Strokes

COMMON CARD .75 2.00
SEMISTARS 1.00 2.50
UNLISTED STARS 1.25 3.00
*AMETHYST/99: 1.5X TO 4X BASIC
*JADE/25: 3X TO 8X BASIC
1 Dejounte Murray 1.50 4.00
2 Shai Gilgeous-Alexander 6.00 15.00
3 DeMar DeRozan 1.50 4.00
4 RJ Barrett 2.00 5.00
5 Kawhi Leonard 3.00 8.00
6 Tyrese Maxey 2.50 6.00
7 James Harden 2.50 6.00
8 Damian Lillard 3.00 8.00
9 Ja Morant 4.00 10.00
10 Jayson Tatum 5.00 12.00
11 LeBron James 10.00 25.00
12 Tyrese Haliburton 2.50 6.00
13 Trae Young 3.00 8.00
14 Jamal Murray 2.00 5.00
15 Cade Cunningham 4.00 10.00
16 Jalen Green 4.00 10.00
17 De'Aaron Fox 2.50 6.00
18 Fred VanVleet 1.50 4.00
19 Paul George 2.00 5.00
20 CJ McCollum 1.25 3.00
21 Anthony Edwards 6.00 15.00
22 Devin Booker 3.00 8.00
23 Stephen Curry 10.00 25.00
24 Kevin Durant 4.00 10.00
25 Darius Garland 2.00 5.00
26 LaMelo Ball 3.00 8.00
27 Kyrie Irving 2.50 6.00
28 Jaylen Brown 2.50 6.00
29 Donovan Mitchell 2.50 6.00
30 Luka Doncic 8.00 20.00

2022-23 Court Kings Paint by Number

1 Trae Young 25.00 60.00
2 Ja Morant 60.00 150.00
3 Jayson Tatum 75.00 200.00
4 Giannis Antetokounmpo 75.00 200.00
5 LaMelo Ball 60.00 150.00
6 LeBron James 125.00 300.00
7 Kevin Durant 50.00 120.00
8 Stephen Curry 125.00 300.00
9 Luka Doncic 100.00 250.00
10 Zion Williamson 50.00 120.00

2022-23 Court Kings Rookie Exclusive

1 Paolo Banchero 125.00 300.00

2022-23 Court Kings Rookie Expression Memorabilia

COMMON CARD 1.25 3.00
SEMISTARS 1.50 4.00
UNLISTED STARS 2.00 5.00
*PRIME/25: 1.5X TO 4X BASIC
1 Jake LaRavia 2.00 5.00
2 Bennedict Mathurin 6.00 15.00
3 Dalen Terry 2.00 5.00
4 TyTy Washington Jr. 2.00 5.00
5 Jaden Ivey 6.00 15.00
6 Kennedy Chandler 2.00 5.00
7 Johnny Davis 2.00 5.00
8 MarJon Beauchamp 2.00 5.00
9 Christian Braun 5.00 12.00
10 Peyton Watson 3.00 8.00
11 Ousmane Dieng 2.50 6.00
12 Tari Eason 5.00 12.00
13 Christian Koloko 2.00 5.00
14 Jabari Smith Jr. 6.00 15.00
15 Jaden Hardy 3.00 8.00
16 Max Christie 5.00 12.00
17 Wendell Moore Jr. 2.00 5.00
18 Trevor Keels 1.50 4.00
19 Blake Wesley 2.00 5.00
20 E.J. Liddell 2.00 5.00
21 Isaiah Mobley 2.00 5.00
22 Chet Holmgren 10.00 25.00
23 Jalen Duren 6.00 15.00
24 David Roddy 2.50 6.00
25 Dyson Daniels 5.00 12.00
26 Moussa Diabate 2.00 5.00
27 Patrick Baldwin Jr. 2.00 5.00
28 Mark Williams 4.00 10.00
29 Shaedon Sharpe 8.00 20.00
30 Ochai Agbaji 2.50 6.00
31 Keegan Murray 5.00 12.00
32 Malaki Branham 2.00 5.00
33 Jeremy Sochan 6.00 15.00
34 AJ Griffin 1.50 4.00
35 Andrew Nembhard 4.00 10.00
36 Jalen Williams 10.00 25.00
37 Caleb Houstan 2.00 5.00
38 Walker Kessler 4.00 10.00
39 Nikola Jovic 4.00 10.00
40 Paolo Banchero 12.00 30.00

2022-23 Court Kings Water Color

COMMON CARD .60 1.50
SEMISTARS .75 2.00
UNLISTED STARS 1.00 2.50
*RUBY/149: 1.25X TO 3X BASIC
*VIOLET/49: 2.5X TO 6X BASIC
*SAPPHIRE/25: 5X TO 12X BASIC
1 Nikola Jokic 5.00 12.00
2 Stephen Curry 8.00 20.00
3 Allen Iverson 2.50 6.00
4 Ja Morant 3.00 8.00
5 Dirk Nowitzki 2.50 6.00
6 Luka Doncic 6.00 15.00
7 Josh Giddey 1.50 4.00
8 Damian Lillard 2.50 6.00
9 James Harden 2.00 5.00
10 Kyrie Irving 2.00 5.00
11 Anthony Edwards 5.00 12.00
12 Zion Williamson 2.50 6.00
13 Charles Barkley 2.50 6.00
14 Kevin Garnett 2.50 6.00
15 Kevin Durant 3.00 8.00
16 Larry Bird 4.00 10.00
17 Devin Booker 2.50 6.00
18 Cade Cunningham 3.00 8.00
19 Zach LaVine 2.00 5.00
20 LaMelo Ball 2.50 6.00
21 Kawhi Leonard 2.50 6.00
22 Anthony Davis 2.50 6.00
23 Jalen Green 3.00 8.00
24 Jayson Tatum 4.00 10.00
25 Bradley Beal 1.25 3.00
26 Giannis Antetokounmpo 5.00 12.00
27 Donovan Mitchell 2.00 5.00
28 LeBron James 8.00 20.00
29 Trae Young 2.50 6.00
30 Scottie Barnes 1.50 4.00

2022-23 Court Kings Works in Progress

COMMON CARD .60 1.50
SEMISTARS .75 2.00
UNLISTED STARS 1.00 2.50
*RUBY/149: 1.25X TO 3X BASIC
*VIOLET/49: 2.5X TO 6X BASIC
*SAPPHIRE/25: 5X TO 12X BASIC
1 Chet Holmgren 5.00 12.00
2 Shaedon Sharpe 4.00 10.00
3 Jake LaRavia 1.00 2.50
4 Patrick Baldwin Jr. 1.00 2.50
5 Jabari Smith Jr. 3.00 8.00
6 Nikola Jovic 2.00 5.00
7 David Roddy 1.25 3.00
8 Jaden Ivey 3.00 8.00
9 Dalen Terry 1.00 2.50
10 Wendell Moore Jr. 1.00 2.50
11 Ousmane Dieng 1.25 3.00
12 Jalen Williams 5.00 12.00
13 Blake Wesley 1.00 2.50
14 Malaki Branham 1.00 2.50
15 Keegan Murray 2.50 6.00
16 Dyson Daniels 2.50 6.00
17 Mark Williams 2.00 5.00
18 AJ Griffin .75 2.00
19 Jalen Duren 3.00 8.00
20 Christian Braun 2.50 6.00
21 TyTy Washington Jr. 1.00 2.50
22 Paolo Banchero 6.00 15.00
23 Peyton Watson 1.50 4.00
24 Jeremy Sochan 3.00 8.00
25 Bennedict Mathurin 3.00 8.00
26 Johnny Davis 1.00 2.50
27 MarJon Beauchamp 1.00 2.50
28 Tari Eason 2.50 6.00
29 Jaden Hardy 1.50 4.00
30 Ochai Agbaji 1.25 3.00

2023-24 Court Kings

*ARTIST PROOF: .75X TO 2X BASIC
*STEALTH: .75X TO 2X BASIC
*RUBY/149: 2X TO 5X BASIC
*AMETHYST/99: 2.5X TO 6X BASIC
*PINK/99: 2.5X TO 6X BASIC
*AMBER/75: 2.5X TO 6X BASIC
*VIOLET/49: 3X TO 8X BASIC
*JADE/25: 4X TO 10X BASIC
*SAPPHIRE/25: 4X TO 10X BASIC
1 Jrue Holiday .60 1.50
2 Bradley Beal .60 1.50
3 Trae Young 1.00 2.50
4 Jayson Tatum 2.00 5.00
5 Keegan Murray .60 1.50
6 Jalen Williams 1.00 2.50
7 Stephen Curry 4.00 10.00
8 Donovan Mitchell 1.00 2.50
9 Jalen Green .75 2.00
10 Jalen Brunson 1.00 2.50
11 Cade Cunningham 1.25 3.00
12 Pascal Siakam .75 2.00
13 Keldon Johnson .60 1.50
14 Chet Holmgren 1.25 3.00
15 Darius Garland .75 2.00
16 Jamal Murray 1.00 2.50
17 Shai Gilgeous-Alexander 2.50 6.00
18 Jaren Jackson Jr. .75 2.00
19 Bam Adebayo .75 2.00
20 Anthony Davis 1.25 3.00
21 Tyrese Maxey 1.00 2.50
22 Paul George .75 2.00
23 Jimmy Butler .75 2.00
24 De'Aaron Fox 1.00 2.50
25 Mikal Bridges .60 1.50
26 Kevin Durant 1.50 4.00
27 Lauri Markkanen .75 2.00
28 Domantas Sabonis .75 2.00
29 Dejounte Murray .60 1.50
30 DeMar DeRozan .75 2.00
31 Spencer Dinwiddie .40 1.00
32 Brandon Ingram .60 1.50
33 Khris Middleton .50 1.25
34 Austin Reaves 1.25 3.00
35 James Harden 1.00 2.50
36 Nikola Jokic 2.50 6.00
37 Zach LaVine .75 2.00
38 Kawhi Leonard 1.25 3.00
39 Tyrese Haliburton 1.25 3.00
40 Kristaps Porzingis .60 1.50
41 Jabari Smith Jr. .75 2.00
42 Bennedict Mathurin .75 2.00
43 Chris Paul .75 2.00
44 Jaden Ivey .60 1.50
45 Jaylen Brown 1.00 2.50
46 Damian Lillard 1.25 3.00
47 Zion Williamson 1.25 3.00
48 Jordan Clarkson .50 1.25
49 Anthony Edwards 2.50 6.00
50 Julius Randle .60 1.50
51 Klay Thompson 1.25 3.00
52 LeBron James 4.00 10.00
53 Josh Giddey .60 1.50
54 Joel Embiid 1.25 3.00
55 Terry Rozier III .60 1.50
56 Karl-Anthony Towns .75 2.00
57 Giannis Antetokounmpo 2.50 6.00
58 LaMelo Ball 1.25 3.00
59 Luka Doncic 3.00 8.00
60 Russell Westbrook .75 2.00
61 Alperen Sengun .75 2.00
62 Scottie Barnes .60 1.50
63 Desmond Bane .60 1.50
64 Ja Morant 1.50 4.00
65 Kyrie Irving 1.00 2.50
66 Shaedon Sharpe 1.00 2.50
67 Devin Booker 1.25 3.00
68 Jaime Jaquez Jr. RC 1.50 4.00
69 Jalen Hood-Schifino RC 1.00 2.50
70 Anthony Black RC 2.00 5.00
71 Jordan Hawkins RC 1.50 4.00
72 Jett Howard RC 1.25 3.00
73 Victor Wembanyama RC 25.00 60.00
74 Taylor Hendricks RC 1.00 2.50
75 Scoot Henderson RC 3.00 8.00
76 Nick Smith Jr. RC 1.25 3.00
77 Jarace Walker RC 2.00 5.00
78 Gradey Dick RC 2.00 5.00
79 Cam Whitmore RC 2.50 6.00
80 Brandon Miller RC 4.00 10.00
81 Amen Thompson RC 5.00 12.00
82 Keyonte George RC 3.00 8.00
83 Ausar Thompson RC 2.50 6.00
84 Kobe Bufkin RC 1.25 3.00
85 Bilal Coulibaly RC 2.50 6.00
86 Noah Clowney RC 1.25 3.00
87 Marcus Sasser RC 1.50 4.00
88 Ben Sheppard RC 1.00 2.50
89 Julian Strawther RC 1.25 3.00
90 James Nnaji RC .75 2.00
91 Kobe Brown RC 1.00 2.50
92 Brice Sensabaugh RC 1.50 4.00
93 Cason Wallace RC 2.00 5.00
94 Dereck Lively II RC 2.00 5.00
95 Jalen Pickett RC .75 2.00
96 Brandin Podziemski RC 3.00 8.00
97 Leonard Miller RC 1.00 2.50
98 Dariq Whitehead RC 1.25 3.00
99 Kris Murray RC 1.00 2.50
100 Olivier-Maxence Prosper RC 1.00 2.50
101 Jaime Jaquez Jr. 3.00 8.00
102 Jalen Hood-Schifino 2.00 5.00
103 Anthony Black 4.00 10.00
104 Jordan Hawkins 3.00 8.00
105 Jett Howard 2.50 6.00
106 Victor Wembanyama 100.00 250.00
107 Taylor Hendricks 2.00 5.00
108 Scoot Henderson 6.00 15.00
109 Nick Smith Jr. 2.50 6.00
110 Jarace Walker 4.00 10.00
111 Gradey Dick 4.00 10.00
112 Cam Whitmore 5.00 12.00
113 Brandon Miller 8.00 20.00
114 Amen Thompson 10.00 25.00
115 Keyonte George 6.00 15.00
116 Ausar Thompson 5.00 12.00
117 Kobe Bufkin 2.50 6.00
118 Bilal Coulibaly 5.00 12.00
119 Noah Clowney 2.50 6.00
120 Marcus Sasser 3.00 8.00
121 Ben Sheppard 2.00 5.00
122 Julian Strawther 2.50 6.00
123 James Nnaji 1.50 4.00
124 Kobe Brown 2.00 5.00
125 Brice Sensabaugh 3.00 8.00
126 Cason Wallace 4.00 10.00
127 Dereck Lively II 4.00 10.00
128 Jalen Pickett 1.50 4.00
129 Brandin Podziemski 6.00 15.00
130 Leonard Miller 2.00 5.00
131 Dariq Whitehead 2.50 6.00
132 Kris Murray 2.00 5.00
133 Olivier-Maxence Prosper 2.00 5.00
134 Jaime Jaquez Jr. 8.00 20.00
135 Jalen Hood-Schifino 5.00 12.00
136 Anthony Black 10.00 25.00
137 Jordan Hawkins 8.00 20.00
138 Jett Howard 6.00 15.00
139 Victor Wembanyama 200.00 500.00
140 Taylor Hendricks 5.00 12.00
141 Scoot Henderson 15.00 40.00
142 Nick Smith Jr. 6.00 15.00
143 Jarace Walker 10.00 25.00
144 Gradey Dick 10.00 25.00
145 Cam Whitmore 12.00 30.00
146 Brandon Miller 20.00 50.00
147 Amen Thompson 25.00 60.00
148 Keyonte George 15.00 40.00
149 Ausar Thompson 12.00 30.00
150 Kobe Bufkin 6.00 15.00
151 Bilal Coulibaly 12.00 30.00
152 Noah Clowney 6.00 15.00
153 Marcus Sasser 8.00 20.00
154 Ben Sheppard 5.00 12.00
155 Julian Strawther 6.00 15.00
156 James Nnaji 4.00 10.00
157 Kobe Brown 5.00 12.00
158 Brice Sensabaugh 8.00 20.00
159 Cason Wallace 10.00 25.00
160 Dereck Lively II 10.00 25.00
161 Jalen Pickett 4.00 10.00
162 Brandin Podziemski 15.00 40.00
163 Leonard Miller 5.00 12.00
164 Dariq Whitehead 6.00 15.00
165 Kris Murray 5.00 12.00
166 Olivier-Maxence Prosper 5.00 12.00
167 Jaime Jaquez Jr. 40.00 100.00
168 Jalen Hood-Schifino 25.00 60.00
169 Anthony Black 50.00 125.00
170 Jordan Hawkins 40.00 100.00
171 Jett Howard 30.00 80.00
172 Victor Wembanyama 1,000.00 2,000.00
173 Taylor Hendricks 25.00 60.00
174 Scoot Henderson 80.00 200.00
175 Nick Smith Jr. 30.00 80.00
176 Jarace Walker 50.00 125.00
177 Gradey Dick 50.00 125.00
178 Cam Whitmore 60.00 150.00
179 Brandon Miller 100.00 250.00
180 Amen Thompson 120.00 300.00
181 Keyonte George 80.00 200.00
182 Ausar Thompson 60.00 150.00
183 Kobe Bufkin 30.00 80.00
184 Bilal Coulibaly 60.00 150.00
185 Noah Clowney 30.00 80.00
186 Marcus Sasser 40.00 100.00
187 Ben Sheppard 25.00 60.00
188 Julian Strawther 30.00 80.00
189 James Nnaji 20.00 50.00
190 Kobe Brown 25.00 60.00
191 Brice Sensabaugh 40.00 100.00
192 Cason Wallace 50.00 125.00
193 Dereck Lively II 50.00 125.00
194 Jalen Pickett 20.00 50.00
195 Brandin Podziemski 80.00 200.00
196 Leonard Miller 25.00 60.00
197 Dariq Whitehead 30.00 80.00
198 Kris Murray 25.00 60.00
199 Olivier-Maxence Prosper 25.00 60.00

2023-24 Court Kings Acetate Rookies

1 Brandin Podziemski 5.00 12.00
2 Gradey Dick 3.00 8.00
3 Jarace Walker 3.00 8.00
4 Victor Wembanyama 50.00 120.00
5 Kris Murray 1.50 4.00
6 Jaime Jaquez Jr. 2.50 6.00
7 Anthony Black 3.00 8.00
8 Jalen Hood-Schifino 1.50 4.00
9 Taylor Hendricks 1.50 4.00
10 Olivier-Maxence Prosper 1.50 4.00
11 Keyonte George 5.00 12.00
12 Marcus Sasser 2.50 6.00
13 Cam Whitmore 4.00 10.00
14 Jett Howard 2.00 5.00
15 Bilal Coulibaly 4.00 10.00
16 Scoot Henderson 5.00 12.00
17 Kobe Bufkin 2.00 5.00
18 Noah Clowney 2.00 5.00
19 Dereck Lively II 3.00 8.00
20 Cason Wallace 3.00 8.00
21 Brandon Miller 6.00 15.00
22 Ausar Thompson 4.00 10.00
23 Jordan Hawkins 2.50 6.00
24 Amen Thompson 8.00 20.00
25 Dariq Whitehead 2.00 5.00

2023-24 Court Kings Art Nouveau Jerseys

1 Victor Wembanyama 60.00 150.00
2 Amen Thompson 12.00 30.00
3 Bilal Coulibaly 6.00 15.00
4 Ausar Thompson 6.00 15.00
5 Keyonte George 8.00 20.00
6 Brandon Miller 10.00 25.00
7 Dariq Whitehead 3.00 8.00
8 Anthony Black 5.00 12.00
9 Cason Wallace 5.00 12.00
10 Kobe Bufkin 3.00 8.00
11 Taylor Hendricks 2.50 6.00
12 Cam Whitmore 6.00 15.00
13 Jett Howard 3.00 8.00
14 Jarace Walker 5.00 12.00
15 Scoot Henderson 8.00 20.00
16 Tyler Herro 4.00 10.00
17 Klay Thompson 6.00 15.00
18 RJ Barrett 4.00 10.00
19 Karl-Anthony Towns 4.00 10.00
20 Khris Middleton 2.50 6.00
21 Domantas Sabonis 4.00 10.00
22 Keldon Johnson 3.00 8.00
23 Franz Wagner 4.00 10.00
24 Anfernee Simons 3.00 8.00
25 Tyrese Maxey 5.00 12.00
26 Tobias Harris 2.50 6.00
27 Bam Adebayo 4.00 10.00
28 Cameron Thomas 3.00 8.00
29 Norman Powell 2.50 6.00
30 DeMar DeRozan 4.00 10.00
31 Alperen Sengun 4.00 10.00
32 Buddy Hield 2.50 6.00
33 Deandre Ayton 2.50 6.00
34 D'Angelo Russell 2.50 6.00
35 Dejounte Murray 3.00 8.00
36 LeBron James 30.00 80.00
37 Jimmy Butler 4.00 10.00
38 Jamal Murray 5.00 12.00
39 Brandon Ingram 3.00 8.00
40 Darius Garland 4.00 10.00

2023-24 Court Kings Art Nouveau Jerseys Prime

*PRIME/25: 1.25X TO 3X BASIC
1 Victor Wembanyama/25 400.00 800.00

2023-24 Court Kings Artistic Endeavors Jerseys

1 Joel Embiid 5.00 12.00
2 Jimmy Butler 3.00 8.00
3 Jaylen Brown 4.00 10.00
4 Devin Booker 5.00 12.00
5 LeBron James 30.00 80.00
6 Kawhi Leonard 5.00 12.00
7 Giannis Antetokounmpo 10.00 25.00
8 Kevin Durant 6.00 15.00
9 Jalen Hood-Schifino 2.00 5.00
10 Jarace Walker 4.00 10.00
11 Jett Howard 2.50 6.00
12 Jaime Jaquez Jr. 3.00 8.00
13 Brandon Miller 8.00 20.00
14 Ausar Thompson 5.00 12.00
15 Anthony Black 4.00 10.00
16 Bilal Coulibaly 5.00 12.00
17 Cam Whitmore 5.00 12.00
18 Amen Thompson 10.00 25.00
19 Scoot Henderson 6.00 15.00
20 Victor Wembanyama 30.00 80.00

2023-24 Court Kings Artistry in Motion

*AMETHYST/99: 1.5X TO 4X BASIC
*JADE/25: 3X TO 8X BASIC
1 Shaquille O'Neal 2.50 6.00
2 Giannis Antetokounmpo 4.00 10.00
3 Nikola Jokic 4.00 10.00
4 Stephen Curry 6.00 15.00
5 Dirk Nowitzki 2.00 5.00
6 Pau Gasol 1.25 3.00
7 Ausar Thompson 2.00 5.00
8 Donovan Mitchell 1.50 4.00
9 Chet Holmgren 2.00 5.00
10 Kevin Durant 2.50 6.00
11 Tyrese Haliburton 1.50 4.00
12 Victor Wembanyama 25.00 60.00
13 Anthony Edwards 4.00 10.00
14 De'Aaron Fox 1.50 4.00
15 LeBron James 6.00 15.00
16 Cason Wallace 1.50 4.00
17 Damian Lillard 2.00 5.00
18 Allen Iverson 2.00 5.00
19 Brandon Miller 3.00 8.00
20 Joel Embiid 2.00 5.00
21 Paolo Banchero 2.00 5.00
22 Zion Williamson 2.00 5.00
23 Jayson Tatum 3.00 8.00
24 Bilal Coulibaly 2.00 5.00
25 Amen Thompson 4.00 10.00
26 Ja Morant 2.50 6.00
27 Scoot Henderson 2.50 6.00
28 Luka Doncic 5.00 12.00
29 Trae Young 1.50 4.00
30 Shai Gilgeous-Alexander 4.00 10.00

2023-24 Court Kings Aurora

1 Amen Thompson 50.00 120.00
2 Brandon Miller 75.00 200.00
3 Keyonte George 50.00 120.00
4 Ausar Thompson 50.00 120.00
5 Bilal Coulibaly 40.00 100.00
6 Scoot Henderson 60.00 150.00
7 Anthony Black 30.00 80.00
8 Victor Wembanyama 500.00 1,000.00
9 Cason Wallace 40.00 100.00
10 Taylor Hendricks 25.00 60.00
11 LeBron James 125.00 300.00
12 Luka Doncic 75.00 200.00
13 Stephen Curry 125.00 300.00
14 Giannis Antetokounmpo 50.00 120.00
15 Jayson Tatum 50.00 120.00
16 Nikola Jokic 50.00 120.00
17 Trae Young 30.00 80.00

2023-24 Court Kings Brush Strokes Autographs

STATED PRINT RUN 49-75 SER.#'d SETS
*JADE: .4X TO 1X BASIC
*RUBY/49: .5X TO 1.25X BASIC
*VIOLET/35: .6X TO 1.5X BASIC
*SAPPHIRE/25: .6X TO 1.5X BASIC
1 Derek Fisher/75 6.00 15.00
2 Nick Van Exel/75 6.00 15.00
3 Gary Payton/75 15.00 40.00
4 Steve Kerr/75 8.00 20.00
5 Tyrese Haliburton/75 50.00 120.00
6 Jordan Poole/75 10.00 25.00
7 Immanuel Quickley/75 6.00 15.00
8 Ayo Dosunmu/75 6.00 15.00
9 Alperen Sengun/75 10.00 25.00
10 Desmond Bane/49 8.00 20.00
11 Bob Pettit/49 8.00 20.00
12 Artis Gilmore/75 8.00 20.00
13 Rayan Rupert/75 6.00 15.00
14 Jrue Holiday/75 12.00 30.00
15 Jalen Wilson/75 6.00 15.00
17 Bennedict Mathurin/75 10.00 25.00
18 Brice Sensabaugh/75 10.00 25.00
19 Maxwell Lewis/75 5.00 12.00
20 Amen Thompson/75 40.00 100.00
21 Ausar Thompson/75 20.00 50.00
22 Bilal Coulibaly/75 15.00 40.00
23 Cason Wallace/75 12.00 30.00
24 Dereck Lively II/75 12.00 30.00
25 Deandre Ayton/49 6.00 15.00
26 Keyonte George/75 40.00 100.00
27 Brandin Podziemski/75 40.00 100.00
28 Noah Clowney/75 8.00 20.00
29 Dariq Whitehead/75 8.00 20.00
30 Jordan Clarkson/75 6.00 15.00

2023-24 Court Kings Debut Showcase Memorabilia

*PRIME/25: 1.5X TO 4X BASIC
1 Kobe Brown 2.00 5.00
2 Leonard Miller 2.00 5.00
3 Marcus Sasser 3.00 8.00
4 Bilal Coulibaly 5.00 12.00
5 Scoot Henderson 6.00 15.00
6 James Nnaji 1.50 4.00
7 Ben Sheppard 2.00 5.00
8 Julian Phillips 2.00 5.00
9 Gradey Dick 4.00 10.00
10 Dariq Whitehead 2.50 6.00
11 Jordan Walsh 2.00 5.00
12 Jordan Hawkins 3.00 8.00
13 Jaime Jaquez Jr. 3.00 8.00
14 Colby Jones 2.00 5.00
15 Maxwell Lewis 1.50 4.00
16 Taylor Hendricks 2.00 5.00
17 Jarace Walker 4.00 10.00
18 Brandin Podziemski 6.00 15.00
19 Nick Smith Jr. 2.50 6.00
20 Cason Wallace 4.00 10.00
21 Jalen Pickett 1.50 4.00
22 Victor Wembanyama 40.00 100.00
23 Brandon Miller 8.00 20.00
24 Julian Strawther 2.50 6.00
25 Kris Murray 2.00 5.00
26 Andre Jackson Jr. 3.00 8.00
27 Brice Sensabaugh 3.00 8.00
28 Ausar Thompson 5.00 12.00
29 Amen Thompson 10.00 25.00
30 Hunter Tyson 2.00 5.00
31 Jalen Hood-Schifino 2.00 5.00
32 Noah Clowney 2.50 6.00
33 Jett Howard 2.50 6.00
34 Dereck Lively II 4.00 10.00
35 Anthony Black 4.00 10.00
36 Kobe Bufkin 2.50 6.00
37 Keyonte George 6.00 15.00
38 Cam Whitmore 5.00 12.00
39 Olivier-Maxence Prosper 2.00 5.00
40 GG Jackson II 4.00 10.00

2023-24 Court Kings Double Exposure

*AMETHYST/99: 1.5X TO 4X BASIC
*JADE/25: 3X TO 8X BASIC
1 Donovan Mitchell 1.50 4.00

Tyrese Haliburton 1.50 4.00
Kyrie Irving 1.50 4.00
Stephen Curry 6.00 15.00
Vince Carter 1.50 4.00
Joel Embiid 2.00 5.00
Anthony Black 1.50 4.00
James Harden 1.50 4.00
LaMelo Ball 2.00 5.00
0 Jayson Tatum 3.00 8.00
1 Keyonte George 2.50 6.00
2 Zion Williamson 2.00 5.00
3 Carmelo Anthony 1.25 3.00
4 Ausar Thompson 2.00 5.00
5 Ja Morant 2.50 6.00
6 Dwyane Wade 1.50 4.00
7 Trae Young 1.50 4.00
8 Amen Thompson 4.00 10.00
9 Victor Wembanyama 25.00 60.00
0 Brandon Miller 3.00 8.00
1 Bilal Coulibaly 2.00 5.00
2 Scoot Henderson 2.50 6.00
3 Anfernee Hardaway 2.00 5.00
4 Damian Lillard 2.00 5.00
5 LeBron James 6.00 15.00
6 Devin Booker 2.00 5.00
7 Jaylen Brown 1.50 4.00
8 Anthony Edwards 4.00 10.00
9 Giannis Antetokounmpo 4.00 10.00
0 Nikola Jokic 4.00 10.00

2023-24 Court Kings Dressed to Impress

AMETHYST/99: 1.5X TO 4X BASIC
*JADE/25: 3X TO 8X BASIC
1 LeBron James 6.00 15.00
2 Shai Gilgeous-Alexander 4.00 10.00
3 Luka Doncic 5.00 12.00
4 Jayson Tatum 3.00 8.00
5 Victor Wembanyama 25.00 60.00
6 Scoot Henderson 2.50 6.00
7 Brandon Miller 3.00 8.00
8 Amen Thompson 4.00 10.00
9 Ausar Thompson 2.00 5.00
10 Bilal Coulibaly 2.00 5.00

2023-24 Court Kings First Steps

*RUBY/149: .75X TO 2X BASIC
*VIOLET/49: 1.25X TO 3X BASIC
*SAPPHIRE/25: 2X TO 5X BASIC
1 Victor Wembanyama 40.00 100.00
2 Brandon Miller 6.00 15.00
3 Scoot Henderson 5.00 12.00
4 Amen Thompson 8.00 20.00
5 Ausar Thompson 4.00 10.00
6 Anthony Black 3.00 8.00
7 Cason Wallace 3.00 8.00
8 Gradey Dick 3.00 8.00
9 Bilal Coulibaly 4.00 10.00
10 Dereck Lively II 3.00 8.00

2023-24 Court Kings Fresh Paint Autographs

STATED PRINT RUN 99-125 SER.#'d SETS
*JADE: .4X TO 1X BASIC
*RUBY/75-99: .4X TO 1X BASIC
*AMBER/49-75: .5X TO 1.2X BASIC
*VIOLET/25-49: .6X TO 1.5X BASIC
*SAPPHIRE/15-25: .75X TO 2X BASIC
1 Amen Thompson/125 30.00 80.00
2 Ausar Thompson/125 15.00 40.00
3 Keyonte George/125 20.00 50.00
4 Cason Wallace/125 12.00 30.00
5 Dariq Whitehead/125 8.00 20.00
6 GG Jackson II/125 12.00 30.00
7 Chris Livingston/125 6.00 15.00
8 Brice Sensabaugh/125 10.00 25.00
9 Brandin Podziemski/125 25.00 60.00
10 Bilal Coulibaly/125 15.00 40.00
11 Dereck Lively II/125 12.00 30.00
12 Kobe Bufkin/125 8.00 20.00
13 Noah Clowney/125 8.00 20.00
14 Kris Murray/125 6.00 15.00
15 Olivier-Maxence Prosper/125 6.00 15.00
16 Marcus Sasser/125 10.00 25.00
17 Ben Sheppard/125 6.00 15.00
18 Julian Strawther/125 8.00 20.00
19 Kobe Brown/125 6.00 15.00
20 James Nnaji/125 5.00 12.00
21 Jalen Pickett/125 5.00 12.00
22 Leonard Miller/125 6.00 15.00
23 Colby Jones/125 6.00 15.00
24 Julian Phillips/125 6.00 15.00
25 Andre Jackson Jr./125 10.00 25.00
26 Hunter Tyson/125 6.00 15.00
27 Jordan Walsh/125 6.00 15.00
28 Maxwell Lewis/125 5.00 12.00
29 Tristan Vukcevic/125 6.00 15.00
30 Rayan Rupert/125 6.00 15.00
31 Keyontae Johnson/125 6.00 15.00
32 Jalen Wilson/125 6.00 15.00
33 Toumani Camara/125 12.00 30.00
34 Jordan Miller/125 8.00 20.00
35 Mouhamed Gueye/125 6.00 15.00
36 Seth Lundy/125 5.00 12.00
37 Filip Petrusev/125 6.00 15.00
38 Jalen Slawson/99 6.00 15.00
39 Sidy Cissoko/125 6.00 15.00
40 Jaylen Clark/125 6.00 15.00
41 Isaiah Wong/125 6.00 15.00
42 Trayce Jackson-Davis/125 8.00 20.00
43 Terquavion Smith/125 6.00 15.00
44 Ricky Council IV/99 8.00 20.00
45 Markquis Nowell/99 6.00 15.00

2023-24 Court Kings Heir Apparent Autographs

STATED PRINT RUN 99-125 SER.#'d SETS
*JADE: .4X TO 1X BASIC
*RUBY/75-99: .4X TO 1X BASIC
*AMBER/49-75: .5X TO 1.2X BASIC
*VIOLET/25-49: .6X TO 1.5X BASIC
*SAPPHIRE/15-25: .75X TO 2X BASIC
1 James Nnaji 5.00 12.00
2 Andre Jackson Jr. 10.00 25.00
3 Ben Sheppard 6.00 15.00
4 Filip Petrusev 6.00 15.00
5 Jalen Pickett 5.00 12.00
6 Keyontae Johnson 6.00 15.00
7 Julian Phillips 6.00 15.00
8 Marcus Sasser 10.00 25.00
9 Ausar Thompson 15.00 40.00
10 Seth Lundy 5.00 12.00
11 Olivier-Maxence Prosper 6.00 15.00
12 Toumani Camara 12.00 30.00
13 Amen Thompson 30.00 80.00
14 Kobe Brown 6.00 15.00
15 Markquis Nowell 6.00 15.00
16 Colby Jones 6.00 15.00
17 Terquavion Smith 6.00 15.00
18 Jordan Walsh 6.00 15.00
19 Cason Wallace 12.00 30.00
20 Kobe Bufkin 8.00 20.00
21 Leonard Miller 6.00 15.00
22 Noah Clowney 8.00 20.00
23 Isaiah Wong 6.00 15.00
24 Hunter Tyson 6.00 15.00
25 Maxwell Lewis 5.00 12.00
26 GG Jackson II 30.00 80.00
27 Rayan Rupert 6.00 15.00
28 Dariq Whitehead 8.00 20.00
29 Tristan Vukcevic 6.00 15.00
30 Trayce Jackson-Davis 20.00 50.00
32 Kris Murray 6.00 15.00
33 Jalen Wilson 6.00 15.00
34 Sidy Cissoko 6.00 15.00
35 Jordan Miller 8.00 20.00
36 Julian Strawther 8.00 20.00
37 Dereck Lively II 12.00 30.00
38 Keyonte George 25.00 60.00
39 Mouhamed Gueye 6.00 15.00
40 Brice Sensabaugh 10.00 25.00
41 Brandin Podziemski 25.00 60.00
42 Adama Sanogo 6.00 15.00
43 Jalen Slawson 6.00 15.00
44 Bilal Coulibaly 15.00 40.00
45 Chris Livingston 6.00 15.00

2023-24 Court Kings Impressionist Ink

STATED PRINT RUN 49-99 SER.#'d SETS
*JADE: .4X TO 1X BASIC
*RUBY/49: .5X TO 1.25X BASIC
*VIOLET/35: .5X TO 1.5X BASIC
*SAPPHIRE/25: .6X TO 1.5X BASIC
1 Keegan Murray/99 8.00 20.00
2 Jerry Stackhouse/99 6.00 15.00
3 Jordan Clarkson/49 6.00 15.00
5 Robert Horry/99 6.00 15.00
6 Ray Allen/49 20.00 50.00
7 Anthony Edwards/99 125.00 300.00
8 Ochai Agbaji/99 6.00 15.00
10 Zach Randolph/99 6.00 15.00
11 Bobby Portis/99 8.00 20.00
12 Obi Toppin/99 6.00 15.00
13 Jonathan Kuminga/99 15.00 40.00
14 Khris Middleton/99 6.00 15.00
15 Brandon Ingram/99 8.00 20.00
18 Shaedon Sharpe/99 12.00 30.00
19 Seth Curry/75 6.00 15.00
20 Immanuel Quickley/99 6.00 15.00
21 Onyeka Okongwu/99 5.00 12.00
22 Devin Vassell/99 8.00 20.00
23 Kevin Huerter/75 5.00 12.00
24 Kobe Brown/99 6.00 15.00
25 Rick Fox/49 6.00 15.00
26 Desmond Bane/75 8.00 20.00
27 Ben Sheppard/99 6.00 15.00
28 Deandre Ayton/75 6.00 15.00
29 Julian Strawther/99 8.00 20.00
30 Isaac Okoro/75 5.00 12.00

2023-24 Court Kings Legacy Portrait Signatures

STATED PRINT RUN 75 SER.#'d SETS
*AMBER/49: .5X TO 1.2X BASIC
*RUBY/25: .6X TO 1.5X BASIC
*VIOLET/15: .75X TO 2X BASIC
1 Ja Morant 100.00 250.00
2 Russell Westbrook 75.00 200.00
3 Luka Doncic 300.00 600.00
4 Paul George 50.00 120.00
5 Dirk Nowitzki 75.00 200.00
6 Kevin Garnett 60.00 150.00
7 Steve Nash 50.00 120.00
8 Manu Ginobili 40.00 100.00
9 Magic Johnson 40.00 100.00
10 Nikola Jokic 100.00 250.00

2023-24 Court Kings Masterstrokes Autographs

STATED PRINT RUN 49-99 SER.#'d SETS
*JADE: .4X TO 1X BASIC
*RUBY/49: .5X TO 1.25X BASIC
*VIOLET/35: .6X TO 1.5X BASIC
*SAPPHIRE/25: .6X TO 1.5X BASIC
1 Bradley Beal/99 8.00 20.00
2 Rudy Gobert/99 8.00 20.00
3 Lauri Markkanen/99 10.00 25.00
4 Austin Reaves/75 40.00 100.00
6 Alperen Sengun/99 10.00 25.00
8 Jaren Jackson Jr./99 12.00 30.00
9 Josh Giddey/99 12.00 30.00
10 Cole Anthony/99 6.00 15.00
11 D'Angelo Russell/99 6.00 15.00
12 Gary Trent Jr./99 6.00 15.00
13 Seth Curry/99 6.00 15.00
14 Karl-Anthony Towns/99 12.00 30.00
15 Leonard Miller/99 6.00 15.00
16 Malik Monk/99 8.00 20.00
17 Alex English/75 8.00 20.00
19 Stephen Jackson/75 5.00 12.00
20 Carlos Boozer/75 5.00 12.00
21 Mo Bamba/99 5.00 12.00
22 Jason Williams/75 15.00 40.00
23 Ayo Dosunmu/99 6.00 15.00
24 Kris Murray/99 6.00 15.00
25 Amar'e Stoudemire/49 8.00 20.00
26 Marcus Smart/49 8.00 20.00
27 Peja Stojakovic/99 6.00 15.00
28 Olivier-Maxence Prosper/99 6.00 15.00
29 RJ Barrett/99 10.00 25.00
31 Derrick White/99 12.00 30.00
32 Bojan Bogdanovic/99 6.00 15.00
33 Ivica Zubac/99 6.00 15.00
34 Marcus Sasser/99 10.00 25.00
35 Colby Jones/99 6.00 15.00
36 Kentavious Caldwell-Pope/99 12.00 30.00
37 Metta World Peace/99 6.00 15.00
38 Ralph Sampson/99 6.00 15.00
40 Dale Ellis/75 6.00 15.00

2023-24 Court Kings Modern Strokes

*AMETHYST/99: 1.5X TO 4X BASIC
*JADE/25: 3X TO 8X BASIC
1 Jayson Tatum 4.00 10.00
2 Gradey Dick 2.00 5.00
3 Trae Young 2.00 5.00
4 Anthony Edwards 5.00 12.00
5 Kyrie Irving 2.00 5.00
6 Donovan Mitchell 2.00 5.00
7 LaMelo Ball 2.50 6.00
8 Bilal Coulibaly 2.50 6.00
9 Kevin Durant 3.00 8.00
10 Nikola Jokic 5.00 12.00
11 Amen Thompson 5.00 12.00
12 Luka Doncic 6.00 15.00
13 Ausar Thompson 2.50 6.00
14 Tyrese Haliburton 2.00 5.00
15 Ja Morant 3.00 8.00
16 Brandon Miller 4.00 10.00
17 Anthony Davis 2.50 6.00
18 LeBron James 8.00 20.00
19 Devin Booker 2.50 6.00
20 Scoot Henderson 3.00 8.00
21 Cason Wallace 2.00 5.00
22 Jordan Hawkins 1.50 4.00
23 Kobe Bufkin 1.25 3.00
24 Stephen Curry 8.00 20.00
25 Damian Lillard 2.50 6.00
26 Giannis Antetokounmpo 5.00 12.00
27 Victor Wembanyama 20.00 50.00
28 Jett Howard 1.25 3.00
29 Shai Gilgeous-Alexander 5.00 12.00
30 Keyonte George 3.00 8.00

2023-24 Court Kings Paint by Number

1 Victor Wembanyama 400.00 800.00
2 Cason Wallace 40.00 100.00
3 Scoot Henderson 40.00 100.00
4 Gradey Dick 30.00 80.00
5 Jordan Hawkins 25.00 60.00
6 Amen Thompson 50.00 120.00
7 Ausar Thompson 40.00 100.00
8 Bilal Coulibaly 40.00 100.00
9 Brandon Miller 75.00 200.00
10 Jarace Walker 20.00 50.00
11 Ja Morant 50.00 120.00
12 Kyrie Irving 50.00 120.00
13 LeBron James 100.00 250.00
14 Luka Doncic 60.00 150.00
15 Stephen Curry 75.00 200.00
16 Giannis Antetokounmpo 50.00 120.00
17 Anthony Edwards 50.00 120.00
18 Nikola Jokic 50.00 120.00
19 Joel Embiid 30.00 80.00
20 Damian Lillard 30.00 80.00

2023-24 Court Kings Rookie Exclusive

1 Victor Wembanyama 500.00 1,000.00

2023-24 Court Kings Self Expression

*RUBY/149: 1.5X TO 4X BASIC
*VIOLET/49: 2.5X TO 6X BASIC
*SAPPHIRE/25: 4X TO 10X BASIC
1 Gradey Dick 2.00 5.00
2 Paul Pierce 1.50 4.00
3 Jimmy Butler 1.50 4.00
4 Cam Whitmore 2.50 6.00
5 Brandon Miller 4.00 10.00
6 Dereck Lively II 2.00 5.00
7 Victor Wembanyama 30.00 80.00
8 Dariq Whitehead 1.25 3.00
9 Trae Young 2.00 5.00
10 LeBron James 8.00 20.00
11 Charles Barkley 2.50 6.00
12 Luka Doncic 6.00 15.00
13 Jayson Tatum 4.00 10.00
14 Giannis Antetokounmpo 5.00 12.00
15 Magic Johnson 4.00 10.00
16 Kobe Bufkin 1.25 3.00
17 Jarace Walker 2.00 5.00
18 Allen Iverson 2.50 6.00
19 Anthony Black 2.00 5.00
20 Bilal Coulibaly 2.50 6.00
21 Cason Wallace 2.00 5.00
22 Ausar Thompson 2.50 6.00
23 Joel Embiid 2.50 6.00
24 Amen Thompson 5.00 12.00
25 Keyonte George 3.00 8.00
26 Kevin Durant 3.00 8.00
27 Nikola Jokic 5.00 12.00
28 Stephen Curry 8.00 20.00
29 Scoot Henderson 3.00 8.00
30 Shaquille O'Neal 3.00 8.00

2023-24 Court Kings State of the Art

1 Stephen Curry 125.00 300.00
2 Giannis Antetokounmpo 100.00 250.00
3 LeBron James 125.00 300.00
4 Kevin Durant 60.00 150.00
5 Jayson Tatum 75.00 200.00
6 Brandon Miller 100.00 250.00
7 Amen Thompson 75.00 200.00
8 Ausar Thompson 60.00 150.00
9 Scoot Henderson 75.00 200.00
10 Victor Wembanyama 400.00 800.00

2023-24 Court Kings Water Color

*RUBY/149: 1.5X TO 4X BASIC
*VIOLET/49: 1.5X TO 6X BASIC
*SAPPHIRE/25: 4X TO 10X BASIC
1 Victor Wembanyama 30.00 80.00
2 Ja Morant 3.00 8.00
3 Donovan Mitchell 2.00 5.00
4 LeBron James 8.00 20.00
5 Ausar Thompson 2.50 6.00
6 Anthony Edwards 5.00 12.00
7 Jayson Tatum 4.00 10.00
8 Bilal Coulibaly 2.50 6.00
9 Shai Gilgeous-Alexander 5.00 12.00
10 Kobe Bufkin 1.25 3.00
11 Tim Duncan 2.50 6.00
12 Luka Doncic 6.00 15.00
13 Anthony Black 2.00 5.00
14 Carmelo Anthony 1.50 4.00
15 Scoot Henderson 3.00 8.00
16 Brandon Miller 4.00 10.00
17 Stephen Curry 8.00 20.00
18 Yao Ming 2.50 6.00
19 Hakeem Olajuwon 2.00 5.00
20 Dirk Nowitzki 2.50 6.00
21 Damian Lillard 2.50 6.00
22 Keyonte George 3.00 8.00
23 Joel Embiid 2.50 6.00
24 Nikola Jokic 5.00 12.00
25 Kyrie Irving 2.00 5.00
26 Giannis Antetokounmpo 5.00 12.00
27 Cason Wallace 2.00 5.00
28 Trae Young 2.00 5.00
29 Kevin Durant 3.00 8.00
30 Amen Thompson 5.00 12.00

2023-24 Court Kings Works in Progress

*RUBY/149: 1.5X TO 4X BASIC
*VIOLET/49: 2.5X TO 6X BASIC
*SAPPHIRE/25: 4X TO 10X BASIC
1 Jordan Hawkins 1.50 4.00
2 Victor Wembanyama 25.00 60.00
3 Brandon Miller 4.00 10.00
4 Ausar Thompson 2.50 6.00
5 Jalen Hood-Schifino 1.00 2.50
6 Jarace Walker 2.00 5.00
7 Dariq Whitehead 1.25 3.00
8 Bilal Coulibaly 2.50 6.00
9 Jaime Jaquez Jr. 1.50 4.00
10 Taylor Hendricks 1.00 2.50
11 Keyonte George 3.00 8.00
12 Amen Thompson 5.00 12.00
13 Rayan Rupert 1.00 2.50
14 Julian Strawther 1.25 3.00
15 Brandin Podziemski 3.00 8.00
16 Brice Sensabaugh 1.50 4.00
17 Kris Murray 1.00 2.50
18 Anthony Black 2.00 5.00
19 Jett Howard 1.25 3.00
20 Kobe Bufkin 1.25 3.00
21 Scoot Henderson 3.00 8.00
22 Gradey Dick 2.00 5.00
23 Cam Whitmore 2.50 6.00
24 Ben Sheppard 1.00 2.50
25 Cason Wallace 2.00 5.00
26 Noah Clowney 1.25 3.00
27 Marcus Sasser 1.50 4.00
28 Olivier-Maxence Prosper 1.00 2.50
29 Nick Smith Jr. 1.25 3.00
30 Dereck Lively II 2.00 5.00

2024-25 Court Kings

*CANVAS: .75X TO 2X BASIC
*RED & BLUE: .75X TO 2X BASIC
*ARTIST PROOF: 1.25X TO 3X BASIC
*RUBY/149: 1.5X TO 4X BASIC
*BURGUNDY/125: 2X TO 5X BASIC
*PINK/99: 2.5X TO 6X BASIC
*AMBER/75: 3X TO 8X BASIC
*VIOLET/49: 4X TO 10X BASIC
*JADE/25: 5X TO 15X BASIC
*SAPPHIRE/25: 5X TO 12X BASIC
1 Klay Thompson 1.25 3.00
2 Tyler Herro .75 2.00
3 Domantas Sabonis .75 2.00
4 Jalen Johnson .60 1.50
5 Miles Bridges .40 1.00
6 Fred VanVleet .50 1.25
7 Russell Westbrook .75 2.00
8 Keldon Johnson .40 1.00
9 Donovan Mitchell 1.00 2.50
10 Julius Randle .50 1.25
11 Jarrett Allen .40 1.00
12 Jalen Williams 1.00 2.50
13 CJ McCollum .40 1.00
14 DeMar DeRozan .60 1.50
15 Kristaps Porzingis .60 1.50
16 Luka Doncic 3.00 8.00
17 Immanuel Quickley .40 1.00
18 John Collins .40 1.00
19 Joel Embiid .75 2.00
20 Naz Reid .50 1.25
21 Devin Vassell .60 1.50
22 Evan Mobley .75 2.00
23 Chris Paul .75 2.00
24 Brandon Ingram .50 1.25
25 Karl-Anthony Towns .75 2.00
26 Keyonte George .60 1.50
27 Scottie Barnes .60 1.50
28 Chet Holmgren .75 2.00
29 Cameron Thomas .50 1.25
30 Coby White .50 1.25
31 Lauri Markkanen .50 1.25
32 Jimmy Butler .75 2.00
33 Jalen Green 1.00 2.50
34 Shai Gilgeous-Alexander 2.50 6.00
35 LaMelo Ball 1.00 2.50
36 Trae Young 1.00 2.50
37 Jalen Duren .50 1.25
38 Anthony Edwards 2.50 6.00
39 Paul George .75 2.00
40 Draymond Green .60 1.50
41 Desmond Bane .50 1.25
42 RJ Barrett .60 1.50
43 Jaylen Brown .75 2.00
44 Bradley Beal .60 1.50
45 Mikal Bridges .50 1.25
46 Scoot Henderson .60 1.50
47 Myles Turner .40 1.00
48 Jamal Murray .75 2.00
49 Zach LaVine .75 2.00
50 Jrue Holiday .60 1.50
51 Jalen Brunson 1.00 2.50
52 Kevin Durant 1.50 4.00
53 Pascal Siakam .60 1.50
54 Jayson Tatum 1.50 4.00
55 Khris Middleton .50 1.25
56 Gary Trent Jr. .40 1.00
57 Jaden Ivey .60 1.50
58 Deandre Ayton .40 1.00
59 Zion Williamson 1.25 3.00
60 Paolo Banchero 1.25 3.00
61 Stephen Curry 4.00 10.00
62 De'Aaron Fox 1.00 2.50
63 Andrew Wiggins .60 1.50
64 Ja Morant 1.50 4.00
65 Derrick White .50 1.25
66 Bojan Bogdanovic .40 1.00
67 Kawhi Leonard 1.00 2.50
68 Anthony Davis 1.25 3.00
69 Brandon Miller .75 2.00
70 Nikola Vucevic .40 1.00
71 Austin Reaves .60 1.50
72 Devin Booker 1.25 3.00
73 Tyrese Maxey 1.00 2.50
74 Bam Adebayo .60 1.50
75 LeBron James 4.00 10.00
76 Cade Cunningham 1.25 3.00
77 Franz Wagner .75 2.00
78 Tyrese Haliburton 1.00 2.50
79 Josh Giddey .60 1.50
80 Donte DiVincenzo .50 1.25
81 Michael Porter Jr. .50 1.25
82 James Harden 1.00 2.50
83 Alperen Sengun .75 2.00
84 Darius Garland .60 1.50
85 Kyle Kuzma .40 1.00
86 Dejounte Murray .50 1.25
87 Jordan Poole .50 1.25
88 Jonathan Kuminga .60 1.50
89 Anfernee Simons .50 1.25
90 Jonas Valanciunas .40 1.00
91 Ivica Zubac .50 1.25
92 Damian Lillard 1.25 3.00
93 Shaedon Sharpe .60 1.50
94 Kyrie Irving 1.25 3.00
95 Cameron Johnson .40 1.00
96 Giannis Antetokounmpo 2.00 5.00
97 Jaren Jackson Jr. .75 2.00
98 Victor Wembanyama 4.00 10.00
99 GG Jackson II .50 1.25
100 Nikola Jokic 2.50 6.00
101 Rob Dillingham RC 2.50 6.00
102 Ron Holland II RC 2.00 5.00
103 Nikola Topic RC 3.00 8.00
104 Baylor Scheierman RC 1.25 3.00
105 Cody Williams RC 1.25 3.00
106 Bobi Klintman RC 1.25 3.00
107 Tyler Smith RC 1.25 3.00
108 Matas Buzelis RC 5.00 12.00
109 Jaylen Wells RC 3.00 8.00
110 Tidjane Salaun RC 1.00 2.50
111 Ja'Kobe Walter RC 1.25 3.00
112 Isaiah Collier RC 2.00 5.00
113 Yves Missi RC 2.50 6.00
114 Devin Carter RC 2.00 5.00
115 Donovan Clingan RC 2.50 6.00
116 Stephon Castle RC 6.00 15.00
117 Kel'el Ware RC 2.50 6.00
118 Kyle Filipowski RC 2.50 6.00
119 Reed Sheppard RC 3.00 8.00
120 Jaylon Tyson RC 1.00 2.50
121 Jared McCain RC 4.00 10.00
122 Bub Carrington RC 2.50 6.00
123 Terrence Shannon Jr. RC 2.00 5.00
124 Bronny James Jr. RC 3.00 8.00
125 Zach Edey RC 3.00 8.00
126 Dalton Knecht RC 3.00 8.00
127 Adem Bona RC 1.25 3.00
128 Johnny Furphy RC 1.50 4.00
129 Alexandre Sarr RC 3.00 8.00
130 Tyler Kolek RC 1.50 4.00
131 Antonio Reeves RC 1.00 2.50
132 Tristan da Silva RC 2.50 6.00
133 Zaccharie Risacher RC 3.00 8.00
134 Rob Dillingham 5.00 12.00
135 Ron Holland II 4.00 10.00
136 Nikola Topic 6.00 15.00
137 Baylor Scheierman 2.50 6.00
138 Cody Williams 2.50 6.00
139 Bobi Klintman 2.50 6.00
140 Tyler Smith 2.50 6.00
141 Matas Buzelis 10.00 25.00
142 Jaylen Wells 6.00 15.00
143 Tidjane Salaun 2.00 5.00
144 Ja'Kobe Walter 2.50 6.00
145 Isaiah Collier 4.00 10.00
146 Yves Missi 5.00 12.00
147 Devin Carter 2.50 6.00
148 Donovan Clingan 5.00 12.00
149 Stephon Castle 12.00 30.00
150 Kel'el Ware 5.00 12.00
151 Kyle Filipowski 5.00 12.00
152 Reed Sheppard 6.00 15.00
153 Jaylon Tyson 2.00 5.00
154 Jared McCain 8.00 20.00
155 Bub Carrington 5.00 12.00
156 Terrence Shannon Jr. 4.00 10.00
157 Bronny James Jr. 6.00 15.00
158 Zach Edey 6.00 15.00
159 Dalton Knecht 6.00 15.00
160 Adem Bona 2.50 6.00
161 Johnny Furphy 3.00 8.00
162 Alexandre Sarr 6.00 15.00
163 Tyler Kolek 3.00 8.00
164 Antonio Reeves 2.00 5.00
165 Tristan da Silva 5.00 12.00
166 Zaccharie Risacher 6.00 15.00
167 Rob Dillingham 12.00 30.00
168 Ron Holland II 10.00 25.00
169 Nikola Topic 15.00 40.00
170 Baylor Scheierman 6.00 15.00
171 Cody Williams 6.00 15.00
172 Bobi Klintman 6.00 15.00
173 Tyler Smith 6.00 15.00
174 Matas Buzelis 25.00 60.00
175 Jaylen Wells 15.00 40.00
176 Tidjane Salaun 5.00 12.00
177 Ja'Kobe Walter 6.00 15.00
178 Isaiah Collier 10.00 25.00
179 Yves Missi 12.00 30.00
180 Devin Carter 6.00 15.00
181 Donovan Clingan 12.00 30.00
182 Stephon Castle 30.00 80.00
183 Kel'el Ware 12.00 30.00
184 Kyle Filipowski 12.00 30.00
185 Reed Sheppard 15.00 40.00
186 Jaylon Tyson 5.00 12.00
187 Jared McCain 20.00 50.00
188 Bub Carrington 12.00 30.00
189 Terrence Shannon Jr. 10.00 25.00
190 Bronny James Jr. 15.00 40.00
191 Zach Edey 15.00 40.00
192 Dalton Knecht 15.00 40.00
193 Adem Bona 6.00 15.00
194 Johnny Furphy 8.00 20.00
195 Alexandre Sarr 15.00 40.00
196 Tyler Kolek 8.00 20.00
197 Antonio Reeves 5.00 12.00
198 Tristan da Silva 12.00 30.00
199 Zaccharie Risacher 15.00 40.00
200 Rob Dillingham 60.00 150.00
201 Ron Holland II 50.00 125.00
202 Nikola Topic 80.00 200.00
203 Baylor Scheierman 30.00 80.00
204 Cody Williams 30.00 80.00
205 Bobi Klintman 30.00 80.00
206 Tyler Smith 30.00 80.00
207 Matas Buzelis 120.00 300.00
208 Jaylen Wells 80.00 200.00
209 Tidjane Salaun 25.00 60.00
210 Ja'Kobe Walter 30.00 80.00
211 Isaiah Collier 50.00 125.00
212 Yves Missi 60.00 150.00
213 Devin Carter 30.00 80.00
214 Donovan Clingan 60.00 150.00
215 Stephon Castle 150.00 400.00
216 Kel'el Ware 60.00 150.00
217 Kyle Filipowski 60.00 150.00
218 Reed Sheppard 80.00 200.00
219 Jaylon Tyson 25.00 60.00
220 Jared McCain 100.00 250.00
221 Bub Carrington 60.00 150.00
222 Terrence Shannon Jr. 50.00 125.00
223 Bronny James Jr. 80.00 200.00
224 Zach Edey 80.00 200.00
225 Dalton Knecht 80.00 200.00
226 Adem Bona 30.00 80.00
227 Johnny Furphy 40.00 100.00
228 Alexandre Sarr 80.00 200.00
229 Tyler Kolek 40.00 100.00
230 Antonio Reeves 25.00 60.00
231 Tristan da Silva 60.00 150.00
232 Zaccharie Risacher 80.00 200.00
233 Rob Dillingham 80.00 200.00
234 Ron Holland II 60.00 150.00
235 Nikola Topic 100.00 250.00
236 Baylor Scheierman 40.00 100.00
237 Cody Williams 40.00 100.00
238 Bobi Klintman 40.00 100.00
239 Tyler Smith 40.00 100.00
240 Matas Buzelis 150.00 400.00
241 Jaylen Wells 100.00 250.00
242 Tidjane Salaun 30.00 80.00
243 Ja'Kobe Walter 40.00 100.00
244 Isaiah Collier 60.00 150.00
245 Yves Missi 80.00 200.00
246 Devin Carter 40.00 100.00
247 Donovan Clingan 80.00 200.00
248 Stephon Castle 200.00 500.00
249 Kel'el Ware 80.00 200.00
250 Kyle Filipowski 80.00 200.00
251 Reed Sheppard 100.00 250.00
252 Jaylon Tyson 30.00 80.00
253 Jared McCain 120.00 300.00
254 Bub Carrington 80.00 200.00
255 Terrence Shannon Jr. 60.00 150.00
256 Bronny James Jr. 100.00 250.00
257 Zach Edey 100.00 250.00
258 Dalton Knecht 100.00 250.00
259 Adem Bona 40.00 100.00
260 Johnny Furphy 50.00 125.00
261 Alexandre Sarr 100.00 250.00
262 Tyler Kolek 50.00 125.00
263 Antonio Reeves 30.00 80.00
264 Tristan da Silva 80.00 200.00
265 Zaccharie Risacher 100.00 250.00

2024-25 Court Kings Acetate Rookies

1 Ja'Kobe Walter 2.00 5.00
2 Kel'el Ware 4.00 10.00
3 Dillon Jones 1.50 4.00
4 Alexandre Sarr 5.00 12.00
5 Jonathan Mogbo 2.50 6.00
6 Harrison Ingram 1.50 4.00
7 Baylor Scheierman 2.00 5.00
8 Nikola Topic 5.00 12.00
9 Stephon Castle 10.00 25.00
10 Tristan da Silva 4.00 10.00
11 AJ Johnson 3.00 8.00
12 Rob Dillingham 4.00 10.00
13 Matas Buzelis 8.00 20.00
14 Jared McCain 6.00 15.00
15 Cody Williams 2.00 5.00
16 Pacome Dadiet 2.00 5.00
17 Bub Carrington 4.00 10.00
18 Tidjane Salaun 1.50 4.00
19 Zach Edey 5.00 12.00
20 Terrence Shannon Jr. 3.00 8.00
21 Donovan Clingan 4.00 10.00
22 Zaccharie Risacher 5.00 12.00
23 Tyler Kolek 2.50 6.00
24 Jaylon Tyson 1.50 4.00
25 Reed Sheppard 5.00 12.00
26 Ryan Dunn 2.00 5.00
27 Isaiah Collier 3.00 8.00
28 Ron Holland II 3.00 8.00
29 Yves Missi 4.00 10.00
30 Bronny James Jr. 5.00 12.00
31 Dalton Knecht 5.00 12.00
32 Kyshawn George 2.50 6.00
33 Devin Carter 2.00 5.00

2024-25 Court Kings Art Nouveau Jerseys

*SAPPHIRE/25: 1.25X TO 3X BASIC
1 Nikola Jokic 12.00 30.00
2 Paul George 4.00 10.00
3 Luka Doncic 15.00 40.00
4 Joel Embiid 4.00 10.00
5 Victor Wembanyama 20.00 50.00
6 Paolo Banchero 6.00 15.00
7 De'Aaron Fox 5.00 12.00
8 Kevin Durant 8.00 20.00
9 Shai Gilgeous-Alexander 12.00 30.00
10 Kristaps Porzingis 3.00 8.00
11 Kawhi Leonard 5.00 12.00
12 Jaylen Brown 4.00 10.00
13 Devin Booker 6.00 15.00
14 Jalen Green 5.00 12.00
15 LeBron James 30.00 80.00
16 Dejounte Murray 2.50 6.00
17 Zaccharie Risacher 8.00 20.00
18 Alexandre Sarr 8.00 20.00
19 Reed Sheppard 8.00 20.00
20 Stephon Castle 15.00 40.00
21 Ron Holland II 5.00 12.00
22 Matas Buzelis 12.00 30.00
23 Bronny James Jr. 8.00 20.00
24 Bub Carrington 6.00 15.00
25 Kel'el Ware 6.00 15.00

2024-25 Court Kings Artistic Endeavors Jerseys

1 Russell Westbrook 4.00 10.00
2 Darius Garland 3.00 8.00
3 Zion Williamson 6.00 15.00
4 Karl-Anthony Towns 4.00 10.00
5 Jimmy Butler 4.00 10.00
6 Stephen Curry 30.00 80.00
7 Jayson Tatum 8.00 20.00
8 Trae Young 5.00 12.00
9 Scottie Barnes 3.00 8.00
10 Klay Thompson 6.00 15.00
11 Bam Adebayo 3.00 8.00
12 RJ Barrett 3.00 8.00
13 Zaccharie Risacher 8.00 20.00
14 Alexandre Sarr 8.00 20.00
15 Donovan Clingan 6.00 15.00
16 Dalton Knecht 8.00 20.00
17 Rob Dillingham 6.00 15.00
18 Zach Edey 6.00 15.00
19 Cody Williams 3.00 8.00
20 Jared McCain 10.00 25.00

2024-25 Court Kings Artistry in Motion

*BURGUNDY/125: 1.25X TO 3X BASIC
*AMBER/99: 1.5X TO 4X BASIC
*JADE/49: 2X TO 5X BASIC
1 Giannis Antetokounmpo 5.00 12.00
2 Nikola Jokic 6.00 15.00
3 Shai Gilgeous-Alexander 6.00 15.00
4 Stephen Curry 10.00 25.00
5 Jayson Tatum 4.00 10.00
6 Ja Morant 4.00 10.00
7 LeBron James 10.00 25.00
8 Anthony Edwards 6.00 15.00
9 Victor Wembanyama 10.00 25.00
10 Luka Doncic 8.00 20.00
11 Kevin Durant 4.00 10.00
12 Trae Young 2.50 6.00
13 Reed Sheppard 4.00 10.00
14 Stephon Castle 8.00 20.00
15 Bub Carrington 3.00 8.00
16 Zaccharie Risacher 4.00 10.00
17 Jared McCain 5.00 12.00
18 Alexandre Sarr 4.00 10.00
19 Cody Williams 1.50 4.00
20 Bronny James Jr. 4.00 10.00
21 David Robinson 2.50 6.00
22 Shaquille O'Neal 3.00 8.00
23 Dirk Nowitzki 3.00 8.00
24 Yao Ming 2.50 6.00
25 Vince Carter 2.50 6.00
26 Larry Bird 4.00 10.00
27 Tim Duncan 3.00 8.00
28 Charles Barkley 3.00 8.00
29 Pete Maravich 3.00 8.00
30 Brandon Roy 2.00 5.00

2024-25 Court Kings Aurora

1 Damian Lillard 25.00 60.00
2 Jalen Brunson 20.00 50.00
3 Anthony Edwards 50.00 125.00
4 Jared McCain 40.00 100.00
5 Dalton Knecht 30.00 80.00
6 Trae Young 20.00 50.00
7 Donovan Mitchell 20.00 50.00
8 Zaccharie Risacher 30.00 80.00
9 Giannis Antetokounmpo 40.00 100.00
10 Alexandre Sarr 30.00 80.00
11 Kyrie Irving 25.00 60.00
12 Shai Gilgeous-Alexander 75.00 200.00
13 Ron Holland II 20.00 50.00
14 Kevin Durant 30.00 80.00
15 Bub Carrington 25.00 60.00
16 Donovan Clingan 25.00 60.00
17 Kawhi Leonard 25.00 60.00
18 Jayson Tatum 30.00 80.00
19 Victor Wembanyama 100.00 250.00
20 Matas Buzelis 50.00 120.00
21 Luka Doncic 75.00 200.00
22 Tyrese Maxey 20.00 50.00
23 Stephen Curry 100.00 250.00
24 Reed Sheppard 30.00 80.00
25 Chet Holmgren 15.00 40.00
26 Ja Morant 30.00 80.00
27 Zion Williamson 25.00 60.00
28 Nikola Jokic 50.00 125.00
29 LeBron James 100.00 250.00
30 Stephon Castle 75.00 200.00

2024-25 Court Kings Blank Slate

1 Kevin Durant 125.00 300.00
2 Jayson Tatum 200.00 500.00
3 Ja Morant 200.00 500.00
4 Shai Gilgeous-Alexander 400.00 800.00
5 Giannis Antetokounmpo 200.00 500.00
6 Nikola Jokic 300.00 600.00
7 Anthony Edwards 400.00 800.00
8 Victor Wembanyama 500.00 1,000.00
9 LeBron James 500.00 1,000.00
10 Stephen Curry 400.00 800.00
11 Luka Doncic 400.00 800.00
12 Trae Young 200.00 500.00
13 Rob Dillingham 100.00 250.00
14 Stephon Castle 500.00 1,000.00
15 Matas Buzelis 400.00 800.00
16 Alexandre Sarr 150.00 400.00
17 Reed Sheppard 150.00 400.00
18 Dalton Knecht 150.00 400.00
19 Zaccharie Risacher 150.00 400.00
20 Bronny James Jr. 200.00 500.00
21 Larry Bird 150.00 400.00
22 Kevin Garnett 150.00 400.00
23 Julius Erving 125.00 300.00
24 Yao Ming 150.00 400.00
25 Dirk Nowitzki 150.00 400.00
26 Dwyane Wade 150.00 400.00

27 Magic Johnson 150.00 400.00
28 Tracy McGrady 150.00 400.00
29 Tim Duncan 150.00 400.00
30 Shaquille O'Neal 150.00 400.00

2024-25 Court Kings Debut Showcase Memorabilia

*SAPPHIRE/25: 1.25X TO 3X BASIC
1 Matas Buzelis 10.00 25.00
2 Bronny James Jr. 6.00 15.00
3 Zach Edey 6.00 15.00
4 Terrence Shannon Jr. 4.00 10.00
5 Jared McCain 8.00 20.00
6 Rob Dillingham 5.00 12.00
7 Ron Holland II 4.00 10.00
8 Zaccharie Risacher 6.00 15.00
9 Cody Williams 2.50 6.00
10 Kyle Filipowski 5.00 12.00
11 Bub Carrington 5.00 12.00
12 Devin Carter 2.50 6.00
13 AJ Johnson 4.00 10.00
14 Jaylon Tyson 2.00 5.00
15 Alexandre Sarr 6.00 15.00
16 Dalton Knecht 6.00 15.00
17 Pacome Dadiet 2.50 6.00
18 Tyler Smith 2.50 6.00
19 Yves Missi 5.00 12.00
20 Ja'Kobe Walter 2.50 6.00
21 Tristan da Silva 5.00 12.00
22 Ryan Dunn 2.50 6.00
23 Stephon Castle 12.00 30.00
24 Tidjane Salaun 2.00 5.00
25 Reed Sheppard 6.00 15.00
26 Dillon Jones 2.00 5.00
27 Kel'el Ware 5.00 12.00
28 Nikola Topic 6.00 15.00
29 Donovan Clingan 5.00 12.00
30 Kyshawn George 3.00 8.00

2024-25 Court Kings Double Exposure

*BURGUNDY/125: 1.25X TO 3X BASIC
*AMBER/99: 1.5X TO 4X BASIC
*JADE/49: 2X TO 5X BASIC
1 Luka Doncic 5.00 12.00
2 Donovan Clingan 2.00 5.00
3 Ron Holland II 1.50 4.00
4 Zaccharie Risacher 2.50 6.00
5 Damian Lillard 2.00 5.00
6 Jayson Tatum 2.50 6.00
7 Giannis Antetokounmpo 3.00 8.00
8 Ja Morant 2.50 6.00
9 Victor Wembanyama 6.00 15.00
10 Trae Young 1.50 4.00
11 LeBron James 6.00 15.00
12 Kevin Durant 2.50 6.00
13 Donovan Mitchell 1.50 4.00
14 Chet Holmgren 1.25 3.00
15 Shai Gilgeous-Alexander 4.00 10.00
16 Jalen Brunson 1.50 4.00
17 Cody Williams 1.00 2.50
18 Anthony Edwards 4.00 10.00
19 Stephen Curry 6.00 15.00
20 Dalton Knecht 2.50 6.00
21 Zion Williamson 2.00 5.00
22 Kel'el Ware 2.00 5.00
23 Reed Sheppard 2.50 6.00
24 James Harden 1.50 4.00
25 Stephon Castle 5.00 12.00
26 Matas Buzelis 4.00 10.00
27 Alexandre Sarr 2.50 6.00
28 Zach Edey 2.50 6.00
29 Nikola Jokic 4.00 10.00
30 Rob Dillingham 2.00 5.00

2024-25 Court Kings Dressed to Impress

*BURGUNDY/125: 1.25X TO 3X BASIC
*AMBER/99: 1.5X TO 4X BASIC
*JADE/49: 2X TO 5X BASIC
1 Shai Gilgeous-Alexander 4.00 10.00
2 LeBron James 6.00 15.00
3 Luka Doncic 5.00 12.00
4 Victor Wembanyama 6.00 15.00
5 Zaccharie Risacher 2.50 6.00
6 Stephon Castle 5.00 12.00
7 Ron Holland II 1.50 4.00
8 Ja'Kobe Walter 1.00 2.50
9 Jared McCain 3.00 8.00
10 Rob Dillingham 2.00 5.00

2024-25 Court Kings First Steps

*RUBY/149: 1.25X TO 3X BASIC
*PINK/99: 1.5X TO 4X BASIC
*VIOLET/49: 2X TO 5X BASIC
*SAPPHIRE/25: 2.5X TO 6X BASIC
1 Rob Dillingham 3.00 8.00
2 Donovan Clingan 3.00 8.00
3 Bronny James Jr. 4.00 10.00
4 Zaccharie Risacher 4.00 10.00
5 Matas Buzelis 6.00 15.00
6 Ron Holland II 2.50 6.00
7 Dalton Knecht 4.00 10.00
8 Stephon Castle 8.00 20.00
9 Reed Sheppard 4.00 10.00
10 Alexandre Sarr 4.00 10.00

2024-25 Court Kings Fresh Paint Autographs

STATED PRINT RUN 125 SER.#'d SETS
*JADE: .4X TO 1X BASIC
*RUBY/99: .5X TO 1.2X BASIC
*AMBER/75: .6X TO 1.5X BASIC
*VIOLET/49: .75X TO 2X BASIC
*SAPPHIRE/25: 1X TO 2.5X BASIC
1 Reed Sheppard 20.00 50.00
2 Zach Edey 20.00 50.00
3 Jonathan Mogbo 10.00 25.00
4 Donovan Clingan 15.00 40.00
5 Tyler Kolek 10.00 25.00
6 Jaylen Wells 20.00 50.00
7 Dalton Knecht 20.00 50.00
8 Jared McCain 25.00 60.00
9 Oso Ighodaro 8.00 20.00
10 Tidjane Salaun 6.00 15.00
11 Adem Bona 8.00 20.00
12 Johnny Furphy 10.00 25.00
13 Bub Carrington 15.00 40.00
14 Devin Carter 8.00 20.00
15 KJ Simpson Jr. 6.00 15.00
16 Nikola Durisic 8.00 20.00
17 Bobi Klintman 8.00 20.00
18 Pelle Larsson 8.00 20.00
19 Jamal Shead 8.00 20.00
20 Cam Christie 8.00 20.00
21 Jaylon Tyson 6.00 15.00
22 Ja'Kobe Walter 8.00 20.00
23 Ajay Mitchell 10.00 25.00
25 Tristan da Silva 15.00 40.00
26 Harrison Ingram 6.00 15.00
27 Matas Buzelis 30.00 80.00
28 Tristen Newton 6.00 15.00
29 Terrence Shannon Jr. 12.00 30.00
31 Yongxi Jacky Cui 12.00 30.00
32 Dillon Jones 6.00 15.00
33 Pacome Dadiet 8.00 20.00
34 Cam Spencer 6.00 15.00
35 Anton Watson 5.00 12.00
36 Kyshawn George 10.00 25.00
37 Kevin McCullar Jr. 6.00 15.00
38 AJ Johnson 12.00 30.00
39 DaRon Holmes II 8.00 20.00
40 Yves Missi 15.00 40.00
41 Ulrich Chomche 5.00 12.00
42 Ariel Hukporti 5.00 12.00
43 Trey Alexander 5.00 12.00
44 Trentyn Flowers 5.00 12.00
45 Baylor Scheierman 8.00 20.00

2024-25 Court Kings Heir Apparent Autographs

STATED PRINT RUN 125 SER.#'d SETS
*JADE: .4X TO 1X BASIC
*RUBY/99: .5X TO 1.2X BASIC
*AMBER/75: .6X TO 1.5X BASIC
*VIOLET/49: .75X TO 2X BASIC
*SAPPHIRE/25: 1X TO 2.5X BASIC
1 Donovan Clingan 15.00 40.00
2 Dalton Knecht 20.00 50.00
3 Jared McCain 25.00 60.00
4 Reed Sheppard 20.00 50.00
5 Bub Carrington 15.00 40.00
6 Tidjane Salaun 6.00 15.00
7 Zach Edey 20.00 50.00
8 Tristan da Silva 15.00 40.00
9 Jaylon Tyson 6.00 15.00
10 Matas Buzelis 30.00 80.00
11 Devin Carter 8.00 20.00
12 Ja'Kobe Walter 8.00 20.00
13 DaRon Holmes II 8.00 20.00
14 Yves Missi 15.00 40.00
15 Ajay Mitchell 10.00 25.00
16 Cam Spencer 6.00 15.00
17 Anton Watson 5.00 12.00
18 Keshad Johnson 5.00 12.00
19 Ariel Hukporti 5.00 12.00
20 Ulrich Chomche 5.00 12.00
21 KJ Simpson Jr. 6.00 15.00
22 Nikola Durisic 8.00 20.00
23 AJ Johnson 12.00 30.00
24 Kyshawn George 10.00 25.00
25 Kevin McCullar Jr. 6.00 15.00
26 Jaylen Wells 20.00 50.00
27 Jalen Bridges 5.00 12.00
28 Pelle Larsson 8.00 20.00
29 Cam Christie 8.00 20.00
30 Judah Mintz 5.00 12.00
31 Pacome Dadiet 8.00 20.00
32 Dillon Jones 6.00 15.00
33 Terrence Shannon Jr. 12.00 30.00
34 Oso Ighodaro 8.00 20.00
35 Adem Bona 8.00 20.00
36 Tyler Kolek 10.00 25.00
37 Harrison Ingram 6.00 15.00
38 Tristen Newton 6.00 15.00
39 Jamal Shead 8.00 20.00
40 Johnny Furphy 10.00 25.00
42 Yongxi Jacky Cui 12.00 30.00
43 Bobi Klintman 8.00 20.00
45 Jonathan Mogbo 10.00 25.00

2024-25 Court Kings La Cinque Piu Belle

1 Victor Wembanyama 600.00 1,200.00
2 Luka Doncic 500.00 1,000.00
3 LeBron James 600.00 1,200.00
4 Anthony Edwards 400.00 800.00
5 Stephen Curry 600.00 1,200.00

2024-25 Court Kings Legacy Portrait Signatures

STATED PRINT RUN 25-35 SER.#'d SETS
*JADE: .4X TO 1X BASIC
*AMBER/25: .4X TO 1X BASIC
*VIOLET/15: .4X TO 1X BASIC
1 Stephen Curry/25 400.00 800.00
2 Shai Gilgeous-Alexander/35 400.00 800.00
3 Anthony Edwards/25 300.00 600.00
4 Luka Doncic/25 400.00 800.00
5 Kevin Durant/35 125.00 300.00
6 Manu Ginobili/35 60.00 150.00
7 John Stockton/35 50.00 120.00
8 Carmelo Anthony/25 100.00 250.00
9 Allen Iverson/25 100.00 250.00
10 Kareem Abdul-Jabbar/35 100.00 250.00

2024-25 Court Kings Masterstrokes

STATED PRINT RUN 49-99 SER.#'d SETS
*JADE: .4X TO 1X BASIC
*RUBY/75: .5X TO 1.2X BASIC
*AMBER/49: .6X TO 1.5X BASIC
*VIOLET/35: .75X TO 2X BASIC
1 Tidjane Salaun 8.00 20.00
2 Zach Edey 25.00 60.00
3 Devin Carter 10.00 25.00
4 Tristan da Silva 20.00 50.00
5 DaRon Holmes II 10.00 25.00
6 Pacome Dadiet 10.00 25.00
7 Jaden Hardy 8.00 20.00
8 Jalen Duren 8.00 20.00
9 Cason Wallace 10.00 25.00
10 Andrew Nembhard 6.00 15.00
11 Jalen Suggs 8.00 20.00
12 Ausar Thompson 12.00 30.00
13 Ben Simmons 8.00 20.00
14 Christian Braun 10.00 25.00
15 Jalen Green 15.00 40.00
17 Deandre Ayton 6.00 15.00
18 Shaedon Sharpe 10.00 25.00
19 Bennedict Mathurin 10.00 25.00
20 Franz Wagner 12.00 30.00
21 Trayce Jackson-Davis 8.00 20.00
22 Max Christie 8.00 20.00
23 Cade Cunningham 40.00 100.00
24 Dillon Jones 8.00 20.00
25 Johnny Furphy 12.00 30.00
26 Jonathan Mogbo 12.00 30.00
28 Adem Bona 10.00 25.00
29 Jaylen Wells 25.00 60.00
30 Pelle Larsson 10.00 25.00
31 Tristen Newton 8.00 20.00
32 Rasheed Wallace 15.00 40.00
34 Jabari Smith Jr. 12.00 30.00
35 Zydrunas Ilgauskas 6.00 15.00
36 Jeremy Lin 60.00 150.00
37 Lance Stephenson 6.00 15.00
38 Shawn Kemp 12.00 30.00
39 Michael Cooper 8.00 20.00
40 Steve Francis 8.00 20.00

2024-25 Court Kings Modern Strokes

*BURGUNDY/125: 1.25X TO 3X BASIC
*AMBER/99: 1.5X TO 4X BASIC
*JADE/49: 2X TO 5X BASIC
1 Nikola Jokic 4.00 10.00
2 Luka Doncic 5.00 12.00
3 Zaccharie Risacher 2.50 6.00
4 Stephen Curry 6.00 15.00
5 De'Aaron Fox 1.50 4.00
6 Trae Young 1.50 4.00
7 Ja Morant 2.50 6.00
8 Stephon Castle 5.00 12.00
9 Anthony Edwards 4.00 10.00
10 Shai Gilgeous-Alexander 4.00 10.00
11 Zion Williamson 2.00 5.00
12 LeBron James 6.00 15.00
13 Joel Embiid 1.25 3.00
14 Alexandre Sarr 2.50 6.00
15 Tyrese Maxey 1.50 4.00
16 Kevin Durant 2.50 6.00
17 Paolo Banchero 2.00 5.00
18 Giannis Antetokounmpo 3.00 8.00
19 Victor Wembanyama 6.00 15.00
20 Rob Dillingham 2.00 5.00
21 Matas Buzelis 4.00 10.00
22 Tidjane Salaun .75 2.00
23 Tyrese Haliburton 1.50 4.00
24 Jayson Tatum 2.50 6.00
25 Damian Lillard 2.00 5.00
26 Ron Holland II 1.50 4.00
27 Jalen Brunson 1.50 4.00
28 Donovan Clingan 2.00 5.00
29 Reed Sheppard 2.50 6.00
30 Dalton Knecht 2.50 6.00

2024-25 Court Kings Paint by Number

1 Jalen Brunson 20.00 50.00
2 Trae Young 20.00 50.00
3 Zach Edey 30.00 80.00
4 Zion Williamson 25.00 60.00
5 Jaylen Brown 15.00 40.00
6 Giannis Antetokounmpo 40.00 100.00
7 Zaccharie Risacher 30.00 80.00
8 Jayson Tatum 30.00 80.00
9 LeBron James 80.00 200.00
10 Damian Lillard 25.00 60.00
11 Rob Dillingham 25.00 60.00
12 Luka Doncic 60.00 150.00
13 Stephon Castle 60.00 150.00
14 Alexandre Sarr 30.00 80.00
15 Stephen Curry 80.00 200.00
16 Kevin Durant 30.00 80.00
17 Matas Buzelis 50.00 120.00
18 Anthony Edwards 60.00 150.00
19 Nikola Jokic 50.00 125.00
20 Paolo Banchero 25.00 60.00
21 Reed Sheppard 50.00 120.00
22 Ja Morant 30.00 80.00
23 Bronny James Jr. 30.00 80.00
24 Shai Gilgeous-Alexander 60.00 150.00
25 Victor Wembanyama 75.00 200.00

2024-25 Court Kings Rookie Swatches

*SAPPHIRE/25: 1.25X TO 3X BASIC
1 Jaylen Wells 6.00 15.00
2 Ron Holland II 6.00 15.00
3 Reed Sheppard 6.00 15.00
4 Jared McCain 8.00 20.00
5 Stephon Castle 12.00 30.00
6 Zach Edey 6.00 15.00
7 Ja'Kobe Walter 2.50 6.00
8 Baylor Scheierman 2.50 6.00
9 Cody Williams 2.50 6.00
10 Rob Dillingham 5.00 12.00
11 Bronny James Jr. 6.00 15.00
12 Isaiah Collier 4.00 10.00
13 Matas Buzelis 10.00 25.00
14 Zaccharie Risacher 6.00 15.00
15 Bub Carrington 5.00 12.00
16 Tyler Kolek 3.00 8.00
17 Tristan da Silva 5.00 12.00
18 Kel'el Ware 5.00 12.00
19 Donovan Clingan 5.00 12.00
20 Alexandre Sarr 6.00 15.00
21 Bobi Klintman 2.50 6.00
22 Tidjane Salaun 2.00 5.00
23 Dalton Knecht 6.00 15.00
24 Antonio Reeves 2.00 5.00
25 Johnny Furphy 3.00 8.00

2024-25 Court Kings Self Expression

*RUBY/149: 1.25X TO 3X BASIC
*PINK/99: 1.5X TO 4X BASIC
*VIOLET/49: 2X TO 5X BASIC
*SAPPHIRE/25: 2.5X TO 6X BASIC
1 Damian Lillard 2.00 5.00
2 James Harden 1.50 4.00
3 Devin Booker 2.00 5.00
4 Reed Sheppard 2.50 6.00
5 Dalton Knecht 2.50 6.00
6 Donovan Clingan 2.00 5.00
7 Trae Young 1.50 4.00
8 LeBron James 6.00 15.00
9 Anthony Davis 2.00 5.00
10 Giannis Antetokounmpo 3.00 8.00
11 Luka Doncic 5.00 12.00
12 Victor Wembanyama 6.00 15.00
13 Kevin Durant 2.50 6.00
14 Jared McCain 3.00 8.00
15 Cody Williams 1.00 2.50
16 Ron Holland II 1.50 4.00
17 Bub Carrington 2.00 5.00
18 Zion Williamson 2.00 5.00
19 Zaccharie Risacher 2.50 6.00
20 Anthony Edwards 4.00 10.00
21 Jalen Brunson 1.50 4.00
22 Donovan Mitchell 1.50 4.00
23 Stephen Curry 6.00 15.00
24 Ja Morant 2.50 6.00
25 Alexandre Sarr 2.50 6.00
26 Nikola Jokic 4.00 10.00
27 Shai Gilgeous-Alexander 4.00 10.00
28 Jayson Tatum 2.50 6.00
29 Rob Dillingham 2.00 5.00
30 Jaylen Brown 1.25 3.00

2024-25 Court Kings State of the Art

1 Stephen Curry 125.00 300.00
2 Anthony Edwards 75.00 200.00
3 Shai Gilgeous-Alexander 75.00 200.00
4 Luka Doncic 75.00 200.00
5 LeBron James 125.00 300.00
6 Jayson Tatum 75.00 200.00
7 Victor Wembanyama 150.00 400.00
8 Zaccharie Risacher 40.00 100.00
9 Reed Sheppard 40.00 100.00
10 Matas Buzelis 60.00 150.00

2024-25 Court Kings Water Color

*RUBY/149: 1.25X TO 3X BASIC
*PINK/99: 1.5X TO 4X BASIC
*VIOLET/49: 2X TO 5X BASIC
*SAPPHIRE/25: 2.5X TO 6X BASIC
1 Jayson Tatum 3.00 8.00
2 Ja Morant 3.00 8.00
3 Shai Gilgeous-Alexander 5.00 12.00
4 Anthony Edwards 5.00 12.00
5 Victor Wembanyama 8.00 20.00
6 Stephen Curry 8.00 20.00
7 Giannis Antetokounmpo 4.00 10.00
8 Nikola Jokic 5.00 12.00
9 Luka Doncic 6.00 15.00
10 LeBron James 8.00 20.00
11 Kevin Durant 3.00 8.00
12 Paolo Banchero 2.50 6.00
13 Zaccharie Risacher 3.00 8.00
14 Alexandre Sarr 3.00 8.00
15 Reed Sheppard 3.00 8.00
16 Stephon Castle 6.00 15.00
17 Tidjane Salaun 1.00 2.50
18 Matas Buzelis 5.00 12.00
19 Zach Edey 3.00 8.00
20 Bronny James Jr. 3.00 8.00
21 Tim Duncan 2.50 6.00
22 Shaquille O'Neal 2.50 6.00
23 Kevin Garnett 2.50 6.00
24 Dirk Nowitzki 2.50 6.00
25 Julius Erving 2.50 6.00
26 Larry Bird 3.00 8.00
27 Karl Malone 2.00 5.00
28 Magic Johnson 3.00 8.00
29 Steve Nash 2.00 5.00
30 Dwyane Wade 2.00 5.00

2024-25 Court Kings Works in Progress

*RUBY/149: 1.25X TO 3X BASIC
*PINK/99: 1.5X TO 4X BASIC
*VIOLET/49: 2X TO 5X BASIC
*SAPPHIRE/25: 2.5X TO 6X BASIC
1 Cody Williams 1.00 2.50
2 Terrence Shannon Jr. 1.50 4.00
3 Jaylon Tyson .75 2.00
4 Dalton Knecht 2.50 6.00
5 Donovan Clingan 2.00 5.00
6 Ja'Kobe Walter 1.00 2.50
7 Zaccharie Risacher 2.50 6.00
8 Reed Sheppard 2.50 6.00
9 Isaiah Collier 1.50 4.00
10 Bronny James Jr. 2.50 6.00
11 Devin Carter 1.00 2.50
12 Tyler Kolek 1.25 3.00
13 Zach Edey 2.50 6.00
14 Yves Missi 2.00 5.00
15 Tristan da Silva 2.00 5.00
16 Nikola Topic 2.50 6.00
17 Bub Carrington 2.00 5.00
18 Jared McCain 3.00 8.00
19 Matas Buzelis 4.00 10.00
20 Kel'el Ware 2.00 5.00
21 Rob Dillingham 2.00 5.00
22 Jaylen Wells 2.50 6.00
23 Stephon Castle 5.00 12.00
24 Antonio Reeves .75 2.00
25 Johnny Furphy 1.25 3.00
26 Baylor Scheierman 1.00 2.50
27 Kyle Filipowski 2.00 5.00
28 Ron Holland II 1.50 4.00
29 Alexandre Sarr 2.50 6.00
30 Tidjane Salaun .75 2.00

1991 Cousy Collection Preview

COMPLETE SET (5) 2.00 5.00
COMMON CARD (1-5) .60 1.50
1 Rookie Card 1.00 2.50

1992 Cousy Collection

COMPLETE SET (25) 2.50 6.00
COMMON CARD (1-25) .20 .50
1 Rookie Card 1.00 2.50
7 Double Trouble w/Bill Sharman .40 1.00
9 Stan the Man 1955 1.00 2.50
10 Timely Idea 1955 .40 1.00
14 Four Plan 1958-1959 w/Bill Sharman .40 1.00
16 Victory Watch/1961-1962 (With Red Auerbach and Tom Heinsohn) .40 1.00
17 Visit with J.F.K./1961-1962 (With Red Auerbach) .60 1.50
21 Author 1965 (With Howard Cosell) .40 1.00
22 Podnuhs 1965 .40 1.00

2009-10 Crown Royale

COMP.SET w/o SPs (100) 60.00 120.00
101-140 RC PRINT RUNS LISTED BELOW
1 Kevin Garnett 4.00 10.00
2 Paul Pierce 2.50 6.00
3 Rasheed Wallace 2.00 5.00
4 Ray Allen 2.50 6.00
5 Brook Lopez 1.50 4.00
6 Devin Harris 1.00 2.50
7 Yi Jianlian 2.00 5.00
8 Al Harrington 1.25 3.00
9 Danilo Gallinari 1.25 3.00
10 David Lee 1.00 2.50
11 Nate Robinson 1.25 3.00
12 Allen Iverson 3.00 8.00
13 Andre Iguodala 1.50 4.00
14 Elton Brand 1.25 3.00
15 Louis Williams 1.50 4.00
16 Andrea Bargnani 1.00 2.50
17 Chris Bosh 2.00 5.00
18 Hedo Turkoglu 1.25 3.00
19 Dirk Nowitzki 4.00 10.00
20 J.J. Barea 1.50 4.00
21 Jason Kidd 2.50 6.00
22 Jason Terry 1.25 3.00
23 Aaron Brooks 1.00 2.50
24 Carl Landry 1.00 2.50
25 Trevor Ariza 1.00 2.50
26 O.J. Mayo 1.00 2.50
27 Rudy Gay 1.50 4.00
28 Zach Randolph 1.50 4.00
29 Chris Paul 3.00 8.00
30 David West 1.25 3.00
31 Peja Stojakovic 1.25 3.00
32 Manu Ginobili 3.00 8.00
33 Tim Duncan 4.00 10.00
34 Tony Parker 2.50 6.00
35 Derrick Rose 2.50 6.00
36 John Salmons 1.25 3.00
37 Luol Deng 1.25 3.00
38 LeBron James 15.00 40.00
39 Mo Williams 1.25 3.00
40 Shaquille O'Neal 5.00 12.00
41 Ben Gordon 1.25 3.00
42 Charlie Villanueva 1.00 2.50
43 Richard Hamilton 1.50 4.00
44 Rodney Stuckey 1.00 2.50
45 Dahntay Jones 1.00 2.50
46 Danny Granger 1.00 2.50
47 Troy Murphy 1.00 2.50
48 Andrew Bogut 1.25 3.00
49 Hakim Warrick 1.00 2.50
50 Luke Ridnour 1.25 3.00
51 Carmelo Anthony 2.50 6.00
52 Chauncey Billups 2.00 5.00
53 J.R. Smith 1.50 4.00
54 Nene 1.25 3.00
55 Al Jefferson 1.25 3.00
56 Corey Brewer 1.00 2.50
57 Kevin Love 1.50 4.00
58 Andre Miller 1.50 4.00
59 Brandon Roy 2.00 5.00
60 LaMarcus Aldridge 1.50 4.00
61 Jeff Green 1.25 3.00
62 Kevin Durant 6.00 15.00
63 Russell Westbrook 3.00 8.00
64 Carlos Boozer 1.25 3.00
65 Deron Williams 1.25 3.00
66 Mehmet Okur 1.00 2.50
67 Al Horford 1.50 4.00
68 Jamal Crawford 1.50 4.00
69 Joe Johnson 1.50 4.00
70 Josh Smith 1.00 2.50
71 Gerald Wallace 1.25 3.00
72 Raymond Felton 1.00 2.50
73 Stephen Jackson 1.00 2.50
74 Dwyane Wade 3.00 8.00
75 Jermaine O'Neal 1.50 4.00
76 Michael Beasley 1.00 2.50
77 Dwight Howard 2.00 5.00
78 J.J. Redick 1.50 4.00
79 Rashard Lewis 1.25 3.00
80 Vince Carter 3.00 8.00
81 Antawn Jamison 1.25 3.00
82 Caron Butler 1.25 3.00
83 Randy Foye 1.00 2.50
84 Corey Maggette 1.25 3.00
85 Kelenna Azubuike 1.00 2.50
86 Monta Ellis 1.25 3.00
87 Al Thornton 1.00 2.50
88 Baron Davis 1.25 3.00
89 Chris Kaman 1.25 3.00
90 Eric Gordon 1.25 3.00
91 Andrew Bynum 1.00 2.50
92 Kobe Bryant 15.00 40.00
93 Pau Gasol 2.50 6.00
94 Ron Artest 1.50 4.00
95 Amare Stoudemire 1.25 3.00
96 Jason Richardson 1.50 4.00
97 Steve Nash 3.00 8.00
98 Beno Udrih 1.00 2.50
99 Jason Thompson 1.00 2.50
100 Kevin Martin 1.25 3.00
101 Tyreke Evans AU/399 RC 3.00 8.00
102 Brandon Jennings AU/399 RC 4.00 10.00
103 Stephen Curry AU/399 RC 2,500.00 5,000.00
104 James Harden AU/399 RC 300.00 600.00
105 Jonny Flynn AU/149 RC 2.50 6.00
106 Ty Lawson AU/599 RC 5.00 12.00
107 DeJuan Blair AU/699 RC 3.00 8.00
108 Blake Griffin AU/399 RC 30.00 80.00
109 Hasheem Thabeet AU/149 RC 2.50 6.00
110 Omri Casspi AU/650 RC 2.50 6.00
111 Gerald Henderson AU/599 RC 2.50 6.00
112 Taj Gibson AU/599 RC 3.00 8.00
113 Jrue Holiday AU/599 RC 12.00 30.00
114 Rodrigue Beaubois AU/599 RC 2.50 6.00
115 Jeff Teague AU/599 RC 3.00 8.00
116 Earl Clark AU/599 RC 2.50 6.00
117 Chase Budinger AU/699 RC 2.50 6.00
118 Jordan Hill AU/599 RC 2.50 6.00
119 Terrence Williams AU/599 RC 2.50 6.00
120 Tyler Hansbrough AU/612 RC 3.00 8.00
121 Austin Daye AU/599 RC 2.50 6.00
122 Wayne Ellington AU/658 RC 3.00 8.00
123 Darren Collison AU/599 RC 4.00 10.00
124 James Johnson AU/593 RC 3.00 8.00
125 B.J. Mullens AU/699 RC 2.50 6.00
126 Toney Douglas AU/699 RC 2.50 6.00
127 DeMarre Carroll AU/699 RC 3.00 8.00
128 DaJuan Summers AU/699 RC 2.50 6.00
129 Jodie Meeks AU/699 RC 2.50 6.00
130 DeMar DeRozan AU/599 RC 125.00 300.00
131 Jermaine Taylor AU/699 RC 2.50 6.00
132 Jon Brockman AU/699 RC 2.50 6.00
133 Marcus Thornton AU/669 RC 3.00 8.00
134 Jonas Jerebko AU/699 RC 3.00 8.00
135 Sam Young AU/149 RC 2.50 6.00
136 Wesley Matthews AU/699 RC 4.00 10.00
137 Jeff Pendergraph AU/149 RC 2.50 6.00
138 Serge Ibaka AU/699 RC 8.00 20.00
139 David Andersen AU/149 RC 2.50 6.00
140 Dante Cunningham AU/699 RC 2.50 6.00

2009-10 Crown Royale All-Stars

COMPLETE SET (25) 15.00 40.00
1 Kobe Bryant 6.00 15.00
2 LeBron James 6.00 15.00
3 Allen Iverson 1.50 4.00
4 Kevin Garnett 2.00 5.00
5 Rajon Rondo 1.00 2.50
6 Al Horford .75 2.00
7 Brook Lopez .75 2.00
8 Chauncey Billups 1.00 2.50
9 Danny Granger .50 1.25
10 David Lee .50 1.25
11 Gerald Wallace .60 1.50
12 Pau Gasol 1.25 3.00
13 Tony Parker 1.25 3.00
14 Zach Randolph .75 2.00
15 Aaron Brooks .50 1.25
16 Al Jefferson .50 1.25
17 Antawn Jamison .60 1.50
18 Chris Kaman .60 1.50
19 Corey Maggette .60 1.50
20 David West .60 1.50
21 Kevin Martin .60 1.50
22 O.J. Mayo .50 1.25
23 Rashard Lewis .60 1.50
24 Rodney Stuckey .50 1.25
25 Stephen Jackson .60 1.50

2009-10 Crown Royale All-Stars Materials

STATED PRINT RUN 25 TO 599 SER.#'d SETS
1 Kobe Bryant/599 12.00 30.00
2 LeBron James/99 25.00 60.00
3 Allen Iverson/100 5.00 12.00
4 Kevin Garnett/599 6.00 15.00
5 Rajon Rondo/599 3.00 8.00
6 Al Horford/599 2.50 6.00
7 Brook Lopez/599 2.50 6.00
8 Chauncey Billups/100 3.00 8.00
9 Danny Granger/599 1.50 4.00
11 Gerald Wallace/599 2.00 5.00
12 Pau Gasol/299 4.00 10.00
13 Tony Parker/599 4.00 10.00
15 Aaron Brooks/25 3.00 8.00
16 Al Jefferson/599 1.50 4.00
19 Corey Maggette/599 2.00 5.00
20 David West/599 2.00 5.00
21 Kevin Martin/599 2.00 5.00
22 O.J. Mayo/599 1.50 4.00
23 Rashard Lewis/399 2.00 5.00
24 Rodney Stuckey/599 1.50 4.00
25 Stephen Jackson/599 2.00 5.00

2009-10 Crown Royale All-Stars Materials Prime

PRIME: 1.25X TO 3X BASE HI
STATED PRINT RUN ONE TO 25 SER.#'d SETS
3 Allen Iverson/25 20.00 50.00

2009-10 Crown Royale King on the Court

COMPLETE SET (10) 15.00 30.00
1 LeBron James 8.00 20.00
2 Joakim Noah .60 1.50
3 Tim Duncan 2.50 6.00
4 Chris Paul 2.00 5.00
5 Kevin Durant 4.00 10.00
6 Dwyane Wade 2.00 5.00
7 Paul Pierce 1.50 4.00
8 Chris Bosh 1.25 3.00
9 Tyreke Evans .75 2.00
10 Kobe Bryant 8.00 20.00

2009-10 Crown Royale King on the Court Materials

STATED PRINT RUN 149 SER.#'d SETS
1 LeBron James 10.00 25.00
2 Joakim Noah 2.00 5.00
3 Tim Duncan 8.00 20.00
4 Chris Paul 6.00 15.00
5 Kevin Durant 8.00 20.00
6 Dwyane Wade 6.00 15.00
7 Paul Pierce 5.00 12.00
8 Chris Bosh 4.00 10.00
9 Tyreke Evans 2.50 6.00
10 Kobe Bryant 12.00 30.00

2009-10 Crown Royale Living Legends

COMPLETE SET (25) 25.00 50.00
1 Bob Love 1.50 4.00
2 Brad Daugherty 1.50 4.00
3 Alex English 2.00 5.00
4 Ricky Pierce 1.00 2.50
5 Patrick Ewing 2.50 6.00
6 Chris Webber 2.00 5.00
7 Magic Johnson 6.00 15.00
8 Phil Jackson 2.00 5.00
9 Lafayette Lever 1.50 4.00
10 Larry Bird 6.00 15.00
11 Mark Aguirre 1.25 3.00
12 Mychal Thompson 1.50 4.00
13 Brad Davis 1.00 2.50
14 Oscar Robertson 2.00 5.00
15 M.L. Carr 1.50 4.00
16 Karl Malone 2.00 5.00
17 David Robinson 3.00 8.00
18 Elgin Baylor 4.00 10.00
19 Maurice Lucas 1.50 4.00
20 Scottie Pippen 4.00 10.00
21 Jerry West 2.50 6.00
22 Dan Majerle 1.25 3.00
23 Hakeem Olajuwon 2.00 5.00
24 John Stockton 2.50 6.00
25 George Gervin 2.00 5.00

2009-10 Crown Royale Living Legends Materials

STATED PRINT RUN 25 TO 499 SER.#'d SETS
3 Alex English/499 5.00 12.00
5 Patrick Ewing/299 6.00 15.00
6 Chris Webber/499 5.00 12.00
7 Magic Johnson/99 15.00 40.00
10 Larry Bird/25 10.00 25.00
16 Karl Malone/499 5.00 12.00
19 Maurice Lucas/499 4.00 10.00
20 Scottie Pippen/499 6.00 15.00
21 Jerry West/25 8.00 20.00
23 Hakeem Olajuwon/499 5.00 12.00
24 John Stockton/199 5.00 12.00

2009-10 Crown Royale Living Legends Materials Prime

*PRIME: .75X TO 2X BASE HI
STATED PRINT RUN 5 TO 25 SER.#'d SETS
3 Alex English/25 12.00 30.00
5 Patrick Ewing/25 15.00 30.00
7 Magic Johnson/25 15.00 40.00
20 Scottie Pippen/25 20.00 50.00
24 John Stockton/25 15.00 40.00
25 George Gervin/25 10.00 25.00

2009-10 Crown Royale Majestic Signatures

STATED PRINT RUN 10 TO 99 SER.#'d SETS
AA Alvan Adams/199 6.00 15.00
AB Andrew Bogut/199 6.00 15.00
AI Allen Iverson/25 150.00 400.00
AM Alonzo Mourning/99 20.00 50.00
BD Bob Dandridge/199 6.00 15.00
BJ Bobby Jackson/199 6.00 15.00
BR Bill Russell/49 500.00 1,000.00
CA Chris Andersen/99 12.00 30.00
CR Cazzie Russell/196 6.00 15.00
CV Charlie Villanueva/199 6.00 15.00
DA D.J. Augustin/199 6.00 15.00
DF Derek Fisher/199 10.00 25.00
DG Danny Granger/99 6.00 15.00
DH Devin Harris/199 6.00 15.00
DL David Lee/199 6.00 15.00
DLM Dan Majerle/199 6.00 15.00
DMW Deron Williams/99 6.00 15.00
DR Doc Rivers/199 10.00 25.00
DS Detlef Schrempf/199 8.00 20.00
DT David Thompson/199 6.00 15.00
EG Eric Gordon/198 6.00 15.00
EO Emeka Okafor/99 6.00 15.00
GM George McGinnis/199 6.00 15.00
GP Gary Payton/99 20.00 50.00
HH Hersey Hawkins/199 6.00 15.00
JB J.J. Barea/199 10.00 25.00
JH John Havlicek/25 30.00 80.00
JK Jason Kidd/49 25.00 60.00
JO Jermaine O'Neal/99 6.00 15.00
JR Jalen Rose/199 6.00 15.00
KB Kobe Bryant/199 500.00 1,000.00
KL Kevin Love/99 12.00 30.00
LB Larry Bird/25 125.00 300.00
LO Lamar Odom/99 12.00 30.00
MB Michael Beasley/99 8.00 20.00
MJ Magic Johnson/23 75.00 200.00
MW Mo Williams/99 6.00 15.00
OR Oscar Robertson/25 75.00 200.00
PG Pau Gasol/30 30.00 80.00
RA Ray Allen/49 30.00 80.00
RH Robert Horry/99 25.00 60.00
RR Rajon Rondo/199 15.00 40.00
RW Russell Westbrook/99 50.00 120.00
SB Shawn Bradley/199 6.00 15.00
SE Sean Elliott/199 8.00 20.00
SH Spencer Haywood/199 6.00 15.00
SN Steve Nash/96 60.00 150.00
SO Shaquille O'Neal/25 150.00 400.00
SP Scottie Pippen/99 75.00 200.00
TM Tracy McGrady/25 30.00 80.00
TP Tony Parker/99 15.00 40.00
VC Vince Carter/99 40.00 100.00
AI2 Andre Iguodala/199 6.00 15.00

2009-10 Crown Royale Nothing But Net

COMPLETE SET (10) 6.00 15.00
1 Danilo Gallinari .75 2.00
2 Channing Frye .60 1.50
3 Aaron Brooks .60 1.50
4 Peja Stojakovic .75 2.00
5 Martell Webster .60 1.50
6 Rashard Lewis .75 2.00
7 Mo Williams .75 2.00
8 Jason Kidd 1.50 4.00
9 LeBron James 8.00 20.00
10 Chauncey Billups 1.25 3.00

2009-10 Crown Royale Nothing But Net Materials

STATED PRINT RUN 25 TO 499 SER.#'d SETS
*PRIME: .75X TO 2X HI COLUMN
PRIME PRINT RUN ONE TO 25 SETS
3 Aaron Brooks/25 3.00 8.00
4 Peja Stojakovic/499 2.50 6.00
6 Rashard Lewis/299 2.50 6.00
8 Jason Kidd/399 5.00 12.00
9 LeBron James/99 10.00 25.00
10 Chauncey Billups/100 4.00 10.00

2009-10 Crown Royale Rookie Royalty

COMPLETE SET (10) 8.00 20.00
1 Jennings/Curry/Evans 75.00 200.00
2 Collison/Flynn/Lawson 1.00 2.50
3 Griffin/Blair/Gibson 4.00 10.00
4 Budinger/DeRozan/Harden 6.00 15.00
5 Daye/Clark/Casspi .60 1.50
6 Maynor/Teague/Holiday 3.00 8.00
7 Griffin/Thabeet/Harden 6.00 15.00
8 Lawson/Hansbrough/Ellington .75 2.00
9 Carroll/Thabeet/Young .75 2.00
10 Johnson/Pendergraph/Hill .75 2.00

2009-10 Crown Royale Rookie Royalty Materials

STATED PRINT RUN 499 SER.#'d SETS
1 Jennings/Curry/Evans 150.00 400.00
2 Collison/Flynn/Lawson 4.00 10.00
3 Griffin/Blair/Gibson 10.00 25.00
4 Budinger/DeRozan/Harden 15.00 40.00
5 Daye/Clark/Casspi 4.00 10.00

6 Maynor/Teague/Holiday 5.00 12.00
7 Griffin/Thabeet/Harden 8.00 20.00
8 Lawson/Hansbrough/Ellington 5.00 12.00
9 Carroll/Thabeet/Young 4.00 10.00
10 Johnson/Pendergraph/Hill 4.00 10.00

2009-10 Crown Royale Rookie Royalty Materials Prime

*PRIME: .75X TO 2X BASE HI
STATED PRINT RUN 25 SER.#'d SETS
1 Jennings/Curry/Evans 400.00 800.00
2 Collison/Flynn/Lawson 20.00 50.00
3 Griffin/Blair/Gibson 25.00 60.00
4 Budinger/DeRozan/Harden 60.00 150.00
6 Maynor/Teague/Holiday 12.50 30.00
7 Griffin/Thabeet/Harden 15.00 40.00
8 Lawson/Hansbrough/Ellington 20.00 50.00

2009-10 Crown Royale Royalty

COMPLETE SET (20) 15.00 30.00
1 Kobe Bryant 6.00 15.00
2 LeBron James 6.00 15.00
3 Dwyane Wade 1.50 4.00
4 Carmelo Anthony 1.25 3.00
5 Kevin Durant 3.00 8.00
6 Monta Ellis .60 1.50
7 Dirk Nowitzki 2.00 5.00
8 Chris Bosh 1.00 2.50
9 Brandon Roy 1.00 2.50
10 Joe Johnson .75 2.00
11 Dwight Howard 1.00 2.50
12 Steve Nash 1.50 4.00
13 Chris Paul 1.50 4.00
14 Tim Duncan 2.00 5.00
15 Paul Pierce 1.25 3.00
16 Shaquille O'Neal 2.50 6.00
17 Amare Stoudemire .60 1.50
18 Derrick Rose 1.25 3.00
19 Deron Williams .60 1.50
20 Vince Carter 1.50 4.00

2009-10 Crown Royale Royalty Materials

STATED PRINT RUN 99 TO 499 SER.#'d SETS
1 Kobe Bryant/499 40.00 100.00
2 LeBron James/99 40.00 100.00
4 Carmelo Anthony/499 5.00 12.00
5 Kevin Durant/499 12.00 30.00
7 Dirk Nowitzki/499 8.00 20.00
8 Chris Bosh/499 4.00 10.00
9 Brandon Roy/499 4.00 10.00
10 Joe Johnson/499 3.00 8.00
11 Dwight Howard/499 4.00 10.00
13 Chris Paul/499 6.00 15.00
14 Tim Duncan/499 8.00 20.00
15 Paul Pierce/499 5.00 12.00
16 Shaquille O'Neal/499 10.00 25.00
18 Derrick Rose/499 5.00 12.00
19 Deron Williams/499 2.50 6.00
20 Vince Carter/499 6.00 15.00

2009-10 Crown Royale Royalty Materials Prime

PRIME: 1X TO 2.5X BASE HI
STATED PRINT RUN 5 TO 25 SER.#'d SETS
3 Dwyane Wade/25 15.00 40.00

2010 Crown Royale National Convention VIP

COMPLETE SET (6) 5.00 12.00
VIP1 Kobe Bryant 3.00 8.00
VIP2 Carmelo Anthony .75 2.00
VIP3 Derrick Rose 2.00 5.00
VIP4 Brandon Jennings .60 1.50
VIP5 Wesley Johnson .60 1.50
VIP6 Evan Turner .60 1.50

2010 Crown Royale National Convention VIP Blue

COMPLETE SET (6) 40.00 80.00
*BLUE: 2X TO 5X BASE HI
ANNOUNCED PRINT RUN 25 SETS

2010 Crown Royale National Convention VIP Green

COMPLETE SET (6) 10.00 25.00
*GREEN: .75X TO 2X BASE HI
ANNOUNCED PRINT RUN 50 SETS

2017-18 Crown Royale

JSY AU PRINT RUN 199 SER.#'d SETS
1 Kemba Walker .30 .75
2 Elfrid Payton .25 .60
3 Wesley Matthews .25 .60
4 Damian Lillard 1.00 2.50
5 Stephen Curry 3.00 8.00
6 DeMar DeRozan .50 1.25
7 Blake Griffin .40 1.00
8 Josh Richardson .30 .75
9 Dennis Schroder .30 .75
10 Rajon Rondo .50 1.25
11 Nicolas Batum .25 .60
12 Evan Fournier .30 .75
13 Harrison Barnes .30 .75
14 CJ McCollum .40 1.00
15 Klay Thompson 1.00 2.50
16 Kyle Lowry .40 1.00
17 Markelle Fultz RC 1.25 3.00
18 Goran Dragic .30 .75
19 Lonzo Ball RC 2.00 5.00
20 Jrue Holiday .50 1.25
21 Michael Kidd-Gilchrist .25 .60
22 Aaron Gordon .40 1.00
23 Dirk Nowitzki 1.00 2.50
24 Al-Farouq Aminu .25 .60
25 Kevin Durant 1.50 4.00
26 Serge Ibaka .30 .75
27 DeAndre Jordan .30 .75
28 Jayson Tatum RC 6.00 15.00
29 Taurean Prince .25 .60
30 Anthony Davis 1.00 2.50
31 Josh Jackson RC .60 1.50
32 Nikola Vucevic .30 .75
33 De'Aaron Fox RC 4.00 10.00
34 Jusuf Nurkic .30 .75
35 Draymond Green .50 1.25
36 Jonas Valanciunas .30 .75
37 Lou Williams .30 .75
38 Tyler Johnson .25 .60
39 Ersan Ilyasova .25 .60
40 DeMarcus Cousins .50 1.25
41 Dwight Howard .50 1.25
42 Jonathon Simmons .25 .60
43 J.J. Barea .30 .75
44 Evan Turner .25 .60
45 Andre Iguodala .40 1.00
46 Delon Wright .25 .60
47 Danilo Gallinari .30 .75
48 Hassan Whiteside .30 .75
49 Dewayne Dedmon .25 .60
50 E'Twaun Moore .25 .60
51 Jeremy Lamb .25 .60
52 Terrence Ross .30 .75
53 Dwight Powell .25 .60
54 Maurice Harkless .25 .60
55 Zaza Pachulia .25 .60
56 Pascal Siakam .75 2.00
57 Patrick Beverley .25 .60
58 Justise Winslow .25 .60
59 Marco Belinelli .25 .60
60 Jameer Nelson .25 .60
61 Kris Dunn .25 .60
62 Ben Simmons .40 1.00
63 Gary Harris .30 .75
64 George Hill .30 .75
65 Chris Paul .60 1.50
66 Ricky Rubio .30 .75
67 Brandon Ingram .50 1.25
68 Giannis Antetokounmpo 2.00 5.00
69 Kyrie Irving .75 2.00
70 Tim Hardaway Jr. .30 .75
71 Robin Lopez .25 .60
72 JJ Redick .40 1.00
73 Will Barton .25 .60
74 Willie Cauley-Stein .25 .60
75 Eric Gordon .30 .75
76 Joe Ingles .30 .75
77 Kentavious Caldwell-Pope .30 .75
78 Khris Middleton .50 1.25
79 Jaylen Brown 1.00 2.50
80 Kristaps Porzingis .50 1.25
81 Denzel Valentine .25 .60
82 Dario Saric .30 .75
83 Nikola Jokic 2.50 6.00
84 Zach Randolph .40 1.00
85 Trevor Ariza .25 .60
86 Rudy Gobert .50 1.25
87 Julius Randle .40 1.00
88 Eric Bledsoe .30 .75
89 Al Horford .40 1.00
90 Courtney Lee .25 .60
91 Nikola Mirotic .25 .60
92 Robert Covington .25 .60
93 Wilson Chandler .30 .75
94 Buddy Hield .40 1.00
95 Ryan Anderson .25 .60
96 Rodney Hood .25 .60
97 Jordan Clarkson .40 1.00
98 Malcolm Brogdon .30 .75
99 Marcus Smart .40 1.00
100 Jarrett Jack .30 .75
101 Zach LaVine .60 1.50
102 Joel Embiid .75 2.00
103 Paul Millsap .30 .75
104 Skal Labissiere .25 .60
105 Clint Capela .30 .75
106 Derrick Favors .30 .75
107 Brook Lopez .30 .75
108 John Henson .25 .60
109 Marcus Morris .25 .60
110 Enes Kanter .30 .75
111 Bobby Portis .30 .75
112 Jerryd Bayless .25 .60
113 Jamal Murray .60 1.50
114 Vince Carter .75 2.00
115 James Harden .75 2.00
116 Joe Johnson .30 .75
117 Larry Nance Jr. .30 .75
118 Thon Maker .25 .60
119 Aron Baynes .25 .60
120 Jonathan Isaac RC 1.25 3.00
121 Isaiah Thomas .30 .75
122 Devin Booker 1.00 2.50
123 Tobias Harris .30 .75
124 Tony Parker .60 1.50
125 Darren Collison .25 .60
126 Bradley Beal .50 1.25
127 Marc Gasol .40 1.00
128 Jeff Teague .25 .60
129 DeMarre Carroll .25 .60
130 Russell Westbrook .60 1.50
131 LeBron James 3.00 8.00
132 TJ Warren .30 .75
133 Andre Drummond .30 .75
134 Manu Ginobili .75 2.00
135 Victor Oladipo .30 .75
136 John Wall .50 1.25
137 Mike Conley .30 .75
138 Jimmy Butler .60 1.50
139 Allen Crabbe .25 .60
140 Paul George .60 1.50
141 Kevin Love .40 1.00
142 Tyson Chandler .30 .75
143 Avery Bradley .25 .60
144 Kawhi Leonard 1.00 2.50
145 Bojan Bogdanovic .30 .75
146 Otto Porter Jr. .30 .75
147 Tyreke Evans .25 .60
148 Andrew Wiggins .50 1.25
149 Rondae Hollis-Jefferson .25 .60
150 Carmelo Anthony .60 1.50
151 Dwyane Wade .75 2.00
152 Lauri Markkanen RC 3.00 8.00
153 Frank Ntilikina RC .60 1.50
154 Rudy Gay .30 .75
155 Thaddeus Young .25 .60
156 Dennis Smith Jr. RC .60 1.50
157 Zach Collins RC .75 2.00
158 Taj Gibson .25 .60
159 Spencer Dinwiddie .30 .75
160 Steven Adams .30 .75
161 Malik Monk 1.00 2.50
163 Reggie Jackson .30 .75
164 LaMarcus Aldridge .40 1.00
165 Myles Turner .40 1.00
166 Luke Kennard RC 1.00 2.50
167 Donovan Mitchell RC 5.00 12.00
168 Karl-Anthony Towns .60 1.50
169 D'Angelo Russell .30 .75
170 Kyle Kuzma RC 2.00 5.00
171 JR Smith .30 .75
172 Bam Adebayo RC 3.00 8.00
173 John Collins RC 1.25 3.00
174 Pau Gasol .60 1.50
175 Jordan Bell RC .50 1.25
176 Frank Mason III RC .50 1.25
177 Milos Teodosic RC .60 1.50
178 Jamal Crawford .40 1.00
179 Jeremy Lin .60 1.50
180 Bogdan Bogdanovic RC 1.25 3.00
181 Kobe Bryant 3.00 8.00
182 Shaquille O'Neal 1.25 3.00
183 Allen Iverson 1.00 2.50
184 Reggie Miller .75 2.00
185 Julius Erving 1.00 2.50
186 John Stockton .75 2.00
187 Magic Johnson 1.50 4.00
188 Larry Bird 1.50 4.00
189 Wilt Chamberlain 1.25 3.00
190 Tim Duncan 1.00 2.50
191 Kevin Garnett 1.00 2.50
192 Patrick Ewing .60 1.50
193 Pete Maravich 1.00 2.50
194 Steve Nash .60 1.50
195 Drazen Petrovic .40 1.00
196 Chris Webber .60 1.50
197 Scottie Pippen 1.00 2.50
198 Karl Malone .75 2.00
199 Kareem Abdul-Jabbar 1.25 3.00
200 Oscar Robertson .75 2.00
201 D.J. Wilson JSY AU RC 3.00 8.00
202 Frank Mason III JSY AU 3.00 8.00
203 Jonathan Isaac JSY AU 10.00 25.00
205 Luke Kennard JSY AU 6.00 15.00
206 Frank Jackson JSY AU RC 3.00 8.00
208 Dennis Smith Jr. JSY AU 4.00 10.00
209 Markelle Fultz JSY AU 20.00 50.00
210 Caleb Swanigan JSY AU RC 3.00 8.00
211 TJ Leaf JSY AU RC 3.00 8.00
212 Semi Ojeleye JSY AU RC 4.00 10.00
213 Frank Ntilikina JSY AU 4.00 10.00
215 Donovan Mitchell JSY AU 125.00 300.00
217 Jarrett Allen JSY AU RC 8.00 20.00
219 Lonzo Ball JSY AU 25.00 60.00
220 Tony Bradley JSY AU RC 3.00 8.00
221 John Collins JSY AU 8.00 20.00
222 Jawun Evans JSY AU RC 3.00 8.00
223 Zach Collins JSY AU 5.00 12.00
225 Bam Adebayo JSY AU 20.00 50.00
227 OG Anunoby JSY AU RC 6.00 15.00
228 Wayne Selden JSY AU RC 3.00 8.00
229 Jayson Tatum JSY AU 300.00 600.00
231 Harry Giles JSY AU RC 3.00 8.00
232 Tyler Dorsey JSY AU RC 3.00 8.00
234 Kyle Kuzma JSY AU 12.00 30.00
235 Justin Patton JSY AU RC 3.00 8.00
236 Ante Zizic JSY AU RC 4.00 10.00
237 Tyler Lydon JSY AU RC 3.00 8.00
238 Josh Jackson JSY AU 4.00 10.00
239 De'Aaron Fox JSY AU 30.00 80.00
240 Davon Reed JSY AU RC 3.00 8.00

2017-18 Crown Royale Crystal

*CRYSTAL: 1.5X TO 4X BASIC
*CRYSTAL RC: .75X TO 2X BASIC RC
STATED PRINT RUN 99 SER.#'d SETS
28 Jayson Tatum 40.00 100.00
131 LeBron James 20.00 50.00
167 Donovan Mitchell 20.00 50.00

2017-18 Crown Royale Crystal Purple

*CRSTL PRPLE: 4X TO 10X BASIC
*CRSTL PRPLE RC: 2X TO 5X BASIC RC
STATED PRINT RUN 25 SER.#'d SETS
28 Jayson Tatum 100.00 250.00
131 LeBron James 50.00 120.00
167 Donovan Mitchell 50.00 120.00

2017-18 Crown Royale Autograph Relic Silhouettes

PRINT RUNS B/WN 25-49 COPIES PER
1 Damian Lillard/25 25.00 60.00
2 Kyrie Irving/25 60.00 150.00
4 Giannis Antetokounmpo/25 100.00 250.00
5 Karl-Anthony Towns/25 30.00 80.00
7 Ricky Rubio/25 10.00 25.00
8 Kristaps Porzingis/49 20.00 50.00
12 Aaron Gordon/49 8.00 20.00
13 Al Horford/49 8.00 20.00
14 Harrison Barnes/49 6.00 15.00
15 Kevin Durant/25 75.00 200.00
16 David Robinson/25 20.00 50.00
17 Kobe Bryant/25 1,000.00 2,000.00
18 Shaquille O'Neal/25 75.00 200.00
19 Grant Hill/49 20.00 50.00
20 Julius Erving/25 50.00 120.00

2017-18 Crown Royale Crown Autographs

PRINT RUNS B/WN 49-99 COPIES PER
*BLUE/25: .6X TO 1.5X p/r 75-99
*BLUE/25: .5X TO 1.2X p/r 49
1 Latrell Sprewell/99 5.00 12.00
2 Ricky Rubio/49 6.00 15.00
3 Nick Young/99 4.00 10.00
4 Kemba Walker/75 6.00 15.00
5 B.J. Armstrong/99 5.00 12.00
6 Tyson Chandler/99 3.00 8.00
7 Myles Turner/99 4.00 10.00
8 Magic Johnson/49 25.00 60.00
9 Rick Fox/99 3.00 8.00
10 Jerry West/49 15.00 40.00
11 Danny Manning/99 3.00 8.00
12 Anfernee Hardaway/75 15.00 40.00
13 Kyle Korver/99 3.00 8.00
14 Rudy Gobert/75 5.00 12.00
15 Allan Houston/99 4.00 10.00
16 Kentavious Caldwell-Pope/99 3.00 8.00
17 Jrue Holiday/99 5.00 12.00
18 Reggie Miller/49 30.00 80.00
19 Nerlens Noel/99 2.50 6.00
20 Giannis Antetokounmpo/49 60.00 150.00
21 Frank Ramsey/99 10.00 25.00
22 Dennis Rodman/75 20.00 50.00
23 TJ Warren/99 3.00 8.00
24 Sam Jones/75 12.00 30.00
25 Danny Green/99 3.00 8.00
26 Aaron Gordon/99 5.00 12.00
27 Joe Johnson/99 3.00 8.00
28 Allen Iverson/49 30.00 80.00
29 Robert Horry/99 4.00 10.00
30 Alonzo Mourning/49 12.00 30.00
31 Ben Wallace/99 8.00 20.00
32 Gary Payton/75 10.00 25.00
33 Iman Shumpert/99 2.50 6.00
34 Christian Laettner/75 6.00 15.00
35 DeMarre Carroll/99 2.50 6.00
36 Harrison Barnes/75 3.00 8.00
37 Justise Winslow/99 2.50 6.00
38 Kyrie Irving/49 25.00 60.00
39 Cliff Hagan/99 5.00 12.00
40 Karl-Anthony Towns/49 12.00 30.00
41 Ralph Sampson/99 4.00 10.00
42 Jeremy Lin/75 10.00 25.00
43 Malcolm Brogdon/99 3.00 8.00
44 Richard Hamilton/75 5.00 12.00
45 Antawn Jamison/99 3.00 8.00
46 Avery Bradley/99 2.50 6.00
47 Michael Kidd-Gilchrist/99 2.50 6.00
48 Damian Lillard/49 15.00 40.00
49 Elfrid Payton/99 2.50 6.00
50 Hakeem Olajuwon/49 12.00 30.00
51 Channing Frye/99 2.50 6.00
52 Kristaps Porzingis/75 12.00 30.00
53 Terrence Ross/99 3.00 8.00
55 Evan Turner/99 2.50 6.00
56 Elvin Hayes/99 5.00 12.00
57 Clint Capela/99 3.00 8.00
58 Karl Malone/49 12.00 30.00
59 Jermaine O'Neal/99 4.00 10.00
61 Gerald Green/99 3.00 8.00
62 James Worthy/75 8.00 20.00
63 Zaza Pachulia/99 2.50 6.00
64 Artis Gilmore/99 5.00 12.00
65 Darren Collison/99 2.50 6.00
66 Nate Archibald/75 5.00 12.00
67 Trevor Ariza/99 2.50 6.00
68 Blake Griffin/49 10.00 25.00
69 Lenny Wilkens/99 5.00 12.00
70 Clyde Drexler/49 12.00 30.00
71 Thaddeus Young/99 2.50 6.00
72 Gordon Hayward/75 10.00 25.00
73 Nene/99 3.00 8.00
74 Al Horford/99 4.00 10.00
75 Juwan Howard/99 3.00 8.00

2017-18 Crown Royale Crown Autographs Rookies

STATED PRINT RUN 199 SER.#'d SETS
*BLUE/25: .6X TO 1.5X BASIC
1 Markelle Fultz 12.00 30.00
2 Lonzo Ball 20.00 50.00
3 Jayson Tatum 50.00 120.00
4 De'Aaron Fox 30.00 80.00
5 Jonathan Isaac 8.00 20.00
6 Frank Ntilikina 3.00 8.00
7 Zach Collins 4.00 10.00
8 Malik Monk 10.00 25.00
9 Luke Kennard 5.00 12.00
10 Donovan Mitchell 60.00 150.00
11 Bam Adebayo 6.00 15.00
12 Justin Patton 2.50 6.00
13 D.J. Wilson 2.50 6.00
14 TJ Leaf 2.50 6.00
15 John Collins 10.00 25.00
16 Bogdan Bogdanovic 6.00 15.00
17 Dillon Brooks 8.00 20.00
18 Josh Hart 6.00 15.00
19 Milos Teodosic 3.00 8.00
20 Cedi Osman 5.00 12.00
21 Tyler Cavanaugh 2.50 6.00
23 Lauri Markkanen 40.00 100.00
24 Maxi Kleber 4.00 10.00
25 Justin Jackson 2.50 6.00

2017-18 Crown Royale Jerseys

PRINT RUNS B/WN 99-249 COPIES PER
1 Danny Granger/249 2.00 5.00
2 Kristaps Porzingis/249 4.00 10.00
3 Tim Duncan/249 8.00 20.00
4 Rondae Hollis-Jefferson/249 2.00 5.00
5 Trevor Ariza/249 2.00 5.00
6 Andrew Wiggins/249 4.00 10.00
7 JR Smith/249 2.50 6.00
8 Zach LaVine/249 5.00 12.00
9 Kobe Bryant/249 10.00 25.00
10 Serge Ibaka/249 2.50 6.00
11 David Robinson/249 6.00 15.00
12 Al-Farouq Aminu/249 2.00 5.00
13 Magic Johnson/99 6.00 15.00
14 Harrison Barnes/249 2.50 6.00
15 Steven Adams/249 2.50 6.00
16 Karl-Anthony Towns/249 5.00 12.00
17 Klay Thompson/249 8.00 20.00
18 Pau Gasol/249 2.50 6.00
19 Shaquille O'Neal/249 6.00 15.00
20 Wesley Matthews/249 2.00 5.00
21 Larry Bird/99 6.00 15.00
22 Terrence Ross/249 2.50 6.00
23 Jerry West/99 6.00 15.00
24 Kris Dunn/249 2.00 5.00
25 Damian Lillard/249 8.00 20.00
26 Dirk Nowitzki/249 8.00 20.00
27 Kenneth Faried/249 2.50 6.00
28 Kevin Love/249 3.00 8.00
29 Paul Pierce/249 5.00 12.00
30 DeAndre Jordan/249 2.50 6.00
31 Shawn Marion/249 2.50 6.00
32 Nikola Jokic/249 20.00 50.00
33 Julius Erving/99 8.00 20.00
34 Blake Griffin/249 3.00 8.00
35 John Wall/249 4.00 10.00
36 Rudy Gobert/249 4.00 10.00
37 Draymond Green/249 4.00 10.00
38 Joe Johnson/249 2.00 5.00
39 Grant Hill/249 5.00 12.00
40 Jusuf Nurkic/249 2.50 6.00
41 Karl Malone/99 6.00 15.00
42 Rodney Hood/249 2.00 5.00
43 Kareem Abdul-Jabbar/99 10.00 25.00
44 Kevin Durant/249 6.00 15.00
45 Anthony Davis/249 8.00 20.00
46 Gordon Hayward/249 2.50 6.00
48 Al Jefferson/249 2.50 6.00
49 Scottie Pippen/249 8.00 20.00
50 Evan Turner/249 2.00 5.00
51 Ray Allen/249 5.00 12.00
52 LeBron James/249 10.00 25.00
53 Elgin Baylor/99 5.00 12.00
54 Elfrid Payton/249 2.00 5.00
55 Nicolas Batum/249 2.00 5.00
56 Derrick Favors/249 2.00 5.00
57 Kevin Garnett/249 8.00 20.00
58 Carmelo Anthony/249 5.00 12.00
59 Clyde Drexler/249 5.00 12.00
60 Maurice Harkless/249 2.00 5.00

2017-18 Crown Royale Mamba's Choice

STATED PRINT RUN 99 SER.#'d SETS
MC1 Russell Westbrook 12.00 30.00
MC2 LeBron James 150.00 400.00
MC3 Chris Paul 15.00 40.00
MC4 Kevin Durant 20.00 50.00
MC5 Anthony Davis 12.00 30.00
MC6 Stephen Curry 100.00 250.00
7 Giannis Antetokounmpo 50.00 120.00
MC8 Kawhi Leonard 12.00 30.00
MC9 John Wall 10.00 25.00
MC10 James Harden 12.00 30.00

2017-18 Crown Royale Mamba's Choice Blue

*BLUE: .6X TO 1.5X BASIC
STATED PRINT RUN 25 SER.#'d SETS
MC8 Kawhi Leonard 20.00 50.00

2017-18 Crown Royale Mamba's Choice Red

*RED: .5X TO 1.2X BASIC
STATED PRINT RUN 75 SER.#'d SETS

2017-18 Crown Royale Pacific Marquee

1 De'Aaron Fox 20.00 50.00
2 Jayson Tatum 125.00 300.00
3 Dwight Howard 5.00 12.00
4 Damian Lillard 15.00 40.00
5 Gordon Hayward 3.00 8.00
6 Josh Jackson 3.00 8.00
7 CJ McCollum 4.00 10.00
8 Kyrie Irving 20.00 50.00
9 Kemba Walker 3.00 8.00
10 Devin Booker 25.00 60.00
11 James Harden 8.00 20.00
12 Frank Ntilikina 3.00 8.00
13 Paul George 6.00 15.00
14 Draymond Green 5.00 12.00
15 Kristaps Porzingis 5.00 12.00
16 Klay Thompson 30.00 80.00
17 Chris Paul 12.00 30.00
18 DeMarcus Cousins 3.00 8.00
19 Russell Westbrook 6.00 15.00
20 Kevin Durant 40.00 100.00
21 John Wall 5.00 12.00
22 Lauri Markkanen 15.00 40.00
23 Dwyane Wade 15.00 40.00
24 DeMar DeRozan 12.00 30.00
25 LeBron James 125.00 300.00
26 Tony Parker 15.00 40.00
27 Donovan Mitchell 100.00 250.00
28 Malik Monk 12.00 30.00
29 Kevin Love 4.00 10.00
30 Kawhi Leonard 10.00 25.00
31 Goran Dragic 3.00 8.00
32 Jonathan Isaac 6.00 15.00
33 Joel Embiid 12.00 30.00
34 Brandon Ingram 5.00 12.00
35 Ben Simmons 4.00 10.00
36 Blake Griffin 4.00 10.00
37 Dillon Brooks 8.00 20.00
38 Carmelo Anthony 6.00 15.00
39 Markelle Fultz 6.00 15.00
40 Lonzo Ball 40.00 100.00
41 Anthony Davis 10.00 25.00
42 Dirk Nowitzki 15.00 40.00
43 Stephen Curry 100.00 250.00
44 Karl-Anthony Towns 6.00 15.00
45 Dennis Smith Jr. 3.00 8.00
46 Giannis Antetokounmpo 40.00 100.00
47 Andrew Wiggins 5.00 12.00
48 Bogdan Bogdanovic 6.00 15.00
49 Kyle Kuzma 10.00 25.00
50 Jimmy Butler 6.00 15.00

2017-18 Crown Royale Panini's Choice

STATED PRINT RUN 99 SER.#'d SETS
*RED/75: .5X TO 1.2X BASIC
1 Josh Jackson 2.00 5.00
2 Klay Thompson 8.00 20.00
3 Tony Parker 4.00 10.00
4 Blake Griffin 2.50 6.00
5 Giannis Antetokounmpo 12.00 30.00
6 Kyrie Irving 5.00 12.00
7 DeMarcus Cousins 2.00 5.00
8 Malik Monk 6.00 15.00
9 Carmelo Anthony 4.00 10.00
10 Bogdan Bogdanovic 4.00 10.00
11 Devin Booker 6.00 15.00
12 Kevin Durant 10.00 25.00
13 Kawhi Leonard 6.00 15.00
14 Lonzo Ball 6.00 15.00
15 Jimmy Butler 4.00 10.00
16 Jayson Tatum 60.00 150.00
17 Frank Ntilikina 2.50 6.00
18 Lauri Markkanen 10.00 25.00
19 Jonathan Isaac 4.00 10.00
20 Dirk Nowitzki 6.00 15.00
21 Damian Lillard 6.00 15.00
22 Draymond Green 3.00 8.00
23 DeMar DeRozan 3.00 8.00
24 Brandon Ingram 3.00 8.00
25 Karl-Anthony Towns 4.00 10.00
26 Gordon Hayward 3.00 8.00
27 Kristaps Porzingis 3.00 8.00
28 LeBron James 30.00 80.00
29 Ben Simmons 2.50 6.00
30 Dennis Smith Jr. 2.00 5.00
31 CJ McCollum 2.50 6.00
32 Chris Paul 4.00 10.00
33 Donovan Mitchell 40.00 100.00
34 Dillon Brooks 5.00 12.00
35 Andrew Wiggins 3.00 8.00
36 Kemba Walker 2.00 5.00
37 Russell Westbrook 4.00 10.00
38 Kevin Love 2.50 6.00
39 Markelle Fultz 4.00 10.00
40 Luke Kennard 3.00 8.00
41 De'Aaron Fox 12.00 30.00
42 James Harden 5.00 12.00
43 John Wall 3.00 8.00
44 Goran Dragic 2.00 5.00
45 Anthony Davis 6.00 15.00
46 Dwight Howard 3.00 8.00
47 Paul George 4.00 10.00
48 Dwyane Wade 8.00 20.00
49 Joel Embiid 8.00 20.00
50 Stephen Curry 30.00 80.00

2017-18 Crown Royale Panini's Choice Blue

*BLUE: .6X TO 1.5X BASIC
STATED PRINT RUN 25 SER.#'d SETS
33 Donovan Mitchell 60.00 150.00

2017-18 Crown Royale Power in the Paint

1 Patrick Ewing 15.00 40.00
2 Giannis Antetokounmpo 75.00 200.00
3 Blake Griffin 4.00 10.00
4 LeBron James 100.00 250.00
5 Kareem Abdul-Jabbar 40.00 100.00
6 Andre Drummond 3.00 8.00
7 Shaquille O'Neal 40.00 100.00
8 DeMarcus Cousins 3.00 8.00
9 David Robinson 40.00 100.00
10 Dwight Howard 5.00 12.00
11 Dennis Rodman 40.00 100.00
12 Anthony Davis 15.00 40.00
13 Dirk Nowitzki 40.00 100.00
14 Wilt Chamberlain 40.00 100.00
100 Hakeem Olajuwon 40.00 100.00
16 DeAndre Jordan 3.00 8.00
17 Tim Duncan 40.00 100.00
18 Karl-Anthony Towns 6.00 15.00
19 Kevin Garnett 40.00 100.00
20 Kevin Love 4.00 10.00
21 Kristaps Porzingis 5.00 12.00
22 Joel Embiid 40.00 100.00
23 Kevin Durant 15.00 40.00
24 Bill Russell 40.00 100.00
25 Charles Barkley 40.00 100.00

2017-18 Crown Royale Regents of Roundball

1 Pete Maravich 25.00 60.00
2 Allen Iverson 40.00 100.00
3 Karl Malone 25.00 60.00
4 Larry Bird 40.00 100.00
5 Kareem Abdul-Jabbar 40.00 100.00
6 Kobe Bryant 150.00 400.00
7 Scottie Pippen 10.00 25.00
8 Dennis Rodman 30.00 80.00
9 Kevin Garnett 40.00 100.00
10 Tim Duncan 40.00 100.00
11 Oscar Robertson 25.00 60.00
12 John Havlicek 25.00 60.00
13 Wilt Chamberlain 40.00 100.00
14 Chris Webber 30.00 80.00
15 Magic Johnson 40.00 100.00
16 Shaquille O'Neal 40.00 100.00
17 John Stockton 25.00 60.00
18 Paul Pierce 12.00 30.00
19 Hakeem Olajuwon 40.00 100.00
20 Reggie Miller 30.00 80.00
21 David Robinson 30.00 80.00
22 Bill Russell 40.00 100.00
23 Patrick Ewing 15.00 40.00
24 Julius Erving 40.00 100.00
25 Charles Barkley 40.00 100.00

2017-18 Crown Royale Rookie Jersey Autographs

STATED PRINT RUN 199 SER.#'d SETS
1 Terrance Ferguson 3.00 8.00
3 Markelle Fultz 20.00 50.00
4 Semi Ojeleye 4.00 10.00
5 Jonathan Isaac 8.00 20.00
7 Luke Kennard 6.00 15.00
8 Ante Zizic 4.00 10.00
9 D.J. Wilson 3.00 8.00
11 Jarrett Allen 8.00 20.00
13 Lonzo Ball 25.00 60.00
14 Frank Jackson 3.00 8.00
15 Frank Ntilikina 4.00 10.00
17 Donovan Mitchell 75.00 200.00
18 Ike Anigbogu 3.00 8.00
19 TJ Leaf 3.00 8.00
20 Frank Mason III 3.00 8.00
21 OG Anunoby 15.00 40.00
23 Jayson Tatum 100.00 250.00
24 Derrick White 12.00 30.00
25 Zach Collins 5.00 12.00
27 Bam Adebayo 20.00 50.00
28 Wayne Selden 3.00 8.00
29 John Collins 12.00 30.00
30 Jawun Evans 3.00 8.00
31 Tyler Lydon 3.00 8.00
32 Dennis Smith Jr. 4.00 10.00
33 De'Aaron Fox 25.00 60.00
34 Wes Iwundu 3.00 8.00
36 Sterling Brown 3.00 8.00
37 Justin Patton 3.00 8.00
38 Caleb Swanigan 3.00 8.00

2017-18 Crown Royale Rookie Jerseys

STATED PRINT RUN 249 SER.#'d SETS
*PRIME/25: 1X TO 2.5X BASIC
1 Dwayne Bacon 1.25 3.00
2 Malik Monk 5.00 12.00
3 Tyler Dorsey 1.25 3.00
4 Zach Collins 2.00 5.00
5 John Collins 3.00 8.00
6 Lonzo Ball 6.00 15.00
7 Derrick White 5.00 12.00
8 Markelle Fultz 4.00 10.00
9 Sterling Brown 1.25 3.00
10 De'Aaron Fox 10.00 25.00
11 Wes Iwundu 1.25 3.00
12 Jonathan Isaac 3.00 8.00
13 Sindarius Thornwell 1.25 3.00
14 OG Anunoby 6.00 15.00
15 Justin Patton 1.25 3.00
16 Donovan Mitchell 12.00 30.00
17 Terrance Ferguson 1.25 3.00
18 Frank Ntilikina 1.50 4.00
19 Jarrett Allen 3.00 8.00
20 Josh Jackson 1.50 4.00
21 Davon Reed 1.25 3.00
22 Bam Adebayo 8.00 20.00
23 Tyler Lydon 1.25 3.00
24 TJ Leaf 1.25 3.00
25 Tony Bradley 1.25 3.00
26 Jayson Tatum 15.00 40.00
27 Jawun Evans 1.25 3.00
28 Dennis Smith Jr. 1.50 4.00
29 Ivan Rabb 1.25 3.00
30 Luke Kennard 2.50 6.00
31 D.J. Wilson 1.25 3.00
32 Harry Giles 1.25 3.00
33 Lauri Markkanen 8.00 20.00
34 Josh Hart 3.00 8.00
35 Caleb Swanigan 1.25 3.00
36 Kyle Kuzma 5.00 12.00
37 Semi Ojeleye 1.50 4.00
38 Jordan Bell 1.25 3.00
39 Frank Jackson 1.25 3.00
40 Frank Mason III 1.25 3.00

2017-18 Crown Royale Roundball Royalty

STATED PRINT RUN 99 SER.#'d SETS
*RED/75: .4X TO 1X BASIC
1 Kobe Bryant 15.00 40.00
2 Tracy McGrady 3.00 8.00
3 Bob Pettit 2.00 5.00
4 Shaquille O'Neal 6.00 15.00
5 Dennis Rodman 5.00 12.00
6 Paul Pierce 3.00 8.00
7 Ben Wallace 1.50 4.00
8 Tim Duncan 5.00 12.00
9 Reggie Miller 4.00 10.00
10 Allen Iverson 5.00 12.00
11 Ray Allen 3.00 8.00
12 George Mikan 5.00 12.00
13 John Havlicek 4.00 10.00
14 Gary Payton 3.00 8.00
15 Bill Russell 6.00 15.00
16 Rick Barry 2.50 6.00
17 Chris Webber 3.00 8.00
18 Julius Erving 5.00 12.00
19 Kareem Abdul-Jabbar 6.00 15.00
20 Magic Johnson 8.00 20.00
21 Jason Kidd 3.00 8.00
22 Alonzo Mourning 3.00 8.00
23 Patrick Ewing 3.00 8.00
24 Scottie Pippen 5.00 12.00
25 John Stockton 4.00 10.00
26 Bill Bradley 2.50 6.00
27 Dominique Wilkins 3.00 8.00
28 Kevin Garnett 5.00 12.00
29 Hakeem Olajuwon 4.00 10.00
30 Pete Maravich 5.00 12.00
31 Oscar Robertson 4.00 10.00
32 Steve Nash 3.00 8.00
33 David Robinson 4.00 10.00
34 Karl Malone 4.00 10.00
35 Wilt Chamberlain 6.00 15.00
36 Yao Ming 4.00 10.00
37 Anfernee Hardaway 5.00 12.00
38 Clyde Drexler 3.00 8.00
39 Stephon Marbury 1.50 4.00
40 Charles Barkley 5.00 12.00

2017-18 Crown Royale Roundball Royalty Blue

*BLUE: .6X TO 1.5X BASIC
STATED PRINT RUN 25 SER.#'d SETS
4 Shaquille O'Neal 15.00 40.00
5 Dennis Rodman 15.00 40.00
8 Tim Duncan 12.00 30.00
9 Reggie Miller 10.00 25.00
10 Allen Iverson 10.00 25.00
17 Chris Webber 15.00 40.00
22 Alonzo Mourning 12.00 30.00
28 Kevin Garnett 10.00 25.00
32 Steve Nash 12.00 30.00
33 David Robinson 10.00 25.00
35 Wilt Chamberlain 12.00 30.00
36 Yao Ming 10.00 25.00
40 Charles Barkley 20.00 50.00

2017-18 Crown Royale Silhouettes Rookies Prime

*PRIME: 2.5X TO 6X BASE
STATED PRINT RUN 25 SER.#'d SETS
203 Jonathan Isaac 125.00 300.00
215 Donovan Mitchell 1,000.00 3,000.00
217 Jarrett Allen 75.00 200.00
221 John Collins 200.00 400.00
227 OG Anunoby 150.00 400.00
229 Jayson Tatum 2,000.00 4,000.00
239 De'Aaron Fox 400.00 800.00

2018-19 Crown Royale

JSY AU PRINT RUN 199 SER.#'d SETS
EXCHANGE DEADLINE 7/23/2020
1 Bojan Bogdanovic .30 .75
2 Lou Williams .30 .75
3 Mikal Bridges RC 2.00 5.00
4 Eric Bledsoe .30 .75
5 Russell Westbrook .60 1.50
6 Kent Bazemore .25 .60
7 Damian Lillard 1.00 2.50
8 Kris Dunn .25 .60
9 Jonas Valanciunas .40 1.00
10 Reggie Jackson .30 .75
11 Jalen Brunson RC 3.00 8.00
12 Tobias Harris .30 .75
13 Gary Trent Jr. RC .75 2.00
14 Malcolm Brogdon .40 1.00
15 Dennis Schroder .30 .75
16 Taurean Prince .25 .60
17 CJ McCollum .40 1.00
18 Zach LaVine .60 1.50
19 Ricky Rubio .30 .75
20 Luke Kennard .30 .75
21 Jerome Robinson RC .40 1.00
22 Danilo Gallinari .30 .75
23 Troy Brown Jr. RC .50 1.25

24 Khris Middleton .40 1.00
25 Paul George .60 1.50
26 John Collins .40 1.00
27 Evan Turner .25 .60
28 Lauri Markkanen .60 1.50
29 Donovan Mitchell 1.25 3.00
30 Stanley Johnson .25 .60
31 Bruce Brown RC .75 2.00
32 Marcin Gortat .25 .60
33 De'Anthony Melton RC .75 2.00
34 Giannis Antetokounmpo 2.00 5.00
35 Steven Adams .30 .75
36 Jeremy Lin .60 1.50
37 Al-Farouq Aminu .25 .60
38 Jabari Parker .25 .60
39 Joe Ingles .30 .75
40 Blake Griffin .40 1.00
41 Donte DiVincenzo RC 1.00 2.50
42 Avery Bradley .25 .60
43 Kevin Huerter RC .75 2.00
44 John Henson .25 .60
45 Nerlens Noel .25 .60
46 Vince Carter .75 2.00
47 Jusuf Nurkic .30 .75
48 Robin Lopez .25 .60
49 Derrick Favors .25 .60
50 Andre Drummond .30 .75
51 Grayson Allen RC .75 2.00
52 Lonzo Ball .40 1.00
53 Aaron Holiday RC .60 1.50
54 Derrick Rose .75 2.00
55 Evan Fournier .30 .75
56 Kyrie Irving 1.00 2.50
57 De'Aaron Fox .75 2.00
58 George Hill .30 .75
59 Rudy Gobert .50 1.25
60 Stephen Curry 3.00 8.00
61 Deandre Ayton RC 1.25 3.00
62 LeBron James 3.00 8.00
63 Luka Doncic RC 12.00 30.00
64 Jimmy Butler .60 1.50
65 Terrence Ross .30 .75
66 Jaylen Brown .60 1.50
67 Bogdan Bogdanovic .40 1.00
68 JR Smith .40 1.00
69 John Wall .50 1.25
70 Klay Thompson 1.00 2.50
71 Moritz Wagner RC .75 2.00
72 Brandon Ingram .40 1.00
73 Robert Williams III RC .75 2.00
74 Andrew Wiggins .50 1.25
75 Aaron Gordon .40 1.00
76 Jayson Tatum 1.50 4.00
77 Buddy Hield .40 1.00
78 Kyle Korver .30 .75
79 Bradley Beal .50 1.25
80 Kevin Durant 1.50 4.00
81 Trae Young RC 3.00 8.00
82 Kyle Kuzma .40 1.00
83 Wendell Carter Jr. RC 1.00 2.50
84 Taj Gibson .25 .60
85 Nikola Vucevic .30 .75
86 Al Horford .40 1.00
87 Zach Randolph .30 .75
88 Kevin Love .30 .75
89 Otto Porter Jr. .30 .75
90 Draymond Green .50 1.25
91 Dzanan Musa RC .40 1.00
92 Kentavious Caldwell-Pope .25 .60
93 Elie Okobo RC .40 1.00
94 Karl-Anthony Towns .60 1.50
95 Jonathan Isaac .40 1.00
96 Gordon Hayward .40 1.00
97 Willie Cauley-Stein .25 .60
98 Tristan Thompson .25 .60
99 Kelly Oubre Jr. .40 1.00
100 DeMarcus Cousins .30 .75
101 Kevin Knox RC .50 1.25
102 Mike Conley .30 .75
103 Shai Gilgeous-Alexander RC 4.00 10.00
104 Elfrid Payton .30 .75
105 Ben Simmons .40 1.00
106 Spencer Dinwiddie .30 .75
107 DeMar DeRozan .50 1.25
108 Dennis Smith Jr. .25 .60
109 Dwight Howard .50 1.25
110 Chris Paul .75 2.00
111 Devonte' Graham RC .60 1.50
112 MarShon Brooks .25 .60
113 Miles Bridges 6.00 15.00
114 Jrue Holiday .50 1.25
115 JJ Redick .40 1.00
116 D'Angelo Russell .40 1.00
117 Pau Gasol .60 1.50
118 Wesley Matthews .25 .60
119 Kyle Anderson .25 .60
120 James Harden .75 2.00
121 Michael Porter Jr. RC 1.50 4.00
122 Dillon Brooks .40 1.00
123 Keita Bates-Diop RC .50 1.25
124 Julius Randle .40 1.00
125 Joel Embiid 1.00 2.50
126 DeMarre Carroll .25 .60
127 LaMarcus Aldridge .40 1.00
128 Harrison Barnes .30 .75
129 Fred VanVleet .50 1.25
130 Carmelo Anthony .60 1.50
131 Hamidou Diallo RC .60 1.50
132 JaMychal Green .25 .60
133 Zhaire Smith RC .40 1.00
134 Nikola Mirotic .25 .60
135 Markelle Fultz .30 .75
136 Jarrett Allen .40 1.00
137 Rudy Gay .40 1.00
138 Dirk Nowitzki 1.00 2.50
139 Dwight Powell .25 .60
140 Clint Capela .30 .75
141 Lonnie Walker IV RC .75 2.00
142 Marc Gasol .40 1.00
143 Josh Okogie RC .60 1.50
144 Anthony Davis 1.00 2.50
145 Dario Saric .30 .75
146 Rondae Hollis-Jefferson .25 .60
147 Dejounte Murray .50 1.25
148 DeAndre Jordan .30 .75
149 Will Barton .25 .60
150 Eric Gordon .30 .75
151 Chandler Hutchison RC .50 1.25
152 Goran Dragic .30 .75
153 Anfernee Simons RC 2.00 5.00
154 Tim Hardaway Jr. .25 .60
155 Devin Booker 1.00 2.50
156 Kemba Walker .30 .75
157 Kyle Lowry .40 1.00
158 Jamal Murray .75 2.00
159 Robert Covington .30 .75
160 Tyreke Evans .25 .60
161 Marvin Bagley III RC .60 1.50
162 Dion Waiters .25 .60
163 Jaren Jackson Jr. RC 3.00 8.00
164 Frank Ntilikina .25 .60
165 T.J. Warren .30 .75
166 Nicolas Batum .25 .60
167 Danny Green .30 .75
168 Isaiah Thomas .30 .75
169 Larry Nance Jr. .25 .60
170 Victor Oladipo .30 .75
171 Landry Shamet RC .60 1.50
172 James Johnson .25 .60
173 Jacob Evans III RC .40 1.00
174 Kristaps Porzingis .50 1.25
175 Trevor Ariza .25 .60
176 Michael Kidd-Gilchrist .25 .60
177 Kawhi Leonard 1.00 2.50
178 Gary Harris .30 .75
179 Terry Rozier .30 .75
180 Darren Collison .25 .60
181 Mo Bamba RC .60 1.50
182 Hassan Whiteside .30 .75
183 Collin Sexton RC 1.25 3.00
184 Enes Kanter .30 .75
185 Josh Jackson .25 .60
186 Cody Zeller .25 .60
187 Svi Mykhailiuk RC .50 1.25
188 Paul Millsap .30 .75
189 Jerami Grant .40 1.00
190 Thaddeus Young .25 .60
191 Omari Spellman RC .40 1.00
192 Bam Adebayo .60 1.50
193 Jevon Carter RC .60 1.50
194 Mario Hezonja .25 .60
195 Ryan Anderson .25 .60
196 Tony Parker .60 1.50
197 Serge Ibaka .30 .75
198 Nikola Jokic 2.00 5.00
199 Jeremy Lamb .25 .60
200 Myles Turner .40 1.00
201 Jalen Brunson JSY AU 25.00 60.00
202 Jerome Robinson JSY AU 3.00 8.00
203 Bruce Brown JSY AU 6.00 15.00
204 Donte DiVincenzo JSY AU 8.00 20.00
205 Grayson Allen JSY AU 6.00 15.00
206 Deandre Ayton JSY AU 40.00 100.00
207 Moritz Wagner JSY AU 6.00 15.00
208 Trae Young JSY AU 300.00 600.00
209 Dzanan Musa JSY AU 3.00 8.00
210 Kevin Knox JSY AU 4.00 10.00
211 Devonte' Graham JSY AU 5.00 12.00
212 Michael Porter Jr. JSY AU 75.00 200.00
213 Hamidou Diallo JSY AU 6.00 15.00
214 Lonnie Walker IV JSY AU 15.00 40.00
215 Chandler Hutchison JSY AU 4.00 10.00
216 Marvin Bagley III JSY AU 5.00 12.00
217 Landry Shamet JSY AU 6.00 15.00
218 Mo Bamba JSY AU 10.00 25.00
219 Omari Spellman JSY AU 3.00 8.00
220 Mikal Bridges JSY AU 15.00 40.00
221 Gary Trent Jr. JSY AU 6.00 15.00
222 Troy Brown Jr. JSY AU 4.00 10.00
223 De'Anthony Melton JSY AU 6.00 15.00
224 Kevin Huerter JSY AU 12.00 30.00
225 Aaron Holiday JSY AU 5.00 12.00
226 Luka Doncic JSY AU 600.00 1,200.00
227 Robert Williams III JSY AU 6.00 15.00
228 Wendell Carter Jr. JSY AU 20.00 50.00
229 Elie Okobo JSY AU 3.00 8.00
230 Shai Gilgeous-Alexander JSY AU 600.00 1,200.00
231 Jarred Vanderbilt JSY AU 6.00 15.00
232 Keita Bates-Diop JSY AU 4.00 10.00
233 Zhaire Smith JSY AU 3.00 8.00
234 Josh Okogie JSY AU 5.00 12.00
235 Anfernee Simons JSY AU 75.00 200.00
236 Jaren Jackson Jr. JSY AU 125.00 300.00
237 Jacob Evans III JSY AU 3.00 8.00
238 Collin Sexton JSY AU 10.00 25.00
239 Jevon Carter JSY AU 5.00 12.00
240 Svi Mykhailiuk JSY AU 4.00 10.00

2018-19 Crown Royale Crystal

*CRYSTAL: 1.2X TO 3X BASIC
*CRYSTAL RC: .75X TO 2X BASIC RC
STATED PRINT RUN 99 SER.#'d SETS
62 LeBron James 10.00 25.00
63 Luka Doncic 40.00 100.00

2018-19 Crown Royale Crystal Purple

*CRSTL PRPLE: 4X TO 10X BASIC
*CRSTL PRPLE RC: 2.5X TO 6X BASIC RC
STATED PRINT RUN 25 SER.#'d SETS
62 LeBron James 60.00 150.00
63 Luka Doncic 300.00 600.00

2018-19 Crown Royale Crystal Red

*CRSTL RED: 1.5X TO 4X BASIC
*CRSTL RED RC: 1X TO 2.5X BASIC RC
STATED PRINT RUN 49 SER.#'d SETS
62 LeBron James 20.00 50.00
63 Luka Doncic 150.00 400.00

2018-19 Crown Royale Autograph Relic Silhouettes

PRINT RUNS B/WN 25-99 COPIES PER
EXCHANGE DEADLINE 7/23/2020
1 Myles Turner/99 5.00 12.00
2 Dirk Nowitzki/25 EXCH 50.00 120.00
3 Charles Barkley/25 EXCH 150.00 400.00
4 Karl-Anthony Towns/49 15.00 40.00
5 Hakeem Olajuwon/49 EXCH 15.00 40.00
6 Stephen Curry/25 500.00 1,000.00
7 Kristaps Porzingis/99 12.00 30.00
8 Shaquille O'Neal/25 EXCH 60.00 150.00
9 Andrew Wiggins/49 8.00 20.00
10 Larry Bird/25 50.00 120.00
11 Enes Kanter/99 4.00 10.00
12 Julius Erving/25 40.00 100.00
13 Jason Kidd/49 20.00 50.00
14 Joel Embiid/49 EXCH 30.00 80.00
15 David Robinson/49 20.00 50.00
16 Kevin Durant/25 60.00 150.00
17 Harrison Barnes/99 4.00 10.00
18 Allen Iverson/25 60.00 150.00
19 Goran Dragic/99 4.00 10.00
20 Damian Lillard/25 20.00 50.00

2018-19 Crown Royale Crown Autographs

PRINT RUNS B/WN 49-99 COPIES PER
EXCHANGE DEADLINE 7/23/2020
*RED/40-49: .5X TO 1.2X p/r 60-99
*RED/40-49: .4X TO 1X p/r 49
*BLUE/35: .5X TO 1.2X p/r 60-99
*BLUE/35: .4X TO 1X p/r 49
*PURPLE/25: .6X TO 1.5X p/r 60-99
*PURPLE/25: .5X TO 1.2X p/r 49
1 Larry Bird/49 125.00 300.00
2 Horace Grant/99 8.00 20.00
3 Paul Pierce/49 30.00 80.00
4 Mark Aguirre/99 4.00 10.00
5 Dragan Bender/60 3.00 8.00
6 Toni Kukoc/99 8.00 20.00
7 JJ Redick/99 6.00 15.00
8 Gerald Green/99 4.00 10.00
9 Derrick Favors/99 3.00 8.00
10 Terry Rozier/99 6.00 15.00
11 Kobe Bryant/49 1,000.00 2,000.00
12 DeMarre Carroll/99 3.00 8.00
13 Jeremy Lin/60 12.00 30.00
14 Kevin Willis/99 4.00 10.00
15 Paul Millsap/99 4.00 10.00
16 Alex English/99 5.00 12.00
17 Nikola Mirotic/60 3.00 8.00
18 Marvin Williams/99 3.00 8.00
19 Mario Hezonja/99 3.00 8.00
20 Ralph Sampson/99 4.00 10.00
21 Kawhi Leonard/49 60.00 150.00
22 Ryan Anderson/99 3.00 8.00
23 Marcus Smart/99 5.00 12.00
24 Bill Cartwright/99 4.00 10.00
25 George Gervin/60 12.00 30.00
26 Tom Heinsohn/99 25.00 60.00
27 Tyson Chandler/60 4.00 10.00
28 Donovan Mitchell/49 30.00 80.00
29 Jalen Rose/99 8.00 20.00
30 Myles Turner/99 5.00 12.00
31 Alonzo Mourning/49 20.00 50.00
32 John Collins/99 5.00 12.00
33 Jerry Lucas/99 6.00 15.00
34 Mitch Richmond/99 8.00 20.00
35 Nick Van Exel/60 12.00 30.00
36 David Thompson/99 6.00 15.00
37 Danilo Gallinari/99 4.00 10.00
38 Patrick Beverley/99 3.00 8.00
39 Avery Johnson/99 4.00 10.00
40 Michael Kidd-Gilchrist/60 3.00 8.00
41 Andrew Wiggins/49 12.00 30.00
42 Frank Kaminsky/99 3.00 8.00
43 Zach Randolph/99 4.00 10.00
44 T.J. Warren/99 4.00 10.00
45 Kentavious Caldwell-Pope/99 3.00 8.00
46 Alvan Adams/99 4.00 10.00
47 Al Horford/60 5.00 12.00
48 Jayson Tatum/99 75.00 200.00
49 Chauncey Billups/60 6.00 15.00
50 Trevor Ariza/99 3.00 8.00
51 Ray Allen/49 25.00 60.00
52 Lauri Markkanen/99 6.00 15.00
53 Walt Frazier/99 12.00 30.00
54 Stephen Jackson/99 4.00 10.00
55 Eric Bledsoe/99 4.00 10.00
56 Thaddeus Young/60 3.00 8.00
57 Michael Carter-Williams/99 3.00 8.00
58 J.J. Barea/99 5.00 12.00
59 Marquese Chriss/99 3.00 8.00
60 Iman Shumpert/99 3.00 8.00

2018-19 Crown Royale Crown Autographs Rookies

STATED PRINT RUN 149 SER.#'d SETS
EXCHANGE DEADLINE 7/23/2020
*BLUE/49: .5X TO 1.2X BASIC
1 Gary Trent Jr. 6.00 15.00
2 Jarred Vanderbilt 6.00 15.00
3 Elie Okobo 3.00 8.00
4 Svi Mykhailiuk 4.00 10.00
5 Collin Sexton 10.00 25.00
6 Wendell Carter Jr. 8.00 20.00
7 Luka Doncic 800.00 1,500.00
8 Anfernee Simons 60.00 150.00
9 Zhaire Smith 3.00 8.00
10 De'Anthony Melton 6.00 15.00
11 Jalen Brunson 15.00 40.00
12 Devonte' Graham 5.00 12.00
13 Dzanan Musa 3.00 8.00
14 Mikal Bridges 15.00 40.00
15 Mo Bamba 5.00 12.00
16 Trae Young 200.00 500.00
19 Hamidou Diallo 5.00 12.00
20 Bruce Brown 6.00 15.00
21 Aaron Holiday 5.00 12.00
22 Jaren Jackson Jr. 60.00 150.00
23 Josh Okogie 5.00 12.00
24 Kevin Huerter 6.00 15.00
25 Troy Brown Jr. 4.00 10.00
26 Keita Bates-Diop 4.00 10.00
27 Shai Gilgeous-Alexander 150.00 400.00
28 Jevon Carter 5.00 12.00
29 Jacob Evans III 3.00 8.00
30 Robert Williams III 6.00 15.00
31 Grayson Allen 6.00 15.00
32 Marvin Bagley III 5.00 12.00
33 Lonnie Walker IV 6.00 15.00
34 Donte DiVincenzo 8.00 20.00
36 Michael Porter Jr. 12.00 30.00
37 Kevin Knox 4.00 10.00
38 Omari Spellman 3.00 8.00
40 Moritz Wagner 6.00 15.00

2018-19 Crown Royale Crown Autographs Rookies Purple

*PURPLE: .75X TO 2X BASIC
STATED PRINT RUN 25 SER.#'d SETS
EXCHANGE DEADLINE 7/23/2020
7 Luka Doncic 2,000.00 4,000.00
16 Trae Young 500.00 1,000.00
17 Deandre Ayton 60.00 150.00

2018-19 Crown Royale Crown Autographs Rookies Red

*RED: .4X TO 1X BASIC
STATED PRINT RUN 99 SER.#'d SETS
EXCHANGE DEADLINE 7/23/2020
16 Trae Young 300.00 600.00
17 Deandre Ayton 40.00 100.00

2018-19 Crown Royale Jerseys

1 Bradley Beal 3.00 8.00
2 Enes Kanter 2.00 5.00
3 Rodney Hood 2.00 5.00
4 Derrick Rose 5.00 12.00
5 Chris Webber 3.00 8.00
6 Jimmy Butler 4.00 10.00
7 Alvin Robertson 2.00 5.00
8 Dominique Wilkins 4.00 10.00
9 Kareem Abdul-Jabbar 15.00 40.00
10 Harrison Barnes 2.00 5.00
11 John Stockton 5.00 12.00
12 Tim Duncan 10.00 25.00
13 James Johnson 1.50 4.00
14 Rondae Hollis-Jefferson 1.50 4.00
15 Shaquille O'Neal 12.00 30.00
16 Lance Stephenson 2.00 5.00
17 Ben Simmons 2.50 6.00
18 Gordon Hayward 2.50 6.00
19 Magic Johnson 10.00 25.00
20 Jeff Teague 1.50 4.00
21 Larry Bird 10.00 25.00
22 Derrick Favors 1.50 4.00
23 Dennis Smith Jr. 1.50 4.00
24 Wesley Matthews 1.50 4.00
25 Reggie Miller 10.00 25.00
26 Karl-Anthony Towns 4.00 10.00
27 Nate Thurmond 2.00 5.00
28 Courtney Lee 1.50 4.00
29 Jamaal Wilkes 2.50 6.00
30 Paul Pierce 4.00 10.00
31 Russell Westbrook 4.00 10.00
32 Devin Harris 1.50 4.00
33 Pau Gasol 4.00 10.00
34 Kevin Garnett 10.00 25.00
35 Frank Ntilikina 1.50 4.00
36 J.J. Barea 2.50 6.00
37 Elvin Hayes 3.00 8.00
38 Rudy Gobert 3.00 8.00
39 Julius Erving 10.00 25.00
40 Caris LeVert 2.50 6.00
41 Jarrett Allen 2.50 6.00
42 George Hill 2.00 5.00
43 Grant Hill 4.00 10.00
44 Kris Dunn 1.50 4.00
45 Peja Stojakovic 2.00 5.00
46 Jamal Crawford 2.50 6.00
47 Artis Gilmore 3.00 8.00
48 Steven Adams 2.00 5.00
49 Dan Issel 3.00 8.00
50 DeMarre Carroll 1.50 4.00
51 Markelle Fultz 2.00 5.00
52 Dirk Nowitzki 10.00 25.00
53 Anfernee Hardaway 6.00 15.00
54 LeBron James 20.00 50.00
55 Stephon Marbury 3.00 8.00
56 Andrew Wiggins 3.00 8.00
57 John Havlicek 8.00 20.00
58 Dion Waiters 1.50 4.00
59 Isiah Thomas 8.00 20.00
60 Taj Gibson 1.50 4.00

2018-19 Crown Royale Kaboom!

1 Kevin Durant 400.00 800.00
2 LeBron James 1,500.00 3,000.00
3 Donovan Mitchell 150.00 400.00
4 Stephen Curry 500.00 1,000.00
5 Giannis Antetokounmpo 400.00 800.00
6 Kyrie Irving 150.00 400.00
7 Russell Westbrook 150.00 400.00
8 Anthony Davis 125.00 300.00
9 Damian Lillard 125.00 300.00
10 James Harden 125.00 300.00
11 DeMar DeRozan 125.00 300.00
12 Jimmy Butler 75.00 200.00
13 Ben Simmons 150.00 400.00
14 Jayson Tatum 500.00 1,000.00
15 Chris Paul 200.00 500.00
16 Kawhi Leonard 500.00 1,000.00
17 Joel Embiid 200.00 500.00
18 Lonzo Ball 125.00 300.00
19 Devin Booker 300.00 600.00
20 Kristaps Porzingis 75.00 200.00
21 Deandre Ayton 300.00 600.00
22 Marvin Bagley III 30.00 80.00
23 Luka Doncic 8,000.00 12,000.00
24 Jaren Jackson Jr. 200.00 500.00
25 Trae Young 1,000.00 2,000.00

2018-19 Crown Royale Mamba's Choice

STATED PRINT RUN 99 SER.#'d SETS
*RED/75: .5X TO 1.2X BASIC
*BLUE/49: .6X TO 1.5X BASIC
*PURPLE/25: 1X TO 2.5X BASIC
1 Deandre Ayton 5.00 12.00
2 Marvin Bagley III 2.50 6.00
3 Luka Doncic 200.00 500.00
4 Jaren Jackson Jr. 15.00 40.00
5 Trae Young 125.00 300.00
6 Mo Bamba 2.50 6.00
7 Wendell Carter Jr. 4.00 10.00
8 Collin Sexton 5.00 12.00
9 Kevin Knox 2.00 5.00
10 Mikal Bridges 8.00 20.00

2018-19 Crown Royale Pacific Marquee

1 Jaren Jackson Jr. 20.00 50.00
2 Jimmy Butler 6.00 15.00
3 De'Aaron Fox 8.00 20.00
4 Klay Thompson 10.00 25.00
5 Kevin Knox 3.00 8.00
6 Paul George 6.00 15.00
7 Dennis Smith Jr. 2.50 6.00
8 John Wall 5.00 12.00
9 Deandre Ayton 8.00 20.00
10 Devin Booker 15.00 40.00
11 Ben Simmons 4.00 10.00
12 Lauri Markkanen 6.00 15.00
13 Wendell Carter Jr. 6.00 15.00
14 James Harden 8.00 20.00
15 Victor Oladipo 3.00 8.00
16 CJ McCollum 4.00 10.00
17 Joel Embiid 10.00 25.00
18 Giannis Antetokounmpo 25.00 60.00
19 Kyrie Irving 10.00 25.00
20 Stephen Curry 75.00 200.00
21 Trae Young 75.00 200.00
22 Russell Westbrook 6.00 15.00
23 Collin Sexton 8.00 20.00
24 LeBron James 100.00 250.00
25 Mikal Bridges 12.00 30.00
26 Kevin Durant 40.00 100.00
27 Andre Drummond 3.00 8.00
28 Jaylen Brown 6.00 15.00
29 Marvin Bagley III 4.00 10.00
30 Chris Paul 8.00 20.00
31 Mo Bamba 4.00 10.00
32 DeAndre Jordan 3.00 8.00
33 Draymond Green 5.00 12.00
34 Andrew Wiggins 5.00 12.00
35 Jayson Tatum 15.00 40.00
36 Kawhi Leonard 10.00 25.00
37 DeMar DeRozan 5.00 12.00
38 Kristaps Porzingis 5.00 12.00
39 Luka Doncic 300.00 600.00
40 Bradley Beal 5.00 12.00
41 Blake Griffin 4.00 10.00
42 Damian Lillard 10.00 25.00
43 Donovan Mitchell 12.00 30.00
44 Kevin Love 3.00 8.00
45 Anthony Davis 10.00 25.00
46 Carmelo Anthony 6.00 15.00
47 DeMarcus Cousins 3.00 8.00
48 Dirk Nowitzki 10.00 25.00
49 Karl-Anthony Towns 6.00 15.00
50 Lonzo Ball 4.00 10.00

2018-19 Crown Royale Panini's Choice

STATED PRINT RUN 99 SER.#'d SETS
*RED/75: .5X TO 1.2X BASIC
*BLUE/49: .6X TO 1.5X BASIC
1 Marc Gasol 2.00 5.00
2 Kyrie Irving 5.00 12.00
3 Karl-Anthony Towns 3.00 8.00
4 Zach LaVine 3.00 8.00
5 Ben Simmons 2.00 5.00
6 Blake Griffin 2.00 5.00
7 De'Aaron Fox 4.00 10.00
8 Draymond Green 2.50 6.00
9 Donovan Mitchell 6.00 15.00
10 Victor Oladipo 1.50 4.00
11 Goran Dragic 1.50 4.00
12 Jayson Tatum 12.00 30.00
13 Anthony Davis 5.00 12.00
14 Dennis Smith Jr. 1.25 3.00
15 Joel Embiid 8.00 20.00
16 Andre Drummond 1.50 4.00
17 DeMar DeRozan 2.50 6.00
18 DeMarcus Cousins 1.50 4.00
19 John Wall 2.50 6.00
20 Lou Williams 1.50 4.00
21 Giannis Antetokounmpo 12.00 30.00
22 Jaylen Brown 6.00 15.00
23 Kristaps Porzingis 2.50 6.00
24 Dirk Nowitzki 8.00 20.00
25 Devin Booker 12.00 30.00
26 Stephen Curry 20.00 50.00
27 LaMarcus Aldridge 2.00 5.00
28 Chris Paul 8.00 20.00
29 Bradley Beal 2.50 6.00
30 Lonzo Ball 3.00 8.00
31 Jimmy Butler 3.00 8.00
32 Lauri Markkanen 3.00 8.00
33 Russell Westbrook 3.00 8.00
34 DeAndre Jordan 1.50 4.00
35 Damian Lillard 5.00 12.00
36 Klay Thompson 10.00 25.00
37 Kyle Lowry 2.00 5.00
38 James Harden 4.00 10.00
39 Aaron Gordon 2.00 5.00
40 LeBron James 20.00 50.00
41 Andrew Wiggins 2.50 6.00
42 Kevin Love 1.50 4.00
43 Paul George 3.00 8.00
44 Nikola Jokic 10.00 25.00
45 CJ McCollum 2.00 5.00
46 Kevin Durant 12.00 30.00
47 Kawhi Leonard 12.00 30.00
48 Carmelo Anthony 3.00 8.00
49 Nikola Vucevic 1.50 4.00
50 Kyle Kuzma 2.00 5.00

2018-19 Crown Royale Panini's Choice Purple

*PURPLE: .75X TO 2X BASIC
STATED PRINT RUN 25 SER.#'d SETS
100 LeBron James 40.00 100.00

2018-19 Crown Royale Power in the Paint

1 Deandre Ayton 6.00 15.00
2 Marvin Bagley III 15.00 40.00
3 Jaren Jackson Jr. 15.00 40.00
4 Mo Bamba 8.00 20.00
5 Wendell Carter Jr. 5.00 12.00
6 DeMarcus Cousins 2.50 6.00
7 Karl-Anthony Towns 5.00 12.00
8 Marc Gasol 3.00 8.00
9 Nikola Jokic 15.00 40.00
10 Rudy Gobert 4.00 10.00
11 Hassan Whiteside 2.50 6.00
12 DeAndre Jordan 2.50 6.00
13 Joel Embiid 8.00 20.00
14 Andre Drummond 2.50 6.00
15 Anthony Davis 8.00 20.00
16 Kareem Abdul-Jabbar 10.00 25.00
17 Shaquille O'Neal 10.00 25.00
18 Hakeem Olajuwon 4.00 10.00
19 Wilt Chamberlain 10.00 25.00
20 Bill Russell 10.00 25.00
21 David Robinson 6.00 15.00
22 Patrick Ewing 5.00 12.00
23 Charles Barkley 20.00 50.00
24 Tim Duncan 10.00 25.00
25 Kevin Garnett 10.00 25.00

2018-19 Crown Royale Rookie Autograph Relic Silhouettes Prime

*PRIME: 3X TO 8X BASE
STATED PRINT RUN 25 SER.#'d SETS
EXCHANGE DEADLINE 7/23/2020
205 Grayson Allen 60.00 150.00
206 Deandre Ayton 300.00 600.00
208 Trae Young 3,000.00 6,000.00
211 Devonte' Graham 40.00 100.00
212 Michael Porter Jr. 1,000.00 2,000.00
220 Mikal Bridges 100.00 250.00
226 Luka Doncic 20,000.00 40,000.00
230 Shai Gilgeous-Alexander 2,500.00 5,000.00
235 Anfernee Simons 200.00 500.00
236 Jaren Jackson Jr. 1,000.00 2,000.00
238 Collin Sexton 400.00 800.00

2018-19 Crown Royale Rookie Jersey Autographs

STATED PRINT RUN 199 SER.#'d SETS
EXCHANGE DEADLINE 7/23/2020
*PRIME/25: .75X TO 2X BASIC
1 Zhaire Smith 2.50 6.00
2 Hamidou Diallo 4.00 10.00
3 Jacob Evans III 2.50 6.00
4 Landry Shamet 4.00 10.00
5 Gary Trent Jr. 5.00 12.00
6 Jalen Brunson 20.00 50.00
7 Aaron Holiday 4.00 10.00
8 Grayson Allen 5.00 12.00
9 Elie Okobo 2.50 6.00
10 Dzanan Musa 2.50 6.00
11 Josh Okogie 6.00 15.00
12 Lonnie Walker IV 10.00 25.00
13 Collin Sexton 8.00 20.00
14 Mo Bamba 10.00 25.00
15 Troy Brown Jr. 3.00 8.00
16 Jerome Robinson 2.50 6.00
17 Luka Doncic 1,000.00 2,000.00
18 Deandre Ayton 30.00 80.00
19 Shai Gilgeous-Alexander 500.00 1,000.00
20 Kevin Knox 3.00 8.00
21 Anfernee Simons 60.00 150.00
22 Chandler Hutchison 3.00 8.00
23 Jevon Carter 4.00 10.00
24 Omari Spellman 2.50 6.00
25 De'Anthony Melton 5.00 12.00
26 Bruce Brown 5.00 12.00
27 Robert Williams III 5.00 12.00
28 Moritz Wagner 5.00 12.00
29 Jarred Vanderbilt 5.00 12.00
30 Devonte' Graham 4.00 10.00
31 Jaren Jackson Jr. 150.00 400.00
32 Marvin Bagley III 4.00 10.00
33 Svi Mykhailiuk 3.00 8.00
34 Mikal Bridges 12.00 30.00
35 Kevin Huerter 6.00 15.00
36 Donte DiVincenzo 6.00 15.00
37 Wendell Carter Jr. 10.00 25.00
38 Trae Young 150.00 400.00
39 Keita Bates-Diop 3.00 8.00
40 Michael Porter Jr. 40.00 100.00

2018-19 Crown Royale Rookie Jerseys

1 Zhaire Smith 1.25 3.00
2 Hamidou Diallo 2.00 5.00
3 Jacob Evans III 1.25 3.00
4 Landry Shamet 2.00 5.00
5 Gary Trent Jr. 2.50 6.00
6 Jalen Brunson 10.00 25.00
7 Aaron Holiday 2.00 5.00
8 Grayson Allen 2.50 6.00
9 Elie Okobo 1.25 3.00
10 Dzanan Musa 1.25 3.00
11 Josh Okogie 2.00 5.00
12 Lonnie Walker IV 2.50 6.00
13 Collin Sexton 2.50 6.00
14 Mo Bamba 2.00 5.00
15 Troy Brown Jr. 1.50 4.00
16 Jerome Robinson 1.25 3.00
17 Luka Doncic 20.00 50.00
18 Deandre Ayton 5.00 12.00
19 Shai Gilgeous-Alexander 2.50 6.00
20 Kevin Knox 1.50 4.00
21 Anfernee Simons 6.00 15.00
22 Chandler Hutchison 1.50 4.00
23 Jevon Carter 2.00 5.00
24 Omari Spellman 1.25 3.00
25 De'Anthony Melton 2.50 6.00
26 Bruce Brown 2.50 6.00
27 Robert Williams III 2.50 6.00
28 Moritz Wagner 2.50 6.00
29 Jarred Vanderbilt 2.50 6.00
30 Devonte' Graham 2.00 5.00
31 Jaren Jackson Jr. 4.00 10.00
32 Marvin Bagley III 4.00 10.00
33 Svi Mykhailiuk 1.50 4.00
34 Mikal Bridges 6.00 15.00
35 Kevin Huerter 2.50 6.00
36 Donte DiVincenzo 3.00 8.00
37 Wendell Carter Jr. 3.00 8.00
38 Trae Young 5.00 12.00
39 Keita Bates-Diop 1.50 4.00
40 Michael Porter Jr. 5.00 12.00

2018-19 Crown Royale Rookie Royalty

STATED PRINT RUN 99 SER.#'d SETS
*RED/75: .5X TO 1.2X BASIC
*BLUE/49: .6X TO 1.5X BASIC
*PURPLE/25: 1.2X TO 3X BASIC
1 Gary Trent Jr. 1.50 4.00
2 Jalen Brunson 6.00 15.00
3 Aaron Holiday 1.25 3.00
4 Grayson Allen 1.50 4.00
5 Elie Okobo .75 2.00
6 Dzanan Musa .75 2.00
7 Zhaire Smith .75 2.00
8 Hamidou Diallo 1.25 3.00
9 Jacob Evans III .75 2.00
10 Landry Shamet 1.25 3.00
11 Troy Brown Jr. 1.00 2.50
12 Jerome Robinson .75 2.00
13 Luka Doncic 60.00 150.00
14 Deandre Ayton 2.50 6.00
15 Shai Gilgeous-Alexander 8.00 20.00
16 Kevin Knox 1.00 2.50
17 Josh Okogie 1.25 3.00
18 Lonnie Walker IV 1.50 4.00
19 Collin Sexton 2.50 6.00
20 Mo Bamba 1.25 3.00
21 De'Anthony Melton 1.50 4.00
22 Bruce Brown 1.50 4.00
23 Robert Williams III 1.50 4.00
24 Moritz Wagner 1.50 4.00
25 Jarred Vanderbilt 1.50 4.00
26 Devonte' Graham 1.25 3.00
27 Anfernee Simons 4.00 10.00
28 Chandler Hutchison 1.00 2.50
29 Omari Spellman .75 2.00
30 Jevon Carter 1.25 3.00
31 Kevin Huerter 1.50 4.00
32 Donte DiVincenzo 2.00 5.00
33 Wendell Carter Jr. 2.00 5.00
34 Trae Young 40.00 100.00
35 Keita Bates-Diop 1.00 2.50
36 Michael Porter Jr. 3.00 8.00
37 Jaren Jackson Jr. 6.00 15.00
38 Marvin Bagley III 1.25 3.00
39 Miles Bridges 2.00 5.00
40 Mikal Bridges 4.00 10.00

2019-20 Crown Royale

JSY AU PRINT RUN 49-199 SER.#'d SETS
1 Cameron Johnson RC 1.00 2.50
2 Chris Paul .75 2.00
3 Darius Bazley RC .40 1.00
4 CJ McCollum .40 1.00
5 Kevin Durant 1.25 3.00
6 Mike Conley .30 .75
7 Kristaps Porzingis .50 1.25
8 Russell Westbrook .60 1.50
9 Darius Garland RC 1.50 4.00
10 Goran Dragic .30 .75
11 PJ Washington Jr. RC 1.25 3.00
12 Steven Adams .30 .75
13 Ty Jerome RC .75 2.00
14 Hassan Whiteside .25 .60
15 DeAndre Jordan .30 .75
16 Donovan Mitchell .75 2.00
17 Jamal Murray .60 1.50
18 James Harden .75 2.00
19 Zion Williamson RC 40.00 100.00
20 Jimmy Butler .75 2.00
21 Tyler Herro RC 2.00 5.00
22 Aaron Gordon .40 1.00
23 Nassir Little RC .60 1.50
24 De'Aaron Fox .60 1.50
25 Terry Rozier .30 .75
26 Rudy Gobert .50 1.25
27 Paul Millsap .30 .75
28 Victor Oladipo .30 .75
29 Ja Morant RC 20.00 50.00
30 Giannis Antetokounmpo 2.00 5.00
31 Romeo Langford RC .40 1.00
32 Nikola Vucevic .30 .75
33 Keldon Johnson RC 1.25 3.00
34 Buddy Hield .30 .75
35 Miles Bridges .40 1.00
36 John Wall .50 1.25
37 Nikola Jokic 2.00 5.00
38 Malcolm Brogdon .30 .75
39 RJ Barrett RC 1.50 4.00
40 Khris Middleton .40 1.00
41 Sekou Doumbouya RC .40 1.00
42 Ben Simmons .40 1.00
43 Kevin Porter Jr. RC .75 2.00
44 Marvin Bagley III .30 .75
45 Zach LaVine .60 1.50
46 Bradley Beal .50 1.25
47 Blake Griffin .40 1.00
48 Paul George .60 1.50
49 De'Andre Hunter RC 1.50 4.00
50 Andrew Wiggins .50 1.25
51 Carsen Edwards RC .50 1.25
52 Joel Embiid .75 2.00
53 Trae Young 1.00 2.50
54 DeMar DeRozan .50 1.25
55 Lauri Markkanen .50 1.25
56 Isaiah Thomas .30 .75
57 Andre Drummond .30 .75
58 Kawhi Leonard 1.00 2.50
59 Jarrett Culver RC .40 1.00
60 Karl-Anthony Towns .60 1.50
61 Nickeil Alexander-Walker RC .60 1.50
62 Josh Richardson .25 .60
63 John Collins .40 1.00
64 LaMarcus Aldridge .40 1.00
65 Wendell Carter Jr. .40 1.00
66 Ricky Rubio .30 .75
67 Stephen Curry 3.00 8.00
68 LeBron James 3.00 8.00
69 Coby White RC 1.25 3.00
70 Brandon Ingram .40 1.00
71 Goga Bitadze RC .60 1.50
72 Devin Booker .10 .25
73 Kemba Walker .30 .75
74 Pascal Siakam .60 1.50
75 Collin Sexton .50 1.25
76 Tobias Harris .30 .75
77 Klay Thompson 1.00 2.50
78 Anthony Davis 1.00 2.50
79 Jaxson Hayes RC .60 1.50
80 Lonzo Ball .40 1.00
81 Luka Samanic RC .50 1.25
82 Deandre Ayton .40 1.00
83 Jayson Tatum 1.50 4.00
84 Marc Gasol .40 1.00
85 Kevin Love .40 1.00
86 Dennis Smith Jr. .25 .60
87 D'Angelo Russell .30 .75
88 Jaren Jackson Jr. .60 1.50
89 Rui Hachimura RC 1.50 4.00
90 Kevin Knox II .25 .60
91 Matisse Thybulle RC .75 2.00
92 Damian Lillard 1.00 2.50
93 Kyrie Irving .75 2.00
94 Kyle Lowry .40 1.00
95 Luka Doncic 2.50 6.00
96 Jrue Holiday .50 1.25
97 Draymond Green .50 1.25
98 Jonas Valanciunas .30 .75
99 Cam Reddish RC .60 1.50

00 Julius Randle .50 1.25
01 Isaiah Roby JSY AU/199 4.00 10.00
02 Keldon Johnson JSY AU/199 10.00 25.00
03 Mfiondu Kabengele JSY AU/199 4.00 10.00
04 Bol Bol JSY AU/199 8.00 20.00
05 Admiral Schofield JSY AU/199 4.00 10.00
06 Dylan Windler JSY AU/199 4.00 10.00
07 Ty Jerome JSY AU/199 6.00 15.00
08 Bruno Fernando JSY AU/199 4.00 10.00
09 KZ Okpala JSY AU/199 4.00 10.00
10 Q.Weatherspoon JSY AU/199 3.00 8.00
111 Goga Bitadze JSY AU/199 5.00 12.00
112 Jaxson Hayes JSY AU/199 5.00 12.00
113 Jarrett Culver JSY AU/199 3.00 8.00
114 N.Alexander-Walker JSY AU/199 5.00 12.00
115 Sekou Doumbouya JSY AU/199 3.00 8.00
116 De'Andre Hunter JSY AU/199 12.00 30.00
117 Ja Morant JSY AU/199 200.00 500.00
118 PJ Washington Jr. JSY AU/199 10.00 25.00
119 Cam Reddish JSY AU/199 5.00 12.00
120 Matisse Thybulle JSY AU/199 6.00 15.00
121 Grant Williams JSY AU/199 5.00 12.00
122 Cody Martin JSY AU/199 5.00 12.00
123 Carsen Edwards JSY AU/199 4.00 10.00
124 Tremont Waters JSY AU/199 4.00 10.00
125 Ignas Brazdeikis JSY AU/199 4.00 10.00
126 Kevin Porter Jr. JSY AU/199 6.00 15.00
127 Jordan Poole JSY AU/199 12.00 30.00
128 Jaylen Nowell JSY AU/199 4.00 10.00
129 Eric Paschall JSY AU/199 4.00 10.00
130 Nassir Little JSY AU/199 5.00 12.00
131 Zion Williamson JSY AU/49 1,000.00 3,000.00
132 Tyler Herro JSY AU/199 125.00 300.00
133 C.Johnson JSY AU/199 8.00 20.00
134 Brandon Clarke JSY AU/199 20.00 50.00
136 Rui Hachimura JSY AU/199 60.00 150.00
137 Coby White JSY AU/199 60.00 150.00
138 Chuma Okeke JSY AU/199 5.00 12.00
139 R.Langford JSY AU/199 3.00 8.00
140 RJ Barrett JSY AU/199 40.00 100.00

2019-20 Crown Royale Crystal
*CRYSTAL: .75X TO 2X BASIC
*CRYSTAL RC: .5X TO 1.2X BASIC RC
30 Giannis Antetokounmpo 6.00 15.00
68 LeBron James 40.00 100.00
95 Luka Doncic 10.00 25.00

2019-20 Crown Royale Crystal Blue
*CRYSTAL BLUE: 1.2X TO 3X BASIC
*CRYSTAL BLUE RC: .75X TO 2X BASIC RC
STATED PRINT RUN 99 SER.#'d SETS
30 Giannis Antetokounmpo 10.00 25.00
68 LeBron James 60.00 150.00
95 Luka Doncic 15.00 40.00

2019-20 Crown Royale Crystal Purple
*CRSTL PRPLE: 3X TO 8X BASIC
STATED PRINT RUN 25 SER.#'d SETS
30 Giannis Antetokounmpo 30.00 80.00
68 LeBron James 200.00 500.00
95 Luka Doncic 50.00 120.00

2019-20 Crown Royale Crystal Red
*CRSTL RED: 1.5X TO 4X BASIC
*CRSTL RED RC: 1X TO 2.5X BASIC RC
STATED PRINT RUN 49 SER.#'d SETS
30 Giannis Antetokounmpo 12.00 30.00
68 LeBron James 100.00 250.00
95 Luka Doncic 20.00 50.00

2019-20 Crown Royale Air to the Throne
STATED PRINT RUN 99 SER.#'d SETS
*BLUE/75: .5X TO 1.2X BASIC
*RED/49: .6X TO 1.5X BASIC
*PURPLE/25: 1.2X TO 3X BASIC
1 Giannis/Hachimura 12.00 30.00
2 Allen/Hayes 1.25 3.00
3 Fox/Morant 30.00 80.00
4 Hunter/Leonard 3.00 8.00
5 Porter Jr./LaVine 2.00 5.00
6 Garland/Irving 3.00 8.00
7 Culver/George 2.00 5.00
8 White/Nash 8.00 20.00
9 James/Williamson 200.00 500.00
10 Harden/Barrett 8.00 20.00

2019-20 Crown Royale Autograph Relic Silhouettes
PRINT RUNS B/WN 25-99 COPIES PER
EXCHANGE DEADLINE 7/29/2021
1 Jaren Jackson Jr./25 8.00 20.00
2 Damian Lillard/25 12.00 30.00
3 Kyrie Irving/25 10.00 25.00
4 Anthony Davis/25 12.00 30.00
5 Karl-Anthony Towns/25 8.00 20.00
6 Lonzo Ball/49 15.00 40.00
7 Donovan Mitchell/49 10.00 25.00
8 Kevin Love/49 5.00 12.00
9 Ersan Ilyasova/49 3.00 8.00
10 Tony Parker/49 8.00 20.00
11 Kristaps Porzingis/49 10.00 25.00
13 LaMarcus Aldridge/49 5.00 12.00
14 Mike Conley/49 4.00 10.00
15 Lauri Markkanen/49 6.00 15.00
16 Nikola Jokic/99 150.00 400.00
17 Khris Middleton/99 8.00 20.00
18 Danilo Gallinari/99 4.00 10.00
19 Julius Randle/99 6.00 15.00
20 Nikola Vucevic/99 4.00 10.00
21 Wendell Carter Jr./99 5.00 12.00
22 Malcolm Brogdon/99 4.00 10.00
23 Willie Cauley-Stein/99 3.00 8.00
24 Collin Sexton/99 6.00 15.00
25 Myles Turner/99 5.00 12.00
26 Caris LeVert/99 10.00 25.00
27 Thaddeus Young/99 3.00 8.00
28 J.J. Barea/99 4.00 10.00
29 De'Aaron Fox/49 15.00 40.00
30 Jarrett Allen/99 5.00 12.00

2019-20 Crown Royale Coat of Arms Materials
1 Donovan Mitchell 4.00 10.00
2 James Harden 4.00 10.00
3 Victor Oladipo 1.50 4.00
4 Trae Young 5.00 12.00
5 Terry Rozier 1.50 4.00
6 Jimmy Butler 4.00 10.00
7 Stephen Curry 40.00 100.00
8 Russell Westbrook 3.00 8.00
9 Paul George 3.00 8.00
10 Joel Embiid 4.00 10.00
11 Giannis Antetokounmpo 20.00 50.00
12 John Wall 2.50 6.00
13 Anthony Davis 5.00 12.00
14 Ben Simmons 2.00 5.00
15 LeBron James 40.00 100.00
16 Kyrie Irving 4.00 10.00
17 Kristaps Porzingis 2.50 6.00
18 Kevin Love 2.00 5.00
19 Kemba Walker 1.50 4.00
20 Kawhi Leonard 5.00 12.00

2019-20 Crown Royale Crown Autographs
STATED PRINT RUN 49 SER.#'d SETS
EXCHANGE DEADLINE 7/29/2021
*BLUE/25: .5X TO 1.2X BASIC
1 DeMarcus Cousins 4.00 10.00
2 Alex English 6.00 15.00
3 Artis Gilmore 6.00 15.00
4 Joe Harris 4.00 10.00
5 Jason Terry 4.00 10.00
6 Sarunas Marciulionis 3.00 8.00
7 Robert Parish 6.00 15.00
8 Allonzo Trier 3.00 8.00
9 Magic Johnson 15.00 40.00
10 Shane Battier 4.00 10.00
11 Trae Young 125.00 300.00
12 Toni Kukoc 6.00 15.00
13 Nikola Vucevic 4.00 10.00
14 Jarrett Allen 5.00 12.00
15 Malcolm Brogdon 4.00 10.00
16 Mychal Thompson 3.00 8.00
17 Louie Dampier 5.00 12.00
18 Wesley Matthews 3.00 8.00
19 Jerry West 8.00 20.00
20 Michael Porter Jr. 8.00 20.00
21 Lauri Markkanen 6.00 15.00
22 Robert Covington 3.00 8.00
23 Kentavious Caldwell-Pope 4.00 10.00
24 Rashard Lewis 4.00 10.00
25 Pascal Siakam 8.00 20.00
26 Antonio McDyess 4.00 10.00
27 Lenny Wilkens 6.00 15.00
28 Montrezl Harrell 4.00 10.00
29 Andrew Wiggins 4.00 10.00
30 Elvin Hayes 6.00 15.00
31 P.J. Tucker 4.00 10.00
32 Glen Rice 4.00 10.00
33 Eric Bledsoe 4.00 10.00
34 Paul Silas 4.00 10.00
35 Jalen Rose 4.00 10.00
36 Rudy Tomjanovich 4.00 10.00
37 Kevin Knox II 3.00 8.00
38 Thaddeus Young 3.00 8.00
39 Hakeem Olajuwon 12.00 30.00
40 Nate McMillan 4.00 10.00
41 Christian Laettner 5.00 12.00
42 Gary Clark 3.00 8.00
43 Julius Randle 6.00 15.00
44 Sam Perkins 4.00 10.00
45 Willie Cauley-Stein 3.00 8.00
46 Larry Johnson 6.00 15.00
47 George Gervin 8.00 20.00
48 Carlos Boozer 4.00 10.00
49 David Robinson 10.00 25.00
50 Ersan Ilyasova 3.00 8.00
51 Luka Doncic 200.00 500.00
52 Quinn Cook 4.00 10.00
53 Otto Porter Jr. 3.00 8.00
54 Charlie Ward 4.00 10.00
55 Latrell Sprewell 6.00 15.00
56 Terrence Ross 5.00 12.00
57 Danny Green 4.00 10.00
58 Josh Hart 4.00 10.00
59 Chris Bosh 6.00 15.00
60 Sam Cassell 4.00 10.00

2019-20 Crown Royale Crown Jewel Signatures
STATED PRINT RUN 25 SER.#'d SETS
EXCHANGE DEADLINE 7/29/2021
1 Kobe Bryant 500.00 1,000.00
2 Kevin Durant 60.00 150.00
3 Kyrie Irving 30.00 80.00
4 Anthony Davis 40.00 100.00
5 Damian Lillard 30.00 80.00
6 Charles Barkley 75.00 200.00
7 Magic Johnson 50.00 120.00
8 Larry Bird 50.00 120.00
9 Julius Erving 40.00 100.00
10 Shaquille O'Neal 60.00 150.00

2019-20 Crown Royale Crown Rookie Autographs
STATED PRINT RUN 49-99 SER.#'d SETS
*BLUE/25-75: .5X TO 1.2X BASIC
*BLUE/25: .75X TO 1X BASIC
*PURPLE/25: .75X TP 2X BASIC
*RED/49: .6X TO 1.5X BASIC
*RED/20: .75X TO 2X BASIC
1 KZ Okpala/99 4.00 10.00
2 Quinndary Weatherspoon/99 3.00 8.00
3 Isaiah Roby/99 4.00 10.00
4 Keldon Johnson/99 10.00 25.00
5 Mfiondu Kabengele/99 4.00 10.00
6 Bol Bol/99 10.00 25.00
7 Admiral Schofield/99 4.00 10.00
8 Dylan Windler/99 4.00 10.00
9 Ty Jerome/99 6.00 15.00
10 Bruno Fernando/99 4.00 10.00
11 Cam Reddish/49 5.00 12.00
12 Matisse Thybulle/99 8.00 20.00
13 Goga Bitadze/99 5.00 12.00
14 Jaxson Hayes/99 5.00 12.00
15 Jarrett Culver/49 3.00 8.00
16 Nickeil Alexander-Walker/99 5.00 12.00
17 Sekou Doumbouya/99 3.00 8.00
18 De'Andre Hunter/49 12.00 30.00
19 Ja Morant/49 200.00 500.00
20 PJ Washington Jr./99 10.00 25.00
21 Eric Paschall/99 4.00 10.00
22 Nassir Little/99 5.00 12.00
23 Grant Williams/99 5.00 12.00
24 Cody Martin/99 5.00 12.00
25 Carsen Edwards/99 4.00 10.00
26 Tremont Waters/99 4.00 10.00
27 Ignas Brazdeikis/99 4.00 10.00
28 Kevin Porter Jr./99 6.00 15.00
29 Jordan Poole/99 10.00 25.00
30 Jaylen Nowell/99 4.00 10.00
31 Romeo Langford/99 3.00 8.00
32 RJ Barrett/49 40.00 100.00
33 Zion Williamson/99 500.00 1,000.00
34 Tyler Herro/99 20.00 50.00
35 Cameron Johnson/99 8.00 20.00
36 Brandon Clarke/99 6.00 15.00
37 Luka Samanic/99 4.00 10.00
38 Rui Hachimura/49 12.00 30.00
39 Coby White/49 10.00 25.00
40 Chuma Okeke/99 5.00 12.00

2019-20 Crown Royale Hall of Fame Memorabilia
1 Allen Iverson 8.00 20.00
2 Patrick Ewing 5.00 12.00
3 Scottie Pippen 8.00 20.00
4 Clyde Drexler 5.00 12.00
5 Yao Ming 8.00 20.00
6 Grant Hill 5.00 12.00
7 Hakeem Olajuwon 6.00 15.00
8 Shaquille O'Neal 12.00 30.00
9 Karl Malone 6.00 15.00
10 Larry Bird 12.00 30.00

2019-20 Crown Royale Heirs to the Throne Materials
1 RJ Barrett 5.00 12.00
2 Romeo Langford 1.25 3.00
3 Ignas Brazdeikis 1.50 4.00
4 Cody Martin 2.00 5.00
5 Coby White 4.00 10.00
6 Chuma Okeke 2.00 5.00
7 Dylan Windler 1.50 4.00
8 Eric Paschall 1.50 4.00
9 Darius Bazley 1.25 3.00
10 Jarrett Culver 1.25 3.00
11 Isaiah Roby 1.50 4.00
12 KZ Okpala 1.50 4.00
13 Goga Bitadze 2.00 5.00
14 Bol Bol 3.00 8.00
15 Cam Reddish 2.00 5.00
16 Sekou Doumbouya 1.25 3.00
17 De'Andre Hunter 5.00 12.00
18 Rui Hachimura 5.00 12.00
19 Ty Jerome 2.50 6.00
20 Keldon Johnson 4.00 10.00
21 Bruno Fernando 1.50 4.00
22 Ja Morant 12.00 30.00
23 Tyler Herro 6.00 15.00
24 Matisse Thybulle 2.50 6.00
25 Nickeil Alexander-Walker 2.00 5.00
26 Jaxson Hayes 2.00 5.00
27 Nassir Little 2.00 5.00
28 Cameron Johnson 3.00 8.00
29 Jordan Poole 5.00 12.00
30 Grant Williams 2.00 5.00
31 Admiral Schofield 1.50 4.00
32 Kyle Guy 1.50 4.00
33 Luka Samanic 1.50 4.00
34 Carsen Edwards 1.50 4.00
35 Brandon Clarke 2.50 6.00
36 Zion Williamson 20.00 50.00
37 Quinndary Weatherspoon 1.25 3.00
38 Mfiondu Kabengele 1.50 4.00
39 Kevin Porter Jr. 2.50 6.00
40 PJ Washington Jr. 4.00 10.00

2019-20 Crown Royale Kaboom!
1 Kyrie Irving 200.00 500.00
2 De'Andre Hunter 400.00 800.00
3 James Harden 100.00 250.00
4 Coby White 100.00 250.00
5 Ben Simmons 100.00 250.00
6 Charles Barkley 200.00 500.00
7 Paul George 125.00 300.00
8 Damian Lillard 200.00 500.00
9 LeBron James 1,500.00 3,000.00
10 Ja Morant 2,000.00 4,000.00
11 Giannis Antetokounmpo 300.00 600.00
12 Jarrett Culver 100.00 250.00
13 Russell Westbrook 75.00 200.00
14 Rui Hachimura 200.00 500.00
15 Luka Doncic 2,000.00 4,000.00
16 Kobe Bryant 1,500.00 3,000.00
17 Kawhi Leonard 125.00 300.00
18 Zion Williamson 2,500.00 5,000.00
19 Stephen Curry 400.00 800.00
20 RJ Barrett 500.00 1,000.00
21 Anthony Davis 300.00 600.00
22 Darius Garland 200.00 500.00
23 Kevin Garnett 150.00 400.00
24 Cam Reddish 125.00 300.00
25 Trae Young 300.00 800.00

2019-20 Crown Royale Knights of the Round Table Jersey Autographs
PRINT RUNS B/WN 49-99 COPIES PER
EXCHANGE DEADLINE 7/29/2021
1 Reggie Jackson/99 5.00 12.00
2 TJ Leaf/99 4.00 10.00
3 Andrew Wiggins/49 8.00 20.00
4 Terrence Ross/99 6.00 15.00
5 Chris Bosh/49 8.00 20.00
6 Nemanja Bjelica/99 4.00 10.00
7 Khris Middleton/79 6.00 15.00
8 Dwight Powell/99 4.00 10.00
9 Derrick Favors/99 4.00 10.00
10 Larry Johnson/99 10.00 25.00
11 Michael Kidd-Gilchrist/99 4.00 10.00
12 Wesley Matthews/99 4.00 10.00
13 Hakeem Olajuwon/49 15.00 40.00
14 Evan Turner/99 4.00 10.00
15 DeMarcus Cousins/49 5.00 12.00
16 Markelle Fultz/99 5.00 12.00
17 Nikola Vucevic/99 5.00 12.00
18 Joe Harris/99 4.00 10.00
19 Otto Porter Jr./99 4.00 10.00
20 Josh Okogie/99 5.00 12.00
21 Kevin Knox II/99 4.00 10.00
22 Thaddeus Young/99 4.00 10.00
23 David Robinson/49 15.00 40.00
24 Dario Saric/99 5.00 12.00
25 Lauri Markkanen/99 8.00 20.00
26 Tyus Jones/99 4.00 10.00
27 Eric Bledsoe/99 5.00 12.00
28 Jarrett Allen/99 6.00 15.00
29 Nerlens Noel/99 4.00 10.00
30 Gorgui Dieng/99 4.00 10.00

2019-20 Crown Royale Knights of the Round Table Materials
1 Kyrie Irving 4.00 10.00
2 James Harden 4.00 10.00
3 Anthony Davis 5.00 12.00
4 Jarrett Culver 1.25 3.00
5 Donovan Mitchell 4.00 10.00
6 RJ Barrett 5.00 12.00
7 Devin Booker .50 1.25
8 LeBron James 20.00 50.00
9 Stephen Curry 15.00 40.00
10 Kemba Walker 1.50 4.00
11 Karl-Anthony Towns 3.00 8.00
12 Damian Lillard 5.00 12.00
13 Russell Westbrook 3.00 8.00
14 D'Angelo Russell 1.50 4.00
15 Ja Morant 12.00 30.00
16 Kevin Love 2.00 5.00
17 Zion Williamson 15.00 40.00
18 Jaxson Hayes 2.00 5.00
19 De'Andre Hunter 5.00 12.00
20 Giannis Antetokounmpo 10.00 25.00
21 Jimmy Butler 4.00 10.00
22 Kevin Durant 6.00 15.00
23 Tyler Herro 6.00 15.00
24 Rui Hachimura 5.00 12.00
25 Hassan Whiteside 1.25 3.00
26 Coby White 4.00 10.00
27 Chris Paul 4.00 10.00
28 Nikola Jokic 10.00 25.00
29 Cam Reddish 2.00 5.00
30 Blake Griffin 2.00 5.00

2019-20 Crown Royale Lineage Scripts
STATED PRINT RUN 49 SER.#'d SETS
EXCHANGE DEADLINE 7/29/2021
1 KZ Okpala 6.00 15.00
2 Cam Reddish 8.00 20.00
3 Eric Paschall 6.00 15.00
4 Romeo Langford 5.00 12.00
5 Isaiah Roby 6.00 15.00
6 Goga Bitadze 8.00 20.00
7 Grant Williams 8.00 20.00
8 Zion Williamson 800.00 1,500.00
9 Mfiondu Kabengele 6.00 15.00
10 Jarrett Culver 5.00 12.00
11 Carsen Edwards 6.00 15.00
12 Cameron Johnson 12.00 30.00
13 Admiral Schofield 6.00 15.00
14 Sekou Doumbouya 5.00 12.00
15 Ignas Brazdeikis 6.00 15.00
17 Ty Jerome 10.00 25.00
18 Ja Morant 300.00 600.00
19 Jordan Poole 20.00 50.00
20 Coby White 15.00 40.00
21 Bruno Fernando 6.00 15.00
22 PJ Washington Jr. 15.00 40.00
23 Jaylen Nowell 6.00 15.00
24 Chuma Okeke 8.00 20.00
25 Quinndary Weatherspoon 5.00 12.00
26 Matisse Thybulle 10.00 25.00
27 Nassir Little 8.00 20.00
28 RJ Barrett 40.00 100.00
29 Keldon Johnson 15.00 40.00
30 Jaxson Hayes 8.00 20.00
31 Cody Martin 8.00 20.00
32 Tyler Herro 25.00 60.00
33 Bol Bol 12.00 30.00
34 Nickeil Alexander-Walker 8.00 20.00
35 Tremont Waters 6.00 15.00
36 Brandon Clarke 10.00 25.00
37 Dylan Windler 6.00 15.00
38 De'Andre Hunter 20.00 50.00
39 Kevin Porter Jr. 10.00 25.00
40 Rui Hachimura 20.00 50.00

2019-20 Crown Royale Lords of the Court
STATED PRINT RUN 99 SER.#'d SETS
*BLUE/75: .5X TO 1.2X BASIC
*RED/49: .6X TO 1.5X BASIC
*PURPLE/25: .75X TO 2X BASIC
1 RJ Barrett 4.00 10.00
2 Russell Westbrook 2.50 6.00
3 Jarrett Culver 1.00 2.50
4 Ben Simmons 1.50 4.00
5 Paul George 2.50 6.00
6 LeBron James 40.00 100.00
7 Derrick Rose 3.00 8.00
8 Kyrie Irving 3.00 8.00
9 Zion Williamson 60.00 150.00
10 Joel Embiid 3.00 8.00
11 De'Andre Hunter 4.00 10.00
12 Jimmy Butler 3.00 8.00
13 Darius Garland 4.00 10.00
14 Luka Doncic 15.00 40.00
15 Kawhi Leonard 4.00 10.00
16 Stephen Curry 12.00 30.00
17 Trae Young 4.00 10.00
18 Giannis Antetokounmpo 12.00 30.00
19 Ja Morant 30.00 80.00
20 James Harden 3.00 8.00
21 Cam Reddish 1.50 4.00

2019-20 Crown Royale Regal Achievement Signatures
STATED PRINT RUN 25-49 SER.#'d SETS
EXCHANGE DEADLINE 7/29/2021
1 Karl Malone/25 12.00 30.00
2 Goran Dragic/49 5.00 12.00
3 Karl-Anthony Towns/25 12.00 30.00
5 Allen Iverson/25 40.00 100.00
6 Lou Williams/49 6.00 15.00
7 Trae Young/35 100.00 250.00
8 LaMarcus Aldridge/35 6.00 15.00
9 Kobe Bryant/25 800.00 1,500.00
10 Zach LaVine/49 10.00 25.00
11 Damian Lillard/25 15.00 40.00
12 Pascal Siakam/49 10.00 25.00
13 David Robinson/35 15.00 40.00
14 Zach LaVine/49 10.00 25.00
15 Ralph Sampson/35 5.00 12.00
16 Jarrett Allen/49 6.00 15.00
17 De'Aaron Fox/35 15.00 40.00
18 Nikola Jokic/49 125.00 300.00
19 Shaquille O'Neal /25 50.00 120.00
20 Kyle Kuzma/49 8.00 20.00

2019-20 Crown Royale Rookie Royalty
STATED PRINT RUN 99 SER.#'d SETS
*BLUE/75: .5X TO 1.2X BASIC
*RED/49: .6X TO 1.5X BASIC
*PURPLE/25: 1.2X TO 3X BASIC
1 Carsen Edwards 1.00 2.50
2 PJ Washington Jr. 2.50 6.00
3 Admiral Schofield 1.00 2.50
4 Ignas Brazdeikis 1.00 2.50
5 Matisse Thybulle 1.50 4.00
6 Ty Jerome 1.50 4.00
7 Zion Williamson 75.00 200.00
8 Jordan Poole 3.00 8.00
9 Coby White 2.50 6.00
10 Bruno Fernando 1.00 2.50
11 Tyler Herro 4.00 10.00
12 Jaylen Nowell 1.00 2.50
13 Nickeil Alexander-Walker 1.25 3.00
14 Quinndary Weatherspoon .75 2.00
15 Brandon Clarke 1.50 4.00
16 Nassir Little 1.25 3.00
17 RJ Barrett 3.00 8.00
18 Keldon Johnson 2.50 6.00
19 Jaxson Hayes 1.25 3.00
20 Cody Martin 1.25 3.00
21 Romeo Langford .75 2.00
22 Bol Bol 2.00 5.00
23 Goga Bitadze 1.25 3.00
24 Tremont Waters 1.00 2.50
25 Grant Williams 1.25 3.00
26 Dylan Windler 1.00 2.50
27 De'Andre Hunter 3.00 8.00
28 Kevin Porter Jr. 1.50 4.00
29 Cam Reddish 1.25 3.00
30 Eric Paschall 1.00 2.50
31 Sekou Doumbouya .75 2.00
32 Isaiah Roby 1.00 2.50
33 Luka Samanic 1.00 2.50
34 Kyle Guy 1.00 2.50
35 Darius Bazley .75 2.00
36 Mfiondu Kabengele 1.00 2.50
37 Jarrett Culver .75 2.00
38 KZ Okpala 1.00 2.50
39 Cameron Johnson 2.00 5.00

2019-20 Crown Royale Rookie Silhouettes Prime
*PRIME: 3X TO 8X BASE
STATED PRINT RUN 25 SER.#'d SETS
EXCHANGE DEADLINE 7/29/2021
104 Bol Bol 400.00 800.00
112 Jaxson Hayes 125.00 300.00
114 Nickeil Alexander-Walker 75.00 200.00
116 De'Andre Hunter 125.00 300.00
117 Ja Morant 2,500.00 5,000.00
118 PJ Washington Jr. 75.00 200.00
120 Matisse Thybulle 125.00 300.00
126 Kevin Porter Jr. 50.00 120.00
127 Jordan Poole 100.00 250.00
131 Zion Williamson 4,000.00 6,000.00
132 Tyler Herro 2,000.00 4,000.00
134 Brandon Clarke 200.00 500.00
136 Rui Hachimura 400.00 800.00
137 Coby White 150.00 400.00
140 RJ Barrett 400.00 800.00

2019-20 Crown Royale Royal Signatures
STATED PRINT RUN 25-49 SER.#'d SETS
EXCHANGE DEADLINE 7/29/2021
1 Bernard King/49 8.00 20.00
2 Shaquille O'Neal /25 50.00 120.00
3 Louie Dampier/49 6.00 15.00
4 Kevin Garnett/25 50.00 120.00
5 Gail Goodrich/49 6.00 15.00
6 Chris Bosh/35 8.00 20.00
7 Shane Battier/49 5.00 12.00
8 Grant Hill/35 25.00 60.00
9 John Starks/49 6.00 15.00
10 Dominique Wilkins/35 8.00 20.00
11 Derek Fisher/49 6.00 15.00
12 Allen Iverson/25 50.00 120.00
13 Danny Manning/49 5.00 12.00
14 Kareem Abdul-Jabbar/25 50.00 120.00
15 Bill Walton/49 20.00 50.00
16 Paul Pierce/35 10.00 25.00
17 B.J. Armstrong/49 6.00 15.00
18 Pat Riley/35 20.00 50.00
19 Alvan Adams/49 4.00 10.00
20 Bob Lanier/49 8.00 20.00
21 Jalen Rose/49 8.00 20.00
22 John Stockton/25 40.00 100.00
23 Ralph Sampson/49 5.00 12.00
24 Hakeem Olajuwon/35 20.00 50.00
25 George McGinnis/49 6.00 15.00
26 Clyde Drexler/35 15.00 40.00
27 Luke Walton/49 5.00 12.00
28 Elgin Baylor/35 12.00 30.00
29 Alex English/49 8.00 20.00
30 Artis Gilmore/49 8.00 20.00

2019-20 Crown Royale The Kings Court
STATED PRINT RUN 99 SER.#'d SETS
*BLUE/75: .5X TO 1.2X BASIC
*RED/49: .6X TO 1.5X BASIC
*PURPLE/25: .75X TO 2X BASIC
1 McCo/Lill/White 6.00 15.00
2 Rssll/Drmnd Grn/Crry 20.00 50.00
3 Lwry/Gsl/Skm 4.00 10.00
4 KLnrd/LWlms/PGgr 6.00 15.00
5 Drgic/JButlr/THrro 8.00 20.00
6 JBrown/Tatum/Kemba 10.00 25.00
7 Ingrm/JHayes/Zion 25.00 60.00
8 MBrdgs/PJ Was/TRzr 5.00 12.00
9 AGrdn/EFrnr/NVuc 2.50 6.00
10 KPzing/Luka/THrdy Jr. 15.00 40.00
11 BHield/DFox/MBgly III 4.00 10.00
12 Caplg/J Hrdn/RWstbrk 5.00 12.00
13 DMtchll/M Cnly/RGbert 5.00 12.00
14 Davis/Kuzma/James 20.00 50.00
15 EBldso/GAnte/KMddltn 12.00 30.00
16 DJordan/Harrs/Irvng 5.00 12.00
17 DSmth Jr./KKnx II/RJ Bar 6.00 15.00
18 CWhite/Mrkkn/ LaVine 5.00 12.00
19 BSmns/JEbid/JRchrdsn 5.00 12.00
20 Hrris/ Mrray/Jokic 12.00 30.00
21 Rozan/ Aldrdg/Gay 3.00 8.00
22 Sabon/ Brogdn/Oldipo 3.00 8.00
23 Beal/Wall/Rui 6.00 15.00
24 BClark/Ja Mrnt/Jcksn Jr. 15.00 40.00
25 Wiggin/JCulvr/Towns 4.00 10.00
26 Redish/Hunt/Young 6.00 15.00
27 Paul/ Gil-Alxnd/Adams 12.00 30.00
28 Sextn/Garlnd/Love 6.00 15.00
29 CJohn/Ayton/DBook 4.00 10.00
30 ADrum/BGfin/Rose 5.00 12.00

2020-21 Crown Royale
JSY AU PRINT RUN 199 SER.#'d SETS
EXCHANGE DEADLINE 11/05/2022
1 Joel Embiid 1.25 3.00
2 Nikola Vucevic .50 1.25
3 RJ Barrett .75 2.00
4 Ja Morant 8.00 20.00
5 Pascal Siakam .75 2.00
6 Kyrie Irving 1.00 2.50
7 Kawhi Leonard 1.25 3.00
8 Victor Oladipo .40 1.00
9 Blake Griffin .50 1.25
10 Zion Williamson 4.00 10.00
11 Miles Bridges .50 1.25
12 Derrick Rose .75 2.00
13 Kemba Walker .50 1.25
14 Jrue Holiday .50 1.25
15 Bradley Beal .60 1.50
16 Chris Paul 1.00 2.50
17 Trae Young 1.25 3.00
18 LeBron James 10.00 25.00
19 Devin Booker 1.25 3.00
20 Kevin Durant 2.00 5.00
21 Donovan Mitchell 1.00 2.50
22 Coby White .60 1.50
23 Carmelo Anthony .75 2.00
24 Tyler Herro 1.00 2.50
25 Domantas Sabonis .60 1.50
26 Deandre Ayton .50 1.25
27 Bogdan Bogdanovic .50 1.25
28 Jaylen Brown .75 2.00
29 Kyle Kuzma .60 1.50
30 LaMarcus Aldridge .50 1.25
31 Kevin Love .50 1.25
32 Damian Lillard 1.25 3.00
33 John Wall .60 1.50
34 Bam Adebayo .75 2.00
35 Myles Turner .50 1.25
36 Giannis Antetokounmpo 2.50 6.00
37 Shai Gilgeous-Alexander 2.50 6.00
38 Stephen Curry 6.00 15.00
39 Steven Adams .50 1.25
40 Julius Randle .50 1.25
41 CJ McCollum .50 1.25
42 Paul George .75 2.00
43 Luka Doncic 12.00 30.00
44 De'Aaron Fox .75 2.00
45 John Collins .50 1.25
46 DeMar DeRozan .60 1.50
47 Michael Porter Jr. .60 1.50
48 James Harden 1.00 2.50
49 Kyle Lowry .60 1.50
50 D'Angelo Russell .50 1.25
51 Marvin Bagley III .40 1.00
52 Karl-Anthony Towns .75 2.00
53 Mitchell Robinson .50 1.25
54 Zach LaVine .75 2.00
55 Russell Westbrook 1.00 2.50
56 Andre Drummond .50 1.25
57 Jayson Tatum 2.00 5.00
58 Rudy Gobert .60 1.50
59 Anthony Davis 1.25 3.00
60 Kristaps Porzingis .60 1.50
61 Fred VanVleet .75 2.00
62 Jaren Jackson Jr. .75 2.00
63 Brandon Ingram .60 1.50
64 Davis Bertans .40 1.00
65 Ben Simmons .50 1.25
66 Collin Sexton .50 1.25
67 Devonte' Graham .40 1.00
68 Khris Middleton .60 1.50
69 Jamal Murray .75 2.00
70 Aaron Gordon .50 1.25
71 Andrew Wiggins .60 1.50
72 Jimmy Butler 1.00 2.50
73 Wendell Carter Jr. .40 1.00
74 Klay Thompson 1.25 3.00
75 Nikola Jokic 2.50 6.00
76 Onyeka Okongwu RC 1.50 4.00
77 Aaron Nesmith RC 1.50 4.00
78 Payton Pritchard RC 2.50 6.00
79 LaMelo Ball RC 50.00 120.00
80 Patrick Williams RC 2.00 5.00
81 Isaac Okoro RC 1.25 3.00
82 Josh Green RC 1.50 4.00
83 RJ Hampton RC .75 2.00
84 Isaiah Stewart RC 1.50 4.00
85 Killian Hayes RC .75 2.00
86 James Wiseman RC 1.00 2.50
87 Xavier Tillman RC 1.00 2.50
88 Precious Achiuwa RC 1.50 4.00
89 Anthony Edwards RC 20.00 50.00
90 Jae'Sean Tate RC 1.00 2.50
91 Kira Lewis Jr. RC .75 2.00
92 Obi Toppin RC 1.50 4.00
93 Immanuel Quickley RC 2.00 5.00
94 Aleksej Pokusevski RC 1.00 2.50
95 Cole Anthony RC 2.00 5.00
96 Tyrese Maxey RC 6.00 15.00
97 Jalen Smith RC 1.50 4.00
98 Tyrese Haliburton RC 6.00 15.00
99 Devin Vassell RC 2.50 6.00
100 Deni Avdija RC 2.00 5.00
101 Onyeka Okongwu JSY AU/199 12.00 30.00
102 Aaron Nesmith JSY AU/199 12.00 30.00
103 Payton Pritchard JSY AU/199 30.00 80.00
104 LaMelo Ball JSY AU/199 500.00 1,000.00
105 Vernon Carey Jr. JSY AU/199 6.00 15.00
106 Patrick Williams JSY AU/199 40.00 100.00
107 Isaac Okoro JSY AU/199 10.00 25.00
108 Josh Green JSY AU/199 12.00 30.00
109 Tyrell Terry JSY AU/199 5.00 12.00
110 Jahmi'us Ramsey JSY AU/199 6.00 15.00
111 Zeke Nnaji JSY AU/199 8.00 20.00
112 RJ Hampton JSY AU/199 6.00 15.00
113 Isaiah Stewart JSY AU/199 12.00 30.00
114 Saddiq Bey JSY AU/199 60.00 150.00
115 Killian Hayes JSY AU/199 6.00 15.00
116 James Wiseman JSY AU/199 8.00 20.00
117 Nico Mannion JSY AU/199 8.00 20.00
118 Daniel Oturu JSY AU/199 6.00 15.00
119 Desmond Bane JSY AU/199 50.00 120.00
120 Xavier Tillman JSY AU/199 8.00 20.00
121 Precious Achiuwa JSY AU/199 12.00 30.00
122 Jordan Nwora JSY AU/199 8.00 20.00
123 Anthony Edwards JSY AU/199 300.00 600.00
124 CJ Elleby JSY AU/199 6.00 15.00
125 Jaden McDaniels JSY AU/199 30.00 80.00
126 Kira Lewis Jr. JSY AU/199 6.00 15.00
127 Obi Toppin JSY AU/199 40.00 100.00
128 Immanuel Quickley JSY AU/199 15.00 40.00
129 Aleksej Pokusevski JSY AU/199 8.00 20.00
130 Theo Maledon JSY AU/199 6.00 15.00
131 Cole Anthony JSY AU/199 60.00 150.00
132 Tyrese Maxey JSY AU/199 125.00 300.00
133 Jalen Smith JSY AU/199 12.00 30.00
134 Tyrese Haliburton JSY AU/199 100.00 250.00
135 Robert Woodard II JSY AU/199 6.00 15.00
136 Tre Jones JSY AU/199 10.00 25.00
137 Devin Vassell JSY AU/199 25.00 60.00
138 Malachi Flynn JSY AU/199 6.00 15.00
139 Udoka Azubuike JSY AU/199 8.00 20.00
140 Deni Avdija JSY AU/199 40.00 100.00

2020-21 Crown Royale Crystal
*CRYSTAL: .75X TO 2X BASIC
*CRYSTAL RC: .5X TO 1.2X BASIC RC
18 LeBron James 30.00 80.00
98 Tyrese Haliburton 15.00 40.00

2020-21 Crown Royale Crystal Blue
*CRYSTAL BLUE: 1.2X TO 3X BASIC
STATED PRINT RUN 99 SER.#'d SETS
18 LeBron James 50.00 120.00
79 LaMelo Ball 200.00 500.00
80 Patrick Williams 20.00 50.00
93 Immanuel Quickley 20.00 50.00
98 Tyrese Haliburton 40.00 100.00

2020-21 Crown Royale Crystal Green
*CRSTL GREEN: 3X TO 8X BASIC
STATED PRINT RUN 21 SER.#'d SETS
17 Trae Young 30.00 80.00
18 LeBron James 125.00 300.00
19 Devin Booker 25.00 60.00
21 Donovan Mitchell 25.00 60.00
38 Stephen Curry 75.00 200.00
57 Jayson Tatum 40.00 100.00
75 Nikola Jokic 25.00 60.00
79 LaMelo Ball 600.00 1,200.00
80 Patrick Williams 60.00 150.00
93 Immanuel Quickley 50.00 120.00
98 Tyrese Haliburton 100.00 250.00

2020-21 Crown Royale Crystal Purple
*CRSTL PRPLE: 3X TO 8X BASIC
STATED PRINT RUN 25 SER.#'d SETS
17 Trae Young 30.00 80.00
18 LeBron James 125.00 300.00
19 Devin Booker 25.00 60.00
21 Donovan Mitchell 25.00 60.00
38 Stephen Curry 75.00 200.00
57 Jayson Tatum 40.00 100.00
75 Nikola Jokic 25.00 60.00
79 LaMelo Ball 600.00 1,200.00
80 Patrick Williams 60.00 150.00
93 Immanuel Quickley 50.00 120.00
98 Tyrese Haliburton 100.00 250.00

2020-21 Crown Royale Crystal Red
STATED PRINT RUN 49 SER.#'d SETS
17 Trae Young 15.00 40.00
18 LeBron James 60.00 150.00
19 Devin Booker 12.00 30.00
21 Donovan Mitchell 12.00 30.00
38 Stephen Curry 40.00 100.00
57 Jayson Tatum 20.00 50.00
75 Nikola Jokic 12.00 30.00
79 LaMelo Ball 300.00 600.00
80 Patrick Williams 25.00 60.00
93 Immanuel Quickley 25.00 60.00
98 Tyrese Haliburton 50.00 120.00

2020-21 Crown Royale FOTL Green Crystal
*FOTL GREEN CRSTL: 3X TO 8X BASIC
STATED PRINT RUN 21 SER.#'d SETS
17 Trae Young 30.00 80.00
18 LeBron James 125.00 300.00
19 Devin Booker 25.00 60.00
21 Donovan Mitchell 25.00 60.00
38 Stephen Curry 75.00 200.00
57 Jayson Tatum 40.00 100.00
75 Nikola Jokic 25.00 60.00
79 LaMelo Ball 600.00 1,200.00
80 Patrick Williams 60.00 150.00
93 Immanuel Quickley 50.00 120.00
98 Tyrese Haliburton 100.00 250.00

2020-21 Crown Royale Air to the Throne
STATED PRINT RUN 99 SER.#'d SETS
*BLUE/75: .5X TO 1.2X BASIC
*RED/49: .6X TO 1.5X BASIC
*PURPLE/25: 1.2X TO 3X BASIC
1 A.Edwards/Z.Williamson 75.00 200.00
2 J.Wiseman/S.Curry 15.00 40.00
3 L.Ball/L.Ball 150.00 400.00
4 L.James/O.Toppin 60.00 150.00
5 D.Avdija/L.Doncic 40.00 100.00
6 K.Hayes/T.Parker 3.00 8.00
7 K.Leonard/P.Williams 20.00 50.00
8 B.Adebayo/O.Okongwu 3.00 8.00
9 T.Herro/T.Maxey 12.00 30.00
10 D.Fox/T.Haliburton 40.00 100.00

2020-21 Crown Royale Coat of Arms Materials
1 Karl-Anthony Towns 3.00 8.00
2 Derrick Rose 8.00 20.00
3 Kevin Garnett 12.00 30.00
4 LeBron James 40.00 100.00
5 Nikola Jokic 20.00 50.00
6 Anfernee Hardaway 12.00 30.00
7 Shaquille O'Neal 12.00 30.00

8 Jamal Murray 3.00 8.00
9 Draymond Green 2.50 6.00
10 Kyle Lowry 2.50 6.00
11 Anthony Davis 5.00 12.00
12 Charles Barkley 15.00 40.00
13 Coby White 2.50 6.00
14 Chris Webber 10.00 25.00
15 Kyrie Irving 4.00 10.00
16 Tim Duncan 12.00 30.00
17 Kawhi Leonard 5.00 12.00
18 Dirk Nowitzki 12.00 30.00
19 Luka Doncic 40.00 100.00
20 Rudy Gobert 2.50 6.00

2020-21 Crown Royale Crown Autographs

STATED PRINT RUN 49-99 SER.#'d SETS
EXCHANGE DEADLINE 11/05/2022
*BLUE/49-75: .5X TO 1.2X BASIC
*RED/32-49: .6X TO 1.5X BASIC
*PURPLE/25: 1.5X TO 3X BASIC
1 RJ Barrett/99 20.00 50.00
2 Devonte' Graham/99 4.00 10.00
4 Alvin Robertson/99 4.00 10.00
5 Jaxson Hayes/99 4.00 10.00
6 Nate McMillan/99 3.00 8.00
7 Shawn Kemp/99 30.00 80.00
8 Ray Allen/99 30.00 80.00
9 Magic Johnson/49 60.00 150.00
10 Alex Caruso/99 20.00 50.00
11 Ricky Rubio/99 8.00 20.00
13 Dave Bing/99 12.00 30.00
14 Kyle Kuzma/99 10.00 25.00
15 Baron Davis/99 5.00 12.00
16 Eric Bledsoe/99 4.00 10.00
17 Boban Marjanovic/99 8.00 20.00
18 John Collins/99 8.00 20.00
19 Jason Williams/99 40.00 100.00
20 Nate Archibald/99 6.00 15.00
21 Jerry West/49 30.00 80.00
22 Derrick Coleman/99 5.00 12.00
23 Stephon Marbury/99 12.00 30.00
24 Robert Horry/99 8.00 20.00
25 Mychal Thompson/99 4.00 10.00
26 Spud Webb/99 5.00 12.00
27 David Thompson/99 6.00 15.00
28 Xavier McDaniel/99 4.00 10.00
29 J.J. Barea/99 8.00 20.00
30 Vlade Divac/99 4.00 10.00
31 Steve Francis/99 8.00 20.00
32 Jrue Holiday/99 8.00 20.00
33 Tom Heinsohn/99 12.00 30.00
34 Gheorghe Muresan/99 4.00 10.00
35 Al Horford/99 12.00 30.00
36 Jamal Mashburn/99 4.00 10.00
37 Pat Riley/99 8.00 20.00
38 Juwan Howard/99 4.00 10.00
39 JJ Redick/99 8.00 20.00
40 Otto Porter Jr./99 3.00 8.00
41 Malcolm Brogdon/99 5.00 12.00
42 Rudy Tomjanovich/99 5.00 12.00
43 Sarunas Marciulionis/99 5.00 12.00
44 Luc Longley/99 4.00 10.00
45 B.J. Armstrong/99 4.00 10.00
46 Doc Rivers/99 5.00 12.00
47 Calvin Murphy/99 5.00 12.00
48 John Starks/99 4.00 10.00
49 Jason Richardson/99 5.00 12.00
50 Eric Gordon/99 4.00 10.00
51 Hedo Turkoglu/99 4.00 10.00
52 Muggsy Bogues/99 12.00 30.00
53 Rik Smits/99 4.00 10.00
54 Jerome Williams/99 3.00 8.00
55 Tim Hardaway/99 15.00 40.00
56 Karl-Anthony Towns/49 15.00 40.00
57 Dwight Howard/99 15.00 40.00
59 Alex English/99 5.00 12.00
60 Bogdan Bogdanovic/99 8.00 20.00

2020-21 Crown Royale Crown Jewel Signatures

STATED PRINT RUN 49 SER.#'d SETS
3 Dirk Nowitzki 125.00 300.00
4 Kevin Durant 150.00 400.00
5 Stephen Curry 500.00 1,000.00
7 Luka Doncic 600.00 1,200.00
9 Dwyane Wade 75.00 200.00
10 Anthony Davis 75.00 200.00

2020-21 Crown Royale Hall of Fame Memorabilia

1 Larry Bird 15.00 40.00
2 John Stockton 6.00 15.00
3 Magic Johnson 15.00 40.00
4 Shaquille O'Neal 15.00 40.00
5 Tracy McGrady 8.00 20.00
6 Arvydas Sabonis 4.00 10.00
7 Grant Hill 6.00 15.00
8 Dikembe Mutombo 5.00 12.00
9 Julius Erving 10.00 25.00
10 Karl Malone 6.00 15.00

2020-21 Crown Royale Heirs to the Throne Materials

1 Aaron Nesmith 3.00 8.00
2 LaMelo Ball 30.00 80.00
3 Patrick Williams 4.00 10.00
4 Josh Green 3.00 8.00
5 Jahmi'us Ramsey 1.50 4.00
6 RJ Hampton 1.50 4.00
7 Saddiq Bey 3.00 8.00
8 James Wiseman 2.00 5.00
9 Daniel Oturu 1.50 4.00
10 Xavier Tillman 2.00 5.00
11 Jordan Nwora 2.00 5.00
12 CJ Elleby 1.50 4.00
13 Kira Lewis Jr. 1.50 4.00
14 Immanuel Quickley 4.00 10.00
15 Theo Maledon 1.50 4.00
16 Tyrese Maxey 12.00 30.00
17 Tyrese Haliburton 12.00 30.00
18 Tre Jones 2.50 6.00
19 Malachi Flynn 1.50 4.00
20 Deni Avdija 4.00 10.00
21 Udoka Azubuike 2.00 5.00
22 Devin Vassell 5.00 12.00
23 Robert Woodard II 1.50 4.00
24 Jalen Smith 3.00 8.00
25 Cole Anthony 4.00 10.00
26 Aleksej Pokusevski 2.00 5.00
27 Obi Toppin 3.00 8.00
28 Jaden McDaniels 5.00 12.00
29 Anthony Edwards 25.00 60.00
30 Precious Achiuwa 3.00 8.00
31 Desmond Bane 5.00 12.00
32 Nico Mannion 1.50 4.00
33 Killian Hayes 1.50 4.00
34 Isaiah Stewart 3.00 8.00
35 Zeke Nnaji 2.00 5.00
36 Tyrell Terry 1.25 3.00
37 Isaac Okoro 2.50 6.00
38 Vernon Carey Jr. 1.50 4.00
39 Payton Pritchard 5.00 12.00
40 Onyeka Okongwu 3.00 8.00

2020-21 Crown Royale Kaboom!

1 Luka Doncic 2,000.00 4,000.00
2 Ja Morant 600.00 1,200.00
3 Anthony Davis 200.00 500.00
4 LeBron James 1,250.00 2,500.00
5 James Harden 400.00 800.00
6 Donovan Mitchell 200.00 500.00
7 Dirk Nowitzki 300.00 600.00
8 Kawhi Leonard 200.00 500.00
9 Vince Carter 350.00 700.00
10 Damian Lillard 200.00 500.00
11 Nikola Jokic 500.00 1,000.00
12 Trae Young 300.00 600.00
13 Ben Simmons 150.00 400.00
14 Jimmy Butler 200.00 500.00
15 Dwyane Wade 300.00 600.00
16 Tim Duncan 300.00 600.00
17 Allen Iverson 400.00 800.00
18 Jayson Tatum 500.00 1,000.00
19 Zion Williamson 300.00 600.00
20 Giannis Antetokounmpo 400.00 800.00
21 Anthony Edwards 3,000.00 6,000.00
22 James Wiseman 60.00 150.00
23 LaMelo Ball 1,000.00 2,000.00
24 Obi Toppin 300.00 600.00
25 Deni Avdija 200.00 500.00

2020-21 Crown Royale Knights of the Round Table Jersey Autographs

PRINT RUNS B/WN 25-99 COPIES PER
EXCHANGE DEADLINE 11/05/2022
1 Tobias Harris/99 8.00 20.00
2 RJ Barrett/49 25.00 60.00
4 Spencer Dinwiddie/99 5.00 12.00
6 Alvin Robertson/99 5.00 12.00
7 John Salmons/99 4.00 10.00
8 Shawn Kemp/99 40.00 100.00
9 Mike Miller/99 5.00 12.00
10 Jarrett Allen/99 6.00 15.00
11 De'Andre Hunter/99 6.00 15.00
12 Magic Johnson/49 60.00 150.00
13 Andrea Bargnani/99 4.00 10.00
14 Ricky Rubio/99 6.00 15.00
15 Matt Bonner/99 4.00 10.00
16 Eric Bledsoe/99 5.00 12.00
17 Boban Marjanovic/99 10.00 25.00
18 John Collins/99 6.00 15.00
19 T.J. Ford/99 4.00 10.00
20 Arron Afflalo/99 4.00 10.00
21 Deron Williams/99 5.00 12.00
22 Jarrett Culver/99 4.00 10.00
23 Chris Kaman/99 4.00 10.00
24 J.J. Barea/99 12.00 30.00
25 Aaron Holiday/99 5.00 12.00
26 Doug McDermott/99 5.00 12.00
27 Pat Riley/49 10.00 25.00
28 Mo Bamba/99 6.00 15.00
29 Wendell Carter Jr./99 5.00 12.00

2020-21 Crown Royale Knights of the Round Table Materials

1 Rudy Gobert 2.50 6.00
2 Andrew Wiggins 2.50 6.00
3 Kevin Love 2.00 5.00
4 Kawhi Leonard 5.00 12.00
5 Marcus Smart 2.00 5.00
6 Jamal Murray 3.00 8.00
7 Brandon Clarke 2.00 5.00
8 Miles Bridges 2.00 5.00
9 Ricky Rubio 2.00 5.00
10 Kevin Porter Jr. 1.50 4.00
11 Vince Carter 4.00 10.00
12 Giannis Antetokounmpo 12.00 30.00
13 Bradley Beal 2.50 6.00
14 Jarrett Culver 1.25 3.00
15 Steven Adams 2.00 5.00
16 Rui Hachimura 2.50 6.00
17 Jarrett Allen 2.00 5.00
18 Markelle Fultz 1.50 4.00
19 Myles Turner 2.00 5.00
20 Karl-Anthony Towns 3.00 8.00
21 Anthony Edwards 20.00 50.00
22 James Wiseman 2.00 5.00
23 LaMelo Ball 40.00 100.00
24 Obi Toppin 3.00 8.00
25 Deni Avdija 4.00 10.00
26 Patrick Williams 10.00 25.00
27 Tyrese Haliburton 15.00 40.00
28 Cole Anthony 4.00 10.00
29 Killian Hayes 1.50 4.00
30 Onyeka Okongwu 3.00 8.00

2020-21 Crown Royale Regal Achievements Signatures

STATED PRINT RUN 49 SER.#'d SETS
EXCHANGE DEADLINE 11/05/2022
1 Vince Carter 60.00 150.00
3 Nikola Jokic 125.00 300.00
5 PJ Washington Jr. 15.00 40.00
6 Trae Young 125.00 300.00
8 Caris LeVert 20.00 50.00
9 Domantas Sabonis 20.00 50.00
10 Shai Gilgeous-Alexander 300.00 600.00
11 Anthony Davis 60.00 150.00
12 Karl-Anthony Towns 15.00 40.00
13 Stephen Curry 600.00 1,200.00
14 Dirk Nowitzki 125.00 300.00
15 Jayson Tatum 125.00 300.00
16 Dwyane Wade 75.00 200.00
18 Zach LaVine 40.00 100.00
19 Luka Doncic 800.00 1,500.00
20 Ja Morant 300.00 600.00

2020-21 Crown Royale Rookie Crown Autographs

STATED PRINT RUN 99 SER.#'d SETS
EXCHANGE DEADLINE 11/05/2022
*BLUE/75: .5X TO 1.2X BASIC
*RED/49: .6X TO 1.5X BASIC
*PURPLE/25: 1.5X TO 3X BASIC
1 Deni Avdija 10.00 25.00
2 Udoka Azubuike 5.00 12.00
3 Malachi Flynn 4.00 10.00
4 Devin Vassell 20.00 50.00
5 Tre Jones 6.00 15.00
6 Robert Woodard II 4.00 10.00
7 Tyrese Haliburton 75.00 200.00
8 Jalen Smith 8.00 20.00
9 Tyrese Maxey 75.00 200.00
10 Cole Anthony 25.00 60.00
11 Theo Maledon 4.00 10.00
12 Aleksej Pokusevski 5.00 12.00
13 Immanuel Quickley 10.00 25.00
14 Obi Toppin 25.00 60.00
15 Kira Lewis Jr. 4.00 10.00
16 Jaden McDaniels 20.00 50.00
17 Caleb Martin 8.00 20.00
18 Anthony Edwards 150.00 400.00
19 Jordan Nwora 5.00 12.00
20 Precious Achiuwa 8.00 20.00
21 Xavier Tillman 5.00 12.00
22 Desmond Bane 40.00 100.00
23 Daniel Oturu 4.00 10.00
24 Nico Mannion 4.00 10.00
25 James Wiseman 5.00 12.00
26 Killian Hayes 5.00 12.00
27 Saddiq Bey 30.00 80.00
28 Isaiah Stewart 8.00 20.00
29 RJ Hampton 4.00 10.00
30 Zeke Nnaji 5.00 12.00
31 Tyler Bey 4.00 10.00
32 Tyrell Terry 3.00 8.00
33 Josh Green 8.00 20.00
34 Isaac Okoro 6.00 15.00
35 Patrick Williams 40.00 100.00
36 Vernon Carey Jr. 4.00 10.00
37 LaMelo Ball 400.00 800.00
38 Payton Pritchard 12.00 30.00
39 Aaron Nesmith 8.00 20.00
40 Onyeka Okongwu 8.00 20.00

2020-21 Crown Royale Rookie Royalty

STATED PRINT RUN 99 SER.#'d SETS
*ASIA GOLD: .4X TO 1X BASIC
*ASIA RED: .4X TO 1X BASIC
*BLUE/75: .5X TO 1.2X BASIC
*RED/49: .6X TO 1.5X BASIC
*PURPLE/25: .75X TO 2X BASIC
1 Elijah Hughes 3.00 8.00
2 Udoka Azubuike 4.00 10.00
3 Saddiq Bey 6.00 15.00
4 Devin Vassell 10.00 25.00
5 Zeke Nnaji 4.00 10.00
6 Tyrese Haliburton 25.00 60.00
7 Jalen Smith 6.00 15.00
8 Cole Anthony 8.00 20.00
9 Josh Green 6.00 15.00
10 LaMelo Ball 25.00 60.00
11 Immanuel Quickley 8.00 20.00
12 Obi Toppin 6.00 15.00
13 Aaron Nesmith 6.00 15.00
14 Malachi Flynn 3.00 8.00
15 Jordan Nwora 4.00 10.00
16 Precious Achiuwa 6.00 15.00
17 Cassius Winston 3.00 8.00
18 Desmond Bane 10.00 25.00
19 Deni Avdija 8.00 20.00
20 Nico Mannion 3.00 8.00
21 James Wiseman 4.00 10.00
22 Tyrese Maxey 25.00 60.00
23 Kira Lewis Jr. 3.00 8.00
24 Killian Hayes 3.00 8.00
25 Isaiah Stewart 6.00 15.00
26 RJ Hampton 3.00 8.00
27 Tyler Bey 3.00 8.00
28 Tyrell Terry 2.50 6.00
29 Isaac Okoro 5.00 12.00
30 Patrick Williams 8.00 20.00
31 Anthony Edwards 30.00 80.00
32 Tre Jones 5.00 12.00
33 Payton Pritchard 10.00 25.00
34 Onyeka Okongwu 6.00 15.00
35 Kenyon Martin Jr. 5.00 12.00
36 Cassius Stanley 3.00 8.00
37 Daniel Oturu 3.00 8.00
38 Aleksej Pokusevski 4.00 10.00
39 Theo Maledon 4.00 10.00
40 Jaden McDaniels 10.00 25.00

2020-21 Crown Royale Rookie Silhouettes Material Autographs Prime

*ROOKIE SILHOUETTES PRIME: 2X TO 5X BASE
STATED PRINT RUN 25 SER.#'d SETS
EXCHANGE DEADLINE 11/05/2022

2020-21 Crown Royale Royal Signatures

STATED PRINT RUN 49 SER.#'d SETS
EXCHANGE DEADLINE 11/05/2022
1 Oscar Robertson 75.00 200.00
2 Bill Walton 25.00 60.00
3 David Robinson 40.00 100.00
4 Adrian Dantley 6.00 15.00
5 Elgin Baylor 25.00 60.00
6 Rick Barry 12.00 30.00
8 Nate Archibald 8.00 20.00
9 Magic Johnson 100.00 250.00
10 Robert Parish 8.00 20.00
11 Jerry West 40.00 100.00
12 Joe Dumars 15.00 40.00
13 Grant Hill 15.00 40.00
15 Gary Payton 40.00 100.00
16 Jerry Lucas 8.00 20.00
17 Allen Iverson 15.00 40.00
18 Elvin Hayes 12.00 30.00
19 Julius Erving 75.00 200.00
20 Lenny Wilkens 6.00 15.00
21 Hakeem Olajuwon 60.00 150.00
22 Ralph Sampson 5.00 12.00
23 Ray Allen 40.00 100.00
24 David Thompson 8.00 20.00
25 Dominique Wilkins 30.00 80.00
26 George Gervin 15.00 40.00
27 Larry Bird 100.00 250.00
28 Dave Cowens 8.00 20.00
29 Kareem Abdul-Jabbar 100.00 250.00
30 Gail Goodrich 12.00 30.00

2020-21 Crown Royale Silhouettes Material Autographs

STATED PRINT RUN 13-99 SER.#'d SETS
EXCHANGE DEADLINE 11/05/2022
1 Hakeem Olajuwon/49 100.00 250.00
2 Andrea Bargnani/99 6.00 15.00
3 Clyde Drexler/49 40.00 100.00
4 Robert Covington/99 8.00 20.00
5 Nikola Jokic/99 150.00 400.00
6 Al Horford/99 10.00 25.00
8 Joe Harris/99 8.00 20.00
9 Anthony Davis/49 125.00 300.00
10 Steven Adams/99 10.00 25.00
12 Domantas Sabonis/99 40.00 100.00
13 Vince Carter/49 100.00 250.00
14 Roy Hibbert/99 6.00 15.00
16 Nikola Vucevic/99 20.00 50.00
17 Dirk Nowitzki/49 150.00 400.00
18 Deron Williams/93 8.00 20.00
19 Kevin Garnett/49 150.00 400.00
20 Jarrett Allen/99 10.00 25.00
21 Grant Hill/49 40.00 100.00
22 J.J. Barea/99 20.00 50.00
23 Brandon Clarke/49 10.00 25.00
24 Mike Miller/99 8.00 20.00
25 Andrew Wiggins/99 25.00 60.00
26 Brook Lopez/99 8.00 20.00
28 Lou Williams/99 10.00 25.00
29 Karl-Anthony Towns/49 25.00 60.00
30 Chris Kaman/99 5.00 12.00

2020-21 Crown Royale Sno Globe

STATED PRINT RUN 99 SER.#'d SETS
*BLUE/75: .5X TO 1.2X BASIC
*RED/49: .6X TO 1.5X BASIC
*PURPLE/25: .75X TO 2X BASIC
1 Trae Young 25.00 60.00
2 Stephen Curry 60.00 150.00
3 LeBron James 60.00 150.00
4 Giannis Antetokounmpo 30.00 80.00
5 Anthony Davis 10.00 25.00
6 Luka Doncic 60.00 150.00
7 Jayson Tatum 30.00 80.00
8 Donovan Mitchell 20.00 50.00
9 Jimmy Butler 12.00 30.00
10 Jamal Murray 15.00 40.00
11 Kyrie Irving 15.00 40.00
12 Damian Lillard 20.00 50.00
13 Zion Williamson 50.00 120.00
14 Ja Morant 50.00 120.00
15 Pascal Siakam 8.00 20.00
16 James Harden 12.00 30.00
17 Joel Embiid 30.00 80.00
18 Paul George 12.00 30.00
19 Bradley Beal 8.00 20.00
20 Kemba Walker 3.00 8.00
21 Devin Booker 25.00 60.00
22 Russell Westbrook 10.00 25.00
23 Bam Adebayo 10.00 25.00
24 Kawhi Leonard 20.00 50.00
25 Karl-Anthony Towns 10.00 25.00
26 RJ Barrett 15.00 40.00
27 John Wall 10.00 25.00
28 Kyle Lowry 10.00 25.00
29 Chris Paul 12.00 30.00
30 Ben Simmons 10.00 25.00

2020-21 Crown Royale Test of Time

STATED PRINT RUN 99 SER.#'d SETS
*BLUE/75: .5X TO 1.2X BASIC
*RED/49: .6X TO 1.5X BASIC
*PURPLE/25: 1.25X TO 3X BASIC
1 Giannis Antetokounmpo 20.00 50.00
2 Anthony Davis 15.00 40.00
3 Kawhi Leonard 15.00 40.00
4 Jayson Tatum 20.00 50.00
5 Kevin Durant 15.00 40.00
6 LeBron James 60.00 150.00
7 Nikola Jokic 15.00 40.00
8 Jimmy Butler 8.00 20.00
9 Devin Booker 25.00 60.00
10 Damian Lillard 15.00 40.00
11 Stephen Curry 40.00 100.00
12 Ben Simmons 8.00 20.00
13 Russell Westbrook 10.00 25.00
14 Ja Morant 30.00 80.00
15 Zion Williamson 40.00 100.00
16 James Harden 15.00 40.00
17 Luka Doncic 60.00 150.00
18 Kyrie Irving 15.00 40.00
19 Donovan Mitchell 20.00 50.00
20 Trae Young 20.00 50.00

2021-22 Crown Royale

COMMON CARD (1-100) .30 .75
SEMISTARS .40 1.00
UNLISTED STARS .50 1.25
COMMON RC (1-100) .60 1.50
RC SEMIS .75 2.00
RC UNLISTED 1.00 2.50
COMMON JSY AU (101-140) 6.00 15.00
JSY AU SEMIS 8.00 20.00
JSY AU UNLISTED 10.00 25.00
JSY AU PRINT RUN 199 SER.#'d SETS
EXCHANGE DEADLINE 11/11/2023
*ASIA RED: .5X TO 1.2X BASIC
*CRYSTAL: .75X TO 2X BASIC
*ROOKIE SILHOUETTES PRIME/25: 2X TO 5X BASE
1 Jalen Suggs RC 2.50 6.00
2 Malcolm Brogdon .40 1.00
3 Corey Kispert RC 1.25 3.00
4 Giannis Antetokounmpo 2.50 6.00
5 Quentin Grimes RC 2.00 5.00
6 Ben Simmons .50 1.25
7 Isaiah Livers RC 1.00 2.50
8 Fred VanVleet .60 1.50
9 Kevin Durant 1.50 4.00
10 Collin Sexton .50 1.25
11 Josh Giddey RC 3.00 8.00
12 Domantas Sabonis .60 1.50
13 Alperen Sengun RC 3.00 8.00
14 Khris Middleton .50 1.25
15 Bones Hyland RC 1.25 3.00
16 Joel Embiid 1.25 3.00
17 Brandon Boston Jr. RC 1.00 2.50
18 Mike Conley .40 1.00
19 Kyrie Irving 1.00 2.50
20 Luka Doncic 3.00 8.00
21 Jonathan Kuminga RC 3.00 8.00
22 Paul George .75 2.00
23 Trey Murphy III RC 3.00 8.00
24 Karl-Anthony Towns .75 2.00
25 Cameron Thomas RC 2.00 5.00
26 Chris Paul 1.00 2.50
27 Luka Garza RC 1.00 2.50
28 Donovan Mitchell 1.00 2.50
29 LaMelo Ball 1.25 3.00
30 Kristaps Porzingis .60 1.50
31 Franz Wagner RC 3.00 8.00
32 Kawhi Leonard 1.25 3.00
33 Tre Mann RC 1.50 4.00
34 Anthony Edwards 2.50 6.00
35 Jaden Springer RC 1.00 2.50
36 Devin Booker 1.25 3.00
37 JT Thor RC 1.00 2.50
38 Rudy Gobert .60 1.50
39 Terry Rozier III .40 1.00
40 Jamal Murray .75 2.00
41 Davion Mitchell RC 1.00 2.50
42 Russell Westbrook .75 2.00
43 Kai Jones RC .75 2.00
44 Zion Williamson 1.25 3.00
45 Day'Ron Sharpe RC 1.00 2.50
46 Damian Lillard 1.25 3.00
47 Isaiah Todd .40 1.00
48 Bradley Beal .60 1.50
49 Zach LaVine .75 2.00
50 Nikola Jokic 2.50 6.00
51 Ziaire Williams RC 1.25 3.00
52 LeBron James 4.00 10.00
53 Jalen Johnson RC 3.00 8.00
54 Brandon Ingram .60 1.50
55 Santi Aldama RC 1.25 3.00
56 CJ McCollum .40 1.00
57 Juan Toscano-Anderson .50 1.25
58 Carmelo Anthony .75 2.00
59 Nikola Vucevic .50 1.25
60 Jerami Grant .50 1.25
61 James Bouknight RC .75 2.00
62 Anthony Davis 1.25 3.00
63 Keon Johnson RC 1.00 2.50
64 Julius Randle .60 1.50
65 Jeremiah Robinson-Earl RC 1.00 2.50
66 De'Aaron Fox .75 2.00
67 Trae Young 1.25 3.00
68 Lonzo Ball .50 1.25
69 Cade Cunningham RC 6.00 15.00
70 Stephen Curry 3.00 8.00
71 Joshua Primo RC .75 2.00
72 Ja Morant 1.50 4.00
73 Isaiah Jackson RC 1.00 2.50
74 Kemba Walker .50 1.25
75 Miles McBride RC 1.50 4.00
76 Tyrese Haliburton 1.00 2.50
77 Jayson Tatum 2.00 5.00
78 Gordon Hayward .40 1.00
79 Jalen Green RC 5.00 12.00
80 James Wiseman .40 1.00
81 Chris Duarte RC .75 2.00
82 Jimmy Butler .75 2.00
83 Usman Garuba RC .75 2.00
84 Shai Gilgeous-Alexander 2.50 6.00
85 Ayo Dosunmu RC 2.00 5.00
86 Dejounte Murray .50 1.25
87 Jaylen Brown .75 2.00
88 Michael Porter Jr. .60 1.50
89 Evan Mobley RC 4.00 10.00
90 John Wall .60 1.50
91 Moses Moody RC 2.00 5.00
92 Bam Adebayo .75 2.00
93 Josh Christopher RC .75 2.00
94 Cole Anthony .60 1.50
95 Jared Butler RC 1.00 2.50
96 Pascal Siakam .75 2.00
97 James Harden 1.00 2.50
98 Derrick Rose .75 2.00
99 Scottie Barnes RC 3.00 8.00
100 Christian Wood .40 1.00
101 Jaden Springer JSY AU/199 10.00 25.00
102 Bones Hyland JSY AU/199 12.00 30.00
103 Davion Mitchell JSY AU/199 10.00 25.00
104 Isaiah Livers JSY AU/199 10.00 25.00
105 Chris Duarte JSY AU/199 8.00 20.00
106 Usman Garuba JSY AU/199 8.00 20.00
107 Miles McBride JSY AU/199 15.00 40.00
108 Santi Aldama JSY AU/199 12.00 30.00
109 Scottie Lewis JSY AU/199 RC 8.00 20.00
110 Luka Garza JSY AU/199 10.00 25.00
111 Franz Wagner JSY AU/199 75.00 200.00
112 Josh Giddey JSY AU/199 75.00 200.00
113 Keon Johnson JSY AU/199 10.00 25.00
114 Corey Kispert JSY AU/199 12.00 30.00
115 Quentin Grimes JSY AU/199 20.00 50.00
116 Evan Mobley JSY AU/199 125.00 300.00
117 Joshua Primo JSY AU/199 8.00 20.00
118 Ziaire Williams JSY AU/199 12.00 30.00
119 Jalen Johnson JSY AU/199 30.00 80.00
120 Tre Mann JSY AU/199 15.00 40.00
121 Day'Ron Sharpe JSY AU/199 10.00 25.00
122 Jeremiah Robinson-Earl JSY AU/199 10.00 25.00
123 Ayo Dosunmu JSY AU/199 20.00 50.00
124 Charles Bassey JSY AU/199 RC 10.00 25.00
125 Brandon Boston Jr. JSY AU/199 10.00 25.00
126 Cameron Thomas JSY AU/199 20.00 50.00
127 Greg Brown III JSY AU/199 RC 8.00 20.00
128 Jared Butler JSY AU/199 10.00 25.00
129 Josh Christopher JSY AU/199 8.00 20.00
130 Isaiah Jackson JSY AU/199 10.00 25.00
131 Trey Murphy III JSY AU/199 30.00 80.00
132 James Bouknight JSY AU/199 8.00 20.00
133 Cade Cunningham JSY AU/199 200.00 500.00
134 Kai Jones JSY AU/199 8.00 20.00
135 Jalen Suggs JSY AU/199 25.00 60.00
136 Jonathan Kuminga JSY AU/199 75.00 200.00
137 Alperen Sengun JSY AU/199 75.00 200.00
138 Moses Moody JSY AU/199 20.00 50.00
139 Scottie Barnes JSY AU/199 100.00 250.00
140 Jalen Green JSY AU/199 125.00 300.00

2021-22 Crown Royale Crystal Purple

*CRYSTAL PURPLE: 3X TO 8X BASIC
STATED PRINT RUN 25 SER.#'d SETS
20 Luka Doncic 50.00 120.00
29 LaMelo Ball 50.00 120.00
34 Anthony Edwards 40.00 100.00
44 Zion Williamson 30.00 80.00
52 LeBron James 50.00 120.00
69 Cade Cunningham 125.00 300.00
70 Stephen Curry 50.00 120.00
72 Ja Morant 50.00 120.00

2021-22 Crown Royale Crystal Red

*CRYSTAL RED: 2X TO 5X BASIC
STATED PRINT RUN 49 SER.#'d SETS

2021-22 Crown Royale Coat of Arms Materials

COMMON CARD 1.25 3.00
SEMISTARS 1.50 4.00
UNLISTED STARS 2.00 5.00
1 Gordon Hayward 1.50 4.00
2 John Collins 2.00 5.00
3 Karl-Anthony Towns 3.00 8.00
4 Joel Embiid 5.00 12.00
5 Bam Adebayo 3.00 8.00
6 Seth Curry 1.50 4.00
7 Joe Ingles 1.50 4.00
8 Chris Paul 4.00 10.00
9 Lou Williams 2.00 5.00
10 Brook Lopez 1.50 4.00
11 Terry Rozier III 1.50 4.00
12 Kendrick Perkins 1.50 4.00
13 Jamal Murray 3.00 8.00
14 Josh Jackson 1.25 3.00
15 Elton Brand 2.00 5.00
16 Al Harrington 1.50 4.00
17 Kristaps Porzingis 2.50 6.00
18 Immanuel Quickley 2.00 5.00
19 LaMarcus Aldridge 2.00 5.00
20 Kyle Lowry 2.00 5.00

2021-22 Crown Royale Crown Autographs

COMMON CARD 4.00 10.00
SEMISTARS 5.00 12.00
UNLISTED STARS 6.00 15.00
STATED PRINT RUN 44-99 SER.#'d SETS
*BLUE/75: .4X TO 1X BASIC
1 CJ McCollum/99 5.00 12.00
2 Jason Terry/99 5.00 12.00
3 Kenny Sky Walker/99 4.00 10.00
4 Al Attles/99 6.00 15.00
5 Marcus Camby/99 5.00 12.00
6 Bill Laimbeer/99 6.00 15.00
7 Ralph Sampson/99 6.00 15.00
8 Danny Manning/99 5.00 12.00
9 Stephen Jackson/99 5.00 12.00
10 Felipe Lopez/99 5.00 12.00
12 Jason Williams/99 30.00 80.00
13 Dwight Howard/99 30.00 80.00
14 Andre Miller/99 5.00 12.00
15 Mark Aguirre/99 5.00 12.00
16 Bob Dandridge/99 6.00 15.00
17 Rex Chapman/99 5.00 12.00
18 Darrell Griffith/99 6.00 15.00
19 T.J. McConnell/99 5.00 12.00
20 George McGinnis/99 6.00 15.00
22 Mark Eaton/99 6.00 15.00
23 Kiki Vandeweghe/99 5.00 12.00
24 Arvydas Sabonis/99 8.00 20.00
25 Mark Price/99 6.00 15.00
26 Caris LeVert/99 5.00 12.00
27 Rick Fox/99 6.00 15.00
28 David Thompson/99 8.00 20.00
29 Udonis Haslem/99 4.00 10.00
30 Glen Rice/99 6.00 15.00
31 Tony Parker/99 15.00 40.00
32 JJ Redick/99 6.00 15.00
33 Kurt Rambis/99 5.00 12.00
34 Avery Johnson/91 5.00 12.00
35 Maurice Cheeks/99 5.00 12.00
36 Carlos Boozer/99 5.00 12.00
37 Ron Mercer/99 5.00 12.00
38 Detlef Schrempf/99 6.00 15.00
39 Dennis Rodman/99 40.00 100.00
40 Hedo Turkoglu/99 5.00 12.00
41 Pat Riley/99 20.00 50.00
42 Joe Harris/99 5.00 12.00
43 Kurt Thomas/99 5.00 12.00
44 B.J. Armstrong/99 6.00 15.00
45 Michael Porter Jr./99 8.00 20.00
46 Chris Boucher/99 6.00 15.00
47 Roy Hibbert/99 5.00 12.00
48 Elton Brand/99 6.00 15.00
49 Khris Middleton/99 6.00 15.00
50 Herb Williams/99 4.00 10.00
51 Kawhi Leonard/44 75.00 200.00
52 Jonas Valanciunas/99 5.00 12.00
53 Louie Dampier/99 6.00 15.00
54 Ben Wallace/99 20.00 50.00
55 Nate McMillan/99 5.00 12.00
56 Clint Capela/99 6.00 15.00
57 Rudy Gay/99 6.00 15.00
58 Elvin Hayes/99 8.00 20.00
59 Jamal Murray/99 15.00 40.00
60 Jae'Sean Tate/99 6.00 15.00

2021-22 Crown Royale Crown Autographs Purple

*PURPLE: .6X TO 1.5X BASIC
STATED PRINT RUN 25 SER.#'d SETS
11 Anfernee Hardaway 60.00 150.00

2021-22 Crown Royale Crown Autographs Red

*RED: .5X TO 1.2X BASIC
STATED PRINT RUN 49 SER.#'d SETS
11 Anfernee Hardaway 50.00 120.00

2021-22 Crown Royale Future Kings Signatures

STATED PRINT RUN 49 SER.#'d SETS
EXCHANGE DEADLINE 11/11/2023
*FOTL/17: .5X TO 1.2X BASIC
1 Day'Ron Sharpe 10.00 25.00
2 Davion Mitchell 10.00 25.00
3 Ayo Dosunmu 20.00 50.00
4 Chris Duarte 8.00 20.00
5 Brandon Boston Jr. 10.00 25.00
6 Trey Murphy III 30.00 80.00
7 Keon Johnson 10.00 25.00
8 Cade Cunningham 150.00 400.00
9 Quentin Grimes 20.00 50.00
10 Jalen Suggs 25.00 60.00
11 Santi Aldama 12.00 30.00
12 Ziaire Williams 12.00 30.00
13 Jared Butler 10.00 25.00
14 Moses Moody 20.00 50.00
15 Luka Garza 10.00 25.00
16 Tre Mann 15.00 40.00
17 Isaiah Jackson 10.00 25.00
18 Jalen Green 100.00 250.00
19 Bones Hyland 12.00 30.00
20 Josh Giddey 60.00 150.00
21 Jeremiah Robinson-Earl 10.00 25.00
22 James Bouknight 8.00 20.00
23 Isaiah Livers 10.00 25.00
24 Corey Kispert 12.00 30.00
25 Charles Bassey 10.00 25.00
26 Kai Jones 8.00 20.00
27 Usman Garuba 8.00 20.00
28 Evan Mobley 75.00 200.00
29 Cameron Thomas 20.00 50.00
30 Jonathan Kuminga 75.00 200.00
31 Miles McBride 15.00 40.00
32 Joshua Primo 8.00 20.00
33 Greg Brown III 8.00 20.00
34 Alperen Sengun 75.00 200.00
35 Scottie Lewis 8.00 20.00
36 Jalen Johnson 30.00 80.00
37 Josh Christopher 8.00 20.00
38 Scottie Barnes 75.00 200.00
39 Jaden Springer 10.00 25.00
40 Franz Wagner 60.00 150.00

2021-22 Crown Royale Hall of Fame Memorabilia

COMMON CARD 2.50 6.00
SEMISTARS 3.00 8.00
UNLISTED STARS 4.00 10.00
1 Clyde Drexler 6.00 15.00
2 James Worthy 6.00 15.00
3 Dominique Wilkins 6.00 15.00
4 Ralph Sampson 4.00 10.00
5 Tim Duncan 10.00 25.00
6 Patrick Ewing 6.00 15.00
7 David Robinson 8.00 20.00
8 Steve Nash 8.00 20.00
9 Alonzo Mourning 6.00 15.00
10 Ray Allen 6.00 15.00

2021-22 Crown Royale Heirs to the Throne Materials

COMMON CARD 1.50 4.00
SEMISTARS 2.00 5.00
UNLISTED STARS 2.50 6.00
*PRIME: 1.5X TO 4X BASIC
1 Chris Duarte 2.00 5.00
2 Kessler Edwards 2.50 6.00
3 Scottie Lewis 2.00 5.00
4 Cade Cunningham 15.00 40.00
5 Keon Johnson 2.50 6.00
6 Aaron Wiggins 3.00 8.00
7 Joshua Primo 2.00 5.00
8 Day'Ron Sharpe 2.50 6.00
9 Jaden Springer 2.50 6.00
10 Brandon Boston Jr. 2.50 6.00
11 JT Thor 2.50 6.00
12 Isaiah Jackson 2.50 6.00
13 Neemias Queta 2.50 6.00
14 Kai Jones 2.00 5.00
15 Corey Kispert 3.00 8.00
16 Moses Moody 5.00 12.00
17 Ziaire Williams 3.00 8.00
18 Jeremiah Robinson-Earl 2.50 6.00
19 Bones Hyland 3.00 8.00
20 Cameron Thomas 5.00 12.00
21 Miles McBride 4.00 10.00
22 Trey Murphy III 8.00 20.00
23 Franz Wagner 8.00 20.00
24 Jalen Suggs 6.00 15.00
25 Quentin Grimes 5.00 12.00
26 Scottie Barnes 8.00 20.00
27 Jalen Johnson 8.00 20.00
28 Ayo Dosunmu 5.00 12.00
29 Davion Mitchell 2.50 6.00
30 Greg Brown III 2.00 5.00
31 Santi Aldama 3.00 8.00
32 James Bouknight 2.00 5.00
33 Josh Giddey 8.00 20.00
34 Jonathan Kuminga 8.00 20.00
35 Evan Mobley 10.00 25.00
36 Jalen Green 12.00 30.00
37 Tre Mann 4.00 10.00
38 Charles Bassey 2.50 6.00
39 Joe Wieskamp 2.00 5.00
40 Jared Butler 2.50 6.00

2021-22 Crown Royale Kaboom

1 Luka Doncic 800.00 1,500.00
2 LeBron James 1,250.00 2,500.00
3 Stephen Curry 1,250.00 2,500.00
4 Zion Williamson 300.00 600.00
5 Giannis Antetokounmpo 500.00 1,000.00
6 Kevin Durant 300.00 600.00
7 Ja Morant 500.00 1,000.00
8 Damian Lillard 300.00 600.00
9 Trae Young 200.00 500.00
10 Jayson Tatum 500.00 1,000.00
11 LaMelo Ball 300.00 600.00
12 James Harden 200.00 500.00
13 Kareem Abdul-Jabbar 200.00 500.00
14 Tracy McGrady 400.00 800.00
15 Ben Wallace 200.00 500.00
16 Bill Russell 300.00 600.00
17 Jason Williams 200.00 500.00
18 James Bouknight 40.00 100.00
19 Jonathan Kuminga 500.00 1,000.00
20 Davion Mitchell 100.00 250.00
21 Cade Cunningham 1,000.00 2,000.00
22 Jalen Green 500.00 1,000.00
23 Evan Mobley 500.00 1,000.00
24 Jalen Suggs 125.00 300.00
25 Scottie Barnes 500.00 1,000.00

2021-22 Crown Royale Knights of the Round Table Jersey Autographs

COMMON CARD 4.00 10.00
SEMISTARS 5.00 12.00
UNLISTED STARS 6.00 15.00
PRINT RUNS 99 COPIES PER
EXCHANGE DEADLINE 11/11/2023
1 Tom Gugliotta 5.00 12.00
2 Rick Fox 6.00 15.00
3 T.J. McConnell 5.00 12.00
4 Drew Gooden 5.00 12.00
5 Danny Manning 5.00 12.00
6 Bill Laimbeer 6.00 15.00
7 Hedo Turkoglu 5.00 12.00
8 Mark Price 6.00 15.00
9 Ralph Sampson 6.00 15.00
10 Maurice Cheeks 5.00 12.00
11 Mark Aguirre 5.00 12.00
12 Caris LeVert 5.00 12.00
13 Arvydas Sabonis 8.00 20.00
14 Elton Brand 6.00 15.00
15 Fat Lever 5.00 12.00
16 Ben Wallace 40.00 100.00
17 Udonis Haslem 4.00 10.00
18 Kenny Smith 5.00 12.00
19 Carlos Boozer 5.00 12.00
20 Joe Harris 5.00 12.00
21 Jason Williams 40.00 100.00
22 Kurt Thomas 5.00 12.00
23 Andre Miller 5.00 12.00
24 Mark Eaton 6.00 15.00
25 Marcus Camby 5.00 12.00
26 Michael Porter Jr. 8.00 20.00
27 Jason Terry 5.00 12.00
28 Chris Boucher 6.00 15.00
29 Alvan Adams 5.00 12.00
30 David Thompson 8.00 20.00

2021-22 Crown Royale Knights of the Round Table Materials

COMMON CARD 1.25 3.00
SEMISTARS 1.50 4.00
UNLISTED STARS 2.00 5.00
1 Tyrese Maxey 5.00 12.00
2 Kevin Knox II 1.25 3.00
3 Paul Pierce 3.00 8.00
4 DeMar DeRozan 2.50 6.00
5 Aaron Gordon 2.00 5.00
6 Derrick Rose 3.00 8.00
7 Josh Richardson 1.50 4.00
8 Carmelo Anthony 3.00 8.00
9 D'Angelo Russell 2.00 5.00
10 Ben Simmons 2.00 5.00
11 Kemba Walker 2.00 5.00
12 Shai Gilgeous-Alexander 10.00 25.00
13 OG Anunoby 2.00 5.00
14 Tyler Herro 3.00 8.00
15 Onyeka Okongwu 2.00 5.00
16 Paul George 3.00 8.00
17 Marcus Smart 2.00 5.00
18 Jamal Crawford 2.00 5.00
19 Devin Vassell 3.00 8.00
20 Giannis Antetokounmpo 15.00 40.00
21 Enes Freedom 1.50 4.00
22 Jeff Teague 1.25 3.00
23 LeBron James 25.00 60.00
24 Bojan Bogdanovic 1.50 4.00
25 Vince Carter 4.00 10.00
26 Mitchell Robinson 2.00 5.00
27 Jimmy Butler 3.00 8.00
28 Deandre Ayton 2.00 5.00
29 Julius Randle 2.50 6.00
30 Rudy Gobert 2.50 6.00

2021-22 Crown Royale Pivotal Players

COMMON CARD 2.00 5.00
SEMISTARS 2.50 6.00
UNLISTED STARS 3.00 8.00
STATED PRINT RUN 99 SER.#'d SETS
*BLUE/75: .5X TO 1.2X BASIC
*RED/49: .6X TO 1.5X BASIC
*PURPLE/25: 1.25X TO 3X BASIC
1 Giannis Antetokounmpo 15.00 40.00
2 Stephen Curry 20.00 50.00
3 Zion Williamson 8.00 20.00
4 Trae Young 8.00 20.00
5 Luka Doncic 20.00 50.00
6 Kawhi Leonard 8.00 20.00
7 Kevin Durant 10.00 25.00
8 Jayson Tatum 12.00 30.00
9 LeBron James 25.00 60.00
10 Devin Booker 8.00 20.00

2021-22 Crown Royale Regal Achievements Signatures

COMMON CARD 5.00 12.00
SEMISTARS 6.00 15.00
UNLISTED STARS 8.00 20.00
STATED PRINT RUN 49 SER.#'d SETS
1 Nikola Jokic 200.00 500.00
3 Jrue Holiday 12.00 30.00
4 Kevin Durant 200.00 500.00
5 Brook Lopez 6.00 15.00
6 Khris Middleton 8.00 20.00
7 Thaddeus Young 5.00 12.00
8 Jayson Tatum 200.00 500.00
9 Jamal Murray 40.00 100.00
10 Enes Freedom 6.00 15.00
11 Clint Capela 8.00 20.00
12 Andre Drummond 6.00 15.00
13 Luka Doncic 600.00 1,200.00
14 T.J. McConnell 6.00 15.00
15 Myles Turner 8.00 20.00
16 Tim Hardaway Jr. 5.00 12.00
17 Danilo Gallinari 6.00 15.00
18 Joe Harris 6.00 15.00
19 Jonas Valanciunas 6.00 15.00
20 Collin Sexton 15.00 40.00

2021-22 Crown Royale Rookie Crown Autographs

COMMON CARD 4.00 10.00
SEMISTARS 5.00 12.00
UNLISTED STARS 6.00 15.00
STATED PRINT RUN 75-99 SER.#'d SETS
EXCHANGE DEADLINE 11/11/2023
*BLUE/75: .5X TO 1.2X BASIC
*RED/49: .6X TO 1.5X BASIC
*PURPLE/25: .75X TO 2X BASIC
1 Day'Ron Sharpe/99 6.00 15.00
2 Jaden Springer/99 6.00 15.00
3 Brandon Boston Jr./99 6.00 15.00
4 Chris Duarte/99 5.00 12.00
5 Josh Christopher/99 5.00 12.00
6 Scottie Lewis/99 5.00 12.00
7 Cade Cunningham/75 200.00 500.00
8 Keon Johnson/99 6.00 15.00
9 Alperen Sengun/99 20.00 50.00
10 Joshua Primo/99 5.00 12.00
11 Jeremiah Robinson-Earl/99 6.00 15.00
12 Bones Hyland/99 8.00 20.00
13 Cameron Thomas/99 12.00 30.00
15 Isaiah Jackson/99 6.00 15.00
16 Luka Garza/99 6.00 15.00
18 Corey Kispert/99 8.00 20.00
19 Moses Moody/99 12.00 30.00
20 Ziaire Williams/99 8.00 20.00
21 Ayo Dosunmu/99 12.00 30.00
22 Davion Mitchell/99 6.00 15.00
23 Greg Brown III/99 5.00 12.00
24 Miles McBride/99 10.00 25.00
26 Franz Wagner/99 40.00 100.00
27 Jalen Suggs/75 50.00 120.00
28 Quentin Grimes/99 12.00 30.00
29 Scottie Barnes/99 125.00 300.00
30 Jalen Johnson/99 20.00 50.00
31 Charles Bassey/99 6.00 15.00
32 Isaiah Livers/99 6.00 15.00
33 Jared Butler/99 6.00 15.00
34 Santi Aldama/99 8.00 20.00
36 Josh Giddey/99 100.00 250.00
37 Jonathan Kuminga/99 100.00 250.00
38 Evan Mobley/75 125.00 300.00
39 Jalen Green/75 150.00 400.00
40 Tre Mann/99 10.00 25.00

2021-22 Crown Royale Rookie Royalty

COMMON CARD 2.50 6.00
SEMISTARS 3.00 8.00
UNLISTED STARS 4.00 10.00
STATED PRINT RUN 99 SER.#'d SETS
*ASIA RED: .4X TO 1X BASIC
*BLUE/75: .5X TO 1.2X BASIC
*RED/49: .6X TO 1.5X BASIC
*PURPLE/25: .75X TO 2X BASIC
1 Jalen Green 20.00 50.00
2 Scottie Barnes 12.00 30.00
3 Moses Moody 8.00 20.00
4 Alperen Sengun 12.00 30.00
5 Jonathan Kuminga 12.00 30.00
6 Jalen Suggs 10.00 25.00
7 Kai Jones 3.00 8.00
8 Cade Cunningham 25.00 60.00
9 James Bouknight 3.00 8.00
10 Trey Murphy III 12.00 30.00
11 Isaiah Jackson 4.00 10.00
12 Josh Christopher 3.00 8.00
13 Jared Butler 4.00 10.00
14 Greg Brown III 3.00 8.00
15 Cameron Thomas 8.00 20.00
16 Brandon Boston Jr. 4.00 10.00
17 Charles Bassey 4.00 10.00
18 Ayo Dosunmu 8.00 20.00
19 Jeremiah Robinson-Earl 4.00 10.00
20 Day'Ron Sharpe 4.00 10.00
21 Tre Mann 6.00 15.00
22 Jalen Johnson 12.00 30.00
23 Ziaire Williams 5.00 12.00
24 Joshua Primo 3.00 8.00
25 Evan Mobley 15.00 40.00
26 Quentin Grimes 8.00 20.00
27 Corey Kispert 5.00 12.00
28 Keon Johnson 4.00 10.00
29 Josh Giddey 12.00 30.00
30 Franz Wagner 12.00 30.00
31 Luka Garza 4.00 10.00
32 Scottie Lewis 3.00 8.00
33 Santi Aldama 5.00 12.00
34 Miles McBride 6.00 15.00
35 Usman Garuba 3.00 8.00
36 Chris Duarte 3.00 8.00
37 Isaiah Livers 4.00 10.00
38 Davion Mitchell 4.00 10.00
39 Bones Hyland 5.00 12.00
40 Jaden Springer 4.00 10.00

2021-22 Crown Royale Royal Signatures

COMMON CARD 5.00 12.00
SEMISTARS 6.00 15.00
UNLISTED STARS 8.00 20.00
STATED PRINT RUN 49 SER.#'d SETS
1 Anthony Edwards 200.00 500.00
2 Anthony Davis 60.00 150.00
3 Jae'Sean Tate 8.00 20.00
4 Trae Young 100.00 250.00
5 Enes Freedom 6.00 15.00
6 Frank Kaminsky 5.00 12.00
8 Taj Gibson 5.00 12.00
9 Tim Hardaway Jr. 5.00 12.00
10 Grant Williams 8.00 20.00
11 Nikola Jokic 150.00 400.00
13 Roy Hibbert 6.00 15.00
14 Kevin Johnson 15.00 40.00
15 Luka Doncic 600.00 1,200.00
16 Andre Drummond 6.00 15.00
18 Stephen Jackson 6.00 15.00
19 Steve Kerr 40.00 100.00
20 Nate Archibald 8.00 20.00
21 James Wiseman 6.00 15.00
23 Ray Allen 40.00 100.00
24 Vince Carter 75.00 200.00
25 Chauncey Billups 15.00 40.00
26 Mark Aguirre 6.00 15.00
27 Richard Hamilton 12.00 30.00
28 Larry Bird 100.00 250.00
29 Magic Johnson 100.00 250.00

2021-22 Crown Royale Silhouettes Material Autographs

COMMON CARD 5.00 12.00
SEMISTARS 6.00 15.00
UNLISTED STARS 8.00 20.00
PRINT RUNS BTWN 25-99 COPIES PER
EXCHANGE DEADLINE 11/11/2023
2 Anthony Davis/25 150.00 400.00
4 Roy Hibbert/99 6.00 15.00
5 Vince Carter/49 100.00 250.00
7 Elton Brand/99 8.00 20.00
8 David Lee/99 6.00 15.00
9 CJ McCollum/49 6.00 15.00
10 Rudy Gay/99 8.00 20.00
14 Nikola Vucevic/99 8.00 20.00
15 Karl-Anthony Towns/49 40.00 100.00
16 Grant Williams/99 8.00 20.00
19 T.J. Warren/99 5.00 12.00
20 Lonnie Walker IV/99 6.00 15.00
21 Thaddeus Young/99 5.00 12.00
22 Nikola Jokic/49 200.00 500.00
24 Luka Doncic/25 1,000.00 2,000.00
26 Eric Gordon/99 6.00 15.00
27 Coby White/99 8.00 20.00
28 Jamal Murray/49 75.00 200.00
29 Cam Reddish/99 8.00 20.00
30 Gordon Hayward/49 6.00 15.00

2021-22 Crown Royale Sno Globe

COMMON CARD 2.50 6.00
SEMISTARS 3.00 8.00
UNLISTED STARS 4.00 10.00
STATED PRINT RUN 99 SER.#'d SETS
*ASIA RED: .4X TO 1X BASIC
*BLUE/75: .5X TO 1.2X BASIC
*RED/49: .6X TO 1.5X BASIC
*PURPLE/25: .75X TO 2X BASIC
1 Luka Doncic 40.00 100.00
2 Giannis Antetokounmpo 20.00 50.00
3 LeBron James 40.00 100.00
4 James Harden 8.00 20.00
5 Stephen Curry 40.00 100.00
6 Trae Young 10.00 25.00
7 Ja Morant 30.00 80.00
8 LaMelo Ball 30.00 80.00
9 Kawhi Leonard 10.00 25.00
10 Zion Williamson 30.00 80.00
11 Anthony Davis 10.00 25.00
12 Devin Booker 10.00 25.00
13 Nikola Jokic 20.00 50.00
14 Joel Embiid 10.00 25.00
15 Kevin Durant 12.00 30.00
16 Damian Lillard 10.00 25.00
17 Jayson Tatum 15.00 40.00
18 Anthony Edwards 30.00 80.00
19 Tim Duncan 10.00 25.00
20 Shaquille O'Neal 12.00 30.00
21 Magic Johnson 12.00 30.00
22 Larry Bird 12.00 30.00
23 Dwyane Wade 8.00 20.00
24 Dirk Nowitzki 10.00 25.00
25 Cade Cunningham 50.00 120.00
26 Jalen Green 40.00 100.00
27 Jonathan Kuminga 25.00 60.00
28 Jalen Suggs 10.00 25.00
29 Evan Mobley 25.00 60.00
30 Davion Mitchell 4.00 10.00

2021-22 Crown Royale Test of Time

COMMON CARD 2.50 6.00
SEMISTARS 3.00 8.00
UNLISTED STARS 4.00 10.00
STATED PRINT RUN 99 SER.#'d SETS
*ASIA RED: .4X TO 1X BASIC
*BLUE/75: .5X TO 1.2X BASIC
*RED/49: .6X TO 1.5X BASIC
*PURPLE/25: .75X TO 2X BASIC
1 LeBron James 30.00 80.00
2 Chris Paul 8.00 20.00
3 Kyle Lowry 4.00 10.00
4 Stephen Curry 25.00 60.00
5 Carmelo Anthony 6.00 15.00
6 Robert Parish 5.00 12.00
7 Vince Carter 8.00 20.00
8 Dikembe Mutombo 5.00 12.00
9 Kareem Abdul-Jabbar 12.00 30.00
10 Karl Malone 8.00 20.00
11 Paul George 6.00 15.00
12 Russell Westbrook 6.00 15.00
13 Jimmy Butler 6.00 15.00
14 Damian Lillard 10.00 25.00
15 Kevin Durant 12.00 30.00
16 Dirk Nowitzki 10.00 25.00
17 Grant Hill 6.00 15.00
18 Steve Nash 8.00 20.00
19 Tim Duncan 10.00 25.00
20 Kevin Garnett 10.00 25.00

2022-23 Crown Royale

COMMON CARD (1-100) .30 .75
SEMISTARS .40 1.00
UNLISTED STARS .50 1.25
COMMON RC (1-100) .60 1.50
RC SEMIS .75 2.00
RC UNLISTED 1.00 2.50
COMMON JSY AU (101-140) 6.00 15.00
JSY AU SEMIS 8.00 20.00
JSY AU UNLISTED 10.00 25.00
JSY AU PRINT RUN 199 SER.#'d SETS
EXCHANGE DEADLINE 11/17/2024
*ASIA RED: .6X TO 1.5X BASIC
*CRYSTAL: .5X TO 1.2X BASIC
*CRYSTAL BLUE/99: 1.5X TO 4X BASIC
*CRYSTAL PINK/75: 1.5X TO 4X BASIC
*CRYSTAL RED/49: 2X TO 5X BASIC
*CRYSTAL PURPLE/25: 3X TO 8X BASIC
*ROOKIE SILHOUETTES PRIME/25: 2X TO 5X BASE
1 Nikola Jokic 2.50 6.00
2 Walker Kessler RC 2.00 5.00
3 Dejounte Murray .60 1.50
4 Dyson Daniels RC 2.50 6.00
5 Jalen Suggs .60 1.50
6 Jabari Smith Jr. RC 3.00 8.00
7 Kristaps Porzingis .60 1.50
8 Dalen Terry RC 1.00 2.50
9 Tari Eason RC 2.50 6.00
10 DeMar DeRozan .60 1.50
11 Darius Garland .75 2.00
12 TyTy Washington Jr. RC 1.00 2.50
13 Wendell Moore Jr. RC 1.00 2.50
14 Damian Lillard 1.25 3.00
15 Jimmy Butler 1.00 2.50
16 Jake LaRavia RC 1.00 2.50
17 Tyrese Maxey 1.00 2.50
18 Andrew Wiggins .60 1.50
19 David Roddy RC 1.25 3.00
20 Malcolm Brogdon .40 1.00
21 Karl-Anthony Towns .75 2.00
22 De'Aaron Fox 1.00 2.50
23 Rudy Gobert .60 1.50
24 Jaden Ivey RC 3.00 8.00
25 Michael Porter Jr. .60 1.50
26 Buddy Hield .50 1.25
27 Jrue Holiday .60 1.50
28 Ochai Agbaji RC 1.25 3.00
29 Paul George .75 2.00
30 Anthony Davis 1.25 3.00
31 Cade Cunningham 1.50 4.00
32 Keegan Murray RC 2.50 6.00
33 Kyle Kuzma .60 1.50
34 Jalen Duren RC 3.00 8.00
35 Klay Thompson 1.25 3.00
36 Tyrese Haliburton 1.00 2.50
37 Ayo Dosunmu .60 1.50
38 Jalen Brunson 1.00 2.50
39 Paolo Banchero RC 6.00 15.00
40 MarJon Beauchamp RC 1.00 2.50
41 Collin Sexton .60 1.50
42 Zion Williamson 1.25 3.00
43 James Harden 1.00 2.50
44 LeBron James 4.00 10.00
45 Stephen Curry 4.00 10.00
46 AJ Griffin RC .75 2.00
47 Khris Middleton .60 1.50
48 Shaedon Sharpe RC 4.00 10.00
49 Christian Wood .30 .75
50 Kyrie Irving 1.00 2.50
51 Ousmane Dieng RC 1.25 3.00
52 Donovan Mitchell 1.00 2.50
53 Jeremy Sochan RC 3.00 8.00
54 Jaylen Brown 1.00 2.50
55 RJ Barrett .75 2.00
56 Zach LaVine 1.00 2.50
57 Marcus Smart .60 1.50
58 Fred VanVleet .60 1.50
59 Kevin Durant 1.50 4.00
60 Bennedict Mathurin RC 3.00 8.00
61 Devin Booker 1.25 3.00
62 Jamal Murray .75 2.00
63 Julius Randle .60 1.50
64 LaMelo Ball 1.25 3.00
65 Anfernee Simons .60 1.50
66 Tyler Herro .75 2.00
67 Christian Braun RC 2.50 6.00
68 Evan Mobley 1.25 3.00
69 Lauri Markkanen .75 2.00
70 Anthony Edwards 2.50 6.00
71 Blake Wesley RC 1.00 2.50
72 Terry Rozier III .60 1.50
73 Joel Embiid .75 2.00
74 Pascal Siakam .75 2.00
75 Johnny Davis RC 1.00 2.50
76 Nikola Jovic RC 2.00 5.00
77 Kevin Porter Jr. .40 1.00
78 Chris Paul .75 2.00
79 Jaden Hardy RC 1.50 4.00
80 Luka Doncic 3.00 8.00
81 Jalen Green 1.50 4.00
82 Jalen Williams RC 5.00 12.00
83 Scottie Barnes .75 2.00
84 Patrick Baldwin Jr. RC 1.00 2.50
85 Chet Holmgren RC 5.00 12.00
86 Keldon Johnson .60 1.50
87 Jayson Tatum 2.00 5.00
88 Cole Anthony .50 1.25
89 Shai Gilgeous-Alexander 2.50 6.00
90 Bam Adebayo .75 2.00
91 Ja Morant 1.50 4.00
92 Brandon Ingram .60 1.50
93 Josh Giddey .75 2.00
94 Giannis Antetokounmpo 2.50 6.00
95 Bradley Beal .60 1.50
96 Desmond Bane .60 1.50
97 Domantas Sabonis .60 1.50
98 Devin Vassell .60 1.50
99 Kawhi Leonard 1.25 3.00
100 Trae Young 1.25 3.00
101 Chet Holmgren JSY AU 150.00 400.00
102 MarJon Beauchamp JSY AU 10.00 25.00
103 Christian Braun JSY AU 25.00 60.00
104 Jabari Smith Jr. JSY AU 60.00 150.00
105 TyTy Washington Jr. JSY AU 10.00 25.00
106 Christian Koloko JSY AU 10.00 25.00
107 Caleb Houstan JSY AU 10.00 25.00
108 Blake Wesley JSY AU 10.00 25.00
109 Mark Williams JSY AU 20.00 50.00
110 Andrew Nembhard JSY AU 20.00 50.00
111 Kennedy Chandler JSY AU 10.00 25.00
112 Shaedon Sharpe JSY AU 60.00 150.00
113 Wendell Moore Jr. JSY AU 10.00 25.00
114 Jake LaRavia JSY AU 10.00 25.00
115 E.J. Liddell JSY AU 10.00 25.00
116 Malaki Branham JSY AU 10.00 25.00
117 Peyton Watson JSY AU 15.00 40.00
118 Patrick Baldwin Jr. JSY AU 10.00 25.00
119 Keegan Murray JSY AU 60.00 150.00
120 Johnny Davis JSY AU 10.00 25.00
121 Trevor Keels JSY AU 8.00 20.00
122 Isaiah Mobley JSY AU 10.00 25.00
123 Moussa Diabate JSY AU 10.00 25.00
124 Jaden Ivey JSY AU 30.00 80.00
125 Jalen Williams JSY AU 75.00 200.00
126 Walker Kessler JSY AU 20.00 50.00
127 Nikola Jovic JSY AU 20.00 50.00
128 Jeremy Sochan JSY AU 30.00 80.00
129 Ousmane Dieng JSY AU 12.00 30.00
130 Dalen Terry JSY AU 10.00 25.00
131 Paolo Banchero JSY AU 150.00 400.00
132 David Roddy JSY AU 12.00 30.00
133 Ochai Agbaji JSY AU 12.00 30.00
134 Max Christie JSY AU 25.00 60.00
135 Jaden Hardy JSY AU 15.00 40.00
136 Tari Eason JSY AU 25.00 60.00
137 Bennedict Mathurin JSY AU 30.00 80.00
138 Dyson Daniels JSY AU 25.00 60.00
139 Jalen Duren JSY AU 30.00 80.00
140 AJ Griffin JSY AU 8.00 20.00

2022-23 Crown Royale Coat of Arms Relics

COMMON CARD 1.25 3.00
SEMISTARS 1.50 4.00
UNLISTED STARS 2.00 5.00
*PRIME/25: 1.5X TO 4X BASIC
1 LaMelo Ball 5.00 12.00
2 Paul George 3.00 8.00
3 Devin Booker 5.00 12.00
4 Zach LaVine 4.00 10.00
5 Jimmy Butler 4.00 10.00
6 Pascal Siakam 3.00 8.00
7 Jaylen Brown 4.00 10.00
8 Karl-Anthony Towns 3.00 8.00
9 Brandon Ingram 2.50 6.00
10 James Harden 4.00 10.00
11 RJ Barrett 3.00 8.00
12 Josh Giddey 3.00 8.00
13 Carmelo Anthony 3.00 8.00
15 Jamal Murray 3.00 8.00
16 Rudy Gobert 2.50 6.00
17 Chris Paul 4.00 10.00
18 Anfernee Simons 2.50 6.00
19 Bradley Beal 2.50 6.00
20 Franz Wagner 5.00 12.00

2022-23 Crown Royale Crown Autographs

COMMON CARD 4.00 10.00
SEMISTARS 5.00 12.00
UNLISTED STARS 6.00 15.00
STATED PRINT RUN 75-99 SER.#'d SETS
EXCHANGE DEADLINE 11/17/2024
*BLUE/75: .4X TO 1X BASIC
*PINK/49: .5X TO 1.2X BASIC
*RED/35: .5X TO 1.2X BASIC
*PURPLE/25: .6X TO 1.5X BASIC
1 Jalen McDaniels/99 6.00 15.00
2 Greg Anthony/99 5.00 12.00
3 Lenny Wilkens/99 8.00 20.00
4 Dennis Scott/99 5.00 12.00
5 Jamal Crawford/99 6.00 15.00
6 Spencer Dinwiddie/99 5.00 12.00
7 Alex Caruso/99 12.00 30.00
8 John Lucas/99 6.00 15.00
9 Moses Moody/99 8.00 20.00
10 Danny Green/99 5.00 12.00
11 Lonnie Walker IV/99 5.00 12.00
13 Marcus Smart/99 12.00 30.00
14 Jason Terry/99 5.00 12.00
15 Tim Hardaway Jr./99 5.00 12.00
16 Anfernee Simons/99 12.00 30.00
17 De'Aaron Fox/99 25.00 60.00
18 Dale Ellis/99 6.00 15.00
19 Kenyon Martin/99 6.00 15.00
20 Shawn Kemp/99 15.00 40.00
21 Bernard King/99 8.00 20.00
22 Scottie Barnes/99 25.00 60.00
23 Franz Wagner/99 25.00 60.00
24 Jalen Brunson/99 40.00 100.00
25 Malik Monk/99 6.00 15.00
26 Aaron Nesmith/99 6.00 15.00
27 T.J. McConnell/99 5.00 12.00
28 Caris LeVert/99 5.00 12.00
29 Jordan Clarkson/99 12.00 30.00
30 Tyrese Haliburton/99 40.00 100.00
31 Alperen Sengun/99 20.00 50.00
32 Bones Hyland/99 5.00 12.00
33 Sam Cassell/99 6.00 15.00
34 Pau Gasol/99 25.00 60.00
35 Brook Lopez/99 6.00 15.00
36 Michael Porter Jr./99 8.00 20.00
37 Josh Giddey/99 40.00 100.00
38 Davion Mitchell/99 5.00 12.00
39 Gail Goodrich/99 6.00 15.00
40 Grant Hill/99 20.00 50.00
41 Kevin Garnett/75 50.00 120.00
42 Jose Alvarado/99 6.00 15.00
43 Glen Rice/99 6.00 15.00
44 Jack Sikma/99 8.00 20.00
45 Jerry Stackhouse/99 8.00 20.00
46 Jalen Green/99 40.00 100.00
47 Evan Fournier/99 5.00 12.00
48 James Worthy/99 15.00 40.00
49 Wendell Carter Jr./99 6.00 15.00
50 Calvin Murphy/99 6.00 15.00
51 Joakim Noah/99 5.00 12.00
52 Chris Paul/75 40.00 100.00
53 Ayo Dosunmu/99 8.00 20.00
54 Grant Williams/99 5.00 12.00
55 Robert Covington/99 4.00 10.00
56 Kendrick Perkins/99 4.00 10.00
57 Juwan Howard/99 6.00 15.00
58 Luguentz Dort/99 6.00 15.00
59 PJ Washington Jr./99 6.00 15.00
60 Will Barton/99 4.00 10.00

2022-23 Crown Royale Future Kings Signatures

COMMON CARD 5.00 12.00
SEMISTARS 6.00 15.00
UNLISTED STARS 8.00 20.00
STATED PRINT RUN 49 SER.#'d SETS
EXCHANGE DEADLINE 11/17/2024
1 AJ Griffin 6.00 15.00
2 Jaden Hardy 40.00 100.00
3 Tari Eason 20.00 50.00
4 Bennedict Mathurin 75.00 200.00
5 Dyson Daniels 20.00 50.00
6 Jalen Duren 25.00 60.00
7 Jeremy Sochan 25.00 60.00
8 Ousmane Dieng 10.00 25.00
9 Dalen Terry 8.00 20.00
10 Paolo Banchero 200.00 500.00
11 David Roddy 10.00 25.00
12 Ochai Agbaji 10.00 25.00
13 Max Christie 40.00 100.00
14 Chet Holmgren 150.00 400.00
15 MarJon Beauchamp 8.00 20.00
16 Christian Braun 20.00 50.00
17 Caleb Houstan 8.00 20.00
18 Jabari Smith Jr. 75.00 200.00
19 Blake Wesley 8.00 20.00
20 Mark Williams 15.00 40.00
21 Andrew Nembhard 15.00 40.00
22 Johnny Davis 8.00 20.00
23 Trevor Keels 6.00 15.00
24 Isaiah Mobley 8.00 20.00
25 Moussa Diabate 8.00 20.00
26 Jaden Ivey 75.00 200.00
27 Jalen Williams 75.00 200.00
28 Walker Kessler 15.00 40.00
29 Nikola Jovic 15.00 40.00
30 Kennedy Chandler 8.00 20.00
31 Shaedon Sharpe 100.00 250.00
32 Wendell Moore Jr. 8.00 20.00
33 Jake LaRavia 8.00 20.00
34 E.J. Liddell 8.00 20.00
35 Malaki Branham 8.00 20.00
36 Patrick Baldwin Jr. 8.00 20.00
37 Keegan Murray 75.00 200.00
38 TyTy Washington Jr. 8.00 20.00
39 Christian Koloko 8.00 20.00
40 Peyton Watson 12.00 30.00

2022-23 Crown Royale Hand Crafted

STATED PRINT RUN 99 SER.#'d SETS
*ASIA RED: .4X TO 1X BASIC
*BLUE/75: .5X TO 1.2X BASIC
*RED/49: 6X TO 1.5X BASIC
*PURPLE/25: .75X TO 2X BASIC
1 Magic Johnson 20.00 50.00
2 Larry Bird 20.00 50.00
3 Kareem Abdul-Jabbar 15.00 40.00
4 LeBron James 60.00 150.00
5 Stephen Curry 60.00 150.00
6 Tim Duncan 15.00 40.00
7 Dennis Rodman 40.00 100.00
8 Dwyane Wade 15.00 40.00
9 Shaquille O'Neal 20.00 50.00
10 Kawhi Leonard 15.00 40.00

2022-23 Crown Royale Heirs to the Throne Relics

COMMON CARD 1.25 3.00
SEMISTARS 1.50 4.00
UNLISTED STARS 2.00 5.00
*PRIME/25: 1.5X TO 4X BASIC
1 Wendell Moore Jr. 2.00 5.00
2 Jaden Hardy 3.00 8.00
3 AJ Griffin 1.50 4.00
4 Dalen Terry 2.00 5.00
5 Johnny Davis 2.00 5.00
6 Nikola Jovic 4.00 10.00
7 Mark Williams 4.00 10.00
8 David Roddy 2.50 6.00
9 Jaden Ivey 6.00 15.00
10 Peyton Watson 3.00 8.00
11 Keegan Murray 5.00 12.00
12 Jabari Smith Jr. 6.00 15.00
13 Jake LaRavia 2.00 5.00
14 Isaiah Mobley 2.00 5.00
15 Patrick Baldwin Jr. 2.00 5.00
16 TyTy Washington Jr. 2.00 5.00
17 Christian Koloko 2.00 5.00
18 Jeremy Sochan 6.00 15.00
19 Dyson Daniels 5.00 12.00
20 Tari Eason 5.00 12.00
21 Christian Braun 5.00 12.00
22 E.J. Liddell 2.00 5.00
23 Ochai Agbaji 2.50 6.00
24 Moussa Diabate 2.00 5.00
25 Paolo Banchero 12.00 30.00
26 Caleb Houstan 2.00 5.00
27 MarJon Beauchamp 2.00 5.00
28 Jalen Williams 10.00 25.00
29 Blake Wesley 2.00 5.00
30 Chet Holmgren 10.00 25.00
31 Malaki Branham 2.00 5.00
32 Jalen Duren 6.00 15.00
33 Shaedon Sharpe 8.00 20.00
34 Walker Kessler 4.00 10.00
35 Ousmane Dieng 2.50 6.00
36 Max Christie 5.00 12.00
37 Trevor Keels 1.50 4.00
38 Kennedy Chandler 2.00 5.00
39 Andrew Nembhard 4.00 10.00
40 Bennedict Mathurin 6.00 15.00

2022-23 Crown Royale Kaboom

1 Luka Doncic 600.00 1,200.00
2 LeBron James 1,250.00 2,500.00
3 Trae Young 350.00 700.00
4 Kevin Durant 200.00 500.00
5 LaMelo Ball 300.00 600.00
6 Jayson Tatum 500.00 1,000.00
7 Ja Morant 400.00 800.00
8 Giannis Antetokounmpo 500.00 1,000.00
9 Damian Lillard 200.00 500.00
10 Cade Cunningham 350.00 700.00
11 Stephen Curry 1,500.00 3,000.00
12 Anthony Edwards 500.00 1,000.00
13 Zion Williamson 300.00 600.00
14 Jalen Green 300.00 600.00
15 Larry Bird 300.00 600.00
16 Tracy McGrady 300.00 600.00
17 Dennis Rodman 350.00 700.00
18 Manu Ginobili 300.00 600.00
19 Shaquille O'Neal 400.00 800.00
20 Paolo Banchero 1,000.00 2,000.00
21 Chet Holmgren 800.00 1,500.00
22 Jabari Smith Jr. 400.00 800.00
23 Keegan Murray 400.00 800.00
24 Jaden Ivey 500.00 1,000.00
25 Bennedict Mathurin 500.00 1,000.00

2022-23 Crown Royale Kings Court Jersey Autographs

COMMON CARD 5.00 12.00
SEMISTARS 6.00 15.00
UNLISTED STARS 8.00 20.00
STATED PRINT RUN 25-99 SER.#'d SETS
EXCHANGE DEADLINE 11/17/2024
2 Davion Mitchell/99 6.00 15.00
3 Dirk Nowitzki/49 100.00 250.00
4 Joe Dumars/99 10.00 25.00
6 Jaren Jackson Jr./99 50.00 120.00
7 Bogdan Bogdanovic/99 8.00 20.00
8 Bradley Beal/49 10.00 25.00
9 Marcus Smart/99 25.00 60.00
10 Steve Francis/99 8.00 20.00
11 Maxi Kleber/99 6.00 15.00
12 Bill Laimbeer/99 8.00 20.00
13 Antawn Jamison/99 8.00 20.00
16 Brandon Clarke/99 6.00 15.00
18 Isiah Thomas/49 20.00 50.00
19 Onyeka Okongwu/99 8.00 20.00
22 Jrue Holiday/99 10.00 25.00
23 Georges Niang/99 6.00 15.00
24 Brandon Ingram/99 25.00 60.00
25 Mike Conley/99 6.00 15.00
26 Caron Butler/99 6.00 15.00
27 Kyrie Irving/25 75.00 200.00
28 Gordon Hayward/99 6.00 15.00
29 Cameron Johnson/99 6.00 15.00
30 Dorian Finney-Smith/99 6.00 15.00

2022-23 Crown Royale Knights of the Round Table Relics

COMMON CARD 1.25 3.00
SEMISTARS 1.50 4.00
UNLISTED STARS 2.00 5.00
*PRIME/25: 1.5X TO 4X BASIC
1 Tyrese Maxey 4.00 10.00
2 Anthony Davis 5.00 12.00
3 DeMar DeRozan 2.50 6.00
4 Tyler Herro 3.00 8.00
5 Fred VanVleet 2.50 6.00
6 Klay Thompson 5.00 12.00
7 Ben Simmons 2.00 5.00
8 Darius Garland 3.00 8.00
9 Saddiq Bey 1.50 4.00
10 Donovan Mitchell 4.00 10.00
11 D'Angelo Russell 1.50 4.00
12 Kawhi Leonard 5.00 12.00
13 Julius Randle 2.50 6.00
14 Christian Wood 1.25 3.00
15 Deandre Ayton 2.00 5.00
16 Keldon Johnson 2.50 6.00
18 Bam Adebayo 3.00 8.00
19 Russell Westbrook 3.00 8.00
20 Terry Rozier III 2.50 6.00
21 CJ McCollum 2.00 5.00
22 Derrick Rose 4.00 10.00
23 De'Andre Hunter 2.00 5.00
24 Jerami Grant 2.50 6.00
25 Draymond Green 2.50 6.00
26 Buddy Hield 2.00 5.00
27 Shai Gilgeous-Alexander 10.00 25.00
28 Domantas Sabonis 2.50 6.00
29 John Collins 2.00 5.00
30 OG Anunoby 2.50 6.00

2022-23 Crown Royale Majestic Signatures

COMMON CARD 5.00 12.00
SEMISTARS 6.00 15.00
UNLISTED STARS 8.00 20.00
STATED PRINT RUN 49 SER.#'d SETS
EXCHANGE DEADLINE 11/17/2024
1 Luka Doncic 500.00 1,000.00
2 Paul Pierce 40.00 100.00
3 Anfernee Hardaway 100.00 250.00
4 Vince Carter 100.00 250.00
5 Ja Morant 150.00 400.00
6 Anthony Edwards 150.00 400.00
8 John Stockton 50.00 120.00
10 Cade Cunningham 100.00 250.00
11 Stephen Curry 1,250.00 2,500.00
12 Jayson Tatum 150.00 400.00
13 Jerry West 40.00 100.00
14 Jason Kidd 40.00 100.00
15 Dominique Wilkins 30.00 80.00
17 Clyde Drexler 30.00 80.00
18 Ray Allen 50.00 120.00
19 Kevin Garnett 150.00 400.00
20 Isiah Thomas 30.00 80.00

2022-23 Crown Royale Monarch Memorabilia

COMMON CARD 1.25 3.00
SEMISTARS 1.50 4.00
UNLISTED STARS 2.00 5.00
1 LeBron James 25.00 60.00
2 Giannis Antetokounmpo 10.00 25.00
3 Kevin Durant 6.00 15.00
4 Zion Williamson 5.00 12.00
5 Stephen Curry 25.00 60.00
6 Damian Lillard 5.00 12.00
7 Trae Young 5.00 12.00
8 Nikola Jokic 10.00 25.00
9 Jayson Tatum 8.00 20.00
10 Joel Embiid 3.00 8.00

2022-23 Crown Royale Pillars of the Game

STATED PRINT RUN 99 SER.#'d SETS
*ASIA RED: .4X TO 1X BASIC
*BLUE/75: .5X TO 1.2X BASIC
*RED/49: 6X TO 1.5X BASIC
*PURPLE/25: .75X TO 2X BASIC
1 LeBron James 25.00 60.00
2 Stephen Curry 25.00 60.00
3 Kevin Durant 10.00 25.00
4 Giannis Antetokounmpo 15.00 40.00
5 Luka Doncic 20.00 50.00
6 Vince Carter 6.00 15.00
7 Oscar Robertson 6.00 15.00
8 Kareem Abdul-Jabbar 10.00 25.00
9 Larry Bird 12.00 30.00
10 Wilt Chamberlain 10.00 25.00
11 Jerry West 6.00 15.00
12 Dirk Nowitzki 8.00 20.00
13 Allen Iverson 8.00 20.00
14 Magic Johnson 12.00 30.00
15 Shaquille O'Neal 12.00 30.00

2022-23 Crown Royale Regal Achievements Signatures

COMMON CARD 6.00 15.00
SEMISTARS 8.00 20.00
UNLISTED STARS 10.00 25.00
STATED PRINT RUN 49 SER.#'d SETS
EXCHANGE DEADLINE 11/17/2024
1 Ja Morant 150.00 400.00
2 Stephen Curry 1,250.00 2,500.00
3 Evan Mobley 25.00 60.00
5 Anthony Edwards 150.00 400.00
6 Jalen Green 100.00 250.00
7 RJ Barrett 20.00 50.00
8 Jayson Tatum 150.00 400.00
9 Dwyane Wade 125.00 300.00
10 Larry Bird 100.00 250.00

2022-23 Crown Royale Rookie Crown Autographs

COMMON CARD
SEMISTARS
STATED PRINT RUN 49-99 SER.#'d SETS
EXCHANGE DEADLINE 11/17/2024
*BLUE/75: .4X TO 1X BASIC
*PINK/49: .5X TO 1.2X BASIC

- *RED/35: 5X TO 1.2X BASIC
- *PURPLE/25: 6X TO 1.5X BASIC
- 1 TyTy Washington Jr. 6.00 15.00
- 2 Dyson Daniels 15.00 40.00
- 3 Chet Holmgren 125.00 300.00
- 4 Jabari Smith Jr. 50.00 120.00
- 5 Jaden Ivey 50.00 120.00
- 6 Paolo Banchero 125.00 300.00
- 7 Jaden Hardy 10.00 25.00
- 8 AJ Griffin 5.00 12.00
- 9 Bennedict Mathurin 50.00 120.00
- 10 Jalen Duren 20.00 50.00
- 11 Johnny Davis 6.00 15.00
- 12 Shaedon Sharpe 60.00 150.00
- 13 Keegan Murray 50.00 120.00
- 14 Jeremy Sochan 40.00 100.00
- 15 Blake Wesley 6.00 15.00
- 16 Ousmane Dieng 8.00 20.00
- 17 Ochai Agbaji 8.00 20.00
- 18 Mark Williams 12.00 30.00
- 19 Wendell Moore Jr. 6.00 15.00
- 20 Jake LaRavia 6.00 15.00
- 21 E.J. Liddell 6.00 15.00
- 22 Malaki Branham 6.00 15.00
- 23 MarJon Beauchamp 6.00 15.00
- 24 Christian Braun 15.00 40.00
- 25 David Roddy 8.00 20.00
- 27 Max Christie 25.00 60.00
- 28 Christian Koloko 6.00 15.00
- 29 Caleb Houstan 6.00 15.00
- 30 Andrew Nembhard 12.00 30.00
- 31 Trevor Keels 5.00 12.00
- 32 Isaiah Mobley 6.00 15.00
- 33 Moussa Diabate 6.00 15.00
- 34 Scotty Pippen Jr. 8.00 20.00
- 35 Vlatko Cancar 8.00 20.00
- 36 Ryan Rollins 6.00 15.00
- 37 Kenneth Lofton Jr. 8.00 20.00
- 38 Jabari Walker 5.00 12.00
- 39 Collin Gillespie 6.00 15.00
- 40 Bryce McGowens 6.00 15.00

2022-23 Crown Royale Rookie Royalty

- COMMON CARD 2.50 6.00
- SEMISTARS 3.00 8.00
- UNLISTED STARS 4.00 10.00
- STATED PRINT RUN 99 SER.#'d SETS
- *ASIA RED: .4X TO 1X BASIC
- *BLUE/75: .5X TO 1.2X BASIC
- *RED/49: .6X TO 1.5X BASIC
- *PURPLE/25: .75X TO 2X BASIC
- 1 Paolo Banchero 25.00 60.00
- 2 Chet Holmgren 20.00 50.00
- 3 Jabari Smith Jr. 12.00 30.00
- 4 Keegan Murray 10.00 25.00
- 5 Jaden Ivey 12.00 30.00
- 6 Bennedict Mathurin 12.00 30.00
- 7 Shaedon Sharpe 15.00 40.00
- 8 Dyson Daniels 10.00 25.00
- 9 Jeremy Sochan 12.00 30.00
- 10 Johnny Davis 4.00 10.00
- 11 Ousmane Dieng 5.00 12.00
- 12 Jalen Williams 20.00 50.00
- 13 Jalen Duren 12.00 30.00
- 14 Ochai Agbaji 5.00 12.00
- 15 Mark Williams 8.00 20.00
- 16 AJ Griffin 3.00 8.00
- 17 Tari Eason 10.00 25.00
- 18 Dalen Terry 4.00 10.00
- 19 Jake LaRavia 4.00 10.00
- 20 Malaki Branham 4.00 10.00
- 21 Christian Braun 10.00 25.00
- 22 Walker Kessler 8.00 20.00
- 23 David Roddy 5.00 12.00
- 24 MarJon Beauchamp 4.00 10.00
- 25 Blake Wesley 4.00 10.00
- 26 Wendell Moore Jr. 4.00 10.00
- 27 Nikola Jovic 8.00 20.00
- 28 Patrick Baldwin Jr. 4.00 10.00
- 29 TyTy Washington Jr. 4.00 10.00
- 30 Peyton Watson 6.00 15.00
- 31 Andrew Nembhard 8.00 20.00
- 32 Caleb Houstan 4.00 10.00
- 33 Christian Koloko 4.00 10.00
- 34 Max Christie 10.00 25.00
- 35 Jaden Hardy 6.00 15.00
- 36 Kennedy Chandler 4.00 10.00
- 37 Moussa Diabate 4.00 10.00
- 38 E.J. Liddell 4.00 10.00
- 39 Trevor Keels 3.00 8.00
- 40 Isaiah Mobley 4.00 10.00

2022-23 Crown Royale Royal Signatures

- COMMON CARD 6.00 15.00
- SEMISTARS 8.00 20.00
- UNLISTED STARS 10.00 25.00
- STATED PRINT RUN 49 SER.#'d SETS
- EXCHANGE DEADLINE 11/17/2024
- 1 Jason Williams 40.00 100.00
- 2 Ray Allen 50.00 120.00
- 3 Jason Kidd 40.00 100.00
- 4 RJ Barrett 20.00 50.00
- 6 Shai Gilgeous-Alexander 300.00 600.00
- 7 Dirk Nowitzki 150.00 400.00
- 8 Hakeem Olajuwon 60.00 150.00
- 9 Jonathan Kuminga 25.00 60.00
- 11 Collin Sexton 12.00 30.00
- 12 Dennis Rodman 125.00 300.00
- 13 Jamal Murray 40.00 100.00
- 14 Walt Frazier 15.00 40.00
- 15 Al Horford 10.00 25.00
- 16 Joe Dumars 12.00 30.00
- 17 Lenny Wilkens 12.00 30.00
- 18 CJ McCollum 10.00 25.00

2022-23 Crown Royale Silhouettes Material Autographs

- COMMON CARD 6.00 15.00
- SEMISTARS 8.00 20.00
- UNLISTED STARS 10.00 25.00
- STATED PRINT RUN 49-149 SER.#'d SETS
- EXCHANGE DEADLINE 11/17/2024
- 2 RJ Barrett/99 15.00 40.00
- 3 Jonathan Kuminga/99 25.00 60.00
- 5 Jamal Crawford/99 10.00 25.00
- 7 Myles Turner/149 10.00 25.00
- 8 Elton Brand/149 10.00 25.00
- 9 Carmelo Anthony/49 125.00 300.00
- 12 Zach Randolph/149 10.00 25.00
- 13 Stephen Curry/49 1,000.00 2,000.00
- 15 Mike Miller/149 8.00 20.00
- 16 Adrian Dantley/99 10.00 25.00
- 17 Paul Pierce/75 50.00 120.00
- 20 Sam Cassell/99 10.00 25.00
- 21 Shai Gilgeous-Alexander/99 400.00 800.00
- 22 Charles Barkley/49 125.00 300.00
- 24 Caron Butler/99 8.00 20.00
- 25 Kristaps Porzingis/99 12.00 30.00
- 28 Rudy Gobert/99 12.00 30.00
- 29 Manu Ginobili/49 75.00 200.00
- 30 Vince Carter/75 75.00 200.00

2022-23 Crown Royale Sno Globe

- COMMON CARD 1.50 4.00
- SEMISTARS 2.00 5.00
- UNLISTED STARS 2.50 6.00
- STATED PRINT RUN 99 SER.#'d SETS
- *ASIA RED: .4X TO 1X BASIC
- *BLUE/75: .5X TO 1.2X BASIC
- *RED/49: .6X TO 1.5X BASIC
- *PURPLE/25: .75X TO 2X BASIC
- 1 Jayson Tatum 10.00 25.00
- 2 Zion Williamson 6.00 15.00
- 3 LeBron James 20.00 50.00
- 4 Kevin Durant 8.00 20.00
- 5 Ja Morant 8.00 20.00
- 6 Stephen Curry 20.00 50.00
- 7 Trae Young 6.00 15.00
- 8 Giannis Antetokounmpo 12.00 30.00
- 9 LaMelo Ball 6.00 15.00
- 10 Anthony Edwards 12.00 30.00
- 11 Cade Cunningham 8.00 20.00
- 12 Scottie Barnes 4.00 10.00
- 13 Nikola Jokic 12.00 30.00
- 14 Luka Doncic 15.00 40.00
- 15 Paolo Banchero 15.00 40.00
- 16 Chet Holmgren 12.00 30.00
- 17 Jabari Smith Jr. 8.00 20.00
- 18 Keegan Murray 6.00 15.00
- 19 Jaden Ivey 8.00 20.00
- 20 Bennedict Mathurin 8.00 20.00

2022-23 Crown Royale Test of Time

- COMMON CARD 1.50 4.00
- SEMISTARS 2.00 5.00
- UNLISTED STARS 2.50 6.00
- STATED PRINT RUN 99 SER.#'d SETS
- *ASIA RED: .4X TO 1X BASIC
- *BLUE/75: .5X TO 1.2X BASIC
- *RED/49: .6X TO 1.5X BASIC
- *PURPLE/25: .75X TO 2X BASIC
- 1 James Harden 5.00 12.00
- 2 Shaquille O'Neal 10.00 25.00
- 3 Chris Paul 5.00 12.00
- 4 Kareem Abdul-Jabbar 8.00 20.00
- 5 Stephen Curry 20.00 50.00
- 6 Kevin Durant 8.00 20.00
- 7 LeBron James 20.00 50.00
- 8 Damian Lillard 6.00 15.00
- 9 Tim Duncan 6.00 15.00
- 10 Vince Carter 5.00 12.00
- 11 Kyle Lowry 3.00 8.00
- 12 Paul George 4.00 10.00
- 13 Dirk Nowitzki 6.00 15.00
- 14 Karl Malone 5.00 12.00
- 15 Jimmy Butler 5.00 12.00

2023-24 Crown Royale

- *CRYSTAL: .6X TO 1.5X BASIC
- *INTL RED: .6X TO 1.5X BASIC
- *CRYSTAL BLUE/99: 1.5X TO 4X BASIC
- *CRYSTAL PINK/75: 1.5X TO 4X BASIC
- *CRYSTAL RED/49: 2X TO 5X BASIC
- *CRYSTAL PURPLE/25: 3X TO 8X BASIC
- *CRYSTAL FOTL GREEN/21: 4X TO 10X BASIC
- *ROOKIE SILHOUETTES PRIME/25: 2X TO 5X BASE
- 1 Cason Wallace RC 2.00 5.00
- 2 Brandon Ingram .60 1.50
- 3 Julius Randle .60 1.50
- 4 Jarace Walker RC 2.00 5.00
- 5 Dereck Lively II RC 2.00 5.00
- 6 Paul George .75 2.00
- 7 Mikal Bridges .60 1.50
- 8 Dariq Whitehead RC 1.25 3.00
- 9 Nick Smith Jr. RC 1.25 3.00
- 10 Bam Adebayo .75 2.00
- 11 Khris Middleton .50 1.25
- 12 Karl-Anthony Towns .75 2.00
- 13 Deandre Ayton .50 1.25
- 14 Kobe Bufkin RC 1.25 3.00
- 15 Brice Sensabaugh RC 1.50 4.00
- 16 Jaren Jackson Jr. .75 2.00
- 17 Darius Garland .75 2.00
- 18 Jabari Smith Jr. .75 2.00
- 19 Dejounte Murray .60 1.50
- 20 Klay Thompson 1.25 3.00
- 21 Zion Williamson 1.25 3.00
- 22 James Harden 1.00 2.50
- 23 Chris Paul 1.00 2.50
- 24 Kristaps Porzingis .60 1.50
- 25 Damian Lillard 1.25 3.00
- 26 Jaylen Brown 1.00 2.50
- 27 Jaden Ivey .60 1.50
- 28 GG Jackson II RC 2.00 5.00
- 29 Russell Westbrook .75 2.00
- 30 Pascal Siakam .75 2.00
- 31 Anthony Black RC 2.00 5.00
- 32 Scoot Henderson RC 3.00 8.00
- 33 Stephen Curry 4.00 10.00
- 34 Kris Murray RC 1.00 2.50
- 35 Jeremy Sochan .60 1.50
- 36 Jordan Poole .75 2.00
- 37 Marcus Sasser RC 1.50 4.00
- 38 Tyrese Maxey 1.00 2.50
- 39 Colby Jones RC 1.00 2.50
- 40 Jaime Jaquez Jr. RC 1.50 4.00
- 41 Donovan Mitchell 1.00 2.50
- 42 Cade Cunningham 1.25 3.00
- 43 Jalen Williams 1.00 2.50
- 44 Jayson Tatum 2.00 5.00
- 45 Lauri Markkanen .75 2.00
- 46 Bradley Beal .60 1.50
- 47 Gradey Dick RC 2.00 5.00
- 48 Victor Wembanyama RC 40.00 100.00
- 49 Kyle Kuzma .60 1.50
- 50 Julian Strawther RC 1.25 3.00
- 51 Kawhi Leonard 1.25 3.00
- 52 LaMelo Ball 1.25 3.00
- 53 Cam Whitmore RC 2.50 6.00
- 54 Bennedict Mathurin .75 2.00
- 55 Jamal Murray 1.00 2.50
- 56 Julian Phillips RC 1.00 2.50
- 57 Ben Sheppard RC 1.00 2.50
- 58 Zach LaVine .75 2.00
- 59 Giannis Antetokounmpo 2.50 6.00
- 60 Ausar Thompson RC 2.50 6.00
- 61 Tyler Herro .75 2.00
- 62 Anthony Davis 1.25 3.00
- 63 Austin Reaves 1.25 3.00
- 64 Taylor Hendricks RC 1.00 2.50
- 65 Amen Thompson RC 5.00 12.00
- 66 Scottie Barnes .60 1.50
- 67 Ja Morant 1.50 4.00
- 68 Keldon Johnson .60 1.50
- 69 Tyrese Haliburton 1.00 2.50
- 70 De'Aaron Fox 1.00 2.50
- 71 Devin Booker 1.25 3.00
- 72 Noah Clowney RC 1.25 3.00
- 73 Paolo Banchero 1.25 3.00
- 74 Kevin Durant 1.50 4.00
- 75 Keegan Murray .60 1.50
- 76 Brandin Podziemski RC 3.00 8.00
- 77 Joel Embiid 1.25 3.00
- 78 Jalen Brunson 1.00 2.50
- 79 Nikola Jokic 2.50 6.00
- 80 Olivier-Maxence Prosper RC 1.00 2.50
- 81 Kyrie Irving 1.00 2.50
- 82 Luka Doncic 3.00 8.00
- 83 Jett Howard RC 1.25 3.00
- 84 Jordan Hawkins RC 1.50 4.00
- 85 Shai Gilgeous-Alexander 2.50 6.00
- 86 Jimmy Butler .75 2.00
- 87 Jordan Walsh RC 1.00 2.50
- 88 Andre Jackson Jr. RC 1.50 4.00
- 89 Franz Wagner .75 2.00
- 90 DeMar DeRozan .60 1.50
- 91 RJ Barrett .75 2.00
- 92 Keyonte George RC 3.00 8.00
- 93 Trae Young 1.00 2.50
- 94 Brandon Miller RC 4.00 10.00
- 95 LeBron James 4.00 10.00
- 96 Leonard Miller RC 1.00 2.50
- 97 Bilal Coulibaly RC 2.50 6.00
- 98 Anthony Edwards 2.50 6.00
- 99 Chet Holmgren 1.25 3.00
- 100 Jalen Hood-Schifino RC 1.00 2.50
- 101 Amen Thompson JSY AU/99 60.00 150.00
- 102 Ausar Thompson JSY AU/99 30.00 80.00
- 103 Bilal Coulibaly JSY AU/99 30.00 80.00
- 104 Cason Wallace JSY AU/99 25.00 60.00
- 105 Dereck Lively II JSY AU/125 25.00 60.00
- 106 Kobe Bufkin JSY AU/125 15.00 40.00
- 107 Keyonte George JSY AU/99 40.00 100.00
- 108 Brandin Podziemski JSY AU/125 40.00 100.00
- 109 Noah Clowney JSY AU/125 15.00 40.00
- 110 Dariq Whitehead JSY AU/125 15.00 40.00
- 111 Kris Murray JSY AU/125 12.00 30.00
- 112 Olivier-Maxence Prosper JSY AU/125 12.00 30.00
- 113 Marcus Sasser JSY AU/125 20.00 50.00
- 114 Ben Sheppard JSY AU/125 12.00 30.00
- 115 Brice Sensabaugh JSY AU/125 20.00 50.00
- 116 Julian Strawther JSY AU/125 15.00 40.00
- 117 Kobe Brown JSY AU/125 RC 12.00 30.00
- 118 Sasha Vezenkov JSY AU/125 RC 10.00 25.00
- 119 Jalen Pickett JSY AU/125 RC 10.00 25.00
- 120 Leonard Miller JSY AU/125 12.00 30.00
- 121 Julian Phillips JSY AU/125 12.00 30.00
- 122 Jordan Hawkins JSY AU/125 20.00 50.00
- 123 Andre Jackson Jr. JSY AU/125 20.00 50.00
- 125 Jordan Walsh JSY AU/125 12.00 30.00
- 126 Maxwell Lewis JSY AU/125 RC 10.00 25.00
- 127 Chris Livingston JSY AU/125 RC 12.00 30.00
- 128 Rayan Rupert JSY AU/125 RC 12.00 30.00
- 129 GG Jackson II JSY AU/125 25.00 60.00
- 131 Jalen Wilson JSY AU/125 RC 12.00 30.00
- 134 Markquis Nowell JSY AU/125 RC 12.00 30.00
- 136 Sidy Cissoko JSY AU/125 RC 12.00 30.00
- 137 Jaylen Clark JSY AU/125 RC 12.00 30.00
- 138 Isaiah Wong JSY AU/125 RC 12.00 30.00
- 139 Trayce Jackson-Davis JSY AU/125 RC 15.00 40.00
- 140 Toumani Camara JSY AU/125 RC 25.00 60.00

2023-24 Crown Royale Coat of Arms Jerseys

- *PRIME/10-25: 1.5X TO 4X BASIC
- 1 Domantas Sabonis 4.00 10.00
- 2 DeMar DeRozan 4.00 10.00
- 3 Jalen Green 4.00 10.00
- 4 Jimmy Butler 4.00 10.00
- 5 Julius Randle 3.00 8.00
- 6 Pascal Siakam 4.00 10.00
- 7 Shai Gilgeous-Alexander 12.00 30.00
- 8 Darius Garland 4.00 10.00
- 9 Jaylen Brown 5.00 12.00
- 10 LaMelo Ball 6.00 15.00
- 11 Kawhi Leonard 6.00 15.00
- 12 Kevin Durant 8.00 20.00
- 13 Lauri Markkanen 4.00 10.00
- 14 Deandre Ayton 2.50 6.00
- 15 Klay Thompson 6.00 15.00
- 16 Scottie Barnes 3.00 8.00
- 17 Cade Cunningham 6.00 15.00
- 18 Mikal Bridges 3.00 8.00
- 19 Tyrese Maxey 5.00 12.00
- 20 Tyler Herro 4.00 10.00

2023-24 Crown Royale Crown Autographs

- STATED PRINT RUN 75-125 SER.#'d SETS
- *BLUE/35-75: .5X TO 1.2X BASIC
- *PINK/25-49: .6X TO 1.5X BASIC
- *RED/25-35: .75X TO 2X BASIC
- *PURPLE/15-25: .75X TO 2X BASIC
- 1 Max Christie 5.00 12.00
- 2 Peyton Watson 5.00 12.00
- 3 MarJon Beauchamp 4.00 10.00
- 4 Christian Braun 5.00 12.00
- 5 Nikola Jovic 5.00 12.00
- 6 Walker Kessler 5.00 12.00
- 7 Karl Malone 30.00 80.00
- 8 Ousmane Dieng 5.00 12.00
- 9 Ochai Agbaji 5.00 12.00
- 10 Tari Eason 6.00 15.00
- 11 Nicolas Batum 3.00 8.00
- 12 Bruce Brown 5.00 12.00
- 13 Kentavious Caldwell-Pope 4.00 10.00
- 14 Wendell Moore Jr. 4.00 10.00
- 15 Keldon Johnson 6.00 15.00
- 16 Franz Wagner 8.00 20.00
- 18 Oscar Robertson 30.00 80.00
- 19 Scottie Barnes 6.00 15.00
- 20 Jordan Clarkson 5.00 12.00
- 21 Jonathan Kuminga 12.00 30.00
- 22 Patrick Ewing 60.00 150.00
- 23 Bradley Beal 6.00 15.00
- 24 Jose Alvarado 5.00 12.00
- 25 Stephen Jackson 4.00 10.00
- 26 Dell Curry 5.00 12.00
- 27 Rolando Blackman 4.00 10.00
- 28 Jabari Smith Jr. 8.00 20.00
- 29 Tom Chambers 5.00 12.00
- 30 Wally Szczerbiak 4.00 10.00
- 31 Monte Morris 5.00 12.00
- 32 Alperen Sengun 20.00 50.00
- 33 Boban Marjanovic 5.00 12.00
- 34 James Wiseman 4.00 10.00
- 35 Bob Dandridge 5.00 12.00
- 36 Mark Aguirre 4.00 10.00
- 37 John Starks 5.00 12.00
- 38 Isiah Thomas 15.00 40.00
- 39 Jeremy Sochan 6.00 15.00
- 40 Steve Francis 5.00 12.00
- 41 Precious Achiuwa 4.00 10.00
- 42 Dorian Finney-Smith 4.00 10.00
- 43 Jalen McDaniels 4.00 10.00
- 44 Juan Toscano-Anderson 4.00 10.00
- 46 Jason Kidd 15.00 40.00
- 47 Goran Dragic 4.00 10.00
- 48 Max Strus 5.00 12.00
- 49 Dillon Brooks 5.00 12.00
- 50 Caleb Martin 4.00 10.00
- 52 Cameron Thomas 6.00 15.00
- 53 Ivica Zubac 5.00 12.00
- 54 Moses Moody 6.00 15.00
- 55 Georges Niang 3.00 8.00
- 56 Jeff Hornacek 4.00 10.00
- 57 Chris Paul 25.00 60.00
- 59 Maurice Cheeks 5.00 12.00
- 60 Kendrick Perkins 3.00 8.00

2023-24 Crown Royale Crown Jewel Signatures

- 1 Amen Thompson 60.00 150.00
- 2 Zion Williamson 125.00 300.00
- 3 Stephen Curry 500.00 1,000.00
- 4 Ausar Thompson 50.00 120.00
- 5 Hakeem Olajuwon 75.00 200.00
- 6 Carmelo Anthony 75.00 200.00
- 7 Magic Johnson 60.00 150.00
- 8 Dwyane Wade 75.00 200.00
- 9 Charles Barkley 60.00 150.00
- 10 Paul George 60.00 150.00

2023-24 Crown Royale Future Kings Signatures

- STATED PRINT RUN 49 SER.#'d SETS
- *FOTL/17: .75X TO 2X BASIC
- 1 Amen Thompson 60.00 150.00
- 2 Ausar Thompson 30.00 80.00
- 3 Bilal Coulibaly 30.00 80.00
- 4 Cason Wallace 25.00 60.00
- 5 Dereck Lively II 25.00 60.00
- 6 Kobe Bufkin 15.00 40.00
- 7 Keyonte George 40.00 100.00
- 8 Brandin Podziemski 40.00 100.00
- 11 Olivier-Maxence Prosper 12.00 30.00
- 12 Marcus Sasser 20.00 50.00
- 13 Ben Sheppard 12.00 30.00
- 14 Brice Sensabaugh 20.00 50.00
- 15 Julian Strawther 15.00 40.00
- 16 Kobe Brown 12.00 30.00
- 17 Sasha Vezenkov 10.00 25.00
- 18 Jalen Pickett 10.00 25.00
- 19 Leonard Miller 12.00 30.00
- 21 Julian Phillips 12.00 30.00
- 22 Andre Jackson Jr. 20.00 50.00
- 24 Jordan Walsh 12.00 30.00
- 26 Chris Livingston 12.00 30.00
- 27 Rayan Rupert 12.00 30.00
- 28 GG Jackson II 25.00 60.00
- 30 Jalen Wilson 12.00 30.00
- 33 Mike Miles Jr. 10.00 25.00
- 35 Sidy Cissoko 12.00 30.00
- 36 Isaiah Wong 12.00 30.00
- 37 Trayce Jackson-Davis 15.00 40.00
- 38 Markquis Nowell 12.00 30.00
- 39 Jaylen Clark 12.00 30.00
- 40 Toumani Camara 25.00 60.00

2023-24 Crown Royale Hand Crafted

- STATED PRINT RUN 99 SER.#'d SETS
- *INTL RED: .4X TO 1X BASIC
- *BLUE/75: .5X TO 1.2X BASIC
- *RED/49: .6X TO 1.5X BASIC
- *PURPLE/25: .75X TO 2X BASIC
- 1 Kevin Garnett 10.00 25.00
- 2 Tim Duncan 10.00 25.00
- 3 Larry Bird 15.00 40.00
- 4 Pau Gasol 6.00 15.00
- 5 Dirk Nowitzki 10.00 25.00
- 6 Nikola Jokic 20.00 50.00
- 7 Giannis Antetokounmpo 20.00 50.00
- 8 LeBron James 30.00 80.00
- 9 Hakeem Olajuwon 8.00 20.00
- 10 Stephen Curry 30.00 80.00

2023-24 Crown Royale Heirs to the Throne Jerseys

- *PRIME/25: 1.5X TO 4X BASIC
- 1 Kris Murray 1.50 4.00
- 2 Olivier-Maxence Prosper 1.50 4.00
- 3 Scoot Henderson 5.00 12.00
- 4 Marcus Sasser 2.50 6.00
- 5 Dereck Lively II 3.00 8.00
- 6 Julian Strawther 2.00 5.00
- 7 Gradey Dick 3.00 8.00
- 8 Andre Jackson Jr. 2.50 6.00
- 9 Victor Wembanyama 50.00 120.00
- 10 Brice Sensabaugh 2.50 6.00
- 11 Jett Howard 2.00 5.00
- 12 Amari Bailey 1.50 4.00
- 13 Anthony Black 3.00 8.00
- 14 Bilal Coulibaly 4.00 10.00
- 15 Jalen Pickett 1.25 3.00
- 16 Brandin Podziemski 5.00 12.00
- 17 Brandon Miller 6.00 15.00
- 18 Kobe Brown 1.50 4.00
- 19 Keyonte George 5.00 12.00
- 20 Noah Clowney 2.00 5.00
- 21 Kobe Bufkin 2.00 5.00
- 22 Maxwell Lewis 1.25 3.00
- 23 Jordan Walsh 1.50 4.00
- 24 Taylor Hendricks 1.50 4.00
- 25 Leonard Miller 1.50 4.00
- 26 Jalen Hood-Schifino 1.50 4.00
- 27 Dariq Whitehead 2.00 5.00
- 28 Hunter Tyson 1.50 4.00
- 29 Colby Jones 1.50 4.00
- 30 Jaime Jaquez Jr. 2.50 6.00
- 31 Craig Porter Jr. 2.00 5.00
- 32 Julian Phillips 1.50 4.00
- 33 Jordan Hawkins 2.50 6.00
- 34 Cason Wallace 3.00 8.00
- 35 Ausar Thompson 4.00 10.00
- 36 Ben Sheppard 1.50 4.00
- 37 Nick Smith Jr. 2.00 5.00
- 38 Jarace Walker 3.00 8.00
- 39 Cam Whitmore 4.00 10.00
- 40 Amen Thompson 8.00 20.00

2023-24 Crown Royale Kaboom

- 1 Tim Duncan 350.00 700.00
- 2 LeBron James 1,250.00 2,500.00
- 3 Jayson Tatum 500.00 1,000.00
- 4 Ja Morant 400.00 800.00
- 5 Scoot Henderson 400.00 800.00
- 6 Stephen Curry 1,250.00 2,500.00
- 7 Giannis Antetokounmpo 400.00 800.00
- 8 Julius Erving 200.00 500.00
- 9 Nikola Jokic 400.00 800.00
- 10 Yao Ming 400.00 800.00
- 11 Victor Wembanyama 4,000.00 8,000.00
- 12 Luka Doncic 1,000.00 2,000.00
- 13 Keyonte George 500.00 1,000.00
- 14 Gradey Dick 200.00 500.00
- 15 Bilal Coulibaly 300.00 600.00
- 16 Brandon Miller 1,000.00 2,000.00
- 17 Jordan Hawkins 300.00 600.00
- 18 Damian Lillard 300.00 600.00
- 19 Anthony Edwards 1,000.00 2,000.00
- 20 Cason Wallace 300.00 600.00
- 21 Ausar Thompson 350.00 700.00
- 22 Cam Whitmore 350.00 700.00
- 23 Anthony Black 200.00 500.00
- 24 Kobe Bufkin 150.00 400.00
- 25 Amen Thompson 500.00 1,000.00

2023-24 Crown Royale Kings Court Jersey Autographs

- STATED PRINT RUN 25-99 SER.#'d SETS
- 1 Keegan Murray/99 10.00 25.00
- 2 Shaquille O'Neal/25 125.00 300.00
- 3 Immanuel Quickley/99 8.00 20.00
- 4 Davion Mitchell/99 6.00 15.00
- 5 Desmond Bane/99 10.00 25.00
- 6 Franz Wagner/99 12.00 30.00
- 7 Charles Barkley/25 75.00 200.00
- 8 Jaden Hardy/99 10.00 25.00
- 10 Keldon Johnson/99 10.00 25.00
- 11 Onyeka Okongwu/99 6.00 15.00
- 12 Jordan Clarkson/99 8.00 20.00
- 13 Markelle Fultz/99 6.00 15.00
- 14 Shaedon Sharpe/99 15.00 40.00
- 15 Russell Westbrook/49 50.00 120.00
- 16 RJ Barrett/49 12.00 30.00
- 17 Norman Powell/99 8.00 20.00
- 18 Nicolas Batum/99 5.00 12.00
- 19 Isaiah Stewart/49 8.00 20.00
- 20 Caris LeVert/99 8.00 20.00
- 22 Myles Turner/99 8.00 20.00
- 23 Domantas Sabonis/99 12.00 30.00
- 24 Max Christie/99 8.00 20.00
- 25 Peyton Watson/99 8.00 20.00
- 26 Walker Kessler/99 8.00 20.00
- 27 Ousmane Dieng/99 8.00 20.00
- 29 De'Aaron Fox/99 15.00 40.00
- 30 Nikola Jovic/99 8.00 20.00

2023-24 Crown Royale Knights of the Round Table Jerseys

- *PRIME/10-25: 1.5X TO 4X BASIC
- 1 Cole Anthony 2.00 5.00
- 2 D'Angelo Russell 2.00 5.00
- 3 Anfernee Simons 2.50 6.00
- 4 CJ McCollum 2.00 5.00
- 5 Quentin Grimes 2.00 5.00
- 6 Zach LaVine 3.00 8.00
- 7 Fred VanVleet 3.00 8.00
- 8 Jalen Suggs 2.50 6.00
- 9 Keldon Johnson 2.50 6.00
- 10 Draymond Green 2.50 6.00
- 11 Kristaps Porzingis 2.50 6.00
- 12 OG Anunoby 2.50 6.00
- 13 Rudy Gobert 2.50 6.00
- 14 Terry Rozier III 2.50 6.00
- 15 Tobias Harris 2.00 5.00
- 16 Jarred Vanderbilt 1.50 4.00
- 17 Bones Hyland 1.50 4.00
- 18 Brook Lopez 1.50 4.00
- 19 Buddy Hield 2.00 5.00
- 20 Davion Mitchell 1.50 4.00
- 21 John Collins 2.00 5.00
- 22 Jonas Valanciunas 1.50 4.00
- 23 Cameron Thomas 2.50 6.00
- 24 De'Andre Hunter 2.00 5.00
- 25 Derrick Rose 3.00 8.00
- 26 Gordon Hayward 2.00 5.00
- 27 Kyle Kuzma 2.50 6.00
- 29 Myles Turner 2.00 5.00
- 30 Norman Powell 2.00 5.00

2023-24 Crown Royale Majestic Signatures

- STATED PRINT RUN 25-49 SER.#'d SETS
- *FOTL/17: .5X TO 1.2X BASIC
- 1 Luka Doncic/49 400.00 800.00
- 2 Donovan Mitchell/49 60.00 150.00
- 3 Shaquille O'Neal/25 200.00 500.00
- 4 Anthony Edwards/49 350.00 700.00
- 5 Charles Barkley/49 75.00 200.00
- 6 Paolo Banchero/49 75.00 200.00
- 7 Chet Holmgren/49 125.00 300.00
- 8 Clyde Drexler/49 50.00 120.00
- 9 Brandon Roy/49 50.00 120.00
- 10 Steve Nash/25 100.00 250.00
- 11 Yao Ming/49 200.00 500.00
- 12 Tyrese Maxey/49 100.00 250.00
- 13 Russell Westbrook/49 75.00 200.00
- 14 Amen Thompson/49 60.00 150.00
- 15 Ausar Thompson/49 60.00 150.00
- 16 Kobe Bufkin/49 15.00 40.00
- 17 Ja Morant/49 150.00 400.00
- 18 Nikola Jokic/49 150.00 400.00
- 19 Tyrese Haliburton/49 75.00 200.00
- 20 Paul George/49 75.00 200.00

2023-24 Crown Royale Noblemen

- STATED PRINT RUN 49-99 SER.#'d SETS
- 1 Jaden Hardy 8.00 20.00
- 2 Shaedon Sharpe 12.00 30.00
- 3 Keegan Murray 8.00 20.00
- 4 Bennedict Mathurin 10.00 25.00
- 5 Gilbert Arenas 6.00 15.00
- 6 Jalen Williams 12.00 30.00
- 7 Arvydas Sabonis 8.00 20.00
- 8 Devin Vassell 8.00 20.00
- 9 John Wall 8.00 20.00
- 10 Austin Reaves 30.00 80.00
- 12 Marcus Smart 8.00 20.00
- 13 Jrue Holiday 15.00 40.00
- 14 Cade Cunningham 40.00 100.00
- 15 Evan Mobley 10.00 25.00
- 17 Jalen Suggs 8.00 20.00
- 18 Jalen Green 30.00 80.00
- 19 Jordan Clarkson 6.00 15.00
- 20 Deandre Ayton 6.00 15.00
- 21 James Wiseman 5.00 12.00
- 22 Desmond Bane 8.00 20.00
- 23 Scottie Barnes 8.00 20.00
- 24 Ayo Dosunmu 6.00 15.00
- 25 Jaren Jackson Jr. 10.00 25.00
- 27 Davion Mitchell 5.00 12.00
- 28 Bruce Brown 6.00 15.00
- 29 Johnny Davis 5.00 12.00
- 30 Jalen Duren 8.00 20.00

2023-24 Crown Royale Pillars of the Game

- STATED PRINT RUN 99 SER.#'d SETS
- *INTL RED: .4X TO 1X BASIC
- *BLUE/75: .5X TO 1.2X BASIC
- *RED/49: .6X TO 1.5X BASIC
- *PURPLE/25: .75X TO 2X BASIC
- 1 Scoot Henderson 12.00 30.00
- 2 Amen Thompson 20.00 50.00
- 3 Nikola Jokic 20.00 50.00
- 4 Cason Wallace 8.00 20.00
- 5 Gradey Dick 8.00 20.00
- 6 Bilal Coulibaly 10.00 25.00
- 7 Jett Howard 5.00 12.00
- 8 Jarace Walker 8.00 20.00
- 9 Kevin Durant 12.00 30.00
- 10 Luka Doncic 25.00 60.00
- 11 Ausar Thompson 10.00 25.00
- 12 Brandon Miller 15.00 40.00
- 13 LeBron James 30.00 80.00
- 14 Ja Morant 12.00 30.00
- 15 Victor Wembanyama 125.00 300.00

2023-24 Crown Royale Regal Achievements Signatures

- 1 Nikola Jokic/25 300.00 600.00
- 2 Paolo Banchero/49 125.00 300.00
- 3 Stephen Curry/49 800.00 1,500.00
- 4 Donovan Mitchell/25 100.00 250.00
- 5 Ja Morant/49 150.00 400.00
- 6 Luka Doncic/49 500.00 1,000.00
- 7 Tracy McGrady/49 125.00 300.00
- 8 Allen Iverson/49 150.00 400.00
- 9 Kevin Garnett/49 125.00 300.00
- 10 Tim Duncan/25 800.00 1,500.00

2023-24 Crown Royale Rookie Crown Autographs

- STATED PRINT RUN 99-125 SER.#'d SETS
- *BLUE/75: .4X TO 1X BASIC
- *PINK/49: .5X TO 1.2X BASIC
- *RED/35: .6X TO 1.5X BASIC
- *PURPLE/25: .6X TO 1.5X BASIC
- 1 Amen Thompson/99 30.00 80.00
- 2 Ausar Thompson/99 15.00 40.00
- 3 Bilal Coulibaly/99 15.00 40.00
- 4 Cason Wallace/99 12.00 30.00
- 5 Dereck Lively II/99 12.00 30.00
- 6 Kobe Bufkin/99 8.00 20.00
- 7 Keyonte George/99 20.00 50.00
- 8 Brandin Podziemski/99 20.00 50.00
- 9 Noah Clowney/99 8.00 20.00
- 10 Dariq Whitehead/99 8.00 20.00
- 11 Kris Murray/99 6.00 15.00
- 12 Olivier-Maxence Prosper/99 6.00 15.00
- 13 Marcus Sasser/125 10.00 25.00
- 14 Ben Sheppard/99 6.00 15.00
- 15 Brice Sensabaugh/99 10.00 25.00
- 16 Julian Strawther/99 8.00 20.00
- 17 Kobe Brown/99 6.00 15.00
- 18 Amari Bailey/99 6.00 15.00
- 19 Jalen Pickett/99 5.00 12.00
- 20 Leonard Miller/99 6.00 15.00
- 21 Colby Jones/99 6.00 15.00
- 22 Julian Phillips/99 6.00 15.00
- 23 Andre Jackson Jr./99 10.00 25.00
- 24 Hunter Tyson/99 6.00 15.00
- 25 Jordan Walsh/125 6.00 15.00
- 26 Maxwell Lewis/99 5.00 12.00
- 27 Stanley Umude/99 6.00 15.00
- 28 Rayan Rupert/99 6.00 15.00
- 29 GG Jackson II/99 12.00 30.00
- 30 Keyontae Johnson/99 6.00 15.00
- 31 Jalen Wilson/99 6.00 15.00
- 32 Mouhamed Gueye/99 6.00 15.00
- 34 Chris Livingston/125 6.00 15.00
- 35 Jalen Slawson/99 6.00 15.00
- 36 Sidy Cissoko/99 6.00 15.00
- 37 Toumani Camara/99 12.00 30.00
- 38 Isaiah Wong/99 6.00 15.00
- 39 Trayce Jackson-Davis/99 8.00 20.00
- 40 Jaylen Clark/99 6.00 15.00

2023-24 Crown Royale Rookie Royalty

- STATED PRINT RUN 99 SER.#'d SETS
- *INTL RED: .4X TO 1X BASIC
- *BLUE/75: .5X TO 1.2X BASIC
- *RED/49: .6X TO 1.5X BASIC
- *PURPLE/25: .75X TO 2X BASIC
- 1 Olivier-Maxence Prosper 4.00 10.00
- 2 Hunter Tyson 4.00 10.00
- 3 Cason Wallace 8.00 20.00
- 4 Amen Thompson 20.00 50.00
- 5 Marcus Sasser 6.00 15.00
- 6 Gradey Dick 8.00 20.00
- 7 Jarace Walker 8.00 20.00
- 8 Kobe Bufkin 5.00 12.00
- 9 Bilal Coulibaly 10.00 25.00
- 10 Victor Wembanyama 125.00 300.00
- 11 Rayan Rupert 4.00 10.00
- 12 Jordan Walsh 4.00 10.00
- 13 Cam Whitmore 10.00 25.00
- 14 Maxwell Lewis 3.00 8.00
- 15 Scoot Henderson 12.00 30.00
- 16 Andre Jackson Jr. 6.00 15.00
- 17 Julian Phillips 4.00 10.00
- 18 Leonard Miller 4.00 10.00
- 19 Nick Smith Jr. 5.00 12.00
- 20 Jalen Pickett 3.00 8.00
- 21 Ben Sheppard 4.00 10.00
- 22 Kris Murray 4.00 10.00
- 23 Jaime Jaquez Jr. 6.00 15.00
- 24 GG Jackson II 8.00 20.00
- 25 Amari Bailey 4.00 10.00
- 26 Colby Jones 4.00 10.00
- 27 Brandin Podziemski 12.00 30.00
- 28 Dereck Lively II 8.00 20.00
- 29 Jett Howard 5.00 12.00
- 30 Kobe Brown 4.00 10.00
- 31 Jalen Hood-Schifino 4.00 10.00
- 32 Brice Sensabaugh 6.00 15.00
- 33 Anthony Black 8.00 20.00
- 34 Noah Clowney 5.00 12.00
- 35 Taylor Hendricks 4.00 10.00
- 36 Dariq Whitehead 5.00 12.00
- 37 Julian Strawther 5.00 12.00
- 38 Ausar Thompson 10.00 25.00
- 39 Jordan Hawkins 6.00 15.00
- 40 Brandon Miller 15.00 40.00

2023-24 Crown Royale Royal Rookie Showcase

- STATED PRINT RUN 25-49 SER.#'d SETS
- 1 Amen Thompson/25 60.00 150.00
- 2 Ausar Thompson/25 30.00 80.00
- 3 Bilal Coulibaly/49 30.00 80.00
- 4 Cason Wallace/49 25.00 60.00
- 5 Dereck Lively II/49 25.00 60.00
- 6 Kobe Bufkin/49 15.00 40.00
- 7 Keyonte George/49 40.00 100.00
- 8 Brandin Podziemski/49 40.00 100.00
- 9 Noah Clowney/49 15.00 40.00
- 10 Dariq Whitehead/49 15.00 40.00
- 11 Kris Murray/49 12.00 30.00
- 12 Olivier-Maxence Prosper/49 12.00 30.00
- 13 Marcus Sasser/49 20.00 50.00
- 14 Ben Sheppard/49 12.00 30.00
- 15 Brice Sensabaugh/49 20.00 50.00
- 16 Julian Strawther/49 15.00 40.00
- 17 Kobe Brown/49 12.00 30.00
- 18 Dru Smith/49 10.00 25.00
- 19 Jalen Pickett/49 10.00 25.00
- 20 Leonard Miller/49 12.00 30.00
- 21 Colby Jones/49 12.00 30.00
- 22 Julian Phillips/49 12.00 30.00
- 23 Hunter Tyson/49 12.00 30.00
- 24 Maxwell Lewis/49 10.00 25.00
- 25 Craig Porter Jr./49 15.00 40.00
- 26 Rayan Rupert/49 12.00 30.00
- 27 GG Jackson II/49 25.00 60.00
- 28 Keyontae Johnson/49 12.00 30.00
- 30 Isaiah Wong/49 12.00 30.00
- 31 Andre Jackson Jr./49 20.00 50.00
- 32 Jordan Walsh/49 12.00 30.00
- 33 Jalen Wilson/49 12.00 30.00
- 34 Mouhamed Gueye/49 12.00 30.00
- 35 Chris Livingston/49 12.00 30.00
- 36 Jalen Slawson/49 12.00 30.00
- 38 Toumani Camara/49 25.00 60.00
- 39 Amari Bailey/49 12.00 30.00
- 40 Jaylen Clark/49 12.00 30.00

2023-24 Crown Royale Royal Signatures

- 1 Carmelo Anthony/49 75.00 200.00
- 2 Shaquille O'Neal/25 200.00 500.00
- 3 Jabari Smith Jr./49 40.00 100.00
- 4 Jaden Ivey/49 30.00 80.00
- 5 Brandon Ingram/49 50.00 120.00
- 7 Keyonte George/49 100.00 250.00
- 8 Cason Wallace/49 40.00 100.00
- 9 Jalen Brunson/49 75.00 200.00
- 10 Bilal Coulibaly/49 30.00 80.00
- 11 James Harden/49 125.00 300.00
- 12 Dirk Nowitzki/49 125.00 300.00
- 13 Luka Doncic/49 400.00 800.00
- 14 Paul Pierce/49 50.00 120.00
- 15 Brandon Roy/49 50.00 120.00
- 16 Anthony Edwards/49 300.00 600.00
- 17 Trae Young/49 100.00 250.00
- 18 Russell Westbrook/49 60.00 150.00
- 19 Donovan Mitchell/49 50.00 120.00
- 20 Julius Erving/49 50.00 120.00

2023-24 Crown Royale Silhouettes Material Autographs

- NO PRICING ON QTY 10
- STATED PRINT RUN 10-99 SER.#'d SETS
- 2 Ja Morant/25 300.00 600.00
- 3 James Harden/25 150.00 400.00
- 4 Zion Williamson/25 150.00 400.00
- 6 Jordan Clarkson/99 30.00 80.00
- 7 Jrue Holiday/49 60.00 150.00
- 9 Alperen Sengun/99 40.00 100.00
- 13 Onyeka Okongwu/99 12.00 30.00
- 14 Lauri Markkanen/49 50.00 120.00
- 15 Deandre Ayton/99 30.00 80.00
- 16 Jalen Brunson/49 125.00 300.00
- 17 Brandon Ingram/99 60.00 150.00
- 19 Joakim Noah/99 20.00 50.00
- 21 Markelle Fultz/49 20.00 50.00

22 Jalen Duren/49 40.00 100.00
24 Bennedict Mathurin/99 50.00 120.00
25 Stephen Curry/25 800.00 1,500.00
26 Jalen Williams/99 100.00 250.00
28 Jaden Ivey/99 50.00 120.00
29 Paolo Banchero/99 100.00 250.00
30 Devin Vassell/99 40.00 100.00

2023-24 Crown Royale Sno Globe

STATED PRINT RUN 99 SER.#'d SETS
*INTNL RED: .4X TO 1X BASIC
*BLUE/75: .5X TO 1.2X BASIC
*RED/49: .6X TO 1.5X BASIC
*PURPLE/25: .75X TO 2X BASIC
1 Brandon Miller 15.00 40.00
2 Nick Smith Jr. 5.00 12.00
3 Jordan Hawkins 6.00 15.00
4 Stephen Curry 30.00 80.00
5 Bilal Coulibaly 10.00 25.00
6 Keyonte George 12.00 30.00
7 Luka Doncic 25.00 60.00
8 Scoot Henderson 12.00 30.00
9 Amen Thompson 20.00 50.00
10 Jayson Tatum 15.00 40.00
11 Anthony Black 8.00 20.00
12 LeBron James 30.00 80.00
13 Jaleh Hood-Schifino 4.00 10.00
14 Cam Whitmore 10.00 25.00
15 Giannis Antetokounmpo 20.00 50.00
16 Ausar Thompson 10.00 25.00
17 Taylor Hendricks 4.00 10.00
18 Dereck Lively II 8.00 20.00
19 Victor Wembanyama 125.00 300.00
20 Jaime Jaquez Jr. 6.00 15.00

2023-24 Crown Royale Test of Time

STATED PRINT RUN 99 SER.#'d SETS
*INTNL RED: .4X TO 1X BASIC
*BLUE/75: .5X TO 1.2X BASIC
*RED/49: .6X TO 1.5X BASIC
*PURPLE/25: .75X TO 2X BASIC
1 Tracy McGrady 6.00 15.00
2 Jayson Tatum 15.00 40.00
3 Carmelo Anthony 6.00 15.00
4 Luka Doncic 25.00 60.00
5 Stephen Curry 30.00 80.00
6 Nikola Jokic 20.00 50.00
7 Charles Barkley 10.00 25.00
8 LeBron James 30.00 80.00
9 Dwyane Wade 8.00 20.00
10 Yao Ming 10.00 25.00
11 Ja Morant 12.00 30.00
12 Magic Johnson 15.00 40.00
13 Giannis Antetokounmpo 20.00 50.00
14 Dirk Nowitzki 10.00 25.00
15 Kevin Durant 12.00 30.00

2023-24 Crown Royale Treasured Autographs

1 Stephen Curry/49 500.00 1,000.00
2 Nikola Jokic/49 75.00 200.00
3 Shaquille O'Neal/25 100.00 250.00
4 Kevin Garnett/49 40.00 100.00
5 Dwyane Wade/49 50.00 120.00
6 Magic Johnson/49 40.00 100.00
7 Julius Erving/49 40.00 100.00
8 Dirk Nowitzki/49 100.00 250.00
9 Kareem Abdul-Jabbar/49 75.00 200.00
10 Manu Ginobili/49 40.00 100.00
11 Pau Gasol/49 40.00 100.00
12 Rasheed Wallace/49 20.00 50.00
13 Tony Parker/49 30.00 80.00
14 Hakeem Olajuwon/49 40.00 100.00
15 Dennis Rodman/49 60.00 150.00
16 Clyde Drexler/49 20.00 50.00
17 James Worthy/49 20.00 50.00
18 Ben Wallace/49 20.00 50.00
19 Metta World Peace/49 12.00 30.00
20 Bill Walton/49 25.00 60.00
21 Derek Fisher/49 15.00 40.00
22 Richard Hamilton/49 20.00 50.00
23 Jason Williams/49 20.00 50.00
24 Chauncey Billups/49 20.00 50.00
25 Robert Horry/49 15.00 40.00
26 Khris Middleton/49 12.00 30.00
27 Ray Allen/49 60.00 150.00
28 Michael Porter Jr./25 12.00 30.00
29 Larry Bird/49 75.00 200.00
30 B.J. Armstrong/49 8.00 20.00

2002-03 Dakota Wizards CBA

COMPLETE SET (15) 1.50 4.00
1 Shawn Daniels .15 .40
2 Khalid El-Amin .30 .75
3 Rico Hill .15 .40
4 Courtney James .15 .40
5 Dave Joerger CO .30 .75
6 Ken Johnson .15 .40
7 Mike Johnson .15 .40
8 Casey Owens ACO .15 .40
9 Chris Porter .30 .75
10 Kevin Rice .15 .40
11 Miles Simon .15 .40
12 Marketing Team .15 .40
13 President/Vice President .15 .40
14 Dance Team .15 .40
15 Mascot .15 .40

1991-92 David Robinson Fan Club

COMPLETE SET (2) 4.00 10.00
COMMON CARD (1-2) 2.00 5.00

1977-78 Dell Flipbooks

COMPLETE SET (6) 40.00 80.00
1 Kareem Abdul-Jabbar 7.50 15.00
2 Dave Cowens 6.00 12.00
3 Julius Erving 7.50 15.00
4 Pete Maravich 20.00 40.00
5 David Thompson 6.00 12.00
6 Bill Walton 6.00 12.00

1970 Detroit Free Press

COMPLETE SET (6) 30.00 60.00
1 Dave Bing 12.50 25.00
2 Howard Komives 3.00 8.00
3 Eddie Miles 3.00 8.00
4 Ralph Simpson 6.00 12.00
5 Rudy Tomjanovich 10.00 20.00
6 Jimmy Walker 5.00 10.00

2010-11 Donruss

COMPLETE SET (295) 75.00 200.00
EXCHANGE EXP: 6/20/2012
1 Rajon Rondo .50 1.25
2 Kevin Garnett 1.00 2.50
3 Shaquille O'Neal 1.50 4.00
4 Ray Allen .60 1.50
5 Paul Pierce .60 1.50
6 Kendrick Perkins .25 .60
7 Nate Robinson .30 .75
8 Jermaine O'Neal .40 1.00
9 Jordan Farmar .25 .60
10 Brook Lopez .30 .75
11 Terrence Williams .25 .60
12 Devin Harris .25 .60
13 Troy Murphy .25 .60
14 Anthony Morrow .25 .60
15 Danilo Gallinari .30 .75
16 Amare Stoudemire .40 1.00
17 Raymond Felton .25 .60
18 Toney Douglas .25 .60
19 Wilson Chandler .30 .75
20 Anthony Randolph .25 .60
21 Kelenna Azubuike .25 .60
22 Jrue Holiday .50 1.25
23 Andres Nocioni .25 .60
24 Elton Brand .30 .75
25 Andre Iguodala .40 1.00
26 Spencer Hawes .25 .60
27 Thaddeus Young .25 .60
28 Louis Williams .30 .75
29 Jason Kapono .25 .60
30 Leandro Barbosa .30 .75
31 Andrea Bargnani .25 .60
32 Jose Calderon .25 .60
33 Jarrett Jack .25 .60
34 DeMar DeRozan .60 1.50
35 Amir Johnson .25 .60
36 Sonny Weems .25 .60
37 Derrick Rose .75 2.00
38 Taj Gibson .25 .60
39 Joakim Noah .40 1.00
40 Luol Deng .30 .75
41 C.J. Watson .25 .60
42 Kyle Korver .30 .75
43 James Johnson .25 .60
44 Carlos Boozer .30 .75
45 Mo Williams .30 .75
46 Antawn Jamison .30 .75
47 Daniel Gibson .25 .60
48 Anderson Varejao .25 .60
49 Ramon Sessions .25 .60
50 Anthony Parker .25 .60
51 Ryan Hollins .25 .60
52 Ben Gordon .25 .60
53 Tracy McGrady .60 1.50
54 Jonas Jerebko .25 .60
55 Richard Hamilton .50 1.25
56 Ben Wallace .50 1.25
57 Charlie Villanueva .25 .60
58 Tayshaun Prince .40 1.00
59 Mike Dunleavy .25 .60
60 Dahntay Jones .25 .60
61 T.J. Ford .25 .60
62 Roy Hibbert .25 .60
63 Darren Collison .25 .60
64 Danny Granger .25 .60
65 Tyler Hansbrough .25 .60
66 Brandon Rush .25 .60
67 Andrew Bogut .25 .60
68 Brandon Jennings .25 .60
69 John Salmons .25 .60
70 Corey Maggette .25 .60
71 Carlos Delfino .25 .60
72 Michael Redd .30 .75
73 Drew Gooden .25 .60
74 Rodrigue Beaubois .25 .60
75 Dirk Nowitzki 1.00 2.50
76 Caron Butler .30 .75
77 Tyson Chandler .30 .75
78 Jason Kidd .60 1.50
79 Shawn Marion .40 1.00
80 Brendan Haywood .25 .60
81 Jason Terry .30 .75
82 Aaron Brooks .25 .60
83 Yao Ming .75 2.00
84 Jordan Hill .25 .60
85 Courtney Lee .25 .60
86 Kevin Martin .30 .75
87 Shane Battier .30 .75
88 Luis Scola .30 .75
89 Brad Miller .30 .75
90 O.J. Mayo .30 .75
91 Marc Gasol .40 1.00
92 Rudy Gay .40 1.00
93 Zach Randolph .40 1.00
94 Sam Young .25 .60
95 Mike Conley Jr. .30 .75
96 Hasheem Thabeet .25 .60
97 Darrell Arthur .25 .60
98 Chris Paul .75 2.00
99 David West .30 .75
100 Trevor Ariza .25 .60
101 Emeka Okafor .30 .75
102 Marcus Thornton .25 .60
103 Peja Stojakovic .30 .75
104 Marco Belinelli .25 .60
105 DeJuan Blair .25 .60
106 Tim Duncan 1.00 2.50
107 George Hill .30 .75
108 Antonio McDyess .30 .75
109 Richard Jefferson .30 .75
110 Tony Parker .60 1.50
111 Manu Ginobili .75 2.00
112 Carmelo Anthony .60 1.50
113 Chris Andersen .40 1.00
114 Ty Lawson .25 .60
115 Chauncey Billups .50 1.25
116 Al Harrington .30 .75
117 Nene' .30 .75
118 Kenyon Martin .40 1.00
119 J.R. Smith .40 1.00
120 Michael Beasley .25 .60
121 Jonny Flynn .25 .60
122 Kevin Love .40 1.00
123 Luke Ridnour .25 .60
124 Darko Milicic .25 .60
125 Anthony Tolliver .25 .60
126 Corey Brewer .25 .60
127 Marcus Camby .30 .75
128 LaMarcus Aldridge .40 1.00
129 Rudy Fernandez .25 .60
130 Brandon Roy .50 1.25
131 Andre Miller .30 .75
132 Greg Oden .25 .60
133 Nicolas Batum .30 .75
134 Kevin Durant 1.50 4.00
135 Jeff Green .30 .75
136 Russell Westbrook .60 1.50
137 Serge Ibaka .30 .75
138 James Harden 1.00 2.50
139 Nenad Krstic .25 .60
140 Daequan Cook .25 .60
141 Eric Maynor .25 .60
142 Deron Williams .30 .75
143 Al Jefferson .25 .60
144 C.J. Miles .25 .60
145 Raja Bell .30 .75
146 Paul Millsap .30 .75
147 Mehmet Okur .25 .60
148 Andrei Kirilenko .30 .75
149 Joe Johnson .40 1.00
150 Jeff Teague .30 .75
151 Mike Bibby .40 1.00
152 Josh Smith .25 .60
153 Al Horford .40 1.00
154 Marvin Williams .30 .75
155 Jamal Crawford .40 1.00
156 Maurice Evans .25 .60
157 Gerald Wallace .30 .75
158 Gerald Henderson .25 .60
159 D.J. Augustin .25 .60
160 Eduardo Najera .25 .60
161 Stephen Jackson .30 .75
162 Tyrus Thomas .25 .60
163 Boris Diaw .30 .75
164 Derrick Brown .25 .60
165 LeBron James 3.00 8.00
166 Dwyane Wade .75 2.00
167 Chris Bosh .50 1.25
168 Mike Miller .30 .75
169 Mario Chalmers .25 .60
170 Udonis Haslem .25 .60
171 Juwan Howard .30 .75
172 Carlos Arroyo .25 .60
173 Dwight Howard .50 1.25
174 Vince Carter .75 2.00
175 Chris Duhon .25 .60
176 Jason Williams .50 1.25
177 J.J. Redick .40 1.00
178 Quentin Richardson .25 .60
179 Jameer Nelson .25 .60
180 Rashard Lewis .30 .75
181 Al Thornton .30 .75
182 Kirk Hinrich .30 .75
183 Josh Howard .30 .75
184 Yi Jianlian .40 1.00
185 Nick Young .25 .60
186 Gilbert Arenas .30 .75
187 Andray Blatche .25 .60
188 JaVale McGee .30 .75
189 Stephen Curry 8.00 20.00
190 Monta Ellis .30 .75
191 David Lee .25 .60
192 Andris Biedrins .25 .60
193 Reggie Williams RC .30 .75
194 Charlie Bell .25 .60
195 Vladimir Radmanovic .25 .60
196 Eric Gordon .30 .75
197 Blake Griffin .40 1.00
198 Chris Kaman .25 .60
199 Baron Davis .40 1.00
200 Craig Smith .25 .60
201 Ryan Gomes .25 .60
202 Rasual Butler .25 .60
203 Kobe Bryant 3.00 8.00
204 Derek Fisher .40 1.00
205 Lamar Odom .30 .75
206 Pau Gasol .60 1.50
207 Andrew Bynum .25 .60
208 Shannon Brown .25 .60
209 Ron Artest .40 1.00
210 Luke Walton .25 .60
211 Sasha Vujacic .25 .60
212 Steve Nash .75 2.00
213 Hedo Turkoglu .30 .75
214 Channing Frye .25 .60
215 Robin Lopez .25 .60
216 Earl Clark .25 .60
217 Grant Hill .60 1.50
218 Jared Dudley .25 .60
219 Jason Richardson .40 1.00
220 Tyreke Evans .30 .75
221 Carl Landry .25 .60
222 Francisco Garcia .25 .60
223 Omri Casspi .25 .60
224 Jason Thompson .25 .60
225 Samuel Dalembert .25 .60
226 Beno Udrih .25 .60
227 Antoine Wright .25 .60
228 John Wall RC 2.00 5.00
229 Evan Turner RC .50 1.25
230 Derrick Favors RC .60 1.50
231 Wesley Johnson RC .40 1.00
232 DeMarcus Cousins RC 1.25 3.00
233 Ekpe Udoh RC .30 .75
234 Greg Monroe RC .50 1.25
235 Al-Farouq Aminu RC .50 1.25
236 Gordon Hayward RC 1.50 4.00
237 Paul George RC 8.00 20.00
238 Cole Aldrich RC .40 1.00
239 Xavier Henry RC .40 1.00
240 Ed Davis RC .50 1.25
241 Patrick Patterson RC .50 1.25
242 Larry Sanders RC .40 1.00
243 Luke Babbitt RC .40 1.00
244 Kevin Seraphin RC .40 1.00
245 Eric Bledsoe RC .75 2.00
246 Avery Bradley RC .60 1.50
247 James Anderson RC .40 1.00
248 Craig Brackins RC .40 1.00
249 Elliot Williams RC .40 1.00
250 Trevor Booker RC .40 1.00
251 Damion James RC .40 1.00
252 Dominique Jones RC .40 1.00
253 Quincy Pondexter RC .40 1.00
254 Jordan Crawford RC .40 1.00
255 Greivis Vasquez RC .40 1.00
256 Daniel Orton RC .40 1.00
257 Lazar Hayward RC .40 1.00
258 Dexter Pittman RC .40 1.00
259 Hassan Whiteside RC .75 2.00
260 Andy Rautins RC .40 1.00
261 Luke Harangody RC .40 1.00
262 Timofey Mozgov RC .50 1.25
263 Boston Celtics CL .60 1.50
264 New Jersey Nets CL .40 1.00
265 New York Knicks CL .40 1.00
266 Philadelphia 76ers CL .40 1.00
267 Toronto Raptors CL .40 1.00
268 Chicago Bulls CL
Joakim Noah
Luol Deng
Derrick Rose
Carlos Boozer .40 1.00
269 Cleveland Cavaliers CL .40 1.00
270 Detroit Pistons CL .40 1.00
271 Indiana Pacers CL .40 1.00
272 Milwaukee Bucks CL .40 1.00
273 Atlanta Hawks CL .40 1.00
274 Charlotte Bobcats CL .40 1.00
275 Miami Heat CL .60 1.50
276 Orlando Magic CL .40 1.00
277 Washington Wizards CL .75 2.00
278 Dallas Mavericks CL .40 1.00
279 Houston Rockets CL .40 1.00
280 Memphis Grizzlies CL .40 1.00
281 New Orleans Hornets CL .40 1.00
282 San Antonio Spurs CL .40 1.00
283 Denver Nuggets CL .40 1.00
284 Minnesota Timberwolves CL .40 1.00
285 Portland Trail Blazers CL .40 1.00
286 Oklahoma City Thunder CL .40 1.00
287 Utah Jazz CL .40 1.00
288 Golden State Warriors CL .40 1.00
289 Los Angeles Clippers CL .40 1.00
290 Los Angeles Lakers CL .60 1.50
291 Phoenix Suns CL .40 1.00
292 Sacramento Kings CL .40 1.00
293 Kobe Bryant CL 3.00 8.00
294 Chris Bosh CL .50 1.25
295 Kevin Durant CL 1.50 4.00

2010-11 Donruss Die Cuts Emerald

*VETS/CL: 1X TO 2.5X BASE HI
*ROOKIES: .6X TO 1.5X BASE HI

2010-11 Donruss Die Cuts Ruby

*VETS/CL: 5X TO 12X BASE HI
*ROOKIES: 2.5X TO 6X BASE HI
*PL CL 293-295: 10X TO 25X BASE HI
STATED PRINT RUN 25 SER.#'d SETS

2010-11 Donruss Die Cuts Sapphire

*VETS/CL: 3X TO 8X BASE HI
*ROOKIES: 2X TO 5X BASE HI
*PL CL 293-295: 6X TO 15X BASE HI
STATED PRINT RUN 49 SER.#'d SETS

2010-11 Donruss Press Proofs

*VETS/CL: 2.5X TO 6X BASE HI
*ROOKIES: 1.5X TO 4X BASE HI
*PL CL 293-295: 5X TO 12X BASE HI
STATED PRINT RUN 100 SER.#'d SETS
134 Kevin Durant 25.00 60.00
165 LeBron James 100.00 250.00
203 Kobe Bryant 100.00 250.00
228 John Wall 50.00 120.00
237 Paul George 75.00 200.00

2010-11 Donruss Craftsmen

COMPLETE SET (15) 12.50 25.00
STATED PRINT RUN 999 SER.#'d SETS
*DC EMERALD: .5X TO 1.25X HI
*DC RUBY: 2X TO 5X HI
DC RUBY PRINT RUN 25 SETS
*DC SAPPHIRE: 1.5X TO 4X HI
DC SAPPHIRE PRINT RUN 49 SETS
*PRESS PROOFS: 1.25X TO 3X HI
PRESS PROOFS PRINT RUN 100 SETS
1 Kobe Bryant 6.00 15.00
2 Kevin Durant 3.00 8.00
3 LeBron James 6.00 15.00
4 Dwight Howard 1.00 2.50
5 Carmelo Anthony 1.00 2.50
6 Dwyane Wade 1.50 4.00
7 Dirk Nowitzki 2.00 5.00
8 Amare Stoudemire 1.00 2.50
9 Steve Nash 1.50 4.00
10 Deron Williams .60 1.50
11 Andrew Bogut .60 1.50
12 Joe Johnson .75 2.00
13 Brandon Roy 1.00 2.50
14 Pau Gasol 1.25 3.00
15 Tim Duncan 2.00 5.00

2010-11 Donruss Craftsmen Materials

STATED PRINT RUN 99 TO 299 SER.#'d SETS
*PRIME: .75X TO 2X HI
PRIME PRINT RUN 5 TO 25 SER.#'d SETS
1 Kobe Bryant/299 25.00 60.00
2 Kevin Durant/299 12.00 30.00
3 LeBron James/299 25.00 60.00
4 Dwight Howard/299 4.00 10.00
5 Carmelo Anthony/99 5.00 12.00
6 Dwyane Wade/299 6.00 15.00
7 Dirk Nowitzki/299 8.00 20.00
8 Amare Stoudemire/299 3.00 8.00
9 Steve Nash/299 6.00 15.00
10 Deron Williams/299 2.50 6.00
11 Andrew Bogut/99 2.50 6.00
12 Joe Johnson/299 3.00 8.00
13 Brandon Roy/99 4.00 10.00
14 Pau Gasol/299 5.00 12.00
15 Tim Duncan/299 8.00 20.00

2010-11 Donruss Craftsmen Materials Signatures

STATED PRINT RUN ONE TO 25 SER.#'d SETS
1 Kobe Bryant/25 1,500.00 3,000.00
8 Amare Stoudemire/25 25.00 60.00
11 Andrew Bogut/25 12.00 30.00
12 Joe Johnson/25 10.00 25.00

2010-11 Donruss Craftsmen Signatures

STATED PRINT RUN ONE TO 49 SER.#'d SETS
1 Kobe Bryant/49 1,500.00 3,000.00
8 Amare Stoudemire/25 12.00 30.00
11 Andrew Bogut/25 10.00 25.00
12 Joe Johnson/25 6.00 15.00

2010-11 Donruss Duos

COMPLETE SET (5) 7.50 15.00
1 K.Bryant/L.James 30.00 80.00
2 L.Bird/M.Johnson 5.00 12.00
3 A.Stoudemire/D.Howard 1.25 3.00
4 B.Griffin/J.Wall 3.00 8.00
5 D.Wade/K.Durant 4.00 10.00

2010-11 Donruss Gamers

COMPLETE SET (25) 15.00 40.00
STATED PRINT RUN 999 SER.#'d SETS
*DC EMERALD: .5X TO 1.25X HI
*DC RUBY: 2X TO 5X HI
DC RUBY PRINT RUN 25 SETS
*DC SAPPHIRE: 1.5X TO 4X HI
DC SAPPHIRE PRINT RUN 49 SETS
*PRESS PROOFS: 1.25X TO 3X HI
PRESS PROOFS PRINT RUN 100 SETS
1 Derrick Rose 1.50 4.00
2 Kobe Bryant 6.00 15.00
3 LeBron James 6.00 15.00
4 Kevin Garnett 2.00 5.00
5 Dwight Howard 1.00 2.50
6 Brook Lopez .60 1.50
7 Robin Lopez .50 1.25
8 Eric Gordon .60 1.50
9 David Lee .50 1.25
10 Al Jefferson .50 1.25
11 Russell Westbrook 1.25 3.00
12 Marcus Camby .60 1.50
13 Jonny Flynn .50 1.25
14 Carmelo Anthony 1.25 3.00
15 Manu Ginobili 1.50 4.00
16 David West .60 1.50
17 Zach Randolph .75 2.00
18 Luis Scola .60 1.50
19 Jason Terry .60 1.50
20 Stephen Jackson .60 1.50
21 Josh Smith .50 1.25
22 Ben Wallace 1.00 2.50
23 Anderson Varejao .50 1.25
24 Andre Iguodala .75 2.00
25 Amare Stoudemire .75 2.00

2010-11 Donruss Gamers Materials

STATED PRINT RUN 99 TO 299 SER.#'d SETS
*PRIME: .75X TO 2X HI
PRIME PRINT RUN 5 TO 49 SER.#'d SETS
1 Derrick Rose/299 6.00 15.00
2 Kobe Bryant/299 30.00 80.00
3 LeBron James/299 30.00 80.00
4 Kevin Garnett/299 8.00 20.00
5 Dwight Howard/299 4.00 10.00
6 Brook Lopez/299 2.50 6.00
7 Robin Lopez/299 2.00 5.00
8 Eric Gordon/299 2.50 6.00
9 David Lee/299 2.00 5.00
10 Al Jefferson/299 2.00 5.00
11 Russell Westbrook/299 5.00 12.00
12 Marcus Camby/99 2.50 6.00
13 Jonny Flynn/299 2.00 5.00
14 Carmelo Anthony/99 5.00 12.00
15 Manu Ginobili/299 6.00 15.00
16 David West/299 2.50 6.00
17 Zach Randolph/299 3.00 8.00
18 Luis Scola/199 2.50 6.00
19 Jason Terry/299 2.50 6.00
20 Stephen Jackson/299 2.50 6.00
21 Josh Smith/99 2.00 5.00
24 Andre Iguodala/299 3.00 8.00
25 Amare Stoudemire/299 3.00 8.00

2010-11 Donruss Gamers Materials Prime

*PRIME: .75X TO 2X BASE HI
STATED PRINT RUN 5 TO 49 SER.#'d SETS
4 Kevin Garnett/49 20.00 50.00

2010-11 Donruss Gamers Materials Signatures

STATED PRINT RUN 5 TO 49 SER.#'d SETS
2 Kobe Bryant/25 1,500.00 3,000.00
6 Brook Lopez/25 8.00 20.00
7 Robin Lopez/49 5.00 12.00
9 David Lee/25 8.00 20.00
10 Al Jefferson/25 10.00 25.00
11 Russell Westbrook/25 60.00 150.00
13 Jonny Flynn/25 5.00 12.00
25 Amare Stoudemire/25 12.00 30.00

2010-11 Donruss Gamers Materials Signatures Prime

STATED PRINT RUN 5 TO 25 SER.#'d SETS
7 Robin Lopez/25 6.00 15.00
13 Jonny Flynn/25 6.00 15.00

2010-11 Donruss Gamers Signatures

STATED PRINT RUN 5 TO 99 SER.#'d SETS
2 Kobe Bryant/49 1,500.00 3,000.00
6 Brook Lopez/25 5.00 12.00
7 Robin Lopez/99 4.00 10.00
9 David Lee/25 6.00 15.00
10 Al Jefferson/49 4.00 10.00
11 Russell Westbrook/25 50.00 120.00
13 Jonny Flynn/49 4.00 10.00
25 Amare Stoudemire/25 20.00 50.00

2010-11 Donruss Jersey Kings

COMPLETE SET (25) 15.00 40.00
STATED PRINT RUN 999 SER.#'d SETS
*DC EMERALD: .5X TO 1.25X HI
*DC RUBY: 1.5X TO 4X HI
DC RUBY PRINT RUN 25 SETS
*DC SAPPHIRE: 1X TO 2.5X HI
DC SAPPHIRE PRINT RUN 49 SETS
*PRESS PROOFS: .75X TO 2X HI
PRESS PROOFS PRINT RUN 100 SETS
1 Allen Iverson 2.50 6.00
2 Andre Miller 1.00 2.50
3 Ben Gordon 1.00 2.50
4 Xavier McDaniel 1.00 2.50
5 Vince Carter 2.50 6.00
6 Luis Scola 1.00 2.50
7 J.J. Redick 1.25 3.00
8 Thaddeus Young .75 2.00
9 Baron Davis 1.25 3.00
10 Kevin Love 1.25 3.00
11 Danilo Gallinari 1.00 2.50
12 Joe Dumars 1.25 3.00
13 Maurice Cheeks 1.00 2.50
14 Dennis Rodman 2.50 6.00
15 Tayshaun Prince 1.25 3.00
16 Andrew Bogut 1.00 2.50
17 Cedric Maxwell 1.25 3.00
18 Jonny Flynn .75 2.00
19 LaMarcus Aldridge 1.25 3.00
20 Mitch Richmond 1.50 4.00
21 Toni Kukoc 1.25 3.00
22 Luol Deng 1.00 2.50
23 Al Horford 1.25 3.00
24 Richard Hamilton 1.50 4.00
25 Dan Majerle 1.00 2.50

2010-11 Donruss Jersey Kings Materials

STATED PRINT RUN 99 TO 299 SER.#'d SETS
*PRIME: .75X TO 2X HI
PRIME PRINT RUN 5 TO 49 SER.#'d SETS
1 Allen Iverson/99 12.00 30.00
2 Andre Miller/299 2.50 6.00
3 Ben Gordon/299 2.50 6.00
4 Xavier McDaniel/299 2.50 6.00
5 Vince Carter/299 8.00 20.00
6 Luis Scola/199 2.50 6.00
7 J.J. Redick/299 3.00 8.00
8 Thaddeus Young/299 2.00 5.00
9 Baron Davis/99 3.00 8.00
10 Kevin Love/299 3.00 8.00
11 Danilo Gallinari/299 2.50 6.00
12 Joe Dumars/199 3.00 8.00
13 Maurice Cheeks/299 2.50 6.00
14 Dennis Rodman/299 12.00 30.00
15 Tayshaun Prince/299 3.00 8.00
16 Andrew Bogut/99 2.50 6.00
18 Jonny Flynn/299 2.00 5.00
19 LaMarcus Aldridge/299 3.00 8.00
20 Mitch Richmond/299 4.00 10.00
21 Toni Kukoc/299 3.00 8.00
22 Luol Deng/299 2.50 6.00
23 Al Horford/299 3.00 8.00
24 Richard Hamilton/299 4.00 10.00
25 Dan Majerle/299 2.50 6.00

2010-11 Donruss Jersey Kings Materials Signatures

STATED PRINT RUN 10 TO 49 SER.#'d SETS
3 Ben Gordon/25 6.00 15.00
4 Xavier McDaniel/49 6.00 15.00
7 J.J. Redick/25 10.00 25.00
10 Kevin Love/25 10.00 25.00
11 Danilo Gallinari/49 8.00 20.00
12 Joe Dumars/49 12.00 30.00
13 Maurice Cheeks/49 8.00 20.00
14 Dennis Rodman/49 25.00 60.00
16 Andrew Bogut/25 8.00 20.00
18 Jonny Flynn/49 5.00 12.00
21 Toni Kukoc/49 15.00 40.00
24 Richard Hamilton/25 12.00 30.00
25 Dan Majerle/49 12.00 30.00

2010-11 Donruss Jersey Kings Materials Signatures Prime

STATED PRINT RUN 5 TO 25 SER.#'d SETS
4 Xavier McDaniel/25 10.00 25.00
7 J.J. Redick/25 15.00 40.00
10 Kevin Love/25 15.00 40.00
12 Joe Dumars/25 20.00 50.00
13 Maurice Cheeks/25 10.00 25.00
14 Dennis Rodman/25 40.00 100.00
18 Jonny Flynn/25 8.00 20.00
21 Toni Kukoc/25 20.00 50.00
25 Dan Majerle/25 20.00 50.00

2010-11 Donruss Jersey Kings Signatures

STATED PRINT RUN 10 TO 99 SER.#'d SETS
3 Ben Gordon/25 5.00 12.00
4 Xavier McDaniel/75 5.00 12.00
7 J.J. Redick/49 8.00 20.00
10 Kevin Love/25 8.00 20.00
11 Danilo Gallinari/25 6.00 15.00
12 Joe Dumars/25 10.00 25.00
13 Maurice Cheeks/49 6.00 15.00
14 Dennis Rodman/49 20.00 50.00
16 Andrew Bogut/25 6.00 15.00
17 Cedric Maxwell/49 4.00 10.00
18 Jonny Flynn/49 4.00 10.00
21 Toni Kukoc/25 12.00 30.00
24 Richard Hamilton/49 10.00 25.00
25 Dan Majerle/99 10.00 25.00

2010-11 Donruss Magicians

COMPLETE SET (10) 7.50 15.00
STATED PRINT RUN 999 SER.#'d SETS
*DC EMERALD: .5X TO 1.25X HI
*DC RUBY: 2X TO 5X HI
DC RUBY PRINT RUN 25 SETS
*DC SAPPHIRE: 1.5X TO 4X HI
DC SAPPHIRE PRINT RUN 49 SETS
*PRESS PROOFS: 1.25X TO 3X HI
PRESS PROOFS PRINT RUN 100 SETS
1 Steve Nash 2.00 5.00
2 Jason Kidd 1.50 4.00
3 Chris Paul 2.00 5.00
4 Deron Williams .75 2.00
5 Rajon Rondo 1.25 3.00
6 Stephen Curry 8.00 20.00
7 Derrick Rose 2.00 5.00
8 John Stockton 1.50 4.00
9 Pete Maravich 2.50 6.00
10 Isiah Thomas 1.50 4.00

2010-11 Donruss Magicians Materials

STATED PRINT RUN 299 SER.#'d SETS
1 Steve Nash 6.00 15.00
2 Jason Kidd 5.00 12.00
3 Chris Paul 6.00 15.00
4 Deron Williams 2.50 6.00
5 Rajon Rondo 4.00 10.00
6 Stephen Curry 40.00 100.00
7 Derrick Rose 6.00 15.00
8 John Stockton 5.00 12.00

2010-11 Donruss Magicians Materials Prime

STATED PRINT RUN 10 TO 49 SER.#'d SETS
1 Steve Nash/25 8.00 20.00
8 John Stockton/49 10.00 25.00
10 Isiah Thomas/49 10.00 25.00

2010-11 Donruss Masters

COMPLETE SET (10) 7.50 15.00
STATED PRINT RUN 999 SER.#'d SETS
*DC EMERALD: .5X TO 1.25X HI
*DC RUBY: 2X TO 5X HI
DC RUBY PRINT RUN 25 SETS
*DC SAPPHIRE: 1.5X TO 4X HI
DC SAPPHIRE PRINT RUN 49 SETS
*PRESS PROOFS: 1.25X TO 3X HI
PRESS PROOFS PRINT RUN 100 SETS
1 Magic Johnson 4.00 10.00
2 Larry Bird 4.00 10.00
3 Artis Gilmore 1.25 3.00
4 Chris Mullin 1.25 3.00
5 Clyde Drexler 1.50 4.00
6 Kevin McHale 1.50 4.00
7 Patrick Ewing 1.50 4.00
8 Rolando Blackman .75 2.00
9 Scottie Pippen 2.50 6.00
10 Walt Frazier 1.50 4.00

2010-11 Donruss Masters Materials

STATED PRINT RUN 49 TO 299 SER.#'d SETS
*PRIME: .75X TO 2X BASE HI
1 Magic Johnson/299 12.00 30.00
2 Larry Bird/299 12.00 30.00
3 Artis Gilmore/49 4.00 10.00
4 Chris Mullin/299 4.00 10.00
5 Clyde Drexler/299 5.00 12.00
6 Kevin McHale/299 5.00 12.00
7 Patrick Ewing/299 5.00 12.00
8 Rolando Blackman/49 2.50 6.00
9 Scottie Pippen/299 8.00 20.00

2010-11 Donruss Masters Materials Prime

STATED PRINT RUN 5 TO 49 SER.#'d SETS

2010-11 Donruss Masters Materials Signatures

STATED PRINT RUN ONE TO 49 SER.#'d SETS
3 Artis Gilmore/49 10.00 25.00
4 Chris Mullin/49 10.00 25.00
5 Clyde Drexler/49 15.00 40.00
8 Rolando Blackman/49 8.00 20.00

2010-11 Donruss Masters Materials Signatures Prime

STATED PRINT RUN ONE TO 25 SER.#'d SETS
3 Artis Gilmore/25 20.00 50.00
4 Chris Mullin/25 20.00 50.00
5 Clyde Drexler/25 30.00 80.00
8 Rolando Blackman/25 15.00 40.00

2010-11 Donruss Masters Signatures

STATED PRINT RUN ONE TO 99 SER.#'d SETS
3 Artis Gilmore/49 10.00 25.00
4 Chris Mullin/99 12.00 30.00
5 Clyde Drexler/25 20.00 50.00
8 Rolando Blackman/25 6.00 15.00

2010-11 Donruss Production Line

COMPLETE SET (100) 50.00 100.00
STATED PRINT RUN 999 SER.#'d SETS
*DC EMERALD: .5X TO 1.25X HI
*DC RUBY: 1.5X TO 4X HI
DC RUBY PRINT RUN 25 SETS
*DC SAPPHIRE: 1X TO 2.5X HI
DC SAPPHIRE PRINT RUN 49 SETS
*PRESS PROOFS: .75X TO 2X HI
PRESS PROOFS PRINT RUN 100 SETS
*RACK PACK: .5X TO 1.2X BASE HI
1 Kevin Durant 3.00 8.00
2 LeBron James 6.00 15.00
3 Carmelo Anthony 1.25 3.00
4 Kobe Bryant 6.00 15.00
5 Dwyane Wade 1.50 4.00
6 Monta Ellis .60 1.50
7 Dirk Nowitzki 2.00 5.00
8 Danny Granger .50 1.25
9 Chris Bosh 1.00 2.50
10 Amare Stoudemire .75 2.00
11 Gilbert Arenas .60 1.50
12 Brandon Roy 1.00 2.50
13 Joe Johnson .75 2.00
14 Derrick Rose 1.50 4.00
15 Zach Randolph .75 2.00
16 Stephen Jackson .60 1.50
17 Kevin Martin .60 1.50
18 David Lee .50 1.25
19 Tyreke Evans .60 1.50
20 Corey Maggette .60 1.50
21 Dwight Howard 1.00 2.50
22 Marcus Camby .60 1.50
23 Zach Randolph .75 2.00
24 David Lee .50 1.25
25 Pau Gasol 1.25 3.00
26 Carlos Boozer .60 1.50
27 Joakim Noah .75 2.00
28 Kevin Love .75 2.00
29 Chris Bosh 1.00 2.50
30 Troy Murphy .50 1.25
31 Andrew Bogut .60 1.50
32 Tim Duncan 2.00 5.00
33 Gerald Wallace .60 1.50
34 Al Horford .75 2.00
35 Lamar Odom .60 1.50
36 Samuel Dalembert .50 1.25
37 Kenyon Martin .75 2.00
38 Brendan Haywood .50 1.25
39 Marc Gasol .75 2.00
40 Chris Kaman .50 1.25
41 Steve Nash 1.50 4.00
42 Chris Paul 1.50 4.00
43 Deron Williams .60 1.50
44 Rajon Rondo 1.00 2.50
45 Jason Kidd 1.25 3.00
46 LeBron James 6.00 15.00
47 Baron Davis .75 2.00
48 Russell Westbrook 1.25 3.00
49 Gilbert Arenas .60 1.50
50 Devin Harris .50 1.25
51 Dwyane Wade 1.50 4.00
52 Derrick Rose 1.50 4.00

53 Jose Calderon .50 1.25
54 Stephen Curry 6.00 15.00
55 Andre Iguodala .75 2.00
56 Tyreke Evans .60 1.50
57 Brandon Jennings .50 1.25
58 Darren Collison .50 1.25
59 Tony Parker 1.25 3.00
60 Dwight Howard 1.00 2.50
61 Andrew Bogut .60 1.50
62 Greg Oden .50 1.25
63 Josh Smith .50 1.25
64 Brendan Haywood .50 1.25
65 Marcus Camby .60 1.50
66 Chris Andersen .75 2.00
67 Samuel Dalembert .50 1.25
68 Pau Gasol 1.25 3.00
69 Brook Lopez .60 1.50
70 Kendrick Perkins .50 1.25
71 JaVale McGee .60 1.50
72 Roy Hibbert .60 1.50
73 Marc Gasol .75 2.00
74 Tyrus Thomas .50 1.25
75 Joakim Noah .75 2.00
76 Rajon Rondo 1.00 2.50
77 Monta Ellis .60 1.50
78 Chris Paul 1.50 4.00
79 Stephen Curry 6.00 15.00
80 Dwyane Wade 1.50 4.00
81 Jason Kidd 1.25 3.00
82 Trevor Ariza .50 1.25
83 Andre Iguodala .75 2.00
84 Baron Davis .75 2.00
85 LeBron James 6.00 15.00
86 Stephen Jackson .60 1.50
87 Josh Smith .50 1.25
88 C.J. Watson .50 1.25
89 Ronnie Brewer .50 1.25
90 Caron Butler .60 1.50
91 Aaron Brooks .50 1.25
92 Danilo Gallinari .60 1.50
93 Jason Kidd 1.25 3.00
94 Channing Frye .50 1.25
95 Rashard Lewis .60 1.50
96 Stephen Curry 6.00 15.00
97 Jamal Crawford .75 2.00
98 Mo Williams .60 1.50
99 Danny Granger .50 1.25
100 J.R. Smith .75 2.00

2010-11 Donruss Production Line Materials

STATED PRINT RUN 49 TO 399 SER.#'d SETS
*STAT DC: .4X TO 1X BASE HI
STAT DC PRINT RUN 49 TO 399 SER.#'d SETS
*PRIME: .75X TO 2X HI
PRIME PRINT RUN 5 TO 49 SER.#'d SETS
*STAT DC PRIME: .75X TO 2X HI
STAT DC PRIME PRINT RUN 5 TO 49 SETS
1 Kevin Durant/399 12.00 30.00
2 LeBron James/399 25.00 60.00
3 Carmelo Anthony/299 5.00 12.00
4 Kobe Bryant/399 25.00 60.00
5 Dwyane Wade/399 6.00 15.00
7 Dirk Nowitzki/399 8.00 20.00
9 Chris Bosh/399 4.00 10.00
10 Amare Stoudemire/399 3.00 8.00
11 Gilbert Arenas/399 2.50 6.00
12 Brandon Roy/99 4.00 10.00
13 Joe Johnson/399 3.00 8.00
14 Derrick Rose/399 6.00 15.00
15 Zach Randolph/399 3.00 8.00
16 Stephen Jackson/399 2.50 6.00
18 David Lee/399 2.00 5.00
19 Tyreke Evans/399 2.50 6.00
20 Corey Maggette/49 2.50 6.00
21 Dwight Howard/399 4.00 10.00
22 Marcus Camby/49 2.50 6.00
23 Zach Randolph/399 3.00 8.00
24 David Lee/399 2.00 5.00
25 Pau Gasol/399 5.00 12.00
26 Carlos Boozer/299 2.50 6.00
27 Joakim Noah/199 3.00 8.00
28 Kevin Love/399 3.00 8.00
29 Chris Bosh/399 4.00 10.00
31 Andrew Bogut/199 2.50 6.00
32 Tim Duncan/399 8.00 20.00
33 Gerald Wallace/399 2.50 6.00
34 Al Horford/299 3.00 8.00
35 Lamar Odom/399 2.50 6.00
36 Samuel Dalembert/299 2.00 5.00
37 Kenyon Martin/399 3.00 8.00
38 Brendan Haywood/199 2.00 5.00
39 Marc Gasol/399 3.00 8.00
40 Chris Kaman/399 2.00 5.00
41 Steve Nash/399 6.00 15.00
42 Chris Paul/399 6.00 15.00
43 Deron Williams/399 2.50 6.00
44 Rajon Rondo/399 4.00 10.00
45 Jason Kidd/399 5.00 12.00
46 LeBron James/399 25.00 60.00
47 Baron Davis/99 3.00 8.00
48 Russell Westbrook/399 5.00 12.00
49 Gilbert Arenas/399 2.50 6.00
51 Dwyane Wade/399 6.00 15.00
52 Derrick Rose/399 6.00 15.00
53 Jose Calderon/399 2.00 5.00
54 Stephen Curry/399 60.00 150.00
55 Andre Iguodala/299 3.00 8.00
56 Tyreke Evans/399 2.50 6.00
57 Brandon Jennings/399 2.00 5.00
58 Darren Collison/199 2.00 5.00
59 Tony Parker/99 5.00 12.00
60 Dwight Howard/399 4.00 10.00
61 Andrew Bogut/199 2.50 6.00
62 Greg Oden/299 2.00 5.00
63 Josh Smith/99 2.00 5.00
64 Brendan Haywood/199 2.00 5.00
65 Marcus Camby/49 2.50 6.00
66 Chris Andersen/399 3.00 8.00
67 Samuel Dalembert/299 2.00 5.00
68 Pau Gasol/399 5.00 12.00
69 Brook Lopez/399 2.50 6.00
73 Marc Gasol/399 3.00 8.00
75 Joakim Noah/199 3.00 8.00
76 Rajon Rondo/399 4.00 10.00
78 Chris Paul/399 6.00 15.00
79 Stephen Curry/399 25.00 60.00
80 Dwyane Wade/399 6.00 15.00
81 Jason Kidd/399 5.00 12.00
83 Andre Iguodala/299 3.00 8.00
84 Baron Davis/99 3.00 8.00
85 LeBron James/399 25.00 60.00
86 Stephen Jackson/399 2.50 6.00
87 Josh Smith/99 2.00 5.00
90 Caron Butler/99 2.50 6.00
92 Danilo Gallinari/399 2.50 6.00
93 Jason Kidd/399 5.00 12.00
94 Channing Frye/74 2.00 5.00
95 Rashard Lewis/399 2.50 6.00
96 Stephen Curry/399 25.00 60.00
100 J.R. Smith/399 3.00 8.00

2010-11 Donruss Production Line Materials Signatures

STATED PRINT RUN ONE TO 25 SER.#'d SETS
4 Kobe Bryant/25 1,500.00 3,000.00
9 Chris Bosh/25 20.00 50.00
10 Amare Stoudemire/25 25.00 60.00
13 Joe Johnson/25 15.00 40.00
18 David Lee/25 8.00 20.00
19 Tyreke Evans/25 15.00 40.00
24 David Lee/25 8.00 20.00
27 Joakim Noah/25 12.00 30.00
28 Kevin Love/25 12.00 30.00
29 Chris Bosh/25 12.00 30.00
31 Andrew Bogut/25 8.00 20.00
39 Marc Gasol/25 12.00 30.00
48 Russell Westbrook/25 60.00 150.00
56 Tyreke Evans/25 15.00 40.00
59 Tony Parker/25 10.00 25.00
61 Andrew Bogut/25 8.00 20.00
66 Chris Andersen/25 20.00 50.00
69 Brook Lopez/25 8.00 20.00
73 Marc Gasol/25 12.00 30.00
75 Joakim Noah/25 12.00 30.00
90 Caron Butler/15 10.00 25.00
92 Danilo Gallinari/25 8.00 20.00
94 Channing Frye/25 8.00 20.00
100 J.R. Smith/25 12.00 30.00

2010-11 Donruss Production Line Materials Signatures Prime

STATED PRINT RUN ONE TO 49 SER.#'d SETS
50 Devin Harris/49 10.00 25.00
90 Caron Butler/15 12.50 30.00
94 Channing Frye/25 10.00 25.00
100 J.R. Smith/25 10.00 25.00

2010-11 Donruss Production Line Signatures

STATED PRINT RUN ONE TO 99 SER.#'d SETS
4 Kobe Bryant/49 1,500.00 3,000.00
8 Danny Granger/25 6.00 15.00
9 Chris Bosh/25 12.00 30.00
10 Amare Stoudemire/25 20.00 50.00
13 Joe Johnson/25 8.00 20.00
18 David Lee/25 6.00 15.00
19 Tyreke Evans/49 6.00 15.00
24 David Lee/25 6.00 15.00
27 Joakim Noah/25 10.00 25.00
28 Kevin Love/25 10.00 25.00
29 Chris Bosh/25 12.00 30.00
31 Andrew Bogut/25 6.00 15.00
39 Marc Gasol/25 10.00 25.00
48 Russell Westbrook/25 50.00 120.00
50 Devin Harris/25 6.00 15.00
56 Tyreke Evans/49 6.00 15.00
58 Darren Collison/25 6.00 15.00
59 Tony Parker/25 6.00 15.00
61 Andrew Bogut/25 6.00 15.00
66 Chris Andersen/25 12.00 30.00
69 Brook Lopez/25 4.00 10.00
73 Marc Gasol/25 10.00 25.00
75 Joakim Noah/25 10.00 25.00
89 Ronnie Brewer/99 4.00 10.00
90 Caron Butler/15 6.00 15.00
91 Aaron Brooks/99 4.00 10.00
92 Danilo Gallinari/49 4.00 10.00
94 Channing Frye/25 4.00 10.00
98 Mo Williams/25 4.00 10.00
99 Danny Granger/25 6.00 15.00
100 J.R. Smith/49 12.00 30.00

2010-11 Donruss Production Line Stat Die Cuts Materials

STATED PRINT RUN 5 TO 49 SER.#'d SETS
1 Kevin Durant/399 6.00 15.00
2 LeBron James/399 8.00 20.00
3 Carmelo Anthony/299 5.00 12.00
4 Kobe Bryant/399 8.00 20.00
5 Dwyane Wade/399 6.00 15.00
7 Dirk Nowitzki/399 8.00 20.00
9 Chris Bosh/399 4.00 10.00
10 Amare Stoudemire/399 3.00 8.00
11 Gilbert Arenas/399 2.50 6.00
12 Brandon Roy/99 4.00 10.00
13 Joe Johnson/399 3.00 8.00
14 Derrick Rose/399 8.00 20.00
15 Zach Randolph/399 3.00 8.00
16 Stephen Jackson/399 2.50 6.00
18 David Lee/399 2.00 5.00
19 Tyreke Evans/399 2.50 6.00
20 Corey Maggette/49 2.50 6.00
21 Dwight Howard/399 4.00 10.00
22 Marcus Camby/49 2.50 6.00
23 Zach Randolph/399 3.00 8.00
24 David Lee/399 2.00 5.00
25 Pau Gasol/399 5.00 12.00
26 Carlos Boozer/299 2.50 6.00
27 Joakim Noah/199 3.00 8.00
28 Kevin Love/399 3.00 8.00
29 Chris Bosh/399 4.00 10.00
31 Andrew Bogut/199 2.50 6.00
32 Tim Duncan/399 8.00 20.00
33 Gerald Wallace/399 2.50 6.00
34 Al Horford/299 3.00 8.00
35 Lamar Odom/399 2.50 6.00
36 Samuel Dalembert/299 2.00 5.00
37 Kenyon Martin/399 2.00 5.00
38 Brendan Haywood/199 2.00 5.00
39 Marc Gasol/399 3.00 8.00
40 Chris Kaman/399 2.00 5.00
41 Steve Nash/399 6.00 15.00
42 Chris Paul/399 6.00 15.00
43 Deron Williams/399 2.50 6.00
44 Rajon Rondo/399 4.00 10.00
45 Jason Kidd/399 5.00 12.00
46 LeBron James/399 8.00 20.00
47 Baron Davis/99 3.00 8.00
48 Russell Westbrook/399 5.00 12.00
49 Gilbert Arenas/399 2.50 6.00
51 Dwyane Wade/399 6.00 15.00
52 Derrick Rose/399 8.00 20.00
53 Jose Calderon/399 2.00 5.00
54 Stephen Curry/399 25.00 60.00
55 Andre Iguodala/299 3.00 8.00
56 Tyreke Evans/399 2.50 6.00
57 Brandon Jennings/399 2.00 5.00
58 Darren Collison/199 2.00 5.00
59 Tony Parker/99 5.00 12.00
60 Dwight Howard/399 4.00 10.00
61 Andrew Bogut/199 2.50 6.00
62 Greg Oden/299 2.00 5.00
63 Josh Smith/99 2.00 5.00
64 Brendan Haywood/199 2.00 5.00
65 Marcus Camby/49 2.50 6.00
66 Chris Andersen/399 3.00 8.00
67 Samuel Dalembert/299 2.00 5.00
68 Pau Gasol/399 5.00 12.00
69 Brook Lopez/399 2.50 6.00
73 Marc Gasol/399 3.00 8.00
75 Joakim Noah/199 3.00 8.00
76 Rajon Rondo/99 4.00 10.00
78 Chris Paul/399 6.00 15.00
79 Stephen Curry/399 25.00 60.00
80 Dwyane Wade/399 6.00 15.00
81 Jason Kidd/399 5.00 12.00
83 Andre Iguodala/299 3.00 8.00
84 Baron Davis/99 3.00 8.00
85 LeBron James/399 8.00 20.00
87 Josh Smith/99 2.00 5.00
90 Caron Butler/399 2.50 6.00
92 Danilo Gallinari/399 2.50 6.00
93 Jason Kidd/399 5.00 12.00
94 Channing Frye/99 2.00 5.00
95 Rashard Lewis/399 2.50 6.00
96 Stephen Curry/399 25.00 60.00
100 J.R. Smith/399 3.00 8.00

2010-11 Donruss Signatures

STATED PRINT RUN ONE TO 599 SER.#'d SETS
6 Kendrick Perkins/49 3.00 8.00
10 Brook Lopez/25 4.00 10.00
11 Terrence Williams/199 3.00 8.00
12 Devin Harris/49 3.00 8.00
15 Danilo Gallinari/25 4.00 10.00
18 Toney Douglas/199 3.00 8.00
20 Anthony Randolph/49 3.00 8.00
22 Jrue Holiday/199 12.00 30.00
31 Andrea Bargnani/49 3.00 8.00
34 DeMar DeRozan/99 25.00 60.00
36 Sonny Weems/99 3.00 8.00
39 Joakim Noah/25 4.00 10.00
45 Mo Williams/25 4.00 10.00
52 Ben Gordon/25 4.00 10.00
54 Jonas Jerebko/199 3.00 8.00
55 Richard Hamilton/25 10.00 25.00
57 Charlie Villanueva/49 3.00 8.00
59 Mike Dunleavy/49 3.00 8.00
61 T.J. Ford/49 3.00 8.00
63 Darren Collison/25 3.00 8.00
64 Danny Granger/25 3.00 8.00
65 Tyler Hansbrough/99 3.00 8.00
67 Andrew Bogut/25 8.00 20.00
74 Rodrigue Beaubois/199 3.00 8.00
76 Caron Butler/25 4.00 10.00
82 Aaron Brooks/49 3.00 8.00
84 Jordan Hill/49 3.00 8.00
91 Marc Gasol/49 10.00 25.00
94 Sam Young/299 3.00 8.00
96 Hasheem Thabeet/199 3.00 8.00
101 Emeka Okafor/49 3.00 8.00
102 Marcus Thornton/199 3.00 8.00
105 DeJuan Blair/99 3.00 8.00
110 Tony Parker/25 15.00 40.00
113 Chris Andersen/25 12.00 30.00
114 Ty Lawson/149 3.00 8.00
115 Chauncey Billups/25 12.00 30.00
119 J.R. Smith/49 5.00 12.00
121 Jonny Flynn/99 3.00 8.00
122 Kevin Love/25 10.00 25.00
136 Russell Westbrook/25 50.00 120.00
138 James Harden/49 60.00 150.00
141 Eric Maynor/199 3.00 8.00
143 Al Jefferson/49 3.00 8.00
149 Joe Johnson/25 5.00 12.00
150 Jeff Teague/199 3.00 8.00
151 Mike Bibby/25 5.00 12.00
158 Gerald Henderson/99 3.00 8.00
159 D.J. Augustin/49 3.00 8.00
164 Derrick Brown/399 3.00 8.00
167 Chris Bosh/25 12.00 30.00
177 J.J. Redick/49 10.00 25.00
181 Al Thornton/49 3.00 8.00
183 Josh Howard/49 4.00 10.00
191 David Lee/25 3.00 8.00
197 Blake Griffin/25 10.00 25.00
203 Kobe Bryant/49 1,500.00 3,000.00
214 Channing Frye/25 3.00 8.00
215 Robin Lopez/49 3.00 8.00
216 Earl Clark/199 3.00 8.00
220 Tyreke Evans/49 4.00 10.00
221 Carl Landry/49 3.00 8.00
223 Omri Casspi/199 3.00 8.00
228 John Wall/299 25.00 60.00
229 Evan Turner/199 4.00 10.00
230 Derrick Favors/299 5.00 12.00
231 Wesley Johnson/99 3.00 8.00
232 DeMarcus Cousins/299 25.00 60.00
233 Ekpe Udoh/399 3.00 8.00
234 Greg Monroe/399 4.00 10.00
235 Al-Farouq Aminu/399 4.00 10.00
236 Gordon Hayward/299 12.00 30.00
237 Paul George/399 60.00 150.00
238 Cole Aldrich/399 3.00 8.00
239 Xavier Henry/399 3.00 8.00
240 Ed Davis/399 4.00 10.00
241 Patrick Patterson/499 4.00 10.00
242 Larry Sanders/399 3.00 8.00
243 Luke Babbitt/399 3.00 8.00
244 Kevin Seraphin/399 3.00 8.00
245 Eric Bledsoe/399 6.00 15.00
246 Avery Bradley/399 5.00 12.00
247 James Anderson/499 3.00 8.00
248 Craig Brackins/499 3.00 8.00
249 Elliot Williams/499 3.00 8.00
250 Trevor Booker/499 3.00 8.00
251 Damion James/399 3.00 8.00
252 Dominique Jones/399 3.00 8.00
253 Quincy Pondexter/599 3.00 8.00
254 Jordan Crawford/499 3.00 8.00
255 Greivis Vasquez/599 3.00 8.00
256 Daniel Orton/499 3.00 8.00
257 Lazar Hayward/599 3.00 8.00
258 Dexter Pittman/599 3.00 8.00
259 Hassan Whiteside/599 6.00 15.00
260 Andy Rautins/499 3.00 8.00
261 Luke Harangody/499 3.00 8.00
262 Timofey Mozgov/599 4.00 10.00

2014-15 Donruss

COMP.SET w/o RCs (200) 12.00 30.00
1 Al Horford .40 1.00
2 Rajon Rondo .50 1.25
3 Brook Lopez .40 1.00
4 Michael Kidd-Gilchrist .25 .60
5 Taj Gibson .25 .60
6 Kyrie Irving .75 2.00
7 Dirk Nowitzki 1.00 2.50
8 JaVale McGee .30 .75
9 Greg Monroe .25 .60
10 Klay Thompson 1.00 2.50
11 Dwight Howard .50 1.25
12 Roy Hibbert .30 .75
13 DeAndre Jordan .30 .75
14 Steve Nash .75 2.00
15 Zach Randolph .40 1.00
16 Dwyane Wade .75 2.00
17 O.J. Mayo .25 .60
18 Thaddeus Young .25 .60
19 Tyreke Evans .30 .75
20 Amar'e Stoudemire .40 1.00
21 Russell Westbrook .60 1.50
22 Brandon Knight .25 .60
23 Victor Oladipo .30 .75
24 Luc Mbah a Moute .25 .60
25 Eric Bledsoe .30 .75
26 LaMarcus Aldridge .40 1.00
27 DeMarcus Cousins .30 .75
28 Tony Parker .60 1.50
29 Kyle Lowry .50 1.25
30 Derrick Favors .25 .60
31 Marcin Gortat .25 .60
32 Jeff Teague .25 .60
33 Jeff Green .30 .75
34 Kevin Garnett 1.00 2.50
35 Lance Stephenson .30 .75
36 Jimmy Butler .60 1.50
37 Kevin Love .40 1.00
38 Tyson Chandler .40 1.00
39 Ty Lawson .25 .60
40 Brandon Jennings .25 .60
41 Andre Iguodala .40 1.00
42 Trevor Ariza .25 .60
43 Paul George .60 1.50
44 Chris Paul .60 1.50
45 Kobe Bryant 3.00 8.00
46 Marc Gasol .40 1.00
47 Chris Bosh .50 1.25
48 Larry Sanders .25 .60
49 Nikola Pekovic .25 .60
50 Anthony Davis 1.00 2.50
51 Carmelo Anthony .60 1.50
52 Kevin Durant 1.25 3.00
53 Channing Frye .25 .60
54 Michael Carter-Williams .25 .60
55 Marcus Morris .25 .60
56 Wesley Matthews .25 .60
57 Rudy Gay .40 1.00
58 Tim Duncan 1.00 2.50
59 Landry Fields .25 .60
60 Gordon Hayward .30 .75
61 Nene .30 .75
62 Brandon Bass .25 .60
63 DeMarre Carroll .25 .60
64 Mirza Teletovic .25 .60
65 Pau Gasol .60 1.50
66 Mike Dunleavy .25 .60
67 Dion Waiters .25 .60
68 Raymond Felton .25 .60
69 J.J. Hickson .25 .60
70 Stephen Curry 3.00 8.00
71 James Harden .75 2.00
72 George Hill .30 .75
73 Jamal Crawford .40 1.00
74 Nick Young .30 .75
75 Courtney Lee .25 .60
76 Norris Cole .25 .60
77 Anthony Bennett .25 .60
78 Omer Asik .25 .60
79 Iman Shumpert .25 .60
80 Serge Ibaka .30 .75
81 Nikola Vucevic .30 .75
82 Nerlens Noel .25 .60
83 Goran Dragic .40 1.00
84 Isaiah Thomas .30 .75
85 C.J. McCollum .40 1.00
86 Darren Collison .25 .60
87 Tiago Splitter .25 .60
88 Jonas Valanciunas .30 .75
89 Enes Kanter .30 .75
90 John Wall .50 1.25
91 Patrick Patterson .25 .60
92 Danny Green .30 .75
93 Steve Blake .25 .60
94 Alexey Shved .25 .60
95 Nick Collison .30 .75
96 Jose Calderon .25 .60
97 Corey Brewer .25 .60
98 Giannis Antetokounmpo 2.50 6.00
99 Luol Deng .30 .75
100 Tayshaun Prince .40 1.00
101 Jeremy Lin .75 2.00
102 Rodney Stuckey .25 .60
103 Jason Terry .30 .75
104 Andrew Bogut .30 .75
105 Andre Drummond .30 .75
106 Monta Ellis .30 .75
107 Anderson Varejao .25 .60
108 Joakim Noah .40 1.00
109 Andrei Kirilenko .30 .75
110 Tyler Zeller .25 .60
111 Avery Bradley .25 .60
112 Paul Millsap .25 .60
113 Chandler Parsons .25 .60
114 Tristan Thompson .25 .60
115 Arron Afflalo .25 .60
116 Jonas Jerebko .25 .60
117 Terrence Jones .25 .60
118 J.J. Redick .40 1.00
119 Ed Davis .25 .60
120 Chris Andersen .30 .75
121 Ricky Rubio .30 .75
122 Samuel Dalembert .25 .60
123 Tobias Harris .30 .75
124 Miles Plumlee .25 .60
125 Ben McLemore .25 .60
126 Cory Joseph .25 .60
127 Trey Burke .25 .60
128 Glen Rice Jr. .25 .60
129 Damian Lillard 1.00 2.50
130 Tony Wroten .25 .60
131 Tim Hardaway Jr. .30 .75
132 Eric Gordon .30 .75
133 Vince Carter .75 2.00
134 Carlos Boozer .30 .75
135 Reggie Bullock .25 .60
136 Isaiah Canaan .25 .60
137 Draymond Green .50 1.25
138 Kentavious Caldwell-Pope .30 .75
139 Jameer Nelson .25 .60
140 Shawn Marion .30 .75
141 Kemba Walker .40 1.00
142 Joe Johnson .30 .75
143 Dennis Schroder .40 1.00
144 Derrick Rose .75 2.00
145 Mike Miller .30 .75
146 Josh Smith .25 .60
147 David Lee .25 .60
148 Patrick Beverley .25 .60
149 Matt Barnes .30 .75
150 Mike Conley .30 .75
151 John Henson .25 .60
152 Ryan Anderson .25 .60
153 Reggie Jackson .30 .75
154 Hollis Thompson .25 .60
155 Nicolas Batum .30 .75
156 Manu Ginobili .75 2.00
157 Amir Johnson .25 .60
158 Paul Pierce .60 1.50
159 Carl Landry .25 .60
160 Markieff Morris .25 .60
161 Maurice Harkless .25 .60
162 Kendrick Perkins .25 .60
163 Jrue Holiday .50 1.25
164 Kevin Martin .30 .75
165 Mario Chalmers .30 .75
166 Jordan Hill .25 .60
167 Blake Griffin .40 1.00
168 Harrison Barnes .30 .75
169 Devin Harris .25 .60
170 LeBron James 3.00 8.00
171 Cody Zeller .25 .60
172 Mason Plumlee .25 .60
173 Jared Sullinger .25 .60
174 Kyle Korver .30 .75
175 Gerald Henderson .25 .60
176 Kirk Hinrich .30 .75
177 Kenneth Faried .30 .75
178 Luis Scola .30 .75
179 Josh McRoberts .25 .60
180 Shabazz Muhammad .25 .60
181 Austin Rivers .25 .60
182 J.R. Smith .40 1.00
183 Steven Adams .50 1.25
184 Robin Lopez .25 .60
185 Boris Diaw .25 .60
186 Terrence Ross .30 .75
187 Otto Porter .30 .75
188 Evan Fournier .30 .75
189 Ersan Ilyasova .25 .60
190 David West .25 .60
191 Danilo Gallinari .25 .60
192 Al Jefferson .25 .60
193 Deron Williams .30 .75
194 Kelly Olynyk .25 .60
195 Derrick Williams .25 .60
196 Kawhi Leonard 1.00 2.50
197 DeMar DeRozan .50 1.25
198 Rudy Gobert .60 1.50
199 Bradley Beal .60 1.50
200 Alec Burks .30 .75
201 Andrew Wiggins RC 2.50 6.00
202 Jabari Parker RC .60 1.50
203 Joel Embiid RC 5.00 12.00
204 Dante Exum RC .75 2.00
205 Cory Jefferson RC .50 1.25
206 Elfrid Payton RC .75 2.00
207 Marcus Smart RC 2.00 5.00
208 James Young RC .50 1.25
209 Aaron Gordon RC 2.50 6.00
210 Jusuf Nurkic RC 1.50 4.00
211 Doug McDermott RC .75 2.00
212 Damjan Rudez RC .50 1.25
213 Kostas Papanikolaou RC .50 1.25
214 P.J. Hairston RC .50 1.25
215 Shabazz Napier RC .60 1.50
216 Rodney Hood RC .60 1.50
217 Nik Stauskas RC .50 1.25
218 Jordan Clarkson RC 2.00 5.00
219 Nikola Mirotic RC .75 2.00
220 Cleanthony Early RC .50 1.25
221 Zach LaVine RC 3.00 8.00
222 James Ennis RC .50 1.25
223 Kyle Anderson RC .75 2.00
224 Julius Randle RC 2.50 6.00
225 T.J. Warren RC .75 2.00
226 Noah Vonleh RC .40 1.00
227 Glenn Robinson III RC .60 1.50
228 Gary Harris RC .75 2.00
229 Spencer Dinwiddie RC .75 2.00
230 Russ Smith RC .50 1.25
231 K.J. McDaniels RC .50 1.25
232 Jarnell Stokes RC .50 1.25
233 Bruno Caboclo RC .60 1.50
234 Erick Green RC .50 1.25
235 Tarik Black RC .50 1.25
236 Joe Harris RC .75 2.00
237 Tyler Ennis RC .50 1.25
238 Langston Galloway RC .75 2.00
239 Markel Brown RC .50 1.25

2014-15 Donruss Press Proofs Blue

*VETS: 1.5X TO 4X BASE HI
*ROOKIES: 1.5X TO 4X BASE HI
STATED PRINT RUN 99 SER.#'d SETS

2014-15 Donruss Press Proofs Purple

*VETS: 1.2X TO 3X BASE HI
*ROOKIES: 1.2X TO 3X BASE HI
STATED PRINT RUN 199 SER.#'d SETS

2014-15 Donruss Press Proofs Silver

*VETS: 4X TO 10X BASE HI
*ROOKIES: 4X TO 10X BASE HI
STATED PRINT RUN 25 SER.#'d SETS

2014-15 Donruss Rated Rookies Artists Proofs

*ROOKIES AP: .6X TO 1.5X BASE HI
STATED PRINT RUN 99 SER.#'d SETS
201 Andrew Wiggins 10.00 25.00

2014-15 Donruss Rated Rookies Jersey Numbers

STATED PRINT RUN B/WN 1-44 COPIES PER
NO PRICING ON QTY 19 OR LESS
201 Andrew Wiggins/22 60.00 150.00
203 Joel Embiid/21 400.00 800.00
207 Marcus Smart/36 40.00 100.00

2014-15 Donruss Stat Line Career

*CAREER: 3X TO 8X BASE HI
STATED PRINT RUN B/WN 43-440 COPIES PER

2014-15 Donruss Stat Line Season

*SEASON: 2.5X TO 6X BASE HI
STATED PRINT RUN B/WN 76-485 COPIES PER

2014-15 Donruss Swirlorama

*VETS: 1.2X TO 3X BASE HI
*ROOKIES: 1.25X TO 3X BASE HI
45 Kobe Bryant 20.00 50.00
70 Stephen Curry 20.00 50.00
170 LeBron James 20.00 50.00

2014-15 Donruss Court Kings

*PURPLE/199: 1.5X TO 4X BASE HI
*BLUE/99: 2X TO 5X BASE HI
*SILVER/25: 5X TO 12X BASE HI
*CAREER: 1.5X TO 4X BASE HI
*SEASON: .1.5X TO 4X BASE HI
1 Blake Griffin .50 1.25
2 Pau Gasol .75 2.00
3 James Harden 1.00 2.50
4 Zach Randolph .50 1.25
5 Paul Millsap .40 1.00
6 Damian Lillard 1.25 3.00
7 LeBron James 4.00 10.00
8 Dwyane Wade 1.00 2.50
9 Greg Monroe .30 .75
10 Rajon Rondo .60 1.50
11 Tim Duncan 1.25 3.00
12 Andre Iguodala .50 1.25
13 Ricky Rubio .40 1.00
14 Roy Hibbert .40 1.00
15 Carmelo Anthony .75 2.00
16 Derrick Rose 1.00 2.50
17 Chris Paul .75 2.00
18 Goran Dragic .50 1.25
19 Dirk Nowitzki 1.25 3.00
20 Nikola Vucevic .40 1.00
21 Ty Lawson .30 .75
22 Kobe Bryant 4.00 10.00
23 Tony Parker .75 2.00
24 Deron Williams .40 1.00
25 Kevin Durant 1.50 4.00
26 Kevin Love .50 1.25
27 Marc Gasol .50 1.25
28 Al Horford .50 1.25
29 Dwight Howard .60 1.50
30 Josh Smith .30 .75
31 DeMarcus Cousins .40 1.00
32 Al Jefferson .30 .75
33 Iman Shumpert .30 .75
34 Jeremy Lin 1.00 2.50
35 Tyson Chandler .50 1.25
36 Chris Bosh .60 1.50
37 Serge Ibaka .40 1.00
38 Stephen Curry 4.00 10.00
39 Thaddeus Young .30 .75
40 Michael Carter-Williams .30 .75
41 Lance Stephenson .40 1.00
42 DeMar DeRozan .60 1.50
43 Anthony Davis 1.25 3.00
44 John Wall .60 1.50
45 Brandon Knight .30 .75
46 Paul Pierce .75 2.00
47 Nicolas Batum .40 1.00
48 Gordon Hayward .40 1.00
49 Eric Bledsoe .40 1.00
50 Rudy Gay .50 1.25

2014-15 Donruss Game Threads

1 Kobe Bryant 40.00 100.00
2 Brook Lopez 2.00 5.00
3 Al Jefferson 1.25 3.00
4 Dirk Nowitzki 5.00 12.00
5 Harrison Barnes 1.50 4.00
6 Paul George 3.00 8.00
7 Zach Randolph 2.00 5.00
8 Larry Sanders 1.25 3.00
9 Eric Gordon 1.50 4.00
10 Victor Oladipo 1.50 4.00
11 Kevin Durant 6.00 15.00
12 Eric Bledsoe 1.50 4.00
13 Michael Kidd-Gilchrist 1.25 3.00
14 Kenneth Faried 1.25 3.00
15 Andrew Bogut 1.50 4.00
16 Roy Hibbert 1.50 4.00
17 Mike Conley 1.50 4.00
18 Nikola Pekovic 1.25 3.00
19 Russell Westbrook 3.00 8.00
20 Damian Lillard 5.00 12.00
21 LeBron James 40.00 100.00
22 Paul Pierce 3.00 8.00
23 Jimmy Butler 3.00 8.00
25 Stephen Curry 40.00 100.00
26 Blake Griffin 2.00 5.00
27 Chris Bosh 2.50 6.00
29 Tobias Harris 1.50 4.00
30 LaMarcus Aldridge 2.00 5.00
31 Kevin Love 2.00 5.00
32 Ben Gordon 1.50 4.00
33 Joakim Noah 2.00 5.00
34 Andre Drummond 1.50 4.00
35 Terrence Jones 1.25 3.00
36 Nick Young 1.25 3.00
38 Austin Rivers 1.25 3.00
40 Tim Duncan 5.00 12.00
41 Kevin Garnett 5.00 12.00
43 Nazr Mohammed 1.25 3.00
44 Josh Smith 1.25 3.00
45 Luis Scola 1.50 4.00

2014-15 Donruss Game Threads Prime

*PRIME: 1.5X TO 4X BASE HI
STATED PRINT RUN B/WN 18-20 COPIES PER

2014-15 Donruss Gamers Jerseys

*PRIME/15-20: 1.25X TO 3X BASE HI
1 Tim Duncan 5.00 12.00
2 DeMarcus Cousins 1.50 4.00
3 DeMar DeRozan 2.50 6.00
4 Hakeem Olajuwon 4.00 10.00
5 Chris Kaman 1.50 4.00
6 Dwyane Wade 4.00 10.00
7 Shaquille O'Neal 8.00 20.00
8 Scottie Pippen 5.00 12.00
9 Greg Monroe 1.25 3.00
10 Danny Manning 1.50 4.00
11 Gordon Hayward 1.50 4.00
12 Larry Bird 8.00 20.00
13 Karl Malone 4.00 10.00
14 Ty Lawson 1.25 3.00
15 George Hill 1.50 4.00
16 Derrick Favors 1.25 3.00
17 Kyle Korver 1.50 4.00
18 John Stockton 4.00 10.00
19 Wilson Chandler 1.25 3.00
20 Ben McLemore 1.25 3.00
21 Jimmy Butler 3.00 8.00
22 Serge Ibaka 1.50 4.00
23 Jonas Valanciunas 1.50 4.00
24 Monta Ellis 1.50 4.00
25 Carl Landry 1.25 3.00
26 Kemba Walker 2.00 5.00
27 Kevin Durant 6.00 15.00
28 Gary Payton 3.00 8.00
29 Dirk Nowitzki 5.00 12.00
30 Chris Mullin 2.50 6.00
31 Paul Pierce 3.00 8.00
32 Kobe Bryant 40.00 100.00
33 Kawhi Leonard 5.00 12.00
34 Chris Bosh 2.50 6.00
35 Andre Iguodala 2.50 6.00
36 Robert Parish 2.50 6.00
37 John Wall 2.50 6.00
38 Tony Parker 3.00 8.00
39 LeBron James 40.00 100.00
40 Stephen Curry 40.00 100.00
41 Jeff Green 1.50 4.00
42 Bradley Beal 3.00 8.00
43 Kyle Lowry 2.50 6.00
44 Paul Millsap 1.50 4.00
45 Clyde Drexler 3.00 8.00

2014-15 Donruss Jersey Kings

*PRIME: 1.5X TO 4X BASE HI
1 Kobe Bryant 40.00 100.00
2 Kyrie Irving 4.00 10.00
3 Carmelo Anthony 3.00 8.00
4 LeBron James 40.00 100.00
5 Rajon Rondo 2.50 6.00
6 Dirk Nowitzki 5.00 12.00
7 Tim Duncan 5.00 12.00
10 Michael Carter-Williams 1.25 3.00
12 DeMar DeRozan 2.50 6.00
13 LaMarcus Aldridge 2.00 5.00
14 Al Jefferson 1.25 3.00
15 Marc Gasol 2.00 5.00
16 Kevin Garnett 5.00 12.00
18 Damian Lillard 5.00 12.00
19 Stephen Curry 40.00 100.00
21 Blake Griffin 2.00 5.00
22 Eric Bledsoe 1.50 4.00
23 Anthony Davis 5.00 12.00
25 Kenneth Faried 1.25 3.00
26 Kawhi Leonard 5.00 12.00

2014-15 Donruss Production Line Assists

*PURPLE/199: 1.25X TO 3X BASE HI
*BLUE/99: 1.5X TO 4X BASE HI
*SILVER/25: 4X TO 10X BASE HI
*CAREER: 1.5X TO 4X BASE HI
*SEASON: 1.5X TO 4X BASE HI
*SWIRLORAMA: 1X TO 2.5X BASE HI
1 Chris Paul 1.00 2.50
2 Kendall Marshall .40 1.00
3 John Wall .75 2.00
4 Ty Lawson .40 1.00
5 Ricky Rubio .50 1.25
6 Stephen Curry 5.00 12.00
7 Brandon Jennings .40 1.00
8 Kyle Lowry .75 2.00
9 Jameer Nelson .40 1.00
10 Jeff Teague .40 1.00

2014-15 Donruss Production Line Rebounds

*PURPLE/199: 1.25X TO 3X BASE HI
*BLUE/99: 1.5X TO 4X BASE HI
*SILVER: 4X TO 10X BASE HI
*CAREER: 1.25X TO 3X BASE HI
*SEASON: 1.25X TO 3X BASE HI
*SWIRLORAMA: 1X TO 2.5X BASE HI
1 DeAndre Jordan .50 1.25
2 Andre Drummond .50 1.25
3 Kevin Love .60 1.50
4 Dwight Howard .75 2.00
5 DeMarcus Cousins .50 1.25
6 Joakim Noah .60 1.50
7 LaMarcus Aldridge .60 1.50
8 Al Jefferson .40 1.00
9 Zach Randolph .60 1.50
10 Anthony Davis 1.50 4.00

2014-15 Donruss Production Line Scoring
*PURPLE/199: 1.2X TO 3X BASE HI
*BLUE/99: 1.5X TO 4X BASE HI
*SILVER/25: 4X TO 10X BASE HI
*SWIRLORAMA: 1X TO 2.5X BASE HI
1 Kevin Durant 2.00 5.00
2 Carmelo Anthony 1.00 2.50
3 LeBron James 5.00 12.00
4 Kevin Love .60 1.50
5 James Harden 1.25 3.00
6 Blake Griffin .60 1.50
7 Stephen Curry 5.00 12.00
8 LaMarcus Aldridge .60 1.50
9 DeMarcus Cousins .50 1.25
10 DeMar DeRozan .75 2.00

2014-15 Donruss Rated Rookie Signature Patches
1 Aaron Gordon 20.00 50.00
2 Adreian Payne 4.00 10.00
3 Andrew Wiggins 20.00 50.00
4 Bruno Caboclo 5.00 12.00
5 C.J. Wilcox 4.00 10.00
6 Cleanthony Early 4.00 10.00
7 Cory Jefferson 4.00 10.00
8 Damien Inglis 4.00 10.00
9 Doug McDermott 6.00 15.00
10 Elfrid Payton 6.00 15.00
11 Gary Harris 6.00 15.00
12 Glenn Robinson III 5.00 12.00
13 Jabari Parker 5.00 12.00
14 James Young 4.00 10.00
15 Jarnell Stokes 4.00 10.00
16 Jerami Grant 20.00 50.00
17 Joe Harris 6.00 15.00
18 Joel Embiid 100.00 250.00
19 Johnny O'Bryant 4.00 10.00
20 Jordan Adams 4.00 10.00
21 Julius Randle 20.00 50.00
22 K.J. McDaniels 4.00 10.00
23 Kyle Anderson 6.00 15.00
24 Marcus Smart 15.00 40.00
25 Markel Brown 4.00 10.00
26 Mitch McGary 4.00 10.00
27 Nik Stauskas 4.00 10.00
28 Noah Vonleh 4.00 10.00
29 P.J. Hairston 4.00 10.00
30 Rodney Hood 5.00 12.00
31 Russ Smith 4.00 10.00
32 Shabazz Napier 5.00 12.00
33 Spencer Dinwiddie 6.00 15.00
34 James Ennis 4.00 10.00
35 T.J. Warren 6.00 15.00
36 Tyler Ennis 4.00 10.00
37 Zach LaVine 40.00 100.00

2014-15 Donruss Rookie Autographs
STATED PRINT RUN B/WN 99-199 COPIES PER
1 Devyn Marble/199 3.00 8.00
2 Elfrid Payton/149 5.00 12.00
3 Andrew Wiggins/99 15.00 40.00
4 Jabari Parker/99 4.00 10.00
5 Joel Embiid/99 150.00 400.00
6 James Ennis/199 3.00 8.00
7 K.J. McDaniels/199 3.00 8.00
8 Jerami Grant/199 15.00 40.00
9 Kyle Anderson/199 5.00 12.00
10 Glenn Robinson III/149 4.00 10.00
11 Jordan Adams/199 3.00 8.00
12 Erick Green/199 3.00 8.00
13 Dwight Powell/199 4.00 10.00
14 Joe Harris/199 5.00 12.00
15 Marcus Smart/99 12.00 30.00
16 Alex Kirk/199 3.00 8.00
17 James Young/149 3.00 8.00
18 Markel Brown/199 3.00 8.00
19 Lucas Nogueira/199 3.00 8.00
20 Russ Smith/199 3.00 8.00
21 Damjan Rudez/199 3.00 8.00
22 Doug McDermott/149 5.00 12.00
23 T.J. Warren/149 5.00 12.00
24 Aaron Gordon/99 15.00 40.00
25 Spencer Dinwiddie/199 5.00 12.00
26 Jordan Clarkson/199 12.00 30.00
27 P.J. Hairston/199 3.00 8.00
28 Zach LaVine/149 40.00 100.00
29 Jusuf Nurkic/149 10.00 25.00
30 Gary Harris/149 5.00 12.00
31 Shabazz Napier/149 4.00 10.00
32 Mitch McGary/199 3.00 8.00
33 Rodney Hood/199 4.00 10.00

2014-15 Donruss Rookie Autographs Die-Cuts
*DIE CUTS: .6X TO 1.5X BASE HI
STATED PRINT RUN 49 SER.#'d SETS

2014-15 Donruss Scoring Kings
*PURPLE: .8X TO 2X BASE HI
*BLUE: 1X TO 2.5X BASE HI
*SILVER: 1.25X TO 3X BASE HI
1 Kevin Durant 2.00 5.00
2 Kobe Bryant 5.00 12.00
3 Dwyane Wade 1.25 3.00
4 Allen Iverson 1.50 4.00
5 Kevin Garnett 1.50 4.00
6 Paul Pierce 1.00 2.50
7 James Harden 1.25 3.00
8 Shaquille O'Neal 2.50 6.00
9 David Robinson 1.25 3.00
10 Alex English .75 2.00
11 Adrian Dantley .60 1.50
12 George Gervin 1.00 2.50
13 Pete Maravich 2.00 5.00
14 Bob McAdoo .50 1.25
15 Kareem Abdul-Jabbar 2.00 5.00
16 Elvin Hayes .60 1.50
17 Rick Barry .75 2.00
18 Karl Malone 1.25 3.00
19 Tracy McGrady 1.00 2.50
20 LeBron James 5.00 12.00
21 Vince Carter 1.25 3.00
22 Dominique Wilkins 1.00 2.50
23 Dirk Nowitzki 1.50 4.00
24 Carmelo Anthony 1.00 2.50
25 Kiki Vandeweghe .50 1.25
26 Hakeem Olajuwon 1.25 3.00
27 Patrick Ewing 1.00 2.50
28 Moses Malone 1.00 2.50
29 Tim Duncan 1.50 4.00
30 Mitch Richmond .75 2.00
31 Larry Bird 2.00 5.00
32 Julius Erving 1.50 4.00
33 Chris Mullin .75 2.00
34 Bernard King .75 2.00
35 Clyde Drexler 1.50 4.00
36 World B. Free .50 1.25
37 Dale Ellis .50 1.25
38 Blake Griffin .50 1.25
39 Stephen Curry 5.00 12.00
40 Oscar Robertson 1.25 3.00
41 Wilt Chamberlain 2.00 5.00
42 Bob Pettit .60 1.50
43 Mark Aguirre .50 1.25
44 Glen Rice .60 1.50
45 Amar'e Stoudemire .60 1.50
46 John Havlicek 1.25 3.00
47 David Thompson .60 1.50
48 Jerry West 1.50 4.00
49 Walt Bellamy .50 1.25
50 Gary Payton 1.00 2.50

2014-15 Donruss Scoring Kings Stat Line Career
*CAREER: 1X TO 2.5X BASE HI
STATED PRINT RUN B/WN 157-303 COPIES PER
1 Kevin Durant/274 3.00 8.00
2 Kobe Bryant/254 4.00 10.00
10 Alex English/215 3.00 8.00
20 LeBron James/275 4.00 10.00
31 Larry Bird/243 6.00 15.00

2014-15 Donruss Scoring Kings Stat Line Season
*SEASON: 1X TO 2.5X BASE HI
STATED PRINT RUN B/WN 25-302 COPIES PER
8 Shaquille O'Neal/61 5.00 12.00
24 Carmelo Anthony/62 5.00 12.00

2014-15 Donruss Signature Stars
STATED PRINT RUN 40 SER.#'d SETS
1 Andrew Wiggins 25.00 60.00
2 Jabari Parker 6.00 15.00
3 Joel Embiid 125.00 300.00
4 Dante Exum 8.00 20.00
5 Grant Hill 20.00 50.00
6 Allen Iverson 60.00 150.00
7 Chris Webber 60.00 150.00
8 Carmelo Anthony 40.00 100.00
9 Paul George 20.00 50.00
11 Kevin Durant 75.00 200.00
12 Blake Griffin 8.00 20.00
13 Kareem Abdul-Jabbar 100.00 250.00
14 Shaquille O'Neal 75.00 200.00
15 Magic Johnson 60.00 150.00
16 Bill Russell 400.00 800.00
17 Karl Malone 20.00 50.00
18 David Robinson 30.00 80.00
19 Jerry West 30.00 80.00
20 Dwight Howard 10.00 25.00
21 Yao Ming 75.00 200.00
22 Jason Kidd 30.00 80.00
23 Dwyane Wade 40.00 100.00
24 John Wall 10.00 25.00
25 Bradley Beal 12.00 30.00
27 Steve Nash 40.00 100.00
28 Kevin Love 12.00 30.00
29 Tony Parker 20.00 50.00
30 Manu Ginobili 40.00 100.00
31 Chris Bosh 15.00 40.00
32 Julius Randle 25.00 60.00
33 Elfrid Payton 8.00 20.00

2014-15 Donruss The Rookies
*PRESS PROOF PURPLE/199: 1.25X TO 3X BASE HI
*ARTIST PROOFS/99: 1.5X TO 4X BASE HI
*PRESS PROOF BLUE/99: 1.5X TO 4X BASE HI
*PRESS PROOF SILVER/25: 4X TO 10X BASE HI
1 Andrew Wiggins 2.50 6.00
2 Jabari Parker .60 1.50
3 Joel Embiid 5.00 12.00
4 Dante Exum .75 2.00
5 Marcus Smart 2.00 5.00
6 Julius Randle 2.50 6.00
7 Zach LaVine 3.00 8.00
8 Aaron Gordon 2.50 6.00
9 Elfrid Payton .75 2.00
10 Doug McDermott .75 2.00
11 James Young .50 1.25
12 Nik Stauskas .50 1.25
13 Shabazz Napier .60 1.50
14 Noah Vonleh .50 1.25
15 T.J. Warren .75 2.00
16 Glenn Robinson III .60 1.50
17 Rodney Hood .60 1.50
18 Gary Harris .75 2.00
19 Cleanthony Early .50 1.25
20 Mitch McGary .50 1.25
21 Kyle Anderson .75 2.00
22 Bruno Caboclo .60 1.50
23 Tyler Ennis .50 1.25
24 Russ Smith .50 1.25
25 Jarnell Stokes .50 1.25
26 Adreian Payne .50 1.25
27 James Ennis .50 1.25
28 Spencer Dinwiddie .75 2.00
29 C.J. Wilcox .50 1.25
30 K.J. McDaniels .50 1.25

2014-15 Donruss The Rookies Swirlorama
*SWIRLORAMA: 1.2X TO 3X BASE HI

2014-15 Donruss Timeless Treasures Jersey Autographs
STATED PRINT RUN 99 SER.#'d SETS
2 Kevin Durant 50.00 120.00
3 Kyrie Irving 40.00 100.00
5 Stephen Curry 300.00 600.00
6 Andrew Wiggins 30.00 80.00
7 Jabari Parker 12.00 30.00
9 Marcus Smart 15.00 40.00
10 Julius Randle 20.00 50.00

2014-15 Donruss Timeless Treasures Jersey Autographs Prime
*PRIME: .6X TO 1.5X BASE HI
STATED PRINT RUN B/WN 15-25 COPIES PER

2015-16 Donruss
COMPLETE SET (250) 60.00 150.00
COMP.SET w/o RCs (200) 12.00 30.00
1 Gorgui Dieng .25 .60
2 Chris Paul .75 2.00
3 Wesley Matthews .25 .60
4 Darren Collison .25 .60
5 Vince Carter .75 2.00
6 Jodie Meeks .25 .60
7 Tiago Splitter .25 .60
8 David Lee .25 .60
9 Tobias Harris .30 .75
10 Hollis Thompson .25 .60
11 Serge Ibaka .30 .75
12 Paul Pierce .60 1.50
13 Devin Harris .25 .60
14 Rajon Rondo .50 1.25
15 Anthony Davis 1.00 2.50
16 Reggie Jackson .30 .75
17 Paul Millsap .30 .75
18 Tyler Zeller .25 .60
19 Nikola Vucevic .30 .75
20 Nik Stauskas .25 .60
21 Dion Waiters .25 .60
22 Lance Stephenson .30 .75
23 Deron Williams .30 .75
24 Ben McLemore .25 .60
25 Ryan Anderson .25 .60
26 Brandon Jennings .25 .60
27 Cody Zeller .25 .60
28 Avery Bradley .25 .60
29 Nene .30 .75
30 Tony Wroten .25 .60
31 Russell Westbrook .60 1.50
32 DeAndre Jordan .30 .75
33 J.J. Barea .30 .75
34 Marco Belinelli .25 .60
35 Omer Asik .25 .60
36 Marcus Morris .25 .60
37 Nicolas Batum .25 .60
38 Marcus Smart .50 1.25
39 Bradley Beal .50 1.25
40 Isaiah Canaan .25 .60
41 Kevin Durant 1.50 4.00
42 Brandon Bass .25 .60
43 Chandler Parsons .25 .60
44 Pau Gasol .60 1.50
45 Quincy Pondexter .25 .60
46 Andre Drummond .40 1.00
47 Jeremy Lamb .25 .60
48 Evan Turner .25 .60
49 John Wall .50 1.25
50 Patrick Patterson .25 .60
51 Enes Kanter .25 .60
52 Julius Randle .50 1.25
53 Zaza Pachulia .25 .60
54 Taj Gibson .25 .60
55 Tyreke Evans .30 .75
56 Jordan Hill .25 .60
57 Kemba Walker .40 1.00
58 Isaiah Thomas .30 .75
59 Otto Porter Jr. .30 .75
60 Luis Scola .30 .75
61 Steven Adams .30 .75
62 Kobe Bryant 3.00 8.00
63 Terrence Jones .25 .60
64 Nikola Mirotic .25 .60
65 Jrue Holiday .50 1.25
66 Monta Ellis .30 .75
67 Jeremy Lin .75 2.00
68 Jarrett Jack .30 .75
69 Marcin Gortat .30 .75
70 DeMar DeRozan .50 1.25
71 Gerald Henderson .25 .60
72 Jordan Clarkson .40 1.00
73 James Harden .75 2.00
74 Jimmy Butler .75 2.00
75 Eric Gordon .30 .75
76 George Hill .30 .75
77 Michael Kidd-Gilchrist .25 .60
78 Bojan Bogdanovic .30 .75
79 Jared Dudley .25 .60
80 Terrence Ross .30 .75
81 Damian Lillard 1.00 2.50
82 Nick Young .25 .60
83 Ty Lawson .25 .60
84 Derrick Rose .60 1.50
85 Tony Parker .60 1.50
86 Rodney Stuckey .25 .60
87 Al Jefferson .25 .60
88 Thaddeus Young .25 .60
89 Kenneth Faried .30 .75
90 Kyle Lowry .40 1.00
91 Al-Farouq Aminu .25 .60
92 Roy Hibbert .30 .75
93 Trevor Ariza .25 .60
94 Mike Dunleavy .25 .60
95 Kawhi Leonard 1.25 3.00
96 Paul George .60 1.50
97 Chris Bosh .50 1.25
98 Brook Lopez .40 1.00
99 Randy Foye .25 .60
100 DeMarre Carroll .25 .60
101 Mason Plumlee .25 .60
102 Markieff Morris .25 .60
103 Corey Brewer .25 .60
104 Joakim Noah .25 .60
105 Tim Duncan 1.00 2.50
106 Solomon Hill .25 .60
107 Dwyane Wade .75 2.00
108 Joe Johnson .30 .75
109 Gary Harris .30 .75
110 Jonas Valanciunas .30 .75
111 Noah Vonleh .25 .60
112 Mirza Teletovic .25 .60
113 Dwight Howard .50 1.25
114 Kevin Love .40 1.00
115 LaMarcus Aldridge .40 1.00
116 Chase Budinger .25 .60
117 Gerald Green .25 .60
118 Andrea Bargnani .25 .60
119 Jameer Nelson .25 .60
120 Stephen Curry 3.00 8.00
121 Ed Davis .25 .60
122 Eric Bledsoe .30 .75
123 Donatas Motiejunas .25 .60
124 Iman Shumpert .25 .60
125 David West .30 .75
126 Jabari Parker .25 .60
127 Goran Dragic .40 1.00
128 Arron Afflalo .25 .60
129 Danilo Gallinari .30 .75
130 Klay Thompson 1.00 2.50
131 Alec Burks .25 .60
132 Brandon Knight .25 .60
133 Mike Conley .40 1.00
134 Kyrie Irving .75 2.00
135 Danny Green .30 .75
136 Khris Middleton .50 1.25
137 Mario Chalmers .30 .75
138 Jose Calderon .25 .60
139 Wilson Chandler .30 .75
140 Draymond Green .50 1.25
141 Trey Burke .25 .60
142 P.J. Tucker .25 .60
143 Tony Allen .25 .60
144 LeBron James 3.00 8.00
145 Manu Ginobili .75 2.00
146 O.J. Mayo .25 .60
147 Luol Deng .30 .75
148 Langston Galloway .25 .60
149 Jusuf Nurkic .30 .75
150 Andrew Bogut .30 .75
151 Gordon Hayward .40 1.00
152 Tyson Chandler .30 .75
153 Jeff Green .25 .60
154 Timofey Mozgov .25 .60
155 Kyle Korver .30 .75
156 Michael Carter-Williams .25 .60
157 Hassan Whiteside .30 .75
158 Carmelo Anthony .60 1.50
159 Kevin Garnett 1.00 2.50
160 Harrison Barnes .30 .75
161 Rudy Gobert .50 1.25
162 Alex Len .25 .60
163 Marc Gasol .40 1.00
164 Mo Williams .30 .75
165 Tim Hardaway Jr. .30 .75
166 Greivis Vasquez .25 .60
167 Channing Frye .25 .60
168 Robin Lopez .25 .60
169 Kevin Martin .30 .75
170 Andre Iguodala .40 1.00
171 Derrick Favors .30 .75
172 DeMarcus Cousins .40 1.00
173 Zach Randolph .40 1.00
174 Anderson Varejao .25 .60
175 Jeff Teague .25 .60
176 Giannis Antetokounmpo 2.00 5.00
177 Aaron Gordon .40 1.00
178 Derrick Williams .25 .60
179 Zach LaVine 1.00 2.50
180 Blake Griffin .40 1.00
181 Rodney Hood .30 .75
182 Kosta Koufos .25 .60
183 Brandan Wright .25 .60
184 Ersan Ilyasova .25 .60
185 Thabo Sefolosha .25 .60
186 Greg Monroe .30 .75
187 Victor Oladipo .30 .75
188 Nerlens Noel .25 .60
189 Ricky Rubio .30 .75
190 Josh Smith .25 .60
191 Dante Exum .30 .75
192 Rudy Gay .40 1.00
193 Courtney Lee .25 .60
194 Kentavious Caldwell-Pope .30 .75
195 Al Horford .40 1.00
196 Dirk Nowitzki 1.00 2.50
197 Elfrid Payton .30 .75
198 Robert Covington .30 .75
199 Andrew Wiggins .50 1.25
200 J.J. Redick .40 1.00
201 Anthony Brown RC .50 1.25
202 Myles Turner RC 2.00 5.00
203 Joe Young RC .50 1.25
204 Terry Rozier RC 2.00 5.00
205 Nemanja Bjelica RC .75 2.00
206 Justin Anderson RC .50 1.25
207 Branden Dawson RC .50 1.25
208 Karl-Anthony Towns RC 4.00 10.00
209 Larry Nance Jr. RC 1.00 2.50
210 Willie Cauley-Stein RC .60 1.50
211 Rakeem Christmas RC .50 1.25
212 Trey Lyles RC .60 1.50
213 T.J. McConnell RC 2.00 5.00
214 Rashad Vaughn RC .50 1.25
215 Nikola Jokic RC 75.00 200.00
216 Bobby Portis RC 1.25 3.00
217 Aaron Harrison RC .60 1.50
218 D'Angelo Russell RC 2.00 5.00
219 R.J. Hunter RC .50 1.25
220 Justise Winslow RC .75 2.00
221 Emmanuel Mudiay RC .60 1.50
222 Richaun Holmes RC .75 2.00
223 Devin Booker RC 12.00 30.00
224 Boban Marjanovic RC 1.50 4.00
225 Sam Dekker RC .50 1.25
226 Raul Neto RC .50 1.25
227 Rondae Hollis-Jefferson RC .60 1.50
228 Jonathon Simmons RC .60 1.50
229 Jahlil Okafor RC .60 1.50
230 Chris McCullough RC .50 1.25
231 Stanley Johnson RC .60 1.50
232 Pat Connaughton RC .75 2.00
233 Cameron Payne RC .75 2.00
234 Walter Tavares RC .50 1.25
235 Jerian Grant RC .50 1.25
236 Josh Richardson RC .75 2.00
237 Tyus Jones RC .60 1.50
238 Christian Wood RC .75 2.00
239 Kristaps Porzingis RC 4.00 10.00
240 Montrezl Harrell RC 1.50 4.00
241 Frank Kaminsky RC .60 1.50
242 Marcelo Huertas RC .50 1.25
243 Kelly Oubre Jr. RC 1.50 4.00
244 Kevon Looney RC 1.50 4.00
245 Delon Wright RC .60 1.50
246 Cliff Alexander RC .50 1.25
247 Jarell Martin RC .50 1.25
248 Josh Huestis RC .50 1.25
249 Mario Hezonja RC .60 1.50
250 Jordan Mickey RC .50 1.25

2015-16 Donruss Assists
*ASSIST p/r 100-102: 1.5X TO 4X BASIC
*ASSIST p/r 51-96: 2X TO 5X BASIC
*ASSIST p/r 26-49: 2.5X TO 6X BASIC
*ASSIST p/r 20-25: 3X TO 8X BASIC
PRINT RUNS B/WN 20-102 COPIES PER

2015-16 Donruss Holo
*HOLO: 1.5X TO 4X BASIC
*HOLO RC: 1.5X TO 4X BASIC RC
STATED PRINT RUN 199 SER.#'d SETS

2015-16 Donruss Inspirations
*INSP: 2.5X TO 6X BASIC
*INSP RC: 1.25X TO 3X BASIC RC
PRINT RUNS B/WN 12-99 COPIES PER
NO PRICING ON QTY 12
208 Karl-Anthony Towns/68 20.00 50.00
215 Nikola Jokic/85 800.00 1,500.00
223 Devin Booker/99 75.00 200.00

2015-16 Donruss Points
*POINTS p/r 126-281: 1.2X TO 3X BASIC
*POINTS p/r 101-124: 1.5X TO 4X BASIC
*POINTS p/r 52-99: 2X TO 5X BASIC
*POINTS p/r 33-48: 2.5X TO 6X BASIC
PRINT RUNS B/WN 33-281 COPIES PER

2015-16 Donruss Rebounds
*RBNDS p/r 127-150: 1.2X TO 3X BASIC
*RBNDS p/r 100-118: 1.5X TO 4X BASIC
*RBNDS p/r 51-98: 2X TO 5X BASIC
*RBNDS p/r 26-49: 2.5X TO 6X BASIC
*RBNDS p/r 20-25: 3X TO 8X BASIC
PRINT RUNS B/WN 12-150 COPIES PER
NO PRICING ON QTY 19 OR LESS

2015-16 Donruss Status
*RBNDS p/r 50-88: 2X TO 5X BASIC
*RBNDS RC p/r 50-88: 1X TO 2.5X BASIC RC
*RBNDS p/r 26-44: 2.5X TO 6X BASIC
*RBNDS RC p/r 26-44: 1.2X TO 3X BASIC RC
*RBNDS p/r 20-25: 3X TO 8X BASIC
*RBNDS RC p/r 20-25: 1.5X TO 4X BASIC RC
PRINT RUNS B/WN 1-88 COPIES PER
NO PRICING ON QTY 18 OR LESS
62 Kobe Bryant/24 25.00 60.00
105 Tim Duncan/21 10.00 25.00
144 LeBron James/23 25.00 60.00
202 Myles Turner/33 6.00 15.00
208 Karl-Anthony Towns/32 15.00 40.00
238 Christian Wood/35 1.50 4.00

2015-16 Donruss Back to the Future Materials
PRINT RUNS B/WN 11-99 COPIES PER
NO PRICING ON QTY 11
*PRIME/21-25: 1X TO 2.5X BASIC
1 Aaron Brooks/99 2.00 5.00
2 Al Jefferson/99 2.00 5.00
3 Al-Farouq Aminu/75 2.00 5.00
4 Amar'e Stoudemire/99 3.00 8.00
5 Arron Afflalo/99 2.00 5.00
7 Boris Diaw/99 2.50 6.00
8 Brandon Bass/99 2.00 5.00
10 Caron Butler/99 2.50 6.00
11 Danilo Gallinari/99 2.50 6.00
13 Darren Collison/99 2.00 5.00
14 David West/99 2.50 6.00
15 Metta World Peace/99 2.50 6.00
16 Evan Turner/99 2.00 5.00
18 Isaiah Thomas/99 2.50 6.00
19 J.J. Redick/99 3.00 8.00
20 J.R. Smith/99 3.00 8.00
21 Jameer Nelson/99 2.00 5.00
22 Jason Richardson/99 3.00 8.00
23 Jeremy Lin/99 6.00 15.00
25 Jose Calderon/99 2.00 5.00
26 Jrue Holiday/99 4.00 10.00
27 Kevin Love/99 3.00 8.00
28 Kevin Martin/99 2.50 6.00
29 LeBron James/99 8.00 20.00
30 Luis Scola/99 2.50 6.00
31 Luol Deng/99 2.50 6.00
32 Matt Barnes/99 2.00 5.00
33 Monta Ellis/99 2.50 6.00
35 Nick Young/99 2.00 5.00
36 Nikola Vucevic/99 2.50 6.00
37 Pau Gasol/99 5.00 12.00
39 Paul Pierce/99 5.00 12.00
40 Rajon Rondo/99 4.00 10.00
41 Raymond Felton/99 2.00 5.00
42 Rudy Gay/99 3.00 8.00
43 Ryan Anderson/99 2.00 5.00
44 Spencer Hawes/99 2.00 5.00
45 Thaddeus Young/99 2.00 5.00
46 Tobias Harris/99 2.50 6.00
47 Tyson Chandler/99 2.50 6.00
48 Wilson Chandler/99 2.50 6.00
49 Chandler Parsons/99 2.00 5.00
50 Channing Frye/99 2.00 5.00

2015-16 Donruss Elite Dominator
STATED PRINT RUN 999 SER.#'d SETS
1 Pau Gasol 1.00 2.50
2 James Harden 1.25 3.00
3 Tim Duncan 1.50 4.00
4 Vince Carter 1.25 3.00
5 Tony Parker 1.00 2.50
6 Kevin Garnett 1.50 4.00
7 Damian Lillard 1.50 4.00
8 Kobe Bryant 5.00 12.00
9 Chris Bosh .75 2.00
10 Kyrie Irving 1.25 3.00
11 Derrick Rose 1.00 2.50
12 Stephen Curry 5.00 12.00
13 Dwight Howard .75 2.00
14 Andrew Wiggins .75 2.00
15 Russell Westbrook 1.00 2.50
16 Dwyane Wade 1.25 3.00
17 Klay Thompson 1.50 4.00
18 Kevin Durant 2.50 6.00
19 Dirk Nowitzki 1.50 4.00
20 Anthony Davis 1.50 4.00
21 Carmelo Anthony 1.00 2.50
22 LeBron James 5.00 12.00
23 Manu Ginobili 1.25 3.00
24 Chris Paul 1.25 3.00
25 Jabari Parker .40 1.00

2015-16 Donruss Elite Dominator Signatures
PRINT RUNS B/WN 25-49 COPIES PER
EXCHANGE DEADLINE 8/19/2017
EDSAD Anthony Davis/25 40.00 100.00
EDSAI Allen Iverson/25 50.00 120.00
EDSAW Andrew Wiggins/25 20.00 50.00
EDSCP Chris Paul/25 40.00 100.00
EDSDR D'Angelo Russell/25 25.00 60.00
EDSDR Dennis Rodman/25 20.00 50.00
EDSDW Dwyane Wade/25 40.00 100.00
EDSDW Dominique Wilkins/49 10.00 25.00
EDSEM Emmanuel Mudiay/49 3.00 8.00
EDSGH Grant Hill/49 10.00 25.00
EDSGP Gary Payton/49 8.00 20.00
EDSJO Jahlil Okafor/25 30.00 80.00
EDSJP Jabari Parker/25 15.00 40.00
EDSJW John Wall/25 15.00 40.00
EDSKB Kobe Bryant/25 500.00 1,000.00
EDSKD Kevin Durant/25 EXCH 50.00 120.00
EDSKI Kyrie Irving/25 EXCH 30.00 80.00
EDSKP Kristaps Porzingis/49 60.00 150.00
EDSKT Karl-Anthony Towns/25 150.00 250.00
EDSLS Latrell Sprewell/25 12.00 30.00
EDSMG Manu Ginobili/25 15.00 40.00
EDSMH Mario Hezonja/49 10.00 25.00
EDSOR Oscar Robertson/25 30.00 80.00
EDSPG Paul George/25 25.00 60.00

2015-16 Donruss Elite Hall Dominator
STATED PRINT RUN 999 SER.#'d SETS
1 Pete Maravich 1.50 4.00
2 Wilt Chamberlain 2.50 6.00
3 Larry Bird 2.50 6.00
4 Kareem Abdul-Jabbar 2.00 5.00
5 Hakeem Olajuwon 1.25 3.00
6 David Robinson 1.25 3.00
7 Gary Payton 1.00 2.50
8 Drazen Petrovic .60 1.50
9 Karl Malone 1.00 2.50
10 Alonzo Mourning 1.00 2.50
11 Dominique Wilkins 1.00 2.50
12 Magic Johnson 2.50 6.00
13 Scottie Pippen 1.50 4.00
14 Jerry West 1.00 2.50
15 Julius Erving 1.50 4.00
16 James Worthy 1.00 2.50
17 Oscar Robertson 1.50 4.00
18 Moses Malone 1.00 2.50
19 George Mikan 1.25 3.00
20 John Stockton 1.25 3.00
21 Elgin Baylor 1.25 3.00
22 Clyde Drexler 1.00 2.50
23 Dennis Rodman 1.50 4.00
24 Bill Russell 2.00 5.00
25 Patrick Ewing 1.00 2.50

2015-16 Donruss Elite Rookie Dominator
STATED PRINT RUN 999 SER.#'d SETS
1 Bobby Portis 1.00 2.50
2 Rondae Hollis-Jefferson .60 1.50
3 Devin Booker 6.00 15.00
4 Emmanuel Mudiay .60 1.50
5 Terry Rozier 2.00 5.00
6 Justise Winslow .75 2.00
7 Jerian Grant .50 1.25
8 Karl-Anthony Towns 3.00 8.00
9 Jahlil Okafor .60 1.50
10 Mario Hezonja .60 1.50
11 Cameron Payne .75 2.00
12 Stanley Johnson .60 1.50
13 Rashad Vaughn .50 1.25
14 Myles Turner 2.00 5.00
15 Delon Wright .60 1.50
16 D'Angelo Russell 2.00 5.00
17 Kristaps Porzingis 3.00 8.00
18 Willie Cauley-Stein .60 1.50
19 Kelly Oubre Jr. 1.50 4.00
20 Frank Kaminsky .60 1.50
21 Sam Dekker .50 1.25
22 Tyus Jones .60 1.50
23 Trey Lyles .60 1.50
24 Justin Anderson .50 1.25
25 Larry Nance Jr. 1.00 2.50

2015-16 Donruss Innovative Ink
1 Aaron Gordon 5.00 12.00
2 Adreian Payne 3.00 8.00
3 Andrew Wiggins 15.00 40.00
4 Bruno Caboclo 3.00 8.00
5 C.J. Wilcox 3.00 8.00
6 Cleanthony Early 3.00 8.00
7 Cory Jefferson 3.00 8.00
8 Damien Inglis 3.00 8.00
9 Doug McDermott 4.00 10.00
10 Elfrid Payton 4.00 10.00
11 Gary Harris 4.00 10.00
12 Glenn Robinson III 3.00 8.00
13 Jabari Parker 3.00 8.00
14 James Young 3.00 8.00
15 Jarnell Stokes 3.00 8.00
16 Jerami Grant 5.00 12.00
17 Joe Harris 4.00 10.00
19 Johnny O'Bryant 3.00 8.00
20 Jordan Adams 3.00 8.00
21 Josh Huestis 3.00 8.00
22 Julius Randle 10.00 25.00
23 K.J. McDaniels 3.00 8.00
24 Kyle Anderson 3.00 8.00
25 Marcus Smart 6.00 15.00
26 Markel Brown 3.00 8.00
27 Mitch McGary 3.00 8.00
28 Nik Stauskas 3.00 8.00
29 Noah Vonleh 3.00 8.00
30 Rodney Hood 4.00 10.00
31 Russ Smith 3.00 8.00
32 Shabazz Napier 3.00 8.00
33 Spencer Dinwiddie 4.00 10.00
34 T.J. Warren 5.00 12.00
36 Tyler Ennis 3.00 8.00
37 Zach LaVine 20.00 50.00

2015-16 Donruss Newly Crowned Rookie Jerseys
STATED PRINT RUN 149 SER.#'d SETS
*PRIME/25: .75X TO 2X BASIC
1 Jerian Grant 2.00 5.00
2 Emmanuel Mudiay 2.50 6.00
3 Bobby Portis 5.00 12.00
4 Justise Winslow 3.00 8.00
5 R.J. Hunter 2.00 5.00
6 Devin Booker 4.00 10.00
7 Jordan Mickey 2.00 5.00
8 Karl-Anthony Towns 10.00 25.00
9 Terry Rozier 8.00 20.00
10 Kristaps Porzingis 6.00 15.00
11 Delon Wright 2.50 6.00
12 Stanley Johnson 2.50 6.00
13 Rondae Hollis-Jefferson 2.50 6.00
14 Myles Turner 8.00 20.00
15 Chris McCullough 2.00 5.00
16 Cameron Payne 3.00 8.00
17 Anthony Brown 2.00 5.00
18 D'Angelo Russell 4.00 10.00
19 Joe Young 2.00 5.00
20 Mario Hezonja 2.50 6.00
21 Justin Anderson 2.00 5.00
22 Frank Kaminsky 2.50 6.00
23 Jarell Martin 2.00 5.00
24 Trey Lyles 2.50 6.00
25 Montrezl Harrell 6.00 15.00
26 Kelly Oubre Jr. 6.00 15.00
27 Rakeem Christmas 2.00 5.00
28 Jahlil Okafor 2.50 6.00
29 Sam Dekker 2.00 5.00
30 Willie Cauley-Stein 2.50 6.00

2015-16 Donruss Passing Kings
COMPLETE SET (30) 12.00 30.00
*CAR p/r 105-112: 1X TO 2.5X BASIC
*CAR p/r 52-99: 1.2X TO 3X BASIC
1 Oscar Robertson 1.25 3.00
2 Russell Westbrook .75 2.00
3 John Wall .60 1.50
4 Mark Price .50 1.25
5 Rajon Rondo .60 1.50
6 Lenny Wilkens .50 1.25
7 Bob Cousy .75 2.00
8 Damon Stoudamire .50 1.25
9 Magic Johnson 2.00 5.00
10 Tony Parker .75 2.00
11 Isiah Thomas .50 1.25
12 LeBron James 4.00 10.00
13 Deron Williams .40 1.00
14 Gary Payton .75 2.00
15 Tim Hardaway .60 1.50
16 Jerry West .75 2.00
17 Nate Archibald .60 1.50
18 Damian Lillard 1.25 3.00
19 John Stockton 1.00 2.50
20 Tyreke Evans .40 1.00
21 Jason Kidd .75 2.00
22 Stephen Curry 4.00 10.00
23 Steve Nash .75 2.00
24 Maurice Cheeks .40 1.00
25 Muggsy Bogues .40 1.00
26 Nick Van Exel .50 1.25
27 Baron Davis .40 1.00
28 Ty Lawson .30 .75
29 Chris Paul 1.00 2.50
30 Kyle Lowry .50 1.25

2015-16 Donruss Promising Pros Jumbo Swatches
STATED PRINT RUN 149 SER.#'d SETS
*PRIME/25: .75X TO 2X BASIC
1 Rakeem Christmas 2.00 5.00
2 Devin Booker 4.00 10.00
3 Kevon Looney 6.00 15.00
4 Karl-Anthony Towns 10.00 25.00
5 Terry Rozier 8.00 20.00
6 Kristaps Porzingis 5.00 12.00
7 Jerian Grant 2.00 5.00
8 Emmanuel Mudiay 2.50 6.00
9 Bobby Portis 5.00 12.00
10 Justise Winslow 3.00 8.00
11 Pat Connaughton 3.00 8.00
12 Cameron Payne 3.00 8.00
13 Josh Richardson 3.00 8.00
14 D'Angelo Russell 6.00 15.00
15 Jordan Mickey 2.00 5.00
16 Mario Hezonja 2.50 6.00
17 Delon Wright 2.50 6.00
18 Stanley Johnson 2.50 6.00
19 Rondae Hollis-Jefferson 2.50 6.00
20 Myles Turner 8.00 20.00
21 Joe Young 2.00 5.00
22 Kelly Oubre Jr. 6.00 15.00
23 Josh Huestis 2.00 5.00
24 Jahlil Okafor 6.00 15.00
25 Sam Dekker 2.00 5.00
26 Willie Cauley-Stein 2.50 6.00
27 Justin Anderson 2.00 5.00
28 Frank Kaminsky 2.50 6.00
29 Jarell Martin 2.00 5.00
30 Trey Lyles 2.50 6.00

2015-16 Donruss Rated Rookie Signature Patches
EXCHANGE DEADLINE 8/19/2017
1 Anthony Brown 3.00 8.00
2 Myles Turner 12.00 30.00
3 Joe Young 3.00 8.00
4 Terry Rozier 12.00 30.00
5 Justin Anderson 3.00 8.00
6 Karl-Anthony Towns 60.00 150.00
7 Willie Cauley-Stein 12.00 30.00
8 Rakeem Christmas 3.00 8.00
9 Trey Lyles 5.00 12.00
11 Rashad Vaughn 3.00 8.00
12 Bobby Portis 8.00 20.00
13 D'Angelo Russell 25.00 60.00
14 R.J. Hunter 3.00 8.00
15 Justise Winslow 10.00 25.00
16 Emmanuel Mudiay 4.00 10.00
17 Richaun Holmes 5.00 12.00
18 Devin Booker 300.00 600.00
20 Sam Dekker 3.00 8.00
21 Rondae Hollis-Jefferson 4.00 10.00
22 Jahlil Okafor 20.00 50.00
23 Chris McCullough 3.00 8.00
24 Stanley Johnson 10.00 25.00
25 Pat Connaughton 5.00 12.00
26 Cameron Payne 5.00 12.00
27 Walter Tavares 3.00 8.00
28 Jerian Grant 3.00 8.00

29 Josh Richardson 5.00 12.00
30 Tyus Jones 4.00 10.00
31 Kristaps Porzingis 50.00 120.00
32 Montrezl Harrell 10.00 25.00
33 Frank Kaminsky 6.00 15.00
34 Kelly Oubre Jr. 10.00 25.00
35 Kevon Looney 8.00 20.00
36 Delon Wright 4.00 10.00
37 Jarell Martin 3.00 8.00
38 Josh Huestis 3.00 8.00
39 Jordan Mickey 3.00 8.00
40 Mario Hezonja 10.00 25.00

2015-16 Donruss Rebounding Kings

*CAR p/r 127-229: .75X TO 2X BASIC
*CAR p/r 100-123: 1X TO 2.5X BASIC
*CAR p/r 84-98: 1.2X TO 3X BASIC
1 Kevin Love .60 1.50
2 Bill Laimbeer .60 1.50
3 Tim Duncan 1.50 4.00
4 Shawn Kemp 1.00 2.50
5 Wilt Chamberlain 2.50 6.00
6 Pau Gasol 1.00 2.50
7 Wes Unseld .75 2.00
8 Dikembe Mutombo 1.00 2.50
9 Dennis Rodman 1.50 4.00
10 Larry Bird 2.50 6.00
11 Kareem Abdul-Jabbar 2.00 5.00
12 Rony Seikaly .50 1.25
13 Shaquille O'Neal 2.00 5.00
14 Zach Randolph .60 1.50
15 Bill Russell 2.00 5.00
16 DeAndre Jordan .50 1.25
17 Dave Cowens .75 2.00
18 Kevin Garnett 1.50 4.00
19 Dwight Howard .75 2.00
20 Patrick Ewing 1.00 2.50
21 Hakeem Olajuwon 1.25 3.00
22 Robert Parish .75 2.00
23 David Robinson 1.25 3.00
24 Joakim Noah .40 1.00
25 Nate Thurmond .75 2.00
26 DeMarcus Cousins .60 1.50
27 Elgin Baylor 1.25 3.00
28 Karl Malone 1.25 3.00
29 Moses Malone 1.00 2.50
30 Chris Webber .75 2.00

2015-16 Donruss Rookie Material Signatures

PRINT RUNS B/WN 149 COPIES PER
EXCHANGE DEADLINE 8/19/2017
*PRIME/25: .6X TO 1.5X BASIC
1 Karl-Anthony Towns 75.00 200.00
2 D'Angelo Russell 30.00 80.00
3 Jahlil Okafor 20.00 50.00
4 Kristaps Porzingis 40.00 100.00
5 Mario Hezonja 8.00 20.00
6 Willie Cauley-Stein 5.00 12.00
7 Emmanuel Mudiay 5.00 12.00
8 Stanley Johnson 10.00 25.00
9 Frank Kaminsky 5.00 12.00
10 Justise Winslow 6.00 15.00
11 Myles Turner 10.00 25.00
12 Trey Lyles 5.00 12.00
13 Devin Booker 300.00 600.00
14 Cameron Payne 6.00 15.00
15 Kelly Oubre Jr. 12.00 30.00
16 Terry Rozier 15.00 40.00
17 Rashad Vaughn 4.00 10.00
18 Sam Dekker 4.00 10.00
19 Jerian Grant 4.00 10.00
20 Delon Wright 5.00 12.00
21 Justin Anderson 4.00 10.00
22 Bobby Portis 10.00 25.00
23 Rondae Hollis-Jefferson 5.00 12.00
24 Jarell Martin 4.00 10.00
25 R.J. Hunter 4.00 10.00
26 Chris McCullough 4.00 10.00
27 Montrezl Harrell 12.00 30.00
28 Jordan Mickey 4.00 10.00
29 Anthony Brown 4.00 10.00
30 Rakeem Christmas 4.00 10.00
31 Pat Connaughton 6.00 15.00
32 Joe Young 4.00 10.00
33 Kevon Looney 12.00 30.00
34 Josh Richardson 6.00 15.00
35 Walter Tavares 4.00 10.00

2015-16 Donruss Scoring Kings

*CAR p/r 250-301: .6X TO 1.5X BASIC
*CAR p/r 176-248: .75X TO 2X BASIC
1 Jerry West .75 2.00
2 Hakeem Olajuwon 1.00 2.50
3 Carmelo Anthony .75 2.00
4 Rick Barry .60 1.50
5 Patrick Ewing .75 2.00
6 Clyde Drexler .75 2.00
7 Julius Erving 1.25 3.00
8 LaMarcus Aldridge .50 1.25
9 Wilt Chamberlain 2.00 5.00
10 Kyrie Irving 1.00 2.50
11 Allen Iverson 1.25 3.00
12 Russell Westbrook .75 2.00
13 George Gervin .75 2.00
14 John Havlicek .60 1.50
15 Moses Malone .75 2.00
16 Larry Bird 2.00 5.00
17 Dwyane Wade 1.00 2.50
18 Elgin Baylor 1.00 2.50
19 Chris Bosh .60 1.50
20 Anthony Davis 1.25 3.00
21 Oscar Robertson 1.25 3.00
22 David Robinson 1.00 2.50
23 Karl Malone .75 2.00
24 Paul Pierce .75 2.00
25 Adrian Dantley .50 1.25
26 Tim Duncan 1.25 3.00
27 Shaquille O'Neal 1.50 4.00
28 Chris Paul 1.00 2.50
29 LeBron James 4.00 10.00
30 John Wall .60 1.50
31 Kobe Bryant 4.00 10.00
32 Mitch Richmond .60 1.50
33 Dominique Wilkins .75 2.00
34 Chris Webber .60 1.50
35 Pete Maravich 1.25 3.00
36 Vince Carter 1.00 2.50
37 Dirk Nowitzki 1.25 3.00
38 Stephen Curry 4.00 10.00
39 Kevin Durant 2.00 5.00
40 James Harden 1.00 2.50

2015-16 Donruss Signature Series

EXCHANGE DEADLINE 8/19/2017
1 Kobe Bryant 800.00 1,500.00
2 Dwyane Wade 25.00 60.00
3 Allen Iverson 40.00 100.00
4 Anthony Davis 40.00 100.00
6 Kyrie Irving 40.00 100.00
7 Karl-Anthony Towns 50.00 120.00
8 D'Angelo Russell 12.00 30.00
9 Jahlil Okafor 4.00 10.00
10 Emmanuel Mudiay 4.00 10.00
11 Alex Len 3.00 8.00
12 Kristaps Porzingis 25.00 60.00
13 Mario Hezonja 4.00 10.00
14 Justise Winslow 5.00 12.00
15 Willie Cauley-Stein 4.00 10.00
16 Stanley Johnson 4.00 10.00
17 Frank Kaminsky 4.00 10.00
18 Devin Booker 200.00 500.00
19 Myles Turner 12.00 30.00
20 Trey Lyles 4.00 10.00
21 Scott Wedman 4.00 10.00
22 Sleepy Floyd 3.00 8.00
23 Mo Williams 4.00 10.00
24 Keith Van Horn 4.00 10.00
25 Michael Cage 3.00 8.00
26 James Jones 3.00 8.00
27 Micheal Ray Richardson 4.00 10.00
28 Jerian Grant 3.00 8.00
29 Phil Chenier 3.00 8.00
30 Tony Allen 3.00 8.00
31 Hubert Davis 3.00 8.00
32 Cameron Payne 5.00 12.00
33 Rashad Vaughn 3.00 8.00
34 E'Twaun Moore 3.00 8.00
35 Kelly Oubre Jr. 10.00 25.00
36 Terry Rozier 12.00 30.00
37 Sam Dekker 3.00 8.00
38 Damien Inglis 3.00 8.00
39 Donatas Motiejunas 3.00 8.00
40 JaKarr Sampson 3.00 8.00
41 Kyle O'Quinn 3.00 8.00
42 Robert Sacre 3.00 8.00
43 Josh Huestis 3.00 8.00
44 Ray McCallum 3.00 8.00
45 Dwight Powell 3.00 8.00
46 Brian Roberts 3.00 8.00
47 Isaiah Canaan 3.00 8.00
48 Andre Roberson 3.00 8.00
49 Johnny O'Bryant 3.00 8.00
50 Jarnell Stokes 3.00 8.00
51 Solomon Hill 3.00 8.00
52 Lamar Patterson 3.00 8.00
53 Cameron Bairstow 3.00 8.00
54 Mike Muscala 3.00 8.00
55 Boban Marjanovic 10.00 25.00
56 Nikola Jokic 500.00 1,000.00
57 Robert Covington 4.00 10.00
58 James Ennis 3.00 8.00
59 Norman Powell 6.00 15.00
60 Ryan Kelly 3.00 8.00
61 James Michael McAdoo 3.00 8.00
62 Hollis Thompson 3.00 8.00
63 Seth Curry 5.00 12.00

2015-16 Donruss Studio Series Rookie Jerseys

*PRIME/25: .75X TO 2X BASIC
1 Mario Hezonja 2.50 6.00
2 Myles Turner 8.00 20.00
3 Emmanuel Mudiay 2.50 6.00
4 Devin Booker 5.00 12.00
5 Frank Kaminsky 2.50 6.00
6 Kelly Oubre Jr. 6.00 15.00
7 Karl-Anthony Towns 6.00 15.00
8 Montrezl Harrell 6.00 15.00
9 Jahlil Okafor 5.00 12.00
10 Jerian Grant 2.00 5.00
11 Willie Cauley-Stein 2.50 6.00
12 Trey Lyles 2.50 6.00
13 Stanley Johnson 2.50 6.00
14 Cameron Payne 3.00 8.00
15 Justise Winslow 3.00 8.00
16 Terry Rozier 8.00 20.00
17 D'Angelo Russell 5.00 12.00
18 Sam Dekker 2.00 5.00
19 Kristaps Porzingis 6.00 15.00
20 Justin Anderson 2.00 5.00

2015-16 Donruss Superstar Swatches

PRINT RUNS B/WN 49-149 COPIES PER
*PRIME/25: .75X TO 2X BASIC
1 Dwight Howard/149 4.00 10.00
2 Anthony Davis/149 5.00 12.00
3 Blake Griffin/149 3.00 8.00
4 Tony Parker/149 5.00 12.00
5 Dwyane Wade/149 5.00 12.00
6 Kawhi Leonard/149 10.00 25.00
7 Carmelo Anthony/149 5.00 12.00
8 Kobe Bryant/149 10.00 25.00
9 Derrick Rose/149 5.00 12.00
10 Kyrie Irving/149 5.00 12.00
11 Chris Paul/149 6.00 15.00
12 Damian Lillard/149 5.00 12.00
13 Russell Westbrook/149 5.00 12.00
14 Tim Duncan/149 8.00 20.00
15 John Wall/149 4.00 10.00
16 Chris Bosh/149 4.00 10.00
17 Paul George/49 5.00 12.00
18 Kevin Durant/49 6.00 15.00
19 James Harden/149 6.00 15.00
20 Stephen Curry/149 12.00 30.00

2015-16 Donruss Swatch Kings

STATED PRINT RUN 149 SER.#'d SETS
*PRIME/25: .75X TO 2X BASIC
1 Kenneth Faried 2.50 6.00
2 Cody Zeller 2.00 5.00
3 Mario Chalmers 2.50 6.00
4 David West 2.50 6.00
5 Reggie Jackson 2.50 6.00
6 Doug McDermott 2.50 6.00
7 Tobias Harris 2.50 6.00
8 Aaron Gordon 3.00 8.00
9 J.J. Hickson 2.00 5.00
10 Bojan Bogdanovic 2.50 6.00
11 Kentavious Caldwell-Pope 2.50 6.00
12 Danilo Gallinari 2.50 6.00
13 Markieff Morris 2.00 5.00
14 DeMar DeRozan 4.00 10.00
15 Robert Sacre 2.00 5.00
16 Eric Bledsoe 2.50 6.00
17 Trey Burke 2.00 5.00
18 Alec Burks 2.00 5.00
19 Jeff Teague 2.00 5.00
20 Boris Diaw 2.50 6.00
21 Kyle Korver 2.50 6.00
22 Danny Green 2.50 6.00
23 Mike Conley 3.00 8.00
24 Dennis Schroder 3.00 8.00
25 Serge Ibaka 2.50 6.00
26 Eric Gordon 2.50 6.00
27 Tristan Thompson 3.00 8.00
28 Alex Len 2.00 5.00
29 Jimmy Butler 6.00 15.00
30 Bradley Beal 4.00 10.00
31 Manu Ginobili 6.00 15.00
32 Dante Exum 2.50 6.00
33 Mo Williams 2.50 6.00
34 Derrick Favors 2.50 6.00
35 Steven Adams 2.50 6.00
36 George Hill 2.50 6.00
37 Victor Oladipo 2.50 6.00
38 Anderson Varejao 2.00 5.00
39 John Henson 2.00 5.00
40 Brandon Jennings 2.00 5.00
41 Marc Gasol 3.00 8.00
42 Darren Collison 2.00 5.00
43 Paul Millsap 2.50 6.00
44 Donatas Motiejunas 2.00 5.00
45 Terrence Ross 2.50 6.00
46 Gordon Hayward 3.00 8.00
47 Zach Randolph 3.00 8.00
48 Andre Drummond 3.00 8.00
49 Jonas Valanciunas 2.50 6.00
50 C.J. McCollum 3.00 8.00

2015-16 Donruss The Rookies

*HOLO/199: 1.5X TO 4X BASIC
*INSP/56-99: 2X TO 5X BASIC
*INSP/45: 2X TO 5X BASIC
*STATUS/55-88: 1.2X TO 3X BASIC
*STATUS/28-44: 1.5X TO 4X BASIC
*STATUS/20-25: 2X TO 5X BASIC
1 Justin Anderson .50 1.25
2 Josh Richardson .75 2.00
3 Rakeem Christmas .50 1.25
4 Frank Kaminsky .60 1.50
5 Bobby Portis 1.25 3.00
6 Cliff Alexander .50 1.25
7 Emmanuel Mudiay .60 1.50
8 Raul Neto .50 1.25
9 Anthony Brown .50 1.25
10 Stanley Johnson .60 1.50
11 Branden Dawson .50 1.25
12 Tyus Jones .60 1.50
13 Trey Lyles .60 1.50
14 T.J. McConnell 2.00 5.00
15 Aaron Harrison .60 1.50
16 Jarell Martin .50 1.25
17 Richaun Holmes .75 2.00
18 Rondae Hollis-Jefferson .60 1.50
19 Myles Turner 2.00 5.00
20 Pat Connaughton .75 2.00
21 Karl-Anthony Towns 3.00 8.00
22 Boban Marjanovic 1.50 4.00
23 Christian Wood .75 2.00
24 Kelly Oubre Jr. 1.50 4.00
25 D'Angelo Russell 2.00 5.00
26 Josh Huestis .50 1.25
27 Devin Booker 12.00 30.00
28 Jonathon Simmons .60 1.50
29 Joe Young .50 1.25
30 Cameron Payne .75 2.00
31 Larry Nance Jr. 1.00 2.50
32 Kristaps Porzingis 3.00 8.00
33 Rashad Vaughn .50 1.25
34 Kevon Looney 1.50 4.00
35 R.J. Hunter .50 1.25
36 Mario Hezonja .60 1.50
37 Marcelo Huertas .50 1.25
38 Jahlil Okafor .60 1.50
39 Terry Rozier 2.00 5.00
40 Walter Tavares .50 1.25
41 Willie Cauley-Stein .60 1.50
42 Montrezl Harrell 1.50 4.00
43 Nikola Jokic 60.00 150.00
44 Delon Wright .60 1.50
45 Justise Winslow .75 2.00
46 Jordan Mickey .50 1.25
47 Sam Dekker .50 1.25
48 Chris McCullough .50 1.25
49 Nemanja Bjelica .75 2.00
50 Jerian Grant .50 1.25

2015-16 Donruss Timeless Treasures Jersey Autographs

PRINT RUNS B/WN 49-99 COPIES PER
EXCHANGE DEADLINE 8/19/2017
*PRIME/25: .5X TO 1.2X BASIC
1 Willie Cauley-Stein/75 6.00 15.00
2 Andrew Wiggins/49 25.00 60.00
3 David Thompson/75 10.00 25.00
4 Grant Hill/75 30.00 80.00
5 John Starks/75 15.00 40.00
6 Kobe Bryant/49 1,000.00 2,000.00
7 Mario Hezonja/49 6.00 15.00
8 Kyrie Irving/49 60.00 150.00
9 Danny Manning/75 6.00 15.00
10 Karl-Anthony Towns/75 40.00 100.00
11 Stanley Johnson/75 6.00 15.00
12 Jahlil Okafor/75 6.00 15.00
13 Tony Parker/49 20.00 50.00
14 Kristaps Porzingis/75 40.00 100.00
15 Clifford Robinson/75 8.00 20.00
16 Kevin Durant/49 125.00 300.00
17 Justise Winslow/49 8.00 20.00
18 John Wall/49 15.00 40.00
19 Kenny Smith/49 6.00 15.00
20 D'Angelo Russell/75 20.00 50.00
21 Frank Kaminsky/99 6.00 15.00
22 Emmanuel Mudiay/75 6.00 15.00
23 Devin Booker/99 125.00 300.00
24 Steve Kerr/49 20.00 50.00
25 Rik Smits/75 6.00 15.00

2016-17 Donruss

COMPLETE SET (200) 20.00 50.00
*GRN/YLW LSR: 1.5X TO 4X BASIC
*ORANGE LSR: 1.5X TO 4X BASIC
*PP SILVER/299: 1.5X TO 4X BASIC
*PP PURPLE/199: 1.5X TO 4X BASIC
*GREEN LSR/99: 2X TO 5X BASIC
*RED LSR/99: 2X TO 5X BASIC
*PP RED/75: 2X TO 5X BASIC
*BLUE LSR/49: 2.5X TO 6X BASIC
*YELLOW LSR/25: 4X TO 10X BASIC
*PP BLUE/25: 4X TO 10X BASIC
1 Joel Embiid .75 2.00
2 Jahlil Okafor .20 .50
3 Nerlens Noel .20 .50
4 T.J. McConnell .25 .60
5 Giannis Antetokounmpo 1.50 4.00
6 Jabari Parker .20 .50
7 Khris Middleton .30 .75
8 Matthew Dellavedova .25 .60
9 John Henson .20 .50
10 Jimmy Butler .60 1.50
11 Rajon Rondo .40 1.00
12 Dwyane Wade .60 1.50
13 Nikola Mirotic .20 .50
14 Bobby Portis .30 .75
15 LeBron James 2.50 6.00
16 Kevin Love .30 .75
17 Kyrie Irving .60 1.50
18 Richard Jefferson .20 .50
19 Tristan Thompson .25 .60
20 Isaiah Thomas .25 .60
21 Avery Bradley .20 .50
22 Al Horford .30 .75
23 Marcus Smart .40 1.00
24 Jordan Mickey .20 .50
25 Chris Paul .50 1.25
26 DeAndre Jordan .25 .60
27 Blake Griffin .30 .75
28 Jamal Crawford .30 .75
29 J.J. Redick .30 .75
30 Mike Conley .25 .60
31 Chandler Parsons .20 .50
32 Marc Gasol .30 .75
33 Zach Randolph .30 .75
34 Dennis Schroder .25 .60
35 Paul Millsap .25 .60
36 Dwight Howard .40 1.00
37 Kent Bazemore .20 .50
38 Kyle Korver .25 .60
39 Justise Winslow .25 .60
40 Josh Richardson .25 .60
41 Goran Dragic .30 .75
42 Chris Bosh .40 1.00
43 Hassan Whiteside .25 .60
44 Kemba Walker .25 .60
45 Nicolas Batum .25 .60
46 Frank Kaminsky .20 .50
47 Jeremy Lamb .20 .50
48 Aaron Harrison .20 .50
49 Alec Burks .25 .60
50 Rudy Gobert .40 1.00
51 George Hill .25 .60
52 Gordon Hayward .30 .75
53 Rodney Hood .25 .60
54 DeMarcus Cousins .25 .60
55 Ben McLemore .20 .50
56 Willie Cauley-Stein .25 .60
57 Rudy Gay .30 .75
58 Omri Casspi .25 .60
59 Carmelo Anthony .50 1.25
60 Kristaps Porzingis .50 1.25
61 Joakim Noah .20 .50
62 Derrick Rose .50 1.25
63 Larry Nance Jr. .20 .50
64 D'Angelo Russell .40 1.00
65 Julius Randle .25 .60
66 Lou Williams .30 .75
67 Serge Ibaka .25 .60
68 Jeff Green .20 .50
69 Mario Hezonja .20 .50
70 Evan Fournier .25 .60
71 Aaron Gordon .30 .75
72 Bismack Biyombo .20 .50
73 Nikola Vucevic .30 .75
74 Harrison Barnes .25 .60
75 Andrew Bogut .30 .75
76 J.J. Barea .25 .60
77 Dirk Nowitzki .75 2.00
78 Deron Williams .25 .60
79 Wesley Matthews .20 .50
80 Brook Lopez .25 .60
81 Rondae Hollis-Jefferson .20 .50
82 Bojan Bogdanovic .25 .60
83 Jeremy Lin .60 1.50
84 Chris McCullough .20 .50
85 Emmanuel Mudiay .20 .50
86 Kenneth Faried .25 .60
87 Danilo Gallinari .25 .60
88 Will Barton .20 .50
89 Wilson Chandler .25 .60
90 Nikola Jokic 1.50 4.00
91 Jeff Teague .20 .50
92 Myles Turner .30 .75
93 Paul George .50 1.25
94 Monta Ellis .25 .60
95 C.J. Miles .20 .50
96 Thaddeus Young .20 .50
97 Anthony Davis 1.00 2.50
98 Tyreke Evans .25 .60
99 Jrue Holiday .40 1.00
100 Stanley Johnson .20 .50
101 Marcus Morris .20 .50
102 Kentavious Caldwell-Pope .25 .60
103 Reggie Jackson .25 .60
104 Andre Drummond .30 .75
105 DeMar DeRozan .40 1.00
106 Kyle Lowry .30 .75
107 Jonas Valanciunas .25 .60
108 DeMarre Carroll .20 .50
109 Norman Powell .30 .75
110 James Harden .60 1.50
111 Trevor Ariza .20 .50
112 Clint Capela .25 .60
113 Sam Dekker .20 .50
114 Patrick Beverley .20 .50
115 LaMarcus Aldridge .30 .75
116 Kawhi Leonard .75 2.00
117 Tony Parker .50 1.25
118 Manu Ginobili .60 1.50
119 Pau Gasol .50 1.25
120 Eric Bledsoe .25 .60
121 Devin Booker 1.25 3.00
122 Brandon Knight .25 .60
123 Alex Len .20 .50
124 Tyson Chandler .25 .60
125 Andrew Wiggins .40 1.00
126 Zach LaVine .60 1.50
127 Ricky Rubio .25 .60
128 Karl-Anthony Towns .60 1.50
129 Kevin Garnett .75 2.00
130 C.J. McCollum .30 .75
131 Damian Lillard .75 2.00
132 Evan Turner .20 .50
133 Al-Farouq Aminu .20 .50
134 Mason Plumlee .25 .60
135 Stephen Curry 2.50 6.00
136 Klay Thompson .75 2.00
137 Kevin Durant 1.25 3.00
138 Draymond Green .40 1.00
139 Andre Iguodala .30 .75
140 John Wall .40 1.00
141 Markieff Morris .20 .50
142 Marcin Gortat .20 .50
143 Bradley Beal .40 1.00
144 Kelly Oubre Jr. .40 1.00
145 Russell Westbrook .50 1.25
146 Victor Oladipo .25 .60
147 Steven Adams .25 .60
148 Cameron Payne .30 .75
149 Andre Roberson .20 .50
150 Jordan Clarkson .30 .75
151 Ben Simmons RC 1.25 3.00
152 Brandon Ingram RC 1.50 4.00
153 Jaylen Brown RC 6.00 15.00
154 Dragan Bender RC .40 1.00
155 Kris Dunn RC .60 1.50
156 Buddy Hield RC 1.25 3.00
157 Jamal Murray RC 3.00 8.00
158 Marquese Chriss RC .50 1.25
159 Jakob Poeltl RC .75 2.00
160 Thon Maker RC .50 1.25
161 Domantas Sabonis RC 2.50 6.00
162 Taurean Prince RC .50 1.25
163 Denzel Valentine RC .40 1.00
164 Wade Baldwin IV RC .40 1.00
165 Henry Ellenson RC .40 1.00
166 Malik Beasley RC .75 2.00
167 Caris LeVert RC 1.00 2.50
168 DeAndre' Bembry RC .60 1.50
169 Malachi Richardson RC .40 1.00
170 Brice Johnson RC .40 1.00
171 Pascal Siakam RC 2.50 6.00
172 Skal Labissiere RC .40 1.00
173 Dejounte Murray RC 2.00 5.00
174 Damian Jones RC .40 1.00
175 Deyonta Davis RC .40 1.00
176 Ivica Zubac RC 1.00 2.50
177 Cheick Diallo RC .40 1.00
178 Tyler Ulis RC .50 1.25
179 Malcolm Brogdon RC 1.25 3.00
180 Chinanu Onuaku RC .40 1.00
181 Patrick McCaw RC .40 1.00
182 Diamond Stone RC .40 1.00
183 Stephen Zimmerman RC .40 1.00
184 Isaiah Whitehead RC .40 1.00
185 Demetrius Jackson RC .40 1.00
186 A.J. Hammons RC .40 1.00
187 Jake Layman RC .50 1.25
188 Michael Gbinije RC .40 1.00
189 Georges Niang RC .60 1.50
190 Ben Bentil RC .40 1.00
191 Joel Bolomboy RC .40 1.00
192 Kay Felder RC .40 1.00
193 Marcus Paige RC .40 1.00
194 Daniel Hamilton RC .40 1.00
195 Georgios Papagiannis RC .40 1.00
196 Isaiah Cousins .40 1.00
197 Tyrone Wallace RC .40 1.00
198 Gary Payton II RC 1.00 2.50
199 Sheldon McClellan RC .40 1.00
200 Ron Baker RC .40 1.00

2016-17 Donruss All Stars

*PROOF: .6X TO 1.5X BASIC
*PROOF BLUE/99: 1X TO 2.5X BASIC
1 Kobe Bryant 4.00 10.00
2 Larry Bird 2.00 5.00
3 Magic Johnson 2.00 5.00
4 Shaquille O'Neal 1.50 4.00
5 Grant Hill .60 1.50
6 Scottie Pippen 1.00 2.50
7 Isiah Thomas .75 2.00
8 Allen Iverson .75 2.00
9 Wilt Chamberlain 1.50 4.00
10 Steve Nash .75 2.00
11 Dwyane Wade 1.00 2.50
12 Kyle Lowry .50 1.25
13 LeBron James 4.00 10.00
14 Paul George .75 2.00
15 Carmelo Anthony .75 2.00
16 John Wall .60 1.50
17 Paul Millsap .40 1.00
18 DeMar DeRozan .60 1.50
19 Andre Drummond .50 1.25
20 Isaiah Thomas .40 1.00
21 Stephen Curry 4.00 10.00
22 Russell Westbrook .75 2.00
23 Kobe Bryant 4.00 10.00
24 Kevin Durant 2.00 5.00
25 Kawhi Leonard 1.25 3.00
26 Chris Paul .75 2.00
27 LaMarcus Aldridge .50 1.25
28 James Harden 1.00 2.50
29 Anthony Davis 1.50 4.00
30 Draymond Green .60 1.50

2016-17 Donruss Back to the Future Materials

PRINT RUNS B/WN 150-199 COPIES PER
1 Brandon Jennings/199 1.50 4.00
2 Pau Gasol/199 4.00 10.00
3 Chris Paul/199 4.00 10.00
4 Carmelo Anthony/150 4.00 10.00
5 Markieff Morris/199 1.50 4.00
6 Rajon Rondo/199 3.00 8.00
7 Vince Carter/199 5.00 12.00
8 Kevin Garnett/199 6.00 15.00
9 Reggie Jackson/199 2.00 5.00
10 Wesley Matthews/199 1.50 4.00
11 LaMarcus Aldridge/199 2.50 6.00
12 Monta Ellis/199 2.00 5.00
13 Paul Pierce/199 4.00 10.00
14 Danilo Gallinari/199 2.00 5.00
15 LeBron James/199 20.00 50.00

2016-17 Donruss Court Kings

*PROOF: .6X TO 1.5X BASIC
*PROOF ORNG/125: .75X TO 2X BASIC
*PROOF BLUE/99: 1X TO 2.5X BASIC
1 LeBron James 4.00 10.00
2 Stephen Curry 4.00 10.00
3 Dwyane Wade 1.00 2.50
4 Dirk Nowitzki 1.25 3.00
5 Chris Paul .75 2.00
6 Anthony Davis 1.50 4.00
7 Kyrie Irving 1.00 2.50
8 Kevin Durant 2.00 5.00
9 James Harden 1.00 2.50
10 Paul George .75 2.00
11 Jimmy Butler 1.00 2.50
12 Carmelo Anthony .75 2.00
13 DeMarcus Cousins .40 1.00
14 Blake Griffin .50 1.25
15 Karl-Anthony Towns 1.00 2.50
16 John Wall .60 1.50
17 Derrick Rose .75 2.00
18 Kawhi Leonard 1.25 3.00
19 Russell Westbrook .75 2.00
20 Klay Thompson 1.25 3.00
21 DeMar DeRozan .60 1.50
22 Damian Lillard 1.25 3.00
23 Kristaps Porzingis .75 2.00
24 Giannis Antetokounmpo 2.50 6.00
25 Andrew Wiggins .60 1.50
26 Isaiah Thomas .40 1.00
27 Jeremy Lin 1.00 2.50
28 Victor Oladipo .40 1.00
29 Eric Bledsoe .40 1.00
30 Kyle Lowry .50 1.25
31 Andre Drummond .50 1.25
32 Kemba Walker .40 1.00
33 Mike Conley .40 1.00
34 Dennis Schroder .50 1.25
35 Justise Winslow .40 1.00
36 Jordan Clarkson .40 1.00
37 Serge Ibaka .40 1.00
38 Gordon Hayward .50 1.25
39 Emmanuel Mudiay .30 .75
40 Jahlil Okafor .30 .75

2016-17 Donruss Crashers

*PROOF: .6X TO 1.5X BASIC
*PROOF BLUE/99: 1X TO 2.5X BASIC
1 DeAndre Jordan .40 1.00
2 Hassan Whiteside .40 1.00
3 Pau Gasol .75 2.00
4 Andre Drummond .50 1.25
5 Dwight Howard .60 1.50
6 DeMarcus Cousins .40 1.00
7 Rudy Gobert .60 1.50
8 Karl-Anthony Towns 1.00 2.50
9 Anthony Davis 1.50 4.00
10 Julius Randle .60 1.50
11 Kevin Love .50 1.25
12 Marcin Gortat .30 .75
13 Draymond Green .60 1.50
14 Kenneth Faried .40 1.00
15 LaMarcus Aldridge .50 1.25

2016-17 Donruss Dimes

*PROOF: .6X TO 1.5X BASIC
*PROOF BLUE/99: 1X TO 2.5X BASIC
1 Chris Paul .75 2.00
2 John Wall .60 1.50
3 Ricky Rubio .40 1.00
4 James Harden 1.00 2.50
5 Russell Westbrook .75 2.00
6 Damian Lillard 1.25 3.00
7 Goran Dragic .50 1.25
8 Stephen Curry 4.00 10.00
9 Kyle Lowry .50 1.25
10 Isaiah Thomas .40 1.00

2016-17 Donruss Dominator Signatures

PRINT RUNS B/WN 25-49 COPIES PER
1 Karl-Anthony Towns/49 30.00 80.00
2 Kristaps Porzingis/49 60.00 150.00
4 Justise Winslow/49 4.00 10.00
5 Nikola Jokic/25 150.00 400.00
6 Jabari Parker/49 15.00 40.00
7 Victor Oladipo/25 4.00 10.00
9 Kevin Durant/49 50.00 120.00
10 Kyrie Irving/49 25.00 60.00
11 John Wall/49 15.00 40.00
12 Bobby Portis/49 5.00 12.00
13 Dwyane Wade/49 30.00 80.00
14 Jordan Clarkson/49 5.00 12.00
15 Eric Bledsoe/25 4.00 10.00
16 Carmelo Anthony/25 20.00 50.00
18 Isaiah Thomas/49 20.00 50.00
19 Kyle Lowry/25 12.00 30.00
21 Draymond Green/25 12.00 30.00
22 Mike Conley/25 12.00 30.00
23 Marcus Smart/25 20.00 50.00
26 Goran Dragic/25 8.00 20.00
27 Allen Iverson/49 30.00 80.00
28 Latrell Sprewell/25 15.00 40.00
29 James Worthy/25 12.00 30.00
30 Nick Van Exel/25 20.00 50.00
32 Steve Francis/25 10.00 25.00
33 Jalen Rose/25 4.00 10.00
34 John Starks/25 5.00 12.00
35 Bill Russell/49 400.00 800.00
36 Ray Allen/49 15.00 40.00
37 John Stockton/49 15.00 40.00
38 Julius Erving/49 30.00 80.00
40 Anfernee Hardaway/25 30.00 80.00

2016-17 Donruss Elite Series

*PROOF: .6X TO 1.5X BASIC
*PROOF BLUE/99: 1X TO 2.5X BASIC
1 Dirk Nowitzki 1.25 3.00
2 Stephen Curry 4.00 10.00
3 Kevin Durant 2.00 5.00
4 Derrick Rose .75 2.00
5 Dwyane Wade 1.00 2.50
6 Al Horford .50 1.25
7 Russell Westbrook .75 2.00
8 Damian Lillard 1.25 3.00
9 LeBron James 4.00 10.00
10 Anthony Davis 1.50 4.00
11 James Harden 1.00 2.50
12 Chris Paul .75 2.00
13 Kawhi Leonard 1.25 3.00
14 LaMarcus Aldridge .50 1.25
15 John Wall .60 1.50
16 Jimmy Butler 1.00 2.50
17 Kyrie Irving 1.00 2.50
18 Klay Thompson 1.25 3.00
19 Blake Griffin .50 1.25
20 Kyle Lowry .50 1.25
21 Pau Gasol .75 2.00
22 Marc Gasol .50 1.25
23 Carmelo Anthony .75 2.00
24 Mike Conley .40 1.00
25 Jordan Clarkson .50 1.25

2016-17 Donruss Elite Signatures

PRINT RUNS B/WN 25-99 COPIES PER
1 Kevin Durant/99 40.00 100.00
2 C.J. Miles/25 3.00 8.00
3 T.J. McConnell/99 4.00 10.00
4 Allen Crabbe/25 3.00 8.00
5 Marcelo Huertas/99 3.00 8.00
6 Deron Williams/25 4.00 10.00
7 Jordan McRae/99 3.00 8.00
9 Carmelo Anthony/25 20.00 50.00
10 Alan Anderson/25 3.00 8.00
11 Kyrie Irving/99 25.00 60.00
12 Aaron Harrison/99 3.00 8.00
13 Mike Muscala/25 10.00 25.00
14 Karl-Anthony Towns/25 40.00 100.00
15 Dirk Nowitzki/49 50.00 120.00
16 Bob Dandridge/49 5.00 12.00
17 Walter Tavares/49 3.00 8.00
18 Draymond Green/25 12.00 30.00
19 Vin Baker/49 4.00 10.00
20 Seth Curry/25 12.00 30.00
21 Mark Price/49 5.00 12.00
22 Luis Montero/99 3.00 8.00
23 Dan Majerle/25 6.00 15.00
24 D'Angelo Russell/25 10.00 25.00
25 Jim Jackson/25 6.00 15.00
26 E'Twaun Moore/49 3.00 8.00
27 Langston Galloway/25 3.00 8.00
28 Glen Rice/25 5.00 12.00
29 C.J. Wilcox/49 3.00 8.00
30 Jamal Mashburn/25 4.00 10.00
31 Rashad Vaughn/25 3.00 8.00
32 Dennis Scott/25 3.00 8.00
33 Noah Vonleh/99 3.00 8.00
34 Dell Curry/25 10.00 25.00
35 Kelly Olynyk/25 3.00 8.00
36 Vinny Del Negro/25 4.00 10.00
37 Anthony Bennett/99 3.00 8.00
38 Glenn Robinson III/25 3.00 8.00
39 Bill Laimbeer/25 5.00 12.00
40 Dikembe Mutombo/25 8.00 20.00
41 James Ennis/99 3.00 8.00
42 Jeff Hornacek/25 8.00 20.00
43 Robert Covington/25 4.00 10.00
45 Jalen Rose/25 4.00 10.00
46 C.J. McCollum/49 5.00 12.00
47 Tim Hardaway/25 12.00 30.00
48 Michael Kidd-Gilchrist/99 3.00 8.00
49 Latrell Sprewell/25 15.00 40.00
50 Dwight Powell/99 3.00 8.00
51 Bobby Portis/25 5.00 12.00
52 Raef LaFrentz/25 3.00 8.00
53 Jonas Valanciunas/25 10.00 25.00
54 Larry Nance/25 4.00 10.00
55 Cody Zeller/99 3.00 8.00
56 Festus Ezeli/25 3.00 8.00
57 Jo Jo White/25 20.00 50.00
58 JaKarr Sampson/99 3.00 8.00
59 P.J. Tucker/25 3.00 8.00
60 Chauncey Billups/25 6.00 15.00
62 Mark Aguirre/25 4.00 10.00
63 Avery Johnson/25 4.00 10.00
64 Reggie Bullock/99 3.00 8.00
65 Marcus Camby/25 4.00 10.00
66 Antonio McDyess/25 4.00 10.00
67 Steve Novak/49 3.00 8.00
68 Dee Brown/25 3.00 8.00
69 Michael Carter-Williams/49 3.00 8.00
71 Kevon Looney/49 5.00 12.00
72 Rolando Blackman/25 4.00 10.00
73 Steve Smith/25 12.00 30.00
74 Jeff Withey/49 3.00 8.00
75 Scott Skiles/25 4.00 10.00
76 Tyronn Lue/25 15.00 40.00
77 Ian Clark/99 3.00 8.00
78 Jerry Stackhouse/25 4.00 10.00
79 Devin Harris/25 4.00 10.00
80 Mark Jackson/25 4.00 10.00
81 Tristan Thompson/49 4.00 10.00
82 Mike Bibby/25 4.00 10.00
83 Matthew Dellavedova/49 4.00 10.00
84 B.J. Armstrong/25 15.00 40.00
85 Kyle O'Quinn/99 3.00 8.00
86 Rick Fox/25 4.00 10.00
87 Clifford Robinson/25 12.00 30.00
88 Lamar Patterson/99 3.00 8.00
89 Terry Porter/25 3.00 8.00
90 Kenny Anderson/25 4.00 10.00
92 Tom Gugliotta/25 10.00 25.00
93 Tony Delk/25 3.00 8.00
94 Alex Len/99 3.00 8.00
95 Kendall Gill/25 5.00 12.00
97 Sam Bowie/25 3.00 8.00
98 Troy Daniels/99 3.00 8.00

99 Juwan Howard/25 4.00 10.00
100 Josh Huestis/99 3.00 8.00

2016-17 Donruss Hall Dominator Signatues

PRINT RUNS B/WN 25-49 COPIES PER
1 Dan Issel/49 6.00 15.00
2 Artis Gilmore/49 6.00 15.00
3 Adrian Dantley/49 5.00 12.00
4 Tom Heinsohn/49 20.00 50.00
5 Elvin Hayes/49 6.00 15.00
6 Jamaal Wilkes/49 5.00 12.00
7 Satch Sanders/49 8.00 20.00
8 David Robinson/49 15.00 40.00
9 Rick Barry/49 6.00 15.00
10 Bob Lanier/25 6.00 15.00
11 Dennis Rodman/49 25.00 60.00
12 David Thompson/49 6.00 15.00
13 John Stockton/49 15.00 40.00
14 Alex English/25 8.00 20.00
15 Bernard King/25 10.00 25.00
16 Oscar Robertson/49 40.00 100.00
17 Hakeem Olajuwon/25 20.00 50.00
18 Kevin McHale/25 12.00 30.00
19 Earl Lloyd/25 40.00 100.00
20 Calvin Murphy/25 6.00 15.00
21 Nate Thurmond/25 4.00 10.00
22 Cliff Hagan/25 10.00 25.00
23 Robert Parish/25 6.00 15.00
24 Wes Unseld/25 8.00 20.00
25 Earl Monroe/25 8.00 20.00
26 Gary Payton/25 8.00 20.00
27 Gail Goodrich/25 12.00 30.00
28 Willis Reed/25 40.00 100.00
29 Arvydas Sabonis/25 8.00 20.00
30 Dominique Wilkins/25 20.00 50.00

2016-17 Donruss Hall Kings

*PROOF: .6X TO 1.5X BASIC
*PROOF ORNG/125: .75X TO 2X BASIC
*PROOF BLUE/99: 1X TO 2.5X BASIC
1 Shaquille O'Neal 2.00 5.00
2 Allen Iverson 1.00 2.50
3 Yao Ming 1.50 4.00
4 Alonzo Mourning 1.00 2.50
5 Gary Payton 1.00 2.50
6 Bernard King .75 2.00
7 Ralph Sampson .50 1.25
8 Jamaal Wilkes .60 1.50
9 Artis Gilmore .75 2.00
10 Chris Mullin .60 1.50
11 Dennis Rodman 1.25 3.00
12 Karl Malone 1.00 2.50
13 Scottie Pippen 1.25 3.00
14 David Robinson 1.25 3.00
15 John Stockton 1.00 2.50
16 Adrian Dantley .60 1.50
17 Patrick Ewing .75 2.00
18 Hakeem Olajuwon 1.25 3.00
19 Joe Dumars .60 1.50
20 Dominique Wilkins .75 2.00
21 Clyde Drexler 1.00 2.50
22 Robert Parish .75 2.00
23 James Worthy .75 2.00
24 Magic Johnson 2.50 6.00
25 Drazen Petrovic .60 1.50
26 Moses Malone 1.00 2.50
27 Isiah Thomas 1.00 2.50
28 Bob McAdoo .75 2.00
29 Kevin McHale 1.00 2.50
30 Larry Bird 2.50 6.00

2016-17 Donruss Jersey Kings

1 Jabari Parker 1.50 4.00
2 Jimmy Butler 5.00 12.00
3 LeBron James 40.00 100.00
4 Isaiah Thomas 2.00 5.00
5 DeAndre Jordan 2.00 5.00
6 Marc Gasol 2.50 6.00
7 Paul Millsap 2.00 5.00
8 Kemba Walker 2.00 5.00
9 DeMarcus Cousins 2.00 5.00
10 Carmelo Anthony 4.00 10.00
11 Jordan Clarkson 2.50 6.00
12 Brook Lopez 2.00 5.00
13 Danilo Gallinari 2.00 5.00
14 Paul George 4.00 10.00
15 Jrue Holiday 3.00 8.00
16 Andre Drummond 2.50 6.00
17 DeMar DeRozan 3.00 8.00
18 Karl-Anthony Towns 5.00 12.00
19 Kawhi Leonard 6.00 15.00
20 Gordon Hayward 2.50 6.00
21 Andrew Wiggins 3.00 8.00
22 Damian Lillard 6.00 15.00
23 Stephen Curry 40.00 100.00
24 John Wall 3.00 8.00
25 Russell Westbrook 4.00 10.00

2016-17 Donruss Jersey Series

1 Jusuf Nurkic 2.00 5.00
2 Al Horford 2.50 6.00
3 Zach LaVine 5.00 12.00
4 Ben McLemore 1.50 4.00
5 Bojan Bogdanovic 2.00 5.00
6 Bradley Beal 3.00 8.00
7 Brook Lopez 2.00 5.00
8 Carmelo Anthony 4.00 10.00
9 Chandler Parsons 1.50 4.00
10 Chris Bosh 3.00 8.00
11 Cody Zeller 1.50 4.00
12 Danilo Gallinari 2.00 5.00
13 Danny Green 2.00 5.00
14 DeMarcus Cousins 2.00 5.00
15 DeMarre Carroll 1.50 4.00
16 Derrick Rose 4.00 10.00
17 Dirk Nowitzki 6.00 15.00
18 Donatas Motiejunas 1.50 4.00
19 Dwight Howard 3.00 8.00
20 Dwyane Wade 5.00 12.00
21 Eric Gordon 2.00 5.00
22 George Hill 2.00 5.00
23 Gorgui Dieng 1.50 4.00
24 Terrence Ross 2.00 5.00
25 Jabari Parker 1.50 4.00
26 Jared Sullinger 1.50 4.00
27 Jeff Teague 1.50 4.00
28 John Henson 1.50 4.00
29 John Wall 3.00 8.00
30 Jonas Valanciunas 2.00 5.00
31 Jrue Holiday 3.00 8.00
32 Karl-Anthony Towns 5.00 12.00
33 Kemba Walker 2.00 5.00
34 Kenneth Faried 2.00 5.00
35 Kevin Durant 10.00 25.00
36 Kevin Garnett 6.00 15.00
37 Kevin Love 2.50 6.00
38 Kyle Lowry 2.50 6.00
39 Kyrie Irving 5.00 12.00
40 LeBron James 40.00 100.00
41 Marc Gasol 2.50 6.00
42 Marcin Gortat 1.50 4.00
43 Matthew Dellavedova 1.50 4.00
44 Mike Conley 2.00 5.00
45 Nerlens Noel 1.50 4.00
46 Otto Porter 2.00 5.00
47 Patrick Beverley 1.50 4.00
48 Ricky Rubio 2.00 5.00
49 Shabazz Muhammad 1.50 4.00
50 Andrew Bogut 2.50 6.00

2016-17 Donruss Newly Crowned Rookie Jerseys

2 Brandon Ingram 6.00 15.00
3 Jaylen Brown 12.00 30.00
4 Dragan Bender 1.50 4.00
5 Kris Dunn 2.50 6.00
6 Buddy Hield 5.00 12.00
7 Jamal Murray 12.00 30.00
8 Marquese Chriss 2.00 5.00
9 Jakob Poeltl 3.00 8.00
10 Thon Maker 2.00 5.00
11 Taurean Prince 2.00 5.00
12 Denzel Valentine 1.50 4.00
13 Wade Baldwin IV 1.50 4.00
14 Henry Ellenson 1.50 4.00
15 Malik Beasley 3.00 8.00
16 Caris LeVert 4.00 10.00
17 DeAndre' Bembry 2.50 6.00
18 Malachi Richardson 1.50 4.00
19 T. Luwawu-Cabarrot 2.50 6.00
20 Brice Johnson 1.50 4.00
21 Pascal Siakam 10.00 25.00
22 Skal Labissiere 1.50 4.00
23 Dejounte Murray 8.00 20.00
24 Damian Jones 1.50 4.00
25 Deyonta Davis 1.50 4.00
26 Ivica Zubac 4.00 10.00
28 Gary Payton II 4.00 10.00
29 Cheick Diallo 1.50 4.00
30 Tyler Ulis 2.00 5.00
31 Malcolm Brogdon 5.00 12.00
32 Patrick McCaw 1.50 4.00
33 Kay Felder 1.50 4.00
34 Diamond Stone 1.50 4.00
35 Isaiah Whitehead 1.50 4.00

2016-17 Donruss Next Day Autographs

1 Brandon Ingram 200.00 500.00
2 Jaylen Brown 400.00 800.00
3 Dragan Bender 6.00 15.00
4 Kris Dunn 10.00 25.00
5 Buddy Hield 20.00 50.00
6 Jamal Murray 200.00 500.00
7 Marquese Chriss 8.00 20.00
8 Jakob Poeltl 20.00 50.00
9 Thon Maker 8.00 20.00
10 Taurean Prince 8.00 20.00
11 Georgios Papagiannis 6.00 15.00
12 Denzel Valentine 6.00 15.00
13 Juan Hernangomez 12.00 30.00
14 Wade Baldwin IV 6.00 15.00
15 Henry Ellenson 6.00 15.00
16 Caris LeVert 15.00 40.00
17 DeAndre' Bembry 10.00 25.00
18 Malachi Richardson 6.00 15.00
19 T. Luwawu-Cabarrot 10.00 25.00
20 Brice Johnson 6.00 15.00
21 Pascal Siakam 100.00 250.00
22 Skal Labissiere 6.00 15.00
23 Dejounte Murray 200.00 500.00
24 Damian Jones 6.00 15.00
25 Deyonta Davis 6.00 15.00
26 Cheick Diallo 6.00 15.00
27 Tyler Ulis 8.00 20.00
28 Patrick McCaw 6.00 15.00
29 Malcolm Brogdon 50.00 120.00
30 Isaiah Whitehead 6.00 15.00
31 Demetrius Jackson 6.00 15.00
32 Kay Felder 6.00 15.00
33 Gary Payton II 75.00 200.00
34 Diamond Stone 6.00 15.00
35 Ivica Zubac 20.00 50.00
36 Chinanu Onuaku 6.00 15.00
37 Stephen Zimmerman 6.00 15.00
38 A.J. Hammons 6.00 15.00
39 Malik Beasley 12.00 30.00

2016-17 Donruss Optic Preview

1 Ben Simmons 6.00 15.00
2 Nerlens Noel 2.00 5.00
3 Jahlil Okafor 2.00 5.00
4 Damian Lillard 15.00 40.00
5 C.J. McCollum 3.00 8.00
6 Allen Crabbe 2.00 5.00
7 Greg Monroe 2.00 5.00
8 Jabari Parker 10.00 25.00
9 Thon Maker 2.50 6.00
10 Dwyane Wade 15.00 40.00
11 Jimmy Butler 6.00 15.00
12 Rajon Rondo 4.00 10.00
13 LeBron James 40.00 100.00
14 Ben Simmons 15.00 40.00
15 Kevin Love 10.00 25.00
16 Tristan Thompson 2.50 6.00
17 Isaiah Thomas 2.50 6.00
18 Jared Sullinger 2.00 5.00
20 Chris Paul 10.00 25.00
21 Blake Griffin 10.00 25.00
22 DeAndre Jordan 2.50 6.00
23 J.J. Redick 3.00 8.00
24 Vince Carter 6.00 15.00
25 Mike Conley 2.50 6.00
26 Zach Randolph 3.00 8.00
27 Marc Gasol 3.00 8.00
28 Chandler Parsons 2.00 5.00
29 Dennis Schroder 3.00 8.00
30 Al Horford 3.00 8.00
31 Paul Millsap 2.50 6.00
32 Chris Bosh 4.00 10.00
33 Joe Johnson 3.00 8.00
34 Hassan Whiteside 2.50 6.00
35 Nicolas Batum 2.50 6.00
36 Al Jefferson 2.00 5.00
37 Michael Kidd-Gilchrist 2.00 5.00
38 Derrick Favors 2.00 5.00
39 Gordon Hayward 3.00 8.00
40 Rudy Gobert 4.00 10.00
41 DeMarcus Cousins 2.50 6.00
42 Willie Cauley-Stein 2.50 6.00
43 Rudy Gay 3.00 8.00
44 Carmelo Anthony 10.00 25.00
45 Kristaps Porzingis 15.00 40.00
46 Derrick Rose 12.00 30.00
47 Jordan Clarkson 3.00 8.00
48 Julius Randle 4.00 10.00
49 D'Angelo Russell 10.00 25.00
50 Brandon Ingram 40.00 100.00
51 Elfrid Payton 2.50 6.00
52 Aaron Gordon 3.00 8.00
53 Serge Ibaka 2.50 6.00
54 Dirk Nowitzki 10.00 25.00
55 Harrison Barnes 2.50 6.00
56 Wesley Matthews 2.00 5.00
57 Jeremy Lin 6.00 15.00
58 Brook Lopez 2.50 6.00
59 Kenneth Faried 2.50 6.00
60 Emmanuel Mudiay 2.00 5.00
61 Jamal Murray 20.00 50.00
62 Paul George 10.00 25.00
63 Jeff Teague 2.00 5.00
64 Myles Turner 3.00 8.00
65 Anthony Davis 15.00 40.00
66 Buddy Hield 15.00 40.00
67 Tyreke Evans 2.50 6.00
68 Andre Drummond 3.00 8.00
69 Stanley Johnson 2.00 5.00
70 Tobias Harris 3.00 8.00
71 DeMar DeRozan 4.00 10.00
72 Kyle Lowry 3.00 8.00
73 Terrence Ross 2.50 6.00
74 Jakob Poeltl 4.00 10.00
75 James Harden 6.00 15.00
76 Dwight Howard 4.00 10.00
77 LaMarcus Aldridge 3.00 8.00
78 Manu Ginobili 6.00 15.00
79 Kawhi Leonard 12.00 30.00
80 Tony Parker 5.00 12.00
81 Eric Bledsoe 2.50 6.00
82 Devin Booker 12.00 30.00
83 Brandon Knight 2.50 6.00
84 Dragan Bender 10.00 25.00
85 Marquese Chriss 10.00 25.00
86 Russell Westbrook 15.00 40.00
87 Enes Kanter 2.00 5.00
88 Victor Oladipo 2.50 6.00
89 Zach LaVine 6.00 15.00
90 Andrew Wiggins 12.00 30.00
91 Ricky Rubio 2.50 6.00
92 Karl-Anthony Towns 20.00 50.00
93 Kris Dunn 3.00 8.00
94 Stephen Curry 40.00 100.00
95 Kevin Durant 20.00 50.00
96 Klay Thompson 10.00 25.00
97 Andre Iguodala 3.00 8.00
98 John Wall 10.00 25.00
99 Bradley Beal 4.00 10.00
100 Marcin Gortat 2.00 5.00

2016-17 Donruss Rookie Dominator Signatures

PRINT RUNS B/WN 50-65 COPIES PER
1 Stephen Zimmerman/50 3.00 8.00
2 Marquese Chriss/65 4.00 10.00
3 Buddy Hield/65 10.00 25.00
4 Henry Ellenson/65 3.00 8.00
5 Georges Niang/65 5.00 12.00
6 Demetrius Jackson/65 3.00 8.00
7 Isaiah Whitehead/50 3.00 8.00
8 Thon Maker/65 4.00 10.00
9 Domantas Sabonis/65 20.00 50.00
10 Dragan Bender/65 3.00 8.00
11 T. Luwawu-Cabarrot/65 5.00 12.00
12 Ivica Zubac/65 8.00 20.00
13 Damian Jones/65 3.00 8.00
14 Tyler Ulis/65 4.00 10.00
15 Kris Dunn/50 5.00 12.00
16 Deyonta Davis/65 3.00 8.00
17 Brandon Ingram/50 12.00 30.00
18 Jamal Murray/65 60.00 150.00
19 Denzel Valentine/65 3.00 8.00
20 Jakob Poeltl/65 6.00 15.00
21 Skal Labissiere/50 3.00 8.00
22 Caris LeVert/65 8.00 20.00
23 Diamond Stone/65 3.00 8.00
24 Chinanu Onuaku/65 3.00 8.00
25 Brice Johnson/65 3.00 8.00
26 Malik Beasley/65 6.00 15.00
27 Wade Baldwin IV/65 3.00 8.00
28 Daniel Hamilton/60 3.00 8.00
29 Kay Felder/65 3.00 8.00
30 Michael Gbinije/50 3.00 8.00

2016-17 Donruss Rookie Jerseys

*PRIME/25: 1X TO 2.5X BASIC
1 Brandon Ingram 5.00 12.00
2 Jaylen Brown 4.00 10.00
3 Dragan Bender 1.50 4.00
4 Kris Dunn 2.50 6.00
5 Buddy Hield 4.00 10.00
6 Jamal Murray 12.00 30.00
7 Marquese Chriss 2.00 5.00
8 Jakob Poeltl 2.00 5.00
9 Thon Maker 2.00 5.00
10 Taurean Prince 2.00 5.00
11 Denzel Valentine 1.50 4.00
12 Wade Baldwin IV 1.50 4.00
13 Henry Ellenson 1.50 4.00
14 Malik Beasley 3.00 8.00
15 Caris LeVert 4.00 10.00
16 DeAndre' Bembry 2.50 6.00
17 Malachi Richardson 1.50 4.00
18 T. Luwawu-Cabarrot 2.50 6.00
19 Brice Johnson 1.50 4.00
20 Pascal Siakam 10.00 25.00
21 Skal Labissiere 1.50 4.00
22 Dejounte Murray 8.00 20.00
23 Gary Payton II 4.00 10.00
24 Damian Jones 1.50 4.00
25 Deyonta Davis 1.50 4.00
26 Ivica Zubac 4.00 10.00
28 Cheick Diallo 1.50 4.00
29 Tyler Ulis 2.00 5.00
30 Malcolm Brogdon 5.00 12.00
31 Patrick McCaw 1.50 4.00
32 Kay Felder 1.50 4.00
33 Diamond Stone 1.50 4.00
34 Isaiah Whitehead 1.50 4.00
35 Brandon Ingram 5.00 12.00
36 Dragan Bender 1.50 4.00
37 Buddy Hield 4.00 10.00
38 Jamal Murray 12.00 30.00
39 Marquese Chriss 2.00 5.00
40 Jakob Poeltl 3.00 8.00
41 Thon Maker 2.00 5.00
42 Taurean Prince 2.00 5.00
43 Denzel Valentine 1.50 4.00
44 Wade Baldwin IV 1.50 4.00
45 Henry Ellenson 1.50 4.00
46 Malik Beasley 3.00 8.00
47 Caris LeVert 4.00 10.00
48 DeAndre' Bembry 2.50 6.00
49 Malachi Richardson 1.50 4.00
50 T. Luwawu-Cabarrot 2.50 6.00
51 Brice Johnson 1.50 4.00
52 Pascal Siakam 10.00 25.00
53 Skal Labissiere 1.50 4.00
54 Dejounte Murray 8.00 20.00
55 Gary Payton II 4.00 10.00
56 Damian Jones 1.50 4.00
57 Deyonta Davis 1.50 4.00
58 Ivica Zubac 4.00 10.00
60 Cheick Diallo 1.50 4.00
61 Tyler Ulis 2.00 5.00
62 Malcolm Brogdon 5.00 12.00
63 Patrick McCaw 1.50 4.00
64 Kay Felder 1.50 4.00
65 Diamond Stone 1.50 4.00
66 Isaiah Whitehead 1.50 4.00
67 Jaylen Brown 4.00 10.00
68 Brandon Ingram 5.00 12.00
69 Jaylen Brown 4.00 10.00
70 Dragan Bender 1.50 4.00
71 Kris Dunn 2.50 6.00
72 Buddy Hield 4.00 10.00
73 Jamal Murray 8.00 20.00
74 Marquese Chriss 2.00 5.00
75 Jakob Poeltl 3.00 8.00
76 Thon Maker 2.00 5.00
77 Taurean Prince 2.00 5.00
78 Denzel Valentine 1.50 4.00
79 Wade Baldwin IV 1.50 4.00
80 Henry Ellenson 1.50 4.00
81 Malik Beasley 3.00 8.00
82 Caris LeVert 4.00 10.00
83 DeAndre' Bembry 2.50 6.00
84 Malachi Richardson 1.50 4.00
85 T. Luwawu-Cabarrot 2.50 6.00
86 Brice Johnson 1.50 4.00
87 Pascal Siakam 10.00 25.00
88 Skal Labissiere 1.50 4.00
89 Dejounte Murray 8.00 20.00
90 Gary Payton II 4.00 10.00
91 Damian Jones 1.50 4.00
92 Deyonta Davis 1.50 4.00
93 Ivica Zubac 4.00 10.00
95 Cheick Diallo 1.50 4.00
96 Tyler Ulis 2.00 5.00
97 Malcolm Brogdon 5.00 12.00
98 Patrick McCaw 1.50 4.00
99 Diamond Stone 1.50 4.00
100 Kris Dunn 2.50 6.00

2016-17 Donruss Rookie Kings

*PROOF: .6X TO 1.5X BASIC
*PROOF ORNG/125: 1.5X TO 4X BASIC
*PROOF BLUE/99: 1X TO 2.5X BASIC
1 Brandon Ingram 1.50 4.00
2 Ben Simmons 1.25 3.00
3 Jaylen Brown 3.00 8.00
4 Dragan Bender .40 1.00
5 Kris Dunn .60 1.50
6 Buddy Hield 1.25 3.00
7 Jamal Murray 3.00 8.00
8 Marquese Chriss .50 1.25
9 Jakob Poeltl .75 2.00
10 Thon Maker .50 1.25
11 Domantas Sabonis 2.50 6.00
12 Taurean Prince .50 1.25
13 Denzel Valentine .40 1.00
14 Wade Baldwin IV .40 1.00
15 Henry Ellenson .40 1.00
16 Malik Beasley .75 2.00
17 Caris LeVert 1.00 2.50
18 DeAndre' Bembry .60 1.50
19 Malachi Richardson .40 1.00
20 T. Luwawu-Cabarrot .60 1.50
21 Brice Johnson .40 1.00
22 Pascal Siakam 2.50 6.00
23 Skal Labissiere .40 1.00
24 Dejounte Murray 2.00 5.00
25 Damian Jones .40 1.00
26 Isaiah Whitehead .40 1.00
27 Deyonta Davis .40 1.00
28 Kay Felder .40 1.00
29 A.J. Hammons .40 1.00
30 Dario Saric .60 1.50

2016-17 Donruss Rookie Materials Signatures

STATED PRINT RUN 75 SER.#'d SETS
1 Brandon Ingram 60.00 150.00
2 Jaylen Brown 100.00 250.00
3 Dragan Bender 5.00 12.00
4 Kris Dunn 8.00 20.00
5 Buddy Hield 15.00 40.00
6 Jamal Murray 75.00 200.00
7 Marquese Chriss 6.00 15.00
8 Jakob Poeltl 10.00 25.00
9 Thon Maker 6.00 15.00
10 Taurean Prince 6.00 15.00
11 Denzel Valentine 5.00 12.00
12 Wade Baldwin IV 5.00 12.00
13 Henry Ellenson 5.00 12.00
14 Malik Beasley 10.00 25.00
15 Caris LeVert 12.00 30.00
16 DeAndre' Bembry 8.00 20.00
17 Malachi Richardson 5.00 12.00
18 T. Luwawu-Cabarrot 8.00 20.00
19 Brice Johnson 5.00 12.00
20 Pascal Siakam 40.00 100.00
21 Skal Labissiere 5.00 12.00
22 Dejounte Murray 100.00 250.00
23 Damian Jones 5.00 12.00
24 Deyonta Davis 5.00 12.00
25 Ivica Zubac 12.00 30.00
26 Cheick Diallo 5.00 12.00
27 Tyler Ulis 6.00 15.00
28 Isaiah Whitehead 5.00 12.00
29 Demetrius Jackson 5.00 12.00
30 Kay Felder 5.00 12.00
31 Gary Payton II 12.00 30.00
32 Diamond Stone 5.00 12.00
33 Malcolm Brogdon 15.00 40.00
34 Chinanu Onuaku 5.00 12.00
35 Patrick McCaw 5.00 12.00

2016-17 Donruss Signature Series

1 Cody Zeller 3.00 8.00
2 C.J. McCollum 5.00 12.00
3 Ian Clark 3.00 8.00
4 Dwight Powell 3.00 8.00
5 Josh Huestis 3.00 8.00
6 T.J. McConnell 4.00 10.00
7 James Ennis 3.00 8.00
8 Walter Tavares 3.00 8.00
9 Alex Len 3.00 8.00
10 Allen Crabbe 3.00 8.00
11 Noah Vonleh 3.00 8.00
12 Aaron Harrison 3.00 8.00
13 Kevon Looney 5.00 12.00
14 Tristan Thompson 4.00 10.00
15 C.J. Miles 3.00 8.00
16 Dirk Nowitzki 100.00 250.00
17 Kyle O'Quinn 3.00 8.00
18 Jeff Withey 3.00 8.00
19 Jonas Valanciunas 4.00 10.00
20 Rashad Vaughn 3.00 8.00
21 Seth Curry 12.00 30.00
22 Deron Williams 4.00 10.00
23 D'Angelo Russell 6.00 15.00
24 Kelly Olynyk 3.00 8.00
25 Michael Carter-Williams 3.00 8.00
26 Devin Harris 3.00 8.00
27 Matthew Dellavedova 4.00 10.00
28 Montrezl Harrell 5.00 12.00
29 Draymond Green 20.00 50.00
30 Langston Galloway 3.00 8.00
31 Glenn Robinson III 3.00 8.00
32 Robert Covington 4.00 10.00
33 Bobby Portis 5.00 12.00
34 Festus Ezeli 3.00 8.00
35 Jared Dudley 3.00 8.00
36 Justise Winslow 4.00 10.00
37 Shabazz Muhammad 3.00 8.00
38 Jarell Martin 3.00 8.00
39 Terrence Jones 3.00 8.00
40 Timofey Mozgov 3.00 8.00
41 Al-Farouq Aminu 3.00 8.00
42 Khris Middleton 5.00 12.00
43 Tyus Jones 3.00 8.00
44 Rodney Stuckey 3.00 8.00
45 Luc Mbah a Moute 3.00 8.00
46 Brandon Rush 3.00 8.00
47 James Young 3.00 8.00
48 Avery Bradley 3.00 8.00
49 Kristaps Porzingis 15.00 40.00
50 Anthony Bennett 3.00 8.00

2016-17 Donruss Swatch Kings Jumbo

STATED PRINT RUN 99 SER.#'d SETS
1 Nerlens Noel 1.50 4.00
2 Russell Westbrook 4.00 10.00
3 Dwyane Wade 5.00 12.00
4 Kyrie Irving 5.00 12.00
5 Marcus Smart 3.00 8.00
6 J.J. Redick 2.50 6.00
7 Chandler Parsons 1.50 4.00
8 Kent Bazemore 1.50 4.00
9 Goran Dragic 2.50 6.00
10 Nicolas Batum 2.00 5.00
11 Jeremy Lin 5.00 12.00
12 Paul George 4.00 10.00
13 Marcus Morris 1.50 4.00
14 Kyle Lowry 2.50 6.00
15 Derrick Rose 4.00 10.00
16 Patrick Beverley 1.50 4.00
17 Tony Parker 3.00 8.00
18 Damian Lillard 6.00 15.00
19 Kevin Durant 10.00 25.00
20 Karl-Anthony Towns 5.00 12.00
21 Zach LaVine 5.00 12.00
22 Kevin Love 2.50 6.00
23 Jordan Clarkson 2.50 6.00
24 Kentavious Caldwell-Pope 2.00 5.00
25 Nikola Vucevic 2.50 6.00

2016-17 Donruss The Champ Is Here

*PROOF: .6X TO 1.5X BASIC
*PROOF BLUE/99: 1X TO 2.5X BASIC
1 LeBron James 5.00 12.00
2 Stephen Curry 5.00 12.00
3 Kyrie Irving 1.25 3.00
4 Klay Thompson 1.50 4.00
5 Dwyane Wade 1.25 3.00
6 Shaquille O'Neal 2.00 5.00
7 Kobe Bryant 5.00 12.00
8 Alonzo Mourning 1.00 2.50
9 Dirk Nowitzki 1.50 4.00
10 Tony Parker 1.00 2.50
11 Kevin Garnett 1.50 4.00
12 Manu Ginobili 1.25 3.00
13 Scottie Pippen 1.25 3.00
14 Larry Bird 2.50 6.00
15 Magic Johnson 2.50 6.00

2016-17 Donruss The Rookies

*PROOF: .6X TO 1.5X BASIC
*PROOF BLUE/99: 1X TO 2.5X BASIC
1 Brandon Ingram 1.50 4.00
2 Ben Simmons 1.25 3.00
3 Kris Dunn .60 1.50
4 Buddy Hield 1.25 3.00
5 Marquese Chriss .50 1.25

2016-17 Donruss Timeless Treasures Materials Signatures

PRINT RUNS B/WN 49-99 COPIES PER
*PRIME/25: .75X TO 2X BASIC
1 Brandon Ingram/99 40.00 100.00
2 Kris Dunn/99 6.00 15.00
3 Buddy Hield/99 12.00 30.00
4 Jaylen Brown/99 75.00 200.00
5 Jamal Murray/99 40.00 100.00
6 Marquese Chriss/99 5.00 12.00
7 Thon Maker/99 5.00 12.00
8 Denzel Valentine/99 4.00 10.00
9 Wade Baldwin IV/99 4.00 10.00
10 Malachi Richardson/99 4.00 10.00
11 Dragan Bender/99 4.00 10.00
12 Kevin Durant/49 60.00 150.00
13 Kyrie Irving/49 25.00 60.00
14 Carmelo Anthony/49 20.00 50.00
15 D'Angelo Russell/49 15.00 40.00
16 Karl-Anthony Towns/49 50.00 120.00
17 Dirk Nowitzki/49 40.00 100.00
18 Mark Price/49 10.00 25.00
19 Dan Issel/49 12.00 30.00
20 Jim Jackson/49 5.00 12.00
21 Glen Rice/49 6.00 15.00
22 Dennis Scott/49 4.00 10.00
23 Bill Laimbeer/49 6.00 15.00
24 Dikembe Mutombo/49 10.00 25.00
25 Jeff Hornacek/49 5.00 12.00

2017-18 Donruss

COMPLETE SET (200) 30.00 80.00
1 DeAndre' Bembry .25 .60
2 Dennis Schroder .30 .75
3 Taurean Prince .25 .60
4 Malcolm Delaney .25 .60
5 Ersan Ilyasova .25 .60
6 Jaylen Brown 1.00 2.50
7 Al Horford .40 1.00
8 Marcus Morris .25 .60
9 Isaiah Thomas .30 .75
10 Gordon Hayward .30 .75
11 D'Angelo Russell .30 .75
12 Trevor Booker .25 .60
13 Jeremy Lin .60 1.50
14 Rondae Hollis-Jefferson .25 .60
15 DeMarre Carroll .25 .60
16 Kemba Walker .30 .75
17 Nicolas Batum .25 .60
18 Michael Kidd-Gilchrist .25 .60
19 Dwight Howard .50 1.25
20 Jeremy Lamb .25 .60
21 Kris Dunn .25 .60
22 Zach LaVine .60 1.50
23 Bobby Portis .25 .60
24 Denzel Valentine .25 .60
25 Dwyane Wade .75 2.00
26 Kyrie Irving .75 2.00
27 LeBron James 3.00 8.00
28 Kevin Love .40 1.00
29 Derrick Rose .60 1.50
30 J.R. Smith .30 .75
31 Harrison Barnes .30 .75
32 Seth Curry .40 1.00
33 Wesley Matthews .25 .60
34 Dirk Nowitzki 1.00 2.50
35 J.J. Barea .30 .75
36 Gary Harris .30 .75
37 Nikola Jokic 2.50 6.00
38 Paul Millsap .30 .75
39 Jamal Murray .60 1.50
40 Emmanuel Mudiay .25 .60
41 Reggie Jackson .30 .75
42 Tobias Harris .30 .75
43 Andre Drummond .30 .75
44 Avery Bradley .25 .60
45 Stanley Johnson .25 .60
46 Stephen Curry 3.00 8.00
47 Kevin Durant 1.50 4.00
48 Draymond Green .50 1.25
49 Klay Thompson 1.00 2.50
50 Andre Iguodala .40 1.00
51 James Harden .75 2.00
52 Chris Paul .60 1.50
53 Eric Gordon .30 .75
54 Trevor Ariza .25 .60
55 Ryan Anderson .25 .60
56 Victor Oladipo .25 .60
57 Domantas Sabonis .75 2.00
58 Myles Turner .40 1.00
59 Thaddeus Young .25 .60
60 Darren Collison .25 .60
61 Patrick Beverley .25 .60
62 Danilo Gallinari .30 .75
63 Blake Griffin .40 1.00
64 DeAndre Jordan .30 .75
65 Lou Williams .30 .75
66 Jordan Clarkson .40 1.00
67 Brandon Ingram .50 1.25
68 Brook Lopez .30 .75
69 Julius Randle .40 1.00
70 Larry Nance Jr. .30 .75
71 Mario Chalmers .30 .75
72 Mike Conley .30 .75
73 Marc Gasol .40 1.00
74 Ben McLemore .25 .60
75 Chandler Parsons .25 .60
76 Goran Dragic .30 .75
77 James Johnson .25 .60
78 Justise Winslow .25 .60
79 Dion Waiters .25 .60
80 Hassan Whiteside .30 .75
81 Giannis Antetokounmpo 2.00 5.00
82 Greg Monroe .25 .60
83 Malcolm Brogdon .30 .75
84 Khris Middleton .50 1.25
85 Jabari Parker .25 .60
86 Jimmy Butler .60 1.50
87 Jamal Crawford .40 1.00
88 Andrew Wiggins .50 1.25
89 Karl-Anthony Towns .60 1.50
90 Jeff Teague .25 .60
91 Anthony Davis 1.00 2.50
92 DeMarcus Cousins .30 .75
93 Jrue Holiday .50 1.25
94 Rajon Rondo .50 1.25
95 E'Twaun Moore .25 .60
96 Carmelo Anthony .60 1.50
97 Tim Hardaway Jr. .30 .75
98 Kristaps Porzingis .50 1.25
99 Willy Hernangomez .25 .60
100 Courtney Lee .25 .60
101 Russell Westbrook .60 1.50
102 Paul George .60 1.50
103 Steven Adams .30 .75
104 Enes Kanter .30 .75
105 Doug McDermott .25 .60
106 Aaron Gordon .40 1.00
107 Terrence Ross .30 .75
108 Nikola Vucevic .30 .75
109 Jonathon Simmons .25 .60
110 Elfrid Payton .25 .60
111 Robert Covington .25 .60
112 Joel Embiid .75 2.00
113 JJ Redick .40 1.00
114 Ben Simmons .40 1.00
115 Amir Johnson .25 .60
116 Eric Bledsoe .30 .75
117 Devin Booker 1.00 2.50
118 Marquese Chriss .25 .60
119 Tyler Ulis .25 .60
120 T.J. Warren .30 .75
121 Al-Farouq Aminu .25 .60
122 Damian Lillard 1.00 2.50
123 C.J. McCollum .40 1.00
124 Evan Turner .25 .60
125 Jusuf Nurkic .30 .75
126 Vince Carter .75 2.00
127 Willie Cauley-Stein .25 .60
128 Buddy Hield .40 1.00
129 George Hill .30 .75
130 Zach Randolph .40 1.00
131 LaMarcus Aldridge .40 1.00
132 Pau Gasol .60 1.50
133 Rudy Gay .30 .75
134 Kawhi Leonard 1.00 2.50
135 Dejounte Murray .40 1.00
136 DeMar DeRozan .50 1.25
137 Serge Ibaka .30 .75
138 Kyle Lowry .40 1.00
139 Pascal Siakam .75 2.00
140 Delon Wright .25 .60
141 Alec Burks .25 .60
142 Rudy Gobert .50 1.25
143 Rodney Hood .25 .60
144 Joe Johnson .30 .75
145 Ricky Rubio .30 .75
146 Markieff Morris .25 .60
147 John Wall .50 1.25
148 Otto Porter Jr. .30 .75
149 Marcin Gortat .25 .60
150 Bradley Beal .50 1.25
151 Zhou Qi RR RC 1.00 2.50
152 Dillon Brooks RR RC 1.50 4.00
153 Wayne Selden Jr. RR RC .50 1.25
154 Guerschon Yabusele RR RC .50 1.25
155 Rade Zagorac RR RC .50 1.25
156 Ivan Rabb RR RC .50 1.25
157 Tyler Dorsey RR RC .50 1.25
158 Justin Jackson RR RC .50 1.25
159 Lauri Markkanen RR RC 3.00 8.00
160 Thomas Bryant RR RC .75 2.00
161 Dwayne Bacon RR RC .50 1.25
162 Jawun Evans RR RC .50 1.25
163 Jordan Bell RR RC .60 1.50
164 Semi Ojeleye RR RC .60 1.50
165 Sterling Brown RR RC .50 1.25
166 Damyean Dotson RR RC .60 1.50
167 Frank Mason III RR RC .50 1.25
168 Wesley Iwundu RR RC .50 1.25
169 Davon Reed RR RC .50 1.25
170 Frank Jackson RR RC .50 1.25
171 Josh Hart RR RC 1.25 3.00
172 Derrick White RR RC 2.00 5.00
173 Tony Bradley RR RC .50 1.25
174 Kyle Kuzma RR RC 2.00 5.00
175 Caleb Swanigan RR RC .50 1.25
176 Ike Anigbogu RR RC .50 1.25
177 Tyler Lydon RR RC .50 1.25
178 OG Anunoby RR RC 2.50 6.00
179 Jarrett Allen RR RC 1.25 3.00
180 Terrance Ferguson RR RC .50 1.25
181 Harry Giles RR RC .50 1.25
182 John Collins RR RC 1.25 3.00
183 T.J. Leaf RR RC .50 1.25
184 D.J. Wilson RR RC .50 1.25
185 Justin Patton RR RC .50 1.25
186 Ante Zizic RR RC .60 1.50
187 Bam Adebayo RR RC 3.00 8.00
188 Donovan Mitchell RR RC 5.00 12.00
189 Luke Kennard RR RC 1.00 2.50
190 Malik Monk RR RC 2.00 5.00
191 Zach Collins RR RC .75 2.00
192 Dennis Smith Jr. RR RC .60 1.50
193 Frank Ntilikina RR RC .60 1.50
194 Sindarius Thornwell RR RC .50 1.25
195 Jonathan Isaac RR RC 1.25 3.00
196 De'Aaron Fox RR RC 4.00 10.00
197 Josh Jackson RR RC .60 1.50
198 Jayson Tatum RR RC 20.00 50.00
199 Lonzo Ball RR RC 2.00 5.00
200 Markelle Fultz RR RC 1.25 3.00

2017-18 Donruss Green Flood

*GRN FLD: 1.2X TO 3X BASIC
*GRN FLD RC: 1.2X TO 3X BASIC

2017-18 Donruss Holo Laser Blue

*HOLO LSR BLUE: 3X TO 8X BASIC
*HOLO LSR BLUE RC: 3X TO 8X BASIC
STATED PRINT RUN 49 SER.#'d SETS

2017-18 Donruss Holo Laser Green

*HOLO LSR GRN: 2X TO 5X BASIC
*HOLO LSR GRN RC: 2X TO 5X BASIC
STATED PRINT RUN 99 SER.#'d SETS
198 Jayson Tatum RR 125.00 300.00

2017-18 Donruss Holo Laser Green and Yellow

*HOLO GRN YLLW: 1X TO 2.5X BASIC
*HOLO GRN YLLW RC: 1X TO 2.5X BASIC

2017-18 Donruss Holo Laser Orange
*HOLO ORNGE: 1.2X TO 3X BASIC
*HOLO ORNGE RC: 1.2X TO 3X BASIC

2017-18 Donruss Holo Laser Red
*HOLO LSR RED: 2X TO 5X BASIC
*HOLO LSR RED RC: 2X TO 5X BASIC
STATED PRINT RUN 99 SER.#'d SETS

2017-18 Donruss Holo Laser Yellow
*HOLO LSR YLLW: 5X TO 12X BASIC
*HOLO LSR YLLW RC: 5X TO 12X BASIC
STATED PRINT RUN 25 SER.#'d SETS
198 Jayson Tatum RR 500.00 1,000.00

2017-18 Donruss All Clear for Takeoff
COMPLETE SET (15) 5.00 12.00
*GREEN FLOOD: .5X TO 1.2X BASIC
*PROOF: .6X TO 1.5X BASIC
*PROOF BLUE/125: 1X TO 2.5X BASIC
1 Aaron Gordon .50 1.25
2 Norman Powell .50 1.25
3 Glenn Robinson III .30 .75
4 Giannis Antetokounmpo 2.50 6.00
5 Jamal Murray .75 2.00
6 Jaylen Brown 1.25 3.00
7 DeMar DeRozan .60 1.50
8 Andrew Wiggins .60 1.50
9 Kevin Durant 2.00 5.00
10 James Harden 1.00 2.50
11 Russell Westbrook .75 2.00
12 Blake Griffin .50 1.25
13 Zach LaVine .75 2.00
14 Larry Nance Jr. .40 1.00
15 Malcolm Brogdon .40 1.00

2017-18 Donruss All-Stars
COMPLETE SET (30) 12.00 30.00
*GREEN FLOOD: .5X TO 1.2X BASIC
*PROOF: .6X TO 1.5X BASIC
*PROOF BLUE/125: 1X TO 2.5X BASIC
1 Stephen Curry 4.00 10.00
2 James Harden 1.00 2.50
3 Kevin Durant 2.00 5.00
4 Kawhi Leonard 1.25 3.00
5 Anthony Davis 1.25 3.00
6 Russell Westbrook .75 2.00
7 DeMarcus Cousins .40 1.00
8 Klay Thompson 1.25 3.00
9 Draymond Green .60 1.50
10 Marc Gasol .50 1.25
11 DeAndre Jordan .40 1.00
12 Gordon Hayward .40 1.00
13 Kyrie Irving 1.00 2.50
14 DeMar DeRozan .60 1.50
15 LeBron James 4.00 10.00
16 Giannis Antetokounmpo 2.50 6.00
17 Jimmy Butler .75 2.00
18 Isaiah Thomas .40 1.00
19 John Wall .60 1.50
20 Tim Duncan 1.25 3.00
21 Kyle Lowry .50 1.25
22 Paul George .75 2.00
23 Kemba Walker .40 1.00
24 Paul Millsap .40 1.00
25 Carmelo Anthony .75 2.00
26 Kobe Bryant 4.00 10.00
27 Grant Hill .75 2.00
28 Shawn Kemp .75 2.00
29 Larry Bird 2.00 5.00
30 Magic Johnson 2.00 5.00

2017-18 Donruss Back to the Future Materials
1 Vince Carter 5.00 12.00
2 Marco Belinelli 1.50 4.00
3 Nicolas Batum 1.50 4.00
4 Markieff Morris 1.50 4.00
5 Nerlens Noel 1.50 4.00
6 Victor Oladipo 2.00 5.00
7 Boris Diaw 2.00 5.00
8 Joffrey Lauvergne 5.00 12.00
9 Greg Monroe 1.50 4.00
10 Kent Bazemore 1.50 4.00
11 Jeremy Lin 4.00 10.00
12 David West 2.00 5.00
13 Josh McRoberts 1.50 4.00
14 Trevor Booker 1.50 4.00
15 Trevor Ariza 1.50 4.00

2017-18 Donruss Court Kings
COMPLETE SET (40) 20.00 50.00
*GREEN FLOOD: .5X TO 1.2X BASIC
*PROOF: .6X TO 1.5X BASIC
*PROOF BLUE/125: 1X TO 2.5X BASIC
*PRF ORNGE/99: 1.2X TO 3X BASIC
1 Ben Simmons .50 1.25
2 Joel Embiid 1.00 2.50
3 Giannis Antetokounmpo 2.50 6.00
4 Dwyane Wade 1.00 2.50
5 LeBron James 4.00 10.00
6 Isaiah Thomas .40 1.00
7 Blake Griffin .50 1.25
8 Mike Conley .40 1.00
9 Dennis Schroder .40 1.00
10 Hassan Whiteside .40 1.00
11 Kemba Walker .40 1.00
12 Rudy Gobert .40 1.00
13 Buddy Hield .50 1.25
14 Kristaps Porzingis .60 1.50
15 Brandon Ingram .60 1.50
16 Aaron Gordon .50 1.25
17 Dirk Nowitzki 1.25 3.00
18 Harrison Barnes .40 1.00
19 Jeremy Lin .75 2.00
20 Gary Harris .40 1.00
21 Myles Turner .50 1.25
22 Anthony Davis 1.25 3.00
23 DeMarcus Cousins .40 1.00
24 Reggie Jackson .40 1.00
25 DeMar DeRozan .60 1.50
26 Kyle Lowry .50 1.25
27 James Harden 1.00 2.50
28 Kawhi Leonard 1.25 3.00
29 Devin Booker 1.25 3.00
30 Russell Westbrook .75 2.00
31 Andrew Wiggins .60 1.50
32 Karl-Anthony Towns .75 2.00
33 Damian Lillard 1.25 3.00
34 C.J. McCollum .50 1.25
35 Stephen Curry 4.00 10.00
36 Kevin Durant 2.00 5.00
37 Klay Thompson 1.25 3.00
38 John Wall .60 1.50
39 Otto Porter Jr. .40 1.00
40 Nikola Jokic 3.00 8.00

2017-18 Donruss Dominators Signatures
PRINT RUNS B/WN 25-40 COPIES PER
1 Bernard King/40 8.00 20.00
2 Hakeem Olajuwon/40 25.00 60.00
3 Shaquille O'Neal/40 75.00 200.00
4 Alex English/40 8.00 20.00
5 Calvin Murphy/40 6.00 15.00
6 Louie Dampier/40 6.00 15.00
7 Allen Iverson/40 60.00 150.00
8 John Stockton/40 30.00 80.00
9 Pau Gasol/40 20.00 50.00
10 Bill Russell/25 200.00 500.00
11 Larry Bird/40 100.00 250.00
12 George Hill/40 5.00 12.00
13 Andre Drummond/40 5.00 12.00
14 Frank Ramsey/40 6.00 15.00
15 Kobe Bryant/40 800.00 1,500.00
16 Andrei Kirilenko/40 5.00 12.00
17 Vin Baker/40 5.00 12.00
18 Juwan Howard/40 5.00 12.00
19 Cedric Ceballos/40 4.00 10.00
20 Jason Kidd/40 10.00 25.00
21 Marcus Smart/40 8.00 20.00
22 Jason Terry/40 8.00 20.00
23 Carmelo Anthony/40 40.00 100.00
24 T.J. Warren/40 5.00 12.00
25 Jordan Clarkson/40 6.00 15.00
26 Dwyane Wade/40 40.00 100.00
27 Clint Capela/40 5.00 12.00
29 Norman Powell/40 6.00 15.00
30 Jonas Valanciunas/40 5.00 12.00
31 Nikola Vucevic/40 5.00 12.00
32 Chris Bosh/30 15.00 40.00
33 Emmanuel Mudiay/40 4.00 10.00
34 Gordon Hayward/40 5.00 12.00
35 Kyrie Irving/40 75.00 200.00
36 Harrison Barnes/40 5.00 12.00
37 DeMarcus Cousins/40 5.00 12.00
38 Victor Oladipo/40 5.00 12.00
39 Will Barton/40 4.00 10.00
40 Nikola Mirotic/40 4.00 10.00

2017-18 Donruss Hall Dominators Signatures
PRINT RUNS B/WN 40-99 COPIES PER
1 Adrian Dantley/99 6.00 15.00
2 Alex English/50 8.00 20.00
3 Alonzo Mourning/99 20.00 50.00
4 Artis Gilmore/99 8.00 20.00
5 Arvydas Sabonis/99 8.00 20.00
6 Bernard King/65 8.00 20.00
7 Bob McAdoo/99 8.00 20.00
8 Calvin Murphy/40 6.00 15.00
9 Dan Issel/99 8.00 20.00
10 Dave Cowens/40 10.00 25.00
11 David Robinson/99 20.00 50.00
12 David Thompson/99 8.00 20.00
13 Dennis Rodman/99 40.00 100.00
14 Dikembe Mutombo/99 15.00 40.00
15 Dominique Wilkins/99 15.00 40.00
16 Gail Goodrich/99 6.00 15.00
17 Gary Payton/75 15.00 40.00
18 George Gervin/99 10.00 25.00
19 Jerry West/75 30.00 80.00
20 Joe Dumars/75 8.00 20.00
21 Karl Malone/75 40.00 100.00
22 Louie Dampier/40 6.00 15.00
23 Magic Johnson/99 60.00 150.00
24 Nate Archibald/99 8.00 20.00
25 Oscar Robertson/99 30.00 80.00
26 Ralph Sampson/99 6.00 15.00
27 Rick Barry/99 8.00 20.00
28 Robert Parish/99 8.00 20.00
29 Walt Frazier/99 20.00 50.00
30 Willis Reed/99 20.00 50.00

2017-18 Donruss Hall Kings
COMPLETE SET (30) 12.00 30.00
*GREEN FLOOD: .5X TO 1.2X BASIC
*PROOF: .6X TO 1.5X BASIC
*PROOF BLUE/125: 1X TO 2.5X BASIC
*PRF ORNGE/99: 1.2X TO 3X BASIC
1 Kareem Abdul-Jabbar 1.50 4.00
2 Elgin Baylor .75 2.00
3 Larry Bird 2.00 5.00
4 Wilt Chamberlain 1.50 4.00
5 Julius Erving 1.25 3.00
6 John Havlicek 1.00 2.50
7 Magic Johnson 2.00 5.00
8 George Mikan 1.25 3.00
9 Oscar Robertson 1.00 2.50
10 Bill Russell 1.50 4.00
11 Isiah Thomas .75 2.00
12 Jerry West 1.00 2.50
13 Wes Unseld .50 1.25
14 Rick Barry .60 1.50
15 Pete Maravich 1.25 3.00
16 Patrick Ewing .75 2.00
17 Tracy McGrady .75 2.00
18 Allen Iverson 1.25 3.00
19 Shaquille O'Neal 1.50 4.00
20 Yao Ming 1.00 2.50
21 Jo Jo White .50 1.25
22 Dikembe Mutombo .60 1.50
23 Mitch Richmond .60 1.50
24 Alonzo Mourning .75 2.00
25 Reggie Miller 1.00 2.50
26 Gary Payton .75 2.00
27 Artis Gilmore .60 1.50
28 Arvydas Sabonis .60 1.50
29 Dennis Rodman 1.25 3.00
30 Scottie Pippen 1.25 3.00

2017-18 Donruss Jersey Kings
1 Kyrie Irving 10.00 25.00
2 Juan Hernangomez 2.50 6.00
3 C.J. McCollum 2.50 6.00
4 LaMarcus Aldridge 2.50 6.00
5 J.J. Barea 2.00 5.00
6 Stephen Curry 20.00 50.00
7 Rondae Hollis-Jefferson 1.50 4.00
8 Kemba Walker 2.00 5.00
9 Brandon Knight 2.00 5.00
10 DeMar DeRozan 3.00 8.00
11 Denzel Valentine 1.50 4.00
12 Dirk Nowitzki 6.00 15.00
13 Blake Griffin 2.50 6.00
14 Jaylen Brown 6.00 15.00
15 Steven Adams 2.00 5.00
16 John Wall 3.00 8.00
17 Kevin Love 2.50 6.00
18 Mike Conley 2.00 5.00
19 Carmelo Anthony 4.00 10.00
20 DeAndre' Bembry 1.50 4.00
21 Rudy Gobert 3.00 8.00
22 Malik Beasley 2.00 5.00
23 Goran Dragic 2.00 5.00
24 Jrue Holiday 3.00 8.00
25 LeBron James 30.00 80.00

2017-18 Donruss Jersey Series
1 DeAndre' Bembry 1.50 4.00
2 Jaylen Brown 6.00 15.00
3 Marcus Smart 2.50 6.00
4 Rondae Hollis-Jefferson 1.50 4.00
5 Brook Lopez 2.00 5.00
6 Caris LeVert 2.50 6.00
7 Frank Kaminsky 1.50 4.00
8 Kemba Walker 2.00 5.00
9 Denzel Valentine 1.50 4.00
10 LeBron James 8.00 20.00
11 Kyrie Irving 10.00 25.00
12 Kevin Love 2.50 6.00
13 Dirk Nowitzki 6.00 15.00
14 J.J. Barea 2.00 5.00
15 Malik Beasley 2.00 5.00
16 Juan Hernangomez 2.50 6.00
17 Stanley Johnson 1.50 4.00
18 Andre Drummond 2.00 5.00
19 Draymond Green 3.00 8.00
20 Stephen Curry 20.00 50.00
21 Trevor Ariza 1.50 4.00
22 Clint Capela 2.00 5.00
23 George Hill 2.00 5.00
24 Blake Griffin 2.50 6.00
25 DeAndre Jordan 2.00 5.00
26 Brandon Ingram 3.00 8.00
27 Mike Conley 2.00 5.00
28 Goran Dragic 2.00 5.00
29 John Henson 1.50 4.00
30 Kris Dunn 1.50 4.00
31 Jrue Holiday 3.00 8.00
32 Anthony Davis 3.00 8.00
33 Carmelo Anthony 4.00 10.00
34 Ron Baker 1.50 4.00
35 Steven Adams 2.00 5.00
36 Russell Westbrook 4.00 10.00
37 Nikola Vucevic 2.00 5.00
38 Timothe Luwawu-Cabarrot 1.50 4.00
39 Brandon Knight 2.00 5.00
40 C.J. McCollum 2.50 6.00
41 Malachi Richardson 1.50 4.00
42 Skal Labissiere 1.50 4.00
43 LaMarcus Aldridge 2.50 6.00
44 Kyle Anderson 1.50 4.00
45 DeMar DeRozan 3.00 8.00
46 Kyle Lowry 2.50 6.00
47 Alec Burks 1.50 4.00
48 Rudy Gobert 3.00 8.00
49 John Wall 3.00 8.00
50 Otto Porter Jr. 2.00 5.00

2017-18 Donruss Newly Crowned Rookie Jerseys
1 Markelle Fultz 6.00 15.00
2 Lonzo Ball 10.00 25.00
3 Jayson Tatum 20.00 50.00
4 Josh Jackson 2.00 5.00
5 De'Aaron Fox 10.00 25.00
6 Jonathan Isaac 4.00 10.00
7 Ivan Rabb 1.50 4.00
8 Frank Ntilikina 2.00 5.00
9 Dennis Smith Jr. 2.00 5.00
10 Zach Collins 2.50 6.00
11 Malik Monk 6.00 15.00
12 Luke Kennard 3.00 8.00
13 Donovan Mitchell 12.00 30.00
14 Bam Adebayo 10.00 25.00
15 Ante Zizic 2.00 5.00
16 Justin Patton 1.50 4.00
17 D.J. Wilson 1.50 4.00
18 T.J. Leaf 1.50 4.00
19 John Collins 6.00 15.00
20 Harry Giles 1.50 4.00
21 Terrance Ferguson 1.50 4.00
22 Jarrett Allen 4.00 10.00
23 OG Anunoby 8.00 20.00
24 Tyler Lydon 1.50 4.00
25 Kyle Kuzma 6.00 15.00
26 Tony Bradley 1.50 4.00
27 Derrick White 6.00 15.00
28 Josh Hart 4.00 10.00
29 Frank Jackson 1.50 4.00
30 Davon Reed 1.50 4.00
31 Frank Mason III 1.50 4.00
32 Semi Ojeleye 2.00 5.00
33 Jordan Bell 4.00 10.00
34 Jawun Evans 1.50 4.00
35 Dwayne Bacon 1.50 4.00

2017-18 Donruss Next Day Autographs
1 Markelle Fultz 40.00 100.00
2 Lonzo Ball 60.00 150.00
3 Jayson Tatum 1,000.00 2,000.00
4 Josh Jackson 5.00 12.00
5 De'Aaron Fox 300.00 600.00
6 Jonathan Isaac 40.00 100.00
7 Tyler Dorsey 4.00 10.00
8 Frank Ntilikina 5.00 12.00
9 Dennis Smith Jr. 5.00 12.00
10 Zach Collins 6.00 15.00
11 Malik Monk 40.00 100.00
12 Luke Kennard 8.00 20.00
13 Donovan Mitchell 400.00 800.00
14 Bam Adebayo 75.00 200.00
15 Ante Zizic 5.00 12.00
16 Justin Patton 4.00 10.00
17 D.J. Wilson 4.00 10.00
18 T.J. Leaf 4.00 10.00
19 John Collins 25.00 60.00
20 Harry Giles 4.00 10.00
21 Terrance Ferguson 4.00 10.00
22 Jarrett Allen 40.00 100.00
23 OG Anunoby 100.00 250.00
24 Tyler Lydon 4.00 10.00
25 Sindarius Thornwell 4.00 10.00
26 Caleb Swanigan 4.00 10.00
27 Kyle Kuzma 60.00 150.00
28 Tony Bradley 4.00 10.00
29 Derrick White 125.00 300.00
30 Josh Hart 75.00 200.00
31 Frank Jackson 4.00 10.00
32 Davon Reed 4.00 10.00
33 Wesley Iwundu 4.00 10.00
34 Frank Mason III 4.00 10.00
35 Ivan Rabb 4.00 10.00
36 Sterling Brown 4.00 10.00
37 Semi Ojeleye 5.00 12.00
38 Jordan Bell 4.00 10.00
39 Jawun Evans 4.00 10.00
40 Dwayne Bacon 4.00 10.00

2017-18 Donruss Retro Series
COMPLETE SET (25) 12.00 30.00
*GREEN FLOOD: .5X TO 1.2X BASIC
*PROOF: .6X TO 1.5X BASIC
*PROOF BLUE/125: 1X TO 2.5X BASIC
1 Tracy McGrady .75 2.00
2 Alonzo Mourning .75 2.00
3 Bill Russell 1.50 4.00
4 Wilt Chamberlain 1.50 4.00
5 Rick Barry .60 1.50
6 Gary Payton .75 2.00
7 Dan Issel .60 1.50
8 Norm Nixon .30 .75
9 Bob McAdoo .60 1.50
10 Glen Rice .40 1.00
11 Jim Jackson .30 .75
12 George Gervin .75 2.00
13 Reggie Miller 1.00 2.50
14 Scottie Pippen 1.25 3.00
15 Dave DeBusschere .50 1.25
16 Dave Bing .50 1.25
17 Oscar Robertson 1.00 2.50
18 Clyde Drexler .75 2.00
19 Paul Westphal .50 1.25
20 Shaquille O'Neal 1.50 4.00
21 Shareef Abdur-Rahim .40 1.00
22 Jason Kidd .75 2.00
23 John Stockton 1.00 2.50
24 Chauncey Billups .60 1.50
25 Walt Frazier .75 2.00

2017-18 Donruss Rookie Dominators Signatures
STATED PRINT RUN 99 SER.#'d SETS
1 Markelle Fultz 8.00 20.00
2 Lonzo Ball 12.00 30.00
3 Jayson Tatum 200.00 500.00
4 Jordan Bell 3.00 8.00
5 De'Aaron Fox 60.00 150.00
6 Jonathan Isaac 8.00 20.00
7 Lauri Markkanen 25.00 60.00
8 Frank Ntilikina 4.00 10.00
9 Dennis Smith Jr. 4.00 10.00
10 Zach Collins 5.00 12.00
11 Malik Monk 12.00 30.00
12 Luke Kennard 6.00 15.00
13 Donovan Mitchell 100.00 250.00
15 Justin Jackson 3.00 8.00
16 Justin Patton 3.00 8.00
17 D.J. Wilson 3.00 8.00
18 T.J. Leaf 3.00 8.00
19 John Collins 8.00 20.00
20 Frank Mason III 3.00 8.00
21 Terrance Ferguson 3.00 8.00
22 Jarrett Allen 8.00 20.00
23 OG Anunoby 15.00 40.00
24 Dwayne Bacon 3.00 8.00
25 Frank Jackson 3.00 8.00
26 Davon Reed 3.00 8.00
27 Kyle Kuzma 12.00 30.00
28 Tony Bradley 3.00 8.00
29 Derrick White 15.00 40.00
30 Josh Hart 8.00 20.00

2017-18 Donruss Rookie Jerseys
*PRIME/25: .75X TO 2X BASIC
1 Markelle Fultz 6.00 15.00
2 Markelle Fultz 6.00 15.00
3 Markelle Fultz 6.00 15.00
4 Lonzo Ball 10.00 25.00
5 Lonzo Ball 10.00 25.00
6 Lonzo Ball 10.00 25.00
7 Donovan Mitchell 12.00 30.00
8 Donovan Mitchell 12.00 30.00
9 Donovan Mitchell 12.00 30.00
10 Bam Adebayo 10.00 25.00
11 Bam Adebayo 10.00 25.00
12 Bam Adebayo 10.00 25.00
13 Jarrett Allen 4.00 10.00
14 Jarrett Allen 4.00 10.00
15 Jarrett Allen 4.00 10.00
16 OG Anunoby 8.00 20.00
17 OG Anunoby 8.00 20.00
18 OG Anunoby 8.00 20.00
19 Dwayne Bacon 1.50 4.00
20 Dwayne Bacon 1.50 4.00
21 Dwayne Bacon 1.50 4.00
22 Jordan Bell 1.50 4.00
23 Jordan Bell 1.50 4.00
24 Jordan Bell 1.50 4.00
25 De'Aaron Fox 10.00 25.00
26 De'Aaron Fox 10.00 25.00
27 De'Aaron Fox 10.00 25.00
28 Jonathan Isaac 6.00 15.00
29 Jonathan Isaac 6.00 15.00
30 Jonathan Isaac 6.00 15.00
31 Justin Patton 1.50 4.00
32 Justin Patton 1.50 4.00
33 Justin Patton 1.50 4.00
34 D.J. Wilson 1.50 4.00
35 D.J. Wilson 1.50 4.00
36 D.J. Wilson 1.50 4.00
37 T.J. Leaf 1.50 4.00
38 T.J. Leaf 1.50 4.00
39 T.J. Leaf 1.50 4.00
40 Frank Jackson 1.50 4.00
41 Frank Jackson 1.50 4.00
42 Frank Jackson 1.50 4.00
43 Davon Reed 1.50 4.00
44 Davon Reed 1.50 4.00
45 Davon Reed 1.50 4.00
46 Kyle Kuzma 6.00 15.00
47 Kyle Kuzma 6.00 15.00
48 Kyle Kuzma 6.00 15.00
49 Frank Ntilikina 2.00 5.00
50 Frank Ntilikina 2.00 5.00
51 Frank Ntilikina 2.00 5.00
52 Dennis Smith Jr. 2.00 5.00
53 Dennis Smith Jr. 2.00 5.00
54 Dennis Smith Jr. 2.00 5.00
55 John Collins 6.00 15.00
56 John Collins 6.00 15.00
57 John Collins 6.00 15.00
58 Frank Mason III 1.50 4.00
59 Frank Mason III 1.50 4.00
60 Frank Mason III 1.50 4.00
61 Terrance Ferguson 1.50 4.00
62 Terrance Ferguson 1.50 4.00
63 Terrance Ferguson 1.50 4.00
64 Tony Bradley 1.50 4.00
65 Tony Bradley 1.50 4.00
66 Tony Bradley 1.50 4.00
67 Derrick White 6.00 15.00
68 Derrick White 6.00 15.00
69 Derrick White 6.00 15.00
70 Josh Hart 4.00 10.00
71 Josh Hart 4.00 10.00
72 Josh Hart 4.00 10.00
73 Josh Jackson 2.00 5.00
74 Josh Jackson 2.00 5.00
75 Josh Jackson 2.00 5.00
76 Zach Collins 2.50 6.00
77 Zach Collins 2.50 6.00
78 Zach Collins 2.50 6.00
79 Malik Monk 6.00 15.00
80 Malik Monk 6.00 15.00
81 Malik Monk 6.00 15.00
82 Harry Giles 1.50 4.00
83 Harry Giles 1.50 4.00
84 Harry Giles 1.50 4.00
85 Luke Kennard 3.00 8.00
86 Luke Kennard 3.00 8.00
87 Luke Kennard 3.00 8.00
88 Sterling Brown 1.50 4.00
89 Sterling Brown 1.50 4.00
90 Sterling Brown 1.50 4.00
91 Tyler Lydon 1.50 4.00
92 Tyler Lydon 1.50 4.00
93 Tyler Lydon 1.50 4.00
94 Jayson Tatum 25.00 60.00
95 Jayson Tatum 25.00 60.00
96 Jayson Tatum 25.00 60.00
97 Ante Zizic 2.00 5.00
98 Ante Zizic 2.00 5.00
99 Ante Zizic 2.00 5.00
100 Josh Jackson 2.00 5.00

2017-18 Donruss Rookie Kings
COMPLETE SET (30) 20.00 50.00
*GREEN FLOOD: .5X TO 1.2X BASIC
*PROOF: .6X TO 1.5X BASIC
*PROOF BLUE/125: 1X TO 2.5X BASIC
*PRF ORNGE/99: 1.2X TO 3X BASIC
1 Markelle Fultz 1.00 2.50
2 Lonzo Ball 1.50 4.00
3 Jayson Tatum 5.00 12.00
4 Josh Jackson .50 1.25
5 De'Aaron Fox 3.00 8.00
6 Jonathan Isaac 1.00 2.50
7 Ivan Rabb .40 1.00
8 Frank Ntilikina .50 1.25
9 Dennis Smith Jr. .50 1.25
10 Zach Collins .60 1.50
11 Malik Monk 1.50 4.00
12 Luke Kennard .75 2.00
13 Donovan Mitchell 4.00 10.00
14 Bam Adebayo 2.50 6.00
15 Caleb Swanigan .40 1.00
16 Derrick White 1.50 4.00
17 D.J. Wilson .40 1.00
18 T.J. Leaf .40 1.00
19 John Collins 1.00 2.50
20 Harry Giles .40 1.00
21 Terrance Ferguson .40 1.00
22 Jarrett Allen 1.00 2.50
23 OG Anunoby 2.00 5.00
24 Wayne Selden Jr. .40 1.00
25 Kyle Kuzma 1.50 4.00
26 Josh Hart 1.00 2.50
27 Frank Jackson .40 1.00
28 Frank Mason III .40 1.00
29 Jordan Bell .40 1.00
30 Dwayne Bacon .40 1.00

2017-18 Donruss Rookie Materials Signatures
PRINT RUNS B/WN 75-150 COPIES PER
1 Markelle Fultz/75 50.00 120.00
2 Lonzo Ball/75 75.00 200.00
3 Jayson Tatum/75 400.00 800.00
4 Donovan Mitchell/75 200.00 500.00
6 Ivan Rabb/75 4.00 10.00
7 Jarrett Allen/75 15.00 40.00
8 OG Anunoby/75 20.00 50.00
9 Dwayne Bacon/75 4.00 10.00
10 Jordan Bell/75 4.00 10.00
11 De'Aaron Fox/75 100.00 250.00
12 Jonathan Isaac/75 10.00 25.00
13 Justin Patton/75 4.00 10.00
14 D.J. Wilson/75 4.00 10.00
15 T.J. Leaf/150 4.00 10.00
16 Frank Jackson/75 6.00 15.00
17 Davon Reed/75 6.00 15.00
18 Kyle Kuzma/75 15.00 40.00
19 Tyler Dorsey/75 4.00 10.00
20 Frank Ntilikina/75 5.00 12.00
21 Dennis Smith Jr./75 5.00 12.00
22 John Collins/75 10.00 25.00
23 Frank Mason III/75 4.00 10.00
24 Terrance Ferguson/75 4.00 10.00
25 Tony Bradley/75 4.00 10.00
26 Derrick White/75 12.00 30.00
27 Josh Hart/75 10.00 25.00
29 Zach Collins/75 6.00 15.00
30 Malik Monk/75 15.00 40.00
31 Harry Giles/75 4.00 10.00
32 Jawun Evans/75 4.00 10.00
33 Luke Kennard/75 8.00 20.00
34 Sterling Brown/75 4.00 10.00
35 Tyler Lydon/75 4.00 10.00

2017-18 Donruss Signature Series
1 Evan Turner 3.00 8.00
2 Kristaps Porzingis 15.00 40.00
3 Karl-Anthony Towns 25.00 60.00
4 Andrew Wiggins 10.00 25.00
5 Mindaugas Kuzminskas 3.00 8.00
6 DeAndre' Bembry 3.00 8.00
7 Malcolm Delaney 3.00 8.00
8 Yogi Ferrell 3.00 8.00
9 Kelly Oubre Jr. 5.00 12.00
10 Emmanuel Mudiay 3.00 8.00
11 Georgios Papagiannis 3.00 8.00
12 Damian Jones 3.00 8.00
13 Wade Baldwin IV 3.00 8.00
14 Taurean Prince 3.00 8.00
15 Rodney McGruder 3.00 8.00
16 Kay Felder 3.00 8.00
17 Arvydas Sabonis 12.00 30.00
18 Dikembe Mutombo 12.00 30.00
19 Ralph Sampson 5.00 12.00
20 Gail Goodrich 5.00 12.00
21 Bob McAdoo 6.00 15.00
22 Artis Gilmore 6.00 15.00
23 Adrian Dantley 5.00 12.00
24 Robert Parish 6.00 15.00
25 George Gervin 8.00 20.00
26 Nate Archibald 6.00 15.00
27 Tom "Satch" Sanders 5.00 12.00
28 Dave Cowens 8.00 20.00
29 Jawun Evans 3.00 8.00
30 James Worthy 6.00 15.00
31 Jerry West 15.00 40.00
34 Kyrie Irving 60.00 150.00
35 James Johnson 3.00 8.00
36 Tyler Johnson 3.00 8.00
37 T.J. Warren 4.00 10.00
38 Boban Marjanovic 12.00 30.00
39 Jarrett Allen 8.00 20.00
40 Justin Patton 3.00 8.00
41 John Collins 20.00 50.00
42 Jayson Tatum 200.00 500.00
43 Lonzo Ball 75.00 200.00
44 Edmond Sumner 5.00 12.00
45 Luke Kennard 6.00 15.00
46 Frank Mason III 3.00 8.00
47 Wayne Selden Jr. 3.00 8.00
48 Justin Jackson 3.00 8.00
50 Marcus Smart 5.00 12.00
SSKD Kevin Durant 75.00 200.00

2017-18 Donruss Significant Signatures
1 Damian Lillard 30.00 80.00
2 Carmelo Anthony 15.00 40.00
3 Kyrie Irving 30.00 80.00
4 Anthony Davis 30.00 80.00
5 Karl-Anthony Towns 25.00 60.00
6 Goran Dragic 4.00 10.00
7 Jason Kidd 12.00 30.00
8 Julius Randle 5.00 12.00
10 Doug McDermott 3.00 8.00
11 Alan Williams 3.00 8.00
13 DeAndre' Bembry 3.00 8.00
14 Nikola Jokic 125.00 300.00
15 Harrison Barnes 4.00 10.00
16 George Hill 4.00 10.00
17 Jeff Teague 3.00 8.00
18 Jabari Parker 3.00 8.00
19 Jonas Valanciunas 4.00 10.00
20 Kent Bazemore 3.00 8.00
21 Wade Baldwin IV 3.00 8.00
22 Zydrunas Ilgauskas 4.00 10.00
23 Tristan Thompson 3.00 8.00
24 Kenny Anderson 4.00 10.00
25 Danny Manning 4.00 10.00
26 Enes Kanter 4.00 10.00
27 Clint Capela 4.00 10.00
28 Theo Ratliff 3.00 8.00
29 Emmanuel Mudiay 3.00 8.00
30 Malcolm Delaney 3.00 8.00
31 Zach Randolph 5.00 12.00
32 Jim Chones 3.00 8.00
33 Gorgui Dieng 3.00 8.00
34 Bob Dandridge 5.00 12.00
35 Andrei Kirilenko 4.00 10.00
36 Marc Gasol 5.00 12.00
37 E'Twaun Moore 3.00 8.00
38 Danilo Gallinari 4.00 10.00
39 Anfernee Hardaway 30.00 80.00
40 Kelly Tripucka 4.00 10.00
41 C.J. McCollum 8.00 20.00
42 Dante Exum 3.00 8.00
43 Yogi Ferrell 3.00 8.00
44 Taurean Prince 3.00 8.00
45 Robin Lopez 3.00 8.00
46 Pau Gasol 8.00 20.00
47 Andrew Wiggins 10.00 25.00
48 Tyler Johnson 3.00 8.00
49 Andrew Harrison 3.00 8.00
50 Gordon Hayward 15.00 40.00
51 Brice Johnson 4.00 10.00
52 Nikola Mirotic 3.00 8.00
53 Solomon Hill 3.00 8.00
54 Boban Marjanovic 3.00 8.00
55 Evan Fournier 4.00 10.00
56 Allen Crabbe 3.00 8.00
57 Ricky Rubio 6.00 15.00
58 Tony Delk 3.00 8.00
59 Walter Berry 3.00 8.00
60 Marcus Smart 5.00 12.00
61 Dwyane Wade 20.00 50.00
62 Sidney Moncrief 4.00 10.00
63 Rodney McGruder 3.00 8.00
64 Rick Fox 4.00 10.00
65 Mel Davis 3.00 8.00
66 Blake Griffin 10.00 25.00
67 Bill Laimbeer 5.00 12.00
68 Nikola Vucevic 4.00 10.00
69 Marcus Camby 4.00 10.00
70 Walter McCarty 3.00 8.00
71 J.J. Barea 12.00 30.00
72 John Wall 12.00 30.00
73 Michael Kidd-Gilchrist 3.00 8.00
74 Mario Hezonja 3.00 8.00
75 Ray Allen 15.00 40.00
76 Khris Middleton 6.00 15.00
77 Justise Winslow 3.00 8.00
78 Jordan Clarkson 5.00 12.00
79 D'Angelo Russell 4.00 10.00
80 Vin Baker 4.00 10.00
81 Victor Oladipo 6.00 15.00
82 Mindaugas Kuzminskas 3.00 8.00
83 Frank Kaminsky 3.00 8.00
84 Andre Drummond 4.00 10.00
85 Maurice Harkless 3.00 8.00
86 Juwan Howard 4.00 10.00
87 Jeremy Lin 15.00 40.00
88 Dell Curry 3.00 8.00
89 Jason Terry 4.00 10.00
90 James Johnson 3.00 8.00
91 Damon Stoudamire 5.00 12.00
92 Cedric Ceballos 3.00 8.00
93 Eric Gordon 4.00 10.00
94 Tim Hardaway Jr. 4.00 10.00
95 Will Barton 3.00 8.00
96 Hersey Hawkins 3.00 8.00
97 Dorian Finney-Smith 3.00 8.00
98 Noah Vonleh 3.00 8.00
99 Sean Kilpatrick 3.00 8.00
100 Marcin Gortat 3.00 8.00

2017-18 Donruss Swatch Kings Jumbo
1 Dirk Nowitzki 6.00 15.00
2 Damian Lillard 6.00 15.00
3 Carmelo Anthony 4.00 10.00
4 Kris Dunn 1.50 4.00
5 Draymond Green 3.00 8.00
6 Andre Drummond 2.00 5.00
7 C.J. McCollum 2.50 6.00
8 LeBron James 30.00 80.00
9 DeMar DeRozan 3.00 8.00
10 Kyle Lowry 2.50 6.00
11 Brandon Knight 2.00 5.00
12 Caris LeVert 2.50 6.00
13 Jrue Holiday 3.00 8.00
14 Marcus Smart 2.50 6.00
15 Mike Conley 2.00 5.00
16 Trevor Ariza 1.50 4.00
17 Kevin Love 2.50 6.00
18 John Wall 3.00 8.00
19 Rudy Gobert 3.00 8.00
20 Steven Adams 2.00 5.00
21 Frank Kaminsky 1.50 4.00
22 Rondae Hollis-Jefferson 1.50 4.00
23 Blake Griffin 2.50 6.00
24 George Hill 2.00 5.00
25 Denzel Valentine 1.50 4.00

2017-18 Donruss Swishful Thinking
COMPLETE SET (10) 6.00 15.00
*GREEN FLOOD: .5X TO 1.2X BASIC
*PROOF: .6X TO 1.5X BASIC
*PROOF BLUE/125: 1X TO 2.5X BASIC
1 Klay Thompson 1.25 3.00
2 Isaiah Thomas .40 1.00
3 Devin Booker 1.25 3.00
4 Russell Westbrook .75 2.00
5 James Harden 1.00 2.50
6 Giannis Antetokounmpo 2.50 6.00
7 Stephen Curry 4.00 10.00
8 Kemba Walker .40 1.00
9 Kyle Lowry .50 1.25
10 Kristaps Porzingis .60 1.50

2017-18 Donruss The Champ is Here
COMPLETE SET (15) 6.00 15.00
*GREEN FLOOD: .5X TO 1.2X BASIC
*PROOF: .6X TO 1.5X BASIC
*PROOF BLUE/125: 1X TO 2.5X BASIC
1 Kevin Durant 2.00 5.00
2 Kyrie Irving 1.00 2.50
3 David Robinson 1.00 2.50
4 Dennis Rodman 1.25 3.00
5 Stephen Curry 4.00 10.00
6 Kobe Bryant 4.00 10.00
7 Shaquille O'Neal 1.50 4.00
8 Dwyane Wade 1.00 2.50
9 Jason Kidd .75 2.00
10 Peja Stojakovic .40 1.00
11 Tim Duncan 1.25 3.00
12 Robert Horry .50 1.25
13 Ray Allen .75 2.00
14 David West .40 1.00
15 Shawn Marion .40 1.00

2017-18 Donruss The Rookies
COMPLETE SET (5) 12.00 30.00
*GREEN FLOOD: .5X TO 1.2X BASIC
*PROOF: .6X TO 1.5X BASIC
*PROOF BLUE/125: 1X TO 2.5X BASIC
1 Markelle Fultz 1.00 2.50
2 Lonzo Ball 1.50 4.00
3 Jayson Tatum 15.00 40.00
4 Josh Jackson .50 1.25
5 De'Aaron Fox 3.00 8.00

2017-18 Donruss Timeless Treasures Materials Signatures
PRINT RUNS B/WN 23-99 COPIES PER
1 Kobe Bryant/40 1,000.00 2,000.00
3 Allen Iverson/30 75.00 200.00
4 Kyrie Irving/50 60.00 150.00
5 Karl Malone/30 40.00 100.00
6 Dirk Nowitzki/30 150.00 400.00
7 Magic Johnson/25 75.00 200.00
8 Karl-Anthony Towns/50 20.00 50.00
9 David Robinson/30 40.00 100.00
10 Ricky Rubio/30 8.00 20.00
11 Marc Gasol/30 10.00 25.00
12 Ray Allen/30 60.00 150.00
13 Chris Bosh/30 15.00 40.00
14 Jeremy Lin/30 75.00 200.00
15 Dominique Wilkins/30 15.00 40.00
16 Anfernee Hardaway/30 75.00 200.00
17 C.J. McCollum/30 10.00 25.00
18 Andre Drummond/30 8.00 20.00
19 Tristan Thompson/30 6.00 15.00

20 Joe Dumars/30 15.00 40.00
21 Robert Horry/49 12.00 30.00
22 Taurean Prince/99 6.00 15.00
23 Tim Hardaway/23 15.00 40.00
24 Marcus Smart/49 12.00 30.00
25 Bill Laimbeer/49 10.00 25.00

2018-19 Donruss

COMPLETE SET (200)
1 Damian Lillard 1.00 2.50
2 Stephen Curry 3.00 8.00
3 Kyle Lowry .40 1.00
4 Patrick Beverley .25 .60
5 Goran Dragic .30 .75
6 Dennis Schroder .30 .75
7 Elfrid Payton .30 .75
8 Kemba Walker .30 .75
9 D.J. Augustin .25 .60
10 Dennis Smith Jr. .25 .60
11 CJ McCollum .40 1.00
12 Klay Thompson 1.00 2.50
13 DeMar DeRozan .50 1.25
14 Lou Williams .30 .75
15 Dwyane Wade .75 2.00
16 Jeremy Lin .60 1.50
17 Jrue Holiday .50 1.25
18 Nicolas Batum .25 .60
19 Evan Fournier .30 .75
20 Wesley Matthews .25 .60
21 Evan Turner .25 .60
22 Kevin Durant 1.50 4.00
23 OG Anunoby .40 1.00
24 Avery Bradley .25 .60
25 James Johnson .25 .60
26 Taurean Prince .25 .60
27 Nikola Mirotic .25 .60
28 Malik Monk .40 1.00
29 Terrence Ross .30 .75
30 Harrison Barnes .30 .75
31 Zach Collins .30 .75
32 Draymond Green .50 1.25
33 Serge Ibaka .30 .75
34 Tobias Harris .30 .75
35 Dion Waiters .25 .60
36 John Collins .40 1.00
37 Julius Randle .40 1.00
38 Michael Kidd-Gilchrist .25 .60
39 Aaron Gordon .40 1.00
40 Dirk Nowitzki 1.00 2.50
41 Jusuf Nurkic .30 .75
42 DeMarcus Cousins .30 .75
43 Jonas Valanciunas .40 1.00
44 Marcin Gortat .25 .60
45 Hassan Whiteside .30 .75
46 Dewayne Dedmon .25 .60
47 Anthony Davis 1.00 2.50
48 Tony Parker .60 1.50
49 Nikola Vucevic .30 .75
50 DeAndre Jordan .30 .75
51 De'Aaron Fox .75 2.00
52 Chris Paul .75 2.00
53 Ricky Rubio .30 .75
54 Lonzo Ball .40 1.00
55 Eric Bledsoe .30 .75
56 Kyrie Irving 1.00 2.50
57 Frank Ntilikina .25 .60
58 Kris Dunn .25 .60
59 Ben Simmons .40 1.00
60 Jamal Murray .75 2.00
61 Bogdan Bogdanovic .40 1.00
62 Clint Capela .30 .75
63 Donovan Mitchell 1.25 3.00
64 Brandon Ingram .40 1.00
65 Malcolm Brogdon .40 1.00
66 Jaylen Brown .60 1.50
67 Tim Hardaway Jr. .25 .60
68 Zach LaVine .60 1.50
69 Markelle Fultz .30 .75
70 Gary Harris .30 .75
71 Buddy Hield .40 1.00
72 James Harden .75 2.00
73 Joe Ingles .30 .75
74 Rajon Rondo .50 1.25
75 Khris Middleton .40 1.00
76 Jayson Tatum 1.50 4.00
77 Mario Hezonja .25 .60
78 Denzel Valentine .25 .60
79 JJ Redick .40 1.00
80 Will Barton .25 .60
81 Zach Randolph .30 .75
82 Ryan Anderson .25 .60
83 Derrick Favors .25 .60
84 Kyle Kuzma .40 1.00
85 Giannis Antetokounmpo 2.00 5.00
86 Gordon Hayward .40 1.00
87 Kristaps Porzingis .50 1.25
88 Lauri Markkanen .60 1.50
89 Dario Saric .30 .75
90 Paul Millsap .30 .75
91 Willie Cauley-Stein .25 .60
92 Eric Gordon .30 .75
93 Rudy Gobert .50 1.25
94 LeBron James 3.00 8.00
95 Matthew Dellavedova .30 .75
96 Al Horford .40 1.00
97 Enes Kanter .30 .75
98 Robin Lopez .25 .60
99 Joel Embiid 1.00 2.50
100 Nikola Jokic 2.00 5.00
101 Dejounte Murray .50 1.25
102 Tyreke Evans .25 .60
103 John Wall .50 1.25
104 Mike Conley .30 .75
105 Jeff Teague .25 .60
106 Spencer Dinwiddie .30 .75
107 Russell Westbrook .60 1.50
108 George Hill .30 .75
109 Brandon Knight .25 .60
110 Reggie Jackson .25 .60
111 Danny Green .30 .75
112 Victor Oladipo .30 .75
113 Bradley Beal .50 1.25
114 MarShon Brooks .25 .60
115 Jimmy Butler .60 1.50
116 D'Angelo Russell .40 1.00
117 Paul George .60 1.50
118 JR Smith .40 1.00
119 Devin Booker 1.00 2.50
120 Luke Kennard .30 .75
121 Kawhi Leonard 1.00 2.50
122 Bojan Bogdanovic .30 .75
123 Otto Porter Jr. .30 .75
124 Dillon Brooks .40 1.00
125 Derrick Rose .75 2.00
126 DeMarre Carroll .25 .60
127 Carmelo Anthony .60 1.50
128 Kyle Korver .30 .75
129 TJ Warren .25 .60
130 Stanley Johnson .25 .60
131 LaMarcus Aldridge .40 1.00
132 Thaddeus Young .25 .60
133 Jeff Green .25 .60
134 JaMychal Green .25 .60
135 Andrew Wiggins .50 1.25
136 Rondae Hollis-Jefferson .25 .60
137 Steven Adams .30 .75
138 Kevin Love .30 .75
139 Josh Jackson .25 .60
140 Blake Griffin .40 1.00
141 Pau Gasol .60 1.50
142 Myles Turner .40 1.00
143 Dwight Howard .50 1.25
144 Marc Gasol .40 1.00
145 Karl-Anthony Towns .60 1.50
146 Jarrett Allen .40 1.00
147 Nerlens Noel .25 .60
148 Tristan Thompson .25 .60
149 Trevor Ariza .25 .60
150 Andre Drummond .30 .75
151 Jarred Vanderbilt RR RC 1.00 2.50
152 Jerome Robinson RR RC .50 1.25
153 Melvin Frazier Jr. RR RC .50 1.25
154 Zhaire Smith RR RC .50 1.25
155 Rodions Kurucs RR RC .60 1.50
156 Grayson Allen RR RC 1.00 2.50
157 Deandre Ayton RR RC 1.50 4.00
158 Landry Shamet RR RC .75 2.00
159 Elie Okobo RR RC .50 1.25
160 Mo Bamba RR RC .75 2.00
161 Bruce Brown RR RC 1.00 2.50
162 Shai Gilgeous-Alexander RR RC 12.00 30.00
163 Mitchell Robinson RR RC 1.25 3.00
164 Donte DiVincenzo RR RC 1.25 3.00
165 Vincent Edwards RR RC .50 1.25
166 Chandler Hutchison RR RC .60 1.50
167 Robert Williams III RR RC 1.00 2.50
168 Marvin Bagley III RR RC .75 2.00
169 Jevon Carter RR RC .75 2.00
170 Wendell Carter Jr. RR RC 1.25 3.00
171 Hamidou Diallo RR RC .75 2.00
172 Miles Bridges RR RC 1.25 3.00
173 Khyri Thomas RR RC .50 1.25
174 Lonnie Walker IV RR RC 1.00 2.50
175 Allonzo Trier RR RC .50 1.25
176 Aaron Holiday RR RC .75 2.00
177 Luka Doncic RR RC 20.00 50.00
178 Jacob Evans III RR RC .50 1.25
179 Jalen Brunson RR RC 4.00 10.00
180 Collin Sexton RR RC 1.50 4.00
181 De'Anthony Melton RR RC 1.00 2.50
182 Michael Porter Jr. RR RC 2.00 5.00
183 Justin Jackson RR RC .50 1.25
184 Kevin Huerter RR RC 1.00 2.50
185 Kostas Antetokounmpo RR RC .60 1.50
186 Anfernee Simons RR RC 2.50 6.00
187 Dzanan Musa RR RC .50 1.25
188 Jaren Jackson Jr. RR RC 4.00 10.00
189 Devonte' Graham RR RC 1.25 3.00
190 Kevin Knox RR RC .60 1.50
191 Keita Bates-Diop RR RC .60 1.50
192 Troy Brown Jr. RR RC .60 1.50
193 Svi Mykhailiuk RR RC .60 1.50
194 Josh Okogie RR RC .75 2.00
195 Chimezie Metu RR RC .60 1.50
196 Omari Spellman RR RC .50 1.25
197 Moritz Wagner RR RC 1.00 2.50
198 Trae Young RR RC 4.00 10.00
199 Gary Trent Jr. RR RC 1.00 2.50
200 Mikal Bridges RR RC 2.50 6.00

2018-19 Donruss Green Flood

*GRN FLD: 1X TO 2.5X BASIC
*GRN FLD RC: .5X TO 1.2X BASIC
85 Giannis Antetokounmpo 6.00 15.00
94 LeBron James 6.00 15.00
162 Shai Gilgeous-Alexander RR 25.00 60.00
177 Luka Doncic RR 40.00 100.00
198 Trae Young RR 40.00 100.00

2018-19 Donruss Holo Green and Yellow Laser

*HOLO GRN YLW LSR: 1X TO 2.5X BASIC
*HOLO GRN YLW LSR RC: 1X TO 2.5X BASIC

2018-19 Donruss Holo Green Laser

*HOLO GRN LSR: 2X TO 5X BASIC
*HOLO GRN LSR RC: 2X TO 5X BASIC
STATED PRINT RUN 99 SER.#'d SETS

2018-19 Donruss Holo Orange Laser

*HOLO ORNG LSR: 1.25X TO 3X BASIC
*HOLO ORNG LSR RC: 1.25X TO 3X BASIC

2018-19 Donruss Holo Pink Laser

*HOLO PNK LSR: 2.5X TO 6X BASIC
*HOLO PNK LSR RC: 2.5X TO 6X BASIC
STATED PRINT RUN 79 SER.#'d SETS

2018-19 Donruss Holo Yellow Laser

*HOLO YLW LSR: 5X TO 12X BASIC
*HOLO YLW LSR RC: 5X TO 12X BASIC
STATED PRINT RUN 25 SER.#'d SETS
177 Luka Doncic RR 1,500.00 3,000.00

2018-19 Donruss Press Proof Blue Laser

*PRESS BLUE LSR: 3X TO 8X BASIC
*PRESS BLUE LSR RC: 3X TO 8X BASIC
STATED PRINT RUN 49 SER.#'d SETS
177 Luka Doncic RR 800.00 1,500.00

2018-19 Donruss Press Proof Purple

*PRESS PURP: 1.5X TO 4X BASIC
*PRESS PURP RC: 1.5X TO 4X BASIC
STATED PRINT RUN 199 SER.#'d SETS

2018-19 Donruss Press Proof Red Laser

*PRESS RED LSR: 2X TO 5X BASIC
*PRESS RED LSR RC: 2X TO 5X BASIC
STATED PRINT RUN 99 SER.#'d SETS
177 Luka Doncic RR 400.00 800.00

2018-19 Donruss Press Proof Silver

*PRESS SLVR: 1.2X TO 3X BASIC
*PRESS SLVR RC: 1.25X TO 3X BASIC
STATED PRINT RUN 349 SER.#'d SETS

2018-19 Donruss All Clear for Takeoff

COMPLETE SET (15)
*PRESS: .5X TO 1.2X BASIC
1 LeBron James 4.00 10.00
2 Victor Oladipo .40 1.00
3 Dominique Wilkins .75 2.00
4 Larry Nance Jr. .30 .75
5 Zach LaVine .75 2.00
6 Russell Westbrook .75 2.00
7 Spud Webb .50 1.25
8 Dwight Howard .60 1.50
9 Shawn Kemp .75 2.00
10 Tracy McGrady .75 2.00
11 Blake Griffin .50 1.25
12 Donovan Mitchell 1.50 4.00
13 Julius Erving 1.25 3.00
14 Dennis Smith Jr. .30 .75
15 Kobe Bryant 4.00 10.00

2018-19 Donruss All Heart

COMPLETE SET (20)
*PRESS: .5X TO 1.2X BASIC
1 Allen Iverson 1.25 3.00
2 Jimmy Butler .75 2.00
3 Dwyane Wade 1.00 2.50
4 Giannis Antetokounmpo 2.50 6.00
5 Kevin Durant 2.00 5.00
6 Draymond Green .60 1.50
7 Paul Pierce .75 2.00
8 James Harden 1.00 2.50
9 Kevin Garnett 1.25 3.00
10 Russell Westbrook .75 2.00
11 Dirk Nowitzki 1.25 3.00
12 Andrew Wiggins .60 1.50
13 LeBron James 4.00 10.00
14 Dennis Rodman 1.25 3.00
15 Donovan Mitchell 1.50 4.00
16 Chris Paul 1.00 2.50
17 John Wall .60 1.50
18 Rudy Gay .50 1.25
19 Kobe Bryant 4.00 10.00
20 Stephen Curry 4.00 10.00

2018-19 Donruss All-Stars

COMPLETE SET (20)
*PRESS: .5X TO 1.2X BASIC
1 LeBron James 4.00 10.00
2 Kevin Durant 2.00 5.00
3 Russell Westbrook .75 2.00
4 Kyrie Irving 1.25 3.00
5 Anthony Davis 1.25 3.00
6 Paul George .75 2.00
7 Andre Drummond .40 1.00
8 Bradley Beal .60 1.50
9 Victor Oladipo .40 1.00
10 Kemba Walker .40 1.00
11 James Harden 1.00 2.50
12 DeMar DeRozan .60 1.50
13 Stephen Curry 4.00 10.00
14 Giannis Antetokounmpo 2.50 6.00
15 Joel Embiid 1.25 3.00
16 Kyle Lowry .50 1.25
17 Klay Thompson 1.25 3.00
18 Damian Lillard 1.25 3.00
19 Draymond Green .60 1.50
20 Karl-Anthony Towns .75 2.00

2018-19 Donruss Court Kings

COMPLETE SET (40)
*GREEN FLOOD: .5X TO 1.2X BASIC
*PRESS: .6X TO 1.5X BASIC
*PRESS ORANGE/125: .8X TO 2X BASIC
*PRESS RED/99: 1X TO 2.5X BASIC
*PRESS BLUE/49: 1.2X TO 3X BASIC
*PRESS PURPLE/49: 1.2X TO 3X BASIC
1 James Harden 1.00 2.50
2 Ben Simmons .50 1.25
3 Kyle Kuzma .50 1.25
4 CJ McCollum .50 1.25
5 Bradley Beal .60 1.50
6 Dennis Smith Jr. .30 .75
7 Kyrie Irving 1.25 3.00
8 Kyle Lowry .50 1.25
9 John Wall .60 1.50
10 Dwight Howard .60 1.50
11 DeMarcus Cousins .40 1.00
12 Dirk Nowitzki 1.25 3.00
13 Damian Lillard 1.25 3.00
14 Donovan Mitchell 1.50 4.00
15 Victor Oladipo .40 1.00
16 Marc Gasol .50 1.25
17 LaMarcus Aldridge .50 1.25
18 Russell Westbrook .75 2.00
19 LeBron James 4.00 10.00
20 Giannis Antetokounmpo 2.50 6.00
21 Stephen Curry 4.00 10.00
22 Lonzo Ball .50 1.25
23 Rudy Gobert .50 1.25
24 Goran Dragic .40 1.00
25 Jayson Tatum 2.00 5.00
26 Jimmy Butler .75 2.00
27 Kevin Durant 2.00 5.00
28 Dwyane Wade 1.00 2.50
29 Blake Griffin .50 1.25
30 Zach LaVine .75 2.00
31 Joel Embiid 1.25 3.00
32 D'Angelo Russell .50 1.25
33 Karl-Anthony Towns .75 2.00
34 Paul George .75 2.00
35 Chris Paul 1.00 2.50
36 Klay Thompson 1.25 3.00
37 Kristaps Porzingis .60 1.50
38 Andrew Wiggins .60 1.50
39 DeMar DeRozan .60 1.50
40 Anthony Davis 1.25 3.00

2018-19 Donruss Dominator Signatures

COMPLETE SET (39)
1 Aaron Gordon/99 5.00 12.00
2 Stephen Curry/49 500.00 1,000.00
4 Kyrie Irving/99 25.00 60.00
6 Kawhi Leonard/25 40.00 100.00
11 Eric Gordon/99 4.00 10.00
12 Dwyane Wade/25 40.00 100.00
13 JJ Redick/99 5.00 12.00
14 Dirk Nowitzki/25 75.00 200.00
15 Elfrid Payton/99 4.00 10.00
16 Giannis Antetokounmpo/45 100.00 250.00
17 Trevor Ariza/99 3.00 8.00
18 Jeremy Lin/49 30.00 80.00
19 Malcolm Brogdon/99 5.00 12.00
20 Brook Lopez/99 4.00 10.00
21 Goran Dragic/99 4.00 10.00
22 Chris Paul/25 40.00 100.00
23 Reggie Jackson/25 6.00 15.00
25 Jrue Holiday/99 6.00 15.00
26 Karl-Anthony Towns/49 10.00 25.00
27 JR Smith/99 5.00 12.00
28 LaMarcus Aldridge/49 6.00 15.00
29 Thon Maker/99 3.00 8.00
30 Rodney Hood/99 4.00 10.00
31 Eric Bledsoe/99 4.00 10.00
32 Damian Lillard/25 40.00 100.00
33 Michael Kidd-Gilchrist/99 3.00 8.00
34 Blake Griffin/25 8.00 20.00
35 Myles Turner/99 5.00 12.00
36 Joel Embiid/49 75.00 200.00
37 Kyle Korver/99 4.00 10.00
38 Gordon Hayward/99 5.00 12.00
39 Gerald Green/99 4.00 10.00
40 Al Horford/99 5.00 12.00

2018-19 Donruss Express Lane

COMPLETE SET (25)
*GREEN FLOOD: .5X TO 1.2X BASIC
*HOLO RED LSR/99: 1X TO 2.5X BASIC
*HOLO YLW LSR/25: 1.5X TO 4X BASIC
1 Jrue Holiday .60 1.50
2 Isiah Thomas .75 2.00
3 Ben Simmons .50 1.25
4 LeBron James 4.00 10.00
5 Kobe Bryant 4.00 10.00
6 Russell Westbrook .75 2.00
7 Lonzo Ball .50 1.25
8 CJ McCollum .50 1.25
9 Brandon Ingram .50 1.25
10 Chris Paul 1.00 2.50
11 Harrison Barnes .40 1.00
12 Allen Iverson 1.25 3.00
13 Victor Oladipo .40 1.00
14 Dwyane Wade 1.00 2.50
15 Bradley Beal .60 1.50
16 Isaiah Thomas .40 1.00
17 Devin Booker 1.25 3.00
18 Stephen Curry 4.00 10.00
19 Damian Lillard 1.25 3.00
20 Kevin Johnson .50 1.25
21 Jimmy Butler .75 2.00
22 Tony Parker .75 2.00
23 Giannis Antetokounmpo 2.50 6.00
24 Gary Payton .60 1.50
25 Klay Thompson 1.25 3.00

2018-19 Donruss Fantasy Stars

COMPLETE SET (5)
*GREEN FLOOD: .5X TO 1.2X BASIC
*HOLO RED LSR/99: 1X TO 2.5X BASIC
*HOLO YLW LSR/25: 1.5X TO 4X BASIC
1 Anthony Davis 1.25 3.00
2 LeBron James 4.00 10.00
3 James Harden 1.00 2.50
4 Karl-Anthony Towns .75 2.00
5 Kevin Durant 2.00 5.00

2018-19 Donruss Franchise Features

COMPLETE SET (30)
*GREEN FLOOD: .5X TO 1.2X BASIC
*HOLO RED LSR/99: 1X TO 2.5X BASIC
*HOLO YLW LSR/25: 1.5X TO 4X BASIC
1 Taurean Prince .30 .75
2 Kyrie Irving 1.25 3.00
3 D'Angelo Russell .50 1.25
4 Kemba Walker .40 1.00
5 Lauri Markkanen .75 2.00
6 LeBron James 4.00 10.00
7 Dennis Smith Jr. .30 .75
8 Nikola Jokic 2.50 6.00
9 Andre Drummond .40 1.00
10 Stephen Curry 4.00 10.00
11 James Harden 1.00 2.50
12 Victor Oladipo .40 1.00
13 Lou Williams .40 1.00
14 Kevin Love .40 1.00
15 Marc Gasol .50 1.25
16 Dwyane Wade 1.00 2.50
17 Giannis Antetokounmpo 2.50 6.00
18 Karl-Anthony Towns .75 2.00
19 Anthony Davis 1.25 3.00
20 Kristaps Porzingis .60 1.50
21 Russell Westbrook .75 2.00
22 Aaron Gordon .50 1.25
23 Ben Simmons .50 1.25
24 Devin Booker 1.25 3.00
25 Damian Lillard 1.25 3.00
26 De'Aaron Fox 1.00 2.50
27 LaMarcus Aldridge .50 1.25
28 Kyle Lowry .50 1.25
29 Donovan Mitchell 1.50 4.00
30 John Wall .60 1.50

2018-19 Donruss Hall Dominator Signatures

COMPLETE SET (30)
1 Jamaal Wilkes/99 5.00 12.00
2 Willis Reed/99 15.00 40.00
3 David Thompson/99 6.00 15.00
4 Artis Gilmore/99 6.00 15.00
5 Elvin Hayes/99 6.00 15.00
6 Karl Malone/25 30.00 80.00
7 Lenny Wilkens/99 6.00 15.00
8 Julius Erving/25 30.00 80.00
9 Louie Dampier/99 5.00 12.00
10 David Robinson/49 20.00 50.00
11 Tom Heinsohn/99 20.00 50.00
12 Bob Lanier/99 6.00 15.00
13 Bob McAdoo/99 6.00 15.00
14 George Gervin/99 8.00 20.00
15 Robert Parish/99 8.00 20.00
16 John Stockton/25 25.00 60.00
17 Bill Walton/99 15.00 40.00
18 Oscar Robertson/25 30.00 80.00
19 Dikembe Mutombo/99 15.00 40.00
20 Clyde Drexler/49 20.00 50.00
21 Adrian Dantley/99 4.00 10.00
22 Sam Jones/99 12.00 30.00
23 Dan Issel/99 6.00 15.00
24 Calvin Murphy/99 4.00 10.00
25 Gail Goodrich/99 5.00 12.00
26 Magic Johnson/25 40.00 100.00
27 Ralph Sampson/99 4.00 10.00
28 Alonzo Mourning/49 15.00 40.00
29 George McGinnis/99 6.00 15.00
30 Dennis Rodman/49 40.00 100.00

2018-19 Donruss Hall Kings

COMPLETE SET (30)
*GREEN FLOOD: .5X TO 1.2X BASIC
*PRESS: .6X TO 1.5X BASIC
*PRESS ORANGE/125: .8X TO 2X BASIC
*PRESS RED/99: 1X TO 2.5X BASIC
*PRESS BLUE/49: 1.2X TO 3X BASIC
*PRESS PURPLE/49: 1.2X TO 3X BASIC
1 Dikembe Mutombo .75 2.00
2 Robert Parish .75 2.00
3 Clyde Drexler .75 2.00
4 Karl Malone 1.00 2.50
5 Wilt Chamberlain 1.50 4.00
6 Gary Payton .60 1.50
7 Rick Barry .60 1.50
8 Ray Allen .60 1.50
9 Bill Russell 1.50 4.00
10 Hakeem Olajuwon .60 1.50
11 Patrick Ewing .75 2.00
12 Kareem Abdul-Jabbar 1.50 4.00
13 Dominique Wilkins .75 2.00
14 Jason Kidd .75 2.00
15 Oscar Robertson 1.00 2.50
16 Artis Gilmore .60 1.50
17 John Havlicek .75 2.00
18 David Robinson 1.00 2.50
19 Magic Johnson 2.00 5.00
20 Steve Nash 1.00 2.50
21 Scottie Pippen 1.25 3.00
22 John Stockton 1.00 2.50
23 Charles Barkley 1.00 2.50
24 Reggie Miller 1.00 2.50
25 Grant Hill .75 2.00
26 Elvin Hayes .60 1.50
27 Isiah Thomas .75 2.00
28 Julius Erving 1.25 3.00
29 Larry Bird 2.00 5.00
30 Shaquille O'Neal 1.50 4.00

2018-19 Donruss Jersey Series

COMPLETE SET (60)
1 John Wall 3.00 8.00
2 DeAndre Jordan 2.00 5.00
3 Scottie Pippen 6.00 15.00
4 Michael Redd 2.00 5.00
5 Anthony Davis 6.00 15.00
6 Dennis Schroder 2.00 5.00
7 Nikola Vucevic 2.00 5.00
8 LeBron James 12.00 30.00
9 Jonas Valanciunas 2.50 6.00
10 Andre Drummond 2.00 5.00
11 Bradley Beal 3.00 8.00
12 Blake Griffin 2.50 6.00
13 Wesley Matthews 1.50 4.00
14 Andrew Wiggins 3.00 8.00
15 Jrue Holiday 3.00 8.00
16 Larry Bird 10.00 25.00
17 CJ McCollum 2.50 6.00
18 Dirk Nowitzki 6.00 15.00
19 Rudy Gobert 3.00 8.00
20 Klay Thompson 6.00 15.00
21 Marcin Gortat 1.50 4.00
22 Kobe Bryant 20.00 50.00
23 Shawn Marion 2.00 5.00
24 Karl-Anthony Towns 4.00 10.00
25 Kristaps Porzingis 3.00 8.00
26 Rondae Hollis-Jefferson 1.50 4.00
27 Damian Lillard 6.00 15.00
28 Dwight Powell 1.50 4.00
29 Rodney Hood 2.00 5.00
30 Trevor Ariza 1.50 4.00
31 DeAndre' Bembry 1.50 4.00
32 Shaquille O'Neal 8.00 20.00
33 Harrison Barnes 2.00 5.00
34 Gorgui Dieng 1.50 4.00
35 Tim Hardaway Jr. 1.50 4.00
36 Nicolas Batum 1.50 4.00
37 Willie Cauley-Stein 1.50 4.00
38 J.J. Barea 2.50 6.00
39 Enes Kanter 2.00 5.00
40 Eric Gordon 2.00 5.00
41 Yogi Ferrell 1.50 4.00
42 Thon Maker 1.50 4.00
43 Stephen Curry 20.00 50.00
44 Kevin Garnett 6.00 15.00
45 Steven Adams 2.00 5.00
46 Kevin Love 2.00 5.00
47 David Robinson 5.00 12.00
48 Grant Hill 4.00 10.00
49 Karl Malone 5.00 12.00
50 Danny Granger 1.50 4.00
51 Jimmy Butler 4.00 10.00
52 Carmelo Anthony 4.00 10.00
53 Kris Dunn 2.00 5.00
54 Pau Gasol 4.00 10.00
55 Lance Stephenson 2.00 5.00
56 Rudy Gay 2.50 6.00
57 Nerlens Noel 1.50 4.00
58 Goran Dragic 2.00 5.00
59 DeMarcus Cousins 2.00 5.00
60 Ryan Anderson 1.50 4.00

2018-19 Donruss League Leaders

COMPLETE SET (10)
*GREEN FLOOD: .5X TO 1.2X BASIC
*HOLO RED LSR/99: 1X TO 2.5X BASIC
*HOLO YLW LSR/25: 1.5X TO 4X BASIC
1 James Harden 1.00 2.50
2 Andre Drummond .40 1.00
3 Russell Westbrook .75 2.00
4 Victor Oladipo .40 1.00
5 Anthony Davis 1.25 3.00
6 James Harden 1.00 2.50
7 Darren Collison .30 .75
8 Stephen Curry 4.00 10.00
9 LeBron James 4.00 10.00
10 Clint Capela .40 1.00

2018-19 Donruss Lock it Up

COMPLETE SET (10)
*GREEN FLOOD: .5X TO 1.2X BASIC
*HOLO RED LSR/99: 1X TO 2.5X BASIC
*HOLO YLW LSR/25: 1.5X TO 4X BASIC
1 Jimmy Butler .75 2.00
2 Victor Oladipo .40 1.00
3 Rudy Gobert .60 1.50
4 Giannis Antetokounmpo 2.50 6.00
5 Anthony Davis 1.25 3.00
6 Paul George .75 2.00
7 John Wall .60 1.50
8 Draymond Green .60 1.50
9 Chris Paul 1.00 2.50
10 Karl-Anthony Towns .75 2.00

2018-19 Donruss Next Day Autographs

COMPLETE SET (40)
1 Moritz Wagner 10.00 25.00
2 Mikal Bridges 100.00 250.00
3 Jacob Evans III 5.00 12.00
4 Jerome Robinson 5.00 12.00
5 Zhaire Smith 5.00 12.00
6 Deandre Ayton 75.00 200.00
7 Kevin Huerter 20.00 50.00
8 Jaren Jackson Jr. 400.00 800.00
9 Chandler Hutchison 6.00 15.00
10 Wendell Carter Jr. 12.00 30.00
11 Landry Shamet 8.00 20.00
12 Shai Gilgeous-Alexander 1,500.00 3,000.00
13 Dzanan Musa 5.00 12.00
14 Michael Porter Jr. 125.00 300.00
15 Donte DiVincenzo 60.00 150.00
16 Marvin Bagley III 20.00 50.00
17 Josh Okogie 8.00 20.00
18 Trae Young 1,500.00 3,000.00
19 Aaron Holiday 8.00 20.00
20 Collin Sexton 50.00 120.00
21 Robert Williams III 40.00 100.00
22 Svi Mykhailiuk 6.00 15.00
23 Omari Spellman 5.00 12.00
24 Troy Brown Jr. 6.00 15.00
25 Lonnie Walker IV 20.00 50.00
26 Luka Doncic 3,000.00 6,000.00
27 Grayson Allen 25.00 60.00
28 Mo Bamba 15.00 40.00
29 Anfernee Simons 75.00 200.00
30 Kevin Knox 6.00 15.00
31 Elie Okobo 5.00 12.00
32 Jevon Carter 8.00 20.00
33 Jalen Brunson 400.00 800.00
34 Devonte' Graham 8.00 20.00
35 Gary Trent Jr. 20.00 50.00
36 Jarred Vanderbilt 15.00 40.00
37 Bruce Brown 15.00 40.00
38 Hamidou Diallo 8.00 20.00
39 De'Anthony Melton 20.00 50.00
40 Keita Bates-Diop 6.00 15.00

2018-19 Donruss Retro Series

COMPLETE SET (30)
*PRESS: .5X TO 1.2X BASIC
1 Baron Davis .40 1.00
2 Paul Pierce .75 2.00
3 Kevin Garnett 1.25 3.00
4 John Stockton 1.00 2.50
5 Allen Iverson 1.25 3.00
6 Amar'e Stoudemire .50 1.25
7 Larry Bird 2.00 5.00
8 Stephon Marbury .60 1.50
9 Ray Allen .60 1.50
10 Shaquille O'Neal 1.50 4.00
11 Tim Duncan 1.25 3.00
12 Scottie Pippen 1.25 3.00
13 Anfernee Hardaway 1.25 3.00
14 Karl Malone 1.00 2.50
15 Dennis Johnson .50 1.25
16 Charles Barkley 1.00 2.50
17 Oscar Robertson 1.00 2.50
18 Tracy McGrady .75 2.00
19 Manute Bol .50 1.25
20 Gary Payton .60 1.50
21 Julius Erving 1.25 3.00
22 Dennis Rodman 1.25 3.00
23 Kobe Bryant 4.00 10.00
24 Grant Hill .75 2.00
25 Magic Johnson 2.00 5.00
26 Reggie Miller 1.00 2.50
27 Pete Maravich 1.25 3.00
28 Steve Nash 1.00 2.50
29 Wilt Chamberlain 1.50 4.00
30 Drazen Petrovic .60 1.50

2018-19 Donruss Rookie Dominator Signatures

COMPLETE SET (30)
STATED PRINT RUN 99 SER.#'d SETS
1 Moritz Wagner 6.00 15.00
2 Mikal Bridges 15.00 40.00
3 Jacob Evans III 3.00 8.00
4 Jerome Robinson 3.00 8.00
5 Zhaire Smith 3.00 8.00
6 Deandre Ayton 10.00 25.00
7 Kevin Huerter 6.00 15.00
8 Jaren Jackson Jr. 75.00 200.00
9 Chandler Hutchison 4.00 10.00
10 Wendell Carter Jr. 8.00 20.00
11 Landry Shamet 5.00 12.00
12 Shai Gilgeous-Alexander 300.00 600.00
13 Dzanan Musa 3.00 8.00
14 Michael Porter Jr. 12.00 30.00
15 Donte DiVincenzo 8.00 20.00
16 Marvin Bagley III 5.00 12.00
17 Josh Okogie 5.00 12.00
18 Trae Young 300.00 600.00
19 Aaron Holiday 5.00 12.00
20 Collin Sexton 10.00 25.00
21 Robert Williams III 6.00 15.00
22 Jalen Brunson 40.00 100.00
23 Omari Spellman 3.00 8.00
24 Troy Brown Jr. 4.00 10.00
25 Lonnie Walker IV 6.00 15.00
26 Luka Doncic 800.00 1,500.00
27 Grayson Allen 6.00 15.00
28 Mo Bamba 5.00 12.00
29 Anfernee Simons 15.00 40.00
30 Kevin Knox 4.00 10.00

2018-19 Donruss Rookie Jerseys

COMPLETE SET (40)
*PRIME/25: .75X TO 2X BASIC
1 Moritz Wagner 3.00 8.00
2 Mikal Bridges 8.00 20.00
3 Jacob Evans III 1.50 4.00
4 Jerome Robinson 1.50 4.00
5 Zhaire Smith 1.50 4.00
6 Deandre Ayton 5.00 12.00
7 Kevin Huerter 3.00 8.00
8 Jaren Jackson Jr. 12.00 30.00
9 Chandler Hutchison 2.00 5.00
10 Wendell Carter Jr. 4.00 10.00
11 Landry Shamet 2.50 6.00
12 Shai Gilgeous-Alexander 15.00 40.00
13 Dzanan Musa 1.50 4.00
14 Michael Porter Jr. 6.00 15.00
15 Donte DiVincenzo 4.00 10.00
16 Marvin Bagley III 2.50 6.00
17 Josh Okogie 2.50 6.00
18 Trae Young 15.00 40.00
19 Aaron Holiday 2.50 6.00
20 Collin Sexton 5.00 12.00
21 Robert Williams III 3.00 8.00
22 Svi Mykhailiuk 2.00 5.00
23 Omari Spellman 1.50 4.00
24 Troy Brown Jr. 2.00 5.00
25 Lonnie Walker IV 3.00 8.00
26 Luka Doncic 25.00 60.00
27 Grayson Allen 3.00 8.00
28 Mo Bamba 2.50 6.00
29 Anfernee Simons 8.00 20.00
30 Kevin Knox 2.00 5.00
31 Elie Okobo 1.50 4.00
32 Jevon Carter 2.50 6.00
33 Jalen Brunson 12.00 30.00
34 Devonte' Graham 2.50 6.00
35 Gary Trent Jr. 3.00 8.00
36 Jarred Vanderbilt 3.00 8.00
37 Bruce Brown 3.00 8.00
38 Hamidou Diallo 2.50 6.00
39 De'Anthony Melton 3.00 8.00
40 Keita Bates-Diop 2.00 5.00

2018-19 Donruss Rookie Kings

COMPLETE SET (30)
*GREEN FLOOD: .5X TO 1.2X BASIC
*PRESS: .6X TO 1.5X BASIC
*PRESS ORANGE/125: .8X TO 2X BASIC
*PRESS RED/99: 1X TO 2.5X BASIC
*PRESS BLUE/49: 1.2X TO 3X BASIC
*PRESS PURPLE/49: 1.2X TO 3X BASIC
1 Wendell Carter Jr. 1.00 2.50
2 Mo Bamba .60 1.50
3 Dzanan Musa .40 1.00
4 Marvin Bagley III .60 1.50
5 Moritz Wagner .75 2.00
6 Aaron Holiday .60 1.50
7 Jerome Robinson .40 1.00
8 Miles Bridges 1.00 2.50
9 Kevin Huerter .75 2.00
10 Lonnie Walker IV .75 2.00
11 Landry Shamet .60 1.50
12 Anfernee Simons 2.00 5.00
13 Michael Porter Jr. 1.50 4.00
14 Josh Okogie .75 2.00
15 Mikal Bridges 2.00 5.00
16 Collin Sexton 1.25 3.00
17 Zhaire Smith .40 1.00
18 Omari Spellman .40 1.00
19 Jaren Jackson Jr. 3.00 8.00
20 Luka Doncic 6.00 15.00
21 Shai Gilgeous-Alexander 4.00 10.00
22 Kevin Knox .50 1.25
23 Donte DiVincenzo 1.00 2.50
24 Trae Young 8.00 20.00
25 Jacob Evans III .40 1.00
26 Robert Williams III .75 2.00
27 Deandre Ayton 1.25 3.00
28 Troy Brown Jr. .50 1.25
29 Chandler Hutchison .50 1.25
30 Grayson Allen .75 2.00

2018-19 Donruss Rookie Materials Signatures

COMPLETE SET (39)
STATED PRINT RUN 99 SER.#'d SETS
1 Robert Williams III 8.00 20.00
2 Moritz Wagner 8.00 20.00
3 Lonnie Walker IV 15.00 40.00
4 Zhaire Smith 4.00 10.00
5 Anfernee Simons 20.00 50.00
6 Chandler Hutchison 5.00 12.00
7 Jalen Brunson 30.00 80.00
8 Dzanan Musa 4.00 10.00
9 Bruce Brown 8.00 20.00
10 Josh Okogie 6.00 15.00
11 Svi Mykhailiuk 5.00 12.00
12 Mikal Bridges 20.00 50.00
13 Luka Doncic 400.00 800.00
14 Deandre Ayton 12.00 30.00
15 Kevin Knox 6.00 15.00
16 Wendell Carter Jr. 10.00 25.00
17 Devonte' Graham 6.00 15.00
18 Michael Porter Jr. 12.00 30.00
19 Hamidou Diallo 6.00 15.00
RMS-TYG Trae Young 100.00 250.00
21 Omari Spellman 4.00 10.00
22 Jacob Evans III 4.00 10.00
23 Grayson Allen 8.00 20.00
24 Kevin Huerter 8.00 20.00
25 Elie Okobo 4.00 10.00
26 Landry Shamet 6.00 15.00
27 Gary Trent Jr. 8.00 20.00
28 Donte DiVincenzo 10.00 25.00
29 De'Anthony Melton 8.00 20.00
30 Aaron Holiday 6.00 15.00
31 Troy Brown Jr. 5.00 12.00
32 Jerome Robinson 4.00 10.00
33 Mo Bamba 6.00 15.00
34 Jaren Jackson Jr. 60.00 150.00
36 Shai Gilgeous-Alexander 500.00 1,000.00
37 Jarred Vanderbilt 8.00 20.00
38 Marvin Bagley III 6.00 15.00

39 Keita Bates-Diop 5.00 12.00
40 Collin Sexton 12.00 30.00

2018-19 Donruss Signature Series
COMPLETE SET (99)
1 Luke Kornet 3.00 8.00
2 LaMarcus Aldridge 5.00 12.00
3 Bryn Forbes 4.00 10.00
4 Michael Carter-Williams 3.00 8.00
5 Marquese Chriss 3.00 8.00
6 Tyson Chandler 4.00 10.00
7 Tony Snell 3.00 8.00
8 Kentavious Caldwell-Pope 3.00 8.00
9 Devin Robinson 3.00 8.00
10 Alonzo Mourning 10.00 25.00
11 Zhou Qi 3.00 8.00
12 Jrue Holiday 6.00 15.00
13 Tyrone Wallace 3.00 8.00
14 Rodney Hood 4.00 10.00
15 Tyler Cavanaugh 3.00 8.00
16 Al Horford 5.00 12.00
17 Derrick Favors 3.00 8.00
18 Antonio Blakeney 5.00 12.00
19 Alize Johnson 5.00 12.00
20 David Robinson 10.00 25.00
21 Lorenzo Brown 3.00 8.00
22 Christian Laettner 5.00 12.00
23 Furkan Korkmaz 4.00 10.00
24 Calvin Murphy 4.00 10.00
25 Daryl Macon 3.00 8.00
26 George Gervin 8.00 20.00
27 TJ Warren 3.00 8.00
28 John Stockton 12.00 30.00
29 Jairus Lyles 4.00 10.00
30 Dennis Rodman 12.00 30.00
31 Kadeem Allen 3.00 8.00
32 Dragan Bender 3.00 8.00
33 Ian Clark 3.00 8.00
34 Nikola Mirotic 3.00 8.00
35 Billy Preston 3.00 8.00
36 Nick Van Exel 5.00 12.00
37 Trey Lyles 3.00 8.00
38 Kawhi Leonard 25.00 60.00
39 Isaac Bonga 4.00 10.00
40 Jeremy Lin 8.00 20.00
41 Wade Baldwin IV 3.00 8.00
42 Brook Lopez 4.00 10.00
43 Jarell Martin 3.00 8.00
44 Eric Bledsoe 4.00 10.00
45 Bismack Biyombo 3.00 8.00
46 Nate Archibald 6.00 15.00
47 Marcus Paige 3.00 8.00
48 Magic Johnson 20.00 50.00
49 Edmond Sumner 3.00 8.00
50 Michael Porter Jr. 12.00 30.00
51 Grayson Allen 6.00 15.00
52 Jaren Jackson Jr. 125.00 300.00
53 Bruce Brown 6.00 15.00
54 Svi Mykhailiuk 4.00 10.00
55 Chandler Hutchison 4.00 10.00
56 Trae Young 25.00 60.00
57 Hamidou Diallo 5.00 12.00
58 Aaron Holiday 5.00 12.00
59 Jerome Robinson 3.00 8.00
60 Justin Jackson 3.00 8.00
61 Deandre Ayton 25.00 60.00
62 Devonte' Graham 5.00 12.00
63 Shai Gilgeous-Alexander 400.00 800.00
64 Josh Okogie 5.00 12.00
65 Robert Williams III 6.00 15.00
66 Gary Trent Jr. 6.00 15.00
67 J.P. Macura 4.00 10.00
68 Luka Doncic 500.00 1,000.00
69 Melvin Frazier Jr. 3.00 8.00
70 Kevin Huerter 6.00 15.00
71 Landry Shamet 5.00 12.00
72 Kevin Knox 4.00 10.00
73 Mitchell Robinson 8.00 20.00
74 Chimezie Metu 4.00 10.00
75 Marvin Bagley III 5.00 12.00
76 Mikal Bridges 15.00 40.00
77 Khyri Thomas 3.00 8.00
78 Jacob Evans III 3.00 8.00
79 Zhaire Smith 3.00 8.00
80 Kostas Antetokounmpo 4.00 10.00
81 Elie Okobo 3.00 8.00
82 Keita Bates-Diop 4.00 10.00
83 Donte DiVincenzo 4.00 10.00
84 Omari Spellman 3.00 8.00
85 Jevon Carter 5.00 12.00
86 Lonnie Walker IV 6.00 15.00
87 Jalen Brunson 25.00 60.00
88 Trevon Bluiett 3.00 8.00
89 Anfernee Simons 15.00 40.00
90 Mo Bamba 5.00 12.00
91 Troy Brown Jr. 4.00 10.00
92 Vincent Edwards 3.00 8.00
93 Moritz Wagner 6.00 15.00
94 Wendell Carter Jr. 8.00 20.00
95 Yante Maten 3.00 8.00
96 Collin Sexton 10.00 25.00
97 De'Anthony Melton 6.00 15.00
98 Dzanan Musa 3.00 8.00
99 Rodions Kurucs 4.00 10.00

2018-19 Donruss Significant Signatures
COMPLETE SET (99)
EXCHANGE DEADLINE 5/07/2020
1 David Robinson 8.00 20.00
2 Antoine Walker 4.00 10.00
3 Christian Laettner 5.00 12.00
4 Otis Birdsong 4.00 10.00
5 Kentavious Caldwell-Pope 3.00 8.00
6 Hersey Hawkins 3.00 8.00
7 George Gervin 8.00 20.00
8 Rafer Alston 4.00 10.00
9 John Stockton 8.00 20.00
10 TJ Warren 3.00 8.00
11 Dennis Rodman 12.00 30.00
12 Sam Perkins 4.00 10.00
13 Dragan Bender 3.00 8.00
14 Kerry Kittles 3.00 8.00
15 Nikola Mirotic 3.00 8.00
16 Detlef Schrempf 5.00 12.00
17 Nick Van Exel 5.00 12.00
18 Tariq Abdul-Wahad 3.00 8.00
19 Kawhi Leonard 20.00 50.00
20 Paul Silas 5.00 12.00
21 Jeremy Lin 40.00 100.00
22 Joe Smith 4.00 10.00
23 Brook Lopez 4.00 10.00
24 Doug Collins 5.00 12.00
25 Charles Barkley 125.00 300.00
26 Chris Whitney 3.00 8.00
27 Derrick Favors 3.00 8.00
28 Zydrunas Ilgauskas 4.00 10.00
29 Magic Johnson 15.00 40.00
30 Fat Lever 4.00 10.00
31 LaMarcus Aldridge 5.00 12.00
32 Nazr Mohammed 3.00 8.00
33 Kobe Bryant EXCH 300.00 600.00
34 Dino Radja 3.00 8.00
35 Tyson Chandler 4.00 10.00
36 Mark Price 5.00 12.00
37 Calvin Murphy 4.00 10.00
38 Erick Dampier 3.00 8.00
39 Alonzo Mourning 8.00 20.00
40 Andrei Kirilenko 4.00 10.00
41 Jrue Holiday 6.00 15.00
42 Isaiah Rider 4.00 10.00
43 Kevin Durant EXCH 30.00 80.00
44 Sam Bowie 3.00 8.00
45 Al Horford 5.00 12.00
46 Jim Barnett 3.00 8.00
47 Jeff Hornacek 4.00 10.00
48 Jack Sikma 4.00 10.00
49 Kevin Hervey 3.00 8.00
50 Michael Porter Jr. 12.00 30.00
51 Grayson Allen 6.00 15.00
52 Jaren Jackson Jr. 125.00 300.00
53 Bruce Brown 6.00 15.00
54 Svi Mykhailiuk 4.00 10.00
55 Chandler Hutchison 4.00 10.00
56 Trae Young 25.00 60.00
57 Hamidou Diallo 5.00 12.00
58 Aaron Holiday 5.00 12.00
59 Jerome Robinson 3.00 8.00
60 Justin Jackson 3.00 8.00
61 Deandre Ayton 10.00 25.00
62 Devonte' Graham 5.00 12.00
63 Shai Gilgeous-Alexander 400.00 800.00
64 Josh Okogie 5.00 12.00
65 Robert Williams III 6.00 15.00
66 Gary Trent Jr. 6.00 15.00
67 Allonzo Trier 3.00 8.00
68 Luka Doncic 500.00 1,000.00
69 Melvin Frazier Jr. 3.00 8.00
70 Kevin Huerter 6.00 15.00
71 Landry Shamet 5.00 12.00
72 Kevin Knox 4.00 10.00
74 Chimezie Metu 4.00 10.00
75 Marvin Bagley III 5.00 12.00
76 Mikal Bridges 15.00 40.00
77 Khyri Thomas 3.00 8.00
78 Jacob Evans III 3.00 8.00
79 Zhaire Smith 3.00 8.00
80 Kostas Antetokounmpo 4.00 10.00
81 Elie Okobo 3.00 8.00
82 Keita Bates-Diop 4.00 10.00
83 Donte DiVincenzo 8.00 20.00
84 Omari Spellman 3.00 8.00
85 Jevon Carter 5.00 12.00
86 Lonnie Walker IV 6.00 15.00
87 Jalen Brunson 25.00 60.00
88 Trevon Bluiett 3.00 8.00
89 Anfernee Simons 15.00 40.00
90 Mo Bamba 5.00 12.00
91 Troy Brown Jr. 4.00 10.00
92 Vincent Edwards 3.00 8.00
93 Moritz Wagner 6.00 15.00
94 Wendell Carter Jr. 8.00 20.00
95 Billy Preston 3.00 8.00
96 Collin Sexton 10.00 25.00
97 De'Anthony Melton 6.00 15.00
98 Dzanan Musa 3.00 8.00

2018-19 Donruss Swishful Thinking
COMPLETE SET (10)
*PRESS: .5X TO 1.2X BASIC
1 Larry Bird 2.00 5.00
2 Klay Thompson 1.25 3.00
3 Kyle Lowry .50 1.25
4 Reggie Miller 1.00 2.50
5 Ray Allen .60 1.50
6 Steve Kerr .60 1.50
7 James Harden 1.00 2.50
8 Paul George .75 2.00
9 Stephen Curry 4.00 10.00
10 Kemba Walker .60 1.50

2018-19 Donruss The Rookies
COMPLETE SET (5)
*PRESS: .5X TO 1.2X BASIC
1 Deandre Ayton 1.00 2.50
2 Marvin Bagley III .50 1.25
3 Luka Doncic 30.00 80.00
4 Jaren Jackson Jr. 2.50 6.00
5 Trae Young 10.00 25.00

2018-19 Donruss The Rookies Press Proof
*PRESS: .5X TO 1.2X BASIC
3 Luka Doncic 60.00 150.00
5 Trae Young 15.00 40.00

2018-19 Donruss Timeless Treasures Materials Signatures
COMPLETE SET (39)
1 Calvin Murphy/99 5.00 12.00
2 J.J. Barea/99 6.00 15.00
3 John Stockton/25 20.00 50.00
4 Seth Curry/99 5.00 12.00
5 World B. Free/99 5.00 12.00
6 Andrew Wiggins/49 10.00 25.00
7 Jason Kidd/49 12.00 30.00
8 Spencer Dinwiddie/99 5.00 12.00
9 Shaquille O'Neal/25 40.00 100.00
10 Nick Van Exel/99 6.00 15.00
11 Alonzo Mourning/49 10.00 25.00
12 Dirk Nowitzki/16 40.00 100.00
13 Gordon Hayward/99 6.00 15.00
14 Alvan Adams/99 5.00 12.00
15 Karl Malone/25 20.00 50.00
16 Karl-Anthony Towns/49 12.00 30.00
17 Willie Cauley-Stein/99 4.00 10.00
18 Stephen Jackson/99 5.00 12.00
19 Tony Parker/49 12.00 30.00
20 Rik Smits/99 5.00 12.00
22 Dzanan Musa/99 4.00 10.00
23 Jarred Vanderbilt/99 8.00 20.00
24 Josh Okogie/99 6.00 15.00
25 Collin Sexton/99 12.00 30.00
26 Moritz Wagner/99 8.00 20.00
27 Troy Brown Jr./99 5.00 12.00
28 Zhaire Smith/99 4.00 10.00
29 Mo Bamba/99 6.00 15.00
30 Chandler Hutchison/99 5.00 12.00
31 Jalen Brunson/99 30.00 80.00
32 Michael Porter Jr./99 15.00 40.00
33 Bruce Brown/99 8.00 20.00
34 Trae Young/99 125.00 300.00
35 Robert Williams III/99 8.00 20.00
36 Mikal Bridges/99 20.00 50.00
37 Lonnie Walker IV/99 12.00 30.00
38 Deandre Ayton/99 12.00 30.00
39 Anfernee Simons/99 20.00 50.00
40 Keita Bates-Diop/99 5.00 12.00
41 Devonte' Graham/99 6.00 15.00
42 Donte DiVincenzo/99 10.00 25.00
43 Hamidou Diallo/99 6.00 15.00
44 Aaron Holiday/99 6.00 15.00
45 Svi Mykhailiuk/99 5.00 12.00
46 Jacob Evans III/99 4.00 10.00
47 Luka Doncic/99 500.00 1,000.00
48 Kevin Huerter/99 8.00 20.00
49 Kevin Knox/99 5.00 12.00
50 Landry Shamet/99 6.00 15.00
51 Gary Trent Jr./99 8.00 20.00
52 Marvin Bagley III/99 8.00 20.00
53 De'Anthony Melton/99 8.00 20.00
54 Wendell Carter Jr./99 10.00 25.00
55 Omari Spellman/99 4.00 10.00
56 Jerome Robinson/99 4.00 10.00
57 Grayson Allen/99 6.00 15.00
58 Jaren Jackson Jr./99 75.00 200.00
59 Elie Okobo/99 4.00 10.00
60 Shai Gilgeous-Alexander/99 200.00 500.00

2018-19 Donruss Winner Stays
COMPLETE SET (20)
*GREEN FLOOD: .5X TO 1.2X BASIC
*HOLO RED LSR/99: 1X TO 2.5X BASIC
*HOLO YLW LSR/25: 1.5X TO 4X BASIC
1 Dwyane Wade 1.00 2.50
2 Kobe Bryant 4.00 10.00
3 Dirk Nowitzki 1.25 3.00
4 Robert Parish .75 2.00
5 Kevin Durant 2.00 5.00
6 Dennis Rodman 1.25 3.00
7 Klay Thompson 1.25 3.00
8 Bill Russell 1.50 4.00
9 Tony Parker .75 2.00
10 Kareem Abdul-Jabbar 1.50 4.00
11 LeBron James 4.00 10.00
12 Tim Duncan 1.25 3.00
13 J.J. Barea .50 1.25
14 Shaquille O'Neal 1.50 4.00
15 Stephen Curry 4.00 10.00
16 Robert Horry .50 1.25
17 Kevin Love .40 1.00
18 Magic Johnson 2.00 5.00
19 Jerry West 1.00 2.50
20 Scottie Pippen 1.25 3.00

2019-20 Donruss
COMPLETE SET (250)
1 Trae Young .75 2.00
2 John Collins .30 .75
3 Kevin Huerter .30 .75
4 Vince Carter .60 1.50
5 Allen Crabbe .20 .50
6 Dewayne Dedmon .20 .50
7 Alex Len .20 .50
8 Jaylen Brown .50 1.25
9 Gordon Hayward .25 .60
10 Al Horford .30 .75
11 Kyrie Irving .60 1.50
12 Terry Rozier .25 .60
13 Marcus Smart .25 .60
14 Jayson Tatum 1.25 3.00
15 Robert Williams III .20 .50
16 Jarrett Allen .30 .75
17 DeMarre Carroll .20 .50
18 Taurean Prince .20 .50
19 Spencer Dinwiddie .25 .60
20 Joe Harris .25 .60
21 D'Angelo Russell .25 .60
22 Caris LeVert .25 .60
23 Dwayne Bacon .20 .50
24 Nicolas Batum .20 .50
25 Miles Bridges .30 .75
26 Kemba Walker .25 .60
27 Malik Monk .30 .75
28 Michael Kidd-Gilchrist .20 .50
29 Marvin Williams .20 .50
30 Wendell Carter Jr. .30 .75
31 Chandler Hutchison .20 .50
32 Kris Dunn .20 .50
33 Zach LaVine .50 1.25
34 Robin Lopez .20 .50
35 Lauri Markkanen .40 1.00
36 Otto Porter Jr. .20 .50
37 Jordan Clarkson .30 .75
38 Matthew Dellavedova .25 .60
39 Kevin Love .30 .75
40 Larry Nance Jr. .25 .60
41 Collin Sexton .40 1.00
42 JR Smith .20 .50
43 Tristan Thompson .20 .50
44 T.J. Warren .25 .60
45 Jalen Brunson .75 2.00
46 Luka Doncic 2.00 5.00
47 Tim Hardaway Jr. .20 .50
48 Justin Jackson .20 .50
49 Kristaps Porzingis .40 1.00
50 Courtney Lee .20 .50
51 Will Barton .20 .50
52 Malik Beasley .25 .60
53 Torrey Craig .20 .50
54 Gary Harris .25 .60
55 Nikola Jokic 1.50 4.00
56 Jamal Murray .50 1.25
57 Michael Porter Jr. .50 1.25
58 Andre Drummond .25 .60
59 Blake Griffin .30 .75
60 Luke Kennard .25 .60
61 Thon Maker .20 .50
62 Seth Curry .20 .50
63 Reggie Jackson .25 .60
64 Stephen Curry 2.50 6.00
65 DeMarcus Cousins .25 .60
66 Kevin Durant 1.00 2.50
67 Alfonzo McKinnie .20 .50
68 Quinn Cook .25 .60
69 Draymond Green .40 1.00
70 Andre Iguodala .25 .60
71 Klay Thompson .75 2.00
72 Kevon Looney .25 .60
73 Clint Capela .25 .60
74 Eric Gordon .25 .60
75 Jeff Green .20 .50
76 James Harden .60 1.50
77 Chris Paul .60 1.50
78 P.J. Tucker .25 .60
79 Bojan Bogdanovic .25 .60
80 Anthony Davis .75 2.00
81 Aaron Holiday .25 .60
82 Victor Oladipo .25 .60
83 Domantas Sabonis .40 1.00
84 Myles Turner .30 .75
85 Thaddeus Young .20 .50
86 Shai Gilgeous-Alexander 1.50 4.00
87 Danilo Gallinari .25 .60
88 Montrezl Harrell .25 .60
89 Landry Shamet .25 .60
90 Lou Williams .30 .75
91 Ivica Zubac .25 .60
92 Kentavious Caldwell-Pope .25 .60
93 Trevor Ariza .20 .50
94 LeBron James 2.50 6.00
95 Kyle Kuzma .40 1.00
96 Rajon Rondo .40 1.00
97 Mike Conley .25 .60
98 Avery Bradley .20 .50
99 Jae Crowder .20 .50
100 Bruno Caboclo .20 .50
101 Jeremy Lamb .20 .50
102 Jaren Jackson Jr. .50 1.25
103 Jonas Valanciunas .25 .60
104 Chandler Parsons .20 .50
105 Kyle Anderson .20 .50
106 Bam Adebayo .50 1.25
107 Goran Dragic .25 .60
108 Derrick Jones Jr. .20 .50
109 Josh Richardson .20 .50
110 Hassan Whiteside .20 .50
111 Justise Winslow .20 .50
112 Dion Waiters .20 .50
113 Giannis Antetokounmpo 1.50 4.00
114 Eric Bledsoe .25 .60
115 Pau Gasol .50 1.25
116 Malcolm Brogdon .25 .60
117 Khris Middleton .30 .75
118 Brook Lopez .20 .50
119 Nerlens Noel .20 .50
120 Josh Okogie .20 .50
121 Derrick Rose .60 1.50
122 Jeff Teague .20 .50
123 Karl-Anthony Towns .50 1.25
124 Andrew Wiggins .40 1.00
125 Robert Covington .20 .50
126 Lonzo Ball .30 .75
127 Brandon Ingram .30 .75
128 Josh Hart .25 .60
129 Jrue Holiday .40 1.00
130 Jahlil Okafor .20 .50
131 Julius Randle .40 1.00
132 Elfrid Payton .20 .50
133 Mario Hezonja .20 .50
134 DeAndre Jordan .25 .60
135 Kevin Knox II .25 .60
136 Frank Ntilikina .20 .50
137 Mitchell Robinson .30 .75
138 Allonzo Trier .20 .50
139 Steven Adams .20 .50
140 Hamidou Diallo .25 .60
141 Paul George .50 1.25
142 Russell Westbrook .50 1.25
143 Andre Roberson .20 .50
144 Terrance Ferguson .20 .50
145 Mo Bamba .25 .60
146 Evan Fournier .25 .60
147 D.J. Augustin .20 .50
148 Markelle Fultz .25 .60
149 Aaron Gordon .30 .75
150 Jonathan Isaac .30 .75
151 Nikola Vucevic .25 .60
152 Jimmy Butler .60 1.50
153 Joel Embiid .60 1.50
154 Tobias Harris .25 .60
155 Ben Simmons .30 .75
156 JJ Redick .30 .75
157 Zhaire Smith .20 .50
158 Deandre Ayton .30 .75
159 Devin Booker .07 .20
160 Tyler Johnson .20 .50
161 Josh Jackson .20 .50
162 Kelly Oubre Jr. .25 .60
163 Damian Lillard .75 2.00
164 CJ McCollum .30 .75
165 Jusuf Nurkic .25 .60
166 Evan Turner .20 .50
167 Enes Kanter .20 .50
168 Rodney Hood .25 .60
169 Marvin Bagley III .25 .60
170 Harrison Barnes .25 .60
171 Bogdan Bogdanovic .30 .75
172 Willie Cauley-Stein .25 .60
173 De'Aaron Fox .50 1.25
174 Harry Giles .25 .60
175 Buddy Hield .30 .75
176 LaMarcus Aldridge .30 .75
177 DeMar DeRozan .40 1.00
178 Rudy Gay .25 .60
179 Patty Mills .30 .75
180 Dejounte Murray .30 .75
181 Lonnie Walker IV .25 .60
182 Derrick White .30 .75
183 OG Anunoby .25 .60
184 Marc Gasol .30 .75
185 Danny Green .25 .60
186 Serge Ibaka .25 .60
187 Kawhi Leonard .75 2.00
188 Kyle Lowry .30 .75
189 Pascal Siakam .50 1.25
190 Fred VanVleet .40 1.00
191 Rudy Gobert .40 1.00
192 Derrick Favors .20 .50
193 Donovan Mitchell .60 1.50
194 Ricky Rubio .25 .60
195 Bradley Beal .40 1.00
196 Troy Brown Jr. .20 .50
197 Thomas Bryant .25 .60
198 Isaiah Thomas .25 .60
199 Jabari Parker .20 .50
200 John Wall .40 1.00
201 Zion Williamson RR RC 3.00 8.00
202 Ja Morant RR RC 4.00 10.00
203 RJ Barrett RR RC 1.50 4.00
204 De'Andre Hunter RR RC 1.50 4.00
205 Jarrett Culver RR RC .40 1.00
206 Coby White RR RC 1.25 3.00
207 Jaxson Hayes RR RC .60 1.50
208 Rui Hachimura RR RC 1.50 4.00
209 Cam Reddish RR RC .60 1.50
210 Cameron Johnson RR RC 1.00 2.50
211 PJ Washington Jr. RR RC 1.25 3.00
212 Tyler Herro RR RC 2.00 5.00
213 Romeo Langford RR RC .40 1.00
214 Sekou Doumbouya RR RC .40 1.00
215 Chuma Okeke RR RC .60 1.50
216 Nickeil Alexander-Walker RR RC .60 1.50
217 Goga Bitadze RR RC .50 1.25
218 Luka Samanic RR RC .50 1.25
219 Matisse Thybulle RR RC .75 2.00
220 Brandon Clarke RR RC .75 2.00
221 Grant Williams RR RC .60 1.50
222 Ty Jerome RR RC .75 2.00
223 Nassir Little RR RC .60 1.50
224 Dylan Windler RR RC .50 1.25
225 Mfiondu Kabengele RR RC .50 1.25
226 Jordan Poole RR RC 1.50 4.00
227 Keldon Johnson RR RC 1.25 3.00
228 Kevin Porter Jr. RR RC .75 2.00
229 Nicolas Claxton RR RC .50 1.25
230 KZ Okpala RR RC .50 1.25
231 Carsen Edwards RR RC .50 1.25
232 Bruno Fernando RR RC .50 1.25
233 Cody Martin RR RC .60 1.50
234 Bol Bol RR RC 1.00 2.50
235 Isaiah Roby RR RC .50 1.25
236 Daniel Gafford RR RC .75 2.00
237 Alen Smailagic RR RC .40 1.00
238 Eric Paschall RR RC .50 1.25
239 Admiral Schofield RR RC .50 1.25
240 Jaylen Nowell RR RC .50 1.25
241 Ignas Brazdeikis RR RC .50 1.25
242 Terance Mann RR RC .75 2.00
243 Quinndary Weatherspoon RR RC .40 1.00
244 Tremont Waters RR RC .50 1.25
245 Kyle Guy RR RC .50 1.25
246 Jordan Bone RR RC .40 1.00
247 Jalen McDaniels RR RC 1.00 2.50
248 Talen Horton-Tucker RR RC .60 1.50
249 Darius Bazley RR RC .60 1.50
250 Darius Garland RR RC 1.50 4.00

2019-20 Donruss Green Flood
*GRN FLD: 1X TO 2.5X BASIC
*GRN FLD RC: .5X TO 1.2X BASIC
94 LeBron James 12.00 30.00
201 Zion Williamson RR 30.00 80.00
202 Ja Morant RR 40.00 100.00

2019-20 Donruss Holo Green and Yellow Laser
*HOLO GRN YLW LSR: 1X TO 2.5X BASIC
*HOLO GRN YLW LSR RC: .75X TO 2X BASIC
94 LeBron James 20.00 50.00
201 Zion Williamson RR 50.00 120.00
202 Ja Morant RR 75.00 200.00
212 Tyler Herro RR 20.00 50.00
226 Jordan Poole RR 20.00 50.00

2019-20 Donruss Holo Green Laser
*HOLO GRN LSR: 1.5X TO 4X BASIC
*HOLO GRN LSR RC: 1.25X TO 3X BASIC
STATED PRINT RUN 99 SER.#'d SETS
94 LeBron James 100.00 250.00
201 Zion Williamson RR 75.00 200.00
202 Ja Morant RR 125.00 300.00
212 Tyler Herro RR 30.00 80.00
226 Jordan Poole RR 30.00 80.00

2019-20 Donruss Holo Orange Laser
*HOLO ORNG LSR: 1X TO 2.5X BASIC
*HOLO ORNG LSR RC: .75X TO 2X BASIC
201 Zion Williamson RR 50.00 120.00
202 Ja Morant RR 75.00 200.00
212 Tyler Herro RR 20.00 50.00
226 Jordan Poole RR 20.00 50.00

2019-20 Donruss Holo Pink Laser
*HOLO PINK LSR: 2.5X TO 6X BASIC
*HOLO PINK LSR RC: 2X TO 5X BASIC
STATED PRINT RUN 50 SER.#'d SETS
94 LeBron James 150.00 400.00
201 Zion Williamson RR 125.00 300.00
202 Ja Morant RR 200.00 500.00
212 Tyler Herro RR 50.00 120.00
226 Jordan Poole RR 50.00 120.00

2019-20 Donruss Holo Yellow Laser
*HOLO YLW LSR: 4X TO 10X BASIC
*HOLO YLW LSR RC: 3X TO 8X BASIC
STATED PRINT RUN 25 SER.#'d SETS
94 LeBron James 300.00 600.00
201 Zion Williamson RR 200.00 500.00
202 Ja Morant RR 400.00 800.00
212 Tyler Herro RR 75.00 200.00
226 Jordan Poole RR 75.00 200.00

2019-20 Donruss Infinite
*INFINITE RC: .5X TO 1.2X BASIC
201 Zion Williamson RR 50.00 120.00
202 Ja Morant RR 30.00 80.00
212 Tyler Herro RR 25.00 60.00

2019-20 Donruss Infinite Blue
*INFINITE BLUE: 3X TO 8X BASIC
*INFINITE BLUE RC: 1.5X TO 4X BASIC
STATED PRINT RUN 35 SER.#'d SETS
94 LeBron James 200.00 500.00
201 Zion Williamson RR 200.00 500.00
202 Ja Morant RR 125.00 300.00
212 Tyler Herro RR 125.00 300.00

2019-20 Donruss Infinite Red
*INFINITE RED: 2X TO 5X BASIC
*INFINITE RED RC: 1X TO 2.5X BASIC
STATED PRINT RUN 99 SER.#'d SETS
94 LeBron James 100.00 250.00
201 Zion Williamson RR 150.00 400.00
202 Ja Morant RR 60.00 150.00
212 Tyler Herro RR 40.00 100.00

2019-20 Donruss Press Proof Blue Laser
*PRESS BLUE LSR: 2.5X TO 6X BASIC
*PRESS BLUE LSR RC: 2X TO 5X BASIC
STATED PRINT RUN 49 SER.#'d SETS
94 LeBron James 150.00 400.00
201 Zion Williamson RR 125.00 300.00
202 Ja Morant RR 200.00 500.00
212 Tyler Herro RR 50.00 120.00
226 Jordan Poole RR 50.00 120.00

2019-20 Donruss Press Proof Purple
*PRESS PRPL: 1.25X TO 3X BASIC
*PRESS PRPL RC: 1X TO 2.5X BASIC
STATED PRINT RUN 199 SER.#'d SETS
94 LeBron James 75.00 200.00
201 Zion Williamson RR 60.00 150.00
202 Ja Morant RR 100.00 250.00
212 Tyler Herro RR 25.00 60.00
226 Jordan Poole RR 25.00 60.00

2019-20 Donruss Press Proof Red Laser
*PRESS RED LSR: 1.5X TO 4X BASIC
*PRESS RED LSR RC: 1.25X TO 3X BASIC
STATED PRINT RUN 99 SER.#'d SETS
94 LeBron James 100.00 250.00
201 Zion Williamson RR 75.00 200.00
202 Ja Morant RR 125.00 300.00
212 Tyler Herro RR 30.00 80.00
226 Jordan Poole RR 30.00 80.00

2019-20 Donruss Press Proof Silver
*PRESS SLVR: 1X TO 2.5X BASIC
*PRESS SLVR RC: .75X TO 2X BASIC
STATED PRINT RUN 349 SER.#'d SETS
94 LeBron James 60.00 150.00
201 Zion Williamson RR 50.00 120.00
202 Ja Morant RR 75.00 200.00
212 Tyler Herro RR 20.00 50.00
226 Jordan Poole RR 20.00 50.00

2019-20 Donruss Changing Stripes
*GREEN FLOOD: .5X TO 1.2X BASIC
*HOLO RED LSR/99: 1.25X TO 3X BASIC
*HOLO YLW LSR/25: 2X TO 5X BASIC
1 Jimmy Butler 1.00 2.50
2 Kemba Walker .40 1.00
3 Anthony Davis 1.25 3.00
4 Kevin Durant 1.50 4.00
5 D'Angelo Russell .40 1.00
6 Kyrie Irving 1.00 2.50
7 Kawhi Leonard 1.25 3.00
8 Paul George .75 2.00
9 Derrick Rose 1.00 2.50
10 Al Horford .50 1.25

2019-20 Donruss Changing Stripes Holo Yellow Laser
*HOLO YLW LSR/25: 2X TO 5X BASIC
STATED PRINT RUN 25 SER.#'d SETS

2019-20 Donruss Complete Players
*GREEN FLOOD: .5X TO 1.2X BASIC
1 Bradley Beal .60 1.50
2 Karl-Anthony Towns .75 2.00
3 Clint Capela .40 1.00
4 Damian Lillard 1.25 3.00
5 Pascal Siakam .75 2.00
6 Nikola Vucevic .40 1.00
7 Stephen Curry 4.00 10.00
8 James Harden 1.00 2.50
9 Kevin Durant 1.50 4.00
10 Nikola Jokic 2.50 6.00
11 Luka Doncic 3.00 8.00
12 Russell Westbrook .75 2.00
13 LaMarcus Aldridge .50 1.25
14 Paul George .75 2.00
15 Joel Embiid 1.00 2.50
16 LeBron James 4.00 10.00
17 Blake Griffin .50 1.25
18 Giannis Antetokounmpo 2.50 6.00
19 Kemba Walker .40 1.00
20 Rudy Gobert .60 1.50

2019-20 Donruss Complete Players Holo Red Laser
*HOLO RED LSR/99: 1X TO 2.5X BASIC
STATED PRINT RUN 99 SER.#'d SETS
11 Luka Doncic 12.00 30.00
16 LeBron James 25.00 60.00

2019-20 Donruss Complete Players Holo Yellow Laser
*HOLO YLW LSR/25: 1.5X TO 4X BASIC
STATED PRINT RUN 25 SER.#'d SETS
7 Stephen Curry 12.00 30.00
11 Luka Doncic 40.00 100.00
16 LeBron James 75.00 200.00
18 Giannis Antetokounmpo 12.00 30.00

2019-20 Donruss Crunch Time
*PRESS: .75X TO 2X BASIC
1 Paul George 1.00 2.50
2 LeBron James 20.00 50.00
3 Nikola Jokic 3.00 8.00
4 Giannis Antetokounmpo 8.00 20.00
5 Draymond Green .75 2.00
6 James Harden 1.25 3.00
7 Victor Oladipo .50 1.25
8 Kevin Durant 6.00 15.00
9 Bradley Beal .75 2.00
10 Luka Doncic 20.00 50.00
11 Damian Lillard 6.00 15.00
12 Stephen Curry 10.00 25.00
13 Chris Paul 1.25 3.00
14 Joel Embiid 1.25 3.00
15 Rudy Gobert .75 2.00
16 Russell Westbrook 1.00 2.50
17 Kemba Walker .50 1.25
18 Ben Simmons .60 1.50
19 Karl-Anthony Towns 1.00 2.50
20 Trae Young 1.50 4.00

2019-20 Donruss Dominator Signatures
STATED PRINT RUN 99 SER.#'d SETS
EXCHANGE DEADLINE 6/13/2021
1 Montrezl Harrell 4.00 10.00
2 Otto Porter Jr. 3.00 8.00
3 Robert Covington 3.00 8.00
4 Cedi Osman 4.00 10.00
5 Thaddeus Young 3.00 8.00
6 Monte Morris 5.00 12.00
7 Malcolm Brogdon 4.00 10.00
8 Danny Green 4.00 10.00
9 Terrence Ross 5.00 12.00
10 Lauri Markkanen 6.00 15.00
11 Pascal Siakam 12.00 30.00
12 Jalen Brunson 12.00 30.00
13 Willie Cauley-Stein 3.00 8.00
14 Andrew Wiggins 8.00 20.00
15 Nikola Vucevic 4.00 10.00
16 Allonzo Trier 3.00 8.00
17 Michael Porter Jr. 8.00 20.00
18 Jarrett Allen 5.00 12.00
19 Trae Young 75.00 200.00
20 Julius Randle 6.00 15.00
21 Kevin Knox II 3.00 8.00
22 Deandre Ayton 25.00 60.00
23 Khris Middleton 5.00 12.00
24 Rudy Gobert 6.00 15.00
25 Vince Carter 30.00 80.00
26 Harry Giles 3.00 8.00
27 Jeff Teague 3.00 8.00
28 Kawhi Leonard EXCH 30.00 80.00
29 Kyrie Irving 15.00 40.00
30 Kevin Durant EXCH 30.00 80.00

2019-20 Donruss Fantasy Stars
*GREEN FLOOD: .5X TO 1.2X BASIC
1 Giannis Antetokounmpo 2.50 6.00
2 James Harden 1.00 2.50
3 Karl-Anthony Towns .75 2.00
4 LeBron James 4.00 10.00
5 Joel Embiid 1.00 2.50

2019-20 Donruss Fantasy Stars Holo Red Laser
*HOLO RED LSR/99: 1X TO 2.5X BASIC
STATED PRINT RUN 99 SER.#'d SETS
4 LeBron James 20.00 50.00

2019-20 Donruss Fantasy Stars Holo Yellow Laser
*HOLO YLW LSR/25: 1.5X TO 4X BASIC
STATED PRINT RUN 25 SER.#'d SETS
1 Giannis Antetokounmpo 12.00 30.00
4 LeBron James 50.00 120.00

2019-20 Donruss Franchise Features
*GREEN FLOOD: .5X TO 1.2X BASIC
1 Miles Bridges .50 1.25
2 Goran Dragic .40 1.00
3 Lou Williams .50 1.25
4 Kyle Lowry .50 1.25
5 Donovan Mitchell 1.00 2.50
6 John Wall .60 1.50
7 Joel Embiid 1.00 2.50
8 Jaren Jackson Jr. .75 2.00
9 Trae Young 1.25 3.00
10 Kevin Love .50 1.25
11 Joe Harris .40 1.00
12 Stephen Curry 4.00 10.00
13 Jrue Holiday .60 1.50
14 Giannis Antetokounmpo 2.50 6.00
15 Lauri Markkanen .60 1.50
16 Blake Griffin .50 1.25
17 Devin Booker .12 .30
18 Jayson Tatum 2.00 5.00
19 De'Aaron Fox .75 2.00
20 Karl-Anthony Towns .75 2.00
21 Nikola Jokic 2.50 6.00
22 Steven Adams .40 1.00
23 Aaron Gordon .50 1.25
24 Damian Lillard 1.25 3.00
25 Victor Oladipo .40 1.00
26 James Harden 1.00 2.50
27 LeBron James 4.00 10.00
28 Kevin Knox II .30 .75
29 Luka Doncic 3.00 8.00
30 DeMar DeRozan .60 1.50

2019-20 Donruss Franchise Features Holo Red Laser
*HOLO RED LSR/99: 1X TO 2.5X BASIC
STATED PRINT RUN 99 SER.#'d SETS
27 LeBron James 25.00 60.00
29 Luka Doncic 10.00 25.00

2019-20 Donruss Franchise Features Holo Yellow Laser
*HOLO YLW LSR/25: 1.5X TO 4X BASIC
STATED PRINT RUN 25 SER.#'d SETS
27 LeBron James 75.00 200.00
29 Luka Doncic 25.00 60.00

2019-20 Donruss Great X-Pectations
1 De'Andre Hunter 1.25 3.00
2 Brandon Clarke .60 1.50
3 Jaxson Hayes .50 1.25
4 Nassir Little .50 1.25
5 Cameron Johnson .75 2.00
6 Romeo Langford .30 .75
7 Zion Williamson 8.00 20.00
8 Chuma Okeke .50 1.25
9 RJ Barrett 1.25 3.00
10 Goga Bitadze .50 1.25
11 Jarrett Culver .30 .75
12 Grant Williams .50 1.25
13 Rui Hachimura 1.25 3.00
14 Dylan Windler .40 1.00
15 PJ Washington Jr. 1.00 2.50
16 Sekou Doumbouya .30 .75
17 Ja Morant 3.00 8.00
18 Nickeil Alexander-Walker .50 1.25
19 Darius Garland 1.25 3.00
20 Luka Samanic .40 1.00
21 Coby White 1.00 2.50
22 Ty Jerome .60 1.50

23 Cam Reddish .50 1.25
24 Mfiondu Kabengele .40 1.00
25 Tyler Herro 1.50 4.00

2019-20 Donruss Great X-Pectations Green Flood

*GREEN FLOOD: .5X TO 1.2X BASIC
7 Zion Williamson 15.00 40.00
17 Ja Morant 10.00 25.00

2019-20 Donruss Great X-Pectations Holo Red Laser

*HOLO RED LSR/99: 1X TO 2.5X BASIC
STATED PRINT RUN 99 SER.#'d SETS
7 Zion Williamson 75.00 200.00
9 RJ Barrett 6.00 15.00
17 Ja Morant 30.00 80.00
25 Tyler Herro 6.00 15.00

2019-20 Donruss Great X-Pectations Holo Yellow Laser

*HOLO YLW LSR/25: 1.5X TO 4X BASIC
STATED PRINT RUN 25 SER.#'d SETS
7 Zion Williamson 150.00 400.00
9 RJ Barrett 10.00 25.00
17 Ja Morant 75.00 200.00
21 Coby White 20.00 50.00
25 Tyler Herro 15.00 40.00

2019-20 Donruss Hall Dominator Signatures

STATED PRINT RUN 99 SER.#'d SETS
EXCHANGE DEADLINE 6/13/2021
1 Magic Johnson 20.00 50.00
2 Hakeem Olajuwon 12.00 30.00
3 Robert Parish 6.00 15.00
4 Louie Dampier 6.00 15.00
5 Calvin Murphy 5.00 12.00
6 Jerry West 12.00 30.00
7 Elvin Hayes 6.00 15.00
8 Lenny Wilkens 6.00 15.00
9 Alex English 6.00 15.00
10 Artis Gilmore 6.00 15.00
11 David Robinson 12.00 30.00
12 Sarunas Marciulionis 3.00 8.00
13 George Gervin 8.00 20.00
14 Jamaal Wilkes 5.00 12.00
15 Dave Cowens 6.00 15.00
16 Dennis Rodman 15.00 40.00
17 Dan Issel 6.00 15.00
18 Tom Satch Sanders 6.00 15.00
19 Nate Archibald 5.00 12.00
20 Bernard King 6.00 15.00
21 Tom Heinsohn 12.00 30.00
22 Clyde Drexler 10.00 25.00
23 David Thompson 5.00 12.00
24 Shaquille O'Neal EXCH 50.00 120.00
25 Allen Iverson 25.00 60.00
26 Larry Bird 20.00 50.00
27 Cliff Hagan 4.00 10.00
28 Tracy McGrady 15.00 40.00
29 Kobe Bryant EXCH 400.00 800.00
30 Charles Barkley EXCH 60.00 150.00

2019-20 Donruss Jersey Kings

STATED PRINT RUN 75 SER.#'d SETS
1 Damian Lillard 6.00 15.00
2 Kemba Walker 2.00 5.00
3 Kobe Bryant 20.00 50.00
4 Draymond Green 3.00 8.00
5 James Harden 5.00 12.00
6 Vince Carter 5.00 12.00
7 Larry Bird 10.00 25.00
8 CJ McCollum 2.50 6.00
9 David Robinson 5.00 12.00
10 Derrick Rose 5.00 12.00
11 LeBron James 15.00 40.00
12 Scottie Pippen 15.00 40.00
13 Victor Oladipo 2.00 5.00
14 Hassan Whiteside 1.50 4.00
15 Chris Paul 5.00 12.00
16 Karl Malone 5.00 12.00
17 Steven Adams 2.00 5.00
18 Anthony Davis 6.00 15.00
19 Nikola Jokic 12.00 30.00
20 Zach LaVine 4.00 10.00
21 Jimmy Butler 5.00 12.00
22 Andre Drummond 2.00 5.00
23 Klay Thompson 6.00 15.00
24 Karl-Anthony Towns 4.00 10.00
25 Bradley Beal 3.00 8.00
26 Giannis Antetokounmpo 12.00 30.00
27 Kyle Lowry 2.50 6.00
28 Kawhi Leonard 6.00 15.00
29 Kyle Kuzma 3.00 8.00
30 Grant Hill 10.00 25.00
31 Kevin Garnett 6.00 15.00
32 Hakeem Olajuwon 5.00 12.00
33 Clyde Drexler 4.00 10.00
34 Andrew Wiggins 3.00 8.00
35 Myles Turner 2.50 6.00
36 Nikola Vucevic 2.00 5.00
37 LaMarcus Aldridge 2.50 6.00
38 Blake Griffin 2.50 6.00
39 Paul George 4.00 10.00
40 Rudy Gay 2.00 5.00
41 Devin Booker .60 1.50
42 Kyrie Irving 5.00 12.00
43 Kevin Love 2.50 6.00
44 Goran Dragic 2.00 5.00
45 Kevin Durant 8.00 20.00
46 Joel Embiid 5.00 12.00
47 Paul Pierce 4.00 10.00
48 Donovan Mitchell 5.00 12.00
49 Mike Conley 2.00 5.00
50 D'Angelo Russell 2.00 5.00
51 Shaquille O'Neal 10.00 25.00
52 Dennis Smith Jr. 1.50 4.00
53 Kristaps Porzingis 3.00 8.00
54 Khris Middleton 2.50 6.00
55 Jamal Murray 4.00 10.00
56 Rudy Gobert 3.00 8.00
57 Aaron Gordon 2.50 6.00
58 John Wall 3.00 8.00
59 Caris LeVert 2.00 5.00
60 Stephen Curry 10.00 25.00

2019-20 Donruss Jersey Series

1 Dirk Nowitzki 6.00 15.00
2 Karl-Anthony Towns 4.00 10.00
3 Andrew Wiggins 3.00 8.00
4 Vince Carter 5.00 12.00
5 Kevin Love 2.50 6.00
6 Zach LaVine 4.00 10.00
7 DeAndre Jordan 2.00 5.00
8 Jarrett Allen 2.50 6.00
9 Ricky Rubio 2.00 5.00
10 Enes Kanter 1.50 4.00
11 Bradley Beal 3.00 8.00
12 Rondae Hollis-Jefferson 1.50 4.00
13 Pau Gasol 4.00 10.00
14 Kyrie Irving 5.00 12.00
15 Shaquille O'Neal 10.00 25.00
16 Rudy Gobert 3.00 8.00
17 Thaddeus Young 1.50 4.00
18 Jimmy Butler 5.00 12.00
19 John Wall 3.00 8.00
20 Eric Gordon 2.00 5.00
21 Harrison Barnes 2.00 5.00
22 Evan Turner 1.50 4.00
23 Dwyane Wade 5.00 12.00
24 Joe Harris 2.00 5.00
25 Derrick Rose 5.00 12.00
26 Gorgui Dieng 1.50 4.00
27 Stephen Curry 5.00 12.00
28 Allen Crabbe 1.50 4.00
29 Serge Ibaka 2.00 5.00
30 DeMarre Carroll 1.50 4.00
31 Kyle Lowry 2.50 6.00
32 CJ McCollum 2.50 6.00
33 Kristaps Porzingis 3.00 8.00
34 Nerlens Noel 1.50 4.00
35 Kevin Garnett 6.00 15.00
36 Andre Drummond 2.00 5.00
37 Victor Oladipo 2.00 5.00
38 LeBron James 20.00 50.00
39 Kris Dunn 1.50 4.00
JS-PML Paul Millsap 2.00 5.00
41 Kobe Bryant 20.00 50.00
42 Anthony Davis 6.00 15.00
43 Goran Dragic 2.00 5.00
44 Nikola Vucevic 2.00 5.00
45 Kevin Durant 8.00 20.00
46 Terrence Ross 2.50 6.00
47 Rudy Gay 2.00 5.00
48 Steven Adams 2.00 5.00
49 Dwight Powell 1.50 4.00
50 Darius Bazley 1.50 4.00
51 Dennis Smith Jr. 1.50 4.00
52 DeMarcus Cousins 2.00 5.00
53 LaMarcus Aldridge 2.50 6.00
54 Aaron Gordon 2.50 6.00
55 Blake Griffin 2.50 6.00
56 Al Horford 2.50 6.00
57 Caris LeVert 2.00 5.00
58 Klay Thompson 6.00 15.00
59 Chris Paul 5.00 12.00
60 Kevin Knox II 1.50 4.00
61 Zion Williamson 12.00 30.00
62 Ja Morant 12.00 30.00
63 RJ Barrett 6.00 15.00
64 De'Andre Hunter 6.00 15.00
65 Jarrett Culver 1.50 4.00
66 Coby White 5.00 12.00
67 Jaxson Hayes 2.50 6.00
68 Rui Hachimura 6.00 15.00
69 Cam Reddish 2.50 6.00
70 Cameron Johnson 4.00 10.00
71 PJ Washington Jr. 5.00 12.00
72 Tyler Herro 8.00 20.00
73 Romeo Langford 1.50 4.00
74 Sekou Doumbouya 1.50 4.00
75 Chuma Okeke 2.50 6.00
76 Nickeil Alexander-Walker 2.50 6.00
77 Goga Bitadze 2.50 6.00
78 Luka Samanic 2.00 5.00
79 Brandon Clarke 3.00 8.00
80 Grant Williams 2.50 6.00
81 Ty Jerome 3.00 8.00
82 Nassir Little 2.50 6.00
83 Dylan Windler 2.00 5.00
84 Mfiondu Kabengele 2.00 5.00
85 Jordan Poole 6.00 15.00
86 Keldon Johnson 5.00 12.00
87 Kevin Porter Jr. 3.00 8.00
88 KZ Okpala 2.00 5.00
89 Carsen Edwards 2.00 5.00
90 Bruno Fernando 2.00 5.00
91 Cody Martin 2.50 6.00
92 Eric Paschall 2.00 5.00
93 Admiral Schofield 2.00 5.00
94 Jaylen Nowell 2.00 5.00
95 Bol Bol 4.00 10.00
96 Isaiah Roby 2.00 5.00
97 Ignas Brazdeikis 2.00 5.00
98 Quinndary Weatherspoon 1.50 4.00
99 Tremont Waters 2.00 5.00
100 Matisse Thybulle 3.00 8.00

2019-20 Donruss League Leaders

*GREEN FLOOD: .5X TO 1.2X BASIC
*HOLO RED LSR/99: 1X TO 2.5X BASIC
*HOLO YLW LSR/25: 1.5X TO 4X BASIC
1 James Harden 1.00 2.50
2 Andre Drummond .40 1.00
3 Russell Westbrook .75 2.00
4 Paul George .75 2.00
5 Myles Turner .50 1.25
6 Rudy Gobert .60 1.50
7 Joe Harris .40 1.00
8 Malcolm Brogdon .40 1.00
9 Bradley Beal .60 1.50
10 James Harden 1.00 2.50

2019-20 Donruss Net Marvels

COMMON CARD .60 1.50
SEMISTARS .75 2.00
UNLISTED STARS 1.00 2.50
*PRESS: .75X TO 2X BASIC
1 Nikola Jokic 25.00 60.00
2 Rudy Gobert 12.00 30.00
3 Draymond Green 20.00 50.00
4 Zion Williamson 75.00 200.00
5 Coby White 15.00 40.00
6 Karl-Anthony Towns 12.00 30.00
7 Bradley Beal 12.00 30.00
8 Damian Lillard 30.00 80.00
9 Ja Morant 75.00 200.00
10 RJ Barrett 20.00 50.00
11 Giannis Antetokounmpo 40.00 100.00
12 Cam Reddish 1.00 2.50
13 James Harden 15.00 40.00
14 Ben Simmons 15.00 40.00
15 Jarrett Culver 10.00 25.00
16 Trae Young 30.00 80.00
17 Luka Doncic 75.00 200.00
18 Stephen Curry 75.00 200.00
19 LeBron James 100.00 250.00
20 Joel Embiid 30.00 80.00

2019-20 Donruss Next Day Autographs

EXCHANGE DEADLINE 6/13/2021
1 Zion Williamson 350.00 700.00
2 Ja Morant 1,000.00 2,000.00
3 RJ Barrett 150.00 400.00
4 De'Andre Hunter 50.00 120.00
5 Jarrett Culver 12.00 30.00
6 Coby White 75.00 200.00
7 Jaxson Hayes 20.00 50.00
ND-RHM Rui Hachimura 125.00 300.00
9 Cam Reddish 40.00 100.00
10 Cameron Johnson 40.00 100.00
11 PJ Washington Jr. 40.00 100.00
12 Tyler Herro 150.00 400.00
13 Romeo Langford 12.00 30.00
14 Sekou Doumbouya 12.00 30.00
15 Chuma Okeke 20.00 50.00
16 Nickeil Alexander-Walker 20.00 50.00
17 Goga Bitadze 20.00 50.00
18 Luka Samanic 15.00 40.00
19 Brandon Clarke 25.00 60.00
20 Grant Williams 20.00 50.00
21 Ty Jerome 25.00 60.00
22 Nassir Little 20.00 50.00
23 Dylan Windler 15.00 40.00
24 Mfiondu Kabengele 15.00 40.00
25 Jordan Poole 125.00 300.00
26 Keldon Johnson 125.00 300.00
27 Kevin Porter Jr. 25.00 60.00
28 KZ Okpala 15.00 40.00
29 Carsen Edwards 15.00 40.00
30 Bruno Fernando 15.00 40.00
31 Cody Martin 20.00 50.00
32 Eric Paschall 15.00 40.00
33 Admiral Schofield 15.00 40.00
34 Jaylen Nowell 15.00 40.00
35 Bol Bol 30.00 80.00
36 Isaiah Roby 15.00 40.00
37 Ignas Brazdeikis 15.00 40.00
38 Quinndary Weatherspoon 12.00 30.00
39 Tremont Waters 15.00 40.00
40 Matisse Thybulle 25.00 60.00
41 Darius Bazley 12.00 30.00
42 Kyle Guy 15.00 40.00

2019-20 Donruss Rated Rookies Signatures

EXCHANGE DEADLINE 6/13/2021
201 Zion Williamson 125.00 300.00
202 Ja Morant 150.00 400.00
203 RJ Barrett 25.00 60.00
204 De'Andre Hunter 12.00 30.00
205 Jarrett Culver 3.00 8.00
206 Coby White 10.00 25.00
207 Jaxson Hayes 5.00 12.00
208 Rui Hachimura 12.00 30.00
209 Cam Reddish 12.00 30.00
210 Cameron Johnson 8.00 20.00
211 PJ Washington Jr. 10.00 25.00
212 Tyler Herro 15.00 40.00
213 Romeo Langford 3.00 8.00
214 Sekou Doumbouya 3.00 8.00
215 Chuma Okeke 5.00 12.00
216 Nickeil Alexander-Walker 5.00 12.00
217 Goga Bitadze 5.00 12.00
218 Luka Samanic 4.00 10.00
219 Matisse Thybulle 6.00 15.00
220 Brandon Clarke 6.00 15.00
221 Grant Williams 6.00 15.00
222 Ty Jerome 6.00 15.00
223 Nassir Little 5.00 12.00
224 Dylan Windler 4.00 10.00
225 Mfiondu Kabengele 4.00 10.00
226 Jordan Poole 25.00 60.00
227 Keldon Johnson 10.00 25.00
228 Kevin Porter Jr. 6.00 15.00
229 Nicolas Claxton 6.00 15.00
230 KZ Okpala 4.00 10.00
231 Carsen Edwards 4.00 10.00
232 Bruno Fernando 4.00 10.00
233 Cody Martin 5.00 12.00
234 Bol Bol 8.00 20.00
235 Isaiah Roby 4.00 10.00
236 Daniel Gafford 6.00 15.00
237 Alen Smailagic 3.00 8.00
238 Eric Paschall 4.00 10.00
239 Admiral Schofield 4.00 10.00
240 Jaylen Nowell 4.00 10.00
241 Ignas Brazdeikis 4.00 10.00
242 Terance Mann 6.00 15.00
243 Quinndary Weatherspoon 3.00 8.00
244 Tremont Waters 4.00 10.00
245 Kyle Guy 4.00 10.00
246 Jordan Bone 3.00 8.00
247 Jalen McDaniels 8.00 20.00

2019-20 Donruss Rated Rookies Signatures Blue Infinite

*BLUE INFINITE: .6X TO 1.5X BASIC
STATED PRINT RUN 35 SER.#'d SETS
201 Zion Williamson 200.00 500.00
202 Ja Morant 300.00 600.00
204 De'Andre Hunter 20.00 50.00
208 Rui Hachimura 20.00 50.00
212 Tyler Herro 25.00 60.00
220 Brandon Clarke 10.00 25.00
226 Jordan Poole 40.00 100.00

2019-20 Donruss Rated Rookies Signatures Green and Yellow Laser

*GRN YLW LSR: .5X TO 1.2X BASIC

2019-20 Donruss Rated Rookies Signatures Green Flood

*GRN FLOOD: .5X TO 1.2X BASIC

2019-20 Donruss Rated Rookies Signatures Holo Orange Laser

*HOLO ORNG LSR: .5X TO 1.2X BASIC

2019-20 Donruss Rated Rookies Signatures Holo Purple and Green Laser

*HOLO PRPL GRN LSR: .5X TO 1.2X BASIC

2019-20 Donruss Rated Rookies Signatures Holo Yellow Laser

*HOLO YLW LSR: .5X TO 1.2X BASIC

2019-20 Donruss Rookie Dominator Signatures

PRINT RUN BTW 25-99 COPIES PER
EXCHANGE DEADLINE 6/13/2021
1 Zion Williamson/25 400.00 800.00
2 Ja Morant/99 150.00 400.00
3 RJ Barrett/99 30.00 80.00
4 De'Andre Hunter/99 12.00 30.00
5 Jarrett Culver/99 3.00 8.00
6 Coby White/99 40.00 100.00
7 Jaxson Hayes/99 10.00 25.00
8 Rui Hachimura/99 40.00 100.00
9 Cam Reddish/99 5.00 12.00
10 Cameron Johnson/99 8.00 20.00
11 PJ Washington Jr./99 10.00 25.00
12 Tyler Herro/99 125.00 300.00
13 Romeo Langford/99 3.00 8.00
14 Sekou Doumbouya/99 3.00 8.00
15 Chuma Okeke/99 5.00 12.00
16 Nickeil Alexander-Walker/99 5.00 12.00
17 Goga Bitadze/99 5.00 12.00
18 Luka Samanic/99 4.00 10.00
19 Brandon Clarke/99 6.00 15.00
20 Grant Williams/99 5.00 12.00
21 Ty Jerome/99 6.00 15.00
22 Nassir Little/99 5.00 12.00
23 Dylan Windler/99 4.00 10.00
24 Mfiondu Kabengele/99 4.00 10.00
25 Jordan Poole/99 12.00 30.00
26 Keldon Johnson/99 10.00 25.00
27 Kevin Porter Jr./99 6.00 15.00
28 KZ Okpala/99 4.00 10.00
29 Carsen Edwards/99 4.00 10.00
30 Bruno Fernando/99 4.00 10.00
31 Cody Martin/99 5.00 12.00
32 Eric Paschall/99 4.00 10.00
33 Admiral Schofield/99 4.00 10.00
34 Jaylen Nowell/99 4.00 10.00
35 Bol Bol/99 8.00 20.00
36 Isaiah Roby/99 4.00 10.00
37 Ignas Brazdeikis/99 4.00 10.00
38 Quinndary Weatherspoon/99 3.00 8.00
39 Tremont Waters/99 4.00 10.00
40 Matisse Thybulle/99 6.00 15.00

2019-20 Donruss Rookie Jersey Kings

COMMON CARD 1.50 4.00
SEMISTARS 2.00 5.00
UNLISTED STARS 2.50 6.00
PRINT RUN B/TW 75-99 COPIES PER
*PRIME/25: .75X TO 2X BASIC
1 Zion Williamson/99 12.00 30.00
2 Ja Morant/99 25.00 60.00
3 RJ Barrett/99 6.00 15.00
4 De'Andre Hunter/99 6.00 15.00
5 Jarrett Culver/99 1.50 4.00
6 Coby White/99 4.00 10.00
7 Jaxson Hayes/99 2.50 6.00
8 Rui Hachimura/99 6.00 15.00
9 Cam Reddish/99 2.50 6.00
10 Cameron Johnson/99 4.00 10.00
11 PJ Washington Jr./99 5.00 12.00
12 Tyler Herro/99 8.00 20.00
13 Romeo Langford/99 1.50 4.00
14 Sekou Doumbouya/99 1.50 4.00
15 Chuma Okeke/99 2.50 6.00
16 Nickeil Alexander-Walker/99 2.50 6.00
17 Goga Bitadze/99 2.50 6.00
18 Luka Samanic/99 2.00 5.00
19 Brandon Clarke/99 3.00 8.00
20 Grant Williams/99 2.50 6.00
21 Ty Jerome/75 3.00 8.00
22 Nassir Little/75 2.50 6.00
23 Dylan Windler/75 2.00 5.00
24 Mfiondu Kabengele/75 2.00 5.00
25 Jordan Poole/75 6.00 15.00
26 Keldon Johnson/75 5.00 12.00
27 Kevin Porter Jr./75 3.00 8.00
28 KZ Okpala/75 2.00 5.00
29 Carsen Edwards/75 2.00 5.00
30 Bruno Fernando/75 2.00 5.00
31 Cody Martin/75 2.50 6.00
32 Eric Paschall/75 2.00 5.00
33 Admiral Schofield/75 2.00 5.00
34 Jaylen Nowell/75 2.00 5.00
35 Bol Bol/75 4.00 10.00
36 Isaiah Roby/75 2.00 5.00
37 Ignas Brazdeikis/75 2.00 5.00
38 Quinndary Weatherspoon/75 1.50 4.00
39 Tremont Waters/75 2.00 5.00
40 Matisse Thybulle/75 3.00 8.00

2019-20 Donruss The Rookies

COMMON CARD .30 .75
SEMISTARS .40 1.00
UNLISTED STARS .50 1.25
*PRESS: .5X TO 1.2X BASIC
1 Zion Williamson 2.50 6.00
2 Ja Morant 6.00 15.00
3 RJ Barrett 1.25 3.00
4 De'Andre Hunter 1.25 3.00
5 Jarrett Culver .30 .75

2020-21 Donruss

1 Jonas Valanciunas .30 .75
2 Gary Harris .30 .75
3 Nikola Vucevic .40 1.00
4 Kelly Oubre Jr. .40 1.00
5 Christian Wood .30 .75
6 Donte DiVincenzo .40 1.00
7 Nikola Jokic 2.00 5.00
8 Kristaps Porzingis .50 1.25
9 Fred VanVleet .60 1.50
10 DeMar DeRozan .50 1.25
11 Langston Galloway .25 .60
12 LeBron James 3.00 8.00
13 Luka Doncic 2.50 6.00
14 Bam Adebayo .60 1.50
15 James Johnson .25 .60
16 Trevor Ariza .25 .60
17 Jaren Jackson Jr. .60 1.50
18 Josh Jackson .25 .60
19 Devonte' Graham .30 .75
20 Karl-Anthony Towns .60 1.50
21 LaMarcus Aldridge .40 1.00
22 Chris Paul .75 2.00
23 Otto Porter Jr. .25 .60
24 Marvin Bagley III .30 .75
25 Aaron Gordon .40 1.00
26 Michael Porter Jr. .50 1.25
27 Enes Kanter .30 .75
28 Damian Lillard 1.00 2.50
29 Andrew Wiggins .50 1.25
30 Dwight Powell .25 .60
31 Deandre Ayton .40 1.00
32 Klay Thompson 1.00 2.50
33 Josh Hart .30 .75
34 Markelle Fultz .30 .75
35 Aron Baynes .25 .60
36 Bojan Bogdanovic .30 .75
37 James Harden .75 2.00
38 Lou Williams .40 1.00
39 Sekou Doumbouya .25 .60
40 Julius Randle .40 1.00
41 Stephen Curry 3.00 8.00
42 Cody Zeller .25 .60
43 Jaxson Hayes .30 .75
44 Lonzo Ball .50 1.25
45 Terry Rozier .40 1.00
46 Norman Powell .30 .75
47 Dillon Brooks .40 1.00
48 Pascal Siakam .60 1.50
49 John Wall .50 1.25
50 Terrence Ross .30 .75
51 OG Anunoby .40 1.00
52 Jarrett Culver .25 .60
53 Thon Maker .25 .60
54 John Collins .40 1.00
55 Paul George .60 1.50
56 Darius Garland .60 1.50
57 JJ Redick .40 1.00
58 De'Aaron Fox .60 1.50
59 Kyrie Irving .75 2.00
60 Derrick Rose .60 1.50
61 Eric Gordon .30 .75
62 Dwight Howard .50 1.25
63 PJ Washington Jr. .30 .75
64 Russell Westbrook .75 2.00
65 Davis Bertans .30 .75
66 Hassan Whiteside .30 .75
67 Eric Paschall .30 .75
68 Torrey Craig .30 .75
69 Blake Griffin .40 1.00
70 Marcus Smart .40 1.00
71 Joel Embiid 1.00 2.50
72 Grant Williams .30 .75
73 Dejounte Murray .40 1.00
74 Matisse Thybulle .30 .75
75 Jordan Clarkson .40 1.00
76 Domantas Sabonis .50 1.25
77 Collin Sexton .40 1.00
78 Bismack Biyombo .25 .60
79 Dorian Finney-Smith .30 .75
80 Robert Covington .30 .75
81 Goran Dragic .40 1.00
82 Kevin Huerter .30 .75
83 Dennis Schroder .40 1.00
84 Steven Adams .40 1.00
85 Shake Milton .30 .75
86 Kevin Love .40 1.00
87 Anfernee Simons .50 1.25
88 Patty Mills .40 1.00
89 Seth Curry .40 1.00
90 Tim Hardaway Jr. .25 .60
91 CJ McCollum .40 1.00
92 Ricky Rubio .40 1.00
93 Kevin Durant 1.50 4.00
94 Kemba Walker .40 1.00
95 Dwayne Bacon .25 .60
96 Jamal Murray .60 1.50
97 Alex Caruso .60 1.50
98 Mikal Bridges .50 1.25
99 Dennis Smith Jr. .25 .60
100 Josh Richardson .30 .75
101 D'Angelo Russell .40 1.00
102 Derrick Jones Jr. .30 .75
103 Bryn Forbes .30 .75
104 Giannis Antetokounmpo 2.00 5.00
105 T.J. Warren .30 .75
106 Serge Ibaka .30 .75
107 Ja Morant 1.25 3.00
108 Montrezl Harrell .40 1.00
109 Nemanja Bjelica .25 .60
110 Mo Bamba .40 1.00
111 Carmelo Anthony .60 1.50
112 Devin Booker 1.00 2.50
113 Jeff Teague .50 1.25
114 Rudy Gobert .50 1.25
115 Doug McDermott .30 .75
116 De'Andre Hunter .40 1.00
117 Luke Kennard .30 .75
118 Clint Capela .40 1.00
119 Wesley Matthews .25 .60
120 Cam Reddish .50 1.25
121 Taurean Prince .25 .60
122 Harrison Barnes .30 .75
123 Bogdan Bogdanovic .40 1.00
124 Danuel House Jr. .30 .75
125 Harry Giles III .25 .60
126 Malik Beasley .30 .75
127 Jae Crowder .25 .60
128 Donovan Mitchell .75 2.00
129 Mike Conley .30 .75
130 Bobby Portis .40 1.00
131 Joe Harris .30 .75
132 Kyle Kuzma .50 1.25
133 Ivica Zubac .40 1.00
134 Kentavious Caldwell-Pope .30 .75
135 Jonathan Isaac .40 1.00
136 Will Barton .25 .60
137 Gordon Hayward .40 1.00
138 Spencer Dinwiddie .30 .75
139 Danny Green .30 .75
140 Jarrett Allen .40 1.00
141 Evan Fournier .30 .75
142 Marquese Chriss .25 .60
143 Malcolm Brogdon .40 1.00
144 Marc Gasol .40 1.00
145 Jeff Green .25 .60
146 Kawhi Leonard 1.00 2.50
147 Zion Williamson 1.25 3.00
148 Coby White .50 1.25
149 Nerlens Noel .25 .60
150 Tristan Thompson .25 .60
151 Troy Brown Jr. .30 .75
152 Keldon Johnson .60 1.50
153 Trae Young 1.00 2.50
154 Brandon Ingram .50 1.25
155 Joe Ingles .30 .75
156 Kevin Porter Jr. .30 .75
157 Brook Lopez .30 .75
158 Duncan Robinson .40 1.00
159 Jordan Poole .60 1.50
160 Juancho Hernangomez .40 1.00
161 Jaylen Brown .60 1.50
162 Mitchell Robinson .40 1.00
163 Draymond Green .50 1.25
164 Marcus Morris Sr. .25 .60
165 Landry Shamet .30 .75
166 Jayson Tatum 1.50 4.00
167 Thomas Bryant .30 .75
168 Anthony Davis 1.00 2.50
169 Zach LaVine .60 1.50
170 Al Horford .30 .75
171 Eric Bledsoe .30 .75
172 Myles Turner .40 1.00
173 Matthew Dellavedova .30 .75
174 RJ Barrett .60 1.50
175 Kendrick Nunn .30 .75
176 Ben Simmons .40 1.00
177 Caris LeVert .40 1.00
178 Tobias Harris .40 1.00
179 Shabazz Napier .25 .60
180 Buddy Hield .40 1.00
181 Jrue Holiday .40 1.00
182 Elfrid Payton .30 .75
183 Wendell Carter Jr. .30 .75
184 Andre Drummond .40 1.00
185 Khris Middleton .50 1.25
186 Paul Millsap .30 .75
187 Tyler Herro .75 2.00
188 Lauri Markkanen .50 1.25
189 Jimmy Butler .75 2.00
190 Miles Bridges .40 1.00
191 Kris Dunn .25 .60
192 Brandon Clarke .40 1.00
193 Victor Oladipo .30 .75
194 Bradley Beal .50 1.25
195 Shai Gilgeous-Alexander 2.00 5.00
196 Kyle Lowry .40 1.00
197 Lonnie Walker IV .40 1.00
198 Rui Hachimura .50 1.25
199 Danilo Gallinari .30 .75
200 Derrick White .40 1.00
201 Anthony Edwards RR RC 5.00 12.00
202 LaMelo Ball RR RC 4.00 10.00
203 Isaac Okoro RR RC .75 2.00
204 Killian Hayes RR RC .50 1.25
205 Deni Avdija RR RC 1.25 3.00
206 Devin Vassell RR RC 1.50 4.00
207 Kira Lewis Jr. RR RC .50 1.25
208 Cole Anthony RR RC 1.25 3.00
209 Aleksej Pokusevski RR RC .60 1.50
210 Saddiq Bey RR RC 1.00 2.50
211 Tyrese Maxey RR RC 4.00 10.00
212 Caleb Martin RR RC 1.00 2.50
213 Immanuel Quickley RR RC 1.25 3.00
214 Udoka Azubuike RR RC .60 1.50
215 Malachi Flynn RR RC .50 1.25
216 Tyrell Terry RR RC .40 1.00
217 Daniel Oturu RR RC .50 1.25
218 Xavier Tillman RR RC .60 1.50
219 Robert Woodard II RR RC .50 1.25
220 Jordan Nwora RR RC .60 1.50
221 Saben Lee RR RC .50 1.25
222 Nick Richards RR RC .60 1.50
223 CJ Elleby RR RC .50 1.25
224 Kenyon Martin Jr. RR RC .75 2.00
225 Cassius Stanley RR RC .50 1.25
226 James Wiseman RR RC .60 1.50
227 Patrick Williams RR RC 1.25 3.00
228 Onyeka Okongwu RR RC 1.00 2.50
229 Obi Toppin RR RC 1.00 2.50
230 Jalen Smith RR RC 1.00 2.50
231 Tyrese Haliburton RR RC 4.00 10.00
232 Aaron Nesmith RR RC 1.00 2.50
233 Isaiah Stewart RR RC 1.00 2.50
234 Josh Green RR RC 1.00 2.50
235 Precious Achiuwa RR RC 1.00 2.50
236 Zeke Nnaji RR RC .60 1.50
237 RJ Hampton RR RC .50 1.25
238 Payton Pritchard RR RC 1.50 4.00
239 Jaden McDaniels RR RC 1.50 4.00
240 Desmond Bane RR RC 1.50 4.00
241 Vernon Carey Jr. RR RC .50 1.25
242 Theo Maledon RR RC .50 1.25
243 Tyler Bey RR RC .50 1.25
244 Tre Jones RR RC .75 2.00
245 Nico Mannion RR RC .50 1.25
246 Elijah Hughes RR RC .50 1.25
247 Jahmi'us Ramsey RR RC .50 1.25
248 Skylar Mays RR RC .50 1.25
249 Cassius Winston RR RC .50 1.25
250 Grant Riller RR RC .50 1.25

2020-21 Donruss Choice

*CHOICE: .75X TO 2X BASIC
201 Anthony Edwards RR 40.00 100.00
202 LaMelo Ball RR 75.00 200.00
203 Isaac Okoro RR 8.00 20.00
211 Tyrese Maxey RR 12.00 30.00
227 Patrick Williams RR 12.00 30.00
231 Tyrese Haliburton RR 15.00 40.00

2020-21 Donruss Choice Blue

STATED PRINT RUN 49 SER.#'d SETS
201 Anthony Edwards RR 75.00 200.00

2020-21 Donruss Green Flood

*GREEN FLOOD: 1.25X TO 3X BASIC
201 Anthony Edwards RR 25.00 60.00

2020-21 Donruss Holo Blue Laser

*HOLO BLUE LSR: 4X TO 10X BASIC
STATED PRINT RUN 49 SER.#'d SETS
201 Anthony Edwards RR 75.00 200.00

2020-21 Donruss Holo Green and Yellow Laser

*HOLO GRN YLW LSR: 1.5X TO 4X BASIC
201 Anthony Edwards RR 30.00 80.00

2020-21 Donruss Holo Green Laser

*HOLO GREEN LSR: 1.25X TO 3X BASIC
201 Anthony Edwards RR 25.00 60.00

2020-21 Donruss Holo Light Blue Laser

*HOLO LIGHT BLUE LSR: 1.5X TO 4X BASIC
201 Anthony Edwards RR 30.00 80.00

2020-21 Donruss Holo Orange Laser

*HOLO ORNG LSR: 1.5X TO 4X BASIC
201 Anthony Edwards RR 30.00 80.00

2020-21 Donruss Holo Purple Laser

*HOLO PURPLE LSR: 3X TO 8X BASIC
STATED PRINT RUN 99 SER.#'d SETS
201 Anthony Edwards RR 60.00 150.00

2020-21 Donruss Holo Red and Gold Laser

*HOLO RED GOLD LSR: 1.5X TO 4X BASIC
201 Anthony Edwards RR 30.00 80.00

2020-21 Donruss Holo Red Laser

*HOLO RED LSR/99: 1.5X TO 4X BASIC
STATED PRINT RUN 99 SER.#'d SETS
12 LeBron James 50.00 120.00
13 Luka Doncic 50.00 120.00
41 Stephen Curry 15.00 40.00
107 Ja Morant 25.00 60.00
147 Zion Williamson 30.00 80.00
201 Anthony Edwards RR 125.00 300.00
202 LaMelo Ball RR 200.00 500.00
203 Isaac Okoro RR 15.00 40.00
205 Deni Avdija RR 20.00 50.00
210 Saddiq Bey RR 20.00 50.00
211 Tyrese Maxey RR 30.00 80.00
213 Immanuel Quickley RR 12.00 30.00
227 Patrick Williams RR 25.00 60.00
229 Obi Toppin RR 15.00 40.00
231 Tyrese Haliburton RR 200.00 500.00
237 RJ Hampton RR 2.50 6.00
238 Payton Pritchard RR 25.00 60.00
239 Jaden McDaniels RR 25.00 60.00
240 Desmond Bane RR 8.00 20.00

2020-21 Donruss Holo Yellow Laser

*HOLO YLW LSR: 6X TO 15X BASIC
STATED PRINT RUN 25 SER.#'d SETS
201 Anthony Edwards RR 125.00 300.00

2020-21 Donruss Press Proof Purple

*PRESS PURPLE: 2.5X TO 6X BASIC
STATED PRINT RUN 199 SER.#'d SETS
201 Anthony Edwards RR 50.00 120.00

2020-21 Donruss Press Proof Silver

*PRESS SLVR: 2X TO 5X BASIC
STATED PRINT RUN 349 SER.#'d SETS
201 Anthony Edwards RR 40.00 100.00

2020-21 Donruss Yellow Flood

*YELLOW FLOOD: 1.25X TO 3X BASIC
201 Anthony Edwards RR 25.00 60.00

2020-21 Donruss All Time League Leaders

1 Kareem Abdul-Jabbar 1.50 4.00
2 LeBron James 4.00 10.00
3 Robert Parish .60 1.50
4 Ray Allen .75 2.00
5 Oscar Robertson 1.25 3.00
6 Bill Russell 1.50 4.00
7 Dirk Nowitzki 1.25 3.00
8 John Stockton 1.00 2.50
9 Wilt Chamberlain 1.50 4.00
10 Vince Carter 1.00 2.50

2020-21 Donruss All Time League Leaders Green Flood

*GREEN FLOOD: .75X TO 2X BASIC
2 LeBron James 15.00 40.00

2020-21 Donruss All Time League Leaders Holo Red Laser

*HOLO RED LSR/99: 1.5X TO 4X BASIC
STATED PRINT RUN 99 SER.#'d SETS
1 Kareem Abdul-Jabbar 20.00 50.00
2 LeBron James 60.00 150.00
5 Oscar Robertson 15.00 40.00
6 Bill Russell 15.00 40.00
7 Dirk Nowitzki 15.00 40.00
9 Wilt Chamberlain 25.00 60.00
10 Vince Carter 15.00 40.00

2020-21 Donruss All Time League Leaders Holo Yellow Laser

*HOLO YELLOW LSR/25: 2.5X TO 6X BASIC
STATED PRINT RUN 25 SER.#'d SETS
1 Kareem Abdul-Jabbar 30.00 80.00
2 LeBron James 100.00 250.00
5 Oscar Robertson 25.00 60.00
6 Bill Russell 25.00 60.00
7 Dirk Nowitzki 25.00 60.00
10 Vince Carter 25.00 60.00

2020-21 Donruss Choice Signatures

STATED PRINT RUN 49 SER.#'d SETS
EXCHANGE DEADLINE 8/24/2022
1 B.J. Armstrong 6.00 15.00
2 David Lee 5.00 12.00
3 Allan Houston 8.00 20.00
4 Doc Rivers 8.00 20.00
5 Jermaine O'Neal 10.00 25.00
6 Dwyane Wade 60.00 150.00
7 Chauncey Billups 15.00 40.00
8 Stephon Marbury 15.00 40.00
9 Jason Richardson 12.00 30.00
10 Nick Van Exel 12.00 30.00
11 Danny Granger 5.00 12.00
12 Avery Johnson 6.00 15.00
13 Kevin Martin 6.00 15.00
14 Rick Fox 15.00 40.00
15 World B. Free 8.00 20.00
16 Kevin Garnett 75.00 200.00
17 Danny Manning 6.00 15.00
18 Kenny Smith 6.00 15.00

19 Glen Rice 6.00 15.00
20 Gerald Wallace 6.00 15.00
21 Michael Cooper 6.00 15.00
22 Steve Francis 8.00 20.00
23 Ron Harper 8.00 20.00
24 Jalen Rose 8.00 20.00
25 Latrell Sprewell 15.00 40.00
26 Paul Pierce 50.00 120.00
27 Robert Horry 15.00 40.00
28 Baron Davis 8.00 20.00
29 Andrea Bargnani 5.00 12.00
30 Peja Stojakovic 8.00 20.00
31 Antawn Jamison 6.00 15.00
32 Jason Terry 6.00 15.00
33 Derrick Coleman 8.00 20.00
34 Vinny Del Negro 6.00 15.00
35 Jason Williams 50.00 120.00
36 Pat Riley 15.00 40.00
37 Shawn Kemp 30.00 80.00
38 Derek Fisher 10.00 25.00
39 Chris Kaman 5.00 12.00
40 Deron Williams 6.00 15.00

2020-21 Donruss Complete Players

1 Kawhi Leonard 1.25 3.00
2 Joel Embiid 1.25 3.00
3 Trae Young 1.25 3.00
4 LeBron James 4.00 10.00
5 Pascal Siakam .75 2.00
6 Stephen Curry 4.00 10.00
7 Ben Simmons .50 1.25
8 James Harden 1.00 2.50
9 Zion Williamson 1.50 4.00
10 Rudy Gobert .60 1.50
11 Kyrie Irving 1.00 2.50
12 Giannis Antetokounmpo 2.50 6.00
13 Zach LaVine .75 2.00
14 Jayson Tatum 2.00 5.00
15 Russell Westbrook 1.00 2.50
16 Luka Doncic 3.00 8.00
17 Ja Morant 1.50 4.00
18 Anthony Davis 1.25 3.00
19 Paul George .75 2.00
20 Nikola Jokic 2.50 6.00

2020-21 Donruss Complete Players Green Flood

*GREEN FLOOD: .75X TO 2X BASIC
4 LeBron James 15.00 40.00
9 Zion Williamson 12.00 30.00
16 Luka Doncic 15.00 40.00
17 Ja Morant 6.00 15.00

2020-21 Donruss Complete Players Holo Red Laser

*HOLO RED LSR/99: 1.5X TO 4X BASIC
STATED PRINT RUN 99 SER.#'d SETS
4 LeBron James 60.00 150.00
6 Stephen Curry 15.00 40.00
9 Zion Williamson 50.00 120.00
12 Giannis Antetokounmpo 15.00 40.00
16 Luka Doncic 60.00 150.00
17 Ja Morant 25.00 60.00

2020-21 Donruss Complete Players Holo Yellow Laser

*HOLO YELLOW LSR/25: 2.5X TO 6X BASIC
STATED PRINT RUN 25 SER.#'d SETS
4 LeBron James 125.00 300.00
6 Stephen Curry 40.00 100.00
9 Zion Williamson 125.00 300.00
12 Giannis Antetokounmpo 40.00 100.00
13 Zach LaVine 12.00 30.00
16 Luka Doncic 125.00 300.00
17 Ja Morant 50.00 120.00
20 Nikola Jokic 20.00 50.00

2020-21 Donruss Craftsmen

1 Russell Westbrook 1.00 2.50
2 Jayson Tatum 2.00 5.00
3 Ja Morant 1.50 4.00
4 Luka Doncic 3.00 8.00
5 Kawhi Leonard 1.25 3.00
6 Anthony Davis 1.25 3.00
7 Joel Embiid 1.25 3.00
8 Giannis Antetokounmpo 2.50 6.00
9 Trae Young 1.25 3.00
10 LeBron James 4.00 10.00
11 Ben Simmons .50 1.25
12 Stephen Curry 4.00 10.00
13 Zion Williamson 1.50 4.00
14 James Harden 1.00 2.50
15 Kyrie Irving 1.00 2.50

2020-21 Donruss Craftsmen Press Proof

PRESS PROOF: 1.25X TO 3X BASIC
4 Luka Doncic 15.00 40.00
10 LeBron James 15.00 40.00
13 Zion Williamson 12.00 30.00

2020-21 Donruss Crunch Time

*PRESS: 1.25X TO 3X BASIC
1 RJ Barrett 1.00 2.50
2 James Harden 1.25 3.00
3 Trae Young 1.50 4.00
4 Kawhi Leonard 1.50 4.00
5 Pascal Siakam 1.00 2.50
6 Joel Embiid 1.50 4.00
7 Ben Simmons .60 1.50
8 LeBron James 15.00 40.00
9 Zion Williamson 15.00 40.00
10 Stephen Curry 8.00 20.00
11 Rui Hachimura .75 2.00
12 Luka Doncic 15.00 40.00
13 Paul George 1.00 2.50
14 Anthony Davis 1.50 4.00
15 Zach LaVine 1.00 2.50
16 Kyrie Irving 1.25 3.00
17 Russell Westbrook 1.25 3.00
18 Giannis Antetokounmpo 6.00 15.00
19 Ja Morant 8.00 20.00
20 Jayson Tatum 2.50 6.00

2020-21 Donruss Dominator Signatures

STATED PRINT RUN 49 SER.#'d SETS
EXCHANGE DEADLINE 8/24/2022
1 Devonte' Graham 5.00 12.00
2 Lauri Markkanen 8.00 20.00
3 Jaren Jackson Jr. 12.00 30.00
4 Stephen Curry 300.00 800.00
5 Jrue Holiday 6.00 15.00
6 Karl-Anthony Towns 12.00 30.00
7 Spencer Dinwiddie 5.00 12.00
8 De'Aaron Fox 12.00 30.00
9 Danilo Gallinari 5.00 12.00
10 Kristaps Porzingis 8.00 20.00
11 Jonas Valanciunas 5.00 12.00
13 Zach LaVine 20.00 50.00
14 Giannis Antetokounmpo 300.00 600.00
15 Al Horford 6.00 15.00
16 Trae Young 40.00 100.00
17 Dwight Howard 8.00 20.00
18 Vince Carter 40.00 100.00
19 Ricky Rubio 6.00 15.00
20 Mike Conley 5.00 12.00
21 Michael Kidd-Gilchrist 4.00 10.00
22 Gordon Hayward 6.00 15.00
23 John Collins 6.00 15.00
24 Kawhi Leonard 150.00 400.00
25 Eric Bledsoe 5.00 12.00
26 Donovan Mitchell 40.00 100.00
27 Kyle Kuzma 8.00 20.00
28 Lonzo Ball 12.00 30.00
29 Eric Gordon 5.00 12.00
30 Jayson Tatum 75.00 200.00

2020-21 Donruss Fantasy Stars

*GREEN FLOOD: .75X TO 2X BASIC
1 LeBron James 4.00 10.00
2 Nikola Jokic 2.50 6.00
3 James Harden 1.00 2.50
4 Ben Simmons .50 1.25
5 Luka Doncic 3.00 8.00

2020-21 Donruss Fantasy Stars Holo Red Laser

*HOLO RED LSR/99: 1.5X TO 4X BASIC
STATED PRINT RUN 99 SER.#'d SETS

2020-21 Donruss Fantasy Stars Holo Yellow Laser

STATED PRINT RUN 25 SER.#'d SETS

2020-21 Donruss Franchise Features

1 Trae Young 1.25 3.00
2 Jayson Tatum 2.00 5.00
3 Kyrie Irving 1.00 2.50
4 Devonte' Graham .40 1.00
5 Zach LaVine .75 2.00
6 Darius Garland .75 2.00
7 Luka Doncic 3.00 8.00
8 Nikola Jokic 2.50 6.00
9 Derrick Rose .75 2.00
10 Stephen Curry 4.00 10.00
11 James Harden 1.00 2.50
12 Domantas Sabonis .60 1.50
13 Kawhi Leonard 1.25 3.00
14 LeBron James 4.00 10.00
15 Ja Morant 1.50 4.00
16 Tyler Herro 1.00 2.50
17 Giannis Antetokounmpo 2.50 6.00
18 Karl-Anthony Towns .75 2.00
19 Zion Williamson 1.50 4.00
20 RJ Barrett .75 2.00
21 Shai Gilgeous-Alexander 2.50 6.00
22 Nikola Vucevic .50 1.25
23 Joel Embiid 1.25 3.00
24 Devin Booker 1.25 3.00
25 Damian Lillard 1.25 3.00
26 De'Aaron Fox .75 2.00
27 DeMar DeRozan .60 1.50
28 Pascal Siakam .75 2.00
29 Donovan Mitchell 1.00 2.50
30 Bradley Beal .60 1.50

2020-21 Donruss Franchise Features Green Flood

7 Luka Doncic 15.00 40.00
10 Stephen Curry 8.00 20.00
14 LeBron James 15.00 40.00
15 Ja Morant 10.00 25.00
17 Giannis Antetokounmpo 8.00 20.00
19 Zion Williamson 15.00 40.00

2020-21 Donruss Franchise Features Holo Red Laser

STATED PRINT RUN 99 SER.#'d SETS
7 Luka Doncic 60.00 150.00
10 Stephen Curry 20.00 50.00
14 LeBron James 60.00 150.00
15 Ja Morant 40.00 100.00
17 Giannis Antetokounmpo 20.00 50.00
19 Zion Williamson 60.00 150.00

2020-21 Donruss Franchise Features Holo Yellow Laser

STATED PRINT RUN 25 SER.#'d SETS
2 Jayson Tatum 20.00 50.00
3 Kyrie Irving 15.00 40.00
7 Luka Doncic 125.00 300.00
8 Nikola Jokic 20.00 50.00
10 Stephen Curry 40.00 100.00
14 LeBron James 125.00 300.00
17 Giannis Antetokounmpo 40.00 100.00
19 Zion Williamson 125.00 300.00
23 Joel Embiid 12.00 30.00
25 Damian Lillard 12.00 30.00

2020-21 Donruss Great X-Pectations

1 Anthony Edwards 6.00 15.00
2 James Wiseman .75 2.00
3 LaMelo Ball 15.00 40.00
4 Patrick Williams 1.50 4.00
5 Isaac Okoro 1.00 2.50
6 Onyeka Okongwu 1.50 4.00
7 Killian Hayes .60 1.50
8 Obi Toppin 1.25 3.00
9 Deni Avdija 1.50 4.00
10 Jalen Smith 1.25 3.00
11 Devin Vassell 2.00 5.00
12 Tyrese Haliburton 5.00 12.00
13 Kira Lewis Jr. .60 1.50
14 Aaron Nesmith 1.25 3.00
15 Cole Anthony 1.50 4.00
16 Isaiah Stewart 1.25 3.00
17 Aleksej Pokusevski .75 2.00
18 Josh Green 1.25 3.00
19 Saddiq Bey 1.25 3.00
20 Precious Achiuwa 1.25 3.00
21 Tyrese Maxey 5.00 12.00
22 Zeke Nnaji .75 2.00
23 Nico Mannion .60 1.50
24 RJ Hampton .60 1.50
25 Immanuel Quickley 1.50 4.00

2020-21 Donruss Great X-Pectations Green Flood

*GREEN FLOOD: .75X TO 2X BASIC
1 Anthony Edwards 20.00 50.00
3 LaMelo Ball 40.00 100.00

2020-21 Donruss Great X-Pectations Holo Red Laser

*HOLO RED LSR/99: 1.5X TO 4X BASIC
STATED PRINT RUN 99 SER.#'d SETS
1 Anthony Edwards 125.00 300.00
3 LaMelo Ball 300.00 600.00
7 Killian Hayes 15.00 40.00
8 Obi Toppin 15.00 40.00
9 Deni Avdija 15.00 40.00
12 Tyrese Haliburton 75.00 200.00
13 Kira Lewis Jr. 15.00 40.00
15 Cole Anthony 20.00 50.00
19 Saddiq Bey 20.00 50.00
21 Tyrese Maxey 20.00 50.00
24 RJ Hampton 2.50 6.00
25 Immanuel Quickley 40.00 100.00

2020-21 Donruss Great X-Pectations Holo Yellow Laser

*HOLO YELLOW LSR/25: 2.5X TO 6X BASIC
STATED PRINT RUN 25 SER.#'d SETS
1 Anthony Edwards 200.00 500.00
3 LaMelo Ball 500.00 1,000.00
7 Killian Hayes 40.00 100.00
8 Obi Toppin 40.00 100.00
9 Deni Avdija 40.00 100.00
12 Tyrese Haliburton 125.00 300.00
13 Kira Lewis Jr. 40.00 100.00
15 Cole Anthony 50.00 120.00
19 Saddiq Bey 50.00 120.00
21 Tyrese Maxey 50.00 120.00
24 RJ Hampton 4.00 10.00
25 Immanuel Quickley 100.00 250.00

2020-21 Donruss Hall Dominator Signatures

STATED PRINT RUN 49 SER.#'d SETS
EXCHANGE DEADLINE 8/24/2022
1 George Gervin 12.00 30.00
2 Allen Iverson 100.00 250.00
3 Bill Walton 25.00 60.00
4 Julius Erving 40.00 100.00
5 Dave Cowens 8.00 20.00
6 Hakeem Olajuwon 40.00 100.00
8 Grant Hill 12.00 30.00
9 Vlade Divac 5.00 12.00
10 Dennis Rodman 40.00 100.00
11 Nate Archibald 8.00 20.00
12 Larry Bird 75.00 200.00
13 Joe Dumars 8.00 20.00
14 Oscar Robertson 20.00 50.00
15 Louie Dampier 6.00 15.00
16 David Robinson 20.00 50.00
17 David Thompson 15.00 40.00
18 Gary Payton 15.00 40.00
19 Sarunas Marciulionis 6.00 15.00
20 Jerry Lucas 8.00 20.00
21 Elvin Hayes 8.00 20.00
22 Magic Johnson 75.00 200.00
23 Lenny Wilkens 6.00 15.00
24 Jerry West 30.00 80.00
25 Gail Goodrich 12.00 30.00
26 Ray Allen 15.00 40.00
27 Dino Radja 5.00 12.00
28 Rick Barry 12.00 30.00
29 Calvin Murphy 8.00 20.00
30 Dave Bing 12.00 30.00

2020-21 Donruss Jersey Kings

1 Karl-Anthony Towns 4.00 10.00
2 John Wall 3.00 8.00
3 Nikola Jokic 12.00 30.00
4 Anthony Davis 6.00 15.00
5 Zach LaVine 4.00 10.00
6 Anfernee Hardaway 25.00 60.00
7 Steve Nash 12.00 30.00
8 Tim Duncan 12.00 30.00
9 Ben Simmons 2.50 6.00
10 Devin Booker 8.00 20.00
11 Domantas Sabonis 3.00 8.00
12 Charles Barkley 25.00 60.00
13 PJ Washington Jr. 2.50 6.00
14 David Robinson 12.00 30.00
15 Larry Bird 25.00 60.00
16 Shaquille O'Neal 25.00 60.00
17 Kareem Abdul-Jabbar 25.00 60.00
18 Derrick Rose 4.00 10.00
19 Sekou Doumbouya 1.50 4.00
20 Tony Parker 4.00 10.00
21 Shai Gilgeous-Alexander 12.00 30.00
22 Ja Morant 40.00 100.00
23 Draymond Green 3.00 8.00
24 Jamal Murray 4.00 10.00
25 Damian Lillard 15.00 40.00
26 CJ McCollum 2.50 6.00
27 Kevin Love 2.50 6.00
28 Alonzo Mourning 12.00 30.00
29 Giannis Antetokounmpo 20.00 50.00
30 Shawn Kemp 15.00 40.00
31 Jayson Tatum 15.00 40.00
32 Terry Rozier 2.50 6.00
33 Clyde Drexler 4.00 10.00
34 Dwyane Wade 12.00 30.00
35 Kevin Johnson 2.50 6.00
36 Mike Bibby 2.50 6.00
37 Chris Paul 5.00 12.00
38 Kemba Walker 2.50 6.00
39 Grant Hill 4.00 10.00
40 LeBron James 75.00 200.00
41 Victor Oladipo 2.00 5.00
42 Bradley Beal 3.00 8.00
43 Blake Griffin 2.50 6.00
44 RJ Barrett 4.00 10.00
45 Buddy Hield 2.50 6.00
46 Chris Mullin 3.00 8.00
47 Tyler Herro 5.00 12.00
48 James Harden 8.00 20.00
49 Coby White 3.00 8.00
50 Zion Williamson 75.00 200.00
51 Fred VanVleet 4.00 10.00
52 James Worthy 4.00 10.00
53 De'Aaron Fox 4.00 10.00
54 Allen Iverson 6.00 15.00
55 Kevin Garnett 12.00 30.00
56 Kevin McHale 3.00 8.00
57 Patrick Ewing 8.00 20.00
58 Magic Johnson 20.00 50.00
59 Jason Kidd 4.00 10.00
60 Robert Parish 3.00 8.00

2020-21 Donruss Jersey Series

1 Ben Simmons 2.50 6.00
2 Scottie Pippen 5.00 12.00
3 Giannis Antetokounmpo 20.00 50.00
4 Grant Hill 4.00 10.00
5 Coby White 3.00 8.00
6 Tobias Harris 2.50 6.00
7 Jason Kidd 4.00 10.00
8 Karl-Anthony Towns 4.00 10.00
9 Domantas Sabonis 3.00 8.00
10 Shai Gilgeous-Alexander 12.00 30.00
11 Lauri Markkanen 3.00 8.00
12 Malik Monk 2.50 6.00
13 Jayson Tatum 15.00 40.00
14 Marvin Bagley III 2.00 5.00
15 Alex English 2.50 6.00
16 Aaron Holiday 2.00 5.00
17 Victor Oladipo 2.00 5.00
18 Andrew Wiggins 3.00 8.00
19 Fred VanVleet 4.00 10.00
20 Taj Gibson 1.50 4.00
21 Nikola Jokic 12.00 30.00
22 Hakeem Olajuwon 8.00 20.00
23 Draymond Green 3.00 8.00
24 Clyde Drexler 4.00 10.00
25 Anfernee Simons 3.00 8.00
26 Blake Griffin 2.50 6.00
27 De'Aaron Fox 4.00 10.00
28 Zach LaVine 4.00 10.00
29 Mikal Bridges 3.00 8.00
30 Larry Bird 20.00 50.00
31 Reggie Jackson 2.00 5.00
32 Damian Lillard 6.00 15.00
33 Bernard King 3.00 8.00
34 Clyde Drexler 4.00 10.00
35 Kevin Johnson 2.50 6.00
36 Buddy Hield 2.50 6.00
37 Kevin Garnett 12.00 30.00
38 Josh Okogie 2.00 5.00
39 Steve Nash 8.00 20.00
40 Jeff Teague 1.50 4.00
41 Kareem Abdul-Jabbar 12.00 30.00
42 Kevin Love 2.50 6.00
43 Dennis Johnson 2.50 6.00
44 Chris Paul 5.00 12.00
45 Tyler Herro 5.00 12.00
46 Patrick Ewing 3.00 8.00
47 Tim Duncan 8.00 20.00
48 Derrick Rose 4.00 10.00
49 Steve Nash 8.00 20.00
50 Luke Kennard 2.00 5.00
51 Alonzo Mourning 3.00 8.00
52 Kemba Walker 2.50 6.00
53 James Harden 5.00 12.00
54 Magic Johnson 20.00 50.00
55 OG Anunoby 2.50 6.00
56 Devin Booker 8.00 20.00
57 Tony Parker 4.00 10.00
58 Carmelo Anthony 4.00 10.00
59 Moses Malone 3.00 8.00
60 Shawn Kemp 15.00 40.00
61 Reggie Lewis 12.00 30.00
62 Malcolm Brogdon 2.50 6.00
63 Myles Turner 2.50 6.00
64 Charles Barkley 20.00 50.00
65 Zion Williamson 40.00 100.00
66 Robert Parish 3.00 8.00
67 Mo Bamba 2.50 6.00
68 John Wall 3.00 8.00
69 Moses Malone 8.00 20.00
70 Shawn Kemp 12.00 30.00
71 Lou Williams 2.50 6.00
72 Andre Drummond 2.50 6.00
73 Eric Gordon 2.00 5.00
74 Charles Barkley 6.00 15.00
75 Ja Morant 25.00 60.00
76 Terry Rozier 2.50 6.00
77 Dennis Schroder 2.50 6.00
78 Bradley Beal 3.00 8.00
79 James Worthy 4.00 10.00
80 Anthony Davis 6.00 15.00
81 Aaron Gordon 2.50 6.00
82 David Robinson 8.00 20.00
83 Jamal Murray 4.00 10.00
84 Dwyane Wade 8.00 20.00
85 RJ Barrett 4.00 10.00
86 Allen Iverson 8.00 20.00
87 Anfernee Hardaway 20.00 50.00
88 Shaquille O'Neal 20.00 50.00
89 Yao Ming 15.00 40.00
90 CJ McCollum 2.50 6.00
91 Mike Bibby 2.50 6.00
92 Tyus Jones 2.00 5.00
93 Bobby Portis 2.50 6.00
94 Jrue Holiday 2.50 6.00
95 Matisse Thybulle 2.00 5.00
96 Chris Mullin 3.00 8.00
97 Kevin McHale 3.00 8.00
98 Shaquille O'Neal 20.00 50.00
99 Jonathan Isaac 2.50 6.00
100 Scottie Pippen 5.00 12.00

2020-21 Donruss Net Marvels

PRESS PROOF: 1.25X TO 3X BASIC
1 Trae Young 12.00 30.00
2 Zach LaVine 8.00 20.00
3 Pascal Siakam 3.00 8.00
4 Russell Westbrook 4.00 10.00
5 Ben Simmons 6.00 15.00
6 Ja Morant 40.00 100.00
7 Zion Williamson 20.00 50.00
8 Rui Hachimura 2.50 6.00
9 RJ Barrett 3.00 8.00
10 Paul George 3.00 8.00
11 Kawhi Leonard 10.00 25.00
12 Kyrie Irving 10.00 25.00
13 Joel Embiid 10.00 25.00
14 Giannis Antetokounmpo 20.00 50.00
15 LeBron James 40.00 100.00
16 Jayson Tatum 8.00 20.00
17 Stephen Curry 25.00 60.00
18 Luka Doncic 40.00 100.00
19 James Harden 8.00 20.00
20 Anthony Davis 5.00 12.00

2020-21 Donruss Power in the Paint

1 Rudy Gobert .60 1.50
2 Nikola Jokic 2.50 6.00
3 Bam Adebayo .75 2.00
4 Nikola Vucevic .50 1.25
5 Joel Embiid 1.25 3.00
6 Karl-Anthony Towns .75 2.00
7 Andre Drummond .50 1.25
8 Jarrett Allen .50 1.25
9 Steven Adams .50 1.25
10 Hassan Whiteside .40 1.00

2020-21 Donruss Power in the Paint Green Flood

*GREEN FLOOD: .75X TO 2X BASIC
2 Nikola Jokic 6.00 15.00
5 Joel Embiid 6.00 15.00

2020-21 Donruss Power in the Paint Holo Red Laser

*HOLO RED LSR/99: 1.5X TO 4X BASIC
STATED PRINT RUN 99 SER.#'d SETS
2 Nikola Jokic 12.00 30.00
5 Joel Embiid 12.00 30.00

2020-21 Donruss Power in the Paint Holo Yellow Laser

*HOLO YELLOW LSR/25: 2.5X TO 6X BASIC
STATED PRINT RUN 25 SER.#'d SETS
2 Nikola Jokic 30.00 80.00
5 Joel Embiid 30.00 80.00

2020-21 Donruss Rated Rookies Signatures

EXCHANGE DEADLINE 8/24/2022
*CHOICE: .5X TO 1.2X BASIC
*GRN FLOOD: .5X TO 1.2X BASIC
*GRN YLW LSR: .5X TO 1.2X BASIC
*HOLO LIGHT BLUE LSR: .5X TO 1.2X BASIC
*HOLO ORNG LSR: .5X TO 1.2X BASIC
*HOLO RED GOLD LSR: .5X TO 1.2X BASIC
*HOLO YLW LSR: .5X TO 1.2X BASIC
*CHOICE RED/99: .6X TO 1.5X BASE
*CHOICE BLUE/49: .75X TO 2X BASE
*HOLO RED LSR/49: .75X TO 2X BASIC
*HOLO BLUE LSR/25: 1.25X TO 3X BASIC
*HOLO RED & BLUE LSR/20: 1.25X TO 3X BASIC
201 Anthony Edwards 300.00 600.00
202 LaMelo Ball 100.00 250.00
203 Isaac Okoro 8.00 20.00
204 Killian Hayes 5.00 12.00
205 Deni Avdija 12.00 30.00
206 Devin Vassell 15.00 40.00
207 Kira Lewis Jr. 5.00 12.00
208 Cole Anthony 12.00 30.00
209 Aleksej Pokusevski 6.00 15.00
210 Saddiq Bey 10.00 25.00
211 Tyrese Maxey 75.00 200.00
212 Caleb Martin 10.00 25.00
213 Immanuel Quickley 12.00 30.00
214 Udoka Azubuike 6.00 15.00
215 Malachi Flynn 5.00 12.00
216 Tyrell Terry 4.00 10.00
217 Daniel Oturu 5.00 12.00
218 Xavier Tillman 6.00 15.00
219 Robert Woodard II 6.00 15.00
220 Jordan Nwora 6.00 15.00
221 Saben Lee 5.00 12.00
222 Nick Richards 6.00 15.00
223 CJ Elleby 5.00 12.00
224 Kenyon Martin Jr. 8.00 20.00
225 Cassius Stanley 5.00 12.00
226 James Wiseman 6.00 15.00
227 Patrick Williams 12.00 30.00
228 Onyeka Okongwu 10.00 25.00
229 Obi Toppin 10.00 25.00
230 Jalen Smith 10.00 25.00
231 Tyrese Haliburton 100.00 250.00
232 Aaron Nesmith 10.00 25.00
233 Isaiah Stewart 10.00 25.00
234 Josh Green 10.00 25.00
235 Precious Achiuwa 10.00 25.00
236 Zeke Nnaji 6.00 15.00
237 RJ Hampton 5.00 12.00
238 Payton Pritchard 15.00 40.00
239 Jaden McDaniels 15.00 40.00
240 Desmond Bane 15.00 40.00
241 Vernon Carey Jr. 5.00 12.00
242 Theo Maledon 5.00 12.00
243 Tyler Bey 5.00 12.00
244 Tre Jones 8.00 20.00
245 Nico Mannion 5.00 12.00
246 Elijah Hughes 5.00 12.00
247 Jahmi'us Ramsey 5.00 12.00
248 Skylar Mays 5.00 12.00
249 Cassius Winston 5.00 12.00
250 Grant Riller 5.00 12.00

2020-21 Donruss Retro Series

*PRESS: .75X TO 2X BASIC
1 Ray Allen .75 2.00
2 Anfernee Hardaway 1.25 3.00
3 Dennis Rodman 1.25 3.00
4 Tracy McGrady .75 2.00
5 Shaquille O'Neal 2.00 5.00
6 Drazen Petrovic .50 1.25
7 Charles Barkley 1.25 3.00
8 Bill Bradley .50 1.25
9 Jerry West 1.00 2.50
10 Tim Duncan 1.25 3.00
11 Jason Kidd .75 2.00
12 Moses Malone .60 1.50
13 Bill Russell 1.50 4.00
14 Alonzo Mourning .60 1.50
15 Allen Iverson 1.25 3.00
16 Amar'e Stoudemire .50 1.25
17 Dwyane Wade 1.00 2.50
18 Wilt Chamberlain 1.50 4.00
19 Oscar Robertson 1.25 3.00
20 Patrick Ewing .60 1.50
21 Stephon Marbury .60 1.50
22 Pete Maravich 1.25 3.00
23 Paul Pierce .75 2.00
24 Steve Nash 1.00 2.50
25 Karl Malone 1.00 2.50
26 Chris Webber .60 1.50
27 Magic Johnson 2.00 5.00
28 Darryl Dawkins .40 1.00
29 David Robinson 1.00 2.50
30 Kevin Garnett 1.25 3.00

2020-21 Donruss Rookie Jersey Kings

*PRIME/25: .75X TO 2X BASIC
1 Anthony Edwards 75.00 200.00
2 Isaac Okoro 4.00 10.00
3 Deni Avdija 12.00 30.00
4 Kira Lewis Jr. 2.50 6.00
5 Aleksej Pokusevski 3.00 8.00
6 Tyrese Maxey 20.00 50.00
7 Immanuel Quickley 30.00 80.00
8 Malachi Flynn 2.50 6.00
9 Daniel Oturu 2.50 6.00
10 Robert Woodard II 2.50 6.00
11 James Wiseman 3.00 8.00
12 Onyeka Okongwu 5.00 12.00
13 Jalen Smith 5.00 12.00
14 Aaron Nesmith 5.00 12.00
15 Josh Green 5.00 12.00
16 Zeke Nnaji 3.00 8.00
17 Payton Pritchard 12.00 30.00
18 Desmond Bane 8.00 20.00
19 Theo Maledon 2.50 6.00
20 Tre Jones 4.00 10.00
21 LaMelo Ball 150.00 400.00
22 Killian Hayes 2.50 6.00
23 Devin Vassell 8.00 20.00
24 Cole Anthony 6.00 15.00
25 Saddiq Bey 5.00 12.00
26 Caleb Martin 5.00 12.00
27 Udoka Azubuike 3.00 8.00
28 Tyrell Terry 2.00 5.00
29 Xavier Tillman 3.00 8.00
30 Jordan Nwora 3.00 8.00
31 Patrick Williams 20.00 50.00
32 Obi Toppin 5.00 12.00
33 Tyrese Haliburton 40.00 100.00
34 Isaiah Stewart 5.00 12.00
35 Precious Achiuwa 5.00 12.00
36 RJ Hampton 2.50 6.00
37 Jaden McDaniels 8.00 20.00
38 Vernon Carey Jr. 2.50 6.00
39 Tyler Bey 2.50 6.00
40 Nico Mannion 2.50 6.00

2020-21 Donruss Signature Series

EXCHANGE DEADLINE 8/24/2022
1 Zion Williamson 300.00 600.00
2 Otis Birdsong 4.00 10.00
3 Dennis Rodman 40.00 100.00
4 Hamidou Diallo 4.00 10.00
5 Alex Caruso 20.00 50.00
6 Isaac Bonga 3.00 8.00
7 Tony Delk 4.00 10.00
8 Langston Galloway 3.00 8.00
9 Terry Cummings 5.00 12.00
10 Micheal Ray Richardson 3.00 8.00
11 Dwyane Wade 75.00 200.00
12 Jonas Valanciunas 4.00 10.00
13 RJ Barrett 8.00 20.00
14 Ricky Pierce 3.00 8.00
15 Alvin Robertson 4.00 10.00
16 Monte Morris 3.00 8.00
17 Shawn Kemp 15.00 40.00
18 Devonte' Graham 4.00 10.00
19 Jakob Poeltl 4.00 10.00
20 Gerald Green 3.00 8.00
21 Magic Johnson 75.00 200.00
22 DeAndre' Bembry 3.00 8.00
23 Ja Morant 300.00 600.00
24 Slick Watts 4.00 10.00
25 Jevon Carter 4.00 10.00
26 Dale Ellis 4.00 10.00
27 Darius Miles 3.00 8.00
28 Ricky Davis 8.00 20.00
29 Tony Snell 3.00 8.00
30 Dick Barnett 4.00 10.00
31 Kevin Garnett 75.00 200.00
32 Kevon Looney 4.00 10.00
33 Ray Allen 40.00 100.00
34 Bob Love 5.00 12.00
35 Danuel House Jr. 4.00 10.00
36 Damian Jones 3.00 8.00
37 Mason Plumlee 3.00 8.00
38 Larry Nance Jr. 4.00 10.00
39 Dave Bing 12.00 30.00
40 Mikal Bridges 6.00 15.00
41 Jerry West 30.00 80.00
42 Spencer Dinwiddie 4.00 10.00
43 Trae Young 75.00 200.00
44 Meyers Leonard 3.00 8.00
45 Spencer Haywood 5.00 12.00
46 Ben McLemore 3.00 8.00
47 Quentin Richardson 3.00 8.00
48 Brian Scalabrine 3.00 8.00
49 Craig Ehlo 4.00 10.00
50 Archie Clark 4.00 10.00
51 Anthony Edwards 300.00 600.00
52 Patrick Williams 40.00 100.00
53 Killian Hayes 4.00 10.00
54 Jalen Smith 8.00 20.00
55 Kira Lewis Jr. 4.00 10.00
56 Isaiah Stewart 8.00 20.00
57 Saddiq Bey 30.00 80.00
58 Zeke Nnaji 5.00 12.00
59 Immanuel Quickley 40.00 100.00
60 Jaden McDaniels 25.00 60.00
61 Tyrell Terry 3.00 8.00
62 Theo Maledon 4.00 10.00
63 Robert Woodard II 4.00 10.00
64 Nico Mannion 4.00 10.00
65 James Wiseman 5.00 12.00
66 Isaac Okoro 15.00 40.00
67 Obi Toppin 30.00 80.00
68 Devin Vassell 12.00 30.00
69 Aaron Nesmith 5.00 12.00
70 Aleksej Pokusevski 5.00 12.00
71 Precious Achiuwa 8.00 20.00
72 Caleb Martin 8.00 20.00
73 Payton Pritchard 12.00 30.00
74 Malachi Flynn 4.00 10.00
75 Vernon Carey Jr. 4.00 10.00
76 Xavier Tillman 5.00 12.00
77 Tre Jones 6.00 15.00
78 LaMelo Ball 500.00 1,000.00
79 Onyeka Okongwu 8.00 20.00
80 Deni Avdija 10.00 25.00
81 Tyrese Haliburton 75.00 200.00
82 Cole Anthony 40.00 100.00
83 Josh Green 8.00 20.00
84 Tyrese Maxey 75.00 200.00
85 RJ Hampton 4.00 10.00
86 Udoka Azubuike 5.00 12.00
88 Daniel Oturu 4.00 10.00
89 Tyler Bey 4.00 10.00
90 Jordan Nwora 15.00 40.00
91 Saben Lee 4.00 10.00
92 Elijah Hughes 4.00 10.00
93 Nick Richards 5.00 12.00
94 Jahmi'us Ramsey 4.00 10.00
95 CJ Elleby 4.00 10.00
96 Skylar Mays 4.00 10.00
98 Cassius Winston 4.00 10.00
99 Cassius Stanley 4.00 10.00
100 Grant Riller 4.00 10.00

2020-21 Donruss The Rookies

1 LaMelo Ball 20.00 50.00
2 Anthony Edwards 12.00 30.00
3 James Wiseman .75 2.00
4 Obi Toppin 1.25 3.00
5 Tyrese Haliburton 6.00 15.00

2020-21 Donruss Zero Gravity

1 Dominique Wilkins .75 2.00
2 LeBron James 8.00 20.00
3 Shawn Kemp .75 2.00
4 Donovan Mitchell 1.00 2.50
5 Zion Williamson 8.00 20.00
6 Zach LaVine .75 2.00
7 Anthony Davis 1.25 3.00
8 Giannis Antetokounmpo 2.50 6.00
9 Julius Erving 1.25 3.00
10 Blake Griffin .50 1.25

2020-21 Donruss Zero Gravity Press Proof

PRESS PROOF: 1.25X TO 3X BASIC
2 LeBron James 50.00 120.00
5 Zion Williamson 30.00 80.00
8 Giannis Antetokounmpo 15.00 40.00

2021-22 Donruss

COM CARD (1-200) .20 .50
SEMISTARS .25 .60
UNLISTED STARS .30 .75
COMMON RC (201-250) .40 1.00
RC SEMIS .50 1.25
RC UNLISTED .60 1.50
*PRESS PROOF SILVER: .5X TO 1.2X BASIC
*YELLOW FLOOD: 1X TO 2.5X BASIC
*HOLO GRN LSR: 1.25X TO 3X BASIC
*HOLO GRN YLW LSR: 1.25X TO 3X BASIC
*HOLO ORANGE LSR: 1.25X TO 3X BASIC
*HOLO PINK LSR: 1.25X TO 3X BASIC
*RED & GOLD LSR: 1.25X TO 3X BASIC
*PRESS PROOF PRPL/199: 1.5X TO 4X BASIC
*HOLO LSR/149: 2X TO 5X BASIC
*CHOICE RED/99: 2.5X TO 6X BASIC
*HOLO PRPL LSR/99: 2.5X TO 6X BASIC
*HOLO RED LSR/99: 2.5X TO 6X BASIC
*75TH ANN/75: 3X TO 8X BASIC
*HOLO LT BLUE LSR/60: 4X TO 10X BASIC
*CHOICE BLUE/49: 5X TO 12X BASIC
*HOLO BLUE LSR/49: 5X TO 12X BASIC
*HOLO YLW LSR/25: 8X TO 20X BASIC
1 Joel Embiid .75 2.00
2 Payton Pritchard .30 .75
3 Davis Bertans .20 .50
4 Kevin Huerter .25 .60
5 Ben Simmons .30 .75
6 Immanuel Quickley .30 .75
7 Thomas Bryant .20 .50
8 Kevin Durant 1.00 2.50
9 Domantas Sabonis .40 1.00
10 Tristan Thompson .20 .50
11 Zach LaVine .50 1.25
12 LeBron James 2.50 6.00
13 Jordan Poole .50 1.25
14 Gary Trent Jr. .25 .60
15 Devin Vassell .50 1.25
16 Saben Lee .25 .60
17 Darius Bazley .20 .50
18 Kira Lewis Jr. .20 .50
19 Jalen Brunson .60 1.50
20 Aaron Gordon .30 .75
21 DeMar DeRozan .40 1.00
22 Derrick White .30 .75
23 Shai Gilgeous-Alexander 1.50 4.00
24 Precious Achiuwa .30 .75
25 Lonnie Walker IV .25 .60
26 Andrew Wiggins .40 1.00
27 Andre Drummond .25 .60
28 Nikola Jokic 1.50 4.00
29 Brandon Ingram .40 1.00
30 Evan Fournier .25 .60
31 Robert Covington .20 .50
32 Paul George .50 1.25
33 Clint Capela .30 .75
34 Myles Turner .30 .75
35 Blake Griffin .30 .75
36 Chuma Okeke .30 .75
37 Eric Gordon .25 .60
38 Fred VanVleet .40 1.00
39 Enes Freedom .25 .60
40 Bogdan Bogdanovic .30 .75
41 PJ Washington Jr. .30 .75
42 Aleksej Pokusevski .25 .60
43 Tyrese Haliburton .60 1.50
44 Desmond Bane .60 1.50
45 Derrick Rose .50 1.25
46 Jonas Valanciunas .25 .60
47 Theo Maledon .25 .60
48 Tyrese Maxey .75 2.00
49 Patty Mills .30 .75
50 Dillon Brooks .30 .75
51 Ricky Rubio .30 .75
52 Al Horford .30 .75
53 Harrison Barnes .25 .60

54 Jerami Grant .30 .75
55 Draymond Green .40 1.00
56 Trae Young .75 2.00
57 Kristaps Porzingis .40 1.00
58 Malik Easley .25 .60
59 Reggie Jackson .25 .60
60 Jayson Tatum 1.25 3.00
61 Richaun Holmes .20 .50
62 Goran Dragic .25 .60
63 Monte Morris .25 .60
64 James Harden .60 1.50
65 Royce O'Neale .25 .60
66 Bryn Forbes .25 .60
67 Kemba Walker .30 .75
68 Stephen Curry 2.00 5.00
69 Christian Wood .25 .60
70 Boban Marjanovic .30 .75
71 Cameron Johnson .30 .75
72 Russell Westbrook .50 1.25
73 Klay Thompson .75 2.00
74 Devonte' Graham .25 .60
75 Karl-Anthony Towns .50 1.25
76 Ja Morant 1.00 2.50
77 Luka Doncic 2.00 5.00
78 Jaden McDaniels .30 .75
79 Lonzo Ball .30 .75
80 Seth Curry .25 .60
81 Bradley Beal .40 1.00
82 D'Angelo Russell .30 .75
83 RJ Barrett .50 1.25
84 Kendrick Nunn .25 .60
85 Jaren Jackson Jr. .50 1.25
86 P.J. Tucker .25 .60
87 Miles Bridges .25 .60
88 Brook Lopez .25 .60
89 Spencer Dinwiddie .25 .60
90 Thaddeus Young .20 .50
91 Rui Hachimura .30 .75
92 Alec Burks .20 .50
93 Pascal Siakam .50 1.25
94 Donte DiVincenzo .30 .75
95 Jimmy Butler .50 1.25
96 Damian Lillard .75 2.00
97 Kenyon Martin Jr. .30 .75
98 Jae Crowder .20 .50
99 Michael Porter Jr. .40 1.00
100 Deni Avdija .30 .75
101 Eric Bledsoe .25 .60
102 Norman Powell .25 .60
103 Carmelo Anthony .50 1.25
104 Keldon Johnson .40 1.00
105 John Collins .30 .75
106 Will Barton .20 .50
107 Duncan Robinson .25 .60
108 Jrue Holiday .40 1.00
109 Darius Garland .50 1.25
110 CJ McCollum .30 .75
111 LaMelo Ball .75 2.00
112 Joe Harris .25 .60
113 Isaiah Stewart .30 .75
114 Tyler Herro .50 1.25
115 James Wiseman .25 .60
116 T.J. Warren .20 .50
117 Ty Jerome .25 .60
118 Obi Toppin .30 .75
119 Kyle Lowry .30 .75
120 Jae'Sean Tate .30 .75
121 Jamal Murray .50 1.25
122 Kelly Olynyk .20 .50
123 Jusuf Nurkic .25 .60
124 Collin Sexton .30 .75
125 Caris LeVert .25 .60
126 De'Aaron Fox .50 1.25
127 Patrick Williams .30 .75
128 Jordan Clarkson .30 .75
129 Reggie Bullock .20 .50
130 Dennis Schroder .30 .75
131 Jarrett Allen .30 .75
132 Buddy Hield .25 .60
133 Tobias Harris .25 .60
134 Marvin Bagley III .25 .60
135 Chris Boucher .30 .75
136 Kawhi Leonard .75 2.00
137 Kelly Oubre Jr. .30 .75
138 Terry Rozier .25 .60
139 Dorian Finney-Smith .20 .50
140 Marcus Smart .30 .75
141 Facundo Campazzo .30 .75
142 John Wall .40 1.00
143 Daniel Gafford .25 .60
144 Wendell Carter Jr. .30 .75
145 Killian Hayes .30 .75
146 Luke Kennard .25 .60
147 Cameron Payne .30 .75
148 Mike Conley .25 .60
149 Lauri Markkanen .40 1.00
150 Maxi Kleber .20 .50
151 Markelle Fultz .20 .50
152 Luguentz Dort .30 .75
153 Malachi Flynn .20 .50
154 Bam Adebayo .50 1.25
155 Nikola Vucevic .30 .75
156 Terance Mann .30 .75
157 Dejounte Murray .30 .75
158 Doug McDermott .25 .60
159 Donovan Mitchell .60 1.50
160 Cole Anthony .40 1.00
161 Josh Jackson .20 .50
162 Deandre Ayton .30 .75
163 Terrence Ross .25 .60
164 Jaylen Brown .50 1.25
165 Coby White .30 .75
166 Kyle Kuzma .40 1.00
167 Talen Horton-Tucker .30 .75
168 Joe Ingles .25 .60
169 Mikal Bridges .40 1.00
170 Nickeil Alexander-Walker .25 .60
171 Kevin Love .30 .75
172 Anthony Davis .75 2.00
173 Kyle Anderson .20 .50
174 Matisse Thybulle .25 .60
175 Anthony Edwards 1.50 4.00
176 Danny Green .25 .60
177 Giannis Antetokounmpo 1.50 4.00
178 Chris Paul .60 1.50
179 Kyrie Irving .60 1.50
180 Onyeka Okongwu .30 .75
181 Montrezl Harrell .25 .60
182 Rudy Gobert .40 1.00
183 Tim Hardaway Jr. .20 .50
184 Malcolm Brogdon .25 .60
185 RJ Hampton .20 .50
186 Danilo Gallinari .25 .60
187 Cedi Osman .25 .60
188 Patrick Beverley .20 .50
189 Zion Williamson .75 2.00
190 Bojan Bogdanovic .25 .60
191 Kevin Porter Jr. .25 .60
192 Julius Randle .40 1.00
193 Steven Adams .25 .60
194 Ivica Zubac .30 .75
195 Saddiq Bey .25 .60
196 Isaac Okoro .25 .60
197 OG Anunoby .30 .75
198 Gordon Hayward .25 .60
199 Khris Middleton .30 .75
200 Devin Booker .75 2.00
201 James Bouknight RR RC .50 1.25
202 Josh Giddey RR RC 2.00 5.00
203 Cameron Thomas RR RC 1.25 3.00
204 Kessler Edwards RR RC .60 1.50
205 Davion Mitchell RR RC .60 1.50
206 Neemias Queta RR RC .60 1.50
207 Herbert Jones RR RC .75 2.00
208 Sharife Cooper RR RC .50 1.25
209 Jalen Green RR RC 3.00 8.00
210 Jason Preston RR RC .50 1.25
211 Cade Cunningham RR RC 4.00 10.00
212 Joshua Primo RR RC .50 1.25
213 Charles Bassey RR RC .60 1.50
214 Luka Garza RR RC .60 1.50
215 Day'Ron Sharpe RR RC .60 1.50
216 Quentin Grimes RR RC 1.25 3.00
217 Isaiah Jackson RR RC .60 1.50
218 Tre Mann RR RC 1.00 2.50
219 Alperen Sengun RR RC 2.00 5.00
220 Jeremiah Robinson-Earl RR RC .60 1.50
221 Ayo Dosunmu RR RC 1.25 3.00
222 JT Thor RR RC .60 1.50
223 Chris Duarte RR RC .50 1.25
224 Miles McBride RR RC 1.00 2.50
225 Evan Mobley RR RC 2.50 6.00
226 Santi Aldama RR RC .75 2.00
227 Isaiah Livers RR RC .60 1.50
228 Trey Murphy III RR RC 2.00 5.00
229 Jalen Suggs RR RC 1.50 4.00
230 Joe Wieskamp RR RC .50 1.25
231 Jalen Johnson RR RC 2.00 5.00
232 Kai Jones RR RC .50 1.25
233 Corey Kispert RR RC .75 2.00
234 Moses Moody RR RC 1.25 3.00
235 Franz Wagner RR RC 2.00 5.00
236 Scottie Barnes RR RC 2.00 5.00
237 Isaiah Todd RR RC .50 1.25
238 Usman Garuba RR RC .50 1.25
239 Brandon Boston Jr. RR RC .60 1.50
240 Jonathan Kuminga RR RC 2.00 5.00
241 Aaron Wiggins RR RC .75 2.00
242 Keon Johnson RR RC .60 1.50
243 David Johnson RR RC .50 1.25
244 Bones Hyland RR RC .75 2.00
245 Greg Brown III RR RC .50 1.25
246 Scottie Lewis RR RC .50 1.25
247 Jaden Springer RR RC .60 1.50
248 Ziaire Williams RR RC .75 2.00
249 Jared Butler RR RC .60 1.50
250 Josh Christopher RR RC .50 1.25

2021-22 Donruss Choice

*CHOICE: 1.25X TO 3X BASIC
202 Josh Giddey RR 30.00 80.00
209 Jalen Green RR 30.00 80.00
211 Cade Cunningham RR 40.00 100.00
219 Alperen Sengun RR 10.00 25.00
225 Evan Mobley RR 30.00 80.00
236 Scottie Barnes RR 30.00 80.00
240 Jonathan Kuminga RR 30.00 80.00

2021-22 Donruss Complete Players

COMMON CARD .30 .75
SEMISTARS .40 1.00
UNLISTED STARS .50 1.25
*HOLO GRN ICE: .75X TO 2X BASIC
*HOLO PINK LSR: .75X TO 2X BASIC
*HOLO TEAL LSR: .75X TO 2X BASIC
*HOLO RED LSR/99: 1.5X TO 4X BASIC
*HOLO YELLOW LSR/25: 4X TO 10X BASIC
1 LeBron James 4.00 10.00
2 LaMelo Ball 1.25 3.00
3 Luka Doncic 3.00 8.00
4 Russell Westbrook .75 2.00
5 Kevin Durant 1.50 4.00
6 Trae Young 1.25 3.00
7 Stephen Curry 3.00 8.00
8 James Harden 1.00 2.50
9 Giannis Antetokounmpo 2.50 6.00
10 Kawhi Leonard 1.25 3.00
11 Anthony Davis 1.25 3.00
12 Bradley Beal .60 1.50
13 Jayson Tatum 2.00 5.00
14 Damian Lillard 1.25 3.00
15 Zion Williamson 1.25 3.00
16 Julius Randle .60 1.50
17 Nikola Jokic 2.50 6.00
18 Jimmy Butler .75 2.00
19 Kyrie Irving 1.00 2.50
20 Chris Paul 1.00 2.50

2021-22 Donruss Craftsmen

COMMON CARD .30 .75
SEMISTARS .40 1.00
UNLISTED STARS .50 1.25
*PRESS PROOF: .75X TO 2X BASIC
*PRESS PROOF PRPL: .75X TO 2X BASIC
1 LaMelo Ball 1.25 3.00
2 Luka Doncic 3.00 8.00
3 LeBron James 4.00 10.00
4 Ja Morant 1.50 4.00
5 Stephen Curry 3.00 8.00
6 Nikola Jokic 2.50 6.00
7 Russell Westbrook .75 2.00
8 Chris Paul 1.00 2.50
9 Damian Lillard 1.25 3.00
10 Donovan Mitchell 1.00 2.50
11 Trae Young 1.25 3.00
12 De'Aaron Fox .75 2.00
13 Kyrie Irving 1.00 2.50
14 James Harden 1.00 2.50
15 Jayson Tatum 2.00 5.00

2021-22 Donruss Crunch Time

COMMON CARD .30 .75
SEMISTARS .40 1.00
UNLISTED STARS .50 1.25
*PRESS PROOF: .75X TO 2X BASIC
*PRESS PROOF PRPL: .75X TO 2X BASIC
1 Trae Young 1.25 3.00
2 Zion Williamson 1.25 3.00
3 Stephen Curry 3.00 8.00
4 Giannis Antetokounmpo 2.50 6.00
5 Luka Doncic 3.00 8.00
6 LaMelo Ball 1.25 3.00
7 Kevin Durant 1.50 4.00
8 Kawhi Leonard 1.25 3.00
9 Anthony Edwards 2.50 6.00
10 LeBron James 4.00 10.00
11 Bradley Beal .60 1.50
12 Zach LaVine .75 2.00
13 Devin Booker 1.25 3.00
14 Donovan Mitchell 1.00 2.50
15 Jayson Tatum 2.00 5.00
16 Ja Morant 1.50 4.00
17 Damian Lillard 1.25 3.00
18 Joel Embiid 1.25 3.00
19 James Harden 1.00 2.50
20 Chris Paul 1.00 2.50

2021-22 Donruss Duos

COMMON CARD .30 .75
SEMISTARS .40 1.00
UNLISTED STARS .50 1.25
*PRESS PROOF: .75X TO 2X BASIC
*PRESS PROOF PRPL: .75X TO 2X BASIC
1 LeBron James
Zion Williamson 4.00 10.00
2 Trae Young
Luka Doncic 3.00 8.00
3 Stephen Curry
Damian Lillard 3.00 8.00
4 Kevin Durant
Giannis Antetokounmpo 2.50 6.00
5 Donovan Mitchell
Ja Morant 1.50 4.00

2021-22 Donruss Franchise Features

COMMON CARD .30 .75
SEMISTARS .40 1.00
UNLISTED STARS .50 1.25
*HOLO PINK LSR: .75X TO 2X BASIC
*HOLO TEAL LSR: .75X TO 2X BASIC
*HOLO RED LSR/99: 1.5X TO 4X BASIC
*HOLO YELLOW LSR/25: 4X TO 10X BASIC
1 Luka Doncic 3.00 8.00
2 Giannis Antetokounmpo 2.50 6.00
3 Trae Young 1.25 3.00
4 Ja Morant 1.50 4.00
5 De'Aaron Fox .75 2.00
6 Bradley Beal .60 1.50
7 Collin Sexton .50 1.25
8 Joel Embiid 1.25 3.00
9 Pascal Siakam .75 2.00
10 Paul George .75 2.00
11 Jayson Tatum 2.00 5.00
12 Jimmy Butler .75 2.00
13 Jerami Grant .50 1.25
14 Damian Lillard 1.25 3.00
15 Julius Randle .60 1.50
16 Karl-Anthony Towns .75 2.00
17 Nikola Jokic 2.50 6.00
18 Stephen Curry 3.00 8.00
19 Zach LaVine .75 2.00
20 LeBron James 4.00 10.00
21 Cole Anthony .60 1.50
22 Zion Williamson 1.25 3.00
23 LaMelo Ball 1.25 3.00
24 Kevin Porter Jr. .40 1.00
25 Shai Gilgeous-Alexander 2.50 6.00
26 Domantas Sabonis .60 1.50
27 Dejounte Murray .50 1.25
28 Kevin Durant 1.50 4.00
29 Devin Booker 1.25 3.00
30 Donovan Mitchell 1.00 2.50

2021-22 Donruss Great X-Pectations

*HOLO GREEN ICE: .75X TO 2X BASIC
*HOLO PINK LSR: .75X TO 2X BASIC
*HOLO TEAL LSR: .75X TO 2X BASIC
*HOLO RED LSR/99: 2X TO 5X BASIC
*HOLO YELLOW LSR/25: 5X TO 12X BASIC
1 Davion Mitchell .75 2.00
2 Moses Moody 1.50 4.00
3 Joshua Primo .60 1.50
4 Jonathan Kuminga 2.50 6.00
5 Tre Mann 1.25 3.00
6 Ziaire Williams 1.00 2.50
7 Evan Mobley 3.00 8.00
8 Jalen Suggs 2.00 5.00
9 James Bouknight .60 1.50
10 Kai Jones .60 1.50
11 Jalen Green 4.00 10.00
12 Franz Wagner 2.50 6.00
13 Quentin Grimes 1.50 4.00
14 Keon Johnson .75 2.00
15 Alperen Sengun 2.50 6.00
16 Josh Christopher .60 1.50
17 Trey Murphy III 2.50 6.00
18 Jalen Johnson 2.50 6.00
19 Josh Giddey 2.50 6.00
20 Corey Kispert 1.00 2.50
21 Cade Cunningham 5.00 12.00
22 Scottie Barnes 2.50 6.00
23 Isaiah Jackson .75 2.00
24 Bones Hyland 1.00 2.50
25 Chris Duarte .60 1.50

2021-22 Donruss Jersey Kings

COMMON CARD 2.00 5.00
SEMISTARS 2.50 6.00
UNLISTED STARS 3.00 8.00
1 Lonzo Ball 3.00 8.00
2 D'Angelo Russell 3.00 8.00
3 CJ McCollum 2.50 6.00
4 Rudy Gay 3.00 8.00
5 Giannis Antetokounmpo 15.00 40.00
6 Kevin Durant 10.00 25.00
7 Josh Richardson 2.50 6.00
8 Karl-Anthony Towns 5.00 12.00
9 Collin Sexton 3.00 8.00
10 Derrick Rose 5.00 12.00
11 Mitchell Robinson 3.00 8.00
12 Steven Adams 2.50 6.00
13 Fred VanVleet 4.00 10.00
14 Paul George 5.00 12.00
15 LaMelo Ball 8.00 20.00
16 Lou Williams 3.00 8.00
17 Brandon Clarke 3.00 8.00
18 Vince Carter 6.00 15.00
19 Khris Middleton 3.00 8.00
20 Kevin Love 3.00 8.00
21 De'Andre Hunter 3.00 8.00
22 Roy Hibbert 2.50 6.00
23 Klay Thompson 8.00 20.00
24 Kawhi Leonard 8.00 20.00
25 Anthony Edwards 15.00 40.00
26 Mike Conley 2.50 6.00
27 Buddy Hield 2.50 6.00
28 Carmelo Anthony 5.00 12.00
29 Trae Young 8.00 20.00
30 Ricky Rubio 3.00 8.00
31 Paul Pierce 5.00 12.00
32 Harrison Barnes 2.50 6.00
33 Jason Kidd 5.00 12.00
34 Anthony Davis 8.00 20.00
35 Isaac Okoro 2.50 6.00
36 Julius Randle 4.00 10.00
37 Myles Turner 3.00 8.00
38 Zach LaVine 5.00 12.00
39 Markelle Fultz 2.00 5.00
40 Brook Lopez 2.50 6.00
41 Larry Johnson 4.00 10.00
42 Jonas Valanciunas 2.50 6.00
43 Patrick Williams 3.00 8.00
44 LeBron James 25.00 60.00
45 Damian Lillard 8.00 20.00
46 Zion Williamson 8.00 20.00
47 De'Aaron Fox 5.00 12.00
48 Bojan Bogdanovic 2.50 6.00
49 Lamar Odom 3.00 8.00
50 Kristaps Porzingis 4.00 10.00
51 Donovan Mitchell 6.00 15.00
52 Kyle Lowry 3.00 8.00
53 Obi Toppin 3.00 8.00
54 Luka Doncic 20.00 50.00
55 Jayson Tatum 12.00 30.00
56 DeMar DeRozan 4.00 10.00
57 Stephen Curry 20.00 50.00
58 Kyrie Irving 6.00 15.00
59 Darius Bazley 2.00 5.00
60 Rudy Gobert 4.00 10.00

2021-22 Donruss Magicians

COMMON CARD .30 .75
SEMISTARS .40 1.00
UNLISTED STARS .50 1.25
*HOLO GREEN ICE: .75X TO 2X BASIC
*HOLO PINK LSR: .75X TO 2X BASIC
*HOLO TEAL LSR: .75X TO 2X BASIC
*HOLO RED LSR/99: 1.5X TO 4X BASIC
*HOLO YELLOW LSR/25: 4X TO 10X BASIC
1 Giannis Antetokounmpo 2.50 6.00
2 Kyrie Irving 1.00 2.50
3 LeBron James 4.00 10.00
4 Anthony Davis 1.25 3.00
5 Luka Doncic 3.00 8.00
6 Jayson Tatum 2.00 5.00
7 Kevin Durant 1.50 4.00
8 Zion Williamson 1.25 3.00
9 Stephen Curry 3.00 8.00
10 Nikola Jokic 2.50 6.00

2021-22 Donruss Next Day Autographs

COMMON CARD 12.00 30.00
SEMISTARS 15.00 40.00
UNLISTED STARS 20.00 50.00
EXCHANGE DEADLINE 8/25/2023
1 Jalen Green 300.00 600.00
2 Chris Duarte 15.00 40.00
3 Cameron Thomas 100.00 250.00
4 Jaden Springer 20.00 50.00
5 Isaiah Jackson 20.00 50.00
6 Cade Cunningham 500.00 1,000.00
7 Ayo Dosunmu 40.00 100.00
8 Evan Mobley 200.00 500.00
9 Davion Mitchell 20.00 50.00
10 Jalen Suggs 150.00 400.00
11 Jared Butler 20.00 50.00
12 Moses Moody 125.00 300.00
13 Luka Garza 20.00 50.00
14 Ziaire Williams 25.00 60.00
15 Trey Murphy III 125.00 300.00
16 Keon Johnson 20.00 50.00
17 Joshua Primo 15.00 40.00
18 Scottie Barnes 200.00 500.00
19 Quentin Grimes 125.00 300.00
20 Jonathan Kuminga 200.00 500.00
21 Alperen Sengun 200.00 500.00
22 Franz Wagner 200.00 500.00
23 Day'Ron Sharpe 20.00 50.00
24 James Bouknight 15.00 40.00
25 Jalen Johnson 125.00 300.00
26 Corey Kispert 60.00 150.00
27 Charles Bassey 20.00 50.00
28 Isaiah Livers 20.00 50.00
29 Greg Brown III 15.00 40.00
30 Brandon Boston Jr. 20.00 50.00
31 Josh Giddey 150.00 400.00
32 Scottie Lewis 15.00 40.00
33 Santi Aldama 25.00 60.00
34 Josh Christopher 15.00 40.00
35 Jeremiah Robinson-Earl 20.00 50.00
36 Bones Hyland 25.00 60.00
37 Miles McBride 60.00 150.00
38 Usman Garuba 15.00 40.00
39 Tre Mann 75.00 200.00
40 Kai Jones 15.00 40.00

2021-22 Donruss Power in the Paint

COMMON CARD .30 .75
SEMISTARS .40 1.00
UNLISTED STARS .50 1.25
*HOLO PINK LSR: .75X TO 2X BASIC
*HOLO TEAL LSR: .75X TO 2X BASIC
*HOLO RED LSR/99: 1.5X TO 4X BASIC
*HOLO YELLOW LSR/25: 4X TO 10X BASIC
1 Wilt Chamberlain 1.50 4.00
2 Kareem Abdul-Jabbar 1.50 4.00
3 Giannis Antetokounmpo 2.50 6.00
4 Bam Adebayo .75 2.00
5 Karl-Anthony Towns .75 2.00
6 Bill Russell 1.50 4.00
7 Charles Barkley 1.25 3.00
8 Deandre Ayton .50 1.25
9 Shaquille O'Neal 1.50 4.00
10 Joel Embiid 1.25 3.00

2021-22 Donruss Production Line

COMMON CARD .30 .75
SEMISTARS .40 1.00
UNLISTED STARS .50 1.25
*PRESS PROOF: .5X TO 1.2X BASIC
*PRESS PROOF PURPLE: .5X TO 1.2X BASIC
1 Russell Westbrook .75 2.00
2 Stephen Curry 3.00 8.00
3 Clint Capela .50 1.25
4 Jimmy Butler .75 2.00
5 Rudy Gobert .60 1.50
6 Damian Lillard 1.25 3.00
7 LeBron James 4.00 10.00
8 Ben Simmons .50 1.25
9 Bradley Beal .60 1.50
10 Trae Young 1.25 3.00

2021-22 Donruss Rated Rookies Signatures

COMMON CARD 4.00 10.00
SEMISTARS 5.00 12.00
UNLISTED STARS 6.00 15.00
EXCHANGE DEADLINE 8/25/2023
*CHOICE: .5X TO 1.2X BASIC
*HOLO GRN/YLLW LSR: .5X TO 1.2X BASIC
*HOLO LIGHT BLUE LSR: .5X TO 1.2X BASIC
*HOLO ORANGE LSR: .5X TO 1.2X BASIC
*HOLO PINK LSR: .5X TO 1.2X BASIC
*HOLO RED & GOLD LSR: .5X TO 1.2X BASIC
*HOLO TEAL LSR: .5X TO 1.2X BASIC
*HOLO YELLOW LSR: .5X TO 1.2X BASIC
*CHOICE RED/99: .6X TO 1.5X BASIC
*HOLO LASER/99: .6X TO 1.5X BASIC
*CHOICE BLUE/49: .75X TO 2X BASIC
*HOLO RED LSR/49: .75X TO 2X BASIC
*HOLO BLUE LASER/25: 1.25X TO 3X BASIC
201 James Bouknight 5.00 12.00
202 Josh Giddey 20.00 50.00
203 Cameron Thomas 12.00 30.00
204 Kessler Edwards 6.00 15.00
205 Davion Mitchell 6.00 15.00
206 Neemias Queta 6.00 15.00
207 Herbert Jones 8.00 20.00
209 Jalen Green 60.00 150.00
210 Jason Preston 5.00 12.00
211 Cade Cunningham 100.00 250.00
212 Joshua Primo 5.00 12.00
213 Charles Bassey 6.00 15.00
214 Luka Garza 6.00 15.00
215 Day'Ron Sharpe 6.00 15.00
216 Quentin Grimes 12.00 30.00
217 Isaiah Jackson 6.00 15.00
218 Tre Mann 10.00 25.00
219 Alperen Sengun 20.00 50.00
220 Jeremiah Robinson-Earl 6.00 15.00
221 Ayo Dosunmu 12.00 30.00
222 JT Thor 6.00 15.00
223 Chris Duarte 5.00 12.00
224 Miles McBride 10.00 25.00
225 Evan Mobley 25.00 60.00
226 Santi Aldama 8.00 20.00
227 Isaiah Livers 6.00 15.00
228 Trey Murphy III 20.00 50.00
229 Jalen Suggs 15.00 40.00
230 Joe Wieskamp 5.00 12.00
231 Jalen Johnson 20.00 50.00
232 Kai Jones 5.00 12.00
233 Corey Kispert 8.00 20.00
234 Moses Moody 12.00 30.00
235 Franz Wagner 20.00 50.00
236 Scottie Barnes 20.00 50.00
237 Isaiah Todd 5.00 12.00
238 Usman Garuba 5.00 12.00
239 Brandon Boston Jr. 6.00 15.00
240 Jonathan Kuminga 20.00 50.00
241 Aaron Wiggins 8.00 20.00
242 Keon Johnson 6.00 15.00
243 David Johnson 5.00 12.00
244 Bones Hyland 8.00 20.00
245 Greg Brown III 5.00 12.00
246 Scottie Lewis 5.00 12.00
247 Jaden Springer 6.00 15.00
248 Ziaire Williams 8.00 20.00
249 Jared Butler 6.00 15.00
250 Josh Christopher 5.00 12.00

2021-22 Donruss Retro Series

COMMON CARD .25 .60
SEMISTARS .30 .75
UNLISTED STARS .40 1.00
*PRESS PROOF: .5X TO 1.2X BASIC
*PRESS PROOF PURPLE: .75X TO 2X BASIC
1 Shaquille O'Neal 1.25 3.00
2 Dirk Nowitzki 1.00 2.50
3 Larry Bird 1.25 3.00
4 Ben Wallace .50 1.25
5 Tracy McGrady .60 1.50
6 Magic Johnson 1.25 3.00
7 Kevin Garnett 1.00 2.50
8 Charles Barkley 1.00 2.50
9 Drazen Petrovic .50 1.25
10 Isiah Thomas .60 1.50
11 Ray Allen .60 1.50
12 Rasheed Wallace .50 1.25
13 Jason Kidd .60 1.50
14 Tony Parker .60 1.50
15 Dikembe Mutombo .50 1.25
16 Vince Carter .75 2.00
17 Dwyane Wade .75 2.00
18 Hakeem Olajuwon .75 2.00
19 Bill Russell 1.25 3.00
20 Dominique Wilkins .60 1.50
21 Tim Duncan 1.00 2.50
22 Allen Iverson 1.00 2.50
23 Paul Pierce .60 1.50
24 Chris Webber .50 1.25
25 Karl Malone .75 2.00
26 Patrick Ewing .60 1.50
27 Jason Williams .50 1.25
28 Steve Nash .75 2.00
29 Gary Payton .60 1.50
30 Clyde Drexler .60 1.50

2021-22 Donruss Rookie Jersey Kings

COMMON CARD .75 2.00
SEMISTARS 1.00 2.50
UNLISTED STARS 1.25 3.00
*PRIME/25: 1.25X TO 3X BASIC
1 Davion Mitchell 1.25 3.00
2 Quentin Grimes 2.50 6.00
3 Greg Brown III 1.00 2.50
4 Tre Mann 2.00 5.00
5 Jalen Green 6.00 15.00
6 Jared Butler 1.25 3.00
7 Alperen Sengun 4.00 10.00
8 Josh Giddey 4.00 10.00
9 Cameron Thomas 2.50 6.00
10 Luka Garza 1.25 3.00
11 Day'Ron Sharpe 1.25 3.00
12 Santi Aldama 1.50 4.00
13 Isaiah Jackson 1.25 3.00
14 Trey Murphy III 4.00 10.00
15 Jalen Johnson 4.00 10.00
16 Jeremiah Robinson-Earl 1.25 3.00
17 Ayo Dosunmu 2.50 6.00
18 Joshua Primo 1.00 2.50
19 Charles Bassey 1.25 3.00
20 Miles McBride 2.00 5.00
21 Evan Mobley 5.00 12.00
22 Scottie Barnes 4.00 10.00
23 Isaiah Livers 1.25 3.00
24 Usman Garuba 1.00 2.50
25 Jalen Suggs 3.00 8.00
26 Jonathan Kuminga 4.00 10.00
27 Brandon Boston Jr. 1.25 3.00
28 Kai Jones 1.00 2.50
29 Chris Duarte 1.00 2.50
30 Moses Moody 2.50 6.00
31 Franz Wagner 4.00 10.00
32 Scottie Lewis 1.00 2.50
33 Jaden Springer 1.25 3.00
34 Ziaire Williams 1.50 4.00
35 James Bouknight 1.00 2.50
36 Josh Christopher 1.00 2.50
37 Cade Cunningham 8.00 20.00
38 Keon Johnson 1.25 3.00
39 Corey Kispert 1.50 4.00
40 Bones Hyland 1.50 4.00

2021-22 Donruss Signature Series

COMMON CARD 4.00 10.00
SEMISTARS 5.00 12.00
UNLISTED STARS 6.00 15.00
EXCHANGE DEADLINE 8/16/2023
1 Langston Galloway 5.00 12.00
2 Thurl Bailey 5.00 12.00
3 Will Barton 4.00 10.00
4 Drew Gooden 5.00 12.00
5 Luke Kennard 5.00 12.00
6 Bobby Portis 5.00 12.00
7 Jack Sikma 6.00 15.00
8 Dick Van Arsdale 6.00 15.00
9 John Salley 5.00 12.00
10 Luka Doncic 400.00 800.00
11 Doug Christie 5.00 12.00
12 Lawrence Funderburke 4.00 10.00
13 Thomas Bryant 4.00 10.00
14 Doug McDermott 5.00 12.00
15 Rod Strickland 5.00 12.00
16 Tyus Jones 5.00 12.00
17 Dan Issel 6.00 15.00
18 Len Elmore 5.00 12.00
19 Caron Butler 5.00 12.00
20 Kevin Durant 100.00 250.00
21 Rick Fox 6.00 15.00
22 Major Jones 6.00 15.00
23 Monte Morris 5.00 12.00
24 Luguentz Dort 6.00 15.00
25 Tom Gugliotta 5.00 12.00
26 Mark Eaton 6.00 15.00
27 Shawn Bradley 5.00 12.00
28 Norm Nixon 5.00 12.00
29 James Ennis III 4.00 10.00
31 Alex Caruso 6.00 15.00
32 Vernon Maxwell 5.00 12.00
33 Quinndary Weatherspoon 4.00 10.00
34 Aron Baynes 4.00 10.00
35 Tomas Satoransky 4.00 10.00
36 Daniel House Jr. 5.00 12.00
37 Gheorghe Muresan 4.00 10.00
38 Scott Brooks 5.00 12.00
39 Rick Mahorn 5.00 12.00
40 Magic Johnson 60.00 150.00
41 Darius Bazley 4.00 10.00
42 Stanley Johnson 5.00 12.00
43 Micheal Ray Richardson 5.00 12.00
44 Terence Davis II 5.00 12.00
45 Dennis Rodman 40.00 100.00
46 Daniel Theis 5.00 12.00
47 Frank Jackson 4.00 10.00
48 Steve Smith 6.00 15.00
49 Torrey Craig 5.00 12.00
51 Aaron Wiggins 8.00 20.00
52 Quentin Grimes 12.00 30.00
53 Scottie Lewis 5.00 12.00
54 Ayo Dosunmu 12.00 30.00
55 Santi Aldama 8.00 20.00
57 Jalen Johnson 20.00 50.00
58 Neemias Queta 6.00 15.00
59 Scottie Barnes 20.00 50.00
60 Cade Cunningham 100.00 250.00
61 Keon Johnson 6.00 15.00
62 Isaiah Jackson 6.00 15.00
63 Jaden Springer 6.00 15.00
64 JT Thor 6.00 15.00
65 Isaiah Livers 6.00 15.00
66 Josh Giddey 20.00 50.00
67 Kai Jones 5.00 12.00
68 Herbert Jones 8.00 20.00
69 Marcus Zegarowski 5.00 12.00
70 Joshua Primo 5.00 12.00
71 David Johnson 5.00 12.00
72 Tre Mann 10.00 25.00
73 Ziaire Williams 8.00 20.00
74 Chris Duarte 5.00 12.00
75 Trey Murphy III 20.00 50.00
76 Cameron Thomas 12.00 30.00
77 Corey Kispert 8.00 20.00
78 Sandro Mamukelashvili 8.00 20.00
80 Charles Bassey 6.00 15.00
81 Bones Hyland 8.00 20.00
82 Alperen Sengun 20.00 50.00
83 Jared Butler 6.00 15.00
84 Miles McBride 10.00 25.00
85 Jalen Suggs 15.00 40.00
86 Kessler Edwards 6.00 15.00
87 Moses Moody 12.00 30.00
88 Jalen Green 60.00 150.00
89 Brandon Boston Jr. 6.00 15.00
90 Luka Garza 6.00 15.00
91 Greg Brown III 5.00 12.00
92 Jeremiah Robinson-Earl 6.00 15.00
93 Josh Christopher 5.00 12.00
94 Evan Mobley 25.00 60.00
95 Joe Wieskamp 5.00 12.00
96 Davion Mitchell 6.00 15.00
97 Franz Wagner 20.00 50.00
98 Jason Preston 5.00 12.00
99 Jonathan Kuminga 20.00 50.00
100 Day'Ron Sharpe 6.00 15.00

2021-22 Donruss The Rookies

COMMON CARD .40 1.00
SEMISTARS .50 1.25
UNLISTED STARS .60 1.50
*HOLO PINK LSR: .75X TO 2X BASIC
*HOLO TEAL LSR: .75X TO 2X BASIC
*HOLO GRN ICE: 1.2X TO 3X BASIC
*HOLO RED LSR/99: 2X TO 5X BASIC
*HOLO YELLOW LSR/25: 5X TO 12X BASIC
1 Cade Cunningham 4.00 10.00
2 Jalen Green 3.00 8.00
3 Evan Mobley 2.50 6.00
4 Scottie Barnes 2.00 5.00
5 Jalen Suggs 1.50 4.00

2022-23 Donruss

COM CARD (1-200) .20 .50
SEMISTARS .25 .60
UNLISTED STARS .30 .75
COMMON RC (201-250) .40 1.00
RC SEMIS .50 1.25
RC UNLISTED .60 1.50
*PRESS PROOF SILVER: .5X TO 1.2X BASIC
*YELLOW FLOOD: 1X TO 2.5X BASIC
*RED & GOLD LSR: 1.25X TO 3X BASIC
*PRESS PROOF PRPL/199: 1.5X TO 4X BASIC
1 Jayson Tatum 1.25 3.00
2 Jaylen Brown .60 1.50
3 Robert Williams III .25 .60
4 Al Horford .30 .75
5 Marcus Smart .40 1.00
6 Kevin Durant 1.00 2.50
7 Kyrie Irving .60 1.50
8 Cameron Thomas .50 1.25
9 Joe Harris .25 .60
10 Seth Curry .25 .60
11 Ben Simmons .30 .75
12 Obi Toppin .30 .75
13 RJ Barrett .50 1.25
14 Evan Fournier .25 .60
15 Jalen Brunson .60 1.50
16 Cam Reddish .25 .60
17 Julius Randle .40 1.00
18 Tyrese Maxey .60 1.50
19 James Harden .60 1.50
20 Tobias Harris .25 .60
21 Joel Embiid .50 1.25
22 De'Anthony Melton .25 .60
23 Pascal Siakam .50 1.25
24 Fred VanVleet .40 1.00
25 Scottie Barnes .50 1.25
26 OG Anunoby .40 1.00
27 Armoni Brooks .25 .60
28 Gary Trent Jr. .30 .75
29 Lonzo Ball .30 .75
30 Zach LaVine .60 1.50
31 DeMar DeRozan .40 1.00
32 Nikola Vucevic .30 .75
33 Coby White .25 .60
34 Ayo Dosunmu .40 1.00
35 Darius Garland .50 1.25
36 Evan Mobley .75 2.00
37 Caris LeVert .25 .60
38 Collin Sexton .40 1.00
39 Isaac Okoro .25 .60
40 Jarrett Allen .30 .75
41 Cade Cunningham 1.00 2.50
42 Saddiq Bey .25 .60
43 Marvin Bagley III .25 .60
44 Isaiah Stewart .25 .60
45 Hamidou Diallo .25 .60
46 Killian Hayes .20 .50
47 Tyrese Haliburton .60 1.50
48 Chris Duarte .25 .60
49 Myles Turner .30 .75
50 Buddy Hield .30 .75
51 T.J. McConnell .25 .60
52 Isaiah Jackson .30 .75
53 Giannis Antetokounmpo 1.50 4.00
54 Khris Middleton .40 1.00
55 Jrue Holiday .40 1.00
56 Bobby Portis .30 .75
57 Grayson Allen .30 .75
58 Pat Connaughton .25 .60
59 Trae Young .75 2.00
60 John Collins .30 .75
61 Dejounte Murray .40 1.00
62 Justin Holiday .20 .50
63 Bogdan Bogdanovic .30 .75
64 De'Andre Hunter .30 .75
65 Gordon Hayward .25 .60
66 Terry Rozier III .40 1.00
67 LaMelo Ball .75 2.00
68 Kelly Oubre Jr. .30 .75
69 Cody Martin .25 .60
70 PJ Washington Jr. .30 .75
71 Jimmy Butler .60 1.50
72 Bam Adebayo .50 1.25

73 Kyle Lowry .40 1.00
74 Victor Oladipo .25 .60
75 Tyler Herro .50 1.25
76 Caleb Martin .30 .75
77 Franz Wagner .75 2.00
78 Markelle Fultz .25 .60
79 Wendell Carter Jr. .30 .75
80 Gary Harris .25 .60
81 Jalen Suggs .40 1.00
82 Cole Anthony .30 .75
83 Bradley Beal .40 1.00
84 Kristaps Porzingis .40 1.00
85 Kyle Kuzma .40 1.00
86 Rui Hachimura .30 .75
87 Corey Kispert .30 .75
88 Will Barton .20 .50
89 Nikola Jokic 1.50 4.00
90 Jamal Murray .50 1.25
91 Michael Porter Jr. .40 1.00
92 Aaron Gordon .30 .75
93 Bones Hyland .25 .60
94 Rudy Gobert .40 1.00
95 Karl-Anthony Towns .50 1.25
96 Anthony Edwards 1.50 4.00
97 D'Angelo Russell .25 .60
98 Jaden McDaniels .30 .75
99 Jaylen Nowell .30 .75
100 Shai Gilgeous-Alexander 1.50 4.00
101 Luguentz Dort .30 .75
102 Josh Giddey .50 1.25
103 Tre Mann .25 .60
104 Darius Bazley .20 .50
105 Aleksej Pokusevski .30 .75
106 Damian Lillard .75 2.00
107 Anfernee Simons .40 1.00
108 Jusuf Nurkic .30 .75
109 Josh Hart .30 .75
110 Gary Payton II .25 .60
111 Donovan Mitchell .60 1.50
112 Mike Conley .25 .60
113 Jae Crowder .20 .50
114 Jordan Clarkson .30 .75
115 Rudy Gay .30 .75
116 Stephen Curry 2.50 6.00
117 Klay Thompson .75 2.00
118 Draymond Green .40 1.00
119 James Wiseman .25 .60
120 Jordan Poole .50 1.25
121 Andrew Wiggins .40 1.00
122 Paul George .50 1.25
123 Kawhi Leonard .75 2.00
124 Norman Powell .30 .75
125 Terance Mann .25 .60
126 Luke Kennard .25 .60
127 Russell Westbrook .50 1.25
128 LeBron James 2.50 6.00
129 Anthony Davis .75 2.00
130 Talen Horton-Tucker .25 .60
131 Kendrick Nunn .25 .60
132 Devin Booker .75 2.00
133 Deandre Ayton .30 .75
134 Chris Paul .60 1.50
135 Mikal Bridges .40 1.00
136 Bojan Bogdanovic .30 .75
137 Cameron Johnson .25 .60
138 De'Aaron Fox .60 1.50
139 Domantas Sabonis .40 1.00
140 Harrison Barnes .25 .60
141 Malik Monk .30 .75
142 Davion Mitchell .25 .60
143 Luka Doncic 2.00 5.00
144 Spencer Dinwiddie .25 .60
145 Christian Wood .20 .50
146 Tim Hardaway Jr. .25 .60
147 Dorian Finney-Smith .25 .60
148 Davis Bertans .20 .50
149 Eric Gordon .25 .60
150 Jalen Green 1.00 2.50
151 Jae'Sean Tate .20 .50
152 Kevin Porter Jr. .25 .60
153 Alperen Sengun .40 1.00
154 Josh Christopher .20 .50
155 Jaren Jackson Jr. .50 1.25
156 Ja Morant 1.00 2.50
157 Dillon Brooks .30 .75
158 Tyus Jones .25 .60
159 Danny Green .25 .60
160 Ziaire Williams .25 .60
161 CJ McCollum .30 .75
162 Brandon Ingram .40 1.00
163 Jonas Valanciunas .25 .60
164 Zion Williamson .75 2.00
165 Herbert Jones .30 .75
166 Devonte' Graham .25 .60
167 Doug McDermott .20 .50
168 Josh Richardson .25 .60
169 Keldon Johnson .40 1.00
170 Devin Vassell .40 1.00
171 Joshua Primo .20 .50
172 Jakob Poeltl .25 .60
173 Derrick White .30 .75
174 Patty Mills .30 .75
175 Immanuel Quickley .30 .75
176 Lauri Markkanen .50 1.25
177 Max Strus .30 .75
178 Deni Avdija .30 .75
179 Jonathan Kuminga .75 2.00
180 Moses Moody .40 1.00
181 Marcus Morris Sr. .20 .50
182 Trey Lyles .25 .60
183 Reggie Bullock .25 .60
184 Brandon Clarke .25 .60
185 Trey Murphy III .40 1.00
186 Danilo Gallinari .25 .60
187 Georges Niang .25 .60
188 Nassir Little .30 .75
189 Malcolm Brogdon .25 .60
190 P.J. Tucker .25 .60
191 Kentavious Caldwell-Pope .25 .60
192 Jerami Grant .40 1.00
193 Malik Beasley .25 .60
194 John Wall .40 1.00
195 Lonnie Walker IV .25 .60
196 Kevin Huerter .30 .75
197 Andre Drummond .30 .75
198 Joe Ingles .25 .60
199 Monte Morris .20 .50
200 Bruce Brown .30 .75
201 Paolo Banchero RR RC 4.00 10.00
202 Chet Holmgren RR RC 3.00 8.00
203 Jabari Smith Jr. RR RC 2.00 5.00
204 Keegan Murray RR RC 1.50 4.00
205 Jaden Ivey RR RC 2.00 5.00
206 Bennedict Mathurin RR RC 2.00 5.00
207 Shaedon Sharpe RR RC 2.50 6.00
208 Dyson Daniels RR RC 1.50 4.00
209 Jeremy Sochan RR RC 2.00 5.00
210 Johnny Davis RR RC .60 1.50
211 Ousmane Dieng RR RC .75 2.00
212 Jalen Williams RR RC 3.00 8.00
213 Jalen Duren RR RC 2.00 5.00
214 Ochai Agbaji RR RC .75 2.00
215 Mark Williams RR RC 1.25 3.00
216 AJ Griffin RR RC .50 1.25
217 Tari Eason RR RC 1.50 4.00
218 Dalen Terry RR RC .60 1.50
219 Jake LaRavia RR RC .60 1.50
220 Malaki Branham RR RC .60 1.50
221 Christian Braun RR RC 1.50 4.00
222 Walker Kessler RR RC 1.25 3.00
223 David Roddy RR RC .75 2.00
224 MarJon Beauchamp RR RC .60 1.50
225 Blake Wesley RR RC .60 1.50
226 Wendell Moore Jr. RR RC .60 1.50
227 Nikola Jovic RR RC 1.25 3.00
228 Patrick Baldwin Jr. RR RC .60 1.50
229 TyTy Washington Jr. RR RC .60 1.50
230 Peyton Watson RR RC 1.00 2.50
231 Andrew Nembhard RR RC 1.25 3.00
232 Caleb Houstan RR RC .60 1.50
233 Christian Koloko RR RC .60 1.50
234 Max Christie RR RC 1.50 4.00
235 Jaden Hardy RR RC 1.00 2.50
236 Kennedy Chandler RR RC .60 1.50
237 Moussa Diabate RR RC .60 1.50
238 E.J. Liddell RR RC .60 1.50
239 Trevor Keels RR RC .50 1.25
240 Isaiah Mobley RR RC .60 1.50
241 Jaylin Williams RR RC .75 2.00
242 Bryce McGowens RR RC .60 1.50
243 Tyrese Martin RR RC .50 1.25
244 Ryan Rollins RR RC .60 1.50
245 Josh Minott RR RC .60 1.50
246 Vince Williams Jr. RR RC .75 2.00
247 Kendall Brown RR RC .50 1.25
248 Luke Travers RR RC .50 1.25
249 Jabari Walker RR RC .50 1.25
250 Kenneth Lofton Jr. RR RC .75 2.00

2022-23 Donruss Basketball

*BASKETBALL: 3X TO 8X BASIC
STATED PRINT RUN 75 COPIES PER
201 Paolo Banchero RR 100.00 250.00
206 Bennedict Mathurin RR 50.00 120.00

2022-23 Donruss Choice Blue

*CHOICE BLUE: 4X TO 10X BASIC
STATED PRINT RUN 49 COPIES PER

2022-23 Donruss Choice Red

*CHOICE RED: 3X TO 8X BASIC
STATED PRINT RUN 99 COPIES PER

2022-23 Donruss Holo Blue Laser

*HOLO BLUE LSR: 4X TO 10X BASIC
STATED PRINT RUN 49 COPIES PER

2022-23 Donruss Holo Green Laser

*HOLO GRN LASER: 1.5X TO 4X BASIC

2022-23 Donruss Holo Laser

*HOLO LSR: 2.5X TO 6X BASIC
STATED PRINT RUN 149 COPIES PER

2022-23 Donruss Holo Light Blue Laser

*HOLO LGT BLUE LSR: 6X TO 15X BASIC
STATED PRINT RUN 25 COPIES PER

2022-23 Donruss Holo Pink Laser

*HOLO PINK LSR: 4X TO 10X BASIC
STATED PRINT RUN 50 COPIES PER

2022-23 Donruss Holo Purple Laser

*HOLO PRPL LSR: 3X TO 8X BASIC
STATED PRINT RUN 99 COPIES PER

2022-23 Donruss Holo Red Laser

*HOLO RED LSR: 3X TO 8X BASIC
STATED PRINT RUN 99 COPIES PER

2022-23 Donruss Holo Yellow Laser

*HOLO YELLOW LSR: 6X TO 15X BASIC
STATED PRINT RUN 25 COPIES PER

2022-23 Donruss Animation

1 Giannis Antetokounmpo 300.00 600.00
2 LeBron James 500.00 1,000.00
3 Stephen Curry 400.00 800.00
4 Luka Doncic 400.00 800.00
5 Nikola Jokic 300.00 600.00
6 Jayson Tatum 350.00 700.00
7 Ja Morant 200.00 500.00
8 Jaden Ivey 125.00 300.00
9 Paolo Banchero 400.00 800.00
10 Chet Holmgren 400.00 800.00

2022-23 Donruss Bomb Squad

COMMON CARD .30 .75
SEMISTARS .40 1.00
UNLISTED STARS .50 1.25
*HOLO PRPL LSR/99: 3X TO 8X BASIC
*HOLO PINK LSR/50: 4X TO 10X BASIC
*HOLO YLW LSR/25: 6X TO 15X BASIC
1 Anthony Edwards 2.50 6.00
2 Ja Morant 1.50 4.00
3 LeBron James 4.00 10.00
4 Stephen Curry 4.00 10.00
5 Giannis Antetokounmpo 2.50 6.00
6 Luka Doncic 3.00 8.00
7 Zion Williamson 1.25 3.00
8 Jalen Green 1.50 4.00
9 Cade Cunningham 1.50 4.00
10 LaMelo Ball 1.25 3.00
11 Trae Young 1.25 3.00
12 Evan Mobley 1.25 3.00
13 Donovan Mitchell 1.00 2.50
14 Jayson Tatum 2.00 5.00
15 Zach LaVine 1.00 2.50
16 Shaquille O'Neal 2.00 5.00
17 Dwyane Wade 1.00 2.50
18 Vince Carter 1.00 2.50
19 Dominique Wilkins .75 2.00
20 Shawn Kemp .75 2.00

2022-23 Donruss Complete Players

COMMON CARD .30 .75
SEMISTARS .40 1.00
UNLISTED STARS .50 1.25
*HOLO PRPL LSR/99: 2X TO 5X BASIC
*HOLO PINK LSR/50: 2.5X TO 6X BASIC
*HOLO YLW LSR/25: 4X TO 10X BASIC
1 LeBron James 4.00 10.00
2 Luka Doncic 3.00 8.00
3 Stephen Curry 4.00 10.00
4 Giannis Antetokounmpo 2.50 6.00
5 Paul George .75 2.00
6 Nikola Jokic 2.50 6.00
7 Anthony Edwards 2.50 6.00
8 Damian Lillard 1.25 3.00
9 Kevin Durant 1.50 4.00
10 Trae Young 1.25 3.00

2022-23 Donruss Craftsmen

COMMON CARD .40 1.00
SEMISTARS .50 1.25
UNLISTED STARS .60 1.50
*PRESS PROOF: .75X TO 2X BASIC
*PRESS PROOF PRPL: .75X TO 2X BASIC
*DIAMOND: 1.25X TO 3X BASIC
1 LaMelo Ball 1.50 4.00
2 Luka Doncic 4.00 10.00
3 LeBron James 5.00 12.00
4 Stephen Curry 5.00 12.00
5 Nikola Jokic 3.00 8.00
6 Chris Paul 1.25 3.00
7 Trae Young 1.50 4.00
8 Kyrie Irving 1.25 3.00
9 Damian Lillard 1.50 4.00
10 Jayson Tatum 2.50 6.00
11 Ja Morant 2.00 5.00
12 Jalen Green 2.00 5.00
13 James Harden 1.25 3.00
14 Bradley Beal .75 2.00
15 Donovan Mitchell 1.25 3.00

2022-23 Donruss Crunch Time

COMMON CARD .30 .75
SEMISTARS .40 1.00
UNLISTED STARS .50 1.25
*PRESS PROOF: .5X TO 1.2X BASIC
*PRESS PROOF PRPL: .6X TO 1.5X BASIC
*DIAMOND: 2.5X TO 6X BASIC
1 Luka Doncic 3.00 8.00
2 Trae Young 1.25 3.00
3 Zion Williamson 1.25 3.00
4 Stephen Curry 4.00 10.00
5 Giannis Antetokounmpo 2.50 6.00
6 LaMelo Ball 1.25 3.00
7 Kawhi Leonard 1.25 3.00
8 Kevin Durant 1.50 4.00
9 Anthony Edwards 2.50 6.00
10 LeBron James 4.00 10.00
11 Jayson Tatum 2.00 5.00
12 Jimmy Butler 1.00 2.50
13 Damian Lillard 1.25 3.00
14 Devin Booker 1.25 3.00
15 Ja Morant 1.50 4.00

2022-23 Donruss Franchise Features

COMMON CARD .30 .75
SEMISTARS .40 1.00
UNLISTED STARS .50 1.25
*HOLO PRPL LSR/99: 2X TO 5X BASIC
*HOLO PINK LSR/50: 2.5X TO 6X BASIC
*HOLO YLW LSR/25: 4X TO 10X BASIC
1 Jayson Tatum 2.00 5.00
2 Kevin Durant 1.50 4.00
3 RJ Barrett .75 2.00
4 Joel Embiid .75 2.00
5 Pascal Siakam .75 2.00
6 Zach LaVine 1.00 2.50
7 Evan Mobley 1.25 3.00
8 Cade Cunningham 1.50 4.00
9 Tyrese Haliburton 1.00 2.50
10 Giannis Antetokounmpo 2.50 6.00
11 Trae Young 1.25 3.00
12 LaMelo Ball 1.25 3.00
13 Jimmy Butler 1.00 2.50
14 Cole Anthony .50 1.25
15 Bradley Beal .60 1.50
16 Nikola Jokic 2.50 6.00
17 Anthony Edwards 2.50 6.00
18 Shai Gilgeous-Alexander 2.50 6.00
19 Damian Lillard 1.25 3.00
20 Jordan Clarkson .50 1.25
21 Stephen Curry 4.00 10.00
22 Kawhi Leonard 1.25 3.00
23 LeBron James 4.00 10.00
24 Devin Booker 1.25 3.00
25 De'Aaron Fox 1.00 2.50
26 Luka Doncic 3.00 8.00
27 Jalen Green 1.50 4.00
28 Ja Morant 1.50 4.00
29 Zion Williamson 1.25 3.00
30 Keldon Johnson .60 1.50

2022-23 Donruss Great X-Pectations

COMMON CARD .30 .75
SEMISTARS .40 1.00
UNLISTED STARS .50 1.25
*HOLO PRPL LSR/99: 3X TO 8X BASIC
*HOLO PINK LSR/50: 4X TO 10X BASIC
*HOLO YLW LSR/25: 6X TO 15X BASIC
1 Keegan Murray 1.25 3.00
2 Bennedict Mathurin 1.50 4.00
3 Shaedon Sharpe 2.00 5.00
4 Jaden Ivey 1.50 4.00
5 Chet Holmgren 2.50 6.00
6 Jabari Smith Jr. 1.50 4.00
7 Paolo Banchero 3.00 8.00
8 Dyson Daniels 1.25 3.00
9 Jeremy Sochan 1.50 4.00
10 Johnny Davis .50 1.25
11 Ousmane Dieng .60 1.50
12 Jalen Williams 2.50 6.00
13 Ochai Agbaji .60 1.50
14 AJ Griffin .40 1.00
15 Malaki Branham .50 1.25
16 Nikola Jovic 1.00 2.50
17 Mark Williams 1.00 2.50
18 Jalen Duren 1.50 4.00
19 Dalen Terry .50 1.25
20 Jaden Hardy .75 2.00
21 Christian Braun 1.25 3.00
22 Blake Wesley .50 1.25
23 Wendell Moore Jr. .50 1.25
24 TyTy Washington Jr. .50 1.25
25 Peyton Watson .75 2.00

2022-23 Donruss Magicians

COMMON CARD .30 .75
SEMISTARS .40 1.00
UNLISTED STARS .50 1.25
*HOLO PRPL LSR/99: 3X TO 8X BASIC
*HOLO PINK LSR/50: 4X TO 10X BASIC
*HOLO YLW LSR/25: 6X TO 15X BASIC
1 LeBron James 4.00 10.00
2 Luka Doncic 3.00 8.00
3 Stephen Curry 4.00 10.00
4 Nikola Jokic 2.50 6.00
5 Kyrie Irving 1.00 2.50
6 Ja Morant 1.50 4.00
7 Trae Young 1.25 3.00
8 Zion Williamson 1.25 3.00
9 LaMelo Ball 1.25 3.00
10 Anthony Edwards 2.50 6.00

2022-23 Donruss Net Marvels

COMMON CARD .30 .75
SEMISTARS .40 1.00
UNLISTED STARS .50 1.25
*PRESS PROOF: .5X TO 1.2X BASIC
*PRESS PROOF PRPL: .6X TO 1.5X BASIC
*DIAMOND: 2.5 TO 6X BASIC
1 Kawhi Leonard 1.25 3.00
2 Giannis Antetokounmpo 2.50 6.00
3 LeBron James 4.00 10.00
4 Stephen Curry 4.00 10.00
5 Ja Morant 1.50 4.00
6 Cade Cunningham 1.50 4.00
7 LaMelo Ball 1.25 3.00
8 Anthony Edwards 2.50 6.00
9 Jalen Green 1.50 4.00
10 Kevin Durant 1.50 4.00
11 Zion Williamson 1.25 3.00
12 Bradley Beal .60 1.50
13 Nikola Jokic 2.50 6.00
14 Devin Booker 1.25 3.00
15 Damian Lillard 1.25 3.00
16 James Harden 1.00 2.50
17 Luka Doncic 3.00 8.00
18 Jayson Tatum 2.00 5.00
19 Scottie Barnes .75 2.00
20 Zach LaVine 1.00 2.50

2022-23 Donruss Next Day Autographs

1 Paolo Banchero 500.00 1,000.00
2 Chet Holmgren 500.00 1,000.00
3 Jabari Smith Jr. 150.00 400.00
4 Keegan Murray 200.00 500.00
5 Jaden Ivey 150.00 400.00
6 Bennedict Mathurin 200.00 500.00
7 Shaedon Sharpe 300.00 600.00
8 Dyson Daniels 40.00 100.00
9 Jeremy Sochan 125.00 300.00
10 Johnny Davis 25.00 60.00
11 Ousmane Dieng 25.00 60.00
12 Jalen Williams 400.00 800.00
13 Jalen Duren 125.00 300.00
14 Ochai Agbaji 60.00 150.00
15 Mark Williams 60.00 150.00
16 AJ Griffin 30.00 80.00
17 Tari Eason 125.00 300.00
18 Dalen Terry 30.00 80.00
19 Jake LaRavia 12.00 30.00
20 Malaki Branham 40.00 100.00
21 Christian Braun 75.00 200.00
22 Walker Kessler 75.00 200.00
23 David Roddy 25.00 60.00
24 MarJon Beauchamp 25.00 60.00
25 Blake Wesley 20.00 50.00
26 Wendell Moore Jr. 20.00 50.00
27 Nikola Jovic 75.00 200.00
28 Patrick Baldwin Jr. 25.00 60.00
29 Peyton Watson 50.00 120.00
31 Andrew Nembhard 50.00 120.00
32 Caleb Houstan 20.00 50.00
33 Christian Koloko 12.00 30.00
34 Max Christie 100.00 250.00
35 Jaden Hardy 150.00 400.00
36 Kennedy Chandler 15.00 40.00
37 Moussa Diabate 15.00 40.00
38 E.J. Liddell 12.00 30.00
39 Trevor Keels 12.00 30.00
40 Isaiah Mobley 12.00 30.00

2022-23 Donruss Night Moves

1 Paolo Banchero 300.00 600.00
2 Chet Holmgren 150.00 400.00
3 Jabari Smith Jr. 150.00 400.00
4 Keegan Murray 150.00 400.00
5 Jaden Ivey 150.00 400.00
6 Bennedict Mathurin 150.00 400.00
7 Shaedon Sharpe 150.00 400.00
8 Dyson Daniels 75.00 200.00
9 Jeremy Sochan 150.00 400.00
10 Johnny Davis 40.00 100.00
11 Ousmane Dieng 60.00 150.00
12 Jalen Williams 200.00 500.00
13 LaMelo Ball 100.00 250.00
14 Cade Cunningham 100.00 250.00
15 Jalen Green 125.00 300.00
16 Giannis Antetokounmpo 200.00 500.00
17 LeBron James 350.00 700.00
18 Stephen Curry 350.00 700.00
19 Luka Doncic 300.00 600.00
20 Nikola Jokic 150.00 400.00
21 Jayson Tatum 200.00 500.00
22 Ja Morant 60.00 150.00
23 Kevin Durant 100.00 250.00
24 Zion Williamson 100.00 250.00
25 Shaquille O'Neal 100.00 250.00
26 Allen Iverson 150.00 400.00
27 Dwyane Wade 75.00 200.00
28 Charles Barkley 75.00 200.00
29 Dirk Nowitzki 125.00 300.00
30 Kevin Garnett 125.00 300.00

2022-23 Donruss Production Line

COMMON CARD .30 .75
SEMISTARS .40 1.00
UNLISTED STARS .50 1.25
*PRESS PROOF: .5X TO 1.2X BASIC
*PRESS PROOF PRPL: .6X TO 1.5X BASIC
*DIAMOND: 1.5X TO 4X BASIC
1 LeBron James 4.00 10.00
2 Stephen Curry 4.00 10.00
3 Trae Young 1.25 3.00
4 Darius Garland .75 2.00
5 Nikola Jokic 2.50 6.00
6 Anthony Davis 1.25 3.00
7 Giannis Antetokounmpo 2.50 6.00
8 Devin Booker 1.25 3.00
9 Luka Doncic 3.00 8.00
10 Jayson Tatum 2.00 5.00

2022-23 Donruss Rated Rookies Signatures

COMMON CARD 4.00 10.00
SEMISTARS 5.00 12.00
UNLISTED STARS 6.00 15.00
*CHOICE: .5X TO 1.2X BASIC
*HOLO PINK LSR: .5X TO 1.2X BASIC
*HOLO RED & GOLD LSR: .5X TO 1.2X BASIC
*CHOICE RED/99: .5X TO 1.2X BASIC
*HOLO LASER/99: .5X TO 1.2X BASIC
*HOLO FRAME/75: .5X TO 1.2X BASIC
*CHOICE BLUE/49: .6X TO 1.5X BASIC
*HOLO RED LSR/49: .6X TO 1.5X BASIC
*HOLO PRPL LASER/30: .75X TO 2X BASIC
*HOLO BLUE LASER/25: .75X TO 2X BASIC
201 Paolo Banchero 75.00 200.00
202 Chet Holmgren 125.00 300.00
203 Jabari Smith Jr. 20.00 50.00
204 Keegan Murray 15.00 40.00
205 Jaden Ivey 20.00 50.00
206 Bennedict Mathurin 20.00 50.00
207 Shaedon Sharpe 25.00 60.00
208 Dyson Daniels 15.00 40.00
209 Jeremy Sochan 20.00 50.00
210 Johnny Davis 6.00 15.00
211 Ousmane Dieng 8.00 20.00
212 Jalen Williams 50.00 120.00
213 Jalen Duren 20.00 50.00
214 Ochai Agbaji 8.00 20.00
215 Mark Williams 12.00 30.00
216 AJ Griffin 5.00 12.00
217 Tari Eason 15.00 40.00
218 Dalen Terry 6.00 15.00
219 Jake LaRavia 6.00 15.00
220 Malaki Branham 6.00 15.00
221 Christian Braun 15.00 40.00
222 Walker Kessler 12.00 30.00
223 David Roddy 8.00 20.00
224 MarJon Beauchamp 6.00 15.00
225 Blake Wesley 6.00 15.00
226 Wendell Moore Jr. 6.00 15.00
227 Nikola Jovic 12.00 30.00
228 Patrick Baldwin Jr. 6.00 15.00
229 TyTy Washington Jr. 6.00 15.00
230 Peyton Watson 10.00 25.00
231 Andrew Nembhard 12.00 30.00
232 Caleb Houstan 6.00 15.00
233 Christian Koloko 6.00 15.00
234 Max Christie 15.00 40.00
235 Jaden Hardy 10.00 25.00
236 Kennedy Chandler 6.00 15.00
237 Moussa Diabate 6.00 15.00
238 E.J. Liddell 6.00 15.00
239 Trevor Keels 5.00 12.00
241 Jaylin Williams 8.00 20.00
242 Bryce McGowens 6.00 15.00
243 Tyrese Martin 5.00 12.00
244 Ryan Rollins 6.00 15.00
245 Josh Minott 6.00 15.00
246 Vince Williams Jr. 8.00 20.00
247 Kendall Brown 5.00 12.00
248 Luke Travers 5.00 12.00
249 Jabari Walker 5.00 12.00
250 Kenneth Lofton Jr. 8.00 20.00

2022-23 Donruss Retro Series

COMMON CARD .30 .75
SEMISTARS .40 1.00
UNLISTED STARS .50 1.25
*PRESS PROOF: .5X TO 1.2X BASIC
*PRESS PROOF PRPL: .6X TO 1.5X BASIC
*DIAMOND: 2X TO 5X BASIC
1 Larry Bird 2.00 5.00
2 Shaquille O'Neal 2.00 5.00
3 Dirk Nowitzki 1.25 3.00
4 Tracy McGrady .75 2.00
5 Magic Johnson 2.00 5.00
6 Kevin Garnett 1.25 3.00
7 Charles Barkley 1.25 3.00
8 Isiah Thomas .75 2.00
9 Ray Allen .75 2.00
10 Jason Kidd .75 2.00
11 Tony Parker .75 2.00
12 Vince Carter 1.00 2.50
13 Dwyane Wade 1.00 2.50
14 Hakeem Olajuwon 1.00 2.50
15 Dominique Wilkins .75 2.00
16 Tim Duncan 1.25 3.00
17 Allen Iverson 1.25 3.00
18 Karl Malone 1.00 2.50
19 Grant Hill .75 2.00
20 Clyde Drexler .75 2.00
21 Steve Nash 1.00 2.50
22 Jason Williams .75 2.00
23 Paul Pierce .75 2.00
24 Chris Webber .60 1.50
25 Patrick Ewing .75 2.00

2022-23 Donruss Signature Series

COMMON CARD 4.00 10.00
SEMISTARS 5.00 12.00
UNLISTED STARS 6.00 15.00
1 Paolo Banchero 300.00 600.00
2 Chet Holmgren 150.00 400.00
3 Jabari Smith Jr. 75.00 200.00
4 Keegan Murray 75.00 200.00
5 Jaden Ivey 75.00 200.00
6 Bennedict Mathurin 75.00 200.00
7 Shaedon Sharpe 60.00 150.00
8 Dyson Daniels 25.00 60.00
9 Jeremy Sochan 75.00 200.00
10 Johnny Davis 6.00 15.00
11 Ousmane Dieng 8.00 20.00
12 Jalen Williams 75.00 200.00
13 Jalen Duren 25.00 60.00
14 Ochai Agbaji 20.00 50.00
15 Mark Williams 12.00 30.00
16 AJ Griffin 5.00 12.00
17 Tari Eason 20.00 50.00
18 Dalen Terry 6.00 15.00
19 Jake LaRavia 6.00 15.00
20 Malaki Branham 20.00 50.00
21 Christian Braun 15.00 40.00
22 Walker Kessler 40.00 100.00
23 David Roddy 8.00 20.00
24 MarJon Beauchamp 6.00 15.00
25 Blake Wesley 6.00 15.00
26 Wendell Moore Jr. 6.00 15.00
27 Nikola Jovic 12.00 30.00
29 TyTy Washington Jr. 6.00 15.00
30 Peyton Watson 12.00 30.00
31 Andrew Nembhard 20.00 50.00
32 Caleb Houstan 6.00 15.00
33 Christian Koloko 6.00 15.00
34 Max Christie 12.00 30.00
35 Jaden Hardy 75.00 200.00
36 Kennedy Chandler 6.00 15.00
37 Moussa Diabate 6.00 15.00
38 E.J. Liddell 6.00 15.00
39 Trevor Keels 5.00 12.00
40 Isaiah Mobley 6.00 15.00
41 Jaylin Williams 8.00 20.00
42 Bryce McGowens 6.00 15.00
43 Tyrese Martin 5.00 12.00
44 Scotty Pippen Jr. 8.00 20.00
45 Josh Minott 6.00 15.00
46 Vince Williams Jr. 8.00 20.00
47 Kendall Brown 5.00 12.00
48 Mac McClung 125.00 300.00
49 Jabari Walker 5.00 12.00
50 Kenneth Lofton Jr. 20.00 50.00
53 Anthony Davis 40.00 100.00
54 Gabe Vincent 6.00 15.00
55 Frank Ntilikina 4.00 10.00
56 Will Barton 4.00 10.00
57 Garrison Mathews 6.00 15.00
58 Royce O'Neale 5.00 12.00
59 De'Anthony Melton 5.00 12.00
60 Chuma Okeke 6.00 15.00
61 Xavier Tillman 6.00 15.00
62 Vernon Carey Jr. 6.00 15.00
63 Justin Holiday 4.00 10.00
64 Khem Birch 5.00 12.00
65 Nerlens Noel 4.00 10.00
66 Robin Lopez 5.00 12.00
67 Nassir Little 6.00 15.00
68 Luke Kennard 5.00 12.00
69 Reggie Jackson 5.00 12.00
70 Aaron Nesmith 6.00 15.00
71 Gary Harris 5.00 12.00
72 Doug McDermott 4.00 10.00
73 Danny Green 5.00 12.00
74 Anfernee Simons 12.00 30.00
75 Jordan Clarkson 12.00 30.00
76 Onyeka Okongwu 6.00 15.00
77 Jalen Brunson 12.00 30.00
78 Keita Bates-Diop 5.00 12.00
79 Terence Davis II 5.00 12.00
80 John Konchar 6.00 15.00
81 Damian Jones 4.00 10.00
82 Wayne Ellington 5.00 12.00
83 Ty Jerome 5.00 12.00
84 Ish Smith 5.00 12.00
85 Michael Porter Jr. 8.00 20.00
86 Collin Sexton 8.00 20.00
87 Dejounte Murray 12.00 30.00
88 RJ Barrett 12.00 30.00
89 Jonas Valanciunas 5.00 12.00
90 Sleepy Floyd 6.00 15.00
91 Muggsy Bogues 12.00 30.00
92 Rolando Blackman 5.00 12.00
93 Jeff Malone 5.00 12.00
94 Tim Hardaway 8.00 20.00
95 Elton Brand 6.00 15.00
96 Sam Cassell 6.00 15.00
97 Jamaal Wilkes 6.00 15.00
98 Jason Kidd 20.00 50.00
99 Walt Frazier 10.00 25.00
100 Vince Carter 60.00 150.00

2022-23 Donruss The Rookies

*HOLO PRPL LSR/99: 2.5X TO 6X BASIC
*HOLO PINK LSR/50: 3X TO 8X BASIC
*HOLO YLW LSR/25: 5X TO 12X BASIC
1 Paolo Banchero 5.00 12.00
2 Chet Holmgren 4.00 10.00
3 Jabari Smith Jr. 2.50 6.00
4 Keegan Murray 2.00 5.00
5 Jaden Ivey 2.50 6.00

2022-23 Donruss Unleashed

COMMON CARD .30 .75
SEMISTARS .40 1.00
UNLISTED STARS .50 1.25
*PRESS PROOF: .6X TO 1.5X BASIC
*PRESS PROOF PRPL: .6X TO 1.5X BASIC
*DIAMOND: 1.5X TO 4X BASIC
1 Luka Doncic 3.00 8.00
2 Ja Morant 1.50 4.00
3 LeBron James 4.00 10.00
4 Stephen Curry 4.00 10.00
5 Damian Lillard 1.25 3.00
6 Trae Young 1.25 3.00
7 Kevin Durant 1.50 4.00
8 Kawhi Leonard 1.25 3.00
9 LaMelo Ball 1.25 3.00
10 Jayson Tatum 2.00 5.00
11 Giannis Antetokounmpo 2.50 6.00
12 Zion Williamson 1.25 3.00
13 Anthony Edwards 2.50 6.00
14 Jalen Green 1.50 4.00
15 Cade Cunningham 1.50 4.00

2023-24 Donruss

1 Bones Hyland .30 .75
2 LeBron James 3.00 8.00
3 Derrick White .50 1.25
4 Tobias Harris .40 1.00
5 Harrison Barnes .30 .75
6 Collin Sexton .50 1.25
7 Cameron Payne .30 .75
8 Tyrese Haliburton .75 2.00
9 Desmond Bane .50 1.25
10 Richaun Holmes .25 .60
11 Cade Cunningham 1.00 2.50
12 Myles Turner .40 1.00
13 Mike Conley .30 .75
14 Kenneth Lofton Jr. .40 1.00
15 Trae Young .75 2.00
16 Rudy Gobert .50 1.25
17 Malcolm Brogdon .40 1.00
18 Austin Reaves 1.00 2.50
19 Bradley Beal .50 1.25
20 Malik Monk .50 1.25
21 Immanuel Quickley .40 1.00
22 Jake LaRavia .30 .75
23 Seth Curry .40 1.00
24 De'Andre Hunter .40 1.00
25 Trey Murphy III .50 1.25
26 Peyton Watson .40 1.00
27 Tyler Herro .60 1.50
28 Zach LaVine .60 1.50
29 Kawhi Leonard 1.00 2.50
30 Brandon Ingram .50 1.25
31 Dejounte Murray .50 1.25
32 Keegan Murray .50 1.25
33 Kristaps Porzingis .50 1.25
34 Gordon Hayward .40 1.00
35 Kevin Durant 1.25 3.00
36 Lauri Markkanen .60 1.50
37 Rui Hachimura .40 1.00
38 Aaron Gordon .40 1.00
39 Darius Garland .60 1.50
40 Shai Gilgeous-Alexander 2.00 5.00
41 Julius Randle .50 1.25
42 Ochai Agbaji .40 1.00
43 Devin Booker 1.00 2.50
44 Damian Lillard 1.00 2.50
45 Spencer Dinwiddie .30 .75
46 Scottie Barnes .50 1.25
47 Devin Vassell .50 1.25
48 Kyrie Irving .75 2.00
49 Talen Horton-Tucker .30 .75
50 Keldon Johnson .50 1.25
51 Deni Avdija .40 1.00
52 Matisse Thybulle .30 .75
53 Cam Reddish .30 .75
54 Herbert Jones .40 1.00
55 Ziaire Williams .40 1.00
56 P.J. Washington Jr. .40 1.00
57 RJ Barrett .60 1.50
58 Nikola Jokic 2.00 5.00
59 Devonte' Graham .30 .75
60 Eric Gordon .30 .75
61 Draymond Green .50 1.25
62 Christian Wood .30 .75
63 James Harden .75 2.00
64 Jimmy Butler .60 1.50
65 Stephen Curry 3.00 8.00
66 Isaiah Mobley .25 .60
67 Onyeka Okongwu .30 .75
68 Gabe Vincent .40 1.00
69 Cameron Thomas .50 1.25
70 Mikal Bridges .50 1.25
71 Bam Adebayo .60 1.50
72 Jeandre Ayton .40 1.00
73 Kyle Lowry .50 1.25
74 Patrick Beverley .30 .75
75 Derrick Rose .60 1.50
76 Jalen Williams .75 2.00
77 Jose Alvarado .40 1.00
78 Chris Paul .75 2.00
79 Terance Mann .30 .75
80 Walker Kessler .40 1.00
81 Robert Williams III .40 1.00
82 Domantas Sabonis .60 1.50
83 Max Strus .40 1.00
84 Moses Moody .50 1.25
85 Luguentz Dort .40 1.00
86 Naz Reid .40 1.00
87 LaMelo Ball 1.00 2.50
88 Davion Mitchell .30 .75
89 Franz Wagner .60 1.50
90 Chris Duarte .30 .75
91 Clint Capela .30 .75
92 Tari Eason .50 1.25
93 AJ Griffin .30 .75
94 Tim Hardaway Jr. .30 .75
95 CJ McCollum .40 1.00
96 Malaki Branham .30 .75
97 Anfernee Simons .50 1.25
98 Jabari Smith Jr. .60 1.50
99 Blake Wesley .25 .60
100 Quentin Grimes .40 1.00
101 Bennedict Mathurin .60 1.50
102 Jerami Grant .50 1.25
103 Caris LeVert .40 1.00
104 Jalen Duren .50 1.25
105 Marvin Bagley III .30 .75
106 Kyle Kuzma .50 1.25
107 Ivica Zubac .40 1.00
108 Jaren Jackson Jr. .60 1.50
109 Buddy Hield .40 1.00
110 Joel Embiid 1.00 2.50
111 Nikola Jovic .40 1.00
112 Alperen Sengun .60 1.50
113 Jordan Clarkson .40 1.00
114 Grant Williams .30 .75
115 Nikola Vucevic .40 1.00
116 Jalen Green .60 1.50
117 Max Christie .40 1.00
118 D'Angelo Russell .40 1.00
119 Ousmane Dieng .40 1.00
120 Terry Rozier III .50 1.25
121 Duncan Robinson .30 .75
122 Zion Williamson 1.00 2.50
123 Chet Holmgren 1.00 2.50
124 Shaedon Sharpe .75 2.00
125 Mark Williams .40 1.00
126 De'Aaron Fox .75 2.00
127 Markelle Fultz .30 .75
128 Jaylen Brown .75 2.00
129 Josh Green .30 .75
130 Anthony Davis 1.00 2.50
131 Ja Morant 1.25 3.00
132 Pascal Siakam .60 1.50

133 Bojan Bogdanovic .40 1.00
134 Josh Giddey .50 1.25
135 Jaden Ivey .50 1.25
136 Norman Powell .40 1.00
137 Anthony Edwards 2.00 5.00
138 Khris Middleton .40 1.00
139 Jamal Murray .75 2.00
140 Donovan Mitchell .75 2.00
141 Luka Doncic 2.50 6.00
142 Jrue Holiday .50 1.25
143 Simone Fontecchio .40 1.00
144 Gary Trent Jr. .40 1.00
145 Russell Westbrook .60 1.50
146 James Wiseman .30 .75
147 Bogdan Bogdanovic .40 1.00
148 Jonathan Kuminga 1.00 2.50
149 Dyson Daniels .50 1.25
150 Shake Milton .30 .75
151 OG Anunoby .50 1.25
152 Tyrese Maxey .75 2.00
153 Fred VanVleet .60 1.50
154 Michael Porter Jr. .50 1.25
155 Karl-Anthony Towns .60 1.50
156 Jabari Walker .25 .60
157 Xavier Tillman .40 1.00
158 Steven Adams .40 1.00
159 Kenyon Martin Jr. .40 1.00
160 Christian Braun .40 1.00
161 Tre Jones .40 1.00
162 Kevin Huerter .30 .75
163 Cole Anthony .40 1.00
164 Ben Simmons .40 1.00
165 Cameron Johnson .40 1.00
166 Kevin Love .40 1.00
167 Paul George .60 1.50
168 Jeremy Sochan .50 1.25
169 Marcus Smart .50 1.25
170 Andrew Wiggins .50 1.25
171 Jae'Sean Tate .40 1.00
172 Jalen Suggs .50 1.25
173 Victor Oladipo .30 .75
174 Josh Hart .40 1.00
175 Saddiq Bey .40 1.00
176 Reggie Bullock .25 .60
177 Jordan Poole .60 1.50
178 Jaylin Williams .40 1.00
179 DeAndre Jordan .30 .75
180 Jonas Valanciunas .30 .75
181 Dillon Brooks .40 1.00
182 Caleb Martin .30 .75
183 Bruce Brown .30 .75
184 John Collins .40 1.00
185 Klay Thompson 1.00 2.50
186 Jarrett Allen .40 1.00
187 David Roddy .30 .75
188 Giannis Antetokounmpo 2.00 5.00
189 Jalen Brunson .75 2.00
190 E.J. Liddell .30 .75
191 Alex Caruso .40 1.00
192 Gary Payton II .30 .75
193 Kentavious Caldwell-Pope .30 .75
194 Jarred Vanderbilt .30 .75
195 Evan Mobley .60 1.50
196 Jaden Hardy .50 1.25
197 Jayson Tatum 1.50 4.00
198 Kelly Oubre Jr. .40 1.00
199 DeMar DeRozan .60 1.50
200 Paolo Banchero 1.00 2.50
201 Hunter Tyson RC .75 2.00
202 Anthony Black RC 1.50 4.00
203 Kris Murray RC .75 2.00
204 Kobe Bufkin RC 1.00 2.50
205 Emoni Bates RC 1.00 2.50
206 Amen Thompson RC 4.00 10.00
207 Jarace Walker RC 1.50 4.00
208 Taylor Hendricks RC .75 2.00
209 Leonard Miller RC .75 2.00
210 Andre Jackson Jr. RC 1.25 3.00
211 Cam Whitmore RC 2.00 5.00
212 Jett Howard RC 1.00 2.50
213 Jaime Jaquez Jr. RC 1.25 3.00
214 Brice Sensabaugh RC 1.25 3.00
215 James Nnaji RC .60 1.50
216 Jalen Hood-Schifino RC .75 2.00
217 Jalen Pickett RC .60 1.50
218 Rayan Rupert RC .75 2.00
219 Jordan Hawkins RC 1.25 3.00
220 Victor Wembanyama RC 6.00 15.00
221 Colby Jones RC .75 2.00
222 Marcus Sasser RC 1.25 3.00
223 Sidy Cissoko RC .75 2.00
224 Jalen Wilson RC .75 2.00
225 Bilal Coulibaly RC 2.00 5.00
226 Brandon Miller RC 3.00 8.00
227 Julian Phillips RC .75 2.00
228 Ausar Thompson RC 2.00 5.00
229 Jordan Walsh RC .75 2.00
230 Tristan Vukcevic RC .75 2.00
231 Cason Wallace RC 1.50 4.00
232 GG Jackson II RC 1.50 4.00
233 Dereck Lively II RC 1.50 4.00
234 Noah Clowney RC 1.00 2.50
235 Maxwell Lewis RC .60 1.50
236 Jordan Miller RC 1.00 2.50
237 Keyontae Johnson RC .75 2.00
238 Markquis Nowell RC .75 2.00
239 Kobe Brown RC .75 2.00
240 Dariq Whitehead RC 1.00 2.50
241 Olivier-Maxence Prosper RC .75 2.00
242 Julian Strawther RC 1.00 2.50
243 Mouhamed Gueye RC .75 2.00
244 Keyonte George RC 2.50 6.00
245 Toumani Camara RC 1.50 4.00
246 Ben Sheppard RC .75 2.00
247 Gradey Dick RC 1.50 4.00
248 Nick Smith Jr. RC 1.00 2.50
249 Brandin Podziemski RC 2.50 6.00
250 Scoot Henderson RC 2.50 6.00

2023-24 Donruss Choice
*CHOICE: 1.5X TO 4X BASIC
220 Victor Wembanyama 75.00 200.00

2023-24 Donruss Choice Blue
*CHOICE BLUE: 4X TO 10X BASIC
STATED PRINT RUN 49 SER.#'d SETS
220 Victor Wembanyama 500.00 1,000.00
226 Brandon Miller 75.00 200.00

2023-24 Donruss Choice Red
*CHOICE RED: 2.5X TO 6X BASIC
STATED PRINT RUN 99 SER.#'d SETS
220 Victor Wembanyama 300.00 600.00
226 Brandon Miller 50.00 120.00

2023-24 Donruss Holo Blue and Green Laser
*HOLO BLUE & GRN LASER: 5X TO 12X BASIC
STATED PRINT RUN 35 SER.#'d SETS
220 Victor Wembanyama 600.00 1,200.00
226 Brandon Miller 100.00 250.00

2023-24 Donruss Holo Blue Laser
*HOLO BLUE LASER: 4X TO 10X BASIC
STATED PRINT RUN 49 SER.#'d SETS
220 Victor Wembanyama 500.00 1,000.00
226 Brandon Miller 75.00 200.00

2023-24 Donruss Holo Green Laser
*HOLO GRN LASER: 1.25X TO 3X BASIC
220 Victor Wembanyama 100.00 250.00

2023-24 Donruss Holo Laser
*HOLO LASER: 2X TO 5X BASIC
STATED PRINT RUN 149 SER.#'d SETS
220 Victor Wembanyama 200.00 500.00
226 Brandon Miller 40.00 100.00

2023-24 Donruss Holo Light Blue Laser
*HOLO LGT BLUE LSR: 6X TO 15X BASIC
STATED PRINT RUN 25 SER.#'d SETS
220 Victor Wembanyama 800.00 1,500.00
226 Brandon Miller 125.00 300.00

2023-24 Donruss Holo Orange Laser
*HOLO ORNG LASER: 2X TO 5X BASIC
STATED PRINT RUN 125 SER.#'d SETS
220 Victor Wembanyama 200.00 500.00
226 Brandon Miller 40.00 100.00

2023-24 Donruss Holo Teal Laser
*HOLO TEAL LSR: 6X TO 15X BASIC
STATED PRINT RUN 20 SER.#'d SETS
220 Victor Wembanyama 800.00 1,500.00
226 Brandon Miller 125.00 300.00

2023-24 Donruss Holo Yellow Laser
*HOLO YLW LSR: 6X TO 15X BASIC
STATED PRINT RUN 25 SER.#'d SETS
220 Victor Wembanyama 800.00 1,500.00
226 Brandon Miller 125.00 300.00

2023-24 Donruss Press Proof Silver
*PRESS PROOF SILVER: .5X TO 1.2X BASIC
220 Victor Wembanyama 20.00 50.00

2023-24 Donruss Yellow Flood
*YELLOW FLOOD: .75X TO 2X BASIC
220 Victor Wembanyama 25.00 60.00

2023-24 Donruss Animation
1 LeBron James 350.00 700.00
2 Stephen Curry 350.00 700.00
3 Luka Doncic 350.00 700.00
4 Victor Wembanyama 1,250.00 2,500.00
5 Scoot Henderson 150.00 400.00
6 Brandon Miller 200.00 500.00
7 Amen Thompson 75.00 200.00
8 Ausar Thompson 40.00 100.00
9 Jayson Tatum 300.00 600.00
10 Bilal Coulibaly 60.00 120.00

2023-24 Donruss Bomb Squad
*HOLO PRPL LSR/99: 3X TO 8X BASIC
*HOLO RED & GRN LSR/75: 4X TO 10X BASIC
*HOLO PINK LSR/50: 5X TO 12X BASIC
*HOLO BLUE & GRN LSR/35: 6X TO 15X BASIC
*HOLO YLW LSR/25: 8X TO 20X BASIC
1 Stephen Curry 4.00 10.00
2 Ja Morant 1.50 4.00
3 Luka Doncic 3.00 8.00
4 Kyrie Irving 1.00 2.50
5 Devin Booker 1.25 3.00
6 Anthony Edwards 2.50 6.00
7 LeBron James 4.00 10.00
8 Anthony Davis 1.25 3.00
9 Zion Williamson 1.25 3.00
10 Shai Gilgeous-Alexander 2.50 6.00
11 Donovan Mitchell 1.00 2.50
12 Damian Lillard 1.25 3.00
13 LaMelo Ball 1.25 3.00
14 Jayson Tatum 2.00 5.00
15 Giannis Antetokounmpo 2.00 5.00
16 Dirk Nowitzki 1.25 3.00
17 Dwyane Wade 1.00 2.50
18 Yao Ming 1.25 3.00
19 Vince Carter 1.00 2.50
20 Magic Johnson 2.00 5.00

2023-24 Donruss Complete Players
*HOLO PRPL LSR/99: 2.5X TO 6X BASIC
*HOLO RED & GRN LSR/75: 3X TO 8X BASIC
*HOLO PINK LSR/50: 4X TO 10X BASIC
*HOLO BLUE & GRN LSR/35: 5X TO 12X BASIC
*HOLO YLW LSR/25: 6X TO 15X BASIC
1 LeBron James 4.00 10.00
2 Giannis Antetokounmpo 2.50 6.00
3 Nikola Jokic 2.50 6.00
4 Trae Young 1.00 2.50
5 Luka Doncic 3.00 8.00
6 Kawhi Leonard 1.25 3.00
7 Damian Lillard 1.25 3.00
8 Kyrie Irving 1.00 2.50
9 Kevin Durant 1.50 4.00
10 Jayson Tatum 2.00 5.00

2023-24 Donruss Crunch Time
*PRESS PROOF: .5X TO 1.2X BASIC
*PRESS PROOF PRPL: .6X TO 1.5X BASIC
*DIAMOND: 1.5X TO 4X BASIC
*HOLO LASER/99: 2.5X TO 6X BASIC
1 Luka Doncic 3.00 8.00
2 LeBron James 4.00 10.00
3 De'Aaron Fox 1.00 2.50
4 Anthony Edwards 2.50 6.00
5 LaMelo Ball 1.25 3.00
6 Stephen Curry 4.00 10.00
7 Ja Morant 1.50 4.00
8 Kawhi Leonard 1.25 3.00
9 Jalen Green .75 2.00
10 Jayson Tatum 2.00 5.00
11 Devin Booker 1.25 3.00
12 Cade Cunningham 1.25 3.00
13 Shai Gilgeous-Alexander 2.50 6.00
14 Trae Young 1.00 2.50
15 Giannis Antetokounmpo 2.50 6.00

2023-24 Donruss Dominators Autographs
STATED PRINT RUN 25-99 SER.#'d SETS
3 Larry Bird/49 75.00 200.00
4 Deandre Ayton/99 6.00 15.00
5 Jalen Williams/99 20.00 50.00
7 Immanuel Quickley/99 6.00 15.00
8 Shaedon Sharpe/99 25.00 60.00
9 Desmond Bane/49 8.00 20.00
10 Keegan Murray/99 20.00 50.00
11 Stephen Curry/25 500.00 1,000.00
12 Ja Morant/30 125.00 300.00
13 Walker Kessler/99 6.00 15.00
14 Jalen Duren/99 8.00 20.00
16 Kareem Abdul-Jabbar/25 75.00 200.00
17 Kevin Garnett/49 50.00 120.00
18 Isaiah Stewart/99 6.00 15.00
19 Karl Malone/25 25.00 60.00
20 Lonnie Walker IV/99 6.00 15.00
21 Jalen Green/99 10.00 25.00
22 Luka Doncic/49 350.00 700.00
23 Tari Eason/99 8.00 20.00
24 Cole Anthony/99 6.00 15.00
25 Alperen Sengun/99 10.00 25.00

2023-24 Donruss Dominators Autographs Holo Red and Gold Laser
*HOLO RED & GOLD LSR: .4X TO 1X BASIC
1 Saddiq Bey 6.00 15.00
2 RJ Barrett 10.00 25.00
6 Nikola Vucevic 6.00 15.00
15 James Wiseman 5.00 12.00

2023-24 Donruss Franchise Features Holo Blue and Green Laser
*HOLO BLUE GRN LSR: 5X TO 12X BASIC
STATED PRINT RUN 35 SER.#'d SETS
29 Victor Wembanyama 300.00 600.00

2023-24 Donruss Franchise Features Holo Pink Laser
*HOLO PINK LSR: 4X TO 10X BASIC
STATED PRINT RUN 50 SER.#'d SETS
29 Victor Wembanyama 200.00 500.00

2023-24 Donruss Franchise Features Holo Purple Laser
*HOLO PRPL LSR: 2.5X TO 6X BASIC
STATED PRINT RUN 99 SER.#'d SETS
29 Victor Wembanyama 125.00 300.00

2023-24 Donruss Franchise Features Holo Red and Green Laser
*HOLO RED GRN LSR: 3X TO 8X BASIC
STATED PRINT RUN 75 SER.#'d SETS
29 Victor Wembanyama 150.00 400.00

2023-24 Donruss Franchise Features Holo Yellow Laser
*HOLO YLW LSR: 6X TO 15X BASIC
STATED PRINT RUN 25 SER.#'d SETS
29 Victor Wembanyama 400.00 800.00

2023-24 Donruss Great X-Pectations
*HOLO PRPL LSR/99: 2X TO 5X BASIC
*HOLO RED GRN LSR/75: 2.5X TO 6X BASIC
*HOLO PINK LSR/50: 3X TO 8X BASIC
*HOLO BLUE GRN LSR/35: 4X TO 10X BASIC
*HOLO YLW LSR/25: 5X TO 12X BASIC
1 Anthony Black 1.00 2.50
2 Brandon Miller 2.00 5.00
3 Cam Whitmore 1.25 3.00
4 Gradey Dick 1.00 2.50
5 Jarace Walker 1.00 2.50
6 Jordan Hawkins .75 2.00
7 Nick Smith Jr. .60 1.50
8 Scoot Henderson 1.50 4.00
9 Taylor Hendricks .50 1.25
10 Victor Wembanyama 20.00 50.00
11 Jett Howard .60 1.50
12 Jalen Hood-Schifino .50 1.25
13 Jaime Jaquez Jr. .75 2.00
14 Amen Thompson 2.50 6.00
15 Ausar Thompson 1.25 3.00
16 Bilal Coulibaly 1.25 3.00
17 Keyonte George 1.50 4.00
18 Cason Wallace 1.00 2.50
19 Dariq Whitehead .60 1.50
20 Dereck Lively II 1.00 2.50
21 Kobe Bufkin .60 1.50
22 Brandin Podziemski 1.50 4.00
23 Kris Murray .50 1.25
24 Noah Clowney .60 1.50
25 Marcus Sasser .75 2.00

2023-24 Donruss Hardwood Masters Diamond
*DIAMOND: 1.5X TO 4X BASIC
3 Victor Wembanyama 150.00 400.00
5 Scoot Henderson 25.00 60.00
7 Brandon Miller 25.00 60.00

2023-24 Donruss Hardwood Masters Holo Laser
*HOLO LSR: 2.5X TO 6X BASIC
STATED PRINT RUN 99 SER.#'d SETS
3 Victor Wembanyama 200.00 500.00
5 Scoot Henderson 40.00 100.00
7 Brandon Miller 40.00 100.00

2023-24 Donruss Magicians
1 Victor Wembanyama 15.00 40.00
2 Scoot Henderson 1.25 3.00
3 Amen Thompson 2.00 5.00
4 Ausar Thompson 1.00 2.50
5 Brandon Miller 1.50 4.00
6 Trae Young .75 2.00
7 Nikola Jokic 2.00 5.00
8 Kyrie Irving .75 2.00
9 Stephen Curry 3.00 8.00
10 LeBron James 3.00 8.00

2023-24 Donruss Magicians Holo Blue and Green Laser
*HOLO BLUE GRN LSR: 8X TO 20X BASIC
STATED PRINT RUN 35 SER.#'d SETS
1 Victor Wembanyama 500.00 1,000.00
5 Brandon Miller 75.00 200.00

2023-24 Donruss Magicians Holo Pink Laser
*HOLO PINK LSR: 6X TO 15X BASIC
STATED PRINT RUN 50 SER.#'d SETS
1 Victor Wembanyama 400.00 800.00
5 Brandon Miller 60.00 150.00

2023-24 Donruss Magicians Holo Purple Laser
*HOLO PRPL LSR: 4X TO 10X BASIC
STATED PRINT RUN 99 SER.#'d SETS
1 Victor Wembanyama 200.00 500.00
5 Brandon Miller 40.00 100.00

2023-24 Donruss Magicians Holo Red and Green Laser
*HOLO RED GRN LSR: 5X TO 12X BASIC
STATED PRINT RUN 75 SER.#'d SETS
1 Victor Wembanyama 300.00 600.00
5 Brandon Miller 50.00 120.00

2023-24 Donruss Magicians Holo Yellow Laser
*HOLO YLW LSR: 10X TO 25X BASIC
STATED PRINT RUN 25 SER.#'d SETS
1 Victor Wembanyama 600.00 1,200.00
5 Brandon Miller 100.00 250.00

2023-24 Donruss Net Marvels
*PRESS PROOF: .5X TO 1.2X BASIC
*PRESS PROOF PRPL: .6X TO 1.5X BASIC
*DIAMOND: 3X TO 8X BASIC
*HOLO LSR/99: 3X TO 8X BASIC
1 Nikola Jokic 2.50 6.00
2 Joel Embiid 1.25 3.00
3 Damian Lillard 1.25 3.00
4 Jaylen Brown 1.00 2.50
5 Devin Booker 1.25 3.00
6 Kyrie Irving 1.00 2.50
7 Luka Doncic 3.00 8.00
8 Jamal Murray 1.00 2.50
9 LeBron James 4.00 10.00
10 Anthony Edwards 2.50 6.00
11 Kawhi Leonard 1.25 3.00
12 Ja Morant 1.50 4.00
13 LaMelo Ball 1.25 3.00
14 Stephen Curry 4.00 10.00
15 Donovan Mitchell 1.00 2.50
16 Jimmy Butler .75 2.00
17 Shai Gilgeous-Alexander 2.50 6.00
18 Trae Young 1.00 2.50
19 Kevin Durant 1.50 4.00
20 Cade Cunningham 1.25 3.00

2023-24 Donruss Rated Rookies Signatures
*CHOICE: .5X TO 1.2X BASIC
*HOLO PINK LSR: .5X TO 1.2X BASIC
*HOLO RED & GOLD LSR: .5X TO 1.2X BASIC
*CHOICE RED/99: .5X TO 1.2X BASIC
*HOLO LASER/99: .5X TO 1.2X BASIC
*CHOICE BLUE/49: .6X TO 1.5X BASIC
*HOLO RED LSR/49: .6X TO 1.5X BASIC
*HOLO PRPL LASER/30: .75X TO 2X BASIC
*HOLO BLUE LASER/25: .75X TO 2X BASIC
252 Vasilije Micic 5.00 12.00
253 Amen Thompson 25.00 60.00
254 Cason Wallace 10.00 25.00
255 Ricky Council IV 6.00 15.00
257 Tristan Vukcevic 5.00 12.00
258 GG Jackson II 10.00 25.00
259 Azuolas Tubelis 4.00 10.00
260 Adama Sanogo 5.00 12.00
261 Chris Livingston 5.00 12.00
263 Jalen Wilson 5.00 12.00
264 Andre Jackson Jr. 8.00 20.00
265 Jordan Walsh 5.00 12.00
266 Marcus Sasser 8.00 20.00
267 Trayce Jackson-Davis 6.00 15.00
268 Kobe Brown 5.00 12.00
269 Kris Murray 5.00 12.00
271 Jalen Slawson 5.00 12.00
272 Bilal Coulibaly 12.00 30.00
273 Leonard Miller 5.00 12.00
274 James Nnaji 4.00 10.00
275 Rayan Rupert 5.00 12.00
276 Sidy Cissoko 5.00 12.00
277 Toumani Camara 10.00 25.00
278 Ausar Thompson 12.00 30.00
279 Kobe Bufkin 6.00 15.00
280 Colby Jones 5.00 12.00
281 Dereck Lively II 10.00 25.00
282 Markquis Nowell 5.00 12.00
283 Isaiah Wong 5.00 12.00
284 Colin Castleton 4.00 10.00
285 Ben Sheppard 5.00 12.00
286 Keyonte George 15.00 40.00
287 Julian Phillips 5.00 12.00
288 Olivier-Maxence Prosper 5.00 12.00
289 Sir'Jabari Rice 4.00 10.00
290 Brandin Podziemski 15.00 40.00
291 Sasha Vezenkov 4.00 10.00
292 Brice Sensabaugh 8.00 20.00
293 Julian Strawther 6.00 15.00
294 Seth Lundy 4.00 10.00
295 Jalen Pickett 4.00 10.00
296 Noah Clowney 6.00 15.00
297 Filip Petrusev 5.00 12.00
298 Maxwell Lewis 4.00 10.00
299 Dariq Whitehead 6.00 15.00
300 Mouhamed Gueye 5.00 12.00

2023-24 Donruss Retro Series
PRESS PROOF: .5X TO 1.2X BASIC
Victor Wembanyama 8.00 20.00
2 Anthony Black 1.00 2.50
3 Brandon Miller 2.00 5.00
4 Amen Thompson 2.50 6.00
5 Ausar Thompson 1.25 3.00
6 Scoot Henderson 1.50 4.00
7 Cam Whitmore 1.25 3.00
8 Keyonte George 1.50 4.00
9 Cason Wallace 1.00 2.50
10 Bilal Coulibaly 1.25 3.00
11 Jett Howard .60 1.50
12 Taylor Hendricks .50 1.25
13 LeBron James 4.00 10.00
14 Stephen Curry 4.00 10.00
15 Luka Doncic 3.00 8.00
16 Ja Morant 1.50 4.00
17 Nikola Jokic 2.50 6.00
18 Joel Embiid 1.25 3.00
19 Damian Lillard 1.25 3.00
20 Donovan Mitchell 1.00 2.50
21 Jayson Tatum 2.00 5.00
22 Trae Young 1.00 2.50
23 Giannis Antetokounmpo 2.50 6.00
24 Jimmy Butler .75 2.00
25 Kevin Durant 1.50 4.00

2023-24 Donruss Retro Series Diamond
*DIAMOND: 1.5X TO 4X BASIC
1 Victor Wembanyama 50.00 120.00

2023-24 Donruss Retro Series Holo Laser
*HOLO PRPL LASER: 2.5X TO 6X BASIC
STATED PRINT RUN 99 SER.#'d SETS
1 Victor Wembanyama 125.00 300.00
3 Brandon Miller 20.00 50.00
6 Scoot Henderson 20.00 50.00

2023-24 Donruss Retro Series Press Proof Purple
1 Victor Wembanyama 20.00 50.00

2023-24 Donruss Rookie Dominators Autographs
STATED PRINT RUN 99 SER.#'d SETS
*HOLO RED GOLD LASER: .4X TO 1X BASIC
1 Julian Strawther 10.00 25.00
2 Noah Clowney 10.00 25.00
3 Olivier-Maxence Prosper 8.00 20.00
4 Jordan Walsh 25.00 60.00
5 Leonard Miller 8.00 20.00
6 Kris Murray 8.00 20.00
7 Dariq Whitehead 10.00 25.00
8 Marcus Sasser 12.00 30.00
9 Colby Jones 8.00 20.00
10 Cason Wallace 15.00 40.00
11 Amen Thompson 40.00 100.00
12 Ben Sheppard 8.00 20.00
13 Tristan Vukcevic 8.00 20.00
14 Dereck Lively II 15.00 40.00
15 Bilal Coulibaly 40.00 100.00
16 GG Jackson II 15.00 40.00
17 Brice Sensabaugh 12.00 30.00
19 Brandin Podziemski 40.00 100.00
20 Maxwell Lewis 6.00 15.00
21 Ausar Thompson 40.00 100.00
23 Kobe Bufkin 10.00 25.00
24 Rayan Rupert 8.00 20.00
25 Keyonte George 40.00 100.00

2023-24 Donruss Signature Series
*GREEN LASER/75: .5X TO 1.2X BASIC
*HOLO RED BLUE LSR/25: .75X TO 2X BASIC
*HOLO PINK LSR/20: .75X TO 2X BASIC
1 Adama Sanogo 5.00 12.00
2 Brandin Podziemski 50.00 120.00
3 Kobe Bufkin 6.00 15.00
6 Jordan Walsh 20.00 50.00
7 Dereck Lively II 10.00 25.00
8 Markquis Nowell 5.00 12.00
9 Brice Sensabaugh 8.00 20.00
11 GG Jackson II 10.00 25.00
12 Marcus Sasser 8.00 20.00
13 Jalen Pickett 4.00 10.00
14 Amen Thompson 25.00 60.00
15 Colin Castleton 4.00 10.00
16 Dariq Whitehead 6.00 15.00
17 Azuolas Tubelis 4.00 10.00
19 Bilal Coulibaly 20.00 50.00
20 Maxwell Lewis 4.00 10.00
21 Filip Petrusev 5.00 12.00
22 Sidy Cissoko 5.00 12.00
23 Mouhamed Gueye 5.00 12.00
24 Kris Murray 5.00 12.00
25 Noah Clowney 6.00 15.00
27 Olivier-Maxence Prosper 5.00 12.00
28 Jalen Slawson 5.00 12.00
29 Rayan Rupert 5.00 12.00
31 Cason Wallace 20.00 50.00
32 Trayce Jackson-Davis 6.00 15.00
33 Keyonte George 50.00 120.00
35 Jalen Wilson 5.00 12.00
36 Jalen McDaniels 4.00 10.00
37 Ricky Council IV 6.00 15.00
38 Julian Strawther 6.00 15.00
39 Tristan Vukcevic 5.00 12.00
40 Georges Niang 3.00 8.00
42 Isaiah Wong 5.00 12.00
43 Sir'Jabari Rice 4.00 10.00
44 Kobe Brown 5.00 12.00
45 Vasilije Micic 5.00 12.00
46 Ben Sheppard 5.00 12.00
48 Colby Jones 5.00 12.00
49 Ausar Thompson 40.00 100.00
51 Nick Richards 4.00 10.00
52 Jose Alvarado 5.00 12.00
53 Monte Morris 5.00 12.00
56 Max Strus 5.00 12.00
58 Terry Cummings 5.00 12.00
59 Gary Harris 4.00 10.00
61 Daniel Gafford 5.00 12.00
62 Calvin Natt 3.00 8.00
63 Mo Bamba 4.00 10.00
64 Ayo Dosunmu 5.00 12.00
65 Ty Jerome 3.00 8.00
66 Rolando Blackman 4.00 10.00
67 LaSalle Thompson 3.00 8.00
68 Markelle Fultz 4.00 10.00
69 Kenneth Lofton Jr. 5.00 12.00
70 Jaylin Williams 5.00 12.00
71 Jabari Walker 3.00 8.00
73 Tyrese Martin 4.00 10.00
74 Julian Champagnie 5.00 12.00
75 Precious Achiuwa 4.00 10.00
77 Bryce McGowens 5.00 12.00
78 Moussa Diabate 4.00 10.00
79 David Roddy 4.00 10.00
80 Evan Fournier 4.00 10.00
81 James Donaldson 4.00 10.00
82 Craig Hodges 4.00 10.00
83 Josh Minott 5.00 12.00
84 Scotty Pippen Jr. 5.00 12.00
85 Rick Mahorn 4.00 10.00
86 Ricky Pierce 4.00 10.00
87 Xavier McDaniel 5.00 12.00
88 Rod Strickland 5.00 12.00
89 Larry Nance 5.00 12.00
90 Bob Dandridge 5.00 12.00
91 Tom Chambers 5.00 12.00
92 Fred Brown 4.00 10.00
94 Quentin Richardson 4.00 10.00
95 Simone Fontecchio 5.00 12.00
97 Dalen Terry 5.00 12.00
98 Nikola Jovic 5.00 12.00
99 Toumani Camara 10.00 25.00
100 Isaiah Roby 3.00 8.00

2023-24 Donruss The Rookies
1 Victor Wembanyama 10.00 25.00
2 Scoot Henderson 2.50 6.00
3 Brandon Miller 3.00 8.00
4 Amen Thompson 4.00 10.00
5 Ausar Thompson 2.00 5.00

2023-24 Donruss The Rookies Holo Blue and Green Laser
*HOLO BLUE GRN LSR: 5X TO 12X BASIC
STATED PRINT RUN 35 SER.#'d SETS
1 Victor Wembanyama 400.00 800.00
3 Brandon Miller 75.00 200.00

2023-24 Donruss The Rookies Holo Pink Laser
STATED PRINT RUN 50 SER.#'d SETS
1 Victor Wembanyama 300.00 600.00
3 Brandon Miller 60.00 150.00

2023-24 Donruss The Rookies Holo Purple Laser
*HOLO PRPL LASER: 2.5X TO 6X BASIC
STATED PRINT RUN 99 SER.#'d SETS
1 Victor Wembanyama 150.00 400.00
3 Brandon Miller 40.00 100.00

2023-24 Donruss The Rookies Holo Red and Green Laser
*HOLO RED GRN LSR: 3X TO 8X BASIC
STATED PRINT RUN 75 SER.#'d SETS
1 Victor Wembanyama 200.00 500.00
3 Brandon Miller 50.00 120.00

2023-24 Donruss The Rookies Holo Yellow Laser
*HOLO YLW LSR: 6X TO 15X BASIC
STATED PRINT RUN 25 SER.#'d SETS
1 Victor Wembanyama 500.00 1,000.00
3 Brandon Miller 100.00 250.00

2023-24 Donruss Unleashed
*PRESS PROOF: .5X TO 1.2X BASIC
*PRESS PROOF PRPL: .6X TO 1.5X BASIC
*DIAMOND: 1.5X TO 4X BASIC
1 LeBron James 4.00 10.00
2 Paul George .75 2.00
3 Jimmy Butler .75 2.00
4 Zion Williamson 1.25 3.00
5 Jayson Tatum 2.00 5.00
6 Ja Morant 1.50 4.00
7 Stephen Curry 4.00 10.00
8 Giannis Antetokounmpo 2.50 6.00
9 Damian Lillard 1.25 3.00
10 Joel Embiid 1.25 3.00
11 Jamal Murray 1.00 2.50
12 Kevin Durant 1.50 4.00
13 Tyrese Haliburton 1.00 2.50
14 DeMar DeRozan .75 2.00
15 Luka Doncic 3.00 8.00

2023-24 Donruss Zero Gravity
*PRESS PROOF: .5X TO 1.2X BASIC
*PRESS PROOF PRPL: .6X TO 1.5X BASIC
*DIAMOND: 1.5X TO 4X BASIC
1 Ja Morant 1.50 4.00
2 Jayson Tatum 2.00 5.00
3 De'Aaron Fox 1.00 2.50
4 Donovan Mitchell 1.00 2.50
5 Zion Williamson 1.25 3.00
6 Jalen Green .75 2.00
7 Giannis Antetokounmpo 2.50 6.00
8 Paul George .75 2.00
9 LeBron James 4.00 10.00
10 Zach LaVine .75 2.00

2024-25 Donruss
*WINTER: 4X TO 1X BASIC
*PRESS PROOF SILVER: .5X TO 1.2X BASIC
*DISCO: .75X TO 2X BASIC
*HOLO GRN LASER: .75X TO 2X BASIC
*HOLO WINTER: .75X TO 2X BASIC
*INTERNATIONAL: .75X TO 2X BASIC
*INL HOLO MAROON LASER: .75X TO 2X BASIC
*YELLOW FLOOD: .75X TO 2X BASIC
*STORM/299: 1.5X TO 4X BASIC
*PRESS PROOF PURPLE/199: 1.5X TO 4X BASIC
*CUBIC/175: 2X TO 5X BASIC
*HOLO LASER/149: 2X TO 5X BASIC
*RED DISCO/149: 2X TO 5X BASIC
*TEAL EXPLOSION/149: 2X TO 5X BASIC
*CRYSTALS/125: 2.5X TO 6X BASIC
*HOLO ORANGE LASER/125: 2.5X TO 6X BASIC
*HYPER/125: 2.5X TO 6X BASIC
*INT RED STARS/125: 2.5X TO 6X BASIC
*CHOICE RED/99: 3X TO 8X BASIC
*HOLO PURPLE LASER/99: 3X TO 8X BASIC
*HOLO RED & GRN LASER/99: 3X TO 8X BASIC
*RED HOLO LASER/99: 3X TO 8X BASIC
*DOTS/85: 3X TO 8X BASIC
*INT BLUE FIREWORKS/85: 3X TO 8X BASIC
*BLUE DISCO/75: 4X TO 10X BASIC
*BLUE WEDGES/75: 4X TO 10X BASIC
*SILVER PRESS PROOF DIE CUT/75: 4X TO 10X BASIC
*WINTER BLUE/75: 4X TO 10X BASIC
*HOLO PINK LASER/50: 5X TO 12X BASIC
*CHECKERBOARD/49: 5X TO 12X BASIC
*CHOICE BLUE/49: 5X TO 12X BASIC
*HOLO BLUE LASER/49: 5X TO 12X BASIC
*BLUE EXPLOSION/45: 5X TO 12X BASIC
*HOLO BLUE & GREEN LASER/30: 6X TO 15X BASIC
*PRESS PROOF GOLD DIE CUT/25: 8X TO 20X BASIC
*HOLO TEAL LASER/25: 8X TO 20X BASIC
*HOLO YELLOW LASER/25: 8X TO 20X BASIC
*PINK DISCO/25: 8X TO 20X BASIC
1 Daniel Gafford .25 .60
2 Paolo Banchero .75 2.00
3 Anthony Davis .75 2.00
4 Trey Murphy III .40 1.00
5 Kentavious Caldwell-Pope .20 .50
6 Victor Wembanyama 2.50 6.00
7 Marcus Smart .30 .75
8 Karl-Anthony Towns .50 1.25
9 Marcus Sasser .25 .60
10 Max Strus .25 .60
11 Cole Anthony .30 .75
12 LaMelo Ball .60 1.50
13 Saddiq Bey .25 .60
14 Aaron Nesmith .25 .60
15 Derrick Jones Jr. .20 .50
16 Norman Powell .30 .75
17 Coby White .30 .75
18 Jarrett Allen .25 .60
19 LeBron James 2.50 6.00
20 Jalen Williams .60 1.50
21 James Harden .60 1.50
22 Brandin Podziemski .40 1.00
23 Harrison Barnes .25 .60
24 Luguentz Dort .25 .60
25 Jaylen Brown .50 1.25
26 De'Aaron Fox .60 1.50
27 RJ Barrett .40 1.00
28 Joel Embiid .50 1.25
29 Myles Turner .25 .60
30 Cam Reddish .20 .50
31 Toumani Camara .30 .75
32 Bilal Coulibaly .40 1.00
33 Kris Murray .20 .50
34 Dillon Brooks .25 .60
35 Alex Caruso .30 .75
36 Jaden McDaniels .30 .75
37 Miles Bridges .25 .60
38 Chris Paul .50 1.25
39 Jaden Ivey .40 1.00
40 Julius Randle .30 .75
41 Grayson Allen .25 .60
42 Kelly Olynyk .20 .50
43 Tyler Herro .50 1.25
44 Jae Crowder .20 .50
45 Domantas Sabonis .50 1.25
46 Draymond Green .40 1.00
47 Keyonte George .40 1.00
48 John Collins .25 .60
49 Jayson Tatum 1.00 2.50
50 Jaden Hardy .30 .75
51 Nicolas Batum .20 .50
52 Grant Williams .20 .50
53 DeMar DeRozan .40 1.00
54 Kevin Durant 1.00 2.50
55 Collin Sexton .30 .75
56 Bol Bol .20 .50
57 Jabari Smith Jr. .30 .75
58 Fred VanVleet .30 .75
59 Jalen Suggs .30 .75
60 Anthony Black .40 1.00
61 Vince Williams Jr. .25 .60
62 Jamal Murray .50 1.25
63 Jaren Jackson Jr. .50 1.25
64 Stephen Curry 2.50 6.00
65 Derrick Rose .75 2.00
66 Ja Morant 1.00 2.50
67 Evan Mobley .50 1.25
68 Immanuel Quickley .25 .60
69 Isaiah Hartenstein .25 .60
70 Caris LeVert .25 .60
71 Jonas Valanciunas .25 .60
72 Jordan Poole .30 .75
73 Brook Lopez .25 .60
74 Markelle Fultz .20 .50
75 Jrue Holiday .40 1.00
76 Khris Middleton .30 .75
77 Donte DiVincenzo .30 .75
78 Buddy Hield .25 .60
79 Aaron Gordon .30 .75
80 Deandre Ayton .25 .60
81 Malik Beasley .25 .60
82 Luka Doncic 2.00 5.00
83 Jimmy Butler III .50 1.25
84 Taylor Hendricks .30 .75
85 Andrew Nembhard .25 .60
86 Jalen Green .60 1.50
87 Malaki Branham .25 .60
88 Bogdan Bogdanovic .25 .60
89 Lauri Markkanen .30 .75
90 Dejounte Murray .30 .75
91 Mitchell Robinson .25 .60
92 Bam Adebayo .40 1.00
93 Trae Young .60 1.50
94 Mike Conley .25 .60
95 Rudy Gobert .30 .75
96 Patrick Williams .25 .60
97 Bradley Beal .30 .75
98 Brandon Ingram .30 .75
99 Pascal Siakam .40 1.00
100 Michael Porter Jr. .30 .75
101 Taurean Prince .20 .50
102 CJ McCollum .25 .60
103 Amen Thompson .75 2.00
104 Nick Smith Jr. .25 .60
105 Cason Wallace .40 1.00
106 D'Angelo Russell .25 .60
107 Kobe Bufkin .25 .60
108 Jalen Johnson .40 1.00
109 Kyrie Irving .75 2.00
110 Donovan Mitchell .60 1.50
111 Ben Simmons .30 .75
112 Spencer Dinwiddie .20 .50
113 Gradey Dick .40 1.00
114 Anfernee Simons .30 .75
115 Devin Booker .75 2.00
116 Shaedon Sharpe .40 1.00
117 Paul George .50 1.25
118 Ivica Zubac .30 .75
119 Deni Avdija .30 .75
120 Alperen Sengun .50 1.25
121 Naz Reid .30 .75
122 Chet Holmgren .50 1.25
123 Shai Gilgeous-Alexander 1.50 4.00
124 Zach LaVine .50 1.25
125 Damian Lillard .75 2.00
126 Malik Monk .30 .75
127 Bennedict Mathurin .40 1.00

128 Jalen Brunson .60 1.50
129 Zion Williamson .75 2.00
130 Jakob Poeltl .25 .60
131 Nicolas Claxton .25 .60
132 Desmond Bane .30 .75
133 Ayo Dosunmu .25 .60
134 Klay Thompson .75 2.00
135 Cameron Johnson .25 .60
136 Marvin Bagley III .20 .50
137 Payton Pritchard .30 .75
138 Jalen Duren .30 .75
139 Keegan Murray .25 .60
140 Jaime Jaquez Jr. .30 .75
141 Kyle Kuzma .25 .60
142 Clint Capela .25 .60
143 Scoot Henderson .40 1.00
144 Derrick White .30 .75
145 Keldon Johnson .25 .60
146 Nikola Vucevic .25 .60
147 Jordan Clarkson .30 .75
148 Tari Eason .30 .75
149 Jordan Hawkins .25 .60
150 Al Horford .30 .75
151 Jonathan Kuminga .40 1.00
152 Dennis Schroder .30 .75
153 Scottie Barnes .40 1.00
154 Jusuf Nurkic .25 .60
155 Kyle Anderson .20 .50
156 Dorian Finney-Smith .20 .50
157 Isaac Okoro .20 .50
158 Russell Westbrook .50 1.25
159 Herbert Jones .25 .60
160 Bobby Portis .25 .60
161 Tobias Harris .25 .60
162 Vasilije Micic .25 .60
163 Austin Reaves .40 1.00
164 GG Jackson II .30 .75
165 Anthony Edwards 1.50 4.00
166 Dereck Lively II .30 .75
167 Cam Whitmore .30 .75
168 Obi Toppin .25 .60
169 Andrew Wiggins .40 1.00
170 Darius Garland .40 1.00
171 Kawhi Leonard .60 1.50
172 Giannis Antetokounmpo 1.25 3.00
173 Isaiah Stewart .25 .60
174 Cade Cunningham .75 2.00
175 De'Andre Hunter .30 .75
176 Kristaps Porzingis .40 1.00
177 Rui Hachimura .30 .75
178 Josh Hart .25 .60
179 Franz Wagner .50 1.25
180 Jeremy Sochan .30 .75
181 T.J. McConnell .25 .60
182 Julian Strawther .30 .75
183 Kelly Oubre Jr. .25 .60
184 Gary Trent Jr. .25 .60
185 OG Anunoby .25 .60
186 Trayce Jackson-Davis .30 .75
187 Cameron Thomas .30 .75
188 Nikola Jokic 1.50 4.00
189 Jerami Grant .25 .60
190 Josh Giddey .40 1.00
191 Tyrese Haliburton .60 1.50
192 Tyrese Maxey .60 1.50
193 Kyle Lowry .30 .75
194 Devin Vassell .40 1.00
195 P.J. Washington Jr. .25 .60
196 Duncan Robinson .25 .60
197 Brandon Miller .50 1.25
198 Terry Rozier III .25 .60
199 Mikal Bridges .30 .75
200 Ausar Thompson .50 1.25
201 Oso Ighodaro RR RC .75 2.00
202 Reed Sheppard RR RC 2.00 5.00
203 Tristan da Silva RR RC 1.50 4.00
204 Rob Dillingham RR RC 1.50 4.00
205 Adem Bona RR RC .75 2.00
206 Jaylon Tyson RR RC .60 1.50
207 Bobi Klintman RR RC .75 2.00
208 Nikola Topic RR RC 2.00 5.00
209 Jonathan Mogbo RR RC 1.00 2.50
210 Devin Carter RR RC .75 2.00
211 Pacome Dadiet RR RC .75 2.00
212 Tyler Smith RR RC .75 2.00
213 DaRon Holmes II RR RC .75 2.00
214 Ryan Dunn RR RC .75 2.00
215 Alexandre Sarr RR RC 2.00 5.00
216 Tristen Newton RR RC .60 1.50
217 Yves Missi RR RC 1.50 4.00
218 Ajay Mitchell RR RC 1.00 2.50
219 Zaccharie Risacher RR RC 2.00 5.00
220 Bub Carrington RR RC 1.50 4.00
221 Kel'el Ware RR RC 1.50 4.00
222 AJ Johnson RR RC 1.25 3.00
223 Donovan Clingan RR RC 1.50 4.00
224 Baylor Scheierman RR RC .75 2.00
225 Kyshawn George RR RC 1.00 2.50
226 Terrence Shannon Jr. RR RC 1.25 3.00
227 Dalton Knecht RR RC 2.00 5.00
228 Jared McCain RR RC 2.50 6.00
229 Tidjane Salaun RR RC .60 1.50
230 Cody Williams RR RC .75 2.00
231 Ja'Kobe Walter RR RC .75 2.00
232 Antonio Reeves RR RC .60 1.50
233 Kyle Filipowski RR RC 1.50 4.00
234 Harrison Ingram RR RC .60 1.50
235 Cam Spencer RR RC .60 1.50
236 Ron Holland II RR RC 1.25 3.00
237 Isaiah Collier RR RC 1.25 3.00
238 Melvin Ajinca RR RC .50 1.25
239 Zach Edey RR RC 2.00 5.00
240 Matas Buzelis RR RC 3.00 8.00
241 Cam Christie RR RC .75 2.00
242 Johnny Furphy RR RC 1.00 2.50
243 Bronny James Jr. RR RC 2.00 5.00
244 Stephon Castle RR RC 4.00 10.00
245 Jaylen Wells RR RC 2.00 5.00
246 Jamal Shead RR RC .75 2.00
247 KJ Simpson Jr. RR RC .60 1.50
248 Kevin McCullar Jr. RR RC .60 1.50
249 Tyler Kolek RR RC 1.00 2.50
250 Dillon Jones RR RC .60 1.50
251 Reed Sheppard RR AU 20.00 50.00
252 Tidjane Salaun RR AU 5.00 12.00
253 Donovan Clingan RR AU 12.00 30.00
254 Zach Edey RR AU 15.00 40.00
255 Matas Buzelis RR AU 30.00 80.00
256 Devin Carter RR AU 6.00 15.00
257 Bub Carrington RR AU 12.00 30.00
258 Jared McCain RR AU 20.00 50.00
259 Dalton Knecht RR AU 20.00 50.00
260 Tristan da Silva RR AU 12.00 30.00
261 Ja'Kobe Walter RR AU 6.00 15.00
262 Jaylon Tyson RR AU 5.00 12.00
263 Yves Missi RR AU 12.00 30.00
264 DaRon Holmes II RR AU 6.00 15.00
265 AJ Johnson RR AU 10.00 25.00
266 Kyshawn George RR AU 8.00 20.00
267 Pacome Dadiet RR AU 6.00 15.00
268 Dillon Jones RR AU 5.00 12.00
269 Terrence Shannon Jr. RR AU 10.00 25.00
270 Baylor Scheierman RR AU 6.00 15.00
271 Jonathan Mogbo RR AU 8.00 20.00
272 Tyler Kolek RR AU 8.00 20.00
273 Johnny Furphy RR AU 8.00 20.00
274 Bobi Klintman RR AU 6.00 15.00
275 Ajay Mitchell RR AU 8.00 20.00
276 Jaylen Wells RR AU 15.00 40.00
277 Oso Ighodaro RR AU 6.00 15.00
278 Adem Bona RR AU 6.00 15.00
279 KJ Simpson Jr. RR AU 5.00 12.00
280 Cam Christie RR AU 6.00 15.00
281 Antonio Reeves RR AU 5.00 12.00
282 Tristen Newton RR AU 5.00 12.00
283 Melvin Ajinca RR AU 4.00 10.00
284 Harrison Ingram RR AU 5.00 12.00
285 Cam Spencer RR AU 5.00 12.00
286 Kevin McCullar Jr. RR AU 5.00 12.00
287 Ariel Hukporti RR AU RC 4.00 10.00
288 Jalen Bridges RR AU RC 4.00 10.00
289 Judah Mintz RR AU RC 4.00 10.00
290 Keshad Johnson RR AU RC 4.00 10.00
291 Nikola Durisic RR AU RC 6.00 15.00
292 Pelle Larsson RR AU RC 6.00 15.00
293 PJ Hall RR AU RC 4.00 10.00
294 Trey Alexander RR AU RC 4.00 10.00
295 Ulrich Chomche RR AU RC 4.00 10.00
296 Enrique Freeman RR AU RC 4.00 10.00
297 Anton Watson RR AU RC 4.00 10.00
298 Quinten Post RR AU RC 10.00 25.00
299 Trentyn Flowers RR AU RC 4.00 10.00
300 Jamal Shead RR AU 6.00 15.00

2024-25 Donruss Animation

1 Dalton Knecht 100.00 250.00
2 Ja Morant 150.00 400.00
3 Victor Wembanyama 400.00 800.00
4 Anthony Edwards 200.00 500.00
5 Kevin Durant 125.00 300.00
6 Reed Sheppard 125.00 300.00
7 Stephen Curry 300.00 600.00
8 Shai Gilgeous-Alexander 200.00 500.00
9 Giannis Antetokounmpo 150.00 400.00
10 Jayson Tatum 125.00 300.00
11 Donovan Clingan 60.00 150.00
12 LeBron James 300.00 600.00
13 Bronny James Jr. 125.00 300.00
14 Nikola Jokic 150.00 400.00
15 Luka Doncic 200.00 500.00

2024-25 Donruss Around the World

1 Luka Doncic 300.00 600.00
2 Nikola Jokic 150.00 400.00
3 Manu Ginobili 40.00 100.00
4 Rudy Gobert 6.00 15.00
5 Deandre Ayton 5.00 12.00
6 Jeremy Lin 75.00 200.00
7 Sun Yue 15.00 40.00
8 J.J. Barea 5.00 12.00
9 Yuta Tabuse 8.00 20.00
10 Ben Simmons 6.00 15.00
11 Shai Gilgeous-Alexander 300.00 600.00
12 Kristaps Porzingis 20.00 50.00
13 Josh Green 5.00 12.00
14 Peja Stojakovic 6.00 15.00
15 Jakob Poeltl 5.00 12.00

2024-25 Donruss Bomb Squad

*WINTER: 4X TO 1X BASIC
*DISCO: 1.25X TO 3X BASIC
*HOLO PRPL LSR/99: 3X TO 8X BASIC
*BLUE DISCO/75: 3X TO 8X BASIC
*BLUE WINTER/75: 3X TO 8X BASIC
*HOLO RED & GRN LSR/75: 4X TO 10X BASIC
*HOLO PINK LSR/50: 5X TO 12X BASIC
*HOLO BLUE & GRN LSR/35: 6X TO 15X BASIC
*CHECKERBOARD/30: 8X TO 20X BASIC
*HOLO YLW LSR/25: 8X TO 20X BASIC
*PINK DISCO/25: 8X TO 20X BASIC
*HOLO RED & BLUE LSR/15: 10X TO 25X BASIC
1 Stephen Curry 3.00 8.00
2 Nikola Jokic 2.00 5.00
3 Ja Morant 1.25 3.00
4 Zion Williamson 1.00 2.50
5 Giannis Antetokounmpo 1.50 4.00
6 Victor Wembanyama 3.00 8.00
7 LeBron James 3.00 8.00
8 Donovan Clingan 1.00 2.50
9 Alexandre Sarr 1.25 3.00
10 Trae Young .75 2.00
11 Zaccharie Risacher 1.25 3.00
12 Shai Gilgeous-Alexander 2.00 5.00
13 Anthony Edwards 2.00 5.00
14 Bronny James Jr. 1.25 3.00
15 Dalton Knecht 1.25 3.00
16 Luka Doncic 2.50 6.00
17 Jayson Tatum 1.25 3.00
18 Kevin Durant 1.25 3.00
19 Anthony Davis 1.00 2.50
20 Reed Sheppard 1.25 3.00

2024-25 Donruss Crunch Time

*PRESS PROOF: .5X TO 1.2X BASIC
*PRESS PROOF PRPL: .5X TO 1.2X BASIC
*DIAMOND: 1.25X TO 3X BASIC
*HOLO LSR/99: 3X TO 8X BASIC
*INT BLUE STARS/99: 3X TO 8X BASIC
*DIAMOND RED/75: 4X TO 10X BASIC
*INT RED FIREWORKS/55: 5X TO 12X BASIC
*HOLO BLUE LSR/49: 5X TO 12X BASIC
*HYPER/25: 8X TO 20X BASIC
1 Zaccharie Risacher 1.25 3.00
2 Victor Wembanyama 3.00 8.00
3 Jayson Tatum 1.25 3.00
4 LeBron James 3.00 8.00
5 Stephen Curry 3.00 8.00
6 Devin Booker 1.00 2.50
7 Ron Holland II .75 2.00
8 Luka Doncic 2.50 6.00
9 Reed Sheppard 1.25 3.00
10 Nikola Jokic 2.00 5.00
11 Ja Morant 1.25 3.00
12 Giannis Antetokounmpo 1.50 4.00
13 Tyrese Maxey .75 2.00
14 Shai Gilgeous-Alexander 2.00 5.00
15 Anthony Edwards 2.00 5.00

2024-25 Donruss Dominators Autographs

STATED PRINT RUN 25-99 SER.#'d SETS
1 Jalen Suggs/99 8.00 20.00
2 Jalen Duren/99 8.00 20.00
3 Russell Westbrook/25 75.00 200.00
4 Evan Mobley/99 12.00 30.00
5 Jabari Smith Jr./99 8.00 20.00
6 Paolo Banchero/99 40.00 100.00
7 Mark Williams/99 6.00 15.00
8 Cade Cunningham/49 60.00 150.00
9 James Wiseman/99 5.00 12.00
10 Davion Mitchell/99 6.00 15.00
11 Bennedict Mathurin/99 10.00 25.00
12 Jonathan Kuminga/25 15.00 40.00
13 RJ Barrett/49 12.00 30.00
14 P.J. Washington Jr./99 6.00 15.00
15 Chris Paul/25 40.00 100.00
16 Steven Adams/99 6.00 15.00
17 Bogdan Bogdanovic/99 6.00 15.00
18 Ben Simmons/99 8.00 20.00
19 Josh Hart/99 6.00 15.00
20 Deandre Ayton/99 6.00 15.00
21 Khris Middleton/25 12.00 30.00
22 Amen Thompson/49 25.00 60.00
23 Ausar Thompson/49 15.00 40.00
24 Keyonte George/49 12.00 30.00
25 GG Jackson II/49 10.00 25.00

2024-25 Donruss Dominators Autographs Choice

1 Jalen Suggs 8.00 20.00
2 Jalen Duren 8.00 20.00
3 Russell Westbrook 50.00 120.00
4 Evan Mobley 12.00 30.00
5 Jabari Smith Jr. 8.00 20.00
6 Paolo Banchero 40.00 100.00
7 Mark Williams 6.00 15.00
8 Cade Cunningham 50.00 120.00
9 James Wiseman 5.00 12.00
10 Davion Mitchell 6.00 15.00
11 Bennedict Mathurin 10.00 25.00
12 Jonathan Kuminga 10.00 25.00
13 RJ Barrett 10.00 25.00
14 P.J. Washington Jr. 6.00 15.00
15 Chris Paul 25.00 60.00
16 Steven Adams 6.00 15.00
17 Bogdan Bogdanovic 6.00 15.00
18 Ben Simmons 8.00 20.00
19 Josh Hart 6.00 15.00
20 Deandre Ayton 6.00 15.00
21 Khris Middleton 8.00 20.00
22 Amen Thompson 20.00 50.00
23 Ausar Thompson 12.00 30.00
24 Keyonte George 10.00 25.00
25 GG Jackson II 8.00 20.00

2024-25 Donruss Dominators Autographs International

1 Jalen Suggs 8.00 20.00
2 Jalen Duren 8.00 20.00
3 Russell Westbrook 50.00 120.00
4 Evan Mobley 12.00 30.00
5 Jabari Smith Jr. 8.00 20.00
6 Paolo Banchero 40.00 100.00
7 Mark Williams 6.00 15.00
8 Cade Cunningham 50.00 120.00
9 James Wiseman 5.00 12.00
10 Davion Mitchell 6.00 15.00
11 Bennedict Mathurin 10.00 25.00
12 Jonathan Kuminga 10.00 25.00
13 RJ Barrett 10.00 25.00
14 P.J. Washington Jr. 6.00 15.00
15 Chris Paul 25.00 60.00
16 Steven Adams 6.00 15.00
17 Bogdan Bogdanovic 6.00 15.00
18 Ben Simmons 8.00 20.00
19 Josh Hart 6.00 15.00
20 Deandre Ayton 6.00 15.00
21 Khris Middleton 8.00 20.00
22 Amen Thompson 20.00 50.00
23 Ausar Thompson 12.00 30.00
24 Keyonte George 10.00 25.00
25 GG Jackson II 8.00 20.00

2024-25 Donruss Fadeaway

1 Kevin Durant 30.00 80.00
2 Giannis Antetokounmpo 40.00 100.00
3 Ja Morant 30.00 80.00
4 Alexandre Sarr 30.00 80.00
5 Zaccharie Risacher 30.00 80.00
6 Stephen Curry 80.00 200.00
7 Matas Buzelis 50.00 120.00
8 Kawhi Leonard 20.00 50.00
9 De'Aaron Fox 20.00 50.00
10 Jayson Tatum 30.00 80.00
11 Reed Sheppard 30.00 80.00
12 Anthony Edwards 50.00 125.00
13 Luka Doncic 60.00 150.00
14 Cody Williams 12.00 30.00
15 Kyrie Irving 25.00 60.00
16 Nikola Jokic 50.00 125.00
17 Trae Young 20.00 50.00
18 LeBron James 80.00 200.00
19 Shai Gilgeous-Alexander 50.00 125.00
20 Victor Wembanyama 80.00 200.00

2024-25 Donruss Franchise Features

*WINTER: .4X TO 1X BASIC
*DISCO: 1.25X TO 3X BASIC
*HOLO PRPL LSR/99: 3X TO 8X BASIC
*BLUE DISCO/75: 3X TO 8X BASIC
*BLUE WINTER/75: 3X TO 8X BASIC
*HOLO RED & GRN LSR/75: 4X TO 10X BASIC
*HOLO PINK LSR/50: 5X TO 12X BASIC
*HOLO BLUE & GRN LSR/35: 6X TO 15X BASIC
*CHECKERBOARD/30: 8X TO 20X BASIC
*HOLO YLW LSR/25: 8X TO 20X BASIC
*PINK DISCO/25: 8X TO 20X BASIC
*HOLO RED & BLUE LSR/15: 10X TO 25X BASIC
1 Tyrese Maxey .75 2.00
2 Donovan Clingan 1.00 2.50
3 Giannis Antetokounmpo 1.50 4.00
4 Matas Buzelis 2.00 5.00
5 Donovan Mitchell .75 2.00
6 Jayson Tatum 1.25 3.00
7 Kawhi Leonard .75 2.00
8 Ja Morant 1.25 3.00
9 Trae Young .75 2.00
10 Jimmy Butler III .60 1.50
11 Tidjane Salaun .40 1.00
12 Cody Williams .50 1.25
13 De'Aaron Fox .75 2.00
14 Jalen Brunson .75 2.00
15 LeBron James 3.00 8.00
16 Paolo Banchero 1.00 2.50
17 Luka Doncic 2.50 6.00
18 Cameron Thomas .40 1.00
19 Nikola Jokic 2.00 5.00
20 Tyrese Haliburton .75 2.00
21 Zion Williamson 1.00 2.50
22 Cade Cunningham 1.00 2.50
23 Ja'Kobe Walter .50 1.25
24 Reed Sheppard 1.25 3.00
25 Victor Wembanyama 3.00 8.00
26 Kevin Durant 1.25 3.00
27 Shai Gilgeous-Alexander 2.00 5.00
28 Anthony Edwards 2.00 5.00
29 Stephen Curry 3.00 8.00
30 Alexandre Sarr 1.25 3.00

2024-25 Donruss Great X-Pectations

*WINTER: .4X TO 1X BASIC
*DISCO: 1.25X TO 3X BASIC
*HOLO PRPL LSR/99: 3X TO 8X BASIC
*BLUE DISCO/75: 3X TO 8X BASIC
*BLUE WINTER/75: 3X TO 8X BASIC
*HOLO RED & GRN LSR/75: 4X TO 10X BASIC
*HOLO PINK LSR/50: 5X TO 12X BASIC
*HOLO BLUE & GRN LSR/35: 6X TO 15X BASIC
*CHECKERBOARD/30: 8X TO 20X BASIC
*HOLO YLW LSR/25: 8X TO 20X BASIC
*PINK DISCO/25: 8X TO 20X BASIC
*HOLO RED & BLUE LSR/15: 10X TO 25X BASIC
1 Stephon Castle 2.50 6.00
2 Cody Williams .50 1.25
3 Dalton Knecht 1.25 3.00
4 Jaylon Tyson .40 1.00
5 Jared McCain 1.50 4.00
6 AJ Johnson .75 2.00
7 Ron Holland II .75 2.00
8 Tidjane Salaun .40 1.00
9 Devin Carter .50 1.25
10 Ja'Kobe Walter .50 1.25
11 Kel'el Ware 1.00 2.50
12 Nikola Topic 1.25 3.00
13 Zach Edey 1.25 3.00
14 Bronny James Jr. 1.25 3.00
15 Reed Sheppard 1.25 3.00
16 Tristan da Silva 1.00 2.50
17 Rob Dillingham 1.00 2.50
18 Bub Carrington 1.00 2.50
19 Matas Buzelis 2.00 5.00
20 Alexandre Sarr 1.25 3.00
21 Donovan Clingan 1.00 2.50
22 Yves Missi 1.00 2.50
23 Terrence Shannon Jr. .75 2.00
24 Kyshawn George .60 1.50
25 Zaccharie Risacher 1.25 3.00

2024-25 Donruss Hardwood Masters

*PRESS PROOF: .5X TO 1.2X BASIC
*PRESS PROOF PRPL: .5X TO 1.2X BASIC
*DIAMOND: 1.25X TO 3X BASIC
*HOLO LSR/99: 3X TO 8X BASIC
*INT BLUE STARS/99: 3X TO 8X BASIC
*DIAMOND RED/75: 4X TO 10X BASIC
*INT RED FIREWORKS/55: 5X TO 12X BASIC
*HOLO BLUE LSR/49: 5X TO 12X BASIC
*HYPER/25: 8X TO 20X BASIC
1 Victor Wembanyama 3.00 8.00
2 Jimmy Butler III .60 1.50
3 Nikola Jokic 2.00 5.00
4 Ja Morant 1.25 3.00
5 Anthony Edwards 2.00 5.00
6 Kevin Durant 1.25 3.00
7 LeBron James 3.00 8.00
8 Jayson Tatum 1.25 3.00
9 Trae Young .75 2.00
10 Stephen Curry 3.00 8.00
11 Shai Gilgeous-Alexander 2.00 5.00
12 Luka Doncic 2.50 6.00
13 Jaylen Brown .60 1.50
14 Damian Lillard 1.00 2.50
15 Giannis Antetokounmpo 1.50 4.00

2024-25 Donruss Magicians

*WINTER: .4X TO 1X BASIC
*DISCO: 1.25X TO 3X BASIC
*HOLO PRPL LSR/99: 3X TO 8X BASIC
*BLUE DISCO/75: 3X TO 8X BASIC
*BLUE WINTER/75: 3X TO 8X BASIC
*HOLO RED & GRN LSR/75: 4X TO 10X BASIC
*HOLO PINK LSR/50: 5X TO 12X BASIC
*HOLO BLUE & GRN LSR/35: 6X TO 15X BASIC
*CHECKERBOARD/30: 8X TO 20X BASIC
*HOLO YLW LSR/25: 8X TO 20X BASIC
*PINK DISCO/25: 8X TO 20X BASIC
*HOLO RED & BLUE LSR/15: 10X TO 25X BASIC
1 LeBron James 3.00 8.00
2 Anthony Edwards 2.00 5.00
3 Shai Gilgeous-Alexander 2.00 5.00
4 Jayson Tatum 1.25 3.00
5 Kevin Durant 1.25 3.00
6 Stephen Curry 3.00 8.00
7 Ja Morant 1.25 3.00
8 Luka Doncic 2.50 6.00
9 Victor Wembanyama 3.00 8.00
10 Nikola Jokic 2.00 5.00

2024-25 Donruss Net Marvels

*PRESS PROOF: .5X TO 1.2X BASIC
*PRESS PROOF PRPL: .5X TO 1.2X BASIC
*DIAMOND: 1.25X TO 3X BASIC
*HOLO LSR/99: 3X TO 8X BASIC
*INT BLUE STARS/99: 3X TO 8X BASIC
*DIAMOND RED/75: 4X TO 10X BASIC
*INT RED FIREWORKS/55: 5X TO 12X BASIC
*HOLO BLUE LSR/49: 5X TO 12X BASIC
*HYPER/25: 8X TO 20X BASIC
1 Donovan Clingan 1.50 4.00
2 Nikola Jokic 3.00 8.00
3 Dalton Knecht 2.00 5.00
4 Paolo Banchero 1.50 4.00
5 Anthony Edwards 3.00 8.00
6 Ja Morant 2.00 5.00
7 Donovan Mitchell 1.25 3.00
8 Alexandre Sarr 2.00 5.00
9 Stephen Curry 5.00 12.00
10 Tyrese Haliburton 1.25 3.00
11 Bronny James Jr. 2.00 5.00
12 Shai Gilgeous-Alexander 3.00 8.00
13 LeBron James 5.00 12.00
14 Zaccharie Risacher 2.00 5.00
15 Reed Sheppard 2.00 5.00
16 Luka Doncic 4.00 10.00
17 Giannis Antetokounmpo 2.50 6.00
18 Zion Williamson 1.50 4.00
19 Trae Young 1.25 3.00
20 Cody Williams .75 2.00
21 Victor Wembanyama 5.00 12.00
22 Kevin Durant 2.00 5.00
23 Stephon Castle 4.00 10.00
24 Jayson Tatum 2.00 5.00
25 Jalen Brunson 1.25 3.00

2024-25 Donruss Net Marvels Signatures

*CHOICE: .4X TO 1X BASIC
*INTERNATIONAL: .4X TO 1X BASIC
1 Cade Cunningham/49 125.00 300.00
2 Stephen Curry/15 1,000.00 2,000.00
3 Chet Holmgren/49 75.00 200.00
4 Trae Young/49 75.00 200.00
5 Shai Gilgeous-Alexander/15 500.00 1,000.00
6 Alperen Sengun/99 50.00 120.00
7 Josh Giddey/99 40.00 100.00
8 Kevin Durant/15 200.00 500.00
9 Ja Morant/15 200.00 500.00
10 Damian Lillard/15 125.00 300.00
11 Paolo Banchero/99 125.00 300.00
12 Jabari Smith Jr./99 25.00 60.00
13 Jalen Green/49 60.00 150.00
14 Shaedon Sharpe/99 40.00 100.00
15 Donovan Clingan/99 60.00 150.00
16 Zach Edey/99 75.00 200.00
17 Matas Buzelis/99 125.00 300.00
18 Devin Carter/99 25.00 60.00
19 Bub Carrington/99 60.00 150.00
20 Jared McCain/99 75.00 200.00
21 Dalton Knecht/99 75.00 200.00
22 Tristan da Silva/99 40.00 100.00
23 Ja'Kobe Walter/99 40.00 100.00
24 Reed Sheppard/99 60.00 150.00
25 Tidjane Salaun/99 25.00 60.00

2024-25 Donruss Next Day

1 Zaccharie Risacher 30.00 80.00
2 Alexandre Sarr 30.00 80.00
4 Stephon Castle 100.00 250.00
5 Ron Holland II 15.00 40.00
8 Rob Dillingham 15.00 40.00
10 Cody Williams 10.00 25.00
12 Nikola Topic 15.00 40.00
15 Kel'el Ware 20.00 50.00
28 Ryan Dunn 12.00 30.00
29 Isaiah Collier 12.00 30.00
45 Bronny James Jr. 20.00 50.00
46 Kyle Filipowski 12.00 30.00
47 Tyler Smith 12.00 30.00

2024-25 Donruss Next Day Autographs

3 Reed Sheppard 200.00 500.00
6 Tidjane Salaun 50.00 120.00
7 Donovan Clingan 125.00 300.00
9 Zach Edey 150.00 400.00
11 Matas Buzelis 350.00 700.00
13 Devin Carter 50.00 120.00
14 Bub Carrington 100.00 250.00
16 Jared McCain 300.00 600.00
17 Dalton Knecht 300.00 600.00
18 Tristan da Silva 75.00 200.00
19 Ja'Kobe Walter 75.00 200.00
20 Jaylon Tyson 40.00 100.00
21 Yves Missi 50.00 120.00
22 DaRon Holmes II 40.00 100.00
23 AJ Johnson 100.00 250.00
24 Kyshawn George 75.00 200.00
25 Pacome Dadiet 40.00 100.00
26 Dillon Jones 20.00 50.00
27 Terrence Shannon Jr. 75.00 200.00
30 Baylor Scheierman 60.00 150.00
31 Jonathan Mogbo 50.00 120.00
32 Tyler Kolek 40.00 100.00
33 Johnny Furphy 50.00 120.00
34 Bobi Klintman 30.00 80.00
35 Ajay Mitchell 60.00 150.00
36 Jaylen Wells 100.00 250.00
37 Oso Ighodaro 30.00 80.00
38 Adem Bona 40.00 100.00
39 KJ Simpson Jr. 30.00 80.00
40 Jamal Shead 50.00 120.00
41 Cam Christie 30.00 80.00
42 Antonio Reeves 40.00 100.00
43 Tristen Newton 20.00 50.00
44 Melvin Ajinca 20.00 50.00
48 Harrison Ingram 20.00 50.00
49 Cam Spencer 20.00 50.00
50 Kevin McCullar Jr. 20.00 50.00

2024-25 Donruss Night Moves

1 Donovan Mitchell 15.00 40.00
2 Dalton Knecht 25.00 60.00
3 Damian Lillard 20.00 50.00
4 Alexandre Sarr 25.00 60.00
5 Anthony Davis 20.00 50.00
6 Zaccharie Risacher 25.00 60.00
7 Paolo Banchero 20.00 50.00
8 Luka Doncic 50.00 120.00
9 Giannis Antetokounmpo 30.00 80.00
10 Jalen Brunson 15.00 40.00
11 Stephon Castle 50.00 125.00
12 Trae Young 15.00 40.00
13 Ja Morant 25.00 60.00
14 Bronny James Jr. 25.00 60.00
15 Reed Sheppard 25.00 60.00
16 Donovan Clingan 20.00 50.00
17 Stephen Curry 60.00 150.00
18 Rob Dillingham 20.00 50.00
19 Jayson Tatum 25.00 60.00
20 Jaylen Brown 12.00 30.00
21 Zion Williamson 20.00 50.00
22 Tyrese Haliburton 15.00 40.00
23 Victor Wembanyama 75.00 200.00
24 LeBron James 60.00 150.00
25 Anthony Edwards 40.00 100.00
26 Nikola Jokic 40.00 100.00
27 Ron Holland II 15.00 40.00
28 Kevin Durant 25.00 60.00
29 Jared McCain 30.00 80.00
30 Shai Gilgeous-Alexander 40.00 100.00

2024-25 Donruss Pass the Rock

*WINTER: .4X TO 1X BASIC
*DISCO: 1.25X TO 3X BASIC
*HOLO PRPL LSR/99: 3X TO 8X BASIC
*BLUE DISCO/75: 3X TO 8X BASIC
*BLUE WINTER/75: 3X TO 8X BASIC
*HOLO RED & GRN LSR/75: 4X TO 10X BASIC
*HOLO PINK LSR/50: 5X TO 12X BASIC
*HOLO BLUE & GRN LSR/35: 6X TO 15X BASIC
*CHECKERBOARD/30: 8X TO 20X BASIC
*HOLO YLW LSR/25: 8X TO 20X BASIC
*PINK DISCO/25: 8X TO 20X BASIC
*HOLO RED & BLUE LSR/15: 10X TO 25X BASIC
1 Damian Lillard 1.00 2.50
2 Tyrese Haliburton .75 2.00
3 Kyrie Irving 1.00 2.50
4 LeBron James 3.00 8.00
5 Stephen Curry 3.00 8.00
6 De'Aaron Fox .75 2.00
7 Shai Gilgeous-Alexander 2.00 5.00
8 Nikola Jokic 2.00 5.00
9 Trae Young .75 2.00
10 Luka Doncic 2.50 6.00

2024-25 Donruss PlayMakers

1 Tidjane Salaun 5.00 12.00
2 Anthony Edwards 25.00 60.00
3 LeBron James 40.00 100.00
4 James Harden 10.00 25.00
5 Joel Embiid 8.00 20.00
6 Nikola Jokic 25.00 60.00
7 Ja Morant 15.00 40.00
8 Luka Doncic 30.00 80.00
9 Devin Booker 12.00 30.00
10 Shai Gilgeous-Alexander 25.00 60.00
11 Victor Wembanyama 75.00 200.00
12 Alexandre Sarr 15.00 40.00
13 Jayson Tatum 15.00 40.00
14 Zaccharie Risacher 15.00 40.00
15 Reed Sheppard 15.00 40.00
16 Giannis Antetokounmpo 20.00 50.00
17 Chet Holmgren 8.00 20.00
18 Stephen Curry 40.00 100.00
19 Stephon Castle 30.00 80.00
20 Tyrese Maxey 10.00 25.00

2024-25 Donruss Retro Rated Rookie Box Topper

2 Kevin Durant 12.00 30.00
3 Trae Young 8.00 20.00
4 Jayson Tatum 12.00 30.00
5 LeBron James 30.00 80.00
6 Stephen Curry 30.00 80.00
7 Tyrese Haliburton 8.00 20.00
8 Luka Doncic 25.00 60.00
9 James Harden 8.00 20.00
10 Kawhi Leonard 8.00 20.00
11 Tyrese Maxey 8.00 20.00
12 Kyrie Irving 10.00 25.00
13 Zion Williamson 10.00 25.00
14 Damian Lillard 10.00 25.00
15 Jalen Brunson 8.00 20.00
16 De'Aaron Fox 8.00 20.00
17 Donovan Mitchell 8.00 20.00
18 Anthony Davis 8.00 20.00
19 Ja Morant 12.00 30.00
20 Shai Gilgeous-Alexander 20.00 50.00
21 Giannis Antetokounmpo 15.00 40.00
22 Nikola Jokic 20.00 50.00
23 Joel Embiid 6.00 15.00
24 Devin Booker 10.00 25.00
25 Paul George 6.00 15.00

2024-25 Donruss Signature Series

*WINTER: .4X TO 1X BASIC
*HOLO GRN LSR/75: .5X TO 1.2X BASIC
*HOLO RED & BLUE LSR/25: .75X TO 2X BASIC
*HOLO PINK LSR/25: .75X TO 2X BASIC
1 Jaden Hardy 6.00 15.00
2 Jalen Duren 6.00 15.00
3 Cason Wallace 8.00 20.00
4 Cade Cunningham 40.00 100.00
6 Jabari Smith Jr. 6.00 15.00
7 Jalen Suggs 6.00 15.00
8 Trendon Watford 5.00 12.00
9 Kendall Brown 5.00 12.00
10 Greg Brown III 4.00 10.00
11 E.J. Liddell 5.00 12.00
12 Garrett Temple 5.00 12.00
13 Chimezie Metu 5.00 12.00
14 AJ Lawson 4.00 10.00
15 Dalano Banton 6.00 15.00
16 Julian Champagnie 5.00 12.00
17 Vit Krejci 5.00 12.00
18 Jordan Miller 5.00 12.00
19 Ryan Rollins 6.00 15.00
20 Josh Christopher 4.00 10.00
21 Kessler Edwards 5.00 12.00
23 Lindy Waters III 5.00 12.00
24 Sam Merrill 5.00 12.00
25 Usman Garuba 4.00 10.00
26 Paolo Banchero 15.00 40.00
27 Sandro Mamukelashvili 8.00 20.00
28 Keon Ellis 5.00 12.00
29 Orlando Robinson 4.00 10.00
30 Trevelin Queen 5.00 12.00
31 Wendell Moore Jr. 5.00 12.00
32 Tosan Evbuomwan 4.00 10.00
33 Jason Preston 4.00 10.00
34 Pete Nance 4.00 10.00
35 Cole Swider 5.00 12.00
36 Jared Butler 5.00 12.00
37 Buddy Boeheim 5.00 12.00
38 Collin Gillespie 5.00 12.00
39 RaiQuan Gray 5.00 12.00
40 Johnny Juzang 5.00 12.00
41 Ruben Patterson 5.00 12.00
42 Otis Thorpe 6.00 15.00
43 Jerome Williams 5.00 12.00
44 Calvin Natt 4.00 10.00
45 Malik Rose 5.00 12.00
46 Don Buse 5.00 12.00
47 Sam Mitchell 5.00 12.00
48 John Long 4.00 10.00
49 Joe Smith 5.00 12.00
50 John Lucas 5.00 12.00
52 Cam Spencer 6.00 15.00
53 Nikola Durisic 8.00 20.00
55 Devin Carter 8.00 20.00
56 Antonio Reeves 6.00 15.00
57 DaRon Holmes II 8.00 20.00
58 Kevin McCullar Jr. 6.00 15.00
59 Matas Buzelis 30.00 80.00
60 Ariel Hukporti 5.00 12.00
61 Tidjane Salaun 6.00 15.00
62 Jamal Shead 8.00 20.00
63 Bobi Klintman 8.00 20.00
65 Judah Mintz 5.00 12.00
66 Jaylen Wells 20.00 50.00
67 Ulrich Chomche 5.00 12.00
68 Donovan Clingan 15.00 40.00
69 Harrison Ingram 6.00 15.00
70 Jared McCain 25.00 60.00
71 Ja'Kobe Walter 8.00 20.00
72 Armando Bacot 5.00 12.00
73 Baylor Scheierman 8.00 20.00
74 Pacome Dadiet 8.00 20.00
75 PJ Hall 5.00 12.00
76 Terrence Shannon Jr. 12.00 30.00
77 Kyshawn George 10.00 25.00
78 Keshad Johnson 5.00 12.00
79 KJ Simpson Jr. 6.00 15.00
80 Oso Ighodaro 8.00 20.00
81 Trey Alexander 5.00 12.00
82 Cam Christie 8.00 20.00
83 Dalton Knecht 20.00 50.00
84 Pelle Larsson 8.00 20.00
85 Dillon Jones 6.00 15.00
86 AJ Johnson 12.00 30.00
87 Anton Watson 5.00 12.00
88 Jonathan Mogbo 10.00 25.00
89 Reed Sheppard 20.00 50.00
91 Adem Bona 8.00 20.00
92 Tristen Newton 6.00 15.00
93 Bub Carrington 15.00 40.00
94 Tristan da Silva 15.00 40.00
95 Enrique Freeman 5.00 12.00
97 Jalen Bridges 5.00 12.00
98 Tyler Kolek 10.00 25.00
99 Jaylon Tyson 6.00 15.00
100 Yves Missi 15.00 40.00

2024-25 Donruss Snow Globe

*BLUE WINTER/75: 4X TO 10X BASIC
1 Stephen Curry 3.00 8.00
2 Jalen Brunson .75 2.00
3 Paolo Banchero 1.00 2.50
4 Giannis Antetokounmpo 1.50 4.00
5 Tyrese Maxey .75 2.00
6 Tyrese Haliburton .75 2.00
7 Nikola Jokic 2.00 5.00
8 Luka Doncic 2.50 6.00
9 Zion Williamson 1.00 2.50
10 LeBron James 3.00 8.00
11 Trae Young .75 2.00
12 Anthony Edwards 2.00 5.00
13 Shai Gilgeous-Alexander 2.00 5.00
14 Victor Wembanyama 3.00 8.00
15 Kevin Durant 1.25 3.00
16 Jayson Tatum 1.25 3.00
17 Ja Morant 1.25 3.00
18 Damian Lillard 1.00 2.50
19 Devin Booker 1.00 2.50
20 Donovan Mitchell .75 2.00
21 Zaccharie Risacher 1.25 3.00
22 Alexandre Sarr 1.25 3.00
23 Reed Sheppard 1.25 3.00
24 Stephon Castle 2.50 6.00
25 Ron Holland II .75 2.00
26 Tidjane Salaun .40 1.00
27 Donovan Clingan 1.00 2.50
28 Rob Dillingham 1.00 2.50
29 Zach Edey 1.25 3.00
30 Cody Williams .50 1.25
31 Matas Buzelis 2.00 5.00
32 Nikola Topic 1.25 3.00
33 Devin Carter .50 1.25
34 Bub Carrington 1.00 2.50
35 Kel'el Ware 1.00 2.50
36 Jared McCain 1.50 4.00
37 Dalton Knecht 1.25 3.00
38 Tristan da Silva 1.00 2.50
39 Ja'Kobe Walter .50 1.25
40 Bronny James Jr. 1.25 3.00
41 Kevin Garnett 1.00 2.50
42 Allen Iverson 1.00 2.50
43 Karl Malone .75 2.00
44 Shaquille O'Neal 1.00 2.50
45 Tim Duncan 1.00 2.50
46 Yao Ming .75 2.00
47 Larry Bird 1.25 3.00
48 Dirk Nowitzki 1.00 2.50
49 Magic Johnson 1.25 3.00
50 Dwyane Wade .75 2.00

2024-25 Donruss Swish

*PRESS PROOF: .5X TO 1.2X BASIC
*PRESS PROOF PRPL: .5X TO 1.2X BASIC
*DIAMOND: 1.25X TO 3X BASIC
*HOLO LSR/99: 3X TO 8X BASIC
*INT BLUE STARS/99: 3X TO 8X BASIC
*DIAMOND RED/75: 4X TO 10X BASIC
*INT RED FIREWORKS/55: 5X TO 12X BASIC
*HOLO BLUE LSR/49: 5X TO 12X BASIC
*HYPER/25: 8X TO 20X BASIC
1 Shai Gilgeous-Alexander 2.00 5.00
2 Jalen Brunson .75 2.00
3 Stephen Curry 3.00 8.00

4 Matas Buzelis 2.00 5.00
5 LeBron James 3.00 8.00
6 Kyrie Irving 1.00 2.50
7 Jayson Tatum 1.25 3.00
8 Alexandre Sarr 1.25 3.00
9 Trae Young .75 2.00
10 Luka Doncic 2.50 6.00
11 Zaccharie Risacher 1.25 3.00
12 Damian Lillard 1.00 2.50
13 Dalton Knecht 1.25 3.00
14 Reed Sheppard 1.25 3.00
15 Victor Wembanyama 3.00 8.00
16 Nikola Jokic 2.00 5.00
17 Kevin Durant 1.25 3.00
18 Anthony Edwards 2.00 5.00
19 Rob Dillingham 1.00 2.50
20 Ja Morant 1.25 3.00

2024-25 Donruss The Rookies
*WINTER: .4X TO 1X BASIC
*DISCO: 1.25X TO 3X BASIC
*HOLO PRPL LSR/99: 3X TO 8X BASIC
*BLUE DISCO/75: 3X TO 8X BASIC
*BLUE WINTER/75: 3X TO 8X BASIC
*HOLO RED & GRN LSR/75: 4X TO 10X BASIC
*HOLO PINK LSR/50: 5X TO 12X BASIC
*HOLO BLUE & GRN LSR/35: 6X TO 15X BASIC
*CHECKERBOARD/30: 8X TO 20X BASIC
*HOLO YLW LSR/25: 8X TO 20X BASIC
*PINK DISCO/25: 8X TO 20X BASIC
*HOLO RED & BLUE LSR/15: 10X TO 25X BASIC
1 Matas Buzelis 2.50 6.00
2 Tidjane Salaun .50 1.25
3 Dalton Knecht 1.50 4.00
4 Reed Sheppard 1.50 4.00
5 Donovan Clingan 1.25 3.00

2024-25 Donruss Treasured Materials Signatures
STATED PRINT RUN 99 SER.#'d SETS
1 Max Christie/99 10.00 25.00
2 Scottie Barnes/99 12.00 30.00
3 Walker Kessler/99 8.00 20.00
4 Donte DiVincenzo/99 10.00 25.00
5 T.J. McConnell/99 8.00 20.00
7 Ivica Zubac/99 10.00 25.00
8 Clint Capela/99 8.00 20.00
9 Dyson Daniels/99 12.00 30.00
10 Moses Moody/99 10.00 25.00
11 Franz Wagner/99 15.00 40.00
12 Jaden Hardy/99 10.00 25.00
13 Cole Anthony/99 10.00 25.00
14 Cason Wallace/99 12.00 30.00
15 Onyeka Okongwu/99 10.00 25.00
16 Anfernee Simons/99 10.00 25.00
17 Jonathan Kuminga/25 12.00 30.00
18 Mark Williams/99 8.00 20.00
19 Trey Murphy III/99 12.00 30.00
20 Cameron Thomas/99 10.00 25.00
21 Nikola Jovic/99 10.00 25.00
22 Bobby Portis/99 8.00 20.00
23 Jalen Duren/99 10.00 25.00
24 Jeremy Sochan/99 10.00 25.00
25 Jarrett Allen/99 8.00 20.00

2024-25 Donruss Unleashed
*PRESS PROOF: .5X TO 1.2X BASIC
*PRESS PROOF PRPL: .5X TO 1.2X BASIC
*DIAMOND: 1.25X TO 3X BASIC
*HOLO LSR/99: 3X TO 8X BASIC
*INT BLUE STARS/99: 3X TO 8X BASIC
*DIAMOND RED/75: 4X TO 10X BASIC
*INT RED FIREWORKS/55: 5X TO 12X BASIC
*HOLO BLUE LSR/49: 5X TO 12X BASIC
*HYPER/25: 8X TO 20X BASIC
1 Nikola Jokic 2.00 5.00
2 Giannis Antetokounmpo 1.50 4.00
3 Anthony Davis 1.00 2.50
4 Anthony Edwards 2.00 5.00
5 Ja Morant 1.25 3.00
6 Alexandre Sarr 1.25 3.00
7 Stephen Curry 3.00 8.00
8 Jayson Tatum 1.25 3.00
9 Luka Doncic 2.50 6.00
10 Tidjane Salaun .40 1.00
11 Shai Gilgeous-Alexander 2.00 5.00
12 Zion Williamson 1.00 2.50
13 Donovan Clingan 1.00 2.50
14 LeBron James 3.00 8.00
15 Victor Wembanyama 3.00 8.00

2024-25 Donruss Zero Gravity
*PRESS PROOF: .5X TO 1.2X BASIC
*PRESS PROOF PRPL: .5X TO 1.2X BASIC
*DIAMOND: 1.25X TO 3X BASIC
*HOLO LSR/99: 3X TO 8X BASIC
*INT BLUE STARS/99: 3X TO 8X BASIC
*DIAMOND RED/75: 4X TO 10X BASIC
*INT RED FIREWORKS/55: 5X TO 12X BASIC
*HOLO BLUE LSR/49: 5X TO 12X BASIC
*HYPER/25: 8X TO 20X BASIC
1 Jayson Tatum 1.25 3.00
2 Shai Gilgeous-Alexander 2.00 5.00
3 LeBron James 3.00 8.00
4 Stephen Curry 3.00 8.00
5 Nikola Jokic 2.00 5.00
6 Giannis Antetokounmpo 1.50 4.00
7 Anthony Edwards 2.00 5.00
8 Luka Doncic 2.50 6.00
9 Ja Morant 1.25 3.00
10 Victor Wembanyama 3.00 8.00

2016-17 Donruss Optic
COMPLETE SET (200) 30.00 80.00
1 Joel Embiid 1.00 2.50
2 Jahlil Okafor .25 .60
3 Nerlens Noel .25 .60
4 T.J. McConnell .30 .75
5 Giannis Antetokounmpo 2.00 5.00
6 Jabari Parker .25 .60
7 Khris Middleton .40 1.00
8 Matthew Dellavedova .30 .75
9 John Henson .25 .60
10 Jimmy Butler .75 2.00
11 Rajon Rondo .50 1.25
12 Dwyane Wade .75 2.00
13 Nikola Mirotic .25 .60
14 Bobby Portis .40 1.00
15 LeBron James 8.00 20.00
16 Kevin Love .40 1.00
17 Kyrie Irving .75 2.00
18 Richard Jefferson .30 .75
19 Tristan Thompson .30 .75
20 Isaiah Thomas .30 .75
21 Avery Bradley .25 .60
22 Al Horford .40 1.00
23 Marcus Smart .50 1.25
24 Jordan Mickey .25 .60
25 Chris Paul .60 1.50
26 DeAndre Jordan .30 .75
27 Blake Griffin .40 1.00
28 Jamal Crawford .40 1.00
29 J.J. Redick .40 1.00
30 Mike Conley .30 .75
31 Chandler Parsons .25 .60
32 Marc Gasol .40 1.00
33 Zach Randolph .40 1.00
34 Dennis Schroder .40 1.00
35 Paul Millsap .30 .75
36 Dwight Howard .50 1.25
37 Kent Bazemore .25 .60
38 Kyle Korver .30 .75
39 Justise Winslow .30 .75
40 Josh Richardson .30 .75
41 Goran Dragic .40 1.00
42 Tyler Johnson .25 .60
43 Hassan Whiteside .30 .75
44 Kemba Walker .30 .75
45 Nicolas Batum .30 .75
46 Frank Kaminsky .25 .60
47 Jeremy Lamb .25 .60
48 Aaron Harrison .25 .60
49 Joe Johnson .40 1.00
50 Rudy Gobert .50 1.25
51 George Hill .30 .75
52 Gordon Hayward .40 1.00
53 Rodney Hood .30 .75
54 DeMarcus Cousins .30 .75
55 Ben McLemore .25 .60
56 Willie Cauley-Stein .30 .75
57 Rudy Gay .40 1.00
58 Omri Casspi .25 .60
59 Carmelo Anthony .60 1.50
60 Kristaps Porzingis .60 1.50
61 Joakim Noah .25 .60
62 Derrick Rose .60 1.50
63 Larry Nance Jr. .25 .60
64 D'Angelo Russell .50 1.25
65 Julius Randle .50 1.25
66 Lou Williams .40 1.00
67 Serge Ibaka .30 .75
68 Jeff Green .25 .60
69 Mario Hezonja .25 .60
70 Evan Fournier .30 .75
71 Aaron Gordon .40 1.00
72 Bismack Biyombo .25 .60
73 Nikola Vucevic .40 1.00
74 Harrison Barnes .30 .75
75 Andrew Bogut .40 1.00
76 J.J. Barea .30 .75
77 Dirk Nowitzki 1.00 2.50
78 Deron Williams .30 .75
79 Wesley Matthews .25 .60
80 Brook Lopez .30 .75
81 Rondae Hollis-Jefferson .25 .60
82 Bojan Bogdanovic .30 .75
83 Jeremy Lin .75 2.00
84 Chris McCullough .25 .60
85 Emmanuel Mudiay .25 .60
86 Kenneth Faried .30 .75
87 Danilo Gallinari .30 .75
88 Will Barton .25 .60
89 Wilson Chandler .30 .75
90 Nikola Jokic 4.00 10.00
91 Jeff Teague .25 .60
92 Myles Turner .40 1.00
93 Paul George .60 1.50
94 Monta Ellis .30 .75
95 C.J. Miles .25 .60
96 Thaddeus Young .25 .60
97 Anthony Davis 1.25 3.00
98 Tyreke Evans .30 .75
99 Jrue Holiday .50 1.25
100 Stanley Johnson .25 .60
101 Marcus Morris .25 .60
102 Kentavious Caldwell-Pope .30 .75
103 Reggie Jackson .30 .75
104 Andre Drummond .40 1.00
105 DeMar DeRozan .50 1.25
106 Kyle Lowry .40 1.00
107 Jonas Valanciunas .30 .75
108 DeMarre Carroll .25 .60
109 Norman Powell .40 1.00
110 James Harden .75 2.00
111 Trevor Ariza .25 .60
112 Clint Capela .30 .75
113 Sam Dekker .25 .60
114 Patrick Beverley .30 .75
115 LaMarcus Aldridge .40 1.00
116 Kawhi Leonard 1.00 2.50
117 Tony Parker .60 1.50
118 Manu Ginobili .75 2.00
119 Pau Gasol .60 1.50
120 Eric Bledsoe .30 .75
121 Devin Booker 1.50 4.00
122 Brandon Knight .30 .75
123 Alex Len .25 .60
124 Tyson Chandler .25 .60
125 Andrew Wiggins .50 1.25
126 Zach LaVine .75 2.00
127 Ricky Rubio .30 .75
128 Karl-Anthony Towns .75 2.00
129 Gorgui Dieng .25 .60
130 C.J. McCollum .40 1.00
131 Damian Lillard 1.00 2.50
132 Evan Turner .25 .60
133 Al-Farouq Aminu .25 .60
134 Mason Plumlee .25 .60
135 Stephen Curry 3.00 8.00
136 Klay Thompson 1.00 2.50
137 Kevin Durant 1.50 4.00
138 Draymond Green .50 1.25
139 Andre Iguodala .40 1.00
140 John Wall .50 1.25
141 Markieff Morris .25 .60
142 Marcin Gortat .25 .60
143 Bradley Beal .50 1.25
144 Kelly Oubre Jr. .50 1.25
145 Russell Westbrook .60 1.50
146 Victor Oladipo .30 .75
147 Steven Adams .30 .75
148 Cameron Payne .40 1.00
149 Andre Roberson .25 .60
150 Jordan Clarkson .40 1.00
151 Ben Simmons RC 1.50 4.00
152 Brandon Ingram RC 2.00 5.00
153 Jaylen Brown RC 6.00 15.00
154 Dragan Bender RC .50 1.25
155 Kris Dunn RC .75 2.00
156 Buddy Hield RC 1.50 4.00
157 Jamal Murray RC 4.00 10.00
158 Marquese Chriss RC .60 1.50
159 Jakob Poeltl RC 1.00 2.50
160 Thon Maker RC .60 1.50
161 Domantas Sabonis RC 3.00 8.00
162 Taurean Prince RC .60 1.50
163 Denzel Valentine RC .50 1.25
164 Wade Baldwin IV RC .50 1.25
165 Henry Ellenson RC .50 1.25
166 Malik Beasley RC 1.00 2.50
167 Caris LeVert RC 1.25 3.00
168 DeAndre' Bembry RC .75 2.00
169 Malachi Richardson RC .50 1.25
170 Brice Johnson RC .50 1.25
171 Pascal Siakam RC 3.00 8.00
172 Skal Labissiere RC .50 1.25
173 Dejounte Murray RC 2.50 6.00
174 Damian Jones RC .50 1.25
175 Deyonta Davis RC .50 1.25
176 Ivica Zubac RC 1.25 3.00
177 Cheick Diallo RC .50 1.25
178 Tyler Ulis RC .60 1.50
179 Malcolm Brogdon RC 1.50 4.00
180 Chinanu Onuaku RC .50 1.25
181 Patrick McCaw RC .50 1.25
182 Diamond Stone RC .50 1.25
183 Stephen Zimmerman RC .50 1.25
184 Isaiah Whitehead RC .50 1.25
185 Demetrius Jackson RC .50 1.25
186 A.J. Hammons RC .50 1.25
187 Jake Layman RC .60 1.50
188 Michael Gbinije RC .50 1.25
189 Georges Niang RC .75 2.00
190 Tomas Satoransky RC .75 2.00
191 Joel Bolomboy RC .50 1.25
192 Kay Felder RC .50 1.25
193 Paul Zipser RC .50 1.25
194 Mindaugas Kuzminskas RC .50 1.25
195 Georgios Papagiannis RC .50 1.25
196 Alex Abrines RC .60 1.50
197 Willy Hernangomez RC .60 1.50
198 Marshall Plumlee RC .50 1.25
199 Sheldon McClellan RC .50 1.25
200 Ron Baker RC .50 1.25

2016-17 Donruss Optic Aqua
*AQUA: 8X TO 20X BASIC
STATED PRINT RUN 25 SER. #'D SETS
12 Dwyane Wade 40.00 100.00
15 LeBron James 300.00 600.00
90 Nikola Jokic 125.00 300.00
157 Jamal Murray 150.00 400.00

2016-17 Donruss Optic Blue
*BLUE: 4X TO 10X BASIC
STATED PRINT RUN 49 SER. #'D SETS
12 Dwyane Wade 20.00 50.00
15 LeBron James 125.00 300.00
90 Nikola Jokic 60.00 150.00
157 Jamal Murray 75.00 200.00

2016-17 Donruss Optic Checkerboard
*CHECKER: 4X TO 10X BASIC
*CHECKER RC: 4X TO 10X BASIC RC
12 Dwyane Wade 20.00 50.00
15 LeBron James 125.00 300.00
90 Nikola Jokic 60.00 150.00
157 Jamal Murray 75.00 200.00

2016-17 Donruss Optic Holo
*HOLO: 1.5X TO 4X BASIC
12 Dwyane Wade 8.00 20.00
90 Nikola Jokic 25.00 60.00

2016-17 Donruss Optic Orange
*ORANGE: 2.5X TO 6X BASIC
STATED PRINT RUN 199 SER. #'D SETS
12 Dwyane Wade 12.00 30.00
15 LeBron James 75.00 200.00
157 Jamal Murray 50.00 120.00

2016-17 Donruss Optic Pink
*PINK: 8X TO 20X BASIC
STATED PRINT RUN 25 SER. #'D SETS
12 Dwyane Wade 40.00 100.00
15 LeBron James 300.00 600.00
90 Nikola Jokic 125.00 300.00
157 Jamal Murray 150.00 400.00

2016-17 Donruss Optic Purple
*PURPLE: 1X TO 2.5X BASIC

2016-17 Donruss Optic Red
*RED: 3X TO 8X BASIC
STATED PRINT RUN 99 SER. #'D SETS
12 Dwyane Wade 15.00 40.00
15 LeBron James 100.00 250.00
157 Jamal Murray 60.00 150.00

2016-17 Donruss Optic White Sparkle
*WHITE SPARKLE: 6X TO 15X BASIC
*WHITE SPARKLE RC: 6X TO 15X BASIC RC
1 Joel Embiid 12.00 30.00
5 Giannis Antetokounmpo 20.00 50.00
15 LeBron James 300.00 500.00
20 Isaiah Thomas 25.00 60.00
62 Derrick Rose 20.00 50.00
110 James Harden 20.00 50.00
116 Kawhi Leonard 40.00 100.00
121 Devin Booker 40.00 100.00
125 Andrew Wiggins 15.00 4.00
126 Zach LaVine 6.00 15.00
128 Karl-Anthony Towns 60.00 150.00
135 Stephen Curry 40.00 100.00
136 Klay Thompson 20.00 50.00
137 Kevin Durant 40.00 100.00
138 Draymond Green 20.00 50.00
145 Russell Westbrook 40.00 100.00
152 Brandon Ingram 250.00 500.00
154 Dragan Bender 40.00 100.00
155 Kris Dunn 10.00 25.00
156 Buddy Hield 100.00 250.00
157 Jamal Murray 100.00 250.00
158 Marquese Chriss 40.00 100.00
161 Domantas Sabonis 400.00 800.00
162 Taurean Prince 20.00 50.00
163 Denzel Valentine 20.00 50.00
164 Wade Baldwin IV 15.00 40.00
165 Henry Ellenson 12.00 30.00
167 Caris LeVert 15.00 40.00
168 DeAndre' Bembry 12.00 30.00
169 Malachi Richardson 30.00 80.00
170 Brice Johnson 20.00 50.00
172 Skal Labissiere 60.00 150.00
173 Dejounte Murray 125.00 300.00
178 Tyler Ulis 40.00 100.00
179 Malcolm Brogdon 125.00 300.00
197 Willy Hernangomez 12.00 30.00

2017-18 Donruss Optic Fast Break Blue
*FB BLUE: 5X TO 12X BASIC
*FB BLUE RC: 5X TO 12X BASIC RC
STATED PRINT RUN 50 SER. #'D SETS
37 Nikola Jokic 40.00 100.00

2017-18 Donruss Optic Fast Break Holo
*FB HOLO: 1.25X TO 3X BASIC
*FB HOLO RC: 1.25X TO 3X BASIC RC

2017-18 Donruss Optic Fast Break Pink
*FB PINK: 8X TO 20X BASIC
*FB PINK RC: 8X TO 20X BASIC RC
STATED PRINT RUN 20 SER. #'D SETS
27 LeBron James 100.00 250.00
37 Nikola Jokic 75.00 200.00
46 Stephen Curry 75.00 200.00
188 Donovan Mitchell RR 150.00 400.00
196 De'Aaron Fox RR 150.00 400.00
198 Jayson Tatum RR 800.00 1,500.00

2017-18 Donruss Optic Fast Break Signatures
1 Kobe Bryant 500.00 1,000.00
2 Kevin Durant 100.00 250.00
3 Shaquille O'Neal 60.00 150.00
4 Allen Iverson 60.00 150.00
5 Reggie Miller 60.00 150.00
6 Chris Paul 40.00 100.00
7 Damian Lillard 40.00 100.00
8 Kyrie Irving 25.00 60.00
9 John Stockton 20.00 50.00
10 Larry Bird 40.00 100.00
11 Magic Johnson 40.00 100.00
12 Jerry West 25.00 60.00
13 Alonzo Mourning 15.00 40.00
14 Markelle Fultz 8.00 20.00
15 Josh Jackson 4.00 10.00
16 Lonzo Ball 12.00 30.00
17 Jayson Tatum 200.00 500.00
18 Sam Jones 6.00 15.00
19 Artis Gilmore 6.00 15.00
20 Elvin Hayes 6.00 15.00
21 De'Aaron Fox 75.00 200.00
22 Milos Teodosic 4.00 10.00
23 Myles Turner 5.00 12.00
24 Nate Thurmond 5.00 12.00
25 Jermaine O'Neal 5.00 12.00
26 Jonathan Isaac 8.00 20.00
27 Channing Frye 3.00 8.00
28 Lauri Markkanen 20.00 50.00
29 Cody Zeller 3.00 8.00
30 Enes Kanter 4.00 10.00
31 Frank Ntilikina 4.00 10.00
32 Nene 4.00 10.00
33 Antawn Jamison 4.00 10.00
34 Dennis Smith Jr. 4.00 10.00
35 Zach Collins 5.00 12.00
36 Courtney Lee 3.00 8.00
37 Jerami Grant 4.00 10.00
38 Thaddeus Young 3.00 8.00
39 Jamaal Wilkes 5.00 12.00
40 Kenny "Sky" Walker 3.00 8.00
41 Guerschon Yabusele 3.00 8.00
42 Malik Monk 12.00 30.00
43 Matthew Dellavedova 4.00 10.00
44 Bogdan Bogdanovic 8.00 20.00
45 Luke Kennard 6.00 15.00
46 Maxi Kleber 5.00 12.00
47 Ed Davis 3.00 8.00
48 Lou Williams 4.00 10.00
49 Aaron McKie 3.00 8.00
50 Damon Stoudamire 5.00 12.00
51 Tom Gugliotta 3.00 8.00
52 Donovan Mitchell 100.00 250.00
53 Bam Adebayo 20.00 50.00
54 Daniel Theis 6.00 15.00
55 Darrell Arthur 3.00 8.00
56 Antoine Walker 4.00 10.00
57 Brian Scalabrine 3.00 8.00
58 Cedric Ceballos 3.00 8.00
59 Corey Maggette 4.00 10.00
60 Eric Snow 3.00 8.00
61 Fat Lever 4.00 10.00
62 Michael Adams 3.00 8.00
63 P.J. Brown 3.00 8.00
64 Purvis Short 3.00 8.00
65 Sam Bowie 3.00 8.00
66 Chris Herren 4.00 10.00
67 Ante Zizic 4.00 10.00
68 D.J. Wilson 3.00 8.00
69 Justin Jackson 3.00 8.00
70 Justin Patton 3.00 8.00
71 Terry Rozier 4.00 10.00
72 Abdel Nader 4.00 10.00
73 Brandon Paul 3.00 8.00
74 Cedi Osman 6.00 15.00
75 Harry Giles 3.00 8.00
76 John Collins 8.00 20.00
77 TJ Leaf 3.00 8.00
78 Trevor Booker 3.00 8.00
79 David Nwaba 3.00 8.00
80 Jarrett Allen 8.00 20.00
81 OG Anunoby 15.00 40.00
82 Terrance Ferguson 3.00 8.00
83 Tyler Lydon 3.00 8.00
84 Zhou Qi 20.00 50.00
85 Alex Caruso 30.00 80.00
86 Antonio Blakeney 5.00 12.00
87 Derrick White 15.00 40.00
88 Josh Hart 8.00 20.00
89 Kyle Kuzma 12.00 30.00
90 Matt Costello 4.00 10.00
91 Ryan Arcidiacono 12.00 30.00
92 Tony Bradley 3.00 8.00
93 Dwight Buycks 3.00 8.00
94 Dwayne Bacon 3.00 8.00
95 Frank Mason III 3.00 8.00
96 Ivan Rabb 3.00 8.00
97 Wes Iwundu 3.00 8.00
98 Ish Smith 3.00 8.00
99 Johnathan Motley 3.00 8.00
100 James Ennis 3.00 8.00

2016-17 Donruss Optic All-Stars
1 Kobe Bryant 5.00 12.00
2 Larry Bird 2.50 6.00
3 Magic Johnson 2.50 6.00
4 Shaquille O'Neal 2.00 5.00
5 Grant Hill .75 2.00
6 Scottie Pippen 1.25 3.00
7 Isiah Thomas 1.00 2.50
8 Allen Iverson 1.00 2.50
9 Wilt Chamberlain 2.00 5.00
10 Steve Nash 1.00 2.50
11 Dwyane Wade 1.25 3.00
12 Kyle Lowry .60 1.50
13 LeBron James 5.00 12.00
14 Paul George 1.00 2.50
15 Carmelo Anthony 1.00 2.50
16 John Wall .75 2.00
17 Paul Millsap .50 1.25
18 DeMar DeRozan .75 2.00
19 Andre Drummond .60 1.50
20 Isaiah Thomas .50 1.25
21 Stephen Curry 5.00 12.00
22 Russell Westbrook 1.00 2.50
23 Kobe Bryant 5.00 12.00
24 Kevin Durant 2.50 6.00
25 Kawhi Leonard 1.50 4.00
26 Chris Paul 1.00 2.50
27 LaMarcus Aldridge .60 1.50
28 James Harden 1.25 3.00
29 Anthony Davis 2.00 5.00
30 Draymond Green .75 2.00

2016-17 Donruss Optic Court Kings
COMPLETE SET (40) 15.00 40.00
1 LeBron James 4.00 10.00
2 Stephen Curry 4.00 10.00
3 Dwyane Wade 1.00 2.50
4 Dirk Nowitzki 1.25 3.00
5 Chris Paul .75 2.00
6 Anthony Davis 1.50 4.00
7 Kyrie Irving 1.00 2.50
8 Kevin Durant 2.00 5.00
9 James Harden 1.00 2.50
10 Paul George .75 2.00
11 Jimmy Butler 1.00 2.50
12 Carmelo Anthony .75 2.00
13 DeMarcus Cousins .40 1.00
14 Blake Griffin .50 1.25
15 Karl-Anthony Towns 1.00 2.50
16 John Wall .60 1.50
17 Derrick Rose .75 2.00
18 Kawhi Leonard 1.25 3.00
19 Russell Westbrook .75 2.00
20 Klay Thompson 1.25 3.00
21 DeMar DeRozan .60 1.50
22 Damian Lillard 1.25 3.00
23 Kristaps Porzingis .75 2.00
24 Giannis Antetokounmpo 2.50 6.00
25 Andrew Wiggins .60 1.50
26 Isaiah Thomas .40 1.00
27 Jeremy Lin 1.00 2.50
28 Victor Oladipo .40 1.00
29 Eric Bledsoe .40 1.00
30 Kyle Lowry .50 1.25
31 Andre Drummond .50 1.25
32 Kemba Walker .40 1.00
33 Mike Conley .40 1.00
34 Dennis Schroder .50 1.25
35 Justise Winslow .40 1.00
36 Jordan Clarkson .50 1.25
37 Serge Ibaka .40 1.00
38 Gordon Hayward .50 1.25
39 Emmanuel Mudiay .30 .75
40 Jahlil Okafor .30 .75

2016-17 Donruss Optic Court Kings Aqua
*AQUA: 2.5X TO 6X BASIC
STATED PRINT RUN 25 SER. #'D SETS
1 LeBron James 75.00 200.00
2 Stephen Curry 40.00 100.00
24 Giannis Antetokounmpo 50.00 120.00

2016-17 Donruss Optic Court Kings Blue
*BLUE: 1.2X TO 3X BASIC
STATED PRINT RUN 49 SER. #'D SETS
1 LeBron James 40.00 100.00
2 Stephen Curry 20.00 50.00
24 Giannis Antetokounmpo 25.00 60.00

2016-17 Donruss Optic Court Kings Holo
*HOLO: .75X TO 2X BASIC
1 LeBron James 30.00 80.00
2 Stephen Curry 8.00 20.00
24 Giannis Antetokounmpo 15.00 40.00

2016-17 Donruss Optic Court Kings Orange
*ORANGE: .75X TO 2X BASIC
STATED PRINT RUN 199 SER. #'D SETS
1 LeBron James 25.00 60.00
2 Stephen Curry 10.00 25.00
24 Giannis Antetokounmpo 20.00 50.00

2016-17 Donruss Optic Court Kings Pink
*PINK: 2.5X TO 6X BASIC
STATED PRINT RUN 25 SER. #'D SETS
1 LeBron James 75.00 200.00
2 Stephen Curry 40.00 100.00
24 Giannis Antetokounmpo 50.00 120.00

2016-17 Donruss Optic Court Kings Purple
*PURPLE: .6X TO 1.5X BASIC
1 LeBron James 20.00 50.00
2 Stephen Curry 6.00 15.00
24 Giannis Antetokounmpo 8.00 20.00

2016-17 Donruss Optic Court Kings Red
*RED: .75X TO 2X BASIC
STATED PRINT RUN 99 SER. #'D SETS
1 LeBron James 25.00 60.00
2 Stephen Curry 12.00 30.00
24 Giannis Antetokounmpo 20.00 50.00

2016-17 Donruss Optic Crashers
*HOLO: 2X TO 5X BASIC
*RED/99: 3X TO 8X BASIC
*BLUE/49: 4X TO 10X BASIC
1 DeAndre Jordan .50 1.25
2 Hassan Whiteside .50 1.25
3 Pau Gasol 1.00 2.50
4 Andre Drummond .60 1.50
5 Dwight Howard .75 2.00
6 DeMarcus Cousins .50 1.25
7 Rudy Gobert .75 2.00
8 Karl-Anthony Towns 1.25 3.00
9 Anthony Davis 2.00 5.00
10 Julius Randle .75 2.00
11 Kevin Love .60 1.50
12 Marcin Gortat .40 1.00
13 Draymond Green .75 2.00
14 Kenneth Faried .50 1.25
15 LaMarcus Aldridge .60 1.50

2016-17 Donruss Optic Dimes
*HOLO: 2X TO 5X BASIC
*RED/99: 3X TO 8X BASIC
*BLUE/49: 4X TO 10X BASIC
1 Chris Paul 1.00 2.50
2 John Wall .75 2.00
3 Ricky Rubio .50 1.25
4 James Harden 1.25 3.00
5 Russell Westbrook 1.00 2.50
6 Damian Lillard 1.50 4.00
7 Goran Dragic .60 1.50
8 Stephen Curry 5.00 12.00
9 Kyle Lowry .60 1.50
10 Isaiah Thomas .60 1.50

2016-17 Donruss Optic Dimes Blue
*BLUE: 4X TO 10X BASIC
STATED PRINT RUN 49 SER. #'D SETS
8 Stephen Curry 50.00 125.00

2016-17 Donruss Optic Dominator Signatures
PRINT RUNS B/WN 25-99 COPIES PER
1 Karl-Anthony Towns/25 50.00 120.00
3 Devin Booker/99 40.00 100.00
4 Justise Winslow/99 4.00 10.00
5 Dirk Nowitzki/25 60.00 150.00
6 Jabari Parker/25 12.00 30.00
7 Victor Oladipo/99 12.00 30.00
8 Andrew Wiggins/25 25.00 60.00
9 Kevin Durant/25 75.00 200.00
10 Kyrie Irving/25 30.00 80.00
11 John Wall/25 25.00 60.00
13 Dwyane Wade/25 30.00 80.00
14 Jordan Clarkson/99 5.00 12.00
15 Eric Bledsoe/99 4.00 10.00
16 Carmelo Anthony/25 12.00 30.00
17 Jeremy Lin/99 20.00 50.00
18 Isaiah Thomas/99 12.00 30.00
19 D'Angelo Russell/25 12.00 30.00
20 Klay Thompson/99 20.00 50.00
22 Paul Millsap/25 6.00 15.00
23 Pau Gasol/25 10.00 25.00
24 Chris Paul/25 40.00 100.00
25 Blake Griffin/99 12.00 30.00
26 Goran Dragic/99 5.00 12.00
27 Allen Iverson/25 50.00 120.00
28 Latrell Sprewell/25 8.00 20.00
29 James Worthy/25 10.00 25.00
30 Vin Baker/25 6.00 15.00
31 George Gervin/25 15.00 40.00
32 Spud Webb/25 8.00 20.00
33 Jalen Rose/50 5.00 12.00
34 John Starks/99 5.00 12.00
35 Bill Russell/25 500.00 1,000.00
36 Shawn Kemp/25 25.00 60.00
37 Sean Elliott/25 6.00 15.00
38 Kobe Bryant/25 500.00 1,000.00
39 Jason Kidd/25 12.00 30.00
40 Anfernee Hardaway/25 25.00 60.00

2016-17 Donruss Optic Elite Series
1 Dirk Nowitzki 1.50 4.00
2 Stephen Curry 5.00 12.00
3 Kevin Durant 2.50 6.00
4 Derrick Rose 1.00 2.50
5 Dwyane Wade 1.25 3.00
6 Al Horford .60 1.50
7 Russell Westbrook 1.00 2.50
8 Damian Lillard 1.50 4.00
9 LeBron James 5.00 12.00
10 Anthony Davis 2.00 5.00
11 James Harden 1.25 3.00
12 Chris Paul 1.00 2.50
13 Kawhi Leonard 1.50 4.00
14 LaMarcus Aldridge .60 1.50
15 John Wall .75 2.00
16 Jimmy Butler 1.25 3.00
17 Kyrie Irving 1.25 3.00
18 Klay Thompson 1.50 4.00
19 Blake Griffin .60 1.50
20 Kyle Lowry .60 1.50
21 Pau Gasol 1.00 2.50
22 Marc Gasol .60 1.50
23 Carmelo Anthony 1.00 2.50
24 Mike Conley .50 1.25
25 Jordan Clarkson .50 1.25

2016-17 Donruss Optic Hall Dominator Signatures
PRINT RUNS B/WN 25-99 COPIES PER
1 Dan Issel/99 6.00 15.00
2 Artis Gilmore/50 8.00 20.00
3 Adrian Dantley/99 5.00 12.00
4 Tom Heinsohn/99 12.00 30.00
5 Elvin Hayes/50 8.00 20.00
6 Jamaal Wilkes/99 5.00 12.00
7 Tom Sanders/99 10.00 25.00
8 David Robinson/25 15.00 40.00
9 Rick Barry/50 8.00 20.00
10 Bob Lanier/99 6.00 15.00
11 Dennis Rodman/50 15.00 40.00
12 Scottie Pippen/25 60.00 150.00
14 Alex English/99 4.00 10.00
15 Bernard King/99 6.00 15.00
16 Alonzo Mourning/25 15.00 40.00
17 Hakeem Olajuwon/50 12.00 30.00
18 Karl Malone/25 25.00 60.00
19 Earl Lloyd/50 12.00 30.00
20 Calvin Murphy/50 6.00 15.00
21 Shaquille O'Neal/50 50.00 120.00
22 Cliff Hagan/50 6.00 15.00
23 James Worthy/25 10.00 25.00
24 Joe Dumars/50 6.00 15.00
25 Nate Archibald/25 8.00 20.00
26 Magic Johnson/25 25.00 60.00
27 Walt Frazier/50 6.00 15.00
28 Oscar Robertson/25 20.00 50.00
29 Louie Dampier/50 5.00 12.00
30 Dominique Wilkins/25 10.00 25.00

2016-17 Donruss Optic Hall Kings
*HOLO: .5X TO 1.2X BASIC
*PURPLE: .5X TO 1.2X BASIC
*ORANGE/199: .75X TO 2X BASIC
*RED/99: .75X TO 2X BASIC
*BLUE/49: 1.2X TO 3X BASIC
*AQUA/25: 2.5X TO 6X BASIC
*PINK/25: 2.5X TO 6X BASIC
1 Shaquille O'Neal 1.50 4.00
2 Allen Iverson .75 2.00
3 Yao Ming 1.25 3.00
4 Alonzo Mourning .75 2.00
5 Gary Payton .75 2.00
6 Bernard King .60 1.50
7 Ralph Sampson .40 1.00
8 Jamaal Wilkes .50 1.25
9 Artis Gilmore .60 1.50
10 Chris Mullin .50 1.25
11 Dennis Rodman 1.00 2.50
12 Karl Malone .75 2.00
13 Scottie Pippen 1.00 2.50
14 David Robinson 1.00 2.50
15 John Stockton .75 2.00
16 Adrian Dantley .50 1.25
17 Patrick Ewing .60 1.50
18 Hakeem Olajuwon 1.00 2.50
19 Joe Dumars .50 1.25
20 Dominique Wilkins .60 1.50
21 Clyde Drexler .75 2.00
22 Robert Parish .60 1.50
23 James Worthy .60 1.50
24 Magic Johnson 2.00 5.00
25 Drazen Petrovic .50 1.25
26 Moses Malone .75 2.00
27 Isiah Thomas .75 2.00
28 Bob McAdoo .60 1.50
29 Kevin McHale .75 2.00
30 Larry Bird 2.00 5.00

2016-17 Donruss Optic Rookie Dominator Signatures
PRINT RUNS B/WN 25-99 COPIES PER
1 Patrick McCaw/99 3.00 8.00
2 Marquese Chriss/25 6.00 15.00
3 Buddy Hield/25 15.00 40.00
4 Henry Ellenson/99 3.00 8.00
5 Georges Niang/99 5.00 12.00
6 Demetrius Jackson/50 4.00 10.00
7 Dario Saric/25 8.00 20.00
8 Thon Maker/25 6.00 15.00
9 Domantas Sabonis/25 100.00 250.00
10 Dragan Bender/25 5.00 12.00
11 T. Luwawu-Cabarrot/99 5.00 12.00
12 Ivica Zubac/99 8.00 20.00
13 Damian Jones/50 4.00 10.00
15 Kris Dunn/25 8.00 20.00
16 Deyonta Davis/50 4.00 10.00
17 Brandon Ingram/25 75.00 200.00
18 Jamal Murray/25 125.00 300.00
19 Denzel Valentine/50 4.00 10.00
20 Jakob Poeltl/25 10.00 25.00
21 Skal Labissiere/50 4.00 10.00
22 Jake Layman/50 5.00 12.00
23 Diamond Stone/99 3.00 8.00
24 Chinanu Onuaku/99 3.00 8.00
25 Brice Johnson/99 3.00 8.00
26 Malik Beasley/50 8.00 20.00
27 Wade Baldwin IV/25 5.00 12.00
28 Taurean Prince/25 6.00 15.00
29 Kay Felder/99 3.00 8.00
30 Juan Hernangomez/50 8.00 20.00

2016-17 Donruss Optic Rookie Kings
*PURPLE: .75X TO 2X BASIC
*HOLO: 1X TO 2.5X BASIC
*ORANGE/199: 1.5X TO 4X BASIC
*RED/99: 2X TO 5X BASIC
*BLUE/49: 2.5X TO 6X BASIC
*AQUA/25: 4X TO 10X BASIC
*PINK/25: 4X TO 10X BASIC
1 Brandon Ingram 1.50 4.00
2 Ben Simmons 1.25 3.00
3 Jaylen Brown 6.00 15.00
4 Dragan Bender .40 1.00
5 Kris Dunn .60 1.50
6 Buddy Hield 1.25 3.00
7 Jamal Murray 8.00 20.00
8 Marquese Chriss .50 1.25
9 Jakob Poeltl .75 2.00
10 Thon Maker .50 1.25
11 Domantas Sabonis 2.50 6.00
12 Taurean Prince .50 1.25
13 Denzel Valentine .40 1.00
14 Wade Baldwin IV .40 1.00
15 Henry Ellenson .40 1.00
16 Malik Beasley .75 2.00
17 Caris LeVert 1.00 2.50
18 DeAndre' Bembry .60 1.50
19 Malachi Richardson .40 1.00
20 Timothe Luwawu-Cabarrot .60 1.50
21 Brice Johnson .40 1.00

22 Pascal Siakam 2.50 6.00
23 Skal Labissiere .40 1.00
24 Dejounte Murray 2.00 5.00
25 Damian Jones .40 1.00
26 Isaiah Whitehead .40 1.00
27 Deyonta Davis .40 1.00
28 Kay Felder .40 1.00
29 A.J. Hammons .40 1.00
30 Dario Saric .60 1.50

2016-17 Donruss Optic Rookie Signatures

*BLUE/25: .75X TO 2X BASIC
*PINK/25: .75X TO 2X BASIC
1 Brandon Ingram 10.00 25.00
2 Jaylen Brown 125.00 300.00
3 Kris Dunn 4.00 10.00
4 Buddy Hield 8.00 20.00
5 Jakob Poeltl 5.00 12.00
6 Jamal Murray 60.00 150.00
7 Patrick McCaw 2.50 6.00
8 Malcolm Brogdon 8.00 20.00
9 Wade Baldwin IV 2.50 6.00
10 Deyonta Davis 2.50 6.00
11 Kay Felder 2.50 6.00
12 Dario Saric 4.00 10.00
13 Timothe Luwawu-Cabarrot 4.00 10.00
14 Paul Zipser 2.50 6.00
15 Diamond Stone 2.50 6.00
16 Brice Johnson 2.50 6.00
17 Taurean Prince 3.00 8.00
18 DeAndre' Bembry 4.00 10.00
19 Joel Bolomboy 2.50 6.00
20 Skal Labissiere 2.50 6.00
22 Georgios Papagiannis 2.50 6.00
23 Ron Baker 2.50 6.00
24 Willy Hernangomez 3.00 8.00
25 Mindaugas Kuzminskas 2.50 6.00
26 Ivica Zubac 6.00 15.00
27 Stephen Zimmerman 2.50 6.00
31 Juan Hernangomez 5.00 12.00
32 Malik Beasley 5.00 12.00
33 Cheick Diallo 2.50 6.00
34 Henry Ellenson 2.50 6.00
35 Pascal Siakam 15.00 40.00
36 Chinanu Onuaku 2.50 6.00
37 Yogi Ferrell 3.00 8.00
39 Marquese Chriss 3.00 8.00
40 Dragan Bender 2.50 6.00
41 Domantas Sabonis 15.00 40.00
42 Jake Layman 3.00 8.00
43 Damian Jones 2.50 6.00
44 Sheldon McClellan 2.50 6.00
46 Denzel Valentine 2.50 6.00
47 Demetrius Jackson 2.50 6.00
48 Thon Maker 3.00 8.00
49 Georges Niang 4.00 10.00
50 Fred VanVleet 50.00 120.00

2016-17 Donruss Optic Rookie Signatures Holo

*HOLO: .5X TO 1.2X BASIC

2016-17 Donruss Optic Rookie Signatures Purple

*PURPLE: .5X TO 1.2X BASIC
28 A.J. Hammons 3.00 8.00

2016-17 Donruss Optic Signature Series

*HOLO: .4X TO 1X BASIC
*PURPLE: .4X TO 1X BASIC
1 Cody Zeller 2.50 6.00
2 C.J. McCollum 6.00 15.00
3 Ian Clark 2.50 6.00
4 Dwight Powell 2.50 6.00
5 E'Twaun Moore 2.50 6.00
7 James Ennis 2.50 6.00
8 Justin Hamilton 2.50 6.00
9 Alex Len 2.50 6.00
10 Allen Crabbe 2.50 6.00
11 Noah Vonleh 2.50 6.00
12 Spud Webb 4.00 10.00
13 Kevon Looney 4.00 10.00
14 Maurice Harkless 2.50 6.00
15 C.J. Miles 2.50 6.00
16 Dirk Nowitzki 100.00 250.00
17 Kyle O'Quinn 2.50 6.00
18 Jeff Withey 2.50 6.00
19 Mario Hezonja 2.50 6.00
20 Rashad Vaughn 2.50 6.00
21 Jordan McRae 2.50 6.00
22 Deron Williams 3.00 8.00
23 Jason Terry 3.00 8.00
24 Glen Rice 4.00 10.00
25 Michael Carter-Williams 2.50 6.00
26 Jason Smith 2.50 6.00
27 Jeremy Lin 40.00 100.00
28 Vin Baker 3.00 8.00
29 Norman Powell 4.00 10.00
30 Langston Galloway 2.50 6.00
31 Glenn Robinson III 2.50 6.00
32 Will Barton 2.50 6.00
33 Michael Kidd-Gilchrist 2.50 6.00
35 Steve Novak 2.50 6.00
36 James Johnson 2.50 6.00
37 Mike Muscala 2.50 6.00
38 Reggie Bullock 2.50 6.00
39 Troy Daniels 2.50 6.00
40 Alan Anderson 2.50 6.00
41 Rondae Hollis-Jefferson 2.50 6.00
42 Karl-Anthony Towns 25.00 60.00
43 John Wall 12.00 30.00
44 Justise Winslow 3.00 8.00
45 Marc Gasol 6.00 15.00
48 Devin Booker 125.00 300.00
49 Isaiah Canaan 2.50 6.00
50 Justin Anderson 2.50 6.00

2016-17 Donruss Optic Signature Series Blue

*BLUE: .75X TO 2X BASIC
STATED PRINT RUN 25 SER. #'D SETS
6 T.J. McConnell 6.00 15.00

2016-17 Donruss Optic Signature Series Pink

*PINK/25: .75X TO 2X BASIC
STATED PRINT RUN 25 SER. #'D SETS
6 T.J. McConnell 6.00 15.00

2016-17 Donruss Optic The Champ is Here

*HOLO: 1.25X TO 3X BASIC
1 LeBron James 5.00 12.00
2 Stephen Curry 5.00 12.00
3 Kyrie Irving 1.25 3.00
4 Klay Thompson 1.50 4.00
5 Dwyane Wade 1.25 3.00
6 Shaquille O'Neal 2.00 5.00
7 Kobe Bryant 5.00 12.00
8 Alonzo Mourning 1.00 2.50
9 Dirk Nowitzki 1.50 4.00
10 Tony Parker 1.00 2.50
11 Kevin Garnett 1.50 4.00
12 Manu Ginobili 1.25 3.00
13 Scottie Pippen 1.25 3.00
14 Larry Bird 2.50 6.00
15 Magic Johnson 2.50 6.00

2016-17 Donruss Optic The Champ is Here Blue

*BLUE: 4X TO 10X BASIC
STATED PRINT RUN 49 SER. #'D SETS
1 LeBron James 125.00 300.00
2 Stephen Curry 125.00 300.00
3 Kyrie Irving 12.00 30.00
4 Klay Thompson 15.00 40.00
5 Dwyane Wade 12.00 30.00
6 Shaquille O'Neal 20.00 50.00
7 Kobe Bryant 125.00 300.00
9 Dirk Nowitzki 15.00 40.00
10 Tony Parker 10.00 25.00
11 Kevin Garnett 15.00 40.00
12 Manu Ginobili 12.00 30.00
13 Scottie Pippen 12.00 30.00
14 Larry Bird 25.00 60.00
15 Magic Johnson 25.00 60.00

2016-17 Donruss Optic The Champ is Here Holo

*HOLO: 1.2X TO 3X BASIC
1 LeBron James 40.00 100.00
2 Stephen Curry 40.00 100.00
3 Kyrie Irving 4.00 10.00
4 Klay Thompson 5.00 12.00
5 Dwyane Wade 4.00 10.00
6 Shaquille O'Neal 6.00 15.00
7 Kobe Bryant 40.00 100.00
8 Alonzo Mourning 3.00 8.00
9 Dirk Nowitzki 5.00 12.00
10 Tony Parker 3.00 8.00
11 Kevin Garnett 5.00 12.00
12 Manu Ginobili 4.00 10.00
13 Scottie Pippen 4.00 10.00
14 Larry Bird 8.00 20.00
15 Magic Johnson 8.00 20.00

2016-17 Donruss Optic The Champ is Here Red

*RED: 2.5X TO 6X BASIC
STATED PRINT RUN 99 SER. #'D SETS
1 LeBron James 75.00 200.00
2 Stephen Curry 75.00 200.00
3 Kyrie Irving 8.00 20.00
4 Klay Thompson 10.00 25.00
5 Dwyane Wade 8.00 20.00
6 Shaquille O'Neal 12.00 30.00
7 Kobe Bryant 75.00 200.00
9 Dirk Nowitzki 10.00 25.00
10 Tony Parker 6.00 15.00
11 Kevin Garnett 10.00 25.00
12 Manu Ginobili 8.00 20.00
13 Scottie Pippen 8.00 20.00
14 Larry Bird 15.00 40.00
15 Magic Johnson 15.00 40.00

2016-17 Donruss Optic The Rookies

1 Brandon Ingram 2.00 5.00
2 Ben Simmons 1.50 4.00
3 Kris Dunn .75 2.00
4 Buddy Hield 1.50 4.00
5 Marquese Chriss .60 1.50

2017-18 Donruss Optic

1 DeAndre' Bembry .25 .60
2 Dennis Schroder .30 .75
3 Taurean Prince .30 .75
4 Malcolm Delaney .25 .60
5 Ersan Ilyasova .25 .60
6 Jaylen Brown 1.00 2.50
7 Al Horford .40 1.00
8 Marcus Morris .25 .60
9 Isaiah Thomas .30 .75
10 Gordon Hayward .30 .75
11 D'Angelo Russell .30 .75
12 Trevor Booker .25 .60
13 Jeremy Lin .60 1.50
14 Rondae Hollis-Jefferson .25 .60
15 DeMarre Carroll .25 .60
16 Kemba Walker .30 .75
17 Nicolas Batum .25 .60
18 Michael Kidd-Gilchrist .25 .60
19 Dwight Howard .50 1.25
20 Jeremy Lamb .25 .60
21 Kris Dunn .25 .60
22 Zach LaVine .60 1.50
23 Bobby Portis .25 .60
24 Denzel Valentine .25 .60
25 Dwyane Wade .75 2.00
26 Kyrie Irving .75 2.00
27 LeBron James 3.00 8.00
28 Kevin Love .40 1.00
29 Derrick Rose .60 1.50
30 JR Smith .30 .75
31 Harrison Barnes .30 .75
32 Seth Curry .40 1.00
33 Wesley Matthews .25 .60
34 Dirk Nowitzki 1.00 2.50
35 J.J. Barea .30 .75
36 Gary Harris .30 .75
37 Nikola Jokic 2.50 6.00
38 Paul Millsap .30 .75
39 Jamal Murray .60 1.50
40 Emmanuel Mudiay .25 .60
41 Reggie Jackson .30 .75
42 Tobias Harris .30 .75
43 Andre Drummond .30 .75
44 Avery Bradley .25 .60
45 Stanley Johnson .25 .60
46 Stephen Curry 3.00 8.00
47 Kevin Durant 1.50 4.00
48 Draymond Green .50 1.25
49 Klay Thompson 1.00 2.50
50 Andre Iguodala .40 1.00
51 James Harden .75 2.00
52 Chris Paul .60 1.50
53 Eric Gordon .30 .75
54 Trevor Ariza .25 .60
55 Ryan Anderson .25 .60
56 Victor Oladipo .30 .75
57 Domantas Sabonis .75 2.00
58 Myles Turner .40 1.00
59 Thaddeus Young .25 .60
60 Darren Collison .25 .60
61 Patrick Beverley .25 .60
62 Danilo Gallinari .30 .75
63 Blake Griffin .40 1.00
64 DeAndre Jordan .30 .75
65 Lou Williams .30 .75
66 Jordan Clarkson .40 1.00
67 Brandon Ingram .50 1.25
68 Brook Lopez .30 .75
69 Julius Randle .40 1.00
70 Larry Nance Jr. .30 .75
71 Mario Chalmers .30 .75
72 Mike Conley .30 .75
73 Marc Gasol .40 1.00
74 Ben McLemore .25 .60
75 Chandler Parsons .25 .60
76 Goran Dragic .30 .75
77 James Johnson .25 .60
78 Justise Winslow .25 .60
79 Dion Waiters .25 .60
80 Hassan Whiteside .30 .75
81 Giannis Antetokounmpo 2.00 5.00
82 Greg Monroe .25 .60
83 Malcolm Brogdon .30 .75
84 Khris Middleton .50 1.25
85 Jabari Parker .25 .60
86 Jimmy Butler .60 1.50
87 Jamal Crawford .40 1.00
88 Andrew Wiggins .50 1.25
89 Karl-Anthony Towns .60 1.50
90 Jeff Teague .25 .60
91 Anthony Davis 1.00 2.50
92 DeMarcus Cousins .50 1.25
93 Jrue Holiday .50 1.25
94 Rajon Rondo .50 1.25
95 E'Twaun Moore .25 .60
96 Carmelo Anthony .60 1.50
97 Tim Hardaway Jr. .30 .75
98 Kristaps Porzingis .50 1.25
99 Willy Hernangomez .25 .60
100 Courtney Lee .25 .60
101 Russell Westbrook .60 1.50
102 Paul George .60 1.50
103 Steven Adams .30 .75
104 Enes Kanter .30 .75
105 Doug McDermott .25 .60
106 Aaron Gordon .40 1.00
107 Terrence Ross .30 .75
108 Nikola Vucevic .30 .75
109 Jonathon Simmons .25 .60
110 Elfrid Payton .25 .60
111 Robert Covington .25 .60
112 Joel Embiid .75 2.00
113 JJ Redick .40 1.00
114 Ben Simmons .40 1.00
115 Amir Johnson .25 .60
116 Eric Bledsoe .30 .75
117 Devin Booker 1.00 2.50
118 Marquese Chriss .25 .60
119 Tyler Ulis .25 .60
120 TJ Warren .30 .75
121 Al-Farouq Aminu .25 .60
122 Damian Lillard 1.00 2.50
123 CJ McCollum .40 1.00
124 Evan Turner .25 .60
125 Jusuf Nurkic .30 .75
126 Vince Carter .75 2.00
127 Willie Cauley-Stein .25 .60
128 Buddy Hield .40 1.00
129 George Hill .30 .75
130 Zach Randolph .40 1.00
131 LaMarcus Aldridge .40 1.00
132 Pau Gasol .60 1.50
133 Rudy Gay .30 .75
134 Kawhi Leonard 1.00 2.50
135 Dejounte Murray .40 1.00
136 DeMar DeRozan .50 1.25
137 Serge Ibaka .30 .75
138 Kyle Lowry .40 1.00
139 Pascal Siakam .75 2.00
140 Delon Wright .25 .60
141 Alec Burks .25 .60
142 Rudy Gobert .50 1.25
143 Rodney Hood .25 .60
144 Joe Johnson .30 .75
145 Ricky Rubio .30 .75
146 Markieff Morris .25 .60
147 John Wall .50 1.25
148 Otto Porter Jr. .30 .75
149 Marcin Gortat .25 .60
150 Bradley Beal .50 1.25
151 Zhou Qi RR RC 1.00 2.50
152 Dillon Brooks RR RC 1.50 4.00
153 Wayne Selden RR RC .50 1.25
154 Guerschon Yabusele RR RC .50 1.25
155 Milos Teodosic RR RC .60 1.50
156 Ivan Rabb RR RC .50 1.25
157 Tyler Dorsey RR RC .50 1.25
158 Justin Jackson RR RC .50 1.25
159 Lauri Markkanen RR RC 3.00 8.00
160 Thomas Bryant RR RC .75 2.00
161 Dwayne Bacon RR RC .50 1.25
162 Jawun Evans RR RC .50 1.25
163 Jordan Bell RR RC .50 1.25
164 Semi Ojeleye RR RC .60 1.50
165 Sterling Brown RR RC .50 1.25
166 Damyean Dotson RR RC .60 1.50
167 Frank Mason III RR RC .50 1.25
168 Wes Iwundu RR RC .50 1.25
169 Davon Reed RR RC .50 1.25
170 Frank Jackson RR RC .50 1.25
171 Josh Hart RR RC 1.25 3.00
172 Derrick White RR RC 2.00 5.00
173 Tony Bradley RR RC .50 1.25
174 Kyle Kuzma RR RC 2.00 5.00
175 Caleb Swanigan RR RC .50 1.25
176 Ike Anigbogu RR RC .50 1.25
177 Tyler Lydon RR RC .50 1.25
178 OG Anunoby RR RC 2.50 6.00
179 Jarrett Allen RR RC 1.25 3.00
180 Terrance Ferguson RR RC .50 1.25
181 Harry Giles RR RC .60 1.50
182 John Collins RR RC 1.25 3.00
183 TJ Leaf RR RC .50 1.25
184 D.J. Wilson RR RC .50 1.25
185 Justin Patton RR RC .50 1.25
186 Ante Zizic RR RC .60 1.50
187 Bam Adebayo RR RC 3.00 8.00
188 Donovan Mitchell RR RC 5.00 12.00
189 Luke Kennard RR RC 1.00 2.50
190 Malik Monk RR RC 2.00 5.00
191 Zach Collins RR RC .75 2.00
192 Dennis Smith Jr. RR RC .60 1.50
193 Frank Ntilikina RR RC .60 1.50
194 Sindarius Thornwell RR RC .50 1.25
195 Jonathan Isaac RR RC 1.25 3.00
196 De'Aaron Fox RR RC 4.00 10.00
197 Josh Jackson RR RC .60 1.50
198 Jayson Tatum RR RC 15.00 40.00
199 Lonzo Ball RR RC 2.00 5.00
200 Markelle Fultz RR RC 1.25 3.00

2017-18 Donruss Optic Aqua

*AQUA: 8X TO 20X BASIC
*AQUA RC: 8X TO 20X BASIC RC
STATED PRINT RUN 25 SER. #'D SETS
27 LeBron James 100.00 250.00
37 Nikola Jokic 75.00 200.00
46 Stephen Curry 75.00 200.00
188 Donovan Mitchell RR 150.00 400.00
196 De'Aaron Fox RR 150.00 400.00
198 Jayson Tatum RR 800.00 1,500.00

2017-18 Donruss Optic Black Velocity

*BLK VEL: 3X TO 8X BASIC
*BLK VEL RC: 3X TO 8X BASIC RC
STATED PRINT RUN 39 SER. #'D SETS
27 LeBron James 75.00 200.00
46 Stephen Curry 60.00 150.00
47 Kevin Durant 50.00 120.00
81 Giannis Antetokounmpo 60.00 150.00
174 Kyle Kuzma RR 12.00 30.00
179 Jarrett Allen RR 30.00 80.00
187 Bam Adebayo RR 60.00 150.00
188 Donovan Mitchell RR 200.00 500.00
196 De'Aaron Fox RR 75.00 200.00
198 Jayson Tatum RR 400.00 800.00
199 Lonzo Ball RR 75.00 200.00

2017-18 Donruss Optic Blue

*BLUE: 5X TO 12X BASIC
*BLUE RC: 5X TO 12X BASIC RC
STATED PRINT RUN 49 SER. #'D SETS
37 Nikola Jokic 40.00 100.00

2017-18 Donruss Optic Pink

*PINK: 8X TO 20X BASIC
*PINK RC: 8X TO 20X BASIC RC
STATED PRINT RUN 25 SER. #'D SETS
27 LeBron James 100.00 250.00
37 Nikola Jokic 75.00 200.00
46 Stephen Curry 75.00 200.00
188 Donovan Mitchell RR 150.00 400.00
196 De'Aaron Fox RR 150.00 400.00
198 Jayson Tatum RR 800.00 1,500.00

2017-18 Donruss Optic White Sparkle

*WHITE SPKL: X TO X BASIC
*WHITE SPKL RC: X TO X BASIC RC

2017-18 Donruss Press Proof Blue

*PROOF BLUE: 4X TO 10X BASIC
*PROOF BLUE RC: 2X TO 5X BASIC
STATED PRINT RUN 25 SER. #'d SETS
27 LeBron James 75.00 200.00
159 Lauri Markkanen RR 25.00 60.00
174 Kyle Kuzma RR 6.00 15.00
187 Bam Adebayo RR 50.00 120.00
188 Donovan Mitchell RR 75.00 200.00
190 Malik Monk RR 12.00 30.00
196 De'Aaron Fox RR 40.00 100.00
198 Jayson Tatum RR 200.00 500.00
199 Lonzo Ball RR 25.00 60.00
200 Markelle Fultz RR 25.00 60.00

2017-18 Donruss Press Proof Purple

*PRF PRPLE: 1.2X TO 3X BASIC
*PRF PURPLE RC: .6X TO 1.5X BASIC
STATED PRINT RUN 199 SER. #'d SETS
27 LeBron James 20.00 50.00
174 Kyle Kuzma RR 2.00 5.00
187 Bam Adebayo RR 15.00 40.00
188 Donovan Mitchell RR 25.00 60.00
196 De'Aaron Fox RR 10.00 25.00
198 Jayson Tatum RR 50.00 120.00
199 Lonzo Ball RR 8.00 20.00
200 Markelle Fultz RR 4.00 10.00

2017-18 Donruss Press Proof Red

*PROOF RED: 2X TO 5X BASIC
*PROOF RED RC: 1X TO 2.5X BASIC
STATED PRINT RUN 75 SER. #'d SETS
27 LeBron James 30.00 80.00
159 Lauri Markkanen RR 12.00 30.00
174 Kyle Kuzma RR 3.00 8.00
187 Bam Adebayo RR 25.00 60.00
188 Donovan Mitchell RR 40.00 100.00
190 Malik Monk RR 6.00 15.00
196 De'Aaron Fox RR 15.00 40.00
198 Jayson Tatum RR 75.00 200.00
199 Lonzo Ball RR 12.00 30.00
200 Markelle Fultz RR 6.00 15.00

2017-18 Donruss Press Proof Silver

*PRF SLVR: 1X TO 2.5X BASIC
*PRF SLVR RC: .5X TO 1.2X BASIC
STATED PRINT RUN 299 SER. #'d SETS
27 LeBron James 15.00 40.00
174 Kyle Kuzma RR 1.50 4.00
187 Bam Adebayo RR 12.00 30.00
188 Donovan Mitchell RR 20.00 50.00
196 De'Aaron Fox RR 8.00 20.00
198 Jayson Tatum RR 40.00 100.00
199 Lonzo Ball RR 6.00 15.00
200 Markelle Fultz RR 3.00 8.00

2017-18 Donruss Optic All Clear for Takeoff

COMPLETE SET (15) 8.00 20.00
*HOLO: .5X TO 1.2X BASIC
*FB HOLO: .5X TO 1.2X BASIC
*LIME GRN/175: 1.5X TO 4X BASIC
*RED/99: 2X TO 5X BASIC
*BLUE/49: 2.5X TO 6X BASIC
1 Aaron Gordon .50 1.25
2 Norman Powell .50 1.25
3 Andre Drummond .40 1.00
4 Giannis Antetokounmpo 2.50 6.00
5 Jamal Murray .75 2.00
6 Jaylen Brown 1.25 3.00
7 DeMar DeRozan .60 1.50
8 Andrew Wiggins .60 1.50
9 Kevin Durant 2.00 5.00
10 James Harden 1.00 2.50
11 Russell Westbrook .75 2.00
12 Blake Griffin .50 1.25
13 Zach LaVine .75 2.00
14 Larry Nance Jr. .40 1.00
15 Malcolm Brogdon .40 1.00

2017-18 Donruss Optic All Stars

COMPLETE SET (30) 15.00 40.00
*HOLO: .5X TO 1.2X BASIC
*FB HOLO: .5X TO 1.2X BASIC
*LIME GRN/175: 1.5X TO 4X BASIC
*RED/99: 2X TO 5X BASIC
*BLUE/49: 2.5X TO 6X BASIC
1 Stephen Curry 4.00 10.00
2 James Harden 1.00 2.50
3 Kevin Durant 2.00 5.00
4 Kawhi Leonard 1.25 3.00
5 Anthony Davis 1.25 3.00
6 Russell Westbrook .75 2.00
7 DeMarcus Cousins .40 1.00
8 Klay Thompson 1.25 3.00
9 Draymond Green .60 1.50
10 Marc Gasol .50 1.25
11 DeAndre Jordan .40 1.00
12 Gordon Hayward .40 1.00
13 Kyrie Irving 1.00 2.50
14 DeMar DeRozan .60 1.50
15 LeBron James 4.00 10.00
16 Giannis Antetokounmpo 2.50 6.00
17 Jimmy Butler .75 2.00
18 Isaiah Thomas .40 1.00
19 John Wall .60 1.50
20 Tim Duncan 1.25 3.00
21 Kyle Lowry .50 1.25
22 Paul George .75 2.00
23 Kemba Walker .40 1.00
24 Paul Millsap .40 1.00
25 Carmelo Anthony .75 2.00
26 Kobe Bryant 4.00 10.00
27 Grant Hill .75 2.00
28 Shawn Kemp .75 2.00
29 Larry Bird 2.00 5.00
30 Magic Johnson 2.00 5.00

2017-18 Donruss Optic Court Kings

COMPLETE SET (40) 15.00 40.00
*PURPLE: 75X TO 2X BASIC
*HOLO: 1.5X TO 4X BASIC
*LIME GRN/149: 3X TO 8X BASIC
*BLUE/85: 4X TO 10X BASIC
*AQUA/25: 6X TO 15X BASIC
*PINK/25: 6 TO 15X BASIC
1 Ben Simmons .50 1.25
2 Joel Embiid 1.00 2.50
3 Giannis Antetokounmpo 2.50 6.00
4 Dwyane Wade 1.00 2.50
5 LeBron James 4.00 10.00
6 Isaiah Thomas .40 1.00
7 Blake Griffin .50 1.25
8 Mike Conley .40 1.00
9 Dennis Schroder .40 1.00
10 Hassan Whiteside .40 1.00
11 Kemba Walker .40 1.00
12 Rudy Gobert .60 1.50
13 Buddy Hield .50 1.25
14 Kristaps Porzingis .60 1.50
15 Brandon Ingram .60 1.50
16 Aaron Gordon .50 1.25
17 Dirk Nowitzki 1.25 3.00
18 Harrison Barnes .40 1.00
19 Jeremy Lin .75 2.00
20 Gary Harris .40 1.00
21 Myles Turner .50 1.25
22 Anthony Davis 1.25 3.00
23 DeMarcus Cousins .40 1.00
24 Reggie Jackson .40 1.00
25 DeMar DeRozan .60 1.50
26 Kyle Lowry .50 1.25
27 James Harden 1.00 2.50
28 Kawhi Leonard 1.25 3.00
29 Devin Booker 1.25 3.00
30 Russell Westbrook .75 2.00
31 Andrew Wiggins .60 1.50
32 Karl-Anthony Towns .75 2.00
33 Damian Lillard 1.25 3.00
34 CJ McCollum .50 1.25
35 Stephen Curry 4.00 10.00
36 Kevin Durant 2.00 5.00
37 Klay Thompson 1.25 3.00
38 John Wall .60 1.50
39 Otto Porter Jr. .40 1.00
40 Nikola Jokic 3.00 8.00

2017-18 Donruss Optic Dominators Signatures

PRINT RUNS B/WN 25-49 COPIES PER
1 Bernard King/49 8.00 20.00
2 Hakeem Olajuwon/25 25.00 60.00
3 Shaquille O'Neal/49 60.00 150.00
4 Alex English/49 8.00 20.00
5 Calvin Murphy/49 6.00 15.00
6 Louie Dampier/49 10.00 25.00
7 Allen Iverson/49 60.00 150.00
8 John Stockton/49 20.00 50.00
9 Pau Gasol/49 15.00 40.00
10 Bill Russell/49 300.00 600.00
11 Larry Bird/49 50.00 120.00
12 George Hill/49 5.00 12.00
13 Andre Drummond/49 5.00 12.00
14 Frank Ramsey/49 6.00 15.00
15 Kobe Bryant/49 EXCH 500.00 1,000.00
16 Andrei Kirilenko/49 5.00 12.00
17 Vin Baker/49 5.00 12.00
18 Juwan Howard/49 5.00 12.00
19 Cedric Ceballos/49 4.00 10.00
20 Jason Kidd/29 20.00 50.00
21 Marcus Smart/49 6.00 15.00
22 Jason Terry/49 5.00 12.00
23 Reggie Miller/49 60.00 150.00
24 TJ Warren/35 6.00 15.00
25 Jordan Clarkson/49 6.00 15.00
26 Dwyane Wade/45 40.00 100.00
27 Clint Capela/49 5.00 12.00
28 Kevin Durant/49 EXCH 125.00 300.00
29 Norman Powell/49 6.00 15.00
30 Jonas Valanciunas/49 5.00 12.00
31 Nikola Vucevic/49 5.00 12.00
32 Chris Bosh/49 15.00 40.00
33 Emmanuel Mudiay/25 5.00 12.00
34 Gordon Hayward/49 5.00 12.00
35 Kyrie Irving/30 40.00 100.00
36 Harrison Barnes/49 5.00 12.00
38 Victor Oladipo/49 5.00 12.00
40 Nikola Mirotic/49 4.00 10.00

2017-18 Donruss Optic Hall Dominators Signatures

PRINT RUNS B/WN 25-49 COPIES PER
1 Adrian Dantley/49 8.00 20.00
3 Alonzo Mourning/49 20.00 50.00
4 Artis Gilmore/49 10.00 25.00
5 Arvydas Sabonis/49 10.00 25.00
6 Bernard King/49 10.00 25.00
7 Bob McAdoo/49 10.00 25.00
8 Calvin Murphy/49 8.00 20.00
9 Dan Issel/49 10.00 25.00
10 Dave Cowens/49 12.00 30.00
11 David Robinson/49 30.00 80.00
12 David Thompson/49 10.00 25.00
13 Dennis Rodman/49 40.00 100.00
14 Dikembe Mutombo/49 15.00 40.00
15 Dominique Wilkins/49 15.00 40.00
16 Gail Goodrich/49 8.00 20.00
17 Gary Payton/25 20.00 50.00
18 George Gervin/49 12.00 30.00
19 Jerry West/49 40.00 100.00
20 Joe Dumars/49 10.00 25.00
21 Karl Malone/49 40.00 100.00
22 Louie Dampier/49 8.00 20.00
23 Magic Johnson/49 75.00 200.00
24 Nate Archibald/49 10.00 25.00
25 Oscar Robertson/49 25.00 60.00
26 Ralph Sampson/49 8.00 20.00
27 Rick Barry/49 10.00 25.00
28 Robert Parish/49 10.00 25.00
29 Walt Frazier/49 15.00 40.00
30 Willis Reed/49 20.00 50.00

2017-18 Donruss Optic Hall Kings

COMPLETE SET (30) 15.00 40.00
*HOLO: .75X TO 2X BASIC
*PURPLE: .75X TO 2X BASIC
*LIME GRN/149: 1.2X TO 3X BASIC
*BLUE/85: 1.2X TO 3X BASIC
*AQUA/25: 2X TO 5X BASIC
*PINK/25: 2X TO 5X BASIC
1 Kareem Abdul-Jabbar 1.50 4.00
2 Elgin Baylor .75 2.00
3 Larry Bird 2.00 5.00
4 Wilt Chamberlain 1.50 4.00
5 Julius Erving 1.25 3.00
6 John Havlicek 1.00 2.50
7 Magic Johnson 2.00 5.00
8 George Mikan 1.25 3.00
9 Oscar Robertson 1.00 2.50
10 Bill Russell 1.50 4.00
11 Isiah Thomas .75 2.00
12 Jerry West 1.00 2.50
13 Wes Unseld .50 1.25
14 Rick Barry .60 1.50
15 Pete Maravich 1.25 3.00
16 Patrick Ewing .75 2.00
17 Tracy McGrady .75 2.00
18 Allen Iverson 1.25 3.00
19 Shaquille O'Neal 1.50 4.00
20 Yao Ming 1.00 2.50
21 Jo Jo White .50 1.25
22 Dikembe Mutombo .60 1.50
23 Mitch Richmond .60 1.50
24 Alonzo Mourning .75 2.00
25 Reggie Miller 1.00 2.50
26 Gary Payton .75 2.00
27 Artis Gilmore .60 1.50
28 Arvydas Sabonis .60 1.50
29 Dennis Rodman 1.25 3.00
30 Scottie Pippen 1.25 3.00

2017-18 Donruss Optic Rated Rookies Signatures

*FB: .5X TO 1.2X
*HOLO: .5X TO 1.2X
*PURPLE: .5X TO 1.2X
*BLUE/49: .75X TO 2X
151 Zhou Qi 25.00 60.00
152 Dillon Brooks 10.00 25.00
153 Wayne Selden 3.00 8.00
154 Guerschon Yabusele 3.00 8.00
155 Milos Teodosic 4.00 10.00
156 Ivan Rabb 3.00 8.00
157 Tyler Dorsey 3.00 8.00
158 Justin Jackson 3.00 8.00
159 Lauri Markkanen 30.00 80.00
160 Thomas Bryant 5.00 12.00
161 Dwayne Bacon 3.00 8.00
162 Jawun Evans 3.00 8.00
163 Jordan Bell 3.00 8.00
164 Semi Ojeleye 4.00 10.00
165 Sterling Brown 3.00 8.00
166 Damyean Dotson 4.00 10.00
167 Frank Mason III 3.00 8.00
168 Wes Iwundu 3.00 8.00
169 Davon Reed 3.00 8.00
170 Frank Jackson 3.00 8.00
171 Josh Hart 15.00 40.00
172 Derrick White 20.00 50.00
173 Tony Bradley 3.00 8.00
174 Kyle Kuzma EXCH 12.00 30.00
175 Caleb Swanigan 3.00 8.00
176 Ike Anigbogu 3.00 8.00
177 Tyler Lydon 3.00 8.00
178 OG Anunoby 15.00 40.00
179 Jarrett Allen 8.00 20.00
180 Terrance Ferguson 3.00 8.00
181 Harry Giles 3.00 8.00
182 John Collins 8.00 20.00
183 TJ Leaf 3.00 8.00
184 D.J. Wilson 3.00 8.00
185 Justin Patton 3.00 8.00
186 Ante Zizic 4.00 10.00
187 Bam Adebayo 40.00 100.00
188 Donovan Mitchell EXCH 125.00 300.00
189 Luke Kennard 6.00 15.00
190 Malik Monk 12.00 30.00
191 Zach Collins 5.00 12.00
192 Dennis Smith Jr. 4.00 10.00
193 Frank Ntilikina 4.00 10.00
194 Sindarius Thornwell 3.00 8.00
195 Jonathan Isaac 8.00 20.00
196 De'Aaron Fox 60.00 150.00
197 Josh Jackson 4.00 10.00
198 Jayson Tatum 300.00 600.00
199 Lonzo Ball 12.00 30.00
200 Markelle Fultz 8.00 20.00

2017-18 Donruss Optic Rated Rookies Signatures Fast Break Pink

*FB PINK: 1.25X TO 3X
STATED PRINT RUN 20 SER. #'D SETS
188 Donovan Mitchell EXCH 800.00 1,500.00
198 Jayson Tatum 1,250.00 2,500.00

2017-18 Donruss Optic Rated Rookies Signatures Pink

*PINK: 1.25X TO 3X
STATED PRINT RUN 25 SER. #'D SETS

2017-18 Donruss Optic Rated Rookies Signatures Premium

*PREMIUM: X TO X
ONE INCL. IN PREMIUM BOXES
STATED PRINT RUN 25 SER. #'D SETS

2017-18 Donruss Optic Retro Series

COMPLETE SET (25) 25.00 60.00
*FB HOLO: .6X TO 1.5X BASIC
*HOLO: .6X TO 1.5X BASIC
*LIME GRN/175: 1.25X TO 3X BASIC
*RED/99: 2X TO 5X BASIC
*BLUE/49: 2.5X TO 6X BASIC
1 Tracy McGrady .75 2.00
2 Alonzo Mourning .75 2.00
3 Bill Russell 1.50 4.00
4 Wilt Chamberlain 1.50 4.00
5 Rick Barry .60 1.50
6 Gary Payton .75 2.00
7 Dan Issel .60 1.50
8 Norm Nixon .30 .75
9 Bob McAdoo .60 1.50
10 Glen Rice .40 1.00
11 Jim Jackson .30 .75
12 George Gervin .75 2.00
13 Reggie Miller 1.00 2.50
14 Scottie Pippen 15.00 40.00
15 Dave DeBusschere .50 1.25
16 Dave Bing .50 1.25
17 Oscar Robertson 1.00 2.50
18 Clyde Drexler .75 2.00
19 Paul Westphal .50 1.25
20 Shaquille O'Neal 1.50 4.00
21 Shareef Abdur-Rahim .40 1.00
22 Jason Kidd .75 2.00
23 John Stockton 1.00 2.50
24 Chauncey Billups .60 1.50
25 Walt Frazier .75 2.00

2017-18 Donruss Optic Rookie Dominators Signatures

STATED PRINT RUN 49 SER. #'d SETS
1 Markelle Fultz 10.00 25.00
2 Lonzo Ball 15.00 40.00
3 Jayson Tatum 300.00 600.00
4 Jordan Bell 4.00 10.00
5 De'Aaron Fox 60.00 150.00
6 Jonathan Isaac 10.00 25.00
7 Lauri Markkanen 25.00 60.00
8 Frank Ntilikina 5.00 12.00
9 Dennis Smith Jr. 5.00 12.00
10 Zach Collins 6.00 15.00
11 Malik Monk 15.00 40.00
12 Luke Kennard 8.00 20.00
13 Donovan Mitchell 150.00 400.00
14 Bam Adebayo 75.00 200.00
15 Justin Jackson 4.00 10.00
16 Justin Patton 4.00 10.00
17 D.J. Wilson 4.00 10.00
18 TJ Leaf 4.00 10.00
19 John Collins 10.00 25.00
20 Frank Mason III 4.00 10.00
21 Terrance Ferguson 4.00 10.00
22 Jarrett Allen 10.00 25.00
23 OG Anunoby 20.00 50.00
24 Dwayne Bacon 4.00 10.00
25 Frank Jackson 4.00 10.00
26 Davon Reed 4.00 10.00
27 Kyle Kuzma 15.00 40.00
28 Tony Bradley 4.00 10.00
29 Derrick White 15.00 40.00
30 Josh Hart 10.00 25.00

2017-18 Donruss Optic Rookie Kings

COMPLETE SET (30) 20.00 50.00
*HOLO: .75X TO 2X BASIC
*PURPLE: .75X TO 2X BASIC
*LIME GRN/149: 1.25X TO 3X BASIC
*BLUE/85: 2X TO 5X BASIC
*AQUA/25: 5X TO 12X BASIC
*PINK/25: 5X TO 12X BASIC
1 Markelle Fultz 1.25 3.00
2 Lonzo Ball 2.00 5.00
3 Jayson Tatum 12.00 30.00
4 Josh Jackson .60 1.50
5 De'Aaron Fox 4.00 10.00
6 Jonathan Isaac 1.25 3.00
7 Ivan Rabb .50 1.25
8 Frank Ntilikina .60 1.50
9 Dennis Smith Jr. .60 1.50

) Zach Collins .75 2.00
Malik Monk 2.00 5.00
2 Luke Kennard 1.00 2.50
3 Donovan Mitchell 5.00 12.00
4 Bam Adebayo 3.00 8.00
5 Caleb Swanigan .50 1.25
6 Derrick White 2.00 5.00
7 D.J. Wilson .50 1.25
8 TJ Leaf .50 1.25
9 John Collins 1.25 3.00
0 Harry Giles .50 1.25
1 Terrance Ferguson .50 1.25
2 Jarrett Allen 1.25 3.00
3 OG Anunoby 2.50 6.00
4 Wayne Selden .50 1.25
5 Kyle Kuzma 2.00 5.00
6 Josh Hart 1.25 3.00
7 Frank Jackson .50 1.25
8 Frank Mason III .50 1.25
9 Jordan Bell .50 1.25
0 Dwayne Bacon .50 1.25

2017-18 Donruss Optic Rookie Kings Purple

PURPLE: .75X TO 2X BASIC

2017-18 Donruss Optic Signature Series

HOLO: .6X TO 1.5X
PURPLE: .6X TO 1.5X
Abdel Nader 3.00 8.00
Alec Peters 2.50 6.00
Ante Zizic 3.00 8.00
Bogdan Bogdanovic 6.00 15.00
Edmond Sumner 4.00 10.00
Guerschon Yabusele 2.50 6.00
0 Ike Anigbogu 2.50 6.00
1 Kadeem Allen 2.50 6.00
2 Thomas Bryant 10.00 25.00
3 Treveon Graham 3.00 8.00
5 Zhou Qi 30.00 80.00
6 Lonzo Ball 20.00 50.00
7 Markelle Fultz 20.00 50.00
8 Jayson Tatum 125.00 300.00
9 Dennis Smith Jr. 3.00 8.00
20 Amir Johnson 2.50 6.00
21 Caris LeVert 4.00 10.00
22 Ish Smith 2.50 6.00
23 Chris McCullough 2.50 6.00
24 Clint Capela 3.00 8.00
25 D.J. Augustin 2.50 6.00
26 Dakari Johnson 2.50 6.00
27 D'Angelo Russell 3.00 8.00
28 Daniel Hamilton 2.50 6.00
29 Dwight Buycks 2.50 6.00
30 Dwight Powell 2.50 6.00
31 Evan Turner 2.50 6.00
32 Ian Clark 2.50 6.00
33 John Henson 2.50 6.00
34 Josh Huestis 2.50 6.00
35 Kelly Oubre Jr. 4.00 10.00
36 Luis Montero 2.50 6.00
37 Manu Ginobili 15.00 40.00
38 Marcus Paige 2.50 6.00
39 Marvin Williams 2.50 6.00
40 Matthew Dellavedova 3.00 8.00
41 Mike Muscala 2.50 6.00
42 Raul Neto 2.50 6.00
43 Sheldon Mac 2.50 6.00
44 Spencer Dinwiddie 3.00 8.00
45 Taurean Prince 2.50 6.00
46 Timothe Luwawu-Cabarrot 2.50 6.00
47 Troy Daniels 2.50 6.00
48 Willie Cauley-Stein 2.50 6.00
49 Kevin Durant 60.00 150.00
50 Artis Gilmore 5.00 12.00
51 Bernard King 5.00 12.00
52 Clyde Drexler 15.00 40.00
53 Magic Johnson 50.00 120.00
54 Reggie Miller 50.00 120.00
55 Ronny Turiaf 2.50 6.00
56 Rick Fox 3.00 8.00
57 Caron Butler 3.00 8.00
58 Damon Jones 2.50 6.00
59 Maurice Taylor 2.50 6.00
60 Mario Elie 2.50 6.00
61 Tree Rollins 2.50 6.00
62 Ricky Pierce 3.00 8.00
63 Terry Dehere 2.50 6.00
64 Byron Scott 4.00 10.00
65 James Posey 2.50 6.00
66 Dana Barros 2.50 6.00
67 Tom Gugliotta 2.50 6.00
68 Jared Jeffries 2.50 6.00
69 Bobby Jones 4.00 10.00
70 Kenny "Sky" Walker 2.50 6.00
71 Michael Cage 3.00 8.00
72 Chucky Brown 2.50 6.00
73 Keith Van Horn 3.00 8.00
74 Brian Grant 2.50 6.00
75 Kurt Thomas 2.50 6.00
76 Walter McCarty 2.50 6.00
77 Cazzie Russell 4.00 10.00
78 Marques Johnson 3.00 8.00
79 Bill Laimbeer 8.00 20.00
80 Tom Chambers 4.00 10.00
81 Junior Bridgeman 3.00 8.00
82 B.J. Armstrong 4.00 10.00
83 Larry Hughes 3.00 8.00
84 Stephen Jackson 3.00 8.00
85 Derek Harper 3.00 8.00
86 Bob Dandridge 4.00 10.00
87 Kobe Bryant 400.00 800.00
88 Lauri Markkanen 30.00 80.00
89 Tyrone Wallace 2.50 6.00
90 Frank Mason III 2.50 6.00
91 Matt Costello 3.00 8.00
92 David Nwaba 2.50 6.00
93 Tyler Cavanaugh 2.50 6.00
94 Brandon Paul 2.50 6.00
95 Alex Caruso 25.00 60.00
96 Ryan Arcidiacono 4.00 10.00
97 Royce O'Neale 3.00 8.00
98 Maxi Kleber 4.00 10.00
99 Semi Ojeleye 3.00 8.00
100 Alfonzo McKinnie 4.00 10.00

2017-18 Donruss Optic Signature Series Blue

*BLUE: 1X TO 2.5X
STATED PRINT RUN 25 SER. #'D SETS
18 Jayson Tatum 500.00 1,000.00
49 Kevin Durant 200.00 500.00

2017-18 Donruss Optic Signature Series Holo

*HOLO: .6X TO 1.5X

2017-18 Donruss Optic Signature Series Pink

*PINK: 1X TO 2.5X
STATED PRINT RUN 25 SER. #'D SETS
18 Jayson Tatum 500.00 1,000.00
49 Kevin Durant 200.00 500.00

2017-18 Donruss Optic Signature Series Purple

*PURPLE: .6X TO 1.5X

2017-18 Donruss Optic Swishful Thinking

COMPLETE SET (10) 10.00 25.00
*HOLO: 1.5X TO 4X BASIC
*FB HOLO: 1.5X TO 4X BASIC
*LIME GRN/175: 2.5X TO 6X BASIC
*RED/99: 3X TO 8X BASIC
*BLUE/49: 4X TO 10X BASIC
1 Klay Thompson 1.25 3.00
2 Kevin Durant 2.00 5.00
3 Devin Booker 1.25 3.00
4 Russell Westbrook .75 2.00
5 James Harden 1.00 2.50
6 Giannis Antetokounmpo 2.50 6.00
7 Stephen Curry 4.00 10.00
8 Kemba Walker .40 1.00
9 Kyle Lowry .50 1.25
10 Kristaps Porzingis .60 1.50

2017-18 Donruss Optic The Champ is Here

COMPLETE SET (15) 12.00 30.00
*HOLO: .6X TO 1.5X BASIC
*FB HOLO: .6X TO 1.5X BASIC
*LIME GRN/175: 1.25X TO 3X BASIC
*RED/99: 2X TO 5X BASIC
*BLUE/49: 2.5X TO 6X BASIC
1 Kevin Durant 2.50 6.00
2 Kyrie Irving 1.25 3.00
3 David Robinson 1.25 3.00
4 Dennis Rodman 1.50 4.00
5 Stephen Curry 5.00 12.00
6 Kobe Bryant 5.00 12.00
7 Shaquille O'Neal 2.00 5.00
8 Dwyane Wade 1.25 3.00
9 Jason Kidd 1.00 2.50
10 Peja Stojakovic .50 1.25
11 Tim Duncan 1.50 4.00
12 Robert Horry .60 1.50
13 Ray Allen 1.00 2.50
14 David West .50 1.25
15 Shawn Marion .50 1.25

2017-18 Donruss Optic The Rookies

COMPLETE SET (5) 10.00 25.00
1 Markelle Fultz 1.25 3.00
2 Lonzo Ball 2.00 5.00
3 Jayson Tatum 15.00 40.00
4 Josh Jackson .60 1.50
5 De'Aaron Fox 4.00 10.00

2017-18 Donruss Optic The Rookies Blue

*BLUE: 2.5X TO 6X BASIC
STATED PRINT RUN 49 SER. #'D SETS
3 Jayson Tatum 150.00 400.00

2017-18 Donruss Optic The Rookies Fast Break Holo

*FB HOLO: .75X TO 2X BASIC
1 Markelle Fultz 2.50 6.00
2 Lonzo Ball 4.00 10.00
3 Jayson Tatum 50.00 120.00
4 Josh Jackson 1.25 3.00
5 De'Aaron Fox 8.00 20.00

2017-18 Donruss Optic The Rookies Holo

*HOLO: .75X TO 2X BASIC
1 Markelle Fultz 2.50 6.00
2 Lonzo Ball 4.00 10.00
3 Jayson Tatum 50.00 120.00
4 Josh Jackson 1.25 3.00
5 De'Aaron Fox 8.00 20.00

2017-18 Donruss Optic The Rookies Lime Green

*LIME GRN: 1.25X TO 3X BASIC
STATED PRINT RUN 175 SER. #'D SETS
3 Jayson Tatum 75.00 200.00

2017-18 Donruss Optic The Rookies Red

*RED: 2X TO 5X BASIC
STATED PRINT RUN 99 SER. #'D SETS
3 Jayson Tatum 125.00 300.00

2018-19 Donruss Optic

COMPLETE SET (200) 150.00 400.00
1 Damian Lillard 1.00 2.50
2 Stephen Curry 3.00 8.00
3 Kyle Lowry .40 1.00
4 Patrick Beverley .25 .60
5 Goran Dragic .30 .75
6 Dennis Schroder .30 .75
7 Elfrid Payton .30 .75
8 Kemba Walker .30 .75
9 D.J. Augustin .25 .60
10 Dennis Smith Jr. .25 .60
11 CJ McCollum .40 1.00
12 Klay Thompson 1.00 2.50
13 DeMar DeRozan .50 1.25
14 Lou Williams .30 .75
15 Dwyane Wade .75 2.00
16 Jeremy Lin .60 1.50
17 Jrue Holiday .50 1.25
18 Nicolas Batum .25 .60
19 Evan Fournier .30 .75
20 Wesley Matthews .25 .60
21 Evan Turner .25 .60
22 Kevin Durant 1.50 4.00
23 OG Anunoby .40 1.00
24 Avery Bradley .25 .60
25 James Johnson .25 .60
26 Taurean Prince .25 .60
27 Nikola Mirotic .25 .60
28 Malik Monk .40 1.00
29 Terrence Ross .30 .75
30 Harrison Barnes .30 .75
31 Zach Collins .30 .75
32 Draymond Green .50 1.25
33 Serge Ibaka .30 .75
34 Tobias Harris .30 .75
35 Dion Waiters .25 .60
36 John Collins .40 1.00
37 Julius Randle .40 1.00
38 Michael Kidd-Gilchrist .25 .60
39 Aaron Gordon .40 1.00
40 Dirk Nowitzki 1.00 2.50
41 Jusuf Nurkic .30 .75
42 DeMarcus Cousins .30 .75
43 Jonas Valanciunas .40 1.00
44 Marcin Gortat .25 .60
45 Hassan Whiteside .30 .75
46 Dewayne Dedmon .25 .60
47 Anthony Davis 1.00 2.50
48 Tony Parker .60 1.50
49 Nikola Vucevic .30 .75
50 DeAndre Jordan .30 .75
51 De'Aaron Fox .75 2.00
52 Chris Paul .75 2.00
53 Ricky Rubio .30 .75
54 Lonzo Ball .40 1.00
55 Eric Bledsoe .30 .75
56 Kyrie Irving 1.00 2.50
57 Frank Ntilikina .25 .60
58 Kris Dunn .25 .60
59 Ben Simmons .40 1.00
60 Jamal Murray .75 2.00
61 Bogdan Bogdanovic .40 1.00
62 Clint Capela .30 .75
63 Donovan Mitchell 1.25 3.00
64 Brandon Ingram .40 1.00
65 Malcolm Brogdon .40 1.00
66 Jaylen Brown .60 1.50
67 Tim Hardaway Jr. .25 .60
68 Zach LaVine .60 1.50
69 Markelle Fultz .30 .75
70 Gary Harris .30 .75
71 Buddy Hield .40 1.00
72 James Harden .75 2.00
73 Joe Ingles .30 .75
74 Rajon Rondo .50 1.25
75 Khris Middleton .40 1.00
76 Jayson Tatum 1.50 4.00
77 Mario Hezonja .25 .60
78 Denzel Valentine .25 .60
79 JJ Redick .40 1.00
80 Will Barton .25 .60
81 Zach Randolph .30 .75
82 Ryan Anderson .25 .60
83 Derrick Favors .25 .60
84 Kyle Kuzma .40 1.00
85 Giannis Antetokounmpo 2.00 5.00
86 Gordon Hayward .40 1.00
87 Kristaps Porzingis .50 1.25
88 Lauri Markkanen .60 1.50
89 Dario Saric .30 .75
90 Paul Millsap .30 .75
91 Willie Cauley-Stein .25 .60
92 Eric Gordon .30 .75
93 Rudy Gobert .50 1.25
94 LeBron James 3.00 8.00
95 Matthew Dellavedova .30 .75
96 Al Horford .40 1.00
97 Enes Kanter .30 .75
98 Robin Lopez .25 .60
99 Joel Embiid 1.00 2.50
100 Nikola Jokic 2.00 5.00
101 Rudy Gay .40 1.00
102 Tyreke Evans .25 .60
103 John Wall .50 1.25
104 Mike Conley .30 .75
105 Jeff Teague .25 .60
106 Spencer Dinwiddie .30 .75
107 Russell Westbrook .60 1.50
108 George Hill .30 .75
109 Brandon Knight .25 .60
110 Reggie Jackson .30 .75
111 Danny Green .30 .75
112 Victor Oladipo .30 .75
113 Bradley Beal .30 .75
114 MarShon Brooks .25 .60
115 Jimmy Butler .60 1.50
116 D'Angelo Russell .50 1.25
117 Paul George .60 1.50
118 JR Smith .40 1.00
119 Devin Booker 1.00 2.50
120 Luke Kennard .40 1.00
121 Kawhi Leonard 1.00 2.50
122 Bojan Bogdanovic .30 .75
123 Otto Porter Jr. .30 .75
124 Dillon Brooks .40 1.00
125 Derrick Rose .75 2.00
126 DeMarre Carroll .25 .60
127 Carmelo Anthony .60 1.50
128 Kyle Korver .50 1.25
129 T.J. Warren .40 1.00
130 Stanley Johnson .25 .60
131 LaMarcus Aldridge .50 1.25
132 Thaddeus Young .25 .60
133 Jeff Green .25 .60
134 JaMychal Green .25 .60
135 Andrew Wiggins .50 1.25
136 Rondae Hollis-Jefferson .25 .60
137 Steven Adams .30 .75
138 Kevin Love .50 1.25
139 Josh Jackson .25 .60
140 Blake Griffin .60 1.50
141 Pau Gasol .60 1.50
142 Myles Turner .50 1.25
143 Dwight Howard .50 1.25
144 Marc Gasol .40 1.00
145 Karl-Anthony Towns .60 1.50
146 Jarrett Allen .40 1.00
147 Nerlens Noel .25 .60
148 Tristan Thompson .25 .60
149 Trevor Ariza .25 .60
150 Andre Drummond .30 .75
151 Jarred Vanderbilt RR RC 1.00 2.50
152 Jerome Robinson RR RC .50 1.25
153 Melvin Frazier Jr. RR RC .50 1.25
154 Zhaire Smith RR RC .50 1.25
155 Rodions Kurucs RR RC .60 1.50
156 Grayson Allen RR RC 1.00 2.50
157 Deandre Ayton RR RC 1.50 4.00
158 Landry Shamet RR RC .75 2.00
159 Elie Okobo RR RC .50 1.25
160 Mo Bamba RR RC .75 2.00
161 Bruce Brown RR RC .75 2.00
162 Shai Gilgeous-Alexander RR RC 12.00 30.00
163 Mitchell Robinson RR RC 1.25 3.00
164 Donte DiVincenzo RR RC 1.25 3.00
165 Vincent Edwards RR RC .50 1.25
166 Chandler Hutchison RR RC .60 1.50
167 Robert Williams III RR RC 1.00 2.50
168 Marvin Bagley III RR RC .75 2.00
169 Jevon Carter RR RC .75 2.00
170 Wendell Carter Jr. RR RC 1.25 3.00
171 Hamidou Diallo RR RC .75 2.00
172 Miles Bridges RR RC 1.25 3.00
173 Khyri Thomas RR RC .50 1.25
174 Lonnie Walker IV RR RC 1.00 2.50
175 Allonzo Trier RR RC .50 1.25
176 Aaron Holiday RR RC .75 2.00
177 Luka Doncic RR RC 25.00 60.00
178 Jacob Evans III RR RC .50 1.25
179 Jalen Brunson RR RC 4.00 10.00
180 Collin Sexton RR RC 1.50 4.00
181 De'Anthony Melton RR RC 1.00 2.50
182 Michael Porter Jr. RR RC 2.00 5.00
183 Justin Jackson RR RC .50 1.25
184 Kevin Huerter RR RC 1.00 2.50
185 Kostas Antetokounmpo RR RC .60 1.50
186 Anfernee Simons RR RC 2.50 6.00
187 Dzanan Musa RR RC .50 1.25
188 Jaren Jackson Jr. RR RC 4.00 10.00
189 Devonte' Graham RR RC .75 2.00
190 Kevin Knox RR RC .60 1.50
191 Keita Bates-Diop RR RC .60 1.50
192 Troy Brown Jr. RR RC .60 1.50
193 Svi Mykhailiuk RR RC .60 1.50
194 Josh Okogie RR RC .75 2.00
195 Chimezie Metu RR RC .60 1.50
196 Omari Spellman RR RC .50 1.25
197 Moritz Wagner RR RC 1.00 2.50
198 Trae Young RR RC 4.00 10.00
199 Gary Trent Jr. RR RC 1.00 2.50
200 Mikal Bridges RR RC 2.50 6.00

2018-19 Donruss Optic Black Velocity

*BLK VEL: 5X TO 15X BASIC
*BLK VEL RC: 6X TO 15X BASIC RC
STATED PRINT RUN 39 SER. #'D SETS
2 Stephen Curry 125.00 300.00
94 LeBron James 200.00 500.00
162 Shai Gilgeous-Alexander RR 1,000.00 2,000.00
177 Luka Doncic RR 2,500.00 5,000.00
179 Jalen Brunson RR 150.00 400.00
198 Trae Young RR 200.00 500.00

2018-19 Donruss Optic Blue

*BLUE: 2.5X TO 6X BASIC
*BLUE RC: 3X TO 8X BASIC RC
STATED PRINT RUN 49 SER. #'D SETS
2 Stephen Curry 50.00 120.00
94 LeBron James 100.00 250.00
162 Shai Gilgeous-Alexander RR 400.00 800.00
172 Miles Bridges RR 40.00 100.00
177 Luka Doncic RR 2,000.00 4,000.00
180 Collin Sexton RR 150.00 400.00
182 Michael Porter Jr. RR 200.00 500.00
188 Jaren Jackson Jr. RR 60.00 150.00
198 Trae Young RR 400.00 800.00

2018-19 Donruss Optic Blue Velocity

*BLUE VEL: 1X TO 2.5X BASIC
*BLUE VEL RC: 1X TO 2.5X BASIC RC
162 Shai Gilgeous-Alexander RR 50.00 120.00
177 Luka Doncic RR 125.00 300.00

2018-19 Donruss Optic Holo

*HOLO: 1.25X TO 3X BASIC
*HOLO RC: 1.25X TO 3X BASIC RC
162 Shai Gilgeous-Alexander RR 100.00 250.00
177 Luka Doncic RR 150.00 400.00
179 Jalen Brunson RR 15.00 40.00
198 Trae Young RR 20.00 50.00

2018-19 Donruss Optic Hyper Pink

*HYPER PINK: .75X TO 2X BASIC
*HYPER PINK RC: .75X TO 2X BASIC RC
94 LeBron James 12.00 30.00
162 Shai Gilgeous-Alexander RR 50.00 120.00
177 Luka Doncic RR 125.00 300.00

2018-19 Donruss Optic Lime Green

*LIME GRN: 1.5X TO 4X BASIC
*LIME GRN RC: 1.5X TO 4X BASIC RC
STATED PRINT RUN 149 SER. #'D SETS
2 Stephen Curry 40.00 100.00
94 LeBron James 60.00 150.00
162 Shai Gilgeous-Alexander RR 150.00 400.00
177 Luka Doncic RR 600.00 1,200.00
180 Collin Sexton RR 20.00 50.00
182 Michael Porter Jr. RR 25.00 60.00
186 Anfernee Simons RR 20.00 50.00
188 Jaren Jackson Jr. RR 20.00 50.00
198 Trae Young RR 125.00 300.00

2018-19 Donruss Optic Orange

*ORANGE: 1.5X TO 4X BASIC
*ORANGE RC: 1.5X TO 4X BASIC RC
STATED PRINT RUN 199 SER. #'D SETS
2 Stephen Curry 30.00 80.00
94 LeBron James 60.00 150.00
162 Shai Gilgeous-Alexander RR 125.00 300.00
177 Luka Doncic RR 500.00 1,000.00
180 Collin Sexton RR 15.00 40.00
182 Michael Porter Jr. RR 25.00 60.00
186 Anfernee Simons RR 20.00 50.00
188 Jaren Jackson Jr. RR 20.00 50.00
198 Trae Young RR 125.00 300.00

2018-19 Donruss Optic Pink

*PINK: 4X TO 10X BASIC
*PINK RC: 5X TO 12X BASIC RC
STATED PRINT RUN 125 SER. #'D SETS
2 Stephen Curry 20.00 50.00
85 Giannis Antetokounmpo 60.00 150.00
94 LeBron James 600.00 1,200.00
157 Deandre Ayton RR 50.00 120.00
160 Mo Bamba RR 12.00 30.00
162 Shai Gilgeous-Alexander RR 1,000.00 2,000.00
168 Marvin Bagley III RR 60.00 150.00
172 Miles Bridges RR 150.00 400.00
174 Lonnie Walker IV RR 15.00 40.00
177 Luka Doncic RR 3,000.00 6,000.00
180 Collin Sexton RR 300.00 600.00
182 Michael Porter Jr. RR 400.00 800.00
184 Kevin Huerter RR 12.00 30.00
188 Jaren Jackson Jr. RR 50.00 120.00
198 Trae Young RR 300.00 600.00

2018-19 Donruss Optic Pink Velocity

*PINK VEL: 2X TO 5X BASIC
*PINK VEL RC: 2.5X TO 6X BASIC RC
STATED PRINT RUN 79 SER. #'D SETS
85 Giannis Antetokounmpo 60.00 150.00
94 LeBron James 400.00 800.00
162 Shai Gilgeous-Alexander RR 300.00 600.00
168 Marvin Bagley III RR 12.00 30.00
172 Miles Bridges RR 60.00 150.00
177 Luka Doncic RR 1,000.00 2,000.00
180 Collin Sexton RR 100.00 250.00
182 Michael Porter Jr. RR 150.00 400.00
188 Jaren Jackson Jr. RR 10.00 25.00
198 Trae Young RR 125.00 300.00

2018-19 Donruss Optic Purple

*PURPLE: 1X TO 2.5X BASIC
*PURPLE RC: 1X TO 2.5X BASIC RC
162 Shai Gilgeous-Alexander RR 50.00 120.00
177 Luka Doncic RR 125.00 300.00

2018-19 Donruss Optic Red

*RED: 2X TO 5X BASIC
*RED RC: 2X TO 5X BASIC RC
STATED PRINT RUN 99 SER. #'D SETS
2 Stephen Curry 50.00 120.00
94 LeBron James 75.00 200.00
162 Shai Gilgeous-Alexander RR 200.00 500.00
177 Luka Doncic RR 800.00 1,500.00
182 Michael Porter Jr. RR 30.00 80.00
186 Anfernee Simons RR 30.00 80.00
188 Jaren Jackson Jr. RR 25.00 60.00
198 Trae Young RR 200.00 500.00

2018-19 Donruss Optic Shock

*SHOCK RC: .75X TO 2X BASIC RC
162 Shai Gilgeous-Alexander RR 50.00 120.00
177 Luka Doncic RR 60.00 150.00

2018-19 Donruss Optic All Clear for Takeoff

COMPLETE SET (15) 6.00 15.00
1 LeBron James 4.00 10.00
2 Victor Oladipo .40 1.00
3 Dominique Wilkins .75 2.00
4 Larry Nance Jr. .30 .75
5 Zach LaVine .75 2.00
6 Russell Westbrook .75 2.00
7 Spud Webb .50 1.25
8 Dwight Howard .60 1.50
9 Shawn Kemp .75 2.00
10 Tracy McGrady .75 2.00
11 Blake Griffin .50 1.25
12 Donovan Mitchell 1.50 4.00
13 Julius Erving 1.25 3.00
14 Dennis Smith Jr. .30 .75
15 Kobe Bryant 4.00 10.00

2018-19 Donruss Optic All Clear for Takeoff Blue

*BLUE: 2X TO 5X BASIC
STATED PRINT RUN 49 SER. #'D SETS
1 LeBron James 50.00 120.00
15 Kobe Bryant 40.00 100.00

2018-19 Donruss Optic All Clear for Takeoff Fast Break Holo

*FB HOLO: .75X TO 2X BASIC
1 LeBron James 20.00 50.00
15 Kobe Bryant 15.00 40.00

2018-19 Donruss Optic All Clear for Takeoff Holo

*HOLO: .75X TO 2X BASIC
1 LeBron James 20.00 50.00
15 Kobe Bryant 15.00 40.00

2018-19 Donruss Optic All Clear for Takeoff Red

*RED: 1.5X TO 4X BASIC
STATED PRINT RUN 99 SER. #'D SETS
1 LeBron James 40.00 100.00
15 Kobe Bryant 30.00 80.00

2018-19 Donruss Optic All Heart

COMPLETE SET (20) 10.00 25.00
*HOLO: .6X TO 1.5X BASIC
*FB HOLO: .6X TO 1.5X BASIC
1 Allen Iverson 1.25 3.00
2 Jimmy Butler .75 2.00
3 Dwyane Wade 1.00 2.50
4 Giannis Antetokounmpo 2.50 6.00
5 Kevin Durant 2.00 5.00
6 Draymond Green .60 1.50
7 Paul Pierce .75 2.00
8 James Harden 1.00 2.50
9 Kevin Garnett 1.25 3.00
10 Russell Westbrook .75 2.00
11 Dirk Nowitzki 1.25 3.00
12 Andrew Wiggins .60 1.50
13 LeBron James 4.00 10.00
14 Dennis Rodman 1.25 3.00
15 Donovan Mitchell 1.50 4.00
16 Chris Paul 1.00 2.50
17 John Wall .60 1.50
18 Rudy Gay .50 1.25
19 Kobe Bryant 4.00 10.00
20 Stephen Curry 4.00 10.00

2018-19 Donruss Optic All Heart Blue

*BLUE: 2X TO 5X BASIC
STATED PRINT RUN 49 SER. #'D SETS
13 LeBron James 75.00 200.00
19 Kobe Bryant 60.00 150.00
20 Stephen Curry 50.00 120.00

2018-19 Donruss Optic All Heart Fast Break Holo

*FB HOLO: .75X TO 2X BASIC
13 LeBron James 25.00 60.00
19 Kobe Bryant 20.00 50.00
20 Stephen Curry 15.00 40.00

2018-19 Donruss Optic All Heart Holo

*HOLO: .75X TO 2X BASIC
13 LeBron James 25.00 60.00
19 Kobe Bryant 20.00 50.00
20 Stephen Curry 12.00 30.00

2018-19 Donruss Optic All Heart Red

*RED: 1.5X TO 4X BASIC
STATED PRINT RUN 99 SER. #'D SETS
13 LeBron James 60.00 150.00
19 Kobe Bryant 50.00 120.00
20 Stephen Curry 40.00 100.00

2018-19 Donruss Optic All Stars

COMPLETE SET (20) 12.00 30.00
1 LeBron James 4.00 10.00
2 Kevin Durant 2.00 5.00
3 Russell Westbrook .75 2.00
4 Kyrie Irving 1.25 3.00
5 Anthony Davis 1.25 3.00
6 Paul George .75 2.00
7 Andre Drummond .40 1.00
8 Bradley Beal .60 1.50
9 Victor Oladipo .40 1.00
10 Kemba Walker .40 1.00
11 James Harden 1.00 2.50
12 DeMar DeRozan .60 1.50
13 Stephen Curry 4.00 10.00
14 Giannis Antetokounmpo 2.50 6.00
15 Joel Embiid 1.25 3.00
16 Kyle Lowry .50 1.25
17 Klay Thompson 1.25 3.00
18 Damian Lillard 1.25 3.00
19 Draymond Green .60 1.50
20 Karl-Anthony Towns .75 2.00

2018-19 Donruss Optic All Stars Blue

*BLUE: 2X TO 5X BASIC
STATED PRINT RUN 49 SER. #'D SETS
1 LeBron James 50.00 120.00
13 Stephen Curry 50.00 120.00

2018-19 Donruss Optic All Stars Fast Break Holo

*FB HOLO: .75X TO 2X BASIC
1 LeBron James 15.00 40.00
13 Stephen Curry 15.00 40.00

2018-19 Donruss Optic All Stars Holo

*HOLO: .75X TO 2X BASIC
1 LeBron James 15.00 40.00
13 Stephen Curry 15.00 40.00

2018-19 Donruss Optic All Stars Red

*RED: 1.5X TO 4X BASIC
STATED PRINT RUN 99 SER. #'D SETS
1 LeBron James 30.00 80.00
13 Stephen Curry 30.00 80.00

2018-19 Donruss Optic Choice

*CHOICE RC: 1.2X TO 3X BASIC RC
162 Shai Gilgeous-Alexander RR 75.00 200.00
177 Luka Doncic RR 150.00 400.00

2018-19 Donruss Optic Choice Red

*CH.RED: 2X TO 5X BASIC
*CH.RED RC: 2X TO 5X BASIC RC
STATED PRINT RUN 88 SER. #'D SETS
2 Stephen Curry 50.00 120.00
94 LeBron James 75.00 200.00
162 Shai Gilgeous-Alexander RR 300.00 600.00
177 Luka Doncic RR 800.00 1,500.00
180 Collin Sexton RR 25.00 60.00
182 Michael Porter Jr. RR 30.00 80.00
186 Anfernee Simons RR 30.00 80.00
188 Jaren Jackson Jr. RR 25.00 60.00
198 Trae Young RR 150.00 400.00

2018-19 Donruss Optic Dominator Signatures

PRINT RUNS B/WN 25-60 COPIES PER
EXCHANGE DEADLINE 7/30/2020
1 Aaron Gordon/45 6.00 15.00
2 Stephen Curry/25 600.00 1,200.00
3 Avery Bradley/45 4.00 10.00
4 Kyrie Irving/25 30.00 80.00
5 Clint Capela/60 5.00 12.00
6 Kawhi Leonard/25 75.00 200.00
7 Nerlens Noel/60 4.00 10.00
8 Marc Gasol/45 6.00 15.00
9 Danny Green/60 5.00 12.00
10 Buddy Hield/45 6.00 15.00
11 Eric Gordon/45 5.00 12.00
12 Dwyane Wade/25 40.00 100.00
13 JJ Redick/45 12.00 30.00
14 Dirk Nowitzki/25 75.00 200.00
15 Elfrid Payton/60 5.00 12.00
16 Giannis Antetokounmpo/25 150.00 400.00
17 Trevor Ariza/60 4.00 10.00
18 Jeremy Lin/45 75.00 200.00
19 Malcolm Brogdon/60 6.00 15.00
20 Brook Lopez/45 5.00 12.00
21 Goran Dragic/45 5.00 12.00
22 Chris Paul/25 50.00 120.00
23 Reggie Jackson/60 5.00 12.00
25 Jrue Holiday/60 8.00 20.00
26 Karl-Anthony Towns/25 20.00 50.00
27 JR Smith/60 6.00 15.00
29 Thon Maker/60 4.00 10.00
30 Rodney Hood/45 5.00 12.00
31 Eric Bledsoe/45 5.00 12.00
32 Damian Lillard/50 75.00 200.00
33 Michael Kidd-Gilchrist/60 4.00 10.00
34 Blake Griffin/25 12.00 30.00
35 Myles Turner/60 6.00 15.00
36 Joel Embiid/25 75.00 200.00
37 Kyle Korver/60 5.00 12.00
38 Gordon Hayward/45 6.00 15.00
39 Gerald Green/60 5.00 12.00
40 Al Horford/45 6.00 15.00

2018-19 Donruss Optic Express Lane

COMPLETE SET (25) 15.00 40.00
*HOLO: .75X TO 2X BASIC
*PURPLE: .75X TO 2X BASIC
*LIME GREEN/149: 1.25X TO 3X BASIC
*BLUE/85: 2X TO 5X BASIC
*ORANGE/39: 3X TO 8X BASIC
*PINK/25: 4X TO 10X BASIC
1 Jrue Holiday .60 1.50
2 Isiah Thomas .75 2.00
3 Ben Simmons .50 1.25
4 LeBron James 4.00 10.00
5 Kobe Bryant 4.00 10.00
6 Russell Westbrook .75 2.00
7 Lonzo Ball .50 1.25
8 CJ McCollum .50 1.25
9 Brandon Ingram .50 1.25
10 Chris Paul 1.00 2.50
11 Harrison Barnes .40 1.00
12 Allen Iverson 1.25 3.00
13 Victor Oladipo .40 1.00
14 Dwyane Wade 1.00 2.50
15 Bradley Beal .60 1.50
16 Isaiah Thomas .40 1.00
17 Devin Booker 1.25 3.00
18 Stephen Curry 4.00 10.00
19 Damian Lillard 1.25 3.00
20 Kevin Johnson .50 1.25
21 Jimmy Butler .75 2.00
22 Tony Parker .75 2.00
23 Giannis Antetokounmpo 2.50 6.00
24 Gary Payton .60 1.50
25 Klay Thompson 1.25 3.00

2018-19 Donruss Optic Express Lane Pink

*PINK: 4X TO 10X BASIC
STATED PRINT RUN 25 SER. #'D SETS

2018-19 Donruss Optic Fantasy Stars

COMPLETE SET (5) 3.00 8.00
*HOLO: .75X TO 2X BASIC
*PURPLE: .75X TO 2X BASIC
*LIME GREEN/149: 1.25X TO 3X BASIC
*BLUE/85: 2X TO 5X BASIC
*ORANGE/39: 3X TO 8X BASIC
*PINK/25: 4X TO 10X BASIC
1 Anthony Davis 1.25 3.00
2 LeBron James 4.00 10.00
3 James Harden 1.00 2.50
4 Karl-Anthony Towns .75 2.00
5 Kevin Durant 2.00 5.00

2018-19 Donruss Optic Fantasy Stars Orange

*ORANGE: 3X TO 8X BASIC
STATED PRINT RUN 39 SER. #'D SETS

2018-19 Donruss Optic Fast Break Blue

2017-18 Donruss Optic Fast Break Blue
2017-18 Donruss Optic Fast Break Blue
2017-18 Donruss Optic Fast Break Blue
2017-18 Donruss Optic Fast Break Blue
2 Stephen Curry 50.00 120.00
94 LeBron James 100.00 250.00
162 Shai Gilgeous-Alexander RR 25.00 60.00
172 Miles Bridges RR 40.00 100.00
177 Luka Doncic RR 2,000.00 4,000.00
182 Michael Porter Jr. RR 25.00 60.00
188 Jaren Jackson Jr. RR 20.00 50.00
198 Trae Young RR 75.00 200.00

2018-19 Donruss Optic Fast Break Holo

*FB HOLO: 1.2X TO 3X BASIC
*FB HOLO RC: 1.2X TO 3X BASIC RC
85 Giannis Antetokounmpo 12.00 30.00
94 LeBron James 40.00 100.00
157 Deandre Ayton RR 15.00 40.00
162 Shai Gilgeous-Alexander RR 25.00 60.00
172 Miles Bridges RR 25.00 60.00
177 Luka Doncic RR 200.00 500.00
180 Collin Sexton RR 12.00 30.00
182 Michael Porter Jr. RR 25.00 60.00
198 Trae Young RR 75.00 200.00

2018-19 Donruss Optic Fast Break Pink

*FB PINK: 5X TO 12X BASIC
*PINK RC: 5X TO 12X BASIC RC
STATED PRINT RUN 20 SER. #'D SETS
2 Stephen Curry 25.00 60.00
85 Giannis Antetokounmpo 60.00 150.00
94 LeBron James 800.00 1,500.00
157 Deandre Ayton RR 60.00 150.00
160 Mo Bamba RR 15.00 40.00
162 Shai Gilgeous-Alexander RR 50.00 120.00
168 Marvin Bagley III RR 75.00 200.00
172 Miles Bridges RR 200.00 500.00
174 Lonnie Walker IV RR 20.00 50.00
177 Luka Doncic RR 4,000.00 8,000.00
180 Collin Sexton RR 25.00 60.00
182 Michael Porter Jr. RR 50.00 120.00
184 Kevin Huerter RR 15.00 40.00
188 Jaren Jackson Jr. RR 60.00 150.00
198 Trae Young RR 150.00 400.00

2018-19 Donruss Optic Fast Break Purple

*FB PURPLE: 2X TO 5X BASIC
*FB PURPLE RC: 2X TO 5X BASIC RC
STATED PRINT RUN 95 SER. #'D SETS
85 Giannis Antetokounmpo 20.00 50.00
94 LeBron James 400.00 800.00
162 Shai Gilgeous-Alexander RR 20.00 50.00
168 Marvin Bagley III RR 12.00 30.00
172 Miles Bridges RR 50.00 120.00
177 Luka Doncic RR 1,250.00 2,500.00
182 Michael Porter Jr. RR 10.00 25.00
188 Jaren Jackson Jr. RR 10.00 25.00
198 Trae Young RR 60.00 150.00

2018-19 Donruss Optic Fast Break Red

*FB.RED: 2X TO 5X BASIC
*FB.RED RC: 2X TO 5X BASIC RC
STATED PRINT RUN 85 SER. #'D SETS
85 Giannis Antetokounmpo 20.00 50.00
94 LeBron James 400.00 800.00
162 Shai Gilgeous-Alexander RR 20.00 50.00
168 Marvin Bagley III RR 12.00 30.00
172 Miles Bridges RR 60.00 150.00
177 Luka Doncic RR 1,500.00 3,000.00
182 Michael Porter Jr. RR 10.00 25.00
188 Jaren Jackson Jr. RR 10.00 25.00
198 Trae Young RR 60.00 150.00

2018-19 Donruss Optic Franchise Features

COMPLETE SET (30) 15.00 40.00
*HOLO: .75X TO 2X BASIC

*PURPLE: .75X TO 2X BASIC
*LIME GREEN/149: 1.25X TO 3X BASIC
*BLUE/85: 2X TO 5X BASIC
*ORANGE/39: 3X TO 8X BASIC
*PINK/25: 4X TO 10X BASIC
1 Taurean Prince .30 .75
2 Kyrie Irving 1.25 3.00
3 D'Angelo Russell .50 1.25
4 Kemba Walker .40 1.00
5 Lauri Markkanen .75 2.00
6 LeBron James 4.00 10.00
7 Dennis Smith Jr. .30 .75
8 Nikola Jokic 2.50 6.00
9 Andre Drummond .40 1.00
10 Stephen Curry 4.00 10.00
11 James Harden 1.00 2.50
12 Victor Oladipo .40 1.00
13 Lou Williams .40 1.00
14 Kevin Love .40 1.00
15 Marc Gasol .50 1.25
16 Dwyane Wade 1.00 2.50
17 Giannis Antetokounmpo 2.50 6.00
18 Karl-Anthony Towns .75 2.00
19 Anthony Davis 1.25 3.00
20 Kristaps Porzingis .60 1.50
21 Russell Westbrook .75 2.00
22 Aaron Gordon .50 1.25
23 Ben Simmons .50 1.25
24 Devin Booker 1.25 3.00
25 Damian Lillard 1.25 3.00
26 De'Aaron Fox 1.00 2.50
27 LaMarcus Aldridge .50 1.25
28 Kyle Lowry .50 1.25
29 Donovan Mitchell 1.50 4.00
30 John Wall .60 1.50

2018-19 Donruss Optic Franchise Features Pink

*PINK: 4X TO 10X BASIC
STATED PRINT RUN 25 SER.#'D SETS

2018-19 Donruss Optic Hall Dominator Signatures

STATED PRINT RUN 40 SER.#'d SETS
EXCHANGE DEADLINE 7/30/2020
1 Jamaal Wilkes 5.00 12.00
2 Willis Reed 40.00 100.00
3 David Thompson 6.00 15.00
4 Artis Gilmore 6.00 15.00
5 Elvin Hayes 6.00 15.00
6 Karl Malone 20.00 50.00
7 Lenny Wilkens 6.00 15.00
8 Julius Erving 20.00 50.00
9 Louie Dampier 5.00 12.00
10 David Robinson 12.00 30.00
11 Tom Heinsohn 10.00 25.00
12 Bob Lanier 6.00 15.00
13 Bob McAdoo 6.00 15.00
14 George Gervin 6.00 15.00
15 Robert Parish 6.00 15.00
16 John Stockton 12.00 30.00
17 Bill Walton 20.00 50.00
18 Oscar Robertson 20.00 50.00
19 Dikembe Mutombo 12.00 30.00
20 Clyde Drexler 12.00 30.00
21 Adrian Dantley 4.00 10.00
22 Sam Jones 12.00 30.00
23 Dan Issel 6.00 15.00
24 Calvin Murphy 4.00 10.00
25 Gail Goodrich 5.00 12.00
26 Magic Johnson 20.00 50.00
27 Ralph Sampson 4.00 10.00
28 Alonzo Mourning 10.00 25.00
29 George McGinnis 6.00 15.00
30 Dennis Rodman 12.00 30.00

2018-19 Donruss Optic League Leaders

COMPLETE SET (10) 5.00 12.00
*HOLO: .75X TO 2X BASIC
*PURPLE: .75X TO 2X BASIC
*LIME GREEN/149: 1.25X TO 3X BASIC
*BLUE/85: 2X TO 5X BASIC
*ORANGE/39: 3X TO 8X BASIC
*PINK/25: 4X TO 10X BASIC
1 James Harden 1.00 2.50
2 Andre Drummond .40 1.00
3 Russell Westbrook .75 2.00
4 Victor Oladipo .40 1.00
5 Anthony Davis 1.25 3.00
6 James Harden 1.00 2.50
7 Darren Collison .30 .75
8 Stephen Curry 4.00 10.00
9 LeBron James 4.00 10.00
10 Clint Capela .40 1.00

2018-19 Donruss Optic League Leaders Blue

*BLUE: 2X TO 5X BASIC
STATED PRINT RUN 85 SER. #'D SETS

2018-19 Donruss Optic League Leaders Orange

*ORANGE: 3X TO 8X BASIC
STATED PRINT RUN 39 SER. #'D SETS

2018-19 Donruss Optic League Leaders Pink

*PINK: 4X TO 10X BASIC
STATED PRINT RUN 25 SER. #'D SETS

2018-19 Donruss Optic Lock it Up

COMPLETE SET (10) 5.00 12.00
*HOLO: .75X TO 2X BASIC
*PURPLE: .75X TO 2X BASIC
*LIME GRN/149: 1.25X TO 3X BASIC
*BLUE/85: 2X TO 5X BASIC
*ORANGE/39: 3X TO 8X BASIC
*PINK/25: 4X TO 10X BASIC
1 Jimmy Butler .75 2.00
2 Victor Oladipo .40 1.00
3 Rudy Gobert .60 1.50
4 Giannis Antetokounmpo 2.50 6.00
5 Anthony Davis 1.25 3.00
6 Paul George .75 2.00
7 John Wall .60 1.50
8 Draymond Green .60 1.50
9 Chris Paul 1.00 2.50
10 Karl-Anthony Towns .75 2.00

2018-19 Donruss Optic Rated Rookies Signatures

EXCHANGE DEADLINE 7/30/2020
151 Jarred Vanderbilt 6.00 15.00
153 Melvin Frazier Jr. 3.00 8.00
154 Zhaire Smith 3.00 8.00
155 Rodions Kurucs 4.00 10.00
156 Grayson Allen 6.00 15.00
157 Deandre Ayton 40.00 100.00
158 Landry Shamet EXCH 5.00 12.00
159 Elie Okobo 3.00 8.00
160 Mo Bamba 12.00 30.00
161 Bruce Brown 6.00 15.00
162 Shai Gilgeous-Alexander 500.00 1,000.00
163 Mitchell Robinson 8.00 20.00
164 Donte DiVincenzo 12.00 30.00
166 Chandler Hutchison 4.00 10.00
168 Marvin Bagley III 5.00 12.00
169 Jevon Carter 5.00 12.00
170 Wendell Carter Jr. 8.00 20.00
172 Isaac Bonga 4.00 10.00
173 Khyri Thomas 3.00 8.00
174 Lonnie Walker IV EXCH 6.00 15.00
175 Allonzo Trier 3.00 8.00
176 Aaron Holiday 5.00 12.00
177 Luka Doncic 1,000.00 2,000.00
178 Jacob Evans III 3.00 8.00
179 Jalen Brunson 30.00 80.00
180 Collin Sexton 10.00 25.00
181 De'Anthony Melton 6.00 15.00
182 Michael Porter Jr. 40.00 100.00
183 Justin Jackson EXCH 3.00 8.00
184 Kevin Huerter 6.00 15.00
186 Anfernee Simons 50.00 120.00
187 Dzanan Musa 3.00 8.00
188 Jaren Jackson Jr. 150.00 400.00
189 Devonte' Graham 5.00 12.00
190 Kevin Knox EXCH 4.00 10.00
192 Troy Brown Jr. 4.00 10.00
193 Svi Mykhailiuk 4.00 10.00
194 Josh Okogie 8.00 20.00
195 Chimezie Metu 4.00 10.00
196 Omari Spellman 3.00 8.00
197 Moritz Wagner 6.00 15.00
198 Trae Young 400.00 800.00
199 Gary Trent Jr. 6.00 15.00
200 Mikal Bridges 30.00 80.00

2018-19 Donruss Optic Rated Rookies Signatures Blue

*BLUE: .75X TO 2X BASIC
STATED PRINT RUN 49 SER.#'d SETS
EXCHANGE DEADLINE 7/30/2020
165 Vincent Edwards 6.00 15.00
167 Robert Williams III 25.00 60.00
171 Hamidou Diallo 10.00 25.00
177 Luka Doncic 3,000.00 6,000.00

2018-19 Donruss Optic Rated Rookies Signatures Choice

*CHOICE: .6X TO 1.5X BASIC
EXCHANGE DEADLINE 7/30/2020
165 Vincent Edwards 5.00 12.00
167 Robert Williams III 20.00 50.00
171 Hamidou Diallo 8.00 20.00
177 Luka Doncic 2,500.00 5,000.00
185 Kostas Antetokounmpo EXCH 10.00 25.00
191 Keita Bates-Diop 6.00 15.00
198 Trae Young 600.00 1,200.00

2018-19 Donruss Optic Rated Rookies Signatures Fast Break

*FB: .4X TO 1X BASIC
EXCHANGE DEADLINE 7/30/2020
165 Vincent Edwards 5.00 12.00
167 Robert Williams III 20.00 50.00
171 Hamidou Diallo 8.00 20.00
177 Luka Doncic 2,500.00 5,000.00
191 Keita Bates-Diop 6.00 15.00
198 Trae Young 600.00 1,200.00

2018-19 Donruss Optic Rated Rookies Signatures Fast Break Pink

*FB PINK: 1.25X TO 3X BASIC
STATED PRINT RUN 20 SER.#'d SETS
EXCHANGE DEADLINE 7/30/2020
165 Vincent Edwards 10.00 25.00
167 Robert Williams III 40.00 100.00
171 Hamidou Diallo 15.00 40.00
177 Luka Doncic 5,000.00 10,000.00

2018-19 Donruss Optic Rated Rookies Signatures Holo

*HOLO: .4X TO 1X BASIC
EXCHANGE DEADLINE 7/30/2020
165 Vincent Edwards 5.00 12.00
167 Robert Williams III 20.00 50.00
171 Hamidou Diallo 8.00 20.00
177 Luka Doncic 2,500.00 5,000.00
188 Jaren Jackson Jr. 300.00 600.00

2018-19 Donruss Optic Rated Rookies Signatures Pink

*PINK: .75X TO 2X BASIC
STATED PRINT RUN 25 SER.#'d SETS
EXCHANGE DEADLINE 7/30/2020
162 Shai Gilgeous-Alexander 1,500.00 3,000.00
177 Luka Doncic 5,000.00 10,000.00

2018-19 Donruss Optic Rated Rookies Signatures Purple

*PURPLE: .5X TO 1.2X BASIC
EXCHANGE DEADLINE 7/30/2020
177 Luka Doncic 2,000.00 4,000.00
198 Trae Young 800.00 1,500.00

2018-19 Donruss Optic Retro Series

COMPLETE SET (30) 12.00 30.00
*HOLO: .6X TO 1.5X BASIC
*FB HOLO: .6X TO 1.5X BASIC
*RED/99: .75X TO 2X BASIC
*BLUE/49: 1X TO 2.5X BASIC
1 Baron Davis .30 .75
2 Paul Pierce .60 1.50
3 Kevin Garnett 1.00 2.50
4 John Stockton .75 2.00
5 Allen Iverson 1.00 2.50
6 Amar'e Stoudemire .40 1.00
7 Larry Bird 1.50 4.00
8 Stephon Marbury .50 1.25
9 Ray Allen .50 1.25
10 Shaquille O'Neal 1.25 3.00
11 Tim Duncan 1.00 2.50
12 Scottie Pippen 1.00 2.50
13 Anfernee Hardaway 1.00 2.50
14 Karl Malone .75 2.00
15 Dennis Johnson .40 1.00
16 Charles Barkley .75 2.00
17 Oscar Robertson .75 2.00
18 Tracy McGrady .60 1.50
19 Manute Bol .40 1.00
20 Gary Payton .50 1.25
21 Julius Erving 1.00 2.50
22 Dennis Rodman 1.00 2.50
23 Kobe Bryant 3.00 8.00
24 Grant Hill .60 1.50
25 Magic Johnson 1.50 4.00
26 Reggie Miller .75 2.00
27 Pete Maravich 1.00 2.50
28 Steve Nash .75 2.00
29 Wilt Chamberlain 1.25 3.00
30 Drazen Petrovic .50 1.25

2018-19 Donruss Optic Rookie Dominator Signatures

STATED PRINT RUN 50 SER.#'d SETS
EXCHANGE DEADLINE 7/30/2020
1 Moritz Wagner 8.00 20.00
2 Mikal Bridges 20.00 50.00
3 Jacob Evans III 4.00 10.00
4 Jerome Robinson 4.00 10.00
5 Zhaire Smith 4.00 10.00
6 Deandre Ayton 12.00 30.00
7 Kevin Huerter 8.00 20.00
8 Jaren Jackson Jr. 100.00 250.00
9 Chandler Hutchison 5.00 12.00
10 Wendell Carter Jr. 10.00 25.00
11 Landry Shamet 4.00 10.00
12 Shai Gilgeous-Alexander 500.00 1,000.00
13 Dzanan Musa 4.00 10.00
14 Michael Porter Jr. 50.00 120.00
15 Donte DiVincenzo 10.00 25.00
16 Marvin Bagley III 6.00 15.00
17 Josh Okogie 6.00 15.00
18 Trae Young 400.00 800.00
19 Aaron Holiday 6.00 15.00
20 Collin Sexton 12.00 30.00
21 Robert Williams III 8.00 20.00
22 Jalen Brunson 30.00 80.00
23 Omari Spellman 4.00 10.00
24 Troy Brown Jr. 5.00 12.00
25 Lonnie Walker IV 8.00 20.00
26 Luka Doncic 1,250.00 2,500.00
27 Grayson Allen 8.00 20.00
28 Mo Bamba 6.00 15.00
29 Anfernee Simons 20.00 50.00
30 Kevin Knox 5.00 12.00

2018-19 Donruss Optic Signature Series

EXCHANGE DEADLINE 7/30/2020
2 LaMarcus Aldridge 6.00 15.00
4 Michael Carter-Williams 2.50 6.00
5 Marquese Chriss 2.50 6.00
6 Tyson Chandler 3.00 8.00
8 Kentavious Caldwell-Pope 2.50 6.00
9 Kevin Durant EXCH 60.00 150.00
10 Alonzo Mourning 15.00 40.00
11 Kobe Bryant 500.00 1,000.00
12 Jrue Holiday 5.00 12.00
14 Rodney Hood 3.00 8.00
16 Al Horford 4.00 10.00
17 Derrick Favors 2.50 6.00
19 Alize Johnson 4.00 10.00
20 David Robinson 15.00 40.00
22 Christian Laettner 4.00 10.00
24 Calvin Murphy 3.00 8.00
25 Daryl Macon 2.50 6.00
26 George Gervin 6.00 15.00
27 T.J. Warren 3.00 8.00
28 John Stockton 20.00 50.00
29 Jairus Lyles 3.00 8.00
30 Dennis Rodman 30.00 80.00
32 Dragan Bender 2.50 6.00
34 Nikola Mirotic 2.50 6.00
35 Billy Preston 2.50 6.00
36 Nick Van Exel 4.00 10.00
38 Kawhi Leonard 60.00 150.00
39 Isaac Bonga 3.00 8.00
40 Jeremy Lin 25.00 60.00
41 Wade Baldwin IV 2.50 6.00
42 Brook Lopez 3.00 8.00
43 Eric Bledsoe 3.00 8.00
46 Nate Arcibald 5.00 12.00
48 Magic Johnson 40.00 100.00
50 Michael Porter Jr. 25.00 60.00
51 Grayson Allen 5.00 12.00
52 Jaren Jackson Jr. 125.00 300.00
54 Svi Mykhailiuk 3.00 8.00
55 Chandler Hutchison 3.00 8.00
56 Trae Young 300.00 600.00
57 Hamidou Diallo 4.00 10.00
58 Aaron Holiday 4.00 10.00
61 Deandre Ayton 20.00 50.00
62 Devonte' Graham 4.00 10.00
63 Shai Gilgeous-Alexander 300.00 600.00
64 Josh Okogie 4.00 10.00
65 Robert Williams III 5.00 12.00
66 Gary Trent Jr. 5.00 12.00
67 J.P. Macura 3.00 8.00
68 Luka Doncic 500.00 1,000.00
70 Kevin Huerter 5.00 12.00
71 Landry Shamet 4.00 10.00
72 Kevin Knox 3.00 8.00
73 Mitchell Robinson 10.00 25.00
74 Chimezie Metu 3.00 8.00
76 Mikal Bridges 12.00 30.00
77 Khyri Thomas 2.50 6.00
78 Jacob Evans III 2.50 6.00
79 Zhaire Smith 2.50 6.00
81 Elie Okobo 2.50 6.00
82 Keita Bates-Diop 3.00 8.00
83 Donte DiVincenzo 6.00 15.00
84 Omari Spellman 2.50 6.00
85 Jevon Carter 4.00 10.00
86 Lonnie Walker IV 5.00 12.00
87 Jalen Brunson 20.00 50.00
88 Trevon Bluiett 2.50 6.00
89 Anfernee Simons 40.00 100.00
90 Mo Bamba 8.00 20.00
91 Troy Brown Jr. 3.00 8.00
92 Vincent Edwards 2.50 6.00
93 Moritz Wagner 5.00 12.00
94 Wendell Carter Jr. 6.00 15.00
95 Yante Maten 2.50 6.00
97 De'Anthony Melton 5.00 12.00
98 Dzanan Musa 2.50 6.00
100 Charles Barkley EXCH 75.00 200.00

2018-19 Donruss Optic Signature Series Blue

*BLUE: .75X TO 2X BASIC
STATED PRINT RUN 25 SER.#'d SETS
EXCHANGE DEADLINE 7/30/2020
1 Luke Kornet 5.00 12.00
3 Bryn Forbes 6.00 15.00
7 Tony Snell 5.00 12.00
13 Tyrone Wallace 5.00 12.00
15 Tyler Cavanaugh 5.00 12.00
18 Antonio Blakeney 8.00 20.00
21 Lorenzo Brown 5.00 12.00
23 Furkan Korkmaz 6.00 15.00
31 Kadeem Allen 5.00 12.00
33 Ian Clark 5.00 12.00
37 Trey Lyles 5.00 12.00
43 Jarell Martin 5.00 12.00
45 Bismack Biyombo 5.00 12.00
47 Marcus Paige 5.00 12.00
49 Edmond Sumner 5.00 12.00
50 Michael Porter Jr. 500.00 1,000.00
53 Bruce Brown 10.00 25.00
60 Justin Jackson 5.00 12.00
68 Luka Doncic 3,000.00 6,000.00
69 Melvin Frazier Jr. 5.00 12.00
80 Kostas Antetokounmpo 25.00 60.00
96 Collin Sexton 20.00 50.00
99 Rodions Kurucs 10.00 25.00

2018-19 Donruss Optic Signature Series Choice

*CHOICE: .6X TO 1.5X BASIC
EXCHANGE DEADLINE 7/30/2020
1 Luke Kornet 4.00 10.00
3 Bryn Forbes 5.00 12.00
7 Tony Snell 4.00 10.00
13 Tyrone Wallace 4.00 10.00
15 Tyler Cavanaugh 4.00 10.00
18 Antonio Blakeney 6.00 15.00
21 Lorenzo Brown 4.00 10.00
23 Furkan Korkmaz 5.00 12.00
31 Kadeem Allen 4.00 10.00
33 Ian Clark 4.00 10.00
37 Trey Lyles 4.00 10.00
43 Jarell Martin 4.00 10.00
45 Bismack Biyombo 4.00 10.00
47 Marcus Paige 4.00 10.00
49 Edmond Sumner 4.00 10.00
50 Michael Porter Jr. 40.00 100.00
53 Bruce Brown 8.00 20.00
59 Jerome Robinson 4.00 10.00
60 Justin Jackson 4.00 10.00
69 Melvin Frazier Jr. 4.00 10.00
80 Kostas Antetokounmpo 12.00 30.00
96 Collin Sexton 20.00 50.00
99 Rodions Kurucs 5.00 12.00

2018-19 Donruss Optic Signature Series Holo

*HOLO: .4X TO 1X BASIC
EXCHANGE DEADLINE 7/30/2020
1 Luke Kornet 2.50 6.00
3 Bryn Forbes 3.00 8.00
7 Tony Snell 2.50 6.00
13 Tyrone Wallace 2.50 6.00
15 Tyler Cavanaugh 2.50 6.00
18 Antonio Blakeney 4.00 10.00
21 Lorenzo Brown 2.50 6.00
23 Furkan Korkmaz 3.00 8.00
31 Kadeem Allen 2.50 6.00
33 Ian Clark 2.50 6.00
37 Trey Lyles 2.50 6.00
43 Jarell Martin 2.50 6.00
47 Marcus Paige 2.50 6.00
49 Edmond Sumner 2.50 6.00
50 Michael Porter Jr. 200.00 500.00
60 Justin Jackson 2.50 6.00
68 Luka Doncic 1,500.00 3,000.00
69 Melvin Frazier Jr. 2.50 6.00
99 Rodions Kurucs 5.00 12.00

2018-19 Donruss Optic Signature Series Pink

*PINK: .75X TO 2X BASIC
STATED PRINT RUN 25 SER.#'d SETS
EXCHANGE DEADLINE 7/30/2020
1 Luke Kornet 5.00 12.00
3 Bryn Forbes 6.00 15.00
7 Tony Snell 5.00 12.00
13 Tyrone Wallace 5.00 12.00
15 Tyler Cavanaugh 5.00 12.00
18 Antonio Blakeney 8.00 20.00
21 Lorenzo Brown 5.00 12.00
23 Furkan Korkmaz 6.00 15.00
31 Kadeem Allen 5.00 12.00
33 Ian Clark 5.00 12.00
37 Trey Lyles 5.00 12.00
43 Jarell Martin 5.00 12.00
45 Bismack Biyombo 5.00 12.00
47 Marcus Paige 5.00 12.00
49 Edmond Sumner 5.00 12.00
50 Michael Porter Jr. 500.00 1,000.00
53 Bruce Brown 10.00 25.00
60 Justin Jackson 5.00 12.00
68 Luka Doncic 3,000.00 6,000.00
69 Melvin Frazier Jr. 5.00 12.00
96 Collin Sexton 20.00 50.00
99 Rodions Kurucs 10.00 25.00

2018-19 Donruss Optic Signature Series Purple

*PURPLE: .5X TO 1.2X BASIC
EXCHANGE DEADLINE 7/30/2020
1 Luke Kornet 3.00 8.00
3 Bryn Forbes 4.00 10.00
7 Tony Snell 3.00 8.00
13 Tyrone Wallace 3.00 8.00
15 Tyler Cavanaugh 3.00 8.00
18 Antonio Blakeney 5.00 12.00
21 Lorenzo Brown 3.00 8.00
23 Furkan Korkmaz 4.00 10.00
31 Kadeem Allen 3.00 8.00
33 Ian Clark 3.00 8.00
37 Trey Lyles 3.00 8.00
43 Jarell Martin 3.00 8.00
47 Marcus Paige 3.00 8.00
49 Edmond Sumner 3.00 8.00
50 Michael Porter Jr. 300.00 600.00
53 Bruce Brown 6.00 15.00
60 Justin Jackson 3.00 8.00
68 Luka Doncic 2,000.00 4,000.00
69 Melvin Frazier Jr. 3.00 8.00
96 Collin Sexton 12.00 30.00
99 Rodions Kurucs 6.00 15.00

2018-19 Donruss Optic Swishful Thinking

COMPLETE SET (10) 5.00 12.00
*HOLO: .75X TO 2X BASIC
*FB HOLO: .6X TO 1.5X BASIC
*RED/99: 1.5X TO 4X BASIC
*BLUE/49: 2X TO 5X BASIC
1 Larry Bird 2.00 5.00
2 Klay Thompson 1.25 3.00
3 Kyle Lowry .50 1.25
4 Reggie Miller 1.00 2.50
5 Ray Allen .60 1.50
6 Steve Kerr .60 1.50
7 James Harden 1.00 2.50
8 Paul George .75 2.00
9 Stephen Curry 4.00 10.00
10 Kemba Walker .40 1.00

2018-19 Donruss Optic Winner Stays

COMPLETE SET (20) 12.00 30.00
*HOLO: .75X TO 2X BASIC
*PURPLE: .75X TO 2X BASIC
*LIME GREEN/149: 1.25X TO 3X BASIC
*BLUE/85: 2X TO 5X BASIC
*ORANGE/39: 3X TO 8X BASIC
*PINK/25: 4X TO 10X BASIC
1 Dwyane Wade 1.00 2.50
2 Kobe Bryant 4.00 10.00
3 Dirk Nowitzki 1.25 3.00
4 Robert Parish .75 2.00
5 Kevin Durant 2.00 5.00
6 Dennis Rodman 1.25 3.00
7 Klay Thompson 1.25 3.00
8 Bill Russell 1.50 4.00
9 Tony Parker .75 2.00
10 Kareem Abdul-Jabbar 1.50 4.00
11 LeBron James 4.00 10.00
12 Tim Duncan 1.25 3.00
13 J.J. Barea .50 1.25
14 Shaquille O'Neal 1.50 4.00
15 Stephen Curry 4.00 10.00
16 Robert Horry .50 1.25
17 Kevin Love .40 1.00
18 Magic Johnson 2.00 5.00
19 Jerry West 1.00 2.50
20 Scottie Pippen 1.25 3.00

2019-20 Donruss Optic

*BLUE VEL: 1X TO 2.5X BASIC
*PURPLE: 1X TO 2.5X BASIC
1 Goran Dragic .30 .75
2 Trae Young 1.00 2.50
3 Lonzo Ball .40 1.00
4 Terry Rozier .30 .75
5 D.J. Augustin .25 .60
6 Delon Wright .25 .60
7 Damian Lillard 1.00 2.50
8 Stephen Curry 3.00 8.00
9 Fred VanVleet .50 1.25
10 Lou Williams .40 1.00
11 Jimmy Butler .75 2.00
12 Allen Crabbe .25 .60
13 Jrue Holiday .50 1.25
14 Malik Monk .40 1.00
15 Evan Fournier .30 .75
16 Luka Doncic 2.50 6.00
17 CJ McCollum .40 1.00
18 Klay Thompson 1.00 2.50
19 Pascal Siakam .60 1.50
20 Paul George .60 1.50
21 Justise Winslow .25 .60
22 John Collins .40 1.00
23 Brandon Ingram .40 1.00
24 Nicolas Batum .25 .60
25 Aaron Gordon .40 1.00
26 Tim Hardaway Jr. .25 .60
27 Kent Bazemore .25 .60
28 D'Angelo Russell .30 .75
29 Serge Ibaka .30 .75
30 Kawhi Leonard 1.00 2.50
31 Kelly Olynyk .25 .60
32 Alex Len .25 .60
33 Derrick Favors .25 .60
34 Miles Bridges .40 1.00
35 Nikola Vucevic .30 .75
36 Kristaps Porzingis .50 1.25
37 Pau Gasol .60 1.50
38 Draymond Green .50 1.25
39 Marc Gasol .40 1.00
40 Montrezl Harrell .30 .75
41 Bam Adebayo .60 1.50
42 Jabari Parker .30 .75
43 JJ Redick .40 1.00
44 Cody Zeller .25 .60
45 Mo Bamba .30 .75
46 Dwight Powell .25 .60
47 Hassan Whiteside .25 .60
48 Willie Cauley-Stein .25 .60
49 Mike Conley .30 .75
50 Ivica Zubac .30 .75
51 Eric Bledsoe .30 .75
52 Kemba Walker .30 .75
53 Dennis Smith Jr. .25 .60
54 Kris Dunn .25 .60
55 Ben Simmons .40 1.00
56 Jamal Murray .60 1.50
57 De'Aaron Fox .60 1.50
58 Russell Westbrook .60 1.50
59 Donovan Mitchell .75 2.00
60 LeBron James 8.00 20.00
61 Wesley Matthews .25 .60
62 Marcus Smart .30 .75
63 Kevin Knox II .25 .60
64 Zach LaVine .60 1.50
65 Josh Richardson .25 .60
66 Gary Harris .25 .60
67 Buddy Hield .30 .75
68 James Harden .75 2.00
69 Joe Ingles .30 .75
70 Danny Green .30 .75
71 Khris Middleton .40 1.00
72 Jaylen Brown .60 1.50
73 Julius Randle .50 1.25
74 Otto Porter Jr. .25 .60
75 Tobias Harris .30 .75
76 Will Barton .25 .60
77 Harrison Barnes .30 .75
78 Eric Gordon .30 .75
79 Bojan Bogdanovic .30 .75
80 Kyle Kuzma .50 1.25
81 Giannis Antetokounmpo 2.00 5.00
82 Jayson Tatum 1.50 4.00
83 Mitchell Robinson .40 1.00
84 Lauri Markkanen .50 1.25
85 Al Horford .40 1.00
86 Paul Millsap .30 .75
87 Marvin Bagley III .30 .75
88 Gerald Green .30 .75
89 Rudy Gobert .50 1.25
90 Anthony Davis 1.00 2.50
91 Brook Lopez .30 .75
92 Enes Kanter .25 .60
93 Allonzo Trier .25 .60
94 Wendell Carter Jr. .40 1.00
95 Joel Embiid .75 2.00
96 Nikola Jokic 2.00 5.00
97 Bogdan Bogdanovic .40 1.00
98 Clint Capela .30 .75
99 John Wall .50 1.25
100 Rajon Rondo .50 1.25
101 Jeff Teague .25 .60
102 Kyrie Irving .75 2.00
103 Chris Paul .75 2.00
104 Collin Sexton .50 1.25
105 Ricky Rubio .30 .75
106 Reggie Jackson .30 .75
107 Dejounte Murray .40 1.00
108 Malcolm Brogdon .30 .75
109 Bradley Beal .50 1.25
110 Jaren Jackson Jr. .60 1.50
111 Andrew Wiggins .50 1.25
112 Kevin Durant 1.25 3.00
113 Shai Gilgeous-Alexander 2.00 5.00
114 Cedi Osman .30 .75
115 Devin Booker .10 .25
116 Derrick Rose .75 2.00
117 DeMarre Carroll .25 .60
118 Jeremy Lamb .25 .60
119 Isaiah Thomas .30 .75
120 Markelle Fultz .30 .75
121 Robert Covington .25 .60
122 Joe Harris .30 .75
123 Steven Adams .30 .75
124 Kevin Love .40 1.00
125 Mikal Bridges .60 1.50
126 Luke Kennard .40 1.00
127 DeMar DeRozan .50 1.25
128 Justin Holiday .25 .60
129 Thomas Bryant .30 .75
130 Jonas Valanciunas .30 .75
131 Karl-Anthony Towns .60 1.50
132 DeAndre Jordan .30 .75
133 Dennis Schroder .30 .75
134 Tristan Thompson .25 .60
135 Dario Saric .30 .75
136 Blake Griffin .40 1.00
137 Rudy Gay .30 .75
138 Domantas Sabonis .50 1.25
139 Ish Smith .25 .60
140 Dillon Brooks .30 .75
141 Shabazz Napier .25 .60
142 Jarrett Allen .40 1.00
143 Danilo Gallinari .30 .75
144 Jordan Clarkson .40 1.00
145 Deandre Ayton .40 1.00
146 Andre Drummond .30 .75
147 LaMarcus Aldridge .40 1.00
148 Myles Turner .40 1.00
149 Kyle Lowry .40 1.00
150 Jae Crowder .25 .60
151 Talen Horton-Tucker RR RC .75 2.00
152 PJ Washington Jr. RR RC 1.50 4.00
153 Daniel Gafford RR RC 1.00 2.50
154 Nassir Little RR RC .75 2.00
155 Jaylen Nowell RR RC .60 1.50
156 Darius Bazley RR RC .50 1.25
157 Grant Williams RR RC .60 1.50
158 Zion Williamson RR RC 4.00 10.00
159 Mfiondu Kabengele RR RC .60 1.50
160 Jarrett Culver RR RC .60 1.50
161 Tacko Fall RR RC .60 1.50
162 Bol Bol RR RC 1.25 3.00
163 Nicolo Melli RR RC .60 1.50
164 Sekou Doumbouya RR RC .50 1.25
165 Terance Mann RR RC 1.00 2.50
166 Goga Bitadze RR RC .75 2.00
167 Ty Jerome RR RC 1.00 2.50
168 Ja Morant RR RC 5.00 12.00
169 Jordan Poole RR RC 2.00 5.00
170 Cam Reddish RR RC .75 2.00
171 Nicolas Claxton RR RC 1.00 2.50
172 Tyler Herro RR RC 2.50 6.00
173 Ignas Brazdeikis RR RC .60 1.50
174 Justin Robinson RR RC .50 1.25
175 Quinndary Weatherspoon RR RC .50 1.25
176 Luka Samanic RR RC UER
Missing name .60 1.50
177 Bruno Fernando RR RC .60 1.50
178 RJ Barrett RR RC 2.00 5.00
179 Kevin Porter Jr. RR RC 2.50 6.00
180 Coby White RR RC 1.50 4.00
181 Cody Martin RR RC .75 2.00
182 Romeo Langford RR RC .50 1.25
183 Kyle Guy RR RC .60 1.50
184 Nickeil Alexander-Walker RR RC .75 2.00
185 Tremont Waters RR RC .60 1.50
186 Keldon Johnson RR RC 1.50 4.00
187 Admiral Schofield RR RC .60 1.50
188 Rui Hachimura RR RC 2.00 5.00
189 KZ Okpala RR RC .60 1.50
190 Jaxson Hayes RR RC .75 2.00
191 Isaiah Roby RR RC .60 1.50
192 Matisse Thybulle RR RC 1.00 2.50
193 Kendrick Nunn RR RC UER
Missing name .75 2.00
194 Brandon Clarke RR RC 1.00 2.50
195 Darius Garland RR RC 2.00 5.00
196 Carsen Edwards RR RC .60 1.50
197 Dylan Windler RR RC .60 1.50
198 De'Andre Hunter RR RC 2.00 5.00
199 Eric Paschall RR RC .60 1.50
200 Cameron Johnson RR RC 1.25 3.00

2019-20 Donruss Optic Black Velocity

*BLACK VEL: 6X TO 15X BASIC
*BLACK VEL RC: 6X TO 15X BASIC RC
STATED PRINT RUN 39 SER. #'D SETS
8 Stephen Curry 125.00 300.00
16 Luka Doncic 150.00 400.00
60 LeBron James 200.00 500.00
158 Zion Williamson RR 300.00 600.00
168 Ja Morant RR 400.00 800.00

2019-20 Donruss Optic Blue

*BLUE: 4X TO 10X BASIC
*BLUE RC: 4X TO 10X BASIC RC
STATED PRINT RUN 59 SER. #'D SETS
158 Zion Williamson RR 125.00 300.00
168 Ja Morant RR 150.00 400.00

2019-20 Donruss Optic Choice

*CHOICE RC: 1.2X TO 3X BASIC RC
158 Zion Williamson RR 75.00 200.00
168 Ja Morant RR 100.00 250.00
169 Jordan Poole RR 40.00 100.00
172 Tyler Herro RR 60.00 150.00
178 RJ Barrett RR 20.00 50.00

2019-20 Donruss Optic Choice Red

*CHOICE RED: 1.5X TO 4X BASIC
*CHOICE RED RC: 2X TO 5X BASIC RC
STATED PRINT RUN 88 SER. #'D SETS
16 Luka Doncic 75.00 200.00
60 LeBron James 200.00 500.00
158 Zion Williamson RR 300.00 600.00
168 Ja Morant RR 300.00 600.00
169 Jordan Poole RR 75.00 200.00
172 Tyler Herro RR 75.00 200.00
178 RJ Barrett RR 30.00 80.00
180 Coby White RR 15.00 40.00
188 Rui Hachimura RR 25.00 60.00

2019-20 Donruss Optic Fast Break Blue

*FB BLUE: 2X TO 5X BASIC
*FB BLUE RC: 2.5X TO 6X BASIC RC
STATED PRINT RUN 50 SER. #'D SETS
16 Luka Doncic 100.00 250.00
60 LeBron James 300.00 600.00
90 Anthony Davis 75.00 200.00
158 Zion Williamson RR 400.00 800.00
168 Ja Morant RR 350.00 700.00
172 Tyler Herro RR 300.00 600.00
178 RJ Barrett RR 40.00 100.00
180 Coby White RR 20.00 50.00
188 Rui Hachimura RR 50.00 120.00

2019-20 Donruss Optic Fast Break Holo

*FB HOLO: .75X TO 2X BASIC
*FB HOLO RC: 1X TO 2.5X BASIC RC
60 LeBron James 75.00 200.00
90 Anthony Davis 20.00 50.00
158 Zion Williamson RR 60.00 150.00
172 Tyler Herro RR 60.00 150.00

2019-20 Donruss Optic Fast Break Pink

*FB PINK: 4X TO 10X BASIC
*FB PINK RC: 5X TO 12X BASIC RC
STATED PRINT RUN 20 SER. #'D SETS
16 Luka Doncic 300.00 600.00
60 LeBron James 1,250.00 2,500.00
90 Anthony Davis 150.00 400.00
158 Zion Williamson RR 800.00 1,500.00
168 Ja Morant RR 800.00 1,500.00
172 Tyler Herro RR 600.00 1,200.00
178 RJ Barrett RR 125.00 300.00
180 Coby White RR 40.00 100.00
188 Rui Hachimura RR 100.00 250.00

2019-20 Donruss Optic Fast Break Purple

*FB PURPLE: 1.5X TO 4X BASIC
*FB PURPLE RC: 2X TO 5X BASIC RC
STATED PRINT RUN 95 SER. #'D SETS
16 Luka Doncic 75.00 200.00
60 LeBron James 200.00 500.00
90 Anthony Davis 60.00 150.00
158 Zion Williamson RR 300.00 600.00
168 Ja Morant RR 300.00 600.00
172 Tyler Herro RR 200.00 500.00
178 RJ Barrett RR 30.00 80.00
180 Coby White RR 15.00 40.00
188 Rui Hachimura RR 40.00 100.00

2019-20 Donruss Optic Fast Break Red

*FB RED: 1.5X TO 4X BASIC
*FB RED RC: 2X TO 5X BASIC RC
STATED PRINT RUN 85 SER. #'D SETS
16 Luka Doncic 75.00 200.00
60 LeBron James 200.00 500.00
90 Anthony Davis 60.00 150.00
158 Zion Williamson RR 300.00 600.00
164 Sekou Doumbouya RR 2.00 5.00
168 Ja Morant RR 300.00 600.00
169 Jordan Poole RR 75.00 200.00
172 Tyler Herro RR 75.00 200.00
178 RJ Barrett RR 30.00 80.00
180 Coby White RR 15.00 40.00
188 Rui Hachimura RR 25.00 60.00

2019-20 Donruss Optic Green Wave

158 Zion Williamson RR 75.00 200.00
168 Ja Morant RR 75.00 200.00
169 Jordan Poole RR 20.00 50.00
172 Tyler Herro RR 60.00 150.00

2019-20 Donruss Optic Holo

*HOLO: 1.2X TO 3X BASIC

*HOLO RC: 1X TO 2.5X BASIC RC
158 Zion Williamson RR 20.00 50.00
168 Ja Morant RR 25.00 60.00

2019-20 Donruss Optic Lime Green

16 Luka Doncic 50.00 120.00
60 LeBron James 125.00 300.00
90 Anthony Davis 40.00 100.00
158 Zion Williamson RR 200.00 500.00
168 Ja Morant RR 200.00 500.00
169 Jordan Poole RR 125.00 300.00
172 Tyler Herro RR 150.00 400.00
178 RJ Barrett RR 20.00 50.00
188 Rui Hachimura RR 25.00 60.00

2019-20 Donruss Optic Orange

*ORNG: 2X TO 5X BASIC
*ORNG RC: 2X TO 5X BASIC RC
STATED PRINT RUN 199 SER. #'D SETS
158 Zion Williamson RR 40.00 100.00
168 Ja Morant RR 50.00 120.00

2019-20 Donruss Optic Pink

*PINK: 3X TO 8X BASIC
*PINK RC: 4X TO 10X BASIC RC
STATED PRINT RUN 25 SER. #'D SETS
16 Luka Doncic 150.00 400.00
60 LeBron James 1,000.00 2,000.00
90 Anthony Davis 125.00 300.00
158 Zion Williamson RR 600.00 1,200.00
168 Ja Morant RR 600.00 1,200.00
169 Jordan Poole RR 400.00 800.00
172 Tyler Herro RR 500.00 1,000.00
178 RJ Barrett RR 100.00 250.00
180 Coby White RR 30.00 80.00
188 Rui Hachimura RR 75.00 200.00

2019-20 Donruss Optic Pink Velocity

*PINK VEL: 1.5X TO 4X BASIC
*PINK VEL RC: 2X TO 5X BASIC RC
STATED PRINT RUN 79 SER. #'D SETS
16 Luka Doncic 75.00 200.00
60 LeBron James 200.00 500.00
90 Anthony Davis 60.00 150.00
158 Zion Williamson RR 300.00 600.00
168 Ja Morant RR 300.00 600.00
169 Jordan Poole RR 125.00 300.00
172 Tyler Herro RR 200.00 500.00
178 RJ Barrett RR 30.00 80.00
180 Coby White RR 15.00 40.00
188 Rui Hachimura RR 40.00 100.00

2019-20 Donruss Optic Premium Box Set

*PREM: 1.2X TO 3X BASIC
*PREM RC: 1.5X TO 4X BASIC RC
STATED PRINT RUN 249 SER. #'D SETS
16 Luka Doncic 50.00 120.00
60 LeBron James 125.00 300.00
90 Anthony Davis 40.00 100.00
158 Zion Williamson RR 150.00 400.00
168 Ja Morant RR 200.00 500.00
169 Jordan Poole RR 75.00 200.00
172 Tyler Herro RR 100.00 250.00
178 RJ Barrett RR 20.00 50.00
188 Rui Hachimura RR 25.00 60.00

2019-20 Donruss Optic Purple Shock

*PRPL SHOCK: .75X TO 2X BASIC
*PRPL SHOCK RC: 1X TO 2.5X BASIC RC
60 LeBron James 25.00 60.00
90 Anthony Davis 15.00 40.00
158 Zion Williamson RR 60.00 150.00
172 Tyler Herro RR 60.00 150.00

2019-20 Donruss Optic Purple Stars

*PRPL STRS VEL: 3X TO 8X BASIC
*PRPL STRS RC: 4X TO 10X BASIC RC
STATED PRINT RUN 29 SER. #'D SETS
16 Luka Doncic 150.00 400.00
60 LeBron James 1,000.00 2,000.00
158 Zion Williamson RR 600.00 1,200.00
168 Ja Morant RR 600.00 1,200.00
169 Jordan Poole RR 400.00 800.00
178 RJ Barrett RR 100.00 250.00
180 Coby White RR 30.00 80.00
188 Rui Hachimura RR 75.00 200.00

2019-20 Donruss Optic Red

*RED: 1.5X TO 4X BASIC
*RED RC: 2X TO 5X BASIC RC
STATED PRINT RUN 99 SER. #'D SETS
16 Luka Doncic 40.00 100.00
60 LeBron James 200.00 500.00
158 Zion Williamson RR 300.00 600.00
168 Ja Morant RR 300.00 600.00
169 Jordan Poole RR 75.00 200.00
172 Tyler Herro RR 75.00 200.00
178 RJ Barrett RR 30.00 80.00
188 Rui Hachimura RR 25.00 60.00

2019-20 Donruss Optic All Clear for Takeoff

1 Donovan Mitchell 1.00 2.50
2 LeBron James 4.00 10.00
3 Victor Oladipo .40 1.00
4 Russell Westbrook .75 2.00
5 John Wall .60 1.50
6 Giannis Antetokounmpo 2.50 6.00
7 Ben Simmons .50 1.25
8 Aaron Gordon .50 1.25
9 Andrew Wiggins .60 1.50
10 Zach LaVine .75 2.00
11 Paul George .75 2.00
12 Blake Griffin .50 1.25
13 DeAndre Jordan .40 1.00
14 Zion Williamson 8.00 20.00
15 Ja Morant 8.00 20.00

2019-20 Donruss Optic All Clear for Takeoff Blue

*BLUE: 2.5X TO 6X BASIC
STATED PRINT RUN 49 SER. #'D SETS
14 Zion Williamson 75.00 200.00
15 Ja Morant 75.00 200.00

2019-20 Donruss Optic All Clear for Takeoff Holo Fast Break

*FB HOLO: .75X TO 2X BASIC

2019-20 Donruss Optic All Clear for Takeoff Red

*RED: 2X TO 5X BASIC
STATED PRINT RUN 99 SER. #'D SETS
14 Zion Williamson 50.00 120.00
15 Ja Morant 50.00 120.00

2019-20 Donruss Optic All Stars

1 Giannis Antetokounmpo 2.50 6.00
2 Paul George .75 2.00
3 Joel Embiid 1.00 2.50
4 Stephen Curry 4.00 10.00
5 Kemba Walker .40 1.00
6 Khris Middleton .50 1.25
7 Blake Griffin .50 1.25
8 Russell Westbrook .75 2.00
9 Nikola Jokic 2.50 6.00
10 Dirk Nowitzki 1.25 3.00
11 LeBron James 4.00 10.00
12 Kawhi Leonard 1.25 3.00
13 Kevin Durant 1.50 4.00
14 James Harden 1.00 2.50
15 Kyrie Irving 1.00 2.50
16 Damian Lillard 1.25 3.00
17 Klay Thompson 1.25 3.00
18 Bradley Beal .60 1.50
19 Ben Simmons .50 1.25
20 Dwyane Wade 1.00 2.50

2019-20 Donruss Optic All Stars Blue

*BLUE: 1X TO 2.5X BASIC
STATED PRINT RUN 49 SER. #'D SETS
4 Stephen Curry 40.00 100.00
11 LeBron James 40.00 100.00

2019-20 Donruss Optic All Stars Red

*RED: 2X TO 5X BASIC
STATED PRINT RUN 99 SER. #'D SETS
4 Stephen Curry 25.00 60.00
11 LeBron James 25.00 60.00

2019-20 Donruss Optic Dominators Signatures

PRINT RUN BTW 49-99 COPIES PER
EXCHANGE DEADLINE 8/5/2021
*PRPL STARS: .6X TO 1.5X BASIC
1 Kevin Durant/99 EXCH 75.00 200.00
2 Chris Paul/99 50.00 120.00
3 Kyrie Irving/99 EXCH 25.00 60.00
4 Damian Lillard/99 25.00 60.00
5 Anthony Davis/99 60.00 150.00
6 Karl-Anthony Towns/99 12.00 30.00
7 Andrew Wiggins/99 6.00 15.00
8 DeMarcus Cousins/99 4.00 10.00
9 Wesley Matthews/49 3.00 8.00
10 Otto Porter Jr./49 3.00 8.00
11 Montrezl Harrell/49 4.00 10.00
12 Robert Covington/49 3.00 8.00
13 Dario Saric/49 4.00 10.00
14 Noah Vonleh/49 3.00 8.00
15 Thaddeus Young/49 3.00 8.00
16 Al-Farouq Aminu/49 3.00 8.00
17 Malcolm Brogdon/49 4.00 10.00
18 Danny Green/49 4.00 10.00
19 Terrence Ross/49 5.00 12.00
20 Lauri Markkanen/49 6.00 15.00
21 Pascal Siakam/49 8.00 20.00
22 Ersan Ilyasova/49 3.00 8.00
23 Willie Cauley-Stein/49 3.00 8.00
24 Tyus Jones/49 3.00 8.00
25 Kelly Olynyk/49 3.00 8.00
26 Danilo Gallinari/99 4.00 10.00
27 Nikola Vucevic/99 4.00 10.00
28 Nemanja Bjelica/49 3.00 8.00
29 Cedi Osman/49 4.00 10.00
30 Trae Young/99 60.00 150.00
31 Michael Porter Jr./49 8.00 20.00
32 Jarrett Allen/49 5.00 12.00
33 Julius Randle/99 12.00 30.00
34 CJ McCollum/99 12.00 30.00
35 Khris Middleton/99 5.00 12.00
36 Kevin Knox II/99 3.00 8.00
37 Rodney McGruder/49 3.00 8.00
38 Avery Bradley/49 3.00 8.00
39 P.J. Tucker/49 4.00 10.00
40 Rudy Gobert/49 10.00 25.00

2019-20 Donruss Optic Elite Dominators

*HOLO: .6X TO 1.5X BASIC
*FB HOLO: .6X TO 1.5X BASIC
*RED/99: .75X TO 2X BASIC
*BLUE/49: 1X TO 2.5X BASIC
1 Kawhi Leonard 1.00 2.50
2 Russell Westbrook .60 1.50
3 Joel Embiid .75 2.00
4 Nikola Jokic 2.00 5.00
5 Paul George .60 1.50
6 D'Angelo Russell .30 .75
7 Anthony Davis 1.00 2.50
8 Kemba Walker .30 .75
9 De'Aaron Fox .60 1.50
10 Luka Doncic 2.50 6.00
11 Donovan Mitchell .75 2.00
12 Jayson Tatum 1.50 4.00
13 Trae Young 1.00 2.50
14 Damian Lillard 1.00 2.50
15 James Harden .75 2.00
16 Stephen Curry 3.00 8.00
17 Giannis Antetokounmpo 2.00 5.00
18 Ben Simmons .40 1.00
19 LeBron James 8.00 20.00
20 Bradley Beal .50 1.25
21 DeMar DeRozan .50 1.25
22 Marc Gasol .40 1.00
23 Marvin Bagley III .30 .75
24 Kristaps Porzingis .50 1.25
25 Devin Booker .10 .25

2019-20 Donruss Optic Express Lane

*HOLO: .75X TO 2X BASIC
*PURPLE: .75X TO 2X BASIC
*RED WAVE: 1X TO 2.5X BASIC
*GOLD WAVE: 1.25X TO 3X BASIC
*LIME GREEN/149: 1.25X TO 3X BASIC
*BLUE/85: 1.5X TO 4X BASIC
*ORANGE/39: 2.5X TO 6X BASIC
*PINK/25: 4X TO 10X BASIC
1 James Harden 1.00 2.50
2 Isiah Thomas 1.00 2.50
3 Damian Lillard 1.25 3.00
4 Ricky Rubio .40 1.00
5 DeMar DeRozan .60 1.50
6 Mike Conley .40 1.00
7 Russell Westbrook .75 2.00
8 John Stockton 1.00 2.50
9 Ben Simmons .50 1.25
10 Steve Nash 1.00 2.50
11 Kyle Lowry .50 1.25
12 Devin Booker .12 .30
13 Jrue Holiday .60 1.50
14 Lou Williams .50 1.25
15 Chris Paul 1.00 2.50
16 Stephen Curry 4.00 10.00
17 Trae Young 1.25 3.00
18 Jason Kidd .75 2.00
19 De'Aaron Fox .75 2.00
20 Magic Johnson 1.50 4.00
21 D'Angelo Russell .40 1.00
22 Eric Bledsoe .40 1.00
23 Kemba Walker .40 1.00
24 Jamal Murray .75 2.00
25 Kyrie Irving 1.00 2.50

2019-20 Donruss Optic Fantasy Stars

1 Karl-Anthony Towns .60 1.50
2 Kyrie Irving .75 2.00
3 Joel Embiid .75 2.00
4 Bradley Beal .50 1.25
5 Nikola Jokic 2.00 5.00
6 Paul George .60 1.50
7 Nikola Vucevic .30 .75
8 Anthony Davis 1.00 2.50
9 Damian Lillard 1.00 2.50
10 Kawhi Leonard 1.00 2.50
11 James Harden .75 2.00
12 Jimmy Butler .75 2.00
13 Stephen Curry 3.00 8.00
14 LeBron James 3.00 8.00
15 Giannis Antetokounmpo 2.00 5.00

2019-20 Donruss Optic Fantasy Stars Blue

*BLUE: .75X TO 2X BASIC
STATED PRINT RUN 85 SER. #'D SETS
14 LeBron James 60.00 150.00

2019-20 Donruss Optic Fantasy Stars Holo

*HOLO: .6X TO 1.5X BASIC
14 LeBron James 15.00 40.00

2019-20 Donruss Optic Fantasy Stars Lime Green

*LIME GREEN: .75X TO 2X BASIC
STATED PRINT RUN 149 SER.#'d SETS
14 LeBron James 60.00 150.00

2019-20 Donruss Optic Fantasy Stars Orange

*ORANGE: 1.5X TO 4X BASIC
STATED PRINT RUN 39 SER. #'D SETS
14 LeBron James 125.00 300.00

2019-20 Donruss Optic Fantasy Stars Pink

*PINK: 2.5X TO 6X BASIC
STATED PRINT RUN 25 SER. #'D SETS
14 LeBron James 200.00 500.00

2019-20 Donruss Optic Fantasy Stars Purple

*PURPLE: .75X TO 2X BASIC
14 LeBron James 15.00 40.00

2019-20 Donruss Optic Fast Break Signatures

EXCHANGE DEADLINE 8/5/2021
1 Goga Bitadze 4.00 10.00
2 Chauncey Billups 5.00 12.00
3 Jordan Poole 10.00 25.00
4 Montrezl Harrell 3.00 8.00
5 Cameron Johnson 6.00 15.00
6 Charles Barkley EXCH 50.00 120.00
7 Matisse Thybulle 5.00 12.00
8 Chris Bosh 5.00 12.00
9 Quinn Cook 3.00 8.00
10 Danilo Gallinari 3.00 8.00
11 Keldon Johnson 8.00 20.00
12 Reggie Jackson 3.00 8.00
13 KZ Okpala 3.00 8.00
14 Thaddeus Young 2.50 6.00
15 Dario Saric 3.00 8.00
17 Romeo Langford 2.50 6.00
18 DeMarcus Cousins 3.00 8.00
19 Bob Dandridge 2.50 6.00
20 Coby White 30.00 80.00
21 Luka Samanic 3.00 8.00
22 Chandler Hutchison 2.50 6.00
23 Mfiondu Kabengele 3.00 8.00
24 Al-Farouq Aminu 2.50 6.00
25 Ersan Ilyasova 2.50 6.00
26 Zion Williamson 500.00 1,200.00
27 Robert Covington 2.50 6.00
28 Markelle Fultz 3.00 8.00
29 Kelly Olynyk 2.50 6.00
30 Nikola Vucevic 3.00 8.00
31 Grant Williams 4.00 10.00
32 Latrell Sprewell 8.00 20.00
33 Cody Martin 4.00 10.00
34 Terrence Ross 4.00 10.00
35 Kenny Sky Walker 3.00 8.00
36 Kevin Durant EXCH 30.00 80.00
37 Cedi Osman 3.00 8.00
39 Joe Harris 3.00 8.00
40 Julius Randle 5.00 12.00
41 Admiral Schofield 3.00 8.00
42 Robert Parish 5.00 12.00
43 Ignas Brazdeikis 3.00 8.00
44 Mario Hezonja 2.50 6.00
45 Sam Cassell 3.00 8.00
46 Ja Morant 150.00 400.00
47 Calvin Murphy 4.00 10.00
48 Trae Young 75.00 200.00
49 M.L. Carr 4.00 10.00
50 Otto Porter Jr. 2.50 6.00
51 Ty Jerome 5.00 12.00
52 Louie Dampier 4.00 10.00
53 Isaiah Roby 3.00 8.00
54 Luke Walton 3.00 8.00
55 Tom Chambers 4.00 10.00
56 Magic Johnson 25.00 60.00
57 Darius Bazley 2.50 6.00
58 Lauri Markkanen 5.00 12.00
59 Tree Rollins 2.50 6.00
60 Jason Terry 3.00 8.00
61 Bruno Fernando 3.00 8.00
62 Lenny Wilkens 5.00 12.00
63 Kyle Guy 3.00 8.00
64 Shane Battier 3.00 8.00
65 Nemanja Bjelica 2.50 6.00
66 Jerry West 20.00 50.00
67 Brandon Clarke 5.00 12.00
68 De'Andre Hunter 10.00 25.00
69 Jarrett Allen 4.00 10.00
70 Malcolm Brogdon 3.00 8.00
71 Eric Paschall 3.00 8.00
72 Danny Green 3.00 8.00
73 Quinndary Weatherspoon 2.50 6.00
74 Michael Porter Jr. 6.00 15.00
75 D.J. Augustin 2.50 6.00
76 Andrew Wiggins 5.00 12.00
77 Chuma Okeke 4.00 10.00
78 Christian Laettner 4.00 10.00
79 Rashard Lewis 3.00 8.00
80 Pascal Siakam 6.00 15.00
81 Dylan Windler 3.00 8.00
82 Jaxson Hayes 4.00 10.00
83 Jaylen Nowell 3.00 8.00
84 PJ Washington Jr. 8.00 20.00
85 Tyler Herro EXCH 25.00 60.00
86 RJ Barrett 25.00 60.00
87 Nickeil Alexander-Walker 4.00 10.00
88 Jarrett Culver 2.50 6.00
89 Joe Smith 3.00 8.00
90 Jalen Rose 3.00 8.00
91 Kevin Porter Jr. 5.00 12.00
92 Wesley Matthews 2.50 6.00
93 Tremont Waters 3.00 8.00
94 Bol Bol 6.00 15.00
95 Nassir Little 4.00 10.00
96 Hakeem Olajuwon 20.00 50.00
97 Sekou Doumbouya 2.50 6.00
98 Cam Reddish 4.00 10.00
99 Carsen Edwards 3.00 8.00
100 Willie Cauley-Stein 2.50 6.00

2019-20 Donruss Optic My House

1 Luka Doncic 6.00 15.00
2 Karl-Anthony Towns .60 1.50
3 DeMar DeRozan .50 1.25
4 Joel Embiid .75 2.00
5 Giannis Antetokounmpo 2.00 5.00
6 Nikola Jokic 2.00 5.00
7 Ja Morant 10.00 25.00
8 Nikola Vucevic .30 .75
9 Coby White .75 2.00
10 Damian Lillard 1.00 2.50
11 Jayson Tatum 1.50 4.00
12 Pascal Siakam .60 1.50
13 LeBron James 8.00 20.00
14 Bradley Beal .50 1.25
15 Zion Williamson 10.00 25.00
16 Donovan Mitchell .75 2.00
17 RJ Barrett 1.00 2.50
18 Trae Young 1.00 2.50
19 Jarrett Culver .25 .60
20 Kyle Lowry .40 1.00

2019-20 Donruss Optic My House Blue

*BLUE: 1.25X TO 3X BASIC
STATED PRINT RUN 85 SER. #'D SETS
1 Luka Doncic 75.00 200.00
7 Ja Morant 100.00 250.00
13 LeBron James 100.00 250.00
15 Zion Williamson 100.00 250.00
18 Trae Young 40.00 100.00

2019-20 Donruss Optic My House Holo

*HOLO: .75X TO 2X BASIC
1 Luka Doncic 15.00 40.00
5 Giannis Antetokounmpo 10.00 25.00
7 Ja Morant 25.00 60.00
13 LeBron James 60.00 150.00
15 Zion Williamson 15.00 40.00
18 Trae Young 10.00 25.00

2019-20 Donruss Optic My House Lime Green

*LIME GREEN: 1.25X TO 3X BASIC
STATED PRINT RUN 149 SER.#'d SETS
1 Luka Doncic 60.00 150.00
7 Ja Morant 75.00 200.00
13 LeBron James 75.00 200.00
15 Zion Williamson 60.00 150.00
18 Trae Young 40.00 100.00

2019-20 Donruss Optic My House Orange

*ORANGE: 1.5X TO 4X BASIC
STATED PRINT RUN 39 SER. #'D SETS
1 Luka Doncic 125.00 300.00
7 Ja Morant 150.00 400.00
13 LeBron James 150.00 400.00
15 Zion Williamson 400.00 800.00
18 Trae Young 50.00 120.00

2019-20 Donruss Optic My House Pink

*PINK: 2.5X TO 6X BASIC
STATED PRINT RUN 25 SER. #'D SETS
1 Luka Doncic 200.00 500.00
7 Ja Morant 300.00 600.00
13 LeBron James 400.00 800.00
15 Zion Williamson 500.00 1,000.00
18 Trae Young 75.00 200.00

2019-20 Donruss Optic My House Purple

*PURPLE: .75X TO 2X BASIC
13 LeBron James 60.00 150.00
15 Zion Williamson 25.00 60.00

2019-20 Donruss Optic My House Red Wave

*RED WAVE: 1.25X TO 3X BASIC
1 Luka Doncic 50.00 120.00
5 Giannis Antetokounmpo 20.00 50.00
7 Ja Morant 75.00 200.00
11 Jayson Tatum 15.00 40.00
13 LeBron James 60.00 150.00
15 Zion Williamson 75.00 200.00
17 RJ Barrett 12.00 30.00
18 Trae Young 15.00 40.00

2019-20 Donruss Optic Rainmakers

*HOLO: .6X TO 1.5X BASIC
*FB HOLO: .6X TO 1.5X BASIC
*RED/99: .75X TO 2X BASIC
*BLUE/49: 1X TO 2.5X BASIC
1 JJ Redick .40 1.00
2 Joe Harris .30 .75
3 D'Angelo Russell .30 .75
4 Stephen Curry 3.00 8.00
5 Bradley Beal .50 1.25
6 Malcolm Brogdon .30 .75
7 Paul Pierce .60 1.50
8 Kyrie Irving .75 2.00
9 Dirk Nowitzki 1.00 2.50
10 Paul George .60 1.50
11 Damian Lillard 1.00 2.50
12 Danny Green .30 .75
13 Eric Gordon .30 .75
14 Buddy Hield .30 .75
15 Ray Allen .60 1.50
16 Vince Carter .75 2.00
17 Jason Kidd .60 1.50
18 James Harden .75 2.00
19 Kobe Bryant 3.00 8.00
20 Kemba Walker .30 .75

2019-20 Donruss Optic Rated Rookies Signatures

EXCHANGE DEADLINE 8/5/2021
*CHOICE: .5X TO 1.2X BASIC
*FB: .5X TO 1.2X BASIC
*HOLO: .5X TO 1.2X BASIC
*PURPLE: .5X TO 1.2X BASIC
*BLUE/49: .6X TO 1.5X BASIC
*PRPL STARS/49: .6X TO 1.5X BASIC
*PINK/25: 1X TO 2.5X BASIC
151 Talen Horton-Tucker 5.00 12.00
152 PJ Washington Jr. 10.00 25.00
153 Daniel Gafford 6.00 15.00
154 Nassir Little 5.00 12.00
155 Jaylen Nowell EXCH 4.00 10.00
156 Darius Bazley 3.00 8.00
157 Grant Williams 5.00 12.00
158 Zion Williamson EXCH 125.00 300.00
159 Mfiondu Kabengele 4.00 10.00
160 Jarrett Culver 3.00 8.00
161 Tacko Fall 4.00 10.00
162 Bol Bol EXCH 8.00 20.00
163 Alen Smailagic 3.00 8.00
164 Sekou Doumbouya 3.00 8.00
165 Terance Mann 6.00 15.00
166 Goga Bitadze 5.00 12.00
167 Ty Jerome 6.00 15.00
168 Ja Morant 150.00 400.00
169 Jordan Poole 25.00 60.00
170 Cam Reddish EXCH 5.00 12.00
171 Nicolas Claxton 6.00 15.00
172 Tyler Herro EXCH 15.00 40.00
173 Ignas Brazdeikis 4.00 10.00
174 Chuma Okeke 5.00 12.00
175 Quinndary Weatherspoon 3.00 8.00
176 Luka Samanic 4.00 10.00
177 Bruno Fernando 4.00 10.00
178 RJ Barrett 25.00 60.00
179 Kevin Porter Jr. 6.00 15.00
180 Coby White 10.00 25.00
181 Cody Martin 5.00 12.00
182 Romeo Langford EXCH 3.00 8.00
183 Kyle Guy 4.00 10.00
184 Nickeil Alexander-Walker 5.00 12.00
185 Tremont Waters 4.00 10.00
186 Keldon Johnson 10.00 25.00
187 Admiral Schofield 4.00 10.00
188 Rui Hachimura 12.00 30.00
189 KZ Okpala 4.00 10.00
190 Jaxson Hayes 5.00 12.00
191 Isaiah Roby 4.00 10.00
192 Matisse Thybulle 6.00 15.00
193 Jalen McDaniels 8.00 20.00
194 Brandon Clarke 6.00 15.00
195 Jordan Bone 3.00 8.00
196 Carsen Edwards 4.00 10.00
197 Dylan Windler 4.00 10.00
198 De'Andre Hunter 12.00 30.00
199 Eric Paschall 4.00 10.00
200 Cameron Johnson 8.00 20.00

2019-20 Donruss Optic Retro Series Signatures

PRINT RUN BTW 49-99 COPIES PER
EXCHANGE DEADLINE 8/5/2021
*PRPL STARS: .6X TO 1.5X BASIC
1 Jason Terry/99 4.00 10.00
2 Luke Walton/49 4.00 10.00
3 Jalen Rose/99 4.00 10.00
4 Chris Bosh/99 6.00 15.00
5 Bob Dandridge/49 3.00 8.00
6 Kenny Sky Walker/49 4.00 10.00
7 Magic Johnson/99 20.00 50.00
8 Sam Cassell/49 4.00 10.00
9 Chauncey Billups/99 6.00 15.00
10 Tom Chambers/49 6.00 15.00
11 Alvan Adams/49 3.00 8.00
12 M.L. Carr/49 5.00 12.00
13 Shane Battier/49 4.00 10.00
14 Latrell Sprewell/99 6.00 15.00
15 Hakeem Olajuwon/99 25.00 60.00
16 Robert Parish/99 6.00 15.00
17 Louie Dampier/99 5.00 12.00
18 Calvin Murphy/99 5.00 12.00
19 Lenny Wilkens/99 6.00 15.00
20 Kenny Smith/99 4.00 10.00
21 Charlie Ward/49 4.00 10.00
22 Jerry West/99 25.00 60.00
23 Charlie Scott/49 4.00 10.00
24 Artis Gilmore/99 6.00 15.00
25 Toni Kukoc/49 6.00 15.00
26 Antonio McDyess/49 4.00 10.00
27 David Robinson/99 20.00 50.00
28 Michael Cooper/49 5.00 12.00
29 George Gervin/99 8.00 20.00
30 Glen Rice/49 4.00 10.00

2019-20 Donruss Optic Rookie Dominators Signatures

PRINT RUN BTW 49-99 COPIES PER
EXCHANGE DEADLINE 8/5/2021
1 De'Andre Hunter/99 12.00 30.00
2 Nassir Little/49 5.00 12.00
3 Jaxson Hayes/49 EXCH 15.00 40.00
4 Jordan Poole/49 12.00 30.00
5 Cameron Johnson/49 8.00 20.00
6 KZ Okpala/49 4.00 10.00
7 Romeo Langford/49 EXCH 3.00 8.00
8 Nickeil Alexander-Walker/49 5.00 12.00
9 Zion Williamson/49 500.00 1,000.00
10 Brandon Clarke/49 12.00 30.00
11 Jarrett Culver/99 3.00 8.00
12 Dylan Windler/49 4.00 10.00
13 Rui Hachimura/99 30.00 80.00
14 Keldon Johnson/49 10.00 25.00
15 PJ Washington Jr./49 10.00 25.00
16 Carsen Edwards/49 4.00 10.00
17 Sekou Doumbouya/49 3.00 8.00
18 Goga Bitadze/49 5.00 12.00
19 Ja Morant/99 200.00 400.00
20 Grant Williams/49 5.00 12.00
21 Coby White/99 40.00 100.00
22 Mfiondu Kabengele/49 4.00 10.00
23 Cam Reddish/99 5.00 12.00
24 Kevin Porter Jr./49 6.00 15.00
25 Tyler Herro/49 30.00 80.00
26 Bruno Fernando/49 4.00 10.00
27 Chuma Okeke/49 5.00 12.00
28 Luka Samanic/49 4.00 10.00
29 RJ Barrett/99 30.00 80.00
30 Ty Jerome/49 6.00 15.00

2019-20 Donruss Optic Rookie Dominators Signatures Purple Stars

*PRPL STARS: .6X TO 1.5X BASIC
STATED PRINT RUN 29 SER.#'d SETS
EXCHANGE DEADLINE 8/5/2021
9 Zion Williamson 600.00 1,200.00
17 Sekou Doumbouya 5.00 12.00
25 Tyler Herro 60.00 150.00
27 Chuma Okeke 15.00 40.00

2019-20 Donruss Optic Signature Series

EXCHANGE DEADLINE 8/5/2021
44 Chris Bosh 5.00 12.00
45 Darius Bazley 2.50 6.00
46 Kobe Bryant EXCH 500.00 1,000.00
47 Kevin Durant EXCH 100.00 250.00
48 Magic Johnson 60.00 150.00
49 Charles Barkley EXCH 60.00 150.00
60 RJ Barrett 30.00 80.00
61 Nassir Little 4.00 10.00
62 Coby White 8.00 20.00
63 PJ Washington Jr. 8.00 20.00
64 Carsen Edwards 3.00 8.00
65 Matisse Thybulle 5.00 12.00
66 Jarrett Culver 2.50 6.00
67 Quinndary Weatherspoon 2.50 6.00
68 Grant Williams 4.00 10.00
69 Eric Paschall 3.00 8.00
70 Dylan Windler 3.00 8.00
71 Admiral Schofield 3.00 8.00
72 Brandon Clarke 5.00 12.00
73 Cam Reddish 4.00 10.00
74 Kevin Porter Jr. 5.00 12.00
75 Ja Morant 400.00 800.00
76 Rui Hachimura 25.00 60.00
77 Ty Jerome 5.00 12.00
78 Bol Bol 12.00 30.00
79 Bruno Fernando 3.00 8.00
80 Cameron Johnson 6.00 15.00
81 Cody Martin 4.00 10.00
82 De'Andre Hunter 10.00 25.00
83 Goga Bitadze 4.00 10.00
84 Ignas Brazdeikis 3.00 8.00
85 Isaiah Roby 3.00 8.00
86 Jaylen Nowell 3.00 8.00
87 Jordan Poole 75.00 200.00
88 Keldon Johnson 40.00 100.00
89 Kyle Guy 3.00 8.00
90 KZ Okpala 3.00 8.00
91 Luka Samanic 3.00 8.00
92 Mfiondu Kabengele 3.00 8.00
93 Romeo Langford 2.50 6.00
94 Jaxson Hayes 4.00 10.00
95 Chuma Okeke 4.00 10.00
96 Tremont Waters 3.00 8.00
97 Tyler Herro EXCH 40.00 100.00
98 Nickeil Alexander-Walker 4.00 10.00
99 Sekou Doumbouya 2.50 6.00
100 Zion Williamson 400.00 800.00

2019-20 Donruss Optic Signature Series Blue

*BLUE: .75X TO 2X BASIC
STATED PRINT RUN 25 SER.#'d SETS
EXCHANGE DEADLINE 8/5/2021
2 Ricky Davis 6.00 15.00
3 Jordan Bone 5.00 12.00
4 Gary Clark 5.00 12.00
5 Alize Johnson 5.00 12.00
10 Otis Birdsong 8.00 20.00
11 Daryl Macon 5.00 12.00
12 Damian Jones 5.00 12.00
15 Wesley Matthews 5.00 12.00
16 Drew Eubanks 6.00 15.00
17 Daniel Gafford 10.00 25.00
18 Chimezie Metu 5.00 12.00
19 Ryan Broekhoff 8.00 20.00
20 Jarred Vanderbilt 5.00 12.00
21 Terence Davis 8.00 20.00
22 Max Strus 50.00 120.00
23 Jonah Bolden 8.00 20.00
26 Otto Porter Jr. 5.00 12.00
27 Theo Pinson 5.00 12.00
28 Duncan Robinson 75.00 200.00
29 Chandler Hutchison 5.00 12.00
30 Montrezl Harrell 6.00 15.00
32 Robert Covington 6.00 15.00
33 Dario Saric 6.00 15.00
34 Kadeem Allen 5.00 12.00
35 Semi Ojeleye 5.00 12.00
36 Cedi Osman 6.00 15.00
37 De'Anthony Melton 5.00 12.00
38 Nicolo Melli 6.00 15.00
39 Edmond Sumner 5.00 12.00
40 Noah Vonleh 5.00 12.00
41 Jason Terry 6.00 15.00
42 Luke Walton 6.00 15.00
43 Jalen Rose 6.00 15.00
50 Bob Dandridge 5.00 12.00
51 Nicolas Claxton 10.00 25.00
52 Marial Shayok 5.00 12.00
53 Alen Smailagic 5.00 12.00
54 Dewan Hernandez 5.00 12.00
55 Terance Mann 10.00 25.00
56 Justin Wright-Foreman 5.00 12.00
57 Jalen Lecque 5.00 12.00
59 Miye Oni 5.00 12.00
60 RJ Barrett 75.00 200.00

2019-20 Donruss Optic Signature Series Choice

*CHOICE: .5X TO 1.2X BASIC
EXCHANGE DEADLINE 8/5/2021
15 Wesley Matthews 3.00 8.00
26 Otto Porter Jr. 3.00 8.00
30 Montrezl Harrell 4.00 10.00
32 Robert Covington 3.00 8.00
33 Dario Saric 4.00 10.00
41 Jason Terry 4.00 10.00
42 Luke Walton 4.00 10.00
43 Jalen Rose 4.00 10.00
50 Bob Dandridge 3.00 8.00

2019-20 Donruss Optic Signature Series Green

*GREEN: .5X TO 1.2X BASIC
EXCHANGE DEADLINE 8/5/2021
2 Ricky Davis 4.00 10.00
3 Jordan Bone 3.00 8.00
4 Gary Clark 3.00 8.00
5 Alize Johnson 3.00 8.00
10 Otis Birdsong 5.00 12.00
11 Daryl Macon 3.00 8.00
12 Damian Jones 3.00 8.00
15 Wesley Matthews 3.00 8.00
16 Drew Eubanks 4.00 10.00
17 Daniel Gafford 6.00 15.00
18 Chimezie Metu 3.00 8.00
19 Ryan Broekhoff 5.00 12.00
20 Jarred Vanderbilt 3.00 8.00
21 Terence Davis 5.00 12.00
23 Jonah Bolden 5.00 12.00
26 Otto Porter Jr. 3.00 8.00
27 Theo Pinson 3.00 8.00
28 Duncan Robinson 50.00 120.00
29 Chandler Hutchison 3.00 8.00
30 Montrezl Harrell 4.00 10.00
32 Robert Covington 3.00 8.00
33 Dario Saric 4.00 10.00
34 Kadeem Allen 3.00 8.00
35 Semi Ojeleye 3.00 8.00
36 Cedi Osman 4.00 10.00
37 De'Anthony Melton 3.00 8.00
38 Nicolo Melli 4.00 10.00
39 Edmond Sumner 3.00 8.00
40 Noah Vonleh 3.00 8.00
41 Jason Terry 4.00 10.00
42 Luke Walton 4.00 10.00
43 Jalen Rose 4.00 10.00
50 Bob Dandridge 3.00 8.00
51 Nicolas Claxton 6.00 15.00
52 Marial Shayok 3.00 8.00
53 Alen Smailagic 3.00 8.00
54 Dewan Hernandez 3.00 8.00
55 Terance Mann 6.00 15.00
56 Justin Wright-Foreman 3.00 8.00
57 Jalen Lecque 3.00 8.00
59 Miye Oni 3.00 8.00

2019-20 Donruss Optic Signature Series Holo

*HOLO: .5X TO 1.2X BASIC
EXCHANGE DEADLINE 8/5/2021
2 Ricky Davis 4.00 10.00
3 Jordan Bone 3.00 8.00
4 Gary Clark 3.00 8.00
5 Alize Johnson 3.00 8.00
10 Otis Birdsong 5.00 12.00
11 Daryl Macon 3.00 8.00
12 Damian Jones 3.00 8.00
15 Wesley Matthews 3.00 8.00
16 Drew Eubanks 4.00 10.00
17 Daniel Gafford 6.00 15.00
18 Chimezie Metu 3.00 8.00
19 Ryan Broekhoff 5.00 12.00
20 Jarred Vanderbilt 3.00 8.00
21 Terence Davis 5.00 12.00
22 Max Strus 15.00 40.00
23 Jonah Bolden 5.00 12.00
26 Otto Porter Jr. 3.00 8.00
27 Theo Pinson 3.00 8.00
28 Duncan Robinson 40.00 100.00
29 Chandler Hutchison 3.00 8.00
30 Montrezl Harrell 4.00 10.00
32 Robert Covington 3.00 8.00
33 Dario Saric 4.00 10.00
34 Kadeem Allen 3.00 8.00
35 Semi Ojeleye 3.00 8.00
36 Cedi Osman 4.00 10.00
37 De'Anthony Melton 3.00 8.00
38 Nicolo Melli 4.00 10.00
39 Edmond Sumner 3.00 8.00
40 Noah Vonleh 3.00 8.00
41 Jason Terry 4.00 10.00
42 Luke Walton 4.00 10.00
43 Jalen Rose 4.00 10.00
50 Bob Dandridge 3.00 8.00
51 Nicolas Claxton 6.00 15.00
52 Marial Shayok 3.00 8.00
53 Alen Smailagic 3.00 8.00
54 Dewan Hernandez 3.00 8.00
55 Terance Mann 6.00 15.00
56 Justin Wright-Foreman 3.00 8.00
57 Jalen Lecque 3.00 8.00
59 Miye Oni 3.00 8.00

2019-20 Donruss Optic Signature Series Pink

*PINK: .75X TO 2X BASIC
STATED PRINT RUN 25 SER.#'d SETS
EXCHANGE DEADLINE 8/5/2021
2 Ricky Davis 6.00 15.00
3 Jordan Bone 5.00 12.00
4 Gary Clark 5.00 12.00
5 Alize Johnson 5.00 12.00
10 Otis Birdsong 8.00 20.00
11 Daryl Macon 5.00 12.00
12 Damian Jones 5.00 12.00
15 Wesley Matthews 5.00 12.00
16 Drew Eubanks 6.00 15.00

17 Daniel Gafford 10.00 25.00
18 Chimezie Metu 5.00 12.00
19 Ryan Broekhoff 8.00 20.00
20 Jarred Vanderbilt 5.00 12.00
21 Terence Davis 8.00 20.00
22 Max Strus 50.00 120.00
23 Jonah Bolden 8.00 20.00
26 Otto Porter Jr. 5.00 12.00
27 Theo Pinson 5.00 12.00
28 Duncan Robinson 75.00 200.00
29 Chandler Hutchison 5.00 12.00
30 Montrezl Harrell 6.00 15.00
32 Robert Covington 5.00 12.00
33 Dario Saric 6.00 15.00
34 Kadeem Allen 5.00 12.00
35 Semi Ojeleye 5.00 12.00
36 Cedi Osman 6.00 15.00
37 De'Anthony Melton 5.00 12.00
38 Nicolo Melli 6.00 15.00
39 Edmond Sumner 5.00 12.00
40 Noah Vonleh 5.00 12.00
41 Jason Terry 6.00 15.00
42 Luke Walton 6.00 15.00
43 Jalen Rose 6.00 15.00
50 Bob Dandridge 5.00 12.00
51 Nicolas Claxton 10.00 25.00
52 Marial Shayok 5.00 12.00
53 Alen Smailagic 5.00 12.00
54 Dewan Hernandez 5.00 12.00
55 Terance Mann 10.00 25.00
56 Justin Wright-Foreman 5.00 12.00
57 Jalen Lecque 5.00 12.00
59 Miye Oni 5.00 12.00
60 RJ Barrett 75.00 200.00

2019-20 Donruss Optic Signature Series Purple

*PURPLE: .5X TO 1.2X BASIC
EXCHANGE DEADLINE 8/5/2021
2 Ricky Davis 4.00 10.00
3 Jordan Bone 3.00 8.00
4 Gary Clark 3.00 8.00
5 Alize Johnson 3.00 8.00
10 Otis Birdsong 5.00 12.00
11 Daryl Macon 3.00 8.00
12 Damian Jones 3.00 8.00
15 Wesley Matthews 3.00 8.00
16 Drew Eubanks 4.00 10.00
17 Daniel Gafford 6.00 15.00
18 Chimezie Metu 3.00 8.00
19 Ryan Broekhoff 5.00 12.00
20 Jarred Vanderbilt 3.00 8.00
21 Terence Davis 5.00 12.00
22 Max Strus 15.00 40.00
23 Jonah Bolden 5.00 12.00
26 Otto Porter Jr. 3.00 8.00
27 Theo Pinson 3.00 8.00
28 Duncan Robinson 40.00 100.00
29 Chandler Hutchison 3.00 8.00
30 Montrezl Harrell 4.00 10.00
32 Robert Covington 3.00 8.00
33 Dario Saric 4.00 10.00
34 Kadeem Allen 3.00 8.00
35 Semi Ojeleye 3.00 8.00
36 Cedi Osman 4.00 10.00
37 De'Anthony Melton 3.00 8.00
38 Nicolo Melli 4.00 10.00
39 Edmond Sumner 3.00 8.00
40 Noah Vonleh 3.00 8.00
41 Jason Terry 4.00 10.00
42 Luke Walton 4.00 10.00
43 Jalen Rose 4.00 10.00
50 Bob Dandridge 3.00 8.00
51 Nicolas Claxton 6.00 15.00
52 Marial Shayok 3.00 8.00
53 Alen Smailagic 3.00 8.00
54 Dewan Hernandez 3.00 8.00
55 Terance Mann 6.00 15.00
56 Justin Wright-Foreman 3.00 8.00
57 Jalen Lecque 3.00 8.00
59 Miye Oni 3.00 8.00

2019-20 Donruss Optic Star Gazing

1 Stephen Curry 3.00 8.00
2 Karl-Anthony Towns .60 1.50
3 Anthony Davis 1.00 2.50
4 Donovan Mitchell .75 2.00
5 Paul George .60 1.50
6 Ben Simmons .40 1.00
7 Damian Lillard 1.00 2.50
8 Joel Embiid .75 2.00
9 LeBron James 3.00 8.00
10 Kyrie Irving .75 2.00
11 Kawhi Leonard 1.00 2.50
12 Nikola Jokic 2.00 5.00
13 Russell Westbrook .60 1.50
14 Giannis Antetokounmpo 2.00 5.00
15 James Harden .75 2.00

2019-20 Donruss Optic Star Gazing Blue

*BLUE: 1X TO 2.5X BASIC
STATED PRINT RUN 49 SER. #'D SETS
9 LeBron James 300.00 600.00

2019-20 Donruss Optic Star Gazing Holo

*HOLO: .6X TO 1.5X BASIC
9 LeBron James 100.00 250.00

2019-20 Donruss Optic Star Gazing Holo Fast Break

*FB HOLO: .6X TO 1.5X BASIC
9 LeBron James 40.00 100.00

2019-20 Donruss Optic Star Gazing Red

*RED: .75X TO 2X BASIC
STATED PRINT RUN 99 SER. #'D SETS
9 LeBron James 100.00 250.00

2019-20 Donruss Optic T-Minus 3, 2, 1

1 Joel Embiid .75 2.00
2 Anthony Davis 1.00 2.50
3 Paul George .60 1.50
4 James Harden .75 2.00
5 Kawhi Leonard 1.00 2.50
6 Stephen Curry 3.00 8.00
7 Damian Lillard 1.00 2.50
8 Giannis Antetokounmpo 2.00 5.00
9 LeBron James 3.00 8.00
10 Karl-Anthony Towns .60 1.50

2019-20 Donruss Optic T-Minus 3, 2, 1 Blue

*BLUE: .75X TO 2X BASIC
STATED PRINT RUN 85 SER. #'D SETS
9 LeBron James 40.00 100.00

2019-20 Donruss Optic T-Minus 3, 2, 1 Holo

*HOLO: .6X TO 1.5X BASIC
9 LeBron James 15.00 40.00

2019-20 Donruss Optic T-Minus 3, 2, 1 Lime Green

*LIME GREEN: .75X TO 2X BASIC
STATED PRINT RUN 149 SER.#'d SETS
9 LeBron James 30.00 80.00

2019-20 Donruss Optic T-Minus 3, 2, 1 Orange

*ORANGE: 1.5X TO 4X BASIC
STATED PRINT RUN 39 SER. #'D SETS
9 LeBron James 125.00 300.00

2019-20 Donruss Optic T-Minus 3, 2, 1 Purple

*PURPLE: .75X TO 2X BASIC
9 LeBron James 15.00 40.00

2019-20 Donruss Optic The Rookies

1 Zion Williamson 10.00 25.00
2 Ja Morant 12.00 30.00
3 RJ Barrett 1.00 2.50
4 De'Andre Hunter 1.00 2.50
5 Rui Hachimura 1.00 2.50

2019-20 Donruss Optic The Rookies Blue

*BLUE: 1X TO 2.5X BASIC
STATED PRINT RUN 49 SER. #'D SETS
1 Zion Williamson 125.00 300.00
2 Ja Morant 150.00 400.00

2019-20 Donruss Optic The Rookies Holo

*HOLO: .6X TO 1.5X BASIC
1 Zion Williamson 20.00 50.00
2 Ja Morant 25.00 60.00

2019-20 Donruss Optic The Rookies Holo Fast Break

*FB HOLO: .6X TO 1.5X BASIC
1 Zion Williamson 20.00 50.00
2 Ja Morant 25.00 60.00

2019-20 Donruss Optic The Rookies Red

*RED: .75X TO 2X BASIC
STATED PRINT RUN 99 SER. #'D SETS
1 Zion Williamson 75.00 200.00
2 Ja Morant 100.00 250.00

2019-20 Donruss Optic Winner Stays

1 Magic Johnson 1.25 3.00
2 Dirk Nowitzki 1.00 2.50
3 Kareem Abdul-Jabbar 1.25 3.00
4 Paul Pierce .60 1.50
5 Joe Dumars .40 1.00
6 Kawhi Leonard 1.00 2.50
7 Tim Duncan 1.00 2.50
8 Kawhi Leonard 1.00 2.50
9 Hakeem Olajuwon .75 2.00
10 LeBron James 3.00 8.00
11 Larry Bird 1.50 4.00
12 Kobe Bryant 3.00 8.00
13 Moses Malone .60 1.50
14 Tony Parker .50 1.25
15 James Worthy .60 1.50
16 Dwyane Wade .75 2.00
17 Shaquille O'Neal 1.50 4.00
18 Kevin Durant 1.25 3.00
19 Isiah Thomas .75 2.00
20 LeBron James 3.00 8.00

2019-20 Donruss Optic Winner Stays Blue

*BLUE: 1.25X TO 3X BASIC
STATED PRINT RUN 85 SER. #'D SETS
10 LeBron James 40.00 100.00
20 LeBron James 40.00 100.00

2019-20 Donruss Optic Winner Stays Holo

*HOLO: .75X TO 2X BASIC
10 LeBron James 12.00 30.00
12 Kobe Bryant 12.00 30.00
20 LeBron James 12.00 30.00

2019-20 Donruss Optic Winner Stays Lime Green

*LIME GREEN: 1.25X TO 3X BASIC
STATED PRINT RUN 149 SER.#'d SETS
10 LeBron James 30.00 80.00
20 LeBron James 30.00 80.00

2019-20 Donruss Optic Winner Stays Orange

*ORANGE: 1.5X TO 4X BASIC
STATED PRINT RUN 39 SER. #'D SETS
10 LeBron James 60.00 150.00
20 LeBron James 60.00 150.00

2019-20 Donruss Optic Winner Stays Pink

*PINK: 2.5X TO 6X BASIC
STATED PRINT RUN 25 SER. #'D SETS
10 LeBron James 125.00 300.00
20 LeBron James 125.00 300.00

2019-20 Donruss Optic Winner Stays Purple

*PURPLE: .6X TO 1.5X BASIC
10 LeBron James 8.00 20.00
12 Kobe Bryant 8.00 20.00
20 LeBron James 8.00 20.00

2020-21 Donruss Optic

*BLUE VELOCITY: 1.25X TO 3X BASIC
*PURPLE: 1.25X TO 3X BASIC
*PURPLE SHOCK: 1.25X TO 3X BASIC
*BLUE PULSAR: 1.5X TO 4X BASIC
1 Josh Richardson .30 .75
2 Trae Young 1.00 2.50
3 Paul George .60 1.50
4 Jerami Grant .40 1.00
5 Brandon Clarke .40 1.00
6 Jamal Murray .60 1.50
7 Danilo Gallinari .30 .75
8 Kyle Kuzma .50 1.25
9 Markelle Fultz .30 .75
10 Keldon Johnson .60 1.50
11 Christian Wood .30 .75
12 Devonte' Graham .30 .75
13 LeBron James 3.00 8.00
14 Lou Williams .40 1.00
15 Thomas Bryant .30 .75
16 Jaren Jackson Jr. .60 1.50
17 Stephen Curry 3.00 8.00
18 Kevin Huerter .30 .75
19 Sekou Doumbouya .25 .60
20 Joel Embiid 1.00 2.50
21 Miles Bridges .40 1.00
22 Al Horford .40 1.00
23 De'Aaron Fox .60 1.50
24 T.J. Warren .30 .75
25 Carmelo Anthony .60 1.50
26 Cody Zeller .25 .60
27 Goran Dragic .40 1.00
28 Rudy Gobert .50 1.25
29 Giannis Antetokounmpo 2.00 5.00
30 Donovan Mitchell .75 2.00
31 Brook Lopez .30 .75
32 JJ Redick .40 1.00
33 Jimmy Butler .75 2.00
34 Wendell Carter Jr. .30 .75
35 Harrison Barnes .30 .75
36 DeMar DeRozan .50 1.25
37 Steven Adams .40 1.00
38 Myles Turner .40 1.00
39 Tim Hardaway Jr. .25 .60
40 Zion Williamson 1.25 3.00
41 Marcus Smart .40 1.00
42 Anthony Davis 1.00 2.50
43 Spencer Dinwiddie .30 .75
44 Jusuf Nurkic .40 1.00
45 Dwight Powell .25 .60
46 Eric Paschall .30 .75
47 Marvin Bagley III .30 .75
48 Duncan Robinson .40 1.00
49 Klay Thompson 1.00 2.50
50 Norman Powell .30 .75
51 Eric Bledsoe .30 .75
52 Bam Adebayo .60 1.50
53 John Wall .50 1.25
54 Mikal Bridges .50 1.25
55 Khris Middleton .50 1.25
56 Montrezl Harrell .40 1.00
57 D'Angelo Russell .40 1.00
58 Brandon Ingram .50 1.25
59 Malcolm Brogdon .40 1.00
60 Buddy Hield .40 1.00
61 Tyler Herro .75 2.00
62 RJ Barrett .60 1.50
63 Kyle Lowry .60 1.50
64 Joe Ingles .30 .75
65 Luke Kennard .30 .75
66 Jonathan Isaac .40 1.00
67 Rui Hachimura .50 1.25
68 Donte DiVincenzo .40 1.00
69 Victor Oladipo .30 .75
70 Russell Westbrook .75 2.00
71 LaMarcus Aldridge .40 1.00
72 Terry Rozier .40 1.00
73 Kevin Knox II .25 .60
74 Josh Jackson .25 .60
75 Michael Porter Jr. .50 1.25
76 Kevin Love .40 1.00
77 Jayson Tatum 1.50 4.00
78 Cam Reddish .50 1.25
79 Karl-Anthony Towns .60 1.50
80 Otto Porter Jr. .25 .60
81 Mo Bamba .40 1.00
82 Kristaps Porzingis .50 1.25
83 Lonnie Walker IV .40 1.00
84 De'Andre Hunter .40 1.00
85 Lauri Markkanen .50 1.25
86 Luka Doncic 2.50 6.00
87 Bradley Beal .50 1.25
88 Bojan Bogdanovic .30 .75
89 Julius Randle .40 1.00
90 Deandre Ayton .40 1.00
91 Serge Ibaka .30 .75
92 Caris LeVert .40 1.00
93 Dejounte Murray .40 1.00
94 Luguentz Dort .60 1.50
95 Kemba Walker .40 1.00
96 Nikola Jokic 2.00 5.00
97 Jaxson Hayes .30 .75
98 Alex Caruso .40 1.00
99 Mitchell Robinson .40 1.00
100 Chris Paul .75 2.00
101 Kyrie Irving .75 2.00
102 Derrick Rose .60 1.50
103 Pascal Siakam .60 1.50
104 Bogdan Bogdanovic .40 1.00
105 Elfrid Payton .30 .75
106 Jrue Holiday .40 1.00
107 Rajon Rondo .40 1.00
108 P.J. Tucker .30 .75
109 Paul Millsap .30 .75
110 Josh Okogie .30 .75
111 Ben Simmons .40 1.00
112 Rudy Gay .40 1.00
113 Seth Curry .40 1.00
114 Danuel House Jr. .30 .75
115 Kevin Porter Jr. .30 .75
116 Zach LaVine .60 1.50
117 Ja Morant 1.25 3.00
118 Jarrett Allen .40 1.00
119 Aaron Gordon .40 1.00
120 Andre Drummond .40 1.00
121 Blake Griffin .40 1.00
122 Devin Booker 1.00 2.50
123 Mike Conley .30 .75
124 Zach Collins .30 .75
125 Kawhi Leonard 1.00 2.50
126 Coby White .50 1.25
127 Jaylen Brown .60 1.50
128 Jonas Valanciunas .30 .75
129 Darius Garland .60 1.50
130 Nikola Vucevic .40 1.00
131 Fred VanVleet .60 1.50
132 Kelly Oubre Jr. .40 1.00
133 Landry Shamet .30 .75
134 James Harden .75 2.00
135 CJ McCollum .40 1.00
136 Kevin Durant 1.50 4.00
137 PJ Washington Jr. .40 1.00
138 Ricky Rubio .40 1.00
139 John Collins .40 1.00
140 Gordon Hayward .40 1.00
141 Davis Bertans .30 .75
142 Domantas Sabonis .50 1.25
143 Shai Gilgeous-Alexander 2.00 5.00
144 Damian Lillard 1.00 2.50
145 Tobias Harris .40 1.00
146 Andrew Wiggins .50 1.25
147 Eric Gordon .30 .75
148 Collin Sexton .40 1.00
149 Draymond Green .50 1.25
150 Jarrett Culver .25 .60
151 Anthony Edwards RR RC 8.00 20.00
152 James Wiseman RR RC .75 2.00
153 LaMelo Ball RR RC 5.00 12.00
154 Patrick Williams RR RC 1.50 4.00
155 Isaac Okoro RR RC 1.00 2.50
156 Onyeka Okongwu RR RC 1.25 3.00
157 Killian Hayes RR RC .60 1.50
158 Obi Toppin RR RC 1.25 3.00
159 Deni Avdija RR RC 1.50 4.00
160 Jalen Smith RR RC 1.25 3.00
161 Devin Vassell RR RC 2.00 5.00
162 Tyrese Haliburton RR RC 5.00 12.00
163 Kira Lewis Jr. RR RC .60 1.50
164 Aaron Nesmith RR RC 1.25 3.00
165 Cole Anthony RR RC 1.50 4.00
166 Isaiah Stewart RR RC 1.25 3.00
167 Aleksej Pokusevski RR RC .75 2.00
168 Josh Green RR RC 1.25 3.00
169 Saddiq Bey RR RC 1.25 3.00
170 Precious Achiuwa RR RC 1.25 3.00
171 Tyrese Maxey RR RC 5.00 12.00
172 Zeke Nnaji RR RC .75 2.00
173 Devon Dotson RR RC .60 1.50
174 RJ Hampton RR RC .60 1.50
175 Immanuel Quickley RR RC 1.50 4.00
176 Payton Pritchard RR RC 2.00 5.00
177 Udoka Azubuike RR RC .75 2.00
178 Jaden McDaniels RR RC 2.00 5.00
179 Malachi Flynn RR RC .60 1.50
180 Desmond Bane RR RC 2.00 5.00
181 Tyrell Terry RR RC .50 1.25
182 Vernon Carey Jr. RR RC .60 1.50
183 Daniel Oturu RR RC .60 1.50
184 Theo Maledon RR RC .60 1.50
185 Xavier Tillman RR RC .75 2.00
186 Tyler Bey RR RC .60 1.50
187 Robert Woodard II RR RC .60 1.50
188 Tre Jones RR RC 1.00 2.50
189 Jordan Nwora RR RC .75 2.00
190 Nico Mannion RR RC .60 1.50
191 Saben Lee RR RC .60 1.50
192 Elijah Hughes RR RC .60 1.50
193 Nick Richards RR RC .75 2.00
194 Jahmius Ramsey RR RC .60 1.50
195 CJ Elleby RR RC .60 1.50
196 Skylar Mays RR RC .60 1.50
197 Kenyon Martin Jr. RR RC 1.00 2.50
198 Cassius Winston RR RC .60 1.50
199 Cassius Stanley RR RC .60 1.50
200 Grant Riller RR RC .60 1.50

2020-21 Donruss Optic Blue

*BLUE: 4X TO 10X BASIC
STATED PRINT RUN 59 SER. #'D SETS
151 Anthony Edwards RR 300.00 600.00
153 LaMelo Ball RR 400.00 800.00
154 Patrick Williams RR 20.00 50.00
162 Tyrese Haliburton RR 125.00 300.00
165 Cole Anthony RR 20.00 50.00
171 Tyrese Maxey RR 150.00 400.00
180 Desmond Bane RR 25.00 60.00

2020-21 Donruss Optic Checkerboard

*CHKRBRD: 2.5X TO 6X BASIC
2 Trae Young 30.00 80.00
13 LeBron James 100.00 250.00
17 Stephen Curry 100.00 250.00
29 Giannis Antetokounmpo 30.00 80.00
30 Donovan Mitchell 12.00 30.00
40 Zion Williamson 75.00 200.00
49 Klay Thompson 20.00 50.00
61 Tyler Herro 12.00 30.00
77 Jayson Tatum 40.00 100.00
86 Luka Doncic 75.00 200.00
90 Deandre Ayton 10.00 25.00
100 Chris Paul 12.00 30.00
102 Derrick Rose 8.00 20.00
116 Zach LaVine 10.00 25.00
117 Ja Morant 75.00 200.00
118 Jarrett Allen 10.00 25.00
122 Devin Booker 20.00 50.00
127 Jaylen Brown 10.00 25.00
131 Fred VanVleet 10.00 25.00
134 James Harden 10.00 25.00
136 Kevin Durant 25.00 60.00
143 Shai Gilgeous-Alexander 10.00 25.00
151 Anthony Edwards RR 300.00 600.00
153 LaMelo Ball RR 1,000.00 2,000.00
154 Patrick Williams RR 100.00 250.00
157 Killian Hayes RR 30.00 80.00
158 Obi Toppin RR 75.00 200.00
159 Deni Avdija RR 50.00 120.00
161 Devin Vassell RR 40.00 100.00
162 Tyrese Haliburton RR 125.00 300.00
164 Aaron Nesmith RR 30.00 80.00
165 Cole Anthony RR 200.00 500.00
171 Tyrese Maxey RR 200.00 500.00
174 RJ Hampton RR 5.00 12.00
175 Immanuel Quickley RR 50.00 120.00
176 Payton Pritchard RR 50.00 120.00
178 Jaden McDaniels RR 20.00 50.00
180 Desmond Bane RR 50.00 120.00
189 Jordan Nwora RR 40.00 100.00
191 Saben Lee RR 15.00 40.00
197 Kenyon Martin Jr. RR 25.00 60.00

2020-21 Donruss Optic Choice

*CHOICE: 1.5X TO 4X BASIC
153 LaMelo Ball RR 300.00 600.00
171 Tyrese Maxey RR 30.00 80.00
189 Jordan Nwora RR 20.00 50.00

2020-21 Donruss Optic Choice Red

*CHOICE RED: 3X TO 8X BASIC
STATED PRINT RUN 88 SER. #'D SETS
151 Anthony Edwards RR 200.00 500.00
153 LaMelo Ball RR 75.00 200.00
162 Tyrese Haliburton RR 75.00 200.00
171 Tyrese Maxey RR 60.00 150.00

2020-21 Donruss Optic Choice Red and Green

*CHOICE RD & GRN: 1.5X TO 4X BASIC
13 LeBron James 20.00 50.00
86 Luka Doncic 20.00 50.00
153 LaMelo Ball RR 800.00 1,500.00
171 Tyrese Maxey RR 30.00 80.00
189 Jordan Nwora RR 20.00 50.00

2020-21 Donruss Optic Fast Break Blue

*FB BLUE: 4X TO 10X BASIC
STATED PRINT RUN 50 SER. #'D SETS
13 LeBron James 150.00 400.00
17 Stephen Curry 60.00 150.00
86 Luka Doncic 100.00 250.00
117 Ja Morant 50.00 120.00
151 Anthony Edwards RR 400.00 800.00
153 LaMelo Ball RR 1,500.00 3,000.00
154 Patrick Williams RR 75.00 200.00
162 Tyrese Haliburton RR 100.00 250.00
165 Cole Anthony RR 125.00 300.00
171 Tyrese Maxey RR 125.00 300.00
180 Desmond Bane RR 100.00 250.00
189 Jordan Nwora RR 50.00 120.00

2020-21 Donruss Optic Fast Break Holo

*HOLO: 1.5X TO 4X BASIC
13 LeBron James 20.00 50.00
153 LaMelo Ball RR 200.00 500.00
161 Devin Vassell RR 12.00 30.00
189 Jordan Nwora RR 25.00 60.00

2020-21 Donruss Optic Fast Break Pink

*FB PINK: 6X TO 15X BASIC
STATED PRINT RUN 20 SER. #'D SETS
13 LeBron James 300.00 600.00
17 Stephen Curry 100.00 250.00
86 Luka Doncic 150.00 400.00
117 Ja Morant 75.00 200.00
151 Anthony Edwards RR 600.00 1,200.00
153 LaMelo Ball RR 2,500.00 5,000.00
154 Patrick Williams RR 125.00 300.00
162 Tyrese Haliburton RR 150.00 40.00
165 Cole Anthony RR 200.00 500.00
171 Tyrese Maxey RR 200.00 500.00
180 Desmond Bane RR 150.00 400.00
189 Jordan Nwora RR 75.00 200.00

2020-21 Donruss Optic Fast Break Purple

*FB PURPLE: 3X TO 8X BASIC
STATED PRINT RUN 95 SER. #'D SETS
13 LeBron James 125.00 300.00
17 Stephen Curry 50.00 120.00
86 Luka Doncic 75.00 200.00
151 Anthony Edwards RR 200.00 500.00
153 LaMelo Ball RR 1,000.00 2,000.00
154 Patrick Williams RR 60.00 150.00
162 Tyrese Haliburton RR 75.00 200.00
165 Cole Anthony RR 100.00 250.00
171 Tyrese Maxey RR 100.00 250.00
180 Desmond Bane RR 75.00 200.00
189 Jordan Nwora RR 40.00 100.00

2020-21 Donruss Optic Fast Break Red

*FB RED: 3X TO 8X BASIC
STATED PRINT RUN 85 SER. #'D SETS
13 LeBron James 125.00 300.00
17 Stephen Curry 50.00 120.00
86 Luka Doncic 75.00 200.00
151 Anthony Edwards RR 200.00 500.00
153 LaMelo Ball RR 1,000.00 2,000.00
154 Patrick Williams RR 60.00 150.00
162 Tyrese Haliburton RR 75.00 200.00
165 Cole Anthony RR 100.00 250.00
171 Tyrese Maxey RR 100.00 250.00
180 Desmond Bane RR 75.00 200.00
189 Jordan Nwora RR 40.00 100.00

2020-21 Donruss Optic Holo

*HOLO: 1.5X TO 4X BASIC
153 LaMelo Ball RR 60.00 150.00

2020-21 Donruss Optic Hyper Pink

153 LaMelo Ball RR 60.00 150.00

2020-21 Donruss Optic Lime Green

*LIME GREEN: 2.5X TO 6X BASIC
STATED PRINT RUN 149 SER. #'D SETS
151 Anthony Edwards RR 200.00 500.00
153 LaMelo Ball RR 200.00 500.00
162 Tyrese Haliburton RR 60.00 150.00
171 Tyrese Maxey RR 75.00 200.00

2020-21 Donruss Optic Orange

*ORNG: 2X TO 5X BASIC
STATED PRINT RUN 199 SER. #'D SETS
151 Anthony Edwards RR 150.00 400.00
153 LaMelo Ball RR 200.00 500.00
162 Tyrese Haliburton RR 60.00 150.00
171 Tyrese Maxey RR 75.00 200.00

2020-21 Donruss Optic Pink

*PINK: 6X TO 15X BASIC
STATED PRINT RUN 25 SER. #'D SETS
13 LeBron James 300.00 600.00
17 Stephen Curry 100.00 250.00
86 Luka Doncic 150.00 400.00
117 Ja Morant 75.00 200.00
151 Anthony Edwards RR 600.00 1,200.00
153 LaMelo Ball RR 2,500.00 5,000.00
154 Patrick Williams RR 125.00 300.00
162 Tyrese Haliburton RR 150.00 400.00
165 Cole Anthony RR 200.00 500.00
171 Tyrese Maxey RR 200.00 500.00
180 Desmond Bane RR 150.00 400.00
189 Jordan Nwora RR 75.00 200.00

2020-21 Donruss Optic Pink Velocity

*PINK VELOCITY: 4X TO 10X BASIC
STATED PRINT RUN 75 SER. #'D SETS
13 LeBron James 150.00 400.00
17 Stephen Curry 60.00 150.00
86 Luka Doncic 100.00 250.00
117 Ja Morant 50.00 120.00
151 Anthony Edwards RR 300.00 600.00
153 LaMelo Ball RR 1,500.00 3,000.00
154 Patrick Williams RR 75.00 200.00
162 Tyrese Haliburton RR 100.00 250.00
165 Cole Anthony RR 125.00 300.00
171 Tyrese Maxey RR 125.00 300.00
180 Desmond Bane RR 100.00 250.00
189 Jordan Nwora RR 50.00 120.00

2020-21 Donruss Optic Red

*RED: 3X TO 8X BASIC
STATED PRINT RUN 99 SER. #'D SETS
13 LeBron James 125.00 300.00
17 Stephen Curry 50.00 120.00
86 Luka Doncic 75.00 200.00
151 Anthony Edwards RR 200.00 500.00
153 LaMelo Ball RR 1,000.00 2,000.00
154 Patrick Williams RR 60.00 150.00
162 Tyrese Haliburton RR 75.00 200.00
165 Cole Anthony RR 100.00 250.00
171 Tyrese Maxey RR 100.00 250.00
180 Desmond Bane RR 75.00 200.00
189 Jordan Nwora RR 40.00 100.00

2020-21 Donruss Optic Red Pulsar

*RED PULSAR: 1.5X TO 4X BASIC
13 LeBron James 20.00 50.00
86 Luka Doncic 20.00 50.00
153 LaMelo Ball RR 300.00 600.00
171 Tyrese Maxey RR 30.00 80.00
189 Jordan Nwora RR 20.00 50.00

2020-21 Donruss Optic Target Purple Pulsar

*PURPLE PULSAR: .75X TO 2X BASIC
151 Anthony Edwards RR 75.00 200.00
153 LaMelo Ball RR 150.00 400.00

2020-21 Donruss Optic Air Defense

*PURPLE: .6X TO 1.5X BASIC
*HOLO: .75X TO 2X BASIC
*RED WAVE: 1.5X TO 4X BASIC
*LIME GREEN/149: 2X TO 5X BASIC
*BLUE/85: 2.5X TO 6X BASIC
*ORANGE/39: 4X TO 10X BASIC
*PINK/25: 5X TO 12X BASIC
1 Giannis Antetokounmpo 2.50 6.00
2 Bam Adebayo .75 2.00
3 LeBron James 4.00 10.00
4 Kawhi Leonard 1.25 3.00
5 Anthony Davis 1.25 3.00

2020-21 Donruss Optic All Stars

*HOLO: .75X TO 2X BASIC
*FB: 1.25X TO 3X BASIC
*BLUE PULSAR: 1.25X TO 3X BASIC
*RED PULSAR: 1.25X TO 3X BASIC
*RED/99: 2.5X TO 6X BASIC
*BLUE/49: 4X TO 10X BASIC
1 Kawhi Leonard 1.25 3.00
2 LeBron James 4.00 10.00
3 Anthony Davis 1.25 3.00
4 Luka Doncic 3.00 8.00
5 James Harden 1.00 2.50
6 Ben Simmons .50 1.25
7 Russell Westbrook 1.00 2.50
8 Chris Paul 1.00 2.50
9 Devin Booker 1.25 3.00
10 Jayson Tatum 2.00 5.00
11 Giannis Antetokounmpo 2.50 6.00
12 Kemba Walker .50 1.25
13 Trae Young 1.25 3.00
14 Donovan Mitchell 1.00 2.50
15 Jimmy Butler 1.00 2.50
16 Brandon Ingram .60 1.50
17 Joel Embiid 1.25 3.00
18 Nikola Jokic 2.50 6.00
19 Pascal Siakam .75 2.00
20 Khris Middleton .60 1.50

2020-21 Donruss Optic Dominators Signatures

PRINT RUN BTW 25-99 COPIES PER
EXCHANGE DEADLINE 2/27/2023
1 Otto Porter Jr./99 3.00 8.00
2 Kevin Huerter/99 4.00 10.00
3 Bradley Beal/49 20.00 50.00
4 Shake Milton/99 4.00 10.00
5 Jarrett Allen/99 5.00 12.00
6 Markelle Fultz/99 4.00 10.00
7 Zach Collins/99 4.00 10.00
8 Cam Reddish/99 12.00 30.00
9 Kyle Kuzma/99 6.00 15.00
10 Joe Harris/99 4.00 10.00
11 Lauri Markkanen/99 6.00 15.00
12 Mike Conley/99 4.00 10.00
13 J.J. Barea/99 4.00 10.00
14 LaMarcus Aldridge/49 5.00 12.00
15 Myles Turner/99 5.00 12.00
16 Devonte' Graham/99 4.00 10.00
17 Lou Williams/99 5.00 12.00
18 Domantas Sabonis/49 6.00 15.00
19 Trae Young/49 75.00 200.00
20 Mo Bamba/99 5.00 12.00
21 Gordon Hayward/49 5.00 12.00
22 Thomas Bryant/99 4.00 10.00
23 Jarrett Culver/99 3.00 8.00
24 Spencer Dinwiddie/99 4.00 10.00
25 Kelly Oubre Jr./99 5.00 12.00
26 Jayson Tatum/25 100.00 250.00
27 Cameron Johnson/99 6.00 15.00
28 Bam Adebayo/99 8.00 20.00
29 Kelly Olynyk/99 3.00 8.00
30 Lonzo Ball/99 12.00 30.00
31 Kawhi Leonard/25 75.00 200.00
32 Duncan Robinson/99 5.00 12.00
33 Jrue Holiday/99 12.00 30.00
34 John Collins/99 5.00 12.00
35 Donovan Mitchell/49 40.00 100.00
36 Tobias Harris/99 5.00 12.00
37 Patrick Beverley/99 3.00 8.00
38 Boban Marjanovic/99 10.00 25.00
39 Anfernee Simons/99 6.00 15.00
40 Donte DiVincenzo/99 5.00 12.00

2020-21 Donruss Optic Elite Dominators

*BLUE PULSAR: .75X TO 2X BASIC
*RED PULSAR: .75X TO 2X BASIC
*HOLO: .75X TO 2X BASIC
*FAST BREAK: 1.25X TO 3X BASIC
*RED/99: 2.5X TO 6X BASIC
*BLUE/49: 3X TO 8X BASIC
1 Luka Doncic 3.00 8.00
2 Pascal Siakam .75 2.00
3 LeBron James 4.00 10.00
4 Russell Westbrook 1.00 2.50
5 James Harden 1.00 2.50
6 Anthony Davis 1.25 3.00
7 Kawhi Leonard 1.25 3.00
8 Kyrie Irving 1.00 2.50
9 Damian Lillard 1.25 3.00
10 Trae Young 1.25 3.00
11 Paul George .75 2.00
12 Giannis Antetokounmpo 2.50 6.00
13 Stephen Curry 4.00 10.00
14 Devin Booker 1.25 3.00
15 Donovan Mitchell 1.00 2.50
16 Kemba Walker .50 1.25
17 Jimmy Butler 1.00 2.50
18 Jayson Tatum 2.00 5.00
19 Nikola Jokic 2.50 6.00
20 Jamal Murray .75 2.00
21 Ja Morant 1.50 4.00
22 Zion Williamson 1.50 4.00
23 Ben Simmons .50 1.25
24 Kevin Durant 2.00 5.00
25 Joel Embiid 1.25 3.00

2020-21 Donruss Optic Elite Dominators Red

STATED PRINT RUN 99 SER.#'d SETS

2020-21 Donruss Optic Express Lane

*PURPLE: .6X TO 1.5X BASIC
*HOLO: .75X TO 2X BASIC
*LIME GREEN/149: 2X TO 5X BASIC
*BLUE/85: 2.5X TO 6X BASIC
*ORANGE/39: 4X TO 10X BASIC
*PINK/25: 5X TO 12X BASIC
1 Ja Morant 1.50 4.00
2 John Stockton 1.00 2.50
3 Stephen Curry 4.00 10.00
4 Jason Williams .75 2.00
5 De'Aaron Fox .75 2.00
6 Pete Maravich 1.25 3.00
7 Kyle Lowry .60 1.50
8 Damian Lillard 1.25 3.00
9 Allen Iverson 1.25 3.00
10 Kyrie Irving 1.00 2.50
11 Trae Young 1.25 3.00
12 Devin Booker 1.25 3.00
13 Luka Doncic 3.00 8.00
14 Donovan Mitchell 1.00 2.50
15 Gary Payton .75 2.00
16 John Wall .60 1.50
17 Anfernee Hardaway 1.25 3.00
18 Jamal Murray .75 2.00
19 Dwyane Wade 1.00 2.50
20 Steve Nash 1.00 2.50
21 Isiah Thomas .75 2.00
22 Ben Simmons .50 1.25
23 Kemba Walker .50 1.25
24 Chris Paul 1.00 2.50
25 James Harden 1.00 2.50

2020-21 Donruss Optic Express Lane Blue

*BLUE: 2.5X TO 6X BASIC
STATED PRINT RUN 85 SER.#'d SETS

2020-21 Donruss Optic Express Lane Lime Green

*LIME GREEN: 2X TO 5X BASIC
STATED PRINT RUN 149 SER.#'d SETS

2020-21 Donruss Optic Express Lane Orange

*ORANGE: 4X TO 10X BASIC
STATED PRINT RUN 39 SER.#'d SETS

2020-21 Donruss Optic Express Lane Pink

*PINK: 5X TO 12X BASIC
STATED PRINT RUN 25 SER.#'d SETS

2020-21 Donruss Optic Fast Break Signatures

EXCHANGE DEADLINE 2/27/2023
1 Allen Iverson 75.00 200.00
2 Jarrett Culver 3.00 8.00
3 Caron Butler 4.00 10.00
4 Donte DiVincenzo 5.00 12.00
5 Daniel Gibson 3.00 8.00
6 Facundo Campazzo 5.00 12.00
7 Mike Bibby 5.00 12.00
8 Kevin Garnett 75.00 200.00
9 Boban Marjanovic 10.00 25.00
10 Magic Johnson 60.00 150.00
11 Tobias Harris 5.00 12.00
12 Dillon Brooks 5.00 12.00
13 Jordan Poole 40.00 100.00
14 Udonis Haslem 4.00 10.00
15 Gordon Hayward 10.00 25.00
16 Kyle Kuzma 6.00 15.00
17 Jrue Holiday 5.00 12.00
18 Kenyon Martin 5.00 12.00
19 Lenny Wilkens 5.00 12.00
20 Deron Williams 4.00 10.00
21 Pat Riley 20.00 50.00
22 Mo Bamba 5.00 12.00
23 Dave Bing 12.00 30.00
24 Danilo Gallinari 4.00 10.00
25 Buddy Hield 5.00 12.00
26 Karl Malone 40.00 100.00
27 Keith Van Horn 4.00 10.00
28 Dominique Wilkins 15.00 40.00
29 Antoine Walker 5.00 12.00
30 Lonzo Ball 25.00 60.00
31 Toni Kukoc 12.00 30.00
32 Sarunas Marciulionis 5.00 12.00
33 Hakeem Olajuwon 40.00 100.00

4 Karl-Anthony Towns 20.00 50.00
5 Stephon Marbury 12.00 30.00
6 Wendell Carter Jr. 4.00 10.00
7 Steve Francis 5.00 12.00
8 Joe Harris 4.00 10.00
9 Robert Horry 12.00 30.00
0 Cam Reddish 20.00 50.00
1 Zach Collins 4.00 10.00
2 Chuma Okeke 5.00 12.00
3 Bradley Beal 20.00 50.00
4 Jerry West 30.00 80.00
5 Josh Hart 4.00 10.00
6 Tim Hardaway 12.00 30.00
7 Otto Porter Jr. 3.00 8.00
8 Robert Covington 4.00 10.00
9 Michael Porter Jr. 6.00 15.00
0 Shawn Kemp 30.00 80.00
1 Anthony Edwards 300.00 600.00
2 LaMelo Ball 500.00 1,000.00
4 Patrick Williams 40.00 100.00
5 Isaac Okoro 6.00 15.00
6 Onyeka Okongwu 8.00 20.00
7 Killian Hayes 4.00 10.00
8 Obi Toppin 8.00 20.00
9 Deni Avdija 10.00 25.00
0 Jalen Smith 8.00 20.00
1 Devin Vassell 12.00 30.00
2 Tyrese Haliburton 50.00 120.00
3 Kira Lewis Jr. 4.00 10.00
4 Aaron Nesmith 15.00 40.00
5 Cole Anthony 50.00 120.00
6 Isaiah Stewart 8.00 20.00
7 Aleksej Pokusevski 5.00 12.00
8 Josh Green 8.00 20.00
9 Saddiq Bey 8.00 20.00
0 Precious Achiuwa 8.00 20.00
1 Tyrese Maxey 50.00 120.00
2 Zeke Nnaji 5.00 12.00
3 Caleb Martin 8.00 20.00
4 RJ Hampton 4.00 10.00
5 Immanuel Quickley 20.00 50.00
6 Payton Pritchard 12.00 30.00
7 Udoka Azubuike 5.00 12.00
8 Jaden McDaniels 12.00 30.00
9 Malachi Flynn 4.00 10.00
0 Desmond Bane 25.00 60.00
1 Tyrell Terry 3.00 8.00
2 Vernon Carey Jr. 4.00 10.00
3 Daniel Oturu 4.00 10.00
4 Theo Maledon 4.00 10.00
85 Xavier Tillman 5.00 12.00
86 Tyler Bey 4.00 10.00
87 Robert Woodard II 4.00 10.00
88 Tre Jones 6.00 15.00
89 Jordan Nwora 25.00 60.00
0 Nico Mannion 4.00 10.00
1 Saben Lee 4.00 10.00
2 Elijah Hughes 4.00 10.00
3 Nick Richards 5.00 12.00
4 Jahmi'us Ramsey 4.00 10.00
5 CJ Elleby 4.00 10.00
6 Skylar Mays 4.00 10.00
7 Kenyon Martin Jr. 6.00 15.00
8 Cassius Winston 4.00 10.00
9 Cassius Stanley 4.00 10.00
100 Grant Riller 4.00 10.00

2020-21 Donruss Optic Lights Out

1 James Harden 1.00 2.50
2 Bradley Beal .60 1.50
3 Damian Lillard 1.25 3.00
4 Trae Young 1.25 3.00
5 Devin Booker 1.25 3.00
6 Donovan Mitchell 1.00 2.50
7 Jamal Murray .75 2.00
8 Kevin Durant 2.00 5.00
9 Ja Morant 1.50 4.00
10 Luka Doncic 3.00 8.00
11 Giannis Antetokounmpo 2.50 6.00
12 Brandon Ingram .60 1.50
13 Zach LaVine .75 2.00
14 Anthony Davis 1.25 3.00
15 Paul George .75 2.00

2020-21 Donruss Optic Lights Out Blue

STATED PRINT RUN 49 SER.#'d SETS
4 Trae Young 20.00 50.00
9 Ja Morant 30.00 80.00
10 Luka Doncic 60.00 150.00
11 Giannis Antetokounmpo 20.00 50.00

2020-21 Donruss Optic Lights Out Blue Pulsar

9 Ja Morant 12.00 30.00
10 Luka Doncic 25.00 60.00

2020-21 Donruss Optic Lights Out Fast Break

9 Ja Morant 12.00 30.00
10 Luka Doncic 15.00 60.00

2020-21 Donruss Optic Lights Out Holo

9 Ja Morant 12.00 30.00
10 Luka Doncic 25.00 60.00

2020-21 Donruss Optic Lights Out Red

9 Ja Morant 25.00 60.00
10 Luka Doncic 50.00 120.00

2020-21 Donruss Optic Lights Out Red Pulsar

9 Ja Morant 12.00 30.00
10 Luka Doncic 25.00 60.00

2020-21 Donruss Optic My House

*PURPLE: .6X TO 1.5X BASIC
*HOLO: .75X TO 2X BASIC
1 Jayson Tatum 4.00 10.00
2 Giannis Antetokounmpo 5.00 12.00
3 Ja Morant 3.00 8.00
4 LeBron James 8.00 20.00
5 Stephen Curry 8.00 20.00
6 Jimmy Butler 2.00 5.00
7 Damian Lillard 2.50 6.00
8 Kyrie Irving 2.00 5.00
9 Nikola Jokic 5.00 12.00
10 Donovan Mitchell 2.00 5.00
11 Paul George 1.50 4.00
12 James Harden 2.00 5.00
13 Luka Doncic 6.00 15.00
14 Russell Westbrook 2.00 5.00
15 Devin Booker 2.50 6.00
16 Bam Adebayo 1.50 4.00
17 Trae Young 2.50 6.00
18 Zion Williamson 3.00 8.00
19 Kawhi Leonard 2.50 6.00
20 Anthony Davis 2.50 6.00

2020-21 Donruss Optic My House Blue

*BLUE: 2X TO 5X BASIC
STATED PRINT RUN 85 SER.#'d SETS
1 Jayson Tatum 40.00 100.00
2 Giannis Antetokounmpo 60.00 150.00
3 Ja Morant 75.00 200.00
4 LeBron James 125.00 300.00
5 Stephen Curry 75.00 200.00
10 Donovan Mitchell 25.00 60.00
12 James Harden 25.00 60.00
13 Luka Doncic 125.00 300.00
17 Trae Young 40.00 100.00
18 Zion Williamson 50.00 120.00

2020-21 Donruss Optic My House Lime Green

*LIME GREEN: 1.5X TO 4X BASIC
STATED PRINT RUN 149 SER.#'d SETS
1 Jayson Tatum 30.00 80.00
2 Giannis Antetokounmpo 50.00 120.00
3 Ja Morant 60.00 150.00
4 LeBron James 100.00 250.00
5 Stephen Curry 60.00 150.00
10 Donovan Mitchell 20.00 50.00
12 James Harden 20.00 50.00
13 Luka Doncic 100.00 250.00
17 Trae Young 30.00 80.00
18 Zion Williamson 40.00 100.00

2020-21 Donruss Optic My House Pink

*PINK: 4X TO 10X BASIC
STATED PRINT RUN 25 SER.#'d SETS
1 Jayson Tatum 100.00 250.00
2 Giannis Antetokounmpo 125.00 300.00
3 Ja Morant 150.00 400.00
4 LeBron James 350.00 700.00
5 Stephen Curry 150.00 400.00
6 Jimmy Butler 25.00 60.00
8 Kyrie Irving 40.00 100.00
9 Nikola Jokic 40.00 100.00
10 Donovan Mitchell 50.00 120.00
12 James Harden 50.00 120.00
13 Luka Doncic 350.00 700.00
17 Trae Young 75.00 200.00
18 Zion Williamson 100.00 250.00

2020-21 Donruss Optic Raining 3s

1 Ray Allen 1.50 4.00
2 Allen Iverson 2.50 6.00
3 Tyler Herro 2.00 5.00
4 JJ Redick 1.00 2.50
5 Stephen Curry 8.00 20.00
6 Joe Harris .75 2.00
7 Damian Lillard 2.50 6.00
8 Trae Young 2.50 6.00
9 Seth Curry 1.00 2.50
10 James Harden 2.00 5.00
11 Devin Booker 2.50 6.00
12 Khris Middleton 1.25 3.00
13 Buddy Hield 1.00 2.50
14 Paul George 1.50 4.00
15 Duncan Robinson 1.00 2.50
16 D'Angelo Russell 1.00 2.50
17 Bradley Beal 1.25 3.00
18 Carmelo Anthony 1.50 4.00
19 Chauncey Billups 1.25 3.00
20 Steve Nash 2.00 5.00

2020-21 Donruss Optic Raining 3s Blue

*BLUE: 2.5X TO 6X BASIC
STATED PRINT RUN 49 SER.#'d SETS
5 Stephen Curry 60.00 150.00

2020-21 Donruss Optic Raining 3s Blue Pulsar

*BLUE PULSAR: .75X TO 2X BASIC
5 Stephen Curry 20.00 50.00

2020-21 Donruss Optic Raining 3s Fast Break

*FB: .75X TO 2X BASIC
5 Stephen Curry 20.00 50.00

2020-21 Donruss Optic Raining 3s Holo

*HOLO: .75X TO 2X BASIC
5 Stephen Curry 20.00 50.00

2020-21 Donruss Optic Raining 3s Red

*RED: 2X TO 5X BASIC
STATED PRINT RUN 99 SER.#'d SETS
5 Stephen Curry 50.00 120.00

2020-21 Donruss Optic Raining 3s Red Pulsar

*RED PULSAR: .75X TO 2X BASIC
5 Stephen Curry 20.00 50.00

2020-21 Donruss Optic Rated Rookies Signatures

EXCHANGE DEADLINE 2/27/2023
151 Anthony Edwards 500.00 1,000.00
152 James Wiseman 5.00 12.00
153 LaMelo Ball 125.00 300.00
154 Patrick Williams 60.00 150.00
155 Isaac Okoro 6.00 15.00
156 Onyeka Okongwu 8.00 20.00
157 Killian Hayes 4.00 10.00
158 Obi Toppin 40.00 100.00
159 Deni Avdija 10.00 25.00
160 Jalen Smith 8.00 20.00
161 Devin Vassell 30.00 80.00
162 Tyrese Haliburton 125.00 300.00
163 Kira Lewis Jr. 4.00 10.00
164 Aaron Nesmith 8.00 20.00
165 Cole Anthony 125.00 300.00
166 Isaiah Stewart 8.00 20.00
167 Aleksej Pokusevski 5.00 12.00
168 Josh Green 8.00 20.00
169 Saddiq Bey 30.00 80.00
170 Precious Achiuwa 8.00 20.00
171 Tyrese Maxey 100.00 250.00
172 Zeke Nnaji 5.00 12.00
173 Devon Dotson 4.00 10.00
174 RJ Hampton 4.00 10.00
175 Immanuel Quickley 40.00 [illegible]
176 Payton Pritchard 30.00 [illegible]
177 Udoka Azubuike 5.00 [illegible]
178 Jaden McDaniels 20.00 [illegible]
179 Malachi Flynn 4.00 [illegible]
180 Desmond Bane 40.00 [illegible]
181 Tyrell Terry 3.00 8.00
182 Vernon Carey Jr. 4.00 [illegible]
183 Daniel Oturu 4.00 [illegible]
184 Theo Maledon 4.00 [illegible]
185 Xavier Tillman 5.00 [illegible]
186 Tyler Bey 4.00 [illegible]
187 Robert Woodard II 4.00 [illegible]
188 Tre Jones 6.00 [illegible]
189 Jordan Nwora 30.00 [illegible]
190 Nico Mannion 4.00 [illegible]
191 Saben Lee 4.00 [illegible]
192 Elijah Hughes 4.00 10.00
193 Nick Richards 5.00 12.00
194 Jahmi'us Ramsey 4.00 10.00
195 CJ Elleby 4.00 10.00
196 Skylar Mays 4.00 10.00
197 Kenyon Martin Jr. 20.00 [illegible]
198 Cassius Winston 4.00 10.00
199 Cassius Stanley 4.00 10.00
200 Grant Riller 4.00 10.00

2020-21 Donruss Optic Rated Rookies Signatures Blue

*BLUE: 1.2X TO 3X BASIC
PRINT RUN 49 COPIES PER
EXCHANGE DEADLINE 2/27/2023
151 Anthony Edwards 2,000.00 [illegible]
153 LaMelo Ball 4,000.00 [illegible]
158 Obi Toppin 150.00 [illegible]

2020-21 Donruss Optic Rated Rookies Signatures Choice

*CHOICE: .6X TO 1.5X BASIC
EXCHANGE DEADLINE 2/27/2023
151 Anthony Edwards 1,000.00 [illegible]
153 LaMelo Ball 2,000.00 [illegible]

2020-21 Donruss Optic Rated Rookies Signatures Fast Break Pink

*FB PINK: 1.5X TO 4X BASIC
PRINT RUN 20 COPIES PER
EXCHANGE DEADLINE 2/27/2023
151 Anthony Edwards 2,500.00 [illegible]
153 LaMelo Ball 5,000.00 [illegible]
158 Obi Toppin 200.00 [illegible]

2020-21 Donruss Optic Rated Rookies Signatures Holo

*HOLO: .6X TO 1.5X BASIC
EXCHANGE DEADLINE 2/27/2023
151 Anthony Edwards 1,000.00 [illegible]
153 LaMelo Ball 2,000.00 [illegible]

2020-21 Donruss Optic Rated Rookies Signatures Pink

*PINK: 1.5X TO 4X BASIC
PRINT RUN 25 COPIES PER
EXCHANGE DEADLINE 2/27/2023
151 Anthony Edwards 2,500.00 [illegible]
153 LaMelo Ball 5,000.00 [illegible]
158 Obi Toppin 200.00 [illegible]

2020-21 Donruss Optic Rated Rookies Signatures Purple

*PURPLE: .6X TO 1.5X BASIC
EXCHANGE DEADLINE 2/27/2023
151 Anthony Edwards 1,000.00 [illegible]
153 LaMelo Ball 2,000.00 [illegible]

2020-21 Donruss Optic Retro Series Signatues

PRINT RUN BTW 49-99 COPIES PER
EXCHANGE DEADLINE 2/27/2023
1 Shawn Kemp/99 25.00 [illegible]
2 Jack Sikma/99 5.00 [illegible]
3 Baron Davis/99 5.00 [illegible]
4 Kenny Walker/99 4.00 [illegible]
5 Rod Strickland/99 4.00 [illegible]
6 Alex English/99 5.00 [illegible]
7 Magic Johnson/99 75.00 [illegible]
8 Dino Radja/99 4.00 [illegible]
9 Robert Horry/99 5.00 [illegible]
10 Isaiah Rider/99 4.00 [illegible]
11 Ray Allen/49 25.00 [illegible]
12 Al Harrington/99 3.00 [illegible]
13 B.J. Armstrong/99 4.00 [illegible]
14 Toni Kukoc/99 6.00 [illegible]
15 Rik Smits/99 4.00 [illegible]
16 Michael Cooper/99 4.00 [illegible]
17 Paul Pierce/99 25.00 [illegible]
18 Chris Mullin/49 6.00 [illegible]
19 Elgin Baylor/49 40.00 [illegible]
20 Allen Iverson/49 75.00 [illegible]
21 Rick Barry/99 6.00 [illegible]
22 Nate Archibald/99 6.00 [illegible]
23 Terry Porter/99 4.00 [illegible]
24 Jason Williams/99 30.00 [illegible]
25 Calvin Murphy/99 5.00 [illegible]
26 Wally Szczerbiak/99 4.00 [illegible]
27 Kevin Garnett/49 75.00 [illegible]
28 Mehmet Okur/99 3.00 [illegible]
29 Xavier McDaniel/99 4.00 [illegible]
30 Jerry West/99 30.00 [illegible]

2020-21 Donruss Optic Rookie Dominators Signatures

PRINT RUN 99 COPIES PER
EXCHANGE DEADLINE 2/27/2023
1 Anthony Edwards 300.00 [illegible]
2 James Wiseman 6.00 [illegible]
3 LaMelo Ball 500.00 [illegible]
4 Patrick Williams 40.00 [illegible]
5 Isaac Okoro 8.00 [illegible]
6 Onyeka Okongwu 10.00 [illegible]
7 Killian Hayes 5.00 [illegible]
8 Obi Toppin 10.00 [illegible]
9 Deni Avdija 12.00 [illegible]
11 Devin Vassell 15.00 [illegible]
12 Tyrese Haliburton 75.00 [illegible]
13 Kira Lewis Jr. 5.00 [illegible]
14 Aaron Nesmith 10.00 [illegible]
15 Cole Anthony 50.00 [illegible]
16 Isaiah Stewart 10.00 [illegible]
17 Aleksej Pokusevski 6.00 [illegible]
18 Josh Green 10.00 [illegible]
19 Saddiq Bey 10.00 [illegible]
20 Precious Achiuwa 10.00 25.00
21 Tyrese Maxey 50.00 120.00
22 Jae'Sean Tate 6.00 15.00
23 RJ Hampton 5.00 12.00
24 Immanuel Quickley 25.00 60.00
25 Payton Pritchard 15.00 40.00
26 Udoka Azubuike 6.00 15.00
27 Malachi Flynn 5.00 12.00
28 Desmond Bane 30.00 80.00
29 Daniel Oturu 5.00 12.00
30 Jordan Nwora 25.00 60.00

2020-21 Donruss Optic Signature Series Blue

*BLUE: .75X TO 2X BASIC
PRINT RUN 25 COPIES PER
EXCHANGE DEADLINE 2/27/2023
14 Michael Porter Jr. 12.00 30.00
53 LaMelo Ball 1,500.00 3,000.00

2020-21 Donruss Optic Signature Series Choice

*CHOICE: .5X TO 1.2X BASIC
53 LaMelo Ball 800.00 1,500.00

2020-21 Donruss Optic Signature Series Green

*GREEN: .4X TO 1X BASIC
53 LaMelo Ball 600.00 1,200.00

2020-21 Donruss Optic Signature Series Holo

*HOLO: .5X TO 1.2X BASIC
EXCHANGE DEADLINE 2/27/2023
53 LaMelo Ball 800.00 1,500.00

2020-21 Donruss Optic Signature Series Pink

*PINK: .75X TO 2X BASIC
PRINT RUN 25 COPIES PER
EXCHANGE DEADLINE 2/27/2023
14 Michael Porter Jr. 12.00 30.00
53 LaMelo Ball 1,500.00 3,000.00

2020-21 Donruss Optic Signature Series Purple

*PURPLE: .4X TO 1X BASIC
53 LaMelo Ball 600.00 1,200.00

2020-21 Donruss Optic Splash

*PURPLE: .6X TO 1.5X BASIC
1 James Harden 1.25 3.00
2 Jamal Murray 1.00 2.50
3 Stephen Curry 5.00 12.00
4 Tyler Herro 1.25 3.00
5 Damian Lillard 1.50 4.00
6 Khris Middleton .75 2.00
7 D'Angelo Russell .60 1.50
8 Bradley Beal .75 2.00
9 Buddy Hield .60 1.50
10 Kemba Walker .60 1.50
11 Trae Young 1.50 4.00
12 Devin Booker 1.50 4.00
13 LeBron James 5.00 12.00
14 Jayson Tatum 2.50 6.00
15 Luka Doncic 4.00 10.00

2020-21 Donruss Optic Splash Blue

*BLUE: 2X TO 5X BASIC
STATED PRINT RUN 85 SER.#'d SETS
3 Stephen Curry 50.00 120.00
13 LeBron James 50.00 120.00
14 Jayson Tatum 20.00 50.00
15 Luka Doncic 50.00 120.00

2020-21 Donruss Optic Splash Holo

*HOLO: .75X TO 2X BASIC
3 Stephen Curry 15.00 40.00
13 LeBron James 15.00 40.00
15 Luka Doncic 15.00 40.00

2020-21 Donruss Optic Splash Lime Green

*LIME GREEN: 1.5X TO 4X BASIC
STATED PRINT RUN 149 SER.#'d SETS
3 Stephen Curry 40.00 100.00
13 LeBron James 40.00 100.00
14 Jayson Tatum 15.00 40.00
15 Luka Doncic 40.00 100.00

2020-21 Donruss Optic Splash Orange

*ORANGE: 2.5X TO 6X BASIC
STATED PRINT RUN 39 SER.#'d SETS
3 Stephen Curry 60.00 150.00
13 LeBron James 60.00 150.00
14 Jayson Tatum 25.00 60.00
15 Luka Doncic 60.00 150.00

2020-21 Donruss Optic Splash Pink

*PINK: 4X TO 10X BASIC
STATED PRINT RUN 25 SER.#'d SETS
3 Stephen Curry 100.00 250.00
13 LeBron James 100.00 250.00
14 Jayson Tatum 40.00 100.00
15 Luka Doncic 100.00 250.00

2020-21 Donruss Optic Star Gazing

1 Ja Morant 2.50 6.00
2 Zion Williamson 2.50 6.00
3 LeBron James 6.00 15.00
4 Luka Doncic 5.00 12.00
5 Giannis Antetokounmpo 4.00 10.00
6 Kevin Durant 3.00 8.00
7 Damian Lillard 2.00 5.00
8 Stephen Curry 6.00 15.00
9 James Harden 1.50 4.00
10 Donovan Mitchell 1.50 4.00
11 Ben Simmons .75 2.00
12 Kawhi Leonard 2.00 5.00
13 Nikola Jokic 4.00 10.00
14 Chris Paul 1.50 4.00
15 Jimmy Butler 1.50 4.00

2020-21 Donruss Optic Star Gazing Blue

*BLUE: 2.5X TO 6X BASIC
STATED PRINT RUN 49 SER.#'d SETS
3 LeBron James 75.00 200.00
4 Luka Doncic 75.00 200.00
8 Stephen Curry 50.00 120.00

2020-21 Donruss Optic Star Gazing Blue Pulsar

*BLUE PULSAR: .75X TO 2X BASIC
3 LeBron James 25.00 60.00
4 Luka Doncic 25.00 60.00
8 Stephen Curry 15.00 40.00

2020-21 Donruss Optic Star Gazing Holo

*HOLO: .75X TO 2X BASIC
3 LeBron James 25.00 60.00
4 Luka Doncic 25.00 60.00
8 Stephen Curry 15.00 40.00

2020-21 Donruss Optic Star Gazing Red

*RED: 2X TO 5X BASIC
STATED PRINT RUN 99 SER.#'d SETS
3 LeBron James 60.00 150.00
4 Luka Doncic 60.00 150.00
8 Stephen Curry 40.00 100.00

2020-21 Donruss Optic Star Gazing Red Pulsar

*RED PULSAR: .75X TO 2X BASIC
3 LeBron James 25.00 60.00
4 Luka Doncic 25.00 60.00
8 Stephen Curry 15.00 40.00

2020-21 Donruss Optic T-Minus 3 2 1

*PURPLE: .6X TO 1.5X BASIC
*HOLO: .75X TO 2X BASIC
1 Stephen Curry 4.00 10.00
2 Anthony Davis 1.25 3.00
3 Kawhi Leonard 1.25 3.00
4 Jamal Murray .75 2.00
5 Jimmy Butler 1.00 2.50
6 Donovan Mitchell 1.00 2.50
7 James Harden 1.00 2.50
8 Zion Williamson 1.50 4.00
9 LeBron James 4.00 10.00
10 Luka Doncic 3.00 8.00
11 Jayson Tatum 2.00 5.00
12 Devin Booker 1.25 3.00
13 Joel Embiid 1.25 3.00
14 Damian Lillard 1.25 3.00
15 Giannis Antetokounmpo 2.50 6.00

2020-21 Donruss Optic T-Minus 3 2 1 Blue

*BLUE: 2X TO 5X BASIC
STATED PRINT RUN 85 SER.#'d SETS
1 Stephen Curry 30.00 80.00
9 LeBron James 30.00 80.00
10 Luka Doncic 30.00 80.00
15 Giannis Antetokounmpo 15.00 40.00

2020-21 Donruss Optic T-Minus 3 2 1 Lime Green

*LIME GREEN: 1.5X TO 4X BASIC
STATED PRINT RUN 149 SER.#'d SETS
1 Stephen Curry 25.00 60.00
9 LeBron James 25.00 60.00
10 Luka Doncic 25.00 60.00

2020-21 Donruss Optic T-Minus 3 2 1 Orange

*ORANGE: 2.5X TO 6X BASIC
STATED PRINT RUN 39 SER.#'d SETS
1 Stephen Curry 50.00 120.00
9 LeBron James 50.00 120.00
10 Luka Doncic 50.00 120.00
15 Giannis Antetokounmpo 20.00 50.00

2020-21 Donruss Optic T-Minus 3 2 1 Pink

*PINK: 4X TO 10X BASIC
STATED PRINT RUN 25 SER.#'d SETS
1 Stephen Curry 75.00 200.00
9 LeBron James 75.00 200.00
10 Luka Doncic 75.00 200.00
15 Giannis Antetokounmpo 30.00 80.00

2020-21 Donruss Optic The Rookies

*BLUE PULSAR: 1.25X TO 3X BASIC
*FAST BREAK: 1.25X TO 3X BASIC
*HOLO: 1.25X TO 3X BASIC
*RED PULSAR: 1.25X TO 3X BASIC
1 LaMelo Ball 10.00 25.00
2 James Wiseman 1.00 2.50
3 Deni Avdija 2.00 5.00
4 Obi Toppin 1.50 4.00
5 Anthony Edwards 6.00 15.00

2020-21 Donruss Optic The Rookies Blue

STATED PRINT RUN 49 SER.#'d SETS
1 LaMelo Ball 300.00 600.00
5 Anthony Edwards 150.00 400.00

2020-21 Donruss Optic The Rookies Red

STATED PRINT RUN 99 SER.#'d SETS
1 LaMelo Ball 150.00 400.00
5 Anthony Edwards 100.00 250.00

2020-21 Donruss Optic Winner Stays

*PURPLE: .6X TO 1.5X BASIC
*HOLO: .75X TO 2X BASIC
1 Shaquille O'Neal 2.00 5.00
2 Kyrie Irving 1.00 2.50
3 Stephen Curry 4.00 10.00
4 Jason Williams .75 2.00
5 Kyle Lowry .60 1.50
6 Kawhi Leonard 1.25 3.00
7 Klay Thompson 1.25 3.00
8 Dirk Nowitzki 1.25 3.00
9 Toni Kukoc .60 1.50
10 David Robinson 1.00 2.50
11 Ben Wallace .60 1.50
12 Jason Kidd .75 2.00
13 Pascal Siakam .75 2.00
14 Gary Payton .75 2.00
15 Tim Duncan 1.25 3.00
16 Dwyane Wade 1.00 2.50
17 Ray Allen .75 2.00
18 Kevin Durant 2.00 5.00
19 Larry Bird 2.00 5.00
20 LeBron James 4.00 10.00

2020-21 Donruss Optic Winner Stays Lime Green

*LIME GREEN: 1.5X TO 4X BASIC
STATED PRINT RUN 149 SER.#'d SETS
3 Stephen Curry 25.00 60.00
8 Dirk Nowitzki 8.00 20.00
10 David Robinson 8.00 20.00
15 Tim Duncan 8.00 20.00
16 Dwyane Wade 8.00 20.00
19 Larry Bird 8.00 20.00
20 LeBron James 25.00 60.00

2020-21 Donruss Optic Winner Stays Orange

*ORANGE: 2.5X TO 6X BASIC
STATED PRINT RUN 39 SER.#'d SETS
3 Stephen Curry 50.00 120.00
8 Dirk Nowitzki 12.00 30.00
10 David Robinson 12.00 30.00
15 Tim Duncan 12.00 30.00
16 Dwyane Wade 12.00 30.00
19 Larry Bird 12.00 30.00
20 LeBron James 50.00 120.00

2020-21 Donruss Optic Winner Stays Pink

*PINK: 4X TO 10X BASIC
STATED PRINT RUN 25 SER.#'d SETS
1 Shaquille O'Neal 20.00 50.00
3 Stephen Curry 75.00 200.00
8 Dirk Nowitzki 15.00 40.00
10 David Robinson 15.00 40.00
15 Tim Duncan 15.00 40.00
16 Dwyane Wade 15.00 40.00
19 Larry Bird 15.00 40.00
20 LeBron James 75.00 200.00

2021-22 Donruss Optic

COMMON CARD (1-150) .30 .75
SEMISTARS .40 1.00
UNLISTED STARS .50 1.25
COMMON RC (151-200) .60 1.50
RC SEMIS .75 2.00
RC UNLISTED 1.00 2.50
*BLUE VELOCITY: 1.25X TO 3X BASIC
*PURPLE: 1.25X TO 3X BASIC
*PURPLE SHOCK: 1.25X TO 3X BASIC
*HOLO: 1.5X TO 4X BASIC
*CHOICE RED & GREEN: 2X TO 5X BASIC
*ORANGE/199: 2.5X TO 6X BASIC
*LIME GREEN/149: 2.5X TO 6X BASIC
*RED/99: 3X TO 8X BASIC
*CHOICE RED/88: 3X TO 8X BASIC
1 Fred VanVleet .60 1.50
2 Andre Drummond .40 1.00
3 Rudy Gobert .60 1.50
4 Derrick White .50 1.25
5 Kelly Olynyk .30 .75
6 Kyle Lowry .50 1.25
7 Michael Porter Jr. .60 1.50
8 Jimmy Butler .75 2.00
9 Deandre Ayton .50 1.25
10 Paul George .75 2.00
11 Kevin Durant 1.50 4.00
12 Isaiah Stewart .50 1.25
13 De'Andre Hunter .50 1.25
14 Kevin Porter Jr. .40 1.00
15 Kyle Kuzma .60 1.50
16 Lonnie Walker IV .40 1.00
17 Patrick Williams .50 1.25
18 Kristaps Porzingis .60 1.50
19 Jaylen Brown .75 2.00
20 Killian Hayes .50 1.25
21 Bryn Forbes .40 1.00
22 Terry Rozier III .40 1.00
23 Malcolm Brogdon .40 1.00
24 Wendell Carter Jr. .50 1.25
25 Jayson Tatum 2.00 5.00
26 LaMelo Ball 1.25 3.00
27 Darius Bazley .30 .75
28 DeMar DeRozan .60 1.50
29 Draymond Green .60 1.50
30 Bobby Portis .40 1.00
31 Giannis Antetokounmpo 2.50 6.00
32 Bogdan Bogdanovic .50 1.25
33 Derrick Favors .30 .75
34 Cameron Johnson .50 1.25
35 Terrence Ross .40 1.00
36 Myles Turner .50 1.25
37 Al Horford .50 1.25
38 Tyrese Haliburton 1.00 2.50
39 Bojan Bogdanovic .40 1.00
40 Jrue Holiday .50 1.25
41 LeBron James 4.00 10.00
42 Tim Hardaway Jr. .30 .75
43 Jamal Murray .75 2.00
44 T.J. Warren .30 .75
45 Donovan Mitchell 1.00 2.50
46 Gary Trent Jr. .40 1.00
47 Kemba Walker .50 1.25
48 Jonathan Isaac .50 1.25
49 Kenyon Martin Jr. .50 1.25
50 Desmond Bane 1.00 2.50
51 Trae Young 1.25 3.00
52 Jusuf Nurkic .40 1.00
53 Joe Ingles .40 1.00
54 Spencer Dinwiddie .40 1.00
55 Eric Gordon .40 1.00
56 D'Angelo Russell .50 1.25
57 Collin Sexton .50 1.25
58 Theo Maledon .40 1.00
59 Nikola Jokic 2.50 6.00
60 Brandon Ingram .60 1.50
61 Will Barton .30 .75
62 Clint Capela .50 1.25
63 RJ Barrett .75 2.00
64 Mitchell Robinson .50 1.25
65 Darius Garland .75 2.00
66 Marcus Smart .50 1.25
67 Victor Oladipo .40 1.00
68 Ivica Zubac .40 1.00
69 Caris LeVert .40 1.00
70 Malik Beasley .40 1.00
71 Jonas Valanciunas .50 1.25
72 Terance Mann .50 1.25
73 Eric Bledsoe .40 1.00
74 Bradley Beal .60 1.50
75 Jarrett Allen .50 1.25
76 Russell Westbrook .75 2.00
77 Jakob Poeltl .40 1.00
78 Luguentz Dort .50 1.25
79 Rui Hachimura .50 1.25
80 Josh Hart .40 1.00
81 Chuma Okeke .50 1.25
82 Brandon Clarke .50 1.25
83 Anthony Edwards ERR
Partial stats back 2.50 6.00
83 Anthony Edwards COR
Full stats back 2.50 6.00
84 Ben Simmons .50 1.25
85 De'Aaron Fox .75 2.00
86 Jordan Clarkson .50 1.25
87 Karl-Anthony Towns .75 2.00
88 Joel Embiid 1.25 3.00
89 Duncan Robinson .40 1.00
90 Donte DiVincenzo .50 1.25
91 Seth Curry .40 1.00
92 Deni Avdija .50 1.25
93 Christian Wood .40 1.00
94 Domantas Sabonis .60 1.50
95 Zion Williamson 1.25 3.00
96 Kyrie Irving 1.00 2.50
97 Jalen Brunson 1.00 2.50
98 Buddy Hield .40 1.00
99 Isaac Okoro .40 1.00
100 Julius Randle .60 1.50
101 Luka Doncic 3.00 8.00
102 Blake Griffin .50 1.25
103 Talen Horton-Tucker .50 1.25
104 Richaun Holmes .30 .75
105 Zach LaVine .75 2.00
106 James Harden 1.00 2.50
107 Miles Bridges .40 1.00
108 Dennis Schroder .50 1.25
109 Carmelo Anthony .75 2.00
110 PJ Washington Jr. .50 1.25
111 Harrison Barnes .40 1.00
112 Josh Okogie .30 .75
113 Andrew Wiggins .60 1.50
114 Lonzo Ball .50 1.25
115 Chris Paul 1.00 2.50
116 Dejounte Murray .50 1.25
117 John Wall .60 1.50
118 Damian Lillard 1.25 3.00
119 OG Anunoby .50 1.25
120 Devonte' Graham .40 1.00
121 Norman Powell .40 1.00
122 Jerami Grant .50 1.25
123 Pascal Siakam .75 2.00
124 Klay Thompson 1.25 3.00
125 Reggie Bullock .30 .75
126 Saddiq Bey .40 1.00
127 Derrick Rose .75 2.00
128 Stephen Curry 3.00 8.00
129 John Collins .50 1.25
130 Mikal Bridges .60 1.50
131 CJ McCollum .40 1.00
132 Gordon Hayward .40 1.00
133 Anthony Davis 1.25 3.00
134 Ricky Rubio .50 1.25
135 James Wiseman .40 1.00
136 Dillon Brooks .50 1.25
137 Steven Adams .40 1.00
138 Joe Harris .40 1.00
139 Goran Dragic .40 1.00
140 Aaron Gordon .50 1.25
141 Nikola Vucevic .50 1.25
142 Devin Booker 1.25 3.00
143 Khris Middleton .50 1.25
144 Ja Morant 1.50 4.00
145 Kawhi Leonard 1.25 3.00
146 Cole Anthony .60 1.50
147 Shai Gilgeous-Alexander 2.50 6.00
148 Bam Adebayo .75 2.00
149 Robert Covington .30 .75
150 Matisse Thybulle .40 1.00
151 James Bouknight RC .75 2.00
152 Josh Giddey RC 3.00 8.00
153 Cameron Thomas RC 2.00 5.00
154 Kessler Edwards RC 1.00 2.50
155 Davion Mitchell RC 1.00 2.50
156 Neemias Queta RC 1.00 2.50
157 Herbert Jones RC 1.25 3.00
158 Sharife Cooper RC .75 2.00
159 Jalen Green RC 5.00 12.00
160 Jason Preston RC .75 2.00
161 Cade Cunningham RC 6.00 15.00
162 Joshua Primo RC .75 2.00
163 Charles Bassey RC 1.00 2.50
164 Luka Garza RC 1.00 2.50
165 Day'Ron Sharpe RC 1.00 2.50
166 Quentin Grimes RC 2.00 5.00
167 Isaiah Jackson RC 1.00 2.50
168 Tre Mann RC 1.50 4.00
169 Alperen Sengun RC 3.00 8.00
170 Jeremiah Robinson-Earl RC 1.00 2.50
171 Ayo Dosunmu RC 2.00 5.00
172 JT Thor RC 1.00 2.50
173 Chris Duarte RC .75 2.00
174 Miles McBride RC 1.50 4.00
175 Evan Mobley RC 4.00 10.00
176 Santi Aldama RC 1.25 3.00
177 Isaiah Livers RC 1.00 2.50
178 Trey Murphy III RC 1.25 3.00
179 Jalen Suggs RC 2.50 6.00
180 Joe Wieskamp RC .75 2.00
181 Jalen Johnson RC 3.00 8.00
182 Kai Jones RC .75 2.00
183 Corey Kispert RC 1.25 3.00
184 Moses Moody RC 2.00 5.00
185 Franz Wagner RC 3.00 8.00
186 Scottie Barnes RC 3.00 8.00
187 Isaiah Todd RC .75 2.00
188 Usman Garuba RC .75 2.00
189 Brandon Boston Jr. RC 1.00 2.50
190 Jonathan Kuminga RC 3.00 8.00
191 Aaron Wiggins RC 1.25 3.00
192 Keon Johnson RC 1.00 2.50
193 David Johnson RC .75 2.00
194 Bones Hyland RC 1.25 3.00
195 Greg Brown III RC .75 2.00
196 Scottie Lewis RC .75 2.00
197 Jaden Springer RC 1.00 2.50
198 Ziaire Williams RC 1.25 3.00
199 Jared Butler RC 1.00 2.50
200 Josh Christopher RC .75 2.00

2021-22 Donruss Optic Blue

*BLUE: 5X TO 12X BASIC
STATED PRINT RUN 59 SER. #'D SETS
152 Josh Giddey 300.00 600.00
159 Jalen Green 350.00 700.00
161 Cade Cunningham 400.00 800.00
171 Ayo Dosunmu 100.00 250.00
175 Evan Mobley 300.00 600.00
184 Moses Moody 100.00 250.00

185 Franz Wagner 150.00 400.00
186 Scottie Barnes 350.00 700.00
190 Jonathan Kuminga 150.00 400.00
194 Bones Hyland 75.00 200.00

2021-22 Donruss Optic Blue Pulsar

*BLUE PULSAR: 1.5X TO 4X BASIC
159 Jalen Green 50.00 120.00
161 Cade Cunningham 60.00 150.00
175 Evan Mobley 40.00 100.00
186 Scottie Barnes 50.00 120.00

2021-22 Donruss Optic Blue Velocity

*BLUE VELOCITY: 1.25X TO 3X BASIC
159 Jalen Green 25.00 60.00
161 Cade Cunningham 30.00 80.00
175 Evan Mobley 20.00 50.00
186 Scottie Barnes 25.00 60.00

2021-22 Donruss Optic Choice

*CHOICE: 2X TO 5X BASIC

2021-22 Donruss Optic Fast Break Blue

*FB BLUE: 5X TO 12X BASIC
STATED PRINT RUN 50 SER. #'D SETS
152 Josh Giddey 300.00 600.00
159 Jalen Green 350.00 700.00
161 Cade Cunningham 400.00 800.00
171 Ayo Dosunmu 100.00 250.00
175 Evan Mobley 300.00 600.00
184 Moses Moody 100.00 250.00
185 Franz Wagner 150.00 400.00
186 Scottie Barnes 350.00 700.00
190 Jonathan Kuminga 150.00 400.00
194 Bones Hyland 75.00 200.00

2021-22 Donruss Optic Fast Break Holo

*FB HOLO: 1.5X TO 4X BASIC
159 Jalen Green 40.00 100.00
161 Cade Cunningham 50.00 120.00
175 Evan Mobley 30.00 80.00
186 Scottie Barnes 40.00 100.00

2021-22 Donruss Optic Fast Break Purple

*FB PURPLE: 3X TO 8X BASIC
STATED PRINT RUN 95 SER. #'D SETS
152 Josh Giddey 150.00 400.00
159 Jalen Green 200.00 500.00
161 Cade Cunningham 300.00 600.00
171 Ayo Dosunmu 60.00 150.00
175 Evan Mobley 150.00 400.00
184 Moses Moody 60.00 150.00
185 Franz Wagner 100.00 250.00
186 Scottie Barnes 200.00 500.00
190 Jonathan Kuminga 100.00 250.00
194 Bones Hyland 50.00 120.00

2021-22 Donruss Optic Fast Break Red

*FB RED: 3X TO 8X BASIC
STATED PRINT RUN 85 SER. #'D SETS
152 Josh Giddey 150.00 400.00
159 Jalen Green 200.00 500.00
161 Cade Cunningham 300.00 600.00
171 Ayo Dosunmu 60.00 150.00
175 Evan Mobley 150.00 400.00
184 Moses Moody 60.00 150.00
185 Franz Wagner 100.00 250.00
186 Scottie Barnes 200.00 500.00
190 Jonathan Kuminga 100.00 250.00
194 Bones Hyland 50.00 120.00

2021-22 Donruss Optic Pink Velocity

*PINK VELOCITY: 4X TO 10X BASIC
STATED PRINT RUN 79 SER. #'D SETS
152 Josh Giddey 200.00 500.00
159 Jalen Green 300.00 600.00
161 Cade Cunningham 350.00 700.00
171 Ayo Dosunmu 75.00 200.00
175 Evan Mobley 200.00 500.00
185 Franz Wagner 125.00 300.00
186 Scottie Barnes 300.00 600.00
190 Jonathan Kuminga 125.00 300.00
194 Bones Hyland 60.00 150.00

2021-22 Donruss Optic Purple

*PURPLE: 1.25X TO 3X BASIC
159 Jalen Green 30.00 80.00
161 Cade Cunningham 40.00 100.00
175 Evan Mobley 25.00 60.00
186 Scottie Barnes 30.00 80.00

2021-22 Donruss Optic Red Pulsar

*RED PULSAR: 1.5X TO 4X BASIC
159 Jalen Green 50.00 120.00
161 Cade Cunningham 60.00 150.00
175 Evan Mobley 40.00 100.00
186 Scottie Barnes 50.00 120.00

2021-22 Donruss Optic Air Defense

COMMON CARD .40 1.00
SEMISTARS .50 1.25
UNLISTED STARS .60 1.50
*PURPLE: .6X TO 1.5X BASIC
*HOLO: .75X TO 2X BASIC
*RED WAVE: 1.5X TO 4X BASIC
*LIME GREEN/149: 2X TO 5X BASIC
*BLUE/85: 2.5X TO 6X BASIC
*ORANGE/39: 4X TO 10X BASIC
*PINK/25: 5X TO 12X BASIC
1 Rudy Gobert .75 2.00
2 Anthony Davis 1.50 4.00
3 Giannis Antetokounmpo 3.00 8.00
4 Bam Adebayo 1.00 2.50
5 Joel Embiid 1.50 4.00

2021-22 Donruss Optic All-Stars

COMMON CARD .40 1.00
SEMISTARS .50 1.25
UNLISTED STARS .60 1.50
*HOLO: .75X TO 2X BASIC
*FB: .75X TO 2X BASIC
*BLUE PULSAR: 1.25X TO 3X BASIC
*RED PULSAR: 1.25X TO 3X BASIC
*RED/99: 2.5X TO 6X BASIC
*BLUE/49: 4X TO 10X BASIC
1 LeBron James
Zion Williamson 5.00 12.00
2 Bradley Beal
Stephen Curry 4.00 10.00
3 Nikola Jokic
Nikola Vucevic 3.00 8.00
4 Jayson Tatum
Paul George 2.50 6.00
5 Damian Lillard
Donovan Mitchell 1.50 4.00
6 Jaylen Brown
Zach LaVine 1.00 2.50
7 Mike Conley
Rudy Gobert .75 2.00
8 Domantas Sabonis
Julius Randle .75 2.00
9 Isiah Thomas
Magic Johnson 2.00 5.00
10 Tracy McGrady
Vince Carter 1.25 3.00
11 Luka Doncic
Trae Young 4.00 10.00
12 Dirk Nowitzki
Dwyane Wade 1.50 4.00
13 Larry Bird
Magic Johnson 2.00 5.00
14 Charles Barkley
Karl Malone 1.50 4.00
15 Allen Iverson
Tim Duncan 1.50 4.00
16 Anthony Davis
Giannis Antetokounmpo 3.00 8.00
17 James Harden
Kyrie Irving 1.25 3.00
18 Carmelo Anthony
Dwight Howard 1.00 2.50
19 Kawhi Leonard
Pascal Siakam 1.50 4.00
20 Derrick Rose
Kevin Durant 2.00 5.00

2021-22 Donruss Optic Dominators Signatures

COMMON CARD 4.00 10.00
SEMISTARS 5.00 12.00
UNLISTED STARS 6.00 15.00
STATED PRINT RUN 49-99 SER.#'d SETS
EXCHANGE DEADLINE 3/02/2024
1 CJ McCollum/99 5.00 12.00
2 Mike Conley/99 5.00 12.00
3 Wendell Carter Jr./99 6.00 15.00
4 T.J. Warren/99 4.00 10.00
5 Brandon Clarke/99 6.00 15.00
6 Spencer Dinwiddie/99 5.00 12.00
7 Elfrid Payton/99 4.00 10.00
8 Willie Cauley-Stein/99 4.00 10.00
9 Caris LeVert/99 5.00 12.00
10 Trevor Ariza/99 4.00 10.00
11 Thaddeus Young/99 4.00 10.00
12 Cody Zeller/99 4.00 10.00
13 Al-Farouq Aminu/99 4.00 10.00
14 Lonnie Walker IV/99 5.00 12.00
15 Doug McDermott/99 5.00 12.00
16 Devonte' Graham/99 5.00 12.00
17 Terrence Ross/99 5.00 12.00
18 JaVale McGee/99 5.00 12.00
19 Taj Gibson/99 4.00 10.00
20 Dario Saric/99 4.00 10.00
21 Austin Rivers/99 5.00 12.00
22 Bruce Brown/99 5.00 12.00
23 Sekou Doumbouya/99 4.00 10.00
24 Udonis Haslem/99 4.00 10.00
25 Matthew Dellavedova/99 6.00 15.00
26 Luka Doncic/49 400.00 800.00
29 Ja Morant/49 300.00 600.00
30 Trae Young/99 150.00 400.00
31 Nikola Jokic/99 125.00 300.00
32 DeMarcus Cousins/97 5.00 12.00
33 Rui Hachimura/99 12.00 30.00
34 Kristaps Porzingis/99 8.00 20.00
35 Khris Middleton/90 6.00 15.00
36 Rajon Rondo/99 8.00 20.00
38 Lauri Markkanen/99 8.00 20.00
39 Andre Drummond/99 5.00 12.00
40 Julius Randle/99 8.00 20.00

2021-22 Donruss Optic Elite Dominators

COMMON CARD
SEMISTARS
*HOLO: .75X TO 2X BASIC
*FB: .75X TO 2X BASIC
*BLUE PULSAR: 1.25X TO 3X BASIC
*RED PULSAR: 1.25X TO 3X BASIC
*RED/99: 2.5X TO 6X BASIC
*BLUE/49: 4X TO 10X BASIC
1 Zion Williamson 1.50 4.00
2 Stephen Curry 4.00 10.00
3 James Harden 1.25 3.00
4 Joel Embiid 1.50 4.00
5 Giannis Antetokounmpo 3.00 8.00
6 LeBron James 5.00 12.00
7 Kevin Durant 2.00 5.00
8 LaMelo Ball 1.50 4.00
9 Damian Lillard 1.50 4.00
10 Bradley Beal .75 2.00
11 Trae Young 1.50 4.00
12 Jayson Tatum 2.50 6.00
13 Donovan Mitchell 1.25 3.00
14 Julius Randle .75 2.00
15 Nikola Jokic 3.00 8.00
16 Ja Morant 2.00 5.00
17 Luka Doncic 4.00 10.00
18 Devin Booker 1.50 4.00
19 Kawhi Leonard 1.50 4.00
20 Anthony Edwards 3.00 8.00
21 Zach LaVine 1.00 2.50
22 Russell Westbrook 1.00 2.50
23 Anthony Davis 1.50 4.00
24 Jimmy Butler 1.00 2.50
25 Khris Middleton .60 1.50

2021-22 Donruss Optic Express Lane

COMMON CARD .40 1.00
SEMISTARS .50 1.25
UNLISTED STARS .60 1.50
*PURPLE: .6X TO 1.5X BASIC
*HOLO: .75X TO 2X BASIC
*RED WAVE: 1.5X TO 4X BASIC
*LIME GREEN/149: 2X TO 5X BASIC
*BLUE/85: 2.5X TO 6X BASIC
*ORANGE/39: 4X TO 10X BASIC
*PINK/25: 5X TO 12X BASIC
1 Ja Morant 2.00 5.00
2 Damian Lillard 1.50 4.00
3 Giannis Antetokounmpo 3.00 8.00
4 Stephen Curry 4.00 10.00
5 Trae Young 1.50 4.00
6 LeBron James 5.00 12.00
7 Luka Doncic 4.00 10.00
8 Donovan Mitchell 1.25 3.00
9 Chris Paul 1.25 3.00
10 De'Aaron Fox 1.00 2.50
11 Kyrie Irving 1.25 3.00
12 Zion Williamson 1.50 4.00
13 James Harden 1.25 3.00
14 Russell Westbrook 1.00 2.50
15 Ben Simmons .60 1.50
16 LaMelo Ball 1.50 4.00
17 Shai Gilgeous-Alexander 3.00 8.00
18 Devin Booker 1.50 4.00
19 Anthony Davis 1.50 4.00
20 Bradley Beal .75 2.00
21 Paul George 1.00 2.50
22 Zach LaVine 1.00 2.50
23 Jayson Tatum 2.50 6.00
24 Kawhi Leonard 1.50 4.00
25 Kevin Durant 2.00 5.00

2021-22 Donruss Optic Fast Break Signatures

COMMON CARD 4.00 10.00
SEMISTARS 5.00 12.00
UNLISTED STARS 6.00 15.00
EXCHANGE DEADLINE 3/02/2024
1 Spencer Dinwiddie 5.00 12.00
2 Jamal Murray 20.00 50.00
3 Joakim Noah 5.00 12.00
4 Mike Conley 5.00 12.00
5 Isiah Thomas 25.00 60.00
6 Charles Barkley 100.00 250.00
7 Wendell Carter Jr. 6.00 15.00
8 Ja Morant 300.00 600.00
9 T.J. Warren 4.00 10.00
10 Damian Lillard 75.00 200.00
11 Brandon Clarke 6.00 15.00
12 CJ McCollum 5.00 12.00
13 Louie Dampier 6.00 15.00
14 Jrue Holiday 12.00 30.00
15 Bob Lanier 8.00 20.00
16 Luka Doncic 400.00 800.00
17 Chris Mullin 8.00 20.00
18 Oscar Robertson 30.00 80.00
19 Baron Davis 6.00 15.00
20 Jason Kidd 20.00 50.00
21 Onyeka Okongwu 6.00 15.00
22 Tony Parker 20.00 50.00
23 Wang Zhi-zhi 50.00 120.00
24 Jerry Lucas 8.00 20.00
25 Artis Gilmore 8.00 20.00
27 Bernard King 8.00 20.00
28 Zion Williamson 200.00 500.00
29 Derek Fisher 12.00 30.00
30 Ray Allen 30.00 80.00
31 Peja Stojakovic 5.00 12.00
32 Josh Jackson 4.00 10.00
33 Juwan Howard 5.00 12.00
34 Dominique Wilkins 20.00 50.00
35 Danilo Gallinari 5.00 12.00
36 Anthony Davis 60.00 150.00
37 Ralph Sampson 6.00 15.00
38 Anthony Edwards 150.00 400.00
39 Nick Van Exel 12.00 30.00
40 David Robinson 25.00 60.00
41 Jalen Rose 5.00 12.00
42 Gordon Hayward 5.00 12.00
43 Mark Jackson 5.00 12.00
44 Metta World Peace 12.00 30.00
45 Walt Frazier 12.00 30.00
46 Larry Bird 100.00 250.00
47 Jason Williams 25.00 60.00
48 Trae Young 200.00 500.00
49 Nate Archibald 6.00 15.00
50 Dennis Rodman 40.00 100.00
51 Joe Wieskamp 5.00 12.00
52 Charles Bassey 6.00 15.00
53 Quentin Grimes 12.00 30.00
54 Trey Murphy III 20.00 50.00
55 Jalen Johnson 20.00 50.00
56 Isaiah Todd 5.00 12.00
57 Jalen Suggs 40.00 100.00
58 Joshua Primo 5.00 12.00
59 Day'Ron Sharpe 6.00 15.00
60 Isaiah Livers 6.00 15.00
61 Kessler Edwards 6.00 15.00
62 Bones Hyland 8.00 20.00
63 Jaden Springer 6.00 15.00
64 Josh Giddey 100.00 250.00
65 Davion Mitchell 6.00 15.00
66 Greg Brown III 5.00 12.00
67 Cameron Thomas 12.00 30.00
68 David Johnson 5.00 12.00
69 Leandro Bolmaro 6.00 15.00
70 James Bouknight 5.00 12.00
71 Franz Wagner 40.00 100.00
72 Tre Mann 10.00 25.00
73 Ayo Dosunmu 12.00 30.00
74 Corey Kispert 8.00 20.00
75 Scottie Barnes 150.00 400.00
76 Alperen Sengun 20.00 50.00
77 Moses Moody 40.00 100.00
78 Isaiah Jackson 6.00 15.00
79 Jeremiah Robinson-Earl 6.00 15.00
80 Kai Jones 5.00 12.00
81 Austin Reaves 30.00 80.00
82 Jared Butler 6.00 15.00
83 T.J. McConnell 5.00 12.00
84 Herbert Jones 8.00 20.00
85 Cade Cunningham 300.00 600.00
86 Josh Christopher 5.00 12.00
87 Jalen Green 200.00 500.00
88 Ziaire Williams 8.00 20.00
89 Jericho Sims 8.00 20.00
90 Neemias Queta 6.00 15.00
91 Aaron Wiggins 8.00 20.00
92 Chris Duarte 6.00 15.00
93 Santi Aldama 8.00 20.00
94 Brandon Boston Jr. 6.00 15.00
95 Keon Johnson 6.00 15.00
96 Miles McBride 10.00 25.00
97 Jonathan Kuminga 75.00 200.00
98 JT Thor 6.00 15.00
99 Evan Mobley 125.00 300.00
100 Usman Garuba 5.00 12.00

2021-22 Donruss Optic Light It Up

COMMON CARD .40 1.00
SEMISTARS .50 1.25
UNLISTED STARS .60 1.50
*HOLO: .75X TO 2X BASIC
*FB: .75X TO 2X BASIC
*BLUE PULSAR: 1.25X TO 3X BASIC
*RED PULSAR: 1.25X TO 3X BASIC
*RED/99: 2.5X TO 6X BASIC
*BLUE/49: 4X TO 10X BASIC
1 Kyrie Irving 1.25 3.00
2 Stephen Curry 4.00 10.00
3 Trae Young 1.50 4.00
4 Kevin Durant 2.00 5.00
5 Devin Booker 1.50 4.00
6 Ja Morant 2.00 5.00
7 Damian Lillard 1.50 4.00
8 Bradley Beal .75 2.00
9 Jayson Tatum 2.50 6.00
10 Luka Doncic 4.00 10.00
11 LeBron James 5.00 12.00
12 Zach LaVine 1.00 2.50
13 Russell Westbrook 1.00 2.50
14 Donovan Mitchell 1.25 3.00
15 Khris Middleton .60 1.50

2021-22 Donruss Optic My House

COMMON CARD .40 1.00
SEMISTARS .50 1.25
UNLISTED STARS .60 1.50
*PURPLE: .6X TO 1.5X BASIC
*HOLO .75X TO 2X BASIC
*RED WAVE: 1.5X TO 4X BASIC
*LIME GREEN/149: 2X TO 5X BASIC
*BLUE/85: 2.5X TO 6X BASIC
*ORANGE/39: 4X TO 10X BASIC
*PINK/25: 5X TO 12X BASIC
1 Luka Doncic 4.00 10.00
2 Donovan Mitchell 1.25 3.00
3 Stephen Curry 4.00 10.00
4 Giannis Antetokounmpo 3.00 8.00
5 Kevin Durant 2.00 5.00
6 LeBron James 5.00 12.00
7 Kawhi Leonard 1.50 4.00
8 LaMelo Ball 1.50 4.00
9 Anthony Edwards 3.00 8.00
10 Zion Williamson 1.50 4.00
11 Anthony Davis 1.50 4.00
12 Ja Morant 2.00 5.00
13 James Harden 1.25 3.00
14 Trae Young 1.50 4.00
15 Damian Lillard 1.50 4.00
16 Cade Cunningham 8.00 20.00
17 Jalen Green 6.00 15.00
18 Evan Mobley 2.50 6.00
19 Scottie Barnes 6.00 15.00
20 Jalen Suggs 1.50 4.00

2021-22 Donruss Optic Opti-Graphs

COMMON CARD 4.00 10.00
SEMISTARS 5.00 12.00
UNLISTED STARS 6.00 15.00
STATED PRINT RUN 25-99 SER.#'d SETS
EXCHANGE DEADLINE 3/02/2024
*CHOICE: .4X TO 1X BASIC
1 Jae'Sean Tate/99 6.00 15.00
2 Rasheed Wallace/99 25.00 60.00
3 Damian Lillard/99 75.00 200.00
4 Metta World Peace/99 12.00 30.00
5 Manu Ginobili/99 60.00 150.00
6 Kendrick Perkins/99 5.00 12.00
7 Latrell Sprewell/99 12.00 30.00
9 Ralph Sampson/99 6.00 15.00
10 Larry Bird/25 100.00 250.00
11 Dario Saric/99 4.00 10.00
12 Larrar Odom/99 6.00 15.00
13 Al-Farouq Aminu/99 4.00 10.00
14 Tony Allen/99 4.00 10.00
15 Tyus Jones/99 5.00 12.00
16 Matt Barnes/99 5.00 12.00
17 Maurice Cheeks/99 5.00 12.00
18 Luka Doncic/25 400.00 800.00
19 Ray Allen/99 30.00 80.00
20 Ja Morant/25 350.00 700.00
21 Paul Pressey/99 5.00 12.00
22 David Lee/99 5.00 12.00
23 Elfrid Payton/87 4.00 10.00
24 Raymond Felton/99 4.00 10.00
25 Austin Rivers/99 5.00 12.00
26 Nate McMillan/99 5.00 12.00
27 Dennis Rodman/99 30.00 80.00
29 George McGinnis/99 6.00 15.00
30 Oscar Robertson/25 40.00 100.00
31 Udonis Haslem/99 4.00 10.00
32 Josh Howard/99 5.00 12.00
33 Willie Cauley-Stein/70 4.00 10.00
34 Wang Zhi-zhi/99 50.00 120.00
35 Trevor Ariza/99 5.00 12.00
36 Rolando Blackman/99 5.00 12.00
37 Bob Dandridge/99 6.00 15.00
39 Dan Issel/99 6.00 15.00
40 Anthony Edwards/25 150.00 400.00
41 Cody Zeller/99 4.00 10.00
42 Joakim Noah/49 5.00 12.00
43 Caris LeVert/99 5.00 12.00
44 Juwan Howard/99 5.00 12.00
45 Shawn Kemp/99 30.00 80.00
46 Kurt Rambis/99 6.00 15.00
47 Dominique Wilkins/99 15.00 40.00
49 Nate Archibald/99 6.00 15.00
50 Trae Young/25 150.00 400.00
51 Joshua Primo/99 5.00 12.00
52 David Johnson/99 5.00 12.00
53 Isaiah Jackson/99 6.00 15.00
54 Ziaire Williams/99 8.00 20.00
55 JT Thor/99 6.00 15.00
56 Isaiah Livers/49 6.00 15.00
58 Kai Jones/49 5.00 12.00
59 Neemias Queta/49 6.00 15.00
60 Usman Garuba/49 5.00 12.00
61 Charles Bassey/49 5.00 15.00
62 Bones Hyland/49 8.00 20.00
63 Tre Mann/49 10.00 25.00
64 Jared Butler/49 6.00 15.00
65 Chris Duarte/49 5.00 12.00
66 Trey Murphy III/49 20.00 50.00
67 Josh Giddey/49 100.00 250.00
68 Corey Kispert/49 8.00 20.00
69 Herbert Jones/49 8.00 20.00
70 Brandon Boston Jr./49 6.00 15.00
71 Isaiah Todd/99 5.00 12.00
72 Greg Brown III/99 5.00 12.00
73 Alperen Sengun/99 20.00 50.00
74 Josh Christopher/99 5.00 12.00
75 Miles McBride/99 10.00 25.00
76 Jalen Suggs/25 60.00 150.00
77 Cameron Thomas/99 12.00 30.00
78 Moses Moody/99 40.00 100.00
79 Jalen Green/25 200.00 500.00
80 Jonathan Kuminga/25 75.00 200.00
81 Day'Ron Sharpe/99 6.00 15.00
82 Leandro Bolmaro/99 6.00 15.00
83 Jeremiah Robinson-Earl/99 6.00 15.00
84 Jericho Sims/99 8.00 20.00
85 Evan Mobley/25 125.00 300.00
86 Joe Wieskamp/99 5.00 12.00
87 Kessler Edwards/99 6.00 15.00
88 Franz Wagner/99 50.00 120.00
89 Austin Reaves/99 30.00 80.00
90 Aaron Wiggins/99 8.00 20.00
91 Quentin Grimes/99 12.00 30.00
92 Jaden Springer/99 6.00 15.00
93 Ayo Dosunmu/99 12.00 30.00
94 T.J. McConnell/99 5.00 12.00
95 Santi Aldama/99 8.00 20.00
96 Jalen Johnson/99 20.00 50.00
97 Davion Mitchell/99 6.00 15.00
98 Scottie Barnes/99 150.00 400.00
99 Cade Cunningham/25 300.00 600.00
100 Keon Johnson/99 6.00 15.00

2021-22 Donruss Optic Raining 3s

COMMON CARD .40 1.00
SEMISTARS .50 1.25
UNLISTED STARS .60 1.50
*HOLO: .75X TO 2X BASIC
*FB: .75X TO 2X BASIC
*BLUE PULSAR: 1.25X TO 3X BASIC
*RED PULSAR: 1.25X TO 3X BASIC
*RED/99: 2.5X TO 6X BASIC
*BLUE/49: 4X TO 10X BASIC
1 Trae Young 1.50 4.00
2 Stephen Curry 4.00 10.00
3 Khris Middleton .60 1.50
4 Luka Doncic 4.00 10.00
5 James Harden 1.25 3.00
6 Desmond Bane 1.25 3.00
7 Buddy Hield .50 1.25
8 Donovan Mitchell 1.25 3.00
9 Damian Lillard 1.50 4.00
10 Kevin Durant 2.00 5.00
11 Saddiq Bey .50 1.25
12 Fred VanVleet .75 2.00
13 Duncan Robinson .50 1.25
14 Joe Harris .50 1.25
15 Klay Thompson 1.50 4.00
16 Steve Nash 1.25 3.00
17 Peja Stojakovic .50 1.25
18 Dirk Nowitzki 1.50 4.00
19 Paul George 1.00 2.50
20 Ray Allen 1.00 2.50

2021-22 Donruss Optic Rated Rookie Signatures

COMMON CARD 4.00 10.00
SEMISTARS 5.00 12.00
UNLISTED STARS 6.00 15.00
EXCHANGE DEADLINE 3/02/2024
*FAST BREAK: .4X TO 1X BASIC
*PURPLE: .4X TO 1X BASIC
*CHOICE: .6X TO 1.5X BASIC
*HOLO: .6X TO 1.5X BASIC
*BLUE/49: .75X TO 2X BASIC
151 James Bouknight 5.00 12.00
152 Josh Giddey 150.00 400.00
153 Cameron Thomas 25.00 60.00
154 Kessler Edwards 6.00 15.00
155 Davion Mitchell 40.00 100.00
156 Neemias Queta 6.00 15.00
157 Herbert Jones 8.00 20.00
159 Jalen Green 300.00 600.00
160 Jason Preston 5.00 12.00
161 Cade Cunningham 400.00 800.00
162 Joshua Primo 5.00 12.00
163 Charles Bassey 6.00 15.00
164 Luka Garza 6.00 15.00
165 Day'Ron Sharpe 6.00 15.00
166 Quentin Grimes 25.00 60.00
167 Isaiah Jackson 6.00 15.00
168 Tre Mann 40.00 100.00
169 Alperen Sengun 50.00 120.00
170 Jeremiah Robinson-Earl 6.00 15.00
171 Ayo Dosunmu 75.00 200.00
172 JT Thor 6.00 15.00
173 Chris Duarte 5.00 12.00
174 Miles McBride 10.00 25.00
175 Evan Mobley 200.00 500.00
176 Santi Aldama 8.00 20.00
177 Isaiah Livers 6.00 15.00
178 Trey Murphy III 30.00 80.00
179 Jalen Suggs 60.00 150.00
180 Joe Wieskamp 5.00 12.00
181 Jalen Johnson 20.00 50.00
182 Kai Jones 5.00 12.00
183 Corey Kispert 8.00 20.00
184 Moses Moody 50.00 120.00
185 Franz Wagner 100.00 250.00
186 Scottie Barnes 200.00 500.00
187 Isaiah Todd 5.00 12.00
188 Usman Garuba 5.00 12.00
189 Brandon Boston Jr. 6.00 15.00
190 Jonathan Kuminga 100.00 250.00
191 Aaron Wiggins 8.00 20.00
192 Keon Johnson 6.00 15.00
193 David Johnson 5.00 12.00
194 Bones Hyland 50.00 120.00
195 Greg Brown III 5.00 12.00
196 Scottie Lewis 5.00 12.00
197 Jaden Springer 6.00 15.00
198 Ziaire Williams 8.00 20.00
199 Jared Butler 6.00 15.00
200 Josh Christopher 5.00 12.00

2021-22 Donruss Optic Retro Series Signatues

COMMON CARD 4.00 10.00
SEMISTARS 5.00 12.00
UNLISTED STARS 6.00 15.00
STATED PRINT RUN 99 SER.#'d SETS
EXCHANGE DEADLINE 3/02/2024
1 Rasheed Wallace 25.00 60.00
2 David Lee 5.00 12.00
3 Harold Miner 6.00 15.00
4 Joakim Noah 5.00 12.00
5 Josh Howard 5.00 12.00
6 Juwan Howard 5.00 12.00
7 Kendrick Perkins 5.00 12.00
8 Lamar Odom 6.00 15.00
9 Matt Barnes 5.00 12.00
10 Metta World Peace 15.00 40.00
11 Raymond Felton 4.00 10.00
12 Tony Allen 4.00 10.00
13 Tony Parker 15.00 40.00
14 Wang Zhi-zhi 60.00 150.00
15 Adrian Dantley 6.00 15.00
16 Artis Gilmore 8.00 20.00
17 Bob Dandridge 6.00 15.00
18 Chris Mullin 12.00 30.00
19 David Thompson 8.00 20.00
20 Dennis Rodman 40.00 100.00
21 Dominique Wilkins 15.00 40.00
22 Isiah Thomas 15.00 40.00
23 Maurice Cheeks 5.00 12.00
24 Nate Archibald 6.00 15.00
25 Ralph Sampson 6.00 15.00
26 Ray Allen 30.00 80.00
27 Robert Parish 8.00 20.00
28 Tom "Satch" Sanders 6.00 15.00
29 Walt Frazier 12.00 30.00
30 Jason Williams 30.00 80.00

2021-22 Donruss Optic Signature Series

COMMON CARD 4.00 10.00
SEMISTARS 5.00 12.00
UNLISTED STARS 6.00 15.00
EXCHANGE DEADLINE 3/02/2024
*HOLO: .5X TO 1.2X BASIC
*GREEN SHOCK: .5X TO 1.2X BASIC
*BLUE/25: .6X TO 1.5X BASIC
*PINK/25: .6X TO 1.5X BASIC
1 Oshae Brissett 5.00 12.00
2 Taj Gibson 4.00 10.00
3 Joel Ayayi 5.00 12.00
4 Charles Oakley 5.00 12.00
5 Benoit Benjamin 4.00 10.00
7 Nick Richards 5.00 12.00
8 Metta World Peace 12.00 30.00
9 Max Strus 6.00 15.00
10 Bob Dandridge 6.00 15.00
11 Duane Washington Jr. 6.00 15.00
12 Raymond Felton 4.00 10.00
13 Sam Hauser 15.00 40.00
14 Jose Alvarado 15.00 40.00
15 Wayne Ellington 4.00 10.00
17 Garfield Heard 5.00 12.00
18 Kendrick Perkins 5.00 12.00
19 David Duke Jr. 6.00 15.00
20 Sterling Brown 4.00 10.00
21 Malik Fitts 5.00 12.00
22 Brent Barry 5.00 12.00
23 Enes Freedom 5.00 12.00
25 Leonard "Truck" Robinson 5.00 12.00
26 Karl Malone 40.00 100.00
27 Purvis Short 5.00 12.00
28 Matt Barnes 5.00 12.00
29 Jay Scrubb 5.00 12.00
30 Jaylen Nowell 4.00 10.00
31 Alize Johnson 6.00 15.00
32 Kenny "Sky" Walker 4.00 10.00
33 Calvin Natt 5.00 12.00
35 Danny Schayes 5.00 12.00
36 Larry Bird 100.00 250.00
37 Michael Adams 5.00 12.00
38 Dennis Rodman 30.00 80.00
39 DaQuan Jeffries 5.00 12.00
40 Kwame Brown 5.00 12.00
41 Tyler Cook 5.00 12.00
42 Dan Issel 6.00 15.00
43 Spencer Haywood 5.00 12.00
45 Reggie Theus 5.00 12.00
46 Anthony Edwards 150.00 400.00
47 James Donaldson 5.00 12.00
48 Shawn Kemp 15.00 40.00
49 Amir Coffey 5.00 12.00
50 Luke Kennard 5.00 12.00
51 Franz Wagner 20.00 50.00
52 Alperen Sengun 20.00 50.00
53 Joe Wieskamp 5.00 12.00
54 Austin Reaves 30.00 80.00
55 Isaiah Todd 5.00 12.00
56 Josh Christopher 5.00 12.00
57 Kessler Edwards 6.00 15.00
58 Aaron Wiggins 8.00 20.00
59 Greg Brown III 5.00 12.00
60 Miles McBride 10.00 25.00
61 Tre Mann 10.00 25.00
62 Moses Moody 12.00 30.00
63 Charles Bassey 6.00 15.00
64 Jared Butler 6.00 15.00
65 Jalen Suggs 15.00 40.00
66 Jalen Green 75.00 200.00
67 Bones Hyland 8.00 20.00
68 Chris Duarte 5.00 12.00
69 Cameron Thomas 12.00 30.00
70 Jonathan Kuminga 20.00 50.00
71 Ayo Dosunmu 12.00 30.00
72 Isaiah Jackson 6.00 15.00
73 Quentin Grimes 12.00 30.00
74 Markus Howard 6.00 15.00
75 Joshua Primo 5.00 12.00
76 Ziaire Williams 8.00 20.00
77 Jaden Springer 6.00 15.00
78 Santi Aldama 8.00 20.00
79 David Johnson 5.00 12.00
80 JT Thor 6.00 15.00
81 Corey Kispert 8.00 20.00
82 Jeremiah Robinson-Earl 6.00 15.00
83 Trey Murphy III 20.00 50.00
84 Herbert Jones 8.00 20.00
85 Day'Ron Sharpe 6.00 15.00
86 Jericho Sims 8.00 20.00
87 Josh Giddey 20.00 50.00
88 Brandon Boston Jr. 6.00 15.00
89 Leandro Bolmaro 6.00 15.00
90 Evan Mobley 25.00 60.00
91 Scottie Barnes 20.00 50.00
92 Kai Jones 5.00 12.00
93 Jalen Johnson 20.00 50.00
94 Cade Cunningham 125.00 300.00
95 Isaiah Livers 6.00 15.00
96 Neemias Queta 6.00 15.00
97 Davion Mitchell 6.00 15.00
98 Keon Johnson 6.00 15.00
100 Usman Garuba 5.00 12.00

2021-22 Donruss Optic Splash!

COMMON CARD .40 1.00
SEMISTARS .50 1.25
UNLISTED STARS .60 1.50
*PURPLE: .6X TO 1.5X BASIC
*HOLO .75X TO 2X BASIC
*GREEN SHOCK: 1X TO 2.5X BASIC
*RED WAVE: 1.5X TO 4X BASIC
*LIME GREEN/149: 2X TO 5X BASIC
*BLUE/85: 2.5X TO 6X BASIC
*ORANGE/39: 4X TO 10X BASIC
*PINK/25: 5X TO 12X BASIC
1 Stephen Curry 4.00 10.00
2 Klay Thompson 1.50 4.00
3 James Harden 1.25 3.00
4 Luka Doncic 4.00 10.00
5 Trae Young 1.50 4.00
6 Damian Lillard 1.50 4.00
7 Kevin Durant 2.00 5.00
8 Zach LaVine 1.00 2.50
9 Khris Middleton .60 1.50
10 Bradley Beal .75 2.00
11 LeBron James 5.00 12.00
12 Jayson Tatum 2.50 6.00
13 Devin Booker 1.50 4.00
14 Donovan Mitchell 1.25 3.00
15 Kawhi Leonard 1.50 4.00

2021-22 Donruss Optic Star Gazing

COMMON CARD .40 1.00
SEMISTARS .50 1.25
UNLISTED STARS .60 1.50
*HOLO .75X TO 2X BASIC
*FB: .75X TO 2X BASIC
*BLUE PULSAR: 1.25X TO 3X BASIC
*RED PULSAR: 1.25X TO 3X BASIC
*RED/99: 2.5X TO 6X BASIC
*BLUE/49: 4X TO 10X BASIC
1 Luka Doncic 4.00 10.00
2 Stephen Curry 4.00 10.00
3 Giannis Antetokounmpo 3.00 8.00
4 Zion Williamson 1.50 4.00
5 Nikola Jokic 3.00 8.00
6 LeBron James 5.00 12.00
7 Kevin Durant 2.00 5.00
8 Anthony Davis 1.50 4.00
9 LaMelo Ball 1.50 4.00
10 Damian Lillard 1.50 4.00
11 Donovan Mitchell 1.25 3.00
12 Chris Paul 1.25 3.00
13 Kawhi Leonard 1.50 4.00
14 Trae Young 1.50 4.00
15 James Harden 1.25 3.00

2021-22 Donruss Optic T-Minus 3...2...1...

COMMON CARD .40 1.00
SEMISTARS .50 1.25
UNLISTED STARS .60 1.50
*PURPLE: .6X TO 1.5X BASIC
*HOLO: .75X TO 2X BASIC
*RED WAVE: 1.5X TO 4X BASIC
*LIME GREEN/149: 2X TO 5X BASIC
*BLUE/85: 2.5X TO 6X BASIC
*ORANGE/39: 4X TO 10X BASIC
*PINK/25: 5X TO 12X BASIC
1 Zion Williamson 1.50 4.00
2 LeBron James 5.00 12.00
3 Giannis Antetokounmpo 3.00 8.00
4 Anthony Davis 1.50 4.00
5 Donovan Mitchell 1.25 3.00
6 Kevin Durant 2.00 5.00
7 Luka Doncic 4.00 10.00
8 Zach LaVine 1.00 2.50
9 Paul George 1.00 2.50
10 Ja Morant 2.00 5.00
11 Anthony Edwards 3.00 8.00
12 Stephen Curry 4.00 10.00
13 Trae Young 1.50 4.00
14 Kyrie Irving 1.25 3.00
15 Devin Booker 1.50 4.00

2021-22 Donruss Optic The Rookies

*FAST BREAK: 1X TO 2.5X BASIC
*HOLO: 1X TO 2.5X BASIC
*BLUE PULSAR: 1.25X TO 3X BASIC
*RED PULSAR: 1.25X TO 3X BASIC
*RED/99: 2.5X TO 6X BASIC
*BLUE/49: 4X TO 10X BASIC
1 Cade Cunningham 6.00 15.00
2 Jalen Green 5.00 12.00
3 Evan Mobley 4.00 10.00
4 Scottie Barnes 3.00 8.00
5 Jalen Suggs 2.50 6.00

2021-22 Donruss Optic Winner Stays

COMMON CARD .40 1.00
SEMISTARS .50 1.25
UNLISTED STARS .60 1.50
*PURPLE: .6X TO 1.5X BASIC
*HOLO: .75X TO 2X BASIC
*RED WAVE: 1.5X TO 4X BASIC
*LIME GREEN/149: 2X TO 5X BASIC
*BLUE/85: 2.5X TO 6X BASIC
*ORANGE/39: 4X TO 10X BASIC
*PINK/25: 5X TO 12X BASIC
1 Giannis Antetokounmpo 3.00 8.00
2 Khris Middleton .60 1.50
3 LeBron James 5.00 12.00
4 Stephen Curry 4.00 10.00

Ray Allen 1.00 2.50
Dennis Rodman 1.50 4.00
Anthony Davis 1.50 4.00
Chauncey Billups .75 2.00
Shaquille O'Neal 2.00 5.00
0 Dwyane Wade 1.25 3.00
1 Kevin Garnett 1.50 4.00
2 Wilt Chamberlain 2.00 5.00
3 Bill Walton 1.00 2.50
4 Draymond Green .75 2.00
5 Clyde Drexler 1.00 2.50
6 Magic Johnson 2.00 5.00
7 Kevin Durant 2.00 5.00
8 Kawhi Leonard 1.50 4.00
9 Tim Duncan 1.50 4.00
20 Dirk Nowitzki 1.50 4.00

2022-23 Donruss Optic

COMMON CARD (1-200) .25 6.00
SEMISTARS .30 .75
UNLISTED STARS .40 1.00
COMMON RC (201-250) .50 1.25
RC SEMIS .60 1.50
RC UNLISTED .75 2.00
*PURPLE: 1.25X TO 3X BASIC
*FB HOLO: 1.5X TO 4X BASIC
*GREEN SHOCK: 1.5X TO 4X BASIC
*HOLO: 1.5X TO 4X BASIC
*HYPER PINK: 1.5X TO 4X BASIC
*PURPLE SHOCK: 1.5X TO 4X BASIC
*RED WAVE: 1.5X TO 4X BASIC
1 OG Anunoby .50 1.25
2 Quentin Grimes .30 .75
3 Jalen Brunson .75 2.00
4 Gary Trent Jr. .40 1.00
5 Michael Porter Jr. .50 1.25
6 Otto Porter Jr. .25 .60
7 Kentavious Caldwell-Pope .30 .75
8 Jayson Tatum 1.50 4.00
9 Kevin Durant 1.25 3.00
10 Fred VanVleet .50 1.25
11 Malcolm Brogdon .30 .75
12 Marcus Smart .50 1.25
13 Tobias Harris .30 .75
14 P.J. Tucker .30 .75
15 Obi Toppin .40 1.00
16 Ben Simmons .40 1.00
17 Grant Williams .30 .75
18 Cameron Thomas .60 1.50
19 Pascal Siakam .60 1.50
20 Scottie Barnes .60 1.50
21 Bones Hyland .30 .75
22 James Harden .75 2.00
23 Julius Randle .50 1.25
24 Robert Williams III .30 .75
25 Al Horford .40 1.00
26 Tyrese Maxey .75 2.00
27 Joel Embiid .60 1.50
28 RJ Barrett .60 1.50
29 Seth Curry .30 .75
30 Cam Reddish .30 .75
31 Kyrie Irving .75 2.00
32 Jaylen Brown .75 2.00
33 Evan Fournier .30 .75
34 T.J. Warren .30 .75
35 De'Anthony Melton .30 .75
36 Jordan Clarkson .40 1.00
37 Collin Sexton .50 1.25
38 Bojan Bogdanovic .40 1.00
39 Luguentz Dort .40 1.00
40 Mike Conley .30 .75
41 Gary Payton II .30 .75
42 Jamal Murray .60 1.50
43 Josh Giddey .60 1.50
44 Shai Gilgeous-Alexander 2.00 5.00
45 Anthony Edwards 2.00 5.00
46 Bruce Brown .40 1.00
47 Tre Mann .30 .75
48 Nikola Jokic 2.00 5.00
49 Damian Lillard 1.00 2.50
50 Karl-Anthony Towns .60 1.50
51 Zach LaVine .75 2.00
52 Anfernee Simons .50 1.25
53 Jerami Grant .50 1.25
54 Alex Caruso .40 1.00
55 Josh Hart .40 1.00
56 Aaron Wiggins .30 .75
57 D'Angelo Russell .30 .75
58 Lonzo Ball .40 1.00
59 Talen Horton-Tucker .30 .75
60 Nikola Vucevic .40 1.00
61 Austin Rivers .25 .60
62 Jusuf Nurkic .40 1.00
63 Ayo Dosunmu .50 1.25
64 Darius Bazley .25 .60
65 DeMar DeRozan .50 1.25
66 Malik Beasley .30 .75
67 Jaden McDaniels .40 1.00
68 Aaron Gordon .40 1.00
69 Lauri Markkanen .60 1.50
70 Rudy Gobert .50 1.25
71 Klay Thompson 1.00 2.50
72 Donovan Mitchell .75 2.00
73 Oshae Brissett .30 .75
74 Pat Connaughton .30 .75
75 Giannis Antetokounmpo 2.00 5.00
76 Jarrett Allen .40 1.00
77 Isaiah Stewart .30 .75
78 Kevin Love .40 1.00
79 Draymond Green .50 1.25
80 James Wiseman .30 .75
81 T.J. McConnell .30 .75
82 Khris Middleton .50 1.25
83 Grayson Allen .40 1.00
84 Andrew Wiggins .50 1.25
85 Caris LeVert .30 .75
86 Isaac Okoro .30 .75
87 Joe Ingles .30 .75
88 Moses Moody .50 1.25
89 Myles Turner .40 1.00
90 Coby White .30 .75
91 Jrue Holiday .50 1.25
92 Cade Cunningham 1.25 3.00
93 Evan Mobley 1.00 2.50
94 Saddiq Bey .30 .75
95 Buddy Hield .40 1.00
96 Stephen Curry 3.00 8.00
97 Hamidou Diallo .30 .75
98 Darius Garland .60 1.50
99 Tyrese Haliburton .75 2.00
100 Jordan Poole .60 1.50
101 Bobby Portis .40 1.00
102 Jonathan Kuminga 1.00 2.50
103 Marvin Bagley III .30 .75
104 Alec Burks .30 .75
105 Chris Duarte .30 .75
106 Norman Powell .40 1.00
107 Patrick Beverley .25 .60
108 Mikal Bridges .50 1.25
109 Harrison Barnes .30 .75
110 Paul George .60 1.50
111 Dennis Schroder .40 1.00
112 De'Andre Hunter .40 1.00
113 Jae Crowder .25 .60
114 John Wall .50 1.25
115 Bogdan Bogdanovic .40 1.00
116 LeBron James 3.00 8.00
117 Domantas Sabonis .50 1.25
118 Kawhi Leonard 1.00 2.50
119 Marcus Morris Sr. .25 .60
120 Terance Mann .30 .75
121 Reggie Jackson .30 .75
122 Anthony Davis 1.00 2.50
123 Kendrick Nunn .30 .75
124 Davion Mitchell .30 .75
125 Chris Paul .75 2.00
126 Deandre Ayton .40 1.00
127 Trae Young 1.00 2.50
128 Malik Monk .40 1.00
129 Justin Holiday .25 .60
130 De'Aaron Fox .75 2.00
131 Cameron Johnson .30 .75
132 Luke Kennard .30 .75
133 Russell Westbrook .60 1.50
134 Devin Booker 1.00 2.50
135 Kevin Huerter .40 1.00
136 Austin Reaves 1.00 2.50
137 John Collins .40 1.00
138 Dejounte Murray .50 1.25
139 Richaun Holmes .25 .60
140 Jason Preston .30 .75
141 Deni Avdija .40 1.00
142 Dorian Finney-Smith .30 .75
143 Terry Rozier III .50 1.25
144 Kyle Lowry .50 1.25
145 Cole Anthony .40 1.00
146 Kevin Porter Jr. .30 .75
147 Jalen Green 1.25 3.00
148 Cody Martin .30 .75
149 Kristaps Porzingis .50 1.25
150 LaMelo Ball 1.00 2.50
151 Tyler Herro .60 1.50
152 Christian Wood .25 .60
153 Mo Bamba .30 .75
154 Clint Capela .40 1.00
155 Kyle Kuzma .50 1.25
156 Davis Bertans .25 .60
157 Markelle Fultz .30 .75
158 Victor Oladipo .30 .75
159 Jalen Suggs .50 1.25
160 Luka Doncic 2.50 6.00
161 Franz Wagner 1.00 2.50
162 Duncan Robinson .40 1.00
163 Bradley Beal .50 1.25
164 Gordon Hayward .30 .75
165 Gary Harris .30 .75
166 Will Barton .25 .60
167 Tim Hardaway Jr. .30 .75
168 Max Strus .40 1.00
169 Monte Morris .25 .60
170 Rui Hachimura .40 1.00
171 Jimmy Butler .75 2.00
172 PJ Washington Jr. .40 1.00
173 Kelly Oubre Jr. .40 1.00
174 Bam Adebayo .60 1.50
175 Spencer Dinwiddie .40 1.00
176 Ja Morant 1.25 3.00
177 Alperen Sengun .50 1.25
178 Trey Murphy III .50 1.25
179 CJ McCollum .40 1.00
180 Josh Christopher .25 .60
181 Zion Williamson 1.00 2.50
182 Herbert Jones .40 1.00
183 Eric Gordon .30 .75
184 Tyus Jones .30 .75
185 Brandon Ingram .50 1.25
186 Keldon Johnson .50 1.25
187 Jakob Poeltl .30 .75
188 Ziaire Williams .30 .75
189 Jaren Jackson Jr. .60 1.50
190 Desmond Bane .50 1.25
191 Jae'Sean Tate .25 .60
192 Danny Green .30 .75
193 Jonas Valanciunas .30 .75
194 Devonte' Graham .30 .75
195 Kenyon Martin Jr. .40 1.00
196 Devin Vassell .50 1.25
197 Doug McDermott .25 .60
198 Josh Richardson .30 .75
199 Tre Jones .40 1.00
200 Dillon Brooks .40 1.00
201 Wendell Moore Jr. RR RC .75 2.00
202 Kenneth Lofton Jr. RR RC 1.00 2.50
203 Tari Eason RR RC 2.00 5.00
204 AJ Griffin RR RC .60 1.50
205 Ochai Agbaji RR RC 1.00 2.50
206 Johnny Davis RR RC .75 2.00
207 E.J. Liddell RR RC .75 2.00
208 Chet Holmgren RR RC 4.00 10.00
209 Bennedict Mathurin RR RC 2.50 6.00
210 MarJon Beauchamp RR RC .75 2.00
211 Ryan Rollins RR RC .75 2.00
212 Christian Koloko RR RC .75 2.00
213 Walker Kessler RR RC 1.50 4.00
214 Keegan Murray RR RC 2.00 5.00
215 Blake Wesley RR RC .75 2.00
216 Jake LaRavia RR RC .75 2.00
217 Kendall Brown RR RC .60 1.50
218 Patrick Baldwin Jr. RR RC .75 2.00
219 Kennedy Chandler RR RC .75 2.00
220 Ousmane Dieng RR RC 1.00 2.50
221 Paolo Banchero RR RC 5.00 12.00
222 Malaki Branham RR RC .75 2.00
223 Peyton Watson RR RC 1.25 3.00
224 Nikola Jovic RR RC 1.50 4.00
225 David Roddy RR RC 1.00 2.50
226 Vince Williams Jr. RR RC 1.00 2.50
227 Jalen Duren RR RC 2.50 6.00
228 Scotty Pippen Jr. RR RC 1.00 2.50
229 Caleb Houstan RR RC .75 2.00
230 Andrew Nembhard RR RC 1.50 4.00
231 TyTy Washington Jr. RR RC .75 2.00
232 Dalen Terry RR RC .75 2.00
233 Max Christie RR RC 2.00 5.00
234 Tyrese Martin RR RC .60 1.50
235 Jalen Williams RR RC 4.00 10.00
236 Jeremy Sochan RR RC 2.50 6.00
237 Isaiah Mobley RR RC .75 2.00
238 Christian Braun RR RC 2.00 5.00
239 Bryce McGowens RR RC .75 2.00
240 Jabari Smith Jr. RR RC 2.50 6.00
241 Jaden Ivey RR RC 2.50 6.00
242 Jabari Walker RR RC .60 1.50
243 Trevor Keels RR RC .60 1.50
244 Josh Minott RR RC .75 2.00
245 Mark Williams RR RC 1.50 4.00
246 Jaylin Williams RR RC 1.00 2.50
247 Moussa Diabate RR RC .75 2.00
248 Jaden Hardy RR RC 1.25 3.00
249 Shaedon Sharpe RR RC 3.00 8.00
250 Dyson Daniels RR RC 2.00 5.00

2022-23 Donruss Optic Basketballs Parallel

*BASKETBALL: 2.5X TO 6X BASIC
208 Chet Holmgren RR 50.00 120.00
221 Paolo Banchero RR 75.00 200.00

2022-23 Donruss Optic Black Velocity

*BLACK VELOCITY: 10X TO 25X BASIC
STATED PRINT RUN 39 SER. #'D SETS
208 Chet Holmgren RR 200.00 500.00
221 Paolo Banchero RR 400.00 800.00

2022-23 Donruss Optic Blue

*BLUE: 6X TO 15X BASIC
STATED PRINT RUN 49 SER. #'D SETS
208 Chet Holmgren RR 125.00 300.00
221 Paolo Banchero RR 200.00 500.00

2022-23 Donruss Optic Blue Sparkle

*BLUE SPARKLE: 2.5X TO 6X BASIC
STATED PRINT RUN 180 SER. #'D SETS
208 Chet Holmgren RR 50.00 120.00
221 Paolo Banchero RR 75.00 200.00

2022-23 Donruss Optic Choice Blue Mojo

*CHOICE BLUE MOJO: 10X TO 25X BASIC
STATED PRINT RUN 24 SER. #'D SETS
208 Chet Holmgren RR 300.00 500.00
221 Paolo Banchero RR 500.00 1,000.00

2022-23 Donruss Optic Choice Red

*CHOICE RED: 4X TO 10X BASIC
STATED PRINT RUN 88 SER. #'D SETS
208 Chet Holmgren RR 40.00 100.00
221 Paolo Banchero RR 50.00 125.00

2022-23 Donruss Optic Copper Glitter

*COPPER GLITTER: 4X TO 10X BASIC
STATED PRINT RUN 99 SER. #'D SETS
208 Chet Holmgren RR 75.00 200.00
221 Paolo Banchero RR 125.00 300.00

2022-23 Donruss Optic Fast Break Blue

*FB BLUE: 6X TO 15X BASIC
STATED PRINT RUN 49 SER. #'D SETS
208 Chet Holmgren RR 125.00 300.00
221 Paolo Banchero RR 200.00 500.00

2022-23 Donruss Optic Fast Break Pink

*FB PINK: 10X TO 25X BASIC
STATED PRINT RUN 25 SER. #'D SETS
208 Chet Holmgren RR 200.00 500.00
221 Paolo Banchero RR 400.00 800.00

2022-23 Donruss Optic Fast Break Purple

*FB PURPLE: 4X TO 10X BASIC
STATED PRINT RUN 99 SER. #'D SETS
208 Chet Holmgren RR 75.00 200.00
221 Paolo Banchero RR 125.00 300.00

2022-23 Donruss Optic Fast Break Red

*FB RED: 5X TO 12X BASIC
STATED PRINT RUN 75 SER. #'D SETS
208 Chet Holmgren RR 100.00 250.00
221 Paolo Banchero RR 150.00 400.00

2022-23 Donruss Optic Gold Sparkle

*GOLD SPARKLE: 10X TO 25X BASIC
STATED PRINT RUN 24 SER. #'D SETS
208 Chet Holmgren RR 300.00 600.00
221 Paolo Banchero RR 500.00 1,000.00

2022-23 Donruss Optic Lime Green

*LIME GREEN: 3X TO 8X BASIC
STATED PRINT RUN 149 SER. #'D SETS
208 Chet Holmgren RR 60.00 150.00
221 Paolo Banchero RR 100.00 250.00

2022-23 Donruss Optic Orange

*ORANGE: 2.5X TO 6X BASIC
STATED PRINT RUN 199 SER. #'D SETS
208 Chet Holmgren RR 50.00 120.00
221 Paolo Banchero RR 75.00 200.00

2022-23 Donruss Optic Pink Velocity

*PINK VELOCITY: 5X TO 12X BASIC
STATED PRINT RUN 79 SER. #'D SETS
208 Chet Holmgren RR 75.00 200.00
221 Paolo Banchero RR 75.00 200.00

2022-23 Donruss Optic Premium Box Set

*PREMIUM BOX SET: 2.5X TO 6X BASIC
STATED PRINT RUN 249 SER. #'D SETS
208 Chet Holmgren RR 40.00 100.00
221 Paolo Banchero RR 60.00 150.00

2022-23 Donruss Optic Red

*RED: 3X TO 8X BASIC
STATED PRINT RUN 99 SER. #'D SETS
208 Chet Holmgren RR 60.00 150.00
221 Paolo Banchero RR 100.00 250.00

2022-23 Donruss Optic Red and Gold Wave

*RED & GOLD WAVE: 4X TO 10X BASIC
STATED PRINT RUN 99 SER. #'D SETS
208 Chet Holmgren RR 75.00 200.00
221 Paolo Banchero RR 125.00 300.00

2022-23 Donruss Optic All-Stars

COMMON CARD .50 1.25
SEMISTARS .60 1.50
UNLISTED STARS .75 2.00
*HOLO: .75X TO 2X BASIC
*FB: .75X TO 2X BASIC
*RED WAVE: 1X TO 2.5X BASIC
*RED/99: 2X TO 5X BASIC
*RED & GOLD WAVE/99: 2X TO 5X BASIC
*BLUE/49: 2.5X TO 6X BASIC
1 LeBron James
Luka Doncic 15.00 40.00
2 Stephen Curry
Trae Young 4.00 10.00
3 Ja Morant
LaMelo Ball 1.50 4.00
4 DeMar DeRozan
Devin Booker 1.25 3.00
5 Jayson Tatum
Zach LaVine 2.00 5.00
6 Giannis Antetokounmpo
Nikola Jokic 2.50 6.00
7 Andrew Wiggins
Khris Middleton .60 1.50
8 Dejounte Murray
Jimmy Butler 1.00 2.50
9 Joel Embiid
Karl-Anthony Towns .75 2.00
10 Darius Garland
Fred VanVleet .75 2.00
11 Kevin Durant
Kyrie Irving 1.50 4.00
12 Anthony Davis
Dirk Nowitzki 1.25 3.00
13 David Robinson
Tim Duncan 1.25 3.00
14 Hakeem Olajuwon
Shaquille O'Neal 2.00 5.00
15 Draymond Green
Kawhi Leonard 1.25 3.00
16 Jimmy Butler
Klay Thompson 1.25 3.00
17 Julius Randle
Zion Williamson 1.25 3.00
18 Dwyane Wade
Manu Ginobili 1.00 2.50
19 Allen Iverson
Vince Carter 1.25 3.00
20 Anfernee Hardaway
Grant Hill 1.25 3.00

2022-23 Donruss Optic Dominators Signatures

COMMON CARD 4.00 10.00
SEMISTARS 5.00 12.00
UNLISTED STARS 6.00 15.00
STATED PRINT RUN 49-99 SER.#'d SETS
1 Jalen Brunson/99 40.00 100.00
2 RJ Hampton/99 5.00 12.00
3 Rudy Gobert/99 8.00 20.00
4 Anthony Edwards/49 75.00 200.00
6 Brandon Clarke/99 5.00 12.00
7 Jalen Green/99 40.00 100.00
9 Andre Drummond/99 6.00 15.00
10 Davion Mitchell/99 5.00 12.00
11 Manu Ginobili/99 30.00 80.00
12 Duncan Robinson/99 15.00 40.00
13 Jason Kidd/99 15.00 40.00
14 Seth Curry/99 5.00 12.00
15 Clint Capela/99 6.00 15.00
16 Ben Wallace/99 15.00 40.00
18 James Worthy/99 10.00 25.00
19 Ayo Dosunmu/99 8.00 20.00
20 Bones Hyland/99 5.00 12.00
21 Gordon Hayward/99 5.00 12.00
22 Pau Gasol/99 30.00 80.00
23 Tyrese Haliburton/99 25.00 60.00
24 Lauri Markkanen/99 12.00 30.00
25 Tobias Harris/99 5.00 12.00
26 Jaden McDaniels/99 6.00 15.00
27 Deni Avdija/99 6.00 15.00
28 Patrick Beverley/99 4.00 10.00
29 Evan Fournier/99 5.00 12.00
30 Bobby Portis/99 6.00 15.00
31 Steven Adams/99 6.00 15.00
33 Trae Young/49 150.00 400.00
34 Derek Harper/99 5.00 12.00
35 Kenyon Martin/99 6.00 15.00
36 Glen Rice/99 6.00 15.00
37 Evan Mobley/99 25.00 60.00
38 Alperen Sengun/99 15.00 40.00
39 Juan Toscano-Anderson/99 4.00 10.00
40 Boban Marjanovic/99 6.00 15.00

2022-23 Donruss Optic Elite Dominators

COMMON CARD .30 .75
SEMISTARS .40 1.00
UNLISTED STARS .50 1.25
*HOLO: .75X TO 2X BASIC
*FB: .75X TO 2X BASIC
*RED WAVE: 2X TO 5X BASIC
*RED/99: 2X TO 5X BASIC
*RED & GOLD WAVE/99: 2X TO 5X BASIC
*BLUE/49: 2.5X TO 6X BASIC
1 Devin Booker 1.25 3.00
2 James Harden 1.00 2.50
3 Zion Williamson 1.25 3.00
4 Luka Doncic 3.00 8.00
5 Ja Morant 1.50 4.00
6 Anthony Davis 1.25 3.00
7 Stephen Curry 4.00 10.00
8 Donovan Mitchell 1.00 2.50
9 Joel Embiid .75 2.00
10 Damian Lillard 1.25 3.00
11 LaMelo Ball 1.25 3.00
12 Dejounte Murray .60 1.50
13 DeMar DeRozan .60 1.50
14 Darius Garland .75 2.00
15 Jayson Tatum 2.00 5.00
16 Shai Gilgeous-Alexander 2.50 6.00
17 Trae Young 1.25 3.00
18 Kawhi Leonard 1.25 3.00
19 Nikola Jokic 2.50 6.00
20 Cade Cunningham 1.50 4.00
21 Giannis Antetokounmpo 2.50 6.00
22 LeBron James 4.00 10.00
23 Anthony Edwards 2.50 6.00
24 Jimmy Butler 1.00 2.50
25 Kevin Durant 1.50 4.00

2022-23 Donruss Optic Express Lane

COMMON CARD .30 .75
SEMISTARS .40 1.00
UNLISTED STARS .50 1.25
*PURPLE: .6X TO 1.5X BASIC
*HOLO: .75X TO 2X BASIC
*GREEN SHOCK: X TO X BASIC
*LIME GREEN/149: 1.5X TO 4X BASIC
*BLUE/85: 2X TO 5X BASIC
1 Ja Morant 1.50 4.00
2 Stephen Curry 4.00 10.00
3 Trae Young 1.25 3.00
4 LeBron James 4.00 10.00
5 Luka Doncic 3.00 8.00
6 Donovan Mitchell 1.00 2.50
7 Chris Paul 1.00 2.50
8 Kyrie Irving 1.00 2.50
9 Zion Williamson 1.25 3.00
10 Giannis Antetokounmpo 2.50 6.00
11 LaMelo Ball 1.25 3.00
12 Damian Lillard 1.25 3.00
13 Bradley Beal .60 1.50
14 De'Aaron Fox 1.00 2.50
15 Zach LaVine 1.00 2.50
16 James Harden 1.00 2.50
17 Cade Cunningham 1.50 4.00
18 Jalen Green 1.50 4.00
19 Scottie Barnes .75 2.00
20 Jimmy Butler 1.00 2.50
21 Jaylen Brown 1.00 2.50
22 Anthony Davis 1.25 3.00
23 Jayson Tatum 2.00 5.00
24 Josh Giddey .75 2.00
25 Kevin Durant 1.50 4.00

2022-23 Donruss Optic Fast Break Signatures

COMMON CARD 4.00 10.00
SEMISTARS 5.00 12.00
UNLISTED STARS 6.00 15.00
1 Jordan Poole 25.00 60.00
2 Calvin Murphy 6.00 15.00
4 Jarrett Allen 6.00 15.00
5 Luka Doncic 300.00 600.00
6 Bones Hyland 5.00 12.00
8 Ja Morant 100.00 250.00
10 Jordan Clarkson 15.00 40.00
11 Dominique Wilkins 10.00 25.00
12 Chris Paul 60.00 150.00
13 Anthony Edwards 75.00 200.00
14 Jamal Crawford 6.00 15.00
15 Stephen Curry 400.00 800.00
16 Karl-Anthony Towns 10.00 25.00
17 Trae Young 100.00 250.00
19 Jonas Valanciunas 5.00 12.00
20 Jason Kidd 20.00 50.00
22 Steven Adams 6.00 15.00
24 Joe Harris 5.00 12.00
25 Caris LeVert 5.00 12.00
26 Shawn Kemp 25.00 60.00
29 De'Aaron Fox 25.00 60.00
30 Rudy Gobert 8.00 20.00
31 Chris Mullin 8.00 20.00
32 Evan Mobley 15.00 40.00
34 Spencer Dinwiddie 5.00 12.00
36 Luguentz Dort 6.00 15.00
37 Jayson Tatum 125.00 300.00
39 Nikola Vucevic 6.00 15.00
40 Jalen Suggs 8.00 20.00
41 Davion Mitchell 5.00 12.00
42 Jalen Brunson 30.00 80.00
44 Franz Wagner 15.00 40.00
46 Joe Dumars 8.00 20.00
48 John Stockton 30.00 80.00
49 Jalen Green 50.00 120.00
50 Lenny Wilkens 8.00 20.00
51 Chet Holmgren 100.00 250.00
52 Jabari Smith Jr. 20.00 50.00
53 Jaden Ivey 60.00 150.00
54 Paolo Banchero 150.00 400.00
55 Jaden Hardy 10.00 25.00
56 Jalen Duren 20.00 50.00
57 Johnny Davis 6.00 15.00
58 Keegan Murray 40.00 100.00
59 Shaedon Sharpe 60.00 150.00
61 Bennedict Mathurin 40.00 100.00
62 TyTy Washington Jr. 6.00 15.00
63 Dyson Daniels 15.00 40.00
64 Jeremy Sochan 20.00 50.00
65 Ochai Agbaji 8.00 20.00
66 Blake Wesley 6.00 15.00
67 Ousmane Dieng 8.00 20.00
68 Tari Eason 15.00 40.00
69 Mark Williams 12.00 30.00
70 Jalen Williams 30.00 80.00
71 Walker Kessler 12.00 30.00
72 Kennedy Chandler 6.00 15.00
73 Nikola Jovic 12.00 30.00
74 Dalen Terry 6.00 15.00
75 Wendell Moore Jr. 6.00 15.00
76 E.J. Liddell 6.00 15.00
77 Jake LaRavia 6.00 15.00
78 Malaki Branham 6.00 15.00
79 MarJon Beauchamp 6.00 15.00
80 Kendall Brown 5.00 12.00
81 David Roddy 8.00 20.00
82 Christian Braun 15.00 40.00
85 Max Christie 15.00 40.00
86 Bryce McGowens 6.00 15.00
87 Christian Koloko 6.00 15.00
88 Caleb Houstan 6.00 15.00
89 Andrew Nembhard 12.00 30.00
90 Jabari Walker 5.00 12.00
91 Jaylin Williams 8.00 20.00
92 Ryan Rollins 6.00 15.00
93 Vince Williams Jr. 8.00 20.00
94 Scotty Pippen Jr. 8.00 20.00
95 Tyrese Martin 5.00 12.00
97 Jabari Walker 5.00 12.00
98 Josh Minott 6.00 15.00
99 Moussa Diabate 6.00 15.00
100 Kenneth Lofton Jr. 8.00 20.00

2022-23 Donruss Optic Lights Out

COMMON CARD .30 .75
SEMISTARS .40 1.00
UNLISTED STARS .50 1.25
*HOLO: .75X TO 2X BASIC
*FB: .75X TO 2X BASIC
*RED WAVE: 2X TO 5X BASIC
*RED/99: 2X TO 5X BASIC
*RED & GOLD WAVE/99: 2X TO 5X BASIC
*BLUE/49: 3X TO 8X BASIC
1 Jayson Tatum 2.00 5.00
2 Ja Morant 1.50 4.00
3 LaMelo Ball 1.25 3.00
4 Kevin Durant 1.50 4.00
5 Nikola Jokic 2.50 6.00
6 LeBron James 4.00 10.00
7 Dejounte Murray .60 1.50
8 Trae Young 1.25 3.00
9 James Harden 1.00 2.50
10 Luka Doncic 3.00 8.00
11 Cade Cunningham 1.50 4.00
12 Anthony Edwards 2.50 6.00
13 Stephen Curry 4.00 10.00
14 Donovan Mitchell 1.00 2.50
15 DeMar DeRozan .60 1.50

2022-23 Donruss Optic My House

COMMON CARD .30 .75
SEMISTARS .40 1.00
UNLISTED STARS .50 1.25
*PURPLE: .6X TO 1.5X BASIC
*HOLO: .75X TO 2X BASIC
*GREEN SHOCK: X TO X BASIC
*LIME GREEN/149: 1.5X TO 4X BASIC
*BLUE/85: 2X TO 5X BASIC
1 Donovan Mitchell 1.00 2.50
2 Damian Lillard 1.25 3.00
3 Luka Doncic 3.00 8.00
4 LeBron James 4.00 10.00
5 James Harden 1.00 2.50
6 Giannis Antetokounmpo 2.50 6.00
7 Trae Young 1.25 3.00
8 Chet Holmgren 2.50 6.00
9 Jaden Ivey 1.50 4.00
10 Stephen Curry 4.00 10.00
11 Paolo Banchero 3.00 8.00
12 Keegan Murray 1.25 3.00
13 Jabari Smith Jr. 1.50 4.00
14 Devin Booker 1.25 3.00
15 Kevin Durant 1.50 4.00
16 LaMelo Ball 1.25 3.00
17 Jayson Tatum 2.00 5.00
18 Ja Morant 1.50 4.00
19 Anthony Edwards 2.50 6.00
20 Zion Williamson 1.25 3.00

2022-23 Donruss Optic Opti-Graphs

COMMON CARD 4.00 10.00
SEMISTARS 5.00 12.00
UNLISTED STARS 6.00 15.00
STATED PRINT RUN 49-99 SER.#'d SETS
10 Ja Morant/25 75.00 200.00
11 Steve Kerr/99 12.00 30.00
12 Stephen Curry/25 500.00 1,000.00
13 Muggsy Bogues/99 12.00 30.00
14 Dino Radja/99 5.00 12.00
16 Moses Moody/99 8.00 20.00
17 Ziaire Williams/99 5.00 12.00
18 Glen Rice/99 6.00 15.00
20 Andrew Bogut/99 6.00 15.00
21 Oscar Robertson/49 30.00 80.00
22 Dale Ellis/99 6.00 15.00
24 Larry Bird/49 75.00 200.00
25 John Stockton/49 30.00 80.00
27 Tony Parker/75 15.00 40.00
28 Wendell Carter Jr./99 6.00 15.00
30 Victor Oladipo/99 5.00 12.00
31 Derrick White/99 15.00 40.00
33 Kevin Porter Jr./99 5.00 12.00
35 Cameron Thomas/99 10.00 25.00
36 Chris Duarte/99 5.00 12.00
37 RJ Barrett/99 10.00 25.00
39 Luka Doncic/25 400.00 800.00
40 Corey Kispert/99 6.00 15.00
41 Herbert Jones/99 6.00 15.00
42 Doug Collins/99 6.00 15.00
43 Greg Anthony/99 6.00 15.00

2022-23 Donruss Optic Optical Illusions

COMMON CARD .30 .75
SEMISTARS .40 1.00
UNLISTED STARS .50 1.25
*PURPLE: .6X TO 1.5X BASIC
*HOLO: .75X TO 2X BASIC
*GREEN SHOCK: X TO X BASIC
*LIME GREEN/149: 1.5X TO 4X BASIC
*BLUE/85: 2X TO 5X BASIC
1 James Harden
Joel Embiid 1.00 2.50
2 Jaylen Brown
Jayson Tatum 2.00 5.00
3 Anthony Davis
LeBron James 4.00 10.00
4 Kawhi Leonard
Paul George 1.25 3.00
5 Kyrie Irving
Luka Doncic 3.00 8.00

2022-23 Donruss Optic Raining 3s

COMMON CARD .30 .75
SEMISTARS .40 1.00
UNLISTED STARS .50 1.25
*HOLO: .75X TO 2X BASIC
*FB: .75X TO 2X BASIC
*RED WAVE: 2X TO 5X BASIC
*RED/99: 2X TO 5X BASIC
*RED & GOLD WAVE/99: 2X TO 5X BASIC
*BLUE/49: 3X TO 8X BASIC
1 Stephen Curry 4.00 10.00
2 Anthony Edwards 2.50 6.00
3 Buddy Hield .50 1.25
4 Donovan Mitchell 1.00 2.50
5 Desmond Bane .60 1.50
6 Zach LaVine 1.00 2.50
7 Luka Doncic 3.00 8.00
8 Trae Young 1.25 3.00
9 Devin Booker 1.25 3.00
10 Fred VanVleet .60 1.50
11 Duncan Robinson .50 1.25
12 LaMelo Ball 1.25 3.00
13 Jayson Tatum 2.00 5.00
14 Damian Lillard 1.25 3.00
15 Saddiq Bey .40 1.00
16 Jordan Poole .75 2.00
17 Steve Kerr .60 1.50
18 Larry Bird 2.00 5.00
19 Dirk Nowitzki 1.25 3.00
20 Chris Mullin .60 1.50

2022-23 Donruss Optic Rated Rookies Signatures

COMMON CARD 5.00 12.00
SEMISTARS 6.00 15.00
UNLISTED STARS 8.00 20.00
*CHOICE: .6X TO 1.5X BASIC
*FAST BREAK: .5X TO 1.2X BASIC
*HOLO: .6X TO 1.5X BASIC
*PURPLE: .6X TO 1.5X BASIC
*BLUE/49: .75X TO 2X BASIC
*FB PINK/25: 1.25X TO 3X BASIC
*BLACK PANDORA/25: 1.5X TO 4X BASIC
201 Wendell Moore Jr. 8.00 20.00
202 Kenneth Lofton Jr. 10.00 25.00
203 Tari Eason 20.00 50.00
204 AJ Griffin 6.00 15.00
205 Ochai Agbaji 10.00 25.00
206 Johnny Davis 8.00 20.00
207 E.J. Liddell 8.00 20.00
208 Chet Holmgren 150.00 400.00
209 Bennedict Mathurin 60.00 150.00
210 MarJon Beauchamp 8.00 20.00
211 Ryan Rollins 8.00 20.00
212 Christian Koloko 8.00 20.00
213 Walker Kessler 40.00 100.00
214 Keegan Murray 60.00 150.00
215 Blake Wesley 8.00 20.00
216 Jake LaRavia 8.00 20.00
217 Kendall Brown 6.00 15.00
218 Patrick Baldwin Jr. 8.00 20.00
219 Kennedy Chandler 8.00 20.00
220 Ousmane Dieng 10.00 25.00
221 Paolo Banchero 300.00 600.00
222 Malaki Branham 8.00 20.00
223 Peyton Watson 12.00 30.00
224 Nikola Jovic 15.00 40.00
225 David Roddy 10.00 25.00
226 Vince Williams Jr. 10.00 25.00
227 Jalen Duren 25.00 60.00
228 Scotty Pippen Jr. 10.00 25.00
229 Caleb Houstan 8.00 20.00
230 Andrew Nembhard 15.00 40.00
231 TyTy Washington Jr. 8.00 20.00
232 Dalen Terry 8.00 20.00
233 Max Christie 20.00 50.00
234 Tyrese Martin 6.00 15.00
235 Jalen Williams 40.00 100.00
236 Jeremy Sochan 25.00 60.00
237 Isaiah Mobley 8.00 20.00
238 Christian Braun 20.00 50.00
239 Bryce McGowens 8.00 20.00
240 Jabari Smith Jr. 25.00 60.00
241 Jaden Ivey 75.00 200.00
242 Jabari Walker 6.00 15.00
243 Trevor Keels 6.00 15.00
244 Josh Minott 8.00 20.00
245 Mark Williams 15.00 40.00
246 Jaylin Williams 10.00 25.00
247 Moussa Diabate 8.00 20.00
248 Jaden Hardy 12.00 30.00
249 Shaedon Sharpe 75.00 200.00
250 Dyson Daniels 20.00 50.00

2022-23 Donruss Optic Retro Series Signatures

COMMON CARD 4.00 10.00
SEMISTARS 5.00 12.00
UNLISTED STARS 6.00 15.00
STATED PRINT RUN 49-99 SER.#'d SETS
*CHOICE: .4X TO 1X BASIC
*GREEN WAVE: .4X TO 1X BASIC
1 Dale Ellis/99 6.00 15.00
3 Lenny Wilkens/99 8.00 20.00
5 Tim Hardaway/99 12.00 30.00
6 Mitch Richmond/99 8.00 20.00
7 Walt Frazier/99 12.00 30.00
8 Steve Francis/99 6.00 15.00
10 Shawn Kemp/99 20.00 50.00
11 Earl Monroe/49 12.00 30.00

2022-23 Donruss Optic Rookie Dominators Signatures

COMMON CARD 4.00 10.00
SEMISTARS 5.00 12.00
UNLISTED STARS 6.00 15.00
STATED PRINT RUN 25-99 SER.#'d SETS
1 Chet Holmgren/25 125.00 300.00
2 Kennedy Chandler/99 6.00 15.00
3 Jalen Williams/49 40.00 100.00
4 Walker Kessler/99 12.00 30.00
5 Nikola Jovic/99 12.00 30.00
6 MarJon Beauchamp/99 6.00 15.00
7 Jaden Ivey/25 40.00 100.00
8 Trevor Keels/99 5.00 12.00
10 Ryan Rollins/99 6.00 15.00
11 Johnny Davis/49 6.00 15.00
12 Keegan Murray/25 60.00 150.00
14 Andrew Nembhard/99 12.00 30.00
15 Caleb Houstan/99 6.00 15.00
16 Christian Koloko/99 6.00 15.00
17 Blake Wesley/99 6.00 15.00
18 Jabari Smith Jr./25 40.00 100.00
19 Dalen Terry/99 6.00 15.00
20 Wendell Moore Jr./99 6.00 15.00
21 Jake LaRavia/99 6.00 15.00
22 E.J. Liddell/99 6.00 15.00
23 David Roddy/99 8.00 20.00
24 Tari Eason/99 15.00 40.00
25 Christian Braun/99 15.00 40.00
26 Max Christie/99 15.00 40.00
27 Paolo Banchero/25 125.00 300.00

28 Jaylin Williams/99 8.00 20.00
29 Moussa Diabate/99 6.00 15.00
31 Collin Gillespie/99 6.00 15.00
32 Shaedon Sharpe/49 60.00 150.00
34 Bennedict Mathurin/49 40.00 100.00
35 TyTy Washington Jr./99 6.00 15.00
36 Dyson Daniels/99 15.00 40.00
37 Jeremy Sochan/49 20.00 50.00
38 Ousmane Dieng/99 8.00 20.00
39 Ochai Agbaji/99 8.00 20.00
40 Scotty Pippen Jr./99 8.00 20.00

2022-23 Donruss Optic Rookie Optics Autographs

COMMON CARD 5.00 12.00
SEMISTARS 6.00 15.00
UNLISTED STARS 8.00 20.00
STATED PRINT RUN 25-99 SER.#'d SETS
*CHOICE: .4X TO 1X BASIC
*GREEN WAVE: .4X TO 1X BASIC
1 Chet Holmgren/25 125.00 300.00
2 Kennedy Chandler/99 8.00 20.00
3 Jalen Williams/99 40.00 100.00
4 Walker Kessler/99 15.00 40.00
5 Nikola Jovic/99 15.00 40.00
6 MarJon Beauchamp/99 8.00 20.00
7 Jaden Ivey/25 25.00 60.00
8 Bennedict Mathurin/25 25.00 60.00
10 Jalen Duren/99 25.00 60.00
11 Johnny Davis/49 8.00 20.00
12 Keegan Murray/49 20.00 50.00
13 Shaedon Sharpe/49 30.00 80.00
14 Andrew Nembhard/99 15.00 40.00
15 Caleb Houstan/99 8.00 20.00
16 TyTy Washington Jr./99 8.00 20.00
17 Blake Wesley/99 8.00 20.00
18 Jabari Smith Jr./25 25.00 60.00
19 Dalen Terry/99 8.00 20.00
20 Wendell Moore Jr./99 8.00 20.00
21 Ousmane Dieng/99 10.00 25.00
23 David Roddy/99 10.00 25.00
24 Tari Eason/99 20.00 50.00
25 Dyson Daniels/99 20.00 50.00
26 Max Christie/99 20.00 50.00
27 Paolo Banchero /25 125.00 300.00
28 Jaden Hardy/99 12.00 30.00
29 Ochai Agbaji/99 10.00 25.00
30 Vlatko Cancar/99 10.00 25.00

2022-23 Donruss Optic Signature Series

COMMON CARD 3.00 8.00
SEMISTARS 4.00 10.00
UNLISTED STARS 5.00 12.00
*GREEN: .6X TO 1.5X BASIC
*GREEN SHOCK: .6X TO 1.5X BASIC
*HOLO: .6X TO 1.5X BASIC
*BLUE/25: 1.25X TO 3X BASIC
1 Jose Alvarado 5.00 12.00
2 Maxi Kleber 4.00 10.00
3 Kevin Huerter 5.00 12.00
4 Kenyon Martin Jr. 5.00 12.00
5 Jordan Nwora 5.00 12.00
6 Aaron Nesmith 5.00 12.00
7 T.J. McConnell 4.00 10.00
8 Nerlens Noel 3.00 8.00
9 Monte Morris 3.00 8.00
10 Kyle Anderson 4.00 10.00
11 Ben McLemore 4.00 10.00
12 Daniel Gafford 5.00 12.00
13 Nicolas Claxton 5.00 12.00
14 Corey Kispert 5.00 12.00
15 Keon Johnson 3.00 8.00
16 Royce O'Neale 4.00 10.00
17 Daniel Theis 4.00 10.00
18 Darius Miles 4.00 10.00
19 Austin Reaves 30.00 80.00
20 Max Strus 5.00 12.00
21 Landry Shamet 3.00 8.00
22 Payton Pritchard 5.00 12.00
23 Jeff Green 3.00 8.00
24 Herbert Jones 5.00 12.00
25 Jack Sikma 6.00 15.00
26 Wally Szczerbiak 4.00 10.00
27 Quentin Richardson 4.00 10.00
28 Luka Doncic 200.00 500.00
29 Ayo Dosunmu 6.00 15.00
30 John Lucas 5.00 12.00
31 Scotty Pippen Jr. 6.00 15.00
32 Dennis Scott 4.00 10.00
33 Eddy Curry 4.00 10.00
34 Julian Champagnie 6.00 15.00
35 Craig Hodges 4.00 10.00
36 Josh Christopher 3.00 8.00
37 Sleepy Floyd 5.00 12.00
38 Jabari Smith Jr. 15.00 40.00
39 Jaden Ivey 15.00 40.00
40 Paolo Banchero 150.00 400.00
41 Jaden Hardy 8.00 20.00
42 Jalen Duren 15.00 40.00
43 Johnny Davis 5.00 12.00
44 Keegan Murray 12.00 30.00
45 Shaedon Sharpe 40.00 100.00
46 AJ Griffin 4.00 10.00
47 Bennedict Mathurin 15.00 40.00
48 Brandon Boston Jr. 3.00 8.00
49 Alton Lister 3.00 8.00
50 Cazzie Russell 6.00 15.00
51 Mason Plumlee 4.00 10.00
52 Tre Mann 4.00 10.00
53 Brad Miller 4.00 10.00
54 Rolando Blackman 4.00 10.00
55 Gabe Vincent 12.00 30.00
56 Usman Garuba 3.00 8.00
57 Ricky Pierce 4.00 10.00
58 Jared Butler 4.00 10.00
59 Andre Drummond 5.00 12.00
60 Jonathan Kuminga 12.00 30.00
61 Anthony Edwards 60.00 150.00
62 Jalen Green 40.00 100.00
63 Anthony Gill 4.00 10.00
64 TyTy Washington Jr. 5.00 12.00
65 Dyson Daniels 12.00 30.00
66 Jeremy Sochan 15.00 40.00
67 Ochai Agbaji 6.00 15.00
68 Blake Wesley 5.00 12.00
69 Ousmane Dieng 6.00 15.00
70 Tari Eason 12.00 30.00
71 Mark Williams 10.00 25.00
72 Jalen Williams 25.00 60.00
73 Walker Kessler 10.00 25.00
74 Kennedy Chandler 5.00 12.00
75 Nikola Jovic 10.00 25.00
76 Malik Monk 5.00 12.00
77 Mychal Thompson 4.00 10.00
78 Bernard King 6.00 15.00
79 Deni Avdija 5.00 12.00
80 RJ Hampton 4.00 10.00
81 Mark Price 5.00 12.00
82 Andrew Nembhard 10.00 25.00
83 Trevor Keels 4.00 10.00
84 Jaylin Williams 6.00 15.00
85 Ryan Rollins 5.00 12.00
86 Vince Williams Jr. 6.00 15.00
87 Johnny Juzang 6.00 15.00
88 Tyrese Martin 4.00 10.00
89 Isaiah Mobley 5.00 12.00
90 Jabari Walker 4.00 10.00
91 Josh Minott 5.00 12.00
92 Moussa Diabate 5.00 12.00
93 Kenneth Lofton Jr. 6.00 15.00
94 Billy Knight 5.00 12.00
95 Aaron Wiggins 4.00 10.00
96 Charlie Ward 5.00 12.00
97 Willie Green 5.00 12.00
98 Nick Richards 4.00 10.00
99 Juan Toscano-Anderson 3.00 8.00
100 Collin Gillespie 5.00 12.00

2022-23 Donruss Optic Splash!

COMMON CARD .30 .75
SEMISTARS .40 1.00
UNLISTED STARS .50 1.25
*PURPLE: .6X TO 1.5X BASIC
*HOLO: .75X TO 2X BASIC
*GREEN SHOCK: X TO X BASIC
*LIME GREEN/149: 1.5X TO 4X BASIC
*BLUE/85: 2X TO 5X BASIC
1 LaMelo Ball 1.25 3.00
2 Anthony Edwards 2.50 6.00
3 Donovan Mitchell 1.00 2.50
4 Kevin Durant 1.50 4.00
5 Bradley Beal .60 1.50
6 Damian Lillard 1.25 3.00
7 Jayson Tatum 2.00 5.00
8 Kawhi Leonard 1.25 3.00
9 Trae Young 1.25 3.00
10 Stephen Curry 4.00 10.00
11 Luka Doncic 3.00 8.00
12 Devin Booker 1.25 3.00
13 James Harden 1.00 2.50
14 Zach LaVine 1.00 2.50
15 LeBron James 4.00 10.00

2022-23 Donruss Optic Star Gazing

COMMON CARD .30 .75
SEMISTARS .40 1.00
UNLISTED STARS .50 1.25
*HOLO: .75X TO 2X BASIC
*FB: .75X TO 2X BASIC
*RED WAVE: 2X TO 5X BASIC
*RED/99: 2X TO 5X BASIC
*RED & GOLD WAVE/99: 2X TO 5X BASIC
*BLUE/49: 3X TO 8X BASIC
1 Giannis Antetokounmpo 2.50 6.00
2 Jalen Green 1.50 4.00
3 Trae Young 1.25 3.00
4 Ja Morant 1.50 4.00
5 Zion Williamson 1.25 3.00
6 Luka Doncic 3.00 8.00
7 Nikola Jokic 2.50 6.00
8 LaMelo Ball 1.25 3.00
9 Kevin Durant 1.50 4.00
10 Stephen Curry 4.00 10.00
11 James Harden 1.00 2.50
12 LeBron James 4.00 10.00
13 Jayson Tatum 2.00 5.00
14 Anthony Edwards 2.50 6.00
15 Cade Cunningham 1.50 4.00

2022-23 Donruss Optic T-Minus 3...2...1...

COMMON CARD .30 .75
SEMISTARS .40 1.00
UNLISTED STARS .50 1.25
*PURPLE: .6X TO 1.5X BASIC
*HOLO: .75X TO 2X BASIC
*GREEN SHOCK: X TO X BASIC
*LIME GREEN/149: 1.5X TO 4X BASIC
*BLUE/85: 2X TO 5X BASIC
1 DeMar DeRozan .60 1.50
2 Kevin Durant 1.50 4.00
3 Russell Westbrook .75 2.00
4 Jayson Tatum 2.00 5.00
5 Trae Young 1.25 3.00
6 Giannis Antetokounmpo 2.50 6.00
7 Luka Doncic 3.00 8.00
8 Cade Cunningham 1.50 4.00
9 Ja Morant 1.50 4.00
10 Stephen Curry 4.00 10.00
11 Anthony Edwards 2.50 6.00
12 Kawhi Leonard 1.25 3.00
13 Jalen Green 1.50 4.00
14 Zion Williamson 1.25 3.00
15 LeBron James 4.00 10.00

2022-23 Donruss Optic The Elite Series Signatures

COMMON CARD 4.00 10.00
SEMISTARS 5.00 12.00
UNLISTED STARS 6.00 15.00
STATED PRINT RUN 49-99 SER.#'d SETS
1 Grant Hill/99 20.00 50.00
4 Jordan Clarkson/99 15.00 40.00
6 Hakeem Olajuwon/99 25.00 60.00
7 Dwyane Wade/49 12.00 30.00
8 Ray Allen/99 25.00 60.00
9 Jamal Crawford/99 6.00 15.00
10 Joe Harris/99 5.00 12.00
11 Scottie Barnes/99 10.00 25.00
12 RJ Barrett/99 10.00 25.00
13 Bernard King/99 8.00 20.00
15 Chauncey Billups/99 8.00 20.00
16 Maurice Cheeks/99 6.00 15.00
17 Marcus Smart/99 15.00 40.00
18 Adrian Dantley/99 6.00 15.00
19 Josh Giddey/99 25.00 60.00

2022-23 Donruss Optic The Rookies

*HOLO: 1X TO 2.5X BASIC
*FB: 1X TO 2.5X BASIC
*RED WAVE: 2.5X TO 6X BASIC
*RED/99: 2.5X TO 6X BASIC
*RED & GOLD WAVE/99: 2.5X TO 6X BASIC
*BLUE/49: 4X TO 10X BASIC
1 Paolo Banchero 5.00 12.00
2 Chet Holmgren 4.00 10.00
3 Jabari Smith Jr. 2.50 6.00
4 Keegan Murray 2.00 5.00
5 Jaden Ivey 2.50 6.00

2022-23 Donruss Optic Winner Stays

COMMON CARD .30 .75
SEMISTARS .40 1.00
UNLISTED STARS .50 1.25
*PURPLE: .6X TO 1.5X BASIC
*HOLO: .75X TO 2X BASIC
*GREEN SHOCK: X TO X BASIC
*LIME GREEN/149: 1.5X TO 4X BASIC
*BLUE/85: 2X TO 5X BASIC
1 Klay Thompson 1.25 3.00
2 LeBron James 4.00 10.00
3 Pascal Siakam .75 2.00
4 Tim Duncan 1.25 3.00
5 Dwyane Wade 1.00 2.50
6 Fred VanVleet .60 1.50
7 Dirk Nowitzki 1.25 3.00
8 Anthony Davis 1.25 3.00
9 Dennis Rodman 1.25 3.00
10 Khris Middleton .60 1.50
11 Shaquille O'Neal 2.00 5.00
12 Giannis Antetokounmpo 2.50 6.00
13 Kyrie Irving 1.00 2.50
14 Kevin Durant 1.50 4.00
15 Larry Bird 2.00 5.00
16 Manu Ginobili 1.00 2.50
17 Kareem Abdul-Jabbar 1.50 4.00
18 Stephen Curry 4.00 10.00
19 Magic Johnson 2.00 5.00
20 Paul Pierce .75 2.00

2023-24 Donruss Optic

*AU RC PURPLE: .5X TO 1.2X BASIC
*AU RC CHOICE: .6X TO 1.5X BASIC
*AU RC FAST BREAK: .6X TO 1.5X BASIC
*AU RC GRN INTER: .6X TO 1.5X BASIC
*AU RC HOLO: .6X TO 1.5X BASIC
*AU RC PINK VELOCITY/79: .75X TO 2X BASIC
*AU RC BLUE/49: 1X TO 2.5X BASIC
*AU RC BLK PANDORA/25: 1.5X TO 4X BASIC
*AU RC FB PINK/25: 1.5X TO 4X BASIC
*AU RC PINK/25: 1.5X TO 4X BASIC
*AU RC CHOICE BLUE/24: 1.5X TO 4X BASIC
1 RJ Barrett .60 1.50
2 Mitchell Robinson .40 1.00
3 Andrew Nembhard .40 1.00
4 Damian Lillard 1.00 2.50
5 Clint Capela .30 .75
6 Luguentz Dort .40 1.00
7 Brandon Ingram .50 1.25
8 Jusuf Nurkic .40 1.00
9 Cameron Thomas .50 1.25
10 Derrick White .50 1.25
11 Khris Middleton .40 1.00
12 Scottie Barnes .50 1.25
13 Bam Adebayo .60 1.50
14 Dejounte Murray .50 1.25
15 Brook Lopez .30 .75
16 Ivica Zubac .40 1.00
17 Obi Toppin .40 1.00
18 D'Angelo Russell .40 1.00
19 Nikola Jokic 2.00 5.00
20 Davion Mitchell .30 .75
21 Saddiq Bey .40 1.00
22 Kyrie Irving .75 2.00
23 Zach LaVine .60 1.50
24 Ayo Dosunmu .40 1.00
25 Walker Kessler .40 1.00
26 Donovan Mitchell .75 2.00
27 Tyrese Haliburton .75 2.00
28 Rudy Gobert .50 1.25
29 LaMelo Ball 1.00 2.50
30 Jordan Clarkson .40 1.00
31 Darius Garland .60 1.50
32 Ben Simmons .40 1.00
33 Josh Giddey .50 1.25
34 Derrick Rose .60 1.50
35 Zion Williamson 1.00 2.50
36 Gabe Vincent .40 1.00
37 Jonathan Isaac .30 .75
38 Max Strus .40 1.00
39 Bruce Brown .40 1.00
40 Julius Randle .50 1.25
41 Kevin Durant 1.25 3.00
42 Buddy Hield .40 1.00
43 DeMar DeRozan .60 1.50
44 Devin Booker 1.00 2.50
45 Evan Mobley .60 1.50
46 Quentin Grimes .40 1.00
47 Harrison Barnes .30 .75
48 Gordon Hayward .40 1.00
49 Gary Trent Jr. .40 1.00
50 Bones Hyland .30 .75
51 Malaki Branham .30 .75
52 De'Aaron Fox .75 2.00
53 Giannis Antetokounmpo 2.00 5.00
54 Paolo Banchero 1.00 2.50
55 Jaden Hardy .50 1.25
56 Jeremy Sochan .50 1.25
57 Draymond Green .50 1.25
58 Alex Caruso .40 1.00
59 Anthony Edwards 2.00 5.00
60 Christian Braun .40 1.00
61 Markelle Fultz .30 .75
62 Kelly Oubre Jr. .40 1.00
63 Jerami Grant .50 1.25
64 Duncan Robinson .40 1.00
65 LeBron James 3.00 8.00
66 Christian Wood .30 .75
67 Luka Doncic 2.50 6.00
68 Tim Hardaway Jr. .30 .75
69 Dorian Finney-Smith .30 .75
70 Tyrese Maxey .75 2.00
71 Terance Mann .30 .75
72 Jarrett Allen .40 1.00
73 Herbert Jones .40 1.00
74 Kyle Kuzma .50 1.25
75 Malcolm Brogdon .40 1.00
76 Al Horford .40 1.00
77 Mike Conley .30 .75
78 Josh Green .30 .75
79 Jalen McDaniels .30 .75
80 Gary Payton II .30 .75
81 Russell Westbrook .60 1.50
82 Dillon Brooks .40 1.00
83 Immanuel Quickley .40 1.00
84 Marvin Bagley III .30 .75
85 Alperen Sengun .60 1.50
86 Terry Rozier III .50 1.25
87 Robert Williams III .40 1.00
88 Max Christie .40 1.00
89 Wendell Carter Jr. .40 1.00
90 Cade Cunningham 1.00 2.50
91 Collin Sexton .50 1.25
92 P.J. Washington Jr. .40 1.00
93 Jordan Poole .60 1.50
94 Jakob Poeltl .30 .75
95 Kawhi Leonard 1.00 2.50
96 Malik Monk .50 1.25
97 Keegan Murray .50 1.25
98 Josh Richardson .25 .60
99 Grayson Allen .40 1.00
100 Devonte' Graham .30 .75
101 Pascal Siakam .60 1.50
102 Michael Porter Jr. .50 1.25
103 Grant Williams .30 .75
104 Shai Gilgeous-Alexander 2.00 5.00
105 CJ McCollum .40 1.00
106 Dennis Schroder .40 1.00
107 Lonnie Walker IV .40 1.00
108 Spencer Dinwiddie .30 .75
109 Franz Wagner .60 1.50
110 Bogdan Bogdanovic .40 1.00
111 Jamal Murray .75 2.00
112 Keldon Johnson .50 1.25
113 Jaylen Brown .75 2.00
114 Chet Holmgren 1.00 2.50
115 Josh Hart .40 1.00
116 Jonas Valanciunas .30 .75
117 Jrue Holiday .50 1.25
118 Jaden McDaniels .40 1.00
119 MarJon Beauchamp .30 .75
120 Kristaps Porzingis .50 1.25
121 Kentavious Caldwell-Pope .30 .75
122 Bennedict Mathurin .60 1.50
123 Tari Eason .50 1.25
124 Joel Embiid 1.00 2.50
125 Coby White .40 1.00
126 Danilo Gallinari .30 .75
127 Nikola Vucevic .40 1.00
128 Lauri Markkanen .60 1.50
129 Zach Collins .30 .75
130 Kyle Lowry .50 1.25
131 Bradley Beal .50 1.25
132 Kenyon Martin Jr. .40 1.00
133 Kevin Huerter .30 .75
134 Bojan Bogdanovic .40 1.00
135 Trae Young .75 2.00
136 Tobias Harris .40 1.00
137 Tre Jones .40 1.00
138 Daniel Gafford .40 1.00
139 Jarred Vanderbilt .30 .75
140 Jayson Tatum 1.50 4.00
141 Deandre Ayton .40 1.00
142 Domantas Sabonis .60 1.50
143 Jonathan Kuminga 1.00 2.50
144 Anthony Davis 1.00 2.50
145 Jose Alvarado .40 1.00
146 John Collins .40 1.00
147 Chris Paul .75 2.00
148 Nicolas Claxton .40 1.00
149 Talen Horton-Tucker .30 .75
150 Jaylin Williams .40 1.00
151 Jalen Green .60 1.50
152 Marcus Smart .50 1.25
153 Anfernee Simons .50 1.25
154 Jimmy Butler .60 1.50
155 Aaron Gordon .40 1.00
156 Ochai Agbaji .40 1.00
157 Paul George .60 1.50
158 Jalen Brunson .75 2.00
159 Bobby Portis .50 1.25
160 Austin Reaves 1.00 2.50
161 Norman Powell .40 1.00
162 Rui Hachimura .40 1.00
163 Onyeka Okongwu .30 .75
164 Jabari Smith Jr. .60 1.50
165 Jaden Ivey .50 1.25
166 Cameron Johnson .40 1.00
167 Reggie Jackson .25 .60
168 Patrick Beverley .30 .75
169 Robert Covington .30 .75
170 Shaedon Sharpe .75 2.00
171 Desmond Bane .50 1.25
172 Jalen Suggs .50 1.25
173 Matisse Thybulle .30 .75
174 James Harden .75 2.00
175 Mark Williams .40 1.00
176 Patrick Williams .30 .75
177 Isaiah Stewart .40 1.00
178 Myles Turner .40 1.00
179 Karl-Anthony Towns .60 1.50
180 Tyler Herro .60 1.50
181 Jaren Jackson Jr. .60 1.50
182 Tyus Jones .30 .75
183 Bol Bol .40 1.00
184 Devin Vassell .50 1.25
185 P.J. Tucker .30 .75
186 Dyson Daniels .50 1.25
187 Jalen Duren .50 1.25
188 Jalen Williams .75 2.00
189 Klay Thompson 1.00 2.50
190 Ja Morant 1.25 3.00
191 OG Anunoby .50 1.25
192 Naz Reid .40 1.00
193 Seth Curry .40 1.00
194 De'Andre Hunter .40 1.00
195 Kyle Anderson .30 .75
196 Donte DiVincenzo .40 1.00
197 Fred VanVleet .60 1.50
198 Stephen Curry 3.00 8.00
199 Mikal Bridges .50 1.25
200 Andrew Wiggins .50 1.25
201 Hunter Tyson RR RC .75 2.00
202 Olivier-Maxence Prosper RR RC .75 2.00
203 Brandin Podziemski RR RC 2.50 6.00
204 Toumani Camara RR RC 1.50 4.00
205 Noah Clowney RR RC 1.00 2.50
206 Jalen Wilson RR RC .75 2.00
207 Anthony Black RR RC 1.50 4.00
208 Vasilije Micic RR RC .75 2.00
209 Brice Sensabaugh RR RC 1.25 3.00
210 Amari Bailey RR RC .75 2.00
211 Maxwell Lewis RR RC .60 1.50
212 Gradey Dick RR RC 1.50 4.00
213 Kris Murray RR RC .75 2.00
214 Jalen Hood-Schifino RR RC .75 2.00
215 Jalen Pickett RR RC .60 1.50
216 Jaime Jaquez Jr. RR RC 1.25 3.00
217 Cam Whitmore RR RC 2.00 5.00
218 Cason Wallace RR RC 1.50 4.00
219 Brandon Miller RR RC 3.00 8.00
220 Kobe Bufkin RR RC 1.00 2.50
221 Ben Sheppard RR RC .75 2.00
222 Chris Livingston RR RC .75 2.00
223 Keyonte George RR RC 2.50 6.00
224 Nick Smith Jr. RR RC 1.00 2.50
225 Victor Wembanyama RR RC 8.00 20.00
226 Jarace Walker RR RC 1.50 4.00
227 Jordan Walsh RR RC .75 2.00
228 GG Jackson II RR RC 1.50 4.00
229 Amen Thompson RR RC 4.00 10.00
230 Dariq Whitehead RR RC 1.00 2.50
231 Julian Phillips RR RC .75 2.00
232 Kobe Brown RR RC .75 2.00
233 Taylor Hendricks RR RC .75 2.00
234 Leonard Miller RR RC .75 2.00
235 Ausar Thompson RR RC 2.00 5.00
236 Markquis Nowell RR RC .75 2.00
237 Keyontae Johnson RR RC .75 2.00
238 Jordan Hawkins RR RC 1.25 3.00
239 Scoot Henderson RR RC 2.50 6.00
240 Jett Howard RR RC 1.00 2.50
241 Emoni Bates RR RC 1.00 2.50
242 Marcus Sasser RR RC 1.25 3.00
243 Bilal Coulibaly RR RC 2.00 5.00
244 Sasha Vezenkov RR RC .60 1.50
245 Dereck Lively II RR RC 1.50 4.00
246 Colby Jones RR RC .75 2.00
247 Julian Strawther RR RC 1.00 2.50
248 Rayan Rupert RR RC .75 2.00
249 Andre Jackson Jr. RR RC 1.25 3.00
250 Jordan Miller RR RC 1.00 2.50
251 Trayce Jackson-Davis RR AU RC 10.00 25.00
252 Maxwell Lewis RR AU 6.00 15.00
253 Seth Lundy RR AU RC 6.00 15.00
254 James Nnaji RR AU RC 6.00 15.00
255 Ausar Thompson RR AU 20.00 50.00
256 Brandin Podziemski RR AU 25.00 60.00
257 Noah Clowney RR AU 10.00 25.00
258 Marcus Sasser RR AU 12.00 30.00
259 Vasilije Micic RR AU 8.00 20.00
260 GG Jackson II RR AU 15.00 40.00
261 Sidy Cissoko RR AU RC 8.00 20.00
262 Jalen Pickett RR AU 6.00 15.00
263 Jaylen Clark RR AU RC 8.00 20.00
264 Markquis Nowell RR AU 8.00 20.00
265 Kobe Bufkin RR AU 10.00 25.00
266 Lester Quinones RR AU RC 6.00 15.00
267 Sir'Jabari Rice RR AU RC 6.00 15.00
268 Colby Jones RR AU 8.00 20.00
269 Cason Wallace RR AU 15.00 40.00
270 Mouhamed Gueye RR AU RC 8.00 20.00
271 Sasha Vezenkov RR AU 6.00 15.00
272 Keyontae Johnson RR AU 8.00 20.00
273 Tristan Vukcevic RR AU RC 8.00 20.00
274 Olivier-Maxence Prosper RR AU 8.00 20.00
275 Kris Murray RR AU 8.00 20.00
276 Julian Phillips RR AU 8.00 20.00
277 Dariq Whitehead RR AU 10.00 25.00
278 Oscar Tshiebwe RR AU RC 10.00 25.00
279 Jordan Miller RR AU 10.00 25.00
280 Rayan Rupert RR AU 8.00 20.00
281 Dereck Lively II RR AU 15.00 40.00
282 Toumani Camara RR AU 15.00 40.00
283 Julian Strawther RR AU 10.00 25.00
284 Kobe Brown RR AU 8.00 20.00
285 Ricky Council IV RR AU RC 10.00 25.00
286 Leonard Miller RR AU 8.00 20.00
287 Amen Thompson RR AU 40.00 100.00
288 Brice Sensabaugh RR AU 12.00 30.00
289 Jalen Slawson RR AU RC 8.00 20.00
290 Keyonte George RR AU 25.00 60.00
291 Jalen Wilson RR AU 8.00 20.00
292 Hunter Tyson RR AU 8.00 20.00
293 Andre Jackson Jr. RR AU 12.00 30.00
294 Ben Sheppard RR AU 8.00 20.00
295 Bilal Coulibaly RR AU 20.00 50.00
296 Chris Livingston RR AU 8.00 20.00
297 Isaiah Wong RR AU RC 8.00 20.00
298 Jordan Walsh RR AU 8.00 20.00
300 D'Moi Hodge RR AU RC 6.00 15.00

2023-24 Donruss Optic Aqua

*AQUA: 2.5X TO 6X BASIC
STATED PRINT RUN 249 SER. #'D SETS
219 Brandon Miller RR 75.00 200.00
225 Victor Wembanyama RR 500.00 1,000.00
228 GG Jackson II RR 40.00 100.00

2023-24 Donruss Optic Black Velocity

*BLACK VELOCITY: 8X TO 20X BASIC
STATED PRINT RUN 39 SER. #'D SETS
219 Brandon Miller RR 300.00 600.00
225 Victor Wembanyama RR 2,500.00 5,000.00
228 GG Jackson II RR 125.00 300.00

2023-24 Donruss Optic Blue

*BLUE: 6X TO 15X BASIC
STATED PRINT RUN 49 SER. #'D SETS
219 Brandon Miller RR 200.00 500.00
225 Victor Wembanyama RR 1,500.00 3,000.00
228 GG Jackson II RR 100.00 250.00

2023-24 Donruss Optic Blue Seismic

*BLUE SEISMIC: 2.5X TO 6X BASIC
STATED PRINT RUN 249 SER. #'D SETS
219 Brandon Miller RR 75.00 200.00
225 Victor Wembanyama RR 500.00 1,000.00
228 GG Jackson II RR 40.00 100.00

2023-24 Donruss Optic Choice

*CHOICE (201-250): 3X TO 8X BASIC
225 Victor Wembanyama RR 150.00 400.00

2023-24 Donruss Optic Choice Blue Mojo

*CHOICE BLUE MOJO: 10X TO 25X BASIC
STATED PRINT RUN 24 SER. #'D SETS
219 Brandon Miller RR 400.00 800.00
225 Victor Wembanyama RR 3,000.00 6,000.00
228 GG Jackson II RR 150.00 400.00

2023-24 Donruss Optic Choice Red

*CHOICE RED: 4X TO 10X BASIC
STATED PRINT RUN 88 SER. #'D SETS
219 Brandon Miller RR 125.00 300.00
225 Victor Wembanyama RR 1,000.00 2,000.00
228 GG Jackson II RR 60.00 150.00

2023-24 Donruss Optic Choice Red and Green

*CHOICE RED & GREEN: 2X TO 5X BASIC
225 Victor Wembanyama RR 400.00 800.00

2023-24 Donruss Optic Copper Glitter

*COPPER GLITTER: 4X TO 10X BASIC
STATED PRINT RUN 99 SER. #'D SETS
219 Brandon Miller RR 125.00 300.00
225 Victor Wembanyama RR 1,000.00 2,000.00
228 GG Jackson II RR 60.00 150.00

2023-24 Donruss Optic Fast Break Blue

*FB BLUE: 6X TO 15X BASIC
STATED PRINT RUN 49 SER. #'D SETS
219 Brandon Miller RR 200.00 500.00
225 Victor Wembanyama RR 1,500.00 3,000.00
228 GG Jackson II RR 100.00 250.00

2023-24 Donruss Optic Fast Break Holo

*FAST BREAK HOLO: 1.5X TO 4X BASIC
225 Victor Wembanyama RR 150.00 400.00

2023-24 Donruss Optic Fast Break Pink

*FB PINK (1-250): 10X TO 25X BASIC
STATED PRINT RUN 25 SER. #'D SETS
219 Brandon Miller RR 400.00 800.00
225 Victor Wembanyama RR 3,000.00 6,000.00
228 GG Jackson II RR 150.00 400.00

2023-24 Donruss Optic Fast Break Purple

*FB PURPLE: 4X TO 10X BASIC
STATED PRINT RUN 99 SER. #'D SETS
219 Brandon Miller RR 125.00 300.00
225 Victor Wembanyama RR 1,000.00 2,000.00
228 GG Jackson II RR 60.00 150.00

2023-24 Donruss Optic Fast Break Red

*FB RED: 5X TO 12X BASIC
STATED PRINT RUN 75 SER. #'D SETS
219 Brandon Miller RR 150.00 400.00
225 Victor Wembanyama RR 1,250.00 2,500.00
228 GG Jackson II RR 75.00 200.00

2023-24 Donruss Optic Green Glitter

*GREEN GLITTER: 5X TO 12X BASIC
STATED PRINT RUN 77 SER. #'D SETS
219 Brandon Miller RR 150.00 400.00
225 Victor Wembanyama RR 1,250.00 2,500.00
228 GG Jackson II RR 75.00 200.00

2023-24 Donruss Optic Green International

*GREEN INTER (1-250): 5X TO 12X BASIC
STATED PRINT RUN 65 SER. #'D SETS
219 Brandon Miller RR 150.00 400.00
225 Victor Wembanyama RR 1,250.00 2,500.00
228 GG Jackson II RR 75.00 200.00

2023-24 Donruss Optic Green Shock

*GREEN SHOCK: 1.5X TO 4X BASIC
225 Victor Wembanyama RR 150.00 400.00

2023-24 Donruss Optic Green Velocity

*GREEN VELOCITY: 6X TO 15X BASIC
STATED PRINT RUN 49 SER. #'D SETS
219 Brandon Miller RR 200.00 500.00
225 Victor Wembanyama RR 1,500.00 3,000.00
228 GG Jackson II RR 100.00 250.00

2023-24 Donruss Optic Holo

*HOLO (1-250): 1.5X TO 4X BASIC
225 Victor Wembanyama RR 50.00 120.00

2023-24 Donruss Optic Hyper Orange

*HYPER ORANGE: 4X TO 10X BASIC
STATED PRINT RUN 99 SER. #'D SETS
219 Brandon Miller RR 125.00 300.00
225 Victor Wembanyama RR 1,000.00 2,000.00
228 GG Jackson II RR 60.00 150.00

2023-24 Donruss Optic Hyper Pink

*HYPER PINK: 1X TO 2.5X BASIC
225 Victor Wembanyama RR 75.00 200.00

2023-24 Donruss Optic Jazz

*JAZZ: 5X TO 12X BASIC
219 Brandon Miller RR 125.00 300.00
225 Victor Wembanyama RR 800.00 1,500.00
228 GG Jackson II RR 60.00 150.00

2023-24 Donruss Optic Lime Green

*LIME GREEN: 3X TO 8X BASIC
STATED PRINT RUN 149 SER. #'D SETS
219 Brandon Miller RR 100.00 250.00
225 Victor Wembanyama RR 600.00 1,200.00
228 GG Jackson II RR 50.00 120.00

2023-24 Donruss Optic Orange

*ORANGE: 2.5X TO 6X BASIC
STATED PRINT RUN 199 SER. #'D SETS
219 Brandon Miller RR 75.00 200.00
225 Victor Wembanyama RR 500.00 1,000.00
228 GG Jackson II RR 40.00 100.00

2023-24 Donruss Optic Photon

*PHOTON: 5X TO 12X BASIC
219 Brandon Miller RR 125.00 300.00
225 Victor Wembanyama RR 800.00 1,500.00
228 GG Jackson II RR 60.00 150.00

2023-24 Donruss Optic Pink

*PINK (1-250): 10X TO 25X BASIC
STATED PRINT RUN 25 SER. #'D SETS
219 Brandon Miller RR 400.00 800.00
225 Victor Wembanyama RR 3,000.00 6,000.00
228 GG Jackson II RR 150.00 400.00

2023-24 Donruss Optic Pink Velocity

*PINK VELOCITY (1-250): 5X TO 12X BASIC
STATED PRINT RUN 79 SER. #'D SETS
219 Brandon Miller RR 150.00 400.00
225 Victor Wembanyama RR 1,250.00 2,500.00
228 GG Jackson II RR 75.00 200.00

2023-24 Donruss Optic Premium Box Set

*PREMIUM BOX SET: 2.5X TO 6X BASIC
STATED PRINT RUN 249 SER. #'D SETS
219 Brandon Miller RR 75.00 200.00
225 Victor Wembanyama RR 500.00 1,000.00
228 GG Jackson II RR 40.00 100.00

2023-24 Donruss Optic Purple

*PURPLE (1-250): 1X TO 2.5X BASIC
225 Victor Wembanyama RR 30.00 80.00

2023-24 Donruss Optic Purple Shock

*PURPLE SHOCK: 1X TO 2.5X BASIC
225 Victor Wembanyama RR 75.00 200.00

2023-24 Donruss Optic Red

*RED: 4X TO 10X BASIC
STATED PRINT RUN 99 SER. #'D SETS
219 Brandon Miller RR 125.00 300.00
225 Victor Wembanyama RR 1,000.00 2,000.00
228 GG Jackson II RR 60.00 150.00

2023-24 Donruss Optic Red and Gold International

*RED & GOLD INTER: 4X TO 10X BASIC
STATED PRINT RUN 99 SER. #'D SETS
219 Brandon Miller RR 125.00 300.00
225 Victor Wembanyama RR 1,000.00 2,000.00
228 GG Jackson II RR 60.00 150.00

2023-24 Donruss Optic Red Glitter

*RED GLITTER: 5X TO 12X BASIC
STATED PRINT RUN 75 SER. #'D SETS
219 Brandon Miller RR 150.00 400.00
225 Victor Wembanyama RR 1,250.00 2,500.00
228 GG Jackson II RR 75.00 200.00

2023-24 Donruss Optic Red Seismic

*RED SEISMIC: 4X TO 10X BASIC
STATED PRINT RUN 130 SER. #'D SETS
219 Brandon Miller RR 100.00 250.00
225 Victor Wembanyama RR 600.00 1,200.00
228 GG Jackson II RR 50.00 120.00

2023-24 Donruss Optic Red Velocity

*RED VELOCITY: 2X TO 5X BASIC
STATED PRINT RUN 299 SER. #'D SETS
219 Brandon Miller RR 60.00 150.00
225 Victor Wembanyama RR 400.00 800.00
228 GG Jackson II RR 30.00 80.00

2023-24 Donruss Optic Alter Ego

1 Luka Doncic 300.00 600.00
2 Giannis Antetokounmpo 200.00 500.00
3 Karl Malone 100.00 250.00
4 Victor Wembanyama 2,500.00 5,000.00
5 Shaquille O'Neal 150.00 400.00
6 Stephen Curry 400.00 800.00
7 Magic Johnson 125.00 300.00
8 Nikola Jokic 200.00 500.00
9 LeBron James 500.00 1,000.00
10 Dennis Rodman 150.00 400.00

2023-24 Donruss Optic Dominators Signatures

STATED PRINT RUN 25-99 SER.#'d SETS
1 Dillon Brooks/99 6.00 15.00
2 Jalen Green/99 10.00 25.00
3 Nikola Jokic/25 125.00 300.00
4 Gilbert Arenas/99 6.00 15.00
5 Ray Allen/49 30.00 80.00
6 Tracy McGrady/49 30.00 80.00
7 Jaren Jackson Jr./99 10.00 25.00
8 Coby White/99 6.00 15.00
9 Josh Giddey/99 8.00 20.00
10 Immanuel Quickley/99 6.00 15.00
11 Keegan Murray/99 8.00 20.00
12 Ayo Dosunmu/99 6.00 15.00
13 Nicolas Batum/99 4.00 10.00
14 Zion Williamson/25 100.00 250.00
15 Russell Westbrook/25 75.00 200.00
16 Manu Ginobili/49 20.00 50.00
17 James Harden/25 75.00 200.00
19 Evan Mobley/49 10.00 25.00
20 Brandon Ingram/49 8.00 20.00
21 John Wall/99 8.00 20.00
22 Tyrese Maxey/49 30.00 80.00
23 Paul Pierce/49 25.00 60.00
24 Nate Archibald/99 8.00 20.00
25 Juwan Howard/99 6.00 15.00
26 Chet Holmgren/25 75.00 200.00
27 Jabari Smith Jr./49 10.00 25.00
28 Bennedict Mathurin/49 10.00 25.00
29 Nikola Jovic/99 6.00 15.00
30 Malik Monk/99 8.00 20.00
31 Isaac Okoro/99 5.00 12.00
32 JaVale McGee/99 5.00 12.00
33 Jose Alvarado/99 6.00 15.00
34 Keldon Johnson/99 8.00 20.00
35 Bojan Bogdanovic/99 6.00 15.00
36 Caris LeVert/99 6.00 15.00
37 Luguentz Dort/99 6.00 15.00
38 Malik Beasley/99 6.00 15.00
39 Dirk Nowitzki/25 75.00 200.00
40 Dorian Finney-Smith/99 5.00 12.00

2023-24 Donruss Optic Elite Dominators Blue

*BLUE: 2.5X TO 6X BASIC
STATED PRINT RUN 49 SER. #'D SETS
18 Victor Wembanyama 300.00 600.00

2023-24 Donruss Optic Elite Dominators Holo

*HOLO: .75X TO 2X BASIC
18 Victor Wembanyama 25.00 60.00

2023-24 Donruss Optic Elite Dominators Holo Fast Break

*HOLO FB: .75X TO 2X BASIC
18 Victor Wembanyama 25.00 60.00

2023-24 Donruss Optic Elite Dominators Pink Velocity

*PINK VELOCITY: 2X TO 5X BASIC

STATED PRINT RUN 79 SER. #'D SETS
18 Victor Wembanyama 150.00 400.00

2023-24 Donruss Optic Elite Dominators Red

*RED: 2X TO 5X BASIC
STATED PRINT RUN 99 SER. #'D SETS
18 Victor Wembanyama 150.00 400.00

2023-24 Donruss Optic Elite Dominators Red and Gold International

*RED & GOLD INTER: 2X TO 5X BASIC
STATED PRINT RUN 99 SER. #'D SETS
18 Victor Wembanyama 150.00 400.00

2023-24 Donruss Optic Express Lane

*PURPLE: .6X TO 1.5X BASIC
*HOLO: .75X TO 2X BASIC
1 Kyrie Irving .75 2.00
2 Amen Thompson 2.00 5.00
3 Brandon Miller 1.50 4.00
4 Kawhi Leonard 1.00 2.50
5 Damian Lillard 1.00 2.50
6 LaMelo Ball 1.00 2.50
7 Cam Whitmore 1.00 2.50
8 Victor Wembanyama 6.00 15.00
9 LeBron James 3.00 8.00
10 Jarace Walker .75 2.00
11 Zion Williamson 1.00 2.50
12 Jayson Tatum 1.50 4.00
13 Luka Doncic 2.50 6.00
14 Scoot Henderson 1.25 3.00
15 Paul George .60 1.50
16 De'Aaron Fox .75 2.00
17 Ja Morant 1.25 3.00
18 Ausar Thompson 1.00 2.50
19 Donovan Mitchell .75 2.00
20 Jaime Jaquez Jr. .60 1.50
21 Joel Embiid 1.00 2.50
22 Trae Young .75 2.00
23 Giannis Antetokounmpo 2.00 5.00
24 Anthony Edwards 2.00 5.00
25 Stephen Curry 3.00 8.00

2023-24 Donruss Optic Express Lane Blue

*BLUE: 3X TO 8X BASIC
STATED PRINT RUN 85 SER. #'D SETS
8 Victor Wembanyama 150.00 400.00

2023-24 Donruss Optic Express Lane Green Shock

*GREEN SHOCK: 1X TO 2.5X BASIC
8 Victor Wembanyama 25.00 60.00

2023-24 Donruss Optic Express Lane Lime Green

*LIME GREEN: 2X TO 5X BASIC
STATED PRINT RUN 149 SER. #'D SETS
8 Victor Wembanyama 75.00 200.00

2023-24 Donruss Optic Express Lane Orange

*ORANGE: 5X TO 12X BASIC
STATED PRINT RUN 39 SER. #'D SETS
8 Victor Wembanyama 300.00 600.00

2023-24 Donruss Optic Express Lane Pink

*PINK: 6X TO 15X BASIC
STATED PRINT RUN 25 SER. #'D SETS
8 Victor Wembanyama 400.00 800.00

2023-24 Donruss Optic Fast Break Signatures

* FB PINK/25: .75X TO 2X BASIC
1 Ja Morant 100.00 250.00
2 Stephen Curry 400.00 800.00
3 Zion Williamson 100.00 250.00
4 Luka Doncic 350.00 700.00
5 Dirk Nowitzki 75.00 200.00
6 Russell Westbrook 40.00 100.00
7 Nikola Jokic 100.00 250.00
8 Cade Cunningham 40.00 100.00
9 Jabari Smith Jr. 10.00 25.00
10 Amen Thompson 30.00 80.00
11 Ausar Thompson 15.00 40.00
12 Donovan Mitchell 30.00 80.00
13 Evan Mobley 10.00 25.00
14 Allen Iverson 75.00 200.00
15 Dariq Whitehead 8.00 20.00
16 Keyonte George 20.00 50.00
17 CJ McCollum 6.00 15.00
18 Jalen Green 10.00 25.00
19 Clyde Drexler 20.00 50.00
20 John Wall 8.00 20.00
21 Brandon Ingram 8.00 20.00
22 Dominique Wilkins 10.00 25.00
23 Tyrese Maxey 12.00 30.00
24 Jaren Jackson Jr. 10.00 25.00
25 Cason Wallace 12.00 30.00
26 Michael Porter Jr. 8.00 20.00
27 Shaedon Sharpe 12.00 30.00
28 Keegan Murray 8.00 20.00
29 GG Jackson II 12.00 30.00
30 Desmond Bane 8.00 20.00
31 Scottie Barnes 8.00 20.00
32 Josh Giddey 8.00 20.00
33 Al Horford 6.00 15.00
34 Bilal Coulibaly 15.00 40.00
35 Brice Sensabaugh 10.00 25.00
36 Kobe Bufkin 8.00 20.00
37 Franz Wagner 10.00 25.00
38 Keldon Johnson 8.00 20.00
39 Jason Terry 6.00 15.00
40 Rayan Rupert 6.00 15.00
41 Maxwell Lewis 5.00 12.00
42 Steve Francis 6.00 15.00
43 Dereck Lively II 12.00 30.00
44 Carlos Boozer 5.00 12.00
45 Christian Wood 5.00 12.00
46 Bobby Portis 8.00 20.00
47 Ousmane Dieng 6.00 15.00
48 Brandin Podziemski 20.00 50.00
49 Leonard Miller 6.00 15.00
50 Caleb Martin 5.00 12.00
51 Cameron Payne 5.00 12.00
52 Rolando Blackman 5.00 12.00
53 Julian Strawther 8.00 20.00
54 Colby Jones 6.00 15.00
55 Walker Kessler 6.00 15.00
56 Noah Clowney 8.00 20.00
57 Bruce Brown 6.00 15.00
58 Mike Bibby 6.00 15.00
59 Dell Curry 6.00 15.00
60 Austin Reaves 15.00 40.00
61 Herbert Jones 6.00 15.00
62 Evan Fournier 5.00 12.00
63 Luke Kennard 5.00 12.00
64 Sidy Cissoko 6.00 15.00
65 Jalen Wilson 6.00 15.00
66 Dru Smith 5.00 12.00
67 Jalen McDaniels 5.00 12.00
68 Larry Nance Jr. 4.00 10.00
69 Norman Powell 6.00 15.00
70 Nikola Jovic 6.00 15.00
71 Trayce Jackson-Davis 8.00 20.00
72 Julian Phillips 6.00 15.00
73 Kris Murray 6.00 15.00
74 Andre Jackson Jr. 10.00 25.00
75 Jordan Walsh 6.00 15.00
76 Chris Livingston 6.00 15.00
77 Isaiah Wong 6.00 15.00
78 Christian Braun 6.00 15.00
79 Marcus Sasser 10.00 25.00
80 Ben Sheppard 6.00 15.00
81 Hunter Tyson 6.00 15.00
82 Craig Porter Jr. 8.00 20.00
83 Jaylen Clark 6.00 15.00
84 Ricky Council IV 8.00 20.00
85 Keyontae Johnson 6.00 15.00
86 Mouhamed Gueye 6.00 15.00
87 Moussa Diabate 5.00 12.00
88 Toumani Camara 12.00 30.00
89 Zach LaVine 10.00 25.00
90 Jordan Miller 8.00 20.00
91 Seth Lundy 5.00 12.00
92 Jalen Slawson 6.00 15.00
93 D'Moi Hodge 5.00 12.00
94 Markquis Nowell 6.00 15.00
95 Ben Simmons 6.00 15.00
96 Duop Reath 6.00 15.00
97 Vasilije Micic 6.00 15.00
98 Colin Castleton 5.00 12.00
99 Sasha Vezenkov 5.00 12.00
100 Bruce Bowen 5.00 12.00

2023-24 Donruss Optic Lights Out

*HOLO: .75X TO 2X BASIC
*HOLO FB: .75X TO 2X BASIC
1 Damian Lillard 1.25 3.00
2 Brandon Miller 2.00 5.00
3 Luka Doncic 3.00 8.00
4 Victor Wembanyama 10.00 25.00
5 Nikola Jokic 2.50 6.00
6 Stephen Curry 4.00 10.00
7 Jayson Tatum 2.00 5.00
8 Giannis Antetokounmpo 2.50 6.00
9 Donovan Mitchell 1.00 2.50
10 LeBron James 4.00 10.00
11 Zion Williamson 1.25 3.00
12 Ja Morant 1.50 4.00
13 Ausar Thompson 1.25 3.00
14 Scoot Henderson 1.50 4.00
15 Amen Thompson 2.50 6.00

2023-24 Donruss Optic Lights Out Blue

*BLUE: 2.5X TO 6X BASIC
STATED PRINT RUN 49 SER. #'D SETS
4 Victor Wembanyama 200.00 500.00

2023-24 Donruss Optic Lights Out Pink Velocity

*PINK VELOCITY: 2X TO 5X BASIC
STATED PRINT RUN 79 SER. #'D SETS
4 Victor Wembanyama 150.00 400.00

2023-24 Donruss Optic Lights Out Red

*RED: 2X TO 5X BASIC
STATED PRINT RUN 99 SER. #'D SETS
4 Victor Wembanyama 125.00 300.00

2023-24 Donruss Optic Lights Out Red and Gold International

*RED & GOLD INTER: 2X TO 5X BASIC
STATED PRINT RUN 99 SER. #'D SETS
4 Victor Wembanyama 125.00 300.00

2023-24 Donruss Optic My House

*PURPLE: .6X TO 1.5X BASIC
*HOLO: .75X TO 2X BASIC
*GREEN SHOCK: 1X TO 2.5X BASIC
1 Luka Doncic 3.00 8.00
2 LeBron James 4.00 10.00
3 Anthony Black 1.00 2.50
4 Keyonte George 1.50 4.00
5 Brandon Miller 2.00 5.00
6 Victor Wembanyama 12.00 30.00
7 Jayson Tatum 2.00 5.00
8 Trae Young 1.00 2.50
9 Anthony Edwards 2.50 6.00
10 Kevin Durant 1.50 4.00
11 Giannis Antetokounmpo 2.50 6.00
12 Cam Whitmore 1.25 3.00
13 Donovan Mitchell 1.00 2.50
14 Jett Howard .60 1.50
15 Ja Morant 1.50 4.00
16 Bilal Coulibaly 1.25 3.00
17 Stephen Curry 4.00 10.00
18 Ausar Thompson 1.25 3.00
19 Amen Thompson 2.50 6.00
20 Scoot Henderson 1.50 4.00

2023-24 Donruss Optic My House Blue

*BLUE: 4X TO 10X BASIC
STATED PRINT RUN 85 SER. #'D SETS
6 Victor Wembanyama 200.00 500.00

2023-24 Donruss Optic My House Lime Green

*LIME GREEN: 2.5X TO 6X BASIC
STATED PRINT RUN 149 SER. #'D SETS
6 Victor Wembanyama 125.00 300.00

2023-24 Donruss Optic My House Orange

*ORANGE: 6X TO 15X BASIC
STATED PRINT RUN 39 SER. #'D SETS
6 Victor Wembanyama 400.00 800.00

2023-24 Donruss Optic My House Pink

*PINK: 8X TO 20X BASIC
STATED PRINT RUN 25 SER. #'D SETS
6 Victor Wembanyama 500.00 1,000.00

2023-24 Donruss Optic Opti-Graphs Holo

*CHOICE: .4X TO 1X BASIC
*GREEN INTER: .4X TO 1X BASIC
1 Stephen Curry 400.00 300.00
2 Luka Doncic 350.00 700.00
3 Donovan Mitchell 40.00 100.00
4 Ja Morant 100.00 250.00
5 Al Horford 10.00 25.00
6 Jalen Brunson 40.00 100.00
7 Anthony Edwards 150.00 400.00
10 Cade Cunningham 40.00 100.00
11 De'Aaron Fox 25.00 60.00
12 Desmond Bane 8.00 20.00
13 Austin Reaves 25.00 60.00
14 Pau Gasol 25.00 60.00
15 Tony Parker 20.00 50.00
16 Devonte' Graham 5.00 12.00
17 Lonnie Walker IV 6.00 15.00
18 Gary Harris 5.00 12.00
19 Cole Anthony 6.00 15.00
20 Jalen Suggs 8.00 20.00
22 Deandre Ayton 6.00 15.00
23 Jrue Holiday 25.00 60.00
25 Dejounte Murray 8.00 20.00
26 Dave Bing 8.00 20.00
27 Alex English 8.00 20.00
28 Dale Ellis 6.00 15.00
29 Mike Miller 5.00 12.00
30 Paolo Banchero 75.00 200.00
31 Jaden Hardy 8.00 20.00
32 Jeremy Sochan 8.00 20.00
33 Jalen Williams 12.00 30.00
34 Moses Moody 8.00 20.00
35 Norman Powell 6.00 15.00
36 Damian Lillard 75.00 200.00
37 James Wiseman 5.00 12.00
38 Seth Curry 6.00 15.00
39 Alperen Sengun 10.00 25.00
40 Franz Wagner 10.00 25.00
41 Ayo Dosunmu 6.00 15.00
42 Nickeil Alexander-Walker 4.00 10.00
43 Corey Kispert 5.00 12.00
44 Tim Hardaway Jr. 5.00 12.00
45 Max Strus 6.00 15.00
46 Jaden Ivey 8.00 20.00
47 Markelle Fultz 5.00 12.00
49 Victor Oladipo 5.00 12.00
50 Steve Kerr 12.00 30.00

2023-24 Donruss Optic Optical Illusions

*PURPLE: .6X TO 1.5X BASIC
*HOLO: .75X TO 2X BASIC
*GREEN SHOCK: 1X TO 2.5X BASIC
*LIME GREEN/149: 2X TO 5X BASIC
*BLUE/85: 3X TO 8X BASIC
*ORANGE/39: 5X TO 12X BASIC
*PINK/25: 6X TO 15X BASIC
1 Anthony Davis
LeBron James 3.00 8.00
2 Jaylen Brown
Jayson Tatum 1.50 4.00
3 Jamal Murray
Nikola Jokic 2.00 5.00
4 Kyrie Irving
Luka Doncic 2.50 6.00
5 Chris Paul
Stephen Curry 3.00 8.00

2023-24 Donruss Optic Phases

1 Donovan Mitchell 25.00 60.00
2 Jordan Hawkins 20.00 50.00
3 Cam Whitmore 30.00 80.00
4 Cason Wallace 25.00 60.00
5 De'Aaron Fox 25.00 60.00
6 Jett Howard 15.00 40.00
7 Amen Thompson 60.00 150.00
8 Paolo Banchero 30.00 80.00
9 Victor Wembanyama 800.00 1,500.00
10 Shai Gilgeous-Alexander 60.00 150.00
11 Bilal Coulibaly 30.00 80.00
12 Brandon Miller 50.00 120.00
13 Allen Iverson 30.00 80.00
14 Jayson Tatum 50.00 120.00
15 Trae Young 25.00 60.00
16 LeBron James 100.00 250.00
17 Ja Morant 40.00 100.00
18 Giannis Antetokounmpo 60.00 150.00
19 Gradey Dick 25.00 60.00
20 LaMelo Ball 30.00 80.00
21 Damian Lillard 30.00 80.00
22 Stephen Curry 100.00 250.00
23 Scoot Henderson 40.00 100.00
24 Magic Johnson 50.00 120.00
25 Anthony Edwards 60.00 150.00
26 Nikola Jokic 60.00 150.00
27 Luka Doncic 80.00 200.00
28 Larry Bird 50.00 120.00
29 Anthony Black 25.00 60.00
30 Ausar Thompson 30.00 80.00

2023-24 Donruss Optic Raining 3s

*HOLO: .75X TO 2X BASIC
*FB: .75X TO 2X BASIC
*RED INTER: X TO X BASIC
*RED/99: 2X TO 5X BASIC
*RED & GOLD INTER/99: 2X TO 5X BASIC
*PINK VELOCITY/79: 2X TO 5X BASIC
*BLUE/49: 2.5X TO 6X BASIC
1 Larry Bird 1.50 4.00
2 Damian Lillard 1.00 2.50
3 Jamal Murray .75 2.00
4 James Harden .75 2.00
5 Ray Allen .60 1.50
6 Paul George .60 1.50
7 Klay Thompson 1.00 2.50
8 Donovan Mitchell .75 2.00
9 Stephen Curry 3.00 8.00
10 Dirk Nowitzki 1.00 2.50
11 Kyrie Irving .75 2.00
12 LaMelo Ball 1.00 2.50
13 Carmelo Anthony .60 1.50
14 Kevin Durant 1.25 3.00
15 Luka Doncic 2.50 6.00
16 Paul Pierce .60 1.50
17 Devin Booker 1.00 2.50
18 Jayson Tatum 1.50 4.00
19 Trae Young .75 2.00
20 Steve Nash .75 2.00

2023-24 Donruss Optic Red Hot Rookies

*HOLO: .75X TO 2X BASIC
*HOLO FB: .75X TO 2X BASIC
1 Cam Whitmore 2.00 5.00
2 Victor Wembanyama 12.00 30.00
3 Brandon Miller 3.00 8.00
4 Keyonte George 2.50 6.00
5 Jordan Hawkins 1.25 3.00
6 Kobe Bufkin 1.00 2.50
7 Cason Wallace 1.50 4.00
8 Ausar Thompson 2.00 5.00
9 Scoot Henderson 2.50 6.00
10 Anthony Black 1.50 4.00
11 Bilal Coulibaly 2.00 5.00
12 Jett Howard 1.00 2.50
13 Gradey Dick 1.50 4.00
14 Amen Thompson 4.00 10.00
15 Dereck Lively II 1.50 4.00

2023-24 Donruss Optic Red Hot Rookies Blue

*BLUE: 3X TO 8X BASIC
STATED PRINT RUN 49 SER. #'D SETS
2 Victor Wembanyama 200.00 500.00

2023-24 Donruss Optic Red Hot Rookies Pink Velocity

*PINK VELOCITY: 2.5X TO 6X BASIC
STATED PRINT RUN 79 SER. #'D SETS
2 Victor Wembanyama 150.00 400.00

2023-24 Donruss Optic Red Hot Rookies Red

*RED: 2X TO 5X BASIC
STATED PRINT RUN 99 SER. #'D SETS
2 Victor Wembanyama 125.00 300.00

2023-24 Donruss Optic Red Hot Rookies Red and Gold International

*RED & GOLD INTER: 2X TO 5X BASIC
STATED PRINT RUN 99 SER. #'D SETS
2 Victor Wembanyama 125.00 300.00

2023-24 Donruss Optic Retro Series Signatures Holo

*CHOICE: .4X TO 1X BASIC
*GREEN INTER: .4X TO 1X BASIC
1 Joakim Noah 6.00 15.00
2 Julius Erving 50.00 120.00
3 Chauncey Billups 12.00 30.00
4 Dell Curry 6.00 15.00
5 Ben Wallace 20.00 50.00
6 Steve Nash 60.00 150.00
7 Jason Kidd 30.00 80.00
8 Mike Bibby 6.00 15.00
9 Lenny Wilkens 8.00 20.00
10 Cazzie Russell 6.00 15.00
11 Dennis Rodman 50.00 120.00
12 Dave Bing 8.00 20.00
14 Gary Payton 25.00 60.00
15 Nate Archibald 8.00 20.00
16 Dick Barnett 6.00 15.00
17 Rasheed Wallace 15.00 40.00
18 Isiah Thomas 25.00 60.00
19 Hakeem Olajuwon 40.00 100.00
20 Jason Williams 30.00 80.00

2023-24 Donruss Optic Rising Suns

*HOLO: .75X TO 2X BASIC
*FB: .75X TO 2X BASIC
1 Anthony Black 1.00 2.50
2 Ja Morant 1.50 4.00
3 LeBron James 4.00 10.00
4 Brandon Miller 2.00 5.00
5 Anthony Edwards 2.50 6.00
6 Stephen Curry 4.00 10.00
7 Damian Lillard 1.25 3.00
8 Trae Young 1.00 2.50
9 Ausar Thompson 1.25 3.00
10 Kevin Durant 1.50 4.00
11 Victor Wembanyama 12.00 30.00
12 Donovan Mitchell 1.00 2.50
13 Nikola Jokic 2.50 6.00
14 Luka Doncic 3.00 8.00
15 Amen Thompson 2.50 6.00
16 Giannis Antetokounmpo 2.50 6.00
17 Scoot Henderson 1.50 4.00
18 Zion Williamson 1.25 3.00
19 Jayson Tatum 2.00 5.00
20 Jaime Jaquez Jr. .75 2.00

2023-24 Donruss Optic Rising Suns Blue

*BLUE: 3X TO 8X BASIC
STATED PRINT RUN 49 SER. #'D SETS
11 Victor Wembanyama 200.00 500.00

2023-24 Donruss Optic Rising Suns Pink Velocity

*PINK VELOCITY: 2.5X TO 6X BASIC
STATED PRINT RUN 79 SER. #'D SETS
11 Victor Wembanyama 150.00 400.00

2023-24 Donruss Optic Rising Suns Red

*RED: 2X TO 5X BASIC
STATED PRINT RUN 99 SER. #'D SETS
11 Victor Wembanyama 125.00 300.00

2023-24 Donruss Optic Rising Suns Red and Gold International

*RED & GOLD INTER: 2X TO 5X BASIC
STATED PRINT RUN 99 SER. #'D SETS
11 Victor Wembanyama 125.00 300.00

2023-24 Donruss Optic Rookie Dominators Signatures

STATED PRINT RUN 25-99 SER.#'d SETS
1 Amen Thompson/25 30.00 80.00
2 Ausar Thompson/25 15.00 40.00
3 Bilal Coulibaly/25 15.00 40.00
4 Cason Wallace/25 12.00 30.00
5 Dereck Lively II/99 12.00 30.00
6 Kobe Bufkin/49 8.00 20.00
7 Keyonte George/49 20.00 50.00
8 Brandin Podziemski/49 20.00 50.00
9 Noah Clowney/99 8.00 20.00
10 Dariq Whitehead/99 8.00 20.00
11 Kris Murray/99 6.00 15.00
12 Olivier-Maxence Prosper/99 6.00 15.00
13 Marcus Sasser/99 10.00 25.00
14 Ben Sheppard/99 6.00 15.00
15 Brice Sensabaugh/99 10.00 25.00
16 Julian Strawther/99 8.00 20.00
17 Kobe Brown/99 6.00 15.00
18 Amari Bailey/99 6.00 15.00
19 Jalen Pickett/99 5.00 12.00
20 Leonard Miller/99 6.00 15.00
21 Colby Jones/99 6.00 15.00
22 Julian Phillips/99 6.00 15.00
24 Hunter Tyson/99 6.00 15.00
25 Jordan Walsh/99 6.00 15.00
26 Maxwell Lewis/99 5.00 12.00
27 Dru Smith/99 5.00 12.00
28 Rayan Rupert/99 6.00 15.00
29 GG Jackson II/99 12.00 30.00
30 Keyontae Johnson/99 6.00 15.00
31 Jalen Wilson/99 6.00 15.00
32 Chris Livingston/99 6.00 15.00
33 Toumani Camara/99 12.00 30.00
34 D'Moi Hodge/99 5.00 12.00
35 Mouhamed Gueye/99 6.00 15.00
36 Seth Lundy/99 5.00 12.00
37 Jalen Slawson/99 6.00 15.00
39 Jaylen Clark/99 6.00 15.00
40 Isaiah Wong/99 6.00 15.00

2023-24 Donruss Optic Rookie Dual Signatures Holo

1 Amen Thompson
Ausar Thompson 75.00 200.00
2 Bilal Coulibaly
Cason Wallace 75.00 200.00
3 Kobe Bufkin
Keyonte George 75.00 200.00
4 Brandin Podziemski
Marcus Sasser 75.00 200.00

2023-24 Donruss Optic Rookie Optics Autographs Holo

*CHOICE: .4X TO 1X BASIC
*GREEN INTER: .4X TO 1X BASIC
1 Bilal Coulibaly 15.00 40.00
2 Brandin Podziemski 20.00 50.00
3 Dariq Whitehead 8.00 20.00
4 Ben Sheppard 6.00 15.00
5 Kobe Bufkin 8.00 20.00
6 Noah Clowney 8.00 20.00
7 Brice Sensabaugh 10.00 25.00
8 Colby Jones 6.00 15.00
9 Leonard Miller 6.00 15.00
10 Julian Phillips 6.00 15.00
11 Amen Thompson 30.00 80.00
12 Stanley Umude 5.00 12.00
13 Julian Strawther 8.00 20.00
14 Keyonte George 40.00 100.00
15 Ausar Thompson 30.00 80.00
16 Rayan Rupert 6.00 15.00
17 Cason Wallace 12.00 30.00
18 Jalen Wilson 6.00 15.00
19 Dereck Lively II 12.00 30.00
20 Kris Murray 6.00 15.00
21 GG Jackson II 12.00 30.00
22 Keyontae Johnson 6.00 15.00
24 Jordan Walsh 6.00 15.00
25 Jalen Pickett 5.00 12.00

2023-24 Donruss Optic Signature Series

*GREEN: .5X TO 1.2X BASIC
*GREEN SHOCK: .5X TO 1.2X BASIC
*HOLO: .5X TO 1.2X BASIC
*BLUE/25: 1X TO 2.5X BASIC
*PINK/25: 1X TO 2.5X BASIC
1 Amen Thompson 25.00 60.00
2 Ausar Thompson 12.00 30.00
3 Bilal Coulibaly 12.00 30.00
4 Cason Wallace 10.00 25.00
5 Dereck Lively II 10.00 25.00
6 Kobe Bufkin 6.00 15.00
7 Keyonte George 15.00 40.00
8 Brandin Podziemski 15.00 40.00
9 Noah Clowney 6.00 15.00
10 Dariq Whitehead 6.00 15.00
11 Kris Murray 5.00 12.00
12 Olivier-Maxence Prosper 5.00 12.00
13 Marcus Sasser 8.00 20.00
15 Brice Sensabaugh 8.00 20.00
16 Julian Strawther 6.00 15.00
17 Kobe Brown 5.00 12.00
18 Jalen Pickett 4.00 10.00
19 Leonard Miller 5.00 12.00
20 Colby Jones 5.00 12.00
23 Hunter Tyson 5.00 12.00
24 Jordan Walsh 5.00 12.00
25 Mouhamed Gueye 5.00 12.00
26 Maxwell Lewis 4.00 10.00
27 Rayan Rupert 5.00 12.00
29 GG Jackson II 10.00 25.00
31 Jordan Miller 6.00 15.00
32 Keyontae Johnson 5.00 12.00
33 Jalen Wilson 5.00 12.00
34 Toumani Camara 10.00 25.00
36 Jalen Slawson 5.00 12.00
37 Trayce Jackson-Davis 6.00 15.00
38 Chris Livingston 5.00 12.00
39 Markquis Nowell 5.00 12.00
40 D'Moi Hodge 4.00 10.00
41 Jaden Springer 4.00 10.00
42 Colin Castleton 4.00 10.00
43 Filip Petrusev 5.00 12.00
44 Leaky Black 4.00 10.00
45 Amari Bailey 5.00 12.00
46 Robin Lopez 4.00 10.00
47 Brandon Boston Jr. 4.00 10.00
48 Davion Mitchell 4.00 10.00
49 Corey Kispert 4.00 10.00
50 Jalen McDaniels 4.00 10.00
51 Justin Lewis 4.00 10.00
52 Dalen Terry 5.00 12.00
53 Sam Hauser 5.00 12.00
54 Tre Mann 5.00 12.00
55 Sam Merrill 5.00 12.00
56 Jose Alvarado 5.00 12.00
57 Julian Champagnie 5.00 12.00
58 Scotty Pippen Jr. 5.00 12.00
59 Bruno Fernando 3.00 8.00
60 Xavier Tillman 5.00 12.00
61 Torrey Craig 4.00 10.00
62 Georges Niang 3.00 8.00
63 Kessler Edwards 4.00 10.00
64 Daniel Theis 4.00 10.00
66 Ziaire Williams 5.00 12.00
67 Garrison Mathews 5.00 12.00
68 Chris Duarte 4.00 10.00
69 Dick Van Arsdale 5.00 12.00
70 Brian Scalabrine 4.00 10.00
71 Wally Szczerbiak 4.00 10.00
72 Udonis Haslem 5.00 12.00
73 Tom Van Arsdale 5.00 12.00
74 Sandro Mamukelashvili 5.00 12.00
75 Dale Ellis 5.00 12.00
76 Ty Jerome 3.00 8.00
77 Miles McBride 5.00 12.00
78 Jake LaRavia 4.00 10.00
79 Moussa Diabate 4.00 10.00
80 Tyus Jones 4.00 10.00
81 Bryce McGowens 5.00 12.00
82 Jericho Sims 3.00 8.00
84 Delon Wright 3.00 8.00
86 Vasilije Micic 5.00 12.00
87 Usman Garuba 4.00 10.00
88 Aaron Wiggins 4.00 10.00
89 Isaiah Livers 4.00 10.00
90 Luka Garza 4.00 10.00
91 E.J. Liddell 4.00 10.00
92 Dan Majerle 5.00 12.00
93 Cuttino Mobley 4.00 10.00
94 Santi Aldama 4.00 10.00
95 JT Thor 4.00 10.00
96 Day'Ron Sharpe 4.00 10.00
97 Amir Coffey 3.00 8.00
98 Chuma Okeke 4.00 10.00
99 Jock Landale 4.00 10.00
100 Oshae Brissett 4.00 10.00

2023-24 Donruss Optic Slammy!

1 Joel Embiid 125.00 300.00
2 Damian Lillard 125.00 300.00
3 Brandon Miller 400.00 800.00
4 Anthony Edwards 200.00 500.00
5 Keyonte George 150.00 400.00
6 Tim Duncan 125.00 300.00
7 Anthony Black 75.00 200.00
8 LeBron James 500.00 1,000.00
9 Shaquille O'Neal 125.00 300.00
10 Zion Williamson 100.00 250.00
11 Ja Morant 400.00 800.00
12 Kobe Bufkin 75.00 200.00
13 Kevin Durant 125.00 300.00
14 Jimmy Butler 100.00 250.00
15 Jett Howard 75.00 200.00
16 Charles Barkley 125.00 300.00
17 Luka Doncic 400.00 800.00
18 Scoot Henderson 200.00 500.00
19 Jayson Tatum 200.00 500.00
20 Stephen Curry 400.00 800.00
21 Bilal Coulibaly 100.00 250.00
22 Amen Thompson 150.00 400.00
23 Gradey Dick 100.00 250.00
24 Victor Wembanyama 1,500.00 3,000.00
25 Nikola Jokic 150.00 400.00
26 Cason Wallace 100.00 250.00
27 Giannis Antetokounmpo 150.00 400.00
28 Jaylen Brown 150.00 400.00
29 Kyrie Irving 125.00 300.00
30 Ausar Thompson 150.00 400.00

2023-24 Donruss Optic Splash

1 Trae Young .75 2.00
2 Devin Booker 1.00 2.50
3 Jayson Tatum 1.50 4.00
4 Damian Lillard 1.00 2.50
5 Luka Doncic 2.50 6.00
6 Victor Wembanyama 6.00 15.00
7 Paul George .60 1.50
8 Stephen Curry 3.00 8.00
9 Gradey Dick .75 2.00
10 Jordan Hawkins .60 1.50
11 Brandon Miller 1.50 4.00
12 Jett Howard .50 1.25
13 Anthony Black .75 2.00
14 Jalen Hood-Schifino .40 1.00
15 Scoot Henderson 1.25 3.00

2023-24 Donruss Optic Splash Blue

*BLUE: 4X TO 10X BASIC
STATED PRINT RUN 85 SER. #'D SETS
6 Victor Wembanyama 150.00 400.00
11 Brandon Miller 40.00 100.00

2023-24 Donruss Optic Splash Green Shock

*GREEN SHOCK: 1.25X TO 3X BASIC
6 Victor Wembanyama 40.00 100.00

2023-24 Donruss Optic Splash Holo

*HOLO: .75X TO 2X BASIC
6 Victor Wembanyama 15.00 40.00

2023-24 Donruss Optic Splash Lime Green

*LIME GREEN: 3X TO 8X BASIC
STATED PRINT RUN 149 SER. #'D SETS
6 Victor Wembanyama 125.00 300.00
11 Brandon Miller 30.00 80.00

2023-24 Donruss Optic Splash Orange

*ORANGE: 6X TO 15X BASIC
STATED PRINT RUN 39 SER. #'D SETS
6 Victor Wembanyama 300.00 600.00
11 Brandon Miller 60.00 150.00

2023-24 Donruss Optic Splash Pink

*PINK: 8X TO 20X BASIC
STATED PRINT RUN 25 SER. #'D SETS
6 Victor Wembanyama 400.00 800.00
11 Brandon Miller 75.00 200.00

2023-24 Donruss Optic Splash Purple

*PURPLE: .6X TO 1.5X BASIC
6 Victor Wembanyama 12.00 30.00

2023-24 Donruss Optic The Elite Series Signatues

STATED PRINT RUN 49-99 SER.#'d SETS
1 Trae Young/49 75.00 200.00
2 Scottie Barnes/99 20.00 50.00
3 Carmelo Anthony/49 40.00 100.00
4 Chris Paul/49 25.00 60.00
5 Rui Hachimura/99 25.00 60.00
6 Amar'e Stoudemire/99 8.00 20.00
7 Dwyane Wade/99 50.00 120.00
8 Jordan Poole/99 10.00 25.00
9 RJ Barrett/99 10.00 25.00
10 Deandre Ayton/99 6.00 15.00
11 Jordan Clarkson/99 6.00 15.00
12 Devin Vassell/99 8.00 20.00
13 Nikola Vucevic/99 6.00 15.00
14 Karl-Anthony Towns/49 10.00 25.00
15 Paul Pierce/49 30.00 80.00
16 De'Aaron Fox/49 25.00 60.00
17 Marcus Smart/99 8.00 20.00
18 Obi Toppin/99 6.00 15.00
19 Andre Drummond/99 5.00 12.00

2023-24 Donruss Optic The Rookies

1 Brandon Miller 3.00 8.00
2 Amen Thompson 4.00 10.00
3 Scoot Henderson 2.50 6.00
4 Victor Wembanyama 12.00 30.00
5 Ausar Thompson 2.00 5.00

2023-24 Donruss Optic The Rookies Blue

*BLUE: 4X TO 10X BASIC
STATED PRINT RUN 49 SER. #'D SETS
1 Brandon Miller 75.00 200.00
4 Victor Wembanyama 600.00 1,200.00

2023-24 Donruss Optic The Rookies Holo

*HOLO: .75X TO 2X BASIC
4 Victor Wembanyama 75.00 200.00

2023-24 Donruss Optic The Rookies Holo Fast Break

*HOLO FB: .75X TO 2X BASIC
4 Victor Wembanyama 75.00 200.00

2023-24 Donruss Optic The Rookies Pink Velocity

*PINK VELOCITY: 3X TO 8X BASIC
STATED PRINT RUN 79 SER. #'D SETS
1 Brandon Miller 60.00 150.00
4 Victor Wembanyama 500.00 1,000.00

2023-24 Donruss Optic The Rookies Red

*RED: 2.5X TO 6X BASIC
STATED PRINT RUN 99 SER. #'D SETS
1 Brandon Miller 50.00 120.00
4 Victor Wembanyama 400.00 800.00

2023-24 Donruss Optic The Rookies Red and Gold International

*RED INTER: 2.5X TO 6X BASIC
STATED PRINT RUN 99 SER. #'D SETS
1 Brandon Miller 50.00 120.00
4 Victor Wembanyama 400.00 800.00

2023-24 Donruss Optic White Hot Rookies

1 Anthony Black 1.25 3.00
2 Victor Wembanyama 8.00 20.00
3 Cason Wallace 1.25 3.00
4 Bilal Coulibaly 1.50 4.00
5 Cam Whitmore 1.50 4.00
6 Jalen Hood-Schifino .60 1.50
7 Kobe Bufkin .75 2.00
8 Dereck Lively II 1.25 3.00
9 Amen Thompson 3.00 8.00
10 Brandon Miller 2.50 6.00
11 Ausar Thompson 1.50 4.00
12 Keyonte George 2.00 5.00
13 Jaime Jaquez Jr. 1.00 2.50
14 Brandin Podziemski 2.00 5.00
15 Scoot Henderson 2.00 5.00

2023-24 Donruss Optic White Hot Rookies Blue

STATED PRINT RUN 85 SER. #'D SETS
2 Victor Wembanyama 150.00 400.00

2023-24 Donruss Optic White Hot Rookies Green Shock

*GREEN SHOCK: 1X TO 2.5X BASIC
2 Victor Wembanyama 30.00 80.00

2023-24 Donruss Optic White Hot Rookies Holo

*HOLO: .75X TO 2X BASIC
2 Victor Wembanyama 25.00 60.00

2023-24 Donruss Optic White Hot Rookies Lime Green

*LIME GRN: 2.5X TO 6X BASIC
STATED PRINT RUN 149 SER. #'D SETS
2 Victor Wembanyama 125.00 300.00

2023-24 Donruss Optic White Hot Rookies Orange

*ORANGE: 5X TO 12X BASIC
STATED PRINT RUN 39 SER. #'D SETS
2 Victor Wembanyama 300.00 600.00

2023-24 Donruss Optic White Hot Rookies Pink

STATED PRINT RUN 25 SER. #'D SETS
2 Victor Wembanyama 400.00 800.00

2023-24 Donruss Optic White Hot Rookies Purple

2 Victor Wembanyama 15.00 40.00

2023-24 Donruss Optic Winner Stays

*PURPLE: .6X TO 1.5X BASIC
*HOLO: .75X TO 2X BASIC
*GREEN SHOCK: 1X TO 2.5X BASIC
*LIME GREEN/149: 2X TO 5X BASIC
*BLUE/85: 3X TO 8X BASIC
*ORANGE/39: 5X TO 12X BASIC
*PINK/25: 6X TO 15X BASIC
1 Giannis Antetokounmpo 2.00 5.00
2 LeBron James 3.00 8.00
3 Larry Bird 1.50 4.00
4 Dirk Nowitzki 1.00 2.50
5 Tim Duncan 1.00 2.50
6 Nikola Jokic 2.00 5.00
7 Pau Gasol .60 1.50
8 Jamal Murray .75 2.00
9 Jrue Holiday .50 1.25
10 Kyrie Irving .75 2.00
11 Magic Johnson 1.50 4.00
12 Hakeem Olajuwon .75 2.00
13 Kevin Durant 1.25 3.00
14 Isiah Thomas .60 1.50
15 Tony Parker .60 1.50

16 Stephen Curry 3.00 8.00
17 Shaquille O'Neal 1.25 3.00
18 Kawhi Leonard 1.00 2.50
19 Anthony Davis 1.00 2.50
20 Dwyane Wade .75 2.00

2023-24 Donruss Optic Turkish Airlines EuroLeague

1 Vanja Marinkovic .75 2.00
2 Rodrigue Beaubois .60 1.50
3 Matt Thomas .60 1.50
4 Konstantinos Mitoglou .75 2.00
5 Jordan Loyd .75 2.00
6 Shane Larkin .60 1.50
7 Elijah Bryant .60 1.50
8 Johannes Thiemann .60 1.50
9 Alpha Diallo .60 1.50
10 Matthew Costello .60 1.50
11 Khalifa Koumadje .60 1.50
12 Gabriele Procida .60 1.50
13 Will Clyburn .60 1.50
14 Elie Okobo .60 1.50
15 Luka Mitrovic .60 1.50
16 Justin Bean .60 1.50
17 Tibor Pleiss .60 1.50
18 Khalifa Diop .60 1.50
19 Tamir Blatt .60 1.50
20 Matteo Spagnolo 1.00 2.50
21 Donta Hall .75 2.00
22 Donatas Motiejunas .75 2.00
23 Markus Howard .75 2.00
24 Codi Miller-McIntyre .60 1.50
25 Darius Thompson .75 2.00
26 Sterling Brown .75 2.00
27 Kemba Walker .75 2.00
28 Billy Baron .60 1.50
29 Shaquielle McKissic .60 1.50
30 Walter Tavares .75 2.00
31 Isaiah Canaan .60 1.50
32 Achille Polonara .75 2.00
33 Kassius Robertson .60 1.50
34 Boris Dallo .60 1.50
35 Leandro Bolmaro .75 2.00
36 Bonzie Colson .75 2.00
37 Kostas Papanikolaou .75 2.00
38 Devin Booker (F) 2.00 5.00
39 Kyle Hines .60 1.50
40 Brady Manek .75 2.00
41 Giannoulis Larentzakis .60 1.50
42 Sylvain Francisco .60 1.50
43 Isaac Bonga .60 1.50
44 Alec Peters .60 1.50
45 Marco Belinelli .75 2.00
46 Mathias Lessort 1.00 2.50
47 Kostas Sloukas 1.00 2.50
48 Gabriel Deck .60 1.50
49 Nigel Williams-Goss .60 1.50
50 James Webb III .60 1.50
51 Jan Vesely .75 2.00
52 Edgaras Ulanovas .60 1.50
53 Perry Dozier Jr .75 2.00
54 Semi Ojeleye .75 2.00
55 Paris Lee .60 1.50
56 Bryant Dunston .60 1.50
57 Fabien Causeur .60 1.50
58 Thomas Walkup .75 2.00
59 John DiBartolomeo .60 1.50
60 Nikola Kalinic (BK) .75 2.00
61 James Nunnally .60 1.50
62 Luke Sikma .60 1.50
63 Ignas Brazdeikis .75 2.00
64 Victor Claver .60 1.50
65 Scottie Wilbekin .75 2.00
66 Ioannis Papapetrou .75 2.00
67 Brandon Davies .60 1.50
68 Alen Smailagic .75 2.00
69 Marius Grigonis .75 2.00
70 Guerschon Yabusele .75 2.00
71 Maodo Lo .60 1.50
72 Sergio Llull .75 2.00
73 Yam Madar .75 2.00
74 Nick Calathes .75 2.00
75 Tomas Satoransky .75 2.00
76 Zach LeDay .75 2.00
77 Wade Baldwin IV .60 1.50
78 Marko Guduric .75 2.00
79 Jabari Parker .75 2.00
80 Nando De Colo .75 2.00
81 Devontae Cacok .75 2.00
82 Kevin Punter .75 2.00
83 Kostas Antetokounmpo .75 2.00
84 Andreas Obst .75 2.00
85 Carsen Edwards .75 2.00
86 Joffrey Lauvergne .75 2.00
87 Justin Anderson .60 1.50
88 Sergio Rodriguez .75 2.00
89 Jordan Mickey .75 2.00
90 Mario Hezonja .75 2.00
91 Xabi Lopez-Arostegui .60 1.50
92 Facundo Campazzo .75 2.00
93 Willy Hernangomez .75 2.00
94 Sertac Sanli .60 1.50
95 Milos Teodosic .75 2.00
96 Vladimir Lucic .60 1.50
97 Chris Jones .60 1.50
98 Rokas Jokubaitis .75 2.00
99 Tyler Dorsey .75 2.00
100 Shabazz Napier .75 2.00
101 Keenan Evans .75 2.00
102 Iffe Lundberg .60 1.50
103 Rudy Fernandez .75 2.00
104 Nigel Hayes-Davis .75 2.00
105 Shavon Shields .60 1.50
106 Nikola Milutinov .75 2.00
107 Mike Scott .60 1.50
108 Nicolas Laprovittola .75 2.00
109 Alex Abrines .75 2.00
110 Lukas Lekavicius .60 1.50
111 Frank Kaminsky .75 2.00
112 Lorenzo Brown .60 1.50
113 Dzanan Musa .75 2.00
114 Jaleen Smith .60 1.50
115 Melih Mahmutoglu .60 1.50
116 Daniel Hackett .75 2.00
117 Nicolo Melli .75 2.00
118 Vincent Poirier .75 2.00
119 Luca Vildoza .60 1.50
120 Rokas Giedraitis .60 1.50
121 Kevin Pangos .60 1.50
122 Kevarrius Hayes .60 1.50
123 Moustapha Fall .75 2.00
124 Nemanja Nedovic .75 2.00
125 Tadas Sedekerskis .75 2.00
126 Kendrick Nunn .75 2.00
127 Yago Dos Santos .75 2.00
128 Mike James .75 2.00
129 Nikolaos Rogkavopoulos .60 1.50
130 Mike Tobey .60 1.50
131 Mateusz Ponitka .60 1.50
132 Juancho Hernangomez 1.00 2.50
133 Timothe Luwawu-Cabarrot .75 2.00
134 Dyshawn Pierre .60 1.50
135 Martin Hermannsson .60 1.50
136 Adam Hanga .60 1.50
137 James Nnaji .60 1.50
138 Marko Simonovic .75 2.00
139 Jared Harper .75 2.00
140 Chima Moneke .60 1.50
141 Jerian Grant .75 2.00
142 Jasiel Rivero .60 1.50
143 Tornike Shengelia .75 2.00
144 Naz Mitrou-Long .60 1.50
145 Tyrique Jones .60 1.50
146 Youssoupha Fall .75 2.00
147 David Lighty .60 1.50
148 Antonius Cleveland .75 2.00
149 Devon Hall .60 1.50
150 Georgios Papagiannis .60 1.50
151 Serge Ibaka .75 2.00
152 Aleksa Avramovic .75 2.00
153 Johannes Voigtmann .60 1.50
154 Johnathan Motley .75 2.00
155 Nikola Mirotic .75 2.00
156 Matteo Spagnolo RP 1.25 3.00
157 Omer Mayer RP 2.00 5.00
158 Ismaila Diagne RP 1.00 2.50
159 Nikola Topic RP 2.50 6.00
160 Alexandros Samontourov RP 1.25 3.00
161 Victor Wembanyama LEG 6.00 15.00
162 Antonis Fotsis LEG .60 1.50
163 Ramunas Siskauskas LEG .75 2.00
164 Alexey Shved LEG .60 1.50
165 Fragiskos Alvertis LEG .60 1.50
166 Luka Doncic LEG 5.00 12.00
167 Nikola Vujcic LEG .75 2.00
168 Bogdan Bogdanovic LEG .75 2.00
169 Kostas Tsartsaris LEG .60 1.50
170 Pau Gasol LEG 1.25 3.00
171 Andrey Vorontsevich LEG .75 2.00
172 Georgios Printezis LEG .75 2.00
173 Erazem Lorbek LEG .75 2.00
174 Theodoros Papaloukas LEG .60 1.50
175 JR Holden LEG .60 1.50
176 Andrei Kirilenko LEG .75 2.00
177 Felipe Reyes LEG .75 2.00
178 Dimitris Diamantidis LEG .75 2.00
179 Andres Nocioni LEG .75 2.00
180 Sasha Vezenkov LEG .60 1.50
181 David Andersen LEG .60 1.50
182 Tiago Splitter LEG .60 1.50
183 Mike Batiste LEG .75 2.00
184 Milos Vujanic LEG .75 2.00
185 Ekpe Udoh LEG .60 1.50
186 Trajan Langdon LEG .60 1.50
187 Tyrese Rice LEG .60 1.50
188 Ricky Rubio LEG .60 1.50
189 Juan Carlos Navarro LEG .75 2.00
190 Matjaz Smodis LEG .75 2.00
191 Sofoklis Schortsanitis LEG .60 1.50
192 Vassilis Spanoulis LEG .75 2.00
193 Viktor Khryapa LEG .60 1.50
194 Vasilije Micic LEG .75 2.00
195 Paulius Jankunas LEG .60 1.50
196 Walter Tavares FT .75 2.00
197 Mathias Lessort FT 1.00 2.50
198 Lorenzo Brown FT .60 1.50
199 Dzanan Musa FT .75 2.00
200 Sasha Vezenkov FT .60 1.50

2023-24 Donruss Optic Turkish Airlines EuroLeague Holo

*OPTIC HOLO: .75X TO 2X BASIC
161 Victor Wembanyama LEG 30.00 80.00

2023-24 Donruss Optic Turkish Airlines EuroLeague Red

*OPTIC RED: 2.6X TO 6X BASIC
STATED PRINT RUN 99 SER.#'d SETS
161 Victor Wembanyama LEG 100.00 250.00

2019 Donruss Optic WNBA

*HOLO: 2X TO 5X BASIC
1 Angel McCoughtry .75 2.00
2 Chelsea Gray .75 2.00
3 Kelsey Mitchell 1.25 3.00
4 Jordin Canada .60 1.50
5 Shavonte Zellous .60 1.50
6 Morgan Tuck .60 1.50
7 Sylvia Fowles .75 2.00
8 Yvonne Turner .60 1.50
9 A'ja Wilson 2.50 6.00
10 Cheyenne Parker .60 1.50
11 Brittney Sykes 1.25 3.00
12 Essence Carson .50 1.25
13 Natalie Achonwa .60 1.50
14 Kaleena Mosqueda-Lewis .40 1.00
15 Sugar Rodgers .60 1.50
16 Shekinna Stricklen .40 1.00
17 Tanisha Wright .60 1.50
18 Ariel Atkins .75 2.00
19 Carolyn Swords .50 1.25
20 Courtney Vandersloot .75 2.00
21 Elizabeth Williams .60 1.50
22 Nneka Ogwumike 1.00 2.50
23 Tiffany Mitchell .75 2.00
24 Natasha Howard .75 2.00
25 Tina Charles 1.25 3.00
26 Allisha Gray 1.00 2.50
27 Briann January .50 1.25
28 Elena Delle Donne 2.00 5.00
29 Kayla McBride .75 2.00
30 Diamond DeShields .60 1.50
31 Jessica Breland .50 1.25
32 Odyssey Sims .60 1.50
33 Victoria Vivians .75 2.00
34 Sue Bird 2.50 6.00
35 Cecilia Zandalasini .60 1.50
36 Azura Stevens .60 1.50
37 Brittney Griner 2.00 5.00
38 Kristi Toliver .60 1.50
39 Kelsey Bone .50 1.25
40 Gabby Williams .75 2.00
41 Renee Montgomery .50 1.25
42 Riquna Williams .60 1.50
43 Bria Hartley .50 1.25
44 Alyssa Thomas 1.25 3.00
45 Danielle Robinson .60 1.50
46 Glory Johnson .60 1.50
47 DeWanna Bonner 1.00 2.50
48 LaToya Sanders .60 1.50
49 Kelsey Plum 1.50 4.00
50 Jamierra Faulkner .50 1.25
51 Tiffany Hayes .60 1.50
52 Alysha Clark .50 1.25
53 Brittany Boyd .60 1.50
54 Chiney Ogwumike .60 1.50
55 Karima Christmas-Kelly .60 1.50
56 Kaela Davis .60 1.50
57 Diana Taurasi 2.50 6.00
58 Tianna Hawkins .40 1.00
59 Nia Coffey .60 1.50
60 Stefanie Dolson .60 1.50
61 Candice Dupree .60 1.50
62 Breanna Stewart 2.50 6.00
63 Epiphanny Prince .50 1.25
64 Courtney Williams .60 1.50
65 Erlana Larkins .50 1.25
66 Kayla Thornton .60 1.50
67 Leilani Mitchell .50 1.25
68 Natasha Cloud .75 2.00
69 Tamera Young .60 1.50
70 Alana Beard .60 1.50
71 Cappie Pondexter .75 2.00
72 Crystal Langhorne .50 1.25
73 Kia Nurse .75 2.00
74 Jasmine Thomas .60 1.50
75 Rebekkah Brunson .60 1.50
76 Liz Cambage .75 2.00
77 Sancho Lyttle .50 1.25
78 Tierra Ruffin-Pratt .50 1.25
79 Alex Bentley .60 1.50
80 Candace Parker 1.50 4.00
81 Erica Wheeler .60 1.50
82 Jewell Loyd 1.25 3.00
83 Kia Vaughn .60 1.50
84 Jonquel Jones 1.50 4.00
85 Seimone Augustus 1.00 2.50
86 Skylar Diggins-Smith 1.25 3.00
87 Stephanie Talbot .60 1.50
88 Allie Quigley .50 1.25
89 Kristine Anigwe RR 1.25 3.00
90 Jackie Young RR 10.00 25.00
91 Kiara Leslie RR 1.50 4.00
92 Teaira McCowan RR 1.25 3.00
93 Arike Ogunbowale RR 10.00 25.00
94 Han Xu RR 2.50 6.00
95 Napheesa Collier RR 40.00 100.00
96 Asia Durr RR 1.50 4.00
97 Kalani Brown RR 1.50 4.00
98 Katie Lou Samuelson RR 3.00 8.00
99 Alanna Smith RR 3.00 8.00
100 Brianna Turner RR 2.00 5.00

2009-10 Donruss Elite

COMP.SET w/o SPs (120) 25.00 50.00
121-160 PRINT RUN 499 SER.#'d SETS
161-200 PRINT RUN 499 SER.#'d SETS
1 Joe Johnson .50 1.25
2 Jamal Crawford .50 1.25
3 Josh Smith .30 .75
4 Mike Bibby .50 1.25
5 Paul Pierce .75 2.00
6 Kevin Garnett 1.25 3.00
7 Ray Allen .75 2.00
8 Rajon Rondo .60 1.50
9 Gerald Wallace .40 1.00
10 Boris Diaw .40 1.00
11 Raymond Felton .30 .75
12 Derrick Rose .75 2.00
13 John Salmons .40 1.00
14 Brad Miller .40 1.00
15 Tyrus Thomas .30 .75
16 LeBron James 4.00 10.00
17 Shaquille O'Neal 1.50 4.00
18 Mo Williams .40 1.00
19 Delonte West .30 .75
20 Dirk Nowitzki 1.25 3.00
21 Jason Kidd .75 2.00
22 Jason Terry .40 1.00
23 Shawn Marion .50 1.25
24 Carmelo Anthony .75 2.00
25 Chauncey Billups .60 1.50
26 Kenyon Martin .40 1.00
27 Nene .40 1.00
28 Ben Gordon .40 1.00
29 Richard Hamilton .50 1.25
30 Charlie Villanueva .30 .75
31 Tayshaun Prince .50 1.25
32 Stephen Jackson .40 1.00
33 Monta Ellis .40 1.00
34 Corey Maggette .40 1.00
35 Kelenna Azubuike .30 .75
36 Tracy McGrady 1.00 2.50
37 Shane Battier .50 1.25
38 Luis Scola .40 1.00
39 Trevor Ariza .30 .75
40 Danny Granger .30 .75
41 Mike Dunleavy .30 .75
42 Troy Murphy .30 .75
43 T.J. Ford .30 .75
44 Eric Gordon .40 1.00
45 Al Thornton .30 .75
46 Baron Davis .40 1.00
47 Marcus Camby .40 1.00
48 Kobe Bryant 4.00 10.00
49 Ron Artest .50 1.25
50 Pau Gasol .75 2.00
51 Andrew Bynum .30 .75
52 Zach Randolph .50 1.25
53 Rudy Gay .50 1.25
54 O.J. Mayo .30 .75
55 Marc Gasol .50 1.25
56 Dwyane Wade 1.00 2.50
57 Michael Beasley .30 .75
58 Jermaine O'Neal .50 1.25
59 Daequan Cook .30 .75
60 Quentin Richardson .30 .75
61 Michael Redd .40 1.00
62 Hakim Warrick .30 .75
63 Andrew Bogut .40 1.00
64 Luke Ridnour .30 .75
65 Al Jefferson .30 .75
66 Ryan Gomes .30 .75
67 Kevin Love .50 1.25
68 Devin Harris .30 .75
69 Brook Lopez .50 1.25
70 Yi Jianlian .60 1.50
71 Rafer Alston .30 .75
72 Chris Paul 1.00 2.50
73 David West .40 1.00
74 Peja Stojakovic .40 1.00
75 James Posey .30 .75
76 Emeka Okafor .40 1.00
77 Nate Robinson .40 1.00
78 David Lee .30 .75
79 Al Harrington .40 1.00
80 Larry Hughes .40 1.00
81 Kevin Durant 2.00 5.00
82 Russell Westbrook 1.00 2.50
83 Jeff Green .40 1.00
84 Nenad Krstic .30 .75
85 Dwight Howard .60 1.50
86 Vince Carter 1.00 2.50
87 Rashard Lewis .40 1.00
88 Jameer Nelson .30 .75
89 Elton Brand .40 1.00
90 Andre Iguodala .50 1.25
91 Thaddeus Young .30 .75
92 Amare Stoudemire .40 1.00
93 Steve Nash 1.00 2.50
94 Jason Richardson .50 1.25
95 Grant Hill .30 .75
96 Brandon Roy .60 1.50
97 LaMarcus Aldridge .50 1.25
98 Steve Blake .30 .75
99 Andre Miller .50 1.25
100 Greg Oden .30 .75
101 Kevin Martin .40 1.00
102 Andres Nocioni .30 .75
103 Francisco Garcia .30 .75
104 Spencer Hawes .30 .75
105 Tony Parker .75 2.00
106 Tim Duncan 1.25 3.00
107 Manu Ginobili 1.00 2.50
108 Richard Jefferson .40 1.00
109 Chris Bosh .60 1.50
110 Jose Calderon .30 .75
111 Andrea Bargnani .30 .75
112 Hedo Turkoglu .40 1.00
113 Deron Williams .40 1.00
114 Mehmet Okur .30 .75
115 Andrei Kirilenko .40 1.00
116 Carlos Boozer .40 1.00
117 Antawn Jamison .40 1.00
118 Caron Butler .40 1.00
119 Gilbert Arenas .40 1.00
120 Randy Foye .30 .75
121 Willis Reed 1.25 3.00
122 Chris Mullin 1.00 2.50
123 Kevin Johnson .75 2.00
124 Spencer Haywood .50 1.25
125 David Robinson 1.50 4.00
126 Phil Jackson 1.00 2.50
127 Magic Johnson 3.00 8.00
128 Paul Westphal .75 2.00
129 Alex English 1.00 2.50
130 Kareem Abdul-Jabbar 2.50 6.00
131 Glen Rice .60 1.50
132 Nate McMillan .50 1.25
133 Bob Cousy 2.00 5.00
134 Mitch Richmond .75 2.00
135 Kelly Tripucka .50 1.25
136 Cedric Maxwell .75 2.00
137 Lenny Wilkens .75 2.00
138 Bill Russell 2.50 6.00
139 Sean Elliott .60 1.50
140 Hersey Hawkins .50 1.25
141 Clyde Drexler 1.25 3.00
142 Larry Bird 3.00 8.00
143 Connie Hawkins 1.00 2.50
144 Lou Hudson .75 2.00
145 Oscar Robertson 1.00 2.50
146 Jerry Lucas .75 2.00
147 Kevin McHale 1.25 3.00
148 Michael Cage .50 1.25
149 Vlade Divac .75 2.00
150 Jerry West 1.25 3.00
151 Bill Walton 1.25 3.00
152 Rick Barry .60 1.50
153 Artis Gilmore 1.00 2.50
154 Earl Monroe 1.00 2.50
155 Xavier McDaniel .50 1.25
156 Jalen Rose .60 1.50
157 Walt Frazier 1.25 3.00
158 Isiah Thomas .75 2.00
159 James Worthy 1.00 2.50
160 Karl Malone 1.00 2.50
161 Blake Griffin AU RC 20.00 50.00
162 Hasheem Thabeet AU RC 3.00 8.00
163 James Harden/479 AU RC 100.00 250.00
164 Tyreke Evans AU RC 4.00 10.00
165 Jonny Flynn AU RC 3.00 8.00
166 Stephen Curry AU RC 600.00 1,200.00
167 Jordan Hill AU RC 3.00 8.00
168 Danny Green AU RC 5.00 12.00
169 Brandon Jennings AU RC 5.00 12.00
170 Terrence Williams AU RC 3.00 8.00
171 Gerald Henderson AU RC 3.00 8.00
172 Tyler Hansbrough AU RC 4.00 10.00
173 Earl Clark AU RC 3.00 8.00
174 Austin Daye AU RC 3.00 8.00
175 James Johnson AU RC 4.00 10.00
176 Jrue Holiday AU RC 15.00 40.00
177 Ty Lawson AU RC 4.00 10.00
178 Jeff Teague AU RC 4.00 10.00
179 Eric Maynor/199 AU RC 3.00 8.00
180 Darren Collison/199 AU RC 5.00 12.00
181 Omri Casspi AU RC 3.00 8.00
182 B.J. Mullens AU RC 3.00 8.00
183 Rodrigue Beaubois AU RC 3.00 8.00
184 Taj Gibson/199 AU RC 4.00 10.00
185 DeMarre Carroll AU RC 4.00 10.00
186 Wayne Ellington/199 AU RC 4.00 10.00
187 Toney Douglas AU RC 3.00 8.00
188 Jeff Pendergraph AU RC 3.00 8.00
189 Jermaine Taylor AU RC 3.00 8.00
190 D.Cunningham/199 AU RC 3.00 8.00
191 DaJuan Summers AU RC 3.00 8.00
192 Sam Young/199 AU RC 3.00 8.00
193 DeJuan Blair AU RC 4.00 10.00
194 Jon Brockman AU RC 3.00 8.00
195 A.J. Price AU RC 3.00 8.00
196 Derrick Brown/199 AU RC 3.00 8.00
197 Jodie Meeks AU RC 3.00 8.00
198 Marcus Thornton/199 AU RC 4.00 10.00
199 Chase Budinger AU RC 3.00 8.00
200 Taylor Griffin AU RC 3.00 8.00

2009-10 Donruss Elite Aspirations

*1-120/10-29: 3X TO 8X BASE HI
*1-120/30-55: 2X TO 5X BASE HI
*121-160/10-29: 1.5X TO 4X BASE HI
*121-160/30-55: 1.25X TO 3X BASE HI
PRINT RUNS LISTED IN CHECKLIST
7 Ray Allen/20 5.00 12.00
93 Steve Nash/13 6.00 15.00
95 Grant Hill/33 12.50 30.00
161 Blake Griffin/32 50.00 120.00
162 Hasheem Thabeet/34 1.25 3.00
166 Stephen Curry/30 500.00 1,000.00
167 Jordan Hill/43 1.25 3.00
171 Gerald Henderson/15 2.50 6.00
172 Tyler Hansbrough/50 1.50 4.00
173 Earl Clark/55 1.25 3.00
175 James Johnson/16 3.00 8.00
181 Omri Casspi/18 2.50 6.00
182 B.J. Mullens/23 2.50 6.00
184 Taj Gibson/22 3.00 8.00
186 Wayne Ellington/19 3.00 8.00
187 Toney Douglas/23 2.50 6.00
190 Dante Cunningham/33 1.25 3.00
191 DaJuan Summers/35 1.25 3.00
193 DeJuan Blair/45 1.50 4.00
194 Jon Brockman/40 1.25 3.00
195 A.J. Price/22 2.50 6.00
197 Jodie Meeks/23 2.50 6.00
200 Taylor Griffin/32 1.25 3.00

2009-10 Donruss Elite Status

*1-120/45-75: 1.5X TO 4X BASE HI
*1-120/76-99: 1.25X TO 3X BASE HI
*121-160/45-75: 1.25X TO 3X BASE HI
*121-160/76-99: .75X TO 2X BASE HI
PRINT RUNS LISTED IN CHECKLIST
95 Grant Hill/67 6.00 15.00
161 Blake Griffin/68 30.00 80.00
162 Hasheem Thabeet/66 1.25 3.00
163 James Harden/87 30.00 80.00
164 Tyreke Evans/87 1.50 4.00
165 Jonny Flynn/90 1.25 3.00
166 Stephen Curry/70 400.00 800.00
167 Jordan Hill/57 1.25 3.00
168 Danny Green/86 2.00 5.00
169 Brandon Jennings/97 2.00 5.00
170 Terrence Williams/92 1.25 3.00
171 Gerald Henderson/85 1.25 3.00
172 Tyler Hansbrough/50 1.50 4.00
173 Earl Clark/45 1.25 3.00
174 Austin Daye/95 1.25 3.00
175 James Johnson/84 1.50 4.00
176 Jrue Holiday/89 6.00 15.00
177 Ty Lawson/97 1.50 4.00
178 Jeff Teague/99 1.50 4.00
179 Eric Maynor/97 1.25 3.00
180 Darren Collison/98 2.00 5.00
181 Omri Casspi/82 1.25 3.00
182 B.J. Mullens/77 1.25 3.00
183 Rodrigue Beaubois/97 1.25 3.00
184 Taj Gibson/78 1.50 4.00
185 DeMarre Carroll/99 1.50 4.00
186 Wayne Ellington/81 1.50 4.00
187 Toney Douglas/77 1.25 3.00
188 Jeff Pendergraph/96 1.25 3.00
189 Jermaine Taylor/92 1.25 3.00
190 Dante Cunningham/67 1.25 3.00
191 DaJuan Summers/65 1.25 3.00
192 Sam Young/96 1.25 3.00
193 DeJuan Blair/55 1.50 4.00
194 Jon Brockman/60 1.25 3.00
195 A.J. Price/78 1.25 3.00
196 Derrick Brown/96 1.25 3.00
197 Jodie Meeks/77 1.25 3.00
198 Marcus Thornton/95 1.50 4.00
199 Chase Budinger/90 1.25 3.00
200 Taylor Griffin/68 1.25 3.00

2009-10 Donruss Elite Status Gold

*1-120: 4X TO 10X BASE HI
*121-160: 2X TO 5X BASE HI
GOLD PRINT RUN 24 SER.#'d SETS
93 Steve Nash 6.00 15.00
95 Grant Hill 12.00 30.00
125 David Robinson 8.00 20.00
161 Blake Griffin 125.00 250.00
162 Hasheem Thabeet 3.00 8.00
163 James Harden 30.00 80.00
164 Tyreke Evans 4.00 10.00
165 Jonny Flynn 3.00 8.00
166 Stephen Curry 1,000.00 2,000.00
167 Jordan Hill 3.00 8.00
168 Danny Green 5.00 12.00
169 Brandon Jennings 5.00 12.00
170 Terrence Williams 3.00 8.00
171 Gerald Henderson 3.00 8.00
172 Tyler Hansbrough 4.00 10.00
173 Earl Clark 3.00 8.00
174 Austin Daye 3.00 8.00
175 James Johnson 4.00 10.00
176 Jrue Holiday 15.00 40.00
177 Ty Lawson 4.00 10.00
178 Jeff Teague 4.00 10.00
179 Eric Maynor 3.00 8.00
180 Darren Collison 5.00 12.00
181 Omri Casspi 3.00 8.00
182 B.J. Mullens 3.00 8.00
183 Rodrigue Beaubois 3.00 8.00
184 Taj Gibson 4.00 10.00
185 DeMarre Carroll 4.00 10.00
186 Wayne Ellington 4.00 10.00
187 Toney Douglas 3.00 8.00
188 Jeff Pendergraph 3.00 8.00
189 Jermaine Taylor 3.00 8.00
190 Dante Cunningham 3.00 8.00
191 DaJuan Summers 3.00 8.00
192 Sam Young 3.00 8.00
193 DeJuan Blair 4.00 10.00
194 Jon Brockman 3.00 8.00
195 A.J. Price 3.00 8.00
196 Derrick Brown 3.00 8.00
197 Jodie Meeks 3.00 8.00
198 Marcus Thornton 4.00 10.00
199 Chase Budinger 3.00 8.00
200 Taylor Griffin 3.00 8.00

2009-10 Donruss Elite Status Gold Autographs

STATED PRINT RUN 5 TO 24 SER.#'d SETS
4 Mike Bibby 8.00 20.00
20 Dirk Nowitzki 50.00 125.00
21 Jason Kidd 15.00 40.00
30 Charlie Villanueva 8.00 20.00
37 Shane Battier 8.00 20.00
40 Danny Granger 8.00 20.00
51 Andrew Bynum 10.00 25.00
57 Michael Beasley 12.00 30.00
67 Kevin Love 15.00 40.00
68 Devin Harris 10.00 25.00
90 Andre Iguodala 8.00 20.00
116 Carlos Boozer 8.00 20.00
121 Willis Reed 75.00 200.00
122 Chris Mullin 20.00 50.00
124 Spencer Haywood 8.00 20.00
129 Alex English 8.00 20.00
133 Bob Cousy 12.00 30.00
137 Lenny Wilkens 8.00 20.00
138 Bill Russell 500.00 1,000.00
139 Sean Elliott 25.00 60.00
143 Connie Hawkins 10.00 25.00
145 Oscar Robertson 30.00 80.00
150 Jerry West 30.00 80.00
151 Bill Walton 10.00 25.00
152 Rick Barry 8.00 20.00
153 Artis Gilmore 10.00 25.00
157 Walt Frazier 12.00 30.00
161 Blake Griffin 175.00 350.00
162 Hasheem Thabeet 6.00 15.00
163 James Harden 100.00 250.00
164 Tyreke Evans 50.00 120.00
165 Jonny Flynn 6.00 15.00
166 Stephen Curry 2,000.00 4,000.00
167 Jordan Hill 6.00 15.00
168 Danny Green 50.00 125.00
169 Brandon Jennings 25.00 60.00
170 Terrence Williams 6.00 15.00
171 Gerald Henderson 6.00 15.00
172 Tyler Hansbrough 15.00 40.00
173 Earl Clark 6.00 15.00
174 Austin Daye 6.00 15.00
175 James Johnson 8.00 20.00
176 Jrue Holiday 25.00 60.00
177 Ty Lawson 20.00 50.00
178 Jeff Teague 8.00 20.00
179 Eric Maynor 6.00 15.00
180 Darren Collison 10.00 25.00
181 Omri Casspi 6.00 15.00
182 B.J. Mullens 6.00 15.00
183 Rodrigue Beaubois 6.00 15.00
184 Taj Gibson 8.00 20.00
185 DeMarre Carroll 8.00 20.00
186 Wayne Ellington 8.00 20.00
187 Toney Douglas 6.00 15.00
188 Jeff Pendergraph 6.00 15.00
189 Jermaine Taylor 6.00 15.00
190 Dante Cunningham 6.00 15.00
191 DaJuan Summers 6.00 15.00
192 Sam Young 6.00 15.00
193 DeJuan Blair 8.00 20.00
194 Jon Brockman 6.00 15.00
195 A.J. Price 6.00 15.00
196 Derrick Brown 6.00 15.00
197 Jodie Meeks 6.00 15.00
198 Marcus Thornton 8.00 20.00
199 Chase Budinger 6.00 15.00
200 Taylor Griffin 6.00 15.00

2009-10 Donruss Elite ARCeologists

COMPLETE SET (15) 6.00 15.00
*BLACK: 2X TO 5X BASE HI
BLACK PRINT RUN 25 SER.#'d SETS
*GOLD: 1.25X TO 3X BASE HI
GOLD PRINT RUN 100 SER.#'d SETS
*GREEN: .4X TO 1X BASE HI
*RED: .6X TO 1.5X BASE HI
RED PRINT RUN 249 SER.#'d SETS
1 Ray Allen 1.25 3.00
2 Steve Nash 1.50 4.00
3 Roger Mason .50 1.25
4 Chauncey Billups 1.00 2.50
5 Rashard Lewis .60 1.50
6 Ben Gordon .60 1.50
7 Kobe Bryant 6.00 15.00
8 Troy Murphy .50 1.25
9 Jason Kidd 1.25 3.00
10 Mike Bibby .75 2.00
11 Daequan Cook .50 1.25
12 Vince Carter 1.50 4.00
13 Peja Stojakovic .60 1.50
14 Michael Finley .75 2.00
15 O.J. Mayo .50 1.25

2009-10 Donruss Elite ARCeologists Autographs

STATED PRINT RUN 25 TO 50 SER.#'d SETS
7 Kobe Bryant/47 500.00 1,000.00
9 Jason Kidd/25 15.00 40.00
10 Mike Bibby/50 8.00 20.00

2009-10 Donruss Elite ARCeologists Jerseys

STATED PRINT RUN 99 TO 299 SER.#'d SETS
1 Ray Allen/299 5.00 12.00
5 Rashard Lewis/299 2.50 6.00
7 Kobe Bryant/99 15.00 40.00
9 Jason Kidd/299 5.00 12.00
10 Mike Bibby/299 3.00 8.00
13 Peja Stojakovic/299 2.50 6.00
15 O.J. Mayo/140 2.00 5.00

2009-10 Donruss Elite ARCeologists Jerseys Prime

*PRIME: .75X TO 2X BASE HI
STATED PRINT RUN 24-50 SER.#'d SETS
2 Steve Nash/25 10.00 25.00
7 Kobe Bryant/24 20.00 50.00

2009-10 Donruss Elite Clutch Performers

COMPLETE SET (20) 15.00 30.00
*BLACK: 1.5X TO 4X BASE HI
PRINT RUN 25 SER.#'d SETS
*GOLD: 1X TO 2.5X BASE HI
GOLD PRINT RUN 100 SER.#'d SETS
*GREEN: .4X TO 1X BASE HI
*RED: .5X TO 1.25X BASE HI
RED PRINT RUN 249 SER.#'d SETS
1 Paul Pierce 1.50 4.00
2 LeBron James 8.00 20.00
3 Jason Terry .75 2.00
4 Manu Ginobili 2.00 5.00
5 Kobe Bryant 8.00 20.00
6 Brandon Roy 1.25 3.00
7 Dwyane Wade 2.00 5.00
8 Deron Williams .75 2.00
9 Andre Iguodala 1.00 2.50
10 Carmelo Anthony 1.50 4.00
11 Chris Paul 2.00 5.00
12 Tracy McGrady 2.00 5.00
13 Ray Allen 1.50 4.00
14 Stephen Jackson .75 2.00
15 Devin Harris .60 1.50
16 Gilbert Arenas .75 2.00
17 Al Jefferson .60 1.50
18 Richard Hamilton 1.00 2.50
19 Dirk Nowitzki 2.50 6.00
20 Joe Johnson 1.00 2.50

2009-10 Donruss Elite Clutch Performers Jerseys

STATED PRINT RUN 35 TO 299 SER.#'d SETS
1 Paul Pierce/299 5.00 12.00
2 LeBron James/199 10.00 25.00
3 Jason Terry/299 2.50 6.00
5 Kobe Bryant/99 8.00 20.00
6 Brandon Roy/125 4.00 10.00
7 Dwyane Wade/199 5.00 12.00
8 Deron Williams/299 2.50 6.00
9 Andre Iguodala/299 3.00 8.00
10 Carmelo Anthony/199 5.00 12.00
11 Chris Paul/199 6.00 15.00
12 Tracy McGrady/299 6.00 15.00
13 Ray Allen/299 5.00 12.00
14 Stephen Jackson/299 2.50 6.00
15 Devin Harris/70 2.00 5.00
17 Al Jefferson/299 2.00 5.00
19 Dirk Nowitzki/35 6.00 15.00
20 Joe Johnson/299 3.00 8.00

2009-10 Donruss Elite Clutch Performers Jerseys Prime

*PRIME: .75X TO 2X BASE HI
STATED PRINT RUN 10 TO 50 SER.#'d SETS
2 LeBron James/23 30.00 80.00
4 Manu Ginobili/50 12.00 30.00
7 Dwyane Wade/15 12.00 30.00

2009-10 Donruss Elite In the Zone

COMPLETE SET (20) 20.00 40.00
*BLACK: 1.5X TO 4X BASE HI
BLACK PRINT RUN 25 SER.#'d SETS
*GOLD: 1X TO 2.5X BASE HI
GOLD PRINT RUN 100 SER.#'d SETS
*GREEN: .4X TO 1X BASE HI
*RED: .5X TO 1.25X BASE HI
RED PRINT RUN 249 SER.#'d SETS
1 Shaquille O'Neal 3.00 8.00
2 Nene .75 2.00
3 Dwight Howard 1.25 3.00
4 Pau Gasol 1.50 4.00
5 Emeka Okafor .75 2.00
6 David Lee .60 1.50
7 Yao Ming 2.50 6.00
8 Amare Stoudemire .75 2.00
9 Kevin Garnett 2.50 6.00
10 Al Horford 1.00 2.50
11 Tony Parker 1.50 4.00
12 Rajon Rondo 1.25 3.00
13 Tim Duncan 2.50 6.00
14 Steve Nash 2.00 5.00
15 Chris Paul 2.00 5.00
16 Jose Calderon .60 1.50
17 Al Jefferson .60 1.50
18 Dwyane Wade 2.00 5.00
19 LeBron James 8.00 20.00
20 LaMarcus Aldridge 1.00 2.50

2009-10 Donruss Elite In the Zone Jerseys

PRINT RUNS 199 TO 299 SER.#'d SETS
*PRIME: .75X TO 2X BASE HI
PRIME PRINT RUNS 15 TO 50 SER.#'d SETS
3 Dwight Howard 4.00 10.00
4 Pau Gasol/199 5.00 12.00
6 David Lee 2.00 5.00
7 Yao Ming 8.00 20.00
8 Amare Stoudemire 2.50 6.00
9 Kevin Garnett 8.00 20.00
10 Al Horford 3.00 8.00
12 Rajon Rondo 4.00 10.00
13 Tim Duncan 8.00 20.00
15 Chris Paul/199 6.00 15.00
16 Jose Calderon 2.00 5.00
17 Al Jefferson 2.00 5.00
18 Dwyane Wade/199 6.00 15.00
19 LeBron James/199 8.00 20.00
20 LaMarcus Aldridge 3.00 8.00

2009-10 Donruss Elite Jerseys

STATED PRINT RUN 99 SER.#'d SETS
3 Josh Smith 2.00 5.00
4 Mike Bibby 3.00 8.00
5 Paul Pierce 5.00 12.00
6 Kevin Garnett 8.00 20.00
8 Rajon Rondo 4.00 10.00
16 LeBron James 10.00 25.00
21 Jason Kidd 5.00 12.00
22 Jason Terry 2.50 6.00

26 Kenyon Martin 2.50 6.00
41 Tayshaun Prince 3.00 8.00
42 Stephen Jackson 2.50 6.00
46 Tracy McGrady 6.00 15.00
47 Shane Battier 3.00 8.00
48 Luis Scola 2.50 6.00
49 Kobe Bryant 12.00 30.00
50 Pau Gasol 5.00 12.00
51 Andrew Bynum 2.00 5.00
56 Dwyane Wade 6.00 15.00
57 Michael Beasley 2.00 5.00
58 Jermaine O'Neal 3.00 8.00
63 Andrew Bogut 2.50 6.00
65 Al Jefferson 2.00 5.00
67 Kevin Love 3.00 8.00
72 Chris Paul 6.00 15.00
74 Peja Stojakovic 2.50 6.00
77 Nate Robinson 2.50 6.00
78 David Lee 2.00 5.00
85 Dwight Howard 4.00 10.00
87 Rashard Lewis 2.50 6.00
89 Elton Brand 2.50 6.00
91 Thaddeus Young 2.00 5.00
97 LaMarcus Aldridge 3.00 8.00
102 Andres Nocioni 2.00 5.00
106 Tim Duncan 8.00 20.00
109 Chris Bosh 4.00 10.00
110 Jose Calderon 2.00 5.00
111 Andrea Bargnani 2.00 5.00
113 Deron Williams 2.50 6.00
114 Mehmet Okur 2.00 5.00
115 Andrei Kirilenko 2.50 6.00
116 Carlos Boozer 2.50 6.00
122 Chris Mullin 4.00 10.00
123 Kevin Johnson 3.00 8.00
141 Clyde Drexler 5.00 12.00
142 Larry Bird 12.00 30.00
147 Kevin McHale 5.00 12.00
157 Walt Frazier 5.00 12.00
158 Isiah Thomas 3.00 8.00
160 Karl Malone 4.00 10.00

2009-10 Donruss Elite Jerseys Prime

*PRIME: .75X TO 2X BASE HI
STATED PRINT RUN 15 TO 50 SER.#'d SETS
56 Dwyane Wade/15 15.00 40.00
142 Larry Bird/50 20.00 40.00
147 Kevin McHale/50 10.00 25.00
158 Isiah Thomas/50 8.00 20.00

2009-10 Donruss Elite Passing the Torch

COMPLETE SET (15) 20.00 50.00
*BLACK: 1.5X TO 4X BASE HI
BLACK PRINT RUN 25 SER.#'d SETS
*GOLD: .75X TO 2X BASE HI
GOLD PRINT RUN 100 SER.#'d SETS
*GREEN: .4X TO 1X BASE HI
*RED: .6X TO 1.5X BASE HI
RED PRINT RUN 249 SER.#'d SETS
1 M.Johnson/K.Bryant 4.00 10.00
2 B.Russell/R.Parish 3.00 8.00
3 L.Bird/R.Allen 3.00 8.00
4 B.Walton/L.Walton 2.00 5.00
5 M.Malone/Y.Ming 2.00 5.00
6 D.Thompson/V.Carter 2.00 5.00
7 D.Rodman/C.Andersen 2.50 6.00
8 M.Malone/S.O'Neal 3.00 8.00
9 D.Robinson/T.Duncan 3.00 8.00
10 D.Curry/S.Curry 40.00 100.00
11 T.Hansbrough/B.Griffin 2.50 6.00
12 D.Majerle/C.Kaman 2.00 5.00
13 G.Gervin/T.Parker 2.50 6.00
14 G.McGinnis/T.Hansbrough 2.00 5.00
15 K.Abdul-Jabbar/K.Bryant 4.00 10.00

2009-10 Donruss Elite Passing the Torch Autographs

STATED PRINT RUN 25 SER.#'d SETS
1 M.Johnson/K.Bryant 1,000.00 2,000.00
2 B.Russell/R.Parish 600.00 1,200.00
3 L.Bird/R.Allen 150.00 400.00
10 D.Curry/S.Curry 1,500.00 3,000.00
11 T.Hansbrough/B.Griffin 40.00 100.00
12 D.Majerle/C.Kaman 15.00 40.00
13 G.Gervin/T.Parker 40.00 100.00
14 G.McGinnis/T.Hansbrough 15.00 40.00
15 K.Abdul-Jabbar/K.Bryant 1,000.00 2,000.00

2009-10 Donruss Elite Prime Targets

COMPLETE SET (20) 10.00 25.00
*BLACK: 2X TO 5X BASE HI
BLACK PRINT RUN 25 SER.#'d SETS
*GOLD: 1.25X TO 3X BASE HI
GOLD PRINT RUN 100 SER.#'d SETS
*GREEN: .4X TO 1X BASE HI
*RED: .6X TO 1.5X BASE HI
RED PRINT RUN 249 SER.#'d SETS
1 Dwyane Wade 1.50 4.00
2 Kobe Bryant 6.00 15.00
3 Dirk Nowitzki 2.00 5.00
4 LeBron James 6.00 15.00
5 Antawn Jamison .60 1.50
6 Joe Johnson .75 2.00
7 Kevin Durant 3.00 8.00
8 Vince Carter 1.50 4.00
9 Brandon Roy 1.00 2.50
10 Ben Gordon .60 1.50
11 David West .60 1.50
12 O.J. Mayo .50 1.25
13 Danny Granger .50 1.25
14 Chris Bosh 1.00 2.50
15 Tony Parker 1.25 3.00
16 Rudy Gay .75 2.00
17 Chris Paul 1.50 4.00
18 LaMarcus Aldridge .75 2.00
19 Al Harrington .60 1.50
20 Raymond Felton .50 1.25

2009-10 Donruss Elite Prime Targets Jerseys

STATED PRINT RUN 99 TO 299 SER.#'d SETS
1 Dwyane Wade/199 6.00 15.00
2 Kobe Bryant/99 10.00 25.00
4 LeBron James/199 8.00 20.00
6 Joe Johnson/299 3.00 8.00
12 O.J. Mayo/299 2.00 5.00
14 Chris Bosh/299 4.00 10.00
17 Chris Paul/199 6.00 15.00
18 LaMarcus Aldridge/299 3.00 8.00
19 Al Harrington/145 2.50 6.00

2009-10 Donruss Elite Prime Targets Jerseys Prime

*PRIME: .75X TO 2X BASE HI
STATED PRINT RUN 2 TO 50 SER.#'d SETS
7 Kevin Durant/25 15.00 30.00
9 Brandon Roy/50 8.00 20.00
15 Tony Parker/15 10.00 25.00

2009-10 Donruss Elite Series

COMPLETE SET (20) 25.00 50.00
*BLACK: 1.5X TO 4X BASE HI
BLACK PRINT RUN 25 SER.#'d SETS
*GOLD: 1X TO 2.5X BASE HI
GOLD PRINT RUN 100 SER.#'d SETS
*GREEN: .4X TO 1X BASE HI
*RED: .6X TO 1.5X BASE HI
RED PRINT RUN 249 SER.#'d SETS
1 Joe Johnson 1.00 2.50
2 Paul Pierce 1.50 4.00
3 Gerald Wallace .75 2.00
4 Derrick Rose 1.50 4.00
5 LeBron James 8.00 20.00
6 Dirk Nowitzki 2.50 6.00
7 Carmelo Anthony 1.50 4.00
8 Richard Hamilton 1.00 2.50
9 Stephen Jackson .75 2.00
10 Yao Ming 2.50 6.00
11 Danny Granger .60 1.50
12 Marcus Camby .75 2.00
13 Kobe Bryant 8.00 20.00
14 O.J. Mayo .60 1.50
15 Dwyane Wade 2.00 5.00
16 Michael Redd .75 2.00
17 Al Jefferson .60 1.50
18 Devin Harris .60 1.50
19 Chris Paul 2.00 5.00
20 David Lee .60 1.50
21 Kevin Durant 4.00 10.00
22 Dwight Howard 1.25 3.00
23 Andre Iguodala 1.00 2.50
24 Amare Stoudemire .75 2.00
25 Brandon Roy 1.25 3.00
26 Kevin Martin .75 2.00
27 Tim Duncan 2.50 6.00
28 Chris Bosh 1.25 3.00
29 Deron Williams .75 2.00
30 Antawn Jamison .75 2.00

2009-10 Donruss Elite Series Jerseys

STATED PRINT RUN 5 TO 299 SER.#'d SETS
1 Joe Johnson/225 3.00 8.00
2 Paul Pierce/299 5.00 12.00
5 LeBron James/199 8.00 20.00
9 Stephen Jackson/299 2.50 6.00
10 Yao Ming/149 8.00 20.00
13 Kobe Bryant/99 12.50 30.00
14 O.J. Mayo/299 2.00 5.00
15 Dwyane Wade/199 6.00 15.00
16 Michael Redd/249 2.50 6.00
17 Al Jefferson/299 2.00 5.00
19 Chris Paul/199 6.00 15.00
20 David Lee/299 2.00 5.00
22 Dwight Howard/299 4.00 10.00
23 Andre Iguodala/299 3.00 8.00
25 Brandon Roy/299 4.00 10.00
27 Tim Duncan/299 8.00 20.00
28 Chris Bosh/299 4.00 10.00
29 Deron Williams/299 2.50 6.00

2009-10 Donruss Elite Series Jerseys Prime

*PRIME: .75X TO 2X BASE HI
STATED PRINT RUN 10 TO 50 SER.#'d SETS
18 Devin Harris/50 4.00 10.00
19 Chris Paul/15 12.00 30.00
21 Kevin Durant/25 15.00 30.00
24 Amare Stoudemire/50 5.00 12.00
26 Kevin Martin/25 5.00 12.00
27 Tim Duncan/50 15.00 40.00

2009-10 Donruss Elite Teamwork Combos

*BLACK: 1.5X TO 4X BASE HI
BLACK PRINT RUN 25 SER.#'d SETS
*GOLD: 1X TO 2.5X BASE HI
GOLD PRINT RUN 100 SER.#'d SETS
*GREEN: .4X TO 1X BASE HI
*RED: .5X TO 1.25X BASE HI
RED PRINT RUN 249 SER.#'d SETS
1 J.Johnson/M.Bibby 1.00 2.50
2 K.Garnett/P.Pierce 2.50 6.00
3 G.Henderson/R.Felton .60 1.50
4 D.Rose/J.Salmons 1.50 4.00
5 L.James/S.O'Neal 8.00 20.00
6 D.Nowitzki/J.Kidd 2.50 6.00
7 C.Anthony/C.Billups 1.50 4.00
8 B.Gordon/R.Hamilton 1.00 2.50
9 M.Ellis/S.Jackson .75 2.00
10 S.Battier/T.McGrady 2.00 5.00
11 D.Granger/M.Dunleavy .60 1.50
12 A.Thornton/E.Gordon .75 2.00
13 K.Bryant/P.Gasol 8.00 20.00
14 O.Mayo/Z.Randolph 1.00 2.50
15 D.Wade/M.Beasley 2.00 5.00
16 A.Bogut/M.Redd .75 2.00
17 A.Jefferson/R.Gomes .60 1.50
18 B.Lopez/D.Harris 1.00 2.50
19 C.Paul/D.West 2.00 5.00
20 D.Lee/N.Robinson .75 2.00
21 K.Durant/R.Westbrook 4.00 10.00
22 D.Howard/V.Carter 2.00 5.00
23 A.Iguodala/E.Brand 1.00 2.50
24 A.Stoudemire/S.Nash 2.00 5.00
25 A.Miller/B.Roy 1.25 3.00
26 A.Nocioni/K.Martin .75 2.00
27 T.Duncan/T.Parker 2.50 6.00
28 A.Bargnani/J.Calderon .60 1.50
29 D.Williams/M.Okur .75 2.00
30 A.Jamison/G.Arenas .75 2.00

2009-10 Donruss Elite Teamwork Combos Autographs

STATED PRINT RUN 50 SER.#'d SETS
6 D.Nowitzki/J.Kidd 75.00 200.00
13 K.Bryant/P.Gasol 500.00 1,000.00
23 A.Iguodala/E.Brand 10.00 25.00

2009-10 Donruss Elite Threads

STATED PRINT RUN 15 TO 99 SER.#'d SETS
1 Joe Johnson/99 3.00 8.00
2 Mike Bibby/99 3.00 8.00
3 Al Horford/99 3.00 8.00
4 Kevin Garnett/99 8.00 20.00
5 Ray Allen/99 5.00 12.00
6 Gerald Wallace/99 2.50 6.00
7 Derrick Rose/99 5.00 12.00
8 LeBron James/99 10.00 25.00
9 Josh Howard/99 2.50 6.00
10 Dirk Nowitzki/99 8.00 20.00
11 Jason Kidd/99 5.00 12.00
12 Jason Terry/99 2.50 6.00
13 Carmelo Anthony/99 5.00 12.00
14 Kenyon Martin/99 2.50 6.00
15 Austin Daye/99 2.50 6.00
17 Stephen Jackson/99 2.50 6.00
18 Tracy McGrady/99 6.00 15.00
19 Tyler Hansbrough/99 2.50 6.00
20 Blake Griffin/99 15.00 40.00
21 Kobe Bryant/99 10.00 25.00
22 Andrew Bynum/99 2.00 5.00
23 Pau Gasol/99 5.00 12.00
25 O.J. Mayo/99 2.00 5.00
26 Dwyane Wade/99 6.00 15.00
27 Michael Beasley/99 2.00 5.00
28 Michael Redd/99 2.50 6.00
29 Al Jefferson/99 2.00 5.00
31 Chris Paul/99 6.00 15.00
32 David West/99 2.50 6.00
33 Nate Robinson/99 2.50 6.00
35 Dwight Howard/99 4.00 10.00
37 Elton Brand/99 2.50 6.00
38 Andre Iguodala/99 3.00 8.00
39 Amare Stoudemire/99 2.50 6.00
40 Steve Nash/15 8.00 20.00
41 Brandon Roy/99 4.00 10.00
42 Tyreke Evans/99 2.50 6.00
44 Tim Duncan/99 8.00 20.00
45 Manu Ginobili/45 6.00 15.00
46 Chris Bosh/99 4.00 10.00
47 Deron Williams/99 2.50 6.00
48 Carlos Boozer/99 2.50 6.00
49 Andrei Kirilenko/99 2.50 6.00
50 Tayshaun Prince/99 3.00 8.00

2009-10 Donruss Elite Threads Autographs

STATED PRINT RUN 25 SER.#'d SETS
2 Mike Bibby 6.00 15.00
10 Dirk Nowitzki 50.00 120.00
11 Jason Kidd 15.00 40.00
15 Austin Daye 6.00 15.00
19 Tyler Hansbrough 12.50 30.00
20 Blake Griffin 100.00 200.00
21 Kobe Bryant 800.00 1,500.00
38 Andre Iguodala 6.00 15.00
42 Tyreke Evans 25.00 60.00
48 Carlos Boozer 6.00 15.00

2009-10 Donruss Elite Threads Prime

*PRIME: .75X TO 2X BASE HI
STATED PRINT RUN 10 TO 50 SER.#'d SETS
30 Devin Harris/50 4.00 10.00
34 Kevin Durant/25 25.00 60.00
40 Steve Nash/25 10.00 25.00
43 Tony Parker/50 8.00 20.00

2009-10 Donruss Elite Retail

COMPLETE SET (120) 10.00 25.00
*RETAIL: .2X TO .5X HOBBY

2007 Donruss Elite Extra Edition College Ties

STATED PRINT RUN 1500 SER.#'d SETS
*GOLD: .6X TO 1.5X BASIC
GOLD PRINT RUN 500 SER.#'d SETS
*RED: 1X TO 2.5X BASIC
RED PRINT RUN 100 SER.#'d SETS
OVERALL INSERT ODDS 1:4
5 T.Green/M.LaPorta .60 1.50
7 J.Boeheim/D.Nichols 1.00 2.50
11 D.Cook/C.Luebke .40 1.00
12 D.Strawberry/B.Cecil .60 1.50

2007 Donruss Elite Extra Edition College Ties Autographs

OVERALL AUTO/MEM ODDS 1:5
PRINT RUNS B/WN 50-100 COPIES PER
EXCHANGE DEADLINE 07/01/2009
5 T.Green/M.LaPorta 5.00 12.00
7 J.Boeheim/D.Nichols EXCH 8.00 20.00
11 D.Cook/C.Luebke 3.00 8.00
12 D.Strawberry/B.Cecil EXCH 5.00 12.00

2008 Donruss Elite Extra Edition

COMP.SET w/o AU's (100) 10.00 25.00
COMMON CARD (1-100) .20 .50
COMMON AU (101-200) 3.00 8.00
PRINT RUNS B/WN 99-1495
EXCH DEADLINE 5/26/2010
196 Derrick Rose AU/99 15.00 40.00
199 Michael Beasley AU/99 4.00 10.00
200 O.J. Mayo AU/99 4.00 10.00

2008 Donruss Elite Extra Edition Aspirations

*ASP 1-100: 2.5X TO 6X BASIC
STATED PRINT RUN 150 SER.#'d SETS
198 Derrick Rose 12.00 30.00
199 Michael Beasley 3.00 8.00
200 O.J. Mayo 3.00 8.00

2008 Donruss Elite Extra Edition Status

*STATUS 1-100: 4X TO 10X BASIC
*STATUS 101-200: .6X TO 1.5X ASP
STATED PRINT RUN 50 SER.#'d SETS
198 Derrick Rose 8.00 20.00
199 Michael Beasley 1.50 4.00
200 O.J. Mayo 6.00 15.00

2008 Donruss Elite Extra Edition School Colors

OVERALL INSERT ODDS 1:2
STATED PRINT RUN 1500 SER.#'d SET
4 O.J. Mayo 1.25 3.00
7 Michael Beasley 1.25 3.00
9 Derrick Rose 2.50 6.00

2008 Donruss Elite Extra Edition School Colors Autographs

OVERALL AUTO/MEM ODDS 1:5
PRINT RUNS B/WN 25-50 COPIES PER
NO PRICING ON QTY 25 OR LESS
EXCH DEADLINE 5/26/2010
4 O.J. Mayo/25 6.00 15.00
7 Michael Beasley/25 6.00 15.00
9 Derrick Rose/25 25.00 60.00

2008 Donruss Elite Extra Edition School Colors Materials

OVERALL AU/MEM ODDS 1:5
STATED PRINT RUN 100 SER.#'d SETS
4 O.J. Mayo 4.00 10.00
7 Michael Beasley 4.00 10.00
9 Derrick Rose 6.00 15.00

2008 Donruss Elite Extra Edition Signature Aspirations

OVERALL AUTO/MEM ODDS 1:5
PRINT RUN B/WN 5-100 COPIES PER
NO PRICING ON QTY 25 OR LESS
EXCH DEADLINE 5/26/2010
200 O.J. Mayo/25 6.00 15.00

2008 Donruss Elite Extra Edition Signature Status

OVERALL AUTO/MEM ODDS 1:5
PRINT RUN B/WN 5-50 COPIES PER
NO PRICING ON QTY 25 OR LESS
EXCH DEADLINE 5/26/2010

2008 Donruss Elite Extra Edition Signature Turn of the Century

OVERALL AUTO/MEM ODDS 1:5
PRINT RUNS B/WN 8-999 COPIES PER
EXCH DEADLINE 5/26/2010
198 Derrick Rose/25 25.00 60.00
199 Michael Beasley/25 6.00 15.00
200 O.J. Mayo/25 6.00 15.00

2008 Donruss Elite Extra Edition Throwback Threads

OVERALL AU/MEM ODDS 1:5
PRINT RUNS B/WN 15-500 COPIES PER
NO PRICING ON QTY 15 OR LESS
10 Derrick Rose/500 4.00 10.00
11 Michael Beasley/500 3.00 8.00
12 O.J. Mayo/400 3.00 8.00

2008 Donruss Elite Extra Edition Throwback Threads Prime

OVERALL AU/MEM ODDS 1:5
PRINT RUNS B/WN 1-50 COPIES PER
NO PRICING ON QTY 10 OR LESS

2008 Donruss Elite Extra Edition Throwback Threads Autographs

OVERALL AUTO/MEM ODDS 1:5
PRINT RUNS B/WN 4-100 COPIES PER
NO PRICING ON QTY 25 OR LESS
EXCH DEADLINE 5/26/2010
10 Derrick Rose/25 40.00 100.00
11 Michael Beasley/25 12.00 30.00
12 O.J. Mayo/25 6.00 15.00

2008 Donruss Elite Extra Edition Throwback Threads Autographs Prime

OVERALL AUTO/MEM ODDS 1:5
PRINT RUNS B/WN 1-25 COPIES PER
EXCH DEADLINE 5/26/2010

1996 Donruss Kazaam Promo

NNO Shaquille O'Neal
(as Kazaam) 1.50 4.00

2008 Donruss Sports Legends Signature Connection Triples

STATED PRINT RUN 25-250
1 Bird/Parish/McHale/25 150.00 250.00
3 Wdrd/Hyns/Gbsn/50 30.00 60.00

2008 Donruss Threads Diamond Kings

*GOLD: .6X TO 1.5X BASIC
GOLD PRINT RUN 100 SER.#'d SETS
FRM.BLK.PRINT RUN 10 SER.#'d SETS
NO FRM.BLK PRINCING AVAILABLE
*FRM.BLUE: .75X TO 2X BASIC
FRM.BLUE PRINT RUN 50 SER.#'d SETS
FRM.GRN.PRINT RUN 25 SER.#'d SETS
NO FRM.GRN PRINCING AVAILABLE
*FRM.RED: .6X TO 1.5X BASIC
FRM.RED PRINT RUN 100 SER.#'d SETS
PLAT.PRINT RUN 25 SER.#'d SETS
NO PLAT.PRINCING AVAILABLE
*SILVER: .5X TO 1.2X BASIC
SILVER PRINT RUN 250 SER.#'d SETS
53 Derrick Rose 1.50 4.00
54 Michael Beasley 1.50 4.00
55 O.J. Mayo 1.50 4.00

2008 Donruss Threads Diamond Kings Signatures

PRINT RUNS B/WN 5-500 COPIES PER
NO PRICING ON QTY 25 OR LESS
53 Derrick Rose/60 100.00 200.00

2023-24 Donruss Turkish Airlines EuroLeague

*PRESS PROOF SILVER: .75X TO 2X BASIC
1 Vanja Marinkovic .60 1.50
2 Rodrigue Beaubois .50 1.25
3 Matt Thomas .50 1.25
4 Konstantinos Mitoglou .60 1.50
5 Jordan Loyd .60 1.50
6 Shane Larkin .50 1.25
7 Elijah Bryant .50 1.25
8 Johannes Thiemann .50 1.25
9 Alpha Diallo .50 1.25
10 Matthew Costello .50 1.25
11 Khalifa Koumadje .50 1.25
12 Gabriele Procida .50 1.25
13 Will Clyburn .50 1.25
14 Elie Okobo .50 1.25
15 Luka Mitrovic .50 1.25
16 Justin Bean .50 1.25
17 Tibor Pleiss .50 1.25
18 Khalifa Diop .50 1.25
19 Tamir Blatt .50 1.25
20 Matteo Spagnolo .75 2.00
21 Donta Hall .60 1.50
22 Donatas Motiejunas .60 1.50
23 Markus Howard .60 1.50
24 Codi Miller-McIntyre .50 1.25
25 Darius Thompson .60 1.50
26 Sterling Brown .60 1.50
27 Kemba Walker .60 1.50
28 Billy Baron .50 1.25
29 Shaquielle McKissic .50 1.25
30 Walter Tavares .60 1.50
31 Isaiah Canaan .50 1.25
32 Achille Polonara .60 1.50
33 Kassius Robertson .50 1.25
34 Boris Dallo .50 1.25
35 Leandro Bolmaro .60 1.50
36 Bonzie Colson .60 1.50
37 Kostas Papanikolaou .60 1.50
39 Kyle Hines .50 1.25
40 Brady Manek .60 1.50
41 Giannoulis Larentzakis .50 1.25
42 Sylvain Francisco .50 1.25
43 Isaac Bonga .50 1.25
44 Alec Peters .50 1.25
45 Marco Belinelli .60 1.50
46 Mathias Lessort .75 2.00
47 Kostas Sloukas .75 2.00
48 Gabriel Deck .50 1.25
49 Nigel Williams-Goss .50 1.25
50 James Webb III .50 1.25
51 Jan Vesely .60 1.50
52 Edgaras Ulanovas .50 1.25
53 Perry Dozier Jr .60 1.50
54 Semi Ojeleye .60 1.50
55 Paris Lee .50 1.25
56 Bryant Dunston .50 1.25
57 Fabien Causeur .50 1.25
58 Thomas Walkup .60 1.50
59 John DiBartolomeo .50 1.25
60 Nikola Kalinic (BK) .50 1.25
61 James Nunnally .50 1.25
62 Luke Sikma .50 1.25
63 Ignas Brazdeikis .60 1.50
64 Victor Claver .50 1.25
65 Scottie Wilbekin .60 1.50
66 Ioannis Papapetrou .60 1.50
67 Brandon Davies .60 1.50
68 Alen Smailagic .60 1.50
69 Marius Grigonis .60 1.50
70 Guerschon Yabusele .60 1.50
71 Maodo Lo .60 1.50
72 Sergio Llull .60 1.50
73 Yam Madar .60 1.50
74 Nick Calathes .60 1.50
75 Tomas Satoransky .60 1.50
76 Zach LeDay .60 1.50
77 Wade Baldwin IV .60 1.50
78 Marko Guduric .60 1.50
79 Jabari Parker .60 1.50
80 Nando De Colo .60 1.50
81 Devontae Cacok .60 1.50
82 Kevin Punter .60 1.50
83 Kostas Antetokounmpo .60 1.50
84 Andreas Obst .60 1.50
85 Carsen Edwards .60 1.50
86 Joffrey Lauvergne .60 1.50
87 Justin Anderson .60 1.50
88 Sergio Rodriguez .60 1.50
89 Jordan Mickey .60 1.50
90 Mario Hezonja .60 1.50
91 Xabi Lopez-Arostegui .50 1.25
92 Facundo Campazzo .60 1.50
93 Willy Hernangomez .60 1.50
94 Sertac Sanli .50 1.25
95 Milos Teodosic .60 1.50
96 Vladimir Lucic .50 1.25
97 Chris Jones .50 1.25
98 Rokas Jokubaitis .60 1.50
99 Tyler Dorsey .60 1.50
100 Shabazz Napier .60 1.50
101 Keenan Evans .60 1.50
102 Iffe Lundberg .60 1.50
103 Rudy Fernandez .60 1.50
104 Nigel Hayes-Davis .60 1.50
105 Shavon Shields .60 1.50
106 Nikola Milutinov .60 1.50
107 Mike Scott .60 1.50
108 Nicolas Laprovittola .60 1.50
109 Alex Abrines .60 1.50
110 Lukas Lekavicius .50 1.25
111 Frank Kaminsky .60 1.50
112 Lorenzo Brown .50 1.25
113 Dzanan Musa .60 1.50
114 Jaleen Smith .50 1.25
115 Melih Mahmutoglu .50 1.25
116 Daniel Hackett .60 1.50
117 Nicolo Melli .60 1.50
118 Vincent Poirier .60 1.50
119 Luca Vildoza .50 1.25
120 Rokas Giedraitis .50 1.25
121 Kevin Pangos .50 1.25
122 Kevarrius Hayes .50 1.25
123 Moustapha Fall .50 1.25
124 Nemanja Nedovic .60 1.50
125 Tadas Sedekerskis .60 1.50
126 Kendrick Nunn .60 1.50
127 Yago Dos Santos .60 1.50
128 Mike James .60 1.50
129 Nikolaos Rogkavopoulos .50 1.25
130 Mike Tobey .50 1.25
131 Mateusz Ponitka .50 1.25
132 Juancho Hernangomez .75 2.00
133 Timothe Luwawu-Cabarrot .60 1.50
134 Dyshawn Pierre .50 1.25
135 Martin Hermannsson .50 1.25
136 Adam Hanga .50 1.25
137 James Nnaji .50 1.25
138 Marko Simonovic .60 1.50
139 Jared Harper .50 1.25
140 Chima Moneke .50 1.25
141 Jerian Grant .50 1.25
142 Jasiel Rivero .50 1.25
143 Tornike Shengelia .50 1.25
144 Naz Mitrou-Long .50 1.25
145 Tyrique Jones .50 1.25
146 Youssoupha Fall .60 1.50
147 David Lighty .50 1.25
148 Antonius Cleveland .60 1.50
149 Devon Hall .50 1.25
150 Georgios Papagiannis .50 1.25
151 Serge Ibaka .60 1.50
152 Aleksa Avramovic .60 1.50
153 Johannes Voigtmann .50 1.25
154 Johnathan Motley .60 1.50
155 Nikola Mirotic .60 1.50
156 Matteo Spagnolo RP 1.00 2.50
157 Omer Mayer RP 1.50 4.00
158 Ismaila Diagne RP .75 2.00
159 Nikola Topic RP 2.00 5.00
160 Alexandros Samontourov RP 1.00 2.50
161 Victor Wembanyama LEG 5.00 12.00
162 Antonis Fotsis LEG .50 1.25
163 Ramunas Siskauskas LEG .60 1.50
164 Alexey Shved LEG .50 1.25
165 Fragiskos Alvertis LEG .50 1.25
166 Luka Doncic LEG 4.00 10.00
167 Nikola Vujcic LEG .60 1.50
168 Bogdan Bogdanovic LEG .60 1.50
169 Kostas Tsartsaris LEG .50 1.25
170 Pau Gasol LEG 1.00 2.50
171 Andrey Vorontsevich LEG .50 1.25
172 Georgios Printezis LEG .60 1.50
173 Erazem Lorbek LEG .50 1.25
174 Theodoros Papaloukas LEG .50 1.25
175 JR Holden LEG .50 1.25
176 Andrei Kirilenko LEG .60 1.50
177 Felipe Reyes LEG .60 1.50
178 Dimitris Diamantidis LEG .60 1.50
179 Andres Nocioni LEG .60 1.50
180 Sasha Vezenkov LEG .50 1.25
181 David Andersen LEG .50 1.25
182 Tiago Splitter LEG .50 1.25
183 Mike Batiste LEG .60 1.50
184 Milos Vujanic LEG .50 1.25
185 Ekpe Udoh LEG .50 1.25
186 Trajan Langdon LEG .50 1.25
187 Tyrese Rice LEG .50 1.25
188 Ricky Rubio LEG .60 1.50
189 Juan Carlos Navarro LEG .60 1.50
190 Matjaz Smodis LEG .50 1.25
191 Sofoklis Schortsanitis LEG .50 1.25
192 Vassilis Spanoulis LEG .60 1.50
193 Viktor Khryapa LEG .50 1.25
194 Vasilije Micic LEG .60 1.50
195 Paulius Jankunas LEG .50 1.25
196 Walter Tavares FT .60 1.50
197 Mathias Lessort FT .75 2.00
198 Lorenzo Brown FT .50 1.25
199 Dzanan Musa FT .60 1.50
200 Sasha Vezenkov FT .50 1.25

2023-24 Donruss Turkish Airlines EuroLeague Holo Laser

*HOLO LASER: 1.5X TO 4X BASIC
STATED PRINT RUN 149 SER.#'d SETS
161 Victor Wembanyama LEG 60.00 150.00

2023-24 Donruss Turkish Airlines EuroLeague Neon Green Flood

*NEON GREEN FLOOD: 5X TO 12X BASIC
STATED PRINT RUN 25 SER.#'d SETS
161 Victor Wembanyama LEG 300.00 600.00

2023-24 Donruss Turkish Airlines EuroLeague Press Proof Purple

*PRESS PROOF PURPLE: 1.25X TO 3X BASIC
STATED PRINT RUN 249 SER.#'d SETS
161 Victor Wembanyama LEG 50.00 120.00

2023-24 Donruss Turkish Airlines EuroLeague Purple Laser

*PURPLE LASER: 2X TO 5X BASIC
STATED PRINT RUN 99 SER.#'d SETS
161 Victor Wembanyama LEG 75.00 200.00

2023-24 Donruss Turkish Airlines EuroLeague Yellow Flood

*YELLOW FLOOD: 1X TO 2.5X BASIC
161 Victor Wembanyama LEG 30.00 80.00

2023-24 Donruss Turkish Airlines EuroLeague Club Edition

*PRESS PROOF: .75X TO 2X BASIC
*PURPLE LSR/99: 2X TO 5X BASIC
1 Thomas Walkup .75 2.00
2 Sterling Brown .75 2.00
3 Perry Dozier Jr .75 2.00
4 Facundo Campazzo .75 2.00
5 Kemba Walker .75 2.00
6 Will Clyburn .60 1.50
7 Wade Baldwin IV .60 1.50
8 Markus Howard .75 2.00
9 Johnathan Motley .75 2.00
10 Shabazz Napier .75 2.00
11 Nikola Mirotic .75 2.00
12 Willy Hernangomez .75 2.00
13 Carsen Edwards .75 2.00
14 Timothe Luwawu-Cabarrot .75 2.00
15 Kostas Sloukas 1.00 2.50
16 Chris Jones .60 1.50
17 Marco Belinelli .75 2.00
18 Keenan Evans .75 2.00

2023-24 Donruss Turkish Airlines EuroLeague Crunch Time

*PRESS PROOF: .75X TO 2X BASIC
*PURPLE LSR/99: 2X TO 5X BASIC
1 Walter Tavares .75 2.00
2 Kemba Walker .75 2.00
3 Juancho Hernangomez 1.00 2.50
4 Mike James .75 2.00
5 Frank Kaminsky .75 2.00
6 Shabazz Napier .75 2.00
7 Will Clyburn .60 1.50
8 Nikola Mirotic .75 2.00
9 Nikola Milutinov .75 2.00
10 Kostas Sloukas 1.00 2.50
11 Willy Hernangomez .75 2.00
12 Wade Baldwin IV .60 1.50
13 Kevin Punter .75 2.00
14 Jabari Parker .75 2.00
15 Shane Larkin .60 1.50
16 Carsen Edwards .75 2.00
17 Facundo Campazzo .75 2.00
18 Lorenzo Brown .60 1.50
19 Keenan Evans .75 2.00
20 Chris Jones .60 1.50

2023-24 Donruss Turkish Airlines EuroLeague Dominators Signatures

*PURPLE LSR/25: 1X TO 2.5X BASIC
1 Jordan Loyd 5.00 12.00
2 Keenan Evans 5.00 12.00
3 Balsa Koprivica 5.00 12.00
4 Alpha Diallo 4.00 10.00
5 Mike James 15.00 40.00
7 Brady Manek 5.00 12.00
8 Andrea Bargnani 5.00 12.00
9 Juancho Hernangomez 15.00 40.00
10 Wade Baldwin IV 4.00 10.00
11 Billy Baron 4.00 10.00
12 Perry Dozier Jr 5.00 12.00
13 Uros Trifunovic 5.00 12.00
14 Paris Lee 4.00 10.00
15 Shaquielle McKissic 4.00 10.00
16 Marko Simonovic 5.00 12.00
17 Andreas Obst 5.00 12.00
18 Kyle Hines 4.00 10.00
19 Yam Madar 5.00 12.00
20 Vanja Marinkovic 8.00 20.00

2023-24 Donruss Turkish Airlines EuroLeague EuroLeague Leaders

*PRESS PROOF: .75X TO 2X BASIC
*PURPLE LSR/99: 2X TO 5X BASIC
1 Sasha Vezenkov .60 1.50
2 Darius Thompson .75 2.00
3 Markus Howard .75 2.00
4 Mathias Lessort 1.00 2.50
5 Walter Tavares .75 2.00

2023-24 Donruss Turkish Airlines EuroLeague Highlights

*PRESS PROOF: .75X TO 2X BASIC
*PURPLE LSR/99: 2X TO 5X BASIC
1 Luka Doncic 5.00 12.00
2 Sergio Llull .75 2.00
3 Vasilije Micic .75 2.00
4 Vassilis Spanoulis .75 2.00
5 Dimitris Diamantidis .75 2.00

2023-24 Donruss Turkish Airlines EuroLeague Net Marvels

*PRESS PROOF: .75X TO 2X BASIC
*PURPLE LSR/99: 2X TO 5X BASIC
1 Victor Wembanyama 15.00 40.00
2 Darius Thompson 1.00 2.50
3 Donta Hall 1.00 2.50
4 Jordan Loyd 1.00 2.50
5 Yago Dos Santos 1.00 2.50
6 Nicolo Melli 1.00 2.50
7 Jan Vesely 1.00 2.50
8 Walter Tavares 1.00 2.50
9 Jabari Parker 1.00 2.50
10 Serge Ibaka 1.00 2.50
11 Shabazz Napier 1.00 2.50
12 Leandro Bolmaro 1.00 2.50
13 Johnathan Motley 1.00 2.50
14 Nikola Milutinov 1.00 2.50
15 Juancho Hernangomez 1.25 3.00
16 Frank Kaminsky 1.00 2.50
17 Sergio Rodriguez 1.00 2.50
18 Daniel Hackett 1.00 2.50
19 Ricky Rubio 1.00 2.50
20 Ramunas Siskauskas 1.00 2.50
21 Nikola Vujcic 1.00 2.50
22 Georgios Printezis 1.00 2.50
23 Vasilije Micic 1.00 2.50
24 Mike Batiste 1.00 2.50
25 Luka Doncic 6.00 15.00

2023-24 Donruss Turkish Airlines EuroLeague Night Moves

1 Sterling Brown 12.00 30.00
2 Will Clyburn 10.00 25.00
3 Markus Howard 12.00 30.00
4 Luka Doncic 80.00 200.00
5 Luka Mitrovic 10.00 25.00
6 Tomas Satoransky 12.00 30.00
7 Carsen Edwards 12.00 30.00
8 Pau Gasol 20.00 50.00
9 Nick Calathes 12.00 30.00
10 Kemba Walker 12.00 30.00
11 Victor Wembanyama 350.00 700.00
12 Nikola Mirotic 12.00 30.00
13 Dzanan Musa 12.00 30.00
14 Wade Baldwin IV 10.00 25.00
15 Mathias Lessort 15.00 40.00
16 Perry Dozier Jr 12.00 30.00
17 Facundo Campazzo 12.00 30.00
18 Thomas Walkup 12.00 30.00
19 Tornike Shengelia 12.00 30.00
20 Nemanja Nedovic 12.00 30.00
21 Dimitris Diamantidis 12.00 30.00
22 Tiago Splitter 10.00 25.00
23 Andrei Kirilenko 12.00 30.00
24 Vassilis Spanoulis 12.00 30.00
25 Bogdan Bogdanovic 12.00 30.00

2023-24 Donruss Turkish Airlines EuroLeague Reigning 3s

*PRESS PROOF: .75X TO 2X BASIC
*PURPLE LSR/99: 2X TO 5X BASIC
1 Markus Howard .75 2.00
2 Andreas Obst .75 2.00
3 Vasilije Micic .75 2.00
4 Mike James .75 2.00
5 Scottie Wilbekin .75 2.00
6 Kevin Punter .75 2.00
7 Milos Teodosic .75 2.00
8 Mario Hezonja .75 2.00
9 Juan Carlos Navarro .75 2.00
10 Dimitris Diamantidis .75 2.00
11 Vassilis Spanoulis .75 2.00
12 Sasha Vezenkov .60 1.50

2023-24 Donruss Turkish Airlines EuroLeague Retro Series

*PRESS PROOF: .75X TO 2X BASIC
*PURPLE LSR/99: 2X TO 5X BASIC
1 Luka Doncic 5.00 12.00
2 Sasha Vezenkov .60 1.50
3 Pau Gasol 1.25 3.00
4 Juan Carlos Navarro .75 2.00
5 Vasilije Micic .75 2.00
6 Rudy Fernandez .75 2.00
7 Sofoklis Schortsanitis .60 1.50
8 Andrei Kirilenko .75 2.00
9 Mike Batiste .75 2.00
10 Bogdan Bogdanovic .75 2.00
11 Ricky Rubio .75 2.00
12 Dimitris Diamantidis .75 2.00
13 Theodoros Papaloukas .60 1.50

14 Vassilis Spanoulis .75 2.00
15 Tiago Splitter .60 1.50

2023-24 Donruss Turkish Airlines EuroLeague Retro Series Signatures

*PURPLE LSR/25: 1X TO 2.5X BASIC
1 Xabi Lopez-Arostegui 5.00 12.00
2 Daniel Hackett 6.00 15.00
3 Brandon Davies 5.00 12.00
4 Marko Simonovic 6.00 15.00
5 Khalifa Diop 5.00 12.00
6 Mario Hezonja 6.00 15.00
7 Shabazz Napier 6.00 15.00
8 Khalifa Koumadje 5.00 12.00
9 Maik Kotsar 10.00 25.00
10 Mateusz Ponitka 5.00 12.00
11 Kevarrius Hayes 5.00 12.00
12 Matt Thomas 5.00 12.00
13 Alen Smailagic 6.00 15.00
14 Bonzie Colson 6.00 15.00
15 Sertac Sanli 5.00 12.00
16 Zach LeDay 6.00 15.00
17 Joffrey Lauvergne 6.00 15.00
18 Victor Claver 5.00 12.00
19 Nigel Williams-Goss 5.00 12.00
20 Darius Thompson 6.00 15.00

2023-24 Donruss Turkish Airlines EuroLeague Signature Series

*PURPLE LSR/25: 1X TO 2.5X BASIC
1 Sterling Brown 6.00 15.00
2 Shavon Shields 5.00 12.00
3 Jabari Parker 6.00 15.00
4 Keith Langford 5.00 12.00
5 James Nunnally 5.00 12.00
6 Jared Harper 6.00 15.00
8 Jerian Grant 6.00 15.00
9 Codi Miller-McIntyre 5.00 12.00
11 Krunoslav Simon 6.00 15.00
12 Sergio Rodriguez 6.00 15.00
13 Kevin Punter 6.00 15.00
14 Thomas Walkup 6.00 15.00
15 Frank Kaminsky 6.00 15.00
16 Mathias Lessort 8.00 20.00
17 Devon Hall 5.00 12.00
18 Nando De Colo 6.00 15.00
19 Jan Vesely 6.00 15.00
20 Carsen Edwards 6.00 15.00
21 Tamir Blatt 5.00 12.00
22 Donatas Motiejunas 6.00 15.00
23 Scottie Wilbekin 6.00 15.00
24 Josh Nebo 5.00 12.00
25 Paulius Jankunas 5.00 12.00
26 Johannes Thiemann 5.00 12.00
27 Yam Madar 6.00 15.00
28 Stratos Perperoglou 6.00 15.00
29 Isaac Bonga 5.00 12.00
30 Marco Belinelli 6.00 15.00
31 Bryant Dunston 5.00 12.00
32 Semi Ojeleye 6.00 15.00
33 Luca Vildoza 6.00 15.00
34 Elijah Bryant 5.00 12.00
35 Boris Dallo 5.00 12.00
36 Khalifa Diop 5.00 12.00
37 Nicolo Melli 6.00 15.00
38 Leandro Bolmaro 6.00 15.00
39 Marko Guduric 6.00 15.00
40 Kevin Pangos 5.00 12.00
41 Marko Simonovic 6.00 15.00
42 Markus Howard 6.00 15.00
43 Vladimir Lucic 5.00 12.00
44 Maik Kotsar 8.00 20.00
45 Mike Batiste 6.00 15.00
46 Will Clyburn 6.00 15.00
47 Johnathan Motley 6.00 15.00
48 Chris Jones 5.00 12.00
49 Justin Bean 5.00 12.00
50 Matthew Costello 5.00 12.00

2019 Donruss WNBA

*PRESS PROOF SILVER/199: 2X TO 5X BASIC
*PRESS PROOF PURPLE/99: 2.5X TO 6X BASIC
1 Angel McCoughtry .50 1.25
2 Chelsea Gray .50 1.25
3 Kelsey Mitchell .75 2.00
4 Jordin Canada .40 1.00
5 Shavonte Zellous .40 1.00
6 Morgan Tuck .40 1.00
7 Sylvia Fowles .50 1.25
8 Yvonne Turner .40 1.00
9 A'ja Wilson 1.50 4.00
10 Cheyenne Parker .40 1.00
11 Brittney Sykes .75 2.00
12 Essence Carson .30 .75
13 Natalie Achonwa .40 1.00
14 Kaleena Mosqueda-Lewis .25 .60
15 Sugar Rodgers .40 1.00
16 Shekinna Stricklen .25 .60
17 Tanisha Wright .40 1.00
18 Ariel Atkins .50 1.25
19 Carolyn Swords .30 .75
20 Courtney Vandersloot .50 1.25
21 Elizabeth Williams .40 1.00
22 Nneka Ogwumike .60 1.50
23 Tiffany Mitchell .50 1.25
24 Natasha Howard .50 1.25
25 Tina Charles .75 2.00
26 Allisha Gray .60 1.50
27 Briann January .30 .75
28 Elena Delle Donne 1.25 3.00
29 Kayla McBride .50 1.25
30 Diamond DeShields .40 1.00
31 Jessica Breland .30 .75
32 Odyssey Sims .40 1.00
33 Victoria Vivians .50 1.25
34 Sue Bird 1.50 4.00
35 Cecilia Zandalasini .40 1.00
36 Azura Stevens .40 1.00
37 Brittney Griner 1.25 3.00
38 Kristi Toliver .40 1.00
39 Kelsey Bone .30 .75
40 Gabby Williams .50 1.25
41 Renee Montgomery .30 .75
42 Riquna Williams .40 1.00
43 Bria Hartley .30 .75
44 Alyssa Thomas .75 2.00
45 Danielle Robinson .30 .75
46 Glory Johnson .40 1.00
47 DeWanna Bonner .60 1.50
48 LaToya Sanders .40 1.00
49 Kelsey Plum 1.00 2.50
50 Jamierra Faulkner .30 .75
51 Tiffany Hayes .40 1.00
52 Alysha Clark .30 .75
53 Brittany Boyd .40 1.00
54 Chiney Ogwumike .40 1.00
55 Karima Christmas-Kelly .40 1.00
56 Kaela Davis .40 1.00
57 Diana Taurasi 1.50 4.00
58 Tianna Hawkins .25 .60
59 Nia Coffey .40 1.00
60 Stefanie Dolson .40 1.00
61 Candice Dupree .40 1.00
62 Breanna Stewart 1.50 4.00
63 Epiphanny Prince .30 .75
64 Courtney Williams .40 1.00
65 Erlana Larkins .30 .75
66 Kayla Thornton .40 1.00
67 Leilani Mitchell .30 .75
68 Natasha Cloud .50 1.25
69 Tamera Young .40 1.00
70 Alana Beard .40 1.00
71 Cappie Pondexter .50 1.25
72 Crystal Langhorne .30 .75
73 Kia Nurse .50 1.25
74 Jasmine Thomas .40 1.00
75 Rebekkah Brunson .40 1.00
76 Liz Cambage .50 1.25
77 Sancho Lyttle .30 .75
78 Tierra Ruffin-Pratt .30 .75
79 Alex Bentley .40 1.00
80 Candace Parker 1.00 2.50
81 Erica Wheeler .40 1.00
82 Jewell Loyd .75 2.00
83 Kia Vaughn .40 1.00
84 Jonquel Jones 1.00 2.50
85 Seimone Augustus .60 1.50
86 Skylar Diggins-Smith .75 2.00
87 Stephanie Talbot .40 1.00
88 Allie Quigley .30 .75
89 Kristine Anigwe RC 1.00 2.50
90 Jackie Young RC 5.00 12.00
91 Kiara Leslie RC 1.00 2.50
92 Teaira McCowan RC .75 2.00
93 Arike Ogunbowale RC 4.00 10.00
94 Han Xu RC 1.50 4.00
95 Napheesa Collier RC 15.00 40.00
96 Asia Durr RC 1.00 2.50
97 Kalani Brown RC 1.00 2.50
98 Katie Lou Samuelson RC 2.00 5.00
99 Alanna Smith RC 2.00 5.00
100 Brianna Turner RC 1.25 3.00

2019 Donruss WNBA All-Stars

*PRESS PROOF/199: 1.5X TO 4X BASIC
*PRESS PROOF PURPLE/99: 2X TO 5X BASIC
1 Candace Parker 1.00 2.50
2 Liz Cambage .50 1.25
3 Angel McCoughtry .50 1.25
4 Chelsea Gray .50 1.25
5 Skylar Diggins-Smith .75 2.00
6 Chiney Ogwumike .40 1.00
7 Allie Quigley .30 .75
8 Jewell Loyd .75 2.00
9 Tina Charles .75 2.00
10 Rebekkah Brunson .40 1.00
11 Elena Delle Donne 1.25 3.00
12 Breanna Stewart 1.50 4.00
13 Sylvia Fowles .50 1.25
14 Diana Taurasi 1.50 4.00
15 Sue Bird 1.50 4.00
16 Kristi Toliver .40 1.00
17 Kayla McBride .50 1.25
18 DeWanna Bonner .60 1.50
19 Seimone Augustus .60 1.50
20 Brittney Griner 1.25 3.00
21 A'ja Wilson 1.50 4.00
22 Maya Moore 1.00 2.50

2019 Donruss WNBA Express Lane

*PRESS PROOF/199: 1.5X TO 4X BASIC
*PRESS PROOF PURPLE/99: 2X TO 5X BASIC
1 Lynette Woodard .60 1.50
2 Brittany Boyd .40 1.00
3 Teresa Edwards .60 1.50
4 Natasha Cloud .50 1.25
5 Danielle Robinson .30 .75
6 Courtney Vandersloot .50 1.25
7 Cynthia Cooper-Dyke .60 1.50
8 Skylar Diggins-Smith .75 2.00
9 Katie Smith .50 1.25
10 Chelsea Gray .50 1.25
11 Nancy Lieberman .75 2.00
12 Kristi Toliver .40 1.00
13 Allie Quigley .30 .75
14 Jordin Canada .40 1.00
15 Becky Hammon 1.00 2.50
16 Sue Bird 1.50 4.00
17 Cappie Pondexter .50 1.25
18 Diana Taurasi 1.50 4.00
19 Lindsay Whalen .50 1.25
20 Jasmine Thomas .40 1.00
21 Sheryl Swoopes 1.00 2.50
22 Erica Wheeler .40 1.00

2019 Donruss WNBA Franchise Features

*PRESS PROOF/199: 1.5X TO 4X BASIC
*PRESS PROOF PURPLE/99: 2X TO 5X BASIC
1 Sylvia Fowles .50 1.25
2 Diana Taurasi 1.50 4.00
3 Elena Delle Donne 1.25 3.00
4 Tina Charles .75 2.00
5 Breanna Stewart 1.50 4.00
6 Tiffany Hayes .40 1.00
7 Skylar Diggins-Smith .75 2.00
8 Allie Quigley .30 .75
9 Candice Dupree .40 1.00
10 Candace Parker 1.00 2.50
11 A'ja Wilson 1.50 4.00
12 Jasmine Thomas .40 1.00

2019 Donruss WNBA League Leaders

*PRESS PROOF/199: 1.5X TO 4X BASIC
*PRESS PROOF PURPLE/99: 2X TO 5X BASIC
1 Liz Cambage .50 1.25
2 Sylvia Fowles .50 1.25
3 Courtney Vandersloot .50 1.25
4 Maya Moore 1.00 2.50
5 Brittney Griner 1.25 3.00
6 Diana Taurasi 1.50 4.00
7 Briann January .30 .75
8 Diana Taurasi 1.50 4.00
9 Skylar Diggins-Smith .75 2.00
10 Sylvia Fowles .50 1.25

2019 Donruss WNBA Retro Series

*PRESS PROOF/199: 1.5X TO 4X BASIC
*PRESS PROOF PURPLE/99: 2X TO 5X BASIC
1 Rebecca Lobo .75 2.00
2 Cynthia Cooper-Dyke .60 1.50
3 Ticha Penicheiro .50 1.25
4 Lynette Woodard .60 1.50
5 Nancy Lieberman .75 2.00
6 Sheryl Swoopes 1.00 2.50
7 Becky Hammon 1.00 2.50
8 Teresa Edwards .60 1.50
9 Tamika Catchings .60 1.50
10 Katie Smith .50 1.25
11 Lindsay Whalen .50 1.25
12 Lisa Leslie 1.00 2.50

2019 Donruss WNBA Signature Series

*PRESS PROOF/99-199: .5X TO 1.2X BASIC
*PRESS PROOF PURPLE/49-99: .6X TO 1.5X BASIC
1 Rebecca Lobo 10.00 25.00
2 A'ja Wilson 50.00 120.00
3 Alana Beard 5.00 12.00
4 Tamika Catchings 8.00 20.00
5 Angel McCoughtry 6.00 15.00
6 Breanna Stewart 20.00 50.00
7 Brittney Griner 15.00 40.00
8 Candace Parker 12.00 30.00
9 Candice Dupree 5.00 12.00
10 Cappie Pondexter 6.00 15.00
11 Chelsea Gray 6.00 15.00
12 Chiney Ogwumike 5.00 12.00
13 Courtney Vandersloot 6.00 15.00
14 DeWanna Bonner 8.00 20.00
15 Diana Taurasi 20.00 50.00
16 Elena Delle Donne 15.00 40.00
17 Jewell Loyd 10.00 25.00
18 Kayla McBride 6.00 15.00
19 Kristi Toliver 5.00 12.00
20 Liz Cambage 6.00 15.00
21 Maya Moore 12.00 30.00
22 Nneka Ogwumike 8.00 20.00
23 Rebekkah Brunson 5.00 12.00
24 Seimone Augustus 8.00 20.00
25 Skylar Diggins-Smith 10.00 25.00
26 Sue Bird 20.00 50.00
27 Sylvia Fowles 6.00 15.00
28 Teresa Edwards 8.00 20.00
29 Tina Charles 10.00 25.00
30 Becky Hammon 12.00 30.00
31 Cheryl Miller 12.00 30.00
32 Cynthia Cooper-Dyke 8.00 20.00
34 Nancy Lieberman 10.00 25.00
35 Sheryl Swoopes 12.00 30.00
36 Ticha Penicheiro 6.00 15.00
37 Katie Smith 6.00 15.00
38 Lynette Woodard 8.00 20.00
39 Lindsay Whalen 6.00 15.00
40 Jackie Young 30.00 80.00
41 Asia Durr 6.00 15.00
42 Arike Ogunbowale 20.00 50.00
43 Lisa Leslie 12.00 30.00

2019 Donruss WNBA Swishful Thinking

*PRESS PROOF/199: 1.5X TO 4X BASIC
*PRESS PROOF PURPLE/99: 2X TO 5X BASIC
1 Renee Montgomery .30 .75
2 Diana Taurasi 1.50 4.00
3 Victoria Vivians .50 1.25
4 Jewell Loyd .75 2.00
5 Kelsey Mitchell .75 2.00
6 Briann January .30 .75
7 Kristi Toliver .40 1.00
8 Allie Quigley .30 .75
9 Breanna Stewart 1.50 4.00
10 Skylar Diggins-Smith .75 2.00
11 Sue Bird 1.50 4.00
12 Elena Delle Donne 1.25 3.00

2019 Donruss WNBA The Rookies

*PRESS PROOF/199: 1.5X TO 4X BASIC
*PRESS PROOF PURPLE/99: 2X TO 5X BASIC
1 Asia Durr 1.00 2.50
2 Kristine Anigwe 1.00 2.50
3 Katie Lou Samuelson 2.00 5.00
4 Teaira McCowan .75 2.00
5 Arike Ogunbowale 4.00 10.00
6 Han Xu 1.50 4.00
7 Napheesa Collier 12.00 30.00
8 Kalani Brown 1.00 2.50
9 Jackie Young 5.00 12.00
10 Alanna Smith 2.00 5.00

1990 88's Calgary WBL

COMPLETE SET (24) 15.00 40.00
1 David Boone .60 1.50
2 Scott Hicks .60 1.50
3 Dwayne McClain 1.25 3.00
4 Chip Engelland (Driving to hoop) 2.00 5.00
5 Perry Young 1.25 3.00
6 Chip Engelland 1.50 4.00
7 Steve Smith .60 1.50
8 Jim Thomas (Setting up play) .75 2.00
9 George Jackson (Dunking) .60 1.50
10 George Jackson .60 1.50
11 Perry Young .60 1.50
12 Carlos Clark (Dribbling) 1.25 3.00
13 Dave Henderson (Shooting) .60 1.50
14 Carlos Clark 1.25 3.00
15 John Hegwood .60 1.50
16 Perry Young (Shooting) .60 1.50
17 Chip Engelland (Shooting) 1.50 4.00
18 Sean Chambers .60 1.50
19 Carlos Clark (Shooting) 1.25 3.00
20 1989 WBL Playoffs (Jim Thomas) .75 2.00
21 1989 WBL Playoffs (Final Standings on back) .60 1.50
22 Jim Thomas .75 2.00
23 Team Photo .60 1.50
24 Perry Young (Rebounding) .60 1.50

2012-13 Elite

COMPLETE SET (300) 75.00 200.00
COMP.SET w/o RCs (200) 20.00 50.00
RC PRINT RUN 599 SER.#'d SETS
1 Kobe Bryant 3.00 8.00
2 Kevin Durant 1.50 4.00
3 Dwyane Wade .75 2.00
4 Dirk Nowitzki 1.00 2.50
5 Carmelo Anthony .60 1.50
6 LeBron James 3.00 8.00
7 Derrick Rose .60 1.50
8 Kevin Love .40 1.00
9 Blake Griffin .40 1.00
10 Deron Williams .30 .75
11 Dwight Howard .50 1.25
12 Tim Duncan 1.00 2.50
13 Marcin Gortat .25 .60
14 Paul George .60 1.50
15 Chauncey Billups .50 1.25
16 Devin Harris .25 .60
17 John Salmons .30 .75
18 Andrew Bynum .25 .60
19 Toney Douglas .25 .60
20 Charlie Villanueva .25 .60
21 Mike Conley .30 .75
22 Nate Robinson .25 .60
23 Luke Babbitt .25 .60
24 Beno Udrih .25 .60
25 Andrew Bogut .30 .75
26 Raymond Felton .25 .60
27 Hedo Turkoglu .25 .60
28 James Harden .75 2.00
29 Linas Kleiza .25 .60
30 Danilo Gallinari .25 .60
31 Jason Terry .30 .75
32 Elton Brand .30 .75
33 Pau Gasol .60 1.50
34 Carlos Boozer .30 .75
35 Travis Outlaw .25 .60
36 Rodney Stuckey .25 .60
37 Ray Allen .60 1.50
38 Cory Higgins .25 .60
39 Brook Lopez .30 .75
40 Al Horford .40 1.00
41 Jermaine O'Neal .30 .75
42 Danny Granger .25 .60
43 Steve Nash .75 2.00
44 Jason Richardson .40 1.00
45 J.J. Barea .30 .75
46 Darren Collison .25 .60
47 Ed Davis .25 .60
48 Marc Gasol .40 1.00
49 Ekpe Udoh .25 .60
50 Manu Ginobili .75 2.00
51 Rasheed Wallace .50 1.25
52 Stephen Curry 3.00 8.00
53 Tayshaun Prince .40 1.00
54 Aaron Brooks .25 .60
55 Joakim Noah .30 .75
56 J.J. Redick .40 1.00
57 Caron Butler .30 .75
58 Brandon Bass .25 .60
59 Hakim Warrick .25 .60
60 Jordan Hill .25 .60
61 Omri Casspi .25 .60
62 Serge Ibaka .30 .75
63 Tyler Hansbrough .25 .60
64 Paul Millsap .30 .75
65 Chris Bosh .50 1.25
66 Gerald Wallace .25 .60
67 Vince Carter .75 2.00
68 Kyle Korver .30 .75
69 Luis Scola .30 .75
70 Luol Deng .30 .75
71 Andre Iguodala .40 1.00
72 Chase Budinger .25 .60
73 Greg Monroe .25 .60
74 Rudy Gay .40 1.00
75 Carl Landry .25 .60
76 Tyson Chandler .30 .75
77 Brandon Jennings .25 .60
78 J.J. Hickson .25 .60
79 Evan Turner .25 .60
80 Tyrus Thomas .25 .60
81 O.J. Mayo .25 .60
82 George Hill .30 .75
83 Al Jefferson .30 .75
84 Kyle Lowry .40 1.00
85 Avery Bradley .25 .60
86 Carlos Delfino .25 .60
87 Jameer Nelson .25 .60
88 Jonas Jerebko .25 .60
89 Richard Jefferson .30 .75
90 Josh Smith .30 .75
91 Kendrick Perkins .25 .60
92 Daniel Gibson .25 .60
93 Shane Battier .30 .75
94 Danny Green .30 .75
95 Kirk Hinrich .30 .75
96 Andrei Kirilenko .30 .75
97 Ersan Ilyasova .25 .60
98 Grant Hill .60 1.50
99 Jason Kidd .60 1.50
100 Ty Lawson .25 .60
101 Antawn Jamison .25 .60
102 Kevin Garnett 1.00 2.50
103 Gordon Hayward .40 1.00
104 Al Harrington .30 .75
105 Jrue Holiday .50 1.25
106 Zach Randolph .40 1.00
107 Joe Johnson .30 .75
108 Shawn Marion .40 1.00
109 Mario Chalmers .30 .75
110 Robin Lopez .25 .60
111 Roy Hibbert .40 1.00
112 Nicolas Batum .30 .75
113 Stephen Jackson .30 .75
114 DeShawn Stevenson .25 .60
115 Brandon Roy .30 .75
116 DeMar DeRozan .50 1.25
117 Thabo Sefolosha .25 .60
118 Monta Ellis .30 .75
119 Jeremy Lin .60 1.50
120 Francisco Garcia .25 .60
121 Austin Daye .25 .60
122 Metta World Peace .30 .75
123 Ramon Sessions .25 .60
124 Andre Miller .30 .75
125 David Lee .30 .75
126 Richard Hamilton .40 1.00
127 Derrick Favors .30 .75
128 DeAndre Jordan .30 .75
129 Udonis Haslem .30 .75
130 Goran Dragic .40 1.00
131 Amare Stoudemire .40 1.00
132 Tony Parker .60 1.50
133 Glen Davis .25 .60
134 Marreese Speights .25 .60
135 C.J. Miles .25 .60
136 Eric Gordon .30 .75
137 Louis Williams .30 .75
138 Chris Kaman .30 .75
139 Thaddeus Young .25 .60
140 Wesley Matthews .25 .60
141 Mike Dunleavy .25 .60
142 Tyreke Evans .30 .75
143 Paul Pierce .60 1.50
144 Timofey Mozgov .25 .60
145 Lamar Odom .30 .75
146 Kris Humphries .25 .60
147 Jose Calderon .25 .60
148 Omer Asik .25 .60
149 Russell Westbrook .60 1.50
150 Rashard Lewis .40 1.00
151 Michael Beasley .25 .60
152 David West .30 .75
153 Ricky Rubio .30 .75
154 Brendan Haywood .25 .60
155 Jodie Meeks .25 .60
156 Tiago Splitter .25 .60
157 Will Bynum .25 .60
158 DeMarcus Cousins .40 1.00
159 Brandon Rush .25 .60
160 Samuel Dalembert .25 .60
161 Arron Afflalo .25 .60
162 Chris Paul .75 2.00
163 Taj Gibson .25 .60
164 Tony Allen .25 .60
165 Raja Bell .30 .75
166 Anderson Varejao .25 .60
167 LaMarcus Aldridge .40 1.00
168 Lance Stephenson .30 .75
169 Anthony Randolph .30 .75
170 Jerry Stackhouse .30 .75
171 Ryan Anderson .25 .60
172 Ben Gordon .30 .75
173 Andrea Bargnani .25 .60
174 Kevin Martin .30 .75
175 Rajon Rondo .50 1.25
176 Wilt Chamberlain 1.25 3.00
177 Bill Russell 1.25 3.00
178 Oscar Robertson .75 2.00
179 Magic Johnson 1.25 3.00
180 Larry Bird 1.25 3.00
181 Julius Erving 1.00 2.50
182 Pete Maravich .75 2.00
183 Scottie Pippen 1.00 2.50
184 Shaquille O'Neal 1.25 3.00
185 Patrick Ewing .60 1.50
186 Clyde Drexler .60 1.50
187 John Stockton .75 2.00
188 Allen Iverson .60 1.50
189 Dominique Wilkins .50 1.25
190 Kareem Abdul-Jabbar 1.25 3.00
191 Gary Payton .50 1.25
192 George Gervin .60 1.50
193 Dennis Rodman 1.00 2.50
194 David Thompson .40 1.00
195 Karl Malone .60 1.50
196 Robert Parish .60 1.50
197 Alonzo Mourning .60 1.50
198 Isiah Thomas .75 2.00
199 David Robinson .60 1.50
200 Jerry West .75 2.00
201 Kyrie Irving RC 8.00 20.00
202 Derrick Williams RC .75 2.00
203 Enes Kanter RC 1.25 3.00
204 Tristan Thompson RC 1.25 3.00
205 Jonas Valanciunas RC 1.50 4.00
206 Jan Vesely RC .60 1.50
207 Bismack Biyombo RC 1.00 2.50
208 Brandon Knight RC 1.00 2.50
209 Kemba Walker RC 3.00 8.00
210 Jimmer Fredette RC 1.25 3.00
211 Klay Thompson RC 30.00 80.00
212 Alec Burks RC 1.25 3.00
213 Markieff Morris RC 1.25 3.00
214 Marcus Morris RC 1.25 3.00
215 Kawhi Leonard RC 40.00 100.00
216 Nikola Vucevic RC 3.00 8.00
217 Iman Shumpert RC 1.00 2.50
218 Chris Singleton RC .75 2.00
219 Tobias Harris RC 2.50 6.00
220 Nolan Smith RC .75 2.00
221 Kenneth Faried RC 1.00 2.50
222 Reggie Jackson RC 1.25 3.00
223 MarShon Brooks RC .75 2.00
224 Pablo Prigioni RC .75 2.00
225 Norris Cole RC .75 2.00
226 Cory Joseph RC 1.00 2.50
227 Jimmy Butler RC 8.00 20.00
228 Mirza Teletovic RC 1.00 2.50
229 Kyle Singler RC .75 2.00
230 Tornike Shengelia RC .75 2.00
231 Tyler Honeycutt RC .75 2.00
232 Fab Melo RC .75 2.00
233 Trey Thompkins RC .75 2.00
234 Chandler Parsons RC 1.00 2.50
235 Jeremy Tyler RC .75 2.00
236 Jon Leuer RC .75 2.00
237 Darius Morris RC 1.00 2.50
238 Brian Roberts RC .75 2.00
239 Malcolm Lee RC .75 2.00
240 Charles Jenkins RC .75 2.00
241 Josh Harrellson RC .75 2.00
242 Alexey Shved RC .75 2.00
243 Josh Selby RC .75 2.00
244 Lavoy Allen RC .75 2.00
245 DeAndre Liggins RC .75 2.00
246 E'Twaun Moore RC 1.00 2.50
247 Isaiah Thomas RC 1.50 4.00
248 Ivan Johnson RC .75 2.00
249 Greg Stiemsma RC .75 2.00
250 Jeremy Pargo RC .75 2.00
251 Lance Thomas RC .75 2.00
252 Anthony Davis RC 40.00 100.00
253 Michael Kidd-Gilchrist RC 1.00 2.50
254 Bradley Beal RC 6.00 15.00
255 Dion Waiters RC 1.00 2.50
256 Thomas Robinson RC .75 2.00
257 Damian Lillard RC 40.00 100.00
258 Harrison Barnes RC 1.50 4.00
259 Terrence Ross RC 2.00 5.00
260 Andre Drummond RC 2.00 5.00
261 Austin Rivers RC 1.25 3.00
262 Meyers Leonard RC 1.00 2.50
263 Jeremy Lamb RC 1.25 3.00
264 Kendall Marshall RC .75 2.00
265 John Henson RC 1.00 2.50
266 Maurice Harkless RC 1.00 2.50
267 Royce White RC .75 2.00
268 Tyler Zeller RC .75 2.00
269 Terrence Jones RC .75 2.00
270 Andrew Nicholson RC .75 2.00
271 Evan Fournier RC 1.25 3.00
272 Jared Sullinger RC .75 2.00
273 Chris Copeland RC .75 2.00
274 John Jenkins RC .75 2.00
275 Jared Cunningham RC .75 2.00
276 Tony Wroten RC .75 2.00
277 Miles Plumlee RC .75 2.00
278 Arnett Moultrie RC .75 2.00
279 Perry Jones RC .75 2.00
280 Marquis Teague RC .75 2.00
281 Festus Ezeli RC .75 2.00
282 Jeff Taylor RC .75 2.00
283 Luke Zeller RC .75 2.00
284 Bernard James RC .75 2.00
285 Jae Crowder RC 1.50 4.00
286 Draymond Green RC 5.00 12.00
287 Orlando Johnson RC .75 2.00
288 Quincy Acy RC .75 2.00
289 Diante Garrett RC .75 2.00
290 Khris Middleton RC 4.00 10.00
291 Will Barton RC 1.50 4.00
292 Tyshawn Taylor RC .75 2.00
293 Doron Lamb RC .75 2.00
294 Mike Scott RC 1.00 2.50
295 Kim English RC .75 2.00
296 Darius Miller RC 1.00 2.50
297 Kevin Murphy RC .75 2.00
298 DeQuan Jones RC .75 2.00
299 Robert Sacre RC .75 2.00
300 Nando De Colo RC .75 2.00

2012-13 Elite Aspirations

*VETS: 3X TO 8X BASE HI
*ROOKIES: 1X TO 2.5X BASE HI
STATED PRINT RUN 6 TO 99 SER.#'d SETS
1 Kobe Bryant/76 40.00 100.00
2 Kevin Durant/65 15.00 40.00
6 LeBron James/94 100.00 250.00
98 Grant Hill/67 8.00 20.00
211 Klay Thompson/89 125.00 300.00

2012-13 Elite Status

*VETS P/R 30 AND LESS: 6X TO 15X BASE HI
*VETS P/R 31 AND MORE: 5X TO 12X BASE HI
*ROOKIES P/R 30 AND LESS: 2X TO 5X BASE HI
*ROOKIES P/R 31 AND MORE: 1.5X TO 4X BASE HI
STATED PRINT RUN ONE TO 94 SER.#'d SETS
1 Kobe Bryant/24 30.00 80.00
2 Kevin Durant/35 20.00 50.00
12 Tim Duncan/21 12.00 30.00
37 Ray Allen/34 8.00 20.00
98 Grant Hill/33 10.00 25.00
111 Roy Hibbert/55 3.00 8.00
170 Jerry Stackhouse/42 12.00 30.00
182 Pete Maravich/44 20.00 50.00
183 Scottie Pippen/33 12.00 30.00
185 Patrick Ewing/33 20.00 50.00
271 Evan Fournier/94 5.00 12.00

2012-13 Elite Status Gold

*VETS: 6X TO 15X BASE HI
*ROOKIES: 2X TO 5X BASE HI
STATED PRINT RUN 24 SER.#'d SETS
1 Kobe Bryant 50.00 120.00
2 Kevin Durant 25.00 60.00
6 LeBron James 60.00 150.00
37 Ray Allen 8.00 20.00
98 Grant Hill 12.00 30.00
149 Russell Westbrook 12.00 30.00
153 Ricky Rubio 20.00 50.00
170 Jerry Stackhouse 15.00 40.00
183 Scottie Pippen 15.00 40.00
185 Patrick Ewing 20.00 50.00
187 John Stockton 15.00 40.00
188 Allen Iverson 15.00 40.00
215 Kawhi Leonard 300.00 600.00

2012-13 Elite All-Star Salute Materials

1 Kobe Bryant 25.00 60.00
2 Dwight Howard 4.00 10.00
3 Al Horford 3.00 8.00
4 Carmelo Anthony 5.00 12.00
5 Chris Paul 6.00 15.00
6 Rajon Rondo 4.00 10.00
7 Paul Pierce 5.00 12.00
8 Dwyane Wade 6.00 15.00
9 Blake Griffin 3.00 8.00
10 Russell Westbrook 5.00 12.00
11 Deron Williams 2.50 6.00
12 Kevin Love 3.00 8.00
13 Kevin Garnett 8.00 20.00
14 Derrick Rose 5.00 12.00
15 Manu Ginobili 6.00 15.00
16 Joe Johnson 2.50 6.00
17 Tim Duncan 8.00 20.00
18 Dirk Nowitzki 8.00 20.00
19 Kevin Durant 12.00 30.00
20 Ray Allen 5.00 12.00
21 Shaquille O'Neal 10.00 25.00
22 Chris Bosh 4.00 10.00
23 LeBron James 25.00 60.00
24 Amare Stoudemire 3.00 8.00
25 Zach Randolph 3.00 8.00

2012-13 Elite All-Star Salute Materials Prime

*PRIME: 1.5X TO 4X BASE HI
STATED PRINT RUN 25 SER.#'d SETS

2012-13 Elite All-Time Greats Signatures

STATED PRINT RUN 25 TO 199 SER.#'d SETS
1 Magic Johnson/49 40.00 100.00
2 Larry Bird/49 40.00 100.00
3 Julius Erving/49 30.00 80.00
4 Alonzo Mourning/49 20.00 50.00
5 Walt Frazier/49 10.00 25.00
6 Bill Walton/49 6.00 15.00
7 Isiah Thomas/49 10.00 25.00
8 Clyde Drexler/49 20.00 50.00
9 Dikembe Mutombo/99 10.00 25.00
10 Rick Barry/49 10.00 25.00
11 Pat Riley/49 12.00 30.00
12 David Robinson/49 15.00 40.00
13 Gail Goodrich/199 6.00 15.00
14 Dominique Wilkins/49 12.00 30.00
15 Jerry West/49 20.00 50.00
16 Larry Johnson/199 6.00 15.00
17 Scottie Pippen/49 40.00 100.00
18 John Stockton/49 30.00 60.00
19 Gary Payton/49 12.00 30.00
20 Robert Parish/49 6.00 15.00
21 Hakeem Olajuwon/49 10.00 25.00
22 Bob Lanier/49 8.00 20.00
23 Dan Majerle/199 6.00 15.00
24 Kobe Bryant/99 500.00 1,000.00
25 Bill Russell/25 500.00 1,000.00

2012-13 Elite Back to the Future Materials

1 LeBron James 25.00 60.00
2 Grant Hill 8.00 20.00
3 Steve Nash 6.00 15.00
4 Vince Carter 6.00 15.00
5 Kevin Garnett 8.00 20.00
6 Ray Allen 5.00 12.00
7 Amare Stoudemire 3.00 8.00
8 Carmelo Anthony 5.00 12.00
9 Joe Johnson 2.50 6.00
10 David West 2.50 6.00
11 Chris Paul 6.00 15.00
12 Dwight Howard 4.00 10.00
13 Nate Robinson 2.00 5.00
14 Antawn Jamison 2.50 6.00
15 James Harden 6.00 15.00
16 Nene 2.50 6.00
17 Eric Gordon 2.50 6.00
18 Jeff Green 2.00 5.00
19 Shane Battier 2.50 6.00
20 Derek Fisher 2.50 6.00
21 Lamar Odom 2.50 6.00
22 Brandon Roy 2.50 6.00
23 Jermaine O'Neal 2.50 6.00
24 Jason Terry 2.50 6.00
25 Andrei Kirilenko 2.50 6.00

2012-13 Elite Back to the Future Materials Prime

*PRIME: 1X TO 2.5X BASE HI
STATED PRINT RUN 25 SER.#'d SETS

2012-13 Elite Craftsmen

COMPLETE SET (25) 15.00 40.00
*GOLD: 2.5X TO 6X HI COLUMN
GOLD STATED PRINT RUN 24 SETS
1 Dwight Howard 1.00 2.50
2 Tyreke Evans .60 1.50
3 Dwyane Wade 1.50 4.00
4 Serge Ibaka .60 1.50
5 Raymond Felton .50 1.25
6 LeBron James 6.00 15.00
7 Darren Collison .50 1.25
8 Steve Novak .50 1.25
9 Kevin Durant 3.00 8.00
10 Grant Hill 1.25 3.00
11 Antawn Jamison .60 1.50
12 Derrick Rose 1.25 3.00
13 Zach Randolph .75 2.00
14 Kevin Garnett 2.00 5.00
15 Blake Griffin .75 2.00
16 Roy Hibbert .60 1.50
17 Jeremy Lin 1.25 3.00
18 Steve Nash 1.50 4.00
19 Ty Lawson .50 1.25
20 Brandon Jennings .50 1.25
21 Ricky Rubio .60 1.50
22 Rajon Rondo 1.00 2.50
23 Brook Lopez .60 1.50
24 Kobe Bryant 6.00 15.00
25 Dirk Nowitzki 2.00 5.00

2012-13 Elite Dominators Materials

1 Blake Griffin 3.00 8.00
2 Marc Gasol 3.00 8.00
3 Tim Duncan 8.00 20.00
4 Amare Stoudemire 3.00 8.00
5 Derrick Rose 5.00 12.00
6 LeBron James 25.00 60.00
7 Kevin Durant 12.00 30.00
8 Paul Pierce 5.00 12.00
9 Brook Lopez 2.50 6.00
10 Zach Randolph 3.00 8.00
11 Kevin Garnett 8.00 20.00
12 Al Horford 3.00 8.00
13 Stephen Curry 12.00 30.00
14 Channing Frye 2.00 5.00
15 Tony Parker 5.00 12.00
16 John Wall 4.00 10.00
17 Raymond Felton 2.00 5.00
18 Thaddeus Young 2.00 5.00
19 Al Jefferson 2.00 5.00
20 Metta World Peace 2.50 6.00
21 LaMarcus Aldridge 3.00 8.00
22 Carlos Boozer 2.50 6.00
23 Chris Bosh 4.00 10.00
24 Carmelo Anthony 5.00 12.00
25 Tayshaun Prince 3.00 8.00

2012-13 Elite Dominators Materials Prime

*PRIME: 1X TO 2.5X BASE HI
STATED PRINT RUN 25 SER.#'d SETS

2012-13 Elite Passing the Torch Autographs

STATED PRINT RUN 20 TO 49 SER.#'d SETS
1 K.Bryant/K.Durant/49 800.00 1,500.00
2 S.Nash/G.Dragic/25 40.00 100.00
3 J.Kidd/D.Collison/25 12.00 30.00
4 J.Harden/J.Starks/49 60.00 150.00
5 D.Majerle/R.Allen/25 20.00 50.00
6 B.Walton/L.Aldridge/49 20.00 50.00
7 J.Erving/B.Griffin/25 60.00 120.00
8 D.Thompson/Iguodala/49 8.00 20.00
9 H.Olajuwon/S.Ibaka/25 30.00 80.00
10 Thomas/Paul/25 EXCH 75.00 200.00
11 B.Laimbeer/M.Gortat/49 8.00 20.00
12 D.Rodman/K.Love/25 75.00 200.00
13 G.Gervin/K.Durant/25 75.00 200.00
14 L.Bird/D.Nowitzki/25 150.00 300.00
15 K.Irving/G.Hill/25 60.00 150.00
16 E.Hayes/K.Love/25 15.00 40.00
17 D.Rivers/A.Rivers/49 30.00 60.00
18 S.Curry/D.Curry/49 300.00 600.00
19 Mullin/Lee/49 EXCH 25.00 60.00
20 W.Reed/T.Chandler/25 60.00 150.00
21 R.Sampson/R.Hibbert/49 12.00 30.00
22 W.Free/M.Peace/49 15.00 40.00
23 M.Johnson/S.Nash/25 75.00 200.00
24 K.Irving/A.Davis/25 500.00 1,000.00
25 S.Pippen/G.Hill/25 200.00 500.00

2012-13 Elite Prime Numbers

COMPLETE SET (25) 20.00 50.00
*GOLD: 2X TO 5X HI COLUMN
GOLD STATED PRINT RUN 24 SETS
1 Blake Griffin 1.00 2.50
2 Shaquille O'Neal 3.00 8.00
3 John Stockton 2.00 5.00
4 LeBron James 8.00 20.00
5 Gary Payton 1.25 3.00
6 Kareem Abdul-Jabbar 3.00 8.00
7 Ray Allen 1.50 4.00
8 Dennis Rodman 2.50 6.00
9 Kevin Love 1.00 2.50
10 Jason Terry .75 2.00
11 Oscar Robertson 2.00 5.00
12 Elvin Hayes 1.25 3.00
13 Larry Bird 3.00 8.00
14 Jerry West 2.00 5.00
15 Bill Russell 3.00 8.00
16 Adrian Dantley .75 2.00
17 Jason Kidd 1.50 4.00
18 Mark Eaton .75 2.00
19 Magic Johnson 3.00 8.00
20 Robert Parish 1.50 4.00
21 David Robinson 1.50 4.00
22 Hakeem Olajuwon 2.00 5.00
23 Scott Skiles .75 2.00
24 Kobe Bryant 8.00 20.00
25 Dirk Nowitzki 2.50 6.00

2012-13 Elite Rookie Inscriptions

1 Kyrie Irving 50.00 120.00
2 Bismack Biyombo 3.00 8.00
3 Alec Burks 4.00 10.00
4 Iman Shumpert 3.00 8.00
5 MarShon Brooks 2.50 6.00
6 Kyle Singler 2.50 6.00
7 Chandler Parsons 3.00 8.00
8 Malcolm Lee 2.50 6.00
9 E'Twaun Moore 3.00 8.00
10 Anthony Davis 150.00 400.00
11 Harrison Barnes 5.00 12.00
12 Jeremy Lamb EXCH 4.00 10.00
13 Tyler Zeller 2.50 6.00
14 Miles Plumlee EXCH 2.50 6.00
15 Quincy Acy 2.50 6.00
16 Robert Sacre 2.50 6.00
17 Kim English 2.50 6.00
18 Tyshawn Taylor 2.50 6.00
19 Khris Middleton 12.00 30.00
20 Draymond Green 15.00 40.00
21 Bernard James 2.50 6.00
22 Festus Ezeli 2.50 6.00
23 Perry Jones 2.50 6.00
24 Jared Cunningham 2.50 6.00
25 Jared Sullinger 2.50 6.00
26 Andrew Nicholson 2.50 6.00
27 Royce White 2.50 6.00
28 John Henson 3.00 8.00
29 Austin Rivers 4.00 10.00
30 Terrence Ross 6.00 15.00
31 Dion Waiters 3.00 8.00
32 Jeremy Pargo 2.50 6.00
33 Ivan Johnson 2.50 6.00
34 Lavoy Allen 2.50 6.00
35 Josh Harrellson 2.50 6.00
36 Kent Bazemore 4.00 10.00
37 Jon Leuer 2.50 6.00
38 Trey Thompkins 2.50 6.00
39 Jimmy Butler 15.00 40.00
40 Norris Cole 2.50 6.00
41 Reggie Jackson 4.00 10.00
42 Tobias Harris 8.00 20.00
43 Kawhi Leonard 75.00 200.00
44 Markieff Morris EXCH 4.00 10.00
45 Jimmer Fredette 4.00 10.00
46 Brandon Knight 4.00 10.00
47 Jan Vesely 2.50 6.00
48 Derrick Williams 2.50 6.00
49 Tristan Thompson 4.00 10.00
50 Kemba Walker 20.00 50.00
51 Marcus Morris 4.00 10.00
52 Chris Singleton 2.50 6.00
53 Kenneth Faried 3.00 8.00
54 Cory Joseph 3.00 8.00
55 Donatas Motiejunas 3.00 8.00
56 Darius Morris 3.00 8.00
57 Isaiah Thomas 5.00 12.00
58 Michael Kidd-Gilchrist 3.00 8.00
59 Kyle O'Quinn 3.00 8.00
60 Meyers Leonard 3.00 8.00
61 Maurice Harkless 3.00 8.00
62 Evan Fournier 4.00 10.00
63 John Jenkins 2.50 6.00
64 Arnett Moultrie 2.50 6.00
65 Jeff Taylor 2.50 6.00
66 Jae Crowder 5.00 12.00
67 Quincy Miller 2.50 6.00
68 Doron Lamb 2.50 6.00
69 Darius Miller 3.00 8.00
70 Kris Joseph 2.50 6.00
71 Kevin Murphy 2.50 6.00
72 Will Barton 5.00 12.00
73 Tony Wroten 2.50 6.00
74 Terrence Jones 2.50 6.00
75 Andre Drummond 6.00 15.00
76 Lance Thomas 2.50 6.00
77 DeAndre Liggins 2.50 6.00
78 Jeremy Tyler 2.50 6.00
79 Nolan Smith 2.50 6.00
80 Klay Thompson 25.00 60.00
81 Jonas Valanciunas 5.00 12.00
82 Enes Kanter 4.00 10.00
83 Nikola Vucevic 10.00 25.00
84 Tyler Honeycutt 2.50 6.00
85 Charles Jenkins 2.50 6.00
86 Josh Selby 2.50 6.00
87 Greg Stiemsma 2.50 6.00
88 Bradley Beal 12.00 30.00
89 Thomas Robinson EXCH 2.50 6.00
90 Kendall Marshall 2.50 6.00
91 Fab Melo 2.50 6.00
92 Marquis Teague 2.50 6.00
93 Orlando Johnson 2.50 6.00
94 Mike Scott 3.00 8.00
95 Darius Johnson-Odom 2.50 6.00
96 Chris Copeland 2.50 6.00
97 Victor Claver 2.50 6.00
98 Nando De Colo 2.50 6.00
99 DeQuan Jones 2.50 6.00

2012-13 Elite Series Inserts

COMPLETE SET (30) 20.00 50.00
*GOLD: 2X TO 5X HI COLUMN
GOLD STATED PRINT RUN 24 SETS
1 Blake Griffin 1.00 2.50
2 Kevin Durant 4.00 10.00
3 Carmelo Anthony 1.50 4.00
4 Paul Pierce 1.50 4.00
5 LeBron James 8.00 20.00
6 Chris Paul 2.00 5.00
7 Amare Stoudemire 1.00 2.50
8 Dirk Nowitzki 2.50 6.00
9 Tim Duncan 2.50 6.00
10 Steve Nash 2.00 5.00
11 Derrick Rose 1.50 4.00
12 Deron Williams .75 2.00
13 Andre Iguodala 1.00 2.50
14 Danny Granger .60 1.50
15 Russell Westbrook 1.50 4.00
16 LaMarcus Aldridge 1.00 2.50
17 Kevin Love 1.00 2.50
18 Marcin Gortat .60 1.50
19 Joe Johnson .75 2.00
20 Ray Allen 1.50 4.00
21 Ricky Rubio .75 2.00
22 Dwyane Wade 2.00 5.00
23 DeMarcus Cousins 1.00 2.50
24 Kobe Bryant 8.00 20.00
25 Tyson Chandler .75 2.00
26 Dwight Howard 1.25 3.00
27 Tony Parker 1.50 4.00
28 Rajon Rondo 1.25 3.00
29 James Harden 2.00 5.00
30 Marc Gasol .75 2.00

2012-13 Elite Rookie Elite Series

COMPLETE SET (20) 25.00 60.00
*GOLD: 2X TO 5X HI COLUMN
GOLD STATED PRINT RUN 24 SETS
1 Kyrie Irving 6.00 15.00
2 Anthony Davis 8.00 20.00
3 Kawhi Leonard 12.00 30.00
4 Kenneth Faried .75 2.00
5 Iman Shumpert .75 2.00
6 Michael Kidd-Gilchrist .75 2.00
7 Jared Sullinger .60 1.50
8 Isaiah Thomas 1.25 3.00
9 Kemba Walker 2.50 6.00
10 Markieff Morris .60 1.50
11 Derrick Williams .60 1.50
12 Bradley Beal 5.00 12.00
13 Chandler Parsons .75 2.00
14 Brandon Knight .75 2.00
15 Austin Rivers 1.00 2.50
16 Damian Lillard 40.00 100.00
17 MarShon Brooks .60 1.50
18 Thomas Robinson .60 1.50
19 Tristan Thompson 1.00 2.50
20 Lavoy Allen .60 1.50

2012-13 Elite Signatures

STATED PRINT RUN 49 TO 199 SER.#'d SETS
1 Kobe Bryant/197 400.00 800.00
2 Mario Chalmers/49 4.00 10.00
3 Grant Hill/99 10.00 25.00
4 Kevin Martin/49 4.00 10.00
5 Ryan Anderson/52 4.00 10.00
6 Andrei Kirilenko/99 4.00 10.00
7 Stephen Curry/199 300.00 600.00
8 Zach Randolph/99 4.00 10.00
9 Ty Lawson/199 4.00 10.00
10 Roy Hibbert/53 4.00 10.00
11 Steve Nash/49 20.00 50.00
12 Jason Kidd/49 12.00 30.00
14 Taj Gibson/49 4.00 10.00
15 James Harden/99 40.00 100.00
16 Danny Green/199 4.00 10.00
17 Kevin Love/49 12.00 30.00
18 Jeff Green/49 4.00 10.00
19 Steve Novak/49 4.00 10.00
20 J.J. Hickson/199 4.00 10.00
21 Udonis Haslem/199 4.00 10.00
22 Kevin Durant/49 75.00 200.00
23 Joakim Noah/49 4.00 10.00
24 Luis Scola/49 4.00 10.00
25 Serge Ibaka/98 4.00 10.00
26 Vince Carter/49 6.00 15.00
27 Hedo Turkoglu/49 4.00 10.00
28 Kris Humphries/49 4.00 10.00
29 Marcin Gortat/199 4.00 10.00
30 LaMarcus Aldridge/99 5.00 12.00
31 Jason Richardson/49 4.00 10.00
32 Devin Harris/49 4.00 10.00
33 Luc Mbah a Moute/199 4.00 10.00
34 Rashard Lewis/199 4.00 10.00
35 Tayshaun Prince/49 4.00 10.00
36 Gerald Wallace/49 4.00 10.00
37 Jrue Holiday/199 4.00 10.00
38 Andrew Bynum/49 4.00 10.00
39 Thabo Sefolosha/49 4.00 10.00
40 Luol Deng/49 4.00 10.00
41 Blake Griffin/49 12.00 30.00
42 David West/49 4.00 10.00
43 O.J. Mayo/49 4.00 10.00
45 Ray Allen/49 20.00 50.00
46 Goran Dragic/199 20.00 50.00
47 Nick Collison/199 4.00 10.00
48 Antawn Jamison/49 4.00 10.00
49 Gordon Hayward/199 8.00 20.00
50 Darren Collison/49 4.00 10.00

2012-13 Elite Throwback Threads

1 Patrick Ewing 5.00 12.00
2 Allen Iverson 8.00 20.00
3 John Stockton 6.00 15.00
4 Shaquille O'Neal 10.00 25.00
5 Dennis Rodman 8.00 20.00
6 Kevin McHale 4.00 10.00
7 Ron Harper 3.00 8.00
8 Alonzo Mourning 6.00 15.00
9 Alex English 4.00 10.00
10 Julius Erving 8.00 20.00
11 Kelly Tripucka 2.50 6.00
12 Earl Monroe 4.00 10.00
13 Glen Rice 2.50 6.00
14 Xavier McDaniel 2.00 5.00
15 Tom Chambers 3.00 8.00
16 Kiki Vandeweghe 2.50 6.00
17 Lou Hudson 2.50 6.00
18 Shawn Kemp 8.00 20.00
19 Zydrunas Ilgauskas 2.50 6.00
20 Chris Webber 3.00 8.00
21 Artis Gilmore 4.00 10.00
22 Rick Mahorn 2.00 5.00
23 Manute Bol 5.00 12.00
24 Kenny Anderson 2.50 6.00
25 Slater Martin 5.00 12.00

2012-13 Elite Throwback Threads Prime

*PRIME: 1.25X TO 3X BASE HI
STATED PRINT RUN 25 SER.#'d SETS
3 John Stockton 20.00 50.00

2012-13 Elite Turn of the Century Autographs

STATED PRINT RUN 25 TO 199 SER.#'d SETS
2 Muggsy Bogues/199 6.00 15.00
3 Dwyane Wade/49 25.00 60.00
4 Steve Kerr/49 10.00 25.00
5 Anthony Mason/199 6.00 15.00
6 Anfernee Hardaway/25 75.00 150.00
7 Tim Hardaway/199 6.00 15.00
8 Danny Manning/49 4.00 10.00
9 Mitch Richmond/149 5.00 12.00
10 Trevor Booker/199 2.50 6.00
11 Brook Lopez/25 3.00 8.00
13 George Hill/199 3.00 8.00
14 Greg Monroe/149 2.50 6.00
15 Rodney Stuckey/149 2.50 6.00
16 Marvin Williams/199 2.50 6.00
17 Zaza Pachulia/199 2.50 6.00
18 Andrew Bogut/99 6.00 15.00
19 Stephen Curry/25 500.00 1,000.00
20 Kevin Durant/49 50.00 120.00
21 Bill Cartwright/149 4.00 10.00
22 Brandon Bass/149 2.50 6.00
24 Kobe Bryant/199 400.00 800.00
26 DeMarcus Cousins/25 12.00 30.00
27 Tiago Splitter/199 2.50 6.00
28 Monta Ellis/25 3.00 8.00
29 Tyreke Evans/25 3.00 8.00
31 Gerald Henderson/149 2.50 6.00
32 Chris Bosh/25 5.00 12.00
34 Marcus Thornton/199 2.50 6.00
36 Nick Young/149 2.50 6.00
37 Rick Fox/25 3.00 8.00
38 Steve Novak/99 2.50 6.00
39 Dorell Wright/199 2.50 6.00
40 Blake Griffin/49 15.00 40.00
41 Ty Lawson/49 2.50 6.00
42 Chase Budinger/199 2.50 6.00
43 Udonis Haslem/199 3.00 8.00
44 Zydrunas Ilgauskas/199 4.00 10.00
45 Wesley Matthews/199 2.50 6.00
46 Tyler Hansbrough/25 2.50 6.00
47 Gordon Hayward/199 5.00 12.00
49 Anthony Morrow/199 2.50 6.00
51 Kyle Lowry/199 4.00 10.00
52 Richard Jefferson/49 3.00 8.00
53 Danilo Gallinari/25 8.00 20.00
54 Grant Hill/25 30.00 80.00
55 Ronny Turiaf/149 2.50 6.00
58 Al-Farouq Aminu/199 2.50 6.00
59 Paul George/199 25.00 60.00
60 Ronnie Price/199 2.50 6.00
61 Rolando Blackman/199 4.00 10.00
62 Mike Conley/49 EXCH 4.00 10.00
63 Marreese Speights/199 2.50 6.00
65 Luke Ridnour/199 3.00 8.00
67 Louis Williams/199 4.00 10.00
69 Austin Rivers/25 8.00 20.00
70 Markieff Morris/199 EXCH 4.00 10.00
71 Draymond Green/199 10.00 25.00
72 Kenneth Faried/199 3.00 8.00
73 Kawhi Leonard/199 100.00 250.00
74 Chandler Parsons/199 3.00 8.00
75 Isaiah Thomas/199 5.00 12.00
76 Tyshawn Taylor/199 2.50 6.00
78 Tyler Zeller/199 2.50 6.00
79 Perry Jones/199 2.50 6.00
80 Jared Sullinger/25 2.50 6.00
81 Doron Lamb/199 2.50 6.00
82 Jrue Holiday/49 5.00 12.00
83 Meyers Leonard/199 3.00 8.00
84 Jimmer Fredette/199 4.00 10.00
85 Landry Fields/199 2.50 6.00
86 Andrea Bargnani/25 2.50 6.00
87 JaVale McGee/149 4.00 10.00
88 Jeff Teague/199 2.50 6.00
89 Carlos Delfino/199 4.00 10.00
90 Patrick Patterson/199 2.50 6.00
92 Nikola Pekovic/199 2.50 6.00
93 Norris Cole/199 2.50 6.00
94 Sean Elliott/199 6.00 15.00
95 Shannon Brown/199 2.50 6.00
96 Samardo Samuels/199 2.50 6.00
97 Reggie Evans/149 2.50 6.00
98 Rashard Lewis/199 4.00 10.00
99 Marquis Teague/199 2.50 6.00
100 Bradley Beal/25 20.00 50.00

2013-14 Elite

ROOKIE PRINT RUN 999 SER.#'d SETS
RETIRED PRINT RUN 999 SER.#'d SETS
1 Raymond Felton .25 .60
2 Elton Brand .30 .75
3 Nate Robinson .25 .60
4 Rajon Rondo .50 1.25
5 Josh Smith .25 .60
6 John Wall .50 1.25
7 Ray Allen .60 1.50
8 Louis Williams .30 .75
9 MarShon Brooks .25 .60
10 Tyler Hansbrough .25 .60
11 Taj Gibson .25 .60
12 Josh McRoberts .25 .60
13 Kendrick Perkins .25 .60
14 John Salmons .30 .75
15 Kyle Lowry .40 1.00
16 Metta World Peace .30 .75
17 JaVale McGee .30 .75
18 DeMar DeRozan .50 1.25
19 Andrei Kirilenko .40 1.00
20 Klay Thompson 1.25 3.00
21 Jeff Green .25 .60
22 O.J. Mayo .25 .60
23 Damian Lillard 1.25 3.00
24 Joakim Noah .40 1.00
25 Andre Iguodala .40 1.00
26 Al Horford .40 1.00
27 Jamal Crawford .40 1.00
28 James Harden .75 2.00
29 Greivis Vasquez .25 .60
30 David West .30 .75
31 Amar'e Stoudemire .40 1.00
32 Eric Gordon .30 .75
33 Tony Allen .25 .60
34 Chris Paul .75 2.00
35 Jan Vesely .25 .60
36 Vince Carter .75 2.00
37 Isaiah Thomas .30 .75
38 Thabo Sefolosha .30 .75
39 Andrew Bynum .25 .60
40 Ryan Anderson .25 .60
41 J.R. Smith .40 1.00
42 Kyle Korver .30 .75
43 Tyson Chandler .30 .75
44 Udonis Haslem .30 .75
45 Jason Richardson .40 1.00
46 Danny Granger .25 .60
47 Michael Kidd-Gilchrist .25 .60
48 Tayshaun Prince .40 1.00
49 Gerald Henderson .25 .60
50 J.J. Redick .40 1.00
51 Gerald Wallace .30 .75
52 Kawhi Leonard 1.25 3.00
53 Deron Williams .30 .75
54 Jordan Hill .25 .60
55 Thaddeus Young .25 .60
56 Tony Parker .60 1.50
57 J.J. Hickson .25 .60
58 Luol Deng .30 .75
59 Kemba Walker .40 1.00
60 Kyrie Irving 1.25 3.00
61 Nikola Vucevic .50 1.25
62 Kevin Garnett 1.00 2.50
63 Boris Diaw .30 .75
64 Markieff Morris .25 .60
65 Kevin Durant 1.25 3.00
66 Shawn Marion .30 .75
67 Brandon Jennings .25 .60
68 Andrew Bogut .30 .75
69 Marcus Thornton .25 .60
70 Zach Randolph .30 .75
71 Omer Asik .25 .60
72 J.J. Barea .30 .75
73 Matt Barnes .25 .60
74 Dwyane Wade .75 2.00
75 Jason Maxiell .25 .60
76 Manu Ginobili .75 2.00
77 Chris Kaman .30 .75
78 Kirk Hinrich .30 .75
79 George Hill .30 .75
80 Glen Davis .25 .60
81 Marcus Morris .30 .75
82 Robin Lopez .25 .60
83 Jeremy Lin .60 1.50
84 Paul George .60 1.50
85 Michael Beasley .25 .60
86 Serge Ibaka .30 .75
87 Luke Ridnour .30 .75
88 Joe Johnson .30 .75
89 Derrick Williams .25 .60
90 Trevor Ariza .25 .60
91 Andre Miller .30 .75
92 Paul Millsap .30 .75
93 Kevin Love .40 1.00
94 Mike Conley .40 1.00
95 Orlando Johnson .25 .60
96 David Lee .25 .60
97 Jonas Valanciunas .30 .75
98 Steve Nash .75 2.00
99 Wilson Chandler .30 .75
100 Miles Plumlee .25 .60
101 Tiago Splitter .25 .60
102 Brandon Knight .30 .75
103 Wesley Matthews .25 .60
104 Earl Clark .25 .60
105 Stephen Curry 3.00 8.00
106 Dirk Nowitzki 1.00 2.50
107 Ben Gordon .30 .75
108 Jeff Teague .25 .60
109 Nicolas Batum .30 .75
110 LeBron James 3.00 8.00
111 Bradley Beal .60 1.50
112 Evan Turner .25 .60
113 Russell Westbrook .60 1.50
114 Matt Bonner .25 .60
115 Arron Afflalo .25 .60
116 Dwight Howard .50 1.25
117 Nikola Pekovic .25 .60
118 Kenneth Faried .30 .75
119 Harrison Barnes .40 1.00
120 Greg Monroe .25 .60
121 Dion Waiters .25 .60
122 Spencer Hawes .25 .60
123 Kosta Koufos .25 .60
124 Corey Brewer .25 .60
125 Wayne Ellington .25 .60
126 Andre Drummond .40 1.00
127 Danny Green .30 .75
128 Carlos Boozer .30 .75
129 Roy Hibbert .25 .60
130 Mike Miller .30 .75
131 Nick Young .25 .60
132 Reggie Evans .25 .60
133 DeAndre Jordan .30 .75
134 Carmelo Anthony .60 1.50
135 Draymond Green .60 1.50
136 Jimmer Fredette .40 1.00
137 Al-Farouq Aminu .25 .60
138 Marcin Gortat .25 .60
139 Thomas Robinson .25 .60
140 Lance Stephenson .30 .75
141 Ricky Rubio .30 .75
142 Anthony Davis 1.25 3.00
143 Pau Gasol .60 1.50
144 Alec Burks .30 .75
145 Luis Scola .30 .75
146 Rudy Gay .30 .75
147 Avery Bradley .25 .60
148 Shane Battier .30 .75
149 LaMarcus Aldridge .40 1.00
150 Paul Pierce .60 1.50
151 Marc Gasol .40 1.00
152 Richard Jefferson .30 .75
153 Iman Shumpert .25 .60
154 Gordon Hayward .30 .75
155 Nene .30 .75
156 Kevin Martin .30 .75
157 Monta Ellis .30 .75
158 Tony Wroten .25 .60
159 Martell Webster .25 .60
160 Mario Chalmers .30 .75
161 Byron Mullens .25 .60
162 DeMarcus Cousins .40 1.00
163 Amir Johnson .25 .60
164 Danilo Gallinari .30 .75
165 Lavoy Allen .25 .60
166 Chris Andersen .30 .75
167 Tyreke Evans .30 .75
168 Jameer Nelson .25 .60
169 Larry Sanders .25 .60
170 Eric Bledsoe .30 .75
171 Derrick Rose .60 1.50
172 Andray Blatche .25 .60
173 Andrea Bargnani .25 .60
174 Derrick Favors .25 .60
175 Chauncey Billups .50 1.25
176 John Henson .25 .60
177 Blake Griffin .40 1.00
178 Brandon Bass .25 .60
179 Anderson Varejao .25 .60
180 Channing Frye .25 .60
181 Marvin Williams .25 .60
182 Brook Lopez .40 1.00
183 Rodney Stuckey .25 .60
184 Goran Dragic .30 .75
185 Derek Fisher .30 .75
186 Chandler Parsons .25 .60
187 C.J. Miles .25 .60
188 Ersan Ilyasova .25 .60
189 Jrue Holiday .50 1.25
190 Aaron Brooks .25 .60
191 Tristan Thompson .25 .60
192 Kris Humphries .25 .60
193 Jimmy Butler .75 2.00
194 Kobe Bryant 3.00 8.00
195 Tim Duncan 1.00 2.50
196 Jose Calderon .25 .60
197 Al Jefferson .25 .60
198 Ty Lawson .25 .60
199 Chris Bosh .50 1.25
200 Enes Kanter .30 .75
201 Anthony Bennett RC 1.00 2.50
202 Isaiah Canaan RC 1.00 2.50
203 Nate Wolters RC 1.00 2.50
204 Shane Larkin RC 1.00 2.50
205 Vitor Faverani RC 1.00 2.50
206 Tony Snell RC 1.25 3.00
207 Carrick Felix RC 1.00 2.50
208 Pero Antic RC 1.00 2.50
209 Jeff Withey RC 1.00 2.50
210 Gal Mekel RC 1.00 2.50
211 Andre Roberson RC 1.25 3.00
212 Cody Zeller RC 1.25 3.00
213 Kentavious Caldwell-Pope RC 1.50 4.00
214 Reggie Bullock RC 1.25 3.00
215 Tony Mitchell RC 1.00 2.50
216 Dennis Schroder RC 3.00 8.00
217 Ricky Ledo RC 1.00 2.50
218 Sergey Karasev RC 1.00 2.50
219 Luigi Datome RC 1.00 2.50
220 Erik Murphy RC 1.00 2.50
221 Allen Crabbe RC 1.00 2.50
222 Ben McLemore RC 1.25 3.00
223 M.Carter-Williams RC 1.25 3.00
224 Ryan Kelly RC 1.00 2.50
225 Gorgui Dieng RC 1.25 3.00
226 Steven Adams RC 2.50 6.00
227 Peyton Siva RC 1.00 2.50
228 Mason Plumlee RC 1.25 3.00
229 G.Antetokounmpo RC 125.00 300.00
230 Archie Goodwin RC 1.00 2.50
231 Glen Rice Jr. RC 1.00 2.50
232 Kelly Olynyk RC 1.25 3.00
233 Otto Porter RC 1.50 4.00
234 Shabazz Muhammad RC 1.00 2.50
235 Trey Burke RC 1.25 3.00
236 Nemanja Nedovic RC 1.00 2.50
237 Victor Oladipo RC 2.50 6.00
238 Jamaal Franklin RC 1.00 2.50
239 Alex Len RC 1.25 3.00
240 Dwight Buycks RC 1.00 2.50
241 Tim Hardaway Jr. RC 2.00 5.00
242 Solomon Hill RC 1.25 3.00
243 Nerlens Noel RC 1.25 3.00
244 C.J. McCollum RC 4.00 10.00
245 Phil Pressey RC 1.00 2.50
246 Larry Bird 5.00 12.00
247 Drazen Petrovic 1.50 4.00
248 Dikembe Mutombo 2.00 5.00
249 Jack Sikma 1.25 3.00
250 Calvin Murphy 1.00 2.50
251 World B. Free 1.00 2.50
252 Chris Mullin 1.50 4.00
253 Elvin Hayes 1.50 4.00
254 Kareem Abdul-Jabbar 4.00 10.00
255 Bill Russell 4.00 10.00
256 George Gervin 2.00 5.00
257 Gary Payton 2.00 5.00
258 Artis Gilmore 1.50 4.00
259 Bob Cousy 3.00 8.00
260 Willis Reed 2.00 5.00
261 Rick Barry 1.50 4.00
262 Bill Walton 2.00 5.00
263 Hakeem Olajuwon 2.50 6.00
264 Alonzo Mourning 2.00 5.00
265 Magic Johnson 5.00 12.00
266 John Stockton 2.50 6.00
267 Robert Parish 1.50 4.00
268 George Mikan 4.00 10.00
269 Michael Finley 1.25 3.00
270 Fat Lever 1.00 2.50
271 Dennis Rodman 3.00 8.00
272 Kevin McHale 2.00 5.00
273 Oscar Robertson 2.00 5.00
274 David Robinson 2.50 6.00
275 Isiah Thomas 2.00 5.00
276 Yao Ming 2.50 6.00
277 Scottie Pippen 3.00 8.00
278 Maurice Cheeks 1.00 2.50
279 Shawn Kemp 2.00 5.00
280 Robert Horry 1.25 3.00
281 Kevin Johnson 1.25 3.00
282 James Worthy 1.50 4.00
283 John Havlicek 3.00 8.00
284 Karl Malone 2.50 6.00
285 Shaquille O'Neal 5.00 12.00
286 Julius Erving 3.00 8.00
287 Walt Frazier 2.00 5.00
288 Anfernee Hardaway 3.00 8.00
289 Dolph Schayes 1.25 3.00
290 Moses Malone 2.00 5.00
291 Dave Twardzik .75 2.00
292 Dan Issel 1.50 4.00
293 Grant Hill 2.00 5.00
294 Wilt Chamberlain 4.00 10.00
295 Dominique Wilkins 2.00 5.00
296 Dan Majerle 1.00 2.50
297 Nate Archibald 1.50 4.00
298 Jerry West 3.00 8.00
299 Clyde Drexler 2.00 5.00
300 Bob Pettit 1.25 3.00

2013-14 Elite Status

*STATUS 1-200 p/r 15-25: 5X TO 12X BASE
*STATUS 1-200 p/r 26-49: 4X TO 10X BASE
*STATUS 1-200 p/r 50-99: 3X TO 8X BASE
*STATUS 201-245 p/r 15-25: 1.2X TO 3X BASE
*STATUS 201-245 p/r 26-49: 1X TO 2.5X BASE
*STATUS 246-300 p/r 15-25: 1.5X TO 4X BASE
*STATUS 246-300 p/r 26-49: 1.2X TO 3X BASE
*STATUS 246-300 p/r 50-99: 1X TO 2.5X BASE
PRINT RUNS B/WN 1-99 COPIES PER
NO PRICING ON QTY 14 OR LESS
194 Kobe Bryant/24 125.00 300.00
229 Giannis Antetokounmpo/34 800.00 1,500.00
293 Grant Hill/33 20.00 50.00

2013-14 Elite Status Gold

*STATUS 1-200: 5X TO 12X BASE
*STATUS 201-245: 1.2X TO 3X BASE
*STATUS 246-300: 1.5X TO 4X BASE
STATED PRINT RUN 24 SER.#'d SETS
65 Kevin Durant 30.00 80.00
110 LeBron James 40.00 100.00
194 Kobe Bryant 40.00 100.00
229 Giannis Antetokounmpo 600.00 1,200.00
264 Alonzo Mourning 75.00 150.00
288 Anfernee Hardaway 15.00 40.00
293 Grant Hill 15.00 40.00

2013-14 Elite All-Time Greats Autographs

PRINT RUNS B/WN 10-199 COPIES PER
NO PRICING ON QTY 10
EXCHANGE DEADLINE 7/29/2015
1 Gail Goodrich/99 6.00 15.00
2 Christian Laettner/99 6.00 15.00
4 Scottie Pippen/49 75.00 200.00
5 Magic Johnson/49 75.00 200.00
6 Bob Lanier/49 8.00 20.00
7 Elgin Baylor/15 30.00 80.00
8 George McGinnis/149 6.00 15.00
9 Bill Sharman/75 30.00 80.00
10 Steve Francis/99 5.00 12.00
11 Joe Dumars/75 8.00 20.00
12 Clyde Drexler/25 20.00 50.00
13 Karl Malone/25 40.00 100.00
14 Buck Williams/199 5.00 12.00
15 Ralph Sampson/75 5.00 12.00
16 Alonzo Mourning/49 20.00 50.00
17 Jerry West/25 30.00 80.00
18 Artis Gilmore/25 8.00 20.00
19 Tom Heinsohn/75 40.00 100.00
20 Sam Cassell/75 5.00 12.00
21 Kelly Tripucka/25 5.00 12.00
23 David Thompson/199 6.00 15.00
24 Elvin Hayes/25 12.00 30.00
25 Mitch Richmond/75 8.00 20.00

2013-14 Elite Aspirations

*STATUS 1-200 p/r 23: 5X TO 12X BASE
*STATUS 1-200 p/r 26-49: 4X TO 10X BASE
*STATUS 1-200 p/r 50-99: 3X TO 8X BASE
*STATUS 201-245: .75X TO 2X BASE
*STATUS 246-300 p/r 26-49: 1.2X TO 3X BASE
*STATUS 246-300 p/r 50-99: 1X TO 2.5X BASE
PRINT RUNS B/WN 1-99 COPIES PER
NO PRICING ON QTY 12 OR LESS
229 GAntetokounmpo/66 300.00 600.00
288 Anfernee Hardaway/99 10.00 25.00
293 Grant Hill/67 10.00 25.00

2013-14 Elite Back to the Future Materials

1 Ray Allen 5.00 12.00
2 Jason Richardson 3.00 8.00
3 Greg Oden 2.00 5.00
4 Rashard Lewis 2.50 6.00
5 John Salmons 2.50 6.00
6 Vince Carter 6.00 15.00
7 Kevin Martin 2.50 6.00
8 Michael Beasley 2.00 5.00
9 Andre Miller 2.50 6.00
10 Danilo Gallinari 2.50 6.00
11 Juwan Howard 2.50 6.00
12 Chris Paul 4.00 10.00
13 Mike Miller 2.50 6.00
14 Ben Gordon 2.50 6.00
15 O.J. Mayo 2.00 5.00
16 Elton Brand 2.50 6.00
17 Andrei Kirilenko 3.00 8.00
18 Darren Collison 2.00 5.00
19 Steve Nash 6.00 15.00
20 Jose Calderon 2.00 5.00
21 Andre Iguodala 3.00 8.00
22 Dwight Howard 4.00 10.00
23 Andrew Bynum 2.00 5.00
24 Jeff Green 2.00 5.00
25 Ryan Anderson 2.00 5.00
26 Kevin Durant 6.00 15.00
27 Chris Andersen 2.50 6.00
28 Chris Bosh 4.00 10.00
29 LeBron James 12.00 30.00
30 Monta Ellis 2.50 6.00

2013-14 Elite Back to the Future Materials Prime

*PRIME: .75X TO 2X BASIC
PRINT RUNS B/WN 5-25 COPIES PER
NO PRICING ON QTY 10 OR LESS

2013-14 Elite Dominators Materials

1 Carmelo Anthony 5.00 12.00
2 Kevin Martin 2.50 6.00
3 Chris Bosh 4.00 10.00
4 Blake Griffin 4.00 10.00
5 Paul Pierce 5.00 12.00
6 Shaquille O'Neal 5.00 12.00
7 Robert Parish 4.00 10.00
8 Kevin Garnett 4.00 10.00
9 Ray Allen 5.00 12.00
10 Kevin Durant 6.00 15.00
11 Kemba Walker 3.00 8.00
12 Tracy McGrady 5.00 12.00
13 Kobe Bryant 6.00 15.00
14 Derrick Rose 4.00 10.00
15 Patrick Ewing 5.00 12.00
16 Kenneth Faried 2.50 6.00
17 Kyrie Irving 5.00 12.00
18 Chris Paul 4.00 10.00
19 Clyde Drexler 5.00 12.00
20 Tim Duncan 8.00 20.00
21 Pau Gasol 5.00 12.00
22 David Robinson 6.00 15.00
23 Dirk Nowitzki 8.00 20.00
24 Dominique Wilkins 5.00 12.00
25 Dwyane Wade 4.00 10.00
26 Tony Parker 5.00 12.00
27 Deron Williams 2.50 6.00
28 Grant Hill 5.00 12.00
29 Joe Dumars 4.00 10.00
30 Ralph Sampson 2.50 6.00

2013-14 Elite Dominators Materials Prime

*PRIME: .75X TO 2X BASIC
PRINT RUNS B/WN 1-25 COPIES PER
NO PRICING ON QTY 10 OR LESS

2013-14 Elite Face 2 Face

1 D.Wade/T.Parker 1.50 4.00
2 K.Bryant/L.James 6.00 15.00
3 C.Bosh/T.Duncan 2.00 5.00
4 M.Gasol/S.Ibaka .75 2.00
5 J.Harden/K.Durant 2.50 6.00
6 B.Griffin/Z.Randolph .75 2.00
7 S.Curry/T.Lawson 6.00 15.00
8 K.Leonard/K.Thompson 2.50 6.00
9 C.Anthony/P.George 1.25 3.00
10 D.Rose/J.Wall 1.25 3.00
11 A.Davis/N.Vucevic 2.50 6.00
12 K.Irving/R.Felton 2.50 6.00
13 C.Paul/D.Williams 1.50 4.00
14 R.Rubio/R.Westbrook 1.25 3.00
15 G.Hill/J.Teague .60 1.50
16 B.Beal/J.Fredette 1.25 3.00
17 D.DeRozan/D.Waiters 1.00 2.50
18 D.Lillard/J.Lin 2.50 6.00
19 K.Faried/L.Aldridge .75 2.00
20 A.Drummond/T.Thompson .75 2.00

2013-14 Elite Face 2 Face Gold

*GOLD: 1.5X TO 4X BASIC
STATED PRINT RUN 24 SER.#'d SETS
2 K.Bryant/L.James 75.00 200.00

2013-14 Elite Franchise Future

1 Kyrie Irving 2.50 6.00
2 Andre Drummond .75 2.00
3 Trey Burke .60 1.50
4 Alex Len .60 1.50
5 Victor Oladipo 1.25 3.00
6 Terrence Ross .60 1.50
7 Kawhi Leonard 2.50 6.00
8 Isaiah Thomas .60 1.50
9 Shane Larkin .50 1.25
10 Jimmy Butler 1.50 4.00
11 Anthony Davis 2.50 6.00
12 Kenneth Faried .60 1.50
13 Cody Zeller .60 1.50
14 Bradley Beal 1.25 3.00
15 Michael Carter-Williams .60 1.50
16 Larry Sanders .50 1.25
17 Damian Lillard 2.50 6.00
18 Harrison Barnes .75 2.00
19 Chandler Parsons .50 1.25
20 Kelly Olynyk .60 1.50

2013-14 Elite Franchise Future Gold
*GOLD: 2.5X TO 6X BASIC
STATED PRINT RUN 24 SER.#'d SETS

2013-14 Elite New Breed Autograph Jerseys
PRINT RUNS B/WN 149-599 COPIES PER
EXCHANGE DEADLINE 7/29/2015
1 Victor Oladipo/149 15.00 40.00
2 Ricky Ledo/599 3.00 8.00
3 Reggie Bullock/499 4.00 10.00
4 Jeff Withey/599 3.00 8.00
5 Erik Murphy/599 3.00 8.00
6 Peyton Siva/599 3.00 8.00
7 Solomon Hill/499 4.00 10.00
8 Cody Zeller/149 4.00 10.00
9 Tim Hardaway Jr./499 6.00 15.00
10 Dennis Schroder/499 10.00 25.00
11 Nerlens Noel/175 4.00 10.00
12 Trey Burke/199 4.00 10.00
13 Jamaal Franklin/599 3.00 8.00
14 Andre Roberson/599 4.00 10.00
15 Kelly Olynyk/499 4.00 10.00
16 Isaiah Canaan/599 3.00 8.00
17 C.J. McCollum/199 20.00 50.00
18 Glen Rice Jr./499 3.00 8.00
19 G.Antetokounmpo/299 300.00 600.00
20 Otto Porter/149 5.00 12.00
21 Nate Wolters/499 3.00 8.00
22 M.Carter-Williams/175 4.00 10.00
23 Kentavious Caldwell-Pope/175 5.00 12.00
24 Allen Crabbe/499 3.00 8.00
25 Anthony Bennett/149 3.00 8.00
26 Mason Plumlee/199 4.00 10.00
27 Tony Mitchell/599 3.00 8.00
28 Alex Len/149 4.00 10.00
29 Shane Larkin/399 3.00 8.00
30 Steven Adams/199 15.00 40.00
31 Shabazz Muhammad/199 3.00 8.00
32 Ryan Kelly/599 3.00 8.00
33 Archie Goodwin/599 3.00 8.00
34 Tony Snell/499 4.00 10.00
35 Ben McLemore/175 4.00 10.00

2013-14 Elite New Breed Autograph Jerseys Prime
*PRIME: 1X TO 2.5X BASIC
STATED PRINT RUN 25 SER.#'d SETS
EXCHANGE DEADLINE 7/29/2015
1 Victor Oladipo 75.00 200.00
19 Giannis Antetokounmpo 1,000.00 2,000.00

2013-14 Elite Passing The Torch
1 J.Harden/K.Bryant 6.00 15.00
2 G.Gervin/K.Durant 2.50 6.00
3 A.Mourning/A.Davis 2.50 6.00
4 B.Griffin/B.McAdoo 1.00 2.50
5 J.Stockton/K.Irving 2.50 6.00
6 C.Anthony/W.Frazier 1.25 3.00
7 C.Paul/I.Thomas 1.50 4.00
8 G.Payton/R.Westbrook 1.25 3.00
9 M.Gasol/T.Duncan 2.00 5.00
10 D.Wade/S.Curry 6.00 15.00
11 D.Williams/J.Kidd 1.25 3.00
12 D.Mutombo/S.Ibaka 1.25 3.00
13 D.Rodman/K.Faried 2.00 5.00
14 C.Drexler/D.Lillard 2.50 6.00
15 K.Leonard/M.Ginobili 2.50 6.00
16 H.Olajuwon/R.Hibbert 1.50 4.00
17 G.Dragic/S.Nash 1.50 4.00
18 O.Robertson/R.Rondo 1.25 3.00
19 D.Cousins/V.Divac .75 2.00
20 D.Majerle/K.Thompson 2.50 6.00

2013-14 Elite Passing The Torch Autographs
PRINT RUNS B/WN 10-49 COPIES PER
NO PRICING ON QTY 10
EXCHANGE DEADLINE 7/29/2015
1 J.Harden/K.Bryant/25 500.00 1,000.00
2 H.Williams/R.Hibbert/49 5.00 12.00
3 Griffin/Cage/25 EXCH 25.00 60.00
4 K.Walker/T.Ross/25 6.00 15.00
5 D.Green/S.Elliott/49 8.00 20.00
6 A.Miller/T.Lawson/25 6.00 15.00
7 G.Rice/G.Rice Jr./49 6.00 15.00
8 C.Laettner/G.Henderson/25 10.00 25.00
9 M.Finley/M.Ellis/25 8.00 20.00
10 A.Jamison/H.Barnes/49 8.00 20.00
11 A.Horford/K.Willis/49 8.00 20.00
12 I.Thomas/M.Bogues/49 8.00 20.00
13 A.Hardaway/V.Oladipo/49 40.00 100.00
14 D.Howard/H.Olajuwon/49 25.00 60.00
16 A.Iguodala/C.Mullin/49 15.00 40.00
20 Terry/Thompson/25 EXCH 25.00 60.00
21 A.Mason/J.Smith/49 8.00 20.00
22 J.Lucas/J.Lucas III/49 6.00 15.00
24 M.Richardson/M.Conley/49 8.00 20.00
25 Hardaway/Hardaway Jr./49 20.00 50.00

2013-14 Elite Passing The Torch Gold
*GOLD: 1.5X TO 4X BASIC
STATED PRINT RUN 24 SER.#'d SETS
17 G.Dragic/S.Nash 40.00 100.00

2013-14 Elite Rookie Essentials Autograph Jerseys
PRINT RUNS B/WN 149-599 COPIES PER
EXCHANGE DEADLINE 7/29/2015
1 Ben McLemore/175 4.00 10.00
2 Tony Snell/499 4.00 10.00
3 Archie Goodwin/599 3.00 8.00
4 Ryan Kelly/599 3.00 8.00
5 Shabazz Muhammad/199 3.00 8.00
6 Steven Adams/199 8.00 20.00
7 Shane Larkin/499 3.00 8.00
8 Alex Len/149 4.00 10.00
9 Tony Mitchell/599 3.00 8.00
10 Mason Plumlee/299 4.00 10.00
11 Victor Oladipo/149 15.00 40.00
12 Jeff Withey/599 3.00 8.00
13 Tim Hardaway Jr./499 6.00 15.00
14 Nerlens Noel/175 4.00 10.00
15 Kelly Olynyk/449 4.00 10.00
16 Glen Rice Jr./299 3.00 8.00
17 C.J. McCollum/199 15.00 40.00
18 Otto Porter/149 5.00 12.00
19 Kentavious Caldwell-Pope/175 5.00 12.00
20 Anthony Bennett/149 3.00 8.00
21 Ricky Ledo/599 3.00 8.00
22 Erik Murphy/599 3.00 8.00
23 Cody Zeller/149 4.00 10.00
24 Trey Burke/199 4.00 10.00
25 Isaiah Canaan/599 3.00 8.00
26 Dennis Schroder/499 5.00 12.00
27 G.Antetokounmpo/299 200.00 500.00
28 Nate Wolters/599 3.00 8.00
29 M.Carter-Williams/175 4.00 10.00
30 Allen Crabbe/499 3.00 8.00
31 Reggie Bullock/299 4.00 10.00
32 Peyton Siva/599 3.00 8.00
33 Solomon Hill/599 4.00 10.00
34 Jamaal Franklin/599 3.00 8.00
35 Andre Roberson/599 4.00 10.00

2013-14 Elite Rookie Essentials Autograph Jerseys Prime
*PRIME: 1X TO 2.5X BASIC
STATED PRINT RUN 25 SER.#'d SETS
EXCHANGE DEADLINE 7/29/2015

2013-14 Elite Series Inserts
1 Kevin Durant 2.50 6.00
2 Dwight Howard 1.00 2.50
3 Tim Duncan 2.00 5.00
4 Damian Lillard 2.50 6.00
5 Anfernee Hardaway 2.00 5.00
6 Vince Carter 1.50 4.00
7 Kyrie Irving 2.50 6.00
8 Alonzo Mourning 1.25 3.00
9 Rajon Rondo 1.00 2.50
10 Carmelo Anthony 1.25 3.00
11 Pau Gasol 1.25 3.00
12 Metta World Peace .60 1.50
13 Isiah Thomas 1.25 3.00
14 Ricky Rubio .60 1.50
15 Ray Allen 1.25 3.00
16 Manu Ginobili 1.50 4.00
17 Magic Johnson 3.00 8.00
18 Tony Parker 1.25 3.00
19 Paul Pierce 1.25 3.00
20 Wilt Chamberlain 2.50 6.00
21 Kobe Bryant 6.00 15.00
22 John Wall 1.00 2.50
23 Shaquille O'Neal 3.00 8.00
24 Steve Nash 1.50 4.00
25 Anthony Davis 2.50 6.00
26 Drazen Petrovic 1.00 2.50
27 Russell Westbrook 1.25 3.00
28 Dwyane Wade 1.50 4.00
29 Larry Bird 3.00 8.00
30 Dirk Nowitzki 2.00 5.00
31 Chris Paul 1.50 4.00
32 Paul George 1.25 3.00
33 Julius Erving 2.00 5.00
34 Derrick Rose 1.25 3.00
35 LeBron James 6.00 15.00
36 Blake Griffin .75 2.00
37 George Gervin 1.25 3.00
38 Amar'e Stoudemire .75 2.00
39 Kevin Garnett 2.00 5.00
40 Chris Bosh 1.00 2.50

2013-14 Elite Series Inserts Gold
*GOLD: 2X TO 5X BASIC
STATED PRINT RUN 24 SER.#'d SETS

2013-14 Elite Signatures
PRINT RUNS B/WN 10-199 COPIES PER
NO PRICING ON QTY 10
EXCHANGE DEADLINE 7/29/2015
1 Kevin Durant/99 75.00 200.00
3 Nikola Pekovic/125 3.00 8.00
5 Meyers Leonard/49 3.00 8.00
6 Brandon Bass/50 3.00 8.00
7 Rodney Stuckey/49 3.00 8.00
8 MarShon Brooks/75 3.00 8.00
9 Anthony Davis/49 50.00 100.00
12 Greivis Vasquez/149 EXCH 3.00 8.00
15 Isaiah Thomas/199 12.00 30.00
16 Tiago Splitter/199 3.00 8.00
18 D.J. Augustin/199 3.00 8.00
21 Kyle Korver/149 4.00 10.00
22 Tony Parker/49 12.00 30.00
23 Harrison Barnes/49 5.00 12.00
28 Draymond Green/149 10.00 25.00
30 Stephen Curry/49 400.00 800.00
34 Kobe Bryant/75 400.00 800.00
35 Andre Iguodala/25 12.00 30.00
36 Blake Griffin/49 EXCH 20.00 50.00
37 Luis Scola/150 4.00 10.00
38 J.J. Redick/49 5.00 12.00
39 Josh Smith/99 3.00 8.00
40 Nikola Vucevic/49 6.00 15.00
42 Kyrie Irving/99 EXCH 30.00 80.00
46 Raymond Felton/149 3.00 8.00
47 Nando De Colo/99 3.00 8.00
48 John Salmons/99 4.00 10.00
50 Patrick Patterson/99 3.00 8.00

2013-14 Elite Throwback Threads
1 Robert Parish 4.00 10.00
2 Artis Gilmore 4.00 10.00
3 Larry Bird 12.00 30.00
4 Danny Manning 2.50 6.00
5 Kiki Vandeweghe 2.50 6.00
6 Earl Monroe 5.00 12.00
7 Hakeem Olajuwon 6.00 15.00
8 Magic Johnson 12.00 30.00
9 David Robinson 6.00 15.00
10 Larry Nance 2.50 6.00
11 Robert Horry 3.00 8.00
12 Danny Ainge 3.00 8.00
13 Jeff Hornacek 2.50 6.00
14 Jalen Rose 2.50 6.00
15 Jamal Mashburn 2.50 6.00
16 Reggie Lewis 8.00 20.00
17 Clyde Drexler 5.00 12.00
18 Patrick Ewing 5.00 12.00
19 Xavier McDaniel 2.50 6.00
20 Calvin Murphy 2.50 6.00
21 Buck Williams 2.50 6.00
22 Robert Parish 4.00 10.00
23 Alex English 4.00 10.00
24 Kevin McHale 5.00 12.00
25 Shaquille O'Neal 5.00 12.00
26 Larry Johnson 4.00 10.00
27 Joe Dumars 4.00 10.00
28 Jalen Rose 2.50 6.00
29 Anfernee Hardaway 6.00 15.00
30 Dominique Wilkins 5.00 12.00
31 Larry Nance 2.50 6.00
32 Moses Malone 5.00 12.00
33 Ralph Sampson 2.50 6.00
34 Isiah Thomas 5.00 12.00
35 Bernard King 4.00 10.00
36 Alex English 4.00 10.00
37 Karl Malone 6.00 15.00
38 Shaquille O'Neal 5.00 12.00
39 Fat Lever 2.50 6.00
40 Jeff Hornacek 2.50 6.00

2013-14 Elite Throwback Threads Autographs
PRINT RUNS B/WN 25-299 COPIES PER
EXCHANGE DEADLINE 7/29/2015
3 World B. Free/49 4.00 10.00
5 Joe Dumars/49 10.00 25.00
9 Scottie Pippen/49 50.00 120.00
11 Toni Kukoc/149 12.00 30.00
12 Ralph Sampson/25 4.00 10.00
13 Mitch Richmond/75 15.00 40.00
15 Sean Elliott/299 5.00 12.00
17 Grant Hill/99 20.00 50.00
18 Buck Williams/299 4.00 10.00
19 Jerry West/49 15.00 40.00
21 Alex English/99 8.00 20.00
22 Bill Laimbeer/299 5.00 12.00
23 Clyde Drexler/25 20.00 50.00
24 David Robinson/49 20.00 50.00
25 Fat Lever/299 4.00 10.00
27 Eddie Johnson/199 3.00 8.00
28 Larry Bird/49 30.00 80.00
29 Nick Anderson/199 4.00 10.00
30 Jamal Mashburn/299 4.00 10.00

2013-14 Elite Throwback Threads Autographs Prime
*PRIME: 1X TO 2.5X BASIC
PRINT RUNS B/WN 3-25 COPIES PER
NO PRICING ON QTY 10 OR LESS
EXCHANGE DEADLINE 7/29/2015

2013-14 Elite Throwback Threads Prime
*PRIME: 1X TO 2.5X BASIC
PRINT RUNS B/WN 3-25 COPIES PER
NO PRICING ON QTY 10 OR LESS

2013-14 Elite Turn of the Century Autographs
PRINT RUNS B/WN 5-100 COPIES PER
NO PRICING ON QTY 10 OR LESS
EXCHANGE DEADLINE 7/29/2015
1 Jason Terry/50 5.00 12.00
2 Donatas Motiejunas/75 5.00 12.00
3 Andray Blatche/100 4.00 10.00
4 Marcus Thornton/75 4.00 10.00
5 Harrison Barnes/75 6.00 15.00
6 Nikola Vucevic/100 8.00 20.00
7 Shane Battier/25 5.00 12.00
8 Steve Novak/50 4.00 10.00
9 Brandon Knight/49 5.00 12.00
10 Eric Gordon/25 5.00 12.00
11 Kevin Martin/15 5.00 12.00
12 Austin Rivers/25 5.00 12.00
13 Kawhi Leonard/100 75.00 200.00
14 Marcin Gortat/75 4.00 10.00
15 Anthony Davis/49 50.00 120.00
17 Zaza Pachulia/100 4.00 10.00
18 Lavoy Allen/100 4.00 10.00
19 Draymond Green/75 20.00 50.00
20 Brandon Bass/25 4.00 10.00
21 Joe Johnson/25 5.00 12.00
22 Nikola Pekovic/100 4.00 10.00
23 Andrei Kirilenko/100 6.00 15.00
25 Kobe Bryant/100 EXCH 800.00 1,500.00
26 Gordon Hayward/50 5.00 12.00
27 J.R. Smith/100 6.00 15.00
28 Andrew Bogut/75 5.00 12.00
29 Brandon Rush/50 4.00 10.00
30 Luc Mbah a Moute/100 EXCH 4.00 10.00
31 Jeff Green/50 4.00 10.00
32 Jrue Holiday/50 8.00 20.00
33 Kevin Love/50 6.00 15.00
34 Monta Ellis/50 EXCH 5.00 12.00
35 DeAndre Jordan/25 5.00 12.00
36 Luis Scola/50 5.00 12.00
37 Raymond Felton/75 4.00 10.00
38 Tristan Thompson/25 4.00 10.00
39 Tony Allen/25 4.00 10.00
40 Patrick Patterson/100 4.00 10.00
41 Thomas Robinson/25 4.00 10.00
42 Caron Butler/25 5.00 12.00
44 Courtney Lee/100 4.00 10.00
45 Vince Carter/50 40.00 100.00
46 Ben Gordon/25 5.00 12.00
47 MarShon Brooks/100 4.00 10.00
48 D.J. Augustin/100 4.00 10.00
49 Enes Kanter/75 5.00 12.00
50 Kyle Korver/50 5.00 12.00
52 DeMarcus Cousins/25 6.00 15.00
53 Kevin Durant/75 EXCH 125.00 300.00
54 Ramon Sessions/100 4.00 10.00
55 Mario Chalmers/50 5.00 12.00
57 Nick Young/25 4.00 10.00
58 Klay Thompson/50 60.00 150.00
59 Byron Mullens/75 4.00 10.00
60 Tayshaun Prince/49 6.00 15.00
61 Jared Sullinger/49 4.00 10.00
62 Iman Shumpert/50 4.00 10.00
63 Lance Stephenson/75 5.00 12.00
64 Jerryd Bayless/100 EXCH 4.00 10.00
65 Nando De Colo/100 4.00 10.00
66 Stephen Curry/50 500.00 1,000.00
67 Josh Smith/25 4.00 10.00
68 Steve Blake/100 4.00 10.00
69 Andre Drummond/50 6.00 15.00
70 Taj Gibson/50 4.00 10.00
71 Randy Foye/50 4.00 10.00
72 Andrea Bargnani/25 4.00 10.00
73 Chase Budinger/50 4.00 10.00
74 Kyle Singler/100 4.00 10.00
75 Blake Griffin/50 EXCH 6.00 15.00
76 Greivis Vasquez/25 4.00 10.00
77 Tiago Splitter/75 4.00 10.00
78 John Salmons/100 5.00 12.00
79 Michael Kidd-Gilchrist/25 4.00 10.00
80 Trevor Booker/75 4.00 10.00
81 Dorell Wright/100 4.00 10.00
82 Kyle Lowry/100 6.00 15.00
83 Joel Anthony/100 4.00 10.00
84 Jan Vesely/100 4.00 10.00
85 Jose Calderon/50 4.00 10.00
86 Kent Bazemore/100 4.00 10.00
87 Darren Collison/50 4.00 10.00
88 Tyreke Evans/50 5.00 12.00
89 Kyrie Irving/100 50.00 120.00
90 Andre Iguodala/25 15.00 40.00
91 Isaiah Thomas/75 5.00 12.00
92 Meyers Leonard/100 4.00 10.00
93 Rodney Stuckey/49 4.00 10.00
94 J.J. Redick/50 6.00 15.00
95 Ekpe Udoh/100 4.00 10.00
96 J.J. Hickson/100 4.00 10.00
97 Al Horford/25 6.00 15.00
98 Jonas Valanciunas/50 5.00 12.00
99 Anthony Morrow/75 4.00 10.00
100 E'Twaun Moore/100 4.00 10.00

2014-15 Elite
1 Derrick Favors .40 1.00
2 Kevin Durant 2.00 5.00
3 Wesley Matthews .40 1.00
4 Russell Westbrook 1.00 2.50
5 Thaddeus Young .40 1.00
6 Kevin Love .60 1.50
7 John Wall .75 2.00
8 Stephen Curry 5.00 12.00
9 Andre Drummond .50 1.25
10 Roy Hibbert .50 1.25
11 James Harden 1.25 3.00
12 Klay Thompson 1.50 4.00
13 Tony Parker 1.00 2.50
14 Monta Ellis .50 1.25
15 Goran Dragic .60 1.50
16 Tiago Splitter .40 1.00
17 Joakim Noah .60 1.50
18 Kyle Korver .50 1.25
19 Marc Gasol .60 1.50
20 Deron Williams .50 1.25
21 Paul Millsap .50 1.25
22 Kenneth Faried .40 1.00
23 Kobe Bryant 5.00 12.00
24 Josh Smith .40 1.00
25 Kyrie Irving 1.25 3.00
26 Nicolas Batum .50 1.25
27 Danilo Gallinari .40 1.00
28 Luol Deng .50 1.25
29 Dirk Nowitzki 1.50 4.00
30 DeMar DeRozan .75 2.00
31 Kawhi Leonard 1.50 4.00
32 Lance Stephenson .50 1.25
33 Blake Griffin .60 1.50
34 Pau Gasol 1.00 2.50
35 Al Horford .60 1.50
36 Paul Pierce 1.00 2.50
37 Andrew Bogut .50 1.25
38 Dwight Howard .75 2.00
39 DeAndre Jordan .50 1.25
40 Tyreke Evans .50 1.25
41 Dwyane Wade 1.25 3.00
42 Rajon Rondo .75 2.00
43 Joe Johnson .50 1.25
44 Carmelo Anthony 1.00 2.50
45 Zach Randolph .60 1.50
46 David Lee .40 1.00
47 Damian Lillard 1.50 4.00
48 Ty Lawson .40 1.00
49 Nene .50 1.25
50 Tim Duncan 1.50 4.00
51 Mike Conley .50 1.25
52 Gordon Hayward .50 1.25
53 Chris Bosh .75 2.00
54 David West .50 1.25
55 Al Jefferson .40 1.00
56 Omer Asik .40 1.00
57 LaMarcus Aldridge .60 1.50
58 Rudy Gay .60 1.50
59 Derrick Rose 1.25 3.00
60 Brook Lopez .60 1.50
61 Chandler Parsons .40 1.00
62 Anthony Davis 1.50 4.00
63 Bradley Beal 1.00 2.50
64 Kyle Lowry .75 2.00
65 Nikola Pekovic .40 1.00
66 Serge Ibaka .50 1.25
67 Manu Ginobili 1.25 3.00
68 Jonas Valanciunas .50 1.25
69 DeMarcus Cousins .50 1.25
70 Jrue Holiday .75 2.00
71 Greg Monroe .40 1.00
72 Chris Paul 1.00 2.50
73 Tyson Chandler .60 1.50
74 Marcin Gortat .40 1.00
75 Eric Bledsoe .50 1.25
76 Ricky Rubio .50 1.25
77 Andre Iguodala .60 1.50
78 Arron Afflalo .40 1.00
79 Ryan Anderson .40 1.00
80 LeBron James 5.00 12.00
81 Scottie Pippen 1.50 4.00
82 John Stockton 1.25 3.00
83 Julius Erving 1.50 4.00
84 Moses Malone 1.00 2.50
85 Hakeem Olajuwon 1.25 3.00
86 Jerry West 1.50 4.00
87 Oscar Robertson 1.25 3.00
88 Karl Malone 1.25 3.00
89 Shaquille O'Neal 2.50 6.00
90 Kevin McHale 1.00 2.50
91 Bill Russell 2.00 5.00
92 Kareem Abdul-Jabbar 2.00 5.00
93 Allen Iverson 1.50 4.00
94 Larry Bird 2.50 6.00
95 Patrick Ewing 1.00 2.50
96 Dennis Rodman 1.50 4.00
97 Magic Johnson 2.50 6.00
98 David Robinson 1.25 3.00
99 Isiah Thomas 1.00 2.50
100 Wilt Chamberlain 2.00 5.00

2014-15 Elite Blue
*BLUE: 1.25X TO 3X BASE HI
STATED PRINT RUN 99 SER.#'d SETS

2014-15 Elite Purple
*PURPLE: 1X TO 2.5X BASE HI
STATED PRINT RUN 199 SER.#'d SETS

2014-15 Elite Red
*RED: 2.5X TO 6X BASE HI
STATED PRINT RUN 25 SER.#'d SETS

2014-15 Elite Status
*STATUS: 2X TO 5X BASE HI
STATED PRINT RUN B/WN 9-99 COPIES PER
NO PRICING ON QTY 12 OR LESS

2014-15 Elite Status Signatures
STATED PRINT RUN B/WN 125-249 COPIES PER
1 Andrew Wiggins/125 15.00 40.00
2 Jabari Parker/125 4.00 10.00
3 K.J. McDaniels/249 3.00 8.00
4 Johnny O'Bryant/249 3.00 8.00
5 Damien Inglis/249 3.00 8.00
6 Jordan Adams/249 3.00 8.00
7 Lucas Nogueira/249 3.00 8.00
8 Joe Harris/249 5.00 12.00
9 Alex Kirk/249 3.00 8.00
10 James Young/125 3.00 8.00
11 Markel Brown/249 3.00 8.00
12 Russ Smith/249 3.00 8.00
13 Damjan Rudez/249 3.00 8.00
14 T.J. Warren/125 5.00 12.00
15 Devyn Marble/249 3.00 8.00
16 Zach LaVine/199 20.00 50.00
17 Jusuf Nurkic/199 10.00 25.00
18 James Ennis/249 3.00 8.00
19 Cameron Bairstow/249 3.00 8.00
20 Jerami Grant/249 15.00 40.00
21 Nikola Mirotic/125 5.00 12.00
22 Cory Jefferson/249 3.00 8.00
23 Elfrid Payton/125 5.00 12.00
24 Joel Embiid/125 125.00 300.00
25 Aaron Gordon/125 15.00 40.00
26 Nik Stauskas/125 3.00 8.00
27 Bojan Bogdanovic/249 5.00 12.00
28 Zoran Dragic/249 4.00 10.00
30 Doug McDermott/125 5.00 12.00
31 Kyle Anderson/249 5.00 12.00
32 Glenn Robinson III/199 4.00 10.00
33 Jarnell Stokes/249 3.00 8.00
34 Gary Harris/125 5.00 12.00
35 Adreian Payne/249 3.00 8.00
36 Glen Rice/125 5.00 12.00
37 Isiah Thomas/125 8.00 20.00
38 Adrian Dantley/125 5.00 12.00
39 Toni Kukoc/125 6.00 15.00
40 Dikembe Mutombo/125 8.00 20.00
41 Baron Davis/125 5.00 12.00
42 Dee Brown/125 4.00 10.00
43 Fred Brown/199 3.00 8.00
44 Rolando Blackman/125 4.00 10.00
45 Anfernee Hardaway/125 20.00 50.00
46 Jimmy Jones/125 3.00 8.00
47 Freddie Lewis/125 3.00 8.00
48 Rod Strickland/199 4.00 10.00
49 Tracy McGrady/125 25.00 60.00
50 Rudy Tomjanovich/199 5.00 12.00
51 John Starks/125 5.00 12.00
52 Latrell Sprewell/125 20.00 50.00
53 Cedric Maxwell/125 4.00 10.00
54 Brian Grant/199 4.00 10.00
55 Michael Cooper/199 5.00 12.00
56 Rick Fox/125 4.00 10.00
57 Allan Houston/125 5.00 12.00
58 Mark Price/249 5.00 12.00
59 Spud Webb/249 5.00 12.00
60 Vlade Divac/249 5.00 12.00
61 Muggsy Bogues/249 5.00 12.00
62 Eddie Jones/199 5.00 12.00
63 Josh Smith/125 3.00 8.00
64 Caron Butler/125 3.00 8.00
65 Chris Kaman/125 4.00 10.00
66 Andre Iguodala/125 5.00 12.00
67 Brook Lopez/125 5.00 12.00
68 Isaiah Canaan/249 3.00 8.00
69 Andrea Bargnani/125 3.00 8.00
70 Steve Blake/199 3.00 8.00
71 C.J. Watson/125 3.00 8.00
72 Jose Calderon/125 3.00 8.00
73 Gorgui Dieng/249 3.00 8.00
74 Richard Jefferson/125 4.00 10.00
75 Tristan Thompson/125 3.00 8.00
76 Amir Johnson/125 3.00 8.00
77 Gerald Henderson/125 3.00 8.00
78 Alexey Shved/199 3.00 8.00
79 Jason Thompson/125 3.00 8.00
80 Ryan Anderson/125 3.00 8.00
81 Chris Copeland/249 3.00 8.00
82 Timofey Mozgov/199 3.00 8.00
83 Kyle Korver/249 4.00 10.00
84 Greg Smith/125 3.00 8.00
85 Jason Terry/125 4.00 10.00
86 Rasual Butler/199 3.00 8.00
87 Chris Douglas-Roberts/199 3.00 8.00
88 Kevin Martin/125 4.00 10.00
89 Taj Gibson/125 3.00 8.00
90 Dennis Schroder/249 5.00 12.00
91 Troy Daniels/249 3.00 8.00
92 Solomon Hill/249 3.00 8.00
93 Ryan Kelly/249 3.00 8.00
94 Maurice Harkless/199 3.00 8.00
95 Brandon Knight/125 3.00 8.00
96 C.J. Miles/249 3.00 8.00
97 Lance Thomas/249 3.00 8.00
98 Phil Pressey/249 3.00 8.00
99 Mathew Dellavedova/249 4.00 10.00
100 Mike Muscala/249 3.00 8.00

2014-15 Elite Status Signatures Blue
*BLUE: .8X TO 2X BASE HI
STATED PRINT RUN 49 SER.#'d SETS
50 Rudy Tomjanovich 10.00 25.00

2014-15 Elite Status Signatures Bronze
*BRONZE: 1X TO 2.5X BASE HI
STATED PRINT RUN 25 SER.#'d SETS
LACK OF PRICING DUE TO MARKET INFO

2014-15 Elite Status Signatures Purple
*PURPLE: .6X TO 1.5X BASE HI
STATED PRINT RUN 74 SER.#'d SETS

2014-15 Elite Status Signatures Red
*RED: .5X TO 1.2X BASE HI
STATED PRINT RUN 99 SER.#'d SETS

2014-15 Elite Dominators
STATED PRINT RUN 999 SER.#'d SETS
1 Kevin Love 1.50 4.00
2 Kevin Durant 5.00 12.00
3 John Wall 2.00 5.00
4 Russell Westbrook 2.50 6.00
5 Stephen Curry 12.00 30.00
6 Andre Drummond 1.25 3.00
7 Roy Hibbert 1.25 3.00
8 James Harden 3.00 8.00
9 Klay Thompson 4.00 10.00
10 Tony Parker 2.50 6.00
11 DeMarcus Cousins 1.25 3.00
12 Anthony Davis 4.00 10.00
13 Al Jefferson 1.00 2.50
14 Kyle Lowry 2.00 5.00
15 Goran Dragic 1.50 4.00
16 Kobe Bryant 12.00 30.00
17 Joakim Noah 1.50 4.00
18 Kyrie Irving 3.00 8.00
19 Marc Gasol 1.50 4.00
20 Serge Ibaka 1.25 3.00
21 Paul Millsap 1.25 3.00
22 Dirk Nowitzki 4.00 10.00
23 DeMar DeRozan 2.00 5.00
24 Kawhi Leonard 4.00 10.00
25 Dwight Howard 2.00 5.00
26 Dwyane Wade 3.00 8.00
27 Rajon Rondo 2.00 5.00
28 Luol Deng 1.25 3.00
29 Blake Griffin 1.50 4.00
30 Pau Gasol 2.50 6.00
31 Carmelo Anthony 2.50 6.00
32 Damian Lillard 4.00 10.00
33 Tim Duncan 4.00 10.00
34 Chris Bosh 2.00 5.00
35 LaMarcus Aldridge 1.50 4.00
36 Chris Paul 2.50 6.00
37 LeBron James 12.00 30.00
38 DeAndre Jordan 1.25 3.00
39 Zach Randolph 1.50 4.00
40 Derrick Rose 3.00 8.00
41 Julius Erving 4.00 10.00
42 John Stockton 3.00 8.00
43 Oscar Robertson 3.00 8.00
44 Karl Malone 3.00 8.00
45 Shaquille O'Neal 6.00 15.00
46 Scottie Pippen 4.00 10.00
47 Bill Russell 5.00 12.00
48 Kareem Abdul-Jabbar 5.00 12.00
49 Allen Iverson 4.00 10.00
50 Magic Johnson 6.00 15.00

2014-15 Elite Dominators Signatures
STATED PRINT RUN B/WN 50-149 COPIES PER
1 Alex English/50 8.00 20.00
2 Jamaal Wilkes/50 6.00 15.00
3 Dan Issel/99 8.00 20.00
4 Dolph Schayes/50 6.00 15.00
5 Walt Frazier/50 10.00 25.00
6 George Gervin/50 10.00 25.00
7 Glen Rice/50 6.00 15.00
8 David Thompson/50 6.00 15.00
9 Maurice Cheeks/149 5.00 12.00
10 John Starks/99 6.00 15.00
11 Tom Chambers/50 6.00 15.00
12 Bill Cartwright/50 6.00 15.00
13 Norm Nixon/149 5.00 12.00
14 Rod Strickland/149 5.00 12.00
15 Cazzie Russell/149 6.00 15.00
16 Mahmoud Abdul-Rauf/149 5.00 12.00
17 Larry Nance/149 5.00 12.00
18 Billy Paultz/149 5.00 12.00
19 Dale Ellis/50 5.00 12.00
20 Paul Westphal/149 6.00 15.00
21 Fat Lever/149 5.00 12.00
22 Bob Dandridge/149 6.00 15.00
23 Vernon Maxwell/149 5.00 12.00
24 Cedric Ceballos/149 5.00 12.00
25 Dee Brown/149 5.00 12.00
26 Rolando Blackman/99 5.00 12.00
27 Fred Brown/149 4.00 10.00
28 Bo Kimble/149 5.00 12.00
29 Christian Laettner/50 6.00 15.00
30 Byron Scott/50 6.00 15.00
31 Baron Davis/50 5.00 12.00
32 Steve Smith/149 5.00 12.00
33 Bill Laimbeer/149 6.00 15.00
34 Bill Walton/50 12.00 30.00
35 Chris Webber/50 50.00 120.00
36 Mark Aguirre/50 5.00 12.00
38 Mitch Richmond/50 8.00 20.00
39 Jason Kidd/50 20.00 50.00
40 Darryl Dawkins/99 6.00 15.00
41 Rudy Tomjanovich/149 6.00 15.00
42 Jack Sikma/149 6.00 15.00
43 Brad Davis/149 5.00 12.00
44 Peja Stojakovic/50 5.00 12.00
45 Mychal Thompson/149 5.00 12.00
46 Spencer Haywood/149 6.00 15.00
47 Dikembe Mutombo/50 10.00 25.00
48 Alonzo Mourning/50 25.00 60.00
49 Tim Hardaway/149 8.00 20.00
50 Tracy McGrady/149 40.00 100.00

2014-15 Elite Jersey Number Die Cuts
*DIE CUTS: 1.5X TO 4X BASE HI
STATED PRINT RUN B/WN 1-91 COPIES PER
NO PRICING ON QTY 19 OR LESS
23 Kobe Bryant/24 30.00 80.00
26 Nicolas Batum/88 5.00 12.00
50 Tim Duncan/21 10.00 25.00
62 Anthony Davis/23 20.00 50.00
80 LeBron James/23 40.00 100.00
90 Kevin McHale/32 5.00 12.00

2019-20 Elite
RC (101-150) STATED PRINT RUN 299 SER. #'d SETS
1 Kyrie Irving .75 2.00
2 Nikola Vucevic .30 .75
3 Will Barton .25 .60
4 John Collins .40 1.00
5 Robert Covington .25 .60
6 Dillon Brooks .30 .75
7 Derrick Rose .75 2.00
8 Kawhi Leonard 1.00 2.50
9 Pascal Siakam .60 1.50
10 Harrison Barnes .30 .75
11 Spencer Dinwiddie .30 .75
12 Evan Fournier .30 .75
13 Shai Gilgeous-Alexander 2.00 5.00
14 Jabari Parker .25 .60
15 Giannis Antetokounmpo 2.00 5.00
16 Jonas Valanciunas .30 .75
17 Andre Drummond .30 .75
18 Paul George .60 1.50
19 Kyle Lowry .40 1.00
20 Marvin Bagley III .30 .75
21 Marcus Morris Sr. .25 .60
22 Devonte' Graham .30 .75
23 Danilo Gallinari .30 .75
24 James Harden .75 2.00
25 Khris Middleton .40 1.00
26 DeMar DeRozan .50 1.25
27 Luke Kennard .30 .75
28 Lou Williams .40 1.00
29 Fred VanVleet .50 1.25
30 Stephen Curry 3.00 8.00
31 Julius Randle .50 1.25
32 Terry Rozier .30 .75
33 Dennis Schroder .30 .75
34 Russell Westbrook .60 1.50
35 Eric Bledsoe .30 .75
36 LaMarcus Aldridge .40 1.00
37 Blake Griffin .40 1.00
38 Montrezl Harrell .30 .75
39 Kemba Walker .30 .75
40 Klay Thompson 1.00 2.50
41 Kevin Knox II .25 .60
42 Miles Bridges .40 1.00
43 Chris Paul .75 2.00
44 Eric Gordon .30 .75
45 T.J. Warren .30 .75
46 Rudy Gay .30 .75
47 Collin Sexton .50 1.25
48 Devin Booker .10 .25
49 Jayson Tatum 1.50 4.00
50 Draymond Green .50 1.25
51 Donovan Mitchell .75 2.00
52 Bradley Beal .50 1.25
53 Damian Lillard 1.00 2.50
54 Vince Carter .75 2.00
55 Domantas Sabonis .50 1.25
56 Bryn Forbes .30 .75
57 Kevin Love .40 1.00
58 Kelly Oubre Jr. .30 .75
59 Jaylen Brown .60 1.50
60 D'Angelo Russell .30 .75
61 Bojan Bogdanovic .30 .75
62 John Wall .50 1.25
63 CJ McCollum .40 1.00
64 Luka Doncic 2.50 6.00
65 Malcolm Brogdon .30 .75
66 Brandon Ingram .40 1.00
67 Tristan Thompson .25 .60
68 Deandre Ayton .40 1.00
69 Joel Embiid .75 2.00
70 Jimmy Butler .75 2.00
71 Rudy Gobert .50 1.25
72 Christian Wood .30 .75
73 Carmelo Anthony .60 1.50
74 Kristaps Porzingis .50 1.25
75 Zach LaVine .60 1.50
76 Jrue Holiday .50 1.25
77 Anthony Davis 1.00 2.50
78 Ricky Rubio .30 .75
79 Tobias Harris .30 .75
80 Bam Adebayo .60 1.50
81 Nikola Jokic 2.00 5.00
82 Davis Bertans .25 .60
83 Andrew Wiggins .50 1.25
84 Tim Hardaway Jr. .25 .60
85 Lauri Markkanen .50 1.25
86 JJ Redick .40 1.00
87 LeBron James 3.00 8.00
88 Buddy Hield .30 .75
89 Ben Simmons .40 1.00
90 Goran Dragic .30 .75
91 Jamal Murray .60 1.50
92 Trae Young 1.00 2.50
93 Karl-Anthony Towns .60 1.50
94 Jaren Jackson Jr. .60 1.50
95 Wendell Carter Jr. .40 1.00
96 Lonzo Ball .40 1.00
97 Kyle Kuzma .50 1.25
98 De'Aaron Fox .60 1.50
99 Kevin Durant 1.25 3.00
100 Aaron Gordon .40 1.00
101 Jaylen Nowell RC 1.25 3.00
102 Cameron Johnson RC 2.50 6.00
103 Tremont Waters RC 1.25 3.00
104 Nickeil Alexander-Walker RC 1.50 4.00
105 Terence Davis RC 1.50 4.00
106 Grant Williams RC 1.50 4.00
107 Mfiondu Kabengele RC 1.25 3.00
108 Zion Williamson RC 125.00 300.00
109 Carsen Edwards RC 1.25 3.00
110 Darius Garland RC 4.00 10.00
111 Bol Bol RC 8.00 20.00
112 PJ Washington Jr. RC 8.00 20.00
113 Kyle Guy RC 1.25 3.00
114 Goga Bitadze RC 1.50 4.00
115 Nicolo Melli RC 1.25 3.00
116 Darius Bazley RC 1.00 2.50
117 Jordan Poole RC 4.00 10.00
118 Ja Morant RC 100.00 250.00
119 Bruno Fernando RC 1.25 3.00
120 Coby White RC 20.00 50.00
121 Isaiah Roby RC 1.25 3.00
122 Tyler Herro RC 30.00 80.00
123 Kendrick Nunn RC 1.50 4.00
124 Luka Samanic RC 1.25 3.00
125 Daniel Gafford RC 2.00 5.00
126 Ty Jerome RC 2.00 5.00
127 Keldon Johnson RC 8.00 20.00
128 RJ Barrett RC 10.00 25.00
129 Cody Martin RC 1.50 4.00
130 Jaxson Hayes RC 1.50 4.00
131 Ignas Brazdeikis RC 1.25 3.00
132 Romeo Langford RC 1.00 2.50

133 Ky Bowman RC 1.25 3.00
134 Matisse Thybulle RC 2.00 5.00
135 Luguentz Dort RC 12.00 30.00
136 Nassir Little RC 1.50 4.00
137 Kevin Porter Jr. RC 2.00 5.00
138 De'Andre Hunter RC 4.00 10.00
139 Eric Paschall RC 1.25 3.00
140 Rui Hachimura RC 4.00 10.00
141 Quindary Weatherspoon RC 1.00 2.50
142 Sekou Doumbouya RC 1.00 2.50
143 Tacko Fall RC 1.25 3.00
144 Brandon Clarke RC 2.00 5.00
145 Terance Mann RC 2.00 5.00
146 Dylan Windler RC 1.25 3.00
147 KZ Okpala RC 1.25 3.00
148 Jarrett Culver RC 1.00 2.50
149 Admiral Schofield RC 1.25 3.00
150 Cam Reddish RC 1.50 4.00

2019-20 Elite Aspirations
*ASPIRATIONS: .75X TO 2X BASIC
PRINT RUN BTWN 1-99 SER.#'d SETS
15 Giannis Antetokounmpo/66 10.00 25.00
30 Stephen Curry/70 8.00 20.00
49 Jayson Tatum/99 8.00 20.00
64 Luka Doncic/23 75.00 200.00
77 Anthony Davis/97 10.00 25.00
80 Bam Adebayo/87 4.00 10.00
87 LeBron James/77 75.00 200.00
99 Kevin Durant/93 8.00 20.00

2019-20 Elite Blue
*BLUE: .75X TO 2X BASIC
PRINT RUN 99 SER.#'d SETS
15 Giannis Antetokounmpo 8.00 20.00
30 Stephen Curry 8.00 20.00
49 Jayson Tatum 8.00 20.00
64 Luka Doncic 75.00 200.00
77 Anthony Davis 10.00 25.00
80 Bam Adebayo 4.00 10.00
87 LeBron James 75.00 200.00
99 Kevin Durant 8.00 20.00

2019-20 Elite Purple
*PURPLE: 1X TO 2.5X BASIC
PRINT RUN 49 SER.#'d SETS
15 Giannis Antetokounmpo 12.00 30.00
30 Stephen Curry 12.00 30.00
49 Jayson Tatum 10.00 25.00
64 Luka Doncic 100.00 250.00
77 Anthony Davis 12.00 30.00
80 Bam Adebayo 5.00 12.00
87 LeBron James 100.00 250.00
99 Kevin Durant 10.00 25.00

2019-20 Elite Red
*RED 1-100: .5X TO 1.2X BASIC
*RED 101-150: .4X TO 1X BASIC
64 Luka Doncic 25.00 60.00
77 Anthony Davis 8.00 20.00
87 LeBron James 25.00 60.00

2019-20 Elite Court Vision
1 Shai Gilgeous-Alexander 3.00 8.00
2 James Harden 1.25 3.00
3 Kemba Walker .50 1.25
4 Trae Young 1.50 4.00
5 Jimmy Butler 1.25 3.00
6 Devin Booker .15 .40
7 Derrick Rose 1.25 3.00
8 LeBron James 10.00 25.00
9 Kyle Lowry .60 1.50
10 Anthony Davis 1.50 4.00
11 Nikola Jokic 3.00 8.00
12 Damian Lillard 1.50 4.00
13 Jayson Tatum 2.50 6.00
14 Luka Doncic 10.00 25.00
15 Chris Paul 1.25 3.00
16 Donovan Mitchell 1.25 3.00
17 Joel Embiid 1.25 3.00
18 Brandon Ingram .60 1.50
19 Nikola Vucevic .50 1.25
20 Russell Westbrook 1.00 2.50
21 CJ McCollum .60 1.50
22 Giannis Antetokounmpo 3.00 8.00
23 Pascal Siakam 1.00 2.50
24 Zach LaVine 1.00 2.50
25 Karl-Anthony Towns 1.00 2.50
26 Bradley Beal .75 2.00
27 Ben Simmons .60 1.50
28 DeMar DeRozan .75 2.00
29 Rudy Gobert .75 2.00
30 Kawhi Leonard 1.50 4.00

2019-20 Elite Passing the Torch Signatures
STATED PRINT RUN 10-99 SER.#'d SETS
EXCHANGE DEADLINE 1/08/2022
2 Austin Rivers
Doc Rivers/99 12.00 30.00
4 Artis Gilmore
Coby White/99 40.00 100.00
6 Bill Walton
Luke Walton/99 20.00 50.00
8 Larry Johnson
PJ Washington Jr./99 30.00 80.00
9 Domantas Sabonis
Arvydas Sabonis/99 25.00 60.00
10 Gerald Henderson Sr.
Gerald Henderson/99 8.00 20.00

2019-20 Elite Pen Pals
STATED PRINT RUN 75-99 SER.#'d SETS
EXCHANGE DEADLINE 1/08/2022
*RED: .5X TO 1.25X BASIC
*BLUE: .6X TO 1.5X BASIC
*PURPLE: .75X TO 2X BASIC
2 KZ Okpala/99 5.00 12.00
3 Tyler Herro/99 100.00 250.00
4 Talen Horton-Tucker/99 6.00 15.00
5 Brandon Clarke/99 25.00 60.00
6 Darius Bazley/99 4.00 10.00
7 Zion Williamson/75 500.00 1,000.00
8 Carsen Edwards/99 5.00 12.00
9 De'Andre Hunter/99 15.00 40.00
10 Grant Williams/75 6.00 15.00
11 PJ Washington Jr./99 12.00 30.00
12 Eric Paschall/99 5.00 12.00
13 Matisse Thybulle/99 8.00 20.00
14 Nicolo Melli/99 5.00 12.00
15 Nickeil Alexander-Walker/99 6.00 15.00
16 Goga Bitadze/99 6.00 15.00
17 Ja Morant/99 350.00 700.00
18 Ty Jerome/99 8.00 20.00
19 Cam Reddish/99 6.00 15.00
20 Dylan Windler/99 5.00 12.00
21 Cameron Johnson/99 15.00 40.00
22 Tacko Fall/99 5.00 12.00
23 Nassir Little/99 6.00 15.00
24 Kyle Guy/99 12.00 30.00
25 Chuma Okeke/75 25.00 60.00
26 Luka Samanic/99 5.00 12.00
27 RJ Barrett/99 50.00 120.00
28 Bruno Fernando/99 5.00 12.00
29 Jarrett Culver/99 4.00 10.00
30 Mfiondu Kabengele/99 5.00 12.00
31 Bol Bol/99 20.00 50.00
32 Kendrick Nunn/99 6.00 15.00
33 Romeo Langford/75 4.00 10.00
34 Cody Martin/99 6.00 15.00
35 Sekou Doumbouya/99 4.00 10.00
36 Keldon Johnson/75 15.00 40.00
37 Rui Hachimura/99 15.00 40.00
38 Nicolas Claxton/99 8.00 20.00
39 Coby White/99 50.00 120.00
40 Kevin Porter Jr./99 8.00 20.00

2019-20 Elite Primary Colors
1 Damian Lillard 2.00 5.00
2 Russell Westbrook 1.25 3.00
3 Luka Doncic 5.00 12.00
4 Trae Young 2.00 5.00
5 James Harden 1.50 4.00
6 Giannis Antetokounmpo 4.00 10.00
7 LeBron James 6.00 15.00
8 Jayson Tatum 3.00 8.00
9 Anthony Davis 2.00 5.00
10 Kawhi Leonard 2.00 5.00

2019-20 Elite Signatures
STATED PRINT RUN 15-60 SER.#'d SETS
EXCHANGE DEADLINE 1/08/2022
*RED: .5X TO 1.25X BASIC
*BLUE: .6X TO 1.5X BASIC
*PURPLE: .75X TO 2X BASIC
1 Gary Payton/25 25.00 60.00
2 Andrea Bargnani/60 5.00 12.00
3 JJ Redick/49 8.00 20.00
4 Robert Parish/49 10.00 25.00
6 Derrick Coleman/60 6.00 15.00
8 Hedo Turkoglu/60 6.00 15.00
9 Jerry West/25 30.00 80.00
10 Alvin Robertson/60 6.00 15.00
11 Jrue Holiday/49 10.00 25.00
12 Chris Kaman/60 5.00 12.00
13 Elvin Hayes/49 10.00 25.00
14 Shawn Kemp/60 25.00 60.00
16 Bogdan Bogdanovic/60 8.00 20.00
18 Jack Sikma/60 8.00 20.00
19 Dennis Rodman/25 30.00 80.00
20 Devonte' Graham/60 6.00 15.00
21 Brook Lopez/49 6.00 15.00
22 Kirk Hinrich /60 5.00 12.00
23 Steve Francis/49 8.00 20.00
24 Domantas Sabonis/60 10.00 25.00

2019-20 Elite Spellbound
1 LeBron James 40.00 100.00
2 LeBron James 40.00 100.00
3 LeBron James 40.00 100.00
4 LeBron James 40.00 100.00
5 LeBron James 40.00 100.00
6 Giannis Antetokounmpo 25.00 60.00
7 Giannis Antetokounmpo 25.00 60.00
8 Giannis Antetokounmpo 25.00 60.00
9 Giannis Antetokounmpo 25.00 60.00
10 Giannis Antetokounmpo 25.00 60.00
11 Giannis Antetokounmpo 25.00 60.00
12 Giannis Antetokounmpo 25.00 60.00
13 Giannis Antetokounmpo 25.00 60.00
14 Giannis Antetokounmpo 25.00 60.00
15 Giannis Antetokounmpo 25.00 60.00
16 Giannis Antetokounmpo 25.00 60.00
17 Giannis Antetokounmpo 25.00 60.00
18 Giannis Antetokounmpo 25.00 60.00
19 Stephen Curry 40.00 100.00
20 Stephen Curry 40.00 100.00
21 Stephen Curry 40.00 100.00
22 Stephen Curry 40.00 100.00
23 Stephen Curry 40.00 100.00
24 Luka Doncic 30.00 80.00
25 Luka Doncic 30.00 80.00
26 Luka Doncic 30.00 80.00
27 Luka Doncic 30.00 80.00
28 Luka Doncic 30.00 80.00
29 Luka Doncic 30.00 80.00
30 Anthony Davis 12.00 30.00
31 Anthony Davis 12.00 30.00
32 Anthony Davis 12.00 30.00
33 Anthony Davis 12.00 30.00
34 Anthony Davis 12.00 30.00
35 James Harden 10.00 25.00
36 James Harden 10.00 25.00
37 James Harden 10.00 25.00
38 James Harden 10.00 25.00
39 James Harden 10.00 25.00
40 James Harden 10.00 25.00

2019-20 Elite Star Status
1 Derrick Rose 2.00 5.00
2 Pascal Siakam 1.50 4.00
3 Anthony Davis 2.50 6.00
4 Karl-Anthony Towns 1.50 4.00
5 Damian Lillard 2.50 6.00
6 Ben Simmons 1.00 2.50
7 Luka Doncic 10.00 25.00
8 Joel Embiid 2.00 5.00
9 James Harden 2.00 5.00
10 CJ McCollum 1.00 2.50
11 LeBron James 10.00 25.00
12 Zach LaVine 1.50 4.00
13 Nikola Jokic 5.00 12.00
14 Bradley Beal 1.25 3.00
15 Jayson Tatum 4.00 10.00
16 Kawhi Leonard 2.50 6.00
17 Donovan Mitchell 2.00 5.00
18 Russell Westbrook 1.50 4.00
19 Trae Young 6.00 15.00
20 Giannis Antetokounmpo 5.00 12.00

2019-20 Elite Turn of the Century Signatures
STATED PRINT RUN 15-60 SER.#'d SETS
EXCHANGE DEADLINE 1/08/2022
*RED: .5X TO 1.25X BASIC
*BLUE: .6X TO 1.5X BASIC
*PURPLE: .75X TO 2X BASIC
1 Charles Oakley/60 6.00 15.00
3 Gheorghe Muresan/60 5.00 12.00
4 Andrew Wiggins/49 10.00 25.00
5 Kevin Martin/60 5.00 12.00
6 Eric Bledsoe/49 6.00 15.00
7 Dave Cowens/49 10.00 25.00
9 Jason Richardson/60 8.00 20.00
11 Luke Kennard/60 6.00 15.00
12 Magic Johnson/25 25.00 60.00
13 Boban Marjanovic/60 12.00 30.00
14 Al Horford/49 8.00 20.00
15 Boris Diaw/60 6.00 15.00
16 Joe Dumars/49 8.00 20.00
17 Larry Johnson/49 12.00 30.00
19 Fred VanVleet/60 15.00 40.00
21 Vlade Divac/60 8.00 20.00
22 Stephon Marbury/25 12.00 30.00
23 Deron Williams/49 6.00 15.00
24 Eric Gordon/49 6.00 15.00
25 Arron Afflalo/60 5.00 12.00

2020-21 Elite
RC (101-150) STATED PRINT RUN 299 SER.#'d SETS
1 Ben Simmons .50 1.25
2 Dillon Brooks .50 1.25
3 Luka Doncic 3.00 8.00
4 Brandon Ingram .60 1.50
5 Terry Rozier .50 1.25
6 De'Andre Hunter .50 1.25
7 Devonte' Graham .40 1.00
8 Gordon Hayward .50 1.25
9 Clint Capela .40 1.00
10 Tobias Harris .50 1.25
11 Jimmy Butler 1.00 2.50
12 Kemba Walker .50 1.25
13 Malcolm Brogdon .50 1.25
14 Russell Westbrook 1.00 2.50
15 Darius Garland .75 2.00
16 Jerami Grant .50 1.25
17 Julius Randle .50 1.25
18 James Harden 1.00 2.50
19 Kawhi Leonard 1.25 3.00
20 Jarrett Allen .50 1.25
21 Dejounte Murray .50 1.25
22 Myles Turner .50 1.25
23 Michael Porter Jr. .60 1.50
24 Delon Wright .30 .75
25 Giannis Antetokounmpo 2.50 6.00
26 Stephen Curry 4.00 10.00
27 Christian Wood .40 1.00
28 Fred VanVleet .75 2.00
29 Kyle Lowry .60 1.50
30 Marcus Smart .50 1.25
31 Nikola Jokic 2.50 6.00
32 De'Aaron Fox .75 2.00
33 Brandon Clarke .50 1.25
34 Victor Oladipo .40 1.00
35 Kristaps Porzingis .60 1.50
36 Carmelo Anthony .75 2.00
37 LeBron James 4.00 10.00
38 Anthony Davis 1.25 3.00
39 Draymond Green .60 1.50
40 Al Horford .50 1.25
41 Jayson Tatum 2.00 5.00
42 CJ McCollum .50 1.25
43 Buddy Hield .50 1.25
44 Trae Young 1.25 3.00
45 DeMar DeRozan .60 1.50
46 Donovan Mitchell 1.00 2.50
47 Derrick Rose .75 2.00
48 Paul George .75 2.00
49 Harrison Barnes .40 1.00
50 Joe Harris .40 1.00
51 LaMarcus Aldridge .50 1.25
52 Zach LaVine .75 2.00
53 Duncan Robinson .50 1.25
54 Khris Middleton .60 1.50
55 D'Angelo Russell .50 1.25
56 Lou Williams .50 1.25
57 Chris Paul 1.00 2.50
58 Rui Hachimura .60 1.50
59 RJ Barrett .75 2.00
60 Shai Gilgeous-Alexander 2.50 6.00
61 Devin Booker 1.25 3.00
62 John Collins .50 1.25
63 Evan Fournier .40 1.00
64 Nikola Vucevic .50 1.25
65 Kevin Durant 2.00 5.00
66 Kyrie Irving 1.00 2.50
67 Mike Conley .40 1.00
68 Jordan Clarkson .50 1.25
69 Kyle Kuzma .60 1.50
70 Kelly Oubre Jr. .50 1.25
71 Deandre Ayton .50 1.25
72 Joel Embiid 1.25 3.00
73 Coby White .60 1.50
74 Jrue Holiday .50 1.25
75 Andrew Wiggins .60 1.50
76 Bam Adebayo .75 2.00
77 Ja Morant 1.50 4.00
78 Aaron Gordon .50 1.25
79 Jalen Brunson .75 2.00
80 Dennis Schroder .50 1.25
81 Pascal Siakam .75 2.00
82 Damian Lillard 1.25 3.00
83 Blake Griffin .50 1.25
84 Jamal Murray .75 2.00
85 Ricky Rubio .50 1.25
86 Collin Sexton .50 1.25
87 Keldon Johnson .75 2.00
88 John Wall .60 1.50
89 Lonzo Ball .60 1.50
90 Rudy Gobert .60 1.50
91 Zion Williamson 1.50 4.00
92 Lauri Markkanen .60 1.50
93 Kendrick Nunn .40 1.00
94 Karl-Anthony Towns .75 2.00
95 Gary Trent Jr. .50 1.25
96 Tyler Herro 1.00 2.50
97 Bradley Beal .60 1.50
98 Domantas Sabonis .60 1.50
99 Luguentz Dort .75 2.00
100 Jaylen Brown .75 2.00
101 Obi Toppin RC 4.00 10.00
102 Udoka Azubuike RC 2.50 6.00
103 Saddiq Bey RC 4.00 10.00
104 James Wiseman RC 2.50 6.00
105 Tyrese Haliburton RC 15.00 40.00
106 Reggie Perry RC 2.00 5.00
107 Paul Reed RC 2.50 6.00
108 Patrick Williams RC 5.00 12.00
109 Payton Pritchard RC 6.00 15.00
110 Tyrese Maxey RC 15.00 40.00
111 CJ Elleby RC 2.00 5.00
112 Killian Hayes RC 2.00 5.00
113 Isaiah Stewart RC 4.00 10.00
114 Robert Woodard II RC 2.00 5.00
115 Tyrell Terry RC 1.50 4.00
116 Vernon Carey Jr. RC 2.00 5.00
117 Theo Maledon RC 2.00 5.00
118 Jordan Nwora RC 2.50 6.00
119 Zeke Nnaji RC 2.50 6.00
120 Skylar Mays RC 2.00 5.00
121 Desmond Bane RC 6.00 15.00
122 Aaron Nesmith RC 4.00 10.00
123 Immanuel Quickley RC 5.00 12.00
124 Kira Lewis Jr. RC 2.00 5.00
125 Cassius Stanley RC 2.00 5.00
126 Saben Lee RC 2.00 5.00
127 Josh Green RC 4.00 10.00
128 Mason Jones RC 1.50 4.00
129 RJ Hampton RC 2.00 5.00
130 Jalen Smith RC 4.00 10.00
131 Devon Dotson RC 2.00 5.00
132 Facundo Campazzo RC 2.50 6.00
133 Onyeka Okongwu RC 4.00 10.00
134 LaMelo Ball RC 15.00 40.00
135 Anthony Edwards RC 60.00 150.00
136 Deni Avdija RC 5.00 12.00
137 Kenyon Martin Jr. RC 3.00 8.00
138 Jae'Sean Tate RC 2.50 6.00
139 Jaden McDaniels RC 6.00 15.00
140 Sam Merrill RC 3.00 8.00
141 Devin Vassell RC 6.00 15.00
142 Tre Jones RC 3.00 8.00
143 Lamar Stevens RC 2.50 6.00
144 Isaiah Joe RC 2.50 6.00
145 Precious Achiuwa RC 4.00 10.00
146 Malachi Flynn RC 2.00 5.00
147 Cole Anthony RC 5.00 12.00
148 Isaac Okoro RC 3.00 8.00
149 Xavier Tillman RC 2.50 6.00
150 Aleksej Pokusevski RC 2.50 6.00

2020-21 Elite Aspirations
PRINT RUN BTWN 6-99 SER.#'d SETS

2020-21 Elite Blue
PRINT RUN 99 SER.#'d SETS

2020-21 Elite Purple
PRINT RUN 49 SER.#'d SETS

2020-21 Elite Status
PRINT RUN 1-94 SER.#'d SETS
NO PRICING ON QTY 20 & BELOW
1 Ben Simmons/25 15.00 40.00
2 Dillon Brooks/24 8.00 20.00
3 Luka Doncic/77 60.00 150.00
26 Stephen Curry/30 40.00 100.00
30 Marcus Smart/36 4.00 10.00
46 Donovan Mitchell/45 15.00 40.00
54 Khris Middleton/22 8.00 20.00
95 Gary Trent Jr./33 5.00 12.00

2020-21 Elite Passing the Torch Signatures
STATED PRINT RUN 25 SER.#'d SETS
EXCHANGE DEADLINE 1/07/2023
1 A.Edwards/J.Morant 600.00 1,200.00
2 P.Williams/Z.LaVine 40.00 100.00
3 L.Ball/L.Ball 200.00 500.00
4 J.Murray/M.Porter Jr. 50.00 120.00
5 A.Hardaway/C.Anthony 125.00 300.00
6 F.Campazzo/J.Williams 20.00 50.00
7 I.Quickley/R.Barrett 75.00 200.00
8 K.Towns/K.Garnett 150.00 400.00
9 C.Sexton/I.Okoro 15.00 40.00
10 D.Avdija/L.Doncic 800.00 1,500.00

2020-21 Elite Pen Pals
STATED PRINT RUN 75-99 SER.#'d SETS
EXCHANGE DEADLINE 1/07/2023
*RED/49: .5X TO 1.2X BASIC
*BLUE/35: .6X TO 1.5X BASIC
*PURPLE/25: .75X TO 2X BASIC
1 Facundo Campazzo/99 6.00 15.00
2 Paul Reed/99 6.00 15.00
3 Tyrese Haliburton/99 75.00 200.00
4 Payton Pritchard/99 15.00 40.00
5 Anthony Edwards/99 300.00 600.00
6 RJ Hampton/99 5.00 12.00
7 Cassius Winston/99 5.00 12.00
8 Kira Lewis Jr./99 5.00 12.00
9 James Wiseman/99 6.00 15.00
10 Killian Hayes/99 5.00 12.00
11 Zeke Nnaji/99 6.00 15.00
12 Mychal Mulder/99 5.00 12.00
13 Isaiah Stewart/99 10.00 25.00
14 Deni Avdija/75 12.00 30.00
15 Isaiah Joe/99 6.00 15.00
16 Josh Green/99 10.00 25.00
17 Immanuel Quickley/99 12.00 30.00
18 Onyeka Okongwu/99 10.00 25.00
19 Cole Anthony/99 12.00 30.00
20 Tyrese Maxey/99 60.00 150.00
21 Theo Maledon/99 5.00 12.00
22 Saddiq Bey/99 10.00 25.00
23 Jordan Nwora/99 6.00 15.00
25 Robert Woodard II/99 5.00 12.00
26 Precious Achiuwa/99 10.00 25.00
27 LaMelo Ball/75 75.00 200.00
28 Jaden McDaniels/99 15.00 40.00
29 Devon Dotson/99 5.00 12.00
30 Daniel Oturu/99 5.00 12.00
31 Xavier Tillman/99 6.00 15.00
32 Devin Vassell/99 15.00 40.00
33 Saben Lee/99 5.00 12.00
34 Patrick Williams/99 12.00 30.00
35 Isaac Okoro/99 8.00 20.00
36 Skylar Mays/99 5.00 12.00
37 Jahmi'us Ramsey/99 5.00 12.00
38 Lamar Stevens/99 6.00 15.00
39 Obi Toppin/99 10.00 25.00
40 Jae'Sean Tate/99 6.00 15.00

2020-21 Elite Power Formulas
1 Damian Lillard 2.00 5.00
2 Donovan Mitchell 1.50 4.00
3 Luka Doncic 5.00 12.00
4 Kawhi Leonard 2.00 5.00
5 Kevin Durant 3.00 8.00
6 James Harden 1.50 4.00
7 Joel Embiid 2.00 5.00
8 Giannis Antetokounmpo 4.00 10.00
9 Bradley Beal 1.00 2.50
10 LeBron James 6.00 15.00
11 Stephen Curry 6.00 15.00
12 Devin Booker 2.00 5.00
13 Jayson Tatum 3.00 8.00
14 Zion Williamson 2.50 6.00
15 Nikola Jokic 4.00 10.00
16 Anthony Davis 2.00 5.00
17 Trae Young 2.00 5.00
18 Ben Simmons .75 2.00
19 Ja Morant 2.50 6.00
20 Jaylen Brown 1.25 3.00
21 Kyrie Irving 1.50 4.00
22 Paul George 1.25 3.00
23 Zach LaVine 1.25 3.00
24 Chris Paul 1.50 4.00
25 Pascal Siakam 1.25 3.00
26 Russell Westbrook 1.50 4.00
27 Julius Randle .75 2.00
28 Collin Sexton .75 2.00
29 De'Aaron Fox 1.25 3.00
30 Jimmy Butler 1.50 4.00

2020-21 Elite Primary Colors
1 Joel Embiid 2.50 6.00
2 LeBron James 8.00 20.00
3 Damian Lillard 2.50 6.00
4 Luka Doncic 6.00 15.00
5 Kevin Durant 4.00 10.00
6 Donovan Mitchell 2.00 5.00
7 Zion Williamson 3.00 8.00
8 Stephen Curry 8.00 20.00
9 Devin Booker 2.50 6.00
10 Giannis Antetokounmpo 5.00 12.00

2020-21 Elite Signatures
STATED PRINT RUN 25-60 SER.#'d SETS
EXCHANGE DEADLINE 1/07/2023
*RED/49: .5X TO 1.2X BASIC
*BLUE/25: .6X TO 1.5X BASIC
1 Montrezl Harrell/60 8.00 20.00
2 Luke Kennard/60 6.00 15.00
3 Clint Capela/60 6.00 15.00
4 Ja Morant/25 300.00 600.00
5 Malcolm Brogdon/60 8.00 20.00
6 Cam Reddish/60 10.00 25.00
7 Luka Doncic/25 600.00 1,200.00
8 Luguentz Dort/60 12.00 30.00
9 PJ Washington Jr./60 8.00 20.00
10 Zion Williamson/25 200.00 500.00
11 Ivica Zubac/60 8.00 20.00
12 Bogdan Bogdanovic/60 8.00 20.00
13 Julius Randle/60 8.00 20.00
14 CJ McCollum/60 8.00 20.00
15 Talen Horton-Tucker/60 8.00 20.00
16 Duncan Robinson/49 20.00 50.00
17 Mason Plumlee/60 5.00 12.00
18 Terrence Ross/60 6.00 15.00
19 P.J. Tucker/60 6.00 15.00
20 Coby White/49 10.00 25.00
21 De'Aaron Fox/49 25.00 60.00
22 Boban Marjanovic/60 6.00 15.00
23 Jarrett Culver/60 5.00 12.00
24 Jaren Jackson Jr./49 12.00 30.00
25 Myles Turner/60 8.00 20.00

2020-21 Elite Spellbound
1 Zion Williamson 12.00 30.00
2 Zion Williamson 12.00 30.00
3 Zion Williamson 12.00 30.00
4 Zion Williamson 12.00 30.00
5 LaMelo Ball 25.00 60.00
6 LaMelo Ball 25.00 60.00
7 LaMelo Ball 25.00 60.00
8 LaMelo Ball 25.00 60.00
9 LaMelo Ball 25.00 60.00
10 LaMelo Ball 25.00 60.00
11 LeBron James 30.00 80.00
12 LeBron James 30.00 80.00
13 LeBron James 30.00 80.00
14 LeBron James 30.00 80.00
15 LeBron James 30.00 80.00
16 Luka Doncic 25.00 60.00
17 Luka Doncic 25.00 60.00
18 Luka Doncic 25.00 60.00
19 Luka Doncic 25.00 60.00
20 Trae Young 10.00 25.00
21 Trae Young 10.00 25.00
22 Trae Young 10.00 25.00
23 Trae Young 10.00 25.00
24 Stephen Curry 30.00 80.00
25 Stephen Curry 30.00 80.00
26 Stephen Curry 30.00 80.00
27 Stephen Curry 30.00 80.00
28 Stephen Curry 30.00 80.00
29 Anthony Edwards 30.00 80.00
30 Anthony Edwards 30.00 80.00
31 Anthony Edwards 30.00 80.00
32 Anthony Edwards 30.00 80.00
33 Anthony Edwards 30.00 80.00
34 Anthony Edwards 30.00 80.00
35 Anthony Edwards 30.00 80.00
36 Ja Morant 12.00 30.00
37 Ja Morant 12.00 30.00
38 Obi Toppin 6.00 15.00
39 Obi Toppin 6.00 15.00
40 Obi Toppin 6.00 15.00

2020-21 Elite Star Status
1 Luka Doncic 12.00 30.00
2 LeBron James 15.00 40.00
3 Nikola Jokic 10.00 25.00
4 Joel Embiid 5.00 12.00
5 James Harden 4.00 10.00
6 Stephen Curry 15.00 40.00
7 Bradley Beal 2.50 6.00
8 Anthony Davis 5.00 12.00
9 Donovan Mitchell 4.00 10.00
10 Damian Lillard 5.00 12.00
11 Jayson Tatum 8.00 20.00
12 Kawhi Leonard 5.00 12.00
13 Giannis Antetokounmpo 10.00 25.00
14 Devin Booker 5.00 12.00
15 Zion Williamson 6.00 15.00
16 Kyrie Irving 4.00 10.00
17 Ja Morant 6.00 15.00
18 Ben Simmons 2.00 5.00
19 Zach LaVine 3.00 8.00
20 Kevin Durant 8.00 20.00

2020-21 Elite Turn of the Century Signatures
STATED PRINT RUN 25-60 SER.#'d SETS
EXCHANGE DEADLINE 1/07/2023
*RED/49: .5X TO 1.2X BASIC
*BLUE/25: .6X TO 1.5X BASIC
1 Rasheed Wallace/49 75.00 200.00
2 Horace Grant/60 8.00 20.00
3 Glen Rice/60 6.00 15.00
4 Mike Bibby/60 8.00 20.00
5 Mitch Richmond/60 15.00 40.00
6 Oscar Robertson/49 40.00 100.00
7 Robert Parish/49 12.00 30.00
8 Adrian Dantley/49 8.00 20.00
9 Baron Davis/60 8.00 20.00
10 Shawn Kemp/60 50.00 120.00
11 Richard Hamilton/60 12.00 30.00
12 Lamar Odom/60 12.00 30.00
13 Dikembe Mutombo/60 12.00 30.00
14 David Robinson/49 50.00 120.00
15 Gary Payton/49 15.00 40.00
16 Dominique Wilkins/49 15.00 40.00
17 Kenny Smith/60 6.00 15.00
18 Harold Miner/60 8.00 20.00
19 Hakeem Olajuwon/49 50.00 120.00
20 Chris Mullin/60 12.00 30.00
21 Isiah Thomas/49 40.00 100.00
22 Rex Chapman/60 12.00 30.00
23 Magic Johnson/25 60.00 150.00
24 John Salley/60 6.00 15.00
25 B.J. Armstrong/60 6.00 15.00

2021-22 Elite
COMMON CARD (1-200) .30 .75
SEMISTARS .40 1.00
UNLISTED STARS .50 1.25
COMMON ROOKIE (201-250) 1.50 4.00
ROOKIE SEMISTARS 2.00 5.00
ROOKIE UNLISTED 2.50 6.00
RC (201-250) STATED PRINT RUN 999 SER.#'d SETS
1 Anthony Edwards 2.50 6.00
2 LeBron James 4.00 10.00
3 Richaun Holmes .30 .75
4 Dillon Brooks .50 1.25
5 Chris Boucher .50 1.25
6 Lonzo Ball .50 1.25
7 Naz Reid .50 1.25
8 Tyrese Haliburton 1.00 2.50
9 Joel Embiid 1.25 3.00
10 Lou Williams .50 1.25
11 Marcus Smart .50 1.25
12 Rudy Gay .50 1.25
13 Terrence Ross .40 1.00
14 Brandon Ingram .60 1.50
15 Kevin Huerter .40 1.00
16 Ja Morant 1.50 4.00
17 Joe Ingles .40 1.00
18 Austin Rivers .40 1.00
19 Isaiah Stewart .50 1.25
20 Markieff Morris .40 1.00
21 PJ Washington Jr. .50 1.25
22 Cameron Payne .50 1.25
23 Zach LaVine .75 2.00
24 Desmond Bane 1.00 2.50
25 Spencer Dinwiddie .40 1.00
26 Karl-Anthony Towns .75 2.00
27 Jae Crowder .30 .75
28 Damian Lillard 1.25 3.00
29 Mason Plumlee .30 .75
30 Coby White .50 1.25
31 LaMelo Ball 1.25 3.00
32 Cedi Osman .40 1.00
33 Deandre Ayton .50 1.25
34 Derrick White .50 1.25
35 Obi Toppin .50 1.25
36 Christian Wood .40 1.00
37 Danilo Gallinari .40 1.00
38 Jimmy Butler .75 2.00
39 Davis Bertans .30 .75
40 John Wall .60 1.50
41 Brook Lopez .40 1.00
42 Carmelo Anthony .75 2.00
43 Devin Vassell .75 2.00
44 Khris Middleton .50 1.25
45 Keldon Johnson .60 1.50
46 Ben Simmons .50 1.25
47 Michael Porter Jr. .60 1.50
48 Seth Curry .40 1.00
49 Domantas Sabonis .60 1.50
50 Jayson Tatum 2.00 5.00
51 Immanuel Quickley .50 1.25
52 Moses Brown .30 .75
53 Rudy Gobert .60 1.50
54 Tyrese Maxey 1.25 3.00
55 Kenyon Martin Jr. .50 1.25
56 Lonnie Walker IV .40 1.00
57 Anfernee Simons .75 2.00
58 Killian Hayes .50 1.25
59 Yuta Watanabe .50 1.25
60 Dorian Finney-Smith .30 .75
61 Josh Hart .40 1.00
62 Bojan Bogdanovic .40 1.00
63 Jarrett Allen .50 1.25
64 Goran Dragic .40 1.00
65 Paul Millsap .40 1.00
66 Danny Green .40 1.00
67 Malcolm Brogdon .40 1.00
68 Ricky Rubio .50 1.25
69 Jordan Poole .75 2.00
70 Myles Turner .50 1.25
71 Patrick Beverley .30 .75
72 Kevin Durant 1.50 4.00
73 Jaylen Brown .75 2.00
74 Cole Anthony .60 1.50
75 Darius Bazley .30 .75
76 Cameron Johnson .50 1.25
77 Jalen Brunson 1.00 2.50
78 John Collins .50 1.25
79 DeMar DeRozan .60 1.50
80 Russell Westbrook .75 2.00
81 Kristaps Porzingis .60 1.50
82 Reggie Bullock .30 .75
83 Boban Marjanovic .50 1.25
84 Kevin Love .50 1.25
85 Victor Oladipo .40 1.00
86 Steven Adams .40 1.00
87 Mo Bamba .40 1.00
88 Chuma Okeke .50 1.25
89 T.J. Warren .30 .75
90 CJ McCollum .40 1.00
91 Andrew Wiggins .60 1.50
92 Thomas Bryant .30 .75
93 Lauri Markkanen .60 1.50
94 OG Anunoby .50 1.25
95 Malik Beasley .40 1.00
96 Theo Maledon .40 1.00
97 Buddy Hield .40 1.00
98 De'Andre Hunter .50 1.25
99 Jerami Grant .50 1.25
100 RJ Barrett .75 2.00
101 Donovan Mitchell 1.00 2.50
102 Kyle Anderson .30 .75
103 Tobias Harris .40 1.00
104 Julius Randle .60 1.50
105 Collin Sexton .50 1.25
106 Caris LeVert .40 1.00
107 Nickeil Alexander-Walker .40 1.00
108 Nikola Vucevic .50 1.25
109 Luka Doncic 3.00 8.00
110 Joe Harris .40 1.00
111 Marvin Bagley III .40 1.00
112 Shake Milton .40 1.00
113 Mikal Bridges .60 1.50
114 Dejounte Murray .50 1.25
115 Donte DiVincenzo .50 1.25
116 Jae'Sean Tate .50 1.25
117 Wendell Carter Jr. .50 1.25
118 Jusuf Nurkic .40 1.00
119 Isaac Okoro .40 1.00
120 Jalen McDaniels .40 1.00
121 Cam Reddish .50 1.25
122 Miles Bridges .40 1.00
123 James Harden 1.00 2.50
124 RJ Hampton .30 .75
125 Trae Young 1.25 3.00
126 Blake Griffin .50 1.25
127 Darius Garland .75 2.00
128 Patrick Williams .50 1.25
129 Markelle Fultz .30 .75
130 Bryn Forbes .40 1.00
131 Stephen Curry 3.00 8.00
132 Marcus Morris Sr. .30 .75
133 Kawhi Leonard 1.25 3.00
134 Evan Fournier .40 1.00
135 Jordan Clarkson .50 1.25
136 Klay Thompson 1.25 3.00
137 Royce O'Neale .40 1.00
138 Jarrett Culver .30 .75
139 James Wiseman .40 1.00
140 Ivica Zubac .50 1.25
141 Zion Williamson 1.25 3.00
142 Harrison Barnes .40 1.00
143 Daniel Gafford .40 1.00
144 Eric Gordon .40 1.00
145 Clint Capela .50 1.25
146 Dennis Schroder .50 1.25
147 Anthony Davis 1.25 3.00
148 Bam Adebayo .75 2.00
149 Duncan Robinson .40 1.00
150 Rui Hachimura .50 1.25
151 Kelly Olynyk .30 .75
152 Tyler Herro .75 2.00
153 Thaddeus Young .30 .75
154 Deni Avdija .50 1.25
155 Nicolas Claxton .50 1.25
156 Jaren Jackson Jr. .75 2.00
157 Jonathan Isaac .50 1.25
158 Brandon Clarke .50 1.25
159 Derrick Rose .75 2.00
160 Robert Covington .30 .75
161 Tim Hardaway Jr. .30 .75
162 Devin Booker 1.25 3.00
163 Aaron Gordon .50 1.25
164 Shai Gilgeous-Alexander 2.50 6.00
165 Payton Pritchard .50 1.25
166 Terry Rozier .40 1.00
167 Facundo Campazzo .50 1.25
168 Bobby Portis .40 1.00
169 Doug McDermott .40 1.00
170 Bradley Beal .60 1.50
171 Pascal Siakam .60 1.50
172 Paul George .60 1.50
173 Giannis Antetokounmpo 2.50 6.00
174 Kyrie Irving 1.00 2.50
175 Sekou Doumbouya .30 .75
176 Jrue Holiday .60 1.50
177 Kyle Kuzma .60 1.50
178 Terance Mann .50 1.25
179 Kyle Lowry .50 1.25
180 Talen Horton-Tucker .50 1.25
181 De'Aaron Fox .75 2.00
182 Draymond Green .60 1.50
183 Nikola Jokic 2.50 6.00
184 Kendrick Nunn .40 1.00
185 D'Angelo Russell .50 1.25
186 Josh Richardson .40 1.00
187 Devonte' Graham .40 1.00
188 Andre Drummond .40 1.00
189 Aleksej Pokusevski .40 1.00
190 Kevin Porter Jr. .40 1.00
191 Bol Bol .40 1.00
192 Bogdan Bogdanovic .50 1.25
193 Chris Paul 1.00 2.50
194 Kelly Oubre Jr. .50 1.25
195 Fred VanVleet .60 1.50

196 Jamal Murray .75 2.00
197 Luguentz Dort .50 1.25
198 Saddiq Bey .40 1.00
199 Norman Powell .40 1.00
200 Kemba Walker .50 1.25
201 Juan Toscano-Anderson RC 2.50 6.00
202 Greg Brown III RC 2.00 5.00
203 Sharife Cooper RC 2.00 5.00
204 Jericho Sims RC 3.00 8.00
205 David Johnson RC 2.00 5.00
206 Aaron Wiggins RC 3.00 8.00
207 Joe Wieskamp RC 2.00 5.00
208 Jason Preston RC 2.00 5.00
209 Isaiah Todd RC 2.00 5.00
210 JT Thor RC 2.50 6.00
211 Santi Aldama RC 3.00 8.00
212 Jeremiah Robinson-Earl RC 2.50 6.00
213 Luka Garza RC 2.50 6.00
214 Brandon Boston Jr. RC 2.50 6.00
215 Charles Bassey RC 2.50 6.00
216 Scottie Lewis RC 2.00 5.00
217 Isaiah Livers RC 2.50 6.00
218 Jared Butler RC 2.50 6.00
219 Miles McBride RC 4.00 10.00
220 Day'Ron Sharpe RC 2.50 6.00
221 Jaden Springer RC 2.50 6.00
222 Cameron Thomas RC 5.00 12.00
223 Bones Hyland RC 3.00 8.00
224 Quentin Grimes RC 5.00 12.00
225 Josh Christopher RC 2.00 5.00
226 Usman Garuba RC 2.00 5.00
227 Isaiah Jackson RC 2.50 6.00
228 Keon Johnson RC 2.50 6.00
229 Jalen Johnson RC 8.00 20.00
230 Kai Jones RC 2.00 5.00
231 Tre Mann RC 4.00 10.00
232 Trey Murphy III RC 8.00 20.00
233 Alperen Sengun RC 8.00 20.00
234 Corey Kispert RC 3.00 8.00
235 Moses Moody RC 5.00 12.00
236 Chris Duarte RC 2.00 5.00
237 Joshua Primo RC 2.00 5.00
238 James Bouknight RC 2.00 5.00
239 Ziaire Williams RC 3.00 8.00
240 Davion Mitchell RC 2.50 6.00
241 Franz Wagner RC 8.00 20.00
242 Jonathan Kuminga RC 8.00 20.00
243 Josh Giddey RC 8.00 20.00
244 Jalen Suggs RC 6.00 15.00
245 Scottie Barnes RC 8.00 20.00
246 Evan Mobley RC 10.00 25.00
247 Jalen Green RC 12.00 30.00
248 Cade Cunningham RC 15.00 40.00
249 Ayo Dosunmu RC 5.00 12.00
250 Herbert Jones RC 3.00 8.00

2021-22 Elite Blue

*BLUE 1-200: 2.5X TO 6X BASIC
*BLUE 201-250: 1.25X TO 3X BASIC
STATED PRINT RUN 99 COPIES PER
2 LeBron James 60.00 150.00
109 Luka Doncic 40.00 100.00
131 Stephen Curry 60.00 150.00
173 Giannis Antetokounmpo 40.00 100.00
248 Cade Cunningham 75.00 200.00

2021-22 Elite Orange

*ORANGE: 1.5X TO 4X BASIC
*ORANGE RC: .75X TO 2X BASIC
ORANGE 201-250 PRINT RUN 210 SER.#'d SETS

2021-22 Elite Purple

*PURPLE 1-200: 2.5X TO 6X BASIC
*PURPLE 201-250: 1.5X TO 4X BASIC
STATED PRINT RUN 49 COPIES PER
2 LeBron James 75.00 200.00
109 Luka Doncic 50.00 120.00
131 Stephen Curry 75.00 200.00
173 Giannis Antetokounmpo 50.00 120.00
248 Cade Cunningham 100.00 250.00

2021-22 Elite Clarity

COMMON CARD .50 1.25
SEMISTARS .60 1.50
UNLISTED STARS .75 2.00
1 Nikola Jokic 4.00 10.00
2 Kevin Durant 2.50 6.00
3 Zion Williamson 2.00 5.00
4 Chris Paul 1.50 4.00
5 Bradley Beal 1.00 2.50
6 Jaylen Brown 1.25 3.00
7 Kawhi Leonard 2.00 5.00
8 Damian Lillard 2.00 5.00
9 Anthony Davis 2.00 5.00
10 Carmelo Anthony 1.25 3.00
11 Julius Randle 1.00 2.50
12 Stephen Curry 5.00 12.00
13 Pascal Siakam 1.25 3.00
14 Russell Westbrook 1.25 3.00
15 Jayson Tatum 3.00 8.00
16 Zach LaVine 1.25 3.00
17 LaMelo Ball 2.00 5.00
18 James Harden 1.50 4.00
19 Jimmy Butler 1.50 4.00
20 Brandon Ingram 1.00 2.50
21 Collin Sexton .75 2.00
22 De'Aaron Fox 1.25 3.00
23 Joel Embiid 2.00 5.00
24 Donovan Mitchell 1.50 4.00
25 Kyrie Irving 1.50 4.00
26 Luka Doncic 5.00 12.00
27 Giannis Antetokounmpo 4.00 10.00
28 Trae Young 2.00 5.00
29 Devin Booker 2.00 5.00
30 Ben Simmons .75 2.00

2021-22 Elite Deck

COMMON CARD .50 1.25
SEMISTARS .60 1.50
UNLISTED STARS .75 2.00
1 Anthony Davis 2.50 6.00
2 Jimmy Butler 1.50 4.00
3 Devin Booker 2.50 6.00
4 Nikola Jokic 5.00 12.00
5 Julius Randle 1.25 3.00
6 Collin Sexton 1.00 2.50
7 Zion Williamson 2.50 6.00
8 Fred VanVleet 1.25 3.00
9 Joel Embiid 2.50 6.00
10 Bradley Beal 1.25 3.00
11 Jayson Tatum 4.00 10.00
12 Kyrie Irving 2.00 5.00
13 Kawhi Leonard 2.50 6.00
14 LaMelo Ball 2.50 6.00
15 Giannis Antetokounmpo 5.00 12.00
16 Damian Lillard 2.50 6.00
17 James Harden 2.00 5.00
18 Trae Young 2.50 6.00
19 Carmelo Anthony 1.50 4.00
20 Brandon Ingram 1.25 3.00
21 Ben Simmons 1.00 2.50
22 Kevin Durant 3.00 8.00
23 Stephen Curry 6.00 15.00
24 De'Aaron Fox 1.50 4.00
25 Chris Paul 2.00 5.00
26 Russell Westbrook 1.50 4.00
27 Donovan Mitchell 2.00 5.00
28 Jaylen Brown 1.50 4.00
29 Zach LaVine 1.50 4.00
30 Luka Doncic 6.00 15.00

2021-22 Elite Dimensions

COMMON CARD 20.00 50.00
SEMISTARS 25.00 60.00
UNLISTED STARS 30.00 80.00
1 Russell Westbrook 30.00 80.00
2 Kyrie Irving 40.00 100.00
3 Jayson Tatum 80.00 200.00
4 LeBron James 200.00 500.00
5 Zion Williamson 50.00 120.00
6 Kevin Durant 60.00 150.00
7 Damian Lillard 50.00 120.00
8 Stephen Curry 150.00 400.00
9 Trae Young 50.00 120.00
10 Giannis Antetokounmpo 125.00 300.00
11 Nikola Jokic 100.00 250.00
12 Anthony Davis 50.00 120.00
13 James Harden 40.00 100.00
14 Luka Doncic 150.00 400.00
15 Jimmy Butler 30.00 80.00

2021-22 Elite Glass Cleaners

COMMON CARD .50 1.25
SEMISTARS .60 1.50
UNLISTED STARS .75 2.00
1 Giannis Antetokounmpo 4.00 10.00
2 Clint Capela .75 2.00
3 Nikola Jokic 4.00 10.00
4 Rudy Gobert 1.00 2.50
5 Joel Embiid 2.00 5.00
6 Domantas Sabonis 1.00 2.50
7 Julius Randle 1.00 2.50
8 Nikola Vucevic .75 2.00
9 Deandre Ayton .75 2.00
10 Russell Westbrook 1.25 3.00

2021-22 Elite Impact Impressions

COMMON CARD 4.00 10.00
SEMISTARS 5.00 12.00
UNLISTED STARS 6.00 15.00
EXCHANGE DEADLINE 08/16/2023
1 Purvis Short 5.00 12.00
2 Mark Eaton 6.00 15.00
3 Darius Bazley 4.00 10.00
4 Charles Barkley 75.00 200.00
5 Drew Gooden 5.00 12.00
6 Kevin Garnett 75.00 200.00
7 Desmond Mason 5.00 12.00
8 Kristaps Porzingis 8.00 20.00
9 Jeff Malone 5.00 12.00
10 Eric Bledsoe 5.00 12.00
11 Rick Mahorn 5.00 12.00
12 Danny Manning 5.00 12.00
13 Shawn Kemp 25.00 60.00
14 Luka Doncic 500.00 1,000.00
15 Luke Kennard 5.00 12.00
16 Larry Bird 125.00 300.00
17 Doug Christie 5.00 12.00
18 Buddy Hield 5.00 12.00
19 John Salley 5.00 12.00
20 Ralph Sampson 6.00 15.00
21 Ricky Pierce 5.00 12.00
22 Joakim Noah 5.00 12.00
23 Doug McDermott 5.00 12.00
24 Zion Williamson 150.00 400.00
25 T.J. McConnell 5.00 12.00
26 Ja Morant 300.00 600.00
27 Frank Jackson 4.00 10.00
28 Artis Gilmore 8.00 20.00
29 LaPhonso Ellis 5.00 12.00
30 JJ Redick 6.00 15.00
31 Rod Strickland 5.00 12.00
32 Juwan Howard 5.00 12.00
33 Harold Miner 6.00 15.00
34 Kevin Durant 125.00 300.00
35 Dan Issel 6.00 15.00
36 Oscar Robertson 12.00 30.00
37 Gheorghe Muresan 4.00 10.00
38 Eric Gordon 5.00 12.00
39 Mario Chalmers 5.00 12.00
40 Michael Porter Jr. 8.00 20.00
41 Tom Gugliotta 5.00 12.00
42 Mark Jackson 5.00 12.00
43 Luguentz Dort 6.00 15.00
44 Anthony Davis 50.00 120.00
45 Alvin Robertson 5.00 12.00
46 Dennis Rodman 40.00 100.00
47 Jack Sikma 6.00 15.00
48 Kenny Smith 5.00 12.00
49 Michael Adams 5.00 12.00
50 Kevin Johnson 6.00 15.00
51 Tomas Satoransky 4.00 10.00
52 Avery Johnson 5.00 12.00
53 Thomas Bryant 4.00 10.00
54 Allen Iverson 75.00 200.00
55 Caron Butler 5.00 12.00
56 Jerry West 30.00 80.00
57 James Donaldson 5.00 12.00
58 Rick Fox 6.00 15.00
59 Micheal Ray Richardson 5.00 12.00
60 Elvin Hayes 8.00 20.00

2021-22 Elite Next Up

COMMON CARD 20.00 50.00
SEMISTARS 25.00 60.00
UNLISTED STARS 30.00 80.00
1 Cade Cunningham 75.00 200.00
2 Jalen Green 75.00 200.00
3 Evan Mobley 60.00 150.00
4 Scottie Barnes 60.00 150.00
5 Jalen Suggs 25.00 60.00
6 Josh Giddey 60.00 150.00
7 Jonathan Kuminga 40.00 100.00
8 Davion Mitchell 20.00 50.00
9 James Bouknight 4.00 10.00
10 Joshua Primo 8.00 20.00

2021-22 Elite Passing the Torch Signatures

1 Cunningham/Doncic/49 1,500.00 3,000.00
2 Green/Drexler/49 300.00 600.00
3 Davis/Mobley/49 300.00 600.00
4 Kuminga/Mutombo/149 200.00 500.00
5 Suggs/Stockton/49 150.00 400.00
8 Wagner/Nowitzki/49 1,000.00 2,000.00
9 Hield/Mitchell/159 60.00 150.00
10 Bouknight/Allen/149 50.00 120.00

2021-22 Elite Past and Present

COMMON CARD 20.00 50.00
SEMISTARS 25.00 60.00
UNLISTED STARS 30.00 80.00
1 LeBron James 300.00 600.00
2 Kevin Durant 100.00 250.00
3 Derrick Rose 50.00 120.00
4 James Harden 60.00 150.00
5 Stephen Curry 200.00 500.00

2021-22 Elite Pen Pals

COMMON CARD 5.00 12.00
SEMISTARS 6.00 15.00
UNLISTED STARS 8.00 20.00
STATED PRINT RUN 149 SER.#'d SETS
EXCHANGE DEADLINE 8/16/2023
*RED/49: .5X TO 1.2X BASIC
*BLUE/35: .5X TO 1.2X BASIC
*PURPLE/25: .6X TO 1.5X BASIC
1 Greg Brown III 6.00 15.00
2 Santi Aldama 10.00 25.00
3 Jeremiah Robinson-Earl 8.00 20.00
4 Luka Garza 8.00 20.00
5 Brandon Boston Jr. 8.00 20.00
6 Charles Bassey 8.00 20.00
7 Scottie Lewis 6.00 15.00
8 Isaiah Livers 8.00 20.00
9 Jared Butler 8.00 20.00
10 Miles McBride 12.00 30.00
11 Day'Ron Sharpe 8.00 20.00
12 Jaden Springer 8.00 20.00
13 Cameron Thomas 15.00 40.00
14 Bones Hyland 10.00 25.00
15 Quentin Grimes 15.00 40.00
16 Josh Christopher 6.00 15.00
17 Usman Garuba 6.00 15.00
18 Isaiah Jackson 8.00 20.00
19 Keon Johnson 8.00 20.00
20 Jalen Johnson 25.00 60.00
21 Kai Jones 6.00 15.00
22 Tre Mann 12.00 30.00
23 Trey Murphy III 25.00 60.00
24 Alperen Sengun 50.00 120.00
25 Corey Kispert 10.00 25.00
26 Moses Moody 15.00 40.00
27 Chris Duarte 6.00 15.00
28 Joshua Primo 6.00 15.00
29 James Bouknight 6.00 15.00
30 Ziaire Williams 10.00 25.00
31 Davion Mitchell 8.00 20.00
32 Franz Wagner 75.00 200.00
33 Jonathan Kuminga 25.00 60.00
34 Josh Giddey 125.00 300.00
35 Jalen Suggs 20.00 50.00
36 Scottie Barnes 100.00 250.00
37 Evan Mobley 125.00 300.00
38 Jalen Green 150.00 400.00
39 Cade Cunningham 150.00 400.00
40 Ayo Dosunmu 15.00 40.00

2021-22 Elite Power Formulas

COMMON CARD .50 1.25
SEMISTARS .60 1.50
UNLISTED STARS .75 2.00
*ORANGE DIE CUT: .6X TO 1.5X BASIC
*BLUE/99: 1.5X TO 4X BASIC
*PURPLE/49: 2X TO 5X BASIC
1 Joel Embiid 2.00 5.00
2 Carmelo Anthony 1.25 3.00
3 Zach LaVine 1.25 3.00
4 Anthony Davis 2.00 5.00
5 Jayson Tatum 3.00 8.00
6 Ben Simmons .75 2.00
7 Devin Booker 2.00 5.00
8 Kawhi Leonard 2.00 5.00
9 Stephen Curry 5.00 12.00
10 Julius Randle 1.00 2.50
11 Giannis Antetokounmpo 4.00 10.00
12 Chris Paul 1.50 4.00
13 Zion Williamson 2.00 5.00
14 James Harden 1.50 4.00
15 Donovan Mitchell 1.50 4.00
16 Fred VanVleet 1.00 2.50
17 Trae Young 2.00 5.00
18 Jaylen Brown 1.25 3.00
19 Bradley Beal 1.00 2.50
20 Brandon Ingram 1.00 2.50
21 Luka Doncic 5.00 12.00
22 Jimmy Butler 1.25 3.00
23 Kyrie Irving 1.50 4.00
24 Kevin Durant 2.50 6.00
25 Nikola Jokic 4.00 10.00
26 LaMelo Ball 2.00 5.00
27 De'Aaron Fox 1.25 3.00
28 Collin Sexton .75 2.00
29 Damian Lillard 2.00 5.00
30 Russell Westbrook 1.25 3.00

2021-22 Elite Primary Colors

COMMON CARD .50 1.25
SEMISTARS .60 1.50
UNLISTED STARS .75 2.00
*ORANGE DIE CUT: .6X TO 1.5X BASIC
*BLUE/99: 1.5X TO 4X BASIC
*PURPLE/49: 2X TO 5X BASIC
1 Kyrie Irving 1.50 4.00
2 LeBron James 6.00 15.00
3 Anthony Davis 2.00 5.00
4 Luka Doncic 5.00 12.00
5 Jayson Tatum 3.00 8.00
6 Kevin Durant 2.50 6.00
7 Zion Williamson 2.00 5.00
8 Stephen Curry 5.00 12.00
9 Trae Young 2.00 5.00
10 Giannis Antetokounmpo 4.00 10.00

2021-22 Elite Prime Numbers

COMMON CARD .50 1.25
SEMISTARS .60 1.50
UNLISTED STARS .75 2.00
1 James Harden 1.50 4.00
2 Kawhi Leonard 2.00 5.00
3 LeBron James 6.00 15.00
4 Bradley Beal 1.00 2.50
5 Kyrie Irving 1.50 4.00
6 De'Aaron Fox 1.25 3.00
7 Pascal Siakam 1.25 3.00
8 Kevin Durant 2.50 6.00
9 Paul George 1.25 3.00
10 Trae Young 2.00 5.00

2021-22 Elite Rookie Yearbook Autographs

COMMON CARD 4.00 10.00
SEMISTARS 5.00 12.00
UNLISTED STARS 6.00 15.00
EXCHANGE DEADLINE 8/16/2023
1 Cade Cunningham 350.00 700.00
2 Jalen Green 150.00 400.00
3 Evan Mobley 200.00 500.00
4 Scottie Barnes 200.00 500.00
5 Jalen Suggs 75.00 200.00
6 Josh Giddey 200.00 500.00
7 Jonathan Kuminga 200.00 500.00
8 Franz Wagner 60.00 150.00
9 Jared Butler 12.00 30.00
10 Davion Mitchell 50.00 120.00
11 Ziaire Williams 30.00 80.00
12 Miles McBride 25.00 60.00
13 Ayo Dosunmu 75.00 200.00
14 Day'Ron Sharpe 6.00 15.00
15 Jaden Springer 6.00 15.00
16 Cameron Thomas 40.00 100.00
17 Bones Hyland 50.00 120.00
18 Quentin Grimes 12.00 30.00
19 Josh Christopher 5.00 12.00
20 Usman Garuba 5.00 12.00
21 Isaiah Jackson 6.00 15.00
22 Keon Johnson 6.00 15.00
23 Jalen Johnson 20.00 50.00
24 Kai Jones 6.00 15.00
25 Tre Mann 10.00 25.00
26 Trey Murphy III 20.00 50.00
27 Alperen Sengun 40.00 100.00
28 Corey Kispert 8.00 20.00
29 Moses Moody 40.00 100.00
30 Chris Duarte 25.00 60.00
31 Joshua Primo 5.00 12.00
32 James Bouknight 5.00 12.00
33 Greg Brown III 5.00 12.00
34 Santi Aldama 8.00 20.00
35 Jeremiah Robinson-Earl 6.00 15.00
36 Luka Garza 20.00 50.00
37 Brandon Boston Jr. 30.00 80.00
38 Charles Bassey 6.00 15.00
39 Scottie Lewis 5.00 12.00
40 Isaiah Livers 6.00 15.00

2021-22 Elite Signatures

COMMON CARD 4.00 10.00
SEMISTARS 5.00 12.00
UNLISTED STARS 6.00 15.00
STATED PRINT RUN 99-149 SER.#'d SETS
EXCHANGE DEADLINE 8/16/2023
*RED/49: .5X TO 1.2X BASIC
*BLUE/35: .6X TO 1.5X BASIC
*PURPLE/25: .75X TO 2X BASIC
1 Shawn Kemp/149 25.00 60.00
2 Anthony Davis/99 40.00 100.00
3 Alex Caruso/149 6.00 15.00
4 Larry Bird/99 75.00 200.00
5 Luguentz Dort/149 6.00 15.00
6 Rex Chapman/149 5.00 12.00
7 Luke Kennard/149 5.00 12.00
8 Charles Barkley/99 60.00 150.00
9 Tomas Satoransky/149 4.00 10.00
10 Zion Williamson/99 200.00 500.00
11 Caron Butler/149 5.00 12.00
12 Allen Iverson/99 60.00 150.00
13 Desmond Mason/149 5.00 12.00
14 Trae Young/99 100.00 250.00
15 Bill Laimbeer/149 6.00 15.00
16 Mitch Kupchak/149 5.00 12.00
17 Tom Gugliotta/149 5.00 12.00
18 Luka Doncic/99 400.00 800.00
19 Jack Sikma/149 6.00 15.00
20 Shaquille O'Neal/99 75.00 200.00
21 T.J. McConnell/149 5.00 12.00
22 Kevin Garnett/99 60.00 150.00
23 Doug McDermott/149 5.00 12.00
24 Ja Morant/99 300.00 600.00
25 Charles Oakley/149 5.00 12.00

2021-22 Elite Spellbound

COMMON CARD .50 1.25
SEMISTARS .60 1.50
UNLISTED STARS .75 2.00
*ORANGE DIE CUT: .6X TO 1.5X BASIC
*BLUE/99: 2X TO 5X BASIC
*PURPLE/49: 2.5X TO 6X BASIC
1 LeBron James 6.00 15.00
2 LeBron James 6.00 15.00
3 LeBron James 6.00 15.00
4 LeBron James 6.00 15.00
5 LeBron James 6.00 15.00
6 LeBron James 6.00 15.00
7 Giannis Antetokounmpo 4.00 10.00
8 Giannis Antetokounmpo 4.00 10.00
9 Giannis Antetokounmpo 4.00 10.00
10 Giannis Antetokounmpo 4.00 10.00
11 Giannis Antetokounmpo 4.00 10.00
12 Giannis Antetokounmpo 4.00 10.00
13 Giannis Antetokounmpo 4.00 10.00
14 Ja Morant 2.50 6.00
15 Ja Morant 2.50 6.00
16 Ja Morant 2.50 6.00
17 Ja Morant 2.50 6.00
18 Ja Morant 2.50 6.00
19 Ja Morant 2.50 6.00
20 Stephen Curry 5.00 12.00
21 Stephen Curry 5.00 12.00
22 Stephen Curry 5.00 12.00
23 Stephen Curry 5.00 12.00
24 Stephen Curry 5.00 12.00
25 Stephen Curry 5.00 12.00
26 Stephen Curry 5.00 12.00
27 Zion Williamson 2.00 5.00
28 Zion Williamson 2.00 5.00
29 Zion Williamson 2.00 5.00
30 Zion Williamson 2.00 5.00
31 Zion Williamson 2.00 5.00
32 Zion Williamson 2.00 5.00
33 Zion Williamson 2.00 5.00
34 Zion Williamson 2.00 5.00
35 Zion Williamson 2.00 5.00
36 Zion Williamson 2.00 5.00
37 Chris Paul 1.50 4.00
38 Chris Paul 1.50 4.00
39 Chris Paul 1.50 4.00
40 Chris Paul 1.50 4.00

2021-22 Elite Star Status

COMMON CARD .50 1.25
SEMISTARS .60 1.50
UNLISTED STARS .75 2.00
*ORANGE DIE CUT: .6X TO 1.5X BASIC
*BLUE/99: 1.5X TO 4X BASIC
*PURPLE/49: 2X TO 5X BASIC
1 Joel Embiid 2.00 5.00
2 James Harden 1.50 4.00
3 Jimmy Butler 1.25 3.00
4 LeBron James 6.00 15.00
5 Kawhi Leonard 2.00 5.00
6 Kevin Durant 2.50 6.00
7 Russell Westbrook 1.25 3.00
8 Giannis Antetokounmpo 4.00 10.00
9 Chris Paul 1.50 4.00
10 Anthony Davis 2.00 5.00
11 Bradley Beal 1.00 2.50
12 Zion Williamson 2.00 5.00
13 Damian Lillard 2.00 5.00
14 Luka Doncic 5.00 12.00
15 Trae Young 2.00 5.00
16 Stephen Curry 5.00 12.00
17 Nikola Jokic 4.00 10.00
18 Kyrie Irving 1.50 4.00
19 Devin Booker 2.00 5.00
20 Jayson Tatum 3.00 8.00

2021-22 Elite Title Waves

COMMON CARD .50 1.25
SEMISTARS .60 1.50
UNLISTED STARS .75 2.00
1 Giannis Antetokounmpo 4.00 10.00
2 Khris Middleton .75 2.00
3 LeBron James 6.00 15.00
4 Anthony Davis 2.00 5.00
5 Kawhi Leonard 2.00 5.00
6 Pascal Siakam 1.25 3.00
7 Kevin Durant 2.50 6.00
8 Stephen Curry 5.00 12.00
9 Klay Thompson 2.00 5.00
10 Draymond Green 1.00 2.50
11 LeBron James 6.00 15.00
12 Kyrie Irving 1.50 4.00
13 Tim Duncan 2.00 5.00
14 Tony Parker 1.25 3.00
15 Kawhi Leonard 2.00 5.00
16 LeBron James 6.00 15.00
17 Dwyane Wade 1.50 4.00
18 Paul Pierce 1.25 3.00
19 Ray Allen 1.25 3.00
20 Kevin Garnett 2.00 5.00

2021-22 Elite Turn of the Century Signatures

COMMON CARD 4.00 10.00
SEMISTARS 5.00 12.00
UNLISTED STARS 6.00 15.00
STATED PRINT RUN 99-149 SER.#'d SETS
EXCHANGE DEADLINE 8/16/2023
*RED/49: .5X TO 1.2X BASIC
*BLUE/35: .6X TO 1.5X BASIC
*PURPLE/25: .75X TO 2X BASIC
1 Khris Middleton/99 6.00 15.00
2 Gheorghe Muresan/149 4.00 10.00
3 Rasheed Wallace/99 30.00 80.00
4 LaPhonso Ellis/149 5.00 12.00
5 CJ McCollum/99 5.00 12.00
6 Bobby Portis/149 5.00 12.00
7 Mark Price/149 6.00 15.00
8 Jeff Malone/149 5.00 12.00
9 Joakim Noah/149 5.00 12.00
10 Dennis Rodman/99 30.00 80.00
11 Ben Wallace/99 30.00 80.00
12 Alvin Robertson/149 5.00 12.00
13 Jamal Murray/99 12.00 30.00
14 Thomas Bryant/149 4.00 10.00
15 Anfernee Hardaway/99 40.00 100.00
16 Mark Eaton/149 6.00 15.00
17 Hedo Turkoglu/149 5.00 12.00
18 Rod Strickland/149 5.00 12.00
19 Ralph Sampson/149 6.00 15.00
20 Harold Miner/149 6.00 15.00
21 Clint Capela/149 6.00 15.00
22 Mario Chalmers/149 5.00 12.00
23 Jason Williams/149 25.00 60.00
24 Micheal Ray Richardson/149 5.00 12.00
25 Tony Parker/99 12.00 30.00

2022-23 Elite

*HYPER RED & GRN: .75X TO 2X BASIC
*ORANGE: .75X TO 2X BASIC
1 Quentin Grimes .40 1.00
2 De'Anthony Melton .40 1.00
3 Patty Mills .50 1.25
4 Derrick White .50 1.25
5 Jaylen Brown 1.00 2.50
6 Kyrie Irving 1.00 2.50
7 Kevin Durant 1.50 4.00
8 Jalen Brunson 1.00 2.50
9 Jayson Tatum 2.00 5.00
10 Evan Fournier .40 1.00
11 RJ Barrett .75 2.00
12 James Harden 1.00 2.50
13 Joel Embiid .75 2.00
14 Cameron Thomas .75 2.00
15 Ben Simmons .50 1.25
16 Robert Williams III .40 1.00
17 Seth Curry .40 1.00
18 Al Horford .50 1.25
19 Obi Toppin .50 1.25
20 Malcolm Brogdon .40 1.00
21 Julius Randle .60 1.50
22 Tobias Harris .40 1.00
23 Tyrese Maxey 1.00 2.50
24 Marcus Smart .60 1.50
25 Cam Reddish .40 1.00
26 P.J. Tucker .40 1.00
27 Aaron Gordon .50 1.25
28 Rudy Gobert .60 1.50
29 Trendon Watford .50 1.25
30 Anthony Edwards 2.50 6.00
31 Josh Hart .50 1.25
32 Jerami Grant .60 1.50
33 Bruce Brown .50 1.25
34 Nikola Jokic 2.50 6.00
35 Pascal Siakam .75 2.00
36 Damian Lillard 1.25 3.00
37 Jamal Murray .75 2.00
38 Gary Payton II .40 1.00
39 Scottie Barnes .75 2.00
40 Gary Trent Jr. .50 1.25
41 Michael Porter Jr. .60 1.50
42 Jeff Green .30 .75
43 Jusuf Nurkic .50 1.25
44 OG Anunoby .60 1.50
45 Jaden McDaniels .50 1.25
46 D'Angelo Russell .40 1.00
47 Anfernee Simons .60 1.50
48 Karl-Anthony Towns .75 2.00
49 Bones Hyland .40 1.00
50 Fred VanVleet .60 1.50
51 Bojan Bogdanovic .50 1.25
52 Kelly Olynyk .40 1.00
53 Caris LeVert .40 1.00
54 Jarrett Allen .50 1.25
55 Lauri Markkanen .75 2.00
56 Ayo Dosunmu .60 1.50
57 Marvin Bagley III .40 1.00
58 Collin Sexton .60 1.50
59 Jaylen Nowell .50 1.25
60 Coby White .40 1.00
61 Donovan Mitchell 1.00 2.50
62 Saddiq Bey .40 1.00
63 Jordan Clarkson .50 1.25
64 Isaiah Stewart .40 1.00
65 Evan Mobley 1.25 3.00
66 Zach LaVine 1.00 2.50
67 DeMar DeRozan .60 1.50
68 Malik Beasley .40 1.00
69 Cade Cunningham 1.50 4.00
70 Kevin Love .50 1.25
71 Nikola Vucevic .50 1.25
72 Alex Caruso .50 1.25
73 Lonzo Ball .50 1.25
74 Darius Garland .75 2.00
75 Mike Conley .40 1.00
76 Grayson Allen .50 1.25
77 Brook Lopez .50 1.25
78 Joe Ingles .40 1.00
79 Reggie Jackson .40 1.00
80 Chris Duarte .40 1.00
81 Khris Middleton .60 1.50
82 Draymond Green .60 1.50
83 Bobby Portis .50 1.25
84 Andrew Wiggins .60 1.50
85 Jordan Poole .75 2.00
86 Kawhi Leonard 1.25 3.00
87 Jrue Holiday .60 1.50
88 Aaron Nesmith .50 1.25
89 Myles Turner .50 1.25
90 Jonathan Kuminga 1.25 3.00
91 James Wiseman .40 1.00
92 Moses Moody .60 1.50
93 Buddy Hield .50 1.25
94 Giannis Antetokounmpo 2.50 6.00
95 Norman Powell .50 1.25
96 Klay Thompson 1.25 3.00
97 Paul George .75 2.00
98 Stephen Curry 4.00 10.00
99 John Wall .60 1.50
100 Tyrese Haliburton 1.00 2.50
101 Trae Young 1.25 3.00
102 Domantas Sabonis .60 1.50
103 Chris Paul 1.00 2.50
104 Kevin Huerter .50 1.25
105 Cameron Johnson .40 1.00
106 Anthony Davis 1.25 3.00
107 Mikal Bridges .60 1.50
108 Ivica Zubac .50 1.25
109 Patrick Beverley .30 .75
110 Russell Westbrook .75 2.00
111 Derrick Rose 1.00 2.50
112 Lonnie Walker IV .40 1.00
113 Davion Mitchell .40 1.00
114 Harrison Barnes .40 1.00
115 Deandre Ayton .50 1.25
116 Marcus Morris Sr. .30 .75
117 Dejounte Murray .60 1.50
118 De'Aaron Fox 1.00 2.50
119 Jae Crowder .30 .75
120 Justin Holiday .30 .75
121 Devin Booker 1.25 3.00
122 LeBron James 4.00 10.00
123 Kendrick Nunn .40 1.00
124 Carmelo Anthony .75 2.00
125 RJ Hampton .40 1.00
126 Markelle Fultz .40 1.00
127 Kelly Oubre Jr. .50 1.25
128 Victor Oladipo .40 1.00
129 Bam Adebayo .75 2.00
130 Franz Wagner 1.25 3.00
131 Jalen Suggs .60 1.50
132 LaMelo Ball 1.25 3.00
133 PJ Washington Jr. .50 1.25
134 De'Andre Hunter .50 1.25
135 Bogdan Bogdanovic .50 1.25
136 Bol Bol .50 1.25
137 Wendell Carter Jr. .50 1.25
138 Clint Capela .50 1.25
139 Gary Harris .40 1.00
140 Montrezl Harrell .50 1.25
141 Kyle Lowry .60 1.50
142 Tyler Herro .75 2.00
143 Gordon Hayward .40 1.00
144 Duncan Robinson .50 1.25
145 Max Strus .50 1.25
146 Jimmy Butler 1.00 2.50
147 Terry Rozier III .60 1.50
148 John Collins .60 1.50
149 Cole Anthony .50 1.25
150 Corey Kispert .50 1.25
151 Desmond Bane .60 1.50
152 Christian Wood .30 .75
153 Eric Gordon .40 1.00
154 Davis Bertans .30 .75
155 Kyle Kuzma .60 1.50
156 Dillon Brooks .50 1.25
157 Deni Avdija .50 1.25
158 Maxi Kleber .40 1.00
159 Tim Hardaway Jr. .40 1.00
160 Monte Morris .30 .75
161 Alperen Sengun .60 1.50
162 Jalen Green 1.50 4.00
163 Kenyon Martin Jr. .50 1.25
164 Kevin Porter Jr. .40 1.00
165 Kristaps Porzingis .60 1.50
166 Jalen Smith .50 1.25
167 Luka Doncic 3.00 8.00
168 Will Barton .30 .75
169 Jae'Sean Tate .30 .75
170 Dorian Finney-Smith .40 1.00
171 Reggie Bullock .40 1.00
172 Bradley Beal .60 1.50
173 Rui Hachimura .50 1.25
174 Spencer Dinwiddie .40 1.00
175 Jakob Poeltl .40 1.00
176 Ziaire Williams .40 1.00
177 Josh Richardson .40 1.00
178 Jaren Jackson Jr. .75 2.00
179 Aaron Wiggins .40 1.00
180 CJ McCollum .50 1.25
181 Tre Mann .40 1.00
182 Doug McDermott .30 .75
183 Josh Giddey .75 2.00
184 Devin Vassell .60 1.50
185 Shai Gilgeous-Alexander 2.50 6.00
186 Zion Williamson 1.25 3.00
187 Darius Bazley .30 .75
188 Brandon Clarke .40 1.00
189 Keldon Johnson .60 1.50
190 Devonte' Graham .40 1.00
191 Ja Morant 1.50 4.00
192 Tre Jones .50 1.25
193 Jonas Valanciunas .40 1.00
194 Tyus Jones .40 1.00
195 Trey Murphy III .60 1.50
196 Luguentz Dort .50 1.25
197 Danny Green .40 1.00
198 Brandon Ingram .60 1.50
199 Herbert Jones .50 1.25
200 Malik Monk .50 1.25
201 Wendell Moore Jr. RC 1.00 2.50
202 Christian Braun RC 2.50 6.00
203 Ryan Rollins RC 1.00 2.50
204 Tyrese Martin RC .75 2.00
205 Trevor Keels RC .75 2.00
206 Ousmane Dieng RC 1.25 3.00
207 Jabari Smith Jr. RC 3.00 8.00
208 Max Christie RC 2.50 6.00
209 Keegan Murray RC 2.50 6.00
210 Bryce McGowens RC 1.00 2.50
211 Tari Eason RC 2.50 6.00
212 Johnny Davis RC 1.00 2.50
213 Jalen Williams RC 5.00 12.00
214 Bennedict Mathurin RC 3.00 8.00
215 Blake Wesley RC 1.00 2.50
216 Walker Kessler RC 2.00 5.00
217 Jabari Walker RC .75 2.00
218 Kenneth Lofton Jr. RC 1.25 3.00
219 Kendall Brown RC .75 2.00
220 Kennedy Chandler RC 1.00 2.50
221 Scotty Pippen Jr. RC 1.25 3.00
222 Jaden Hardy RC 1.50 4.00
223 Vince Williams Jr. RC 1.25 3.00
224 AJ Griffin RC .75 2.00
225 Mark Williams RC 2.00 5.00
226 Dyson Daniels RC 2.50 6.00
227 TyTy Washington Jr. RC 1.00 2.50
228 Jalen Duren RC 3.00 8.00
229 Jaylin Williams RC 1.00 2.50
230 Josh Minott RC 1.00 2.50
231 Patrick Baldwin Jr. RC 1.00 2.50
232 Jeremy Sochan RC 3.00 8.00
233 Jake LaRavia RC 1.00 2.50
234 Andrew Nembhard RC 2.00 5.00
235 Isaiah Mobley RC 1.00 2.50
236 Malaki Branham RC 1.00 2.50
237 David Roddy RC 1.25 3.00
238 Dalen Terry RC 1.00 2.50
239 Christian Koloko RC 1.00 2.50
240 Moussa Diabate RC 1.00 2.50
241 Chet Holmgren RC 5.00 12.00
242 Ochai Agbaji RC 1.25 3.00
243 Jaden Ivey RC 3.00 8.00
244 Shaedon Sharpe RC 4.00 10.00
245 Peyton Watson RC 1.50 4.00
246 E.J. Liddell RC 1.00 2.50
247 Nikola Jovic RC 2.00 5.00
248 Caleb Houstan RC 1.00 2.50
249 MarJon Beauchamp RC 1.00 2.50
250 Paolo Banchero RC 6.00 15.00

2022-23 Elite Asia Hyper Red

*ASIA HYPER RED: 1.5X TO 4X BASIC
STATED PRINT RUN 88 COPIES PER
98 Stephen Curry 30.00 80.00
122 LeBron James 30.00 80.00

2022-23 Elite Aspirations

*ASPIRATIONS: 3X TO 8X BASIC
STATED PRINT RUN 1-99 COPIES PER
98 Stephen Curry/70 50.00 120.00
122 LeBron James/94 50.00 120.00
250 Paolo Banchero/95 125.00 300.00

2022-23 Elite Blue

*BLUE: 1.5X TO 4X BASIC
STATED PRINT RUN 99 COPIES PER
98 Stephen Curry 30.00 80.00
122 LeBron James 30.00 80.00

2022-23 Elite Purple
*PURPLE: 3X TO 8X BASIC
STATED PRINT RUN 49 COPIES PER
38 Stephen Curry 50.00 120.00
122 LeBron James 50.00 120.00
250 Paolo Banchero 125.00 300.00

2022-23 Elite Back to the Future
COMMON CARD .60 1.50
SEMISTARS .75 2.00
UNLISTED STARS 1.00 2.50
*ASIA RED: .6X TO 1.5X BASIC
1 Larry Bird 4.00 10.00
2 Magic Johnson 4.00 10.00
3 Shaquille O'Neal 4.00 10.00
4 Allen Iverson 2.50 6.00
5 Tracy McGrady 1.50 4.00
6 Charles Barkley 2.50 6.00
7 Hakeem Olajuwon 2.00 5.00
8 Karl Malone 2.00 5.00
9 Kevin Garnett 2.50 6.00
10 Dirk Nowitzki 2.50 6.00

2022-23 Elite Clarity
COMMON CARD
SEMISTARS .60 1.50
UNLISTED STARS .75 2.00
*ASIA RED: .75X TO 2X BASIC 1.00 2.50
1 Ja Morant 3.00 8.00
2 Kawhi Leonard 2.50 6.00
3 Anthony Edwards 5.00 12.00
4 Darius Garland 1.50 4.00
5 Bradley Beal 1.25 3.00
6 Nikola Jokic 5.00 12.00
7 Jayson Tatum 4.00 10.00
8 Zion Williamson 2.50 6.00
9 Stephen Curry 8.00 20.00
10 Kevin Durant 3.00 8.00
11 Chris Paul 2.00 5.00
12 Anthony Davis 2.50 6.00
13 Zach LaVine 2.00 5.00
14 LaMelo Ball 2.50 6.00
15 Jimmy Butler 2.00 5.00
16 Luka Doncic 6.00 15.00
17 Donovan Mitchell 2.00 5.00
18 Trae Young 2.50 6.00
19 Giannis Antetokounmpo 5.00 12.00
20 James Harden 2.00 5.00
21 Joel Embiid 1.50 4.00
22 Cade Cunningham 3.00 8.00
23 Jalen Green 3.00 8.00
24 Josh Giddey 1.50 4.00
25 Julius Randle 1.25 3.00
26 Devin Booker 2.50 6.00
27 Kyrie Irving 2.00 5.00
28 DeMar DeRozan 1.25 3.00
29 Brandon Ingram 1.25 3.00
30 Pascal Siakam 1.50 4.00

2022-23 Elite Deck
COMMON CARD .60 1.50
SEMISTARS .75 2.00
UNLISTED STARS 1.00 2.50
*ASIA RED: .5X TO 1.2X BASIC
1 Luka Doncic 6.00 15.00
2 Stephen Curry 8.00 20.00
3 Jayson Tatum 4.00 10.00
4 LeBron James 8.00 20.00
5 Giannis Antetokounmpo 5.00 12.00
6 Zion Williamson 2.50 6.00
7 Devin Booker 2.50 6.00
8 Bradley Beal 1.25 3.00
9 Kevin Durant 3.00 8.00
10 RJ Barrett 1.50 4.00
11 James Harden 2.00 5.00
12 Scottie Barnes 1.50 4.00
13 Zach LaVine 2.00 5.00
14 Evan Mobley 2.50 6.00
15 Cade Cunningham 3.00 8.00
16 Kyrie Irving 2.00 5.00
17 Trae Young 2.50 6.00
18 LaMelo Ball 2.50 6.00
19 Jimmy Butler 2.00 5.00
20 Nikola Jokic 5.00 12.00
21 Anthony Edwards 5.00 12.00
22 Josh Giddey 1.50 4.00
23 Damian Lillard 2.50 6.00
24 Donovan Mitchell 2.00 5.00
25 Kawhi Leonard 2.50 6.00
26 De'Aaron Fox 2.00 5.00
27 Jalen Green 3.00 8.00
28 Ja Morant 3.00 8.00
29 Jaylen Brown 2.00 5.00
30 Franz Wagner 2.50 6.00

2022-23 Elite Dimensions
1 Kevin Durant 60.00 150.00
2 Stephen Curry 125.00 300.00
3 Jayson Tatum 60.00 150.00
4 Nikola Jokic 60.00 150.00
5 LeBron James 125.00 300.00
6 Giannis Antetokounmpo 125.00 300.00
7 Trae Young 50.00 120.00
8 Luka Doncic 125.00 300.00
9 Anthony Davis 60.00 150.00
10 Zion Williamson 60.00 150.00
11 Cade Cunningham 60.00 150.00
12 Josh Giddey 60.00 150.00
13 Jalen Green 60.00 150.00
14 Ja Morant 100.00 250.00
15 Anthony Edwards 60.00 150.00

2022-23 Elite Elite Signatures
COMMON CARD 5.00 12.00
SEMISTARS 6.00 15.00
UNLISTED STARS 8.00 20.00
*RED/49: .6X TO 1.5X BASIC
*BLUE/25: .75X TO 2X BASIC
1 Alex English 10.00 25.00
2 John Collins 8.00 20.00
3 Jaren Jackson Jr. 30.00 80.00
4 Julius Randle 10.00 25.00
5 Jamal Murray 20.00 50.00
6 Jerry West 30.00 80.00
7 Larry Bird 75.00 200.00
8 Victor Oladipo 6.00 15.00
9 Robert Williams III 6.00 15.00
10 Isiah Thomas 20.00 50.00
11 Jason Williams 30.00 80.00
12 Dejounte Murray 10.00 25.00
13 Elvin Hayes 10.00 25.00
14 Pau Gasol 20.00 50.00
15 Robert Parish 10.00 25.00
16 John Stockton 40.00 100.00
17 Jrue Holiday 15.00 40.00
18 Glen Rice 8.00 20.00
19 Jason Richardson 8.00 20.00
20 Grant Hill 20.00 50.00
21 Collin Sexton 10.00 25.00
22 CJ McCollum 8.00 20.00
23 T.J. Warren 6.00 15.00
24 Cade Cunningham 75.00 200.00
25 Amar'e Stoudemire 8.00 20.00

2022-23 Elite Full Throttle
COMMON CARD .50 1.25
SEMISTARS .60 1.50
UNLISTED STARS .75 2.00
*ASIA RED & GRN: .5X TO 1.2X BASIC
*ORNG DIE CUT: .5X TO 1.2X BASIC
*BLUE/99: 1.5X TO 4X BASIC
PURPLE/49: 2X TO 5X BASIC
1 Stephen Curry 6.00 15.00
2 Anthony Edwards 4.00 10.00
3 LaMelo Ball 2.00 5.00
4 Kyrie Irving 1.50 4.00
5 Trae Young 2.00 5.00
6 Damian Lillard 2.00 5.00
7 Ja Morant 2.50 6.00
8 Donovan Mitchell 1.50 4.00
9 Jayson Tatum 3.00 8.00
10 LeBron James 6.00 15.00

2022-23 Elite GenreGraphs
RED/49: .5X TO 1.2X BASIC
BLUE/25: .6X TO 1.5X BASIC
1 Jayson Tatum 200.00 500.00
2 Luka Doncic 600.00 1,200.00
3 Ja Morant 200.00 500.00
4 Anthony Edwards 200.00 500.00
6 Stephen Curry 800.00 1,500.00
7 Anfernee Hardaway 125.00 300.00
9 Jamal Murray 60.00 150.00
10 Shai Gilgeous-Alexander 400.00 800.00
11 Tony Parker 40.00 100.00
12 Dirk Nowitzki 150.00 400.00
13 Dwyane Wade 100.00 250.00
14 RJ Barrett 40.00 100.00
15 Tyrese Haliburton 125.00 300.00
16 Karl-Anthony Towns 40.00 100.00
17 Chris Paul 75.00 200.00
18 Allen Iverson 150.00 400.00
19 Paul Pierce 50.00 120.00
20 Ray Allen 100.00 250.00
21 Jason Kidd 40.00 100.00
22 Hakeem Olajuwon 60.00 150.00
23 Cade Cunningham 100.00 250.00
24 Manu Ginobili 75.00 200.00
25 Dominique Wilkins 100.00 250.00

2022-23 Elite Glass Masters
COMMON CARD .50 1.25
SEMISTARS .60 1.50
UNLISTED STARS .75 2.00
*ASIA RED: .75X TO 2X BASIC
1 Rudy Gobert 1.00 2.50
2 Nikola Jokic 4.00 10.00
3 Domantas Sabonis 1.00 2.50
4 Clint Capela .75 2.00
5 Joel Embiid 1.25 3.00
6 Giannis Antetokounmpo 4.00 10.00
7 Jonas Valanciunas .60 1.50
8 Nikola Vucevic .75 2.00
9 Deandre Ayton .75 2.00
10 Christian Wood .50 1.25

2022-23 Elite Impact Impressions Autographs
COMMON CARD 4.00 10.00
SEMISTARS 5.00 12.00
UNLISTED STARS 6.00 15.00
*ASIA RED & GRN: .4X TO 1X BASIC
RED/49: .5X TO 1.2X BASIC
BLUE/25: .6X TO 1.5X BASIC
1 Luguentz Dort 6.00 15.00
2 Spencer Dinwiddie 5.00 12.00
3 Jalen Brunson 15.00 40.00
4 Kristaps Porzingis 8.00 20.00
5 Scottie Barnes 30.00 80.00
6 Jordan Clarkson 20.00 50.00
7 Franz Wagner 20.00 50.00
8 Eric Gordon 5.00 12.00
9 Josh Giddey 30.00 80.00
10 Reggie Jackson 5.00 12.00
11 Ayo Dosunmu 8.00 20.00
12 Danny Green 5.00 12.00
13 Juan Toscano-Anderson 4.00 10.00
14 Chris Duarte 5.00 12.00
15 Jordan Nwora 6.00 15.00
16 Alperen Sengun 15.00 40.00
17 Herbert Jones 6.00 15.00
18 Ray Allen 40.00 100.00
19 Kevin Porter Jr. 5.00 12.00
20 RJ Hampton 5.00 12.00
21 Desmond Bane 8.00 20.00
22 Keon Johnson 4.00 10.00
23 Keldon Johnson 8.00 20.00
24 Juwan Howard 6.00 15.00
25 Jaren Jackson Jr. 15.00 40.00
26 De'Anthony Melton 5.00 12.00
27 Moses Moody 8.00 20.00
28 Jerry Stackhouse 8.00 20.00
29 Jose Alvarado 6.00 15.00
30 Pau Gasol 12.00 30.00
31 Jalen Green 60.00 150.00
32 Derek Fisher 6.00 15.00
33 Davion Mitchell 5.00 12.00
34 Mark Jackson 6.00 15.00
35 Sam Cassell 6.00 15.00
36 Grayson Allen 6.00 15.00
37 Muggsy Bogues 6.00 15.00
38 Cazzie Russell 8.00 20.00
39 Bill Laimbeer 6.00 15.00
40 Caron Butler 5.00 12.00
41 Christian Wood 4.00 10.00
42 Anfernee Simons 8.00 20.00
43 Lonnie Walker IV 5.00 12.00
44 Rudy Gobert 8.00 20.00
45 Derrick Coleman 6.00 15.00
46 Cameron Payne 5.00 12.00
47 Artis Gilmore 8.00 20.00
48 Richard Hamilton 8.00 20.00
49 Kelly Oubre Jr. 6.00 15.00
50 Louie Dampier 6.00 15.00
51 Glen Rice 6.00 15.00
52 Kevin Huerter 6.00 15.00
53 Wendell Carter Jr. 6.00 15.00
54 Jonas Valanciunas 5.00 12.00
55 Avery Johnson 5.00 12.00
56 Aaron Nesmith 6.00 15.00
57 Derek Harper 5.00 12.00
58 Larry Johnson 20.00 50.00
59 Eddy Curry 5.00 12.00
60 Bradley Beal 8.00 20.00

2022-23 Elite New Breed Autographs
COMMON CARD 4.00 10.00
SEMISTARS 5.00 12.00
UNLISTED STARS 6.00 15.00
*ASIA RED & GRN: .4X TO 1X BASIC
RED/49: .5X TO 1.2X BASIC
BLUE/25: .6X TO 1.5X BASIC
1 Jaden Ivey 100.00 250.00
2 Dalen Terry 6.00 15.00
3 MarJon Beauchamp 6.00 15.00
4 AJ Griffin 5.00 12.00
5 Blake Wesley 6.00 15.00
6 Johnny Davis 6.00 15.00
7 Paolo Banchero 300.00 600.00
8 Chet Holmgren 150.00 400.00
9 TyTy Washington Jr. 6.00 15.00
10 Jaden Hardy 75.00 200.00
11 Peyton Watson 10.00 25.00
12 Keegan Murray 100.00 250.00
13 Isaiah Mobley 6.00 15.00
14 Kenneth Lofton Jr. 8.00 20.00
15 Collin Gillespie 6.00 15.00
16 Tari Eason 15.00 40.00
17 Jabari Smith Jr. 75.00 200.00
18 Jalen Williams 125.00 300.00
19 Patrick Baldwin Jr. 6.00 15.00
20 Jalen Duren 25.00 60.00
21 Ochai Agbaji 20.00 50.00
22 Ousmane Dieng 8.00 20.00
23 Bennedict Mathurin 100.00 250.00
24 Jeremy Sochan 100.00 250.00
25 Dyson Daniels 25.00 60.00
26 Nikola Jovic 12.00 30.00
27 Wendell Moore Jr. 6.00 15.00
28 Mark Williams 12.00 30.00
29 Jake LaRavia 6.00 15.00
30 David Roddy 8.00 20.00
31 Walker Kessler 40.00 100.00
32 Shaedon Sharpe 100.00 250.00
33 Christian Koloko 6.00 15.00
34 Caleb Houstan 6.00 15.00
35 Andrew Nembhard 20.00 50.00
36 Bryce McGowens 6.00 15.00
37 Tyrese Martin 5.00 12.00
38 Ryan Rollins 6.00 15.00
39 Josh Minott 6.00 15.00
40 Vince Williams Jr. 8.00 20.00
41 Scotty Pippen Jr. 8.00 20.00
42 Jabari Walker 5.00 12.00
43 Kendall Brown 5.00 12.00
44 Kennedy Chandler 6.00 15.00
45 Malaki Branham 20.00 50.00
46 Christian Braun 15.00 40.00
47 Jaylin Williams 8.00 20.00
48 Max Christie 15.00 40.00
49 E.J. Liddell 6.00 15.00
50 Trevor Keels 5.00 12.00

2022-23 Elite Next Up
1 Paolo Banchero 150.00 400.00
2 Chet Holmgren 125.00 300.00
3 Jabari Smith Jr. 100.00 250.00
4 Keegan Murray 100.00 250.00
5 Jaden Ivey 100.00 250.00
6 Bennedict Mathurin 100.00 250.00
7 Shaedon Sharpe 100.00 250.00
8 Dyson Daniels 40.00 100.00
9 Johnny Davis 20.00 50.00
10 Jalen Williams 100.00 250.00

2022-23 Elite Passing the Torch Signatures
1 P.Banchero/S.O'Neal 1,000.00 2,000.00
2 C.Holmgren/D.Nowitzki 800.00 1,500.00
3 C.Barkley/J.Smith Jr. 400.00 800.00
5 G.Hill/J.Ivey 200.00 500.00
6 J.Tatum/P.Pierce 400.00 800.00
7 A.Iverson/J.Morant 600.00 1,200.00
8 C.Paul/J.Kidd 200.00 500.00
9 A.Edwards/D.Wilkins 200.00 500.00
10 S.Sharpe/S.Gilgeous-Alexander 1,000.00 2,000.00

2022-23 Elite Pen Pals
COMMON CARD 5.00 12.00
SEMISTARS 6.00 15.00
UNLISTED STARS 8.00 20.00
RED/49: .5X TO 1.2X BASIC
BLUE/49: .6X TO 1.5X BASIC
1 Chet Holmgren 150.00 400.00
2 Keegan Murray 100.00 250.00
3 Jaden Hardy 75.00 200.00
4 Jalen Duren 25.00 60.00
5 AJ Griffin 6.00 15.00
6 Mark Williams 15.00 40.00
7 Jabari Smith Jr. 100.00 250.00
8 Christian Braun 20.00 50.00
9 Dalen Terry 8.00 20.00
10 Isaiah Mobley 8.00 20.00
11 Max Christie 20.00 50.00
12 Jaden Ivey 100.00 250.00
13 Jalen Williams 125.00 300.00
14 Tari Eason 20.00 50.00
15 Paolo Banchero 300.00 600.00
16 Shaedon Sharpe 100.00 250.00
17 Blake Wesley 8.00 20.00
18 Walker Kessler 40.00 100.00
19 MarJon Beauchamp 8.00 20.00
20 Kennedy Chandler 8.00 20.00
21 TyTy Washington Jr. 8.00 20.00
22 Dyson Daniels 40.00 100.00
23 Moussa Diabate 8.00 20.00
24 David Roddy 10.00 25.00
25 Peyton Watson 12.00 30.00
26 Bennedict Mathurin 100.00 250.00
27 Patrick Baldwin Jr. 8.00 20.00
28 Ochai Agbaji 50.00 120.00
29 Andrew Nembhard 20.00 50.00
30 E.J. Liddell 8.00 20.00
31 Wendell Moore Jr. 8.00 20.00
32 Nikola Jovic 15.00 40.00
33 Jake LaRavia 8.00 20.00
34 Malaki Branham 25.00 60.00
35 Ousmane Dieng 10.00 25.00
36 Trevor Keels 6.00 15.00
37 Caleb Houstan 8.00 20.00
38 Jeremy Sochan 100.00 250.00
39 Christian Koloko 8.00 20.00
40 Johnny Davis 8.00 20.00

2022-23 Elite Power Formulas
COMMON CARD .50 1.20
SEMISTARS .60 1.50
UNLISTED STARS .75 2.00
*ASIA RED & GRN: .5X TO 1.2X BASIC
*ORNG DIE CUT: .5X TO 1.2X BASIC
*BLUE/99: 1.5X TO 4X BASIC
PURPLE/49: 2X TO 5X BASIC
1 Jayson Tatum 3.00 8.00
2 Kevin Durant 2.50 6.00
3 James Harden 1.50 4.00
4 Pascal Siakam 1.25 3.00
5 Nikola Jokic 4.00 10.00
6 Anthony Edwards 4.00 10.00
7 Josh Giddey 1.25 3.00
8 Damian Lillard 2.00 5.00
9 Donovan Mitchell 1.50 4.00
10 Zach LaVine 1.50 4.00
11 Darius Garland 1.25 3.00
12 Cade Cunningham 2.50 6.00
13 Tyrese Haliburton 1.50 4.00
14 Giannis Antetokounmpo 4.00 10.00
15 Stephen Curry 6.00 15.00
16 Kawhi Leonard 2.00 5.00
17 LeBron James 6.00 15.00
18 Devin Booker 2.00 5.00
19 De'Aaron Fox 1.50 4.00
20 Trae Young 2.00 5.00
21 LaMelo Ball 2.00 5.00
22 Jimmy Butler 1.50 4.00
23 Bradley Beal 1.00 2.50
24 Luka Doncic 5.00 12.00
25 Jalen Green 2.50 6.00
26 Ja Morant 2.50 6.00
27 Zion Williamson 2.00 5.00
28 Jaylen Brown 1.50 4.00
29 Kyrie Irving 1.50 4.00
30 Anthony Davis 2.00 5.00

2022-23 Elite Rookie Yearbook Autographs
COMMON CARD 4.00 10.00
SEMISTARS 5.00 12.00
UNLISTED STARS 6.00 15.00
*ASIA RED & GRN: .4X TO 1X BASIC
RED/49: .5X TO 1.2X BASIC
BLUE/25: .6X TO 1.5X BASIC
1 Jalen Duren 20.00 50.00
2 AJ Griffin 5.00 12.00
3 Mark Williams 12.00 30.00
4 Jabari Smith Jr. 75.00 200.00
5 Christian Braun 15.00 40.00
6 Dalen Terry 6.00 15.00
7 Isaiah Mobley 6.00 15.00
8 Max Christie 15.00 40.00
9 Jaden Ivey 75.00 200.00
10 Jalen Williams 75.00 200.00
11 Tari Eason 15.00 40.00
12 Bennedict Mathurin 75.00 200.00
13 Patrick Baldwin Jr. 6.00 15.00
14 Ochai Agbaji 20.00 50.00
15 Trevor Keels 5.00 12.00
16 Caleb Houstan 6.00 15.00
17 Jeremy Sochan 75.00 200.00
18 Christian Koloko 6.00 15.00
19 Johnny Davis 6.00 15.00
20 Nikola Jovic 12.00 30.00
21 Jake LaRavia 6.00 15.00
22 Malaki Branham 6.00 15.00
23 Ousmane Dieng 8.00 20.00
24 Paolo Banchero 200.00 500.00
25 Shaedon Sharpe 75.00 200.00
26 Blake Wesley 6.00 15.00
27 Walker Kessler 40.00 100.00
28 MarJon Beauchamp 20.00 50.00
29 Kennedy Chandler 6.00 15.00
30 TyTy Washington Jr. 6.00 15.00
31 Dyson Daniels 20.00 50.00
32 Moussa Diabate 6.00 15.00
33 David Roddy 8.00 20.00
34 Peyton Watson 10.00 25.00
35 Andrew Nembhard 20.00 50.00
36 E.J. Liddell 6.00 15.00
37 Wendell Moore Jr. 6.00 15.00
38 Chet Holmgren 125.00 300.00
39 Keegan Murray 75.00 200.00
40 Jaden Hardy 60.00 150.00

2022-23 Elite Spellbound
COMMON CARD .50 1.20
SEMISTARS .60 1.50
UNLISTED STARS .75 2.00
*ASIA RED & GRN: .75X TO 2X BASIC
*ORNG DIE CUT: .75X TO 2X BASIC
*BLUE/99: 1.5X TO 4X BASIC
PURPLE/49: 2X TO 5X BASIC
1 LeBron James 6.00 15.00
2 LeBron James 6.00 15.00
3 LeBron James 6.00 15.00
4 LeBron James 6.00 15.00
5 LeBron James 6.00 15.00
6 LeBron James 6.00 15.00
7 Ja Morant 2.50 6.00
8 Ja Morant 2.50 6.00
9 Ja Morant 2.50 6.00
10 Ja Morant 2.50 6.00
11 Ja Morant 2.50 6.00
12 Ja Morant 2.50 6.00
13 Luka Doncic 5.00 12.00
14 Luka Doncic 5.00 12.00
15 Luka Doncic 5.00 12.00
16 Luka Doncic 5.00 12.00
17 Luka Doncic 5.00 12.00
18 Luka Doncic 5.00 12.00
19 Trae Young 2.00 5.00
20 Trae Young 2.00 5.00
21 Trae Young 2.00 5.00
22 Trae Young 2.00 5.00
23 Zion Williamson 2.00 5.00
24 Zion Williamson 2.00 5.00
25 Zion Williamson 2.00 5.00
26 Zion Williamson 2.00 5.00
27 Anthony Edwards 4.00 10.00
28 Anthony Edwards 4.00 10.00
29 Anthony Edwards 4.00 10.00
30 Anthony Edwards 4.00 10.00
31 Anthony Edwards 4.00 10.00
32 Anthony Edwards 4.00 10.00
33 Anthony Edwards 4.00 10.00
34 Stephen Curry 6.00 15.00
35 Stephen Curry 6.00 15.00
36 Stephen Curry 6.00 15.00
37 Stephen Curry 6.00 15.00
38 Stephen Curry 6.00 15.00
39 Stephen Curry 6.00 15.00
40 Stephen Curry 6.00 15.00

2022-23 Elite Star Status
COMMON CARD .50 1.20
SEMISTARS .60 1.50
UNLISTED STARS .75 2.00
*ASIA RED & GRN: .5X TO 1.2X BASIC
*ORNG DIE CUT: .5X TO 1.2X BASIC
*BLUE/99: 1.5X TO 4X BASIC
PURPLE/49: 2X TO 5X BASIC
1 Jayson Tatum 3.00 8.00
2 LeBron James 6.00 15.00
3 Kevin Durant 2.50 6.00
4 James Harden 1.50 4.00
5 Kawhi Leonard 2.00 5.00
6 Zion Williamson 2.00 5.00
7 Luka Doncic 5.00 12.00
8 Stephen Curry 6.00 15.00
9 Nikola Jokic 4.00 10.00
10 Devin Booker 2.00 5.00
11 Anthony Edwards 4.00 10.00
12 LaMelo Ball 2.00 5.00
13 Kyrie Irving 1.50 4.00
14 Anthony Davis 2.00 5.00
15 Trae Young 2.00 5.00
16 Jimmy Butler 1.50 4.00
17 Giannis Antetokounmpo 4.00 10.00
18 Damian Lillard 2.00 5.00
19 Ja Morant 2.50 6.00
20 Donovan Mitchell 1.50 4.00

2022-23 Elite Title Waves
COMMON CARD .50 1.25
SEMISTARS .60 1.50
UNLISTED STARS .75 2.00
*ASIA RED: .75X TO 2X BASIC
1 Stephen Curry 6.00 15.00
2 Klay Thompson 2.00 5.00
3 Draymond Green 1.00 2.50
4 Andrew Wiggins 1.00 2.50
5 Giannis Antetokounmpo 4.00 10.00
6 Khris Middleton 1.00 2.50
7 LeBron James 6.00 15.00
8 Anthony Davis 2.00 5.00
9 Kawhi Leonard 2.00 5.00
10 Pascal Siakam 1.25 3.00
11 LeBron James 6.00 15.00
12 Kyrie Irving 1.50 4.00
13 Kevin Love .75 2.00
14 Dirk Nowitzki 2.00 5.00
15 Jason Kidd 1.25 3.00
16 Tim Duncan 2.00 5.00
17 Tony Parker 1.25 3.00
18 Manu Ginobili 1.50 4.00
19 Richard Hamilton 1.00 2.50
20 Chauncey Billups 1.00 2.50

2022-23 Elite Turn of the Century Signatures
COMMON CARD 4.00 10.00
SEMISTARS 5.00 12.00
UNLISTED STARS 6.00 15.00
*ASIA RED & GRN: .5X TO 1.2X BASIC
RED/49: .5X TO 1.2X BASIC
BLUE/25: .6X TO 1.5X BASIC
1 Elton Brand 6.00 15.00
2 Hedo Turkoglu 6.00 15.00
3 Adrian Dantley 6.00 15.00
4 Jason Richardson 6.00 15.00
5 Gail Goodrich 6.00 15.00
6 Dave Bing 8.00 20.00
7 Bobby Portis 6.00 15.00
8 B.J. Armstrong 6.00 15.00
9 Jae'Sean Tate 4.00 10.00
10 Dale Ellis 6.00 15.00
11 Kenyon Martin 6.00 15.00
12 Mark Aguirre 6.00 15.00
13 Jack Sikma 8.00 20.00
14 Maurice Cheeks 6.00 15.00
15 Tim Hardaway 8.00 20.00
16 Jason Terry 5.00 12.00
17 Grant Hill 15.00 40.00
18 Vince Carter 40.00 100.00
19 Walt Frazier 10.00 25.00
20 Calvin Murphy 6.00 15.00
21 Joe Dumars 8.00 20.00
22 Steve Francis 6.00 15.00
23 Jalen Rose 6.00 15.00
24 Chris Mullin 8.00 20.00
25 Dan Issel 8.00 20.00
26 Brandon Clarke 5.00 12.00
27 Michael Porter Jr. 8.00 20.00
28 Rick Fox 6.00 15.00
29 Carlos Boozer 5.00 12.00
30 Bob McAdoo 8.00 20.00
31 Earl Monroe 10.00 25.00
32 Cameron Thomas 10.00 25.00
33 Jeff Hornacek 6.00 15.00
34 Evan Fournier 5.00 12.00
35 Jamal Crawford 6.00 15.00
36 Collin Sexton 8.00 20.00
37 Bogdan Bogdanovic 6.00 15.00
38 Brook Lopez 12.00 30.00
39 Grant Williams 5.00 12.00
40 Chris Boucher 6.00 15.00
41 Dino Radja 5.00 12.00
42 Detlef Schrempf 6.00 15.00
43 Mitch Richmond 8.00 20.00
44 Kenny Walker 5.00 12.00
45 Rick Barry 8.00 20.00
46 Jonathan Kuminga 15.00 40.00
47 Julius Randle 8.00 20.00
48 Coby White 5.00 12.00
49 Duncan Robinson 6.00 15.00
50 Christian Wood 4.00 10.00

2023-24 Elite
*INTERNATIONAL: .5X TO 1.2X BASIC
*INTERNATIONAL RED & GREEN: .75X TO 2X BASIC
*ORANGE: .75X TO 2X BASIC
1 PJ Washington Jr. .50 1.25
2 Nikola Vucevic .50 1.25
3 LaMelo Ball 1.25 3.00
4 Dirk Nowitzki 1.25 3.00
5 Jordan Poole .75 2.00
6 Jalen Williams 1.00 2.50
7 Jrue Holiday .60 1.50
8 Bradley Beal .60 1.50
9 Allen Iverson 1.25 3.00
10 Khris Middleton .50 1.25
11 James Harden 1.00 2.50
12 Klay Thompson 1.25 3.00
13 John Collins .50 1.25
14 Chet Holmgren 1.25 3.00
15 Lauri Markkanen .75 2.00
16 Obi Toppin .50 1.25
17 Paul George .75 2.00
18 Malcolm Brogdon .50 1.25
19 Collin Sexton .60 1.50
20 Tracy McGrady .75 2.00
21 Grant Williams .40 1.00
22 Buddy Hield .50 1.25
23 Anthony Edwards 2.50 6.00
24 Chris Paul 1.00 2.50
25 Devin Vassell .60 1.50
26 Trey Murphy III .60 1.50
27 Blake Griffin .50 1.25
28 Jaden Ivey .60 1.50
29 Jabari Smith Jr. .75 2.00
30 Bojan Bogdanovic .50 1.25
31 Tyler Herro .75 2.00
32 Max Strus .50 1.25
33 Alperen Sengun .75 2.00
34 Davion Mitchell .40 1.00
35 Marvin Bagley III .40 1.00
36 Shaquille O'Neal 1.50 4.00
37 Jeremy Sochan .60 1.50
38 Tim Hardaway Jr. .40 1.00
39 Kentavious Caldwell-Pope .40 1.00
40 Julius Randle .60 1.50
41 Jamal Murray 1.00 2.50
42 Jarrett Allen .50 1.25
43 Deandre Ayton .50 1.25
44 Walker Kessler .50 1.25
45 Caleb Martin .40 1.00
46 Dennis Rodman 1.25 3.00
47 Karl-Anthony Towns .75 2.00
48 Kyle Anderson .40 1.00
49 Tobias Harris .50 1.25
50 Josh Hart .50 1.25
51 Mike Conley .40 1.00
52 Duncan Robinson .50 1.25
53 Derrick Jones Jr. .40 1.00
54 Eric Gordon .40 1.00
55 CJ McCollum .50 1.25
56 Jaden Hardy .60 1.50
57 Ochai Agbaji .50 1.25
58 Larry Bird 2.00 5.00
59 Shaedon Sharpe 1.00 2.50
60 Jonathan Kuminga 1.25 3.00
61 Magic Johnson 2.00 5.00
62 Bogdan Bogdanovic .50 1.25
63 James Wiseman .40 1.00
64 Derrick White .60 1.50
65 Rudy Gobert .60 1.50
66 Bones Hyland .40 1.00
67 Ben Simmons .50 1.25
68 Max Christie .50 1.25
69 Isaiah Stewart .50 1.25
70 Giannis Antetokounmpo 2.50 6.00
71 Josh Giddey .60 1.50
72 Patrick Williams .40 1.00
73 Desmond Bane .60 1.50
74 John Stockton 1.00 2.50
75 Jerami Grant .60 1.50
76 Donovan Mitchell 1.00 2.50
77 Dwyane Wade 1.00 2.50
78 Tyrese Maxey 1.00 2.50
79 Jaren Jackson Jr. .75 2.00
80 Kevin Love .50 1.25
81 Marcus Smart .60 1.50
82 Johnny Davis .40 1.00
83 Andrew Nembhard .50 1.25
84 Kyle Kuzma .60 1.50
85 Vince Carter 1.00 2.50
86 Bruce Brown .50 1.25
87 Karl Malone 1.00 2.50
88 Kyle Lowry .60 1.50
89 Myles Turner .60 1.50
90 Kelly Oubre Jr. .50 1.25
91 Terry Rozier III .60 1.50
92 Damian Lillard 1.25 3.00
93 Anthony Davis 1.25 3.00
94 Markelle Fultz .40 1.00
95 Harrison Barnes .40 1.00
96 Kevin Garnett 1.25 3.00
97 Hakeem Olajuwon 1.00 2.50
98 Jalen Brunson 1.00 2.50
99 Josh Green .40 1.00
100 Darius Garland .75 2.00
101 Pau Gasol .75 2.00
102 Russell Westbrook .75 2.00
103 Domantas Sabonis .75 2.00
104 Jimmy Butler .75 2.00
105 Caris LeVert .50 1.25
106 Alex Caruso .50 1.25
107 Tari Eason .60 1.50
108 Robert Williams III .50 1.25
109 Bobby Portis .60 1.50
110 D'Angelo Russell .50 1.25
111 Brook Lopez .40 1.00
112 Jalen Duren .60 1.50
113 Keegan Murray .60 1.50
114 DeMar DeRozan .75 2.00
115 Cameron Johnson .50 1.25
116 Andrew Wiggins .60 1.50
117 Steve Nash 1.00 2.50
118 Tyrese Haliburton 1.00 2.50
119 Ja Morant 1.50 4.00
120 Paolo Banchero 1.25 3.00
121 Anfernee Simons .60 1.50
122 Clint Capela .40 1.00
123 Kevin Durant 1.50 4.00
124 Grayson Allen .50 1.25
125 Jordan Clarkson .50 1.25
126 Pascal Siakam .75 2.00
127 Gabe Vincent .50 1.25
128 Coby White .50 1.25
129 Jalen Suggs .60 1.50
130 Cole Anthony .50 1.25
131 Ayo Dosunmu .50 1.25
132 Stephen Curry 4.00 10.00
133 Zion Williamson 1.25 3.00
134 Malik Monk .60 1.50
135 Fred VanVleet .75 2.00
136 Brandon Ingram .60 1.50
137 Paul Pierce .75 2.00
138 Gilbert Arenas .50 1.25
139 Mark Williams .50 1.25
140 Aaron Gordon .50 1.25
141 Dorian Finney-Smith .40 1.00
142 Kawhi Leonard 1.25 3.00
143 Moses Moody .60 1.50
144 Quentin Grimes .50 1.25
145 Devin Booker 1.25 3.00
146 Naz Reid .50 1.25
147 Gordon Hayward .50 1.25
148 Yao Ming 1.25 3.00
149 Austin Reaves 1.25 3.00
150 OG Anunoby .60 1.50
151 Dillon Brooks .50 1.25
152 MarJon Beauchamp .40 1.00
153 LeBron James 4.00 10.00
154 Lonnie Walker IV .50 1.25
155 Jaden McDaniels .50 1.25
156 Jalen Green .75 2.00
157 De'Andre Hunter .50 1.25
158 De'Aaron Fox 1.00 2.50
159 AJ Griffin .40 1.00
160 Bam Adebayo .75 2.00
161 Jaylen Brown 1.00 2.50
162 Shai Gilgeous-Alexander 2.50 6.00
163 Joel Embiid 1.25 3.00
164 Jayson Tatum 2.00 5.00
165 Keldon Johnson .60 1.50
166 Trae Young 1.00 2.50
167 Kristaps Porzingis .60 1.50
168 Franz Wagner .75 2.00
169 Carmelo Anthony .75 2.00
170 Luka Doncic 3.00 8.00
171 Kyrie Irving 1.00 2.50
172 Matisse Thybulle .40 1.00
173 Kareem Abdul-Jabbar 1.50 4.00
174 Draymond Green .60 1.50
175 Onyeka Okongwu .40 1.00
176 Saddiq Bey .50 1.25
177 Rui Hachimura .50 1.25
178 Terance Mann .40 1.00
179 Julius Erving 1.25 3.00
180 Ousmane Dieng .50 1.25
181 Evan Fournier .40 1.00
182 Spencer Dinwiddie .40 1.00
183 Evan Mobley .75 2.00
184 Charles Barkley 1.25 3.00
185 Cameron Thomas .60 1.50
186 Ivica Zubac .50 1.25
187 Scottie Barnes .60 1.50
188 Bennedict Mathurin .75 2.00
189 Reggie Jackson .30 .75
190 Norman Powell .50 1.25
191 Nikola Jokic 2.50 6.00
192 Donte DiVincenzo .50 1.25
193 Kenyon Martin Jr. .50 1.25
194 Zach LaVine .75 2.00
195 Deni Avdija .50 1.25
196 Christian Braun .50 1.25
197 Dejounte Murray .60 1.50
198 Cade Cunningham 1.25 3.00
199 Gary Trent Jr. .50 1.25
200 Mikal Bridges .60 1.50
201 Noah Clowney RC 1.25 3.00
202 Gradey Dick RC 2.00 5.00
203 GG Jackson II RC 2.00 5.00
204 Jett Howard RC 1.25 3.00
205 Jordan Walsh RC 1.00 2.50
206 Marcus Sasser RC 1.50 4.00
207 Olivier-Maxence Prosper RC 1.00 2.50
208 Brandin Podziemski RC 3.00 8.00
209 Amari Bailey RC 1.00 2.50
210 Colby Jones RC 1.00 2.50
211 Tristan Vukcevic RC 1.00 2.50
212 Jarace Walker RC 2.00 5.00
213 Keyontae Johnson RC 1.00 2.50
214 Maxwell Lewis RC .75 2.00
215 Jalen Wilson RC 1.00 2.50
216 Taylor Hendricks RC 1.00 2.50
217 Bilal Coulibaly RC 2.50 6.00
218 Ausar Thompson RC 2.50 6.00
219 Cason Wallace RC 2.00 5.00
220 Julian Strawther RC 1.25 3.00
221 Keyonte George RC 3.00 8.00
222 Jalen Hood-Schifino RC 1.00 2.50
223 Emoni Bates RC 1.25 3.00
224 Kobe Brown RC 1.00 2.50
225 Ben Sheppard RC 1.00 2.50
226 Cam Whitmore RC 2.50 6.00
227 Mouhamed Gueye RC 1.00 2.50
228 Nick Smith Jr. RC 1.25 3.00
229 Dereck Lively II RC 2.00 5.00
230 Jordan Hawkins RC 1.50 4.00
231 Victor Wembanyama RC 8.00 20.00
232 Julian Phillips RC 1.00 2.50
233 Scoot Henderson RC 3.00 8.00
234 Brice Sensabaugh RC 1.50 4.00
235 Leonard Miller RC 1.00 2.50
236 Hunter Tyson RC 1.00 2.50
237 Jaime Jaquez Jr. RC 1.50 4.00

238 Chris Livingston RC 1.00 2.50
239 Rayan Rupert RC 1.00 2.50
240 Anthony Black RC 2.00 5.00
241 Isaiah Wong RC 1.00 2.50
242 Dariq Whitehead RC 1.25 3.00
243 James Nnaji RC .75 2.00
244 Brandon Miller RC 4.00 10.00
245 Jalen Pickett RC .75 2.00
246 Amen Thompson RC 5.00 12.00
247 Trayce Jackson-Davis RC 1.25 3.00
248 Kris Murray RC 1.00 2.50
249 Kobe Bufkin RC 1.25 3.00
250 Andre Jackson Jr. RC 1.50 4.00

2023-24 Elite Mixorama

*MIXORAMA: 5X TO 12X BASIC
132 Stephen Curry 100.00 250.00
153 LeBron James 100.00 250.00
231 Victor Wembanyama 1,000.00 2,000.00
244 Brandon Miller 125.00 300.00

2023-24 Elite Neon Green

*NEON GREEN: 2X TO 5X BASIC
STATED PRINT RUN 75 COPIES PER
153 LeBron James 40.00 100.00
231 Victor Wembanyama 400.00 800.00
244 Brandon Miller 30.00 80.00

2023-24 Elite Purple

*PURPLE: 2.5X TO 6X BASIC
STATED PRINT RUN 49 COPIES PER
153 LeBron James 50.00 120.00
231 Victor Wembanyama 500.00 1,000.00
244 Brandon Miller 40.00 100.00

2023-24 Elite Clarity

*INTERNATIONAL RED: .75X TO 2X BASIC
1 LeBron James 8.00 20.00
2 Jayson Tatum 4.00 10.00
3 Ja Morant 3.00 8.00
4 Stephen Curry 8.00 20.00
5 Nikola Jokic 5.00 12.00
6 Kevin Durant 3.00 8.00
7 Damian Lillard 2.50 6.00
8 Luka Doncic 6.00 15.00
9 Giannis Antetokounmpo 5.00 12.00
10 Trae Young 2.00 5.00
11 Kobe Bufkin 1.25 3.00
12 Cason Wallace 2.00 5.00
13 Bilal Coulibaly 2.50 6.00
14 Keyonte George 3.00 8.00
15 Ausar Thompson 2.50 6.00
16 Jaime Jaquez Jr. 1.50 4.00
17 Jalen Hood-Schifino 1.00 2.50
18 Anthony Black 2.00 5.00
19 Brandon Miller 4.00 10.00
20 Victor Wembanyama 30.00 80.00
21 Scoot Henderson 3.00 8.00
22 Brandin Podziemski 3.00 8.00
23 Taylor Hendricks 1.00 2.50
24 Nick Smith Jr. 1.25 3.00
25 Gradey Dick 2.00 5.00
26 Jordan Hawkins 1.50 4.00
27 Jett Howard 1.25 3.00
28 Cam Whitmore 2.50 6.00
29 Jarace Walker 2.00 5.00
30 Amen Thompson 5.00 12.00

2023-24 Elite Clear Path

*INTERNATIONAL RED: .75X TO 2X BASIC
1 Amen Thompson 5.00 12.00
2 Ausar Thompson 2.50 6.00
3 Keyonte George 3.00 8.00
4 Victor Wembanyama 30.00 80.00
5 Scoot Henderson 3.00 8.00
6 Brandon Miller 4.00 10.00
7 Bilal Coulibaly 2.50 6.00
8 Cason Wallace 2.00 5.00
9 Anthony Black 2.00 5.00
10 Jarace Walker 2.00 5.00
11 LeBron James 8.00 20.00
12 Ja Morant 3.00 8.00
13 Luka Doncic 6.00 15.00
14 Stephen Curry 8.00 20.00
15 Giannis Antetokounmpo 5.00 12.00
16 Jayson Tatum 4.00 10.00
17 Kevin Durant 3.00 8.00
18 Donovan Mitchell 2.00 5.00
19 Nikola Jokic 5.00 12.00
20 Trae Young 2.00 5.00

2023-24 Elite Deck

*INTERNATIONAL RED: .5X TO 1.2X BASIC
1 Stephen Curry 8.00 20.00
2 Kevin Durant 3.00 8.00
3 LeBron James 8.00 20.00
4 Kyrie Irving 2.00 5.00
5 Jayson Tatum 4.00 10.00
6 LaMelo Ball 2.50 6.00
7 Anthony Edwards 5.00 12.00
8 Tyrese Haliburton 2.00 5.00
9 Giannis Antetokounmpo 5.00 12.00
10 Nikola Jokic 5.00 12.00
11 Damian Lillard 2.50 6.00
12 Kawhi Leonard 2.50 6.00
13 Trae Young 2.00 5.00
14 James Harden 2.00 5.00
15 Devin Booker 2.50 6.00
16 Bradley Beal 1.25 3.00
17 Anthony Davis 2.50 6.00
18 Joel Embiid 2.50 6.00
19 Jimmy Butler 1.50 4.00
20 Ja Morant 3.00 8.00
21 Donovan Mitchell 2.00 5.00
22 Shai Gilgeous-Alexander 5.00 12.00
23 Cade Cunningham 2.50 6.00
24 Zach LaVine 1.50 4.00
25 DeMar DeRozan 1.50 4.00
26 De'Aaron Fox 2.00 5.00
27 Lauri Markkanen 1.50 4.00
28 Jalen Brunson 2.00 5.00
29 Paul George 1.50 4.00
30 Jamal Murray 2.00 5.00

2023-24 Elite Dimensions

1 Ja Morant 60.00 150.00
2 Luka Doncic 60.00 150.00
3 LeBron James 125.00 300.00
4 Jayson Tatum 60.00 150.00
5 Giannis Antetokounmpo 60.00 150.00
6 Kevin Durant 40.00 100.00
7 Nikola Jokic 60.00 150.00
8 Trae Young 30.00 80.00
9 Stephen Curry 125.00 300.00
10 Anthony Edwards 60.00 150.00
11 Kyrie Irving 40.00 100.00
12 Shai Gilgeous-Alexander 60.00 150.00
13 Donovan Mitchell 30.00 80.00
14 De'Aaron Fox 40.00 100.00
15 Joel Embiid 40.00 100.00

2023-24 Elite Elite Series

*INTERNATIONAL RED & GRN: .75X TO 2X BASIC
*ORANGE DIE CUT: .75X TO 2X BASIC
*BLUE/99: 1.25X TO 3X BASIC
*NEON GREEN/75: 1.5X TO 4X BASIC
*PURPLE/49: 2X TO 5X BASIC
1 LeBron James 5.00 12.00
2 Luka Doncic 4.00 10.00
3 Kevin Durant 2.00 5.00
4 Stephen Curry 5.00 12.00
5 Trae Young 1.25 3.00
6 Giannis Antetokounmpo 3.00 8.00
7 Ja Morant 2.00 5.00
8 Nikola Jokic 3.00 8.00
9 Joel Embiid 1.50 4.00
10 Damian Lillard 1.50 4.00
11 Donovan Mitchell 1.25 3.00
12 Tyrese Haliburton 1.25 3.00
13 Shai Gilgeous-Alexander 3.00 8.00
14 Anthony Edwards 3.00 8.00
15 LaMelo Ball 1.50 4.00
16 Jayson Tatum 2.50 6.00
17 Devin Booker 1.50 4.00
18 Jimmy Butler 1.00 2.50
19 De'Aaron Fox 1.25 3.00
20 Kyrie Irving 1.25 3.00

2023-24 Elite Elite Signatures

RED/49: .5X TO 1.2X BASIC
BLUE/15-25: .6X TO 1.5X BASIC
1 Bojan Bogdanovic 6.00 15.00
3 Bob Dandridge 6.00 15.00
4 Richard Hamilton 8.00 20.00
5 Karl-Anthony Towns 10.00 25.00
6 CJ McCollum 6.00 15.00
7 De'Aaron Fox 30.00 80.00
8 Shaedon Sharpe 12.00 30.00
9 Austin Reaves 20.00 50.00
11 Peja Stojakovic 6.00 15.00
12 Obi Toppin 6.00 15.00
13 Tyrese Haliburton 60.00 150.00
14 Max Strus 6.00 15.00
15 Marcus Smart 8.00 20.00
16 Clyde Drexler 20.00 50.00
17 Kareem Abdul-Jabbar 40.00 100.00
18 Jason Williams 25.00 60.00
19 Hakeem Olajuwon 25.00 60.00
20 Alperen Sengun 20.00 50.00
21 Metta World Peace 6.00 15.00
22 Steve Kerr 12.00 30.00
23 Immanuel Quickley 6.00 15.00
24 Alex English 8.00 20.00
25 RJ Barrett 10.00 25.00

2023-24 Elite Glass Masters

*INTERNATIONAL RED: .75X TO 2X BASIC
1 Nikola Jokic 4.00 10.00
2 Joel Embiid 2.00 5.00
3 Giannis Antetokounmpo 4.00 10.00
4 Domantas Sabonis 1.25 3.00
5 Bam Adebayo 1.25 3.00
6 Anthony Davis 2.00 5.00
7 Rudy Gobert 1.00 2.50
8 Victor Wembanyama 25.00 60.00
9 Jarace Walker 1.50 4.00
10 Dereck Lively II 1.50 4.00

2023-24 Elite Impact Impressions

*INTRNTL RED & GRN: .5X TO 1.2X BASIC
RED/25-49: .6X TO 1.5X BASIC
BLUE/25: .6X TO 1.5X BASIC
1 Keegan Murray 6.00 15.00
2 Max Christie 5.00 12.00
3 Kevin Huerter 4.00 10.00
4 Max Strus 5.00 12.00
5 Jabari Smith Jr. 8.00 20.00
6 Shaedon Sharpe 10.00 25.00
8 Bennedict Mathurin 8.00 20.00
10 Alperen Sengun 12.00 30.00
11 Ayo Dosunmu 5.00 12.00
12 Bobby Portis 6.00 15.00
13 Isaiah Stewart 5.00 12.00
14 Boban Marjanovic 5.00 12.00
15 Landry Shamet 3.00 8.00
16 Jose Alvarado 5.00 12.00
17 Jalen McDaniels 4.00 10.00
18 Walker Kessler 5.00 12.00
19 Jalen Williams 20.00 50.00
20 Nicolas Batum 3.00 8.00
21 Evan Fournier 4.00 10.00
22 Bruce Brown 5.00 12.00
23 Torrey Craig 4.00 10.00
24 Jaden Hardy 6.00 15.00
25 Jordan Clarkson 5.00 12.00
27 MarJon Beauchamp 4.00 10.00
28 Patty Mills 5.00 12.00
30 Dorian Finney-Smith 4.00 10.00
31 Jalen Green 20.00 50.00
32 Kevon Looney 5.00 12.00
34 Drew Eubanks 3.00 8.00
35 Will Barton 4.00 10.00
36 Jaylin Williams 5.00 12.00
37 John Wall 6.00 15.00
38 Antoine Carr 4.00 10.00
39 Brian Scalabrine 4.00 10.00
40 Isaiah Rider 5.00 12.00
41 Fat Lever 5.00 12.00
42 Eddy Curry 3.00 8.00
43 Xavier McDaniel 5.00 12.00
44 Bob McAdoo 6.00 15.00
45 Lenny Wilkens 6.00 15.00
46 Calvin Murphy 5.00 12.00
47 Tony Allen 3.00 8.00
48 Artis Gilmore 6.00 15.00
49 Ricky Davis 4.00 10.00
50 Vin Baker 4.00 10.00
51 Lauri Markkanen 8.00 20.00
52 Kenny "Sky" Walker 4.00 10.00
53 Dale Ellis 5.00 12.00
54 Carlos Boozer 4.00 10.00
55 George McGinnis 5.00 12.00
56 Mark Aguirre 4.00 10.00
57 Kevin Willis 4.00 10.00
58 Juwan Howard 5.00 12.00
59 Gary Harris 4.00 10.00
60 Gilbert Arenas 5.00 12.00

2023-24 Elite New Breed Autographs

*INTRNTL RED & GRN: .5X TO 1.2X BASIC
RED/49: .6X TO 1.5X BASIC
BLUE/25: .6X TO 1.5X BASIC
1 Marcus Sasser 8.00 20.00
2 Trayce Jackson-Davis 20.00 50.00
3 Chris Livingston 5.00 12.00
4 Colby Jones 5.00 12.00
5 Tari Eason 6.00 15.00
6 Oscar Tshiebwe 6.00 15.00
7 Jordan Walsh 5.00 12.00
8 Jaylen Clark 5.00 12.00
9 Jake LaRavia 4.00 10.00
10 Walker Kessler 5.00 12.00
11 Julian Phillips 5.00 12.00
12 Noah Clowney 6.00 15.00
13 Bilal Coulibaly 15.00 40.00
14 Rayan Rupert 5.00 12.00
15 Jeremy Sochan 6.00 15.00
16 Brandin Podziemski 25.00 60.00
17 Maxwell Lewis 4.00 10.00
18 Julian Strawther 6.00 15.00
19 Mouhamed Gueye 5.00 12.00
20 Leonard Miller 5.00 12.00
21 Jalen Wilson 5.00 12.00
22 GG Jackson II 25.00 60.00
23 Toumani Camara 10.00 25.00
24 Andre Jackson Jr. 8.00 20.00
25 Ausar Thompson 12.00 30.00
26 Brice Sensabaugh 8.00 20.00
27 Dereck Lively II 10.00 25.00
28 Tristan Vukcevic 5.00 12.00
30 Kobe Bufkin 6.00 15.00
31 Jalen Slawson 5.00 12.00
32 Olivier-Maxence Prosper 5.00 12.00
33 Isaiah Wong 5.00 12.00
34 Christian Braun 5.00 12.00
35 Jalen Pickett 4.00 10.00
36 Keyontae Johnson 5.00 12.00
37 Ben Sheppard 5.00 12.00
38 Hunter Tyson 5.00 12.00
39 Amen Thompson 25.00 60.00
40 Cason Wallace 10.00 25.00
41 Bryce McGowens 5.00 12.00
42 Dariq Whitehead 6.00 15.00
43 Dalen Terry 5.00 12.00
44 Nikola Jovic 5.00 12.00
45 Keyonte George 15.00 40.00
46 Kobe Brown 5.00 12.00
47 Kris Murray 5.00 12.00
49 Sidy Cissoko 5.00 12.00
50 James Nnaji 4.00 10.00

2023-24 Elite Next Up

1 Amen Thompson 60.00 140.00
2 Ausar Thompson 40.00 100.00
3 Victor Wembanyama 350.00 700.00
4 Scoot Henderson 60.00 150.00
5 Brandon Miller 100.00 250.00
6 Bilal Coulibaly 50.00 120.00
7 Taylor Hendricks 30.00 80.00
8 Cason Wallace 40.00 100.00
9 Keyonte George 60.00 150.00
10 Anthony Black 50.00 120.00

2023-24 Elite Passing the Torch Signatures

1 Amen Thompson
Dwyane Wade 150.00 400.00
2 Ausar Thompson
Dennis Rodman 150.00 400.00
4 Cason Wallace
Shai Gilgeous-Alexander 400.00 800.00
5 Jaren Jackson Jr.
Zach Randolph 125.00 300.00
6 Allen Iverson
Stephen Curry 1,500.00 3,000.00
7 Dirk Nowitzki
Luka Doncic 800.00 1,500.00
8 Nikola Jokic
Shaquille O'Neal 500.00 1,000.00
9 Carmelo Anthony
Nikola Jokic 350.00 700.00
10 Carmelo Anthony
Paul George 200.00 500.00

2023-24 Elite Pen Pals

RED/49: .5X TO 1.25X BASIC
1 Amen Thompson 30.00 80.00
2 Ausar Thompson 15.00 40.00
3 Bilal Coulibaly 20.00 50.00
4 Cason Wallace 12.00 30.00
5 Dereck Lively II 12.00 30.00
6 Kobe Bufkin 8.00 20.00
7 Keyonte George 30.00 80.00
8 Brandin Podziemski 30.00 80.00
9 Noah Clowney 8.00 20.00
10 Dariq Whitehead 8.00 20.00
11 Kris Murray 6.00 15.00
12 Olivier-Maxence Prosper 6.00 15.00
13 Marcus Sasser 10.00 25.00
14 Ben Sheppard 6.00 15.00
15 Brice Sensabaugh 10.00 25.00
16 Julian Strawther 8.00 20.00
17 Kobe Brown 6.00 15.00
18 James Nnaji 5.00 12.00
19 Jalen Pickett 5.00 12.00
20 Leonard Miller 6.00 15.00
21 Colby Jones 6.00 15.00
22 Julian Phillips 6.00 15.00
23 Andre Jackson Jr. 10.00 25.00
24 Hunter Tyson 6.00 15.00
25 Jordan Walsh 6.00 15.00
26 Maxwell Lewis 5.00 12.00
28 Rayan Rupert 6.00 15.00
29 GG Jackson II 30.00 80.00
30 Keyontae Johnson 6.00 15.00
31 Jalen Wilson 6.00 15.00
32 Toumani Camara 12.00 30.00
33 Isaiah Wong 6.00 15.00
34 Mouhamed Gueye 6.00 15.00
35 Chris Livingston 6.00 15.00
36 Mike Miles Jr. 5.00 12.00
37 Jalen Slawson 6.00 15.00
38 Sidy Cissoko 6.00 15.00
39 Jaylen Clark 6.00 15.00
40 Trayce Jackson-Davis 25.00 60.00

2023-24 Elite Rookie Yearbook Autographs

*INTRNTL RED & GRN: .5X TO 1.2X BASIC
RED/49: .6X TO 1.5X BASIC
BLUE/25: .75X TO 2X BASIC
1 Mouhamed Gueye 5.00 12.00
2 Rayan Rupert 5.00 12.00
3 Trayce Jackson-Davis 20.00 50.00
4 Julian Strawther 6.00 15.00
5 Jordan Miller 6.00 15.00
6 Jalen Slawson 5.00 12.00
7 Isaiah Wong 5.00 12.00
8 Ben Sheppard 5.00 12.00
9 Tristan Vukcevic 5.00 12.00
10 Keyontae Johnson 5.00 12.00
11 Jalen Wilson 5.00 12.00
12 Jalen Pickett 4.00 10.00
13 Jaylen Clark 5.00 12.00
14 Olivier-Maxence Prosper 5.00 12.00
15 Cason Wallace 10.00 25.00
16 Sidy Cissoko 5.00 12.00
17 Dariq Whitehead 6.00 15.00
18 Amen Thompson 25.00 60.00
19 Marcus Sasser 8.00 20.00
20 Toumani Camara 10.00 25.00
21 Kris Murray 5.00 12.00
22 Brandin Podziemski 25.00 60.00
23 Colby Jones 5.00 12.00
24 Keyonte George 15.00 40.00
25 Andre Jackson Jr. 8.00 20.00
26 Leonard Miller 5.00 12.00
27 Hunter Tyson 5.00 12.00
28 Kobe Brown 5.00 12.00
29 Noah Clowney 6.00 15.00
30 Maxwell Lewis 4.00 10.00
31 Jordan Walsh 5.00 12.00
32 Dereck Lively II 10.00 25.00
33 GG Jackson II 25.00 60.00
34 Kobe Bufkin 6.00 15.00
35 Ausar Thompson 12.00 30.00
36 Bilal Coulibaly 15.00 40.00
37 Julian Phillips 5.00 12.00
38 Brice Sensabaugh 8.00 20.00
39 James Nnaji 4.00 10.00
40 Seth Lundy 4.00 10.00

2023-24 Elite Spellbound

*INTERNATIONAL RED & GRN: .75X TO 2X BASIC
*ORNG DIE CUT: .75X TO 2X BASIC
1 Victor Wembanyama 10.00 25.00
2 Victor Wembanyama 10.00 25.00
3 Victor Wembanyama 10.00 25.00
4 Victor Wembanyama 10.00 25.00
5 Victor Wembanyama 10.00 25.00
6 Victor Wembanyama 10.00 25.00
7 Victor Wembanyama 10.00 25.00
8 Victor Wembanyama 10.00 25.00
9 Victor Wembanyama 10.00 25.00
10 Victor Wembanyama 10.00 25.00
11 Scoot Henderson 2.00 5.00
12 Scoot Henderson 2.00 5.00
13 Scoot Henderson 2.00 5.00
14 Scoot Henderson 2.00 5.00
15 Scoot Henderson 2.00 5.00
16 Amen Thompson 3.00 8.00
17 Amen Thompson 3.00 8.00
18 Amen Thompson 3.00 8.00
19 Amen Thompson 3.00 8.00
20 Ausar Thompson 1.50 4.00
21 Ausar Thompson 1.50 4.00
22 Ausar Thompson 1.50 4.00
23 Ausar Thompson 1.50 4.00
24 Ausar Thompson 1.50 4.00
25 Luka Doncic 4.00 10.00
26 Luka Doncic 4.00 10.00
27 Luka Doncic 4.00 10.00
28 Luka Doncic 4.00 10.00
29 Luka Doncic 4.00 10.00
30 Luka Doncic 4.00 10.00
31 Stephen Curry 5.00 12.00
32 Stephen Curry 5.00 12.00
33 Stephen Curry 5.00 12.00
34 Stephen Curry 5.00 12.00
35 Stephen Curry 5.00 12.00
36 LeBron James 5.00 12.00
37 LeBron James 5.00 12.00
38 LeBron James 5.00 12.00
39 LeBron James 5.00 12.00
40 LeBron James 5.00 12.00

2023-24 Elite Turn of the Century Signatures

*INTRNTL RED & GRN: .5X TO 1.2X BASIC
RED/25-49: .6X TO 1.5X BASIC
BLUE/15-25: .6X TO 1.5X BASIC
1 Ousmane Dieng 5.00 12.00
2 Mark Williams 5.00 12.00
3 Malaki Branham 4.00 10.00
4 Isaac Okoro 4.00 10.00
5 Isaiah Mobley 3.00 8.00
6 Ivica Zubac 5.00 12.00
7 Tim Hardaway Jr. 4.00 10.00
8 Doug McDermott 4.00 10.00
9 Mo Bamba 4.00 10.00
10 Mason Plumlee 4.00 10.00
11 Herbert Jones 5.00 12.00
12 Larry Nance Jr. 3.00 8.00
13 Georges Niang 3.00 8.00
14 Isaiah Roby 3.00 8.00
15 Daniel Gafford 5.00 12.00
17 TyTy Washington Jr. 4.00 10.00
18 Blake Wesley 3.00 8.00
19 Goran Dragic 4.00 10.00
20 Michael Porter Jr. 6.00 15.00
21 Dyson Daniels 6.00 15.00
23 Thomas Bryant 4.00 10.00
24 Monte Morris 5.00 12.00
25 Juan Toscano-Anderson 4.00 10.00
26 Ty Jerome 3.00 8.00
27 Chuma Okeke 4.00 10.00
28 Jason Terry 5.00 12.00
29 Mike Miller 4.00 10.00
30 Harold Miner 5.00 12.00
31 Charlie Ward 4.00 10.00
32 Terry Cummings 5.00 12.00
33 Glen Rice 5.00 12.00
34 Walter McCarty 4.00 10.00
35 Patrick Ewing 50.00 120.00
36 Kiki Vandeweghe 4.00 10.00
37 Nick Anderson 5.00 12.00
38 Theo Ratliff 4.00 10.00
39 Tree Rollins 4.00 10.00
40 Jerome Williams 3.00 8.00
41 Craig Hodges 4.00 10.00
42 Derek Harper 4.00 10.00
43 Malik Rose 4.00 10.00
44 Herb Williams 3.00 8.00
45 Greg Anthony 4.00 10.00
46 Jeff Hornacek 4.00 10.00
47 Dino Radja 4.00 10.00
48 Rasheed Wallace 12.00 30.00
49 Fred Brown 4.00 10.00
50 James Donaldson 4.00 10.00

2010-11 Elite Black Box

STATED PRINT RUN 99 SER.#'d SETS
1 LeBron James 15.00 40.00
2 Dirk Nowitzki 5.00 12.00
3 Kevin Durant 8.00 20.00
4 Kobe Bryant 15.00 40.00
5 Carmelo Anthony 3.00 8.00
6 LaMarcus Aldridge 2.00 5.00
7 Al Horford 2.00 5.00
8 Kevin Garnett 5.00 12.00
9 Chris Paul 4.00 10.00
10 Dwight Howard 2.50 6.00
11 Dwyane Wade 4.00 10.00
12 Blake Griffin 2.00 5.00
13 Andrea Bargnani 1.25 3.00
14 Kevin Love 2.00 5.00
15 Zach Randolph 2.00 5.00
16 Ray Allen 3.00 8.00
17 Derrick Rose 4.00 10.00
18 Monta Ellis 1.50 4.00
19 Danny Granger 1.50 4.00
20 Ty Lawson 1.25 3.00
21 Tony Parker 3.00 8.00
22 Brook Lopez 1.50 4.00
23 Eric Gordon 1.50 4.00
24 Russell Westbrook 3.00 8.00
25 Tyson Chandler 1.50 4.00
26 Vince Carter 4.00 10.00
27 Amare Stoudemire 2.00 5.00
28 Kevin Martin 1.50 4.00
29 Joe Johnson 2.00 5.00
30 Stephen Jackson 1.50 4.00
31 JaVale McGee 1.50 4.00
32 Chauncey Billups 2.50 6.00
33 Paul Pierce 3.00 8.00
34 Darren Collison 1.25 3.00
35 Serge Ibaka 1.50 4.00
36 J.J. Barea 1.50 4.00
37 Chris Bosh 2.50 6.00
38 Al Jefferson 1.25 3.00
39 Rudy Gay 2.00 5.00
40 Deron Williams 2.50 6.00
41 David West 1.50 4.00
42 Luis Scola 1.50 4.00
43 Antawn Jamison 1.50 4.00
44 Brandon Jennings 1.25 3.00
45 Stephen Curry 15.00 40.00
46 Steve Nash 4.00 10.00
47 Chris Kaman 1.25 3.00
48 Andre Iguodala 2.00 5.00
49 Joakim Noah 2.00 5.00
50 Brandon Roy 2.50 6.00
51 Andrei Kirilenko 1.50 4.00
52 Jameer Nelson 1.25 3.00
53 Jrue Holiday 2.50 6.00
54 Ben Gordon 1.50 4.00
55 Marc Gasol 2.00 5.00
56 Gerald Wallace 1.50 4.00
57 Rajon Rondo 2.50 6.00
58 Tim Duncan 5.00 12.00
59 Pau Gasol 3.00 8.00
60 Michael Beasley 1.25 3.00
61 Tyreke Evans 1.50 4.00
62 David Lee 1.25 3.00
63 DeMar DeRozan 3.00 8.00
64 Wesley Matthews 1.25 3.00
65 Josh Smith 1.25 3.00
66 Juwan Howard 1.50 4.00
67 Nene 1.50 4.00
68 James Harden 5.00 12.00
69 Devin Harris 1.25 3.00
70 Elton Brand 1.50 4.00
71 Emeka Okafor 1.50 4.00
72 Jason Terry 1.50 4.00
73 Luol Deng 1.50 4.00
74 Nick Young 1.25 3.00
75 Danilo Gallinari 1.50 4.00
76 Carlos Boozer 1.50 4.00
77 Andrew Bogut 1.50 4.00
78 Raymond Felton 1.25 3.00
79 Baron Davis 2.00 5.00
80 Manu Ginobili 4.00 10.00
81 Jamal Crawford 2.00 5.00
82 Ben Wallace 2.50 6.00
83 Jason Kidd 3.00 8.00
84 Trevor Ariza 1.25 3.00
85 Kendrick Perkins 1.25 3.00
86 Andrew Bynum 1.25 3.00
87 Aaron Brooks 1.25 3.00
88 Roy Hibbert 1.50 4.00
89 Nick Collison 1.25 3.00
90 J.J. Redick 2.00 5.00
91 J.R. Smith 2.00 5.00
92 Kris Humphries 1.25 3.00
93 Jonny Flynn 1.25 3.00
94 Brandon Bass 1.25 3.00
95 Taj Gibson 1.25 3.00
96 Gerald Henderson 1.25 3.00
97 Glen Davis 1.25 3.00
98 DeJuan Blair 1.25 3.00
99 Tracy McGrady 3.00 8.00
100 Samuel Dalembert 1.25 3.00
101 Wilt Chamberlain 5.00 12.00
102 Karl Malone 4.00 10.00
103 Julius Erving 4.00 10.00
104 Jalen Rose 1.50 4.00
105 Alex English 1.50 4.00
106 Alonzo Mourning 3.00 8.00
107 David Robinson 4.00 10.00
108 Kevin Johnson 2.00 5.00
109 Kevin McHale 3.00 8.00
110 Shaquille O'Neal 8.00 20.00
111 Wes Unseld 2.50 6.00
112 Walt Frazier 3.00 8.00
113 George Gervin 3.00 8.00
114 Gary Payton 3.00 8.00
115 Elgin Baylor 4.00 10.00
116 Bob McAdoo 2.50 6.00
117 Dominique Wilkins 3.00 8.00
118 George Mikan 6.00 15.00
119 Lenny Wilkens 2.00 5.00
120 Jerry West 4.00 10.00
121 Hakeem Olajuwon 4.00 10.00
122 Kenny Smith 1.50 4.00
123 Clyde Drexler 3.00 8.00
124 Nate Thurmond 2.50 6.00
125 John Havlicek 4.00 10.00
126 Darryl Dawkins 2.00 5.00
127 Darrell Griffith 1.25 3.00
128 Danny Manning 1.50 4.00
129 Dan Issel 2.50 6.00
130 Larry Bird 8.00 20.00
131 Sam Perkins 1.25 3.00
132 Bill Laimbeer 1.50 4.00
133 Shawn Bradley 1.25 3.00
134 James Worthy 2.50 6.00
135 Cedric Maxwell 2.00 5.00
136 Bailey Howell 2.00 5.00
137 Magic Johnson 8.00 20.00
138 Kelly Tripucka 1.25 3.00
139 Dikembe Mutombo 3.00 8.00
140 Christian Laettner 2.00 5.00
141 Bob Lanier 3.00 8.00
142 Mark Eaton 2.00 5.00
143 Toni Kukoc 2.00 5.00
144 Earl Monroe 2.00 5.00
145 Glen Rice 2.00 5.00
146 Larry Johnson 2.50 6.00
147 Kiki Vandeweghe 1.50 4.00
148 Chris Webber 2.50 6.00
149 Ron Harper 2.00 5.00
150 Kareem Abdul-Jabbar 6.00 15.00
151 Sam Jones 2.50 6.00
152 Spencer Haywood 2.00 5.00
153 Dennis Scott 1.25 3.00
154 Elvin Hayes 2.50 6.00
155 Robert Horry 2.00 5.00
156 Manute Bol 2.00 5.00
157 Kevin Willis 1.25 3.00
158 Chris Mullin 2.50 6.00
159 Isiah Thomas 3.00 8.00
160 Dave Cowens 3.00 8.00
161 Oscar Robertson 5.00 12.00
162 Rick Barry 2.50 6.00
163 Alvan Adams 1.25 3.00
164 Xavier McDaniel 1.50 4.00
165 Sleepy Floyd 1.25 3.00
166 Mark Aguirre 1.50 4.00
167 Mark Price 2.00 5.00
168 Bernard King 2.50 6.00
169 Joe Dumars 2.00 5.00
170 Reggie Lewis 2.00 5.00
171 Michael Cooper 2.00 5.00
172 Robert Parish 3.00 8.00
173 Danny Ainge 2.00 5.00
174 Maurice Cheeks 1.50 4.00
175 Sidney Moncrief 1.25 3.00
176 Artis Gilmore 2.50 6.00
177 Jeff Hornacek 2.00 5.00
178 Dennis Rodman 8.00 20.00
179 Tom Chambers 2.00 5.00
180 Tim Hardaway 2.50 6.00
181 Mitch Richmond 2.50 6.00
182 Pete Maravich 5.00 12.00
183 Patrick Ewing 3.00 8.00
184 Walt Bellamy 2.50 6.00
185 Vlade Divac 2.00 5.00
186 Steve Smith 1.50 4.00
187 Rolando Blackman 1.50 4.00
188 M.L. Carr 2.00 5.00
189 Kurt Rambis 1.25 3.00
190 Kenny Walker 2.00 5.00
191 Jamal Mashburn 1.25 3.00
192 Connie Hawkins 2.50 6.00
193 Dan Majerle 1.50 4.00
194 Adrian Dantley 2.00 5.00
195 Al Attles 2.00 5.00
196 Ralph Sampson 1.50 4.00
197 Walter Berry 1.25 3.00
198 Bill Russell 6.00 15.00
199 Bill Walton 3.00 8.00
200 World B. Free 1.50 4.00

2010-11 Elite Black Box All-Star Matchups Materials Prime

STATED PRINT RUN 25 SER.#'d SETS
1 Bosh/Wade/KD/Wstbrk 125.00 250.00
2 Duncan/Yao/Howard/KG 40.00 100.00
3 Iverson/Carter/KG/Shaq 75.00 150.00
4 Malone/Kemp/Dmrs/Hard 100.00 200.00
5 English/Magic/Dr.J/Parish 40.00 100.00

2010-11 Elite Black Box All-Star Matchups Signatures

STATED PRINT RUN 5 TO 25 SER.#'d SETS
1 PP/Allen/Kobe/Gasol/25 1,000.00 2,000.00
3 VC/Hill/D.Rob/Payton/25 200.00 500.00
4 Mllr/Drxlr/Wilkins/Pytn/25 100.00 200.00
5 Frzr/Unsld/Barry/Hywd/25 50.00 120.00

2010-11 Elite Black Box All-Time Matchups Materials Prime

STATED PRINT RUN 10 TO 25 SER.#'d SETS
2 Erving/M.Johnson/25 40.00 100.00
3 K.Malone/Olajuwon/25 40.00 100.00
4 D.Robinson/Ewing/25 60.00 150.00
5 Abdul-Jabbar/Parish/25 35.00 70.00

2010-11 Elite Black Box All-Time Matchups Signatures

STATED PRINT RUN 10 TO 25 SER.#'d SETS
3 Abdul-Jabbar/Hayes/25 40.00 100.00
4 Drexler/Wilkins/25 40.00 100.00
5 Baylor/Thurmond/25 20.00 50.00

2010-11 Elite Black Box Award Winners Materials Prime

STATED PRINT RUN 15 TO 25 SER.#'d SETS
1 Rose/LJ/Kobe/Dirk/25 200.00 500.00
2 Bird/Moses/Dr.J/KAJ/15 75.00 150.00
3 KM/D.Rob/Olaj/Magic/25 75.00 150.00

2010-11 Elite Black Box Award Winners Signatures

STATED PRINT RUN 5 TO 25 SER.#'d SETS
3 Unsld/Mnr/Brry/Reed/25 100.00 250.00

2010-11 Elite Black Box Black and Blue Signatures

STATED PRINT RUN 10 TO 40 SER.#'d SETS
1 Kobe Bryant/37 1,500.00 3,000.00
2 Blake Griffin/25 100.00 200.00
5 Zach Randolph/39 10.00 25.00
6 Monta Ellis/39 10.00 25.00
7 Kevin Martin/49 10.00 25.00
8 LaMarcus Aldridge/39 12.00 30.00
9 Tyreke Evans/25 10.00 25.00
10 Stephen Curry/39 1,000.00 2,000.00
11 Kevin Love/40 20.00 50.00
12 Eric Gordon/39 10.00 25.00
13 Paul Pierce/25 EXCH 25.00 60.00
14 Joe Johnson/25 10.00 25.00
15 Andrea Bargnani/39 10.00 25.00
18 Oscar Robertson/25 30.00 80.00

2010-11 Elite Black Box Champions Materials Prime

STATED PRINT RUN ONE TO 25 SER.#'d SETS
1 Los Angeles Lakers/25 125.00 300.00
2 Boston Celtics/25 60.00 150.00
3 San Antonio Spurs/25 100.00 200.00
4 Chicago Bulls/25 200.00 350.00

2010-11 Elite Black Box Champions Signatures

STATED PRINT RUN 10 TO 25 SER.#'d SETS
4 Boston Celtics/25 200.00 500.00
5 Detroit Pistons/25 75.00 150.00

2010-11 Elite Black Box Crusade

STATED PRINT RUN 25 SER.#'d SETS
1 Derrick Rose 8.00 20.00
2 John Wall 12.00 30.00
3 Dwyane Wade 10.00 25.00
4 Chauncey Billups 5.00 12.00
5 Kevin Garnett 10.00 25.00
6 LeBron James 40.00 100.00
7 Carmelo Anthony 6.00 15.00
8 Deron Williams 3.00 8.00
9 Rajon Rondo 5.00 12.00
10 David Lee 2.50 6.00
11 Brook Lopez 3.00 8.00
12 Dwight Howard 5.00 12.00
13 Steve Nash 8.00 20.00
14 Jameer Nelson 2.50 6.00
15 Al Horford 4.00 10.00
16 Pau Gasol 6.00 15.00
17 Anderson Varejao 2.50 6.00
18 Marc Gasol 4.00 10.00
19 Beno Udrih 2.50 6.00
20 Ray Allen 6.00 15.00
21 Tim Duncan 8.00 20.00
22 Rudy Gay 4.00 10.00
23 Jason Richardson 4.00 10.00
24 Kobe Bryant 30.00 80.00
25 Al Jefferson 2.50 6.00
26 Chris Kaman 2.50 6.00
27 Danny Granger 2.50 6.00
28 Elton Brand 3.00 8.00
29 Emeka Okafor 3.00 8.00
30 Stephen Curry 30.00 80.00
31 Jason Terry 3.00 8.00
32 Blake Griffin 4.00 10.00
33 Grant Hill 10.00 25.00
34 Paul Pierce 6.00 15.00
35 Kevin Durant 15.00 40.00
36 Boris Diaw 3.00 8.00
37 Nene 3.00 8.00
38 David West 3.00 8.00
39 Paul Millsap 3.00 8.00
40 Andre Miller 3.00 8.00
41 Dirk Nowitzki 8.00 20.00
42 Kevin Love 4.00 10.00
43 Kris Humphries 2.50 6.00
44 Tayshaun Prince 4.00 10.00
45 J.J. Hickson 2.50 6.00
46 Manu Ginobili 8.00 20.00
47 Raymond Felton 2.50 6.00
48 Andrew Bynum 2.50 6.00
49 John Salmons 2.50 6.00
50 Zach Randolph 4.00 10.00
51 DeMarcus Cousins 8.00 20.00
52 D.J. Augustin 2.50 6.00
53 Tyreke Evans 3.00 8.00
54 James Harden 10.00 25.00
55 Roy Hibbert 3.00 8.00
56 Luke Ridnour 2.50 6.00
57 Joakim Noah 4.00 10.00
58 Kevin Martin 3.00 8.00
59 LaMarcus Aldridge 4.00 10.00
60 Jrue Holiday 5.00 12.00
61 Mike Conley Jr. 3.00 8.00
62 DeMar DeRozan 6.00 15.00
63 Eric Gordon 3.00 8.00
64 Andre Iguodala 4.00 10.00
65 Tony Parker 6.00 15.00
66 Luol Deng 3.00 8.00
67 Michael Beasley 2.50 6.00
68 Monta Ellis 3.00 8.00
69 Jose Calderon 2.50 6.00
70 Danilo Gallinari 3.00 8.00
71 Channing Frye 2.50 6.00
72 Andrea Bargnani 2.50 6.00
73 Lamar Odom 3.00 8.00
74 Kyle Lowry 4.00 10.00
75 Andray Blatche 2.50 6.00
76 Andrew Bogut 3.00 8.00
77 Devin Harris 2.50 6.00
78 Josh Smith 2.50 6.00
79 Carlos Boozer 3.00 8.00
80 Antawn Jamison 3.00 8.00
81 Luis Scola 3.00 8.00

82 Caron Butler 3.00 8.00
83 Gerald Wallace 3.00 8.00
84 Chris Paul 8.00 20.00
85 Baron Davis 4.00 10.00
86 Ramon Sessions 2.50 6.00
87 Brandon Jennings 2.50 6.00
88 Rodney Stuckey 2.50 6.00
89 Wesley Matthews 2.50 6.00
90 Joe Johnson 4.00 10.00
91 Mo Williams 3.00 8.00
92 Darren Collison 2.50 6.00
93 Jason Kidd 6.00 15.00
94 Dorell Wright 2.50 6.00
95 Chris Bosh 5.00 12.00
96 Nick Young 2.50 6.00
97 Amare Stoudemire 4.00 10.00
98 Stephen Jackson 3.00 8.00
99 Shawn Marion 4.00 10.00
100 Russell Westbrook 6.00 15.00

2010-11 Elite Black Box Crusade Materials

STATED PRINT RUN 99 SER.#'d SETS
1 Derrick Rose 8.00 20.00
2 John Wall 8.00 20.00
3 Dwyane Wade 8.00 20.00
4 Chauncey Billups 5.00 12.00
5 Kevin Garnett 10.00 25.00
6 LeBron James 15.00 40.00
7 Carmelo Anthony 6.00 15.00
8 Deron Williams 3.00 8.00
9 Rajon Rondo 5.00 12.00
10 David Lee 2.50 6.00
11 Brook Lopez 3.00 8.00
12 Dwight Howard 5.00 12.00
13 Steve Nash 8.00 20.00
14 Jameer Nelson 2.50 6.00
15 Al Horford 4.00 10.00
16 Pau Gasol 6.00 15.00
17 Anderson Varejao 2.50 6.00
18 Marc Gasol 4.00 10.00
19 Beno Udrih 2.50 6.00
20 Ray Allen 6.00 15.00
21 Tim Duncan 10.00 25.00
22 Rudy Gay 4.00 10.00
23 Jason Richardson 4.00 10.00
24 Kobe Bryant 12.00 30.00
25 Al Jefferson 2.50 6.00
26 Chris Kaman 2.50 6.00
27 Danny Granger 2.50 6.00
28 Elton Brand 3.00 8.00
29 Emeka Okafor 2.50 6.00
30 Stephen Curry 30.00 80.00
31 Jason Terry 3.00 8.00
32 Blake Griffin 4.00 10.00
33 Grant Hill 10.00 25.00
34 Paul Pierce 6.00 15.00
35 Kevin Durant 15.00 40.00
36 Boris Diaw 3.00 8.00
37 Nene 3.00 8.00
38 David West 3.00 8.00
39 Paul Millsap 3.00 8.00
40 Andre Miller 3.00 8.00
41 Dirk Nowitzki 10.00 25.00
42 Kevin Love 4.00 10.00
44 Tayshaun Prince 4.00 10.00
46 Manu Ginobili 8.00 20.00
48 Andrew Bynum 2.50 6.00
49 John Salmons 2.50 6.00
50 Zach Randolph 4.00 10.00
51 DeMarcus Cousins 5.00 12.00
52 D.J. Augustin 2.50 6.00
53 Tyreke Evans 3.00 8.00
54 James Harden 10.00 25.00
55 Roy Hibbert 3.00 8.00
56 Luke Ridnour 2.50 6.00
57 Joakim Noah 4.00 10.00
58 Kevin Martin 3.00 8.00
59 LaMarcus Aldridge 4.00 10.00
60 Jrue Holiday 5.00 12.00
61 Mike Conley Jr. 3.00 8.00
62 DeMar DeRozan 6.00 15.00
63 Eric Gordon 3.00 8.00
64 Andre Iguodala 4.00 10.00
65 Tony Parker 6.00 15.00
66 Luol Deng 3.00 8.00
67 Michael Beasley 2.50 6.00
68 Monta Ellis 3.00 8.00
69 Jose Calderon 2.50 6.00
70 Danilo Gallinari 3.00 8.00
71 Channing Frye 2.50 6.00
72 Andrea Bargnani 2.50 6.00
73 Lamar Odom 3.00 8.00
74 Kyle Lowry 4.00 10.00
76 Andrew Bogut 3.00 8.00
77 Devin Harris 2.50 6.00
78 Josh Smith 2.50 6.00
79 Carlos Boozer 3.00 8.00
80 Antawn Jamison 3.00 8.00
81 Luis Scola 3.00 8.00
82 Caron Butler 3.00 8.00
84 Chris Paul 8.00 20.00
86 Ramon Sessions 2.50 6.00
87 Brandon Jennings 2.50 6.00
89 Wesley Matthews 2.50 6.00
90 Joe Johnson 4.00 10.00
91 Mo Williams 3.00 8.00
92 Darren Collison 2.50 6.00
93 Jason Kidd 6.00 15.00
95 Chris Bosh 5.00 12.00
96 Nick Young 2.50 6.00
97 Amare Stoudemire 4.00 10.00
98 Stephen Jackson 3.00 8.00
99 Shawn Marion 4.00 10.00
100 Russell Westbrook 6.00 15.00

2010-11 Elite Black Box Crusade Materials Signatures

STATED PRINT RUN 5 TO 25 SER.#'d SETS
10 David Lee/25 5.00 12.00
11 Brook Lopez/25 8.00 20.00
14 Jameer Nelson/25 5.00 12.00
15 Al Horford/25 6.00 15.00
17 Anderson Varejao/25 5.00 12.00
19 Beno Udrih/25 5.00 12.00
22 Rudy Gay/25 8.00 20.00
24 Kobe Bryant/25 1,250.00 2,500.00
25 Al Jefferson/25 6.00 15.00
26 Chris Kaman/25 5.00 12.00
27 Danny Granger/25 8.00 20.00
29 Emeka Okafor/25 5.00 12.00
30 Stephen Curry/25 600.00 1,200.00
31 Jason Terry/25 10.00 25.00
33 Grant Hill/25 75.00 150.00
36 Boris Diaw/25 5.00 12.00
39 Paul Millsap/25 10.00 25.00
40 Andre Miller/25 6.00 15.00
50 Zach Randolph/25 12.00 30.00
51 DeMarcus Cousins/25 20.00 50.00
52 D.J. Augustin/25 5.00 12.00
53 Tyreke Evans/25 6.00 15.00
54 James Harden/25 20.00 50.00
55 Roy Hibbert/25 5.00 12.00
56 Luke Ridnour/25 5.00 12.00
57 Joakim Noah/25 EXCH 10.00 25.00
58 Kevin Martin/25 5.00 12.00
59 LaMarcus Aldridge/25 10.00 25.00
60 Jrue Holiday/25 5.00 12.00
61 Mike Conley Jr./25 8.00 20.00
62 DeMar DeRozan/25 60.00 150.00
63 Eric Gordon/25 8.00 20.00
64 Andre Iguodala/25 8.00 20.00
68 Monta Ellis/25 12.00 30.00
69 Jose Calderon/25 10.00 25.00
70 Danilo Gallinari/25 5.00 12.00
71 Channing Frye/20 5.00 12.00
72 Andrea Bargnani/25 6.00 15.00
76 Andrew Bogut/25 12.00 30.00
77 Devin Harris/25 6.00 15.00
78 Josh Smith/25 10.00 25.00
79 Carlos Boozer/25 EXCH 10.00 25.00
80 Antawn Jamison/25 5.00 12.00
81 Luis Scola/25 EXCH 5.00 12.00
82 Caron Butler/25 8.00 20.00
87 Brandon Jennings/25 10.00 25.00
89 Wesley Matthews/25 8.00 20.00
90 Joe Johnson/25 8.00 20.00
91 Mo Williams/25 5.00 12.00
92 Darren Collison/25 5.00 12.00
98 Stephen Jackson/25 5.00 12.00
100 Russell Westbrook/25 50.00 120.00

2010-11 Elite Black Box Crusade Signatures

STATED PRINT RUN 5 TO 149 SER.#'d SETS
10 David Lee/25 10.00 25.00
11 Brook Lopez/25 10.00 25.00
14 Jameer Nelson/25 8.00 20.00
17 Anderson Varejao/49 5.00 12.00
19 Beno Udrih/99 5.00 12.00
22 Rudy Gay/49 6.00 15.00
24 Kobe Bryant/149 1,000.00 2,000.00
26 Chris Kaman/49 5.00 12.00
30 Stephen Curry/49 500.00 1,000.00
31 Jason Terry/25 EXCH 12.00 30.00
36 Boris Diaw/99 5.00 12.00
39 Paul Millsap/99 6.00 15.00
40 Andre Miller/49 5.00 12.00
43 Kris Humphries/99 5.00 12.00
47 Raymond Felton/49 5.00 12.00
50 Zach Randolph/49 5.00 12.00
51 DeMarcus Cousins/25 40.00 100.00
52 D.J. Augustin/25 8.00 20.00
54 James Harden/25 25.00 60.00
55 Roy Hibbert/99 5.00 12.00
56 Luke Ridnour/49 5.00 12.00
58 Kevin Martin/59 5.00 12.00
59 LaMarcus Aldridge/25 8.00 20.00
60 Jrue Holiday/99 8.00 20.00
61 Mike Conley Jr./49 5.00 12.00
62 DeMar DeRozan/25 40.00 100.00
63 Eric Gordon/49 8.00 20.00
64 Andre Iguodala/25 6.00 15.00
68 Monta Ellis/49 6.00 15.00
69 Jose Calderon/49 10.00 25.00
71 Channing Frye/49 5.00 12.00
72 Andrea Bargnani/25 6.00 15.00
77 Devin Harris/25 6.00 15.00
78 Josh Smith/25 12.00 30.00
79 Carlos Boozer/49 12.00 30.00
80 Antawn Jamison/49 6.00 15.00
81 Luis Scola/49 8.00 20.00
82 Caron Butler/25 12.00 30.00
83 Gerald Wallace/25 12.00 30.00
87 Brandon Jennings/25 15.00 40.00
89 Wesley Matthews/99 5.00 12.00
92 Darren Collison/99 6.00 15.00
95 Chris Bosh/20 12.00 30.00
98 Stephen Jackson/99 5.00 12.00
100 Russell Westbrook/25 50.00 120.00

2010-11 Elite Black Box Draft Classes Materials Prime

STATED PRINT RUN 15 TO 99 SER.#'d SETS
1 Magic/Eaton/Laimbeer/99 12.50 30.00
2 Aguirre/Thomas/Ro/15 15.00 40.00
3 Worthy/Wilkins/Floyd/99 10.00 25.00
5 Griffin/Curry/Collison/99 75.00 200.00

2010-11 Elite Black Box Draft Classes Signatures

STATED PRINT RUN 10 TO 49 SER.#'d SETS
2 Aguirre/Thomas/Ro/49 EXCH 20.00 50.00
3 Worthy/Wilkins/Floyd/25 30.00 80.00
4 D.Rob/Smith/Johnson/25 40.00 100.00
5 Griffin/Curry/Collison/25 500.00 1,000.00

2010-11 Elite Black Box Dream Team Materials Prime

STATED PRINT RUN 99 SER.#'d SETS
1 Drexler/Stockton/Magic 30.00 80.00
2 Mullin/Bird/Robinson 30.00 80.00

2010-11 Elite Black Box Elite Series Materials Prime

STATED PRINT RUN ONE TO 49 SER.#'d SETS
1 Julius Erving/25 12.00 30.00
2 Magic Johnson/49 25.00 60.00
3 Chris Mullin/49 8.00 20.00
5 Kevin McHale/49 10.00 25.00
6 Nate Thurmond/25 25.00 60.00
10 Mark Price/49 10.00 25.00
11 David Robinson/49 12.00 30.00
12 Michael Cooper/49 6.00 15.00
14 Charles Oakley/49 8.00 20.00
18 Spencer Haywood/49 12.50 30.00
19 Robert Parish/25 10.00 25.00
20 Mark Eaton/49 6.00 15.00
21 Bill Laimbeer/25 5.00 12.00
23 Bernard King/25 8.00 20.00
24 Dennis Rodman/25 20.00 50.00
26 Kareem Abdul-Jabbar/25 20.00 50.00
29 Dominique Wilkins/25 10.00 25.00
30 Gary Payton/25 10.00 25.00
31 Jalen Rose/49 5.00 12.00
34 Alex English/25 5.00 12.00
35 Alonzo Mourning/25 25.00 60.00
37 Dan Issel/25 8.00 20.00
38 Kelly Tripucka/49 4.00 10.00
39 Larry Johnson/49 20.00 50.00
40 Mitch Richmond/25 15.00 40.00
42 Sam Perkins/25 8.00 20.00
44 George Gervin/25 10.00 25.00
46 Hakeem Olajuwon/49 12.00 30.00
48 Maurice Cheeks/25 5.00 12.00
49 Nick Van Exel/49 8.00 20.00
50 Robert Horry/25 6.00 15.00
51 Kobe Bryant/25 40.00 100.00
52 Kevin Durant/25 25.00 60.00
53 Blake Griffin/49 20.00 50.00
55 Kevin Love/25 6.00 15.00
56 Zach Randolph/25 6.00 15.00
57 Derrick Rose/25 30.00 80.00
59 Tony Parker/25 10.00 25.00
60 Paul Pierce/25 10.00 25.00
61 Lamar Odom/25 5.00 12.00
63 Eric Gordon/25 5.00 12.00
64 Carlos Boozer/25 5.00 12.00
65 Danny Granger/25 5.00 12.00
66 Jason Kidd/25 10.00 25.00
67 Kevin Martin/25 5.00 12.00
68 LaMarcus Aldridge/25 6.00 15.00
69 Pau Gasol/15 10.00 25.00
70 Ray Allen/25 10.00 25.00
71 Rudy Gay/25 6.00 15.00
72 Stephen Curry/25 50.00 125.00
73 Ben Gordon/15 5.00 12.00
74 Brandon Jennings/25 4.00 10.00
76 Tyreke Evans/25 4.00 10.00
77 Ty Lawson/25 4.00 10.00
78 Joe Johnson/25 6.00 15.00
79 Andre Miller/25 6.00 15.00
80 Chris Bosh/25 8.00 20.00
81 Chauncey Billups/25 8.00 20.00
84 Jeff Teague/25 4.00 10.00
88 Marc Gasol/25 6.00 15.00
89 Samuel Dalembert/25 4.00 10.00
91 Grant Hill/25 20.00 50.00
93 DeMar DeRozan/25 10.00 25.00
94 Caron Butler/25 5.00 12.00
95 Monta Ellis/25 5.00 12.00
96 Taj Gibson/25 4.00 10.00
97 O.J. Mayo/25 4.00 10.00
98 Trevor Ariza/25 4.00 10.00
99 Jrue Holiday/25 8.00 20.00
100 Steve Nash/25 10.00 25.00

2010-11 Elite Black Box Flag Patches Signatures

STATED PRINT RUN 5 TO 149 SER.#'d SETS
4 Toni Kukoc/99 15.00 40.00
7 Peja Stojakovic/25 25.00 60.00
11 Dikembe Mutombo/99 6.00 15.00
12 Al Horford/25 8.00 20.00
14 Boris Diaw/99 6.00 15.00
15 Shawn Bradley/149 6.00 15.00
16 Chris Kaman/25 10.00 25.00
17 Detlef Schrempf/149 6.00 15.00
19 Andrea Bargnani/25 10.00 25.00
20 Roy Hibbert/149 6.00 15.00
21 Serge Ibaka/99 10.00 25.00
22 Vlade Divac/149 EXCH 8.00 20.00
23 Nenad Krstic/149 6.00 15.00
24 Darko Milicic/149 6.00 15.00
25 Goran Dragic/149 20.00 50.00
26 Jose Calderon/49 8.00 20.00
29 Hedo Turkoglu/49 6.00 15.00
34 Kobe Bryant/49 1,000.00 2,000.00
49 Bill Walton/25 20.00 50.00
50 Brook Lopez/25 6.00 15.00
51 Byron Scott/149 6.00 15.00
52 Caron Butler/25 10.00 25.00
56 Dan Majerle/149 6.00 15.00
57 Dave Cowens/25 10.00 25.00
58 David Lee/25 8.00 20.00
59 Dell Curry/149 6.00 15.00
62 Elgin Baylor/25 15.00 40.00
74 Larry Johnson/149 8.00 20.00
75 Lenny Wilkens/25 15.00 40.00
76 Mark Price/149 8.00 20.00
77 Monta Ellis/99 6.00 15.00
83 Robert Horry/49 6.00 15.00
84 Shane Battier/49 6.00 15.00
85 Stephen Curry/49 800.00 1,500.00
86 Tim Hardaway/149 8.00 20.00
87 Tyson Chandler/25 10.00 25.00
88 A.C. Green/99 8.00 20.00
89 Adrian Dantley/99 6.00 15.00
90 Bernard King/99 8.00 20.00
91 Bill Laimbeer/149 6.00 15.00
92 Cedric Maxwell/149 6.00 15.00
93 Darryl Dawkins/149 6.00 15.00
94 Gail Goodrich/25 12.50 30.00
95 Glen Rice/99 10.00 25.00
96 Jeff Hornacek/149 8.00 20.00
97 Nate Archibald/25 6.00 15.00
98 Nate Thurmond/25 12.00 30.00
99 Sam Perkins/99 6.00 15.00
100 Sean Elliott/149 8.00 20.00

2010-11 Elite Black Box Hall of Fame Materials Prime

STATED PRINT RUN 99 SER.#'d SETS
3 Worthy/English/Wilkins 12.50 30.00
4 Dumars/Drexler/D.Rob 25.00 60.00

2010-11 Elite Black Box Hall of Fame Signatures

STATED PRINT RUN 10 TO 49 SER.#'d SETS
3 Worthy/English/Wilkins/25 25.00 60.00
6 Jones/Thrmnd/Cngham/49 25.00 60.00
7 Gervin/Howell/Risen/49 25.00 60.00
8 Mullin/Gilmore/Rod/25 60.00 150.00

2010-11 Elite Black Box Materials

STATED PRINT RUN 2 TO 99 SER.#'d SETS
1 LeBron James/99 12.00 30.00
2 Dirk Nowitzki/99 10.00 25.00
3 Kevin Durant/99 15.00 40.00
4 Kobe Bryant/99 12.00 30.00
5 Carmelo Anthony/99 6.00 15.00
6 LaMarcus Aldridge/99 4.00 10.00
7 Al Horford/99 4.00 10.00
8 Kevin Garnett/99 10.00 25.00
9 Chris Paul/99 8.00 20.00
10 Dwight Howard/99 5.00 12.00
11 Dwyane Wade/99 8.00 20.00
12 Blake Griffin/99 4.00 10.00
13 Andrea Bargnani/99 2.50 6.00
14 Kevin Love/99 4.00 10.00
15 Zach Randolph/99 4.00 10.00
16 Ray Allen/99 6.00 15.00
17 Derrick Rose/99 8.00 20.00
18 Monta Ellis/99 3.00 8.00
19 Danny Granger/99 2.50 6.00
20 Ty Lawson/99 2.50 6.00
21 Tony Parker/99 6.00 15.00
22 Brook Lopez/99 3.00 8.00
23 Eric Gordon/99 3.00 8.00
24 Russell Westbrook/99 6.00 15.00
25 Tyson Chandler/99 3.00 8.00
26 Vince Carter/99 8.00 20.00
27 Amare Stoudemire/99 4.00 10.00
28 Kevin Martin/99 3.00 8.00
29 Joe Johnson/99 4.00 10.00
30 Stephen Jackson/99 3.00 8.00
31 JaVale McGee/99 3.00 8.00
32 Chauncey Billups/99 5.00 12.00
33 Paul Pierce/99 6.00 15.00
34 Darren Collison/99 2.50 6.00
35 Serge Ibaka/99 3.00 8.00
36 J.J. Barea/99 3.00 8.00
37 Chris Bosh/99 5.00 12.00
38 Al Jefferson/99 2.50 6.00
39 Rudy Gay/99 4.00 10.00
40 Deron Williams/99 3.00 8.00
41 David West/99 3.00 8.00
42 Luis Scola/99 3.00 8.00
43 Antawn Jamison/99 3.00 8.00
44 Brandon Jennings/99 2.50 6.00
45 Stephen Curry/99 30.00 80.00
46 Steve Nash/99 8.00 20.00
47 Chris Kaman/99 2.50 6.00
48 Andre Iguodala/99 4.00 10.00
49 Joakim Noah/99 4.00 10.00
50 Brandon Roy/99 5.00 12.00
51 Andrei Kirilenko/99 3.00 8.00
52 Jameer Nelson/99 2.50 6.00
53 Jrue Holiday/99 5.00 12.00
54 Ben Gordon/99 3.00 8.00
55 Marc Gasol/99 4.00 10.00
56 Gerald Wallace/99 3.00 8.00
57 Rajon Rondo/99 5.00 12.00
58 Tim Duncan/99 10.00 25.00
59 Pau Gasol/99 6.00 15.00
60 Michael Beasley/99 2.50 6.00
61 Tyreke Evans/99 3.00 8.00
62 David Lee/99 2.50 6.00
63 DeMar DeRozan/99 6.00 15.00
64 Wesley Matthews/99 2.50 6.00
65 Josh Smith/99 2.50 6.00
67 Nene/99 3.00 8.00
68 James Harden/99 10.00 25.00
69 Devin Harris/99 2.50 6.00
70 Elton Brand/99 3.00 8.00
71 Emeka Okafor/99 2.50 6.00
72 Jason Terry/99 3.00 8.00
73 Luol Deng/99 3.00 8.00
74 Nick Young/99 2.50 6.00
75 Danilo Gallinari/99 3.00 8.00
76 Carlos Boozer/99 3.00 8.00
77 Andrew Bogut/99 3.00 8.00
80 Manu Ginobili/99 8.00 20.00
82 Ben Wallace/99 5.00 12.00
83 Jason Kidd/99 6.00 15.00
84 Trevor Ariza/99 2.50 6.00
86 Andrew Bynum/99 2.50 6.00
88 Roy Hibbert/99 3.00 8.00
90 J.J. Redick/99 4.00 10.00
91 J.R. Smith/99 4.00 10.00
93 Jonny Flynn/99 2.50 6.00
94 Brandon Bass/99 2.50 6.00
95 Taj Gibson/99 2.50 6.00
97 Glen Davis/99 2.50 6.00
98 DeJuan Blair/99 2.50 6.00
99 Tracy McGrady/99 6.00 15.00
100 Samuel Dalembert/99 2.50 6.00
102 Karl Malone/99 8.00 20.00
103 Julius Erving/49 8.00 20.00
104 Jalen Rose/99 3.00 8.00
105 Alex English/99 3.00 8.00
106 Alonzo Mourning/99 6.00 15.00
107 David Robinson/99 6.00 15.00
108 Kevin Johnson/99 5.00 12.00
109 Kevin McHale/99 6.00 15.00
110 Shaquille O'Neal/99 15.00 40.00
114 Gary Payton/25 8.00 20.00
117 Dominique Wilkins/99 6.00 15.00
118 George Mikan/49 10.00 25.00
120 Jerry West/25 8.00 20.00
121 Hakeem Olajuwon/99 8.00 20.00
123 Clyde Drexler/99 6.00 15.00
124 Nate Thurmond/25 5.00 12.00
127 Darrell Griffith/99 2.50 6.00
128 Danny Manning/99 3.00 8.00
129 Dan Issel/99 4.00 10.00
130 Larry Bird/99 15.00 40.00
132 Bill Laimbeer/99 3.00 8.00
133 Shawn Bradley/99 2.50 6.00
134 James Worthy/99 5.00 12.00
135 Cedric Maxwell/99 4.00 10.00
136 Bailey Howell/25 4.00 10.00
137 Magic Johnson/25 15.00 40.00
138 Kelly Tripucka/99 2.50 6.00
139 Dikembe Mutombo/99 6.00 15.00
142 Mark Eaton/99 4.00 10.00
143 Toni Kukoc/99 4.00 10.00
144 Earl Monroe/99 4.00 10.00
145 Glen Rice/99 4.00 10.00
146 Larry Johnson/99 6.00 15.00
147 Kiki Vandeweghe/99 3.00 8.00
148 Chris Webber/99 5.00 12.00
149 Ron Harper/99 4.00 10.00
150 Kareem Abdul-Jabbar/49 12.00 30.00
151 Sam Jones/49 5.00 12.00
152 Spencer Haywood/49 4.00 10.00
153 Dennis Scott/99 2.50 6.00
155 Robert Horry/49 4.00 10.00
156 Manute Bol/99 4.00 10.00
157 Kevin Willis/99 2.50 6.00
158 Chris Mullin/49 5.00 12.00
159 Isiah Thomas/99 6.00 15.00
163 Alvan Adams/99 2.50 6.00
164 Xavier McDaniel/99 3.00 8.00
165 Sleepy Floyd/99 2.50 6.00
166 Mark Aguirre/99 3.00 8.00
167 Mark Price/25 6.00 15.00
168 Bernard King/25 5.00 12.00
169 Joe Dumars/99 4.00 10.00
170 Reggie Lewis/99 12.50 30.00
171 Michael Cooper/99 4.00 10.00
172 Robert Parish/99 6.00 15.00
173 Danny Ainge/99 4.00 10.00
174 Maurice Cheeks/99 3.00 8.00
177 Jeff Hornacek/25 3.00 8.00
179 Tom Chambers/99 4.00 10.00
181 Mitch Richmond/99 5.00 12.00
183 Patrick Ewing/99 8.00 20.00
186 Steve Smith/99 3.00 8.00
193 Dan Majerle/99 3.00 8.00

2010-11 Elite Black Box Passing the Torch Materials

STATED PRINT RUN 5 TO 99 SER.#'d SETS
1 J.West/K.Bryant/25 400.00 800.00
2 S.Kemp/K.Durant/99 75.00 200.00
5 J.Erving/A.Iguodala/99 15.00 40.00
6 M.Richmond/M.Ellis/99 8.00 20.00
8 C.Drexler/K.Martin/99 20.00 50.00
9 C.Mullin/D.Lee/75 12.00 30.00
10 D.Wilkins/J.Johnson/99 15.00 40.00
13 J.Rose/D.Collison/99 6.00 15.00
15 D.Rodman/K.Love/99 40.00 100.00
16 M.Eaton/A.Bogut/99 12.00 30.00
18 J.Dumars/G.Monroe/99 8.00 20.00
20 A.Mourning/C.Bosh/99 40.00 100.00
22 K.Johnson/S.Nash/99 40.00 100.00
24 R.Parish/M.Camby/99 12.00 30.00
26 R.Allen/S.Curry/99 2,000.00 4,000.00
27 G.Payton/E.Gordon/99 10.00 25.00
28 G.Payton/R.Westbrook/99 40.00 100.00
30 D.Robinson/A.Bynum/99 40.00 100.00
31 J.Stockton/J.Barea/99 25.00 60.00
32 G.Gervin/K.Durant/75 60.00 150.00
34 K.Bryant/A.Iguodala/99 400.00 800.00
36 E.Baylor/K.Bryant/25 400.00 800.00
38 T.Kukoc/J.Noah/99 12.00 30.00
39 J.Havlicek/P.Pierce/25 75.00 200.00
41 D.Griffith/D.Harris/99 6.00 15.00
42 I.Thomas/B.Gordon/99 15.00 40.00
45 A.English/J.Smith/25 12.00 30.00
48 D.Mutombo/J.Smith/99 8.00 20.00
49 K.Tripucka/D.Favors/99 6.00 15.00
50 G.Rice/S.Jackson/85 8.00 20.00

2010-11 Elite Black Box Passing the Torch Signatures

STATED PRINT RUN 3 TO 149 SER.#'d SETS
4 W.Frazier/C.Billups/25 15.00 40.00
6 Richmond/M.Ellis/149 EXCH 12.00 30.00
9 C.Mullin/D.Lee/149 15.00 40.00
11 A.Dantley/G.Monroe/149 10.00 25.00
13 J.Rose/Collison/149 10.00 25.00
16 M.Eaton/A.Bogut/149 10.00 25.00
17 S.Perkins/Z.Randolph/99 10.00 25.00
18 J.Dumars/G.Monroe/149 12.00 30.00
19 N.Archibald/B.Jennings/49 10.00 25.00
21 E.Hayes/L.Aldridge/25 15.00 40.00
24 R.Parish/M.Camby/99 12.00 30.00
25 W.Free/M.Ellis/99 10.00 25.00
26 R.Allen/S.Curry/25 4,000.00 8,000.00
29 D.Thompson/Crawford/99 10.00 25.00
33 Archibald/Fisher/99 EXCH 10.00 25.00
34 K.Bryant/A.Iguodala/99 800.00 1,500.00
36 Baylor/K.Bryant/99 EXCH 800.00 1,500.00
37 S.Perkins/T.Chandler/25 12.00 30.00
38 Kukoc/J.Noah/25 EXCH 30.00 80.00
41 D.Griffith/D.Harris/99 10.00 25.00
43 B.King/L.Fields/149 8.00 20.00
44 Dawkins/B.Lopez/49 EXCH 10.00 25.00
45 A.English/J.Smith/99 10.00 25.00
46 Blackman/J.Terry/49 EXCH 12.00 30.00
48 D.Mutombo/J.Smith/99 15.00 40.00
49 K.Tripucka/D.Favors/99 10.00 25.00
50 G.Rice/S.Jackson/99 10.00 25.00

2010-11 Elite Black Box Private Signings

STATED PRINT RUN 10 TO 199 SER.#'d SETS
2 Artis Gilmore/148 6.00 15.00
3 Dirk Nowitzki/51 150.00 400.00
4 Gail Goodrich/49 5.00 12.00
5 Jack Twyman/99 15.00 40.00
6 Bill Laimbeer/148 5.00 12.00
7 Rolando Blackman/149 6.00 15.00
8 Sean Elliott/199 6.00 15.00
9 Mark Eaton/199 5.00 12.00

2010-11 Elite Black Box Reigning Threes Materials Prime

STATED PRINT RUN 24 TO 49 SER.#'d SETS
1 Kobe Bryant/24 60.00 150.00
2 Kevin Durant/49 15.00 40.00
3 Stephen Curry/49 150.00 400.00
4 Ty Lawson/49 5.00 12.00
5 Ray Allen/49 12.00 30.00
6 Channing Frye/49 5.00 12.00
7 Jason Terry/49 6.00 15.00
8 Danny Granger/49 5.00 12.00
9 Kevin Martin/49 6.00 15.00
10 Toney Douglas/49 5.00 12.00

2010-11 Elite Black Box Reigning Threes Signatures

STATED PRINT RUN 10 TO 99 SER.#'d SETS
1 Kobe Bryant/99 1,000.00 2,000.00
3 Stephen Curry/99 1,000.00 2,000.00
4 Ty Lawson/99 6.00 15.00
6 Channing Frye/99 5.00 12.00
7 Jason Terry/49 EXCH 6.00 15.00
8 Danny Granger/49 5.00 12.00
9 Kevin Martin/99 5.00 12.00
10 Toney Douglas/49 5.00 12.00

2010-11 Elite Black Box Signatures

STATED PRINT RUN 5 TO 149 SER.#'d SETS
4 Kobe Bryant/99 1,000.00 2,000.00
6 LaMarcus Aldridge/24 8.00 20.00
7 Al Horford/24 6.00 15.00
13 Andrea Bargnani/24 4.00 10.00
14 Kevin Love/24 15.00 40.00
15 Zach Randolph/24 8.00 20.00
18 Monta Ellis/149 8.00 20.00
19 Danny Granger/24 6.00 15.00
20 Ty Lawson/149 5.00 12.00
22 Brook Lopez/24 5.00 12.00
23 Eric Gordon/149 6.00 15.00
24 Russell Westbrook/24 30.00 80.00
25 Tyson Chandler/24 6.00 15.00
28 Kevin Martin/149 4.00 10.00
30 Stephen Jackson/49 4.00 10.00
31 JaVale McGee/149 4.00 10.00
34 Darren Collison/149 4.00 10.00
35 Serge Ibaka/149 6.00 15.00
36 J.J. Barea/149 10.00 25.00
39 Rudy Gay/49 EXCH 5.00 12.00
43 Antawn Jamison/49 4.00 10.00
45 Stephen Curry/49 500.00 1,000.00
47 Chris Kaman/24 4.00 10.00
48 Andre Iguodala/24 5.00 12.00
51 Andrei Kirilenko/24 6.00 15.00
52 Jameer Nelson/24 4.00 10.00
53 Jrue Holiday/49 8.00 20.00
56 Gerald Wallace/24 10.00 25.00
62 David Lee/24 5.00 12.00
63 DeMar DeRozan/24 40.00 100.00
64 Wesley Matthews/99 5.00 12.00
65 Josh Smith/24 8.00 20.00
66 Juwan Howard/99 4.00 10.00
68 James Harden/24 15.00 40.00
69 Devin Harris/24 4.00 10.00
76 Carlos Boozer/24 6.00 15.00
77 Andrew Bogut/149 8.00 20.00
78 Raymond Felton/24 4.00 10.00
79 Baron Davis/24 5.00 12.00
84 Trevor Ariza/24 4.00 10.00
85 Kendrick Perkins/49 6.00 15.00
86 Andrew Bynum/24 8.00 20.00
87 Aaron Brooks/49 4.00 10.00
88 Roy Hibbert/149 6.00 15.00
90 J.J. Redick/99 10.00 25.00
92 Kris Humphries/99 4.00 10.00
93 Jonny Flynn/99 4.00 10.00
95 Taj Gibson/99 5.00 12.00
96 Gerald Henderson/149 4.00 10.00
98 DeJuan Blair/149 4.00 10.00
100 Samuel Dalembert/99 4.00 10.00
105 Alex English/99 4.00 10.00
111 Wes Unseld/24 4.00 10.00
112 Walt Frazier/24 10.00 25.00
113 George Gervin/24 8.00 20.00
115 Elgin Baylor/24 EXCH 10.00 25.00
116 Bob McAdoo/99 8.00 20.00
119 Lenny Wilkens/24 6.00 15.00
122 Kenny Smith/24 4.00 10.00
124 Nate Thurmond/24 6.00 15.00
126 Darryl Dawkins/149 4.00 10.00
127 Darrell Griffith/149 4.00 10.00
128 Danny Manning/24 8.00 20.00
129 Dan Issel/149 6.00 15.00
131 Sam Perkins/99 5.00 12.00
132 Bill Laimbeer/149 4.00 10.00
133 Shawn Bradley/149 4.00 10.00
135 Cedric Maxwell/149 4.00 10.00
136 Bailey Howell/99 8.00 20.00
138 Kelly Tripucka/149 4.00 10.00
139 Dikembe Mutombo/99 10.00 25.00
142 Mark Eaton/149 4.00 10.00
143 Toni Kukoc/99 8.00 20.00
144 Earl Monroe/24 12.00 30.00
145 Glen Rice/49 10.00 25.00
146 Larry Johnson/149 6.00 15.00
147 Kiki Vandeweghe/149 4.00 10.00
149 Ron Harper/149 10.00 25.00
151 Sam Jones/24 10.00 25.00
152 Spencer Haywood/149 4.00 10.00
154 Elvin Hayes/24 5.00 12.00
155 Robert Horry/99 10.00 25.00
156 Manute Bol/99 15.00 40.00
157 Kevin Willis/149 6.00 15.00
158 Chris Mullin/99 8.00 20.00
159 Isiah Thomas/24 EXCH 10.00 25.00
160 Dave Cowens/24 6.00 15.00
162 Rick Barry/24 8.00 20.00
163 Alvan Adams/99 4.00 10.00
164 Xavier McDaniel/149 4.00 10.00
165 Sleepy Floyd/149 5.00 12.00
166 Mark Aguirre/149 6.00 15.00
167 Mark Price/149 6.00 15.00
168 Bernard King/99 4.00 10.00
169 Joe Dumars/99 10.00 25.00
171 Michael Cooper/99 6.00 15.00
172 Robert Parish/24 6.00 15.00
174 Maurice Cheeks/149 4.00 10.00
175 Sidney Moncrief/149 4.00 10.00
176 Artis Gilmore/24 8.00 20.00
177 Jeff Hornacek/149 4.00 10.00
180 Tim Hardaway/99 8.00 20.00
181 Mitch Richmond/99 EXCH 12.50 30.00
184 Walt Bellamy/24 5.00 12.00
185 Vlade Divac/149 8.00 20.00
186 Steve Smith/149 4.00 10.00
187 Rolando Blackman/149 4.00 10.00
188 M.L. Carr/149 6.00 15.00
189 Kurt Rambis/149 10.00 25.00
190 Kenny Walker/99 10.00 25.00
191 Jamal Mashburn/149 10.00 25.00
192 Connie Hawkins/99 8.00 20.00
193 Dan Majerle/149 EXCH 6.00 15.00
194 Adrian Dantley/99 4.00 10.00
195 Al Attles/149 4.00 10.00
196 Ralph Sampson/149 5.00 12.00
197 Walter Berry/149 4.00 10.00
199 Bill Walton/24 20.00 50.00
200 World B. Free/24 6.00 15.00

2010-11 Elite Black Box Teammates Materials Prime

STATED PRINT RUN 49 SER.#'d SETS
1 KD/Westbrook/Ibaka 40.00 100.00
2 Griffin/Gordon/Williams 20.00 50.00
3 Pierce/Allen/Rondo 20.00 50.00
4 James/Wade/Bosh 200.00 400.00
5 Bryant/Gasol/Fisher 200.00 500.00
6 Abdul-Jabbar/Magic/Worthy 30.00 80.00
8 Bird/McHale/Parish 25.00 60.00

2010-11 Elite Black Box Teammates Signatures

STATED PRINT RUN 10 TO 25 SER.#'d SETS
2 Griffin/Gordon/Mo/25 20.00 50.00
5 Bryant/Gasol/Fish/25 600.00 1,200.00
10 Olaj/Drexler/Horry/25 75.00 150.00

2010-11 Elite Black Box The Rookies Materials Dual Prime

STATED PRINT RUN 20 TO 25 SER.#'d SETS
1 J.Wall/D.Cousins/25 20.00 50.00
2 L.Fields/J.Wall/25 15.00 40.00
4 W.Johnson/L.Hayward/20 8.00 20.00
5 D.Cousins/L.Fields/25 10.00 25.00
7 B.Griffin/J.Wall/25 25.00 60.00
9 G.Hayward/D.Favors/25 15.00 40.00
10 W.Johnson/E.Turner/25 10.00 25.00

2010-11 Elite Black Box The Rookies Materials Prime

STATED PRINT RUN 15 TO 99 SER.#'d SETS
1 John Wall/99 12.00 30.00
2 Landry Fields/99 2.50 6.00
3 DeMarcus Cousins/99 8.00 20.00
4 Greg Monroe/99 3.00 8.00
5 Gary Neal/35 3.00 8.00
6 Eric Bledsoe/37 6.00 15.00
7 Paul George/20 25.00 60.00
8 Gordon Hayward/99 10.00 25.00
9 Greivis Vasquez/15 3.00 8.00

2010-11 Elite Black Box The Rookies Materials Triple

STATED PRINT RUN 49 SER.#'d SETS
1 Griffin/Wall/Cousins 20.00 50.00
2 Turner/Favors/Johnson 10.00 25.00
3 Udoh/Monroe/Aminu 8.00 20.00
4 Hayward/George/Davis 6.00 15.00
6 Griffin/Aminu/Warren 12.00 30.00
7 Fields/Neal/Monroe 10.00 25.00
9 Wall/Fields/Monroe 12.50 30.00

2010-11 Elite Black Box The Rookies Signatures

STATED PRINT RUN 10 TO 149 SER.#'d SETS
1 John Wall/25 75.00 150.00
2 Landry Fields/149 3.00 8.00
3 DeMarcus Cousins/49 15.00 40.00
4 Greg Monroe/149 4.00 10.00
5 Gary Neal/149 4.00 10.00
6 Eric Bledsoe/149 6.00 15.00
7 Paul George/149 40.00 100.00
8 Gordon Hayward/149 12.00 30.00
9 Greivis Vasquez/149 3.00 8.00

2010-11 Elite Black Box The Rookies Signatures Dual

STATED PRINT RUN 10 TO 99 SER.#'d SETS
3 E.Bledsoe/A.Aminu/99 6.00 15.00
4 W.Johnson/L.Hayward/25 10.00 25.00
5 D.Cousins/L.Fields/25 20.00 50.00
6 E.Davis/P.George/25 15.00 40.00
9 G.Hayward/D.Favors/49 12.00 30.00

2010-11 Elite Black Box The Rookies Signatures Triple

STATED PRINT RUN 49 SER.#'d SETS
1 Griffin/Wall/Cousins EXCH 200.00 350.00
2 Turner/Favors/Johnson 15.00 40.00
3 Udoh/Monroe/Aminu 15.00 40.00
4 Hayward/George/Davis 30.00 80.00
5 Wall/Cousins/Bldse EXCH 60.00 150.00
6 Griffin/Aminu/Warren 30.00 60.00
7 Fields/Neal/Monroe 15.00 40.00
8 Favors/Hayward/Evans 15.00 40.00
9 Wall/Fields/Monroe EXCH 60.00 150.00
10 Cousins/Neal/Evans 15.00 40.00

2010-11 Elite Black Box Thunderstruck Signatures

COMMON CARD (1-10) 125.00 300.00
STATED PRINT RUN 10 SER.#'d SETS

2010-11 Elite Black Box USA Basketball Materials Prime Signatures

STATED PRINT RUN 25 TO 49 SER.#'d SETS
1 Alonzo Mourning/25 40.00 80.00
2 Carlos Boozer/25 12.50 30.00
3 Christian Laettner/49 30.00 80.00
4 Clyde Drexler/25 50.00 125.00
5 Dan Majerle/49 25.00 60.00
6 Dominique Wilkins/25 40.00 100.00
7 Joe Dumars/49 15.00 40.00
8 Kevin Johnson/49 25.00 60.00
9 Larry Johnson/49 20.00 50.00
10 Steve Smith/49 12.50 30.00

2010-11 Elite Black Box USA Basketball Materials Signatures

STATED PRINT RUN 25 TO 49 SER.#'d SETS
1 Alonzo Mourning/25 40.00 100.00
2 Carlos Boozer/25 12.50 30.00
3 Christian Laettner/49 20.00 50.00
5 Dan Majerle/49 12.50 30.00
6 Dominique Wilkins/25 25.00 60.00
7 Joe Dumars/49 10.00 25.00
9 Larry Johnson/49 20.00 50.00
10 Steve Smith/49 10.00 25.00

2010-11 Elite Black Box USA Basketball Patches Signatures

STATED PRINT RUN 5 TO 49 SER.#'d SETS
2 Chris Mullin/49 20.00 50.00
6 Isiah Thomas/49 EXCH 15.00 40.00
11 Kevin Love/25 15.00 40.00
12 Kobe Bryant/49 1,000.00 2,000.00
17 Sean Elliott/49 12.00 30.00
18 Tyson Chandler/25 12.00 30.00
20 Walt Bellamy/25 12.00 30.00

2015-16 Elite Extra Edition

COMPLETE SET (40) 8.00 20.00

*PROD/286: .6X TO 1.5X BASIC
*PROD/127-239: .75X TO 2X BASIC
*PROD/100-120: 1X TO 2.5X BASIC
*PROD/56-99: 1.2X TO 3X BASIC
*PROD/39-42: 1.5X TO 4X BASIC
*PROD/23: 2X TO 5X BASIC
1 Derrick Rose .75 2.00
2 Damian Lillard 1.25 3.00
3 Dirk Nowitzki 1.25 3.00
4 Tony Parker .75 2.00
5 Klay Thompson 1.25 3.00
6 Dwyane Wade 1.00 2.50
7 Blake Griffin .50 1.25
8 Anthony Davis 1.25 3.00
9 DeMar DeRozan .60 1.50
10 Elfrid Payton .40 1.00
11 Jimmy Butler 1.00 2.50
12 DeMarcus Cousins .50 1.25
13 Kenneth Faried .50 1.25
14 Tim Duncan 1.25 3.00
15 James Harden 1.00 2.50
16 Chris Bosh .60 1.50
17 Chris Paul 1.00 2.50
18 Carmelo Anthony .75 2.00
19 Al Horford .50 1.25
20 Nikola Vucevic .40 1.00
21 LeBron James 4.00 10.00
22 John Wall .60 1.50
23 Andre Drummond .60 1.50
24 LaMarcus Aldridge .50 1.25
25 Dwight Howard .60 1.50
26 Jabari Parker .30 .75
27 Kobe Bryant 4.00 10.00
28 Kevin Durant 2.00 5.00
29 Marcus Smart .60 1.50
30 Nerlens Noel .30 .75
31 Kyrie Irving 1.00 2.50
32 Bradley Beal .60 1.50
33 Stephen Curry 4.00 10.00
34 Gordon Hayward .50 1.25
35 Paul George .75 2.00
36 Andrew Wiggins .60 1.50
37 Mike Conley .50 1.25
38 Russell Westbrook .75 2.00
39 Kemba Walker .50 1.25
40 Eric Bledsoe .40 1.00

2015-16 Elite Franchise Futures

*PROD/253: .6X TO 1.5X BASIC
*PROD/173-233: .75X TO 2X BASIC
*PROD/52-97: 1.2X TO 3X BASIC
*PROD/48: 1.5X TO 4X BASIC
1 Karl-Anthony Towns 2.00 5.00
2 D'Angelo Russell 1.25 3.00
3 Jahlil Okafor .40 1.00
4 Kristaps Porzingis 2.00 5.00
5 Mario Hezonja .40 1.00
6 Willie Cauley-Stein .40 1.00
7 Emmanuel Mudiay .40 1.00
8 Stanley Johnson .40 1.00
9 Frank Kaminsky .40 1.00
10 Justise Winslow .50 1.25
11 Myles Turner 1.25 3.00
12 Trey Lyles .40 1.00
13 Devin Booker 4.00 10.00
14 Cameron Payne .50 1.25
15 Kelly Oubre Jr. 1.00 2.50
16 Terry Rozier 1.25 3.00
17 Rashad Vaughn .30 .75
18 Sam Dekker .30 .75
19 Jerian Grant .30 .75
20 Justin Anderson .30 .75

2015-16 Elite Series Inserts

COMPLETE SET (40) 8.00 20.00
*PROD/258-376: .6X TO 1.5X BASIC
*PROD/139-231: .75X TO 2X BASIC
*PROD/100-121: 1X TO 2.5X BASIC
*PROD/29-41: 1.5X TO 4X BASIC
1 Isiah Thomas .50 1.25
2 Chris Paul 1.00 2.50
3 Dominique Wilkins .75 2.00
4 Julius Erving 1.25 3.00
5 Grant Hill .75 2.00
6 Oscar Robertson 1.25 3.00
7 Chris Webber .60 1.50
8 Kobe Bryant 4.00 10.00
9 Karl Malone .75 2.00
10 Stephen Curry 4.00 10.00
11 Scottie Pippen 1.25 3.00
12 LeBron James 4.00 10.00
13 Gary Payton .75 2.00
14 Wilt Chamberlain 2.00 5.00
15 Shawn Kemp .75 2.00
16 David Robinson 1.00 2.50
17 Jerry West .75 2.00
18 Kevin Durant 2.00 5.00
19 John Havlicek .60 1.50
20 Russell Westbrook .75 2.00
21 Clyde Drexler .75 2.00
22 Magic Johnson 2.00 5.00
23 Tracy McGrady .75 2.00
24 Pete Maravich 1.25 3.00
25 Anfernee Hardaway 1.25 3.00
26 Bill Russell 1.50 4.00
27 Alonzo Mourning .75 2.00
28 Kyrie Irving 1.00 2.50
29 Patrick Ewing .75 2.00
30 Blake Griffin .50 1.25
31 Allen Iverson 1.25 3.00
32 Larry Bird 2.00 5.00
33 Kareem Abdul-Jabbar 1.50 4.00
34 Hakeem Olajuwon 1.00 2.50
35 Shaquille O'Neal 1.50 4.00
36 John Stockton 1.00 2.50
37 George Mikan 1.00 2.50
38 Anthony Davis 1.25 3.00
39 Jason Kidd .75 2.00
40 Tim Duncan 1.25 3.00

2015-16 Elite Signatures

PRINT RUNS B/WN 25-49 COPIES PER
EXCHANGE DEADLINE 8/19/2017
*RED/20-25: .5X TO 1.2X BASIC
ESAFA Al-Farouq Aminu/49 2.50 6.00
ESAD Anthony Davis/49 20.00 50.00
ESAD Andre Drummond/49 4.00 10.00
ESAG Artis Gilmore/49 5.00 12.00
ESAH Anfernee Hardaway/49 12.00 30.00
ESAH Allan Houston/49 3.00 8.00
ESAI Allen Iverson/49 40.00 100.00
ESAJ Amir Johnson/49 2.50 6.00
ESAL Alex Len/49 2.50 6.00
ESAM Antonio McDyess/49 3.00 8.00
ESAR Andre Roberson/49 2.50 6.00
ESAW Andrew Wiggins/49 12.00 30.00
ESBB Brandon Bass/49 2.50 6.00
ESBB Bojan Bogdanovic/49 3.00 8.00
ESBG Blake Griffin/49 6.00 15.00
ESBK Brandon Knight/49 2.50 6.00
ESBK Bernard King/49 5.00 12.00
ESBM Bob McAdoo/49 5.00 12.00
ESCD Clyde Drexler/49 12.00 30.00
ESCH Cliff Hagan/49 4.00 10.00
ESCK Clark Kellogg/49 4.00 10.00
ESCM Calvin Murphy/49 3.00 8.00
ESCM Chris Mullin/49 5.00 12.00
ESDC Dave Cowens/49 5.00 12.00
ESDE Dante Exum/49 6.00 15.00
ESDG Danilo Gallinari/49 3.00 8.00
ESDM Donatas Motiejunas/49 2.50 6.00
ESDM Danny Manning/49 3.00 8.00
ESDM Dikembe Mutombo/49 6.00 15.00
ESDR Dennis Rodman/49 10.00 25.00
ESDR Dino Radja/49 10.00 25.00
ESDS Damon Stoudamire/49 4.00 10.00
ESDW Dominique Wilkins/49 10.00 25.00
ESDW Dwyane Wade/49 12.00 30.00
ESEH Elvin Hayes/49 6.00 15.00
ESGG Gail Goodrich/49 4.00 10.00
ESGG George Gervin/49 8.00 20.00
ESGH Grant Hill/49 15.00 40.00
ESGP Gary Payton/49 8.00 20.00
ESJC Jordan Clarkson/49 4.00 10.00
ESJD Joe Dumars/49 5.00 12.00
ESJL Jerry Lucas/49 5.00 12.00
ESJN Jusuf Nurkic/49 3.00 8.00
ESJR Julius Randle/49 6.00 15.00
ESJS Josh Smith/49 2.50 6.00
ESJS Jerry Stackhouse/49 8.00 20.00
ESJW James Worthy/49 8.00 20.00
ESJW Jamaal Wilkes/49 4.00 10.00
ESKB Kobe Bryant/49 400.00 800.00
ESKD Kevin Durant/49 EXCH 40.00 100.00
ESKI Kyrie Irving/49 EXCH 30.00 80.00
ESKK Kyle Korver/49 3.00 8.00
ESKM K.J. McDaniels/49 2.50 6.00
ESKM Kevin McHale/49 10.00 25.00
ESKR Kurt Rambis/49 3.00 8.00
ESKV Keith Van Horn/49 3.00 8.00
ESKW Kenny Walker/49 2.50 6.00
ESLD Luol Deng/49 3.00 8.00
ESLP Lamar Patterson/49 2.50 6.00
ESLS Latrell Sprewell/49 15.00 40.00
ESLW Lenny Wilkens/49 4.00 10.00
ESMA Mahmoud Abdul-Rauf/49 2.50 6.00
ESMC Michael Carter-Williams/49 2.50 6.00
ESMD Matthew Dellavedova/49 4.00 10.00
ESMG Manu Ginobili/25 20.00 50.00
ESMH Maurice Harkless/49 2.50 6.00
ESMP Mason Plumlee/49 2.50 6.00
ESMR Mitch Richmond/49 5.00 12.00
ESNN Nerlens Noel/25 2.50 6.00
ESNS Nik Stauskas/49 2.50 6.00
ESNV Nick Van Exel/49 4.00 10.00
ESOR Oscar Robertson/49 15.00 40.00
ESPG Pau Gasol/49 6.00 15.00
ESRA Rafer Alston/49 2.50 6.00
ESRA Ray Allen/49 12.00 30.00
ESRA Ryan Anderson/49 2.50 6.00
ESRF Rick Fox/49 3.00 8.00
ESRG Rudy Gobert/49 8.00 20.00
ESRH Roy Hibbert/49 3.00 8.00
ESRH Richard Hamilton/49 4.00 10.00
ESRM Ray McCallum/49 2.50 6.00
ESRP Robert Parish/49 5.00 12.00
ESRS Rik Smits/49 3.00 8.00
ESRS Ralph Sampson/49 3.00 8.00
ESRS Rony Seikaly/49 3.00 8.00
ESSB Shawn Bradley/39 2.50 6.00
ESSB Sam Bowie/49 2.50 6.00
ESSC Stephen Curry/49 400.00 800.00
ESSC Seth Curry/49 4.00 10.00
ESSF Steve Francis/49 4.00 10.00
ESTA Tony Allen/49 2.50 6.00
ESTB Trey Burke/49 2.50 6.00
ESTC Tom Chambers/49 3.00 8.00
ESTD Tony Delk/49 2.50 6.00
ESTM Tracy McGrady/49 12.00 30.00
ESTM Timofey Mozgov/49 2.50 6.00
ESVO Victor Oladipo/49 6.00 15.00

2012-13 Elite Series

1-200 PRINT RUN 275 SER.#'d SETS
201-275 PRINT RUN 249 SER.#'d SETS
1 Cartier Martin 1.50 4.00
2 Emeka Okafor 1.25 3.00
3 John Wall 2.00 5.00
4 Jordan Crawford 1.00 2.50
5 Trevor Ariza 1.00 2.50
6 Trevor Booker 1.00 2.50
7 Al Jefferson 1.00 2.50
8 Derrick Favors 1.25 3.00
9 Gordon Hayward 1.50 4.00
10 Jamaal Tinsley 1.00 2.50
11 Marvin Williams 1.00 2.50
12 Mo Williams 1.25 3.00
13 Alan Anderson 1.00 2.50
14 Amir Johnson 1.00 2.50
15 Andrea Bargnani 1.00 2.50
16 Ed Davis 1.00 2.50
17 Jose Calderon 1.00 2.50
18 Kyle Lowry 1.50 4.00
19 Landry Fields 1.00 2.50
20 Linas Kleiza 1.00 2.50
21 Boris Diaw 1.00 2.50
22 Danny Green 1.25 3.00
23 DeJuan Blair 1.00 2.50
24 Manu Ginobili 3.00 8.00
25 Stephen Jackson 1.25 3.00
26 Tiago Splitter 1.00 2.50
27 Tim Duncan 4.00 10.00
28 Tony Parker 2.50 6.00
29 DeMarcus Cousins 1.50 4.00
30 Francisco Garcia 1.25 3.00
31 James Johnson 1.00 2.50
32 Jason Thompson 1.00 2.50
33 John Salmons 1.25 3.00
34 Marcus Thornton 1.00 2.50
35 Tyreke Evans 1.25 3.00
36 Elliot Williams 1.00 2.50
37 J.J. Hickson 1.00 2.50
38 Joel Freeland 1.00 2.50
39 LaMarcus Aldridge 1.50 4.00
40 Nicolas Batum 1.25 3.00
41 Goran Dragic 1.50 4.00
42 Marcin Gortat 1.00 2.50
43 Michael Beasley 1.00 2.50
44 Shannon Brown 1.00 2.50
45 Wesley Johnson 1.00 2.50
46 Andrew Bynum 1.00 2.50
47 Evan Turner 1.00 2.50
48 Jason Richardson 1.50 4.00
49 Jrue Holiday 2.00 5.00
50 Kwame Brown 1.00 2.50
51 Nick Young 1.00 2.50
52 Spencer Hawes 1.00 2.50
53 Thaddeus Young 1.00 2.50
54 Al Harrington 1.25 3.00
55 Arron Afflalo 1.00 2.50
56 Glen Davis 1.00 2.50
57 Hedo Turkoglu 1.25 3.00
58 J.J. Redick 1.50 4.00
59 Jameer Nelson 1.00 2.50
60 Hasheem Thabeet 1.00 2.50
61 Kendrick Perkins 1.00 2.50
62 Kevin Durant 6.00 15.00
63 Kevin Martin 1.25 3.00
64 Nick Collison 1.00 2.50
65 Russell Westbrook 2.50 6.00
66 Serge Ibaka 1.25 3.00
67 Thabo Sefolosha 1.00 2.50
68 Amar'e Stoudemire 1.50 4.00
69 Carmelo Anthony 2.50 6.00
70 J.R. Smith 1.50 4.00
71 Jason Kidd 2.50 6.00
72 Marcus Camby 1.50 4.00
73 Rasheed Wallace 2.00 5.00
74 Raymond Felton 1.00 2.50
75 Ronnie Brewer 1.00 2.50
76 Tyson Chandler 1.25 3.00
77 Al-Farouq Aminu 1.00 2.50
78 Greivis Vasquez 1.00 2.50
79 Robin Lopez 1.00 2.50
80 Ryan Anderson 1.00 2.50
81 Andrei Kirilenko 1.25 3.00
82 Chase Budinger 1.00 2.50
83 J.J. Barea 1.25 3.00
84 Kevin Love 1.50 4.00
85 Luke Ridnour 1.25 3.00
86 Nikola Pekovic 1.00 2.50
87 Ricky Rubio 1.25 3.00
88 Brandon Jennings 1.00 2.50
89 Drew Gooden 1.25 3.00
90 Ersan Ilyasova 1.00 2.50
91 Larry Sanders 1.00 2.50
92 Luc Mbah a Moute 1.00 2.50
93 Mike Dunleavy 1.00 2.50
94 Monta Ellis 1.25 3.00
95 Chris Bosh 2.00 5.00
96 Dwyane Wade 3.00 8.00
97 Udonis Haslem 1.25 3.00
98 Joel Anthony 1.00 2.50
99 LeBron James 12.00 30.00
100 Mario Chalmers 1.25 3.00
101 Rashard Lewis 1.50 4.00
102 Ray Allen 2.50 6.00
103 Shane Battier 1.25 3.00
104 Marc Gasol 1.50 4.00
105 Marreese Speights 1.00 2.50
106 Mike Conley 1.25 3.00
107 Rudy Gay 1.50 4.00
108 Tony Allen 1.00 2.50
109 Zach Randolph 1.50 4.00
110 Antawn Jamison 1.25 3.00
111 Devin Ebanks 1.00 2.50
112 Earl Clark 1.00 2.50
113 Kobe Bryant 12.00 30.00
114 Metta World Peace 1.25 3.00
115 Pau Gasol 2.50 6.00
116 Steve Blake 1.00 2.50
117 Steve Nash 3.00 8.00
118 Blake Griffin 1.50 4.00
119 Chauncey Billups 2.00 5.00
120 Chris Paul 3.00 8.00
121 DeAndre Jordan 1.25 3.00
122 Eric Bledsoe 1.25 3.00
123 Grant Hill 2.50 6.00
124 Jamal Crawford 1.50 4.00
125 Lamar Odom 1.25 3.00
126 Matt Barnes 1.00 2.50
127 Ronny Turiaf 1.00 2.50
128 Danny Granger 1.00 2.50
129 David West 1.25 3.00
130 George Hill 1.25 3.00
131 Ian Mahinmi 1.00 2.50
132 Paul George 2.50 6.00
133 Tyler Hansbrough 1.00 2.50
134 Carlos Delfino 1.00 2.50
135 James Harden 3.00 8.00
136 Jeremy Lin 2.50 6.00
137 Omer Asik 1.00 2.50
138 Patrick Patterson 1.00 2.50
139 Andrew Bogut 1.25 3.00
140 Andris Biedrins 1.00 2.50
141 Brandon Rush 1.00 2.50
142 David Lee 1.00 2.50
143 Stephen Curry 12.00 30.00
144 Austin Daye 1.00 2.50
145 Greg Monroe 1.00 2.50
146 Jonas Jerebko 1.00 2.50
147 Rodney Stuckey 1.00 2.50
148 Tayshaun Prince 1.50 4.00
149 Will Bynum 1.00 2.50
150 Andre Iguodala 1.50 4.00
151 Andre Miller 1.25 3.00
152 Corey Brewer 1.00 2.50
153 Danilo Gallinari 1.00 2.50
154 Ty Lawson 1.00 2.50
155 Darren Collison 1.00 2.50
156 Dirk Nowitzki 4.00 10.00
157 Elton Brand 1.25 3.00
158 O.J. Mayo 1.00 2.50
159 Shawn Marion 1.50 4.00
160 Vince Carter 3.00 8.00
161 Alonzo Gee 1.00 2.50
162 Anderson Varejao 1.00 2.50
163 Daniel Gibson 1.00 2.50
164 Carlos Boozer 1.25 3.00
165 Derrick Rose 2.50 6.00
166 Joakim Noah 1.25 3.00
167 Kirk Hinrich 1.25 3.00
168 Luol Deng 1.25 3.00
169 Marco Belinelli 1.00 2.50
170 Richard Hamilton 1.50 4.00
171 Taj Gibson 1.00 2.50
172 Ben Gordon 1.25 3.00
173 Brendan Haywood 1.00 2.50
174 Byron Mullens 1.00 2.50
175 Gerald Henderson 1.00 2.50
176 Ramon Sessions 1.00 2.50
177 Tyrus Thomas 1.00 2.50
178 Andray Blatche 1.00 2.50
179 Brook Lopez 1.25 3.00
180 C.J. Watson 1.00 2.50
181 Deron Williams 1.25 3.00
182 Gerald Wallace 1.25 3.00
183 Jerry Stackhouse 1.25 3.00
184 Joe Johnson 1.25 3.00
185 Kris Humphries 1.00 2.50
186 Reggie Evans 1.00 2.50
187 Avery Bradley 1.00 2.50
188 Brandon Bass 1.00 2.50
189 Courtney Lee 1.00 2.50
190 Jason Terry 1.25 3.00
191 Jeff Green 1.25 3.00
192 Kevin Garnett 4.00 10.00
193 Leandro Barbosa 1.25 3.00
194 Paul Pierce 2.50 6.00
195 Rajon Rondo 2.00 5.00
196 Al Horford 1.50 4.00
197 Devin Harris 1.00 2.50
198 Josh Smith 1.50 4.00
199 Louis Williams 1.25 3.00
200 Zaza Pachulia 1.00 2.50
201 Damian Lillard RC 20.00 50.00
202 MarShon Brooks RC 1.25 3.00
203 Kyrie Irving RC 12.00 30.00
204 Brandon Knight RC 1.50 4.00
205 Orlando Johnson RC 1.25 3.00
206 Anthony Davis RC 20.00 50.00
207 E'Twaun Moore RC 1.50 4.00
208 Will Barton RC 2.50 6.00
209 Terrence Ross RC 3.00 8.00
210 Nando De Colo RC 1.25 3.00
211 Reggie Jackson RC 2.00 5.00
212 Lavoy Allen RC 1.25 3.00
213 Jordan Hamilton RC 1.25 3.00
214 Kent Bazemore RC 2.00 5.00
215 Darius Morris RC 1.50 4.00
216 Tony Wroten RC 1.25 3.00
217 Jimmy Butler RC 12.00 30.00
218 Marquis Teague RC 1.25 3.00
219 Jan Vesely RC 1.25 3.00
220 Quincy Acy RC 1.25 3.00
221 Jared Sullinger RC 1.25 3.00
222 Tristan Thompson RC 2.00 5.00
223 Kyle Singler RC 1.25 3.00
224 Norris Cole RC 1.25 3.00
225 Austin Rivers RC 2.00 5.00
226 Maurice Harkless RC 1.50 4.00
227 Isaiah Thomas RC 2.50 6.00
228 Alec Burks RC 2.00 5.00
229 Marcus Morris RC 2.00 5.00
230 John Jenkins RC 1.25 3.00
231 Tornike Shengelia RC 1.25 3.00
232 Tyler Zeller RC 1.25 3.00
233 Draymond Green RC 8.00 20.00
234 Robert Sacre RC 1.25 3.00
235 Brian Roberts RC 1.25 3.00
236 Nikola Vucevic RC 5.00 12.00
237 Jimmer Fredette RC 2.00 5.00
238 Bradley Beal RC 10.00 25.00
239 Bernard James RC 1.25 3.00
240 Mike Scott RC 1.50 4.00
241 Jeff Taylor RC 1.25 3.00
242 Jae Crowder RC 2.50 6.00
243 Harrison Barnes RC 2.50 6.00
244 John Henson RC 1.50 4.00
245 Lance Thomas RC 1.25 3.00
246 Kendall Marshall RC 1.25 3.00
247 Thomas Robinson RC 1.25 3.00
248 Mirza Teletovic RC 1.50 4.00
249 Pablo Prigioni RC 1.25 3.00
250 Festus Ezeli RC 1.25 3.00
251 Kemba Walker RC 5.00 12.00
252 Evan Fournier RC 2.00 5.00
253 Chandler Parsons RC 1.50 4.00
254 Tobias Harris RC 4.00 10.00
255 Chris Copeland RC 1.25 3.00
256 Greg Stiemsma RC 1.25 3.00
257 Kawhi Leonard RC 40.00 100.00
258 Tyshawn Taylor RC 1.25 3.00
259 Viacheslav Kravtsov RC 1.25 3.00
260 Jeremy Lamb RC 2.00 5.00
261 Michael Kidd-Gilchrist RC 1.50 4.00
262 Kenneth Faried RC 1.50 4.00
263 Terrence Jones RC 1.25 3.00
264 Alexey Shved RC 1.25 3.00
265 Iman Shumpert RC 1.50 4.00
266 Nolan Smith RC 1.25 3.00
267 Jonas Valanciunas RC 2.50 6.00
268 Klay Thompson RC 60.00 150.00
269 Markieff Morris RC 6.00 15.00
270 Perry Jones RC 1.25 3.00
271 Dion Waiters RC 1.50 4.00
272 Andre Drummond RC 3.00 8.00
273 Miles Plumlee RC 1.25 3.00
274 Derrick Williams RC 1.25 3.00
275 Andrew Nicholson RC 1.25 3.00

2012-13 Elite Series Aspirations Autographs

PRINT RUNS B/WN 45-99 COPIES PER
EXCHANGE DEADLINE 02/21/2015
1 Bradley Beal/97 12.00 30.00
2 Alec Burks/90 5.00 12.00
3 Derrick Favors/85 4.00 10.00
4 Gordon Hayward/80 5.00 12.00
5 Jamaal Tinsley/94 3.00 8.00
6 Marvin Williams/98 3.00 8.00
7 Andrea Bargnani/93 3.00 8.00
8 Ed Davis/68 3.00 8.00
9 Jonas Valanciunas/83 6.00 15.00
10 Kyle Lowry/97 5.00 12.00
11 Terrence Ross/69 8.00 20.00
12 George Gervin/56 8.00 20.00
13 Nando De Colo/75 3.00 8.00
14 Tiago Splitter/78 3.00 8.00
15 Isaiah Thomas/78 6.00 15.00
16 Jimmer Fredette/93 5.00 12.00
17 John Salmons/95 4.00 10.00
18 Kyrie Irving/98 60.00 150.00
19 J.J. Hickson/79 EXCH 3.00 8.00
20 Nolan Smith/96 3.00 8.00
21 Jared Dudley/97 3.00 8.00
22 Nick Young/99 3.00 8.00
23 Kwame Brown/46 3.00 8.00
24 Arron Afflalo/96 EXCH 3.00 8.00
25 E'Twaun Moore/45 4.00 10.00
27 Maurice Harkless/79 4.00 10.00
28 Nikola Vucevic/91 12.00 30.00
29 Kevin Durant/65 EXCH 50.00 120.00
30 Kevin Martin/77 4.00 10.00
31 Reggie Jackson/85 5.00 12.00
32 Thabo Sefolosha/98 3.00 8.00
33 Marcus Camby/77 5.00 12.00
34 Raymond Felton/98 3.00 8.00
35 Ronnie Brewer/92 3.00 8.00
36 Austin Rivers/75 5.00 12.00
37 Brian Roberts/78 3.00 8.00
38 Eric Gordon/90 4.00 10.00
39 Greivis Vasquez/79 3.00 8.00
40 Lance Thomas/58 3.00 8.00
41 Chase Budinger/90 3.00 8.00
42 Beno Udrih/81 EXCH 3.00 8.00
43 Ekpe Udoh/87 3.00 8.00
44 Ersan Ilyasova/93 3.00 8.00
45 John Henson/69 4.00 10.00
46 Monta Ellis/89 4.00 10.00
47 Mario Chalmers/85 4.00 10.00
48 Rashard Lewis/91 EXCH 5.00 12.00
49 Udonis Haslem/60 4.00 10.00
50 Antawn Jamison/96 4.00 10.00
51 Bob McAdoo/89 10.00 25.00
52 Kobe Bryant/76 400.00 800.00
53 Michael Cooper/79 5.00 12.00
54 Blake Griffin/68 15.00 40.00
55 Caron Butler/95 4.00 10.00
56 Grant Hill/67 15.00 40.00
57 Danny Granger/67 3.00 8.00
58 Lance Stephenson/99 4.00 10.00
59 Orlando Johnson/89 3.00 8.00
60 Terrence Jones/94 EXCH 3.00 8.00
61 Andrew Bogut/88 4.00 10.00
62 Brandon Rush/96 3.00 8.00
63 Carl Landry/93 3.00 8.00
64 Harrison Barnes/60 6.00 15.00
65 Stephen Curry/70 500.00 1,000.00
66 Andre Drummond/99 12.00 30.00
67 Austin Daye/95 EXCH 3.00 8.00
68 Brandon Knight/93 4.00 10.00
69 Charlie Villanueva/69 3.00 8.00
70 Isiah Thomas/89 8.00 20.00
71 Rodney Stuckey/97 3.00 8.00
72 Will Bynum/88 3.00 8.00
73 Alex English/98 6.00 15.00
74 Andre Iguodala/91 EXCH 5.00 12.00
75 Danilo Gallinari/92 3.00 8.00
76 David Thompson/57 4.00 10.00
77 Chris Kaman/65 4.00 10.00
78 Jared Cunningham/99 3.00 8.00
79 Anderson Varejao/83 3.00 8.00
80 Jon Leuer/70 3.00 8.00
81 Tristan Thompson/87 5.00 12.00
82 Tyler Zeller/60 3.00 8.00
83 Zydrunas Ilgauskas/89 4.00 10.00
84 Carlos Boozer/95 EXCH 4.00 10.00
85 Joakim Noah/87 4.00 10.00
86 Kirk Hinrich/88 4.00 10.00
87 Marquis Teague/75 3.00 8.00
88 Taj Gibson/78 3.00 8.00
89 Larry Johnson/98 6.00 15.00
90 Michael Kidd-Gilchrist/79 4.00 10.00
91 Jeff Taylor/56 3.00 8.00
92 Kemba Walker/85 15.00 40.00
93 Brook Lopez/89 4.00 10.00
94 Anthony Davis/77 200.00 500.00
95 Tornike Shengelia/80 3.00 8.00
96 Brandon Bass/70 3.00 8.00
97 Courtney Lee/89 3.00 8.00
98 Jared Sullinger/93 3.00 8.00
99 Anthony Morrow/77 EXCH 3.00 8.00
100 Zaza Pachulia/73 3.00 8.00

2012-13 Elite Series Class Masters

STATED PRINT RUN 99 SER.#'d SETS
1 Yao Ming 5.00 12.00
2 Tim Duncan 6.00 15.00
3 Shawn Marion 2.50 6.00
4 Shaquille O'Neal 8.00 20.00
5 Ray Allen 4.00 10.00
6 Paul Pierce 4.00 10.00
7 Pau Gasol 4.00 10.00
8 LeBron James 400.00 800.00
9 Larry Johnson 3.00 8.00
10 Kobe Bryant 20.00 50.00
11 Kevin Garnett 6.00 15.00
12 Kevin Durant 10.00 25.00
13 John Wall 3.00 8.00
14 Gary Payton 3.00 8.00
15 Elton Brand 2.00 5.00
16 Dwight Howard 3.00 8.00
17 Dirk Nowitzki 6.00 15.00
18 Derrick Rose 4.00 10.00
19 David Robinson 4.00 10.00
20 Carmelo Anthony 4.00 10.00
21 Blake Griffin 2.50 6.00
22 Andrew Bogut 2.00 5.00
23 Andrea Bargnani 1.50 4.00
24 Amar'e Stoudemire 2.50 6.00
25 Allen Iverson 4.00 10.00

2012-13 Elite Series Court Kings Autographs

PRINT RUNS B/WN 25-249 COPIES PER
EXCHANGE DEADLINE 02/21/2015
1 Al Horford/25 15.00 40.00
2 Devin Harris/25 8.00 20.00
3 Dominique Wilkins/99 10.00 25.00
4 Steve Smith/249 4.00 10.00
5 Zaza Pachulia/249 3.00 8.00
6 Jeff Teague/249 EXCH 3.00 8.00
7 Maurice Cheeks/249 4.00 10.00
8 Brook Lopez/25 10.00 25.00
9 Andray Blatche/249 EXCH 3.00 8.00
10 Antoine Walker/249 4.00 10.00
11 Bill Russell/25 1,000.00 2,000.00
12 Brandon Bass/99 3.00 8.00
13 Courtney Lee/249 3.00 8.00
14 J.Sullinger/99 3.00 8.00
16 Leandro Barbosa/249 4.00 10.00
17 Byron Mullens/249 3.00 8.00
18 K.Walker/99 EXCH 12.00 30.00
19 M.Kidd-Gilchrist/81 4.00 10.00
20 Bob Love/249 5.00 12.00
21 Marco Belinelli/249 EXCH 3.00 8.00
22 Scottie Pippen/25 125.00 300.00
23 Toni Kukoc/99 6.00 15.00
24 Zydrunas Ilgauskas/249 4.00 10.00
25 Alonzo Gee/249 3.00 8.00
26 Jim Jackson/249 4.00 10.00
27 Vince Carter/249 10.00 25.00
28 Corey Brewer/249 3.00 8.00
29 Dikembe Mutombo/99 12.00 30.00
30 Andre Miller/99 4.00 10.00
31 Danilo Gallinari/25 10.00 25.00
32 Fat Lever/249 4.00 10.00
33 Andre Drummond/99 15.00 40.00
35 Joe Dumars/25 12.00 30.00
36 Greg Monroe/99 3.00 8.00
37 Carl Landry/99 3.00 8.00
38 Stephen Curry/25 500.00 1,000.00
39 Brandon Rush/249 3.00 8.00
40 Andrew Bogut/99 8.00 20.00
41 Hakeem Olajuwon/25 25.00 60.00
42 George Hill/99 EXCH 4.00 10.00
44 Grant Hill/99 12.00 30.00
45 Caron Butler/25 4.00 10.00
46 Blake Griffin/25 50.00 100.00
47 James Worthy/99 15.00 40.00
48 Antawn Jamison/99 6.00 15.00
49 Kobe Bryant/99 400.00 800.00
50 Magic Johnson/25 60.00 150.00
51 Bob McAdoo/99 4.00 10.00
52 Jerry West/25 40.00 80.00
53 Mike Conley/99 6.00 15.00
55 Alonzo Mourning/99 15.00 40.00
56 Norris Cole/249 EXCH 3.00 8.00
57 Udonis Haslem/249 4.00 10.00
58 Mario Chalmers/99 EXCH 4.00 10.00
59 Larry Sanders/249 3.00 8.00
60 Ersan Ilyasova/249 3.00 8.00
61 Sidney Moncrief/99 3.00 8.00
62 Kevin Love/25 20.00 50.00
63 Chase Budinger/99 3.00 8.00
64 Anthony Davis/25 300.00 600.00
65 Al-Farouq Aminu/249 3.00 8.00
66 Larry Johnson/249 6.00 15.00
67 Ronnie Brewer/249 3.00 8.00
68 Chris Copeland/249 EXCH 3.00 8.00
69 Allan Houston/99 10.00 25.00
71 Kendrick Perkins/99 EXCH 3.00 8.00
72 Kevin Durant/25 75.00 150.00
73 Nick Collison/249 3.00 8.00
74 Kevin Martin/25 10.00 25.00
75 Hedo Turkoglu/99 EXCH 4.00 10.00
76 Nick Anderson/249 4.00 10.00
77 Darryl Dawkins/249 6.00 15.00
78 Jason Richardson/99 EXCH 5.00 12.00
79 Nick Young/99 3.00 8.00
80 Jared Dudley/99 3.00 8.00
81 Kendall Marshall/249 3.00 8.00
82 Bill Walton/25 12.00 30.00
83 LaMarcus Aldridge/25 20.00 50.00
84 Clyde Drexler/25 60.00 120.00
85 J.Crawford/99 EXCH 10.00 25.00
86 Jimmer Fredette/99 5.00 12.00
87 John Salmons/249 4.00 10.00
88 David Robinson/25 75.00 150.00
89 Stephen Jackson/99 4.00 10.00
90 George Gervin/25 10.00 25.00
91 Gary Payton/99 10.00 25.00
92 Sam Perkins/99 4.00 10.00
93 Alan Anderson/249 3.00 8.00
94 Ed Davis/249 EXCH 3.00 8.00
95 Jose Calderon/99 3.00 8.00
96 John Stockton/25 75.00 150.00
97 Gordon Hayward/249 5.00 12.00
98 Marvin Williams/249 3.00 8.00
99 Jordan Crawford/249 EXCH 3.00 8.00
100 Bradley Beal/99 15.00 40.00

2012-13 Elite Series Court Vision

STATED PRINT RUN 49 SER.#'d SETS
1 Andre Miller 3.00 8.00
2 Brandon Jennings 2.50 6.00
3 Brandon Knight 2.50 6.00
4 Chris Paul 8.00 20.00
5 Damian Lillard 60.00 150.00
6 Darren Collison 2.50 6.00
7 Deron Williams 3.00 8.00
8 Derrick Rose 6.00 15.00
9 George Hill 3.00 8.00
10 Goran Dragic 4.00 10.00
11 Jason Kidd 6.00 15.00
12 Jeff Teague 2.50 6.00
13 Jeremy Lin 6.00 15.00
14 Jose Calderon 2.50 6.00
15 Jrue Holiday 5.00 12.00
16 Kobe Bryant 30.00 80.00
17 LeBron James 30.00 80.00
18 Mike Conley 3.00 8.00
19 Rajon Rondo 5.00 12.00
20 Ricky Rubio 3.00 8.00
21 Russell Westbrook 6.00 15.00
22 Stephen Curry 30.00 80.00
23 Steve Nash 8.00 20.00
24 Tony Parker 6.00 15.00
25 Ty Lawson 2.50 6.00

2012-13 Elite Series Electrifying

STATED PRINT RUN 125 SER.#'d SETS
1 Allen Iverson 4.00 10.00
2 Blake Griffin 2.50 6.00
3 Carmelo Anthony 4.00 10.00
4 Chris Bosh 3.00 8.00
5 Chris Paul 5.00 12.00
6 DeMar DeRozan 3.00 8.00
7 Dominique Wilkins 3.00 8.00
8 Harrison Barnes 3.00 8.00
9 James Harden 5.00 12.00
10 John Wall 3.00 8.00
11 Julius Erving 6.00 15.00
12 Kemba Walker 6.00 15.00
13 Kevin Durant 10.00 25.00
14 Kobe Bryant 15.00 40.00
15 LeBron James 25.00 60.00
16 Magic Johnson 8.00 20.00
17 Manu Ginobili 5.00 12.00
18 O.J. Mayo 1.50 4.00
19 Rajon Rondo 3.00 8.00
20 Russell Westbrook 4.00 10.00
21 Stephen Curry 20.00 50.00
23 Tyreke Evans 2.00 5.00
24 Tyson Chandler 2.00 5.00
25 Vince Carter 5.00 12.00

2012-13 Elite Series Elite Glass

1 Kobe Bryant 40.00 100.00
2 Kyrie Irving 12.00 30.00
3 James Harden 4.00 10.00
4 Kevin Durant 8.00 20.00
5 Anthony Davis 60.00 150.00
6 Blake Griffin 2.00 5.00
7 Damian Lillard 60.00 150.00
8 Dwight Howard 2.50 6.00
9 Dirk Nowitzki 5.00 12.00
10 LeBron James 40.00 100.00
11 Kevin Love 2.00 5.00
12 Tim Duncan 5.00 12.00
13 Rajon Rondo 2.50 6.00
14 Derrick Rose 3.00 8.00
15 Carmelo Anthony 3.00 8.00
16 Chris Paul 4.00 10.00
17 Paul Pierce 3.00 8.00
18 Tyson Chandler 1.50 4.00
19 Dwyane Wade 4.00 10.00
20 Russell Westbrook 8.00 20.00
21 Deron Williams 1.50 4.00
22 Joakim Noah 1.50 4.00
23 David Lee 1.25 3.00
24 Kevin Garnett 5.00 12.00
25 Brook Lopez 1.50 4.00

2012-13 Elite Series Elite Glass Gold

*GOLD: .1X TO 2.5X BASIC
1 Kobe Bryant 300.00 600.00
5 Anthony Davis 400.00 800.00
7 Damian Lillard 400.00 800.00
10 LeBron James 300.00 600.00

2012-13 Elite Series Elite Signings

PRINT RUNS B/WN 25-249 COPIES PER
EXCHANGE DEADLINE 02/21/2015
1 Anderson Varejao/25 3.00 8.00
4 Arron Afflalo/25 5.00 12.00
5 Blake Griffin/49 20.00 50.00
6 Bob McAdoo/149 6.00 15.00
7 Brook Lopez/25 4.00 10.00
8 Carlos Boozer/25 6.00 15.00
10 Courtney Lee/25 3.00 8.00
11 Dan Majerle/149 6.00 15.00
12 Derrick Favors/25 4.00 10.00
13 Dikembe Mutombo/149 8.00 20.00
15 George Gervin/25 8.00 20.00
16 George Hill/149 4.00 10.00
17 Grant Hill/49 40.00 80.00
18 Greivis Vasquez/249 3.00 8.00
19 Kevin Love/49 15.00 40.00
20 Hedo Turkoglu/49 EXCH 4.00 10.00
21 Isiah Thomas/25 8.00 20.00
22 Jamaal Tinsley/249 3.00 8.00
23 Jeff Green/49 3.00 8.00
24 Jeff Teague/249 3.00 8.00
25 Joakim Noah/25 4.00 10.00
26 John Henson/25 4.00 10.00
27 Jose Calderon/25 8.00 20.00
28 Kevin Durant/49 60.00 150.00
29 Kirk Hinrich/149 EXCH 4.00 10.00
30 Kyle Lowry/249 5.00 12.00
31 Larry Sanders/249 EXCH 3.00 8.00
32 Leandro Barbosa/249 4.00 10.00
33 Marcus Camby/249 5.00 12.00
34 Mark Aguirre/249 4.00 10.00
35 Marvin Williams/249 3.00 8.00
36 Mitch Richmond/149 10.00 25.00
38 Nick Young/99 3.00 8.00
39 Patrick Patterson/249 3.00 8.00
40 Ralph Sampson/249 4.00 10.00
41 Randy Foye/99 3.00 8.00
42 Raymond Felton/25 3.00 8.00
43 Rolando Blackman/249 4.00 10.00
44 Stephen Curry/25 500.00 1,000.00
45 Thabo Sefolosha/49 3.00 8.00
46 Tristan Thompson/25 5.00 12.00
47 Tyreke Evans/25 4.00 10.00
48 Wesley Matthews/149 3.00 8.00
49 Zach Randolph/25 12.00 30.00
50 Zaza Pachulia/249 EXCH 3.00 8.00

2012-13 Elite Series Glass Masters

1 Blake Griffin 1.25 3.00
2 Kobe Bryant 40.00 100.00
3 Kevin Durant 5.00 12.00
4 Shaquille O'Neal 4.00 10.00
5 Dwyane Wade 2.50 6.00
6 Grant Hill 2.00 5.00
7 Magic Johnson 4.00 10.00
8 Larry Bird 4.00 10.00
9 David Robinson 2.00 5.00
10 LeBron James 40.00 100.00
11 Anfernee Hardaway 3.00 8.00
12 Steve Nash 2.50 6.00
13 Jeremy Lin 2.00 5.00
14 Ricky Rubio 1.00 2.50
15 John Wall 1.50 4.00
16 Hakeem Olajuwon 2.50 6.00

17 Patrick Ewing 2.00 5.00
18 Yao Ming 2.50 6.00
19 LaMarcus Aldridge 1.25 3.00
20 Amar'e Stoudemire 1.25 3.00
21 Drazen Petrovic 1.25 3.00
22 Kyrie Irving 8.00 20.00
23 Anthony Davis 60.00 150.00
24 Damian Lillard 60.00 150.00

2012-13 Elite Series Glass Masters Gold

*GOLD: 1X TO 2.5X BASIC

2012-13 Elite Series Passing the Torch Autographs

PRINT RUNS B/WN 10-25 COPIES PER
EXCHANGE DEADLINE 02/21/2015
1 Durant/Bryant EXCH 400.00 700.00
2 A.Shved/A.Kirilenko 6.00 15.00
3 S.Curry/T.Hardaway 150.00 300.00
4 Drummond/Laimbeer 30.00 60.00
6 Rodman/M.W.Peace 40.00 80.00
7 B.Knight/I.Thomas 12.00 30.00
8 H.Barnes/V.Carter 75.00 150.00
10 Valanciunas/Ilgauskas 10.00 25.00
11 Parsons/Drexler EXCH 30.00 60.00
12 G.Hill/K.Irving 400.00 600.00
13 T.Robinson/R.Sampson 6.00 15.00
14 English/Iguodala EXCH 20.00 50.00
15 A.Mourning/A.Davis 90.00 150.00
16 J.Sullinger/R.Parish 12.00 30.00
17 D.Wilkins/J.Smith 12.00 30.00
18 Hickson/L.Aldridge 8.00 20.00
19 D.Williams/W.Frazier 12.00 30.00
20 I.Shumpert/J.Starks 6.00 15.00
21 A.Bargnani/D.Gallinari 5.00 12.00
22 A.Hardaway/T.Evans 60.00 120.00
23 B.Beal/R.Allen 90.00 150.00
25 M.Jackson/R.Felton 6.00 15.00

2012-13 Elite Series Rookie Elite Series

STATED PRINT RUN 199 SER.#'d SETS
1 Damian Lillard 40.00 100.00
2 Kyrie Irving 12.00 30.00
3 Brandon Knight 1.50 4.00
4 Anthony Davis 20.00 50.00
5 Jared Sullinger 1.25 3.00
6 Tristan Thompson 2.00 5.00
7 Dion Waiters 1.50 4.00
8 Klay Thompson 40.00 100.00
9 Jonas Valanciunas 2.50 6.00
10 Isaiah Thomas 2.50 6.00
11 Thomas Robinson 1.25 3.00
12 Kemba Walker 5.00 12.00
13 Nikola Vucevic 5.00 12.00
14 Jimmer Fredette 2.00 5.00
15 Bradley Beal 10.00 25.00
16 Harrison Barnes 2.50 6.00
17 John Henson 1.50 4.00
18 Chandler Parsons 1.50 4.00
19 Kenneth Faried 1.50 4.00
20 Chris Copeland 1.25 3.00
21 Alexey Shved 1.25 3.00
22 Derrick Williams 1.25 3.00
23 Andre Drummond 3.00 8.00
24 Michael Kidd-Gilchrist 1.50 4.00
25 Kawhi Leonard 20.00 50.00

2012-13 Elite Series Rookie Inscriptions Autographs

EXCHANGE DEADLINE 02/21/2015
1 MarShon Brooks 2.50 6.00
2 Jared Sullinger 2.50 6.00
4 Jeff Taylor 2.50 6.00
5 Kemba Walker EXCH 10.00 25.00
6 Michael Kidd-Gilchrist 3.00 8.00
7 Dion Waiters EXCH 3.00 8.00
8 Kyrie Irving 75.00 200.00
9 Tristan Thompson 4.00 10.00
10 Tyler Zeller 2.50 6.00
11 Jae Crowder 5.00 12.00
12 Evan Fournier 4.00 10.00
13 Kenneth Faried 3.00 8.00
14 Andre Drummond 6.00 15.00
15 Brandon Knight 3.00 8.00
16 Kyle Singler 2.50 6.00
17 Draymond Green 20.00 50.00
18 Harrison Barnes 5.00 12.00
19 Chandler Parsons 3.00 8.00
20 Terrence Jones 2.50 6.00
22 Orlando Johnson 2.50 6.00
23 Robert Sacre 2.50 6.00
24 Norris Cole EXCH 2.50 6.00
25 John Henson 3.00 8.00
26 Tobias Harris 8.00 20.00
27 Alexey Shved 2.50 6.00
28 Derrick Williams 2.50 6.00
29 Anthony Davis 150.00 400.00
30 Austin Rivers EXCH 4.00 10.00
31 Brian Roberts 2.50 6.00
33 Chris Copeland 2.50 6.00
34 Iman Shumpert EXCH 3.00 8.00
35 Andrew Nicholson 2.50 6.00
36 E'Twaun Moore 3.00 8.00
37 Maurice Harkless 3.00 8.00
38 Nikola Vucevic 10.00 25.00
39 Kendall Marshall 2.50 6.00
40 Greg Stiemsma 2.50 6.00
41 Nolan Smith 2.50 6.00
42 Will Barton EXCH 5.00 12.00
43 Isaiah Thomas 5.00 12.00
44 Jimmer Fredette 4.00 10.00
45 Thomas Robinson EXCH 2.50 6.00
46 Kawhi Leonard 60.00 150.00
47 Jonas Valanciunas 5.00 12.00
48 Terrence Ross EXCH 6.00 15.00
49 Alec Burks 4.00 10.00
50 Bradley Beal 12.00 30.00

2012-13 Elite Series Status Autographs

PRINT RUNS B/WN 1-55 COPIES PER
NO PRICING ON QTY 24 OR LESS
EXCHANGE DEADLINE 02/21/2015
8 Ed Davis/32 4.00 10.00
11 Terrence Ross/31 4.00 10.00
12 George Gervin/44 12.00 30.00
13 Nando De Colo/25 8.00 20.00
14 Tiago Splitter/22 12.00 30.00
15 Isaiah Thomas/22 60.00 150.00
23 Kwame Brown/54 4.00 10.00
25 E'Twaun Moore/55 4.00 10.00
36 Austin Rivers/25 8.00 20.00
40 Lance Thomas/42 4.00 10.00
45 John Henson/31 8.00 20.00
49 Udonis Haslem/40 6.00 15.00
52 Kobe Bryant/24 150.00 400.00
54 Blake Griffin/32 50.00 100.00
56 Grant Hill/33 25.00 60.00
57 Danny Granger/33 10.00 25.00
64 Harrison Barnes/40 40.00 80.00
65 Stephen Curry/30 500.00 1,000.00
69 Charlie Villanueva/31 4.00 10.00
76 David Thompson/33 4.00 10.00
77 Chris Kaman/35 6.00 15.00
80 Jon Leuer/30 4.00 10.00
82 Tyler Zeller/40 4.00 10.00
87 Marquis Teague/25 6.00 15.00
91 Jeff Taylor/44 4.00 10.00
96 Brandon Bass/30 4.00 10.00
100 Zaza Pachulia/27 4.00 10.00

2012-13 Elite Series Turn of the Century

STATED PRINT RUN 99 SER.#'d SETS
1 Tyson Chandler 2.00 5.00
2 Zach Randolph 1.50 4.00
3 Yao Ming 3.00 8.00
4 Vlade Divac 1.50 4.00
5 Vince Carter 3.00 8.00
6 Steve Nash 3.00 8.00
7 Dirk Nowitzki 4.00 10.00
8 Kevin Garnett 4.00 10.00
9 Ray Allen 2.50 6.00
10 Pau Gasol 2.50 6.00
11 Paul Pierce 2.50 6.00
12 Lamar Odom 1.25 3.00
13 Kobe Bryant 12.00 30.00
14 Andre Miller 1.25 3.00
15 Elton Brand 1.25 3.00
16 Steve Francis 1.25 3.00
17 Shaquille O'Neal 5.00 12.00
18 Alonzo Mourning 2.50 6.00
19 Tim Duncan 4.00 10.00
20 Marcus Camby 1.50 4.00
21 Jerry Stackhouse 1.25 3.00
22 Grant Hill 2.50 6.00
23 Michael Finley 1.50 4.00
24 Antawn Jamison 1.25 3.00
25 Jason Kidd 2.50 6.00

2012-13 Elite Series Veteran Elite Series

STATED PRINT RUN 199 SER.#'d SETS
1 Blake Griffin 2.00 5.00
2 Chris Paul 4.00 10.00
3 Dirk Nowitzki 5.00 12.00
4 Kobe Bryant 15.00 40.00
5 Steve Nash 4.00 10.00
6 Dwight Howard 2.50 6.00
7 James Harden 4.00 10.00
8 David Lee 1.25 3.00
9 Stephen Curry 15.00 40.00
10 Zach Randolph 2.00 5.00
11 Derrick Rose 3.00 8.00
12 Dwyane Wade 4.00 10.00
13 LeBron James 15.00 40.00
14 Kevin Love 2.00 5.00
15 Deron Williams 1.50 4.00
16 Carmelo Anthony 3.00 8.00
17 Kevin Durant 8.00 20.00
18 Russell Westbrook 3.00 8.00
19 LaMarcus Aldridge 2.00 5.00
20 Tim Duncan 5.00 12.00
21 Tony Parker 3.00 8.00
22 John Wall 2.50 6.00
24 Paul Pierce 3.00 8.00
25 Rajon Rondo 2.50 6.00

2012-13 Elite Series Veteran Inscriptions Autographs

PRINT RUNS B/WN 25-249 COPIES PER
EXCHANGE DEADLINE 02/21/2015
1 Anthony Morrow/249 3.00 8.00
3 Jason Terry/25 6.00 15.00
4 Larry Bird/99 40.00 100.00
6 Gerald Henderson/49 3.00 8.00
7 Larry Johnson/249 6.00 15.00
8 Taj Gibson/49 3.00 8.00
10 Z.Ilgauskas/249 4.00 10.00
12 Vince Carter/49 15.00 40.00
13 Rodney Stuckey/49 3.00 8.00
14 Stephen Curry/25 500.00 1,000.00
15 Chris Mullin/99 10.00 25.00
16 James Harden/25 50.00 120.00
17 S.Francis/49 EXCH 10.00 25.00
18 Hakeem Olajuwon/99 15.00 40.00
19 Sam Cassell/99 4.00 10.00
20 D.Granger/25 EXCH 3.00 8.00
21 George Hill/49 EXCH 4.00 10.00
22 Grant Hill/99 12.00 30.00
23 Blake Griffin/99 20.00 50.00
24 Kobe Bryant/99 400.00 800.00
25 Magic Johnson/99 25.00 60.00
26 R.Horry/49 EXCH 6.00 15.00
27 Antawn Jamison/25 10.00 25.00
28 A.C. Green/49 10.00 25.00
29 Zach Randolph/25 5.00 12.00
31 Udonis Haslem/149 4.00 10.00
32 Glen Rice/25 12.00 30.00
33 Kevin Love/99 8.00 20.00
34 Greivis Vasquez/249 3.00 8.00
35 Ryan Anderson/49 3.00 8.00
36 M.Camby/149 EXCH 6.00 15.00
37 Kevin Durant/99 60.00 150.00
38 LaMarcus Aldridge/25 8.00 20.00
39 J.J. Hickson/149 3.00 8.00
41 David Robinson/99 15.00 40.00
42 Danny Green/249 4.00 10.00
43 Tiago Splitter/149 3.00 8.00
44 Gary Payton/99 15.00 40.00
45 Kyle Lowry/149 5.00 12.00
46 Landry Fields/149 3.00 8.00
48 Bill Laimbeer/249 6.00 15.00
49 J.Crawford/249 EXCH 12.00 30.00
50 Trevor Booker/249 3.00 8.00

1994-95 Embossed

COMPLETE SET (121) 10.00 25.00
1 Stacey Augmon .20 .50
2 Mookie Blaylock .25 .60
3 Ken Norman .15 .40
4 Steve Smith .20 .50
5 Dee Brown .20 .50
6 Blue Edwards .15 .40
7 Dino Radja .15 .40
8 Dominique Wilkins .40 1.00
9 Muggsy Bogues .20 .50
10 Dell Curry .15 .40
11 Larry Johnson .30 .75
12 Alonzo Mourning .40 1.00
13 B.J. Armstrong .25 .60
14 Ron Harper .20 .50
15 Toni Kukoc .30 .75
16 Scottie Pippen .60 1.50
17 Tyrone Hill .15 .40
18 Mark Price .25 .60
19 John Williams .15 .40
20 Jim Jackson .20 .50
21 Popeye Jones .15 .40
22 Jamal Mashburn .25 .60
23 Mahmoud Abdul-Rauf .15 .40
24 LaPhonso Ellis .15 .40
25 Dikembe Mutombo .40 1.00
26 Rodney Rogers .15 .40
27 Joe Dumars .25 .60
28 Lindsey Hunter .15 .40
29 Oliver Miller .15 .40
30 Terry Mills .15 .40
31 Tom Gugliotta .15 .40
32 Tim Hardaway .30 .75
33 Chris Mullin .30 .75
34 Latrell Sprewell .30 .75
35 Sam Cassell FOIL .25 .60
36 Robert Horry FOIL .25 .60
37 Vernon Maxwell FOIL .15 .40
38 Hakeem Olajuwon FOIL .50 1.25
39 Otis Thorpe FOIL .15 .40
40 Mark Jackson .20 .50
41 Reggie Miller .50 1.25
42 Rik Smits .20 .50
43 Terry Dehere .15 .40
44 Stanley Roberts .15 .40
45 Loy Vaught .15 .40
46 Vlade Divac .25 .60
47 George Lynch .15 .40
48 Nick Van Exel .25 .60
49 Billy Owens .15 .40
50 Glen Rice .25 .60
51 Kevin Willis .20 .50
52 Vin Baker .25 .60
53 Todd Day .15 .40
54 Eric Murdock .15 .40
55 Christian Laettner .20 .50
56 Isaiah Rider .25 .60
57 Micheal Williams .15 .40
58 Kenny Anderson .20 .50
59 P.J. Brown .15 .40
60 Derrick Coleman .25 .60
61 Chris Morris .15 .40
62 Patrick Ewing .40 1.00
63 Derek Harper .20 .50
64 Anthony Mason .20 .50
65 Charles Oakley .25 .60
66 John Starks .25 .60
67 Horace Grant .25 .60
68 Anfernee Hardaway .50 1.25
69 Shaquille O'Neal 1.00 2.50
70 Dennis Scott .20 .50
71 Shawn Bradley .15 .40
72 Jeff Malone .15 .40
73 Clarence Weatherspoon .15 .40
74 Charles Barkley .60 1.50
75 Kevin Johnson .25 .60
76 Dan Majerle .25 .60
77 Danny Manning .20 .50
78 Wayman Tisdale .15 .40
79 Clyde Drexler .40 1.00
80 Clifford Robinson .20 .50
81 Rod Strickland .15 .40
82 Bobby Hurley .15 .40
83 Olden Polynice .15 .40
84 Mitch Richmond .30 .75
85 Spud Webb .20 .50
86 Sean Elliott .20 .50
87 Chuck Person .20 .50
88 David Robinson .50 1.25
89 Dennis Rodman .60 1.50
90 Kendall Gill .15 .40
91 Shawn Kemp .40 1.00
92 Sarunas Marciulionis .15 .40
93 Gary Payton .40 1.00
94 Detlef Schrempf .25 .60
95 Jeff Hornacek .25 .60
96 Karl Malone .50 1.25
97 John Stockton .50 1.25
98 Don MacLean .15 .40
99 Scott Skiles .15 .40
100 Chris Webber .50 1.25
101 Glenn Robinson FOIL RC .50 1.25
102 Jason Kidd FOIL RC 1.25 3.00
103 Grant Hill FOIL RC 1.25 3.00
104 Donyell Marshall FOIL RC .25 .60
105 Juwan Howard FOIL RC .40 1.00
106 Sharone Wright FOIL RC .20 .50
107 Lamond Murray FOIL RC .20 .50
108 Brian Grant FOIL RC .40 1.00
109 Eric Montross FOIL RC .20 .50
110 Eddie Jones FOIL RC .75 2.00
111 Carlos Rogers FOIL RC .20 .50
112 Khalid Reeves FOIL RC .20 .50
113 Jalen Rose FOIL RC .60 1.50
114 Yinka Dare FOIL RC .15 .40
115 Eric Piatkowski FOIL RC .15 .40
116 Clifford Rozier FOIL RC .15 .40
117 Aaron McKie FOIL RC .15 .40
118 Eric Mobley FOIL RC .15 .40
119 Tony Dumas FOIL RC .20 .50
120 B.J. Tyler FOIL RC .15 .40
121 Michael Jordan 4.00 10.00

1994-95 Embossed Golden Idols

COMPLETE SET (121) 25.00 60.00
*GOLD: .8X TO 2X BASIC CARDS
121 Michael Jordan 12.00 30.00

1994-95 Emotion

COMPLETE SET (121) 12.00 30.00
1 Stacey Augmon .30 .75
2 Mookie Blaylock .40 1.00
3 Steve Smith .30 .75
4 Greg Minor RC .40 1.00
5 Eric Montross RC .30 .75
6 Dino Radja .25 .60
7 Dominique Wilkins .60 1.50
8 Muggsy Bogues .30 .75
9 Larry Johnson .50 1.25
10 Alonzo Mourning .60 1.50
11 B.J. Armstrong .40 1.00
12 Toni Kukoc .50 1.25
13 Scottie Pippen 1.00 2.50
14 Dickey Simpkins RC .30 .75
15 Tyrone Hill .25 .60
16 Chris Mills .30 .75
17 Mark Price .40 1.00
18 Tony Dumas RC .30 .75
19 Jim Jackson .30 .75
20 Jason Kidd RC 2.00 5.00
21 Jamal Mashburn .40 1.00
22 LaPhonso Ellis .25 .60
23 Dikembe Mutombo .60 1.50
24 Rodney Rogers .25 .60
25 Jalen Rose RC 1.00 2.50
26 Bill Curley RC .25 .60
27 Joe Dumars .40 1.00
28 Grant Hill RC 2.00 5.00
29 Tim Hardaway .50 1.25
30 Donyell Marshall RC .40 1.00
31 Chris Mullin .50 1.25
32 Carlos Rogers RC .30 .75
33 Clifford Rozier RC .25 .60
34 Latrell Sprewell .50 1.25
35 Sam Cassell .40 1.00
36 Clyde Drexler .60 1.50
37 Robert Horry .40 1.00
38 Hakeem Olajuwon .75 2.00
39 Mark Jackson .30 .75
40 Reggie Miller .75 2.00
41 Rik Smits .30 .75
42 Lamond Murray RC .40 1.00
43 Eric Piatkowski RC .40 1.00
44 Loy Vaught .25 .60
45 Cedric Ceballos .30 .75
46 Eddie Jones RC 1.25 3.00
47 George Lynch .25 .60
48 Nick Van Exel .40 1.00
49 Harold Miner .25 .60
50 Khalid Reeves RC .30 .75
51 Glen Rice .40 1.00
52 Kevin Willis .30 .75
53 Vin Baker .40 1.00
54 Eric Mobley RC .25 .60
55 Eric Murdock .25 .60
56 Glenn Robinson RC .75 2.00
57 Tom Gugliotta .30 .75
58 Christian Laettner .40 1.00
59 Isaiah Rider .40 1.00
60 Kenny Anderson .30 .75
61 Derrick Coleman .40 1.00
62 Yinka Dare RC .25 .60
63 Patrick Ewing .60 1.50
64 John Starks .30 .75
65 Charlie Ward RC .40 1.00
66 Monty Williams RC .50 1.25
67 Nick Anderson .25 .60
68 Horace Grant .40 1.00
69 Anfernee Hardaway .75 2.00
70 Shaquille O'Neal 1.50 4.00
71 Brooks Thompson RC .30 .75
72 Dana Barros .25 .60
73 Shawn Bradley .25 .60
74 B.J. Tyler RC .25 .60
75 Clarence Weatherspoon .25 .60
76 Sharone Wright RC .30 .75
77 Charles Barkley 1.00 2.50
78 Kevin Johnson .40 1.00
79 Dan Majerle .40 1.00
80 Danny Manning .40 1.00
81 Wesley Person RC .30 .75
82 Aaron McKie RC .40 1.00
83 Clifford Robinson .30 .75
84 Rod Strickland .25 .60
85 Brian Grant RC .60 1.50
86 Bobby Hurley .25 .60
87 Mitch Richmond .50 1.25
88 Sean Elliott .30 .75
89 David Robinson .75 2.00
90 Dennis Rodman 1.00 2.50
91 Shawn Kemp .60 1.50
92 Gary Payton .60 1.50
93 Dontonio Wingfield RC .40 1.00
94 Jeff Hornacek .30 .75
95 Karl Malone .75 2.00
96 John Stockton .75 2.00
97 Calbert Cheaney .25 .60
98 Juwan Howard RC .60 1.50
99 Chris Webber .75 2.00
100 Michael Jordan 10.00 25.00
101 Brian Grant ROO .60 1.50
102 Grant Hill ROO 2.00 5.00
103 Juwan Howard ROO .60 1.50
104 Eddie Jones ROO 1.25 3.00
105 Jason Kidd ROO 2.00 5.00
106 Eric Montross ROO .30 .75
107 Lamond Murray ROO .40 1.00
108 Wesley Person ROO .40 1.00
109 Glenn Robinson ROO .75 2.00
110 Sharone Wright ROO .30 .75
111 Anfernee Hardaway MAS .75 2.00
112 Shawn Kemp MAS .60 1.50
113 Karl Malone MAS .75 2.00
114 Alonzo Mourning MAS .60 1.50
115 Shaquille O'Neal MAS 1.50 4.00
116 Hakeem Olajuwon MAS .75 2.00
117 Scottie Pippen MAS 1.00 2.50
118 David Robinson MAS .75 2.00
119 Latrell Sprewell MAS .50 1.25
120 Chris Webber MAS .75 2.00
121 Checklist .25 .60
NNO Grant Hill
David Robinson Promo 1.00 2.50
NNO G.Hill SkyMotion Exch. 20.00 50.00

1994-95 Emotion N-Tense

COMPLETE SET (10) 125.00 300.00
STATED ODDS 1:18
1 Charles Barkley 10.00 25.00
2 Patrick Ewing 5.00 12.00
3 Michael Jordan 125.00 300.00
4 Shawn Kemp 5.00 12.00
5 Karl Malone 6.00 15.00
6 Alonzo Mourning 5.00 12.00
7 Shaquille O'Neal 15.00 40.00
8 Hakeem Olajuwon 10.00 25.00
9 David Robinson 10.00 25.00
10 Glenn Robinson 6.00 15.00

1994-95 Emotion X-Cited

COMPLETE SET (20) 10.00 25.00
STATED ODDS 1:4
X1 Kenny Anderson .50 1.25
X2 Anfernee Hardaway 1.25 3.00
X3 Tim Hardaway .75 2.00
X4 Grant Hill 3.00 8.00
X5 Jim Jackson .50 1.25
X6 Eddie Jones 2.00 5.00
X7 Jason Kidd 3.00 8.00
X8 Dan Majerle .60 1.50
X9 Jamal Mashburn .60 1.50
X10 Lamond Murray .60 1.50
X11 Gary Payton 1.00 2.50
X12 Wesley Person .60 1.50
X13 Scottie Pippen 1.50 4.00
X14 Mark Price .75 2.00
X15 Mitch Richmond .75 2.00
X16 Isaiah Rider .60 1.50
X17 Latrell Sprewell .75 2.00
X18 John Stockton 1.25 3.00
X19 Rod Strickland .40 1.00
X20 Nick Van Exel .60 1.50

2001 eTopps

1 Darius Miles/795 1.00 2.50
2 Glenn Robinson/474 3.00 8.00
3 Allen Iverson/4368 1.00 2.50
4 Derek Anderson/635 1.00 2.50
5 David Robinson/931 4.00 10.00
6 Gary Payton/640 2.50 6.00
7 Baron Davis/521 2.50 6.00
8 Antoine Walker/763 1.25 3.00
9 Jerry Stackhouse/400 6.00 15.00
10 Vince Carter/2871 1.00 2.50
11 Shawn Marion/2000 1.00 2.50
12 Grant Hill/542 2.50 6.00
13 Kenyon Martin/646 1.50 4.00
14 Eddie Jones/572 1.00 2.50
15 Kobe Bryant/5000 6.00 15.00
16 Michael Finley/1880 1.00 2.50
17 Andre Miller/688 1.25 3.00
18 Peja Stojakovic/1151 1.00 2.50
19 Richard Hamilton/1237 1.00 2.50
20 Steve Francis/841 1.50 4.00
21 Tracy McGrady/758 1.50 4.00
22 Jason Kidd/722 1.25 3.00
23 Lamar Odom/497 1.50 4.00
24 Antawn Jamison/451 2.50 6.00
25 Paul Pierce/797 1.50 4.00
26 Alonzo Mourning/519 2.50 6.00
27 Marcus Camby/810 1.25 3.00
28 Stephon Marbury/418 15.00 30.00
29 Morris Peterson/642 1.25 3.00
30 Tim Duncan/608 5.00 12.00
31 Jason Terry/605 1.25 3.00
32 Reggie Miller/678 6.00 15.00
33 Patrick Ewing/1497 1.25 3.00
34 Shaquille O'Neal/2270 1.50 4.00
35 Ray Allen/1153 1.25 3.00
36 Allan Houston/459 2.50 6.00
37 Dikembe Mutombo/532 2.00 5.00
38 Mike Bibby/638 1.25 3.00
39 Karl Malone/1015 8.00 20.00
40 Chris Webber/473 2.50 6.00
41 Wang Zhizhi/927 1.50 4.00
42 Elton Brand/648 1.50 4.00
43 Antonio McDyess/424 4.00 10.00
44 Shareef Abdur-Rahim/531 2.50 6.00
45 Jamal Mashburn/490 2.00 5.00
46 Jermaine O'Neal/561 2.50 6.00
47 Latrell Sprewell/1009 1.00 2.50
48 Mike Miller/625 2.50 6.00
49 John Stockton/797 2.50 6.00
50 Kevin Garnett/855 4.00 10.00
51 Hakeem Olajuwon/422 8.00 20.00
52 Dirk Nowitzki/1051 3.00 8.00
53 Rasheed Wallace/664 1.25 3.00
54 Kwame Brown/2640 1.00 2.50
55 Tyson Chandler/953 1.00 2.50
56 Pau Gasol/2262 1.25 3.00
57 Eddy Curry/894 1.00 2.50
58 Jason Richardson/1689 1.00 2.50
59 Shane Battier/1784 1.00 2.50
60 Eddie Griffin/869 15.00 40.00
61 Desagana Diop/649 1.00 2.50
62 Rodney White/491 1.50 4.00
63 Joe Johnson/2005 1.00 2.50
64 Kedrick Brown/573 1.25 3.00
65 Vladimir Radmanovic/711 1.00 2.50
66 Richard Jefferson/1915 1.00 2.50
67 Troy Murphy/545 1.25 3.00
68 Joseph Forte/640 1.25 3.00
69 Gerald Wallace/906 1.25 3.00
70 Tony Parker/2165 1.25 3.00
71 Jamaal Tinsley/2423 1.00 2.50
72 Loren Woods/594 1.00 2.50

2002 eTopps

1 Shaquille O'Neal/2273 2.00 5.00
2 Richard Jefferson/1349 1.00 2.50
3 Tracy McGrady/2090 1.00 2.50
4 Steve Francis/1075 1.00 2.50
5 Dirk Nowitzki/2140 1.25 3.00
6 Paul Pierce/1500 1.00 2.50
7 Ben Wallace/1682 1.00 2.50
8 Ray Allen/1129 1.00 2.50
9 Kevin Garnett/1707 1.00 2.50
10 Jermaine O'Neal/1177 1.00 2.50
11 Vince Carter/1889 1.00 2.50
12 Tim Duncan/1089 1.25 3.00
13 Nikoloz Tskitishvili/1468 1.00 2.50
14 Juan Dixon/3000 1.00 2.50
15 Marcus Haislip/1801 1.00 2.50
16 Mike Dunleavy/2859 1.00 2.50
17 Dan Dickau/2000 1.00 2.50
18 Nene Hilario/3000 1.00 2.50
19 Kareem Rush/2000 1.00 2.50
20 Caron Butler/3000 1.00 2.50
21 Jason Terry/1500 1.00 2.50
22 Elton Brand/801 1.00 2.50
23 Shane Battier/1415 1.00 2.50
24 Kenyon Martin/1087 1.00 2.50
25 Jerry Stackhouse/911 1.00 2.50
26 Eddy Curry/1500 1.00 2.50
27 Allen Iverson/1212 1.00 2.50
28 Chris Webber/1500 1.00 2.50
29 Gary Payton/1089 1.00 2.50
30 Mike Bibby/1280 1.00 2.50
31 Wally Szczerbiak/1072 1.50 4.00
32 Shawn Marion/1906 1.00 2.50
33 Jared Jeffries/1875 1.00 2.50
34 Fred Jones/2000 1.00 2.50
35 Drew Gooden/4000 1.00 2.50
36 Jay Williams/3000 1.00 2.50
37 Frank Williams/1864 1.00 2.50
38 Qyntel Woods/2000 1.00 2.50
39 Chris Wilcox/2000 1.00 2.50
40 Casey Jacobsen/1973 1.00 2.50
41 John Stockton/1500 1.00 2.50
42 Rasheed Wallace/762 1.00 2.50
43 Baron Davis/1000 1.00 2.50
44 Grant Hill/1093 1.00 2.50
45 Kobe Bryant/2000 6.00 15.00
46 Jason Richardson/1370 1.00 2.50
47 Andre Miller/722 1.00 2.50
48 Antoine Walker/1585 1.00 2.50
49 Shareef Abdur-Rahim/700 1.00 2.50
50 Tony Parker/1378 2.00 5.00
51 Jason Kidd/1266 1.00 2.50
52 Darius Miles/1108 1.00 2.50
53 Yao Ming/6000 1.00 2.50
54 Manu Ginobili/2000 1.00 2.50
55 John Salmons/1268 1.00 2.50
56 Melvin Ely/1611 1.00 2.50
57 Dajuan Wagner/4000 1.00 2.50
58 Amare Stoudemire/4000 1.00 2.50
59 Bostjan Nachbar/1851 1.00 2.50
60 Marko Jaric/1533 1.00 2.50
61 Antonio McDyess/951 1.00 2.50
62 Pau Gasol/1097 1.00 2.50
63 Steve Nash/2675 1.00 2.50
64 Karl Malone/1500 1.00 2.50
65 Richard Hamilton/738 1.00 2.50
66 Peja Stojakovic/1507 1.00 2.50
67 Jamal Mashburn/641 2.00 5.00
68 Glenn Robinson/1034 1.25 3.00
69 Jamaal Tinsley/1034 1.25 3.00
70 Tyson Chandler/1500 1.00 2.50
71 Jerome Williams/1219 1.00 2.50
72 Latrell Sprewell/1000 1.00 2.50
73 Scottie Pippen/1050 1.50 4.00
74 Ricky Davis/1145 1.00 2.50
75 Carlos Boozer/2309 1.00 2.50
76 Andrei Kirilenko/1254 1.00 2.50
77 Gordan Giricek 1.00 2.50
78 Gilbert Arenas/2000 1.00 2.50

2003 eTopps

1 Tim Duncan/740 1.50 4.00
2 Michael Redd/853 1.00 2.50
3 Antawn Jamison/500 1.00 2.50
4 Allan Houston/523 1.00 2.50
5 Kobe Bryant/1371 25.00 60.00
6 Matt Harpring/635 1.25 3.00
7 Kevin Garnett/664 2.50 6.00
8 Dirk Nowitzki/1000 1.00 2.50
10 Jason Richardson/764 1.00 2.50
11 Amare Stoudemire/554 2.00 5.00
12 Chris Webber/589 2.50 6.00
13 Larry Hughes/717 1.00 2.50
14 Alonzo Mourning/1000 1.00 2.50
15 Yao Ming/1105 1.50 4.00
16 Ron Artest/450 2.50 6.00
17 Kenyon Martin/760 1.00 2.50
19 Stephon Marbury/509 1.25 3.00
20 Shaquille O'Neal/1070 20.00 50.00
21 Jermaine O'Neal/934 1.25 3.00
22 Drew Gooden/392 1.25 3.00
23 Tony Parker/626 3.00 8.00
24 Vince Carter/622 1.25 3.00
25 Jason Kidd/693 4.00 10.00
26 Caron Butler/602 1.50 4.00
27 Paul Pierce/775 1.25 3.00
28 Steve Nash/615 1.00 2.50
29 Al Harrington/642 1.00 2.50
30 Allen Iverson/949 15.00 40.00
31 Troy Hudson/803 1.00 2.50
32 Troy Murphy/607 1.00 2.50
33 Nene/744 1.00 2.50
34 Zydrunas Ilgauskas/558 1.00 2.50
35 Steve Francis/675 2.00 5.00
36 Ray Allen/900 1.00 2.50
37 Bobby Jackson/562 1.00 2.50
38 Ben Wallace/1000 1.00 2.50
39 Quentin Richardson/605 1.00 2.50
40 Tracy McGrady/812 1.00 2.50
41 Shareef Abdur-Rahim/546 1.25 3.00
42 Gary Payton/1000 1.50 4.00
43 LeBron James/10000 400.00 800.00
44 Darko Milicic/1789 1.00 2.50
45 Carmelo Anthony/5000 60.00 150.00
46 Chris Bosh/1571 15.00 40.00
47 Dwyane Wade/1208 500.00 1,000.00
48 Chris Kaman/641 1.00 2.50
49 Kirk Hinrich/686 1.25 3.00
50 T.J. Ford/1500 1.00 2.50
51 Mike Sweetney/910 1.00 2.50
52 Jarvis Hayes/922 1.00 2.50
53 Mickael Pietrus/902 1.00 2.50
54 Nick Collison/1000 1.00 2.50
55 Marcus Banks/687 1.00 2.50
56 Luke Ridnour/874 1.00 2.50
57 Reece gaines/982 1.00 2.50
58 Troy Bell/821 1.00 2.50
59 Zarko Cabarkapa/641 1.00 2.50
60 David West/876 1.00 2.50
61 Aleksandar Pavlovic/618 1.00 2.50
62 Dahntay Jones/798 1.00 2.50
63 Boris Diaw/701 1.00 2.50
64 Zoran Planinic/573 1.00 2.50
65 Travis Outlaw/798 1.00 2.50
66 Brian Cook/768 1.00 2.50
67 Ndudi Ebi/1000 1.00 2.50
68 Kendrick Perkins/857 1.00 2.50
69 Jason Kapono/547 1.00 2.50
70 Luke Walton/1203 1.00 2.50
71 Leandro Barbosa/1000 1.00 2.50
72 Steve Blake/690 1.00 2.50
73 Josh Howard/1000 1.00 2.50
74 Carlos Arroyo/1000 1.00 2.50
75 Zach Randolph/1250 1.00 2.50
76 Brad Miller/1000 1.00 2.50
77 Desmond Mason/918 1.00 2.50
78 Chauncey Billups/977 1.50 4.00
79 Sam Cassell/1000 1.00 2.50
80 Rashard Lewis/923 1.00 2.50

2004 eTopps

1 Miami Heat/1000 1.00 2.50
2 Detroit Pistons/1000 1.00 2.50
3 Cleveland Cavaliers/1000 6.00 15.00
4 Denver Nuggets/1000 1.00 2.50
5 New York Knicks/605 1.00 2.50
6 Dallas Mavericks/1000 1.00 2.50
7 Minnesota Timberwolves/928 1.00 2.50
8 Phoenix Suns/945 1.00 2.50
9 Toronto Raptors/559 2.00 5.00
10 Seattle Supersonics/925 1.50 4.00
11 Utah Jazz/748 1.50 4.00
12 Boston Celtics/688 1.00 2.50
13 Sacramento Kings/766 1.00 2.50
14 Orlando Magic/770 1.00 2.50
15 Indiana Pacers/745 1.00 2.50
16 San Antonio Spurs/950 1.00 2.50
17 Memphis Grizzlies/640 1.00 2.50
18 Los Angeles Lakers/850 5.00 12.00
19 Charlotte Bobcats/950 1.00 2.50
20 Houston Rockets/511 1.50 4.00
21 Golden State Warriors/531 2.00 5.00
22 Chicago Bulls/750 1.50 4.00
23 Atlanta Hawks/499 8.00 20.00
24 Los Angeles Clippers/719 1.00 2.50
25 Milwaukee Bucks/654 1.00 2.50
26 New Jersey Nets/673 1.00 2.50
27 New Orleans Hornets/688 1.00 2.50
28 Philadelphia 76ers/700 1.00 2.50
29 Portland Trail Blazers/700 1.00 2.50
30 Washington Wizards/700 1.00 2.50
31 Tracy McGrady/1000 1.00 2.50
32 Kenyon Martin/1000 1.00 2.50
33 LeBron James/2000 12.00 30.00
34 Carmelo Anthony/2000 1.00 2.50
35 Dwight Howard/3000 4.00 10.00
36 Emeka Okafor/3000 1.00 2.50
37 Shaquille O'Neal/2000 1.00 2.50
38 Ben Gordon/2000 1.00 2.50
39 Devin Harris/1362 1.00 2.50
40 Kris Humphries/839 1.00 2.50
41 Andre Iguodala/982 1.50 4.00
42 Luke Jackson/1366 1.00 2.50
43 Al Jefferson/1000 1.00 2.50
44 Josh Childress/1220 1.00 2.50
45 Jameer Nelson/1000 2.00 5.00
46 Kobe Bryant/1000 8.00 20.00
47 Kirk Snyder/896 1.00 2.50
48 Sebastian Telfair/1756 1.00 2.50
49 Andris Biedrins/668 1.50 4.00
50 Shaun Livingston/2000 1.00 2.50
51 Robert Swift/813 1.00 2.50
52 Rafael Araujo/877 1.00 2.50
53 Lamar Odom/560 1.00 2.50
54 Luol Deng/1000 1.00 2.50
55 J.R. Smith/1000 1.00 2.50
56 Trevor Ariza/1000 1.00 2.50
57 Dwyane Wade/2000 4.00 10.00
58 Peter John Ramos/626 1.00 2.50
59 Carlos Arroyo/633 1.00 2.50
60 Amare Stoudemire/1000 1.00 2.50
61 Jamal Crawford/739 1.00 2.50
62 Quentin Richardson/548 1.00 2.50
63 Marquis Daniels/688 1.00 2.50
64 Corey Maggette/672 1.00 2.50
65 Yao Ming/1000 1.25 3.00
66 Samuel Dalembert/578 1.50 4.00
67 David Harrison/814 1.00 2.50
68 Chris Duhon/963 1.00 2.50
69 Bonzi Wells/580 1.00 2.50
70 Kevin Garnett/1000 1.00 2.50
71 Dirk Nowitzki/800 1.00 2.50
72 Josh Smith/800 2.00 5.00
73 Allen Iverson/604 1.00 2.50
74 Tim Duncan/1000 1.25 3.00
75 Kyle Korver/800 1.00 2.50
76 Rashard Lewis/800 1.00 2.50
78 Stephon Marbury/800 1.00 2.50

2005 eTopps

1 Al Harrington/463 1.25 3.00
2 Paul Pierce/527 3.00 8.00
3 Emeka Okafor/672 1.00 2.50
4 Kirk Hinrich/690 1.00 2.50
5 Lebron James/1000 15.00 40.00
6 Dirk Nowitzki/577 1.50 4.00
7 Carmelo Anthony/1000 1.00 2.50
8 Ben Wallace/605 1.00 2.50
9 Baron Davis/594 1.00 2.50
10 Yao Ming/695 2.00 5.00
11 Jermaine O'Neal/602 2.00 5.00
12 Elton Brand/620 1.00 2.50
13 Kobe Bryant/1000 8.00 20.00
14 Pau Gasol/551 1.00 2.50
15 Dwyane Wade/1500 1.25 3.00
16 Desmond Mason/461 1.50 4.00
17 Kevin Garnett/1000 1.25 3.00
18 Vince Carter/645 1.00 2.50
19 J.R. Smith/534 3.00 8.00
20 Stephon Marbury/529 1.00 2.50
21 Dwight Howard/937 1.25 3.00
22 Allen Iverson/905 1.00 2.50
23 Steve Nash/641 1.00 2.50
24 Zach Randolph/481 1.25 3.00
25 Mike Bibby/564 1.00 2.50

26 Tim Duncan/983 1.25 3.00
27 Ray Allen/602 1.25 3.00
28 Chris Bosh/525 1.50 4.00
29 Carlos Boozer/490 1.25 3.00
30 Gilbert Arenas/702 1.00 2.50
31 Bobby Simmons/504 1.00 2.50
32 Andres Nocioni/590 1.00 2.50
33 Udonis Haslem/544 1.00 2.50
34 Tayshaun Prince/685 1.00 2.50
35 Primoz Brezec/512 1.00 2.50
36 Nenad Krstic/554 1.00 2.50
37 Rafer Alston/493 1.00 2.50
38 Damon Jones/528 1.00 2.50
39 Brent Barry/525 1.00 2.50
40 Earl Boykins/500 1.50 4.00
41 Gerald Green/1500 1.00 2.50
42 Francisco Garcia/1000 1.00 2.50
43 Joey Graham/579 1.00 2.50
44 Deron Williams/1334 2.00 5.00
45 Andrew Bogut/2000 1.00 2.50
46 Chris Paul/2000 75.00 200.00
47 Hakim Warrick/1000 1.00 2.50
48 Antoine Wright/662 1.00 2.50
49 Rashad McCants/1000 1.00 2.50
50 Sarunas Jasikevicius/847 1.00 2.50
51 Channing Frye/1000 1.00 2.50
52 Ike Diogu/945 1.00 2.50
53 Danny Granger/1000 3.00 8.00
54 Charlie Villanueva/906 1.00 2.50
55 Andrew Bynum/844 4.00 10.00
56 Marvin Williams/2000 1.00 2.50
57 Raymond Felton/1156 1.00 2.50
58 Martell Webster/1000 1.00 2.50
59 Sean May/1000 1.00 2.50
60 Julius Hodge/565 1.00 2.50

2005 eTopps Autographs

AI1 Allen Iverson
2001 eTopps/40* 50.00 125.00
AI2 Allen Iverson
2002 eTopps/40* 50.00 125.00
AI3 Allen Iverson
2003 eTopps/40* 50.00 125.00
DW1 Dwyane Wade
2003 eTopps/63* 75.00 150.00
ES1 Steve Nash
Dwyane Wade
2005 eTopps Event Series 200.00 350.00

2005 eTopps Classic

1 Bill Russell/1500 2.50 6.00
2 Elgin Baylor/925 3.00 8.00
4 Oscar Robertson/934 3.00 8.00
5 Willis Reed/672 2.50 6.00
6 Spud Webb/506 2.50 6.00
7 Bill Walton/768 3.00 8.00
8 Chris Mullin/525 3.00 8.00
9 Darryl Dawkins/537 3.00 8.00
10 Earl Monroe/562 3.00 8.00
11 Hal Greer/563 3.00 8.00
12 John Havlicek/759 3.00 8.00
13 Moses Malone/670 2.50 6.00
14 Phil Jackson/589 3.00 8.00
15 Robert Parish/586 2.50 6.00
16 Gail Goodrich/485 5.00 12.00
17 Dolph Schayes/579 2.50 6.00
18 Manute Bol/519 2.50 6.00
19 Bob Pettit/496 4.00 10.00
20 Tom Heinsohn/592 3.00 8.00
21 Magic Johnson/1000 4.00 10.00
22 Dominique Wilkins/635 3.00 8.00
23 Isiah Thomas/941 3.00 8.00
24 Dennis Rodman/849 4.00 10.00

2005 eTopps Playoffs

1 Suns and Heat Sweep/514 1.25 3.00
2 Steve Nash/679 .75 2.00
3 Reggie Miller/1000 2.50 6.00
4 Tony Parker/706 .75 2.00
5 Rasheed Wallace/560 1.00 2.50
6 Robert Horry/609 1.25 3.00
7 Spurs Regain the Throne/1000 .75 2.00
8 Tim Duncan/950 1.25 3.00

2006 eTopps

1 Dwyane Wade/999 1.50 4.00
2 Amare Stoudemire/425 2.50 6.00
2 Chris Paul/999 25.00 60.00
3 Andrea Bargnani/1499 1.00 2.50
4 Randy Foye/999 1.00 2.50
5 Craig Smith/799 1.00 2.50
6 Allen Iverson/655 1.00 2.50
7 Lebron James/999 15.00 40.00
8 Tyrus Thomas/799 1.00 2.50
9 Adam Morrison/999 1.00 2.50
10 Jordan Farmar/799 1.00 2.50
11 Marcus Williams/799 1.00 2.50
12 Brandon Roy/799 2.50 6.00
13 Dirk Nowitzki/499 2.50 6.00
14 Kevin Garnett/799 1.25 3.00
15 Rudy Gay/999 1.25 3.00
16 Rajon Rondo/1025 4.00 10.00
17 Shelden Williams/799 1.00 2.50
19 Kobe Bryant/999 8.00 20.00
20 Lamarcus Aldridge/799 2.50 6.00
21 Allan Ray/799 1.00 2.50
22 J.J. Redick/799 1.00 2.50
23 Rodney Carney/799 1.00 2.50
24 Tim Duncan/405 4.00 10.00
25 Vince Carter/699 1.00 2.50
26 Tracy McGrady/699 1.00 2.50
27 Renaldo Balkman/699 1.00 2.50
28 Josh Boone/699 1.00 2.50
29 Daniel Gibson/699 1.00 2.50
30 Shaquille O'Neal/413 6.00 15.00
31 Carmelo Anthony/699 1.00 2.50
32 Ronnie Brewer/699 1.00 2.50
33 Patrick O'Bryant/699 1.00 2.50
34 Hilton Armstrong/699 1.00 2.50
35 Alexander Johnson/699 1.00 2.50
36 Steve Nash/434 2.00 5.00
37 David Lee/499 1.50 4.00
38 Paul Millsap/699 1.00 2.50
39 Thabo Sefolosha/699 1.00 2.50
40 Kyle Lowry/599 1.50 4.00
41 Jorge Garbajosa/699 1.00 2.50
42 Yao Ming/399 6.00 15.00

2006 eTopps Playoffs

9 Dwyane Wade/1161 1.00 2.50

2006 eTopps Autographs

CA1 Carmelo Anthony 2006
eTopps McDonald's/72 25.00 60.00
CP1 Chris Paul 2006
eTopps McDonald's/112 200.00 500.00
DR1 Dennis Rodman 2005
eTopps Classic/50 20.00 50.00

2006 eTopps McDonald's

1 Jermaine O'Neal 2.00 5.00
2 Chris Paul 25.00 60.00
3 Kenny Smith 3.00 8.00
4 Carmelo Anthony 2.50 6.00
5 Shaheen Holloway 3.00 8.00
6 Shaquille O'Neal 1.50 4.00
7 Magic Johnson 1.50 4.00
10 Elton Brand 2.00 5.00
11 Chris Collins 2.00 5.00
12 Tommy Amaker 2.00 5.00
13 Richard Hamilton 1.50 4.00
14 Vince Carter 1.50 4.00
15 Corey Maggette 1.50 4.00
16 Charlie Villanueva 1.50 4.00

2007 eTopps

1 Jermaine O'Neal/699 1.25 3.00
2 Rashard Lewis/699 1.00 2.50
3 Al Horford/999 1.50 4.00
4 Luis Scola/799 1.00 2.50
5 Mike Conley/999 1.00 2.50
6 Kevin Garnett/544 2.00 5.00
7 Chris Paul/699 20.00 50.00
8 Yi Jianlian/999 1.00 2.50
9 Sean Williams/699 1.00 2.50
10 Ray Allen/699 1.00 2.50
11 Greg Oden/1499 1.25 3.00
12 Javaris Crittenton/599 1.00 2.50
13 Dwight Howard/749 1.25 3.00
14 Carmelo Anthony/699 1.25 3.00
15 Glen Davis/749 1.25 3.00
16 Nick Young/749 1.25 3.00
17 Jason Richardson/699 1.00 2.50
18 Kobe Bryant/999 10.00 25.00
19 Kevin Durant/1499 600.00 1,200.00
20 Zach Randolph/352 8.00 20.00
21 Julian Wright/749 1.00 2.50
22 Joakim Noah/749 1.50 4.00
23 Deron Williams/699 1.25 3.00
24 Chris Bosh/699 1.00 2.50
25 Rodney Stuckey/749 1.00 2.50
26 D.J. Strawberry/749 1.00 2.50
27 Dwyane Wade/899 1.50 4.00
28 Arron Afflalo/699 1.00 2.50
29 Al Thornton/1060 1.00 2.50
30 Tony Parker/499 2.00 5.00
31 Shaquille O'Neal/499 2.00 5.00
32 Brandan Wright/699 1.00 2.50
33 Acie Law/499 1.00 2.50
34 LeBron James/999 15.00 40.00
35 Allen Iverson/649 1.00 2.50
36 Dirk Nowitzki/649 1.00 2.50
37 Corey Brewer/699 1.00 2.50
38 Jeff Green/699 1.25 3.00
39 Jason Kidd/439 2.00 5.00
40 Vince Carter/599 1.00 2.50
41 Thaddeus Young/749 1.00 2.50
42 Jason Smith/799 1.00 2.50
43 Spencer Hawes/499 6.00 15.00
44 Daequan Cook/699 1.00 2.50

2007 eTopps Autographs

BR1 Bill Russell
2005 eTopps Classic/50 125.00 250.00
VC5 Vince Carter
2006 eTopps McDonald's/75 25.00 60.00

1995-96 E-XL

COMPLETE SET (100) 15.00 40.00
1 Stacey Augmon .30 .75
2 Mookie Blaylock .30 .75
3 Christian Laettner .30 .75
4 Dana Barros .30 .75
5 Dino Radja .25 .60
6 Eric Williams RC .40 1.00
7 Kenny Anderson .30 .75
8 Larry Johnson .50 1.25
9 Glen Rice .40 1.00
10 Michael Jordan 8.00 20.00
11 Toni Kukoc .50 1.25
12 Scottie Pippen .75 2.00
13 Dennis Rodman .75 2.00
14 Terrell Brandon .30 .75
15 Bobby Phills .30 .75
16 Bob Sura RC .30 .75
17 Jim Jackson .30 .75
18 Jason Kidd .60 1.50
19 Jamal Mashburn .40 1.00
20 Mahmoud Abdul-Rauf .30 .75
21 Antonio McDyess RC .50 1.25
22 Dikembe Mutombo .60 1.50
23 Joe Dumars .40 1.00
24 Grant Hill .60 1.50
25 Allan Houston .30 .75
26 Joe Smith RC .50 1.25
27 Latrell Sprewell .40 1.00
28 Kevin Willis .25 .60
29 Sam Cassell .40 1.00
30 Clyde Drexler .60 1.50
31 Robert Horry .40 1.00
32 Hakeem Olajuwon .75 2.00
33 Derrick McKey .25 .60
34 Reggie Miller .75 2.00
35 Rik Smits .30 .75
36 Brent Barry RC .60 1.50
37 Loy Vaught .25 .60
38 Brian Williams .25 .60
39 Cedric Ceballos .30 .75
40 Magic Johnson 1.25 3.00
41 Nick Van Exel .40 1.00
42 Tim Hardaway .50 1.25
43 Alonzo Mourning .60 1.50
44 Kurt Thomas RC .40 1.00
45 Walt Williams .25 .60
46 Vin Baker .30 .75
47 Shawn Respert RC .30 .75
48 Glenn Robinson .40 1.00
49 Kevin Garnett RC 8.00 20.00
50 Tom Gugliotta .25 .60
51 Isaiah Rider .40 1.00
52 Shawn Bradley .25 .60
53 Chris Childs .25 .60
54 Ed O'Bannon RC .30 .75
55 Patrick Ewing .60 1.50
56 Anthony Mason .25 .60
57 Charles Oakley .30 .75
58 Horace Grant .30 .75
59 Anfernee Hardaway 1.00 2.50
60 Shaquille O'Neal 1.50 4.00
61 Derrick Coleman .30 .75
62 Jerry Stackhouse RC 1.25 3.00
63 Clarence Weatherspoon .25 .60
64 Charles Barkley 1.00 2.50
65 Michael Finley RC 1.00 2.50
66 Kevin Johnson .40 1.00
67 Clifford Robinson .40 1.00
68 Arvydas Sabonis RC .75 2.00
69 Rod Strickland .25 .60
70 Tyus Edney RC .40 1.00
71 Billy Owens .25 .60
72 Mitch Richmond .50 1.25
73 Sean Elliott .30 .75
74 Avery Johnson .30 .75
75 David Robinson .75 2.00
76 Shawn Kemp .60 1.50
77 Gary Payton .60 1.50
78 Detlef Schrempf .30 .75
79 Tracy Murray .25 .60
80 Damon Stoudamire RC 1.00 2.50
81 Sharone Wright .25 .60
82 Jeff Hornacek .30 .75
83 Karl Malone .75 2.00
84 John Stockton .75 2.00
85 Greg Anthony .25 .60
86 Bryant Reeves RC .30 .75
87 Byron Scott .40 1.00
88 Juwan Howard .40 1.00
89 Gheorghe Muresan .25 .60
90 Rasheed Wallace RC 1.25 3.00
91 Steve Smith UNT .15 .40
92 Dikembe Mutombo UNT .30 .75
93 Brent Barry UNT .30 .75
94 Glenn Robinson UNT .20 .50
95 Armon Gilliam UNT .12 .30
96 Nick Anderson UNT .15 .40
97 Gary Trent UNT .15 .40
98 Brian Grant UNT .15 .40
99 Bryant Reeves UNT .15 .40
100 Checklist .25 .60
NNO Grant Hill Promo 1.00 2.50

1995-96 E-XL Blue

COMPLETE SET (100) 30.00 80.00
*BLUE: .75X TO 2X BASE CARD HI
ONE OR MORE BLUES PER PACK

1995-96 E-XL A Cut Above

COMPLETE SET (10) 60.00 120.00
STATED ODDS 1:130
1 Scottie Pippen 12.00 30.00
2 Jason Kidd 12.00 30.00
3 Grant Hill 8.00 20.00
4 Joe Smith 3.00 8.00
5 Hakeem Olajuwon 12.00 30.00
6 Magic Johnson 15.00 40.00
7 Shaquille O'Neal 20.00 50.00
8 Jerry Stackhouse 8.00 20.00
9 Charles Barkley 12.00 30.00
10 David Robinson 12.00 30.00

1995-96 E-XL Natural Born Thrillers

COMPLETE SET (10) 500.00 1,000.00
STATED ODDS 1:48
1 Michael Jordan 400.00 800.00
2 Antonio McDyess 4.00 10.00
3 Grant Hill 12.00 30.00
4 Clyde Drexler 8.00 20.00
5 Kevin Garnett 75.00 200.00
6 Anfernee Hardaway 30.00 80.00
7 Jerry Stackhouse 10.00 25.00
8 Michael Finley 8.00 20.00
9 Shawn Kemp 8.00 20.00
10 Damon Stoudamire 8.00 20.00
NNO Jerry Stackhouse PROMO 2.50 6.00

1995-96 E-XL No Boundaries

COMPLETE SET (10) 30.00 80.00
STATED ODDS 1:18 HOBBY
1 Michael Jordan 50.00 120.00
2 Antonio McDyess 1.25 3.00
3 Hakeem Olajuwon 4.00 10.00
4 Magic Johnson 6.00 15.00
5 Vin Baker 1.50 4.00
6 Patrick Ewing 3.00 8.00
7 Anfernee Hardaway 5.00 12.00
8 Jerry Stackhouse 3.00 8.00
9 Gary Payton 3.00 8.00
10 Damon Stoudamire 2.50 6.00

1995-96 E-XL Unstoppable

COMPLETE SET (20) 20.00 50.00
STATED ODDS 1:6
1 Alan Henderson 1.25 3.00
2 Glen Rice 1.25 3.00
3 Scottie Pippen 3.00 8.00
4 Dennis Rodman 2.50 6.00
5 Terrell Brandon 1.00 2.50
6 Jason Kidd 2.00 5.00
7 Grant Hill 2.00 5.00
8 Joe Smith 1.50 4.00
9 Sam Cassell 1.25 3.00
10 Reggie Miller 2.50 6.00
11 Alonzo Mourning 2.00 5.00
12 Shaquille O'Neal 5.00 12.00
13 Charles Barkley 3.00 8.00
14 Clifford Robinson 1.25 3.00
15 Sean Elliott 1.00 2.50
16 David Robinson 2.50 6.00
17 Shawn Kemp 2.00 5.00
18 Karl Malone 2.50 6.00
19 John Stockton 2.50 6.00
20 Juwan Howard 1.25 3.00

1996-97 E-X2000

COMPLETE SET (82) 600.00 1,200.00
EMERALD EXCH: STATED ODDS 1:500
1 Christian Laettner 1.00 2.50
2 Dikembe Mutombo 1.50 4.00
3 Steve Smith .75 2.00
4 Antoine Walker RC 1.50 4.00
5 David Wesley .60 1.50
6 Tony Delk RC 1.00 2.50
7 Anthony Mason .75 2.00
8 Glen Rice 1.00 2.50
9 Michael Jordan 50.00 120.00
10 Scottie Pippen 2.50 6.00
11 Dennis Rodman 2.50 6.00
12 Terrell Brandon .75 2.00
13 Chris Mills .60 1.50
14 Shawn Bradley .60 1.50
15 Michael Finley 1.00 2.50
16 Dale Ellis .75 2.00
17 Antonio McDyess 1.00 2.50
18 Joe Dumars 1.25 3.00
19 Grant Hill 1.50 4.00
20 Chris Mullin 1.25 3.00
21 Joe Smith .75 2.00
22 Latrell Sprewell 1.00 2.50
23 Charles Barkley 2.50 6.00
24 Clyde Drexler 1.50 4.00
25 Hakeem Olajuwon 2.00 5.00
26 Erick Dampier RC 1.00 2.50
27 Reggie Miller 2.00 5.00
28 Loy Vaught .60 1.50
29 Lorenzen Wright RC .75 2.00
30 Kobe Bryant RC 150.00 400.00
31 Eddie Jones 1.00 2.50
32 Shaquille O'Neal 4.00 10.00
33 Nick Van Exel 1.00 2.50
34 Tim Hardaway 1.25 3.00
35 Jamal Mashburn .75 2.00
36 Alonzo Mourning 1.50 4.00
37 Ray Allen RC 8.00 20.00
38 Vin Baker .75 2.00
39 Glenn Robinson 1.00 2.50
40 Kevin Garnett 3.00 8.00
41 Tom Gugliotta .60 1.50
42 Stephon Marbury RC 3.00 8.00
43 Kendall Gill .60 1.50
44 Jim Jackson .60 1.50
45 Kerry Kittles RC 1.00 2.50
46 Patrick Ewing 1.50 4.00
47 Larry Johnson 1.25 3.00
48 John Wallace RC .75 2.00
49 Nick Anderson .60 1.50
50 Horace Grant 1.00 2.50
51 Anfernee Hardaway 2.50 6.00
52 Derrick Coleman .75 2.00
53 Allen Iverson RC 40.00 100.00
54 Jerry Stackhouse 1.25 3.00
55 Cedric Ceballos .75 2.00
56 Kevin Johnson 1.00 2.50
57 Jason Kidd 1.50 4.00
58 Clifford Robinson 1.00 2.50
59 Arvydas Sabonis 1.00 2.50
60 Rasheed Wallace 1.25 3.00
61 Mahmoud Abdul-Rauf .75 2.00
62 Brian Grant .75 2.00
63 Mitch Richmond 1.25 3.00
64 Sean Elliott 1.00 2.50
65 David Robinson 2.00 5.00
66 Dominique Wilkins 1.50 4.00
67 Shawn Kemp 1.50 4.00
68 Gary Payton 1.50 4.00
69 Detlef Schrempf .75 2.00
70 Marcus Camby RC 1.50 4.00
71 Damon Stoudamire 1.00 2.50
72 Walt Williams .60 1.50
73 Shandon Anderson RC .75 2.00
74 Karl Malone 2.00 5.00
75 John Stockton 2.00 5.00
76 Shareef Abdur-Rahim RC 1.50 4.00
77 Bryant Reeves .60 1.50
78 Roy Rogers RC .75 2.00
79 Juwan Howard 1.00 2.50
80 Chris Webber 1.25 3.00
81 Checklist .25 .60
82 Checklist .25 .60
NNO Grant Hill
Blow-Up/3000 10.00 25.00
NNO Grant Hill AU Ball/75 100.00 250.00
NNO Grant Hill PROMO 1.25 3.00

1996-97 E-X2000 Credentials

*STARS: 12X TO 30X BASE CARD HI
*RCs: 12X TO 30X BASE HI
STATED PRINT RUN 499 SERIAL #'d SETS
2 Dikembe Mutombo 150.00 400.00
9 Michael Jordan 6,000.00 12,000.00
10 Scottie Pippen 500.00 1,000.00
11 Dennis Rodman 400.00 800.00
15 Michael Finley 50.00 120.00
16 Dale Ellis 50.00 120.00
17 Antonio McDyess 50.00 120.00
18 Joe Dumars 75.00 200.00
19 Grant Hill 150.00 400.00
20 Chris Mullin 100.00 250.00
22 Latrell Sprewell 75.00 200.00
23 Charles Barkley 400.00 800.00
24 Clyde Drexler 125.00 300.00
25 Hakeem Olajuwon 200.00 500.00
27 Reggie Miller 200.00 500.00
30 Kobe Bryant 15,000.00 30,000.00
31 Eddie Jones 75.00 200.00
32 Shaquille O'Neal 800.00 1,500.00
33 Nick Van Exel 75.00 200.00
34 Tim Hardaway 75.00 200.00
36 Alonzo Mourning 150.00 400.00
37 Ray Allen 200.00 500.00
39 Glenn Robinson 60.00 150.00
40 Kevin Garnett 150.00 400.00
42 Stephon Marbury 125.00 300.00
46 Patrick Ewing 150.00 400.00
47 Larry Johnson 100.00 250.00
50 Horace Grant 75.00 200.00
51 Anfernee Hardaway 200.00 500.00
53 Allen Iverson 1,500.00 3,000.00
54 Jerry Stackhouse 60.00 150.00
57 Jason Kidd 125.00 300.00
59 Arvydas Sabonis 100.00 250.00
60 Rasheed Wallace 100.00 250.00
63 Mitch Richmond 100.00 250.00
65 David Robinson 200.00 500.00
66 Dominique Wilkins 200.00 500.00
67 Shawn Kemp 200.00 500.00
68 Gary Payton 200.00 500.00
69 Detlef Schrempf 75.00 200.00
71 Damon Stoudamire 60.00 150.00
73 Shandon Anderson 40.00 100.00
74 Karl Malone 200.00 500.00
75 John Stockton 200.00 500.00
76 Shareef Abdur-Rahim 50.00 120.00
80 Chris Webber 125.00 300.00

1996-97 E-X2000 A Cut Above

COMPLETE SET (10) 4,000.00 8,000.00
STATED ODDS 1:288
1 Kevin Garnett 150.00 400.00
2 Anfernee Hardaway 300.00 600.00
3 Grant Hill 125.00 300.00
4 Allen Iverson 400.00 800.00
5 Michael Jordan 3,000.00 6,000.00
6 Shawn Kemp 125.00 300.00
7 Hakeem Olajuwon 150.00 400.00
8 Shaquille O'Neal 400.00 800.00
9 Glenn Robinson 75.00 200.00
10 Dennis Rodman 300.00 600.00

1996-97 E-X2000 Net Assets

COMPLETE SET (20) 400.00 800.00
STATED ODDS 1:20
1 Ray Allen 15.00 40.00
2 Charles Barkley 15.00 40.00
3 Patrick Ewing 12.00 30.00
4 Kevin Garnett 15.00 40.00
5 Anfernee Hardaway 15.00 40.00
6 Grant Hill 15.00 40.00
7 Allen Iverson 25.00 60.00
8 Michael Jordan 350.00 700.00
9 Jason Kidd 10.00 25.00
10 Kerry Kittles 3.00 8.00
11 Karl Malone 12.00 30.00
12 Alonzo Mourning 10.00 25.00
13 Shaquille O'Neal 20.00 50.00
14 Gary Payton 10.00 25.00
15 Bryant Reeves 2.00 5.00
16 David Robinson 12.00 30.00
17 Dennis Rodman 20.00 50.00
18 Joe Smith 8.00 20.00
19 Damon Stoudamire 8.00 20.00
20 Chris Webber 10.00 25.00

1996-97 E-X2000 Star Date 2000

COMPLETE SET (15) 500.00 1,000.00
STATED ODDS 1:9
1 Shareef Abdur-Rahim 5.00 12.00
2 Ray Allen 15.00 40.00
3 Kobe Bryant 400.00 800.00
4 Marcus Camby 5.00 12.00
5 Erick Dampier 3.00 8.00
6 Juwan Howard 3.00 8.00
7 Allen Iverson 60.00 150.00
8 Jason Kidd 5.00 12.00
9 Kerry Kittles 3.00 8.00
10 Stephon Marbury 10.00 25.00
11 Jamal Mashburn 3.00 8.00
12 Antonio McDyess 3.00 8.00
13 Joe Smith 2.50 6.00
14 Damon Stoudamire 3.00 8.00
15 Antoine Walker 5.00 12.00

1997-98 E-X2001

COMPLETE SET (82) 60.00 150.00
1 Grant Hill .75 2.00
2 Kevin Garnett 1.25 3.00
3 Allen Iverson 1.50 4.00
4 Anfernee Hardaway 1.25 3.00
5 Dennis Rodman 1.25 3.00
6 Shawn Kemp .75 2.00
7 Shaquille O'Neal 1.50 4.00
8 Kobe Bryant 12.00 30.00
9 Michael Jordan 60.00 150.00
10 Marcus Camby .50 1.25
11 Scottie Pippen 1.25 3.00
12 Antoine Walker .50 1.25
13 Stephon Marbury .60 1.50
14 Shareef Abdur-Rahim .50 1.25
15 Jerry Stackhouse .50 1.25
16 Eddie Jones .50 1.25
17 Charles Barkley 1.25 3.00
18 David Robinson 1.00 2.50
19 Karl Malone 1.00 2.50
20 Damon Stoudamire .50 1.25
21 Patrick Ewing .75 2.00
22 Kerry Kittles .40 1.00
23 Gary Payton .75 2.00
24 Glenn Robinson .50 1.25
25 Hakeem Olajuwon 1.00 2.50
26 John Starks .50 1.25
27 John Stockton 1.00 2.50
28 Vin Baker .40 1.00
29 Reggie Miller 1.00 2.50
30 Clyde Drexler .75 2.00
31 Alonzo Mourning .75 2.00
32 Juwan Howard .40 1.00
33 Ray Allen 1.00 2.50
34 Christian Laettner .50 1.25
35 Terrell Brandon .40 1.00
36 Sean Elliott .40 1.00
37 Rod Strickland .40 1.00
38 Rodney Rogers .40 1.00
39 Donyell Marshall .30 .75
40 David Wesley .40 1.00
41 Sam Cassell .40 1.00
42 Cedric Ceballos .40 1.00
43 Mahmoud Abdul-Rauf .30 .75
44 Rik Smits .40 1.00
45 Lindsey Hunter .30 .75
46 Michael Finley .50 1.25
47 Steve Smith .40 1.00
48 Larry Johnson .60 1.50
49 Dikembe Mutombo .75 2.00
50 Tom Gugliotta .40 1.00
51 Joe Dumars .60 1.50
52 Glen Rice .50 1.25
53 Bryant Reeves .30 .75
54 Tim Hardaway .60 1.50
55 Isaiah Rider .40 1.00
56 Rasheed Wallace .60 1.50
57 Jason Kidd .75 2.00
58 Joe Smith .40 1.00
59 Chris Webber .60 1.50
60 Mitch Richmond .60 1.50
61 Antonio McDyess .50 1.25
62 Bobby Jackson RC .75 2.00
63 Derek Anderson RC .60 1.50
64 Kelvin Cato RC .50 1.25
65 Jacque Vaughn RC .50 1.25
66 Tariq Abdul-Wahad RC .50 1.25
67 Johnny Taylor RC .40 1.00
68 Chris Anstey RC .40 1.00
69 Maurice Taylor RC .50 1.25
70 Antonio Daniels RC .60 1.50
71 Chauncey Billups RC 2.00 5.00
72 Austin Croshere RC .50 1.25
73 Brevin Knight RC .60 1.50
74 Keith Van Horn RC 1.00 2.50
75 Tim Duncan RC 25.00 60.00
76 Danny Fortson RC .60 1.50
77 Tim Thomas RC .75 2.00
78 Tony Battie RC .60 1.50
79 Tracy McGrady RC 12.00 30.00
80 Ron Mercer RC .75 2.00
81 Checklist (1-82) .30 .75
82 Checklist (inserts) .30 .75
S1 Grant Hill SAMPLE 1.25 3.00

1997-98 E-X2001 Essential Credentials Future

*VETS #'d 20-80: 40X TO 100X BASE HI
LOWER PRINT RUNS UNPRICED
1 Grant Hill/80 800.00 1,500.00
2 Kevin Garnett/79 1,500.00 3,000.00
3 Allen Iverson/78 2,500.00 5,000.00
4 Anfernee Hardaway/77 1,500.00 3,000.00
5 Dennis Rodman/76 2,500.00 5,000.00
6 Shawn Kemp/75 1,000.00 2,000.00
7 Shaquille O'Neal/74 2,500.00 5,000.00
8 Kobe Bryant/73 10,000.00 20,000.00
9 Michael Jordan/72 20,000.00 40,000.00
11 Scottie Pippen/70 1,000.00 2,000.00
13 Stephon Marbury/68 200.00 500.00
15 Jerry Stackhouse/66 40.00 100.00
17 Charles Barkley/64 2,500.00 5,000.00
18 David Robinson/63 1,000.00 2,000.00
19 Karl Malone/62 125.00 300.00
21 Patrick Ewing/60 1,000.00 2,000.00
23 Gary Payton/58 300.00 600.00
24 Glenn Robinson/57 125.00 300.00
25 Hakeem Olajuwon/56 1,000.00 2,000.00
29 Reggie Miller/52 1,000.00 2,000.00
30 Clyde Drexler/51 800.00 1,500.00
31 Alonzo Mourning/50 1,000.00 2,000.00
33 Ray Allen/48 1,000.00 2,000.00
56 Rasheed Wallace/25 1,000.00 2,000.00
57 Jason Kidd/24 300.00 600.00
59 Chris Webber/22 300.00 600.00
60 Mitch Richmond/21 200.00 500.00
61 Antonio McDyess/20 80.00 200.00

1997-98 E-X2001 Essential Credentials Now

*VETS #'d 20-61: 40X TO 100X BASE HI
*VETS #'d 51-61: 25X TO 60X BASE HI
*RCs #'d 62-80: 12X TO 30X BASE HI
LOWER PRINT RUNS UNPRICED
21 Patrick Ewing/21 300.00 600.00
23 Gary Payton/23 300.00 600.00
25 Hakeem Olajuwon/25 300.00 600.00
27 John Stockton/27 300.00 600.00
29 Reggie Miller/29 1,000.00 2,000.00
30 Clyde Drexler/30 150.00 400.00
31 Alonzo Mourning/31 600.00 1,200.00
33 Ray Allen/33 300.00 600.00
36 Sean Elliott/36 125.00 300.00
47 Steve Smith/47 100.00 250.00
52 Glen Rice/52 30.00 80.00
56 Rasheed Wallace/56 400.00 800.00
57 Jason Kidd/57 200.00 500.00
59 Chris Webber/59 100.00 200.00
60 Mitch Richmond/60 50.00 100.00
66 Tariq Abdul-Wahad/66 40.00 100.00
68 Chris Anstey/68 20.00 50.00
71 Chauncey Billups/71 200.00 500.00
74 Keith Van Horn/74 125.00 300.00
75 Tim Duncan/75 1,500.00 3,000.00
79 Tracy McGrady/79 400.00 800.00

1997-98 E-X2001 Gravity Denied

COMPLETE SET (20) 150.00 400.00
STATED ODDS 1:24
1 Vin Baker 1.25 3.00
2 Charles Barkley 4.00 10.00
3 Tony Battie 1.00 2.50
4 Kobe Bryant 60.00 150.00
5 Patrick Ewing 2.50 6.00
6 Kevin Garnett 4.00 10.00
7 Anfernee Hardaway 4.00 10.00
8 Grant Hill 2.50 6.00
9 Michael Jordan 125.00 300.00
10 Shawn Kemp 2.50 6.00
11 Kerry Kittles 1.25 3.00
12 Karl Malone 3.00 8.00
13 Tracy McGrady 5.00 12.00
14 Hakeem Olajuwon 3.00 8.00
15 Shaquille O'Neal 10.00 25.00
16 Scottie Pippen 4.00 10.00
17 Jerry Stackhouse 1.50 4.00
18 Tim Thomas 1.25 3.00
19 Antoine Walker 1.50 4.00
20 Chris Webber 2.00 5.00

1997-98 E-X2001 Jambalaya

STATED ODDS 1:720
1 Allen Iverson 800.00 1,500.00
2 Anfernee Hardaway 1,000.00 2,000.00
3 Dennis Rodman 800.00 1,500.00
4 Grant Hill 400.00 800.00
5 Kevin Garnett 800.00 1,500.00
6 Michael Jordan 40,000.00 60,000.00
7 Shaquille O'Neal 800.00 1,500.00
8 Tim Duncan 1,250.00 2,500.00
9 Keith Van Horn 150.00 400.00
10 Stephon Marbury 200.00 500.00
11 Shareef Abdur-Rahim 125.00 300.00
12 Kobe Bryant 20,000.00 40,000.00
13 Damon Stoudamire 150.00 400.00
14 Scottie Pippen 500.00 1,000.00
15 Eddie Jones 150.00 400.00

1997-98 E-X2001 Star Date 2001

COMPLETE SET (15) 50.00 120.00
STATED ODDS 1:12
1 Shareef Abdur-Rahim .75 2.00
2 Tony Battie .50 1.25
3 Kobe Bryant 50.00 120.00
4 Antonio Daniels .50 1.25
5 Tim Duncan 3.00 8.00
6 Adonal Foyle .40 1.00
7 Allen Iverson 2.50 6.00
8 Matt Maloney .50 1.25
9 Stephon Marbury 1.00 2.50
10 Tracy McGrady 2.50 6.00
11 Ron Mercer .60 1.50
12 Tim Thomas .60 1.50
13 Keith Van Horn .75 2.00
14 Jacque Vaughn .40 1.00
15 Antoine Walker .75 2.00

1997-98 E-X2001 Grant Hill Hawaii

S1 Grant Hill 6.00 15.00

1998-99 E-X Century

COMPLETE SET (1-90) 15.00 40.00
RC STATED ODDS 1:1.5
1 Keith Van Horn .40 1.00
2 Scottie Pippen 1.00 2.50
3 Tim Thomas .30 .75
4 Stephon Marbury .50 1.25
5 Allen Iverson 1.00 2.50
6 Grant Hill .60 1.50
7 Tim Duncan 1.00 2.50
8 Latrell Sprewell .50 1.25
9 Ron Mercer .30 .75
10 Kobe Bryant 3.00 8.00
11 Antoine Walker .40 1.00
12 Reggie Miller .75 2.00
13 Kevin Garnett 1.00 2.50
14 Shaquille O'Neal 1.50 4.00
15 Karl Malone .75 2.00
16 Dennis Rodman 1.00 2.50
17 Tracy McGrady .60 1.50
18 Anfernee Hardaway 1.00 2.50
19 Shareef Abdur-Rahim .40 1.00
20 Marcus Camby .30 .75
21 Eddie Jones .40 1.00
22 Vin Baker .30 .75
23 Charles Barkley 1.00 2.50
24 Patrick Ewing .60 1.50
25 Jason Kidd .60 1.50
26 Mitch Richmond .50 1.25
27 Tim Hardaway .50 1.25
28 Glen Rice .40 1.00
29 Shawn Kemp .60 1.50
30 John Stockton .75 2.00
31 Ray Allen .60 1.50
32 Brevin Knight .25 .60
33 David Robinson .75 2.00
34 Juwan Howard .30 .75
35 Alonzo Mourning .60 1.50
36 Hakeem Olajuwon .75 2.00
37 Gary Payton .60 1.50
38 Damon Stoudamire .40 1.00
39 Steve Smith .30 .75
40 Chris Webber .50 1.25
41 Michael Finley .40 1.00
42 Jayson Williams .25 .60
43 Maurice Taylor .30 .75
44 Jalen Rose .30 .75
45 Sam Cassell .30 .75
46 Jerry Stackhouse .40 1.00
47 Toni Kukoc .40 1.00
48 Charles Oakley .30 .75
49 Jim Jackson .25 .60
50 Dikembe Mutombo .60 1.50
51 Wesley Person .25 .60
52 Antonio Daniels .25 .60
53 Isaiah Rider .30 .75
54 Tom Gugliotta .30 .75
55 Antonio McDyess .30 .75
56 Jeff Hornacek .30 .75
57 Joe Dumars .40 1.00
58 Jamal Mashburn .30 .75
59 Donyell Marshall .25 .60
60 Glenn Robinson .40 1.00
61 Jelani McCoy RC .75 2.00
62 Peja Stojakovic RC 2.00 5.00
63 Randell Jackson RC 1.00 2.50
64 Brad Miller RC 2.50 6.00
65 Corey Benjamin RC .60 1.50
66 Toby Bailey RC .75 2.00
67 Nazr Mohammed RC 1.00 2.50
68 Dirk Nowitzki RC 4.00 10.00
69 Andrae Patterson RC .75 2.00
70 Michael Dickerson RC 1.00 2.50
71 Cory Carr RC .75 2.00
72 Brian Skinner RC .75 2.00
73 Pat Garrity RC .75 2.00
74 Ricky Davis RC 1.50 4.00
75 Roshown McLeod RC .60 1.50
76 Matt Harpring RC 1.00 2.50
77 Jason Williams RC 3.00 8.00
78 Keon Clark RC 1.00 2.50
79 Al Harrington RC 1.25 3.00
80 Felipe Lopez RC .60 1.50
81 Michael Doleac RC .75 2.00
82 Paul Pierce RC 4.00 10.00
83 Robert Traylor RC 1.00 2.50
84 Raef LaFrentz RC 1.25 3.00
85 Michael Olowokandi RC 1.25 3.00
86 Mike Bibby RC 2.00 5.00
87 Antawn Jamison RC 1.50 4.00
88 Bonzi Wells RC 1.00 2.50
89 Vince Carter RC 5.00 12.00
90 Larry Hughes RC 1.50 4.00

1998-99 E-X Century Essential Credentials Future

*VETS #'d 71-90: 20X TO 50X BASE HI
*VETS #'d 41-70: 25X TO 60X BASE HI
*VETS #'d 31-40: 30X TO 80X BASE HI
*RCs #'d 15-30: 6X TO 15X BASE HI
LOWER PRINT RUNS UNPRICED
2 Scottie Pippen/89 150.00 400.00
5 Allen Iverson/86 200.00 500.00
6 Grant Hill/85 125.00 300.00
7 Tim Duncan/84 300.00 600.00
10 Kobe Bryant/81 5,000.00 10,000.00

13 Kevin Garnett/78 300.00 600.00
14 Shaquille O'Neal/77 600.00 1,200.00
16 Dennis Rodman/75 125.00 250.00
17 Tracy McGrady/74 40.00 100.00
18 Anfernee Hardaway/73 200.00 500.00
19 Shareef Abdur-Rahim/72 40.00 100.00
20 Marcus Camby/71 30.00 80.00
23 Charles Barkley/68 75.00 200.00
24 Patrick Ewing/67 125.00 300.00
26 Mitch Richmond/65 40.00 100.00
29 Shawn Kemp/62 50.00 100.00
30 John Stockton/61 40.00 100.00
31 Ray Allen/60 40.00 100.00
33 David Robinson/58 200.00 500.00
35 Alonzo Mourning/56 150.00 400.00
36 Hakeem Olajuwon/55 75.00 150.00
37 Gary Payton/54 125.00 300.00
40 Chris Webber/51 50.00 120.00
46 Jerry Stackhouse/45 40.00 100.00
47 Toni Kukoc/44 100.00 250.00
68 Dirk Nowitzki/23 1,000.00 2,000.00

1998-99 E-X Century Essential Credentials Now

*VETS #'d 16-30: 40X TO 100X BASE HI
*VETS #'d 31-40: 30X TO 80X BASE HI
*VETS #'d 41-60: 25X TO 60X BASE HI
*RCs #'d 61-90: 4X TO 10X BASE HI
LOWER PRINT RUNS UNPRICED
16 Dennis Rodman/16 300.00 600.00
17 Tracy McGrady/17 100.00 200.00
18 Anfernee Hardaway/18 150.00 300.00
21 Eddie Jones/21 75.00 150.00
26 Mitch Richmond/26 125.00 300.00
29 Shawn Kemp/29 150.00 400.00
30 John Stockton/30 75.00 150.00
31 Ray Allen/31 100.00 250.00
35 Alonzo Mourning/35 75.00 200.00
36 Hakeem Olajuwon/36 125.00 300.00
37 Gary Payton/37 125.00 300.00
40 Chris Webber/40 300.00 600.00
47 Toni Kukoc/47 100.00 175.00
48 Charles Oakley/48 30.00 80.00
68 Dirk Nowitzki/68 300.00 600.00
77 Jason Williams/77 40.00 100.00
82 Paul Pierce/82 300.00 600.00
86 Mike Bibby/86 40.00 80.00
87 Antawn Jamison/87 25.00 60.00
89 Vince Carter/89 150.00 400.00

1998-99 E-X Century Authen-Kicks

PRINT RUNS LISTED BELOW
1 Antawn Jamison/225 15.00 40.00
2 Tracy McGrady/225 40.00 100.00
3 Ron Mercer/180 15.00 40.00
4 Antoine Walker/125 20.00 50.00
5 Mike Bibby/165 25.00 50.00
6 Michael Dickerson/230 15.00 40.00
7 Larry Hughes/115 30.00 60.00
8 Raef LaFrentz/160 15.00 40.00
9 Keith Van Horn/125 25.00 60.00
9AU Keith Van Horn AU/44 40.00 100.00
10 Tim Thomas/215 15.00 40.00
11 Allen Iverson/165 50.00 120.00
12 Robert Traylor/215 15.00 40.00

1998-99 E-X Century Dunk 'N Go Nuts

COMPLETE SET (20)
STATED ODDS 1:36
1 Tim Thomas 12.00 30.00
2 Grant Hill 75.00 200.00
3 Shareef Abdur-Rahim 30.00 80.00
4 Tim Duncan 125.00 300.00
5 Allen Iverson 150.00 400.00
6 Kobe Bryant 800.00 1,500.00
7 Antoine Walker 20.00 50.00
8 Kevin Garnett 125.00 300.00
9 Shaquille O'Neal 125.00 300.00
10 Tracy McGrady 100.00 250.00
11 Antawn Jamison 30.00 80.00
12 Vince Carter 100.00 250.00
13 Robert Traylor 15.00 40.00
14 Scottie Pippen 125.00 300.00
15 Michael Jordan 1,000.00 2,000.00
16 Michael Olowokandi 12.00 30.00
17 Anfernee Hardaway 100.00 250.00
18 Michael Dickerson 15.00 40.00
19 Ron Mercer 15.00 40.00
20 Felipe Lopez 12.00 30.00

1998-99 E-X Century Generation E-X

COMPLETE SET (15) 12.50 30.00
STATED ODDS 1:18
1 Larry Hughes .75 2.00
2 Michael Olowokandi .60 1.50
3 Tim Duncan 2.00 5.00
4 Vince Carter 2.50 6.00
5 Antawn Jamison .75 2.00
6 Kevin Garnett 2.00 5.00
7 Al Harrington .60 1.50
8 Mike Bibby 1.00 2.50
9 Raef LaFrentz .60 1.50
10 Ron Mercer .60 1.50
11 Tracy McGrady 1.25 3.00
12 Kobe Bryant 6.00 15.00
13 Keith Van Horn .75 2.00
14 Stephon Marbury 1.00 2.50
15 Allen Iverson 2.00 5.00

1999-00 E-X

COMPLETE SET (90) 40.00 100.00
COMPLETE SET w/o RC (60) 15.00 30.00
RC PRINT RUN 3499 SERIAL #'d SETS
1 Stephon Marbury .50 1.25
2 Antawn Jamison .40 1.00
3 Patrick Ewing .50 1.25
4 Nick Anderson .25 .60
5 Charles Barkley 1.00 2.50
6 Marcus Camby .30 .75
7 Ron Mercer .30 .75
8 Avery Johnson .30 .75
9 Maurice Taylor .25 .60
10 Isaiah Rider .30 .75
11 Dirk Nowitzki 1.25 3.00
12 Damon Stoudamire .40 1.00
13 Alonzo Mourning .60 1.50
14 Jason Kidd .60 1.50
15 Juwan Howard .30 .75
16 Vince Carter 1.00 2.50
17 Tim Duncan 1.00 2.50
18 Paul Pierce .75 2.00
19 Tim Hardaway .60 1.50
20 Grant Hill .60 1.50
21 Keith Van Horn .30 .75
22 Shaquille O'Neal 1.50 4.00
23 Jason Williams .60 1.50
24 Shareef Abdur-Rahim .40 1.00
25 Kobe Bryant 3.00 8.00
26 David Robinson .75 2.00
27 Anfernee Hardaway 1.00 2.50
28 Vin Baker .30 .75
29 Hakeem Olajuwon .75 2.00
30 Michael Olowokandi .25 .60
31 Mike Bibby .40 1.00
32 Tracy McGrady .60 1.50
33 Antoine Walker .40 1.00
34 Larry Hughes .30 .75
35 Chris Webber .50 1.25
36 Ray Allen .60 1.50
37 Danny Fortson .25 .60
38 Shawn Kemp .60 1.50
39 Michael Doleac .25 .60
40 Gary Payton .60 1.50
41 Toni Kukoc .50 1.25
42 Kevin Garnett 1.00 2.50
43 Steve Smith .30 .75
44 Scottie Pippen 1.00 2.50
45 Allen Iverson 1.00 2.50
46 Latrell Sprewell .50 1.25
47 Matt Harpring .25 .60
48 Lindsey Hunter .25 .60
49 Karl Malone .75 2.00
50 Michael Finley .40 1.00
51 Jerry Stackhouse .40 1.00
52 Cedric Ceballos .25 .60
53 Brent Barry .30 .75
54 Elden Campbell .25 .60
55 Glenn Robinson .30 .75
56 Eddie Jones .40 1.00
57 Reggie Miller .75 2.00
58 Mitch Richmond .50 1.25
59 Raef LaFrentz .30 .75
60 John Starks .40 1.00
61 Elton Brand RC 1.50 4.00
62 William Avery RC .50 1.25
63 Cal Bowdler RC .50 1.25
64 Dion Glover RC .50 1.25
65 Lamar Odom RC 1.50 4.00
66 Richard Hamilton RC 2.00 5.00
67 Kenny Thomas RC .75 2.00
68 Shawn Marion RC 1.50 4.00
69 Baron Davis RC 2.00 5.00
70 Wally Szczerbiak RC 1.25 3.00
71 Scott Padgett RC .60 1.50
72 Jason Terry RC 1.25 3.00
73 Trajan Langdon RC .50 1.25
74 Andre Miller RC 1.50 4.00
75 Jeff Foster RC .50 1.25
76 Tim James RC .50 1.25
77 A.Radojevic RC .50 1.25
78 Quincy Lewis RC .50 1.25
79 James Posey RC .75 2.00
80 Steve Francis RC 1.50 4.00
81 Jonathan Bender RC .75 2.00
82 Corey Maggette RC 1.00 2.50
83 Obinna Ekezie RC .50 1.25
84 Laron Profit RC .50 1.25
85 Devean George RC .60 1.50
86 Ron Artest RC 2.00 5.00
87 Rafer Alston RC 1.00 2.50
88 Vonteego Cummings RC .50 1.25
89 Evan Eschmeyer RC .60 1.50
90 Jumaine Jones RC .50 1.25
S16 Vince Carter PROMO 1.25 3.00

1999-00 E-X Essential Credentials Future

*VETS #'d 36-60: 20X TO 50X BASE HI
*VETS #'d 21-35: 25X TO 60X BASE HI
*RC #'d 21-30: 8X TO 20X BASE HI
LOWER PRINT RUNS UNPRICED
11 Dirk Nowitzki/50 300.00 600.00
17 Tim Duncan/44 200.00 500.00
20 Grant Hill/41 40.00 100.00
25 Kobe Bryant/36 500.00 1,000.00
35 Chris Webber/26 60.00 150.00
36 Ray Allen/25 40.00 100.00
38 Shawn Kemp/23 50.00 120.00

1999-00 E-X Essential Credentials Now

*VETS #'d 36-60: 20X TO 50X BASE HI
*VETS #'d 21-35: 25X TO 60X BASE HI
*RCs #'d 21-30: 8X TO 20X BASE HI
LOWER PRINT RUNS UNPRICED
22 Shaquille O'Neal/22 200.00 500.00
25 Kobe Bryant/25 300.00 600.00
27 Anfernee Hardaway/27 50.00 120.00
29 Hakeem Olajuwon/29 40.00 100.00
32 Tracy McGrady/32 60.00 150.00
35 Chris Webber/35 50.00 120.00
36 Ray Allen/36 30.00 80.00
38 Shawn Kemp/38 100.00 250.00
40 Gary Payton/40 30.00 80.00
42 Kevin Garnett/42 200.00 500.00
44 Scottie Pippen/44 125.00 300.00
45 Allen Iverson/45 125.00 300.00
57 Reggie Miller/57 60.00 150.00

1999-00 E-X E-Xceptional Red

COMPLETE SET (15) 75.00 150.00
STATED ODDS 1:16
*GREEN: 1X TO 2.5X HI COLUMN
GREEN: PRINT RUN 500 SERIAL #'d SETS
XC1 Jason Williams 5.00 12.00
XC2 Kevin Garnett 8.00 20.00
XC3 Allen Iverson 8.00 20.00
XC4 Paul Pierce 6.00 15.00
XC5 Keith Van Horn 2.50 6.00
XC6 Grant Hill 5.00 12.00
XC7 Scottie Pippen 8.00 20.00
XC8 Stephon Marbury 4.00 10.00
XC9 Tim Duncan 8.00 20.00
XC10 Kobe Bryant 15.00 40.00
XC11 Vince Carter 8.00 20.00
XC12 Shaquille O'Neal 12.00 30.00
XC13 Steve Francis 3.00 8.00
XC14 Elton Brand 3.00 8.00
XC15 Lamar Odom 3.00 8.00

1999-00 E-X E-Xceptional Blue

*BLUE STARS: 2.5X TO 6X HI COLUMN
*BLUE RCs: 2X TO 5X HI COLUMN
STATED PRINT RUN 250 SERIAL #'d SETS
XC1 Jason Williams 30.00 80.00
XC10 Kobe Bryant 125.00 300.00

1999-00 E-X E-Xciting

COMPLETE SET (10) 15.00 40.00
STATED ODDS 1:24
XCT1 Jason Williams 4.00 10.00
XCT2 Vince Carter 3.00 8.00
XCT3 Allen Iverson 3.00 8.00
XCT4 Kevin Garnett 3.00 8.00
XCT5 Shaquille O'Neal 5.00 12.00
XCT6 Larry Hughes 1.00 2.50
XCT7 Tim Duncan 3.00 8.00
XCT8 Kobe Bryant 10.00 25.00
XCT9 Grant Hill 2.00 5.00
XCT10 Paul Pierce 2.50 6.00

1999-00 E-X E-Xplosive

STATED PRINT RUN 1999 SERIAL #'d SETS
FIRST 99 ARE AUTOGRAPHED
XP1 William Avery .50 1.25
XP1A William Avery AU 5.00 12.00
XP2 Baron Davis 2.00 5.00
XP2A Baron Davis AU 20.00 50.00
XP3 Richard Hamilton 2.00 5.00
XP3A Richard Hamilton AU 20.00 50.00
XP4 Trajan Langdon .60 1.50
XP4A Trajan Langdon AU 6.00 15.00
XP5 Wally Szczerbiak 1.25 3.00
XP5A Wally Szczerbiak AU 12.00 30.00
XP6 Jason Terry 1.25 3.00
XP6A Jason Terry AU 12.00 30.00
XP7 Shawn Marion 1.50 4.00
XP7A Shawn Marion AU 15.00 40.00
XP8 James Posey .75 2.00
XP8A James Posey AU 8.00 20.00
XP9 Lamar Odom 1.50 4.00
XP9A Lamar Odom AU 15.00 40.00
XP10 Quincy Lewis .50 1.25
XP10A Quincy Lewis AU 5.00 12.00

1999-00 E-X Generation E-X

COMPLETE SET (15) 8.00 20.00
STATED ODDS 1:8
GX1 Michael Olowokandi .40 1.00
GX2 Kobe Bryant 5.00 12.00
GX3 Allen Iverson 1.50 4.00
GX4 Tim Duncan 1.50 4.00
GX5 Vince Carter 1.50 4.00
GX6 Paul Pierce 1.25 3.00
GX7 Jason Williams 1.00 2.50
GX8 Steve Francis 1.25 3.00
GX9 Lamar Odom 1.25 3.00
GX10 Elton Brand 1.25 3.00
GX11 Larry Hughes .50 1.25
GX12 Antawn Jamison .60 1.50
GX13 Mike Bibby .60 1.50
GX14 Keith Van Horn .60 1.50
GX15 Raef LaFrentz .50 1.25

1999-00 E-X Genuine Coverage

STATED ODDS 1:72
GC1 Shaquille O'Neal 10.00 25.00
GC2 Vince Carter 6.00 15.00
GC3 Jason Kidd 4.00 10.00
GC4 Karl Malone 5.00 12.00
GC5 Joe Smith 2.00 5.00
GC6 Terrell Brandon 1.50 4.00
GC7 John Stockton 4.00 10.00
GC8 Lamar Odom 5.00 12.00
GC9 Shareef Abdur-Rahim 2.50 6.00
GC10 David Robinson 5.00 12.00
GC11 Larry Hughes 2.00 5.00
GC12 Michael Olowokandi 1.50 4.00
GC13 Antonio McDyess 2.00 5.00
GC14 Mike Bibby 2.50 6.00
GC15 Stephon Marbury 3.00 8.00
GC16 Michael Finley 2.50 6.00
GC17 Gary Payton 4.00 10.00
GC18 Keith Van Horn 2.00 5.00
GC19 Jamal Mashburn 2.00 5.00
GC20 Grant Hill 4.00 10.00

2000-01 E-X

COMPLETE SET w/o RC (100) 12.50 30.00
101-110: PRINT RUN 1000 #'d SETS
111-120: PRINT RUN 1250 #'d SETS
121-130: PRINT RUN 1500 #'d SETS
1 Dikembe Mutombo .60 1.50
2 Jim Jackson .30 .75
3 Jason Terry .40 1.00
4 Kenny Anderson .30 .75
5 Antoine Walker .40 1.00
6 Paul Pierce .60 1.50
7 Jamal Mashburn .30 .75
8 Baron Davis .40 1.00
9 Derrick Coleman .40 1.00
10 Elton Brand .40 1.00
11 Ron Artest .40 1.00
12 Andre Miller .30 .75
13 Brevin Knight .25 .60
14 Trajan Langdon .25 .60
15 Lamond Murray .25 .60
16 Dirk Nowitzki 1.00 2.50
17 Michael Finley .40 1.00
18 Nick Van Exel .40 1.00
19 Antonio McDyess .30 .75
20 Raef LaFrentz .30 .75
21 Tariq Abdul-Wahad .25 .60
22 Cedric Ceballos .30 .75
23 Jerry Stackhouse .40 1.00
24 Jerome Williams .25 .60
25 Larry Hughes .40 1.00
26 Antawn Jamison .40 1.00
27 Mookie Blaylock .40 1.00
28 Steve Francis .40 1.00
29 Hakeem Olajuwon .75 2.00
30 Maurice Taylor .25 .60
31 Jonathan Bender .25 .60
32 Reggie Miller .75 2.00
33 Austin Croshere .25 .60
34 Travis Best .25 .60
35 Jalen Rose .30 .75
36 Lamar Odom .40 1.00
37 Corey Maggette .30 .75
38 Shaquille O'Neal 1.50 4.00
39 Kobe Bryant 3.00 8.00
40 Horace Grant .40 1.00
41 Isaiah Rider .30 .75
42 Brian Grant .30 .75
43 Eddie Jones .40 1.00
44 Tim Hardaway .50 1.25
45 Anthony Mason .40 1.00
46 Glenn Robinson .40 1.00
47 Ray Allen .60 1.50
48 Sam Cassell .30 .75
49 Tim Thomas .25 .60
50 Kevin Garnett 1.00 2.50
51 Terrell Brandon .30 .75
52 Joe Smith .30 .75
53 Wally Szczerbiak .30 .75
54 Chauncey Billups .50 1.25
55 Stephon Marbury .50 1.25
56 Keith Van Horn .30 .75
57 Kerry Kittles .30 .75
58 Allan Houston .40 1.00
59 Latrell Sprewell .50 1.25
60 Larry Johnson .50 1.25
61 Glen Rice .40 1.00
62 Grant Hill .60 1.50
63 Tracy McGrady .75 2.00
64 Darrell Armstrong .25 .60
65 Allen Iverson 1.00 2.50
66 Toni Kukoc .50 1.25
67 Theo Ratliff .25 .60
68 Jason Kidd .60 1.50
69 Anfernee Hardaway .60 1.50
70 Tom Gugliotta .30 .75
71 Clifford Robinson .40 1.00
72 Shawn Kemp .60 1.50
73 Scottie Pippen 1.00 2.50
74 Rasheed Wallace .50 1.25
75 Steve Smith .40 1.00
76 Chris Webber .50 1.25
77 Jason Williams .60 1.50
78 Peja Stojakovic .30 .75
79 Tim Duncan 1.00 2.50
80 David Robinson .75 2.00
81 Sean Elliott .30 .75
82 Derek Anderson .30 .75
83 Vin Baker .30 .75
84 Rashard Lewis .30 .75
85 Gary Payton .60 1.50
86 Patrick Ewing .60 1.50
87 Vince Carter .75 2.00
88 Mark Jackson .30 .75
89 Antonio Davis .30 .75
90 Karl Malone .75 2.00
91 John Stockton .75 2.00
92 Bryon Russell .25 .60
93 Donyell Marshall .30 .75
94 Shareef Abdur-Rahim .40 1.00
95 Mike Bibby .40 1.00
96 Michael Dickerson .25 .60
97 Mitch Richmond .50 1.25
98 Juwan Howard .30 .75
99 Richard Hamilton .50 1.25
100 Rod Strickland .25 .60
101 DerMarr Johnson RC 1.00 2.50
102 Kenyon Martin RC 3.00 8.00
103 Marcus Fizer RC 1.25 3.00
104 Courtney Alexander RC 1.00 2.50
105 Stromile Swift RC 1.25 3.00
106 Darius Miles RC 1.50 4.00
107 Mike Miller RC 2.50 6.00
108 Jamal Crawford RC 4.00 10.00
109 Speedy Claxton RC 1.25 3.00
110 Quentin Richardson RC 1.25 3.00
111 Keyon Dooling RC 1.25 3.00
112 Desmond Mason RC 2.00 5.00
113 Mateen Cleaves RC 1.50 4.00
114 Morris Peterson RC 1.50 4.00
115 Hedo Turkoglu RC 2.50 6.00
116 Donnell Harvey RC 1.00 2.50
117 Jerome Moiso RC 1.00 2.50
118 Jason Collier RC 1.50 4.00
119 Jamaal Magloire RC 1.50 4.00
120 Erick Barkley RC 1.00 2.50
121 Etan Thomas RC 1.25 3.00
122 DeShawn Stevenson RC 1.50 4.00
123 Dan Langhi RC 1.00 2.50
124 Mark Madsen RC 1.50 4.00
125 Khalid El-Amin RC 1.00 2.50
126 Lavor Postell RC 1.00 2.50
127 Eddie House RC 1.25 3.00
128 Michael Redd RC 4.00 10.00
129 Chris Porter RC 1.00 2.50
130 Mike Smith RC 1.00 2.50

2000-01 E-X Essential Credentials

*STARS: 8X TO 20X BASE CARD HI
*RCs: 5X TO 12X BASE HI
STARS: PRINT RUN 201 SERIAL #'d SETS
RCs: PRINT RUN 21 SERIAL #'d SETS
STATED ODDS 1:42
32 Reggie Miller 20.00 50.00
39 Kobe Bryant 400.00 800.00
50 Kevin Garnett 30.00 80.00
69 Anfernee Hardaway 15.00 40.00
72 Shawn Kemp 40.00 100.00
73 Scottie Pippen 15.00 40.00
77 Jason Williams 25.00 60.00
79 Tim Duncan 75.00 200.00
80 David Robinson 15.00 40.00
85 Gary Payton 12.00 30.00
87 Vince Carter 20.00 50.00
108 Jamal Crawford 75.00 200.00

2000-01 E-X Rookie Memorabilia

STATED PRINT RUN 250 TO 500 SETS
EXCH.DEADLINE 3/01/02
101 DerMarr Johnson JSY/275 2.00 5.00
102 Kenyon Martin JSY/275 6.00 15.00
103 Marcus Fizer BALL/275 2.50 6.00
104 Courtney Alexander AU/500 2.00 5.00
105 Stromile Swift JSY/275 2.50 6.00
106 Darius Miles JSY/275 3.00 8.00
107 Mike Miller JSY/275 5.00 12.00
108 Jamal Crawford AU/250 12.00 30.00
109 Speedy Claxton JSY/275 3.00 8.00
110 Quentin Richardson JSY/275 2.50 6.00
111 Keyon Dooling AU/250 2.50 6.00
112 Desmond Mason AU/500 4.00 10.00
113 Mateen Cleaves AU/500 2.50 6.00
114 Morris Peterson JSY/275 3.00 8.00
115 Hedo Turkoglu AU/250 5.00 12.00
116 Donnell Harvey AU/250 2.50 6.00
117 Jerome Moiso JSY/275 2.00 5.00
118 Jason Collier AU/250 3.00 8.00
120 Erick Barkley AU/250 2.00 5.00
121 Etan Thomas JSY/275 2.50 6.00
122 DeShawn Stevenson JSY/275 3.00 8.00
123 Dan Langhi AU/500 2.00 5.00
125 Khalid El-Amin AU/500 2.00 5.00
126 Lavor Postell AU/500 2.00 5.00
127 Eddie House AU/500 2.50 6.00
128 Michael Redd AU/500 3.00 8.00
129 Chris Porter AU/500 2.00 5.00
130 Mike Smith AU/500 2.00 5.00

2000-01 E-X Vince Carter Rookie Remnants

NNO Vince Carter FLR JSY/15 20.00 50.00
NNO Vince Carter FLR/100 12.50 30.00

2000-01 E-X Generation E-X

STATED ODDS 1:24
GE1 Vince Carter 2.00 5.00
GE2 Grant Hill 1.50 4.00
GE3 Lamar Odom 1.00 2.50
GE4 Allen Iverson 2.50 6.00
GE5 Keith Van Horn .75 2.00
GE6 Shareef Abdur-Rahim 1.00 2.50
GE7 Dirk Nowitzki 2.50 6.00
GE8 Morris Peterson 1.00 2.50
GE9 Mike Miller 1.50 4.00
GE10 Darius Miles 1.00 2.50
GE11 Speedy Claxton 1.00 2.50
GE12 Kenyon Martin 2.00 5.00
GE13 Stromile Swift .75 2.00
GE14 Courtney Alexander .60 1.50
GE15 V.Carter/M.Peterson 2.00 5.00
GE16 G.Hill/M.Miller 1.50 4.00
GE17 L.Odom/D.Miles 1.00 2.50
GE18 A.Iverson/S.Claxton 2.50 6.00
GE19 K.Van Horn/K.Martin 2.00 5.00
GE20 S.Abdur-Rahim/S.Swift 1.00 2.50
GE21 D.Nowitzki/C.Alexander 2.50 6.00

2000-01 E-X Generation E-X Game Jerseys

OVERALL STATED ODDS 1:85
SINGLE GJ EXCH: PRINT RUN 600 #'d SETS
DUAL GJ EXCH: PRINT RUN 100 #'d SETS
1 Shareef Abdur-Rahim 3.00 8.00
2 S.Abdur-Rahim/S.Swift 4.00 10.00
3 Vince Carter 6.00 15.00
4 Speedy Claxton 2.50 6.00
5 Grant Hill 5.00 12.00
6 G.Hill/M.Miller 6.00 15.00
7 Allen Iverson 8.00 20.00
8 A.Iverson/S.Claxton 6.00 15.00
9 Kenyon Martin 5.00 12.00
10 Darius Miles 2.50 6.00
11 Mike Miller 4.00 10.00
12 Dirk Nowitzki 8.00 20.00
13 Lamar Odom 3.00 8.00
14 L.Odom/D.Miles 4.00 10.00
16 Stromile Swift 2.00 5.00
17 Keith Van Horn 2.50 6.00
18 K.Van Horn/K.Martin 6.00 15.00

2000-01 E-X Gravity Denied

COMPLETE SET (10) 20.00 50.00
STATED ODDS 1:48
GD1 Vince Carter 4.00 10.00
GD2 Jason Kidd 3.00 8.00
GD3 Eddie Jones 2.00 5.00
GD4 Tracy McGrady 4.00 10.00
GD5 Kobe Bryant 15.00 40.00
GD6 Grant Hill 3.00 8.00
GD7 Lamar Odom 2.00 5.00
GD8 Steve Francis 2.00 5.00
GD9 Kevin Garnett 5.00 12.00
GD10 Allen Iverson 5.00 12.00

2000-01 E-X NBA Debut Postmarks

STATED ODDS 1:288
PM1 Kenyon Martin 6.00 15.00
PM3 Darius Miles 3.00 8.00
PM4 Marcus Fizer 2.50 6.00
PM5 Mike Miller 5.00 12.00
PM6 Dermarr Johnson 2.00 5.00
PM7 Jamal Crawford 8.00 20.00
PM8 Jerome Moiso 2.00 5.00
PM9 Courtney Alexander 2.00 5.00
PM11 Hedo Turkoglu 5.00 12.00
PM13 Jamaal Magloire 3.00 8.00
PM14 Keyon Dooling 2.50 6.00

2000-01 E-X Net Assets

COMPLETE SET (20) 15.00 30.00
STATED ODDS 1:8
NA1 Vince Carter 1.50 4.00
NA2 Reggie Miller 1.50 4.00
NA3 Karl Malone 1.50 4.00
NA4 Ray Allen 1.25 3.00
NA5 Dirk Nowitzki 2.00 5.00
NA6 Scottie Pippen 2.00 5.00
NA7 Tracy McGrady 1.50 4.00
NA8 Kobe Bryant 6.00 15.00
NA9 Larry Hughes .75 2.00
NA10 Shareef Abdur-Rahim .75 2.00
NA11 Tim Duncan 2.00 5.00
NA12 Gary Payton 1.25 3.00
NA13 Eddie Jones .75 2.00
NA14 Steve Francis .75 2.00
NA15 Antoine Walker .75 2.00
NA16 Kevin Garnett 2.00 5.00
NA17 Chris Webber 1.00 2.50
NA18 Shaquille O'Neal 3.00 8.00
NA19 Jason Kidd 1.25 3.00
NA20 Elton Brand .75 2.00

2000-01 E-X No Boundaries

COMPLETE SET (10) 10.00 25.00
STATED ODDS 1:12
NB1 Vince Carter 1.50 4.00
NB2 Shareef Abdur-Rahim .75 2.00
NB3 Elton Brand .75 2.00
NB4 Shaquille O'Neal 3.00 8.00
NB5 Kobe Bryant 6.00 15.00
NB6 Allen Iverson 2.00 5.00
NB7 Tim Duncan 2.00 5.00
NB8 Steve Francis .75 2.00
NB9 Kevin Garnett 2.00 5.00
NB10 Grant Hill 1.25 3.00

2001-02 E-X

COMPLETE SET (130) 75.00 150.00
COMP.SET w/o SP's (100) 15.00 40.00
1 Shareef Abdur-Rahim .30 .75
2 DerMarr Johnson .25 .60
3 Jason Terry .40 1.00
4 Paul Pierce .60 1.50
5 Antoine Walker .30 .75
6 Baron Davis .40 1.00
7 Jamal Mashburn .30 .75
8 Chris Mihm .25 .60
9 Andre Miller .30 .75
10 Dirk Nowitzki 1.00 2.50
11 Michael Finley .40 1.00
12 Raef LaFrentz .25 .60
13 Antonio McDyess .30 .75
14 Jerry Stackhouse .40 1.00
15 Antawn Jamison .30 .75
16 Steve Francis .40 1.00
17 Jalen Rose .30 .75
18 Elton Brand .30 .75
19 Darius Miles .25 .60
20 Lamar Odom .30 .75
21 Mitch Richmond .50 1.25
22 Michael Dickerson .25 .60
23 Stromile Swift .25 .60
24 Alonzo Mourning .60 1.50
25 Courtney Alexander .25 .60
26 Ray Allen .60 1.50
27 Glenn Robinson .40 1.00
28 Terrell Brandon .30 .75
29 Wally Szczerbiak .30 .75
30 Joe Smith .30 .75
31 Jason Kidd .60 1.50
32 Kenyon Martin .40 1.00
33 Keith Van Horn .30 .75
34 Grant Hill .60 1.50
35 Tracy McGrady .60 1.50
36 Mike Miller .30 .75
37 Allen Iverson 1.00 2.50
38 Speedy Claxton .25 .60
39 Dikembe Mutombo .60 1.50
40 Tom Gugliotta .25 .60
41 Penny Hardaway 1.00 2.50
42 Stephon Marbury .50 1.25
43 Shawn Marion .40 1.00
44 Rasheed Wallace .50 1.25
45 Peja Stojakovic .30 .75
46 Mike Bibby .40 1.00
47 Chris Webber .50 1.25
48 David Robinson .75 2.00
49 Vin Baker .30 .75
50 Rashard Lewis .30 .75
51 Desmond Mason .30 .75
52 Gary Payton .60 1.50
53 Vince Carter .75 2.00
54 Antonio Davis .30 .75
55 Hakeem Olajuwon .75 2.00
56 Morris Peterson .25 .60
57 Karl Malone .75 2.00
58 DeShawn Stevenson .25 .60
59 John Stockton .75 2.00
60 Richard Hamilton .50 1.25
61 Corey Maggette .30 .75
62 Steve Smith .30 .75
63 Tim Thomas .25 .60
64 Lindsey Hunter .25 .60
65 Jermaine O'Neal .30 .75
66 Cuttino Mobley .30 .75
67 Nick Van Exel .40 1.00
68 Juwan Howard .30 .75
69 James Posey .25 .60
70 David Wesley .25 .60
71 Marcus Fizer .25 .60
72 Jumaine Jones .25 .60
73 Tim Hardaway .50 1.25
74 Danny Fortson .25 .60
75 Jonathan Bender .25 .60
76 Quentin Richardson .25 .60
77 Eddie House .25 .60
78 Kurt Thomas .25 .60
79 Anthony Mason .40 1.00
80 Theo Ratliff .25 .60
81 Allan Houston .40 1.00
82 Latrell Sprewell .50 1.25
83 Jason Williams .60 1.50
84 Eddie Jones .40 1.00
85 Damon Stoudamire .40 1.00
86 Sam Cassell .30 .75
87 Cliff Robinson .30 .75
88 Patrick Ewing .60 1.50
89 Tim Duncan 1.00 2.50
90 Marcus Camby .30 .75
91 Brian Grant .25 .60
92 Kobe Bryant 3.00 8.00
93 Ron Mercer .25 .60
94 Reggie Miller .75 2.00
95 Shaquille O'Neal 1.50 4.00
96 Kevin Garnett 1.00 2.50
97 Scottie Pippen 1.00 2.50
98 Michael Jordan 6.00 15.00
99 Steve Nash .75 2.00
100 Derek Anderson .25 .60
101 Kedrick Brown/1750 RC .50 1.25
102 Joseph Forte/1750 RC .50 1.25
103 Joe Johnson/1250 RC 1.50 4.00
104 Kirk Haston/1750 RC .50 1.25
105 Tyson Chandler/750 RC 2.50 6.00
106 Eddy Curry/1250 RC 1.00 2.50
107 DeSagana Diop/1750 RC .50 1.25
108 Trenton Hassell/1250 RC .60 1.50
109 Zeljko Rebraca/1250 RC 1.00 2.50
110 Rodney White/1750 RC .50 1.25
111 Troy Murphy/1250 RC .75 2.00
112 Jason Richardson/750 RC 2.50 6.00
113 Eddie Griffin/750 RC 1.25 3.00
114 Terence Morris/1750 RC .50 1.25
115 Oscar Torres/1250 RC 1.00 2.50
116 Jamaal Tinsley/750 RC 1.25 3.00
117 Pau Gasol/750 RC 6.00 15.00
118 Shane Battier/750 RC 3.00 8.00
119 Brandon Armstrong/1250 RC .60 1.50
120 Richard Jefferson/750 RC 2.00 5.00
121 Steven Hunter/1250 RC .60 1.50
122 Samuel Dalembert/1750 RC .75 2.00
123 Zach Randolph/1250 RC 2.00 5.00
124 Gerald Wallace/1750 RC 1.00 2.50
125 Tony Parker/750 RC 6.00 15.00
126 V.Radmanovic/1250 RC .75 2.00
127 Michael Bradley/1750 RC .50 1.25
128 Jarron Collins/1750 RC .75 2.00
129 Andrei Kirilenko/750 RC 2.50 6.00
130 Kwame Brown/750 RC 1.50 4.00

2001-02 E-X Essential Credentials Future

*STARS #'d 21-40: 10X TO 25X BASE CARD HI
*STARS #'d 41-60: 6X TO 15X BASE CARD HI
*STARS #'d 61-70: 5X TO 12X BASE CARD HI
PRINT RUNS BETWEEN 1 AND 70
LOWER PRINT RUNS NOT PRICED
89 Tim Duncan/42 40.00 100.00
95 Shaquille O'Neal/36 100.00 250.00
103 Joe Johnson/28 30.00 80.00
105 Tyson Chandler/26 30.00 80.00

2001-02 E-X Essential Credentials Future Memorabilia

*STARS #'d 21-40: 10X TO 25X BASE CARD HI
*STARS #'d 41-60: 12X TO 30X BASE HI
PRINT RUNS BETWEEN 1 AND 60
LOWER PRINT RUNS NOT PRICED
26 Ray Allen/35 15.00 40.00

2001-02 E-X Essential Credentials Now

*STARS #'d 21-40: 10X TO 25X BASE CARD HI
*STARS #'d 41-60: 6X TO 15X BASE CARD HI
PRINT RUNS BETWEEN 1 AND 70
LOWER PRINT RUNS NOT PRICED
89 Tim Duncan/29 60.00 150.00
98 Michael Jordan/38 200.00 500.00
103 Joe Johnson/43 20.00 50.00
104 Kirk Haston/44 8.00 20.00
105 Tyson Chandler/45 20.00 50.00
106 Eddy Curry/46 12.00 30.00
107 DeSagana Diop/47 8.00 20.00
108 Trenton Hassell/48 8.00 20.00
109 Zeljko Rebraca/49 12.00 30.00
110 Rodney White/50 8.00 20.00
111 Troy Murphy/51 10.00 25.00
112 Jason Richardson/52 20.00 50.00
113 Eddie Griffin/53 10.00 25.00
114 Terence Morris/54 8.00 20.00
115 Oscar Torres/55 12.00 30.00
116 Jamaal Tinsley/56 10.00 25.00
117 Pau Gasol/57 50.00 125.00
118 Shane Battier/58 25.00 60.00
119 Brandon Armstrong/59 8.00 20.00
120 Richard Jefferson/60 12.00 30.00
121 Steven Hunter/61 8.00 20.00
122 Samuel Dalembert/62 12.00 30.00
123 Zach Randolph/63 25.00 60.00
124 Gerald Wallace/64 15.00 40.00
125 Tony Parker/65 50.00 125.00
126 Vladimir Radmanovic/66 10.00 25.00
127 Michael Bradley/67 8.00 20.00
128 Jarron Collins/68 12.00 30.00
129 Andrei Kirilenko/69 20.00 50.00
130 Kwame Brown/70 12.00 30.00

2001-02 E-X Essential Credentials Now Memorabilia

*STARS #'d 21-40: 12X TO 30X BASE CARD HI
*STARS #'d 41-60: 10X TO 25X BASE HI
PRINT RUNS BETWEEN 1 AND 60
LOWER PRINT RUNS NOT PRICED
26 Ray Allen/26 15.00 40.00
34 Grant Hill/34 30.00 80.00
47 Chris Webber/47 20.00 50.00
48 David Robinson/48 50.00 120.00
59 John Stockton/59 15.00 40.00

2001-02 E-X Behind the Numbers

STATED ODDS 1:288
1 Larry Bird 25.00 60.00
2 Allen Iverson 15.00 40.00
3 David Robinson 12.00 30.00
4 Karl Malone 12.00 30.00
5 Tracy McGrady 10.00 25.00
6 Steve Francis 6.00 15.00
7 Jason Terry 6.00 15.00
8 Antoine Walker 5.00 12.00
9 Grant Hill 10.00 25.00
10 Michael Finley 6.00 15.00
11 Jason Kidd 10.00 25.00
12 Alonzo Mourning 10.00 25.00
13 Darius Miles 4.00 10.00
14 Ray Allen 10.00 25.00
15A Vince Carter 12.00 30.00
15B Vince Carter AU 15.00 40.00

2001-02 E-X Behind the Numbers Jerseys

STATED ODDS 1:24
1 Larry Bird 12.00 30.00
2 Vince Carter 6.00 15.00
3 Baron Davis 3.00 8.00
4 Michael Finley 3.00 8.00
5 Steve Francis 3.00 8.00
6 Grant Hill 5.00 12.00
7 Allen Iverson 8.00 20.00
8 Jason Kidd 5.00 12.00
9 Karl Malone 6.00 15.00
10 Kenyon Martin 3.00 8.00
11 Tracy McGrady 5.00 12.00
12 Darius Miles 2.00 5.00
13 Alonzo Mourning 6.00 15.00
14 Dirk Nowitzki 8.00 20.00
15 Gary Payton 5.00 12.00
16 Paul Pierce 5.00 12.00
17 Jason Terry 3.00 8.00
18 Antoine Walker 2.50 6.00

2001-02 E-X Behind the Numbers Jerseys Autographs

PRINT RUNS LISTED BELOW
1 Larry Bird/33 125.00 250.00
2 Vince Carter/15 75.00 200.00

2001-02 E-X Box Office Draws
COMPLETE SET (20) 15.00 40.00
STATED ODDS 1:24
1 Shareef Abdur-Rahim 1.00 2.50
2 John Stockton 2.50 6.00
3 Peja Stojakovic 1.00 2.50
4 Elton Brand 1.00 2.50
5 Stephon Marbury 1.50 4.00
6 Eddie Jones 1.25 3.00
7 Baron Davis 1.25 3.00
8 Keith Van Horn 1.00 2.50
9 Paul Pierce 2.00 5.00
10 Gary Payton 2.00 5.00
11 Grant Hill 2.00 5.00
12 Chris Webber 1.50 4.00
13 Latrell Sprewell 1.50 4.00
14 Jerry Stackhouse 1.25 3.00
15 Vince Carter 2.50 6.00
16 Allen Iverson 3.00 8.00
17 Dirk Nowitzki 3.00 8.00
18 Shawn Marion 1.25 3.00
19 Steve Francis 1.25 3.00
20 Richard Hamilton 1.50 4.00

2001-02 E-X Box Office Draws Memorabilia
STATED ODDS 1:33
1 Shareef Abdur-Rahim Warm 3.00 8.00
2 Elton Brand Warm 3.00 8.00
3 Vince Carter Shorts 8.00 20.00
4 Michael Finley Shorts 4.00 10.00
5 Steve Francis Shorts 4.00 10.00
6 Richard Hamilton Shorts 5.00 12.00
7 Grant Hill Shorts 6.00 15.00
8 Allen Iverson Shorts 10.00 25.00
9 Stephon Marbury Warm 5.00 12.00
10 Shawn Marion Shorts 4.00 10.00
11 Tracy McGrady Shorts 6.00 15.00
12 Dirk Nowitzki Shorts 10.00 25.00
13 Lamar Odom Shorts 3.00 8.00
14 Paul Pierce Warm 6.00 15.00
15 Jerry Stackhouse Warm 4.00 10.00
16 John Stockton Warm 8.00 20.00
17 Peja Stojakovic Warm 3.00 8.00
18 Keith Van Horn Warm 3.00 8.00
19 Chris Webber Warm 5.00 12.00

2001-02 E-X Net Assets
STATED ODDS 1:12
1 Kobe Bryant 6.00 15.00
2 Kwame Brown .75 2.00
3 Kevin Garnett 2.00 5.00
4 Eddie Griffin .60 1.50
5 Shaquille O'Neal 3.00 8.00
6 Tim Duncan 2.00 5.00
7 Tyson Chandler 1.25 3.00
8 Allen Iverson 2.00 5.00
9 Grant Hill 1.25 3.00
10 Michael Jordan 6.00 15.00
11 Ray Allen 1.25 3.00
12 Jason Richardson 1.25 3.00
13 Eddy Curry .75 2.00
14 Dirk Nowitzki 2.00 5.00
15 Vince Carter 1.50 4.00

2003-04 E-X
COMP.SET w/o SP's (72) 20.00 50.00
1 Shareef Abdur-Rahim .50 1.25
2 Ray Allen .75 2.00
3 Gilbert Arenas .50 1.25
4 Ron Artest .50 1.25
5 Mike Bibby .50 1.25
6 Chauncey Billups .60 1.50
7 Elton Brand .40 1.00
8 Kwame Brown .30 .75
9 Kobe Bryant 12.00 30.00
10 Caron Butler .40 1.00
11 Vince Carter 1.00 2.50
12 Eddy Curry .30 .75
13 Ricky Davis .40 1.00
14 Baron Davis .50 1.25
15 Tim Duncan 1.25 3.00
16 Michael Finley .50 1.25
17 Steve Francis .50 1.25
18 Kevin Garnett 1.25 3.00
19 Pau Gasol .75 2.00
20 Manu Ginobili 1.00 2.50
21 Drew Gooden .40 1.00
22 Nene .40 1.00
23 Grant Hill .60 1.50
24 Allan Houston .50 1.25
25 Juwan Howard .40 1.00
26 Zydrunas Ilgauskas .40 1.00
27 Allen Iverson 1.25 3.00
28 Antawn Jamison .50 1.25
29 Richard Jefferson .40 1.00
30 Eddie Jones .50 1.25
31 Jason Kidd .75 2.00
32 Andrei Kirilenko .40 1.00
33 Rashard Lewis .40 1.00
34 Corey Maggette .40 1.00
35 Karl Malone 1.00 2.50
36 Stephon Marbury .60 1.50
37 Shawn Marion .50 1.25
38 Kenyon Martin .50 1.25
39 Jamal Mashburn .40 1.00
40 Tracy McGrady .75 2.00
41 Reggie Miller 1.00 2.50
42 Mike Miller .40 1.00
43 Yao Ming 1.25 3.00
44 Cuttino Mobley .30 .75
45 Steve Nash 1.00 2.50
46 Dirk Nowitzki 1.25 3.00
47 Jermaine O'Neal .50 1.25
48 Shaquille O'Neal 2.00 5.00
49 Tony Parker .75 2.00
50 Gary Payton .75 2.00
51 Morris Peterson .30 .75
52 Paul Pierce .75 2.00
53 Scottie Pippen 1.25 3.00
54 Tayshaun Prince .30 .75
55 Vladimir Radmanovic .30 .75
56 Michael Redd .50 1.25
57 Jason Richardson .50 1.25
58 Glenn Robinson .40 1.00
59 Jalen Rose .40 1.00
60 Latrell Sprewell .60 1.50
61 Jerry Stackhouse .60 1.50
62 Peja Stojakovic .40 1.00
63 Amare Stoudemire .60 1.50
64 Wally Szczerbiak .40 1.00
65 Jason Terry .40 1.00
66 Keith Van Horn .40 1.00
67 Dajuan Wagner .30 .75
68 Antoine Walker .50 1.25
69 Ben Wallace .60 1.50
70 Rasheed Wallace .60 1.50
71 Chris Webber .60 1.50
72 Bonzi Wells .30 .75
73 Carmelo Anthony RC 15.00 40.00
74 Ndudi Ebi RC 2.00 5.00
75 Luke Ridnour RC 3.00 8.00
76 Josh Howard RC 3.00 8.00
77 Marcus Banks RC 2.00 5.00
78 Zarko Cabarkapa RC 2.00 5.00
79 Kendrick Perkins RC 2.50 6.00
80 Leandro Barbosa RC 3.00 8.00
81 David West RC 4.00 10.00
82 Boris Diaw RC 3.00 8.00
83 Carlos Delfino RC 2.50 6.00
84 Mickael Pietrus RC 2.50 6.00
85 Troy Bell RC 2.00 5.00
86 Reece Gaines RC 2.00 5.00
87 Brian Cook RC 2.00 5.00
88 Kirk Hinrich RC 3.00 8.00
89 Travis Outlaw RC 2.50 6.00
90 Dwyane Wade RC 25.00 60.00
91 Luke Walton RC 3.00 8.00
92 Chris Bosh RC 10.00 25.00
93 Jarvis Hayes RC 2.00 5.00
94 Maciej Lampe RC 2.00 5.00
95 Mike Sweetney RC 2.00 5.00
96 Sofoklis Schortsanitis RC 2.00 5.00
97 Dahntay Jones RC 2.50 6.00
98 Nick Collison RC 2.50 6.00
99 Chris Kaman RC 3.00 8.00
100 Darko Milicic RC 2.50 6.00
101 T.J. Ford RC 2.50 6.00
102 LeBron James RC 600.00 1,200.00

2003-04 E-X Essential Credentials Future
*SINGLES #'d 25-30: 2.5X TO 6X BASE HI
*SINGLES #'d 31-40: 10X TO 25X BASE HI
*SINGLES #'d 41-60: 8X TO 20X BASE HI
*SINGLES #'d 61-80: 6X TO 15X BASE HI
*SINGLES #'d 81-102: 5X TO 12X BASE HI
STATED ODDS 1:28
2 Ray Allen/101 75.00 200.00
3 Gilbert Arenas/100 12.00 30.00
4 Ron Artest/98 12.00 30.00
5 Mike Bibby/98 12.00 30.00
6 Chauncey Billups/97 40.00 100.00
9 Kobe Bryant/94 1,000.00 2,000.00
11 Vince Carter/92 150.00 400.00
14 Baron Davis/89 12.00 30.00
15 Tim Duncan/88 200.00 500.00
18 Kevin Garnett/85 200.00 500.00
19 Pau Gasol/84 30.00 80.00
20 Manu Ginobili/83 125.00 300.00
23 Grant Hill/80 150.00 400.00
31 Jason Kidd/72 40.00 100.00
35 Karl Malone/68 125.00 300.00
36 Stephon Marbury/67 40.00 100.00
40 Tracy McGrady/63 125.00 300.00
41 Reggie Miller/62 125.00 300.00
43 Yao Ming/60 300.00 600.00
45 Steve Nash/58 125.00 300.00
46 Dirk Nowitzki/57 150.00 400.00
48 Shaquille O'Neal/55 50.00 120.00
49 Tony Parker/54 20.00 50.00
50 Gary Payton/53 30.00 80.00
52 Paul Pierce/51 150.00 400.00
53 Scottie Pippen/50 200.00 500.00
61 Jerry Stackhouse/42 15.00 40.00
69 Ben Wallace/34 40.00 100.00
70 Rasheed Wallace/33 75.00 200.00
71 Chris Webber/32 100.00 250.00
73 Carmelo Anthony/30 500.00 1,000.00

2003-04 E-X Essential Credentials Now
*SINGLES #'d 25-40: 12.5X TO 30X BASE HI
*SINGLES #'d 41-60: 10X TO 25X BASE HI
*SINGLES #'d 61-72: 6X TO 15X BASE HI
*SINGLES #'d 73-102: 1.5X TO 4X BASE HI
STATED ODDS 1:28
20 Manu Ginobili/20 400.00 800.00
27 Allen Iverson/27 1,500.00 3,000.00
35 Karl Malone/35 100.00 250.00
40 Tracy McGrady/40 125.00 300.00
41 Reggie Miller/41 125.00 300.00
43 Yao Ming/43 300.00 600.00
45 Steve Nash/45 125.00 300.00
46 Dirk Nowitzki/46 150.00 400.00
48 Shaquille O'Neal/48 400.00 800.00
49 Tony Parker/49 50.00 120.00
50 Gary Payton/50 75.00 200.00
52 Paul Pierce/52 150.00 400.00
53 Scottie Pippen/53 200.00 500.00
70 Rasheed Wallace/70 60.00 150.00
71 Chris Webber/71 75.00 200.00
73 Carmelo Anthony/73 1,000.00 2,000.00
90 Dwyane Wade/90 1,500.00 3,000.00
92 Chris Bosh/92 150.00 400.00
102 LeBron James/102 20,000.00 40,000.00

2003-04 E-X Behind the Numbers
COMPLETE SET (15) 15.00 30.00
STATED ODDS 1:80
1 Dirk Nowitzki 3.00 8.00
2 Antoine Walker 1.25 3.00
3 Tayshaun Prince 1.25 3.00
4 Jason Kidd 2.00 5.00
5 Tracy McGrady 2.00 5.00
6 Allen Iverson 3.00 8.00
7 Pau Gasol 2.00 5.00
8 Eddy Curry .75 2.00
9 Elton Brand 1.00 2.50
10 Amare Stoudemire 1.50 4.00
11 Manu Ginobili 2.50 6.00
12 Andrei Kirilenko 1.00 2.50
13 Kevin Garnett 3.00 8.00
14 Peja Stojakovic 1.00 2.50
15 Kenyon Martin 1.25 3.00

2003-04 E-X Behind the Numbers Game-Used
STATED ODDS 1:10
*GOLD: .5X TO 1.25X BASE HI
GOLD PRINT RUN 150 SER.#'d SETS
1 Dirk Nowitzki 6.00 15.00
2 Antoine Walker 2.50 6.00
3 Tayshaun Prince 2.50 6.00
4 Jason Kidd 4.00 10.00
5 Tracy McGrady 4.00 10.00
6 Allen Iverson 6.00 15.00
7 Pau Gasol 4.00 10.00
8 Eddy Curry 1.50 4.00
9 Elton Brand 2.00 5.00
10 Amare Stoudemire 3.00 8.00
11 Manu Ginobili 5.00 12.00
12 Andrei Kirilenko 2.00 5.00
13 Kevin Garnett 6.00 15.00
14 Peja Stojakovic 2.00 5.00
15 Kenyon Martin 2.50 6.00
16 Tyson Chandler 2.50 6.00
17 Latrell Sprewell 3.00 8.00
18 Caron Butler 2.00 5.00
19 Drew Gooden 2.00 5.00
20 Marcus Haislip 2.00 5.00
21 Kwame Brown 2.00 5.00
22 Vince Carter 5.00 12.00
23 Jermaine O'Neal 2.50 6.00
24 Joe Johnson 2.00 5.00
25 Yao Ming 6.00 15.00

2003-04 E-X Buzzer Beaters
COMPLETE SET (10) 40.00 80.00
STATED ODDS 1:240
1 Vince Carter 8.00 20.00
2 Ben Wallace 5.00 12.00
3 Amare Stoudemire 5.00 12.00
4 Tony Parker 6.00 15.00
5 Kenyon Martin 4.00 10.00
6 Tracy McGrady 6.00 15.00
7 Dirk Nowitzki 10.00 25.00
8 Gilbert Arenas 4.00 10.00
9 Kevin Garnett 10.00 25.00
10 Elton Brand 3.00 8.00

2003-04 E-X Buzzer Beaters Autographs
STATED PRINT RUN 99 TO 299 SETS
1 Ben Wallace/299 40.00 100.00
2 Amare Stoudemire/99 25.00 60.00
5 Tracy McGrady/299 60.00 150.00
6 Gilbert Arenas/99 15.00 40.00
7 Carmelo Anthony/299 75.00 200.00
8 Mike Sweetney/299 8.00 20.00
9 Chris Bosh/299 40.00 100.00
10 Dwyane Wade/299 125.00 300.00

2003-04 E-X Jambalaya
STATED ODDS 1:480
1 LeBron James 8,000.00 15,000.00
2 Carmelo Anthony 500.00 1,000.00
3 Dwyane Wade 1,500.00 3,000.00
4 Darko Milicic 20.00 50.00
5 T.J. Ford 20.00 50.00
6 Chris Bosh 300.00 600.00
7 Mike Sweetney 8.00 20.00
8 Kobe Bryant 4,000.00 8,000.00
9 Jermaine O'Neal 20.00 50.00
10 Vince Carter 300.00 600.00
11 Allen Iverson 300.00 600.00
12 Tracy McGrady 200.00 500.00
13 Yao Ming 200.00 500.00
14 Shaquille O'Neal 500.00 1,000.00
15 Tim Duncan 300.00 600.00

2003-04 E-X Net Assets
COMPLETE SET (10) 8.00 20.00
STATED ODDS 1:32
1 Kobe Bryant 6.00 15.00
2 Jason Richardson .75 2.00
3 Tim Duncan 2.00 5.00
4 Chris Webber 1.00 2.50
5 Jason Kidd 1.25 3.00
6 Steve Nash 1.50 4.00
7 Allen Iverson 2.00 5.00
8 Steve Francis .75 2.00
9 Paul Pierce 1.25 3.00
10 Shaquille O'Neal 3.00 8.00

2003-04 E-X Net Assets Game-Used
STATED ODDS 1:12
1 Chris Webber 3.00 8.00
2 Jason Kidd 4.00 10.00
3 Steve Nash 5.00 12.00
4 Allen Iverson 6.00 15.00
5 Steve Francis 2.50 6.00
6 Paul Pierce 4.00 10.00
7 Jerry Stackhouse 3.00 8.00
8 Reggie Miller 5.00 12.00
9 Bonzi Wells 1.50 4.00
10 Shane Battier 2.00 5.00
11 Dajuan Wagner 1.50 4.00
12 Andre Miller 2.00 5.00
13 Nene Hilario 2.00 5.00
14 Tony Parker 4.00 10.00
15 Jamal Mashburn 2.00 5.00

2003-04 E-X Net Assets Patch
*PATCH: 1.25X TO 3X BASE GU HI
STATED PRINT RUN 75 SERIAL #'d SETS
1 Chris Webber 12.00 30.00
4 Allen Iverson 15.00 40.00
8 Reggie Miller 15.00 40.00

2004-05 E-XL
COMP.SET w/o SP's (70) 15.00 40.00
71-94 PRINT RUN 399 SER.#'d SETS
95-110 PRINT RUN 899 SER.#'d SETS
1 Dwyane Wade 1.50 4.00
2 Kobe Bryant 3.00 8.00
3 Mike Bibby .40 1.00
4 Michael Finley .40 1.00
5 Jamal Mashburn .40 1.00
6 Carmelo Anthony .75 2.00
7 Jason Kidd .60 1.50
8 Andrei Kirilenko .40 1.00
9 Ron Artest .40 1.00
10 Peja Stojakovic .40 1.00
11 Yao Ming 1.00 2.50
12 Shawn Marion .40 1.00
13 Desmond Mason .30 .75
14 Paul Pierce .60 1.50
15 Pau Gasol .60 1.50
16 Tim Duncan 1.00 2.50
17 Andre Miller .30 .75
18 Allan Houston .40 1.00
19 Ben Wallace .50 1.25
20 Stephon Marbury .50 1.25
21 Gilbert Arenas .40 1.00
22 Luke Walton .30 .75
23 Rashard Lewis .30 .75
24 Elton Brand .30 .75
25 Zach Randolph .40 1.00
26 Eddy Curry .25 .60
27 Richard Jefferson .30 .75
28 Kirk Hinrich .40 1.00
29 Jason Terry .30 .75
30 Ray Allen .60 1.50
31 Mike Dunleavy .25 .60
32 Glenn Robinson .30 .75
33 Darko Milicic .25 .60
34 Steve Francis .40 1.00
35 Antawn Jamison .40 1.00
36 Jason Williams .30 .75
37 Tracy McGrady .60 1.50
38 Steve Nash .75 2.00
39 Gary Payton .60 1.50
40 Sam Cassell .30 .75
41 Gerald Wallace .30 .75
42 Shaquille O'Neal 1.50 4.00
43 Tony Parker .60 1.50
44 Richard Hamilton .50 1.25
45 Kenyon Martin .40 1.00
46 Baron Davis .40 1.00
47 Jarvis Hayes .25 .60
48 Chris Kaman .30 .75
49 Manu Ginobili .75 2.00
50 Jermaine O'Neal .30 .75
51 Amare Stoudemire .40 1.00
52 Latrell Sprewell .50 1.25
53 LeBron James 3.00 8.00
54 Michael Redd .30 .75
55 Chris Bosh .60 1.50
56 Juwan Howard .30 .75
57 Jason Richardson .40 1.00
58 Allen Iverson 1.00 2.50
59 Antoine Walker .40 1.00
60 Eddie Jones .40 1.00
61 Carlos Arroyo .25 .60
62 Lamar Odom .40 1.00
63 Chris Webber .50 1.25
64 Drew Gooden .25 .60
65 Jamaal Magloire .25 .60
66 Dirk Nowitzki 1.00 2.50
67 Kevin Garnett 1.00 2.50
68 Vince Carter .75 2.00
69 Reggie Miller .75 2.00
70 Shareef Abdur-Rahim .40 1.00
71 Emeka Okafor RC 2.00 5.00
72 Pavel Podkolzin RC 1.50 4.00
73 Kirk Snyder RC 1.50 4.00
74 Ben Gordon RC 2.50 6.00
75 Devin Harris RC 2.00 5.00
76 Josh Childress RC 1.50 4.00
77 Dorell Wright RC 2.00 5.00
78 Dwight Howard RC 8.00 20.00
79 Andre Iguodala RC 4.00 10.00
80 Viktor Khryapa RC 1.50 4.00
81 Al Jefferson RC 2.50 6.00
82 Kevin Martin RC 3.00 8.00
83 Delonte West RC 2.00 5.00
84 Josh Smith RC 2.50 6.00
85 Luol Deng RC 2.50 6.00
86 Kris Humphries RC 2.00 5.00
87 Sebastian Telfair RC 2.00 5.00
88 Rafael Araujo RC 1.50 4.00
89 Jameer Nelson RC 2.50 6.00
90 Shaun Livingston RC 2.50 6.00
91 Andris Biedrins RC 1.50 4.00
92 Robert Swift RC 1.50 4.00
93 Luke Jackson RC 1.50 4.00
94 J.R. Smith RC 2.50 6.00
95 Tony Allen RC 1.50 4.00
96 Sasha Vujacic RC 1.25 3.00
97 David Harrison RC 1.00 2.50
98 Anderson Varejao RC 1.25 3.00
99 Jackson Vroman RC 1.00 2.50
100 Peter John Ramos RC 1.00 2.50
101 Lionel Chalmers RC 1.25 3.00
102 Donta Smith RC 1.00 2.50
103 Andre Emmett RC 1.00 2.50
104 Trevor Ariza RC 1.50 4.00
105 Tim Pickett RC 1.25 3.00
106 Bernard Robinson RC 1.00 2.50
107 Matt Freije RC 1.00 2.50

2004-05 E-XL Essential Credentials Future
*SINGLES #'d 81-107: 4X TO 10X BASE HI
*SINGLES #'d 61-80: 5X TO 12X BASE HI
*SINGLES #'d 38-60: 6X TO 15X BASE HI
*RCs #'d 26-37: 1.5X TO 4X BASE HI
*RCs #'d 15-25: 2X TO 5X BASE HI
1 Dwyane Wade/107 40.00 100.00
2 Kobe Bryant/106 200.00 500.00
14 Paul Pierce/94 15.00 40.00
16 Tim Duncan/92 20.00 50.00
30 Ray Allen/78 6.00 15.00
44 Richard Hamilton/64 15.00 40.00
53 LeBron James/55 1,000.00 2,000.00
63 Chris Webber/45 8.00 20.00
66 Dirk Nowitzki/42 40.00 100.00
67 Kevin Garnett/41 40.00 100.00
68 Vince Carter/40 40.00 100.00
69 Reggie Miller/39 20.00 50.00

2004-05 E-XL Essential Credentials Now
*SINGLES #'d 15-25: 10X TO 25X BASE HI
*SINGLES #'d 26-40: 8X TO 20X BASE HI
*SINGLES #'d 41-60: 6X TO 15X BASE HI
*SINGLES #'d 60-70: 5X TO 12X BASE HI
*RCs #'d 71-94: .6X TO 1.5X BASE HI
*RCs #'d 95-107: .5 TO 1.25 BASE HI
30 Ray Allen/30 20.00 50.00
38 Steve Nash/38 20.00 50.00
43 Tony Parker/43 20.00 50.00
52 Latrell Sprewell/52 10.00 25.00
53 LeBron James/53 600.00 1,200.00
58 Allen Iverson/58 50.00 120.00
63 Chris Webber/63 15.00 40.00
66 Dirk Nowitzki/66 25.00 60.00
67 Kevin Garnett/67 25.00 60.00

2004-05 E-XL Rookies Die Cuts
*DIE CUTS: .4X TO 1X BASE HI
71-94 STATED PRINT RUN 399 SETS
95-107 STATED PRINT RUN 899 SETS

2004-05 E-XL ConnEXions Autographs
PRINT RUNS LISTED IN CHECKLIST
1 J.Howard/M.Daniels/100 8.00 20.00
2 A.Kirilenko/S.Monia 6.00 15.00
4 T.Prince/C.Billups/20 15.00 40.00
5 Z.Randolph/J-Rich/20 20.00 50.00
10 M.Pietrus/T.Parker 12.50 30.00
13 M.Ginobili/C.Arroyo 60.00 120.00
14 V.Carter/A.Jamison/100 20.00 50.00
17 J.Richardson/F.Jones 15.00 40.00
18 J.Smith/J.R.Smith/20 30.00 80.00
19 B.Gordon/J.Nelson 12.50 30.00
20 E.Brand/C.Boozer/50 20.00 50.00

2004-05 E-XL ConnEXions Jerseys
PRINT RUN 22 SER.#'d SETS
1 D.Wade/C.Anthony 20.00 50.00
2 A.Jamison/V.Carter 15.00 40.00
3 M.Bibby/P.Stojakovic 15.00 40.00
4 D.Wade/S.O'Neal 25.00 60.00
6 S.Marbury/S.Telfair 10.00 25.00
7 J.Mashburn/J.Magloire 10.00 25.00
8 C.Anthony/K.Martin 10.00 25.00
9 S.O'Neal/T.Duncan 25.00 60.00
11 K.Garnett/A.Stoudemire 12.50 30.00
14 B.Gordon/L.Deng 12.50 30.00
22 Y.Ming/T.McGrady 15.00 40.00
23 B.Wallace/R.Wallace 10.00 25.00
26 T.McGrady/V.Carter 30.00 80.00

2004-05 E-XL Court Authentics
PRINT RUN 500 SER.#'d SETS
DIE CUTS PRINT RUN 75 SER.#'d SETS
PATCH PRINT RUN 70 SER.#'d SETS
PATCH 50 PRINT RUN 50 SER.#'d SETS
PATCH DUAL PRINT RUN 22 SER.#'d SETS
PATCH/JSY PRINT RUN 35 SER.#'d SETS
PAT/WARM PRINT RUN 44 SER.#'d SETS
AI Allen Iverson 6.00 15.00
AS Amare Stoudemire 2.50 6.00
BD Baron Davis 2.50 6.00
BG Ben Gordon 2.50 6.00
BW Ben Wallace 3.00 8.00
CA Carmelo Anthony 5.00 12.00
CB Chris Bosh 4.00 10.00
CW Chris Webber 3.00 8.00
DH Dwight Howard 8.00 20.00
DH2 Devin Harris 2.00 5.00
DM Darko Milicic 2.00 5.00
DN Dirk Nowitzki 6.00 15.00
DW Dwyane Wade 10.00 25.00
EB Elton Brand 2.00 5.00
JK Jason Kidd 4.00 10.00
JO Jermaine O'Neal 2.00 5.00
JR Jason Richardson 2.50 6.00
KG Kevin Garnett 6.00 15.00
KH Kirk Hinrich 2.50 6.00
KM Kenyon Martin 2.50 6.00
LD Luol Deng 2.50 6.00
MB Mike Bibby 2.50 6.00
PP Paul Pierce 4.00 10.00
RA Ray Allen 4.00 10.00
SF Steve Francis 2.50 6.00
SL Shaun Livingston 2.50 6.00
SM Stephon Marbury 3.00 8.00
SM2 Shawn Marion 2.50 6.00
SN Steve Nash 5.00 12.00
SO Shaquille O'Neal 10.00 25.00
TD Tim Duncan 6.00 15.00
TM Tracy McGrady 4.00 10.00
TP Tony Parker 4.00 10.00
VC Vince Carter 5.00 12.00
YM Yao Ming 6.00 15.00

2004-05 E-XL Court Authentics Signatures
COMMON CARD 4.00 10.00
PRINT RUN 100 TO 200 SETS
AE Andre Emmett/200 2.50 6.00
AJ Al Jefferson/100 4.00 10.00
CD Carlos Delfino/200 2.50 6.00
JC Josh Childress/100 2.50 6.00
LC Lionel Chalmers/200 3.00 8.00
LD Luol Deng/200 4.00 10.00
NC Nick Collison/100 4.00 10.00

2004-05 E-XL Court Authentics Signatures Jerseys
PRINT RUN 50 TO 70 SER.#'d SETS
*SIG.JSY/WARM: .5X TO 1.25X BASE HI
SIG.JSY/WARM PRINT RUN 30 SETS
AB Andris Biedrins 3.00 8.00
BD Baron Davis 5.00 12.00
BG Ben Gordon 5.00 12.00
CA Carmelo Anthony 20.00 50.00
CB Chris Bosh 10.00 25.00
DH Devin Harris 8.00 20.00
DW Dwyane Wade 40.00 100.00
JC Josh Childress 3.00 8.00
JK Jason Kidd 15.00 40.00
JN Jameer Nelson 5.00 12.00
JO Jermaine O'Neal/67 10.00 25.00
LD Luol Deng 5.00 12.00
LJ Luke Jackson 3.00 8.00
LO Lamar Odom 12.50 30.00
MB Mike Bibby 10.00 25.00
PP Paul Pierce 12.50 30.00
RA Ray Allen 15.00 40.00
RJ Richard Jefferson 10.00 25.00
SL Shaun Livingston 5.00 12.00
SM Stephon Marbury 12.00 30.00
TF T.J. Ford/50 10.00 25.00
VC Vince Carter 12.00 30.00

2004-05 E-XL E-Xceptional
COMPLETE SET (10) 30.00 80.00
STATED ODDS 1:54
*XL PARALLEL: .75X TO 2X BASE
1 Shaquille O'Neal 8.00 20.00
2 LeBron James 15.00 40.00
3 Vince Carter 4.00 10.00
4 Kobe Bryant 15.00 40.00
5 Dwyane Wade 8.00 20.00
6 Kevin Garnett 5.00 12.00
7 Allen Iverson 5.00 12.00
8 Tim Duncan 5.00 12.00
9 Jason Kidd 3.00 8.00
10 Yao Ming 5.00 12.00

2004-05 E-XL Jambalaya
STATED ODDS 1:216
*XL: .6X TO 1.5X BASE HI
XL STATED ODDS 1:2160
1 Carmelo Anthony 125.00 300.00
2 Shaquille O'Neal 200.00 500.00
3 Kobe Bryant 2,000.00 4,000.00
4 Vince Carter 150.00 400.00
5 Tracy McGrady 150.00 400.00
6 Kevin Garnett 200.00 500.00
7 Amare Stoudemire 100.00 250.00
8 Allen Iverson 200.00 500.00
9 LeBron James 2,500.00 5,000.00
10 Tim Duncan 200.00 500.00

2004-05 E-XL Signings of the Times
PRINT RUN 100 SER.#'d SETS
*SIGS 50: .5X TO 1.25X BASE HI
*SIGS 25: .6X TO 1.5X BASE HI
AB Andris Biedrins 4.00 10.00
AJ Al Jefferson 6.00 15.00
AV Anderson Varejao 5.00 12.00
BG Ben Gordon 6.00 15.00
CD Chris Duhon 5.00 12.00
DH David Harrison 4.00 10.00
DH Devin Harris 5.00 12.00
DW Dorell Wright 5.00 12.00
DW Delonte West 5.00 12.00
JC Josh Childress 4.00 10.00
JN Jameer Nelson 6.00 15.00
JS Josh Smith 6.00 15.00
JS2 J.R. Smith 6.00 15.00
KS Kirk Snyder 4.00 10.00
LC Lionel Chalmers 5.00 12.00
LD Luol Deng 6.00 15.00
LJ Luke Jackson 4.00 10.00
PP Pavel Podkolzin 4.00 10.00
RA Rafael Araujo 4.00 10.00
RS Robert Swift 4.00 10.00
SL Shaun Livingston 6.00 15.00
ST Sebastian Telfair 5.00 12.00
TA Tony Allen 6.00 15.00

2006-07 E-X
COMP.SET w/o RC's (40) 75.00 200.00
41-46 RC PRINT RUN 99 SER.#'d SETS
47-63 RC PRINT RUN 899 SER.#'d SETS
64-74 RC PRINT RUN 399 SER.#'d SETS
75-80 RC PRINT RUN 199 SER.#'d SETS
1 Joe Johnson .50 1.25
2 Paul Pierce .75 2.00
3 Emeka Okafor .40 1.00
4 Michael Jordan 40.00 100.00
5 Ben Gordon .40 1.00
6 LeBron James 30.00 80.00
7 Dirk Nowitzki 1.25 3.00
8 Jason Terry .40 1.00
9 Carmelo Anthony 1.25 3.00
10 Chauncey Billups .60 1.50
11 Ben Wallace .60 1.50
12 Baron Davis .50 1.25
13 Jason Richardson .50 1.25
14 Yao Ming 1.25 3.00
15 Jermaine O'Neal .50 1.25
16 Elton Brand .40 1.00
17 Kobe Bryant 15.00 40.00
18 Pau Gasol .75 2.00
19 Tracy McGrady .75 2.00
20 Shaquille O'Neal 2.00 5.00
21 Dwyane Wade 1.00 2.50
22 Andrew Bogut .40 1.00
23 Kevin Garnett 1.25 3.00
24 Vince Carter 1.00 2.50
25 Jason Kidd .75 2.00
26 Chris Paul 3.00 8.00
27 Stephon Marbury .60 1.50
28 Dwight Howard .60 1.50
29 Allen Iverson 1.25 3.00
30 Steve Nash 1.00 2.50
31 Shawn Marion .50 1.25
32 Martell Webster .40 1.00
33 Mike Bibby .50 1.25
34 Ron Artest .50 1.25
35 Tim Duncan 1.25 3.00
36 Manu Ginobili 1.00 2.50
37 Ray Allen .75 2.00
38 Chris Bosh .60 1.50
39 Andrei Kirilenko .40 1.00
40 Gilbert Arenas .50 1.25
41 J.J. Redick/99 RC 12.00 30.00
42 Adam Morrison/99 RC 5.00 12.00
43 Jorge Garbajosa/99 RC 5.00 12.00
44 Saer Sene/99 RC 4.00 10.00
45 Renaldo Balkman/99 RC 5.00 12.00
46 Thabo Sefolosha/99 RC 5.00 12.00
47 Kevin Pittsnogle/899 AU RC 3.00 8.00
48 Daniel Gibson/899 AU RC 3.00 8.00
49 Dee Brown/899 AU RC 2.50 6.00
50 Sergio Rodriguez/899 AU RC 3.00 8.00
51 Bobby Jones/899 AU RC 2.50 6.00
52 Craig Smith/899 AU RC 3.00 8.00
53 David Noel/899 AU RC 2.50 6.00
54 Denham Brown/899 AU RC 2.50 6.00
55 James White/899 AU RC 2.50 6.00
56 Paul Davis/899 AU RC 2.50 6.00
57 P.J. Tucker/899 AU RC 4.00 10.00
58 Solomon Jones/899 AU RC 2.50 6.00
59 Steve Novak/899 AU RC 3.00 8.00
60 Allan Ray/899 AU RC 2.50 6.00
61 Jordan Farmar/899 AU RC 3.00 8.00
62 Josh Boone/899 AU RC 2.50 6.00
63 Mardy Collins/899 AU RC 2.50 6.00
64 Rodney Carney/399 AU RC 4.00 10.00
65 Quincy Douby/399 AU RC 4.00 10.00
66 Shannon Brown/399 AU RC 4.00 10.00
67 Rajon Rondo/399 AU RC 12.00 30.00
68 Maurice Ager/399 AU RC 4.00 10.00
69 Ronnie Brewer/399 AU RC 6.00 15.00
70 Marcus Williams/399 AU RC 4.00 10.00
71 Kyle Lowry/399 AU RC 20.00 50.00
72 Cedric Simmons/399 AU RC 4.00 10.00
73 Patrick O'Bryant/399 AU RC 4.00 10.00
74 Hilton Armstrong/399 AU RC 4.00 10.00
75 Rudy Gay/199 AU RC 8.00 20.00
76 Brandon Roy/199 AU RC 12.00 30.00
77 Shelden Williams/199 AU RC 4.00 10.00
78 Tyrus Thomas/199 AU RC 5.00 12.00
79 LaMarcus Aldridge/199 AU RC 15.00 40.00
80 Andrea Bargnani/199 AU RC 5.00 12.00

2006-07 E-X Behind the Numbers
APPROXIMATE ODDS 1:8
BNAI Andre Iguodala 3.00 8.00
BNBD Baron Davis 3.00 8.00
BNBH Brendan Haywood 2.00 5.00
BNBM Brad Miller 2.50 6.00
BNBW Ben Wallace 4.00 10.00
BNCA Carmelo Anthony 5.00 12.00
BNCB Chauncey Billups 4.00 10.00
BNCM Corey Maggette 2.50 6.00
BNCW Chris Webber 4.00 10.00
BNDW David West 2.50 6.00
BNGA Gilbert Arenas 3.00 8.00
BNJG Joey Graham 2.00 5.00
BNJR Jason Richardson 3.00 8.00
BNJS J.R. Smith 3.00 8.00
BNKB Kobe Bryant 50.00 120.00
BNKH Kirk Hinrich 2.50 6.00
BNKK Kyle Korver 2.50 6.00
BNLJ LeBron James 15.00 40.00
BNLW Luke Walton 2.00 5.00
BNMA Sean May 2.00 5.00
BNPP Paul Pierce 5.00 12.00
BNRI Royal Ivey 2.00 5.00
BNSL Shaun Livingston 2.50 6.00
BNSM Shawn Marion 3.00 8.00
BNSN Steve Nash 6.00 15.00
BNTC Tyson Chandler 2.50 6.00
BNTP Tony Parker 5.00 12.00
BNWS Wally Szczerbiak 2.50 6.00
BNZI Zydrunas Ilgauskas 2.50 6.00

2006-07 E-X Behind the Numbers Autographs
CARDS #'d TO PLAYER JERSEY NUMBER
BNCA Carmelo Anthony/15 30.00 80.00
BNJG Joey Graham/14 8.00 20.00
BNLJ LeBron James/23 2,000.00 4,000.00
BNPP Paul Pierce/34 20.00 50.00
BNSN Steve Nash/13 40.00 100.00

2006-07 E-X Clearly Authentics Autographs
APPROXIMATE ODDS 1:8
CAAAB Andrew Bogut 8.00 20.00
CAAAI Andre Iguodala 4.00 10.00
CAAAJ Al Jefferson 3.00 8.00
CAAAM Amir Johnson 3.00 8.00
CAAAU James Augustine 3.00 8.00
CAABA Brent Barry 5.00 12.00
CAABB Brandon Bass 3.00 8.00
CAABD Baron Davis SP 6.00 15.00
CAABG Ben Gordon SP 12.50 30.00
CAABI Chauncey Billups 8.00 20.00
CAABJ Bobby Jackson 3.00 8.00
CAABO Bruce Bowen 5.00 12.00
CAABS Bobby Simmons 3.00 8.00
CAACA Carmelo Anthony SP 20.00 40.00
CAACB Charlie Bell 3.00 8.00
CAACD Chris Duhon 3.00 8.00
CAACH Chuck Hayes 3.00 8.00
CAACK Chris Kaman 3.00 8.00
CAACM Cedric Maxwell 6.00 15.00
CAACP Chris Paul SP 100.00 250.00
CAADA Damir Markota 3.00 8.00
CAADB Dee Brown 3.00 8.00
CAADD Dan Dickau 3.00 8.00
CAADG Danny Granger 3.00 8.00
CAADH Dwight Howard 12.50 30.00
CAADO Donyell Marshall 3.00 8.00
CAAEC Eddy Curry 3.00 8.00
CAAEI Ersan Ilyasova 3.00 8.00
CAAFG Francisco Garcia 3.00 8.00
CAAGG Gerald Green 3.00 8.00
CAAGW Gerald Wallace 3.00 8.00
CAAHA Hassan Adams 3.00 8.00
CAAIU Ime Udoka 10.00 25.00
CAAJA Antawn Jamison 3.00 8.00
CAAJC Josh Childress 3.00 8.00
CAAJG Joey Graham 3.00 8.00
CAAJK Jason Kapono 3.00 8.00
CAAJR Jalen Rose 4.00 10.00
CAAJS J.R. Smith 3.00 8.00
CAAKD Keyon Dooling 3.00 8.00
CAAKG Kevin Garnett 50.00 120.00
CAAKH Kirk Hinrich 3.00 8.00
CAAKI Jason Kidd SP 15.00 40.00
CAAKK Kyle Korver 5.00 12.00
CAALH Larry Hughes 3.00 8.00
CAALJ LeBron James SP 1,250.00 2,500.00
CAALR Lawrence Roberts 3.00 8.00
CAALW Louis Williams 3.00 8.00
CAAMB Mike Bibby 3.00 8.00
CAAMD Marquis Daniels 3.00 8.00
CAAMM Chris Mihm 3.00 8.00
CAAMO Cuttino Mobley 3.00 8.00
CAAMW Martell Webster 3.00 8.00
CAAPO Patrick O'Bryant 3.00 8.00
CAAPP Paul Pierce 15.00 40.00
CAAPS Peja Stojakovic 5.00 12.00
CAAQR Quentin Richardson 3.00 8.00
CAARF Raymond Felton 3.00 8.00
CAARI Luke Ridnour 3.00 8.00
CAARM Rashad McCants 3.00 8.00
CAARW Mile Ilic 3.00 8.00
CAASA Shareef Abdur-Rahim 3.00 8.00
CAASC Speedy Claxton 3.00 8.00
CAASG Stephen Graham 3.00 8.00
CAASI James Singleton 3.00 8.00
CAASL Shaun Livingston 3.00 8.00
CAASN Steve Nash SP 60.00 120.00
CAASS Salim Stoudamire 3.00 8.00
CAAST DeShawn Stevenson 3.00 8.00
CAATA Tony Allen 3.00 8.00
CAATE Sebastian Telfair 3.00 8.00
CAATF T.J. Ford 3.00 8.00
CAATM Tracy McGrady SP 15.00 40.00

CAATP Tayshaun Prince 3.00 8.00
CAAWB Will Blalock 3.00 8.00
CAAWI Marvin Williams 3.00 8.00
CAAWL Damien Wilkins 3.00 8.00
CAAWM Maurice Williams 3.00 8.00
CAAYM Yao Ming SP 50.00 120.00

2006-07 E-X Clearly Authentics Patches

PRINT RUN 75 SER.#'d SETS
CAAB Andrew Bogut 4.00 10.00
CAAI Andre Iguodala 5.00 12.00
CAAJ Al Jefferson 3.00 8.00
CAAL Ray Allen 8.00 20.00
CAAS Amare Stoudemire 5.00 12.00
CABD Baron Davis 5.00 12.00
CABI Chauncey Billups 6.00 15.00
CABM Brad Miller 4.00 10.00
CABO Bruce Bowen 4.00 10.00
CABR Kobe Bryant 75.00 200.00
CABW Ben Wallace 6.00 15.00
CACA Carmelo Anthony 8.00 20.00
CACB Carlos Boozer 4.00 10.00
CACF Channing Frye 3.00 8.00
CACM Corey Maggette 4.00 10.00
CACP Chris Paul 10.00 25.00
CACW Chris Webber 6.00 15.00
CADG Danny Granger 3.00 8.00
CADH Dwight Howard 6.00 15.00
CADM Donyell Marshall 3.00 8.00
CADN Dirk Nowitzki 12.00 30.00
CADW Deron Williams 4.00 10.00
CAEB Elton Brand 4.00 10.00
CAEC Eddy Curry 4.00 10.00
CAEI Ersan Ilyasova 3.00 8.00
CAEO Emeka Okafor 4.00 10.00
CAFG Francisco Garcia 3.00 8.00
CAGG Gerald Green 4.00 10.00
CAGH Grant Hill 20.00 50.00
CAGO Drew Gooden 4.00 10.00
CAHA Devin Harris 3.00 8.00
CAHE Luther Head 3.00 8.00
CAHW Hakim Warrick 3.00 8.00
CAID Ike Diogu 3.00 8.00
CAIV Royal Ivey 3.00 8.00
CAJA Antawn Jamison 4.00 10.00
CAJC Josh Childress 3.00 8.00
CAJG Joey Graham 3.00 8.00
CAJK Jason Kidd 8.00 20.00
CAJM Jamaal Magloire 3.00 8.00
CAJO Jermaine O'Neal 5.00 12.00
CAJR Jalen Rose 4.00 10.00
CAJS J.R. Smith 5.00 12.00
CAJT Jason Terry 4.00 10.00
CAKB Kwame Brown 3.00 8.00
CAKG Kevin Garnett 12.00 30.00
CAKH Kirk Hinrich 4.00 10.00
CAKK Kyle Korver 4.00 10.00
CALB Leandro Barbosa 4.00 10.00
CALD Luol Deng 4.00 10.00
CALH Larry Hughes 4.00 10.00
CALJ LeBron James 40.00 100.00
CALO Lamar Odom 4.00 10.00
CALR Luke Ridnour 4.00 10.00
CAMA Stephon Marbury 6.00 15.00
CAMB Mike Bibby 5.00 12.00
CAMD Marquis Daniels 3.00 8.00
CAMG Manu Ginobili 10.00 25.00
CAMR Michael Redd 4.00 10.00
CAMW Martell Webster 4.00 10.00
CANE Nene 4.00 10.00
CANR Nate Robinson 4.00 10.00
CAPG Pau Gasol 8.00 20.00
CAPP Paul Pierce 8.00 20.00
CAPS Peja Stojakovic 4.00 10.00
CAPT Tayshaun Prince 5.00 12.00
CAQR Quentin Richardson 3.00 8.00
CARA Ron Artest 5.00 12.00
CARF Raymond Felton 3.00 8.00
CARH Richard Hamilton 5.00 12.00
CARI Jason Richardson 5.00 12.00
CARJ Richard Jefferson 4.00 10.00
CARM Rashad McCants 3.00 8.00
CASI Wayne Simien 3.00 8.00
CASJ Sarunas Jasikevicius 4.00 10.00
CASL Shaun Livingston 4.00 10.00
CASM Sean May 3.00 8.00
CASN Steve Nash 10.00 25.00
CASO Shaquille O'Neal 20.00 50.00
CASS Stromile Swift 3.00 8.00
CAST Sebastian Telfair 3.00 8.00
CATC Tyson Chandler 4.00 10.00
CATM Tracy McGrady 8.00 20.00
CATP Tony Parker 8.00 20.00
CAVC Vince Carter 10.00 25.00
CAWE Delonte West 3.00 8.00
CAWS Wally Szczerbiak 4.00 10.00
CAYM Yao Ming 12.00 30.00
CAZI Zydrunas Ilgauskas 4.00 10.00

2006-07 E-X Clearly Authentics Patches Autographs

PRINT RUN 25 SER.#'d SETS
CAAB Andrew Bogut 12.00 30.00
CAAI Andre Iguodala 12.00 30.00
CAAJ Al Jefferson 8.00 20.00
CABD Baron Davis 8.00 20.00
CABI Chauncey Billups 10.00 25.00
CABO Bruce Bowen 8.00 20.00
CACA Carmelo Anthony 40.00 100.00
CACB Carlos Boozer 8.00 20.00
CACF Channing Frye 8.00 20.00
CADG Danny Granger 8.00 20.00
CADH Dwight Howard 20.00 50.00
CADM Donyell Marshall 8.00 20.00
CADW Deron Williams 8.00 20.00
CAEC Eddy Curry 8.00 20.00
CAEI Ersan Ilyasova 8.00 20.00
CAEO Emeka Okafor 8.00 20.00
CAFG Francisco Garcia 8.00 20.00
CAGG Gerald Green 8.00 20.00
CAHW Hakim Warrick 8.00 20.00
CAJA Antawn Jamison 8.00 20.00
CAJC Josh Childress 8.00 20.00
CAJG Joey Graham 8.00 20.00
CAJK Jason Kidd 12.00 30.00
CAJS J.R. Smith 8.00 20.00
CAKH Kirk Hinrich 8.00 20.00
CAKK Kyle Korver 10.00 25.00
CALB Leandro Barbosa 8.00 20.00
CALH Larry Hughes 8.00 20.00
CALJ LeBron James 2,000.00 4,000.00
CALR Luke Ridnour 8.00 20.00
CAMB Mike Bibby 10.00 25.00
CAMW Martell Webster 8.00 20.00
CANR Nate Robinson 8.00 20.00
CAPP Paul Pierce 25.00 60.00
CAPS Peja Stojakovic 10.00 25.00
CAPT Tayshaun Prince 8.00 20.00
CAQR Quentin Richardson 8.00 20.00
CARA Ron Artest 8.00 20.00
CARF Raymond Felton 8.00 20.00
CARJ Richard Jefferson 8.00 20.00
CARM Rashad McCants 8.00 20.00
CASI Wayne Simien 8.00 20.00
CASL Shaun Livingston 8.00 20.00
CASM Sean May 8.00 20.00
CASN Steve Nash 75.00 200.00
CAST Sebastian Telfair 8.00 20.00
CATC Tyson Chandler 8.00 20.00
CATM Tracy McGrady 60.00 150.00
CAVC Vince Carter 75.00 200.00
CAYM Yao Ming 60.00 150.00

2006-07 E-X ConnEXions

PRINT RUN 199 SER.#'d SETS
CNAR R.Allen/L.Ridnour 3.00 8.00
CNBG C.Bosh/J.Graham 3.00 8.00
CNBO L.Odom/K.Brown 3.00 8.00
CNBW C.Boozer/D.Williams 5.00 12.00
CNCK V.Carter/N.Krstic 8.00 20.00
CNDN L.Deng/A.Nocioni 3.00 8.00
CNDP T.Duncan/T.Parker 6.00 15.00
CNGJ D.Granger/S.Jasikevicius 3.00 8.00
CNGM K.Garnett/R.McCants 5.00 12.00
CNHB R.Hamilton/C.Billups 3.00 8.00
CNIJ Z.Ilgauskas/L.James 10.00 25.00
CNJA A.Jamison/G.Arenas 3.00 8.00
CNJW D.Jones/H.Warrick 3.00 8.00
CNMB C.Maggette/E.Brand 3.00 8.00
CNMM T.McGrady/Y.Ming 5.00 12.00
CNNB A.Bogut/D.Noel 3.00 8.00
CNNH D.Nowitzki/D.Harris 4.00 10.00
CNNM S.Nash/S.Marion 5.00 12.00
CNOF E.Okafor/R.Felton 3.00 8.00
CNRF Q.Richardson/C.Frye 3.00 8.00
CNRR Q.Richardson/N.Robinson 3.00 8.00
CNSH S.Swift/H.Warrick 3.00 8.00
CNSJ J.Smith/R.Ivey 3.00 8.00
CNSO W.Simien/S.O'Neal 5.00 12.00
CNSW J.Smith/M.Williams 3.00 8.00
CNTH J.Terry/D.Harris 3.00 8.00
CNTW B.Wallace/T.Thomas 4.00 10.00
CNWI C.Webber/A.Iguodala 3.00 8.00
CNWP D.West/C.Paul 4.00 10.00
CNWS W.Szczerbiak/D.West 3.00 8.00

2006-07 E-X ConnEXions Autographs

PRINT RUN 25 SER.#'d SETS
CNBG C.Bosh/J.Graham 20.00 50.00
CNBW C.Boozer/D.Williams 25.00 60.00
CNMM T.McGrady/Y.Ming 40.00 100.00
CNNB D.Noel/A.Bogut 12.00 30.00
CNOF E.Okafor/R.Felton 8.00 20.00
CNRF Q.Richardson/C.Frye 8.00 20.00
CNRR Q.Richardson/N.Robinson 8.00 20.00

2006-07 E-X Essential Credentials Future

1 Joe Johnson/80 12.00 30.00
2 Paul Pierce/79 20.00 50.00
3 Emeka Okafor/78 10.00 25.00
4 Michael Jordan/77 6,000.00 12,000.00
5 Ben Gordon/76 10.00 25.00
6 LeBron James/75 5,000.00 10,000.00
7 Dirk Nowitzki/74 40.00 100.00
8 Jason Terry/73 20.00 50.00
9 Carmelo Anthony/72 40.00 100.00
10 Chauncey Billups/71 15.00 40.00
11 Ben Wallace/70 15.00 40.00
12 Baron Davis/69 12.00 30.00
13 Jason Richardson/68 12.00 30.00
14 Yao Ming/67 400.00 800.00
15 Jermaine O'Neal/66 12.00 30.00
16 Elton Brand/65 10.00 25.00
17 Kobe Bryant/64 4,000.00 8,000.00
18 Pau Gasol/63 20.00 50.00
19 Tracy McGrady/62 50.00 120.00
20 Shaquille O'Neal/61 40.00 100.00
21 Dwyane Wade/60 200.00 500.00
22 Andrew Bogut/59 10.00 25.00
23 Kevin Garnett/58 300.00 600.00
24 Vince Carter/57 125.00 300.00
25 Jason Kidd/56 60.00 150.00
26 Chris Paul/55 125.00 300.00
27 Stephon Marbury/54 20.00 50.00
28 Dwight Howard/53 25.00 60.00
29 Allen Iverson/52 150.00 400.00
30 Steve Nash/51 150.00 400.00
31 Shawn Marion/50 12.00 30.00
32 Martell Webster/49 10.00 25.00
33 Mike Bibby/48 12.00 30.00
34 Ron Artest/47 12.00 30.00
35 Tim Duncan/46 150.00 400.00
36 Manu Ginobili/45 75.00 200.00
37 Ray Allen/44 75.00 200.00
38 Chris Bosh/43 15.00 40.00
39 Andrei Kirilenko/42 10.00 25.00
40 Gilbert Arenas/41 12.00 30.00
41 J.J. Redick/40 75.00 200.00
42 Adam Morrison/39 10.00 25.00
43 Jorge Garbajosa/38 10.00 25.00
44 Saer Sene/37 8.00 20.00
45 Renaldo Balkman/36 10.00 25.00
46 Thabo Sefolosha/35 10.00 25.00
47 Kevin Pittsnogle AU/34 6.00 15.00
48 Daniel Gibson AU/33 6.00 15.00
49 Dee Brown AU/32 5.00 12.00
50 Sergio Rodriguez AU/31 6.00 15.00
52 Craig Smith AU/29 6.00 15.00
53 David Noel AU/28 5.00 12.00
54 Denham Brown AU/27 5.00 12.00
55 James White AU/26 5.00 12.00
56 Paul Davis AU/25 5.00 12.00
57 P.J. Tucker AU/24 8.00 20.00
58 Solomon Jones AU/23 5.00 12.00
59 Steve Novak AU/22 6.00 15.00
60 Allan Ray AU/21 5.00 12.00
61 Jordan Farmar AU/20 6.00 15.00
62 Josh Boone AU/19 5.00 12.00
63 Mardy Collins AU/18 5.00 12.00
64 Rodney Carney AU/17 5.00 12.00
65 Quincy Douby AU/16 5.00 12.00
66 Shannon Brown AU/15 5.00 12.00

2006-07 E-X Essential Credentials Now

15 Jermaine O'Neal/15 15.00 40.00
16 Elton Brand/16 12.00 30.00
18 Pau Gasol/18 25.00 60.00
19 Tracy McGrady/19 125.00 300.00
20 Shaquille O'Neal/20 150.00 400.00
21 Dwyane Wade/21 125.00 300.00
22 Andrew Bogut/22 12.00 30.00
23 Kevin Garnett/23 40.00 100.00
24 Vince Carter/24 30.00 80.00
25 Jason Kidd/25 25.00 60.00
26 Chris Paul/26 150.00 400.00
27 Stephon Marbury/27 20.00 50.00
28 Dwight Howard/28 20.00 50.00
29 Allen Iverson/29 25.00 60.00
30 Steve Nash/30 25.00 60.00
31 Shawn Marion/31 15.00 40.00
32 Martell Webster/32 8.00 20.00
33 Mike Bibby/33 12.00 30.00
34 Ron Artest/34 10.00 25.00
35 Tim Duncan/35 200.00 500.00
36 Manu Ginobili/36 125.00 300.00
37 Ray Allen/37 75.00 200.00
38 Chris Bosh/38 30.00 80.00
39 Andrei Kirilenko/39 25.00 60.00
40 Gilbert Arenas/40 10.00 25.00
41 J.J. Redick/41 30.00 80.00
42 Adam Morrison/42 8.00 20.00
43 Jorge Garbajosa/43 8.00 20.00
44 Saer Sene/44 6.00 15.00
45 Renaldo Balkman/45 8.00 20.00
46 Thabo Sefolosha/46 8.00 20.00
47 Kevin Pittsnogle AU/47 5.00 12.00
48 Daniel Gibson AU/48 5.00 12.00
49 Dee Brown AU/49 4.00 10.00
50 Sergio Rodriguez AU/50 5.00 12.00
51 Bobby Jones AU/51 4.00 10.00
52 Craig Smith AU/52 5.00 12.00
53 David Noel AU/53 4.00 10.00
54 Denham Brown AU/54 4.00 10.00
55 James White AU/55 4.00 10.00
56 Paul Davis AU/56 4.00 10.00
57 P.J. Tucker AU/57 6.00 15.00
58 Solomon Jones AU/58 4.00 10.00
59 Steve Novak AU/59 5.00 12.00
60 Allan Ray AU/60 4.00 10.00
61 Jordan Farmar AU/61 5.00 12.00
62 Josh Boone AU/62 4.00 10.00
63 Mardy Collins AU/63 4.00 10.00
64 Rodney Carney AU/64 4.00 10.00
65 Quincy Douby AU/65 4.00 10.00
66 Shannon Brown AU/66 4.00 10.00
67 Rajon Rondo AU/67 25.00 60.00
68 Maurice Ager AU/68 4.00 10.00
69 Ronnie Brewer AU/69 6.00 15.00
70 Marcus Williams AU/70 4.00 10.00
71 Kyle Lowry AU/71 30.00 80.00
72 Cedric Simmons AU/72 4.00 10.00
73 Patrick O'Bryant AU/73 4.00 10.00
74 Hilton Armstrong AU/74 4.00 10.00
75 Rudy Gay AU/75 20.00 50.00
76 Brandon Roy AU/76 6.00 15.00
77 Shelden Williams AU/77 4.00 10.00
78 Tyrus Thomas AU/78 5.00 12.00
79 LaMarcus Aldridge AU/79 30.00 80.00
80 Andrea Bargnani AU/80 5.00 12.00

2006-07 E-X Jambalaya

APPROXIMATE ODDS 1:48
JAI Allen Iverson 200.00 500.00
JBR Bill Russell 200.00 500.00
JCD Clyde Drexler 125.00 300.00
JDH Dwight Howard 75.00 200.00
JDR David Robinson 150.00 400.00
JDW Dwyane Wade 125.00 300.00
JHO Hakeem Olajuwon 125.00 300.00
JJE Julius Erving 150.00 400.00
JJK Jason Kidd 60.00 150.00
JJO Magic Johnson 200.00 500.00
JJS John Stockton 125.00 300.00
JLB Larry Bird 200.00 500.00
JLJ LeBron James 2,000.00 4,000.00
JMG Manu Ginobili 200.00 500.00
JMJ Michael Jordan 3,000.00 5,000.00
JPP Paul Pierce 125.00 300.00
JPS Peja Stojakovic 25.00 60.00
JSM Stephon Marbury 75.00 200.00
JTD Tim Duncan 150.00 400.00
JTM Tracy McGrady 125.00 300.00

2003-04 Exquisite Collection

1-42 PRINT RUN 225 SER.#'d SETS
44-73 RC PRINT RUN 225 SER.#'d SETS
43, 74-78 RC PRINT RUN 99 SER.#'d SETS
1 Jason Terry 12.00 30.00
2 Paul Pierce 75.00 200.00
3 Michael Jordan 2,500.00 5,000.00
4 Kirk Hinrich RC 30.00 80.00
5 Dajuan Wagner 10.00 25.00
6 Dirk Nowitzki 75.00 200.00
7 Steve Nash 60.00 150.00
8 Andre Miller 12.00 30.00
9 Ben Wallace 30.00 80.00
10 Jason Richardson 15.00 40.00
11 Steve Francis 15.00 40.00
12 Yao Ming 125.00 300.00
13 Jermaine O'Neal 15.00 40.00
14 Elton Brand 12.00 30.00
15 Kobe Bryant 1,500.00 3,000.00
16 Gary Payton 40.00 100.00
17 Shaquille O'Neal 125.00 300.00
18 Pau Gasol 60.00 150.00
19 Lamar Odom 12.00 30.00
20 T.J. Ford RC 12.00 30.00
21 Kevin Garnett 100.00 250.00
22 Latrell Sprewell 20.00 50.00
23 Jason Kidd 30.00 80.00
24 Richard Jefferson 12.00 30.00
25 Baron Davis 25.00 60.00
26 Allan Houston 15.00 40.00
27 Stephon Marbury 20.00 50.00
28 Tracy McGrady 75.00 200.00
29 Allen Iverson 125.00 300.00
30 Shawn Marion 15.00 40.00
31 Amare Stoudemire 20.00 50.00
32 Shareef Abdur-Rahim 15.00 40.00
33 Mike Bibby 15.00 40.00
34 Chris Webber 60.00 150.00
35 Tim Duncan 125.00 300.00
36 Manu Ginobili 75.00 200.00
37 Ray Allen 50.00 120.00
38 Nick Collison RC 40.00 100.00
39 Vince Carter 100.00 250.00
40 Andrei Kirilenko 12.00 30.00
41 Gilbert Arenas 15.00 40.00
42 Jerry Stackhouse 20.00 50.00
43 Udonis Haslem JSY AU RC 125.00 300.00
44 Mo Williams JSY AU RC 50.00 120.00
45 Keith Bogans JSY AU RC 15.00 40.00
46 Travis Hansen JSY AU RC 15.00 40.00
47 Jason Kapono JSY AU RC 50.00 120.00
48 Zaza Pachulia JSY AU RC 50.00 120.00
49 Z.Cabarkapa JSY AU RC 15.00 40.00
50 Kyle Korver AU RC 125.00 300.00
51 Luke Walton JSY AU RC 100.00 250.00
52 Maciej Lampe JSY AU RC 25.00 60.00
53 Josh Howard JSY AU RC 60.00 150.00
54 Leandro Barbosa JSY AU RC 75.00 200.00
55 Kendrick Perkins JSY AU RC 50.00 120.00
56 Ndudi Ebi JSY AU RC 15.00 40.00
57 Jerome Beasley JSY AU RC 15.00 40.00
58 Brian Cook JSY AU RC 60.00 150.00
59 Travis Outlaw JSY AU RC 40.00 100.00
60 Zoran Planinic JSY AU RC 15.00 40.00
61 Boris Diaw JSY AU RC 75.00 200.00
62 Steve Blake JSY AU RC 75.00 200.00
63 A.Pavlovic JSY AU RC 20.00 50.00
64 David West JSY AU RC 75.00 200.00
65 Mike Sweetney JSY AU RC 15.00 40.00
66 Troy Bell JSY AU RC 15.00 40.00
67 Reece Gaines JSY AU RC 15.00 40.00
68 Luke Ridnour JSY AU RC 60.00 150.00
69 Marcus Banks JSY AU RC 15.00 40.00
70 Dahntay Jones JSY AU RC 20.00 50.00
71 Mickael Pietrus JSY AU RC 20.00 50.00
72 Chris Kaman JSY AU RC 60.00 150.00
73 Jarvis Hayes JSY AU RC 15.00 40.00
74 Dwyane Wade JSY AU RC 20,000.00 40,000.00
75 Chris Bosh JSY AU RC 1,000.00 2,000.00
76 C.Anthony JSY AU RC 5,000.00 10,000.00
77 Darko Milicic JSY AU RC 200.00 500.00
78 LeBron James JSY AU RC 250,000.00 500,000.00

2003-04 Exquisite Collection Gold

*GOLD 1-42: 1X TO 2.5X BASE HI
PRINT RUN 25 SER.#'d SETS
GOLD RCs DO NOT CONTAIN AU OR PATCH
3 Michael Jordan 8,000.00 15,000.00
43 Udonis Haslem 100.00 250.00
44 Mo Williams 40.00 100.00
45 Keith Bogans 12.00 30.00
46 Travis Hansen 12.00 30.00
47 Jason Kapono 40.00 100.00
48 Zaur Pachulia 40.00 100.00
49 Zarko Cabarkapa 12.00 30.00
50 Kyle Korver 100.00 250.00
51 Luke Walton 75.00 200.00
52 Maciej Lampe 12.00 30.00
53 Josh Howard 50.00 120.00
54 Leandro Barbosa 60.00 150.00
55 Kendrick Perkins 40.00 100.00
56 Ndudi Ebi 12.00 30.00
57 Jerome Beasley 12.00 30.00
58 Brian Cook 50.00 120.00
59 Travis Outlaw 30.00 80.00
60 Zoran Planinic 12.00 30.00
61 Boris Diaw 60.00 150.00
62 Steve Blake 60.00 150.00
63 Aleksandar Pavlovic 15.00 40.00
64 David West 60.00 150.00
65 Mike Sweetney 12.00 30.00
66 Troy Bell 12.00 30.00
67 Reece Gaines 12.00 30.00
68 Luke Ridnour 50.00 120.00
69 Marcus Banks 12.00 30.00
70 Dahntay Jones 15.00 40.00
71 Mickael Pietrus 15.00 40.00
72 Chris Kaman 50.00 120.00
73 Jarvis Hayes 12.00 30.00
74 Dwyane Wade 10,000.00 15,000.00
75 Chris Bosh 100.00 250.00
76 Carmelo Anthony 3,000.00 6,000.00
77 Darko Milicic 30.00 80.00
78 LeBron James 150,000.00 300,000.00

2003-04 Exquisite Collection Jersey Parallel

*JERSEY: .5X TO 1.2X BASE HI
PRINT RUN 25 SER.#'d SETS
4J, 20J, 38J, 39J NOT RELEASED
34J Chris Webber 125.00 300.00
36J Manu Ginobili 125.00 300.00

2003-04 Exquisite Collection Rookie Patch Parallel

CARD #'d TO PLAYER JERSEY
43 Udonis Haslem/40 100.00 250.00
44 Mo Williams/25 125.00 250.00
47 Jason Kapono/24 15.00 40.00
48 Zaur Pachulia/27 50.00 120.00
50 Kyle Korver/26 150.00 300.00
55 Kendrick Perkins/43 50.00 120.00
56 Ndudi Ebi/44 15.00 40.00
57 Jerome Beasley/24 15.00 40.00
59 Travis Outlaw/25 20.00 50.00
61 Boris Diaw/32 100.00 200.00
64 David West/30 150.00 300.00
65 Mike Sweetney/50 15.00 40.00
67 Reece Gaines/22 30.00 80.00
70 Dahntay Jones/30 20.00 50.00
72 Chris Kaman/35 75.00 200.00
73 Jarvis Hayes/24 30.00 80.00
76 Carmelo Anthony/15 15,000.00 30,000.00
77 Darko Milicic/31 100.00 250.00
78 LeBron James/23 30,000.00 50,000.00

2003-04 Exquisite Collection Emblems of Endorsement

COMMON CARD 100.00 200.00
PRINT RUN 15 SER.#'d SETS
SOME NOT PRICED DUE TO LACK OF SALES INFO
CA Carmelo Anthony 2,500.00 5,000.00
GP Gary Payton 1,000.00 2,000.00
KG Kevin Garnett 2,500.00 5,000.00
LB Larry Bird 2,500.00 5,000.00
RJ Richard Jefferson 200.00 500.00
RM Reggie Miller 2,000.00 4,000.00
SM Stephon Marbury 1,000.00 2,000.00
TM Tracy McGrady 2,000.00 4,000.00
YM Yao Ming 3,000.00 6,000.00

2003-04 Exquisite Collection Extra Exquisite

PRINT RUN 75 SER.#'d SETS
*DUAL: .6X TO 1.5X BASE HI
DUAL PRINT RUN 25 SER.#'d SETS
AI Allen Iverson 125.00 300.00
AK Andrei Kirilenko 15.00 40.00
AM Alonzo Mourning 30.00 80.00
AS Amare Stoudemire 20.00 50.00
BD Baron Davis 15.00 40.00
CA Carmelo Anthony 60.00 150.00
CB Chris Bosh 30.00 80.00
CW Chris Webber 60.00 150.00
DN Dirk Nowitzki 75.00 200.00
DR David Robinson 40.00 100.00
DW Dwyane Wade 200.00 500.00
GP Gary Payton 20.00 50.00
IT Isiah Thomas 30.00 80.00
JE Julius Erving 75.00 200.00
JH Jarvis Hayes 15.00 40.00
JK Jason Kidd 40.00 100.00
JO Jermaine O'Neal 15.00 40.00
JR Jason Richardson 15.00 40.00
JS John Stockton 40.00 100.00
KA Kareem Abdul-Jabbar 30.00 80.00
KB Kobe Bryant 500.00 1,000.00
KB1 Kobe Bryant 500.00 1,000.00
KG Kevin Garnett 60.00 150.00
LB Larry Bird 75.00 200.00
LJ LeBron James 5,000.00 10,000.00
LJ1 LeBron James 5,000.00 10,000.00
MA Magic Johnson 40.00 100.00
MJ Michael Jordan 1,500.00 3,000.00
MJ1 Michael Jordan 1,500.00 3,000.00
PG Pau Gasol 15.00 40.00
PP Paul Pierce 50.00 120.00
RA Ray Allen 50.00 120.00
SF Steve Francis 20.00 50.00
SH Shawn Marion 20.00 50.00
SM Stephon Marbury 30.00 80.00
SN Steve Nash 40.00 100.00
SO Shaquille O'Neal 75.00 200.00
TD Tim Duncan 75.00 200.00
TM Tracy McGrady 50.00 120.00
WA Ben Wallace 15.00 40.00
WC Wilt Chamberlain 300.00 600.00
YM Yao Ming 75.00 200.00

2003-04 Exquisite Collection Limited Logos

PRINT RUN 75 SER.#'d SETS
AJ Antawn Jamison 75.00 200.00
AM Andre Miller 75.00 200.00
AS Amare Stoudemire 200.00 500.00
BD Baron Davis 400.00 800.00
CA1 Carmelo Anthony 1,000.00 2,000.00
CA2 C.Anthony Throwback 1,000.00 2,000.00
CM Corey Maggette 75.00 200.00
DA David Robinson 1,000.00 2,000.00
DM Darko Milicic 75.00 200.00
DR Dennis Rodman 2,000.00 4,000.00
DY Dwyane Wade 3,000.00 6,000.00
GA Gilbert Arenas 125.00 300.00
GP Gary Payton 500.00 1,000.00
JK Jason Kidd 500.00 1,000.00
JM John Stockton 600.00 1,000.00
KB Kobe Bryant 100,000.00 200,000.00
KG Kevin Garnett 1,000.00 3,000.00
LB Larry Bird 800.00 1,500.00
LJ LeBron James 150,000.00 300,000.00
MA Magic Johnson 2,000.00 4,000.00
MJ Michael Jordan 100,000.00 200,000.00
PE Patrick Ewing 1,000.00 2,000.00
PP Paul Pierce 1,000.00 2,000.00
PS Peja Stojakovic 125.00 300.00
SA Shareef Abdur-Rahim 200.00 500.00
SC Sam Cassell 75.00 200.00
SM Shawn Marion 100.00 250.00
ST Stephon Marbury 1,000.00 2,000.00
TM Tracy McGrady 2,000.00 4,000.00
ZO Alonzo Mourning 1,000.00 2,000.00

2003-04 Exquisite Collection Noble Nameplates

PRINT RUN 25 SER.#'d SETS
AH Al Harrington 75.00 200.00
AJ Antawn Jamison 75.00 200.00
AK Andrei Kirilenko 100.00 200.00
AS Amare Stoudemire 125.00 300.00
BD Baron Davis 125.00 300.00
CA Carmelo Anthony 1,000.00 2,000.00
CB Chris Bosh 400.00 800.00
CM Corey Maggette 40.00 100.00
DM Darko Milicic 50.00 125.00
DY Dwyane Wade 1,500.00 3,000.00
GA Gilbert Arenas 75.00 200.00
GP Gary Payton 500.00 1,000.00
GR Glenn Robinson 100.00 250.00
IT Isiah Thomas 300.00 600.00
JK Jason Kidd 300.00 600.00
KB Kobe Bryant 4,000.00 8,000.00
KG Kevin Garnett 2,000.00 4,000.00
LJ LeBron James 80,000.00 120,000.00
MJ Michael Jordan 20,000.00 40,000.00
PE Patrick Ewing 500.00 1,000.00
PP Paul Pierce 500.00 1,000.00
PS Peja Stojakovic 100.00 250.00
RJ Richard Jefferson 75.00 200.00
RM Reggie Miller 1,000.00 2,000.00
SA Shareef Abdur-Rahim 200.00 500.00
SM Shawn Marion 200.00 500.00
ST Stephon Marbury 500.00 1,000.00
TM Tracy McGrady 1,000.00 2,000.00
TP Tony Parker 500.00 1,000.00
ZO Alonzo Mourning 500.00 1,000.00

2003-04 Exquisite Collection Number Piece Autographs

STATED PRINT RUN ONE TO 91 SETS
AJ Antawn Jamison/33 40.00 100.00
AK Andrei Kirilenko/47 100.00 200.00
AM Alonzo Mourning/33 200.00 500.00
AS Amare Stoudemire/32 125.00 250.00
CA Carmelo Anthony/15 2,000.00 4,000.00
DA David Robinson/50 400.00 800.00
DM Darius Miles/23 40.00 100.00
DR Dennis Rodman/91 500.00 1,000.00
GP Gary Payton/20 250.00 500.00
KG Kevin Garnett/21 3,000.00 5,000.00
LB Larry Bird/33 600.00 1,200.00
LJ LeBron James/23 80,000.00 120,000.00
MA Magic Johnson/32 600.00 1,200.00
MJ Michael Jordan/23 20,000.00 40,000.00
PE Patrick Ewing/33 1,200.00 2,200.00
PP Paul Pierce/34 600.00 1,200.00
RJ Richard Jefferson/24 40.00 100.00
RM Reggie Miller/31 2,000.00 4,000.00
SM Shawn Marion/31 300.00 600.00

2003-04 Exquisite Collection Patches Autographs

PRINT RUN 100 SER.#'d SETS
AK Andrei Kirilenko 25.00 60.00
AM Antonio McDyess 40.00 100.00
AS Amare Stoudemire 100.00 250.00
BD Baron Davis 125.00 300.00
BR Bill Russell 2,000.00 4,000.00
CA Carmelo Anthony 500.00 1,000.00
CB Chris Bosh 200.00 500.00
CM Corey Maggette 25.00 60.00
DA David Robinson 300.00 600.00
DM Darius Miles 25.00 60.00
DR Dennis Rodman 500.00 1,000.00
EG Manu Ginobili 300.00 600.00
GA Gilbert Arenas 125.00 300.00
GP Gary Payton 150.00 400.00
GR Glenn Robinson 100.00 250.00
JE Julius Erving 600.00 1,200.00
JK Jason Kidd 300.00 600.00
JS John Stockton 300.00 600.00
JY Jerry Stackhouse 75.00 200.00
KB Kobe Bryant 6,000.00 12,000.00
KG Kevin Garnett 500.00 1,000.00
LB Larry Bird 500.00 1,000.00
LJ L.James 50,000.00 100,000.00
LO Lamar Odom 125.00 300.00
MA Magic Johnson 1,000.00 2,000.00
MB Mike Bibby 150.00 400.00
MJ M.Jordan 15,000.00 30,000.00
PE Patrick Ewing 500.00 1,000.00
PP Paul Pierce 300.00 600.00
PS Peja Stojakovic 100.00 200.00
RH Richard Hamilton 100.00 250.00
RJ Richard Jefferson 40.00 100.00
RM Reggie Miller 600.00 1,200.00
SA Shareef Abdur-Rahim 125.00 300.00
SC Sam Cassell 100.00 250.00
SH Shawn Marion 100.00 250.00
ST Stephon Marbury 100.00 250.00
TM Tracy McGrady 300.00 600.00
TP Tony Parker 150.00 400.00
YM Yao Ming 1,000.00 2,000.00
ZR Zach Randolph 100.00 250.00

2003-04 Exquisite Collection Scripted Swatches

PRINT RUN 25 SER.#'d SETS
AS Amare Stoudemire 150.00 400.00
CA Carmelo Anthony 1,000.00 2,000.00
CM Corey Maggette 75.00 200.00
JK Jason Kidd 800.00 1,500.00
JS John Stockton 800.00 1,500.00
KG Kevin Garnett 2,000.00 4,000.00
LJ L.James 100,000.00 150,000.00
MJ M.Jordan 15,000.00 20,000.00
PE Patrick Ewing 800.00 1,500.00
RM Reggie Miller 2,000.00 4,000.00
TM Tracy McGrady 500.00 1,000.00
YM Yao Ming 1,000.00 3,000.00

2004-05 Exquisite Collection

1-84 PRINT RUN 225 SER.#'d SETS
85-90 HAVE BOTH PATCH AND AUTO
1 Al Harrington 5.00 12.00
2 Paul Pierce 20.00 50.00
3 Emeka Okafor RC 5.00 12.00
4 Michael Jordan 500.00 1,000.00
5 LeBron James 150.00 400.00
6 Dirk Nowitzki 30.00 80.00
7 Carmelo Anthony 12.00 30.00
8 Kenyon Martin 6.00 15.00
9 Richard Hamilton 8.00 20.00
10 Ben Wallace 8.00 20.00
11 Jason Richardson 6.00 15.00
12 Yao Ming 30.00 80.00
13 Tracy McGrady 30.00 80.00
14 Reggie Miller 20.00 50.00
15 Corey Maggette 5.00 12.00
16 Kobe Bryant 150.00 400.00
17 Lamar Odom 6.00 15.00
18 Pau Gasol 10.00 25.00
19 Dwyane Wade 25.00 60.00
20 Shaquille O'Neal 60.00 150.00
21 Michael Redd 5.00 12.00
22 Kevin Garnett 30.00 80.00
23 Vince Carter 30.00 80.00
24 Jason Kidd 10.00 25.00
25 Baron Davis 6.00 15.00
26 Jamaal Magloire 4.00 10.00
27 Stephon Marbury 8.00 20.00
28 Steve Francis 6.00 15.00
29 Allen Iverson 30.00 80.00
30 Amare Stoudemire 6.00 15.00
31 Shawn Marion 6.00 15.00
32 Shareef Abdur-Rahim 6.00 15.00
33 Peja Stojakovic 5.00 12.00
34 Mike Bibby 6.00 15.00
35 Tim Duncan 30.00 80.00
36 Tony Parker 10.00 25.00
37 Ray Allen 10.00 25.00
38 Chris Bosh 10.00 25.00
39 Andrei Kirilenko 5.00 12.00
40 Carlos Boozer 5.00 12.00
41 Gilbert Arenas 6.00 15.00
42 Antawn Jamison 5.00 12.00
43 Andre Emmett JSY AU RC 12.00 30.00
44 Jameer Nelson JSY AU RC 40.00 100.00
45 S.Livingston JSY AU RC 50.00 120.00
46 Delonte West JSY AU RC 15.00 40.00
47 Trevor Ariza AU RC 20.00 50.00
48 Tony Allen JSY AU RC 20.00 50.00
49 Luke Jackson JSY AU RC 12.00 30.00
50 Dorell Wright JSY AU RC 15.00 40.00
51 Nenad Krstic JSY AU RC 15.00 40.00
52 Al Jefferson JSY RC 20.00 50.00
53 J.R. Smith JSY AU RC 60.00 150.00
54 Rafael Araujo JSY AU RC 12.00 30.00
55 Andris Biedrins JSY AU RC 12.00 30.00
56 Josh Smith JSY AU RC 40.00 100.00
57 Ha Seung-Jin JSY AU RC 20.00 50.00
58 B.Robinson JSY AU RC 12.00 30.00
59 Kevin Martin JSY AU RC 75.00 200.00
60 David Harrison JSY AU RC 12.00 30.00
61 Kris Humphries JSY AU RC 15.00 40.00
62 A.Varejao JSY AU RC 15.00 40.00
63 Jackson Vroman JSY AU RC 12.00 30.00
64 Sebastian Telfair JSY AU RC 15.00 40.00
65 Chris Duhon JSY AU RC 15.00 40.00
66 Kirk Snyder JSY AU RC 12.00 30.00
67 Andres Nocioni AU RC 20.00 50.00
68 Antonio Burks AU RC 12.00 30.00
69 Beno Udrih AU RC 15.00 40.00
70 D.J. Mbenga AU RC 12.00 30.00
71 Lionel Chalmers JSY AU RC 15.00 40.00
72 Robert Swift AU RC 12.00 30.00
73 Sasha Vujacic JSY AU RC 15.00 40.00
74 Donta Smith AU RC 12.00 30.00
75 Peter John Ramos AU RC 12.00 30.00
76 Justin Reed AU RC 12.00 30.00
77 Pape Sow AU RC 12.00 30.00
78 Pavel Podkolzin AU RC 12.00 30.00
79 Viktor Khryapa AU RC 12.00 30.00
80 John Edwards AU RC 12.00 30.00
81 Royal Ivey AU RC 12.00 30.00
82 Damien Wilkins AU RC 15.00 40.00
83 Erik Daniels AU RC 15.00 40.00
84 Luis Flores AU RC 15.00 40.00
85 Andre Iguodala JSY AU RC 150.00 400.00
86 Josh Childress JSY AU RC 12.00 30.00
87 Devin Harris JSY AU RC 15.00 40.00
88 Ben Gordon JSY AU RC 75.00 200.00
89 Luol Deng JSY AU RC 125.00 300.00
90 Dwight Howard JSY AU RC 500.00 1,000.00

2004-05 Exquisite Collection Jersey Parallel

*JSY PARALLEL: 1.25X TO 3X BASE HI
PRINT RUN 25 SER.#'d SETS
2 Paul Pierce 30.00 80.00
4 Michael Jordan 2,500.00 5,000.00
5 LeBron James 200.00 500.00
7 Carmelo Anthony 40.00 100.00
16 Kobe Bryant 300.00 600.00
20 Shaquille O'Neal 50.00 125.00
38 Chris Bosh 15.00 40.00

2004-05 Exquisite Collection Platinum

*1-42 PLATINUM: 1.25X TO 3X BASE HI
43-90 DO NOT HAVE JSY OR AU
PRINT RUN 25 SER.#'d SETS
43 Andre Emmett 10.00 25.00
44 Jameer Nelson 15.00 40.00
45 Shaun Livingston 40.00 100.00
46 Delonte West 12.00 30.00
47 Trevor Ariza 15.00 40.00
48 Tony Allen 15.00 40.00
49 Luke Jackson 10.00 25.00
50 Dorell Wright 12.00 30.00
51 Nenad Krstic 12.00 30.00
52 Al Jefferson 15.00 40.00
53 J.R. Smith 50.00 120.00
54 Rafael Araujo 10.00 25.00
55 Andris Biedrins 10.00 25.00
56 Josh Smith 30.00 80.00
57 Ha Seung-Jin 15.00 40.00
58 Bernard Robinson 10.00 25.00
59 Kevin Martin 60.00 150.00
60 David Harrison 10.00 25.00
61 Kris Humphries 12.00 30.00
62 Anderson Varejao 12.00 30.00
63 Jackson Vroman 10.00 25.00
64 Sebastian Telfair 12.00 30.00
65 Chris Duhon 12.00 30.00
66 Kirk Snyder 10.00 25.00
67 Andres Nocioni 15.00 40.00
68 Antonio Burks 10.00 25.00
69 Beno Udrih 12.00 30.00
70 D.J. Mbenga 10.00 25.00
71 Lionel Chalmers 12.00 30.00
72 Robert Swift 10.00 25.00
73 Sasha Vujacic 12.00 30.00
74 Donta Smith 10.00 25.00
75 Peter John Ramos 10.00 25.00
76 Justin Reed 10.00 25.00
77 Pape Sow 10.00 25.00
78 Pavel Podkolzin 10.00 25.00
79 Viktor Khryapa 10.00 25.00
80 John Edwards 10.00 25.00
81 Royal Ivey 10.00 25.00
82 Damien Wilkins 12.00 30.00
83 Erik Daniels 12.00 30.00
84 Luis Flores 12.00 30.00
85 Andre Iguodala 125.00 300.00
86 Josh Childress 10.00 25.00
87 Devin Harris 12.00 30.00
88 Ben Gordon 60.00 150.00
89 Luol Deng 100.00 250.00
90 Dwight Howard 400.00 800.00

2004-05 Exquisite Collection Rookie Parallel

PRINT RUNS LISTED IN CHECKLIST
44 Jameer Nelson JSY AU/14 50.00 120.00
45 Shaun Livingston JSY AU/14 60.00 150.00
47 Trevor Ariza AU/21 25.00 60.00
48 Tony Allen JSY AU/42 25.00 60.00
49 Luke Jackson JSY AU/33 15.00 40.00
54 Rafael Araujo JSY AU/55 15.00 40.00
55 Andris Biedrins JSY AU/15 15.00 40.00

58 Bernard Robinson JSY/21 15.00 40.00
59 Kevin Martin JSY AU/23 100.00 250.00
61 Kris Humphries JSY AU/43 20.00 50.00
62 Anderson Varejao JSY AU/17 20.00 50.00
64 Sebastian Telfair JSY AU/31 30.00 80.00
65 Chris Duhon JSY AU/21 40.00 100.00
69 Beno Udrih AU/14 40.00 100.00
70 D.J. Mbenga AU/28 15.00 40.00
72 Robert Swift AU/31 15.00 40.00
73 Sasha Vujacic JSY AU/18 50.00 100.00
74 Donta Smith AU/15 15.00 40.00
75 Peter John Ramos AU/34 15.00 40.00
78 Pavel Podkolzin AU/24 15.00 40.00
79 Viktor Khryapa AU/38 15.00 40.00
80 John Edwards AU/54 15.00 40.00
81 Royal Ivey AU/36 15.00 40.00
83 Erik Daniels AU/15 20.00 50.00
87 Devin Harris JSY AU/34 30.00 80.00

2004-05 Exquisite Collection Dual Signature Shots

PRINT RUN 25 SER.#'d SETS
GD B.Gordon/L.Deng 75.00 150.00
HC D.Harris/J.Childress 30.00 80.00
HN D.Howard/J.Nelson 50.00 120.00
IS A.Iguodala/J.R.Smith 30.00 80.00
KB A.Kirilenko/C.Boozer 40.00 100.00
LT S.Livingston/S.Telfair 15.00 40.00

2004-05 Exquisite Collection Enshrinements Autographs

PRINT RUN 25 SER.#'d SETS
ENAS1 A.Stoudemire Purple 40.00 100.00
ENAS2 A.Stoudemire Orange 75.00 150.00
ENBG Ben Gordon 50.00 120.00
ENBR1 Bill Russell Posed 2,000.00 4,000.00
ENBR2 Bill Russell Dunk 2,000.00 4,000.00
ENBW Ben Wallace 40.00 100.00
ENCA1 C.Anthony Dribble 125.00 300.00
ENCA2 C.Anthony Dunk 125.00 300.00
ENDH Dwight Howard 125.00 300.00
ENDH2 Dwight Howard 125.00 300.00
ENDR David Robinson 200.00 500.00
ENHO Hakeem Olajuwon 150.00 400.00
ENIT Isiah Thomas 150.00 400.00
ENJE1 Julius Erving Red 150.00 400.00
ENJE2 Julius Erving White 150.00 400.00
ENJK Jason Kidd 125.00 300.00
ENJS Josh Smith 40.00 100.00
ENJS1 John Stockton Black 150.00 400.00
ENJS2 John Stockton White 150.00 400.00
ENKB1 Kobe Bryant Yellow 500.00 1,000.00
ENKB2 Kobe Bryant Purple 500.00 1,000.00
ENKG Kevin Garnett 1,000.00 2,000.00
ENLB1 Larry Bird Green 150.00 400.00
ENLB2 Larry Bird White 125.00 300.00
ENLD Luol Deng 40.00 100.00
ENLJ1 LeBron James Red 3,000.00 5,000.00
ENLJ2 LeBron James White 3,000.00 5,000.00
ENMA1 Magic Johnson 150.00 400.00
ENMA2 Magic Johnson 150.00 400.00
ENMJ1 Michael Jordan Red 3,000.00 6,000.00
ENMJ2 Michael Jordan White 3,000.00 6,000.00
ENPP Paul Pierce 125.00 300.00
ENRA Ray Allen 125.00 300.00
ENRO Dennis Rodman 200.00 500.00
ENSN Steve Nash 200.00 500.00
ENSP S.Pippen Straight 400.00 800.00
ENSP2 S.Pippen Head Right 400.00 800.00
ENST Stephon Marbury 100.00 250.00
ENTM1 Tracy McGrady Red 150.00 400.00
ENTM2 Tracy McGrady White 150.00 400.00
ENYM1 Yao Ming Red 600.00 1,200.00
ENYM2 Yao Ming White 600.00 1,200.00

2004-05 Exquisite Collection Extra Exquisite Jerseys

PRINT RUN 25 SER.#'d SETS
AI Allen Iverson 60.00 150.00
AK Andrei Kirilenko 12.00 30.00
AN Andre Iguodala 25.00 60.00
AS Amare Stoudemire 15.00 40.00
BD Baron Davis 15.00 40.00
BG Ben Gordon 15.00 40.00
BW Ben Wallace 20.00 50.00
CA Carmelo Anthony 30.00 80.00
CB Chris Bosh 25.00 60.00
DE Devin Harris 12.00 30.00
DH Dwight Howard 50.00 120.00
DN Dirk Nowitzki 60.00 150.00
DR David Robinson 50.00 120.00
IT Isiah Thomas 25.00 60.00
JE Julius Erving 60.00 150.00
JK Jason Kidd 25.00 60.00
JO Josh Smith 15.00 40.00
JS John Stockton 50.00 120.00
KB1 Kobe Bryant Purple 200.00 500.00
KB2 Kobe Bryant White 200.00 500.00
KG Kevin Garnett 75.00 200.00
LB Larry Bird 60.00 150.00
LD Luol Deng 15.00 40.00
LJ1 LeBron James Red 300.00 600.00
LJ2 LeBron James White 300.00 600.00
MA Magic Johnson 60.00 150.00
MG Manu Ginobili 50.00 120.00
MJ1 Michael Jordan White 400.00 800.00
MJ2 Michael Jordan Red 400.00 800.00
PP Paul Pierce 40.00 100.00
RA Ray Allen 30.00 80.00
RM Reggie Miller 75.00 200.00
RO Dennis Rodman 75.00 200.00
SF Steve Francis 15.00 40.00
SL Shaun Livingston 15.00 40.00
SN Steve Nash 30.00 80.00
SO Shaquille O'Neal 60.00 150.00
SP Scottie Pippen 100.00 250.00
ST Stephon Marbury 20.00 50.00
TD Tim Duncan 75.00 200.00
TM Tracy McGrady 75.00 200.00
YM Yao Ming 100.00 250.00

2004-05 Exquisite Collection Limited Logos

PRINT RUN 50 SER.#'d SETS
AK Andrei Kirilenko 75.00 200.00
AS Amare Stoudemire 125.00 300.00
BD Baron Davis 100.00 250.00
BG Ben Gordon 50.00 120.00
BW Ben Wallace 20.00 50.00
CA Carmelo Anthony 300.00 600.00
CB Carlos Boozer 50.00 120.00
CM Corey Maggette 50.00 120.00
DH1 Dwight Howard Blue 300.00 600.00
DH2 Dwight Howard White 300.00 600.00
DR David Robinson 300.00 600.00
GA Gilbert Arenas 75.00 200.00
HO Hakeem Olajuwon 300.00 600.00
IT Isiah Thomas 200.00 500.00
JK Jason Kidd 300.00 600.00
JS John Stockton 400.00 800.00
JW Jason Williams 400.00 800.00
KB1 Kobe Bryant Purple 6,000.00 10,000.00
KB2 Kobe Bryant Yellow 6,000.00 10,000.00
KG1 Kevin Garnett Black 500.00 1,000.00
KG2 Kevin Garnett Blue 500.00 1,000.00
KH Kirk Hinrich 50.00 120.00
LB Larry Bird 600.00 1,200.00
LD Luol Deng 60.00 150.00
LJ1 LJames Red 10,000.00 15,000.00
LJ2 LJames White 10,000.00 15,000.00
LO Lamar Odom 75.00 200.00
MA Magic Johnson 600.00 1,200.00
MJ Michael Jordan 15,000.00 20,000.00
MR Michael Redd 50.00 120.00
PG Pau Gasol 200.00 500.00
PP Paul Pierce 400.00 800.00
PS Peja Stojakovic 400.00 800.00
RA Ray Allen 400.00 800.00
RJ Richard Jefferson 50.00 120.00
RO Dennis Rodman 500.00 1,000.00
SM Shawn Marion 125.00 300.00
SN Steve Nash 400.00 800.00
ST Stephon Marbury 125.00 300.00
TM Tracy McGrady 500.00 1,000.00
TP Tony Parker 500.00 1,000.00
YM Yao Ming 800.00 1,500.00

2004-05 Exquisite Collection Number Pieces Autographs

PRINT RUNS LISTED IN CHECKLIST
AK Andrei Kirilenko/47 20.00 50.00
AS Amare Stoudemire/32 50.00 125.00
CA Carmelo Anthony/15 250.00 500.00
CM Corey Maggette/50 20.00 50.00
DE Devin Harris/34 25.00 60.00
DR David Robinson/50 100.00 250.00
HO Hakeem Olajuwon/34 100.00 250.00
KG Kevin Garnett/21 400.00 800.00
LB Larry Bird/33 300.00 600.00
LJ LeBron James/23 1,500.00 3,000.00
MA Magic Johnson/34 300.00 600.00
MJ Michael Jordan/23 10,000.00 15,000.00
PG Pau Gasol/16 75.00 150.00
PP Paul Pierce/34 125.00 250.00
PS Peja Stojakovic/16 60.00 150.00
RA Ray Allen/34 100.00 200.00
RJ Richard Jefferson/24 20.00 50.00
RO Dennis Rodman/91 100.00 200.00
SM Shawn Marion/31 20.00 50.00
SP Scottie Pippen/33 600.00 1,200.00

2004-05 Exquisite Collection Patches Autographs

PRINT RUN 50 TO 100 SER.#'d SETS
AJ Antawn Jamison/100 75.00 200.00
AK Andrei Kirilenko/100 75.00 200.00
AS Amare Stoudemire/100 75.00 200.00
BD Baron Davis/100 75.00 200.00
BG Ben Gordon/100 40.00 100.00
BR Bill Russell/75 2,500.00 5,000.00
BW Ben Wallace/100 350.00 700.00
CA Carmelo Anthony/100 400.00 800.00
CB Carlos Boozer/100 20.00 50.00
DE Devin Harris/100 20.00 50.00
DH Dwight Howard/100 300.00 600.00
DR David Robinson/100 400.00 800.00
GP Gary Payton/100 300.00 600.00
HO Hakeem Olajuwon/50 400.00 800.00
IT Isiah Thomas/100 150.00 400.00
JE Julius Erving/50 1,000.00 2,000.00
JK Jason Kidd/100 150.00 400.00
JS John Stockton/100 200.00 500.00
KB Kobe Bryant/100 15,000.00 30,000.00
KG Kevin Garnett/100 800.00 1,500.00
KH Kirk Hinrich/100 40.00 100.00
LB Larry Bird/100 1,000.00 2,000.00
LD Luol Deng/100 40.00 100.00
LJ LeBron James/100 15,000.00 30,000.00
MA Magic Johnson/100 1,000.00 2,000.00
MB Mike Bibby/100 75.00 200.00
MJ Michael Jordan/100 20,000.00 40,000.00
MR Michael Redd/100 40.00 100.00
PG Pau Gasol/100 100.00 250.00
PP Paul Pierce/100 200.00 500.00
PS Peja Stojakovic/100 75.00 200.00
RA Ray Allen/100 200.00 500.00
RH Richard Hamilton/100 100.00 250.00
RJ Richard Jefferson/100 40.00 100.00
RO Dennis Rodman/100 500.00 1,000.00
SA Shareef Abdur-Rahim/100 75.00 200.00
SM Shawn Marion/100 75.00 200.00
SP Scottie Pippen/100 1,000.00 2,000.00
ST Stephon Marbury/100 100.00 250.00
TM Tracy McGrady/100 300.00 600.00
TP Tony Parker/100 300.00 800.00
YM Yao Ming/100 1,500.00 3,000.00

2004-05 Exquisite Collection Signature Shots Patches

PRINT RUN 100 SER.#'d SETS
AI Andre Iguodala 20.00 50.00
AK Andrei Kirilenko 15.00 40.00
BG Ben Gordon 15.00 40.00
BM Brad Miller 12.00 30.00
CB Carlos Boozer 12.00 30.00
DE Devin Harris 12.00 30.00
DH Dwight Howard 50.00 120.00
JC Josh Childress 12.00 30.00
JN Jameer Nelson 12.00 30.00
JR J.R. Smith 20.00 50.00
LD Luol Deng 12.00 30.00
SL Shaun Livingston 15.00 40.00
SM Shawn Marion 12.00 30.00
ST Sebastian Telfair 12.00 30.00

2005-06 Exquisite Collection

1-42 PRINT RUN 225 SER.#'d SETS
43-48 JSY AU RC PRINT RUN 99 SETS
49-82 JSY AU RC PRINT RUN 225 SETS
83-96 AU RC PRINT RUN 225 SER.#'d SETS
1 Joe Johnson 3.00 8.00
2 Paul Pierce 6.00 15.00
3 Emeka Okafor 3.00 8.00
4 Ben Gordon 3.00 8.00
5 Michael Jordan 500.00 1,000.00
6 LeBron James 150.00 400.00
7 Dirk Nowitzki 12.00 30.00
8 Carmelo Anthony 6.00 15.00
9 Kenyon Martin 3.00 8.00
10 Chauncey Billups 5.00 12.00
11 Ben Wallace 5.00 12.00
12 Jason Richardson 4.00 10.00
13 Tracy McGrady 25.00 60.00
14 Yao Ming 40.00 100.00
15 Jermaine O'Neal 3.00 8.00
16 Elton Brand 3.00 8.00
17 Kobe Bryant 150.00 400.00
18 Pau Gasol 6.00 15.00
19 Shaquille O'Neal 12.00 30.00
20 Dwyane Wade 15.00 40.00
21 Michael Redd 3.00 8.00
22 Kevin Garnett 10.00 25.00
23 Vince Carter 12.00 30.00
24 Jason Kidd 6.00 15.00
25 J.R. Smith 4.00 10.00
26 Stephon Marbury 5.00 12.00
27 Quentin Richardson 2.50 6.00
28 Steve Francis 4.00 10.00
29 Dwight Howard 5.00 12.00
30 Allen Iverson 30.00 80.00
31 Chris Webber 15.00 40.00
32 Steve Nash 12.00 30.00
33 Amare Stoudemire 4.00 10.00
34 Zach Randolph 4.00 10.00
35 Mike Bibby 4.00 10.00
36 Peja Stojakovic 3.00 8.00
37 Tim Duncan 15.00 40.00
38 Tony Parker 6.00 15.00
39 Ray Allen 6.00 15.00
40 Chris Bosh 5.00 12.00
41 Andrei Kirilenko 3.00 8.00
42 Gilbert Arenas 4.00 10.00
43 Andrew Bogut JSY AU/99 RC 60.00 150.00
44 M.Williams JSY AU/99 RC 15.00 40.00
45 D.Williams JSY AU/99 RC 100.00 250.00
46 Chris Paul JSY AU/99 RC 2,000.00 4,000.00
47 R.Felton JSY AU RC/99 30.00 80.00
48 C.Frye JSY AU/99 RC 15.00 40.00
49 M.Webster JSY AU RC 12.00 30.00
50 C.Villanueva JSY AU RC 5.00 12.00
51 Ike Diogu JSY AU RC 5.00 12.00
52 Andrew Bynum JSY AU RC 20.00 50.00
53 Sean May JSY AU RC 5.00 12.00
54 Rashad McCants JSY AU RC 20.00 50.00
55 Antoine Wright JSY AU RC 6.00 15.00
56 Joey Graham JSY AU RC 6.00 15.00
57 Danny Granger JSY AU RC 8.00 20.00
58 Gerald Green JSY AU RC 40.00 100.00
59 Hakim Warrick JSY AU RC 6.00 15.00
60 Julius Hodge JSY AU RC 5.00 12.00
61 Nate Robinson JSY AU RC 8.00 20.00
62 Jarrett Jack JSY AU RC 10.00 25.00
63 Francisco Garcia JSY AU RC 5.00 12.00
64 Luther Head JSY AU RC 5.00 12.00
65 Johan Petro JSY AU RC 5.00 12.00
66 Jason Maxiell JSY AU RC 6.00 15.00
67 Linas Kleiza JSY AU RC 6.00 15.00
68 Wayne Simien JSY AU RC 5.00 12.00
69 David Lee JSY AU RC 8.00 20.00
70 Salim Stoudamire JSY AU RC 6.00 15.00
71 Daniel Ewing JSY AU RC 6.00 15.00
72 Brandon Bass JSY AU RC 6.00 15.00
73 C.J. Miles JSY AU RC 6.00 15.00
74 Ersan Ilyasova JSY AU RC 15.00 40.00
75 Travis Diener JSY AU RC 5.00 12.00
76 Monta Ellis JSY AU RC 30.00 80.00
77 Chris Taft JSY AU RC 5.00 12.00
78 M.Andriuskevicius JSY AU RC 5.00 12.00
79 Louis Williams JSY AU RC 40.00 100.00
80 Andray Blatche JSY AU RC 8.00 20.00
81 Ryan Gomes JSY AU RC 6.00 15.00
82 S.Jasikevicius JSY AU RC 8.00 20.00
83 Yaroslav Korolev AU RC 4.00 10.00
85 Von Wafer AU RC 4.00 10.00
86 Orien Greene AU RC 5.00 12.00
87 Robert Whaley AU RC 4.00 10.00
88 Dijon Thompson AU RC 4.00 10.00
89 Bracey Wright AU RC 4.00 10.00
90 Amir Johnson AU RC 6.00 15.00
91 Ronny Turiaf AU RC 6.00 15.00
92 James Singleton AU RC 4.00 10.00
93 Alex Acker AU RC 4.00 10.00
94 Chuck Hayes AU RC 6.00 15.00
95 Lawrence Roberts AU RC 4.00 10.00
96 Stephen Graham AU RC 5.00 12.00

2005-06 Exquisite Collection Gold

*1-42 GOLD: 1.25X TO 3X BASE HI
GOLD PRINT RUN 25 SER.#'d SETS
20 Dwyane Wade 75.00 200.00
26 Stephon Marbury 12.00 30.00
43 Andrew Bogut 25.00 60.00
44 Marvin Williams 15.00 40.00
45 Deron Williams 40.00 100.00
46 Chris Paul 200.00 500.00
47 Raymond Felton 12.00 30.00
48 Channing Frye 12.00 30.00
49 Martell Webster 12.00 30.00
50 Charlie Villanueva 12.00 30.00
51 Ike Diogu 10.00 25.00
52 Andrew Bynum 12.00 30.00
53 Sean May 10.00 25.00
54 Rashad McCants 10.00 25.00
55 Antoine Wright 12.00 30.00
56 Joey Graham 12.00 30.00
57 Danny Granger 15.00 40.00
58 Gerald Green 15.00 40.00
59 Hakim Warrick 12.00 30.00
60 Julius Hodge 10.00 25.00
61 Nate Robinson 15.00 40.00
62 Jarrett Jack 15.00 40.00
63 Francisco Garcia 10.00 25.00
64 Luther Head 10.00 25.00
65 Johan Petro 10.00 25.00
66 Jason Maxiell 12.00 30.00
67 Linas Kleiza 12.00 30.00
68 Wayne Simien 10.00 25.00
69 David Lee 15.00 40.00
70 Salim Stoudamire 12.00 30.00
71 Daniel Ewing 12.00 30.00
72 Brandon Bass 12.00 30.00
73 C.J. Miles 12.00 30.00
74 Ersan Ilyasova 15.00 40.00
75 Travis Diener 10.00 25.00
76 Monta Ellis 30.00 80.00
77 Chris Taft 10.00 25.00
78 Martynas Andriuskevicius 10.00 25.00
79 Louis Williams 40.00 100.00
80 Andray Blatche 15.00 40.00
81 Ryan Gomes 12.00 30.00
82 Sarunas Jasikevicius 15.00 40.00
83 Yaroslav Korolev 10.00 25.00
84 Jose Calderon 15.00 40.00
85 Von Wafer 10.00 25.00
86 Orien Greene 12.00 30.00
87 Robert Whaley 10.00 25.00
88 Dijon Thompson 10.00 25.00
89 Bracey Wright 10.00 25.00
90 Amir Johnson 15.00 40.00
91 Ronny Turiaf 15.00 40.00
92 James Singleton 10.00 25.00
93 Alex Acker 10.00 25.00
94 Chuck Hayes 15.00 40.00
95 Lawrence Roberts 10.00 25.00
96 Stephen Graham 12.00 30.00

2005-06 Exquisite Collection Jerseys

*JERSEY: 1.25X TO 3X BASE HI
PRINT RUN 25 SER.#'d SETS

2005-06 Exquisite Collection Rookie Parallel

PRINT RUNS LISTED IN CHECKLIST
44AP Marvin Williams JSY AU/24 40.00 100.00
47AP Raymond Felton JSY AU/20 20.00 50.00
50AP Charlie Villanueva JSY AU/31 20.00 50.00
52AP A.Bynum JSY AU/17 600.00 800.00
53AP Sean May JSY AU/42 15.00 40.00
55AP Antoine Wright JSY AU/21 40.00 100.00
56AP Joey Graham JSY AU/14 20.00 50.00
57AP Danny Granger JSY AU/33 25.00 60.00
59AP Hakim Warrick JSY AU/21 150.00 300.00
60AP Julius Hodge JSY AU/32 15.00 40.00
63AP Francisco Garcia JSY AU/32 15.00 40.00
65AP Johan Petro JSY AU/27 15.00 40.00
66AP Jason Maxiell JSY AU/54 30.00 80.00
67AP Linas Kleiza JSY AU/43 20.00 50.00
68AP Wayne Simien JSY AU/25 15.00 40.00
69AP David Lee JSY AU/42 25.00 60.00
70AP Salim Stoudamire JSY AU/20 20.00 50.00
72AP Brandon Bass JSY AU/33 30.00 80.00
73AP C.J. Miles JSY AU/34 60.00 120.00
74AP Ersan Ilyasova JSY AU/23 20.00 50.00
75AP Travis Diener JSY AU/34 15.00 40.00
77AP Chris Taft JSY AU/21 15.00 40.00
78AP Andriuskevicius JSY AU/15 40.00 100.00
79AP Louis Williams JSY AU/23 125.00 250.00
80AP Andray Blatche JSY AU/32 25.00 60.00
85AP Von Wafer AU/23 15.00 40.00
86AP Orien Greene AU/100 20.00 50.00
87AP Robert Whaley AU/21 15.00 40.00
90AP Amir Johnson AU/25 60.00 120.00
91AP Ronny Turiaf AU/21 100.00 200.00
92AP James Singleton AU/15 15.00 40.00
94AP Chuck Hayes AU/44 25.00 60.00
95AP Lawrence Roberts AU/44 15.00 40.00

2005-06 Exquisite Collection Autographs Patches

PRINT RUN 100 SER.#'d SETS
APAB Andrew Bogut 30.00 80.00
APAN Andrew Bynum 20.00 50.00
APAW Antoine Wright 10.00 25.00
APCA Carmelo Anthony 60.00 150.00
APCB Chris Bosh 30.00 80.00
APCF Channing Frye 10.00 25.00
APCH Chauncey Billups 60.00 150.00
APCP Chris Paul 200.00 400.00
APCV Charlie Villanueva 10.00 25.00
APDE Dennis Rodman 150.00 400.00
APDG Danny Granger 25.00 60.00
APDH Dwight Howard 50.00 120.00
APDL David Lee 25.00 60.00
APDR David Robinson 60.00 150.00
APDW Deron Williams 25.00 60.00
APEB Elton Brand 12.00 30.00
APHW Hakim Warrick 10.00 25.00
APID Ike Diogu 10.00 25.00
APJJ Jarrett Jack 12.00 30.00
APJK Jason Kidd 60.00 150.00
APJR J.R. Smith 12.00 30.00
APJS John Stockton 75.00 200.00
APKG Kevin Garnett 400.00 800.00
APLB Larry Bird 100.00 250.00
APLH Larry Hughes 12.00 30.00
APLJ LeBron James 2,000.00 4,000.00
APLO Lamar Odom 25.00 60.00
APMA Magic Johnson 200.00 400.00
APMB Mike Bibby 12.00 30.00
APMJ Michael Jordan 5,000.00 8,000.00
APMR Martell Webster 10.00 25.00
APMW Marvin Williams 12.00 30.00
APNR Nate Robinson 15.00 40.00
APPS Peja Stojakovic 50.00 120.00
APRF Raymond Felton 10.00 25.00
APSJ Sarunas Jasikevicius 20.00 50.00
APSM Sean May 10.00 25.00
APSP Scottie Pippen 150.00 400.00
APST Stephon Marbury 15.00 40.00
APTM Tracy McGrady 100.00 250.00
APTP Tayshaun Prince 15.00 40.00
APVC Vince Carter 40.00 100.00

2005-06 Exquisite Collection Emblems of Endorsements

PRINT RUN 15 SER.#'d SETS
EMAB Andrew Bogut 150.00 300.00
EMAI Andre Iguodala 60.00 150.00
EMAJ Antawn Jamison 30.00 80.00
EMBW Bill Walton 175.00 350.00
EMCA Carmelo Anthony 150.00 300.00
EMCB Chauncey Billups 100.00 250.00
EMCH Chris Bosh 100.00 250.00
EMCM Corey Maggette 30.00 80.00
EMCP Chris Paul 400.00 700.00
EMDH Dwight Howard 150.00 325.00
EMDR David Robinson 175.00 350.00
EMEB Elton Brand 30.00 80.00
EMEO Emeka Okafor 30.00 80.00
EMHO Hakeem Olajuwon 200.00 500.00
EMJE Julius Erving 175.00 350.00
EMJS John Stockton 1,000.00 2,000.00
EMKG Kevin Garnett 2,000.00 4,000.00
EMKH Kirk Hinrich 30.00 80.00
EMLH Larry Hughes 30.00 80.00
EMLJ LeBron James 4,000.00 6,000.00
EMLO Lamar Odom 30.00 80.00
EMMJ Michael Jordan 10,000.00 15,000.00
EMMW Marvin Williams 30.00 80.00
EMPG Pau Gasol 125.00 300.00
EMPP Paul Pierce 150.00 400.00
EMPS Peja Stojakovic 100.00 250.00
EMRA Ron Artest 30.00 80.00
EMRH Richard Hamilton 75.00 200.00
EMRJ Richard Jefferson 30.00 80.00
EMSA Shareef Abdur-Rahim 30.00 80.00
EMSM Stephon Marbury 30.00 80.00
EMSN Steve Nash 200.00 400.00
EMSP Scottie Pippen 400.00 800.00
EMST Sebastian Telfair 30.00 80.00
EMTM Tracy McGrady 400.00 800.00
EMTP Tayshaun Prince 30.00 80.00
EMVC Vince Carter 150.00 400.00
EMYM Yao Ming 200.00 500.00

2005-06 Exquisite Collection Enshrinements

PRINT RUN 25 SER.#'d SETS
EEAB Andrew Bogut 20.00 50.00
EEAI Andre Iguodala 12.00 30.00
EEAJ Antawn Jamison 15.00 40.00
EEBD Baron Davis 15.00 40.00
EEBR Bill Russell 2,500.00 5,000.00
EECA Carmelo Anthony 75.00 200.00
EECB Chauncey Billups 50.00 120.00
EECF Channing Frye 12.00 30.00
EECH Chris Bosh 50.00 100.00
EECP Chris Paul 150.00 400.00
EEDE Dennis Rodman 300.00 600.00
EEDH Dwight Howard 50.00 120.00
EEDR David Robinson 100.00 250.00
EEDW Deron Williams 50.00 120.00
EEEB Elton Brand 15.00 40.00
EEEO Emeka Okafor 15.00 40.00
EEGG George Gervin 50.00 120.00
EEHO Hakeem Olajuwon 100.00 250.00
EEJE Julius Erving 100.00 250.00
EEJK Jason Kidd 100.00 250.00
EEJS John Stockton 125.00 300.00
EEKA Kareem Abdul-Jabbar 125.00 300.00
EEKG Kevin Garnett 150.00 400.00
EELB Larry Bird 125.00 300.00
EELJ LeBron James 3,000.00 6,000.00
EELO Lamar Odom 20.00 50.00
EEMA Magic Johnson 125.00 300.00
EEMJ Michael Jordan 4,000.00 8,000.00
EEMW Marvin Williams 25.00 60.00
EEPP Paul Pierce 125.00 300.00
EERA Ron Artest 20.00 50.00
EESA Shareef Abdur-Rahim 15.00 40.00
EESM Stephon Marbury 15.00 40.00
EESN Steve Nash 100.00 250.00
EESP Scottie Pippen 200.00 500.00
EETM Tracy McGrady 125.00 300.00
EEVC Vince Carter 125.00 300.00
EEYM Yao Ming 500.00 1,000.00
EELJ2 LeBron James 4,000.00 8,000.00
EEMJ2 Michael Jordan 4,000.00 8,000.00

2005-06 Exquisite Collection Extra Exquisite

PRINT RUN 25 SER.#'d SETS
EXAB Andrew Bogut 12.00 30.00
EXBR Bill Russell 125.00 300.00
EXBW Ben Wallace 12.00 30.00
EXCA Carmelo Anthony 15.00 40.00
EXCB Chris Bosh 20.00 40.00
EXCF Channing Frye 8.00 20.00
EXCP Chris Paul 50.00 120.00
EXCV Charlie Villanueva 8.00 20.00
EXDN Dirk Nowitzki 30.00 80.00
EXDR David Robinson 30.00 60.00
EXDW Deron Williams 15.00 40.00
EXEB Elton Brand 8.00 20.00
EXEO Emeka Okafor 8.00 20.00
EXIT Isiah Thomas 15.00 40.00
EXJO Jermaine O'Neal 8.00 20.00
EXJS John Stockton 25.00 50.00
EXKA Kareem Abdul-Jabbar 20.00 50.00
EXKB Kobe Bryant 500.00 1,000.00
EXKG Kevin Garnett 30.00 60.00
EXLB Larry Bird 40.00 100.00
EXLJ LeBron James 150.00 400.00
EXMA Magic Johnson 25.00 60.00
EXMG Manu Ginobili 15.00 30.00
EXMJ Michael Jordan 200.00 500.00
EXMW Marvin Williams 10.00 25.00
EXPS Peja Stojakovic 8.00 20.00
EXRA Ray Allen 15.00 40.00
EXRF Raymond Felton 8.00 20.00
EXRJ Richard Jefferson 8.00 20.00
EXRO Ron Artest 8.00 20.00
EXSO Shaquille O'Neal 30.00 60.00
EXSP Scottie Pippen 50.00 125.00
EXTD Tim Duncan 25.00 60.00
EXTM Tracy McGrady 25.00 60.00
EXVC Vince Carter 20.00 40.00
EXWC Wilt Chamberlain 150.00 400.00
EXYM Yao Ming 60.00 150.00
EXLJ2 LeBron James 150.00 400.00
EXLJ3 LeBron James 150.00 400.00
EXMJ2 Michael Jordan 200.00 500.00
EXMJ3 Michael Jordan 200.00 500.00
EXMW2 Marvin Williams 10.00 25.00

2005-06 Exquisite Collection Limited Logos

PRINT RUN 28 TO 50 SER.#'d SETS
LLAB Andrew Bogut 60.00 150.00
LLAJ Antawn Jamison 20.00 50.00
LLAL Al Jefferson 25.00 60.00
LLAN Andrew Bynum 40.00 100.00
LLBG Ben Gordon 40.00 100.00
LLBR Bill Russell/28 2,000.00 4,000.00
LLCA Carmelo Anthony 500.00 1,000.00
LLCB Chauncey Billups 400.00 800.00
LLCF Channing Frye 40.00 100.00
LLCH Chris Bosh 150.00 400.00
LLCP Chris Paul 600.00 1,200.00
LLCV Charlie Villanueva 25.00 60.00
LLDE Dennis Rodman 2,000.00 4,000.00
LLDH Dwight Howard 150.00 400.00
LLDR David Robinson 500.00 1,000.00
LLDW Deron Williams 100.00 250.00
LLEB Elton Brand 25.00 60.00
LLID Ike Diogu 25.00 60.00
LLJE Julius Erving 500.00 1,000.00
LLJK Jason Kidd 150.00 400.00
LLKG Kevin Garnett 1,000.00 2,000.00
LLLB Larry Bird 1,500.00 3,000.00
LLLH Larry Hughes 25.00 60.00
LLLJ LeBron James 20,000.00 40,000.00
LLMA Magic Johnson 1,500.00 3,000.00
LLMJ Michael Jordan 30,000.00 60,000.00
LLNR Nate Robinson 40.00 100.00
LLPP Paul Pierce 400.00 800.00
LLRA Ron Artest 75.00 200.00
LLRF Raymond Felton 25.00 60.00
LLRM Rashad McCants 25.00 60.00
LLSA Shareef Abdur-Rahim 60.00 150.00
LLSM Sean May 25.00 60.00
LLSN Steve Nash 500.00 1,000.00
LLSP Scottie Pippen 800.00 1,500.00
LLTC Tyson Chandler 75.00 200.00
LLTM Tracy McGrady 300.00 600.00
LLTP Tayshaun Prince 60.00 150.00
LLVC Vince Carter 400.00 800.00
LLYM Yao Ming 1,000.00 2,000.00
LLMW2 Marvin Williams 30.00 80.00

2005-06 Exquisite Collection Noble Nameplates

PRINT RUN 25 SER.#'d SETS
NNAB Andrew Bogut 40.00 100.00
NNAJ Antawn Jamison 20.00 50.00
NNAN Andrew Bynum 20.00 50.00
NNBK Bernard King 40.00 100.00
NNBR Bill Russell 3,000.00 6,000.00
NNCA Carmelo Anthony 400.00 800.00
NNCB Carlos Boozer 20.00 50.00
NNCF Channing Frye 40.00 100.00
NNCH Chauncey Billups 100.00 250.00
NNCM Corey Maggette 20.00 50.00
NNCP Chris Paul 400.00 800.00
NNCS Chris Bosh 125.00 300.00
NNCV Charlie Villanueva 25.00 60.00
NNDA David Robinson 400.00 800.00
NNDG Danny Granger 40.00 100.00
NNDH Dwight Howard 100.00 250.00
NNDL David Lee 30.00 60.00
NNDR Dennis Rodman 300.00 600.00
NNEB Elton Brand 20.00 50.00
NNEO Emeka Okafor 20.00 50.00
NNGG Gerald Green 40.00 100.00
NNHO Hakeem Olajuwon 400.00 800.00
NNHW Hakim Warrick 20.00 50.00
NNID Ike Diogu 20.00 50.00
NNJE Julius Erving 500.00 1,000.00
NNJJ Joe Johnson 20.00 50.00
NNJK Jason Kidd 150.00 400.00
NNJN Jameer Nelson 20.00 50.00
NNJP Johan Petro 20.00 50.00
NNJR J.R. Smith 75.00 200.00
NNJS John Stockton 400.00 800.00
NNKA Kareem Abdul-Jabbar 1,500.00 3,000.00
NNLB Larry Bird 1,000.00 2,000.00
NNLJ LeBron James 5,000.00 10,000.00
NNMB Mike Bibby 40.00 100.00
NNMJ Magic Johnson 1,000.00 2,000.00
NNMR Michael Redd 20.00 50.00
NNMW Marvin Williams 20.00 50.00
NNNR Nate Robinson 20.00 50.00
NNPP Paul Pierce 200.00 500.00
NNPS Peja Stojakovic 40.00 100.00
NNRA Ron Artest 100.00 250.00
NNRF Raymond Felton 20.00 50.00
NNRH Richard Hamilton 100.00 250.00
NNRJ Richard Jefferson 40.00 100.00
NNRM Rashad McCants 20.00 50.00
NNSA Shareef Abdur-Rahim 60.00 150.00
NNSC Speedy Claxton 20.00 50.00
NNSE Sean May 20.00 50.00
NNSF Stephon Marbury 100.00 250.00
NNSN Steve Nash 300.00 600.00
NNSP Scottie Pippen 300.00 600.00
NNST Sebastian Telfair 20.00 50.00
NNTM Tracy McGrady 200.00 500.00
NNTP Tayshaun Prince 50.00 120.00
NNVC Vince Carter 300.00 600.00
NNWF Walt Frazier 125.00 300.00

2005-06 Exquisite Collection Numbers

STATED PRINT RUN ONE TO 91 SETS
ENCA Carmelo Anthony/15 200.00 500.00
ENDR Dennis Rodman/91 125.00 300.00
ENEB Elton Brand/42 20.00 50.00
ENEO Emeka Okafor/50 20.00 50.00
ENHO Hakeem Olajuwon/34 125.00 300.00
ENKG Kevin Garnett/21 500.00 1,000.00
ENLB Larry Bird/33 300.00 600.00
ENLJ LeBron James/23 2,000.00 4,000.00
ENMA Magic Johnson/32 300.00 600.00
ENMJ Michael Jordan/23 3,000.00 5,000.00
ENMW Marvin Williams/24 40.00 100.00
ENPS Peja Stojakovic/16 50.00 120.00
ENSN Steve Nash/13 200.00 500.00
ENVC Vince Carter/15 300.00 600.00

2005-06 Exquisite Collection Numbers Dual

STATED PRINT RUN 12 TO 50 SETS
DNAB Abdul-Jabbar/Bird/33 200.00 500.00
DNAC C.Anthony/Carter/15 150.00 400.00
DNBM E.Brand/S.May/42 15.00 40.00
DNHS K.Hinrich/Stockton/12 100.00 250.00
DNJH M.Johnson/Hughes/32 125.00 300.00
DNJJ M.Jordan/L.James/23 8,000.00 12,000.00
DNJW Jefferson/Williams/24 15.00 40.00
DNOR Okafor/D.Robinson/50 50.00 125.00
DNPR T.Prince/M.Redd/22 60.00 150.00
DNSJ J.R.Smith/L.James/23 1,000.00 2,000.00
DNWG Warrick/Garnett/21 125.00 300.00

2005-06 Exquisite Collection Scripted Swatches

PRINT RUN 3 TO 25 SER.#'d SETS
SSAB Andrew Bogut/25 20.00 50.00
SSCA Carmelo Anthony/25 100.00 200.00
SSCB Chauncey Billups/25 25.00 60.00
SSCF Channing Frye/25 40.00 100.00
SSCH Chris Bosh/25 25.00 60.00
SSCP Chris Paul/25 500.00 1,000.00
SSCV Charlie Villanueva/25 40.00 100.00
SSDE Dennis Rodman/25 200.00 500.00
SSDH Dwight Howard/25 30.00 80.00
SSDM Desmond Mason/25 25.00 60.00
SSDR David Robinson/25 125.00 300.00
SSDW Deron Williams/25 75.00 150.00
SSEB Elton Brand/25 25.00 60.00
SSJK Jason Kidd/25 125.00 300.00
SSJS John Stockton/25 300.00 600.00
SSKA Kareem Abdul-Jabbar/25 150.00 400.00
SSKG Kevin Garnett/25 400.00 800.00
SSLB Larry Bird/25 200.00 400.00
SSLJ LeBron James/25 1,000.00 3,000.00
SSMA Magic Johnson/25 150.00 400.00
SSMJ Michael Jordan/25 6,000.00 10,000.00
SSMW Marvin Williams/25 25.00 60.00
SSPP Paul Pierce/25 125.00 300.00
SSPS Peja Stojakovic/25 75.00 200.00
SSSN Steve Nash/25 200.00 500.00
SSTM Tracy McGrady/25 125.00 300.00
SSVC Vince Carter/25 150.00 400.00
SSYM Yao Ming/25 200.00 500.00

2006-07 Exquisite Collection

1-42 PRINT RUN 225 SER.#'d SETS
43-48 PRINT RUN 99 SER.#'d SETS
1 Joe Johnson 5.00 12.00
2 Paul Pierce 8.00 20.00
3 Emeka Okafor 4.00 10.00
4 Adam Morrison RC 4.00 10.00
5 Michael Jordan 500.00 1,000.00
6 Kirk Hinrich 4.00 10.00
7 LeBron James 150.00 400.00
8 Dirk Nowitzki 12.00 30.00
9 Carmelo Anthony 8.00 20.00
10 Allen Iverson 12.00 30.00
11 Chauncey Billups 6.00 15.00
12 Richard Hamilton 5.00 12.00
13 Baron Davis 5.00 12.00
14 Yao Ming 30.00 80.00
15 Tracy McGrady 12.00 30.00
16 Jermaine O'Neal 5.00 12.00
17 Elton Brand 4.00 10.00
18 Kobe Bryant 150.00 400.00
19 Lamar Odom 4.00 10.00
20 Pau Gasol 8.00 20.00
21 Dwyane Wade 8.00 20.00
22 Shaquille O'Neal 12.00 30.00
23 Michael Redd 4.00 10.00
24 Kevin Garnett 15.00 40.00
25 Vince Carter 10.00 25.00
26 Jason Kidd 8.00 20.00
27 Chris Paul 10.00 25.00
28 Peja Stojakovic 4.00 10.00
29 Stephon Marbury 6.00 15.00
30 Dwight Howard 6.00 15.00
31 J.J. Redick RC 10.00 25.00
32 Andre Iguodala 5.00 12.00
33 Steve Nash 10.00 25.00
34 Amare Stoudemire 5.00 12.00
35 Jarrett Jack 4.00 10.00
36 Mike Bibby 5.00 12.00
37 Tim Duncan 12.00 30.00
38 Tony Parker 8.00 20.00
39 Ray Allen 8.00 20.00
40 Chris Bosh 6.00 15.00
41 Deron Williams 4.00 10.00
42 Antawn Jamison 4.00 10.00
43 A.Bargnani JSY AU/99 RC 40.00 100.00
44 L.Aldridge JSY AU/99 RC 200.00 400.00
45 T.Thomas JSY AU/99 RC 6.00 15.00
46 Brandon Roy JSY AU/99 RC 75.00 200.00
47 Rudy Gay JSY AU/99 RC 100.00 250.00
48 S.Williams JSY AU/99 RC 5.00 12.00
49 Randy Foye JSY AU RC 6.00 15.00
50 Patrick O'Bryant JSY AU RC 5.00 12.00
51 Saer Sene JSY AU RC 5.00 12.00
52 H.Armstrong JSY AU RC 5.00 12.00
53 T.Sefolosha JSY AU RC 6.00 15.00
54 Ronnie Brewer JSY AU RC 8.00 20.00
55 Cedric Simmons JSY AU RC 5.00 12.00
56 Rodney Carney JSY AU RC 5.00 12.00
57 Shawne Williams JSY AU RC 5.00 12.00
58 Quincy Douby JSY AU RC 5.00 12.00
59 R.Balkman JSY AU RC 6.00 15.00
60 Rajon Rondo JSY AU RC 125.00 300.00
61 Marcus Williams JSY AU RC 5.00 12.00
62 Josh Boone JSY AU RC 5.00 12.00
63 Allan Ray JSY AU RC 5.00 12.00
64 Shannon Brown JSY AU RC 5.00 12.00
65 Jordan Farmar JSY AU RC 6.00 15.00
66 Dee Brown JSY AU RC 5.00 12.00
67 Maurice Ager JSY AU RC 5.00 12.00
68 Mardy Collins JSY AU RC 5.00 12.00
69 James White JSY AU RC 5.00 12.00
70 Steve Novak JSY AU RC 6.00 15.00
71 Solomon Jones JSY AU RC 5.00 12.00
72 Paul Davis JSY AU RC 5.00 12.00
73 P.J. Tucker JSY AU RC 12.00 30.00
74 Craig Smith JSY AU RC 6.00 15.00
75 Bobby Jones JSY AU RC 5.00 12.00
76 David Noel JSY AU RC 5.00 12.00
77 Jorge Garbajosa JSY AU RC 6.00 15.00
78 Daniel Gibson JSY AU RC 6.00 15.00
79 Sergio Rodriguez AU RC 6.00 15.00
80 Paul Millsap AU RC 25.00 60.00
81 Will Blalock AU RC 5.00 12.00
82 Hassan Adams AU RC 5.00 12.00
83 Kyle Lowry AU RC 50.00 120.00
84 James Augustine AU RC 5.00 12.00

2006-07 Exquisite Collection Gold

*1-42 GOLD: 1.5X TO 4X BASE HI
GOLD PRINT RUN 25 SER.#'d SETS
43 Andrea Bargnani 10.00 25.00
44 LaMarcus Aldridge 40.00 100.00

45 Tyrus Thomas 10.00 25.00
46 Brandon Roy 25.00 60.00
47 Rudy Gay 15.00 40.00
48 Shelden Williams 8.00 20.00
49 Randy Foye 10.00 25.00
50 Patrick O'Bryant 8.00 20.00
51 Saer Sene 8.00 20.00
52 Hilton Armstrong 8.00 20.00
53 Thabo Sefolosha 10.00 25.00
54 Ronnie Brewer 12.00 30.00
55 Cedric Simmons 8.00 20.00
56 Rodney Carney 8.00 20.00
57 Shawne Williams 8.00 20.00
58 Quincy Douby 8.00 20.00
59 Renaldo Balkman 10.00 25.00
60 Rajon Rondo 40.00 100.00
61 Marcus Williams 8.00 20.00
62 Josh Boone 8.00 20.00
63 Allan Ray 8.00 20.00
64 Shannon Brown 8.00 20.00
66 Dee Brown 8.00 20.00
67 Maurice Ager 8.00 20.00
68 Mardy Collins 8.00 20.00
69 James White 8.00 20.00
70 Steve Novak 10.00 25.00
71 Solomon Jones 8.00 20.00
72 Paul Davis 8.00 20.00
73 P.J. Tucker 12.00 30.00
74 Craig Smith 10.00 25.00
75 Bobby Jones 8.00 20.00
76 David Noel 8.00 20.00
77 Jorge Garbajosa 10.00 25.00
79 Sergio Rodriguez 10.00 25.00
80 Paul Millsap 15.00 40.00
81 Will Blalock 8.00 20.00
82 Hassan Adams 8.00 20.00
83 Kyle Lowry 40.00 100.00
84 James Augustine 8.00 20.00

2006-07 Exquisite Collection Jerseys

*JERSEYS: 1.25X TO 3X BASE HI
JSY PRINT RUN 25 SER.#'d SETS

2006-07 Exquisite Collection Rookie Parallel

44 L.Aldridge JSY AU/12 300.00 600.00
45 Tyrus Thomas JSY AU/24 20.00 50.00
47 Rudy Gay JSY AU/22 300.00 600.00
48 Shelden Williams JSY AU/33 15.00 40.00
50 Patrick O'Bryant JSY AU/26 15.00 40.00
51 Saer Sene JSY AU/18 40.00 100.00
52 Hilton Armstrong JSY AU/12 40.00 100.00
55 Cedric Simmons JSY AU/22 15.00 40.00
56 Rodney Carney JSY AU/25 15.00 40.00
59 Renaldo Balkman JSY AU/32 20.00 50.00
66 Dee Brown JSY AU/11 15.00 40.00
67 Maurice Ager JSY AU/13 15.00 40.00
68 Mardy Collins JSY AU/25 15.00 40.00
69 James White JSY AU/33 15.00 40.00
70 Steve Novak JSY AU/20 20.00 50.00
71 Solomon Jones JSY AU/44 15.00 40.00
72 Paul Davis JSY AU/40 15.00 40.00
75 Bobby Jones JSY AU/11 75.00 150.00
76 David Noel JSY AU/34 15.00 40.00
77 Jorge Garbajosa JSY AU/15 125.00 250.00
79 Sergio Rodriguez AU/11 30.00 80.00
80 Paul Millsap AU/24 75.00 150.00
83 Kyle Lowry AU/12 100.00 250.00
84 James Augustine AU/40 15.00 40.00

2006-07 Exquisite Collection Autographs Patches

PRINT RUN 100 SER.#'d SETS
APAB Andrea Bargnani 10.00 25.00
APBG Ben Gordon 10.00 25.00
APBJ Bobby Jones 10.00 25.00
APBO Chris Bosh 30.00 80.00
APBR Brandon Roy 30.00 80.00
APCA Carmelo Anthony 75.00 200.00
APCB Chauncey Billups 20.00 50.00
APCP Chris Paul 500.00 1,000.00
APCS Craig Smith 10.00 25.00
APDA Baron Davis 15.00 40.00
APDG Daniel Gibson 10.00 25.00
APDN David Noel 10.00 25.00
APDR Dennis Rodman 50.00 125.00
APEO Emeka Okafor 10.00 25.00
APHO Hakeem Olajuwon 75.00 200.00
APJE Julius Erving 125.00 300.00
APJG Jorge Garbajosa 10.00 25.00
APJO Jermaine O'Neal 12.00 30.00
APJS J.R. Smith 20.00 50.00
APKB Kobe Bryant 3,000.00 6,000.00
APLA LaMarcus Aldridge 75.00 200.00
APLB Larry Bird 100.00 200.00
APLJ LeBron James 5,000.00 10,000.00
APMA Magic Johnson 100.00 250.00
APMJ Michael Jordan 5,000.00 8,000.00
APMW Marcus Williams 10.00 25.00
APPD Paul Davis 10.00 25.00
APRB Renaldo Balkman 10.00 25.00
APRC Rodney Carney 10.00 25.00
APRF Randy Foye 10.00 25.00
APRG Rudy Gay 15.00 40.00
APRJ Richard Jefferson 10.00 25.00
APRO Ronnie Brewer 10.00 25.00
APSB Shannon Brown 10.00 25.00
APSH Shawne Williams 10.00 25.00
APSW Shelden Williams 10.00 25.00
APTF T.J. Ford 10.00 25.00
APTT Tyrus Thomas 10.00 25.00
APVC Vince Carter 125.00 300.00
APWI Marvin Williams 10.00 25.00

2006-07 Exquisite Collection Emblems of Endorsements

PRINT RUN 15 SER.#'d SETS
EMAB Andrea Bargnani 40.00 100.00
EMAI Andre Iguodala 40.00 100.00
EMAJ Antawn Jamison 25.00 60.00
EMAM Alonzo Mourning 125.00 300.00
EMBI Chauncey Billups 40.00 100.00
EMBR Brandon Roy 75.00 200.00
EMCA Carmelo Anthony 150.00 400.00
EMCB Chris Bosh 50.00 120.00
EMCD Clyde Drexler 75.00 200.00
EMCP Chris Paul 500.00 1,000.00
EMDR Dennis Rodman 200.00 500.00
EMDW Deron Williams 75.00 200.00
EMFE Raymond Felton 25.00 60.00
EMHO Hakeem Olajuwon 100.00 250.00
EMJE Julius Erving 150.00 400.00
EMJH Jeff Hornacek 40.00 100.00
EMJK Jason Kidd 125.00 300.00
EMJO Jermaine O'Neal 25.00 60.00
EMJS John Stockton 150.00 400.00
EMKA Kareem Abdul-Jabbar 150.00 400.00
EMKB Kobe Bryant 8,000.00 15,000.00
EMLA LaMarcus Aldridge 150.00 400.00
EMLB Larry Bird 200.00 500.00
EMLJ LeBron James 4,000.00 6,000.00
EMMA Magic Johnson 200.00 500.00
EMMJ Michael Jordan 10,000.00 15,000.00
EMMW Marcus Williams 25.00 60.00
EMPP Paul Pierce 150.00 400.00
EMPS Peja Stojakovic 40.00 100.00
EMRC Rodney Carney 25.00 60.00
EMRF Randy Foye 25.00 60.00
EMRG Rudy Gay 60.00 150.00
EMRJ Richard Jefferson 25.00 60.00
EMRO David Robinson 100.00 200.00
EMSL Shaun Livingston 60.00 150.00
EMSN Steve Nash 200.00 500.00
EMTM Tracy McGrady 150.00 400.00
EMTS Thabo Sefolosha 30.00 80.00
EMTT Tyrus Thomas 25.00 60.00
EMVC Vince Carter 150.00 400.00

2006-07 Exquisite Collection Enshrinements

PRINT RUN 25 SER.#'d SETS
EXAB Andrea Bargnani 15.00 40.00
EXBI Chauncey Billups 75.00 200.00
EXBR Bill Russell 2,000.00 4,000.00
EXCA Carmelo Anthony 200.00 500.00
EXCB Chris Bosh 100.00 250.00
EXCP Chris Paul 400.00 800.00
EXDA David Robinson 400.00 800.00
EXDR Dennis Rodman 400.00 800.00
EXHO Hakeem Olajuwon 400.00 800.00
EXJE Julius Erving 500.00 1,000.00
EXJK Jason Kidd 40.00 100.00
EXJO Jermaine O'Neal 40.00 100.00
EXJS John Stockton 200.00 500.00
EXJW James Worthy 150.00 400.00
EXKA Kareem Abdul-Jabbar 1,500.00 3,000.00
EXKB Kobe Bryant 5,000.00 10,000.00
EXKH Kirk Hinrich 15.00 40.00
EXLA LaMarcus Aldridge 75.00 200.00
EXLB Larry Bird 1,000.00 2,000.00
EXLJ LeBron James 5,000.00 10,000.00
EXLJ2 LeBron James 5,000.00 10,000.00
EXMA Magic Johnson 1,000.00 2,000.00
EXMJ Michael Jordan 10,000.00 20,000.00
EXMJ2 Michael Jordan 10,000.00 20,000.00
EXMW Marcus Williams 15.00 40.00
EXPP Paul Pierce 300.00 600.00
EXPR Tayshaun Prince 60.00 150.00
EXRB Renaldo Balkman 15.00 40.00
EXRC Rodney Carney 15.00 40.00
EXRF Randy Foye 15.00 40.00
EXRG Rudy Gay 75.00 200.00
EXRH Richard Hamilton 75.00 200.00
EXRI Pat Riley 75.00 200.00
EXRO Brandon Roy 75.00 200.00
EXSN Steve Nash 500.00 1,000.00
EXTF T.J. Ford 15.00 40.00
EXTM Tracy McGrady 300.00 600.00
EXTP Tony Parker 125.00 300.00
EXTT Tyrus Thomas 15.00 40.00
EXVC Vince Carter 300.00 600.00
EXWJ John Wooden 300.00 600.00
EXYM Yao Ming 1,000.00 2,000.00

2006-07 Exquisite Collection Extra Exquisite

PRINT RUN 25 SER.#'d SETS
EEAB Andrea Bargnani 6.00 15.00
EEAI Allen Iverson 75.00 200.00
EEAM Alonzo Mourning 30.00 80.00
EEAR Ron Artest 10.00 25.00
EEAS Amare Stoudemire 8.00 20.00
EEBG Ben Gordon 6.00 15.00
EEBK Bernard King 6.00 15.00
EEBO Carlos Boozer 6.00 15.00
EEBR Brandon Roy 15.00 40.00
EEBW Ben Wallace 10.00 25.00
EECA Carmelo Anthony 15.00 40.00
EECB Chris Bosh 10.00 25.00
EECD Clyde Drexler 15.00 40.00
EECM Chris Mullin 10.00 25.00
EECP Chris Paul 20.00 50.00
EEDH Dwight Howard 10.00 25.00
EEDN Dirk Nowitzki 40.00 100.00
EEDR Dennis Rodman 20.00 50.00
EEEB Elton Brand 6.00 15.00
EEEM Earl Monroe 15.00 40.00
EEEO Emeka Okafor 6.00 15.00
EEGH Grant Hill 30.00 80.00
EEHO Hakeem Olajuwon 30.00 80.00
EEIA Andre Iguodala 8.00 20.00
EEIT Isiah Thomas 12.00 30.00
EEJE Julius Erving 30.00 80.00
EEJG Jorge Garbajosa 6.00 15.00
EEJO Jermaine O'Neal 8.00 20.00
EEJR J.J. Redick 15.00 40.00
EEJS John Stockton 15.00 40.00
EEJT Jason Terry 6.00 15.00
EEJW Jerry West 25.00 60.00
EEKA Kareem Abdul-Jabbar 25.00 60.00
EEKM Karl Malone 10.00 25.00
EELA LaMarcus Aldridge 20.00 50.00
EELJ LeBron James 150.00 400.00
EELJ2 LeBron James 150.00 400.00
EEMA Magic Johnson 20.00 50.00
EEMG Manu Ginobili 30.00 80.00
EEMJ Michael Jordan 150.00 400.00
EEMJ2 Michael Jordan 150.00 400.00
EEOR Oscar Robertson 30.00 80.00
EEPM Pete Maravich 75.00 200.00
EEPP Paul Pierce 12.00 30.00
EEPR Pat Riley 12.00 30.00
EERA Ray Allen 12.00 30.00
EERB Bill Russell 100.00 250.00
EERF Randy Foye 6.00 15.00
EERG Rudy Gay 10.00 25.00
EERI Jason Richardson 8.00 20.00
EERO David Robinson 30.00 80.00
EERR Rajon Rondo 30.00 80.00
EESM Shawn Marion 8.00 20.00
EESO Shaquille O'Neal 30.00 80.00
EETM Tracy McGrady 30.00 80.00
EETP Tony Parker 20.00 50.00
EETT Tyrus Thomas 6.00 15.00
EEVC Vince Carter 30.00 80.00
EEWC Wilt Chamberlain 150.00 400.00
EEYM Yao Ming 30.00 80.00

2006-07 Exquisite Collection Limited Logos

PRINT RUN 50 SER.#'d SETS
LLAB Andrea Bargnani 20.00 50.00
LLBG Ben Gordon 20.00 50.00
LLBI Chauncey Billups 30.00 80.00
LLBR Ronnie Brewer 25.00 60.00
LLCA Carmelo Anthony 1,000.00 2,000.00
LLCB Chris Bosh 150.00 400.00
LLCD Clyde Drexler 400.00 800.00
LLCP Chris Paul 500.00 1,000.00
LLCS Craig Smith 15.00 40.00
LLDA Baron Davis 150.00 400.00
LLDE Dennis Rodman 1,000.00 2,000.00
LLDG Daniel Gibson 20.00 50.00
LLDN David Noel 15.00 40.00
LLDR David Robinson 1,000.00 2,000.00
LLEO Emeka Okafor 20.00 50.00
LLHO Hakeem Olajuwon 1,000.00 2,000.00
LLJE Julius Erving 1,000.00 2,000.00
LLJF Jordan Farmar 15.00 40.00
LLJO Jermaine O'Neal 125.00 300.00
LLJS J.R. Smith 125.00 300.00
LLKB Kobe Bryant 10,000.00 20,000.00
LLLA LaMarcus Aldridge 500.00 1,000.00
LLLB Larry Bird 3,000.00 5,000.00
LLLJ L.James 15,000.00 30,000.00
LLMA Magic Johnson 3,000.00 6,000.00
LLMJ M.Jordan 25,000.00 50,000.00
LLMW Marcus Williams 15.00 40.00
LLRB Renaldo Balkman 20.00 50.00
LLRC Rodney Carney 15.00 40.00
LLRF Randy Foye 20.00 50.00
LLRG Rudy Gay 125.00 300.00
LLRJ Richard Jefferson 75.00 200.00
LLRO Brandon Roy 75.00 200.00
LLSN Steve Nash 800.00 1,500.00
LLST John Stockton 800.00 1,500.00
LLSW Shawne Williams 15.00 40.00
LLTT Tyrus Thomas 15.00 40.00
LLVC Vince Carter 1,000.00 2,000.00
LLWI Shelden Williams 15.00 40.00
LLWM Marvin Williams 15.00 40.00

2006-07 Exquisite Collection Noble Nameplates

PRINT RUN 25 SER.#'d SETS
NNAB Andrea Bargnani 20.00 50.00
NNAJ Al Jefferson 10.00 25.00
NNAM Alonzo Mourning 75.00 200.00
NNBD Baron Davis 40.00 100.00
NNBG Ben Gordon 25.00 60.00
NNBO Chris Bosh 40.00 100.00
NNBR Brandon Roy 30.00 80.00
NNCA Carmelo Anthony 75.00 200.00
NNCB Chauncey Billups 25.00 60.00
NNCD Clyde Drexler 50.00 120.00
NNCP Chris Paul 75.00 150.00
NNCS Craig Smith 10.00 25.00
NNDE Dennis Rodman 150.00 400.00
NNDG Danny Granger 10.00 25.00
NNDI Boris Diaw 20.00 50.00
NNDN David Noel 10.00 25.00
NNDR David Robinson 125.00 300.00
NNEO Emeka Okafor 10.00 25.00
NNFE Raymond Felton 10.00 25.00
NNGD Daniel Gibson 20.00 50.00
NNGG Gerald Green 10.00 25.00
NNHO Hakeem Olajuwon 60.00 120.00
NNHW Hakim Warrick 10.00 25.00
NNJB Josh Boone 10.00 25.00
NNJE Julius Erving 150.00 400.00
NNJG Jorge Garbajosa 10.00 25.00
NNJK Jason Kidd 200.00 500.00
NNJO Jermaine O'Neal 25.00 60.00
NNJS J.R. Smith 25.00 60.00
NNJW Jerry West 150.00 400.00
NNKA Kareem Abdul-Jabbar 75.00 150.00
NNKB Kobe Bryant 3,000.00 6,000.00
NNKL Kyle Lowry 40.00 100.00
NNLA LaMarcus Aldridge 50.00 120.00
NNLB Larry Bird 100.00 250.00
NNLJ LeBron James 3,000.00 6,000.00
NNMA Magic Johnson 125.00 300.00
NNMB Mike Bibby 10.00 25.00
NNMJ Michael Jordan 4,000.00 8,000.00
NNMW Marcus Williams 10.00 25.00
NNPP Paul Pierce 40.00 100.00
NNPS Peja Stojakovic 30.00 80.00
NNQD Quincy Douby 10.00 25.00
NNRB Renaldo Balkman 10.00 25.00
NNRC Rodney Carney 10.00 25.00
NNRF Randy Foye 10.00 25.00
NNRG Rudy Gay 50.00 120.00
NNRH Richard Hamilton 25.00 60.00
NNRJ Richard Jefferson 10.00 25.00
NNRO Ronnie Brewer 10.00 25.00
NNSB Shannon Brown 10.00 25.00
NNSI Cedric Simmons 10.00 25.00
NNSN Steve Nash 150.00 400.00
NNST John Stockton 125.00 300.00
NNSW Shelden Williams 10.00 25.00
NNTM Tracy McGrady 150.00 400.00
NNTP Tayshaun Prince 30.00 80.00
NNTT Tyrus Thomas 10.00 25.00
NNVC Vince Carter 75.00 200.00
NNYM Yao Ming 60.00 150.00

2006-07 Exquisite Collection Numbers

PRINT RUNS LISTED IN CHECKLIST
ENAH Al Harrington/32 12.00 30.00
ENAM Alonzo Mourning/33 150.00 400.00
ENCA Carmelo Anthony/15 125.00 250.00
ENCD Clyde Drexler/22 75.00 150.00
ENCM Corey Maggette/50 12.00 30.00
ENDG Danny Granger/33 12.00 30.00
ENDN David Noel/34 12.00 30.00
ENDR David Robinson/50 150.00 400.00
ENEO Emeka Okafor/50 12.00 30.00
ENHO Hakeem Olajuwon/34 150.00 400.00
ENHW Hakim Warrick/21 25.00 60.00
ENKA K.Abdul-Jabbar/33 300.00 600.00
ENKB Kobe Bryant/24 3,000.00 6,000.00
ENLA LaMarcus Aldridge/12 150.00 300.00
ENLB Larry Bird/33 200.00 500.00
ENLH Larry Hughes/32 12.00 30.00
ENLJ LeBron James/23 5,000.00 8,000.00
ENMA Magic Johnson/32 300.00 600.00
ENMJ Michael Jordan/23 5,000.00 8,000.00
ENPO Patrick O'Bryant/26 12.00 30.00
ENPP Paul Pierce/34 200.00 500.00
ENPS Peja Stojakovic/16 50.00 120.00
ENRC Rodney Carney/25 12.00 30.00
ENRE Renaldo Balkman/32 12.00 30.00
ENRG Rudy Gay/22 75.00 200.00
ENRH Richard Hamilton/32 30.00 80.00
ENRJ Richard Jefferson/24 25.00 60.00
ENRO Dennis Rodman/91 125.00 300.00
ENSH Shelden Williams/33 12.00 30.00
ENSI Cedric Simmons/22 12.00 30.00
ENSL Shaun Livingston/14 30.00 60.00
ENTP Tayshaun Prince/22 25.00 60.00
ENTT Tyrus Thomas/24 12.00 30.00
ENVC Vince Carter/15 150.00 400.00
ENWI Marvin Williams/24 15.00 40.00

2006-07 Exquisite Collection Numbers Dual

PRINT RUNS LISTED IN CHECKLIST
DENAA Aldridge/Armstrong/12 75.00 150.00
DENAC Anthony/V.Carter/15 200.00 500.00
DENAW Kareem/S.Williams/33 60.00 150.00
DENBG L.Bird/D.Granger/33 100.00 250.00
DENBH Balkman/Hughes/32 15.00 40.00
DENBJ Bryant/R.Jefferson/24 1,500.00 3,000.00
DENBT Bryant/T.Thomas/24 1,500.00 3,000.00
DENCC Carney/M.Collins/25 15.00 40.00
DENDG C.Drexler/R.Gay/22 100.00 250.00
DENJH M.Johnson/Hamilton/32 100.00 250.00
DENJJ Jordan/L.James/23 10,000.00 15,000.00
DENOP Olajuwon/Pierce/34 150.00 400.00
DENOR Okafor/D.Robinson/50 25.00 60.00
DENPG T.Prince/R.Gay/22 60.00 120.00
DENTW T.Thomas/M.Will/24 50.00 125.00

2006-07 Exquisite Collection Scripted Swatches

PRINT RUN 25 SER.#'d SETS
SSAB Andrea Bargnani 20.00 50.00
SSAD Adrian Dantley 25.00 60.00
SSAH Al Harrington 10.00 25.00
SSAJ Antawn Jamison 20.00 50.00
SSBD Baron Davis 30.00 80.00
SSBG Ben Gordon 15.00 40.00
SSBO Chris Bosh 40.00 100.00
SSBR Brandon Roy 20.00 50.00
SSCA Carmelo Anthony 125.00 225.00
SSCB Chauncey Billups 75.00 200.00
SSCD Clyde Drexler 60.00 150.00
SSCM Corey Maggette 10.00 25.00
SSCP Chris Paul 400.00 800.00
SSCS Cedric Simmons 10.00 25.00
SSDB Dee Brown 10.00 25.00
SSDE Dennis Rodman 200.00 500.00
SSDG Danny Granger 10.00 25.00
SSDR David Robinson 150.00 400.00
SSDW Deron Williams 40.00 100.00
SSER Julius Erving 200.00 500.00
SSFE Raymond Felton 10.00 25.00
SSGG Gerald Green 10.00 25.00
SSGI Daniel Gibson 10.00 25.00
SSHA Hilton Armstrong 10.00 25.00
SSHO Hakeem Olajuwon 125.00 300.00
SSHW Hakim Warrick 10.00 25.00
SSJB Josh Boone 10.00 25.00
SSJE Richard Jefferson 10.00 25.00
SSJK Jason Kidd 125.00 300.00
SSJM Magic Johnson 100.00 250.00
SSJO Jermaine O'Neal 25.00 60.00
SSJS John Stockton 100.00 250.00
SSJW Jerry West 125.00 300.00
SSKA Kareem Abdul-Jabbar 150.00 400.00
SSKB Kobe Bryant 1,000.00 3,000.00
SSKH Kirk Hinrich 40.00 100.00
SSKL Kyle Lowry 25.00 60.00
SSLA LaMarcus Aldridge 60.00 150.00
SSLB Larry Bird 150.00 400.00
SSLJ LeBron James 5,000.00 10,000.00
SSLR Luke Ridnour 10.00 25.00
SSMA Marcus Williams 10.00 25.00
SSMB Mike Bibby 10.00 25.00
SSMC Mardy Collins 10.00 25.00
SSMJ Michael Jordan 6,000.00 10,000.00
SSMP Morris Peterson 10.00 25.00
SSMW Martell Webster 10.00 25.00
SSPS Peja Stojakovic 75.00 200.00
SSPT Tony Parker 75.00 200.00
SSRB Renaldo Balkman 10.00 25.00
SSRC Rodney Carney 10.00 25.00
SSRF Randy Foye 10.00 25.00
SSRG Rudy Gay 100.00 200.00
SSRH Richard Hamilton 25.00 60.00
SSRO Ronnie Brewer 20.00 50.00
SSSB Shannon Brown 10.00 25.00
SSSM Craig Smith 10.00 25.00
SSSN Steve Nash 150.00 400.00
SSST Sebastian Telfair 10.00 25.00
SSSW Shelden Williams 10.00 25.00
SSTM Tracy McGrady 125.00 300.00
SSTP Tayshaun Prince 25.00 60.00
SSTT Tyrus Thomas 10.00 25.00
SSVC Vince Carter 125.00 300.00
SSWI Shawne Williams 10.00 25.00
SSYM Yao Ming 200.00 500.00

2007-08 Exquisite Collection

PRINT RUN 225 SER.#'d SETS
61-93 RC PRINT RUN 225 SER.#'d SETS
94-112 PRINT RUN 99 SER.#'d SETS
1 LeBron James 150.00 400.00
2 Yao Ming 8.00 20.00
3 Kobe Bryant 150.00 400.00
4 Dwyane Wade 15.00 40.00
5 Tracy McGrady 5.00 12.00
6 Allen Iverson 8.00 20.00
7 Shaquille O'Neal 8.00 20.00
8 Kevin Garnett 20.00 50.00
9 Steve Nash 6.00 15.00
10 Dwight Howard 4.00 10.00
11 Gilbert Arenas 3.00 8.00
12 Vince Carter 6.00 15.00
13 Tim Duncan 20.00 50.00
14 Carmelo Anthony 5.00 12.00
15 Dirk Nowitzki 12.00 30.00
16 Amare Stoudemire 3.00 8.00
17 Chris Bosh 4.00 10.00
18 Jermaine O'Neal 3.00 8.00
19 Jason Kidd 5.00 12.00
20 Ben Wallace 4.00 10.00
21 Paul Pierce 5.00 12.00
22 Shawn Marion 3.00 8.00
23 Michael Jordan 300.00 600.00
24 Manu Ginobili 8.00 20.00
25 Tony Parker 5.00 12.00
26 Chauncey Billups 4.00 10.00
27 Chris Paul 6.00 15.00
28 Andre Iguodala 3.00 8.00
29 Stephon Marbury 4.00 10.00
30 Ray Allen 5.00 12.00
31 Lamar Odom 2.50 6.00
32 Jason Terry 2.50 6.00
33 Josh Howard 2.50 6.00
34 Caron Butler 2.50 6.00
35 Emeka Okafor 2.50 6.00
36 Marcus Camby 2.50 6.00
37 Pau Gasol 5.00 12.00
38 Carlos Boozer 2.50 6.00
39 Baron Davis 2.50 6.00
40 Michael Redd 2.50 6.00
41 Ben Gordon 2.50 6.00
42 Richard Hamilton 4.00 10.00
43 Andrew Bogut 2.50 6.00
44 Tyson Chandler 3.00 8.00
45 Eddy Curry 2.00 5.00
46 Larry Hughes 2.50 6.00
47 LaMarcus Aldridge 3.00 8.00
48 Andrea Bargnani 2.00 5.00
49 Mike Bibby 3.00 8.00
50 Elton Brand 2.50 6.00
51 Al Harrington 2.50 6.00
52 Al Jefferson 2.00 5.00
53 Joe Johnson 2.50 6.00
54 Rashard Lewis 2.50 6.00
55 Kevin Martin 2.50 6.00
56 Andre Miller 2.50 6.00
57 Brandon Roy 4.00 10.00
58 Gerald Wallace 2.50 6.00
59 Rasheed Wallace 4.00 10.00
60 Deron Williams 2.50 6.00
61 Arron Afflalo JSY AU RC 6.00 15.00
62 Morris Almond JSY AU RC 5.00 12.00
63 Julian Wright JSY AU RC 5.00 12.00
64 Aaron Brooks JSY AU RC 15.00 40.00
65 Herbert Hill JSY AU RC 5.00 12.00
66 Wilson Chandler JSY AU RC 6.00 15.00
67 Daequan Cook JSY AU RC 6.00 15.00
68 Javaris Crittenton JSY AU RC 5.00 12.00
69 Jermareo Davidson JSY AU RC 5.00 12.00
70 Glen Davis JSY AU RC 6.00 15.00
71 Jared Dudley JSY AU RC 6.00 15.00
72 Corey Brewer JSY AU RC 6.00 15.00
73 Aaron Gray JSY AU RC 5.00 12.00
74 Taurean Green JSY AU RC 5.00 12.00
75 Nick Fazekas JSY AU RC 5.00 12.00
76 Spencer Hawes JSY AU RC 5.00 12.00
77 Al Horford JSY AU RC 40.00 100.00
78 Jeff Green JSY AU RC 6.00 15.00
79 Carl Landry JSY AU RC 5.00 12.00
80 Mike Conley Jr. JSY AU RC 60.00 150.00
81 Acie Law JSY AU RC 5.00 12.00
82 Dominic McGuire JSY AU RC 5.00 12.00
83 Josh McRoberts JSY AU RC 5.00 12.00
84 Demetris Nichols JSY AU RC 5.00 12.00
85 Joakim Noah JSY AU RC 20.00 50.00
86 Gabe Pruitt JSY AU RC 5.00 12.00
87 Chris Richard JSY AU RC 5.00 12.00
88 Jason Smith JSY AU RC 5.00 12.00
89 D.J. Strawberry JSY AU RC 5.00 12.00
90 Rodney Stuckey JSY AU RC 15.00 40.00
91 Sean Williams JSY AU RC 5.00 12.00
92 Al Thornton JSY AU RC 5.00 12.00
93 Alando Tucker JSY AU RC 5.00 12.00
94 K.Durant JSY AU/99 RC 30,000.00 60,000.00
95 M.Belinelli JSY AU/99 RC 6.00 15.00
96 Luis Scola JSY AU/99 RC 15.00 40.00
97 L.Amundson JSY AU/99 RC 5.00 12.00
98 C.J. Watson AU RC 5.00 12.00
99 Cheikh Samb AU RC 4.00 10.00
100 Juan Navarro AU RC 5.00 12.00
101 JamesOn Curry AU RC 4.00 10.00
102 Ramon Sessions AU RC 5.00 12.00
103 Mario West AU RC 5.00 12.00
104 Coby Karl AU RC 4.00 10.00
105 Oleksiy Pecherov AU RC 6.00 15.00
106 Jamario Moon AU RC 5.00 12.00
107 Kyrylo Fesenko RC 4.00 10.00
108 Yi Jianlian RC 100.00 250.00
109 Brandan Wright RC 5.00 12.00
110 Thaddeus Young RC 6.00 15.00
111 Nick Young RC 6.00 15.00
112 Greg Oden RC 10.00 25.00

2007-08 Exquisite Collection Gold

*1-60 GOLD: 2.5X TO 6X BASE HI
PRINT RUN 25 SER.#'d SETS
61 Arron Afflalo 5.00 12.00
62 Morris Almond 4.00 10.00
63 Julian Wright 4.00 10.00
64 Aaron Brooks 40.00 100.00
65 Herbert Hill 4.00 10.00
66 Wilson Chandler 5.00 12.00
67 Daequan Cook 4.00 10.00
68 Javaris Crittenton 4.00 10.00
69 Jermareo Davidson 4.00 10.00
70 Glen Davis 5.00 12.00
71 Jared Dudley 5.00 12.00
72 Corey Brewer 5.00 12.00
73 Aaron Gray 4.00 10.00
74 Taurean Green 4.00 10.00
75 Nick Fazekas 4.00 10.00
76 Spencer Hawes 4.00 10.00
77 Al Horford 20.00 50.00
78 Jeff Green 5.00 12.00
79 Carl Landry 4.00 10.00
80 Mike Conley Jr. 25.00 60.00
81 Acie Law 4.00 10.00
82 Dominic McGuire 4.00 10.00
83 Josh McRoberts 4.00 10.00
84 Demetris Nichols 4.00 10.00
85 Joakim Noah 12.00 30.00
86 Gabe Pruitt 4.00 10.00
87 Chris Richard 4.00 10.00
88 Jason Smith 4.00 10.00
89 D.J. Strawberry 4.00 10.00
90 Rodney Stuckey 4.00 10.00
91 Sean Williams 4.00 10.00
92 Al Thornton 4.00 10.00
93 Alando Tucker 4.00 10.00
94 Kevin Durant 15,000.00 30,000.00
95 Marco Belinelli 5.00 12.00
96 Luis Scola 6.00 15.00
97 Louis Amundson 4.00 10.00
98 C.J. Watson 5.00 12.00
99 Cheikh Samb 4.00 10.00
100 Juan Navarro 5.00 12.00
101 JamesOn Curry 4.00 10.00
102 Ramon Sessions 5.00 12.00
103 Mario West 5.00 12.00
104 Coby Karl 4.00 10.00
105 Oleksiy Pecherov 6.00 15.00
106 Jamario Moon 5.00 12.00
107 Kyrylo Fesenko 4.00 10.00
108 Yi Jianlian 8.00 20.00
109 Brandan Wright 5.00 12.00
110 Thaddeus Young 6.00 15.00
111 Nick Young 6.00 15.00
112 Greg Oden 8.00 20.00

2007-08 Exquisite Collection Autographs Patches

PRINT RUN 35 SER.#'d SETS
EAAH Al Horford 75.00 150.00
EAAI Andre Iguodala 15.00 40.00
EAAJ Al Jefferson 15.00 40.00
EAAM Alonzo Mourning 200.00 500.00
EABG Ben Gordon 15.00 40.00
EABI Chauncey Billups 125.00 300.00
EABO Carlos Boozer 15.00 40.00
EABR Brandon Roy 30.00 60.00
EACA Carmelo Anthony 125.00 300.00
EACB Corey Brewer 15.00 40.00
EACD Clyde Drexler 75.00 200.00
EACH Chris Bosh 75.00 200.00
EACM Corey Maggette 15.00 40.00
EACP Chris Paul 200.00 500.00
EADG Daniel Gibson 15.00 40.00
EADR David Robinson 200.00 500.00
EAEO Emeka Okafor 15.00 40.00
EAHO Hakeem Olajuwon 200.00 500.00
EAJG Jeff Green 30.00 80.00
EAJK Jason Kidd 150.00 400.00
EAJN Joakim Noah 40.00 100.00
EAJO Magic Johnson 1,000.00 2,000.00
EAJS John Stockton 150.00 400.00
EAJW Julian Wright 20.00 50.00
EAKA Kelenna Azubuike 15.00 40.00
EAKD Kevin Durant 15,000.00 30,000.00
EAKG Kevin Garnett 1,000.00 2,000.00
EALB Larry Bird 1,000.00 2,000.00
EALH Larry Hughes 20.00 50.00
EALJ LeBron James 15,000.00 30,000.00
EAMB Mike Bibby 15.00 40.00
EAMC Mike Conley Jr. 60.00 150.00
EAPP Paul Pierce 200.00 500.00
EARA Ray Allen 200.00 500.00
EARF Raymond Felton 15.00 40.00
EARJ Richard Jefferson 15.00 40.00
EASB Shannon Brown 15.00 40.00
EASL Shaun Livingston 15.00 40.00
EATC Tyson Chandler 15.00 40.00
EATP Tayshaun Prince 75.00 200.00
EAVC Vince Carter 200.00 500.00

2007-08 Exquisite Collection Boxes

AH Al Horford/15 100.00 250.00
JJ M.Jordan/L.James/23 4,000.00 8,000.00
KB Kobe Bryant/24 400.00 800.00
KD Kevin Durant/35 3,000.00 6,000.00
LJ LeBron James/23 300.00 550.00
MJ Michael Jordan/23 500.00 700.00
SN Steve Nash/13 125.00 250.00
YM Yao Ming/11 125.00 250.00

2007-08 Exquisite Collection Draft Picks Reservation

A-F PRINT RUN 99 SER.#'d SETS
G-L PRINT RUN 199 SER.#'d SETS
DPA Mayo/Beasley/Rose 40.00 100.00
DPB Mayo/Beasley/Gordon 12.00 30.00
DPC Mayo/Beasley/Bayless 10.00 25.00
DPD Aug/Rose/Westbrk 100.00 250.00
DPE Beasley/Love/Alexander 15.00 40.00
DPF Rose/Gordon/Bayless 40.00 100.00
DPG Lopez/Thmpsn/Alxndr 8.00 20.00
DPH Galli/Love/Westbrk 60.00 150.00
DPI Rush/Gallinari/Westbrk 40.00 100.00
DPJ Augustin/Rush/Bayless 8.00 20.00
DPK Thmpsn/Speights/Alexndr 8.00 20.00
DPL Hibbert/B.Lopez/R.Lopez 8.00 20.00

2007-08 Exquisite Collection Enshrinements

PRINT RUN 25 SER.#'d SETS
ENAE Alex English 20.00 50.00
ENAR Arnie Risen 20.00 50.00
ENBL Bill Laimbeer 20.00 50.00
ENBR Bill Russell 1,500.00 3,000.00
ENBS Bill Sharman 20.00 50.00
ENBW Bill Walton 75.00 200.00
ENCD Clyde Drexler 150.00 400.00
ENCH Connie Hawkins 40.00 100.00
ENDR David Robinson 200.00 500.00
ENDT David Thompson 20.00 40.00
ENDW Dominique Wilkins 125.00 300.00
ENEB Elgin Baylor 125.00 300.00
ENGE George Gervin 100.00 250.00
ENGG Gail Goodrich 40.00 100.00
ENHO Hakeem Olajuwon 200.00 500.00
ENJE Julius Erving 400.00 800.00
ENJH John Havlicek 400.00 800.00
ENJK Jason Kidd 75.00 200.00
ENJL Jerry Lucas 25.00 60.00
ENJO Michael Jordan 20,000.00 40,000.00
ENJS John Stockton 150.00 400.00
ENJW James Worthy 75.00 200.00
ENKA Kareem Abdul-Jabbar 800.00 1,500.00
ENKB Kobe Bryant 15,000.00 30,000.00
ENKG Kevin Garnett 800.00 1,500.00
ENLA Bob Lanier 40.00 100.00
ENLB Larry Bird 800.00 1,500.00
ENLJ LeBron James 15,000.00 30,000.00
ENMJ Magic Johnson 800.00 1,500.00
ENMM Moses Malone 200.00 500.00
ENPP Paul Pierce 150.00 400.00
ENPR Pat Riley 125.00 300.00
ENRB Rick Barry 60.00 150.00
ENRO Dennis Rodman 200.00 500.00
ENRP Robert Parish 60.00 150.00
ENSK Steve Kerr 75.00 200.00
ENSN Steve Nash 800.00 1,500.00
ENTM Tracy McGrady 500.00 1,000.00
ENTP Tony Parker 150.00 400.00
ENVC Vince Carter 500.00 1,000.00
ENWE Jerry West 200.00 500.00
ENWF Walt Frazier 75.00 200.00
ENWU Wes Unseld 60.00 150.00

2007-08 Exquisite Collection Exclusives Autographs

STATED PRINT RUN 5 TO 35 SER.#'d SETS
AH Al Horford/15 25.00 60.00
JG Jeff Green/22 25.00 60.00
JW Julian Wright/32 25.00 60.00
KB Kobe Bryant/24 4,000.00 8,000.00
KD Kevin Durant/35 5,000.00 10,000.00
LJ LeBron James/23 5,000.00 10,000.00
MJ Michael Jordan/23 5,000.00 10,000.00

2007-08 Exquisite Collection Exclusives Autographs Patches

STATED PRINT RUN 5 TO 35 SER.#'d SETS
AH Al Horford/15 50.00 120.00
JN Joakim Noah/13 50.00 120.00
KB Kobe Bryant/24 6,000.00 12,000.00
KD Kevin Durant/35 6,000.00 12,000.00
LJ LeBron James/23 6,000.00 12,000.00
MJ Michael Jordan/23 6,000.00 12,000.00

2007-08 Exquisite Collection Exclusives Autographs Dual

STATED PRINT RUN 23 SER.#'d SETS
AMJLJ M.Jordan/L.James 10,000.00 20,000.00

2007-08 Exquisite Collection Exclusives Autographs Patches Dual

STATED PRINT RUN 23 SER.#'d SETS
PMJLJ M.Jordan/L.James 20,000.00 30,000.00

2007-08 Exquisite Collection Exclusives Memorabilia

STATED PRINT RUN 5 TO 35 SER.#'d SETS
MAH Al Horford/15 12.00 30.00
MJN Joakim Noah/13 25.00 60.00
MJW Julian Wright/32 10.00 25.00
MKB Kobe Bryant/24 500.00 1,000.00
MKD Kevin Durant/35 60.00 150.00
MLJ LeBron James/23 300.00 600.00
MMJ Michael Jordan/23 400.00 800.00
MSN Steve Nash/13 40.00 100.00
MYM Yao Ming/11 40.00 100.00

2007-08 Exquisite Collection Exclusives Memorabilia Dual

STATED PRINT RUN 23 SER.#'d SETS
MMJLJ M.Jordan/L.James 800.00 1,500.00

2007-08 Exquisite Collection Extra Quad Jerseys

PRINT RUN 25 SER.#'d SETS
EQAD Adrian Dantley 5.00 12.00
EQAH Al Harrington 5.00 12.00
EQAI Andre Iguodala 5.00 12.00
EQAJ Al Jefferson 5.00 12.00
EQAM Alonzo Mourning 30.00 80.00
EQBD Baron Davis 5.00 12.00
EQBG Ben Gordon 5.00 12.00
EQBK Bernard King 5.00 12.00
EQBL Bill Laimbeer 5.00 12.00
EQBR Brandon Roy 6.00 15.00
EQCA Carmelo Anthony 8.00 20.00
EQCB Chris Bosh 8.00 20.00
EQCD Clyde Drexler 15.00 30.00
EQCM Corey Maggette 5.00 12.00
EQCP Chris Paul 10.00 25.00
EQDH Dwight Howard 10.00 25.00
EQDR David Robinson 20.00 50.00
EQDW Deron Williams 8.00 20.00
EQEO Emeka Okafor 5.00 12.00
EQFE Raymond Felton 5.00 12.00
EQGG George Gervin 12.00 30.00
EQHO Hakeem Olajuwon 20.00 50.00
EQJA Antawn Jamison 5.00 12.00
EQJE Julius Erving 40.00 100.00
EQJK Jason Kidd 10.00 25.00
EQJO Jermaine O'Neal 5.00 12.00
EQJS John Stockton 20.00 50.00
EQJW Jerry West 40.00 100.00
EQKA Kareem Abdul-Jabbar 40.00 100.00
EQKB Kobe Bryant 400.00 800.00
EQKG Kevin Garnett 40.00 100.00
EQKH Kirk Hinrich 5.00 12.00
EQLA LaMarcus Aldridge 5.00 12.00
EQLB Leandro Barbosa 5.00 12.00
EQLH Larry Hughes 5.00 12.00
EQLJ LeBron James 500.00 1,000.00
EQMA Magic Johnson 40.00 100.00
EQMB Mike Bibby 5.00 12.00
EQME Mark Eaton 6.00 15.00
EQMJ Michael Jordan 1,000.00 2,000.00
EQMM Moses Malone 5.00 12.00
EQMR Micheal Ray Richardson 5.00 12.00
EQMU Chris Mullin 5.00 12.00
EQPP Paul Pierce 12.00 30.00
EQPR Tayshaun Prince 5.00 12.00
EQRF Randy Foye 5.00 12.00
EQRG Rudy Gay 5.00 12.00
EQRJ Richard Jefferson 5.00 12.00
EQRO Dennis Rodman 40.00 100.00
EQRT Reggie Theus 5.00 12.00
EQSB Shannon Brown 5.00 12.00
EQSM Shawn Marion 5.00 12.00

EQSN Steve Nash 40.00 100.00
EQTC Tom Chambers 5.00 12.00
EQTM Tracy McGrady 6.00 15.00
EQTP Tony Parker 12.00 30.00
EQTT Tyrus Thomas 5.00 12.00
EQVC Vince Carter 30.00 80.00
EQWO James Worthy 15.00 40.00
EQYM Yao Ming 40.00 100.00

2007-08 Exquisite Collection Finalists Autographs Dual

PRINT RUN 25 SER.#'d SETS
FABG R.Barry/H.Greer 75.00 200.00
FABK K.Bryant/J.Kidd 4,000.00 8,000.00
FABS K.Bryant/J.Stockton 5,000.00 10,000.00
FACD T.Chambers/C.Drexler 75.00 200.00
FAEJ J.Erving/Abdul-Jabbar 500.00 1,000.00
FAEW J.Erving/B.Walton 75.00 200.00
FAFJ D.Fisher/R.Jefferson 25.00 60.00
FAGC H.Grant/T.Chambers 25.00 60.00
FAGL H.Grant/B.Laimbeer 40.00 100.00
FAHA Havlicek/Abdul-Jabbar 1,000.00 2,000.00
FAJB M.Johnson/L.Bird 2,000.00 4,000.00
FAJP T.Parker/L.James 5,000.00 10,000.00
FAJR M.Jordan/D.Rodman 10,000.00 15,000.00
FALA Laimbeer/Abdul-Jabbar 125.00 300.00
FANP S.Nash/T.Parker 150.00 400.00
FAOP H.Olajuwon/R.Parish 125.00 300.00
FAOR H.Olajuwon/D.Robinson 200.00 500.00
FAPJ T.Prince/L.James 4,000.00 8,000.00
FAPW T.Parker/D.Williams 40.00 100.00
FAWE J.Worthy/J.Erving 125.00 300.00

2007-08 Exquisite Collection Inscriptions

PRINT RUN 25 SER.#'d SETS
IAAB Andrea Bargnani 15.00 40.00
IAAD A.Dantley Z-Time Scoring 40.00 100.00
IAAM Alonzo Mourning ZO 100.00 250.00
IABD Baron Davis BDiddy 40.00 100.00
IABI Larry Bird None 125.00 300.00
IABL Bill Laimbeer Bad Boys 60.00 150.00
IABR Brandon Roy ROY 40.00 100.00
IACP Chris Paul 200.00 500.00
IADA B.Daugherty No 1 Pick 15.00 40.00
IADG Daniel Gibson None 15.00 40.00
IADH D.Howard Superman 150.00 400.00
IADR D.Robinson Admiral 150.00 400.00
IADT D.Thompson Skywalker 20.00 50.00
IADW Dominique Wilkins 50.00 100.00
IAGG George Gervin None 25.00 60.00
IAGO Gail Goodrich None 20.00 50.00
IAHO Hakeem Olajuwon 75.00 200.00
IAJK J.Kidd 6 Time All-NBA 125.00 300.00
IAJW James Worthy 100.00 250.00
IAKA K.Abdul-Jabbar None 60.00 150.00
IAKB Kobe Bryant Mamba 10,000.00 15,000.00
IAKG K.Garnett Big Ticket 2,000.00 4,000.00
IALB Leandro Barbosa #10 15.00 40.00
IALJ L.James Chosen One 3,000.00 6,000.00
IAMC Michael Cooper 25.00 60.00
IAMJ M.Johnson 5 Rings 400.00 800.00
IAMP Morris Peterson MoPete 15.00 40.00
IAPR T.Prince Palace Prince 75.00 200.00
IARD D.Rodman The Worm 200.00 500.00
IARP Robert Parish 60.00 120.00
IASM S.Moncrief Squid 30.00 80.00
IASN Steve Nash None 50.00 125.00
IASP S.Perkins Big Smooth 30.00 80.00
IATM T.McGrady Mac Man 150.00 400.00
IATP Tony Parker 30.00 80.00
IAVC Vince Carter VC 150.00 400.00
IAWA Slick Watts 25.00 50.00
IAWE Jerry West Mr. Clutch 150.00 400.00
IAWF Walt Frazier 60.00 150.00

2007-08 Exquisite Collection Jerseys

PRINT RUN 25 SER.#'d SETS
1 LeBron James 400.00 1,000.00
2 Yao Ming 40.00 100.00
3 Kobe Bryant 500.00 1,000.00
4 Dwyane Wade 25.00 60.00
5 Tracy McGrady 25.00 60.00
6 Allen Iverson 30.00 80.00
7 Shaquille O'Neal 50.00 125.00
8 Kevin Garnett 75.00 200.00
9 Steve Nash 25.00 60.00
10 Dwight Howard 15.00 40.00
11 Gilbert Arenas 12.00 30.00
12 Vince Carter 25.00 60.00
13 Tim Duncan 30.00 80.00
14 Carmelo Anthony 20.00 50.00
15 Dirk Nowitzki 30.00 80.00
16 Amare Stoudemire 12.00 30.00
17 Chris Bosh 15.00 40.00
18 Jermaine O'Neal 12.00 30.00
19 Jason Kidd 20.00 50.00
20 Ben Wallace 15.00 40.00
21 Paul Pierce 20.00 50.00
22 Shawn Marion 12.00 30.00
23 Michael Jordan 250.00 500.00
24 Manu Ginobili 30.00 80.00
25 Tony Parker 20.00 50.00
26 Chauncey Billups 15.00 40.00
27 Chris Paul 25.00 60.00
28 Andre Iguodala 12.00 30.00
29 Stephon Marbury 15.00 40.00
30 Ray Allen 30.00 80.00
31 Lamar Odom 10.00 25.00
32 Jason Terry 10.00 25.00
33 Josh Howard 10.00 25.00
34 Caron Butler 10.00 25.00
35 Emeka Okafor 10.00 25.00
36 Marcus Camby 10.00 25.00
37 Pau Gasol 20.00 50.00
38 Carlos Boozer 10.00 25.00
39 Baron Davis 10.00 25.00
40 Michael Redd 10.00 25.00
41 Ben Gordon 10.00 25.00
42 Richard Hamilton 15.00 40.00
43 Andrew Bogut 10.00 25.00
44 Tyson Chandler 12.00 30.00
45 Eddy Curry 8.00 20.00
46 Larry Hughes 10.00 25.00
47 LaMarcus Aldridge 12.00 30.00
48 Andrea Bargnani 8.00 20.00
49 Mike Bibby 12.00 30.00
50 Elton Brand 10.00 25.00
51 Al Harrington 10.00 25.00
52 Al Jefferson 8.00 20.00
53 Joe Johnson 10.00 25.00
54 Rashard Lewis 10.00 25.00
55 Kevin Martin 10.00 25.00
56 Andre Miller 10.00 25.00
57 Brandon Roy 15.00 40.00
58 Gerald Wallace 10.00 25.00
59 Rasheed Wallace 15.00 40.00
60 Deron Williams 10.00 25.00

2007-08 Exquisite Collection Limited Logos

PRINT RUN 50 SER.#'d SETS
LLAB Andrew Bogut 30.00 80.00
LLAI Andre Iguodala 60.00 150.00
LLAJ Al Jefferson 20.00 50.00
LLAL Al Horford 50.00 120.00
LLAM Alonzo Mourning 300.00 600.00
LLBD Baron Davis 100.00 250.00
LLBG Ben Gordon 20.00 50.00
LLBO Chris Bosh 150.00 400.00
LLBR Brandon Roy 75.00 200.00
LLCA Carmelo Anthony 400.00 800.00
LLCB Carlos Boozer 30.00 80.00
LLCP Chris Paul 500.00 1,000.00
LLDH Dwight Howard 200.00 500.00
LLDW Deron Williams 40.00 100.00
LLGG George Gervin 100.00 250.00
LLHA Al Harrington 20.00 50.00
LLJA Antawn Jamison 20.00 50.00
LLJK Jason Kidd 400.00 800.00
LLKB Kobe Bryant 15,000.00 30,000.00
LLKD Kevin Durant 30,000.00 60,000.00
LLKG Kevin Garnett 1,500.00 3,000.00
LLKH Kirk Hinrich 20.00 50.00
LLLA LaMarcus Aldridge 100.00 250.00
LLLH Larry Hughes 75.00 200.00
LLLJ LeBron James 15,000.00 30,000.00
LLMB Mike Bibby 100.00 250.00
LLNA Nate Archibald 75.00 200.00
LLPA Tony Parker 300.00 600.00
LLPP Paul Pierce 400.00 800.00
LLRF Randy Foye 20.00 50.00
LLRG Rudy Gay 100.00 250.00
LLRJ Richard Jefferson 40.00 100.00
LLRL Rashard Lewis 20.00 50.00
LLSB Shannon Brown 20.00 50.00
LLSL Shaun Livingston 75.00 200.00
LLSW Shelden Williams 20.00 50.00
LLTJ T.J. Ford 20.00 50.00
LLTM Tracy McGrady 500.00 1,000.00
LLTP Tayshaun Prince 75.00 200.00
LLVC Vince Carter 500.00 1,000.00
LLYM Yao Ming 4,000.00 8,000.00

2007-08 Exquisite Collection Noble Nameplates

PRINT RUN 25 SER.#'d SETS
NPAB Andrew Bogut 30.00 80.00
NPAH Al Harrington 15.00 40.00
NPAI Andre Iguodala 75.00 200.00
NPAJ Al Jefferson 15.00 40.00
NPAL Al Horford 30.00 80.00
NPAM Alonzo Mourning 400.00 800.00
NPAS Amare Stoudemire 75.00 200.00
NPBD Baron Davis 75.00 200.00
NPBG Ben Gordon 20.00 50.00
NPBO Chris Bosh 100.00 250.00
NPBR Brandon Roy 75.00 200.00
NPBY Andrew Bynum 15.00 40.00
NPCA Carmelo Anthony 400.00 800.00
NPCB Carlos Boozer 20.00 50.00
NPCO Corey Brewer 15.00 40.00
NPCP Chris Paul 500.00 1,000.00
NPDG Daniel Gibson 15.00 40.00
NPDH Dwight Howard 150.00 400.00
NPDI Boris Diaw 40.00 100.00
NPDR David Robinson 500.00 1,000.00
NPDW Deron Williams 40.00 100.00
NPEC Eddy Curry 15.00 40.00
NPEO Emeka Okafor 15.00 40.00
NPGG George Gervin 75.00 200.00
NPGR Darrell Griffith 15.00 40.00
NPJA Antawn Jamison 15.00 40.00
NPJO Jermaine O'Neal 15.00 40.00
NPKB Kobe Bryant 15,000.00 30,000.00
NPKD Kevin Durant 15,000.00 30,000.00
NPKG Kevin Garnett 1,500.00 3,000.00
NPKH Kirk Hinrich 20.00 50.00
NPKK Jason Kidd 400.00 800.00
NPLA LaMarcus Aldridge 75.00 200.00
NPLH Larry Hughes 15.00 40.00
NPLJ LeBron James 15,000.00 30,000.00
NPMB Mike Bibby 75.00 200.00
NPMM Moses Malone 500.00 1,000.00
NPMP Morris Peterson 15.00 40.00
NPPA Tony Parker 300.00 600.00
NPRF Raymond Felton 15.00 40.00
NPRG Rudy Gay 75.00 200.00
NPRJ Richard Jefferson 15.00 40.00
NPRO Dennis Rodman 1,500.00 3,000.00
NPSB Shane Battier 15.00 40.00
NPSH Shannon Brown 15.00 40.00
NPSL Shaun Livingston 75.00 200.00
NPSN Steve Nash 500.00 1,000.00
NPSS Stromile Swift 15.00 40.00
NPSW Shelden Williams 15.00 40.00
NPTJ T.J. Ford 15.00 40.00
NPTM Tracy McGrady 500.00 1,000.00
NPTP Tayshaun Prince 75.00 200.00
NPTT Tyrus Thomas 15.00 40.00
NPVC Vince Carter 500.00 1,000.00
NPYM Yao Ming 500.00 1,000.00

2007-08 Exquisite Collection Numbers

STATED PRINT RUN ONE TO 50 SER.#'d SETS
ENAH Al Horford/15 50.00 120.00
ENAJ Al Jefferson/25 25.00 60.00
ENAM Alonzo Mourning/33 300.00 600.00
ENAT Alando Tucker/29 20.00 50.00
ENCA Carmelo Anthony/15 300.00 600.00
ENCB Corey Brewer/11 30.00 80.00
ENCD Clyde Drexler/22 150.00 400.00
ENCM Corey Maggette/50 20.00 50.00
ENDC Daequan Cook/14 20.00 50.00
ENDG Danny Granger/33 25.00 60.00
ENDH Dwight Howard/12 150.00 300.00
ENDR David Robinson/50 500.00 1,000.00
ENHO Hakeem Olajuwon/34 1,000.00 2,000.00
ENJG Jeff Green/22 50.00 120.00
ENJN Joakim Noah/13 100.00 225.00
ENJO Magic Johnson/32 1,000.00 2,000.00
ENJS Jason Smith/14 20.00 50.00
ENJW Jerry West/44 400.00 800.00
ENKA K.Abdul-Jabbar/33 1,000.00 2,000.00
ENKB Kobe Bryant/24 20,000.00 40,000.00
ENKD KDurant/35 20,000.00 40,000.00
ENKH Kirk Hinrich/12 40.00 100.00
ENLA LaMarcus Aldridge/12 125.00 300.00
ENLB Larry Bird/33 1,000.00 2,000.00
ENLJ LeBron James/23 20,000.00 40,000.00
ENMA Morris Almond/22 20.00 50.00
ENMB Marco Belinelli/18 30.00 80.00
ENMJ Michael Jordan/23 25,000.00 50,000.00
ENMM Moses Malone/24 400.00 800.00
ENMR Micheal Ray Richardson/20 20.00 50.00
ENPP Paul Pierce/34 400.00 800.00
ENRA Ray Allen/20 400.00 800.00
ENRF Raymond Felton/20 20.00 50.00
ENRG Rudy Gay/22 100.00 250.00
ENRJ Richard Jefferson/24 20.00 50.00
ENRT Reggie Theus/24 20.00 50.00
ENSH Spencer Hawes/31 25.00 60.00
ENSN Steve Nash/13 500.00 1,000.00
ENSW Sean Williams/51 20.00 50.00
ENTC Tom Chambers/24 20.00 50.00
ENTH Al Thornton/12 30.00 80.00
ENTP Tayshaun Prince/22 125.00 300.00
ENTT Tyrus Thomas/24 40.00 100.00
ENVC Vince Carter/15 2,000.00 4,000.00
ENVD Vlade Divac/13 75.00 200.00
ENWC Wilson Chandler/21 40.00 100.00
ENWO James Worthy/42 200.00 500.00
ENWR Julian Wright/32 20.00 50.00
ENYM Yao Ming/11 5,000.00 10,000.00

2007-08 Exquisite Collection Numbers Dual

STATED PRINT RUN ONE TO 44 SER.#'d SETS
AH C.Anthony/A.Horford/15 125.00 300.00
BA L.Bird/K.Abdul-Jabbar/33 2,000.00 4,000.00
BM K.Bryant/M.Malone/24 10,000.00 20,000.00
CH V.Carter/A.Horford/15 125.00 300.00
DH K.Durant/H.Hill/35 800.00 1,500.00
FC T.Ford/M.Conley/11 50.00 100.00
GD D.Griffith/K.Durant/35 1,500.00 3,000.00
GG R.Gay/J.Green/22 75.00 200.00
HA D.Howard/L.Aldridge/12 150.00 400.00
HS K.Hinrich/J.Stockton/12 100.00 250.00
JJ M.Jordan/L.James/23 25,000.00 50,000.00
JT R.Jefferson/T.Thomas/24 30.00 80.00
MD Y.Ming/G.Davis/11 125.00 300.00
NN S.Nash/J.Noah/13 125.00 300.00
NP J.Noah/G.Pruitt/13 30.00 80.00
OP H.Olajuwon/P.Pierce/34 400.00 800.00
PD T.Prince/C.Drexler/22 150.00 400.00
RW J.Wright/C.Richard/32 30.00 80.00
SC J.Smith/D.Cook/14 30.00 80.00
TH D.Howard/A.Thornton/12 75.00 200.00
WG J.West/G.Gervin/44 200.00 500.00

2007-08 Exquisite Collection Rookie Parallel

CARD #'d TO PLAYER JSY #
62 Morris Almond JSY AU/22 12.00 30.00
63 Julian Wright JSY AU/22 12.00 30.00
64 Aaron Brooks JSY AU/10 40.00 100.00
66 Wilson Chandler JSY AU 15.00 40.00
67 Daequan Cook JSY AU/14 15.00 40.00
69 Jermareo Davidson JSY AU/23 12.00 30.00
70 Glen Davis JSY AU/11 15.00 40.00
72 Corey Brewer JSY AU/22 15.00 40.00
73 Aaron Gray JSY AU/34 12.00 30.00
74 Taurean Green JSY AU 12.00 30.00
76 Spencer Hawes JSY AU/31 12.00 30.00
77 Al Horford JSY AU/35 75.00 200.00
78 Jeff Green JSY AU/22 15.00 40.00
79 Carl Landry JSY AU/10 12.00 30.00
80 Mike Conley Jr. JSY AU/11 250.00 500.00
81 Acie Law JSY AU 12.00 30.00
82 Dominic McGuire JSY AU 12.00 30.00
84 Demetris Nichols JSY AU/35 12.00 30.00
85 Joakim Noah JSY AU/13 75.00 200.00
86 Gabe Pruitt JSY AU/13 12.00 30.00
87 Chris Richard JSY AU/32 12.00 30.00
88 Jason Smith JSY AU/14 12.00 30.00
91 Sean Williams JSY AU/51 12.00 30.00
92 Al Thornton JSY AU/12 12.00 30.00
93 Alando Tucker JSY AU/29 12.00 30.00
94 Kevin Durant JSY AU/35 40,000.00 60,000.00
95 Marco Belinelli JSY AU/18 15.00 40.00
96 Luis Scola JSY AU 40.00 100.00
97 Louis Amundson JSY AU/20 12.00 30.00
98 C.J. Watson AU/23 15.00 40.00
99 Cheikh Samb AU/35 12.00 30.00
104 Coby Karl AU/11 12.00 30.00
105 Oleksiy Pecherov AU/14 20.00 50.00
106 Jamario Moon AU/33 15.00 40.00
107 Kyrylo Fesenko/44 12.00 30.00
109 Brandan Wright/32 15.00 40.00
110 Thaddeus Young/21 20.00 50.00
112 Greg Oden/52 30.00 60.00

2007-08 Exquisite Collection Scripted Swatches

PRINT RUN 15 SER.#'d SETS
SSAB Andrew Bogut 20.00 50.00
SSAH Al Harrington 15.00 40.00
SSAI Andre Iguodala 50.00 120.00
SSAJ Al Jefferson 25.00 60.00
SSAM Alonzo Mourning 300.00 600.00
SSBG Ben Gordon 15.00 40.00
SSBI Chauncey Billups 75.00 200.00
SSBO Chris Bosh 75.00 200.00
SSBR Brandon Roy 60.00 150.00
SSCA Carmelo Anthony 300.00 600.00
SSCK Chris Kaman 15.00 40.00
SSCM Chris Mullin 40.00 100.00
SSCO Corey Maggette 20.00 50.00
SSCP Chris Paul 500.00 1,000.00
SSDG Daniel Gibson 15.00 40.00
SSDH Dwight Howard 125.00 300.00
SSDI Boris Diaw 40.00 100.00
SSDM Desmond Mason 15.00 40.00
SSDN David Noel 15.00 40.00
SSDR David Robinson 400.00 800.00
SSDW Deron Williams 25.00 60.00
SSEC Eddy Curry 15.00 40.00
SSEO Emeka Okafor 15.00 40.00
SSFE Raymond Felton 15.00 40.00
SSGG George Gervin 75.00 200.00
SSJA Antawn Jamison 20.00 50.00
SSJF Jordan Farmar 15.00 40.00
SSJH John Havlicek 500.00 1,000.00
SSJK Jason Kidd 300.00 600.00
SSJO Jermaine O'Neal 25.00 50.00
SSJS John Stockton 300.00 600.00
SSKB Kobe Bryant 8,000.00 15,000.00
SSKG Kevin Garnett 500.00 1,000.00
SSKH Kirk Hinrich 25.00 60.00
SSLA LaMarcus Aldridge 60.00 150.00
SSLB Larry Bird 500.00 1,000.00
SSLH Larry Hughes 40.00 100.00
SSLJ LeBron James 8,000.00 15,000.00
SSMA Donyell Marshall 15.00 40.00
SSMB Mike Bibby 40.00 100.00
SSMI Michael Jordan 10,000.00 20,000.00
SSMJ Magic Johnson 500.00 1,000.00
SSMM Moses Malone 500.00 1,000.00
SSMP Morris Peterson 15.00 40.00
SSPA Tony Parker 200.00 500.00
SSPP Paul Pierce 300.00 600.00
SSPR Mark Price 75.00 200.00
SSRC Rodney Carney 15.00 40.00
SSRF Randy Foye 15.00 40.00
SSRG Rudy Gay 30.00 80.00
SSRH Richard Hamilton 75.00 200.00
SSRJ Richard Jefferson 15.00 40.00
SSRL Rashard Lewis 30.00 80.00
SSRO Dennis Rodman 500.00 1,000.00
SSSB Shane Battier 15.00 40.00
SSSH Shannon Brown 20.00 50.00
SSSL Shaun Livingston 40.00 100.00
SSSN Steve Nash 500.00 1,000.00
SSSW Shelden Williams 15.00 40.00
SSTJ T.J. Ford 15.00 40.00
SSTM Tracy McGrady 400.00 800.00
SSTP Tayshaun Prince 75.00 200.00
SSTT Tyrus Thomas 15.00 40.00
SSVC Vince Carter 500.00 1,000.00
SSYM Yao Ming 500.00 1,000.00

2007-08 Exquisite Collection Uncut Sheet Redemptions

COMMON EXCH (1-22) 200.00 300.00
NO ODDS GIVEN

2008-09 Exquisite Collection

1-60 PRINT RUN 125 SER.#'d SETS
STATED PRINT RUN 55 TO 225 SER.#'d SETS
1 Kevin Garnett 20.00 50.00
2 LeBron James 150.00 400.00
3 Dwight Howard 6.00 15.00
4 Kobe Bryant 150.00 400.00
5 Carmelo Anthony 6.00 15.00
6 Tim Duncan 30.00 80.00
7 Yao Ming 15.00 40.00
8 Dwyane Wade 25.00 60.00
9 Dirk Nowitzki 15.00 40.00
10 Jason Kidd 8.00 20.00
11 Allen Iverson 20.00 50.00
12 Tracy McGrady 15.00 40.00
13 Steve Nash 10.00 25.00
14 Ray Allen 8.00 20.00
15 Amare Stoudemire 5.00 12.00
16 Vince Carter 10.00 25.00
17 Shaquille O'Neal 15.00 40.00
18 Chris Bosh 6.00 15.00
19 Gilbert Arenas 5.00 12.00
20 Chauncey Billups 6.00 15.00
21 Paul Pierce 8.00 20.00
22 Chris Paul 10.00 25.00
23 Michael Jordan 125.00 300.00
24 Carlos Boozer 4.00 10.00
25 Manu Ginobili 12.00 30.00
26 Shawn Marion 5.00 12.00
27 Tony Parker 6.00 15.00
28 Baron Davis 5.00 12.00
29 Kevin Durant 40.00 100.00
30 Josh Howard 4.00 10.00
31 Marcus Camby 4.00 10.00
32 Michael Redd 4.00 10.00
33 Caron Butler 4.00 10.00
34 Richard Hamilton 5.00 12.00
35 Andrea Bargnani 4.00 10.00
36 Tyson Chandler 4.00 10.00
37 Andrew Bogut 4.00 10.00
38 Joe Johnson 5.00 12.00
39 T.J. Ford 3.00 8.00
40 Rashard Lewis 4.00 10.00
41 Pau Gasol 6.00 15.00
42 David Lee 3.00 8.00
43 Andre Iguodala 4.00 10.00
44 Greg Oden 3.00 8.00
45 Corey Maggette 4.00 10.00
46 Andrew Bynum 3.00 8.00
47 Mo Williams 4.00 10.00
48 Elton Brand 4.00 10.00
49 Ben Gordon 4.00 10.00
50 Danny Granger 4.00 10.00
51 Richard Jefferson 4.00 10.00
52 Al Horford 5.00 12.00
53 Gerald Wallace 4.00 10.00
54 Rudy Gay 4.00 10.00
55 Deron Williams 4.00 10.00
56 Corey Brewer 4.00 10.00
57 Monta Ellis 4.00 10.00
58 Kevin Martin 4.00 10.00
59 Luol Deng 4.00 10.00
60 Brandon Roy 4.00 10.00
61 Kevin Love JSY AU RC 75.00 200.00
62 Joe Alexander JSY AU RC 6.00 15.00
63 D.J. Augustin JSY AU RC 10.00 25.00
64 Brook Lopez JSY AU RC 30.00 80.00
65 Jason Thompson JSY AU RC 6.00 15.00
66 Brandon Rush JSY AU RC 6.00 15.00
67 A.Randolph JSY AU RC 6.00 15.00
68 Robin Lopez JSY AU RC 8.00 20.00
69 Marreese Speights JSY AU RC 15.00 40.00
70 Roy Hibbert JSY AU RC 8.00 20.00
71 JaVale McGee JSY AU RC 40.00 100.00
72 J.J. Hickson JSY AU RC 10.00 25.00
73 Ryan Anderson JSY AU RC 12.00 30.00
74 Courtney Lee JSY AU RC 8.00 20.00
75 Kosta Koufos JSY AU RC 6.00 15.00
76 George Hill JSY AU RC 15.00 40.00
77 Darrell Arthur JSY AU RC 8.00 20.00
78 Donte Greene JSY AU RC 6.00 15.00
79 D.J. White JSY AU/55 RC 6.00 15.00
80 J.R. Giddens JSY AU RC 6.00 15.00
81 Walter Sharpe JSY AU RC 6.00 15.00
82 Joey Dorsey JSY AU RC 6.00 15.00
83 Mario Chalmers JSY AU RC 20.00 50.00
84 DeAndre Jordan JSY AU RC 40.00 100.00
85 Kyle Weaver JSY AU RC 6.00 15.00
86 Sonny Weems JSY AU RC 6.00 15.00
87 C.Douglas-Roberts JSY AU RC 6.00 15.00
88 Rudy Fernandez JSY AU RC 30.00 80.00
89 Marc Gasol JSY AU/150 RC 50.00 120.00
90 O.J. Mayo JSY AU/99 RC 40.00 100.00
91 M.Beasley JSY AU/99 RC 30.00 80.00
92 D.Rose JSY AU/99 RC 400.00 800.00
93 R.Westbrook JSY AU RC 1,500.00 3,000.00
94 Eric Gordon JSY AU RC 60.00 150.00
95 Nicolas Batum AU/99 RC 60.00 150.00
96 Mike Taylor AU/99 RC 6.00 15.00
97 Alexis Ajinca AU/99 RC 6.00 15.00
98 Luc Mbah A Moute AU/99 RC 8.00 20.00
99 Sean Singletary AU/99 RC 6.00 15.00
100 Danilo Gallinari AU/99 RC 15.00 40.00
NNO Uncut Sheet EXCH 100.00 200.00

2008-09 Exquisite Collection Gold

*1-50 GOLD: .75X TO 2X BASE HI
1-50 PRINT RUN 50 SER.#'d SETS
51-100 PRINT RUN 25 SER.#'d SETS
8 Dwyane Wade 75.00 200.00
14 Ray Allen 15.00 40.00
23 Michael Jordan 800.00 1,500.00
29 Kevin Durant 125.00 250.00
61 Kevin Love 75.00 150.00
62 Joe Alexander 12.00 30.00
63 D.J. Augustin 20.00 50.00
64 Brook Lopez 40.00 100.00
65 Jason Thompson 12.00 30.00
66 Brandon Rush 12.00 30.00
67 Anthony Randolph 12.00 30.00
68 Robin Lopez 15.00 40.00
69 Marreese Speights 30.00 80.00
70 Roy Hibbert 25.00 60.00
71 JaVale McGee 20.00 50.00
72 J.J. Hickson 20.00 50.00
73 Ryan Anderson 15.00 40.00
74 Courtney Lee 15.00 40.00
75 Kosta Koufos 12.00 30.00
76 George Hill 30.00 80.00
77 Darrell Arthur 15.00 40.00
78 Donte Greene 12.00 30.00
79 D.J. White 12.00 30.00
80 J.R. Giddens 12.00 30.00
81 Walter Sharpe 12.00 30.00
82 Joey Dorsey 12.00 30.00
83 Mario Chalmers 20.00 50.00
84 DeAndre Jordan 25.00 60.00
85 Kyle Weaver 12.00 30.00
86 Sonny Weems 12.00 30.00
87 Chris Douglas-Roberts 12.00 30.00
88 Rudy Fernandez 30.00 80.00
89 Marc Gasol 40.00 100.00
90 O.J. Mayo 40.00 100.00
91 Michael Beasley 20.00 50.00
92 Derrick Rose 400.00 700.00
93 Russell Westbrook 1,000.00 2,000.00
94 Eric Gordon 30.00 80.00
95 Nicolas Batum 25.00 60.00
96 Mike Taylor 12.00 30.00
97 Alexis Ajinca 12.00 30.00
98 Luc Mbah A Moute 15.00 40.00
99 Sean Singletary 12.00 30.00
100 Danilo Gallinari 30.00 80.00

2008-09 Exquisite Collection Autographs

STATED PRINT RUN 23 TO 35 SER.#'d SETS
AUTOAD Adrian Dantley/35 10.00 25.00
AUTOAG Artis Gilmore/35 10.00 25.00
AUTOAH Al Horford/35 8.00 20.00
AUTOAM Alonzo Mourning/35 50.00 120.00
AUTOBB Bobby Brown/35 6.00 15.00
AUTOBL Bill Laimbeer/35 10.00 25.00
AUTOBO Bob Lanier/35 10.00 25.00
AUTOBW Bill Walton/35 30.00 80.00
AUTOCB Carlos Boozer/35 10.00 25.00
AUTOCL Clyde Drexler/35 30.00 80.00
AUTODC Daequan Cook/35 6.00 15.00
AUTODE Derrick Rose/35 75.00 200.00
AUTODF Derek Fisher/35 20.00 50.00
AUTODH Dwight Howard/35 40.00 100.00
AUTODO Dominique Wilkins/35 20.00 50.00
AUTODW Deron Williams/35 25.00 50.00
AUTOEG Eric Gordon/35 20.00 50.00
AUTOFE Rudy Fernandez/35 12.00 30.00
AUTOGG George Gervin/35 15.00 40.00
AUTOGW Gerald Wallace/35 6.00 15.00
AUTOJB Jose Barea/35 30.00 80.00
AUTOJH John Havlicek/35 30.00 80.00
AUTOKB Kobe Bryant/24 1,500.00 3,000.00
AUTOKD Kevin Durant/35 300.00 600.00
AUTOKG Kevin Garnett/35 200.00 500.00
AUTOLJ LeBron James/23 3,000.00 6,000.00
AUTOLO Lamar Odom/35 15.00 40.00
AUTOMB Michael Beasley/35 25.00 60.00
AUTOMC Mike Conley Jr./35 10.00 25.00
AUTOMG Marc Gasol/35 20.00 50.00
AUTOOM O.J. Mayo/35 6.00 15.00
AUTOOR Oscar Robertson/35 100.00 250.00
AUTORD Dennis Rodman/35 40.00 100.00
AUTORF Randy Foye/35 6.00 15.00
AUTORO Brandon Roy/35 25.00 60.00
AUTORP Robert Parish/35 10.00 25.00
AUTORS Rodney Stuckey/35 10.00 25.00
AUTORW R. Westbrook/35 400.00 800.00
AUTOSI Jack Sikma/35 10.00 25.00
AUTOSM Sidney Moncrief/35 8.00 20.00
AUTOWF Walt Frazier/35 8.00 20.00

2008-09 Exquisite Collection Big Jersey Autographs

STATED PRINT RUN 10 SER.#'d SETS
BIGBD Baron Davis 40.00 100.00
BIGDH Dwight Howard 125.00 250.00
BIGKB Kobe Bryant 5,000.00 10,000.00
BIGKD Kevin Durant 250.00 500.00
BIGKG Kevin Garnett 150.00 300.00
BIGLJ LeBron James 10,000.00 15,000.00
BIGRS Rodney Stuckey 40.00 100.00
BIGSN Steve Nash 100.00 200.00

2008-09 Exquisite Collection Emblems of Endorsement

STATED PRINT RUN ONE TO 10 SER.#'d SETS
EEAH Al Horford/10 50.00 100.00
EECP Chris Paul/10 2,000.00 4,000.00
EEDE Derrick Rose White/10 1,400.00 2,100.00
EEDR Derrick Rose Red/10 1,400.00 2,100.00
EEDW Deron Williams/10 150.00 300.00
EEGH George Hill/10 100.00 200.00
EEJB Jerryd Bayless/10 125.00 250.00
EEJG Jeff Green/10 100.00 200.00
EEJK Jason Kidd/10 150.00 300.00
EEJS John Stockton/10 150.00 300.00
EEJW Jerry West/10 100.00 200.00
EEKB Kobe Bryant/10 6,000.00 12,000.00
EEKD Kevin Durant/10 250.00 500.00
EEKG Kevin Garnett/10 400.00 750.00
EEMC Mike Conley Jr./10 50.00 100.00
EEMJ Michael Jordan/10 5,000.00 8,000.00
EEOJ O.J. Mayo/10 150.00 300.00
EEOM O.J. Mayo/10 150.00 300.00
EEPP Paul Pierce/10 125.00 250.00
EERF Rudy Fernandez/10 125.00 250.00
EERO David Robinson/10 125.00 250.00
EERS Rodney Stuckey/10 60.00 120.00
EESW Sonny Weems/10 50.00 100.00
EEVC Vince Carter/10 250.00 500.00

2008-09 Exquisite Collection Enshrinements

PRINT RUN 23 TO 25 SER.#'d SETS
ENBR Bill Russell/25 2,500.00 5,000.00
ENCP Chris Paul/25 800.00 1,500.00
ENDR David Robinson/25 500.00 1,000.00
ENDW Dominique Wilkins/25 125.00 300.00
ENHO Hakeem Olajuwon/25 500.00 1,000.00
ENIT Isiah Thomas/25 300.00 600.00
ENJE Julius Erving/25 500.00 1,000.00
ENJO Magic Johnson/25 1,000.00 2,000.00
ENJS John Stockton/25 200.00 500.00
ENJW Jerry West/25 300.00 600.00
ENKA Kareem Abdul-Jabbar/25 1,000.00 2,000.00
ENKB Kobe Bryant/24 3,000.00 6,000.00
ENKG Kevin Garnett/25 600.00 1,200.00
ENLB Larry Bird/25 1,000.00 2,000.00
ENLJ LeBron James/23 5,000.00 10,000.00
ENMJ Michael Jordan/23 4,000.00 8,000.00
ENOR Oscar Robertson/25 300.00 600.00
ENRP Robert Parish/25 75.00 200.00
ENVC Vince Carter/25 150.00 400.00
ENWF Walt Frazier/25 75.00 200.00

2008-09 Exquisite Collection Enshrinements Dual

STATED PRINT RUN 23 TO 25 SER.#'d SETS
ENDBA Kareem/McAdoo/25 300.00 600.00
ENDBJ K.Bryant/L.James/25 10,000.00 20,000.00
ENDBP K.Bryant/Pierce/25 3,000.00 6,000.00
ENDCK Cooper/Kupchak/25 60.00 150.00
ENDCW V.Carter/Wilkins/25 200.00 500.00
ENDGA Gervin/Dantley/25 60.00 150.00
ENDJB Magic/L.Bird/25 2,000.00 4,000.00
ENDJJ Jordan/L.James/23 15,000.00 30,000.00
ENDJR Jordan/Rodman/25 5,000.00 10,000.00
ENDKM Jordan/Bryant/25 15,000.00 30,000.00
ENDMG Mourning/KG/25 1,000.00 2,000.00
ENDMM Yao/McGrady/25 2,000.00 4,000.00
ENDNK J.Kidd/S.Nash/25 1,000.00 2,000.00
ENDOR Olajuwon/D.Rob/25 1,000.00 2,000.00
ENDRH Havlicek/Russell/25 3,000.00 6,000.00
ENDRJ O.Rob/L.James/25 4,000.00 8,000.00
ENDSH Stdmre/D.Howard/25 125.00 300.00
ENDTP I.Thomas/C.Paul/25 125.00 300.00
ENDWG J.West/Goodrich/25 125.00 300.00
ENDWS Stkn/D.Williams/25 100.00 250.00

2008-09 Exquisite Collection Flawless Autographs

STATED PRINT RUN 23 TO 50 SER.#'d SETS
FLAWAB Andrew Bynum/50 15.00 40.00
FLAWAH Al Horford/50 15.00 40.00
FLAWAM Alonzo Mourning/25 125.00 300.00
FLAWBD Baron Davis/50 20.00 50.00
FLAWBR Bill Russell/25 3,000.00 6,000.00
FLAWCD Clyde Drexler/25 125.00 300.00
FLAWCP Chris Paul/25 125.00 300.00
FLAWDF Derek Fisher/47 15.00 40.00
FLAWDW Deron Williams/25 25.00 60.00
FLAWIT Isiah Thomas/25 200.00 500.00
FLAWJE Julius Erving/25 300.00 600.00
FLAWJN Joakim Noah/50 20.00 50.00
FLAWJW Jerry West/25 400.00 800.00
FLAWKA K.Abdul-Jabbar/25 1,000.00 2,000.00
FLAWKB Kobe Bryant/24 2,500.00 5,000.00
FLAWKD Kevin Durant/50 1,000.00 2,000.00
FLAWKG Kevin Garnett/50 800.00 1,500.00
FLAWLJ LeBron James/23 3,000.00 6,000.00
FLAWMC Michael Cooper/50 15.00 40.00
FLAWMJ Michael Jordan/23 4,000.00 8,000.00
FLAWMK Mitch Kupchak/25 25.00 60.00
FLAWOR Oscar Robertson/25 100.00 250.00
FLAWPP Paul Pierce/50 75.00 200.00
FLAWRO Brandon Roy/50 20.00 50.00
FLAWRP Robert Parish/50 20.00 50.00
FLAWRS Rodney Stuckey/50 15.00 40.00
FLAWTM Tracy McGrady/50 125.00 300.00
FLAWVC Vince Carter/50 125.00 300.00

2008-09 Exquisite Collection Inscriptions

STATED PRINT RUN 20 TO 50 SER.#'d SETS
SCRIPTAD A.Dantley/25 12.00 30.00
SCRIPTAH A.Horford/50 15.00 40.00
SCRIPTAI A.Iguodala/25 15.00 40.00
SCRIPTAM A.Mourning #33/25 75.00 200.00
SCRIPTAS A.Stoudemire #1/25 25.00 60.00
SCRIPTBD Baron Davis/50 12.00 30.00
SCRIPTBL Bill Laimbeer/50 15.00 40.00
SCRIPTBM Bob McAdoo/50 15.00 40.00
SCRIPTBR B.Roy #7/50 20.00 50.00
SCRIPTCB C.Billups/50 20.00 40.00
SCRIPTCP Chris Paul CP3/25 200.00 500.00
SCRIPTDC Daequan Cook/50 8.00 20.00
SCRIPTDG D.Griffith Dr. Dunk/25 25.00 60.00
SCRIPTDH Dwight Howard/50 75.00 200.00
SCRIPTDR Rodman Worm/25 150.00 400.00
SCRIPTDW Dom.Wilkins/25 75.00 200.00
SCRIPTGG George Gervin/50 25.00 60.00
SCRIPTGW Gerald Wallace/50 8.00 20.00
SCRIPTHA H.Armstrong #12/50 8.00 20.00
SCRIPTHO H.Olajuwon #34/25 50.00 120.00
SCRIPTJG Jeff Green/50 20.00 50.00
SCRIPTJK Kidd Mr. TD/50 150.00 400.00
SCRIPTJS J.Sikma 7 AS/50 20.00 50.00
SCRIPTJW Jerry West/25 125.00 300.00
SCRIPTKB Kobe Bryant/24 3,000.00 6,000.00
SCRIPTKD Kevin Durant/50 125.00 250.00
SCRIPTKG Kevin Garnett/50 150.00 400.00
SCRIPTMC M.Conley Money Mike/50 60.00 150.00
SCRIPTMW M.Williams #24/50 8.00 20.00
SCRIPTOR O.Robertson/25 150.00 400.00
SCRIPTPA Tony Parker/50 25.00 60.00
SCRIPTPP Pierce The Truth/50 100.00 250.00
SCRIPTRP Robert Parish/50 15.00 40.00
SCRIPTSM Sidney Moncrief/20 8.00 20.00
SCRIPTSN Steve Nash/50 125.00 300.00
SCRIPTTM T.McGrady/50 25.00 50.00
SCRIPTTP T.Prince Palace/25 25.00 60.00
SCRIPTVC V.Carter Sanity/50 75.00 200.00
SCRIPTYM Yao Ming/50 75.00 200.00

2008-09 Exquisite Collection Jerseys

*JERSEY: 1X TO 2.5X BASE HI
STATED PRINT RUN 35 SER.#'d SETS

2008-09 Exquisite Collection Limited Logos

STATED PRINT RUN 23 TO 25 SER.#'d SETS
LLAH Al Horford/25 25.00 50.00
LLAI Andre Iguodala/25 75.00 200.00
LLBD Baron Davis/25 40.00 100.00
LLCP Chris Paul/25 800.00 1,500.00
LLDH Dwight Howard/25 250.00 500.00
LLDL David Lee/25 25.00 50.00
LLDR Derrick Rose/25 400.00 800.00
LLDW David West/25 20.00 50.00
LLEG Eric Gordon/25 75.00 200.00
LLGH George Hill/25 50.00 125.00
LLJG Jeff Green/25 40.00 100.00
LLJK Jason Kidd/25 200.00 500.00
LLJR J.R. Giddens/25 20.00 50.00
LLJS John Stockton/25 125.00 300.00
LLKB Kobe Bryant/24 6,000.00 12,000.00
LLKD Kevin Durant/25 1,000.00 2,000.00
LLKG Kevin Garnett/25 400.00 800.00
LLKL Kevin Love/25 125.00 300.00
LLLJ L.James/23 10,000.00 15,000.00
LLMB Michael Beasley/25 30.00 80.00
LLMJ M.Jordan/23 10,000.00 15,000.00
LLPP Paul Pierce/25 200.00 500.00
LLRF Rudy Fernandez/25 20.00 50.00
LLRJ Richard Jefferson/25 20.00 50.00
LLRP Robert Parish/25 75.00 200.00
LLRS Rodney Stuckey/25 20.00 50.00
LLSB Shane Battier/25 40.00 100.00
LLSN Steve Nash/24 300.00 600.00
LLTC Tom Chambers/25 30.00 80.00
LLVC Vince Carter/25 400.00 800.00
LLVD Vlade Divac/25 100.00 200.00
LLWI Deron Williams/25 60.00 150.00

2008-09 Exquisite Collection Limited Throwback Logo Autographs

STATED PRINT RUN 22 TO 25 SER.#'d SETS
LTAR Anthony Randolph/25 10.00 25.00
LTBL Brook Lopez/25 40.00 100.00
LTBR Brandon Rush/22 10.00 25.00
LTCD Chris Douglas-Roberts/25 10.00 25.00
LTCL Courtney Lee/25 12.00 30.00
LTDA Darrell Arthur/25 12.00 30.00
LTDG Donte Greene/25 10.00 25.00
LTDJ D.J. Augustin/25 20.00 50.00
LTDR Derrick Rose/25 400.00 800.00
LTEG Eric Gordon/25 50.00 120.00
LTGH George Hill/25 15.00 40.00
LTJA Joe Alexander/25 10.00 25.00
LTJB Jerryd Bayless/25 12.00 30.00
LTJD Joey Dorsey/25 10.00 25.00
LTJG J.R. Giddens/25 10.00 25.00
LTJH J.J. Hickson/25 10.00 25.00
LTJM Javale McGee/25 40.00 100.00
LTJT Jason Thompson/25 10.00 25.00
LTKK Kosta Koufos/25 10.00 25.00
LTKL Kevin Love/25 125.00 300.00
LTMB Michael Beasley/25 15.00 40.00
LTMC Mario Chalmers/25 15.00 40.00
LTMS Marreese Speights/25 12.00 30.00
LTOM O.J. Mayo/25 15.00 40.00
LTRA Ryan Anderson/25 12.00 30.00
LTRL Robin Lopez/25 12.00 30.00
LTSW Sonny Weems/25 10.00 25.00
LTWS Walter Sharpe/25 10.00 25.00

2008-09 Exquisite Collection Noble Nameplates

STATED PRINT RUN 5 TO 25 SER.#'d SETS
NAAH Al Horford/25 15.00 40.00
NAAJ Al Jefferson/25 20.00 50.00
NAAL Joe Alexander/25 15.00 40.00
NAAM Alonzo Mourning/25 125.00 300.00
NAAR Anthony Randolph/25 30.00 80.00
NAAT Al Thornton/25 15.00 40.00
NABA Jose Barea/25 75.00 200.00
NABD Baron Davis/25 30.00 80.00
NABG Ben Gordon/25 30.00 80.00
NABI Mike Bibby/25 15.00 40.00
NABR Corey Brewer/25 15.00 40.00
NACB Chauncey Billups/25 125.00 300.00
NACP Chris Paul/25 800.00 1,500.00
NADA D.J. Augustin/25 30.00 80.00
NADH Dwight Howard/25 125.00 300.00
NADR Derrick Rose/25 300.00 600.00
NADW David West/25 20.00 50.00
NAEG Eric Gordon/25 60.00 150.00
NAFE Raymond Felton/10 15.00 40.00
NAFG Francisco Garcia/25 15.00 40.00
NAGH George Hill/25 40.00 100.00
NAGP Gabe Pruitt/25 15.00 40.00
NAHA Al Harrington/18 15.00 40.00
NAJB Jerryd Bayless/25 15.00 40.00

AJG Jeff Green/25 30.00 80.00
AJJ J.J. Hickson/25 25.00 60.00
AJK Jason Kidd/25 75.00 150.00
AJM Jamario Moon/25 15.00 40.00
AJO Jermaine O'Neal/25 15.00 40.00
NAJT Jason Thompson/25 15.00 40.00
NAKB Kobe Bryant/24 6,000.00 12,000.00
NAKD Kevin Durant/25 330.00 600.00
NAKG Kevin Garnett/25 2,000.00 4,000.00
NAKL Kevin Love/25 100.00 250.00
NAKW Kyle Weaver/25 15.00 40.00
NALJ LeBron James/23 10,000.00 15,000.00
NAMB Michael Beasley/25 60.00 150.00
NAMC Mario Chalmers/14 25.00 60.00
NAMI Mike Conley Jr./25 40.00 100.00
NAMJ Michael Jordan/18 6,000.00 12,000.00
NAMP Morris Peterson/25 15.00 40.00
NAOM O.J. Mayo/25 60.00 150.00
NAPP Paul Pierce/25 800.00 1,500.00
NARA Ray Allen/25 200.00 500.00
NARF Rudy Fernandez/25 25.00 60.00
NARJ Richard Jefferson/25 15.00 40.00
NARS Rodney Stuckey/20 15.00 40.00
NARY Ryan Anderson/25 25.00 60.00
NASB Shane Battier/20 15.00 40.00
NASH Spencer Hawes/25 15.00 40.00
NATC Tyson Chandler/25 30.00 80.00
NATM Tracy McGrady/25 1,000.00 3,000.00
NATP Tayshaun Prince/25 20.00 50.00
NAWI Deron Williams/25 40.00 100.00

2008-09 Exquisite Collection Patches
*PATCHES: 2X TO 5X BASE HI
PATCH PRINT RUN 10 SER.#'d SETS
2 LeBron James 200.00 500.00
14 Ray Allen 30.00 80.00
22 Chris Paul 60.00 150.00

2008-09 Exquisite Collection Player Box Autographs
STATED PRINT RUN 5 TO 34 SER.#'d SETS
PBAHO Hakeem Olajuwon/34 25.00 60.00
PBAJO Magic Johnson/32 300.00 600.00
PBAJS John Stockton/12 60.00 120.00
PBAKB Kobe Bryant/24 1,500.00 3,000.00
PBALB Larry Bird/33 125.00 300.00
PBALJ LeBron James/23 5,000.00 10,000.00
PBAMB Michael Beasley/30 30.00 80.00
PBAMJ Michael Jordan/23 2,000.00 4,000.00
PBAOM O.J. Mayo/32 12.00 30.00

2008-09 Exquisite Collection Player Box Base
STATED PRINT RUN 5 TO 34 SER.#'d SETS
PBHO Hakeem Olajuwon/34 8.00 20.00
PBJO Magic Johnson/32 15.00 40.00
PBJS John Stockton/12 12.00 30.00
PBKB Kobe Bryant/24 40.00 100.00
PBLB Larry Bird/33 15.00 30.00
PBLJ LeBron James/23 30.00 80.00
PBMB Michael Beasley/30 6.00 15.00
PBMJ Michael Jordan/23 200.00 500.00
PBOM O.J. Mayo/32 6.00 15.00

2008-09 Exquisite Collection Player Box Memorabilia
STATED PRINT RUN 5 TO 34 SER.#'d SETS
PBMHO Hakeem Olajuwon/34 10.00 25.00
PBMJO Magic Johnson/32 25.00 60.00
PBMJS John Stockton/12 20.00 40.00
PBMKB Kobe Bryant/24 500.00 1,000.00
PBMLB Larry Bird/33 20.00 40.00
PBMMB Michael Beasley/30 10.00 25.00
PBMMJ Michael Jordan/23 300.00 600.00
PBMOM O.J. Mayo/32 10.00 25.00

2008-09 Exquisite Collection Player Box Patches Autographs
STATED PRINT RUN 5 TO 50 SER.#'d SETS
PBAMDR Derrick Rose/50 150.00 400.00
PBAMHO Hakeem Olajuwon/34 75.00 200.00
PBAMJO Magic Johnson/32 300.00 600.00
PBAMJS John Stockton/12 300.00 600.00
PBAMKB Kobe Bryant/24 5,000.00 10,000.00
PBAMLB Larry Bird/33 200.00 500.00
PBAMLJ LeBron James/23 4,000.00 8,000.00
PBAMMB Michael Beasley/30 30.00 80.00
PBAMMJ Michael Jordan/23 4,000.00 6,000.00
PBAMOM O.J. Mayo/32 30.00 80.00

2008-09 Exquisite Collection Prime
STATED PRINT RUN 35 TO 50 SER.#'d SETS
PRMAB Andrew Bynum 10.00 25.00
PRMAI Allen Iverson 100.00 250.00
PRMAM Adam Morrison 10.00 25.00
PRMAN Andrew Bogut 12.00 30.00
PRMAT Al Thornton 10.00 25.00
PRMBC Carlos Boozer 12.00 30.00
PRMBD Baron Davis 15.00 40.00
PRMBE Marco Belinelli 12.00 30.00
PRMBL Brook Lopez 12.00 30.00
PRMBO Chris Bosh 25.00 60.00
PRMBU Caron Butler 12.00 30.00
PRMBY Michael Beasley 15.00 40.00
PRMCB Chauncey Billups 20.00 50.00
PRMCM Corey Maggette 12.00 30.00
PRMCO Corey Brewer 12.00 30.00
PRMCP Chris Paul 50.00 125.00
PRMDA D.J. Augustin 15.00 40.00
PRMDE Derrick Rose 125.00 300.00
PRMDH Dwight Howard/39 40.00 100.00
PRMDN Dirk Nowitzki 60.00 150.00
PRMDR Derrick Rose 125.00 300.00
PRMEB Elton Brand 12.00 30.00
PRMEG Eric Gordon 25.00 60.00
PRMGH Grant Hill 40.00 100.00
PRMHI George Hill 15.00 40.00
PRMJA Joe Alexander 10.00 25.00
PRMJB Jerryd Bayless 12.00 30.00
PRMJK Jason Kidd 30.00 80.00
PRMJT Jason Thompson 10.00 25.00
PRMKD Kevin Durant 125.00 300.00
PRMKG Kevin Garnett 60.00 150.00
PRMKL Kevin Love 30.00 80.00
PRMKM Kevin Martin 12.00 30.00
PRMLJ LeBron James 800.00 1,500.00
PRMMA Stephon Marbury 30.00 80.00
PRMMB Mike Bibby 15.00 40.00
PRMMG Manu Ginobili 40.00 100.00
PRMMI Michael Beasley 15.00 40.00
PRMMS Marreese Speights 12.00 30.00
PRMOJ O.J. Mayo 12.00 30.00
PRMOM O.J. Mayo/35 12.00 30.00
PRMPA Tony Parker 25.00 60.00
PRMPG Pau Gasol 25.00 60.00
PRMPP Paul Pierce 25.00 60.00
PRMRF Rudy Fernandez 12.00 30.00
PRMRJ Richard Jefferson 12.00 30.00
PRMRL Rashard Lewis 12.00 30.00
PRMRO Brandon Roy/43 20.00 50.00
PRMRS Rodney Stuckey 10.00 25.00
PRMRW Rasheed Wallace 20.00 50.00
PRMSB Shane Battier/45 20.00 50.00
PRMSM Shawn Marion 15.00 40.00
PRMSO Shaquille O'Neal 50.00 120.00
PRMTC Tyson Chandler 12.00 30.00
PRMTD Tim Duncan 60.00 150.00
PRMTP Tayshaun Prince 15.00 40.00
PRMTS Thabo Sefolosha 10.00 25.00
PRMWI Deron Williams/40 12.00 30.00
PRMZR Zach Randolph 15.00 40.00

2008-09 Exquisite Collection Rookie Parallel
STATED PRINT RUN ONE TO 44 SER.#'d SETS
61 Kevin Love JSY AU/42 300.00 500.00
62 Joe Alexander JSY AU/11 100.00 200.00
63 D.J. Augustin JSY AU/14 100.00 200.00
64 Brook Lopez JSY AU/11 250.00 400.00
66 Brandon Rush JSY AU/25 30.00 80.00
68 Robin Lopez JSY AU/15 50.00 100.00
69 M.Speights JSY AU/16 75.00 150.00
71 Javale McGee JSY AU/34 100.00 200.00
72 J.J. Hickson JSY AU/21 125.00 250.00
73 Ryan Anderson JSY AU/20 40.00 100.00
74 Courtney Lee JSY AU/11 100.00 200.00
75 Kosta Koufos JSY AU/41 12.00 30.00
78 Donte Greene JSY AU/10 50.00 100.00
81 Walter Sharpe JSY AU/42 12.00 30.00
82 Joey Dorsey JSY AU/15 12.00 30.00
85 Kyle Weaver JSY AU/20 20.00 50.00
86 Sonny Weems JSY AU/13 40.00 100.00
89 Marc Gasol JSY AU/33 60.00 120.00
90 O.J. Mayo JSY AU/32 250.00 500.00
91 Michael Beasley JSY AU/30 30.00 80.00
95 Nicolas Batum AU/12 150.00 300.00
97 Alexis Ajinca AU/21 12.00 30.00
98 Luc Mbah A Moute AU/12 15.00 40.00
99 Sean Singletary AU/44 12.00 30.00
100 Danilo Gallinari AU/44 100.00 200.00

2008-09 Exquisite Collection Scripted Swatches
STATED PRINT RUN 12 TO 25 SER.#'d SETS
SCRPAB Andrew Bynum/25 50.00 125.00
SCRPAD Adrian Dantley/12 40.00 80.00
SCRPAH Al Horford/25 15.00 40.00
SCRPAL Al Jefferson/25 15.00 40.00
SCRPAR Anthony Randolph/25 15.00 40.00
SCRPAS Amare Stoudemire/25 50.00 100.00
SCRPBE Michael Beasley/25 40.00 100.00
SCRPBI Chauncey Billups/25 25.00 60.00
SCRPBL Brook Lopez/25 50.00 120.00
SCRPBR Brandon Roy/25 50.00 120.00
SCRPBY Michael Beasley/25 30.00 80.00
SCRPCL Courtney Lee/25 60.00 120.00
SCRPCM Corey Maggette/25 15.00 40.00
SCRPCP Chris Paul/25 300.00 600.00
SCRPDA Darrell Arthur/25 15.00 40.00
SCRPDE Derrick Rose White/25 300.00 600.00
SCRPDH Dwight Howard/25 125.00 250.00
SCRPDJ D.J. Augustin/25 40.00 80.00
SCRPDL David Lee/25 15.00 40.00
SCRPDO DeAndre Jordan/25 30.00 80.00
SCRPDR Derrick Rose Red/25 300.00 600.00
SCRPEG Eric Gordon Ball Right/25 60.00 150.00
SCRPGG George Gervin/25 15.00 40.00
SCRPGO Eric Gordon Ball Left/25 15.00 40.00
SCRPGR Danny Granger/25 25.00 60.00
SCRPHA Hilton Armstrong/25 15.00 40.00
SCRPHI George Hill/25 40.00 100.00
SCRPHR Al Harrington/25 15.00 40.00
SCRPID Ike Diogu/25 15.00 40.00
SCRPJB Jose Barea/25 75.00 200.00
SCRPJD Joey Dorsey/25 15.00 40.00
SCRPJK Jason Kidd/25 75.00 200.00
SCRPJO Jermaine O'Neal/25 15.00 40.00
SCRPJR J.R. Smith/25 15.00 40.00
SCRPJT Jason Thompson/25 15.00 40.00
SCRPKB Kobe Bryant/24 3,000.00 6,000.00
SCRPKD Kevin Durant/25 500.00 1,000.00
SCRPKG Kevin Garnett/25 1,000.00 2,000.00
SCRPKL Kevin Love/25 150.00 300.00
SCRPLB Larry Bird/25 125.00 300.00
SCRPLH Larry Hughes No Auto/25 15.00 40.00
SCRPLJ LeBron James/23 10,000.00 15,000.00
SCRPMA Desmond Mason/25 15.00 40.00
SCRPMC Mario Chalmers/21 30.00 80.00
SCRPMJ Michael Jordan/16 5,000.00 8,000.00
SCRPOJ O.J. Mayo Blue/25 20.00 50.00
SCRPOM O.J. Mayo White/25 20.00 50.00
SCRPRA Ryan Anderson/25 20.00 50.00
SCRPRF Rudy Fernandez/25 100.00 200.00
SCRPRJ Richard Jefferson/25 15.00 40.00
SCRPRO David Robinson/25 125.00 300.00
SCRPRS Ramon Sessions/25 15.00 40.00
SCRPRW Russell Westbrook/25 1,000.00 2,000.00
SCRPSB Shane Battier/25 30.00 80.00
SCRPSN Steve Nash/25 125.00 300.00
SCRPST John Stockton/25 125.00 300.00
SCRPVC Vince Carter/25 125.00 300.00
SCRPVD Vlade Divac/25 40.00 80.00

2008-09 Exquisite Collection Triple Patches
STATED PRINT RUN 10 SER.#'d SETS
ETPAI Allen Iverson 75.00 150.00
ETPAS Amare Stoudemire 20.00 50.00
ETPCA Carmelo Anthony 40.00 80.00
ETPDH Dwight Howard 60.00 120.00
ETPDN Dirk Nowitzki 50.00 100.00
ETPDR Derrick Rose 200.00 400.00
ETPGA Gilbert Arenas 20.00 50.00
ETPJK Jason Kidd 20.00 50.00
ETPKB Kobe Bryant 500.00 1,000.00
ETPKM Kevin Martin 20.00 50.00
ETPLJ LeBron James 125.00 250.00
ETPLW Luke Walton 20.00 50.00
ETPMB Michael Beasley 40.00 100.00
ETPOM O.J. Mayo 40.00 100.00
ETPRA Ray Allen 25.00 60.00
ETPSN Steve Nash 40.00 80.00
ETPTD Tim Duncan 50.00 120.00
ETPVC Vince Carter 40.00 80.00

2009-10 Exquisite Collection
1-42 PRINT RUN 199 SER.#'d SETS
43-79 PRINT RUN 225 SER.#'d SETS
1 Dwight Howard 12.00 30.00
2 LeBron James 150.00 400.00
3 Kobe Bryant 150.00 400.00
4 Dwyane Wade 50.00 120.00
5 Yao Ming 50.00 120.00
6 Tim Duncan 60.00 150.00
7 Kevin Garnett 60.00 150.00
8 Allen Iverson 50.00 120.00
9 Yi Jianlian 50.00 120.00
10 Tracy McGrady 30.00 30.00
11 Chris Paul 25.00 60.00
12 Shaquille O'Neal 30.00 30.00
13 Carmelo Anthony 15.00 40.00
14 Vince Carter 20.00 50.00
15 Dirk Nowitzki 50.00 120.00
16 Chris Bosh 12.00 30.00
17 Manu Ginobili 40.00 100.00
18 Pau Gasol 15.00 40.00
19 Ray Allen 30.00 80.00
20 Paul Pierce 20.00 50.00
21 Jamal Crawford 30.00 80.00
22 Steve Nash 20.00 50.00
23 Michael Jordan 500.00 1,000.00
24 Gilbert Arenas 8.00 20.00
25 Luke Ridnour 8.00 20.00
26 Derrick Rose 20.00 50.00
27 Jose Calderon 6.00 15.00
28 Brandon Roy 12.00 30.00
29 Joe Johnson 10.00 25.00
30 Danny Granger 6.00 15.00
31 Greg Oden 6.00 15.00
32 Al Jefferson 6.00 15.00
33 Kevin Durant 60.00 150.00
34 Andre Iguodala 10.00 25.00
35 David Lee 6.00 15.00
36 Kevin Martin 8.00 20.00
37 O.J. Mayo 6.00 15.00
38 Zach Randolph 10.00 25.00
39 Gerald Wallace 8.00 20.00
40 Russell Westbrook 25.00 60.00
41 Deron Williams 8.00 20.00
42 Mo Williams 8.00 20.00
43 Blake Griffin RC 75.00 200.00
44 Ricky Rubio AU RC 75.00 200.00
45 James Harden AU RC 1,000.00 2,000.00
46 Tyreke Evans RC 8.00 20.00
47 Brandon Jennings RC 10.00 25.00
48 James Johnson AU RC 8.00 20.00
49 Earl Clark AU RC 6.00 15.00
50 Chase Budinger AU RC 6.00 15.00
51 DeJuan Blair RC 8.00 20.00
52 B.J. Mullens AU RC 6.00 15.00
53 Darren Collison AU RC 10.00 25.00
54 Tyler Hansbrough RC 8.00 20.00
55 Sam Young AU RC 6.00 15.00
56 Marcus Thornton AU RC 8.00 20.00
57 Jeff Teague AU RC 8.00 20.00
58 Jonny Flynn AU RC 6.00 15.00
59 Terrence Williams RC 6.00 15.00
60 Gerald Henderson AU RC 6.00 15.00
61 Hasheem Thabeet RC 6.00 15.00
62 Ty Lawson AU RC 8.00 20.00
63 Eric Maynor AU RC 6.00 15.00
64 Stephen Curry AU RC 6,000.00 12,000.00
65 DeMar DeRozan RC 125.00 300.00
66 Patrick Mills RC 15.00 40.00
67 Jordan Hill RC 6.00 15.00
68 Derrick Brown AU RC 6.00 15.00
69 Wayne Ellington AU RC 8.00 20.00
70 DaJuan Summers AU RC 6.00 15.00
71 Eric Maynor AU RC 6.00 15.00
72 Stephen Curry AU 6,000.00 2,000.00
73 Ricky Rubio AU 75.00 200.00
74 James Harden AU 1,000.00 2,000.00
75 James Johnson AU 8.00 20.00
76 Sam Young AU 6.00 15.00
77 Gerald Henderson AU 6.00 15.00
78 B.J. Mullens AU 6.00 15.00
79 Jonny Flynn AU 6.00 15.00

2009-10 Exquisite Collection Rookie Parallel
STATED PRINT RUN ONE TO 50 SETS
43 Blake Griffin/23 1,000.00 2,000.00
46 Tyreke Evans/12 600.00 1,000.00
48 James Johnson AU/23 25.00 60.00
50 Chase Budinger AU/34 20.00 50.00
51 DeJuan Blair/45 25.00 60.00
52 B.J. Mullens AU/32 20.00 50.00
54 Tyler Hansbrough/50 25.00 60.00
55 Sam Young AU/23 20.00 50.00
60 Gerald Henderson AU/15 20.00 50.00
61 Hasheem Thabeet/34 20.00 50.00
64 Stephen Curry AU/30 15,000.00 30,000.00
66 Patrick Mills/13 50.00 125.00
67 Jordan Hill/43 20.00 50.00
69 Wayne Ellington AU/22 25.00 60.00
72 Stephen Curry AU/31 15,000.00 30,000.00
75 James Johnson AU/23 25.00 60.00
76 Sam Young AU/23 20.00 50.00
77 Gerald Henderson AU/15 20.00 50.00
78 B.J. Mullens AU/32 20.00 50.00

2009-10 Exquisite Collection Autographs Patches
STATED PRINT RUN 50 SER.#'d SETS
PAA Arron Afflalo 12.00 30.00
PAB Andrew Bynum 20.00 50.00
PAJ Al Jefferson 20.00 50.00
PAM Alonzo Mourning 100.00 250.00
PAS Amare Stoudemire 40.00 100.00
PAZ Kelenna Azubuike 12.00 30.00
PBD Baron Davis 60.00 150.00
PBI Mike Bibby 60.00 150.00
PBL Bill Laimbeer 60.00 150.00
PBM Brad Miller 15.00 40.00
PBR Brandon Roy 30.00 80.00
PCD Clyde Drexler 100.00 250.00
PCH Tyson Chandler 20.00 50.00
PCO Corey Brewer 12.00 30.00
PCP Chris Paul 300.00 600.00
PDG Danny Granger 30.00 80.00
PDH Dwight Howard 100.00 250.00
PDM Desmond Mason 20.00 50.00
PDO Donyell Marshall 20.00 50.00
PDR David Robinson 150.00 400.00
PDW David West 12.00 30.00
PER Julius Erving 200.00 500.00
PGR Darrell Griffith 40.00 100.00
PJB Jerryd Bayless 12.00 30.00
PJE Jeff Green 40.00 100.00
PJF Jordan Farmar 12.00 30.00
PJG J.R. Giddens 12.00 30.00
PJK Jason Kidd 125.00 300.00
PJM Jamario Moon 12.00 30.00
PJN Joakim Noah 20.00 50.00
PJO Jermaine O'Neal 40.00 100.00
PJS J.R. Smith 75.00 200.00
PJW Jerry West 200.00 500.00
PKA Kareem Abdul-Jabbar 300.00 600.00
PKG Kevin Garnett 300.00 600.00
PKL Kevin Love 100.00 250.00
PLA LaMarcus Aldridge 100.00 250.00
PLB Larry Bird 500.00 1,000.00
PLH Larry Hughes 12.00 30.00
PLJ LeBron James 3,000.00 6,000.00
PLO Lamar Odom 60.00 150.00
PLW Luke Walton 25.00 60.00
PMA Magic Johnson 500.00 1,000.00
PMC Mike Conley Jr. 25.00 60.00
PMJ Michael Jordan 5,000.00 10,000.00
PMP Mark Price 60.00 150.00
PMW Mo Williams 15.00 40.00
POM O.J. Mayo 15.00 40.00
PPP Paul Pierce 200.00 500.00
PQR Quentin Richardson 12.00 30.00
PRF Randy Foye 12.00 30.00
PRJ Richard Jefferson 12.00 30.00
PRO Derrick Rose 200.00 500.00
PRP Robert Parish 40.00 100.00
PSA Stacey Augmon 12.00 30.00
PSH Spencer Hawes 12.00 30.00
PSN Steve Nash 150.00 400.00
PST John Stockton 150.00 400.00
PTC Tom Chambers 40.00 100.00
PTM Tracy McGrady 200.00 500.00
PTP Tayshaun Prince 8.00 20.00
PVC Vince Carter 200.00 500.00
PVD Vlade Divac 40.00 100.00
PWI Deron Williams 40.00 100.00
PYM Yao Ming 500.00 1,000.00

2009-10 Exquisite Collection Extra Exquisite Jerseys
PRINT RUN 50 SER.#'d SETS
*GOLD: .6X TO 1.5X BASE HI
GOLD PRINT RUN 25 SER.#'d SETS
XAB Andrew Bynum 5.00 12.00
XAI Allen Iverson 12.50 30.00
XAR Ron Artest 8.00 20.00
XAS Amare Stoudemire 6.00 15.00
XAT Al Thornton 5.00 12.00
XBW Brandan Wright 5.00 12.00
XBY Marcus Camby 6.00 15.00
XCA Carmelo Anthony 15.00 40.00
XCB Chris Bosh 10.00 25.00
XCM Chris Mullin/15 10.00 25.00
XDH Devin Harris 5.00 12.00
XDN Dirk Nowitzki 30.00 80.00
XDR Derrick Rose 20.00 50.00
XEB Elton Brand 6.00 15.00
XEG Eric Gordon 6.00 15.00
XGH Grant Hill 20.00 50.00
XHO Josh Howard 6.00 15.00
XIG Andre Iguodala 8.00 20.00
XJC Jose Calderon 5.00 12.00
XJR Jason Richardson 8.00 20.00
XJS Josh Smith 5.00 12.00
XJT Jason Terry 6.00 15.00
XKB Kobe Bryant 60.00 150.00
XKE Kevin Martin 6.00 15.00
XKG Kevin Garnett 20.00 50.00
XKM Karl Malone 10.00 25.00
XLB Leandro Barbosa 6.00 15.00
XLJ LeBron James 200.00 500.00
XLS Luis Scola 6.00 15.00
XLW Luke Walton 6.00 15.00
XMA Kenyon Martin 6.00 15.00
XME Monta Ellis 6.00 15.00
XMG Manu Ginobili 12.00 30.00
XMJ Michael Jordan 300.00 600.00
XMR Michael Redd 6.00 15.00
XOM O.J. Mayo 5.00 12.00
XPE Patrick Ewing 20.00 50.00
XPG Pau Gasol 15.00 30.00
XPP Paul Pierce 12.00 30.00
XPS Peja Stojakovic 8.00 20.00
XRA Ray Allen 12.00 30.00
XRG Rudy Gay 8.00 20.00
XRH Richard Hamilton 8.00 20.00
XRR Rajon Rondo 20.00 50.00
XRW Rasheed Wallace 10.00 25.00
XSM Shawn Marion 8.00 20.00
XSO Shaquille O'Neal 20.00 50.00
XSP Scottie Pippen 40.00 100.00
XST Sebastian Telfair 5.00 12.00
XSV Sasha Vujacic 5.00 12.00
XTD Tim Duncan 60.00 150.00
XTO Travis Outlaw 5.00 12.00
XTY Thaddeus Young 5.00 12.00
XYI Yi Jianlian 25.00 60.00
XZR Zach Randolph 10.00 25.00

2009-10 Exquisite Collection Extra Exquisite Patches
PRINT RUN 15 SER.#'d SETS
XAI Allen Iverson 100.00 200.00
XAR Ron Artest 40.00 100.00
XAS Amare Stoudemire 30.00 80.00
XAT Al Thornton 25.00 60.00
XBW Brandan Wright 25.00 60.00
XBY Marcus Camby 30.00 80.00
XCA Carmelo Anthony 100.00 200.00
XCB Chris Bosh 60.00 150.00
XCM Chris Mullin 50.00 120.00
XDH Devin Harris 25.00 60.00
XDN Dirk Nowitzki 60.00 150.00
XDR Derrick Rose 60.00 150.00
XEB Elton Brand 30.00 80.00
XEG Eric Gordon 30.00 80.00
XGH Grant Hill 100.00 200.00
XHO Josh Howard 30.00 80.00
XIG Andre Iguodala 40.00 100.00
XJC Jose Calderon 25.00 60.00
XJH Jeff Hornacek 30.00 80.00
XJR Jason Richardson 40.00 100.00
XJS Josh Smith 25.00 60.00
XJT Jason Terry 30.00 80.00
XKB Kobe Bryant 400.00 800.00
XKE Kevin Martin 30.00 80.00
XKG Kevin Garnett 100.00 250.00
XKM Karl Malone 50.00 125.00
XLB Leandro Barbosa 30.00 80.00
XLJ LeBron James 400.00 700.00
XLS Luis Scola 30.00 80.00
XLW Luke Walton 30.00 80.00
XMA Kenyon Martin 30.00 80.00
XMC Kevin McHale 60.00 150.00
XME Monta Ellis 30.00 80.00
XMG Manu Ginobili 80.00 200.00
XMJ Michael Jordan 600.00 1,100.00
XMR Michael Redd 30.00 80.00
XNA Nate Archibald 50.00 120.00
XOM O.J. Mayo 25.00 60.00
XOR Oscar Robertson 50.00 120.00
XPE Patrick Ewing 100.00 200.00
XPG Pau Gasol 60.00 150.00
XPP Paul Pierce 60.00 150.00
XPS Peja Stojakovic 30.00 80.00
XRA Ray Allen 50.00 125.00
XRG Rudy Gay 60.00 150.00
XRH Richard Hamilton 40.00 100.00
XRR Rajon Rondo 50.00 120.00
XRW Rasheed Wallace 50.00 120.00
XSM Shawn Marion 50.00 100.00
XSO Shaquille O'Neal 120.00 300.00
XSP Scottie Pippen 125.00 250.00
XST Sebastian Telfair 25.00 60.00
XSV Sasha Vujacic 25.00 60.00
XTD Tim Duncan 125.00 250.00
XTO Travis Outlaw 25.00 60.00
XTY Thaddeus Young 25.00 60.00
XYI Yi Jianlian 50.00 120.00
XZR Zach Randolph 40.00 100.00

2009-10 Exquisite Collection Jerseys
*JERSEYS: .75X TO 2X BASE HI
JERSEY PRINT RUN 25 SER.#'d SETS

2009-10 Exquisite Collection Limited Logos
STATED PRINT RUN 7 TO 25 SER.#'d SETS
LAB Andrew Bynum/13 75.00 200.00
LAS Amare Stoudemire/15 125.00 300.00
LDH Dwight Howard/20 200.00 500.00
LDW David West/17 30.00 80.00
LJB Jerryd Bayless/20 40.00 100.00
LJE Julius Erving/20 1,000.00 2,000.00
LJF Jordan Farmar/20 50.00 120.00
LJG Jeff Green/20 50.00 100.00
LJK Jason Kidd/12 200.00 500.00
LJN Joakim Noah/18 60.00 150.00
LJO Jermaine O'Neal/14 50.00 125.00
LKL Kevin Love/14 150.00 400.00
LLB Larry Bird/16 2,000.00 4,000.00
LLJ LeBron James/16 15,000.00 30,000.00
LLO Lamar Odom/15 125.00 300.00
LLW Luke Walton/13 75.00 200.00
LMJ Magic Johnson/16 2,000.00 4,000.00
LMW Mo Williams/18 30.00 80.00
LQR Quentin Richardson/17 30.00 80.00
LRA Ray Allen/18 300.00 600.00
LRO Derrick Rose/16 300.00 600.00
LSN Steve Nash/19 1,000.00 2,000.00
LTM Tracy McGrady/13 1,000.00 2,000.00
LTP Tayshaun Prince/14 30.00 80.00
LVC Vince Carter/25 1,000.00 2,000.00
LWI Deron Williams/18 125.00 250.00
LYM Yao Ming/11 2,000.00 4,000.00

2009-10 Exquisite Collection Noble Nameplates
STATED PRINT RUN 3 TO 33 SER.#'d SETS
NAB Andrew Bynum/15 30.00 80.00
NBD Baron Davis/19 50.00 120.00
NBL Bill Laimbeer/15 50.00 120.00
NBR Brandon Roy/15 75.00 200.00
NCP Chris Paul/15 400.00 800.00
NDH Dwight Howard/18 125.00 300.00
NDM Desmond Mason/25 25.00 60.00
NDR David Robinson/15 300.00 600.00
NJB Jerryd Bayless/20 25.00 60.00
NJE Julius Erving/17 500.00 1,000.00
NJF Jordan Farmar/26 25.00 60.00
NJG Jeff Green/12 25.00 60.00
NJK Jason Kidd/12 150.00 400.00
NJO Jermaine O'Neal/15 30.00 80.00
NJS J.R. Smith/21 30.00 80.00
NKL Kevin Love/12 100.00 250.00
NLA LaMarcus Aldridge/15 125.00 300.00
NLB Larry Bird/12 1,500.00 3,000.00
NLH Larry Hughes/18 40.00 100.00
NLJ LeBron James/18 10,000.00 20,000.00
NLO Lamar Odom/15 50.00 120.00
NMI Michael Jordan/15 15,000.00 30,000.00
NMJ Magic Johnson/31 1,500.00 3,000.00
NMW Mo Williams/28 25.00 60.00
NPP Paul Pierce/15 400.00 800.00
NQR Quentin Richardson/33 25.00 60.00
NRA Ray Allen/18 200.00 500.00
NRO Derrick Rose/20 300.00 600.00
NRP Robert Parish/15 50.00 120.00
NSA Stacey Augmon/15 40.00 100.00
NSN Steve Nash/16 400.00 800.00
NST John Stockton/15 200.00 500.00
NTC Tom Chambers/15 25.00 60.00
NTM Tracy McGrady/20 400.00 800.00
NTP Tayshaun Prince/12 100.00 250.00
NVC Vince Carter/19 500.00 1,000.00
NWI Deron Williams/26 50.00 120.00

2009-10 Exquisite Collection Numbers
PRINT RUNS B/WN 1-50 COPIES PER
ADJJ M.Jordan/L.James/23 25,000.00 50,000.00
EDJJ M.Jordan/L.James/23 25,000.00 50,000.00
EDMA Mourning/Jabbar/33 800.00 1,500.00
EDRS J.Stockton/P.Riley/12 200.00 500.00
NPAB Andrew Bynum/17 40.00 100.00
NPAM Alonzo Mourning/33 300.00 600.00
NPBL Bill Laimbeer/40 75.00 200.00
NPBW Bill Walton/32 200.00 500.00
NPCD Clyde Drexler/22 300.00 600.00
NPDE Dennis Rodman/50 500.00 1,000.00
NPDH Dwight Howard/12 125.00 300.00
NPDR David Robinson/50 300.00 600.00
NPDW David West/30 40.00 100.00
NPEO Emeka Okafor/50 25.00 60.00
NPGG George Gervin/44 150.00 400.00
NPJG Jeff Green/22 25.00 60.00
NPJN Joakim Noah/13 60.00 150.00
NPJW Jerry West/44 1,000.00 2,000.00
NPKA K.Abdul-Jabbar/33 1,000.00 2,000.00
NPKL Kevin Love/42 75.00 200.00
NPLJ LeBron James/23 10,000.00 20,000.00
NPMP Mark Price/25 125.00 300.00
NPOM O.J. Mayo/32 25.00 60.00
NPPP Paul Pierce/34 300.00 600.00
NPPR Pat Riley/12 200.00 500.00
NPRT Reggie Theus/24 25.00 60.00
NPSN Steve Nash/13 1,000.00 2,000.00
NPST John Stockton/12 300.00 600.00
NPTC Tom Chambers/24 75.00 200.00
NPVC Vince Carter/15 500.00 1,000.00
NPVD Vlade Divac/21 25.00 60.00
NPYM Yao Ming/11 2,000.00 4,000.00

2011-12 Exquisite Collection
1-60 PRINT RUN 99 SER.#'d SETS
AU PRINT RUN 199 SER.#'d SETS
*HOLO 61-85/25: .75X TO 2X BASIC
1 Michael Jordan 50.00 120.00
2 LeBron James 30.00 80.00
3 Walt Frazier 6.00 15.00
4 Hal Greer 4.00 10.00
5 Tim Hardaway 5.00 12.00
6 Alonzo Mourning 6.00 15.00
7 Larry Johnson 5.00 12.00
8 Magic Johnson 15.00 40.00
9 Julius Erving 10.00 25.00
10 Mark Jackson 3.00 8.00
11 Darrell Griffith 4.00 10.00
12 Hakeem Olajuwon 8.00 20.00
13 Clyde Drexler 6.00 15.00
14 David Robinson 8.00 20.00
15 Christian Laettner 4.00 10.00
16 Bill Sharman 4.00 10.00
17 Greg Anthony 2.50 6.00
18 Jim Jackson 3.00 8.00
19 Adrian Dantley 3.00 8.00
20 Jerry West 8.00 20.00
21 John Havlicek 8.00 20.00
22 Dennis Rodman 10.00 25.00
23 Gail Goodrich 4.00 10.00
24 Danny Manning 3.00 8.00
25 Glen Rice 4.00 10.00
26 Anfernee Hardaway 10.00 25.00
27 LeBron James 30.00 80.00
28 Bob McAdoo 5.00 12.00
29 Robert Horry 4.00 10.00
30 Michael Jordan 50.00 120.00
31 Brad Daugherty 3.00 8.00
32 Candace Parker 8.00 20.00
33 Jack Sikma 3.00 8.00
34 Reggie Theus 3.00 8.00
35 Cynthia Cooper 5.00 12.00
36 Bill Laimbeer 4.00 10.00
37 Grant Hill 6.00 15.00
38 Kenny Smith 3.00 8.00
39 Toni Kukoc 5.00 12.00
40 Don Nelson 4.00 10.00
41 Jerry Sloan 4.00 10.00
42 B.J. Armstrong 3.00 8.00
43 Bill Cartwright 3.00 8.00
44 Bobby Hurley 4.00 10.00
45 Terry Porter 3.00 8.00
46 Rudy Tomjanovich 4.00 10.00
47 Lonnie Shelton 2.50 6.00
48 Chet Walker 3.00 8.00
49 Bill Russell 12.00 30.00
50 Micheal Ray Richardson 3.00 8.00
51 Cazzie Russell 4.00 10.00
52 Sam Cassell 3.00 8.00
53 David Thompson 4.00 10.00
54 Freddie Lewis 2.50 6.00
55 James Worthy 6.00 15.00
56 Rick Barry 5.00 12.00
57 Larry Bird 15.00 40.00
58 George Gervin 6.00 15.00
59 Elgin Baylor 6.00 15.00
60 Bill Walton 6.00 15.00
61 Alec Burks AU 8.00 20.00
62 Shelvin Mack AU 5.00 12.00
63 JaJuan Johnson AU 5.00 12.00
64 Klay Thompson AU 150.00 400.00
65 Kawhi Leonard AU 150.00 400.00
66 Nikola Vucevic AU 8.00 20.00
67 Jimmer Fredette AU 15.00 40.00
68 Nolan Smith AU 5.00 12.00
69 Malcolm Lee AU 6.00 15.00
70 Reggie Jackson AU 6.00 15.00
71 Bismack Biyombo AU 6.00 15.00
72 Jordan Williams AU 6.00 15.00
73 Tobias Harris AU 12.00 30.00
74 Marcus Morris AU 8.00 20.00
75 MarShon Brooks AU 6.00 15.00
76 Tristan Thompson AU 8.00 20.00
77 Chris Singleton AU 5.00 12.00
78 Markieff Morris AU 8.00 20.00
79 J.Valanciunas AU 10.00 25.00
80 D.Motiejunas AU 6.00 15.00
81 Norris Cole AU 6.00 15.00
82 Cory Joseph AU 6.00 15.00
83 Tyler Honeycutt AU 5.00 12.00
84 Chandler Parsons AU 6.00 15.00
85 Josh Selby AU 6.00 15.00

2011-12 Exquisite Collection Championship Bling Autographs
STATED PRINT RUN 50 TO 99 SER.#'d SETS
*GOLD: 4X TO 1X BASE HI
CBAM Alonzo Mourning/99 50.00 120.00
CBBD Billy Donovan/50 40.00 100.00
CBBM Bob McAdoo/99 25.00 60.00
CBBR Bill Russell/50 800.00 1,500.00
CBBW Bill Walton/99 60.00 150.00
CBCA Vince Carter/99 125.00 300.00
CBCD Clyde Drexler/50 50.00 120.00
CBCL Christian Laettner/99 60.00 150.00
CBCR Cazzie Russell/99 40.00 100.00
CBDA David Robinson/50 50.00 120.00
CBDG Darrell Griffith/99 25.00 60.00
CBDM Danny Manning/99 20.00 50.00
CBDR David Robinson/50 50.00 120.00
CBDT David Thompson/99 40.00 100.00
CBGG Gail Goodrich/99 20.00 50.00
CBGO Gail Goodrich/99 20.00 50.00
CBGR Glen Rice/99 20.00 50.00
CBHO Hakeem Olajuwon/50 125.00 300.00
CBJA LeBron James/99 1,500.00 3,000.00
CBJB Jim Boeheim/99 75.00 200.00
CBJH John Havlicek/50 125.00 300.00
CBJL LeBron James/99 1,500.00 3,000.00
CBJO Michael Jordan/99 2,000.00 4,000.00
CBJW James Worthy/50 40.00 100.00
CBLA Larry Brown/99 60.00 150.00
CBLB Larry Bird/50 125.00 300.00
CBLE LeBron James/99 1,500.00 3,000.00
CBLJ Larry Johnson/99 50.00 120.00
CBMI Michael Jordan/99 2,000.00 4,000.00
CBMJ Magic Johnson/50 125.00 300.00
CBOL Hakeem Olajuwon/50 125.00 300.00
CBRO David Robinson/50 50.00 120.00
CBRU Bill Russell/50 800.00 1,500.00
CBRW Roy Williams/50 75.00 200.00
CBTI Tom Izzo/99 150.00 400.00
CBVC Vince Carter/50 125.00 300.00
CBWA Bill Walton/99 60.00 150.00
CBWE Jerry West/50 75.00 200.00
CBWI Roy Williams/50 75.00 200.00
CBWO James Worthy/50 40.00 100.00

2011-12 Exquisite Collection Dimensions Autographs
DAH Anfernee Hardaway 60.00 150.00
DAM Alonzo Mourning 40.00 100.00
DBR Bill Russell 800.00 1,500.00
DBW Bill Walton 20.00 50.00
DCD Clyde Drexler 40.00 100.00
DCO DeMarcus Cousins 15.00 40.00
DCR Cazzie Russell 12.00 30.00
DDA David Robinson 50.00 120.00
DDC DeMarcus Cousins 15.00 40.00
DDM Danny Manning 8.00 20.00
DDR David Robinson 40.00 100.00
DDT David Thompson 15.00 40.00
DGG George Gervin 20.00 50.00
DGH Grant Hill 25.00 60.00
DGO Gail Goodrich 10.00 25.00
DGR Glen Rice 10.00 25.00
DHG Hal Greer 20.00 50.00
DHO Hakeem Olajuwon 60.00 150.00
DJA LeBron James 1,500.00 3,000.00
DJE Julius Erving 50.00 120.00
DJN Michael Jordan 2,000.00 4,000.00
DJO Michael Jordan 2,000.00 4,000.00
DJR Michael Jordan 2,000.00 4,000.00
DJW James Worthy 20.00 50.00
DKS Kenny Smith 10.00 25.00
DLA Larry Bird 100.00 250.00
DLB Larry Bird 100.00 250.00
DLE LeBron James 1,500.00 3,000.00
DLJ Larry Johnson 30.00 80.00
DMA Mark Jackson 10.00 25.00
DMC Magic Johnson 100.00 250.00
DMG Magic Johnson 100.00 250.00
DMI Michael Jordan 2,000.00 4,000.00
DMJ Michael Jordan 2,000.00 4,000.00
DML Michael Jordan 2,000.00 4,000.00
DRB Rick Barry 20.00 50.00
DRO Dennis Rodman 75.00 200.00
DST John Starks 20.00 50.00
DWE Jerry West 50.00 120.00
DWF Walt Frazier 40.00 100.00

2011-12 Exquisite Collection Endorsements
STATED PRINT RUN 10 TO 50 SER.#'d SETS
EEAH Anfernee Hardaway/50 75.00 200.00
EEBR Bill Russell/10 500.00 1,000.00
EEBS Bill Sharman/50 40.00 100.00
EEBW Bill Walton/50 20.00 50.00
EEGK George Karl/50 15.00 40.00
EEHG Hal Greer/50 25.00 60.00
EEJA LeBron James/50 1,500.00 3,000.00
EEJN Michael Jordan/50 2,500.00 5,000.00
EEJO Michael Jordan/50 2,500.00 5,000.00
EEJS LeBron James/50 1,500.00 3,000.00
EELB Larry Bird/50 125.00 300.00
EELE LeBron James/50 1,500.00 3,000.00
EEMI Michael Jordan/50 2,500.00 5,000.00
EEMJ Magic Johnson/50 125.00 300.00
EERB Rick Barry/50 12.00 30.00
EEST John Starks/50 40.00 100.00
EEVC Vince Carter/50 125.00 300.00
EEWF Walt Frazier/50 40.00 100.00

2011-12 Exquisite Collection Endorsements Dual
STATED PRINT RUN 10 TO 20 SER.#'d SETS
EE2BH L.Bird/J.Havlicek/20 300.00 600.00
EE2BM D.Manning/L.Brown/20 50.00 120.00
EE2EJ J.Erving/M.Jordan/20 3,000.00 6,000.00
EE2IB T.Izzo/J.Boeheim/20 200.00 500.00
EE2JB M.Jordan/L.Bird/20 3,000.00 6,000.00
EE2JE L.James/J.Erving/20 1,500.00 3,000.00
EE2JH A.Hardaway/L.James/20 1,500.00 3,000.00
EE2JJ M.Jordan/M.Johnson/20 3,000.00 6,000.00
EE2JR L.James/P.Riley/20 1,500.00 3,000.00
EE2LA L.James/A.Mourning/20 1,500.00 3,000.00
EE2MJ L.Johnson/Mourning/20 75.00 200.00
EE2ML L.James/M.Jordan/20 4,000.00 8,000.00
EE2OD C.Drexler/Olajuwon/20 75.00 200.00
EE2RO Olajuwon/Robinson/20 100.00 250.00
EE2WC J.Calhoun/R.Williams/20 200.00 500.00

2011-12 Exquisite Collection Endorsements Triple
STATED PRINT RUN 15 SER.#'d SETS
EE3BRH Havlicek/Russell/Bird 1,500.00 3,000.00
EE3IWC Roy/Izzo/Calhn EXCH 400.00 800.00
EE3JBJ Bird/LeBron/Jordan 4,000.00 8,000.00
EE3JJB Jordan/Magic/Bird 4,000.00 8,000.00
EE3JJE Erving/LeBron/Jordan 4,000.00 8,000.00
EE3JJJ Jordan/Magic/LeBron 4,000.00 8,000.00
EE3JRM LeBron/Riley/Zo 1,500.00 3,000.00
EE3JWW West/Worthy/Magic 200.00 500.00
EE3RRO Olaj/Russell/DRob 1,000.00 2,000.00
EE3WEJ Worthy/Erving/LeBron 1,500.00 3,000.00
EE3WIB Izzo/Roy/Boeheim EXCH 400.00 800.00

2011-12 Exquisite Collection Legacy Autographs
STATED PRINT RUN 10 TO 23 SER.#'d SETS
ELAD Adrian Dantley/15 20.00 50.00
ELBR Bill Russell/15 600.00 1,200.00
ELCD Clyde Drexler/15 50.00 120.00
ELDR David Robinson/15 50.00 120.00
ELHO Hakeem Olajuwon/15 50.00 120.00
ELJE Julius Erving/15 50.00 120.00
ELJH John Havlicek/15 60.00 150.00
ELJN Michael Jordan/23 2,500.00 5,000.00
ELJO Michael Jordan/23 2,500.00 5,000.00
ELJW James Worthy/15 40.00 100.00
ELLB Larry Bird/15 125.00 300.00
ELMI Michael Jordan/23 2,500.00 5,000.00
ELMJ Magic Johnson/15 100.00 250.00
ELWE Jerry West/15 60.00 150.00

2011-12 Exquisite Collection Personal Touch Car
STATED PRINT RUN 30 SER.#'d SETS
PTCAH Anfernee Hardaway 60.00 150.00
PTCAM Alonzo Mourning 40.00 100.00
PTCBC Bill Cartwright 15.00 40.00
PTCBM Bob McAdoo 25.00 60.00
PTCCD Clyde Drexler 50.00 120.00
PTCDM Danny Manning 10.00 25.00
PTCDN Don Nelson 20.00 50.00
PTCDT David Thompson 12.00 30.00
PTCGR Glen Rice 8.00 20.00
PTCJA LeBron James 1,500.00 3,000.00
PTCJE Julius Erving 75.00 200.00
PTCJS Jerry Sloan 40.00 100.00
PTCJW Jerry West 50.00 120.00
PTCLJ Larry Johnson 30.00 80.00
PTCMJ Magic Johnson 125.00 300.00
PTCRH Robert Horry 20.00 50.00
PTCRO Dennis Rodman 75.00 200.00
PTCST John Starks 20.00 50.00
PTCTP Terry Porter 8.00 20.00
PTCVC Vince Carter 75.00 200.00
PTCWF Walt Frazier 40.00 100.00

2011-12 Exquisite Collection Personal Touch Date
STATED PRINT RUN 30 SER.#'d SETS
PTDAD Adrian Dantley 8.00 20.00
PTDAH Anfernee Hardaway 60.00 150.00
PTDAJ Avery Johnson 8.00 20.00
PTDAM Alonzo Mourning 40.00 100.00
PTDBC Bill Cartwright 15.00 40.00
PTDBM Bob McAdoo 25.00 60.00
PTDBW Bill Walton 20.00 50.00
PTDCD Clyde Drexler 50.00 120.00
PTDDM Danny Manning 10.00 25.00
PTDDN Don Nelson 20.00 50.00
PTDDT David Thompson 12.00 30.00
PTDGG George Gervin 15.00 40.00
PTDGR Glen Rice 15.00 40.00
PTDHO Hakeem Olajuwon 50.00 120.00
PTDJA LeBron James 1,500.00 3,000.00
PTDLB Larry Bird 125.00 300.00
PTDLJ Larry Johnson 25.00 60.00
PTDRO Dennis Rodman 75.00 200.00
PTDWF Walt Frazier 40.00 100.00

2011-12 Exquisite Collection Personal Touch Food
STATED PRINT RUN 30 SER.#'d SETS
PTFAD Adrian Dantley 8.00 20.00
PTFAH Anfernee Hardaway 60.00 150.00
PTFAJ Avery Johnson 8.00 20.00
PTFAM Alonzo Mourning 40.00 100.00
PTFBW Bill Walton 20.00 50.00
PTFCD Clyde Drexler 50.00 120.00
PTFDE Dennis Rodman 75.00 200.00
PTFDM Danny Manning 10.00 25.00
PTFDT David Thompson 12.00 30.00
PTFGG George Gervin 15.00 40.00
PTFGK George Karl 15.00 40.00
PTFGR Glen Rice 15.00 40.00
PTFHG Hal Greer 20.00 50.00
PTFHO Hakeem Olajuwon 50.00 120.00
PTFJA LeBron James 1,500.00 3,000.00
PTFJW Jerry West 50.00 120.00
PTFLB Larry Bird 125.00 300.00
PTFLJ Larry Johnson 25.00 60.00
PTFRO David Robinson 50.00 120.00
PTFST John Starks 20.00 50.00
PTFWF Walt Frazier 40.00 100.00

2011-12 Exquisite Collection Personal Touch Musician
STATED PRINT RUN 30 SER.#'d SETS
PTMAH Anfernee Hardaway 60.00 150.00
PTMAJ Avery Johnson 8.00 20.00
PTMAM Alonzo Mourning 40.00 100.00
PTMBM Bob McAdoo 25.00 60.00
PTMBW Bill Walton 20.00 50.00
PTMCD Clyde Drexler 50.00 120.00
PTMCR Cazzie Russell 15.00 40.00
PTMDM Danny Manning 12.00 30.00
PTMDN Don Nelson 20.00 50.00
PTMHG Hal Greer 20.00 50.00
PTMHO Hakeem Olajuwon 50.00 120.00
PTMJA LeBron James 1,500.00 3,000.00
PTMJE Julius Erving 60.00 150.00
PTMKS Kenny Smith 12.00 30.00
PTMLJ Larry Johnson 30.00 80.00
PTMRB Rick Barry 12.00 30.00
PTMRO Dennis Rodman 75.00 200.00
PTMTP Terry Porter 8.00 20.00
PTMVC Vince Carter 75.00 200.00

2011-12 Exquisite Collection UD Black Bio-Scripts
STATED PRINT RUN 10 TO 15 SER.#'d SETS
BSAH Anfernee Hardaway/15 100.00 250.00
BSAM Alonzo Mourning/15 75.00 200.00
BSBW Bill Walton/15 40.00 100.00
BSCP Candace Parker/15 75.00 200.00
BSCR Cazzie Russell/15 20.00 50.00
BSDE Dennis Rodman/15 100.00 250.00
BSDM Danny Manning/15 40.00 100.00
BSDT David Thompson/15 25.00 60.00
BSGR Glen Rice/15 25.00 60.00
BSJA LeBron James/15 2,000.00 4,000.00
BSJJ Jim Jackson/15 30.00 80.00
BSJO Larry Johnson/15 40.00 100.00
BSKS Kenny Smith/15 15.00 40.00
BSLB Larry Brown/15 40.00 100.00
BSLE LeBron James/15 2,000.00 4,000.00
BSLJ LeBron James/15 2,000.00 4,000.00
BSLS Lonnie Shelton/15 20.00 50.00
BSRB Rick Barry/15 30.00 80.00
BSSC Sam Cassell/15 25.00 60.00

2011-12 Exquisite Collection UD Black Blackboard Autographs
STATED PRINT RUN 40 SER.#'d SETS
BBBD Billy Donovan 40.00 100.00
BBBH Ben Howland 15.00 40.00
BBBR Bo Ryan 20.00 50.00
BBBS Bill Self 40.00 100.00
BBCA Jim Calhoun 40.00 100.00
BBGK George Karl 15.00 40.00
BBGW Gary Williams 15.00 40.00
BBHU Bob Huggins 20.00 50.00
BBJB Jim Boeheim 40.00 100.00
BBJS Jerry Sloan 40.00 100.00
BBJW Jay Wright 40.00 100.00
BBLB Larry Brown 40.00 100.00
BBMF Mark Few 25.00 60.00
BBMM Mike Montgomery 8.00 20.00
BBPR Pat Riley 40.00 100.00
BBRM Rick Majerus 40.00 100.00
BBRW Roy Williams 40.00 100.00
BBSF Steve Fisher 12.00 30.00
BBTI Tom Izzo 40.00 100.00
BBTS Tubby Smith 20.00 50.00

2011-12 Exquisite Collection UD Black College Logo Autographs
STATED PRINT RUN 40 SER.#'d SETS
LAM Alonzo Mourning 40.00 100.00
LBH Bob Huggins 20.00 50.00
LBR Bill Russell 500.00 1,000.00
LBW Bill Walton 20.00 50.00
LCD Clyde Drexler 50.00 120.00
LDR David Robinson 50.00 120.00
LGR Glen Rice 10.00 25.00
LHO Hakeem Olajuwon 50.00 120.00
LJB Jim Boeheim 40.00 100.00
LJE Julius Erving 60.00 150.00
LJO Michael Jordan 2,500.00 5,000.00
LLB Larry Bird 100.00 250.00
LLJ LeBron James 1,500.00 3,000.00
LLS Lonnie Shelton 12.00 30.00
LMJ Magic Johnson 100.00 250.00
LTI Tom Izzo 75.00 200.00
LWE Jerry West 50.00 120.00
LWI Roy Williams 40.00 100.00

2011-12 Exquisite Collection UD Black College Vault Autographs
STATED PRINT RUN 60 SER.#'d SETS
VAH Anfernee Hardaway 60.00 150.00
VAM Alonzo Mourning 50.00 120.00
VBA B.J. Armstrong 20.00 50.00
VBH Bob Huggins 20.00 50.00
VBW Bill Walton 20.00 50.00
VCD Clyde Drexler 60.00 150.00
VCP Candace Parker 50.00 120.00
VDA David Robinson 50.00 120.00
VDC DeMarcus Cousins 12.00 30.00
VDR Dennis Rodman 60.00 150.00
VFL Freddie Lewis 12.00 30.00
VGG Gail Goodrich 10.00 25.00
VGR Glen Rice 10.00 25.00
VGW Gary Williams 25.00 60.00
VHO Hakeem Olajuwon 60.00 150.00
VJB Jim Boeheim 40.00 100.00
VJE Julius Erving 50.00 120.00
VJH John Havlicek 75.00 200.00
VJJ Jim Jackson 15.00 40.00
VJO Michael Jordan 2,500.00 5,000.00
VLB Larry Bird 125.00 300.00
VLJ LeBron James 1,500.00 3,000.00
VLS Lonnie Shelton 8.00 20.00
VMJ Magic Johnson 125.00 300.00
VRU Bill Russell 400.00 800.00
VRW Roy Williams 30.00 80.00
VSA Steve Alford 12.00 30.00
VTC Tom Crean 8.00 20.00
VTH Tim Hardaway 20.00 50.00
VTI Tom Izzo 40.00 100.00
VWJ Jerry West 50.00 120.00

2011-12 Exquisite Collection UD Black Dual Patch Autographs
STATED PRINT RUN 23 TO 50 SER.#'d SETS
LP2BH Boeheim/Howland/25 60.00 150.00
LP2BJ M.Jordan/L.Bird/25 2,000.00 4,000.00
LP2BW L.Bird/J.West/25 150.00 400.00
LP2EJ J.Erving/L.James/25 1,500.00 3,000.00
LP2HH Hill/Hardaway/25 EXCH 75.00 200.00
LP2JE J.Erving/M.Jordan/25 2,000.00 4,000.00
LP2JH L.James/A.Hard/50 1,500.00 3,000.00
LP2JJ L.James/M.Jordan/23 4,000.00 8,000.00
LP2JM L.James/Mourning/50 1,500.00 3,000.00
LP2JR D.Rodman/M.Jordan/50 2,000.00 4,000.00
LP2JW M.Johnson/J.West/50 150.00 400.00
LP2MH Mourning/T.Hard/50 40.00 100.00
LP2ML M.Johnson/L.Bird/25 500.00 1,000.00
LP2MM M.Johnson/Jordan/25 2,000.00 4,000.00
LP2OD Drexler/Olajuwon/25 100.00 250.00
LP2OM Olajuwon/Mourning/50 60.00 150.00
LP2OR D.Rob/Olajuwon/50 75.00 200.00
LP2RB B.Russell/L.Bird/25 1,000.00 2,000.00
LP2RR B.Russell/D.Rob/25 600.00 1,200.00
LP2SW B.Self/R.Williams/50 75.00 200.00
LP2TW Walton/Thompson/50 50.00 120.00
LP2WG B.Walton/Goodrich/50 50.00 120.00

2012-13 Exquisite Collection
1-60 PRINT RUN 99 SER.#'d SETS
61-79 AU PRINT RUN 199 SER.#'d SETS
EXCHANGE DEADLINE 10/23/2015
1 Adrian Dantley 2.00 5.00
2 Alonzo Mourning 4.00 10.00
3 Anfernee Hardaway 6.00 15.00
4 Bill Laimbeer 3.00 8.00
5 Bill Russell 8.00 20.00
6 Bill Walton 4.00 10.00
7 Bob McAdoo 2.00 5.00
8 Brad Daugherty 2.00 5.00
9 Christian Laettner 2.50 6.00
10 Clyde Drexler 4.00 10.00
11 Danny Manning 2.00 5.00
12 David Robinson 4.00 10.00
13 David Thompson 2.50 6.00
14 Dennis Rodman 6.00 15.00
15 Tony Gwynn 2.50 6.00
16 Isiah Thomas 5.00 12.00
17 Glen Rice 2.00 5.00
18 Grant Hill 4.00 10.00
19 Hakeem Olajuwon 5.00 12.00
20 Hal Greer 3.00 8.00
21 Julius Erving 6.00 15.00
22 John Havlicek 5.00 12.00
23 Larry Bird 8.00 20.00
24 Larry Johnson 3.00 8.00
25 LeBron James 25.00 60.00
26 Magic Johnson 8.00 20.00
27 Mark A. Jackson 2.00 5.00
28 Michael Jordan 40.00 100.00
29 Micheal Ray Richardson 2.00 5.00
30 Robert Horry 2.50 6.00
31 Tim Hardaway 3.00 8.00
32 Toni Kukoc 2.50 6.00
33 Walt Frazier 4.00 10.00
34 Karl Malone 4.00 10.00
35 Jason Kidd 4.00 10.00
36 Dominique Wilkins 3.00 8.00
37 Sean Elliott 2.00 5.00
38 Mookie Blaylock 1.50 4.00
39 A.C. Green 2.50 6.00
40 Cheryl Miller 2.50 6.00
41 Chris Paul 5.00 12.00
42 Lou Hudson 2.00 5.00
43 Dave Cowens 4.00 10.00
44 Derrick Coleman 2.50 6.00
45 Nick Van Exel 2.50 6.00
46 Vinny Del Negro 1.50 4.00
47 Elvin Hayes 3.00 8.00
48 Gary Payton 3.00 8.00
49 Jamal Mashburn 2.00 5.00
50 Jeff Hornacek 2.00 5.00
51 Fat Lever 2.00 5.00
52 Nate Thurmond 2.50 6.00
53 Swen Nater 2.00 5.00
54 Antoine Walker 2.00 5.00
55 Bernard King 3.00 8.00
56 Allen Iverson 4.00 10.00
57 Spencer Haywood 2.50 6.00
58 Spud Webb 2.00 5.00
59 Wilt Chamberlain 8.00 20.00
60 Ray Allen 4.00 10.00
61 Meyers Leonard AU 4.00 10.00
63 Kendall Marshall AU EXCH 3.00 8.00
64 Moe Harkless AU 4.00 10.00
65 Tyler Zeller AU 3.00 8.00
66 Andrew Nicholson AU 3.00 8.00
67 Evan Fournier AU 5.00 12.00
68 Jared Cunningham AU 3.00 8.00
70 Arnett Moultrie AU 3.00 8.00
71 Bernard James AU 3.00 8.00
72 Jae Crowder AU 6.00 15.00
73 Draymond Green AU 60.00 150.00
74 Quincy Acy AU 3.00 8.00
75 Khris Middleton AU 15.00 40.00
76 Will Barton AU 6.00 15.00
77 Tyshawn Taylor AU 3.00 8.00
78 Darius Miller AU 4.00 10.00
80 Darius Johnson-Odom AU 3.00 8.00
81 Robert Sacre AU 3.00 8.00

2012-13 Exquisite Collection Signatures Silver Spectrum
*SILVER SPECTRUM: .6X TO 1.5X BASIC
STATED PRINT RUN 50 SER.#'d SETS
EXCHANGE DEADLINE 10/23/2015

2012-13 Exquisite Collection 2013-14 Rookies
STATED PRINT RUN 99 SER.#'d SETS
R1 Skylar Diggins 10.00 25.00
R2 Giannis Antetokounmpo 800.00 1,500.00
R3 Lucas Nogueira 4.00 10.00
R4 Dennis Schroeder 6.00 15.00
R5 Shane Larkin 4.00 10.00
R6 Sergey Karasev 4.00 10.00
R7 Tony Snell 4.00 10.00
R8 Mason Plumlee 4.00 10.00
R9 Solomon Hill 4.00 10.00
R10 Tim Hardaway Jr. 5.00 12.00
R11 Reggie Bullock 4.00 10.00
R12 Andre Roberson 4.00 10.00
R13 Rudy Gobert 20.00 50.00
R14 Livio Jean-Charles 4.00 10.00
R15 Archie Goodwin 4.00 10.00
R16 Nemanja Nedovic 4.00 10.00

2012-13 Exquisite Collection Autographs
PRINT RUNS B/WN 30-99 COPIES PER
EXCHANGE DEADLINE 10/23/2015
AG A.C. Green/99 10.00 25.00
AH Anfernee Hardaway/99 60.00 150.00
AI Allen Iverson/30 EXCH 75.00 200.00
AL Allan Houston/99 12.00 30.00
AM Alonzo Mourning/30 40.00 100.00
BO Muggsy Bogues/99 20.00 50.00
BR Bill Russell/30 600.00 1,200.00
CD Clyde Drexler/30 50.00 120.00
DC Dave Cowens/99 12.00 30.00
DR David Robinson/30 50.00 120.00
GH Grant Hill/30 40.00 100.00
GP Gary Payton/99 30.00 80.00
HO Hakeem Olajuwon/30 50.00 120.00
JA LeBron James/30 2,000.00 4,000.00
JE Julius Erving/30 60.00 150.00
JH Jeff Hornacek/99 10.00 25.00
JO Michael Jordan/99 2,000.00 4,000.00
KM Karl Malone/30 50.00 120.00
LB Larry Bird/30 125.00 300.00
LH Lou Hudson/99 10.00 25.00
LJ LeBron James/30 1,500.00 3,000.00
MC Michael Cooper/99 10.00 25.00
MI Michael Jordan/99 2,000.00 4,000.00
MJ Magic Johnson/30 125.00 300.00
MP Mark Price/99 15.00 40.00
NT Nate Thurmond/99 10.00 25.00
RA Ray Allen/99 40.00 100.00
RO Dennis Rodman/30 75.00 200.00
SB Shawn Bradley/99 8.00 20.00
SW Spud Webb/99 15.00 40.00
TK Toni Kukoc/99 20.00 50.00
SJN Michael Jordan
released in 14-15 SP Authentic 2,000.00 4,000.00

2012-13 Exquisite Collection Collegiate Seal Autographs
PRINT RUNS B/WN 45-99 COPIES PER
EXCHANGE DEADLINE 10/23/2015
AH Anfernee Hardaway/99 60.00 150.00
AI Allen Iverson/99 EXCH 75.00 200.00
AW Antoine Walker/99 8.00 20.00
BR Bill Russell/45 500.00 1,000.00
BW Bill Walton/99 30.00 80.00
DM Danny Manning/99 8.00 20.00
DW Dominique Wilkins/45 30.00 80.00
GH Grant Hill/45 30.00 80.00
HG Hal Greer/99 20.00 50.00
HM Harold Miner/99 6.00 15.00
HO Hakeem Olajuwon/45 50.00 120.00
JE Julius Erving/45 50.00 120.00
JH John Havlicek/45 60.00 150.00
JK Jason Kidd/45 40.00 100.00
JO Michael Jordan/99 2,000.00 4,000.00
KM Karl Malone/45 40.00 100.00
LB Larry Bird/45 100.00 250.00
LH Lou Hudson/99 6.00 15.00
MA Mark A. Jackson/99 6.00 15.00
SB Shawn Bradley/99 6.00 15.00
SE Sean Elliott/99 8.00 20.00
VE Nick Van Exel/99 20.00 50.00

2012-13 Exquisite Collection Dimensions Autographs
PRINT RUNS B/WN 25-70 COPIES PER
EXCHANGE DEADLINE 10/23/2015
AH Anfernee Hardaway/70* 60.00 150.00
AI Allen Iverson/25* 100.00 250.00
BR Bill Russell/25* 600.00 1,200.00
CM Cheryl Miller/70* 15.00 40.00
DR David Robinson/70* 50.00 120.00
DW Dominique Wilkins/25* 40.00 100.00
GH Grant Hill/70* 40.00 100.00
GP Gary Payton/70* 40.00 100.00
HM Harold Miner/70 * 6.00 15.00
JA LeBron James/25* 2,000.00 4,000.00
JE Julius Erving/70* 60.00 150.00
JH John Havlicek/70* 75.00 200.00
JK Jason Kidd/25* 40.00 100.00
JN Michael Jordan/25* 3,000.00 6,000.00
JO Magic Johnson/25* 125.00 300.00
KM Karl Malone/25* 50.00 120.00
LB Larry Bird/25* 125.00 300.00
LJ LeBron James/25* 2,000.00 4,000.00
MA Mark A. Jackson/70* 6.00 15.00
MI Michael Jordan/70* 2,000.00 4,000.00
MJ Michael Jordan/70* 2,000.00 4,000.00
OL Hakeem Olajuwon/70* 50.00 120.00
RO Dennis Rodman/70* 75.00 200.00
TK Toni Kukoc/70* 20.00 50.00

2012-13 Exquisite Collection Dream Seasons Autographs
PRINT RUNS B/WN 10-70 COPIES PER
NO PRICING ON QTY 10
EXCHANGE DEADLINE 10/23/2015
AW Antoine Walker/70 10.00 25.00
BR Bill Russell/35 600.00 1,200.00
BW Bill Walton/70 30.00 80.00
CL Christian Laettner/70 12.00 30.00
CM Cheryl Miller/70 15.00 40.00
DM Danny Manning/70 10.00 25.00
DR David Robinson/35 50.00 120.00
DT David Thompson/70 12.00 30.00
GH Grant Hill/70 40.00 100.00
GR Glen Rice/70 8.00 20.00
HG Grant Hill/35 40.00 100.00
HI Grant Hill/35 40.00 100.00
HO Hakeem Olajuwon/35 50.00 120.00
IT Isiah Thomas/70 40.00 100.00
JA LeBron James/10 2,500.00 5,000.00
JH John Havlicek/35 75.00 200.00
JM Michael Jordan/70 2,000.00 4,000.00
JO Magic Johnson/35 125.00 300.00
JS LeBron James/35 1,500.00 3,000.00
KM Karl Malone/35 40.00 100.00
LA Larry Johnson/70 30.00 80.00
LB Larry Bird/35 125.00 300.00
MI Michael Jordan/70 2,000.00 4,000.00
MJ Michael Jordan/70 2,000.00 4,000.00
RU Bill Russell/35 600.00 1,200.00
SE Sean Elliott/70 8.00 20.00
SN Swen Nater/70 6.00 15.00
WA Bill Walton/70 30.00 80.00

2012-13 Exquisite Collection Endorsements
PRINT RUNS B/WN 25-99 COPIES PER
EXCHANGE DEADLINE 10/23/2015
AI Allen Iverson/25 100.00 250.00
AM Alonzo Mourning/99 40.00 100.00
AW Antoine Walker/99 8.00 20.00
BR Bill Russell/25 600.00 1,200.00
BW Bill Walton/99 40.00 100.00
CD Clyde Drexler/99 40.00 100.00
CM Cheryl Miller/99 15.00 40.00
DR David Robinson/25 40.00 100.00
DW Dominique Wilkins/25 30.00 80.00
HA John Havlicek/25 75.00 200.00
HO Hakeem Olajuwon/99 40.00 100.00
IT Isiah Thomas/99 30.00 80.00
JA LeBron James/99 1,500.00 3,000.00
JH Jeff Hornacek/99 8.00 20.00
JK Jason Kidd/99 30.00 80.00
JN Michael Jordan/25 3,000.00 6,000.00
JO Magic Johnson/25 125.00 300.00
JU Julius Erving/25 75.00 200.00
KM Karl Malone/25 50.00 120.00
LA Larry Johnson/25 30.00 80.00
LB Larry Bird/25 125.00 300.00
LH Lou Hudson/99 4.00 10.00
LJ LeBron James/25 2,000.00 4,000.00
NT Nate Thurmond/99 12.00 30.00
RA Ray Allen/99 40.00 100.00
EEMI Michael Jordan
released in 14-15 SP Authentic 2,000.00 4,000.00
EEMJ Michael Jordan
released in 14-15 SP Authentic 2,000.00 4,000.00

2012-13 Exquisite Collection Endorsements Dual
PRINT RUNS B/WN 15-30 COPIES PER
EXCHANGE DEADLINE 10/23/2015
HH A.Hardaway/G.Hill/15 75.00 200.00
HL G.Hill/C.Laettner/30 40.00 100.00
HM G.Hill/J.Mashburn/30 25.00 60.00
JB Magic/L.Bird/15 EXCH 500.00 1,000.00
JE M.Jordan/J.Erving/15 2,000.00 4,000.00
JJ M.Jordan/L.James/30 4,000.00 8,000.00
JM M.Johnson/K.Malone/30 100.00 250.00
JT M.Johnson/I.Thomas/15 100.00 250.00
KI J.Kidd/A.Iverson/15 125.00 300.00
LJ L.James/J.Erving/15 1,500.00 3,000.00
ML M.Jordan/L.Bird/15 2,500.00 5,000.00
MM M.Jordan/M.Johnson/15 2,500.00 5,000.00
MO K.Malone/H.Olajuwon/15 75.00 200.00
OD H.Olajuwon/C.Drexler/30 75.00 200.00
RM D.Robinson/K.Malone/15 75.00 200.00
WM S.Webb/H.Miner/30 15.00 40.00

2012-13 Exquisite Collection Endorsements Triple
PRINT RUNS B/WN 10-35 COPIES PER
NO PRICING ON QTY 10
EXCHANGE DEADLINE 10/23/2015
BEJ Russell/Erving/Magic/35 1,500.00 3,000.00
HHK Hill/Hardaway/Kidd/35 150.00 400.00
JHH Jackson/Penny/Hardaway/35 30.00 80.00
JMR Magic/Malone/Robinson/35 150.00 400.00

2012-13 Exquisite Collection Impressions
PRINT RUNS B/WN 5-20 COPIES PER
NO PRICING ON QTY 5
EXCHANGE DEADLINE 10/23/2015
AG A.C. Green/20 15.00 40.00
AH Anfernee Hardaway/20 125.00 300.00
BL Bill Laimbeer/20 12.00 30.00
BR Bryant Reeves/20 12.00 30.00
CD Clyde Drexler/20 75.00 200.00
DC Dave Cowens/20 40.00 100.00
DT David Thompson/20 25.00 60.00
DW Dominique Wilkins/20 50.00 120.00
EH Elvin Hayes/20 20.00 50.00
GH Grant Hill/14 * 60.00 150.00
GHB G.Hill G-Money/6 * 75.00 200.00
HM Harold Miner/20 40.00 100.00
IT Isiah Thomas/20 75.00 200.00
JM Jamal Mashburn/20 30.00 80.00
NT Nate Thurmond/20 30.00 80.00
RO Dennis Rodman/20 125.00 300.00
TK Toni Kukoc/20 40.00 100.00

2012-13 Exquisite Collection Impressions Dual
STATED PRINT RUN 15 SER.#'d SETS
EXCHANGE DEADLINE 10/23/2015
DH Drexler/Hayes 60.00 150.00
DR Drexler/Robinson 75.00 200.00
HC Havlicek/Cowens 300.00 600.00
HH Hill/Hardaway 60.00 150.00
HK Hardaway/Kidd 75.00 200.00
HM Hardaway/Mashburn 60.00 150.00
JE James/Erving 2,000.00 4,000.00
JH James/Hardaway 2,000.00 4,000.00
MD Malone/Drexler 60.00 150.00
MO Malone/Olajuwon 60.00 150.00
MR Malone/Robinson 60.00 150.00
OD Olajuwon/Drexler 75.00 200.00
OH Olajuwon/Hayes 60.00 150.00
OM Olajuwon/Mourning 75.00 200.00
RK Rodman/Kukoc 75.00 200.00
RL Rodman/Laimbeer 75.00 200.00
RO Robinson/Olajuwon 75.00 200.00
RT Rodman/Thurmond 75.00 200.00
TE Thomas/Erving 75.00 200.00
WO Wilkins/Olajuwon 75.00 200.00

2012-13 Exquisite Collection Limited Logos
PRINT RUNS B/WN 10-25 COPIES PER
EXCHANGE DEADLINE 10/23/2015
ALL VERSIONS EQUALLY PRICED
JM Jamal Mashburn 20.00 50.00
TH Tim Hardaway 30.00 80.00
AD1 Adrian Dantley 15.00 40.00
AD2 Adrian Dantley 15.00 40.00
AD3 Adrian Dantley 15.00 40.00
AD4 Adrian Dantley 15.00 40.00
AG1 A.C. Green 10.00 25.00
AG2 A.C. Green 10.00 25.00
AG3 A.C. Green 10.00 25.00
AG4 A.C. Green 10.00 25.00
AH1 Anfernee Hardaway 200.00 500.00
AH2 Anfernee Hardaway 200.00 500.00
AH3 Anfernee Hardaway 200.00 500.00
AH4 Anfernee Hardaway 200.00 500.00
AI1 Allen Iverson EXCH 200.00 500.00
AI2 Allen Iverson EXCH 200.00 500.00
AI3 Allen Iverson EXCH 200.00 500.00
AI4 Allen Iverson EXCH 200.00 500.00
AM1 Alonzo Mourning 75.00 200.00
AM2 Alonzo Mourning 75.00 200.00
AM3 Alonzo Mourning 75.00 200.00
AM4 Alonzo Mourning 75.00 200.00
BR1 Bill Russell 600.00 1,200.00
BR2 Bill Russell 600.00 1,200.00
BR3 Bill Russell 600.00 1,200.00
BR4 Bill Russell 600.00 1,200.00
CD1 Clyde Drexler 75.00 200.00
CD2 Clyde Drexler 75.00 200.00
CD3 Clyde Drexler 75.00 200.00
CD4 Clyde Drexler 75.00 200.00
DR1 David Robinson 100.00 250.00
DR2 David Robinson 100.00 250.00
DR3 David Robinson 100.00 250.00
DR4 David Robinson 100.00 250.00
DW1 Dominique Wilkins 75.00 200.00
DW2 Dominique Wilkins 75.00 200.00
DW3 Dominique Wilkins 75.00 200.00
DW4 Dominique Wilkins 75.00 200.00
GP1 Gary Payton 100.00 250.00
GP2 Gary Payton 100.00 250.00
GP3 Gary Payton 100.00 250.00
GP4 Gary Payton 100.00 250.00
GR1 Glen Rice 12.00 30.00
GR2 Glen Rice 12.00 30.00
GR3 Glen Rice 12.00 30.00
GR4 Glen Rice 12.00 30.00
HG1 Hal Greer 25.00 60.00
HG2 Hal Greer 25.00 60.00
HG3 Hal Greer 25.00 60.00
HG4 Hal Greer 25.00 60.00
HI1 Grant Hill 75.00 200.00
HI2 Grant Hill 75.00 200.00
HI3 Grant Hill 75.00 200.00
HI4 Grant Hill 75.00 200.00
HO1 Hakeem Olajuwon 100.00 250.00
HO2 Hakeem Olajuwon 100.00 250.00
HO3 Hakeem Olajuwon 100.00 250.00
HO4 Hakeem Olajuwon 100.00 250.00
JA1 LeBron James 1,500.00 3,000.00
JA2 LeBron James 1,500.00 3,000.00
JA3 LeBron James 1,500.00 3,000.00
JA4 LeBron James 1,500.00 3,000.00
JE1 Julius Erving 125.00 300.00
JE2 Julius Erving 125.00 300.00
JE3 Julius Erving 125.00 300.00
JE4 Julius Erving 125.00 300.00
JK1 Jason Kidd 75.00 200.00
JK2 Jason Kidd 75.00 200.00
JK3 Jason Kidd 75.00 200.00
JK4 Jason Kidd 75.00 200.00
JO1 Michael Jordan 2,500.00 5,000.00
JO2 Michael Jordan 2,500.00 5,000.00
JO3 Michael Jordan 2,500.00 5,000.00
JO4 Michael Jordan 2,500.00 5,000.00
KM1 Karl Malone 75.00 200.00
KM2 Karl Malone 75.00 200.00
KM3 Karl Malone 75.00 200.00
KM4 Karl Malone 75.00 200.00
LB1 Larry Bird 200.00 500.00
LB2 Larry Bird 200.00 500.00
LB3 Larry Bird 200.00 500.00
LB4 Larry Bird 200.00 500.00
LH1 Lou Hudson 15.00 40.00
LJ1 Larry Johnson 40.00 100.00
LJ2 Larry Johnson 40.00 100.00
LJ3 Larry Johnson 40.00 100.00
LJ4 Larry Johnson 40.00 100.00
MA1 Danny Manning 20.00 50.00
MA2 Danny Manning 20.00 50.00
MA3 Danny Manning 20.00 50.00
MA4 Danny Manning 20.00 50.00
MG1 Magic Johnson 200.00 500.00
MG2 Magic Johnson 200.00 500.00
MG3 Magic Johnson 200.00 500.00
MG4 Magic Johnson 200.00 500.00
MI1 Michael Jordan 2,500.00 5,000.00
MI2 Michael Jordan 2,500.00 5,000.00
MI3 Michael Jordan 2,500.00 5,000.00
MI4 Michael Jordan 2,500.00 5,000.00
MJ1 Michael Jordan 2,500.00 5,000.00
MJ2 Michael Jordan 2,500.00 5,000.00
MJ3 Michael Jordan 2,500.00 5,000.00
MJ4 Michael Jordan 2,500.00 5,000.00
MP1 Mark Price 12.00 30.00
MP2 Mark Price 12.00 30.00
MP3 Mark Price 12.00 30.00
MP4 Mark Price 12.00 30.00
PG1 Paul George EXCH 75.00 200.00
PG2 Paul George EXCH 75.00 200.00
PG3 Paul George EXCH 75.00 200.00
PG4 Paul George EXCH 75.00 200.00
RO1 Dennis Rodman 100.00 250.00
RO2 Dennis Rodman 100.00 250.00
RO3 Dennis Rodman 100.00 250.00
RO4 Dennis Rodman 100.00 250.00
SB1 Shawn Bradley 10.00 25.00
SB2 Shawn Bradley 10.00 25.00
SB3 Shawn Bradley 10.00 25.00
SB4 Shawn Bradley 10.00 25.00
SE1 Sean Elliott 20.00 50.00
SE2 Sean Elliott 20.00 50.00
SE3 Sean Elliott 20.00 50.00
SE4 Sean Elliott 20.00 50.00

2012-13 Exquisite Collection National Championship Trophy Autographs
PRINT RUNS B/WN 15-50 COPIES PER
EXCHANGE DEADLINE 10/23/2015
BR Bill Russell/15 600.00 1,200.00
DM Danny Manning/50 12.00 30.00
GH Grant Hill/15 50.00 120.00
GR Glen Rice/50 12.00 30.00
HI Grant Hill/15 50.00 120.00
JH John Havlicek/15 100.00 250.00
JO Michael Jordan/50 2,000.00 4,000.00
LA Christian Laettner/50 12.00 30.00
MJ Magic Johnson/15 125.00 300.00
RU Bill Russell/15 600.00 1,200.00
WA Bill Walton/50 30.00 80.00

2012-13 Exquisite Collection UD Black Autographs
PRINT RUNS B/WN 15-99 COPIES PER
EXCHANGE DEADLINE 10/23/2015
AH Anfernee Hardaway/15 60.00 150.00
BR Bill Russell/15 600.00 1,200.00
CD Clyde Drexler/15 50.00 120.00
CM Cheryl Miller/15 20.00 50.00
DR David Robinson/15 50.00 120.00
DW Dominique Wilkins/15 40.00 100.00
EJ Eddie Jones/99 15.00 40.00
GP Gary Payton/15 40.00 100.00
HO Hakeem Olajuwon/15 50.00 120.00
JA LeBron James/15 1,500.00 3,000.00
JE Julius Erving/15 60.00 150.00
JK Jason Kidd/15 40.00 100.00
JO Magic Johnson/15 100.00 250.00
KM Karl Malone/15 50.00 120.00
LB Larry Bird/15 100.00 250.00
LJ LeBron James/15 1,500.00 3,000.00
MI Michael Jordan/75 1,500.00 3,000.00
MJ Michael Jordan/75 1,500.00 3,000.00
MR Michael Ray Richardson/99 8.00 20.00
RO Dennis Rodman/15 60.00 150.00
SB Shawn Bradley/99 8.00 20.00

2012-13 Exquisite Collection UD Black Autographs Dual
PRINT RUNS B/WN 10-35 COPIES PER
NO PRICING ON QTY 10
EXCHANGE DEADLINE 10/23/2015
HH Hardaway/Hardaway/35 15.00 40.00
HL Hill/Laettner/35 40.00 80.00
OD Olajuwon/Drexler/35 40.00 80.00
RK Rodman/Kukoc/35 40.00 80.00
RL Rodman/Laimbeer/35 20.00 50.00
RO Rodman/Olajuwon/35 30.00 80.00

2012-13 Exquisite Collection UD Black Leather Autographs Dual
PRINT RUNS B/WN 20-40 COPIES PER
EXCHANGE DEADLINE 10/23/2015
AJ Walker/Mashburn/40 20.00 50.00
BE Bird/Erving/20 100.00 250.00
BH Bird/John Havlicek/20 100.00 250.00
DR Drexler/Richardson/40 15.00 40.00
EJ LeBron/Erving/20 1,500.00 3,000.00
HH Hill/Penny/40 50.00 120.00
HK Penny/Kidd/40 40.00 100.00
HL Hill/Laettner/40 30.00 80.00
JB Jordan/Bird/40 1,000.00 2,000.00
JE Jordan/Erving/40 1,000.00 2,000.00
JJ Jordan/Magic/40 1,500.00 3,000.00
JM Magic/Erving/20 75.00 200.00
KM Kidd/Mashburn/40 20.00 50.00
LJ LeBron/Magic/20 2,000.00 4,000.00
MJ Mourning/Johnson/40 30.00 80.00
MK Malone/Magic/40 60.00 150.00
MM Jordan/Malone/20 300.00 600.00
MO Malone/Olajuwon/20 30.00 80.00
OD Olajuwon/Drexler/40 30.00 80.00
RJ Jordan/Rodman/40 300.00 600.00
RL Laimbeer/Rodman/40 20.00 50.00
RO Robinson/Olajuwon/20 30.00 80.00
WM Wilkins/Malone/20 40.00 100.00

2012-13 Exquisite Collection UD Black Legendary Lustrous
STATED PRINT RUN 25 SER.#'d SETS
AI Allen Iverson 75.00 150.00

2012-13 Exquisite Collection UD Black Old School Autographs
PRINT RUNS B/WN 25-75 COPIES PER
EXCHANGE DEADLINE 10/23/2015
BR Bill Russell 1,000.00 2,000.00
CW Chet Walker 4.00 10.00
DR Dennis Rodman 20.00 50.00
HO Hakeem Olajuwon 20.00 50.00
JE Julius Erving 40.00 80.00
JH John Havlicek 20.00 50.00
JO Magic Johnson 50.00 120.00
LB Larry Bird 40.00 80.00
LH Lou Hudson 8.00 20.00
MJ Michael Jordan 2,000.00 4,000.00
RT Reggie Theus 5.00 12.00
SN Swen Nater 4.00 10.00
OSMI Michael Jordan
released in 14-15 SP Authentic 2,000.00 4,000.00

2013-14 Exquisite Collection
STATED PRINT RUN 75 SER.#'d SETS
AU PRINT RUN B/WN 60-99 COPIES PER
JSY AU PRINT RUN B/WN 99-199 COPIES PER
EXCHANGE DEADLINE 10/10/2016
1 Michael Jordan 50.00 120.00
2 LeBron James 20.00 50.00
3 Allen Iverson 5.00 12.00
4 Rajon Rondo 3.00 8.00
5 Robert Horry 2.50 6.00
6 Glenn Robinson 2.00 5.00
7 Tony Gwynn 2.50 6.00
8 Dennis Rodman 6.00 15.00
9 Joe Smith 2.00 5.00
10 Elvin Hayes 3.00 8.00
11 Jamal Mashburn 2.00 5.00
12 Alex English 3.00 8.00
13 Antoine Walker 2.00 5.00
14 David Thompson 2.50 6.00
15 Cheryl Miller 2.50 6.00
16 Bill Laimbeer 2.50 6.00
17 Toni Kukoc 3.00 8.00
18 Jerry Stackhouse 2.00 5.00
19 Grant Hill 3.00 8.00
20 Harold Miner 1.50 4.00
21 Allan Houston 2.50 6.00
22 Tim Hardaway 3.00 8.00
23 Alonzo Mourning 4.00 10.00
24 Anfernee Hardaway 6.00 15.00
25 Glen Rice 2.00 5.00
26 Otis Birdsong 2.00 5.00
27 Kenny Anderson 2.00 5.00

28 Micheal Ray Richardson 2.00 5.00
29 Keith Smart 2.50 6.00
30 Christian Laettner 2.50 6.00
31 Isiah Thomas 4.00 10.00
32 Dave Cowens 2.50 6.00
33 Bill Walton 4.00 10.00
34 Danny Manning 2.00 5.00
35 Shawn Bradley 1.50 4.00
36 Paul George 4.00 10.00
37 Bill Russell 8.00 20.00
38 David Robinson 5.00 12.00
39 Derek Harper 2.00 5.00
40 Jerry Lucas 2.50 6.00
41 Hakeem Olajuwon 5.00 12.00
42 Larry Bird 10.00 25.00
43 Jason Kidd 4.00 10.00
44 LaPhonso Ellis 1.50 4.00
45 Jay Williams 1.50 4.00
46 Julius Erving 6.00 15.00
47 Karl Malone 5.00 12.00
48 Larry Johnson 3.00 8.00
49 Dominique Wilkins 4.00 10.00
50 James Harden 5.00 12.00
51 Isaiah Canaan AU/60 4.00 10.00
52 Nemanja Nedovic AU/60 4.00 10.00
54 Mike Muscala AU/60 6.00 15.00
55 Erick Green AU/60 5.00 12.00
56 Ryan Kelly AU/60 4.00 10.00
57 Lorenzo Brown AU/60 4.00 10.00
58 Allen Crabbe JSY AU/199 6.00 15.00
59 Mason Plumlee JSY AU/199 8.00 20.00
60 Rudy Gobert JSY AU/199 40.00 100.00
61 Lucas Nogueira JSY AU/199 6.00 15.00
62 Livio Jean-Charles JSY AU/199 6.00 15.00
63 Reggie Bullock JSY AU/199 8.00 20.00
64 Pierre Jackson JSY AU/199 6.00 15.00
65 Solomon Hill JSY AU/199 8.00 20.00
66 Tony Snell JSY AU/199 8.00 20.00
67 Dennis Schroeder JSY AU/199 20.00 50.00
68 Andre Roberson JSY AU/199 8.00 20.00
69 Sergey Karasev JSY AU/199 6.00 15.00
70 Archie Goodwin JSY AU/199 6.00 15.00
71 Peyton Siva JSY AU/199 6.00 15.00
72 Jamaal Franklin JSY AU/199 6.00 15.00
74 Deshaun Thomas JSY AU/199 6.00 15.00
75 Grant Jerrett JSY AU/199 6.00 15.00
76 G.Antetokounmpo AU/99 1,500.00 3,000.00
77 Skylar Diggins JSY AU/99 12.00 30.00
78 Tim Hardaway Jr. JSY AU/99 12.00 30.00

2013-14 Exquisite Collection Silver

*SILVER: .5X TO 1.2X BASE

2013-14 Exquisite Collection '03-04 Tribute Autographs

STATED PRINT RUN 35 SER.#'d SETS
EXCHANGE DEADLINE 10/10/2016
78DR David Robinson 50.00 120.00
78GH Grant Hill 50.00 120.00
78GL Glenn Robinson 15.00 40.00
78GR Glen Rice 15.00 40.00
78JE Julius Erving 75.00 200.00
78JK Jason Kidd 50.00 120.00
78JM Jamal Mashburn 15.00 40.00
78JS Joe Smith
released in 14-15 SP Authentic 12.00 30.00
78KM Karl Malone 50.00 120.00
78LB Larry Bird 75.00 200.00
78LU Andrew Luck 500.00 1,000.00
78MA Magic Johnson 75.00 200.00
78MJ Michael Jordan 1,000.00 3,000.00
78OL Oscar De La Hoya 100.00 250.00
78RO Dennis Rodman 30.00 80.00
78RR Rajon Rondo 30.00 80.00
78TH Tim Hardaway 25.00 60.00

2013-14 Exquisite Collection '03-04 Tribute Patch Autographs

STATED PRINT RUN 35 SER.#'d SETS
EXCHANGE DEADLINE 10/10/2016
78AH Anfernee Hardaway 125.00 300.00
78AL Allan Houston 20.00 50.00
78AM Alonzo Mourning 60.00 150.00
78BD Brad Daugherty 20.00 50.00
78BW Bill Walton 60.00 150.00
78CL Christian Laettner 40.00 100.00
78CM Danny Manning 30.00 80.00
78CW Corliss Williamson 10.00 25.00
78DM Donyell Marshall 20.00 50.00
78JH James Harden EXCH 500.00 1,000.00
78JL Jerry Lucas 25.00 60.00
78JO Larry Johnson 60.00 150.00
78JW Jay Williams 40.00 100.00
78KA Kenny Anderson 20.00 50.00
78LJ LeBron James 10,000.00 20,000.00
78MR Micheal Ray Richardson 20.00 50.00
78PG Paul George 125.00 300.00
78SP Sam Perkins 30.00 80.00
78ST Jerry Stackhouse 50.00 120.00

2013-14 Exquisite Collection '14-15 Rookie Autographs

STATED PRINT RUN 99 SER.#'d SETS
EXCHANGE DEADLINE 10/10/2016
RAG Aaron Gordon 25.00 60.00
RAP Adreian Payne 6.00 15.00
RCW C.J. Wilcox 6.00 15.00
RDM Doug McDermott 10.00 25.00
RDS Dario Saric 20.00 50.00
REP Elfrid Payton 10.00 25.00
RGH Gary Harris 20.00 50.00
RGR Glenn Robinson III 6.00 15.00
RJA Jordan Adams 6.00 15.00
RJN Jusuf Nurkic 20.00 50.00
RJY James Young 6.00 15.00
RMM Mitch McGary 6.00 15.00
RNM Nikola Mirotic 12.00 30.00
RNS Nik Stauskas 6.00 15.00
RRH Rodney Hood 12.00 30.00
RSN Shabazz Napier 6.00 15.00
RTW T.J. Warren 15.00 40.00
RZL Zach LaVine 40.00 100.00

2013-14 Exquisite Collection '14-15 Rookie Autographs Spectrum

*SPECTRUM: .6X TO 1.5X BASE HI
STATED PRINT RUN 25 SER.#'d SETS
EXCHANGE DEADLINE 10/10/2016
RGH Gary Harris 60.00 150.00
RZL Zach LaVine 75.00 200.00

2013-14 Exquisite Collection Dimensions Autographs

EXCHANGE DEADLINE 10/10/2016
DAE Alex English 12.00 30.00
DAH Anfernee Hardaway 25.00 60.00
DAM Alonzo Mourning 15.00 40.00
DBR Bill Russell 1,000.00 2,000.00
DBW Bill Walton 8.00 20.00
DCL Christian Laettner 10.00 25.00
DDC Dave Cowens 6.00 15.00
DDM Danny Manning 8.00 20.00
DDR Dennis Rodman 10.00 25.00
DDT David Thompson 10.00 25.00
DEH Elvin Hayes 6.00 15.00
DGL Glenn Robinson 6.00 15.00
DGR Glen Rice 8.00 20.00
DHO Hakeem Olajuwon 20.00 50.00
DJH James Harden 20.00 50.00
DJK Jason Kidd 15.00 40.00
DJL Jerry Lucas 10.00 25.00
DJN Michael Jordan 250.00 500.00
DJO Larry Johnson 12.00 30.00
DJS Jerry Stackhouse 20.00 50.00
DKA Kenny Anderson 8.00 20.00
DKM Karl Malone 20.00 50.00
DLB Larry Bird 40.00 100.00
DLJ LeBron James 1,500.00 3,000.00
DMA Magic Johnson 40.00 100.00
DMI Michael Jordan 250.00 500.00
DMJ Michael Jordan 250.00 500.00
DMR Micheal Ray Richardson 6.00 15.00
DPG Paul George 20.00 50.00
DRO David Robinson 20.00 50.00
DSA Stacey Augmon 6.00 15.00
DSP Sam Perkins 10.00 25.00
DTC Toni Kukoc 12.00 30.00
DTH Tim Hardaway 6.00 15.00

2013-14 Exquisite Collection Enshrinements

PRINT RUNS B/WN 23-60 COPIES PER
EXCHANGE DEADLINE 10/10/2016
EEAH Allan Houston/60 6.00 15.00
EEAM Alonzo Mourning/60 12.00 30.00
EEBR Bill Russell/25 1,000.00 2,000.00
EECL Christian Laettner/60 10.00 25.00
EEDC Dave Cowens/60 6.00 15.00
EEDM Danny Manning/60 5.00 12.00
EEDR Dennis Rodman/25 15.00 40.00
EEEH Elvin Hayes/60 8.00 20.00
EEGH Grant Hill/25 20.00 50.00
EEHA Anfernee Hardaway/25 25.00 60.00
EEHM Harold Miner/60 4.00 10.00
EEHO Hakeem Olajuwon/25 15.00 40.00
EEJE Julius Erving/25 60.00 150.00
EEJH James Harden/25 20.00 50.00
EEJK Jason Kidd/25 15.00 40.00
EEJL Jerry Lucas/60 8.00 20.00
EEJM Jamal Mashburn/60 12.00 30.00
EEJO Michael Jordan/23 400.00 800.00
EEJW Jay Williams/60 4.00 10.00
EEKM Karl Malone/25 20.00 50.00
EELB Larry Bird/25 50.00 120.00
EELJ LeBron James/23 1,500.00 3,000.00
EELS Lonnie Shelton/60 4.00 10.00
EEMI Michael Jordan/23 400.00 800.00
EEMJ Magic Johnson/25 30.00 80.00
EEPG Paul George/60 15.00 40.00
EERH Robert Horry/60 6.00 15.00
EERO David Robinson/60 20.00 50.00
EERR Rajon Rondo/60 10.00 25.00
EESP Sam Perkins/60 5.00 12.00
EETH Tim Hardaway/60 8.00 20.00
EETK Toni Kukoc/60 8.00 20.00

2013-14 Exquisite Collection Exquisite Signatures

PRINT RUNS B/WN 23-65 COPIES PER
EXCHANGE DEADLINE 10/10/2016
ESAH Allan Houston/65 6.00 15.00
ESAM Alonzo Mourning/65 15.00 40.00
ESBR Bill Russell/25 1,000.00 2,000.00
ESBW Buck Williams/65 8.00 20.00
ESCC Calbert Cheaney/65 4.00 10.00
ESDC Dave Cowens/65 6.00 15.00
ESDH Derek Harper/65 5.00 12.00
ESDM Donyell Marshall/65 4.00 10.00
ESDR Dennis Rodman/65 20.00 50.00
ESDT David Thompson/65 6.00 15.00
ESGH Grant Hill/65 20.00 50.00
ESGR Glenn Robinson/65 5.00 12.00
ESHA Anfernee Hardaway/65 15.00 40.00
ESHO Hakeem Olajuwon/65 40.00 100.00
ESJE Julius Erving/25 40.00 100.00
ESJH James Harden/25 75.00 200.00
ESJK Jason Kidd/65 15.00 40.00
ESJL Jerry Lucas/65 10.00 25.00
ESJO Michael Jordan/23 1,500.00 3,000.00
ESJW Jay Williams/65 10.00 25.00
ESKA Kenny Anderson/65 5.00 12.00
ESKM Karl Malone/65 12.00 30.00
ESLA Larry Johnson/65 8.00 20.00
ESLB Larry Bird/25 100.00 250.00
ESLJ LeBron James/23 1,500.00 3,000.00
ESMA Magic Johnson/25 40.00 100.00
ESMI Cheryl Miller/65 6.00 15.00
ESMJ Michael Jordan/23 300.00 500.00
ESMR Micheal Ray Richardson/65 5.00 12.00
ESPG Paul George/65 20.00 50.00
ESRI Glen Rice/65 5.00 12.00
ESRR Rajon Rondo/25 25.00 60.00
ESSA Stacey Augmon/65 8.00 20.00
ESSD Skylar Diggins/65 20.00 50.00
ESTH Tim Hardaway/65 8.00 20.00

2013-14 Exquisite Collection Game Face Autograph Booklets

EXCHANGE DEADLINE 10/10/2016
GFAL Allan Houston 6.00 15.00
GFAH Anfernee Hardaway 10.00 25.00
GFAM Alonzo Mourning 12.00 30.00
GFAW Antoine Walker 15.00 40.00
GFBR Bill Russell 600.00 1,200.00
GFBW Bill Walton 10.00 25.00
GFCL Christian Laettner 10.00 25.00
GFDM Danny Manning 10.00 25.00
GFDR David Robinson 15.00 40.00
GFDT David Thompson 6.00 15.00
GFEH Elvin Hayes 8.00 20.00
GFGH Grant Hill 20.00 50.00
GFGL Glenn Robinson 5.00 12.00
GFGR Glen Rice 15.00 40.00
GFHO Hakeem Olajuwon 15.00 40.00
GFJE Julius Erving 30.00 30.00
GFJH James Harden 15.00 40.00
GFJO Larry Johnson 8.00 20.00
GFKA Kenny Anderson 5.00 12.00
GFLB Larry Bird 50.00 100.00
GFLJ LeBron James 1,500.00 3,000.00
GFMI Michael Jordan 400.00 800.00
GFMJ Michael Jordan 400.00 800.00
GFPG Paul George 15.00 40.00
GFRR Rajon Rondo 15.00 40.00
GFSA Stacey Augmon 8.00 20.00
GFTH Tim Hardaway 8.00 20.00

2013-14 Exquisite Collection Game Face Autograph Booklets Dual

EXCHANGE DEADLINE 10/10/2016
GFDHH G.Hill/A.Hardaway 40.00 100.00
GFDJA S.Augmon/L.Johnson 30.00 80.00
GFDJB L.Bird/M.Johnson 100.00 250.00
GFDJR M.Jordan/D.Rodman 200.00 500.00
GFDLL LeBron James
LeBron James 2,500.00 5,000.00
GFDMM Michael Jordan
Michael Jordan 800.00 1,500.00
GFDRO D.Robinson/H.Olajuwon 40.00 100.00
GFDRR D.Robinson/B.Russell 600.00 1,200.00

2013-14 Exquisite Collection Limited Logos

STATED PRINT RUN 25 SER.#'d SETS
LLHJ Tim Hardaway Jr. 30.00 80.00
LLMP Mason Plumlee 20.00 50.00
LLSD Skylar Diggins 30.00 80.00

2013-14 Exquisite Collection Rookie Autographs

STATED PRINT RUN 75 SER.#'d SETS
EXCHANGE DEADLINE 10/10/2016
R1 Reggie Bullock 6.00 15.00
R2 Andre Roberson 6.00 15.00
R3 Solomon Hill 6.00 15.00
R4 Allen Crabbe 5.00 12.00
R5 Jamaal Franklin 5.00 12.00
R6 Mason Plumlee 6.00 15.00
R7 Shane Larkin 5.00 12.00
R8 Lucas Nogueira 5.00 12.00
R9 Livio Jean-Charles 5.00 12.00
R10 Tim Hardaway Jr. 10.00 25.00
R11 Giannis Antetokounmpo 1,000.00 2,000.00
R12 Tony Snell 6.00 15.00
R13 Archie Goodwin 5.00 12.00
R14 Sergey Karasev 5.00 12.00
R15 Skylar Diggins 8.00 20.00
R16 Deshaun Thomas 5.00 12.00
R17 Rudy Gobert 25.00 60.00
R18 Dennis Schroeder 15.00 40.00

2013-14 Exquisite Collection Rookie Autographs Black

*BLACK: .4X TO 1X BASE HI
EXCHANGE DEADLINE 10/10/2016

2013-14 Exquisite Collection Signatures

*VETS: 1.5X TO 4X BASE HI
EXCHANGE DEADLINE 10/10/2016
37 Bill Russell 800.00 1,500.00
41 Hakeem Olajuwon 15.00 40.00
46 Julius Erving 20.00 50.00

2013-14 Exquisite Collection Signatures Black

*BLACK: 2X TO 5X BASE HI
EXCHANGE DEADLINE 10/10/2016
1 Michael Jordan 1,000.00 2,000.00
2 LeBron James 1,500.00 3,000.00
4 Rajon Rondo 15.00 40.00
18 Jerry Stackhouse 25.00 60.00
23 Alonzo Mourning 40.00 100.00
24 Anfernee Hardaway 30.00 80.00
36 Paul George 20.00 50.00
37 Bill Russell 800.00 1,500.00
38 David Robinson 25.00 60.00
41 Hakeem Olajuwon 25.00 60.00
42 Larry Bird 30.00 80.00
43 Jason Kidd 15.00 40.00
45 Jay Williams 8.00 20.00
46 Julius Erving 30.00 80.00
47 Karl Malone 25.00 60.00
48 Larry Johnson 15.00 40.00
50 James Harden 20.00 50.00

2013-14 Exquisite Collection Signature Kicks Foundations

STATED PRINT RUN 35 SER.#'d SETS
*SOLES/35: .4X TO 1X FOUNDATIONS
EXCHANGE DEADLINE 10/10/2016
SFAH Anfernee Hardaway 50.00 120.00
SFBR Bill Russell 1,000.00 2,000.00
SFDR David Robinson 25.00 60.00
SFGH Grant Hill 30.00 80.00
SFHA Anfernee Hardaway 50.00 120.00
SFJA LeBron James 2,000.00 4,000.00
SFJE Julius Erving 40.00 100.00
SFJH James Harden 30.00 80.00
SFJK Jason Kidd 25.00 60.00
SFJO Michael Jordan 800.00 1,500.00
SFLA Larry Johnson 15.00 40.00
SFLB Larry Bird 60.00 150.00
SFLJ LeBron James 2,000.00 4,000.00
SFMA Magic Johnson 40.00 100.00
SFPG Paul George 25.00 60.00
SFRO Dennis Rodman 30.00 80.00
SFTH Tim Hardaway 15.00 40.00

2014 Exquisite Collection

8 Michael Jordan 30.00 80.00

2014 Exquisite Collection Endorsements

STATED PRINT RUN 25-75

2014 Exquisite Collection Signature Masterpieces

GROUP A STATED ODDS 1:37
GROUP B STATED ODDS 1:12
GROUP C STATED ODDS 1:5
GROUP D STATED ODDS 1:2
OVERALL ODDS 1 PER TIN
ESMMJ Michael Jordan A 300.00 400.00

1991 Farley's Fruit Snacks Jordan

COMPLETE SET (4) 6.00 15.00
COMMON CARD (1-4) 2.00 5.00

2009-10 Fathead Tradeables

1 LeBron James 8.00 20.00
2 Kobe Bryant 8.00 20.00
3 Dwight Howard 1.25 3.00
4 Kevin Garnett 2.50 6.00
5 Chauncey Billups 1.25 3.00
6 Al Jefferson .60 1.50
7 Greg Oden .60 1.50
8 Deron Williams .75 2.00
9 Mo Williams .75 2.00
10 Yao Ming 2.50 6.00
11 Chris Paul 2.00 5.00
12 Steve Nash 2.00 5.00
13 Antawn Jamison .75 2.00
14 Manu Ginobili 2.00 5.00
15 Ray Allen 1.50 4.00
16 Baron Davis .75 2.00
17 Elton Brand .75 2.00
18 Joe Johnson 1.00 2.50
19 Kevin Durant 4.00 10.00
20 Tony Parker 1.50 4.00
21 Ben Gordon .75 2.00
22 Gerald Wallace .75 2.00
23 Michael Redd .75 2.00
24 Pau Gasol 1.50 4.00
25 Brandon Roy 1.25 3.00
26 Gilbert Arenas .75 2.00
27 Jason Kidd 1.50 4.00
28 Paul Pierce 1.50 4.00
29 Richard Hamilton 1.00 2.50
30 Amare Stoudemire .75 2.00
31 Kevin Martin .75 2.00
32 Dwyane Wade 2.00 5.00
33 Vince Carter 2.00 5.00
34 Derrick Rose 1.50 4.00
35 Blake Griffin 4.00 10.00
36 Josh Smith .60 1.50
37 Shaquille O'Neal 3.00 8.00
38 Carmelo Anthony 1.50 4.00
39 David Lee .60 1.50
40 Russell Westbrook 2.00 5.00
41 Tayshaun Prince 1.00 2.50
42 Andre Iguodala 1.00 2.50
43 Danny Granger .60 1.50
44 Tracy McGrady 2.00 5.00
45 Monta Ellis .75 2.00
46 O.J. Mayo .60 1.50
47 Dirk Nowitzki 2.50 6.00
48 Devin Harris .60 1.50
49 Chris Bosh 1.25 3.00
50 Tim Duncan 2.50 6.00

2010-11 Fathead Tradeables

1 Kobe Bryant 8.00 20.00
2 Rajon Rondo 1.25 3.00
3 Kevin Durant 4.00 10.00
4 Dwyane Wade 2.00 5.00
5 Dwight Howard 1.25 3.00
6 Derrick Rose 2.00 5.00
7 Dirk Nowitzki 2.50 6.00
8 Antawn Jamison .75 2.00
9 Andre Iguodala 1.00 2.50
10 Carmelo Anthony 1.50 4.00
11 Brandon Jennings .60 1.50
12 Chauncey Billups 1.25 3.00
13 Stephen Curry 8.00 20.00
14 Mo Williams .75 2.00
15 Evan Turner .75 2.00
16 Devin Harris .60 1.50
17 Kevin Garnett 2.50 6.00
18 Jason Kidd 1.50 4.00
19 Brandon Roy 1.25 3.00
20 Kevin Martin .75 2.00
21 Chris Paul 2.00 5.00
22 Rudy Gay 1.00 2.50
23 Vince Carter 2.00 5.00
24 Aaron Brooks .60 1.50
25 Jason Richardson 1.00 2.50
26 Danny Granger .60 1.50
27 LaMarcus Aldridge 1.00 2.50
28 Joe Johnson 1.00 2.50
29 Manu Ginobili 2.00 5.00
30 Deron Williams .75 2.00
31 Ray Allen 1.50 4.00
32 Michael Beasley .60 1.50
33 Eric Gordon .75 2.00
34 Pau Gasol 1.50 4.00
35 Paul Pierce 1.50 4.00
36 Chris Bosh 1.25 3.00
37 Monta Ellis .75 2.00
38 J.J. Hickson .60 1.50
39 Andrea Bargnani .60 1.50
40 Steve Nash 2.00 5.00
41 Joakim Noah 1.00 2.50
42 Tyreke Evans .75 2.00
43 Tim Duncan 2.50 6.00
44 Shaquille O'Neal 4.00 10.00
45 David West .75 2.00
46 Russell Westbrook 1.50 4.00
47 Amare Stoudemire 1.00 2.50
48 Richard Hamilton 1.25 3.00
49 John Wall 3.00 8.00
50 Gerald Wallace .75 2.00

1993-94 Finest

COMPLETE SET (220) 100.00 250.00
1 Michael Jordan 60.00 150.00
2 Larry Bird 6.00 15.00
3 Shaquille O'Neal 2.00 5.00
4 Benoit Benjamin .40 1.00
5 Ricky Pierce .50 1.25
6 Ken Norman .40 1.00
7 Victor Alexander .40 1.00
8 Mark Jackson .50 1.25
9 Mark West .40 1.00
10 Don MacLean .40 1.00
11 Reggie Miller 1.25 3.00
12 Sarunas Marciulionis .60 1.50
13 Craig Ehlo .40 1.00
14 Toni Kukoc RC 1.50 4.00
15 Glen Rice .60 1.50
16 Otis Thorpe .60 1.50
17 Reggie Williams .40 1.00
18 Charles Smith .40 1.00
19 Micheal Williams .40 1.00
20 Tom Chambers .60 1.50
21 David Robinson 1.25 3.00
22 Jamal Mashburn RC 1.25 3.00
23 Clifford Robinson .60 1.50
24 Acie Earl RC .60 1.50
25 Danny Ferry .40 1.00
26 Bobby Hurley RC .60 1.50
27 Eddie Johnson .40 1.00
28 Detlef Schrempf .60 1.50
29 Mike Brown .40 1.00
30 Latrell Sprewell 1.00 2.50
31 Derek Harper .50 1.25
32 Stacey Augmon .50 1.25
33 Pooh Richardson .50 1.25
34 Larry Krystkowiak .40 1.00
35 Pervis Ellison .40 1.00
36 Jeff Malone .50 1.25
37 Sean Elliott .60 1.50
38 John Paxson .60 1.50
39 Robert Parish .75 2.00
40 Mark Aguirre .50 1.25
41 Danny Ainge .60 1.50
42 Brian Shaw .40 1.00
43 LaPhonso Ellis .50 1.25
44 Carl Herrera .40 1.00
45 Terry Cummings .50 1.25
46 Chris Dudley .40 1.00
47 Anthony Mason .50 1.25
48 Chris Morris .40 1.00
49 Todd Day .40 1.00
50 Nick Van Exel RC 1.50 4.00
51 Larry Nance .50 1.25
52 Derrick McKey .50 1.25
53 Muggsy Bogues .60 1.50
54 Andrew Lang .40 1.00
55 Chuck Person .50 1.25
56 Michael Adams .50 1.25
57 Spud Webb .50 1.25
58 Scott Skiles .40 1.00
59 A.C. Green .50 1.25
60 Terry Mills .40 1.00
61 Xavier McDaniel .60 1.50
62 B.J. Armstrong .60 1.50
63 Donald Hodge .40 1.00
64 Gary Grant .40 1.00
65 Billy Owens .50 1.25
66 Greg Anthony .40 1.00
67 Jay Humphries .50 1.25
68 Lionel Simmons .40 1.00
69 Dana Barros .40 1.00
70 Steve Smith .50 1.25
71 Ervin Johnson RC .60 1.50
72 Sleepy Floyd .50 1.25
73 Blue Edwards .40 1.00
74 Clyde Drexler 1.00 2.50
75 Elden Campbell .40 1.00
76 Hakeem Olajuwon 1.25 3.00
77 Clarence Weatherspoon .40 1.00
78 Kevin Willis .50 1.25
79 Isaiah Rider RC 1.00 2.50
80 Derrick Coleman .60 1.50
81 Nick Anderson .50 1.25
82 Bryant Stith .40 1.00
83 Johnny Newman .40 1.00
84 Calbert Cheaney RC .60 1.50
85 Oliver Miller .40 1.00
86 Loy Vaught .40 1.00
87 Isiah Thomas 1.00 2.50
88 Dee Brown .50 1.25
89 Horace Grant .60 1.50
90 Patrick Ewing AF 1.00 2.50
91 Clarence Weatherspoon AF .40 1.00
92 Rony Seikaly AF .50 1.25
93 Dino Radja AF .60 1.50
94 Kenny Anderson AF .50 1.25
95 John Starks AF .60 1.50
96 Tom Gugliotta AF .50 1.25
97 Steve Smith AF .50 1.25
98 Derrick Coleman AF .60 1.50
99 Shaquille O'Neal AF 3.00 8.00
100 Brad Daugherty CF .50 1.25
101 Horace Grant CF .60 1.50
102 Dominique Wilkins CF 1.00 2.50
103 Joe Dumars CF .75 2.00
104 Alonzo Mourning CF 1.00 2.50
105 Scottie Pippen CF 1.50 4.00
106 Reggie Miller CF 1.25 3.00
107 Mark Price CF .60 1.50
108 Ken Norman CF .40 1.00
109 Larry Johnson CF .75 2.00
110 Jamal Mashburn MF 1.25 3.00
111 Christian Laettner MF .60 1.50
112 Karl Malone MF 1.25 3.00
113 Dennis Rodman MF 1.50 4.00
114 Mahmoud Abdul-Rauf MF .50 1.25
115 Hakeem Olajuwon MF 1.25 3.00
116 Jim Jackson MF .50 1.25
117 John Stockton MF 1.25 3.00
118 David Robinson MF 1.25 3.00
119 Dikembe Mutombo MF 1.00 2.50
120 Vlade Divac PF .60 1.50
121 Dan Majerle PF .60 1.50
122 Chris Mullin PF .75 2.00
123 Shawn Kemp PF 1.00 2.50
124 Danny Manning PF .50 1.25
125 Charles Barkley PF 1.50 4.00
126 Mitch Richmond PF .75 2.00
127 Tim Hardaway PF .75 2.00
128 Detlef Schrempf PF .60 1.50
129 Clyde Drexler PF 1.00 2.50
130 Christian Laettner .60 1.50
131 Rodney Rogers RC .60 1.50
132 Rik Smits .50 1.25
133 Chris Mills RC .60 1.50
134 Corie Blount RC .60 1.50
135 Mookie Blaylock .60 1.50
136 Jim Jackson .50 1.25
137 Tom Gugliotta .50 1.25
138 Dennis Scott .40 1.00
139 Vin Baker RC 1.00 2.50
140 Gary Payton .75 2.00
141 Sedale Threatt .40 1.00
142 Orlando Woolridge .40 1.00
143 Avery Johnson .50 1.25
144 Charles Oakley .60 1.50
145 Harvey Grant .50 1.25
146 Bimbo Coles .40 1.00
147 Vernon Maxwell .50 1.25
148 Danny Manning .50 1.25
149 Hersey Hawkins .50 1.25
150 Kevin Gamble .40 1.00
151 Johnny Dawkins .50 1.25
152 Olden Polynice .40 1.00
153 Kevin Edwards .40 1.00
154 Willie Anderson .40 1.00
155 Wayman Tisdale .50 1.25
156 Popeye Jones RC .60 1.50
157 Dan Majerle .60 1.50
158 Rex Chapman .40 1.00
159 Shawn Kemp UER 136 1.00 2.50
160 Eric Murdock .40 1.00
161 Randy White .40 1.00
162 Larry Johnson .75 2.00
163 Dominique Wilkins 1.00 2.50
164 Dikembe Mutombo 1.00 2.50
165 Patrick Ewing 1.00 2.50
166 Jerome Kersey .50 1.25
167 Dale Davis .50 1.25
168 Ron Harper .60 1.50
169 Sam Cassell RC 1.25 3.00
170 Bill Cartwright .50 1.25
171 John Williams .40 1.00
172 Dino Radja RC .60 1.50
173 Dennis Rodman 1.50 4.00
174 Kenny Anderson .50 1.25
175 Robert Horry .60 1.50
176 Chris Mullin .75 2.00
177 John Salley .50 1.25
178 Scott Burrell RC .60 1.50
179 Mitch Richmond .75 2.00
180 Lee Mayberry .40 1.00
181 James Worthy .75 2.00
182 Rick Fox .50 1.25
183 Kevin Johnson .60 1.50
184 Lindsey Hunter RC .60 1.50
185 Marlon Maxey .40 1.00
186 Sam Perkins .50 1.25
187 Kevin Duckworth .50 1.25
188 Jeff Hornacek .50 1.25
189 Anfernee Hardaway RC 8.00 20.00
190 Rex Walters RC .50 1.25
191 Mahmoud Abdul-Rauf .50 1.25
192 Terry Dehere RC .60 1.50
193 Brad Daugherty .50 1.25
194 John Starks .60 1.50
195 Rod Strickland .50 1.25
196 Luther Wright RC .40 1.00
197 Vlade Divac .60 1.50
198 Tim Hardaway .75 2.00
199 Joe Dumars .75 2.00
200 Charles Barkley 1.50 4.00
201 Alonzo Mourning 1.00 2.50
202 Doug West .40 1.00
203 Anthony Avent .40 1.00
204 Lloyd Daniels .40 1.00
205 Mark Price .60 1.50
206 Rumeal Robinson .40 1.00
207 Kendall Gill .50 1.25
208 Scottie Pippen 1.50 4.00
209 Kenny Smith .50 1.25
210 Walt Williams .60 1.50
211 Hubert Davis .50 1.25
212 Chris Webber RC 8.00 20.00
213 Rony Seikaly .50 1.25
214 Sam Bowie .50 1.25
215 Karl Malone 1.25 3.00
216 Malik Sealy .40 1.00
217 Dale Ellis .40 1.00
218 Harold Miner .50 1.25
219 John Stockton 1.25 3.00
220 Shawn Bradley RC .60 1.50

1993-94 Finest Refractors

SP (10/35/40/47/49/53) 2.00 5.00
SP (56/190/204/218) 2.00 5.00
SP (33/36/41/91/116/128) 3.00 8.00
SP (147/155/180/211/217) 3.00 8.00
SP (7/12/48/64/66/105/170/182) 10.00 25.00
*VETS: 2X TO 5X BASIC CARDS
*SUBSETS: 2X TO 5X BASIC CARDS
*ROOKIES: 2X TO 5X BASIC CARDS
STATED ODDS 1:9 HOBBY, 1:4 JUMBO
1 Michael Jordan 800.00 1,500.00
2 Larry Bird 60.00 150.00
3 Shaquille O'Neal SP ! 125.00 300.00
11 Reggie Miller SP 12.00 30.00
12 Sarunas Marciulionis SP 12.00 30.00
14 Toni Kukoc 30.00 80.00
21 David Robinson 20.00 50.00
30 Latrell Sprewell 8.00 20.00
33 Pooh Richardson SP 10.00 25.00
35 Pervis Ellison SP 8.00 20.00
50 Nick Van Exel ! 20.00 50.00
53 Muggsy Bogues SP 8.00 20.00
57 Spud Webb SP 4.00 10.00
74 Clyde Drexler SP 20.00 50.00
76 Hakeem Olajuwon 25.00 60.00
78 Kevin Willis SP 20.00 50.00
84 Calbert Cheaney SP 20.00 50.00
87 Isiah Thomas 15.00 40.00
89 Horace Grant SP 4.00 10.00
90 Patrick Ewing AF 15.00 40.00
99 Shaquille O'Neal AF 40.00 100.00
102 Dominique Wilkins CF 10.00 25.00
104 Alonzo Mourning CF 12.00 30.00
105 Scottie Pippen CF SP 75.00 200.00
106 Reggie Miller CF SP 10.00 25.00
112 Karl Malone MF 12.00 30.00
113 Dennis Rodman MF SP ! 30.00 80.00
115 Hakeem Olajuwon MF 20.00 50.00
117 John Stockton MF 12.00 30.00
118 David Robinson MF SP 20.00 50.00
123 Shawn Kemp PF 15.00 40.00
125 Charles Barkley PF 15.00 40.00
129 Clyde Drexler PF 12.00 30.00
133 Chris Mills SP 8.00 20.00
140 Gary Payton SP 20.00 50.00
142 Orlando Woolridge SP 6.00 15.00
155 Wayman Tisdale SP 12.00 30.00
159 Shawn Kemp UER 136 15.00 40.00
163 Dominique Wilkins 12.00 30.00
165 Patrick Ewing SP 25.00 60.00
170 Bill Cartwright SP 12.00 30.00
172 Dino Radja 6.00 15.00
173 Dennis Rodman SP 30.00 80.00
176 Chris Mullin 4.00 10.00
181 James Worthy 8.00 20.00
189 Anfernee Hardaway 75.00 200.00
198 Tim Hardaway 4.00 10.00
200 Charles Barkley 30.00 80.00
201 Alonzo Mourning 12.00 30.00
208 Scottie Pippen SP 75.00 200.00
211 Hubert Davis SP 5.00 12.00
212 Chris Webber SP ! 75.00 200.00
215 Karl Malone 25.00 60.00
217 Dale Ellis SP 20.00 50.00
219 John Stockton 25.00 60.00

1993-94 Finest Main Attraction

COMPLETE SET (27) 15.00 40.00
ONE PER JUMBO PACK
1 Dominique Wilkins 1.00 2.50
2 Dino Radja .60 1.50
3 Larry Johnson .75 2.00
4 Scottie Pippen 2.00 5.00
5 Mark Price .60 1.50
6 Jamal Mashburn 1.25 3.00
7 Mahmoud Abdul-Rauf .50 1.25
8 Joe Dumars .75 2.00
9 Chris Webber 5.00 12.00
10 Hakeem Olajuwon 1.25 3.00
11 Reggie Miller 1.25 3.00
12 Danny Manning .50 1.25
13 Doug Christie .50 1.25
14 Steve Smith .50 1.25
15 Eric Murdock .40 1.00
16 Isaiah Rider 1.00 2.50
17 Derrick Coleman .60 1.50
18 Patrick Ewing 1.00 2.50
19 Shaquille O'Neal 3.00 8.00
20 Shawn Bradley .60 1.50
21 Charles Barkley 1.50 4.00
22 Clyde Drexler 1.00 2.50
23 Mitch Richmond .75 2.00
24 David Robinson 1.25 3.00
25 Shawn Kemp 1.00 2.50
26 Karl Malone 1.25 3.00
27 Tom Gugliotta .50 1.25

1994-95 Finest

COMPLETE SET (1-331) 40.00 100.00
COMP.SERIES 1 (165) 20.00 50.00
COMP.SERIES 2 (166) 20.00 50.00
1 Chris Mullin CY .40 1.00
2 Anthony Mason CY .25 .60
3 John Salley CY .20 .50
4 Jamal Mashburn CY .30 .75
5 Mark Jackson CY .25 .60
6 Mario Elie CY .20 .50
7 Kenny Anderson CY .25 .60
8 Rod Strickland CY .20 .50
9 Kenny Smith CY .25 .60
10 Olden Polynice CY .20 .50
11 Derek Harper .50 1.25
12 Danny Ainge .60 1.50
13 Dino Radja .40 1.00
14 Eric Murdock .40 1.00
15 Sean Rooks .40 1.00
16 Dell Curry .40 1.00
17 Victor Alexander .40 1.00
18 Rodney Rogers .40 1.00
19 John Salley .40 1.00
20 Brad Daugherty .50 1.25
21 Elmore Spencer .40 1.00
22 Mitch Richmond .75 2.00
23 Rex Walters .40 1.00
24 Antonio Davis .50 1.25
25 B.J. Armstrong .60 1.50
26 Andrew Lang .40 1.00
27 Carl Herrera .40 1.00
28 Kevin Edwards .40 1.00
29 Micheal Williams .40 1.00
30 Clyde Drexler 1.00 2.50
31 Dana Barros .40 1.00
32 Shaquille O'Neal 2.50 6.00
33 Patrick Ewing 1.00 2.50
34 Charles Barkley 1.50 4.00
35 J.R. Reid .40 1.00
36 Lindsey Hunter .40 1.00
37 Jeff Malone .40 1.00
38 Rik Smits .50 1.25
39 Brian Williams .40 1.00
40 Shawn Kemp 1.00 2.50
41 Terry Porter .40 1.00
42 James Worthy .75 2.00
43 Rex Chapman .40 1.00
44 Stanley Roberts .40 1.00
45 Chris Smith .40 1.00
46 Dee Brown .50 1.25
47 Chris Gatling .40 1.00
48 Donald Hodge .40 1.00
49 Bimbo Coles .40 1.00
50 Derrick Coleman .60 1.50
51 Muggsy Bogues CY .25 .60
52 Reggie Williams CY .20 .50
53 David Wingate CY .20 .50
54 Sam Cassell CY .30 .75
55 Sherman Douglas CY .20 .50
56 Keith Jennings .40 1.00
57 Kenny Gattison .40 1.00
58 Brent Price .40 1.00
59 Luc Longley .50 1.25

60 Jamal Mashburn .60 1.50
61 Doug West .40 1.00
62 Walt Williams .40 1.00
63 Tracy Murray .40 1.00
64 Robert Pack .50 1.25
65 Johnny Dawkins .40 1.00
66 Vin Baker .60 1.50
67 Sam Cassell .60 1.50
68 Dale Davis .40 1.00
69 Terrell Brandon .40 1.00
70 Billy Owens .40 1.00
71 Ervin Johnson .40 1.00
72 Allan Houston .60 1.50
73 Craig Ehlo .40 1.00
74 Loy Vaught .40 1.00
75 Scottie Pippen 2.00 5.00
76 Sam Bowie .40 1.00
77 Anthony Mason .50 1.25
78 Felton Spencer .40 1.00
79 P.J. Brown .40 1.00
80 Christian Laettner .50 1.25
81 Todd Day .40 1.00
82 Sean Elliott .50 1.25
83 Grant Long .40 1.00
84 Xavier McDaniel .40 1.00
85 David Benoit .40 1.00
86 Larry Stewart .40 1.00
87 Donald Royal .40 1.00
88 Duane Causwell .40 1.00
89 Vlade Divac .60 1.50
90 Derrick McKey .40 1.00
91 Kevin Johnson .60 1.50
92 LaPhonso Ellis .40 1.00
93 Jerome Kersey .40 1.00
94 Muggsy Bogues .50 1.25
95 Tom Gugliotta .40 1.00
96 Jeff Hornacek .50 1.25
97 Kevin Willis .50 1.25
98 Chris Mills .50 1.25
99 Sam Perkins .40 1.00
100 Alonzo Mourning 1.00 2.50
101 Derrick Coleman CY .30 .75
102 Glen Rice CY .30 .75
103 Kevin Willis CY .25 .60
104 Chris Webber CY .75 2.00
105 Terry Mills CY .20 .50
106 Tim Hardaway CY .40 1.00
107 Nick Anderson CY .20 .50
108 Terry Cummings CY .25 .60
109 Hersey Hawkins CY .20 .50
110 Ken Norman CY .20 .50
111 Nick Anderson .40 1.00
112 Tim Perry .40 1.00
113 Terry Dehere .40 1.00
114 Chris Morris .40 1.00
115 John Williams .40 1.00
116 Jon Barry .40 1.00
117 Rony Seikaly .40 1.00
118 Detlef Schrempf .60 1.50
119 Terry Cummings .50 1.25
120 Chris Webber 1.50 4.00
121 David Wingate .40 1.00
122 Popeye Jones .40 1.00
123 Sherman Douglas .40 1.00
124 Greg Anthony .40 1.00
125 Mookie Blaylock .60 1.50
126 Don MacLean .40 1.00
127 Lionel Simmons .40 1.00
128 Scott Brooks .40 1.00
129 Jeff Turner .40 1.00
130 Bryant Stith .40 1.00
131 Shawn Bradley .40 1.00
132 Byron Scott .50 1.25
133 Doug Christie .50 1.25
134 Dennis Rodman 2.00 5.00
135 Dan Majerle .60 1.50
136 Gary Grant .40 1.00
137 Bryon Russell .40 1.00
138 Will Perdue .40 1.00
139 Gheorghe Muresan .40 1.00
140 Kendall Gill .40 1.00
141 Isaiah Rider .60 1.50
142 Terry Mills .40 1.00
143 Willie Anderson .40 1.00
144 Hubert Davis .40 1.00
145 Lucious Harris .40 1.00
146 Spud Webb .50 1.25
147 Glen Rice .60 1.50
148 Dennis Scott .50 1.25
149 Robert Horry .60 1.50
150 John Stockton 1.25 3.00
151 Stacey Augmon CY .25 .60
152 Chris Mills CY .25 .60
153 Elden Campbell CY .20 .50
154 Jay Humphries CY .20 .50
155 Reggie Miller CY .60 1.50
156 George Lynch .40 1.00
157 Tyrone Hill .40 1.00
158 Lee Mayberry .40 1.00
159 Jon Koncak .40 1.00
160 Joe Dumars .60 1.50
161 Vernon Maxwell .40 1.00
162 Joe Kleine .40 1.00
163 Acie Earl .40 1.00
164 Steve Kerr .50 1.25
165 Rod Strickland .40 1.00
166 Glenn Robinson RC 1.50 4.00
167 Anfernee Hardaway 1.25 3.00
168 Latrell Sprewell .60 1.50
169 Sergei Bazarevich RC .75 2.00
170 Hakeem Olajuwon 1.00 2.50
171 Nick Van Exel .50 1.25
172 Buck Williams .30 .75
173 Antoine Carr .30 .75
174 Corie Blount .30 .75
175 Dominique Wilkins .75 2.00
176 Yinka Dare RC .50 1.25
177 Byron Houston .30 .75
178 LaSalle Thompson .30 .75
179 Doug Smith .30 .75
180 David Robinson 1.00 2.50
181 Eric Piatkowski RC .75 2.00
182 Scott Skiles .30 .75
183 Scott Burrell .30 .75
184 Mark West .30 .75
185 Billy Owens .30 .75
186 Brian Grant RC 1.25 3.00
187 Scott Williams .30 .75
188 Gerald Madkins .30 .75
189 Reggie Williams .30 .75
190 Danny Manning .40 1.00
191 Mike Brown .30 .75
192 Charles Smith .30 .75
193 Elden Campbell .30 .75
194 Ricky Pierce .30 .75
195 Karl Malone 1.00 2.50
196 Brooks Thompson RC .60 1.50
197 Alaa Abdelnaby .30 .75
198 Tyrone Corbin .30 .75
199 Johnny Newman .30 .75
200 Grant Hill CB 2.00 5.00
201 Kenny Anderson CB .20 .50
202 Olden Polynice CB .15 .40
203 Horace Grant CB .25 .60
204 Muggsy Bogues CB .20 .50
205 Mark Price CB .25 .60
206 Tom Gugliotta CB .15 .40
207 Christian Laettner CB .20 .50
208 Eric Montross CB .30 .75
209 Sam Cassell CB .25 .60
210 Charles Oakley .50 1.25
211 Harold Ellis .30 .75
212 Nate McMillan .40 1.00
213 Chuck Person .40 1.00
214 Harold Miner .30 .75
215 Clarence Weatherspoon .30 .75
216 Robert Parish .50 1.25
217 Michael Cage .30 .75
218 Kenny Smith .40 1.00
219 Larry Krystkowiak .30 .75
220 Dikembe Mutombo .75 2.00
221 Wayman Tisdale .30 .75
222 Kevin Duckworth .30 .75
223 Vern Fleming .30 .75
224 Eric Mobley RC .50 1.25
225 Patrick Ewing CB .40 1.00
226 Clifford Robinson CB .20 .50
227 Eric Murdock CB .15 .40
228 Derrick Coleman CB .25 .60
229 Otis Thorpe CB .15 .40
230 Alonzo Mourning CB .40 1.00
231 Donyell Marshall CB .40 1.00
232 Dikembe Mutombo CB .40 1.00
233 Rony Seikaly CB .15 .40
234 Chris Mullin CB .30 .75
235 Reggie Miller 1.00 2.50
236 Benoit Benjamin .30 .75
237 Sean Rooks .30 .75
238 Terry Davis .30 .75
239 Anthony Avent .30 .75
240 Grant Hill RC 6.00 15.00
241 Randy Woods .30 .75
242 Tom Chambers .40 1.00
243 Michael Adams .30 .75
244 Monty Williams RC 1.00 2.50
245 Chris Mullin .60 1.50
246 Bill Wennington .30 .75
247 Mark Jackson .40 1.00
248 Blue Edwards .30 .75
249 Jalen Rose RC 2.00 5.00
250 Glenn Robinson CB .75 2.00
251 Kevin Willis CB .20 .50
252 B.J. Armstrong CB .25 .60
253 Jim Jackson CB .20 .50
254 Steve Smith CB .20 .50
255 Chris Webber CB .60 1.50
256 Glen Rice CB .25 .60
257 Derek Harper CB .20 .50
258 Jalen Rose CB 1.00 2.50
259 Juwan Howard CB .60 1.50
260 Kenny Anderson .40 1.00
261 Calbert Cheaney .40 1.00
262 Bill Cartwright .40 1.00
263 Mario Elie .30 .75
264 Chris Dudley .30 .75
265 Jim Jackson .40 1.00
266 Antonio Harvey .30 .75
267 Bill Curley RC .50 1.25
268 Moses Malone .50 1.25
269 A.C. Green .40 1.00
270 Larry Johnson .60 1.50
271 Marty Conlon .30 .75
272 Greg Graham .30 .75
273 Eric Montross RC .60 1.50
274 Stacey King .30 .75
275 Charles Barkley CB .60 1.50
276 Chris Morris CB .15 .40
277 Robert Horry CB .25 .60
278 Dominique Wilkins CB .40 1.00
279 Latrell Sprewell CB .30 .75
280 Shaquille O'Neal CB 1.25 3.00
281 Wesley Person CB .40 1.00
282 Mahmoud Abdul-Rauf CB .15 .40
283 Jamal Mashburn CB .40 1.00
284 Dale Ellis CB .15 .40
285 Gary Payton .75 2.00
286 Jason Kidd RC 6.00 15.00
287 Ken Norman .30 .75
288 Juwan Howard RC 1.25 3.00
289 Lamond Murray RC .75 2.00
290 Clifford Robinson .40 1.00
291 Frank Brickowski .30 .75
292 Adam Keefe .30 .75
293 Ron Harper .40 1.00
294 Tom Hammonds .30 .75
295 Otis Thorpe .30 .75
296 Rick Mahorn .30 .75
297 Alton Lister .30 .75
298 Vinny Del Negro .30 .75
299 Danny Ferry .30 .75
300 John Starks .50 1.25
301 Duane Ferrell .30 .75
302 Hersey Hawkins .30 .75
303 Khalid Reeves RC .60 1.50
304 Anthony Peeler .30 .75
305 Tim Hardaway .60 1.50
306 Rick Fox .30 .75
307 Jay Humphries .30 .75
308 Brian Shaw .30 .75
309 Danny Schayes .30 .75
310 Stacey Augmon .40 1.00
311 Oliver Miller .30 .75
312 Pooh Richardson .30 .75
313 Donyell Marshall RC .75 2.00
314 Aaron McKie RC .75 2.00
315 Mark Price .50 1.25
316 B.J. Tyler RC .50 1.25
317 Olden Polynice .30 .75
318 Avery Johnson .40 1.00
319 Derek Strong .30 .75
320 Toni Kukoc .60 1.50
321 Charlie Ward RC .75 2.00
322 Wesley Person RC .75 2.00
323 Eddie Jones RC 3.00 8.00
324 Horace Grant .50 1.25
325 Mahmoud Abdul-Rauf .30 .75
326 Sharone Wright RC .60 1.50
327 Kevin Gamble .30 .75
328 Sarunas Marciulionis .30 .75
329 Harvey Grant .30 .75
330 Bobby Hurley .30 .75
331 Michael Jordan 60.00 150.00

1994-95 Finest Refractors

*SER.1 STARS: 2.5X TO 6X BASE CARD HI
*SER.2 SUBSETS: 5X TO 12X BASE HI
*SER.2 STARS: 3X TO 8X BASE HI
*SER.2 SUBSETS: 6X TO 15X BASE HI
*RCs: 3X TO 8X BASE HI
SER.1/2 STATED ODDS 1:12
CONDITION SENSITIVE SET
22 Mitch Richmond 8.00 20.00
30 Clyde Drexler 10.00 25.00
32 Shaquille O'Neal 75.00 200.00
33 Patrick Ewing 15.00 40.00
34 Charles Barkley 20.00 50.00
40 Shawn Kemp 15.00 40.00
42 James Worthy 15.00 40.00
75 Scottie Pippen 12.00 30.00
100 Alonzo Mourning 10.00 25.00
102 Glen Rice CY SP 30.00 80.00
104 Chris Webber CY SP 20.00 50.00
106 Tim Hardaway CY SP 10.00 25.00
120 Chris Webber SP 30.00 80.00
134 Dennis Rodman 40.00 100.00
150 John Stockton SP 15.00 40.00
155 Reggie Miller CY SP 20.00 50.00
160 Joe Dumars 8.00 20.00
166 Glenn Robinson 25.00 60.00
167 Anfernee Hardaway 50.00 120.00
170 Hakeem Olajuwon 20.00 50.00
171 Nick Van Exel 8.00 20.00
175 Dominique Wilkins 8.00 20.00
180 David Robinson 12.00 30.00
195 Karl Malone 10.00 25.00
200 Grant Hill CB 20.00 50.00
230 Alonzo Mourning CB 10.00 25.00
235 Reggie Miller 8.00 20.00
240 Grant Hill 100.00 250.00
244 Monty Williams 12.00 30.00
245 Chris Mullin 8.00 20.00
255 Chris Webber CB 10.00 25.00
275 Charles Barkley CB 10.00 25.00
285 Gary Payton 8.00 20.00
286 Jason Kidd 100.00 250.00
320 Toni Kukoc 12.00 30.00
331 Michael Jordan 400.00 800.00

1994-95 Finest Cornerstone

COMPLETE SET (15) 15.00 40.00
SER.2 STATED ODDS 1:24
CS1 Shaquille O'Neal 10.00 25.00
CS2 Alonzo Mourning 4.00 10.00
CS3 Patrick Ewing 4.00 10.00
CS4 Karl Malone 5.00 12.00
CS5 Kenny Anderson 2.00 5.00
CS6 Latrell Sprewell 3.00 8.00
CS7 Dikembe Mutombo 4.00 10.00
CS8 Charles Barkley 6.00 15.00
CS9 John Stockton 5.00 12.00
CS10 Reggie Miller 5.00 12.00
CS11 Jamal Mashburn 2.50 6.00
CS12 Anfernee Hardaway 6.00 15.00
CS13 Jim Jackson 2.00 5.00
CS14 David Robinson 5.00 12.00
CS15 Hakeem Olajuwon 5.00 12.00

1994-95 Finest Cornerstone Refractors Test

CS1 Shaquille O'Neal 300.00 800.00
CS2 Alonzo Mourning 120.00 300.00
CS3 Patrick Ewing 120.00 300.00
CS4 Karl Malone 150.00 400.00
CS5 Kenny Anderson 60.00 150.00
CS6 Latrell Sprewell 100.00 250.00
CS7 Dikembe Mutombo 120.00 300.00
CS8 Charles Barkley 200.00 500.00
CS9 John Stockton 150.00 400.00
CS10 Reggie Miller 150.00 400.00
CS11 Jamal Mashburn 80.00 200.00
CS12 Anfernee Hardaway 150.00 400.00
CS13 Jim Jackson 60.00 150.00
CS14 David Robinson 150.00 400.00
CS15 Hakeem Olajuwon 150.00 400.00

1994-95 Finest Iron Men

COMPLETE SET (10) 15.00 30.00
SER.1 STATED ODDS 1:24
1 Shaquille O'Neal 6.00 15.00
2 Kenny Anderson 1.50 4.00
3 Jim Jackson 1.50 4.00
4 Clarence Weatherspoon 1.25 3.00
5 Karl Malone 4.00 10.00
6 Dan Majerle 2.00 5.00
7 Anfernee Hardaway 4.00 10.00
8 David Robinson 4.00 10.00
9 Latrell Sprewell 2.50 6.00
10 Hakeem Olajuwon 4.00 10.00

1994-95 Finest Lottery Prize

COMPLETE SET (22) 12.00 30.00
SER.2 STATED ODDS 1:6
LP1 Patrick Ewing 1.50 4.00
LP2 Chris Mullin 1.25 3.00
LP3 David Robinson 2.00 5.00
LP4 Scottie Pippen 2.50 6.00
LP5 Kevin Johnson 1.00 2.50
LP6 Danny Manning .75 2.00
LP7 Mitch Richmond 1.25 3.00
LP8 Derrick Coleman 1.00 2.50
LP9 Gary Payton 1.50 4.00
LP10 Mahmoud Abdul-Rauf .60 1.50
LP11 Larry Johnson 1.25 3.00
LP12 Kenny Anderson .75 2.00
LP13 Dikembe Mutombo 1.50 4.00
LP14 Stacey Augmon .75 2.00
LP15 Shaquille O'Neal 4.00 10.00
LP16 Alonzo Mourning 1.50 4.00
LP17 Clarence Weatherspoon .60 1.50
LP18 Robert Horry 1.00 2.50
LP19 Chris Webber 2.00 5.00
LP20 Anfernee Hardaway 2.00 5.00
LP21 Jamal Mashburn 1.00 2.50
LP22 Vin Baker 1.00 2.50

1994-95 Finest Lottery Prize Refractors Test

LP1 Patrick Ewing 80.00 200.00
LP2 Chris Mullin 60.00 150.00
LP3 David Robinson 100.00 250.00
LP4 Scottie Pippen 120.00 300.00
LP5 Kevin Johnson 50.00 125.00
LP6 Danny Manning 40.00 100.00
LP7 Mitch Richmond 60.00 150.00
LP8 Derrick Coleman 50.00 125.00
LP9 Gary Payton 80.00 200.00
LP10 Mahmoud Abdul-Rauf 30.00 80.00
LP11 Larry Johnson 60.00 150.00
LP12 Kenny Anderson 40.00 100.00
LP13 Dikembe Mutombo 80.00 200.00
LP14 Stacey Augmon 40.00 100.00
LP15 Shaquille O'Neal 200.00 500.00
LP16 Alonzo Mourning 80.00 200.00
LP17 Clarence Weatherspoon 30.00 80.00
LP18 Robert Horry 50.00 125.00
LP19 Chris Webber 100.00 250.00
LP20 Anfernee Hardaway 100.00 250.00
LP21 Jamal Mashburn 50.00 125.00
LP22 Vin Baker 50.00 125.00

1994-95 Finest Marathon Men

COMPLETE SET (20) 20.00 50.00
SER.1 STATED ODDS 1:12
1 Latrell Sprewell 3.00 8.00
2 Gary Payton 3.00 8.00
3 Kenny Anderson 1.50 4.00
4 Jim Jackson 1.50 4.00
5 Lindsey Hunter 1.25 3.00
6 Rod Strickland 1.25 3.00
7 Hersey Hawkins 1.25 3.00
8 Gerald Wilkins 1.25 3.00
9 B.J. Armstrong 2.00 5.00
10 Anfernee Hardaway 5.00 12.00
11 Stacey Augmon 1.50 4.00
12 Eric Murdock 1.25 3.00
13 Clarence Weatherspoon 1.25 3.00
14 Karl Malone 4.00 10.00
15 Charles Oakley 2.00 5.00
16 Rick Fox 1.25 3.00
17 Otis Thorpe 1.25 3.00
18 Dikembe Mutombo 3.00 8.00
19 Mike Brown 1.25 3.00
20 A.C. Green 1.50 4.00

1994-95 Finest Rack Pack

COMPLETE SET (7) 15.00 40.00
SER.2 STATED ODDS 1:72
RP1 Grant Hill 8.00 20.00
RP2 Wesley Person 1.50 4.00
RP3 Juwan Howard 2.50 6.00
RP4 Lamond Murray 1.50 4.00
RP5 Glenn Robinson 3.00 8.00
RP6 Donyell Marshall 1.50 4.00
RP7 Jason Kidd 8.00 20.00

1994-95 Finest Rack Pack Refractors Test

RP1 Grant Hill 100.00 250.00
RP2 Wesley Person 20.00 50.00
RP3 Juwan Howard 30.00 80.00
RP4 Lamond Murray 20.00 50.00
RP5 Glenn Robinson 40.00 100.00
RP6 Donyell Marshall 20.00 50.00
RP7 Jason Kidd 100.00 250.00

1995-96 Finest

COMPLETE SET (251) 75.00 200.00
COMP.SERIES 1 (140) 60.00 150.00
COMP.SERIES 2 (111) 20.00 50.00
1 Hakeem Olajuwon 1.50 4.00
2 Stacey Augmon .60 1.50
3 John Starks .75 2.00
4 Sharone Wright .50 1.25
5 Jason Kidd 1.25 3.00
6 Lamond Murray .50 1.25
7 Kenny Anderson .60 1.50
8 James Robinson .50 1.25
9 Wesley Person .50 1.25
10 Latrell Sprewell .75 2.00
11 Sean Elliott .60 1.50
12 Greg Anthony .50 1.25
13 Kendall Gill .50 1.25
14 Mark Jackson .60 1.50
15 John Stockton 1.50 4.00
16 Steve Smith .60 1.50
17 Bobby Hurley .50 1.25
18 Ervin Johnson .50 1.25
19 Elden Campbell .50 1.25
20 Vin Baker .60 1.50
21 Micheal Williams .50 1.25
22 Steve Kerr .75 2.00
23 Kevin Duckworth .50 1.25
24 Willie Anderson .50 1.25
25 Joe Dumars .75 2.00
26 Dale Ellis .60 1.50
27 Bimbo Coles .50 1.25
28 Nick Anderson .60 1.50
29 Dee Brown .60 1.50
30 Tyrone Hill .50 1.25
31 Reggie Miller 1.50 4.00
32 Shaquille O'Neal 3.00 8.00
33 Brian Grant .60 1.50
34 Charles Barkley 2.00 5.00
35 Cedric Ceballos .50 1.25
36 Rex Walters .50 1.25
37 Kenny Smith .60 1.50
38 Popeye Jones .50 1.25
39 Harvey Grant .50 1.25
40 Gary Payton 1.25 3.00
41 John Williams .50 1.25
42 Sherman Douglas .50 1.25
43 Oliver Miller .50 1.25
44 Kevin Willis .50 1.25
45 Isaiah Rider .75 2.00
46 Gheorghe Muresan .50 1.25
47 Blue Edwards .50 1.25
48 Jeff Hornacek .60 1.50
49 J.R. Reid .50 1.25
50 Glenn Robinson .75 2.00
51 Dell Curry .75 2.00
52 Greg Graham .50 1.25
53 Ron Harper .60 1.50
54 Derek Harper .60 1.50
55 Dikembe Mutombo 1.25 3.00
56 Terry Mills .50 1.25
57 Victor Alexander .50 1.25
58 Malik Sealy .50 1.25
59 Vincent Askew .50 1.25
60 Mitch Richmond 1.00 2.50
61 Duane Ferrell .50 1.25
62 Dickey Simpkins .50 1.25
63 Pooh Richardson .50 1.25
64 Khalid Reeves .50 1.25
65 Dino Radja .50 1.25
66 Lee Mayberry .50 1.25
67 Kenny Gattison .50 1.25
68 Joe Kleine .50 1.25
69 Tony Dumas .50 1.25
70 Nick Van Exel .75 2.00
71 Armon Gilliam .50 1.25
72 Craig Ehlo .50 1.25
73 Adam Keefe .50 1.25
74 Chris Dudley .50 1.25
75 Clyde Drexler 1.25 3.00
76 Jeff Turner .50 1.25
77 Calbert Cheaney .50 1.25
78 Vinny Del Negro .50 1.25
79 Tim Perry .50 1.25
80 Tim Hardaway 1.00 2.50
81 B.J. Armstrong .75 2.00
82 Muggsy Bogues .75 2.00
83 Mark Macon .50 1.25
84 Doug West .50 1.25
85 Jalen Rose 1.00 2.50
86 Chris Mills .50 1.25
87 Charles Oakley .60 1.50
88 Andrew Lang .50 1.25
89 Olden Polynice .50 1.25
90 Sam Cassell .75 2.00
91 Todd Day .50 1.25
92 P.J. Brown .50 1.25
93 Benoit Benjamin .50 1.25
94 Sam Perkins .60 1.50
95 Eddie Jones .75 2.00
96 Robert Parish 1.00 2.50
97 Avery Johnson .60 1.50
98 Lindsey Hunter .60 1.50
99 Billy Owens .50 1.25
100 Shawn Bradley .50 1.25
101 Dale Davis .50 1.25
102 Terry Dehere .50 1.25
103 A.C. Green .60 1.50
104 Christian Laettner .60 1.50
105 Horace Grant .60 1.50
106 Rony Seikaly .50 1.25
107 Reggie Williams .50 1.25
108 Toni Kukoc 1.00 2.50
109 Terrell Brandon .60 1.50
110 Clifford Robinson .60 1.50
111 Joe Smith RC 1.00 2.50
112 Antonio McDyess RC 1.00 2.50
113 Jerry Stackhouse RC 2.50 6.00
114 Rasheed Wallace RC 5.00 12.00
115 Kevin Garnett RC 25.00 60.00
116 Bryant Reeves RC .60 1.50
117 Damon Stoudamire RC 2.00 5.00
118 Shawn Respert RC .60 1.50
119 Ed O'Bannon RC .60 1.50
120 Kurt Thomas RC .75 2.00
121 Gary Trent RC .60 1.50
122 Cherokee Parks RC .60 1.50
123 Corliss Williamson RC .75 2.00
124 Eric Williams RC .75 2.00
125 Brent Barry RC 1.25 3.00
126 Alan Henderson RC .75 2.00
127 Bob Sura RC .60 1.50
128 Theo Ratliff RC 1.25 3.00
129 Randolph Childress RC .60 1.50
130 Jason Caffey RC .75 2.00
131 Michael Finley RC 2.50 6.00
132 George Zidek RC .60 1.50
133 Travis Best RC .75 2.00
134 Loren Meyer RC .75 2.00
135 David Vaughn RC .75 2.00
136 Sherrell Ford RC .60 1.50
137 Mario Bennett RC .60 1.50
138 Greg Ostertag RC .75 2.00
139 Cory Alexander RC .75 2.00
140 Checklist UER #111 .50 1.25
141 Chucky Brown .60 1.50
142 Eric Mobley .60 1.50
143 Tom Hammonds .50 1.25
144 Chris Webber 1.00 2.50
145 Carlos Rogers .50 1.25
146 Chuck Person .60 1.50
147 Brian Williams .50 1.25
148 Kevin Gamble .50 1.25
149 Dennis Rodman 1.50 4.00
150 Pervis Ellison .50 1.25
151 Jayson Williams .50 1.25
152 Buck Williams .60 1.50
153 Allan Houston .60 1.50
154 Tom Gugliotta .60 1.50
155 Charles Smith .50 1.25
156 Chris Gatling .50 1.25
157 Darrin Hancock .50 1.25
158 Blue Edwards .50 1.25
159 Shawn Kemp 1.25 3.00
160 Michael Cage .50 1.25
161 Sedale Threatt .50 1.25
162 Byron Scott .75 2.00
163 Elliot Perry .50 1.25
164 Jim Jackson .60 1.50
165 Wayman Tisdale .50 1.25
166 Vernon Maxwell .50 1.25
167 Brian Shaw .50 1.25
168 Haywoode Workman .50 1.25
169 Mookie Blaylock .75 2.00
170 Donald Royal .50 1.25
171 Lorenzo Williams .50 1.25
172 Eric Piatkowski UER .50 1.25
173 Sarunas Marciulionis .75 2.00
174 Otis Thorpe .60 1.50
175 Rex Chapman .50 1.25
176 Felton Spencer .50 1.25
177 John Salley .50 1.25
178 Pete Chilcutt .50 1.25
179 Scottie Pippen 2.00 5.00
180 Robert Pack .60 1.50
181 Dana Barros .60 1.50
182 Mahmoud Abdul-Rauf .60 1.50
183 Eric Murdock .50 1.25
184 Anthony Mason .50 1.25
185 Will Perdue .60 1.50
186 Jeff Malone .50 1.25
187 Anthony Peeler .50 1.25
188 Chris Childs .50 1.25
189 Glen Rice .75 2.00
190 Grant Hill 1.25 3.00
191 Michael Smith .50 1.25
192 Sean Rooks .50 1.25
193 Clifford Rozier .50 1.25
194 Rik Smits .60 1.50
195 Spud Webb .50 1.25
196 Aaron McKie .50 1.25
197 Nate McMillan .50 1.25
198 Bobby Phills .60 1.50
199 Dennis Scott .50 1.25
200 Mark West .50 1.25
201 George McCloud .50 1.25
202 B.J. Tyler .50 1.25
203 Lionel Simmons .50 1.25
204 Loy Vaught .50 1.25
205 Kevin Edwards .50 1.25
206 Eric Montross .50 1.25
207 Kenny Gattison .50 1.25
208 Mario Elie .50 1.25
209 Karl Malone 1.50 4.00
210 Ken Norman .50 1.25
211 Antonio Davis .50 1.25
212 Doc Rivers .60 1.50
213 Hubert Davis .50 1.25
214 Jamal Mashburn .75 2.00
215 Donyell Marshall .50 1.25
216 Sasha Danilovic RC .75 2.00
217 Danny Manning .60 1.50
218 Scott Burrell .50 1.25
219 Vlade Divac .75 2.00
220 Marty Conlon .50 1.25
221 Clarence Weatherspoon .50 1.25
222 Terry Porter .50 1.25
223 Luc Longley .60 1.50
224 Juwan Howard .75 2.00
225 Danny Ferry .50 1.25
226 Rod Strickland .50 1.25
227 Bryant Stith .50 1.25
228 Derrick McKey .50 1.25
229 Michael Jordan 15.00 40.00
230 Jamie Watson .50 1.25
231 Rick Fox .50 1.25
232 Scott Williams .50 1.25
233 Larry Johnson 1.00 2.50
234 Anfernee Hardaway 2.00 5.00
235 Hersey Hawkins .60 1.50
236 Robert Horry .75 2.00
237 Kevin Johnson .75 2.00
238 Rodney Rogers .60 1.50
239 Detlef Schrempf .75 2.00
240 Derrick Coleman .60 1.50
241 Walt Williams .50 1.25
242 LaPhonso Ellis .60 1.50
243 Patrick Ewing 1.25 3.00
244 Grant Long .50 1.25
245 David Robinson 1.50 4.00
246 Chris Mullin .75 2.00
247 Alonzo Mourning 1.25 3.00
248 Dan Majerle .75 2.00
249 Johnny Newman .50 1.25
250 Chris Morris .50 1.25
252 Magic Johnson 2.50 6.00

1995-96 Finest Refractors

*REF: 2.5X TO 6X HI COLUMN
SER.1/2 STATED ODDS: 1:12 HOB, 1:18 RET
229 Michael Jordan 600.00 1,200.00
252 Magic Johnson 6P 20.00 50.00

1995-96 Finest Dish and Swish

COMPLETE SET (29) 30.00 80.00
SER.1 STATED ODDS 1:24
DS1 M.Blaylock/S.Smith 1.50 4.00
DS2 S.Douglas/D.Radja 1.00 2.50
DS3 M.Bogues/L.Johnson 2.00 5.00
DS4 S.Pippen/M.Jordan 30.00 80.00
DS5 M.Price/C.Mills 1.50 4.00
DS6 J.Kidd/J.Mashburn 2.50 6.00
DS7 M.Abdul-Rauf/D.Mutombo 2.50 6.00
DS8 G.Hill/J.Dumars 3.00 8.00
DS9 T.Hardaway/C.Mullin 2.50 6.00
DS10 C.Drexler/H.Olajuwon 3.00 8.00
DS11 M.Jackson/R.Miller 2.50 6.00
DS12 P.Richardson/L.Murray 1.00 2.50
DS13 N.Van Exel/C.Ceballos 1.50 4.00
DS14 G.Rice/K.Reeves 1.50 4.00
DS15 G.Robinson/Murdock 1.50 4.00
DS16 T.Gugliotta/C.Laettner 1.50 4.00
DS17 K.Anderson/D.Coleman 1.25 3.00
DS18 P.Ewing/D.Harper 2.50 6.00
DS19 A.Hardaway/S.O'Neal 5.00 12.00
DS20 D.Barros/C.Weatherspoon 1.25 3.00
DS21 K.Johnson/C.Barkley 5.00 12.00
DS22 R.Strickland/C.Robinson 1.50 4.00
DS23 Richmond/W.Williams 2.00 5.00
DS24 A.Johnson/D.Rob 2.50 6.00
DS25 G.Payton/S.Kemp 4.00 10.00
DS26 B.J.Armstrong/O.Miller 1.50 4.00
DS27 J.Stockton/K.Malone 3.00 8.00
DS28 G.Anthony/B.Scott 1.50 4.00
DS29 J.Howard/C.Webber 3.00 8.00

1995-96 Finest Hot Stuff

COMPLETE SET (15) 30.00 80.00
SER.1 STATED ODDS 1:9
HS1 Michael Jordan 30.00 80.00
HS2 Grant Hill 2.50 6.00
HS3 Clyde Drexler 2.50 6.00
HS4 Anfernee Hardaway 4.00 10.00
HS5 Sean Elliott 1.25 3.00
HS6 Latrell Sprewell 1.50 4.00
HS7 Larry Johnson 2.00 5.00
HS8 Eddie Jones 1.50 4.00
HS9 Karl Malone 3.00 8.00
HS10 John Starks 1.50 4.00
HS11 Scottie Pippen 4.00 10.00
HS12 Shawn Kemp 2.50 6.00
HS13 Chris Webber 2.00 5.00
HS14 Isaiah Rider 1.50 4.00
HS15 Robert Horry 1.50 4.00

1995-96 Finest Mystery

COMPLETE SET (44) 20.00 45.00
COMP.BORDER SER.1 (22) 12.50 30.00
COMP.BRONZE SER.2 (22) 7.50 15.00
ONE BORDER PER SER.1 PACK
*BDLS./SILVER: 1.5X TO 4X HI COLUMN
*SILVER RCs: 1.25X TO 3X HI
BDLS: SER.1 STATED ODDS 1:24
SILVER: SER.2 STATED ODDS 1:24
M1 Michael Jordan 20.00 50.00
M2 Grant Hill 1.00 2.50
M3 Anfernee Hardaway 1.50 4.00
M4 Shawn Kemp 1.00 2.50
M5 Kenny Anderson .50 1.25
M6 Charles Barkley 1.50 4.00
M7 Latrell Sprewell .60 1.50
M8 Chris Webber .75 2.00
M9 Jason Kidd 1.00 2.50
M10 Glenn Robinson .60 1.50
M11 David Robinson 1.25 3.00
M12 Karl Malone 1.25 3.00
M13 Larry Johnson .75 2.00
M14 Reggie Miller 1.25 3.00
M15 Scottie Pippen 1.50 4.00
M16 Patrick Ewing 1.00 2.50
M17 Mitch Richmond .75 2.00
M18 Glen Rice .60 1.50
M19 Jamal Mashburn .60 1.50
M20 Juwan Howard .60 1.50
M21 Hakeem Olajuwon 1.25 3.00
M22 Shaquille O'Neal 2.50 6.00
M23 Alonzo Mourning .75 2.00
M24 Dennis Rodman 1.00 2.50
M25 Joe Dumars .50 1.25
M26 Tim Hardaway .60 1.50
M27 Clyde Drexler .75 2.00
M28 Jerry Stackhouse 1.50 4.00
M29 John Stockton 1.00 2.50
M30 Derrick Coleman .40 1.00
M31 Michael Finley 1.25 3.00
M32 Glen Rice .50 1.25
M33 Mahmoud Abdul-Rauf .40 1.00
M34 Anthony Mason .30 .75
M35 Nick Van Exel .50 1.25
M36 Vin Baker .40 1.00
M37 Horace Grant .40 1.00
M38 John Starks .50 1.25
M39 Clarence Weatherspoon .30 .75
M40 Kevin Johnson .50 1.25
M41 Joe Smith .60 1.50
M42 Dikembe Mutombo .75 2.00
M43 Damon Stoudamire 1.25 3.00
M44 Antonio McDyess .60 1.50

1995-96 Finest Mystery Borderless Refractors/Gold

*BDLS.REF: 8X TO 20X VALUE
*GOLD STARS: 6X TO 15X VALUE
*GOLD RCs: 4X TO 10X VALUE
BDLS RF: SER.1 STATED ODDS 1:96
GOLD: SER.2 STATED ODDS 1:96

1995-96 Finest Rack Pack

COMPLETE SET (7) 20.00 50.00
SER.2 STATED ODDS 1:72 HOB, 1:96 RET
RP1 Jerry Stackhouse 6.00 15.00
RP2 Brent Barry 3.00 8.00
RP3 Damon Stoudamire 5.00 12.00
RP4 Joe Smith 2.50 6.00
RP5 Michael Finley 5.00 12.00
RP6 Antonio McDyess 2.50 6.00
RP7 Rasheed Wallace 6.00 15.00

1995-96 Finest Rack Pack Refractors Test

RP1 Jerry Stackhouse 50.00 125.00
RP2 Brent Barry 25.00 60.00
RP3 Damon Stoudamire 40.00 100.00
RP4 Joe Smith 20.00 50.00
RP5 Michael Finley 40.00 100.00
RP6 Antonio McDyess 20.00 50.00
RP7 Rasheed Wallace 50.00 125.00

1995-96 Finest Veteran/Rookie

COMPLETE SET (29) 125.00 250.00
SER.2 STATED ODDS 1:24 HOB, 1:18 RET
RV1 J.Smith/L.Sprewell 4.00 10.00
RV2 A.McDyess/Mutombo 5.00 12.00
RV3 Stackhouse/W.Spoon 5.00 12.00
RV4 R.Wallace/C.Webber 8.00 20.00
RV5 K.Garnett/T.Gugliotta 20.00 50.00
RV6 B.Reeves/G.Anthony 3.00 8.00
RV7 Stoudamire/Anderson 4.00 10.00
RV8 S.Respert/V.Baker 2.00 5.00
RV9 E.O'Bannon/A.Gilliam 2.00 5.00
RV10 K.Thomas/Mourning 4.00 10.00
RV11 G.Trent/R.Strickland 2.50 6.00
RV12 C.Parks/J.Mashburn 2.00 5.00
RV13 Williamson/Richmond 3.00 8.00
RV14 E.Williams/D.Radja 2.00 5.00
RV15 B.Barry/L.Vaught 2.50 6.00
RV16 A.Henderson/M.Blaylock 2.50 6.00
RV17 B.Sura/T.Brandon 2.50 6.00
RV18 T.Ratliff/G.Hill 5.00 12.00
RV19 R.Childress/R.Strickland 2.00 5.00
RV20 J.Caffey/M.Jordan 60.00 150.00
RV21 M.Finley/K.Johnson 6.00 15.00
RV22 G.Zidek/L.Johnson 2.50 6.00
RV23 T.Best/R.Miller 4.00 10.00
RV24 L.Meyer/J.Kidd 4.00 10.00

RV25 D.Vaughn/S.O'Neal 15.00 40.00
RV26 S.Ford/S.Kemp 2.50 6.00
RV27 M.Bennett/C.Barkley 4.00 10.00
RV28 G.Ostertag/K.Malone 4.00 10.00
RV29 Alexander/D.Robinson 4.00 10.00

1996-97 Finest

COMPLETE SET (291) 300.00 600.00
COMPLETE SERIES 1 (146) 150.00 350.00
COMPLETE SERIES 2 (145) 150.00 300.00
COMP.BRONZE SET (200) 70.00 140.00
COMP.BRONZE SER.1 (100) 50.00 100.00
COMP.BRONZE SER.2 (100) 20.00 40.00
SILVER: SER.1/2 STATED ODDS 1:4
GOLD: SER.1/2 STATED ODDS 1:24
CARD NUMBERS 7 AND 134 DO NOT EXIST
LAETTNR B EWING G HORNCEK G #'d 136
NUMBER 269 PART OF GOLD SET
NUMBER 289 PART OF SILVER SET
CONDITION SENSITIVE SET
1 Scottie Pippen B 1.00 2.50
2 Tim Legler B .25 .60
3 Rex Walters B .25 .60
4 Calbert Cheaney B .25 .60
5 Dennis Rodman B 1.00 2.50
6 Tyrone Hill B .25 .60
8 Dell Curry B .40 1.00
9 Olden Polynice B .25 .60
10 John Wallace B RC .60 1.50
11 Martin Muursepp B RC .50 1.25
12 Chuck Person B .30 .75
13 Grant Hill B .60 1.50
14 Shawn Kemp B .60 1.50
15 B.J. Armstrong B .30 .75
16 Gary Trent B .25 .60
17 Scott Williams B .25 .60
18 Dino Radja B .25 .60
19 Roy Rogers B RC .60 1.50
20 Tony Delk B RC .75 2.00
21 Clifford Robinson B .40 1.00
22 Ray Allen B RC 10.00 25.00
23 Clyde Drexler B .60 1.50
24 Elliot Perry B .25 .60
25 Gary Payton B .60 1.50
26 Dale Davis B .25 .60
27 Horace Grant B .40 1.00
28 Brian Evans B RC .50 1.25
29 Joe Smith B .40 1.00
30 Reggie Miller B .75 2.00
31 Jermaine O'Neal B RC 1.25 3.00
32 Avery Johnson B .30 .75
33 Ed O'Bannon B .25 .60
34 Cedric Ceballos B .30 .75
35 Jamal Mashburn B .40 1.00
36 Micheal Williams B .25 .60
37 Detlef Schrempf B .40 1.00
38 Damon Stoudamire B .40 1.00
39 Jason Kidd B .60 1.50
40 Tom Gugliotta B .25 .60
41 Arvydas Sabonis B .40 1.00
42 Samaki Walker B RC .25 .60
43 Derek Fisher B RC 1.00 2.50
44 Patrick Ewing B .60 1.50
45 Bryant Reeves B .25 .60
46 Mookie Blaylock B .40 1.00
47 George Zidek B .25 .60
48 Jerry Stackhouse B .50 1.25
49 Vin Baker B .30 .75
50 Michael Jordan B 15.00 40.00
51 Terrell Brandon B .30 .75
52 Karl Malone B .75 2.00
53 Lorenzen Wright B RC .60 1.50
54 Shareef Abdur-Rahim B RC 1.25 3.00
55 Kurt Thomas B .25 .60
56 Glen Rice B .40 1.00
57 Shawn Bradley B .25 .60
58 Todd Fuller B RC .50 1.25
59 Dale Ellis B .30 .75
60 David Robinson B .75 2.00
61 Doug Christie B .25 .60
62 Stephon Marbury B RC 2.50 6.00
63 Hakeem Olajuwon B .75 2.00
64 Lindsey Hunter B .25 .60
65 Anfernee Hardaway B 1.00 2.50
66 Kevin Garnett B 1.25 3.00
67 Kendall Gill B .40 1.00
68 Sean Elliott B .40 1.00
69 Allen Iverson B RC 10.00 25.00
70 Erick Dampier B RC .75 2.00
71 Jerome Williams B RC .60 1.50
72 Charles Jones B .25 .60
73 Danny Manning B .30 .75
74 Kobe Bryant B RC 100.00 250.00
75 Steve Nash B RC 5.00 12.00
76 Sam Perkins B .30 .75
77 Horace Grant B .40 1.00
78 Alonzo Mourning B .60 1.50
79 Kerry Kittles B RC .75 2.00
80 LaPhonso Ellis B .25 .60
81 Michael Finley B .40 1.00
82 Marcus Camby B RC 1.25 3.00
83 Antonio McDyess B .40 1.00
84 Antoine Walker B RC 1.25 3.00
85 Juwan Howard B .40 1.00
86 Bryon Russell B .25 .60
87 Walter McCarty B RC .75 2.00
88 Priest Lauderdale B RC .50 1.25
89 Clarence Weatherspoon B .25 .60
90 John Stockton B .75 2.00
91 Mitch Richmond B .50 1.25
92 Dontae' Jones B RC .60 1.50
93 Michael Smith B .25 .60
94 Brent Barry B .30 .75
95 Chris Mills B .25 .60
96 Dee Brown B .25 .60
97 Terry Dehere B .25 .60
98 Danny Ferry B .25 .60
99 Gheorghe Muresan B .25 .60
100 Checklist B .25 .60
101 Jim Jackson S .60 1.50
102 Cedric Ceballos S .75 2.00
103 Glen Rice S 1.00 2.50
104 Tom Gugliotta S .60 1.50
105 Mario Elie S .60 1.50
106 Nick Anderson S .60 1.50
107 Glenn Robinson S 1.00 2.50
108 Terrell Brandon S .75 2.00
109 Tim Hardaway S 1.25 3.00
110 John Stockton S 2.00 5.00
111 Brent Barry S .75 2.00
112 Mookie Blaylock S 1.00 2.50
113 Tyus Edney S .60 1.50
114 Gary Payton S 1.50 4.00
115 Joe Smith S .75 2.00
116 Karl Malone S 2.00 5.00
117 Dino Radja S .60 1.50
118 Alonzo Mourning S 1.50 4.00
119 Bryant Stith S .60 1.50
120 Derrick McKey S .60 1.50
121 Clyde Drexler S 1.50 4.00
122 Michael Finley S 1.00 2.50
123 Sean Elliott S 1.00 2.50
124 Hakeem Olajuwon S 2.00 5.00
125 Joe Dumars S 1.25 3.00
126 Shawn Bradley S .60 1.50
127 Michael Jordan S 15.00 40.00
128 Latrell Sprewell G 3.00 8.00
129 Anfernee Hardaway G 8.00 20.00
130 Grant Hill G 5.00 12.00
131 Damon Stoudamire G 3.00 8.00
132 David Robinson G 6.00 15.00
133 Scottie Pippen G 8.00 20.00
135 Jason Kidd G 5.00 12.00
136A Jeff Hornacek G 2.50 6.00
136B Patrick Ewing G UER 5.00 12.00
136C Christian Laettner B UER .40 1.00
137 Jerry Stackhouse G 4.00 10.00
138 Kevin Garnett G 10.00 25.00
139 Mitch Richmond G 4.00 10.00
140 Juwan Howard G 3.00 8.00
141 Reggie Miller G 6.00 15.00
142 Christian Laettner G 3.00 8.00
143 Vin Baker G 2.50 6.00
144 Shawn Kemp G 5.00 12.00
145 Dennis Rodman G 8.00 20.00
146 Shaquille O'Neal G 12.00 30.00
147 Mookie Blaylock B .40 1.00
148 Derek Harper B .30 .75
149 Gerald Wilkins B .30 .75
150 Adam Keefe B .25 .60
151 Billy Owens B .25 .60
152 Terrell Brandon B .30 .75
153 Antonio Davis B .25 .60
154 Muggsy Bogues B .40 1.00
155 Cherokee Parks B .25 .60
156 Rasheed Wallace B .50 1.25
157 Lee Mayberry B .25 .60
158 Craig Ehlo B .25 .60
159 Todd Fuller B .25 .60
160 Charles Barkley B 1.00 2.50
161 Glenn Robinson B .40 1.00
162 Charles Oakley B .40 1.00
163 Chris Webber B .50 1.25
164 Frank Brickowski B .25 .60
165 Mark Jackson B .30 .75
166 Jayson Williams B .25 .60
167 Clarence Weatherspoon B .25 .60
168 Toni Kukoc B .40 1.00
169 Alan Henderson B .25 .60
170 Tony Delk B .40 1.00
171 Jamal Mashburn B .40 1.00
172 Vinny Del Negro B .25 .60
173 Greg Ostertag B .25 .60
174 Shawn Bradley B .25 .60
175 Gheorghe Muresan B .25 .60
176 Brent Price B .25 .60
177 Rick Fox B .25 .60
178 Stacey Augmon B .30 .75
179 P.J. Brown B .25 .60
180 Jim Jackson B .25 .60
181 Hersey Hawkins B .25 .60
182 Danny Manning B .30 .75
183 Dennis Scott B .30 .75
184 Tom Gugliotta B .30 .75
185 Tyrone Hill B .30 .75
186 Malik Sealy B .25 .60
187 John Starks B .40 1.00
188 Mark Price B .40 1.00
189 Elden Campbell B .30 .75
190 Mahmoud Abdul-Rauf B .30 .75
191 Will Perdue B .25 .60
192 Nate McMillan B .25 .60
193 Robert Horry B .40 1.00
194 Dino Radja B .25 .60
195 Loy Vaught B .25 .60
196 Dikembe Mutombo B .60 1.50
197 Eric Montross B .25 .60
198 Sasha Danilovic B .25 .60
199 Kenny Anderson B .30 .75
200 Sean Elliott B .40 1.00
201 Mark West B .25 .60
202 Vlade Divac B .40 1.00
203 Joe Dumars B .50 1.25
204 Allan Houston B .40 1.00
205 Kevin Garnett B 1.25 3.00
206 Rod Strickland B .40 1.00
207 Robert Parish B .50 1.25
208 Jalen Rose B .50 1.25
209 Armon Gilliam B .25 .60
210 Kerry Kittles B .40 1.00
211 Derrick Coleman B .25 .60
212 Greg Anthony B .25 .60
213 Joe Smith B .30 .75
214 Steve Smith B .30 .75
215 Tim Hardaway B .50 1.25
216 Tyus Edney B .25 .60
217 Steve Nash B 2.50 6.00
218 Anthony Mason B .30 .75
219 Otis Thorpe B .30 .75
220 Eddie Jones B .40 1.00
221 Rik Smits B .25 .60
222 Isaiah Rider B .30 .75
223 Bobby Phills B .25 .60
224 Antoine Walker B .60 1.50
225 Rod Strickland B .40 1.00
226 Hubert Davis B .25 .60
227 Eric Williams B .25 .60
228 Danny Manning B .30 .75
229 Dominique Wilkins B .60 1.50
230 Brian Shaw B .25 .60
231 Larry Johnson B .50 1.25
232 Kevin Willis B .30 .75
233 Bryant Stith B .25 .60
234 Blue Edwards B .25 .60
235 Robert Pack B .25 .60
236 Brian Grant B .30 .75
237 Latrell Sprewell B .40 1.00
238 Glen Rice B .40 1.00
239 Jerome Williams B .30 .75
240 Allen Iverson B 8.00 20.00
241 Popeye Jones B .25 .60
242 Clifford Robinson B .40 1.00
243 Shaquille O'Neal B 1.50 4.00
244 Vitaly Potapenko B RC .60 1.50
245 Ervin Johnson B .25 .60
246 Checklist .25 .60
247 Scottie Pippen S 2.50 6.00
248 Jason Kidd S 1.50 4.00
249 Antonio McDyess S 1.00 2.50
250 Latrell Sprewell S 1.00 2.50
251 Lorenzen Wright S .50 1.25
252 Ray Allen S 10.00 25.00
253 Stephon Marbury S 2.00 5.00
254 Patrick Ewing S 1.50 4.00
255 Anfernee Hardaway S 2.50 6.00
256 Kenny Anderson S .75 2.00
257 David Robinson S 2.00 5.00
258 Marcus Camby S 1.00 2.50
259 Shareef Abdur-Rahim S 1.00 2.50
260 Dennis Rodman S 2.50 6.00
261 Juwan Howard S 1.00 2.50
262 Damon Stoudamire S 1.00 2.50
263 Shawn Kemp S 1.50 4.00
264 Mitch Richmond S 1.25 3.00
265 Jerry Stackhouse S 1.25 3.00
266 Horace Grant S 1.00 2.50
267 Kerry Kittles S .60 1.50
268 Vin Baker S .75 2.00
269 Kobe Bryant G 800.00 1,500.00
270 Reggie Miller S 2.00 5.00
271 Grant Hill S 1.50 4.00
272 Oliver Miller S .60 1.50
273 Chris Webber S 1.25 3.00
274 Dikembe Mutombo G 5.00 12.00
275 Antonio McDyess G 3.00 8.00
276 Clyde Drexler G 5.00 12.00
277 Brent Barry G 2.50 6.00
278 Tim Hardaway G 4.00 10.00
279 Glenn Robinson G 3.00 8.00
280 Allen Iverson G 15.00 40.00
281 Hakeem Olajuwon G 6.00 15.00
282 Marcus Camby G 3.00 8.00
283 John Stockton G 6.00 15.00
284 Shareef Abdur-Rahim G 3.00 8.00
285 Karl Malone G 6.00 15.00
286 Gary Payton G 5.00 12.00
287 Stephon Marbury G 6.00 15.00
288 Alonzo Mourning G 5.00 12.00
289 Shaquille O'Neal S 4.00 10.00
290 Charles Barkley G 8.00 20.00
291 Michael Jordan G 60.00 150.00

1996-97 Finest Refractors

*BRONZE STARS: 5X TO 12X BASIC CARDS
*BRONZE RCs: 2.5X TO 6X HI
BRONZE: SER.1/2 STATED ODDS 1:12
*SILVER STARS: 2X TO 5X BASIC CARDS
*SILVER RCs: 1.25X TO 3X BASIC CARDS
SILVER: SER.1/2 STATED ODDS 1:48
*GOLD STARS/RCs: 1.25X TO 3X BASIC CARDS
GOLD: SER.1/2 STATED ODDS 1:288
LAETTNR B EWING G HORNCEK G #'d 136
22 Ray Allen B 125.00 300.00
50 Michael Jordan B 150.00 400.00
69 Allen Iverson B 200.00 500.00
74 Kobe Bryant B 1,250.00 2,500.00
75 Steve Nash B 150.00 400.00
127 Michael Jordan S 150.00 400.00
141 Reggie Miller G 15.00 40.00
217 Steve Nash B 75.00 200.00
240 Allen Iverson B 75.00 200.00
252 Ray Allen S 125.00 300.00
280 Allen Iverson G 100.00 250.00
290 Charles Barkley G 20.00 50.00
291 Michael Jordan G 600.00 1,200.00

1997-98 Finest Promos

COMPLETE SET (6) 2.50 6.00
27 Chris Webber .75 2.00
45 Vin Baker .50 1.25
57 Allen Iverson 2.00 5.00
67 Eddie Jones .60 1.50
68 Joe Smith .50 1.25
80 Gary Payton 1.00 2.50

1997-98 Finest

COMPLETE SET (326) 300.00 600.00
COMPLETE SERIES 1 (173) 150.00 300.00
COMPLETE SERIES 2 (153) 150.00 300.00
SILVER: SER.1/2 STATED ODDS 1:4
GOLD: SER.1/2 STATED ODDS 1:24
1 Scottie Pippen B 1.25 3.00
2 Tim Hardaway B .60 1.50
3 Bo Outlaw B .30 .75
4 Rik Smits B .30 .75
5 Dale Ellis B .40 1.00
6 Clyde Drexler B .75 2.00
7 Steve Smith B .40 1.00
8 Nick Anderson B .40 1.00
9 Juwan Howard B .40 1.00
10 Cedric Ceballos B .40 1.00
11 Shawn Bradley B .30 .75
12 Loy Vaught B .30 .75
13 Todd Day B .30 .75
14 Glen Rice B .50 1.25
15 Bryant Stith B .30 .75
16 Bob Sura B .30 .75
17 Derrick McKey B .30 .75
18 Ray Allen B 1.00 2.50
19 Stephon Marbury B .60 1.50
20 David Robinson B 1.00 2.50
21 Anthony Peeler B .30 .75
22 Isaiah Rider B .40 1.00
23 Mookie Blaylock B .50 1.25
24 Damon Stoudamire B .50 1.25
25 Rod Strickland B .40 1.00
26 Glenn Robinson B .50 1.25
27 Chris Webber B .60 1.50
28 Christian Laettner B .50 1.25
29 Joe Dumars B .50 1.25
30 Mark Price B .50 1.25
31 Jamal Mashburn B .40 1.00
32 Danny Manning B .40 1.00
33 John Stockton B 1.00 2.50
34 Detlef Schrempf B .50 1.25
35 Tyus Edney B .30 .75
36 Chris Childs B .30 .75
37 Dana Barros B .30 .75
38 Bobby Phills B .40 1.00
39 Michael Jordan B 15.00 40.00
40 Grant Hill B .75 2.00
41 Brent Barry B .40 1.00
42 Rony Seikaly B .40 1.00
43 Shareef Abdur-Rahim B .50 1.25
44 Dominique Wilkins B .60 1.50
45 Vin Baker B .40 1.00
46 Kendall Gill B .40 1.00
47 Muggsy Bogues B .40 1.00
48 Hakeem Olajuwon B 1.00 2.50
49 Reggie Miller B 1.00 2.50
50 Shaquille O'Neal B 1.50 4.00
51 Antonio McDyess B .50 1.25
52 Michael Finley B .50 1.25
53 Jerry Stackhouse B .50 1.25
54 Brian Grant B .40 1.00
55 Greg Anthony B .40 1.00
56 Patrick Ewing B .75 2.00
57 Allen Iverson B 1.50 4.00
58 Rasheed Wallace B .60 1.50
59 Shawn Kemp B .75 2.00
60 Bryant Reeves B .30 .75
61 Kevin Garnett B 1.25 3.00
62 Allan Houston B .50 1.25
63 Stacey Augmon B .40 1.00
64 Rick Fox B .40 1.00
65 Derek Harper B .40 1.00
66 Lindsey Hunter B .30 .75
67 Eddie Jones B .50 1.25
68 Joe Smith B .40 1.00
69 Alonzo Mourning B .75 2.00
70 LaPhonso Ellis B .40 1.00
71 Tyrone Hill B .40 1.00
72 Charles Barkley B 1.25 3.00
73 Malik Sealy B .40 1.00
74 Shandon Anderson B .30 .75
75 Arvydas Sabonis B .60 1.50
76 Tom Gugliotta B .60 1.50
77 Anfernee Hardaway B 1.25 3.00
78 Sean Elliott B .40 1.00
79 Marcus Camby B .50 1.25
80 Gary Payton B .75 2.00
81 Kerry Kittles B .40 1.00
82 Dikembe Mutombo B .75 2.00
83 Antoine Walker B .50 1.25
84 Terrell Brandon B .40 1.00
85 Otis Thorpe B .40 1.00
86 Mark Jackson B .40 1.00
87 A.C. Green B .40 1.00
88 John Starks B .50 1.25
89 Kenny Anderson B .40 1.00
90 Karl Malone B 1.00 2.50
91 Mitch Richmond B .60 1.50
92 Derrick Coleman B .50 1.25
93 Horace Grant B .50 1.25
94 John Williams B .30 .75
95 Jason Kidd B .75 2.00
96 Mahmoud Abdul-Rauf B .30 .75
97 Walt Williams B .40 1.00
98 Anthony Mason B .40 1.00
99 Latrell Sprewell B .60 1.50
100 Checklist .20 .50
101 Tim Duncan B RC 8.00 20.00
102 Keith Van Horn B RC .75 2.00
103 Chauncey Billups B RC 1.50 4.00
104 Antonio Daniels B RC .50 1.25
105 Tony Battie B RC .50 1.25
106 Tim Thomas B RC .60 1.50
107 Tracy McGrady B RC 2.50 6.00
108 Adonal Foyle B RC .40 1.00
109 Maurice Taylor B RC .40 1.00
110 Austin Croshere B RC .40 1.00
111 Bobby Jackson B RC .60 1.50
112 Olivier Saint-Jean B RC .40 1.00
113 John Thomas B RC .30 .75
114 Derek Anderson B RC .50 1.25
115 Brevin Knight B RC .50 1.25
116 Charles Smith B RC .30 .75
117 Johnny Taylor B RC .30 .75
118 Jacque Vaughn B RC .40 1.00
119 Anthony Parker B RC .50 1.25
120 Paul Grant B RC .30 .75
121 Stephon Marbury S 1.25 3.00
122 Terrell Brandon S .75 2.00
123 Dikembe Mutombo S 1.50 4.00
124 Patrick Ewing S 1.50 4.00
125 Scottie Pippen S 2.50 6.00
126 Antoine Walker S 1.00 2.50
127 Karl Malone S 2.00 5.00
128 Sean Elliott S .75 2.00
129 Chris Webber S 1.25 3.00
130 Shawn Kemp S 1.25 3.00
131 Hakeem Olajuwon S 2.00 5.00
132 Tim Hardaway S 1.25 3.00
133 Glen Rice S 1.00 2.50
134 Vin Baker S .75 2.00
135 Jim Jackson S .75 2.00
136 Kevin Garnett S 2.50 6.00
137 Kobe Bryant S 25.00 60.00
138 Damon Stoudamire S 1.00 2.50
139 Larry Johnson S 1.25 3.00
140 Latrell Sprewell S 1.25 3.00
141 Lorenzen Wright S .60 1.50
142 Toni Kukoc S 1.25 3.00
143 Allen Iverson S 3.00 8.00
144 Elden Campbell S .60 1.50
145 Tom Gugliotta S .75 2.00
146 David Robinson S 2.00 5.00
147 Jayson Williams S 1.00 2.50
148 Shaquille O'Neal S 3.00 8.00
149 Grant Hill S 1.50 4.00
150 Reggie Miller S 2.00 5.00
151 Clyde Drexler S 1.50 4.00
152 Ray Allen S 2.00 5.00
153 Eddie Jones S 1.00 2.50
154 Michael Jordan G 40.00 100.00
155 Dominique Wilkins G 5.00 12.00
156 Charles Barkley G 10.00 25.00
157 Jerry Stackhouse G 4.00 10.00
158 Juwan Howard G 3.00 8.00
159 Marcus Camby G 4.00 10.00
160 Christian Laettner G 4.00 10.00
161 Anthony Mason G 3.00 8.00
162 Joe Smith G 3.00 8.00
163 Kerry Kittles G 3.00 8.00
164 Mitch Richmond G 5.00 12.00
165 Shareef Abdur-Rahim G 4.00 10.00
166 Alonzo Mourning G 6.00 15.00
167 Dennis Rodman G 10.00 25.00
168 Antonio McDyess G 4.00 10.00
169 Shawn Bradley G 2.50 6.00
170 Anfernee Hardaway G 10.00 25.00
171 Jason Kidd G 6.00 15.00
172 Gary Payton G 6.00 15.00
173 John Stockton G 8.00 20.00
174 Allan Houston B .50 1.25
175 Bob Sura B .30 .75
176 Clyde Drexler B .75 2.00
177 Glenn Robinson B .50 1.25
178 Joe Smith B .40 1.00
179 Larry Johnson B .60 1.50
180 Mitch Richmond B .60 1.50
181 Rony Seikaly B .40 1.00
182 Tyrone Hill B .40 1.00
183 Allen Iverson B 1.50 4.00
184 Brent Barry B .40 1.00
185 Damon Stoudamire B .50 1.25
186 Grant Hill B .75 2.00
187 John Stockton B 1.00 2.50
188 Latrell Sprewell B .60 1.50
189 Mookie Blaylock B .50 1.25
190 Samaki Walker B .30 .75
191 Vin Baker B .40 1.00
192 Alonzo Mourning B .75 2.00
193 Brevin Knight B .50 1.25
194 Danny Manning B .40 1.00
195 Hakeem Olajuwon B 1.00 2.50
196 Johnny Taylor B .30 .75
197 Lorenzen Wright B .30 .75
198 Olden Polynice B .30 .75
199 Scottie Pippen B 1.25 3.00
200 Lindsey Hunter B .30 .75
201 Anfernee Hardaway B 1.25 3.00
202 Greg Anthony B .40 1.00
203 David Robinson B 1.00 2.50
204 Horace Grant B .50 1.25
205 Calbert Cheaney B .40 1.00
206 Loy Vaught B .40 1.00
207 Tariq Abdul-Wahad B .40 1.00
208 Sean Elliott B .40 1.00
209 Rodney Rogers B .40 1.00
210 Anthony Mason B .40 1.00
211 Bryant Reeves B .30 .75
212 David Wesley B .40 1.00
213 Isaiah Rider B .40 1.00
214 Karl Malone B 1.00 2.50
215 Mahmoud Abdul-Rauf B .30 .75
216 Patrick Ewing B .75 2.00
217 Shaquille O'Neal B 1.50 4.00
218 Antoine Walker B .50 1.25
219 Charles Barkley B 1.25 3.00
220 Dennis Rodman B 1.25 3.00
221 Jamal Mashburn B .40 1.00
222 Kendall Gill B .40 1.00
223 Malik Sealy B .40 1.00
224 Rasheed Wallace B .60 1.50
225 Shareef Abdur-Rahim B .50 1.25
226 Antonio Daniels B .50 1.25
227 Charles Oakley B .40 1.00
228 Derek Anderson B .50 1.25
229 Jason Kidd B .75 2.00
230 Kenny Anderson B .40 1.00
231 Marcus Camby B .50 1.25
232 Ray Allen B 1.00 2.50
233 Shawn Bradley B .30 .75
234 Antonio McDyess B .50 1.25
235 Chauncey Billups B 1.50 4.00
236 Detlef Schrempf B .50 1.25
237 Jayson Williams B .30 .75
238 Kerry Kittles B .40 1.00
239 Jalen Rose B .40 1.00
240 Reggie Miller B 1.00 2.50
241 Shawn Kemp B .75 2.00
242 Arvydas Sabonis B .60 1.50
243 Tom Gugliotta B .60 1.50
244 Dikembe Mutombo B .75 2.00
245 Jeff Hornacek B .50 1.25
246 Kevin Garnett B 1.25 3.00
247 Matt Maloney B .30 .75
248 Rex Chapman B .30 .75
249 Stephon Marbury B .60 1.50
250 Austin Croshere B .40 1.00
251 Chris Childs B .30 .75
252 Eddie Jones B .50 1.25
253 Jerry Stackhouse B .50 1.25
254 Kevin Johnson B .40 1.00
255 Maurice Taylor B .40 1.00
256 Chris Mullin B .60 1.50
257 Terrell Brandon B .40 1.00
258 Avery Johnson B .40 1.00
259 Chris Webber B .60 1.50
260 Gary Payton B .75 2.00
261 Jim Jackson B .40 1.00
262 Kobe Bryant B 10.00 25.00
263 Michael Finley B .50 1.25
264 Rod Strickland B .40 1.00
265 Tim Hardaway B .60 1.50
266 B.J. Armstrong B .30 .75
267 Christian Laettner B .50 1.25
268 Glen Rice B .50 1.25
269 Joe Dumars B .60 1.50
270 LaPhonso Ellis B .40 1.00
271 Michael Jordan B 12.00 30.00
272 Ron Mercer B RC .60 1.50
273 Checklist S .60 1.50
274 Anfernee Hardaway S 2.50 6.00
275 Dennis Rodman S 2.50 6.00
276 Gary Payton S 1.50 4.00
277 Jamal Mashburn S .75 2.00
278 Shareef Abdur-Rahim S 1.00 2.50
279 Steve Smith S .75 2.00
280 Tony Battie S .60 1.50
281 Alonzo Mourning S 1.50 4.00
282 Bobby Jackson S .75 2.00
283 Christian Laettner S 1.00 2.50
284 Jerry Stackhouse S 1.00 2.50
285 Terrell Brandon S .75 2.00
286 Chauncey Billups S 2.00 5.00
287 Michael Jordan S 25.00 60.00
288 Glenn Robinson S 1.00 2.50
289 Jason Kidd S 1.50 4.00
290 Joe Smith S .75 2.00
291 Michael Finley S 1.00 2.50
292 Rod Strickland S .75 2.00
293 Ron Mercer S .75 2.00
294 Tracy McGrady S 3.00 8.00
295 Adonal Foyle S .50 1.25
296 Marcus Camby S 1.00 2.50
297 John Stockton S 2.00 5.00
298 Kerry Kittles S .75 2.00
299 Mitch Richmond S 1.25 3.00
300 Shawn Bradley S .60 1.50
301 Anthony Mason S .75 2.00
302 Antonio Daniels S .60 1.50
303 Antonio McDyess S 1.00 2.50
304 Charles Barkley S 2.50 6.00
305 Keith Van Horn S 1.00 2.50
306 Tim Duncan S 6.00 15.00
307 Dikembe Mutombo G 6.00 15.00
308 Grant Hill G 6.00 15.00
309 Shaquille O'Neal G 12.00 30.00
310 Keith Van Horn G 4.00 10.00
311 Shawn Kemp G 6.00 15.00
312 Antoine Walker G 4.00 10.00
313 Hakeem Olajuwon G 8.00 20.00
314 Vin Baker G 3.00 8.00
315 Patrick Ewing G 6.00 15.00
316 Tracy McGrady G 12.00 30.00
317 Glen Rice G 4.00 10.00
318 Reggie Miller G 8.00 20.00
319 Kevin Garnett G 10.00 25.00
320 Allen Iverson G 12.00 30.00
321 Karl Malone G 8.00 20.00
322 Scottie Pippen G 10.00 25.00
323 Kobe Bryant G 25.00 60.00
324 Stephon Marbury G 5.00 12.00
325 Tim Duncan G 30.00 80.00
326 Chris Webber G 5.00 12.00

1997-98 Finest Embossed

*SILVER: .5X TO 1.25X BASE HI
*SILVER RCs: .4X TO 1X BASE HI
SILVER: SER.1/2 STATED ODDS 1:16
*GOLD STARS: .6X TO 1.5X BASE HI
*GOLD RCs: .5X TO 1.25X BASE HI
GOLD: SER.1/2 STATED ODDS 1:96
154 Michael Jordan G 100.00 250.00
325 Tim Duncan G 25.00 60.00

1997-98 Finest Embossed Refractors

*SILVER STARS/RCs: 4X TO 10X BASE HI
SILVER: SER.1/2 STATED ODDS 1:192
STATED PRINT RUN 263 SERIAL #'d SETS
ALL SILVER CARDS ARE NON DIE CUT
*GOLD STARS/RCs: 8X TO 20X BASE HI
GOLD: SER.1/2 STATED ODDS 1:1152
STATED PRINT RUN 74 SERIAL #'d SETS
136 Kevin Garnett S 75.00 200.00
137 Kobe Bryant S 500.00 1,000.00
146 David Robinson S 25.00 60.00
148 Shaquille O'Neal S 75.00 200.00
149 Grant Hill S 40.00 100.00
150 Reggie Miller S 40.00 100.00
151 Clyde Drexler S 30.00 80.00
152 Ray Allen S 40.00 100.00
154 Michael Jordan G 25,000.00 50,000.00
156 Charles Barkley G 300.00 600.00
157 Jerry Stackhouse G 150.00 400.00
167 Dennis Rodman G 1,000.00 3,000.00
170 Anfernee Hardaway G 400.00 800.00
274 Anfernee Hardaway S 40.00 100.00
275 Dennis Rodman S 75.00 200.00
276 Gary Payton S 30.00 80.00
286 Chauncey Billups S 75.00 200.00
287 Michael Jordan S 3,000.00 6,000.00
306 Tim Duncan S 125.00 300.00
308 Grant Hill G 200.00 500.00
309 Shaquille O'Neal G 300.00 600.00
311 Shawn Kemp G 200.00 500.00
313 Hakeem Olajuwon G 150.00 400.00
315 Patrick Ewing G 150.00 400.00
318 Reggie Miller G 200.00 500.00
319 Kevin Garnett G 200.00 500.00
320 Allen Iverson G 500.00 1,000.00
321 Karl Malone G 200.00 500.00
322 Scottie Pippen G 200.00 500.00
323 Kobe Bryant G 10,000.00 15,000.00
325 Tim Duncan G 2,000.00 4,000.00
326 Chris Webber G 200.00 500.00

1997-98 Finest Refractors

*BRONZE STARS: 3X TO 8X BASIC CARDS
BRONZE: SER.1/2 STATED ODDS 1:12
*SILVER: 3X TO 8X BASIC CARDS
SILVER: SER.1/2 STATED ODDS 1:48
STATED PRINT RUN 1090 SERIAL #'d SETS
*GOLD STARS/RCs: 2X TO 5X BASIC CARDS
GOLD: SER.1/2 STATED ODDS 1:288
STATED PRINT RUN 289 SERIAL #'d SETS
1 Scottie Pippen B 20.00 50.00
20 David Robinson B 12.00 30.00
39 Michael Jordan B 200.00 500.00
48 Hakeem Olajuwon B 15.00 40.00
49 Reggie Miller B 15.00 40.00
50 Shaquille O'Neal B 30.00 80.00
57 Allen Iverson B 20.00 50.00
61 Kevin Garnett B 20.00 50.00
101 Tim Duncan B 50.00 120.00
125 Scottie Pippen S 25.00 60.00
129 Chris Webber S 20.00 50.00
130 Shawn Kemp S 20.00 50.00
131 Hakeem Olajuwon S 20.00 50.00
136 Kevin Garnett S 40.00 100.00
137 Kobe Bryant S 200.00 500.00
154 Michael Jordan G 2,000.00 4,000.00
166 Alonzo Mourning G 40.00 100.00
167 Dennis Rodman G 125.00 300.00
199 Scottie Pippen B 20.00 50.00
201 Anfernee Hardaway B 15.00 40.00
203 David Robinson B 12.00 30.00
217 Shaquille O'Neal B 20.00 50.00
220 Dennis Rodman B 15.00 40.00
262 Kobe Bryant B 125.00 300.00
271 Michael Jordan B 200.00 500.00
275 Dennis Rodman S 75.00 200.00
276 Gary Payton S 12.00 30.00
287 Michael Jordan S 500.00 1,000.00
304 Charles Barkley S 30.00 80.00
306 Tim Duncan S 125.00 300.00
319 Kevin Garnett G 75.00 200.00
320 Allen Iverson G 125.00 300.00
322 Scottie Pippen G 125.00 300.00
323 Kobe Bryant G 500.00 1,000.00
325 Tim Duncan G 350.00 700.00

1998-99 Finest Promos

COMPLETE SET (6) 2.50 6.00
PP1 Dikembe Mutombo 1.25 3.00
PP2 Antoine Walker .75 2.00
PP3 Reggie Miller 1.50 4.00
PP4 John Stockton 1.50 4.00
PP5 Eddie Jones .75 2.00
PP6 Gary Payton 1.25 3.00

1998-99 Finest

COMPLETE SET (250) 30.00 60.00
COMPLETE SERIES 1 (125) 15.00 30.00
COMPLETE SERIES 2 (125) 15.00 30.00
1 Chris Mills .20 .50
2 Matt Maloney .20 .50
3 Sam Mitchell .20 .50
4 Corliss Williamson .20 .50
5 Bryant Reeves .20 .50
6 Juwan Howard .25 .60
7 Eddie Jones .30 .75
8 Ray Allen .50 1.25
9 Larry Johnson .50 1.25
10 Travis Best .20 .50
11 Isaiah Rider .25 .60
12 Hakeem Olajuwon .60 1.50
13 Gary Trent .20 .50
14 Kevin Garnett .75 2.00
15 Dikembe Mutombo .50 1.25
16 Brevin Knight .20 .50
17 Keith Van Horn .30 .75
18 Theo Ratliff .25 .60
19 Tim Hardaway .40 1.00
20 Blue Edwards .20 .50
21 David Wesley .20 .50
22 Jaren Jackson .20 .50
23 Nick Anderson .20 .50
24 Rodney Rogers .20 .50
25 Antonio Davis .20 .50
26 Clarence Weatherspoon .20 .50
27 Kelvin Cato .20 .50
28 Tracy McGrady .50 1.25
29 Mookie Blaylock .25 .60
30 Ron Harper .25 .60
31 Allan Houston .30 .75
32 Brian Williams .20 .50
33 John Stockton .60 1.50
34 Hersey Hawkins .20 .50
35 Donyell Marshall .20 .50
36 Mark Strickland .20 .50
37 Rod Strickland .20 .50
38 Cedric Ceballos .25 .60
39 Danny Fortson .20 .50
40 Shaquille O'Neal 1.25 3.00
41 Kendall Gill .25 .60
42 Allen Iverson .75 2.00
43 Travis Knight .20 .50
44 Cedric Henderson .20 .50
45 Steve Kerr .25 .60
46 Antonio McDyess .25 .60
47 Darrick Martin .20 .50
48 Shandon Anderson .20 .50
49 Shareef Abdur-Rahim .30 .75
50 Antoine Carr .20 .50
51 Jason Kidd .50 1.25
52 Calbert Cheaney .20 .50
53 Antoine Walker .30 .75
54 Greg Anthony .20 .50
55 Jeff Hornacek .25 .60
56 Reggie Miller .60 1.50
57 Lawrence Funderburke .20 .50
58 Derek Strong .20 .50
59 Robert Horry .25 .60
60 Shawn Bradley .20 .50
61 Matt Bullard .20 .50
62 Terrell Brandon .25 .60
63 Dan Majerle .30 .75
64 Jim Jackson .20 .50
65 Anthony Peeler .20 .50
66 Bo Outlaw .20 .50
67 Khalid Reeves .20 .50
68 Toni Kukoc .30 .75
69 Mario Elie .20 .50
70 Derek Anderson .25 .60
71 Jalen Rose .25 .60
72 Tyrone Corbin .20 .50
73 Anthony Mason .25 .60
74 Lamond Murray .20 .50
75 Tom Gugliotta .25 .60
76 Arvydas Sabonis .25 .60
77 Brian Shaw .20 .50
78 Rick Fox .20 .50
79 Danny Manning .20 .50
80 Lindsey Hunter .20 .50
81 Michael Jordan 3.00 8.00
82 LaPhonso Ellis .20 .50
83 David Robinson .60 1.50
84 Christian Laettner .25 .60
85 Armon Gilliam .20 .50
86 Sherman Douglas .20 .50
87 Charlie Ward .20 .50
88 Shawn Kemp .50 1.25
89 Gary Payton .50 1.25
90 Doug Christie .25 .60
91 Voshon Lenard .20 .50
92 Detlef Schrempf .30 .75
93 Walter McCarty .20 .50
94 Sam Cassell .25 .60
95 Jerry Stackhouse .30 .75
96 Billy Owens .25 .60
97 Matt Geiger .20 .50
98 Avery Johnson .25 .60
99 Bobby Jackson .25 .60
100 Rex Chapman .25 .60

101 Andrew DeClercq .20 .50
102 Vlade Divac .30 .75
103 Erick Strickland .20 .50
104 Dean Garrett .20 .50
105 Grant Long .20 .50
106 Adonal Foyle .20 .50
107 Isaac Austin .20 .50
108 Michael Curry .20 .50
109 Darrell Armstrong .20 .50
110 Aaron McKie .20 .50
111 Stacey Augmon .25 .60
112 Anthony Johnson .20 .50
113 Vinny Del Negro .20 .50
114 Reggie Slater .20 .50
115 Lee Mayberry .20 .50
116 Tracy Murray .20 .50
117 Scottie Pippen .75 2.00
118 Sam Perkins .20 .50
119 Derek Fisher .25 .60
120 Mark Bryant .20 .50
121 Dale Davis .20 .50
122 B.J. Armstrong .20 .50
123 Charles Barkley .75 2.00
124 Horace Grant .30 .75
125 Checklist .20 .50
126 Alonzo Mourning .50 1.25
127 Kerry Kittles .25 .60
128 Eldridge Recasner .20 .50
129 Dell Curry .20 .50
130 Jamal Mashburn .30 .75
131 Eric Piatkowski .20 .50
132 Othella Harrington .20 .50
133 Pete Chilcutt .20 .50
134 Dennis Rodman .75 2.00
135 Patrick Ewing .50 1.25
136 Danny Schayes .20 .50
137 John Williams .20 .50
138 Joe Smith .25 .60
139 Tariq Abdul-Wahad .20 .50
140 Vin Baker .25 .60
141 Elden Campbell .20 .50
142 Chris Carr .20 .50
143 John Starks .30 .75
144 Felton Spencer .20 .50
145 Mark Jackson .25 .60
146 Dana Barros .20 .50
147 Eric Williams .20 .50
148 Wesley Person .20 .50
149 Joe Dumars .30 .75
150 Steve Smith .25 .60
151 Randy Brown .20 .50
152 A.C. Green .25 .60
153 Dee Brown .20 .50
154 Brian Grant .20 .50
155 Tim Thomas .25 .60
156 Howard Eisley .20 .50
157 Malik Sealy .20 .50
158 Maurice Taylor .20 .50
159 Tyrone Hill .20 .50
160 Chris Gatling .20 .50
161 Rodrick Rhodes .20 .50
162 Muggsy Bogues .25 .60
163 Kenny Anderson .25 .60
164 Zydrunas Ilgauskas .30 .75
165 Grant Hill .50 1.25
166 Lorenzen Wright .20 .50
167 Tony Battie .20 .50
168 Bobby Phills .20 .50
169 Michael Finley .30 .75
170 Anfernee Hardaway .75 2.00
171 Terry Porter .20 .50
172 P.J. Brown .20 .50
173 Clifford Robinson .20 .50
174 Olden Polynice .20 .50
175 Kobe Bryant 2.50 6.00
176 Sean Elliott .30 .75
177 Latrell Sprewell .40 1.00
178 Rik Smits .25 .60
179 Darrell Armstrong .20 .50
180 Stephon Marbury .40 1.00
181 Brent Price .20 .50
182 Danny Fortson .20 .50
183 Vitaly Potapenko .20 .50
184 Anthony Parker .20 .50
185 Glenn Robinson .30 .75
186 Erick Dampier .20 .50
187 George McCloud .20 .50
188 Rasheed Wallace .40 1.00
189 Aaron Williams .20 .50
190 Tim Duncan .75 2.00
191 Chauncey Billups .40 1.00
192 Jim McIlvaine .20 .50
193 Chris Mullin .40 1.00
194 George Lynch .20 .50
195 Damon Stoudamire .30 .75
196 Bryon Russell .20 .50
197 Luc Longley .25 .60
198 Ron Mercer .25 .60
199 Alan Henderson .20 .50
200 Jayson Williams .20 .50
201 Ben Wallace .25 .60
202 Elliot Perry .20 .50
203 Walt Williams .20 .50
204 Cherokee Parks .20 .50
205 Brent Barry .25 .60
206 Hubert Davis .20 .50
207 Terry Davis .20 .50
208 Loy Vaught .20 .50
209 Adam Keefe .20 .50
210 Karl Malone .60 1.50
211 Chuck Person .25 .60
212 Chris Childs .20 .50
213 Rony Seikaly .20 .50
214 Ervin Johnson .20 .50
215 Derrick McKey .20 .50
216 Jerome Williams .20 .50
217 Glen Rice .30 .75
218 Steve Nash .60 1.50
219 Nick Van Exel .30 .75
220 Chris Webber .40 1.00
221 Marcus Camby .25 .60
222 Antonio Daniels .20 .50
223 Mitch Richmond .40 1.00
224 Otis Thorpe .20 .50
225 Charles Oakley .25 .60
226 Michael Olowokandi RC .75 2.00
227 Mike Bibby RC 1.25 3.00
228 Raef LaFrentz RC .75 2.00
229 Antawn Jamison RC 1.00 2.50
230 Vince Carter RC 15.00 40.00
231 Robert Traylor RC .60 1.50
232 Jason Williams RC 2.00 5.00
233 Larry Hughes RC 1.00 2.50
234 Dirk Nowitzki RC 20.00 50.00
235 Paul Pierce RC 12.00 30.00
236 Bonzi Wells RC .60 1.50
237 Michael Doleac RC .50 1.25
238 Keon Clark RC .60 1.50
239 Michael Dickerson RC .60 1.50
240 Matt Harpring RC .60 1.50
241 Bryce Drew RC .40 1.00
242 Pat Garrity RC .50 1.25
243 Roshown McLeod RC .40 1.00
244 Ricky Davis RC 1.00 2.50
245 Brian Skinner RC .50 1.25
246 Tyronn Lue RC .75 2.00
247 Felipe Lopez RC .40 1.00
248 Sam Jacobson RC .40 1.00
249 Corey Benjamin RC .40 1.00
250 Nazr Mohammed RC .60 1.50

1998-99 Finest No Protectors

*STARS: 1.5X TO 4X BASE CARD HI
*RCs: .6X TO 1.5X BASE HI
SER.1/2 STATED ODDS 1:4 H/R

1998-99 Finest No Protectors Refractors

*STARS: 6X TO 15X BASE CARD HI
*RCs: 2.5X TO 6X BASE HI
SER.1/2 STATED ODDS 1:24 H/R
81 Michael Jordan 1,500.00 3,000.00
230 Vince Carter 300.00 600.00
232 Jason Williams 75.00 200.00
234 Dirk Nowitzki 400.00 800.00

1998-99 Finest Refractors

*REF.STARS: 3X TO 8X BASE CARD HI
*REF.RCs: 1.5X TO 4X BASE
REF: SER.1/2 STATED ODDS 1:12 H/R
9 Larry Johnson 10.00 25.00
28 Tracy McGrady 12.00 30.00
42 Allen Iverson 12.00 30.00
81 Michael Jordan 400.00 800.00
88 Shawn Kemp 12.00 30.00
89 Gary Payton 12.00 30.00
117 Scottie Pippen 6.00 15.00
134 Dennis Rodman 25.00 60.00
175 Kobe Bryant 300.00 600.00
218 Steve Nash 12.00 30.00
230 Vince Carter 150.00 400.00
232 Jason Williams 50.00 120.00
234 Dirk Nowitzki 200.00 500.00
235 Paul Pierce 75.00 200.00

1998-99 Finest Arena Stars

COMPLETE SET (20) 300.00 600.00
SER.2 STATED ODDS 1:48 H/R
AS1 Shaquille O'Neal 10.00 25.00
AS2 Stephon Marbury 3.00 8.00
AS3 Allen Iverson 6.00 15.00
AS4 John Stockton 5.00 12.00
AS5 Kobe Bryant 75.00 200.00
AS6 Alonzo Mourning 4.00 10.00
AS7 Damon Stoudamire 2.50 6.00
AS8 Scottie Pippen 6.00 15.00
AS9 Tim Hardaway 3.00 8.00
AS10 Karl Malone 5.00 12.00
AS11 Tim Duncan 6.00 15.00
AS12 Gary Payton 4.00 10.00
AS13 Antoine Walker 2.50 6.00
AS14 Keith Van Horn 2.50 6.00
AS15 Juwan Howard 2.00 5.00
AS16 David Robinson 5.00 12.00
AS17 Michael Finley 2.50 6.00
AS18 Shareef Abdur-Rahim 2.50 6.00
AS19 Michael Jordan 300.00 600.00
AS20 Vin Baker 2.00 5.00

1998-99 Finest Centurions

SER.1 STATED ODDS 1:91 H/R
STATED PRINT RUN 500 SERIAL #'d SETS
*REF: 3X TO 8X HI COLUMN
REF: PRINT RUN 75 SERIAL #'d SETS
C1 Grant Hill 6.00 15.00
C2 Tim Thomas 3.00 8.00
C3 Eddie Jones 4.00 10.00
C4 Michael Finley 4.00 10.00
C5 Shaquille O'Neal 12.00 30.00
C6 Kobe Bryant 40.00 100.00
C7 Keith Van Horn 4.00 10.00
C8 Tim Duncan 6.00 15.00
C9 Antoine Walker 4.00 10.00
C10 Shareef Abdur-Rahim 4.00 10.00
C11 Stephon Marbury 5.00 12.00
C12 Kevin Garnett 10.00 25.00
C13 Ray Allen 6.00 15.00
C14 Kerry Kittles 3.00 8.00
C15 Allen Iverson 10.00 25.00
C16 Damon Stoudamire 4.00 10.00
C17 Brevin Knight 2.50 6.00
C18 Bryant Reeves 2.50 6.00
C19 Ron Mercer 3.00 8.00
C20 Zydrunas Ilgauskas 4.00 10.00

1998-99 Finest Court Control

SER.2 STATED ODDS 1:76 H/R
STATED PRINT RUN 750 SERIAL #'d SETS
*REF: 1.25X TO 3X HI COLUMN
REF: PRINT RUN 150 SERIAL #'d SETS
CC1 Shareef Abdur-Rahim 3.00 8.00
CC2 Keith Van Horn 3.00 8.00
CC3 Tim Duncan 8.00 20.00
CC4 Antoine Walker 3.00 8.00
CC5 Stephon Marbury 4.00 10.00
CC6 Kevin Garnett 8.00 20.00
CC7 Grant Hill 5.00 12.00
CC8 Michael Finley 3.00 8.00
CC9 Ron Mercer 2.50 6.00
CC10 Damon Stoudamire 3.00 8.00
CC11 Michael Olowokandi 2.00 5.00
CC12 Mike Bibby 3.00 8.00
CC13 Antawn Jamison 2.50 6.00
CC14 Vince Carter 8.00 20.00
CC15 Jason Williams 5.00 12.00
CC16 Larry Hughes 2.50 6.00
CC17 Paul Pierce 6.00 15.00
CC18 Michael Dickerson 1.50 4.00
CC19 Bryce Drew 1.00 2.50
CC20 Felipe Lopez 1.00 2.50

1998-99 Finest Hardwood Honors

COMPLETE SET (20) 75.00 150.00
SER.1 STATED ODDS 1:33 H/R
H1 Michael Jordan 60.00 150.00
H2 Shaquille O'Neal 10.00 25.00
H3 Karl Malone 5.00 12.00
H4 Eddie Jones 2.50 6.00
H5 Dikembe Mutombo 4.00 10.00
H6 Wesley Person 1.50 4.00
H7 Glen Rice 2.50 6.00
H8 David Robinson 5.00 12.00
H9 Rik Smits 2.00 5.00
H10 Steve Smith 2.00 5.00
H11 Allen Iverson 6.00 15.00
H12 Jayson Williams 1.50 4.00
H13 Nick Anderson 1.50 4.00
H14 Tim Duncan 6.00 15.00
H15 Jason Kidd 4.00 10.00
H16 Alonzo Mourning 4.00 10.00
H17 Sam Cassell 2.00 5.00
H18 Alan Henderson 1.50 4.00
H19 Gary Payton 4.00 10.00
H20 Scottie Pippen 6.00 15.00

1998-99 Finest Mystery Finest

SER.1 STATED ODDS 1:33 H/R
SER.2 STATED ODDS 1:36 H/R
M1 M.Jordan/K.Bryant 25.00 60.00
M2 K.Bryant/S.O'Neal 10.00 25.00
M3 S.O'Neal/D.Robinson 6.00 15.00
M4 D.Robinson/T.Duncan 3.00 8.00
M5 T.Duncan/K.Van Horn 2.00 5.00
M6 K.Van Horn/S.Pippen 2.00 5.00
M7 S.Pippen/S.Abdur-Rahim 4.00 10.00
M8 S.Abdur-Rahim/G.Hill 2.50 6.00
M9 G.Hill/K.Garnett 6.00 15.00
M10 K.Garnett/S.Marbury 4.00 10.00
M11 S.Marbury/G.Payton 1.50 4.00
M12 G.Payton/V.Baker 1.50 4.00
M13 V.Baker/K.Malone 1.50 4.00
M14 K.Malone/S.Kemp 3.00 8.00
M15 S.Kemp/T.Thomas 1.50 4.00
M16 T.Thomas/A.Walker 1.50 4.00
M17 A.Walker/R.Mercer 1.25 3.00
M18 R.Mercer/K.Kittles 1.25 3.00
M19 K.Kittles/E.Jones 1.25 3.00
M20 E.Jones/M.Jordan 12.00 30.00
M21 A.Mourning/S.Pippen 4.00 10.00
M22 S.Pippen/A.Walker 4.00 10.00
M23 A.Walker/S.Abdur-Rahim 2.00 5.00
M24 S.Abdur-Rahim/K.Garnett 4.00 10.00
M25 K.Garnett/K.Van Horn 2.50 6.00
M26 K.Van Horn/T.Thomas 1.25 3.00
M27 T.Thomas/G.Hill 2.00 5.00
M28 G.Hill/A.Hardaway 4.00 10.00
M29 A.Hardaway/K.Kittles 2.50 6.00
M30 K.Kittles/J.Williams 1.25 3.00
M31 J.Williams/K.Malone 1.50 4.00
M32 K.Malone/J.Stockton 2.50 6.00
M33 J.Stockton/G.Payton 2.00 5.00
M34 G.Payton/R.Mercer 1.50 4.00
M35 R.Mercer/S.Marbury 1.50 4.00
M36 S.Marbury/A.Iverson 3.00 8.00
M37 A.Iverson/K.Bryant 6.00 15.00
M38 K.Bryant/T.Duncan 6.00 15.00
M39 T.Duncan/S.O'Neal 5.00 12.00
M40 S.O'Neal/A.Mourning 5.00 12.00

1998-99 Finest Mystery Finest Refractors

*REFRACTORS: .75X TO 2X BASE CARD HI
SER.1 STATED ODDS 1:333 H/R
SER.2 STATED ODDS 1:144 H/R
M1 M.Jordan/K.Bryant 1,500.00 3,000.00
M2 K.Bryant/S.O'Neal 800.00 1,500.00
M4 D.Robinson/T.Duncan 12.00 30.00
M20 E.Jones/M.Jordan 500.00 1,000.00
M37 A.Iverson/K.Bryant 400.00 800.00
M38 K.Bryant/T.Duncan 400.00 800.00

1998-99 Finest Oversized

COMPLETE SET (14) 12.50 30.00
COMPLETE SERIES 1 (7) 10.00 20.00
COMPLETE SERIES 2 (7) 5.00 12.00
SER.1 STATED ODDS 1:3 BOXES
SER.2 STATED ODDS ONE PER BOX
*REF: .75X TO 2X HI COLUMN
REF: SER.1/2 STATED ODDS 1:12 BOXES
1 Kevin Garnett 3.00 8.00
2 Keith Van Horn 1.25 3.00
3 Shaquille O'Neal 5.00 12.00
4 Shareef Abdur-Rahim 1.25 3.00
5 Antoine Walker 1.25 3.00
6 Gary Payton 2.00 5.00
7 Scottie Pippen 3.00 8.00
8 Alonzo Mourning 1.00 2.50
9 Kerry Kittles .50 1.25
10 Kobe Bryant 5.00 12.00
11 Stephon Marbury .75 2.00
12 Tim Duncan 1.50 4.00
13 Ron Mercer .50 1.25
14 Karl Malone 1.25 3.00

1999-00 Finest Promos

COMPLETE SET (6) 2.50 6.00
PP1 Reggie Miller 1.25 3.00
PP2 Corliss Williamson .40 1.00
PP3 Tom Gugliotta .50 1.25
PP4 Tracy McGrady 1.00 2.50
PP5 Anfernee Hardaway 1.50 4.00
PP6 Tim Duncan 1.50 4.00

1999-00 Finest

COMPLETE SET (266) 100.00 250.00
COMPLETE SERIES 1 (133) 25.00 60.00
COMPLETE SERIES 2 (133) 75.00 150.00
COMP.SERIES 2 w/o RC (118) 15.00 40.00
SER.2 RCs STATED ODDS 1:14, 1:6 HTA
SER.2 RCs PRINT RUN 2000 SERIAL #'d SETS
SUBSET CARDS INSERTED ONE PER PACK
1 Shareef Abdur-Rahim .40 1.00
2 Kevin Willis .25 .60
3 Sean Elliott .30 .75
4 Vlade Divac .40 1.00
5 Tom Gugliotta .30 .75
6 Matt Harpring .25 .60
7 Kerry Kittles .30 .75
8 Joe Smith .30 .75
9 Jamal Mashburn .30 .75
10 Tyrone Nesby RC .40 1.00
11 Alan Henderson .25 .60
12 Vitaly Potapenko .25 .60
13 Dickey Simpkins .25 .60
14 Michael Finley .40 1.00
15 Lindsey Hunter .25 .60
16 Antawn Jamison .40 1.00
17 Reggie Miller .75 2.00
18 Maurice Taylor .25 .60
19 Clarence Weatherspoon .25 .60
20 Sam Mitchell .25 .60
21 Latrell Sprewell .50 1.25
22 Michael Doleac .25 .60
23 Rex Chapman .25 .60
24 Peja Stojakovic .40 1.00
25 Vladimir Stepania .25 .60
26 Tracy McGrady .60 1.50
27 Cherokee Parks .25 .60
28 LaPhonso Ellis .25 .60
29 Hakeem Olajuwon .75 2.00
30 Adonal Foyle .25 .60
31 Bryant Stith .25 .60
32 Andrew DeClercq .25 .60
33 Toni Kukoc .50 1.25
34 Kenny Anderson .30 .75
35 Mike Bibby .40 1.00
36 Glen Rice .40 1.00
37 Avery Johnson .30 .75
38 Arvydas Sabonis .30 .75
39 Kornel David RC .40 1.00
40 Hubert Davis .25 .60
41 Grant Hill .60 1.50
42 Donyell Marshall .30 .75
43 Jalen Rose .30 .75
44 Derrick Coleman .30 .75
45 P.J. Brown .25 .60
46 Vin Baker .30 .75
47 Clifford Robinson .30 .75
48 Allan Houston .30 .75
49 Kendall Gill .40 1.00
50 Matt Geiger .25 .60
51 Larry Hughes .30 .75
52 Corliss Williamson .25 .60
53 Darrell Armstrong .25 .60
54 Bobby Jackson .30 .75
55 Bryon Russell .25 .60
56 Juwan Howard .30 .75
57 Dikembe Mutombo .60 1.50
58 Eddie Jones .40 1.00
59 Randy Brown .25 .60
60 Dirk Nowitzki 1.25 3.00
61 Jerome Williams .25 .60
62 Scottie Pippen 1.00 2.50
63 Dale Davis .25 .60
64 Kobe Bryant 3.00 8.00
65 Robert Traylor .25 .60
66 Tim Hardaway .50 1.25
67 Michael Olowokandi .25 .60
68 Walter McCarty .25 .60
69 Damon Stoudamire .40 1.00
70 Othella Harrington .25 .60
71 Chauncey Billups .40 1.00
72 John Starks .40 1.00
73 Ricky Davis .40 1.00
74 Glenn Robinson .30 .75
75 Dean Garrett .25 .60
76 Chris Childs .25 .60
77 Shawn Kemp .60 1.50
78 Allen Iverson 1.00 2.50
79 Brian Grant .25 .60
80 David Robinson .75 2.00
81 Tracy Murray .25 .60
82 Howard Eisley .25 .60
83 Doug Christie .30 .75
84 Gary Payton .60 1.50
85 John Stockton .60 1.50
86 Rod Strickland .30 .75
87 Tyrone Corbin .25 .60
88 Antonio Daniels .25 .60
89 Dee Brown .25 .60
90 Antoine Walker .40 1.00
91 Theo Ratliff .30 .75
92 Larry Johnson .40 1.00
93 Stephon Marbury .50 1.25
94 Brevin Knight .25 .60
95 Antonio McDyess .30 .75
96 Bison Dele .25 .60
97 Cuttino Mobley .25 .60
98 Haywoode Workman .25 .60
99 J.R. Reid .25 .60
100 Travis Best .25 .60
101 Chris Webber GEM .75 2.00
102 Grant Hill GEM 1.00 2.50
103 Kevin Garnett GEM 1.50 4.00
104 Jason Kidd GEM 1.00 2.50
105 Gary Payton GEM 1.00 2.50
106 Shaquille O'Neal GEM 2.50 6.00
107 Alonzo Mourning GEM 1.00 2.50
108 Karl Malone GEM 1.25 3.00
109 John Stockton GEM 1.00 2.50
110 Elton Brand RC 1.25 3.00
111 Baron Davis RC 1.50 4.00
112 A.Radojevic RC .40 1.00
113 Cal Bowdler RC .40 1.00
114 Jumaine Jones RC .40 1.00
115 Jason Terry RC 1.00 2.50
116 Trajan Langdon RC .50 1.25
117 Dion Glover RC .40 1.00
118 Jeff Foster RC .60 1.50
119 Lamar Odom RC 1.25 3.00
120 Wally Szczerbiak RC 1.00 2.50
121 Shawn Marion RC 1.25 3.00
122 Kenny Thomas RC .60 1.50
123 Devean George RC .50 1.25
124 Scott Padgett RC .50 1.25
125 Tim Duncan SEN 1.50 4.00
126 Jason Williams SEN 1.00 2.50
127 Paul Pierce SEN 1.25 3.00
128 Kobe Bryant SEN 5.00 12.00
129 Keith Van Horn SEN .50 1.25
130 Vince Carter SEN 1.50 4.00
131 Matt Harpring SEN .40 1.00
132 Antawn Jamison SEN .60 1.50
133 Tracy McGrady SEN 1.00 2.50
134 Tim Duncan 1.00 2.50
135 Tariq Abdul-Wahad .25 .60
136 Luc Longley .30 .75
137 Steve Smith .30 .75
138 Alonzo Mourning .60 1.50
139 Kevin Garnett 1.00 2.50
140 Christian Laettner .30 .75
141 Rik Smits .30 .75
142 Cedric Henderson .25 .60
143 Jim Jackson .25 .60
144 Dan Majerle .40 1.00
145 Bryant Reeves .25 .60
146 Antonio Davis .25 .60
147 Michael Smith .25 .60
148 Charlie Ward .25 .60
149 Chris Mullin .40 1.00
150 Danny Manning .30 .75
151 Eric Williams .25 .60
152 Hersey Hawkins .25 .60
153 Isaiah Rider .30 .75
154 Shandon Anderson .25 .60
155 Jason Kidd .60 1.50
156 Chris Whitney .25 .60
157 Brent Barry .30 .75
158 Patrick Ewing .50 1.25
159 George Lynch .25 .60
160 Dickey Simpkins .25 .60
161 Derek Anderson .25 .60
162 Ron Mercer .30 .75
163 David Wesley .25 .60
164 Mookie Blaylock .25 .60
165 Terrell Brandon .25 .60
166 Detlef Schrempf .30 .75
167 Olden Polynice .25 .60
168 Jayson Williams .25 .60
169 Eric Piatkowski .25 .60
170 A.C. Green .30 .75
171 Chris Mills .25 .60
172 Chris Webber .50 1.25
173 Jeff Hornacek .30 .75
174 Calbert Cheaney .25 .60
175 Wesley Person .25 .60
176 Corey Benjamin .25 .60
177 Loy Vaught .25 .60
178 Keith Closs .25 .60
179 Bo Outlaw .25 .60
180 Mitch Richmond .50 1.25
181 Charles Oakley .40 1.00
182 Felipe Lopez .25 .60
183 Eric Snow .25 .60
184 Paul Pierce .75 2.00
185 Elden Campbell .25 .60
186 Shaquille O'Neal 1.50 4.00
187 Charles Barkley 1.00 2.50
188 Mark Jackson .30 .75
189 Scott Burrell .25 .60
190 Anfernee Hardaway 1.00 2.50
191 Samaki Walker .25 .60
192 Karl Malone .75 2.00
193 Jermaine O'Neal .30 .75
194 Mario Elie .25 .60
195 Malik Sealy .25 .60
196 Voshon Lenard .25 .60
197 Chris Gatling .25 .60
198 Walt Williams .25 .60
199 Nick Van Exel .30 .75
200 Bimbo Coles .25 .60
201 John Wallace .25 .60
202 Anthony Mason .40 1.00
203 Steve Nash .75 2.00
204 Erick Dampier .25 .60
205 Cedric Ceballos .25 .60
206 Derek Fisher .30 .75
207 Marcus Camby .30 .75
208 Tyrone Hill .25 .60
209 Nick Anderson .25 .60
210 Sam Cassell .30 .75
211 Raef LaFrentz .30 .75
212 Ruben Patterson .25 .60
213 Rick Fox .25 .60
214 Jason Williams .60 1.50
215 Vince Carter 1.00 2.50
216 Michael Dickerson .25 .60
217 Steve Kerr .30 .75
218 Rasheed Wallace .50 1.25
219 Keith Van Horn .30 .75
220 Bob Sura .25 .60
221 Ray Allen .60 1.50
222 Jerry Stackhouse .40 1.00
223 Shawn Bradley .25 .60
224 Horace Grant .30 .75
225 Tim Duncan USA 1.50 4.00
226 Kevin Garnett USA 1.50 4.00
227 Jason Kidd USA 1.00 2.50
228 Steve Smith USA .50 1.25
229 Allan Houston USA .50 1.25
230 Tom Gugliotta USA .50 1.25
231 Gary Payton USA 1.00 2.50
232 Tim Hardaway USA .75 2.00
233 Vin Baker USA .50 1.25
234 Karl Malone CAT 1.25 3.00
235 Vince Carter CAT 1.50 4.00
236 Jason Williams CAT 1.00 2.50
237 Alonzo Mourning CAT 1.00 2.50
238 Anfernee Hardaway CAT 1.50 4.00
239 Mitch Richmond CAT .75 2.00
240 Steve Smith CAT .50 1.25
241 Charles Barkley CAT 1.50 4.00
242 Ron Mercer CAT .50 1.25
243 Shaquille O'Neal EDGE 2.50 6.00
244 Jason Kidd EDGE 1.00 2.50
245 Kevin Garnett EDGE 1.50 4.00
246 Tim Duncan EDGE 1.50 4.00
247 Ray Allen EDGE 1.00 2.50
248 Chris Webber EDGE .75 2.00
249 Jerry Stackhouse EDGE .60 1.50
250 Keith Van Horn EDGE .50 1.25
251 Patrick Ewing EDGE .75 2.00
252 Steve Francis RC 5.00 12.00
253 Jonathan Bender RC 2.50 6.00
254 Richard Hamilton RC 6.00 15.00
255 Andre Miller RC 5.00 12.00
256 Corey Maggette RC 3.00 8.00
257 William Avery RC 1.50 4.00
258 Ron Artest RC 6.00 15.00
259 James Posey RC 2.50 6.00
260 Quincy Lewis RC 1.50 4.00
261 Tim James RC 1.50 4.00
262 Vonteego Cummings RC 1.50 4.00
263 Anthony Carter RC 2.00 5.00
264 Mirsad Turkcan RC 2.50 6.00
265 Adrian Griffin RC 2.00 5.00
266 Ryan Robertson RC 1.50 4.00

1999-00 Finest Refractors

*STARS: 2.5X TO 6X BASE CARD HI
*SUBSETS: 1.5X TO 4X HI
*SER.1 RCs: 1.25X TO 3X HI
*SER.2 RCs: .5X TO 1.25X HI
SER.2 RCs STATED ODDS 1:138, 1:64 HTA
SER.2 RCs: PRINT RUN 200 SERIAL #'d SETS
SER.1/2 STATED ODDS 1:12, 1:5 HTA
64 Kobe Bryant 15.00 40.00
128 Kobe Bryant SEN 15.00 40.00

1999-00 Finest Refractors Gold

*STARS: 8X TO 20X BASE CARD HI
*SER.1 RCs: 4X TO 10X BASE HI
*SER.2 RCs: 1X TO 2.5X BASE HI
*SUBSETS: 5X TO 12X BASE HI
SER.1 STATED ODDS 1:62, 1:28 HTA
SER.2 STATED ODDS 1:31, 1:14 HTA
STATED PRINT RUN 100 SERIAL #'d SETS
77 Shawn Kemp 10.00 25.00
103 Kevin Garnett GEM 25.00 60.00
126 Jason Williams SEN 20.00 50.00
128 Kobe Bryant SEN 150.00 400.00
134 Tim Duncan 40.00 100.00
221 Ray Allen 15.00 40.00
225 Tim Duncan USA 30.00 80.00
226 Kevin Garnett USA 30.00 80.00
236 Jason Williams CAT 25.00 60.00
241 Charles Barkley CAT 20.00 50.00

1999-00 Finest 24-Karat Touch

COMPLETE SET (10) 8.00 20.00
SER.2 STATED ODDS 1:30, 1:15 HTA
*REF: 2X TO 5X HI COLUMN
REF: SER.2 STATED ODDS 1:300, 1:150 HTA
KT1 Reggie Miller 3.00 8.00
KT2 Keith Van Horn 1.25 3.00
KT3 Allan Houston 1.25 3.00
KT4 Patrick Ewing 2.00 5.00
KT5 Anfernee Hardaway 4.00 10.00
KT6 Steve Smith 1.25 3.00
KT7 Glen Rice 1.50 4.00
KT8 Ray Allen 2.50 6.00
KT9 Charles Barkley 4.00 10.00
KT10 Mitch Richmond 2.00 5.00

1999-00 Finest Box Office Draws

COMPLETE SET (10) 12.00 30.00
SER.2 STATED ODDS 1:30, 1:15 HTA
*REF: 2X TO 5X HI COLUMN
REF: SER.2 STATED ODDS 1:300, 1:150 HTA
BOD1 Shaquille O'Neal 6.00 15.00
BOD2 Patrick Ewing 2.00 5.00
BOD3 Karl Malone 3.00 8.00
BOD4 Jason Williams 2.50 6.00
BOD5 Charles Barkley 4.00 10.00
BOD6 Tim Duncan 4.00 10.00
BOD7 Kevin Garnett 4.00 10.00
BOD8 Alonzo Mourning 2.50 6.00
BOD9 Mitch Richmond 2.00 5.00
BOD10 Elton Brand 3.00 8.00

1999-00 Finest Double Double

COMPLETE SET (15) 20.00 50.00
SER.2 STATED ODDS 1:20, 1:10 HTA
*REF: 2X TO 5X HI COLUMN
REF: SER.2 STATED ODDS 1:200, 1:100 HTA
D1 Jason Kidd 2.50 6.00
D2 Kobe Bryant 12.00 30.00
D3 Antoine Walker 1.50 4.00
D4 Chris Webber 2.00 5.00
D5 Anfernee Hardaway 4.00 10.00
D6 Shawn Kemp 2.50 6.00
D7 Tim Duncan 4.00 10.00
D8 Antonio McDyess 1.25 3.00
D9 Grant Hill 2.50 6.00
D10 Karl Malone 3.00 8.00
D11 Shaquille O'Neal 6.00 15.00
D12 Allen Iverson 4.00 10.00
D13 Jayson Williams 1.00 2.50
D14 Keith Van Horn 1.25 3.00
D15 Gary Payton 2.50 6.00

1999-00 Finest Double Feature Right Refractors

COMPLETE SET (14) 15.00 30.00
SER.1 STATED ODDS 1:26, 1:12 HTA
RIGHT/LEFT VARIATIONS EQUAL VALUE
*DUAL REF: 1X TO 2.5X BASE HI
DUAL REFRACTOR SER.1 ODDS 1:78, 1:36 HTA
DF1 H.Olajuwon/S.Pippen 2.50 6.00
DF2 P.Pierce/A.Walker 2.00 5.00
DF3 S.Abdur-Rahim/M.Bibby 1.00 2.50
DF4 A.Mourning/T.Hardaway 1.50 4.00
DF5 G.Robinson/R.Allen 1.50 4.00
DF6 K.Garnett/J.Smith 2.50 6.00
DF7 K.Van Horn/S.Marbury 1.25 3.00
DF8 C.Webber/J.Williams 1.50 4.00
DF9 T.Duncan/D.Robinson 2.50 6.00
DF10 G.Payton/V.Baker 1.50 4.00
DF11 K.Malone/J.Stockton 2.00 5.00
DF12 J.Kidd/T.Gugliotta 1.50 4.00
DF13 M.Richmond/J.Howard 1.25 3.00
DF14 K.Bryant/S.O'Neal 8.00 20.00

1999-00 Finest Dunk Masters

SER.1 STATED ODDS 1:73, 1:34 HTA
STATED PRINT RUN 750 SERIAL #'d SETS
*REFRACTORS: 1.25X TO 3X HI COLUMN
REF: SER.1 ODDS 1:364, 1:168 HTA
REF: PRINT RUN 150 SERIAL #'d SETS
DM1 Kobe Bryant 30.00 80.00
DM2 Shaquille O'Neal 15.00 40.00
DM3 Chris Webber 5.00 12.00
DM4 Antonio McDyess 3.00 8.00
DM5 Michael Finley 4.00 10.00
DM6 Shawn Kemp 6.00 15.00
DM7 Tracy McGrady 6.00 15.00
DM8 Antoine Walker 4.00 10.00
DM9 Alonzo Mourning 6.00 15.00
DM10 Ray Allen 6.00 15.00
DM11 Kevin Garnett 10.00 25.00
DM12 Allen Iverson 10.00 25.00
DM13 Vince Carter 10.00 25.00
DM14 Tim Duncan 10.00 25.00
DM15 Scottie Pippen 10.00 25.00

1999-00 Finest Future's Finest

SER.1 STATED ODDS 1:73, 1:34 HTA
STATED PRINT RUN 750 SERIAL #'d SETS
REF: 1.25X TO 3X HI COLUMN
REF: SER. ODDS 1:364, 1:168 HTA
REF: PRINT RUN 150 SERIAL #'d SETS
FF1 Elton Brand 2.50 6.00
FF2 Steve Francis 2.50 6.00
FF3 Baron Davis 3.00 8.00
FF4 Lamar Odom 2.50 6.00
FF5 Jonathan Bender 1.25 3.00
FF6 Wally Szczerbiak 2.00 5.00
FF7 Richard Hamilton 3.00 8.00
FF8 Andre Miller 2.50 6.00
FF9 Shawn Marion 2.50 6.00
FF10 Jason Terry 2.00 5.00
FF11 Trajan Langdon 1.00 2.50
FF12 Aleksandar Radojevic .75 2.00
FF13 Corey Maggette 1.50 4.00
FF14 William Avery .75 2.00
FF15 Cal Bowdler .75 2.00

1999-00 Finest Heirs to Air

COMPLETE SET (10) 15.00 40.00
SER.2 STATED ODDS 1:36, 1:16 HTA
HA1 Michael Finley 2.00 5.00
HA2 Brent Barry 1.50 4.00
HA3 Corey Maggette 2.50 6.00
HA4 Ron Mercer 1.50 4.00
HA5 Eddie Jones 2.00 5.00
HA6 Tracy McGrady 3.00 8.00
HA7 Vince Carter 5.00 12.00
HA8 Jerry Stackhouse 2.00 5.00
HA9 Ray Allen 3.00 8.00
HA10 Kobe Bryant 15.00 40.00

1999-00 Finest Leading Indicators

COMPLETE SET (10) 10.00 25.00
SER.1 STATED ODDS 1:30, 1:14 HTA
L1 Stephon Marbury 1.50 4.00
L2 Paul Pierce 2.50 6.00
L3 Jason Kidd 2.00 5.00
L4 Gary Payton 2.00 5.00
L5 Keith Van Horn 1.00 2.50
L6 Reggie Miller 2.50 6.00
L7 Jason Williams 2.00 5.00
L8 Vince Carter 3.00 8.00
L9 Ray Allen 2.00 5.00
L10 Kobe Bryant 10.00 25.00

1999-00 Finest New Millennium

SER.1 STATED ODDS 1:55, 1:25 HTA
STATED PRINT RUN 1500 SERIAL #'d SETS
*REF: 1.25X TO 3X HI COLUMN
REF: SER.1 ODDS 1:273, 1:126 HTA
REF: PRINT RUN 300 SERIAL #'d SETS
NM1 Jason Williams 2.50 6.00
NM2 Vince Carter 4.00 10.00
NM3 Paul Pierce 3.00 8.00
NM4 Mike Bibby 1.50 4.00
NM5 Elton Brand 2.00 5.00
NM6 Steve Francis 2.00 5.00
NM7 Baron Davis 2.50 6.00
NM8 Lamar Odom 2.00 5.00
NM9 Jonathan Bender 1.00 2.50
NM10 Wally Szczerbiak 1.50 4.00

1999-00 Finest Next Generation

SER.2 STATED ODDS 1:20, 1:10 HTA
*REF: 1.5X TO 4X HI COLUMN
REF: SER.2 STATED ODDS 1:200, 1:100 HTA
NG1 Steve Francis 1.00 2.50
NG2 Jonathan Bender .50 1.25
NG3 Richard Hamilton 1.25 3.00
NG4 Andre Miller 1.00 2.50
NG5 Corey Maggette .60 1.50
NG6 William Avery .30 .75
NG7 Ron Artest 1.25 3.00
NG8 Wally Szczerbiak .75 2.00
NG9 Quincy Lewis .30 .75
NG10 Devean George .40 1.00
NG11 Vonteego Cummings .30 .75
NG12 Lamar Odom 1.00 2.50
NG13 Shawn Marion 1.00 2.50
NG14 Elton Brand 1.00 2.50
NG15 Baron Davis 1.25 3.00

1999-00 Finest Producers

COMPLETE SET (10) 8.00 20.00
SER.1 STATED ODDS 1:22, 1:10 HTA
*REFRACTORS: 1.25X TO 3X HI COLUMN
REF: SER.1 ODDS 1:109, 1:50 HTA
FP1 Shaquille O'Neal 4.00 10.00
FP2 Chris Webber 1.25 3.00
FP3 Karl Malone 2.00 5.00
FP4 Allen Iverson 2.50 6.00
FP5 Kevin Garnett 2.50 6.00
FP6 Jason Kidd 1.50 4.00
FP7 Grant Hill 1.50 4.00
FP8 Shareef Abdur-Rahim 1.00 2.50
FP9 Gary Payton 1.50 4.00
FP10 Charles Barkley 2.50 6.00

1999-00 Finest Salute

SER.1 STATED ODDS 1:108, 1:50 HTA
REF: SER.1 ODDS 1:5,305, 1:2,333 HTA
GR: SER.1 ODDS 1:16,992, 1:7,423 HTA
SER.2 STATED ODDS 1:100, 1:50 HTA
REF: SER.2 ODDS 1:4,616, 1:2,194 HTA
GR: SER.2 ODDS 1:8,539, 1:3,790 HTA
GR: PRINT RUN 50 SERIAL #'d SETS
FS1 Carter/Duncn/Iversn 1.50 4.00
FS1 Carter/Duncn/Iversn REF 15.00 40.00
FS1 Carter/Duncn/Iversn GR 100.00 250.00
FS2 Draft Picks 1.50 4.00
FS2 Draft Picks REF 25.00 60.00
FS2 Draft Picks GR 75.00 200.00

1999-00 Finest Team Finest Blue

COMPLETE SET (20) 25.00 65.00
COMPLETE SERIES 1 (10) 10.00 25.00
COMPLETE SERIES 2 (10) 15.00 40.00
SER.1 STATED ODDS 1:55, 1:25 HTA
SER.2 STATED ODDS 1:28, 1:13 HTA

STATED PRINT RUN 1500 SERIAL #'d SETS
BLUE REF: 1.5X TO 4X BASIC BLUE
BLUE REF: SER.1 ODDS 1:546, 1:252 HTA
BLUE REF: SER.2 ODDS 1:276, 1:127 HTA
BLUE REF: PRINT RUN 150 SERIAL #'d SETS
RED: .75X TO 2X BASIC BLUE
RED: SER.1 STATED ODDS 1:18 HTA
RED: SER.2 STATED ODDS 1:9 HTA
RED: PRINT RUN 500 SERIAL #'d SETS
GOLD: 1X TO 2.5X BASIC BLUE
GOLD: SER.1 STATED ODDS 1:35 HTA
GOLD: SER.2 STATED ODDS 1:18 HTA
GOLD: PRINT RUN 250 SERIAL #'d SETS
TF1 Shareef Abdur-Rahim 1.50 4.00
TF2 Stephon Marbury 2.00 5.00
TF3 Shawn Kemp 2.50 6.00
TF4 Allen Iverson 4.00 10.00
TF5 Antoine Walker 1.50 4.00
TF6 Hakeem Olajuwon 3.00 8.00
TF7 Tim Duncan 4.00 10.00
TF8 Karl Malone 3.00 8.00
TF9 Grant Hill 2.50 6.00
TF10 Keith Van Horn 1.25 3.00
TF11 Alonzo Mourning 2.50 6.00
TF12 Jason Kidd 2.50 6.00
TF13 Chris Webber 2.00 5.00
TF14 Shaquille O'Neal 6.00 15.00
TF15 Gary Payton 2.50 6.00
TF16 Kevin Garnett 4.00 10.00
TF17 Antonio McDyess 1.25 3.00
TF18 Kobe Bryant 12.00 30.00
TF19 Scottie Pippen 4.00 10.00
TF20 Vince Carter 4.00 10.00

1999-00 Finest Team Finest Gold Refractors

*REFRACTORS: 8X TO 20X HI COLUMN
STATED PRINT RUN 25 SERIAL #'d SETS
TF4 Allen Iverson 125.00 300.00
TF7 Tim Duncan 100.00 250.00
TF14 Shaquille O'Neal 60.00 150.00
TF18 Kobe Bryant 200.00 500.00

1999-00 Finest Team Finest Red Refractors

*REFRACTORS: 3X TO 8X HI COLUMN
STATED PRINT RUN 50 SERIAL #'d SETS
TF16 Kevin Garnett 25.00 60.00
TF18 Kobe Bryant 125.00 300.00
TF19 Scottie Pippen 30.00 80.00

2000-01 Finest

COMPLETE SET (173) 125.00 250.00
COMPLETE SET w/o SP (125) 15.00 40.00
126-150 STATED ODDS 1:18 H, 1:8 HTA
126-150 PRINT RUN 1599 SERIAL #'d SETS
OTM UNLISTED STARS .50 1.25
OTM: STATED ODDS 1:8 H, 1:3 HTA
GEMS: STATED ODDS 1:24 H, 1:5 HTA
1 Shaquille O'Neal 1.50 4.00
2 P.J. Brown .25 .60
3 Joe Smith .30 .75
4 Kendall Gill .40 1.00
5 Corey Maggette .30 .75
6 Marcus Camby .30 .75
7 Toni Kukoc .50 1.25
8 Kobe Bryant 15.00 40.00
9 David Robinson .75 2.00
10 Ruben Patterson .25 .60
11 Allen Iverson 1.00 2.50
12 Glenn Robinson .40 1.00
13 Anthony Carter .25 .60
14 Jonathan Bender .25 .60
15 Vince Carter .75 2.00
16 Jerry Stackhouse .40 1.00
17 Raef LaFrentz .30 .75
18 Dikembe Mutombo .60 1.50
19 Baron Davis .40 1.00
20 Kenny Anderson .30 .75
21 Corey Benjamin .25 .60
22 Andre Miller .30 .75
23 Cedric Ceballos .30 .75
24 Christian Laettner .40 1.00
25 Shandon Anderson .25 .60
26 Rik Smits .25 .60
27 Michael Olowokandi .25 .60
28 Sam Cassell .30 .75
29 Tom Gugliotta .30 .75
30 Jason Williams .60 1.50
31 Avery Johnson .30 .75
32 Karl Malone .75 2.00
33 Grant Hill .60 1.50
34 Paul Pierce .60 1.50
35 Antonio Davis .30 .75
36 Nick Anderson .30 .75
37 Alan Henderson .25 .60
38 Eddie Jones .40 1.00
39 Ron Artest .40 1.00
40 Brevin Knight .25 .60
41 Keon Clark .25 .60
42 Elton Brand .40 1.00
43 Reggie Miller .75 2.00
44 Steve Francis .40 1.00
45 Derek Anderson .30 .75
46 Alonzo Mourning .60 1.50
47 Terrell Brandon .30 .75
48 Larry Johnson .50 1.25
49 Keith Van Horn .30 .75
50 Jason Kidd .60 1.50
51 Scottie Pippen 1.00 2.50
52 Gary Payton .60 1.50
53 Robert Pack .25 .60
54 Adrian Griffin .25 .60
55 Jim Jackson .30 .75
56 Lamond Murray .25 .60
57 Larry Hughes .40 1.00
58 Dirk Nowitzki 1.00 2.50
59 Vonteego Cummings .25 .60
60 Jalen Rose .30 .75
61 Arvydas Sabonis .40 1.00
62 Kerry Kittles .30 .75
63 Kevin Garnett 1.00 2.50
64 Latrell Sprewell .50 1.25
65 Shawn Marion .40 1.00
66 Darrell Armstrong .25 .60
67 Ron Mercer .30 .75
68 Damon Stoudamire .40 1.00
69 Tracy McGrady .75 2.00
70 Theo Ratliff .25 .60
71 Lamar Odom .40 1.00
72 Charlie Ward .30 .75
73 John Amaechi .25 .60
74 Quincy Lewis .25 .60
75 Othella Harrington .25 .60
76 Doug Christie .30 .75
77 Richard Hamilton .50 1.25
78 Donyell Marshall .30 .75
79 Vlade Divac .40 1.00
80 Clifford Robinson .40 1.00
81 Sean Elliott .30 .75
82 Rashard Lewis .30 .75
83 Wally Szczerbiak .30 .75
84 Dale Davis .30 .75
85 Kelvin Cato .25 .60
86 Cuttino Mobley .30 .75
87 Travis Best .25 .60
88 Robert Horry .40 1.00
89 Maurice Taylor .25 .60
90 Jamal Mashburn .30 .75
91 Tim Thomas .25 .60
92 Stephon Marbury .50 1.25
93 Patrick Ewing .60 1.50
94 Eric Snow .25 .60
95 Anfernee Hardaway .60 1.50
96 Steve Smith .40 1.00
97 Chris Webber .50 1.25
98 Rodney Rogers .25 .60
99 John Stockton .75 2.00
100 Tim Duncan 1.00 2.50
101 Ray Allen .60 1.50
102 Glen Rice .40 1.00
103 Bryon Russell .25 .60
104 Tim Hardaway .50 1.25
105 Allan Houston .40 1.00
106 Rasheed Wallace .50 1.25
107 Vin Baker .30 .75
108 Michael Dickerson .25 .60
109 Juwan Howard .30 .75
110 Hakeem Olajuwon .75 2.00
111 Shareef Abdur-Rahim .40 1.00
112 Rod Strickland .25 .60
113 Hersey Hawkins .25 .60
114 Jason Terry .40 1.00
115 Anthony Mason .40 1.00
116 Mike Bibby .40 1.00
117 Shawn Kemp .60 1.50
118 Derrick Coleman .40 1.00
119 Antoine Walker .40 1.00
120 Antawn Jamison .40 1.00
121 Michael Finley .40 1.00
122 Antonio McDyess .30 .75
123 Nick Van Exel .40 1.00
124 Mitch Richmond .50 1.25
125 Lindsey Hunter .25 .60
126 Kenyon Martin RC 4.00 10.00
127 Stromile Swift RC 1.50 4.00
128 Darius Miles RC 2.00 5.00
129 Marcus Fizer RC 1.50 4.00
130 Mike Miller RC 3.00 8.00
131 DerMarr Johnson RC 1.25 3.00
132 Chris Mihm RC 1.25 3.00
133 Jamal Crawford RC 5.00 12.00
134 Joel Przybilla RC 1.50 4.00
135 Keyon Dooling RC 1.50 4.00
136 Jerome Moiso RC 1.25 3.00
137 Etan Thomas RC 1.50 4.00
138 Courtney Alexander RC 1.25 3.00
139 Mateen Cleaves RC 1.50 4.00
140 Jason Collier RC 2.00 5.00
141 Desmond Mason RC 2.50 6.00
142 Quentin Richardson RC 1.50 4.00
143 Jamaal Magloire RC 2.00 5.00
144 Speedy Claxton RC 2.00 5.00
145 Morris Peterson RC 2.00 5.00
146 Donnell Harvey RC 1.50 4.00
147 DeShawn Stevenson RC 2.00 5.00
148 Mamadou N'Diaye RC 1.25 3.00
149 Erick Barkley RC 1.25 3.00
150 Mark Madsen RC 2.00 5.00
151 A.Iverson/S.Marbury OTM 1.25 3.00
152 V.Carter/K.Bryant OTM 12.00 30.00
153 K.Garnett/Abdur-Rahim OTM 1.25 3.00
154 T.McGrady/S.Pippen OTM 1.25 3.00
155 T.Duncan/E.Brand OTM 1.25 3.00
156 S.Francis/G.Payton OTM .75 2.00
157 C.Webber/K.Malone OTM 1.00 2.50
158 A.Mourning/P.Ewing OTM .75 2.00
159 L.Sprewell/E.Jones OTM .60 1.50
160 J.Kidd/J.Stockton OTM 1.00 2.50
161 R.Miller/A.Houston OTM 1.00 2.50
162 R.Wallace/A.Walker OTM .60 1.50
163 J.Stackhouse/J.Rose OTM .50 1.25
164 Shaquille O'Neal GEM 4.00 10.00
165 Kobe Bryant GEM 25.00 60.00
166 Vince Carter GEM 2.00 5.00
167 Kevin Garnett GEM 2.50 6.00
168 Jason Williams GEM 1.50 4.00
169 Tracy McGrady GEM 2.00 5.00
170 Steve Francis GEM 1.00 2.50
171 Tim Duncan GEM 2.50 6.00
172 Elton Brand GEM 1.00 2.50
173 Grant Hill GEM 1.50 4.00

2000-01 Finest Gold Refractors

*STARS: 10X TO 25X BASE CARD HI
*OTM: 8X TO 20X BASE HI
*GEMS: 4X TO 10X BASE HI
*RCs: 1X TO 2.5X BASE HI
VETS: STATED ODDS 1:67 H, 1:19 HTA
RCs: STATED ODDS 1:336 H, 1:93 HTA
GEM: STATED ODDS 1:840 H, 1:233 HTA
OTM: STATED ODDS 1:323 H, 1:90 HTA
STATED PRINT RUN 100 SERIAL #'d SETS
8 Kobe Bryant 800.00 1,500.00
33 Grant Hill 15.00 40.00
43 Reggie Miller 12.00 30.00
51 Scottie Pippen 25.00 60.00
64 Latrell Sprewell 10.00 25.00
152 V.Carter/K.Bryant OTM 500.00 1,000.00
161 R.Miller/A.Houston OTM 25.00 60.00
164 Shaquille O'Neal GEM 30.00 80.00
165 Kobe Bryant GEM 1,000.00 2,000.00
168 Jason Williams GEM 15.00 40.00
173 Grant Hill GEM 15.00 40.00

2000-01 Finest Man to Man

COMPLETE SET (10) 7.50 15.00
STATED ODDS 1:25 H, 1:12 HTA
1A Tim Duncan DUNK 2.00 5.00
1B Elton Brand DUNK .75 2.00
2A Tim Duncan REB 2.00 5.00
2B Elton Brand REB .75 2.00
3A Tim Duncan SH 2.00 5.00
3B Elton Brand SH .75 2.00
4A Tim Duncan BLK 2.00 5.00
4B Elton Brand BLK .75 2.00
5A Tim Duncan PU 2.00 5.00
5B Elton Brand PU .75 2.00

2000-01 Finest Moments

COMPLETE SET (21) 12.50 25.00
STATED ODDS 1:14 H, 1:6 HTA
*REF: .75X TO 2X HI COLUMN
REF: STATED ODDS 1:24 H, 1:11 HTA
FMAC Anthony Carter .50 1.25
FMAH Allan Houston .75 2.00
FMAI Allen Iverson 2.00 5.00
FMEB Elton Brand .75 2.00
FMGP Gary Payton 1.25 3.00
FMGR Glen Rice .75 2.00
FMJK Jason Kidd 1.25 3.00
FMJR Jalen Rose .60 1.50
FMJS John Starks .75 2.00
FMKM Karl Malone 1.50 4.00
FMLH Larry Hughes .75 2.00
FMLJ Larry Johnson 1.00 2.50
FMMC Mateen Cleaves .60 1.50
FMMJ Magic Johnson 1.50 4.00
FMSE Sean Elliott .60 1.50
FMSF Steve Francis .75 2.00
FMSO Shaquille O'Neal 3.00 8.00
FMTD Tim Duncan 2.00 5.00
FMTH Tim Hardaway 1.00 2.50
FMTK Toni Kukoc 1.00 2.50
FMTM Tracy McGrady 1.50 4.00
FMR11 Vince Carter/1000 25.00 60.00

2000-01 Finest Moments Refractors Autographs

GROUP A ODDS 1:258 H, 1:117 HTA
GROUP B ODDS 1:2026 H, 1:921 HTA
GROUP C ODDS 1:355 H, 1:161 HTA
GROUP D ODDS 1:253 H, 1:115 HTA
OVERALL ODDS 1:90 H, 1:41 HTA
FMAH Allan Houston A 8.00 20.00
FMEB Elton Brand A 10.00 20.00
FMEJ Eddie Jones A 40.00 00.00
FMGP Gary Payton A 25.00 60.00
FMGR Glen Rice A 20.00 50.00
FMJR Jalen Rose A 15.00 30.00
FMJS John Starks D 25.00 60.00
FMLH Larry Hughes A 15.00 30.00
FMLJ Larry Johnson A 150.00 300.00
FMMC Mateen Cleaves D 10.00 25.00
FMMJ Magic Johnson C 60.00 50.00
FMMR Mitch Richmond C 40.00 100.00
FMSE Sean Elliott D 15.00 40.00
FMSF Steve Francis B 12.00 30.00
FMSO Shaquille O'Neal C 200.00 500.00
FMSO2 Shaquille O'Neal 200.00 500.00
FMTD Tim Duncan A 2,500.00 5,000.00
FMTM Tracy McGrady D 20.00 50.00

2000-01 Finest Moments Relics

GROUP A 1:617 H, 1:280 HTA
GROUP B 1:127 H, 1:58 HTA
GROUP C 1:236 H, 1:107 HTA
GROUP D 1:430 H, 1:195 HTA
GROUP E 1:411 H, 1:187 HTA
GROUP F 1:394 H, 1:179 HTA
OVERALL STATED ODDS 1:48 H, 1:22 HTA
FMR1 Vin Baker D 3.00 8.00
FMR2 Antonio McDyess F 3.00 8.00
FMR3 Jason Kidd B 6.00 15.00
FMR4 Tim Hardaway B 5.00 12.00
FMR5 Allan Houston B 4.00 10.00
FMR6 Steve Smith C 4.00 10.00
FMR7 Alonzo Mourning E 6.00 15.00
FMR8 Gary Payton A 6.00 15.00
FMR9 Ray Allen B 6.00 15.00
FMR10 Shareef Abdur-Rahim C 4.00 10.00
FMR11 Vince Carter/1000 20.00 50.00
FMR12 Kevin Garnett/1000 10.00 25.00

2000-01 Finest Showmen

COMPLETE SET (10) 4.00 10.00
STATED ODDS 1:13 H, 1:8 HTA
S1 Chris Webber .75 2.00
S2 Elton Brand .60 1.50
S3 Tim Duncan 1.50 4.00
S4 Shareef Abdur-Rahim .60 1.50
S5 Jason Williams 1.00 2.50
S6 Grant Hill 1.00 2.50
S7 Lamar Odom .60 1.50
S8 Larry Hughes .60 1.50
S9 Michael Finley .60 1.50
S10 Latrell Sprewell .75 2.00

2000-01 Finest Title Quest

COMPLETE SET (10) 12.50 30.00
STATED ODDS 1:54 H, 1:27 HTA
APT1 Reggie Miller 3.00 8.00
APT2 Alonzo Mourning 2.50 6.00
APT3 Allen Iverson 4.00 10.00
APT4 Latrell Sprewell 2.00 5.00
APT5 Jalen Rose 1.25 3.00
APT6 Scottie Pippen 4.00 10.00
APT7 Shaquille O'Neal 6.00 15.00
APT8 Kobe Bryant 50.00 120.00
APT9 Chris Webber 2.00 5.00
APT10 Rasheed Wallace 2.00 5.00

2000-01 Finest World's Finest

COMPLETE SET (15) 25.00 60.00
STATED ODDS 1:36 H, 1:18 HTA
WF1 Tim Duncan 5.00 12.00
WF2 Vince Carter 4.00 10.00
WF3 Grant Hill 3.00 8.00
WF4 Kevin Garnett 5.00 12.00
WF5 Scottie Pippen 5.00 12.00
WF6 Karl Malone 4.00 10.00
WF7 Patrick Ewing 3.00 8.00
WF8 Tim Hardaway 2.50 6.00
WF9 Anfernee Hardaway 3.00 8.00
WF10 Reggie Miller 4.00 10.00
WF11 John Stockton 4.00 10.00
WF12 Ray Allen 3.00 8.00
WF13 Hakeem Olajuwon 4.00 10.00
WF14 David Robinson 4.00 10.00
WF15 Steve Smith 2.00 5.00

2002-03 Finest

101-120 AU PRINT RUN 999 SER.#'d SETS
121-156 JSY PRINT RUN 999 SER.#'d SETS
157-177 AU PRINT RUN 999 SER.#'d SETS
1 Dirk Nowitzki 1.00 2.50
2 Jason Terry .30 .75
3 Marcus Camby .30 .75
4 Joe Johnson .30 .75
5 Shawn Marion .40 1.00
6 Andrei Kirilenko .40 1.00
7 Jamal Mashburn .30 .75
8 Andre Miller .30 .75
9 Jason Williams .50 1.25
10 Tony Delk .25 .60
11 Tyson Chandler .40 1.00
12 Jason Richardson .40 1.00
13 Derek Fisher .40 1.00
14 Troy Hudson .25 .60
15 Kerry Kittles .25 .60
16 Peja Stojakovic .30 .75
17 Kurt Thomas .25 .60
18 Jamaal Tinsley .25 .60
19 Matt Harpring .25 .60
20 Kenny Thomas .25 .60
21 Kwame Brown .25 .60
22 Antonio Davis .30 .75
23 David Robinson .75 2.00
24 Keith Van Horn .30 .75
25 Howard Eisley .25 .60
26 Jalen Rose .30 .75
27 Chauncey Billups .40 1.00
28 Corey Maggette .30 .75
29 Pau Gasol .60 1.50
30 Desmond Mason .25 .60
31 Brian Grant .25 .60
32 Eddie Griffin .25 .60
33 Voshon Lenard .25 .60
34 Al Harrington .30 .75
35 Calbert Cheaney .25 .60
36 Malik Rose .25 .60
37 Bonzi Wells .25 .60
38 Pat Garrity .25 .60
39 P.J. Brown .25 .60
40 Ray Allen .60 1.50
41 Karl Malone .75 2.00
42 Steve Nash .75 2.00
43 Antawn Jamison .30 .75
44 Ron Artest .30 .75
45 Shane Battier .40 1.00
46 Gary Payton .60 1.50
47 Kobe Bryant 3.00 8.00
48 Lucious Harris .25 .60
49 Richard Hamilton .50 1.25
50 Darius Miles .25 .60
51 Marcus Fizer .25 .60
52 Antoine Walker .30 .75
53 Juwan Howard .30 .75
54 Eddie Jones .40 1.00
55 Kenyon Martin .40 1.00
56 Derek Anderson .25 .60
57 Stephen Jackson .30 .75
58 Vince Carter .75 2.00
59 Larry Hughes .30 .75
60 Doug Christie .25 .60
61 Derrick Coleman .25 .60
62 Michael Finley .40 1.00
63 Wally Szczerbiak .25 .60
64 David Wesley .25 .60
65 Brad Miller .30 .75
66 Clifford Robinson .40 1.00
67 Shandon Anderson .25 .60
68 Stephon Marbury .50 1.25
69 Bobby Jackson .25 .60
70 Brent Barry .25 .60
71 Ruben Patterson .25 .60
72 Rashard Lewis .30 .75
73 Tony Battie .25 .60
74 Ben Wallace .50 1.25
75 Theo Ratliff .25 .60
76 Ricky Davis .30 .75
77 Nick Van Exel .40 1.00
78 Mike Miller .30 .75
79 Sam Cassell .30 .75
80 Malik Allen .25 .60
81 Mike Bibby .40 1.00
82 Scottie Pippen 1.00 2.50
83 Dikembe Mutombo .60 1.50
84 Latrell Sprewell .40 1.00
85 Predrag Drobnjak .25 .60
86 Joe Smith .25 .60
87 Aaron Mckie .25 .60
88 Jamaal Magloire .25 .60
89 Keon Clark .25 .60
90 Eric Williams .25 .60
91 Raef Lafrentz .30 .75
92 Troy Murphy .30 .75
93 Rick Fox .25 .60
94 Michael Redd .30 .75
95 Radoslav Nesterovic .25 .60
96 Donyell Marshall .25 .60
97 Elton Brand .30 .75
98 Robert Horry .40 1.00
99 Zydrunas Ilgauskas .30 .75
100 Michael Jordan 4.00 10.00
101 Juaquin Hawkins AU RC 2.50 6.00
102 Dan Dickau AU RC 2.50 6.00
103 Vincent Yarbrough AU RC 3.00 8.00
104 John Salmons AU RC 4.00 10.00
105 Tamar Slay AU RC 2.50 6.00
106 Melvin Ely AU RC 3.00 8.00
107 Jared Jeffries AU RC 2.50 6.00
108 Junior Harrington AU RC 2.50 6.00
110 Qyntel Woods AU RC 2.50 6.00
111 Ryan Humphrey AU RC 3.00 8.00
112 J.R. Bremer AU RC 2.50 6.00
113 Antoine Rigaudeau AU RC 4.00 10.00
114 Jay Williams RC 3.00 8.00
115 Pat Burke AU RC 2.50 6.00
116 Smush Parker AU RC 4.00 10.00
117 Juan Dixon AU RC 3.00 8.00
118 Vincent Yarbrough AU RC 2.50 6.00
120 Rasual Butler AU RC 3.00 8.00
121 Baron Davis JSY 4.00 10.00
122 Shareef Abdur-Rahim JSY 4.00 10.00
123 Gilbert Arenas JSY 4.00 10.00
124 Travis Best JSY 2.50 6.00
125 Vlade Divac JSY 3.00 8.00
126 Tim Duncan JSY 10.00 25.00
127 Jason Kidd JSY 6.00 15.00
128 Kevin Garnett JSY 10.00 25.00
129 Anfernee Hardaway JSY 10.00 25.00
130 Allen Iverson JSY 10.00 25.00
131 Cuttino Mobley JSY 2.50 6.00
132 Steve Francis JSY 4.00 10.00
133 Jermaine O'Neal JSY 3.00 8.00
134 Lamar Odom JSY 4.00 10.00
135 Michael Olowokandi JSY 2.50 6.00
136 Paul Pierce JSY 6.00 15.00
137 Reggie Miller JSY 8.00 20.00
138 Chris Webber JSY 5.00 12.00
139 Richard Jefferson JSY 3.00 8.00
140 Allan Houston JSY 4.00 10.00
141 Glenn Robinson JSY 4.00 10.00
142 Jerome Williams JSY 2.50 6.00
143 John Stockton JSY 8.00 20.00
144 Rasheed Wallace JSY 5.00 12.00
145 Eric Snow JSY 2.50 6.00
146 Tracy McGrady JSY 6.00 15.00
147 Shaquille O'Neal JSY 15.00 40.00
148 Jerry Stackhouse JSY 4.00 10.00
149 Morris Peterson JSY 3.00 8.00
150 Darrell Armstrong JSY 2.50 6.00
151 Tony Parker JSY 6.00 15.00
152 Vladimir Radmanovic JSY 2.50 6.00
153 Anthony Mason JSY 3.00 8.00
154 Charles Oakley JSY 3.00 8.00
155 Grant Hill JSY 6.00 15.00
156 Vin Baker JSY 3.00 8.00
157 Chris Jefferies AU RC 2.50 6.00
158 Drew Gooden AU RC 4.00 10.00
159 Casey Jacobsen AU RC 3.00 8.00
160 Kareem Rush AU RC 3.00 8.00
161 Bostjan Nachbar AU RC 3.00 8.00
162 Tayshaun Prince AU RC 8.00 20.00
163 Manu Ginobili RC 40.00 100.00
164 Gordan Giricek AU RC 4.00 10.00
165 Raul Lopez AU RC 4.00 10.00
166 Dan Gadzuric AU RC 3.00 8.00
167 Marko Jaric AU 4.00 10.00
168 Lonny Baxter AU RC 2.50 6.00
169 Yao Ming AU RC 125.00 300.00
170 Mike Dunleavy AU RC 4.00 10.00
171 Caron Butler AU RC 4.00 10.00
172 Nene Hilario AU RC 4.00 10.00
173 Amare Stoudemire AU RC 10.00 25.00
174 Nikoloz Tskitishvili AU RC 2.50 6.00
175 Fred Jones AU RC 3.00 8.00
176 DaJuan Wagner AU RC 3.00 8.00
177 Carlos Boozer AU RC 4.00 10.00
178 LeBron James XRC 800.00 1,500.00
179 Darko Milicic XRC 4.00 10.00
180 Carmelo Anthony XRC 25.00 60.00
181 Chris Bosh XRC 6.00 15.00
182 Dwyane Wade XRC 50.00 120.00
183 Chris Kaman XRC 4.00 10.00
184 Kirk Hinrich XRC 5.00 12.00
185 T.J. Ford XRC 4.00 10.00
186 Mike Sweetney XRC 4.00 10.00
187 Jarvis Hayes XRC 4.00 10.00

2002-03 Finest Refractors

*1-100 STARS: 2.5X TO 6X BASE CARD HI
1-100 STATED ODDS 1:24
1-100 PRINT RUN 250 SER.#'d SETS
*101-120 AU RCs: .6X TO 1.5X BASE CARD HI
101-120 AU RC PRINT RUN 250 SER. #'d SETS
*121-156 JSY: .6X TO 1.5X BASE CARD HI
121-156 JSY PRINT RUN 250 SER.#'d SETS
*157-177 AU RCs: .6X TO 1.5X BASE CARD HI
157-177 AU RC PRINT RUN 250 SER.#'d SETS
*XRC: 1X TO 2.5X BASE CARD HI
1 Dirk Nowitzki 15.00 40.00
40 Ray Allen 5.00 12.00
47 Kobe Bryant 125.00 300.00
100 Michael Jordan 300.00 600.00
113 Anfernee Hardaway JSY 25.00 60.00
163 Manu Ginobili 125.00 300.00
169 Yao Ming AU 300.00 600.00
178 LeBron James 8,000.00 12,000.00
180 Carmelo Anthony 150.00 400.00
182 Dwyane Wade 300.00 600.00

2002-03 Finest Refractors Gold

*GOLD 1-100: 20X TO 50X BASE HI
*GOLD AU RC 101-120: 2X TO 5X HI
*GOLD JSY 121-156: 2X TO 5X HI
*GOLD AU RC 157-177: 2X TO 5X HI
*GOLD XRC 178-187: 3X TO 8X HI
STATED PRINT RUN 25 SER.#'d SETS
1 Dirk Nowitzki 150.00 400.00
40 Ray Allen 125.00 300.00
42 Steve Nash 150.00 400.00
47 Kobe Bryant 1,000.00 2,000.00
58 Vince Carter 150.00 400.00
82 Scottie Pippen 125.00 300.00
100 Michael Jordan 300.00 600.00
126 Tim Duncan JSY 50.00 120.00
163 Manu Ginobili 500.00 1,000.00
178 LeBron James 30,000.00 60,000.00
180 Carmelo Anthony 5,000.00 10,000.00
181 Chris Bosh 150.00 400.00
182 Dwyane Wade 8,000.00 15,000.00

2003-04 Finest

COMP.SET w/o SP's (100) 15.00 40.00
131-143 PRINT RUN 999 SER.#'d SETS
144-172 AU RC PRINT RUN 999 #'d SETS
XRC EXCH STATED ODDS 1:4
1 Zach Randolph .40 1.00
2 Keith Van Horn .30 .75
3 Steve Francis .40 1.00
4 Al Harrington .30 .75
5 Jason Kidd .60 1.50
6 Jamaal Tinsley .25 .60
7 Lamar Odom .30 .75
8 Antoine Walker .40 1.00
9 Tony Parker .60 1.50
10 Jamal Mashburn .30 .75
11 Desmond Mason .30 .75
12 Carlos Arroyo .30 .75
13 Chris Andersen .50 1.25
14 Chris Wilcox .25 .60
15 Vince Carter .75 2.00
16 Peja Stojakovic .30 .75
17 Qyntel Woods .25 .60
18 Mike Dunleavy .30 .75
19 Sam Cassell .30 .75
20 Allan Houston .40 1.00
21 Speedy Claxton .25 .60
22 Rafer Alston .25 .60
23 Michael Finley .40 1.00
24 Richard Jefferson .30 .75
25 Larry Hughes .30 .75
26 Pau Gasol .60 1.50
27 Maurice Taylor .25 .60
28 Donyell Marshall .25 .60
29 Darrell Armstrong .25 .60
30 Latrell Sprewell .50 1.25
31 Reggie Miller .75 2.00
32 Stephon Marbury .50 1.25
33 Antawn Jamison .40 1.00
34 DerMarr Johnson .25 .60
35 Shareef Abdur-Rahim .40 1.00
36 Tony Battie .25 .60
37 Kwame Brown .25 .60
38 Fred Jones .25 .60
39 Jamal Crawford .40 1.00
40 Kurt Thomas .25 .60
41 Eric Snow .25 .60
42 Andre Miller .30 .75
43 Ray Allen .60 1.50
44 Caron Butler .30 .75
45 Corliss Williamson .25 .60
46 Kenny Thomas .25 .60
47 Jason Terry .30 .75
48 Ronald Murray .25 .60
49 Richard Hamilton .50 1.25
50 Elton Brand .30 .75
51 Ron Artest .40 1.00
52 Jerome Williams .25 .60
53 Ricky Davis .30 .75
54 Brent Barry .25 .60
55 Dikembe Mutombo .50 1.25
56 Earl Boykins .25 .60
57 Brad Miller .30 .75
58 Shane Battier .30 .75
59 Tyson Chandler .30 .75
60 Kelvin Cato .25 .60
61 Shawn Marion .40 1.00
62 Bobby Jackson .30 .75
63 Corey Maggette .30 .75
64 Antonio McDyess .30 .75
65 Drew Gooden .30 .75
66 Mike Miller .30 .75
67 Darius Miles .25 .60
68 Stephen Jackson .30 .75
69 Cuttino Mobley .30 .75
70 Gary Payton .60 1.50
71 Toni Kukoc .40 1.00
72 Eddie Jones .40 1.00
73 Gilbert Arenas .40 1.00
74 Matt Harpring .25 .60
75 Marko Jaric .25 .60
76 Bonzi Wells .25 .60
77 Nick Van Exel .40 1.00
78 Quentin Richardson .25 .60
79 Rasho Nesterovic .25 .60
80 Steve Nash .75 2.00
81 Morris Peterson .25 .60
82 Nikoloz Tskitishvili .25 .60
83 Damon Stoudamire .30 .75
84 Bruce Bowen .30 .75
85 Brian Grant .25 .60
86 Jalen Rose .30 .75
87 Jerry Stackhouse .50 1.25
88 Kobe Bryant 3.00 8.00
89 Eddy Curry .25 .60
90 Tim Thomas .25 .60
91 Erick Dampier .25 .60
92 Jason Williams .60 1.50
93 Troy Murphy .25 .60
94 Kerry Kittles .25 .60
95 Zydrunas Ilgauskas .30 .75
96 Theo Ratliff .25 .60
97 Samuel Dalembert .25 .60
98 Jeff McInnis .25 .60
99 Juwan Howard .30 .75
100 Joe Johnson .30 .75
101 Paul Pierce JSY 4.00 10.00
102 Ben Wallace JSY 3.00 8.00
103 Yao Ming JSY 6.00 15.00
104 Jermaine O'Neal JSY 2.50 6.00
105 Rashard Lewis JSY 2.00 5.00
106 Karl Malone JSY 5.00 12.00
107 Allen Iverson JSY 6.00 15.00
108 Mike Bibby JSY 2.50 6.00
109 Rasheed Wallace JSY 3.00 8.00
110 Nene JSY 2.00 5.00
111 Tracy McGrady JSY 4.00 10.00
112 Andrei Kirilenko JSY 2.00 5.00
113 Manu Ginobili JSY 5.00 12.00
114 Kenyon Martin JSY 2.50 6.00
115 Amare Stoudemire JSY 3.00 8.00
116 Baron Davis JSY 2.50 6.00
117 Michael Olowokandi JSY 1.50 4.00
118 Carlos Boozer JSY 2.00 5.00
119 Jason Richardson JSY 2.50 6.00
120 Dirk Nowitzki JSY 6.00 15.00
121 Chauncey Billups JSY 3.00 8.00
122 Chris Webber JSY 3.00 8.00
123 Glenn Robinson JSY/807 2.00 5.00
124 Kevin Garnett JSY 6.00 15.00
125 Michael Redd JSY 2.50 6.00
126 David Wesley JSY 1.50 4.00
127 Tayshaun Prince JSY 2.50 6.00
128 Jamaal Magloire JSY 1.50 4.00
129 Tim Duncan JSY 6.00 15.00
130 Shaquille O'Neal JSY 10.00 25.00
131 Darko Milicic RC 2.00 5.00
132 Chris Kaman RC 2.50 6.00
133 LeBron James RC 600.00 1,200.00
134 Richie Frahm RC 2.50 6.00
135 Steve Blake RC 2.00 5.00
136 Zaza Pachulia RC 2.50 6.00
137 Keith Bogans RC 1.50 4.00
138 Kirk Hinrich AU RC 4.00 10.00
139 Jarvis Hayes RC 1.50 4.00
140 Zarko Cabarkapa AU RC 2.50 6.00
141 Zoran Planinic AU RC 2.50 6.00
142 Udonis Haslem RC 3.00 8.00
143 David West RC 3.00 8.00
144 Boris Diaw AU RC 4.00 10.00
146 Brian Cook AU RC 2.50 6.00
147 Ndudi Ebi AU RC 2.50 6.00
148 Josh Howard AU RC 4.00 10.00
149 Jason Kapono AU RC 2.50 6.00
150 Luke Walton AU RC 4.00 10.00
151 Travis Hansen AU RC 2.50 6.00
152 Willie Green AU RC 4.00 10.00
153 Maurice Williams AU RC 4.00 10.00
154 Francisco Elson AU RC 2.50 6.00
155 Kyle Korver AU RC 5.00 12.00
156 Marquis Daniels AU RC 3.00 8.00
157 Chris Bosh AU RC 12.00 30.00
158 Dwyane Wade AU RC 125.00 300.00
159 Aleksandar Pavlovic AU RC 3.00 8.00
160 Mike Sweetney AU RC 2.50 6.00
161 Marcus Banks AU RC 2.50 6.00
162 Luke Ridnour AU RC 4.00 10.00
163 Carmelo Anthony AU RC 75.00 200.00
164 Mickael Pietrus AU RC 3.00 8.00
165 Reece Gaines AU RC 2.50 6.00
166 Kendrick Perkins AU RC 3.00 8.00
167 Troy Bell AU RC 2.50 6.00
168 Leandro Barbosa AU RC 4.00 10.00
169 Dahntay Jones AU RC 3.00 8.00
170 T.J. Ford AU RC 3.00 8.00
171 Nick Collison AU RC 3.00 8.00
172 Theron Smith AU RC 2.50 6.00
173 Dwight Howard XRC 15.00 40.00
174 Emeka Okafor XRC 4.00 10.00
175 Ben Gordon XRC 5.00 12.00
176 Shaun Livingston XRC 5.00 12.00
177 Devin Harris XRC 5.00 12.00
178 Josh Childress XRC 4.00 10.00
179 Luol Deng XRC 5.00 12.00
180 Rafael Araujo XRC 3.00 8.00
181 Andre Iguodala XRC 6.00 15.00
182 Luke Jackson XRC 3.00 8.00
183 Andris Biedrins XRC 3.00 8.00
184 Robert Swift XRC 3.00 8.00
185 Sebastian Telfair XRC 4.00 10.00

2003-04 Finest Refractors

*1-100 REF.SINGLES: 2.5X TO 6X BASE HI
*131-143 REF.SINGLES: .75X TO 2X BASE HI
*XRC: .75X TO 2X BASE HI
5 Jason Kidd JSY 5.00 12.00
88 Kobe Bryant 400.00 800.00
101 Paul Pierce JSY 5.00 12.00
103 Yao Ming JSY 8.00 20.00
106 Karl Malone JSY 6.00 15.00
107 Allen Iverson JSY 8.00 20.00
111 Tracy McGrady JSY 5.00 12.00
115 Amare Stoudemire JSY 4.00 10.00
120 Dirk Nowitzki JSY 8.00 20.00
124 Kevin Garnett JSY 8.00 20.00
129 Tim Duncan JSY 8.00 20.00
130 Shaquille O'Neal JSY 12.00 30.00
132 Chris Kaman JSY 3.00 8.00
136 Zaza Pachulia JSY 3.00 8.00
138 Kirk Hinrich JSY AU 6.00 15.00
144 Boris Diaw JSY AU 6.00 15.00
150 Luke Walton AU 5.00 12.00
157 Chris Bosh JSY AU 15.00 40.00
162 Luke Ridnour JSY AU 6.00 15.00
164 Mickael Pietrus JSY AU 5.00 12.00
166 Kendrick Perkins JSY AU 5.00 12.00
168 Leandro Barbosa JSY AU 5.00 12.00
170 T.J. Ford JSY AU 5.00 12.00

2003-04 Finest Refractors Gold

*GOLD 1-100: 12X TO 30X BASE HI
*GOLD JSY 101-130: 1.5X TO 4X BASE HI
*GOLD RC 131-143: 2.5X TO 6X BASE HI
*GOLD AU RC 144-172: 1.5X TO 4X BASE HI
*GOLD XRC 173-185: 1.25X TO 3X BASE HI
PRINT RUN 25 SER.#'d SETS
88 Kobe Bryant 3,000.00 6,000.00
92 Jason Williams 40.00 100.00
103 Yao Ming JSY 40.00 100.00
129 Tim Duncan JSY 25.00 60.00
133 LeBron James 60,000.00 100,000.00
157 Chris Bosh AU 150.00 400.00
158 Dwyane Wade AU 1,500.00 3,000.00
163 Carmelo Anthony AU 1,000.00 2,000.00
176 Shaun Livingston 20.00 50.00

2004-05 Finest

COMP.SET w/o SP's (100) 30.00 80.00
131-160 PRINT RUN 400 SER.#'d SETS
161-190 AU RC PRINT RUN 299 #'d SETS
191-220 XRC PRINT RUN 599 #'d SETS
1 Richard Hamilton .50 1.25
2 Mike Dunleavy .25 .60
3 Jamaal Tinsley .25 .60
4 Corey Maggette .30 .75
5 Zach Randolph .40 1.00
6 Desmond Mason .30 .75
7 Marc Jackson .25 .60
8 Kobe Bryant 3.00 8.00
9 Mike Bibby .40 1.00
10 Vince Carter .75 2.00
11 Bonzi Wells .25 .60
12 Ricky Davis .30 .75
13 Steve Nash .75 2.00
14 Rashard Lewis .30 .75
15 Eddy Curry .25 .60
16 Carlos Boozer .30 .75
17 Brad Miller .30 .75
18 Kurt Thomas .25 .60
19 Shareef Abdur-Rahim .40 1.00
20 Grant Hill .50 1.25
21 Jason Hart .25 .60
22 Larry Hughes .30 .75
23 Lebron James 30.00 80.00
24 Udonis Haslem .25 .60
25 David Wesley .25 .60
26 Kenny Thomas .25 .60
27 Marcus Camby .30 .75
28 Michael Redd .30 .75
29 Rasho Nesterovic .25 .60
30 Keith Van Horn .30 .75
31 Reggie Miller .75 2.00

32 Stephon Marbury .50 1.25
33 Donyell Marshall .25 .60
34 Jermaine O'Neal .30 .75
35 Antoine Walker .40 1.00
36 Rasheed Wallace .50 1.25
37 Antonio Daniels .25 .60
38 Damon Jones .25 .60
39 Caron Butler .30 .75
40 Shawn Marion .40 1.00
41 Lee Nailon .25 .60
42 Damon Stoudamire .40 1.00
43 Bob Sura .25 .60
44 Mehmet Okur .30 .75
45 Shane Battier .30 .75
46 Michael Finley .40 1.00
47 Doug Christie .30 .75
48 Eddie Jones .40 1.00
49 Speedy Claxton .25 .60
50 Wally Szczerbiak .30 .75
51 Primoz Brezec .25 .60
52 Marko Jaric .25 .60
53 Antonio McDyess .30 .75
54 Jeff McInnis .25 .60
55 Tony Parker .60 1.50
56 Rafer Alston .25 .60
57 Troy Murphy .25 .60
58 Chris Mihm .25 .60
59 Jarvis Hayes .25 .60
60 Marquis Daniels .25 .60
61 Jamal Crawford .40 1.00
62 Morris Peterson .25 .60
63 Luke Ridnour .30 .75
64 Mike Miller .30 .75
65 Carlos Arroyo .25 .60
66 Gary Payton .60 1.50
67 Joe Johnson .30 .75
68 Latrell Sprewell .50 1.25
69 Allan Houston .40 1.00
70 Earl Boykins .25 .60
71 Brendan Haywood .25 .60
72 Baron Davis .40 1.00
73 Fred Jones .25 .60
74 Joe Smith .30 .75
75 Jalen Rose .30 .75
76 Eddie Griffin .25 .60
77 Lamar Odom .40 1.00
78 Theo Ratliff .30 .75
79 Gordan Giricek .25 .60
80 Maurice Williams .25 .60
81 Tayshaun Prince .40 1.00
82 Kyle Korver .30 .75
83 Andre Miller .30 .75
84 Chris Wilcox .25 .60
85 Alonzo Mourning .50 1.25
86 Gilbert Arenas .40 1.00
87 Zydrunas Ilgauskas .30 .75
88 Jamaal Magloire .25 .60
89 Jason Williams .30 .75
90 Chucky Atkins .25 .60
91 Jeff Foster .25 .60
92 Kareem Rush .25 .60
93 Sam Cassell .30 .75
94 Josh Howard .30 .75
95 Tyronn Lue .25 .60
96 Vladimir Radmanovic .25 .60
97 Chauncey Billups .50 1.25
98 Brent Barry .25 .60
99 Paul Pierce .60 1.50
100 Dwyane Wade 1.50 4.00
101 Al Harrington JSY 2.00 5.00
102 Antawn Jamison JSY 2.00 5.00
103 Kirk Hinrich JSY 2.50 6.00
104 Tim Duncan JSY 6.00 15.00
105 Gerald Wallace JSY 2.00 5.00
106 Dirk Nowitzki JSY 6.00 15.00
107 Chris Webber JSY 3.00 8.00
108 Jason Kidd JSY 4.00 10.00
109 Carmelo Anthony JSY 5.00 12.00
110 Tracy McGrady JSY 4.00 10.00
111 Elton Brand JSY 2.00 5.00
112 Pau Gasol JSY 4.00 10.00
113 Jason Richardson JSY 2.50 6.00
114 Chris Bosh JSY 4.00 10.00
115 Kevin Garnett JSY 6.00 15.00
116 Steve Francis JSY 2.50 6.00
117 Richard Jefferson JSY 2.00 5.00
118 Baron Davis JSY 2.50 6.00
119 Manu Ginobili JSY 5.00 12.00
120 Shaquille O'Neal JSY 10.00 25.00
121 Amare Stoudemire JSY 2.50 6.00
122 Yao Ming JSY 6.00 15.00
123 Kenyon Martin JSY 2.50 6.00
124 Allen Iverson JSY 6.00 15.00
125 Peja Stojakovic JSY 2.00 5.00
126 Drew Gooden JSY 1.50 4.00
127 Ray Allen JSY 4.00 10.00
128 Ben Wallace JSY 3.00 8.00
129 Andrei Kirilenko JSY 2.00 5.00
130 Quentin Richardson JSY 1.50 4.00
131 Larry Bird 8.00 20.00
132 George Gervin 2.00 5.00
133 Walt Frazier 2.50 6.00
134 Oscar Robertson 4.00 10.00
135 Elgin Baylor 2.00 5.00
136 Moses Malone 2.00 5.00
137 Pete Maravich 3.00 8.00
138 Bob Cousy 3.00 8.00
139 Earl Monroe 2.00 5.00
140 Kareem Abdul-Jabbar 3.00 8.00
141 Isiah Thomas 3.00 8.00
142 Kevin McHale 2.50 6.00
143 Bill Walton 2.00 5.00
144 John Havlicek 2.00 5.00
145 Rick Barry 1.50 4.00
146 Wilt Chamberlain 4.00 10.00
147 Bill Russell 3.00 8.00
148 Willis Reed 3.00 8.00
149 Julius Erving 5.00 12.00
150 Drazen Petrovic 3.00 8.00
151 Andre Iguodala RC 3.00 8.00
152 Luke Jackson RC 1.25 3.00
153 Kirk Snyder RC 1.25 3.00
154 Kevin Martin RC 2.50 6.00
155 Antonio Burks RC 1.25 3.00
156 Robert Swift RC 1.25 3.00
157 Dorell Wright RC 1.50 4.00
158 David Harrison RC 1.25 3.00
159 Dwight Howard RC 6.00 15.00
160 Al Jefferson RC 2.00 5.00
161 Justin Reed AU RC 3.00 8.00
162 Shaun Livingston AU RC 5.00 12.00
163 Luol Deng AU RC 5.00 12.00
164 Josh Smith AU RC 5.00 12.00
165 Jameer Nelson AU RC 5.00 12.00
166 Pavel Podkolzin AU RC 3.00 8.00
167 Emeka Okafor AU RC 4.00 10.00
168 Kris Humphries AU RC 4.00 10.00
169 J.R. Smith AU RC 5.00 12.00
170 Sebastian Telfair AU RC 4.00 10.00
171 Sasha Vujacic AU RC 4.00 10.00
172 Tony Allen AU RC 5.00 12.00
173 Romain Sato AU RC 3.00 8.00
174 Ben Gordon AU RC 5.00 12.00
175 Devin Harris AU RC 4.00 10.00
176 Josh Childress AU RC 3.00 8.00
177 Andre Barrett AU RC 3.00 8.00
178 Jackson Vroman AU RC 3.00 8.00
179 Lionel Chalmers AU RC 4.00 10.00
180 Delonte West AU RC 4.00 10.00
181 Nenad Krstic AU RC 4.00 10.00
182 Donta Smith AU RC 3.00 8.00
183 Chris Duhon AU RC 4.00 10.00
184 Peter John Ramos AU RC 3.00 8.00
185 Bernard Robinson AU RC 3.00 8.00
186 Beno Udrih AU RC 4.00 10.00
187 Andris Biedrins AU RC 3.00 8.00
188 Trevor Ariza AU RC 5.00 12.00
189 Rafael Araujo AU RC 3.00 8.00
190 Andres Nocioni AU RC 5.00 12.00
191 Andrew Bogut XRC 5.00 12.00
192 Marvin Williams XRC 5.00 12.00
193 Deron Williams XRC 4.00 10.00
194 Chris Paul XRC 15.00 40.00
195 Raymond Felton XRC 3.00 8.00
196 Martell Webster XRC 3.00 8.00
197 Charlie Villanueva XRC 4.00 10.00
198 Channing Frye XRC 3.00 8.00
199 Ike Diogu XRC 3.00 8.00
200 Andrew Bynum XRC 2.50 6.00
201 Salim Stoudamire XRC 3.00 8.00
202 Yaroslav Korolev XRC 3.00 8.00
203 Sean May XRC 3.00 8.00
204 Rashad McCants XRC 3.00 8.00
205 Antoine Wright XRC 3.00 8.00
206 Joey Graham XRC 3.00 8.00
207 Danny Granger XRC 4.00 10.00
208 Gerald Green XRC 3.00 8.00
209 Hakim Warrick XRC 3.00 8.00
210 Julius Hodge XRC 3.00 8.00
211 Nate Robinson XRC 3.00 8.00
212 Jarrett Jack XRC 3.00 8.00
213 Francisco Garcia XRC 2.50 6.00
214 Luther Head XRC 3.00 8.00
215 Daniel Ewing XRC 3.00 8.00
216 Jason Maxiell XRC 2.50 6.00
217 Linas Kleiza XRC 3.00 8.00
218 Brandon Bass XRC 2.50 6.00
219 Wayne Simien XRC 3.00 8.00
220 David Lee XRC 4.00 10.00

2004-05 Finest Refractors

*1-100 REFRACTORS: 1.25X TO 3X BASE HI
*101-220 REFRACTORS: .5X TO 1.25X BASE HI
1-100 PRINT RUN 249 SER.#'d SETS
101-130 JSY PRINT RUN 179 SER.#'d SETS
131-160 PRINT RUN 249 SER.#'d SETS
161-190 PRINT RUN 179 SER.#'d SETS
191-220 PRINT RUN 359 SER.#'d SETS
8 Kobe Bryant 15.00 40.00
23 LeBron James 125.00 300.00
194 Chris Paul 30.00 80.00

2004-05 Finest Refractors Black

*1-100 REF.BLACK: 8X TO 20X BASE HI
*101-220 REF.BLACK: 1.5X TO 4X BASE HI
1-100 PRINT RUN 29 SER.#'d SETS
101-130 JSY PRINT RUN 19 SER.#'d SETS
161-190 PRINT RUN 19 SER.#'d SETS
191-220 PRINT RUN 39 SER.#'d SETS
8 Kobe Bryant 75.00 200.00
20 Grant Hill 12.00 30.00
23 LeBron James 1,000.00 2,000.00
85 Alonzo Mourning 12.00 30.00
120 Shaquille O'Neal JSY 40.00 100.00
194 Chris Paul 60.00 150.00

2004-05 Finest Refractors Blue

*1-100 REF.BLUE: 4X TO 10X BASE HI
*101-220 REF.BLUE: .75X TO 2X BASE HI
BLUE PRINT RUN 50 SER.#'d SETS
ONE PER BOX AS TOPPER
8 Kobe Bryant 60.00 150.00
20 Grant Hill 6.00 15.00
23 LeBron James 500.00 1,000.00
85 Alonzo Mourning 8.00 20.00
100 Dwyane Wade 15.00 40.00
159 Dwight Howard 15.00 40.00
194 Chris Paul 30.00 80.00

2004-05 Finest Refractors Gold

*1-100 REF.GOLD: 10X TO 25X BASE HI
*101-190 REF.GOLD: 2X TO 5X BASE HI
*191-220 REF.GOLD: 2.5X TO 6X BASE HI
1-100 PRINT RUN 15 SER.#'d SETS
101-130 JSY PRINT RUN 12 SER.#'d SETS
131-160 PRINT RUN 15 SER.#'d SETS
161-190 PRINT RUN 12 SER.#'d SETS
191-220 PRINT RUN 25 SER.#'d SETS
8 Kobe Bryant 100.00 250.00
23 LeBron James 1,500.00 3,000.00
85 Alonzo Mourning 15.00 40.00
120 Shaquille O'Neal JSY 40.00 100.00
194 Chris Paul 100.00 250.00

2004-05 Finest Refractors Green

*1-100 REF.GREEN: 4X TO 10X BASE HI
*101-220 REF.GREEN: .75X TO 2X BASE HI
1-100 PRINT RUN 49 SER.#'d SETS
101-130 JSY PRINT RUN 29 SER.#'d SETS
161-190 PRINT RUN 29 SER.#'d SETS
191-220 PRINT RUN 59 SER.#'d SETS
8 Kobe Bryant 60.00 150.00
23 LeBron James 500.00 1,000.00
85 Alonzo Mourning 8.00 20.00
159 Dwight Howard 15.00 40.00
194 Chris Paul 30.00 80.00

2004-05 Finest Refractors Red

*1-100 REF.RED: 1.5X TO 4X BASE HI
*101-220 REF.RED: .6X TO 1.5X BASE HI
1-100 PRINT RUN 149 SER.#'d SETS
101-130 PRINT RUN 79 SER.#'d SETS
161-190 PRINT RUN 79 SER.#'d SETS
191-220 PRINT RUN 159 SER.#'d SETS
8 Kobe Bryant 25.00 60.00
23 LeBron James 150.00 400.00
159 Dwight Howard 12.00 30.00

2004-05 Finest X-Fractors

*1-100 X-FRAC: 1.5X TO 4X BASE HI
*101-220 X-FRAC: .5X TO 1.25X BASE HI
1-100 PRINT RUN 199 SER.#'d SETS
101-130 JSY PRINT RUN 129 SER.#'d SETS
131-160 PRINT RUN 199 SER.#'d SETS
161-190 PRINT RUN 129 SER.#'d SETS
191-220 PRINT RUN 259 SER.#'d SETS
8 Kobe Bryant 20.00 50.00
23 LeBron James 150.00 400.00

2004-05 Finest X-Fractors Black

1-190 PRINT RUN 9 SER.#'d SETS
*191-220 X-FRAC.BLACK: 2.5X TO 6X BASE HI

2004-05 Finest X-Fractors Blue

*1-100 X-FRAC.BLUE: 10X TO 25X BASE HI
*101-160 X-FRAC.BLUE: 1.5X TO 4X BASE HI
*161-190 X-FRAC.BLUE: 1X TO 2.5X BASE HI
*191-220 X-FRAC.BLUE: 2.5X TO 6X BASE HI
BLUE PRINT RUN 25 SER.#'d SETS
ONE PER BOX AS TOPPER
8 Kobe Bryant 60.00 150.00
23 LeBron James 1,250.00 2,500.00
85 Alonzo Mourning 15.00 40.00

2004-05 Finest X-Fractors Green

*1-100 X-FRAC.GREEN: 8X TO 20X BASE HI
*101-130 X-FRAC.GREEN: 2X TO 5X BASE HI
*131-160 X-FRAC.GREEN: 1.5X TO 4X BASE HI
*191-220 X-FRAC.GREEN: 2X TO 5X BASE HI
1-100 PRINT RUN 19 SER.#'d SETS
161-190 PRINT RUN 15 SER.#'d SETS
191-220 PRINT RUN 30 SER.#'d SETS
8 Kobe Bryant 150.00 300.00
23 LeBron James 1,500.00 3,000.00
85 Alonzo Mourning 20.00 50.00
120 Shaquille O'Neal JSY 50.00 125.00

2004-05 Finest X-Fractors Red

*1-100 X-FRAC.RED: 2.5X TO 6X BASE HI
*101-220 X-FRAC.RED: .6X TO 1.5X BASE HI
8 Kobe Bryant 20.00 50.00
23 LeBron James 300.00 600.00
85 Alonzo Mourning 4.00 10.00
89 Jason Williams 8.00 20.00
100 Dwyane Wade 10.00 25.00

2004-05 Finest Far East Fabrics

PRINT RUN 100 SER.#'d SETS
*REFRACTORS: .6X TO 1.5X BASE HI
REF.PRINT RUN 50 SER.#'d SETS
BJ Bobby Jackson 3.00 8.00
BM Brad Miller 3.00 8.00
BN Bostjan Nachbar 2.50 6.00
CW Chris Webber 5.00 12.00
DC Doug Christie 3.00 8.00
DM Dikembe Mutombo 5.00 12.00
DS Darius Songaila 2.50 6.00
ED Erik Daniels 3.00 8.00
GO Greg Ostertag 2.50 6.00
JH Juwan Howard 3.00 8.00
JJ Jim Jackson 3.00 8.00
KM Kevin Martin 5.00 12.00
MB Matt Barnes 2.50 6.00
ME Maurice Evans 4.00 10.00
MT Maurice Taylor 2.50 6.00
PS Peja Stojakovic 3.00 8.00
RB Ryan Bowen 2.50 6.00
RG Reece Gaines 2.50 6.00
SP Scott Padgett 2.50 6.00
TL Tyronn Lue 2.50 6.00
TM Tracy McGrady 6.00 15.00
YM Yao Ming 10.00 25.00
CWA Charlie Ward 2.50 6.00
MBI Mike Bibby 4.00 10.00

2004-05 Finest Moments Autographs

PRINT RUN 50 SER.#'d SETS
*REFRACTORS: .6X TO 1.5X BASE HI
REF.PRINT RUN 20 SER.#'d SETS
BW Bill Walton 15.00 40.00
CD Clyde Drexler 15.00 40.00
DB Dave Bing 40.00 100.00
DC Dave Cowens 12.00 30.00
DS Detlef Schrempf 15.00 40.00
EB Elgin Baylor 15.00 40.00
EM Earl Monroe 15.00 40.00
GG George Gervin 12.00 30.00
ME Mark Eaton 12.00 30.00
MM Moses Malone 12.00 30.00
RB Rick Barry 12.00 30.00
RP Robert Parish 15.00 40.00

2004-05 Finest Perfect Pairs Autographs

PRINT RUN 50 SER.#'d SETS
*REFRACTORS: .5X TO 1.25X BASE HI
REFRACTOR PRINT RUN 20 SER.#'d SETS
AG C.Anthony/G.Gervin 25.00 60.00
DB L.Deng/E.Baylor 10.00 25.00
DP T.Duncan/R.Parish 75.00 200.00
GB B.Gordon/D.Bing 20.00 50.00
HB R.Hamilton/R.Barry 10.00 25.00
MD T.McGrady/C.Drexler 25.00 60.00
MM S.Marbury/E.Monroe 10.00 25.00
OD S.O'Neal/T.Duncan 150.00 400.00
OH E.Okafor/S.Haywood 10.00 25.00
OL J.O'Neal/B.Lanier 10.00 25.00
SC A.Stoudemire/D.Cowens 25.00 60.00
SS P.Stojakovic/D.Schrempf 25.00 60.00
WE B.Wallace/M.Eaton 10.00 25.00
OHA L.Odom/C.Hawkins 10.00 25.00

2005-06 Finest Refractors

*1-100: 1X TO 2.5X BASE HI
*101-125: .5X TO 1.25X BASE HI
*126-139: SAME VALUE AS BASE
*140-169: .5X TO 1.25X BASE HI
1-100 REF.PRINT RUN 349 SER.#'d SETS
101-125 REF.RC PRINT RUN 249 SER.#'d SETS
126-139 REF.AU RC PRINT RUN 229 SETS
33 Kobe Bryant 200.00 500.00
85 LeBron James 200.00 500.00

2005-06 Finest Refractors Black

*1-100: 6X TO 15X BASE HI
*101-125: 3X TO 8X BASE HI
*126-139: 1.25X TO 3X BASE HI
*140-169: 1.5X TO 4X BASE HI
STATED PRINT RUN 19 SER.#'d SETS
33 Kobe Bryant 1,250.00 2,500.00
85 LeBron James 1,250.00 2,500.00
150 J.J. Redick 75.00 200.00

2005-06 Finest Refractors Gold

*1-100: 5X TO 12X BASE HI
*101-125: 1.5X TO 4X BASE HI
*126-139: 1X TO 2.5X BASE HI
*140-169: 1.25X TO 3X BASE HI
1-125 PRINT RUN 39 SER.#'d SETS
126-139 AU PRINT RUN 59 SER.#'d SETS
33 Kobe Bryant 1,000.00 2,000.00
85 LeBron James 1,000.00 2,000.00
150 J.J. Redick 50.00 120.00

2005-06 Finest Refractors Green

*1-100: 3X TO 8X BASE HI
*101-125: .75X TO 2X BASE HI
*126-139: .5X TO 1.25X BASE HI
*140-169: .75X TO 2X BASE HI
1-125 PRINT RUN 89 SER.#'d SETS
126-139 AU PRINT RUN 99 SER.#'d SETS
33 Kobe Bryant 600.00 1,200.00
85 LeBron James 600.00 1,200.00

2005-06 Finest Refractors Red

*1-100: 2.5X TO 6X BASE HI
*101-125: .6X TO 1.5X BASE HI
*126-139: .4X TO 1X BASE HI
*140-169: .6X TO 1.5X BASE HI
1-125 PRINT RUN 169 SER.#'d SETS
126-139 AU PRINT RUN 199 SER.#'d SETS
33 Kobe Bryant 500.00 1,000.00
85 LeBron James 500.00 1,000.00

2005-06 Finest X-Fractors

*1-100: 2.5X TO 6X BASE HI
*101-125: .75X TO 2X BASE HI
*126-139: .6X TO 1.5X BASE HI
*140-169: .6X TO 1.5X BASE HI
1-100 PRINT RUN 229 SER.#'d SETS
101-125 PRINT RUN 199 SER.#'d SETS
126-139 PRINT RUN 169 SER.#'d SETS
33 Kobe Bryant 400.00 800.00
85 LeBron James 400.00 800.00
106 Chris Paul 15.00 40.00

2005-06 Finest X-Fractors Gold

*1-100: 8X TO 20X BASE HI
*101-125: 2.5X TO 6X BASE HI
*126-139: 1X TO 2.5X BASE HI
*140-169: 1.25X TO 3X BASE HI
1-125 PRINT RUN 29 SER.#'d SETS
126-139 PRINT RUN 39 SER.#'d SETS
33 Kobe Bryant 1,000.00 2,000.00
73 Ray Allen 15.00 40.00
85 LeBron James 1,000.00 2,000.00
150 J.J. Redick 60.00 150.00

2005-06 Finest X-Fractors Green

*1-100: 4X TO 10X BASE HI
*101-125: 1.25X TO 3X BASE HI
*126-139: .75X TO 2X BASE HI
*140-169: 1X TO 2.5X BASE HI
1-125 PRINT RUN 69 SER.#'d SETS
126-139 PRINT RUN 79 SER.#'d SETS
33 Kobe Bryant 600.00 1,200.00
85 LeBron James 600.00 1,200.00
96 Dwyane Wade 25.00 60.00
150 J.J. Redick 30.00 80.00

2005-06 Finest X-Fractors Red

*1-100: 3X TO 8X BASE HI
*101-125: 1X TO 2.5X BASE HI
*126-139: .6X TO 1.5X BASE HI
*140-169: .75X TO 2X BASE HI
1-125 PRINT RUN 169 SER.#'d SETS
126-169 PRINT RUN 149 SER.#'d SETS
33 Kobe Bryant 500.00 1,000.00
85 LeBron James 500.00 1,000.00

2005-06 Finest Boxloaders Celebrity Moments

PRINT RUN 399 SER.#'d SETS
CB1 Christie Brinkley 2.50 6.00
CE1 Carmen Electra 2.50 6.00
JM1 Jenny McCarthy 2.50 6.00
JZ1 Jay-Z 60.00 150.00
SE1 Shannon Elizabeth 2.50 6.00

2005-06 Finest Boxloaders Iverson Moments

COMMON CARD (AI1-AI20) 2.50 6.00
PRINT RUN 399 SER.#'d SETS

2005-06 Finest Boxloaders Wade Moments

COMMON CARD (DW1-DW20) 4.00 10.00
PRINT RUN 399 SER.#'d SETS

2005-06 Finest Dress for Success Relics

PRINT RUN 99 SER.#'d SETS
*REFRACTORS: .6X TO 1.5X BASE HI
REFRACTOR PRINT RUN 29 SER.#'d SETS
AB Andrew Bogut 5.00 12.00
CV Charlie Villanueva 3.00 8.00
DW Dwyane Wade 8.00 20.00
FO Fabricio Oberto 3.00 8.00
JG Joey Graham 3.00 8.00
OG Orien Greene 3.00 8.00

2005-06 Finest Fact

PRINT RUN 1899 SER.#'d SETS
*REFRACTORS: .6X TO 1.5X BASE HI
REFRACTOR PRINT RUN 199 SER.#'d SETS
*X-FRACTORS: .75X TO 2X BASE HI
X-FRACTOR PRINT RUN 99 SER.#'d SETS
FF1 Shawn Marion .75 2.00
FF2 Joey Graham .75 2.00
FF3 Rasheed Wallace 1.00 2.50
FF4 Rashard Lewis .75 2.00
FF5 Pau Gasol 1.50 4.00
FF6 Josh Smith .75 2.00
FF7 Josh Howard .75 2.00
FF8 Sean May .60 1.50
FF9 Hakim Warrick .75 2.00
FF10 Elton Brand .75 2.00
FF11 Antawn Jamison .75 2.00
FF12 Tracy McGrady 1.50 4.00
FF13 Sarunas Jasikevicius 1.00 2.50
FF14 Rashad McCants .60 1.50
FF15 Orien Greene .75 2.00
FF16 Michael Redd .75 2.00
FF17 Gilbert Arenas 1.00 2.50
FF18 Gerald Green 1.00 2.50
FF19 Dwyane Wade 2.00 5.00
FF20 Allen Iverson 2.00 5.00
FF21 Shaquille O'Neal 3.00 8.00
FF22 Chris Paul 25.00 60.00
FF23 LeBron James 25.00 60.00
FF24 Dirk Nowitzki 2.50 6.00
FF25 Tim Duncan 2.50 6.00

2005-06 Finest Fact Autographs

STATED PRINT RUN 30 TO 65 SETS
*REFRACTORS: .6X TO 1.5X BASE AU HI
REF.PRINT RUN 15 TO 25 SETS
AI Allen Iverson 40.00 100.00
CB Christie Brinkley 50.00 100.00
CE Carmen Electra 50.00 100.00
DW Dwyane Wade 60.00 120.00
EO Emeka Okafor 10.00 25.00
JM Jenny McCarthy 50.00 100.00
JZ Jay-Z 800.00 1,500.00
SE Shannon Elizabeth 20.00 50.00
SO Shaquille O'Neal 40.00 80.00
VC Vince Carter 20.00 40.00

2005-06 Finest Fact Relics

PRINT RUNS B/WN 1629-2080 COPIES PER
*REFRACTORS: .6X TO 1.5X BASE HI
REFRACTOR PRINT RUN 199 SER.#'d SETS
*X-FRACTORS: .75X TO 2X BASE HI
X-FRAC.PRINT RUN 49 SER.#'d SETS
AI Allen Iverson/1629 5.00 12.00
AJ Antawn Jamison/1629 2.00 5.00
CP Chris Paul/1629 5.00 12.00
DW Dwyane Wade/1629 5.00 12.00
EB Elton Brand /1629 2.00 5.00
HW Hakim Warrick/1629 2.00 5.00
JG Joey Graham/1629 2.00 5.00
JH Josh Howard/1629 2.00 5.00
JS Josh Smith/1629 2.00 5.00
OG Orien Greene/1629 2.00 5.00
RL Rashard Lewis/1629 2.00 5.00
RM Rashad McCants/1629 1.50 4.00
RW Rasheed Wallace/1629 2.50 6.00
SJ Sarunas Jasikevicius/1629 2.50 6.00
SM Sean May/1629 1.50 4.00
TM Tracy McGrady/2080 4.00 10.00

2005-06 Finest Patchworks

PRINT RUN 30 SER.#'d SETS
*REFRACTORS: .6X TO 1.5X BASE HI
REFRACTOR PRINT RUN 29 SER.#'d SETS
AI Allen Iverson 12.00 30.00
AS Amare Stoudemire 6.00 15.00
DW Dwyane Wade 12.00 30.00
KB Kobe Bryant 75.00 200.00
KG Kevin Garnett 15.00 40.00
RA Ray Allen 10.00 25.00
SN Steve Nash 12.00 30.00
SO Shaquille O'Neal 20.00 50.00
TD Tim Duncan 15.00 40.00
TM Tracy McGrady 10.00 25.00
VC Vince Carter 12.00 30.00
YM Yao Ming 12.00 30.00

2006-07 Finest

COMP.SET w/o SP's (100) 10.00 25.00
XRC PRINT RUN 539 SER.#'d SETS
1 Carmelo Anthony .75 2.00
2 Ben Wallace .60 1.50
3 Baron Davis .50 1.25
4 Jermaine O'Neal .50 1.25
5 Dwyane Wade 1.00 2.50
6 Vince Carter 1.00 2.50
7 Dwight Howard .60 1.50
8 Steve Nash 1.00 2.50
9 Tim Duncan 1.25 3.00
10 Gilbert Arenas .50 1.25
11 Gerald Wallace .40 1.00
12 Dirk Nowitzki 1.25 3.00
13 Chauncey Billups .60 1.50
14 Yao Ming 1.25 3.00
15 Pau Gasol .75 2.00
16 Kevin Garnett 1.25 3.00
17 Chris Paul 1.00 2.50
18 Amare Stoudemire .50 1.25
19 Tony Parker .75 2.00
20 Andrei Kirilenko .40 1.00
21 Paul Pierce .75 2.00
22 LeBron James 4.00 10.00
23 Richard Hamilton .50 1.25
24 Tracy McGrady .75 2.00
25 Kobe Bryant 4.00 10.00
26 Michael Redd .40 1.00
27 Stephon Marbury .60 1.50
28 Andre Iguodala .50 1.25
29 Mike Bibby .50 1.25
30 Chris Bosh .60 1.50
31 Joe Johnson .50 1.25
32 Kirk Hinrich .40 1.00
33 Josh Howard .40 1.00
34 Jason Richardson .50 1.25
35 Elton Brand .40 1.00
36 Shaquille O'Neal 2.00 5.00
37 Jason Kidd .75 2.00
38 Allen Iverson 1.25 3.00
39 Zach Randolph .50 1.25
40 Ray Allen .75 2.00
41 Larry Bird 1.50 4.00
42 Isiah Thomas .75 2.00
43 Dominique Wilkins .75 2.00
44 Willis Reed .75 2.00
45 Robert Parish .60 1.50
46 Chris Mullin .50 1.25
47 Karl Malone .60 1.50
48 Calvin Murphy .40 1.00
49 Xavier McDaniel .30 .75
50 Nate Archibald .40 1.00
51 Steve Novak RC 1.00 2.50
52 Shannon Brown RC .75 2.00
53 Sergio Rodriguez RC .75 2.00
54 Saer Sene RC .75 2.00
55 Ryan Hollins RC .75 2.00
56 Ronnie Brewer RC 1.25 3.00
57 Mile Ilic RC .75 2.00
58 Kyle Lowry RC 4.00 10.00
59 Hilton Armstrong RC .75 2.00
60 Craig Smith RC 1.00 2.50
61 Will Blalock RC .75 2.00
62 Thabo Sefolosha RC 1.00 2.50
63 Rodney Carney RC .75 2.00
64 Quincy Douby RC .75 2.00
65 P.J. Tucker RC 1.25 3.00
66 Josh Boone RC .75 2.00
67 Jordan Farmar RC 1.00 2.50
68 Damir Markota RC .75 2.00
69 Cedric Simmons RC .75 2.00
70 Allan Ray RC .75 2.00
71 Rudy Gay RC 1.50 4.00
72 Rajon Rondo RC 4.00 10.00
73 Patrick O'Bryant RC .75 2.00
74 Marcus Williams RC .75 2.00
75 Marcus Vinicius RC .75 2.00
76 James White RC .75 2.00
77 Dee Brown RC .75 2.00
78 David Noel RC .75 2.00
79 Daniel Gibson RC 1.00 2.50
80 Bobby Jones RC .75 2.00
81 Tyrus Thomas RC 1.00 2.50
82 Shelden Williams RC .75 2.00
83 Pops Mensah-Bonsu RC .75 2.00
84 Paul Davis RC .75 2.00
85 Mardy Collins RC .75 2.00
86 James Augustine RC .75 2.00
87 Hassan Adams RC .75 2.00
88 Chris Quinn RC .75 2.00
89 Brandon Roy RC 2.50 6.00
90 Andrea Bargnani RC 1.00 2.50
91 Solomon Jones RC .75 2.00
92 Shawne Williams RC .75 2.00
93 Renaldo Balkman RC 1.00 2.50
94 Randy Foye RC 1.00 2.50
95 Maurice Ager RC .75 2.00
96 LaMarcus Aldridge RC 3.00 8.00
97 Jorge Garbajosa RC 1.00 2.50
98 J.J. Redick RC 2.50 6.00
99 Alexander Johnson RC .75 2.00
100 Adam Morrison RC 1.00 2.50
101 Greg Oden XRC 3.00 8.00
102 Kevin Durant XRC 50.00 120.00
103 Al Horford XRC 4.00 10.00
104 Mike Conley Jr. XRC 4.00 10.00
105 Jeff Green XRC 3.00 8.00
106 Yi Jianlian XRC 5.00 12.00
107 Corey Brewer XRC 2.50 6.00
108 Brandan Wright XRC 2.50 6.00
109 Joakim Noah XRC 3.00 8.00
110 Spencer Hawes XRC 3.00 8.00
111 Acie Law XRC 2.00 5.00
112 Thaddeus Young XRC 4.00 10.00
113 Julian Wright XRC 2.00 5.00
114 Al Thornton XRC 2.50 6.00
115 Rodney Stuckey XRC 2.50 6.00
116 Nick Young XRC 4.00 10.00
117 Sean Williams XRC 2.50 6.00
118 Marco Belinelli XRC 3.00 8.00
119 Javaris Crittenton XRC 2.50 6.00
120 Jason Smith XRC 3.00 8.00
121 Daequan Cook XRC 2.50 6.00
122 Jared Dudley XRC 2.50 6.00
123 Wilson Chandler XRC 3.00 8.00
124 Carl Landry XRC 3.00 8.00
125 Morris Almond XRC 2.00 5.00
126 Aaron Brooks XRC 3.00 8.00
127 Arron Afflalo XRC 2.50 6.00
128 Gabe Pruitt XRC 2.00 5.00
129 Alando Tucker XRC 2.00 5.00
130 Marcus Williams XRC 2.00 5.00
NNO Rookie Autograph EXCH 75.00 175.00

2006-07 Finest Refractors

*1-50 REF: .75X TO 2X BASE HI
*51-100 REF: .5X TO 1.5X BASE HI
*101-130 XRC REF: .5X TO 1.25X BASE HI
REFRACTOR ODDS 1:6
22 LeBron James 40.00 100.00
25 Kobe Bryant 40.00 100.00
58 Kyle Lowry 12.00 30.00
98 J.J. Redick 10.00 25.00
102 Kevin Durant 100.00 250.00

2006-07 Finest Refractors Black

*1-50 REF.BLACK: 2.5X TO 6X BASE HI
*51-100 REF.BLACK: 1X TO 2.5X BASE HI
*101-130 REF.BLACK: 1X TO 2.5X BASE HI
PRINT RUN 99 SER.#'d SETS
22 LeBron James 400.00 800.00
25 Kobe Bryant 150.00 400.00
58 Kyle Lowry 15.00 40.00
72 Rajon Rondo 15.00 40.00
98 J.J. Redick 20.00 50.00
102 Kevin Durant 300.00 600.00

2006-07 Finest Refractors Blue

*1-50 REF.BLUE: 1X TO 2.5X BASE HI
*51-100 REF.BLUE: .75X TO 2X BASE HI
*101-130 REF.BLUE: .6X TO 1.5X BASE HI
REF.BLUE PRINT RUN 299 SER.#'d SETS
22 LeBron James 200.00 500.00
25 Kobe Bryant 50.00 120.00
58 Kyle Lowry 12.00 30.00
98 J.J. Redick 12.00 30.00
102 Kevin Durant 125.00 300.00

2006-07 Finest Refractors Gold

*1-50 GOLD.REF: 6X TO 15X BASE HI
*51-100 GOLD.REF: 1.5X TO 4X BASE HI
*101-130 GOLD.REF: 1.5X TO 4X BASE HI
PRINT RUN 50 SER.#'d SETS
5 Dwyane Wade 125.00 300.00
14 Yao Ming 40.00 100.00
22 LeBron James 1,000.00 2,000.00
24 Tracy McGrady 40.00 100.00
25 Kobe Bryant 400.00 800.00
40 Ray Allen 30.00 80.00
58 Kyle Lowry 60.00 150.00
72 Rajon Rondo 40.00 100.00
98 J.J. Redick 60.00 150.00
102 Kevin Durant 400.00 800.00
106 Yi Jianlian 125.00 300.00

2006-07 Finest Refractors Green

*1-50 REF.GREEN: 1.25X TO 3X BASE HI
*51-100 REF.GREEN: .75X TO 2X BASE HI
*101-130 REF.GREEN: .75X TO 2X BASE HI
PRINT RUN 199 SER.#'d SETS
22 LeBron James 300.00 600.00
25 Kobe Bryant 60.00 150.00
58 Kyle Lowry 12.00 30.00
98 J.J. Redick 15.00 40.00
102 Kevin Durant 125.00 300.00

2006-07 Finest Refractors Silver

*SILVER: .6X TO 1.5X BASE HI
STATED PRINT RUN 319 SER.#'d SETS
102 Kevin Durant 125.00 300.00

2006-07 Finest X-Fractors

*1-50 X-FRAC: 5X TO 12X BASE HI
*51-100 X-FRAC: 2X TO 5X BASE HI
*101-130 X-FRAC: 2X TO 5X BASE HI
X-FRAC.PRINT RUN 25 SER.#'d SETS
22 LeBron James 1,000.00 2,000.00
25 Kobe Bryant 500.00 1,000.00
58 Kyle Lowry 60.00 150.00
72 Rajon Rondo 30.00 80.00
98 J.J. Redick 75.00 200.00
102 Kevin Durant 400.00 800.00

2006-07 Finest Moments

COMPLETE SET (2) 4.00 10.00
ONE PER BOX AS TOPPER
*REFRACTORS: .75X TO 2X BASE HI
REFRACTORS 1:3 BOXES
AM Adam Morrison 1.25 3.00
LB Larry Bird 3.00 8.00

2006-07 Finest Moments Relics Autographs X-Fractors

AM Adam Morrison/50 20.00 40.00
LB Larry Bird/25 60.00 150.00

2006-07 Finest Moments Relics Refractors

AM Adam Morrison/499 5.00 12.00
LB Larry Bird/299 12.00 30.00

2006-07 Finest Rookie Autographs Refractors

GROUP A ODDS 1:456, GROUP B 1:150
GROUP C 1:66, GROUP D 1:48
GROUP E 1:36, GROUP F 1:36
GROUP G 1:144, GROUP H 1:24
*X-FRACTORS: .75X TO 2X BASE HI
X-FRACTOR PRINT RUN 25 SER.#'d SETS
51 Steve Novak D 2.00 5.00
52 Shannon Brown C 1.50 4.00
53 Sergio Rodriguez H 2.00 5.00
54 Saer Sene H 1.50 4.00
55 Ryan Hollins E 1.50 4.00
56 Ronnie Brewer D 2.50 6.00
57 Mile Ilic E 1.50 4.00
58 Kyle Lowry F 30.00 80.00
59 Hilton Armstrong D 1.50 4.00
60 Craig Smith F 2.00 5.00
61 Will Blalock H 1.50 4.00
62 Thabo Sefolosha D 6.00 15.00
63 Rodney Carney C 1.50 4.00
64 Quincy Douby C 1.50 4.00
66 Josh Boone D 1.50 4.00
67 Jordan Farmar E 2.00 5.00
68 Damir Markota E 1.50 4.00
69 Cedric Simmons B 1.50 4.00
70 Allan Ray E 1.50 4.00
72 Rajon Rondo E 8.00 20.00
73 Patrick O'Bryant C 1.50 4.00
74 Marcus Williams A 1.50 4.00
75 Marcus Vinicius G 1.50 4.00
76 James White E 1.50 4.00
77 Dee Brown F 1.50 4.00
80 Bobby Jones B 1.50 4.00
82 Shelden Williams C 1.50 4.00
83 Pops Mensah-Bonsu H 1.50 4.00
84 Paul Davis B 1.50 4.00
85 Mardy Collins D 1.50 4.00
87 Hassan Adams D 1.50 4.00
90 Andrea Bargnani A 2.00 5.00
91 Solomon Jones C 1.50 4.00
92 Shawne Williams F 1.50 4.00
93 Renaldo Balkman F 2.00 5.00
94 Randy Foye B 2.00 5.00
95 Maurice Ager C 1.50 4.00
97 Jorge Garbajosa H 2.00 5.00
98 J.J. Redick F 40.00 100.00
100 Adam Morrison H 3.00 8.00

2007-08 Finest

COMP.SET w/o DRAFT (100) 25.00 50.00
1 Gilbert Arenas .50 1.25
2 Ray Allen .75 2.00
3 Dwyane Wade 1.00 2.50
4 Dirk Nowitzki 1.25 3.00
5 Manu Ginobili 1.00 2.50
6 Eddy Curry .30 .75
7 Jermaine O'Neal .50 1.25
8 Carlos Boozer .40 1.00
9 Tony Parker .75 2.00
10 Jason Kidd .75 2.00
11 Chris Bosh .60 1.50
12 Al Jefferson .30 .75
13 Steve Nash 1.00 2.50
14 Chris Paul 1.00 2.50
15 Carmelo Anthony .75 2.00
16 Pau Gasol .75 2.00
17 Joe Johnson .40 1.00
18 Chauncey Billups .60 1.50
19 Andre Iguodala .50 1.25
20 Yao Ming 1.25 3.00
21 Tim Duncan 1.25 3.00
22 Michael Redd .40 1.00
23 Allen Iverson 1.25 3.00
24 Kobe Bryant 4.00 10.00
25 Kevin Garnett 1.25 3.00
26 Brandon Roy .60 1.50
27 Luol Deng .40 1.00
28 Deron Williams .40 1.00
29 Amare Stoudemire .50 1.25

30 Vince Carter 1.00 2.50
31 Tracy McGrady .75 2.00
32 Shaquille O'Neal 2.00 5.00
33 Jason Richardson .50 1.25
34 Paul Pierce .75 2.00
35 Baron Davis .40 1.00
36 Dwight Howard .60 1.50
37 Josh Howard .40 1.00
38 Kevin Martin .40 1.00
39 Ben Gordon .40 1.00
40 LeBron James 4.00 10.00
41 Isiah Thomas .50 1.25
42 Dominique Wilkins .75 2.00
43 Magic Johnson 2.00 5.00
44 Bill Russell 1.50 4.00
45 David Robinson 1.00 2.50
46 John Stockton 1.00 2.50
47 Jerry West 1.25 3.00
48 Moses Malone .75 2.00
49 Dennis Rodman 1.25 3.00
50 Larry Bird 2.00 5.00
51 Al Horford RC 2.50 6.00
52 Ramon Sessions RC .75 2.00
53 JamesOn Curry RC .60 1.50
54 Arron Afflalo RC .75 2.00
55 Carl Landry RC .60 1.50
56 Glen Davis RC .75 2.00
57 Jermareo Davidson RC .60 1.50
58 Nick Fazekas RC .60 1.50
59 Taurean Green RC .60 1.50
60 Cheikh Samb RC .60 1.50
61 Mike Conley Jr. RC 2.50 6.00
62 Chris Richard RC .60 1.50
63 Josh McRoberts RC .60 1.50
64 Alando Tucker RC .60 1.50
65 Brandan Wright RC .75 2.00
66 Jamario Moon RC .75 2.00
67 Jared Dudley RC .75 2.00
68 Dominic McGuire RC .60 1.50
69 Sean Williams RC .60 1.50
70 Mario West RC .75 2.00
71 Kevin Durant RC 20.00 50.00
72 Julian Wright RC .60 1.50
73 Yi Jianlian RC 1.25 3.00
74 Coby Karl RC .60 1.50
75 Aaron Brooks RC .75 2.00
76 Kyrylo Fesenko RC .60 1.50
77 Greg Oden RC 1.00 2.50
78 Juan Carlos Navarro RC .75 2.00
79 Nick Young RC .60 1.50
80 Thaddeus Young RC 1.00 2.50
81 Joakim Noah RC 1.00 2.50
82 Luis Scola RC 1.00 2.50
83 Aaron Gray RC .60 1.50
84 Herbert Hill RC .60 1.50
85 Al Thornton RC .60 1.50
86 D.J. Strawberry RC .60 1.50
87 Javaris Crittenton RC .60 1.50
88 Morris Almond RC .60 1.50
89 Spencer Hawes RC .60 1.50
90 C.J. Watson RC .75 2.00
91 Corey Brewer RC .75 2.00
92 Jeff Green RC .75 2.00
93 Marco Belinelli RC .75 2.00
94 Marcin Gortat RC 1.25 3.00
95 Acie Law RC .60 1.50
96 Daequan Cook RC .75 2.00
97 Gabe Pruitt RC .60 1.50
98 Jason Smith RC .60 1.50
99 Rodney Stuckey RC .60 1.50
100 Wilson Chandler RC .75 2.00
101 Derrick Rose XRC 15.00 40.00
102 Michael Beasley XRC 4.00 10.00
103 O.J. Mayo XRC 4.00 10.00
104 Russell Westbrook XRC 25.00 60.00
105 Kevin Love XRC 12.00 30.00
106 Danilo Gallinari XRC 6.00 15.00
107 Eric Gordon XRC 8.00 20.00
108 Joe Alexander XRC 2.50 6.00
109 D.J. Augustin XRC 4.00 10.00
110 Brook Lopez XRC 5.00 12.00
111 Jerryd Bayless XRC 3.00 8.00
112 Jason Thompson XRC 3.00 8.00
113 Brandon Rush XRC 3.00 8.00
114 Anthony Randolph XRC 3.00 8.00
115 Robin Lopez XRC 4.00 10.00
116 Marreese Speights XRC 3.00 8.00
117 Roy Hibbert XRC 4.00 10.00
118 JaVale McGee XRC 4.00 10.00
119 J.J. Hickson XRC 3.00 8.00
120 Alexis Ajinca XRC 2.50 6.00
121 Ryan Anderson XRC 4.00 10.00
122 Courtney Lee XRC 4.00 10.00
123 Kosta Koufos XRC 3.00 8.00
124 Walter Sharpe XRC 3.00 8.00
125 Nicolas Batum XRC 5.00 12.00
126 George Hill XRC 5.00 12.00
127 Darrell Arthur XRC 4.00 10.00
128 Donte Greene XRC 2.50 6.00
129 D.J. White XRC 2.50 6.00
130 J.R. Giddens XRC 2.50 6.00

2007-08 Finest Refractors

*1-100 REF: .6X TO 1.5X BASE HI
*101-130 REF: .5X TO 1.25X BASE HI
1-100 ODDS APPROX. 1:2
101-130 STATED ODDS 1:5
24 Kobe Bryant 12.00 30.00
40 LeBron James 60.00 150.00
71 Kevin Durant 75.00 200.00

2007-08 Finest Refractors Black

*1-50 REF.BLACK: 3X TO 8X BASE HI
*51-100 REF.BLACK: 1.5X TO 4X BASE HI
*101-130 REF.BLACK: 1X TO 2.5X BASE HI
REF.BLACK PRINT RUN 75 SER.#'d SETS
24 Kobe Bryant 50.00 120.00
40 LeBron James 150.00 400.00
71 Kevin Durant 2,000.00 4,000.00

2007-08 Finest Refractors Blue

*1-50 REF.BLUE: 1.25X TO 3X BASE HI
*51-100 REF.BLUE: .75X TO 2X BASE HI
*101-130 REF.BLUE: .6X TO 1.5X BASE HI
REF.BLUE PRINT RUN 199 SER.#'d SETS
24 Kobe Bryant 20.00 50.00
40 LeBron James 100.00 250.00
71 Kevin Durant 1,000.00 2,000.00

2007-08 Finest Refractors Gold

*1-50 REF.GOLD: 10X TO 25X BASE HI
*51-100 REF.GOLD: 3X TO 8X BASE HI
*101-130 REF.GOLD: 1.25X TO 3X BASE HI
PRINT RUN 25 SER.#'d SETS
24 Kobe Bryant 150.00 400.00
40 LeBron James 800.00 1,500.00
71 Kevin Durant 3,000.00 6,000.00
104 Russell Westbrook 300.00 600.00

2007-08 Finest Refractors Green

*1-50 REF.GREEN: 2X TO 5X BASE HI
*51-100 REF.GREEN: 1.25X TO 3X BASE HI
*101-130 REF.GREEN: .75X TO 2X BASE HI
REF.GREEN PRINT RUN 149 SER.#'d SETS
24 Kobe Bryant 30.00 80.00
40 LeBron James 125.00 300.00
71 Kevin Durant 1,500.00 3,000.00

2007-08 Finest Refractors Silver

*SILVER: .5X TO 1.25X BASE HI
STATED PRINT RUN 319 SER.#'d SETS
71 Kevin Durant 800.00 1,500.00

2007-08 Finest X-Fractors

*1-50 X-FRAC: 8X TO 20X BASE HI
*51-100 X-FRAC: 4X TO 10X BASE HI
*101-130 X-FRAC: 1.5X TO 4X BASE HI
STATED PRINT RUN 15 SER.#'d SETS
24 Kobe Bryant 125.00 300.00
40 LeBron James 1,000.00 2,000.00
71 Kevin Durant 4,000.00 8,000.00
104 Russell Westbrook 400.00 800.00

2007-08 Finest Draft Picks Autographs Refractors

STATED ODDS 1:43
102 Michael Beasley 25.00 60.00
103 O.J. Mayo 10.00 25.00
104 Russell Westbrook 200.00 500.00
105 Kevin Love 75.00 200.00
106 Danilo Gallinari 8.00 20.00
107 Eric Gordon 6.00 15.00
108 Joe Alexander 3.00 8.00
109 D.J. Augustin 5.00 12.00
110 Brook Lopez 6.00 15.00
111 Jerryd Bayless 4.00 10.00
112 Jason Thompson 4.00 10.00
113 Brandon Rush 4.00 10.00
114 Anthony Randolph 4.00 10.00
115 Robin Lopez 5.00 12.00
116 Marreese Speights 4.00 10.00
117 Roy Hibbert 5.00 12.00
118 JaVale McGee 5.00 12.00
119 J.J. Hickson 4.00 10.00
120 Alexis Ajinca 3.00 8.00
121 Ryan Anderson 5.00 12.00
122 Courtney Lee 5.00 12.00
123 Kosta Koufos 4.00 10.00
124 Walter Sharpe 3.00 8.00
125 Nicolas Batum 6.00 15.00
126 George Hill 6.00 15.00
127 Darrell Arthur 5.00 12.00
128 Donte Greene 3.00 8.00
129 D.J. White 3.00 8.00
130 J.R. Giddens 3.00 8.00

2007-08 Finest Redemption Autographs

BG Ben Gordon 3.00 8.00
BR Brandon Roy 10.00 25.00

2007-08 Finest Rookie Autographs Refractors

GROUP A ODDS 1:31, GROUP B 1:12
GROUP C ODDS 1:4, GROUP D 1:3
GROUP E ODDS 1:3
53 JamesOn Curry B 2.50 6.00
54 Arron Afflalo C 3.00 8.00
55 Carl Landry C 2.50 6.00
56 Glen Davis D 3.00 8.00
57 Jermareo Davidson E 2.50 6.00
58 Nick Fazekas D 2.50 6.00
59 Taurean Green B 2.50 6.00
63 Josh McRoberts B 2.50 6.00
64 Alando Tucker D 2.50 6.00
65 Brandan Wright A 3.00 8.00
66 Jamario Moon C 3.00 8.00
67 Jared Dudley D 3.00 8.00
68 Dominic McGuire B 2.50 6.00
69 Sean Williams D 2.50 6.00
70 Mario West E 3.00 8.00
73 Yi Jianlian A 5.00 12.00
74 Coby Karl C 2.50 6.00
75 Aaron Brooks D 3.00 8.00
77 Greg Oden A 4.00 10.00
78 Juan Carlos Navarro C 3.00 8.00
79 Nick Young A 4.00 10.00
80 Thaddeus Young A 4.00 10.00
83 Aaron Gray D 2.50 6.00
84 Herbert Hill E 2.50 6.00
85 Al Thornton C 2.50 6.00
86 D.J. Strawberry E 2.50 6.00
87 Javaris Crittenton B 2.50 6.00
88 Morris Almond C 2.50 6.00
89 Spencer Hawes C 2.50 6.00
93 Marco Belinelli A 3.00 8.00
94 Marcin Gortat C 3.00 8.00
95 Acie Law C 2.50 6.00
96 Daequan Cook B 3.00 8.00
97 Gabe Pruitt C 2.50 6.00
98 Jason Smith D 2.50 6.00
99 Rodney Stuckey C 2.50 6.00
100 Wilson Chandler D 3.00 8.00

2008-09 Finest Redemption Autographs

DW Dwyane Wade 20.00 50.00

2021 Finest

COMMON CARD .25 .60
SEMISTARS .30 .75
UNLISTED STARS .40 1.00
*REFRACTOR: 1.25X TO 3X BASIC
*ATOMIC REFRACTOR/299: 1.5X TO 4X BASIC
*PURPLE REFRACTOR/250: 1.5X TO 4X BASIC
*SPECKLE REFRACTOR/199: 2X TO 5X BASIC
*BLUE REFRACTOR/150: 2X TO 5X BASIC
*GREEN REFRACTOR/99: 2.5X TO 6X BASIC
*PINK REFRACTOR/75: 3X TO 8X BASIC
*GOLD REFRACTOR/50: 5X TO 12X BASIC
*WAVE REFRACTOR/30: 8X TO 20X BASIC
*ORANGE REFRACTOR/25: 8X TO 20X BASIC
1 Cole Anthony .60 1.50
2 Allen Iverson 1.00 2.50
3 Greg Anthony .25 .60
4 Joe Dumars .40 1.00
5 Kevin Garnett .75 2.00
6 Larry Johnson .40 1.00
7 Latrell Sprewell .40 1.00
8 Larry Nance Sr. .30 .75
9 Joe Smith .30 .75
10 Dennis Rodman .75 2.00
11 Isiah Thomas .60 1.50
12 Vlade Divac .30 .75
13 Randy Brown .25 .60
14 Ron Harper .40 1.00
15 Allan Houston .40 1.00
16 Jerome Lane .25 .60
17 Kenny Anderson .30 .75
18 Corie Blount .25 .60
19 Anfernee Hardaway .75 2.00
20 Gary Payton .50 1.25
21 Dominique Wilkins .50 1.25
22 Kurt Rambis .30 .75
23 Larry Hughes .30 .75
24 Mike Bibby .30 .75
25 Steve Kerr .40 1.00
26 Isaiah Rider .30 .75
27 Toni Kukoc .40 1.00
28 Glen Rice .30 .75
29 Dennis Hopson .25 .60
30 Dell Curry .30 .75
31 Hersey Hawkins .25 .60
32 Jason Kidd .50 1.25
33 Grant Hill .50 1.25
34 Shaquille O'Neal 1.25 3.00
35 Robert Horry .40 1.00
36 Brad Sellers .25 .60
37 Juwan Howard .30 .75
38 Steve Nash .60 1.50
39 Detlef Schrempf .30 .75
40 Shawn Kemp .50 1.25
41 Dirk Nowitzki .75 2.00
42 James Worthy .50 1.25
43 Danny Manning .30 .75
44 Horace Grant .40 1.00
45 Willie Anderson .25 .60
46 Jason Richardson .40 1.00
47 B.J. Armstrong .30 .75
48 Vinny Del Negro .25 .60
49 Scott Burrell .25 .60
50 Tim Hardaway .50 1.25
51 Steve Smith .30 .75
52 John Starks .30 .75
53 Dan Majerle .30 .75
54 Earl Boykins .25 .60
55 Dikembe Mutombo .50 1.25
56 Gheorghe Muresan .25 .60
57 Damon Stoudamire .40 1.00
58 Vince Carter .50 1.25
59 Jeff Hornacek .30 .75
62 Adonal Foyle .25 .60

2021 Finest Autographs

COMMON CARD 3.00 8.00
SEMISTARS 4.00 10.00
UNLISTED STARS 5.00 12.00
*REFRACTOR/75: .5X TO 1.2X BASIC
*GOLD REFRACTOR/50: .6X TO 1.5X BASIC
*ORANGE REFRACTOR/25: .75X TO 2X BASIC
FAAF Adonal Foyle 3.00 8.00
FAAH Allan Houston 5.00 12.00
FAAI Allen Iverson 75.00 200.00
FABA B.J. Armstrong 4.00 10.00
FABS Brad Sellers 3.00 8.00
FACB Corie Blount 3.00 8.00
FADH Dennis Hopson 3.00 8.00
FADM Dikembe Mutombo 20.00 50.00
FADN Dirk Nowitzki 100.00 250.00
FADR Dennis Rodman 40.00 100.00
FADS Detlef Schrempf 4.00 10.00
FADW Dominique Wilkins 12.00 30.00
FAEB Earl Boykins 3.00 8.00
FAGH Grant Hill 25.00 60.00
FAGM Gheorghe Muresan 3.00 8.00
FAGP Gary Payton 20.00 50.00
FAGR Glen Rice 4.00 10.00
FAHG Horace Grant 5.00 12.00
FAHH Hersey Hawkins 3.00 8.00
FAIT Isiah Thomas 15.00 40.00
FAJB Jud Buechler 3.00 8.00
FAJD Joe Dumars 5.00 12.00
FAJH Jeff Hornacek 4.00 10.00
FAJK Jason Kidd 20.00 50.00
FAJL Jerome Lane 3.00 8.00
FAJS John Starks 4.00 10.00
FAJW James Worthy 12.00 30.00
FAKA Kenny Anderson 4.00 10.00
FAKG Kevin Garnett 75.00 200.00
FAKR Kurt Rambis 4.00 10.00
FALJ Larry Johnson 12.00 30.00
FALN Larry Nance Sr. 4.00 10.00
FALS Latrell Sprewell 15.00 40.00
FAMB Mike Bibby 4.00 10.00
FAMW Mikey Williams 10.00 25.00
FAPH Anfernee Hardaway 50.00 120.00
FARB Randy Brown 3.00 8.00
FARH Ron Harper 5.00 12.00
FASB Scott Burrell 3.00 8.00
FASK Shawn Kemp 30.00 80.00
FASN Steve Nash 50.00 120.00
FASO Shaquille O'Neal 75.00 200.00
FASS Steve Smith 4.00 10.00
FATH Tim Hardaway 8.00 20.00
FATK Toni Kukoc 8.00 20.00
FAVC Vince Carter 50.00 120.00
FAVD Vlade Divac 4.00 10.00
FAWA Willie Anderson 3.00 8.00
FADCR Dell Curry 4.00 10.00
FADMJ Dan Majerle 4.00 10.00
FADST Damon Stoudamire 8.00 20.00
FAJHW Juwan Howard 4.00 10.00
FAJRC Jason Richardson 5.00 12.00
FASKR Steve Kerr 12.00 30.00
FAVDN Vinny Del Negro 3.00 8.00

2023-24 Finest

*CHECKERBOARD REF: 1X TO 2.5X BASIC
*REFRACTOR: 1.25X TO 3X BASIC
1 Nikola Jokic C 1.50 4.00
2 Trae Young C .60 1.50
3 Jaylen Brown C .60 1.50
4 Derrick White C .40 1.00
5 Marcus Smart C .40 1.00
6 Ben Simmons C .30 .75
7 Anfernee Simons C .40 1.00
8 Mark Williams C .30 .75
9 Ayo Dosunmu C .30 .75
10 Zach LaVine C .50 1.25
11 Evan Mobley C .50 1.25
12 Jalen Williams C .60 1.50
13 Aaron Gordon C .30 .75
14 Rip Hamilton C .40 1.00
15 Giannis Antetokounmpo C 1.50 4.00
16 Andrew Wiggins C .40 1.00
17 Draymond Green C .40 1.00
18 Damian Lillard C .75 2.00
19 Buddy Hield C .30 .75
20 Myles Turner C .30 .75
21 Norman Powell C .30 .75
22 Russell Westbrook C .50 1.25
23 Scottie Barnes C .40 1.00
24 Brandon Clarke C .25 .60
25 Tyler Herro C .50 1.25
26 Shaquille O'Neal C 1.00 2.50
27 Jrue Holiday C .40 1.00
28 Karl-Anthony Towns C .50 1.25
29 CJ McCollum C .30 .75
30 Trey Murphy III C .40 1.00
31 Immanuel Quickley C .40 1.00
32 Jalen Brunson C .60 1.50
33 Chet Holmgren C .75 2.00
34 Peja Stojakovic C .30 .75
35 Franz Wagner C .50 1.25
36 Kevin Garnett C .75 2.00
37 James Harden C .60 1.50
38 Tyrese Maxey C .60 1.50
39 Chris Paul C .60 1.50
40 Devin Booker C .75 2.00
41 Allen Iverson C .75 2.00
42 Carmelo Anthony C .50 1.25
43 Kevin Huerter C .25 .60
44 Naz Reid C .30 .75
45 Jakob Poeltl C .25 .60
46 OG Anunoby C .40 1.00
47 Collin Sexton C .40 1.00
48 Larry Bird C 1.25 3.00
49 Al Horford C .30 .75
50 Kelly Oubre C .30 .75
51 Patrick Williams C .25 .60
52 Max Strus C .30 .75
53 Tim Hardaway Jr. C .25 .60
54 Christian Braun C .30 .75
55 Shawn Kemp C .50 1.25
56 Aaron Nesmith C .30 .75
57 Alex English C .40 1.00
58 Jaren Jackson Jr. C .50 1.25
59 Manu Ginobili C .60 1.50
60 Cole Anthony C .30 .75
61 Dennis Rodman C .75 2.00
62 Zach Collins C .25 .60
63 Christian Laettner C .30 .75
64 Lonnie Walker IV C .30 .75
65 Jason Kidd C .50 1.25
66 Kentavious Caldwell-Pope C .25 .60
67 Lenny Wilkens C .40 1.00
68 Anthony Davis C .75 2.00
69 LeBron James C 2.50 6.00
70 Daniel Gafford C .30 .75
71 Josh Hart C .30 .75
72 Jamaal Wilkes C .30 .75
73 Jae'Sean Tate C .30 .75
74 Corey Kispert C .25 .60
75 Elvin Hayes C .40 1.00
76 Victor Wembanyama C RC 2.50 6.00
77 Scoot Henderson C RC 1.00 2.50
78 Jarace Walker C RC .60 1.50
79 Cam Whitmore C RC .75 2.00
80 Taylor Hendricks C RC .50 1.25
81 Jordan Hawkins C RC .50 1.25
82 Brice Sensabaugh C RC .50 1.25
83 Bam Adebayo C .50 1.25
84 Leonard Miller C RC .30 .75
85 Rayan Rupert C RC .30 .75
86 GG Jackson C RC .60 1.50
87 Bilal Coulibaly C RC .75 2.00
88 Noah Clowney C RC .30 .75
89 Marcus Sasser C RC .50 1.25
90 Jalen Wilson C RC .30 .75
91 Trayce Jackson-Davis C RC .40 1.00
92 Brandin Podziemski C RC 1.00 2.50
93 Cameron Johnson C .30 .75
94 Leaky Black C RC .25 .60
95 Dirk Nowitzki C .75 2.00
96 Grant Hill C .50 1.25
97 Amari Bailey C RC .30 .75
98 Fred VanVleet C .50 1.25
99 Jordan Walsh C RC .30 .75
100 Isaiah Wong C RC .30 .75
101 Scoot Henderson UC 1.25 3.00
102 Dejounte Murray UC .50 1.25
103 John Collins UC .40 1.00
104 Jayson Tatum UC 1.50 4.00
105 Mikal Bridges UC .50 1.25
106 Spencer Dinwiddie UC .30 .75
107 Gordon Hayward UC .40 1.00
108 LaMelo Ball UC 1.00 2.50
109 Larry Johnson UC .50 1.25
110 DeMar DeRozan UC .60 1.50
111 Pau Gasol UC .60 1.50
112 Caris LeVert UC .40 1.00
113 Donovan Mitchell UC .75 2.00
114 Rui Hachimura UC .40 1.00
115 Kyrie Irving UC .75 2.00
116 Michael Porter Jr. UC .50 1.25
117 Aaron Gordon UC .40 1.00
118 Cade Cunningham UC 1.00 2.50
119 Rasheed Wallace UC .50 1.25
120 Marcus Sasser UC .60 1.50
121 Klay Thompson UC 1.00 2.50
122 Stephen Curry UC 3.00 8.00
123 Jeff Green UC .25 .60
124 George Gervin UC .60 1.50
125 Obi Toppin UC .40 1.00
126 Tyrese Haliburton UC .75 2.00
127 Jalen Rose UC .40 1.00
128 Paul George UC .60 1.50
129 Jarred Vanderbilt UC .30 .75
130 Austin Reaves UC 1.00 2.50
131 D'Angelo Russell UC .40 1.00
132 Magic Johnson UC 1.50 4.00
133 Paul Pierce UC .60 1.50
134 Carmelo Anthony UC .60 1.50
135 Dwyane Wade UC .75 2.00
136 Maurice Cheeks UC .40 1.00
137 Deron Williams UC .30 .75
138 Karl-Anthony Towns UC .60 1.50
139 Tony Parker UC .60 1.50
140 Rudy Gobert UC .50 1.25
141 C.J. McCollum UC .40 1.00
142 David Robinson UC .75 2.00
143 Zach Randolph UC .40 1.00
144 Jalen Brunson UC .75 2.00
145 Donte DiVincenzo UC .40 1.00
146 Quentin Grimes UC .40 1.00
147 Jalen Williams UC .75 2.00
148 Anfernee Hardaway UC 1.00 2.50
149 Markelle Fultz UC .30 .75
150 Joel Embiid UC 1.00 2.50
151 Tobias Harris UC .40 1.00
152 Evan Fournier UC .30 .75
153 Mike Conley UC .30 .75
154 Kevin Durant UC 1.25 3.00
155 Anfernee Simons UC .50 1.25
156 Jonathan Kuminga UC 1.00 2.50
157 De'Aaron Fox UC .75 2.00
158 Malik Monk UC .50 1.25
159 Devonte' Graham UC .30 .75
160 Robert Parish UC .50 1.25
161 Fred VanVleet UC .60 1.50
162 Pascal Siakam UC .60 1.50
163 Scottie Barnes UC .50 1.25
164 Precious Achiuwa UC .30 .75
165 Jordan Clarkson UC .40 1.00
166 Dominique Wilkins UC .60 1.50
167 Walker Kessler UC .40 1.00
168 Bradley Beal UC .50 1.25
169 Dan Issel UC .50 1.25
170 Clint Capela UC .30 .75
171 Alperen Sengun UC .60 1.50
172 Ray Allen UC .60 1.50
173 Khris Middleton UC .40 1.00
174 Rick Barry UC .50 1.25
175 Isaiah Hartenstein UC .40 1.00
176 Brandon Miller UC RC 1.50 4.00
177 Olivier-Maxence Prosper UC RC .40 1.00
178 Ben Sheppard UC RC .40 1.00
179 Anthony Black UC RC .75 2.00
180 Gradey Dick UC RC .75 2.00
181 Jimmy Butler UC .60 1.50
182 Nick Smith JR. UC RC .50 1.25
183 Jett Howard UC RC .50 1.25
184 Jalen Hood-Schifino UC RC .40 1.00
185 Dereck Lively II UC RC .75 2.00
186 Kris Murray UC RC .40 1.00
187 Kobe Bufkin UC RC .50 1.25
188 Colby Jones UC RC .40 1.00
189 Maxwell Lewis UC RC .30 .75
190 James Nnaji UC RC .30 .75
191 Sidy Cissoko UC RC .40 1.00
192 Jaime Jaquez Jr. UC RC .60 1.50
193 Julian Phillips UC RC .40 1.00
194 Kobe Brown UC RC .40 1.00
195 Julian Strawther UC RC .50 1.25
196 Andre Jackson Jr. UC RC .60 1.50
197 Victor Wembanyama UC 3.00 8.00
198 Jaylen Clark UC RC .40 1.00
199 Pete Nance UC RC .30 .75
200 Keyontae Johnson UC RC .40 1.00
201 Giannis Antetokounmpo R 3.00 8.00
202 Trae Young R 1.25 3.00
203 Dejounte Murray R .75 2.00
204 Jaylen Brown R 1.25 3.00
205 Jayson Tatum R 2.50 6.00
206 Marcus Smart R .75 2.00
207 Mikal Bridges R .75 2.00
208 LaMelo Ball R 1.50 4.00
209 DeMar DeRozan R 1.00 2.50
210 Zach LaVine R 1.00 2.50
211 Donovan Mitchell R 1.25 3.00
212 Evan Mobley R 1.00 2.50
213 Kyrie Irving R 1.25 3.00
214 Kentavious Caldwell-Pope R .50 1.25
215 Michael Porter Jr. R .75 2.00
216 Cade Cunningham R 1.50 4.00
217 Ben Wallace R .75 2.00
218 Draymond Green R .75 2.00
219 Klay Thompson R 1.50 4.00
220 Stephen Curry R 5.00 12.00
221 Myles Turner R .60 1.50
222 Tyrese Haliburton R 1.25 3.00
223 Paul George R 1.00 2.50
224 Russell Westbrook R 1.00 2.50
225 Jaren Jackson Jr. R 1.00 2.50
226 Tyler Herro R 1.00 2.50
227 Jrue Holiday R .75 2.00
228 Khris Middleton R .60 1.50
229 Rudy Gobert R .75 2.00
230 Karl-Anthony Towns R 1.00 2.50
231 Trey Murphy III R .75 2.00
232 CJ McCollum R .60 1.50
233 Jalen Brunson R 1.25 3.00
234 Immanuel Quickley R .60 1.50
235 Chet Holmgren R 1.50 4.00
236 Jalen Williams R 1.25 3.00
237 Franz Wagner R 1.00 2.50
238 James Harden R 1.25 3.00
239 Joel Embiid R 1.50 4.00
240 Devin Booker R 1.50 4.00
241 Kevin Durant R 2.00 5.00
242 De'Aaron Fox R 1.25 3.00
243 Kevin Huerter R .50 1.25
244 Scottie Barnes R .75 2.00
245 OG Anunoby R .75 2.00
246 Collin Sexton R .75 2.00
247 Bradley Beal R .75 2.00
248 Corey Kispert R .50 1.25
249 Aaron Gordon R .60 1.50
250 D'Angelo Russell R .60 1.50
251 Dominique Wilkins R 1.00 2.50
252 Larry Bird R 2.50 6.00
253 Paul Pierce R 1.00 2.50
254 Carmelo Anthony R 1.00 2.50
255 Magic Johnson R 2.50 6.00
256 Dwyane Wade R 1.25 3.00
257 Shaquille O'Neal R 2.00 5.00
258 Anfernee Hardaway R 1.50 4.00
259 Shaedon Sharpe R 1.25 3.00
260 Manu Ginobili R 1.25 3.00
261 Tony Parker R 1.00 2.50
262 David Robinson R 1.25 3.00
263 Larry Johnson R .75 2.00
264 Jason Kidd R 1.00 2.50
265 Rip Hamilton R .75 2.00
266 Shawn Kemp R 1.00 2.50
267 Kevin Garnett R 1.50 4.00
268 Peja Stojakovic R .60 1.50
269 Deron Williams R .50 1.25
270 LeBron James R 5.00 12.00
271 Victor Wembanyama R 5.00 12.00
272 Brandon Miller R 2.50 6.00
273 Scoot Henderson R 2.00 5.00
274 Anthony Black R 1.25 3.00
275 Bilal Coulibaly R 1.50 4.00
276 Jarace Walker R 1.25 3.00
277 Taylor Hendricks R .60 1.50
278 Jett Howard R .75 2.00
279 Dereck Lively II R 1.25 3.00
280 Gradey Dick R 1.25 3.00
281 Jordan Hawkins R 1.00 2.50
282 Kobe Bufkin R .75 2.00
283 Jalen Hood-Schifino R .60 1.50
284 Jaime Jaquez Jr. R 1.00 2.50
285 Brandin Podziemski R 2.00 5.00
286 Cam Whitmore R 1.50 4.00
287 Noah Clowney R .75 2.00
288 Kris Murray R .60 1.50
289 Olivier-Maxence Prosper R .60 1.50
290 Marcus Sasser R 1.00 2.50
291 Ben Sheppard R .60 1.50
292 Nick Smith Jr. R .75 2.00
293 Brice Sensabaugh R 1.00 2.50
294 Julian Strawther R .75 2.00
295 Kobe Brown R .60 1.50
296 James Nnaji R .50 1.25
297 Leonard Miller R .60 1.50
298 Colby Jones R .60 1.50
299 Julian Phillips R .60 1.50
300 Jordan Walsh R .60 1.50

2023-24 Finest Blue Checkerboard Refractors

*BLUE CHKBRD REF: 2.5X TO 6X BASIC
STATED PRINT RUN 49-99 SER.#'d SETS
76 Victor Wembanyama C 40.00 100.00
197 Victor Wembanyama UC 50.00 120.00
271 Victor Wembanyama R 60.00 150.00

2023-24 Finest Checkerboard Blue Refractors

*CHKBRD BLUE REF: 2X TO 5X BASIC
STATED PRINT RUN 150 SER.#'d SETS
76 Victor Wembanyama C 30.00 80.00

2023-24 Finest Die-Cut Refractors

*DC REFRACTOR: 4X TO 10X BASIC
STATED PRINT RUN 25-74 SER.#'d SETS
76 Victor Wembanyama C 60.00 150.00
197 Victor Wembanyama UC 75.00 200.00
271 Victor Wembanyama R 100.00 250.00

2023-24 Finest Gold Refractors

*GOLD REFRACTOR: 5X TO 12X BASIC
STATED PRINT RUN 8-50 SER.#'d SETS
76 Victor Wembanyama C 75.00 200.00
197 Victor Wembanyama UC 100.00 250.00

2023-24 Finest Purple Checkerboard Refractors

*PRPL CHKBRD REF: 2X TO 5X BASIC
STATED PRINT RUN 75-125 SER.#'d SETS
76 Victor Wembanyama C 30.00 80.00
197 Victor Wembanyama UC 40.00 100.00
271 Victor Wembanyama R 50.00 120.00

2023-24 Finest Arrivals

*CHCKRBRD REF: .75X TO 2X BASIC
*REF: 1.25X TO 3X BASIC
*BLUE REF/150: 1.5X TO 4X BASIC
*PRPL CKCKBRD REF/125: 2X TO 5X BASIC
*BLUE CKCKBRD REF/99: 2.5X TO 6X BASIC
*DIE-CUT REF/74: 3X TO 8X BASIC
*GOLD REF/50: 4X TO 10X BASIC
*BLACK REF/25: 5X TO 12X BASIC
A1 Chet Holmgren 1.00 2.50
A2 Cade Cunningham 1.00 2.50
A3 Scottie Barnes .50 1.25
A4 Tyrese Haliburton .75 2.00
A5 Tyrese Maxey .75 2.00
A6 Victor Wembanyama 5.00 12.00
A7 Brandon Miller 1.50 4.00
A8 Scoot Henderson 1.25 3.00
A9 Anthony Black .75 2.00
A10 Bilal Coulibaly 1.00 2.50
A11 Jarace Walker .75 2.00
A12 Taylor Hendricks .40 1.00
A13 Jett Howard .50 1.25
A14 Dereck Lively II .75 2.00
A15 Gradey Dick .75 2.00
A16 Jordan Hawkins .60 1.50
A17 Kobe Bufkin .50 1.25
A18 Jalen Hood-Schifino .40 1.00
A19 Jaime Jaquez Jr. .60 1.50
A20 Brandin Podziemski 1.25 3.00
A21 Cam Whitmore 1.00 2.50
A22 Noah Clowney .50 1.25
A23 Kris Murray .40 1.00
A24 Olivier-Maxence Prosper .40 1.00
A25 Marcus Sasser .60 1.50
A26 Ben Sheppard .40 1.00
A27 Nick Smith Jr. .50 1.25
A28 Brice Sensabaugh .60 1.50
A29 Julian Strawther .50 1.25
A30 Kobe Brown .40 1.00

2023-24 Finest Autographs

*REF: .5X TO 1.2X BASIC
*BLUE GEO REF/99: .5X TO 1.2X BASIC
*GOLD REF/50: .6X TO 1.5X BASIC
*GOLD GEO REF/50: .6X TO 1.5X BASIC
*BLACK REF/25: .75X TO 2X BASIC
*BLACK GEO REF/25: .75X TO 2X BASIC
FAAC Alex Caruso 5.00 12.00
FAAR Austin Reaves 12.00 30.00
FAAS Anfernee Simons 6.00 15.00
FAAW Andrew Wiggins 6.00 15.00
FABW Blake Wesley 3.00 8.00
FACH Chet Holmgren 30.00 80.00
FACK Corey Kispert 4.00 10.00
FACL Caris LeVert 5.00 12.00
FACS Collin Sexton 6.00 15.00
FADH Danuel House Jr 3.00 8.00
FADM Dejounte Murray 6.00 15.00
FADS Day'Ron Sharpe 4.00 10.00
FADW Derrick White 6.00 15.00
FAGH Gordon Hayward 5.00 12.00
FAGW Grant Williams 4.00 10.00
FAIH Isaiah Hartenstein 5.00 12.00
FAJB Jalen Brunson 10.00 25.00
FAJC John Collins 5.00 12.00
FAJG Jalen Green 8.00 20.00
FAJH Jrue Holiday 6.00 15.00
FAJL Jock Landale 4.00 10.00
FAJP Jordan Poole 8.00 20.00
FAJS Jeremy Sochan 6.00 15.00
FAJW Jalen Williams 10.00 25.00
FAKD Kevin Durant 50.00 120.00
FAKK Kyle Kuzma 6.00 15.00
FAKM Khris Middleton 5.00 12.00
FALM Lauri Markkanen 8.00 20.00
FAMF Markelle Fultz 4.00 10.00
FAMM Malik Monk 6.00 15.00
FAMS Marcus Smart 6.00 15.00
FAMT Myles Turner 5.00 12.00
FANV Nikola Vucevic 5.00 12.00
FAOB Oshae Brissett 4.00 10.00
FAOT Obi Toppin 5.00 12.00
FAPM Patty Mills 5.00 12.00
FASM Sandro Mamukelashvili 5.00 12.00
FATM Tyrese Maxey 10.00 25.00
FAWK Walker Kessler 5.00 12.00
FAZC Zach Collins 4.00 10.00
FACJM CJ McCollum 5.00 12.00
FACLC Clint Capela 4.00 10.00
FADBR Dillon Brooks 5.00 12.00
FADSA Domantas Sabonis 8.00 20.00
FAJJJ Jaren Jackson Jr. 8.00 20.00
FAJLA Jake LaRavia 4.00 10.00
FAJPO Jakob Poeltl 4.00 10.00
FAMIB Mikal Bridges 6.00 15.00
FAOGA OG Anunoby 6.00 15.00
FATHJ Tim Hardaway Jr. 4.00 10.00
FATMA Terance Mann 4.00 10.00

2023-24 Finest Centurions

C1 Victor Wembanyama 60.00 150.00
C2 Brandon Miller 6.00 15.00
C3 Scoot Henderson 5.00 12.00
C4 Anthony Black 3.00 8.00
C5 Bilal Coulibaly 4.00 10.00
C6 Jarace Walker 3.00 8.00
C7 Giannis Antetokounmpo 8.00 20.00
C8 Magic Johnson 6.00 15.00
C9 Dereck Lively II 3.00 8.00
C10 Gradey Dick 3.00 8.00
C11 Jaylen Brown 3.00 8.00
C12 Stephen Curry 12.00 30.00
C13 Joel Embiid 4.00 10.00
C14 Kevin Durant 5.00 12.00
C15 Dirk Nowitzki 4.00 10.00
C16 Damian Lillard 4.00 10.00
C17 Allen Iverson 4.00 10.00
C18 Jaime Jaquez Jr. 2.50 6.00
C19 Kevin Garnett 4.00 10.00
C20 Shaquille O'Neal 5.00 12.00

2023-24 Finest Debut

*CKBRD REF: .75X TO 2X BASIC
*REF: 1.25X TO 3X BASIC
*BLUE REF/150: 1.5X TO 4X BASIC
*PRPL CKBRD REF/125: 2X TO 5X BASIC
*BLUE CKBRD REF/99: 2.5X TO 6X BASIC
*DIE-CUT REF/74: 3X TO 8X BASIC
*GOLD REF/50: 4X TO 10X BASIC
*BLACK REF/25: 5X TO 12X BASIC
D1 Victor Wembanyama 5.00 12.00
D2 Brandon Miller 1.50 4.00
D3 Scoot Henderson 1.25 3.00
D4 Anthony Black .75 2.00
D5 Bilal Coulibaly 1.00 2.50
D6 Jarace Walker .75 2.00
D7 Taylor Hendricks .40 1.00
D8 Jett Howard .50 1.25
D9 Dereck Lively II .75 2.00
D10 Gradey Dick .75 2.00
D11 Brandin Podziemski 1.25 3.00
D12 Cam Whitmore 1.00 2.50
D13 Noah Clowney .50 1.25
D14 Kris Murray .40 1.00
D15 Olivier-Maxence Prosper .40 1.00
D16 Marcus Sasser .60 1.50
D17 Ben Sheppard .40 1.00
D18 Nick Smith Jr. .50 1.25
D19 Leonard Miller .40 1.00
D20 Colby Jones .40 1.00
D21 Julian Phillips .40 1.00
D22 Andre Jackson Jr. .60 1.50
D23 Jordan Walsh .40 1.00
D24 Maxwell Lewis .30 .75
D25 Rayan Rupert .40 1.00
D26 Sidy Cissoko .40 1.00
D27 GG Jackson .75 2.00
D28 Amari Bailey .40 1.00
D29 Brice Sensabaugh .60 1.50
D30 Jaime Jaquez Jr. .60 1.50

2023-24 Finest Finishers

*CKBRD REF: .75X TO 2X BASIC
*REF: 1.25X TO 3X BASIC
*BLUE REF/150: 1.5X TO 4X BASIC
*PRPL CKBRD REF/125: 2X TO 5X BASIC
*BLUE CKBRD REF/99: 2.5X TO 6X BASIC
*DIE-CUT REF/74: 3X TO 8X BASIC
*GOLD REF/50: 4X TO 10X BASIC
*BLACK REF/25: 5X TO 12X BASIC

F1 Zach LaVine .60 1.50
F2 Kyrie Irving .75 2.00
F3 Jayson Tatum 1.50 4.00
F4 Jalen Brunson .75 2.00
F5 Devin Booker 1.00 2.50
F6 Stephen Curry 3.00 8.00
F7 Joel Embiid 1.00 2.50
F8 Paul George .60 1.50
F9 Tyrese Haliburton .75 2.00
F10 De'Aaron Fox .75 2.00

2023-24 Finest Flashback Autographs

*REF: .5X TO 1.2X BASIC
*BLUE GEO REF/99: .5X TO 1.2X BASIC
*GOLD REF/50: .6X TO 1.5X BASIC
*GOLD GEO REF/50: .6X TO 1.5X BASIC
*BLACK REF/25: .75X TO 2X BASIC
*BLACK GEO REF/25: .75X TO 2X BASIC
FLAAD Ayo Dosunmu 5.00 12.00
FLAAE Alex English 6.00 15.00
FLAAG Aaron Gordon 5.00 12.00
FLAAS Alperen Sengun 8.00 20.00
FLABC Brandon Clarke 4.00 10.00
FLABM Brandon Miller 40.00 100.00
FLABW Ben Wallace 6.00 15.00
FLACA Carmelo Anthony 40.00 100.00
FLACP Chris Paul 10.00 25.00
FLACW Cam Whitmore 12.00 30.00
FLADD Donte DiVincenzo 5.00 12.00
FLADL Dereck Lively II 10.00 25.00
FLADN Dirk Nowitzki 60.00 150.00
FLADR D'Angelo Russell 5.00 12.00
FLAFW Franz Wagner 8.00 20.00
FLAGD Gradey Dick 10.00 25.00
FLAJH Jett Howard 6.00 15.00
FLAJJ Jaime Jaquez Jr. 8.00 20.00
FLAJK Jason Kidd 8.00 20.00
FLAJS Julian Strawther 6.00 15.00
FLAJW Jerry West 10.00 25.00
FLAKB Kobe Bufkin 6.00 15.00
FLAKH Kevin Huerter 4.00 10.00
FLAKP Kristaps Porzingis 6.00 15.00
FLALB Larry Bird 60.00 150.00
FLALW Lenny Wilkens 6.00 15.00
FLAMC Maurice Cheeks 5.00 12.00
FLAMS Marcus Sasser 8.00 20.00
FLANC Noah Clowney 6.00 15.00
FLAPS Peja Stojakovic 5.00 12.00
FLASC Seth Curry 5.00 12.00
FLASH Scoot Henderson 15.00 40.00
FLASK Shawn Kemp 8.00 20.00
FLATH Taylor Hendricks 5.00 12.00
FLATP Tony Parker 8.00 20.00
FLAVW Victor Wembanyama 500.00 1,000.00
FLAASI Anfernee Simons 6.00 15.00
FLABCO Bilal Coulibaly 12.00 30.00
FLADRO Dennis Rodman 25.00 60.00
FLAJHA Jordan Hawkins 8.00 20.00
FLAJHS Jalen Hood-Schifino 5.00 12.00
FLAJRO Jalen Rose 5.00 12.00
FLAJSH Jerry Stackhouse 5.00 12.00
FLAJST John Stockton 10.00 25.00
FLAJWA Jarace Walker 10.00 25.00
FLAKBO Kobe Brown 5.00 12.00
FLAKMU Kris Murray 5.00 12.00
FLANSJ Nick Smith Jr. 6.00 15.00
FLAOMP Olivier-Maxence Prosper 5.00 12.00
FLATHE Tyler Herro 8.00 20.00

2023-24 Finest Masters Autographs

*REF: .5X TO 1.2X BASIC
*BLUE GEO REF/99: .5X TO 1.2X BASIC
*GOLD REF/50: .6X TO 1.5X BASIC
*GOLD GEO REF/50: .6X TO 1.5X BASIC
*BLACK REF/25: .75X TO 2X BASIC
*BLACK GEO REF/25: .75X TO 2X BASIC
MAAB Anthony Black 10.00 25.00
MAAG Artis Gilmore 6.00 15.00
MAAH Anfernee Hardaway 20.00 50.00
MABB Bradley Beal 6.00 15.00
MABC Bilal Coulibaly 12.00 30.00
MABM Brandon Miller 40.00 100.00
MABP Brandin Podziemski 15.00 40.00
MABS Ben Sheppard 5.00 12.00
MACW Cam Whitmore 12.00 30.00
MADF De'Aaron Fox 10.00 25.00
MADL Dereck Lively II 10.00 25.00
MADM Donovan Mitchell 25.00 60.00
MADR David Robinson 20.00 50.00
MADW Dwyane Wade 20.00 50.00
MAGD Gradey Dick 10.00 25.00
MAHO Hakeem Olajuwon 20.00 50.00
MAJH Jett Howard 6.00 15.00
MAJJ Jaime Jaquez Jr. 8.00 20.00
MAJS Julian Strawther 6.00 15.00
MAJT Jayson Tatum 60.00 150.00
MAKB Kobe Bufkin 6.00 15.00
MAKG Kevin Garnett 30.00 80.00
MALJ Larry Johnson 12.00 30.00
MAMJ Magic Johnson 30.00 80.00
MANC Noah Clowney 6.00 15.00
MAPG Pau Gasol 20.00 50.00
MAPP Paul Pierce 20.00 50.00
MARA Ray Allen 20.00 50.00
MARH Rip Hamilton 6.00 15.00
MARJ Richard Jefferson 4.00 10.00
MARP Robert Parish 6.00 15.00
MASC Stephen Curry 300.00 600.00
MASH Scoot Henderson 15.00 40.00
MASO Shaquille O'Neal 75.00 200.00
MATH Taylor Hendricks 5.00 12.00
MAVC Vince Carter 30.00 80.00
MAVW Victor Wembanyama 500.00 1,000.00
MABSA Brice Sensabaugh 8.00 20.00
MAFVV Fred VanVleet 8.00 20.00
MAJHA Jordan Hawkins 8.00 20.00
MAJWA Jarace Walker 10.00 25.00
MAKAT Karl-Anthony Towns 8.00 20.00
MAKBR Kobe Brown 5.00 12.00
MAKMU Kris Murray 5.00 12.00
MALBJ Lebron James 1,000.00 2,000.00
MAMPJ Michael Porter Jr. 6.00 15.00
MAMSA Marcus Sasser 8.00 20.00
MANSJ Nick Smith Jr. 6.00 15.00
MAOMP Olivier-Maxence Prosper 5.00 12.00
MATHA Tyrese Haliburton 25.00 60.00

2023-24 Finest Rookie Autographs

*REF: .5X TO 1.2X BASIC
*BLUE GEO REF/99: .5X TO 1.2X BASIC
*GOLD REF/50: .6X TO 1.5X BASIC
*GOLD GEO REF/50: .6X TO 1.5X BASIC
*BLACK REF/25: .75X TO 2X BASIC
*BLACK GEO REF/25: .75X TO 2X BASIC
RFAAB Anthony Black 10.00 25.00
RFAAF Alex Fudge 3.00 8.00
RFAAJ Andre Jackson Jr. 8.00 20.00
RFABC Bilal Coulibaly 12.00 30.00
RFABM Brandon Miller 40.00 100.00
RFABP Brandin Podziemski 15.00 40.00
RFABS Ben Sheppard 5.00 12.00
RFACJ Colby Jones 5.00 12.00
RFACL Chris Livingston 5.00 12.00
RFACW Cam Whitmore 12.00 30.00
RFAGD Gradey Dick 10.00 25.00
RFAIW Isaiah Wong 5.00 12.00
RFAJC Jaylen Clark 5.00 12.00
RFAJH Jett Howard 6.00 15.00
RFAJN James Nnaji 4.00 10.00
RFAJP Julian Phillips 5.00 12.00
RFAJS Julian Strawther 6.00 15.00
RFAJT Jacob Toppin 4.00 10.00
RFAJW Jalen Wilson 5.00 12.00
RFAKB Kobe Brown 5.00 12.00
RFAKJ Keyontae Johnson 5.00 12.00
RFAKM Kris Murray 5.00 12.00
RFALB Leaky Black 4.00 10.00
RFALM Leonard Miller 5.00 12.00
RFALR Liam Robbins 4.00 10.00
RFAML Maxwell Lewis 4.00 10.00
RFAMS Marcus Sasser 8.00 20.00
RFANC Noah Clowney 6.00 15.00
RFANS Nick Smith JR. 6.00 15.00
RFARR Rayan Rupert 5.00 12.00
RFASC Sidy Cissoko 5.00 12.00
RFASH Scoot Henderson 15.00 40.00
RFASL Seth Lundy 4.00 10.00
RFATH Taylor Hendricks 5.00 12.00
RFATS Terquavion Smith 5.00 12.00
RFAVW Victor Wembanyama 500.00 1,000.00
RFABA Amari Bailey 5.00 12.00
RFABSE Brice Sensabaugh 8.00 20.00
RFAGJ GG Jackson 10.00 25.00
RFAJAW Jarace Walker 10.00 25.00
RFAJHS Jalen Hood-Schifino 5.00 12.00
RFAJJ Jaime Jaquez JR. 8.00 20.00
RFAJOH Jordan Hawkins 8.00 20.00
RFAJPI Jalen Pickett 4.00 10.00
RFAJWA Jordan Walsh 5.00 12.00
RFAKOB Kobe Bufkin 6.00 15.00
RFAOMP Olivier-Maxence Prosper 5.00 12.00
RFATJD Trayce Jackson-Davis 6.00 15.00
RFADLII Dereck Lively II 10.00 25.00

2023-24 Finest Showstoppers

*CHCKRBRD REF: .75X TO 2X BASIC
*REF: 1.25X TO 3X BASIC
*BLUE REF/150: 1.5X TO 4X BASIC
*PRPL CKCKBRD REF/125: 2X TO 5X BASIC
*BLUE CKCKBRD REF/99: 2.5X TO 6X BASIC
*DIE-CUT REF/74: 3X TO 8X BASIC
*GOLD REF/50: 4X TO 10X BASIC
*BLACK REF/25: 5X TO 12X BASIC
SS1 Tyrese Haliburton .75 2.00
SS2 Jayson Tatum 1.50 4.00
SS3 Trae Young .75 2.00
SS4 Stephen Curry 3.00 8.00
SS5 Kyrie Irving .75 2.00
SS6 Kevin Durant 1.25 3.00
SS7 Joel Embiid 1.00 2.50
SS8 Karl-Anthony Towns .60 1.50
SS9 Paul George .60 1.50
SS10 Donovan Mitchell .75 2.00
SS11 Dwyane Wade .75 2.00
SS12 Shaquille O'Neal 1.25 3.00
SS13 David Robinson .75 2.00
SS14 Carmelo Anthony .60 1.50
SS15 Dirk Nowitzki 1.00 2.50
SS16 Paul Pierce .60 1.50
SS17 Kevin Garnett 1.00 2.50
SS18 Anfernee Hardaway 1.00 2.50
SS19 Shawn Kemp .60 1.50
SS20 Magic Johnson 1.50 4.00
SS21 Victor Wembanyama 5.00 12.00
SS22 Brandon Miller 1.50 4.00
SS23 Scoot Henderson 1.25 3.00
SS24 Anthony Black .75 2.00
SS25 Dereck Lively II .75 2.00
SS26 Jaime Jaquez JR. .60 1.50
SS27 Gradey Dick .75 2.00
SS28 Jalen Hood-Schifino .40 1.00
SS29 Brandin Podziemski 1.25 3.00
SS30 Cam Whitmore 1.00 2.50

2023-24 Finest The Man

TM1 Trae Young 25.00 60.00
TM2 Jayson Tatum 30.00 80.00
TM3 LaMelo Ball 25.00 60.00
TM4 Donovan Mitchell 30.00 80.00
TM5 Kyrie Irving 40.00 100.00
TM6 Larry Bird 60.00 150.00
TM7 Joel Embiid 15.00 40.00
TM8 Stephen Curry 75.00 200.00
TM9 Tyrese Haliburton 40.00 100.00
TM10 Shaquille O'Neal 40.00 100.00
TM11 Nikola Jokic 75.00 200.00
TM12 Karl-Anthony Towns 15.00 40.00
TM13 Chet Holmgren 30.00 80.00
TM14 Dirk Nowitzki 25.00 60.00
TM15 Devin Booker 20.00 50.00
TM16 Kevin Durant 25.00 60.00
TM17 Giannis Antetokounmpo 30.00 80.00
TM18 Victor Wembanyama 400.00 800.00
TM19 Brandon Miller 75.00 200.00
TM20 Scoot Henderson 40.00 100.00

2022-23 Finest Overtime Elite

*REFRACTORS: .75X TO 2X BASIC
*PURPLE REF/250: 2X TO 5X BASIC
*SPECKLE REF/175: 2X TO 5X BASIC
*BLUE REF/150: 2X TO 5X BASIC
*PINK PRISM REF/125: 2.5X TO 6X BASIC
*NEON GREEN/99: 2X TO 6X BASIC
*AQUA WAVE REF/75: 3X TO 8X BASIC
*GOLD REF/50: 4X TO 10X BASIC
*ORANGE REF/25: 6X TO 15X BASIC
1 Jaylen Martin .40 1.00
2 Jalen Lewis .40 1.00
3 Jalen Lewis .40 1.00
4 Amen Thompson 1.00 2.50
5 Izan Almansa .40 1.00
6 Ryan Bewley .40 1.00
7 Bryson Warren .40 1.00
8 Eli Ellis .75 2.00
9 ZZ Clark .40 1.00
10 Bryce Griggs .40 1.00
11 Tyler Bey .40 1.00
12 Kanaan Carlyle .40 1.00
13 Jaylen Martin .40 1.00
14 Bryson Tiller .60 1.50
15 Tudor Somacescu .40 1.00
16 Nassir Cunningham .50 1.25
17 Rob Dillingham 1.25 3.00
18 Jahzare Jackson .40 1.00
19 Ryan Bewley .40 1.00
20 Bryson Warren .40 1.00
21 Tudor Somacescu .40 1.00
22 Tyler Smith .50 1.25
23 Kanaan Carlyle .40 1.00
24 Nassir Cunningham .50 1.25
25 Jazian Gortman .40 1.00
26 Eli Ellis .75 2.00
27 Jayden Williams .50 1.25
28 Rob Dillingham 1.25 3.00
29 Eli Ellis .75 2.00
30 Rob Dillingham 1.25 3.00
31 Bryson Tiller .60 1.50
32 Bryson Tiller .60 1.50
33 Alexandre Sarr 1.25 3.00
34 Amen Thompson 1.00 2.50
35 Nathan Missia-Dio .40 1.00
36 Jazian Gortman .40 1.00
37 Ralph Martino Jr. .50 1.25
38 ZZ Clark .40 1.00
39 Jayden Williams .50 1.25
40 Matt Bewley .40 1.00
41 Jayden Williams .50 1.25
42 ZZ Clark .40 1.00
43 Tyler Bey .40 1.00
44 Jahki Howard .50 1.25
45 Malik Bowman .40 1.00
46 Nassir Cunningham .50 1.25
47 ZZ Clark .40 1.00
48 Izan Almansa .40 1.00
49 Jahki Howard .50 1.25
50 Jahzare Jackson .40 1.00
51 Jalen Lewis .40 1.00
52 Izan Almansa .40 1.00
53 Jahzare Jackson .40 1.00
54 Tyler Smith .50 1.25
55 Jazian Gortman .40 1.00
56 Matt Bewley .40 1.00
57 Jahki Howard .50 1.25
58 Bryce Griggs .40 1.00
59 Amen Thompson 1.00 2.50
60 Kanaan Carlyle .40 1.00
61 Ausar Thompson 1.00 2.50
62 TJ Clark .40 1.00
63 De'Vontes Cobbs .40 1.00
64 Tudor Somacescu .40 1.00
65 Trey Parker .50 1.25
66 Kok Yat .50 1.25
67 Trey Parker .50 1.25
68 Trey Parker .50 1.25
69 Matt Bewley .40 1.00
70 Jayden Williams .50 1.25
71 Eli Ellis .75 2.00
72 Ausar Thompson 1.00 2.50
73 Johned Walker .40 1.00
74 Tyler Bey .40 1.00
75 Tyler Bey .40 1.00
76 Bryson Tiller .60 1.50
77 Rob Dillingham 1.25 3.00
78 Kok Yat .40 1.00
79 Kanaan Carlyle .40 1.00
80 Johned Walker .40 1.00
81 Nassir Cunningham .50 1.25
82 Somto Cyril .50 1.25
83 Ausar Thompson 1.00 2.50
84 Ryan Bewley .40 1.00
85 Trey Parker .50 1.25
86 Somto Cyril .50 1.25
87 Tyler Smith .50 1.25
88 Bryce Griggs .40 1.00
89 Alexandre Sarr 1.25 3.00
90 TJ Clark .40 1.00
91 Malik Bowman .40 1.00
92 Nathan Missia-Dio .40 1.00
93 Jahki Howard .50 1.25
94 Somto Cyril .50 1.25
95 Ralph Martino Jr. .50 1.25
96 De'Vontes Cobbs .40 1.00
97 Malik Bowman .40 1.00
98 Ralph Martino Jr. .50 1.25
99 Bryson Warren .40 1.00
100 Somto Cyril .50 1.25

2022-23 Finest Overtime Elite '96 Finest Apprentices

*AQUA WAVE REF/99: 2.5X TO 6X BASIC
*GOLD RAYWAVE REF/50: 4X TO 10X BASIC
T961 Nassir Cunningham 1.25 3.00
T962 Trey Parker 1.25 3.00
T963 Kanaan Carlyle 1.00 2.50
T964 Bryson Tiller 1.50 4.00
T965 Rob Dillingham 3.00 8.00
T966 ZZ Clark 1.00 2.50
T967 Tyler Bey 1.00 2.50
T968 Jayden Williams 1.25 3.00
T969 Eli Ellis 2.00 5.00
T9610 Somto Cyril 1.25 3.00

2022-23 Finest Overtime Elite Arrivals

*AQUA WAVE REF/99: 2.5X TO 6X BASIC
*GOLD RAYWAVE REF/50: 4X TO 10X BASIC
AR1 Izan Almansa .60 1.50
AR2 Matt Bewley .60 1.50
AR3 Ryan Bewley .60 1.50
AR4 Malik Bowman .60 1.50
AR5 TJ Clark .60 1.50
AR6 De'Vontes Cobbs .60 1.50
AR7 Jazian Gortman .60 1.50
AR8 Bryce Griggs .60 1.50
AR9 Jahzare Jackson .60 1.50
AR10 Jalen Lewis .60 1.50
AR11 Jaylen Martin .60 1.50
AR12 Nathan MissiaDio .60 1.50
AR13 Alexandre Sarr 2.00 5.00
AR14 Tyler Smith .75 2.00
AR15 Tudor Somacescu .60 1.50
AR16 Amen Thompson 1.50 4.00
AR17 Ausar Thompson 1.50 4.00
AR18 Bryson Warren .60 1.50
AR19 Kok Yat .60 1.50
AR20 Naasir Cunningham .75 2.00
AR21 Trey Parker .75 2.00
AR22 Kanaan Carlyle .60 1.50
AR23 Bryson Tiller 1.00 2.50
AR24 Rob Dillingham 2.00 5.00
AR25 ZZ Clark .60 1.50
AR26 Tyler Bey .60 1.50
AR27 Jayden Williams .75 2.00
AR28 Eli Ellis 1.25 3.00
AR29 Somto Cyril .75 2.00
AR30 Johned Walker .60 1.50

2022-23 Finest Overtime Elite Arrivals Autographs

*GOLD REF/50: .5X TO 1.2X BASIC
*ORNG RAYWAVE REF/25: .6X TO 1.5X BASIC
FAAAS Alexandre Sarr 40.00 100.00
FAABG Bryce Griggs 6.00 15.00
FAABT Bryson Tiller 10.00 25.00
FAABW Bryson Warren 6.00 15.00
FAADC De'Vontes Cobbs 6.00 15.00
FAAEE Eli Ellis 12.00 30.00
FAAIA Izan Almansa 6.00 15.00
FAAJG Jazian Gortman 6.00 15.00
FAAJJ Jahzare Jackson 6.00 15.00
FAAJL Jalen Lewis 6.00 15.00
FAAJM Jaylen Martin 6.00 15.00
FAAJW Jayden Williams 8.00 20.00
FAAKC Kanaan Carlyle 6.00 15.00
FAAKY Kok Yat 6.00 15.00
FAAMB Matt Bewley 6.00 15.00
FAANC NAASIR Cunningham 8.00 20.00
FAARB Ryan Bewley 6.00 15.00
FAARD Rob Dillingham 20.00 50.00
FAASC Somto Cyril 8.00 20.00
FAATB Tyler Bey 6.00 15.00
FAATC TJ Clark 6.00 15.00
FAATP Trey Parker 8.00 20.00
FAATS Tyler Smith 8.00 20.00
FAAZC ZZ Clark 6.00 15.00
FAAAMT Amen Thompson 15.00 40.00
FAAAUT Ausar Thompson 15.00 40.00
FAAJWA Johned Walker 6.00 15.00
FAAMBO Malik Bowman 6.00 15.00
FAANMD Nathan MissiaDio 6.00 15.00
FAARMJ Ralph Martino Jr. 8.00 20.00
FAATSO Tudor Somacescu 6.00 15.00

2022-23 Finest Overtime Elite Autographs

*BLUE RAYWAVE REF/150: .5X TO 1.2X BASIC
*GREEN WAVE REF/99: .5X TO 1.2X BASIC
*GOLD REF/50: .6X TO 1.5X BASIC
*ORNG RAYWAVE REF/25: .75X TO 2X BASIC
FAAS Alexandre Sarr 30.00 80.00
FABG Bryce Griggs 5.00 12.00
FABT Bryson Tiller 8.00 20.00
FABW Bryson Warren 5.00 12.00
FADC De'Vontes Cobbs 5.00 12.00
FAEE Eli Ellis 10.00 25.00
FAIA Izan Almansa 5.00 12.00
FAJG Jazian Gortman 5.00 12.00
FAJJ Jahzare Jackson 5.00 12.00
FAJL Jalen Lewis 5.00 12.00
FAJM Jaylen Martin 5.00 12.00
FAJW Jayden Williams 6.00 15.00
FAKC Kanaan Carlyle 5.00 12.00
FAKY Kok Yat 5.00 12.00
FAMB Matt Bewley 5.00 12.00
FANC Naasir Cunningham 6.00 15.00
FARB Ryan Bewley 5.00 12.00
FARD Rob Dillingham 15.00 40.00
FARM Ralph Martino Jr. 6.00 15.00
FASC Somto Cyril 6.00 15.00
FATB Tyler Bey 5.00 12.00
FATC TJ Clark 5.00 12.00
FATP Trey Parker 6.00 15.00
FATS Tyler Smith 6.00 15.00
FAZC ZZ Clark 5.00 12.00
FAAMT Amen Thompson 12.00 30.00
FAAUT Ausar Thompson 12.00 30.00
FAJWA Johned Walker 5.00 12.00
FAMBO Malik Bowman 5.00 12.00
FANMD Nathan MissiaDio 5.00 12.00
FATSO Tudor Somacescu 5.00 12.00

2022-23 Finest Overtime Elite Planet Elite Issue 1

*AQUA WAVE REF/99: 2.5X TO 6X BASIC
*GOLD RAYWAVE REF/50: 4X TO 10X BASIC
PE11 Amen Thompson 1.50 4.00
PE12 Trey Parker .75 2.00
PE13 Kanaan Carlyle .60 1.50
PE14 Jayden Williams .75 2.00
PE15 Ryan Bewley .60 1.50
PE16 Tudor Somacescu .60 1.50
PE17 Jahzare Jackson .60 1.50
PE18 Bryce Griggs .60 1.50
PE19 Izan Almansa .60 1.50
PE110 Somto Cyril .75 2.00

2022-23 Finest Overtime Elite Planet Elite Issue 2

*AQUA WAVE REF/99: 2.5X TO 6X BASIC
*GOLD RAYWAVE REF/50: 4X TO 10X BASIC
PE21 Ausar Thompson 1.50 4.00
PE22 Bryson Tiller 1.00 2.50
PE23 Rob Dillingham 2.00 5.00
PE24 Jazian Gortman .60 1.50
PE25 Malik Bowman .60 1.50
PE26 Jalen Lewis .60 1.50
PE27 De'Vontes Cobbs .60 1.50
PE28 Kok Yat .60 1.50
PE29 Bryson Warren .60 1.50
PE210 Johned Walker .60 1.50

2022-23 Finest Overtime Elite Planet Elite Issue 3

*AQUA WAVE REF/99: 2.5X TO 6X BASIC
*GOLD RAYWAVE REF/50: 4X TO 10X BASIC
PE31 Naasir Cunningham .75 2.00
PE32 ZZ Clark .60 1.50
PE33 Tyler Bey .60 1.50
PE34 Eli Ellis 1.25 3.00
PE35 Matt Bewley .60 1.50
PE36 Alexandre Sarr 2.00 5.00
PE37 Jaylen Martin .60 1.50
PE38 TJ Clark .60 1.50
PE39 Tyler Smith .75 2.00
PE310 Nathan MissiaDio .60 1.50

2001 Fire Fleer WNBA

COMPLETE SET (9) 10.00 25.00
1 Linda Hargrove .40 1.00
2 Sophia Witherspoon .40 1.00
3 Vanessa NyGaard .40 1.00
4 Sylvia Crawley .40 1.00
5 Portland Fire .40 1.00
6 Alisa Burras .40 1.00
7 Jackie Stiles 10.00 25.00
8 Stacey Thomas .40 1.00
9 Spot MASCOT .40 1.00

1991-93 5 Majeur

COMPLETE SET 200.00 500.00
1 Kareem Abdul-Jabbar 3.00 8.00
2 Mahmoud Abdul-Rauf .75 2.00
3 Michael Adams .75 2.00
4 Mark Aguirre 1.25 3.00
5 Danny Ainge 1.50 4.00
6 Greg Anderson .75 2.00
7 Nick Anderson 1.00 2.50
8 B.J. Armstrong White 1.00 2.50
9 B.J. Armstrong Red 1.00 2.50
10 Stacey Augmon .75 2.00
11 Charles Barkley 76ers 4.00 10.00
12 Charles Barkley USA 3.00 8.00
13 Dana Barros .75 2.00
14 Larry Bird 6.00 15.00
15 Larry Bird USA 6.00 15.00
16 Mookie Blaylock 1.00 2.50
17 Muggsy Bogues 1.25 3.00
18 Manute Bol .75 2.00
19 Sam Bowie .75 2.00
20 Frank Brickowski .75 2.00
21 Scott Brooks .75 2.00
22 Dee Brown .75 2.00
23 Antoine Carr .75 2.00
24 Bill Cartwright 1.00 2.50
25 Terry Catledge .75 2.00
26 Wilt Chamberlain 5.00 12.00
27 Tom Chambers 1.50 4.00
28 Rex Chapman 1.25 3.00
29 Maurice Cheeks 1.25 3.00
30 Wayne Cooper .75 2.00
31 Tyrone Corbin .75 2.00
32 Terry Cummings 1.25 3.00
33 Lloyd Daniels .75 2.00
34 Brad Daugherty .75 2.00
35 Vinny Del Negro .75 2.00
36 Vlade Divac 1.50 4.00
37 James Donaldson .75 2.00
38 Clyde Drexler USA 4.00 10.00
39 Joe Dumars 2.00 5.00
40 Mark Eaton .75 2.00
41 Craig Ehlo .75 2.00
42 Sean Elliott 1.25 3.00
43 Dale Ellis .75 2.00
44 Patrick Ewing 2.50 6.00
45 Patrick Ewing USA 2.00 5.00
46 Danny Ferry .75 2.00
47 Vern Fleming .75 2.00
48 Kendall Gill .75 2.00
49 Armon Gilliam .75 2.00
50 Horace Grant 1.25 3.00
51 A.C. Green 1.25 3.00
52 Anfernee Hardaway 3.00 8.00
53 Tim Hardaway 1.50 4.00
54 Derek Harper 1.25 3.00
55 Ron Harper 1.25 3.00
56 Hersey Hawkins 1.25 3.00
57 Carl Herrera .75 2.00
58 Bob Hill CO .75 2.00
59 Jeff Hornacek 1.50 4.00
60 Robert Horry 1.50 4.00
61 Phil Jackson CO 1.50 4.00
62 Kevin Johnson 1.50 4.00
63 Magic Johnson USA 5.00 12.00
64 Vinnie Johnson .75 2.00
65 Michael Jordan White 20.00 40.00
66 Michael Jordan Red 10.00 25.00
67 Michael Jordan USA 15.00 40.00
68 George Karl CO .75 2.00
69 Shawn Kemp 1.50 4.00
70 Jerome Kersey .75 2.00
71 Jon Koncak .75 2.00
72 Christian Laettner USA 1.50 4.00
73 Bill Laimbeer 1.25 3.00
74 Andrew Lang .75 2.00
75 Cliff Levingstone SP .75 2.00
76 Grant Long .75 2.00
77 John Lucas CO .75 2.00
78 Jeff Malone .75 2.00
79 Karl Malone 4.00 10.00
80 Karl Malone USA 3.00 8.00
81 Moses Malone 1.50 4.00
82 Sarunas Marciulionis .75 2.00
83 Vernon Maxwell .75 2.00
84 Rodney McCray .75 2.00
85 Xavier McDaniel .75 2.00
86 Kevin McHale 2.50 6.00
87 Nate McMillan .75 2.00
88 Reggie Miller 3.00 8.00
89 Chris Mullin 1.50 4.00
90 Chris Mullin USA 1.50 4.00
91 Tracy Murray .75 2.00
92 Dikembe Mutombo 1.50 4.00
93 Larry Nance 1.25 3.00
94 Charles Oakley 1.00 2.50
95 Hakeem Olajuwon 3.00 8.00
96 Shaquille O'Neal 6.00 15.00
97 Billy Owens .75 2.00
98 John Paxson White 1.25 3.00
99 John Paxson Red 1.00 2.50
100 Gary Payton 2.50 6.00
101 Will Perdue .75 2.00
102 Sam Perkins 1.25 3.00
103 Drazen Petrovic 3.00 8.00
104 Ricky Pierce .75 2.00
105 Scottie Pippen White 3.00 8.00
106 Scottie Pippen Red 2.50 6.00
107 Scottie Pippen USA 3.00 8.00
108 Olden Polynice .75 2.00
109 Terry Porter 1.00 2.50
110 Paul Pressey .75 2.00
111 Mark Price 1.25 3.00
112 Kurt Rambis 1.25 3.00
113 J.R. Reid .75 2.00
114 Glen Rice 1.25 3.00
115 Pooh Richardson .75 2.00
116 Mitch Richmond 1.50 4.00
117 Fred Roberts .75 2.00
118 David Robinson 4.00 10.00
119 David Robinson USA 3.00 8.00
120 Rumeal Robinson .75 2.00
121 Dennis Rodman 2.00 5.00
122 Donald Royal .75 2.00
123 John Salley 1.00 2.50
124 Detlef Schrempf 1.25 3.00
125 Byron Scott Dribbling 1.25 3.00
126 Byron Scott Shooting 1.25 3.00
127 Dennis Scott .75 2.00
128 Rony Seikaly .75 2.00
129 Scott Skiles 1.25 3.00
130 Kenny Smith .75 2.00
131 John Starks 1.25 3.00
132 John Stockton 5.00 12.00
133 John Stockton USA 4.00 10.00
134 Rod Strickland .75 2.00
135 Isiah Thomas 2.50 6.00
136 Otis Thorpe .75 2.00
137 Sedale Threatt .75 2.00
138 Rudy Tomjanovich CO 1.00 2.50
139 Jeff Turner .75 2.00
140 Spud Webb 1.25 3.00
141 Dominique Wilkins White 3.00 8.00
142 Dominique Wilkins Red 1.50 4.00
143 Lenny Wilkens CO 1.25 3.00
144 Herb Williams .75 2.00
145 John Williams .75 2.00
146 Reggie Williams .75 2.00
147 Scott Williams .75 2.00
148 Kevin Willis White .75 2.00
149 Kevin Willis Red .75 2.00
150 David Wingate .75 2.00
151 Orlando Woolridge .75 2.00

1994-95 Flair

COMPLETE SET (326) 30.00 80.00
COMPLETE SERIES 1 (175) 12.00 30.00
COMPLETE SERIES 2 (151) 20.00 50.00
1 Stacey Augmon .40 1.00
2 Mookie Blaylock .50 1.25
3 Craig Ehlo .30 .75
4 Jon Koncak .30 .75
5 Andrew Lang .30 .75
6 Dee Brown .40 1.00
7 Sherman Douglas .30 .75
8 Acie Earl .30 .75
9 Rick Fox .30 .75
10 Kevin Gamble .30 .75
11 Xavier McDaniel .30 .75
12 Dino Radja .30 .75
13 Tony Bennett .30 .75
14 Dell Curry .30 .75
15 Kenny Gattison .30 .75
16 Hersey Hawkins .30 .75
17 Larry Johnson .60 1.50
18 Alonzo Mourning .75 2.00
19 David Wingate .30 .75
20 B.J. Armstrong .50 1.25
21 Steve Kerr .40 1.00
22 Toni Kukoc .60 1.50
23 Pete Myers .30 .75
24 Scottie Pippen 1.25 3.00
25 Bill Wennington .30 .75
26 Terrell Brandon .30 .75
27 Brad Daugherty .40 1.00
28 Tyrone Hill .30 .75
29 Bobby Phills .30 .75
30 Mark Price .50 1.25
31 Gerald Wilkins .40 1.00
32 John Williams .30 .75
33 Lucious Harris .30 .75
34 Jim Jackson .40 1.00
35 Jamal Mashburn .50 1.25
36 Sean Rooks .30 .75
37 Doug Smith .30 .75
38 Mahmoud Abdul-Rauf .30 .75
39 LaPhonso Ellis .30 .75
40 Dikembe Mutombo .75 2.00
41 Robert Pack .40 1.00
42 Rodney Rogers .30 .75
43 Brian Williams .30 .75
44 Reggie Williams .30 .75
45 Joe Dumars .50 1.25
46 Allan Houston .50 1.25
47 Lindsey Hunter .30 .75
48 Terry Mills .30 .75
49 Victor Alexander .30 .75
50 Chris Gatling .30 .75
51 Billy Owens .30 .75
52 Latrell Sprewell .60 1.50
53 Chris Webber 1.00 2.50
54 Sam Cassell .50 1.25
55 Carl Herrera .30 .75
56 Robert Horry .50 1.25
57 Hakeem Olajuwon 1.00 2.50
58 Kenny Smith .40 1.00
59 Otis Thorpe .30 .75
60 Antonio Davis .40 1.00
61 Dale Davis .30 .75
62 Reggie Miller 1.00 2.50
63 Byron Scott .40 1.00
64 Rik Smits .40 1.00
65 Haywoode Workman .30 .75
66 Terry Dehere .30 .75
67 Harold Ellis .30 .75
68 Gary Grant .30 .75
69 Elmore Spencer .30 .75
70 Loy Vaught .30 .75
71 Elden Campbell .30 .75
72 Doug Christie .40 1.00
73 Vlade Divac .50 1.25
74 George Lynch .30 .75
75 Anthony Peeler .30 .75
76 Nick Van Exel .50 1.25
77 James Worthy .60 1.50
78 Bimbo Coles .30 .75
79 Harold Miner .30 .75
80 John Salley .30 .75
81 Rony Seikaly .30 .75
82 Steve Smith .40 1.00
83 Vin Baker .50 1.25
84 Jon Barry .30 .75
85 Todd Day .30 .75
86 Lee Mayberry .30 .75
87 Eric Murdock .30 .75
88 Mike Brown .30 .75
89 Christian Laettner .40 1.00
90 Isaiah Rider .50 1.25
91 Doug West .30 .75
92 Micheal Williams .30 .75
93 Kenny Anderson .40 1.00
94 Benoit Benjamin .30 .75
95 P.J. Brown .30 .75
96 Derrick Coleman .50 1.25
97 Kevin Edwards .30 .75
98 Hubert Davis .30 .75
99 Patrick Ewing .75 2.00
100 Derek Harper .40 1.00
101 Anthony Mason .40 1.00
102 Charles Oakley .50 1.25
103 Charles Smith .30 .75
104 John Starks .50 1.25
105 Nick Anderson .30 .75
106 Anfernee Hardaway 1.00 2.50
107 Shaquille O'Neal 2.00 5.00
108 Dennis Scott .40 1.00
109 Jeff Turner .30 .75
110 Dana Barros .30 .75
111 Shawn Bradley .30 .75
112 Jeff Malone .30 .75
113 Tim Perry .30 .75
114 Clarence Weatherspoon .30 .75
115 Danny Ainge .50 1.25
116 Charles Barkley 1.25 3.00
117 A.C. Green .40 1.00
118 Kevin Johnson .50 1.25
119 Dan Majerle .50 1.25
120 Clyde Drexler .75 2.00
121 Harvey Grant .30 .75
122 Jerome Kersey .30 .75
123 Clifford Robinson .40 1.00
124 Rod Strickland .30 .75
125 Buck Williams .30 .75
126 Randy Brown .30 .75
127 Olden Polynice .30 .75
128 Mitch Richmond .60 1.50
129 Lionel Simmons .30 .75
130 Spud Webb .40 1.00
131 Walt Williams .30 .75
132 Willie Anderson .30 .75
133 Vinny Del Negro .30 .75
134 Sean Elliott .40 1.00
135 Avery Johnson .40 1.00
136 J.R. Reid .30 .75
137 David Robinson 1.00 2.50
138 Dennis Rodman 1.25 3.00
139 Kendall Gill .30 .75
140 Ervin Johnson .30 .75
141 Shawn Kemp .75 2.00
142 Nate McMillan .40 1.00
143 Gary Payton .75 2.00
144 Sam Perkins .30 .75
145 David Benoit .30 .75
146 Jeff Hornacek .40 1.00
147 Jay Humphries .30 .75
148 Karl Malone 1.00 2.50
149 Bryon Russell .30 .75
150 Felton Spencer .30 .75
151 John Stockton 1.00 2.50
152 Rex Chapman .30 .75
153 Calbert Cheaney .40 1.00
154 Tom Gugliotta .30 .75
155 Don MacLean .30 .75
156 Gheorghe Muresan .30 .75
157 Doug Overton .30 .75
158 Brent Price .30 .75
159 Derrick Coleman USA .50 1.25
160 Joe Dumars USA .50 1.25
161 Tim Hardaway USA .60 1.50
162 Kevin Johnson USA .50 1.25
163 Larry Johnson USA .60 1.50
164 Shawn Kemp USA .75 2.00
165 Dan Majerle USA .50 1.25
166 Reggie Miller USA 1.00 2.50
167 Alonzo Mourning USA .75 2.00
168 Shaquille O'Neal USA 2.00 5.00
169 Mark Price USA .50 1.25
170 Steve Smith USA .40 1.00
171 Isiah Thomas USA .50 1.25
172 Dominique Wilkins USA .75 2.00
173 Checklist .20 .50
174 Checklist .20 .50
175 Checklist .20 .50
176 Tyrone Corbin .30 .75
177 Grant Long .30 .75
178 Ken Norman .30 .75
179 Steve Smith .40 1.00
180 Blue Edwards .30 .75
181 Pervis Ellison .30 .75
182 Greg Minor RC .50 1.25
183 Eric Montross RC .40 1.00
184 Derek Strong .30 .75
185 David Wesley .30 .75
186 Dominique Wilkins .75 2.00
187 Michael Adams .30 .75
188 Muggsy Bogues .40 1.00
189 Scott Burrell .30 .75
190 Darrin Hancock RC .40 1.00
191 Robert Parish .50 1.25
192 Jud Buechler .30 .75
193 Ron Harper .40 1.00
194 Larry Krystkowiak .30 .75

5 Will Perdue .30 .75
6 Dickey Simpkins RC .40 1.00
7 Michael Cage .30 .75
8 Tony Campbell .30 .75
9 Danny Ferry .30 .75
0 Chris Mills .40 1.00
1 Popeye Jones .30 .75
2 Jason Kidd RC 2.50 6.00
3 Roy Tarpley .30 .75
4 Lorenzo Williams .30 .75
5 Dale Ellis .30 .75
6 Tom Hammonds .30 .75
7 Jalen Rose RC 1.25 3.00
8 Reggie Slater .30 .75
9 Bryant Stith .30 .75
0 Rafael Addison .30 .75
1 Bill Curley RC .30 .75
2 Johnny Dawkins .30 .75
3 Grant Hill RC 2.50 6.00
4 Mark Macon .30 .75
5 Oliver Miller .30 .75
6 Ivano Newbill .30 .75
7 Mark West .30 .75
8 Tom Gugliotta .30 .75
9 Tim Hardaway .60 1.50
0 Keith Jennings .30 .75
1 Dwayne Morton .30 .75
2 Chris Mullin .60 1.50
3 Ricky Pierce .30 .75
24 Carlos Rogers RC .40 1.00
25 Clifford Rozier RC .30 .75
26 Rony Seikaly .30 .75
27 Tim Breaux .30 .75
28 Scott Brooks .30 .75
29 Mario Elie .30 .75
30 Vernon Maxwell .30 .75
31 Zan Tabak .30 .75
32 Mark Jackson .40 1.00
33 Derrick McKey .30 .75
34 Tony Massenburg .30 .75
35 Lamond Murray RC .50 1.25
36 Bo Outlaw .50 1.25
37 Eric Piatkowski RC .50 1.25
38 Pooh Richardson .30 .75
39 Malik Sealy .30 .75
40 Cedric Ceballos .40 1.00
41 Eddie Jones RC 1.50 4.00
42 Anthony Miller .50 1.25
43 Tony Smith .30 .75
44 Sedale Threatt .30 .75
45 Ledell Eackles .30 .75
46 Kevin Gamble .30 .75
247 Matt Geiger .30 .75
248 Brad Lohaus .30 .75
249 Billy Owens .30 .75
250 Khalid Reeves RC .40 1.00
251 Glen Rice .50 1.25
252 Kevin Willis .40 1.00
253 Marty Conlon .30 .75
254 Eric Mobley RC .30 .75
255 Johnny Newman .30 .75
256 Ed Pinckney .30 .75
257 Glenn Robinson RC 1.00 2.50
258 Pat Durham .30 .75
259 Howard Eisley .50 1.25
260 Winston Garland .30 .75
261 Stacey King .30 .75
262 Donyell Marshall RC .50 1.25
263 Sean Rooks .30 .75
264 Chris Smith .30 .75
265 Chris Childs RC .40 1.00
266 Sleepy Floyd .30 .75
267 Armon Gilliam .30 .75
268 Sean Higgins .30 .75
269 Rex Walters .30 .75
270 Greg Anthony .30 .75
271 Charlie Ward RC .50 1.25
272 Herb Williams .30 .75
273 Monty Williams RC .60 1.50
274 Anthony Avent .30 .75
275 Anthony Bowie .30 .75
276 Horace Grant .50 1.25
277 Donald Royal .30 .75
278 Brian Shaw .30 .75
279 Brooks Thompson RC .40 1.00
280 Derrick Alston RC .30 .75
281 Willie Burton .30 .75
282 Greg Graham .30 .75
283 B.J. Tyler RC .30 .75
284 Scott Williams .30 .75
285 Sharone Wright RC .40 1.00
286 Joe Kleine .30 .75
287 Danny Manning .40 1.00
288 Elliot Perry .30 .75
289 Wesley Person RC .50 1.25
290 Trevor Ruffin RC .30 .75
291 Wayman Tisdale .30 .75
292 Mark Bryant .30 .75
293 Chris Dudley .30 .75
294 Aaron McKie RC .50 1.25
295 Tracy Murray .30 .75
296 Terry Porter .30 .75
297 James Robinson .30 .75
298 Alaa Abdelnaby .30 .75
299 Duane Causwell .30 .75
300 Brian Grant RC .75 2.00
301 Bobby Hurley .30 .75
302 Michael Smith RC .30 .75
303 Terry Cummings .40 1.00
304 Moses Malone .50 1.25
305 Julius Nwosu .30 .75
306 Chuck Person .40 1.00
307 Doc Rivers .40 1.00
308 Vincent Askew .30 .75
309 Sarunas Marciulionis .30 .75
310 Detlef Schrempf .50 1.25
311 Dontonio Wingfield .50 1.25
312 Antoine Carr .30 .75
313 Tom Chambers .40 1.00
314 John Crotty .30 .75
315 Adam Keefe .30 .75
316 Jamie Watson RC .30 .75
317 Mitchell Butler .30 .75
318 Kevin Duckworth .30 .75
319 Juwan Howard RC .75 2.00
320 Jim McIlvaine RC .40 1.00
321 Scott Skiles .30 .75
322 Anthony Tucker RC .30 .75
323 Chris Webber 1.00 2.50
324 Checklist .20 .50
325 Checklist .20 .50
326 Michael Jordan 8.00 20.00

1994-95 Flair Center Spotlight
COMPLETE SET (6) 10.00 25.00
SER.1 STATED ODDS 1:25
1 Patrick Ewing 2.50 6.00
2 Alonzo Mourning 2.50 6.00
3 Hakeem Olajuwon 3.00 8.00
4 Shaquille O'Neal 6.00 15.00
5 David Robinson 3.00 8.00
6 Chris Webber 3.00 8.00

1994-95 Flair Hot Numbers
COMPLETE SET (20) 15.00 40.00
SER.1 STATED ODDS 1:6
1 Vin Baker 1.00 2.50
2 Sam Cassell 1.00 2.50
3 Patrick Ewing 1.50 4.00
4 Anfernee Hardaway 2.00 5.00
5 Robert Horry 1.00 2.50
6 Shawn Kemp 1.50 4.00
7 Toni Kukoc 1.25 3.00
8 Jamal Mashburn 1.00 2.50
9 Reggie Miller 2.00 5.00
10 Dikembe Mutombo 1.50 4.00
11 Hakeem Olajuwon 2.00 5.00
12 Shaquille O'Neal 4.00 10.00
13 Scottie Pippen 2.50 6.00
14 Isaiah Rider 1.00 2.50
15 David Robinson 2.00 5.00
16 Latrell Sprewell 1.25 3.00
17 John Starks 1.00 2.50
18 John Stockton 2.00 5.00
19 Nick Van Exel 1.00 2.50
20 Chris Webber 2.00 5.00

1994-95 Flair Playmakers
COMPLETE SET (10) 4.00 10.00
SER.2 STATED ODDS 1:4
1 Kenny Anderson .50 1.25
2 Mookie Blaylock .60 1.50
3 Sam Cassell .60 1.50
4 Anfernee Hardaway 1.25 3.00
5 Robert Pack .50 1.25
6 Scottie Pippen 1.50 4.00
7 Mark Price .60 1.50
8 Mitch Richmond .75 2.00
9 John Stockton 1.25 3.00
10 Nick Van Exel .60 1.50

1994-95 Flair Rejectors
COMPLETE SET (6) 12.00 30.00
SER.2 STATED ODDS 1:25
1 Patrick Ewing 3.00 8.00
2 Alonzo Mourning 3.00 8.00
3 Dikembe Mutombo 3.00 8.00
4 Hakeem Olajuwon 4.00 10.00
5 Shaquille O'Neal 8.00 20.00
6 David Robinson 4.00 10.00

1994-95 Flair Scoring Power
COMPLETE SET (10) 8.00 20.00
SER.1 STATED ODDS 1:8
1 Charles Barkley 2.50 6.00
2 Patrick Ewing 1.50 4.00
3 Karl Malone 2.00 5.00
4 Hakeem Olajuwon 2.00 5.00
5 Shaquille O'Neal 3.00 8.00
6 Scottie Pippen 2.50 6.00
7 Mitch Richmond 1.25 3.00
8 David Robinson 2.00 5.00
9 Latrell Sprewell 1.25 3.00
10 Dominique Wilkins 1.50 4.00

1994-95 Flair Wave of the Future
COMPLETE SET (10) 8.00 20.00
SER.2 STATED ODDS 1:7
1 Brian Grant 1.00 2.50
2 Grant Hill 3.00 8.00
3 Juwan Howard 1.00 2.50
4 Eddie Jones 2.00 5.00
5 Jason Kidd 3.00 8.00
6 Donyell Marshall .60 1.50
7 Eric Montross .50 1.25
8 Lamond Murray .60 1.50
9 Wesley Person .60 1.50
10 Glenn Robinson 1.25 3.00

1995-96 Flair
COMPLETE SET (250) 30.00 80.00
COMPLETE SERIES 1 (150) 15.00 40.00
COMPLETE SERIES 2 (100) 15.00 40.00
1 Stacey Augmon .40 1.00
2 Mookie Blaylock .50 1.25
3 Grant Long .30 .75
4 Steve Smith .40 1.00
5 Dee Brown .40 1.00
6 Sherman Douglas .30 .75
7 Eric Montross .30 .75
8 Dino Radja .30 .75
9 David Wesley .30 .75
10 Muggsy Bogues .50 1.25
11 Scott Burrell .30 .75
12 Dell Curry .50 1.25
13 Larry Johnson .60 1.50
14 Alonzo Mourning .75 2.00
15 Michael Jordan 5.00 12.00
16 Steve Kerr .60 1.50
17 Toni Kukoc .60 1.50
18 Scottie Pippen 1.25 3.00
19 Terrell Brandon .40 1.00
20 Tyrone Hill .30 .75
21 Chris Mills .30 .75
22 Bobby Phills .40 1.00
23 Mark Price .50 1.25
24 John Williams .30 .75
25 Jim Jackson .40 1.00
26 Popeye Jones .30 .75
27 Jason Kidd .75 2.00
28 Jamal Mashburn .50 1.25
29 Lorenzo Williams .30 .75
30 Mahmoud Abdul-Rauf .40 1.00
31 Dikembe Mutombo .75 2.00
32 Robert Pack .30 .75
33 Jalen Rose .60 1.50
34 Bryant Stith .30 .75
35 Reggie Williams .30 .75
36 Joe Dumars .50 1.25
37 Grant Hill .75 2.00
38 Allan Houston .40 1.00
39 Lindsey Hunter .30 .75
40 Terry Mills .30 .75
41 Chris Gatling .30 .75
42 Tim Hardaway .60 1.50
43 Donyell Marshall .30 .75
44 Chris Mullin .50 1.25
45 Carlos Rogers .30 .75
46 Clifford Rozier .30 .75
47 Latrell Sprewell .50 1.25
48 Sam Cassell .50 1.25
49 Clyde Drexler .75 2.00
50 Mario Elie .30 .75
51 Robert Horry .50 1.25
52 Hakeem Olajuwon 1.00 2.50
53 Kenny Smith .40 1.00
54 Antonio Davis .30 .75
55 Dale Davis .30 .75
56 Mark Jackson .40 1.00
57 Derrick McKey .30 .75
58 Reggie Miller 1.00 2.50
59 Rik Smits .40 1.00
60 Lamond Murray .30 .75
61 Pooh Richardson .30 .75
62 Malik Sealy .30 .75
63 Loy Vaught .30 .75
64 Elden Campbell .30 .75
65 Cedric Ceballos .40 1.00
66 Vlade Divac .50 1.25
67 Eddie Jones .50 1.25
68 Nick Van Exel .50 1.25
69 Bimbo Coles .30 .75
70 Billy Owens .30 .75
71 Khalid Reeves .30 .75
72 Glen Rice .50 1.25
73 Kevin Willis .30 .75
74 Vin Baker .40 1.00
75 Todd Day .30 .75
76 Eric Murdock .30 .75
77 Glenn Robinson .50 1.25
78 Tom Gugliotta .30 .75
79 Christian Laettner .40 1.00
80 Isaiah Rider .50 1.25
81 Doug West .30 .75
82 Kenny Anderson .40 1.00
83 P.J. Brown .30 .75
84 Derrick Coleman .40 1.00
85 Armon Gilliam .30 .75
86 Chris Morris .30 .75
87 Hubert Davis .30 .75
88 Patrick Ewing .75 2.00
89 Derek Harper .40 1.00
90 Anthony Mason .40 1.00
91 Charles Oakley .40 1.00
92 Charles Smith .30 .75
93 John Starks .50 1.25
94 Nick Anderson .40 1.00
95 Horace Grant .40 1.00
96 Anfernee Hardaway 1.25 3.00
97 Shaquille O'Neal 2.00 5.00
98 Dennis Scott .30 .75
99 Brian Shaw .30 .75
100 Dana Barros .40 1.00
101 Shawn Bradley .30 .75
102 Clarence Weatherspoon .30 .75
103 Sharone Wright .30 .75
104 Charles Barkley 1.25 3.00
105 A.C. Green .40 1.00
106 Kevin Johnson .50 1.25
107 Dan Majerle .50 1.25
108 Danny Manning .40 1.00
109 Elliot Perry .30 .75
110 Wesley Person .30 .75
111 Terry Porter .30 .75
112 Clifford Robinson .50 1.25
113 Rod Strickland .50 1.25
114 Otis Thorpe .40 1.00
115 Buck Williams .40 1.00
116 Brian Grant .40 1.00
117 Bobby Hurley .30 .75
118 Olden Polynice .30 .75
119 Mitch Richmond .60 1.50
120 Walt Williams .30 .75
121 Vinny Del Negro .30 .75
122 Sean Elliott .40 1.00
123 Avery Johnson .40 1.00
124 David Robinson 1.00 2.50
125 Dennis Rodman 1.00 2.50
126 Shawn Kemp .75 2.00
127 Nate McMillan .30 .75
128 Gary Payton .75 2.00
129 Sam Perkins .30 .75
130 Detlef Schrempf .50 1.25
131 B.J. Armstrong .50 1.25
132 Jerome Kersey .30 .75
133 Oliver Miller .30 .75
134 John Salley .40 1.00
135 David Benoit .30 .75
136 Antoine Carr .30 .75
137 Jeff Hornacek .40 1.00
138 Karl Malone 1.00 2.50
139 John Stockton 1.00 2.50
140 Greg Anthony .30 .75
141 Benoit Benjamin .30 .75
142 Blue Edwards .30 .75
143 Byron Scott .50 1.25
144 Calbert Cheaney .30 .75
145 Juwan Howard .50 1.25
146 Gheorghe Muresan .30 .75
147 Scott Skiles .30 .75
148 Chris Webber .60 1.50
149 Checklist .25 .60
150 Checklist .25 .60
151 Stacey Augmon .40 1.00
152 Mookie Blaylock .50 1.25
153 Andrew Lang .30 .75
154 Steve Smith .40 1.00
155 Dana Barros .40 1.00
156 Rick Fox .30 .75
157 Kendall Gill .30 .75
158 Khalid Reeves .30 .75
159 Glen Rice .50 1.25
160 Dennis Rodman 1.00 2.50
161 Dan Majerle .50 1.25
162 Tony Dumas .30 .75
163 Dale Ellis .40 1.00
164 Otis Thorpe .40 1.00
165 Rony Seikaly .30 .75
166 Sam Cassell .50 1.25
167 Clyde Drexler .75 2.00
168 Robert Horry .50 1.25
169 Hakeem Olajuwon 1.00 2.50
170 Ricky Pierce .30 .75
171 Rodney Rogers .40 1.00
172 Brian Williams .30 .75
173 Magic Johnson 1.50 4.00
174 Alonzo Mourning .75 2.00
175 Lee Mayberry .30 .75
176 Terry Porter .30 .75
177 Shawn Bradley .30 .75
178 Jayson Williams .30 .75
179 Gary Grant .30 .75
180 Jon Koncak .30 .75
181 Derrick Coleman .40 1.00
182 Vernon Maxwell .30 .75
183 John Williams .30 .75
184 Aaron McKie .30 .75
185 Michael Smith .30 .75
186 Chuck Person .40 1.00
187 Hersey Hawkins .40 1.00
188 Shawn Kemp .75 2.00
189 Gary Payton .75 2.00
190 Detlef Schrempf .50 1.25
191 Chris Morris .30 .75
192 Robert Pack .30 .75
193 Willie Anderson EXP .15 .40
194 Oliver Miller EXP .15 .40
195 Alvin Robertson EXP .15 .40
196 Greg Anthony EXP .15 .40
197 Blue Edwards EXP .15 .40
198 Byron Scott EXP .25 .60
199 Cory Alexander RC .40 1.00
200 Brent Barry RC .60 1.50
201 Travis Best RC .40 1.00
202 Jason Caffey RC .40 1.00
203 Sasha Danilovic RC .40 1.00
204 Tyus Edney RC .40 1.00
205 Michael Finley RC 1.00 2.50
206 Kevin Garnett RC 6.00 15.00
207 Alan Henderson RC .40 1.00
208 Antonio McDyess RC .50 1.25
209 Loren Meyer RC .25 .60
210 Lawrence Moten RC .40 1.00
211 Ed O'Bannon RC .30 .75
212 Greg Ostertag RC .40 1.00
213 Cherokee Parks RC .30 .75
214 Theo Ratliff RC .60 1.50
215 Bryant Reeves RC .30 .75
216 Shawn Respert RC .30 .75
217 Arvydas Sabonis RC .75 2.00
218 Joe Smith RC .50 1.25
219 Jerry Stackhouse RC 1.25 3.00
220 Damon Stoudamire RC 1.00 2.50
221 Bob Sura RC .30 .75
222 Kurt Thomas RC .40 1.00
223 Gary Trent RC .30 .75
224 David Vaughn RC .30 .75
225 Rasheed Wallace RC 1.25 3.00
226 Eric Williams RC .40 1.00
227 Corliss Williamson RC .40 1.00
228 George Zidek RC .30 .75
229 Vin Baker STY .20 .50
230 Charles Barkley STY .60 1.50
231 Patrick Ewing STY .40 1.00
232 Anfernee Hardaway STY .60 1.50
233 Grant Hill STY .40 1.00
234 Larry Johnson STY .30 .75
235 Michael Jordan STY 2.50 6.00
236 Jason Kidd STY .40 1.00
237 Karl Malone STY .50 1.25
238 Jamal Mashburn STY .25 .60
239 Reggie Miller STY .50 1.25
240 Shaquille O'Neal STY 1.00 2.50
241 Scottie Pippen STY .60 1.50
242 Mitch Richmond STY .30 .75
243 Clifford Robinson STY .25 .60
244 David Robinson STY .50 1.25
245 Glenn Robinson STY .25 .60
246 John Stockton STY .50 1.25
247 Nick Van Exel STY .25 .60
248 Chris Webber STY .30 .75
249 Checklist .25 .60
250 Checklist .25 .60

1995-96 Flair Anticipation
COMPLETE SET (10) 40.00 100.00
SER.2 STATED ODDS 1:36
1 Grant Hill 5.00 12.00
2 Michael Jordan 75.00 200.00
3 Shawn Kemp 5.00 12.00
4 Jason Kidd 5.00 12.00
5 Alonzo Mourning 5.00 12.00
6 Hakeem Olajuwon 6.00 15.00
7 Shaquille O'Neal 12.00 30.00
8 Glenn Robinson 3.00 8.00
9 Joe Smith 2.00 5.00
10 Jerry Stackhouse 5.00 12.00

1995-96 Flair Center Spotlight
COMPLETE SET (6) 8.00 20.00
SER.1 STATED ODDS 1:18
1 Vlade Divac 1.50 4.00
2 Patrick Ewing 2.50 6.00
3 Alonzo Mourning 2.50 6.00
4 Hakeem Olajuwon 3.00 8.00
5 Shaquille O'Neal 6.00 15.00
6 David Robinson 3.00 8.00

1995-96 Flair Class of '95
COMPLETE SET (15) 8.00 20.00
R1 Brent Barry .60 1.50
R2 Kevin Garnett 3.00 8.00
R3 Antonio McDyess .50 1.25
R4 Ed O'Bannon .30 .75
R5 Cherokee Parks .30 .75
R6 Bryant Reeves .30 .75
R7 Shawn Respert .30 .75
R8 Joe Smith .50 1.25
R9 Jerry Stackhouse 1.25 3.00
R10 Damon Stoudamire 1.00 2.50
R11 Kurt Thomas .40 1.00
R12 Gary Trent .30 .75
R13 Rasheed Wallace 1.25 3.00
R14 Eric Williams .40 1.00
R15 Corliss Williamson .40 1.00

1995-96 Flair Hot Numbers
COMPLETE SET (15) 1,000.00 2,000.00
SER.1 STATED ODDS 1:36
1 Charles Barkley 40.00 100.00
2 Grant Hill 20.00 50.00
3 Eddie Jones 20.00 50.00
4 Michael Jordan 500.00 1,000.00
5 Shawn Kemp 25.00 60.00
6 Jason Kidd 20.00 50.00
7 Karl Malone 20.00 50.00
8 Alonzo Mourning 20.00 50.00
9 Dikembe Mutombo 20.00 50.00
10 Hakeem Olajuwon 25.00 60.00
11 Shaquille O'Neal 100.00 250.00
12 Glenn Robinson 12.00 30.00
13 Dennis Rodman 30.00 80.00
14 Latrell Sprewell 15.00 40.00
15 Chris Webber 20.00 50.00

1995-96 Flair New Heights
COMPLETE SET (10) 200.00 500.00
SER.2 STATED ODDS 1:18 HOBBY
1 Anfernee Hardaway 12.00 30.00
2 Grant Hill 8.00 20.00
3 Larry Johnson 6.00 15.00
4 Michael Jordan 200.00 500.00
5 Shawn Kemp 8.00 20.00
6 Karl Malone 10.00 25.00
7 Hakeem Olajuwon 10.00 25.00
8 David Robinson 10.00 25.00
9 Glenn Robinson 5.00 12.00
10 Chris Webber 6.00 15.00

1995-96 Flair Perimeter Power
COMPLETE SET (15) 6.00 15.00
SER.1 STATED ODDS 1:12
1 Dana Barros .60 1.50
2 Clyde Drexler 1.25 3.00
3 Anfernee Hardaway 2.00 5.00
4 Tim Hardaway 1.00 2.50
5 Dan Majerle .75 2.00
6 Jamal Mashburn .75 2.00
7 Reggie Miller 1.50 4.00
8 Gary Payton 1.25 3.00
9 Scottie Pippen 2.00 5.00
10 Glen Rice .75 2.00
11 Mitch Richmond 1.00 2.50
12 Steve Smith .60 1.50
13 John Starks .75 2.00
14 John Stockton 1.50 4.00
15 Nick Van Exel .75 2.00

1995-96 Flair Play Makers
COMPLETE SET (10) 60.00 150.00
SER.2 STATED ODDS 1:54
1 Clyde Drexler 10.00 25.00
2 Anfernee Hardaway 15.00 40.00
3 Jamal Mashburn 6.00 15.00
4 Reggie Miller 12.00 30.00
5 Gary Payton 10.00 25.00
6 Scottie Pippen 15.00 40.00
7 Mitch Richmond 8.00 20.00
8 David Robinson 12.00 30.00
9 Jerry Stackhouse 10.00 25.00
10 Nick Van Exel 6.00 15.00

1995-96 Flair Stackhouse's Scrapbook
COMPLETE SET (2) 3.00 8.00
COMMON CARD (S5-S6) 2.00 5.00
WRAPPER ODDS 1:24

1995-96 Flair Wave of the Future
COMPLETE SET (10) 8.00 20.00
SER.2 STATED ODDS 1:12
1 Tyus Edney .60 1.50
2 Michael Finley 1.50 4.00
3 Kevin Garnett 8.00 20.00
4 Antonio McDyess .75 2.00
5 Ed O'Bannon .50 1.25
6 Arvydas Sabonis 1.25 3.00
7 Joe Smith .75 2.00
8 Jerry Stackhouse 2.00 5.00
9 Damon Stoudamire 1.50 4.00
10 Rasheed Wallace 2.00 5.00

1996-97 Flair Showcase Row 2
COMPLETE SET (90) 25.00 60.00
1-30 ODDS 1.5:1
31-60 ODDS 1:2
61-90 ODDS 1:1.5
1 Anfernee Hardaway 1.25 3.00
2 Mitch Richmond .60 1.50
3 Allen Iverson RC 6.00 15.00
4 Charles Barkley 1.25 3.00
5 Juwan Howard .50 1.25
6 David Robinson 1.00 2.50
7 Gary Payton .75 2.00
8 Kerry Kittles RC .50 1.25
9 Dennis Rodman 1.25 3.00
10 Shaquille O'Neal 2.00 5.00
11 Stephon Marbury RC 1.50 4.00
12 John Stockton 1.00 2.50
13 Glenn Robinson .50 1.25
14 Hakeem Olajuwon 1.00 2.50
15 Jason Kidd .75 2.00
16 Jerry Stackhouse .60 1.50
17 Joe Smith .40 1.00
18 Reggie Miller 1.00 2.50
19 Grant Hill .75 2.00
20 Damon Stoudamire .50 1.25
21 Kevin Garnett 1.50 4.00
22 Clyde Drexler .75 2.00
23 Michael Jordan 12.00 30.00
24 Antonio McDyess .50 1.25
25 Chris Webber .60 1.50
26 Antoine Walker RC .75 2.00
27 Scottie Pippen 1.25 3.00
28 Karl Malone 1.00 2.50
29 Shareef Abdur-Rahim RC .75 2.00
30 Shawn Kemp .75 2.00
31 Kobe Bryant RC 40.00 100.00
32 Derrick Coleman .40 1.00
33 Alonzo Mourning .75 2.00
34 Anthony Mason .40 1.00
35 Ray Allen RC 2.50 6.00
36 Arvydas Sabonis .50 1.25
37 Brian Grant .40 1.00
38 Bryant Reeves .30 .75
39 Christian Laettner .50 1.25
40 Tom Gugliotta .30 .75
41 Latrell Sprewell .50 1.25
42 Erick Dampier RC .50 1.25
43 Gheorghe Muresan .30 .75
44 Glen Rice .50 1.25
45 Patrick Ewing .75 2.00
46 Jim Jackson .30 .75
47 Michael Finley .50 1.25
48 Toni Kukoc .50 1.25
49 Marcus Camby RC .75 2.00
50 Kenny Anderson .40 1.00
51 Mark Price .50 1.25
52 Tim Hardaway .60 1.50
53 Mookie Blaylock .50 1.25
54 Steve Smith .40 1.00
55 Terrell Brandon .40 1.00
56 Lorenzen Wright RC .40 1.00
57 Sasha Danilovic .30 .75
58 Jeff Hornacek .40 1.00
59 Eddie Jones .50 1.25
60 Vin Baker .40 1.00
61 Chris Childs .30 .75
62 Clifford Robinson .50 1.25
63 Anthony Peeler .30 .75
64 Dino Radja .30 .75
65 Joe Dumars .60 1.50
66 Loy Vaught .30 .75
67 Rony Seikaly .40 1.00
68 Vitaly Potapenko RC .40 1.00
69 Chris Gatling .30 .75
70 Dale Ellis .40 1.00
71 Allan Houston .50 1.25
72 Doug Christie .30 .75
73 LaPhonso Ellis .30 .75
74 Kendall Gill .50 1.25
75 Rik Smits .40 1.00
76 Bobby Phills .30 .75
77 Malik Sealy .30 .75
78 Sean Elliott .50 1.25
79 Vlade Divac .50 1.25
80 David Wesley .30 .75
81 Dominique Wilkins .75 2.00
82 Danny Manning .40 1.00
83 Detlef Schrempf .50 1.25
84 Hersey Hawkins .30 .75
85 Lindsey Hunter .30 .75
86 Mahmoud Abdul-Rauf .40 1.00
87 Shawn Bradley .30 .75
88 Horace Grant .50 1.25
89 Cedric Ceballos .40 1.00
90 Jamal Mashburn .50 1.25
NNO Jerry Stackhouse Promo
3-card strip 2.00 5.00

1996-97 Flair Showcase Row 1
*STARS: .75X TO 2X ROW 2
*RCs: .6X TO 1.5X ROW 2
1-30 ODDS 1:2.5
31-60 ODDS 1:2
61-90 ODDS 1:3.5
23 Michael Jordan 50.00 120.00

1996-97 Flair Showcase Row 0
*STARS 1-30: 4X TO 10X ROW 2
*RCs 1-30: 2X TO 5X HI
1-30 ODDS 1:24
*STARS 31-60: 2X TO 5X ROW 2
*RCs 31-60: 1X TO 2.5X ROW 2
31-60 ODDS 1:10
*STARS/RCs 61-90: .6X TO 1.5X ROW 2
61-90 ODDS 1:5
1 Anfernee Hardaway 20.00 50.00
3 Allen Iverson 100.00 250.00
4 Charles Barkley 25.00 60.00
9 Dennis Rodman 25.00 60.00
10 Shaquille O'Neal 25.00 60.00
14 Hakeem Olajuwon 20.00 50.00
18 Reggie Miller 15.00 40.00
19 Grant Hill 12.00 30.00
21 Kevin Garnett 25.00 60.00
23 Michael Jordan 600.00 1,200.00
27 Scottie Pippen 25.00 60.00
30 Shawn Kemp 12.00 30.00
31 Kobe Bryant 400.00 1,000.00
35 Ray Allen 40.00 100.00

1996-97 Flair Showcase Legacy Collection Row 2
*ROW 1/2 STARS: 15X TO 40X HI COLUMN
*ROW 1/2 RCs: 8X TO 20X HI
STATED ODDS 1:30
STATED PRINT RUN 150 SERIAL #'d SETS
LEGACY: ROW 1 AND 2 SAME VALUE
1 Anfernee Hardaway 100.00 250.00
3 Allen Iverson 400.00 800.00
4 Charles Barkley 60.00 150.00
6 David Robinson 40.00 100.00
9 Dennis Rodman 200.00 500.00
10 Shaquille O'Neal 150.00 400.00
11 Stephon Marbury 30.00 80.00
14 Hakeem Olajuwon 40.00 100.00
15 Jason Kidd 60.00 150.00
18 Reggie Miller 75.00 200.00
19 Grant Hill 60.00 150.00
23 Michael Jordan 4,000.00 8,000.00
25 Chris Webber 60.00 150.00
27 Scottie Pippen 200.00 500.00
28 Karl Malone 30.00 80.00
30 Shawn Kemp 25.00 60.00
31 Kobe Bryant 6,000.00 12,000.00
35 Ray Allen 75.00 200.00
41 Latrell Sprewell 30.00 80.00
48 Toni Kukoc 25.00 60.00
81 Dominique Wilkins 25.00 60.00

1996-97 Flair Showcase Legacy Collection Row 0
*STARS: 20X TO 50X HI
*RCs: 10X TO 25X HI
STATED PRINT RUN 150 SER.#'d SETS
1 Anfernee Hardaway 500.00 1,000.00
2 Mitch Richmond 30.00 80.00
3 Allen Iverson 2,000.00 4,000.00
4 Charles Barkley 300.00 600.00
6 David Robinson 125.00 300.00
7 Gary Payton 100.00 250.00
9 Dennis Rodman 500.00 1,000.00
10 Shaquille O'Neal 500.00 1,000.00
11 Stephon Marbury 100.00 250.00
14 Hakeem Olajuwon 125.00 300.00
15 Jason Kidd 100.00 250.00
18 Reggie Miller 125.00 300.00
19 Grant Hill 300.00 600.00
21 Kevin Garnett 500.00 1,000.00
22 Clyde Drexler 40.00 100.00
23 Michael Jordan 2,000.00 4,000.00
25 Chris Webber 100.00 250.00
27 Scottie Pippen 400.00 800.00
28 Karl Malone 100.00 250.00
29 Shareef Abdur-Rahim 30.00 80.00
30 Shawn Kemp 75.00 200.00
31 Kobe Bryant 10,000.00 20,000.00
33 Alonzo Mourning 100.00 250.00
35 Ray Allen 400.00 800.00
41 Latrell Sprewell 60.00 150.00
48 Toni Kukoc 30.00 80.00
49 Marcus Camby 40.00 100.00
71 Allan Houston 25.00 60.00
81 Dominique Wilkins 30.00 80.00

1996-97 Flair Showcase Class of '96
COMPLETE SET (20) 100.00 250.00
STATED ODDS 1:5
1 Shareef Abdur-Rahim 1.50 4.00
2 Ray Allen 5.00 12.00
3 Shandon Anderson .75 2.00
4 Kobe Bryant 200.00 500.00
5 Marcus Camby 1.50 4.00
6 Erick Dampier 1.00 2.50
7 Derek Fisher 1.25 3.00
8 Todd Fuller .60 1.50
9 Othella Harrington .75 2.00
10 Allen Iverson 40.00 100.00
11 Kerry Kittles 1.00 2.50
12 Travis Knight .75 2.00
13 Matt Maloney .75 2.00
14 Stephon Marbury 3.00 8.00
15 Steve Nash 12.00 30.00
16 Jermaine O'Neal 1.50 4.00
17 Vitaly Potapenko .75 2.00
18 Roy Rogers .75 2.00
19 Antoine Walker 1.50 4.00
20 Lorenzen Wright .75 2.00

1996-97 Flair Showcase Hot Shots
STATED ODDS 1:90
1 Michael Jordan 2,000.00 4,000.00
2 Kevin Garnett 125.00 300.00
3 Damon Stoudamire 25.00 60.00
4 Anfernee Hardaway 125.00 300.00
5 Shaquille O'Neal 150.00 400.00
6 Grant Hill 75.00 200.00
7 Dennis Rodman 125.00 300.00
8 Shawn Kemp 60.00 150.00
9 Scottie Pippen 125.00 300.00
10 Juwan Howard 20.00 50.00
11 Jason Kidd 50.00 120.00
12 Hakeem Olajuwon 60.00 150.00
13 Karl Malone 50.00 120.00
14 Joe Smith 20.00 50.00
15 David Robinson 60.00 150.00
16 Jerry Stackhouse 25.00 60.00
17 Antonio McDyess 25.00 60.00
18 Clyde Drexler 50.00 120.00
19 Gary Payton 60.00 150.00
20 Eddie Jones 30.00 80.00

1997-98 Flair Showcase Row 3
COMPLETE SET (80) 12.00 30.00
1-20 STATED ODDS 1:0.9
21-40 STATED ODDS 1:1.1
41-60 STATED ODDS 1:1.5
61-80 STATED ODDS 1:2
1 Michael Jordan 8.00 20.00
2 Grant Hill .75 2.00
3 Allen Iverson 1.50 4.00
4 Kevin Garnett 1.25 3.00
5 Tim Duncan RC 3.00 8.00
6 Shawn Kemp .75 2.00
7 Shaquille O'Neal 1.50 4.00
8 Antoine Walker .50 1.25
9 Shareef Abdur-Rahim .50 1.25
10 Damon Stoudamire .50 1.25
11 Anfernee Hardaway 1.25 3.00
12 Keith Van Horn RC .60 1.50
13 Dennis Rodman 1.25 3.00
14 Ron Mercer RC .50 1.25
15 Stephon Marbury .60 1.50
16 Scottie Pippen 1.00 2.50
17 Kerry Kittles .40 1.00
18 Kobe Bryant 5.00 12.00
19 Marcus Camby .50 1.25
20 Chauncey Billups RC 1.25 3.00
21 Tracy McGrady RC 2.00 5.00
22 Joe Smith .40 1.00
23 Brevin Knight RC .40 1.00
24 Danny Fortson RC .40 1.00
25 Tim Thomas RC .50 1.25
26 Gary Payton .75 2.00
27 David Robinson 1.00 2.50
28 Hakeem Olajuwon 1.00 2.50
29 Antonio Daniels RC .40 1.00
30 Antonio McDyess .50 1.25
31 Eddie Jones .50 1.25
32 Adonal Foyle RC .30 .75
33 Glenn Robinson .50 1.25
34 Charles Barkley 1.25 3.00
35 Vin Baker .40 1.00
36 Jerry Stackhouse .50 1.25
37 Ray Allen 1.00 2.50
38 Derek Anderson RC .40 1.00
39 Isaac Austin .30 .75
40 Tony Battie RC .40 1.00
41 Tariq Abdul-Wahad RC .30 .75
42 Dikembe Mutombo .75 2.00
43 Clyde Drexler .75 2.00
44 Chris Mullin .60 1.50
45 Tim Hardaway .60 1.50
46 Terrell Brandon .40 1.00
47 John Stockton 1.00 2.50
48 Patrick Ewing .75 2.00

49 Horace Grant .50 1.25
50 Tom Gugliotta .40 1.00
51 Mookie Blaylock .50 1.25
52 Mitch Richmond .60 1.50
53 Anthony Mason .40 1.00
54 Michael Finley .50 1.25
55 Jason Kidd .75 2.00
56 Karl Malone 1.00 2.50
57 Reggie Miller 1.00 2.50
58 Steve Smith .40 1.00
59 Glen Rice .50 1.25
60 Bryant Stith .30 .75
61 Loy Vaught .40 1.00
62 Brian Grant .40 1.00
63 Joe Dumars .60 1.50
64 Juwan Howard .40 1.00
65 Rik Smits .40 1.00
66 Alonzo Mourning .75 2.00
67 Allan Houston .50 1.25
68 Chris Webber .60 1.50
69 Kendall Gill .40 1.00
70 Rony Seikaly .40 1.00
71 Kenny Anderson .40 1.00
72 John Wallace .30 .75
73 Bryant Reeves .30 .75
74 Brian Williams .40 1.00
75 Larry Johnson .60 1.50
76 Shawn Bradley .30 .75
77 Kevin Johnson .50 1.25
78 Rod Strickland .40 1.00
79 Rodney Rogers .40 1.00
80 Rasheed Wallace .60 1.50
NNO Grant Hill PROMO 3.00 8.00

1997-98 Flair Showcase Row 2

COMPLETE SET (80) 25.00 60.00
*STARS/RCs: .5X TO 1.25X ROW 3
1-20 STATED ODDS 1:3
21-40 STATED ODDS 1:2.5
41-60 STATED ODDS 1:4
61-80 STATED ODDS 1:3.5

1997-98 Flair Showcase Row 1

COMPLETE SET (80) 80.00 200.00
*STARS/RCs 1-20: 1.25X TO 3X ROW 3
1-20 STATED ODDS 1:16
*STARS/RCs 21-40: 1.5X TO 4X ROW 3
21-40 STATED ODDS 1:24
*STARS/RCs 41-60: .75X TO 2X ROW 3
41-60 STATED ODDS 1:6
*STARS 61-80: 1X TO 2.5X ROW 3
61-80 STATED ODDS 1:10
1 Michael Jordan 60.00 150.00

1997-98 Flair Showcase Row 0

*STARS 1-20: 8X TO 20X ROW 3
*RCs 1-20: 5X TO 12X ROW 3
STATED PRINT RUN 250 SERIAL #'d SETS
*STARS 21-40: 5X TO 12X ROW 3
*RCs 21-40: 4X TO 10X ROW 3
STATED PRINT RUN 500 SERIAL #'d SETS
*STARS 41-60: 4X TO 10X ROW 3
*RCs 41-60: 3X TO 8X ROW 3
STATED PRINT RUN 1000 SERIAL #'d SETS
*STARS 61-80: 2X TO 5X ROW 3
STATED PRINT RUN 2000 SERIAL #'d SETS
1 Michael Jordan 600.00 1,200.00
4 Kevin Garnett 25.00 60.00
5 Tim Duncan 150.00 300.00
11 Anfernee Hardaway 60.00 150.00
13 Dennis Rodman 30.00 80.00
18 Kobe Bryant 500.00 1,000.00

1997-98 Flair Showcase Legacy Collection Row 3

*STARS: 15X TO 40X BASE CARD HI
*RCs: 8X TO 20X BASE HI
STATED PRINT RUN 100 SERIAL #'d SETS
LEGACY: ALL ROWS SAME VALUE
1 Michael Jordan 1,500.00 2,300.00
3 Allen Iverson 150.00 300.00
5 Tim Duncan 300.00 600.00
7 Shaquille O'Neal 125.00 300.00
11 Anfernee Hardaway 100.00 250.00
16 Scottie Pippen 40.00 100.00
18 Kobe Bryant 1,000.00 2,000.00
21 Tracy McGrady 60.00 150.00
26 Gary Payton 25.00 60.00
47 John Stockton 40.00 100.00
57 Reggie Miller 30.00 80.00
66 Alonzo Mourning 40.00 100.00
68 Chris Webber 50.00 120.00

1997-98 Flair Showcase Wave of the Future

COMPLETE SET (12) 10.00 20.00
STATED ODDS 1:20
1 Corey Beck 1.25 3.00
2 Maurice Taylor 1.00 2.50
3 Chris Anstey .75 2.00
4 Keith Booth 1.00 2.50
5 Anthony Parker 1.25 3.00
6 Austin Croshere 1.00 2.50
7 Jacque Vaughn 1.00 2.50
8 God Shammgod 1.25 3.00
9 Bobby Jackson 1.50 4.00
10 Johnny Taylor .75 2.00
11 Ed Gray 1.25 3.00
12 Kelvin Cato 1.00 2.50

1998-99 Flair Showcase Row 3

COMPLETE SET (90) 20.00 50.00
1-30 STATED ODDS 1:0.8
31-60 STATED ODDS 1:1
61-90 STATED ODDS 1:1.2
1 Keith Van Horn .25 .60
1A K.Van Horn PROMO .40 1.00
2 Kobe Bryant 2.00 5.00
3 Tim Duncan .60 1.50
4 Kevin Garnett .60 1.50
5 Grant Hill .40 1.00
6 Allen Iverson .60 1.50
7 Shaquille O'Neal 1.00 2.50
8 Antoine Walker .25 .60
9 Shareef Abdur-Rahim .25 .60
10 Stephon Marbury .30 .75
11 Ray Allen .40 1.00
12 Shawn Kemp .40 1.00
13 Tim Thomas .20 .50
14 Scottie Pippen .60 1.50
15 Latrell Sprewell .30 .75
16 Dirk Nowitzki RC 3.00 8.00
17 Antawn Jamison RC .75 2.00
18 Anfernee Hardaway .60 1.50
19 Larry Hughes RC .75 2.00
20 Robert Traylor RC .50 1.25
21 Kerry Kittles .20 .50
22 Ron Mercer .20 .50
23 Michael Olowokandi RC .60 1.50
24 Jason Kidd .40 1.00
25 Vince Carter RC 2.50 6.00
26 Charles Barkley .60 1.50
27 Antonio McDyess .20 .50
28 Mike Bibby RC 1.00 2.50
29 Paul Pierce RC 2.00 5.00
30 Raef LaFrentz RC .60 1.50
31 Reggie Miller .50 1.25
32 Michael Finley .25 .60
33 Eddie Jones .25 .60
34 Tim Hardaway .30 .75
35 Glenn Robinson .25 .60
36 Brevin Knight .15 .40
37 Gary Payton .40 1.00
38 David Robinson .50 1.25
39 Karl Malone .50 1.25
40 Derek Anderson .20 .50
41 Patrick Ewing .40 1.00
42 Juwan Howard .20 .50
43 Jayson Williams .15 .40
44 Terrell Brandon .20 .50
45 Hakeem Olajuwon .50 1.25
46 Isaac Austin .15 .40
47 Glen Rice .25 .60
48 Maurice Taylor .15 .40
49 Damon Stoudamire .25 .60
50 Brian Skinner RC .40 1.00
51 Nazr Mohammed RC .50 1.25
52 Tom Gugliotta .20 .50
53 Al Harrington RC .60 1.50
54 Pat Garrity RC .40 1.00
55 Jason Williams RC 1.50 4.00
56 Tracy McGrady .40 1.00
57 Keon Clark RC .50 1.25
58 Vin Baker .20 .50
59 Bonzi Wells RC .50 1.25
60 John Stockton .50 1.25
61 Isaiah Rider .20 .50
62 Alonzo Mourning .40 1.00
63 Allan Houston .25 .60
64 Dennis Rodman .60 1.50
65 Felipe Lopez RC .30 .75
66 Joe Smith .20 .50
67 Chris Webber .30 .75
68 Mitch Richmond .30 .75
69 Brent Barry .20 .50
70 Mookie Blaylock .20 .50
71 Donyell Marshall .15 .40
72 Anthony Mason .20 .50
73 Rod Strickland .20 .50
74 Roshown McLeod RC .30 .75
75 Matt Harpring RC .50 1.25
76 Detlef Schrempf .25 .60
77 Michael Dickerson RC .50 1.25
78 Michael Doleac RC .40 1.00
79 John Starks .25 .60
80 Ricky Davis RC .75 2.00
81 Steve Smith .20 .50
82 Voshon Lenard .15 .40
83 Toni Kukoc .25 .60
84 Steve Nash .50 1.25
85 Vlade Divac .25 .60
86 Rasheed Wallace .30 .75
87 Bryon Russell .15 .40
88 Antonio Daniels .15 .40
89 Rik Smits .20 .50
90 Joe Dumars .25 .60

1998-99 Flair Showcase Row 2

COMPLETE SET (90) 60.00 120.00
*STARS: 1X TO 2.5X ROW 3
*RCs: .5X TO 1.25X ROW 3
1-30: STATED ODDS 1:3
31-60: STATED ODDS 1:1.3
61-90: STATED ODDS 1:2
1A K.Van Horn Promo .75 2.00

1998-99 Flair Showcase Row 1

*1-30 STARS: 3X TO 8X ROW 3
*1-30 RCs: 2X TO 5X ROW 3
1-30: PRINT RUN 1500 SERIAL #'d SETS
*31-60 STARS: 2.5X TO 6X ROW 3
*31-60 RCs: 1.5X TO 4X ROW 3
31-60: PRINT RUN 3000 SERIAL #'d SETS
*61-90 STARS: 1.5X TO 4X ROW 3
*61-90 RCs: .75X TO 2X ROW 3
61-90: STATED ODDS 1:6
61-90: PRINT RUN 6000 SERIAL #'d SETS
1A Keith Van Horn Promo 1.25 3.00

1998-99 Flair Showcase Legacy Collection Row 3

*STARS: 25X TO 60X VALUE
*RCs: 8X TO 20X VALUE
STATED PRINT RUN 99 SERIAL #'d SETS
LEGACY: ALL ROWS EQUAL VALUE
2 Kobe Bryant 1,000.00 2,000.00
3 Tim Duncan 100.00 250.00
4 Kevin Garnett 40.00 100.00
5 Grant Hill 30.00 80.00
16 Dirk Nowitzki 125.00 300.00
18 Anfernee Hardaway 75.00 200.00
25 Vince Carter 75.00 200.00
26 Charles Barkley 60.00 150.00
29 Paul Pierce 60.00 150.00
37 Gary Payton 30.00 80.00
38 David Robinson 40.00 100.00
55 Jason Williams 60.00 150.00
56 Tracy McGrady 30.00 80.00
64 Dennis Rodman 125.00 300.00
67 Chris Webber 30.00 80.00

1998-99 Flair Showcase Legacy Collection Row 2

*STARS: 25X TO 60X HI
*RCs: 8X TO 25X HI
2 Kobe Bryant 1,000.00 2,000.00
6 Allen Iverson 75.00 200.00
7 Shaquille O'Neal 75.00 200.00
16 Dirk Nowitzki 125.00 300.00
18 Anfernee Hardaway 75.00 200.00
29 Paul Pierce 60.00 150.00
37 Gary Payton 30.00 80.00
38 David Robinson 40.00 100.00
55 Jason Williams 60.00 150.00
56 Tracy McGrady 30.00 80.00
84 Steve Nash 40.00 100.00

1998-99 Flair Showcase Legacy Collection Row 1

*STARS: 25X TO 60X HI
*RCs: 8X TO 20X HI
2 Kobe Bryant 1,000.00 2,000.00
6 Allen Iverson 75.00 200.00
7 Shaquille O'Neal 75.00 200.00
16 Dirk Nowitzki 125.00 300.00
18 Anfernee Hardaway 75.00 200.00
26 Charles Barkley 60.00 150.00
29 Paul Pierce 60.00 150.00
37 Gary Payton 30.00 80.00
38 David Robinson 40.00 100.00
55 Jason Williams 60.00 150.00
56 Tracy McGrady 30.00 80.00
64 Dennis Rodman 125.00 300.00
84 Steve Nash 40.00 100.00

1998-99 Flair Showcase Class of '98

COMPLETE SET (15) 100.00 250.00
STATED PRINT RUN 500 SERIAL #'d SETS
1 Michael Olowokandi 2.50 6.00
2 Mike Bibby 4.00 10.00
3 Raef LaFrentz 2.50 6.00
4 Antawn Jamison 3.00 8.00
5 Vince Carter 30.00 80.00
6 Robert Traylor 2.00 5.00
7 Jason Williams 25.00 60.00
8 Larry Hughes 3.00 8.00
9 Dirk Nowitzki 60.00 150.00
10 Paul Pierce 25.00 60.00
11 Bonzi Wells 2.00 5.00
12 Michael Doleac 1.50 4.00
13 Michael Dickerson 2.00 5.00
14 Pat Garrity 1.50 4.00
15 Al Harrington 2.50 6.00

1998-99 Flair Showcase takeit2.net

STATED PRINT RUN 1000 SERIAL #'d SETS
1 Scottie Pippen 150.00 400.00
2 Tim Duncan 150.00 400.00
3 Keith Van Horn 15.00 40.00
4 Grant Hill 40.00 100.00
5 Kobe Bryant 1,500.00 3,000.00
6 Antoine Walker 12.00 30.00
7 Kevin Garnett 150.00 400.00
8 Allen Iverson 150.00 400.00
9 Shareef Abdur-Rahim 40.00 100.00
10 Anfernee Hardaway 150.00 400.00
11 Stephon Marbury 40.00 100.00
12 Ron Mercer 25.00 60.00
13 Michael Jordan 3,000.00 6,000.00
14 Shaquille O'Neal 200.00 500.00
15 Shawn Kemp 75.00 200.00

1999-00 Flair Showcase

COMPLETE SET (130) 75.00 150.00
COMPLETE SET w/o RC (100) 20.00 50.00
101-130 PRINT RUN 2000 SERIAL #'d SETS
1 Vince Carter 1.00 2.50
2 Anfernee Hardaway 1.00 2.50
3 Nick Van Exel .30 .75
4 Kerry Kittles .30 .75
5 Michael Doleac .25 .60
6 Sean Elliott .30 .75
7 Shaquille O'Neal 1.50 4.00
8 Avery Johnson .30 .75
9 Brian Grant .25 .60
10 Jerome Williams .25 .60
11 Larry Hughes .40 1.00
12 Jerry Stackhouse .40 1.00
13 Alonzo Mourning .60 1.50
14 Antonio McDyess .30 .75
15 Jason Kidd .60 1.50
16 Bryon Russell .25 .60
17 Hakeem Olajuwon .75 2.00
18 Juwan Howard .30 .75
19 Paul Pierce .75 2.00
20 Vin Baker .30 .75
21 Larry Johnson .40 1.00
22 Gary Trent .25 .60
23 Jayson Williams .25 .60
24 Tim Hardaway .50 1.25
25 Dirk Nowitzki 1.25 3.00
26 Jamal Mashburn .30 .75
27 Glenn Robinson .30 .75
28 Shawn Bradley .25 .60
29 Tom Gugliotta .30 .75
30 Vlade Divac .40 1.00
31 David Robinson .75 2.00
32 Matt Geiger .25 .60
33 Grant Hill .60 1.50
34 Maurice Taylor .25 .60
35 Toni Kukoc .50 1.25
36 Cedric Ceballos .25 .60
37 Patrick Ewing .50 1.25
38 Ray Allen .60 1.50
39 Michael Finley .40 1.00
40 Robert Traylor .25 .60
41 Brevin Knight .25 .60
42 Marcus Camby .30 .75
43 Sam Cassell .30 .75
44 Antawn Jamison .40 1.00
45 Steve Smith .30 .75
46 Darrell Armstrong .25 .60
47 Mookie Blaylock .25 .60
48 Derek Anderson .25 .60
49 Hersey Hawkins .25 .60
50 Kobe Bryant 3.00 8.00
51 Shawn Kemp .60 1.50
52 Scottie Pippen 1.00 2.50
53 Chris Webber .50 1.25
54 Damon Stoudamire .40 1.00
55 Donyell Marshall .30 .75
56 Isaiah Rider .30 .75
57 Karl Malone .75 2.00
58 Kevin Garnett 1.00 2.50
59 Mario Elie .25 .60
60 Michael Dickerson .25 .60
61 Jahidi White .25 .60
62 Joe Smith .30 .75
63 Kenny Anderson .30 .75
64 Reggie Miller .75 2.00
65 Ruben Patterson .25 .60
66 Shareef Abdur-Rahim .40 1.00
67 Allen Iverson 1.00 2.50
68 Glen Rice .40 1.00
69 Nick Anderson .25 .60
70 Rex Chapman .25 .60
71 Ron Mercer .30 .75
72 Tim Duncan 1.00 2.50
73 Al Harrington .40 1.00
74 Brent Barry .30 .75
75 Eddie Jones .40 1.00
76 Mike Bibby .40 1.00
77 Anthony Mason .40 1.00
78 Michael Olowokandi .25 .60
79 Matt Harpring .25 .60
80 Stephon Marbury .50 1.25
81 Tracy McGrady .60 1.50
82 Allan Houston .30 .75
83 Lindsey Hunter .25 .60
84 Tariq Abdul-Wahad .25 .60
85 Antoine Walker .40 1.00
86 Charles Barkley 1.00 2.50
87 Gary Payton .60 1.50
88 John Stockton .60 1.50
89 Mitch Richmond .50 1.25
90 Terrell Brandon .25 .60
91 Charles Oakley .40 1.00
92 Bryant Reeves .25 .60
93 Dikembe Mutombo .60 1.50
94 Elden Campbell .25 .60
95 Jalen Rose .30 .75
96 Jason Williams .60 1.50
97 Keith Van Horn .30 .75
98 Latrell Sprewell .50 1.25
99 Raef LaFrentz .30 .75
100 Rasheed Wallace .50 1.25
101 Cal Bowdler RC .75 2.00
102 Dion Glover RC .75 2.00
103 Jason Terry RC 2.00 5.00
104 Adrian Griffin RC 1.00 2.50
105 Baron Davis RC 3.00 8.00
106 Michael Ruffin RC .75 2.00
107 Elton Brand RC 2.50 6.00
108 Ron Artest RC 3.00 8.00
109 Andre Miller RC 2.50 6.00
110 Trajan Langdon RC 1.00 2.50
111 James Posey RC 1.25 3.00
112 Vonteego Cummings RC .75 2.00
113 Kenny Thomas RC 1.25 3.00
114 Steve Francis RC 2.50 6.00
115 Jonathan Bender RC 1.25 3.00
116 Lamar Odom RC 2.50 6.00
117 Devean George RC 1.00 2.50
118 Tim James RC .75 2.00
119 Anthony Carter RC 1.00 2.50
120 Wally Szczerbiak RC 2.00 5.00
121 William Avery RC .75 2.00
122 Evan Eschmeyer RC 1.00 2.50
123 Corey Maggette RC 1.50 4.00
124 Jumaine Jones RC .75 2.00
125 Shawn Marion RC 2.50 6.00
126 Ryan Robertson RC .75 2.00
127 A.Radojevic RC .75 2.00
128 Quincy Lewis RC .75 2.00
129 Scott Padgett RC 1.00 2.50
130 Richard Hamilton RC 3.00 8.00
P1 Vince Carter PROMO 2.00 5.00

1999-00 Flair Showcase Legacy Collection

*STARS: 30X TO 80X BASE HI
*RCs: 4X TO 10X BASE HI
STATED PRINT RUN 20 SERIAL #'d SETS
33 Grant Hill 75.00 200.00
35 Toni Kukoc 50.00 125.00
51 Shawn Kemp 50.00 125.00
52 Scottie Pippen 100.00 200.00

1999-00 Flair Showcase Ball of Fame

COMPLETE SET (15) 15.00 40.00
STATED ODDS 1:5
BF1 Lamar Odom 2.00 5.00
BF2 Steve Francis 2.00 5.00
BF3 Elton Brand 2.00 5.00
BF4 Wally Szczerbiak 1.50 4.00
BF5 Shawn Marion 2.00 5.00
BF6 Jason Terry 1.50 4.00
BF7 Richard Hamilton 2.50 6.00
BF8 Andre Miller 2.00 5.00
BF9 Corey Maggette 1.25 3.00
BF10 Baron Davis 2.50 6.00
BF11 Vonteego Cummings .60 1.50
BF12 Kenny Thomas 1.00 2.50
BF13 Jumaine Jones .60 1.50
BF14 Trajan Langdon .75 2.00
BF15 Jonathan Bender 1.00 2.50

1999-00 Flair Showcase ConVINCEing

COMPLETE SET (10) 6.00 15.00
COMMON CARD (C1-C10) 1.25 3.00
STATED ODDS 1:10

1999-00 Flair Showcase Elevators

COMPLETE SET (10) 10.00 25.00
STATED ODDS 1:20
E1 Vince Carter 2.00 5.00
E2 Lamar Odom 1.50 4.00
E3 Allen Iverson 2.00 5.00
E4 Kobe Bryant 5.00 12.00
E5 Grant Hill 1.25 3.00
E6 Eddie Jones .75 2.00
E7 Scottie Pippen 2.00 5.00
E8 Kevin Garnett 2.00 5.00
E9 Steve Francis 1.50 4.00
E10 Keith Van Horn .60 1.50

1999-00 Flair Showcase Feel the Game

STATED ODDS 1:120
1 William Avery 1.25 3.00
2 Vince Carter 12.00 30.00
3 Vonteego Cummings 1.25 3.00
4 Patrick Ewing 6.00 15.00
5 Brian Grant 3.00 8.00
6 Karl Malone 10.00 25.00
7 Shawn Marion 4.00 10.00
8 Alonzo Mourning 8.00 20.00
9 Lamar Odom 4.00 10.00
10 Shaquille O'Neal 20.00 50.00
11 Paul Pierce 10.00 25.00
12 David Robinson 10.00 25.00
13 Damon Stoudamire 5.00 12.00
14 Kenny Thomas 2.00 5.00
15 Antoine Walker 5.00 12.00

1999-00 Flair Showcase Fresh Ink

STATED ODDS 1:39
1 Tariq Abdul-Wahad 3.00 8.00
2 Ron Artest 6.00 15.00
3 William Avery 2.00 5.00
4 Tony Battie 2.00 5.00
5 Cal Bowdler 2.00 5.00
6 Vince Carter 15.00 40.00
7 Dion Glover 2.00 5.00
8 Chris Herren 2.50 6.00
9 Juwan Howard 4.00 10.00
10 Eddie Jones 5.00 12.00
11 Jumaine Jones 2.00 5.00
12 Brevin Knight 2.00 5.00
13 Toni Kukoc 6.00 15.00
14 Trajan Langdon 2.50 6.00
15 Quincy Lewis 2.00 5.00
16 Corey Maggette 4.00 10.00
17 Stephon Marbury 8.00 20.00
18 Tracy McGrady 15.00 30.00
19 Ron Mercer 2.50 6.00
20 Andre Miller 6.00 15.00
21 Lamar Odom 6.00 15.00
22 Hakeem Olajuwon 12.00 30.00
23 Scott Padgett 2.50 6.00
24 Scottie Pippen 75.00 200.00
25 James Posey 3.00 8.00
26 Aleksandar Radojevic 2.00 5.00
27 Glen Rice 10.00 25.00
28 Wally Szczerbiak 5.00 12.00
29 Jason Terry 4.00 10.00
30 Kenny Thomas 3.00 8.00
31 Jerome Williams 2.00 5.00

1999-00 Flair Showcase Fresh Ink Rock Steady

STATED PRINT RUN 25 SERIAL #'d SETS
1 Vince Carter 80.00 200.00
2 Chris Herren 10.00 25.00
3 Ron Mercer 6.00 15.00
4 Lamar Odom 60.00 150.00
5 Scottie Pippen 200.00 400.00
6 Aleksandar Radojevic 8.00 20.00
7 Kenny Thomas 12.00 30.00

1999-00 Flair Showcase Guaranteed Fresh

COMPLETE SET (10) 6.00 15.00
STATED ODDS 1:10
GF1 Vince Carter 1.25 3.00
GF2 Shaquille O'Neal 2.00 5.00
GF3 Kevin Garnett 1.25 3.00
GF4 Kobe Bryant 4.00 10.00
GF5 Paul Pierce 1.00 2.50
GF6 Jason Williams .75 2.00
GF7 Stephon Marbury .60 1.50
GF8 Lamar Odom 1.00 2.50
GF9 Keith Van Horn .40 1.00
GF10 Wally Szczerbiak .75 2.00

1999-00 Flair Showcase License to Skill

COMPLETE SET (10) 8.00 20.00
STATED ODDS 1:20
LS1 Vince Carter 2.00 5.00
LS2 Shaquille O'Neal 3.00 8.00
LS3 Tim Duncan 2.00 5.00
LS4 Keith Van Horn .60 1.50
LS5 Grant Hill 1.25 3.00
LS6 Allen Iverson 2.00 5.00
LS7 Antoine Walker .75 2.00
LS8 Scottie Pippen 2.00 5.00
LS9 Kobe Bryant 4.00 10.00
LS10 Lamar Odom 1.50 4.00

1999-00 Flair Showcase Next

COMPLETE SET (20) 6.00 15.00
STATED ODDS 1:2.5
N1 Vince Carter .75 2.00
N2 James Posey .30 .75
N3 Jonathan Bender .30 .75
N4 Corey Maggette .40 1.00
N5 Devean George .25 .60
N6 Trajan Langdon .25 .60
N7 Shawn Marion .60 1.50
N8 William Avery .20 .50
N9 Adrian Griffin .25 .60
N10 Quincy Lewis .20 .50
N11 Kenny Thomas .30 .75
N12 Lamar Odom .60 1.50
N13 Dion Glover .20 .50
N14 Elton Brand .60 1.50
N15 Andre Miller .60 1.50
N16 Jason Terry .50 1.25
N17 Richard Hamilton .75 2.00
N18 Steve Francis .60 1.50
N19 Baron Davis .75 2.00
N20 Wally Szczerbiak .50 1.25

1999-00 Flair Showcase Rookie Showcase Firsts

COMPLETE SET (30) 75.00 150.00
*RC FIRSTS: .75X TO 2X BASE HI
STATED PRINT RUN 500 SERIAL #'d SETS

2001-02 Flair

COMP.SET w/o SP's (90) 12.50 30.00
91-120 PRINT RUN 1500 SERIAL #'d SETS
1 Tracy McGrady .60 1.50
2 Derek Fisher .30 .75
3 Allen Iverson 1.00 2.50
4 Chris Webber .50 1.25
5 Jalen Rose .30 .75
6 Kenyon Martin .40 1.00
7 Jermaine O'Neal .30 .75
8 Kobe Bryant 3.00 8.00
9 Bryon Russell .25 .60
10 Wally Szczerbiak .30 .75
11 Damon Stoudamire .40 1.00
12 John Stockton .75 2.00
13 Glenn Robinson .40 1.00
14 Steve Francis .40 1.00
15 Vince Carter .75 2.00
16 Peja Stojakovic .30 .75
17 Rick Fox .30 .75
18 Allan Houston .40 1.00
19 Danny Fortson .25 .60
20 Gary Payton .60 1.50
21 Darius Miles .25 .60
22 Kevin Garnett 1.00 2.50
23 Marcus Camby .30 .75
24 Desmond Mason .30 .75
25 Tim Duncan 1.00 2.50
26 Jamal Mashburn .30 .75
27 Andre Miller .30 .75
28 Antonio McDyess .30 .75
29 Morris Peterson .30 .75
30 Rasheed Wallace .50 1.25
31 Shawn Marion .40 1.00
32 Karl Malone .75 2.00
33 Grant Hill .60 1.50
34 Shaquille O'Neal 1.50 4.00
35 Hakeem Olajuwon .75 2.00
36 Corliss Williamson .25 .60
37 Paul Pierce .60 1.50
38 Antonio Davis .30 .75
39 Antonio Daniels .25 .60
40 Ray Allen .60 1.50
41 Dirk Nowitzki 1.00 2.50
42 Jerry Stackhouse .40 1.00
43 Donyell Marshall .25 .60
44 Brian Grant .25 .60
45 Raef LaFrentz .25 .60
46 Corey Maggette .30 .75
47 Mike Miller .30 .75
48 Jason Williams .60 1.50
49 Jahidi White .25 .60
50 David Robinson .75 2.00
51 Shareef Abdur-Rahim .30 .75
52 Anfernee Hardaway 1.00 2.50
53 Baron Davis .40 1.00
54 DerMarr Johnson .25 .60
55 Dikembe Mutombo .60 1.50
56 David Wesley .25 .60
57 Chris Mihm .25 .60
58 Michael Finley .40 1.00
59 Eddie House .25 .60
60 Stromile Swift .25 .60
61 Courtney Alexander .25 .60
62 Ron Mercer .25 .60
63 Cuttino Mobley .30 .75
64 Tim Thomas .25 .60
65 Eddie Jones .40 1.00
66 Lamar Odom .30 .75
67 Terrell Brandon .30 .75
68 Rashard Lewis .30 .75
69 Antoine Walker .30 .75
70 Latrell Sprewell .50 1.25
71 Sam Cassell .30 .75
72 Mike Bibby .40 1.00
73 Speedy Claxton .25 .60
74 Steve Nash .75 2.00
75 Mark Jackson .30 .75
76 Ron Artest .30 .75
77 Matt Harpring .25 .60
78 Wang Zhizhi .40 1.00
79 Nazr Mohammed .25 .60
80 Jason Terry .40 1.00
81 Nick Van Exel .40 1.00
82 Reggie Miller .75 2.00
83 Joe Smith .30 .75
84 Jason Kidd .60 1.50
85 Richard Hamilton .50 1.25
86 Antawn Jamison .30 .75
87 Alonzo Mourning .60 1.50
88 Stephon Marbury .50 1.25
89 Scottie Pippen 1.00 2.50
90 Elton Brand .30 .75
91 Kwame Brown RC 1.25 3.00
92 Eddie Griffin RC 1.00 2.50
93 Tyson Chandler RC 2.00 5.00
94 Omar Cook RC 1.25 3.00
95 Loren Woods RC .75 2.00
96 Alton Ford RC 1.25 3.00
97 Shane Battier RC 2.50 6.00
98 Joe Johnson RC 2.00 5.00
99 Rodney White RC .75 2.00
100 Pau Gasol RC 5.00 12.00
101 Zach Randolph RC 2.50 6.00
102 Vladimir Radmanovic RC 1.00 2.50
103 Brendan Haywood RC 1.00 2.50
104 Michael Bradley RC .75 2.00
105 Tony Parker RC 6.00 15.00
106 Jason Richardson RC 2.00 5.00
107 Gerald Wallace RC 1.50 4.00
108 Damone Brown RC .75 2.00
109 Richard Jefferson RC 1.50 4.00
110 Eddy Curry RC 1.25 3.00
111 DeSagana Diop RC .75 2.00
112 Brandon Armstrong RC .75 2.00
113 Troy Murphy RC 1.00 2.50
114 Kedrick Brown RC .75 2.00
115 Kirk Haston RC .75 2.00
116 Gilbert Arenas RC 3.00 8.00
117 Jeryl Sasser RC .75 2.00
118 Jamaal Tinsley RC 1.00 2.50
119 Terence Morris RC .75 2.00
120 Michael Wright RC 1.25 3.00
121 Michael Jordan 6.00 15.00

2001-02 Flair Courting Greatness

COMPLETE SET (20) 50.00 120.00
STATED ODDS 1:23 PACKS
1 Vince Carter 6.00 15.00
2 Dirk Nowitzki 8.00 20.00
3 Allen Iverson 8.00 20.00
4 Tracy McGrady 5.00 12.00
5 Karl Malone 6.00 15.00
6 Antawn Jamison 2.50 6.00
7 Peja Stojakovic 2.50 6.00
8 Eddie Jones 3.00 8.00
9 Jason Williams 5.00 12.00
10 Hakeem Olajuwon 6.00 15.00
11 Antoine Walker 2.50 6.00
12 Jerry Stackhouse 3.00 8.00
13 Chris Webber 4.00 10.00
14 Latrell Sprewell 4.00 10.
15 David Robinson 6.00 15.
16 Stephon Marbury 4.00 10.
17 Grant Hill 5.00 12.
18 Shareef Abdur-Rahim 2.50 6.
19 Jason Kidd 5.00 12.
20 Scottie Pippen 8.00 20.

2001-02 Flair Courting Greatness Ball and Court

PRINT RUN 250 SERIAL #'d SETS
1 Vince Carter 8.00 20.
2 Dirk Nowitzki 10.00 25.
3 Allen Iverson 10.00 25.
4 Tracy McGrady 6.00 15.
5 Karl Malone 8.00 20.
6 Antawn Jamison 3.00 8.
7 Peja Stojakovic 3.00 8.
8 Eddie Jones 4.00 10.
9 Jason Williams 6.00 15.
10 Hakeem Olajuwon 8.00 20.
11 Antoine Walker 3.00 8.
12 Jerry Stackhouse 4.00 10.
13 Chris Webber 5.00 12.
14 Latrell Sprewell 5.00 12.
15 David Robinson 8.00 20.
16 Stephon Marbury 5.00 12.
17 Grant Hill 6.00 15.
18 Shareef Abdur-Rahim 3.00 8.
19 Jason Kidd 6.00 15.
20 Scottie Pippen 10.00 25.

2001-02 Flair Hot Numbers

PRINT RUN 100 SERIAL #'d SETS
1 Darius Miles 5.00 12.00
2 Mike Miller 6.00 15.00
3 Tracy McGrady 12.00 30.00
4 Ray Allen 12.00 30.00
5 Baron Davis 8.00 20.00
6 Dikembe Mutombo 12.00 30.00
7 Kenyon Martin 8.00 20.00
8 Steve Francis 8.00 20.00
9 Patrick Ewing 12.00 30.00
10 Jason Kidd 12.00 30.00
11 Jerome Moiso 5.00 12.00
12 Richard Hamilton 10.00 25.00
13 Vince Carter 15.00 40.00
14 John Stockton 15.00 40.00
15 Mike Bibby 8.00 20.00
16 Reggie Miller 10.00 25.00
17 Jason Terry 8.00 20.00
18 Stephon Marbury 10.00 25.00
19 Chris Webber 10.00 25.00
20 Mitch Richmond 10.00 25.00

2001-02 Flair Jersey Heights

STATED ODDS 1:22
1 Darius Miles 2.50 6.00
2 Mike Miller 3.00 8.00
3 Tracy McGrady 6.00 15.00
4 Ray Allen 6.00 15.00
5 Baron Davis 4.00 10.00
6 Dikembe Mutombo 6.00 15.00
7 Kenyon Martin 4.00 10.00
8 Steve Francis 4.00 10.00
9 Patrick Ewing 6.00 15.00
10 Jason Kidd 6.00 15.00
11 Jerome Moiso 2.50 6.00
12 Richard Hamilton 5.00 12.00
13 Vince Carter 8.00 20.00
14 John Stockton 8.00 20.00
15 Mike Bibby 4.00 10.00
16 Reggie Miller 8.00 20.00
17 Jason Terry 4.00 10.00
18 Stephon Marbury 5.00 12.00
19 Chris Webber 5.00 12.00
20 Mitch Richmond 5.00 12.00

2001-02 Flair Sweet Shots

JSY PRINT RUN 250 SERIAL #'d SETS
AU PRINT RUNS LISTED BELOW
STATED ODDS 1 PER BOX
1 Ray Allen JSY 8.00 20.00
2 Vince Carter JSY 10.00 25.00
3 Baron Davis JSY 5.00 12.00
4 Michael Dickerson JSY 3.00 8.00
5 Steve Francis JSY 5.00 12.00
6 Marc Jackson JSY 3.00 8.00
7 Antawn Jamison JSY 4.00 10.00
8 Rashard Lewis JSY 4.00 10.00
9 Karl Malone JSY 10.00 25.00
10 Shawn Marion JSY 5.00 12.00
11 Kenyon Martin JSY 5.00 12.00
12 Antonio McDyess JSY 4.00 10.00
13 Tracy McGrady JSY 8.00 20.00
14 Darius Miles JSY 3.00 8.00
15 Mike Miller JSY 4.00 10.00
16 Lamar Odom JSY 4.00 10.00
17 Gary Payton JSY 8.00 20.00
18 Morris Peterson JSY 3.00 8.00
19 David Robinson JSY 10.00 25.00
20 John Stockton JSY 10.00 25.00
21 Peja Stojakovic JSY 4.00 10.00
22 Jason Terry JSY 5.00 12.00
23 Antoine Walker JSY 4.00 10.00
24 Chris Webber JSY 6.00 15.00
25 Allen Iverson JSY 12.00 30.00
26 Kwame Brown AU/297 4.00 10.00
27 Eddy Curry AU/368 4.00 10.00
28 Michael Bradley AU/433 2.50 6.00
29 Brendan Haywood AU/345 3.00 8.00
30 Jason Collins AU/390 12.00 30.00
31 Richard Jefferson AU/330 5.00 12.00
32 Kedrick Brown AU/342 2.50 6.00
33 Vince Carter AU/245 20.00 50.00

2001-02 Flair Warming Up

STATED ODDS 1:27
1 Jason Terry 3.00 8.00
2 Shareef Abdur-Rahim 2.50 6.00
3 Antoine Walker 2.50 6.00
4 Paul Pierce 5.00 12.00
5 Andre Miller 2.50 6.00
6 Steve Francis 3.00 8.00
7 Lamar Odom 2.50 6.00
8 Corey Maggette 2.50 6.00
9 Kenyon Martin 3.00 8.00
10 Grant Hill 5.00 12.00
11 Allen Iverson 8.00 20.00

12 Dikembe Mutombo 5.00 12.00
13 Stephon Marbury 4.00 10.00
14 Mike Bibby 3.00 8.00
15 Morris Peterson 2.00 5.00
16 Vince Carter 6.00 15.00
17 Karl Malone 6.00 15.00
18 John Stockton 6.00 15.00
19 Keith Van Horn 2.50 6.00
20 DerMarr Johnson 2.00 5.00

2001-02 Flair Warming Up Dual

STATED ODDS 1:80
1 J.Terry/S.Abdur-Rahim 5.00 12.00
2 A.Walker/P.Pierce 8.00 20.00
3 A.Miller/S.Francis 5.00 12.00
4 L.Odom/C.Maggette 5.00 12.00
5 K.Martin/K.Van Horn 5.00 12.00
6 A.Iverson/D.Mutombo 8.00 20.00
7 S.Marbury/M.Bibby 5.00 12.00
8 M.Peterson/V.Carter 8.00 20.00
9 K.Malone/J.Stockton 15.00 40.00
10 G.Hill/D.Johnson 6.00 15.00

2002-03 Flair

COMP.SET w/o SP's (90) 25.00 50.00
91-120 PRINT RUN 1750 SER.#'d SETS
1 Tracy McGrady .60 1.50
2 Jamal Mashburn .30 .75
3 Allen Iverson 1.00 2.50
4 Alonzo Mourning .60 1.50
5 Joe Smith .30 .75
6 Wang Zhizhi .40 1.00
7 Karl Malone .75 2.00
8 Keith Van Horn .30 .75
9 Joseph Forte .25 .60
10 Peja Stojakovic .30 .75
11 Juwan Howard .30 .75
12 Brian Grant .25 .60
13 Glenn Robinson .40 1.00
14 Antonio McDyess .30 .75
15 Vince Carter .75 2.00
16 Pau Gasol .60 1.50
17 Bonzi Wells .25 .60
18 Chucky Atkins .25 .60
19 Shane Battier .40 1.00
20 Steve Francis .40 1.00
21 Kevin Garnett 1.00 2.50
22 Antawn Jamison .30 .75
23 Hedo Turkoglu .30 .75
24 Kenyon Martin .40 1.00
25 Cuttino Mobley .25 .60
26 Steve Nash .75 2.00
27 Morris Peterson .30 .75
28 Jason Richardson .40 1.00
29 Antoine Walker .30 .75
30 Rasheed Wallace .50 1.25
31 Tim Duncan 1.00 2.50
32 Paul Pierce .60 1.50
33 Ben Wallace .50 1.25
34 Jason Kidd .60 1.50
35 Gary Payton .60 1.50
36 Mike Miller .30 .75
37 Kobe Bryant 3.00 8.00
38 Baron Davis .40 1.00
39 Steve Smith .30 .75
40 Reggie Miller .75 2.00
41 Dirk Nowitzki 1.00 2.50
42 Rashard Lewis .30 .75
43 Andre Miller .30 .75
44 David Wesley .25 .60
45 Ray Allen .60 1.50
46 Tyson Chandler .40 1.00
47 Jamaal Tinsley .25 .60
48 Grant Hill .60 1.50
49 Richard Jefferson .30 .75
50 Latrell Sprewell .40 1.00
51 Jason Terry .30 .75
52 Alvin Williams .25 .60
53 Vin Baker .30 .75
54 Robert Horry .40 1.00
55 Eddie Jones .40 1.00
56 Andrei Kirilenko .30 .75
57 Darius Miles .25 .60
58 Kedrick Brown .25 .60
59 Jermaine O'Neal .30 .75
60 David Robinson .75 2.00
61 Jason Williams .50 1.25
62 Wally Szczerbiak .30 .75
63 Mike Bibby .40 1.00
64 Shawn Marion .40 1.00
65 Shaquille O'Neal 1.50 4.00
66 Michael Redd .30 .75
67 Chris Webber .50 1.25
68 Quentin Richardson .25 .60
69 Michael Jordan 4.00 10.00
70 Jamaal Magloire .25 .60
71 Radoslav Nesterovic .25 .60
72 Eddy Curry .25 .60
73 Michael Finley .40 1.00
74 Eddie Griffin .25 .60
75 Aaron McKie .25 .60
76 Tony Parker .60 1.50
77 Shareef Abdur-Rahim .40 1.00
78 Jalen Rose .30 .75
79 Jerry Stackhouse .40 1.00
80 Jumaine Jones .25 .60
81 Toni Kukoc .40 1.00
82 Vladimir Radmanovic .25 .60
83 Zach Randolph .30 .75
84 John Stockton .75 2.00
85 Mengke Bateer .40 1.00
86 Dikembe Mutombo .60 1.50
87 Elton Brand .30 .75
88 Allan Houston .40 1.00
89 Joe Johnson .30 .75
90 Kwame Brown .25 .60
91 Yao Ming RC 10.00 25.00
92 Jay Williams RC 1.50 4.00
93 Mike Dunleavy RC 2.00 5.00
94 Drew Gooden RC 2.00 5.00
95 DaJuan Wagner RC 1.50 4.00
96 Caron Butler RC 2.50 6.00
97 Jared Jeffries RC 1.50 4.00
98 Nene Hilario RC 2.00 5.00
99 Chris Wilcox RC 1.50 4.00
100 Nikoloz Tskitishvili RC 1.25 3.00
101 Kareem Rush RC 1.50 4.00
102 Curtis Borchardt RC 1.25 3.00
103 Qyntel Woods RC 1.25 3.00
104 Melvin Ely RC 1.50 4.00
105 Marcus Haislip RC 1.25 3.00
106 Carlos Boozer RC 2.00 5.00
107 Bostjan Nachbar RC 1.50 4.00
108 Amare Stoudemire RC 5.00 12.00
109 Frank Williams RC 1.25 3.00
110 Jiri Welsch RC 1.50 4.00
111 Fred Jones RC 1.50 4.00
112 Juan Dixon RC 1.50 4.00
113 Ryan Humphrey RC 1.50 4.00
114 Casey Jacobsen RC 1.50 4.00
115 Tayshaun Prince RC 4.00 10.00
116 Dan Dickau RC 1.25 3.00
117 Chris Jefferies RC 1.25 3.00
118 John Salmons RC 2.00 5.00
119 Manu Ginobili RC 10.00 25.00
120 Gordan Giricek RC 2.00 5.00

2002-03 Flair Row 1

*ROW 1 STARS: 4X TO 10X BASE CARD HI
*ROW 1 RCs: .75X TO 2X BASE CARD HI
PRINT RUN 150 SERIAL #'d SETS

2002-03 Flair Row 2

*ROW 2 STARS: 12X TO 30X BASE HI
*ROW 2 RCs: 3X TO 8X BASE HI
PRINT RUN 25 SERIAL #'d SETS
69 Michael Jordan 125.00 300.00

2002-03 Flair Court Kings

COMPLETE SET (25) 12.00 30.00
STATED ODDS 1:4
1 Kobe Bryant 4.00 10.00
2 Jerry Stackhouse .50 1.25
3 Steve Francis .50 1.25
4 Ray Allen .75 2.00
5 Kevin Garnett 1.25 3.00
6 Elton Brand .40 1.00
7 Jason Kidd .75 2.00
8 Mike Bibby .50 1.25
9 Allen Iverson 1.25 3.00
10 Tracy McGrady .75 2.00
11 Baron Davis .50 1.25
12 Tim Duncan 1.25 3.00
13 Latrell Sprewell .50 1.25
14 Paul Pierce .75 2.00
15 Vince Carter 1.00 2.50
16 Antawn Jamison .50 1.25
17 Eddie Jones .50 1.25
18 Darius Miles .30 .75
19 Dirk Nowitzki 1.25 3.00
20 Karl Malone 1.00 2.50
21 Shaquille O'Neal 2.00 5.00
22 Michael Jordan 5.00 12.00
23 Antoine Walker .40 1.00
24 Kenyon Martin .50 1.25
25 Chris Webber .60 1.50

2002-03 Flair Court Kings Ball and Jersey

PRINT RUN 100 SER.#'d SETS
CKAI Allen Iverson 12.00 30.00
CKAJ Antawn Jamison 5.00 12.00
CKAW Antoine Walker 5.00 12.00
CKBD Baron Davis 6.00 15.00
CKCW Chris Webber 8.00 20.00
CKDM Darius Miles 4.00 10.00
CKDN Dirk Nowitzki 15.00 40.00
CKEB Elton Brand 5.00 12.00
CKEJ Eddie Jones 6.00 15.00
CKJK Jason Kidd 10.00 25.00
CKJS Jerry Stackhouse 6.00 15.00
CKKM Karl Malone 12.00 30.00
CKMB Mike Bibby 6.00 15.00
CKPP Paul Pierce 10.00 25.00
CKPS Peja Stojakovic 5.00 12.00
CKRA Ray Allen 10.00 25.00
CKSF Steve Francis 6.00 15.00
CKSM Stephon Marbury 8.00 20.00
CKTM Tracy McGrady 10.00 25.00
CKVC Vince Carter 12.00 30.00

2002-03 Flair Court Kings Game Used

STATED ODDS 1:20
CKAI Allen Iverson 8.00 20.00
CKAJ Antawn Jamison 2.50 6.00
CKAW Antoine Walker 2.50 6.00
CKBD Baron Davis 3.00 8.00
CKCW Chris Webber 4.00 10.00
CKDN Dirk Nowitzki 8.00 20.00
CKEB Elton Brand 2.50 6.00
CKEJ Eddie Jones 3.00 8.00
CKJK Jason Kidd 5.00 12.00
CKJS Jerry Stackhouse 3.00 8.00
CKLS Latrell Sprewell 3.00 8.00
CKMB Mike Bibby 3.00 8.00
CKPP Paul Pierce 5.00 12.00
CKRA Ray Allen 5.00 12.00
CKVC Vince Carter 6.00 15.00
CKDM1 Darius Miles WU 2.00 5.00
CKDM2 Darius Miles Shorts 2.00 5.00
CKKM1 Karl Malone WU 6.00 15.00
CKKM2 Karl Malone JSY 6.00 15.00
CKKM1 Kenyon Martin WU 3.00 8.00
CKKM2 Kenyon Martin JSY 3.00 8.00
CKSF1 Steve Francis WU 3.00 8.00
CKSF2 Steve Francis Shorts 3.00 8.00
CKTM1 Tracy McGrady Shorts 5.00 12.00
CKTM2 Tracy McGrady Shirt 5.00 12.00

2002-03 Flair Court Kings Game Used Dual

PRINT RUN 250 SER.#'d SETS
BD/SF B.Davis/S.Francis 8.00 20.00
DN/KM D.Nowitzki/K.Malone 12.50 30.00
EB/DM E.Brand/D.Miles 8.00 20.00
EJ/RA E.Jones/R.Allen 8.00 20.00
JK/KM J.Kidd/K.Martin 8.00 20.00
JS/AI J.Stack/A.Iverson 12.50 30.00
MB/CW M.Bibby/C.Webber 12.50 30.00
PP/AW P.Pierce/A.Walker 8.00 20.00
TM/VC T.McGrady/V.Carter 15.00 40.00

2002-03 Flair Hot Numbers Patches

PRINT RUN 100 SER.#'d SETS
HNAI Allen Iverson 20.00 50.00
HNDM Darius Miles 5.00 12.00
HNDN Dirk Nowitzki 20.00 50.00
HNJK Jason Kidd 12.00 30.00
HNPG Pau Gasol 12.00 30.00
HNPP Paul Pierce 12.00 30.00
HNTM Tracy McGrady 12.00 30.00
HNVC Vince Carter 15.00 40.00

2002-03 Flair Jersey Heights

STATED ODDS 1:16
JHAI Allen Iverson 8.00 20.00
JHDM Darius Miles 2.00 5.00
JHDN Dirk Nowitzki 8.00 20.00
JHJK Jason Kidd 5.00 12.00
JHPG Pau Gasol 5.00 12.00
JHPP Paul Pierce 5.00 12.00
JHTM Tracy McGrady 5.00 12.00
JHVC Vince Carter 6.00 15.00

2002-03 Flair New Heights

COMPLETE SET (20) 15.00 40.00
STATED ODDS 1:10
1 Tracy McGrady 1.25 3.00
2 Vince Carter 1.50 4.00
3 Jason Kidd 1.25 3.00
4 Tim Duncan 2.00 5.00
5 Dirk Nowitzki 2.00 5.00
6 Jamaal Tinsley .50 1.25
7 Kobe Bryant 6.00 15.00
8 Eddy Curry .50 1.25
9 Shane Battier .75 2.00
10 Peja Stojakovic .60 1.50
11 Michael Jordan 8.00 20.00
12 Darius Miles .50 1.25
13 Jason Richardson .75 2.00
14 Pau Gasol 1.25 3.00
15 Jerry Stackhouse .75 2.00
16 Shaquille O'Neal 3.00 8.00
17 Paul Pierce 1.25 3.00
18 Eddie Griffin .50 1.25
19 Kwame Brown .50 1.25
20 Allen Iverson 2.00 5.00

2002-03 Flair Sweet Swatch Autographs

SWEET SHOT PACK 1 PER BOX
*GOLD: .75X TO 2X BASE HI
GOLD PRINT RUN 15 SER.#'d SETS
EC Eddy Curry/250 8.00 20.00
GR Glenn Robinson/400 8.00 20.00
JJ Joe Johnson/375 8.00 20.00
KB Kedrick Brown/75 8.00 20.00
MB Michael Bradley/75 8.00 20.00
SA Shareef Abdur-Rahim/500 8.00 20.00
VC Vince Carter/475 15.00 40.00
KBR Kwame Brown/200 8.00 20.00

2002-03 Flair Sweet Swatch Game Used

SWEET SHOT PACK 1 PER BOX
SSAI Allen Iverson/975 12.00 30.00
SSDM Darius Miles/825 3.00 8.00
SSHT Hedo Turkoglu/650 4.00 10.00
SSJK Jason Kidd/800 8.00 20.00
SSJR Jason Richardson/625 5.00 12.00
SSJT Jamaal Tinsley/475 3.00 8.00
SSKM Kenyon Martin/900 5.00 12.00
SSMM Mike Miller/875 4.00 10.00
SSPG Pau Gasol/750 8.00 20.00
SSPP Paul Pierce/625 8.00 20.00
SSPS Peja Stojakovic/725 4.00 10.00
SSRA Ray Allen/850 8.00 20.00
SSSN Steve Nash/625 10.00 25.00
SSTM Tracy McGrady/850 8.00 20.00
SSTP Tony Parker/600 8.00 20.00
SSVC Vince Carter/975 10.00 25.00

2002-03 Flair Sweet Swatch Patches

SWEET SHOT PACK 1 PER BOX
LOWER PRINT RUNS NOT PRICED
SSAI Allen Iverson/33 80.00 200.00
SSDM Darius Miles/26 20.00 50.00
SSJK Jason Kidd/33 40.00 100.00
SSJT Jamaal Tinsley/32 20.00 50.00
SSMM Mike Miller/31 25.00 60.00
SSPG Pau Gasol 50.00 120.00
SSPP Paul Pierce 50.00 120.00
SSRA Ray Allen/49 50.00 120.00
SSTP Tony Parker/32 50.00 120.00
SSVC Vince Carter/35 60.00 150.00

2002-03 Flair Wave of the Future

COMPLETE SET (11) 15.00 40.00
STATED ODDS 1:20
1 Amare Stoudemire 4.00 10.00
2 Caron Butler 1.50 4.00
3 Chris Wilcox 1.25 3.00
4 DaJuan Wagner 1.25 3.00
5 Drew Gooden 1.50 4.00
6 Jared Jeffries 1.25 3.00
7 Jay Williams 1.25 3.00
8 Melvin Ely 1.25 3.00
9 Mike Dunleavy 1.50 4.00
10 Nene Hilario 1.50 4.00
11 Nikoloz Tskitishvili 1.00 2.50

2002-03 Flair Wave of the Future Jerseys

PRINT RUN 100 SERIAL #'D SETS
*PATCHES: .75X TO 2X HI
PATCH PRINT RUN 50 SER.#'d SETS
AS Amare Stoudemire 10.00 25.00
CB Caron Butler 4.00 10.00
CW Chris Wilcox 3.00 8.00
DG Drew Gooden 4.00 10.00
DW DaJuan Wagner 3.00 8.00
JJ Jared Jeffries 3.00 8.00
NH Nene Hilario 4.00 10.00
NT Nikoloz Tskitishvili 2.50 6.00

2003-04 Flair

COMP.SET w/o SP's (90) 15.00 40.00
91-120 PRINT RUN 500 SER.#'d SETS
1 Jerry Stackhouse .40 1.00
2 Eddie Griffin .20 .50
3 Jermaine O'Neal .30 .75
4 Kobe Bryant 2.50 6.00
5 Juwan Howard .25 .60
6 Alonzo Mourning .40 1.00
7 Kenny Thomas .20 .50
8 Chris Webber .40 1.00
9 Radoslav Nesterovic .20 .50
10 Morris Peterson .20 .50
11 DeShawn Stevenson .20 .50
12 Steve Francis .30 .75
13 Andrei Kirilenko .25 .60
14 Kwame Brown .20 .50
15 Tim Duncan .75 2.00
16 Yao Ming .75 2.00
17 Jamaal Tinsley .20 .50
18 Shaquille O'Neal 1.25 3.00
19 Tracy McGrady .75 2.00
20 Dirk Nowitzki .75 2.00
21 Marcus Camby .25 .60
22 Elton Brand .25 .60
23 Latrell Sprewell .40 1.00
24 Grant Hill .40 1.00
25 Shawn Marion .30 .75
26 Rasheed Wallace .40 1.00
27 Ray Allen .50 1.25
28 Antonio Davis .25 .60
29 Antoine Walker .30 .75
30 Ricky Davis .25 .60
31 Jason Kidd .50 1.25
32 Tony Parker .50 1.25
33 Paul Pierce .50 1.25
34 Gary Payton .50 1.25
35 Kenyon Martin .30 .75
36 Dale Davis .20 .50
37 Vladimir Radmanovic .20 .50
38 Matt Harpring .30 .75
39 Shareef Abdur-Rahim .30 .75
40 Antawn Jamison .30 .75
41 Eddie Jones .30 .75
42 Jamaal Magloire .20 .50
43 Jason Richardson .30 .75
44 Jonathan Bender .20 .50
45 Chris Wilcox .20 .50
46 Manu Ginobili .60 1.50
47 Chauncey Billups .40 1.00
48 Jamal Mashburn .25 .60
49 Joe Smith .25 .60
50 Aaron McKie .25 .60
51 Theo Ratliff .20 .50
52 Eddy Curry .25 .60
53 Ron Artest .30 .75
54 Quentin Richardson .20 .50
55 Karl Malone .60 1.50
56 Pau Gasol .30 .75
57 Dan Dickau .20 .50
58 Darius Miles .20 .50
59 Ben Wallace .40 1.00
60 Cuttino Mobley .20 .50
61 Lamar Odom .25 .60
62 Shane Battier .25 .60
63 Allan Houston .30 .75
64 Peja Stojakovic .25 .60
65 Dajuan Wagner .20 .50
66 Caron Butler .25 .60
67 Keith Van Horn .25 .60
68 Vincent Yarbrough .20 .50
69 Tim Thomas .20 .50
70 Troy Hudson .20 .50
71 Amare Stoudemire .40 1.00
72 Bobby Jackson .25 .60
73 Bonzi Wells .20 .50
74 Steve Nash .60 1.50
75 Gilbert Arenas .50 1.25
76 Glenn Robinson .25 .60
77 Jalen Rose .25 .60
78 Michael Finley .30 .75
79 Nene .25 .60
80 Kevin Garnett .75 2.00
81 Richard Jefferson .25 .60
82 Baron Davis .30 .75
83 Mike Bibby .30 .75
84 Tyson Chandler .25 .60
85 Michael Redd .30 .75
86 Mike Dunleavy .25 .60
87 Drew Gooden .25 .60
88 Allen Iverson .75 2.00
89 Vince Carter .60 1.50
90 Larry Hughes .25 .60
91 Josh Howard RC 1.50 4.00
92 Maciej Lampe RC 1.00 2.50
93 Zarko Cabarkapa RC 1.00 2.50
94 LeBron James RC 500.00 1,000.00
95 Reece Gaines RC 1.00 2.50
96 Jarvis Hayes RC 1.00 2.50
97 Mickael Pietrus RC 1.25 3.00
98 T.J. Ford RC 1.25 3.00
99 Zoran Planinic RC 1.25 3.00
100 Luke Ridnour RC 1.50 4.00
101 Boris Diaw RC 1.50 4.00
102 Nick Collison RC 1.25 3.00
103 Travis Outlaw RC 1.25 3.00
104 Carmelo Anthony RC 6.00 15.00
105 Chris Kaman RC 1.50 4.00
106 Mike Sweetney RC 1.00 2.50
107 Kendrick Perkins RC 1.25 3.00
108 Jason Kapono RC 1.00 2.50
109 Troy Bell RC 1.00 2.50
110 Chris Bosh RC 5.00 12.00
111 Jerome Beasley RC 1.00 2.50
112 Darko Milicic RC 1.25 3.00
113 Dwyane Wade RC 8.00 20.00
114 David West RC 2.00 5.00
115 Kirk Hinrich RC 1.25 3.00
116 Dahntay Jones RC 1.25 3.00
117 Leandro Barbosa RC 1.50 4.00
118 Marcus Banks RC 1.00 2.50
119 Luke Walton RC 1.50 4.00
120 Ndudi Ebi RC 1.00 2.50

2003-04 Flair Rookie Jumbos

PRINT RUN 400 SER.#'d SETS
1 LeBron James 400.00 800.00
2 Darko Milicic 1.25 3.00
3 Carmelo Anthony 8.00 20.00
4 Chris Bosh 5.00 12.00
5 Dwyane Wade 75.00 200.00
6 Chris Kaman 1.50 4.00
7 Kirk Hinrich 1.50 4.00
8 T.J. Ford 1.25 3.00
9 Mike Sweetney 1.00 2.50
10 Jarvis Hayes 1.00 2.50
11 Mickael Pietrus 1.25 3.00
12 Nick Collison 1.25 3.00
13 Marcus Banks 1.00 2.50
14 Troy Bell 1.00 2.50
15 David West 2.00 5.00

2003-04 Flair Row 1

*1-90 ROW 1 SINGLES: 4X TO 10X BASE HI
*91-120 ROW 1 RCs: 1.25X TO 3X BASE HI
ROW 1 PRINT RUN 100 SER.#'d SETS
4 Kobe Bryant 20.00 50.00
94 LeBron James 1,500.00 3,000.00

2003-04 Flair A Cut Above

PRINT RUN 500 SER.#'d SETS
*FINAL CUT: 1X TO 2.5X BASE HI
FINAL CUT PRINT RUN 50 SER.#'d SETS
AH Allan Houston 2.50 6.00
AJ Antawn Jamison 2.50 6.00
BD Baron Davis 2.50 6.00
BW Bonzi Wells 2.00 5.00
CB Caron Butler 2.00 5.00
CW Chris Webber 3.00 8.00
DW Dajuan Wagner 2.00 5.00
GP Gary Payton 4.00 10.00
JK Jason Kidd 4.00 10.00
JR Jason Richardson 2.50 6.00
MG Manu Ginobili 5.00 12.00
PG Pau Gasol 4.00 10.00
PS Peja Stojakovic 2.00 5.00
RA Ron Artest 2.50 6.00
RD Ricky Davis 2.00 5.00
RM Reggie Miller 5.00 12.00
SA Shareef Abdur-Rahim 2.50 6.00
SN Steve Nash 5.00 12.00
TP Tayshaun Prince 2.50 6.00
VC Vince Carter 5.00 12.00
YM Yao Ming 6.00 15.00

2003-04 Flair Sweet Swatch

PRINT RUN 250 SER.#'d SETS
*PATCH: 1.25X TO 3X BASE HI
PATCH PRINT RUN 50 SER.#'d SETS
AH Allan Houston 2.50 6.00
AI Allen Iverson 6.00 15.00
AS Amare Stoudemire 3.00 8.00
CA Carmelo Anthony 12.00 30.00
CB Caron Butler 2.00 5.00
DG Drew Gooden 2.00 5.00
DJ Dahntay Jones 2.00 5.00
DN Dirk Nowitzki 6.00 15.00
DW Dwyane Wade 8.00 20.00
KG Kevin Garnett 6.00 15.00
LW Luke Walton 2.50 6.00
MB Marcus Banks 1.50 4.00
MS Mike Sweetney 1.50 4.00
PP Paul Pierce 4.00 10.00
SF Steve Francis 2.50 6.00
SN Steve Nash 5.00 12.00
TM Tracy McGrady 4.00 10.00
TO Travis Outlaw 2.00 5.00
TP Tony Parker 4.00 10.00
VC Vince Carter 5.00 12.00

2003-04 Flair Sweet Swatch Autographs

PRINT RUNS LISTED BELOW
AS Amare Stoudemire/200 8.00 20.00
BC Brian Cook/150 3.00 8.00
CA Carmelo Anthony/271 25.00 60.00
CB Chris Bosh/100 12.00 30.00
DJ Dahntay Jones/200 4.00 10.00
DW Dwyane Wade/145 40.00 100.00
DW David West/200 6.00 15.00
JH Josh Howard 5.00 12.00
JK Jason Kapono/200 3.00 8.00
JO Jermaine O'Neal/20 20.00 50.00
KP Kendrick Perkins/100 4.00 10.00
LR Luke Ridnour/150 5.00 12.00
LW Luke Walton/200 5.00 12.00
MB Marcus Banks/120 3.00 8.00
ML Maciej Lampe/190 3.00 8.00
MP Mickael Pietrus/100 4.00 10.00
MS Mike Sweetney/100 3.00 8.00
PS Peja Stojakovic/15 15.00 40.00
TO Travis Outlaw/200 2.00 5.00
TP Tayshaun Prince/25 15.00 40.00

2003-04 Flair Sweet Swatch Autographs Gold

*GOLD: .75X TO 2X BASE HI
PRINT RUN 25 SER.#'d SETS
CA Carmelo Anthony 100.00 200.00
JO Jermaine O'Neal 12.00 30.00
SF Steve Francis 20.00 50.00
TP Tayshaun Prince 20.00 50.00

2003-04 Flair Sweet Swatch Jumbos Away

AMARE DOES NOT HAVE AWAY VERSION
ONE JUMBO TOPPER PER BOX
*HOME VERSION: .4X TO 1X BASE HI
*PATCH: 1.25X TO 3X BASE HI
PATCH PRINT RUN 30 SER.#'d SETS
AH Allan Houston/187 4.00 10.00
AI Allen Iverson/171 10.00 25.00
CA Carmelo Anthony/125 20.00 50.00
CB Caron Butler/201 3.00 8.00
DG Drew Gooden/165 3.00 8.00
DJ Dahntay Jones/144 3.00 8.00
DN Dirk Nowitzki/87 10.00 25.00
DW Dwyane Wade/116 30.00 80.00
KG Kevin Garnett/190 10.00 25.00
LW Luke Walton/199 4.00 10.00
MB Marcus Banks/135 2.50 6.00
MS Mike Sweetney/173 2.50 6.00
PP Paul Pierce/62 6.00 15.00
SF Steve Francis/187 4.00 10.00
SN Steve Nash/116 8.00 20.00
TM Tracy McGrady/183 6.00 15.00
TO Travis Outlaw/165 3.00 8.00
TP Tony Parker/125 6.00 15.00
VC Vince Carter/139 8.00 20.00

2003-04 Flair Sweet Swatch Jumbos Double

PRINT RUN 50 SER.#'d SETS
1 M.Banks/P.Pierce 15.00 40.00
3 T.McGrady/D.Gooden 12.50 30.00
4 D.Wade/C.Butler 25.00 60.00
5 M.Sweetney/A.Houston 10.00 25.00
6 A.Stoudemire/K.Garnett 15.00 40.00
7 A.Iverson/V.Carter 20.00 50.00
8 D.Jones/L.Walton 10.00 25.00
9 C.Anthony/T.Outlaw 15.00 40.00
10 S.Francis/T.Parker 12.50 30.00

2003-04 Flair Sweet Swatch Jumbos Triple

PRINT RUN 32 SER.#'d SETS
1 Melo/D.Wade/Bosh 125.00 300.00
3 J.O'Neal/Prince/Peja 12.50 30.00
5 Outlaw/West/Cook 12.50 30.00
6 Pietrus/Ridnour/Sweetney 12.50 30.00
7 Howard/Walton/Kapono 12.50 30.00

2003-04 Flair Wave of the Future

COMPLETE SET (15) 25.00 50.00
STATED ODDS 1:20
1 LeBron James 150.00 400.00
2 Darko Milicic .75 2.00
3 Carmelo Anthony 5.00 12.00
4 Chris Bosh 3.00 8.00
5 Dwyane Wade 30.00 80.00
6 Chris Kaman 1.00 2.50
7 Kirk Hinrich 1.00 2.50
8 T.J. Ford .75 2.00
9 Mike Sweetney .60 1.50
10 Jarvis Hayes .60 1.50
11 Mickael Pietrus .75 2.00
12 Nick Collison .75 2.00
13 Marcus Banks .60 1.50
14 Luke Ridnour 1.00 2.50
15 Reece Gaines .60 1.50

2003-04 Flair Wave of the Future Game Used

PRINT RUN 250 SER.#'d SETS
*PATCH: .75X TO 2X BASE HI
PATCH PRINT RUN 50 SER.#'d SETS
CA Carmelo Anthony 12.00 30.00
CB Chris Bosh 8.00 20.00
CK Chris Kaman 2.50 6.00
DW Dwyane Wade 20.00 50.00
DW David West 3.00 8.00
JH Jarvis Hayes 1.50 4.00
LR Luke Ridnour 2.50 6.00
MB Marcus Banks 1.50 4.00
MP Mickael Pietrus 2.00 5.00
MS Mike Sweetney 1.50 4.00
RG Reece Gaines 1.50 4.00
TB Troy Bell 1.50 4.00

2003-04 Flair World Leaders

COMPLETE SET (20) 15.00 30.00
STATED ODDS 1:10
1 Paul Pierce 1.25 3.00
2 Tim Duncan 2.00 5.00
3 Yao Ming 2.00 5.00
4 Shaquille O'Neal 3.00 8.00
5 Tracy McGrady 1.25 3.00
6 Dirk Nowitzki 2.00 5.00
7 Elton Brand .60 1.50
8 Amare Stoudemire 1.00 2.50
9 Kevin Garnett 2.00 5.00
10 Allen Iverson 2.00 5.00
11 Vince Carter 1.50 4.00
12 Steve Francis .75 2.00
13 Tony Parker 1.25 3.00
14 Pau Gasol 1.25 3.00
15 Ben Wallace 1.00 2.50
16 Andrei Kirilenko .60 1.50
17 Gilbert Arenas .75 2.00
18 Jermaine O'Neal .75 2.00
19 Chris Webber 1.00 2.50
20 Drew Gooden .60 1.50

2003-04 Flair World Leaders Game Used

STATED ODDS 1:15
AI Allen Iverson 6.00 15.00
AK Andrei Kirilenko 2.00 5.00
AS Amare Stoudemire 3.00 8.00
BW Ben Wallace 3.00 8.00
CR Chris Webber 3.00 8.00
DG Drew Gooden 2.00 5.00
DR Dirk Nowitzki 6.00 15.00
EB Elton Brand 2.00 5.00
GA Gilbert Arenas 2.50 6.00
JK Jason Kidd 4.00 10.00
KG Kevin Garnett 6.00 15.00
PG Pau Gasol 4.00 10.00
PP Paul Pierce 4.00 10.00
SF Steve Francis 2.50 6.00
SO Shaquille O'Neal 10.00 25.00
TD Tim Duncan 6.00 15.00
TM Tracy McGrady 4.00 10.00
TP Tony Parker 4.00 10.00
VC Vince Carter 5.00 12.00
YM Yao Ming 6.00 15.00

2004 Flair Significant Cuts

OVERALL AU ODDS 1:1 HOBBY
PRINT RUNS B/WN 1-200 COPIES PER
NO PRICING ON QTY OF 10 OR LESS
VC Vince Carter/200 12.00 40.00

2004-05 Flair

COMP.SET w/o SP's (60) 40.00 100.00
61-90 PRINT RUN 799 SER.#'d SETS
1 Gilbert Arenas .60 1.50
2 Richard Hamilton .75 2.00
3 Stephon Marbury .75 2.00
4 Tony Parker 1.00 2.50
5 Michael Redd .50 1.25
6 Latrell Sprewell .75 2.00
7 Willie Green .60 1.50
8 Joe Johnson .50 1.25
9 Lamar Odom .60 1.50
10 Tim Duncan 1.50 4.00
11 Ben Wallace .75 2.00
12 Elton Brand .50 1.25
13 Allen Iverson 1.50 4.00
14 Andrei Kirilenko .50 1.25
15 Dirk Nowitzki 1.50 4.00
16 Paul Pierce 1.00 2.50
17 Mike Dunleavy .40 1.00
18 Zach Randolph .60 1.50
19 David West .50 1.25
20 Corey Maggette .50 1.25
21 Dwyane Wade 2.50 6.00
22 Chris Bosh 1.50 4.00
23 Michael Finley .60 1.50
24 Kevin Garnett 1.25 3.00
25 Allan Houston .60 1.50
26 Antawn Jamison .50 1.25
27 Jermaine O'Neal .50 1.25
28 Alonzo Mourning .75 2.00
29 Gerald Wallace .50 1.25
30 Jason Williams .50 1.25
31 Tyronn Lue .40 1.00
32 Pau Gasol 1.00 2.50
33 Jason Kidd 1.00 2.50
34 Shareef Abdur-Rahim .60 1.50
35 LeBron James 12.00 30.00
36 Shaquille O'Neal 2.50 6.00
37 Jason Richardson .60 1.50
38 Rasheed Wallace .75 2.00
39 Nene .50 1.25
40 Tracy McGrady 1.00 2.50
41 Luke Ridnour .50 1.25
42 Peja Stojakovic .50 1.25
43 Amare Stoudemire .60 1.50
44 Carmelo Anthony 1.25 3.00
45 Steve Francis .60 1.50
46 Antoine Walker .60 1.50
47 Reggie Miller 1.25 3.00
48 Mike Bibby .60 1.50
49 Sam Cassell .60 1.50
50 Richard Jefferson .50 1.25
51 Jason Kapono .40 1.00
52 Dajuan Wagner .40 1.00
53 Kobe Bryant 5.00 12.00
54 Kenyon Martin .60 1.50
55 T.J. Ford .40 1.00
56 Ray Allen 1.00 2.50
57 Vince Carter 1.25 3.00
58 Yao Ming 1.50 4.00
59 Baron Davis .60 1.50
60 Joe Smith .50 1.25
61 Luol Deng RC 1.50 4.00
62 J.R. Smith RC 1.50 4.00
63 Josh Childress RC 1.00 2.50
64 Shaun Livingston RC 1.50 4.00
65 Rafael Araujo RC 1.00 2.50
66 Devin Harris RC 1.50 4.00
67 Kevin Martin RC 2.00 5.00
68 Sasha Vujacic RC 1.25 3.00
69 Robert Swift RC 1.00 2.50
70 Andris Biedrins RC 1.00 2.50
71 Kirk Snyder RC 1.00 2.50
72 Jameer Nelson RC 1.50 4.00
73 Tony Allen RC 1.50 4.00
74 Chris Duhon RC 1.25 3.00
75 David Harrison RC 1.00 2.50
76 Andre Iguodala RC 2.50 6.00
77 Josh Smith RC 1.50 4.00
78 Andre Emmett RC 1.00 2.50
79 Luke Jackson RC 1.00 2.50
80 Dorell Wright RC 1.25 3.00
81 Ben Gordon RC 1.50 4.00
82 Dwight Howard RC 5.00 12.00
83 Kris Humphries RC 1.25 3.00
84 Al Jefferson RC 1.50 4.00
85 Jackson Vroman RC 1.00 2.50
86 Beno Udrih RC 1.25 3.00
87 Trevor Ariza RC 1.50 4.00
88 Sebastian Telfair RC 1.25 3.00
89 Emeka Okafor RC 1.25 3.00
90 Peter John Ramos RC 1.00 2.50

2004-05 Flair Row 1

*1-60 ROW 1: 1X TO 2.5X BASE HI
*61-90 ROW 1 RCs: .5X TO 1.25X BASE HI
PRINT RUN 100 SER.#'d SETS

2004-05 Flair Courting Greatness Jerseys

PRINT RUN 150 SER.#'d SETS
*PATCHES: .75X TO 2X BASE JSY HI
PATCH PRINT RUN 50 SER.#'d SETS
AI Allen Iverson 8.00 20.00
AJ Antawn Jamison 2.50 6.00
AS Amare Stoudemire 3.00 8.00
BW Ben Wallace 4.00 10.00
CB Chauncey Billups 4.00 10.00
DH Dwight Howard 10.00 25.00
DN Dirk Nowitzki 8.00 20.00
DW Dwyane Wade 12.00 30.00
GA Gilbert Arenas 3.00 8.00
GH Grant Hill 4.00 10.00
GP Gary Payton 5.00 12.00
IG Andre Iguodala 4.00 10.00
JK Jason Kidd 5.00 12.00
JR Jason Richardson 3.00 8.00
KG Kevin Garnett 8.00 20.00
LS Latrell Sprewell 4.00 10.00
MB Mike Bibby 3.00 8.00
MD Mike Dunleavy 2.00 5.00
MG Manu Ginobili 6.00 15.00
PP Paul Pierce 5.00 12.00
PS Peja Stojakovic 2.50 6.00
SN Steve Nash 6.00 15.00
TD Tim Duncan 8.00 20.00
TM Tracy McGrady 5.00 12.00
VC Vince Carter 6.00 15.00
HOW Josh Howard 2.50 6.00
SON Shaquille O'Neal 12.00 30.00
YAO Yao Ming 8.00 20.00

2004-05 Flair Courting Greatness Jerseys Dual

PRINT RUN 99 SER.#'d SETS
*PATCH: 1.25X TO 3X BASE HI
PATCH PRINT RUN 15 SER.#'d SETS
AIAI A.Iguodala/A.Iverson 8.00 20.00
CBBW C.Billups/B.Wallace 4.00 10.00
GAAJ G.Arenas/A.Jamison 3.00 8.00
GHDH G.Hill/D.Howard 10.00 25.00
GPPP G.Payton/P.Pierce 5.00 12.00
JHDN J.Howard/D.Nowitzki 8.00 20.00
JKVC J.Kidd/V.Carter 6.00 15.00
KGLS K.Garnett/L.Sprewell 8.00 20.00
MDJR M.Dunleavy/J.Richardson 3.00 8.00
PSMB P.Stojakovic/M.Bibby 3.00 8.00
SNAS S.Nash/A.Stoudemire 6.00 15.00
SODW S.O'Neal/D.Wade 12.00 30.00
TDMG T.Duncan/M.Ginobili 8.00 20.00
TMYM T.McGrady/Y.Ming 8.00 20.00

2004-05 Flair Cuts and Glory Jerseys

STATED PRINT RUN 20 TO 100 SETS

BW Ben Wallace/75 20.00 50.00
JC Josh Childress/100 8.00 20.00
JS Jerry Stackhouse/50 8.00 20.00
PG Pau Gasol/100 8.00 20.00
PS Peja Stojakovic/75 15.00 30.00
RH Richard Hamilton/100 10.00 25.00
SM Stephon Marbury/55 12.00 30.00
TM Tracy McGrady/20 30.00 80.00

2004-05 Flair Cuts and Glory Patches

PRINT RUN 50 SER.#'d SETS
BW Ben Wallace 30.00 80.00
JC Josh Childress 15.00 40.00
PG Pau Gasol 20.00 50.00
PS Peja Stojakovic 15.00 40.00
RH Richard Hamilton 15.00 40.00
SM Stephon Marbury 20.00 50.00

2004-05 Flair Dynasty Foundations Jerseys

PRINT RUN 250 SER.#'d SETS
*PATCHES: .75X TO 2X BASE HI
PATCH PRINT RUN 99 SER.#'d SETS
4 Nuggets Carmelo JSY 6.00 15.00
9 Hornets Smith JSY 3.00 8.00
10 76ers Iverson JSY 6.00 15.00
12 Trailblazers Randolph JSY 5.00 12.00
13 Spurs Duncan JSY 8.00 20.00
15 Raptors Bosh JSY 5.00 12.00
17 Kings Peja JSY 4.00 10.00

2004-05 Flair Dynasty Foundations Jerseys Dual

PRINT RUN 150 SER.#'d SETS
PATCH DUAL PRINT RUN 50 SER.#'d SETS
4 Nuggets Melo/K-Mart JSY 6.00 15.00
9 Hornets Davis/Smith JSY 6.00 15.00
10 76ers Barkley/Iverson JSY 20.00 50.00
12 Blazers Randolph/Telfair JSY 6.00 15.00
13 Spurs Admiral/Duncan JSY 10.00 25.00
17 Kings Webber/Peja JSY 8.00 20.00

2004-05 Flair Dynasty Foundations Patches Dual

4 Nuggets Melo/K-Mart JSY 15.00 40.00
9 Hornets Davis/Smith JSY 15.00 40.00
10 76ers Barkley/Iverson JSY 50.00 120.00
12 Blazers Randolph/Telfair JSY 15.00 40.00
13 Spurs Admiral/Duncan JSY 25.00 60.00
17 Kings Webber/Peja JSY 20.00 50.00

2004-05 Flair Dynasty Foundations Jerseys Triple

PRINT RUN 99 SER.#'d SETS
*PATCH TRIPLE: 1X TO 2.5X BASE HI
PATCH TRIPLE PRINT RUN 25 SER.#'d SETS
9 West/Davis/Smith JSY 10.00 25.00
13 Admiral/Parker/Duncan JSY 20.00 50.00
17 Webber/Bibby/Peja JSY 10.00 25.00

2004-05 Flair Head of the Class Jerseys

STATED PRINT RUN 2 TO 99 SER.#'d SETS
BFD Brand/Francis/B.Davis/99 6.00 15.00
DBM Duncan/Billups/McGrady/97 10.00 25.00
IMA Iverson/Marbury/R.Allen/96 10.00 25.00
NCJ Nowitzki/Carter/Jamison/98 10.00 25.00
OMS Shaq/Mourning/Spree/92 20.00 50.00
RPM Admiral/Pippen/R.Miller/87 30.00 60.00
WHH Webb/Hardway/Houston/93 15.00 40.00

2004-05 Flair Head of the Class Patches

PRINT RUN 33 SER.#'d SETS
BFD Brand/Francis/B.Davis 25.00 60.00
DBM Duncan/Billups/McGrady 40.00 80.00
IMA Iverson/Marbury/R.Allen 60.00 150.00
NCJ Nowitzki/Carter/Jamison 25.00 60.00
OMS Shaq/Mourning/Spree 75.00 200.00
RPM Admiral/Pippen/R.Miller 100.00 225.00
SMB Amare/Ming/Butler 25.00 60.00
SWG Slack/Wallace/Garnett 30.00 80.00
WHH Webb/Hardway/Houston 75.00 200.00

2004-05 Flair Significant Signings

PRINT RUN 44 TO 250 SER.#'d SETS
N Nene/200 5.00 12.00
AJ Antawn Jamison/50 6.00 15.00
AS Amare Stoudemire/150 12.00 30.00
BG Ben Gordon/200 10.00 25.00
BM Brad Miller/150 5.00 12.00
CB Chauncey Billups/44 12.00 30.00
DH David Harrison/150 5.00 12.00
DW David West/200 5.00 12.00
DW Dwyane Wade/75 25.00 60.00
EB Elton Brand/75 6.00 15.00
JH Josh Howard/200 5.00 12.00
JS Josh Smith/200 8.00 20.00
JS2 J.R. Smith/250 10.00 25.00
KH Kris Humphries/200 5.00 12.00
KM Kenyon Martin/50 8.00 20.00
LO Lamar Odom/75 8.00 20.00
MB Mike Bibby/50 10.00 25.00
MG Manu Ginobili/75 15.00 40.00
MP Mickael Pietrus/200 5.00 12.00
RA Rafael Araujo/200 5.00 12.00
RJ Richard Jefferson/50 6.00 15.00

2004-05 Flair Significant Signings 50

PRINT RUN 50 SER.#'d SETS
N Nene 6.00 15.00
AS Amare Stoudemire 15.00 40.00
DW David West 6.00 15.00
DW Dwyane Wade 50.00 120.00
JS Josh Smith 6.00 15.00
JS2 J.R. Smith 6.00 15.00
KH Kris Humphries 6.00 15.00

2004-05 Flair Significant Signings 35

PRINT RUN 35 SER.#'d SETS
N Nene 8.00 20.00
BG Ben Gordon 15.00 40.00
BM Brad Miller 8.00 20.00
EB Elton Brand 10.00 25.00
JH Josh Howard 8.00 20.00
KM Kenyon Martin 12.50 30.00
LO Lamar Odom 12.50 30.00
MG Manu Ginobili 25.00 60.00
RA Rafael Araujo 8.00 20.00

2004-05 Flair Significant Signings 25

PRINT RUN 25 SER.#'d SETS
AS Amare Stoudemire 12.00 30.00
DW Dwyane Wade 50.00 120.00
JH Josh Howard 10.00 25.00
MB Mike Bibby 10.00 25.00
MG Manu Ginobili 20.00 50.00
MP Mickael Pietrus 10.00 25.00
RJ Richard Jefferson 10.00 25.00

2004-05 Flair Significant Signings Die Cuts

STATED PRINT RUN 18 TO 50 SETS
AJ Al Jefferson/24 15.00 40.00
AS Amare Stoudemire/50 15.00 40.00
DW Dwyane Wade/20 25.00 60.00
DW Dorell Wright/18 10.00 25.00
JS Josh Smith/50 12.50 30.00
KH Kris Humphries/50 6.00 15.00

2004-05 Flair Significant Signings Jerseys

PRINT RUN 10 TO 25 SER.#'d SETS
N Nene/25 10.00 25.00
AJ Antawn Jamison/15 15.00 40.00
AS Amare Stoudemire/25 25.00 60.00
DH David Harrison/15 10.00 25.00
DW Dwyane Wade/25 80.00 200.00
DW2 David West/25 10.00 25.00
EB Elton Brand/15 12.00 30.00
JH Josh Howard/25 10.00 25.00
JRS J.R. Smith/25 40.00 100.00
JS Josh Smith/25 40.00 100.00
KH Kris Humphries/25 10.00 25.00
KM Kenyon Martin/15 15.00 40.00
LJ Luke Jackson/50 10.00 25.00
LO Lamar Odom/25 15.00 40.00
MG Manu Ginobili/25 25.00 60.00
MP Mickael Pietrus/25 10.00 25.00
RJ Richard Jefferson/15 12.00 30.00

2003-04 Flair Final Edition

COMP.SET w/o SP's (65) 12.50 30.00
66-90 RC PRINT RUN 799 SER.#'d SETS
1 Allen Iverson .75 2.00
2 Juwan Howard .25 .60
3 Stephen Jackson .25 .60
4 Manu Ginobili .60 1.50
5 Steve Nash .60 1.50
6 Jason Terry .25 .60
7 Tayshaun Prince .30 .75
8 Stephon Marbury .40 1.00
9 Eddie Jones .30 .75
10 Reggie Miller .60 1.50
11 Baron Davis .30 .75
12 Donyell Marshall .20 .50
13 Mike Bibby .30 .75
14 Kobe Bryant 2.50 6.00
15 Jason Richardson .30 .75
16 Cuttino Mobley .20 .50
17 Andre Miller .25 .60
18 Corey Maggette .25 .60
19 Michael Finley .30 .75
20 Jason Kidd .50 1.25
21 Lamar Odom .25 .60
22 Tracy McGrady .50 1.25
23 Peja Stojakovic .25 .60
24 Richard Jefferson .25 .60
25 Rasheed Wallace .40 1.00
26 Eddy Curry .20 .50
27 Ben Wallace .40 1.00
28 Rashard Lewis .25 .60
29 Sam Cassell .25 .60
30 Anfernee Hardaway .75 2.00
31 Carlos Boozer .25 .60
32 Jamal Crawford .30 .75
33 Dirk Nowitzki .75 2.00
34 Steve Francis .30 .75
35 Chris Webber .40 1.00
36 Elton Brand .30 .75
37 Michael Redd .30 .75
38 Jason Williams .50 1.25
39 Nene .25 .60
40 Nick Van Exel .30 .75
41 Amare Stoudemire .40 1.00
42 Latrell Sprewell .40 1.00
43 Tony Parker .50 1.25
44 Keith Van Horn .25 .60
45 Pau Gasol .50 1.25
46 Andrei Kirilenko .25 .60
47 Shareef Abdur-Rahim .30 .75
48 Tim Thomas .20 .50
49 Jerry Stackhouse .40 1.00
50 Jermaine O'Neal .30 .75
51 Jamal Mashburn .25 .60
52 Matt Harpring .20 .50
53 Damon Stoudamire .25 .60
54 Zydrunas Ilgauskas .25 .60
55 Kevin Garnett .75 2.00
56 Tim Duncan .75 2.00
57 Yao Ming .75 2.00
58 Kenyon Martin .30 .75
59 Paul Pierce .50 1.25
60 Ron Artest .30 .75
61 Vince Carter .60 1.50
62 Shaquille O'Neal 1.25 3.00
63 Shawn Marion .30 .75
64 Gilbert Arenas .30 .75
65 Ray Allen .50 1.25
66 Chris Bosh RC 6.00 15.00
67 Brian Cook RC 1.25 3.00
68 Luke Ridnour RC 2.00 5.00
69 Willie Green RC 2.00 5.00
70 Zarko Cabarkapa RC 1.25 3.00
71 Maurice Williams RC 2.00 5.00
72 Luke Walton RC 2.00 5.00
73 David West RC 2.50 6.00
74 Mickael Pietrus RC 1.50 4.00
75 LeBron James RC 400.00 800.00
76 Marcus Banks RC 1.25 3.00
77 Keith Bogans RC 1.25 3.00
78 Darko Milicic RC 1.50 4.00
79 Jarvis Hayes RC 1.25 3.00
80 Josh Howard RC 2.00 5.00
81 Chris Kaman RC 2.00 5.00
82 Mike Sweetney RC 1.25 3.00
83 Carmelo Anthony RC 10.00 25.00
84 Travis Outlaw RC 1.50 4.00
85 Kyle Korver RC 2.50 6.00
86 Boris Diaw RC 2.00 5.00
87 Dwyane Wade RC 15.00 40.00
88 Troy Bell RC 1.25 3.00
89 T.J. Ford RC 1.50 4.00
90 Kirk Hinrich RC 2.00 5.00

2003-04 Flair Final Edition Row 1

*1-65 SINGLES: 2.5X TO 6X BASE CARD HI
*66-90 RC SINGLES: .75X TO 2X BASE HI
PRINT RUN 100 SER.#'d SETS
75 LeBron James 2,000.00 4,000.00
87 Dwyane Wade 25.00 60.00

2003-04 Flair Final Edition Autograph Collection

PRINT RUN 75 TO 200 SER.#'d SETS
*AUTO 25: .75X TO 2X BASE HI
*AUTO 100: .5X TO 1.25X BASE HI
N Nene/200 5.00 12.00
AJ Antawn Jamison/200 6.00 15.00
AK Andrei Kirilenko/200 5.00 12.00
AS Amare Stoudemire/200 8.00 20.00
AW Antoine Walker/200 6.00 15.00
BD Baron Davis/200 6.00 15.00
BM Brad Miller/200 5.00 12.00
CM Corey Maggette/200 5.00 12.00
EG Manu Ginobili/200 15.00 40.00
FJ Fred Jones/200 4.00 10.00
GA Gilbert Arenas/200 6.00 15.00
GP Gary Payton/75 12.00 30.00
JD Juan Dixon/200 4.00 10.00
JJ Joe Johnson/200 5.00 12.00
JS Jerry Stackhouse/200 8.00 20.00
JW Jason Williams/200 15.00 40.00
KB Kwame Brown/200 4.00 10.00
LB Leandro Barbosa/200 5.00 12.00
LR Luke Ridnour/200 5.00 12.00
MP Mickael Pietrus/150 5.00 12.00
PP Paul Pierce/200 15.00 40.00
PS Peja Stojakovic/200 5.00 12.00
RH Richard Hamilton/200 8.00 20.00
RJ Richard Jefferson/200 5.00 12.00
RM Ronald Murray/200 4.00 10.00
SB Shane Battier/75 5.00 12.00
TP Tayshaun Prince/200 6.00 15.00
VC Vince Carter/100 12.00 30.00
WG Willie Green/200 6.00 15.00
CAB Carlos Boozer/200 5.00 12.00
CHB Chris Bosh/200 20.00 50.00
DAW Dajuan Wagner/200 5.00 12.00
DAW David West/150 8.00 20.00
DWW Dwyane Wade/200 20.00 50.00

2003-04 Flair Final Edition Courtside Cuts Jerseys 250

PRINT RUN 250 SER.#'d SETS
*JERSEY 175: .4X TO 1X BASE JSY HI
*JERSEY 125: .5X TO 1.25X BASE JSY HI
*JERSEY 75: .6X TO 1.5X BASE JSY HI
*JERSEY DC: 1X TO 2.5X BASE HI
*JERSEY GREEN: .4X TO 1X BASE HI
JERSEY DIE CUT PRINT RUN 25 SETS
N Nene 2.00 5.00
AI Allen Iverson 6.00 15.00
BD Baron Davis 2.50 6.00
CA Carmelo Anthony 12.00 30.00
CK Chris Kaman 2.50 6.00
CM Cuttino Mobley 1.50 4.00
CW Chris Webber 3.00 8.00
EB Elton Brand 2.00 5.00
GA Gilbert Arenas 2.50 6.00
JS Jerry Stackhouse 3.00 8.00
LO Lamar Odom 2.00 5.00
MF Michael Finley 2.50 6.00
PS Peja Stojakovic 2.00 5.00
RM Reggie Miller 5.00 12.00
SN Steve Nash 5.00 12.00
SN Steve Francis 2.50 6.00
WG Willie Green 2.50 6.00
DAW David West 3.00 8.00
DWW Dwyane Wade 20.00 50.00
JON Jermaine O'Neal 2.50 6.00

2003-04 Flair Final Edition Courtside Cuts Patches

*PATCH: 1.25X TO 3X BASE JSY HI
PRINT RUN 50 SER.#'d SETS

2003-04 Flair Final Edition Courtside Cuts Patches Gold

PRINT RUNS LISTED BELOW
*DIE CUTS: .4X TO 1X BASE HI
N Nene/31 8.00 20.00
CA Carmelo Anthony/15 30.00 80.00
CK Chris Kaman/35 8.00 20.00
DW David West/30 12.00 30.00
EB Elton Brand/42 6.00 15.00
JS Jerry Stackhouse/42 10.00 25.00
RM Reggie Miller/31 20.00 50.00
WG Willie Green/33 8.00 20.00

2003-04 Flair Final Edition Courtside Cuts Patches Platinum

PRINT RUNS LISTED BELOW
*DIE CUTS: .4X TO 1X BASE HI
N Nene/43 6.00 15.00
AI Allen Iverson/33 20.00 50.00
BD Baron Davis/41 8.00 20.00
CA Carmelo Anthony/43 40.00 100.00
CK Chris Kaman/28 8.00 20.00
CM Cuttino Mobley/45 5.00 12.00
CW Chris Webber/55 10.00 25.00
DW Dwyane Wade/42 60.00 150.00
DW David West/51 10.00 25.00
EB Elton Brand/28 6.00 15.00
GA Gilbert Arenas/25 8.00 20.00
JO Jermaine O'Neal/61 8.00 20.00
JS Jerry Stackhouse/25 12.50 30.00
LO Lamar Odom/42 6.00 15.00
MF Michael Finley/42 8.00 20.00
PS Peja Stojakovic/55 6.00 15.00
RM Reggie Miller/61 15.00 40.00
SF Steve Francis/45 8.00 20.00
SN Steve Nash/52 15.00 40.00
WG Willie Green/33 8.00 20.00

2003-04 Flair Final Edition Cuts and Glory Autographs

PRINT RUN 100 SER.#'d SETS
*AUTO 50: .5X TO 1.25X BASE AUTO HI
CA Carmelo Anthony 20.00 50.00
CG Mike Bibby 10.00 25.00
DM Darius Miles 8.00 20.00
DR David Robinson 30.00 80.00
EC Eddy Curry 8.00 20.00
JK Jason Kidd 20.00 50.00
JO Jermaine O'Neal 10.00 25.00
KM Kenyon Martin 10.00 25.00
LO Lamar Odom 10.00 25.00
MB Marcus Banks 8.00 20.00
MS Mike Sweetney 8.00 20.00
RG Reece Gaines 8.00 20.00
RM Reggie Miller 40.00 100.00
TM Tracy McGrady 20.00 50.00
TP Tony Parker 10.00 25.00
VC Vince Carter 20.00 40.00
BEN Ben Wallace 20.00 50.00

2003-04 Flair Final Edition Hot Numbers Jerseys 250

PRINT RUN 250 SER.#'d SETS
*JERSEY 175: .4X TO 1X BASE HI
*JERSEY 125: .5X TO 1.25X BASE HI
*JERSEY 75: .6X TO 1.5X BASE HI
*DIE CUT: 1X TO 2.5X BASE HI
*GREEN: .4X TO 1X BASE HI
DIE CUT PRINT RUN 25 SER.#'d SETS
AI Allen Iverson 6.00 15.00
AS Amare Stoudemire 3.00 8.00
CA Carmelo Anthony 12.00 30.00
CB Chris Bosh 8.00 20.00
CM Corey Maggette 2.00 5.00
DN Dirk Nowitzki 6.00 15.00
DW Dwyane Wade 20.00 50.00
EB Elton Brand 2.00 5.00
JK Jason Kidd 4.00 10.00
JR Jason Richardson 2.50 6.00
KG Kevin Garnett 6.00 15.00
LS Latrell Sprewell 3.00 8.00
MB Mike Bibby 2.50 6.00
MF Michael Finley 2.50 6.00
MG Manu Ginobili 5.00 12.00
MR Michael Redd 2.50 6.00
PG Pau Gasol 4.00 10.00
PP Paul Pierce 4.00 10.00
RA Ray Allen 4.00 10.00
SF Steve Francis 2.50 6.00
TD Tim Duncan 6.00 15.00
TM Tracy McGrady 4.00 10.00
VC Vince Carter 5.00 12.00
JON Jermaine O'Neal 2.50 6.00
KAM Karl Malone 5.00 12.00
KEM Kenyon Martin 2.50 6.00
SHM Shawn Marion 2.50 6.00
SON Shaquille O'Neal 10.00 25.00
STM Stephon Marbury 3.00 8.00
YAO Yao Ming 6.00 15.00

1994 Flair USA

COMPLETE SET (120) 15.00 40.00
1 Don Chaney CO .15 .40
2 Don Chaney CO .15 .40
3 Pete Gillen CO .15 .40
4 Pete Gillen CO .15 .40
5 Rick Majerus CO .20 .50
6 Rick Majerus CO .20 .50
7 Don Nelson CO .20 .50
8 Don Nelson CO .20 .50
9 Derrick Coleman .30 .75
10 Derrick Coleman .30 .75
11 Derrick Coleman .30 .75
12 Derrick Coleman .30 .75
13 Derrick Coleman .30 .75
14 Derrick Coleman .30 .75
15 Derrick Coleman .30 .75
16 Joe Dumars .40 1.00
17 Joe Dumars .40 1.00
18 Joe Dumars .40 1.00
19 Joe Dumars .40 1.00
20 Joe Dumars .40 1.00
21 Joe Dumars .40 1.00
22 Joe Dumars .40 1.00
23 Joe Dumars .40 1.00
24 Joe Dumars .40 1.00
25 Tim Hardaway .40 1.00
26 Tim Hardaway .40 1.00
27 Tim Hardaway .40 1.00
28 Tim Hardaway .40 1.00
29 Tim Hardaway .40 1.00
30 Tim Hardaway .40 1.00
31 Tim Hardaway .40 1.00
32 Tim Hardaway .40 1.00
33 Larry Johnson .40 1.00
34 Larry Johnson .40 1.00
35 Larry Johnson .40 1.00
36 Larry Johnson .40 1.00
37 Larry Johnson .40 1.00
38 Larry Johnson .40 1.00
39 Larry Johnson .40 1.00
40 Larry Johnson .40 1.00
41 Shawn Kemp .40 1.00
42 Shawn Kemp .40 1.00
43 Shawn Kemp .40 1.00
44 Shawn Kemp .40 1.00
45 Shawn Kemp .40 1.00
46 Shawn Kemp .40 1.00
47 Shawn Kemp .40 1.00
48 Shawn Kemp .40 1.00
49 Dan Majerle .30 .75
50 Dan Majerle .30 .75
51 Dan Majerle .30 .75
52 Dan Majerle .30 .75
53 Dan Majerle .30 .75
54 Dan Majerle .30 .75
55 Dan Majerle .30 .75
56 Dan Majerle .30 .75
57 Reggie Miller .50 1.25
58 Reggie Miller .50 1.25
59 Reggie Miller .50 1.25
60 Reggie Miller .50 1.25
61 Reggie Miller .50 1.25
62 Reggie Miller .50 1.25
63 Reggie Miller .50 1.25
64 Reggie Miller .50 1.25
65 Alonzo Mourning .40 1.00
66 Alonzo Mourning .40 1.00
67 Alonzo Mourning .40 1.00
68 Alonzo Mourning .40 1.00
69 Alonzo Mourning .40 1.00
70 Alonzo Mourning .40 1.00
71 Alonzo Mourning .40 1.00
72 Alonzo Mourning .40 1.00
73 Shaquille O'Neal 1.00 2.50
74 Shaquille O'Neal 1.00 2.50
75 Shaquille O'Neal 1.00 2.50
76 Shaquille O'Neal 1.00 2.50
77 Shaquille O'Neal 1.00 2.50
78 Shaquille O'Neal 1.00 2.50
79 Shaquille O'Neal 1.00 2.50
80 Shaquille O'Neal 1.00 2.50
81 Mark Price .30 .75
82 Mark Price .30 .75
83 Mark Price .30 .75
84 Mark Price .30 .75
85 Mark Price .30 .75
86 Mark Price .30 .75
87 Mark Price .30 .75
88 Mark Price .30 .75
89 Steve Smith .25 .60
90 Steve Smith .25 .60
91 Steve Smith .25 .60
92 Steve Smith .25 .60
93 Steve Smith .25 .60
94 Steve Smith .25 .60
95 Steve Smith .25 .60
96 Steve Smith .25 .60
97 Isiah Thomas .50 1.25
98 Isiah Thomas .50 1.25
99 Isiah Thomas .50 1.25
100 Isiah Thomas .50 1.25
101 Isiah Thomas .50 1.25
102 Isiah Thomas .50 1.25
103 Isiah Thomas .50 1.25
104 Isiah Thomas .50 1.25
105 Dominique Wilkins .50 1.25
106 Dominique Wilkins .50 1.25
107 Dominique Wilkins .50 1.25
108 Dominique Wilkins .50 1.25
109 Dominique Wilkins .50 1.25
110 Dominique Wilkins .50 1.25
111 Dominique Wilkins .50 1.25
112 Dominique Wilkins .50 1.25
113 Carol Blazejowski 1.50 4.00
114 Teresa Edwards 1.50 4.00
115 Nancy Lieberman-Cline 4.00 10.00
116 Ann Meyers 1.50 4.00
117 Pat Summitt CO 2.00 5.00
118 Lynette Woodard 1.25 3.00
119 Checklist .15 .40
120 Checklist .15 .40

1994 Flair USA Kevin Johnson

COMPLETE SET (10) 5.00 12.00
COMMON CARD (M1-M8) .50 1.25
119 Team Checklist 1.00 2.50
120 Team Checklist 1.00 2.50

2003-04 Flair Final Edition Hot Numbers Patches

*50 SINGLES: 1.25X TO 3X BASE JSY HI
PRINT RUN 50 SER.#'d SETS
PATCH ONE OF ONE's EXIST

2003-04 Flair Final Edition Hot Numbers Patches Gold

PRINT RUNS LISTED BELOW
AS Amare Stoudemire/32 10.00 25.00
CA Carmelo Anthony/15 40.00 100.00
CM Corey Maggette/50 6.00 15.00
DN Dirk Nowitzki/41 15.00 40.00
EB Elton Brand/42 5.00 12.00
KG Kevin Garnett/21 20.00 50.00
PG Pau Gasol/16 10.00 25.00
PP Paul Pierce/34 10.00 25.00
RA Ray Allen/34 10.00 25.00
TD Tim Duncan/21 15.00 40.00
SHM Shawn Marion/31 8.00 20.00
SON Shaquille O'Neal/34 25.00 60.00

2003-04 Flair Final Edition Hot Numbers Patches Platinum

PRINT RUNS LISTED BELOW
AI Allen Iverson/33 20.00 50.00
AS Amare Stoudemire/29 10.00 25.00
CA Carmelo Anthony/43 15.00 20.00
CB Chris Bosh/33 25.00 60.00
CM Corey Maggette/28 6.00 15.00
DN Dirk Nowitzki/52 20.00 50.00
DW Dwyane Wade/42 60.00 150.00
EB Elton Brand/28 6.00 15.00
JK Jason Kidd/47 12.00 30.00
JR Jason Richardson/37 8.00 20.00
KG Kevin Garnett/58 20.00 50.00
LS Latrell Sprewell/58 10.00 25.00
MB Mike Bibby/55 8.00 20.00
MF Michael Finley/52 8.00 20.00
MG Manu Ginobili/57 15.00 40.00
MR Michael Redd/41 8.00 20.00
PG Pau Gasol/50 12.00 30.00
PP Paul Pierce/36 12.00 30.00
RA Ray Allen/37 12.00 30.00
SF Steve Francis/45 8.00 20.00
TD Tim Duncan/57 20.00 50.00
TM Tracy McGrady/21 12.00 30.00
VC Vince Carter/33 15.00 40.00
JON Jermaine O'Neal/61 8.00 20.00
KAM Karl Malone/56 15.00 40.00
KEM Kenyon Martin/47 8.00 20.00
SHM Shawn Marion/29 8.00 20.00
SON Shaquille O'Neal/56 30.00 80.00
STM Stephon Marbury/39 10.00 25.00
YAO Yao Ming/45 20.00 50.00

2003-04 Flair Final Edition Hot Numbers Retail

PRINT RUN 500 SER.#'d SETS
1 Jason Kidd 2.50 6.00
2 Latrell Sprewell 2.00 5.00
3 Tracy McGrady 2.50 6.00
4 Carmelo Anthony 8.00 20.00
5 Manu Ginobili 3.00 8.00
6 Allen Iverson 4.00 10.00
7 Dirk Nowitzki 4.00 10.00
8 Pau Gasol 2.50 6.00
9 Ray Allen 2.50 6.00
10 Yao Ming 4.00 10.00
11 Michael Redd 1.50 4.00
12 Stephon Marbury 2.00 5.00
13 Amare Stoudemire 2.00 5.00
14 Vince Carter 3.00 8.00
15 Kevin Garnett 4.00 10.00
16 Kenyon Martin 1.50 4.00
17 Ben Wallace 2.00 5.00
18 Dwyane Wade 30.00 80.00
19 Zach Randolph 1.50 4.00
20 Paul Pierce 2.50 6.00
21 Jermaine O'Neal 1.50 4.00
22 Elton Brand 1.25 3.00
23 Steve Francis 1.50 4.00
24 Kirk Hinrich 1.50 4.00
25 Shaquille O'Neal 6.00 15.00
26 Mike Bibby 1.50 4.00
27 Shawn Marion 1.50 4.00
28 Michael Finley 1.50 4.00
29 Tim Duncan 4.00 10.00
30 LeBron James 500.00 1,000.00
31 Karl Malone 3.00 8.00
32 Chris Bosh 5.00 12.00
33 Kobe Bryant 12.00 30.00
34 Jason Richardson 1.50 4.00
35 Corey Maggette 1.25 3.00

2003-04 Flair Final Edition Hot Numbers Retail Gold

CARDS NUMBERED TO PLAYER JERSEY
8 Pau Gasol/16 15.00 40.00
30 LeBron James/23 8,000.00 12,000.00

2003-04 Flair Final Edition Power Game Jersey and Patch

PRINT RUN 50 TO 75 SER.#'d SETS
N Nene/50 6.00 15.00
AJ Antawn Jamison/50 8.00 20.00
AK Andrei Kirilenko/50 6.00 15.00
CW Chris Webber/75 10.00 25.00
DN Dirk Nowitzki/50 15.00 40.00
JH Jarvis Hayes/75 5.00 12.00
KG Kevin Garnett/50 20.00 50.00
KM Kenyon Martin/50 8.00 20.00
MS Mike Sweetney/50 5.00 12.00
PP Paul Pierce/75 12.00 30.00
RW Ben Wallace/50 10.00 25.00
TD Tim Duncan/50 20.00 50.00
VC Vince Carter/50 15.00 40.00
SON Shaquille O'Neal/50 30.00 80.00
YAO Yao Ming/75 20.00 50.00

2003-04 Flair Final Edition Power Game Jersey and Patch Gold

PRINT RUNS LISTED BELOW
AJ Antawn Jamison/33 10.00 25.00
AK Andrei Kirilenko/47 8.00 20.00
DN Dirk Nowitzki/41 25.00 60.00
JH Jarvis Hayes/24 6.00 15.00
KG Kevin Garnett/21 25.00 60.00
MS Mike Sweetney/50 6.00 15.00
PP Paul Pierce/34 15.00 40.00
TD Tim Duncan/21 25.00 60.00
VC Vince Carter/15 20.00 50.00
SON Shaquille O'Neal/34 40.00 100.00

2003-04 Flair Final Edition Power Game Jersey and Patch Platinum

PRINT RUNS LISTED BELOW
N Nene/43 6.00 15.00
AJ Antawn Jamison/52 8.00 20.00
AK Andrei Kirilenko/42 6.00 15.00
CW Chris Webber/55 10.00 25.00
DN Dirk Nowitzki/52 20.00 50.00
JH Jarvis Hayes/25 5.00 12.00
KG Kevin Garnett/58 20.00 50.00
KM Kenyon Martin/47 8.00 20.00
MS Mike Sweetney/39 5.00 12.00
PP Paul Pierce/36 12.00 30.00
RW Ben Wallace/54 10.00 25.00
TD Tim Duncan/57 20.00 50.00
VC Vince Carter/33 15.00 40.00
SON Shaquille O'Neal/56 30.00 80.00
YAO Yao Ming/45 20.00 50.00

2003-04 Flair Final Edition Power Game Jerseys

PRINT RUN 250 SER.#'d SETS
*JERSEY 175: .4X TO 1X BASE HI
*JERSEY 125: .5X TO 1.25X BASE HI
*DIE CUT: 1X TO 2.5X BASE HI
DIE CUT PRINT RUN 25 SER.#'d SETS
N Nene 2.00 5.00
AJ Antawn Jamison 2.50 6.00
AK Andrei Kirilenko 2.00 5.00
CW Chris Webber 3.00 8.00
DN Dirk Nowitzki 6.00 15.00
JH Jarvis Hayes 1.50 4.00
KG Kevin Garnett 6.00 15.00
KM Kenyon Martin 2.50 6.00
MS Mike Sweetney 1.50 4.00
PP Paul Pierce 4.00 10.00
RW Ben Wallace 3.00 8.00
TD Tim Duncan 6.00 15.00
VC Vince Carter 5.00 12.00
SON Shaquille O'Neal 10.00 25.00
YAO Yao Ming 6.00 15.00

2003-04 Flair Final Edition Power Game Patches

*75 PATCHES : 1.25X TO 3X BASE JSY HI
PRINT RUN 75 SER.#'d SETS

2003-04 Flair Final Edition SIGnificant Cuts

PRINT RUNS LISTED BELOW
AJ Antawn Jamison/48 8.00 20.00
AK Andrei Kirilenko/76 15.00 40.00
BW Ben Wallace/50 12.00 30.00
CA Carmelo Anthony/50 30.00 80.00
DR David Robinson/50 50.00 120.00
DW Dwyane Wade/60 40.00 100.00
JK Jason Kidd/25 25.00 60.00
KM Kenyon Martin/60 8.00 20.00
MB Mike Bibby/50 8.00 20.00
PP Paul Pierce/60 20.00 50.00
RM Reggie Miller/49 60.00 120.00
SF Steve Francis/60 12.50 30.00
TM Tracy McGrady/50 12.00 30.00
TP Tony Parker/50 12.50 30.00
UH Udonis Haslem/76 8.00 20.00

1961-62 Fleer

COMPLETE SET (66) 5,000.00 10,000.00
CONDITION SENSITIVE SET
CARDS PRICED IN EX-MT CONDITION
1 Al Attles RC 125.00 300.00
2 Paul Arizin 75.00 200.00
3 Elgin Baylor RC 600.00 1,200.00
4 Walt Bellamy RC 75.00 200.00
5 Arlen Bockhorn 40.00 100.00
6 Bob Boozer RC 40.00 100.00
7 Carl Braun 20.00 50.00
8 Wilt Chamberlain RC 3,000.00 6,000.00
9 Larry Costello 12.00 30.00
10 Bob Cousy 150.00 400.00
11 Walter Dukes 50.00 120.00
12 Wayne Embry RC 30.00 80.00
13 Dave Gambee 15.00 40.00
14 Tom Gola 20.00 50.00
15 Sihugo Green RC 15.00 40.00
16 Hal Greer RC 75.00 200.00
17 Richie Guerin RC 25.00 60.00
18 Cliff Hagan 15.00 40.00
19 Tom Heinsohn 30.00 80.00
20 Bailey Howell RC 40.00 100.00
21 Rod Hundley 25.00 60.00
22 K.C. Jones RC 60.00 150.00
23 Sam Jones RC 75.00 200.00
24 Phil Jordan 15.00 40.00
25 John Kerr 15.00 40.00
26 Rudy LaRusso RC 25.00 60.00
27 George Lee 25.00 60.00
28 Bob Leonard 10.00 25.00
29 Clyde Lovellette 25.00 60.00
30 John McCarthy 25.00 60.00
31 Tom Meschery RC 25.00 60.00
32 Willie Naulls 12.00 30.00
33 Don Ohl RC 12.00 30.00
34 Bob Pettit 50.00 120.00
35 Frank Ramsey 20.00 50.00
36 Oscar Robertson RC 1,000.00 2,000.00
37 Guy Rodgers RC 25.00 60.00
38 Bill Russell ! 500.00 1,000.00
39 Dolph Schayes 50.00 120.00
40 Frank Selvy 20.00 50.00
41 Gene Shue 15.00 40.00
42 Jack Twyman 30.00 80.00
43 Jerry West RC 1,000.00 2,000.00
44 Len Wilkens UER RC 100.00 250.00
45 Paul Arizin IA 30.00 80.00
46 Elgin Baylor IA 125.00 300.00
47 Wilt Chamberlain IA ! 1,000.00 2,000.00
48 Larry Costello IA 20.00 50.00
49 Bob Cousy IA 100.00 250.00
50 Walter Dukes IA 15.00 40.00
51 Tom Gola IA 10.00 25.00
52 Richie Guerin IA 20.00 50.00
53 Cliff Hagan IA 15.00 40.00
54 Tom Heinsohn IA 30.00 80.00
55 Bailey Howell IA 25.00 60.00
56 John Kerr IA 12.00 30.00
57 Rudy LaRusso IA 25.00 60.00
58 Clyde Lovellette IA 25.00 60.00
59 Bob Pettit IA 40.00 100.00
60 Frank Ramsey IA 25.00 60.00
61 Oscar Robertson IA ! 125.00 300.00
62 Bill Russell IA ! 400.00 800.00
63 Dolph Schayes IA 30.00 80.00
64 Gene Shue IA 20.00 50.00
65 Jack Twyman IA 30.00 80.00
66 Jerry West IA ! 200.00 500.00

1973-74 Fleer The Shots

COMPLETE SET (21) 40.00 80.00
COMMON CARD (1-21) 1.50 4.00
21 The Good Shot 2.00 5.00

1974 Fleer Team Patches/Stickers

COMPLETE SET (38) 40.00 80.00
1 NBA Logo 1.00 2.50
2 Atlanta Hawks .75 2.00
3 Boston Celtics 1.00 2.50
4 Buffalo Braves 1.00 2.50
5 Chicago Bulls .75 2.00
6 Cleveland Cavaliers .75 2.00
7 Detroit Pistons .75 2.00
8 Golden State Warriors 1.00 2.50
9 Houston Rockets .75 2.00
10 Kansas City Kings .75 2.00
11 Los Angeles Lakers 1.00 2.50
12 Milwaukee Bucks .75 2.00
13 New Orleans Jazz 1.00 2.50
14 New York Knicks 1.00 2.50
15 Philadelphia 76ers .75 2.00
16 Phoenix Suns .75 2.00
17 Portland Trail Blazers .75 2.00
18 Seattle Supersonics .75 2.00
19 Washington Bullets .75 2.00
20 NBA Logo 1.25 3.00
21 Atlanta Hawks 1.00 2.50
22 Boston Celtics 1.25 3.00
23 Buffalo Braves 1.25 3.00
24 Chicago Bulls 1.00 2.50
25 Cleveland Cavaliers 1.00 2.50
26 Detroit Pistons 1.00 2.50
27 Golden State Warriors 1.00 2.50
28 Houston Rockets 1.00 2.50
29 Kansas City Kings 1.25 3.00
30 Los Angeles Lakers 1.25 3.00
31 Milwaukee Bucks 1.00 2.50
32 New Orleans Jazz 1.25 3.00
33 New York Knicks 1.25 3.00
34 Philadelphia 76ers 1.00 2.50
35 Phoenix Suns 1.00 2.50
36 Portland Trail Blazers 1.00 2.50
37 Seattle Supersonics 1.00 2.50
38 Washington Bullets 1.00 2.50

1977-78 Fleer Team Stickers

COMPLETE SET (22) 7.50 15.00
NNO Atlanta Hawks .30 .75
NNO Boston Celtics .40 1.00
NNO Buffalo Braves .40 1.00
NNO Chicago Bulls .30 .75
NNO Cleveland Cavaliers .30 .75
NNO Denver Nuggets .30 .75

0 Detroit Pistons .30 .75
0 Golden State Warriors .30 .75
0 Houston Rockets .30 .75
0 Indiana Pacers .30 .75
0 Kansas City Kings .40 1.00
0 Los Angeles Lakers .40 1.00
0 Milwaukee Bucks .30 .75
0 New Jersey Nets .30 .75
0 New Orleans Jazz .40 1.00
0 New York Knicks .40 1.00
0 Philadelphia 76ers .30 .75
0 Phoenix Suns .30 .75
0 Portland Trail Blazers .30 .75
0 San Antonio Spurs .30 .75
0 Seattle Supersonics .30 .75
0 Washington Bullets .30 .75

1986-87 Fleer

OMPLETE w/Stickers (143) 10,000.00 15,000.00
OMP.SET (132) 8,000.00 12,000.00
Kareem Abdul-Jabbar 25.00 60.00
Alvan Adams 2.00 5.00
Mark Aguirre RC 8.00 20.00
Danny Ainge RC 8.00 20.00
John Bagley RC 3.00 8.00
Thurl Bailey RC 6.00 15.00
Charles Barkley RC 75.00 200.00
Benoit Benjamin RC 2.00 5.00
Larry Bird ! 30.00 80.00
Otis Birdsong 1.50 4.00
Rolando Blackman RC 4.00 10.00
2 Manute Bol RC 10.00 25.00
3 Sam Bowie RC 4.00 10.00
4 Joe Barry Carroll 1.50 4.00
5 Tom Chambers RC 8.00 20.00
6 Maurice Cheeks 2.00 5.00
7 Michael Cooper 4.00 10.00
8 Wayne Cooper 2.00 5.00
9 Pat Cummings 2.00 5.00
0 Terry Cummings RC 6.00 15.00
1 Adrian Dantley 6.00 15.00
2 Brad Davis RC 4.00 10.00
3 Walter Davis 2.00 5.00
4 Darryl Dawkins 2.00 5.00
5 Larry Drew RC 1.50 4.00
26 Clyde Drexler RC 40.00 100.00
27 Joe Dumars RC 12.00 30.00
28 Mark Eaton RC 5.00 12.00
29 James Edwards 2.50 6.00
30 Alex English 2.00 5.00
31 Julius Erving 20.00 50.00
32 Patrick Ewing 40.00 100.00
33 Vern Fleming RC 2.00 5.00
34 Sleepy Floyd RC 2.00 5.00
35 World B. Free 3.00 8.00
36 George Gervin 5.00 12.00
37 Artis Gilmore 6.00 15.00
38 Mike Gminski 2.00 5.00
39 Rickey Green 2.00 5.00
40 Sidney Green 2.00 5.00
41 David Greenwood 2.50 6.00
42 Darrell Griffith 3.00 8.00
43 Bill Hanzlik 1.50 4.00
44 Derek Harper RC 3.00 8.00
45 Gerald Henderson 1.50 4.00
46 Roy Hinson 5.00 12.00
47 Craig Hodges RC 2.50 6.00
48 Phil Hubbard 1.00 2.50
49 Jay Humphries RC 1.25 3.00
50 Dennis Johnson 6.00 15.00
51 Eddie Johnson RC 4.00 10.00
52 Frank Johnson RC 2.00 5.00
53 Magic Johnson 25.00 60.00
54 Marques Johnson 2.00 5.00
55 Steve Johnson UER 2.00 5.00
56 Vinnie Johnson 2.00 5.00
57 Michael Jordan RC 2,500.00 5,000.00
58 Clark Kellogg RC 8.00 20.00
59 Albert King RC 2.00 5.00
60 Bernard King 1.00 2.50
61 Bill Laimbeer 3.00 8.00
62 Allen Leavell .75 2.00
63 Lafayette Lever RC 3.00 8.00
64 Alton Lister 1.50 4.00
65 Lewis Lloyd 2.00 5.00
66 Maurice Lucas 2.00 5.00
67 Jeff Malone RC 4.00 10.00
68 Karl Malone RC 25.00 60.00
69 Moses Malone 4.00 10.00
70 Cedric Maxwell 2.50 6.00
71 Rodney McCray RC 2.50 6.00
72 Xavier McDaniel RC 4.00 10.00
73 Kevin McHale 5.00 12.00
74 Mike Mitchell 2.00 5.00
75 Sidney Moncrief 3.00 8.00
76 Johnny Moore 6.00 15.00
77 Chris Mullin RC 20.00 50.00
78 Larry Nance RC 4.00 10.00
79 Calvin Natt 2.00 5.00
80 Norm Nixon 3.00 8.00
81 Charles Oakley RC 8.00 20.00
82 Hakeem Olajuwon RC 75.00 200.00
83 Louis Orr 2.00 5.00
84 Robert Parish UER 3.00 8.00
85 Jim Paxson 2.00 5.00
86 Sam Perkins RC 5.00 12.00
87 Ricky Pierce RC 3.00 8.00
88 Paul Pressey RC 2.50 6.00
89 Kurt Rambis RC 4.00 10.00
90 Robert Reid 1.50 4.00
91 Doc Rivers RC 4.00 10.00
92 Alvin Robertson RC 2.50 6.00
93 Cliff Robinson 1.50 4.00
94 Tree Rollins 1.50 4.00
95 Dan Roundfield 1.50 4.00
96 Jeff Ruland 1.50 4.00
97 Ralph Sampson RC 8.00 20.00
98 Danny Schayes RC 1.50 4.00
99 Byron Scott RC 8.00 20.00
100 Purvis Short 2.00 5.00
101 Jerry Sichting 1.50 4.00
102 Jack Sikma 2.00 5.00
103 Derek Smith 1.50 4.00
104 Larry Smith 6.00 15.00
105 Rory Sparrow 1.50 4.00
106 Steve Stipanovich 1.50 4.00
107 Terry Teagle 1.50 4.00
108 Reggie Theus 3.00 8.00
109 Isiah Thomas RC 30.00 80.00
110 LaSalle Thompson RC 2.50 6.00
111 Mychal Thompson 3.00 8.00
112 Sedale Threatt RC 2.00 5.00
113 Wayman Tisdale RC 10.00 25.00
114 Andrew Toney 3.00 8.00
115 Kelly Tripucka RC 2.00 5.00
116 Mel Turpin 2.00 5.00
117 Kiki Vandeweghe RC 6.00 15.00
118 Jay Vincent 2.00 5.00
119 Bill Walton 10.00 25.00
120 Spud Webb RC 25.00 60.00
121 Dominique Wilkins RC 40.00 100.00
122 Gerald Wilkins RC 2.50 6.00
123 Buck Williams RC 3.00 8.00
124 Gus Williams 6.00 15.00
125 Herb Williams RC 3.00 8.00
126 Kevin Willis RC 5.00 12.00
127 Randy Wittman 2.00 5.00
128 Al Wood 2.00 5.00
129 Mike Woodson 2.00 5.00
130 Orlando Woolridge RC 4.00 10.00
131 James Worthy RC 20.00 50.00
132 Checklist 1-132 15.00 40.00

1986-87 Fleer Stickers

COMPLETE SET (11) 800.00 1,500.00
1 Kareem Abdul-Jabbar 30.00 80.00
2 Larry Bird 25.00 60.00
3 Adrian Dantley 20.00 50.00
4 Alex English 20.00 50.00
5 Julius Erving 25.00 60.00
6 Patrick Ewing 20.00 50.00
7 Magic Johnson 25.00 60.00
8 Michael Jordan 600.00 1,200.00
9 Hakeem Olajuwon 30.00 80.00
10 Isiah Thomas 20.00 50.00
11 Dominique Wilkins 20.00 50.00

1987-88 Fleer

COMPLETE w/Stickers (143) 400.00 800.00
COMPLETE SET (132) 200.00 500.00
CONDITION SENSITIVE SET
1 Kareem Abdul-Jabbar 8.00 20.00
2 Alvan Adams .75 2.00
3 Mark Aguirre 1.00 2.50
4 Danny Ainge 1.25 3.00
5 John Bagley .75 2.00
6 Thurl Bailey UER 1.00 2.50
7 Greg Ballard .75 2.00
8 Gene Banks .75 2.00
9 Charles Barkley 8.00 20.00
10 Benoit Benjamin .75 2.00
11 Larry Bird ! 10.00 25.00
12 Rolando Blackman 1.00 2.50
13 Manute Bol 1.50 4.00
14 Tony Brown 1.25 3.00
15 Michael Cage RC 2.00 5.00
16 Joe Barry Carroll .75 2.00
17 Bill Cartwright 1.00 2.50
18 Terry Catledge RC .75 2.00
19 Tom Chambers 1.25 3.00
20 Maurice Cheeks 1.00 2.50
21 Michael Cooper 1.00 2.50
22 Dave Corzine .75 2.00
23 Terry Cummings 1.00 2.50
24 Adrian Dantley 1.00 2.50
25 Brad Daugherty RC 1.50 4.00
26 Walter Davis 1.00 2.50
27 Johnny Dawkins RC 1.50 4.00
28 James Donaldson .75 2.00
29 Larry Drew .75 2.00
30 Clyde Drexler 5.00 12.00
31 Joe Dumars 2.00 5.00
32 Mark Eaton 1.00 2.50
33 Dale Ellis RC 3.00 8.00
34 Alex English 1.25 3.00
35 Julius Erving 5.00 12.00
36 Mike Evans .75 2.00
37 Patrick Ewing 5.00 12.00
38 Vern Fleming 1.00 2.50
39 Sleepy Floyd 1.00 2.50
40 Artis Gilmore 1.25 3.00
41 Mike Gminski UER .75 2.00
42 A.C. Green RC 4.00 10.00
43 Rickey Green 1.00 2.50
44 Sidney Green .75 2.00
45 David Greenwood .75 2.00
46 Darrell Griffith 1.00 2.50
47 Bill Hanzlik .75 2.00
48 Derek Harper 1.00 2.50
49 Ron Harper RC 6.00 15.00
50 Gerald Henderson .75 2.00
51 Roy Hinson .75 2.00
52 Craig Hodges .75 2.00
53 Phil Hubbard .75 2.00
54 Dennis Johnson 1.25 3.00
55 Eddie Johnson .75 2.00
56 Magic Johnson 8.00 20.00
57 Steve Johnson .75 2.00
58 Vinnie Johnson 1.00 2.50
59 Michael Jordan ! 125.00 300.00
60 Jerome Kersey RC 1.25 3.00
61 Bill Laimbeer 1.00 2.50
62 Lafayette Lever UER 1.00 2.50
63 Cliff Levingston RC 1.00 2.50
64 Alton Lister .75 2.00
65 John Long .75 2.00
66 John Lucas .75 2.00
67 Jeff Malone 1.00 2.50
68 Karl Malone 8.00 20.00
69 Moses Malone 1.50 4.00
70 Cedric Maxwell .75 2.00
71 Tim McCormick .75 2.00
72 Rodney McCray 1.00 2.50
73 Xavier McDaniel 1.00 2.50
74 Kevin McHale 1.50 4.00
75 Nate McMillan RC 1.00 2.50
76 Sidney Moncrief 1.25 3.00
77 Chris Mullin 1.50 4.00
78 Larry Nance 1.00 2.50
79 Charles Oakley 1.00 2.50
80 Hakeem Olajuwon 5.00 12.00
81 Robert Parish UER 1.50 4.00
82 Jim Paxson 1.00 2.50
83 John Paxson RC 1.00 2.50
84 Sam Perkins 1.00 2.50
85 Chuck Person RC 1.25 2.50
86 Jim Petersen .75 2.00
87 Ricky Pierce 1.00 2.50
88 Ed Pinckney RC 1.25 3.00
89 Terry Porter RC 1.00 2.50
90 Paul Pressey .75 2.00
91 Robert Reid .75 2.00
92 Doc Rivers 1.25 3.00
93 Alvin Robertson 1.25 3.00
94 Tree Rollins .75 2.00
95 Ralph Sampson 1.00 2.50
96 Mike Sanders RC 1.00 2.50
97 Detlef Schrempf RC 4.00 10.00
98 Byron Scott 1.25 3.00
99 Jerry Sichting .75 2.00
100 Jack Sikma .75 2.00
101 Larry Smith .75 2.00
102 Rory Sparrow .75 2.00
103 Steve Stipanovich .75 2.00
104 Jon Sundvold .75 2.00
105 Reggie Theus 1.00 2.50
106 Isiah Thomas 4.00 10.00
107 LaSalle Thompson .75 2.00
108 Mychal Thompson .75 2.00
109 Otis Thorpe RC 1.50 4.00
110 Sedale Threatt 1.00 2.50
111 Wayman Tisdale 1.00 2.50
112 Kelly Tripucka .75 2.00
113 Trent Tucker RC 1.00 2.50
114 Terry Tyler .75 2.00
115 Darnell Valentine .75 2.00
116 Kiki Vandeweghe 1.00 2.50
117 Darrell Walker RC 1.25 3.00
118 Dominique Wilkins 5.00 12.00
119 Gerald Wilkins 1.25 3.00
120 Buck Williams 1.00 2.50
121 Herb Williams 1.00 2.50
122 John Williams RC .75 2.00
123 Hot Rod Williams RC 1.00 2.50
124 Kevin Willis 1.25 3.00
125 David Wingate RC 1.25 3.00
126 Randy Wittman .75 2.00
127 Leon Wood .75 2.00
128 Mike Woodson .75 2.00
129 Orlando Woolridge 1.00 2.50
130 James Worthy 1.50 4.00
131 Danny Young RC .75 2.00
132 Checklist 1-132 4.00 10.00

1987-88 Fleer Stickers

COMPLETE SET (11) 300.00 600.00
1 Magic Johnson 10.00 25.00
2 Michael Jordan 75.00 200.00
3 Hakeem Olajuwon UER 8.00 20.00
4 Larry Bird 10.00 25.00
5 Kevin McHale 8.00 20.00
6 Charles Barkley 10.00 25.00
7 Dominique Wilkins 8.00 20.00
8 Kareem Abdul-Jabbar 10.00 25.00
9 Mark Aguirre 4.00 10.00
10 Chuck Person 4.00 10.00
11 Alex English 4.00 10.00

1988-89 Fleer

COMPLETE w/Stickers (143) 200.00 500.00
COMPLETE SET (132) 150.00 400.00
1 Antoine Carr RC 1.00 2.50
2 Cliff Levingston .60 1.50
3 Doc Rivers 1.00 2.50
4 Spud Webb 1.00 2.50
5 Dominique Wilkins 1.50 4.00
6 Kevin Willis .75 2.00
7 Randy Wittman .60 1.50
8 Danny Ainge 1.00 2.50
9 Larry Bird 3.00 8.00
10 Dennis Johnson 1.00 2.50
11 Kevin McHale 1.50 4.00
12 Robert Parish 1.50 4.00
13 Muggsy Bogues RC 1.50 4.00
14 Dell Curry RC 1.25 3.00
15 Dave Corzine .60 1.50
16 Horace Grant RC 3.00 8.00
17 Michael Jordan 40.00 100.00
18 Charles Oakley 1.00 2.50
19 John Paxson .75 2.00
20 Scottie Pippen UER RC 25.00 60.00
21 Brad Sellers RC .60 1.50
22 Brad Daugherty .75 2.00
23 Ron Harper 1.00 2.50
24 Larry Nance .75 2.00
25 Mark Price RC 1.50 4.00
26 Hot Rod Williams .60 1.50
27 Mark Aguirre .60 1.50
28 Rolando Blackman .60 1.50
29 James Donaldson .60 1.50
30 Derek Harper .60 1.50
31 Sam Perkins .75 2.00
32 Roy Tarpley RC .75 2.00
33 Michael Adams RC .75 2.00
34 Alex English 1.00 2.50
35 Lafayette Lever .75 2.00
36 Blair Rasmussen RC .60 1.50
37 Danny Schayes .60 1.50
38 Jay Vincent .60 1.50
39 Adrian Dantley .75 2.00
40 Joe Dumars 1.00 2.50
41 Vinnie Johnson .75 2.00
42 Bill Laimbeer 1.00 2.50
43 Dennis Rodman RC 20.00 50.00
44 John Salley RC 1.00 2.50
45 Isiah Thomas 2.00 5.00
46 Winston Garland RC .60 1.50
47 Rod Higgins .60 1.50
48 Chris Mullin 1.25 3.00
49 Ralph Sampson .60 1.50
50 Joe Barry Carroll .60 1.50
51 Sleepy Floyd .60 1.50
52 Rodney McCray .60 1.50
53 Hakeem Olajuwon 2.50 6.00
54 Purvis Short .60 1.50
55 Vern Fleming .60 1.50
56 John Long .60 1.50
57 Reggie Miller RC 15.00 40.00
58 Chuck Person .60 1.50
59 Steve Stipanovich .60 1.50
60 Wayman Tisdale .75 2.00
61 Benoit Benjamin .60 1.50
62 Michael Cage .60 1.50
63 Mike Woodson .50 1.25
64 Kareem Abdul-Jabbar 3.00 8.00
65 Michael Cooper .75 2.00
66 A.C. Green .60 1.50
67 Magic Johnson 3.00 8.00
68 Byron Scott .75 2.00
69 Mychal Thompson .60 1.50
70 James Worthy 1.25 3.00
71 Duane Washington .60 1.50
72 Kevin Williams .60 1.50
73 Randy Breuer RC .60 1.50
74 Terry Cummings .75 2.00
75 Paul Pressey .60 1.50
76 Jack Sikma .75 2.00
77 John Bagley .60 15.00
78 Roy Hinson .60 1.50
79 Buck Williams .75 2.00
80 Patrick Ewing 2.50 6.00
81 Sidney Green .60 1.50
82 Mark Jackson RC 1.25 3.00
83 Kenny Walker RC .75 2.00
84 Gerald Wilkins .60 1.50
85 Charles Barkley 2.50 6.00
86 Maurice Cheeks .75 2.00
87 Mike Gminski .60 1.50
88 Cliff Robinson .60 1.50
89 Armon Gilliam RC .60 1.50
90 Eddie Johnson .60 1.50
91 Mark West RC .60 1.50
92 Clyde Drexler 1.50 4.00
93 Kevin Duckworth RC 1.25 3.00
94 Steve Johnson .60 1.50
95 Jerome Kersey .60 1.50
96 Terry Porter .75 2.00
97 Joe Kleine RC .60 1.50
98 Reggie Theus .60 1.50
99 Otis Thorpe .60 1.50
100 Kenny Smith RC 1.00 2.50
101 Greg Anderson RC .60 1.50
102 Walter Berry RC .60 1.50
103 Frank Brickowski RC .60 1.50
104 Johnny Dawkins .60 1.50
105 Alvin Robertson .60 1.50
106 Tom Chambers .75 2.00
107 Dale Ellis .75 2.00
108 Xavier McDaniel .75 2.00
109 Derrick McKey RC .75 2.00
110 Nate McMillan UER .60 1.50
111 Thurl Bailey .60 1.50
112 Mark Eaton .60 1.50
113 Bobby Hansen RC .60 1.50
114 Karl Malone 2.50 6.00
115 John Stockton RC 15.00 40.00
116 Bernard King 1.00 2.50
117 Jeff Malone .60 1.50
118 Moses Malone 1.25 3.00
119 John Williams .60 1.50
120 Michael Jordan AS 30.00 80.00
121 Mark Jackson AS .75 2.00
122 Byron Scott AS .75 2.00
123 Magic Johnson AS 2.50 6.00
124 Larry Bird AS 2.50 6.00
125 Dominique Wilkins AS 1.25 3.00
126 Hakeem Olajuwon AS 1.25 3.00
127 John Stockton AS 1.25 3.00
128 Alvin Robertson AS .75 2.00
129 Charles Barkley AS 1.25 3.00
130 Patrick Ewing AS 1.25 3.00
131 Mark Eaton AS .75 2.00
132 Checklist 1-132 1.25 3.00

1988-89 Fleer Stickers

COMPLETE SET (11) 75.00 200.00
1 Mark Aguirre 3.00 8.00
2 Larry Bird 10.00 25.00
3 Clyde Drexler 4.00 10.00
4 Alex English 3.00 8.00
5 Patrick Ewing 4.00 10.00
6 Magic Johnson 10.00 25.00
7 Michael Jordan 40.00 100.00
8 Karl Malone 4.00 10.00
9 Kevin McHale 4.00 10.00
10 Isiah Thomas 4.00 10.00
11 Dominique Wilkins 4.00 10.00

1989-90 Fleer

COMPLETE w/Stickers (179) 40.00 100.00
COMPLETE SET (168) 25.00 60.00
1 John Battle RC .60 1.50
2 Jon Koncak RC .40 1.00
3 Cliff Levingston .50 1.25
4 Moses Malone 1.00 2.50
5 Doc Rivers .75 2.00
6 Spud Webb UER .75 2.00
7 Dominique Wilkins 1.25 3.00
8 Larry Bird 2.00 5.00
9 Dennis Johnson .75 2.00
10 Reggie Lewis RC 1.25 3.00
11 Kevin McHale 1.25 3.00
12 Robert Parish .75 2.00
13 Ed Pinckney .40 1.00
14 Brian Shaw RC .60 1.50
15 Rex Chapman RC .75 2.00
16 Kurt Rambis .50 1.25
17 Robert Reid .40 1.00
18 Kelly Tripucka .50 1.25
19 Bill Cartwright UER .50 1.25
20 Horace Grant 1.00 2.50
21 Michael Jordan 12.00 30.00
22 John Paxson .60 1.50
23 Scottie Pippen 4.00 10.00
24 Brad Sellers .40 1.00
25 Brad Daugherty .50 1.25
26 Craig Ehlo RC .60 1.50
27 Ron Harper .75 2.00
28 Larry Nance .60 1.50
29 Mark Price .60 1.50
30 Mike Sanders .40 1.00
31A Hot Rod Williams ERR .40 1.00
31B Hot Rod Williams COR .50 1.25
32 Rolando Blackman UER .50 1.25
33 Adrian Dantley .60 1.50
34 James Donaldson .50 1.25
35 Derek Harper .50 1.25
36 Sam Perkins .50 1.25
37 Herb Williams .50 1.25
38 Michael Adams .50 1.25
39 Walter Davis .60 1.50
40 Alex English .75 2.00
41 Lafayette Lever .60 1.50
42 Blair Rasmussen .40 1.00
43 Danny Schayes .40 1.00
44 Mark Aguirre .50 1.25
45 Joe Dumars .75 2.00
46 James Edwards .50 1.25
47 Vinnie Johnson .50 1.25
48 Bill Laimbeer .75 2.00
49 Dennis Rodman 1.25 3.00
50 Isiah Thomas 1.00 2.50
51 John Salley .50 1.25
52 Manute Bol .75 2.00
53 Winston Garland .40 1.00
54 Rod Higgins .40 1.00
55 Chris Mullin 1.00 2.50
56 Mitch Richmond RC 1.50 4.00
57 Terry Teagle .50 1.25
58 Derrick Chievous UER .40 1.00
59 Sleepy Floyd .50 1.25
60 Tim McCormick .40 1.00
61 Hakeem Olajuwon 1.25 3.00
62 Otis Thorpe .60 1.50
63 Mike Woodson .50 1.25
64 Vern Fleming .50 1.25
65 Reggie Miller 1.25 3.00
66 Chuck Person .40 1.00
67 Detlef Schrempf .50 1.25
68 Rik Smits RC .75 2.00
69 Benoit Benjamin .40 1.00
70 Gary Grant RC .40 1.00
71 Danny Manning RC .75 2.00
72 Ken Norman RC .50 1.25
73 Charles Smith RC .60 1.50
74 Reggie Williams RC .50 1.25
75 Michael Cooper .60 1.50
76 A.C. Green .60 1.50
77 Magic Johnson 2.00 5.00
78 Byron Scott .60 1.50
79 Mychal Thompson .50 1.25
80 James Worthy 1.00 2.50
81 Kevin Edwards RC .50 1.25
82 Grant Long RC .40 1.00
83 Rony Seikaly RC .75 2.00
84 Rory Sparrow .40 1.00
85 Greg Anderson UER .40 1.00
86 Jay Humphries .40 1.00
87 Larry Krystkowiak RC .50 1.25
88 Ricky Pierce .50 1.25
89 Paul Pressey .50 1.25
90 Alvin Robertson .60 1.50
91 Jack Sikma .60 1.50
92 Steve Johnson .40 1.00
93 Rick Mahorn .50 1.25
94 David Rivers .40 1.00
95 Joe Barry Carroll .40 1.00
96 Lester Conner UER .40 1.00
97 Roy Hinson .40 1.00
98 Mike McGee .40 1.00
99 Chris Morris RC .60 1.50
100 Patrick Ewing 1.00 2.50
101 Mark Jackson .60 1.50
102 Johnny Newman RC .40 1.00
103 Charles Oakley .60 1.50
104 Rod Strickland RC 1.00 2.50
105 Trent Tucker .40 1.00
106 Kiki Vandeweghe .50 1.25
107A Gerald Wilkins .50 1.25
107B Gerald Wilkins .50 1.25
108 Terry Catledge .40 1.00
109 Dave Corzine .40 1.00
110 Scott Skiles RC .60 1.50
111 Reggie Theus .50 1.25
112 Ron Anderson RC .50 1.25
113 Charles Barkley 1.25 3.00
114 Scott Brooks RC .50 1.25
115 Maurice Cheeks .50 1.25
116 Mike Gminski .40 1.00
117 Hersey Hawkins UER RC .50 1.25
118 Christian Welp .40 1.00
119 Tom Chambers .60 1.50
120 Armon Gilliam .40 1.00
121 Jeff Hornacek RC 1.00 2.50
122 Eddie Johnson .40 1.00
123 Kevin Johnson RC 1.25 3.00
124 Dan Majerle RC 1.25 3.00
125 Mark West .40 1.00
126 Richard Anderson .40 1.00
127 Mark Bryant RC .40 1.00
128 Clyde Drexler 1.00 2.50
129 Kevin Duckworth .50 1.25
130 Jerome Kersey .50 1.25
131 Terry Porter .50 1.25
132 Buck Williams .60 1.50
133 Danny Ainge .60 1.50
134 Ricky Berry .40 1.00
135 Rodney McCray .50 1.25
136 Jim Petersen .40 1.00
137 Harold Pressley .40 1.00
138 Kenny Smith .50 1.25
139 Wayman Tisdale .60 1.50
140 Willie Anderson RC .50 1.25
141 Frank Brickowski .40 1.00
142 Terry Cummings .50 1.25
143 Johnny Dawkins .50 1.25
144 Vernon Maxwell RC .75 2.00
145 Michael Cage .50 1.25
146 Dale Ellis .50 1.25
147 Alton Lister .40 1.00
148 Xavier McDaniel UER .50 1.25
149 Derrick McKey .50 1.25
150 Nate McMillan .50 1.25
151 Thurl Bailey .50 1.25
152 Mark Eaton .60 1.50
153 Darrell Griffith .50 1.25
154 Eric Leckner .40 1.00
155 Karl Malone 1.25 3.00
156 John Stockton 1.25 3.00
157 Mark Alarie .40 1.00
158 Ledell Eackles RC .40 1.00
159 Bernard King .75 2.00
160 Jeff Malone .50 1.25
161 Darrell Walker .40 1.00
162A John Williams ERR .40 1.00
162B John Williams COR .40 1.00
163 Malone/Stockton/Eaton AS 1.00 2.50
164 H.Olajuwon/C.Drexler AS 1.00 2.50
165 ASG Wilkins/M.Malone 1.00 2.50
166 ASG Daugh/Price/Nance 1.00 2.50
167 ASG Ewing/M.Jackson .60 1.50
168 Checklist 1-168 1.00 2.50

1989-90 Fleer Stickers

COMPLETE SET (11) 20.00 50.00
ONE PER WAX PACK
1 Karl Malone 3.00 8.00
2 Hakeem Olajuwon 3.00 8.00
3 Michael Jordan 10.00 25.00
4 Charles Barkley 3.00 8.00
5 Magic Johnson 4.00 10.00
6 Isiah Thomas 2.50 6.00
7 Patrick Ewing 3.00 8.00
8 Dale Ellis .75 2.00
9 Chris Mullin 2.00 5.00
10 Larry Bird 4.00 10.00
11 Tom Chambers .75 2.00

1990-91 Fleer

COMPLETE SET (198) 10.00 25.00
1 John Battle UER .20 .50
2 Cliff Levingston .20 .50
3 Moses Malone .20 .50
4 Kenny Smith .20 .50
5 Spud Webb .20 .50
6 Dominique Wilkins .40 1.00
7 Kevin Willis 1.00 2.50
8 Larry Bird .75 2.00
9 Dennis Johnson .20 .50
10 Joe Kleine .20 .50
11 Reggie Lewis .20 .50
12 Kevin McHale .40 1.00
13 Robert Parish .20 .50
14 Jim Paxson .20 .50
15 Ed Pinckney .20 .50
16 Muggsy Bogues .20 .50
17 Rex Chapman .20 .50
18 Dell Curry .20 .50
19 Armon Gilliam .20 .50
20 J.R. Reid RC .20 .50
21 Kelly Tripucka .20 .50
22 B.J. Armstrong RC .40 1.00
23A Bill Cartwright ERR .20 .50
23B Bill Cartwright COR .20 .50
24 Horace Grant .20 .50
25 Craig Hodges .20 .50
26 Michael Jordan UER 12.00 30.00
27 Stacey King UER RC .20 .50
28 John Paxson .20 .50
29 Will Perdue .20 .50
30 Scottie Pippen UER .75 2.00
31 Brad Daugherty .20 .50
32 Craig Ehlo .20 .50
33 Danny Ferry RC .20 .50
34 Steve Kerr .60 1.50
35 Larry Nance .20 .50
36 Mark Price UER .20 .50
37 Hot Rod Williams .20 .50
38 Rolando Blackman .20 .50
39A Adrian Dantley ERR .20 .50
39B Adrian Dantley COR .20 .50
40 Brad Davis .20 .50
41 James Donaldson UER .20 .50
42 Derek Harper .20 .50
43 Sam Perkins UER .20 .50
44 Bill Wennington .20 .50
45 Herb Williams .20 .50
46 Michael Adams .20 .50
47 Walter Davis .20 .50
48 Alex English UER .20 .50
49 Bill Hanzlik .20 .50
50 Lafayette Lever UER .20 .50
51 Todd Lichti RC .20 .50
52 Blair Rasmussen .20 .50
53 Danny Schayes .20 .50
54 Mark Aguirre .20 .50
55 Joe Dumars .20 .50
56 James Edwards .20 .50
57 Vinnie Johnson .20 .50
58 Bill Laimbeer .20 .50
59 Dennis Rodman UER .60 1.50
60 John Salley .20 .50
61 Isiah Thomas .60 1.50
62 Manute Bol .20 .50
63 Tim Hardaway RC 1.25 3.00
64 Rod Higgins .20 .50
65 Sarunas Marciulionis RC .40 1.00
66 Chris Mullin .40 1.00
67 Mitch Richmond .40 1.00
68 Terry Teagle .20 .50
69 Anthony Bowie UER RC .20 .50
70 Sleepy Floyd .20 .50
71 Buck Johnson .20 .50
72 Vernon Maxwell .20 .50
73 Hakeem Olajuwon .75 2.00
74 Otis Thorpe .20 .50
75 Mitchell Wiggins .20 .50
76 Vern Fleming .20 .50
77 George McCloud RC .20 .50
78 Reggie Miller .60 1.50
79 Chuck Person .20 .50
80 Mike Sanders .20 .50
81 Detlef Schrempf .20 .50
82 Rik Smits .20 .50
83 LaSalle Thompson .20 .50
84 Benoit Benjamin .20 .50
85 Winston Garland .20 .50
86 Ron Harper .20 .50
87 Danny Manning .20 .50
88 Ken Norman .20 .50
89 Charles Smith .20 .50
90 Michael Cooper .20 .50
91 Vlade Divac RC .40 1.00
92 A.C. Green .20 .50
93 Magic Johnson 1.00 2.50
94 Byron Scott .20 .50
95 Mychal Thompson UER .20 .50
96 Orlando Woolridge .20 .50
97 James Worthy .40 1.00
98 Sherman Douglas RC .20 .50
99 Kevin Edwards .20 .50
100 Grant Long .20 .50
101 Glen Rice RC .40 1.00
102 R.Seikaly/M.Jordan UER .50 1.25
103 Billy Thompson .20 .50
104 Jeff Grayer RC .20 .50
105 Jay Humphries .20 .50
106 Ricky Pierce .20 .50
107 Paul Pressey .20 .50
108 Fred Roberts .20 .50
109 Alvin Robertson .20 .50
110 Jack Sikma .20 .50
111 Randy Breuer .20 .50
112 Tony Campbell .20 .50
113 Tyrone Corbin .20 .50
114 Sam Mitchell UER RC .20 .50
115 Tod Murphy UER .20 .50
116 Pooh Richardson RC .20 .50
117 Mookie Blaylock RC .20 .50
118 Sam Bowie .20 .50
119 Lester Conner .20 .50
120 Dennis Hopson .20 .50
121 Chris Morris .20 .50
122 Charles Shackleford .20 .50
123 Purvis Short .20 .50
124 Maurice Cheeks .20 .50
125 Patrick Ewing .60 1.50
126 Mark Jackson .20 .50
127A Johnny Newman ERR .20 .50
127B Johnny Newman COR .20 .50
128 Charles Oakley .20 .50
129 Trent Tucker .20 .50
130 Kenny Walker .20 .50
131 Gerald Wilkins .20 .50
132 Nick Anderson RC .40 1.00
133 Terry Catledge .20 .50
134 Sidney Green .20 .50
135 Otis Smith .20 .50
136 Reggie Theus .20 .50
137 Sam Vincent .20 .50
138 Ron Anderson .20 .50
139 Charles Barkley UER .75 2.00
140 Scott Brooks UER .20 .50
141 Johnny Dawkins .20 .50
142 Mike Gminski .20 .50
143 Hersey Hawkins .20 .50
144 Rick Mahorn .20 .50
145 Derek Smith .20 .50
146 Tom Chambers .20 .50
147 Jeff Hornacek .20 .50
148 Eddie Johnson .20 .50
149 Kevin Johnson .20 .50
150A Dan Majerle ERR 1988 .30 .75
150B Dan Majerle COR 1989 .20 .50
151 Tim Perry .20 .50
152 Kurt Rambis .20 .50
153 Mark West .20 .50
154 Clyde Drexler .60 1.50
155 Kevin Duckworth .20 .50
156 Byron Irvin .20 .50
157 Jerome Kersey .20 .50
158 Terry Porter .20 .50
159 Clifford Robinson RC .40 1.00
160 Buck Williams .20 .50
161 Danny Young .20 .50
162 Danny Ainge .20 .50
163 Antoine Carr .20 .50
164 Pervis Ellison RC .20 .50
165 Rodney McCray .20 .50
166 Harold Pressley .20 .50
167 Wayman Tisdale .20 .50
168 Willie Anderson .20 .50
169 Frank Brickowski .20 .50
170 Terry Cummings .20 .50
171 Sean Elliott RC .40 1.00
172 David Robinson .75 2.00
173 Rod Strickland .20 .50
174 David Wingate .20 .50
175 Dana Barros RC .20 .50
176 Michael Cage UER .20 .50
177 Dale Ellis .20 .50
178 Shawn Kemp RC 1.25 3.00
179 Xavier McDaniel .20 .50
180 Derrick McKey .20 .50
181 Nate McMillan .20 .50
182 Thurl Bailey .20 .50
183 Mike Brown .20 .50
184 Mark Eaton .20 .50
185 Blue Edwards RC .20 .50
186 Bobby Hansen .20 .50
187 Eric Leckner .20 .50
188 Karl Malone .75 2.00
189 John Stockton .75 2.00
190 Mark Alarie .20 .50
191 Ledell Eackles .20 .50
192A Harvey Grant FFC Black .30 .75
192B Harvey Grant FFC White .20 .50
193 Tom Hammonds RC .20 .50
194 Bernard King .20 .50
195 Jeff Malone .20 .50
196 Darrell Walker .20 .50
197 Checklist 1-99 .20 .50
198 Checklist 100-198 .20 .50

1990-91 Fleer All-Stars

COMPLETE SET (12) 12.00 30.00
1 Charles Barkley 2.00 5.00
2 Larry Bird 2.00 5.00
3 Hakeem Olajuwon 2.00 5.00
4 Magic Johnson 2.00 5.00
5 Michael Jordan 12.00 30.00
6 Isiah Thomas 2.00 5.00
7 Karl Malone 2.00 5.00
8 Tom Chambers .40 1.00
9 John Stockton 2.00 5.00
10 David Robinson 2.00 5.00
11 Clyde Drexler 2.00 5.00
12 Patrick Ewing 2.00 5.00

1990-91 Fleer Rookie Sensations

COMPLETE SET (10) 6.00 15.00
1 David Robinson UER 3.00 8.00
2 Sean Elliott UER .75 2.00
3 Glen Rice 1.50 4.00
4 J.R. Reid .20 .50
5 Stacey King .10 .30
6 Pooh Richardson .20 .50
7 Nick Anderson .60 1.50

8 Tim Hardaway 2.50 6.00
9 Vlade Divac 1.00 2.50
10 Sherman Douglas .20 .50

1990-91 Fleer Update

COMPLETE SET (100) 8.00 20.00
U1 Jon Koncak .20 .50
U2 Tim McCormick .20 .50
U3 Doc Rivers .20 .50
U4 Rumeal Robinson RC .20 .50
U5 Trevor Wilson .20 .50
U6 Dee Brown RC .20 .50
U7 Dave Popson .20 .50
U8 Kevin Gamble .20 .50
U9 Brian Shaw .20 .50
U10 Michael Smith .20 .50
U11 Kendall Gill RC .40 1.00
U12 Johnny Newman .20 .50
U13 Steve Scheffler RC .20 .50
U14 Dennis Hopson .20 .50
U15 Cliff Levingston .20 .50
U16 Chucky Brown RC .20 .50
U17 John Morton RC .20 .50
U18 Gerald Paddio RC .20 .50
U19 Alex English .20 .50
U20 Fat Lever .20 .50
U21 Rodney McCray .20 .50
U22 Roy Tarpley .20 .50
U23 Randy White RC .20 .50
U24 Anthony Cook RC .20 .50
U25 Chris Jackson RC .20 .50
U26 Marcus Liberty RC .20 .50
U27 Orlando Woolridge .20 .50
U28 William Bedford RC .20 .50
U29 Lance Blanks RC .20 .50
U30 Scott Hastings .20 .50
U31 Tyrone Hill RC .20 .50
U32 Les Jepsen .20 .50
U33 Steve Johnson .20 .50
U34 Kevin Pritchard RC .20 .50
U35 Dave Jamerson RC .20 .50
U36 Kenny Smith .20 .50
U37 Greg Dreiling RC .20 .50
U38 Kenny Williams RC .20 .50
U39 Micheal Williams UER .20 .50
U40 Gary Grant .20 .50
U41 Bo Kimble RC .20 .50
U42 Loy Vaught RC .20 .50
U43 Elden Campbell RC .20 .50
U44 Sam Perkins .20 .50
U45 Tony Smith RC .20 .50
U46 Terry Teagle .20 .50
U47 Willie Burton RC .20 .50
U48 Bimbo Coles RC .20 .50
U49 Terry Davis RC .20 .50
U50 Alec Kessler RC .20 .50
U51 Greg Anderson .20 .50
U52 Frank Brickowski .20 .50
U53 Steve Henson RC .20 .50
U54 Brad Lohaus .20 .50
U55 Danny Schayes .20 .50
U56 Gerald Glass RC .20 .50
U57 Felton Spencer RC .20 .50
U58 Doug West RC .20 .50
U59 Jud Buechler RC .20 .50
U60 Derrick Coleman RC .40 1.00
U61 Tate George RC .20 .50
U62 Reggie Theus .20 .50
U63 Greg Grant RC .20 .50
U64 Jerrod Mustaf RC .20 .50
U65 Eddie Lee Wilkins RC .20 .50
U66 Michael Ansley .20 .50
U67 Jerry Reynolds .20 .50
U68 Dennis Scott RC .20 .50
U69 Manute Bol .20 .50
U70 Armon Gilliam .20 .50
U71 Brian Oliver .20 .50
U72 Kenny Payne RC .20 .50
U73 Jayson Williams RC .20 .50
U74 Kenny Battle RC .20 .50
U75 Cedric Ceballos RC .20 .50
U76 Negele Knight RC .20 .50
U77 Xavier McDaniel .20 .50
U78 Alaa Abdelnaby RC .20 .50
U79 Danny Ainge .20 .50
U80 Mark Bryant .20 .50
U81 Drazen Petrovic RC .75 2.00
U82 Anthony Bonner RC .20 .50
U83 Duane Causwell RC .20 .50
U84 Bobby Hansen .20 .50
U85 Eric Leckner .20 .50
U86 Travis Mays RC .20 .50
U87 Lionel Simmons RC .20 .50
U88 Sidney Green .20 .50
U89 Tony Massenburg .20 .50
U90 Paul Pressey .20 .50
U91 Dwayne Schintzius RC .20 .50
U92 Gary Payton RC 4.00 10.00
U93 Olden Polynice .20 .50
U94 Jeff Malone .20 .50
U95 Walter Palmer .20 .50
U96 Delaney Rudd .20 .50
U97 Pervis Ellison .20 .50
U98 A.J. English RC .20 .50
U99 Greg Foster RC .20 .50
U100 Checklist 1-100 .20 .50

1991-92 Fleer

COMPLETE SET (400) 12.00 30.00
COMPLETE SERIES 1 (240) 6.00 15.00
COMPLETE SERIES 2 (160) 6.00 15.00
1 John Battle .20 .50
2 Jon Koncak .20 .50
3 Rumeal Robinson .20 .50
4 Spud Webb .30 .75
5 Bob Weiss CO .20 .50
6 Dominique Wilkins .50 1.25
7 Kevin Willis .25 .60
8 Larry Bird 1.00 2.50
9 Dee Brown .25 .60
10 Chris Ford CO .20 .50
11 Kevin Gamble .20 .50
12 Reggie Lewis .30 .75
13 Kevin McHale .50 1.25
14 Robert Parish .40 1.00
15 Ed Pinckney .25 .60
16 Brian Shaw .25 .60
17 Muggsy Bogues .30 .75
18 Rex Chapman .25 .60
19 Dell Curry .25 .60
20 Kendall Gill .30 .75
21 Eric Leckner .20 .50
22 Gene Littles CO .20 .50
23 Johnny Newman .20 .50
24 J.R. Reid .20 .50
25 B.J. Armstrong .30 .75
26 Bill Cartwright .25 .60
27 Horace Grant .30 .75
28 Phil Jackson CO .40 1.00
29 Michael Jordan 2.50 6.00
30 Cliff Levingston .20 .50
31 John Paxson .25 .60
32 Will Perdue .25 .60
33 Scottie Pippen .75 2.00
34 Brad Daugherty .30 .75
35 Craig Ehlo .25 .60
36 Danny Ferry .25 .60
37 Larry Nance .30 .75
38 Mark Price .30 .75
39 Darnell Valentine .20 .50
40 Hot Rod Williams .20 .50
41 Lenny Wilkens CO .30 .75
42 Richie Adubato CO .20 .50
43 Rolando Blackman .25 .60
44 James Donaldson .20 .50
45 Derek Harper .25 .60
46 Rodney McCray .20 .50
47 Randy White .20 .50
48 Herb Williams .20 .50
49 Chris Jackson .25 .60
50 Marcus Liberty .20 .50
51 Todd Lichti .20 .50
52 Blair Rasmussen .20 .50
53 Paul Westhead CO .20 .50
54 Reggie Williams .25 .60
55 Joe Wolf .20 .50
56 Orlando Woolridge .25 .60
57 Mark Aguirre .25 .60
58 Chuck Daly CO .30 .75
59 Joe Dumars .40 1.00
60 James Edwards .25 .60
61 Vinnie Johnson .30 .75
62 Bill Laimbeer .30 .75
63 Dennis Rodman .60 1.50
64 Isiah Thomas .50 1.25
65 Tim Hardaway .40 1.00
66 Rod Higgins .20 .50
67 Tyrone Hill .25 .60
68 Sarunas Marciulionis .30 .75
69 Chris Mullin .40 1.00
70 Don Nelson CO .30 .75
71 Mitch Richmond .40 1.00
72 Tom Tolbert .20 .50
73 Don Chaney CO .20 .50
74 Eric (Sleepy) Floyd .25 .60
75 Buck Johnson .20 .50
76 Vernon Maxwell .25 .60
77 Hakeem Olajuwon .60 1.50
78 Kenny Smith .25 .60
79 Larry Smith .20 .50
80 Otis Thorpe .25 .60
81 Vern Fleming .25 .60
82 Bob Hill CO RC .20 .50
83 Reggie Miller .50 1.25
84 Chuck Person .25 .60
85 Detlef Schrempf .25 .60
86 Rik Smits .25 .60
87 LaSalle Thompson .20 .50
88 Micheal Williams .20 .50
89 Gary Grant .20 .50
90 Ron Harper .30 .75
91 Bo Kimble .25 .60
92 Danny Manning .30 .75
93 Ken Norman .25 .60
94 Olden Polynice .20 .50
95 Mike Schuler CO .20 .50
96 Charles Smith .25 .60
97 Vlade Divac .25 .60
98 Mike Dunleavy CO .20 .50
99 A.C. Green .25 .60
100 Magic Johnson 1.00 2.50
101 Sam Perkins .25 .60
102 Byron Scott .30 .75
103 Terry Teagle .25 .60
104 James Worthy .40 1.00
105 Willie Burton .20 .50
106 Bimbo Coles .25 .60
107 Sherman Douglas .20 .50
108 Kevin Edwards .20 .50
109 Grant Long .20 .50
110 Kevin Loughery CO .20 .50
111 Glen Rice .30 .75
112 Rony Seikaly .25 .60
113 Frank Brickowski .20 .50
114 Dale Ellis .25 .60
115 Del Harris CO .20 .50
116 Jay Humphries .20 .50
117 Fred Roberts .20 .50
118 Alvin Robertson .20 .50
119 Danny Schayes .20 .50
120 Jack Sikma .30 .75
121 Tony Campbell .20 .50
122 Tyrone Corbin .20 .50
123 Sam Mitchell .20 .50
124 Tod Murphy .20 .50
125 Pooh Richardson .20 .50
126 Jimmy Rodgers CO .20 .50
127 Felton Spencer .20 .50
128 Mookie Blaylock .30 .75
129 Sam Bowie .20 .50
130 Derrick Coleman .25 .60
131 Chris Dudley .20 .50
132 Bill Fitch CO .20 .50
133 Chris Morris .20 .50
134 Drazen Petrovic .40 1.00
135 Maurice Cheeks .25 .60
136 Patrick Ewing .50 1.25
137 Mark Jackson .25 .60
138 Charles Oakley .25 .60
139 Pat Riley CO .40 1.00
140 Trent Tucker .20 .50
141 Kiki Vandeweghe .25 .60
142 Gerald Wilkins .25 .60
143 Nick Anderson .25 .60
144 Terry Catledge .20 .50
145 Matt Guokas CO .20 .50
146 Jerry Reynolds .20 .50
147 Dennis Scott .25 .60
148 Scott Skiles .20 .50
149 Otis Smith .20 .50
150 Ron Anderson .20 .50
151 Charles Barkley .60 1.50
152 Johnny Dawkins .25 .60
153 Armon Gilliam .20 .50
154 Hersey Hawkins .25 .60
155 Jim Lynam CO .20 .50
156 Rick Mahorn .25 .60
157 Brian Oliver .20 .50
158 Tom Chambers .30 .75
159 Cotton Fitzsimmons CO .20 .50
160 Jeff Hornacek .25 .60
161 Kevin Johnson .30 .75
162 Negele Knight .20 .50
163 Dan Majerle .30 .75
164 Xavier McDaniel .25 .60
165 Mark West .25 .60
166 Rick Adelman CO .20 .50
167 Danny Ainge .25 .60
168 Clyde Drexler .50 1.25
169 Kevin Duckworth .25 .60
170 Jerome Kersey .25 .60
171 Terry Porter .25 .60
172 Clifford Robinson .25 .60
173 Buck Williams .25 .60
174 Antoine Carr .20 .50
175 Duane Causwell .20 .50
176 Jim Les RC .20 .50
177 Travis Mays .20 .50
178 Dick Motta CO .20 .50
179 Lionel Simmons .20 .50
180 Rory Sparrow .20 .50
181 Wayman Tisdale .25 .60
182 Willie Anderson .25 .60
183 Larry Brown CO .30 .75
184 Terry Cummings .30 .75
185 Sean Elliott .25 .60
186 Paul Pressey .25 .60
187 David Robinson .60 1.50
188 Rod Strickland .25 .60
189 Benoit Benjamin .20 .50
190 Eddie Johnson .20 .50
191 K.C. Jones CO .30 .75
192 Shawn Kemp .50 1.25
193 Derrick McKey .20 .50
194 Gary Payton .50 1.25
195 Ricky Pierce .25 .60
196 Sedale Threatt .20 .50
197 Thurl Bailey .20 .50
198 Mark Eaton .30 .75
199 Blue Edwards .20 .50
200 Jeff Malone .25 .60
201 Karl Malone .60 1.50
202 Jerry Sloan CO .30 .75
203 John Stockton .60 1.50
204 Ledell Eackles .20 .50
205 Pervis Ellison .20 .50
206 A.J. English .20 .50
207 Harvey Grant .25 .60
208 Bernard King .40 1.00
209 Wes Unseld CO .30 .75
210 Kevin Johnson AS .30 .75
211 Michael Jordan AS 2.50 6.00
212 Dominique Wilkins AS .50 1.25
213 Charles Barkley AS .60 1.50
214 Hakeem Olajuwon AS .60 1.50
215 Patrick Ewing AS .50 1.25
216 Tim Hardaway AS .40 1.00
217 John Stockton AS .60 1.50
218 Chris Mullin AS .40 1.00
219 Karl Malone AS .60 1.50
220 Michael Jordan LL 2.50 6.00
221 John Stockton LL .60 1.50
222 Alvin Robertson LL .25 .60
223 Hakeem Olajuwon LL .60 1.50
224 Buck Williams LL .25 .60
225 David Robinson LL .60 1.50
226 Reggie Miller LL .50 1.25
227 Blue Edwards SD .20 .50
228 Dee Brown SD .25 .60
229 Rex Chapman SD .25 .60
230 Kenny Smith SD .25 .60
231 Shawn Kemp SD .50 1.25
232 Kendall Gill SD .30 .75
233 M.Jordan/Group ASG 2.50 6.00
234 C.Drexler/K.McHale ASG .50 1.25
235 Alvin Robertson ASG .25 .60
236 P.Ewing/K.Malone ASG .60 1.50
237 Superstars/Group ASG 2.50 6.00
238 Michael Jordan ASG 2.50 6.00
239 Checklist 1-120 .20 .50
240 Checklist 121-240 .20 .50
241 Stacey Augmon RC .30 .75
242 Maurice Cheeks .25 .60
243 Paul Graham RC .20 .50
244 Rodney Monroe RC .20 .50
245 Blair Rasmussen .20 .50
246 Alexander Volkov .20 .50
247 John Bagley .20 .50
248 Rick Fox RC .30 .75
249 Rickey Green .25 .60
250 Joe Kleine .20 .50
251 Stojko Vrankovic .20 .50
252 Allan Bristow CO .20 .50
253 Kenny Gattison .20 .50
254 Mike Gminski .20 .50
255 Larry Johnson RC 1.00 2.50
256 Bobby Hansen .20 .50
257 Craig Hodges .25 .60
258 Stacey King .25 .60
259 Scott Williams RC .20 .50
260 John Battle .20 .50
261 Winston Bennett .20 .50
262 Terrell Brandon RC .25 .60
263 Henry James .20 .50
264 Steve Kerr .40 1.00
265 Jimmy Oliver RC .20 .50
266 Brad Davis .20 .50
267 Terry Davis .20 .50
268 Donald Hodge RC .20 .50
269 Mike Iuzzolino RC .20 .50
270 Fat Lever .25 .60
271 Doug Smith RC .20 .50
272 Greg Anderson .20 .50
273 Kevin Brooks RC .20 .50
274 Walter Davis .25 .60
275 Winston Garland .20 .50
276 Mark Macon RC .30 .75
277 Dikembe Mutombo RC 1.25 3.00
277B D.Mutombo 91-92 RC 1.25 3.00
278 William Bedford .20 .50
279 Lance Blanks .20 .50
280 John Salley .25 .60
281 Charles Thomas RC .20 .50
282 Darrell Walker .20 .50
283 Orlando Woolridge .25 .60
284 Victor Alexander RC .20 .50
285 Vincent Askew RC .20 .50
286 Mario Elie RC .30 .75
287 Alton Lister .20 .50
288 Billy Owens RC .30 .75
289 Matt Bullard RC .25 .60
290 Carl Herrera RC .20 .50
291 Tree Rollins .20 .50
292 John Turner .20 .50
293 Dale Davis UER RC .30 .75
294 Sean Green RC .20 .50
295 Kenny Williams .20 .50
296 James Edwards .25 .60
297 LeRon Ellis RC .20 .50
298 Doc Rivers .30 .75
299 Loy Vaught .20 .50
300 Elden Campbell .25 .60
301 Jack Haley .20 .50
302 Keith Owens .20 .50
303 Tony Smith .20 .50
304 Sedale Threatt .20 .50
305 Keith Askins RC .20 .50
306 Alec Kessler .20 .50
307 John Morton .20 .50
308 Alan Ogg .20 .50
309 Steve Smith RC .50 1.25
310 Lester Conner .20 .50
311 Jeff Grayer .20 .50
312 Frank Hamblen CO .20 .50
313 Steve Henson .20 .50
314 Larry Krystkowiak .20 .50
315 Moses Malone .50 1.25
316 Thurl Bailey .25 .60
317 Randy Breuer .20 .50
318 Scott Brooks .20 .50
319 Gerald Glass .20 .50
320 Luc Longley RC .50 1.25
321 Doug West .20 .50
322 Kenny Anderson RC .30 .75
323 Tate George .20 .50
324 Terry Mills RC .20 .50
325 Greg Anthony RC .25 .60
326 Anthony Mason RC .40 1.00
327 Tim McCormick .20 .50
328 Xavier McDaniel .25 .60
329 Brian Quinnett .20 .50
330 John Starks RC 1.00 2.50
331 Stanley Roberts RC .25 .60
332 Jeff Turner .20 .50
333 Sam Vincent .20 .50
334 Brian Williams RC .30 .75
335 Manute Bol .30 .75
336 Kenny Payne .20 .50
337 Charles Shackleford .20 .50
338 Jayson Williams .20 .50
339 Cedric Ceballos .25 .60
340 Andrew Lang .20 .50
341 Jerrod Mustaf .20 .50
342 Tim Perry .20 .50
343 Kurt Rambis .20 .50
344 Alaa Abdelnaby .20 .50
345 Robert Pack RC .25 .60
346 Danny Young .20 .50
347 Anthony Bonner .20 .50
348 Pete Chilcutt RC .20 .50
349 Rex Hughes CO .20 .50
350 Mitch Richmond .40 1.00
351 Dwayne Schintzius .20 .50
352 Spud Webb .30 .75
353 Antoine Carr .25 .60
354 Sidney Green .20 .50
355 Vinnie Johnson .30 .75
356 Greg Sutton RC .20 .50
357 Dana Barros .25 .60
358 Michael Cage .25 .60
359 Marty Conlon RC .20 .50
360 Rich King RC .20 .50
361 Nate McMillan .25 .60
362 David Benoit RC .30 .75
363 Mike Brown .20 .50
364 Tyrone Corbin .20 .50
365 Eric Murdock RC .20 .50
366 Delaney Rudd .20 .50
367 Michael Adams .25 .60
368 Tom Hammonds .20 .50
369 Larry Stewart RC .20 .50
370 Andre Turner .20 .50
371 David Wingate .25 .60
372 Dominique Wilkins TL .50 1.25
373 Larry Bird TL 1.00 2.50
374 Rex Chapman TL .25 .60
375 Michael Jordan TL 2.50 6.00
376 Brad Daugherty TL .30 .75
377 Derek Harper TL .25 .60
378 Dikembe Mutombo TL 1.25 3.00
379 Joe Dumars TL .40 1.00
380 Chris Mullin TL .40 1.00
381 Hakeem Olajuwon TL .60 1.50
382 Chuck Person TL .25 .60
383 Charles Smith TL .25 .60
384 James Worthy TL .40 1.00
385 Glen Rice TL .30 .75
386 Alvin Robertson TL .20 .50
387 Tony Campbell TL .20 .50
388 Derrick Coleman TL .30 .75
389 Patrick Ewing TL .50 1.25
390 Scott Skiles TL .20 .50
391 Charles Barkley TL .60 1.50
392 Kevin Johnson TL .30 .75
393 Clyde Drexler TL .50 1.25
394 Lionel Simmons TL .20 .50
395 David Robinson TL .60 1.50
396 Ricky Pierce TL .25 .60
397 John Stockton TL .60 1.50
398 Michael Adams TL .25 .60
399 Checklist .20 .50
400 Checklist .20 .50
29-3D Michael Jordan 3-D 500.00 1,000.00

1991-92 Fleer Dikembe Mutombo

COMPLETE SET (12) 12.00 30.00
COMMON MUTOMBO (1-12) 1.50 4.00
COMMON AUTOGRAPH (AU) 25.00 60.00

1991-92 Fleer Pro-Visions

COMPLETE SET (6) 6.00 15.00
1 David Robinson 1.00 2.50
2 Michael Jordan 6.00 15.00
3 Charles Barkley 1.00 2.50
4 Patrick Ewing .75 2.00
5 Karl Malone 1.00 2.50
6 Magic Johnson 1.00 2.50

1991-92 Fleer Rookie Sensations

COMPLETE SET (10) 3.00 8.00
1 Lionel Simmons .25 .60
2 Dennis Scott .30 .75
3 Derrick Coleman .40 1.00
4 Kendall Gill .40 1.00
5 Travis Mays .25 .60
6 Felton Spencer .25 .60
7 Willie Burton .25 .60
8 Chris Jackson .30 .75
9 Gary Payton 2.50 6.00
10 Dee Brown .30 .75

1991-92 Fleer Schoolyard

COMPLETE SET (6) 3.00 8.00
1 Chris Mullin .40 1.00
2 Isiah Thomas .50 1.25
3 Kevin McHale .50 1.25
4 Kevin Johnson .30 .75
5 Karl Malone .60 1.50
6 Alvin Robertson .25 .60

1991-92 Fleer Dominique Wilkins

COMPLETE SET (12) 12.00 30.00
COMMON WILKINS (1-12) 1.50 4.00
COMMON AUTOGRAPH (AU) 30.00 80.00

1991-92 Fleer Mutombo/Wilkins Promo

1 Dikembe Mutombo
Dominique Wilkins
With Jeff Massien Fleer VP 8.00 20.00

1991-92 Fleer Tony's Pizza

COMPLETE SET (120) 120.00 300.00
1 Terry Teagle .75 2.00
2 Karl Malone 5.00 12.00
3 Patrick Ewing 3.00 8.00
4 Alvin Robertson .60 1.50
5 Scott Skiles .75 2.00
6 Frank Brickowski .60 1.50
7 Mookie Blaylock .75 2.00
8 Ricky Pierce .60 1.50
9 Gary Payton 3.00 8.00
10 Dennis Scott .75 2.00
11 Derrick McKey .60 1.50
12 Mark West .60 1.50
13 Mark Jackson 1.50 4.00
14 Glen Rice 2.00 5.00
15 Charles Barkley 5.00 12.00
16 David Robinson 4.00 10.00
17 Sam Bowie .75 2.00
18 Ron Harper 1.25 3.00
19 Reggie Miller 4.00 10.00
20 Lionel Simmons .60 1.50
21 Jerome Kersey .75 2.00
22 Rod Strickland .60 1.50
23 Charles Oakley .60 1.50
24 Rony Seikaly .60 1.50
25 Johnny Dawkins .60 1.50
26 Fred Roberts .60 1.50
27 Derrick Coleman .75 2.00
28 Bo Kimble .60 1.50
29 Chuck Person .60 1.50
30 Kiki Vandeweghe 1.25 3.00
31 Jeff Malone .60 1.50
32 Vlade Divac 1.25 3.00
33 Michael Jordan 12.00 30.00
34 Gerald Wilkins .75 2.00
35 Sarunas Marciulionis .75 2.00
36 Pooh Richardson .60 1.50
37 Hakeem Olajuwon 4.00 9.00
38 Rodney McCray .60 1.50
39 Larry Nance .75 2.00
40 Wayman Tisdale .75 2.00
41 Tom Chambers 1.00 2.50
42 A.C. Green 1.00 2.50
43 Bernard King 1.00 2.50
44 Reggie Williams .60 1.50
45 Chris Mullin 1.50 4.00
46 Bill Laimbeer 1.25 3.00
47 Kenny Smith .75 2.00
48 Harvey Grant .60 1.50
49 Mark Price 1.00 2.50
50 Olden Polynice .60 1.50
51 Isiah Thomas 3.00 8.00
52 Magic Johnson 6.00 15.00
53 John Paxson .75 2.00
54 Muggsy Bogues 1.25 3.00
55 Mitch Richmond 3.00 8.00
56 Dennis Rodman 4.00 10.00
57 Otis Thorpe .75 2.00
58 Larry Bird 8.00 20.00
59 Hot Rod Williams .60 1.50
60 Hersey Hawkins .75 2.00
61 Brian Shaw .75 2.00
62 Detlef Schrempf .75 2.00
63 Danny Manning 1.00 2.50
64 Thurl Bailey .60 1.50
65 Benoit Benjamin .60 1.50
66 Nick Anderson .75 2.00
67 Rex Chapman .75 2.00
68 Danny Ainge 1.25 3.00
69 Dee Brown .60 1.50
70 Chris Dudley .60 1.50
71 Kevin McHale 2.00 5.00
72 Dell Curry 1.00 2.50
73 Ken Norman .60 1.50
74 Mark Eaton .60 1.50
75 Shawn Kemp 2.50 6.00
76 Bill Cartwright .75 2.00
77 Terry Cummings .75 2.00
78 Clyde Drexler 4.00 10.00
79 Kevin Johnson 1.25 3.00
80 Dale Ellis .75 2.00
81 Tod Murphy .60 1.50
82 Brad Daugherty .60 1.50
83 Charles Smith .60 1.50
84 Horace Grant 1.25 3.00
85 Vernon Maxwell .60 1.50
86 Todd Lichti .60 1.50
87 Sean Elliott 1.25 3.00
88 Kevin Duckworth .60 1.50
89 Dan Majerle 1.25 3.00
90 James Worthy 1.50 4.00
91 Mark Aguirre .75 2.00
92 Kevin Willis .75 2.00
93 Reggie Lewis 1.25 3.00
94 Rumeal Robinson .60 1.50
95 Terry Porter .75 2.00
96 Rolando Blackman .75 2.00
97 Tony Campbell .60 1.50
98 Sam Perkins 1.25 3.00
99 Willie Burton .60 1.50
100 Joe Dumars 1.50 4.00
101 Felton Spencer .60 1.50
102 Danny Ferry .60 1.50
103 James Donaldson .60 1.50
104 Craig Ehlo .75 2.00
105 Clifford Robinson 1.00 2.50
106 Pervis Ellison .60 1.50
107 Tyrone Corbin .60 1.50
108 Byron Scott 1.25 3.00
109 Sherman Douglas .60 1.50
110 Tim Hardaway 2.00 5.00
111 Kendall Gill .75 2.00
112 J.R. Reid .60 1.50
113 Robert Parish 1.25 3.00
114 Dominique Wilkins 3.00 8.00
115 Buck Williams .75 2.00
116 Scottie Pippen 5.00 12.00
117 Sam Mitchell .60 1.50
118 John Stockton 8.00 20.00
119 Derek Harper .75 2.00
120 Chris Jackson .60 1.50

1991-92 Fleer Wheaties Sheets

COMPLETE SET (8) 40.00 100.00
1 Wheaties Box 1 6.00 15.00
2 Wheaties Box 2 4.00 10.00
3 Wheaties Box 3 3.00 8.00
4 Wheaties Box 4 3.00 8.00
5 Wheaties Box 5 3.00 8.00
6 Wheaties Box 6 15.00 40.00
7 Wheaties Box 7 8.00 20.00
8 Wheaties Box 8 8.00 20.00

1992-93 Fleer

COMPLETE SET (444) 20.00 50.00
COMPLETE SERIES 1 (264) 10.00 25.00
COMPLETE SERIES 2 (180) 10.00 25.00
SLM DNK AUs: SER.2 STATED ODDS 1:5,000
1 Stacey Augmon .40 1.00
2 Duane Ferrell .25 .60
3 Paul Graham .25 .60
4A Jon Koncak
Shooting pose on back .25 .60
4B Jon Koncak
Playing defense on back .25 .60
5 Blair Rasmussen .25 .60
6 Rumeal Robinson .25 .60
7 Bob Weiss CO .25 .60
8 Dominique Wilkins .60 1.50
9 Kevin Willis .30 .75
10 John Bagley .25 .60
11 Larry Bird 1.50 4.00
12 Dee Brown .30 .75
13 Chris Ford CO .25 .60
14 Rick Fox .40 1.00
15 Kevin Gamble .25 .60
16 Reggie Lewis .40 1.00
17 Kevin McHale .60 1.50
18 Robert Parish .50 1.25
19 Ed Pinckney .25 .60
20 Muggsy Bogues .40 1.00
21 Allan Bristow CO .25 .60
22 Dell Curry .30 .75
23 Kenny Gattison .25 .60
24 Kendall Gill .30 .75
25 Larry Johnson .50 1.25
26 Johnny Newman .25 .60
27 J.R. Reid .30 .75
28 B.J. Armstrong .40 1.00
29 Bill Cartwright .30 .75
30 Horace Grant .40 1.00
31 Phil Jackson CO .60 1.50
32 Michael Jordan 3.00 8.00
33 Stacey King .25 .60
34 Cliff Levingston .25 .60
35 John Paxson .30 .75
36 Scottie Pippen 1.00 2.50
37 Scott Williams .25 .60
38 John Battle .25 .60
39 Terrell Brandon .30 .75
40 Brad Daugherty .30 .75
41 Craig Ehlo .30 .75
42 Larry Nance .30 .75
43 Mark Price .40 1.00
44 Mike Sanders .25 .60
45 Lenny Wilkens CO .40 1.00
46 John Hot Rod Williams .25 .60
47 Richie Adubato CO .25 .60
48 Terry Davis .25 .60
49 Derek Harper .30 .75
50 Donald Hodge .25 .60
51 Mike Iuzzolino .25 .60
52 Rodney McCray .25 .60
53 Doug Smith .25 .60
54 Greg Anderson .25 .60
55 Winston Garland .25 .60
56 Dan Issel CO .50 1.25
57 Chris Jackson .30 .75
58 Marcus Liberty .25 .60
59 Mark Macon .25 .60
60 Dikembe Mutombo .60 1.50
61 Reggie Williams .25 .60
62 Mark Aguirre .30 .75
63 Joe Dumars .50 1.25
64 Bill Laimbeer .40 1.00
65 Olden Polynice .25 .60
66 Dennis Rodman 1.00 2.50
67 Ron Rothstein CO .25 .60
68 John Salley .30 .75
69 Isiah Thomas .60 1.50
70 Darrell Walker .25 .60
71 Orlando Woolridge .40 1.00
72 Victor Alexander .25 .60
73 Mario Elie .30 .75
74 Tim Hardaway .50 1.25
75 Tyrone Hill .25 .60
76 Sarunas Marciulionis .40 1.00
77 Chris Mullin .50 1.25
78 Don Nelson CO .50 1.25
79 Billy Owens .30 .75
80 Sleepy Floyd UER .30 .75
81 Avery Johnson .30 .75
82 Buck Johnson .25 .60
83 Vernon Maxwell .30 .75
84 Hakeem Olajuwon .75 2.00
85 Kenny Smith .30 .75
86 Otis Thorpe .30 .75
87 Rudy Tomjanovich CO .50 1.25
88 Dale Davis .25 .60
89 Vern Fleming .30 .75
90 Bob Hill CO .25 .60
91 Reggie Miller .75 2.00
92 Chuck Person .30 .75
93 Detlef Schrempf .40 1.00
94 Rik Smits .30 .75
95 LaSalle Thompson .25 .60
96 Micheal Williams .25 .60
97 Larry Brown CO .40 1.00
98 James Edwards .25 .60
99 Gary Grant .25 .60
100 Ron Harper .40 1.00
101 Danny Manning .30 .75
102 Ken Norman .25 .60
103 Doc Rivers .40 1.00
104 Charles Smith .30 .75
105 Loy Vaught .25 .60
106 Elden Campbell .25 .60
107 Vlade Divac .40 1.00
108 A.C. Green .30 .75
109 Sam Perkins .30 .75
110 Randy Pfund CO RC .25 .60
111 Byron Scott .40 1.00
112 Terry Teagle .25 .60
113 Sedale Threatt .25 .60
114 James Worthy .60 1.50
115 Willie Burton .25 .60
116 Bimbo Coles .25 .60
117 Kevin Edwards .25 .60
118 Grant Long .25 .60
119 Kevin Loughery CO .25 .60
120 Glen Rice .40 1.00
121 Rony Seikaly .30 .75
122 Brian Shaw .25 .60
123 Steve Smith .40 1.00
124 Frank Brickowski .25 .60
125 Mike Dunleavy CO .25 .60
126 Blue Edwards .25 .60
127 Moses Malone .40 1.00
128 Eric Murdock .25 .60
129 Fred Roberts .25 .60
130 Alvin Robertson .30 .75
131 Thurl Bailey .30 .75
132 Tony Campbell .25 .60
133 Gerald Glass .25 .60
134 Luc Longley .40 1.00
135 Sam Mitchell .25 .60
136 Pooh Richardson .25 .60
137 Jimmy Rodgers CO .25 .60
138 Felton Spencer .25 .60
139 Doug West .30 .75
140 Kenny Anderson .30 .75
141 Mookie Blaylock .40 1.00
142 Sam Bowie .30 .75
143 Derrick Coleman .40 1.00
144 Chuck Daly CO .50 1.25
145 Terry Mills .25 .60
146 Chris Morris .30 .75
147 Drazen Petrovic .50 1.25
148 Greg Anthony .30 .75
149 Rolando Blackman .30 .75
150 Patrick Ewing .60 1.50
151 Mark Jackson .40 1.00
152 Anthony Mason .30 .75
153 Xavier McDaniel .30 .75
154 Charles Oakley .40 1.00
155 Pat Riley CO .50 1.25
156 John Starks .40 1.00
157 Gerald Wilkins .30 .75
158 Nick Anderson .30 .75
159 Anthony Bowie .25 .60
160 Terry Catledge .25 .60
161 Matt Guokas CO .25 .60
162 Stanley Roberts .25 .60
163 Dennis Scott .30 .75
164 Scott Skiles .30 .75
165 Brian Williams .30 .75
166 Ron Anderson .25 .60
167 Manute Bol .40 1.00
168 Johnny Dawkins .30 .75
169 Armon Gilliam .25 .60
170 Hersey Hawkins .30 .75
171 Jeff Hornacek .30 .75
172 Andrew Lang .25 .60
173 Doug Moe CO .30 .75
174 Tim Perry .25 .60
175 Jeff Ruland .30 .75
176 Charles Shackleford .25 .60
177 Danny Ainge .40 1.00
178 Charles Barkley 1.00 2.50
179 Cedric Ceballos .30 .75
180 Tom Chambers .40 1.00
181 Kevin Johnson .40 1.00
182 Dan Majerle .40 1.00
183 Mark West UER .30 .75
184 Paul Westphal CO .40 1.00
185 Rick Adelman CO .30 .75
186 Clyde Drexler .60 1.50

187 Kevin Duckworth .30 .75
188 Jerome Kersey .30 .75
189 Robert Pack .25 .60
190 Terry Porter .30 .75
191 Clifford Robinson .30 .75
192 Rod Strickland .30 .75
193 Buck Williams .30 .75
194 Anthony Bonner .25 .60
195 Duane Causwell .25 .60
196 Mitch Richmond .50 1.25
197 Garry St. Jean CO RC .25 .60
198 Lionel Simmons .25 .60
199 Wayman Tisdale .40 1.00
200 Spud Webb .40 1.00
201 Willie Anderson .30 .75
202 Antoine Carr .30 .75
203 Terry Cummings .30 .75
204 Sean Elliott .40 1.00
205 Dale Ellis .30 .75
206 Vinnie Johnson .30 .75
207 David Robinson .75 2.00
208 Jerry Tarkanian CO RC .40 1.00
209 Benoit Benjamin .25 .60
210 Michael Cage .30 .75
211 Eddie Johnson .30 .75
212 George Karl CO .30 .75
213 Shawn Kemp .60 1.50
214 Derrick McKey .30 .75
215 Nate McMillan .30 .75
216 Gary Payton .60 1.50
217 Ricky Pierce .30 .75
218 David Benoit .25 .60
219 Mike Brown .25 .60
220 Tyrone Corbin .30 .75
221 Mark Eaton .40 1.00
222 Jay Humphries .30 .75
223 Larry Krystkowiak .30 .75
224 Jeff Malone .30 .75
225 Karl Malone .75 2.00
226 Jerry Sloan CO .40 1.00
227 John Stockton .75 2.00
228 Michael Adams .30 .75
229 Rex Chapman .30 .75
230 Ledell Eackles .25 .60
231 Pervis Ellison .25 .60
232 A.J. English .25 .60
233 Harvey Grant .25 .60
234 LaBradford Smith .25 .60
235 Larry Stewart .25 .60
236 Wes Unseld CO .50 1.25
237 David Wingate .25 .60
238 Michael Jordan LL 3.00 8.00
239 Dennis Rodman LL 1.00 2.50
240 John Stockton LL .75 2.00
241 Buck Williams LL .30 .75
242 Mark Price LL .40 1.00
243 Dana Barros LL .25 .60
244 David Robinson LL .75 2.00
245 Chris Mullin LL .50 1.25
246 Michael Jordan MVP 3.00 8.00
247 Larry Johnson ROY UER .50 1.25
248 David Robinson POY .75 2.00
249 Detlef Schrempf SM .40 1.00
250 Clyde Drexler PV .60 1.50
251 Tim Hardaway PV .50 1.25
252 Kevin Johnson PV .40 1.00
253 Larry Johnson PV UER .50 1.25
254 Scottie Pippen PV 1.00 2.50
255 Isiah Thomas PV .60 1.50
256 Larry Bird SY 1.50 4.00
257 Brad Daugherty SY .30 .75
258 Kevin Johnson SY .40 1.00
259 Larry Johnson SY .50 1.25
260 Scottie Pippen SY 1.00 2.50
261 Dennis Rodman SY 1.00 2.50
262 Checklist 1 .20 .50
263 Checklist 2 .20 .50
264 Checklist 3 .20 .50
265 Charles Barkley SD 1.00 2.50
266 Shawn Kemp SD .60 1.50
267 Dan Majerle SD .40 1.00
268 Karl Malone SD .75 2.00
269 Buck Williams SD .30 .75
270 Clyde Drexler SD .60 1.50
271 Sean Elliott SD .40 1.00
272 Ron Harper SD .40 1.00
273 Michael Jordan SD 3.00 8.00
274 James Worthy SD .60 1.50
275 Cedric Ceballos SD .30 .75
276 Larry Nance SD .30 .75
277 Kenny Walker SD .25 .60
278 Spud Webb SD .40 1.00
279 Dominique Wilkins SD .60 1.50
280 Terrell Brandon SD .30 .75
281 Dee Brown SD .30 .75
282 Kevin Johnson SD .40 1.00
283 Doc Rivers SD .40 1.00
284 Byron Scott SD .40 1.00
285 Manute Bol SD .40 1.00
286 Dikembe Mutombo SD .60 1.50
287 Robert Parish SD .50 1.25
288 David Robinson SD .75 2.00
289 Dennis Rodman SD 1.00 2.50
290 Blue Edwards SD .25 .60
291 Patrick Ewing SD .60 1.50
292 Larry Johnson SD .50 1.25
293 Jerome Kersey SD .30 .75
294 Hakeem Olajuwon SD .75 2.00
295 Stacey Augmon SD .40 1.00
296 Derrick Coleman SD .40 1.00
297 Kendall Gill SD .30 .75
298 Shaquille O'Neal SD 3.00 8.00
299 Scottie Pippen SD 1.00 2.50
300 Darryl Dawkins SD .30 .75
301 Mookie Blaylock .40 1.00
302 Adam Keefe RC .25 .60
303 Travis Mays .25 .60
304 Morlon Wiley .25 .60
305 Sherman Douglas .30 .75
306 Joe Kleine .25 .60
307 Xavier McDaniel .30 .75
308 Tony Bennett RC .25 .60
309 Tom Hammonds .25 .60
310 Kevin Lynch .25 .60
311 Alonzo Mourning RC 2.00 5.00
312 David Wingate .25 .60
313 Rodney McCray .25 .60
314 Will Perdue .25 .60
315 Trent Tucker .25 .60
316 Corey Williams RC .25 .60
317 Danny Ferry .30 .75
318 Jay Guidinger RC .25 .60
319 Jerome Lane .25 .60
320 Gerald Wilkins .30 .75
321 Steve Bardo RC .25 .60
322 Walter Bond RC .25 .60
323 Brian Howard RC .25 .60
324 Tracy Moore RC .25 .60
325 Sean Rooks RC .25 .60
326 Randy White .25 .60
327 Kevin Brooks .25 .60
328 LaPhonso Ellis RC .40 1.00
329 Scott Hastings .25 .60
330 Todd Lichti .25 .60
331 Robert Pack .25 .60
332 Bryant Stith RC .30 .75
333 Gerald Glass .25 .60
334 Terry Mills .25 .60
335 Isaiah Morris RC .30 .75
336 Mark Randall .25 .60
337 Danny Young .25 .60
338 Chris Gatling .25 .60
339 Jeff Grayer .25 .60
340 Byron Houston RC .25 .60
341 Keith Jennings RC .25 .60
342 Alton Lister .25 .60
343 Latrell Sprewell RC 1.25 3.00
344 Scott Brooks .30 .75
345 Matt Bullard .25 .60
346 Carl Herrera .25 .60
347 Robert Horry RC 1.00 2.50
348 Tree Rollins .30 .75
349 Greg Dreiling .25 .60
350 George McCloud .25 .60
351 Sam Mitchell .25 .60
352 Pooh Richardson .25 .60
353 Malik Sealy RC .30 .75
354 Kenny Williams .25 .60
355 Jaren Jackson RC .25 .60
356 Mark Jackson .40 1.00
357 Stanley Roberts .25 .60
358 Elmore Spencer RC .25 .60
359 Kiki Vandeweghe .30 .75
360 John S. Williams .25 .60
361 Randy Woods RC .25 .60
362 Duane Cooper RC .25 .60
363 James Edwards .25 .60
364 Anthony Peeler RC .30 .75
365 Tony Smith .25 .60
366 Keith Askins .25 .60
367 Matt Geiger RC .25 .60
368 Alec Kessler .25 .60
369 Harold Miner RC .50 1.25
370 John Salley .25 .60
371 Anthony Avent RC .25 .60
372 Todd Day RC .30 .75
373 Blue Edwards .25 .60
374 Brad Lohaus .25 .60
375 Lee Mayberry RC .25 .60
376 Eric Murdock .25 .60
377 Danny Schayes .25 .60
378 Lance Blanks .25 .60
379 Christian Laettner RC 1.25 3.00
380 Bob McCann RC .25 .60
381 Chuck Person .30 .75
382 Brad Sellers .30 .75
383 Chris Smith RC .25 .60
384 Micheal Williams .25 .60
385 Rafael Addison .25 .60
386 Chucky Brown .25 .60
387 Chris Dudley .25 .60
388 Tate George .25 .60
389 Rick Mahorn .30 .75
390 Rumeal Robinson .25 .60
391 Jayson Williams .25 .60
392 Eric Anderson RC .25 .60
393 Rolando Blackman .30 .75
394 Tony Campbell .25 .60
395 Hubert Davis RC .30 .75
396 Doc Rivers .40 1.00
397 Charles Smith .30 .75
398 Herb Williams .30 .75
399 Litterial Green RC .25 .60
400 Greg Kite .25 .60
401 Shaquille O'Neal RC 3.00 8.00
402 Jerry Reynolds .25 .60
403 Jeff Turner .25 .60
404 Greg Grant .25 .60
405 Jeff Hornacek .30 .75
406 Andrew Lang .25 .60
407 Kenny Payne .25 .60
408 Tim Perry .25 .60
409 C.Weatherspoon RC .40 1.00
410 Danny Ainge .40 1.00
411 Charles Barkley 1.00 2.50
412 Negele Knight .25 .60
413 Oliver Miller RC .30 .75
414 Jerrod Mustaf .25 .60
415 Mark Bryant .25 .60
416 Mario Elie .30 .75
417 Dave Johnson RC .25 .60
418 Tracy Murray RC .30 .75
419 Reggie Smith RC .25 .60
420 Rod Strickland .30 .75
421 Randy Brown .25 .60
422 Pete Chilcutt .25 .60
423 Jim Les .25 .60
424 Walt Williams RC .40 1.00
425 Lloyd Daniels RC .30 .75
426 Vinny Del Negro .30 .75
427 Dale Ellis .30 .75
428 Sidney Green .25 .60
429 Avery Johnson .25 .60
430 Dana Barros .25 .60
431 Rich King .25 .60
432 Isaac Austin RC .25 .60
433 John Crotty RC .25 .60
434 Stephen Howard RC .25 .60
435 Jay Humphries .30 .75
436 Larry Krystkowiak .30 .75
437 Tom Gugliotta RC .40 1.00
438 Buck Johnson .25 .60
439 Charles Jones .25 .60
440 Don MacLean RC .30 .75
441 Doug Overton .30 .75
442 Brent Price RC .25 .60
443 Checklist 1 .20 .50
444 Checklist 2 .20 .50
SD266 Shawn Kemp AU 40.00 100.00
SD277 Kenny Walker AU 15.00 40.00
SD300 Darryl Dawkins AU 20.00 50.00
NNO Slam Dunk Wrapper Exch. 3.00 8.00

1992-93 Fleer All-Stars

COMPLETE SET (24) 40.00 100.00
SER.1 STATED ODDS 1:9
1 Michael Adams 1.00 2.50
2 Charles Barkley 3.00 8.00
3 Brad Daugherty 1.00 2.50
4 Joe Dumars 1.50 4.00
5 Patrick Ewing 2.00 5.00
6 Michael Jordan ! 30.00 80.00
7 Reggie Lewis 1.25 3.00
8 Scottie Pippen 3.00 8.00
9 Mark Price 1.25 3.00
10 Dennis Rodman 3.00 8.00
11 Isiah Thomas 2.00 5.00
12 Kevin Willis 1.00 2.50
13 Clyde Drexler 2.00 5.00
14 Tim Hardaway 1.50 4.00
15 Jeff Hornacek 1.00 2.50
16 Dan Majerle 1.25 3.00
17 Karl Malone 2.50 6.00
18 Chris Mullin 1.50 4.00
19 Dikembe Mutombo 2.00 5.00
20 Hakeem Olajuwon 2.50 6.00
21 David Robinson 2.50 6.00
22 John Stockton 2.50 6.00
23 Otis Thorpe 1.00 2.50
24 James Worthy 2.00 5.00

1992-93 Fleer Larry Johnson Promo

NNO Larry Johnson
(With Paul Mullan, CEO of Fleer) 4.00 10.00

1992-93 Fleer Larry Johnson

COMMON L.JOHNSON (1-12) .50 1.25
SER.1 STATED ODDS 1:18
COMMON AUTOGRAPH (AU) 10.00 25.00
COMMON SEND-OFF (13-15) 1.50 4.00
THREE CARDS PER 10 SER.1 WRAPPERS
LJ WRAPPER EXPIRATION: 6/30/93

1992-93 Fleer Rookie Sensations

COMPLETE SET (12) 8.00 20.00
SER.1 STATED ODDS 1:5 CELLO
1 Greg Anthony .60 1.50
2 Stacey Augmon .75 2.00
3 Terrell Brandon .60 1.50
4 Rick Fox .75 2.00
5 Larry Johnson 2.50 6.00
6 Mark Macon .50 1.25
7 Dikembe Mutombo 2.50 6.00
8 Billy Owens .60 1.50
9 Stanley Roberts .50 1.25
10 Doug Smith .50 1.25
11 Steve Smith .75 2.00
12 Larry Stewart .50 1.25

1992-93 Fleer Sharpshooters

COMPLETE SET (18) 8.00 20.00
SER.2 STATED ODDS 1:3
1 Reggie Miller 1.00 2.50
2 Dana Barros .30 .75
3 Jeff Hornacek .40 1.00
4 Drazen Petrovic .60 1.50
5 Glen Rice .50 1.25
6 Terry Porter .40 1.00
7 Mark Price .50 1.25
8 Michael Adams .40 1.00
9 Hersey Hawkins .40 1.00
10 Chuck Person .40 1.00
11 John Stockton 1.00 2.50
12 Dale Ellis .40 1.00
13 Clyde Drexler .75 2.00
14 Mitch Richmond .60 1.50
15 Craig Ehlo .40 1.00
16 Dell Curry .40 1.00
17 Chris Mullin .60 1.50
18 Rolando Blackman .40 1.00

1992-93 Fleer Team Leaders

COMPLETE SET (27) 150.00 400.00
ONE TL OR JOHNSON PER SER.1 RACK PACK
1 Dominique Wilkins 6.00 15.00
2 Reggie Lewis 4.00 10.00
3 Larry Johnson 5.00 12.00
4 Michael Jordan ! 125.00 300.00
5 Mark Price 4.00 10.00
6 Terry Davis 2.50 6.00
7 Dikembe Mutombo 6.00 15.00
8 Isiah Thomas 6.00 15.00
9 Chris Mullin 5.00 12.00
10 Hakeem Olajuwon 8.00 20.00
11 Reggie Miller 8.00 20.00
12 Danny Manning 3.00 8.00
13 James Worthy 6.00 15.00
14 Glen Rice 4.00 10.00
15 Alvin Robertson 3.00 8.00
16 Tony Campbell 2.50 6.00
17 Derrick Coleman 4.00 10.00
18 Patrick Ewing 6.00 15.00
19 Scott Skiles 3.00 8.00
20 Hersey Hawkins 3.00 8.00
21 Kevin Johnson 4.00 10.00
22 Clyde Drexler 6.00 15.00
23 Mitch Richmond 5.00 12.00
24 David Robinson 8.00 20.00
25 Ricky Pierce 3.00 8.00
26 Karl Malone 8.00 20.00
27 Pervis Ellison 2.50 6.00

1992-93 Fleer Total D

COMPLETE SET (15) 75.00 200.00
SER.2 STATED ODDS 1:5 CELLO
1 David Robinson 4.00 10.00
2 Dennis Rodman 5.00 12.00
3 Scottie Pippen 5.00 12.00
4 Joe Dumars 2.50 6.00
5 Michael Jordan ! 60.00 150.00
6 John Stockton 4.00 10.00
7 Patrick Ewing 3.00 8.00
8 Micheal Williams 1.25 3.00
9 Larry Nance 1.50 4.00
10 Buck Williams 1.50 4.00
11 Alvin Robertson 1.50 4.00
12 Dikembe Mutombo 3.00 8.00
13 Mookie Blaylock 2.00 5.00
14 Hakeem Olajuwon 4.00 10.00
15 Rony Seikaly 1.50 4.00

1992-93 Fleer Drake's

COMPLETE SET (55) 40.00 100.00
1 Dominique Wilkins 1.25 3.00
2 Mookie Blaylock .75 2.00
3 Reggie Lewis .75 2.00
4 Dee Brown .60 1.50
5 Alonzo Mourning 4.00 10.00
6 Larry Johnson 1.00 2.50
7 Michael Jordan 6.00 15.00
8 Scottie Pippen 2.00 5.00
9 Mark Price .75 2.00
10 Brad Daugherty .60 1.50
11 Derek Harper .60 1.50
12 Sean Rooks .50 1.25
13 Dikembe Mutombo 1.25 3.00
14 Chris Jackson .60 1.50
15 Isiah Thomas 1.25 3.00
16 Joe Dumars 1.00 2.50
17 Chris Mullin 1.00 2.50
18 Tim Hardaway 1.00 2.50
19 Hakeem Olajuwon 1.50 4.00
20 Kenny Smith .60 1.50
21 Reggie Miller 1.50 4.00
22 Detlef Schrempf .75 2.00
23 Danny Manning .60 1.50
24 Mark Jackson .75 2.00
25 Sedale Threatt .50 1.25
26 James Worthy 1.25 3.00
27 Glen Rice .75 2.00
28 Rony Seikaly .60 1.50
29 Blue Edwards .50 1.25
30 Eric Murdock .50 1.25
31 Christian Laettner 2.50 6.00
32 Micheal Williams .50 1.25
33 Drazen Petrovic 1.00 2.50
34 Derrick Coleman .75 2.00
35 Patrick Ewing 1.25 3.00
36 John Starks .75 2.00
37 Shaquille O'Neal 6.00 15.00
38 Scott Skiles .60 1.50
39 Jeff Hornacek .60 1.50
40 Clarence Weatherspoon .75 2.00
41 Charles Barkley 2.00 5.00
42 Dan Majerle .75 2.00
43 Clyde Drexler 1.25 3.00
44 Terry Porter .60 1.50
45 Mitch Richmond 1.00 2.50
46 Lionel Simmons .50 1.25
47 David Robinson 1.50 4.00
48 Sean Elliott .75 2.00
49 Shawn Kemp 1.25 3.00
50 Gary Payton 1.25 3.00
51 John Stockton 1.50 4.00
52 Karl Malone 1.50 4.00
53 Pervis Ellison .50 1.25
54 Tom Gugliotta .75 2.00
NNO Checklist Card .40 .25

1992-93 Fleer NBA Rising Stars Magazine Sheet

NNO Kendall Gill .40 1.00
NNO Blue Edwards .30 .75
NNO Shaquille O'Neal 4.00 10.00
NNO Clarence Weatherspoon .50 1.25
NNO Gary Payton .75 2.00
NNO Lionel Simmons .30 .75
NNO Kenny Anderson .40 1.00
NNO Complete Sheet 6.00 15.00

1992-93 Fleer Spalding Schoolyard Stars

COMPLETE SET (5) 3.00 8.00
1 Larry Bird 2.00 5.00
2 Kevin Johnson .50 1.25
3 Larry Johnson .60 1.50
4 Scottie Pippen 1.25 3.00
5 Title Card .20 .50

1992-93 Fleer Team Night Sheets

1 Nick Anderson .30 .75
2 B.J. Armstrong .40 1.00
3 Keith Askins .25 .60
4 Anthony Avent .25 .60
5 John Bagley .25 .60
6 Belk
Ad Card .20 .40
7 Tony Bennett .25 .60
8 Muggsy Bogues .40 1.00
9 Walter Bond .25 .60
10 Anthony Bowie .25 .60
11 Frank Brickowski .25 .60
12 Dee Brown .30 .75
13 Willie Burton .25 .60
14 Dexter Cambridge .25 .60
15 Elden Campbell .25 .60
16 Bill Cartwright .30 .75
17 Terry Catledge .25 .60
18 Bimbo Coles .25 .60
19 Duane Cooper .25 .60
20 Dell Curry .30 .75
21 Dale Davis .25 .60
22 Terry Davis .25 .60
23 Todd Day .40 1.00
24 Vlade Divac .40 1.00
25 Sherman Douglas .30 .75
26 Mike Dunleavy CO .25 .60
27 Blue Edwards .25 .60
28 James Edwards .25 .60
29 Kevin Edwards .25 .60
30 Vern Fleming .30 .75
31 Rick Fox .40 1.00
32 Kevin Gamble .25 .60
33 Kenny Gattison .25 .60
34 Kendall Gill .30 .75
35 Mike Gminski .25 .60
36 Gooding's
Ad Card .20 .50
37 Horace Grant .40 1.00
38 A.C. Green .30 .75
39 Derek Harper .30 .75
40 Bob Hill CO .25 .60
41 Donald Hodge .25 .60
42 Hugo (Mascot) .20 .50
43 Mike Iuzzolino .25 .60
44 Jim Jackson .30 .75
45 Larry Johnson .50 1.25
46 Michael Jordan 3.00 8.00
47 Steve Kerr .30 .75
48 Alec Kessler .25 .60
49 Stacey King .25 .60
50 Greg Kite .25 .60
51 Joe Kleine .25 .60
52 Reggie Lewis .40 1.00
53 Brad Lohaus .25 .60
54 Grant Long .25 .60
55 Moses Malone .40 1.00
56 Lee Mayberry .25 .60
57 Lay's Potato Chips
Ad Card .20 .50
58 George McCloud .25 .60
59 Rodney McCray .25 .60
60 Xavier McDaniel .30 .75
61 Kevin McHale .60 1.50
62 Reggie Miller .75 2.00
63 Harold Miner .50 1.25
64 Sam Mitchell .25 .60
65 Alonzo Mourning 2.00 5.00
66 Eric Murdock .25 .60
67 Johnny Newman .25 .60
68 Shaquille O'Neal 3.00 8.00
69 Pacers Gift Shop
Ad Card .20 .50
70 Robert Parish .50 1.25
71 John Paxson .30 .75
72 Anthony Peeler .30 .75
73 Will Perdue .25 .60
74 Sam Perkins .30 .75
75 Ed Pinckney .25 .60
76 Scottie Pippen 1.00 2.50
77 Jerry Reynolds .25 .60
78 Glen Rice .40 1.00
79 Pooh Richardson .25 .60
80 Fred Roberts .25 .60
81 Alvin Robertson .30 .75
82 Sean Rooks .25 .60
83 John Salley .30 .75
84 Dan Schayes .25 .60
85 Detlef Schrempf .40 1.00
86 Byron Scott .40 1.00
87 Dennis Scott .30 .75
88 Malik Sealy .30 .75
89 Rony Seikaly .30 .75
90 Brian Shaw .25 .60
91 Scott Skiles .30 .75
92 Doug Smith .25 .60
93 Steve Smith .40 1.00
94 Rik Smits .30 .75
95 LaSalle Thompson .25 .60
96 Sedale Threatt .25 .60
97 Trent Tucker .25 .60
98 Jeff Turner .25 .60
99 Toyota
Ad Card .20 .50
100 UNO Pizzeria
Ad Card .20 .50
101 Randy White .25 .60
102 Morlon Wiley .25 .60
103 Brian Williams .25 .60
104 Corey Williams .25 .60
105 Scott Williams .25 .60
106 David Wingate .25 .60
107 James Worthy .60 1.50
108 John Bagley
Dee Brown
Sherman Douglas
Rick Fox
Kevin Gamble
Joe Kleine
Reggie Lewis
Xavier McDaniel
Kevin McHale
Robert Parish
Ed Pinckney
UNO Pizzeria (Ad card) .60 1.50
109 Tony Bennett
Muggsy Bogues
Dell Curry
Kenny Gattison
Kendall Gill
Mike Gminski
Hugo (Mascot)
Larry Johnson
Alonzo Mourning
Johnny Newman
David Wingate
Belk (Ad Card) 2.00 5.00
110 B.J. Armstrong
Bill Cartwright
Horace Grant
Michael Jordan
Stacey King
Rodney McCray
John Paxson
Will Perdue
Scottie Pippen
Trent Tucker
Corey Williams
Scott Williams 3.00 8.00
111 Walter Bond
Dexter Cambridge
Terry Davis
Derek Harper
Donald Hodge
Mike Iuzzolino
Jim Jackson
Sean Rooks
Doug Smith
Randy White
Morlon Wiley
Lay's Potato Chips/(Ad card) .30 .75
112 Dale Davis
Vern Fleming
Bob Hill CO
George McCloud
Reggie Miller
Sam Mitchell
Pooh Richardson
Detlef Schrempf
Malik Sealy
Rik Smits
LaSalle Thompson
Pacers Gift Shop/(Ad card) .75 2.00
113 Elden Campbell
Duane Cooper
Vlade Divac
James Edwards
A.C. Green
Anthony Peeler
Sam Perkins
Byron Scott
Sedale Threatt
James Worthy
Toyota (Two ad cards) .60 1.50
114 Keith Askins
Willie Burton
Bimbo Coles
Kevin Edwards
Alec Kessler
Grant Long
Harold Miner
Glen Rice
John Salley
Rony Seikaly
Brian Shaw
Steve Smith .50 1.25
115 Anthony Avent
Frank Brickowski
Todd Day
Mike Dunleavy CO
Blue Edwards
Brad Lohaus
Moses Malone
Lee Mayberry
Eric Murdock
Fred Roberts
Alvin Robertson
Dan Schayes .40 1.00
116 Nick Anderson
Anthony Bowie
Terry Catledge
Steve Kerr
Greg Kite
Shaquille O'Neal
Jerry Reynolds
Dennis Scott
Scott Skiles
Jeff Turner
Brian Williams
Gooding's (Ad card) 3.00 8.00

1992-93 Fleer Tony's Pizza

COMPLETE SET (110) 20.00 50.00
1 Chris Jackson .40 1.00
2 Michael Adams .40 1.00
3 Kenny Anderson .40 1.00
4 Willie Anderson .40 1.00
5 Greg Anthony .40 1.00
6 B.J. Armstrong .50 1.25
7 Stacey Augmon SD .50 1.25
8 Thurl Bailey .40 1.00
9 Charles Barkley SD 1.25 3.00
10 Benoit Benjamin .30 .75
11 Muggsy Bogues .50 1.25
12 Manute Bol SD .50 1.25
13 Sam Bowie .40 1.00
14 Terrell Brandon SD .40 1.00
15 Frank Brickowski .30 .75
16 Dee Brown SD .40 1.00
17 Terry Davis .30 .75
17 Michael Cage .40 1.00
18 Antoine Carr .40 1.00
19 Duane Causwell .30 .75
20 Cedric Ceballos SD .40 1.00
21 Rex Chapman .40 1.00
22 Derrick Coleman SD .50 1.25
23 Tyrone Corbin .40 1.00
24 Brad Daugherty .40 1.00
26 Darryl Dawkins SD .40 1.00
27 Johnny Dawkins .40 1.00
28 Brian Williams .40 1.00
29 Vlade Divac .50 1.25
30 Clyde Drexler SD .75 2.00
31 Joe Dumars .60 1.50
32 Blue Edwards SD .30 .75
33 Craig Ehlo .40 1.00
34 Sean Elliott SD .50 1.25
35 Pervis Ellison .30 .75
36 Patrick Ewing SD .75 2.00
37 Duane Ferrell .30 .75
37 Kevin McHale .75 2.00
38 Vern Fleming .40 1.00
39 Winston Garland .30 .75
40 Kendall Gill SD .40 1.00
41 Horace Grant .50 1.25
42 Tim Hardaway .60 1.50
43 Derek Harper .40 1.00
44 Ron Harper SD .50 1.25
45 Hersey Hawkins .40 1.00
46 Kevin Johnson SD .50 1.25
47 Larry Johnson SD .60 1.50
48 Michael Jordan SD 4.00 10.00
49 Shawn Kemp SD .75 2.00
50 Jerome Kersey SD .40 1.00
51 Stacey King .30 .75
52 Reggie Lewis .50 1.25
53 Dan Majerle SD .50 1.25
54 Jeff Malone .40 1.00
55 Karl Malone SD 1.00 2.50
56 Moses Malone .50 1.25
57 Danny Manning .40 1.00
58 Sarunas Marciulionis .50 1.25
59 Vernon Maxwell .40 1.00
61 Reggie Miller 1.00 2.50
62 Chris Mullin .60 1.50
63 Dikembe Mutombo SD .75 2.00
64 Larry Nance SD .40 1.00
65 Ken Norman .30 .75
66 Charles Oakley .50 1.25
67 Hakeem Olajuwon SD 1.00 2.50
68 Shaquille O'Neal SD 4.00 10.00
69 Billy Owens .40 1.00
70 Robert Parish SD .60 1.50
71 Drazen Petrovic .60 1.50
72 Ricky Pierce .40 1.00
73 Scottie Pippen SD 1.25 3.00
74 J.R. Reid .40 1.00
75 Glen Rice .50 1.25
76 Mitch Richmond .60 1.50
77 Doc Rivers SD .50 1.25
78 Alvin Robertson .40 1.00
79 Clifford Robinson .40 1.00
80 David Robinson SD 1.00 2.50
81 Rumeal Robinson .30 .75
82 Dennis Rodman SD 1.25 3.00
83 Detlef Schrempf .50 1.25
84 Byron Scott SD .50 1.25
85 Dennis Scott .40 1.00
86 Rony Seikaly .40 1.00
87 Charles Shackleford .30 .75
88 Brian Shaw .30 .75
89 Scott Skiles .40 1.00
90 Doug Smith .30 .75
91 Kenny Smith .40 1.00
92 Steve Smith .50 1.25
93 Felton Spencer .30 .75
94 John Stockton 1.00 2.50
95 Isiah Thomas .75 2.00
96 Otis Thorpe .40 1.00
97 Sedale Threatt .30 .75
98 Wayman Tisdale .50 1.25
99 Loy Vaught .30 .75
100 Kenny Walker SD .30 .75
101 Spud Webb SD .50 1.25
102 Doug West .40 1.00
103 Dominique Wilkins SD .75 2.00
104 Buck Williams SD .40 1.00
105 Micheal Williams .30 .75
106 Reggie Williams .30 .75
107 Scott Williams .30 .75
108 Orlando Woolridge .50 1.25
109 James Worthy SD .75 2.00
XX Coupon Card .20 .50

1993-94 Fleer

COMPLETE SET (400) 15.00 40.00
COMPLETE SERIES 1 (240) 8.00 20.00
COMPLETE SERIES 2 (160) 8.00 20.00
1 Stacey Augmon .30 .75
2 Mookie Blaylock .40 1.00
3 Duane Ferrell .25 .60
4 Paul Graham .25 .60
5 Adam Keefe .25 .60
6 Jon Koncak .25 .60
7 Dominique Wilkins .60 1.50
8 Kevin Willis .30 .75
9 Alaa Abdelnaby .25 .60
10 Dee Brown .30 .75
11 Sherman Douglas .25 .60
12 Rick Fox .30 .75
13 Kevin Gamble .25 .60
14 Reggie Lewis .40 1.00
15 Xavier McDaniel .40 1.00
16 Robert Parish .50 1.25
17 Muggsy Bogues .40 1.00
18 Dell Curry .40 1.00
19 Kenny Gattison .25 .60
20 Kendall Gill .30 .75
21 Larry Johnson .50 1.25
22 Alonzo Mourning .60 1.50
23 Johnny Newman .25 .60
24 David Wingate .25 .60
25 B.J. Armstrong .40 1.00
26 Bill Cartwright .30 .75
27 Horace Grant .40 1.00
28 Michael Jordan 4.00 10.00
29 Stacey King .25 .60
30 John Paxson .30 .75
31 Will Perdue .25 .60
32 Scottie Pippen 1.00 2.50
33 Scott Williams .25 .60
34 Terrell Brandon .30 .75
35 Brad Daugherty .30 .75
36 Craig Ehlo .25 .60
37 Danny Ferry .25 .60
38 Larry Nance .30 .75
39 Mark Price .40 1.00
40 Mike Sanders .25 .60
41 Gerald Wilkins .30 .75
42 John Williams .25 .60
43 Terry Davis .25 .60
44 Derek Harper .30 .75
45 Mike Iuzzolino .25 .60
46 Jim Jackson .30 .75
47 Sean Rooks .25 .60
48 Doug Smith .25 .60
49 Randy White .25 .60
50 Mahmoud Abdul-Rauf .30 .75
51 LaPhonso Ellis .30 .75
52 Marcus Liberty .25 .60
53 Mark Macon .25 .60
54 Dikembe Mutombo .60 1.50
55 Robert Pack .25 .60
56 Bryant Stith .25 .60
57 Reggie Williams .25 .60
58 Mark Aguirre .30 .75
59 Joe Dumars .50 1.25
60 Bill Laimbeer .40 1.00
61 Terry Mills .25 .60
62 Olden Polynice .25 .60
63 Alvin Robertson .30 .75
64 Dennis Rodman 1.00 2.50
65 Isiah Thomas .60 1.50
66 Victor Alexander .25 .60
67 Tim Hardaway .50 1.25
68 Tyrone Hill .25 .60
69 Byron Houston .25 .60
70 Sarunas Marciulionis .40 1.00
71 Chris Mullin .50 1.25
72 Billy Owens .30 .75
73 Latrell Sprewell .60 1.50
74 Scott Brooks .25 .60
75 Matt Bullard .25 .60
76 Carl Herrera .25 .60
77 Robert Horry .40 1.00
78 Vernon Maxwell .30 .75
79 Hakeem Olajuwon .75 2.00
80 Kenny Smith .30 .75
81 Otis Thorpe .40 1.00
82 Dale Davis .30 .75
83 Vern Fleming .30 .75

84 George McCloud .25 .60
85 Reggie Miller .75 2.00
86 Sam Mitchell .25 .60
87 Pooh Richardson .30 .75
88 Detlef Schrempf .40 1.00
89 Rik Smits .30 .75
90 Gary Grant .25 .60
91 Ron Harper .40 1.00
92 Mark Jackson .30 .75
93 Danny Manning .30 .75
94 Ken Norman .25 .60
95 Stanley Roberts .25 .60
96 Loy Vaught .25 .60
97 John Williams .25 .60
98 Elden Campbell .25 .60
99 Doug Christie .30 .75
100 Duane Cooper .25 .60
101 Vlade Divac .40 1.00
102 A.C. Green .30 .75
103 Anthony Peeler .30 .75
104 Sedale Threatt .25 .60
105 James Worthy .50 1.25
106 Bimbo Coles .25 .60
107 Grant Long .25 .60
108 Harold Miner .30 .75
109 Glen Rice .40 1.00
110 John Salley .30 .75
111 Rony Seikaly .30 .75
112 Brian Shaw .25 .60
113 Steve Smith .30 .75
114 Anthony Avent .25 .60
115 Jon Barry .25 .60
116 Frank Brickowski .25 .60
117 Todd Day .25 .60
118 Blue Edwards .25 .60
119 Brad Lohaus .25 .60
120 Lee Mayberry .25 .60
121 Eric Murdock .25 .60
122 Thurl Bailey .25 .60
123 Christian Laettner .40 1.00
124 Luc Longley .30 .75
125 Chuck Person .30 .75
126 Felton Spencer .25 .60
127 Doug West .25 .60
128 Micheal Williams .25 .60
129 Rafael Addison .25 .60
130 Kenny Anderson .30 .75
131 Sam Bowie .30 .75
132 Chucky Brown .25 .60
133 Derrick Coleman .40 1.00
134 Chris Dudley .25 .60
135 Chris Morris .25 .60
136 Rumeal Robinson .25 .60
137 Greg Anthony .25 .60
138 Rolando Blackman .30 .75
139 Tony Campbell .25 .60
140 Hubert Davis .30 .75
141 Patrick Ewing .60 1.50
142 Anthony Mason .30 .75
143 Charles Oakley .40 1.00
144 Doc Rivers .30 .75
145 Charles Smith .25 .60
146 John Starks .40 1.00
147 Nick Anderson .30 .75
148 Anthony Bowie .25 .60
149 Shaquille O'Neal 2.00 5.00
150 Donald Royal .25 .60
151 Dennis Scott .25 .60
152 Scott Skiles .25 .60
153 Tom Tolbert .25 .60
154 Jeff Turner .25 .60
155 Ron Anderson .25 .60
156 Johnny Dawkins .30 .75
157 Hersey Hawkins .30 .75
158 Jeff Hornacek .30 .75
159 Andrew Lang .25 .60
160 Tim Perry .25 .60
161 Clarence Weatherspoon .25 .60
162 Danny Ainge .40 1.00
163 Charles Barkley 1.00 2.50
164 Cedric Ceballos .30 .75
165 Tom Chambers .40 1.00
166 Richard Dumas .25 .60
167 Kevin Johnson .40 1.00
168 Negele Knight .25 .60
169 Dan Majerle .40 1.00
170 Oliver Miller .25 .60
171 Mark West .25 .60
172 Mark Bryant .25 .60
173 Clyde Drexler .60 1.50
174 Kevin Duckworth .25 .60
175 Mario Elie .30 .75
176 Jerome Kersey .30 .75
177 Terry Porter .30 .75
178 Clifford Robinson .40 1.00
179 Rod Strickland .40 1.00
180 Buck Williams .30 .75
181 Anthony Bonner .25 .60
182 Duane Causwell .25 .60
183 Mitch Richmond .50 1.25
184 Lionel Simmons .25 .60
185 Wayman Tisdale .25 .60
186 Spud Webb .30 .75
187 Walt Williams .40 1.00
188 Antoine Carr .25 .60
189 Terry Cummings .30 .75
190 Lloyd Daniels .25 .60
191 Vinny Del Negro .25 .60
192 Sean Elliott .40 1.00
193 Dale Ellis .25 .60
194 Avery Johnson .30 .75
195 J.R. Reid .30 .75
196 David Robinson .75 2.00
197 Michael Cage .30 .75
198 Eddie Johnson .25 .60
199 Shawn Kemp .60 1.50
200 Derrick McKey .30 .75
201 Nate McMillan .30 .75
202 Gary Payton .50 1.25
203 Sam Perkins .30 .75
204 Ricky Pierce .30 .75
205 David Benoit .25 .60
206 Tyrone Corbin .25 .60
207 Mark Eaton .40 1.00
208 Jay Humphries .30 .75
209 Larry Krystkowiak .25 .60
210 Jeff Malone .30 .75
211 Karl Malone .75 2.00
212 John Stockton .75 2.00
213 Michael Adams .30 .75
214 Rex Chapman .25 .60
215 Pervis Ellison .25 .60
216 Harvey Grant .30 .75
217 Tom Gugliotta .30 .75
218 Buck Johnson .25 .60
219 LaBradford Smith .25 .60
220 Larry Stewart .25 .60
221 B.J. Armstrong LL .40 1.00
222 Cedric Ceballos LL .30 .75
223 Larry Johnson LL .50 1.25
224 Michael Jordan LL 4.00 10.00
225 Hakeem Olajuwon LL .75 2.00
226 Mark Price LL .40 1.00
227 Dennis Rodman LL 1.00 2.50
228 John Stockton LL .75 2.00
229 Charles Barkley AW 1.00 2.50
230 Hakeem Olajuwon AW .75 2.00
231 Shaquille O'Neal AW 2.00 5.00
232 Clifford Robinson AW .40 1.00
233 Shawn Kemp PV .60 1.50
234 Alonzo Mourning PV .60 1.50
235 Hakeem Olajuwon PV .75 2.00
236 John Stockton PV .75 2.00
237 Dominique Wilkins PV .60 1.50
238 Checklist 1-85 .20 .50
239 Checklist 86-165 .20 .50
240 Checklist 166-240 UER .20 .50
241 Doug Edwards RC .40 1.00
242 Craig Ehlo .25 .60
243 Andrew Lang .25 .60
244 Ennis Whatley .25 .60
245 Chris Corchiani .25 .60
246 Acie Earl RC .40 1.00
247 Jimmy Oliver .25 .60
248 Ed Pinckney .25 .60
249 Dino Radja RC .40 1.00
250 Matt Wenstrom RC .40 1.00
251 Tony Bennett .25 .60
252 Scott Burrell RC .40 1.00
253 LeRon Ellis .25 .60
254 Hersey Hawkins .30 .75
255 Eddie Johnson .25 .60
256 Corie Blount RC .40 1.00
257 Jo Jo English RC .40 1.00
258 Dave Johnson .25 .60
259 Steve Kerr .30 .75
260 Toni Kukoc RC 1.00 2.50
261 Pete Myers .25 .60
262 Bill Wennington .25 .60
263 John Battle .25 .60
264 Tyrone Hill .30 .75
265 Gerald Madkins RC .40 1.00
266 Chris Mills RC .40 1.00
267 Bobby Phills .25 .60
268 Greg Dreiling .25 .60
269 Lucious Harris RC .40 1.00
270 Donald Hodge .25 .60
271 Popeye Jones RC .40 1.00
272 Tim Legler RC .40 1.00
273 Fat Lever .30 .75
274 Jamal Mashburn RC .75 2.00
275 Darren Morningstar RC .40 1.00
276 Tom Hammonds .25 .60
277 Darnell Mee RC .25 .60
278 Rodney Rogers RC .40 1.00
279 Brian Williams .25 .60
280 Greg Anderson .25 .60
281 Sean Elliott .40 1.00
282 Allan Houston RC .75 2.00
283 Lindsey Hunter RC .40 1.00
284 Marcus Liberty .25 .60
285 Mark Macon .25 .60
286 David Wood .25 .60
287 Jud Buechler .25 .60
288 Chris Gatling .25 .60
289 Josh Grant RC .30 .75
290 Jeff Grayer .25 .60
291 Avery Johnson .30 .75
292 Chris Webber RC 2.00 5.00
293 Sam Cassell RC .75 2.00
294 Mario Elie .30 .75
295 Richard Petruska RC .40 1.00
296 Eric Riley RC .40 1.00
297 Antonio Davis RC .50 1.25
298 Scott Haskin RC .25 .60
299 Derrick McKey .30 .75
300 Byron Scott .40 1.00
301 Malik Sealy .30 .75
302 LaSalle Thompson .25 .60
303 Kenny Williams .25 .60
304 Haywoode Workman .25 .60
305 Mark Aguirre .30 .75
306 Terry Dehere RC .40 1.00
307 Bob Martin RC .40 1.00
308 Elmore Spencer .25 .60
309 Tom Tolbert .25 .60
310 Randy Woods .25 .60
311 Sam Bowie .30 .75
312 James Edwards .25 .60
313 Antonio Harvey RC .40 1.00
314 George Lynch RC .40 1.00
315 Tony Smith .25 .60
316 Nick Van Exel RC 1.00 2.50
317 Manute Bol .25 .60
318 Willie Burton .25 .60
319 Matt Geiger .25 .60
320 Alec Kessler .25 .60
321 Vin Baker RC .60 1.50
322 Ken Norman .25 .60
323 Danny Schayes .25 .60
324 Derek Strong RC .30 .75
325 Mike Brown .25 .60
326 Brian Davis RC .40 1.00
327 Tellis Frank .25 .60
328 Marlon Maxey .25 .60
329 Isaiah Rider RC .60 1.50
330 Chris Smith .25 .60
331 Benoit Benjamin .25 .60
332 P.J. Brown RC .40 1.00
333 Kevin Edwards .25 .60
334 Armon Gilliam .25 .60
335 Rick Mahorn .30 .75
336 Dwayne Schintzius .25 .60
337 Rex Walters RC .30 .75
338 David Wesley RC .40 1.00
339 Jayson Williams .25 .60
340 Anthony Bonner .25 .60
341 Herb Williams .25 .60
342 Litterial Green .25 .60
343 Anfernee Hardaway RC 2.00 5.00
344 Greg Kite .25 .60
345 Larry Krystkowiak .25 .60
346 Todd Lichti .25 .60
347 Keith Tower RC .40 1.00
348 Dana Barros .25 .60
349 Shawn Bradley RC .40 1.00
350 Michael Curry RC .40 1.00
351 Greg Graham RC .25 .60
352 Warren Kidd RC .25 .60
353 Moses Malone .60 1.50
354 Orlando Woolridge .25 .60
355 Duane Cooper .25 .60
356 Joe Courtney RC .40 1.00
357 A.C. Green .30 .75
358 Frank Johnson .25 .60
359 Joe Kleine .25 .60
360 Malcolm Mackey RC .25 .60
361 Jerrod Mustaf .25 .60
362 Chris Dudley .25 .60
363 Harvey Grant .30 .75
364 Tracy Murray .25 .60
365 James Robinson RC .40 1.00
366 Reggie Smith .25 .60
367 Kevin Thompson RC .25 .60
368 Randy Breuer .25 .60
369 Randy Brown .25 .60
370 Evers Burns RC .40 1.00
371 Pete Chilcutt .25 .60
372 Bobby Hurley RC .40 1.00
373 Jim Les .25 .60
374 Mike Peplowski RC .25 .60
375 Willie Anderson .25 .60
376 Sleepy Floyd .30 .75
377 Negele Knight .25 .60
378 Dennis Rodman 1.00 2.50
379 Chris Whitney RC .30 .75
380 Vincent Askew .25 .60
381 Kendall Gill .30 .75
382 Ervin Johnson RC .40 1.00
383 Chris King RC .40 1.00
384 Rich King .25 .60
385 Steve Scheffler .25 .60
386 Detlef Schrempf .40 1.00
387 Tom Chambers .40 1.00
388 John Crotty .25 .60
389 Bryon Russell RC .40 1.00
390 Felton Spencer .25 .60
391 Luther Wright RC .25 .60
392 Mitchell Butler RC .40 1.00
393 Calbert Cheaney RC .40 1.00
394 Kevin Duckworth .30 .75
395 Don MacLean .25 .60
396 Gheorghe Muresan RC .40 1.00
397 Doug Overton .25 .60
398 Brent Price .25 .60
399 Checklist .20 .50
400 Checklist .20 .50

1993-94 Fleer All-Stars

COMPLETE SET (24) 12.00 30.00
SER.1 STATED ODDS 1:10 HOBBY
1 Brad Daugherty .50 1.25
2 Joe Dumars .75 2.00
3 Patrick Ewing 1.00 2.50
4 Larry Johnson .75 2.00
5 Michael Jordan 10.00 25.00
6 Larry Nance .50 1.25
7 Shaquille O'Neal 3.00 8.00
8 Scottie Pippen UER 3.00 8.00
9 Mark Price .60 1.50
10 Detlef Schrempf .60 1.50
11 Isiah Thomas 1.00 2.50
12 Dominique Wilkins 1.00 2.50
13 Charles Barkley 1.50 4.00
14 Clyde Drexler 1.00 2.50
15 Sean Elliott .60 1.50
16 Tim Hardaway .75 2.00
17 Shawn Kemp 1.00 2.50
18 Dan Majerle .60 1.50
19 Karl Malone 1.25 3.00
20 Danny Manning .50 1.25
21 Hakeem Olajuwon 1.25 3.00
22 Terry Porter .50 1.25
23 David Robinson 1.25 3.00
24 John Stockton 1.25 3.00

1993-94 Fleer Clyde Drexler

COMPLETE SET (12) 2.50 5.00
COMMON DREXLER (1-12) .20 .50
SER.1 STATED ODDS 1:6
COMMON AUTOGRAPH (AU) 25.00 60.00
DREXLER AU: SER.1 STATED ODDS 1:7,000
COMMON SEND-OFF (13-15) .75 2.00

1993-94 Fleer First Year Phenoms

COMPLETE SET (10) 4.00 10.00
SER.2 STATED ODDS 1:4 HOBBY, 1:3 CELLO
1 Shawn Bradley .40 1.00
2 Anfernee Hardaway 2.00 5.00
3 Lindsey Hunter .40 1.00
4 Bobby Hurley .40 1.00
5 Toni Kukoc 1.00 2.50
6 Jamal Mashburn .75 2.00
7 Dino Radja .40 1.00
8 Isaiah Rider .60 1.50
9 Nick Van Exel 1.00 2.50
10 Chris Webber 2.00 5.00

1993-94 Fleer Internationals

COMPLETE SET (12) 2.50 6.00
SER.1 STATED ODDS 1:10
1 Alaa Abdelnaby .25 .60
2 Vlade Divac .40 1.00
3 Patrick Ewing .60 1.50
4 Carl Herrera .25 .60
5 Luc Longley .30 .75
6 Sarunas Marciulionis .40 1.00
7 Dikembe Mutombo .60 1.50
8 Rumeal Robinson .25 .60
9 Detlef Schrempf .40 1.00
10 Rony Seikaly .30 .75
11 Rik Smits .30 .75
12 Dominique Wilkins .60 1.50

1993-94 Fleer Living Legends

COMPLETE SET (6) 25.00 60.00
SER.2 STATED ODDS 1:37 HOB, 1:24 JUM
1 Charles Barkley 2.50 6.00
2 Larry Bird 4.00 10.00
3 Patrick Ewing 1.50 4.00
4 Michael Jordan 25.00 60.00
5 Hakeem Olajuwon 2.00 5.00
6 Dominique Wilkins 1.50 4.00

1993-94 Fleer Lottery Exchange

COMPLETE SET (11) 6.00 15.00
EXCH.CARD: SER.1 STATED ODDS 1:180
1 Chris Webber 3.00 8.00
2 Shawn Bradley .40 1.00
3 Anfernee Hardaway 2.00 5.00
4 Jamal Mashburn .75 2.00
5 Isaiah Rider .60 1.50
6 Calbert Cheaney .40 1.00
7 Bobby Hurley .40 1.00
8 Vin Baker .60 1.50
9 Rodney Rogers .40 1.00
10 Lindsey Hunter .40 1.00
11 Allan Houston .75 2.00
NNO Expired Exchange Card .20 .50

1993-94 Fleer NBA Superstars

COMPLETE SET (20) 10.00 25.00
1 Mahmoud Abdul-Rauf .50 1.25
2 Charles Barkley 1.50 4.00
3 Derrick Coleman .60 1.50
4 Clyde Drexler 1.00 2.50
5 Joe Dumars .75 2.00
6 Patrick Ewing 1.00 2.50
7 Michael Jordan 8.00 20.00
8 Shawn Kemp 1.00 2.50
9 Christian Laettner .60 1.50
10 Karl Malone 1.25 3.00
11 Danny Manning .50 1.25
12 Reggie Miller 1.25 3.00
13 Alonzo Mourning 1.00 2.50
14 Chris Mullin .75 2.00
15 Hakeem Olajuwon 1.25 3.00
16 Shaquille O'Neal 3.00 8.00
17 Mark Price .60 1.50
18 Mitch Richmond .75 2.00
19 David Robinson 1.25 3.00
20 Dominique Wilkins 1.00 2.50

1993-94 Fleer Rookie Sensations

COMPLETE SET (24) 15.00 40.00
SER.1 STATED ODDS 1:5 CELLO
1 Anthony Avent .40 1.00
2 Doug Christie .50 1.25
3 Lloyd Daniels .40 1.00
4 Hubert Davis .50 1.25
5 Todd Day .40 1.00
6 Richard Dumas .40 1.00
7 LaPhonso Ellis .50 1.25
8 Tom Gugliotta .50 1.25
9 Robert Horry .60 1.50
10 Byron Houston .40 1.00
11 Jim Jackson UER .50 1.25
12 Adam Keefe .40 1.00
13 Christian Laettner .60 1.50
14 Lee Mayberry .40 1.00
15 Oliver Miller .40 1.00
16 Harold Miner .50 1.25
17 Alonzo Mourning 2.50 6.00
18 Shaquille O'Neal 6.00 15.00
19 Anthony Peeler .40 1.00
20 Sean Rooks .40 1.00
21 Latrell Sprewell 1.50 4.00
22 Bryant Stith .40 1.00
23 Clarence Weatherspoon .40 1.00
24 Walt Williams .40 1.00

1993-94 Fleer Sharpshooters

COMPLETE SET (10) 12.00 30.00
1 Tom Gugliotta .50 1.25
2 Jim Jackson .50 1.25
3 Michael Jordan 12.00 30.00
4 Dan Majerle .60 1.50
5 Mark Price .60 1.50
6 Glen Rice .60 1.50
7 Mitch Richmond .75 2.00
8 Latrell Sprewell 1.00 2.50
9 John Starks .60 1.50
10 Dominique Wilkins 1.00 2.50

1993-94 Fleer Towers of Power

COMPLETE SET (30) 15.00 40.00
SER.2 STATED ODDS 2:3 CELLO
1 Charles Barkley 3.00 8.00
2 Shawn Bradley 1.25 3.00
3 Derrick Coleman 1.25 3.00
4 Brad Daugherty 1.00 2.50
5 Dale Davis 1.00 2.50
6 Vlade Divac 1.25 3.00
7 Patrick Ewing 2.00 5.00
8 Horace Grant 1.25 3.00
9 Tom Gugliotta 1.00 2.50
10 Larry Johnson 1.50 4.00
11 Shawn Kemp 2.00 5.00
12 Christian Laettner 1.25 3.00
13 Karl Malone 2.50 6.00
14 Danny Manning 1.00 2.50
15 Jamal Mashburn 2.50 6.00
16 Oliver Miller .75 2.00
17 Alonzo Mourning 2.00 5.00
18 Dikembe Mutombo 2.00 5.00
19 Ken Norman .75 2.00
20 Hakeem Olajuwon 2.50 6.00
21 Shaquille O'Neal 6.00 15.00
22 Robert Parish 1.50 4.00
23 Olden Polynice .75 2.00
24 Clifford Robinson 1.25 3.00
25 David Robinson 2.50 6.00
26 Dennis Rodman 3.00 8.00
27 Rony Seikaly 1.00 2.50
28 Wayman Tisdale 1.00 2.50
29 Chris Webber 6.00 15.00
30 Dominique Wilkins 2.00 5.00

1994-95 Fleer

COMPLETE SET (390) 12.00 30.00
COMPLETE SERIES 1 (240) 6.00 15.00
COMPLETE SERIES 2 (150) 6.00 15.00
1 Stacey Augmon .30 .75
2 Mookie Blaylock .40 1.00
3 Craig Ehlo .25 .60
4 Duane Ferrell .25 .60
5 Adam Keefe .25 .60
6 Jon Koncak .25 .60
7 Andrew Lang .25 .60
8 Danny Manning .30 .75
9 Kevin Willis .30 .75
10 Dee Brown .30 .75
11 Sherman Douglas .25 .60
12 Acie Earl .25 .60
13 Rick Fox .25 .60
14 Kevin Gamble .25 .60
15 Xavier McDaniel .25 .60
16 Robert Parish .40 1.00
17 Ed Pinckney .25 .60
18 Dino Radja .25 .60
19 Muggsy Bogues .30 .75
20 Frank Brickowski .25 .60
21 Scott Burrell .25 .60
22 Dell Curry .25 .60
23 Kenny Gattison .25 .60
24 Hersey Hawkins .25 .60
25 Eddie Johnson .25 .60
26 Larry Johnson .50 1.25
27 Alonzo Mourning .60 1.50
28 David Wingate .25 .60
29 B.J. Armstrong .40 1.00
30 Horace Grant .40 1.00
31 Steve Kerr .30 .75
32 Toni Kukoc .50 1.25
33 Luc Longley .30 .75
34 Pete Myers .25 .60
35 Scottie Pippen 1.00 2.50
36 Bill Wennington .25 .60
37 Scott Williams .25 .60
38 Terrell Brandon .25 .60
39 Brad Daugherty .30 .75
40 Tyrone Hill .25 .60
41 Chris Mills .30 .75
42 Larry Nance .30 .75
43 Bobby Phills .25 .60
44 Mark Price .40 1.00
45 Gerald Wilkins .30 .75
46 John Williams .25 .60
47 Lucious Harris .25 .60
48 Donald Hodge .25 .60
49 Jim Jackson .30 .75
50 Popeye Jones .25 .60
51 Tim Legler .25 .60
52 Fat Lever .40 1.00
53 Jamal Mashburn .40 1.00
54 Sean Rooks .40 1.00
55 Doug Smith .25 .60
56 Mahmoud Abdul-Rauf .25 .60
57 LaPhonso Ellis .25 .60
58 Dikembe Mutombo .60 1.50
59 Robert Pack .30 .75
60 Rodney Rogers .25 .60
61 Bryant Stith .25 .60
62 Brian Williams .25 .60
63 Reggie Williams .25 .60
64 Greg Anderson .25 .60
65 Joe Dumars .40 1.00
66 Sean Elliott .30 .75
67 Allan Houston .40 1.00
68 Lindsey Hunter .25 .60
69 Terry Mills .25 .60
70 Victor Alexander .25 .60
71 Chris Gatling .25 .60
72 Tim Hardaway .50 1.25
73 Keith Jennings .25 .60
74 Avery Johnson .30 .75
75 Chris Mullin .50 1.25
76 Billy Owens .25 .60
77 Latrell Sprewell .50 1.25
78 Chris Webber .75 2.00
79 Scott Brooks .25 .60
80 Sam Cassell .40 1.00
81 Mario Elie .25 .60
82 Carl Herrera .25 .60
83 Robert Horry .40 1.00
84 Vernon Maxwell .25 .60
85 Hakeem Olajuwon .75 2.00
86 Kenny Smith .30 .75
87 Otis Thorpe .25 .60
88 Antonio Davis .30 .75
89 Dale Davis .25 .60
90 Vern Fleming .25 .60
91 Derrick McKey .25 .60
92 Reggie Miller .75 2.00
93 Pooh Richardson .25 .60
94 Byron Scott .30 .75
95 Rik Smits .30 .75
96 Haywoode Workman .25 .60
97 Terry Dehere .25 .60
98 Harold Ellis .25 .60
99 Gary Grant .25 .60
100 Ron Harper .30 .75
101 Mark Jackson .30 .75
102 Stanley Roberts .25 .60
103 Elmore Spencer .25 .60
104 Loy Vaught .25 .60
105 Dominique Wilkins .60 1.50
106 Elden Campbell .25 .60
107 Doug Christie .30 .75
108 Vlade Divac .40 1.00
109 George Lynch .25 .60
110 Anthony Peeler .25 .60
111 Tony Smith .25 .60
112 Sedale Threatt .25 .60
113 Nick Van Exel .40 1.00
114 James Worthy .50 1.25
115 Bimbo Coles .25 .60
116 Grant Long .25 .60
117 Harold Miner .25 .60
118 Glen Rice .40 1.00
119 John Salley .25 .60
120 Rony Seikaly .25 .60
121 Brian Shaw .25 .60
122 Kevin Willis .25 .60
123 Vin Baker .40 1.00
124 Jon Barry .25 .60
125 Todd Day .25 .60
126 Blue Edwards .25 .60
127 Lee Mayberry .25 .60
128 Eric Murdock .25 .60
129 Ken Norman .25 .60
130 Derek Strong .25 .60
131 Thurl Bailey .25 .60
132 Stacey King .25 .60
133 Christian Laettner .30 .75
134 Chuck Person .30 .75
135 Isaiah Rider .40 1.00
136 Chris Smith .25 .60
137 Doug West .25 .60
138 Micheal Williams .25 .60
139 Kenny Anderson .30 .75
140 Benoit Benjamin .25 .60
141 P.J. Brown .25 .60
142 Derrick Coleman .40 1.00
143 Kevin Edwards .25 .60
144 Armon Gilliam .25 .60
145 Chris Morris .25 .60
146 Johnny Newman .25 .60
147 Greg Anthony .25 .60
148 Anthony Bonner .25 .60
149 Hubert Davis .25 .60
150 Patrick Ewing .60 1.50
151 Derek Harper .30 .75
152 Anthony Mason .30 .75
153 Charles Oakley .40 1.00
154 Doc Rivers .30 .75
155 Charles Smith .25 .60
156 John Starks .40 1.00
157 Nick Anderson .25 .60
158 Anthony Avent .25 .60
159 Anfernee Hardaway .75 2.00
160 Shaquille O'Neal 1.50 4.00
161 Donald Royal .25 .60
162 Dennis Scott .30 .75
163 Scott Skiles .25 .60
164 Jeff Turner .25 .60
165 Dana Barros .25 .60
166 Shawn Bradley .25 .60
167 Greg Graham .25 .60
168 Eric Leckner .25 .60
169 Jeff Malone .25 .60
170 Moses Malone .40 1.00
171 Tim Perry .25 .60
172 Clarence Weatherspoon .25 .60
173 Orlando Woolridge .25 .60
174 Danny Ainge .40 1.00
175 Charles Barkley 1.00 2.50
176 Cedric Ceballos .30 .75
177 A.C. Green .30 .75
178 Kevin Johnson .40 1.00
179 Joe Kleine .25 .60
180 Dan Majerle .40 1.00
181 Oliver Miller .25 .60
182 Mark West .25 .60
183 Clyde Drexler .60 1.50
184 Harvey Grant .25 .60
185 Jerome Kersey .25 .60
186 Tracy Murray .25 .60
187 Terry Porter .25 .60
188 Clifford Robinson .30 .75
189 James Robinson .25 .60
190 Rod Strickland .30 .75
191 Buck Williams .25 .60
192 Duane Causwell .25 .60
193 Bobby Hurley .25 .60
194 Olden Polynice .25 .60
195 Mitch Richmond .50 1.25
196 Lionel Simmons .25 .60
197 Wayman Tisdale .25 .60
198 Spud Webb .30 .75
199 Walt Williams .25 .60
200 Trevor Wilson .25 .60
201 Willie Anderson .25 .60
202 Antoine Carr .25 .60
203 Terry Cummings .25 .60
204 Vinny Del Negro .25 .60
205 Dale Ellis .25 .60
206 Negele Knight .25 .60
207 J.R. Reid .25 .60
208 David Robinson .75 2.00
209 Dennis Rodman 1.00 2.50
210 Vincent Askew .25 .60
211 Michael Cage .25 .60
212 Kendall Gill .25 .60
213 Shawn Kemp .60 1.50
214 Nate McMillan .30 .75
215 Gary Payton .60 1.50
216 Sam Perkins .25 .60
217 Ricky Pierce .25 .60
218 Detlef Schrempf .40 1.00
219 David Benoit .25 .60
220 Tom Chambers .25 .60
221 Tyrone Corbin .25 .60
222 Jeff Hornacek .30 .75
223 Jay Humphries .25 .60
224 Karl Malone .75 2.00
225 Bryon Russell .25 .60
226 Felton Spencer .25 .60
227 John Stockton .75 2.00
228 Michael Adams .25 .60
229 Rex Chapman .25 .60
230 Calbert Cheaney .30 .75
231 Kevin Duckworth .25 .60
232 Pervis Ellison .25 .60
233 Tom Gugliotta .30 .75
234 Don MacLean .25 .60
235 Gheorghe Muresan .25 .60
236 Brent Price .25 .60
237 Toronto Raptors Logo .20 .50
238 Checklist .20 .50
239 Checklist .20 .50
240 Checklist .20 .50
241 Sergei Bazarevich RC .40 1.00
242 Tyrone Corbin .25 .60
243 Grant Long .25 .60
244 Ken Norman .25 .60
245 Steve Smith .30 .75
246 Fred Vinson .25 .60
247 Blue Edwards .25 .60
248 Greg Minor RC .40 1.00
249 Eric Montross RC .30 .75
250 Derek Strong .25 .60
251 David Wesley .25 .60
252 Dominique Wilkins .60 1.50
253 Michael Adams .25 .60
254 Tony Bennett .25 .60
255 Darrin Hancock RC .30 .75
256 Robert Horry .40 1.00
257 Corie Blount .25 .60
258 Jud Buechler .25 .60
259 Greg Foster .25 .60
260 Ron Harper .30 .75
261 Larry Krystkowiak .25 .60
262 Will Perdue .25 .60
263 Dickey Simpkins RC .30 .75
264 Michael Cage .25 .60
265 Tony Campbell .25 .60
266 Terry Davis .25 .60
267 Tony Dumas RC .30 .75
268 Jason Kidd RC 2.00 5.00
269 Roy Tarpley .25 .60
270 Morlon Wiley .25 .60
271 Lorenzo Williams .25 .60
272 Dale Ellis .25 .60
273 Tom Hammonds .25 .60
274 Cliff Levingston .25 .60
275 Darnell Mee .25 .60
276 Jalen Rose RC 1.00 2.50
277 Reggie Slater .25 .60
278 Bill Curley RC .25 .60
279 Johnny Dawkins .25 .60
280 Grant Hill RC 2.00 5.00
281 Eric Leckner .25 .60
282 Mark Macon .25 .60
283 Oliver Miller .25 .60
284 Mark West .25 .60
285 Manute Bol .25 .60
286 Tom Gugliotta .25 .60
287 Ricky Pierce .25 .60
288 Carlos Rogers RC .30 .75
289 Clifford Rozier RC .25 .60
290 Rony Seikaly .25 .60
291 Tim Breaux .25 .60
292 Chris Jent .25 .60
293 Eric Riley .25 .60
294 Zan Tabak .25 .60
295 Duane Ferrell .25 .60
296 Mark Jackson .30 .75
297 John Williams .25 .60
298 Matt Fish .25 .60
299 Tony Massenburg .25 .60
300 Lamond Murray RC .40 1.00
301 Bo Outlaw RC .40 1.00
302 Eric Piatkowski RC .40 1.00
303 Pooh Richardson .25 .60
304 Randy Woods .25 .60
305 Sam Bowie .25 .60
306 Cedric Ceballos .30 .75
307 Antonio Harvey .25 .60
308 Eddie Jones RC 1.25 3.00
309 Anthony Miller RC .40 1.00
310 Ledell Eackles .25 .60
311 Kevin Gamble .25 .60
312 Brad Lohaus .25 .60
313 Billy Owens .25 .60
314 Khalid Reeves RC .25 .60
315 Kevin Willis .30 .75
316 Marty Conlon .25 .60
317 Eric Mobley RC .25 .60
318 Johnny Newman .25 .60
319 Ed Pinckney .25 .60
320 Glenn Robinson RC .75 2.00
321 Mike Brown .25 .60
322 Pat Durham .25 .60
323 Howard Eisley RC .40 1.00
324 Andres Guibert .25 .60
325 Donyell Marshall RC .40 1.00
326 Sean Rooks .25 .60
327 Yinka Dare RC .25 .60
328 Sleepy Floyd .25 .60
329 Sean Higgins .25 .60
330 Rick Mahorn .25 .60
331 Rex Walters .25 .60
332 Jayson Williams .25 .60
333 Charlie Ward RC .40 1.00
334 Herb Williams .25 .60
335 Monty Williams RC .50 1.25
336 Anthony Bowie .25 .60
337 Horace Grant .40 1.00
338 Geert Hammink .25 .60
339 Tree Rollins .25 .60
340 Brian Shaw .25 .60
341 Brooks Thompson RC .30 .75
342 Derrick Alston RC .25 .60
343 Willie Burton .25 .60
344 Jaren Jackson .25 .60
345 B.J. Tyler RC .25 .60
346 Scott Williams .25 .60
347 Sharone Wright RC .30 .75
348 Antonio Lang RC .40 1.00
349 Danny Manning .30 .75
350 Elliot Perry .25 .60
351 Wesley Person RC .40 1.00
352 Trevor Ruffin .25 .60
353 Danny Schayes .25 .60
354 Aaron Swinson RC .40 1.00
355 Wayman Tisdale .25 .60
356 Mark Bryant .25 .60
357 Chris Dudley .25 .60
358 James Edwards .25 .60
359 Aaron McKie RC .40 1.00
360 Alaa Abdelnaby .25 .60
361 Frank Brickowski .25 .60
362 Randy Brown .25 .60
363 Brian Grant RC .60 1.50
364 Michael Smith RC .25 .60
365 Henry Turner .25 .60
366 Sean Elliott .30 .75
367 Avery Johnson .30 .75
368 Moses Malone .40 1.00
369 Julius Nwosu .25 .60
370 Chuck Person .30 .75
371 Chris Whitney .25 .60
372 Bill Cartwright .25 .60
373 Byron Houston .25 .60
374 Ervin Johnson .25 .60
375 Sarunas Marciulionis .25 .60
376 Antoine Carr .25 .60
377 John Crotty .25 .60
378 Adam Keefe .25 .60

379 Jamie Watson RC .25 .60
380 Mitchell Butler .25 .60
381 Juwan Howard RC .60 1.50
382 Jim McIlvaine RC .30 .75
383 Doug Overton .25 .60
384 Scott Skiles .25 .60
385 Larry Stewart .25 .60
386 Kenny Walker .25 .60
387 Chris Webber .75 2.00
388 Vancouver Grizzlies .20 .50
389 Checklist .20 .50
390 Checklist .20 .50

1994-95 Fleer All-Defensive
COMPLETE SET (10) 2.50 6.00
SER.1 STATED ODDS 1:9 HOBBY/RETAIL
1 Mookie Blaylock .40 1.00
2 Charles Oakley .40 1.00
3 Hakeem Olajuwon .75 2.00
4 Gary Payton .60 1.50
5 Scottie Pippen 1.00 2.50
6 Horace Grant .40 1.00
7 Nate McMillan .30 .75
8 David Robinson .75 2.00
9 Dennis Rodman 1.00 2.50
10 Latrell Sprewell .50 1.25

1994-95 Fleer All-Stars
COMPLETE SET (26) 10.00 25.00
SER.1 STATED ODDS 1:2 HOBBY
1 Kenny Anderson .50 1.25
2 B.J. Armstrong .60 1.50
3 Mookie Blaylock .60 1.50
4 Derrick Coleman .60 1.50
5 Patrick Ewing 1.00 2.50
6 Horace Grant .60 1.50
7 Alonzo Mourning 1.00 2.50
8 Charles Oakley .60 1.50
9 Shaquille O'Neal 2.50 6.00
10 Scottie Pippen 1.50 4.00
11 Mark Price .60 1.50
12 John Starks .60 1.50
13 Dominique Wilkins 1.00 2.50
14 Charles Barkley 1.50 4.00
15 Clyde Drexler 1.00 2.50
16 Kevin Johnson .60 1.50
17 Shawn Kemp 1.00 2.50
18 Karl Malone 1.25 3.00
19 Danny Manning .50 1.25
20 Hakeem Olajuwon 1.25 3.00
21 Gary Payton 1.00 2.50
22 Mitch Richmond .75 2.00
23 Clifford Robinson .50 1.25
24 David Robinson 1.25 3.00
25 Latrell Sprewell .75 2.00
26 John Stockton 1.25 3.00

1994-95 Fleer Award Winners
COMPLETE SET (4) 1.25 3.00
SER.1 STATED ODDS 1:22 HOBBY/RETAIL
1 Dell Curry .30 .75
2 Don MacLean .30 .75
3 Hakeem Olajuwon 1.00 2.50
4 Chris Webber 1.00 2.50

1994-95 Fleer Career Achievement
COMPLETE SET (6) 5.00 12.00
SER.1 STATED ODDS 1:37 HOBBY/RETAIL
1 Patrick Ewing 2.00 5.00
2 Karl Malone 2.50 6.00
3 Hakeem Olajuwon 2.50 6.00
4 Robert Parish 1.25 3.00
5 Scottie Pippen 3.00 8.00
6 Dominique Wilkins 2.00 5.00

1994-95 Fleer First Year Phenoms
COMPLETE SET (10) 4.00 10.00
SER.2 STATED ODDS 1:5 HOBBY/RETAIL
1 Grant Hill 1.50 4.00
2 Jason Kidd 1.50 4.00
3 Donyell Marshall .30 .75
4 Eric Montross .25 .60
5 Lamond Murray .30 .75
6 Wesley Person .30 .75
7 Khalid Reeves .25 .60
8 Glenn Robinson .60 1.50
9 Jalen Rose .75 2.00
10 Sharone Wright .25 .60

1994-95 Fleer League Leaders
COMPLETE SET (8) 1.50 4.00
SER.1 STATED ODDS 1:11 HOBBY/RETAIL
1 Mahmoud Abdul-Rauf .20 .50
2 Nate McMillan .25 .60
3 Tracy Murray .20 .50
4 Dikembe Mutombo .50 1.25
5 Shaquille O'Neal 1.25 3.00
6 David Robinson .60 1.50
7 Dennis Rodman .75 2.00
8 John Stockton .60 1.50

1994-95 Fleer Lottery Exchange
COMPLETE SET (11) 6.00 15.00
EXCH.CARD: SER.1 STATED ODDS 1:175
1 Glenn Robinson .75 2.00
2 Jason Kidd 2.00 5.00
3 Grant Hill 2.00 5.00
4 Donyell Marshall .40 1.00
5 Juwan Howard .60 1.50
6 Sharone Wright .30 .75
7 Lamond Murray .40 1.00
8 Brian Grant .60 1.50
9 Eric Montross .30 .75
10 Eddie Jones 1.25 3.00
11 Carlos Rogers .30 .75
NNO Expired Exch.Card .40 1.00

1994-95 Fleer Pro-Visions
COMPLETE SET (9) 1.25 3.00
SER.1 STATED ODDS 1:5 HOBBY/RETAIL
1 Jamal Mashburn .25 .60
2 John Starks .25 .60
3 Toni Kukoc .30 .75
4 Derrick Coleman .25 .60
5 Chris Webber .50 1.25
6 Dennis Rodman .60 1.50
7 Gary Payton .40 1.00
8 Anfernee Hardaway .50 1.25
9 Dan Majerle .25 .60

1994-95 Fleer Rookie Sensations
COMPLETE SET (25) 10.00 25.00
SER.1 STATED ODDS 1:3 CELLO
1 Vin Baker 1.00 2.50
2 Shawn Bradley .60 1.50
3 P.J. Brown .60 1.50
4 Sam Cassell 1.00 2.50
5 Calbert Cheaney .75 2.00
6 Antonio Davis .75 2.00
7 Acie Earl .60 1.50
8 Harold Ellis .60 1.50
9 Anfernee Hardaway 2.00 5.00
10 Allan Houston 1.00 2.50
11 Lindsey Hunter .60 1.50
12 Bobby Hurley .60 1.50
13 Popeye Jones .60 1.50
14 Toni Kukoc 1.25 3.00
15 George Lynch .60 1.50
16 Jamal Mashburn 1.00 2.50
17 Chris Mills .75 2.00
18 Gheorghe Muresan .60 1.50
19 Dino Radja .60 1.50
20 Isaiah Rider 1.00 2.50
21 James Robinson .60 1.50
22 Rodney Rogers .60 1.50
23 Bryon Russell .60 1.50
24 Nick Van Exel 1.00 2.50
25 Chris Webber 2.00 5.00

1994-95 Fleer Sharpshooters
COMPLETE SET (10) 5.00 12.00
SER.2 STATED ODDS 1:7 RETAIL
1 Dell Curry .60 1.50
2 Joe Dumars 1.00 2.50
3 Dale Ellis .60 1.50
4 Dan Majerle 1.00 2.50
5 Reggie Miller 2.00 5.00
6 Mark Price 1.00 2.50
7 Glen Rice 1.00 2.50
8 Mitch Richmond 1.25 3.00
9 Dennis Scott .75 2.00
10 Latrell Sprewell 1.25 3.00

1994-95 Fleer Superstars
COMPLETE SET (6) 6.00 15.00
SER.2 STATED ODDS 1:37 HOBBY/RETAIL
1 Charles Barkley 4.00 10.00
2 Patrick Ewing 2.50 6.00
3 Hakeem Olajuwon 3.00 8.00
4 Robert Parish 1.50 4.00
5 Scottie Pippen 4.00 10.00
6 Dominique Wilkins 2.50 6.00

1994-95 Fleer Team Leaders
COMPLETE SET (9) 1.25 3.00
SER.2 STATED ODDS 1:3 HOBBY/RETAIL
1 Blaylock/Wilkins/Mourning .30 .75
2 Pippen/Price/Mashburn .50 1.25
3 Mutom/Dumars/Spree ERR .30 .75
3A Mutom/Dumars/Spree COR .30 .75
4 Olajuwon/R.Miller/Vaught .40 1.00
5 Divac/Rice/Baker .20 .50
6 Rider/Anderson/Ewing .30 .75
7 O'Neal/Weather/Barkley .75 2.00
8 Strick/Richmond/D.Rob .40 1.00
9 Kemp/Stockton/Chapman .40 1.00

1994-95 Fleer Total D
COMPLETE SET (10) 3.00 8.00
SER.2 STATED ODDS 1:7 HOBBY
1 Mookie Blaylock .60 1.50
2 Nate McMillan .50 1.25
3 Dikembe Mutombo 1.00 2.50
4 Charles Oakley .60 1.50
5 Hakeem Olajuwon 1.25 3.00
6 Gary Payton 1.00 2.50
7 Scottie Pippen 1.50 4.00
8 David Robinson 1.25 3.00
9 Latrell Sprewell .75 2.00
10 John Stockton 1.25 3.00

1994-95 Fleer Towers of Power
COMPLETE SET (10) 8.00 20.00
SER.2 STATED ODDS 1:5 CELLO
1 Charles Barkley 2.50 6.00
2 Patrick Ewing 1.50 4.00
3 Shawn Kemp 1.50 4.00
4 Karl Malone 2.00 5.00
5 Alonzo Mourning 1.50 4.00
6 Dikembe Mutombo 1.50 4.00
7 Hakeem Olajuwon 2.00 5.00
8 Shaquille O'Neal 4.00 10.00
9 David Robinson 2.00 5.00
10 Chris Webber 2.00 5.00

1994-95 Fleer Triple Threats
COMPLETE SET (10) 2.00 5.00
SER.1 STATED ODDS 1:9 HOBBY/RETAIL
1 Mookie Blaylock .30 .75
2 Patrick Ewing .50 1.25
3 Shawn Kemp .50 1.25
4 Karl Malone .60 1.50
5 Reggie Miller .60 1.50
6 Hakeem Olajuwon .60 1.50
7 Shaquille O'Neal 1.25 3.00
8 Scottie Pippen .75 2.00
9 David Robinson .60 1.50
10 Latrell Sprewell .40 1.00

1994-95 Fleer Young Lions
COMPLETE SET (6) 1.50 4.00
SER.2 STATED ODDS 1:5 HOBBY/RETAIL
1 Vin Baker .30 .75
2 Anfernee Hardaway .60 1.50
3 Larry Johnson .40 1.00
4 Alonzo Mourning .50 1.25
5 Shaquille O'Neal 1.25 3.00
6 Chris Webber .60 1.50

1995-96 Fleer
COMPLETE SET (350) 15.00 40.00
COMPLETE SERIES 1 (200) 8.00 20.00
COMPLETE SERIES 2 (150) 8.00 20.00
1 Stacey Augmon .30 .75
2 Mookie Blaylock .40 1.00
3 Craig Ehlo .25 .60
4 Andrew Lang .25 .60
5 Grant Long .25 .60
6 Ken Norman .25 .60
7 Steve Smith .30 .75
8 Dee Brown .30 .75
9 Sherman Douglas .25 .60
10 Eric Montross .25 .60
11 Dino Radja .25 .60
12 David Wesley .25 .60
13 Dominique Wilkins .60 1.50
14 Muggsy Bogues .40 1.00
15 Scott Burrell .25 .60
16 Dell Curry .40 1.00
17 Hersey Hawkins .30 .75
18 Larry Johnson .50 1.25
19 Alonzo Mourning .60 1.50
20 Robert Parish .50 1.25
21 B.J. Armstrong .40 1.00
22 Michael Jordan 4.00 10.00
23 Steve Kerr .40 1.00
24 Toni Kukoc .50 1.25
25 Will Perdue .30 .75
26 Scottie Pippen 1.00 2.50
27 Terrell Brandon .30 .75
28 Tyrone Hill .25 .60
29 Chris Mills .25 .60
30 Bobby Phills .30 .75
31 Mark Price .40 1.00
32 John Williams .25 .60
33 Lucious Harris .25 .60
34 Jim Jackson .30 .75
35 Popeye Jones .25 .60
36 Jason Kidd .60 1.50
37 Jamal Mashburn .40 1.00
38 George McCloud .25 .60
39 Roy Tarpley .30 .75
40 Lorenzo Williams .25 .60
41 Mahmoud Abdul-Rauf .30 .75
42 Dale Ellis .30 .75
43 LaPhonso Ellis .30 .75
44 Dikembe Mutombo .60 1.50
45 Robert Pack .25 .60
46 Rodney Rogers .30 .75
47 Jalen Rose .50 1.25
48 Bryant Stith .25 .60
49 Reggie Williams .25 .60
50 Joe Dumars .40 1.00
51 Grant Hill .60 1.50
52 Allan Houston .30 .75
53 Lindsey Hunter .25 .60
54 Oliver Miller .25 .60
55 Terry Mills .25 .60
56 Mark West .25 .60
57 Chris Gatling .25 .60
58 Tim Hardaway .50 1.25
59 Donyell Marshall .25 .60
60 Chris Mullin .40 1.00
61 Carlos Rogers .25 .60
62 Clifford Rozier .25 .60
63 Rony Seikaly .25 .60
64 Latrell Sprewell .40 1.00
65 Sam Cassell .40 1.00
66 Clyde Drexler .60 1.50
67 Mario Elie .25 .60
68 Carl Herrera .25 .60
69 Robert Horry .40 1.00
70 Vernon Maxwell .25 .60
71 Hakeem Olajuwon .75 2.00
72 Kenny Smith .30 .75
73 Dale Davis .25 .60
74 Mark Jackson .30 .75
75 Derrick McKey .25 .60
76 Reggie Miller .75 2.00
77 Sam Mitchell .25 .60
78 Byron Scott .40 1.00
79 Rik Smits .30 .75
80 Terry Dehere .25 .60
81 Tony Massenburg .25 .60
82 Lamond Murray .25 .60
83 Pooh Richardson .25 .60
84 Malik Sealy .25 .60
85 Loy Vaught .25 .60
86 Elden Campbell .25 .60
87 Cedric Ceballos .30 .75
88 Vlade Divac .40 1.00
89 Eddie Jones .40 1.00
90 Anthony Peeler .25 .60
91 Sedale Threatt .25 .60
92 Nick Van Exel .40 1.00
93 Bimbo Coles .25 .60
94 Matt Geiger .25 .60
95 Billy Owens .25 .60
96 Khalid Reeves .25 .60
97 Glen Rice .40 1.00
98 John Salley .25 .60
99 Kevin Willis .25 .60
100 Vin Baker .30 .75
101 Marty Conlon .25 .60
102 Todd Day .25 .60
103 Lee Mayberry .25 .60
104 Eric Murdock .25 .60
105 Glenn Robinson .40 1.00
106 Winston Garland .25 .60
107 Tom Gugliotta .25 .60
108 Christian Laettner .30 .75
109 Isaiah Rider .40 1.00
110 Sean Rooks .25 .60
111 Doug West .25 .60
112 Kenny Anderson .30 .75
113 Benoit Benjamin .25 .60
114 P.J. Brown .25 .60
115 Derrick Coleman .30 .75
116 Armon Gilliam .25 .60
117 Chris Morris .25 .60
118 Rex Walters .25 .60
119 Hubert Davis .25 .60
120 Patrick Ewing .60 1.50
121 Derek Harper .30 .75
122 Anthony Mason .25 .60
123 Charles Oakley .30 .75
124 Charles Smith .25 .60
125 John Starks .40 1.00
126 Nick Anderson .30 .75
127 Anthony Bowie .25 .60
128 Horace Grant .30 .75
129 Anfernee Hardaway 1.00 2.50
130 Shaquille O'Neal 1.50 4.00
131 Donald Royal .25 .60
132 Dennis Scott .25 .60
133 Brian Shaw .25 .60
134 Derrick Alston .25 .60
135 Dana Barros .30 .75
136 Shawn Bradley .25 .60
137 Willie Burton .30 .75
138 Clarence Weatherspoon .25 .60
139 Scott Williams .25 .60
140 Sharone Wright .25 .60
141 Danny Ainge .40 1.00
142 Charles Barkley 1.00 2.50
143 A.C. Green .30 .75
144 Kevin Johnson .40 1.00
145 Dan Majerle .40 1.00
146 Danny Manning .30 .75
147 Elliot Perry .25 .60
148 Wesley Person .25 .60
149 Wayman Tisdale .25 .60
150 Chris Dudley .25 .60
151 Jerome Kersey .25 .60
152 Aaron McKie .30 .75
153 Terry Porter .25 .60
154 Clifford Robinson .40 1.00
155 James Robinson .25 .60
156 Rod Strickland .30 .75
157 Otis Thorpe .30 .75
158 Buck Williams .25 .60
159 Brian Grant .30 .75
160 Bobby Hurley .25 .60
161 Olden Polynice .25 .60
162 Mitch Richmond .50 1.25
163 Michael Smith .25 .60
164 Spud Webb .40 1.00
165 Walt Williams .25 .60
166 Terry Cummings .30 .75
167 Vinny Del Negro .25 .60
168 Sean Elliott .30 .75
169 Avery Johnson .30 .75
170 Chuck Person .30 .75
171 J.R. Reid .25 .60
172 Doc Rivers .30 .75
173 David Robinson .75 2.00
174 Dennis Rodman .75 2.00
175 Vincent Askew .25 .60
176 Kendall Gill .25 .60
177 Shawn Kemp .60 1.50
178 Sarunas Marciulionis .30 .75
179 Nate McMillan .25 .60
180 Gary Payton .60 1.50
181 Sam Perkins .25 .60
182 Detlef Schrempf .40 1.00
183 David Benoit .25 .60
184 Antoine Carr .25 .60
185 Blue Edwards .25 .60
186 Jeff Hornacek .30 .75
187 Adam Keefe .25 .60
188 Karl Malone .75 2.00
189 Felton Spencer .25 .60
190 John Stockton .75 2.00
191 Rex Chapman .25 .60
192 Calbert Cheaney .25 .60
193 Juwan Howard .40 1.00
194 Don MacLean .25 .60
195 Gheorghe Muresan .25 .60
196 Scott Skiles .25 .60
197 Chris Webber .50 1.25
198 Checklist .10 .25
199 Checklist .10 .25
200 Checklist .10 .25
201 Stacey Augmon .30 .75
202 Mookie Blaylock .40 1.00
203 Grant Long .25 .60
204 Ken Norman .25 .60
205 Steve Smith .30 .75
206 Spud Webb .40 1.00
207 Dana Barros .25 .60
208 Rick Fox .25 .60
209 Kendall Gill .25 .60
210 Khalid Reeves .25 .60
211 Glen Rice .40 1.00
212 Luc Longley .30 .75
213 Dennis Rodman .75 2.00
214 Dan Majerle .40 1.00
215 Tony Dumas .25 .60
216 Tom Hammonds .25 .60
217 Elmore Spencer .25 .60
218 Otis Thorpe .30 .75
219 B.J. Armstrong .40 1.00
220 Sam Cassell .40 1.00
221 Clyde Drexler .60 1.50
222 Mario Elie .25 .60
223 Robert Horry .40 1.00
224 Hakeem Olajuwon .75 2.00
225 Kenny Smith .30 .75
226 Antonio Davis .25 .60
227 Eddie Johnson .25 .60
228 Ricky Pierce .25 .60
229 Eric Piatkowski .25 .60
230 Rodney Rogers .25 .60
231 Brian Williams .25 .60
232 Corie Blount .25 .60
233 George Lynch .25 .60
234 Kevin Gamble .25 .60
235 Alonzo Mourning .60 1.50
236 Eric Mobley .25 .60
237 Terry Porter .25 .60
238 Micheal Williams .25 .60
239 Kevin Edwards .25 .60
240 Vern Fleming .25 .60
241 Charlie Ward .30 .75
242 Jon Koncak .25 .60
243 Richard Dumas .25 .60
244 Jeff Malone .25 .60
245 Vernon Maxwell .25 .60
246 John Williams .25 .60
247 Harvey Grant .25 .60
248 Dontonio Wingfield .25 .60
249 Tyrone Corbin .25 .60
250 Sarunas Marciulionis .25 .60
251 Will Perdue .30 .75
252 Hersey Hawkins .30 .75
253 Ervin Johnson .25 .60
254 Shawn Kemp .60 1.50
255 Gary Payton .60 1.50
256 Sam Perkins .25 .60
257 Detlef Schrempf .40 1.00
258 Chris Morris .25 .60
259 Robert Pack .25 .60
260 Willie Anderson ET .25 .60
261 Jimmy King ET .40 1.00
262 Oliver Miller ET .25 .60
263 Tracy Murray ET .25 .60
264 Ed Pinckney ET .25 .60
265 Alvin Robertson ET .25 .60
266 Carlos Rogers ET .25 .60
267 John Salley ET .40 1.00
268 Damon Stoudamire ET 1.00 2.50
269 Zan Tabak ET .25 .60
270 Ashraf Amaya ET .25 .60
271 Greg Anthony ET .25 .60
272 Benoit Benjamin ET .25 .60
273 Blue Edwards ET .25 .60
274 Kenny Gattison ET .25 .60
275 Antonio Harvey ET .25 .60
276 Chris King ET .25 .60
277 Lawrence Moten ET .40 1.00
278 Bryant Reeves ET .30 .75
279 Byron Scott ET .40 1.00
280 Cory Alexander RC .40 1.00
281 Jerome Allen RC .40 1.00
282 Brent Barry RC .60 1.50
283 Mario Bennett RC .30 .75
284 Travis Best RC .40 1.00
285 Junior Burrough RC .40 1.00
286 Jason Caffey RC .40 1.00
287 Randolph Childress RC .30 .75
288 Sasha Danilovic RC .40 1.00
289 Mark Davis RC .40 1.00
290 Tyus Edney RC .40 1.00
291 Michael Finley RC 1.00 2.50
292 Sherrell Ford RC .30 .75
293 Kevin Garnett RC 3.00 8.00
294 Alan Henderson RC .40 1.00
295 Frankie King RC .40 1.00
296 Jimmy King RC .40 1.00
297 Donny Marshall RC .40 1.00
298 Antonio McDyess RC .50 1.25
299 Loren Meyer RC .25 .60
300 Lawrence Moten RC .40 1.00
301 Ed O'Bannon RC .30 .75
302 Greg Ostertag RC .40 1.00
303 Cherokee Parks RC .30 .75
304 Theo Ratliff RC .60 1.50
305 Bryant Reeves RC .30 .75
306 Shawn Respert RC .30 .75
307 Lou Roe RC .40 1.00
308 Arvydas Sabonis RC .75 2.00
309 Joe Smith RC .50 1.25
310 Jerry Stackhouse RC 1.25 3.00
311 Damon Stoudamire RC 1.00 2.50
312 Bob Sura RC .30 .75
313 Kurt Thomas RC .40 1.00
314 Gary Trent RC .30 .75
315 David Vaughn RC .40 1.00
316 Rasheed Wallace RC 1.25 3.00
317 Eric Williams RC .40 1.00
318 Corliss Williamson RC .40 1.00
319 George Zidek RC .30 .75
320 Mookie Blaylock FF .40 1.00
321 Dino Radja FF .25 .60
322 Larry Johnson FF .50 1.25
323 Michael Jordan FF 4.00 10.00
324 Tyrone Hill FF .25 .60
325 Jason Kidd FF .60 1.50
326 Dikembe Mutombo FF .60 1.50
327 Grant Hill FF .60 1.50
328 Joe Smith FF .50 1.25
329 Hakeem Olajuwon FF .75 2.00
330 Reggie Miller FF .75 2.00
331 Loy Vaught FF .25 .60
332 Nick Van Exel FF .40 1.00
333 Alonzo Mourning FF .60 1.50
334 Glenn Robinson FF .40 1.00
335 Kevin Garnett FF 3.00 8.00
336 Kenny Anderson FF .30 .75
337 Patrick Ewing FF .60 1.50
338 Shaquille O'Neal FF 1.50 4.00
339 Jerry Stackhouse FF 1.25 3.00
340 Charles Barkley FF 1.00 2.50
341 Clifford Robinson FF .40 1.00
342 Mitch Richmond FF .50 1.25
343 David Robinson FF .75 2.00
344 Shawn Kemp FF .60 1.50
345 Damon Stoudamire FF 1.00 2.50
346 Karl Malone FF .75 2.00
347 Bryant Reeves FF .30 .75
348 Chris Webber FF .50 1.25
349 Checklist (201-319) .20 .50
350 Checklist (320-350/ins.) .20 .50

1995-96 Fleer All-Stars
COMPLETE SET (13) 2.00 5.00
SER.1 STATED ODDS 1:3 HOBBY/RETAIL
1 G.Hill/C.Barkley .60 1.50
2 S.Pippen/S.Kemp .60 1.50
3 S.O'Neal/H.Olajuwon 1.00 2.50
4 A.Hardaway/D.Majerle .60 1.50
5 R.Miller/L.Sprewell .50 1.25
6 V.Baker/C.Ceballos .20 .50
7 T.Hill/K.Malone .50 1.25
8 L.Johnson/D.Schrempf .30 .75
9 P.Ewing/D.Robinson .50 1.25
10 A.Mourning/D.Mutombo .40 1.00
11 D.Barros/G.Payton .40 1.00
12 J.Dumars/J.Stockton .50 1.25
13 Mitch Richmond .30 .75

1995-96 Fleer Class Encounters
COMPLETE SET (40) 8.00 20.00
SER.2 STATED ODDS 1:2 HOBBY/RETAIL
1 Derrick Alston .25 .60
2 Brian Grant .30 .75
3 Grant Hill .60 1.50
4 Juwan Howard .40 1.00
5 Eddie Jones .40 1.00
6 Jason Kidd .60 1.50
7 Donyell Marshall .25 .60
8 Anthony Miller .25 .60
9 Eric Mobley .25 .60
10 Eric Montross .25 .60
11 Lamond Murray .25 .60
12 Wesley Person .25 .60
13 Eric Piatkowski .25 .60
14 Khalid Reeves .25 .60
15 Glenn Robinson .40 1.00
16 Carlos Rogers .25 .60
17 Jalen Rose .50 1.25
18 Clifford Rozier .25 .60
19 Michael Smith .25 .60
20 Sharone Wright .25 .60
21 Brent Barry .50 1.25
22 Jason Caffey .30 .75
23 Randolph Childress .25 .60
24 Kevin Garnett 2.50 6.00
25 Alan Henderson .30 .75
26 Antonio McDyess .40 1.00
27 Ed O'Bannon .25 .60
28 Cherokee Parks .25 .60
29 Theo Ratliff .50 1.25
30 Bryant Reeves .25 .60
31 Shawn Respert .25 .60
32 Joe Smith .40 1.00
33 Jerry Stackhouse 1.00 2.50
34 Damon Stoudamire .75 2.00
35 Bob Sura .25 .60
36 Kurt Thomas .30 .75
37 Gary Trent .25 .60
38 Rasheed Wallace 1.00 2.50
39 Eric Williams .30 .75
40 Corliss Williamson .30 .75

1995-96 Fleer Double Doubles
COMPLETE SET (12) 1.50 4.00
SER.1 STATED ODDS 1:3 HOBBY/RETAIL
1 Vin Baker .25 .60
2 Vlade Divac .30 .75
3 Patrick Ewing .50 1.25
4 Tyrone Hill .20 .50
5 Popeye Jones .20 .50
6 Shawn Kemp .50 1.25
7 Karl Malone .60 1.50
8 Dikembe Mutombo .50 1.25
9 Hakeem Olajuwon .60 1.50
10 Shaquille O'Neal 1.25 3.00
11 David Robinson .60 1.50
12 John Stockton .60 1.50

1995-96 Fleer End to End
COMPLETE SET (20) 6.00 15.00
SER.2 STATED ODDS 1:4 HOBBY/RETAIL
1 Mookie Blaylock .40 1.00
2 Vlade Divac .40 1.00
3 Clyde Drexler .60 1.50
4 Patrick Ewing .60 1.50
5 Horace Grant .30 .75
6 Anfernee Hardaway 1.00 2.50
7 Grant Hill .60 1.50
8 Eddie Jones .40 1.00
9 Michael Jordan 4.00 10.00
10 Jason Kidd .60 1.50
11 Alonzo Mourning .60 1.50
12 Dikembe Mutombo .60 1.50
13 Hakeem Olajuwon .75 2.00
14 Shaquille O'Neal 1.50 4.00
15 Gary Payton .60 1.50
16 Scottie Pippen 1.00 2.50
17 David Robinson .75 2.00
18 Latrell Sprewell .40 1.00
19 John Stockton .75 2.00
20 Rod Strickland .25 .60

1995-96 Fleer Flair Hardwood Leaders
COMPLETE SET (27) 12.00 30.00
ONE PER SER.1 PACK
1 Mookie Blaylock .50 1.25
2 Dominique Wilkins .75 2.00
3 Alonzo Mourning .75 2.00
4 Michael Jordan 8.00 20.00
5 Mark Price .50 1.25
6 Jim Jackson .40 1.00
7 Dikembe Mutombo .75 2.00
8 Grant Hill .75 2.00
9 Tim Hardaway .60 1.50
10 Hakeem Olajuwon 1.00 2.50
11 Reggie Miller 1.00 2.50
12 Loy Vaught .30 .75
13 Cedric Ceballos .40 1.00
14 Glen Rice .50 1.25
15 Glenn Robinson .50 1.25
16 Christian Laettner .40 1.00
17 Derrick Coleman .40 1.00
18 Patrick Ewing .75 2.00
19 Shaquille O'Neal 2.00 5.00
20 Dana Barros .30 .75
21 Charles Barkley 1.25 3.00
22 Clifford Robinson .50 1.25
23 Mitch Richmond .60 1.50
24 David Robinson 1.00 2.50
25 Gary Payton .75 2.00
26 Karl Malone 1.00 2.50
27 Chris Webber .60 1.50
NNO Uncut Sheet 8.00 20.00

1995-96 Fleer Franchise Futures
COMPLETE SET (9) 12.50 30.00
SER.1 STATED ODDS 1:37 HOBBY/RETAIL
1 Vin Baker 1.50 4.00
2 Anfernee Hardaway 5.00 12.00
3 Jim Jackson 1.50 4.00
4 Jamal Mashburn 2.00 5.00
5 Alonzo Mourning 3.00 8.00
6 Dikembe Mutombo 3.00 8.00
7 Shaquille O'Neal 8.00 20.00
8 Nick Van Exel 2.00 5.00
9 Chris Webber 2.50 6.00

1995-96 Fleer Rookie Phenoms
COMPLETE SET (10) 12.00 30.00
SER.2 STATED ODDS 1:24 HOBBY
HP CARDS: .1X TO .3X HI COLUMN
HP: SER.2 STATED ODDS 1:72 HOBBY
1 Kevin Garnett 6.00 15.00
2 Antonio McDyess 1.00 2.50
3 Ed O'Bannon .60 1.50
4 Bryant Reeves .60 1.50
5 Shawn Respert .60 1.50
6 Joe Smith 1.00 2.50
7 Jerry Stackhouse 2.50 6.00
8 Damon Stoudamire 2.00 5.00
9 Gary Trent .60 1.50
10 Rasheed Wallace 2.50 6.00

1995-96 Fleer Rookie Sensations
COMPLETE SET (15) 10.00 25.00
SER.1 STATED ODDS 1:5 CELLO
1 Brian Grant 1.25 3.00
2 Grant Hill 2.50 6.00
3 Juwan Howard 1.50 4.00
4 Eddie Jones 1.50 4.00
5 Jason Kidd 2.50 6.00
6 Donyell Marshall 1.00 2.50
7 Eric Montross 1.00 2.50
8 Lamond Murray 1.00 2.50
9 Wesley Person 1.00 2.50
10 Khalid Reeves 1.00 2.50
11 Glenn Robinson 1.50 4.00
12 Jalen Rose 2.00 5.00
13 Clifford Rozier 1.00 2.50
14 Michael Smith 1.00 2.50
15 Sharone Wright 1.00 2.50

1995-96 Fleer Stackhouse's Scrapbook
COMPLETE SET (2) 1.50 4.00
COMMON CARD (S1-S2) 1.00 2.50
SER.2 STATED ODDS 1:24 PACKS

1995-96 Fleer Total D
COMPLETE SET (12) 5.00 12.00
SER.1 STATED ODDS 1:5 HOBBY/RETAIL
1 Mookie Blaylock .40 1.00
2 Patrick Ewing .60 1.50
3 Michael Jordan 4.00 10.00
4 Alonzo Mourning .60 1.50
5 Dikembe Mutombo .60 1.50
6 Hakeem Olajuwon .75 2.00
7 Shaquille O'Neal 1.50 4.00
8 Gary Payton .60 1.50
9 Scottie Pippen 1.00 2.50
10 David Robinson .75 2.00
11 Dennis Rodman .75 2.00
12 John Stockton .75 2.00

1995-96 Fleer Total O
COMPLETE SET (10) 10.00 25.00
SER.2 STATED ODDS 1:12 RETAIL
HP CARDS: .25X TO .6X HI COLUMN
HP: SER.2 STATED ODDS 1:72 RETAIL
1 Grant Hill 1.25 3.00
2 Michael Jordan 20.00 50.00
3 Jamal Mashburn .75 2.00
4 Reggie Miller 1.50 4.00
5 Hakeem Olajuwon 1.50 4.00
6 Shaquille O'Neal 3.00 8.00
7 Mitch Richmond 1.00 2.50
8 David Robinson 1.50 4.00
9 Glenn Robinson .75 2.00
10 Jerry Stackhouse 1.25 3.00

1995-96 Fleer Towers of Power
COMPLETE SET (10) 40.00 75.00
SER.2 STATED ODDS 1:54 HOBBY/RETAIL
1 Shawn Kemp 5.00 12.00
2 Karl Malone 6.00 15.00
3 Antonio McDyess 4.00 10.00
4 Alonzo Mourning 5.00 12.00
5 Hakeem Olajuwon 6.00 15.00
6 Shaquille O'Neal 12.00 30.00
7 David Robinson 6.00 15.00
8 Glenn Robinson 3.00 8.00
9 Joe Smith 4.00 10.00
10 Chris Webber 4.00 10.00

1996 Fleer French Kellogg's Frosties
COMPLETE SET (30) 30.00 80.00
1 Kenny Anderson 2.00 5.00
2 Mookie Blaylock 1.50 4.00
3 Muggsy Bogues 2.00 5.00
4 Sam Cassell 2.00 5.00
5 Clyde Drexler 3.00 8.00
6 Brian Grant 2.00 5.00
7 Horace Grant 2.00 5.00
8 Tim Hardaway 2.50 6.00
9 Grant Hill 4.00 10.00
10 Kevin Johnson 2.50 6.00
11 Jim Jackson 1.50 4.00
12 Jason Kidd 4.00 10.00
13 Christian Laettner 2.00 5.00
14 Dan Majerle 2.50 6.00
15 Vernon Maxwell 1.50 4.00
16 Oliver Miller 1.50 4.00
17 Eric Montross 1.50 4.00
18 Gheorghe Muresan 1.50 4.00
19 Lamond Murray 1.50 4.00
20 Dikembe Mutombo 2.50 6.00
21 Charles Oakley 2.00 5.00
22 Hakeem Olajuwon 3.00 8.00
23 Scottie Pippen 4.00 10.00
24 Glen Rice 2.50 6.00
25 Clifford Robinson 2.50 6.00
26 Glenn Robinson 2.00 5.00
27 Byron Scott 2.00 5.00
28 Rik Smits 2.00 5.00
29 John Stockton 3.00 8.00
30 Tony the Tiger .75 2.00

1996 Fleer/Mountain Dew Stackhouse
COMPLETE SET (5) 3.00 8.00
COMMON CARD (1-5) .75 2.00

1996-97 Fleer
COMPLETE SET (300) 25.00 60.00
COMPLETE SERIES 1 (150) 8.00 20.00
COMPLETE SERIES 2 (150) 15.00 40.00
1 Stacey Augmon .25 .60
2 Mookie Blaylock .30 .75
3 Christian Laettner .30 .75
4 Grant Long .20 .50
5 Steve Smith .25 .60
6 Rick Fox .20 .50
7 Dino Radja .20 .50
8 Eric Williams .20 .50
9 Kenny Anderson .25 .60
10 Dell Curry .30 .75
11 Larry Johnson .40 1.00
12 Glen Rice .30 .75
13 Michael Jordan 3.00 8.00
14 Toni Kukoc .30 .75
15 Scottie Pippen .75 2.00
16 Dennis Rodman .75 2.00
17 Terrell Brandon .25 .60
18 Chris Mills .20 .50
19 Bobby Phills .20 .50
20 Bob Sura .20 .50

21 Jim Jackson .20 .50
22 Jason Kidd .50 1.25
23 Jamal Mashburn .30 .75
24 George McCloud .20 .50
25 Mahmoud Abdul-Rauf .25 .60
26 Antonio McDyess .30 .75
27 Dikembe Mutombo .50 1.25
28 Jalen Rose .25 .60
29 Bryant Stith .20 .50
30 Joe Dumars .40 1.00
31 Grant Hill .50 1.25
32 Allan Houston .30 .75
33 Theo Ratliff .20 .50
34 Otis Thorpe .25 .60
35 Chris Mullin .40 1.00
36 Joe Smith .25 .60
37 Latrell Sprewell .30 .75
38 Kevin Willis .25 .60
39 Sam Cassell .25 .60
40 Clyde Drexler .50 1.25
41 Robert Horry .30 .75
42 Hakeem Olajuwon .60 1.50
43 Dale Davis .20 .50
44 Mark Jackson .25 .60
45 Derrick McKey .20 .50
46 Reggie Miller .60 1.50
47 Rik Smits .25 .60
48 Brent Barry .25 .60
49 Malik Sealy .20 .50
50 Loy Vaught .20 .50
51 Brian Williams .20 .50
52 Elden Campbell .20 .50
53 Cedric Ceballos .25 .60
54 Vlade Divac .30 .75
55 Eddie Jones .30 .75
56 Nick Van Exel .30 .75
57 Tim Hardaway .40 1.00
58 Alonzo Mourning .50 1.25
59 Kurt Thomas .20 .50
60 Walt Williams .20 .50
61 Vin Baker .25 .60
62 Sherman Douglas .20 .50
63 Glenn Robinson .30 .75
64 Kevin Garnett 1.00 2.50
65 Tom Gugliotta .20 .50
66 Isaiah Rider .25 .60
67 Shawn Bradley .20 .50
68 Chris Childs .20 .50
69 Armon Gilliam .20 .50
70 Ed O'Bannon .20 .50
71 Patrick Ewing .50 1.25
72 Derek Harper .25 .60
73 Anthony Mason .25 .60
74 Charles Oakley .30 .75
75 John Starks .30 .75
76 Nick Anderson .20 .50
77 Horace Grant .30 .75
78 Anfernee Hardaway .75 2.00
79 Shaquille O'Neal 1.25 3.00
80 Dennis Scott .25 .60
81 Derrick Coleman .25 .60
82 Vernon Maxwell .20 .50
83 Jerry Stackhouse .40 1.00
84 Clarence Weatherspoon .20 .50
85 Charles Barkley .75 2.00
86 Michael Finley .30 .75
87 Kevin Johnson .30 .75
88 Wesley Person .20 .50
89 Clifford Robinson .30 .75
90 Arvydas Sabonis .30 .75
91 Rod Strickland .30 .75
92 Gary Trent .20 .50
93 Tyus Edney .20 .50
94 Brian Grant .25 .60
95 Billy Owens .20 .50
96 Mitch Richmond .40 1.00
97 Vinny Del Negro .20 .50
98 Sean Elliott .30 .75
99 Avery Johnson .25 .60
100 David Robinson .60 1.50
101 Hersey Hawkins .20 .50
102 Shawn Kemp .50 1.25
103 Gary Payton .50 1.25
104 Detlef Schrempf .30 .75
105 Oliver Miller .20 .50
106 Tracy Murray .20 .50
107 Damon Stoudamire .30 .75
108 Sharone Wright .20 .50
109 Jeff Hornacek .25 .60
110 Karl Malone .60 1.50
111 John Stockton .60 1.50
112 Greg Anthony .20 .50
113 Bryant Reeves .20 .50
114 Byron Scott .30 .75
115 Calbert Cheaney .20 .50
116 Juwan Howard .30 .75
117 Gheorghe Muresan .20 .50
118 Rasheed Wallace .40 1.00
119 Chris Webber .40 1.00
120 Mookie Blaylock HL .30 .75
121 Dino Radja HL .20 .50
122 Larry Johnson HL .40 1.00
123 Michael Jordan HL 3.00 8.00
124 Terrell Brandon HL .25 .60
125 Jason Kidd HL .50 1.25
126 Antonio McDyess HL .30 .75
127 Grant Hill HL .50 1.25
128 Latrell Sprewell HL .30 .75
129 Hakeem Olajuwon HL .60 1.50
130 Reggie Miller HL .60 1.50
131 Loy Vaught HL .20 .50
132 Cedric Ceballos HL .25 .60
133 Alonzo Mourning HL .50 1.25
134 Vin Baker HL .25 .60
135 Isaiah Rider HL .25 .60
136 Armon Gilliam HL .20 .50
137 Patrick Ewing HL .50 1.25
138 Shaquille O'Neal HL 1.25 3.00
139 Jerry Stackhouse HL .40 1.00
140 Charles Barkley HL .75 2.00
141 Clifford Robinson HL .30 .75
142 Mitch Richmond HL .40 1.00
143 David Robinson HL .60 1.50
144 Shawn Kemp HL .50 1.25
145 Damon Stoudamire HL .30 .75
146 Karl Malone HL .60 1.50
147 Bryant Reeves HL .20 .50
148 Juwan Howard HL .30 .75
149 Checklist .10 .25
150 Checklist .10 .25
151 Alan Henderson .20 .50
152 Priest Lauderdale RC .20 .50
153 Dikembe Mutombo .50 1.25
154 Dana Barros .20 .50
155 Todd Day .20 .50
156 Brett Szabo RC .30 .75
157 Antoine Walker RC .50 1.25
158 Scott Burrell .20 .50
159 Tony Delk RC .30 .75
160 Vlade Divac .30 .75
161 Matt Geiger .20 .50
162 Anthony Mason .25 .60
163 Malik Rose RC .40 1.00
164 Ron Harper .25 .60
165 Steve Kerr .25 .60
166 Luc Longley .25 .60
167 Danny Ferry .20 .50
168 Tyrone Hill .20 .50
169 Vitaly Potapenko RC .25 .60
170 Tony Dumas .20 .50
171 Chris Gatling .20 .50
172 Oliver Miller .20 .50
173 Eric Montross .20 .50
174 Samaki Walker RC .25 .60
175 Darvin Ham RC .60 1.50
176 Mark Jackson .25 .60
177 Ervin Johnson .20 .50
178 Stacey Augmon .25 .60
179 Joe Dumars .40 1.00
180 Grant Hill .50 1.25
181 Grant Long .20 .50
182 Terry Mills .20 .50
183 Otis Thorpe .25 .60
184 Jerome Williams RC .25 .60
185 B.J. Armstrong .25 .60
186 Todd Fuller RC .20 .50
187 Ray Owes RC .25 .60
188 Mark Price .30 .75
189 Felton Spencer .20 .50
190 Charles Barkley .75 2.00
191 Mario Elie .20 .50
192 Othella Harrington RC .20 .50
193 Matt Maloney RC .25 .60
194 Brent Price .20 .50
195 Kevin Willis .25 .60
196 Travis Best .20 .50
197 Erick Dampier RC .30 .75
198 Antonio Davis .20 .50
199 Jalen Rose .25 .60
200 Pooh Richardson .20 .50
201 Rodney Rogers .20 .50
202 Lorenzen Wright RC .25 .60
203 Kobe Bryant RC 15.00 40.00
204 Derek Fisher RC .40 1.00
205 Travis Knight RC .25 .60
206 Shaquille O'Neal 1.25 3.00
207 Byron Scott .30 .75
208 P.J. Brown .20 .50
209 Sasha Danilovic .20 .50
210 Dan Majerle .30 .75
211 Martin Muursepp RC .20 .50
212 Ray Allen RC 1.50 4.00
213 Armon Gilliam .20 .50
214 Andrew Lang .20 .50
215 Moochie Norris RC .30 .75
216 Kevin Garnett 1.00 2.50
217 Tom Gugliotta .20 .50
218 Shane Heal RC .30 .75
219 Stephon Marbury RC 1.00 2.50
220 Stojko Vrankovic .20 .50
221 Kerry Kittles RC .30 .75
222 Robert Pack .20 .50
223 Jayson Williams .20 .50
224 Allan Houston .30 .75
225 Larry Johnson .40 1.00
226 Dontae' Jones RC .25 .60
227 Walter McCarty RC .30 .75
228 John Wallace RC .30 .75
229 Charlie Ward .20 .50
230 Brian Evans RC .20 .50
231 Amal McCaskill RC .30 .75
232 Brian Shaw .20 .50
233 Mark Davis .20 .50
234 Lucious Harris .20 .50
235 Allen Iverson RC 2.50 6.00
236 Sam Cassell .25 .60
237 Robert Horry .30 .75
238 Danny Manning .25 .60
239 Steve Nash RC 2.00 5.00
240 Kenny Anderson .25 .60
241 Aleksandar Djordjevic RC .30 .75
242 Jermaine O'Neal RC .50 1.25
243 Isaiah Rider .25 .60
244 Rasheed Wallace .40 1.00
245 Mahmoud Abdul-Rauf .25 .60
246 Michael Smith .20 .50
247 Corliss Williamson .20 .50
248 Vernon Maxwell .20 .50
249 Charles Smith .20 .50
250 Dominique Wilkins .50 1.25
251 Craig Ehlo .20 .50
252 Jim McIlvaine .20 .50
253 Sam Perkins .25 .60
254 Marcus Camby RC .50 1.25
255 Popeye Jones .20 .50
256 Donald Whiteside RC .30 .75
257 Walt Williams .20 .50
258 Jeff Hornacek .25 .60
259 Karl Malone .60 1.50
260 Bryon Russell .20 .50
261 John Stockton .60 1.50
262 Shareef Abdur-Rahim RC .50 1.25
263 Anthony Peeler .20 .50
264 Roy Rogers RC .25 .60
265 Tim Legler .20 .50
266 Tracy Murray .20 .50
267 Rod Strickland .30 .75
268 Ben Wallace RC 1.50 4.00
269 Kevin Garnett CB 1.00 2.50
270 Allan Houston CB .30 .75
271 Eddie Jones CB .30 .75
272 Jamal Mashburn CB .30 .75
273 Antonio McDyess CB .30 .75
274 Glenn Robinson CB .30 .75
275 Joe Smith CB .25 .60
276 Steve Smith CB .25 .60
277 Jerry Stackhouse CB .40 1.00
278 Damon Stoudamire CB .30 .75
279 Hakeem Olajuwon AS .60 1.50
280 Charles Barkley AS .75 2.00
281 Patrick Ewing AS .50 1.25
282 Michael Jordan AS 3.00 8.00
283 Clyde Drexler AS .50 1.25
284 Karl Malone AS .60 1.50
285 John Stockton AS .60 1.50
286 David Robinson AS .60 1.50
287 Scottie Pippen AS .75 2.00
288 Shawn Kemp AS .50 1.25
289 Shaquille O'Neal AS 1.25 3.00
290 Mitch Richmond AS .40 1.00
291 Reggie Miller AS .60 1.50
292 Alonzo Mourning AS .50 1.25
293 Gary Payton AS .50 1.25
294 Anfernee Hardaway AS .75 2.00
295 Grant Hill AS .50 1.25
296 Dennis Rodman AS .75 2.00
297 Juwan Howard AS .30 .75
298 Jason Kidd AS .50 1.25
299 Checklist .10 .25
300 Checklist .10 .25

1996-97 Fleer Decade of Excellence

COMPLETE SET (20) 50.00 110.00
COMPLETE SERIES 1 (10) 25.00 60.00
COMPLETE SERIES 2 (10) 25.00 50.00
SER.1/2 STATED ODDS 1:72 HOBBY
1 Clyde Drexler 5.00 12.00
2 Joe Dumars 4.00 10.00
3 Derek Harper 2.50 6.00
4 Michael Jordan 30.00 80.00
5 Karl Malone 6.00 15.00
6 Chris Mullin 4.00 10.00
7 Charles Oakley 3.00 8.00
8 Sam Perkins 2.50 6.00
9 Ricky Pierce 2.50 6.00
10 Buck Williams 3.00 8.00
11 Charles Barkley 8.00 20.00
12 Patrick Ewing 5.00 12.00
13 Eddie Johnson 2.00 5.00
14 Hakeem Olajuwon 6.00 15.00
15 Robert Parish 4.00 10.00
16 Byron Scott 3.00 8.00
17 Wayman Tisdale 2.50 6.00
18 Gerald Wilkins 2.50 6.00
19 Herb Williams 2.00 5.00
20 Kevin Willis 2.50 6.00

1996-97 Fleer Franchise Futures

COMPLETE SET (10) 6.00 15.00
SER.1 STATED ODDS 1:54 HOBBY
1 Kevin Garnett 3.00 8.00
2 Anfernee Hardaway 2.50 6.00
3 Grant Hill 1.50 4.00
4 Juwan Howard 1.00 2.50
5 Jason Kidd 1.50 4.00
6 Antonio McDyess 1.00 2.50
7 Glenn Robinson 1.00 2.50
8 Joe Smith .75 2.00
9 Jerry Stackhouse 1.25 3.00
10 Damon Stoudamire 1.00 2.50

1996-97 Fleer Game Breakers

COMPLETE SET (15) 60.00 150.00
SER.1 STATED ODDS 1:48 RETAIL
1 M.Jordan/S.Pippen 125.00 300.00
2 J.Jackson/J.Kidd 5.00 12.00
3 G.Hill/A.Houston 5.00 12.00
4 J.Smith/L.Sprewell 3.00 8.00
5 C.Drexler/H.Olajuwon 6.00 15.00
6 C.Ceballos/N.Van Exel 3.00 8.00
7 T.Hardaway/A.Mourning 5.00 12.00
8 V.Baker/G.Robinson 3.00 8.00
9 K.Garnett/I.Rider 10.00 25.00
10 A.Hardaway/S.O'Neal 12.00 30.00
11 J.Stackhouse/C.Weatherspoon 4.00 10.00
12 C.Barkley/M.Finley 8.00 20.00
13 S.Elliott/D.Robinson 6.00 15.00
14 S.Kemp/G.Payton 5.00 12.00
15 K.Malone/J.Stockton 6.00 15.00

1996-97 Fleer Lucky 13

COMPLETE SET (13) 25.00 60.00
EXCH.CARDS: SER.1 STATED ODDS 1:30
1 Allen Iverson 8.00 20.00
2 Marcus Camby 1.50 4.00
3 Shareef Abdur-Rahim 1.50 4.00
4 Stephon Marbury 3.00 8.00
5 Ray Allen 5.00 12.00
6 Antoine Walker 1.50 4.00
7 Lorenzen Wright .75 2.00
8 Kerry Kittles 1.00 2.50
9 Samaki Walker .75 2.00
10 Erick Dampier 1.00 2.50
11 Todd Fuller .60 1.50
12 Vitaly Potapenko .75 2.00
13 Kobe Bryant 50.00 120.00
NNO Expired Trade Cards .10 .30

1996-97 Fleer Rookie Rewind

COMPLETE SET (15) 10.00 25.00
SER.1 STATED ODDS 1:24 HOBBY/RETAIL
1 Brent Barry 1.00 2.50
2 Tyus Edney .75 2.00
3 Michael Finley 1.25 3.00
4 Kevin Garnett 4.00 10.00
5 Antonio McDyess 1.25 3.00
6 Bryant Reeves .75 2.00
7 Arvydas Sabonis 1.25 3.00
8 Joe Smith 1.00 2.50
9 Jerry Stackhouse 1.50 4.00
10 Damon Stoudamire 1.25 3.00
11 Bob Sura .75 2.00
12 Kurt Thomas .75 2.00
13 Gary Trent .75 2.00
14 Rasheed Wallace 1.50 4.00
15 Eric Williams .75 2.00

1996-97 Fleer Rookie Sensations

COMPLETE SET (15) 75.00 150.00
SER.2 STATED ODDS 1:90 HOBBY/RETAIL
1 Shareef Abdur-Rahim 3.00 8.00
2 Ray Allen 10.00 25.00
3 Kobe Bryant 200.00 500.00
4 Marcus Camby 3.00 8.00
5 Erick Dampier 2.00 5.00
6 Tony Delk 2.00 5.00
7 Allen Iverson 40.00 100.00
8 Kerry Kittles 2.00 5.00
9 Stephon Marbury 6.00 15.00
10 Steve Nash 8.00 20.00
11 Roy Rogers 1.50 4.00
12 Antoine Walker 3.00 8.00
13 Samaki Walker 1.50 4.00
14 John Wallace 1.50 4.00
15 Lorenzen Wright 1.50 4.00

1996-97 Fleer Stackhouse's All-Fleer

COMPLETE SET (12) 6.00 15.00
SER.1 STATED ODDS 1:12 HOBBY/RETAIL
ONE PER SPECIAL SER.1 RETAIL PACK
1 Charles Barkley 1.00 2.50
2 Anfernee Hardaway 1.00 2.50
3 Grant Hill .60 1.50
4 Michael Jordan 4.00 10.00
5 Shawn Kemp .60 1.50
6 Jason Kidd .60 1.50
7 Karl Malone .75 2.00
8 Hakeem Olajuwon .75 2.00
9 Shaquille O'Neal 1.50 4.00
10 Gary Payton .60 1.50
11 Scottie Pippen 1.00 2.50
12 David Robinson .75 2.00

1996-97 Fleer Stackhouse's Scrapbook

COMPLETE SET (2) 1.50 4.00
COMMON STACK. (S9-S10) 1.00 2.50
SER.1 STATED ODDS 1:24 HOB/RET

1996-97 Fleer Swing Shift

COMPLETE SET (15) 5.00 12.00
SER.2 STATED ODDS 1:6 HOBBY/RETAIL
1 Ray Allen 1.25 3.00
2 Charles Barkley 1.25 3.00
3 Michael Finley .50 1.25
4 Anfernee Hardaway 1.25 3.00
5 Grant Hill .75 2.00
6 Jim Jackson .30 .75
7 Eddie Jones .50 1.25
8 Kerry Kittles .25 .60
9 Reggie Miller 1.00 2.50
10 Gary Payton .75 2.00
11 Scottie Pippen 1.25 3.00
12 Mitch Richmond .60 1.50
13 Steve Smith .40 1.00
14 Latrell Sprewell .50 1.25
15 Jerry Stackhouse .60 1.50

1996-97 Fleer Thrill Seekers

SER.2 STATED ODDS 1:240 HOBBY
1 Shareef Abdur-Rahim 25.00 60.00
2 Charles Barkley 60.00 150.00
3 Anfernee Hardaway 75.00 200.00
4 Grant Hill 60.00 150.00
5 Allen Iverson 300.00 600.00
6 Michael Jordan 1,000.00 2,500.00
7 Shawn Kemp 60.00 150.00
8 Jason Kidd 75.00 200.00
9 Stephon Marbury 30.00 80.00
10 Antonio McDyess 30.00 80.00
11 Reggie Miller 100.00 250.00
12 Alonzo Mourning 75.00 200.00
13 Shaquille O'Neal 75.00 200.00
14 David Robinson 75.00 200.00
15 Damon Stoudamire 30.00 80.00

1996-97 Fleer Total O

COMPLETE SET (10) 200.00 500.00
SER.2 STATED ODDS 1:44 RETAIL
1 Anfernee Hardaway 10.00 25.00
2 Grant Hill 6.00 15.00
3 Juwan Howard 4.00 10.00
4 Michael Jordan 150.00 400.00
5 Shawn Kemp 6.00 15.00
6 Karl Malone 8.00 20.00
7 Alonzo Mourning 6.00 15.00
8 Hakeem Olajuwon 8.00 20.00
9 Shaquille O'Neal 15.00 40.00
10 Jerry Stackhouse 5.00 12.00

1996-97 Fleer Towers of Power

COMPLETE SET (10) 15.00 30.00
SER.2 STATED ODDS 1:30 HOBBY/RETAIL
1 Shareef Abdur-Rahim 1.25 3.00
2 Marcus Camby 1.25 3.00
3 Patrick Ewing 2.50 6.00
4 Kevin Garnett 5.00 12.00
5 Shawn Kemp 2.50 6.00
6 Hakeem Olajuwon 3.00 8.00
7 Shaquille O'Neal 6.00 15.00
8 David Robinson 3.00 8.00
9 Dennis Rodman 4.00 10.00
10 Joe Smith 1.25 3.00

1997-98 Fleer

COMPLETE SET (350) 20.00 50.00
COMPLETE SERIES 1 (200) 10.00 25.00
COMPLETE SERIES 2 (150) 10.00 25.00
1 Anfernee Hardaway 1.00 2.50
2 Mitch Richmond .50 1.25
3 Allen Iverson 1.25 3.00
4 Chris Webber .50 1.25
5 Sasha Danilovic .25 .60
6 Avery Johnson .30 .75
7 Kenny Anderson .30 .75
8 Antoine Walker .40 1.00
9 Nick Van Exel .40 1.00
10 Mookie Blaylock .40 1.00
11 Wesley Person .30 .75
12 Vlade Divac .40 1.00
13 Glenn Robinson .40 1.00
14 Chris Mills .25 .60
15 Latrell Sprewell .50 1.25
16 Jayson Williams .25 .60
17 Travis Best .25 .60
18 Charlie Ward .30 .75
19 Theo Ratliff .30 .75
20 Gary Payton .60 1.50
21 Marcus Camby .40 1.00
22 Clyde Drexler .60 1.50
23 Michael Jordan 4.00 10.00
24 Antonio McDyess .40 1.00
25 Stephon Marbury .50 1.25
26 Isaac Austin .25 .60
27 Shareef Abdur-Rahim .40 1.00
28 Malik Sealy .30 .75
29 Arvydas Sabonis .50 1.25
30 Kerry Kittles .30 .75
31 Reggie Miller .75 2.00
32 Karl Malone .75 2.00
33 Grant Hill .60 1.50
34 Hakeem Olajuwon .75 2.00
35 Danny Ferry .25 .60
36 Dominique Wilkins .50 1.25
37 Armon Gilliam .25 .60
38 Danny Manning .30 .75
39 Larry Johnson .50 1.25
40 Dino Radja .25 .60
41 Jason Caffey .25 .60
42 Jerry Stackhouse .40 1.00
43 Alonzo Mourning .60 1.50
44 Shawn Bradley .25 .60
45 Bo Outlaw .25 .60
46 Bryon Russell .25 .60
47 Doug West .25 .60
48 Lawrence Moten .25 .60
49 Dale Ellis .30 .75
50 Kobe Bryant 4.00 10.00
51 Carlos Rogers .25 .60
52 Todd Fuller .25 .60
53 Tyus Edney .25 .60
54 Horace Grant .40 1.00
55 Dikembe Mutombo .60 1.50
56 Jim McIlvaine .25 .60
57 Harvey Grant .25 .60
58 Dean Garrett .25 .60
59 Samaki Walker .25 .60
60 Johnny Newman .25 .60
61 Antonio Davis .30 .75
62 Jamal Mashburn .30 .75
63 Muggsy Bogues .30 .75
64 Rod Strickland .30 .75
65 Craig Ehlo .25 .60
66 Rex Walters .25 .60
67 Bob Sura .25 .60
68 Travis Knight .25 .60
69 Toni Kukoc .50 1.25
70 Antoine Carr .25 .60
71 Mario Elie .25 .60
72 Popeye Jones .25 .60
73 David Wesley .30 .75
74 John Wallace .25 .60
75 Calbert Cheaney .30 .75
76 Grant Long .25 .60
77 Will Perdue .25 .60
78 Rasheed Wallace .50 1.25
79 Chris Gatling .25 .60
80 Corliss Williamson .25 .60
81 B.J. Armstrong .25 .60
82 Brian Shaw .30 .75
83 Darrick Martin .25 .60
84 Vinny Del Negro .30 .75
85 Tony Delk .30 .75
86 Greg Anthony .30 .75
87 Mark Davis .25 .60
88 Anthony Goldwire .25 .60
89 Rex Chapman .25 .60
90 Stojko Vrankovic .25 .60
91 Dennis Rodman 1.00 2.50
92 Detlef Schrempf .40 1.00
93 Henry James .25 .60
94 Tracy Murray .25 .60
95 Voshon Lenard .25 .60
96 Sharone Wright .25 .60
97 Ed O'Bannon .25 .60
98 Gerald Wilkins .25 .60
99 Kevin Willis .30 .75
100 Shaquille O'Neal 1.25 3.00
101 Jim Jackson .30 .75
102 Mark Price .40 1.00
103 Patrick Ewing .60 1.50
104 Lorenzen Wright .25 .60
105 Tyrone Hill .30 .75
106 Ray Allen .75 2.00
107 Jermaine O'Neal .30 .75
108 Anthony Mason .30 .75
109 Mahmoud Abdul-Rauf .25 .60
110 Terry Mills .25 .60
111 Gheorghe Muresan .25 .60
112 Mark Jackson .25 .60
113 Greg Ostertag .25 .60
114 Kevin Johnson .40 1.00
115 Anthony Peeler .25 .60
116 Rony Seikaly .30 .75
117 Keith Askins .25 .60
118 Todd Day .25 .60
119 Chris Childs .25 .60
120 Chris Carr .25 .60
121 Erick Strickland RC .25 .60
122 Elden Campbell .25 .60
123 Elliot Perry .25 .60
124 Pooh Richardson .25 .60
125 Juwan Howard .30 .75
126 Ervin Johnson .25 .60
127 Eric Montross .25 .60
128 Otis Thorpe .25 .60
129 Hersey Hawkins .30 .75
130 Bimbo Coles .25 .60
131 Olden Polynice .25 .60
132 Christian Laettner .40 1.00
133 Sean Elliott .30 .75
134 Othella Harrington .25 .60
135 Erick Dampier .30 .75
136 Vitaly Potapenko .25 .60
137 Doug Christie .25 .60
138 Luc Longley .40 1.00
139 Clarence Weatherspoon .25 .60
140 Gary Trent .25 .60
141 Shandon Anderson .25 .60
142 Sam Perkins .25 .60
143 Derek Harper .25 .60
144 Robert Horry .40 1.00
145 Roy Rogers .25 .60
146 John Starks .40 1.00
147 Tyrone Corbin .25 .60
148 Andrew Lang .25 .60
149 Derek Strong .25 .60
150 Joe Smith .30 .75
151 Ron Harper .40 1.00
152 Sam Cassell .30 .75
153 Brent Barry .30 .75
154 LaPhonso Ellis .30 .75
155 Matt Geiger .25 .60
156 Steve Nash 1.00 2.50
157 Michael Smith .25 .60
158 Eric Williams .25 .60
159 Tom Gugliotta .30 .75
160 Monty Williams .30 .75
161 Lindsey Hunter .25 .60
162 Oliver Miller .25 .60
163 Brent Price .25 .60
164 Derrick McKey .25 .60
165 Robert Pack .25 .60
166 Derrick Coleman .40 1.00
167 Isaiah Rider .30 .75
168 Dan Majerle .40 1.00
169 Jeff Hornacek .40 1.00
170 Terrell Brandon .30 .75
171 Nate McMillan .25 .60
172 Cedric Ceballos .30 .75
173 Derek Fisher .40 1.00
174 Rodney Rogers .30 .75
175 Blue Edwards .25 .60
176 Brooks Thompson .25 .60
177 Sherman Douglas .25 .60
178 Sam Mitchell .25 .60
179 Charles Oakley .30 .75
180 Greg Minor .25 .60
181 Chris Mullin .50 1.25
182 P.J. Brown .25 .60
183 Stacey Augmon .30 .75
184 Don MacLean .25 .60
185 Aaron McKie .25 .60
186 Dale Davis .30 .75
187 Vernon Maxwell .25 .60
188 Dell Curry .30 .75
189 Kendall Gill .30 .75
190 Billy Owens .25 .60
191 Steve Kerr .50 1.25
192 Matt Maloney .25 .60
193 Dennis Scott .30 .75
194 A.C. Green .30 .75
195 George McCloud .25 .60
196 Walt Williams .30 .75
197 Eldridge Recasner .25 .60
198 Checklist (Hawks/Bucks) .20 .50
199 Checklist (T'wolves/Wizards) .20 .50
200 Checklist (inserts) .20 .50
201 Tim Duncan RC 2.50 6.00
202 Tim Thomas RC .50 1.25
203 Clifford Rozier .25 .60
204 Bryant Reeves .25 .60
205 Glen Rice .40 1.00
206 Darrell Armstrong .25 .60
207 Juwan Howard .30 .75
208 John Stockton .75 2.00
209 Antonio McDyess .40 1.00
210 James Cotton RC .40 1.00
211 Brian Grant .30 .75
212 Chris Whitney .25 .60
213 Antonio Davis .30 .75
214 Kendall Gill .30 .75
215 Adonal Foyle RC .30 .75
216 Dean Garrett .25 .60
217 Dennis Scott .30 .75
218 Zydrunas Ilgauskas .40 1.00
219 Antonio Daniels RC .40 1.00
220 Derek Harper .30 .75
221 Travis Knight .25 .60
222 Bobby Hurley .25 .60
223 Greg Anderson .25 .60
224 Rod Strickland .30 .75
225 David Benoit .25 .60
226 Tracy McGrady RC 2.00 5.00
227 Brian Williams .30 .75
228 James Robinson .25 .60
229 Randy Brown .25 .60
230 Greg Foster .25 .60
231 Reggie Miller .75 2.00
232 Eric Montross .25 .60
233 Malik Rose .25 .60
234 Charles Barkley 1.00 2.50
235 Tony Battie RC .40 1.00
236 Terry Mills .25 .60
237 Jerald Honeycutt RC .40 1.00
238 Bubba Wells RC .25 .60
239 John Wallace .25 .60
240 Jason Kidd .60 1.50
241 Mark Price .40 1.00
242 Ron Mercer RC .50 1.25
243 Derrick Coleman .40 1.00
244 Fred Hoiberg .30 .75
245 Wesley Person .30 .75
246 Eddie Jones .40 1.00
247 Allan Houston .40 1.00
248 Keith Van Horn RC .60 1.50
249 Johnny Newman .25 .60
250 Kevin Garnett 1.00 2.50
251 Latrell Sprewell .50 1.25
252 Tracy Murray .25 .60
253 Charles O'Bannon RC .30 .75
254 Lamond Murray .25 .60
255 Jerry Stackhouse .40 1.00
256 Rik Smits .30 .75
257 Alan Henderson .25 .60
258 Tariq Abdul-Wahad RC .30 .75
259 Nick Anderson .30 .75
260 Calbert Cheaney .30 .75
261 Scottie Pippen 1.00 2.50
262 Rodrick Rhodes RC .30 .75
263 Derek Anderson RC .40 1.00
264 Dana Barros .25 .60
265 Todd Day .25 .60
266 Michael Finley .40 1.00
267 Kevin Edwards .25 .60
268 Terrell Brandon .30 .75
269 Bobby Phills .30 .75
270 Kelvin Cato RC .30 .75
271 Vin Baker .30 .75
272 Eric Washington RC .40 1.00
273 Jim Jackson .30 .75
274 Joe Dumars .50 1.25
275 David Robinson .75 2.00
276 Jayson Williams .25 .60
277 Travis Best .25 .60
278 Kurt Thomas .25 .60
279 Otis Thorpe .30 .75
280 Damon Stoudamire .40 1.00
281 John Williams .25 .60
282 Loy Vaught .30 .75
283 Bo Outlaw .25 .60
284 Todd Fuller .25 .60
285 Terry Dehere .25 .60
286 Clarence Weatherspoon .25 .60
287 Danny Fortson RC .40 1.00
288 Howard Eisley .25 .60
289 Steve Smith .30 .75
290 Chris Webber .50 1.25
291 Shawn Kemp .60 1.50
292 Sam Cassell .30 .75
293 Rick Fox .30 .75
294 Walter McCarty .25 .60
295 Mark Jackson .30 .75
296 Chris Mills .25 .60
297 Jacque Vaughn RC .30 .75
298 Shawn Respert .25 .60
299 Scott Burrell .25 .60
300 Allen Iverson 1.25 3.00
301 Charles Smith RC .30 .75
302 Ervin Johnson .25 .60
303 Hubert Davis .25 .60
304 Eddie Johnson .30 .75
305 Erick Dampier .30 .75
306 Eric Williams .25 .60
307 Anthony Johnson RC .40 1.00
308 David Wesley .30 .75
309 Eric Piatkowski .25 .60
310 Austin Croshere RC .30 .75
311 Malik Sealy .30 .75
312 George McCloud .25 .60
313 Anthony Parker RC .40 1.00
314 Cedric Henderson RC .30 .75
315 John Thomas RC .25 .60
316 Cory Alexander .25 .60
317 Johnny Taylor RC .25 .60
318 Chris Mullin .50 1.25
319 J.R. Reid .30 .75
320 George Lynch .25 .60
321 Lawrence Funderburke RC .30 .75
322 God Shammgod RC .40 1.00
323 Bobby Jackson RC .50 1.25
324 Khalid Reeves .25 .60
325 Zan Tabak .25 .60
326 Chris Gatling .25 .60
327 Alvin Williams RC .40 1.00
328 Scot Pollard RC .30 .75
329 Kerry Kittles .30 .75
330 Tim Hardaway .50 1.25
331 Maurice Taylor RC .30 .75
332 Keith Booth RC .30 .75
333 Chris Morris .25 .60
334 Bryant Stith .25 .60
335 Terry Cummings .30 .75
336 Ed Gray RC .40 1.00
337 Eric Snow .25 .60
338 Clifford Robinson .30 .75
339 Chris Dudley .25 .60
340 Chauncey Billups RC 1.25 3.00
341 Paul Grant RC .25 .60
342 Tyrone Hill .30 .75
343 Joe Smith .30 .75
344 Sean Rooks .25 .60
345 Harvey Grant .25 .60
346 Dale Davis .30 .75
347 Brevin Knight RC .40 1.00
348 Serge Zwikker RC .30 .75
349 Checklist (Hawks/Kings) .20 .50
350 Checklist (Spurs/Wizards/Inserts) .20 .50

1997-98 Fleer Crystal Collection

*STARS: 1.5X TO 4X BASE CARD HI
*RCs: 1.25X TO 3X BASE HI
BOTH SERIES STATED ODDS 1:2 HOBBY
23 Michael Jordan 6.00 15.00
201 Tim Duncan 5.00 12.00

1997-98 Fleer Tiffany Collection

*STARS: 10X TO 25X BASE CARD HI
*RCs: 5X TO 12X BASE HI
SER.1/2 STATED ODDS 1:20 HOBBY
23 Michael Jordan 500.00 1,000.00
50 Kobe Bryant 150.00 400.00
201 Tim Duncan 75.00 200.00
226 Tracy McGrady 40.00 100.00
250 Kevin Garnett 8.00 20.00

1997-98 Fleer Decade of Excellence

SER.1 STATED ODDS 1:36 HOBBY
*RARE TRAD: 1.5X TO 4X HI COLUMN
RARE TRAD: SER.1 STATED ODDS 1:360 HOB
1 Charles Barkley 4.00 10.00
2 Clyde Drexler 2.50 6.00
3 Patrick Ewing 2.50 6.00
4 Kevin Johnson 1.50 4.00
5 Michael Jordan 40.00 100.00
6 Karl Malone 3.00 8.00
7 Reggie Miller 3.00 8.00
8 Hakeem Olajuwon 3.00 8.00
9 Scottie Pippen 4.00 10.00
10 Dennis Rodman 4.00 10.00
11 John Stockton 3.00 8.00
12 Dominique Wilkins 2.00 5.00

1997-98 Fleer Flair Hardwood Leaders

COMPLETE SET (29) 15.00 40.00
SER.1 STATED ODDS 1:6 HOBBY/RETAIL
1 Christian Laettner .60 1.50
2 Antoine Walker .60 1.50
3 Glen Rice .60 1.50
4 Michael Jordan 8.00 20.00
5 Terrell Brandon .50 1.25
6 Michael Finley .60 1.50
7 Antonio McDyess .60 1.50
8 Grant Hill 1.00 2.50
9 Latrell Sprewell .75 2.00
10 Hakeem Olajuwon 1.25 3.00
11 Reggie Miller 1.25 3.00
12 Loy Vaught .50 1.25
13 Shaquille O'Neal 2.00 5.00
14 Alonzo Mourning 1.00 2.50

Vin Baker .50 1.25
Kevin Garnett 1.50 4.00
Kerry Kittles .50 1.25
Patrick Ewing 1.00 2.50
Anfernee Hardaway 1.50 4.00
Jerry Stackhouse .60 1.50
Jason Kidd 1.00 2.50
Kenny Anderson .50 1.25
Mitch Richmond .75 2.00
David Robinson 1.25 3.00
Shawn Kemp 1.00 2.50
Damon Stoudamire .60 1.50
Karl Malone 1.25 3.00
Shareef Abdur-Rahim .60 1.50
Chris Webber .75 2.00

1997-98 Fleer Franchise Futures
COMPLETE SET (10) 8.00 20.00
SER.1 STATED ODDS 1:36 RETAIL
Shareef Abdur-Rahim 1.00 2.50
Ray Allen 2.00 5.00
Kobe Bryant 6.00 15.00
Kevin Garnett 2.50 6.00
Grant Hill 1.50 4.00
Juwan Howard .75 2.00
Allen Iverson 3.00 8.00
Kerry Kittles .75 2.00
Joe Smith .75 2.00
0 Damon Stoudamire 1.00 2.50

1997-98 Fleer Game Breakers
SER.1 STATED ODDS 1:288 HOBBY/RETAIL
1 M.Jordan/D.Rodman 300.00 600.00
2 J.Dumars/G.Hill 12.00 30.00
3 J.Smith/L.Sprewell 10.00 25.00
4 C.Barkley/H.Olajuwon 20.00 50.00
5 E.Jones/S.O'Neal 30.00 80.00
6 K.Garnett/S.Marbury 20.00 50.00
7 N.Anderson/A.Hardaway 15.00 40.00
8 A.Iverson/J.Stackhouse 25.00 60.00
9 S.Kemp/G.Payton 15.00 40.00
10 M.Camby/D.Stoudamire 12.00 30.00
11 K.Malone/J.Stockton 25.00 60.00
12 J.Howard/C.Webber 12.00 30.00

1997-98 Fleer Goudey Greats
COMPLETE SET (15) 4.00 10.00
SER.2 STATED ODDS 1:4 HOBBY/RETAIL
1 Ray Allen .75 2.00
2 Clyde Drexler .60 1.50
3 Patrick Ewing .60 1.50
4 Anfernee Hardaway 1.00 2.50
5 Grant Hill .60 1.50
6 Stephon Marbury .50 1.25
7 Alonzo Mourning .60 1.50
8 Shaquille O'Neal 1.25 3.00
9 Gary Payton .60 1.50
10 Scottie Pippen 1.00 2.50
11 David Robinson .75 2.00
12 Joe Smith .30 .75
13 John Stockton .75 2.00
14 Damon Stoudamire .40 1.00
15 Antoine Walker .40 1.00

1997-98 Fleer Key Ingredient
COMPLETE SET (15) 2.00 5.00
SER.1 STATED ODDS 1:2 RETAIL
*GOLD: 2.5X TO 6X KEY INGRED. HI
GOLD: SER.1 STATED ODDS 1:18 HOB/RET
1 Charles Barkley .50 1.25
2 Marcus Camby .20 .50
3 Anfernee Hardaway .50 1.25
4 Juwan Howard .15 .40
5 Shawn Kemp .30 .75
6 Karl Malone .40 1.00
7 Stephon Marbury .25 .60
8 Alonzo Mourning .30 .75
9 Shaquille O'Neal .60 1.50
10 Scottie Pippen .50 1.25
11 Mitch Richmond .25 .60
12 David Robinson .40 1.00
13 Joe Smith .15 .40
14 Jerry Stackhouse .20 .50
15 Antoine Walker .20 .50

1997-98 Fleer Million Dollar Moments
COMPLETE SET (50) 2.50 6.00
1 Checklist (1-50) .05 .15
2 Mark Jackson .07 .20
3 Charles Barkley .25 .60
4 Terrell Brandon .07 .20
5 Wayman Tisdale .05 .15
6 Clyde Drexler .15 .40
7 Patrick Ewing .15 .40
8 Kevin Garnett .25 .60
9 Tom Gugliotta .07 .20
10 Anfernee Hardaway .25 .60
11 Tim Hardaway .12 .30
12 Grant Hill .15 .40
13 Allen Iverson .30 .75
14 Shawn Kemp .15 .40
15 Jason Kidd .15 .40
16 Charles Oakley .07 .20
17 Karl Malone .20 .50
18 Alonzo Mourning .15 .40
19 Shaquille O'Neal .30 .75
20 Hakeem Olajuwon .20 .50
21 Chris Webber .12 .30
22 Scottie Pippen .25 .60
23 Glen Rice .10 .25
24 Mitch Richmond .12 .30
25 David Robinson .20 .50
26 Dennis Rodman .25 .60
27 Jerry Stackhouse .10 .25
28 John Stockton .20 .50
29 Mookie Blaylock .10 .25
30 Muggsy Bogues .07 .20
31 Kobe Bryant 1.00 2.50
32 Rex Chapman .05 .15
33 Joe Dumars .12 .30
34 Dale Ellis .07 .20
35 Horace Grant .10 .25
36 Jeff Hornacek .10 .25
37 Damon Stoudamire .10 .25
38 Kevin Johnson .10 .25
39 Larry Johnson .12 .30
40 Toni Kukoc .12 .30
41 Danny Manning .07 .20
42 Stephon Marbury .12 .30
43 Reggie Miller .20 .50
44 Chris Mullin .12 .30
45 Dikembe Mutombo .15 .40
46 Gary Payton .15 .40
47 Christian Laettner .10 .25
48 Glenn Robinson .10 .25
49 Nick Van Exel .10 .25
50 Marcus Camby .10 .25

1997-98 Fleer Rookie Rewind
COMPLETE SET (10) 5.00 12.00
SER.1 STATED ODDS 1:4 HOBBY/RETAIL
1 Shareef Abdur-Rahim .60 1.50
2 Ray Allen 1.25 3.00
3 Kobe Bryant 6.00 15.00
4 Marcus Camby .60 1.50
5 Allen Iverson 2.00 5.00
6 Kerry Kittles .50 1.25
7 Matt Maloney .40 1.00
8 Stephon Marbury .75 2.00
9 Roy Rogers .40 1.00
10 Antoine Walker .60 1.50

1997-98 Fleer Rookie Sensations
COMPLETE SET (10) 4.00 10.00
SER.2 STATED ODDS 1:8 HOBBY/RETAIL
1 Derek Anderson .30 .75
2 Tony Battie .30 .75
3 Chauncey Billups 1.00 2.50
4 Austin Croshere .25 .60
5 Antonio Daniels .30 .75
6 Tim Duncan 2.00 5.00
7 Tracy McGrady 1.50 4.00
8 Ron Mercer .40 1.00
9 Tim Thomas .40 1.00
10 Keith Van Horn .50 1.25

1997-98 Fleer Soaring Stars
COMPLETE SET (20) 6.00 15.00
SER.2 STATED ODDS 1:2 RETAIL
*HIGH STARS: 1.5X TO 4X SOARING HI
HIGH FLY: SER.2 STATED ODDS 1:24 H/R
1 Shareef Abdur-Rahim .40 1.00
2 Ray Allen .75 2.00
3 Charles Barkley 1.00 2.50
4 Kobe Bryant 4.00 10.00
5 Marcus Camby .40 1.00
6 Kevin Garnett 1.00 2.50
7 Tim Hardaway .50 1.25
8 Eddie Jones .40 1.00
9 Michael Jordan 60.00 150.00
10 Shawn Kemp .60 1.50
11 Jason Kidd .60 1.50
12 Kerry Kittles .30 .75
13 Karl Malone .75 2.00
14 Antonio McDyess .40 1.00
15 Glen Rice .40 1.00
16 Mitch Richmond .50 1.25
17 Latrell Sprewell .50 1.25
18 Jerry Stackhouse .40 1.00
19 Antoine Walker .40 1.00
20 Chris Webber .50 1.25

1997-98 Fleer Thrill Seekers
SER.2 STATED ODDS 1:288 HOBBY/RETAIL
1 Shareef Abdur-Rahim 10.00 25.00
2 Kobe Bryant 800.00 1,500.00
3 Tim Duncan 150.00 400.00
4 Anfernee Hardaway 60.00 150.00
5 Grant Hill 15.00 40.00
6 Allen Iverson 60.00 150.00
7 Michael Jordan 1,500.00 3,000.00
8 Stephon Marbury 12.00 30.00
9 Dennis Rodman 60.00 150.00
10 Joe Smith 10.00 25.00

1997-98 Fleer Total O
COMPLETE SET (10) 25.00 60.00
SER.2 STATED ODDS 1:18 RETAIL
1 Anfernee Hardaway 4.00 10.00
2 Grant Hill 1.50 4.00
3 Juwan Howard .75 2.00
4 Allen Iverson 4.00 10.00
5 Michael Jordan 100.00 250.00
6 Karl Malone 2.00 5.00
7 Stephon Marbury 1.25 3.00
8 Hakeem Olajuwon 2.00 5.00
9 Shaquille O'Neal 5.00 12.00
10 Damon Stoudamire 1.00 2.50

1997-98 Fleer Towers of Power
COMPLETE SET (12) 12.00 30.00
SER.2 STATED ODDS 1:18 HOBBY/RETAIL
1 Shareef Abdur-Rahim 1.25 3.00
2 Marcus Camby 1.25 3.00
3 Patrick Ewing 2.00 5.00
4 Kevin Garnett 3.00 8.00
5 Shawn Kemp 2.00 5.00
6 Karl Malone 2.50 6.00
7 Hakeem Olajuwon 2.50 6.00
8 Shaquille O'Neal 4.00 10.00
9 Dennis Rodman 3.00 8.00
10 Joe Smith 1.00 2.50
11 Antoine Walker 1.25 3.00
12 Chris Webber 1.50 4.00

1997-98 Fleer Zone
SER.2 STATED ODDS 1:36 HOBBY
1 Shareef Abdur-Rahim 2.50 6.00
2 Kobe Bryant 60.00 150.00
3 Marcus Camby 2.50 6.00
4 Tim Duncan 6.00 15.00
5 Kevin Garnett 6.00 15.00
6 Anfernee Hardaway 6.00 15.00
7 Grant Hill 4.00 10.00
8 Juwan Howard 2.00 5.00
9 Allen Iverson 8.00 20.00
10 Michael Jordan 100.00 250.00
11 Hakeem Olajuwon 5.00 12.00
12 Gary Payton 4.00 10.00
13 Scottie Pippen 6.00 15.00
14 Glen Rice 2.50 6.00
15 Keith Van Horn 4.00 10.00

1998-99 Fleer
COMPLETE SET (150) 12.00 30.00
1 Kobe Bryant 8.00 20.00
2 Corliss Williamson .20 .50
3 Allen Iverson .75 2.00
4 Michael Finley .30 .75
5 Juwan Howard .25 .60
6 Marcus Camby .25 .60
7 Toni Kukoc .30 .75
8 Antoine Walker .30 .75
9 Stephon Marbury .40 1.00
10 Tim Hardaway .40 1.00
11 Zydrunas Ilgauskas .30 .75
12 John Stockton .60 1.50
13 Glenn Robinson .30 .75
14 Isaiah Rider .25 .60
15 Danny Fortson .20 .50
16 Donyell Marshall .20 .50
17 Chris Mullin .40 1.00
18 Shareef Abdur-Rahim .30 .75
19 Bobby Phills .20 .50
20 Gary Payton .50 1.25
21 Derrick Coleman .25 .60
22 Larry Johnson .25 .60
23 Michael Jordan 3.00 8.00
24 Danny Manning .25 .60
25 Nick Anderson .20 .50
26 Chris Gatling .20 .50
27 Steve Smith .25 .60
28 Chris Whitney .20 .50
29 Terrell Brandon .25 .60
30 Rasheed Wallace .40 1.00
31 Reggie Miller .60 1.50
32 Karl Malone .60 1.50
33 Grant Hill .50 1.25
34 Hakeem Olajuwon .60 1.50
35 Erick Dampier .25 .60
36 Vin Baker .25 .60
37 Tim Thomas .25 .60
38 Mark Price .30 .75
39 Shawn Bradley .20 .50
40 Calbert Cheaney .20 .50
41 Glen Rice .30 .75
42 Kevin Willis .25 .60
43 Chris Carr .20 .50
44 Keith Van Horn .30 .75
45 Jamal Mashburn .30 .75
46 Eddie Jones .30 .75
47 Brevin Knight .20 .50
48 Olden Polynice .25 .60
49 Bobby Jackson .25 .60
50 David Robinson .60 1.50
51 Patrick Ewing .50 1.25
52 Samaki Walker .20 .50
53 Antonio Daniels .20 .50
54 Rodney Rogers .20 .50
55 Dikembe Mutombo .50 1.25
56 Tracy McGrady .50 1.25
57 Walt Williams .20 .50
58 Walter McCarty .20 .50
59 Detlef Schrempf .30 .75
60 Ervin Johnson .20 .50
61 Michael Smith .20 .50
62 Clifford Robinson .20 .50
63 Brian Williams .20 .50
64 Shandon Anderson .20 .50
65 P.J. Brown .20 .50
66 Scottie Pippen .75 2.00
67 Anthony Peeler .20 .50
68 Tony Delk .20 .50
69 David Wesley .20 .50
70 John Starks .30 .75
71 Nick Van Exel .30 .75
72 Kerry Kittles .25 .60
73 Tony Battie .20 .50
74 Lamond Murray .20 .50
75 Anfernee Hardaway .75 2.00
76 Jalen Rose .25 .60
77 Derek Anderson .25 .60
78 Avery Johnson .25 .60
79 Michael Stewart .20 .50
80 Brian Shaw .20 .50
81 Chauncey Billups .40 1.00
82 Kenny Anderson .25 .60
83 Bryon Russell .20 .50
84 Jason Kidd .50 1.25
85 Tyrone Hill .20 .50
86 Jim McIlvaine .20 .50
87 Brian Grant .20 .50
88 Bryant Stith .20 .50
89 Brent Price .20 .50
90 John Wallace .20 .50
91 Dennis Rodman .75 2.00
92 Alonzo Mourning .50 1.25
93 Bimbo Coles .20 .50
94 Chris Anstey .20 .50
95 Lindsey Hunter .20 .50
96 Ed Gray .20 .50
97 Chris Mills .20 .50
98 Rick Fox .20 .50
99 Lorenzen Wright .20 .50
100 Kevin Garnett .75 2.00
101 Shawn Kemp .50 1.25
102 Mark Jackson .25 .60
103 Sam Cassell .25 .60
104 Monty Williams .25 .60
105 Ron Mercer .25 .60
106 Bryant Reeves .20 .50
107 Tracy Murray .20 .50
108 Ray Allen .50 1.25
109 Maurice Taylor .20 .50
110 Jerome Williams .20 .50
111 Horace Grant .30 .75
112 Tariq Abdul-Wahad .20 .50
113 Travis Knight .20 .50
114 Kendall Gill .25 .60
115 Aaron McKie .20 .50
116 Dean Garrett .20 .50
117 Jeff Hornacek .25 .60
118 Todd Fuller .20 .50
119 Arvydas Sabonis .30 .75
120 Voshon Lenard .20 .50
121 Steve Nash .60 1.50
122 Cedric Henderson .20 .50
123 Rodrick Rhodes .20 .50
124 Mookie Blaylock .25 .60
125 Hersey Hawkins .20 .50
126 Doug Christie .25 .60
127 Eric Piatkowski .20 .50
128 Sean Elliott .20 .50
129 Anthony Mason .25 .60
130 Allan Houston .30 .75
131 Antonio Davis .20 .50
132 Hubert Davis .20 .50
133 Rod Strickland PF .25 .60
134 Jason Kidd PF .50 1.25
135 Mark Jackson PF .25 .60
136 Marcus Camby PF .25 .60
137 Dikembe Mutombo PF .50 1.25
138 Shawn Bradley PF .20 .50
139 Dennis Rodman PF .75 2.00
140 Jayson Williams PF .20 .50
141 Tim Duncan PF .75 2.00
142 Michael Jordan PF 3.00 8.00
143 Shaquille O'Neal PF 1.25 3.00
144 Karl Malone PF .60 1.50
145 Mookie Blaylock PF .25 .60
146 Brevin Knight PF .20 .50
147 Doug Christie PF .25 .60
148 Checklist .20 .50
149 Checklist .20 .50
150 Checklist .20 .50
S44 Keith Van Horn SAMPLE .75 2.00

1998-99 Fleer Vintage '61
COMPLETE SET (147) 40.00 70.00
*STARS: 1.5X TO 4X BASE CARD HI
ONE PER HOBBY PACK

1998-99 Fleer Classic '61
*STARS: 80X TO 200X BASE CARD HI
STATED PRINT RUN 61 SERIAL #'d SETS
1 Kobe Bryant 500.00 1,000.00
3 Allen Iverson 400.00 800.00
12 John Stockton 75.00 200.00
18 Shareef Abdur-Rahim 40.00 100.00
20 Gary Payton 125.00 300.00
23 Michael Jordan 2,000.00 4,000.00
56 Tracy McGrady 75.00 200.00
66 Scottie Pippen 60.00 150.00
91 Dennis Rodman 200.00 500.00
100 Kevin Garnett 200.00 500.00
141 Tim Duncan PF 200.00 500.00
142 Michael Jordan PF 2,000.00 4,000.00

1998-99 Fleer Electrifying
COMPLETE SET (10) 1,000.00 2,000.00
STATED ODDS 1:72 HOB/RET
1 Kobe Bryant 300.00 600.00
2 Kevin Garnett 40.00 100.00
3 Anfernee Hardaway 40.00 100.00
4 Grant Hill 25.00 60.00
5 Allen Iverson 75.00 200.00
6 Michael Jordan 1,000.00 2,000.00
7 Shawn Kemp 25.00 60.00
8 Stephon Marbury 25.00 60.00
9 Gary Payton 25.00 60.00
10 Dennis Rodman 60.00 150.00

1998-99 Fleer Great Expectations
COMPLETE SET (10) 8.00 20.00
STATED ODDS 1:20 HOB/RET
1 Shareef Abdur-Rahim .75 2.00
2 Ray Allen 1.25 3.00
3 Kobe Bryant 6.00 15.00
4 Tim Duncan 2.00 5.00
5 Kevin Garnett 2.00 5.00
6 Grant Hill 1.25 3.00
7 Allen Iverson 2.00 5.00
8 Stephon Marbury 1.00 2.50
9 Keith Van Horn .75 2.00
10 Antoine Walker .75 2.00

1998-99 Fleer Lucky 13
STATED ODDS 1:96 HOB/RET
1 Michael Olowokandi 3.00 8.00
2 Mike Bibby 6.00 15.00
3 Raef LaFrentz 3.00 8.00
4 Antawn Jamison 12.00 30.00
5 Vince Carter 25.00 60.00
6 Robert Traylor 2.50 6.00
7 Jason Williams 25.00 60.00
8 Larry Hughes 4.00 10.00
9 Dirk Nowitzki 75.00 200.00
10 Paul Pierce 25.00 60.00
11 Bonzi Wells 2.50 6.00
12 Michael Doleac 2.00 5.00
13 Keon Clark 2.50 6.00
NNO Expired Trade Cards .20 .50

1998-99 Fleer Playmakers Theatre
STATED PRINT RUN 100 SERIAL #'d SETS
1 Shareef Abdur-Rahim 300.00 600.00
2 Ray Allen 400.00 800.00
3 Kobe Bryant 4,000.00 8,000.00
4 Tim Duncan 1,000.00 2,000.00
5 Kevin Garnett 1,000.00 2,000.00
6 Anfernee Hardaway 500.00 1,000.00
7 Grant Hill 500.00 1,000.00
8 Allen Iverson 1,000.00 2,000.00
9 Michael Jordan 5,000.00 10,000.00
10 Karl Malone 500.00 1,000.00
11 Stephon Marbury 400.00 800.00
12 Shaquille O'Neal 1,000.00 2,000.00
13 Scottie Pippen 1,000.00 2,000.00
14 Keith Van Horn 150.00 400.00
15 Antoine Walker 150.00 400.00

1998-99 Fleer Rookie Rewind
COMPLETE SET (10) 6.00 15.00
STATED ODDS 1:36 HOB/RET
1 Derek Anderson 1.00 2.50
2 Tim Duncan 3.00 8.00
3 Cedric Henderson .75 2.00
4 Zydrunas Ilgauskas 1.25 3.00
5 Bobby Jackson 1.00 2.50
6 Brevin Knight .75 2.00
7 Ron Mercer 1.00 2.50
8 Maurice Taylor .75 2.00
9 Tim Thomas 1.00 2.50
10 Keith Van Horn 1.25 3.00

1998-99 Fleer Timeless Memories
COMPLETE SET (10) 4.00 10.00
STATED ODDS 1:12 HOB/RET
1 Shareef Abdur-Rahim .60 1.50
2 Ray Allen 1.00 2.50
3 Vin Baker .50 1.25
4 Anfernee Hardaway 1.50 4.00
5 Tim Hardaway .75 2.00
6 Shaquille O'Neal 2.50 6.00
7 Scottie Pippen 1.50 4.00
8 David Robinson 1.25 3.00
9 Dennis Rodman 1.50 4.00
10 Antoine Walker .60 1.50

1999-00 Fleer
COMPLETE SET (220) 20.00 50.00
NNO CL STATED ODDS 1:6
1 Vince Carter 1.00 2.50
2 Kobe Bryant 3.00 8.00
3 Keith Van Horn .30 .75
4 Tim Duncan 1.00 2.50
5 Grant Hill .60 1.50
6 Kevin Garnett 1.00 2.50
7 Anfernee Hardaway 1.00 2.50
8 Jason Williams .60 1.50
9 Paul Pierce .75 2.00
10 Mookie Blaylock .25 .60
11 Shawn Bradley .25 .60
12 Kenny Anderson .30 .75
13 Chauncey Billups .40 1.00
14 Elden Campbell .25 .60
15 Jason Caffey .25 .60
16 Brent Barry .30 .75
17 Charles Barkley 1.00 2.50
18 Derek Anderson .25 .60
19 Darrick Martin .25 .60
20 Bison Dele .25 .60
21 Rick Fox .25 .60
22 Antonio Davis .25 .60
23 Terrell Brandon .25 .60
24 P.J. Brown .25 .60
25 Toby Bailey .25 .60
26 Ray Allen .60 1.50
27 Brian Grant .25 .60
28 Scott Burrell .25 .60
29 Tariq Abdul-Wahad .25 .60
30 Marcus Camby .30 .75
31 John Stockton .60 1.50
32 Nick Anderson .25 .60
33 Antonio Daniels .25 .60
34 Matt Geiger .25 .60
35 Vin Baker .30 .75
36 Dee Brown .25 .60
37 Shandon Anderson .25 .60
38 Calbert Cheaney .25 .60
39 Shareef Abdur-Rahim .40 1.00
40 LaPhonso Ellis .25 .60
41 Cedric Ceballos .25 .60
42 Tony Battie .25 .60
43 Keon Clark .25 .60
44 Derrick Coleman .30 .75
45 Erick Dampier .25 .60
46 Corey Benjamin .25 .60
47 Michael Dickerson .30 .75
48 Cedric Henderson .25 .60
49 Lamond Murray .25 .60
50 Horace Grant .30 .75
51 Shaquille O'Neal 1.50 4.00
52 Dale Davis .25 .60
53 Dean Garrett .25 .60
54 Tim Hardaway .50 1.25
55 Gerald Brown RC .40 1.00
56 Sam Cassell .30 .75
57 Jim Jackson .25 .60
58 Kendall Gill .40 1.00
59 Eric Williams .25 .60
60 Chris Childs .25 .60
61 Vlade Divac .40 1.00
62 Darrell Armstrong .25 .60
63 Mario Elie .25 .60
64 Tyrone Hill .25 .60
65 Dale Ellis .25 .60
66 Doug Christie .30 .75
67 Howard Eisley .25 .60
68 Juwan Howard .30 .75
69 Mike Bibby .40 1.00
70 Alan Henderson .25 .60
71 Michael Finley .40 1.00
72 Dana Barros .25 .60
73 Danny Fortson .25 .60
74 Ricky Davis .40 1.00
75 Adonal Foyle .25 .60
76 Cory Carr .25 .60
77 Bryce Drew .25 .60
78 Shawn Kemp .60 1.50
79 Tyrone Nesby RC .25 .60
80 Lindsey Hunter .25 .60
81 Ruben Patterson .25 .60
82 Al Harrington .40 1.00
83 Bobby Jackson .30 .75
84 Dan Majerle .40 1.00
85 Rex Chapman .25 .60
86 Dell Curry .25 .60
87 Walt Williams .25 .60
88 Kerry Kittles .30 .75
89 Isaiah Rider .30 .75
90 Patrick Ewing .50 1.25
91 Lawrence Funderburke .25 .60
92 Isaac Austin .25 .60
93 Sean Elliott .30 .75
94 Larry Hughes .30 .75
95 Hersey Hawkins .30 .75
96 Tracy McGrady .60 1.50
97 Jeff Hornacek .30 .75
98 Randell Jackson .25 .60
99 J.R. Henderson .25 .60
100 Roshown McLeod .25 .60
101 Steve Nash .75 2.00
102 Ron Mercer .30 .75
103 Raef LaFrentz .30 .75
104 Eddie Jones .40 1.00
105 Antawn Jamison .40 1.00
106 Kornel David RC .25 .60
107 Othella Harrington .25 .60
108 Brevin Knight .25 .60
109 Michael Olowokandi .25 .60
110 Christian Laettner .25 .60
111 J.R. Reid .25 .60
112 Reggie Miller .75 2.00
113 Andrae Patterson .25 .60
114 Jamal Mashburn .30 .75
115 Glenn Robinson .30 .75
116 Pat Garrity .25 .60
117 Stephon Marbury .50 1.25
118 Arvydas Sabonis .30 .75
119 Allan Houston .30 .75
120 Peja Stojakovic .40 1.00
121 Michael Doleac .25 .60
122 Avery Johnson .30 .75
123 Allen Iverson 1.00 2.50
124 Rashard Lewis .30 .75
125 Charles Oakley .40 1.00
126 Karl Malone .75 2.00
127 Tracy Murray .25 .60
128 Felipe Lopez .25 .60
129 Dikembe Mutombo .60 1.50
130 Dirk Nowitzki 1.25 3.00
131 Vitaly Potapenko .25 .60
132 Antonio McDyess .30 .75
133 Anthony Mason .40 1.00
134 Donyell Marshall .30 .75
135 Ron Harper .30 .75
136 Cuttino Mobley .25 .60
137 Wesley Person .25 .60
138 Rodney Rogers .25 .60
139 Jerry Stackhouse .40 1.00
140 Glen Rice .40 1.00
141 Chris Mullin .40 1.00
142 Anthony Peeler .25 .60
143 Alonzo Mourning .60 1.50
144 Tom Gugliotta .30 .75
145 Tim Thomas .30 .75
146 Damon Stoudamire .40 1.00
147 Jayson Williams .25 .60
148 Larry Johnson .40 1.00
149 Chris Webber .50 1.25
150 Matt Harpring .25 .60
151 David Robinson .75 2.00
152 George Lynch .25 .60
153 Gary Payton .60 1.50
154 John Wallace .25 .60
155 Greg Ostertag .25 .60
156 Mitch Richmond .50 1.25
157 Cherokee Parks .25 .60
158 Steve Smith .30 .75
159 Gary Trent .25 .60
160 Antoine Walker .40 1.00
161 Johnny Taylor .25 .60
162 Brad Miller .30 .75
163 Chris Mills .25 .60
164 Charles Jones RC .25 .60
165 Hakeem Olajuwon .75 2.00
166 Bob Sura .25 .60
167 Brian Skinner .25 .60
168 Korleone Young .25 .60
169 Tyronn Lue .25 .60
170 Jalen Rose .30 .75
171 Joe Smith .30 .75
172 Clarence Weatherspoon .25 .60
173 Jason Kidd .60 1.50
174 Robert Traylor .25 .60
175 Rasheed Wallace .50 1.25
176 Latrell Sprewell .50 1.25
177 Corliss Williamson .25 .60
178 Bo Outlaw .25 .60
179 Malik Rose .25 .60
180 Nazr Mohammed .25 .60
181 Olden Polynice .25 .60
182 Kevin Willis .25 .60
183 Bryon Russell .25 .60
184 Bryant Reeves .25 .60
185 Rod Strickland .30 .75
186 Samaki Walker .25 .60
187 Nick Van Exel .30 .75
188 David Wesley .25 .60
189 John Starks .40 1.00
190 Toni Kukoc .50 1.25
191 Scottie Pippen 1.00 2.50
192 Zydrunas Ilgauskas .30 .75
193 Maurice Taylor .25 .60
194 Rik Smits .30 .75
195 Clifford Robinson .25 .60
196 Bonzi Wells .25 .60
197 Charlie Ward .25 .60
198 Detlef Schrempf .30 .75
199 Theo Ratliff .30 .75
200 Rodrick Rhodes .40 1.00
201 Ron Artest RC 1.00 2.50
202 William Avery RC .25 .60
203 Elton Brand RC .75 2.00
204 Baron Davis RC 1.00 2.50
205 Jumaine Jones RC .25 .60
206 Andre Miller RC .75 2.00
207 Lee Nailon RC .40 1.00
208 James Posey RC .40 1.00
209 Jason Terry RC .60 1.50
210 Kenny Thomas RC .40 1.00
211 Steve Francis RC .75 2.00
212 Wally Szczerbiak RC .60 1.50
213 Richard Hamilton RC 1.00 2.50
214 Jonathan Bender RC .40 1.00
215 Shawn Marion RC .75 2.00
216 A.Radojevic RC .25 .60
217 Tim James RC .25 .60
218 Trajan Langdon RC .30 .75
219 Lamar Odom RC .75 2.00
220 Corey Maggette RC 1.25 3.00
NNO Checklist #1 .20 .50
NNO Checklist #3 .20 .50
NNO Checklist #2 .20 .50

1999-00 Fleer Roundball Collection
*ROUND: 1X TO 2.5X BASE CARD HI
ONE PER RETAIL PACK

1999-00 Fleer Supreme Court Collection
*STARS: 50X TO 125X BASE CARD HI
*RCs: 20X TO 50X BASE HI
STATED PRINT RUN 20 SERIAL #'d SETS
2SC Kobe Bryant 500.00 1,000.00
4SC Tim Duncan 75.00 200.00
5SC Grant Hill 100.00 250.00
7SC Anfernee Hardaway 75.00 200.00
51SC Shaquille O'Neal 125.00 300.00

1999-00 Fleer Fresh Ink
STATED PRINT RUN 400 SERIAL #'d SETS
1 Corey Benjamin 4.00 10.00
2 Mike Bibby 6.00 15.00
3 Michael Dickerson 4.00 10.00
4 Michael Doleac 4.00 10.00
5 Bryce Drew 4.00 10.00
6 Pat Garrity 4.00 10.00
7 Matt Harpring 4.00 10.00
8 Larry Hughes 6.00 15.00
9 Antawn Jamison 6.00 15.00
10 Raef LaFrentz 4.00 10.00
11 Felipe Lopez 4.00 10.00
12 Jelani McCoy 4.00 10.00
13 Brad Miller 6.00 15.00
14 Michael Olowokandi 4.00 10.00
15 Robert Traylor 4.00 10.00

1999-00 Fleer Game Breakers
PRINT RUN 100 SERIAL #'d SETS
1 Shareef Abdur-Rahim 125.00 300.00
2 Kobe Bryant 1,500.00 3,000.00
3 Vince Carter 400.00 800.00
4 Tim Duncan 500.00 1,000.00
5 Kevin Garnett 500.00 1,000.00
6 Anfernee Hardaway 500.00 1,000.00
7 Grant Hill 400.00 800.00
8 Allen Iverson 500.00 1,000.00
9 Shawn Kemp 200.00 500.00
10 Stephon Marbury 150.00 400.00
11 Ron Mercer 40.00 100.00
12 Shaquille O'Neal 500.00 1,000.00
13 Keith Van Horn 125.00 300.00
14 Antoine Walker 125.00 300.00
15 Jason Williams 400.00 800.00

1999-00 Fleer Masters of the Hardwood
COMPLETE SET (15) 15.00 30.00
STATED ODDS 1:18
1 Shareef Abdur-Rahim 1.00 2.50
2 Mike Bibby 1.00 2.50
3 Kobe Bryant 8.00 20.00
4 Tim Duncan 2.50 6.00
5 Kevin Garnett 2.50 6.00
6 Anfernee Hardaway 2.50 6.00
7 Grant Hill 1.50 4.00
8 Allen Iverson 2.50 6.00
9 Karl Malone 2.00 5.00
10 Stephon Marbury 1.25 3.00
11 Tracy McGrady 1.50 4.00
12 Ron Mercer .75 2.00
13 Scottie Pippen 2.50 6.00
14 Antoine Walker 1.00 2.50
15 Jason Williams 1.50 4.00

1999-00 Fleer Net Effect
COMPLETE SET (10) 12.00 30.00
STATED ODDS 1:96
1 Kobe Bryant 8.00 20.00
2 Vince Carter 2.50 6.00
3 Tim Duncan 2.50 6.00
4 Kevin Garnett 2.50 6.00
5 Grant Hill 1.50 4.00
6 Allen Iverson 2.50 6.00
7 Shaquille O'Neal 4.00 10.00
8 Paul Pierce 2.00 5.00
9 Scottie Pippen 2.50 6.00
10 Keith Van Horn .75 2.00

1999-00 Fleer Rookie Sensations
COMPLETE SET (20) 8.00 20.00
STATED ODDS 1:5
1 Mike Bibby .75 2.00
2 Vince Carter 2.00 5.00
3 Ricky Davis .75 2.00
4 Michael Dickerson .50 1.25
5 Michael Doleac .50 1.25
6 Matt Harpring .50 1.25
7 Larry Hughes .60 1.50
8 Randell Jackson .50 1.25
9 Antawn Jamison .75 2.00
10 Raef LaFrentz .60 1.50
11 Felipe Lopez .50 1.25
12 Roshown McLeod .50 1.25
13 Brad Miller .60 1.50
14 Cuttino Mobley .60 1.50
15 Dirk Nowitzki 2.50 6.00
16 Michael Olowokandi .50 1.25
17 Paul Pierce 1.50 4.00
18 Peja Stojakovic .75 2.00
19 Robert Traylor .50 1.25
20 Jason Williams 1.25 3.00

2000-01 Fleer
CARTER OSR STCKR: STATED ODDS 1:36
1 Lamar Odom .30 .75
2 Christian Laettner .30 .75
3 Michael Olowokandi .20 .50
4 Anthony Carter .20 .50
5 Steve Francis .30 .75
6 Darvin Ham .25 .60
7 Mitch Richmond .40 1.00
8 Corliss Williamson .20 .50
9 Jason Terry .30 .75
10 Brian Grant .25 .60
11 Peja Stojakovic .25 .60
12 Rick Fox .25 .60
13 Tyrone Hill .20 .50
14 Chauncey Billups .40 1.00
15 Otis Thorpe .25 .60
16 Richard Hamilton .40 1.00
17 Ervin Johnson .20 .50
18 Jim Jackson .25 .60
19 Theo Ratliff .25 .60
20 Doug Christie .25 .60
21 Jalen Rose .25 .60
22 John Wallace .20 .50
23 Ruben Patterson .20 .50
24 Steve Nash .50 1.25
25 Toni Kukoc .40 1.00
26 Anthony Peeler .20 .50
27 Ray Allen .50 1.25
28 Adonal Foyle .20 .50
29 Chris Whitney .20 .50
30 Nick Van Exel .30 .75
31 Sean Elliott .25 .60
32 Erick Strickland .20 .50
33 Jerry Stackhouse .30 .75
34 Antawn Jamison .30 .75
35 Grant Hill .50 1.25
36 Antonio Daniels .20 .50
37 Karl Malone .60 1.50
38 Keith Van Horn .25 .60
39 Ron Harper .30 .75
40 Stephon Marbury .40 1.00
41 Bryon Russell .20 .50

42 Corey Maggette .25 .60
43 Hersey Hawkins .20 .50
44 Vince Carter .60 1.50
45 Paul Pierce .50 1.25
46 Mikki Moore RC .30 .75
47 Othella Harrington .20 .50
48 Erick Dampier .20 .50
49 Jerome Williams .20 .50
50 Nick Anderson .25 .60
51 Tim Hardaway .40 1.00
52 Allan Houston .20 .50
53 Tyrone Nesby .20 .50
54 Brevin Knight .20 .50
55 Chris Mills .20 .50
56 Ron Artest .30 .75
57 Walt Williams .20 .50
58 Duane Causwell .20 .50
59 Bonzi Wells .20 .50
60 Rasheed Wallace .40 1.00
61 Dikembe Mutombo .50 1.25
62 Jahidi White .20 .50
63 Chris Webber .40 1.00
64 Tony Battie .20 .50
65 Mahmoud Abdul-Rauf .20 .50
66 Monty Williams .25 .60
67 Charlie Ward .25 .60
68 David Robinson .60 1.50
69 Eric Snow .20 .50
70 Jermaine O'Neal .25 .60
71 Kurt Thomas .20 .50
72 James Posey .20 .50
73 Travis Best .20 .50
74 Jonathan Bender .20 .50
75 John Stockton .60 1.50
76 Jacque Vaughn .20 .50
77 Ron Mercer .25 .60
78 Shawn Marion .30 .75
79 Larry Johnson .40 1.00
80 Maurice Taylor .20 .50
81 Clifford Robinson .30 .75
82 Scot Pollard .20 .50
83 Patrick Ewing .50 1.25
84 Terrell Brandon .25 .60
85 Horace Grant .30 .75
86 Vin Baker .25 .60
87 Al Harrington .25 .60
88 Larry Hughes .30 .75
89 David Wesley .25 .60
90 Wally Szczerbiak .25 .60
91 Charles Oakley .30 .75
92 Tim Thomas .20 .50
93 Mookie Blaylock .30 .75
94 Jamal Mashburn .25 .60
95 Roshown McLeod .20 .50
96 John Starks .30 .75
97 Rodney Rogers .30 .75
98 Juwan Howard .25 .60
99 Isaiah Rider .25 .60
100 Rashard Lewis .25 .60
101 Dion Glover .20 .50
102 Johnny Newman .20 .50
103 Avery Johnson .25 .60
104 Darrell Armstrong .20 .50
105 Eric Williams .20 .50
106 Gary Payton .50 1.25
107 Antonio Davis .25 .60
108 Dirk Nowitzki .75 2.00
109 Trajan Langdon .20 .50
110 Michael Dickerson .20 .50
111 Joe Smith .25 .60
112 Rod Strickland .20 .50
113 Shawn Kemp .50 1.25
114 Voshon Lenard .20 .50
115 Marcus Camby .25 .60
116 Matt Harpring .20 .50
117 Isaac Austin .20 .50
118 Malik Rose .20 .50
119 Pat Garrity .20 .50
120 Kenny Thomas .20 .50
121 LaPhonso Ellis .25 .60
122 Danny Fortson .25 .60
123 Elton Brand .30 .75
124 Jason Williams .50 1.25
125 Kobe Bryant 2.50 6.00
126 Tariq Abdul-Wahad .20 .50
127 Tracy McGrady .60 1.50
128 Matt Geiger .20 .50
129 Antoine Walker .30 .75
130 Michael Finley .30 .75
131 Andre Miller .25 .60
132 Robert Horry .30 .75
133 Donyell Marshall .25 .60
134 Shareef Abdur-Rahim .30 .75
135 Vonteego Cummings .20 .50
136 Anthony Mason .30 .75
137 Mike Bibby .30 .75
138 Raef LaFrentz .25 .60
139 Glen Rice .30 .75
140 Chris Gatling .20 .50
141 Latrell Sprewell .40 1.00
142 Austin Croshere .20 .50
143 Kenny Anderson .25 .60
144 Elden Campbell .20 .50
145 Jason Kidd .50 1.25
146 Michael Doleac .20 .50
147 Muggsy Bogues .30 .75
148 Tim Duncan .75 2.00
149 Samaki Walker .20 .50
150 Gary Trent .20 .50
151 Kevin Garnett .75 2.00
152 Allen Iverson .75 2.00
153 Anfernee Hardaway .50 1.25
154 Robert Traylor .20 .50
155 Scottie Pippen .75 2.00
156 Shaquille O'Neal 1.25 3.00
157 Vlade Divac .30 .75
158 Lucious Harris .20 .50
159 Keon Clark .20 .50
160 Bo Outlaw .20 .50
161 P.J. Brown .20 .50
162 Derrick Coleman .30 .75
163 Mark Jackson .25 .60
164 Lamond Murray .20 .50
165 Dan Majerle .30 .75
166 Eddie Jones .30 .75
167 Cedric Ceballos .25 .60
168 Kendall Gill .30 .75
169 Tom Gugliotta .25 .60
170 Jeff McInnis .20 .50
171 Steve Smith .30 .75
172 Kevin Willis .20 .50
173 Lindsey Hunter .20 .50
174 Derek Anderson .25 .60
175 Shandon Anderson .20 .50
176 Adrian Griffin .20 .50
177 Baron Davis .30 .75
178 Radoslav Nesterovic .20 .50
179 Glenn Robinson .30 .75
180 Sam Cassell .25 .60
181 Chucky Atkins .20 .50
182 Arvydas Sabonis .30 .75
183 Damon Stoudamire .30 .75
184 Antonio McDyess .25 .60
185 Derek Fisher .30 .75
186 Bryant Reeves .20 .50
187 Hakeem Olajuwon .60 1.50
188 Kerry Kittles .25 .60
189 Alan Henderson .20 .50
190 Sam Perkins .20 .50
191 Felipe Lopez .20 .50
192 Tracy Murray .20 .50
193 Shammond Williams .20 .50
194 Vitaly Potapenko .20 .50
195 John Amaechi .20 .50
196 Quincy Lewis .20 .50
197 Reggie Miller .60 1.50
198 Cuttino Mobley .25 .60
199 Rex Chapman .25 .60
200 Dale Davis .25 .60
201 Andrew DeClercq .20 .50
202 Kelvin Cato .20 .50
203 Jon Barry .20 .50
204 Greg Anthony .20 .50
205 Brent Barry .25 .60
206 Derrick McKey .20 .50
207 Vince Carter UH .60 1.50
208 David Robinson UH .60 1.50
209 Eric Snow UH .20 .50
210 Ray Allen UH .50 1.25
211 Lamar Odom UH .30 .75
212 Dikembe Mutombo UH .50 1.25
213 Brevin Knight UH .20 .50
214 Vin Baker UH .25 .60
215 Antoine Walker UH .30 .75
216 Mitch Richmond UH .40 1.00
217 Elton Brand UH .30 .75
218 Jerome Williams UH .20 .50
219 Keith Van Horn UH .25 .60
220 Nick Van Exel UH .25 .60
221 Shaquille O'Neal UH 1.25 3.00
222 Allan Houston UH .30 .75
223 Shareef Abdur-Rahim UH .30 .75
224 Karl Malone UH .60 1.50
225 Terrell Brandon UH .25 .60
226 Eddie Jones UH .30 .75
227 Stromile Swift RC .25 .60
228 Dalibor Bagaric RC .25 .60
229 Erick Barkley RC .25 .60
230 Mike Miller RC .50 1.25
231 Kenyon Martin RC .60 1.50
232 Michael Redd RC .75 2.00
233 Darius Miles RC .30 .75
234 Chris Mihm RC .30 .75
235 Brian Cardinal RC .20 .50
236 Khalid El-Amin RC .20 .50
237 Hanno Mottola RC .20 .50
238 Jamaal Magloire RC .30 .75
239 Courtney Alexander RC .20 .50
240 Mamadou N'Diaye RC .20 .50
241 Chris Porter RC .20 .50
242 Quentin Richardson RC .25 .60
243 Eddie House RC .25 .60
244 Joel Przybilla RC .25 .60
245 Soumaila Samake RC .20 .50
246 Speedy Claxton RC .30 .75
247 Desmond Mason RC .40 1.00
248 Mike Smith RC .20 .50
249 Lavor Postell RC .20 .50
250 Ruben Garces RC .30 .75
251 DeShawn Stevenson RC .30 .75
252 Hedo Turkoglu RC .50 1.25
253 Keyon Dooling RC .25 .60
254 Dan Langhi RC .20 .50
255 Mateen Cleaves RC .25 .60
256 Donnell Harvey RC .25 .60
257 DerMarr Johnson RC .20 .50
258 Jason Collier RC .30 .75
259 Jake Voskuhl RC .20 .50
260 Mark Madsen RC .30 .75
261 Pepe Sanchez RC .25 .60
262 Morris Peterson RC .30 .75
263 Daniel Santiago RC .30 .75
264 Etan Thomas RC .25 .60
265 A.J. Guyton RC .20 .50
266 Marcus Fizer RC .20 .50
267 Jamal Crawford RC .75 2.00
268 Jerome Moiso RC .20 .50
269 Olumide Oyedeji RC .20 .50
270 Paul McPherson RC .20 .50
271 Eduardo Najera RC .30 .75
272 Dallas Mavericks CL .05 .15
273 Denver Nuggets CL .05 .15
274 Houston Rockets CL .10 .30
275 Minnesota Timberwolves CL .10 .30
276 San Antonio Spurs CL .10 .30
277 Utah Jazz CL .10 .30
278 Vancouver Grizzlies CL .10 .30
279 Golden State Warriors CL .10 .30
280 Los Angeles Clippers CL .10 .30
281 Los Angeles Lakers CL .20 .50
282 Phoenix Suns CL .10 .30
283 Portland Trail Blazers CL .10 .30
284 Sacramento Kings CL .10 .30
285 Seattle Supersonics CL .10 .30
286 Boston Celtics CL .05 .15
287 Miami Heat CL .05 .15
288 New Jersey Nets CL .10 .30
289 New York Knicks CL .10 .30
290 Orlando Magic CL .20 .50
291 Philadelphia 76ers CL .05 .15
292 Washington Wizards CL .05 .15
293 Atlanta Hawks CL .05 .15
294 Charlotte Hornets CL .05 .15
295 Chicago Bulls CL .10 .30
296 Cleveland Cavaliers CL .05 .15
297 Detroit Pistons CL .05 .15
298 Indiana Pacers CL .10 .30
299 Milwaukee Bucks CL .05 .15
300 Toronto Raptors CL .20 .50
NNO Vince Carter OSR Sticker 2.00 5.00
NNO Vince Carter OSR/1986 8.00 20.00
NNO Vince Carter OSR AU/15 20.00 50.00

2000-01 Fleer Stickers

*STARS: 3X TO 8X BASE HI
*RCs: 2X TO 5X BASE HI
*CL: 8X TO 20X BASE HI
STATED ODDS 1:36

2000-01 Fleer Autographics

FOCUS STATED ODDS 1:48
GAME TIME STATED ODDS 1:287
GENUINE STATED ODDS 1:23
GLOSSY: AUTO OR GAME WORN 1:48
GLOSSY STATED ODDS 1:96 RETAIL
HOOPS STATED ODDS 1:72
MYSTIQUE STATED ODDS 1:48
PREMIUM STATED ODDS 1:288
ULTRA STATED ODDS 1:48
NNO CARDS LISTED BELOW ALPHABETICALLY
*GOLD: .75X TO 2X BASE AUTO HI
GOLD PRINT RUN 50 SER.#'d SETS
*SILVER: .5X TO 1.25X BASE AUTO HI
SILVER PRINT RUN 250 SER.#'d SETS
1 Darrell Armstrong 4.00 10.00
2 Ron Artest 10.00 25.00
3 Chucky Atkins 4.00 10.00
4 Travis Best 4.00 10.00
5 Mike Bibby 6.00 15.00
6 Muggsy Bogues 12.00 30.00
7 P.J. Brown 4.00 10.00
8 Elden Campbell 4.00 10.00
9 Vince Carter 125.00 300.00
10 Jason Collier 6.00 15.00
11 Baron Davis 6.00 15.00
12 Andrew DeClercq 4.00 10.00
13 Michael Dickerson 4.00 10.00
14 Vlade Divac 6.00 15.00
15 Michael Doleac 4.00 10.00
16 Dion Glover 4.00 10.00
17 Brian Grant 5.00 12.00
18 Adrian Griffin 4.00 10.00
19 Tom Gugliotta 5.00 12.00
20 Richard Hamilton 12.00 30.00
21 Al Harrington 5.00 12.00
22 Othella Harrington 4.00 10.00
23 Jason Hart 6.00 15.00
24 Allen Iverson 200.00 500.00
25 Antawn Jamison 6.00 15.00
26 Brevin Knight 4.00 10.00
27 Toni Kukoc 12.00 30.00
28 Raef LaFrentz 5.00 12.00
29 Dan Langhi 4.00 10.00
30 Voshon Lenard 4.00 10.00
31 Quincy Lewis 4.00 10.00
32 George Lynch 4.00 10.00
33 Corey Maggette 5.00 12.00
34 Stephon Marbury 12.00 30.00
35 Shawn Marion 6.00 15.00
36 Donyell Marshall 5.00 12.00
37 Jamal Mashburn 5.00 12.00
38 Tracy McGrady 75.00 200.00
39 Ron Mercer 5.00 12.00
40 Andre Miller 5.00 12.00
41 Reggie Miller 75.00 200.00
42 Alonzo Mourning 40.00 100.00
43 Dirk Nowitzki 150.00 400.00
44 Lamar Odom 6.00 15.00
45 Hakeem Olajuwon 75.00 200.00
46 Jermaine O'Neal 5.00 12.00
47 Ruben Patterson 4.00 10.00
48 Scot Pollard 4.00 10.00
49 Theo Ratliff 4.00 10.00
50 Michael Redd 15.00 40.00
51 Eddie Robinson 4.00 10.00
52 Glenn Robinson 10.00 25.00
53 Steve Smith 6.00 15.00
54 Jerry Stackhouse 12.00 30.00
55 Jason Terry 6.00 15.00
56 Kenny Thomas 4.00 10.00
57 Keith Van Horn 5.00 12.00
58 Antoine Walker 6.00 15.00
59 Shareef Abdur-Rahim 6.00 15.00
60 Howard Eisley 4.00 10.00
61 Austin Croshere 4.00 10.00
62 Kurt Thomas 4.00 10.00
63 Pat Garrity 4.00 10.00

2000-01 Fleer Vince Carter Rookie Remnants

NNO Vince Carter FLR/100 15.00 40.00
NNO Vince Carter FLR JSY/15 40.00 100.00

2000-01 Fleer Courting History

COMPLETE SET (10) 6.00 15.00
STATED ODDS 1:18
CH1 Vince Carter 1.00 2.50
CH2 Shaquille O'Neal 2.00 5.00
CH3 Grant Hill .75 2.00
CH4 Kobe Bryant 4.00 10.00
CH5 Tim Duncan 1.25 3.00
CH6 Jason Kidd .75 2.00
CH7 Kevin Garnett 1.25 3.00
CH8 Allen Iverson 1.25 3.00
CH9 Steve Francis .50 1.25
CH10 Elton Brand .50 1.25

2000-01 Fleer Feel the Game

EX STATED ODDS 1:72
FOCUS STATED ODDS 1:48
FUTURES STATED ODDS 1:331
MYSTIQUE STATED ODDS 1:72
PREMIUM STATED ODDS 1:56
SHOWCASE STATED ODDS 1:72
ULTRA STATED ODDS 1:48
NNO CARDS LISTED BELOW ALPHABETICALLY
*GOLD: 1.25X TO 3X BASE HI
GOLD PRINT RUN 50 SER.#'d SETS
*SILVER: .5X TO 1.25X BASE HI
SILVER PRINT RUN 250 SER.#'d SETS
ALL PICTURE VARIATIONS SAME VALUE
1A Shareef Abdur-Rahim White 3.00 8.00
1B Shareef Abdur-Rahim Blue 3.00 8.00
2 Mike Bibby 3.00 8.00
3 Terrell Brandon 2.50 6.00
4 Vince Carter 6.00 15.00
5 Sam Cassell 2.50 6.00
6 Baron Davis 3.00 8.00
7 Michael Finley 3.00 8.00
8 Steve Francis 3.00 8.00
9 Robert Horry 3.00 8.00
10 Allan Houston 3.00 8.00
11A Allen Iverson Black 8.00 20.00
11B Allen Iverson White 8.00 20.00
12 Eddie Jones 3.00 8.00
13 Jason Kidd 5.00 12.00
14 Quincy Lewis 2.00 5.00
15 Tyronn Lue 2.00 5.00
16 George Lynch 2.00 5.00
17 Corey Maggette 2.50 6.00
18A Karl Malone Black 6.00 15.00
18B Karl Malone Purple 6.00 15.00
19A Stephon Marbury Gray 4.00 10.00
19B Stephon Marbury White 4.00 10.00
20 Shawn Marion 3.00 8.00
21 Tracy McGrady 6.00 15.00
22 Reggie Miller 6.00 15.00
23 Alonzo Mourning 5.00 12.00
24A Lamar Odom White 3.00 8.00
24B Lamar Odom Red 3.00 8.00
25 Hakeem Olajuwon 6.00 15.00
26 Michael Olowokandi 2.00 5.00
27A Shaquille O'Neal Purple 12.00 30.00
27B Shaquille O'Neal Yellow 12.00 30.00
27C Shaquille O'Neal Warm-Up 12.00 30.00
28 Scott Padgett 2.00 5.00
29 Gary Payton 5.00 12.00
30 Glenn Robinson 3.00 8.00
31 Joe Smith 2.50 6.00
32 John Stockton 6.00 15.00
33A Jason Terry Red 3.00 8.00
33B Jason Terry Warm-Up 3.00 8.00
34 Keith Van Horn 2.50 6.00
35 Antoine Walker 3.00 8.00
36 Chris Webber 4.00 10.00
37 Jason Williams 5.00 12.00
38 David Robinson SP 6.00 15.00
39 Richard Hamilton 4.00 10.00

2000-01 Fleer Genuine Coverage Nostalgic

STATED ODDS 1:144 HOB, 1:240 RET
1 Courtney Alexander 1.25 3.00
2 Erick Barkley 1.25 3.00
3 Speedy Claxton 2.00 5.00
4 Mateen Cleaves 1.50 4.00
5 Donnell Harvey 1.50 4.00
6 DerMarr Johnson 1.25 3.00
7 Mark Madsen 2.00 5.00
8 Kenyon Martin 4.00 10.00
9 Desmond Mason 2.50 6.00
10 Mike Miller 3.00 8.00
11 Jerome Moiso 1.25 3.00
12 Joel Przybilla 1.50 4.00
13 DeShawn Stevenson 2.00 5.00
14 Stromile Swift 1.50 4.00
15 Etan Thomas 1.50 4.00
16 Hedo Turkoglu 3.00 8.00

2000-01 Fleer Hardcourt Classics

COMPLETE SET (15) 7.50 15.00
STATED ODDS 1:9
HC1 Vince Carter .75 2.00
HC2 Karl Malone .75 2.00
HC3 Kobe Bryant 3.00 8.00
HC4 Tim Duncan 1.00 2.50
HC5 Lamar Odom .40 1.00
HC6 Jason Williams .60 1.50
HC7 Kevin Garnett 1.00 2.50
HC8 Jason Kidd .60 1.50
HC9 Shaquille O'Neal 1.50 4.00
HC10 Chris Webber .50 1.25
HC11 Allen Iverson 1.00 2.50
HC12 Scottie Pippen 1.00 2.50
HC13 Grant Hill .60 1.50
HC14 Elton Brand .40 1.00
HC15 Tracy McGrady .75 2.00

2000-01 Fleer Rookie Retro

COMPLETE SET (20) 8.00 20.00
STATED ODDS 1:36
RR1 Morris Peterson .50 1.25
RR2 DerMarr Johnson .30 .75
RR3 Jerome Moiso .30 .75
RR4 Darius Miles .75 2.00
RR5 Marcus Fizer .40 1.00
RR6 Hedo Turkoglu .75 2.00
RR7 Mateen Cleaves .40 1.00
RR8 Kenyon Martin 1.00 2.50
RR9 Jamaal Magloire .50 1.25
RR10 Keyon Dooling .40 1.00
RR11 DeShawn Stevenson .50 1.25
RR12 Quentin Richardson .40 1.00
RR13 Courtney Alexander .30 .75
RR14 Mark Madsen .50 1.25
RR15 Mike Miller .75 2.00
RR16 Desmond Mason .50 1.25
RR17 Stromile Swift .40 1.00
RR18 Speedy Claxton .50 1.25
RR19 Etan Thomas .40 1.00
RR20 Chris Mihm .30 .75

2000-01 Fleer Sharpshooters

COMPLETE SET (20) 8.00 20.00
STATED ODDS 1:6
SS1 Vince Carter 1.00 2.50
SS2 Wally Szczerbiak .40 1.00
SS3 Kobe Bryant 4.00 10.00
SS4 Eddie Jones .50 1.25
SS5 John Stockton 1.00 2.50
SS6 Ray Allen .75 2.00
SS7 Tracy McGrady 1.00 2.50
SS8 Shareef Abdur-Rahim .50 1.25
SS9 Antoine Walker .50 1.25
SS10 Tim Duncan 1.25 3.00
SS11 Larry Hughes .50 1.25
SS12 Gary Payton .75 2.00
SS13 Dirk Nowitzki 1.25 3.00
SS14 Grant Hill .75 2.00
SS15 Scottie Pippen 1.25 3.00
SS16 Chris Webber .60 1.50
SS17 Stephon Marbury .60 1.50
SS18 Anfernee Hardaway .75 2.00
SS19 Reggie Miller 1.00 2.50
SS20 Steve Francis .50 1.25

2006-07 Fleer

COMPLETE SET (250) 30.00 70.00
COMP.SET w/o RC's (200) 10.00 25.00
RC ODDS APPROXIMATELY ONE PER PACK
ONE ORIGINAL FLEER CARD PER BOX
1 Josh Childress .15 .40
2 Al Harrington .20 .50
3 Joe Johnson .25 .60
4 Tyronn Lue .15 .40
5 Josh Smith .15 .40
6 Salim Stoudamire .15 .40
7 Marvin Williams .15 .40
8 Tony Allen .15 .40
9 Dan Dickau .15 .40
10 Al Jefferson .15 .40
11 Michael Olowokandi .15 .40
12 Paul Pierce .40 1.00
13 Wally Szczerbiak .20 .50
14 Gerald Green .20 .50
15 Raymond Felton .15 .40
16 Brevin Knight .15 .40
17 Sean May .15 .40
18 Emeka Okafor .20 .50
19 Othella Harrington .15 .40
20 Gerald Wallace .20 .50
21 Tyson Chandler .20 .50
22 Luol Deng .20 .50
23 Chris Duhon .15 .40
24 Ben Gordon .20 .50
25 Kirk Hinrich .20 .50
26 Mike Sweetney .15 .40
27 Michael Jordan 2.00 5.00
28 Drew Gooden .20 .50
29 Larry Hughes .20 .50
30 Zydrunas Ilgauskas .20 .50
31 Damon Jones .15 .40
32 LeBron James 2.00 5.00
33 Donyell Marshall .15 .40
34 Anderson Varejao .15 .40
35 Erick Dampier .15 .40
36 Marquis Daniels .15 .40
37 Devin Harris .15 .40
38 Josh Howard .20 .50
39 Dirk Nowitzki .60 1.50
40 Jerry Stackhouse .20 .50
41 Jason Terry .20 .50
42 Carmelo Anthony .40 1.00
43 Marcus Camby .20 .50
44 Reggie Evans .15 .40
45 Kenyon Martin .20 .50
46 Andre Miller .20 .50
47 Eduardo Najera .15 .40
48 Nene .20 .50
49 Chauncey Billups .30 .75
50 Richard Hamilton .25 .60
51 Jason Maxiell .15 .40
52 Antonio McDyess .20 .50
53 Tayshaun Prince .25 .60
54 Ben Wallace .30 .75
55 Rasheed Wallace .30 .75
56 Baron Davis .25 .60
57 Ike Diogu .15 .40
58 Mike Dunleavy .15 .40
59 Derek Fisher .25 .60
60 Adonal Foyle .15 .40
61 Troy Murphy .20 .50
62 Jason Richardson .25 .60
63 Rafer Alston .15 .40
64 Chuck Hayes .15 .40
65 Luther Head .15 .40
66 Juwan Howard .20 .50
67 Tracy McGrady .40 1.00
68 Stromile Swift .15 .40
69 Yao Ming .60 1.50
70 Austin Croshere .15 .40
71 Danny Granger .15 .40
72 Sarunas Jasikevicius .20 .50
73 Stephen Jackson .20 .50
74 Jermaine O'Neal .25 .60
75 Peja Stojakovic .25 .60
76 Jamaal Tinsley .15 .40
77 Elton Brand .20 .50
78 Sam Cassell .20 .50
79 Chris Kaman .15 .40
80 Yaroslav Korolev .15 .40
81 Shaun Livingston .20 .50
82 Corey Maggette .20 .50
83 Cuttino Mobley .20 .50
84 Kwame Brown .15 .40
85 Kobe Bryant 2.00 5.00
86 Andrew Bynum .15 .40
87 Devean George .15 .40
88 Lamar Odom .20 .50
89 Ronny Turiaf .20 .50
90 Luke Walton .15 .40
91 Shane Battier .20 .50
92 Pau Gasol .40 1.00
93 Bobby Jackson .15 .40
94 Mike Miller .20 .50
95 Lawrence Roberts .15 .40
96 Damon Stoudamire .20 .50
97 Hakim Warrick .15 .40
98 Alonzo Mourning .40 1.00
99 Shaquille O'Neal 1.00 2.50
100 Gary Payton .30 .75
101 Wayne Simien .15 .40
102 Dwyane Wade .50 1.25
103 Antoine Walker .25 .60
104 Jason Williams .30 .75
105 Andrew Bogut .20 .50
106 T.J. Ford .15 .40
107 Jamaal Magloire .15 .40
108 Michael Redd .20 .50
109 Bobby Simmons .15 .40
110 Maurice Williams .20 .50
111 Mark Blount .15 .40
112 Ricky Davis .20 .50
113 Kevin Garnett .60 1.50
114 Eddie Griffin .15 .40
115 Troy Hudson .15 .40
116 Rashad McCants .15 .40
117 Vince Carter .50 1.25
118 Jason Collins .15 .40
119 Richard Jefferson .20 .50
120 Jason Kidd .40 1.00
121 Nenad Krstic .15 .40
122 Jeff McInnis .15 .40
123 Antoine Wright .15 .40
124 Brandon Bass .20 .50
125 David West .20 .50
126 Desmond Mason .15 .40
127 Chris Paul .50 1.25
128 J.R. Smith .25 .60
129 Kirk Snyder .15 .40
130 Jamal Crawford .25 .60
131 Steve Francis .25 .60
132 Channing Frye .15 .40
133 Stephon Marbury .30 .75
134 Quentin Richardson .15 .40
135 Nate Robinson .20 .50
136 Jalen Rose .20 .50
137 Carlos Arroyo .15 .40
138 Keyon Dooling .15 .40
139 Grant Hill .40 1.00
140 Dwight Howard .30 .75
141 Darko Milicic .15 .40
142 Jameer Nelson .15 .40
143 DeShawn Stevenson .15 .40
144 Samuel Dalembert .15 .40
145 Steven Hunter .15 .40
146 Andre Iguodala .25 .60
147 Allen Iverson .60 1.50
148 Kyle Korver .20 .50
149 Chris Webber .30 .75
150 Leandro Barbosa .20 .50
151 Raja Bell .20 .50
152 Boris Diaw .20 .50
153 Shawn Marion .25 .60
154 Steve Nash .50 1.25
155 Amare Stoudemire .25 .60
156 Kurt Thomas .15 .40
157 Steve Blake .15 .40
158 Juan Dixon .15 .40
159 Joel Przybilla .15 .40
160 Zach Randolph .25 .60
161 Travis Outlaw .20 .50
162 Sebastian Telfair .15 .40
163 Martell Webster .20 .50
164 Shareef Abdur-Rahim .25 .60
165 Ron Artest .25 .60
166 Mike Bibby .25 .60
167 Francisco Garcia .15 .40
168 Brad Miller .20 .50
169 Kenny Thomas .15 .40
170 Bonzi Wells .15 .40
171 Bruce Bowen .20 .50
172 Tim Duncan .60 1.50
173 Michael Finley .25 .60
174 Manu Ginobili .50 1.25
175 Tony Parker .40 1.00
176 Ray Allen .40 1.00
177 Danny Fortson .15 .40
178 Rashard Lewis .20 .50
179 Luke Ridnour .20 .50
180 Robert Swift .15 .40
181 Chris Wilcox .15 .40
182 Chris Bosh .30 .75
183 Jose Calderon .15 .40
184 Joey Graham .15 .40
185 Pape Sow .15 .40
186 Charlie Villanueva .15 .40
187 Morris Peterson .15 .40
188 Carlos Boozer .20 .50
189 Gordan Giricek .15 .40
190 Kris Humphries .15 .40
191 Andrei Kirilenko .20 .50
192 Mehmet Okur .15 .40
193 Deron Williams .20 .50
194 Gilbert Arenas .25 .60
195 Andray Blatche .15 .40
196 Caron Butler .20 .50
197 Brendan Haywood .15 .40
198 Antawn Jamison .20 .50
199 Etan Thomas .15 .40
200 Antonio Daniels .15 .40
201 Tyrus Thomas RC .50 1.25
202 Adam Morrison RC .50 1.25
203 LaMarcus Aldridge RC 1.50 4.00
204 Rudy Gay RC .75 2.00
205 Andrea Bargnani RC .50 1.25
206 Rodney Carney RC RC .40 1.00
207 Alexander Johnson RC .40 1.00
208 Brandon Roy RC 1.25 3.00
209 Patrick O'Bryant RC .40 1.00
210 Randy Foye RC .50 1.25
211 Ronnie Brewer RC .60 1.50
212 Mardy Collins RC .40 1.00
213 Shelden Williams RC .40 1.00
214 J.J. Redick RC 1.25 3.00
215 Hilton Armstrong RC .40 1.00
216 Marcus Williams RC .40 1.00
217 Rajon Rondo RC 2.00 5.00
218 Cedric Simmons RC .40 1.00
219 Bobby Jones RC .40 1.00
220 Jordan Farmar RC .50 1.25
221 Maurice Ager RC .40 1.00
222 David Noel RC .40 1.00
223 James White RC .40 1.00
224 Leon Powe RC .40 1.00
225 Paul Millsap RC .75 2.00
226 Josh Boone RC .40 1.00
227 Kevin Pittsnogle RC .50 1.25
228 Daniel Gibson RC .50 1.25
229 Hassan Adams RC .40 1.00
230 Kyle Lowry RC 2.00 5.00
231 Renaldo Balkman RC .50 1.25
232 Dee Brown RC .40 1.00
233 Shawne Williams RC .40 1.00
234 P.J. Tucker RC .60 1.50
235 Craig Smith RC .50 1.25
236 Paul Davis RC .40 1.00
237 Pops Mensah-Bonsu RC .40 1.00
238 Denham Brown RC .40 1.00
239 Ryan Hollins RC .40 1.00
240 Allan Ray RC .40 1.00
241 Saer Sene RC .40 1.00
242 Shannon Brown RC .40 1.00
243 Thabo Sefolosha RC .50 1.2
244 Quincy Douby RC .40 1.0
245 Solomon Jones RC .40 1.0
246 Damir Markota RC .40 1.0
247 Steve Novak RC .50 1.2
248 Will Blalock RC .40 1.0
249 Tarence Kinsey RC .40 1.0
250 Vassilis Spanoulis RC .40 1.0
NNO Michael Jordan .40 1.0

2006-07 Fleer Glossy Parallel

*GLOSSY: .75X TO 2X BASE HI
27 Michael Jordan 5.00 12.0

2006-07 Fleer 1986-87 20th Anniversary

APPROXIMATE ODDS 1:2
1 Nene 1.25 3.0
2 Andrea Bargnani 1.25 3.0
3 Maurice Ager 1.00 2.50
4 Allen Iverson 4.00 10.00
5 Antawn Jamison 1.25 3.00
6 Andrei Kirilenko 1.25 3.00
7 Adam Morrison 1.25 3.00
8 Amare Stoudemire 1.50 4.00
9 Shane Battier 1.25 3.0
10 Baron Davis 1.50 4.00
11 Ben Gordon 1.25 3.0
12 Chauncey Billups 2.00 5.00
13 Steve Blake 1.00 2.50
14 Brad Miller 1.25 3.00
15 Andrew Bogut 1.25 3.00
16 Brandon Roy 3.00 8.00
17 Bobby Simmons 1.00 2.50
18 Ben Wallace 40.00 100.00
19 Andrew Bynum 1.00 2.50
20 Carmelo Anthony 15.00 40.00
21 Chris Bosh 12.00 30.00
22 Channing Frye 1.00 2.50
23 Josh Childress 1.00 2.50
24 Chris Kaman 1.00 2.50
25 Cuttino Mobley 1.25 3.00
26 Chris Paul 20.00 50.00
27 Cedric Simmons 1.00 2.50
28 Charlie Villanueva 1.00 2.50
29 Dwight Howard 2.00 5.00
30 Boris Diaw 1.25 3.00
31 Dirk Nowitzki 20.00 50.00
32 Mike Dunleavy 1.00 2.50
33 Dwyane Wade 20.00 50.00
34 Elton Brand 1.25 3.00
35 Eddy Curry 1.25 3.00
36 Fred Jones 1.00 2.50
37 Randy Foye 1.25 3.00
38 Gilbert Arenas 1.50 4.00
39 Gerald Green 1.25 3.00
40 Grant Hill 2.50 6.00
41 Hilton Armstrong 1.00 2.50
42 Hedo Turkoglu 1.50 4.00
43 Larry Hughes 1.25 3.00
44 Hakim Warrick 1.00 2.50
45 Andre Iguodala 1.50 4.00
46 Josh Boone 1.00 2.50
47 Jamal Crawford 1.50 4.00
48 Al Jefferson 1.00 2.50
49 Jordan Farmar 1.25 3.00
50 Josh Howard 1.25 3.00
51 Joe Johnson 1.50 4.00
52 Jason Kidd 2.50 6.00
53 Jermaine O'Neal 1.50 4.00
54 Jason Richardson 1.50 4.00
55 Jerry Stackhouse 1.25 3.00
56 Jason Terry 1.25 3.00
57 Michael Jordan 200.00 500.00
58 Kobe Bryant 100.00 250.00
59 Kevin Garnett 20.00 50.00
60 Kirk Hinrich 1.25 3.00
61 Kyle Korver 1.25 3.00
62 Kyle Lowry 5.00 12.00
63 Kenyon Martin 1.25 3.00
64 Kevin Pittsnogle 1.25 3.00
65 Kirk Snyder 1.00 2.50
66 Kurt Thomas 1.00 2.50
67 LaMarcus Aldridge 4.00 10.00
68 Luol Deng 1.25 3.00
69 Rashard Lewis 1.25 3.00
70 Luther Head 1.00 2.50
71 LeBron James 100.00 250.00
72 Lamar Odom 1.25 3.00
73 Luke Ridnour 1.25 3.00
74 Luke Walton 1.00 2.50
75 Shawn Marion 1.50 4.00
76 Mike Bibby 1.50 4.00
77 Mardy Collins 1.00 2.50
78 Marquis Daniels 1.00 2.50
79 Manu Ginobili 8.00 20.00
80 Andre Miller 1.25 3.00
81 Jason Williams 2.00 5.00
82 Mehmet Okur 1.00 2.50
83 Morris Peterson 1.00 2.50
84 Michael Redd 1.25 3.00
85 Troy Murphy 1.00 2.50
86 Marcus Williams 1.00 2.50
87 Nate Robinson 1.25 3.00
88 Tony Parker 2.50 6.00
89 Pau Gasol 2.50 6.00
90 Patrick O'Bryant 1.00 2.50
91 Paul Pierce 15.00 40.00
92 Peja Stojakovic 1.25 3.00
93 P.J. Tucker 1.50 4.00
94 Quincy Douby 1.00 2.50
95 Ray Allen 2.50 6.00
96 Ronnie Brewer 1.50 4.00
97 Rodney Carney 1.00 2.50
98 Ricky Davis 1.25 3.00
99 J.J. Redick 3.00 8.00
100 Raymond Felton 1.00 2.50
101 Rudy Gay 2.00 5.00
102 Richard Hamilton 1.50 4.00
103 Richard Jefferson 1.25 3.00
104 Raef LaFrentz 1.00 2.50
105 Rashad McCants 1.00 2.50
106 Jalen Rose 1.25 3.00
107 Rajon Rondo 5.00 12.00
108 Rasheed Wallace 2.00 5.00
109 Shannon Brown 1.00 2.50
110 Sam Cassell 1.25 3.00

111 Samuel Dalembert 1.00 2.50
112 Steve Francis 1.50 4.00
113 Sean May 1.00 2.50
114 Steve Nash 20.00 50.00
115 Shaquille O'Neal 20.00 50.00
116 Saer Sene 1.00 2.50
117 Stephon Marbury 2.00 5.00
118 Shelden Williams 1.00 2.50
119 Tyson Chandler 1.25 3.00
120 Tim Duncan 20.00 50.00
121 Tracy McGrady 12.00 30.00
122 Tayshaun Prince 1.50 4.00
123 Thabo Sefolosha 1.25 3.00
124 Tyrus Thomas 1.25 3.00
125 Udonis Haslem 1.00 2.50
126 Vince Carter 3.00 8.00
127 Bonzi Wells 1.00 2.50
128 Deron Williams 1.25 3.00
129 Marvin Williams 1.00 2.50
130 Wally Szczerbiak 1.25 3.00
131 Yao Ming 20.00 50.00
132 Zach Randolph 1.50 4.00

2006-07 Fleer Michael Jordan Buyback Autographs

57 Michael Jordan/23 60,000.00100,000.00

2006-07 Fleer Autographics

AA Alex Acker 5.00 12.00
AB Andrea Bargnani 12.00 30.00
AI Andre Iguodala 8.00 20.00
BB Brent Barry 6.00 15.00
BJ Bobby Jones 5.00 12.00
BO Andrew Bogut SP 6.00 15.00
BS Bobby Simmons 5.00 12.00
CK Chris Kaman SP 6.00 15.00
CP Chris Paul SP 30.00 80.00
CS Cedric Simmons 5.00 12.00
CT Chris Taft 5.00 12.00
DH Dwight Howard SP 15.00 40.00
DN David Noel 5.00 12.00
DW Deron Williams 10.00 25.00
HA Hilton Armstrong 5.00 12.00
JF Jordan Farmar 8.00 20.00
KA Kareem Abdul-Jabbar SP 40.00 100.00
KL Kyle Lowry 6.00 15.00
LA LaMarcus Aldridge 12.00 30.00
LJ LeBron James SP 1,250.00 2,500.00
MA Maurice Ager 5.00 12.00
MC Mardy Collins 5.00 12.00
MW Marcus Williams 5.00 12.00
PM Paul Millsap 8.00 20.00
PS Peja Stojakovic 5.00 12.00
RB Ronnie Brewer 6.00 15.00
RG Rudy Gay 6.00 15.00
RO Brandon Roy 15.00 40.00
RR Rajon Rondo 25.00 60.00
SS Saer Sene 5.00 12.00
TT Tyrus Thomas 10.00 25.00

2006-07 Fleer Autographics Michael Jordan Autographics

COMMON CARD 2,500.00 5,000.00

2006-07 Fleer Jordan's Greatest Moments

COMPLETE SET (10) 20.00 50.00
COMMON CARD 4.00 10.00

2006-07 Fleer Jordan's Platinum Influence

COMPLETE SET (20) 8.00 20.00
APPROXIMATE ODDS 1:3
AH A.J. Hawk 1.00 2.50
BA Renaldo Balkman .75 2.00
BU Reggie Bush 2.50 6.00
HA Hilton Armstrong .60 1.50
JR J.J. Redick 2.00 5.00
LA LaMarcus Aldridge 2.50 6.00
ML Matt Leinart 1.00 2.50
MW Marcus Williams .60 1.50
PO Patrick O'Bryant .60 1.50
QD Quincy Douby .60 1.50
RB Ronnie Brewer 1.00 2.50
RC Rodney Carney .60 1.50
RF Randy Foye .75 2.00
RG Rudy Gay 1.25 3.00
SH Santonio Holmes 1.00 2.50
SW Shelden Williams .60 1.50
TT Tyrus Thomas .75 2.00
VD Vernon Davis 1.00 2.50
VY Vince Young 2.00 5.00
WI Mario Williams 1.00 2.50

2006-07 Fleer Michael Jordan Missing Links

COMMON CARD 80.00 200.00

2006-07 Fleer Rookie Sensations

COMPLETE SET (10) 6.00 15.00
APPROXIMATE ODDS 1:5
AB Andrea Bargnani .50 1.25
AM Adam Morrison .50 1.25
BR Brandon Roy 1.25 3.00
JM Shelden Williams .40 1.00
LA LaMarcus Aldridge 1.50 4.00
PO Patrick O'Bryant .40 1.00
RC Rodney Carney .40 1.00
RF Randy Foye .50 1.25
RG Rudy Gay .75 2.00
TT Tyrus Thomas .50 1.25

2006-07 Fleer Team Leaders

COMPLETE SET (20) 5.00 12.00
APPROXIMATE ODDS 1:2
AI Allen Iverson 1.00 2.50
BD Baron Davis .40 1.00
CB Chauncey Billups .50 1.25
DN Dirk Nowitzki 1.00 2.50
DW Dwyane Wade .75 2.00
EO Emeka Okafor .30 .75
GA Gilbert Arenas .40 1.00
JK Jason Kidd .60 1.50
KB Kobe Bryant 3.00 8.00
KG Kevin Garnett 1.00 2.50
LJ LeBron James 3.00 8.00
MB Mike Bibby .40 1.00
MJ Michael Jordan 3.00 8.00
PP Paul Pierce .60 1.50
RA Ray Allen .60 1.50
SC Sam Cassell .30 .75
SN Steve Nash .75 2.00
SO Shaquille O'Neal 1.50 4.00
TD Tim Duncan 1.00 2.50
TM Tracy McGrady .60 1.50

2006-07 Fleer Throwbacks

APPROXIMATE ODDS ONE PER BOX
BA Renaldo Balkman 2.00 5.00
BJ Bobby Jones 1.50 4.00
CS Craig Smith 2.00 5.00
DB Dee Brown 1.50 4.00
HA Hilton Armstrong 1.50 4.00
JB Josh Boone 1.50 4.00
JF Jordan Farmar 2.00 5.00
JR J.J. Redick 5.00 12.00
JW James White 1.50 4.00
KL Kyle Lowry 8.00 20.00
KP Kevin Pittsnogle 2.00 5.00
LA LaMarcus Aldridge 6.00 15.00
MA Maurice Ager 1.50 4.00
MC Mardy Collins 1.50 4.00
MW Marcus Williams 1.50 4.00
PD Paul Davis 1.50 4.00
PO Patrick O'Bryant 1.50 4.00
PT P.J. Tucker 2.50 6.00
RB Ronnie Brewer 2.50 6.00
RC Rodney Carney 1.50 4.00
RF Randy Foye 2.00 5.00
RG Rudy Gay 3.00 8.00
RR Rajon Rondo 6.00 15.00
SB Shannon Brown 1.50 4.00
SI Cedric Simmons 1.50 4.00
SJ Solomon Jones 1.50 4.00
SN Steve Novak 2.00 5.00
SW Shelden Williams 1.50 4.00
TT Tyrus Thomas 2.00 5.00
WI Shawne Williams 1.50 4.00

2006-07 Fleer Wal-Mart Rookie Exclusive

*WALMART: .6X TO 1.5X BASE HI

2007-08 Fleer

COMPLETE SET (235) 30.00 60.00
ONE ROOKIE PER PACK
ONE JORDAN RELIC PER RETAIL SET
1 Chauncey Billups .40 1.00
2 Amir Johnson .20 .50
3 Richard Hamilton .40 1.00
4 Jason Maxiell .20 .50
5 Tayshaun Prince .30 .75
6 Rasheed Wallace .40 1.00
7 Antonio McDyess .25 .60
8 Daniel Gibson .20 .50
9 Larry Hughes .25 .60
10 Zydrunas Ilgauskas .25 .60
11 Devin Brown .20 .50
12 LeBron James 2.50 6.00
13 Donyell Marshall .20 .50
14 Eric Snow .20 .50
15 Andrea Bargnani .20 .50
16 Chris Bosh .40 1.00
17 T.J. Ford .20 .50
18 Jorge Garbajosa .25 .60
19 Radoslav Nesterovic .20 .50
20 Jose Calderon .20 .50
21 James Posey .20 .50
22 Alonzo Mourning .50 1.25
23 Shaquille O'Neal 1.25 3.00
24 Dwyane Wade .60 1.50
25 Antoine Walker .30 .75
26 Jason Williams .50 1.25
27 Udonis Haslem .20 .50
28 Luol Deng .25 .60
29 Ben Gordon .25 .60
30 Kirk Hinrich .30 .75
31 Ben Wallace .40 1.00
32 Tyrus Thomas .20 .50
33 Thabo Sefolosha .20 .50
34 Chris Duhon .20 .50
35 Vince Carter .60 1.50
36 Jason Collins .20 .50
37 Richard Jefferson .25 .60
38 Jason Kidd .50 1.25
39 Nenad Krstic .20 .50
40 Marcus Williams .20 .50
41 Josh Boone .20 .50
42 Gilbert Arenas .30 .75
43 Caron Butler .25 .60
44 Antawn Jamison .25 .60
45 Brendan Haywood .20 .50
46 Antonio Daniels .20 .50
47 Etan Thomas .20 .50
48 Trevor Ariza .20 .50
49 Dwight Howard .40 1.00
50 Rashard Lewis .25 .60
51 Jameer Nelson .20 .50
52 J.J. Redick .30 .75
53 Hedo Turkoglu .25 .60
54 Carlos Arroyo .20 .50
55 Ike Diogu .20 .50
56 Mike Dunleavy .20 .50
57 Jeff Foster .20 .50
58 Jermaine O'Neal .20 .50
59 Jamaal Tinsley .20 .50
60 Shawne Williams .20 .50
61 Rodney Carney .20 .50
62 Andre Iguodala .30 .75
63 Kyle Korver .30 .75
64 Andre Miller .25 .60
65 Willie Green .20 .50
66 Samuel Dalembert .20 .50
67 Raymond Felton .25 .60
68 Sean May .20 .50
69 Adam Morrison .20 .50
70 Emeka Okafor .25 .60
71 Jason Richardson .30 .75
72 Gerald Wallace .25 .60
73 Ryan Hollins .20 .50
74 David Lee .20 .50
75 Jamal Crawford UER .30 .75
76 Eddy Curry .20 .50
77 Stephon Marbury .40 1.00
78 Zach Randolph .30 .75
79 Nate Robinson .30 .75
80 Quentin Richardson .20 .50
81 Josh Childress .20 .50
82 Joe Johnson .25 .60
83 Tyronn Lue .20 .50
84 Josh Smith .20 .50
85 Marvin Williams .20 .50
86 Shelden Williams .20 .50
87 Salim Stoudamire .20 .50
88 Andrew Bogut .25 .60
89 Bobby Simmons .20 .50
90 David Noel .20 .50
91 Michael Redd .25 .60
92 Charlie Villanueva .20 .50
93 Desmond Mason .20 .50
94 Ray Allen .50 1.25
95 Rajon Rondo .40 1.00
96 Al Jefferson .20 .50
97 Paul Pierce .50 1.25
98 Leon Powe .20 .50
99 Tony Allen .20 .50
100 Pau Gasol .50 1.25
101 Rudy Gay .25 .60
102 Darko Milicic .25 .60
103 Damon Stoudamire .30 .75
104 Hakim Warrick .20 .50
105 Mike Miller .25 .60
106 Johan Petro .20 .50
107 Wally Szczerbiak .25 .60
108 Delonte West .25 .60
109 Luke Ridnour .20 .50
110 Chris Wilcox .20 .50
111 Nick Collison .20 .50
112 LaMarcus Aldridge .30 .75
113 Channing Frye .20 .50
114 Jarrett Jack .25 .60
115 Brandon Roy .40 1.00
116 Martell Webster .25 .60
117 Sergio Rodriguez .20 .50
118 James Jones .20 .50
119 Shareef Abdur-Rahim .30 .75
120 Ron Artest .30 .75
121 Mike Bibby .30 .75
122 Francisco Garcia .20 .50
123 Kevin Martin .25 .60
124 Brad Miller .25 .60
125 Mikki Moore .20 .50
126 Ricky Davis .25 .60
127 Randy Foye .25 .60
128 Kevin Garnett .75 2.00
129 Juwan Howard .30 .75
130 Marko Jaric .20 .50
131 Rashad McCants .20 .50
132 Craig Smith .20 .50
133 Hilton Armstrong .20 .50
134 Tyson Chandler .30 .75
135 Bobby Jackson .20 .50
136 Chris Paul .60 1.50
137 Rasual Butler .20 .50
138 Peja Stojakovic .25 .60
139 Morris Peterson .20 .50
140 Elton Brand .25 .60
141 Sam Cassell .25 .60
142 Paul Davis .20 .50
143 Corey Maggette .25 .60
144 Cuttino Mobley .25 .60
145 Chris Kaman .20 .50
146 Baron Davis .25 .60
147 Monta Ellis .25 .60
148 Al Harrington .25 .60
149 Stephen Jackson .25 .60
150 Matt Barnes .20 .50
151 Andris Biedrins .20 .50
152 Kwame Brown .20 .50
153 Kobe Bryant 2.50 6.00
154 Andrew Bynum .20 .50
155 Jordan Farmar .20 .50
156 Lamar Odom .25 .60
157 Luke Walton .25 .60
158 Maurice Evans .20 .50
159 Carmelo Anthony .50 1.25
160 Marcus Camby .20 .50
161 Allen Iverson .75 2.00
162 Kenyon Martin .25 .60
163 Nene .25 .60
164 J.R. Smith .30 .75
165 Yakhouba Diawara .20 .50
166 Shane Battier .25 .60
167 Luther Head .20 .50
168 Tracy McGrady .50 1.25
169 Yao Ming .75 2.00
170 Rafer Alston .30 .75
171 Bonzi Wells .20 .50
172 Steve Novak .20 .50
173 Carlos Boozer .25 .60
174 Ronnie Brewer .20 .50
175 Andrei Kirilenko .25 .60
176 Paul Millsap .20 .50
177 Mehmet Okur .20 .50
178 Deron Williams .25 .60
179 Jarron Collins .25 .60
180 Tim Duncan .75 2.00
181 Tony Parker .50 1.25
182 Manu Ginobili .60 1.50
183 Bruce Bowen .20 .50
184 Brent Barry .20 .50
185 Robert Horry .30 .75
186 Michael Finley .30 .75
187 Leandro Barbosa .50 1.25
188 Grant Hill .30 .75
189 Shawn Marion .30 .75
190 Steve Nash .60 1.50
191 Amare Stoudemire .30 .75
192 Boris Diaw .25 .60
193 Raja Bell .25 .60
194 Maurice Ager .20 .50
195 Devean George .20 .50
196 Devin Harris .20 .50
197 Josh Howard .25 .60
198 Dirk Nowitzki .75 2.00
199 Jerry Stackhouse .20 .50
200 Jason Terry .25 .60
201 Arron Afflalo RC .30 .75
202 Morris Almond RC .30 .75
203 Marco Belinelli RC .40 1.00
204 Corey Brewer RC .40 1.00
205 Wilson Chandler RC .40 1.00
206 Mike Conley Jr. RC 1.25 3.00
207 Daequan Cook RC .40 1.00
208 Javaris Crittenton RC .30 .75
209 Jermareo Davidson RC .30 .75
210 Glen Davis RC .40 1.00
211 Jared Dudley RC .40 1.00
212 Kevin Durant RC 15.00 40.00
213 Nick Fazekas RC .30 .75
214 Jeff Green RC .40 1.00
215 Taurean Green RC .30 .75
216 Spencer Hawes RC .30 .75
217 Al Horford RC 1.25 3.00
218 Aaron Brooks RC .40 1.00
219 Carl Landry RC .30 .75
220 Acie Law RC .30 .75
221 Josh McRoberts RC .30 .75
222 Joakim Noah RC .50 1.25
223 Greg Oden RC .50 1.25
224 Gabe Pruitt RC .30 .75
225 Jason Smith RC .30 .75
226 Rodney Stuckey RC .30 .75
227 Al Thornton RC .30 .75
228 Alando Tucker RC .30 .75
229 Sean Williams RC .30 .75
230 Yi Jianlian RC .60 1.50
231 Brandan Wright RC .40 1.00
232 Julian Wright RC .30 .75
233 Nick Young RC .50 1.25
234 Thaddeus Young RC .50 1.25
235 Chris Richard RC .30 .75
RCF Michael Jordan Floor 60.00 150.00
COAF M.Jordan Floor AU/23 3,000.00 6,000.00
COFJ M.Jordan JSY Flr/230 125.00 300.00
RCPJ M.Jordan JSY White 75.00 200.00
RCWU M.Jordan JSY Black/250 125.00 300.00

2007-08 Fleer Glossy

*GLOSSY: .75X TO 2X BASE HI

2007-08 Fleer 1961-62

*1961-62 SINGLES: 1.25X TO 3X BASE HI

2007-08 Fleer 1986-87 Rookies

*1986-87 RCs: .6X TO 1.5X BASE HI
APPROXIMATELY ONE PER PACK
*1986-87 RC GLOSSY: .75X TO 2X BASE HI
143 Kevin Durant 25.00 60.00

2007-08 Fleer 1987-88

*1987-88: .75X TO 2X BASE HI
APPROXIMATELY ONE PER PACK
R19 Kobe Bryant 12.00 30.00
R66 LeBron James 12.00 30.00
R71 Michael Jordan 50.00 120.00

2007-08 Fleer Decades of Excellence

COMPLETE SET (20) 25.00 50.00
*GLOSSY: .6X TO 1.5X BASE HI
1 Larry Bird 4.00 10.00
2 Magic Johnson 4.00 10.00
3 Michael Jordan 10.00 25.00
4 Bill Laimbeer .75 2.00
5 David Robinson 2.00 5.00
6 Grant Hill 1.50 4.00
7 Hakeem Olajuwon 2.00 5.00
8 Robert Parish 1.00 2.50
9 John Stockton 2.00 5.00
10 Michael Jordan 10.00 25.00
11 Dennis Rodman 2.50 6.00
12 Shaquille O'Neal 4.00 10.00
13 LeBron James 8.00 20.00
14 Chauncey Billups 1.25 3.00
15 Kobe Bryant 8.00 20.00
16 Steve Nash 2.00 5.00
17 Dwyane Wade 2.00 5.00
18 Allen Iverson 2.50 6.00
19 Baron Davis .75 2.00
20 Tim Duncan 2.50 6.00

2007-08 Fleer Feel The Game

APPROXIMATE ODDS ONE PER BOX
FGAB Andrea Bargnani 1.50 4.00
FGAI Allen Iverson 6.00 15.00
FGAJ Antawn Jamison 2.00 5.00
FGAM Alonzo Mourning 4.00 10.00
FGAS Amare Stoudemire 2.50 6.00
FGBO Carlos Boozer 2.00 5.00
FGBW Ben Wallace 3.00 8.00
FGCA Carmelo Anthony 4.00 10.00
FGCB Chauncey Billups 3.00 8.00
FGCH Chris Bosh 3.00 8.00
FGDH Dwight Howard 3.00 8.00
FGDN Dirk Nowitzki 6.00 15.00
FGDR David Robinson 5.00 12.00
FGEB Elton Brand 2.00 5.00
FGGH Grant Hill 4.00 10.00
FGHO Hakeem Olajuwon 5.00 12.00
FGJJ Joe Johnson 2.00 5.00
FGJK Jason Kidd 4.00 10.00
FGJO Michael Jordan 125.00 300.00
FGKB Kobe Bryant 40.00 100.00
FGKG Kevin Garnett 6.00 15.00
FGLB Larry Bird 10.00 25.00
FGLJ LeBron James 40.00 100.00
FGMJ Magic Johnson 10.00 25.00
FGMR Michael Redd 2.00 5.00
FGO' Jermaine O'Neal 2.50 6.00
FGPG Pau Gasol 4.00 10.00
FGPP Paul Pierce 4.00 10.00
FGPS Peja Stojakovic 2.00 5.00
FGRA Ray Allen 4.00 10.00
FGRH Richard Hamilton 3.00 8.00
FGRO Dennis Rodman 6.00 15.00
FGRW Rasheed Wallace 3.00 8.00
FGSM Stephon Marbury 3.00 8.00
FGSO Shaquille O'Neal 10.00 25.00
FGTD Tim Duncan 6.00 15.00
FGTM Tracy McGrady 4.00 10.00
FGTP Tony Parker 4.00 10.00
FGVC Vince Carter 5.00 12.00
FGYM Yao Ming 6.00 15.00

2007-08 Fleer Michael Jordan Missing Links

COMMON CARD 50.00 125.00

2007-08 Fleer NBA Classics

APPROXIMATELY ONE PER BOX
TTAA Arron Afflalo 2.00 5.00
TTAB Aaron Brooks 2.00 5.00
TTAG Aaron Gray 1.50 4.00
TTAH Al Horford 6.00 15.00
TTAL Acie Law 1.50 4.00
TTAT Al Thornton 1.50 4.00
TTCB Corey Brewer 2.00 5.00
TTCL Carl Landry 1.50 4.00
TTCR Chris Richard 1.50 4.00
TTDM Dominic McGuire 1.50 4.00
TTDU Jared Dudley 2.00 5.00
TTGD Glen Davis 2.00 5.00
TTGP Gabe Pruitt 1.50 4.00
TTHA Adam Haluska 1.50 4.00
TTHH Herbert Hill 1.50 4.00
TTJC Javaris Crittenton 1.50 4.00
TTJD Jermareo Davidson 1.50 4.00
TTJG Jeff Green 2.00 5.00
TTJN Joakim Noah 2.50 6.00
TTJS Jason Smith 1.50 4.00
TTJW Julian Wright 1.50 4.00
TTKD Kevin Durant 10.00 25.00
TTMA Morris Almond 1.50 4.00
TTMC Mike Conley Jr. 6.00 15.00
TTNF Nick Fazekas 1.50 4.00
TTNY Nick Young 2.50 6.00
TTRS Rodney Stuckey 1.50 4.00
TTSH Spencer Hawes 1.50 4.00
TTSW Sean Williams 1.50 4.00
TTTG Taurean Green 1.50 4.00
TTTU Alando Tucker 1.50 4.00
TTTY Thaddeus Young 2.50 6.00
TTWC Wilson Chandler 2.00 5.00

2007-08 Fleer Rookie Sensations

COMPLETE SET (15) 10.00 25.00
*GLOSSY: .6X TO 1.5X BASE HI
RS1 Greg Oden .75 2.00
RS2 Kevin Durant 15.00 40.00
RS3 Al Horford 2.00 5.00
RS4 Mike Conley Jr. 2.00 5.00
RS5 Jeff Green .60 1.50
RS6 Thaddeus Young .75 2.00
RS7 Corey Brewer .60 1.50
RS8 Brandan Wright .60 1.50
RS9 Joakim Noah .75 2.00
RS10 Spencer Hawes .50 1.25
RS11 Acie Law .50 1.25
RS12 Julian Wright .50 1.25
RS13 Al Thornton .50 1.25
RS14 Rodney Stuckey .50 1.25
RS15 Nick Young .75 2.00

2008-09 Fleer

COMPLETE SET (247) 20.00 50.00
ROOKIE STATED ODDS 1:1
TRI-CARD STATED ODDS 1:3
1 Ray Allen .50 1.25
2 Kevin Garnett .75 2.00
3 Paul Pierce .50 1.25
4 Glen Davis .20 .50
5 Rajon Rondo .40 1.00
6 Leon Powe .20 .50
7 James Posey .20 .50
8 Chauncey Billups .40 1.00
9 Richard Hamilton .30 .75
10 Jason Maxiell .20 .50
11 Tayshaun Prince .30 .75
12 Rasheed Wallace .40 1.00
13 Rodney Stuckey .20 .50
14 Antonio McDyess .25 .60
15 Keith Bogans .20 .50
16 Maurice Evans .20 .50
17 Dwight Howard .40 1.00
18 Rashard Lewis .25 .60
19 Jameer Nelson .20 .50
20 Hedo Turkoglu .25 .60
21 Anthony Johnson .20 .50
22 Ben Wallace .40 1.00
23 LeBron James 2.50 6.00
24 Zydrunas Ilgauskas .25 .60
25 Delonte West .20 .50
26 Anderson Varejao .20 .50
27 Daniel Gibson .20 .50
28 Mo Williams .25 .60
29 Gilbert Arenas .30 .75
30 Caron Butler .25 .60
31 Brendan Haywood .20 .50
32 Antawn Jamison .25 .60
33 DeShawn Stevenson .25 .60
34 Nick Young .20 .50
35 Antonio Daniels .20 .50
36 Andrea Bargnani .25 .60
37 Chris Bosh .40 1.00
38 Jose Calderon .20 .50
39 Jermaine O'Neal .30 .75
40 Anthony Parker .20 .50
41 Jamario Moon .20 .50
42 Elton Brand .25 .60
43 Samuel Dalembert .20 .50
44 Willie Green .20 .50
45 Andre Iguodala .25 .60
46 Andre Miller .25 .60
47 Louis Williams .25 .60
48 Thaddeus Young .25 .60
49 Mike Bibby .30 .75
50 Zaza Pachulia .20 .50
51 Al Horford .30 .75
52 Joe Johnson .30 .75
53 Josh Smith .30 .75
54 Marvin Williams .25 .60
55 Acie Law .25 .60
56 Danny Granger .25 .60
57 T.J. Ford .25 .60
58 Mike Dunleavy .20 .50
59 Jamaal Tinsley .20 .50
60 Troy Murphy .20 .50
61 Jeff Foster .20 .50
62 Vince Carter .60 1.50
63 Yi Jianlian .40 1.00
64 Sean Williams .20 .50
65 Devin Harris .20 .50
66 Keyon Dooling .20 .50
67 Josh Boone .20 .50
68 Michael Jordan 2.50 6.00
69 Luol Deng .25 .60
70 Ben Gordon .25 .60
71 Joakim Noah .20 .50
72 Kirk Hinrich .20 .50
73 Andres Nocioni .20 .50
74 Larry Hughes .25 .60
75 Gerald Wallace .25 .60
76 Emeka Okafor .20 .50
77 Jason Richardson .30 .75
78 Raymond Felton .20 .50
79 Adam Morrison .20 .50
80 Jared Dudley .25 .60
81 Nazr Mohammed .20 .50
82 Andrew Bogut .25 .60
83 Charlie Villanueva .20 .50
84 Michael Redd .25 .60
85 Ramon Sessions .20 .50
86 Richard Jefferson .25 .60
87 Charlie Bell .20 .50
88 Jamal Crawford .30 .75
89 Eddy Curry .20 .50
90 Stephon Marbury .30 .75
91 Zach Randolph .30 .75
92 Quentin Richardson .20 .50
93 Nate Robinson .20 .50
94 David Lee .20 .50
95 Dwyane Wade .60 1.50
96 Daequan Cook .20 .50
97 Shawn Marion .30 .75
98 Alonzo Mourning .40 1.00
99 Udonis Haslem .20 .50
100 Dorell Wright .20 .50
101 Kobe Bryant 2.50 6.00
102 Andrew Bynum .20 .50
103 Jordan Farmar .20 .50
104 Pau Gasol .40 1.00
105 Lamar Odom .25 .60
106 Luke Walton .25 .60
107 Sasha Vujacic .20 .50
108 Tyson Chandler .25 .60
109 Chris Paul .60 1.50
110 Hilton Armstrong .20 .50
111 Peja Stojakovic .25 .60
112 Rasual Butler .20 .50
113 Julian Wright .20 .50
114 Morris Peterson .20 .50
115 Tony Parker .40 1.00
116 Tim Duncan .75 2.00
117 Manu Ginobili .60 1.50
118 Michael Finley .30 .75
119 Kurt Thomas .20 .50
120 Bruce Bowen .20 .50
121 Fabricio Oberto .20 .50
122 Mehmet Okur .20 .50
123 Deron Williams .25 .60
124 Carlos Boozer .25 .60
125 Kyle Korver .25 .60
126 Andrei Kirilenko .25 .60
127 Paul Millsap .20 .50
128 Ronnie Brewer .20 .50
129 Shane Battier .25 .60
130 Tracy McGrady .50 1.25
131 Yao Ming .75 2.00
132 Luis Scola .25 .60
133 Luther Head .20 .50
134 Carl Landry .20 .50
135 Ron Artest .30 .75
136 Grant Hill .30 .75
137 Amare Stoudemire .30 .75
138 Steve Nash .60 1.50
139 Shaquille O'Neal 1.00 2.50
140 Leandro Barbosa .25 .60
141 Boris Diaw .25 .60
142 Raja Bell .25 .60
143 Dirk Nowitzki .75 2.00
144 Jason Kidd .50 1.25
145 Josh Howard .25 .60
146 Jerry Stackhouse .30 .75
147 Jason Terry .25 .60
148 Brandon Bass .20 .50
149 Erick Dampier .20 .50
150 Carmelo Anthony .40 1.00
151 Nene .25 .60
152 Allen Iverson .60 1.50
153 Kenyon Martin .25 .60
154 J.R. Smith .30 .75
155 Linas Kleiza .25 .60
156 Corey Maggette .25 .60
157 Monta Ellis .25 .60
158 Stephen Jackson .25 .60
159 Al Harrington .25 .60
160 Andris Biedrins .25 .60
161 Kelenna Azubuike .20 .50
162 C.J. Watson .20 .50
163 LaMarcus Aldridge .30 .75
164 Travis Outlaw .25 .60
165 Greg Oden .25 .60
166 Brandon Roy .20 .50
167 Martell Webster .20 .50
168 Steve Blake .20 .50
169 Bobby Brown .20 .50
170 Beno Udrih .20 .50
171 Kevin Martin .25 .60
172 Francisco Garcia .25 .60
173 Brad Miller .25 .60
174 John Salmons .25 .60
175 Mikki Moore .30 .75
176 Baron Davis .30 .75
177 Chris Kaman .30 .75
178 Shaun Livingston .20 .50
179 Marcus Camby .20 .50
180 Al Thornton .25 .60
181 Cuttino Mobley .25 .60
182 Ricky Davis .25 .60
183 Corey Brewer .25 .60
184 Randy Foye .30 .75
185 Al Jefferson .20 .50
186 Rashad McCants .20 .50
187 Mike Miller .20 .50
188 Sebastian Telfair .60 1.50
189 Mike Conley Jr. .40 1.00
190 Rudy Gay .30 .75
191 Kyle Lowry .20 .50
192 Hakim Warrick .20 .50
193 Marko Jaric .20 .50
194 Javaris Crittenton .20 .50
195 Kevin Durant 1.25 3.00
196 Jeff Green .20 .50
197 Chris Wilcox .20 .50
198 Damien Wilkins .20 .50
199 Earl Watson .20 .50
200 Desmond Mason .20 .50
201 Derrick Rose RC 6.00 15.00
202 Michael Beasley RC .50 1.25
203 O.J. Mayo RC .40 1.00
204 Russell Westbrook RC 8.00 20.00
205 Kevin Love RC 1.00 2.50
206 Danilo Gallinari RC .75 2.00
207 Eric Gordon RC .75 2.00
208 Joe Alexander RC .30 .75
209 D.J. Augustin RC .50 1.25
210 Brook Lopez RC .60 1.50
211 Jerryd Bayless RC .40 1.00
212 Jason Thompson RC .30 .75
213 Brandon Rush RC .30 .75
214 Anthony Randolph RC .30 .75
215 Robin Lopez RC .40 1.00
216 Marreese Speights RC .40 1.00
217 Roy Hibbert RC .40 1.00
218 Javale McGee RC .50 1.25
219 J.J. Hickson RC .30 .75
220 Alexis Ajinca RC .30 .75
221 Ryan Anderson RC .40 1.00
222 Courtney Lee RC .40 1.00
223 Kosta Koufos RC .30 .75
224 George Hill RC .50 1.25
225 Darrell Arthur RC .40 1.00
226 Donte Greene RC .30 .75
227 D.J. White RC .30 .75
228 J.R. Giddens RC .30 .75
229 Walter Sharpe RC .30 .75
230 Joey Dorsey RC .30 .75
231 Mario Chalmers RC .50 1.25
232 Kyle Weaver RC .30 .75
233 Sonny Weems RC .30 .75
234 Chris Douglas-Roberts RC .30 .75
235 Rudy Fernandez RC .40 1.00
236 Rose/Beasley/Mayo 2.00 5.00
237 Westbrook/Love/Gallinari 6.00 15.00
238 Gordon/Alexander/Augustin 1.50 4.00
239 Lopez/Bayless/Thompson 1.50 4.00
240 Rush/Randolph/Lopez 1.50 4.00
241 Speights/Hibbert/McGee 1.50 4.00
242 Hickson/Ajinca/Anderson 1.50 4.00
243 Lee/Koufos/Hill 1.50 4.00
244 Arthur/Greene/White 1.50 4.00
245 Giddens/Sharpe/Dorsey 1.50 4.00
246 Chalmers/Jordan/Weaver 2.00 5.00
247 Weems/Douglas-Roberts/Fernandez 1.50 4.00

2008-09 Fleer Glossy

*GLOSSY: .6X TO 1.5X BASE HI

2008-09 Fleer 1986-87 Rookies

COMPLETE SET (30) 40.00 100.00
STATED ODDS 1:2
*GLOSSY: .75X TO 2X BASE HI
86R163 Derrick Rose 6.00 15.00
86R164 Michael Beasley 1.00 2.50
86R165 O.J. Mayo .75 2.00
86R166 Russell Westbrook 6.00 15.00
86R167 Kevin Love 2.00 5.00
86R168 Eric Gordon 1.50 4.00
86R169 Joe Alexander .60 1.50
86R170 D.J. Augustin 1.00 2.50
86R171 Brook Lopez 1.25 3.00
86R172 Jerryd Bayless .75 2.00
86R173 Jason Thompson .60 1.50
86R174 Brandon Rush .60 1.50
86R175 Anthony Randolph .60 1.50
86R176 Robin Lopez .75 2.00
86R177 Marreese Speights .75 2.00
86R178 Roy Hibbert .75 2.00
86R179 Javale McGee 1.00 2.50
86R180 J.J. Hickson .60 1.50
86R181 Ryan Anderson .75 2.00
86R182 Courtney Lee .75 2.00
86R183 Kosta Koufos .60 1.50
86R184 George Hill 1.00 2.50
86R185 Darrell Arthur .75 2.00
86R186 Donte Greene .60 1.50
86R187 D.J. White .60 1.50
86R188 J.R. Giddens .60 1.50
86R189 Joey Dorsey .60 1.50
86R190 Sonny Weems .60 1.50
86R191 Chris Douglas-Roberts .60 1.50
86R192 Rudy Fernandez .75 2.00

2008-09 Fleer 1988-89

COMPLETE SET (132)
COMMON CARD .60 1.50
SEMISTARS .75 2.00
UNLISTED STARS 1.00 2.50
APPROXIMATE ODDS 1:3
5 Kevin Garnett 12.00 30.00
7 Ray Allen 8.00 20.00
8 Paul Pierce 8.00 20.00
19 LeBron James 60.00 150.00
21 Dirk Nowitzki 12.00 30.00
24 Allen Iverson 12.00 30.00
25 Carmelo Anthony 12.00 30.00
39 Tracy McGrady 8.00 20.00
40 Yao Ming 12.00 30.00
50 Kobe Bryant 60.00 150.00
58 Dwyane Wade 12.00 30.00
71 Vince Carter 12.00 30.00
72 Chris Paul 12.00 30.00
91 Grant Hill 8.00 20.00
93 Shaquille O'Neal 12.00 30.00
94 Steve Nash 12.00 30.00
101 Manu Ginobili 8.00 20.00
103 Tim Duncan 12.00 30.00
104 Tony Parker 6.00 15.00
107 Kevin Durant 60.00 150.00
109 Chris Bosh 8.00 20.00
122 Dwyane Wade AS 12.00 30.00
123 Kevin Garnett AS 12.00 30.00
124 LeBron James AS 40.00 100.00
126 Ray Allen AS 8.00 20.00
127 Kobe Bryant AS 40.00 100.00
128 Allen Iverson AS 12.00 30.00
129 Carmelo Anthony AS 12.00 30.00
130 Tim Duncan AS 12.00 30.00
131 Yao Ming AS 12.00 30.00
132 Chris Paul AS 12.00 30.00

2008-09 Fleer All-Star Sensations

COMPLETE SET (26) 15.00 30.00
AS1 Allen Iverson 1.00 2.50
AS2 David Robinson 1.00 2.50
AS3 Dirk Nowitzki 1.25 3.00
AS4 Dominique Wilkins .75 2.00

AS5 Dwight Howard .60 1.50
AS6 Grant Hill .75 2.00
AS7 Jason Kidd .75 2.00
AS8 Jason Richardson .50 1.25
AS9 John Stockton 1.00 2.50
AS10 Josh Smith .30 .75
AS11 Julius Erving 1.25 3.00
AS12 Kevin Garnett 1.25 3.00
AS13 Kobe Bryant 4.00 10.00
AS14 Larry Bird 1.50 4.00
AS15 LeBron James 4.00 10.00
AS16 Magic Johnson 1.50 4.00
AS17 Michael Jordan 4.00 10.00
AS18 Ray Allen .75 2.00
AS19 Rolando Blackman .40 1.00
AS20 Shaquille O'Neal 1.50 4.00
AS21 Spud Webb .40 1.00
AS22 Tim Duncan 1.25 3.00
AS23 Tom Chambers .40 1.00
AS24 Tracy McGrady .75 2.00
AS25 Vince Carter 1.00 2.50
AS26 Yao Ming 1.25 3.00

2008-09 Fleer Feel the Game

FGCA Carmelo Anthony 3.00 8.00
FGDH Dwight Howard 3.00 8.00
FGGA Gilbert Arenas 2.50 6.00
FGKB Kobe Bryant 40.00 100.00
FGKG Kevin Garnett 6.00 15.00
FGLJ LeBron James 15.00 40.00
FGMJ Michael Jordan 25.00 60.00
FGSN Steve Nash 5.00 12.00
FGSO Shaquille O'Neal 8.00 20.00
FGYM Yao Ming 6.00 15.00

2008-09 Fleer First Year Phenoms

COMPLETE SET (10) 10.00 25.00
PH1 Derrick Rose 4.00 10.00
PH2 Michael Beasley 1.00 2.50
PH3 O.J. Mayo .75 2.00
PH4 Russell Westbrook 5.00 12.00
PH5 Kevin Love 2.00 5.00
PH6 Danilo Gallinari 1.50 4.00
PH7 Eric Gordon 1.50 4.00
PH8 Joe Alexander .60 1.50
PH9 D.J. Augustin 1.00 2.50
PH10 Brook Lopez 1.25 3.00

2008-09 Fleer Genuine Coverage

APPROXIMATE ODDS 1:10
GCAI Andre Iguodala 2.00 5.00
GCAK Andrei Kirilenko 2.00 5.00
GCAS Amare Stoudemire 2.50 6.00
GCBO Chris Bosh 3.00 8.00
GCCA Carmelo Anthony 3.00 8.00
GCCB Chauncey Billups 3.00 8.00
GCCM Corey Maggette 2.00 5.00
GCDH Dwight Howard 3.00 8.00
GCDN Dirk Nowitzki 6.00 15.00
GCEB Elton Brand 2.00 5.00
GCGA Gilbert Arenas 2.50 6.00
GCJK Jason Kidd 4.00 10.00
GCJO Jermaine O'Neal 2.50 6.00
GCKB Kobe Bryant 40.00 100.00
GCKG Kevin Garnett 6.00 15.00
GCLJ LeBron James 10.00 25.00
GCRA Ray Allen 4.00 10.00
GCRH Richard Hamilton 2.50 6.00
GCRW Rasheed Wallace 3.00 8.00
GCSM Shawn Marion 2.50 6.00
GCSO Shaquille O'Neal 8.00 20.00
GCTD Tim Duncan 6.00 15.00
GCTM Tracy McGrady 4.00 10.00
GCVC Vince Carter 5.00 12.00
GCYM Yao Ming 6.00 15.00

2008-09 Fleer Living Legacies

COMPLETE SET (12) 15.00 30.00
LL1 Bill Russell 3.00 8.00
LL2 Bill Walton 1.50 4.00
LL3 Clyde Drexler 1.25 3.00
LL4 Dominique Wilkins 1.50 4.00
LL5 Hakeem Olajuwon 2.00 5.00
LL6 James Worthy 1.00 2.50
LL7 Julius Erving 2.50 6.00
LL8 Larry Bird 3.00 8.00
LL9 Magic Johnson 3.00 8.00
LL10 Michael Jordan 15.00 40.00
LL11 Oscar Robertson 1.00 2.50
LL12 Robert Parish 1.00 2.50

2008-09 Fleer Michael Jordan Retrospective

COMPLETE SET (23) 15.00 40.00
*GLOSSY: .6X TO 1.5X BASE HI

2008-09 Fleer NBA Classics

APPROXIMATE ODDS 1:10
NBAAR Anthony Randolph 1.25 3.00
NBABL Brook Lopez 2.50 6.00
NBABR Brandon Rush 1.25 3.00
NBACD Chris Douglas-Roberts 1.25 3.00
NBACL Courtney Lee 1.50 4.00
NBADA D.J. Augustin 2.00 5.00
NBADG Donte Greene 1.25 3.00
NBADJ DeAndre Jordan 2.50 6.00
NBADR Derrick Rose 8.00 20.00
NBAEG Eric Gordon 3.00 8.00
NBAGH George Hill 2.00 5.00
NBAJA Joe Alexander 1.25 3.00
NBAJB Jerryd Bayless 1.50 4.00
NBAJH J.J. Hickson 1.25 3.00
NBAJM Javale McGee 2.00 5.00
NBAJT Jason Thompson 1.25 3.00
NBAKK Kosta Koufos 1.25 3.00
NBAKL Kevin Love 6.00 15.00
NBAKW Kyle Weaver 1.25 3.00
NBAMB Michael Beasley 2.00 5.00
NBAMC Mario Chalmers 2.00 5.00
NBAMS Marreese Speights 1.50 4.00
NBAOM O.J. Mayo 1.50 4.00
NBAPE Patrick Ewing Jr 1.25 3.00
NBARA Ryan Anderson 1.50 4.00
NBARH Roy Hibbert 1.50 4.00
NBARL Robin Lopez 1.50 4.00
NBASW Sonny Weems 1.25 3.00
NBAWS Walter Sharpe 1.25 3.00

2008-09 Fleer Sharp Shooters

COMPLETE SET (20) 20.00 40.00
SS1 Anthony Parker .75 2.00
SS2 B.J. Armstrong 1.25 3.00
SS3 Ben Gordon 1.00 2.50
SS4 Chauncey Billups 1.50 4.00
SS5 Daniel Gibson .75 2.00
SS6 Jason Kapono .75 2.00
SS7 John Stockton 2.50 6.00
SS8 Kenny Smith 1.00 2.50
SS9 Kevin Martin 1.00 2.50
SS10 Larry Bird 4.00 10.00
SS11 Leandro Barbosa 1.00 2.50
SS12 Manu Ginobili 2.50 6.00
SS13 Mark Price 2.00 5.00
SS14 Michael Redd 1.00 2.50
SS15 Mike Miller 1.00 2.50
SS16 Peja Stojakovic 1.00 2.50
SS17 Rashard Lewis 1.00 2.50
SS18 Ray Allen 2.00 5.00
SS19 Steve Kerr 1.25 3.00
SS20 Steve Nash 2.50 6.00

2008-09 Fleer Signature Approval

APPROXIMATE ODDS 1:15
SAAA Alexis Ajinca 2.50 6.00
SAAB Aaron Brooks 2.50 6.00
SAAJ Al Jefferson 2.50 6.00
SAAM Alonzo Mourning 40.00 100.00
SAAN Carmelo Anthony 12.00 30.00
SAAT Al Thornton 2.50 6.00
SABB Bobby Brown 2.50 6.00
SABD Baron Davis 4.00 10.00
SABE Marco Belinelli 2.50 6.00
SABI Mike Bibby 4.00 10.00
SABR Brad Daugherty 3.00 8.00
SACA ML Carr 6.00 15.00
SACB Corey Brewer 3.00 8.00
SACH Maurice Cheeks 5.00 12.00
SACL Carl Landry 2.50 6.00
SACR Chris Richard 2.50 6.00
SACS Cheikh Samb 2.50 6.00
SADA D.J. Augustin 4.00 10.00
SADC Daequan Cook 2.50 6.00
SADG Danilo Gallinari 8.00 20.00
SADH Dwight Howard 8.00 20.00
SADI Boris Diaw 3.00 8.00
SADJ Darnell Jackson 2.50 6.00
SADM Donyell Marshall 2.50 6.00
SADR Derrick Rose 30.00 80.00
SADS D.J. Strawberry 2.50 6.00
SADW Dominique Wilkins 10.00 25.00
SAGD Glen Davis 2.50 6.00
SAJA Antawn Jamison 3.00 8.00
SAJG Jeff Green 3.00 8.00
SAJN Joakim Noah 2.50 6.00
SAJW Julian Wright 2.50 6.00
SAKB Kobe Bryant 500.00 1,000.00
SAKD Kevin Durant 75.00 200.00
SAKG Kevin Garnett 60.00 150.00
SALJ LeBron James 1,000.00 2,000.00
SALM Luc Richard Mbah A Moute 3.00 8.00
SALO Lamar Odom 3.00 8.00
SALS Luis Scola 3.00 8.00
SAMA Morris Almond 2.50 6.00
SAMB Michael Beasley 4.00 10.00
SAMC Mike Conley Jr. 8.00 20.00
SAMJ Michael Jordan 400.00 800.00
SAOM O.J. Mayo 3.00 8.00
SAPO Patrick O'Bryant 2.50 6.00
SAPR Pat Riley 20.00 50.00
SAQR Quentin Richardson 2.50 6.00
SARH Richard Hendrix 2.50 6.00
SARM Rick Mahorn 2.50 6.00
SARR Rajon Rondo 8.00 20.00
SARS Ramon Sessions 2.50 6.00
SARW Russell Westbrook 125.00 300.00
SAST Rodney Stuckey 2.50 6.00
SASW Sean Williams 2.50 6.00
SAVC Vince Carter 15.00 40.00
SAWC Wilson Chandler 3.00 8.00
SAWH Walter Herrmann 2.50 6.00
SAWI Shelden Williams 2.50 6.00

2002 Fleer All-Star NBA Jam Session

1 Eric Snow .60 1.50

2004 Fleer Authentic Player Autographs

ISSUED FOR UNFULFILLED EXCH
CARDS FROM 2002-2004
BG1 Ben Gordon JSY/100 15.00 40.00
BG2 Ben Gordon/100 12.50 30.00
BG3 Ben Gordon/75 15.00 40.00
BG4 Ben Gordon/50 20.00 50.00
BW Ben Wallace/100 10.00 25.00
DW David West/59 6.00 15.00
DW1 Dwyane Wade JSY/100 30.00 60.00
DW2 Dwyane Wade JSY/25 50.00 100.00
JK Jason Kidd/300 15.00 40.00
JS1 Jerry Stackhouse/126 5.00 12.00
JS2 Jerry Stackhouse/100 6.00 15.00
JS3 Jerry Stackhouse/50 10.00 25.00
MB Marcus Banks/75 10.00 25.00
ST1 Sebastian Telfair/250 6.00 15.00
ST2 Sebastian Telfair/75 8.00 20.00
ST3 Sebastian Telfair/50 10.00 25.00
VC1 Vince Carter/300 15.00 40.00
VC2 Vince Carter/150 20.00 40.00

2005 Fleer Authentic Player Autographs

BG1 Ben Gordon/300 6.00 15.00
BG2 Ben Gordon/150 8.00 20.00
BG3 Ben Gordon/100 10.00 25.00
BG4 Ben Gordon/75 12.50 30.00
DG1 Drew Gooden/300 5.00 12.00
DG2 Drew Gooden/150 6.00 15.00
DW Dwyane Wade/50 25.00 60.00
JK Jason Kidd/225 12.50 30.00
TP Tayshaun Prince/50 8.00 20.00
TP1 Tayshaun Prince/50 6.00 15.00
BGJ1 Ben Gordon JSY/100 8.00 20.00
TPJ Tayshaun Prince JSY/25 10.00 25.00

2001-02 Fleer Authentix

COMP.SET w/o SP'S 12.00 30.00
101-135 PRINT RUN 1250 SER.#'d SETS
1 Vince Carter .60 1.50
2 Terrell Brandon .25 .60
3 Raef LaFrentz .20 .50
4 Iakovos Tsakalidis .20 .50
5 Elton Brand .25 .60
6 David Robinson .60 1.50
7 Lamar Odom .25 .60
8 Larry Hughes .25 .60
9 Gary Payton .50 1.25
10 Rick Fox .25 .60
11 Jamal Mashburn .25 .60
12 Brian Grant .20 .50
13 David Wesley .20 .50
14 Steve Smith .25 .60
15 Corey Maggette .25 .60
16 Michael Jordan 3.00 8.00
17 Wally Szczerbiak .25 .60
18 Antoine Walker .25 .60
19 Marcus Camby .25 .60
20 Rasheed Wallace .40 1.00
21 Travis Best .20 .50
22 Theo Ratliff .20 .50
23 LaPhonso Ellis .20 .50
24 Dirk Nowitzki .75 2.00
25 Kurt Thomas .20 .50
26 Steve Francis .30 .75
27 Tim Duncan .75 2.00
28 Eddie House .20 .50
29 Ron Mercer .20 .50
30 Allan Houston .30 .75
31 Trajan Langdon .20 .50
32 Karl Malone .60 1.50
33 Glenn Robinson .30 .75
34 Wang Zhizhi .30 .75
35 Jason Kidd .50 1.25
36 Maurice Taylor .20 .50
37 Chris Webber .40 1.00
38 Michael Dickerson .20 .50
39 Paul Pierce .50 1.25
40 Bonzi Wells .20 .50
41 Antawn Jamison .25 .60
42 Rashard Lewis .25 .60
43 Reggie Miller .60 1.50
44 Patrick Ewing .50 1.25
45 Marcus Fizer .20 .50
46 Aaron McKie .20 .50
47 Marc Jackson .20 .50
48 Desmond Mason .20 .50
49 Jermaine O'Neal .25 .60
50 DeShawn Stevenson .25 .60
51 John Stockton .60 1.50
52 Tim Thomas .20 .50
53 Andre Miller .25 .60
54 Jumaine Jones .20 .50
55 Nick Van Exel .30 .75
56 Damon Stoudamire .30 .75
57 Stephon Marbury .40 1.00
58 Clifford Robinson .30 .75
59 Hedo Turkoglu .25 .60
60 Kobe Bryant 2.50 6.00
61 Richard Hamilton .40 1.00
62 Stromile Swift .20 .50
63 Chris Mihm .20 .50
64 Tracy McGrady .50 1.25
65 Jalen Rose .25 .60
66 Morris Peterson .20 .50
67 Alonzo Mourning .50 1.25
68 Courtney Alexander .20 .50
69 Michael Finley .30 .75
70 Shawn Marion .30 .75
71 Darius Miles .30 .75
72 Antonio Davis .25 .60
73 Ray Allen .50 1.25
74 Shareef Abdur-Rahim .25 .60
75 Kevin Garnett .75 2.00
76 Latrell Sprewell .40 1.00
77 Antonio McDyess .25 .60
78 Derek Anderson .20 .50
79 Derek Fisher .25 .60
80 Jason Terry .30 .75
81 Eddie Jones .30 .75
82 Hakeem Olajuwon .60 1.50
83 Toni Kukoc .40 1.00
84 Sam Cassell .25 .60
85 Jamal Crawford .30 .75
86 Allen Iverson .75 2.00
87 Steve Nash .60 1.50
88 Dikembe Mutombo .50 1.25
89 Shaquille O'Neal 1.25 3.00
90 Jerome Moiso .20 .50
91 Kenyon Martin .30 .75
92 Chucky Atkins .20 .50
93 Grant Hill .50 1.25
94 Jerry Stackhouse .30 .75
95 Jason Williams .50 1.25
96 Baron Davis .30 .75
97 Mike Miller .25 .60
98 Joe Smith .25 .60
99 Peja Stojakovic .25 .60
100 Cuttino Mobley .25 .60
101 Kwame Brown RC 1.25 3.00
102 Jason Collins RC 1.00 2.50
103 Willie Solomon RC 1.00 2.50
104 Brendan Haywood RC 1.00 2.50
105 Jeff Trepagnier RC .75 2.00
106 Eddie Griffin RC 1.00 2.50
107 Joseph Forte RC .75 2.00
108 Rodney White RC .75 2.00
109 Jeryl Sasser RC .75 2.00
110 Samuel Dalembert RC 1.25 3.00
111 Shane Battier RC 2.50 6.00
112 Tony Parker RC 8.00 20.00
113 DeSagana Diop RC .75 2.00
114 Steven Hunter RC .75 2.00
115 Trenton Hassell RC .75 2.00
116 Michael Bradley RC .75 2.00
117 Brian Scalabrine RC 1.25 3.00
118 Troy Murphy RC 1.00 2.50
119 Brandon Armstrong RC .75 2.00
120 Pau Gasol RC 5.00 12.00
121 Gerald Wallace RC 1.50 4.00
122 Jason Richardson RC 2.00 5.00
123 Joe Johnson RC 2.00 5.00
124 Loren Woods RC .75 2.00
125 Vladimir Radmanovic RC 1.00 2.50
126 Jamaal Tinsley RC 1.00 2.50
127 Omar Cook RC 1.25 3.00
128 Kedrick Brown RC .75 2.00
129 Terence Morris RC .75 2.00
130 Richard Jefferson RC 1.50 4.00
131 Gilbert Arenas RC 3.00 8.00
132 Tyson Chandler RC 2.00 5.00
133 Kirk Haston RC .75 2.00
134 Eddy Curry RC 1.25 3.00
135 Zach Randolph RC 2.50 6.00

2001-02 Fleer Authentix Front Row Parallel

*STARS: 4X TO 10X BASE CARD HI
*RCs: 1.5X TO 4X BASE CARD HI
STATED PRINT RUN 100 SERIAL #'d SETS
16 Michael Jordan 75.00 200.00
60 Kobe Bryant 40.00 100.00

2001-02 Fleer Authentix Second Row Parallel

*STARS: 2.5X TO 6X BASE CARD HI
*RCs: 1X TO 2.5X BASE CARD HI
STATED PRINT RUN 200 SERIAL #'d SETS
16 Michael Jordan 50.00 120.00
60 Kobe Bryant 25.00 60.00

2001-02 Fleer Authentix Autograph Authentix

STATED ODDS 1:639
1 Kwame Brown 8.00 20.00
2 Eddy Curry 6.00 15.00
3 Vince Carter 30.00 80.00

2001-02 Fleer Authentix Autograph Authentix UnRipped

STATED PRINT RUN 25 SER.#'d SETS
1 Kwame Brown 15.00 40.00
2 Eddy Curry 12.00 30.00
3 Vince Carter 60.00 150.00

2001-02 Fleer Authentix Autographed Jersey Authentix

STATED ODDS 1:4971
UNRIPPED SER.#'d TO 1 EXISTS
1 Vince Carter 60.00 150.00

2001-02 Fleer Authentix Courtside Classics

COMPLETE SET (15) 25.00 50.00
STATED ODDS 1:22
1 Steve Francis 1.00 2.50
2 Mike Miller .75 2.00
3 Kenyon Martin 1.00 2.50
4 Vince Carter 2.00 5.00
5 Alonzo Mourning 1.50 4.00
6 Anfernee Hardaway 2.50 6.00
7 Dikembe Mutombo 1.50 4.00
8 Chris Webber 1.25 3.00
9 Glenn Robinson 1.00 2.50
10 Jerry Stackhouse 1.00 2.50
11 Kobe Bryant 12.00 30.00
12 Kevin Garnett 2.50 6.00
13 Tim Duncan 2.50 6.00
14 Shaquille O'Neal 4.00 10.00
15 Michael Jordan 20.00 50.00

2001-02 Fleer Authentix Courtside Classics Memorabilia

STATED ODDS 1:74
*MULT PAR: 1X TO 2.5X BASE HI
MULT PAR PRINT RUN 150 SER.#'d SETS
AH Anfernee Hardaway 12.00 30.00
AM Alonzo Mourning 8.00 20.00
CW Chris Webber 6.00 15.00
DM Dikembe Mutombo 8.00 20.00
GR Glenn Robinson 5.00 12.00
JS Jerry Stackhouse 5.00 12.00
KM Kenyon Martin 5.00 12.00
MM Mike Miller 4.00 10.00
SF Steve Francis 5.00 12.00
VC Vince Carter 10.00 25.00

2001-02 Fleer Authentix Jersey Authentix Ripped

STATED ODDS 1:33
*UNRIPPED: 1.5X TO 3X RIPPED JSY
UNRIPPED PRINT RUN 50 SER.#'d SETS
1 Allen Iverson 10.00 25.00
2 Darius Miles 2.50 6.00
3 Tracy McGrady 6.00 15.00
4 Glenn Robinson 4.00 10.00
5 Rashard Lewis 3.00 8.00
6 Elton Brand 3.00 8.00
7 Andre Miller 3.00 8.00
8 Jason Terry 4.00 10.00
9 Vince Carter 8.00 20.00
10 Karl Malone 8.00 20.00
11 David Robinson 8.00 20.00
12 Lamar Odom 3.00 8.00
13 Antoine Walker 3.00 8.00
14 Shareef Abdur-Rahim 3.00 8.00
15 Jamal Mashburn 3.00 8.00

2001-02 Fleer Authentix Sweet Selections

COMPLETE SET (15) 12.00 30.00
STATED ODDS 1:11
1 Kwame Brown .75 2.00
2 Tyson Chandler 1.25 3.00
3 Pau Gasol 3.00 8.00
4 Eddy Curry .75 2.00
5 Jason Richardson 1.25 3.00
6 Shane Battier 1.50 4.00
7 Eddie Griffin .60 1.50
8 DeSagana Diop .50 1.25
9 Rodney White .50 1.25
10 Joe Johnson 1.25 3.00
11 Kedrick Brown .50 1.25
12 Vladimir Radmanovic .60 1.50
13 Richard Jefferson 1.00 2.50
14 Troy Murphy .60 1.50
15 Steven Hunter .50 1.25

2002-03 Fleer Authentix

COMPLETE SET (135) 30.00 80.00
COMP.SET w/o SP's (100) 8.00 20.00
101-135 PRINT RUN 1250 SER.#'d SETS
1 Vince Carter .75 2.00
2 Bobby Jackson .25 .60
3 Cuttino Mobley .25 .60
4 John Stockton .75 2.00
5 Jamal Mashburn .30 .75
6 Ben Wallace .50 1.25
7 Tim Duncan 1.00 2.50
8 Richard Jefferson .30 .75
9 Clifford Robinson .40 1.00
10 Gary Payton .60 1.50
11 Terrell Brandon .25 .60
12 Michael Finley .40 1.00
13 Rasheed Wallace .50 1.25
14 Jason Williams .50 1.25
15 Andre Miller .30 .75
16 Shawn Marion .40 1.00
17 Kobe Bryant 3.00 8.00
18 Jason Terry .30 .75
19 Latrell Sprewell .40 1.00
20 Jerry Stackhouse .40 1.00
21 Tony Parker .60 1.50
22 Ray Allen .60 1.50
23 Dirk Nowitzki 1.00 2.50
24 Chris Webber .50 1.25
25 Rick Fox .25 .60
26 Jermaine O'Neal .30 .75
27 Karl Malone .75 2.00
28 Allan Houston .40 1.00
29 Jason Richardson .40 1.00
30 Morris Peterson .30 .75
31 Kevin Garnett 1.00 2.50
32 Antawn Jamison .30 .75
33 Rashard Lewis .30 .75
34 Jason Kidd .60 1.50
35 Joe Smith .30 .75
36 David Robinson .75 2.00
37 Brian Grant .25 .60
38 Lamond Murray .25 .60
39 Damon Stoudamire .40 1.00
40 Shane Battier .40 1.00
41 Eddy Curry .25 .60
42 Dikembe Mutombo .60 1.50
43 Jamaal Tinsley .25 .60
44 Courtney Alexander .25 .60
45 Wally Szczerbiak .30 .75
46 Antonio McDyess .30 .75
47 Mike Bibby .40 1.00
48 Alonzo Mourning .60 1.50
49 Tyson Chandler .40 1.00
50 Stephon Marbury .50 1.25
51 Sam Cassell .30 .75
52 Steve Nash .75 2.00
53 Bonzi Wells .25 .60
54 Pau Gasol .60 1.50
55 Rodney Rogers .25 .60
56 Allen Iverson 1.00 2.50
57 Derek Fisher .40 1.00
58 Travis Best .25 .60
59 Aaron McKie .25 .60
60 Darius Miles .25 .60
61 Richard Hamilton .50 1.25
62 Marcus Camby .30 .75
63 Eddie Griffin .25 .60
64 Antonio Davis .30 .75
65 David Wesley .25 .60
66 Stromile Swift .25 .60
67 Brent Barry .25 .60
68 Glenn Robinson .40 1.00
69 Antoine Walker .30 .75
70 Tracy McGrady .60 1.50
71 Steve Smith .30 .75
72 Michael Jordan 4.00 10.00
73 Mike Miller .30 .75
74 DeShawn Stevenson .25 .60
75 Raef LaFrentz .25 .60
76 Al Harrington .30 .75
77 Vlade Divac .30 .75
78 Eddie Jones .40 1.00
79 Wesley Person .25 .60
80 Kenny Anderson .30 .75
81 Elton Brand .30 .75
82 Jalen Rose .30 .75
83 Joe Johnson .30 .75
84 Shaquille O'Neal 1.50 4.00
85 Paul Pierce .60 1.50
86 Grant Hill .60 1.50
87 Steve Francis .40 1.00
88 Keon Clark .25 .60
89 Baron Davis .40 1.00
90 Tim Thomas .25 .60
91 Shareef Abdur-Rahim .40 1.00
92 Kenyon Martin .40 1.00
93 Juwan Howard .30 .75
94 Peja Stojakovic .30 .75
95 Lamar Odom .40 1.00
96 Toni Kukoc .40 1.00
97 Darrell Armstrong .25 .60
98 Reggie Miller .75 2.00
99 Andrei Kirilenko .30 .75
100 Keith Van Horn .30 .75
101 Yao Ming RC 10.00 25.00
102 Jay Williams RC 1.50 4.00
103 Mike Dunleavy RC 2.00 5.00
104 Drew Gooden RC 2.00 5.00
105 Nikoloz Tskitishvili RC 1.25 3.00
106 Caron Butler RC 2.00 5.00
107 Chris Wilcox RC 1.50 4.00
108 DaJuan Wagner RC 1.50 4.00
109 Nene Hilario RC 2.00 5.00
110 Qyntel Woods RC 1.25 3.00
111 Jared Jeffries RC 1.50 4.00
112 Tamar Slay RC 1.25 3.00
113 Marcus Haislip RC 1.25 3.00
114 Kareem Rush RC 1.50 4.00
115 Bostjan Nachbar RC 1.50 4.00
116 Melvin Ely RC 1.50 4.00
117 Jiri Welsch RC 1.50 4.00
118 Amare Stoudemire RC 5.00 12.00
119 Frank Williams RC 1.25 3.00
120 Rasual Butler RC 1.50 4.00
121 Dan Dickau RC 1.25 3.00
122 Carlos Boozer RC 2.00 5.00
123 Roger Mason RC 1.50 4.00
124 Corsley Edwards RC 1.50 4.00
125 Robert Archibald RC 1.25 3.00
126 John Salmons RC 2.00 5.00
127 Rod Grizzard RC 1.25 3.00
128 Dan Gadzuric RC 1.50 4.00
129 Sam Clancy RC 1.50 4.00
130 Fred Jones RC 1.50 4.00
131 Casey Jacobsen RC 1.50 4.00
132 Ryan Humphrey RC 1.50 4.00
133 Vincent Yarbrough RC 1.25 3.00
134 Juan Dixon RC 1.50 4.00
135 Tayshaun Prince RC 4.00 10.00

2002-03 Fleer Authentix Balcony

*BALCONY STARS: 2.5X TO 6X BASE CARD HI
*BALCONY RCs: 1.5X TO 4X BASE CARD HI
PRINT RUN 250 SER.#'d SETS

2002-03 Fleer Authentix Club

*CLUB STARS: 4X TO 10X BASE CARD HI
*CLUB RCs: 2X TO 5X BASE CARD HI
PRINT RUN 100 SER.#'d SETS

2002-03 Fleer Authentix Standing Room Only

*SRO STARS: 15X TO 40X BASE HI
*SRO RCs: 3X TO 8X BASE HI
PRINT RUN 25 SER.#'d SETS
17 Kobe Bryant 150.00 400.00
72 Michael Jordan 300.00 600.00

2002-03 Fleer Authentix Autographed Authentix

STATED ODDS 1:586
1 Vince Carter 75.00 200.00

2002-03 Fleer Authentix Courtside Classics Silver

COMPLETE SET (15) 25.00 60.00
PRINT RUN 750 SERIAL #'D SETS
*GOLD: .4X TO 1X BASE HI
1 Vince Carter 3.00 8.00
2 Tim Duncan 4.00 10.00
3 Ray Allen 2.50 6.00
4 Tony Parker 2.50 6.00
5 Michael Jordan 50.00 120.00
6 Chris Webber 2.00 5.00
7 Shaquille O'Neal 6.00 15.00
8 Kobe Bryant 30.00 80.00
9 Jason Kidd 2.50 6.00
10 Dirk Nowitzki 4.00 10.00
11 Shane Battier 1.50 4.00
12 Kevin Garnett 4.00 10.00
13 Jason Richardson 1.50 4.00
14 Karl Malone 3.00 8.00
15 Pau Gasol 2.50 6.00

2002-03 Fleer Authentix Draft Day Ticket

1 Yao Ming/100 40.00 100.00
2 Drew Gooden 4.00 10.00
3 Amare Stoudemire 10.00 25.00
4 Caron Butler 4.00 10.00
5 Chris Wilcox 3.00 8.00
6 DaJuan Wagner 3.00 8.00
7 Dan Dickau 2.50 6.00
8 Qyntel Woods 2.50 6.00

2002-03 Fleer Authentix Hometown Heroes Silver

COMPLETE SET (20) 25.00 60.00
PRINT RUN 500 SERIAL #'D SETS
*GOLD: .25X TO .6X BASE HI
1 Vince Carter 3.00 8.00
2 Tim Duncan 4.00 10.00
3 Kobe Bryant 12.00 30.00
4 Chris Wilcox 1.25 3.00
5 Jay Williams 1.25 3.00
6 Dirk Nowitzki 4.00 10.00
7 Jared Jeffries 1.25 3.00
8 Kevin Garnett 4.00 10.00
9 Drew Gooden 1.50 4.00
10 Shane Battier 1.50 4.00
11 Juan Dixon 1.25 3.00
12 Allen Iverson 4.00 10.00
13 Jason Richardson 1.50 4.00
14 Mike Dunleavy 1.50 4.00
15 Tracy McGrady 2.50 6.00
16 Michael Jordan 30.00 80.00
17 Shaquille O'Neal 6.00 15.00
18 Paul Pierce 2.50 6.00
19 Steve Francis 1.50 4.00
20 Baron Davis 1.50 4.00

2002-03 Fleer Authentix Jersey Authentix

STATED ODDS 1:17
*UNRIPPED: .75X TO 2X BASE HI
UNRIPPED PRINT RUN 50 SER.#'d SETS
1 Shareef Abdur-Rahim 3.00 8.00
2 Antoine Walker 2.50 6.00
3 Paul Pierce 5.00 12.00
4 Eddy Curry SP 2.00 5.00
5 Glenn Robinson 3.00 8.00
6 Vince Carter SP 6.00 15.00
7 Steve Francis 3.00 8.00
8 Reggie Miller 6.00 15.00
9 Darius Miles 2.00 5.00
10 Elton Brand 2.50 6.00
11 Lamar Odom 3.00 8.00
12 Stromile Swift 2.00 5.00
13 Ray Allen SP 5.00 12.00
14 Jason Kidd 5.00 12.00
15 Richard Jefferson 2.50 6.00
16 Kenyon Martin 3.00 8.00
17 Keith Van Horn 2.50 6.00
18 Baron Davis 3.00 8.00
19 Mike Miller 2.50 6.00
20 Grant Hill 5.00 12.00
21 Tracy McGrady 5.00 12.00
22 Allen Iverson 8.00 20.00
23 Dikembe Mutombo 5.00 12.00
24 Shawn Marion 3.00 8.00
25 Stephon Marbury 4.00 10.00
26 Chris Webber 4.00 10.00
27 Gary Payton 5.00 12.00
28 John Stockton 6.00 15.00
29 Karl Malone 6.00 15.00
30 Richard Hamilton 4.00 10.00

2002-03 Fleer Authentix Jersey Authentix All Star Tickets

DM Dikembe Mutombo 10.00 25.00

2002-03 Fleer Authentix Jersey Authentix Game of the Week

STATED ODDS 1:53
1 J.Kidd/A.Iverson 10.00 25.00
2 S.Marbury/J.Stockton 8.00 20.00
3 S.Abdur-Rahim/D.Miles 4.00 10.00
4 B.Davis/R.Miller 8.00 20.00
5 R.Hamilton/R.Jefferson 5.00 12.00
6 K.Malone/E.Brand 8.00 20.00
7 V.Carter/P.Pierce 8.00 20.00
8 R.Allen/S.Francis 6.00 15.00
9 K.Martin/L.Odom 4.00 10.00
10 A.Walker/C.Webber 5.00 12.00
11 E.Curry/G.Robinson 4.00 10.00
12 G.Hill/G.Payton 6.00 15.00
13 T.McGrady/S.Marion 6.00 15.00
14 M.Miller/K.Van Horn 3.00 8.00
15 S.Swift/D.Mutombo 3.00 8.00

2002-03 Fleer Authentix Ticket for Four

PRINT RUN 200 SERIAL #'D SETS
1 Carter/Davis/Francis/Iverson 15.00 40.00
2 Carter/Jeffrsn/T-Mac/Miles 12.00 30.00
3 Carter/Garnett/Malone/Dirk 12.00 30.00
4 Cartr/Chndlr/Pierce/C-Webb 15.00 40.00
5 Battier/Marion/Bibby/Carter 12.00 30.00
6 Carter/Kidd/Tinsley/Walker 12.00 30.00
7 Allen/Carter/Marbury/Mobley 20.00 50.00
8 Carter/Miller/Richrdsn/Swift 12.00 30.00
9 Brand/Carter/Martin/MoPete 12.00 30.00
10 Rahim/Cartr/Stock/Vn Horn 12.00 30.00

2002-03 Fleer Authentix Tip-Off Ticket

PRINT RUN 15 SER.#'d SETS
1 Yao Ming 60.00 150.00
2 Amare Stoudemire 30.00 80.00
3 Caron Butler 12.00 30.00
4 Chris Wilcox 10.00 25.00
5 Qyntel Woods 8.00 20.00

2003-04 Fleer Authentix

COMP.SET w/o SP's (1-100) 15.00 40.00
1 Vince Carter .60 1.50
2 David Wesley .20 .50
3 Eddie Griffin .20 .50
4 Andrei Kirilenko .25 .60
5 Kerry Kittles .25 .60
6 Tayshaun Prince .30 .75
7 Tim Duncan .75 2.00
8 Troy Hudson .20 .50
9 Ben Wallace .40 1.00
10 Manu Ginobili .60 1.50
11 Gary Payton .50 1.25
12 Dajuan Wagner .20 .50
13 Stephon Marbury .40 1.00
14 Shane Battier .25 .60
15 Zydrunas Ilgauskas .25 .60
16 Eric Snow .20 .50
17 Andre Miller .25 .60
18 Shareef Abdur-Rahim .30 .75
19 Kurt Thomas .20 .50
20 Vincent Yarbrough .20 .50
21 Mike Bibby .30 .75
22 Desmond Mason .25 .60
23 Steve Nash .60 1.50
24 Rasheed Wallace .40 1.00
25 Kobe Bryant 2.50 6.00
26 Cuttino Mobley .20 .50
27 Matt Harpring .20 .50
28 Jamal Mashburn .25 .60
29 Mike Dunleavy .25 .60
30 Antonio Davis .25 .60
31 Michael Redd .30 .75
32 Richard Hamilton .40 1.00
33 Predrag Drobnjak .20 .50
34 Kevin Garnett .75 2.00
35 Nene .25 .60
36 Bobby Jackson .25 .60
37 Jason Williams .50 1.25
38 Ricky Davis .25 .60
39 Shawn Marion .30 .75
40 Kareem Rush .20 .50
41 Eddy Curry .20 .50
42 Gordan Giricek .20 .50
43 Brad Miller .25 .60
44 Kwame Brown .20 .50
45 Sam Cassell .25 .60
46 Juwan Howard .25 .60
47 Peja Stojakovic .25 .60
48 Brian Grant .20 .50
49 Al Harrington .25 .60
50 Allen Iverson .75 2.00
51 Caron Butler .25 .60
52 Dirk Nowitzki .75 2.00
53 Zach Randolph .30 .75
54 Pau Gasol .50 1.25
55 Tony Delk .25 .60
56 Grant Hill .40 1.00
57 Shaquille O'Neal 1.25 3.00
58 Tyson Chandler .25 .60
59 Tracy McGrady .50 1.25
60 Ron Artest .30 .75
61 Jerry Stackhouse .40 1.00
62 Jamaal Magloire .20 .50
63 Jason Richardson .30 .75
64 Morris Peterson .20 .50
65 Richard Jefferson .25 .60
66 Kenny Thomas .20 .50
67 Tony Parker .50 1.25
68 Eddie Jones .30 .75
69 Paul Pierce .50 1.25
70 Drew Gooden .25 .60
71 Jermaine O'Neal .30 .75
72 Juan Dixon .20 .50
73 Baron Davis .30 .75
74 Antawn Jamison .30 .75
75 Rashard Lewis .25 .60
76 Nick Van Exel .30 .75
77 Bonzi Wells .20 .50
78 Speedy Claxton .20 .50
79 Carlos Boozer .25 .60
80 Amare Stoudemire .40 1.00
81 Elton Brand .25 .60
82 Jalen Rose .25 .60
83 Keith Van Horn .25 .60
84 Corey Maggette .25 .60
85 Antoine Walker .30 .75
86 Latrell Sprewell .40 1.00
87 Yao Ming .75 2.00
88 Glenn Robinson .25 .60
89 Jason Kidd .50 1.25
90 Gilbert Arenas .30 .75
91 Ray Allen .50 1.25
92 Wally Szczerbiak .25 .60
93 Michael Finley .30 .75

2008-09 Fleer Feel the Game

4 Chris Webber .40 1.00
5 Reggie Miller .60 1.50
6 Jason Terry .25 .60
7 Allan Houston .30 .75
8 Steve Francis .30 .75
9 Karl Malone .60 1.50
00 Kenyon Martin .30 .75
101 Carmelo Anthony RC 8.00 20.00
102 Troy Bell RC 1.00 2.50
103 T.J. Ford RC 1.25 3.00
104 LeBron James RC 200.00 500.00
105 Travis Outlaw RC 1.25 3.00
106 Mike Sweetney RC 1.00 2.50
107 Aleksandar Pavlovic RC 1.25 3.00
108 Dahntay Jones RC 1.25 3.00
109 Chris Bosh RC 5.00 12.00
110 Boris Diaw RC 1.50 4.00
111 Jarvis Hayes RC 1.00 2.50
112 Brian Cook RC 1.00 2.50
113 Luke Ridnour RC 1.50 4.00
114 David West RC 2.00 5.00
115 Zoran Planinic RC 1.00 2.50
116 Zarko Cabarkapa RC 1.00 2.50
117 Marcus Banks RC 1.00 2.50
118 Kirk Hinrich RC 1.50 4.00
119 Darko Milicic RC 1.25 3.00
120 Sofoklis Schortsanitis RC 1.00 2.50
121 Ndudi Ebi RC 1.00 2.50
122 Kendrick Perkins RC 1.25 3.00
123 Leandro Barbosa RC 1.50 4.00
124 Nick Collison RC 1.25 3.00
125 Reece Gaines RC 1.00 2.50
126 Chris Kaman RC 1.50 4.00
127 Mickael Pietrus RC 1.25 3.00
128 Dwyane Wade RC 12.00 30.00
129 Josh Howard RC 1.50 4.00
130 Carlos Delfino RC 1.25 3.00

2003-04 Fleer Authentix Balcony

*1-100 STARS: 2.5X TO 6X BASE HI
*101-130 RC's: .75X TO 2X BASE HI
PRINT RUN 250 SER.#'d SETS

2003-04 Fleer Authentix Club Box

*1-100 STARS: 4X TO 10X BASE HI
*101-130 RC's: 1.25X TO 3X BASE HI
PRINT RUN 100 SER.#'d SETS
25 Kobe Bryant 40.00 100.00
104 LeBron James 800.00 1,500.00

2003-04 Fleer Authentix Rookie Tickets

*TICKETS: .4X TO 1X BASE HI
ANNOUNCED PRINT RUN 250 SETS

2003-04 Fleer Authentix Standing Room Only

*1-100 STARS: 8X TO 20X BASE HI
*101-130 RCs: 3X TO 8X BASE HI
PRINT RUN 25 SER.#'d SETS
104 LeBron James 5,000.00 10,000.00

2003-04 Fleer Authentix Autographs

PRINT RUNS LISTED BELOW
AABS Amare Stoudemire/225 12.50 30.00
AABW Ben Wallace/225 10.00 25.00
AACA Carmelo Anthony/225 25.00 60.00
AACB Chris Bosh/325 8.00 20.00
AADW Dwyane Wade/325 25.00 60.00
AAJH Josh Howard/225 5.00 12.00
AAKM Kenyon Martin/225 5.00 12.00
AAMS Mike Sweetney/325 5.00 12.00
AATB Troy Bell/225 5.00 12.00
AATP2 Tayshaun Prince/225 5.00 12.00

2003-04 Fleer Authentix Autographs All-Star

PRINT RUN 150 SER.#'d SETS
*PLAYOFF: .5X TO 1.25X ALL STAR HI
PLAYOFF PRINT RUN 50 SER.#'d SETS
AAAM Alonzo Mourning 12.00 30.00
AAAS Amare Stoudemire 15.00 40.00
AABW Ben Wallace 12.00 30.00
AACA Carmelo Anthony 20.00 50.00
AACB Chris Bosh 10.00 25.00
AADW Dwyane Wade 25.00 60.00
AAJH Josh Howard 6.00 15.00
AAKM Kenyon Martin 6.00 15.00
AAMG Manu Ginobili 10.00 25.00
AAMS Mike Sweetney 6.00 15.00
AATB Troy Bell 6.00 15.00
AATP Tony Parker 8.00 20.00
AATP2 Tayshaun Prince 6.00 15.00

2003-04 Fleer Authentix Courtside Classics

COMPLETE SET (10) 8.00 20.00
STATED ODDS 1:12
1 Kevin Garnett 2.00 5.00
2 Vince Carter 1.50 4.00
3 Allen Iverson 2.00 5.00
4 Yao Ming 2.00 5.00
5 Tracy McGrady 1.25 3.00
6 Amare Stoudemire 1.00 2.50
7 Jason Richardson .75 2.00
8 Dirk Nowitzki 2.00 5.00
9 Jason Kidd 1.25 3.00
10 Tony Parker 1.25 3.00

2003-04 Fleer Authentix Courtside Classics Game-Used

STATED ODDS 1:37
1 Kevin Garnett 6.00 15.00
2 Vince Carter 5.00 12.00
3 Allen Iverson 6.00 15.00
4 Yao Ming 6.00 15.00
5 Tracy McGrady 4.00 10.00
6 Amare Stoudemire 3.00 8.00
7 Jason Richardson 2.50 6.00
8 Dirk Nowitzki 6.00 15.00
9 Jason Kidd 4.00 10.00
10 Tony Parker 4.00 10.00

2003-04 Fleer Authentix Draft Day Ticket

PRINT RUN 400 SER.#'d SETS
1 Carmelo Anthony 12.00 30.00
2 Mike Sweetney 1.50 4.00
3 Chris Bosh 8.00 20.00
4 Dwyane Wade 30.00 80.00
5 Chris Kaman 2.50 6.00
6 Kirk Hinrich 2.50 6.00
7 T.J. Ford 2.00 5.00
8 Darko Milicic 2.00 5.00
9 Jarvis Hayes 1.50 4.00
10 Nick Collison 2.00 5.00

2003-04 Fleer Authentix Jersey Authentix Ripped

STATED ODDS 1:37
*AS SINGLES: .75X TO 2X BASE JSY HI
ALL STAR PRINT RUN 80 SER.#'d SETS
*UNRIPPED: 1X TO 2.5X BASE JSY HI
UNRIPPED PRINT RUN 50 SER.#'d SETS
JAN Nene 4.00 10.00
JAAI Allen Iverson 6.00 15.00
JAAS Amare Stoudemire 3.00 8.00
JABW Bonzi Wells 2.00 5.00
JABW Ben Wallace 3.00 8.00
JACB Carlos Boozer 2.00 5.00
JADN Dirk Nowitzki 6.00 15.00
JADW DaJuan Wagner 2.00 5.00
JAEC Eddy Curry 1.50 4.00
JAJK Jason Kidd 4.00 10.00
JAJO Jermaine O'Neal 2.50 6.00
JAJR Jason Richardson 2.50 6.00
JAKG Kevin Garnett 6.00 15.00
JAKM Kenyon Martin 2.50 6.00
JAKM Karl Malone 5.00 12.00
JALS Latrell Sprewell 3.00 8.00
JAPG Pau Gasol 4.00 10.00
JAPP Paul Pierce 4.00 10.00
JARM Reggie Miller 5.00 12.00
JASF Steve Francis 2.50 6.00
JASN Steve Nash 5.00 12.00
JATM Tracy McGrady 4.00 10.00
JATP Tayshaun Prince 2.50 6.00
JAVC Vince Carter 5.00 12.00
JAYM Yao Ming 6.00 15.00

2003-04 Fleer Authentix Jersey Authentix Autographs

PRINT RUN 100 SER.#'d SETS
*AS AUTO: .5X TO 1.25X BASE HI
ALL STAR AU PRINT RUN 50 SER.#'d SETS
*PLAYOFF AUTO: .75X TO 2X BASE HI
PLAYOFF AU PRINT RUN 25 SER.#'d SETS
AJAAM Alonzo Mourning 25.00 60.00
AJAAS Amare Stoudemire 12.00 30.00
AJABW Ben Wallace 20.00 50.00
AJACA Carmelo Anthony 15.00 40.00
AJACB Chris Bosh 8.00 20.00
AJADW Dwyane Wade 30.00 80.00
AJAKM Kenyon Martin 8.00 20.00
AJAMS Mike Sweetney 8.00 20.00
AJATP2 Tayshaun Prince 8.00 20.00

2003-04 Fleer Authentix Jersey Authentix Autographs All-Star

*SINGLES: .5X TO 1.25X BASE AUTO
AJADW Dwyane Wade 75.00 200.00

2003-04 Fleer Authentix Jersey Authentix Autographs Playoff

AJADW Dwyane Wade 125.00 300.00

2003-04 Fleer Authentix Jersey Authentix Game of the Week Ripped

STATED ODDS 1:20
*RIPPED: 1X TO 2.5X BASE JSY HI
RIPPED PRINT RUN 50 SER.#'d SETS
1 T.McGrady/B.Wallace 6.00 15.00
2 Y.Ming/A.Stoudemire 8.00 20.00
3 K.Garnett/J.Kidd 8.00 20.00
4 K.Martin/V.Carter 8.00 20.00
5 D.Nowitzki/P.Gasol 6.00 15.00
6 S.Francis/A.Iverson 6.00 15.00
7 S.Nash/J.Richardson 5.00 12.00
8 Nene/K.Malone 5.00 12.00
9 T.Prince/P.Pierce 5.00 12.00
10 C.Boozer/E.Curry 5.00 12.00

2003-04 Fleer Authentix Ticket for Four

PRINT RUN 100 SERIAL #'d SETS
BGMM Booz/Manu/Marb/Miller 15.00 40.00
BHMB Biby/Hamltn/Marion/Brow 15.00 40.00
JGDR Jeff/Gdn/Baron/GRob 15.00 40.00
KPCW Kidd/Parker/Vince/Web 20.00 50.00
MFIW T-Mac/Frncis/Al/Web 25.00 60.00
NGMN Nene/Gasol/Miller/Nash 15.00 40.00
OPMW J.O'Neal/Princ/Mine/Wallce 15.00 40.00
PRGW Pierce/J-Rich/KG/Wells 25.00 60.00
SBCS Peja/Butler/Chand/Slack 15.00 40.00
WMSC Wagner/Yao/Spree/Curry 15.00 40.00

2003-04 Fleer Authentix Ticket Studs

COMPLETE SET (15) 25.00 60.00
STATED ODDS 1:6
1 LeBron James 20.00 50.00
2 Vince Carter 1.25 3.00
3 Mike Sweetney .40 1.00
4 Chris Webber .75 2.00
5 Chris Bosh 2.00 5.00
6 Kobe Bryant 5.00 12.00
7 Dwyane Wade 5.00 12.00
8 Shaquille O'Neal 2.50 6.00
9 T.J. Ford .50 1.25
10 Kenyon Martin .60 1.50
11 Paul Pierce 1.00 2.50
12 Carmelo Anthony 3.00 8.00
13 Tim Duncan 1.50 4.00
14 Pau Gasol 1.00 2.50
15 Steve Francis .60 1.50

2004-05 Fleer Authentix

COMPLETE SET (137)
COMP.SET w/o SP's (100) 15.00 40.00
130-140 RC PRINT RUN 200 SER.#'d SETS
1 Allen Iverson .75 2.00
2 Allan Houston .30 .75
3 Jermaine O'Neal .25 .60
4 Andrei Kirilenko .25 .60
5 Baron Davis .30 .75
6 Rasheed Wallace .40 1.00
7 Manu Ginobili .60 1.50
8 Kenyon Martin .30 .75
9 Richard Hamilton .40 1.00
10 Tony Parker .50 1.25
11 Keith Van Horn .25 .60
12 Steve Nash .60 1.50
13 Darius Miles .20 .50
14 Jason Williams .25 .60
15 Carlos Boozer .25 .60
16 Amare Stoudemire .30 .75
17 Kobe Bryant 2.50 6.00
18 Jason Terry .25 .60
19 Stephon Marbury .40 1.00
20 Ben Wallace .40 1.00
21 Tim Duncan .75 2.00
22 Michael Redd .25 .60
23 Antoine Walker .30 .75
24 Shareef Abdur-Rahim .30 .75
25 Luke Walton .25 .60
26 Reggie Miller .60 1.50
27 Antawn Jamison .25 .60
28 Anfernee Hardaway .75 2.00
29 Yao Ming .75 2.00
30 Chris Bosh .50 1.25
31 Latrell Sprewell .40 1.00
32 Mike Dunleavy .20 .50
33 Luke Ridnour .25 .60
34 Kevin Garnett .75 2.00
35 Darko Milicic .20 .50
36 Bobby Jackson .25 .60
37 Caron Butler .25 .60
38 Dirk Nowitzki .75 2.00
39 Joe Johnson .20 .50
40 Pau Gasol .50 1.25
41 Kirk Hinrich .30 .75
42 Willie Green .30 .75
43 Jamaal Tinsley .20 .50
44 Jarvis Hayes .20 .50
45 Sam Cassell .25 .60
46 Nene .20 .50
47 Mike Bibby .30 .75
48 Lamar Odom .30 .75
49 LeBron James 2.50 6.00
50 Marquis Daniels .20 .50
51 T.J. Ford .20 .50
52 Michael Finley .30 .75
53 Zach Randolph .30 .75
54 Bonzi Wells .25 .60
56 Stephen Jackson .25 .60
57 Gary Payton .50 1.25
58 Jason Kapono .20 .50
59 Glenn Robinson .25 .60
60 Elton Brand .25 .60
61 Jerry Stackhouse .30 .75
62 Jamaal Magloire .20 .50
63 Tracy McGrady .50 1.25
64 Jalen Rose .25 .60
65 Kerry Kittles .25 .60
66 Nick Van Exel .30 .75
67 Rashard Lewis .25 .60
68 Desmond Mason .25 .60
69 Gerald Wallace .25 .60
70 Drew Gooden .20 .50
71 Corey Maggette .25 .60
72 Gilbert Arenas .30 .75
73 Tim Thomas .20 .50
74 Jason Richardson .30 .75
75 Ray Allen .50 1.25
76 Carmelo Anthony .60 1.50
77 Peja Stojakovic .25 .60
78 Dwyane Wade 1.25 3.00
79 Dajuan Wagner .20 .50
80 Shawn Marion .30 .75
81 Shaquille O'Neal 1.25 3.00
82 Eddy Curry .20 .50
83 Samuel Dalembert .20 .50
84 Karl Malone .60 1.50
85 Ricky Davis .25 .60
86 Steve Francis .30 .75
87 Juwan Howard .25 .60
88 Carlos Arroyo .20 .50
89 Jamal Mashburn .25 .60
90 Mickael Pietrus .20 .50
91 Vince Carter .60 1.50
92 Jason Kidd .50 1.25
93 Andre Miller .25 .60
94 Chris Webber .40 1.00
95 Chris Kaman .25 .60
96 Paul Pierce .50 1.25
97 Cuttino Mobley .25 .60
98 Ron Artest .30 .75
99 Matt Harpring .20 .50
100 Richard Jefferson .25 .60
101 Albert Miralles RC 1.50 4.00
102 Albert Miralles RC 1.25 3.00
103 Chris Duhon RC 1.25 3.00
104 Ha Seung-Jin RC 1.50 4.00
105 Antonio Burks RC 1.00 2.50
106 Andre Emmett RC 1.00 2.50
107 Donta Smith RC 1.00 2.50
108 Lionel Chalmers RC 1.25 3.00
109 Rickey Paulding RC 1.00 2.50
110 Jackson Vroman RC 1.00 2.50
111 Anderson Varejao RC 1.25 3.00
112 Beno Udrih RC 1.25 3.00
113 Sasha Vujacic RC 1.25 3.00
114 Kevin Martin RC 2.00 5.00
115 Tony Allen RC 1.25 3.00
116 Delonte West RC 2.50 6.00
117 Sergei Monia RC 1.00 2.50
118 Romain Sato RC 1.00 2.50
119 Jameer Nelson RC 1.50 4.00
120 Josh Smith RC 1.50 4.00
121 Kirk Snyder RC 1.00 2.50
122 Robert Swift RC 1.00 2.50
123 Andre Iguodala RC 2.50 6.00
124 Rafael Araujo RC 1.00 2.50
125 Luol Deng RC 1.50 4.00
126 Josh Childress RC 1.00 2.50
127 Ben Gordon RC 1.50 4.00
128 Emeka Okafor RC 1.25 3.00
129 Dwight Howard RC 5.00 12.00
130 D.Harrison RC/L.Bird AU 30.00 75.00
131 Livingston RC/E.Baylor AU 10.00 25.00
132 D.Harris RC/D.Nelson AU 10.00 25.00
133 L.Jackson RC/P.Silas AU 6.00 15.00
134 A.Biedrins RC/C.Mullin AU 6.00 15.00
135 S.Telfair RC/M.Cheeks AU 6.00 15.00
136 K.Humphries RC/J.Sloan AU 12.00 30.00
137 A.Jefferson RC/D.Ainge AU 12.00 30.00
138 J.R.Smith RC/B.Scott AU 15.00 40.00
139 D.Wright RC/P.Riley AU 10.00 25.00
140 T.Ariza RC/I.Thomas AU 8.00 20.00

2004-05 Fleer Authentix Parallel 100

*1-100: 2.5X TO 6X BASE CARD HI
*101-129: 1X TO 2.5X BASE CARD HI
STATED PRINT RUN 100 SER.#'d SETS
CARDS 55 & 101 NOT ISSUED
49 LeBron James 25.00 60.00
132 Devin Harris 3.00 8.00
134 Andris Biedrins 2.50 6.00
137 Al Jefferson 4.00 10.00
138 J.R. Smith 4.00 10.00
139 Dorell Wright 3.00 8.00
140 Trevor Ariza 4.00 10.00

2004-05 Fleer Authentix Parallel 75

*1-100: 3X TO 8X BASE CARD HI
*101-129: 1.25X TO 3X BASE CARD HI
CARDS 55 & 101 NOT ISSUED
49 LeBron James 30.00 40.00
132 Devin Harris 4.00 10.00
134 Andris Biedrins 3.00 8.00
137 Al Jefferson 5.00 12.00
138 J.R. Smith 5.00 12.00
139 Dorell Wright 4.00 10.00
140 Trevor Ariza 5.00 12.00

2004-05 Fleer Authentix Parallel 50

*1-100: 4X TO 10X BASE CARD HI
*101-129: 1.5X TO 4X BASE CARD HI
STATED PRINT RUN 50 SER.#'d SETS
CARDS 55 & 101 NOT ISSUED
49 LeBron James 40.00 100.00
132 Devin Harris 5.00 12.00
134 Andris Biedrins 4.00 10.00
137 Al Jefferson 6.00 15.00
138 J.R. Smith 6.00 15.00
139 Dorell Wright 5.00 12.00
140 Trevor Ariza 6.00 15.00

2004-05 Fleer Authentix Parallel 25

*1-100: 6X TO 15X BASE HI
*101-129: 2X TO 5X BASE HI
STATED PRINT RUN 25 SER.#'d SETS
CARDS 55 & 101 NOT ISSUED
26 Reggie Miller 10.00 25.00
49 LeBron James 60.00 150.00
132 Devin Harris 6.00 15.00
134 Andris Biedrins 5.00 12.00
137 Al Jefferson 8.00 20.00
138 J.R. Smith 8.00 20.00
139 Dorell Wright 6.00 15.00
140 Trevor Ariza 8.00 20.00

2004-05 Fleer Authentix Autographs

PRINT RUN 50 SER.#'d SETS
*AUTO 25: .6X TO 1.5X BASE HI
BG Ben Gordon 6.00 15.00
CD Carlos Delfino 6.00 15.00
DH Devin Harris 5.00 12.00
DW Delonte West 5.00 12.00
GA Gilbert Arenas 6.00 15.00
HS Ha Seung-Jin 6.00 15.00
JC Josh Childress 4.00 10.00
JH Josh Howard 6.00 15.00
JS Josh Smith 6.00 15.00
KB Kwame Brown 6.00 15.00
KH Kris Humphries 5.00 12.00
KS Kirk Snyder 4.00 10.00
LD Luol Deng 6.00 15.00
LJ Luke Jackson 4.00 10.00
LO Lamar Odom 10.00 25.00
MB Marcus Banks 6.00 15.00
PP Paul Pierce 10.00 25.00
PS Peja Stojakovic 10.00 25.00
RH Richard Hamilton 10.00 25.00
RS Robert Swift 4.00 10.00
SL Shaun Livingston 6.00 15.00
SM Shawn Marion 8.00 20.00
ST Sebastian Telfair 5.00 12.00
VC Vince Carter 15.00 40.00
YT Yuta Tabuse 6.00 15.00

2004-05 Fleer Authentix Autographs Jerseys

PRINT RUN 50 SER.#'d SETS
*AUTO 25: .6X TO 1.5X BASE HI
AS Amare Stoudemire 15.00 40.00
BD Baron Davis 10.00 25.00
CA Carmelo Anthony 25.00 60.00
CB Chris Bosh 12.50 30.00
CW Dwyane Wade 40.00 100.00
GA Gilbert Arenas 10.00 25.00
HS Ha Seung-Jin 8.00 20.00
JC Josh Childress 5.00 12.00
JK Jason Kidd 15.00 40.00
JO Jermaine O'Neal 10.00 25.00
KB Kwame Brown 8.00 20.00
KM Kenyon Martin 10.00 25.00
LO Lamar Odom 12.50 30.00
PP Paul Pierce 12.50 30.00
PS Peja Stojakovic 15.00 30.00
RG Reece Gaines 8.00 20.00
RH Richard Hamilton 12.50 30.00
SA Shareef Abdur-Rahim 8.00 20.00
SF Steve Francis 8.00 20.00
SM Shawn Marion 10.00 25.00
TO Travis Outlaw 8.00 20.00
VC Vince Carter 15.00 40.00
YT Yuta Tabuse 8.00 20.00
ZR Zach Randolph 8.00 20.00

2004-05 Fleer Authentix Autographs Patches

PRINT RUN 25 SER.#'d SETS
AS Amare Stoudemire 30.00 80.00
BD Baron Davis 20.00 50.00
CA Carmelo Anthony 40.00 100.00
DW Dwyane Wade 80.00 200.00
GA Gilbert Arenas 15.00 40.00
JK Jason Kidd 30.00 80.00
JO Jermaine O'Neal 20.00 50.00
KB Kwame Brown 15.00 40.00
KM Kenyon Martin 20.00 50.00
LO Lamar Odom 25.00 60.00
RG Reece Gaines 15.00 40.00
SA Shareef Abdur-Rahim 15.00 40.00
SF Steve Francis 15.00 40.00
SM Shawn Marion 20.00 50.00
SN Steve Nash 75.00 150.00
TO Travis Outlaw 15.00 40.00
VC Vince Carter 25.00 60.00
ZR Zach Randolph 15.00 40.00

2004-05 Fleer Authentix Draft Night Flashbacks

COMPLETE SET (6) 12.00 30.00
STATED ODDS 1:248 H, 1:480 R
CA Carmelo Anthony 3.00 8.00
CB Chris Bosh 2.50 6.00
DM Darko Milicic 1.00 2.50
DW Dwyane Wade 6.00 15.00
KH Kirk Hinrich 1.50 4.00
LJ LeBron James 12.00 30.00

2004-05 Fleer Authentix Draft Night Tickets

COMPLETE SET (10) 25.00 60.00
STATED ODDS 1:240 H, 1:480 R
AJ Al Jefferson 2.50 6.00
BG Ben Gordon 2.50 6.00
DH Devin Harris 2.00 5.00
DH Dwight Howard 8.00 20.00
EO Emeka Okafor 2.00 5.00
JC Josh Childress 1.50 4.00
LD Luol Deng 2.50 6.00
LJ Luke Jackson 1.50 4.00
SL Shaun Livingston 2.50 6.00
ST Sebastian Telfair 2.00 5.00

2004-05 Fleer Authentix Game of the Week Jerseys

STATED PRINT RUN 10 TO 200 SER.#'d SETS
AM C.Anthony/T.McGrady/120 5.00 12.00
AW C.Anthony/D.Wade/60 10.00 25.00
CM V.Carter/K.Martin/180 5.00 12.00
CM V.Carter/T.McGrady/100 5.00 12.00
DG T.Duncan/K.Garnett/110 6.00 15.00
GS K.Garnett/A.Stoudemire/140 6.00 15.00
IF A.Iverson/S.Francis/90 6.00 15.00
MK S.Marbury/J.Kidd/60 4.00 10.00
MS K.Martin/A.Stoudemire/50 2.50 6.00
NF S.Nash/M.Finley/170 5.00 12.00
OD S.O'Neal/T.Duncan/130 10.00 25.00
PR P.Pierce/J.Richardson/190 4.00 10.00
RA M.Redd/R.Allen/150 4.00 10.00
RW Z.Randolph/B.Wallace/200 3.00 8.00
SN P.Stojakovic/D.Nowitzki/60 6.00 15.00
WH D.Wade/K.Hinrich/160 10.00 25.00
WO B.Wallace/J.O'Neal/30 3.00 8.00
WW C.Webber/R.Wallace/70 3.00 8.00

2004-05 Fleer Authentix Hot Tickets

COMPLETE SET (10) 8.00 20.00
STATED ODDS 1:24 H, 1:48 R
AI Allen Iverson 1.25 3.00
CA Carmelo Anthony 1.00 2.50
KB Kobe Bryant 4.00 10.00
KG Kevin Garnett 1.25 3.00
LJ LeBron James 4.00 10.00
SO Shaquille O'Neal 2.00 5.00
TD Tim Duncan 1.25 3.00
TM Tracy McGrady .75 2.00
VC Vince Carter 1.00 2.50
YM Yao Ming 1.25 3.00

2004-05 Fleer Authentix Hot Tickets Jerseys

PRINT RUN 450 SER.#'d SETS
AI Allen Iverson 6.00 15.00
CA Carmelo Anthony 5.00 12.00
KG Kevin Garnett 6.00 15.00
SO Shaquille O'Neal 10.00 25.00
TD Tim Duncan 6.00 15.00
TM Tracy McGrady 4.00 10.00
VC Vince Carter 5.00 12.00
YM Yao Ming 6.00 15.00

2004-05 Fleer Authentix Jerseys

PRINT RUN 175 SER.#'d SETS
*JERSEY 150: .4X TO 1X BASE HI
*JERSEY 75: .5X TO 1.25X BASE HI
*JERSEY 25: .75X TO 2X BASE HI
*PATCH: .75X TO 2X BASE JSY HI
PATCH PRINT RUN 50 SER.#'d SETS
*PATCH 25: 1.25X TO 3X BASE HI
1 Allen Iverson 6.00 15.00
2 Tim Duncan 6.00 15.00
3 Carmelo Anthony 5.00 12.00
4 Kevin Garnett 6.00 15.00
5 Vince Carter 5.00 12.00
6 Paul Pierce 4.00 10.00
7 Dwyane Wade 10.00 25.00
8 Yao Ming 6.00 15.00
9 Shaquille O'Neal 10.00 25.00
10 Jason Kidd 4.00 10.00
11 Dirk Nowitzki 6.00 15.00
12 Steve Francis 2.50 6.00
13 Tracy McGrady 4.00 10.00
14 Amare Stoudemire 3.00 8.00
15 Stephon Marbury 3.00 8.00
16 Kenyon Martin 2.50 6.00
17 Michael Finley 2.50 6.00
18 Steve Nash 5.00 12.00
19 Jason Richardson 2.50 6.00
20 Chris Webber 3.00 8.00
21 Karl Malone 5.00 12.00
22 Jermaine O'Neal 2.50 6.00
23 Tony Parker 4.00 10.00
24 Peja Stojakovic 3.00 8.00
25 Reggie Miller 5.00 12.00
26 Michael Redd 2.50 6.00
27 Rasheed Wallace 3.00 8.00
28 Ray Allen 4.00 10.00
29 Kirk Hinrich 2.50 6.00
30 Latrell Sprewell 3.00 8.00
31 Baron Davis 2.50 6.00
32 Ben Wallace 3.00 8.00
33 Shawn Marion 2.50 6.00
34 Lamar Odom 2.50 6.00
35 Zach Randolph 2.50 6.00

2004-05 Fleer Authentix Showstoppers

COMPLETE SET (15) 6.00 15.00
STATED ODDS 1:8 H, 1:12 R
1 Shaquille O'Neal 1.25 3.00
2 Kobe Bryant 2.50 6.00
3 Jason Kidd .50 1.25
4 LeBron James 2.50 6.00
5 Carmelo Anthony .60 1.50
6 Mike Bibby .30 .75
7 Amare Stoudemire .30 .75
8 Dwyane Wade 1.25 3.00
9 Kevin Garnett .75 2.00
10 Allen Iverson .75 2.00
11 Tim Duncan .75 2.00
12 Paul Pierce .50 1.25
13 Vince Carter .60 1.50
14 Yao Ming .75 2.00
15 Dirk Nowitzki .75 2.00

2004-05 Fleer Authentix Tip-Off Trios

PRINT RUN 75 SER.#'d SETS
*TRIO 25: 1X TO 2.5X BASE HI
DM Nowitzki/Finley/Terry 10.00 25.00
DN Melo/Nene/A.Miller 10.00 25.00
DP B.Wallace/R.Wallace/Rip 10.00 25.00
HR T-Mac/Yao/J.Howard 10.00 25.00
IP Miller/J.O'Neal/Artest 10.00 25.00
LL Odom/Malone/Walton 10.00 25.00
MB Ford/Mason/Redd 10.00 25.00
MH Jones/Shaq/Wade 25.00 60.00
MT Garnett/Cassell/Spree 12.50 30.00
NH B.Davis/Mash/Magloire 10.00 25.00
NK Houston/Marbury/Crawford 10.00 25.00
OM Hill/Francis/D.Howard 12.50 30.00
PS Nash/Marion/Amare 10.00 25.00
SK Webber/Bibby/Peja 10.00 25.00
SS Duncan/Manu/Parker 12.00 30.00

2002 Fleer Authentix WNBA

COMPLETE SET (120) 30.00 80.00
COMPLETE SET w/o RC's (100) 6.00 15.00
101-120 PRINT RUN 2002 SER.#'d SETS
1 Jackie Stiles 1.25 3.00
2 Taj McWilliams-Franklin .30 .75
3 Allison Feaster .40 1.00
4 Sheryl Swoopes 2.00 5.00
5 Edwina Brown .40 1.00
6 DeLisha Milton .30 .75
7 Tonya Edwards .30 .75
8 Svetlana Abrosimova .30 .75
9 Alicia Thompson .30 .75
10 Kristen Rasmussen .30 .75
11 Marie Ferdinand .30 .75
12 Coco Miller .30 .75
13 Tari Phillips .30 .75
14 Kristin Folkl .50 1.25
15 Annie Burgess RC .30 .75
16 Elaine Powell .30 .75
17 Jamie Redd .30 .75
18 Sophia Witherspoon .50 1.25
19 Shannon Johnson .30 .75
20 Amanda Lassiter .30 .75
21 Dawn Staley .75 2.00
22 Dominique Canty .50 1.25
23 Jessie Hicks .30 .75
24 Mwadi Mabika .30 .75
25 Georgia Schweitzer .30 .75
26 Lauren Jackson 8.00 20.00
27 Natalie Williams .60 1.50
28 Tynesha Lewis .30 .75
29 Rushia Brown .30 .75
30 Tamicha Jackson .30 .75
31 Chasity Melvin .30 .75
32 Chamique Holdsclaw 2.00 5.00
33 Michelle Marciniak .50 1.25
34 Lynn Pride .30 .75
35 Tammy Sutton-Brown .30 .75
36 Sandy Brondello .75 2.00
37 Semeka Randall .30 .75
38 Tammy Jackson .30 .75
39 Ukari Figgs .30 .75
40 Ruthie Bolton 1.00 2.50
41 Lisa Harrison .50 1.25
42 Kate Starbird .50 1.25
43 Katie Douglas .50 1.25
44 Coquese Washington .30 .75
45 Sheri Sam .30 .75
46 Vickie Johnson .50 1.25
47 Latasha Byears .50 1.25
48 Erin Buescher .30 .75
49 Ann Wauters .40 1.00
50 Kedra Holland-Corn .30 .75
51 Astou Ndiaye-Diatta .50 1.25
52 Kara Wolters .40 1.00
53 Tully Bevilaqua .30 .75
54 Simone Edwards RC .30 .75
55 Vicky Bullett .50 1.25
56 Nykesha Sales .50 1.25
57 Crystal Robinson .30 .75
58 Tina Thompson 1.00 2.50
59 Lisa Leslie 1.50 4.00
60 Deanna Nolan .30 .75
61 Jennifer Gillom .75 2.00
62 Nadine Malcolm RC .30 .75
63 Merlakia Jones .50 1.25
64 Rebecca Lobo 1.00 2.50
65 Tamecka Dixon .50 1.25
66 Yolanda Griffith 1.00 2.50
67 Teresa Weatherspoon 1.25 3.00
68 Penny Taylor .50 1.25
69 Brooke Wyckoff .60 1.50
70 Murriel Page .30 .75
71 Adrienne Goodson .30 .75
72 Camille Cooper .30 .75
73 Kamila Vodichkova .30 .75
74 Jennifer Azzi 1.00 2.50
75 Katie Smith 1.00 2.50
76 Kristen Veal .30 .75
77 Tamika Catchings .75 2.00
78 Clarisse Machanguana .30 .75
79 Wendy Palmer .75 2.00
80 Ticha Penicheiro .75 2.00
81 Becky Hammon 2.00 5.00
82 Jennifer Rizzotti .75 2.00
83 Helen Luz .30 .75
84 Adrain Williams .30 .75
85 Tamika Whitmore .30 .75
86 Sylvia Crawley .30 .75
87 Edna Campbell .40 1.00
88 Sonja Henning .30 .75
89 Vedrana Grgin .30 .75
90 Tracy Reid .50 1.25
91 Betty Lennox .75 2.00
92 Andrea Stinson .60 1.50
93 Tangela Smith .30 .75
94 Margo Dydek .50 1.25
95 Nikki McCray .75 2.00
96 Sue Wicks .50 1.25
97 Olympia Scott-Richardson .30 .75
98 Ruth Riley .50 1.25
99 Janeth Arcain .30 .75
100 Rita Williams .40 1.00
101 Sue Bird RC 150.00 400.00
102 Swin Cash RC 20.00 50.00
103 S.Dales-Schuman RC 4.00 10.00
104 Asjha Jones RC 4.00 10.00
105 Nikki Teasley RC 2.50 6.00
106 Tamika Williams RC 4.00 10.00
107 Sheila Lambert RC 2.50 6.00
108 Lindsey Yamasaki RC 2.50 6.00
109 Shaunzinski Gortman RC 2.50 6.00
110 Michelle Snow RC 4.00 10.00
111 Danielle Crockrom RC 3.00 8.00
112 Hamchetou Maiga RC 2.50 6.00
113 Tawana McDonald RC 2.50 6.00
114 LaNeishea Caufield RC 2.50 6.00
115 Tamara Moore RC 8.00 20.00
116 Rosalind Ross RC 2.50 6.00
117 Zuzi Klimesova RC 2.50 6.00
118 Lenae Williams RC 2.50 6.00
119 Iziane Castro-Marques RC 2.50 6.00
120 Ayana Walker RC 3.00 8.00

2002 Fleer Authentix WNBA Front Row

*STARS 1-100: 5X TO 12X BASE HI
*RCs 101-120: .75X TO 2X BASE HI
PRINT RUN 100 SERIAL #'d SETS

2002 Fleer Authentix WNBA Autographed Authentix

PRINT RUNS LISTED BELOW
1A Jackie Stiles AU/90 75.00 200.00
1B Jackie Stiles JSY AU/49 100.00 250.00

2002 Fleer Authentix WNBA Courtside Classics

COMPLETE SET (10) 10.00 25.00
1 Jackie Stiles 2.50 6.00
2 Sheri Sam .60 1.50
3 Betty Lennox 1.50 4.00
4 Teresa Weatherspoon 2.50 6.00
5 Katie Douglas 1.00 2.50
6 DeLisha Milton .60 1.50
7 Lauren Jackson 3.00 8.00
8 Murriel Page .75 2.00
9 Kedra Holland-Corn .60 1.50
10 Tina Thompson 2.00 5.00

2002 Fleer Authentix WNBA Memorabilia Authentix Ripped

STATED ODDS 1:8
*UNRIPPED: 3X TO 8X HI
UNRIPPED PRINT RUN 50 SER.#'d SETS
1 Jackie Stiles 5.00 12.00
2 Jennifer Gillom 3.00 8.00
3 Dawn Staley 3.00 8.00
4 Nikki McCray 3.00 8.00
5 Nykesha Sales 2.00 5.00
6 Becky Hammon 8.00 20.00
7 Sheryl Swoopes 6.00 15.00
8 Yolanda Griffith 4.00 10.00
9 Sue Bird 75.00 200.00
10 Lisa Leslie 6.00 15.00
11 Ruthie Bolton 4.00 10.00
12 Natalie Williams 2.50 6.00
13 Chamique Holdsclaw 6.00 15.00

2002 Fleer Authentix WNBA The Ticket

PRINT RUNS LISTED BELOW
1 Jackie Stiles/500 8.00 20.00
2 Lauren Jackson/575 8.00 20.00
3 Andrea Stinson/320 2.00 5.00
4 Jennifer Rizzotti/500 2.50 6.00
5 Ruth Riley/565 1.50 4.00
6 Deanna Nolan/310 1.00 2.50
7 Tamika Catchings/330 2.50 6.00
8 Sheryl Swoopes/600 6.00 15.00
9 Katie Smith/475 3.00 8.00
10 Becky Hammon/390 30.00 80.00
11 Nykesha Sales/375 1.50 4.00
12 Lisa Harrison/475 1.50 4.00
13 Yolanda Griffith/160 3.00 8.00
14 Natalie Williams/495 2.00 5.00
15 Chamique Holdsclaw/410 6.00 15.00
16 Lisa Leslie/450 5.00 12.00

2000-01 Fleer Authority

COMPLETE SET (141) 80.00 160.00
COMP.SET w/o SP's (110) 10.00 25.00
111-141 PRINT RUN 650 SERIAL #'d SETS
FLEER/BGS REDEMPTION CARD ODDS 1:16
1 Dikembe Mutombo .50 1.25
2 Cuttino Mobley .25 .60
3 Brian Grant .25 .60
4 Grant Hill .50 1.25
5 Jim Jackson .25 .60
6 Derek Anderson .25 .60
7 Jerry Stackhouse .30 .75
8 Eddie Jones .30 .75
9 Tracy McGrady .60 1.50
10 Vin Baker .25 .60
11 Jason Terry .30 .75
12 Jerome Williams .20 .50
13 Tim Hardaway .40 1.00
14 Darrell Armstrong .20 .50
15 Rashard Lewis .25 .60
16 Kenny Anderson .25 .60
17 Larry Hughes .30 .75
18 Anthony Mason .30 .75
19 Allen Iverson .75 2.00
20 Gary Payton .50 1.25
21 Antoine Walker .30 .75
22 Antawn Jamison .30 .75

23 Glenn Robinson .30 .75
24 Toni Kukoc .40 1.00
25 Ruben Patterson .20 .50
26 Paul Pierce .50 1.25
27 Mookie Blaylock .30 .75
28 Ray Allen .50 1.25
29 Theo Ratliff .20 .50
30 Vince Carter .60 1.50
31 Jamal Mashburn .25 .60
32 Steve Francis .30 .75
33 Sam Cassell .25 .60
34 Jason Kidd .50 1.25
35 Mark Jackson .25 .60
36 Baron Davis .30 .75
37 Hakeem Olajuwon .60 1.50
38 Darvin Ham .25 .60
39 Shawn Marion .30 .75
40 Antonio Davis .25 .60
41 Derrick Coleman .30 .75
42 Maurice Taylor .20 .50
43 Kevin Garnett .75 2.00
44 Tom Gugliotta .25 .60
45 Karl Malone .60 1.50
46 Elton Brand .30 .75
47 Jonathan Bender .20 .50
48 Terrell Brandon .25 .60
49 Clifford Robinson .30 .75
50 John Stockton .60 1.50
51 Ron Artest .30 .75
52 Reggie Miller .60 1.50
53 Joe Smith .25 .60
54 Shawn Kemp .50 1.25
55 Bryon Russell .20 .50
56 Andre Miller .25 .60
57 Austin Croshere .20 .50
58 Wally Szczerbiak .25 .60
59 Scottie Pippen .75 2.00
60 Donyell Marshall .25 .60
61 Brevin Knight .20 .50
62 Travis Best .20 .50
63 Chauncey Billups .40 1.00
64 Rasheed Wallace .40 1.00
65 Shareef Abdur-Rahim .30 .75
66 Trajan Langdon .20 .50
67 Jalen Rose .25 .60
68 Stephon Marbury .40 1.00
69 Steve Smith .30 .75
70 Mike Bibby .30 .75
71 Lamond Murray .20 .50
72 Lamar Odom .30 .75
73 Keith Van Horn .25 .60
74 Chris Webber .40 1.00
75 Michael Dickerson .20 .50
76 Dirk Nowitzki .75 2.00
77 Corey Maggette .25 .60
78 Kerry Kittles .25 .60
79 Jason Williams .50 1.25
80 Mitch Richmond .40 1.00
81 Michael Finley .30 .75
82 Shaquille O'Neal 1.25 3.00
83 Allan Houston .30 .75
84 Peja Stojakovic .25 .60
85 Juwan Howard .25 .60
86 Nick Van Exel .30 .75
87 Kobe Bryant 2.50 6.00
88 Latrell Sprewell .40 1.00
89 Tim Duncan .75 2.00
90 Richard Hamilton .40 1.00
91 Antonio McDyess .25 .60
92 Glen Rice .30 .75
93 Larry Johnson .40 1.00
94 David Robinson .60 1.50
95 Rod Strickland .20 .50
96 Raef LaFrentz .25 .60
97 Ron Harper .30 .75
98 Patrick Ewing .50 1.25
99 Sean Elliot .25 .60
100 Tariq Abdul-Wahad .20 .50
101 Chucky Atkins .20 .50
102 Marcus Camby .25 .60
103 Corliss Williamson .20 .50
104 Rodney Rogers .20 .50
105 Othella Harrington .20 .50
106 Alan Henderson .20 .50
107 David Wesley .25 .60
108 Michael Doleac .20 .50
109 Doug Christie .25 .60
110 Vitaly Potapenko .20 .50
111 DerMarr Johnson RC 1.00 2.50
112 Jamal Crawford RC 4.00 10.00
113 Morris Peterson RC 1.50 4.00
114 Erick Barkley RC 1.00 2.50
115 Kenyon Martin RC 3.00 8.00
116 Joel Przybilla RC 1.25 3.00
117 Speedy Claxton RC 1.50 4.00
118 Hedo Turkoglu RC 2.50 6.00
119 Etan Thomas RC 1.25 3.00
120 Eddie House RC 1.25 3.00
121 Marcus Fizer RC 1.25 3.00
122 Quentin Richardson RC 1.25 3.00
123 Donnell Harvey RC 1.25 3.00
124 DeShawn Stevenson RC 1.50 4.00
125 Chris Mihm RC 1.00 2.50
126 Courtney Alexander RC 1.00 2.50
127 Keyon Dooling RC 1.25 3.00
128 Jerome Moiso RC 1.00 2.50
129 Stephen Jackson RC 3.00 8.00
130 Chris Porter RC 1.00 2.50
131 Stromile Swift RC 1.25 3.00
132 Desmond Mason RC 2.00 5.00
133 Jason Collier RC 1.50 4.00
134 Mark Madsen RC 1.50 4.00
135 Mamadou N'Diaye RC 1.00 2.50
136 Dalibor Bagaric RC 1.50 4.00
137 Mateen Cleaves RC 1.25 3.00
138 Jamaal Magloire RC 1.50 4.00
139 Khalid El-Amin RC 1.00 2.50
140 Mike Miller RC 2.50 6.00
141 Marc Jackson RC 1.25 3.00

2000-01 Fleer Authority Rookies 1250

*RC 1250: .2X TO .5X BASE RC
STATED ODDS 1:2 GRADED PACKS
STATED PRINT RUN 1250 SETS

2000-01 Fleer Authority Prominence 125/75

*STARS 1-110: 8X TO 20X BASE HI
1-110 PRINT RUN 125 SERIAL #'d SETS
*ROOKIES 111-141: .6X TO 1.5X BASE HI
111-141 PRINT RUN 75 SERIAL #'d SETS

2000-01 Fleer Authority Prominence 75/25

*STARS 1-110: 10X TO 25X BASE HI
*ROOKIES 111-141: 1.25X TO 3X BASE HI
111-141 PRINT RUN 25 SERIAL #'d SETS

2000-01 Fleer Authority Autographics SSD

SEE 2000-01 FLEER AUTOS FOR PRICES
1 Darrell Armstrong 4.00 10.00
3 Chucky Atkins 4.00 10.00
9 Austin Croshere 4.00 10.00
10 Baron Davis 6.00 15.00
11 Vlade Divac 6.00 15.00
13 Brian Grant 5.00 12.00
15 Tom Gugliotta 5.00 12.00
18 Jason Hart 6.00 15.00
20 Antawn Jamison 6.00 15.00
23 Raef LaFrentz 5.00 12.00
26 Corey Maggette 5.00 12.00
29 Jamal Mashburn 5.00 12.00
32 Andre Miller 5.00 12.00
34 Lamar Odom 6.00 15.00
36 Theo Ratliff 4.00 10.00
38 Steve Smith 6.00 15.00
40 Kurt Thomas 4.00 10.00
42 Antoine Walker 6.00 15.00

2000-01 Fleer Authority Autographics SSD Gold

SEE 2000-01 FLEER AUTO GOLD FOR PRICES

2000-01 Fleer Authority Autographics SSD Silver

SEE 2000-01 FLEER AUTO SILVER FOR PRICES

2000-01 Fleer Authority Vince Carter Rookie Remnants

VCRR1 Vince Carter FLR/100 12.50 30.00
VCRR2 Vince Carter FLR JSY/15 20.00 50.00

2000-01 Fleer Authority Feel the Game

FEEL GAME OR REFLECTION ODDS 1:16
SEE 2000-01 FLEER FEEL GAME FOR PRICES

2000-01 Fleer Authority Figures

COMPLETE SET (15) 10.00 25.00
STATED ODDS 1:16
STATED PRINT RUN 1250 SERIAL #'d SETS
*FIGURES 499: .6X TO 1.5X HI
AF1 C.Alexander/M.Finley .60 1.50
AF2 M.Madsen/K.Bryant 5.00 12.00
AF3 D.Johnson/D.Mutombo 1.00 2.50
AF4 M.Cleaves/J.Stackhouse .60 1.50
AF5 K.Martin/K.Van Horn 1.25 3.00
AF6 M.Peterson/V.Carter 1.25 3.00
AF7 D.Miles/L.Odom .60 1.50
AF8 D.Mason/G.Payton 1.00 2.50
AF9 S.Swift/S.Abdur-Rahim .60 1.50
AF10 S.Claxton/A.Iverson 1.50 4.00
AF11 D.Stevenson/K.Malone 1.25 3.00
AF12 M.Fizer/E.Brand .60 1.50
AF13 H.Turkoglu/C.Webber 1.00 2.50
AF14 J.Collier/S.Francis .60 1.50
AF15 M.Miller/G.Hill 1.00 2.50

2000-01 Fleer Authority Rookie Reflections

FEEL GAME OR REFLECTION ODDS 1:16
RR1 Vince Carter 6.00 15.00
RR2 Grant Hill 5.00 12.00
RR3 Keyon Dooling 2.50 6.00
RR4 Jason Kidd 5.00 12.00
RR5 Chris Mihm 2.00 5.00
RR6 Darius Miles 3.00 8.00
RR7 Mike Miller 5.00 12.00
RR8 Quentin Richardson 2.50 6.00
RR9 Hanno Mottola 2.00 5.00
RR10 Allen Iverson 8.00 20.00
RR11 Desmond Mason 4.00 10.00
RR12 Andre Miller 2.50 6.00
RR13 Tracy McGrady 6.00 15.00
RR14 Shawn Marion 3.00 8.00
RR15 John Stockton 6.00 15.00
RR16 Lamar Odom 3.00 8.00
RR17 V.Carter/D.Miles 8.00 20.00
RR18 G.Hill/D.Mason 4.00 10.00
RR19 J.Kidd/Q.Richardson 5.00 12.00
RR20 A.Iverson/K.Dooling 6.00 15.00
RR21 T.McGrady/M.Miller 6.00 15.00
RR22 A.Miller/C.Mihm 3.00 8.00

2000-01 Fleer Authority Seal of Approval

COMPLETE SET (15) 30.00 60.00
STATED PRINT RUN 250 SERIAL #'d SETS
SA1 Kobe Bryant 12.00 30.00
SA2 Tim Duncan 5.00 12.00
SA3 Jason Kidd 3.00 8.00
SA4 Lamar Odom 2.00 5.00
SA5 Kevin Garnett 5.00 12.00
SA6 Elton Brand 2.00 5.00
SA7 Steve Francis 2.00 5.00
SA8 Stromile Swift 1.50 4.00
SA9 Kenyon Martin 4.00 10.00
SA10 Tracy McGrady 4.00 10.00
SA11 Allen Iverson 5.00 12.00
SA12 Grant Hill 3.00 8.00
SA13 Marcus Fizer 1.50 4.00
SA14 Shaquille O'Neal 8.00 20.00
SA15 Vince Carter 4.00 10.00

2000-01 Fleer Authority With Authority

STATED ODDS 1:16
STATED PRINT RUN 999 SERIAL #'d SETS
*WA 299: .5X TO 1.25X HI
WA1 Dirk Nowitzki 2.50 6.00
WA2 Larry Hughes 1.00 2.50
WA3 Eddie Jones 1.00 2.50
WA4 Chris Webber 1.25 3.00
WA5 Grant Hill 1.50 4.00
WA6 Scottie Pippen 2.50 6.00
WA7 Shareef Abdur-Rahim 1.00 2.50
WA8 Kevin Garnett 2.50 6.00
WA9 Allen Iverson 2.50 6.00
WA10 Karl Malone 2.00 5.00
WA11 Kobe Bryant 8.00 20.00
WA12 Tim Duncan 2.50 6.00
WA13 Stephon Marbury 1.25 3.00
WA14 Shaquille O'Neal 4.00 10.00
WA15 Vince Carter 2.00 5.00
WA16 Tracy McGrady 2.00 5.00
WA17 Gary Payton 1.50 4.00
WA18 Steve Francis 1.00 2.50
WA19 Elton Brand 1.00 2.50
WA20 Ray Allen 1.50 4.00

2003-04 Fleer Avant

COMP.SET w/o SP's 15.00 40.00
57-64 PRINT RUN 699 SER.#'d SETS
65-90 PRINT RUN 699 SER.#'d SETS
1 Ben Wallace .75 2.00
2 Glenn Robinson .50 1.25
3 Pau Gasol 1.00 2.50
4 Keon Clark .40 1.00
5 Kobe Bryant 5.00 12.00
6 Morris Peterson .40 1.00
7 Steve Francis .60 1.50
8 Amare Stoudemire .75 2.00
9 Mike Dunleavy Jr. .50 1.25
10 Kevin Garnett 1.50 4.00
11 Yao Ming 1.50 4.00
12 Stephon Marbury .75 2.00
13 Jason Richardson .60 1.50
14 Rasheed Wallace .75 2.00
15 Tayshaun Prince .60 1.50
16 Steve Nash 1.25 3.00
17 Jamal Mashburn .50 1.25
18 Reggie Miller 1.25 3.00
19 Chris Webber .75 2.00
20 Andre Miller .50 1.25
21 Peja Stojakovic .50 1.25
22 Nene .50 1.25
23 Manu Ginobili 1.25 3.00
24 Bonzi Wells .40 1.00
25 Lamar Odom .60 1.50
26 Kwame Brown .40 1.00
27 Caron Butler .60 1.50
28 Gilbert Arenas .60 1.50
29 Dirk Nowitzki 1.50 4.00
30 Allan Houston .60 1.50
31 Michael Finley .60 1.50
32 Drew Gooden .60 1.50
33 Shareef Abdur-Rahim .60 1.50
34 Michael Redd .60 1.50
35 Jerry Stackhouse .75 2.00
36 Scottie Pippen 1.50 4.00
37 Latrell Sprewell .60 1.50
38 Ron Artest .60 1.50
39 Derrick Coleman .60 1.50
40 Eddy Curry .60 1.50
41 Wally Szczerbiak .50 1.25
42 Dajuan Wagner .40 1.00
43 Baron Davis .60 1.50
44 Karl Malone 1.25 3.00
45 Andrei Kirilenko .50 1.25
46 Paul Pierce 1.00 2.50
47 Desmond Mason .50 1.25
48 Shaquille O'Neal 2.50 6.00
49 Rashard Lewis .60 1.50
50 Ricky Davis .50 1.25
51 Kerry Kittles .50 1.25
52 Quentin Richardson .40 1.00
53 Tony Parker 1.00 2.50
54 Elton Brand .50 1.25
55 Richard Jefferson .50 1.25
56 Kenyon Martin .60 1.50
57 Ray Allen 2.50 6.00
58 Mike Bibby 1.50 4.00
59 Tim Duncan 4.00 10.00
60 Allen Iverson 4.00 10.00
61 Jason Kidd 2.50 6.00
62 Tracy McGrady 2.50 6.00
63 Jermaine O'Neal 1.50 4.00
64 Larry Brown 1.50 4.00
65 LeBron James RC 500.00 1,000.00
66 Darko Milicic RC 1.50 4.00
67 Carmelo Anthony RC 10.00 25.00
68 Chris Bosh RC 6.00 15.00
69 Dwyane Wade RC 60.00 150.00
70 Chris Kaman RC 2.00 5.00
71 Kirk Hinrich RC 2.00 5.00
72 T.J. Ford RC 1.50 4.00
73 Mike Sweetney RC 1.25 3.00
74 Jarvis Hayes RC 1.25 3.00
75 Mickael Pietrus RC 1.50 4.00
76 Travis Hansen RC 1.25 3.00
77 Marcus Banks RC 1.25 3.00
78 Luke Ridnour RC 2.00 5.00
79 Reece Gaines RC 1.25 3.00
80 Troy Bell RC 1.25 3.00
81 Zarko Cabarkapa RC 1.25 3.00
82 David West RC 2.50 6.00
83 Aleksandar Pavlovic RC 1.50 4.00
84 Dahntay Jones RC 1.50 4.00
85 Boris Diaw RC 2.00 5.00
86 Zoran Planinic RC 1.25 3.00
87 Travis Outlaw RC 1.50 4.00
88 Brian Cook RC 1.25 3.00
89 Maciej Lampe RC 1.25 3.00
90 Nick Collison RC 1.50 4.00

2003-04 Fleer Avant Black and White

*1-56 SINGLES: 1.25X TO 3X BASE HI
*57-64 USA SINGLES: .6X TO 1.5X BASE HI
*65-90 RC SINGLES: .6X TO 1.5X BASE HI
B&W PRINT RUN 199 SER.#'d SETS
5 Kobe Bryant 12.00 30.00
65 LeBron James 2,000.00 4,000.00

2003-04 Fleer Avant Candid Collection

PRINT RUN 199 SERIAL #'d SETS
1 Allen Iverson 4.00 10.00
2 Steve Francis 1.50 4.00
3 Amare Stoudemire 2.00 5.00
4 Chris Webber 2.00 5.00
5 Paul Pierce 2.50 6.00
6 Caron Butler 1.25 3.00
7 Yao Ming 4.00 10.00
8 Ben Wallace 2.00 5.00
9 Kevin Garnett 4.00 10.00
10 Tim Duncan 4.00 10.00
11 Dirk Nowitzki 4.00 10.00
12 Carmelo Anthony 8.00 20.00
13 Jason Kidd 2.50 6.00
14 Vince Carter 3.00 8.00
15 Tracy McGrady 2.50 6.00
16 Jermaine O'Neal 1.50 4.00
17 Ray Allen 2.50 6.00
18 Shaquille O'Neal 6.00 15.00
19 Kobe Bryant 15.00 40.00
20 LeBron James 600.00 1,200.00

2003-04 Fleer Avant Candid Collection Memorabilia

PRINT RUN 250 SERIAL #'d SETS
AI Allen Iverson 6.00 15.00
AS Amare Stoudemire 3.00 8.00
BW Ben Wallace 3.00 8.00
DN Dirk Nowitzki 6.00 15.00
JK Jason Kidd 4.00 10.00
KG Kevin Garnett 6.00 15.00
SF Steve Francis 2.50 6.00
TD Tim Duncan 6.00 15.00
TM Tracy McGrady 4.00 10.00
YM Yao Ming 6.00 15.00

2003-04 Fleer Avant Materials

OVERALL MEMORABILIA ODDS 1:6
*BLUE: .4X TO 1X BASE HI
BLUE PRINT RUN 400 SER.#'d SETS
*GOLD: .6X TO 1.5X BASE HI
GOLD PRINT RUN 75 SER.#'d SETS
*PATCH: 1.5X TO 4X BASE HI
PATCH PRINT RUN 25 SER.#'d SETS
BC Brian Cook 1.50 4.00
BD Baron Davis 2.50 6.00
BW Ben Wallace 3.00 8.00
CA Carmelo Anthony 12.00 30.00
CB Chris Bosh 8.00 20.00
CK Chris Kaman 2.50 6.00
DG Drew Gooden 2.00 5.00
DJ Dahntay Jones 2.00 5.00
DW1 Dajuan Wagner 2.00 5.00
DW2 David West 3.00 8.00
DW3 Dwyane Wade 20.00 50.00
JH Jarvis Hayes 1.50 4.00
JK Jason Kidd 4.00 10.00
JO Jermaine O'Neal 2.50 6.00
JR Jason Richardson 2.50 6.00
KG Kevin Garnett 6.00 15.00
LR Luke Ridnour 2.50 6.00
MB1 Marcus Banks 1.50 4.00
MB2 Mike Bibby 2.50 6.00
MD Mike Dunleavy 2.00 5.00
MS Mike Sweetney 1.50 4.00
PG Pau Gasol 4.00 10.00
RA Ray Allen 4.00 10.00
RG Reece Gaines 1.50 4.00
SA Shareef Abdur-Rahim 2.50 6.00
SF Steve Francis 2.50 6.00
SM Stephon Marbury 3.00 8.00
SO Shaquille O'Neal 10.00 25.00
TB Troy Bell 1.50 4.00
TH Travis Hansen 1.50 4.00
TM Tracy McGrady 4.00 10.00
TO Travis Outlaw 2.00 5.00
TP1 Tayshaun Prince 2.50 6.00
WS Wally Szczerbiak 2.00 5.00
YM Yao Ming 6.00 15.00

2003-04 Fleer Avant Stars and Stripes

PRINT RUN 204 SERIAL #'d SETS
1 Ray Allen 6.00 15.00
2 Mike Bibby 4.00 10.00
3 Larry Brown 4.00 10.00
4 Tim Duncan 10.00 25.00
5 Allen Iverson 10.00 25.00
6 Jason Kidd 6.00 15.00
7 Tracy McGrady 6.00 15.00
8 Jermaine O'Neal 4.00 10.00

2003-04 Fleer Avant Stars and Stripes Jerseys

PRINT RUN 500 SER.#'d SETS
*RED SINGLES: .5X TO 1.25X BASE JSY HI
RED PRINT RUN 100 SER.#'d SETS
AI Allen Iverson 12.00 30.00
JK Jason Kidd 8.00 20.00
JO Jermaine O'Neal 5.00 12.00
MB Mike Bibby 5.00 12.00
RA Ray Allen 8.00 20.00
TD Tim Duncan 12.00 30.00
TM Tracy McGrady 8.00 20.00

2003-04 Fleer Avant Work of Heart

PRINT RUN 299 SERIAL #'d SETS
1 Yao Ming 5.00 12.00
2 Allen Iverson 5.00 12.00
3 Jason Kidd 3.00 8.00
4 Tim Duncan 5.00 12.00
5 Vince Carter 4.00 10.00
6 Ben Wallace 2.50 6.00
7 Dirk Nowitzki 5.00 12.00
8 Carmelo Anthony 10.00 25.00
9 Tracy McGrady 3.00 8.00
10 Kevin Garnett 5.00 12.00
11 Shaquille O'Neal 8.00 20.00
12 LeBron James 500.00 1,000.00
13 Kobe Bryant 40.00 100.00
14 Paul Pierce 3.00 8.00
15 Chris Webber 2.50 6.00

2003-04 Fleer Avant Work of Heart Jerseys

PRINT RUN 300 SERIAL #'d SETS
AI Allen Iverson 8.00 20.00
BW Ben Wallace 4.00 10.00
CA Carmelo Anthony 15.00 40.00
DN Dirk Nowitzki 8.00 20.00
JK Jason Kidd 5.00 12.00
KG Kevin Garnett 8.00 20.00
TD Tim Duncan 8.00 20.00
TM Tracy McGrady 5.00 12.00
VC Vince Carter 6.00 15.00
YM Yao Ming 8.00 20.00

2002-03 Fleer Box Score

COMP.SET w/o SP's (135) 12.00 30.00
136-150 PRINT RUN 1999 SER.#'d SETS
1 Kwame Brown .25 .60
2 Eddy Curry .25 .60
3 Allen Iverson 1.00 2.50
4 Elton Brand .30 .75
5 Jason Kidd .60 1.50
6 Kedrick Brown .25 .60
7 Elden Campbell .25 .60
8 Jason Richardson .40 1.00
9 Shawn Marion .40 1.00
10 John Stockton .75 2.00
11 Theo Ratliff .25 .60
12 Marcus Fizer .25 .60
13 Tony Parker .60 1.50
14 Michael Redd .30 .75
15 Vince Carter .75 2.00
16 Aaron McKie .25 .60
17 Michael Finley .40 1.00
18 Rashard Lewis .30 .75
19 Steve Nash .75 2.00
20 Reggie Miller .75 2.00
21 Tim Duncan 1.00 2.50
22 Marcus Camby .30 .75
23 Michael Jordan 4.00 10.00
24 Donnell Harvey .25 .60
25 Michael Dickerson .25 .60
26 James Posey .25 .60
27 Vin Baker .30 .75
28 Antonio McDyess .30 .75
29 Mike Miller .30 .75
30 Karl Malone .75 2.00
31 Corliss Williamson .25 .60
32 Derek Anderson .25 .60
33 Scottie Pippen 1.00 2.50
34 Paul Pierce .60 1.50
35 Steve Francis .40 1.00
36 Terrell Brandon .25 .60
37 Cuttino Mobley .25 .60
38 Ron Artest .30 .75
39 Jonathan Bender .25 .60
40 Ron Mercer .25 .60
41 Dirk Nowitzki 1.00 2.50
42 Jermaine O'Neal .30 .75
43 Ray Allen .60 1.50
44 Jason Terry .30 .75
45 Pau Gasol .60 1.50
46 Lamar Odom .40 1.00
47 P.J. Brown .25 .60
48 Kurt Thomas .25 .60
49 Grant Hill .60 1.50
50 David Robinson .75 2.00
51 Rasheed Wallace .50 1.25
52 Antawn Jamison .30 .75
53 Juwan Howard .30 .75
54 Andre Miller .30 .75
55 Kenyon Martin .40 1.00
56 Jason Williams .50 1.25
57 Travis Best .25 .60
58 Brian Grant .25 .60
59 Keith Van Horn .30 .75
60 Alonzo Mourning .60 1.50
61 Rod Strickland .25 .60
62 Jamaal Tinsley .25 .60
63 Sam Cassell .30 .75
64 Jalen Rose .30 .75
65 Tim Thomas .25 .60
66 Eddie Griffin .25 .60
67 Kevin Garnett 1.00 2.50
68 Darrell Armstrong .25 .60
69 Joe Smith .30 .75
70 Wally Szczerbiak .30 .75
71 Richard Jefferson .30 .75
72 Chauncey Billups .40 1.00
73 Kerry Kittles .25 .60
74 Stromile Swift .25 .60
75 Dikembe Mutombo .60 1.50
76 Courtney Alexander .25 .60
77 Tony Delk .25 .60
78 Baron Davis .40 1.00
79 Ricky Davis .30 .75
80 Vlade Divac .30 .75
81 Allan Houston .40 1.00
82 Richard Hamilton .50 1.25
83 Moochie Norris .25 .60
84 Quentin Richardson .25 .60
85 Charlie Ward .25 .60
86 Troy Hudson .25 .60
87 Pat Garrity .25 .60
88 Kobe Bryant 3.00 8.00
89 Tracy McGrady .60 1.50
90 Clifford Robinson .40 1.00
91 Glenn Robinson .40 1.00
92 Todd MacCulloch .25 .60
93 Lamond Murray .25 .60
94 Eric Snow .25 .60
95 Eddie Jones .40 1.00
96 Tom Gugliotta .25 .60
97 Anfernee Hardaway 1.00 2.50
98 Stephon Marbury .50 1.25
99 Antoine Walker .30 .75
100 Gilbert Arenas .40 1.00
101 Ruben Patterson .25 .60
102 Shane Battier .40 1.00
103 David Wesley .25 .60
104 Damon Stoudamire .40 1.00
105 Shaquille O'Neal 1.50 4.00
106 Bonzi Wells .25 .60
107 Mike Bibby .40 1.00
108 Jamal Mashburn .30 .75
109 Peja Stojakovic .30 .75
110 Latrell Sprewell .40 1.00
111 Chris Webber .50 1.25
112 Alvin Williams .25 .60
113 Trenton Hassell .25 .60
114 Derek Fisher .40 1.00
115 Malik Rose .25 .60
116 Kenny Anderson .30 .75
117 Zydrunas Ilgauskas .30 .75
118 Raef LaFrentz .25 .60
119 Gary Payton .60 1.50
120 Vladimir Radmanovic .25 .60
121 Darius Miles .25 .60
122 Antonio Davis .25 .60
123 Larry Hughes .30 .75
124 Maurice Taylor .25 .60
125 Morris Peterson .30 .75
126 Nick Van Exel .40 1.00
127 Ira Newble .25 .60
128 Eric Williams .25 .60
129 Andrei Kirilenko .30 .75
130 Ben Wallace .50 1.25
131 Tyson Chandler .40 1.00
132 Desmond Mason .30 .75
133 Shareef Abdur-Rahim .40 1.00
134 Danny Fortson .25 .60
135 Jerry Stackhouse .40 1.00
136 Yao Ming RC 8.00 20.00
137 Juan Dixon RC 1.25 3.00
138 Caron Butler RC 1.50 4.00
139 Drew Gooden RC 1.50 4.00
140 DaJuan Wagner RC 1.25 3.00
141 Jared Jeffries RC 1.25 3.00
142 Pat Burke RC 1.00 2.50
143 Kareem Rush RC 1.25 3.00
144 Ryan Humphrey RC 1.25 3.00
145 Manu Ginobili RC 8.00 20.00
146 Predrag Savovic RC 1.25 3.00
147 Marcus Haislip RC 1.00 2.50
148 John Salmons RC 1.50 4.00
149 Fred Jones RC 1.25 3.00
150 Roger Mason RC 1.25 3.00
151 Jay Williams RS RC .75 2.00
152 Mike Dunleavy RS RC 1.00 2.50
153 Carlos Boozer RS RC 1.00 2.50
154 Dan Dickau RS RC .60 1.50
155 Tayshaun Prince RS RC 2.00 5.00
156 Nene Hilario RS RC 1.00 2.50
157 Amare Stoudemire RS RC 2.50 6.00
158 Frank Williams RS RC .60 1.50
159 Chris Wilcox RS RC .75 2.00
160 Robert Archibald RS RC .60 1.50
161 Lonny Baxter RS RC .60 1.50
162 Curtis Borchardt RS RC .60 1.50
163 Sam Clancy RS RC .75 2.00
164 Melvin Ely RS RC .75 2.00
165 Dan Gadzuric RS RC .75 2.00
166 Smush Parker RS RC 1.00 2.50
167 Chris Jefferies RS RC .60 1.50
168 Nikoloz Tskitishvili RS RC .60 1.50
169 Casey Jacobsen RS RC .60 1.50
170 Ronald Murray RS RC 1.00 2.50
171 Gordan Giricek RS RC 1.00 2.50
172 Rasual Butler RS RC .75 2.00
173 Jannero Pargo RS RC .60 1.50
174 Bostjan Nachbar RS RC .75 2.00
175 Jiri Welsch RS RC .75 2.00
176 Qyntel Woods RS RC .60 1.50
177 Vincent Yarbrough RS RC .60 1.50
178 Raul Lopez RS RC 1.00 2.50
179 Mehmet Okur RS RC 1.00 2.50
180 Reggie Evans RS RC .75 2.00
181 Karl Malone AS .75 2.00
182 Michael Jordan AS 4.00 10.00
183 Glen Rice AS .30 .75
184 John Stockton AS .75 2.00
185 David Robinson AS .75 2.00
186 Shaquille O'Neal AS 1.50 4.00
187 Dikembe Mutombo AS .60 1.50
188 Gary Payton AS .60 1.50
189 Alonzo Mourning AS .60 1.50
190 Scottie Pippen AS 1.00 2.50
191 Grant Hill AS .60 1.50
192 Vin Baker AS .30 .75
193 Kevin Garnett AS 1.00 2.50
194 Jason Kidd AS .60 1.50
195 Reggie Miller AS .75 2.00
196 Ray Allen AS .60 1.50
197 Kobe Bryant AS 3.00 8.00
198 Tim Duncan AS 1.00 2.50
199 Chris Webber AS .50 1.25
200 Anfernee Hardaway AS 1.00 2.50
201 Latrell Sprewell AS .40 1.00
202 Vince Carter AS .75 2.00
203 Allen Iverson AS 1.00 2.50
204 Eddie Jones AS .40 1.00
205 Antoine Walker AS .30 .75
206 Michael Finley AS .40 1.00
207 Tracy McGrady AS .60 1.50
208 Jerry Stackhouse AS .40 1.00
209 Glenn Robinson AS .40 1.00
210 Allan Houston AS .40 1.00
211 Baron Davis AW .40 1.00
212 Tony Parker AW .60 1.50
213 Rick Fox AW .40 1.00
214 Steve Nash AW .75 2.00
215 Jamaal Magloire AW .25 .60
216 Wang Zhizhi AW .40 1.00
217 Mengke Bateer AW .40 1.00
218 Dirk Nowitzki AW 1.00 2.50
219 Jake Tsakalidis AW .25 .60
220 Adonal Foyle AW .25 .60
221 Marko Jaric AW .40 1.00
222 Arvydas Sabonis AW .30 .75
223 Eduardo Najera AW .25 .60
224 Michael Olowokandi AW .25 .60
225 Darius Miles AW .25 .60
226 Andrei Kirilenko AW .30 .75
227 Mamadou N'Diaye AW .25 .60
228 DeSagana Diop AW .25 .60
229 Rasho Nesterovic AW .25 .60
230 Pau Gasol AW .60 1.50
231 Vladimir Radmanovic AW .25 .60
232 Hedo Turkoglu AW .30 .75
233 Tim Duncan AW 1.00 2.50
234 Peja Stojakovic AW .30 .75
235 Toni Kukoc AW .40 1.00
236 Zeljko Rebraca AW .25 .60
237 Vlade Divac AW .30 .75
238 Dikembe Mutombo AW .60 1.50
239 Shareef Abdur-Rahim AW .40 1.00
240 Jason Richardson AW .40 1.00

2002-03 Fleer Box Score First Edition

*STARS 1-135: 3X TO 8X BASE CARD HI
*RCs 136-150: 1.25X TO 3X BASE CARD HI
*RCs 151-180: 2X TO 5X BASE HI
*AS 181-210: 3X TO 8X BASE HI
*AW 211-240: 3X TO 8X BASE HI
STATED PRINT RUN 100 SER.#'d SETS

2002-03 Fleer Box Score All-Star Roster Game-Used

ONE PER ALL-STAR EDITION SEALED SET
ASR1 Malone WU/Duncan/C-Webb 4.00 10.00
ASR2 Payton Jsy/Kidd/Stockton 4.00 10.00
ASR3 Hill Jsy/Finley/Allen 4.00 10.00
ASR4 Garnett Jsy/Shaq/Duncan 6.00 15.00
ASR5 Kidd Jsy/Iverson/T-Mac 5.00 12.00
ASR6 Carter Jsy/MJ/Kobe 125.00 300.00
ASR7 Iverson Jsy/MJ/Kobe 125.00 300.00
ASR8 McGrady Jsy/Kobe/Iverson 50.00 120.00
ASR9 Stackhouse Jsy/MJ/Carter 4.00 10.00
ASR10 E.Jones Jsy/Walker/Sprwll 4.00 10.00

2002-03 Fleer Box Score Around the World Memorabilia

ONE PER AROUND THE WORLD SEALED SET
ATWM1 Tony Parker 5.00 12.00
ATWM2 Steve Nash JSY 6.00 15.00
ATWM3 Wang Zhizhi JSY 3.00 8.00
ATWM4 Dirk Nowitzki JSY 8.00 20.00
ATWM5 Michael Olowokandi JSY 2.00 5.00
ATWM6 Andrei Kirilenko Shirt 2.50 6.00
ATWM7 Pau Gasol Jacket 5.00 12.00
ATWM8 Hedo Turkoglu Pants 2.50 6.00
ATWM9 Peja Stojakovic Pants 2.50 6.00
ATWM10 Dikembe Mutombo Jacket 5.00 12.00

2002-03 Fleer Box Score Box Score Debuts

STATED PRINT RUN 2002 SERIAL #'d SETS
1 Yao Ming 6.00 15.00
2 Juan Dixon 1.00 2.50
3 Caron Butler 1.25 3.00
4 Drew Gooden 1.25 3.00
5 DaJuan Wagner 1.00 2.50
6 Jared Jeffries 1.00 2.50
7 Manu Ginobili 6.00 15.00
8 Kareem Rush 1.00 2.50
9 Jay Williams 1.00 2.50
10 Mike Dunleavy 1.25 3.00
11 Chris Wilcox 1.00 2.50
12 Dan Dickau .75 2.00
13 Tayshaun Prince 2.50 6.00
14 Nene Hilario 1.25 3.00
15 Amare Stoudemire 3.00 8.00

2002-03 Fleer Box Score Classic Miniatures

COMP.SEALED SET (31) 15.00 40.00
*1ST EDITION: 1.5X TO 4X MINIATURE HI
1ST EDITION PRINT RUN 100 SETS
1 Glenn Robinson .60 1.50
2 Paul Pierce 1.00 2.50
3 Jalen Rose .50 1.25
4 Darius Miles .40 1.00
5 Dirk Nowitzki 1.50 4.00
6 Jason Richardson .60 1.50
7 Antawn Jamison .50 1.25
8 Steve Francis .60 1.50
9 Reggie Miller 1.25 3.00
10 Jermaine O'Neal .50 1.25
11 Elton Brand .50 1.25
12 Kobe Bryant 5.00 12.00
13 Shaquille O'Neal 2.50 6.00
14 Pau Gasol 1.00 2.50
15 Ray Allen 1.00 2.50
16 Kevin Garnett 1.50 4.00
17 Jason Kidd 1.00 2.50
18 Baron Davis .60 1.50
19 Grant Hill 1.00 2.50
20 Tracy McGrady 1.00 2.50
21 Allen Iverson 1.50 4.00
22 Shawn Marion .60 1.50
23 Mike Bibby .60 1.50
24 Chris Webber .75 2.00
25 Tim Duncan 1.50 4.00
26 David Robinson 1.25 3.00
27 Gary Payton 1.00 2.50
28 Vince Carter 1.25 3.00
29 John Stockton 1.25 3.00
30 Michael Jordan 6.00 15.00

2002-03 Fleer Box Score Classic Miniatures Game-Used

ONE PER SEALED MINI SET
1 Elton Brand JSY 2.50 6.00
2 Steve Francis JSY 3.00 8.00
3 Jason Kidd JSY 5.00 12.00
4 Jermaine O'Neal JSY 2.50 6.00
5 Antawn Jamison Jacket 2.50 6.00
6 Mike Bibby JSY 3.00 8.00
7 Grant Hill JSY 5.00 12.00
8 Dirk Nowitzki JSY 8.00 20.00
9 Paul Pierce JSY 5.00 12.00
10 Allen Iverson JSY 8.00 20.00

2002-03 Fleer Box Score Dish and Swish

COMPLETE SET (20) 10.00 25.00
STATED ODDS 1:9
1 Jason Terry .60 1.50
2 Shareef Abdur-Rahim .75 2.00
3 Andre Miller .60 1.50
4 Elton Brand .60 1.50
5 Tracy McGrady 1.25 3.00
6 Grant Hill 1.25 3.00
7 Allen Iverson 2.00 5.00
8 Keith Van Horn .60 1.50
9 Mike Bibby .75 2.00
10 Chris Webber 1.00 2.50
11 Jason Kidd 1.25 3.00
12 Kenyon Martin .75 2.00
13 Steve Nash 1.50 4.00
14 Dirk Nowitzki 2.00 5.00
15 John Stockton 1.50 4.00
16 Karl Malone 1.50 4.00
17 Paul Pierce 1.25 3.00
18 Antoine Walker .60 1.50
19 Shane Battier .75 2.00
20 Pau Gasol 1.25 3.00

2002-03 Fleer Box Score Dish and Swish Dual

COMPLETE SET (10) 20.00 50.00
STATED ODDS 1:108
1 J.Terry/S.Abdur-Rahim 2.50 6.00
2 A.Miller/E.Brand 2.00 5.00
3 T.McGrady/G.Hill 4.00 10.00
4 A.Iverson/K.Van Horn 6.00 15.00

5 M.Bibby/C.Webber 3.00 8.00
6 J.Kidd/K.Martin 4.00 10.00
7 S.Nash/D.Nowitzki 6.00 15.00
8 J.Stockton/K.Malone 5.00 12.00
9 P.Pierce/A.Walker 4.00 10.00
10 S.Battier/P.Gasol 4.00 10.00

2002-03 Fleer Box Score Dish and Swish Memorabilia

STATED ODDS 1:12
1 Jason Terry JSY 2.50 6.00
2 Shareef Abdur-Rahim Jacket 3.00 8.00
3 Andre Miller Shorts 2.50 6.00
4 Elton Brand Shorts 2.50 6.00
5 Tracy McGrady Jacket 5.00 12.00
6 Grant Hill Pants 5.00 12.00
7 Allen Iverson Shorts 8.00 20.00
8 Keith Van Horn Pants 2.50 6.00
9 Mike Bibby Jacket 3.00 8.00
10 Chris Webber Pants 4.00 10.00
11 Jason Kidd JSY 5.00 12.00
12 Kenyon Martin Shorts 3.00 8.00
13 Steve Nash JSY 6.00 15.00
14 Dirk Nowitzki JSY 8.00 20.00
15 John Stockton Pants 6.00 15.00
16 Karl Malone Jacket 6.00 15.00
17 Paul Pierce JSY 5.00 12.00
18 Antoine Walker JSY 2.50 6.00
19 Shane Battier JSY 3.00 8.00
20 Pau Gasol JSY 5.00 12.00

2002-03 Fleer Box Score Freshman Orientation

ONE PER RISING STARS SEALED SET
FO1 Amare Stoudemire Shirt 8.00 20.00
FO2 Lonny Baxter Shirt 2.00 5.00
FO5 Yao Ming JSY 15.00 40.00
FO6 Gordan Giricek Shirt 3.00 8.00
FO7 Caron Butler Shorts 3.00 8.00
FO8 Drew Gooden Shirt 3.00 8.00
FO9 DaJuan Wagner Shirt 2.50 6.00
FO10 Jared Jeffries Shirt 2.50 6.00

2002-03 Fleer Box Score Press Clippings

COMPLETE SET (15) 12.50 30.00
STATED ODDS 1:18
1 Vince Carter 1.50 4.00
2 Jason Richardson .75 2.00
3 Stephon Marbury 1.00 2.50
4 Steve Francis .75 2.00
5 Ray Allen 1.25 3.00
6 Peja Stojakovic .60 1.50
7 Baron Davis .75 2.00
8 Reggie Miller 1.50 4.00
9 Darius Miles .50 1.25
10 Kevin Garnett 2.00 5.00
11 Tim Duncan 2.00 5.00
12 Michael Jordan 8.00 20.00
13 Shaquille O'Neal 3.00 8.00
14 Latrell Sprewell .75 2.00
15 Kobe Bryant 6.00 15.00

2002-03 Fleer Box Score Press Clippings Memorabilia

STATED ODDS 1:12
*PATCH: 1.5X TO 4X BASE HI
PATCH PRINT RUN 50 SER.#'d SETS
1 Vince Carter JSY 6.00 15.00
2 Jason Richardson Jacket 3.00 8.00
3 Stephon Marbury JSY 4.00 10.00
4 Steve Francis JSY 3.00 8.00
6 Peja Stojakovic JSY 2.50 6.00
7 Baron Davis Shirt 3.00 8.00
8 Reggie Miller Shorts 6.00 15.00
9 Darius Miles JSY 2.00 5.00
10 Kevin Garnett JSY 8.00 20.00

1998-99 Fleer Brilliants

COMPLETE SET (125) 30.00 80.00
COMPLETE SET w/o SP (100) 15.00 40.00
RC: STATED ODDS 1:2
1 Tim Duncan 1.00 2.50
2 Dikembe Mutombo .60 1.50
3 Steve Nash .75 2.00
4 Charles Barkley 1.00 2.50
5 Eddie Jones .40 1.00
6 Ray Allen .60 1.50
7 Stephon Marbury .50 1.25
8 Anfernee Hardaway 1.00 2.50
9 Gary Payton .60 1.50
10 Ron Mercer .30 .75
11 Nick Van Exel .40 1.00
12 Brent Barry .30 .75
13 Allan Houston .40 1.00
14 Avery Johnson .30 .75
15 Shareef Abdur-Rahim .40 1.00
16 Rod Strickland .30 .75
17 Vin Baker .30 .75
18 Patrick Ewing .60 1.50
19 Maurice Taylor .25 .60
20 Shawn Kemp .60 1.50
21 Michael Finley .40 1.00
22 Reggie Miller .75 2.00
23 Joe Smith .30 .75
24 Toni Kukoc .40 1.00
25 Blue Edwards .25 .60
26 Joe Dumars .40 1.00
27 Tom Gugliotta .30 .75
28 Terrell Brandon .30 .75
29 Erick Dampier .25 .60
30 Antonio McDyess .30 .75
31 Donyell Marshall .25 .60
32 Jeff Hornacek .30 .75
33 David Wesley .25 .60
34 Derek Anderson .30 .75
35 Ron Harper .40 1.00
36 John Starks .40 1.00
37 Kenny Anderson .30 .75
38 Anthony Mason .30 .75
39 Brevin Knight .25 .60
40 Antoine Walker .40 1.00
41 Mookie Blaylock .30 .75
42 LaPhonso Ellis .25 .60
43 Tim Hardaway .50 1.25
44 Jim Jackson .25 .60
45 Matt Maloney .25 .60
46 Lamond Murray .25 .60
47 Voshon Lenard .25 .60
48 Isaiah Rider .30 .75
49 Tracy Murray .25 .60
50 Grant Hill .60 1.50
51 Vlade Divac .40 1.00
52 Glenn Robinson .40 1.00
53 Tony Battie .25 .60
54 Bobby Jackson .30 .75
55 Jayson Williams .25 .60
56 Doug Christie .30 .75
57 Glen Rice .40 1.00
58 Tim Thomas .30 .75
59 Lindsey Hunter .25 .60
60 Scottie Pippen 1.00 2.50
61 Marcus Camby .30 .75
61B Keith Van Horn Promo .60 1.50
62 Clifford Robinson .25 .60
63 John Wallace .25 .60
64 Larry Johnson .60 1.50
65 Bryon Russell .25 .60
66 Isaac Austin .25 .60
67 Sam Cassell .30 .75
68 Allen Iverson 1.00 2.50
69 Chauncey Billups .50 1.25
70 Kobe Bryant 3.00 8.00
71 Kevin Willis .25 .60
72 Jason Kidd .60 1.50
73 Chris Webber .50 1.25
74 Rasheed Wallace .50 1.25
75 Karl Malone .75 2.00
76 Shawn Bradley .25 .60
77 Kerry Kittles .30 .75
78 Mitch Richmond .50 1.25
79 Antonio Daniels .25 .60
80 Kevin Garnett 1.00 2.50
81 Nick Anderson .25 .60
82 David Robinson .75 2.00
83 Jamal Mashburn .40 1.00
84 Rodney Rogers .25 .60
85 Michael Stewart .25 .60
86 Rik Smits .30 .75
87 Billy Owens .30 .75
88 Damon Stoudamire .40 1.00
89 Theo Ratliff .30 .75
90 Keith Van Horn .40 1.00
91 Hakeem Olajuwon .75 2.00
92 Alonzo Mourning .60 1.50
93 Steve Smith .30 .75
94 Mark Jackson .30 .75
95 Cedric Ceballos .30 .75
96 Bryant Reeves .25 .60
97 Juwan Howard .30 .75
98 Detlef Schrempf .40 1.00
99 John Stockton .75 2.00
100 Shaquille O'Neal 1.50 4.00
101 Micheal Olowokandi RC 1.00 2.50
102 Mike Bibby RC 1.50 4.00
103 Raef LaFrentz RC 1.00 2.50
104 Antawn Jamison RC 1.25 3.00
105 Vince Carter RC 4.00 10.00
106 Robert Traylor RC .75 2.00
107 Jason Williams RC 2.50 6.00
108 Larry Hughes RC 1.25 3.00
109 Dirk Nowitzki RC 5.00 12.00
110 Paul Pierce RC 3.00 8.00
111 Bonzi Wells RC .75 2.00
112 Michael Doleac RC .60 1.50
113 Keon Clark RC .75 2.00
114 Michael Dickerson RC .75 2.00
115 Matt Harpring RC .75 2.00
116 Bryce Drew RC .50 1.25
117 Pat Garrity RC .60 1.50
118 Roshown McLeod RC .50 1.25
119 Ricky Davis RC 1.25 3.00
120 Rashard Lewis RC 1.25 3.00
121 Tyronn Lue RC 1.00 2.50
122 Al Harrington RC 1.00 2.50
123 Corey Benjamin RC .50 1.25
124 Felipe Lopez RC .50 1.25
125 Korleone Young RC .75 2.00

1998-99 Fleer Brilliants 24-Karat Gold

*STARS: 40X TO 100X BASE CARD HI
*RCs: 10X TO 25X BASE HI
STATED PRINT RUN 24 SERIAL #'d SETS
1 Tim Duncan 200.00 500.00
3 Steve Nash 500.00 1,000.00
4 Charles Barkley 200.00 500.00
8 Anfernee Hardaway 150.00 400.00
15 Shareef Abdur-Rahim 75.00 200.00
20 Shawn Kemp 100.00 250.00
36 John Starks 60.00 150.00
40 Antoine Walker 100.00 250.00
50 Grant Hill 200.00 500.00
60 Scottie Pippen 200.00 500.00
69 Chauncey Billups 100.00 250.00
70 Kobe Bryant 1,000.00 2,000.00
74 Rasheed Wallace 150.00 400.00
75 Karl Malone 150.00 400.00
80 Kevin Garnett 125.00 300.00
91 Hakeem Olajuwon 125.00 300.00
92 Alonzo Mourning 75.00 150.00
100 Shaquille O'Neal 1,000.00 2,000.00
104 Antawn Jamison 60.00 150.00
105 Vince Carter 150.00 400.00
107 Jason Williams 500.00 1,000.00
109 Dirk Nowitzki 600.00 1,200.00
110 Paul Pierce 150.00 400.00

1998-99 Fleer Brilliants Blue

COMPLETE SET (125) 40.00 100.00
*STARS: .6X TO 1.5X BASE CARD HI
*RCs: .5X TO 1.25X BASE
STARS: STATED ODDS 1:3
RCs: STATED ODDS 1:6

1998-99 Fleer Brilliants Gold

*STARS: 15X TO 40X BASE CARD HI
*RCs: 5X TO 12X BASE HI
STATED PRINT RUN 99 SERIAL #'d SETS
4 Charles Barkley 25.00 60.00
105 Vince Carter 60.00 150.00
109 Dirk Nowitzki 100.00 250.00
110 Paul Pierce 40.00 100.00

1998-99 Fleer Brilliants Illuminators

COMPLETE SET (15) 15.00 40.00
STATED ODDS 1:10
1 Michael Olowokandi 1.00 2.50
2 Mike Bibby 1.50 4.00
3 Antawn Jamison 1.25 3.00
4 Vince Carter 4.00 10.00
5 Robert Traylor .75 2.00
6 Larry Hughes 1.25 3.00
7 Paul Pierce 3.00 8.00
8 Raef LaFrentz 1.00 2.50
9 Dirk Nowitzki 5.00 12.00
10 Corey Benjamin .50 1.25
11 Michael Dickerson .75 2.00
12 Roshown McLeod .50 1.25
13 Ricky Davis 1.25 3.00
14 Tyronn Lue 1.00 2.50
15 Al Harrington 1.00 2.50

1998-99 Fleer Brilliants Shining Stars

COMPLETE SET (15) 12.00 30.00
STATED ODDS 1:20
*PULSARS: 4X TO 10X HI COLUMN
PULSARS: STATED ODDS 1:400
1 Tim Thomas 1.00 2.50
2 Antoine Walker 1.25 3.00
3 Tim Duncan 3.00 8.00
4 Keith Van Horn 1.25 3.00
5 Grant Hill 2.00 5.00
6 Shaquille O'Neal 5.00 12.00
7 Kevin Garnett 3.00 8.00
8 Allen Iverson 3.00 8.00
9 Shareef Abdur-Rahim 1.25 3.00
10 Shawn Kemp 2.00 5.00
11 Anfernee Hardaway 3.00 8.00
12 Scottie Pippen 3.00 8.00
13 Stephon Marbury 1.50 4.00
14 Kobe Bryant 10.00 25.00
15 Ron Mercer 1.00 2.50

1994-95 Fleer European

COMPLETE SET (270) 15.00 40.00
1 Stacey Augmon .30 .75
2 Sergei Bazarevich .40 1.00
3 Mookie Blaylock .40 1.00
4 Tyrone Corbin .25 .60
5 Craig Ehlo .25 .60
6 Andrew Lang .25 .60
7 Grant Long .25 .60
8 Ken Norman .25 .60
9 Steve Smith .30 .75
10 Dee Brown .30 .75
11 Sherman Douglas .25 .60
12 Acie Earl .25 .60
13 Blue Edwards .25 .60
14 Rick Fox .25 .60
15 Xavier McDaniel .25 .60
16 Greg Minor .40 1.00
17 Eric Montross .30 .75
18 Dino Radja .25 .60
19 Dominique Wilkins .60 1.50
20 Michael Adams .25 .60
21 Muggsy Bogues .30 .75
22 Scott Burrell .25 .60
23 Dell Curry .25 .60
24 Kenny Gattison .25 .60
25 Hersey Hawkins .25 .60
26 Larry Johnson .50 1.25
27 Alonzo Mourning .60 1.50
28 Robert Parish .40 1.00
29 David Wingate .25 .60
30 B.J. Armstrong .40 1.00
31 Corie Blount .25 .60
32 Steve Kerr .30 .75
33 Larry Krystkowiak .25 .60
34 Toni Kukoc .50 1.25
35 Luc Longley .30 .75
36 Will Perdue .25 .60
37 Scottie Pippen 1.00 2.50
38 Dickey Simpkins .30 .75
39 Terrell Brandon .25 .60
40 Brad Daugherty .30 .75
41 Tyrone Hill .25 .60
42 Chris Mills .30 .75
43 Bobby Phills .25 .60
44 Mark Price .40 1.00
45 Gerald Wilkins .30 .75
46 John Williams .25 .60
47 Tony Dumas .30 .75
48 Jim Jackson .30 .75
49 Popeye Jones .25 .60
50 Jason Kidd 2.00 5.00
51 Jamal Mashburn .40 1.00
52 Doug Smith .25 .60
53 Roy Tarpley .25 .60
54 Mahmoud Abdul-Rauf .25 .60
55 Dale Ellis .25 .60
56 LaPhonso Ellis .25 .60
57 Dikembe Mutombo .60 1.50
58 Robert Pack .30 .75
59 Rodney Rogers .25 .60
60 Jalen Rose 1.00 2.50
61 Bryant Stith .25 .60
62 Brian Williams .25 .60
63 Reggie Williams .25 .60
64 Bill Curley .25 .60
65 Johnny Dawkins .25 .60
66 Joe Dumars .40 1.00
67 Grant Hill 2.00 5.00
68 Allan Houston .40 1.00
69 Lindsey Hunter .25 .60
70 Oliver Miller .25 .60
71 Terry Mills .25 .60
72 Mark West .25 .60
73 Victor Alexander .25 .60
74 Manute Bol .25 .60
75 Chris Gatling .25 .60
76 Tim Hardaway .50 1.25
77 Chris Mullin .50 1.25
78 Ricky Pierce .25 .60
79 Clifford Rozier .25 .60
80 Rony Seikaly .25 .60
81 Latrell Sprewell .50 1.25
82 Chris Webber .75 2.00
83 Scott Brooks .25 .60
84 Sam Cassell .40 1.00
85 Mario Elie .25 .60
86 Carl Herrera .25 .60
87 Robert Horry .40 1.00
88 Vernon Maxwell .25 .60
89 Hakeem Olajuwon .75 2.00
90 Kenny Smith .30 .75
91 Otis Thorpe .25 .60
92 Antonio Davis .30 .75
93 Dale Davis .25 .60
94 Vern Fleming .25 .60
95 Mark Jackson .30 .75
96 Derrick McKey .25 .60
97 Reggie Miller .75 2.00
98 Byron Scott .30 .75
99 Rik Smits .30 .75
100 John Williams .25 .60
101 Haywoode Workman .25 .60
102 Terry Dehere .25 .60
103 Gary Grant .25 .60
104 Lamond Murray .40 1.00
105 Eric Piatkowski .40 1.00
106 Pooh Richardson .25 .60
107 Malik Sealy .25 .60
108 Elmore Spencer .25 .60
109 Loy Vaught .25 .60
110 Elden Campbell .25 .60
111 Cedric Ceballos .30 .75
112 Vlade Divac .40 1.00
113 Eddie Jones 1.25 3.00
114 George Lynch .25 .60
115 Anthony Peeler .25 .60
116 Tony Smith .25 .60
117 Sedale Threatt .25 .60
118 Nick Van Exel .40 1.00
119 Bimbo Coles .25 .60
120 Kevin Gamble .25 .60
121 Harold Miner .25 .60
122 Billy Owens .25 .60
123 Khalid Reeves .30 .75
124 Glen Rice .40 1.00
125 John Salley .25 .60
126 Kevin Willis .30 .75
127 Vin Baker .40 1.00
128 Jon Barry .25 .60
129 Todd Day .25 .60
130 Lee Mayberry .25 .60
131 Eric Mobley .25 .60
132 Eric Murdock .25 .60
133 Johnny Newman .25 .60
134 Glenn Robinson .75 2.00
135 Mike Brown .25 .60
136 Stacey King .25 .60
137 Christian Laettner .30 .75
138 Donyell Marshall .40 1.00
139 Isaiah Rider .40 1.00
140 Sean Rooks .25 .60
141 Doug West .25 .60
142 Micheal Williams .25 .60
143 Kenny Anderson .30 .75
144 Benoit Benjamin .25 .60
145 P.J. Brown .25 .60
146 Derrick Coleman .40 1.00
147 Yinka Dare .25 .60
148 Kevin Edwards .25 .60
149 Sleepy Floyd .25 .60
150 Armon Gilliam .25 .60
151 Chris Morris .25 .60
152 Greg Anthony .25 .60
153 Hubert Davis .25 .60
154 Patrick Ewing .60 1.50
155 Derek Harper .30 .75
156 Anthony Mason .30 .75
157 Charles Oakley .40 1.00
158 Doc Rivers .30 .75
159 Charles Smith .25 .60
160 John Starks .40 1.00
161 Charlie Ward .40 1.00
162 Monty Williams .50 1.25
163 Nick Anderson .25 .60
164 Anthony Avent .25 .60
165 Horace Grant .40 1.00
166 Anfernee Hardaway .75 2.00
167 Shaquille O'Neal 1.50 4.00
168 Donald Royal .25 .60
169 Dennis Scott .30 .75
170 Brooks Thompson .30 .75
171 Jeff Turner .25 .60
172 Dana Barros .25 .60
173 Shawn Bradley .25 .60
174 Jeff Malone .25 .60
175 Tim Perry .25 .60
176 B.J. Tyler .25 .60
177 Clarence Weatherspoon .25 .60
178 Sharone Wright .30 .75
179 Danny Ainge .40 1.00
180 Charles Barkley 1.00 2.50
181 A.C. Green .30 .75
182 Kevin Johnson .40 1.00
183 Joe Kleine .25 .60
184 Dan Majerle .40 1.00
185 Danny Manning .30 .75
186 Wesley Person .40 1.00
187 Wayman Tisdale .25 .60
188 Clyde Drexler .60 1.50
189 Harvey Grant .25 .60
190 Jerome Kersey .25 .60
191 Aaron McKie .40 1.00
192 Tracy Murray .25 .60
193 Terry Porter .25 .60
194 Clifford Robinson .30 .75
195 Rod Strickland .25 .60
196 Buck Williams .25 .60
197 Brian Grant .60 1.50
198 Bobby Hurley .25 .60
199 Olden Polynice .25 .60
200 Mitch Richmond .50 1.25
201 Lionel Simmons .25 .60
202 Spud Webb .30 .75
203 Walt Williams .25 .60
204 Trevor Wilson .25 .60
205 Willie Anderson .25 .60
206 Terry Cummings .30 .75
207 Vinny Del Negro .25 .60
208 Sean Elliott .30 .75
209 Avery Johnson .30 .75
210 Moses Malone .40 1.00
211 J.R. Reid .25 .60
212 David Robinson .75 2.00
213 Dennis Rodman 1.00 2.50
214 Bill Cartwright .30 .75
215 Kendall Gill .25 .60
216 Ervin Johnson .25 .60
217 Shawn Kemp .60 1.50
218 Sarunas Marciulionis .25 .60
219 Nate McMillan .30 .75
220 Gary Payton .60 1.50
221 Sam Perkins .25 .60
222 Detlef Schrempf .40 1.00
223 David Benoit .25 .60
224 Jeff Hornacek .30 .75
225 Jay Humphries .25 .60
226 Karl Malone .75 2.00
227 Bryon Russell .25 .60
228 Felton Spencer .25 .60
229 John Stockton .75 2.00
230 Mitchell Butler .25 .60
231 Rex Chapman .25 .60
232 Calbert Cheaney .30 .75
233 Kevin Duckworth .25 .60
234 Tom Gugliotta .25 .60
235 Don MacLean .25 .60
236 Gheorghe Muresan .25 .60
237 Scott Skiles .25 .60
238 Atlanta Hawks .20 .50
239 Boston Celtics .20 .50
240 Charlotte Hornets .20 .50
241 Chicago Bulls .20 .50
242 Cleveland Cavaliers .20 .50
243 Dallas Mavericks .20 .50
244 Denver Nuggets .20 .50
245 Detroit Pistons .20 .50
246 Golden State Warriors .20 .50
247 Houston Rockets .20 .50
248 Indiana Pacers .20 .50
249 Los Angeles Clippers .20 .50
250 Los Angeles Lakers .20 .50
251 Miami Heat .20 .50
252 Milwaukee Bucks .20 .50
253 Minnesota Timberwolves .20 .50
254 New Jersey Nets .20 .50
255 New York Knicks .20 .50
256 Orlando Magic .20 .50
257 Philadelphia 76ers .20 .50
258 Phoenix Suns .20 .50
259 Portland Trail Blazers .20 .50
260 Sacramento Kings .20 .50
261 San Antonio Spurs .20 .50
262 Seattle Supersonics .20 .50
263 Utah Jazz .20 .50
264 Washington Bullets .20 .50
265 Toronto Raptors .20 .50
266 Vancouver Grizzlies .20 .50
267 NBA Logo .20 .50
268 Checklist 1-103 .20 .50
269 Checklist 104-204 .20 .50
270 Checklist 205-270
(Checklist Insert Sets) .20 .50

1994-95 Fleer European All-Defensive

COMPLETE SET (5) 1.25 3.00
1 Mookie Blaylock
Scottie Pippen 1.00 2.50
2 Horace Grant
Gary Payton .60 1.50
3 Nate McMillan
Dennis Rodman 1.00 2.50
4 Charles Oakley
David Robinson .75 2.00
5 Hakeem Olajuwon
Latrell Sprewell .75 2.00

1994-95 Fleer European Award Winners

COMPLETE SET (2) .60 1.50
1 Dell Curry
Chris Webber .75 2.00
2 Don MacLean
Hakeem Olajuwon .75 2.00

1994-95 Fleer European Career Achievement Awards

COMPLETE SET (2) 1.50 4.00
1 Patrick Ewing
Karl Malone 1.50 4.00
2 Hakeem Olajuwon
Scottie Pippen 2.00 5.00

1994-95 Fleer European League Leaders

COMPLETE SET (4) 1.25 3.00
1 Mahmoud Abdul-Rauf
Dennis Rodman .75 2.00
2 Tracy Murray
Dikembe Mutombo .50 1.25
3 Shaquille O'Neal
David Robinson 1.25 3.00
4 John Stockton
Nate McMillan .60 1.50

1994-95 Fleer European Triple Threats

COMPLETE SET (5) 2.00 5.00
1 Mookie Blaylock
Reggie Miller 1.00 2.50
2 Patrick Ewing
Shaquille O'Neal 2.00 5.00
3 Shawn Kemp
David Robinson 1.00 2.50
4 Karl Malone
Latrell Sprewell 1.00 2.50
5 Hakeem Olajuwon
Scottie Pippen 1.25 3.00

1995-96 Fleer European

COMPLETE SET (499) 20.00 50.00
1 Stacey Augmon .12 .30
2 Mookie Blaylock .15 .40
3 Craig Ehlo .10 .25
4 Andrew Lang .10 .25
5 Grant Long .10 .25
6 Ken Norman .10 .25
7 Steve Smith .12 .30
8 Dee Brown .12 .30
9 Sherman Douglas .10 .25
10 Eric Montross .10 .25
11 Dino Radja .10 .25
12 David Wesley .10 .25
13 Dominique Wilkins .25 .60
14 Muggsy Bogues .15 .40
15 Scott Burrell .10 .25
16 Dell Curry .15 .40
17 Hersey Hawkins .12 .30
18 Larry Johnson .20 .50
19 Alonzo Mourning .25 .60
20 Robert Parish .20 .50
21 B.J. Armstrong .15 .40
22 Michael Jordan 1.50 4.00
23 Steve Kerr .15 .40
24 Toni Kukoc .20 .50
25 Will Perdue .12 .30
26 Scottie Pippen .40 1.00
27 Terrell Brandon .12 .30
28 Tyrone Hill .10 .25
29 Chris Mills .10 .25
30 Bobby Phills .12 .30
31 Mark Price .15 .40
32 John Williams .10 .25
33 Lucious Harris .10 .25
34 Jim Jackson .12 .30
35 Popeye Jones .10 .25
36 Jason Kidd .25 .60
37 Jamal Mashburn .15 .40
38 George McCloud .10 .25
39 Roy Tarpley .12 .30
40 Lorenzo Williams .10 .25
41 Mahmoud Abdul-Rauf .12 .30
42 Dale Ellis .10 .25
43 LaPhonso Ellis .12 .30
44 Dikembe Mutombo .25 .60
45 Robert Pack .10 .25
46 Rodney Rogers .12 .30
47 Jalen Rose .20 .50
48 Bryant Stith .10 .25
49 Reggie Williams .10 .25
50 Joe Dumars .15 .40
51 Grant Hill .25 .60
52 Allan Houston .12 .30
53 Lindsey Hunter .10 .25
54 Oliver Miller .10 .25
55 Terry Mills .10 .25
56 Mark West .10 .25
57 Chris Gatling .10 .25
58 Tim Hardaway .20 .50
59 Donyell Marshall .10 .25
60 Chris Mullin .15 .40
61 Carlos Rogers .10 .25
62 Clifford Rozier .10 .25
63 Rony Seikaly .10 .25
64 Latrell Sprewell .15 .40
65 Sam Cassell .15 .40
66 Clyde Drexler .25 .60
67 Mario Elie .10 .25
68 Carl Herrera .10 .25
69 Robert Horry .15 .40
70 Vernon Maxwell .10 .25
71 Hakeem Olajuwon .30 .75
72 Kenny Smith .12 .30
73 Dale Davis .10 .25
74 Mark Jackson .12 .30
75 Derrick McKey .10 .25
76 Reggie Miller .30 .75
77 Sam Mitchell .15 .40
78 Byron Scott .12 .30
79 Rik Smits .12 .30
80 Terry Dehere .10 .25
81 Tony Massenburg .10 .25
82 Lamond Murray .10 .25
83 Pooh Richardson .10 .25
84 Malik Sealy .10 .25
85 Loy Vaught .10 .25
86 Elden Campbell .10 .25
87 Cedric Ceballos .12 .30
88 Vlade Divac .15 .40
89 Eddie Jones .15 .40
90 Anthony Peeler .10 .25
91 Sedale Threatt .10 .25
92 Nick Van Exel .15 .40
93 Bimbo Coles .10 .25
94 Matt Geiger .10 .25
95 Billy Owens .10 .25
96 Khalid Reeves .10 .25
97 Glen Rice .15 .40
98 John Salley .10 .25
99 Kevin Willis .10 .25
100 Vin Baker .12 .30
101 Marty Conlon .10 .25
102 Todd Day .10 .25
103 Lee Mayberry .10 .25
104 Eric Murdock .10 .25
105 Glenn Robinson .15 .40
106 Winston Garland .10 .25
107 Tom Gugliotta .10 .25
108 Christian Laettner .12 .30
109 Isaiah Rider .15 .40
110 Sean Rooks .10 .25
111 Doug West .10 .25
112 Kenny Anderson .12 .30
113 Benoit Benjamin .10 .25
114 P.J. Brown .10 .25
115 Derrick Coleman .12 .30
116 Armon Gilliam .10 .25
117 Chris Morris .10 .25
118 Rex Walters .10 .25
119 Hubert Davis .10 .25
120 Patrick Ewing .25 .60
121 Derek Harper .12 .30
122 Anthony Mason .10 .25
123 Charles Oakley .12 .30
124 Charles Smith .10 .25
125 John Starks .15 .40
126 Nick Anderson .12 .30
127 Anthony Bowie .10 .25
128 Horace Grant .12 .30
129 Anfernee Hardaway .40 1.00
130 Shaquille O'Neal .60 1.50
131 Donald Royal .10 .25
132 Dennis Scott .10 .25
133 Brian Shaw .10 .25
134 Derrick Alston .10 .25
135 Dana Barros .12 .30
136 Shawn Bradley .10 .25
137 Willie Burton .12 .30
138 Clarence Weatherspoon .10 .25
139 Scott Williams .10 .25
140 Sharone Wright .10 .25
141 Danny Ainge .15 .40
142 Charles Barkley .40 1.00
143 A.C. Green .12 .30
144 Kevin Johnson .15 .40
145 Dan Majerle .15 .40
146 Danny Manning .12 .30
147 Elliot Perry .10 .25
148 Wesley Person .10 .25
149 Wayman Tisdale .10 .25
150 Chris Dudley .10 .25
151 Jerome Kersey .10 .25
152 Aaron McKie .10 .25
153 Terry Porter .10 .25
154 Clifford Robinson .15 .40
155 James Robinson .10 .25
156 Rod Strickland .12 .30
157 Otis Thorpe .12 .30
158 Buck Williams .10 .25
159 Brian Grant .12 .30
160 Bobby Hurley .10 .25
161 Olden Polynice .10 .25
162 Mitch Richmond .20 .50
163 Michael Smith .10 .25
164 Spud Webb .15 .40
165 Walt Williams .10 .25
166 Terry Cummings .12 .30
167 Vinny Del Negro .10 .25
168 Sean Elliott .12 .30
169 Avery Johnson .12 .30
170 Chuck Person .12 .30
171 J.R. Reid .10 .25
172 Doc Rivers .12 .30
173 David Robinson .30 .75
174 Dennis Rodman .30 .75
175 Vincent Askew .10 .25
176 Kendall Gill .10 .25
177 Shawn Kemp .25 .60
178 Sarunas Marciulionis .15 .40
179 Nate McMillan .10 .25
180 Gary Payton .25 .60
181 Sam Perkins .10 .25
182 Detlef Schrempf .15 .40
183 David Benoit .10 .25
184 Antoine Carr .10 .25
185 Blue Edwards .10 .25
186 Jeff Hornacek .12 .30
187 Adam Keefe .10 .25
188 Karl Malone .30 .75
189 Felton Spencer .10 .25
190 John Stockton .30 .75
191 Rex Chapman .10 .25
192 Calbert Cheaney .10 .25
193 Juwan Howard .15 .40
194 Don MacLean .10 .25
195 Gheorghe Muresan .10 .25
196 Scott Skiles .10 .25
197 Chris Webber .20 .50
198 Mookie Blaylock TD .15 .40
199 Patrick Ewing TD .25 .60
200 Michael Jordan TD 1.50 4.00
201 Alonzo Mourning TD .25 .60
202 Dikembe Mutombo TD .25 .60
203 Hakeem Olajuwon TD .30 .75
204 Shaquille O'Neal TD .60 1.50
205 Gary Payton TD .25 .60
206 Scottie Pippen TD .40 1.00
207 David Robinson TD .30 .75
208 Dennis Rodman TD .30 .75
209 John Stockton TD .30 .75
210 Brian Grant RS .12 .30
211 Grant Hill RS .25 .60
212 Juwan Howard RS .15 .40
213 Eddie Jones RS .15 .40
214 Jason Kidd RS .25 .60
215 Donyell Marshall RS .10 .25
216 Eric Montross RS .10 .25
217 Lamond Murray RS .10 .25
218 Wesley Person RS .10 .25
219 Khalid Reeves RS .10 .25
220 Glenn Robinson RS .15 .40
221 Jalen Rose RS .20 .50
222 Clifford Rozier RS .10 .25
223 Michael Smith RS .10 .25
224 Sharone Wright RS .10 .25
225 Grant Hill
Charles Barkley AS .40 1.00
226 Scottie Pippen
Shawn Kemp AS .40 1.00
227 Shaquille O'Neal
Hakeem Olajuwon AS .60 1.50
228 Anfernee Hardaway
Dan Majerle AS .40 1.00
229 Reggie Miller
Latrell Sprewell AS .30 .75
230 Vin Baker
Cedric Ceballos AS .12 .30
231 Tyrone Hill
Karl Malone AS .30 .75
232 Larry Johnson
Detlef Schrempf AS .20 .50
233 Patrick Ewing
David Robinson AS .30 .75
234 Alonzo Mourning
Dikembe Mutombo AS .25 .60
235 Dana Barros
Gary Payton AS .25 .60
236 Joe Dumars
John Stockton AS .30 .75
237 Mitch Richmond MVP .20 .50
238 Atlanta Hawks Logo .10 .25
239 Boston Celtics Logo .10 .25
240 Charlotte Hornets Logo .10 .25
241 Chicago Bulls Logo .10 .25
242 Cleveland Cavaliers Logo .10 .25
243 Dallas Mavericks Logo .10 .25
244 Denver Nuggets Logo .10 .25
245 Detroit Pistons Logo .10 .25
246 Golden State Warriors Logo .10 .25
247 Houston Rockets Logo .10 .25
248 Indiana Pacers Logo .10 .25
249 Los Angeles Clippers Logo .10 .25
250 Los Angeles Lakers Logo .10 .25
251 Miami Heat Logo .10 .25
252 Milwaukee Bucks Logo .10 .25
253 Minnesota Timberwolves Logo .10 .25

254 New Jersey Nets Logo .10 .25
255 New York Knicks Logo .10 .25
256 Orlando Magic Logo .10 .25
257 Philadelphia 76ers Logo .10 .25
258 Phoenix Suns Logo .10 .25
259 Portland Trail Blazers Logo .10 .25
260 Sacramento Kings Logo .10 .25
261 San Antonio Spurs Logo .10 .25
262 Seattle Supersonics Logo .10 .25
263 Toronto Raptors Logo .10 .25
264 Utah Jazz Logo .10 .25
265 Vancouver Grizzlies Logo .10 .25
266 Washington Bullets Logo .10 .25
267 NBA Logo .10 .25
268 Checklist #1 .10 .25
269 Checklist #2 .10 .25
270 Checklist #3 .10 .25
271 Stacey Augmon .12 .30
272 Mookie Blaylock .15 .40
273 Grant Long .10 .25
274 Ken Norman .10 .25
275 Steve Smith .12 .30
276 Spud Webb .15 .40
277 Dana Barros .12 .30
278 Rick Fox .10 .25
279 Kendall Gill .10 .25
280 Khalid Reeves .10 .25
281 Glen Rice .15 .40
282 Luc Longley .12 .30
283 Dennis Rodman .30 .75
284 Dan Majerle .15 .40
285 Tony Dumas .10 .25
286 Elmore Spencer .10 .25
287 Otis Thorpe .12 .30
288 B.J. Armstrong .15 .40
289 Sam Cassell .15 .40
290 Clyde Drexler .25 .60
291 Mario Elie .10 .25
292 Robert Horry .15 .40
293 Hakeem Olajuwon .30 .75
294 Kenny Smith .12 .30
295 Antonio Davis .10 .25
296 Eddie Johnson .10 .25
297 Ricky Pierce .10 .25
298 Eric Piatkowski .10 .25
299 Rodney Rogers .12 .30
300 Brian Williams .10 .25
301 Corie Blount .10 .25
302 George Lynch .10 .25
303 Kevin Gamble .10 .25
304 Alonzo Mourning .25 .60
305 Eric Mobley .10 .25
306 Terry Porter .10 .25
307 Micheal Williams .10 .25
308 Kevin Edwards .10 .25
309 Vern Fleming .10 .25
310 Charlie Ward .12 .30
311 Jon Koncak .10 .25
312 Richard Dumas .10 .25
313 Jeff Malone .10 .25
314 Vernon Maxwell .10 .25
315 John Williams .10 .25
316 Harvey Grant .10 .25
317 Dontonio Wingfield .10 .25
318 Tyrone Corbin .10 .25
319 Sarunas Marciulionis .15 .40
320 Will Perdue .12 .30
321 Hersey Hawkins .12 .30
322 Ervin Johnson .10 .25
323 Shawn Kemp .25 .60
324 Gary Payton .25 .60
325 Sam Perkins .10 .25
326 Detlef Schrempf .15 .40
327 Chris Morris .10 .25
328 Robert Pack .10 .25
329 Willie Anderson ET .10 .25
330 Jimmy King ET .10 .25
331 Oliver Miller ET .10 .25
332 Tracy Murray ET .10 .25
333 Ed Pinckney ET .10 .25
334 Alvin Robertson ET .10 .25
335 Carlos Rogers ET .10 .25
336 John Salley ET .10 .25
337 Damon Stoudamire ET .25 .60
338 Zan Tabak ET .10 .25
339 Ashraf Amaya ET .10 .25
340 Greg Anthony ET .10 .25
341 Benoit Benjamin ET .10 .25
342 Blue Edwards ET .10 .25
343 Kenny Gattison ET .10 .25
344 Antonio Harvey ET .10 .25
345 Chris King ET .10 .25
346 Lawrence Moten ET .10 .25
347 Bryant Reeves ET .07 .20
348 Byron Scott ET .15 .40
349 Cory Alexander .15 .40
350 Jerome Allen .15 .40
351 Brent Barry .25 .60
352 Mario Bennett .12 .30
353 Travis Best .15 .40
354 Junior Burrough .15 .40
355 Jason Caffey .15 .40
356 Randolph Childress .12 .30
357 Sasha Danilovic .15 .40
358 Mark Davis .15 .40
359 Tyus Edney .15 .40
360 Michael Finley .40 1.00
361 Sherrell Ford .12 .30
362 Kevin Garnett 1.25 3.00
363 Alan Henderson .15 .40
364 Frankie King .15 .40
365 Jimmy King .15 .40
366 Donny Marshall .15 .40
367 Antonio McDyess .20 .50
368 Loren Meyer .10 .25
369 Lawrence Moten .15 .40
370 Ed O'Bannon .12 .30
371 Greg Ostertag .15 .40
372 Cherokee Parks .12 .30
373 Theo Ratliff .25 .60
374 Bryant Reeves .12 .30
375 Shawn Respert .12 .30
376 Lou Roe .15 .40
377 Arvydas Sabonis .30 .75
378 Joe Smith .20 .50
379 Jerry Stackhouse .50 1.25
380 Damon Stoudamire .40 1.00
381 Bob Sura .12 .30
382 Kurt Thomas .15 .40
383 Gary Trent .12 .30
384 David Vaughn .15 .40
385 Rasheed Wallace .50 1.25
386 Eric Williams .15 .40
387 Corliss Williamson .15 .40
388 George Zidek .12 .30
389 Checklist .10 .25
390 Checklist .10 .25
391 Mookie Blaylock FF .15 .40
392 Dino Radja FF .10 .25
393 Larry Johnson FF .20 .50
394 Michael Jordan FF 1.50 4.00
395 Tyrone Hill FF .10 .25
396 Jason Kidd FF .25 .60
397 Dikembe Mutombo FF .25 .60
398 Grant Hill FF .25 .60
399 Joe Smith FF .20 .50
400 Hakeem Olajuwon FF .30 .75
401 Reggie Miller FF .30 .75
402 Loy Vaught FF .10 .25
403 Nick Van Exel FF .15 .40
404 Alonzo Mourning FF .25 .60
405 Glenn Robinson FF .15 .40
406 Kevin Garnett FF 1.25 3.00
407 Kenny Anderson FF .12 .30
408 Patrick Ewing FF .25 .60
409 Shaquille O'Neal FF .60 1.50
410 Jerry Stackhouse FF .50 1.25
411 Charles Barkley FF .40 1.00
412 Clifford Robinson FF .15 .40
413 Mitch Richmond FF .20 .50
414 David Robinson FF .30 .75
415 Shawn Kemp FF .25 .60
416 Damon Stoudamire FF .40 1.00
417 Karl Malone FF .30 .75
418 Bryant Reeves FF .12 .30
419 Chris Webber FF .20 .50
420 Shawn Kemp TP .25 .60
421 Karl Malone TP .30 .75
422 Antonio McDyess TP .20 .50
423 Alonzo Mourning TP .25 .60
424 Hakeem Olajuwon TP .30 .75
425 Shaquille O'Neal TP .60 1.50
426 David Robinson TP .30 .75
427 Glenn Robinson TP .15 .40
428 Joe Smith TP .20 .50
429 Chris Webber TP .20 .50
430 Derrick Alston CE .10 .25
431 Brian Grant CE .12 .30
432 Grant Hill CE .25 .60
433 Juwan Howard CE .15 .40
434 Eddie Jones CE .15 .40
435 Jason Kidd CE .25 .60
436 Donyell Marshall CE .10 .25
437 Anthony Miller CE .10 .25
438 Eric Mobley CE .10 .25
439 Eric Montross CE .10 .25
440 Lamond Murray CE .10 .25
441 Wesley Person CE .10 .25
442 Eric Piatkowski CE .10 .25
443 Khalid Reeves CE .10 .25
444 Glenn Robinson CE .15 .40
445 Carlos Rogers CE .10 .25
446 Jalen Rose CE .20 .50
447 Clifford Rozier CE .10 .25
448 Michael Smith CE .10 .25
449 Sharone Wright CE .10 .25
450 Brent Barry CE .25 .60
451 Jason Caffey CE .15 .40
452 Randolph Childress CE .12 .30
453 Kevin Garnett CE 1.25 3.00
454 Alan Henderson CE .15 .40
455 Antonio McDyess CE .20 .50
456 Ed O'Bannon CE .12 .30
457 Cherokee Parks CE .12 .30
458 Theo Ratliff CE .25 .60
459 Bryant Reeves CE .12 .30
460 Shawn Respert CE .12 .30
461 Joe Smith CE .20 .50
462 Jerry Stackhouse CE .50 1.25
463 Damon Stoudamire CE .40 1.00
464 Bob Sura CE .12 .30
465 Kurt Thomas CE .15 .40
466 Gary Trent CE .12 .30
467 Rasheed Wallace CE .50 1.25
468 Eric Williams CE .15 .40
469 Corliss Williamson CE .15 .40
470 Mookie Blaylock EE .15 .40
471 Vlade Divac EE .15 .40
472 Clyde Drexler EE .25 .60
473 Patrick Ewing EE .25 .60
474 Horace Grant EE .12 .30
475 Anfernee Hardaway EE .40 1.00
476 Grant Hill EE .25 .60
477 Eddie Jones EE .15 .40
478 Michael Jordan EE 1.50 4.00
479 Jason Kidd EE .25 .60
480 Alonzo Mourning EE .25 .60
481 Dikembe Mutombo EE .25 .60
482 Hakeem Olajuwon EE .30 .75
483 Shaquille O'Neal EE .60 1.50
484 Gary Payton EE .25 .60
485 Scottie Pippen EE .40 1.00
486 David Robinson EE .30 .75
487 Latrell Sprewell EE .15 .40
488 John Stockton EE .30 .75
489 Rod Strickland EE .10 .25
490 Kevin Garnett RP 1.25 3.00
491 Antonio McDyess RP .20 .50
492 Ed O'Bannon RP .12 .30
493 Bryant Reeves RP .12 .30
494 Shawn Respert RP .12 .30
495 Joe Smith RP .20 .50
496 Jerry Stackhouse RP .50 1.25
497 Damon Stoudamire RP .40 1.00
498 Gary Trent RP .12 .30
499 Rasheed Wallace RP .50 1.25

1996-97 Fleer European

COMPLETE SET (330) 40.00 100.00
COMPLETE SERIES 1 (150) 12.50 30.00
COMPLETE SERIES 2 (150) 25.00 60.00
COMP.TRANSLATION SET (30) 2.50 6.00
1 Stacey Augmon .20 .50
2 Mookie Blaylock .25 .60
3 Christian Laettner .25 .60
4 Grant Long .15 .40
5 Steve Smith .20 .50
6 Rick Fox .15 .40
7 Dino Radja .15 .40
8 Eric Williams .15 .40
9 Kenny Anderson .20 .50
10 Dell Curry .25 .60
11 Larry Johnson .30 .75
12 Glen Rice .25 .60
13 Michael Jordan 2.50 6.00
14 Toni Kukoc .25 .60
15 Scottie Pippen .60 1.50
16 Dennis Rodman .60 1.50
17 Terrell Brandon .20 .50
18 Chris Mills .15 .40
19 Bobby Phills .15 .40
20 Bob Sura .15 .40
21 Jim Jackson .15 .40
22 Jason Kidd .40 1.00
23 Jamal Mashburn .25 .60
24 George McCloud .15 .40
25 Mahmoud Abdul-Rauf .20 .50
26 Antonio McDyess .25 .60
27 Dikembe Mutombo .40 1.00
28 Jalen Rose .20 .50
29 Bryant Stith .15 .40
30 Joe Dumars .30 .75
31 Grant Hill .40 1.00
32 Allan Houston .25 .60
33 Theo Ratliff .15 .40
34 Otis Thorpe .20 .50
35 Chris Mullin .30 .75
36 Joe Smith .20 .50
37 Latrell Sprewell .25 .60
38 Kevin Willis .20 .50
39 Sam Cassell .20 .50
40 Clyde Drexler .40 1.00
41 Robert Horry .25 .60
42 Hakeem Olajuwon .50 1.25
43 Dale Davis .15 .40
44 Mark Jackson .20 .50
45 Derrick McKey .15 .40
46 Reggie Miller .50 1.25
47 Rik Smits .20 .50
48 Brent Barry .20 .50
49 Malik Sealy .15 .40
50 Loy Vaught .15 .40
51 Brian Williams .15 .40
52 Elden Campbell .15 .40
53 Cedric Ceballos .20 .50
54 Vlade Divac .25 .60
55 Eddie Jones .25 .60
56 Nick Van Exel .25 .60
57 Tim Hardaway .30 .75
58 Alonzo Mourning .40 1.00
59 Kurt Thomas .15 .40
60 Walt Williams .15 .40
61 Vin Baker .20 .50
62 Sherman Douglas .15 .40
63 Glenn Robinson .25 .60
64 Kevin Garnett .75 2.00
65 Tom Gugliotta .15 .40
66 Isaiah Rider .20 .50
67 Shawn Bradley .15 .40
68 Chris Childs .15 .40
69 Armon Gilliam .15 .40
70 Ed O'Bannon .15 .40
71 Patrick Ewing .40 1.00
72 Derek Harper .20 .50
73 Anthony Mason .20 .50
74 Charles Oakley .25 .60
75 John Starks .25 .60
76 Nick Anderson .15 .40
77 Horace Grant .25 .60
78 Anfernee Hardaway .60 1.50
79 Shaquille O'Neal 1.00 2.50
80 Dennis Scott .20 .50
81 Derrick Coleman .20 .50
82 Vernon Maxwell .15 .40
83 Jerry Stackhouse .30 .75
84 Clarence Weatherspoon .15 .40
85 Charles Barkley .60 1.50
86 Michael Finley .25 .60
87 Kevin Johnson .25 .60
88 Wesley Person .15 .40
89 Clifford Robinson .25 .60
90 Arvydas Sabonis .25 .60
91 Rod Strickland .25 .60
92 Gary Trent .15 .40
93 Tyus Edney .15 .40
94 Brian Grant .20 .50
95 Billy Owens .15 .40
96 Mitch Richmond .30 .75
97 Vinny Del Negro .15 .40
98 Sean Elliott .25 .60
99 Avery Johnson .20 .50
100 David Robinson .50 1.25
101 Hersey Hawkins .15 .40
102 Shawn Kemp .40 1.00
103 Gary Payton .40 1.00
104 Detlef Schrempf .25 .60
105 Oliver Miller .15 .40
106 Tracy Murray .15 .40
107 Damon Stoudamire .25 .60
108 Sharone Wright .15 .40
109 Jeff Hornacek .20 .50
110 Karl Malone .50 1.25
111 John Stockton .50 1.25
112 Greg Anthony .15 .40
113 Bryant Reeves .15 .40
114 Byron Scott .25 .60
115 Calbert Cheaney .15 .40
116 Juwan Howard .25 .60
117 Gheorghe Muresan .15 .40
118 Rasheed Wallace .30 .75
119 Chris Webber .30 .75
120 Mookie Blaylock HL .25 .60
121 Dino Radja HL .15 .40
122 Larry Johnson HL .30 .75
123 Michael Jordan HL 2.50 6.00
124 Terrell Brandon HL .20 .50
125 Jason Kidd HL .40 1.00
126 Antonio McDyess HL .25 .60
127 Grant Hill HL .40 1.00
128 Latrell Sprewell HL .25 .60
129 Hakeem Olajuwon HL .50 1.25
130 Reggie Miller HL .50 1.25
131 Loy Vaught HL .15 .40
132 Cedric Ceballos HL .20 .50
133 Alonzo Mourning HL .40 1.00
134 Vin Baker HL .20 .50
135 Isaiah Rider HL .20 .50
136 Armon Gilliam HL .15 .40
137 Patrick Ewing HL .40 1.00
138 Shaquille O'Neal HL 1.00 2.50
139 Jerry Stackhouse HL .30 .75
140 Charles Barkley HL .60 1.50
141 Clifford Robinson HL .25 .60
142 Mitch Richmond HL .30 .75
143 David Robinson HL .50 1.25
144 Shawn Kemp HL .40 1.00
145 Damon Stoudamire HL .25 .60
146 Karl Malone HL .50 1.25
147 Bryant Reeves HL .15 .40
148 Juwan Howard HL .30 .75
149 Checklist .15 .40
150 Checklist .15 .40
151 Atlanta Hawks .20 .50
152 Boston Celtics .20 .50
153 Charlotte Hornets .20 .50
154 Chicago Bulls .20 .50
155 Cleveland Cavaliers .20 .50
156 Dallas Mavericks .20 .50
157 Denver Nuggets .20 .50
158 Detroit Pistons .20 .50
159 Golden State Warriors .20 .50
160 Houston Rockets .20 .50
161 Indiana Pacers .20 .50
162 Los Angeles Clippers .20 .50
163 Los Angeles Lakers .20 .50
164 Miami Heat .20 .50
165 Milwaukee Bucks .20 .50
166 Minnesota Timberwolves .20 .50
167 New Jersey Nets .20 .50
168 New York Knicks .20 .50
169 Orlando Magic .20 .50
170 Philadelphia 76ers .20 .50
171 Phoenix Suns .20 .50
172 Portland Trailblazers .20 .50
173 Sacramento Kings .20 .50
174 San Antonio Spurs .20 .50
175 Seattle Supersonics .20 .50
176 Toronto Raptors .20 .50
177 Utah Jazz .20 .50
178 Vancouver Grizzlies .20 .50
179 Washington Bullets .20 .50
180 NBA Logo .20 .50
181 Alan Henderson .15 .40
182 Priest Lauderdale .30 .75
183 Dikembe Mutombo .40 1.00
184 Dana Barros .15 .40
185 Todd Day .15 .40
186 Brett Szabo .50 1.25
187 Antoine Walker .75 2.00
188 Scott Burrell .15 .40
189 Tony Delk .50 1.25
190 Vlade Divac .25 .60
191 Matt Geiger .15 .40
192 Anthony Mason .20 .50
193 Malik Rose .60 1.50
194 Ron Harper .20 .50
195 Steve Kerr .20 .50
196 Luc Longley .20 .50
197 Danny Ferry .15 .40
198 Tyrone Hill .15 .40
199 Vitaly Potapenko .40 1.00
200 Tony Dumas .15 .40
201 Chris Gatling .15 .40
202 Oliver Miller .15 .40
203 Eric Montross .15 .40
204 Samaki Walker .40 1.00
205 Darvin Ham 1.00 2.50
206 Mark Jackson .20 .50
207 Ervin Johnson .15 .40
208 Stacey Augmon .20 .50
209 Joe Dumars .30 .75
210 Grant Hill .40 1.00
211 Grant Long .15 .40
212 Terry Mills .15 .40
213 Otis Thorpe .20 .50
214 Jerome Williams .40 1.00
215 B.J. Armstrong .20 .50
216 Todd Fuller .30 .75
217 Ray Owes .40 1.00
218 Mark Price .25 .60
219 Felton Spencer .15 .40
220 Charles Barkley .60 1.50
221 Mario Elie .15 .40
222 Othella Harrington .40 1.00
223 Matt Maloney .40 1.00
224 Brent Price .15 .40
225 Kevin Willis .20 .50
226 Travis Best .15 .40
227 Erick Dampier .50 1.25
228 Antonio Davis .15 .40
229 Jalen Rose .20 .50
230 Pooh Richardson .15 .40
231 Rodney Rogers .15 .40
232 Lorenzen Wright .40 1.00
233 Kobe Bryant 40.00 100.00
234 Derek Fisher .60 1.50
235 Travis Knight .40 1.00
236 Shaquille O'Neal 1.00 2.50
237 Byron Scott .25 .60
238 P.J. Brown .15 .40
239 Sasha Danilovic .15 .40
240 Dan Majerle .25 .60
241 Martin Muursepp .30 .75
242 Ray Allen 2.50 6.00
243 Armon Gilliam .15 .40
244 Andrew Lang .15 .40
245 Moochie Norris .50 1.25
246 Kevin Garnett .75 2.00
247 Tom Gugliotta .15 .40
248 Shane Heal .50 1.25
249 Stephon Marbury 1.50 4.00
250 Stojko Vrankovic .15 .40
251 Kerry Kittles .50 1.25
252 Robert Pack .15 .40
253 Jayson Williams .15 .40
254 Allan Houston .25 .60
255 Larry Johnson .30 .75
256 Dontae Jones .40 1.00
257 Walter McCarty .50 1.25
258 John Wallace .40 1.00
259 Charlie Ward .15 .40
260 Brian Evans .30 .75
261 Amal McCaskill .50 1.25
262 Brian Shaw .15 .40
263 Mark Davis .15 .40
264 Lucious Harris .15 .40
265 Allen Iverson 4.00 10.00
266 Sam Cassell .20 .50
267 Robert Horry .25 .60
268 Danny Manning .20 .50
269 Steve Nash 3.00 8.00
270 Kenny Anderson .20 .50
271 Aleksandar Djordjevic .50 1.25
272 Jermaine O'Neal .75 2.00
273 Isaiah Rider .20 .50
274 Rasheed Wallace .30 .75
275 Mahmoud Abdul-Rauf .20 .50
276 Michael Smith .15 .40
277 Corliss Williamson .15 .40
278 Vernon Maxwell .15 .40
279 Charles Smith .15 .40
280 Dominique Wilkins .40 1.00
281 Craig Ehlo .15 .40
282 Jim McIlvaine .15 .40
283 Sam Perkins .20 .50
284 Marcus Camby .75 2.00
285 Popeye Jones .15 .40
286 Donald Whiteside .50 1.25
287 Walt Williams .15 .40
288 Jeff Hornacek .20 .50
289 Karl Malone .50 1.25
290 Bryon Russell .15 .40
291 John Stockton .50 1.25
292 Shareef Abdur-Rahim .75 2.00
293 Anthony Peeler .15 .40
294 Roy Rogers .40 1.00
295 Tim Legler .15 .40
296 Tracy Murray .15 .40
297 Rod Strickland .25 .60
298 Ben Wallace 2.50 6.00
299 Kevin Garnett CB .75 2.00
300 Allan Houston CB .25 .60
301 Eddie Jones CB .25 .60
302 Jamal Mashburn CB .25 .60
303 Antonio McDyess CB .25 .60
304 Glenn Robinson CB .25 .60
305 Joe Smith CB .20 .50
306 Steve Smith CB .20 .50
307 Jerry Stackhouse CB .30 .75
308 Damon Stoudamire CB .25 .60
309 Hakeem Olajuwon AS .50 1.25
310 Charles Barkley AS .60 1.50
311 Patrick Ewing AS .40 1.00
312 Michael Jordan AS 2.50 6.00
313 Clyde Drexler AS .40 1.00
314 Karl Malone AS .50 1.25
315 John Stockton AS .50 1.25
316 David Robinson AS .50 1.25
317 Scottie Pippen AS .60 1.50
318 Shawn Kemp AS .40 1.00
319 Shaquille O'Neal AS 1.00 2.50
320 Mitch Richmond AS .30 .75
321 Reggie Miller AS .50 1.25
322 Alonzo Mourning AS .40 1.00
323 Gary Payton AS .40 1.00
324 Anfernee Hardaway AS .60 1.50
325 Grant Hill AS .40 1.00
326 Dennis Rodman AS .60 1.50
327 Juwan Howard AS .25 .60
328 Jason Kidd AS .40 1.00
329 Checklist .15 .40
330 Checklist .15 .40

2001-02 Fleer Exclusive

COMPLETE SET (149) 150.00 300.00
COMP.SET w/o SP's (120) 15.00 40.00
121-149 STATED ODDS 1:24
121-149 HAVE JERSEY PATCH
PRINT RUNS PROVIDED BY FLEER
1 Vince Carter .75 2.00
2 Tracy McGrady .60 1.50
3 Dikembe Mutombo .60 1.50
4 Kobe Bryant 3.00 8.00
5 Baron Davis .40 1.00
6 Alonzo Mourning .60 1.50
7 Allan Houston .40 1.00
8 Paul Pierce .60 1.50
9 Jason Williams .60 1.50
10 Marcus Camby .30 .75
11 Jason Terry .40 1.00
12 Anfernee Hardaway 1.00 2.50
13 Cuttino Mobley .30 .75
14 Kenyon Martin .40 1.00
15 Rashard Lewis .30 .75
16 Darius Miles .25 .60
17 Jamal Mashburn .30 .75
18 Derek Fisher .30 .75
19 Sam Cassell .30 .75
20 Antonio McDyess .30 .75
21 John Stockton .75 2.00
22 Andre Miller .30 .75
23 Shawn Marion .40 1.00
24 Steve Nash .75 2.00
25 Kevin Garnett 1.00 2.50
26 Peja Stojakovic .30 .75
27 Dirk Nowitzki 1.00 2.50
28 Chris Webber .50 1.25
29 Shaquille O'Neal 1.50 4.00
30 Stephon Marbury .50 1.25
31 Eddie Jones .40 1.00
32 Raef LaFrentz .25 .60
33 Wally Szczerbiak .30 .75
34 Richard Hamilton .50 1.25
35 Michael Finley .40 1.00
36 Jason Kidd .60 1.50
37 Courtney Alexander .25 .60
38 Glenn Robinson .40 1.00
39 Tim Duncan 1.00 2.50
40 Steve Francis .40 1.00
41 Stromile Swift .25 .60
42 Desmond Mason .30 .75
43 Shareef Abdur-Rahim .30 .75
44 Terrell Brandon .30 .75
45 Antawn Jamison .30 .75
46 Latrell Sprewell .50 1.25
47 Mateen Cleaves .25 .60
48 Karl Malone .75 2.00
49 Lamar Odom .30 .75
50 Grant Hill .60 1.50
51 Reggie Miller .75 2.00
52 Ray Allen .60 1.50
53 David Robinson .75 2.00
54 Elton Brand .30 .75
55 Jerry Stackhouse .40 1.00
56 Brian Grant .25 .60
57 Hakeem Olajuwon .75 2.00
58 Jalen Rose .30 .75
59 Allen Iverson 1.00 2.50
60 Darrell Armstrong .25 .60
61 Joe Smith .30 .75
62 Anthony Mason .40 1.00
63 Mike Bibby .40 1.00
64 Gary Payton .60 1.50
65 Glen Rice .40 1.00
66 Shandon Anderson .25 .60
67 Antoine Walker .30 .75
68 Tim Thomas .25 .60
69 Patrick Ewing .60 1.50
70 Ben Wallace .50 1.25
71 Corey Maggette .30 .75
72 Larry Hughes .30 .75
73 Scottie Pippen 1.00 2.50
74 Michael Doleac .25 .60
75 Clifford Robinson .40 1.00
76 Aaron McKie .25 .60
77 Marc Jackson .25 .60
78 Tom Gugliotta .25 .60
79 James Posey .25 .60
80 Moochie Norris .25 .60
81 Speedy Claxton .25 .60
82 Michael Redd .40 1.00
83 Rasheed Wallace .50 1.25
84 Juwan Howard .30 .75
85 Nick Van Exel .40 1.00
86 Toni Kukoc .50 1.25
87 Jamaal Magloire .25 .60
88 Jermaine O'Neal .30 .75
89 Anthony Peeler .25 .60
90 Marcus Fizer .25 .60
91 Jumaine Jones .25 .60
92 Kendall Gill .25 .60
93 Antonio Daniels .25 .60
94 DerMarr Johnson .25 .60
95 Mitch Richmond .50 1.25
96 Antonio Davis .30 .75
97 Ron Mercer .25 .60
98 Keyon Dooling .25 .60
99 Morris Peterson .25 .60
100 Derek Anderson .25 .60
101 Allen Iverson MO 1.00 2.50
102 Glenn Robinson MO .40 1.00
103 Tim Duncan MO 1.00 2.50
104 Shaquille O'Neal MO 1.50 4.00
105 Vince Carter MO .75 2.00
106 Tracy McGrady MO .60 1.50
107 Jason Kidd MO .60 1.50
108 Karl Malone MO .75 2.00
109 Michael Jordan MO 6.00 15.00
110 Shareef Abdur-Rahim MO .30 .75
111 Grant Hill MO .60 1.50
112 Stephon Marbury MO .50 1.25
113 Michael Finley MO .40 1.00
114 Antoine Walker MO .30 .75
115 Kobe Bryant MO 3.00 8.00
116 Dirk Nowitzki MO 1.00 2.50
117 Alonzo Mourning MO .60 1.50
118 John Stockton MO .75 2.00
119 Kevin Garnett MO 1.00 2.50
120 Eddie Jones MO .40 1.00
121 Steven Hunter/500 RC 2.00 5.00
122 Tony Parker/500 RC 12.00 30.00
123 Zach Randolph/478 RC 6.00 15.00
124 Richard Jefferson/500 RC 4.00 10.00
125 Kedrick Brown/433 RC 2.00 5.00
126 Kwame Brown/472 RC 3.00 8.00
127 Brandon Armstrong/500 RC 2.00 5.00
128 Pau Gasol/474 RC 12.00 30.00
129 Troy Murphy/500 RC 2.50 6.00
130 Rodney White/500 RC 2.00 5.00
131 Jamaal Tinsley/500 RC 2.50 6.00
132 Jeryl Sasser/500 RC 2.00 5.00
133 Eddie Griffin/500 RC 2.50 6.00
134 Michael Bradley/476 RC 2.00 5.00
135 V.Radmanovic/500 RC 2.50 6.00
136 Jason Richardson/388 RC 5.00 12.00
137 Shane Battier/500 RC 6.00 15.00
138 Joe Johnson/300 RC 5.00 12.00
139 Andrei Kirilenko/500 RC 5.00 12.00
140 Kirk Haston/500 RC 2.00 5.00
141 Jason Collins/500 RC 2.50 6.00
142 Tyson Chandler/500 RC 5.00 12.00
143 DeSagana Diop/499 RC 2.00 5.00
144 Gerald Wallace/467 RC 4.00 10.00
145 Joseph Forte/450 RC 2.00 5.00
146 Brendan Haywood/500 RC 2.50 6.00
147 Samuel Dalembert/360 RC 3.00 8.00
148 Eddy Curry/500 RC 3.00 8.00
149 Primoz Brezec/500 RC 3.00 8.00

2001-02 Fleer Exclusive Game Exclusives

STATED PRINT RUN 100 SER.#'d SETS
*PATCH: 1.25X TO 3X HI
PATCH PRINT RUN 25 SER.#'d SETS
1 Vince Carter 10.00 25.00
2 Allen Iverson 12.00 30.00
3 Alonzo Mourning 8.00 20.00
4 Karl Malone 10.00 25.00
5 Darius Miles 3.00 8.00
6 Antonio McDyess 4.00 10.00
7 Ray Allen 8.00 20.00
8 Steve Francis 5.00 12.00
9 Lamar Odom 4.00 10.00
10 Kenyon Martin 5.00 12.00
11 Andre Miller 4.00 10.00
12 Rashard Lewis 4.00 10.00
13 Stromile Swift 3.00 8.00
14 Antonio Davis 4.00 10.00
15 Latrell Sprewell 6.00 15.00
16 Tracy McGrady 8.00 20.00
17 Jamal Mashburn 4.00 10.00
18 Dikembe Mutombo 8.00 20.00
19 Morris Peterson 3.00 8.00

2001-02 Fleer Exclusive Letter Perfect

COMPLETE SET (25) 10.00 25.00
STATED ODDS 1:8
1 Vince Carter 1.25 3.00
2 Allen Iverson 1.50 4.00
3 Alonzo Mourning 1.00 2.50
4 Karl Malone 1.25 3.00
5 Darius Miles .40 1.00
7 Antonio McDyess .50 1.25
8 Ray Allen 1.00 2.50
9 Steve Francis .60 1.50
10 Lamar Odom .50 1.25
11 Kenyon Martin .60 1.50
12 Andre Miller .50 1.25
13 Rashard Lewis .50 1.25
14 Stromile Swift .40 1.00
15 Antonio Davis .50 1.25
16 Latrell Sprewell .75 2.00
17 Keith Van Horn .50 1.25
18 Tracy McGrady 1.00 2.50
19 Desmond Mason .50 1.25
20 Jason Terry .60 1.50
21 Jamal Mashburn .50 1.25
22 Paul Pierce 1.00 2.50
23 Morris Peterson .40 1.00
24 Baron Davis .60 1.50
25 Antoine Walker .50 1.25
6 Mike Miller .50 1.25

2001-02 Fleer Exclusive Letter Perfect JV

STATED PRINT RUN 100 SER.#'d SETS
*VARSITY: 1.25X TO 3X BASE HI
VARSITY PRINT RUN 25 SER.#'d SETS
1 Vince Carter 10.00 25.00
2 Allen Iverson 12.00 30.00
3 Alonzo Mourning 8.00 20.00
4 Karl Malone 10.00 25.00
5 Darius Miles 3.00 8.00
6 Antonio McDyess 4.00 10.00
7 Ray Allen 8.00 20.00
8 Steve Francis 5.00 12.00
9 Lamar Odom 4.00 10.00
10 Kenyon Martin 5.00 12.00
11 Andre Miller 4.00 10.00
12 Rashard Lewis 4.00 10.00
13 Stromile Swift 3.00 8.00
14 Antonio Davis 4.00 10.00
15 Latrell Sprewell 6.00 15.00
16 Keith Van Horn 4.00 10.00
17 Tracy McGrady 8.00 20.00
18 Desmond Mason 4.00 10.00
19 Jason Terry 5.00 12.00
20 Jamal Mashburn 4.00 10.00
21 Paul Pierce 8.00 20.00
22 Morris Peterson 3.00 8.00
23 Baron Davis 5.00 12.00
24 Antoine Walker 4.00 10.00

2001-02 Fleer Exclusive Team Fleer

CARD #1 STATED ODDS 1:96
2-8 PRINT RUNS LISTED BELOW
1 V.Carter/L.Bird 6.00 15.00
2 V.Carter/L.Bird JSY/500 10.00 25.00
3 Vince Carter JSY/98 10.00 25.00
4 V.Carter JSY Patch/15 20.00 50.00
5 V.Carter JSY AU/100 25.00 60.00
6 Larry Bird JSY/79 25.00 60.00
7 L.Bird JSY Patch/33 50.00 100.00
8 L.Bird JSY AU/100 75.00 200.00

2001-02 Fleer Exclusive Vinsanity Collection

STATED ODDS 1:70
1 Vince Carter UNC Shirt 10.00 25.00
2 Vince Carter Shirt 10.00 25.00
3 Vince Carter Warm 10.00 25.00
4 Vince Carter JSY 10.00 25.00
5 Vince Carter USA 10.00 25.00

2001-02 Fleer Exclusive Vinsanity Collection Autographs

STATED PRINT RUN 30 SER.#'d SETS
1 Vince Carter UNC Shirt 50.00 120.00
2 Vince Carter Shirt 50.00 120.00
3 Vince Carter Warm 50.00 120.00
4 Vince Carter JSY 60.00 150.00
5 Vince Carter USA JSY 60.00 150.00

1999-00 Fleer Focus

COMPLETE SET (150) 75.00 200.00
COMPLETE SET w/o RC (100) 12.00 30.00
101-150 FIRST 999 ARE PORTRAIT PHOTO
101-150 REMAINING 3000 ARE ACTION PHOTO
101-150 PORTRAIT PHOTO LISTED AS SP's
1 Anfernee Hardaway 1.00 2.50
2 Derek Anderson .25 .60
3 Jayson Williams .25 .60
4 Ron Mercer .30 .75
5 Jerry Stackhouse .40 1.00
6 Tariq Abdul-Wahad .25 .60
7 Sean Elliott .30 .75
8 Lindsey Hunter .25 .60
9 Larry Johnson .40 1.00
10 Steve Smith .30 .75
11 Raef LaFrentz .30 .75
12 Jalen Rose .30 .75
13 Stephon Marbury .50 1.25
14 Detlef Schrempf .30 .75
15 Rod Strickland .30 .75
16 Paul Pierce .75 2.00
17 Maurice Taylor .25 .60
18 Allen Iverson 1.00 2.50
19 Mitch Richmond .50 1.25
20 Gary Trent .25 .60
21 Reggie Miller .75 2.00
22 Kerry Kittles .30 .75
23 Rasheed Wallace .50 1.25
24 Steve Nash .75 2.00
25 Scottie Pippen 1.00 2.50
26 Joe Smith .30 .75
27 Jason Williams .60 1.50
28 Michael Finley .40 1.00

9 Hakeem Olajuwon .75 2.00
0 Kevin Garnett 1.00 2.50
1 Darrell Armstrong .25 .60
2 David Robinson .75 2.00
3 Anthony Mason .40 1.00
4 Jamal Mashburn .30 .75
5 Gary Payton .60 1.50
6 Bryon Russell .25 .60
7 Cedric Ceballos .25 .60
8 Michael Dickerson .25 .60
9 Robert Traylor .25 .60
0 Vin Baker .30 .75
1 Shawn Kemp .60 1.50
2 Charles Barkley 1.00 2.50
3 Glenn Robinson .30 .75
4 Vince Carter 1.00 2.50
45 Zydrunas Ilgauskas .30 .75
46 Sam Cassell .30 .75
47 Tracy McGrady .60 1.50
48 Chris Mills .25 .60
49 Antawn Jamison .40 1.00
50 Nick Anderson .25 .60
51 Avery Johnson .30 .75
52 Brent Barry .30 .75
53 Alonzo Mourning .60 1.50
54 Karl Malone .75 2.00
55 Toni Kukoc .50 1.25
56 Ray Allen .60 1.50
57 Charles Oakley .40 1.00
58 Cuttino Mobley .25 .60
59 Kenny Anderson .30 .75
60 Tom Gugliotta .30 .75
61 Antoine Walker .40 1.00
62 Kobe Bryant 3.00 8.00
63 Larry Hughes .30 .75
64 Vlade Divac .40 1.00
65 Juwan Howard .30 .75
66 Isaiah Rider .30 .75
67 Antonio McDyess .30 .75
68 Rik Smits .30 .75
69 Keith Van Horn .30 .75
70 Doug Christie .30 .75
71 Elden Campbell .25 .60
72 Shaquille O'Neal 1.50 4.00
73 Matt Geiger .25 .60
74 Chris Webber .50 1.25
75 Troy Hudson .40 1.00
76 Eddie Jones .40 1.00
77 Tim Hardaway .50 1.25
78 Hersey Hawkins .25 .60
79 Shareef Abdur-Rahim .40 1.00
80 Christian Laettner .30 .75
81 Latrell Sprewell .50 1.25
82 Damon Stoudamire .40 1.00
83 Jason Caffey .25 .60
84 Michael Olowokandi .25 .60
85 Horace Grant .30 .75
86 Grant Hill .60 1.50
87 Patrick Ewing .50 1.25
88 Clifford Robinson .30 .75
89 Ricky Davis .40 1.00
90 Glen Rice .40 1.00
91 Matt Harpring .25 .60
92 Mike Bibby .40 1.00
93 Dikembe Mutombo .60 1.50
94 Chris Mullin .40 1.00
95 Marcus Camby .30 .75
96 Jason Kidd .60 1.50
97 John Starks .40 1.00
98 Terrell Brandon .25 .60
99 Tim Duncan 1.00 2.50
100 John Stockton .60 1.50
101 Ron Artest RC 2.50 6.00
101A Ron Artest SP 4.00 10.00
102 William Avery RC .60 1.50
102A William Avery SP 1.00 2.50
103 Jonathan Bender RC 1.00 2.50
103A Jonathan Bender SP 1.50 4.00
104 Cal Bowdler RC .60 1.50
104A Cal Bowdler SP 1.00 2.50
105 Elton Brand RC 2.00 5.00
105A Elton Brand SP 3.00 8.00
106 Vonteego Cummings RC .60 1.50
106A Vonteego Cummings SP 1.00 2.50
107 Baron Davis RC 2.50 6.00
107A Baron Davis SP 4.00 10.00
108 Jeff Foster RC 1.00 2.50
108A Jeff Foster SP 1.50 4.00
109 Steve Francis RC 2.00 5.00
109A Steve Francis SP 3.00 8.00
110 Devean George RC .75 2.00
110A Devean George SP 1.25 3.00
111 Dion Glover RC .60 1.50
111A Dion Glover SP 1.00 2.50
112 Richard Hamilton RC 2.50 6.00
112A Richard Hamilton SP 4.00 10.00
113 Tim James RC .60 1.50
113A Tim James SP 1.00 2.50
114 Trajan Langdon RC .75 2.00
114A Trajan Langdon SP 1.25 3.00
115 Quincy Lewis RC .60 1.50
115A Quincy Lewis SP 1.00 2.50
116 Corey Maggette RC 1.25 3.00
116A Corey Maggette SP 2.00 5.00
117 Shawn Marion RC 2.00 5.00
117A Shawn Marion SP 3.00 8.00
118 Andre Miller RC 2.00 5.00
118A Andre Miller SP 3.00 8.00
119 Lamar Odom RC 2.00 5.00
119A Lamar Odom SP 3.00 8.00
120 Scott Padgett RC .75 2.00
120A Scott Padgett SP 1.25 3.00
121 James Posey RC 1.00 2.50
121A James Posey SP 1.50 4.00
122 A.Radojevic RC .60 1.50
122A A.Radojevic SP 1.00 2.50
123 Wally Szczerbiak RC 1.50 4.00
123A Wally Szczerbiak SP 2.50 6.00
124 Jason Terry RC 1.50 4.00
124A Jason Terry SP 2.50 6.00
125 Kenny Thomas RC 1.00 2.50
125A Kenny Thomas SP 1.50 4.00
126 Jumaine Jones RC .60 1.50
126A Jumaine Jones SP 1.00 2.50
127 Rick Hughes RC 1.00 2.50
127A Rick Hughes SP 1.50 4.00
128 John Celestand RC .60 1.50
128A John Celestand SP 1.00 2.50
129 Adrian Griffin RC .75 2.00
129A Adrian Griffin SP 1.25 3.00
130 Michael Ruffin RC .60 1.50
130A Michael Ruffin SP 1.00 2.50
131 Chris Herren RC .75 2.00
131A Chris Herren SP 1.25 3.00
132 Evan Eschmeyer RC .60 1.50
132A Evan Eschmeyer SP 1.25 3.00
133 Tim Young RC .60 1.50
133A Tim Young SP 1.00 2.50
134 Obinna Ekezie RC .60 1.50
134A Obinna Ekezie SP 1.00 2.50
135 Laron Profit RC .60 1.50
135A Laron Profit SP 1.00 2.50
136 A.J. Bramlett RC 1.00 2.50
136A A.J. Bramlett SP 1.50 4.00
137 Eddie Robinson RC 1.00 2.50
137A Eddie Robinson SP 1.50 4.00
138 Ryan Bowen RC .75 2.00
138A Ryan Bowen SP 1.25 3.00
139 Chucky Atkins RC .75 2.00
139A Chucky Atkins SP 1.25 3.00
140 Ryan Robertson RC .60 1.50
140A Ryan Robertson SP 1.00 2.50
141 Derrick Dial RC .75 2.00
141A Derrick Dial SP 1.25 3.00
142 Todd MacCulloch RC .75 2.00
142A Todd MacCulloch SP 1.25 3.00
143 DeMarco Johnson RC 1.00 2.50
143A DeMarco Johnson SP 1.50 4.00
144 Anthony Carter RC .75 2.00
144A Anthony Carter SP 1.25 3.00
145 Lazaro Borrell RC 1.00 2.50
145A Lazaro Borrell SP 1.50 4.00
146 Rafer Alston RC 1.25 3.00
146A Rafer Alston SP 2.00 5.00
147 Nikita Morgunov RC 1.00 2.50
147A Nikita Morgunov SP 1.50 4.00
148 Rodney Buford RC 1.00 2.50
148A Rodney Buford SP 1.50 4.00
149 Milt Palacio RC .75 2.00
149A Milt Palacio SP 1.25 3.00
150 Jermaine Jackson RC 1.00 2.50
150A Jermaine Jackson SP 1.50 4.00

1999-00 Fleer Focus Masterpiece Mania

*STARS: 4X TO 10X BASE CARD HI
*RCs: .6X TO 1.5X BASE HI
STATED PRINT RUN 300 SERIAL #'d SETS
42 Charles Barkley 8.00 20.00

1999-00 Fleer Focus Feel the Game

STATED ODDS 1:288
1 Vince Carter 12.00 30.00
2 Kevin Garnett 12.00 30.00
3 Paul Pierce 10.00 25.00
4 Grant Hill 8.00 20.00
5 Tim Hardaway 6.00 15.00
6 Jayson Williams 3.00 8.00
7 Bryon Russell 3.00 8.00
8 Bryant Reeves 3.00 8.00
9 Keith Van Horn 4.00 10.00
10 Vin Baker 4.00 10.00

1999-00 Fleer Focus Focus Pocus

STATED ODDS 1:20
FP1 Vince Carter 8.00 20.00
FP2 Tim Duncan 8.00 20.00
FP3 Shaquille O'Neal 12.00 30.00
FP4 Paul Pierce 6.00 15.00
FP5 Kobe Bryant 25.00 60.00
FP6 Kevin Garnett 8.00 20.00
FP7 Keith Van Horn 2.50 6.00
FP8 Jason Williams 5.00 12.00
FP9 Grant Hill 5.00 12.00
FP10 Allen Iverson 8.00 20.00

1999-00 Fleer Focus Fresh Ink

STATED ODDS 1:96
1 Charles Barkley 500.00 1,000.00
2 Vince Carter 75.00 200.00
3 Obinna Ekezie 2.00 5.00
4 Jeff Foster 3.00 8.00
5 Devean George 2.50 6.00
6 Tim Hardaway 8.00 20.00
7 Matt Harpring 3.00 8.00
8 Al Harrington 3.00 8.00
9 Juwan Howard 5.00 12.00
10 Eddie Jones 12.00 30.00
11 Shawn Kemp 40.00 100.00
12 Brevin Knight 3.00 8.00
13 Trajan Langdon 2.50 6.00
14 Stephon Marbury 12.00 30.00
15 Shawn Marion 6.00 15.00
16 Tracy McGrady 12.00 30.00
17 Roshown McLeod 3.00 8.00
18 Brad Miller 6.00 15.00
19 Alonzo Mourning 60.00 150.00
20 Shaquille O'Neal 150.00 400.00
21 Scott Padgett 2.50 6.00
22 Michael Ruffin 2.00 5.00
23 Damon Stoudamire 12.00 30.00
24 Wally Szczerbiak 5.00 12.00
25 Jason Terry 3.00 8.00
26 Keith Van Horn 5.00 12.00
27 Chris Webber 100.00 250.00

1999-00 Fleer Focus Ray of Light

COMPLETE SET (15) 8.00 20.00
STATED ODDS 1:20
RL1 Andre Miller 1.00 2.50
RL2 Baron Davis 1.25 3.00
RL3 Corey Maggette .60 1.50
RL4 Dion Glover .30 .75
RL5 Elton Brand 1.00 2.50
RL6 Jason Terry 1.00 2.50
RL7 Jonathan Bender .50 1.25
RL8 Lamar Odom 1.00 2.50
RL9 Richard Hamilton 1.25 3.00
RL10 Shawn Marion 1.00 2.50
RL11 Steve Francis 1.00 2.50
RL12 Tim James .30 .75
RL13 Trajan Langdon .40 1.00
RL14 Wally Szczerbiak .75 2.00
RL15 William Avery .30 .75

1999-00 Fleer Focus Sean Elliott Night

1 Sean Elliott .60 1.50

1999-00 Fleer Focus Soar Subjects

COMPLETE SET (15) 6.00 15.00
STATED ODDS 1:6
*VIVID: 50X TO 120X HI COLUMN
VIVID: PRINT RUN 50 SERIAL #'d SETS
SS1 Allen Iverson 1.00 2.50
SS2 Anfernee Hardaway 1.00 2.50
SS3 Paul Pierce .75 2.00
SS4 Antoine Walker .40 1.00
SS5 Grant Hill .60 1.50
SS6 Keith Van Horn .30 .75
SS7 Kevin Garnett 1.00 2.50
SS8 Kobe Bryant 3.00 8.00
SS9 Larry Hughes .30 .75
SS10 Jason Williams .60 1.50
SS11 Scottie Pippen 1.00 2.50
SS12 Shaquille O'Neal 1.50 4.00
SS13 Vince Carter 1.00 2.50
SS14 Stephon Marbury .50 1.25
SS15 Tim Duncan 1.00 2.50

1999-00 Fleer Focus Soar Subjects Vivid

*VIVID: 50X TO 120X HI COLUMN
SS1 Allen Iverson 300.00 600.00
SS8 Kobe Bryant 300.00 600.00
SS11 Scottie Pippen 100.00 250.00
SS13 Vince Carter 100.00 250.00
SS15 Tim Duncan 300.00 600.00

1999-00 Fleer Focus Toni Kukoc Night

1 Toni Kukoc 2.50 6.00

2000-01 Fleer Focus

COMPLETE SET w/o RC (200) 15.00 40.00
RCs A: PRINT RUN 4999 SERIAL #'d SETS
RCs B: PRINT RUN 3499 SERIAL #'d SETS
RCs C: PRINT RUN 2999 SERIAL #'d SETS
RCs D: PRINT RUN 3999 SERIAL #'d SETS
RCs E: PRINT RUN 2499 SERIAL #'d SETS
RCs F: PRINT RUN 1999 SERIAL #'d SETS
SUBSET CARDS HALF VALUE OF BASE CARDS
1 Vince Carter .60 1.50
2 Shawn Marion .30 .75
3 Muggsy Bogues .30 .75
4 Dikembe Mutombo .50 1.25
5 Stephon Marbury .40 1.00
6 Michael Dickerson .20 .50
7 Andre Miller .25 .60
8 Toni Kukoc .40 1.00
9 Nick Van Exel .30 .75
10 Aaron Williams .20 .50
11 Derrick Coleman .30 .75
12 Wally Szczerbiak .25 .60
13 Rodney Rogers .25 .60
14 Tom Gugliotta .25 .60
15 Vonteego Cummings .20 .50
16 Cedric Ceballos .25 .60
17 Malik Rose .20 .50
18 Shawn Bradley .20 .50
19 Shandon Anderson .20 .50
20 Jacque Vaughn .20 .50
21 Jamie Feick .20 .50
22 Shawn Kemp .50 1.25
23 Monty Williams .30 .75
24 Allan Houston .30 .75
25 Chauncey Billups .40 1.00
26 Vlade Divac .30 .75
27 Othella Harrington .20 .50
28 Dale Davis .25 .60
29 Charlie Ward .25 .60
30 Hakeem Olajuwon .60 1.50
31 Ray Allen .50 1.25
32 Lamar Odom .30 .75
33 Shaquille O'Neal 1.25 3.00
34 Chris Childs .20 .50
35 Nick Anderson .25 .60
36 Keon Clark .20 .50
37 Danny Fortson .25 .60
38 Sam Mitchell .20 .50
39 Travis Best .20 .50
40 Chris Webber .40 1.00
41 Brent Barry .25 .60
42 Scottie Pippen .75 2.00
43 Reggie Miller .60 1.50
44 Bryant Reeves .20 .50
45 Bobby Jackson .25 .60
46 Antonio McDyess .25 .60
47 Elden Campbell .20 .50
48 Kenny Anderson .25 .60
49 Christian Laettner .30 .75
50 Darrell Armstrong .20 .50
51 Vinny Del Negro .20 .50
52 Quincy Lewis .20 .50
53 Peja Stojakovic .25 .60
54 Matt Geiger .20 .50
55 Larry Hughes .30 .75
56 Tracy McGrady .60 1.50
57 Tim Hardaway .40 1.00
58 Brevin Knight .20 .50
59 Michael Finley .30 .75
60 Jason Kidd .50 1.25
61 Matt Harpring .30 .75
62 Antawn Jamison .30 .75
63 Wesley Person .20 .50
64 Antonio Davis .25 .60
65 Roshown McLeod .20 .50
66 Anthony Peeler .20 .50
67 Grant Hill .50 1.25
68 Michael Olowokandi .20 .50
69 Kerry Kittles .25 .60
70 Elton Brand .30 .75
71 Tariq Abdul-Wahad .20 .50
72 Aaron McKie .20 .50
73 Andrew DeClercq .20 .50
74 Anfernee Hardaway .50 1.25
75 Bimbo Coles .20 .50
76 Terrell Brandon .25 .60
77 Jalen Rose .25 .60
78 Radoslav Nesterovic .20 .50
79 Howard Eisley .20 .50
80 Steve Smith .30 .75
81 Arvydas Sabonis .30 .75
82 Jim Jackson .25 .60
83 Corey Maggette .25 .60
84 James Posey .20 .50
85 LaPhonso Ellis .25 .60
86 Eric Snow .20 .50
87 Mikki Moore RC .30 .75
88 Baron Davis .30 .75
89 Jason Williams .50 1.25
90 Mike Bibby .30 .75
91 Marcus Camby .25 .60
92 Bryon Russell .20 .50
93 Steve Francis .30 .75
94 Sam Cassell .25 .60
95 Rasheed Wallace .40 1.00
96 Keith Van Horn .25 .60
97 Eddie Jones .30 .75
98 Corliss Williamson .20 .50
99 Ron Mercer .20 .50
100 Sean Elliott .25 .60
101 Shareef Abdur-Rahim .30 .75
102 Glen Rice .30 .75
103 Patrick Ewing .50 1.25
104 Adrian Griffin .20 .50
105 David Robinson .60 1.50
106 Isaac Austin .20 .50
107 Anthony Mason .30 .75
108 P.J. Brown .20 .50
109 Kendall Gill .30 .75
110 Tyrone Nesby .20 .50
111 Damon Stoudamire .30 .75
112 Latrell Sprewell .40 1.00
113 Tim Duncan .75 2.00
114 Glenn Robinson .30 .75
115 John Wallace .20 .50
116 Erick Strickland .20 .50
117 Doug Christie .25 .60
118 Juwan Howard .25 .60
119 Tim Thomas .20 .50
120 Tyrone Hill .20 .50
121 Avery Johnson .25 .60
122 Jerome Williams .20 .50
123 Mitch Richmond .40 1.00
124 Hersey Hawkins .20 .50
125 Donyell Marshall .25 .60
126 Derek Anderson .25 .60
127 Jamal Mashburn .25 .60
128 Richard Hamilton .40 1.00
129 Alonzo Mourning .50 1.25
130 Kelvin Cato .20 .50
131 Lamond Murray .20 .50
132 Bo Outlaw .20 .50
133 Chris Carr .20 .50
134 Jonathan Bender .20 .50
135 Paul Pierce .50 1.25
136 Dan Majerle .30 .75
137 Ron Artest .30 .75
138 Jermaine O'Neal .25 .60
139 Chris Whitney .20 .50
140 Anthony Carter .20 .50
141 Gary Payton .50 1.25
142 Kevin Garnett .75 2.00
143 Kevin Willis .20 .50
144 Charles Oakley .30 .75
145 Larry Johnson .40 1.00
146 Bonzi Wells .20 .50
147 Clifford Robinson .30 .75
148 Chucky Atkins .20 .50
149 Brian Grant .25 .60
150 Voshon Lenard .20 .50
151 Antoine Walker .30 .75
152 Cuttino Mobley .25 .60
153 Robert Horry .30 .75
154 Tracy Murray .20 .50
155 Kobe Bryant 2.50 6.00
156 Joe Smith .25 .60
157 Jaren Jackson .20 .50
158 Scott Williams .20 .50
159 Allen Iverson .75 2.00
160 Rashard Lewis .25 .60
161 Chris Mills .20 .50
162 Karl Malone .60 1.50
163 John Amaechi .20 .50
164 Jason Terry .30 .75
165 Ruben Patterson .20 .50
166 Austin Croshere .20 .50
167 Maurice Taylor .20 .50
168 Rod Strickland .20 .50
169 Clarence Weatherspoon .20 .50
170 Lindsey Hunter .20 .50
171 David Wesley .25 .60
172 Jerry Stackhouse .30 .75
173 Scott Burrell .20 .50
174 John Stockton .60 1.50
175 Vitaly Potapenko .20 .50
176 Dirk Nowitzki .75 2.00
177 Vin Baker .25 .60
178 Rick Fox .25 .60
179 Mookie Blaylock .30 .75
180 Felipe Lopez .20 .50
181 Chris Mihm A RC .25 .60
182 Mamadou N'Diaye A RC .30 .75
183 Joel Przybilla A RC .30 .75
184 Jamaal Magloire A RC .40 1.00
185 Iakovos Tsakalidis A RC .25 .60
186 Etan Thomas A RC .30 .75
187 Mark Madsen B RC .40 1.00
188 Hanno Mottola B RC .30 .75
189 Donnell Harvey B RC .30 .75
190 Jason Collier B RC .40 1.00
191 Eduardo Najera B RC .40 1.00
192 Jerome Moiso B RC .25 .60
193 Mateen Cleaves C RC .50 1.25
194 Keyon Dooling C RC .50 1.25
195 Speedy Claxton C RC .60 1.50
196 Erick Barkley C RC .40 1.00
197 A.J. Guyton C RC .40 1.00
198 Jamal Crawford C RC 1.50 4.00
199 Dan Langhi D RC .25 .60
200 Desmond Mason D RC .50 1.25
201 Chris Porter D RC .25 .60
202 Corey Hightower D RC .40 1.00
203 Morris Peterson D RC .40 1.00
204 Hedo Turkoglu D RC .60 1.50
205 Courtney Alexander E RC .50 1.25
206 Quentin Richardson E RC .60 1.50
207 D.Stevenson E RC .75 2.00
208 Michael Redd E RC 2.00 5.00
209 Chris Carrawell E RC .50 1.25
210 Mark Karcher E RC .50 1.25
211 Kenyon Martin F RC 2.50 6.00
212 Marcus Fizer F RC 1.00 2.50
213 Darius Miles F RC 1.25 3.00
214 Mike Miller F RC 2.00 5.00
215 DerMarr Johnson F RC .75 2.00
216 Stromile Swift F RC 1.00 2.50
217 Shaquille O'Neal 20 .75 2.00
218 Allen Iverson 20 .50 1.25
219 Grant Hill 20 .30 .75
220 Vince Carter 20 .40 1.00
221 Karl Malone 20 .40 1.00
222 Chris Webber 20 .25 .60
223 Gary Payton 20 .30 .75
224 Jerry Stackhouse 20 .20 .50
225 Tim Duncan 20 .50 1.25
226 Kevin Garnett 20 .50 1.25
227 Michael Finley 20 .20 .50
228 Kobe Bryant 20 1.50 4.00
229 Stephon Marbury 20 .25 .60
230 Ray Allen 20 .30 .75
231 Alonzo Mourning 20 .30 .75
232 Glenn Robinson 20 .20 .50
233 Antoine Walker 20 .20 .50
234 Shareef Abdur-Rahim 20 .20 .50
235 Elton Brand 20 .20 .50
236 Eddie Jones 20 .20 .50

2000-01 Fleer Focus Draft Position

*100 STARS: 8X TO 20X BASE CARD HI
*200 STARS: 5X TO 12X BASE HI
*300 STARS: 4X TO 10X BASE HI
PRINT RUN 100, 200 OR 300 #'d SETS
89 Jason Williams/100 12.00 30.00
155 Kobe Bryant/100 25.00 60.00
181 Chris Mihm/100 2.50 6.00
182 Mamadou N'Diaye/100 2.50 6.00
183 Joel Przybilla/100 3.00 8.00
184 Jamaal Magloire/100 4.00 10.00
185 Iakovos Tsakalidis/100 2.50 6.00
186 Etan Thomas/100 3.00 8.00
187 Mark Madsen/100 4.00 10.00
188 Hanno Mottola/200 1.50 4.00
189 Donnell Harvey/100 3.00 8.00
190 Jason Collier/100 4.00 10.00
191 Eduardo Najera/200 2.50 6.00
192 Jerome Moiso/100 2.50 6.00
193 Mateen Cleaves/100 3.00 8.00
194 Keyon Dooling/100 3.00 8.00
195 Speedy Claxton/100 4.00 10.00
196 Erick Barkley/100 2.50 6.00
197 A.J. Guyton/200 1.50 4.00
198 Jamal Crawford/100 10.00 25.00
199 Dan Langhi/200 1.50 4.00
200 Desmond Mason/100 5.00 12.00
201 Chris Porter/200 1.50 4.00
202 Corey Hightower/200 2.50 6.00
203 Morris Peterson/100 4.00 10.00
204 Hedo Turkoglu/100 6.00 15.00
205 Courtney Alexander/100 2.50 6.00
206 Quentin Richardson/100 3.00 8.00
207 DeShawn Stevenson/100 4.00 10.00
208 Michael Redd/200 6.00 15.00
209 Chris Carrawell/200 1.50 4.00
210 Mark Karcher/200 1.50 4.00
211 Kenyon Martin/100 8.00 20.00
212 Marcus Fizer/100 3.00 8.00
213 Darius Miles/100 4.00 10.00
214 Mike Miller/100 6.00 15.00
215 DerMarr Johnson/100 2.50 6.00
216 Stromile Swift/100 3.00 8.00

2000-01 Fleer Focus Arena Vision

COMPLETE SET (15) 8.00 20.00
STATED ODDS 1:12
VIP: PRINT RUN 50 SERIAL #'d SETS
AV1 Vince Carter 1.00 2.50
AV2 Eddie Jones .50 1.25
AV3 Tim Duncan 1.25 3.00
AV4 Kevin Garnett 1.25 3.00
AV5 Steve Francis .50 1.25
AV6 Jason Williams .75 2.00
AV7 Grant Hill .75 2.00
AV8 Elton Brand .50 1.25
AV9 Allen Iverson 1.25 3.00
AV10 Lamar Odom .50 1.25
AV11 Kobe Bryant 4.00 10.00
AV12 Jalen Rose .40 1.00
AV13 Paul Pierce .75 2.00
AV14 Shaquille O'Neal 2.00 5.00
AV15 Stephon Marbury .60 1.50

2000-01 Fleer Focus Vince Carter Rookie Remnants

NNO Vince Carter FLR/100 12.50 30.00
NNO Vince Carter FLR JSY/15 20.00 50.00

2000-01 Fleer Focus Planet Hardwood

COMPLETE SET (10) 12.50 25.00
STATED ODDS 1:24
*VIP: 2.5X TO 6X VALUE
VIP: PRINT RUN 50 SERIAL #'d SETS
PH1 Vince Carter 1.50 4.00
PH2 Tim Duncan 2.00 5.00
PH3 Kevin Garnett 2.00 5.00
PH4 Kobe Bryant 6.00 15.00
PH5 Lamar Odom .75 2.00
PH6 Steve Francis .75 2.00
PH7 Shaquille O'Neal 3.00 8.00
PH8 Tracy McGrady 1.50 4.00
PH9 Grant Hill 1.25 3.00
PH10 Allen Iverson 2.00 5.00

2000-01 Fleer Focus Welcome to the NBA

COMPLETE SET (15) 3.00 8.00
STATED ODDS 1:6
*VIP: 5X TO 12X VALUE
VIP: PRINT RUN 50 SERIAL #'d SETS
WN1 Kenyon Martin .60 1.50
WN2 Stromile Swift .25 .60
WN3 Darius Miles .30 .75
WN4 Marcus Fizer .25 .60
WN5 Mike Miller .50 1.25
WN6 DerMarr Johnson .20 .50
WN7 Chris Mihm .20 .50
WN8 Jamal Crawford .75 2.00
WN9 Keyon Dooling .25 .60
WN10 Jerome Moiso .20 .50
WN11 Etan Thomas .25 .60
WN12 Courtney Alexander .20 .50
WN13 Mateen Cleaves .25 .60
WN14 Jason Collier .30 .75
WN15 Desmond Mason .40 1.00

2001-02 Fleer Focus

COMP.SET w/o SP's (100) 10.00 25.00
101-130 PRINT RUN 1850 SER.#'d SETS
1 Vince Carter .60 1.50
2 Steve Nash .60 1.50
3 Anthony Mason .30 .75
4 Avery Johnson .25 .60
5 Peja Stojakovic .30 .75
6 Shaquille O'Neal 1.25 3.00
7 Jason Kidd .50 1.25
8 Steve Smith .25 .60
9 Kobe Bryant 2.50 6.00
10 Eddie Robinson .20 .50
11 Allan Houston .30 .75
12 Larry Hughes .25 .60
13 Gary Payton .50 1.25
14 Alonzo Mourning .50 1.25
15 Baron Davis .30 .75
16 Speedy Claxton .20 .50
17 Hakeem Olajuwon .60 1.50
18 Anthony Carter .20 .50
19 Raef LaFrentz .20 .50
20 Dikembe Mutombo .50 1.25
21 Moochie Norris .20 .50
22 Karl Malone .60 1.50
23 Darrell Armstrong .20 .50
24 Allen Iverson .75 2.00
25 Danny Fortson .20 .50
26 Antonio Davis .25 .60
27 Eddie Jones .30 .75
28 Patrick Ewing .50 1.25
29 Stephon Marbury .40 1.00
30 Cuttino Mobley .25 .60
31 Morris Peterson .20 .50
32 Glenn Robinson .30 .75
33 Paul Pierce .50 1.25
34 Shawn Marion .30 .75
35 Jermaine O'Neal .25 .60
36 Donyell Marshall .25 .60
37 Chauncey Billups .40 1.00
38 Tracy McGrady .50 1.25
39 Vlade Divac .25 .60
40 Lamar Odom .25 .60
41 Chris Mihm .20 .50
42 Kenyon Martin .30 .75
43 Antonio McDyess .25 .60
44 Mike Bibby .30 .75
45 Darius Miles .20 .50
46 Wesley Person .20 .50
47 Mark Jackson .25 .60
48 Nick Van Exel .30 .75
49 Tim Duncan .75 2.00
50 Sam Cassell .25 .60
51 Jason Terry .30 .75
52 Bonzi Wells .20 .50
53 Al Harrington .25 .60
54 Richard Hamilton .40 1.00
55 Wally Szczerbiak .25 .60
56 Toni Kukoc .40 1.00
57 Rasheed Wallace .40 1.00
58 Reggie Miller .60 1.50
59 Courtney Alexander .20 .50
60 Terrell Brandon .25 .60
61 Dirk Nowitzki .75 2.00
62 Chris Webber .40 1.00
63 Lindsey Hunter .20 .50
64 Andre Miller .25 .60
65 Clifford Robinson .30 .75
66 David Robinson .60 1.50
67 Stromile Swift .20 .50
68 Nazr Mohammed .20 .50
69 Kurt Thomas .20 .50
70 Corliss Williamson .20 .50
71 Rashard Lewis .25 .60
72 Lorenzen Wright .20 .50
73 David Wesley .20 .50
74 Derrick Coleman .25 .60
75 Jerry Stackhouse .30 .75
76 Antonio Daniels .20 .50
77 Mitch Richmond .40 1.00
78 Ron Mercer .20 .50
79 Latrell Sprewell .40 1.00
80 Antawn Jamison .25 .60
81 Desmond Mason .25 .60
82 Jason Williams .50 1.25
83 Jamal Mashburn .25 .60
84 Grant Hill .50 1.25
85 Elton Brand .25 .60
86 Brian Grant .20 .50
87 Antoine Walker .25 .60
88 Anfernee Hardaway .75 2.00
89 Steve Francis .30 .75
90 John Stockton .60 1.50
91 Ray Allen .50 1.25
92 Tim Hardaway .40 1.00
93 Derek Anderson .20 .50
94 Jalen Rose .25 .60
95 Michael Jordan 5.00 12.00
96 Kevin Garnett .75 2.00
97 Shareef Abdur-Rahim .25 .60
98 Tony Delk .25 .60
99 Quentin Richardson .20 .50
100 Michael Finley .30 .75
101 Jamaal Tinsley RC .75 1.50
102 Zach Randolph RC 1.50 4.00
103 Kedrick Brown RC .50 1.25
104 Kirk Haston RC .50 1.25
105 Tyson Chandler RC 1.25 3.00
106 Shane Battier RC 1.50 4.00
107 Richard Jefferson RC 1.00 2.50
108 Gerald Wallace RC 1.00 2.50
109 DeSagana Diop RC .50 1.25
110 Ruben Boumtje-Boumtje RC .60 1.50
111 Rodney White RC .50 1.25
112 Eddie Griffin RC .60 1.50
113 Pau Gasol RC 3.00 8.00
114 Tony Parker RC 3.00 8.00
115 Kwame Brown RC .75 2.00
116 Vladimir Radmanovic RC .60 1.50
117 Troy Murphy RC .60 1.50
118 Loren Woods RC .50 1.25
119 Joe Johnson RC 1.25 3.00
120 Brandon Armstrong RC .50 1.25
121 Trenton Hassell RC .50 1.25
122 Andrei Kirilenko RC 1.25 3.00
123 Jason Richardson RC 1.25 3.00
124 Jason Collins RC .60 1.50
125 Jeryl Sasser RC .50 1.25
126 Michael Bradley RC .50 1.25
127 Eddy Curry RC .75 2.00
128 Joseph Forte RC .50 1.25
129 Brendan Haywood RC .60 1.50
130 Zeljko Rebraca RC .75 2.00

2001-02 Fleer Focus Numbers

*STARS/20: 15X TO 40X BASE CARD HI
*RCs/20: 6X TO 15X BASE CARD HI
*STARS/30:10X TO 25X BASE CARD HI
*RCs/30: 4X TO 10X BASE CARD HI
*STARS/40: 8X TO 20X BASE CARD HI
*RCs/40: 3X TO 8X BASE CARD HI
*STARS/50: 8X TO 20X BASE CARD HI
*RCs/50: 2.5X TO 6X BASE CARD HI
PRINT RUNS BETWEEN 10 AND 50
95 Michael Jordan/30 150.00 400.00

2001-02 Fleer Focus Materialistic Away

STATED ODDS 1:26
*HOME: 2X TO 5X AWAY HI
HOME PRINT RUN 50 SER.#'d SETS
1 Kobe Bryant 20.00 50.00
2 Shaquille O'Neal 10.00 25.00
3 Kevin Garnett 6.00 15.00
4 Tim Duncan 8.00 20.00
5 Michael Jordan 30.00 80.00
6 Allen Iverson 6.00 15.00
7 Dirk Nowitzki 6.00 15.00
8 Kwame Brown 2.50 6.00
9 Tyson Chandler 4.00 10.00
10 Eddie Griffin 2.00 5.00
11 Shane Battier 5.00 12.00
12 Tracy McGrady 4.00 10.00
13 Steve Francis 2.50 6.00
14 Chris Webber 3.00 8.00
15 Vince Carter 5.00 12.00
15A Vince Carter AU 30.00 80.00
16 Jamaal Tinsley 2.00 5.00
17 Grant Hill 4.00 10.00
18 Jason Kidd 4.00 10.00
19 Karl Malone 5.00 12.00
20 Ray Allen 4.00 10.00
21 Pau Gasol 10.00 25.00

2001-02 Fleer Focus ROY Collection

COMPLETE SET (15) 20.00 50.00
STATED ODDS 1:22
1 Vince Carter 2.50 6.00
2 Allen Iverson 3.00 8.00
3 Chris Webber 1.50 4.00
4 David Robinson 2.50 6.00
5 Steve Francis 1.25 3.00
6 Patrick Ewing 2.00 5.00
7 Damon Stoudamire 1.25 3.00
8 Jason Kidd 2.00 5.00
9 Mike Miller 1.00 2.50
10 Larry Bird 5.00 12.00
11 Grant Hill 2.00 5.00
12 Michael Jordan 10.00 25.00
13 Shaquille O'Neal 5.00 12.00
14 Elton Brand 1.00 2.50
15 Tim Duncan 3.00 8.00

2001-02 Fleer Focus ROY Collection Jerseys

COMPLETE SET (9) 40.00 100.00
STATED ODDS 1:55
*PATCHES: 1.25X TO 3X JERSEY HI
PATCH PRINT RUN 99 SER.#'d SETS
1 Vince Carter 8.00 20.00
1A Vince Carter AU/15 60.00 150.00
1B Vince Carter AU/99 30.00 80.00
2 Allen Iverson 10.00 25.00
3 Chris Webber 5.00 12.00
4 David Robinson 8.00 20.00
6 Patrick Ewing 6.00 15.00
8 Jason Kidd 6.00 15.00
9 Mike Miller 3.00 8.00
10 Larry Bird 15.00 40.00
11 Grant Hill 6.00 15.00

2001-02 Fleer Focus Trading Places

COMPLETE SET (15) 15.00 30.00
STATED ODDS 1:12
1 Vince Carter 1.50 4.00
2 Patrick Ewing 1.25 3.00
3 Mike Bibby .75 2.00
4 Jason Kidd 1.25 3.00
5 Stephon Marbury 1.00 2.50
6 Corey Maggette .60 1.50
7 Elton Brand .60 1.50
8 Hakeem Olajuwon 1.50 4.00
9 Dikembe Mutombo 1.25 3.00
10 Eddie Jones .75 2.00
11 Michael Jordan 6.00 15.00
12 Grant Hill 1.25 3.00
13 Chris Webber 1.00 2.50
14 Shaquille O'Neal 3.00 8.00
15 Tracy McGrady 1.25 3.00

2001-02 Fleer Focus Trading Places Jerseys

S.ABDUR-RAHIM HAS JSY VERSIONS ONLY
STATED ODDS 1:51
*PATCHES: 1.5X TO 4X JERSEYS HI
PATCH PRINT RUN 50 SER.#'d SETS
1 Vince Carter 8.00 20.00
2 Patrick Ewing 6.00 15.00
4 Jason Kidd 6.00 15.00
5 Stephon Marbury 5.00 12.00
6 Corey Maggette 3.00 8.00
7 Elton Brand 3.00 8.00

9 Dikembe Mutombo 6.00 15.00
10 Eddie Jones 4.00 10.00
13 Chris Webber 5.00 12.00
TPSA Shareef Abdur-Rahim 3.00 8.00

2003-04 Fleer Focus

COMP.SET w/o SP's 12.50 30.00
1 Allan Houston .30 .75
2 Manu Ginobili .60 1.50
3 Allen Iverson .75 2.00
4 Kenyon Martin .30 .75
5 Rasho Nesterovic .20 .50
6 Tracy McGrady .50 1.25
7 Drew Gooden .25 .60
8 Tony Parker .50 1.25
9 Troy Murphy .20 .50
10 Alonzo Mourning .40 1.00
11 Rasual Butler .20 .50
12 Alvin Williams .20 .50
13 Troy Hudson .20 .50
14 Gary Payton .50 1.25
15 Tyson Chandler .25 .60
16 Ray Allen .50 1.25
17 Amare Stoudemire .40 1.00
18 Chauncey Billups .40 1.00
19 Gilbert Arenas .30 .75
20 Eddie Jones .30 .75
21 Vince Carter .60 1.50
22 Kobe Bryant 2.50 6.00
23 Reggie Miller .60 1.50
24 Vincent Yarbrough .20 .50
25 Kevin Garnett .75 2.00
26 Andre Miller .25 .60
27 Glenn Robinson .25 .60
28 Kurt Thomas .20 .50
29 Vladimir Radmanovic .20 .50
30 Richard Jefferson .25 .60
31 Andrei Kirilenko .25 .60
32 Wally Szczerbiak .25 .60
33 Gordan Giricek .20 .50
34 Kwame Brown .20 .50
35 Yao Ming .75 2.00
36 Devean George .20 .50
37 Richard Hamilton .40 1.00
38 Anfernee Hardaway .75 2.00
39 Grant Hill .40 1.00
40 Zach Randolph .30 .75
41 Dirk Nowitzki .75 2.00
42 Zydrunas Ilgauskas .25 .60
43 Antawn Jamison .30 .75
44 J.R. Bremer .20 .50
45 Latrell Sprewell .40 1.00
46 Ron Artest .30 .75
47 Antoine Walker .30 .75
48 Eddy Curry .20 .50
49 Larry Hughes .25 .60
50 Jalen Rose .25 .60
51 Matt Harpring .25 .60
52 Sam Cassell .25 .60
53 Antonio McDyess .25 .60
54 Jamaal Tinsley .20 .50
55 Mehmet Okur .25 .60
56 Scottie Pippen .75 2.00
57 Antonio Davis .25 .60
58 Jamaal Magloire .20 .50
59 Michael Olowokandi .20 .50
60 Shane Battier .25 .60
61 Desmond Mason .25 .60
62 Baron Davis .30 .75
63 Jamal Mashburn .25 .60
64 Michael Redd .30 .75
65 Shaquille O'Neal 1.25 3.00
66 Ben Wallace .40 1.00
67 Jason Terry .25 .60
68 Michael Finley .30 .75
69 Shareef Abdur-Rahim .30 .75
70 Bobby Jackson .25 .60
71 Jason Williams .50 1.25
72 Mike Bibby .30 .75
73 Shawn Marion .30 .75
74 Ricky Davis .25 .60
75 Bonzi Wells .20 .50
76 Jason Kidd .50 1.25
77 Mike Miller .25 .60
78 Stephen Jackson .25 .60
79 Brad Miller .25 .60
80 Jason Richardson .30 .75
81 Mike Dunleavy Jr. .25 .60
82 Stephon Marbury .40 1.00
83 Brian Grant .20 .50
84 Jay Williams .20 .50
85 Morris Peterson .20 .50
86 Steve Nash .60 1.50
87 Carlos Boozer .25 .60
88 Jermaine O'Neal .30 .75
89 Nene .25 .60
90 Eric Snow .20 .50
91 Steve Francis .30 .75
92 Caron Butler .25 .60
93 Jerry Stackhouse .40 1.00
94 Nick Van Exel .30 .75
95 Tayshaun Prince .30 .75
96 Calbert Cheaney .20 .50
97 Pau Gasol .50 1.25
98 Theo Ratliff .20 .50
99 Chris Webber .40 1.00
100 Juan Dixon .20 .50
101 Paul Pierce .50 1.25
102 Tim Thomas .20 .50
103 Eddie Griffin .20 .50
104 Corey Maggette .25 .60
105 Juwan Howard .25 .60
106 Peja Stojakovic .25 .60
107 Tim Duncan .75 2.00
108 Keith Van Horn .25 .60
109 Cuttino Mobley .20 .50
110 Kareem Rush .20 .50
111 Predrag Drobnjak .20 .50
112 Tony Delk .20 .50
113 Dajuan Wagner .20 .50
114 Karl Malone .60 1.50
115 Rashard Lewis .25 .60
116 David Wesley .20 .50
117 Rasheed Wallace .40 1.00
118 Derrick Coleman .30 .75
119 Donnell Harvey .25 .60
120 Elton Brand .25 .60
121 Carmelo Anthony RC 12.00 30.00
122 Keith Bogans RC 1.50 4.00
123 Leandro Barbosa RC 2.50 6.00
124 Troy Bell RC 1.50 4.00
125 Chris Bosh RC 8.00 20.00
126 Zarko Cabarkapa RC 1.50 4.00
127 Jason Kapono RC 1.50 4.00
128 Nick Collison RC 2.00 5.00
129 Boris Diaw-Riffiod RC 2.50 6.00
130 Marcus Banks RC 1.50 4.00
131 T.J. Ford RC 2.00 5.00
132 Reece Gaines RC 1.50 4.00
133 Travis Hansen RC 1.50 4.00
134 Jarvis Hayes RC 1.50 4.00
135 Kirk Hinrich RC 2.50 6.00
136 Josh Howard RC 2.50 6.00
137 LeBron James RC 400.00 800.00
138 Dahntay Jones RC 2.00 5.00
139 Chris Kaman RC 2.50 6.00
140 Maciej Lampe RC 1.50 4.00
141 Darko Milicic RC 2.00 5.00
142 Travis Outlaw RC 2.00 5.00
143 Mickael Pietrus RC 2.00 5.00
144 Rick Rickert RC 1.50 4.00
145 Luke Ridnour RC 2.50 6.00
146 Sofoklis Schortsanitis RC 1.50 4.00
147 Mike Sweetney RC 1.50 4.00
148 Dwyane Wade RC 25.00 60.00
149 Luke Walton RC 2.50 6.00
150 David West RC 3.00 8.00
151 Zoran Planinic RC 1.50 4.00
152 Ndudi Ebi RC 1.50 4.00
153 Aleksandar Pavlovic RC 2.00 5.00
154 Kendrick Perkins RC 2.00 5.00
155 Maurice Williams RC 2.50 6.00
156 Jerome Beasley RC 1.50 4.00
157 Slavko Vranes RC 1.50 4.00
158 Zaur Pachulia RC 2.50 6.00
159 Carlos Delfino RC 2.00 5.00
160 Brian Cook RC 1.50 4.00

2003-04 Fleer Focus Gold

*GOLD SINGLES: 5X TO 12X BASE HI
*GOLD RCs: 1.25X TO 3X BASE HI
PRINT RUN 50 SERIAL #'d SETS
148 Dwyane Wade 60.00 150.00

2003-04 Fleer Focus Numbers Century

*SINGLES: 4X TO 10X BASE CARD HI
*RCs: .6X TO 1.5X BASE CARD HI
PRINT RUN 100 SERIAL #'d SETS
137 LeBron James 1,000.00 2,000.00
148 Dwyane Wade 30.00 80.00

2003-04 Fleer Focus Silver

*1-120 SILVER: 8X TO 20X BASE HI
*121-160 SILVER RCs: 1.5X TO 4X BASE HI
PRINT RUN 25 SER.#'d SETS
148 Dwyane Wade 80.00 200.00

2003-04 Fleer Focus Auto Focus

PRINT RUN 250 SERIAL #'d SETS
1 Manu Ginobili 3.00 8.00
2 Eddy Curry 1.00 2.50
3 Tracy McGrady 2.50 6.00
4 Drew Gooden 1.25 3.00
5 Caron Butler 1.25 3.00
6 Amare Stoudemire 2.00 5.00
7 Tayshaun Prince 1.50 4.00
8 Vince Carter 3.00 8.00
9 Kevin Garnett 4.00 10.00
10 Dirk Nowitzki 4.00 10.00
11 Ben Wallace 2.00 5.00
12 Tony Parker 2.50 6.00
13 Steve Francis 1.50 4.00
14 Mike Bibby 1.50 4.00
15 Alonzo Mourning 2.00 5.00
16 Carmelo Anthony 8.00 20.00
17 Marcus Banks 1.00 2.50
18 Maciej Lampe 1.00 2.50
19 Mickael Pietrus 1.25 3.00
20 Luke Ridnour 1.50 4.00
21 Dwyane Wade 60.00 150.00
22 David West 2.00 5.00
23 Chris Bosh 5.00 12.00
24 Mike Sweetney 1.00 2.50
25 Troy Bell 1.00 2.50

2003-04 Fleer Focus Auto Focus Autographs

PRINT RUN 100 SERIAL #'d SETS
*AUTO 50: .5X TO 1.25X BASE HI
1 Manu Ginobili 12.50 30.00
2 Eddy Curry 6.00 15.00
3 Steve Francis 6.00 15.00
4 Mike Bibby 12.50 30.00
5 Amare Stoudemire 10.00 25.00
6 Tayshaun Prince 8.00 20.00
7 Tracy McGrady 20.00 50.00
8 Alonzo Mourning 30.00 80.00
9 Ben Wallace 15.00 40.00
11 Carmelo Anthony 30.00 80.00
12 Marcus Banks 6.00 15.00
14 Mickael Pietrus 8.00 20.00
15 Luke Ridnour 8.00 20.00
16 Dwyane Wade 125.00 300.00
17 David West 8.00 20.00
18 Chris Bosh 20.00 50.00
19 Michael Sweetney 6.00 15.00
20 Troy Bell 6.00 15.00
22 Josh Howard 6.00 15.00
23 Leandro Barbosa 6.00 15.00

2003-04 Fleer Focus Autographs

PRINT RUN 100 SERIAL #'d SETS
*AUTO 50: .5X TO 1.25X BASE HI
*AUTO 25: .6X TO 1.5X BASE HI
4 Eddy Curry 6.00 15.00
10 Alonzo Mourning 30.00 80.00
17 Amare Stoudemire 12.00 30.00
91 Steve Francis 12.50 30.00
121 Carmelo Anthony 25.00 60.00
123 Leandro Barbosa 8.00 20.00
124 Troy Bell 6.00 15.00
125 Chris Bosh 12.00 30.00
130 Marcus Banks 6.00 15.00
143 Mickael Pietrus 8.00 20.00
145 Luke Ridnour 8.00 20.00
148 Dwyane Wade 40.00 100.00
150 David West 6.00 15.00
155 Mo Williams 8.00 20.00

2003-04 Fleer Focus Home and Aways

COMPLETE SET (15) 15.00 30.00
PRINT RUN 500 SERIAL #'d SETS
1 Kevin Garnett 3.00 8.00
2 Chris Webber 1.50 4.00
3 Allen Iverson 3.00 8.00
4 Scottie Pippen 3.00 8.00
5 Paul Pierce 2.00 5.00
6 Jason Kidd 2.00 5.00
7 Baron Davis 1.25 3.00
8 Steve Francis 1.25 3.00
9 Stephon Marbury 1.50 4.00
10 Antoine Walker 1.25 3.00
11 Vince Carter 2.50 6.00
12 Latrell Sprewell 1.50 4.00
13 Manu Ginobili 2.50 6.00
14 Caron Butler 1.00 2.50
15 Jason Richardson 1.25 3.00

2003-04 Fleer Focus Home and Aways Dual Jerseys

PRINT RUN 199 SERIAL #'d SETS
HAAI Allen Iverson 12.00 30.00
HAAW Antoine Walker 5.00 12.00
HABD Baron Davis 5.00 12.00
HACB Caron Butler 4.00 10.00
HACW Chris Webber 6.00 15.00
HAJK Jason Kidd 8.00 20.00
HAJR Jason Richardson 5.00 12.00
HAKG Kevin Garnett 12.00 30.00
HALS Latrell Sprewell 6.00 15.00
HAMG Manu Ginobili 10.00 25.00
HAPP Paul Pierce 8.00 20.00
HASF Steve Francis 5.00 12.00
HASP Scottie Pippen 10.00 25.00
HAVC Vince Carter 10.00 25.00

2003-04 Fleer Focus NBA Shirtified

COMPLETE SET (25) 30.00 80.00
PRINT RUN 750 SERIAL #'d SETS
*RED: .25X TO .6X BASIC
1 Tracy McGrady 1.50 4.00
2 Mike Bibby 1.00 2.50
3 Allen Iverson 2.50 6.00
4 Dirk Nowitzki 2.50 6.00
5 Paul Pierce 1.50 4.00
6 Antawn Jamison 1.00 2.50
7 Kenyon Martin 1.00 2.50
8 Shawn Marion 1.00 2.50
9 Rasheed Wallace 1.25 3.00
10 Caron Butler .75 2.00
11 Elton Brand .75 2.00
12 Eddy Curry .60 1.50
13 Michael Finley 1.00 2.50
14 Yao Ming 2.50 6.00
15 Vince Carter 2.00 5.00
16 Amare Stoudemire 1.25 3.00
17 Jermaine O'Neal 1.00 2.50
18 Peja Stojakovic .75 2.00
19 Karl Malone 2.00 5.00
20 Ben Wallace 1.25 3.00
21 Steve Francis 1.00 2.50
22 Baron Davis 1.00 2.50
23 Kobe Bryant 8.00 20.00
24 Shaquille O'Neal 4.00 10.00
25 Tim Duncan 2.50 6.00

2003-04 Fleer Focus NBA Shirtified Jerseys 250

PRINT RUN 250 SERIAL #'d SETS
*150 SINGLES: .5X TO 1.25X BASE HI
*75 SINGLES: .6X TO 1.5X BASE HI
*NAMEPLATES: 1.25X TO 3X BASE HI
NAMPLATES PRINT RUN 50 SER.#'d SETS
*NUMBERS SINGLES: 1X TO 2.5X BASE HI
NUMBERS PRINT RUN 99 SER.#'d SETS
NSAI Allen Iverson 6.00 15.00
NSAJ Antawn Jamison 2.50 6.00
NSAS Amare Stoudemire 3.00 8.00
NSBW Ben Wallace 3.00 8.00
NSDN Dirk Nowitzki 6.00 15.00
NSEB Elton Brand 2.00 5.00
NSEC Eddy Curry 1.50 4.00
NSJO Jermaine O'Neal 2.50 6.00
NSKM Karl Malone 5.00 12.00
NSKM Kenyon Martin 2.50 6.00
NSLS Caron Butler 2.00 5.00
NSMB Mike Bibby 2.50 6.00
NSMF Michael Finley 2.50 6.00
NSPP Paul Pierce 4.00 10.00
NSPS Peja Stojakovic 2.00 5.00
NSRW Rasheed Wallace 3.00 8.00
NSSM Shawn Marion 2.50 6.00
NSTM Tracy McGrady 4.00 10.00
NSVC Vince Carter 5.00 12.00
NSYM Yao Ming 6.00 15.00

2003-04 Fleer Focus Tag Team

PRINT RUN 350 SERIAL #'d SETS
1 J.Kidd/K.Martin 2.00 5.00
2 M.Bibby/P.Stojakovic 1.25 3.00
3 T.Prince/B.Wallace 1.50 4.00
4 A.Houston/L.Sprewell 1.50 4.00
5 K.Garnett/T.Hudson 3.00 8.00
6 S.Francis/Y.Ming 3.00 8.00
7 S.Nash/D.Nowitzki 3.00 8.00
8 P.Pierce/A.Walker 2.00 5.00
9 T.McGrady/D.Gooden 2.00 5.00
10 S.Marbury/A.Stoudemire 1.50 4.00
11 D.Milicic/C.Bosh 4.00 10.00
12 T.Ford/D.Wade 10.00 25.00
13 L.James/C.Anthony 150.00 400.00
14 T.Duncan/T.Parker 3.00 8.00
15 K.Bryant/S.O'Neal 10.00 25.00

2003-04 Fleer Focus Tag Team Jerseys

PRINT RUN 250 SERIAL #'d SETS
1 J.Kidd/K.Martin 5.00 12.00
2 M.Bibby/P.Stojakovic 3.00 8.00
3 T.Prince/B.Wallace 8.00 20.00
4 A.Houston/L.Sprewell 3.00 8.00
5 K.Garnett/T.Hudson 8.00 20.00
6 S.Francis/Y.Ming 10.00 25.00
7 S.Nash/D.Nowitzki 10.00 25.00
8 P.Pierce/A.Walker 5.00 12.00
9 T.McGrady/D.Gooden 5.00 12.00
10 S.Marbury/A.Stoudemire 4.00 10.00

1999-00 Fleer Force

COMPLETE SET (235) 75.00 200.00
COMPLETE SET w/o RC (200) 15.00 40.00
201-235 PRINT RUN 1600 SERIAL #'d SETS
SGT.CARTER CARD: STATED ODDS 1:300
CARTER AU: PRINT RUN 300 SETS
1 Vince Carter 1.00 2.50
2 Kobe Bryant 3.00 8.00
3 Keith Van Horn .30 .75
4 Tim Duncan 1.00 2.50
5 Grant Hill .60 1.50
6 Kevin Garnett 1.00 2.50
7 Anfernee Hardaway 1.00 2.50
8 Jason Williams .60 1.50
9 Paul Pierce .75 2.00
10 Mookie Blaylock .25 .60
11 Shawn Bradley .25 .60
12 Kenny Anderson .30 .75
13 Chauncey Billups .40 1.00
14 Elden Campbell .25 .60
15 Jason Caffey .25 .60
16 Brent Barry .30 .75
17 Charles Barkley 1.00 2.50
18 Derek Anderson .25 .60
19 Darrick Martin .25 .60
20 Michael Curry .25 .60
21 Rick Fox .25 .60
22 Antonio Davis .25 .60
23 Terrell Brandon .25 .60
24 P.J. Brown .25 .60
25 Toby Bailey .25 .60
26 Ray Allen .60 1.50
27 Brian Grant .25 .60
28 Scott Burrell .25 .60
29 Tariq Abdul-Wahad .25 .60
30 Marcus Camby .30 .75
31 John Stockton .60 1.50
32 Nick Anderson .25 .60
33 Jamie Feick RC .25 .60
34 Matt Geiger .25 .60
35 Vin Baker .30 .75
36 Dee Brown .25 .60
37 Shandon Anderson .25 .60
38 Vernon Maxwell .25 .60
39 Shareef Abdur-Rahim .40 1.00
40 LaPhonso Ellis .25 .60
41 Cedric Ceballos .25 .60
42 Tony Battie .25 .60
43 Keon Clark .25 .60
44 Derrick Coleman .30 .75
45 Erick Dampier .25 .60
46 Corey Benjamin .25 .60
47 Michael Dickerson .25 .60
48 Cedric Henderson .25 .60
49 Lamond Murray .25 .60
50 Jerome Williams .25 .60
51 Shaquille O'Neal 1.50 4.00
52 Dale Davis .25 .60
53 Dean Garrett .25 .60
54 Tim Hardaway .50 1.25
55 Dennis Rodman .75 2.00
56 Sam Cassell .30 .75
57 Jim Jackson .25 .60
58 Kendall Gill .40 1.00
59 Eric Williams .25 .60
60 Chris Childs .25 .60
61 Vlade Divac .40 1.00
62 Darrell Armstrong .25 .60
63 Mario Elie .25 .60
64 Jaren Jackson .25 .60
65 Dale Ellis .25 .60
66 Doug Christie .30 .75
67 Howard Eisley .25 .60
68 Juwan Howard .30 .75
69 Mike Bibby .40 1.00
70 Alan Henderson .25 .60
71 Michael Finley .40 1.00
72 Dana Barros .25 .60
73 Troy Hudson .40 1.00
74 Ricky Davis .40 1.00
75 John Amaechi RC .40 1.00
76 Erick Strickland .25 .60
77 Bryce Drew .25 .60
78 Shawn Kemp .60 1.50
79 Tyrone Nesby RC .25 .60
80 Lindsey Hunter .25 .60
81 Ruben Patterson .25 .60
82 Al Harrington .40 1.00
83 Bobby Jackson .30 .75
84 Dan Majerle .30 .75
85 Rex Chapman .25 .60
86 Dell Curry .25 .60
87 Robert Pack .25 .60
88 Kerry Kittles .30 .75
89 Isaiah Rider .30 .75
90 Patrick Ewing .50 1.25
91 Lawrence Funderburke .25 .60
92 Isaac Austin .25 .60
93 Sean Elliott .30 .75
94 Larry Hughes .30 .75
95 Jelani McCoy .25 .60
96 Tracy McGrady .60 1.50
97 Jeff Hornacek .30 .75
98 Jahidi White .25 .60
99 Danny Manning .30 .75
100 Roshown McLeod .25 .60
101 Steve Nash .75 2.00
102 Ron Mercer .30 .75
103 Raef LaFrentz .30 .75
104 Eddie Jones .40 1.00
105 Antawn Jamison .40 1.00
106 Chucky Atkins RC .30 .75
107 Othella Harrington .25 .60
108 Brevin Knight .25 .60
109 Michael Olowokandi .25 .60
110 Christian Laettner .30 .75
111 J.R. Reid .25 .60
112 Reggie Miller .75 2.00
113 Lazaro Borrell RC .40 1.00
114 Jamal Mashburn .30 .75
115 Glenn Robinson .30 .75
116 Pat Garrity .25 .60
117 Stephon Marbury .50 1.25
118 Arvydas Sabonis .30 .75
119 Allan Houston .30 .75
120 Peja Stojakovic .40 1.00
121 Michael Doleac .25 .60
122 Avery Johnson .30 .75
123 Allen Iverson 1.00 2.50
124 Rashard Lewis .30 .75
125 Charles Oakley .40 1.00
126 Karl Malone .75 2.00
127 Tracy Murray .25 .60
128 Felipe Lopez .25 .60
129 Dikembe Mutombo .60 1.50
130 Dirk Nowitzki 1.25 3.00
131 Vitaly Potapenko .25 .60
132 Antonio McDyess .30 .75
133 Anthony Mason .40 1.00
134 Donyell Marshall .30 .75
135 Dickey Simpkins .25 .60
136 Cuttino Mobley .25 .60
137 Wesley Person .25 .60
138 Rodney Rogers .25 .60
139 Jerry Stackhouse .40 1.00
140 Glen Rice .40 1.00
141 Chris Mullin .40 1.00
142 Anthony Peeler .25 .60
143 Alonzo Mourning .60 1.50
144 Tom Gugliotta .30 .75
145 Tim Thomas .30 .75
146 Damon Stoudamire .40 1.00
147 Jayson Williams .25 .60
148 Larry Johnson .40 1.00
149 Chris Webber .50 1.25
150 Matt Harpring .25 .60
151 David Robinson .75 2.00
152 George Lynch .25 .60
153 Gary Payton .60 1.50
154 John Wallace .25 .60
155 Greg Ostertag .25 .60
156 Mitch Richmond .50 1.25
157 Cherokee Parks .25 .60
158 Steve Smith .30 .75
159 Gary Trent .25 .60
160 Antoine Walker .40 1.00
161 Chris Herren RC .30 .75
162 Ron Harper .30 .75
163 Chris Mills .25 .60
164 Fred Hoiberg .25 .60
165 Hakeem Olajuwon .75 2.00
166 Bob Sura .25 .60
167 Brian Skinner .25 .60
168 Loy Vaught .25 .60
169 A.C. Green .30 .75
170 Jalen Rose .30 .75
171 Joe Smith .30 .75
172 Clarence Weatherspoon .25 .60
173 Jason Kidd .60 1.50
174 Robert Traylor .25 .60
175 Rasheed Wallace .50 1.25
176 Latrell Sprewell .50 1.25
177 Corliss Williamson .25 .60
178 Bo Outlaw .25 .60
179 Malik Rose .25 .60
180 Nazr Mohammed .25 .60
181 Eric Murdock .25 .60
182 Kevin Willis .25 .60
183 Bryon Russell .25 .60
184 Bryant Reeves .25 .60
185 Rod Strickland .30 .75
186 Samaki Walker .25 .60
187 Nick Van Exel .30 .75
188 David Wesley .25 .60
189 John Starks .40 1.00
190 Toni Kukoc .50 1.25
191 Scottie Pippen 1.00 2.50
192 Johnny Newman .25 .60
193 Maurice Taylor .25 .60
194 Rik Smits .30 .75
195 Clifford Robinson .30 .75
196 Bonzi Wells .25 .60
197 Charlie Ward .25 .60
198 Detlef Schrempf .30 .75
199 Theo Ratliff .30 .75
200 Kelvin Cato .25 .60
201 Ron Artest RC 4.00 10.00
202 William Avery RC 1.00 2.50
203 Elton Brand RC 3.00 8.00
204 Baron Davis RC 4.00 10.00
205 Jumaine Jones RC 1.00 2.50
206 Andre Miller RC 3.00 8.00
207 Eddie Robinson RC 1.50 4.00
208 James Posey RC 1.50 4.00
209 Jason Terry RC 2.50 6.00
210 Kenny Thomas RC 1.50 4.00
211 Steve Francis RC 3.00 8.00
212 Wally Szczerbiak RC 2.50 6.00
213 Richard Hamilton RC 4.00 10.00
214 Jonathan Bender RC 1.50 4.00
215 Shawn Marion RC 3.00 8.00
216 A.Radojevic RC 1.00 2.50
217 Tim James RC 1.00 2.50
218 Trajan Langdon RC 1.25 3.00
219 Lamar Odom RC 3.00 8.00
220 Corey Maggette RC 2.00 5.00
221 Dion Glover RC 1.00 2.50
222 Cal Bowdler RC 1.00 2.50
223 Vonteego Cummings RC 1.00 2.50
224 Devean George RC 1.25 3.00
225 Anthony Carter RC 1.25 3.00
226 Laron Profit RC 1.00 2.50
227 Quincy Lewis RC 1.00 2.50
228 John Celestand RC 1.00 2.50
229 Obinna Ekezie RC 1.00 2.50
230 Scott Padgett RC 1.25 3.00
231 Michael Ruffin RC 1.00 2.50
232 Jeff Foster RC 1.50 4.00
233 Jermaine Jackson RC 1.50 4.00
234 Adrian Griffin RC 1.25 3.00
235 Todd MacCulloch RC 1.25 3.00
NNO V.Carter Sgt. JSY 8.00 20.00
NNO V.Carter Sgt. AU/300 25.00 60.00

1999-00 Fleer Force Forcefield

*STARS: 1.5X TO 4X BASE CARD HI
*RCs: .1.5X TO 4X BASE HI
STARS: STATED ODDS 1:12
RCs: PRINT RUN 100 SERIAL #'d SETS
2 Kobe Bryant 25.00 60.00

1999-00 Fleer Force Air Force One Five

COMPLETE SET (15) 12.00 30.00
COMMON CARD (AF1-AF15) 1.50 4.00
*FORCEFIELD: 3X TO 8X BASE HI
STATED ODDS 1:24
FF: PRINT RUN 150 SERIAL #'d SETS

1999-00 Fleer Force Attack Force

COMPLETE SET (20) 8.00 20.00
STATED ODDS 1:6
*FF: .75X TO 2X BASE CARD HI
FF: STATED ODDS 1:24
A1 Vince Carter 1.50 4.00
A2 Lamar Odom 1.25 3.00
A3 Stephon Marbury .75 2.00
A4 Jason Terry 1.00 2.50
A5 Richard Hamilton 1.50 4.00
A6 Steve Francis 1.25 3.00
A7 Wally Szczerbiak 1.00 2.50
A8 Tracy McGrady 1.00 2.50
A9 Michael Finley .60 1.50
A10 Baron Davis 1.50 4.00
A11 Shawn Marion 1.25 3.00
A12 Jonathan Bender .60 1.50
A13 Elton Brand 1.25 3.00
A14 Shareef Abdur-Rahim .60 1.50
A15 Keith Van Horn .50 1.25
A16 Jerry Stackhouse .60 1.50
A17 Antonio McDyess .50 1.25
A18 Antoine Walker .60 1.50
A19 Steve Smith .50 1.25
A20 Ron Artest 1.50 4.00

1999-00 Fleer Force Forceful

COMPLETE SET (15) 20.00 50.00
STATED ODDS 1:36
*FF: .75X TO 2X BASE CARD HI
FF: STATED ODDS 1:144
F1 Vince Carter 3.00 8.00
F2 Lamar Odom 2.50 6.00
F3 Shaquille O'Neal 5.00 12.00
F4 Alonzo Mourning 2.00 5.00
F5 Kevin Garnett 3.00 8.00
F6 Tim Duncan 3.00 8.00
F7 Kobe Bryant 10.00 25.00
F8 Allen Iverson 3.00 8.00
F9 Jason Williams 2.00 5.00
F10 Paul Pierce 2.50 6.00
F11 Shareef Abdur-Rahim 1.25 3.00
F12 Stephon Marbury 1.50 4.00
F13 Grant Hill 2.00 5.00
F14 Keith Van Horn 1.00 2.50
F15 Karl Malone 2.50 6.00

1999-00 Fleer Force Mission Accomplished

COMPLETE SET (15) 12.00 30.00
STATED ODDS 1:12
*FF: .75X TO 2X BASE CARD HI
FF: STATED ODDS 1:48
MA1 Vince Carter 2.00 5.00
MA2 Lamar Odom 1.50 4.00
MA3 Allen Iverson 2.00 5.00
MA4 Tim Duncan 2.00 5.00
MA5 Charles Barkley 2.00 5.00
MA6 Jason Kidd 1.25 3.00
MA7 Steve Francis 1.50 4.00
MA8 Elton Brand 1.50 4.00
MA9 Kevin Garnett 2.00 5.00
MA10 Baron Davis 2.00 5.00
MA11 Paul Pierce 1.50 4.00
MA12 Scottie Pippen 2.00 5.00
MA13 Chris Webber 1.00 2.50
MA14 Anfernee Hardaway 2.00 5.00
MA15 David Robinson 1.50 4.00

1999-00 Fleer Force Operation Invasion

COMPLETE SET (15) 20.00 50.00
STATED ODDS 1:24
*FF: .75X TO 2X BASE CARD HI
FF: STATED ODDS 1:96
OI1 Vince Carter 3.00 8.00
OI2 Lamar Odom 2.50 6.00
OI3 Kobe Bryant 15.00 40.00
OI4 Tim Duncan 3.00 8.00
OI5 Paul Pierce 2.50 6.00
OI6 Kevin Garnett 3.00 8.00
OI7 Grant Hill 2.00 5.00
OI8 Allen Iverson 3.00 8.00
OI9 Jason Williams 2.00 5.00
OI10 Ron Mercer 1.00 2.50
OI11 Shaquille O'Neal 5.00 12.00
OI12 Keith Van Horn 1.00 2.50
OI13 Shareef Abdur-Rahim 1.25 3.00
OI14 Alonzo Mourning 2.00 5.00
OI15 Stephon Marbury 1.50 4.00

1999-00 Fleer Force Special Forces

COMPLETE SET (15) 10.00 25.00
STATED ODDS 1:12
*FF: .75X TO 2X BASE CARD HI
FF: STATED ODDS 1:48
SF1 Vince Carter 2.00 5.00
SF2 Lamar Odom 1.50 4.00
SF3 Keith Van Horn .60 1.50
SF4 Stephon Marbury 1.00 2.50
SF5 Scottie Pippen 2.00 5.00
SF6 Ray Allen 1.25 3.00
SF7 Chris Webber 1.00 2.50
SF8 Jason Williams 1.25 3.00
SF9 Karl Malone 1.50 4.00
SF10 Patrick Ewing 1.00 2.50
SF11 Elton Brand 1.50 4.00
SF12 Grant Hill 1.25 3.00
SF13 Eddie Jones .75 2.00
SF14 Shaquille O'Neal 3.00 8.00
SF15 Kobe Bryant 6.00 15.00

2001-02 Fleer Force

COMPLETE SET (180) 75.00 200.00
COMPLETE SET w/o SP's (150) 15.00 40.00
101-130 PRINT RUN 999 SER.#'d SETS
FIRST 300 SER.#'d SETS RC POSTMARKS
1 Vince Carter .75 2.00
2 Allan Houston .40 1.00
3 Steve Francis .40 1.00
4 Karl Malone .75 2.00
5 Joe Smith .30 .7
6 Raef LaFrentz .25 .6
7 David Robinson .75 2.0
8 Tim Thomas .25 .6
9 Antonio McDyess .30 .75
10 Steve Smith .30 .75
11 Eddie Jones .40 1.00
12 Jumaine Jones .25 .60
13 Derek Anderson .25 .60
14 Shaquille O'Neal 1.50 4.00
15 Eddie Robinson .25 .60
16 Stephon Marbury .50 1.25
17 Darius Miles .25 .60
18 Toni Kukoc .50 1.25
19 Latrell Sprewell .50 1.25
20 Wang Zhizhi .40 1.00
21 Tim Duncan 1.00 2.50
22 Eddie House .25 .60
23 Chris Mihm .25 .60
24 Rasheed Wallace .50 1.25
25 Kobe Bryant 3.00 8.00
26 Kenny Thomas .25 .60
27 John Stockton .75 2.00
28 Mike Bibby .40 1.00
29 Larry Hughes .30 .75
30 Antonio Davis .30 .75
31 Ray Allen .60 1.50
32 Corliss Williamson .25 .60
33 Desmond Mason .30 .75
34 Sam Cassell .30 .75
35 Dirk Nowitzki 1.00 2.50
36 Chris Webber .50 1.25
37 Michael Dickerson .25 .60
38 Ron Mercer .25 .60
39 Iakovos Tsakalidis .25 .60
40 Derek Fisher .30 .75
41 Baron Davis .40 1.00
42 Allen Iverson 1.00 2.50
43 Avery Johnson .30 .75
44 Courtney Alexander .25 .60
45 Alonzo Mourning .60 1.50
46 Steve Nash .75 2.00
47 Hedo Turkoglu .30 .75
48 Jason Williams .60 1.50
49 David Wesley .25 .60
50 Dikembe Mutombo .60 1.50
51 LaPhonso Ellis .30 .75
52 Trajan Langdon .25 .60
53 Damon Stoudamire .40 1.00
54 Rick Fox .30 .75
55 Paul Pierce .60 1.50
56 Tracy McGrady .60 1.50
57 Lamar Odom .30 .75
58 Antoine Walker .30 .75
59 Mike Miller .30 .75
60 Jermaine O'Neal .30 .75
61 Michael Jordan 4.00 10.00
62 Jason Kidd .60 1.50
63 Marc Jackson .25 .60
64 Hakeem Olajuwon .75 2.00
65 Kevin Garnett 1.00 2.50
66 Nick Van Exel .40 1.00
67 Rashard Lewis .30 .75
68 Brian Grant .25 .60
69 Keith Van Horn .30 .75
70 Grant Hill .60 1.50
71 Reggie Miller .75 2.00
72 Richard Hamilton .50 1.25
73 Marcus Camby .30 .75
74 Clifford Robinson .40 1.00
75 Gary Payton .60 1.50
76 Andre Miller .30 .75
77 Bonzi Wells .25 .60
78 Stromile Swift .25 .60
79 Marcus Fizer .25 .60
80 Shawn Marion .40 1.00
81 Elton Brand .30 .75
82 Jamal Mashburn .30 .75
83 Aaron McKie .25 .60
84 Corey Maggette .30 .75
85 Jason Terry .40 1.00
86 Anfernee Hardaway 1.00 2.50
87 Antawn Jamison .30 .75
88 Morris Peterson .25 .60
89 Wally Szczerbiak .30 .75
90 Jerry Stackhouse .40 1.00
91 Shareef Abdur-Rahim .30 .75
92 Glenn Robinson .40 1.00
93 Michael Finley .40 1.00
94 Peja Stojakovic .30 .75
95 Jalen Rose .30 .75
96 Theo Ratliff .25 .60
97 Kurt Thomas .25 .60
98 Cuttino Mobley .30 .75
99 DeShawn Stevenson .25 .60
100 Terrell Brandon .30 .75
101 Kwame Brown RC 1.00 2.50
102 Tyson Chandler RC 1.50 4.00
103 Pau Gasol RC 4.00 10.00
104 Eddy Curry RC 1.00 2.50
105 Jason Richardson RC 1.50 4.00
106 Shane Battier RC 2.00 5.00
107 Eddie Griffin RC .75 2.00
108 DeSagana Diop RC .60 1.50
109 Rodney White RC .60 1.50
110 Joe Johnson RC 1.50 4.00
111 Kedrick Brown RC .60 1.50
112 Vladimir Radmanovic RC .75 2.00
113 Richard Jefferson RC 1.25 3.00
114 Troy Murphy RC .75 2.00
115 Steven Hunter RC .60 1.50
116 Kirk Haston RC .60 1.50
117 Michael Bradley RC .60 1.50
118 Jason Collins RC .75 2.00
119 Zach Randolph RC 2.00 5.00
120 Brendan Haywood RC .75 2.00
121 Joseph Forte RC .60 1.50
122 Jeryl Sasser RC .60 1.50
123 Brandon Armstrong RC .60 1.50
124 Andrei Kirilenko RC 1.50 4.00
125 Gerald Wallace RC 1.25 3.00
126 Samuel Dalembert RC 1.00 2.50
127 Jamaal Tinsley RC .75 2.00
128 Tony Parker RC 4.00 10.00
129 Loren Woods RC .60 1.50
130 Primoz Brezec RC 1.00 2.50

131 Dion Glover .25 .60
132 Moochie Norris .25 .60
133 Mark Jackson .30 .75
134 Bryon Russell .25 .60
135 Danny Fortson .25 .60
136 Kenyon Martin .40 1.00
137 Alvin Williams .25 .60
138 Erick Dampier .25 .60
139 Clarence Weatherspoon .25 .60
140 Brent Barry .25 .60
141 Lamond Murray .25 .60
142 Lindsey Hunter .25 .60
143 Speedy Claxton .25 .60
144 James Posey .25 .60
145 Anthony Mason .40 1.00
146 Mateen Cleaves .25 .60
147 Kenny Anderson .30 .75
148 Travis Best .25 .60
149 Patrick Ewing .60 1.50
150 Dana Barros .25 .60
151 Lorenzen Wright .25 .60
152 Rodney Rogers .25 .60
153 Brad Miller .40 1.00
154 Anthony Peeler .25 .60
155 Antonio Daniels .25 .60
156 Tim Hardaway .50 1.25
157 Quentin Richardson .25 .60
158 Darrell Armstrong .25 .60
159 Nazr Mohammad .25 .60
160 Todd MacCulloch .25 .60
161 Ruben Patterson .25 .60
162 Wesley Person .25 .60
163 Jeff McInnis .25 .60
164 Vin Baker .30 .75
165 George McCloud .25 .60
166 Chris Gatling .25 .60
167 Derrick Coleman .30 .75
168 Elden Campbell .25 .60
169 Glen Rice .40 1.00
170 Donyell Marshall .25 .60
171 Juwan Howard .30 .75
172 Mitch Richmond .50 1.25
173 Tom Gugliotta .25 .60
174 Chucky Atkins .25 .60
175 Michael Redd .40 1.00
176 Malik Rose .25 .60
177 Lee Nailon .25 .60
178 Al Harrington .30 .75
179 Matt Harpring .25 .60
180 Tyronn Lue .40 1.00

2001-02 Fleer Force Rookie Postmarks

*RC POSTMARKS: .75X TO 2X BASE RC HI
PRINT RUN FIRST 300 SER.#'d SETS

2001-02 Fleer Force Special Forces

*SF STARS: 4X TO 10X BASE CARD HI
1-100, 131-180 PRINT RUN 250 SER.#'d SETS
*SF ROOKIES: 2.5X TO 6X BASE CARD HI
101-130 PRINT RUN 50 SER.#'d SETS
61 Michael Jordan 40.00 100.00

2001-02 Fleer Force Emblematic

STATED PRINT RUN 399 SER.#'d SETS
1 Vince Carter 3.00 8.00
2 Dikembe Mutombo 2.50 6.00
3 Tracy McGrady 2.50 6.00
4 Lamar Odom 1.25 3.00
5 Jason Kidd 2.50 6.00
6 Ray Allen 2.50 6.00
7 John Stockton 3.00 8.00
8 Paul Pierce 2.50 6.00
9 Baron Davis 1.50 4.00
10 Kenyon Martin 1.50 4.00
11 Richard Hamilton 2.00 5.00
12 Grant Hill 2.50 6.00
13 Morris Peterson 1.00 2.50
14 Shareef Abdur-Rahim 1.25 3.00
15 Peja Stojakovic 1.25 3.00
16 Gary Payton 2.50 6.00
17 Karl Malone 3.00 8.00
18 Keith Van Horn 1.25 3.00
19 Darius Miles 1.00 2.50
20 Allen Iverson 4.00 10.00
21 Michael Jordan 40.00 100.00
22 Kobe Bryant 25.00 60.00
23 Kevin Garnett 4.00 10.00
24 Shaquille O'Neal 6.00 15.00
25 Tim Duncan 4.00 10.00

2001-02 Fleer Force Emblematic Jerseys

STATED PRINT RUN 50 SER.#'d SETS
1 Vince Carter 20.00 50.00
2 Dikembe Mutombo 15.00 40.00
3 Tracy McGrady 15.00 40.00
4 Lamar Odom 8.00 20.00
5 Jason Kidd 15.00 40.00
6 Ray Allen 15.00 40.00
7 John Stockton 20.00 50.00
8 Paul Pierce 15.00 40.00
9 Baron Davis 10.00 25.00
10 Kenyon Martin 10.00 25.00
11 Richard Hamilton 12.00 30.00
12 Grant Hill 15.00 40.00
13 Morris Peterson 6.00 15.00
14 Shareef Abdur-Rahim 8.00 20.00
15 Peja Stojakovic 8.00 20.00
16 Gary Payton 15.00 40.00
17 Karl Malone 20.00 50.00
18 Keith Van Horn 8.00 20.00
19 Darius Miles 6.00 15.00
20 Allen Iverson 25.00 60.00

2001-02 Fleer Force Inside the Game

STATED PRINT RUN 699 SER.#'d SETS
1 Karl Malone 3.00 8.00
2 Keith Van Horn 1.25 3.00
3 Darius Miles 1.00 2.50
4 John Stockton 3.00 8.00
5 Allen Iverson 4.00 10.00
6 Alonzo Mourning 2.50 6.00
7 Dikembe Mutombo 2.50 6.00
8 Tracy McGrady 2.50 6.00
9 Lamar Odom 1.25 3.00
10 Baron Davis 1.50 4.00
11 Michael Jordan 25.00 60.00
12 Kobe Bryant 12.00 30.00
13 Kevin Garnett 4.00 10.00
14 Shaquille O'Neal 6.00 15.00
15 Tim Duncan 4.00 10.00
16 Vince Carter 3.00 8.00
17 Steve Francis 1.50 4.00
18 Dirk Nowitzki 4.00 10.00
19 Chris Webber 2.00 5.00
20 Peja Stojakovic 1.25 3.00
NNO Vince Carter AU/275 60.00 150.00

2001-02 Fleer Force Inside the Game Jerseys

PRINT RUN 399 SER.#'d SETS
*NUMBERS: 1.5X TO 4X JSY HI
NUMBERS PRINT RUN 99 SER.#'d SETS
1 Karl Malone 6.00 15.00
2 Keith Van Horn 2.50 6.00
3 Darius Miles 2.00 5.00
4 John Stockton 6.00 15.00
5 Allen Iverson 8.00 20.00
6 Alonzo Mourning 5.00 12.00
7 Dikembe Mutombo 5.00 12.00
8 Tracy McGrady 5.00 12.00
9 Lamar Odom 2.50 6.00
10 Baron Davis 3.00 8.00
11 Vince Carter 6.00 15.00
12 Steve Francis 3.00 8.00
13 Dirk Nowitzki 8.00 20.00
14 Chris Webber 4.00 10.00
15 Peja Stojakovic 2.50 6.00

2001-02 Fleer Force True Colors Jerseys

PRINT RUN 400 SER.#'d SETS
*FOUR COLOR: 2X TO 5X ONE COLOR HI
FOUR COLOR PRINT RUN 50 SER.#'d SETS
*THREE COLOR: 1.25X TO 3X ONE COLOR HI
THREE COLOR PRINT RUN 100 SER.#'d SETS
*TWO COLOR: .75X TO 2X ONE COLOR HI
TWO COLOR PRINT RUN 200 SER.#'d SETS
1 Vince Carter 6.00 15.00
2 Kenyon Martin 3.00 8.00
3 Baron Davis 3.00 8.00
4 Tracy McGrady 5.00 12.00
5 Mike Miller 2.50 6.00
6 Aaron McKie 2.00 5.00
7 Darius Miles 2.00 5.00
8 Lamar Odom 2.50 6.00
9 Glenn Robinson 3.00 8.00
10 Karl Malone 6.00 15.00
11 John Stockton 6.00 15.00
12 Paul Pierce 5.00 12.00
13 Alonzo Mourning 5.00 12.00
14 Gary Payton 5.00 12.00
15 Stephon Marbury 4.00 10.00
16 Dikembe Mutombo 5.00 12.00
17 Shawn Marion 3.00 8.00
18 Richard Hamilton 4.00 10.00
19 Stromile Swift 2.00 5.00
20 Reggie Miller 15.00 40.00
21 Keith Van Horn 2.50 6.00
22 Steve Francis 3.00 8.00
23 Morris Peterson 2.00 5.00
24 Andre Miller 2.50 6.00
25 Quentin Richardson 2.00 5.00
26 Antonio McDyess 2.50 6.00
27 Anfernee Hardaway 8.00 20.00
28 Jason Williams 5.00 12.00
29 Grant Hill 5.00 12.00
30 Jason Terry 3.00 8.00

2000-01 Fleer Futures

COMPLETE SET (250) 40.00 80.00
COMPLETE SET w/o RCs (200) 10.00 25.00
RCs: STATED ODDS 1:2 FOR EVEN #'s
RCs: STATED ODDS 1:7 FOR ODD #'s
1 Vince Carter .50 1.25
2 Dan Majerle .25 .60
3 George McCloud .15 .40
4 Radoslav Nesterovic .15 .40
5 Corey Maggette .20 .50
6 Derek Anderson .20 .50
7 Ray Allen .40 1.00
8 Greg Ostertag .15 .40
9 Cedric Ceballos .20 .50
10 Danny Fortson .20 .50
11 Roshown McLeod .15 .40
12 Christian Laettner .25 .60
13 Avery Johnson .20 .50
14 Clarence Weatherspoon .15 .40
15 Michael Curry .15 .40
16 Chris Whitney .15 .40
17 Anthony Mason .25 .60
18 Antonio McDyess .25 .60
19 Vitaly Potapenko .15 .40
20 Shaquille O'Neal 1.00 2.50
21 David Robinson .50 1.25
22 Tyrone Hill .15 .40
23 Otis Thorpe .20 .50
24 Reggie Miller .50 1.25
25 Kevin Garnett .60 1.50
26 Michael Dickerson .15 .40
27 John Amaechi .15 .40
28 Jason Kidd .40 1.00
29 Ron Artest .25 .60
30 Muggsy Bogues .25 .60
31 Antawn Jamison .25 .60
32 Brian Grant .20 .50
33 Stephon Marbury .30 .75
34 William Avery .15 .40
35 Paul Pierce .40 1.00
36 Marcus Camby .20 .50
37 Kevin Willis .15 .40
38 Dikembe Mutombo .40 1.00
39 Rashard Lewis .20 .50
40 Allan Houston .25 .60
41 Hakeem Olajuwon .50 1.25
42 Rod Strickland .15 .40
43 Derrick Coleman .15 .40
44 Tariq Abdul-Wahad .15 .40
45 Terrell Brandon .20 .50
46 Michael Olowokandi .15 .40
47 Robert Horry .25 .60
48 Kelvin Cato .15 .40
49 Eric Williams .15 .40
50 Glen Rice .25 .60
51 Carlos Rogers .15 .40
52 Allen Iverson .60 1.50
53 P.J. Brown .15 .40
54 Jalen Rose .20 .50
55 Damon Stoudamire .25 .60
56 Damon Jones RC .25 .60
57 Darrell Armstrong .15 .40
58 Samaki Walker .15 .40
59 John Stockton .50 1.25
60 Chucky Atkins .15 .40
61 Rasheed Wallace .30 .75
62 Jason Terry .25 .60
63 Aaron Williams .15 .40
64 Steve Nash .40 1.00
65 Antoine Walker .25 .60
66 Patrick Ewing .40 1.00
67 Cuttino Mobley .20 .50
68 Aaron McKie .15 .40
69 Jamal Mashburn .20 .50
70 Scottie Pippen .60 1.50
71 Bryant Reeves .15 .40
72 Isaiah Rider .20 .50
73 Jaren Jackson .15 .40
74 Lindsey Hunter .15 .40
75 Jacque Vaughn .15 .40
76 Travis Best .15 .40
77 Vinny Del Negro .15 .40
78 Othella Harrington .15 .40
79 Michael Finley .25 .60
80 Brent Barry .20 .50
81 Brevin Knight .15 .40
82 Kurt Thomas .15 .40
83 Mark Jackson .20 .50
84 Richard Hamilton .30 .75
85 Anthony Carter .15 .40
86 Matt Harpring .15 .40
87 Bobby Jackson .20 .50
88 Jerome Williams .15 .40
89 Jahidi White .15 .40
90 Lorenzen Wright .15 .40
91 Kerry Kittles .20 .50
92 Anthony Peeler .15 .40
93 Kenny Anderson .20 .50
94 Latrell Sprewell .30 .75
95 Maurice Taylor .15 .40
96 Toni Kukoc .30 .75
97 Eddie Robinson .15 .40
98 Voshon Lenard .15 .40
99 Sam Mitchell .15 .40
100 Isaac Austin .15 .40
101 Michael Doleac .15 .40
102 Andre Miller .20 .50
103 Jason Williams .40 1.00
104 Charles Oakley .25 .60
105 Mitch Richmond .30 .75
106 Bruce Bowen .15 .40
107 Keith Van Horn .25 .60
108 Wally Szczerbiak .20 .50
109 Tony Battie .15 .40
110 Larry Johnson .30 .75
111 Shandon Anderson .15 .40
112 Sam Cassell .20 .50
113 David Wesley .20 .50
114 James Posey .20 .50
115 Bonzi Wells .15 .40
116 Mike Bibby .25 .60
117 Andrew DeClercq .15 .40
118 Clifford Robinson .25 .60
119 Corliss Williamson .15 .40
120 Antonio Davis .20 .50
121 Eddie Jones .25 .60
122 Jamie Feick .15 .40
123 Anfernee Hardaway .40 1.00
124 Adrian Griffin .15 .40
125 Erick Strickland .15 .40
126 Doug Christie .20 .50
127 Scot Pollard .15 .40
128 Sam Perkins .15 .40
129 Raef LaFrentz .20 .50
130 Dale Davis .20 .50
131 Tyrone Nesby .15 .40
132 Rick Fox .20 .50
133 Tom Gugliotta .20 .50
134 Glenn Robinson .25 .60
135 Quincy Lewis .15 .40
136 Austin Croshere .15 .40
137 Shawn Kemp .40 1.00
138 Lamar Odom .25 .60
139 Tim Duncan .60 1.50
140 Tim Thomas .15 .40
141 Bryon Russell .15 .40
142 Jermaine O'Neal .20 .50
143 Erick Dampier .15 .40
144 Shareef Abdur-Rahim .20 .50
145 Bo Outlaw .15 .40
146 Gary Payton .40 1.00
147 Chris Gatling .15 .40
148 Vlade Divac .25 .60
149 Ben Wallace .30 .75
150 Larry Hughes .20 .50
151 Ron Mercer .20 .50
152 Karl Malone .50 1.25
153 Jonathan Bender .15 .40
154 Mookie Blaylock .25 .60
155 Jim Jackson .20 .50
156 Chris Crawford .15 .40
157 Vin Baker .20 .50
158 Lamond Murray .15 .40
159 Charlie Ward .20 .50
160 Steve Francis .25 .60
161 Cherokee Parks .15 .40
162 Baron Davis .25 .60
163 Keon Clark .15 .40
164 Ruben Patterson .15 .40
165 Tracy McGrady .50 1.25
166 Antonio Daniels .15 .40
167 Scott Williams .15 .40
168 John Starks .25 .60
169 Jerry Stackhouse .25 .60
170 Vonteego Cummings .15 .40
171 LaPhonso Ellis .20 .50
172 Dirk Nowitzki .60 1.50
173 Horace Grant .25 .60
174 Wesley Person .15 .40
175 Peja Stojakovic .20 .50
176 Eric Snow .15 .40
177 Juwan Howard .20 .50
178 Tim Hardaway .30 .75
179 Kendall Gill .25 .60
180 Chauncey Billups .30 .75
181 Kobe Bryant 2.00 5.00
182 Sean Elliott .20 .50
183 Donyell Marshall .20 .50
184 Al Harrington .20 .50
185 Arvydas Sabonis .25 .60
186 Grant Hill .40 1.00
187 Malik Rose .15 .40
188 Nazr Mohammed .15 .40
189 Elden Campbell .15 .40
190 Nick Van Exel .25 .60
191 Steve Smith .25 .60
192 Sean Rooks .15 .40
193 Monty Williams .20 .50
194 Elton Brand .25 .60
195 Chris Webber .30 .75
196 Mikki Moore RC .25 .60
197 Chris Mills .15 .40
198 Alan Henderson .15 .40
199 Shawn Bradley .15 .40
200 Shawn Marion .25 .60
201 Hedo Turkoglu RC 1.00 2.50
202 Iakovos Tsakalidis RC .15 .40
203 Kenyon Martin RC 1.25 3.00
204 Mamadou N'Diaye RC .15 .40
205 Stromile Swift RC .50 1.25
206 Pepe Sanchez RC .20 .50
207 Chris Mihm RC .40 1.00
208 Lavor Postell RC .15 .40
209 Marcus Fizer RC .50 1.25
210 Ruben Garces RC .25 .60
211 Courtney Alexander RC .40 1.00
212 A.J. Guyton RC .15 .40
213 Darius Miles RC .60 1.50
214 Ademola Okulaja RC .25 .60
215 Jerome Moiso RC .40 1.00
216 Khalid El-Amin RC .15 .40
217 Joel Przybilla RC .50 1.25
218 Mike Smith RC .15 .40
219 DerMarr Johnson RC .40 1.00
220 Soumaila Samake RC .15 .40
221 Mike Miller RC 1.00 2.50
222 Eddie House RC .20 .50
223 Quentin Richardson RC .50 1.25
224 Eduardo Najera RC .25 .60
225 Morris Peterson RC .60 1.50
226 Hanno Mottola RC .15 .40
227 Speedy Claxton RC .60 1.50
228 Ruben Wolkowyski RC .15 .40
229 Keyon Dooling RC .50 1.25
230 Olumide Oyedeji RC .15 .40
231 Mark Madsen RC .60 1.50
232 Mike Penberthy RC .25 .60
233 Mateen Cleaves RC .50 1.25
234 Brian Cardinal RC .15 .40
235 Etan Thomas RC .50 1.25
236 Garth Joseph RC .25 .60
237 Jason Collier RC .60 1.50
238 Paul McPherson RC .15 .40
239 Erick Barkley RC .40 1.00
240 Stephen Jackson RC .50 1.25
241 Desmond Mason RC .75 2.00
242 Jason Hart RC .25 .60
243 Jamal Crawford RC 1.50 4.00
244 Daniel Santiago RC .25 .60
245 DeShawn Stevenson RC .60 1.50
246 S.Medvedenko RC .25 .60
247 Donnell Harvey RC .50 1.25
248 Chris Porter RC .15 .40
249 Jamaal Magloire RC .60 1.50
250 Dalibor Bagaric RC .20 .50

2000-01 Fleer Futures Black Gold

*EVEN RCs: 2.5X TO 6X BASE CARD HI
*ODD RCs: 1X TO 2.5X BASE HI
STATED PRINT RUN 500 SERIAL #'d SETS

2000-01 Fleer Futures Copper

*STARS: 2.5X TO 6X BASE CARD HI
STATED PRINT RUN 750 SERIAL #'d SETS

2000-01 Fleer Futures Gold

*EVEN RCs: 2.5X TO 6X BASE CARD HI
*ODD RCs: 1X TO 2.5X BASE HI
STATED PRINT RUN 500 SERIAL #'d SETS

2000-01 Fleer Futures Autographics On Location

STATED ODDS 1:403
AOL1 Shareef Abdur-Rahim 10.00 25.00
AOL2 Travis Best 10.00 25.00
AOL3 Vince Carter/240 30.00 80.00
AOL4 Austin Croshere/240 10.00 25.00
AOL5 Baron Davis 20.00 50.00
AOL6 Rashard Lewis/240 20.00 50.00
AOL7 Dan Majerle 60.00 120.00
AOL8 Dirk Nowitzki 300.00 600.00
AOL10 Mitch Richmond 20.00 50.00
AOL11 Jalen Rose 10.00 25.00

2000-01 Fleer Futures Vince Carter Rookie Remnants

NNO Vince Carter FLR/100 15.00 40.00
NNO Vince Carter FLR JSY/15 40.00 100.00

2000-01 Fleer Futures Characteristics

COMPLETE SET (10) 12.50 25.00
STATED ODDS 1:28
C1 Vince Carter 2.00 5.00
C2 Kobe Bryant 8.00 20.00
C3 Lamar Odom 1.00 2.50
C4 Kevin Garnett 2.50 6.00
C5 Allen Iverson 2.50 6.00
C6 Grant Hill 1.50 4.00
C7 Tim Duncan 2.50 6.00
C8 Steve Francis 1.00 2.50
C9 Jason Williams 1.50 4.00
C10 Shaquille O'Neal 4.00 10.00

2000-01 Fleer Futures Hot Commodities

COMPLETE SET (10) 10.00 25.00
STATED ODDS 1:28
HC1 Vince Carter 1.50 4.00
HC2 Kobe Bryant 6.00 15.00
HC3 Kevin Garnett 2.00 5.00
HC4 Allen Iverson 2.00 5.00
HC5 Shaquille O'Neal 3.00 8.00
HC6 Steve Francis .75 2.00
HC7 Grant Hill 1.25 3.00
HC8 Tim Duncan 2.00 5.00
HC9 Lamar Odom .75 2.00
HC10 Tracy McGrady 1.50 4.00

2000-01 Fleer Futures Question Air

COMPLETE SET (15) 3.00 8.00
STATED ODDS 1:14
QA1 Kenyon Martin .60 1.50
QA2 Stromile Swift .25 .60
QA3 Chris Mihm .20 .50
QA4 Marcus Fizer .25 .60
QA5 Courtney Alexander .20 .50
QA6 Darius Miles .30 .75
QA7 Jerome Moiso .20 .50
QA8 Desmond Mason .40 1.00
QA9 DerMarr Johnson .20 .50
QA10 Mike Miller .50 1.25
QA11 Quentin Richardson .25 .60
QA12 Morris Peterson .30 .75
QA13 Etan Thomas .25 .60
QA14 Keyon Dooling .25 .60
QA15 Mateen Cleaves .25 .60

2000-01 Fleer Futures Rookie Game Jerseys

*GJ: 1.5X TO 4X BASE HI 2.50 6.00
STATED PRINT RUN 300 SERIAL #'d SETS

2000-01 Fleer Game Time

COMPLETE SET w/o RC (90) 12.50 25.00
RCs: PRINT RUN 2500 SERIAL #'d SETS
CARTER REMNANTS LISTED UNDER FLE.PREM.
1 Vince Carter .60 1.50
2 Raef LaFrentz .25 .60
3 Kobe Bryant 2.50 6.00
4 Toni Kukoc .40 1.00
5 Bonzi Wells .20 .50
6 Rashard Lewis .25 .60
7 Karl Malone .60 1.50
8 Juwan Howard .25 .60
9 Lindsey Hunter .20 .50
10 Alonzo Mourning .50 1.25
11 Larry Hughes .30 .75
12 Austin Croshere .20 .50
13 Charles Oakley .30 .75
14 Patrick Ewing .50 1.25
15 Vlade Divac .30 .75
16 Michael Finley .30 .75
17 Tim Hardaway .40 1.00
18 Jason Kidd .50 1.25
19 Cal Bowdler .20 .50
20 Dirk Nowitzki .75 2.00
21 Terrell Brandon .25 .60
22 Allan Houston .30 .75
23 Theo Ratliff .20 .50
24 Chris Webber .40 1.00
25 Shawn Kemp .50 1.25
26 Jalen Rose .25 .60
27 Bryon Russell .20 .50
28 Jahidi White .20 .50
29 Trajan Langdon .20 .50
30 Baron Davis .30 .75
31 Cuttino Mobley .25 .60
32 Wally Szczerbiak .25 .60
33 Michael Dickerson .25 .60
34 Andre Miller .25 .60
35 Michael Olowokandi .20 .50
36 Ray Allen .50 1.25
37 Latrell Sprewell .40 1.00
38 Jason Williams .50 1.25
39 Mikki Moore RC .30 .75
40 Shawn Marion .30 .75
41 Radoslav Nesterovic .30 .75
42 Ron Artest .30 .75
43 Vonteego Cummings .20 .50
44 Anfernee Hardaway .50 1.25
45 Jerome Williams .20 .50
46 John Stockton .60 1.50
47 Antawn Jamison .30 .75
48 Grant Hill .50 1.25
49 Elden Campbell .20 .50
50 Steve Francis .30 .75
51 Jamie Feick .30 .75
52 Gary Payton .50 1.25
53 Elton Brand .30 .75
54 Eddie Jones .30 .75
55 Tom Gugliotta .25 .60
56 Richard Hamilton .40 1.00
57 Dion Glover .20 .50
58 Shaquille O'Neal 1.25 3.00
59 Kevin Garnett .75 2.00
60 Paul Pierce .50 1.25
61 Brian Grant .25 .60
62 Tim Thomas .20 .50
63 Tracy McGrady .60 1.50
64 Jonathan Bender .20 .50
65 Adrian Griffin .20 .50
66 Lamar Odom .30 .75
67 Rasheed Wallace .40 1.00
68 Mike Bibby .30 .75
69 Glenn Robinson .30 .75
70 Eddie Robinson .20 .50
71 Robert Horry .30 .75
72 Jerry Stackhouse .30 .75
73 Stephon Marbury .40 1.00
74 Marcus Camby .25 .60
75 Scottie Pippen .75 2.00
76 David Robinson .60 1.50
77 Jason Terry .30 .75
78 Reggie Miller .60 1.50
79 Larry Johnson .40 1.00
80 Antonio Daniels .20 .50
81 Shareef Abdur-Rahim .30 .75
82 Ruben Patterson .20 .50
83 Nick Van Exel .30 .75
84 Keith Van Horn .25 .60
85 Antonio Davis .25 .60
86 Antoine Walker .30 .75
87 Allen Iverson .75 2.00
88 Antonio McDyess .25 .60
89 Tim Duncan .75 2.00
90 Hakeem Olajuwon .60 1.50
91 Jamaal Magloire RC .60 1.50
92 DerMarr Johnson RC .40 1.00
93 Jerome Moiso RC .40 1.00
94 Marcus Fizer RC .50 1.25
95 Jamal Crawford RC 1.50 4.00
96 Chris Mihm RC .50 1.25
97 Donnell Harvey RC .50 1.25
98 Courtney Alexander RC .40 1.00
99 Etan Thomas RC .50 1.25
100 Mamadou N'Diaye RC .40 1.00
101 Mateen Cleaves RC .50 1.25
102 Chris Porter RC .40 1.00
103 Jason Collier RC .60 1.50
104 Keyon Dooling RC .60 1.50
105 Darius Miles RC .60 1.50
106 Mark Madsen RC .60 1.50
107 Eddie House RC .50 1.25
108 Joel Przybilla RC .50 1.25
109 Kenyon Martin RC 1.25 3.00
110 Mike Miller RC 1.00 2.50
111 Speedy Claxton RC .60 1.50
112 Iakovos Tsakalidis RC .40 1.00
113 Erick Barkley RC .40 1.00
114 Hedo Turkoglu RC 1.00 2.50
115 Eduardo Najera RC .60 1.50
116 Desmond Mason RC .75 2.00
117 Morris Peterson RC .60 1.50
118 DeShawn Stevenson RC .60 1.50
119 Stromile Swift RC .50 1.25
120 Mike Smith RC .40 1.00

2000-01 Fleer Game Time Extra

*STARS: 1.5X TO 4X BASE CARD HI
*RCs: 1X TO 2.5X BASE HI
STARS: STATED ODDS 1:8
RCs: PRINT RUN 250 SERIAL #'d SETS

2000-01 Fleer Game Time Attack the Rack

COMPLETE SET (20) 7.50 15.00
STATED ODDS 1:4
AR1 Vince Carter .75 2.00
AR2 Lamar Odom .40 1.00
AR3 Kobe Bryant 3.00 8.00
AR4 Shareef Abdur-Rahim .40 1.00
AR5 Allen Iverson 1.00 2.50
AR6 Jason Williams .60 1.50
AR7 Kevin Garnett 1.00 2.50
AR8 Tim Duncan 1.00 2.50
AR9 Latrell Sprewell .50 1.25
AR10 Shaquille O'Neal 1.50 4.00
AR11 Jalen Rose .30 .75
AR12 Antawn Jamison .40 1.00
AR13 Paul Pierce .60 1.50
AR14 Grant Hill .60 1.50
AR15 Eddie Jones .40 1.00
AR16 Karl Malone .75 2.00
AR17 Elton Brand .40 1.00
AR18 Tracy McGrady .75 2.00
AR19 Michael Finley .40 1.00
AR20 Steve Francis .40 1.00

2000-01 Fleer Game Time Vince Carter Rookie Remnants

NNO Vince Carter FLR/100 12.50 30.00
NNO Vince Carter FLR JSY/15 20.00 50.00

2000-01 Fleer Game Time Change the Game

STATED ODDS 1:24
CG1 Vince Carter 2.00 5.00
CG2 Lamar Odom 1.00 2.50
CG3 Kobe Bryant 8.00 20.00
CG4 Allen Iverson 2.50 6.00
CG5 Jason Kidd 1.50 4.00
CG6 Grant Hill 1.50 4.00
CG7 Tim Duncan 2.50 6.00
CG8 Shaquille O'Neal 4.00 10.00
CG9 Kevin Garnett 2.50 6.00
CG10 Elton Brand 1.00 2.50
CG11 Stephon Marbury 1.25 3.00
CG12 Jason Williams 1.50 4.00
CG13 Keith Van Horn .75 2.00
CG14 Steve Francis 1.00 2.50
CG15 Gary Payton 1.50 4.00

2000-01 Fleer Game Time Uniformity

STATED ODDS 1:24
1 Shareef Abdur-Rahim 2.50 6.00
2 Mike Bibby 2.50 6.00
3 Vince Carter 5.00 12.00
4 Baron Davis 2.50 6.00
5 Sean Elliott 2.00 5.00
6 Allen Iverson 6.00 15.00
7 Toni Kukoc 3.00 8.00
8 Karl Malone 5.00 12.00
9 Stephon Marbury 3.00 8.00
10 Shawn Marion 2.50 6.00
11 Alonzo Mourning 4.00 10.00
12 Lamar Odom 2.50 6.00
13 Shaquille O'Neal Gold 10.00 25.00
14 Shaquille O'Neal Purple 10.00 25.00
15 Gary Payton 4.00 10.00
16 Scot Pollard 2.00 5.00
17 Jalen Rose 2.00 5.00
18 John Stockton 5.00 12.00
19 Wally Szczerbiak 2.00 5.00
20 Jason Terry 2.50 6.00
21 Keith Van Horn 2.00 5.00
22 Antoine Walker 2.50 6.00
23 David Wesley 2.00 5.00
GUVI Vince Carter AU/150 25.00 60.00

2000-01 Fleer Game Time Vince and the Revolution

COMPLETE SET (15) 30.00 60.00
COMMON CARD (1-5) 1.00 2.50
1-5 STATED ODDS 1:9
COMMON CARD (6-10) 2.00 5.00
6-10 STATED ODDS 1:24
COMMON CARD (11-15) 5.00 12.00
11-15 STATED ODDS 1:144
6 Vince Carter 2.00 5.00
8 Vince Carter 2.00 5.00
10 Vince Carter 2.00 5.00
12 Vince Carter 5.00 12.00

2000-01 Fleer Genuine

COMPLETE SET w/o RC (100) 20.00 40.00
RCs: PRINT RUN 1500 SERIAL #'d SETS
1 Vince Carter .75 2.00
2 Glenn Robinson .40 1.00
3 Rasheed Wallace .50 1.25
4 Michael Dickerson .25 .60
5 Mikki Moore RC .40 1.00
6 Wally Szczerbiak .30 .75
7 Shawn Marion .40 1.00
8 Dan Majerle .40 1.00
9 Trajan Langdon .25 .60
10 Chauncey Billups .30 .75
11 Jason Kidd .60 1.50
12 Derrick Coleman .40 1.00
13 Jason Terry .40 1.00
14 Eddie Jones .40 1.00
15 Scottie Pippen 1.00 2.50
16 Mike Bibby .40 1.00
17 Ron Mercer .30 .75
18 Hakeem Olajuwon .75 2.00
19 Patrick Ewing .60 1.50
20 Ruben Patterson .25 .60
21 Kenny Anderson .30 .75
22 Alonzo Mourning .60 1.50
23 Steve Smith .40 1.00
24 Juwan Howard .30 .75
25 Antoine Walker .40 1.00
26 Kobe Bryant 3.00 8.00
27 Chris Webber .50 1.25
28 Mitch Richmond .50 1.25
29 Paul Pierce .50 1.25
30 Shaquille O'Neal 1.50 4.00
31 Jason Williams .60 1.50
32 Richard Hamilton .60 1.50
33 Michael Finley .40 1.00
34 Jalen Rose .30 .75
35 Grant Hill .60 1.50
36 John Stockton .75 2.00
37 Vitaly Potapenko .25 .60
38 Glen Rice .40 1.00
39 Vlade Divac .40 1.00
40 Jahidi White .25 .60
41 Baron Davis .40 1.00
42 Michael Olowokandi .25 .60
43 Tim Duncan 1.00 2.50
44 Rod Strickland .25 .60
45 Jamal Mashburn .30 .75
46 Lamar Odom .40 1.00
47 David Robinson .75 2.00
48 Travis Best .25 .60
49 Raef LaFrentz .25 .60
50 Keith Van Horn .30 .75
51 Vonteego Cummings .25 .60
52 Jerome Williams .25 .60
53 Kevin Garnett 1.00 2.50
54 Anfernee Hardaway .60 1.50
55 Antonio McDyess .30 .75
56 Reggie Miller .75 2.00
57 Tracy McGrady .75 2.00
58 Bryon Russell .25 .60
59 Nick Van Exel .40 1.00
60 Allen Iverson 1.00 2.50
61 Karl Malone .75 2.00
62 David Wesley .30 .75
63 Bob Sura .25 .60
64 Stephon Marbury .50 1.25
65 Antonio Daniels .25 .60
66 Shawn Kemp .60 1.50
67 Cuttino Mobley .30 .75
68 Marcus Camby .30 .75
69 Gary Payton .60 1.50
70 Dikembe Mutombo .60 1.50
71 Tim Hardaway .50 1.25
72 Bonzi Wells .25 .60
73 Shareef Abdur-Rahim .40 1.00
74 Brevin Knight .25 .60
75 Steve Francis .40 1.00
76 Allan Houston .40 1.00
77 Dion Glover .25 .60
78 Dirk Nowitzki 1.00 2.50
79 Jonathan Bender .25 .60
80 Darrell Armstrong .25 .60
81 Antonio Davis .30 .75
82 Jerry Stackhouse .40 1.00
83 Terrell Brandon .30 .75
84 Tom Gugliotta .30 .75
85 Sean Elliott .30 .75
86 Elton Brand .40 1.00
87 Larry Hughes .40 1.00
88 Kerry Kittles .30 .75
89 Vin Baker .30 .75
90 Donyell Marshall .30 .75
91 Tim Thomas .30 .75
92 Toni Kukoc .50 1.25
93 Charles Oakley .40 1.00
94 Andre Miller .40 1.00
95 Austin Croshere .25 .60
96 Latrell Sprewell .50 1.25
97 Mark Jackson .30 .75
98 Antawn Jamison .40 1.00
99 Ray Allen .60 1.50
100 Theo Ratliff .25 .60
101 Chris Mihm RC 1.00 2.50
102 Mateen Cleaves RC 1.25 3.00
103 Etan Thomas RC 1.25 3.00
104 Morris Peterson RC 1.50 4.00
105 Jamal Crawford RC 4.00 10.00
106 Darius Miles RC 1.50 4.00
107 Desmond Mason RC 2.00 5.00
108 Joel Przybilla RC 1.25 3.00
109 Mike Miller RC 2.50 6.00
110 Quentin Richardson RC 1.25 3.00
111 Jason Collier RC 1.50 4.00
112 Keyon Dooling RC 1.25 3.00
113 Courtney Alexander RC 1.25 3.00
114 Eddie House RC 1.25 3.00
115 DerMarr Johnson RC 1.25 3.00
116 Michael Redd RC 4.00 10.00
117 Mark Madsen RC 1.50 4.00
118 Stromile Swift RC 1.25 3.00
119 Mamadou N'Diaye RC 1.00 2.50
120 DeShawn Stevenson RC 1.50 4.00
121 Hedo Turkoglu RC 2.50 6.00
122 Stephen Jackson RC 3.00 8.00
123 Marcus Fizer RC 1.25 3.00
124 Khalid El-Amin RC 1.00 2.50
125 Speedy Claxton RC 1.50 4.00
126 Hanno Mottola RC 1.00 2.50
127 Jerome Moiso RC 1.00 2.50
128 Jamaal Magloire RC 1.50 4.00

129 Donnell Harvey RC 1.25 3.00
130 Kenyon Martin RC 3.00 8.00
NNO Vince Carter MM/1500 15.00 40.00
NNO Vince Carter MM AU/15 200.00 400.00

2000-01 Fleer Genuine Formidable

COMPLETE SET (15) 20.00 40.00
STATED ODDS 1:23
F1 Vince Carter 2.00 5.00
F2 Lamar Odom 1.00 2.50
F3 Tracy McGrady 2.00 5.00
F4 Jason Williams 1.50 4.00
F5 Jason Kidd 1.50 4.00
F6 Chris Webber 1.25 3.00
F7 Elton Brand 1.00 2.50
F8 Steve Francis 1.00 2.50
F9 Grant Hill 1.50 4.00
F10 Shaquille O'Neal 4.00 10.00
F11 Allen Iverson 2.50 6.00
F12 Kobe Bryant 8.00 20.00
F13 Tim Duncan 2.50 6.00
F14 Kevin Garnett 2.50 6.00
F15 Latrell Sprewell 1.25 3.00

2000-01 Fleer Genuine Genuine Coverage Plus

STATED PRINT RUN 150 SERIAL #'d SETS
1 Vince Carter 10.00 25.00
2 Karl Malone 10.00 25.00
3 Shawn Marion 5.00 12.00
4 Lamar Odom 5.00 12.00
5 Shaquille O'Neal 20.00 50.00
6 Paul Pierce 8.00 20.00
7 David Robinson 10.00 25.00
8 Antoine Walker 5.00 12.00

2000-01 Fleer Genuine Northern Flights

COMPLETE SET (5) 25.00 60.00
COMMON CARD (NF1-NF5) 6.00 15.00
STATED ODDS 1:22
NNO Vince Carter AU/150 25.00 60.00

2000-01 Fleer Genuine Smooth Operators

COMPLETE SET (15) 15.00 30.00
STATED ODDS 1:23
SO1 Vince Carter 2.00 5.00
SO2 Lamar Odom 1.00 2.50
SO3 Allen Iverson 2.50 6.00
SO4 Kobe Bryant 8.00 20.00
SO5 Kevin Garnett 2.50 6.00
SO6 Tim Duncan 2.50 6.00
SO7 Antawn Jamison 1.00 2.50
SO8 Michael Finley 1.00 2.50
SO9 Ray Allen 1.50 4.00
SO10 Paul Pierce 1.50 4.00
SO11 Karl Malone 2.00 5.00
SO12 Shaquille O'Neal 4.00 10.00
SO13 Elton Brand 1.00 2.50
SO14 Jason Williams 1.50 4.00
SO15 Jalen Rose .75 2.00

2000-01 Fleer Genuine Yes Men

COMPLETE SET (10) 8.00 20.00
STATED ODDS 1:23
Y1 Vince Carter 1.50 4.00
Y2 Lamar Odom .75 2.00
Y3 Kobe Bryant 6.00 15.00
Y4 Kevin Garnett 2.00 5.00
Y5 Tim Duncan 2.00 5.00
Y6 Eddie Jones .75 2.00
Y7 Allan Houston .75 2.00
Y8 Grant Hill 1.25 3.00
Y9 Elton Brand .75 2.00
Y10 Steve Francis .75 2.00

2001-02 Fleer Genuine

COMPLETE SET (150) 75.00 150.00
COMP.SET w/o SP's (120) 12.50 30.00
ROOKIE STATED PRINT RUN 1000 SETS
1 Larry Hughes .30 .75
2 Wally Szczerbiak .30 .75
3 Jahidi White .25 .60
4 Aaron McKie .25 .60
5 Antonio McDyess .30 .75
6 Tom Gugliotta .25 .60
7 Elton Brand .30 .75
8 Lamar Odom .30 .75
9 Chris Webber .50 1.25
10 Ron Artest .30 .75
11 Gary Payton .60 1.50
12 Brian Grant .25 .60
13 Steve Nash .75 2.00
14 DerMarr Johnson .25 .60
15 Vince Carter .75 2.00
16 Kurt Thomas .25 .60
17 Cuttino Mobley .30 .75
18 Marc Jackson .25 .60
19 Stromile Swift .25 .60
20 Grant Hill .60 1.50
21 Raef LaFrentz .25 .60
22 Marcus Fizer .25 .60
23 Antonio Davis .30 .75
24 John Starks .25 .60
25 Trajan Langdon .25 .60
26 Jason Williams .60 1.50
27 Toni Kukoc .50 1.25
28 Morris Peterson .25 .60
29 Allen Iverson 1.00 2.50
30 Andre Miller .30 .75
31 Larry Johnson .40 1.00
32 Vitaly Potapenko .25 .60
33 Tim Thomas .25 .60
34 Eddie House .25 .60
35 Juwan Howard .30 .75
36 Joel Przybilla .25 .60
37 John Stockton .75 2.00
38 Michael Finley .40 1.00
39 Hedo Turkoglu .30 .75
40 Keith Van Horn .30 .75
41 Shawn Marion .40 1.00
42 Derek Fisher .30 .75
43 Terrell Brandon .30 .75
44 Jamal Mashburn .30 .75
45 Shareef Abdur-Rahim .30 .75
46 Brevin Knight .25 .60
47 Antoine Walker .30 .75
48 Mateen Cleaves .25 .60
49 Alonzo Mourning .60 1.50
50 Jermaine O'Neal .30 .75
51 Kenyon Martin .40 1.00
52 Steve Smith .30 .75
53 Jerry Stackhouse .40 1.00
54 Mike Bibby .40 1.00
55 Latrell Sprewell .50 1.25
56 Iakovos Tsakalidis .25 .60
57 Sam Cassell .30 .75
58 Michael Dickerson .25 .60
59 Alan Henderson .25 .60
60 Allan Houston .40 1.00
61 Patrick Ewing .60 1.50
62 Joe Smith .30 .75
63 Rick Fox .30 .75
64 Tracy McGrady .60 1.50
65 Scottie Pippen 1.00 2.50
66 Chauncey Billups .50 1.25
67 Voshon Lenard .25 .60
68 Jalen Rose .30 .75
69 Derrick Coleman .30 .75
70 Shaquille O'Neal 1.50 4.00
71 Anfernee Hardaway 1.00 2.50
72 Derek Anderson .25 .60
73 Travis Best .25 .60
74 Darius Miles .25 .60
75 Glenn Robinson .40 1.00
76 Darrell Armstrong .25 .60
77 Dirk Nowitzki 1.00 2.50
78 Stephon Marbury .50 1.25
79 Tyronn Lue .40 1.00
80 Bonzi Wells .25 .60
81 Mike Miller .30 .75
82 Tim Duncan 1.00 2.50
83 Tim Hardaway .50 1.25
84 Desmond Mason .30 .75
85 Ray Allen .60 1.50
86 Sean Elliott .30 .75
87 David Wesley .25 .60
88 Rasheed Wallace .50 1.25
89 Kevin Garnett 1.00 2.50
90 Dikembe Mutombo .60 1.50
91 Baron Davis .40 1.00
92 Donyell Marshall .25 .60
93 Eddie Jones .40 1.00
94 Vin Baker .30 .75
95 Peja Stojakovic .30 .75
96 Antawn Jamison .30 .75
97 Maurice Taylor .25 .60
98 Courtney Alexander .25 .60
99 Steve Francis .40 1.00
100 Chris Mihm .25 .60
101 Kobe Bryant 3.00 8.00
102 Hakeem Olajuwon .75 2.00
103 Richard Hamilton .50 1.25
104 Karl Malone .75 2.00
105 Chucky Atkins .25 .60
106 Eric Snow .25 .60
107 Ruben Patterson .25 .60
108 David Robinson .75 2.00
109 Bryon Russell .25 .60
110 Jason Terry .40 1.00
111 Jason Kidd .60 1.50
112 Charles Oakley .30 .75
113 Wang Zhizhi .40 1.00
114 Quentin Richardson .25 .60
115 Clarence Weatherspoon .25 .60
116 Nick Van Exel .40 1.00
117 Reggie Miller .75 2.00
118 Marcus Camby .30 .75
119 Corey Maggette .30 .75
120 Paul Pierce .60 1.50
121 Kwame Brown RC 1.25 3.00
122 Eddie Griffin RC 1.00 2.50
123 Eddy Curry RC 1.25 3.00
124 Jamaal Tinsley RC 1.00 2.50
125 Jason Richardson RC 2.00 5.00
126 Shane Battier RC 2.50 6.00
127 Troy Murphy RC 1.00 2.50
128 Richard Jefferson RC 1.50 4.00
129 DeSagana Diop RC .75 2.00
130 Tyson Chandler RC 2.00 5.00
131 Joe Johnson RC 2.00 5.00
132 Zach Randolph RC 2.50 6.00
133 Gerald Wallace RC 1.50 4.00
134 Loren Woods RC .75 2.00
135 Jason Collins RC 1.00 2.50
136 Rodney White RC .75 2.00
137 Jeryl Sasser RC .75 2.00
138 Kirk Haston RC .75 2.00
139 Pau Gasol RC 5.00 12.00
140 Kedrick Brown RC .75 2.00
141 Steven Hunter RC .75 2.00
142 Michael Bradley RC .75 2.00
143 Joseph Forte RC .75 2.00
144 Brandon Armstrong RC .75 2.00
145 Samuel Dalembert RC 1.25 3.00
146 Trenton Hassell RC .75 2.00
147 Gilbert Arenas RC 3.00 8.00
148 Omar Cook RC 1.25 3.00
149 Tony Parker RC 5.00 12.00
150 Terence Morris RC .75 2.00

2001-02 Fleer Genuine At Large

COMPLETE SET (15) 20.00 40.00
STATED ODDS 1:23
AL1 Vince Carter 2.00 5.00
AL2 Dirk Nowitzki 2.50 6.00
AL3 Courtney Alexander .60 1.50
AL4 Jason Williams 1.50 4.00
AL5 Reggie Miller 2.00 5.00
AL6 Chris Webber 1.25 3.00
AL7 Elton Brand .75 2.00
AL8 Peja Stojakovic .75 2.00
AL9 Ray Allen 1.50 4.00
AL10 Shaquille O'Neal 4.00 10.00
AL11 Kevin Garnett 2.50 6.00
AL12 Kobe Bryant 8.00 20.00
AL13 Tim Duncan 2.50 6.00
AL14 Antawn Jamison .75 2.00
AL15 Latrell Sprewell 1.25 3.00

2001-02 Fleer Genuine Coverage Plus

STATED ODDS 1:24
1 Shareef Abdur-Rahim 2.50 6.00
2 Darrell Armstrong 2.00 5.00
3 Mike Bibby 3.00 8.00
4 Vince Carter 6.00 15.00
5 Vince Carter WU 6.00 15.00
6 Michael Dickerson 2.00 5.00
7 Patrick Ewing 5.00 12.00
8 Steve Francis 3.00 8.00
9 Richard Hamilton 4.00 10.00
10 Anfernee Hardaway 8.00 20.00
11 Grant Hill 5.00 12.00
12 DerMarr Johnson 2.00 5.00
13 Jason Kidd 5.00 12.00
14 Rashard Lewis 2.50 6.00
15 Corey Maggette 2.50 6.00
16 Stephon Marbury 4.00 10.00
17 Shawn Marion 3.00 8.00
18 Kenyon Martin 3.00 8.00
19 Tracy McGrady 5.00 12.00
20 Mike Miller 2.50 6.00
21 Lamar Odom 2.50 6.00
22 Quentin Richardson 2.00 5.00
23 Jerry Stackhouse 3.00 8.00
24 Keith Van Horn 2.50 6.00

2001-02 Fleer Genuine Final Cut

STATED ODDS 1:24
1 Shareef Abdur-Rahim 2.50 6.00
2 Vince Carter 6.00 15.00
3 Baron Davis 3.00 8.00
4 Sean Elliott 2.50 6.00
5 Patrick Ewing 5.00 12.00
6 Michael Finley 3.00 8.00
7 Anfernee Hardaway 8.00 20.00
8 Grant Hill 5.00 12.00
9 Allan Houston 3.00 8.00
10 Allen Iverson 8.00 20.00
11 Jason Kidd 5.00 12.00
12 Tyronn Lue 3.00 8.00
13 Karl Malone 6.00 15.00
14 Stephon Marbury 4.00 10.00
15 Shawn Marion 3.00 8.00
16 Kenyon Martin 3.00 8.00
17 Desmond Mason 2.50 6.00
18 Tracy McGrady 5.00 12.00
19 Mike Miller 2.50 6.00
20 Andre Miller 2.50 6.00
21 Alonzo Mourning 6.00 15.00
22 Lamar Odom 2.50 6.00
23 Gary Payton 5.00 12.00
24 Paul Pierce 5.00 12.00
25 Quentin Richardson 2.00 5.00
26 David Robinson 6.00 15.00
27 Glenn Robinson 3.00 8.00
28 John Stockton 6.00 15.00
29 Stromile Swift 2.00 5.00
30 Wally Szczerbiak 2.50 6.00
31 Jason Terry 3.00 8.00
32 Keith Van Horn 2.50 6.00
33 Antoine Walker 2.50 6.00
34 David Wesley 2.00 5.00
35 Jason Williams 5.00 12.00

2001-02 Fleer Genuine Names of the Game

STATED ODDS 1:24
1 Shareef Abdur-Rahim 2.50 6.00
2 Vince Carter 6.00 15.00
3 Steve Francis 3.00 8.00
4 Anfernee Hardaway 8.00 20.00
5 Allen Iverson 8.00 20.00
6 Jason Kidd 5.00 12.00
7 Karl Malone 6.00 15.00
8 Tracy McGrady 5.00 12.00
9 Dikembe Mutombo 5.00 12.00
10 Hakeem Olajuwon 6.00 15.00
11 Gary Payton 5.00 12.00
12 Morris Peterson 2.00 5.00
13 David Robinson 6.00 15.00
14 Glenn Robinson 3.00 8.00
15 Chris Webber 4.00 10.00

2001-02 Fleer Genuine Names of the Game Autographs

STATED PRINT RUN 100 SERIAL #'d SETS
1 Dikembe Mutombo 12.00 30.00
2 Hakeem Olajuwon 25.00 60.00
3 Shareef Abdur-Rahim 8.00 20.00
4 Vince Carter 30.00 80.00

2001-02 Fleer Genuine Skywalkers

COMPLETE SET (15) 15.00 30.00
STATED ODDS 1:23
SW1 Vince Carter 2.00 5.00
SW2 Lamar Odom .75 2.00
SW3 Shawn Marion 1.00 2.50
SW4 Kobe Bryant 8.00 20.00
SW5 Kevin Garnett 2.50 6.00
SW6 Tim Duncan 2.50 6.00
SW7 Antawn Jamison .75 2.00
SW8 Michael Finley 1.00 2.50
SW9 Ray Allen 1.50 4.00
SW10 Paul Pierce 1.50 4.00
SW11 Baron Davis 1.00 2.50
SW12 Antoine Walker .75 2.00
SW13 Desmond Mason .75 2.00
SW14 Jason Williams 1.50 4.00
SW15 Darius Miles .60 1.50

2001-02 Fleer Genuine Unstoppable

STATED ODDS 1:23
US1 Vince Carter 1.50 4.00
US2 Darius Miles .50 1.25
US3 Shaquille O'Neal 3.00 8.00
US4 Jerry Stackhouse .75 2.00
US5 Tim Duncan 2.00 5.00
US6 Eddie Jones .75 2.00
US7 Jason Kidd 1.25 3.00
US8 Glenn Robinson .75 2.00
US9 Elton Brand .60 1.50
US10 Dirk Nowitzki 2.00 5.00

2002-03 Fleer Genuine

COMPLETE SET (135) 100.00 250.00
COMP.SET w/o SP's (100) 20.00 50.00
101-135 PRINT RUN 2002 SER.#'d SETS
1 Shaquille O'Neal 1.50 4.00
2 Allen Iverson 1.00 2.50
3 Jerry Stackhouse .40 1.00
4 Kobe Bryant 3.00 8.00
5 Jason Kidd .60 1.50
6 Andre Miller .30 .75
7 David Robinson .75 2.00
8 John Stockton .75 2.00
9 Glenn Robinson .40 1.00
10 Chauncey Billups .40 1.00
11 Chris Webber .50 1.25
12 Antawn Jamison .30 .75
13 Sam Cassell .30 .75
14 Vlade Divac .30 .75
15 P.J. Brown .25 .60
16 Robert Horry .40 1.00
17 Eric Snow .25 .60
18 Popeye Jones .25 .60
19 Paul Pierce .60 1.50
20 Eddie Griffin .25 .60
21 Marcus Camby .30 .75
22 Gary Payton .60 1.50
23 Michael Jordan 4.00 10.00
24 Shareef Abdur-Rahim .40 1.00
25 Anfernee Hardaway 1.00 2.50
26 Michael Finley .40 1.00
27 Steve Nash .75 2.00
28 Shane Battier .40 1.00
29 Stephon Marbury .50 1.25
30 Dirk Nowitzki 1.00 2.50
31 Pau Gasol .60 1.50
32 Shawn Marion .40 1.00
33 Rodney Rogers .25 .60
34 Steve Smith .30 .75
35 Darrell Armstrong .25 .60
36 Alvin Williams .25 .60
37 Nick Van Exel .40 1.00
38 Jason Williams .50 1.25
39 Ruben Patterson .25 .60
40 Juwan Howard .30 .75
41 Brian Grant .25 .60
42 Damon Stoudamire .40 1.00
43 Antonio McDyess .30 .75
44 Eddie Jones .40 1.00
45 Rasheed Wallace .50 1.25
46 Larry Hughes .30 .75
47 Wally Szczerbiak .30 .75
48 Tony Parker .60 1.50
49 Ron Artest .30 .75
50 Kevin Garnett 1.00 2.50
51 Tim Duncan 1.00 2.50
52 Marcus Fizer .25 .60
53 Darius Miles .25 .60
54 Grant Hill .60 1.50
55 Andrei Kirilenko .30 .75
56 Jalen Rose .30 .75
57 Lamar Odom .40 1.00
58 Tracy McGrady .60 1.50
59 Karl Malone .75 2.00
60 Jason Terry .40 1.00
61 Steve Francis .40 1.00
62 Kenyon Martin .40 1.00
63 Brent Barry .25 .60
64 Antoine Walker .30 .75
65 Reggie Miller .75 2.00
66 Allan Houston .40 1.00
67 Vince Carter .75 2.00
68 Toni Kukoc .40 1.00
69 Lamond Murray .25 .60
70 Jason Richardson .40 1.00
71 Rick Fox .25 .60
72 Kerry Kittles .25 .60
73 Dikembe Mutombo .60 1.50
74 Tyson Chandler .40 1.00
75 Richard Hamilton .50 1.25
76 Elden Campbell .25 .60
77 Jermaine O'Neal .30 .75
78 Mike Miller .30 .75
79 Morris Peterson .30 .75
80 Jamal Mashburn .30 .75
81 Elton Brand .30 .75
82 Kurt Thomas .25 .60
83 Antonio Davis .30 .75
84 Ben Wallace .50 1.25
85 Anthony Mason .30 .75
86 Peja Stojakovic .30 .75
87 Kenny Anderson .30 .75
88 Cuttino Mobley .25 .60
89 Keith Van Horn .30 .75
90 Rashard Lewis .30 .75
91 Clifford Robinson .40 1.00
92 Ray Allen .60 1.50
93 Mike Bibby .40 1.00
94 Baron Davis .40 1.00
95 Jamaal Tinsley .25 .60
96 Latrell Sprewell .40 1.00
97 Jon Barry .25 .60
98 Desmond Mason .30 .75
99 Alonzo Mourning .60 1.50
100 Bonzi Wells .25 .60
101 Jay Williams RC 1.25 3.00
102 Mike Dunleavy RC 1.50 4.00
103 Amare Stoudemire RC 4.00 10.00
104 Caron Butler RC 1.50 4.00
105 Jared Jeffries RC 1.25 3.00
106 Fred Jones RC 1.25 3.00
107 Bostjan Nachbar RC 1.25 3.00
108 Jiri Welsch RC 1.25 3.00
109 Juan Dixon RC 1.25 3.00
110 Curtis Borchardt RC 1.00 2.50
111 Kareem Rush RC 1.00 2.50
112 Qyntel Woods RC 1.00 2.50
113 Casey Jacobsen RC 1.00 2.50
114 Frank Williams RC 1.00 2.50
115 John Salmons RC 1.00 2.50
116 Dan Dickau RC 1.00 2.50
117 DaJuan Wagner RC 1.25 3.00
118 Drew Gooden RC 1.50 4.00
119 Nikoloz Tskitishvili RC 1.00 2.50
120 Yao Ming RC 8.00 20.00
121 Nene Hilario RC 1.50 4.00
122 Chris Wilcox RC 1.25 3.00
123 Melvin Ely RC 1.25 3.00
124 Marcus Haislip RC 1.00 2.50
125 Ryan Humphrey RC 1.25 3.00
126 Tayshaun Prince RC 3.00 8.00
127 Tito Maddox RC 1.00 2.50
128 Chris Jefferies RC 1.00 2.50
129 Manu Ginobili RC 8.00 20.00
130 Roger Mason RC 1.25 3.00
131 Robert Archibald RC 1.00 2.50
132 Vincent Yarbrough RC 1.00 2.50
133 Dan Gadzuric RC 1.25 3.00
134 Carlos Boozer RC 1.50 4.00
135 Rasual Butler RC 1.25 3.00

2002-03 Fleer Genuine Coverage

STATED ODDS 1:24
*GOLD: .6X TO 1.5X HI
GOLD PRINT RUN 100 SER.#'d SETS
1 Vince Carter 6.00 15.00
2 Michael Dickerson 2.00 5.00
3 Keyon Dooling 2.00 5.00
4 Michael Finley 3.00 8.00
5 Tom Gugliotta 2.00 5.00
6 Richard Hamilton 4.00 10.00
7 Anfernee Hardaway 8.00 20.00
8 Grant Hill 5.00 12.00
9 DerMarr Johnson 2.00 5.00
10 Rashard Lewis 2.50 6.00
11 Antonio McDyess 2.50 6.00
12 Desmond Mason 2.50 6.00
13 Lamar Odom 3.00 8.00
14 Keith Van Horn 2.50 6.00
15 Antoine Walker 2.50 6.00

2002-03 Fleer Genuine Global Warning

COMPLETE SET (10) 5.00 12.00
STATED ODDS 1:12
1 Tim Duncan 1.50 4.00
2 Pau Gasol 1.00 2.50
3 Andrei Kirilenko .50 1.25
4 Patrick Ewing .75 2.00
5 Dikembe Mutombo 1.00 2.50
6 Steve Nash 1.25 3.00
7 Hakeem Olajuwon .75 2.00
8 Tony Parker 1.00 2.50
9 Dirk Nowitzki 1.50 4.00
10 Peja Stojakovic .50 1.25

2002-03 Fleer Genuine Global Warning Jersey

STATED ODDS 1:30
1 Pau Gasol 5.00 12.00
2 Andrei Kirilenko 2.50 6.00
3 Patrick Ewing 4.00 10.00
4 Dikembe Mutombo 5.00 12.00
5 Tony Parker 5.00 12.00
6 Peja Stojakovic 2.50 6.00

2002-03 Fleer Genuine Leaders

COMPLETE SET (15) 15.00 40.00
STATED ODDS 1:24
1 Allen Iverson 2.50 6.00
2 Shaquille O'Neal 4.00 10.00
3 Paul Pierce 1.50 4.00
4 Tracy McGrady 1.50 4.00
5 Tim Duncan 2.50 6.00
6 Kobe Bryant 8.00 20.00
7 Vince Carter 2.00 5.00
8 Dirk Nowitzki 2.50 6.00
9 Michael Jordan 10.00 25.00
10 Steve Francis 1.00 2.50
11 Karl Malone 2.00 5.00
12 Elton Brand .75 2.00
13 Andre Miller .75 2.00
14 Jason Kidd 1.50 4.00
15 Baron Davis 1.00 2.50

2002-03 Fleer Genuine Leaders Jerseys

STATED ODDS 1:40
*GOLD: 1.25X TO 3X HI
GOLD PRINT RUN 25 SER.#'d SETS
1 Allen Iverson 8.00 20.00
2 Paul Pierce 5.00 12.00
3 Tracy McGrady 5.00 12.00
4 Vince Carter 6.00 15.00
5 Steve Francis 3.00 8.00
6 Karl Malone 6.00 15.00
7 Elton Brand 2.50 6.00
8 Andre Miller 2.50 6.00
9 Jason Kidd 5.00 12.00
10 Baron Davis 3.00 8.00

2002-03 Fleer Genuine Names of the Game

COMPLETE SET (15) 10.00 25.00
STATED ODDS 1:12
1 Kobe Bryant 5.00 12.00
2 Ray Allen 1.00 2.50
3 Tracy McGrady 1.00 2.50
4 John Stockton 1.25 3.00
5 Paul Pierce 1.00 2.50
6 Allen Iverson 1.50 4.00
7 Michael Jordan 6.00 15.00
8 Vince Carter 1.25 3.00
9 Shaquille O'Neal 2.50 6.00
10 David Robinson 1.25 3.00
11 Kevin Garnett 1.50 4.00
12 Jason Kidd 1.00 2.50
13 Chris Webber .75 2.00
14 Ben Wallace .75 2.00
15 Shawn Marion .60 1.50

2002-03 Fleer Genuine Names of the Game Jerseys

STATED ODDS 1:30
*GOLD: 1X TO 2.5X HI
GOLD: STATED PRINT RUN 50 SER.#'d SETS
1 Ray Allen 4.00 10.00
2 Tracy McGrady 4.00 10.00
3 John Stockton 5.00 12.00
4 Paul Pierce 4.00 10.00
5 Allen Iverson 6.00 15.00
6 Vince Carter 5.00 12.00
7 David Robinson 5.00 12.00
8 Jason Kidd 4.00 10.00
9 Chris Webber 3.00 8.00
10 Shawn Marion 2.50 6.00

2002-03 Fleer Genuine On the Up

COMPLETE SET (15) 5.00 12.00
STATED ODDS 1:12
1 Pau Gasol 1.00 2.50
2 Jamaal Tinsley .40 1.00
3 Jason Richardson .60 1.50
4 Tony Parker 1.00 2.50
5 Shane Battier .60 1.50
6 Andrei Kirilenko .50 1.25
7 Kenyon Martin .60 1.50
8 Gilbert Arenas .60 1.50
9 Mike Miller .50 1.25
10 Darius Miles .40 1.00
11 Stromile Swift .40 1.00
12 Marcus Fizer .40 1.00
13 Iakovos Tsakalidis .40 1.00
14 Richard Jefferson .50 1.25
15 Speedy Claxton .40 1.00

2002-03 Fleer Genuine On the Up Jerseys

STATED ODDS 1:36
1 Jason Richardson 3.00 8.00
2 Shane Battier 3.00 8.00
3 Kenyon Martin 3.00 8.00
4 Mike Miller 2.50 6.00
5 Darius Miles 2.00 5.00
6 Stromile Swift 2.00 5.00
7 Richard Jefferson 2.50 6.00
8 Speedy Claxton 2.00 5.00

2002-03 Fleer Genuine Prime Time Players

COMPLETE SET (10) 40.00 100.00
STATED ODDS 1:288
1 Shaquille O'Neal 10.00 25.00
2 Allen Iverson 6.00 15.00
3 Vince Carter 5.00 12.00
4 Michael Jordan 30.00 80.00
5 Tracy McGrady 4.00 10.00
6 Tim Duncan 6.00 15.00
7 Kevin Garnett 6.00 15.00
8 Dirk Nowitzki 6.00 15.00
9 Paul Pierce 4.00 10.00
10 Kobe Bryant 20.00 50.00

2002-03 Fleer Genuine Prime Time Players Jerseys

STATED ODDS 1:300
1 Allen Iverson 10.00 25.00
2 Vince Carter 8.00 20.00
3 Tracy McGrady 6.00 15.00
4 Dirk Nowitzki 10.00 25.00
5 Paul Pierce 6.00 15.00

2003-04 Fleer Genuine Insider

COMP.SET w/o SP's (100) 12.50 30.00
111-130 RC PRINT RUN 799 SER.#'d SETS
131-140 MINIS FOUND INSIDE 101-110 RC's
MINI PRINT RUN 350 SER.#'d SETS
1 Shareef Abdur-Rahim .30 .75
2 Andre Miller .25 .60
3 Reggie Miller .60 1.50
4 Michael Redd .30 .75
5 Allan Houston .30 .75
6 Mike Bibby .30 .75
7 Kwame Brown .20 .50
8 Earl Boykins .20 .50
9 Ron Artest .20 .50
10 Eddie Jones .30 .75
11 Zach Randolph .30 .75
12 Derek Anderson .25 .60
13 Andrei Kirilenko .25 .60
14 Carlos Boozer .25 .60
15 Yao Ming .75 2.00
16 Pau Gasol .50 1.25
17 Jamal Mashburn .25 .60
18 Shawn Marion .30 .75
19 Vince Carter .60 1.50
20 Eddy Curry .20 .50
21 Mike Dunleavy Jr. .25 .60
22 Kobe Bryant 2.50 6.00
23 Tim Thomas .20 .50
24 Drew Gooden .25 .60
25 Tim Duncan .75 2.00
26 Dajuan Wagner .20 .50
27 Speedy Claxton .20 .50
28 Karl Malone .60 1.50
29 Jason Kidd .50 1.25
30 Kenny Thomas .20 .50
31 Vladimir Radmanovic .20 .50
32 Tyson Chandler .25 .60
33 Jason Richardson .30 .75
34 Quentin Richardson .20 .50
35 Kerry Kittles .20 .50
36 Derrick Coleman .30 .75
37 Manu Ginobili .60 1.50
38 Paul Pierce .50 1.25
39 Ben Wallace .40 1.00
40 Corey Maggette .25 .60
41 Sam Cassell .25 .60
42 Hedo Turkoglu .25 .60
43 Peja Stojakovic .25 .60
44 Gilbert Arenas .30 .75
45 Dirk Nowitzki .75 2.00
46 Al Harrington .25 .60
47 Caron Butler .25 .60
48 Baron Davis .30 .75
49 Rasheed Wallace .40 1.00
50 Morris Peterson .20 .50
51 Steve Nash .60 1.50
52 Steve Francis .30 .75
53 Lamar Odom .25 .60
54 Jamaal Magloire .20 .50
55 Amare Stoudemire .40 1.00
56 Antonio Davis .25 .60
57 Dan Dickau .20 .50
58 Cuttino Mobley .20 .50
59 Jason Williams .50 1.25
60 David Wesley .20 .50
61 Stephon Marbury .40 1.00
62 Ray Allen .50 1.25
63 Scottie Pippen .75 2.00
64 Nick Van Exel .30 .75
65 Shaquille O'Neal 1.25 3.00
66 Richard Jefferson .25 .60
67 Allen Iverson .75 2.00
68 Tony Parker .50 1.25
69 Jason Terry .25 .60
70 Nene .25 .60
71 Marko Jaric .20 .50
72 Troy Hudson .20 .50
73 Malik Rose .20 .50
74 Bobby Jackson .25 .60
75 Jerry Stackhouse .40 1.00
76 Voshon Lenard .20 .50
77 Richard Hamilton .40 1.00
78 Scot Pollard .20 .50
79 Latrell Sprewell .40 1.00
80 Tracy McGrady .50 1.25
81 Chris Webber .40 1.00
82 Raef LaFrentz .20 .50
83 Tayshaun Prince .30 .75
84 Elton Brand .25 .60
85 Kevin Garnett .75 2.00
86 Keon Clark .20 .50
87 Brad Miller .25 .60
88 Alvin Williams .20 .50
89 Michael Finley .30 .75
90 Jermaine O'Neal .30 .75
91 Desmond Mason .25 .60
92 Keith Van Horn .25 .60
93 Bonzi Wells .20 .50
94 Matt Harpring .20 .50
95 Darius Miles .20 .50
96 Eddie Griffin .20 .50
97 Shane Battier .25 .60
98 Kenyon Martin .30 .75
99 Glenn Robinson .25 .60
100 Rashard Lewis .25 .60
101 Carmelo Anthony RC 12.00 30.00
102 Troy Bell RC 1.50 4.00
103 T.J. Ford RC 2.00 5.00
104 LeBron James RC 400.00 800.00
105 Mike Sweetney RC 1.50 4.00
106 Chris Bosh RC 8.00 20.00
107 Jarvis Hayes RC 1.50 4.00
108 Darko Milicic RC 2.00 5.00
109 Chris Kaman RC 2.50 6.00
110 Dwyane Wade RC 20.00 50.00
111 Udonis Haslem RC 2.50 6.00
112 Josh Howard RC 2.00 5.00
113 Mickael Pietrus RC 1.50 4.00
114 Reece Gaines RC 1.25 3.00
115 Nick Collison RC 1.50 4.00
116 Leandrinho Barbosa RC 2.00 5.00
117 Kendrick Perkins RC 1.50 4.00
118 Ndudi Ebi RC 1.25 3.00
119 Willie Green RC 2.00 5.00
120 Kirk Hinrich RC 2.00 5.00
121 Marcus Banks RC 1.25 3.00
122 Zarko Cabarkapa RC 1.25 3.00
123 Zoran Planinic RC 1.25 3.00
124 David West RC 2.50 6.00
125 Luke Ridnour RC 2.00 5.00
126 Brian Cook RC 1.25 3.00
127 Boris Diaw RC 2.00 5.00
128 Dahntay Jones RC 1.50 4.00
129 Maciej Lampe RC 1.25 3.00
130 Travis Outlaw RC 1.50 4.00
131 Ben Handlogten MM RC 1.25 3.00
132 Jerome Beasley MM RC 1.25 3.00
133 Marquis Daniels MM RC 1.50 4.00
134 Luke Walton MM RC 2.00 5.00
135 Aleksandar Pavlovic MM RC 1.50 4.00
136 Matt Carroll MM RC 1.25 3.00
137 Curtis Borchardt MM 1.50 4.00
138 Jason Kapono MM RC 1.25 3.00
139 Steve Blake MM RC 1.50 4.00
140 Keith Bogans MM RC 1.25 3.00

2003-04 Fleer Genuine Insider Reflections

*1-100 REF: 4X TO 10X BASE HI
*101-110 RC REF: .6X TO 1.5X BASE HI
*111-130 RC REF: .75X TO 2X BASE HI
*131-140 RC REF: .75X TO 2X BASE HI
131-140 PRINT RUN 148 SER.#'d SETS

2003-04 Fleer Genuine Insider Genuine Article Insider

PRINT RUN 400 SER.#'d SETS
*PATCH: 1.25X TO 3X BASE HI
PATCH PRINT RUN 50 SER.#'d SETS
1 Baron Davis 2.50 6.00
2 Nene 2.00 5.00
3 Mike Dunleavy 2.00 5.00
4 Tracy McGrady 4.00 10.00
5 Vince Carter 5.00 12.00
6 Allen Iverson 6.00 15.00
7 Jason Kidd 4.00 10.00
8 Shaquille O'Neal 10.00 25.00
9 Yao Ming 6.00 15.00
10 Steve Francis 2.50 6.00
11 Tyson Chandler 2.00 5.00
12 Amare Stoudemire 3.00 8.00
13 Kevin Garnett 6.00 15.00
14 Tim Duncan 6.00 15.00
15 Ben Wallace 3.00 8.00
16 Kenyon Martin 2.50 6.00
17 Peja Stojakovic 2.00 5.00
18 Mike Sweetney 1.50 4.00
19 Carmelo Anthony 12.00 30.00

2003-04 Fleer Genuine Insider Genuine Autograph Insider

STATED ODDS 1:24
2 Carmelo Anthony 15.00 40.00
3 Dwyane Wade 150.00 400.00
5 Amare Stoudemire 10.00 25.00
6 Gilbert Arenas 8.00 20.00
7 Luke Ridnour 4.00 10.00
8 Dajuan Wagner 2.50 6.00
9 Tayshaun Prince 5.00 12.00
10 Earl Boykins 4.00 10.00
12 Maurice Williams 4.00 10.00
13 Travis Outlaw 3.00 8.00
14 Zarko Cabarkapa 2.50 6.00
15 Vince Carter 15.00 40.00

2003-04 Fleer Genuine Insider Scoring Threats

COMPLETE SET (10) 8.00 20.00
STATED ODDS 1:20
1 T.McGrady/V.Carter 1.50 4.00
2 A.Iverson/J.Kidd 2.00 5.00
3 S.O'Neal/Y.Ming 3.00 8.00
4 S.Francis/J.Richardson .75 2.00
5 A.Stoudemire/K.Garnett 2.00 5.00
6 P.Pierce/A.Walker 1.25 3.00
7 D.Nowitzki/P.Gasol 2.00 5.00
8 R.Allen/M.Bibby 1.25 3.00
9 R.Jefferson/K.Martin .75 2.00
10 T.Duncan/J.O'Neal 2.00 5.00

2003-04 Fleer Genuine Insider Scoring Threats Game Used

STATED ODDS 1:48
McGrady/Carter JSY 4.00 10.00
Iverson JSY/Kidd 4.00 10.00
S.O'Neal JSY/Ming 6.00 15.00
Francis JSY/ J.Richardson 2.50 6.00
Stoudemire/Garnett JSY 5.00 12.00
Pierce JSY/Walker 3.00 8.00
Nowitzki JSY/Gasol 4.00 10.00
Allen/Bibby JSY 2.50 6.00
Jefferson/K.Martin JSY 2.50 6.00
0 Duncan JSY/J.O'Neal 4.00 10.00

2003-04 Fleer Genuine Insider Scoring Threats Game Used Dual

PRINT RUN 100 SER.#'d SETS
T.McGrady/V.Carter 10.00 25.00
A.Iverson/J.Kidd 8.00 20.00
A.Stoudemire/K.Garnett 8.00 20.00
D.Nowitzki/P.Gasol 8.00 20.00
T.Duncan/J.O'Neal 10.00 25.00

2003-04 Fleer Genuine Insider Team USA Insider

PRINT RUN 325 SER.#'d SETS
NO JSY FOR LARRY BROWN
1 Ray Allen 10.00 25.00
2 Mike Bibby 6.00 15.00
3 Tim Duncan 15.00 40.00
4 Allen Iverson 15.00 40.00
5 Jason Kidd 10.00 25.00
6 Tracy McGrady 10.00 25.00
7 Jermaine O'Neal 6.00 15.00
8 Larry Brown 8.00 20.00

2003-04 Fleer Genuine Insider Tools of the Game

COMPLETE SET (15) 5.00 12.00
STATED ODDS 1:8
1 Amare Stoudemire .50 1.25
2 Shaquille O'Neal 1.50 4.00
3 Kevin Garnett 1.00 2.50
4 Vince Carter .75 2.00
5 Paul Pierce .60 1.50
6 Yao Ming 1.00 2.50
7 Jason Richardson .40 1.00
8 Chris Webber .50 1.25
9 Antoine Walker .40 1.00
10 Scottie Pippen 1.00 2.50
11 Elton Brand .30 .75
12 Richard Jefferson .30 .75
13 Steve Francis .40 1.00
14 Pau Gasol .60 1.50
15 Stephon Marbury .50 1.25

2003-04 Fleer Genuine Insider Tools of the Game Game Used

PRINT RUN 199 SER.#'d SETS
*DUAL: .6X TO 1.5X BASE HI
DUAL PRINT RUN 99 SER.#'d SETS
*TRIPLE: 1.25X TO 3X BASE HI
TRIPLE PRINT RUN 25 SER.#'d SETS
1 Amare Stoudemire 3.00 8.00
2 Shaquille O'Neal 10.00 25.00
3 Kevin Garnett 6.00 15.00
4 Vince Carter 5.00 12.00
5 Paul Pierce 4.00 10.00
6 Yao Ming 6.00 15.00
7 Jason Richardson 2.50 6.00
8 Chris Webber 3.00 8.00
9 Antoine Walker 2.50 6.00
10 Scottie Pippen 6.00 15.00
11 Elton Brand 2.00 5.00
12 Richard Jefferson 2.00 5.00
13 Steve Francis 2.50 6.00
14 Pau Gasol 4.00 10.00
15 Stephon Marbury 3.00 8.00

2004-05 Fleer Genuine

COMP.SET w/o SP's (100) 15.00 40.00
111-135 RC PRINT RUN 500 SER.#'d SETS
1 Rasheed Wallace .40 1.00
2 Larry Hughes .25 .60
3 Allen Iverson .75 2.00
4 Josh Howard .25 .60
5 Bonzi Wells .20 .50
6 Jamaal Magloire .20 .50
7 Luke Ridnour .25 .60
8 Chauncey Billups .40 1.00
9 Dwyane Wade 1.25 3.00
10 Amare Stoudemire .30 .75
11 Earl Boykins .20 .50
12 Damon Jones .20 .50
13 Marquis Daniels .20 .50
14 Luke Walton .25 .60
15 Jamal Crawford .20 .50
16 Corliss Williamson .20 .50
17 Vince Carter .60 1.50
18 Antoine Walker .30 .75
19 Jason Richardson .30 .75
20 Jason Kidd .50 1.25
21 Peja Stojakovic .25 .60
22 Jeff McInnis .20 .50
23 Lamar Odom .30 .75
24 Allan Houston .30 .75
25 Jalen Rose .25 .60
26 LeBron James 2.50 6.00
27 Caron Butler .25 .60
28 Stephon Marbury .40 1.00
29 Carlos Arroyo .20 .50
30 Zydrunas Ilgauskas .25 .60
31 Kobe Bryant 2.50 6.00
32 Steve Francis .30 .75
33 Carlos Boozer .20 .50
34 Primoz Brezec .20 .50
35 Reggie Miller .60 1.50
36 Sam Cassell .25 .60
37 Ray Allen .50 1.25
38 Drew Gooden .20 .50
39 Chris Wilcox .20 .50
40 Grant Hill .40 1.00
41 Andrei Kirilenko .25 .60
42 Kirk Hinrich .30 .75
43 Corey Maggette .25 .60
44 Cuttino Mobley .25 .60
45 Gilbert Arenas .30 .75
46 Tyson Chandler .25 .60
47 Elton Brand .25 .60
48 Samuel Dalembert .20 .50
49 Jarvis Hayes .20 .50
50 Ben Wallace .40 1.00
51 Shawn Marion .30 .75
52 Michael Redd .25 .60
53 Richard Hamilton .40 1.00
54 Desmond Mason .20 .50
55 Steve Nash .60 1.50
56 Antawn Jamison .25 .60
57 Kareem Rush .20 .50
58 Jermaine O'Neal .25 .60
59 Keith Van Horn .25 .60
60 Rashard Lewis .25 .60
61 Gerald Wallace .25 .60
62 Jamaal Tinsley .20 .50
63 Vladimir Radmanovic .20 .50
64 Predrag Drobnjak .20 .50
65 Mike Dunleavy .20 .50
66 Baron Davis .30 .75
67 Mike Bibby .30 .75
68 Ricky Davis .25 .60
69 Tracy McGrady .50 1.25
70 Richard Jefferson .25 .60
71 Chris Webber .40 1.00
72 Michael Finley .30 .75
73 Pau Gasol .50 1.25
74 David West .25 .60
75 Chris Bosh .50 1.25
76 Gary Payton .50 1.25
77 Yao Ming .75 2.00
78 Wally Szczerbiak .25 .60
79 Tim Duncan .75 2.00
80 Keith Bogans .20 .50
81 Stephen Jackson .25 .60
82 Kevin Garnett .75 2.00
83 Tony Parker .50 1.25
84 Kenyon Martin .30 .75
85 Shaquille O'Neal 1.25 3.00
86 Shareef Abdur-Rahim .30 .75
87 Al Harrington .25 .60
88 Adonal Foyle .20 .50
89 Brian Scalabrine .20 .50
90 Brad Miller .25 .60
91 Carmelo Anthony .60 1.50
92 Udonis Haslem .20 .50
93 Zach Randolph .30 .75
94 Paul Pierce .50 1.25
95 Maurice Taylor .20 .50
96 Latrell Sprewell .40 1.00
97 Manu Ginobili .60 1.50
98 Dirk Nowitzki .75 2.00
99 Jason Williams .25 .60
100 Nick Van Exel .30 .75
101 Charles Barkley 3.00 8.00
102 Jerry West 3.00 8.00
103 Magic Johnson 8.00 20.00
104 Kareem Abdul-Jabbar 3.00 8.00
105 Pete Maravich 3.00 8.00
106 Maurice Cheeks 1.50 4.00
107 Alex English 1.50 4.00
108 George Mikan 4.00 10.00
109 Wilt Chamberlain 4.00 10.00
110 Dominique Wilkins 2.50 6.00
111 Josh Childress RC 1.00 2.50
112 Josh Smith RC 1.50 4.00
113 Al Jefferson RC 1.50 4.00
114 Delonte West RC 1.25 3.00
115 Tony Allen RC 1.50 4.00
116 Emeka Okafor RC 1.25 3.00
117 Chris Duhon RC 1.25 3.00
118 Ben Gordon RC 1.50 4.00
119 Luol Deng RC 1.50 4.00
120 Andres Nocioni RC 1.50 4.00
121 David Harrison RC 1.00 2.50
122 Devin Harris RC 1.25 3.00
123 Shaun Livingston RC 1.50 4.00
124 Dorell Wright RC 1.25 3.00
125 J.R. Smith RC 1.50 4.00
126 Trevor Ariza RC 1.50 4.00
127 Dwight Howard RC 5.00 12.00
128 Jameer Nelson RC 1.50 4.00
129 Andre Iguodala RC 2.50 6.00
130 Sebastian Telfair RC 1.25 3.00
131 Kevin Martin RC 2.00 5.00
132 Ha Seung-Jin RC 1.50 4.00
133 Rafael Araujo RC 1.00 2.50
134 Kirk Snyder RC 1.00 2.50
135 Beno Udrih RC 1.25 3.00

2004-05 Fleer Genuine 100

*1-100: 2.5X TO 6X BASE HI
*101-110: 1.25X TO 3X BASE HI
*111-135: .5X TO 1.25X BASE HI
PRINT RUN 100 SER.#'d SETS
105 Pete Maravich 30.00 80.00

2004-05 Fleer Genuine Article

COMPLETE SET (15) 10.00 25.00
STATED ODDS 1:12 H, 1:15 R
1 Amare Stoudemire .60 1.50
2 LeBron James 5.00 12.00
3 Carmelo Anthony 1.25 3.00
4 Tracy McGrady 1.00 2.50
5 Jermaine O'Neal .50 1.25
6 Kobe Bryant 5.00 12.00
7 Pau Gasol 1.00 2.50
8 Shaquille O'Neal 2.50 6.00
9 Dwyane Wade 2.50 6.00
10 Michael Redd .50 1.25
11 Allen Iverson 1.50 4.00
12 Vince Carter 1.25 3.00
13 Chris Webber .75 2.00
14 Tony Parker 1.00 2.50
15 Andrei Kirilenko .50 1.25

2004-05 Fleer Genuine Article Autographs

STATED PRINT RUN 50 TO 125 SETS
AK Andrei Kirilenko/50 6.00 15.00
CA Carmelo Anthony/50 20.00 50.00
DW Dwyane Wade/50 20.00 50.00
JH Josh Howard/125 5.00 12.00
LJ Luke Jackson/125 5.00 12.00
LR Luke Ridnour/50 5.00 12.00
PG Pau Gasol/50 8.00 20.00
DWE David West 5.00 12.00

2004-05 Fleer Genuine Article Autographs Gold

*GOLD: .5X TO 1.25X BASE HI
STATED PRINT RUN 20 TO 40 SER.#'d SETS
DW Dwyane Wade/20 30.00 [illegible]

2004-05 Fleer Genuine Article Autographs Patches

STATED PRINT RUN 10 TO 30 SETS
AK Andrei Kirilenko/30 12.50 [illegible]
CA Carmelo Anthony/20 50.00 [illegible]
JH Josh Howard/20 12.50 [illegible]
JO Jermaine O'Neal/20 15.00 [illegible]
LR Luke Ridnour/20 12.50 [illegible]
PG Pau Gasol/20 20.00 [illegible]
DWE David West/30 12.50 [illegible]
DWE1 David West/20 12.50 [illegible]

2004-05 Fleer Genuine Article Game Used

STATED ODDS 1:50 H, 1:270 R
*GAME USED 149: .5X TO 1.25X BASE GU HI
PRINT RUN 149 SER.#'d SETS
AI Allen Iverson 6.00 [illegible]
AK Andrei Kirilenko 2.00 [illegible]
AS Amare Stoudemire 2.50 [illegible]
CA Carmelo Anthony 5.00 [illegible]
DW Dwyane Wade 6.00 [illegible]
JO Jermaine O'Neal 2.00 [illegible]
PG Pau Gasol 4.00 [illegible]
SO Shaquille O'Neal 10.00 [illegible]
TM Tracy McGrady 4.00 [illegible]
VC Vince Carter 5.00 [illegible]

2004-05 Fleer Genuine At Large

COMPLETE SET (20) 10.00 [illegible]
STATED ODDS 1:6 H, 1:8 R
1 Corey Maggette .40 [illegible]
2 Steve Francis .50 [illegible]
3 Jason Richardson .50 [illegible]
4 Dwyane Wade 2.00 [illegible]
5 Richard Jefferson .40 [illegible]
6 Ben Wallace .60 [illegible]
7 Carmelo Anthony 1.00 [illegible]
8 Kevin Garnett 1.25 [illegible]
9 Tim Duncan 1.25 [illegible]
10 Yao Ming 1.25 [illegible]
11 Vince Carter 1.00 [illegible]
12 Kobe Bryant 4.00 [illegible]
13 Ray Allen .75 [illegible]
14 Dirk Nowitzki 1.25 [illegible]
15 Shaquille O'Neal 2.00 [illegible]
16 Baron Davis .50 [illegible]
17 Jermaine O'Neal .40 [illegible]
18 Paul Pierce .75 [illegible]
19 LeBron James 4.00 [illegible]
20 Allen Iverson 1.25 [illegible]

2004-05 Fleer Genuine At Large Autographs

STATED PRINT RUN 50 TO 150 SETS
AJ Al Jefferson/150 10.00 25.00
BD Baron Davis 6.00 15.00
BW Ben Wallace/50 10.00 25.00
DW Dwyane Wade/50 50.00 100.00
JR Jason Richardson 6.00 15.00
JS J.R. Smith/150 8.00 20.00
RA Rafael Araujo/150 6.00 15.00
RJ Richard Jefferson/50 6.00 15.00
VC Vince Carter 15.00 40.00

2004-05 Fleer Genuine At Large Autographs Gold

*GOLD: .5X TO 1.25X BASE HI
STATED PRINT RUN 20 TO 40 SETS

2004-05 Fleer Genuine At Large Autographs Patches

STATED PRINT RUN 10 TO 30 SETS
AJ Al Jefferson/30 25.00 [illegible]
BG Ben Gordon/30 15.00 [illegible]
BW Ben Wallace/30 20.00 [illegible]
DW Dwyane Wade/20 40.00 [illegible]
JR Jason Richardson/20 12.50 [illegible]
JS J.R. Smith/30 15.00 [illegible]

2004-05 Fleer Genuine At Large Game Used

STATED ODDS 1:40 H, 1:72 R
*GAME USED 199: .5X TO 1.25X BASE GU HI
PRINT RUN 199 SER.#'d SETS
*PATCH: 1.25X TO 3X BASE HI
PATCH PRINT RUN 25 SER.#'d SETS
AI Allen Iverson 6.00 15.00
BD Baron Davis 2.50 6.00
BW Ben Wallace 3.00 8.00
CA Carmelo Anthony 5.00 12.00
DW Dwyane Wade 10.00 25.00
JO Jermaine O'Neal 2.00 5.00
KG Kevin Garnett 6.00 15.00
PP Paul Pierce 4.00 10.00
RA Ray Allen 4.00 10.00
RJ Richard Jefferson 2.00 5.00
SF Steve Francis 2.50 6.00
SO Shaquille O'Neal 10.00 25.00
TD Tim Duncan 6.00 15.00
VC Vince Carter 5.00 12.00
YM Yao Ming 6.00 15.00

2004-05 Fleer Genuine Big Time

COMPLETE SET (15) 25.00 [illegible]
STATED ODDS 1:99 H, 1:125 R
1 Dwyane Wade 6.00 15.00
2 LeBron James 12.00 30.00
3 Kobe Bryant 12.00 30.00
4 Shaquille O'Neal 6.00 15.00
5 Tim Duncan 4.00 10.00
6 Tracy McGrady 2.50 6.00
7 Richard Hamilton 2.00 5.00
8 Kevin Garnett 4.00 10.00
9 Allen Iverson 4.00 10.00
10 Chris Webber 2.00 5.00
11 Paul Pierce 2.50 6.00
12 Yao Ming 4.00 10.00
13 Pau Gasol 2.50 6.00
14 Carmelo Anthony 3.00 8.00
15 Andrei Kirilenko 1.25 3.00

2004-05 Fleer Genuine Big Time Autographs

*GOLD: .6X TO 1.5X BASE AU HI
GOLD PRINT RUN 25 TO 50 SER.#'d SETS
AB Andris Biedrins 5.00 12.00
AK Andrei Kirilenko 4.00 10.00
AV Anderson Varejao 4.00 10.00
BW Ben Wallace 10.00 25.00
CD Carlos Delfino 4.00 10.00
DW Dorell Wright 8.00 20.00
KS Kirk Snyder 4.00 10.00
LC Lionel Chalmers 4.00 10.00
MP Mickael Pietrus 4.00 10.00
TA Tony Allen 5.00 12.00

2004-05 Fleer Genuine Big Time Autographs Patches

STATED PRINT RUN 10 TO 40 SETS
AB Andris Biedrins/40 8.00 20.00
AK Andrei Kirilenko/20 8.00 20.00
AV Anderson Varejao/40 8.00 20.00
CD Carlos Delfino/40 8.00 20.00
CD1 Carlos Delfino/20 8.00 20.00
DH David Harrison/40 8.00 20.00
DH1 David Harrison/20 8.00 20.00
KS Kirk Snyder/40 8.00 20.00
MP Mickael Pietrus/40 8.00 20.00
TA Tony Allen/20 8.00 20.00

2004-05 Fleer Genuine Big Time Game Used

STATED ODDS 1:60 H, 1:308 R
*GAME USED 49: .6X TO 1.5X BASE HI
PRINT RUN 49 SER.#'d SETS
AI Allen Iverson 6.00 15.00
AK Andrei Kirilenko 2.00 5.00
CA Carmelo Anthony 5.00 12.00
CW Chris Webber 3.00 8.00
DW Dwyane Wade 10.00 25.00
JO Jermaine O'Neal 2.00 5.00
KG Kevin Garnett 6.00 15.00
PG Pau Gasol 4.00 10.00
PP Paul Pierce 4.00 10.00
SO Shaquille O'Neal 10.00 25.00
TD Tim Duncan 6.00 15.00
TM Tracy McGrady 4.00 10.00
TP Tony Parker 4.00 10.00
YM Yao Ming 6.00 15.00
ZR Zach Randolph 2.50 6.00

2004-05 Fleer Genuine Buyback Autographs

STATED ODDS 1:218
38 C.Drexler 88-9Fleer 25.00 60.00
78 M.Johnson 86-7Fleer 50.00 120.00
18 D.Ainge 88-9Fleer 20.00 50.00
26 C.Drexler 86-7Fleer 75.00 150.00
30 C.Drexler 87-8Fleer 30.00 80.00
36 G.Gervin 86-7Fleer 12.50 30.00
68 R.Smits 89-0Fleer 15.00 40.00
119 B.Walton 86-7Fleer 15.00 40.00
133 D.Ainge 89-0Fleer 15.00 40.00
138 D.Robinson 89-0Hoops 40.00 100.00

2000-01 Fleer Glossy

COMP.SET w/o SP's (200) 12.50 30.00
201-210 PRINT RUN 1000 SERIAL #'d SETS
211-235 PRINT RUN 1500 SERIAL #'d SETS
236-245 PRINT RUN 1250 SERIAL #'d SETS
246-251 PRINT RUN 500 SER.#'d SETS
201-251 STATED ODDS AT LEAST 2 PER BOX
1 Lamar Odom .30 .75
2 Christian Laettner .30 .75
3 Michael Olowokandi .20 .50
4 Anthony Carter .20 .50
5 Steve Francis .30 .75
6 Darvin Ham .25 .60
7 Mitch Richmond .40 1.00
8 Corliss Williamson .20 .50
9 Jason Terry .30 .75
10 Brian Grant .25 .60
11 Peja Stojakovic .25 .60
12 Rick Fox .25 .60
13 Tyrone Hill .20 .50
14 Chauncey Billups .40 1.00
15 Otis Thorpe .25 .60
16 Richard Hamilton .40 1.00
17 Ervin Johnson .20 .50
18 Jim Jackson .25 .60
19 Theo Ratliff .20 .50
20 Doug Christie .25 .60
21 Jalen Rose .25 .60
22 John Wallace .20 .50
23 Ruben Patterson .20 .50
24 Steve Nash .50 1.25
25 Toni Kukoc .40 1.00
26 Anthony Peeler .20 .50
27 Ray Allen .50 1.25
28 Adonal Foyle .20 .50
29 Chris Whitney .20 .50
30 Nick Van Exel .30 .75
31 Sean Elliott .25 .60
32 Erick Strickland .20 .50
33 Jerry Stackhouse .30 .75
34 Antawn Jamison .30 .75
35 Grant Hill .50 1.25
36 Antonio Daniels .20 .50
37 Karl Malone .60 1.50
38 Keith Van Horn .25 .60
39 Ron Harper .30 .75
40 Stephon Marbury .40 1.00
41 Bryon Russell .20 .50
42 Corey Maggette .25 .60
43 Hersey Hawkins .20 .50
44 Vince Carter .60 1.50
45 Paul Pierce .50 1.25
46 Mikki Moore RC .30 .75
47 Othella Harrington .20 .50
48 Erick Dampier .20 .50
49 Jerome Williams .20 .50
50 Nick Anderson .25 .60
51 Tim Hardaway .40 1.00
52 Allan Houston .30 .75
53 Tyrone Nesby .20 .50
54 Brevin Knight .20 .50
55 Chris Mills .20 .50
56 Ron Artest .30 .75
57 Walt Williams .20 .50
58 Duane Causwell .20 .50
59 Bonzi Wells .20 .50
60 Rasheed Wallace .40 1.00
61 Dikembe Mutombo .50 1.25
62 Jahidi White .20 .50
63 Chris Webber .40 1.00
64 Tony Battie .20 .50
65 Mahmoud Abdul-Rauf .20 .50
66 Monty Williams .25 .60
67 Charlie Ward .25 .60
68 David Robinson .60 1.50
69 Eric Snow .20 .50
70 Jermaine O'Neal .25 .60
71 Kurt Thomas .20 .50
72 James Posey .20 .50
73 Travis Best .20 .50
74 Jonathan Bender .20 .50
75 John Stockton .60 1.50
76 Jacque Vaughn .20 .50
77 Ron Mercer .25 .60
78 Shawn Marion .30 .75
79 Larry Johnson .40 1.00
80 Maurice Taylor .20 .50
81 Clifford Robinson .30 .75
82 Scot Pollard .20 .50
83 Patrick Ewing .50 1.25
84 Terrell Brandon .25 .60
85 Horace Grant .30 .75
86 Vin Baker .25 .60
87 Al Harrington .25 .60
88 Larry Hughes .30 .75
89 David Wesley .25 .60
90 Wally Szczerbiak .25 .60
91 Charles Oakley .30 .75
92 Tim Thomas .20 .50
93 Mookie Blaylock .30 .75
94 Jamal Mashburn .25 .60
95 Roshown McLeod .20 .50
96 John Starks .30 .75
97 Rodney Rogers .20 .50
98 Juwan Howard .25 .60
99 Isaiah Rider .25 .60
100 Rashard Lewis .25 .60
101 Dion Glover .20 .50
102 Johnny Newman .20 .50
103 Avery Johnson .25 .60
104 Darrell Armstrong .20 .50
105 Eric Williams .20 .50
106 Gary Payton .50 1.25
107 Antonio Davis .25 .60
108 Dirk Nowitzki .75 2.00
109 Trajan Langdon .20 .50
110 Michael Dickerson .20 .50
111 Joe Smith .25 .60
112 Rod Strickland .20 .50
113 Shawn Kemp .50 1.25
114 Voshon Lenard .20 .50
115 Marcus Camby .25 .60
116 Matt Harpring .20 .50
117 Isaac Austin .20 .50
118 Malik Rose .20 .50
119 Pat Garrity .20 .50
120 Kenny Thomas .20 .50
121 LaPhonso Ellis .25 .60
122 Danny Fortson .25 .60
123 Elton Brand .30 .75
124 Jason Williams .50 1.25
125 Kobe Bryant 2.50 6.00
126 Tariq Abdul-Wahad .20 .50
127 Tracy McGrady .60 1.50
128 Matt Geiger .20 .50
129 Antoine Walker .30 .75
130 Michael Finley .30 .75
131 Andre Miller .25 .60
132 Robert Horry .30 .75
133 Donyell Marshall .25 .60
134 Shareef Abdur-Rahim .30 .75
135 Vonteego Cummings .20 .50
136 Anthony Mason .30 .75
137 Mike Bibby .30 .75
138 Raef LaFrentz .25 .60
139 Glen Rice .30 .75
140 Chris Gatling .20 .50
141 Latrell Sprewell .40 1.00
142 Austin Croshere .20 .50
143 Kenny Anderson .25 .60
144 Elden Campbell .20 .50
145 Jason Kidd .50 1.25
146 Michael Doleac .20 .50
147 Muggsy Bogues .30 .75
148 Tim Duncan .75 2.00
149 Samaki Walker .20 .50
150 Gary Trent .20 .50
151 Kevin Garnett .75 2.00
152 Allen Iverson .75 2.00
153 Anfernee Hardaway .50 1.25
154 Robert Traylor .20 .50
155 Scottie Pippen .75 2.00
156 Shaquille O'Neal 1.25 3.00
157 Vlade Divac .30 .75
158 Lucious Harris .20 .50
159 Keon Clark .20 .50
160 Bo Outlaw .20 .50
161 P.J. Brown .20 .50
162 Derrick Coleman .30 .75
163 Mark Jackson .25 .60
164 Lamond Murray .20 .50
165 Dan Majerle .30 .75
166 Eddie Jones .30 .75
167 Cedric Ceballos .25 .60
168 Kendall Gill .30 .75
169 Tom Gugliotta .25 .60
170 Jeff McInnis .20 .50
171 Steve Smith .30 .75
172 Kevin Willis .20 .50
173 Lindsey Hunter .20 .50
174 Derek Anderson .25 .60
175 Shandon Anderson .20 .50
176 Adrian Griffin .20 .50
177 Baron Davis .30 .75
178 Radoslav Nesterovic .20 .50
179 Glenn Robinson .30 .75
180 Sam Cassell .25 .60
181 Chucky Atkins .20 .50
182 Arvydas Sabonis .30 .75
183 Damon Stoudamire .30 .75
184 Antonio McDyess .25 .60
185 Derek Fisher .30 .75
186 Bryant Reeves .20 .50
187 Hakeem Olajuwon .60 1.50
188 Kerry Kittles .25 .60
189 Alan Henderson .20 .50
190 Sam Perkins .20 .50
191 Felipe Lopez .20 .50
192 Tracy Murray .20 .50
193 Shammond Williams .20 .50
194 Vitaly Potapenko .20 .50
195 John Amaechi .20 .50
196 Quincy Lewis .20 .50
197 Reggie Miller .60 1.50
198 Cuttino Mobley .25 .60
199 Rex Chapman .25 .60
200 Dale Davis .25 .60
201 Stromile Swift RC 1.25 3.00
202 Stephen Jackson RC 3.00 8.00
203 Erick Barkley RC 1.00 2.50
204 Mike Miller RC 2.50 6.00
205 Kenyon Martin RC 3.00 8.00
206 Michael Redd RC 4.00 10.00
207 Darius Miles RC 1.50 4.00
208 Chris Mihm RC 1.00 2.50
209 Brian Cardinal RC 1.00 2.50
210 Khalid El-Amin RC 1.00 2.50
211 Hanno Mottola RC .75 2.00
212 Jamaal Magloire RC 1.25 3.00
213 Courtney Alexander RC .75 2.00
214 Mamadou N'Diaye RC .75 2.00
215 Chris Porter RC .75 2.00
216 Quentin Richardson RC 1.00 2.50
217 Eddie House RC 1.00 2.50
218 Joel Przybilla RC 1.00 2.50
219 Soumaila Samake RC .75 2.00
220 Speedy Claxton RC 1.25 3.00
221 Desmond Mason RC 1.50 4.00
222 Mike Smith RC .75 2.00
223 Lavor Postell RC .75 2.00
224 Pepe Sanchez RC 1.00 2.50
225 DeShawn Stevenson RC 1.25 3.00
226 Hedo Turkoglu RC 2.00 5.00
227 Keyon Dooling RC 1.00 2.50
228 Dan Langhi RC .75 2.00
229 Mateen Cleaves RC 1.00 2.50
230 Donnell Harvey RC 1.00 2.50
231 DerMarr Johnson RC .75 2.00
232 Jason Collier RC 1.25 3.00
233 Jake Voskuhl RC .75 2.00
234 Mark Madsen RC 1.25 3.00
235 Jabari Smith RC .75 2.00
236 Morris Peterson RC 1.25 3.00
237 Daniel Santiago RC 1.25 3.00
238 Etan Thomas RC 1.00 2.50
239 A.J. Guyton RC .75 2.00
240 Marcus Fizer RC 1.00 2.50
241 Jamal Crawford RC 3.00 8.00
242 Jerome Moiso RC .75 2.00
243 Olumide Oyedeji RC .75 2.00
244 Paul McPherson RC .75 2.00
245 Eduardo Najera RC 1.25 3.00
246 Marc Jackson AU RC 2.50 6.00
247 Mike Penberthy AU RC 3.00 8.00
248 Dragan Tarlac AU RC 2.00 5.00
249 Ruben Wolkowyski AU RC 2.00 5.00
250 Iakovos Tsakalidis AU RC 2.00 5.00
251 Ruben Garces AU RC 3.00 8.00

2000-01 Fleer Glossy Vince Carter Rookie Remnants

STATED PRINT RUNS LISTED BELOW
NNO Vince Carter FLR/100 12.50 30.00
NNO Vince Carter FLR JSY/15 20.00 50.00

2000-01 Fleer Glossy Class Acts

COMPLETE SET (25) 50.00 120.00
STATED ODDS 1:72
CA1 Hakeem Olajuwon 4.00 10.00
CA2 Karl Malone 4.00 10.00
CA3 Patrick Ewing 3.00 8.00
CA4 Ron Harper 2.00 5.00
CA5 David Robinson 4.00 10.00
CA6 Scottie Pippen 5.00 12.00
CA7 Mitch Richmond 2.50 6.00
CA8 Tim Hardaway 2.50 6.00
CA9 Gary Payton 3.00 8.00
CA10 Larry Johnson 2.50 6.00
CA11 Shaquille O'Neal 8.00 20.00
CA12 Allan Houston 2.00 5.00
CA13 Chris Webber 2.50 6.00
CA14 Jason Kidd 3.00 8.00
CA15 Grant Hill 3.00 8.00
CA16 Kevin Garnett 5.00 12.00
CA17 Allen Iverson 5.00 12.00
CA18 Kobe Bryant 15.00 40.00
CA19 Tracy McGrady 4.00 10.00
CA20 Tim Duncan 5.00 12.00
CA21 Dirk Nowitzki 5.00 12.00
CA22 Larry Hughes 2.00 5.00
CA23 Vince Carter 4.00 10.00
CA24 Elton Brand 2.00 5.00
CA25 Steve Francis 2.00 5.00

2000-01 Fleer Glossy Coach's Corner

STATED ODDS 1:108
1 Pat Riley 15.00 40.00
2 Doc Rivers 6.00 15.00
3 Paul Silas 6.00 15.00
4 Isiah Thomas 6.00 15.00
5 Rudy Tomjanovich 8.00 20.00
6 Jeff Van Gundy 10.00 25.00
7 Lenny Wilkens 10.00 25.00

2000-01 Fleer Glossy Game Breakers

COMPLETE SET (10) 10.00 25.00
STATED ODDS 1:24
1 Allen Iverson 2.00 5.00
2 Elton Brand .75 2.00
3 Grant Hill 1.25 3.00
4 Jason Kidd 1.25 3.00
5 Kevin Garnett 2.00 5.00
6 Kobe Bryant 6.00 15.00
7 Shaquille O'Neal 3.00 8.00
8 Steve Francis .75 2.00
9 Tim Duncan 2.00 5.00
10 Vince Carter 1.50 4.00

2000-01 Fleer Glossy Hardwood Leaders

COMPLETE SET (15) 8.00 20.00
STATED ODDS 1:12
HL1 Allen Iverson 1.25 3.00
HL2 Jason Williams .75 2.00
HL3 Vince Carter 1.00 2.50
HL4 Scottie Pippen 1.25 3.00
HL5 Kevin Garnett 1.25 3.00
HL6 Karl Malone 1.00 2.50
HL7 Grant Hill .75 2.00
HL8 Jason Kidd .75 2.00
HL9 Kobe Bryant 4.00 10.00
HL10 Elton Brand .50 1.25
HL11 Shaquille O'Neal 2.00 5.00
HL12 Tim Duncan 1.25 3.00
HL13 Tracy McGrady 1.00 2.50
HL14 Chris Webber .60 1.50
HL15 Lamar Odom .50 1.25

2000-01 Fleer Glossy Rookie Sensations

COMPLETE SET (25) 6.00 15.00
STATED ODDS 1:6
RS1 Jamaal Magloire .40 1.00
RS2 Etan Thomas .30 .75
RS3 Chris Mihm .25 .60
RS4 Joel Przybilla .30 .75
RS5 Mamadou N'Diaye .25 .60
RS6 Jason Collier .40 1.00
RS7 DerMarr Johnson .25 .60
RS8 Jerome Moiso .25 .60
RS9 Darius Miles .40 1.00
RS10 Marcus Fizer .30 .75
RS11 Kenyon Martin .75 2.00
RS12 Mark Madsen .40 1.00
RS13 Mike Miller .60 1.50
RS14 Desmond Mason .50 1.25
RS15 Morris Peterson .40 1.00
RS16 Hedo Turkoglu .60 1.50
RS17 Mateen Cleaves .30 .75
RS18 Keyon Dooling .30 .75
RS19 DeShawn Stevenson .40 1.00
RS20 Quentin Richardson .30 .75
RS21 Courtney Alexander .25 .60
RS22 Stromile Swift .30 .75
RS23 Stephen Jackson .75 2.00
RS24 Erick Barkley .25 .60
RS25 Khalid El-Amin .25 .60

2000-01 Fleer Glossy Traditional Threads

STATED ODDS 1:63
1 Vince Carter 6.00 15.00
2 Baron Davis 3.00 8.00
3 Trajan Langdon 2.00 5.00
4 Grant Hill 5.00 12.00
5 Allen Iverson 8.00 20.00
6 Jason Kidd 5.00 12.00
7 Karl Malone 6.00 15.00
8 Stephon Marbury 4.00 10.00
9 Shawn Marion 3.00 8.00
10 Tracy McGrady 6.00 15.00
11 Andre Miller 2.50 6.00
12 Dikembe Mutombo 5.00 12.00
13 Lamar Odom 3.00 8.00
14 Shaquille O'Neal 10.00 25.00
15 Gary Payton 5.00 12.00
16 Jason Terry 3.00 8.00
17 John Stockton 6.00 15.00
18 Anfernee Hardaway 5.00 12.00
19 Jason Williams 5.00 12.00
20 Darius Miles 3.00 8.00
21 Chris Mihm 2.00 5.00
22 Desmond Mason 4.00 10.00
23 Keyon Dooling 2.50 6.00
24 DerMarr Johnson 2.00 5.00
25 Speedy Claxton 3.00 8.00
26 Kenyon Martin 6.00 15.00
27 Hanno Mottola 2.00 5.00
28 Mike Miller 5.00 12.00
29 Quentin Richardson 2.50 6.00

2000-01 Fleer Glossy Mutombo Arena

1 Dikembe Mutombo .75 2.00

2001 Fleer Hawaii Bobby Knight

NNO Bobby Knight 15.00 40.00

2006-07 Fleer Hot Prospects

61-70 RC PRINT RUN 150 SER.#'d SETS
71-90 RC PRINT RUN 250 SER.#'d SETS
91-104 PRINT RUN 500 SER.#'d SETS
UNLESS LISTED IN CHECKLIST
105-113 RC PRINT RUN 150 SER.#'d SETS
1 Joe Johnson .40 1.00
2 Marvin Williams .25 .60
3 Tony Allen .25 .60
4 Paul Pierce .60 1.50
5 Raymond Felton .25 .60
6 Emeka Okafor .30 .75
7 Ben Gordon .30 .75
8 Michael Jordan 3.00 8.00
9 Zydrunas Ilgauskas .30 .75
10 LeBron James 3.00 8.00
11 Devin Harris .25 .60
12 Dirk Nowitzki 1.00 2.50
13 Carmelo Anthony .60 1.50
14 Nene .30 .75
15 Chauncey Billups .50 1.25
16 Ben Wallace .50 1.25
17 Baron Davis .40 1.00
18 Troy Murphy .25 .60
19 Tracy McGrady .60 1.50
20 Yao Ming 1.00 2.50
21 Jermaine O'Neal .40 1.00
22 Peja Stojakovic .30 .75
23 Corey Maggette .30 .75
24 Sam Cassell .30 .75
25 Kobe Bryant 3.00 8.00
26 Lamar Odom .30 .75
27 Pau Gasol .60 1.50
28 Hakim Warrick .25 .60
29 Shaquille O'Neal 1.50 4.00
30 Dwyane Wade .75 2.00
31 T.J. Ford .25 .60
32 Michael Redd .30 .75
33 Kevin Garnett 1.00 2.50
34 Troy Hudson .25 .60
35 Vince Carter .75 2.00
36 Jason Kidd .60 1.50
37 Desmond Mason .25 .60

38 Chris Paul .75 2.00
39 Stephon Marbury .50 1.25
40 Nate Robinson .30 .75
41 Grant Hill .60 1.50
42 Darko Milicic .25 .60
43 Andre Iguodala .40 1.00
44 Allen Iverson 1.00 2.50
45 Steve Nash .75 2.00
46 Amare Stoudemire .40 1.00
47 Zach Randolph .40 1.00
48 Sebastian Telfair .25 .60
49 Ron Artest .40 1.00
50 Mike Bibby .40 1.00
51 Tim Duncan 1.00 2.50
52 Manu Ginobili .75 2.00
53 Ray Allen .60 1.50
54 Rashard Lewis .30 .75
55 Chris Bosh .50 1.25
56 Charlie Villanueva .25 .60
57 Andrei Kirilenko .30 .75
58 Deron Williams .30 .75
59 Gilbert Arenas .40 1.00
60 Antawn Jamison .30 .75
61 Ronnie Brewer JSY AU RC 8.00 20.00
62 LaMarcus Aldridge JSY AU RC 30.00 80.00
63 Tyrus Thomas JSY AU RC 6.00 15.00
64 She.Williams JSY AU RC 5.00 12.00
65 Cedric Simmons JSY AU RC 5.00 12.00
66 Randy Foye JSY AU RC 6.00 15.00
67 Rudy Gay JSY AU RC 10.00 25.00
68 Patrick O'Bryant JSY AU RC 5.00 12.00
69 Rodney Carney JSY AU RC 5.00 12.00
70 Hilton Armstrong JSY AU RC 5.00 12.00
71 Denham Brown JSY AU RC 4.00 10.00
72 Dee Brown JSY AU RC 4.00 10.00
73 Allan Ray JSY AU RC 4.00 10.00
74 Shawne Williams JSY AU RC 4.00 10.00
75 Quincy Douby JSY AU RC 4.00 10.00
76 Renaldo Balkman JSY AU RC 5.00 12.00
77 Rajon Rondo JSY AU RC 20.00 50.00
78 Ma.Williams JSY AU RC 4.00 10.00
79 Josh Boone JSY AU RC 4.00 10.00
80 Kyle Lowry JSY AU RC 20.00 50.00
82 Jordan Farmar JSY AU RC 5.00 12.00
83 Maurice Ager JSY AU RC 4.00 10.00
84 Mardy Collins JSY AU RC 4.00 10.00
85 Shannon Brown JSY AU RC 4.00 10.00
86 James White JSY AU RC 4.00 10.00
87 Steve Novak JSY AU RC 5.00 12.00
88 Solomon Jones JSY AU RC 4.00 10.00
89 Paul Davis JSY AU RC 4.00 10.00
90 P.J. Tucker JSY AU RC 6.00 15.00
91 Craig Smith AU RC 4.00 10.00
92 Bobby Jones AU RC 3.00 8.00
93 David Noel AU RC 3.00 8.00
94 A.Bargnani AU/150 RC 6.00 15.00
95 James Augustine AU RC 3.00 8.00
96 Daniel Gibson AU RC 4.00 10.00
97 Brandon Roy AU/150 RC 15.00 40.00
98 Ryan Hollins AU RC 3.00 8.00
99 Hassan Adams AU RC 3.00 8.00
100 Pops Mensah-Bonsu AU RC 3.00 8.00
101 Will Blalock AU RC 3.00 8.00
102 Damir Markota AU RC 3.00 8.00
103 Saer Sene AU RC 3.00 8.00
104 Thabo Sefolosha AU RC 4.00 10.00
105 Leon Powe RC 1.50 4.00
106 J.J. Redick RC 5.00 12.00
107 Adam Morrison RC 2.00 5.00
108 Paul Millsap RC 3.00 8.00
109 J.R. Pinnock RC 1.50 4.00
110 Jorge Garbajosa RC 2.00 5.00
111 Vassilis Spanoulis RC 1.50 4.00
112 Yakhouba Diawara RC 1.50 4.00
113 Alexander Johnson RC 1.50 4.00

2006-07 Fleer Hot Prospects Red Hot

*1-60 RED: 2X TO 5X BASE HI
*61-70/94/97 RC RED: .6X TO 1.5X BASE HI
*71-113 RC RED: .75X TO 2X BASE HI
RED HOT PRINT RUN 50 SER.#'d SETS
10 LeBron James 25.00 60.00

2006-07 Fleer Hot Prospects Alumni Ink

PRINT RUN 10 TO 25 SER.#'d SETS
AF C.Frye/H.Adams/25 6.00 15.00
AW C.Anthony/Warrick/25 20.00 50.00
BA D.Brown/Augustine/25 6.00 15.00
BB C.Boozer/E.Brand/25 6.00 15.00
CJ V.Carter/Jamison/25 25.00 60.00
DW Walton/B.Davis/25 12.00 30.00
EW Shd.Williams/D.Ewing/25 6.00 15.00
FH R.Hollins/Farmar/25 6.00 15.00
FL K.Lowry/R.Foye/25 8.00 20.00
MG D.Marshall/R.Gay/25 6.00 15.00
OD Drexler/Olajuwon/10 100.00 200.00
OG E.Okafor/R.Gay/25 6.00 15.00
PH K.Hinrich/Pierce/25 25.00 60.00
PR R.Rondo/Prince/25 10.00 25.00

2006-07 Fleer Hot Prospects Double Team Memorabilia

PRINT RUN 50 SER.#'d SETS
*RED HOT: .75X TO 2X BASE HI
RED HOT PRINT RUN 25 SER.#'d SETS
AB G.Arenas/C.Butler 4.00 10.00
AI A.Iverson/A.Iguodala 6.00 15.00
AK A.Kirilenko/R.Araujo 4.00 10.00
AL R.Allen/R.Lewis 4.00 10.00
BB K.Bryant/K.Brown 60.00 150.00
BC C.Bosh/J.Calderon 4.00 10.00
BK B.Wallace/K.Hinrich 4.00 10.00
BW A.Bogut/Mv.Williams 4.00 10.00
CB T.Chandler/Kw.Brown 4.00 10.00
CF E.Curry/C.Frye 4.00 10.00
CJ V.Carter/A.Jamison 5.00 12.00
CS T.Chandler/P.Stojakovic 4.00 10.00
CW B.Cook/L.Walton 4.00 10.00
DG T.Duncan/M.Ginobili 6.00 15.00
DI S.Dalembert/A.Iguodala 4.00 10.00
DJ J.Howard/D.Harris 4.00 10.00
DK S.Dalembert/K.Korver 4.00 10.00
FB M.Finley/B.Bowen 5.00 12.00
FM R.Finley/S.May 4.00 10.00
FR S.Francis/Q.Richardson 4.00 10.00
GD L.Deng/B.Gordon 4.00 10.00
HH G.Hill/D.Howard 6.00 15.00
HP R.Hamilton/T.Prince 5.00 12.00
IG Z.Ilgauskas/D.Gooden 4.00 10.00
JD M.Daniels/S.Jasikevicius 4.00 10.00
JH A.Jamison/B.Haywood 4.00 10.00
JI A.Iverson/L.James 12.50 30.00
KC J.Kidd/V.Carter 6.00 15.00
KR K.Garnett/R.Davis 4.00 10.00
KW A.Kirilenko/D.Williams 4.00 10.00
MD J.Magloire/J.Dixon 4.00 10.00
MF R.McCants/R.Felton 4.00 10.00
ML C.Maggette/S.Livingston 4.00 10.00
MM T.McGrady/Y.Ming 5.00 12.00
MP D.Mason/C.Paul 6.00 15.00
MR S.Marbury/N.Robinson 4.00 10.00
MS K.Martin/S.Swift 4.00 10.00
NM S.Nash/S.Marion 5.00 12.00
OH E.Okafor/D.Howard 5.00 12.00
PG T.Parker/M.Ginobili 4.00 10.00
PS P.Pierce/W.Szczerbiak 4.00 10.00
RJ Z.Randolph/J.Jack 4.00 10.00
RV M.Redd/C.Villanueva 4.00 10.00
TS K.Thomas/A.Stoudemire 4.00 10.00
WH D.Williams/L.Head 5.00 12.00
WK N.Krstic/A.Wright 4.00 10.00
WR C.Wilcox/L.Ridnour 4.00 10.00
WS A.Walker/W.Simien 4.00 10.00

2006-07 Fleer Hot Prospects Draft Day Postmarks Autographs

PRINT RUN 100 SER.#'d SETS
AB Andrea Bargnani 6.00 15.00
AD Hassan Adams 4.00 10.00
BA Renaldo Balkman 5.00 12.00
BJ Bobby Jones 4.00 10.00
BR Brandon Roy 15.00 40.00
CS Cedric Simmons 4.00 10.00
DB Denham Brown 4.00 10.00
DE Dee Brown 4.00 10.00
DN David Noel 4.00 10.00
HA Hilton Armstrong 4.00 10.00
JA James Augustine 4.00 10.00
JB Josh Boone 4.00 10.00
JF Jordan Farmar 5.00 12.00
JW James White 4.00 10.00
KL Kyle Lowry 20.00 50.00
LA LaMarcus Aldridge 25.00 60.00
MA Maurice Ager 4.00 10.00
MC Mardy Collins 4.00 10.00
MW Marcus Williams 4.00 10.00
PD Paul Davis 4.00 10.00
PO Patrick O'Bryant 4.00 10.00
PT P.J. Tucker 6.00 15.00
QD Quincy Douby 4.00 10.00
RB Ronnie Brewer 6.00 15.00
RC Rodney Carney 4.00 10.00
RF Randy Foye 5.00 12.00
RG Rudy Gay 8.00 20.00
RH Ryan Hollins 4.00 10.00
RR Rajon Rondo 40.00 80.00
SB Shannon Brown 4.00 10.00
SJ Solomon Jones 4.00 10.00
SM Craig Smith 5.00 12.00
SN Steve Novak 5.00 12.00
SS Saer Sene 4.00 10.00
SW Shelden Williams 4.00 10.00
TS Thabo Sefolosha 5.00 12.00
TT Tyrus Thomas 5.00 12.00
WI Shawne Williams 4.00 10.00

2006-07 Fleer Hot Prospects Draft Rewind

COMPLETE SET (60) 25.00 60.00
APPROXIMATE ODDS TWO PER BOX
AB Andrew Bogut .75 2.00
AI Andre Iguodala 1.00 2.50
AJ Al Jefferson .60 1.50
AS Amare Stoudemire 1.00 2.50
BD Baron Davis 1.00 2.50
BG Ben Gordon 1.00 2.50
BM Brad Miller .75 2.00
BR Kobe Bryant 8.00 20.00
CA Carmelo Anthony 1.50 4.00
CB Chauncey Billups 1.25 3.00
CP Chris Paul 2.00 5.00
DG Drew Gooden .75 2.00
DM Darko Milicic .60 1.50
DN Dirk Nowitzki 2.50 6.00
DW Delonte West .60 1.50
EB Elton Brand .75 2.00
EC Eddy Curry .75 2.00
GA Gilbert Arenas 1.00 2.50
GD Devean George .60 1.50
IV Allen Iverson 2.50 6.00
JA LeBron James 8.00 20.00
JC Jamal Crawford 1.00 2.50
JD Juan Dixon .60 1.50
JK Jason Kidd 1.50 4.00
JM Jamaal Magloire .60 1.50
JO Jermaine O'Neal 1.00 2.50
JR Jason Richardson 1.00 2.50
JT Jason Terry .75 2.00
KB Kwame Brown .60 1.50
KG Kevin Garnett 2.50 6.00
KK Kyle Korver .75 2.00
KM Kenyon Martin .75 2.00
LJ Luke Jackson .60 1.50
LO Lamar Odom .75 2.00
LW Luke Walton .60 1.50
MA Shawn Marion 1.00 2.50
MB Mike Bibby 1.00 2.50
MJ Michael Jordan 8.00 20.00
MM Mike Miller .75 2.00
MP Mickael Pietrus .75 2.00
MS Mike Sweetney .60 1.50
PG Pau Gasol 1.50 4.00
PS Peja Stojakovic .75 2.00
RA Ron Artest 1.00 2.50
RH Richard Hamilton 1.00 2.50
SD Samuel Dalembert .60 1.50
SF Steve Francis 1.00 2.50
SL Shaun Livingston .75 2.00
SM Stephon Marbury 1.25 3.00
SN Steve Nash 2.00 5.00
SO Shaquille O'Neal 4.00 10.00
TC Tyson Chandler .75 2.00
TD Tim Duncan 2.50 6.00
TI Jamaal Tinsley .60 1.50
TM Tracy McGrady 1.50 4.00
TP Tony Parker 1.50 4.00
VC Vince Carter 2.00 5.00
WA Dwyane Wade 2.00 5.00
WS Wally Szczerbiak .75 2.00
YM Yao Ming 2.50 6.00
ZI Zydrunas Ilgauskas .75 2.00

2006-07 Fleer Hot Prospects Draft Rewind Memorabilia

PRINT RUN 50 SER.#'d SETS
*RED HOT: .75X TO 2X BASE HI
RED HOT PRINT RUN 25 SER.#'d SETS
AI Andre Iguodala 3.00 8.00
AS Amare Stoudemire 4.00 10.00
BD Baron Davis 3.00 8.00
BG Ben Gordon 2.50 6.00
BR Kobe Bryant 60.00 150.00
CA Carmelo Anthony 5.00 12.00
DG Drew Gooden 2.50 6.00
DN Dirk Nowitzki 8.00 20.00
DW Delonte West 2.00 5.00
EB Elton Brand 2.50 6.00
EC Eddy Curry 2.50 6.00
GA Gilbert Arenas 3.00 8.00
GD Devean George 2.00 5.00
JA LeBron James 15.00 40.00
JC Jamal Crawford 3.00 8.00
JD Juan Dixon 2.50 6.00
JK Jason Kidd 5.00 12.00
JM Jamaal Magloire 2.00 5.00
JO Jermaine O'Neal 3.00 8.00
JR Jason Richardson 3.00 8.00
KB Kwame Brown 2.50 6.00
KG Kevin Garnett 8.00 20.00
KK Kyle Korver 2.50 6.00
KM Kenyon Martin 2.50 6.00
LJ Luke Jackson 2.50 6.00
LO Lamar Odom 2.50 6.00
LW Luke Walton 2.00 5.00
MA Shawn Marion 3.00 8.00
MB Mike Bibby 3.00 8.00
MP Mickael Pietrus 2.50 6.00
MS Mike Sweetney 2.50 6.00
PS Peja Stojakovic 2.50 6.00
RH Richard Hamilton 3.00 8.00
SD Samuel Dalembert 2.00 5.00
SF Steve Francis 3.00 8.00
SL Shaun Livingston 2.50 6.00
SM Stephon Marbury 4.00 10.00
SN Steve Nash 6.00 15.00
SO Shaquille O'Neal 12.00 30.00
TC Tyson Chandler 2.50 6.00
TD Tim Duncan 8.00 20.00
TI Jamaal Tinsley 2.00 5.00
TM Tracy McGrady 5.00 12.00
TP Tony Parker 5.00 12.00
VC Vince Carter 6.00 15.00
WS Wally Szczerbiak 2.50 6.00
YM Yao Ming 8.00 20.00
ZI Zydrunas Ilgauskas 2.50 6.00

2006-07 Fleer Hot Prospects Hot Materials Jerseys

COMMON CARD 2.50 6.00
PRINT RUN 50 SER.#'d SETS
*RED HOT: .75X TO 2X BASE HI
RED HOT PRINT RUN 25 SER.#'d SETS
AB Andrew Bogut 2.50 6.00
AI Andre Iguodala 3.00 8.00
AS Amare Stoudemire 4.00 10.00
BA Andrea Bargnani 2.50 6.00
BD Baron Davis 3.00 8.00
BG Ben Gordon 2.50 6.00
BM Brad Miller 2.50 6.00
BR Brandon Roy 6.00 15.00
CB Chauncey Billups 4.00 10.00
CP Chris Paul 6.00 15.00
CW Chris Webber 4.00 10.00
DH Dwight Howard 4.00 10.00
DN Dirk Nowitzki 8.00 20.00
EB Elton Brand 2.50 6.00
EO Emeka Okafor 2.50 6.00
JK Jason Kidd 5.00 12.00
KB Kobe Bryant 50.00 120.00
KG Kevin Garnett 8.00 20.00
LA LaMarcus Aldridge 8.00 20.00
LJ LeBron James 10.00 25.00
LO Lamar Odom 2.50 6.00
MG Manu Ginobili 6.00 15.00
MW Marvin Williams 2.50 6.00
PG Pau Gasol 5.00 12.00
PP Paul Pierce 5.00 12.00
PS Peja Stojakovic 2.50 6.00
RB Ronnie Brewer 2.50 6.00
RF Randy Foye 2.50 6.00
RG Rudy Gay 4.00 10.00
RR Rajon Rondo 6.00 15.00
SF Steve Francis 3.00 8.00
SM Shawn Marion 3.00 8.00
SW Shelden Williams 2.00 5.00
TC Tyson Chandler 2.50 6.00
TT Tyrus Thomas 2.50 6.00
WI Chris Wilcox 2.50 6.00
WM Marcus Williams 2.50 6.00
WS Wally Szczerbiak 2.50 6.00
ZI Zydrunas Ilgauskas 2.50 6.00

2006-07 Fleer Hot Prospects Notable Newcomers

COMPLETE SET (20) 12.50 30.00
APPROXIMATE ODDS TWO PER BOX
AB Andrea Bargnani .75 2.00
AD Hassan Adams .60 1.50
BJ Bobby Jones .60 1.50
BR Brandon Roy 2.00 5.00
CS Craig Smith .75 2.00
DN David Noel .60 1.50
HA Hilton Armstrong .60 1.50
JF Jordan Farmar .75 2.00
LA LaMarcus Aldridge 2.50 6.00
MC Mardy Collins .60 1.50
MW Marcus Williams .60 1.50
PO Patrick O'Bryant .60 1.50
QD Quincy Douby .60 1.50
RF Randy Foye .75 2.00
RG Rudy Gay 1.25 3.00
RH Ryan Hollins .60 1.50
RR Rajon Rondo 3.00 8.00
SN Steve Novak .75 2.00
SW Shelden Williams .60 1.50
TT Tyrus Thomas .75 2.00

2006-07 Fleer Hot Prospects Notable Notations

PRINT RUN 50 SER.#'d SETS
AB Andrea Bargnani 4.00 10.00
BA Renaldo Balkman 4.00 10.00
BR Brandon Roy 10.00 25.00
CS Cedric Simmons 3.00 8.00
DB Denham Brown 3.00 8.00
DE Dee Brown 3.00 8.00
DN David Noel 3.00 8.00
JB Josh Boone 3.00 8.00
KP Kevin Pittsnogle 4.00 10.00
LA LaMarcus Aldridge 12.00 30.00
MA Maurice Ager 3.00 8.00
PD Paul Davis 3.00 8.00
QD Quincy Douby 3.00 8.00
RF Randy Foye 8.00 20.00
RG Rudy Gay 12.50 30.00
SB Shannon Brown 3.00 8.00
SC Craig Smith 4.00 10.00
TT Tyrus Thomas 4.00 10.00
WI Shawne Williams 3.00 8.00

2006-07 Fleer Hot Prospects Rookie Materials Letter Autographs

AB Andrea Bargnani 25.00 50.00
BR Brandon Roy 25.00 60.00
CS Cedric Simmons 5.00 12.00
JR Jason Richardson 5.00 12.00
HA Hilton Armstrong 5.00 12.00
JB Josh Boone 5.00 12.00
JF Jordan Farmar 6.00 15.00
LA LaMarcus Aldridge 25.00 50.00
MC Mardy Collins 5.00 12.00
MW Marcus Williams 5.00 12.00
PO Patrick O'Bryant 5.00 12.00
QD Quincy Douby 5.00 12.00
RB Ronnie Brewer 8.00 20.00
RC Rodney Carney 5.00 12.00
RF Randy Foye 10.00 25.00
RG Rudy Gay 25.00 50.00
RR Rajon Rondo 40.00 100.00
SW Shelden Williams 5.00 12.00
TS Thabo Sefolosha 12.50 30.00
TT Tyrus Thomas 10.00 25.00
WI Shawne Williams 5.00 12.00

2006-07 Fleer Hot Prospects Sweet Selections Autographs

PRINT RUN 50 SER.#'d SETS
BR Brandon Roy 12.00 30.00
CA Carmelo Anthony 15.00 40.00
CB Carlos Boozer 5.00 12.00
CM Cuttino Mobley 5.00 12.00
CP Chris Paul 75.00 200.00
CS Cedric Simmons 5.00 12.00
DB Dee Brown 5.00 12.00
DE Denham Brown 5.00 12.00
DM Donyell Marshall 5.00 12.00
FR Randy Foye 5.00 12.00
HW Hakim Warrick 5.00 12.00
ID Ike Diogu 5.00 12.00
JA Antawn Jamison 5.00 12.00
JB Josh Boone 5.00 12.00
JC Josh Childress 5.00 12.00
JJ Joe Johnson 5.00 12.00
JR Jalen Rose 5.00 12.00
KA Kareem Abdul-Jabbar 40.00 80.00
KB Kwame Brown 5.00 12.00
KH Kirk Hinrich 5.00 12.00
KP Kevin Pittsnogle 5.00 12.00
LJ LeBron James 1,250.00 2,500.00
LR Luke Ridnour 5.00 12.00
MA Maurice Ager 5.00 12.00
MW Martell Webster 5.00 12.00
NR Nate Robinson 5.00 12.00
PO Patrick O'Bryant 5.00 12.00
PP Paul Pierce 15.00 40.00
RC Rodney Carney 5.00 12.00
RF Raymond Felton 5.00 12.00
RG Rudy Gay 8.00 20.00
RJ Richard Jefferson 5.00 12.00
RM Rashad McCants 5.00 12.00
SC Craig Smith 5.00 12.00
SN Steve Novak 5.00 12.00
SS Saer Sene 5.00 12.00
TF T.J. Ford 5.00 12.00
TP Tayshaun Prince 6.00 15.00
WS Shelden Williams 5.00 12.00
YM Yao Ming 15.00 40.00

2006-07 Fleer Hot Prospects Sweet Selections Autographs Jerseys

PRINT RUN 25 SER.#'d SETS
CB Carlos Boozer 8.00 20.00
CP Chris Paul 30.00 80.00
CS Cedric Simmons 5.00 12.00
DE Denham Brown 5.00 12.00
DM Donyell Marshall 8.00 20.00
FR Randy Foye 6.00 15.00
HW Hakim Warrick 8.00 20.00
ID Ike Diogu 8.00 20.00
JA Antawn Jamison 10.00 25.00
JB Josh Boone 5.00 12.00
JC Josh Childress 8.00 20.00
JJ Joe Johnson 10.00 25.00
JR Jalen Rose 10.00 25.00
KA Kareem Abdul-Jabbar 75.00 150.00
KB Kwame Brown 8.00 20.00
KH Kirk Hinrich 8.00 20.00
LA LaMarcus Aldridge 20.00 50.00
LJ LeBron James 1,500.00 3,000.00
MA Maurice Ager 5.00 12.00
NR Nate Robinson 10.00 25.00
PP Paul Pierce 12.50 30.00
RC Rodney Carney 5.00 12.00
RF Raymond Felton 10.00 25.00
RG Rudy Gay 10.00 25.00
RJ Richard Jefferson 8.00 20.00
RM Rashad McCants 8.00 20.00
SC Craig Smith 6.00 15.00
SS Saer Sene 5.00 12.00
TP Tayshaun Prince 8.00 20.00
WS Shelden Williams 5.00 12.00
YM Yao Ming 25.00 60.00

2006-07 Fleer Hot Prospects We're #1

COMPLETE SET 6.00 15.00
APPROXIMATE ODDS ONE PER BOX
AB Andrew Bogut .75 2.00
CW Chris Webber 1.25 3.00
DH Dwight Howard 1.25 3.00
EB Elton Brand .75 2.00
KB Kwame Brown .60 1.50
KM Kenyon Martin .75 2.00
LJ LeBron James 8.00 20.00
SO Shaquille O'Neal 4.00 10.00
TD Tim Duncan 2.50 6.00
YM Yao Ming 2.50 6.00
AB2 Andrea Bargnani .75 2.00

2006-07 Fleer Hot Prospects We're #1 Memorabilia

PRINT RUN 50 SER.#'d SETS
*RED HOT: .75X TO 2X BASE HI
RED PRINT RUN 25 SER.#'d SETS
AB Andrew Bogut 2.50 6.00
CW Chris Webber 4.00 10.00
DH Dwight Howard 4.00 10.00
KB Kwame Brown 2.50 6.00
KM Kenyon Martin 2.50 6.00
LJ LeBron James 12.00 30.00
SO Shaquille O'Neal 12.00 30.00
TD Tim Duncan 8.00 20.00
YM Yao Ming 8.00 20.00

2007-08 Fleer Hot Prospects

COMP.SET w/o SP's (60) 10.00 25.00
61-78 PRINT RUN 399 SER.#'d SETS
COMMON CARD (79-84) 3.00 8.00
85-93 RC PRINT RUN 899 SER.#'d SETS
94-121 RC PRINT RUN 599 SER.#'d SETS
122-133 RC PRINT RUN 399 SER.#'d SETS
1 Kobe Bryant 2.50 6.00
2 Carmelo Anthony .50 1.25
3 Gilbert Arenas .30 .75
4 Dwyane Wade .60 1.50
5 LeBron James 2.50 6.00
6 Michael Redd .25 .60
7 Ray Allen .50 1.25
8 Allen Iverson .75 2.00
9 Vince Carter .60 1.50
10 Yao Ming .75 2.00
11 Joe Johnson .25 .60
12 Paul Pierce .50 1.25
13 Tracy McGrady .50 1.25
14 Dirk Nowitzki .75 2.00
15 Zach Randolph .30 .75
16 Chris Bosh .40 1.00
17 Kevin Garnett .75 2.00
18 Rashard Lewis .25 .60
19 Ben Gordon .25 .60
20 Carlos Boozer .25 .60
21 Pau Gasol .50 1.25
22 Elton Brand .25 .60
23 Michael Jordan 3.00 8.00
24 Amare Stoudemire .30 .75
25 Kevin Martin .25 .60
26 Baron Davis .25 .60
27 Tim Duncan .75 2.00
28 Richard Hamilton .40 1.00
29 Eddy Curry .20 .50
30 Jermaine O'Neal .30 .75
31 Caron Butler .25 .60
32 Josh Howard .25 .60
33 Ron Artest .30 .75
34 Luol Deng .25 .60
35 Steve Nash .60 1.50
36 Tony Parker .50 1.25
37 David West .25 .60
38 Andre Iguodala .30 .75
39 Gerald Wallace .25 .60
40 Jamal Crawford .30 .75
41 Dwight Howard .40 1.00
42 Mehmet Okur .20 .50
43 Shawn Marion .30 .75
44 Maurice Williams .25 .60
45 Shaquille O'Neal 1.25 3.00
46 Chris Paul .60 1.50
47 Chauncey Billups .40 1.00
48 Brandon Roy .40 1.00
49 Josh Smith .20 .50
50 Deron Williams .25 .60
51 Jason Richardson .30 .75
52 Al Jefferson .25 .60
53 Lamar Odom .25 .60
54 Raymond Felton .25 .60
55 Andre Miller .25 .60
56 Jason Kidd .50 1.25
57 Zydrunas Ilgauskas .25 .60
58 Andrea Bargnani .20 .50
59 Marcus Camby .25 .60
60 Rudy Gay .25 .60
61 LeBron James 6.00 15.00
62 Amare Stoudemire .75 2.00
63 Vince Carter 1.50 4.00
64 Tim Duncan 2.00 5.00
65 Allen Iverson 2.00 5.00
66 Shaquille O'Neal 2.00 5.00
67 David Robinson 1.50 4.00
68 Michael Jordan 8.00 20.00
69 Darrell Griffith .50 1.25
70 Larry Bird 3.00 8.00
71 Adrian Dantley .60 1.50
72 Bob McAdoo .60 1.50
73 Kareem Abdul-Jabbar 2.50 6.00
74 Wes Unseld 1.00 2.50
75 Dave Bing .75 2.00
76 Willis Reed 1.25 3.00
77 Oscar Robertson .75 2.00
78 Wilt Chamberlain 2.50 6.00
79 Greg Oden RC 3.00 8.00
80 Brandan Wright RC 2.50 6.00
81 Yi Jianlian RC 4.00 10.00
82 Nick Young RC 3.00 8.00
83 Thaddeus Young RC 3.00 8.00
84 Kyrylo Fesenko RC 2.00 5.00
85 Sun Yue AU RC 3.00 8.00
86 Brad Newley AU RC 3.00 8.00
87 Ramon Sessions AU RC 2.50 6.00
88 Sammy Mejia AU RC 2.00 5.00
89 JamesOn Curry AU RC 2.00 5.00
90 Renaldas Seibutis AU RC 3.00 8.00
91 Milovan Rakovic AU RC 3.00 8.00
92 Marco Belinelli AU RC 2.50 6.00
93 Darryl Watkins AU RC 2.00 5.00
94 Demetris Nichols JSY AU RC 4.00 10.00
95 Javaris Crittenton JSY AU RC 4.00 10.00
96 Jason Smith JSY AU RC 4.00 10.00
97 Daequan Cook JSY AU RC 5.00 12.00
98 Jared Dudley JSY AU RC 5.00 12.00
99 Wilson Chandler JSY AU RC 5.00 12.00
100 Morris Almond JSY AU RC 4.00 10.00
101 Aaron Brooks JSY AU RC 5.00 12.00
102 Arron Afflalo JSY AU RC 5.00 12.00
103 Alando Tucker JSY AU RC 4.00 10.00
104 Carl Landry JSY AU RC 4.00 10.00
105 Gabe Pruitt JSY AU RC 4.00 10.00
106 Marcus Williams JSY AU RC 4.00 10.00
107 Nick Fazekas JSY AU RC 4.00 10.00
108 Glen Davis JSY AU RC 5.00 12.00
109 Jermareo Davidson JSY AU RC 4.00 10.00
110 Josh McRoberts JSY AU RC 4.00 10.00
111 Herbert Hill JSY AU RC 4.00 10.00
112 Derrick Byars JSY AU RC 4.00 10.00
113 Adam Haluska JSY AU RC 4.00 10.00
114 Reyshawn Terry JSY AU RC 4.00 10.00
115 Jared Jordan JSY AU RC 4.00 10.00
116 Stephane Lasme JSY AU RC 4.00 10.00
117 Dominic McGuire JSY AU RC 4.00 10.00
118 Aaron Gray JSY AU RC 4.00 10.00
119 Taurean Green JSY AU RC 4.00 10.00
120 D.J. Strawberry JSY AU RC 4.00 10.00
121 Chris Richard JSY AU RC 4.00 10.00
122 Rodney Stuckey JSY AU RC 4.00 10.00
123 Kevin Durant JSY AU RC 500.00 1,000.00
124 Al Thornton JSY AU RC 4.00 10.00
125 Julian Wright JSY AU RC 4.00 10.00
126 Sean Williams JSY AU RC 4.00 10.00
127 Al Horford JSY AU RC 15.00 40.00
128 Mike Conley Jr. JSY AU RC 12.00 30.00
129 Jeff Green JSY AU RC 5.00 12.00
130 Corey Brewer JSY AU RC 5.00 12.00
131 Joakim Noah JSY AU RC 6.00 15.00
132 Spencer Hawes JSY AU RC 4.00 10.00
133 Acie Law JSY AU RC 4.00 10.00

2007-08 Fleer Hot Prospects Red

*1-60 RED: 5X TO 12X BASE HI
*61-78 RED: 1.5X TO 4X BASE HI
*79-93 RC RED: 1X TO 2.5X BASE HI
*94-133 RC RED: .6X TO 1.5X BASE HI
PRINT RUN 25 SER.#'d SETS
68 Michael Jordan 40.00 100.00

2007-08 Fleer Hot Prospects Autographics

APPROXIMATE ODDS ONE PER BOX
CARDS WITH F INSERTED IN FLEER
AA Arron Afflalo 3.00 8.00
AB Aaron Brooks F 3.00 8.00
AG Aaron Gray 2.50 6.00
AH Adam Haluska 2.50 6.00
AH2 Adam Haluska Blue 2.50 6.00
AH3 Al Horford Blue 6.00 15.00
AH4 Al Horford 6.00 15.00
AL Acie Law F 2.50 6.00
AT Al Thornton 2.50 6.00
AT2 Al Thornton Blue 2.50 6.00
AT3 Alando Tucker F 2.50 6.00
CA Carmelo Anthony Blue 15.00 40.00
CB Corey Brewer 3.00 8.00
CB2 Corey Brewer Blue 3.00 8.00
CL Carl Landry 2.50 6.00
CL2 Carl Landry Blue 2.50 6.00
CR Chris Richard 2.50 6.00
CR2 Chris Richard Blue 2.50 6.00
DB Derrick Byars 2.50 6.00
DB2 Derrick Byars Blue 2.50 6.00
DC Daequan Cook 3.00 8.00
DS D.J. Strawberry F 2.50 6.00
DS2 D.J. Strawberry Blue F 2.50 6.00
GD Glen Davis 3.00 8.00
GP Gabe Pruitt F 2.50 6.00
HH Herbert Hill F 2.50 6.00
JC Javaris Crittenton 2.50 6.00
JC2 Javaris Crittenton Blue 2.50 6.00
JD Jared Dudley 3.00 8.00
JD2 Jared Dudley Blue 3.00 8.00
JD3 Jermareo Davidson 2.50 6.00
JG Jeff Green 3.00 8.00
JG2 Jeff Green Blue 3.00 8.00
JM Josh McRoberts 2.50 6.00
JM2 Josh McRoberts Blue 2.50 6.00
JN Joakim Noah 4.00 10.00
JN2 Joakim Noah Blue 4.00 10.00
JS Jason Smith F 2.50 6.00
JW Julian Wright 2.50 6.00
KD Kevin Durant 400.00 800.00
KD2 Kevin Durant Blue 500.00 1,000.00
MA Morris Almond F 2.50 6.00
MB Marco Belinelli Blue F 3.00 8.00
MC Mike Conley Jr. F 10.00 25.00
MC2 Mike Conley Jr. Blue F 10.00 25.00
MW Marcus Williams 2.50 6.00
RS Rodney Stuckey 2.50 6.00
RS2 Rodney Stuckey Green 2.50 6.00
RT Reyshawn Terry 2.50 6.00
RT2 Reyshawn Terry Blue 2.50 6.00
SH Spencer Hawes 2.50 6.00
SH2 Spencer Hawes Blue F 2.50 6.00
SH3 Spencer Hawes Red F 2.50 6.00
SL Stephane Lasme 2.50 6.00
SM Craig Smith F 2.50 6.00
TG Taurean Green 2.50 6.00
TG2 Taurean Green Blue 2.50 6.00
WC Wilson Chandler 3.00 8.00

2007-08 Fleer Hot Prospects Class of

COMPLETE SET (15) 25.00 60.00
PRINT RUNS SAME AS CARD #
1960 Robertson/West/Wilkens 2.50 6.00
1962 DeBusschere/Lucas/Havlicek 2.50 6.00
1967 Frazier/Riley/Jackson 3.00 8.00
1970 Lanier/Maravich/Archibald 5.00 12.00
1972 McAdoo/Westphal/Erving 2.50 6.00
1979 Johnson/Cartwright/Laimbeer 3.00 8.00
1984 Olajuwon/Jordan/Stockton 6.00 15.00
1992 O'Neal/Mourning/Horry 3.00 8.00
1996 Iverson/Bryant/Nash 4.00 10.00
1997 Duncan/Billups/McGrady 3.00 8.00
1998 Carter/Nowitzki/Pierce 3.00 8.00
2001 Gasol/Parker/Arenas 2.50 6.00
2003 James/Anthony/Wade 4.00 10.00
2007A Oden/Durant/Conley 5.00 12.00
2007B Noah/Horford/Brewer 4.00 10.00

2007-08 Fleer Hot Prospects Double Scribble

PRINT RUN 25 SER.#'d SETS
AR L.Aldridge/B.Roy 30.00 60.00
BN S.Nash/K.Bryant 150.00 400.00
FG T.Ford/D.Gibson 10.00 25.00
FL K.Lowry/R.Foye 12.00 30.00
GB D.Gibson/S.Brown 10.00 25.00
GR B.Gordon/R.Rondo 20.00 50.00
GT T.Thomas/H.Grant 50.00 100.00
HA D.Howard/J.Augustine 15.00 40.00
JJ L.James/M.Jordan 4,000.00 8,000.00
JP J.Jack/M.Price 12.00 30.00
PD T.Prince/A.Dantley 12.50 30.00
RC M.Collins/Q.Richardson 10.00 25.00
WB D.Brown/D.Williams 12.50 30.00

2007-08 Fleer Hot Prospects Draft Day Postmarks

PRINT RUN 50 SER.#'d SETS
AA Arron Afflalo 5.00 12.00
AB Aaron Brooks 5.00 12.00
AG Aaron Gray 4.00 10.00
AH Al Horford 15.00 40.00
AL Acie Law 4.00 10.00
AT Al Thornton 4.00 10.00
CB Corey Brewer 5.00 12.00
CL Carl Landry 4.00 10.00
CR Chris Richard 4.00 10.00
DA Jermareo Davidson 4.00 10.00
DB Derrick Byars 4.00 10.00
DC Daequan Cook 8.00 20.00
DN Demetris Nichols 4.00 10.00
DS D.J. Strawberry 4.00 10.00
GD Glen Davis 5.00 12.00
GP Gabe Pruitt 4.00 10.00
HA Adam Haluska 4.00 10.00
JC Javaris Crittenton 4.00 10.00
JC JamesOn Curry 4.00 10.00
JD Jared Dudley 5.00 12.00
JG Jeff Green 12.50 30.00
JM Josh McRoberts 4.00 10.00
JN Joakim Noah 30.00 80.00
JW Julian Wright 8.00 20.00
KD Kevin Durant 500.00 1,000.00
MA Morris Almond 4.00 10.00
MC Mike Conley Jr. 12.50 30.00
MW Marcus Williams 4.00 10.00
NF Nick Fazekas 4.00 10.00
RS Ramon Sessions 6.00 15.00
SH Spencer Hawes 4.00 10.00
SL Stephane Lasme 4.00 10.00
SM Sammy Mejia 4.00 10.00
SW Sean Williams 4.00 10.00
TG Taurean Green 4.00 10.00
TU Alando Tucker 4.00 10.00
WC Wilson Chandler 5.00 12.00
KDP Kevin Durant PROMO 15.00 40.00

2007-08 Fleer Hot Prospects Hot Materials

APPROXIMATE ODDS ONE PER RETAIL BOX
*RED: .75X TO 2X BASE HI
RED PRINT RUN 25 SER.#'d SETS
AH Al Horford 6.00 15.00
AS Amare Stoudemire 2.50 6.00
BL Bill Laimbeer 2.00 5.00
BR Bill Russell 20.00 50.00
CB Corey Brewer 2.00 5.00
CD Clyde Drexler 4.00 10.00
CM Corey Maggette 2.00 5.00
DM Donyell Marshall 2.00 5.00
DN Dirk Nowitzki 6.00 15.00
EB Elton Brand 2.00 5.00
GH Grant Hill 5.00 12.00
HG Horace Grant 2.50 6.00
JE Julius Erving 6.00 15.00
JK Jason Kidd 4.00 10.00
JN Joakim Noah 2.50 6.00
JO Jermaine O'Neal 2.50 6.00
JR Jason Richardson 2.50 6.00
JS John Stockton 5.00 12.00
JT Jamaal Tinsley 2.00 5.00
JW Julian Wright 1.50 4.00
KB Kobe Bryant 60.00 150.00
KD Kevin Durant 40.00 100.00
KG Kevin Garnett 6.00 15.00
LH Larry Hughes 2.00 5.00
LJ LeBron James 6.00 15.00
MC Mike Conley Jr. 6.00 15.00
MP Morris Peterson 1.50 4.00
N Nene 2.00 5.00
RA Ray Allen 4.00 10.00
RL Rashard Lewis 2.00 5.00
RW Rasheed Wallace 3.00 8.00
SM Shawn Marion 2.50 6.00
TC Tyson Chandler 2.50 6.00
TD Tim Duncan 6.00 15.00
TP Tony Parker 4.00 10.00
ZI Zydrunas Ilgauskas 2.00 5.00

2007-08 Fleer Hot Prospects NBA Game Issue

PRINT RUN 99 SER.#'d SETS
*RED: .75X TO 2X BASE HI
RED PRINT RUN 25 SER.#'d SETS
AI Allen Iverson 5.00 12.00
BH Brendan Haywood 3.00 8.00
BL Bill Laimbeer 4.00 10.00
CA Carmelo Anthony 4.00 10.00
CD Clyde Drexler 5.00 12.00
DR David Robinson 8.00 20.00
EB Elton Brand 3.00 8.00
GH Grant Hill 8.00 20.00
HG Horace Grant 3.00 8.00
JE Julius Erving 5.00 12.00
JK Jason Kidd 3.00 8.00

O Jermaine O'Neal 3.00 8.00
S John Stockton 5.00 12.00
3 Kobe Bryant 75.00 200.00
G Kevin Garnett 6.00 15.00
J LeBron James 20.00 50.00
J Michael Jordan 75.00 200.00
A Ray Allen 4.00 10.00
H Richard Hamilton 3.00 8.00
D Tim Duncan 4.00 10.00

2007-08 Fleer Hot Prospects Notable Newcomers

COMPLETE SET (20) 15.00 40.00
APPROXIMATELY TWO PER BOX
N-1 Kevin Durant 20.00 50.00
Joakim Noah 1.00 2.50
Al Horford 2.50 6.00
Corey Brewer .75 2.00
Julian Wright .60 1.50
Mike Conley Jr. 2.50 6.00
Jeff Green .75 2.00
Rodney Stuckey .60 1.50
Spencer Hawes .60 1.50
0 Acie Law .60 1.50
1 Al Thornton .60 1.50
2 Arron Afflalo .75 2.00
3 Marco Belinelli .75 2.00
4 Alando Tucker .60 1.50
5 Aaron Brooks .75 2.00
6 Javaris Crittenton .60 1.50
7 Wilson Chandler .75 2.00
8 Sun Yue 1.00 2.50
9 Taurean Green .60 1.50
20 D.J. Strawberry .60 1.50

2007-08 Fleer Hot Prospects Notable Notations

PRINT RUN 24 TO 50 SER.#'d SETS
*RED: .5X TO 1.25X BASE HI
RED PRINT RUN 25 SER.#'d SETS
AM Alonzo Mourning/50 20.00 50.00
BD Baron Davis/50 6.00 15.00
BL Bill Laimbeer/50 10.00 25.00
DM Dan Majerle/50 15.00 40.00
DR Dennis Rodman/50 25.00 50.00
DT David Thompson/50 6.00 15.00
DW Slick Watts/50 6.00 15.00
HO Hakeem Olajuwon/50 15.00 40.00
JW Jamaal Wilkes/50 6.00 15.00
KB Kobe Bryant/24 150.00 400.00
LB Leandro Barbosa/50 6.00 15.00
LJ LeBron James/50 1,500.00 3,000.00
MP Morris Peterson/25 6.00 15.00
SM Sidney Moncrief/50 10.00 25.00
SP Sam Perkins/50 6.00 15.00
VC Vince Carter/48 15.00 40.00

2007-08 Fleer Hot Prospects Property of

STATED PRINT RUN 149 SER.#'d SETS
*RED: .75X TO 2X BASE HI
RED PRINT RUN 25 SER.#'d SETS
AB Andrew Bogut 2.50 6.00
AK Andrei Kirilenko 2.50 6.00
AS Amare Stoudemire 3.00 8.00
BB Bruce Bowen 2.00 5.00
BR Elton Brand 2.50 6.00
CB Chauncey Billups 4.00 10.00
CF Channing Frye 2.00 5.00
CW Chris Wilcox 2.00 5.00
DB Devin Harris 2.00 5.00
DG Danny Granger 2.00 5.00
DH Dwight Howard 4.00 10.00
DM Desmond Mason 2.00 5.00
DN Dirk Nowitzki 8.00 20.00
DR David Robinson 6.00 15.00
DW Delonte West 2.00 5.00
EJ Eddie Jones 3.00 8.00
GW Gerald Wallace 2.50 6.00
JF Jordan Farmar 2.00 5.00
JM Jamaal Magloire 2.00 5.00
JR Jalen Rose 2.50 6.00
JT Jason Terry 2.50 6.00
KG Kevin Garnett 8.00 20.00
KH Kirk Hinrich 3.00 8.00
LD Luol Deng 2.50 6.00
LJ LeBron James 8.00 20.00
MD Mike Dunleavy 2.00 5.00
MG Manu Ginobili 6.00 15.00
MR Michael Redd 2.50 6.00
PG Pau Gasol 5.00 12.00
PP Paul Pierce 5.00 12.00
PS Peja Stojakovic 2.50 6.00
RA Ron Artest 3.00 8.00
RH Richard Hamilton 4.00 10.00
RJ Richard Jefferson 2.50 6.00
RL Rashard Lewis 2.50 6.00
SB Shane Battier 2.50 6.00
SF Steve Francis 2.50 6.00
SL Shaun Livingston 2.50 6.00
SM Shawn Marion 3.00 8.00
ZI Zydrunas Ilgauskas 2.50 6.00

2007-08 Fleer Hot Prospects Rookie Materials Autographs

AA Arron Afflalo 6.00 15.00
AB Aaron Brooks 6.00 15.00
AG Aaron Gray 5.00 12.00
AH Adam Haluska 5.00 12.00
AL Acie Law 5.00 12.00
AT Al Thornton 5.00 12.00
CB Corey Brewer 6.00 15.00
CL Carl Landry 5.00 12.00
CR Chris Richard 5.00 12.00
DA Jermareo Davidson 5.00 12.00
DB Derrick Byars 5.00 12.00
DM Dominic McGuire 5.00 12.00
GD Glen Davis 6.00 15.00
GP Gabe Pruitt 5.00 12.00
HO Al Horford 20.00 50.00
JA Javaris Crittenton 5.00 12.00
JD Jared Dudley 6.00 15.00
JG Jeff Green 6.00 15.00
JJ Jared Jordan 5.00 12.00
JM Josh McRoberts 5.00 12.00
JN Joakim Noah 8.00 20.00
JS Jason Smith 5.00 12.00
JW Julian Wright 5.00 12.00
KD Kevin Durant 400.00 800.00
MA Morris Almond 5.00 12.00
MB Marco Belinelli 6.00 15.00
MC Mike Conley Jr. 20.00 50.00
MW Marcus Williams 5.00 12.00
NF Nick Fazekas 5.00 12.00
RS Rodney Stuckey 5.00 12.00
RT Reyshawn Terry 5.00 12.00
SH Spencer Hawes 5.00 12.00
SL Stephane Lasme 5.00 12.00
SW Sean Williams 5.00 12.00
TU Alando Tucker 5.00 12.00
WC Wilson Chandler 6.00 15.00

2007-08 Fleer Hot Prospects Rookie Photo Shoot Postmarks

STATED PRINT RUN 50 SER.#'d SETS
AA Arron Afflalo 5.00 12.00
AB Aaron Brooks 5.00 12.00
AG Aaron Gray 4.00 10.00
AH Al Horford 15.00 40.00
AL Acie Law 4.00 10.00
AT Al Thornton 4.00 10.00
CB Corey Brewer 5.00 12.00
CL Carl Landry 4.00 10.00
CR Chris Richard 4.00 10.00
DA Jermareo Davidson 4.00 10.00
DB Derrick Byars 4.00 10.00
DC Daequan Cook 5.00 12.00
DN Demetris Nichols 4.00 10.00
DS D.J. Strawberry 4.00 10.00
GD Glen Davis 5.00 12.00
GP Gabe Pruitt 4.00 10.00
HA Adam Haluska 4.00 10.00
JC Javaris Crittenton 4.00 10.00
JC JamesOn Curry 4.00 10.00
JD Jared Dudley 5.00 12.00
JG Jeff Green 12.50 30.00
JM Josh McRoberts 4.00 10.00
JN Joakim Noah 30.00 80.00
JW Julian Wright 8.00 20.00
KD Kevin Durant 175.00 350.00
MA Morris Almond 4.00 10.00
MC Mike Conley Jr. 12.50 30.00
MW Marcus Williams 4.00 10.00
NF Nick Fazekas 4.00 10.00
RS Ramon Sessions 15.00 40.00
SH Spencer Hawes 4.00 10.00
SL Stephane Lasme 4.00 10.00
SM Sammy Mejia 4.00 10.00
SW Sean Williams 4.00 10.00
TG Taurean Green 4.00 10.00
TU Alando Tucker 4.00 10.00
WC Wilson Chandler 5.00 12.00

2007-08 Fleer Hot Prospects Stat Tracker

COMPLETE SET (35) 20.00 40.00
APPROXIMATELY TWO PER BOX
ST1 A.C. Green .75 2.00
ST2 Adrian Dantley .60 1.50
ST3 Andre Miller .60 1.50
ST4 Andrea Bargnani .50 1.25
ST5 Antawn Jamison .60 1.50
ST6 Artis Gilmore .60 1.50
ST7 B.J. Armstrong .75 2.00
ST8 Baron Davis .60 1.50
ST9 Bill Laimbeer .60 1.50
ST10 Bill Russell 2.50 6.00
ST11 Bill Walton 1.00 2.50
ST12 Brandon Roy 1.00 2.50
ST13 Daniel Gibson .50 1.25
ST14 Dennis Rodman 2.00 5.00
ST15 Deron Williams .60 1.50
ST16 Donyell Marshall .50 1.25
ST17 Emeka Okafor .60 1.50
ST18 Hakeem Olajuwon 1.50 4.00
ST19 Jason Kidd 1.25 3.00
ST20 John Stockton 1.50 4.00
ST21 Kobe Bryant 6.00 15.00
ST22 Kobe Bryant 6.00 15.00
ST23 LeBron James 6.00 15.00
ST24 Magic Johnson 3.00 8.00
ST25 Mark Price .75 2.00
ST26 Michael Jordan 8.00 20.00
ST27 Michael Jordan 8.00 20.00
ST28 Paul Pierce 1.25 3.00
ST29 Robert Parish .75 2.00
ST30 Slick Watts .50 1.25
ST31 Steve Kerr 1.00 2.50
ST32 Steve Nash 1.50 4.00
ST33 Tom Chambers .75 2.00
ST34 Tyson Chandler .75 2.00
ST35 Vince Carter 1.50 4.00

2007-08 Fleer Hot Prospects Stat Tracker Jersey Autographs

PRINT RUN 23 TO 50 SER.#'d SETS
*RED: .5X TO 1.25X BASE HI
RED PRINT RUN 25 SER.#'d SETS
2 Adrian Dantley/50 6.00 15.00
4 Andrea Bargnani/37 6.00 15.00
5 Antawn Jamison/50 6.00 15.00
8 Baron Davis/50 6.00 15.00
10 Bill Russell/50 600.00 1,200.00
11 Bill Walton/50 10.00 25.00
12 Brandon Roy/50 12.00 30.00
13 Daniel Gibson/50 6.00 15.00
14 Dennis Rodman/50 30.00 60.00
15 Deron Williams/50 15.00 30.00
16 Donyell Marshall/50 6.00 15.00
17 Emeka Okafor/50 6.00 15.00
18 Hakeem Olajuwon/50 40.00 100.00
19 Jason Kidd/50 15.00 30.00
20 John Stockton/50 40.00 100.00
21 Kobe Bryant/50 1,000.00 2,000.00
22 Kobe Bryant/24 1,500.00 3,000.00
23 LeBron James/50 1,500.00 3,000.00
24 Magic Johnson/50 40.00 80.00
26 Michael Jordan/23 1,500.00 3,000.00
27 Michael Jordan/23 1,500.00 3,000.00
28 Paul Pierce/50 40.00 100.00
31 Steve Kerr/50 15.00 30.00
32 Steve Nash/50 40.00 100.00
33 Tom Chambers/50 10.00 25.00
34 Tyson Chandler/50 6.00 15.00
35 Vince Carter/50 40.00 100.00

2007-08 Fleer Hot Prospects Supreme Court

COMPLETE SET (30) 15.00 30.00
APPROXIMATELY TWO PER BOX
1 Shareef Abdur-Rahim .75 2.00
2 Leandro Barbosa .60 1.50
3 Rick Barry .60 1.50
4 Mike Bibby .75 2.00
5 Tom Chambers .75 2.00
6 Michael Cooper .75 2.00
7 Chuck Daly .75 2.00
8 Adrian Dantley .60 1.50
9 Brad Daugherty .60 1.50
10 Sean Elliott .60 1.50
11 Walt Frazier 1.25 3.00
12 A.C. Green .75 2.00
13 Connie Hawkins 1.00 2.50
14 Bobby Jackson .50 1.25
15 Antawn Jamison .60 1.50
SC-16 Michael Jordan 8.00 20.00
17 Steve Kerr 1.00 2.50
18 Jason Kidd 1.25 3.00
19 Dan Majerle .60 1.50
20 Donyell Marshall .50 1.25
21 Chris Mihm .50 1.25
22 Andre Miller .60 1.50
23 Don Nelson .60 1.50
24 Robert Parish .75 2.00
25 Tony Parker 1.25 3.00
26 Mark Price .75 2.00
27 Tayshaun Prince .75 2.00
28 Glen Rice .75 2.00
29 Dennis Scott .50 1.25
30 Jerry Sloan .75 2.00

2007-08 Fleer Hot Prospects Supreme Court Autographs

PRINT RUN 15 TO 25 SER.#'d SETS
AJ Antawn Jamison/25 6.00 15.00
AM Andre Miller/25 6.00 15.00
BJ Bobby Jackson/25 6.00 15.00
CH Connie Hawkins/25 15.00 30.00
JK Jason Kidd/25 15.00 30.00
LB Leandro Barbosa/25 6.00 15.00
MJ Michael Jordan/25 1,500.00 3,000.00
MP Mark Price/25 25.00 50.00
PR Tayshaun Prince/25 6.00 15.00
SA Shareef Abdur-Rahim/25 6.00 15.00
SK Steve Kerr/25 15.00 30.00
TC Tom Chambers/25 6.00 15.00
WF Walt Frazier/15 8.00 20.00

2002-03 Fleer Hot Shots

COMP.SET w/o SP's (168) 15.00 40.00
RC PRINT RUN 200 SETS UNLESS NOTED
RC CONTAIN SHOOTING SHIRT UNLESS NOTED
1 Shareef Abdur-Rahim .30 .75
2 Kedrick Brown .20 .50
3 Trenton Hassell .20 .50
4 Raef LaFrentz .20 .50
5 Donnell Harvey .20 .50
6 Danny Fortson .20 .50
7 Maurice Taylor .20 .50
8 Wang Zhizhi .30 .75
9 Malik Allen .20 .50
10 Tim Thomas .20 .50
11 Jason Kidd .50 1.25
12 Jamaal Magloire .20 .50
13 Grant Hill .50 1.25
14 Anfernee Hardaway .75 2.00
15 Bonzi Wells .20 .50
16 Malik Rose .20 .50
17 Antonio Davis .25 .60
18 John Stockton .60 1.50
19 Theo Ratliff .20 .50
20 Paul Pierce .50 1.25
21 Jalen Rose .25 .60
22 Eduardo Najera .25 .60
23 Chauncey Billups .30 .75
24 Antawn Jamison .30 .75
25 Jonathan Bender .20 .50
26 Rick Fox .25 .60
27 Brian Grant .20 .50
28 Kevin Garnett .75 2.00
29 Kenyon Martin .25 .60
30 Allan Houston .30 .75
31 Tracy McGrady .50 1.25
32 Stephon Marbury .40 1.00
33 Mike Bibby .30 .75
34 Predrag Drobnjak .20 .50
35 Lamond Murray .20 .50
36 Kwame Brown .20 .50
37 Glenn Robinson .30 .75
38 Antoine Walker .25 .60
39 Zydrunas Ilgauskas .25 .60
40 Clifford Robinson .30 .75
41 Dirk Nowitzki .75 2.00
42 Troy Murphy .25 .60
43 Al Harrington .25 .60
44 Shaquille O'Neal 1.25 3.00
45 Eddie House .20 .50
46 Troy Hudson .20 .50
47 Rodney Rogers .20 .50
48 Latrell Sprewell .30 .75
49 Allen Iverson .75 2.00
50 Derek Anderson .20 .50
51 Vlade Divac .25 .60
52 Rashard Lewis .25 .60
53 Morris Peterson .25 .60
54 Jerry Stackhouse .30 .75
55 Jason Terry .25 .60
56 Tyson Chandler .30 .75
57 Jumaine Jones .25 .60
58 Nick Van Exel .30 .75
59 Ben Wallace .40 1.00
60 Jason Richardson .30 .75
61 Ron Mercer .20 .50
62 Shane Battier .30 .75
63 Eddie Jones .30 .75
64 Joe Smith .25 .60
65 Courtney Alexander .20 .50
66 Kurt Thomas .20 .50
67 Todd MacCulloch .20 .50
68 Ruben Patterson .20 .50
69 Tim Duncan .75 2.00
70 Gary Payton .50 1.25
71 Jarron Collins .20 .50
72 Vin Baker .25 .60
73 Eddy Curry .20 .50
74 Michael Finley .30 .75
75 Marcus Camby .25 .60
76 Corliss Williamson .20 .50
77 Steve Francis .30 .75
78 Jermaine O'Neal .25 .60
79 Michael Dickerson .20 .50
80 Alonzo Mourning .50 1.25
81 Rod Strickland .20 .50
82 Elden Campbell .20 .50
83 Charlie Ward .20 .50
84 Aaron McKie .20 .50
85 Scottie Pippen .75 2.00
86 Tony Parker .50 1.25
87 Vladimir Radmanovic .20 .50
88 Matt Harpring .20 .50
89 Eddie Griffin .20 .50
90 Michael Olowokandi .20 .50
91 Stromile Swift .20 .50
92 Michael Redd .25 .60
93 Richard Jefferson .25 .60
94 Baron Davis .30 .75
95 Pat Garrity .20 .50
96 Tom Gugliotta .20 .50
97 Arvydas Sabonis .25 .60
98 David Robinson .60 1.50
99 Michael Bradley .20 .50
100 Karl Malone .60 1.50
101 J.Terry/G.Robinson .30 .75
102 T.Delk/P.Pierce .50 1.25
103 J.Rose/M. Fizer .25 .60
104 D.Miles/R.Davis .25 .60
105 S.Nash/D.Nowitzki .75 2.00
106 K.Satterfield/J.Howard .25 .60
107 R.Hamilton/B.Wallace .40 1.00
108 G.Arenas/A.Jamison .30 .75
109 M.Norris/C.Mobley .20 .50
110 J.Tinsley/R.Miller .60 1.50
111 A.Miller/L.Odom .30 .75
112 D.Fisher/K.Bryant 2.50 6.00
113 J.Williams/S.Battier .40 1.00
114 T.Best/E.Jones .30 .75
115 S.Cassell/R.Allen .50 1.25
116 T.Brandon/W.Szczerbiak .25 .60
117 K.Kittles/R.Jefferson .25 .60
118 D.Wesley/J.Mashburn .25 .60
119 L.Sprewell/A.McDyess .30 .75
120 D.Armstrong/M.Miller .25 .60
121 E.Snow/K.Van Horn .20 .50
122 S.Marbury/S.Marion .40 1.00
123 D.Stoudamire/R.Wallace .40 1.00
124 M.Bibby/C.Webber .40 1.00
125 T.Parker/D.Robinson .60 1.50
126 K.Anderson/R.Lewis .25 .60
127 A.Williams/V.Carter .60 1.50
128 J.Stockton/K.Malone .60 1.50
129 L.Hughes/M.Jordan 3.00 8.00
130 Joe Johnson AS .25 .60
131 Andrei Kirilenko AS .25 .60
132 Brendan Haywood AS .20 .50
133 Zeljko Rebraca AS .20 .50
134 Quentin Richardson AS .20 .50
135 Chris Mihm AS .20 .50
136 Darius Miles AS .20 .50
137 Desmond Mason AS .20 .50
138 Hedo Turkoglu AS .25 .60
139 Jason Richardson AS .30 .75
140 Gerald Wallace AS .25 .60
141 Steve Francis AS .30 .75
142 Steve Nash AS .60 1.50
143 Peja Stojakovic AS .25 .60
144 Ray Allen AS .50 1.25
145 Mike Miller AS .25 .60
146 Pau Gasol AS .50 1.25
147 Steve Smith AS .25 .60
148 Paul Pierce AS .50 1.25
149 Derek Fisher AS .30 .75
150 Cuttino Mobley AS .25 .60
151 Dikembe Mutombo AS .50 1.25
152 Vince Carter AS .60 1.50
153 Antoine Walker AS .25 .60
154 Allen Iverson AS .75 2.00
155 Michael Jordan AS 3.00 8.00
156 Shaquille O'Neal AS 1.25 3.00
157 Tim Duncan AS .75 2.00
158 Kevin Garnett AS .75 2.00
159 Kobe Bryant AS 2.50 6.00
160 Shareef Abdur-Rahim AS .30 .75
161 Baron Davis AS .30 .75
162 Jason Kidd AS .50 1.25
163 Tracy McGrady AS .50 1.25
164 Jermaine O'Neal AS .25 .60
165 Elton Brand AS .25 .60
166 Gary Payton AS .50 1.25
167 Wally Szczerbiak AS .25 .60
168 Chris Webber AS .40 1.00
169 Yao Ming JSY/350 RC 20.00 50.00
170 Fred Jones/350 RC 3.00 8.00
171 Ryan Humphrey RC 3.00 8.00
172 Drew Gooden Hat/300 RC 4.00 10.00
173 Nikoloz Tskitishvili RC 2.50 6.00
174 Caron Butler Shorts/350 RC 4.00 10.00
175 Vincent Yarbrough RC 2.50 6.00
176 DaJuan Wagner RC 3.00 8.00
177 Nene Hilario RC 4.00 10.00
178 Qyntel Woods/350 RC 2.50 6.00
179 Jared Jeffries RC 3.00 8.00
180 Casey Jacobsen RC 3.00 8.00
181 Marcus Haislip Hat/300 RC 2.50 6.00
182 Kareem Rush/350 RC 3.00 8.00
183 Predrag Savovic RC 3.00 8.00
184 Melvin Ely RC 3.00 8.00
185 Amare Stoudemire RC 10.00 25.00
186 John Salmons RC 4.00 10.00
187 Chris Jefferies RC 2.50 6.00
188 Juan Dixon RC 3.00 8.00
189 Carlos Boozer RC 4.00 10.00
190 Roger Mason/350 RC 3.00 8.00
191 Ronald Murray/350 RC 4.00 10.00
192 Tayshaun Prince RC 8.00 20.00
193 Chris Wilcox/350 RC 3.00 8.00
194 Sam Clancy RC 3.00 8.00
195 Dan Gadzuric RC 3.00 8.00
196 D.Dickau RC/Carter JSY 4.00 10.00
197 F.Williams RC/Carter JSY 4.00 10.00
198 Dunleavy RC/VC JSY/350 5.00 12.00
199 J.Will RC/Carter JSY/350 5.00 12.00
200 Borchardt RC/VC JSY/350 4.00 10.00
201 Giricek RC/Carter JSY/350 4.00 10.00
202 Pat Burke RC 1.50 4.00
203 Reggie Evans RC 2.00 5.00
204 Rasual Butler RC 2.00 5.00
205 Jiri Welsch RC 2.00 5.00
206 Mehmet Okur RC 2.50 6.00
207 Jannero Pargo RC 1.50 4.00

2002-03 Fleer Hot Shots Hot Hands

*STARS: 3X TO 8X BASE CARD HI
PRINT RUN 199 SERIAL #'d SETS
*RCs 168-201: .5X TO 1.25X BASE CARD HI
*RCs 202-207: .75X TO 2X BASE HI
169-207 PRINT RUN 99 SER.#'d SETS
CARDS DO NOT CONTAIN MEMORABILIA

2002-03 Fleer Hot Shots Rookie Hats Off

*HATS OFF: .4X TO 1X BASE RC HI
CARDS CONTAIN HAT UNLESS NOTED
SKIP NUMBERED SET
PRINT RUN 150 SETS UNLESS NOTED

2002-03 Fleer Hot Shots All-Stars Triple Game-Used

STATED PRINT RUN 25 SER.#'d SETS
1 Carter/T-Mac/Iverson 50.00 120.00
2 Kidd/Pierce/Davis 50.00 100.00
3 Pierce/Stojakovic/Allen 20.00 50.00
4 Gasol/J-Rich/Turkoglu 20.00 50.00
5 J.O'Neal/Mtmbo/A-Rahim 20.00 50.00
6 Szczb/Miller/Gasol 20.00 50.00
7 Brand/Garnett/Webber 75.00 150.00
8 Miles/Johnson/Kirilenko 20.00 50.00
9 Payton/Kidd/Nash 40.00 100.00
10 J-Rich/Mason/Francis 20.00 50.00

2002-03 Fleer Hot Shots En Fuego

COMPLETE SET (12) 6.00 15.00
STATED ODDS 1:12
1 Elton Brand .50 1.25
2 Allen Iverson 1.50 4.00
3 Tracy McGrady 1.00 2.50
4 Jason Richardson .60 1.50
5 Vince Carter 1.25 3.00
6 Karl Malone 1.25 3.00
7 Stephon Marbury .75 2.00
8 Shareef Abdur-Rahim .60 1.50
9 Steve Francis .60 1.50
10 Kenyon Martin .60 1.50
11 Shaquille O'Neal 2.50 6.00
12 Tim Duncan 1.50 4.00

2002-03 Fleer Hot Shots En Fuego Game-Used

*GOLD: .5X TO 1.25X GAME USED HI
GOLD PRINT RUN 150 SER.#'d SETS
AI Allen Iverson 8.00 20.00
EB Elton Brand Shorts 2.50 6.00
JR Jason Richardson 3.00 8.00
KM Kenyon Martin Shorts 3.00 8.00
KM Karl Malone 6.00 15.00
SA Shareef Abdur-Rahim 3.00 8.00
SF Steve Francis 3.00 8.00
SM Stephon Marbury 4.00 10.00
TM Tracy McGrady 5.00 12.00
VC Vince Carter 6.00 15.00

2002-03 Fleer Hot Shots Give and Go Game-Used

STATED PRINT RUN 50 SER.#'d SETS
101 Terry Jkt/G.Robinson Jkt 8.00 20.00
102 Delk Jsy/Pierce Jsy 10.00 25.00
103 Rose Jsy/Fizer Pants 8.00 20.00
104 Miles Jsy/R.Davis Jsy 8.00 20.00
105 Nash Jsy/Nowitzki Jsy 12.00 30.00
106 Satterfield Jsy/Howard Jsy 8.00 20.00
107 Hamilton Shirt/Wallace Jsy 8.00 20.00
108 Arenas Jkt/Jamison Pants 8.00 20.00
109 Norris Jsy/Mobley Jkt 8.00 20.00
110 Tinsley Jsy/R.Miller Jsy 10.00 25.00
111 A.Miller Jsy/Odom Jacket 8.00 20.00
113 J.Williams Jsy/Battier Jsy 12.00 30.00
114 Best Jsy/E.Jones Jsy 8.00 20.00
115 Cassell Shirt/R.Allen Shirt 10.00 25.00
116 T.Brandn Jsy/Szczerb Jsy 8.00 20.00
117 Kittles Jkt/R.Jeffrsn Shts 8.00 20.00
118 Wesley Jsy/Mashburn Jsy 8.00 20.00
119 Spree Shrts/McDyes Jsy 8.00 20.00
120 Armstrong Jsy/M.Miller Jsy 8.00 20.00
121 Snow Jkt/Van Horn Pants 8.00 20.00
122 Marbury Jsy/Marion Jsy 8.00 20.00
123 D-Stoud Jkt/R.Wallce Shrt 8.00 20.00
124 Bibby Jsy/Webber Jsy 10.00 25.00
125 Parker Jsy/D.Robinson Jsy 12.00 30.00
126 K.Andersn Jsy/R.Lewis Jsy 8.00 20.00
127 A.Williams Shirt/V.Carter Jsy 8.00 20.00
128 Stockton Jsy/Malone Jkt 12.00 30.00

2002-03 Fleer Hot Shots Hot Numbers

COMPLETE SET (20) 15.00 40.00
STATED ODDS 1:20
GOLD PRINT RUN 350 SER.#'d SETS
HN1 Vince Carter 1.50 4.00
HN2 Gary Payton 1.25 3.00
HN3 Jason Kidd 1.25 3.00
HN4 Kevin Garnett 2.00 5.00
HN5 Pau Gasol 1.25 3.00
HN6 Darius Miles .50 1.25
HN7 Richard Jefferson .60 1.50
HN8 Corey Maggette .60 1.50
HN9 Kwame Brown .50 1.25
HN10 Antoine Walker .60 1.50
HN11 Shane Battier .75 2.00
HN12 Eddie Jones .75 2.00
HN13 Shawn Marion .75 2.00
HN14 Mike Bibby .75 2.00
HN15 Grant Hill 1.25 3.00
HN16 John Stockton 1.50 4.00
HN17 Lamar Odom .75 2.00
HN18 Keith Van Horn .60 1.50
HN19 Kobe Bryant 6.00 15.00
HN20 Michael Jordan 8.00 20.00

2002-03 Fleer Hot Shots Hot Numbers Game-Used

STATED PRINT RUN 50 SER.#'d SETS
DM Darius Miles 3.00 8.00
JK Jason Kidd 8.00 20.00
KB Kwame Brown 3.00 8.00
KG Kevin Garnett 12.00 30.00
VC Vince Carter 12.00 30.00

2002-03 Fleer Hot Shots Hot Shots Inserts

COMPLETE SET (12) 10.00 25.00
STATED ODDS 1:8
1 Juan Dixon .60 1.50
2 Yao Ming 4.00 10.00
3 Caron Butler .75 2.00
4 Kareem Rush .60 1.50
5 Nene Hilario .75 2.00
6 Jay Williams .60 1.50
7 Jared Jeffries .60 1.50
8 Amare Stoudemire 2.00 5.00
9 Carlos Boozer .75 2.00
10 Drew Gooden .75 2.00
11 DaJuan Wagner .60 1.50
12 Mike Dunleavy .75 2.00

2002-03 Fleer Hot Shots Hot Shots Inserts Game-Used

SWATCHES ARE SHIRT UNLESS NOTED
*GOLD: .75X TO 2X GAME USED HI
GOLD PRINT RUN 150 SER.#'d SETS
AS Amare Stoudemire 6.00 15.00
CB Caron Butler 2.50 6.00
CB Carlos Boozer 2.50 6.00
DG Drew Gooden 2.50 6.00
DW Dajuan Wagner 2.00 5.00
JD Juan Dixon 2.00 5.00
JJ Jared Jeffries 2.00 5.00
KR Kareem Rush 2.00 5.00
NH Nene Hilario 2.00 5.00
YM Yao Ming Jsy 12.00 30.00

2002-03 Fleer Hot Shots Net Burners

COMPLETE SET (10) 8.00 20.00
STATED ODDS 1:24
1 Ray Allen 1.50 4.00
2 Peja Stojakovic .75 2.00
3 Reggie Miller 2.00 5.00
4 Dirk Nowitzki 2.50 6.00
5 Paul Pierce 1.50 4.00
6 Baron Davis 1.00 2.50
7 Steve Nash 2.00 5.00
8 Latrell Sprewell 1.00 2.50
9 Jermaine O'Neal .75 2.00
12 David Robinson 2.00 5.00

2002-03 Fleer Hot Shots Net Burners Game-Used

STATED PRINT RUN 100 SER.#'d SETS
BW Ben Wallace JSY 6.00 15.00
CB Caron Butler Shorts 5.00 12.00
DN Dirk Nowitzki JSY 12.00 30.00
JS Jerry Stackhouse JSY 5.00 12.00
PP Paul Pierce JSY 8.00 20.00

2002-03 Fleer Hot Shots Net Burners Gold

STATED PRINT RUN 105 SER.#'d SETS
1 Michael Finley 3.00 8.00
2 Ben Wallace 4.00 10.00
3 Jerry Stackhouse 3.00 8.00
4 Antawn Jamison 2.50 6.00
5 Jay Williams 2.50 6.00
6 Yao Ming 15.00 40.00
7 Drew Gooden 3.00 8.00
8 Amare Stoudemire 8.00 20.00
9 Caron Butler 3.00 8.00
10 Mike Dunleavy 3.00 8.00

2000-01 Fleer Legacy

COMP.SET w/o SP's (90) 20.00 50.00
91-115 PRINT RUN 799 SERIAL #'d SETS
1 Vince Carter .75 2.00
2 Tim Duncan 1.00 2.50
3 Darrell Armstrong .25 .60
4 Chauncey Billups .50 1.25
5 Shawn Kemp .60 1.50
6 Stephon Marbury .50 1.25
7 Dan Majerle .40 1.00
8 Antawn Jamison .40 1.00
9 Hakeem Olajuwon .75 2.00
10 Kobe Bryant 3.00 8.00
11 Paul Pierce .60 1.50
12 Patrick Ewing .60 1.50
13 Steve Francis .40 1.00
14 Latrell Sprewell .50 1.25
15 Andre Miller .30 .75
16 Gary Payton .60 1.50
17 Michael Finley .40 1.00
18 Brian Grant .30 .75
19 Scottie Pippen 1.00 2.50
20 Antonio Davis .30 .75
21 Jason Williams .60 1.50
22 Chris Gatling .25 .60
23 David Robinson .75 2.00
24 John Stockton .75 2.00
25 Matt Harpring .25 .60
26 Rashard Lewis .30 .75
27 Dirk Nowitzki 1.00 2.50
28 Alan Henderson .25 .60
29 Rasheed Wallace .50 1.25
30 Ben Wallace .50 1.25
31 Chris Webber .50 1.25
32 Elton Brand .40 1.00
33 Anfernee Hardaway .60 1.50
34 Isaiah Rider .30 .75
35 Baron Davis .40 1.00
36 Eric Snow .25 .60
37 Tom Gugliotta .25 .60
38 Grant Hill .60 1.50
39 Lamar Odom .40 1.00
40 Kevin Garnett 1.00 2.50
41 Reggie Miller .75 2.00
42 Gary Payton .75 2.00
43 Ray Allen .60 1.50
44 Derek Anderson .30 .75
45 Glen Rice .40 1.00
46 Antonio McDyess .30 .75
47 Eddie Jones .40 1.00
48 Mitch Richmond .50 1.25
49 Mark Jackson .30 .75
50 Larry Johnson .50 1.25
51 Ron Mercer .30 .75
52 Jason Kidd .60 1.50
53 Voshon Lenard .25 .60
54 Rick Fox .30 .75
55 Rod Strickland .25 .60
56 Jalen Rose .30 .75
57 Tracy McGrady .75 2.00
58 Dikembe Mutombo .60 1.50
59 Richard Hamilton .50 1.25
60 Jerry Stackhouse .40 1.00
61 Peja Stojakovic .30 .75
62 Sam Cassell .30 .75
63 Sean Elliott .30 .75
64 Keith Van Horn .30 .75
65 Mike Bibby .40 1.00
66 Larry Hughes .40 1.00
67 Nick Van Exel .40 1.00
68 Michael Dickerson .25 .60
69 Terrell Brandon .30 .75
70 Chucky Atkins .25 .60
71 John Starks .40 1.00
72 Glenn Robinson .40 1.00
73 Cuttino Mobley .30 .75
74 Shaquille O'Neal 1.50 4.00
75 Shareef Abdur-Rahim .40 1.00
76 Danny Fortson .30 .75
77 Austin Croshere .25 .60
78 Jamal Mashburn .30 .75
79 Kenny Anderson .30 .75
80 Shawn Marion .40 1.00
81 Travis Best .25 .60
82 Derrick Coleman .30 .75
83 Toni Kukoc .50 1.25
84 Allen Iverson 1.00 2.50
85 Allan Houston .40 1.00
86 Antoine Walker .40 1.00
87 Wally Szczerbiak .30 .75
88 Raef LaFrentz .30 .75
89 Tim Hardaway .50 1.25
90 Juwan Howard .30 .75
91 Kenyon Martin JSY RC 6.00 15.00
92 Stromile Swift RC 1.50 4.00
93 Darius Miles JSY RC 3.00 8.00
94 Mike Miller JSY RC 5.00 12.00
95 Marcus Fizer RC 1.50 4.00
96 Jerome Moiso JSY RC 2.00 5.00
97 DerMarr Johnson JSY RC 2.00 5.00
98 Q.Richardson JSY RC 2.50 6.00
99 Morris Peterson JSY RC 3.00 8.00
100 Jamaal Magloire RC 2.00 5.00
101 Mateen Cleaves RC 1.50 4.00
102 Hedo Turkoglu RC 3.00 8.00
103 Chris Mihm JSY RC 2.00 5.00
104 Courtney Alexander RC 1.25 3.00
105 Joel Przybilla RC 1.50 4.00
106 Speedy Claxton JSY RC 3.00 8.00
107 Keyon Dooling JSY RC 2.50 6.00
108 Desmond Mason JSY RC 4.00 10.00
109 Jamal Crawford RC 5.00 12.00
110 DeShawn Stevenson RC 2.00 5.00
111 Stephen Jackson RC 4.00 10.00
112 Marc Jackson RC 1.50 4.00
113 Hanno Mottola JSY RC 2.00 5.00
114 Eduardo Najera RC 2.00 5.00
115 Wang Zhizhi RC 4.00 10.00
WUSA1 Vince Carter/600 30.00 80.00

2000-01 Fleer Legacy Ultimate Legacy

*STARS: 2.5X TO 6X BASE
*RCs: .6X TO 1.5X BASE
*JSY RCs: .4X TO 1X BASE
STATED PRINT RUN 175 SERIAL #'d SETS

2000-01 Fleer Legacy Ball Of Fame

STATED ODDS 1:40
BF1 Vince Carter 6.00 15.00
BF2 Kenyon Martin 6.00 15.00
BF3 Jason Williams 12.00 30.00
BF4 Ray Allen 5.00 12.00
BF5 Lamar Odom 3.00 8.00
BF6 Allen Iverson 8.00 20.00
BF7 Stephon Marbury 4.00 10.00
BF8 Tracy McGrady 6.00 15.00
BF9 Darius Miles 3.00 8.00
BF10 Steve Francis 3.00 8.00
BF11 Stromile Swift 2.50 6.00
BF12 Shawn Marion 3.00 8.00
BF13 Shawn Kemp 6.00 15.00
BF14 Larry Hughes 3.00 8.00
BF15 Baron Davis 3.00 8.00
BF16 Jalen Rose 2.50 6.00
BF17 Patrick Ewing 5.00 12.00
BF18 Karl Malone 6.00 15.00
BF19 Marcus Fizer 2.50 6.00
BF20 Wally Szczerbiak 2.50 6.00

2000-01 Fleer Legacy Floor Generals

STATED ODDS 1:18
FG1 Vince Carter 5.00 12.00
FG2 Allen Iverson 6.00 15.00
FG3 Chris Webber 3.00 8.00
FG4 Shaquille O'Neal 10.00 25.00
FG5 Reggie Miller 5.00 12.00
FG6 Tracy McGrady 5.00 12.00
FG7 David Robinson 5.00 12.00
FG8 Jason Kidd 4.00 10.00
FG9 Latrell Sprewell 3.00 8.00
FG10 Eddie Jones 2.50 6.00
FG11 Michael Finley 2.50 6.00
FG12 Jerry Stackhouse 2.50 6.00
FG13 Karl Malone 5.00 12.00
FG14 Anfernee Hardaway 4.00 10.00
FG15 Gary Payton 4.00 10.00
FG16 Shareef Abdur-Rahim 2.50 6.00
FG17 Tim Hardaway 3.00 8.00
FG18 Ray Allen 4.00 10.00
FG19 Stephon Marbury 3.00 8.00
FG20 John Stockton 5.00 12.00

2000-01 Fleer Legacy NBA Game Issue

STATED ODDS 1:15
GI1 Vince Carter 5.00 12.00
GI2 Baron Davis 2.50 6.00
GI3 Trajan Langdon 2.00 5.00
GI4 Grant Hill 4.00 10.00
GI5 Allen Iverson 8.00 20.00
GI6 Jason Kidd 4.00 10.00
GI7 Karl Malone 5.00 12.00
GI8 Stephon Marbury 3.00 8.00
GI9 Shawn Marion 2.50 6.00
GI10 Tracy McGrady 5.00 12.00
GI11 Andre Miller 2.00 5.00
GI12 Dikembe Mutombo 4.00 10.00
GI13 Lamar Odom 2.50 6.00
GI14 Shaquille O'Neal 10.00 25.00
GI15 Gary Payton 4.00 10.00
GI16 Jason Terry 2.50 6.00
GI17 John Stockton 5.00 12.00
GI18 Patrick Ewing 4.00 10.00
GI19 Anfernee Hardaway 4.00 10.00
GI20 Jason Williams 8.00 20.00
GI21 Darius Miles 2.50 6.00
GI22 Chris Mihm 1.50 4.00
GI23 Desmond Mason 3.00 8.00
GI24 Keyon Dooling 2.00 5.00
GI25 DerMarr Johnson 1.50 4.00
GI26 Speedy Claxton 2.50 6.00
GI27 Kenyon Martin 5.00 12.00
GI28 Hanno Mottola 1.50 4.00
GI29 Mike Miller 4.00 10.00
GI30 Quentin Richardson 2.00 5.00

2000-01 Fleer Legacy Replica Jersey Autographs

STATED ODDS ONE PER BOX
JERSEY ARJ29 DOES NOT EXIST
ARJ1 A.Mourning Black/250 75.00 150.00
ARJ2 A.Walker Green/250 25.00 60.00
ARJ3 C.Alexander Blue/375 20.00 50.00
ARJ4 D.Miles Red/300 20.00 50.00
ARJ5 D.Johnson Red/400 20.00 50.00
ARJ6 D.Mason Red/350 20.00 50.00
ARJ7 D.Mutombo Black/150 50.00 120.00
ARJ8 E.House Black/325 20.00 50.00
ARJ9 E.Jones Black/150 30.00 80.00
ARJ11 J.Crawford Black/400 25.00 60.00
ARJ12 J.Terry Red/500 20.00 50.00
ARJ13 K.Van Horn Black/100 25.00 60.00
ARJ14 K.Martin Blue/300 25.00 60.00
ARJ14A K.Martin Black/250 30.00 80.00
ARJ16 L.Hughes Black/250 20.00 50.00
ARJ17 M.Jackson Black/500 20.00 50.00
ARJ18 M.Camby Blue/400 25.00 60.00
ARJ19 M.Fizer Red/300 20.00 50.00
ARJ19A M.Fizer Black/100 25.00 60.00
ARJ20 M.Cleaves Blue/400 20.00 50.00
ARJ20A M.Cleaves Red/350 20.00 50.00
ARJ21 M.Bibby Black/250 20.00 50.00
ARJ22 P.Pierce Green/500 30.00 80.00
ARJ23 P.Stojakovic Black/150 30.00 80.00
ARJ23A P.Stojakovic Purple/150 30.00 80.00
ARJ24 R.LaFrentz Black/400 20.00 50.00
ARJ25 R.Artest Red/200 30.00 80.00
ARJ26 S.Marion Purple/400 25.00 60.00
ARJ28 S.Francis Blue/400 20.00 50.00
ARJ30 T.Gugliotta Purple/400 20.00 50.00
ARJ31 V.Carter Black/750 50.00 120.00
ARJ31A V.Carter White/250 75.00 150.00
ARJ32 W.Szczerbiak Blue/400 20.00 50.00
ARJ32A W.Szczerbiak Black/200 20.00 50.00

2001-02 Fleer Marquee

COMPLETE SET w/o SPs 12.50 30.00
101-115 PRINT RUN 1500 SER.#'d SETS
116-125 PRINT RUN 2500 SER.#'d SETS
1 DerMarr Johnson .25 .60
2 Darius Miles .25 .60
3 Michael Jordan 5.00 12.00
4 Speedy Claxton .25 .60
5 Stromile Swift .25 .60
6 Michael Finley .40 1.00
7 Kurt Thomas .25 .60
8 Tim Duncan 1.00 2.50
9 Kenyon Martin .40 1.00
10 Jermaine O'Neal .30 .75
11 Elton Brand .30 .75
12 Jamal Mashburn .30 .75
13 Jumaine Jones .25 .60
14 Stephon Marbury .50 1.25
15 Eddie Jones .40 1.00
16 Antonio McDyess .30 .75
17 Tim Thomas .25 .60
18 Gary Payton .60 1.50
19 Latrell Sprewell .50 1.25
20 Grant Hill .60 1.50
21 Jason Terry .40 1.00
22 Marcus Fizer .25 .60
23 Anthony Mason .40 1.00
24 Bonzi Wells .25 .60
25 Sam Cassell .30 .75
26 Jerry Stackhouse .40 1.00
27 Hedo Turkoglu .30 .75
28 Morris Peterson .25 .60
29 John Stockton .75 2.00
30 Dikembe Mutombo .60 1.50
31 Mitch Richmond .50 1.25
32 Andre Miller .30 .75
33 Joe Smith .30 .75
34 Mike Bibby .40 1.00
35 Wally Szczerbiak .30 .75
36 Steve Francis .40 1.00
37 Nazr Mohammed .25 .60
38 Antoine Walker .30 .75
39 Courtney Alexander .25 .60
40 Shawn Marion .40 1.00
41 Jason Williams .60 1.50
42 Steve Nash .75 2.00
43 Antonio Davis .30 .75
44 Steve Smith .30 .75
45 Jason Kidd .60 1.50
46 Reggie Miller .75 2.00
47 Quentin Richardson .25 .60
48 Baron Davis .40 1.00
49 Juwan Howard .30 .75
50 Rasheed Wallace .50 1.25
51 Brian Grant .25 .60
52 Nick Van Exel .40 1.00
53 Donyell Marshall .25 .60
54 Vin Baker .30 .75
55 Allan Houston .40 1.00
56 Mike Miller .30 .75
57 Shaquille O'Neal 1.50 4.00
58 Ron Mercer .25 .60
59 Lindsey Hunter .25 .60
60 Peja Stojakovic .30 .75
61 Ray Allen .60 1.50
62 Antawn Jamison .30 .75
63 Theo Ratliff .25 .60
64 Vince Carter .75 2.00
65 DeShawn Stevenson .25 .60
66 Allen Iverson 1.00 2.50
67 Derek Fisher .30 .75
68 Dirk Nowitzki 1.00 2.50
69 Keith Van Horn .30 .75
70 David Robinson .75 2.00
71 Terrell Brandon .30 .75
72 Cuttino Mobley .30 .75
73 Shareef Abdur-Rahim .30 .75
74 Paul Pierce .60 1.50
75 Elden Campbell .25 .60
76 Anfernee Hardaway 1.00 2.50
77 Alonzo Mourning .60 1.50
78 Raef LaFrentz .25 .60
79 Richard Hamilton .50 1.25
80 Rashard Lewis .30 .75
81 Marcus Camby .30 .75
82 Jalen Rose .30 .75
83 Lamar Odom .30 .75
84 David Wesley .25 .60
85 James Posey .25 .60
86 Derek Anderson .25 .60
87 Glenn Robinson .40 1.00
88 Clifford Robinson .40 1.00
89 Kerry Kittles .25 .60
90 Hakeem Olajuwon .75 2.00
91 Patrick Ewing .60 1.50
92 Tracy McGrady .60 1.50
93 Kobe Bryant 3.00 8.00
94 Chris Mihm .25 .60
95 Lorenzen Wright .25 .60
96 Chris Webber .50 1.25
97 Kevin Garnett 1.00 2.50
98 Larry Hughes .30 .75
99 Keyon Dooling .25 .60
100 Karl Malone .75 2.00
101 Joe Johnson RC 1.25 3.00
102 Tyson Chandler RC 1.25 3.00
103 Eddy Curry RC .75 2.00
104 Jason Richardson RC 1.25 3.00
105 Troy Murphy RC .60 1.50
106 Eddie Griffin RC .60 1.50
107 Jamaal Tinsley RC .60 1.50
108 Pau Gasol RC 3.00 8.00
109 Shane Battier RC 1.50 4.00
110 Richard Jefferson RC 1.00 2.50
111 Steven Hunter RC .50 1.25
112 Tony Parker RC 3.00 8.00
113 Vladimir Radmanovic RC .60 1.50
114 Andrei Kirilenko RC 1.25 3.00
115 Kwame Brown RC .75 2.00
116 S.Dalembert RC/D.Brown RC .75 2.00
117 J.Forte RC/Ke.Brown RC .50 1.25
118 Randolph RC/R.Boumtje RC 1.50 4.00
119 O.Torres RC/T.Morris RC .75 2.00
120 A.Ford RC/K.Satterfield RC .75 2.00
121 R.White RC/Z.Rebraca RC .75 2.00
122 T.Hassell RC/E.Watson RC .60 1.50
123 D.Diop RC/P.Brezec RC .75 2.00
124 E.Brown RC/G.Wallace RC 1.00 2.50
125 L.Woods RC/B.Haywood RC .60 1.50
126 Mengke Bateer RC 1.25 3.00
NNO Vince Carter AU/113 75.00 200.00

2001-02 Fleer Marquee Banner Season

COMPLETE SET (20) 30.00 80.00
STATED ODDS 1:20
1 Vince Carter 2.50 6.00
2 Shaquille O'Neal 5.00 12.00
3 Allen Iverson 3.00 8.00
4 Kevin Garnett 3.00 8.00
5 Dirk Nowitzki 3.00 8.00
6 Tim Duncan 3.00 8.00
7 Michael Jordan 15.00 40.00
8 Steve Francis 1.25 3.00
9 Grant Hill 2.00 5.00
10 Kobe Bryant 10.00 25.00
11 Kenyon Martin 1.25 3.00
12 Shareef Abdur-Rahim 1.00 2.50
13 Ray Allen 2.00 5.00
14 Tracy McGrady 2.00 5.00
15 Baron Davis 1.25 3.00
16 Chris Webber 1.50 4.00
17 Jason Kidd 2.00 5.00
18 Darius Miles .75 2.00
19 Paul Pierce 2.00 5.00
20 Karl Malone 2.50 6.00

2001-02 Fleer Marquee Banner Season Memorabilia

STATED ODDS 1:15
AI Allen Iverson 8.00 20.00
BD Baron Davis 3.00 8.00
CW Chris Webber 4.00 10.00
DM Darius Miles 2.00 5.00
DN Dirk Nowitzki 8.00 20.00
GH Grant Hill 5.00 12.00
JK Jason Kidd 5.00 12.00
KM Kenyon Martin 3.00 8.00
MM Karl Malone 6.00 15.00
PP Paul Pierce 5.00 12.00
RA Ray Allen 5.00 12.00
SF Steve Francis 3.00 8.00
SR Shareef Abdur-Rahim 2.50 6.00
TM Tracy McGrady 5.00 12.00
VC Vince Carter 6.00 15.00

2001-02 Fleer Marquee Co-Stars

STATED ODDS 1:10
1 M.Jordan/K.Brown 3.00 8.00
2 S.Francis/E.Griffin 1.00 2.50
3 T.McGrady/S.Hunter 1.25 3.00
4 K.Malone/A.Kirilenko 1.25 3.00
5 R.Miller/J.Tinsley 1.00 2.50
6 T.Parker/D.Robinson 2.50 6.00
7 S.Battier/P.Gasol 2.00 5.00
8 J.Kidd/R.Jefferson 1.25 3.00
9 A.Jamison/J.Richardson 1.00 2.50
10 R.Mercer/E.Curry 1.00 2.50

2001-02 Fleer Marquee Feature Presentation Film

PRINT RUN 350 SER.#'d SETS
1 Vince Carter 5.00 12.00
1A Vince Carter AU/208 25.00 50.00
2 Darius Miles 1.50 4.00
3 Jason Kidd 4.00 10.00
4 Grant Hill 4.00 10.00
5 Chris Webber 3.00 8.00
6 Dirk Nowitzki 6.00 15.00
7 Allen Iverson 6.00 15.00
8 Tracy McGrady 4.00 10.00
9 Steve Francis 2.50 6.00
10 Karl Malone 5.00 12.00
12 Kevin Garnett 6.00 15.00
13 Kobe Bryant 20.00 50.00
14 Tim Duncan 6.00 15.00
15 Shaquille O'Neal 10.00 25.00

2001-02 Fleer Marquee Feature Presentation Film/Jerseys

*FILM/JSY: 1X TO 2.5X BASE HI 4.00 10.00
PRINT RUN 250 SER.#'d SETS

2001-02 Fleer Marquee Feature Presentation Triples

PRINT RUN 100 SER.#'d SETS
4 Grant Hill 8.00 20.00
5 Chris Webber 12.00 30.00
7 Allen Iverson 12.00 30.00
11 Kevin Garnett 12.00 30.00

2001-02 Fleer Marquee We're Number One

STATED ODDS 1:240
1 Hakeem Olajuwon 5.00 12.00
2 David Robinson 5.00 12.00
3 Shaquille O'Neal 10.00 25.00
4 Chris Webber 3.00 8.00
5 Allen Iverson 6.00 15.00
6 Tim Duncan 6.00 15.00
7 Elton Brand 2.00 5.00
8 Kenyon Martin 2.50 6.00
9 Kwame Brown 2.50 6.00
10 Vince Carter 5.00 12.00
11 Larry Bird 10.00 25.00

2001-02 Fleer Marquee We're Number One Memorabilia

STATED ODDS 1:32
1 Hakeem Olajuwon 10.00 25.00
2 David Robinson 10.00 25.00
3 Allen Iverson 12.00 30.00
4 Elton Brand 4.00 10.00
5 Kenyon Martin 5.00 12.00
6 Kwame Brown 5.00 12.00
6A Kwame Brown AU/101 10.00 25.00
7 Vince Carter 10.00 25.00
7A Vince Carter AU/4 25.00 60.00
8 Larry Bird 20.00 50.00
8A Larry Bird AU/78 60.00 150.00

2001-02 Fleer Maximum

COMPLETE SET (220) 75.00 200.00
COMP.SET w/o SP's (180) 15.00 40.00
181-220 PRINT RUN 1000 SERIAL #'d SETS
1 Ray Allen .60 1.50
2 Elton Brand .30 .75
3 Grant Hill .60 1.50
4 Tracy McGrady .60 1.50
5 Chris Webber .50 1.25
6 Latrell Sprewell .50 1.25
7 Paul Pierce .60 1.50
8 Jason Kidd .60 1.50
9 Shaquille O'Neal 1.50 4.00
10 Stephon Marbury .50 1.25
11 Steve Francis .40 1.00
12 Vince Carter .75 2.00
13 Allen Iverson 1.00 2.50
14 Kevin Garnett 1.00 2.50
15 Eddie Jones .40 1.00
16 Antoine Walker .30 .75
17 Kobe Bryant 3.00 8.00
18 Avery Johnson .30 .75
19 Damon Stoudamire .40 1.00
20 Kurt Thomas .25 .60
21 Aaron McKie .25 .60
22 Chris Whitney .25 .60
23 David Robinson .75 2.00
24 Erick Dampier .25 .60
25 Jumaine Jones .25 .60
26 Radoslav Nesterovic .25 .60
27 Robert Horry .40 1.00
28 Ben Wallace .50 1.25
29 Christian Laettner .30 .75
30 Eddie Robinson .25 .60
31 Alvin Williams .25 .60
32 Matt Harpring .25 .60
33 Terrell Brandon .25 .60
34 Tim Duncan 1.00 2.50
35 Bonzi Wells .25 .60
36 Clarence Weatherspoon .25 .60
37 George McCloud .25 .60
38 Jermaine O'Neal .30 .75
39 Al Harrington .30 .75
40 Antawn Jamison .30 .75
41 John Amaechi .25 .60
42 Rod Strickland .25 .60
43 Stacey Augmon .25 .60
44 Dion Glover .25 .60
45 Michael Dickerson .25 .60
46 Anfernee Hardaway 1.00 2.50
47 Rashard Lewis .30 .75
48 Shawn Bradley .30 .75
49 Todd MacCulloch .25 .60
50 Antonio McDyess .30 .75
51 Darrell Armstrong .25 .60
52 Jalen Rose .30 .75
53 Mike Bibby .40 1.00
54 P.J. Brown .25 .60
55 Quincy Lewis .25 .60
56 Doug Christie .25 .60
57 Elden Campbell .25 .60
58 James Posey .25 .60
59 Karl Malone .75 2.00
60 Patrick Ewing .60 1.50
61 Sam Cassell .30 .75
62 Baron Davis .40 1.00
63 Corey Maggette .30 .75
64 Donyell Marshall .25 .60
65 Ervin Johnson .25 .60
66 Horace Grant .30 .75
67 Nick Van Exel .40 1.00
68 Vlade Divac .30 .75
69 Allan Houston .40 1.00
70 Antonio Davis .30 .75
71 Dale Davis .25 .60
72 Eduardo Najera .25 .60
73 Kenny Anderson .30 .75
74 Kevin Willis .25 .60
75 LaPhonso Ellis .30 .75
76 Anthony Mason .40 1.00
77 Greg Ostertag .25 .60
78 Jamal Mashburn .30 .75
79 Jeff McInnis .25 .60
80 Peja Stojakovic .30 .75
81 Scott Williams .25 .60
82 Bryon Russell .25 .60
83 Chucky Atkins .25 .60
84 Darius Miles .25 .60
85 David Wesley .25 .60
86 Hedo Turkoglu .30 .75
87 Mark Pope .25 .60
88 Dana Barros .25 .60
89 Glenn Robinson .40 1.00
90 John Stockton .75 2.00
91 Lamar Odom .30 .75
92 Mike Miller .30 .75
93 Ron Artest .30 .75
94 Adonal Foyle .25 .60
95 Andre Miller .30 .75
96 Eric Snow .30 .75
97 Stanislav Medvedenko .25 .60
98 Steve Smith .30 .75
99 Wally Szczerbiak .30 .75
100 Chris Mihm .25 .60
101 Danny Fortson .25 .60
102 Dikembe Mutombo .60 1.50
103 Joe Smith .30 .75
104 Lindsey Hunter .25 .60
105 Malik Rose .25 .60
106 Austin Croshere .25 .60
107 Chris Gatling .25 .60
108 Hakeem Olajuwon .75 2.00
109 Mark Jackson .30 .75
110 Milt Palacio .25 .60
111 Ruben Patterson .25 .60
112 Steve Nash .75 2.00
113 Brian Grant .25 .60
114 Dirk Nowitzki 1.00 2.50
115 Jeff Foster .25 .60
116 Morris Peterson .25 .60
117 Scottie Pippen 1.00 2.50
118 Lamond Murray .25 .60
119 Larry Hughes .30 .75
120 Shareef Abdur-Rahim .30 .75
121 Tony Delk .30 .75
122 Vin Baker .30 .75
123 Art Long .25 .60
124 Kenyon Martin .40 1.00
125 Michael Finley .40 1.00
126 Stromile Swift .25 .60
127 Toni Kukoc .50 1.25
128 Alonzo Mourning .60 1.50
129 Charlie Ward .25 .60
130 Eric Williams .25 .60
131 Jerome Williams .25 .60
132 Raef LaFrentz .25 .60
133 Rasheed Wallace .50 1.25
134 Reggie Miller .75 2.00
135 Cuttino Mobley .30 .75
136 Desmond Mason .30 .75
137 Jason Williams .60 1.50
138 Keith Van Horn .30 .75
139 Nazr Mohammed .25 .60
140 Shawn Marion .40 1.00
141 Tim Hardaway .50 1.25
142 Anthony Carter .25 .60
143 Danny Manning .30 .75
144 Derek Anderson .25 .60
145 Jason Terry .40 1.00
146 Kenny Thomas .25 .60
147 Othella Harrington .25 .60
148 Corliss Williamson .25 .60
149 Derek Fisher .30 .75
150 Ricky Davis .30 .75
151 Stephen Jackson .30 .75
152 Tryone Nesby .25 .60
153 Calvin Booth .25 .60
154 Emanual Davis .25 .60
155 Kerry Kittles .25 .60
156 Marc Jackson .25 .60
157 Samaki Walker .25 .60
158 Tom Gugliotta .25 .60
159 Wesley Person .25 .60
160 Antonio Daniels .25 .60
161 Charles Oakley .30 .75
162 Chauncey Billups .50 1.25
163 Derrick Coleman .30 .75
164 Jerry Stackhouse .40 1.00
165 Michael Jordan 4.00 10.00
166 Quentin Richardson .25 .60
167 Gary Payton .60 1.50
168 Iakovos Tsakalidis .25 .60
169 Juwan Howard .30 .75
170 Lorenzen Wright .25 .60
171 Marcus Camby .30 .75
172 Maurice Taylor .25 .60
173 Jacque Vaughn .25 .60
174 Bruce Bowen .25 .60
175 Clifford Robinson .40 1.00
176 Michael Olowokandi .25 .60
177 Richard Hamilton .50 1.25
178 Ron Mercer .25 .60
179 Speedy Claxton .25 .60
180 Tim Thomas .25 .60
181 Joe Johnson HW RC 1.50 4.00
182 Pau Gasol HW RC 4.00 10.00
183 Kwame Brown HW RC 1.00 2.50
184 Zach Randolph HW RC 2.00 5.00
185 Jason Richardson HW RC 1.50 4.00
186 Jamaal Tinsley HW RC .75 2.00
187 Oscar Torres HW RC 1.00 2.50
188 Rodney White HW RC .60 1.50
189 Kedrick Brown HW RC .60 1.50
190 Tony Parker HW RC 4.00 10.00
191 Samuel Dalembert HW RC 1.00 2.50
192 Shane Battier HW RC 2.00 5.00
193 Loren Woods HW RC .60 1.50
194 Richard Jefferson HW RC 1.25 3.00
195 Jeff Trepagnier HW RC .60 1.50
196 Terence Morris HW RC .60 1.50
197 Eddie Griffin TC RC .75 2.00
198 Primoz Brezec TC RC 1.00 2.50
199 V.Radmanovic TC RC .75 2.00
200 Gerald Wallace TC RC 1.25 3.00
201 Alton Ford TC RC 1.00 2.50
202 Steven Hunter TC RC .60 1.50
203 Michael Bradley TC RC .60 1.50
204 Brandon Armstrong TC RC .60 1.50
205 Jamaal Tinsley TC RC .75 2.00
206 Bobby Simmons TC RC 1.00 2.50
207 Zeljko Rebraca TC RC 1.00 2.50
208 Tony Parker TC RC 4.00 10.00
209 Troy Murphy TC RC .75 2.00
210 Kwame Brown TC RC 1.00 2.50
211 Andrei Kirilenko TC RC 1.50 4.00
212 Trenton Hassell TC RC .60 1.50
213 Pau Gasol TC RC 4.00 10.00
214 Tang Hamilton TC RC 1.00 2.50
215 Joseph Forte TC RC .60 1.50
216 Eddy Curry TC RC 1.00 2.50
217 DeSagana Diop TC RC .60 1.50
218 Joe Johnson TC RC 1.50 4.00
219 Tyson Chandler TC RC 1.50 4.00
220 Jason Collins TC RC .75 2.00
NNO Vince Carter AU/375 60.00 150.00

2001-02 Fleer Maximum Big Shots

COMPLETE SET (15) 8.00 20.00
STATED ODDS 1:8
1 Grant Hill 1.00 2.50
2 Ray Allen 1.00 2.50
3 Allen Iverson 1.50 4.00
4 Elton Brand .50 1.25
5 Baron Davis .60 1.50
6 Jason Terry .60 1.50
7 Mike Bibby .60 1.50
8 David Robinson 1.25 3.00
9 Paul Pierce 1.00 2.50
10 Dirk Nowitzki 1.50 4.00
11 Jerry Stackhouse .60 1.50
12 Shawn Marion .60 1.50
13 Tracy McGrady 1.00 2.50
14 Anfernee Hardaway 1.50 4.00
15 Vince Carter 1.25 3.00

2001-02 Fleer Maximum Big Shots Jerseys

STATED ODDS 1:20
1 Grant Hill 5.00 12.00
2 Allen Iverson 8.00 20.00
3 Elton Brand 2.50 6.00
4 Jason Terry 3.00 8.00
5 Mike Bibby 3.00 8.00
6 David Robinson 6.00 15.00
7 Paul Pierce 5.00 12.00
8 Shawn Marion 3.00 8.00
9 Tracy McGrady 5.00 12.00
10 Anfernee Hardaway 8.00 20.00
11 Vince Carter 6.00 15.00

2001-02 Fleer Maximum Floor Score

COMPLETE SET (15) 12.50 30.00
STATED ODDS 1:8
1 Jason Kidd 1.00 2.50
2 Lamar Odom .50 1.25
3 Baron Davis .60 1.50
4 Dirk Nowitzki 1.50 4.00
5 Ray Allen 1.00 2.50
6 Anfernee Hardaway 1.50 4.00
7 Latrell Sprewell .75 2.00
8 Chris Webber .75 2.00
9 Grant Hill 1.00 2.50
10 Vince Carter 1.25 3.00
11 Shaquille O'Neal 2.50 6.00
12 Michael Jordan 5.00 12.00
13 Kobe Bryant 5.00 12.00
14 Kevin Garnett 1.50 4.00
15 Tim Duncan 1.50 4.00

2001-02 Fleer Maximum Floor Score Court

STATED ODDS 1:40
1 Jason Kidd 5.00 12.00
2 Lamar Odom 2.50 6.00
3 Baron Davis 3.00 8.00
4 Dirk Nowitzki 8.00 20.00
5 Ray Allen 5.00 12.00
6 Anfernee Hardaway 8.00 20.00
7 Latrell Sprewell 4.00 10.00
8 Chris Webber 4.00 10.00
9 Grant Hill 5.00 12.00
10 Vince Carter 6.00 15.00

2001-02 Fleer Maximum Performance

STATED PRINT RUN 100 SER.#'d SETS
1 Vince Carter 10.00 25.00
2 Tracy McGrady 8.00 20.00
3 Kobe Bryant 40.00 100.00
4 Michael Jordan 40.00 100.00
5 Shaquille O'Neal 20.00 50.00
6 Allen Iverson 12.00 30.00
7 Grant Hill 8.00 20.00
8 Kevin Garnett 12.00 30.00
9 Steve Francis 5.00 12.00
10 Tim Duncan 12.00 30.00

2001-02 Fleer Maximum Power

COMPLETE SET (15) 15.00 40.00
STATED ODDS 1:16
1 Kobe Bryant 8.00 20.00
2 Michael Jordan 8.00 20.00
3 Shaquille O'Neal 4.00 10.00
4 Kevin Garnett 2.50 6.00
5 Tim Duncan 2.50 6.00
6 Jason Kidd 1.50 4.00
7 Richard Hamilton 1.25 3.00
8 Vince Carter 2.00 5.00
9 Alonzo Mourning 1.50 4.00
10 John Stockton 2.00 5.00
11 Elton Brand .75 2.00
12 Steve Francis 1.00 2.50
13 Keith Van Horn .75 2.00
14 Stephon Marbury 1.25 3.00
15 Darius Miles .60 1.50

2001-02 Fleer Maximum Power Warm-Ups

STATED ODDS 1:20
*GOLD: 2X TO 5X BASE HI
GOLD PRINT RUN 25 SER.#'d SETS
1 Jason Kidd 5.00 12.00
2 Richard Hamilton 4.00 10.00
3 Vince Carter 6.00 15.00
4 Alonzo Mourning 5.00 12.00
5 John Stockton 6.00 15.00
6 Elton Brand 2.50 6.00
7 Steve Francis 3.00 8.00
8 Keith Van Horn 2.50 6.00
9 Stephon Marbury 4.00 10.00
10 Darius Miles 2.00 5.00

2001-02 Fleer Maximum Two Point Shot Jersey/Floor

STATED PRINT RUN 25 SERIAL #'d SETS
1 Vince Carter 40.00 100.00
2 Elton Brand 15.00 40.00
3 Steve Francis 20.00 50.00
4 Jason Kidd 30.00 80.00
5 Allen Iverson 50.00 120.00
6 Tracy McGrady 30.00 80.00
7 Darius Miles 12.00 30.00
8 Paul Pierce 25.00 60.00

2007 Fleer Michael Jordan

COMPLETE SET (100) 25.00 60.00
COMMON CARD (1-100) .40 1.00

2007 Fleer Michael Jordan Award Winners

COMPLETE SET (20) 3.00 8.00
COMMON CARD .40 1.00

2007 Fleer Michael Jordan Playoff Highlights

COMPLETE SET (30) 6.00 15.00
COMMON CARD .40 1.00

2007 Fleer Michael Jordan Season Achievements

COMPLETE SET (50) 12.50 30.00
COMMON CARD .40 1.00

1999-00 Fleer Mystique

COMPLETE SET (150) 75.00 150.00
COMPLETE SET w/o SP (100) 15.00 30.00
101-140 PRINT RUN 2999 SERIAL #'d SETS
141-150 PRINT RUN 2500 SERIAL #'d SETS
1 Allen Iverson 1.00 2.50
2 Grant Hill .60 1.50
3 Antawn Jamison .40 1.00
4 Glenn Robinson .30 .75
5 Kenny Anderson .30 .75
6 Dikembe Mutombo .60 1.50
7 Gary Trent .25 .60
8 Brevin Knight .25 .60
9 Chucky Brown .25 .60
10 Derek Anderson .25 .60
11 Ricky Davis .40 1.00
12 Chris Webber .50 1.25
13 Jalen Rose .30 .75
14 Antoine Walker .40 1.00
15 Michael Dickerson .25 .60
16 Tim Hardaway .50 1.25
17 Toni Kukoc .50 1.25
18 Raef LaFrentz .30 .75
19 Anthony Mason .40 1.00
20 John Stockton .60 1.50
21 Hakeem Olajuwon .75 2.00
22 Shaquille O'Neal 1.50 4.00
23 Scottie Pippen 1.00 2.50
24 Maurice Taylor .25 .60
25 Tariq Abdul-Wahad .25 .60
26 Tracy McGrady .60 1.50
27 Joe Smith .30 .75
28 Rod Strickland .30 .75
29 Ruben Patterson .25 .60
30 Tom Gugliotta .30 .75
31 Ray Allen .60 1.50
32 Elden Campbell .25 .60
33 Lindsey Hunter .25 .60
34 Larry Johnson .40 1.00
35 Michael Olowokandi .25 .60
36 Mario Elie .25 .60
37 Anfernee Hardaway 1.00 2.50
38 Juwan Howard .30 .75
39 Karl Malone .75 2.00
40 Alonzo Mourning .60 1.50
41 Billy Owens .25 .60
42 Mitch Richmond .50 1.25
43 Darrell Armstrong .25 .60
44 Jason Williams .60 1.50
45 Mookie Blaylock .25 .60
46 Gary Payton .60 1.50
47 Brian Grant .25 .60
48 Paul Pierce .75 2.00
49 Michael Finley .40 1.00
50 Reggie Miller .75 2.00
51 Corliss Williamson .25 .60
52 Shandon Anderson .25 .60
53 Stephon Marbury .50 1.25
54 Sam Cassell .30 .75
55 Bryon Russell .25 .60
56 Rasheed Wallace .50 1.25
57 Jayson Williams .25 .60
58 Damon Stoudamire .40 1.00
59 Terrell Brandon .25 .60
60 Loy Vaught .25 .60
61 Kobe Bryant 3.00 8.00
62 Vlade Divac .40 1.00
63 Derek Fisher .30 .75
64 Isaiah Rider .30 .75
65 Eddie Jones .40 1.00
66 Kevin Garnett 1.00 2.50
67 David Robinson .75 2.00
68 Marcus Camby .30 .75
69 Glen Rice .40 1.00
70 Mike Bibby .40 1.00
71 Patrick Ewing .50 1.25
72 Robert Traylor .25 .60
73 Tim Duncan 1.00 2.50
74 Michael Doleac .25 .60
75 Steve Smith .30 .75
76 Allan Houston .30 .75
77 Jamal Mashburn .30 .75
78 Brent Barry .30 .75
79 Charles Barkley 1.00 2.50
80 Ron Mercer .30 .75
81 Jerry Stackhouse .40 1.00
82 Keith Van Horn .30 .75
83 Hersey Hawkins .25 .60
84 Avery Johnson .30 .75
85 Cedric Ceballos .25 .60
86 P.J. Brown .25 .60
87 Doug Christie .30 .75
88 Shawn Kemp .60 1.50
89 Dirk Nowitzki 1.25 3.00
90 Erick Dampier .25 .60
91 Antonio McDyess .30 .75
92 Mark Jackson .30 .75
93 Clifford Robinson .30 .75
94 Vince Carter 1.00 2.50
95 Shareef Abdur-Rahim .40 1.00
96 Vin Baker .30 .75
97 Larry Hughes .30 .75
98 Jason Kidd .60 1.50
99 Kerry Kittles .30 .75
100 Latrell Sprewell .50 1.25
101 Lamar Odom RC 1.50 4.00
102 Elton Brand RC 1.50 4.00
103 Baron Davis RC 2.00 5.00
104 Jason Terry RC 1.25 3.00
105 Corey Maggette RC 1.00 2.50
106 Wally Szczerbiak RC 1.25 3.00
107 Richard Hamilton RC 2.00 5.00
108 Milt Palacio RC .60 1.50
109 Ron Artest RC 2.00 5.00
110 Eddie Robinson RC .75 2.00
111 Jumaine Jones RC .50 1.25
112 Andre Miller RC 1.50 4.00
113 Chucky Atkins RC .60 1.50
114 Kenny Thomas RC .75 2.00
115 Scott Padgett RC .60 1.50
116 Devean George RC .60 1.50
117 Tim Young RC .50 1.25
118 Tim James RC .50 1.25
119 Quincy Lewis RC .50 1.25
120 James Posey RC .75 2.00
121 Shawn Marion RC 1.50 4.00
122 A.Radojevic RC .50 1.25
123 Trajan Langdon RC .60 1.50
124 Laron Profit RC .50 1.25
125 Jonathan Bender RC .75 2.00
126 William Avery RC .50 1.25
127 Cal Bowdler RC .50 1.25
128 Dion Glover RC .50 1.25
129 Jeff Foster RC .75 2.00
130 Steve Francis RC 1.50 4.00
131 Adrian Griffin RC .60 1.50
132 Vonteego Cummings RC .50 1.25
133 Rafer Alston RC 1.00 2.50
134 Michael Ruffin RC .50 1.25
135 Chris Herren RC .60 1.50
136 Jermaine Jackson RC .75 2.00
137 Lazaro Borrell RC .75 2.00
138 Obinna Ekezie RC .50 1.25
139 Rick Hughes RC .75 2.00
140 Todd MacCulloch RC .60 1.50
141 Kobe Bryant STAR 10.00 25.00
142 Vince Carter STAR 3.00 8.00
143 Tim Duncan STAR 3.00 8.00
144 Kevin Garnett STAR 3.00 8.00
145 Allen Iverson STAR 3.00 8.00
146 Keith Van Horn STAR 1.00 2.50
147 Grant Hill STAR 2.00 5.00
148 Stephon Marbury STAR 1.50 4.00
149 Antoine Walker STAR 1.25 3.00
150 Shaquille O'Neal STAR 5.00 12.00

1999-00 Fleer Mystique Gold

*GOLD: 1.25X TO 3X BASE CARD HI
GOLD: STATED ODDS 1:4

1999-00 Fleer Mystique Feel the Game

STATED ODDS 1:120
1 Vince Carter 12.00 30.00
2 Brian Grant 3.00 8.00
3 Raef LaFrentz 4.00 10.00
4 Karl Malone 10.00 25.00
5 Alonzo Mourning 8.00 20.00
6 Shaquille O'Neal 20.00 50.00
7 Gary Payton 8.00 20.00
8 David Robinson 10.00 25.00
9 Glenn Robinson 4.00 10.00
10 Joe Smith 4.00 10.00
11 John Stockton 8.00 20.00

1999-00 Fleer Mystique Fresh Ink

STATED ODDS 1:40
1 Ray Allen 10.00 25.00
2 Ron Artest 8.00 20.00
3 William Avery 2.00 5.00
4 Jonathan Bender 3.00 8.00
5 Mike Bibby 5.00 12.00
6 Cal Bowdler 2.00 5.00
7 Vince Carter 12.00 30.00
8 John Celestand 2.00 5.00
9 Vonteego Cummings 2.00 5.00
10 Baron Davis 6.00 15.00
11 Michael Dickerson 3.00 8.00
12 Michael Doleac 3.00 8.00
13 Evan Eschmeyer 2.50 6.00
14 Michael Finley 6.00 15.00
15 Steve Francis 6.00 15.00
16 Pat Garrity 3.00 8.00
17 Dion Glover 2.00 5.00
18 Brian Grant 3.00 8.00
19 Richard Hamilton 8.00 20.00
20 Tim Hardaway 8.00 20.00
21 Jumaine Jones 2.00 5.00
22 Shawn Kemp 25.00 60.00
23 Raef LaFrentz 3.00 8.00
24 Quincy Lewis 2.00 5.00

25 Stephon Marbury 5.00 12.00
26 Antonio McDyess 3.00 8.00
27 Andre Miller 4.00 10.00
28 Cuttino Mobley 3.00 8.00
29 Alonzo Mourning 25.00 60.00
30 Shaquille O'Neal 50.00 125.00
31 Lamar Odom 10.00 25.00
32 Hakeem Olajuwon 15.00 40.00
33 Michael Olowokandi 3.00 8.00
34 James Posey 3.00 8.00
35 Aleksandar Radojevic 2.00 5.00
36 Kenny Thomas 3.00 8.00
37 Robert Traylor 3.00 8.00
38 Keith Van Horn 5.00 12.00

1999-00 Fleer Mystique Point Perfect

COMPLETE SET (10) 12.00 30.00
STATED PRINT RUN 1999 SERIAL #'d SETS
PP1 Mike Bibby 1.25 3.00
PP2 Stephon Marbury 1.50 4.00
PP3 Jason Williams 4.00 10.00
PP4 Jason Kidd 2.00 5.00
PP5 William Avery .75 2.00
PP6 Allen Iverson 6.00 15.00
PP7 Andre Miller 2.50 6.00
PP8 Baron Davis 3.00 8.00
PP9 Steve Francis 2.50 6.00
PP10 Jason Terry 2.00 5.00

1999-00 Fleer Mystique Raise the Roof

STATED PRINT RUN 100 SERIAL #'d SETS
RR1 Grant Hill 400.00 800.00
RR2 Keith Van Horn 150.00 400.00
RR3 Tim Duncan 500.00 1,000.00
RR4 Kobe Bryant 2,000.00 4,000.00
RR5 Vince Carter 400.00 800.00
RR6 Allen Iverson 400.00 800.00
RR7 Kevin Garnett 400.00 800.00
RR8 Shaquille O'Neal 500.00 1,000.00
RR9 Paul Pierce 300.00 600.00
RR10 Anfernee Hardaway 400.00 800.00

1999-00 Fleer Mystique Slamboree

COMPLETE SET (10) 12.00 30.00
STATED PRINT RUN 999 SERIAL #'d SETS
S1 Antoine Walker 1.50 4.00
S2 Shareef Abdur-Rahim 1.50 4.00
S3 Antawn Jamison 1.50 4.00
S4 Tracy McGrady 8.00 20.00
S5 Larry Hughes 1.25 3.00
S6 Wally Szczerbiak 2.50 6.00
S7 Corey Maggette 2.00 5.00
S8 Lamar Odom 3.00 8.00
S9 Elton Brand 3.00 8.00
S10 Stephon Marbury 2.00 5.00

2000-01 Fleer Mystique

COMPLETE SET w/o RC (100) 15.00 30.00
101-106 A: PRINT RUN 250 SERIAL #'d SETS
107-112 B: PRINT RUN 1000 SERIAL #'d SETS
113-117 C: PRINT RUN 2000 SERIAL #'d SETS
118-124 D: PRINT RUN 3000 SERIAL #'d SETS
125-130 E: PRINT RUN 4000 SERIAL #'d SETS
131-136 F: PRINT RUN 5000 SERIAL #'d SETS
1 Shaquille O'Neal 1.25 3.00
2 Gary Payton .50 1.25
3 Nick Van Exel .30 .75
4 Alonzo Mourning .50 1.25
5 Shawn Marion .30 .75
6 Rod Strickland .20 .50
7 Mookie Blaylock .30 .75
8 Terrell Brandon .25 .60
9 Bryon Russell .20 .50
10 Jerry Stackhouse .30 .75
11 Glenn Robinson .30 .75
12 Rasheed Wallace .40 1.00
13 Tracy McGrady .60 1.50
14 Raef LaFrentz .25 .60
15 P.J. Brown .20 .50
16 Anfernee Hardaway .50 1.25
17 Mike Bibby .30 .75
18 Elden Campbell .20 .50
19 Steve Francis .30 .75
20 Keith Van Horn .25 .60
21 Karl Malone .60 1.50
22 Dirk Nowitzki .75 2.00
23 Glen Rice .30 .75
24 Tom Gugliotta .25 .60
25 Avery Johnson .25 .60
26 Michael Finley .30 .75
27 Theo Ratliff .20 .50
28 Juwan Howard .25 .60
29 Anthony Carter .20 .50
30 Kobe Bryant 2.50 6.00
31 Toni Kukoc .40 1.00
32 Jason Terry .30 .75
33 Elton Brand .30 .75
34 Reggie Miller .60 1.50
35 Latrell Sprewell .40 1.00
36 Adrian Griffin .20 .50
37 Cuttino Mobley .25 .60
38 Maurice Taylor .20 .50
39 Allen Iverson .75 2.00
40 Tim Duncan .75 2.00
41 Andre Miller .25 .60
42 Antonio Davis .25 .60
43 Howard Eisley .20 .50
44 Vlade Divac .30 .75
45 Brevin Knight .20 .50
46 Lamar Odom .30 .75
47 Ron Mercer .25 .60
48 Jason Williams .50 1.25
49 Antawn Jamison .30 .75
50 Wally Szczerbiak .25 .60
51 Chris Webber .40 1.00
52 Larry Hughes .30 .75
53 Kevin Garnett .75 2.00
54 Michael Dickerson .20 .50
55 Chucky Atkins .20 .50
56 Jalen Rose .25 .60
57 John Amaechi .20 .50
58 Shareef Abdur-Rahim .30 .75
59 Shawn Kemp .50 1.25
60 Derek Anderson .25 .60
61 Darrell Armstrong .20 .50
62 Vin Baker .25 .60
63 Paul Pierce .50 1.25
64 Donyell Marshall .25 .60
65 Jamie Feick .20 .50
66 Travis Best .20 .50
67 Baron Davis .30 .75
68 Hakeem Olajuwon .60 1.50
69 Joe Smith .25 .60
70 Ruben Patterson .20 .50
71 Antonio McDyess .25 .60
72 Jamal Mashburn .25 .60
73 Jason Kidd .50 1.25
74 Eddie Jones .30 .75
75 Kenny Thomas .20 .50
76 Marcus Camby .25 .60
77 Doug Christie .25 .60
78 Ron Artest .30 .75
79 Mark Jackson .25 .60
80 Allan Houston .30 .75
81 John Stockton .60 1.50
82 Jerome Williams .20 .50
83 Tim Thomas .20 .50
84 Alan Henderson .20 .50
85 Antoine Walker .30 .75
86 Robert Horry .30 .75
87 Stephon Marbury .40 1.00
88 David Robinson .60 1.50
89 Lindsey Hunter .20 .50
90 Richard Hamilton .40 1.00
91 Damon Stoudamire .30 .75
92 Dikembe Mutombo .50 1.25
93 Anthony Mason .30 .75
94 Austin Croshere .20 .50
95 Patrick Ewing .50 1.25
96 Mitch Richmond .40 1.00
97 Grant Hill .50 1.25
98 Ray Allen .50 1.25
99 Scottie Pippen .75 2.00
100 Vince Carter .60 1.50
101 Kenyon Martin A RC 5.00 12.00
102 Stromile Swift A RC 2.00 5.00
103 Darius Miles A RC 2.50 6.00
104 Marcus Fizer A RC 2.00 5.00
105 Mike Miller A RC 4.00 10.00
106 DerMarr Johnson A RC 1.50 4.00
107 Chris Mihm B RC 1.25 3.00
108 Jamal Crawford B RC 5.00 12.00
109 Joel Przybilla B RC 1.50 4.00
110 Keyon Dooling B RC 1.50 4.00
111 Jerome Moiso B RC 1.25 3.00
112 Etan Thomas B RC 1.50 4.00
113 Courtney Alexander C RC 1.00 2.50
114 Mateen Cleaves C RC 1.25 3.00
115 Jason Collier C RC 1.50 4.00
116 Hedo Turkoglu C RC 2.50 6.00
117 Desmond Mason C RC 2.00 5.00
118 Quentin Richardson C RC 1.25 3.00
119 Jamaal Magloire D RC 1.00 2.50
120 Speedy Claxton D RC 1.00 2.50
121 Morris Peterson D RC 1.00 2.50
122 Donnell Harvey D RC .75 2.00
123 D.Stevenson D RC 1.00 2.50
124 Mark Karcher D RC .60 1.50
125 Mamadou N'Diaye E RC .40 1.00
126 Erick Barkley E RC .40 1.00
127 Mark Madsen E RC .60 1.50
128 Corey Hightower E RC .60 1.50
129 Dan McClintock E RC .60 1.50
130 Soumaila Samake E RC .40 1.00
131 Hanno Mottola F RC .30 .75
132 Chris Carrawell F RC .30 .75
133 Olumide Oyedeji F RC .30 .75
134 Michael Redd F RC 1.25 3.00
135 Chris Porter F RC .30 .75
136 Jabari Smith F RC .30 .75

2000-01 Fleer Mystique Gold

COMPLETE SET (136) 125.00 250.00
*STARS: 1.5X TO 4X BASE CARD HI
*RCs: 2X TO 5X BASE HI
STATED ODDS 1:20

2000-01 Fleer Mystique Vince Carter Rookie Remnants

NNO Vince Carter FLR JSY/15 40.00 100.00
NNO Vince Carter FLR/100 15.00 40.00

2000-01 Fleer Mystique Dial 1

COMPLETE SET (10) 5.00 12.00
STATED ODDS 1:10
1 Jason Kidd 1.00 2.50
2 Stephon Marbury .75 2.00
3 Allen Iverson 1.50 4.00
4 Jason Williams 1.00 2.50
5 Allan Houston .60 1.50
6 Eddie Jones .60 1.50
7 Ray Allen 1.00 2.50
8 Jalen Rose .50 1.25
9 Anfernee Hardaway 1.00 2.50
10 Vince Carter 1.50 4.00

2000-01 Fleer Mystique Film at Eleven

COMPLETE SET (10) 25.00 50.00
STATED ODDS 1:40
1 Vince Carter 3.00 8.00
2 Kobe Bryant 20.00 50.00
3 Allen Iverson 4.00 10.00
4 Kevin Garnett 4.00 10.00
5 Tim Duncan 4.00 10.00
6 Steve Francis 1.50 4.00
7 Lamar Odom 1.50 4.00
8 Elton Brand 1.50 4.00
9 Tracy McGrady 3.00 8.00
10 Jason Williams 2.50 6.00

2000-01 Fleer Mystique Middle Men

COMPLETE SET (10) 5.00 12.00
STATED ODDS 1:10
1 Shaquille O'Neal 2.50 6.00
2 Vince Carter 1.25 3.00
3 Paul Pierce 1.00 2.50
4 Tim Duncan 1.50 4.00
5 Grant Hill .60 1.50
6 David Robinson 1.25 3.00
7 Tracy McGrady 1.25 3.00
8 Jason Williams 1.00 2.50
9 Elton Brand .60 1.50
10 Lamar Odom .60 1.50

2000-01 Fleer Mystique NBAwesome

COMPLETE SET (10) 20.00 50.00
STATED ODDS 1:20
1 Grant Hill 2.00 5.00
2 Steve Francis 1.25 3.00
3 Kobe Bryant 15.00 40.00
4 Elton Brand 1.25 3.00
5 Vince Carter 2.50 6.00
6 Lamar Odom 1.25 3.00
7 Kevin Garnett 3.00 8.00
8 Allen Iverson 3.00 8.00
9 Shareef Abdur-Rahim 1.25 3.00
10 Shaquille O'Neal 5.00 12.00

2000-01 Fleer Mystique Player of the Week

COMPLETE SET (15) 10.00 25.00
STATED ODDS 1:5
1 Sam Cassell .40 1.00
2 Kevin Garnett 1.25 3.00
3 Vince Carter 1.00 2.50
4 Tim Duncan 1.25 3.00
5 Shaquille O'Neal 2.00 5.00
6 Alonzo Mourning .75 2.00
7 Jason Kidd .75 2.00
8 Chris Webber .60 1.50
9 Grant Hill .75 2.00
10 Steve Francis .50 1.25
11 Dikembe Mutombo .75 2.00
12 Michael Finley .50 1.25
13 Karl Malone 1.00 2.50
14 Jalen Rose .40 1.00
15 Kobe Bryant 8.00 20.00

2003-04 Fleer Mystique

COMP.SET w/o SP's (80) 15.00 40.00
81-120 PRINT RUN 999 SER.#'d SETS
1 Eric Williams .20 .50
2 Dirk Nowitzki .75 2.00
3 Jason Richardson .30 .75
4 Corey Maggette .25 .60
5 Troy Hudson .20 .50
6 Tracy McGrady .50 1.25
7 Zach Randolph .30 .75
8 Bobby Jackson .25 .60
9 Dan Gadzuric .20 .50
10 Kevin Garnett .75 2.00
11 Manu Ginobili .60 1.50
12 Andrei Kirilenko .25 .60
13 Richard Hamilton .40 1.00
14 Mike Bibby .30 .75
15 Vince Carter .60 1.50
16 Jermaine O'Neal .30 .75
17 Antoine Walker .30 .75
18 Jalen Rose .25 .60
19 Dajuan Wagner .20 .50
20 Nene .25 .60
21 Jamaal Tinsley .20 .50
22 Kobe Bryant 2.50 6.00
23 Shane Battier .25 .60
24 Allan Houston .30 .75
25 Jerry Stackhouse .40 1.00
26 Eddie Jones .30 .75
27 Morris Peterson .20 .50
28 Richard Jefferson .25 .60
29 Tony Parker .50 1.25
30 Glenn Robinson .25 .60
31 Ron Artest .30 .75
32 Marcus Haislip .20 .50
33 Drew Gooden .25 .60
34 Keith Van Horn .25 .60
35 Shareef Abdur-Rahim .30 .75
36 Michael Redd .30 .75
37 Stephon Marbury .40 1.00
38 Tim Duncan .75 2.00
39 Eddie Griffin .20 .50
40 Kwame Brown .20 .50
41 Steve Francis .30 .75
42 Vladimir Radmanovic .20 .50
43 Kenyon Martin .30 .75
44 Eddy Curry .20 .50
45 Nikoloz Tskitishvili .20 .50
46 Shaquille O'Neal 1.25 3.00
47 Allen Iverson .75 2.00
48 Jason Kidd .50 1.25
49 Ben Wallace .40 1.00
50 Caron Butler .25 .60
51 Dan Dickau .20 .50
52 Baron Davis .30 .75
53 Bruce Bowen .25 .60
54 Amare Stoudemire .40 1.00
55 Michael Finley .30 .75
56 Jamal Mashburn .25 .60
57 Pau Gasol .50 1.25
58 Shawn Marion .30 .75
59 Rasheed Wallace .40 1.00
60 Chris Webber .40 1.00
61 Rodney White .20 .50
62 Tayshaun Prince .30 .75
63 Yao Ming .75 2.00
64 Latrell Sprewell .40 1.00
65 Aaron McKie .20 .50
66 Bonzi Wells .20 .50
67 HedoTurkoglu .25 .60
68 Ray Allen .50 1.25
69 Matt Harpring .20 .50
70 Paul Pierce .50 1.25
71 Darius Miles .20 .50
72 Chris Wilcox .20 .50
73 Steve Nash .60 1.50
74 Antawn Jamison .30 .75
75 Juan Dixon .20 .50
76 Peja Stojakovic .25 .60
77 Antonio Davis .25 .60
78 Kenny Thomas .20 .50
79 Elton Brand .25 .60
80 Gilbert Arenas .30 .75
81 Mickael Pietrus RC 1.50 4.00
82 Keith Bogans RC 1.25 3.00
83 Dahntay Jones RC 1.50 4.00
84 Darko Milicic RC 1.50 4.00
85 Torraye Braggs RC 1.25 3.00
86 Troy Bell RC 1.25 3.00
87 Maciej Lampe RC 1.25 3.00
88 Kendrick Perkins RC 1.50 4.00
89 Kirk Hinrich RC 2.00 5.00
90 Jason Kapono RC 1.25 3.00
91 Udonis Haslem RC 2.50 6.00
92 James Lang RC 1.25 3.00
93 Willie Green RC 2.00 5.00
94 Travis Outlaw RC 1.50 4.00
95 Nick Collison RC 1.50 4.00
96 Jarvis Hayes RC 1.50 4.00
97 Boris Diaw RC 2.00 5.00
98 Chris Bosh RC 6.00 15.00
99 LeBron James RC 1,000.00 2,000.00
100 Zarko Cabarkapa RC 1.25 3.00
101 Travis Hansen RC 1.25 3.00
102 James Jones RC 1.25 3.00
103 Aleksandar Pavlovic RC 1.50 4.00
104 Luke Walton RC 2.00 5.00
105 Maurice Williams RC 2.00 5.00
106 Linton Johnson RC 1.25 3.00
107 David West RC 2.50 6.00
108 Carmelo Anthony RC 10.00 25.00
109 T.J. Ford RC 1.50 4.00
110 Ndudi Ebi RC 1.25 3.00
111 Reece Gaines RC 1.25 3.00
112 Leandro Barbosa RC 2.00 5.00
113 Luke Ridnour RC 2.00 5.00
114 Brian Cook RC 1.25 3.00
115 Marcus Banks RC 1.25 3.00
116 Josh Howard RC 2.00 5.00
117 Chris Kaman RC 2.00 5.00
118 Zoran Planinic RC 1.25 3.00
119 Dwyane Wade RC 20.00 50.00
120 Mike Sweetney RC 1.25 3.00

2003-04 Fleer Mystique Die Cut

*81-120 DC SINGLES: .5X TO 1.25X BASE HI
DIE CUT PRINT RUN 600 SER.#'d SETS

2003-04 Fleer Mystique Gold

*1-80 SINGLES: 2.5X TO 6X BASE HI
1-80 PRINT RUN 150 SER.#'d SETS
*81-120 RCs: 1X TO 2.5X BASE HI
81-120 RC PRINT RUN 50 SER.#'d SETS
1 Eric Williams 1.25 3.00
32 Marcus Haislip 1.25 3.00

2003-04 Fleer Mystique Awe Pairs

PRINT RUN 500 SER.#'d SETS
*GOLD SINGLES/25-40: 1.5X TO 4X BASE HI
*GOLD SINGLES/40-60: 1.25X TO 3X HI COL.
GOLD #'d TO TEAM VICTORIES IN 2002-03
1 S.Battier/P.Gasol 1.50 4.00
2 S.Marion/A.Stoudemire 1.25 3.00
3 P.Pierce/M.Banks 1.50 4.00
4 J.Rose/E.Curry .75 2.00
5 D.Wagner/L.James 75.00 200.00
6 K.Garnett/T.Hudson 2.50 6.00
7 T.Prince/B.Wallace 1.25 3.00
8 Nene/C.Anthony 5.00 12.00
9 K.Bryant/S.O'Neal 8.00 20.00
10 D.Gooden/T.McGrady 1.50 4.00
11 A.Iverson/A.McKie 2.50 6.00
12 C.Butler/D.Wade 8.00 20.00
13 Y.Ming/S.Francis 2.50 6.00
14 E.Brand/C.Kaman 1.00 2.50
15 A.Houston/M.Sweetney 1.00 2.50
16 P.Stojakovic/C.Webber 1.25 3.00
17 J.O'Neal/R.Artest 1.00 2.50
18 T.Duncan/T.Parker 2.50 6.00
19 V.Carter/C.Bosh 3.00 8.00
20 M.Dunleavy/J.Richardson 1.00 2.50

2003-04 Fleer Mystique Awe Pairs Dual Jerseys

PRINT RUN 350 SER.#'d SETS
*JSY/250 SINGLES: .5X TO 1.25X HI COL.
*JSY/35 SINGLES: 2X TO 5X HI COL.
JSY 35 PRINT RUN 35 SER.#'d SETS
AHMS Houston/Sweetney 4.00 10.00
AIAM A.Iverson/A.McKie 5.00 12.00
CBDW C.Butler/D.Wade 8.00 20.00
DGTM D.Gooden/T.McGrady 4.00 10.00
EBCK E.Brand/C.Kaman 4.00 10.00
JONRA J.O'Neal/R.Artest 4.00 10.00
JREC J.Rose/E.Curry 4.00 10.00
KGTH K.Garnett/T.Hudson 5.00 12.00
MDJR M.Dunleavy/J-Rich 4.00 10.00
PPMB P.Pierce/M.Banks 4.00 10.00
PSCW P.Stojakovic/C.Webber 5.00 12.00
SBPG S.Battier/P.Gasol 4.00 10.00
SMAS S.Marion/Amare 5.00 12.00
TDTP T.Duncan/T.Parker 6.00 15.00
TPBW T.Prince/B.Wallace 4.00 10.00
VCCB V.Carter/C.Bosh 6.00 15.00
YMSF Y.Ming/S.Francis 6.00 15.00

2003-04 Fleer Mystique Ink Appeal

PRINT RUNS LISTED BELOW
CA Carmelo Anthony/225 25.00 60.00
DW Dwyane Wade/150 25.00 60.00
JH Josh Howard/100 6.00 15.00
JK Jason Kapono/200 6.00 15.00
LR Luke Ridnour/100 6.00 15.00
MP Mickael Pietrus/150 6.00 15.00
VC Vince Carter/250 12.00 30.00
DWG Dajuan Wagner/125 6.00 15.00

2003-04 Fleer Mystique Ink Appeal Gold

PRINT RUNS LISTED BELOW
CA Carmelo Anthony/15 50.00 125.00
VC Vince Carter/15 20.00 50.00

2003-04 Fleer Mystique Rare Finds

COMPLETE SET (10) 12.50 30.00
PRINT RUN 500 SER.#'d SETS
1 Bryant/Garnett/Amare 3.00 8.00
2 Ginobili/Peja/Kirilenko 2.00 5.00
3 Parker/Francis/Payton 2.00 5.00
4 K-Mart/Kidd/Jefferson 2.00 5.00
5 Nowitzki/Nash/Finley 2.00 5.00
6 McGrady/Iverson/Pierce 2.00 5.00
7 Duncan/Ming/Shaq 5.00 12.00
8 Vince/Slack/Jamison 2.00 5.00
9 Rose/Webber/Howard 2.00 5.00
10 Hamilton/Butler/Allen 2.00 5.00

2003-04 Fleer Mystique Rare Finds 50

PRINT RUN 50 SER.#'d SETS
AS Amare Stoudemire 12.50 30.00
CA Carmelo Anthony 25.00 60.00
DG Drew Gooden 5.00 12.00
TP Tayshaun Prince 5.00 12.00
VC Vince Carter 20.00 40.00

2003-04 Fleer Mystique Rare Finds Jerseys

PRINT RUN 300 SER.#'d SETS
*JERSEY 30: 1X TO 2.5X HI COL.
RFAI Allen Iverson 6.00 15.00
RFAS Amare Stoudemire 3.00 8.00
RFCB Caron Butler 2.00 5.00
RFCW Chris Webber 3.00 8.00
RFDN Dirk Nowitzki 6.00 15.00
RFJK Jason Kidd 4.00 10.00
RFJS Jerry Stackhouse 3.00 8.00
RFKG Kevin Garnett 6.00 15.00
RFMF Michael Finley 2.50 6.00
RFPP Paul Pierce 4.00 10.00
RFPS Peja Stojakovic 2.00 5.00
RFSN Steve Nash 5.00 12.00
RFSO Shaquille O'Neal 10.00 25.00
RFST Steve Francis 2.50 6.00
RFTD Tim Duncan 6.00 15.00
RFTM Tracy McGrady 4.00 10.00
RFTP Tony Parker 4.00 10.00
RFVC Vince Carter 5.00 12.00
RTKM Kenyon Martin 2.50 6.00
RTYM Yao Ming 6.00 15.00

2003-04 Fleer Mystique Rare Finds Jerseys Dual

PRINT RUN 250 SER.#'d SETS
*DUAL 25: 1.25X TO 3X BASE HI
CWJH C.Webber/J.Howard 6.00 15.00
DNMF D.Nowitzki/M.Finley 6.00 15.00
DNSN D.Nowitzki/S.Nash 6.00 15.00
KGAS K.Garnett/Amare 6.00 15.00
KMJK K-Mart/J.Kidd 6.00 15.00
PSAK Stojakovic/Kirilenko 6.00 15.00
SFGP S.Francis/G.Payton 8.00 20.00
TDSO T.Duncan/S.O'Neal 8.00 20.00
TDYM T.Duncan/Y.Ming 8.00 20.00
TMAI T.McGrady/A.Iverson 8.00 20.00
TMPP T.McGrady/P.Pierce 8.00 20.00
TPSF T.Parker/S.Francis 6.00 15.00
VCAJ V.Carter/A.Jamison 6.00 15.00
VCJS V.Carter/J.Stackhouse 6.00 15.00
YMSO Y.Ming/S.O'Neal 10.00 25.00

2003-04 Fleer Mystique Rare Finds Jerseys Triple

PRINT RUN 150 SER.#'d SETS
DSM Nowitzki/Nash/Finley 12.50 30.00
JCJ Rose/Webber/JuHoward 10.00 25.00
KJR K-Mart/Kidd/Jefferson 8.00 20.00
MPA Manu/Peja/Kirilenko 8.00 20.00
RCR Hamilton/Butler/Allen 8.00 20.00
TAP T-Mac/Iverson/Pierce 8.00 20.00
TSG Parker/Francis/Payton 8.00 20.00
TYS Duncan/Yao/Shaq 12.50 30.00
VJA Vince/Stack/Jamison 8.00 20.00

2003-04 Fleer Mystique Secret Weapons

COMPLETE SET (15) 30.00 75.00
PRINT RUN 500 SER.#'d SETS
*GOLD/30-50 SNGLS: .75X TO 2X HI COL.
1 LeBron James 400.00 800.00
2 Carmelo Anthony 8.00 20.00
3 Darko Milicic 1.25 3.00
4 Chris Kaman 1.50 4.00
5 Dwyane Wade 75.00 200.00
6 T.J. Ford 1.25 3.00
7 Chris Bosh 5.00 12.00
8 Kirk Hinrich 1.50 4.00
9 Mike Sweetney 1.00 2.50
10 Jarvis Hayes 1.00 2.50
11 Marcus Banks 1.00 2.50
12 Mickael Pietrus 1.25 3.00
13 Nick Collison 1.25 3.00
14 David West 2.00 5.00
15 Maciej Lampe 1.00 2.50

2003-04 Fleer Mystique Shining Stars

PRINT RUN 500 SER.#'d SETS
*GOLD SINGLES: .75X TO 2X HI COL.
GOLD PRINT RUN 75 SER.#'d SETS
1 Antoine Walker 1.50 4.00
2 Dirk Nowitzki 4.00 10.00
3 Baron Davis 1.50 4.00
4 Peja Stojakovic 1.25 3.00
5 Ray Allen 2.50 6.00
6 Jason Kidd 2.50 6.00
7 Gilbert Arenas 1.50 4.00
8 Jason Richardson 1.50 4.00
9 Tim Duncan 4.00 10.00
10 Vince Carter 3.00 8.00
11 Shaquille O'Neal 6.00 15.00
12 Drew Gooden 1.25 3.00
13 Pau Gasol 2.50 6.00
14 Caron Butler 1.25 3.00
15 Manu Ginobili 3.00 8.00

2003-04 Fleer Mystique Shining Stars Jerseys

PRINT RUN 350 SER.#'d SETS
*JERSEY/250: .4X TO 1X HI COL.
*JERSEY/75: .75X TO 2X HI COL.
*WARM-UPS: .4X TO 1X HI COL.
WARM-UPS PRINT RUN 250 SETS
SSAW Antoine Walker 2.50 6.00
SSBD Baron Davis 2.50 6.00
SSCB Caron Butler 2.00 5.00
SSDG Drew Gooden 2.00 5.00
SSDN Dirk Nowitzki 6.00 15.00
SSJK Jason Kidd 4.00 10.00
SSJR Jason Richardson 2.50 6.00
SSMG Manu Ginobili 5.00 12.00
SSPG Pau Gasol 4.00 10.00
SSPS Peja Stojakovic 2.00 5.00
SSRA Ray Allen 4.00 10.00
SSSO Shaquille O'Neal 10.00 25.00
SSTD Tim Duncan 6.00 15.00
SSVC Vince Carter 5.00 12.00

2003-04 Fleer Mystique Skyview

COMPLETE SET (10) 40.00 80.00
PRINT RUN 100 SER.#'d SETS
*GOLD/30-50: 1X TO 2.5X HI COL.
*GOLD/50-60: .75X TO 2X HI COL.
1 Dirk Nowitzki 8.00 20.00
2 Yao Ming 8.00 20.00
3 Kevin Garnett 8.00 20.00
4 Tracy McGrady 5.00 12.00
5 Allen Iverson 8.00 20.00
6 Steve Francis 3.00 8.00
7 Kobe Bryant 60.00 150.00
8 Amare Stoudemire 4.00 10.00
9 Chris Webber 4.00 10.00
10 Vince Carter 6.00 15.00

2003-04 Fleer Mystique Skyview Jerseys

PRINT RUN 250 SER.#'d SETS
*JERSEY/150: .5X TO 1.25X BASE HI
*JERSEY/25: 2X TO 5X BASE HI
SVAI Allen Iverson 8.00 20.00
SVAS Amare Stoudemire 4.00 10.00
SVCW Chris Webber 4.00 10.00
SVDN Dirk Nowitzki 8.00 20.00
SVKG Kevin Garnett 8.00 20.00
SVSM Steve Francis 3.00 8.00
SVTM Tracy McGrady 5.00 12.00
SVVC Vince Carter 6.00 15.00
SVYM Yao Ming 8.00 20.00

2001-02 Fleer NBA All-Star Jam Session

NNO Eric Snow .40 1.00

1997 Fleer NBA Jam Session Commemorative Sheet

1 Shareef Abdur-Rahim FF
Ray Allen FF
Kobe Bryant FF
Marcus Camby FF
Kerry Kittles FF
Stephon Marbury FF
Charles Barkley AS
Patrick Ewing AS
John Stockton AS
Alonzo Mourning AS
Grant Hill AS
Jason Kidd AS 3.00 8.00

2000 Fleer NBA Jam Session Commemorative Sheet

NNO Vince Carter
Lamar Odom
Stephon Marbury
Keith Van Horn
Antawn Jamison
Allen Iverson
Grant Hill
Jason Williams 4.00 10.00

2003-04 Fleer Patchworks

COMP.SET w/o SP's (90) 12.00 30.00
91-120 PRINT RUN 799 SER.#'d SETS
1 Shareef Abdur-Rahim .30 .75
2 Theo Ratliff .20 .50
3 Jason Terry .25 .60
4 Carlos Boozer .25 .60
5 Paul Pierce .50 1.25
6 Ricky Davis .25 .60
7 Tyson Chandler .25 .60
8 Jamal Crawford .30 .75
9 Eddy Curry .25 .60
10 Darius Miles .25 .60
11 Dajuan Wagner .20 .50
12 Michael Finley .30 .75
13 Steve Nash .60 1.50
14 Dirk Nowitzki .75 2.00
15 Earl Boykins .20 .50
16 Andre Miller .25 .60
17 Nene .25 .60
18 Richard Hamilton .40 1.00
19 Tayshaun Prince .25 .60
20 Ben Wallace .40 1.00
21 Mike Dunleavy .25 .60
22 Troy Murphy .20 .50
23 Jason Richardson .30 .75
24 Steve Francis .30 .75
25 Yao Ming .75 2.00
26 Cuttino Mobley .20 .50
27 Maurice Taylor .20 .50
28 Ron Artest .30 .75
29 Reggie Miller .60 1.50
30 Jermaine O'Neal .30 .75
31 Jamaal Tinsley .20 .50
32 Elton Brand .25 .60
33 Marko Jaric .20 .50
34 Corey Maggette .25 .60
35 Kobe Bryant 2.50 6.00
36 Karl Malone .60 1.50
37 Shaquille O'Neal 1.25 3.00
38 Shane Battier .25 .60
39 Pau Gasol .50 1.25
40 Jason Williams .50 1.25
41 Caron Butler .25 .60
42 Lamar Odom .25 .60
43 Desmond Mason .25 .60
44 Michael Redd .30 .75
45 Tim Thomas .20 .50
46 Sam Cassell .20 .50
47 Kevin Garnett .75 2.00
48 Latrell Sprewell .40 1.00
49 Wally Szczerbiak .25 .60
50 Richard Jefferson .25 .60
51 Jason Kidd .50 1.25
52 Kenyon Martin .30 .75
53 Baron Davis .30 .75
54 Jamal Mashburn .25 .60
55 Jamaal Magloire .20 .50
56 Allan Houston .30 .75
57 Stephon Marbury .40 1.00
58 Kurt Thomas .20 .50
59 Drew Gooden .25 .60
60 Juwan Howard .25 .60
61 Tracy McGrady .50 1.25
62 Allen Iverson .75 2.00
63 Aaron McKie .25 .60
64 Glenn Robinson .25 .60
65 Kenny Thomas .20 .50
66 Shawn Marion .30 .75
67 Antonio McDyess .25 .60
68 Amare Stoudemire .40 1.00
69 Zach Randolph .30 .75
70 Damon Stoudamire .25 .60
71 Rasheed Wallace .40 1.00
72 Qyntel Woods .20 .50
73 Mike Bibby .30 .75
74 Peja Stojakovic .25 .60
75 Chris Webber .40 1.00
76 Tim Duncan .75 2.00
77 Manu Ginobili .60 1.50
78 Tony Parker .50 1.25
79 Malik Rose .20 .50
80 Ray Allen .50 1.25
81 Rashard Lewis .25 .60
82 Vladimir Radmanovic .20 .50
83 Vince Carter .60 1.50
84 Donyell Marshall .20 .50
85 Jalen Rose .25 .60
86 Matt Harpring .20 .50
87 Andrei Kirilenko .25 .60
88 Gilbert Arenas .30 .75
89 Larry Hughes .25 .60
90 Jerry Stackhouse .40 1.00
91 Carmelo Anthony RC 6.00 15.00
92 Marcus Banks RC .75 2.00
93 Troy Bell RC .75 2.00
94 Chris Bosh RC 4.00 10.00
95 Zarko Cabarkapa RC .75 2.00
96 Nick Collison RC 1.00 2.50
97 Boris Diaw RC 1.25 3.00
98 Francisco Elson RC .75 2.00
99 T.J. Ford RC 1.00 2.50
100 Reece Gaines RC .75 2.00
101 Udonis Haslem RC 1.50 4.00
102 Jarvis Hayes RC .75 2.00
103 Kirk Hinrich RC 1.25 3.00
104 Josh Howard RC 1.25 3.00
105 LeBron James RC 200.00 500.00
106 Dahntay Jones RC 1.00 2.50
107 Chris Kaman RC 1.25 3.00
108 Jason Kapono RC .75 2.00
109 Raul Lopez 1.25 3.00
110 Darko Milicic RC 1.00 2.50
111 Zaur Pachulia RC 1.25 3.00
112 Mickael Pietrus RC 1.00 2.50
113 Zoran Planinic RC .75 2.00
114 Luke Ridnour RC 1.25 3.00
115 Darius Songaila .75 2.00
116 Mike Sweetney RC .75 2.00
117 Dwyane Wade RC 10.00 25.00
118 Luke Walton RC 1.25 3.00
119 David West RC 1.50 4.00
120 Maurice Williams RC 1.25 3.00

2003-04 Fleer Patchworks Ruby

*1-90 RUBY SINGLES: 5X TO 12X BASE HI
*91-120 RUBY RCs: 1.5X TO 4X BASE HI
RUBY PRINT RUN 50 SER.#'d SETS

2003-04 Fleer Patchworks By The Numbers

COMPLETE SET (15) 20.00 40.00
STATED ODDS 1:24 H, 1:12 R, 1:24 BLAST
1 Carmelo Anthony 4.00 10.00
2 Steve Francis .75 2.00
3 Shaquille O'Neal 3.00 8.00
4 Kevin Garnett 2.00 5.00
5 Dwyane Wade 6.00 15.00
6 Tracy McGrady 1.25 3.00
7 Allen Iverson 2.00 5.00
8 Chris Webber 1.00 2.50
9 Tim Duncan 2.00 5.00
10 Dirk Nowitzki 2.00 5.00
11 Paul Pierce 1.25 3.00
12 LeBron James 12.00 30.00
13 Kobe Bryant 6.00 15.00
14 Jason Kidd 1.25 3.00
15 Vince Carter 1.50 4.00

2003-04 Fleer Patchworks By The Numbers Jerseys

STATED ODDS 1:300 H, 1:77 R
*PATCHES: .75X TO 2X BASE JSY HI
PATCH PRINT RUN 100 SER.#'d SETS
CA Carmelo Anthony 12.00 30.00
CW Chris Webber 3.00 8.00
DN Dirk Nowitzki 6.00 15.00
DW Dwyane Wade 20.00 50.00
JK Jason Kidd 4.00 10.00
KG Kevin Garnett 6.00 15.00
PP Paul Pierce 4.00 10.00
SF Steve Francis 2.50 6.00
TD Tim Duncan 6.00 15.00
TM Tracy McGrady 4.00 10.00
VC Vince Carter 5.00 12.00
SON Shaquille O'Neal 10.00 25.00

2003-04 Fleer Patchworks Courting Greatness

COMPLETE SET (24) 20.00 40.00
STATED ODDS 1:12 H, 1:6 R, 1:12 BLASTER
1 Dirk Nowitzki 1.50 4.00
2 Jarvis Hayes .40 1.00
3 Tony Parker 1.00 2.50
4 Drew Gooden .50 1.25
5 Yao Ming 1.50 4.00
6 Udonis Haslem .75 2.00
7 Zach Randolph .60 1.50
8 Carmelo Anthony 3.00 8.00
9 Kobe Bryant 5.00 12.00
10 Chris Bosh 2.00 5.00
11 Antawn Jamison .60 1.50
12 Ben Wallace .75 2.00
13 Manu Ginobili 1.25 3.00
14 Baron Davis .60 1.50
15 Vince Carter 1.25 3.00
16 Tayshaun Prince .60 1.50
17 Jermaine O'Neal .60 1.50
18 T.J. Ford .50 1.25
19 Josh Howard .60 1.50
20 Amare Stoudemire .75 2.00
21 Dwyane Wade 5.00 12.00
22 Michael Redd .60 1.50
23 LeBron James 12.00 30.00
24 Jason Richardson .60 1.50
25 Darko Milicic .50 1.25

2003-04 Fleer Patchworks Courting Greatness Jerseys

PRINT RUN 350 SER.#'d SETS
*PATCH: .75X TO 2X BASE JSY HI
PATCH PRINT RUN 150 SER.#'d SETS
AJ Antawn Jamison 2.50 6.00
AS Amare Stoudemire 3.00 8.00
BD Baron Davis 2.50 6.00
BW Ben Wallace 3.00 8.00
CA Carmelo Anthony 12.00 30.00
CB Chris Bosh 8.00 20.00
DG Drew Gooden 2.00 5.00
DN Dirk Nowitzki 6.00 15.00
DW Dwyane Wade 20.00 50.00
JH Josh Howard 2.50 6.00
JH Jarvis Hayes 1.50 4.00
JR Jason Richardson 2.50 6.00
MG Manu Ginobili 5.00 12.00
MR Michael Redd 2.50 6.00
TP Tony Parker 4.00 10.00
TP Tayshaun Prince 2.50 6.00
VC Vince Carter 5.00 12.00
YM Yao Ming 6.00 15.00
ZR Zach Randolph 2.50 6.00
JON Jermaine O'Neal 2.50 6.00

2003-04 Fleer Patchworks Jerseys

PRINT RUN 200 SER.#'d SETS
*DUAL COLOR: .75X TO 2X BASE JSY HI
DUAL PRINT RUN 100 SER.#'d SETS
*MULITICOLOR: 1X TO 2.5X BASE JSY HI
MULTI PRINT RUN 50 SER.#'d SETS
N Nene 2.00 5.00
AI Allen Iverson 6.00 15.00
AK Andrei Kirilenko 2.00 5.00
AS Amare Stoudemire 3.00 8.00
DW DaJuan Wagner 2.00 5.00
GA Gilbert Arenas 2.50 6.00
GR Glenn Robinson 2.00 5.00
KG Kevin Garnett 6.00 15.00
KM Kenyon Martin 2.50 6.00
LR Luke Ridnour 2.50 6.00
MB Marcus Banks 1.50 4.00
MF Michael Finley 2.50 6.00
PS Peja Stojakovic 2.00 5.00
RH Richard Hamilton 3.00 8.00
RM Reggie Miller 5.00 12.00
SB Shane Battier 2.00 5.00
SN Steve Nash 5.00 12.00
TP Tony Parker 4.00 10.00
VC Vince Carter 5.00 12.00
YAO Yao Ming 6.00 15.00

2003-04 Fleer Patchworks Licensed Apparel

PRINT RUN 300 SER.#'d SETS
*NAME: 1.25X TO 3X BASE LIC.APP. HI
NAME PRINT RUN 50 SER.#'d SETS
*NUMBER: .6X TO 1.5X BASE LIC.APP. HI
NUMBER PRINT RUN 100 SER.#'d SETS
*TEAM NAME: .75X TO 2X BASE LIC.APP. HI
TEAM NAME PRINT RUN 150 SER.#'d SETS
AH Allan Houston 2.50 6.00
BD Baron Davis 2.50 6.00
CW Chris Webber 3.00 8.00
EB Elton Brand 2.00 5.00
JR Jason Richardson 2.50 6.00
JS Jerry Stackhouse 3.00 8.00
KM Kenyon Martin 2.50 6.00
KM Karl Malone 5.00 12.00
LS Latrell Sprewell 3.00 8.00
MB Mike Bibby 2.50 6.00
MD Mike Dunleavy 2.00 5.00
MF Michael Finley 2.50 6.00
PG Pau Gasol 4.00 10.00
PP Paul Pierce 4.00 10.00
RA Ray Allen 3.00 8.00
SF Steve Francis 2.50 6.00
SM Stephon Marbury 3.00 8.00
TM Tracy McGrady 4.00 10.00
SAR Shareef Abdur-Rahim 2.50 6.00
SON Shaquille O'Neal 10.00 25.00

2003-04 Fleer Patchworks National Pastime

COMPLETE SET (8) 15.00 30.00
PRINT RUN 250 SER.#'d SETS
1 Jermaine O'Neal 1.50 4.00
2 Jason Kidd 2.50 6.00
3 Tracy McGrady 2.50 6.00
4 Allen Iverson 4.00 10.00
5 Mike Bibby 1.50 4.00
6 Tim Duncan 4.00 10.00
7 Ray Allen 2.50 6.00
8 Larry Brown 1.50 4.00

2003-04 Fleer Patchworks National Patchtime Jerseys NBA

PRINT RUN 350 SER.#'d SETS
*NBA PATCHES: 1.25X TO 3X BASE JSY HI
NBA PATCH PRINT RUN 100 SER.#'d SETS
*USA JERSEY: .6X TO 1.5X BASE JSY HI
*USA PATCHES: 2X TO 5X BASE JSY HI
USA PATCH PRINT RUN 75 SER.#'d SETS
*USA/NBA PATCH: 3X TO 8X BASE HI
USA/NBA PATCH PRINT RUN 25 SETS
AI Allen Iverson 6.00 15.00
JK Jason Kidd 4.00 10.00
MB Mike Bibby 2.50 6.00
RA Ray Allen 4.00 10.00
TD Tim Duncan 6.00 15.00
TM Tracy McGrady 4.00 10.00
JON Jermaine O'Neal 2.50 6.00

2003-04 Fleer Patchworks Vince Carter Autographs

JSY AU PRINT RUN 100 SER.#'d SETS
PATCH AU PRINT RUN 150 SER.#'d SETS
WHITE, PURPLE, RED VERSIONS EXIST
COLORS REFER TO JERSEY IN PICTURE
OVERALL AU STATED ODDS 1:216
VC4 V.Carter JSY AU White 60.00 150.00
VC5 V.Carter JSY AU Purple 60.00 150.00
VC6 V.Carter JSY AU Red 60.00 150.00
VC7 V.Carter Patch AU White 60.00 150.00
VC8 V.Carter Patch AU Purple 60.00 150.00
VC9 V.Carter Patch AU Red 60.00 150.00

2001-02 Fleer Platinum

COMPLETE SET (250) 100.00 200.00
COMP.SET w/o SP's (200) 8.00 20.00
201-220 ODDS 1:6, 1:3 JUMBO, 1:2 RACK
221-250 ODDS 1:6, 1:3 JUMBO, 1:2 RACK
1 Tyrone Hill .25 .60
2 Sam Cassell .30 .75
3 Elton Brand .30 .75
4 Andre Miller .30 .75
5 Vitaly Potapenko .25 .60
6 Lamar Odom .30 .75
7 Mike Bibby .40 1.00
8 Alan Henderson .25 .60
9 Dan Majerle .40 1.00
10 Donyell Marshall .25 .60
11 Jason Williams .60 1.50
12 Glen Rice .40 1.00
13 Kobe Bryant 3.00 8.00
14 Pat Garrity .25 .60
15 Shawn Bradley .25 .60
16 Aaron Williams .25 .60
17 Antonio McDyess .30 .75
18 Jonathan Bender .25 .60
19 Ben Wallace .50 1.25
20 Vince Carter .75 2.00
21 Maurice Taylor .25 .60
22 Antonio Daniels .25 .60
23 Rodney Rogers .25 .60
24 Patrick Ewing .60 1.50
25 Chauncey Billups .50 1.25
26 Steve Smith .30 .75
27 Antawn Jamison .30 .75
28 Mitch Richmond .50 1.25
29 Jumaine Jones .25 .60
30 Glenn Robinson .40 1.00
31 Ron Mercer .25 .60
32 Jelani McCoy .25 .60
33 Paul Pierce .60 1.50
34 Jeff McInnis .25 .60
35 Michael Dickerson .25 .60
36 Toni Kukoc .50 1.25
37 Anthony Mason .40 1.00
38 Jamal Mashburn .30 .75
39 John Stockton .75 2.00
40 Peja Stojakovic .30 .75
41 Charlie Ward .25 .60
42 Donnell Harvey .25 .60
43 Darrell Armstrong .25 .60
44 Michael Finley .40 1.00
45 Kerry Kittles .25 .60
46 Voshon Lenard .25 .60
47 Reggie Miller .75 2.00
48 Joe Smith .30 .75
49 Antonio Davis .30 .75
50 Hakeem Olajuwon .75 2.00
51 David Robinson .75 2.00
52 Tony Delk .30 .75
53 Gary Payton .60 1.50
54 Kevin Garnett 1.00 2.50
55 Arvydas Sabonis .30 .75
56 Larry Hughes .30 .75
57 Richard Hamilton .50 1.25
58 Aaron McKie .25 .60
59 Tim Thomas .25 .60
60 Ron Artest .30 .75
61 Matt Harpring .25 .60
62 Kenny Anderson .30 .75
63 Quentin Richardson .25 .60
64 Damon Jones .25 .60
65 Theo Ratliff .25 .60
66 Brian Grant .25 .60
67 Eddie Robinson .25 .60
68 Karl Malone .75 2.00
69 Bobby Jackson .25 .60
70 Larry Johnson .40 1.00
71 Shareef Abdur-Rahim .30 .75
72 Grant Hill .60 1.50
73 Eduardo Najera .25 .60
74 Keith Van Horn .30 .75
75 Nick Van Exel .40 1.00
76 Jalen Rose .30 .75
77 Jerry Stackhouse .40 1.00
78 Jerome Williams .25 .60
79 Cuttino Mobley .30 .75
80 Derek Anderson .25 .60
81 Anfernee Hardaway 1.00 2.50
82 Rashard Lewis .30 .75
83 Terrell Brandon .30 .75
84 Scottie Pippen 1.00 2.50
85 Danny Fortson .25 .60
86 Jahidi White .25 .60
87 Eric Snow .25 .60
88 Ervin Johnson .25 .60
89 Marcus Fizer .25 .60
90 Lamond Murray .25 .60
91 Antoine Walker .30 .75
92 Keyon Dooling .25 .60
93 Bryant Reeves .25 .60
94 Hanno Mottola .25 .60
95 Tim Hardaway .50 1.25
96 David Wesley .25 .60
97 John Starks .30 .75
98 Hedo Turkoglu .30 .75
99 Allan Houston .40 1.00
100 Rick Fox .30 .75
101 Bo Outlaw .25 .60
102 Juwan Howard .30 .75
103 Kendall Gill .25 .60
104 Raef LaFrentz .25 .60
105 Austin Croshere .25 .60
106 Chucky Atkins .25 .60
107 Morris Peterson .25 .60
108 Shandon Anderson .25 .60
109 Sean Elliott .30 .75
110 Tom Gugliotta .25 .60
111 Vin Baker .30 .75
112 Wally Szczerbiak .30 .75
113 Rasheed Wallace .50 1.25
114 Vonteego Cummings .25 .60
115 Christian Laettner .30 .75
116 Dikembe Mutombo .60 1.50
117 Lindsey Hunter .25 .60
118 Jamal Crawford .40 1.00
119 Jim Jackson .25 .60
120 Bryant Stith .25 .60
121 Corey Maggette .30 .75
122 Mahmoud Abdul-Rauf .25 .60
123 Lorenzen Wright .25 .60
124 Alonzo Mourning .60 1.50
125 Jamaal Magloire .25 .60
126 Bryon Russell .25 .60
127 Vlade Divac .30 .75
128 Marcus Camby .30 .75
129 Derek Fisher .30 .75
130 Mike Miller .30 .75
131 Steve Nash .75 2.00
132 Kenyon Martin .40 1.00
133 James Posey .25 .60
134 Travis Best .25 .60
135 Corliss Williamson .25 .60
136 Alvin Williams .25 .60
137 Walt Williams .25 .60
138 Malik Rose .25 .60
139 Clifford Robinson .40 1.00
140 Ruben Patterson .25 .60
141 LaPhonso Ellis .30 .75
142 Rod Strickland .25 .60
143 Marc Jackson .25 .60
144 Hubert Davis .25 .60
145 Speedy Claxton .25 .60
146 Scott Williams .25 .60
147 Tyronn Lue .40 1.00
148 Chris Mihm .25 .60
149 George Lynch .25 .60
150 Michael Olowokandi .25 .60
151 Nazr Mohammed .25 .60
152 Eddie House .25 .60
153 Elden Campbell .25 .60
154 DeShawn Stevenson .25 .60
155 Doug Christie .25 .60
156 Kurt Thomas .25 .60
157 Robert Horry .40 1.00
158 Radoslav Nesterovic .25 .60
159 Wang Zhizhi .40 1.00
160 Stephen Jackson .30 .75
161 George McCloud .25 .60
162 Jermaine O'Neal .30 .75
163 Mateen Cleaves .25 .60
164 Charles Oakley .30 .75
165 Kenny Thomas .25 .60
166 Terry Porter .25 .60
167 Iakovos Tsakalidis .25 .60
168 Shammond Williams .25 .60
169 Anthony Peeler .25 .60
170 Damon Stoudamire .40 1.00
171 Chris Porter .25 .60
172 Chris Whitney .25 .60
173 Raja Bell RC .50 1.25
174 Darvin Ham .30 .75
175 A.J. Guyton .25 .60
176 Trajan Langdon .25 .60
177 Jerome Moiso .25 .60
178 Anthony Carter .25 .60
179 P.J. Brown .25 .60
180 Danny Manning .30 .75
181 Scot Pollard .25 .60
182 Mark Jackson .30 .75
183 Mark Madsen .25 .60
184 Michael Doleac .25 .60
185 Calvin Booth .25 .60
186 Kevin Willis .25 .60
187 Al Harrington .30 .75
188 Mikki Moore .25 .60
189 Keon Clark .25 .60
190 Moochie Norris .25 .60
191 Ron Harper .30 .75
192 Danny Ferry .25 .60
193 Jacque Vaughn .25 .60
194 Derrick Coleman .30 .75
195 Brent Barry .30 .75
196 Dion Glover .25 .60
197 Felipe Lopez .25 .60
198 Shawn Kemp .40 1.00
199 Mookie Blaylock .25 .60
200 Bonzi Wells .25 .60
201 Vince Carter HL 2.00 5.00
202 Ray Allen HL 1.50 4.00
203 Darius Miles HL .60 1.50
204 Shaquille O'Neal HL 4.00 10.00
205 Stromile Swift HL .60 1.50
206 DerMarr Johnson HL .60 1.50
207 Eddie Jones HL 1.00 2.50
208 Chris Webber HL 1.25 3.00
209 Latrell Sprewell HL 1.25 3.00
210 Tracy McGrady HL 1.50 4.00
211 Dirk Nowitzki HL 2.50 6.00
212 Stephon Marbury HL 1.25 3.00
213 Steve Francis HL 1.00 2.50
214 Tim Duncan HL 2.50 6.00
215 Jason Kidd HL 1.50 4.00
216 Shawn Marion HL 1.00 2.50
217 Desmond Mason HL .75 2.00
218 Courtney Alexander HL .60 1.50
219 Baron Davis HL 1.00 2.50
220 Allen Iverson HL 2.50 6.00
221 Joe Johnson RC 1.50 4.00
222 Kedrick Brown RC .60 1.50
223 Joseph Forte RC .60 1.50
224 Kirk Haston RC .60 1.50
225 Tyson Chandler RC 1.50 4.00
226 Eddy Curry RC 1.00 2.50
227 DeSagana Diop RC .60 1.50
228 Jeff Trepagnier RC .60 1.50
229 Oscar Torres RC 1.00 2.50
230 Rodney White RC .60 1.50
231 Jason Richardson RC 1.50 4.00
232 Troy Murphy RC .75 2.00
233 Eddie Griffin RC .75 2.00
234 Jamaal Tinsley RC .75 2.00
235 Pau Gasol RC 4.00 10.00
236 Shane Battier RC 2.00 5.00
237 Richard Jefferson RC 1.25 3.00
238 Jason Collins RC .75 2.00
239 Brendan Haywood RC .75 2.00
240 Steven Hunter RC .60 1.50
241 Zach Randolph RC 2.00 5.00
242 Gerald Wallace RC 1.25 3.00
243 Tony Parker RC 4.00 10.00
244 Vladimir Radmanovic RC .75 2.00
245 Michael Bradley RC .60 1.50
246 Andrei Kirilenko RC 1.50 4.00
247 Kwame Brown RC 1.00 2.50
248 Alton Ford RC 1.00 2.50
249 Zeljko Rebraca RC 1.00 2.50
250 Trenton Hassell RC .60 1.50

2001-02 Fleer Platinum 15th Anniversary Reprints

COMPLETE SET (25) 60.00 120.00
STATED ODDS 1:12, 1:6 JUMBO, 1:3 RACK
1 Michael Jordan 15.00 40.00
2 Karl Malone 4.00 10.00
3 Hakeem Olajuwon 4.00 10.00
4 Patrick Ewing 3.00 8.00
5 Reggie Miller 4.00 10.00
6 John Stockton 4.00 10.00
7 Scottie Pippen 5.00 12.00
8 David Robinson 4.00 10.00
9 Shaquille O'Neal 8.00 20.00
10 Alonzo Mourning 3.00 8.00
11 Chris Webber 2.50 6.00
12 Grant Hill 3.00 8.00
13 Jason Kidd 3.00 8.00
14 Eddie Jones 2.00 5.00
15 Kevin Garnett 5.00 12.00
16 Kobe Bryant 10.00 25.00
17 Allen Iverson 5.00 12.00
18 Shareef Abdur-Rahim 1.50 4.00
19 Tim Duncan 5.00 12.00
20 Tracy McGrady 3.00 8.00
21 Vince Carter 4.00 10.00
22 Dirk Nowitzki 5.00 12.00
23 Steve Francis 2.00 5.00
24 Darius Miles 1.25 3.00
25 Mike Miller 1.50 4.00

2001-02 Fleer Platinum Anniversary Edition

*ANNIV 1-200: 4X TO 10X BASE CARD HI
*ANNIV 201-250: 6X TO 15X HI
1-200 PRINT RUN 201 SERIAL #'d SETS
201-250 PRINT RUN 21 SERIAL #'d SETS
13 Kobe Bryant 20.00 50.00

2001-02 Fleer Platinum Classic Combinations

1-5 PRINT RUN 1000 SERIAL #'d SETS
6-10 PRINT RUN 500 SERIAL #'d SETS
11-15 PRINT RUN 2000 SERIAL #'d SETS
1 Stockton/Malone/1000 3.00 8.00
2 Iverson/Mutombo/1000 3.00 8.00
3 J.Kidd/G.Hill/1000 3.00 8.00
4 Francis/Brand/1000 3.00 8.00
5 Carter/Jamison/1000 3.00 8.00
6 Olajuwon/Ewing/500 3.00 8.00
7 Carter/McGrady/500 6.00 15.00
8 K.Bryant/S.O'Neal/500 15.00 40.00
9 Duncan/Robinsn/500 4.00 10.00
10 K.Garnett/D.Miles/500 3.00 8.00
11 Nowitzki/Finley/2000 3.00 8.00
12 Walker/Pierce/2000 3.00 8.00
13 Allen/Robinson/2000 3.00 8.00
14 Sprwell/Houston/2000 3.00 8.00
15 Ewing/Mrning/2000 3.00 8.00

2001-02 Fleer Platinum Classic Combinations Jerseys

PRINT RUN 100 SERIAL #'d SETS
1 J.Stockton/K.Malone 12.00 30.00
2 A.Iverson/D.Mutombo 10.00 25.00
3 J.Kidd/G.Hill 10.00 25.00
4 S.Francis/E.Brand 8.00 20.00
5 V.Carter/A.Jamison 10.00 25.00
6 H.Olajuwon/P.Ewing 10.00 25.00
7 V.Carter/T.McGrady 15.00 40.00
11 D.Nowitzki/M.Finley 8.00 20.00
12 A.Walker/P.Pierce 8.00 20.00
13 R.Allen/G.Robinson 8.00 20.00
15 P.Ewing/A.Mourning 15.00 40.00

2001-02 Fleer Platinum Lucky 13

COMPLETE SET (13) 75.00 150.00
PRINT RUN 500 SERIAL #'d SETS
1 Kwame Brown 4.00 10.00
2 Tyson Chandler 6.00 15.00
3 Pau Gasol 15.00 40.00
4 Eddy Curry 4.00 10.00
5 Jason Richardson 6.00 15.00
6 Shane Battier 8.00 20.00
7 Eddie Griffin 3.00 8.00
8 DeSagana Diop 2.50 6.00
9 Rodney White 2.50 6.00
10 Joe Johnson 6.00 15.00
11 Kedrick Brown 2.50 6.00
12 Vladimir Radmanovic 3.00 8.00
13 Richard Jefferson 5.00 12.00

2001-02 Fleer Platinum Nameplates

STATED ODDS 1:12 JUMBO
1 Alonzo Mourning/175 15.00 40.00
2 Hakeem Olajuwon/175 20.00 50.00
3 Allen Iverson/150 25.00 60.00
4 Stephon Marbury/100 12.00 30.00
5 Gary Payton/100 15.00 40.00
6 Glenn Robinson/50 10.00 25.00
7 Shareef Abdur-Rahim/250 8.00 20.00
8 Keith Van Horn/225 8.00 20.00
9 John Stockton/100 20.00 50.00
10 Antoine Walker/100 8.00 20.00
11 David Robinson/125 20.00 50.00
12 Michael Finley/175 10.00 25.00
13 Vince Carter/75 20.00 50.00

2001-02 Fleer Platinum National Patch Time

STATED ODDS 1:24 HOBBY
1 Tom Gugliotta 2.00 5.00
2 Shawn Marion 3.00 8.00
3 Darius Miles 2.00 5.00
4 Mike Miller 2.50 6.00
5 Jason Terry 3.00 8.00
6 Stromile Swift 2.00 5.00
7 Keith Van Horn 2.50 6.00
8 Ray Allen 5.00 12.00
9 Baron Davis 3.00 8.00
10 Shareef Abdur-Rahim 2.50 6.00
11 Stephon Marbury 4.00 10.00
12 Jason Kidd 5.00 12.00
13 Mike Bibby 3.00 8.00
14 Jerome Moiso 2.00 5.00
15 Richard Hamilton 4.00 10.00
16 Paul Pierce 5.00 12.00
17 Dikembe Mutombo 5.00 12.00
18 Gary Payton 5.00 12.00
19 Patrick Ewing 5.00 12.00
20 Vince Carter 6.00 15.00
21 Corey Maggette 2.50 6.00
22 Jacque Vaughn 2.00 5.00
23 Darrell Armstrong 2.00 5.00
24 Mitch Richmond 4.00 10.00
25 Allen Iverson 8.00 20.00
26 Desmond Mason 2.50 6.00

2001-02 Fleer Platinum Stadium Standouts

COMPLETE SET (15) 20.00 50.00
STATED ODDS 1:18, 1:6 JUMBO, 1:3 RACK
1 Vince Carter 2.50 6.00
2 Grant Hill 2.00 5.00
3 Kobe Bryant 10.00 25.00
4 Steve Francis 1.25 3.00
5 Tracy McGrady 2.00 5.00
6 Elton Brand 1.00 2.50
7 Kevin Garnett 3.00 8.00
8 Allen Iverson 3.00 8.00
9 Dirk Nowitzki 3.00 8.00
10 Shaquille O'Neal 5.00 12.00
11 Tim Duncan 3.00 8.00
12 Jason Kidd 2.00 5.00
13 Darius Miles .75 2.00
14 Chris Webber 1.50 4.00
15 Ray Allen 2.00 5.00

2002-03 Fleer Platinum

COMP.SET w/o SP's (160) 20.00 50.00
ODDS 1:1 RACK, 1:2 JUMBO, 1:4 WAX
171-180 PRINT RUN 750 SERIAL #'d SETS
181-190 PRINT RUN 350 SERIAL #'d SETS
181-190 INSERTED ONLY IN JUMBO PACKS
191-200 PRINT RUN 250 SERIAL #'d SETS
191-200 INSERTED ONLY IN RACK PACKS
1 Vince Carter .75 2.00
2 Lamar Odom .40 1.00
3 Darrell Armstrong .25 .60
4 Kwame Brown .25 .60
5 Ron Artest .30 .75
6 Kurt Thomas .25 .60
7 Jerry Stackhouse .40 1.00
8 Eddie Griffin .25 .60
9 David Wesley .25 .60
10 Morris Peterson .30 .75
11 Jon Barry .25 .60
12 Troy Hudson .25 .60
13 Kenny Anderson .30 .75
14 Corliss Williamson .25 .60
15 Kevin Garnett 1.00 2.50
16 Desmond Mason .30 .75
17 Lucious Harris .25 .60
18 Steve Smith .30 .75
19 Nick Van Exel .40 1.00
20 Tyson Chandler .40 1.00
21 Shane Battier .40 1.00
22 Rasheed Wallace .50 1.25
23 Donyell Marshall .25 .60
24 Anfernee Hardaway 1.00 2.50
25 Antoine Walker .30 .75
26 Kobe Bryant 3.00 8.00
27 Keith Van Horn .30 .75
28 Elton Brand .30 .75
29 Grant Hill .60 1.50
30 Elden Campbell .25 .60
31 John Stockton .75 2.00
32 Wally Szczerbiak .30 .75
33 Speedy Claxton .25 .60
34 Voshon Lenard .25 .60
35 Eddie Jones .40 1.00
36 Bonzi Wells .25 .60
37 Jalen Rose .50 1.25
38 Jason Williams .30 .75
39 Tom Gugliotta .25 .60
40 Juwan Howard .30 .75
41 Michael Redd .30 .75
42 David Robinson .75 2.00
43 Steve Nash .75 2.00
44 Vlade Divac .30 .75
45 Avery Johnson .30 .75
46 Scottie Pippen 1.00 2.50
47 Eric Williams .25 .60
48 Derek Fisher .40 1.00
49 Tony Battie .25 .60
50 Rick Fox .25 .60
51 Theo Ratliff .25 .60
52 Corey Maggette .30 .75
53 Jermaine O'Neal .30 .75
54 Bryon Russell .25 .60
55 Steve Francis .40 1.00
56 Jamal Mashburn .30 .75
57 Jerome Williams .25 .60
58 Gilbert Arenas .40 1.00
59 Joe Smith .30 .75
60 Brent Barry .30 .75
61 Marcus Camby .30 .75
62 Toni Kukoc .40 1.00
63 Tim Duncan 1.00 2.50
64 Ira Newble .25 .60
65 Brian Grant .25 .60
66 Jason Terry .30 .75
67 Andre Miller .30 .75
68 Mike Miller .30 .75
69 Troy Murphy .30 .75
70 P.J. Brown .25 .60
71 Jason Richardson .40 1.00
72 Glenn Robinson .40 1.00
73 Richard Jefferson .30 .75
74 Richard Hamilton .50 1.25
75 Jason Kidd .60 1.50
76 Rashard Lewis .30 .75
77 Kenny Satterfield .25 .60
78 Terrell Brandon .25 .60
79 Dirk Nowitzki 1.00 2.50
80 Chris Webber .50 1.25
81 Michael Finley .40 1.00
82 Malik Allen .25 .60
83 Bobby Jackson .25 .60
84 Darius Miles .25 .60
85 Kendall Gill .25 .60
86 Damon Stoudamire .40 1.00
87 Shammond Williams .25 .60
88 Stephon Marbury .50 1.25
89 Shareef Abdur-Rahim .40 1.00
90 Charlie Ward .25 .60
91 Michael Jordan 4.00 10.00
92 Jamaal Magloire .25 .60
93 Karl Malone .75 2.00
94 Kerry Kittles .25 .60
95 Lindsey Hunter .25 .60
96 Gary Payton .60 1.50
97 Travis Best .25 .60
98 Derek Anderson .25 .60
99 Stromile Swift .25 .60
100 Shaquille O'Neal 1.50 4.00
101 Derrick Coleman .30 .75
102 DeShawn Stevenson .25 .60
103 Jamaal Tinsley .25 .60
104 Latrell Sprewell .40 1.00
105 Larry Hughes .30 .75
106 Eddy Curry .25 .60
107 Shawn Marion .40 1.00
108 Paul Pierce .60 1.50
109 Samaki Walker .25 .60
110 Allen Iverson 1.00 2.50
111 Michael Olowokandi .25 .60
112 Tracy McGrady .60 1.50
113 Shawn Bradley .25 .60
114 Reggie Miller .75 2.00
115 Antonio McDyess .30 .75
116 Calbert Cheaney .25 .60
117 Al Harrington .30 .75
118 Allan Houston .40 1.00
119 Andrei Kirilenko .30 .75
120 Courtney Alexander .25 .60
121 Alvin Williams .25 .60
122 Antawn Jamison .30 .75
123 Dikembe Mutombo .60 1.50
124 Tony Parker .60 1.50
125 Raef LaFrentz .25 .60
126 Ray Allen .60 1.50
127 Peja Stojakovic .30 .75
128 Zydrunas Ilgauskas .30 .75
129 Gerald Wallace .30 .75
130 Ruben Patterson .25 .60
131 Pau Gasol .60 1.50
132 Joe Johnson .30 .75
133 Aaron McKie .25 .60
134 Walter McCarty .25 .60
135 Baron Davis .40 1.00
136 Kenyon Martin .40 1.00
137 Antonio Davis .30 .75
138 Ben Wallace .50 1.25
139 Sam Cassell .30 .75
140 Mike Bibby .40 1.00
141 Cuttino Mobley .25 .60
142 LaPhonso Ellis .30 .75
143 Shandon Anderson .25 .60
144 Hedo Turkoglu .30 .75
145 Matt Harpring .25 .60
146 Dion Glover .25 .60
147 Tony Delk .25 .60
148 Ricky Davis .30 .75
149 James Posey .30 .75
150 Chucky Atkins .25 .60
151 Danny Fortson .25 .60
152 Robert Horry .40 1.00
153 Radoslav Nesterovic .25 .60
154 Pat Garrity .25 .60
155 Todd MacCulloch .25 .60
156 Eric Snow .25 .60
157 Malik Rose .25 .60
158 Vladimir Radmanovic .25 .60
159 Trenton Hassell .25 .60
160 Brad Miller .30 .75
161 Kareem Rush RC 1.00 2.50
162 Nikoloz Tskitishvili RC .75 2.00
163 Nene Hilario RC 1.25 3.00
164 Marcus Haislip RC .75 2.00
165 Jiri Welsch RC 1.00 2.50
166 Dan Dickau RC .75 2.00
167 Vincent Yarbrough RC .75 2.00
168 Tito Maddox RC .75 2.00
169 Mike Dunleavy RC 1.25 3.00
170 Chris Wilcox RC 1.00 2.50
171 Jared Jeffries RC 1.50 4.00
172 Bostjan Nachbar RC 1.50 4.00
173 Frank Williams RC 1.25 3.00
174 Reggie Evans RC 1.50 4.00
175 Casey Jacobsen RC 1.50 4.00
176 Tayshaun Prince RC 4.00 10.00
177 Mike Batiste RC 1.25 3.00
178 Drew Gooden RC 2.00 5.00
179 DaJuan Wagner RC 1.50 4.00
180 Tamar Slay RC 1.25 3.00
181 Melvin Ely RC 2.00 5.00
182 Rasual Butler RC 2.00 5.00
183 Dan Gadzuric RC 2.00 5.00
184 Ryan Humphrey RC 2.00 5.00
185 Gordan Giricek RC 2.50 6.00
186 Mehmet Okur RC 2.50 6.00
187 Jay Williams RC 2.00 5.00
188 Caron Butler RC 2.00 5.00
189 Qyntel Woods RC 1.50 4.00
190 Amare Stoudemire RC 6.00 15.00
191 Yao Ming RC 10.00 25.00
192 Carlos Boozer RC 3.00 8.00
193 John Salmons RC 3.00 8.00
194 Fred Jones RC 2.50 6.00
195 Juan Dixon RC 2.50 6.00
196 Manu Ginobili RC 20.00 50.00
197 Pat Burke RC 2.00 5.00
198 Smush Parker RC 3.00 8.00
199 Lonny Baxter RC 2.00 5.00
200 Ronald Murray RC 3.00 8.00

2002-03 Fleer Platinum Finish

*STARS: 4X TO 10X BASE CARD HI
*161-170 RCs: 1.5X TO 4X BASE CARD HI
*171-180 RCs: 1X TO 2.5X BASE CARD HI
*181-190 RCs: .75X TO 2X BASE CARD HI
*191-200 RCs: .6X TO 1.5X BASE CARD HI
PRINT RUN 100 SERIAL #'d SETS
26 Kobe Bryant 125.00 300.00
91 Michael Jordan 200.00 500.00

2002-03 Fleer Platinum Freshman Fabric

STATED ODDS 1:2 RACK PACKS
AS Amare Stoudemire 6.00 15.00
CB Caron Butler 2.50 6.00
CB2 Carlos Boozer 2.50 6.00
CW Chris Wilcox 2.00 5.00
DD Dan Dickau 1.50 4.00
DG Drew Gooden 2.50 6.00
DW DaJuan Wagner 2.00 5.00
EG Manu Ginobili 12.00 30.00
JD Juan Dixon 2.00 5.00
KR Kareem Rush 2.00 5.00
NH Nene Hilario 2.50 6.00
NT Nikoloz Tskitishvili 1.50 4.00
QW Qyntel Woods 1.50 4.00
TP Tayshaun Prince 5.00 12.00
YM Yao Ming 12.00 30.00

2002-03 Fleer Platinum Guts and Glory

COMPLETE SET (10) 6.00 15.00
ODDS: 1:1 RACK, 1:2 JUMBO, 1:4 WAX
1GG Steve Nash 2.00 5.00
2GG Ben Wallace 1.25 3.00
3GG Antawn Jamison .75 2.00
4GG Elton Brand .75 2.00
5GG Kenyon Martin 1.00 2.50
6GG Rasheed Wallace 1.25 3.00
7GG Reggie Miller 2.00 5.00
8GG Andre Miller .75 2.00
9GG Vince Carter 2.00 5.00
10GG Richard Jefferson .75 2.00

2002-03 Fleer Platinum Inside the Playbook

STATED PRINT RUN 400 SERIAL #'d SETS
1PB Paul Pierce 2.50 6.00
2PB Kobe Bryant 25.00 60.00
3PB Caron Butler 1.50 4.00
4PB Tracy McGrady 2.50 6.00
5PB Allen Iverson 4.00 10.00
6PB Tim Duncan 4.00 10.00
7PB Vince Carter 3.00 8.00
8PB Jay Williams 1.25 3.00
9PB Michael Jordan 40.00 100.00
10PB DaJuan Wagner 1.25 3.00
11PB Steve Nash 3.00 8.00
12PB Nene Hilario 1.50 4.00
13PB Ben Wallace 2.00 5.00
14PB Mike Dunleavy 1.50 4.00
15PB Yao Ming 8.00 20.00

2002-03 Fleer Platinum Inside the Playbook Game Used

STATED PRINT RUN 250 SERIAL #'d SETS
INSERTED ONLY IN WAX PACKS
AI Allen Iverson 8.00 20.00
BW Ben Wallace 4.00 10.00
CB Caron Butler 3.00 8.00
DW DaJuan Wagner 2.50 6.00
NH Nene Hilario 3.00 8.00
PP Paul Pierce 5.00 12.00
SN Steve Nash 6.00 15.00
TM Tracy McGrady 5.00 12.00
VC Vince Carter 6.00 15.00
YM Yao Ming 12.00 30.00

2002-03 Fleer Platinum Nameplates

INSERTED ONLY IN JUMBO PACKS
AI Allen Iverson/485 25.00 60.00
AM Andre Miller/260 6.00 15.00
AS Amare Stoudemire/315 6.00 15.00
BD Baron Davis/110 15.00 40.00
BW Ben Wallace/145 12.00 30.00
CB Caron Butler/280 10.00 25.00
DG Drew Gooden/220 10.00 25.00
DM Darius Miles/115 10.00 25.00
DN Dirk Nowitzki/255 25.00 60.00
DR David Robinson/210 15.00 40.00
EB Elton Brand/225 6.00 15.00
JK Jason Kidd/300 12.00 30.00
JO Jermaine O'Neal/135 15.00 40.00
JS John Stockton/230 15.00 40.00
KB Kwame Brown/355 6.00 15.00
KG Kevin Garnett/460 25.00 60.00
KM Kenyon Martin/170 6.00 15.00
LS Latrell Sprewell/190 15.00 40.00
PG Pau Gasol/350 12.00 30.00
PP Paul Pierce/200 15.00 40.00
QW Qyntel Woods/325 6.00 15.00
RA Ray Allen/400 12.00 30.00
SF Steve Francis/385 10.00 25.00
SN Steve Nash/110 20.00 50.00
TC Tyson Chandler/355 6.00 15.00
TM Tracy McGrady/175 15.00 40.00
TP Tony Parker/115 15.00 40.00
VC Vince Carter/545 15.00 40.00
YM Yao Ming/290 40.00 100.00

2002-03 Fleer Platinum Portraits

COMPLETE SET (15) 15.00 40.00
ODDS: 1:4 RACK, 1:8 JUMBO, 1:14 WAX
1PP Vince Carter 2.00 5.00
2PP Jason Kidd 1.50 4.00
3PP Shane Battier 1.00 2.50
4PP Steve Francis 1.00 2.50
5PP Chris Webber 1.25 3.00
6PP Jason Richardson 1.00 2.50
7PP Richard Jefferson .75 2.00
8PP Dirk Nowitzki 2.50 6.00
9PP Kevin Garnett 2.50 6.00
10PP Baron Davis 1.00 2.50
11PP Darius Miles .60 1.50
12PP Tim Duncan 2.50 6.00
13PP Kobe Bryant 8.00 20.00
14PP Shaquille O'Neal 4.00 10.00
15PP Michael Jordan 10.00 25.00

2002-03 Fleer Platinum Portraits Game Worn Jerseys

STATED ODDS 1:21 WAX PACKS
*PATCH: 1X TO 2.5X BASE HI
PATCH STATED PRINT RUN 100 SETS
BD Baron Davis 3.00 8.00
DN Dirk Nowitzki 8.00 20.00
JK Jason Kidd 5.00 12.00
JR Jason Richardson 3.00 8.00
KG Kevin Garnett 8.00 20.00
RJ Richard Jefferson 2.50 6.00
SB Shane Battier 3.00 8.00
SF Steve Francis 3.00 8.00
VC Vince Carter 6.00 15.00

2002-03 Fleer Platinum Vince Carter's All-Stars Game Used

RINT RUN 250 SERIAL #'d SETS
SERTED ONLY IN WAX PACKS
V.Carter/A.Iverson 15.00 40.00
V.Carter/B.Wallace 15.00 40.00
V.Carter/D.Nowitzki 15.00 40.00
V.Carter/J.Kidd 15.00 40.00
V.Carter/K.Garnett 15.00 40.00
V.Carter/T.McGrady 15.00 40.00

2003-04 Fleer Platinum

OMPLETE SET (200) 500.00 1,000.00
OMP.SET w/o SP's (170) 15.00 40.00
TATED ODDS 1:3 WAX, 1:2 JUMBO
31-190 PRINT RUN 750 SER.#'d SETS
31-190 INSERTED IN WAX ONLY
91-200 PRINT RUN 500 SER.#'d SETS
91-200 INSERTED IN JUMBO PACKS ONLY
Shane Battier .25 .60
Brad Miller .25 .60
Jason Kidd .50 1.25
Nick Van Exel .30 .75
David Wesley .20 .50
Corey Maggette .25 .60
Juan Dixon .20 .50
Jamaal Tinsley .20 .50
Stromile Swift .20 .50
Dajuan Wagner .20 .50
Joe Smith .25 .60
2 Jermaine O'Neal .30 .75
3 Steve Nash .60 1.50
4 Karl Malone .60 1.50
5 Vince Carter .60 1.50
6 Antonio McDyess .25 .60
7 Tim Thomas .20 .50
8 Vladimir Radmanovic .20 .50
9 Scottie Pippen .75 2.00
0 Tracy McGrady .50 1.25
Darius Miles .20 .50
2 Toni Kukoc .30 .75
3 Antonio Davis .25 .60
4 Jamal Crawford .30 .75
5 Rasho Nesterovic .20 .50
6 Carlos Boozer .25 .60
7 Cuttino Mobley .20 .50
8 Larry Hughes .25 .60
9 Alvin Williams .20 .50
0 Andre Miller .25 .60
1 Amare Stoudemire .40 1.00
2 Eric Williams .20 .50
3 Pau Gasol .50 1.25
4 Kenyon Martin .30 .75
5 Elton Brand .25 .60
6 Charlie Ward .20 .50
7 Andrei Kirilenko .25 .60
8 Aaron McKie .20 .50
9 Maurice Taylor .20 .50
0 Baron Davis .30 .75
1 Dirk Nowitzki .75 2.00
2 Gary Payton .50 1.25
3 Grant Hill .40 1.00
4 Jalen Rose .25 .60
5 Allan Houston .30 .75
6 Erick Dampier .20 .50
7 Brian Grant .20 .50
8 Wally Szczerbiak .25 .60
9 Greg Ostertag .20 .50
50 Gilbert Arenas .30 .75
51 Kenny Anderson .25 .60
52 Juwan Howard .20 .50
53 Jason Terry .25 .60
54 Raef LaFrentz .20 .50
55 Ricky Davis .25 .60
56 Kobe Bryant 2.50 6.00
57 Chris Webber .40 1.00
58 P.J. Brown .20 .50
59 Nene .25 .60
60 Kenny Thomas .20 .50
61 Mike Bibby .30 .75
62 Chris Wilcox .20 .50
63 Anfernee Hardaway .75 2.00
64 Drew Gooden .25 .60
65 Rodney White .20 .50
66 Shareef Abdur-Rahim .30 .75
67 Quentin Richardson .20 .50
68 Ben Wallace .40 1.00
69 Latrell Sprewell .40 1.00
70 Shaquille O'Neal 1.25 3.00
71 Vin Baker .20 .50
72 Tony Parker .50 1.25
73 Stephen Jackson .25 .60
74 Ray Allen .50 1.25
75 Eric Snow .20 .50
76 Jason Richardson .30 .75
77 Shammond Williams .20 .50
78 Tayshaun Prince .30 .75
79 Antawn Jamison .30 .75
80 Derek Fisher .30 .75
81 Jeff Foster .20 .50
82 Kwame Brown .20 .50
83 Yao Ming .75 2.00
84 Rasheed Wallace .40 1.00
85 Tyson Chandler .25 .60
86 Mike Dunleavy .20 .50
87 Alan Henderson .20 .50
88 Rashard Lewis .25 .60
89 Jamaal Magloire .20 .50
90 Stephon Marbury .40 1.00
91 DeShawn Stevenson .20 .50
92 Damon Stoudamire .25 .60
93 Eddy Curry .20 .50
94 Peja Stojakovic .25 .60
95 Glenn Robinson .25 .60
96 Mike Miller .25 .60
97 Richard Hamilton .40 1.00
98 Kevin Garnett .75 2.00
99 Zach Randolph .30 .75
100 Tony Delk .25 .60
101 Clifford Robinson .20 .50
102 Steve Francis .30 .75
103 Curtis Borchardt .25 .60
104 Jerry Stackhouse .40 1.00
105 Desmond Mason .25 .60
106 Chauncey Billups .40 1.00
107 Sam Cassell .25 .60
108 Michael Finley .30 .75
109 Hedo Turkoglu .25 .60
110 Ronald Murray .20 .50
111 Allen Iverson .75 2.00
112 Richard Jefferson .25 .60
113 Theo Ratliff .20 .50
114 Ron Artest .30 .75
115 Doug Christie .25 .60
116 Lamar Odom .25 .60
117 Lamond Murray .20 .50
118 Bonzi Wells .20 .50
119 Caron Butler .25 .60
120 Marcus Camby .25 .60
121 Manu Ginobili .60 1.50
122 Paul Pierce .50 1.25
123 Troy Hudson .20 .50
124 Jim Jackson .20 .50
125 Keith Van Horn .25 .60
126 Reggie Miller .60 1.50
127 Tim Duncan .75 2.00
128 Shawn Marion .30 .75
129 Eddie Jones .30 .75
130 Matt Harpring .20 .50
131 Elden Campbell .20 .50
132 Marko Jaric .20 .50
133 John Wallace .20 .50
134 Erick Strickland .20 .50
135 Voshon Lenard .20 .50
136 Aaron Williams .20 .50
137 Qyntel Woods .20 .50
138 Kelvin Cato .20 .50
139 Michael Curry .20 .50
140 Vlade Divac .30 .75
141 Jason Hart .20 .50
142 Nazr Mohammed UH .20 .50
143 Mike James UH .20 .50
144 Jerome Williams UH .20 .50
145 Zydrunas Ilgauskas UH .25 .60
146 Antoine Walker UH .30 .75
147 Earl Boykins UH .20 .50
148 Mehmet Okur UH .25 .60
149 Brian Cardinal UH .20 .50
150 Bostjan Nachbar UH .20 .50
151 Al Harrington UH .25 .60
152 Eddie House UH .20 .50
153 Devean George UH .20 .50
154 Jason Williams UH .50 1.25
155 Rafer Alston UH .20 .50
156 Michael Redd UH .30 .75
157 Gary Trent UH .20 .50
158 Kerry Kittles UH .20 .50
159 Jamal Mashburn UH .25 .60
160 Kurt Thomas UH .20 .50
161 Tyronn Lue UH .20 .50
162 Derrick Coleman UH .30 .75
163 Joe Johnson UH .25 .60
164 Dale Davis UH .20 .50
165 Bobby Jackson UH .25 .60
166 Malik Rose UH .20 .50
167 Brent Barry UH .20 .50
168 Donyell Marshall UH .20 .50
169 Carlos Arroyo UH .25 .60
170 Etan Thomas UH .20 .50
171 Zoran Planinic RC .60 1.50
172 Jason Kapono RC .60 1.50
173 Zarko Cabarkapa RC .60 1.50
174 Darko Milicic RC .75 2.00
175 Aleksandar Pavlovic RC .75 2.00
176 Marcus Banks RC .60 1.50
177 Willie Green RC 1.00 2.50
178 Udonis Haslem RC 1.25 3.00
179 Nick Collison RC .75 2.00
180 Chris Kaman RC 1.00 2.50
181 T.J. Ford RC 1.25 3.00
182 Travis Outlaw RC 1.25 3.00
183 LeBron James RC 500.00 1,000.00
184 Troy Bell RC 1.00 2.50
185 Reece Gaines RC 1.00 2.50
186 David West RC 2.00 5.00
187 Kirk Hinrich RC 1.50 4.00
188 Chris Bosh RC 5.00 12.00
189 Leandro Barbosa RC 1.50 4.00
190 Dwyane Wade RC 25.00 60.00
191 Mike Sweetney RC 1.00 2.50
192 Darius Songaila 1.00 2.50
193 Luke Ridnour RC 1.50 4.00
194 Carmelo Anthony RC 15.00 40.00
195 Jarvis Hayes RC 1.00 2.50
196 Mickael Pietrus RC 1.25 3.00
197 Dahntay Jones RC 1.25 3.00
198 Josh Howard RC 1.50 4.00
199 Maciej Lampe RC 1.00 2.50
200 Luke Walton RC 1.50 4.00

2003-04 Fleer Platinum Finish

*1-170 SINGLES: 4X TO 10X BASE HI
*171-180 RCs: 1.25X TO 3X BASE HI
*181-190 RCs: 1.25X TO 3X BASE HI
*191-200 RCs: 1.25X TO 3X BASE HI
PRINT RUN 100 SER.#'d SETS
56 Kobe Bryant 75.00 200.00

2003-04 Fleer Platinum Big Signs

COMPLETE SET (15) 40.00 100.00
STATED ODDS 1:9 H WAX, 1:2 JUMBO 1:8 R
1 Kevin Garnett 1.50 4.00
2 Allen Iverson 1.50 4.00
3 Shaquille O'Neal 2.50 6.00
4 Darko Milicic .50 1.25
5 Kobe Bryant 8.00 20.00
6 Ben Wallace .75 2.00
7 LeBron James 60.00 150.00
8 Dwyane Wade 8.00 20.00
9 Dirk Nowitzki 1.50 4.00
10 Baron Davis .60 1.50
11 Yao Ming 1.50 4.00
12 Carmelo Anthony 3.00 8.00
13 Peja Stojakovic .50 1.25
14 Jermaine O'Neal .60 1.50
15 Vince Carter 1.25 3.00

2003-04 Fleer Platinum Big Signs Autographs

PRINT RUN 50 SER.#'d SETS
BW Ben Wallace 40.00 100.00
DW Dwyane Wade 125.00 300.00
VC Vince Carter 75.00 200.00

2003-04 Fleer Platinum Inscribed

PRINT RUNS LISTED IN CHECKLIST
N Nene/188 4.00 10.00
AK Andrei Kirilenko/193 3.00 8.00
BW Ben Wallace/35 40.00 100.00
CA1 Carmelo Anthony/282 75.00 200.00
CA2 Carmelo Anthony 75.00 200.00
CB Chris Bosh/250 12.00 30.00
DG Drew Gooden/66 3.00 8.00
DR David Robinson/195 30.00 80.00
DW David West/250 5.00 12.00
GA1 Gilbert Arenas/315 4.00 10.00
GA2 Gilbert Arenas/32 15.00 40.00
KK Kyle Korver/87 15.00 30.00
KR Kareem Rush/248 2.50 6.00
LB Leandro Barbosa/196 4.00 10.00
LR Luke Ridnour/197 4.00 10.00
LW Luke Walton/132 4.00 10.00
MB1 Marcus Banks/350 2.50 6.00
MG Manu Ginobili/198 40.00 100.00
ML Maciej Lampe/185 2.50 6.00
MP Mickael Pietrus/249 3.00 8.00
MS Mike Sweetney/264 2.50 6.00
TC Tyson Chandler/195 4.00 10.00
TM Tracy McGrady/99 60.00 150.00
TO Travis Outlaw/276 3.00 8.00
TP Tayshaun Prince/185 6.00 15.00
UH Udonis Haslem/195 5.00 12.00
VC1 Vince Carter/280 75.00 200.00
ZC1 Zarko Cabarkapa/235 2.50 6.00
ZC2 Zarko Cabarkapa/37 2.50 6.00
CAR1 Caron Butler/365 3.00 8.00
CAR2 Caron Butler/28 3.00 8.00
JHO Josh Howard/250 4.00 10.00
SHM Shawn Marion/101 8.00 20.00

2003-04 Fleer Platinum Locker Room Memorabilia

STATED ODDS 1:24 H, 1:96 R
*DUAL SINGLES: 1.25X TO 3X BASE MEM.HI
DUAL PRINT RUN 50 SER.#'d SETS
N Nene 2.50 6.00
AK Andrei Kirilenko 2.50 6.00
BD Baron Davis 3.00 8.00
BW Ben Wallace 4.00 10.00
CB Caron Butler 2.50 [illegible]
EB Elton Brand 2.50 [illegible]
GR Glenn Robinson 2.50 [illegible]
JH Jarvis Hayes 2.00 [illegible]
JK Jason Kidd 5.00 12.00
JR Jason Richardson 3.00 8.00
KM Karl Malone 6.00 15.00
MD Mike Dunleavy 2.50 6.00
MF Michael Finley 3.00 8.00
MG Manu Ginobili 6.00 15.00
MR Michael Redd 3.00 8.00
PP Paul Pierce 5.00 12.00
PS Peja Stojakovic 2.50 6.00
RM Reggie Miller 6.00 15.00
SF Steve Francis 3.00 8.00
SM Stephon Marbury 4.00 10.00
SN Steve Nash 6.00 15.00
JON Jermaine O'Neal 3.00 8.00
SHM Shawn Marion 3.00 8.00
YAO Yao Ming 8.00 20.00
KMAR Kenyon Martin 3.00 8.00

2003-04 Fleer Platinum Nameplates

PRINT RUNS LISTED BELOW
AH Allan Houston/450 8.00 20.00
AJ Antawn Jamison/145 8.00 20.00
BW Ben Wallace/90 8.00 20.00
CA Carmelo Anthony/380 40.00 100.00
CK Chris Kaman/465 8.00 20.00
CW Chris Webber/695 10.00 25.00
DW Dajuan Wagner/585 5.00 12.00
DW Dwyane Wade/465 60.00 150.00
GA Gilbert Arenas/235 8.00 20.00
JC Jamal Crawford/323 8.00 20.00
JH Jarvis Hayes/375 5.00 12.00
LR Luke Ridnour/710 8.00 20.00
LW Luke Walton/215 8.00 20.00
MB Mike Bibby/365 8.00 20.00
MD Mike Dunleavy/250 6.00 15.00
MG Manu Ginobili/195 15.00 40.00
MM Mike Miller/590 6.00 15.00
MP Mickael Pietrus/253 6.00 15.00
MR Michael Redd/725 8.00 20.00
RH Richard Hamilton/170 10.00 25.00
SB Shane Battier/715 6.00 15.00
SP Scottie Pippen/390 20.00 50.00
TD Tim Duncan/725 20.00 50.00
TO Travis Outlaw/590 6.00 15.00
TP Tayshaun Prince/455 8.00 20.00
VC Vince Carter/725 15.00 40.00
ZR Zach Randolph/210 8.00 20.00
SAR Shareef Abdur-Rahim/600 8.00 20.00

2003-04 Fleer Platinum Nameplates Dual

PRINT RUN 25 SER.#'d SETS
AJSN A.Jamison/S.Nash 25.00 60.00
GAJH G.Arenas/J.Hayes 12.00 30.00
GPLW G.Payton/L.Walton 20.00 50.00
JCSP J.Crawford/S.Pippen 30.00 80.00
MBCW M.Bibby/C.Webber 15.00 40.00
MDMP M.Dunleavy/M.Pietrus 10.00 25.00
RHBW R.Hamilton/B.Wallace 15.00 40.00
SBMM S.Battier/M.Miller 10.00 25.00
TDMG T.Duncan/M.Ginobili 30.00 80.00
TOZR T.Outlaw/Z.Randolph 12.00 30.00

2003-04 Fleer Platinum NBA Scouting Report

COMPLETE SET (15) 200.00 500.00
PRINT RUN 400 SER.#'d SETS
1 Shaquille O'Neal 10.00 25.00
2 Tracy McGrady 4.00 10.00
3 Tim Duncan 6.00 15.00
4 Jason Kidd 4.00 10.00
5 Amare Stoudemire 3.00 8.00
6 Kobe Bryant 25.00 60.00
7 Steve Francis 2.50 6.00
8 Kevin Garnett 6.00 15.00
9 Dirk Nowitzki 6.00 15.00
10 Jason Richardson 2.50 6.00
11 Darko Milicic 2.00 5.00
12 Jarvis Hayes 1.50 4.00
13 LeBron James 200.00 500.00
14 Chris Webber 3.00 8.00
15 Chris Bosh 8.00 20.00

2003-04 Fleer Platinum NBA Scouting Report Jerseys

PRINT RUN 250 SER.#'d SETS
INSERTED IN HOBBY WAX AND RETAIL
AS Amare Stoudemire 4.00 10.00
CB Chris Bosh 10.00 25.00
DN Dirk Nowitzki 8.00 20.00
JH Jarvis Hayes 2.00 5.00
JK Jason Kidd 5.00 12.00
KG Kevin Garnett 8.00 20.00
SF Steve Francis 3.00 8.00
SO Shaquille O'Neal 12.00 30.00
TD Tim Duncan 8.00 20.00
TM Tracy McGrady 5.00 12.00

2003-04 Fleer Platinum Portraits

COMPLETE SET (15) 15.00 40.00
STAT.ODDS 1:18 H WAX, 1:4 JUMBO 1:14 R
1 Pau Gasol 2.00 5.00
2 Yao Ming 3.00 8.00
3 Michael Finley 1.25 3.00
4 Tony Parker 2.00 5.00
5 Dwyane Wade 10.00 25.00
6 Darko Milicic 1.00 2.50
7 Tracy McGrady 2.00 5.00
8 Allen Iverson 3.00 8.00
9 Reggie Miller 2.50 6.00
10 Paul Pierce 2.00 5.00
11 Amare Stoudemire 1.50 4.00
12 Steve Nash 2.50 6.00
13 Caron Butler 1.00 2.50
14 Drew Gooden 1.00 2.50
15 Vince Carter 2.50 6.00

2003-04 Fleer Platinum Portraits Jerseys

STATED ODDS 1:40 H WAX, 1:120 R
*PATCHES: 1X TO 2.5X BASE JSY HI
PATCH PRINT RUN 100 SER.#'d SETS
AI Allen Iverson 6.00 15.00
AS Amare Stoudemire 3.00 8.00
DW Dwyane Wade 20.00 50.00
MF Michael Finley 2.50 6.00
PG Pau Gasol 4.00 10.00
RM Reggie Miller 5.00 12.00
TM Tracy McGrady 4.00 10.00
TP Tony Parker 4.00 10.00
VC Vince Carter 5.00 12.00
YAO Yao Ming 6.00 15.00

2003-04 Fleer Platinum Showdown Series

STATED ODDS 1:288 H WAX, 1:480 R
1 A.Iverson/K.Bryant 30.00 80.00
2 J.Kidd/T.Parker 6.00 15.00
3 S.O'Neal/T.Duncan 15.00 40.00
4 P.Pierce/A.Walker 6.00 15.00
5 L.James/C.Anthony 125.00 300.00
6 J.O'Neal/B.Wallace 5.00 12.00
7 V.Carter/T.McGrady 8.00 20.00
8 D.Nowitzki/C.Webber 10.00 25.00
9 K.Garnett/Stoudemire 10.00 25.00
10 N.Collison/K.Hinrich 4.00 10.00

2000-01 Fleer Premium

COMPLETE SET w/o RC (200) 12.50 30.00
RCs: STATED PRINT RUN 1999 SERIAL #'d SETS
217-241: FIRST 250 CONTAIN BALL SWATCH
1 Vince Carter .60 1.50
2 Kobe Bryant 2.50 6.00
3 Jermaine Jackson .20 .50
4 Lamar Odom .30 .75
5 Robert Traylor .20 .50
6 Jason Kidd .50 1.25
7 Rashard Lewis .25 .60
8 Ron Artest .30 .75
9 Grant Hill .50 1.25
10 Kenny Thomas .20 .50
11 Anthony Carter .20 .50
12 Kerry Kittles .25 .60
13 Pat Garrity .20 .50
14 David Robinson .60 1.50
15 Bryant Reeves .20 .50
16 Fred Hoiberg .20 .50
17 Jerry Stackhouse .30 .75
18 Donyell Marshall .25 .60
19 Ron Harper .30 .75
20 Scott Burrell .25 .60
21 Ron Mercer .25 .60
22 Avery Johnson .25 .60
23 Jacque Vaughn .20 .50
24 Adrian Griffin .20 .50
25 Antonio McDyess .25 .60
26 Adonal Foyle .20 .50
27 Derek Fisher .30 .75
28 Terrell Brandon .25 .60
29 Matt Harpring .20 .50
30 Nazr Mohammed .20 .50
31 Tom Gugliotta .25 .60
32 Scott Padgett .20 .50
33 Detlef Schrempf .25 .60
34 Dirk Nowitzki .75 2.00
35 Mookie Blaylock .30 .75
36 James Posey .20 .50
37 Latrell Sprewell .40 1.00
38 Michael Doleac .20 .50
39 Damon Stoudamire .30 .75
40 Tim Duncan .75 2.00
41 John Stockton .60 1.50
42 Danny Fortson .25 .60
43 Raef LaFrentz .25 .60
44 Steve Francis .30 .75
45 Travis Knight .20 .50
46 Kevin Garnett .75 2.00
47 Mitch Richmond .40 1.00
48 Olden Polynice .20 .50
49 Derrick Coleman .30 .75
50 Ervin Johnson .20 .50
51 Shandon Anderson .20 .50
52 Jamal Mashburn .25 .60
53 Joe Smith .25 .60
54 Bo Outlaw .25 .60
55 Clifford Robinson .30 .75
56 Scottie Pippen .75 2.00
57 Chris Webber .40 1.00
58 Doug Christie .25 .60
59 Michael Dickerson .20 .50
60 Anthony Mason .30 .75
61 Shawn Bradley .20 .50
62 Reggie Miller .60 1.50
63 P.J. Brown .20 .50
64 Wally Szczerbiak .25 .60
65 Keon Clark .20 .50
66 Anthony Peeler .20 .50
67 Doug West .20 .50
68 Antoine Walker .30 .75
69 Trajan Langdon .20 .50
70 Mark Jackson .25 .60
71 Sam Cassell .25 .60
72 Kurt Thomas .20 .50
73 Ruben Patterson .20 .50
74 Alvin Williams .20 .50
75 Juwan Howard .25 .60
76 Baron Davis .30 .75
77 Otis Thorpe .25 .60
78 Austin Croshere .20 .50
79 Tony Delk .20 .50
80 William Avery .20 .50
81 Matt Geiger .20 .50
82 Richard Hamilton .40 1.00
83 Ricky Davis .25 .60
84 Hubert Davis .20 .50
85 Jalen Rose .25 .60
86 Theo Ratliff .20 .50
87 Bobby Jackson .25 .60
88 Glenn Robinson .30 .75
89 Kendall Gill .20 .50
90 Laron Profit .20 .50
91 Brad Miller .25 .60
92 Cedric Ceballos .25 .60
93 Arvydas Sabonis .30 .75
94 Vitaly Potapenko .20 .50
95 Rod Strickland .20 .50
96 Erick Dampier .20 .50
97 Ryan Bowen .20 .50
98 Dale Davis .25 .60
99 Larry Johnson .40 1.00
100 John Thomas .20 .50
101 Rodney Rogers .20 .50
102 Ray Allen .50 1.25
103 Isaac Austin .20 .50
104 Radoslav Nesterovic .20 .50
105 Tariq Abdul-Wahad .20 .50
106 Jonathan Bender .20 .50
107 Tim Hardaway .40 1.00
108 Jamie Feick .20 .50
109 Toni Kukoc .40 1.00
110 Tyrone Corbin .20 .50
111 Aleksandar Radojevic .20 .50
112 Tony Battie .20 .50
113 Andre Miller .25 .60
114 Derek Anderson .25 .60
115 Tim Thomas .25 .60
116 Corey Maggette .25 .60
117 Rasheed Wallace .40 1.00
118 Shammond Williams .20 .50
119 Charlie Ward .25 .60
120 Paul Pierce .50 1.25
121 Shawn Kemp .50 1.25
122 Darrell Armstrong .20 .50
123 Fred Vinson .20 .50
124 Jim Jackson .20 .50
125 Steve Nash .50 1.25
126 Michael Stewart .20 .50
127 Maurice Taylor .20 .50
128 Michael Ruffin .20 .50
129 Vlade Divac .30 .75
130 LaPhonso Ellis .25 .60
131 Eddie Jones .30 .75
132 Hakeem Olajuwon .60 1.50
133 Rick Fox .25 .60
134 Patrick Ewing .50 1.25
135 Brian Grant .25 .60
136 Jaren Jackson .20 .50
137 Christian Laettner .30 .75
138 Greg Ostertag .20 .50
139 Anfernee Hardaway .50 1.25
140 Nick Van Exel .30 .75
141 Jason Caffey .20 .50
142 Michael Olowokandi .20 .50
143 Darvin Ham .25 .60
144 Calbert Cheaney .20 .50
145 Steve Smith .30 .75
146 Jason Williams .50 1.25
147 Jelani McCoy .20 .50
148 Karl Malone .60 1.50
149 Dikembe Mutombo .50 1.25
150 Wesley Person .20 .50
151 Kelvin Cato .20 .50
152 Alonzo Mourning .50 1.25
153 Terry Mills .20 .50
154 Allen Iverson .75 2.00
155 Bonzi Wells .20 .50
156 Antonio Daniels .20 .50
157 Shareef Abdur-Rahim .30 .75
158 Randy Brown .20 .50
159 Mike Bibby .30 .75
160 Travis Best .20 .50
161 Dan Majerle .30 .75
162 Aaron McKie .20 .50
163 Jason Terry .30 .75
164 Michael Finley .30 .75
165 Antonio Davis .25 .60
166 Lindsey Hunter .20 .50
167 Cuttino Mobley .25 .60
168 Glen Rice .30 .75
169 Stephon Marbury .40 1.00
170 Sean Elliott .25 .60
171 Cedric Henderson .20 .50
172 Eric Snow .20 .50
173 Othella Harrington .20 .50
174 Vonteego Cummings .20 .50
175 John Amaechi .20 .50
176 Allan Houston .30 .75
177 Shawn Marion .30 .75
178 Scot Pollard .20 .50
179 Elton Brand .30 .75
180 Loy Vaught .20 .50
181 Larry Hughes .30 .75
182 Shaquille O'Neal 1.25 3.00
183 Keith Van Horn .25 .60
184 Terry Porter .20 .50
185 Quincy Lewis .20 .50
186 Alan Henderson .20 .50
187 Brevin Knight .20 .50
188 Walt Williams .20 .50
189 Clarence Weatherspoon .20 .50
190 Marcus Camby .25 .60
191 Corliss Williamson .20 .50
192 Gary Payton .50 1.25
193 Felipe Lopez .20 .50
194 Elden Campbell .20 .50
195 Jerome Williams .20 .50
196 Antawn Jamison .30 .75
197 Gerard King .20 .50
198 Andrae Patterson .20 .50
199 Vin Baker .25 .60
200 Tracy McGrady .60 1.50
201 Chris Carrawell RC .75 2.00
202 Eduardo Najera RC 1.25 3.00
203 Olumide Oyedeji RC .75 2.00
204 Hanno Mottola RC .75 2.00
205 Dan McClintock RC 1.25 3.00
206 Jacquay Walls RC 1.25 3.00
207 Corey Hightower RC 1.25 3.00
208 Jamal Crawford RC 3.00 8.00
209 Soumaila Samake RC .75 2.00
210 Michael Redd RC 3.00 8.00
211 Jason Hart RC 1.25 3.00
212 Mark Karcher RC .75 2.00
213 Chris Porter RC .75 2.00
214 Eddie House RC 1.00 2.50
215 Jabari Smith RC .75 2.00
216 Dan Langhi RC .75 2.00
217 Desmond Mason RC 1.50 4.00
218 Darius Miles RC 1.25 3.00
219 Donnell Harvey RC 1.00 2.50
220 DeShawn Stevenson RC 1.25 3.00
221 Kenyon Martin RC 2.50 6.00
222 Joel Przybilla RC 1.00 2.50
223 Keyon Dooling RC 1.00 2.50
224 Speedy Claxton RC 1.25 3.00
225 Jerome Moiso RC .75 2.00
226 Hedo Turkoglu RC 2.00 5.00
227 Mark Madsen RC 1.25 3.00
228 Morris Peterson RC 1.25 3.00
229 Courtney Alexander RC .75 2.00
230 Etan Thomas RC 1.00 2.50
231 Mateen Cleaves RC 1.00 2.50
232 Stromile Swift RC 1.00 2.50
233 Marcus Fizer RC 1.00 2.50
234 Quentin Richardson RC 1.00 2.50
235 Jason Collier RC 1.25 3.00
236 Jamaal Magloire RC 1.25 3.00
237 Erick Barkley RC .75 2.00
238 DerMarr Johnson RC .75 2.00
239 Chris Mihm RC .75 2.00
240 Mamadou N'Diaye RC .75 2.00
241 Mike Miller RC 2.00 5.00

2000-01 Fleer Premium Rookie Game Balls

*GAME BALL: .6X TO 1.5X HI COLUMN

2000-01 Fleer Premium 10th Anni-VINCE-ry

COMPLETE SET (10) 20.00 40.00
COMMON CARD (AV1-AV10) 2.50 6.00
STATED ODDS 1:24 HOB, 1:20 RET

2000-01 Fleer Premium Vince Carter Rookie Remnants

FLOOR: 100 CARDS IN EACH RELEASE
FLOOR/GJ: 15 CARDS IN EACH RELEASE
FLOOR/GJ AU 1 CARD IN EACH RELEASE
NNO Vince Carter FLR/100 12.50 30.00
NNO Vince Carter FLR JSY/15 20.00 50.00

2000-01 Fleer Premium Name Game

COMPLETE SET (15) 25.00 50.00
STATED ODDS 1:24
NG1 Vince Carter 2.50 6.00
NG2 Allen Iverson 3.00 8.00
NG3 Shaquille O'Neal 5.00 12.00
NG4 Jason Kidd 2.00 5.00
NG5 Jason Williams 2.00 5.00
NG6 Glenn Robinson 1.25 3.00
NG7 Karl Malone 2.50 6.00
NG8 Reggie Miller 2.50 6.00
NG9 Hakeem Olajuwon 2.50 6.00
NG10 Lamar Odom 1.25 3.00
NG11 Tim Duncan 3.00 8.00
NG12 Grant Hill 2.00 5.00
NG13 Kobe Bryant 10.00 25.00
NG14 Tracy McGrady 2.50 6.00
NG15 Kevin Garnett 3.00 8.00

2000-01 Fleer Premium Name Game Premium

STATED PRINT RUN 50 SERIAL #'d SETS
NG1 Vince Carter 30.00 80.00
NG2 Allen Iverson 60.00 150.00
NG3 Shaquille O'Neal 60.00 150.00
NG4 Jason Kidd 25.00 60.00
NG5 Jason Williams 60.00 150.00
NG6 Glenn Robinson 15.00 40.00
NG7 Karl Malone 30.00 80.00
NG8 Reggie Miller 30.00 80.00
NG9 Hakeem Olajuwon 30.00 80.00
NG10 Lamar Odom 15.00 40.00

2000-01 Fleer Premium Skilled Artists

COMPLETE SET (15) 10.00 20.00
STATED ODDS 1:12 HOB, 1:15 RET
SA1 Vince Carter 1.25 3.00
SA2 Steve Francis .60 1.50
SA3 Paul Pierce 1.00 2.50
SA4 Gary Payton 1.00 2.50
SA5 Jason Williams 1.00 2.50
SA6 Larry Hughes .60 1.50
SA7 Tim Duncan 1.50 4.00
SA8 Kobe Bryant 5.00 12.00
SA9 Chris Webber .75 2.00
SA10 Tracy McGrady 1.25 3.00
SA11 Dirk Nowitzki 1.50 4.00
SA12 Elton Brand .60 1.50
SA13 Andre Miller .50 1.25
SA14 Ray Allen 1.00 2.50
SA15 Shareef Abdur-Rahim .60 1.50

2000-01 Fleer Premium Skilled Artists Premium

STATED PRINT RUN 100 SERIAL #'d SETS
SA1 Vince Carter 20.00 50.00
SA2 Steve Francis 10.00 25.00
SA3 Paul Pierce 15.00 40.00
SA4 Gary Payton 15.00 40.00
SA5 Jason Williams 15.00 40.00
SA6 Chris Webber 12.00 30.00

2000-01 Fleer Premium Skylines

COMPLETE SET (10) 25.00 60.00
STATED ODDS 1:144 HOB, 1:288 RET
SL1 Vince Carter 4.00 10.00
SL2 Allen Iverson 5.00 12.00
SL3 Kobe Bryant 15.00 40.00
SL4 Latrell Sprewell 2.50 6.00
SL5 Elton Brand 2.00 5.00
SL6 Grant Hill 3.00 8.00
SL7 Steve Francis 2.00 5.00
SL8 Richard Hamilton 2.50 6.00
SL9 Gary Payton 3.00 8.00
SL10 David Robinson 4.00 10.00

2000-01 Fleer Premium Sole Train

COMPLETE SET (15) 4.00 10.00
STATED ODDS 1:6 HOB, 1:8 RET
ST1 Vince Carter .75 2.00
ST2 Marcus Camby .30 .75
ST3 Wally Szczerbiak .30 .75
ST4 Lamar Odom .40 1.00
ST5 Shaquille O'Neal 1.50 4.00
ST6 Antoine Walker .40 1.00
ST7 Eddie Jones .40 1.00
ST8 Larry Hughes .40 1.00
ST9 Baron Davis .40 1.00
ST10 Mike Bibby .40 1.00
ST11 Elton Brand .40 1.00
ST12 Kevin Garnett 1.00 2.50
ST13 Allen Iverson 1.00 2.50
ST14 Tim Duncan 1.00 2.50
ST15 Grant Hill .60 1.50

2000-01 Fleer Premium Sole Train Premium

STATED PRINT RUN 50 SERIAL #'d SETS
ST1 Vince Carter 15.00 40.00
ST2 Marcus Camby 6.00 15.00
ST3 Wally Szczerbiak 6.00 15.00
ST4 Lamar Odom 8.00 20.00
ST5 Shaquille O'Neal 40.00 100.00
ST6 Antoine Walker 8.00 20.00
ST7 Eddie Jones 8.00 20.00
ST8 Larry Hughes 8.00 20.00
ST9 Baron Davis 8.00 20.00
ST10 Mike Bibby 8.00 20.00

2001-02 Fleer Premium

COMPLETE SET (185) 100.00 200.00
COMP.SET w/o SP's (1-150) 15.00 40.00
151-185 PRINT RUN 1500 SER.#'d SETS
1 Shareef Abdur-Rahim .25 .60
2 Charlie Ward .20 .50
3 Anfernee Hardaway .75 2.00
4 Robert Horry .30 .75
5 Michael Jordan 2.50 6.00
6 Trajan Langdon .20 .50
7 Dan Majerle .30 .75
8 Tracy McGrady .50 1.25
9 Alonzo Mourning .50 1.25
10 Gary Payton .50 1.25
11 Erick Barkley .20 .50
12 Jerry Stackhouse .30 .75
13 Vince Carter .60 1.50
14 Speedy Claxton .20 .50
15 DerMarr Johnson .20 .50
16 Bryon Russell .20 .50
17 Derrick Coleman .25 .60
18 Kevin Willis .20 .50
19 Dirk Nowitzki .75 2.00
20 Derek Anderson .20 .50
21 Tim Hardaway .40 1.00
22 Avery Johnson .25 .60
23 Quincy Lewis .20 .50
24 Shawn Marion .30 .75
25 Joe Smith .25 .60
26 Tim Thomas .20 .50
27 Bonzi Wells .20 .50
28 Ron Artest .25 .60
29 Elton Brand .25 .60
30 Mateen Cleaves .20 .50
31 Marcus Fizer .20 .50
32 Ervin Johnson .20 .50
33 Mark Madsen .20 .50
34 Andre Miller .25 .60
35 Nazr Mohammed .20 .50
36 Dikembe Mutombo .50 1.25
37 Ben Wallace .40 1.00
38 Scottie Pippen .75 2.00
39 Theo Ratliff .20 .50
40 Hedo Turkoglu .25 .60
41 Alvin Williams .20 .50
42 Corey Maggette .25 .60
43 Steve Francis .30 .75
44 Dean Garrett .20 .50
45 Wally Szczerbiak .25 .60
46 Brent Barry .25 .60
47 Vlade Divac .25 .60
48 LaPhonso Ellis .25 .60
49 Tyrone Hill .20 .50
50 Toni Kukoc .40 1.00
51 George Lynch .20 .50
52 Antonio McDyess .25 .60
53 Paul Pierce .50 1.25
54 Mitch Richmond .40 1.00
55 Latrell Sprewell .40 1.00
56 Otis Thorpe .25 .60
57 Ray Allen .50 1.25
58 Mike Bibby .30 .75
59 P.J. Brown .20 .50
60 Allan Houston .30 .75
61 Stephon Marbury .40 1.00
62 Aaron McKie .20 .50
63 Reggie Miller .60 1.50
64 Eduardo Najera .20 .50
65 Eddie Robinson .20 .50

66 John Stockton .60 1.50
67 Chris Webber .40 1.00
68 Kenny Anderson .25 .60
69 Alan Henderson .20 .50
70 Dan Langhi .20 .50
71 Rashard Lewis .25 .60
72 Donyell Marshall .20 .50
73 Charles Oakley .25 .60
74 Stephen Jackson .25 .60
75 Clarence Weatherspoon .20 .50
76 David Wesley .20 .50
77 Kobe Bryant 2.50 6.00
78 Tom Gugliotta .20 .50
79 Darius Miles .20 .50
80 Cuttino Mobley .25 .60
81 Jason Terry .30 .75
82 Shandon Anderson .20 .50
83 Antonio Daniels .20 .50
84 Larry Hughes .25 .60
85 Raef LaFrentz .20 .50
86 Kenyon Martin .30 .75
87 Lamar Odom .25 .60
88 Jermaine O'Neal .25 .60
89 Glenn Robinson .30 .75
90 Damon Stoudamire .30 .75
91 Eddie House .20 .50
92 Antonio Davis .20 .50
93 Rick Fox .25 .60
94 Allen Iverson .75 2.00
95 Chris Mihm .20 .50
96 Hakeem Olajuwon .60 1.50
97 Clifford Robinson .30 .75
98 Derek Fisher .25 .60
99 Joel Przybilla .20 .50
100 Sean Rooks .20 .50
101 Jason Kidd .50 1.25
102 Antoine Walker .25 .60
103 Jason Williams .50 1.25
104 Jamal Mashburn .25 .60
105 Courtney Alexander .20 .50
106 Vin Baker .25 .60
107 Chauncey Billups .40 1.00
108 Marcus Camby .25 .60
109 Kevin Garnett .75 2.00
110 Juwan Howard .25 .60
111 Marc Jackson .20 .50
112 Karl Malone .60 1.50
113 Ricky Davis .25 .60
114 Desmond Mason .25 .60
115 Jerome Moiso .20 .50
116 Steve Nash .60 1.50
117 Quentin Richardson .20 .50
118 Peja Stojakovic .25 .60
119 Rasheed Wallace .40 1.00
120 Travis Best .20 .50
121 Terrell Brandon .25 .60
122 Austin Croshere .20 .50
123 Tony Delk .25 .60
124 Anthony Mason .30 .75
125 Patrick Ewing .50 1.25
126 Brian Grant .20 .50
127 Bobby Jackson .20 .50
128 Eddie Jones .30 .75
129 Popeye Jones .20 .50
130 Brevin Knight .20 .50
131 Mike Miller .25 .60
132 Shaquille O'Neal 1.25 3.00
133 Morris Peterson .20 .50
134 Mookie Blaylock .20 .50
135 David Robinson .60 1.50
136 John Starks .20 .50
137 Stromile Swift .20 .50
138 Nick Van Exel .30 .75
139 Keith Van Horn .25 .60
140 Antawn Jamison .25 .60
141 Kurt Thomas .20 .50
142 Sam Cassell .25 .60
143 Tim Duncan .75 2.00
144 Baron Davis .30 .75
145 Jerome Williams .20 .50
146 Michael Finley .30 .75
147 Richard Hamilton .40 1.00
148 Grant Hill .50 1.25
149 Jalen Rose .25 .60
150 Steve Smith .25 .60
151 Kwame Brown RC 1.25 3.00
152 Jeryl Sasser RC .75 2.00
153 Shane Battier RC 2.50 6.00
154 Gilbert Arenas RC 3.00 8.00
155 Jarron Collins RC 1.25 3.00
156 Jamaal Tinsley RC 1.00 2.50
157 Brandon Armstrong RC .75 2.00
158 Michael Bradley RC .75 2.00
159 Tyson Chandler RC 2.00 5.00
160 Joseph Forte RC .75 2.00
161 Brendan Haywood RC 1.00 2.50
162 Joe Johnson RC 2.00 5.00
163 Vladimir Radmanovic RC 1.00 2.50
164 Gerald Wallace RC 1.50 4.00
165 Steven Hunter RC .75 2.00
166 Richard Jefferson RC 1.50 4.00
167 DeSagana Diop RC .75 2.00
168 Terence Morris RC .75 2.00
169 Jason Richardson RC 2.00 5.00
170 Jeff Trepagnier RC .75 2.00
171 Kirk Haston RC .75 2.00
172 Eddy Curry RC 1.25 3.00
173 Eddie Griffin RC 1.00 2.50
174 Omar Cook RC 1.25 3.00
175 Pau Gasol RC 5.00 12.00
176 Troy Murphy RC 1.00 2.50
177 Trenton Hassell RC .75 2.00
178 Kedrick Brown RC .75 2.00
179 Zeljko Rebraca RC 1.25 3.00
180 Tony Parker RC 5.00 12.00
181 Rodney White RC .75 2.00
182 Jason Collins RC 1.00 2.50
183 Samuel Dalembert RC 1.25 3.00
184 Zach Randolph RC 2.50 6.00
185 Will Solomon RC .75 2.00

2001-02 Fleer Premium Star Rubies

*RUBY STARS: 8X TO 20X BASE CARD HI
1-150 PRINT RUN 100 SER.#'d SETS
*RUBY RCs: 2X TO 5X BASE CARD HI
151-185 PRINT RUN 50 SER.#'d SETS
5 Michael Jordan 150.00 400.00
9 Alonzo Mourning 10.00 25.00
38 Scottie Pippen 15.00 40.00
67 Chris Webber 8.00 20.00
77 Kobe Bryant 60.00 150.00

2001-02 Fleer Premium Commanding Respect

COMPLETE SET (25) 30.00 60.00
STATED ODDS 1:20
1 Shaquille O'Neal 4.00 10.00
2 Tim Duncan 2.50 6.00
3 Marc Jackson .60 1.50
4 Kevin Garnett 2.50 6.00
5 Kobe Bryant 8.00 20.00
6 Chris Webber 1.25 3.00
7 Michael Jordan 8.00 20.00
8 Dirk Nowitzki 2.50 6.00
9 Ray Allen 1.50 4.00
10 Courtney Alexander .60 1.50
11 David Robinson 2.00 5.00
12 Darius Miles .60 1.50
13 Baron Davis 1.00 2.50
14 Tracy McGrady 1.50 4.00
15 Vince Carter 2.00 5.00
16 Antawn Jamison .75 2.00
17 Jerry Stackhouse 1.00 2.50
18 Allen Iverson 2.50 6.00
19 Jason Kidd 1.50 4.00
20 Antoine Walker .75 2.00
21 Karl Malone 2.00 5.00
22 Grant Hill 1.50 4.00
23 Rasheed Wallace 1.25 3.00
24 Anfernee Hardaway 2.50 6.00
25 Steve Francis 1.00 2.50

2001-02 Fleer Premium Commanding Respect Premium Patches

STATED PRINT RUN 75 SER.#'d SETS
AH Anfernee Hardaway 40.00 100.00
AI Allen Iverson 40.00 100.00
AW Antoine Walker 12.00 30.00
BD Baron Davis 15.00 40.00
CW Chris Webber 20.00 50.00
DM Darius Miles 10.00 25.00
GH Grant Hill 25.00 60.00
JK Jason Kidd 25.00 60.00
KM Karl Malone 30.00 80.00
MM Mike Miller 12.00 30.00
RA Ray Allen 25.00 60.00
RW Rasheed Wallace 20.00 50.00
SF Steve Francis 15.00 40.00
TM Tracy McGrady 20.00 50.00
VC Vince Carter 20.00 50.00

2001-02 Fleer Premium Rookie Revolution

COMPLETE SET (10) 8.00 20.00
STATED ODDS 1:10
1 Kwame Brown .75 2.00
2 Eddy Curry .75 2.00
3 Tyson Chandler 1.25 3.00
4 Pau Gasol 3.00 8.00
5 Joe Johnson 1.25 3.00
6 Michael Bradley .50 1.25
7 Jason Richardson 1.25 3.00
8 DeSagana Diop .50 1.25
9 Troy Murphy .60 1.50
10 Jamaal Tinsley .60 1.50

2001-02 Fleer Premium Rookie Revolution Autographs

STATED PRINT RUN 50 SER.#'d SETS
NNO Eddy Curry 10.00 25.00
NNO Joe Johnson 15.00 40.00
NNO Kwame Brown 6.00 15.00
NNO Michael Bradley 4.00 10.00

2001-02 Fleer Premium Solid Performers

COMPLETE SET (30) 30.00 80.00
STATED ODDS 1:20
1 Tracy McGrady 1.50 4.00
2 John Stockton 2.00 5.00
3 Dirk Nowitzki 2.50 6.00
4 Antawn Jamison .75 2.00
5 Scottie Pippen 2.50 6.00
6 Morris Peterson .60 1.50
7 Ray Allen 1.50 4.00
8 Antoine Walker .75 2.00
9 Anfernee Hardaway 2.50 6.00
10 Michael Jordan 8.00 20.00
11 Jerry Stackhouse 1.00 2.50
12 Karl Malone 2.00 5.00
13 Jason Kidd 1.50 4.00
14 Chris Webber 1.25 3.00
15 Vince Carter 2.00 5.00
16 Allen Iverson 2.50 6.00
17 Courtney Alexander .60 1.50
18 Darius Miles .60 1.50
19 Steve Francis 1.00 2.50
20 Grant Hill 1.50 4.00
21 Rasheed Wallace 1.25 3.00
22 Kenyon Martin 1.00 2.50
23 Shawn Marion 1.00 2.50
24 Elton Brand .75 2.00
25 Jason Terry 1.00 2.50
26 Kobe Bryant 8.00 20.00
27 Tim Duncan 2.50 6.00
28 Kevin Garnett 2.50 6.00
29 Reggie Miller 2.00 5.00
30 Shaquille O'Neal 4.00 10.00

2001-02 Fleer Premium Solid Performers Premium Jerseys

STATED ODDS 1:24
AH Anfernee Hardaway 8.00 20.00
AI Allen Iverson 8.00 20.00
AW Antoine Walker 2.50 6.00
CW Chris Webber 4.00 10.00
DM Darius Miles 2.00 5.00
EB Elton Brand 2.50 6.00
GH Grant Hill 5.00 12.00
JK Jason Kidd 5.00 12.00
JS Jerry Stackhouse 3.00 8.00
JS John Stockton 6.00 15.00
JT Jason Terry 3.00 8.00
KM Karl Malone 6.00 15.00
MA Kenyon Martin 3.00 8.00
MM Mike Miller 2.50 6.00
MP Morris Peterson 2.00 5.00
RA Ray Allen 5.00 12.00
RW Rasheed Wallace 4.00 10.00
SF Steve Francis 3.00 8.00
SM Shawn Marion 3.00 8.00
TM Tracy McGrady 5.00 12.00
VC Vince Carter 6.00 15.00

2001-02 Fleer Premium Vertical Heights

COMPLETE SET (25) 15.00 40.00
STATED ODDS 1:10
1 Darius Miles .50 1.25
2 Tracy McGrady 1.25 3.00
3 Allen Iverson 2.00 5.00
4 Baron Davis .75 2.00
5 Desmond Mason .60 1.50
6 Antoine Walker .60 1.50
7 Jerry Stackhouse .75 2.00
8 Michael Finley .75 2.00
9 Eddie Jones .75 2.00
10 Steve Francis .75 2.00
11 David Robinson 1.50 4.00
12 Antawn Jamison .60 1.50
13 Karl Malone 1.50 4.00
14 Michael Jordan 6.00 15.00
15 Vince Carter 1.50 4.00
16 Chris Webber 1.00 2.50
17 Latrell Sprewell 1.00 2.50
18 Ray Allen 1.25 3.00
19 Grant Hill 1.25 3.00
20 Dirk Nowitzki 2.00 5.00
21 Kobe Bryant 6.00 15.00
22 Shaquille O'Neal 3.00 8.00
23 Kevin Garnett 2.00 5.00
24 Tim Duncan 2.00 5.00
25 Stephon Marbury 1.00 2.50

2001-02 Fleer Premium Vertical Heights Shoes

STATED PRINT RUN 100 SER. #'d SETS
NNO Antoine Walker 8.00 20.00
NNO Lamar Odom 8.00 20.00
NNO Jerry Stackhouse 10.00 25.00
NNO Vince Carter 20.00 50.00

2002-03 Fleer Premium

COMP.SET w/o SP's (110) 20.00 50.00
111-140 PRINT RUN 1500 SER.#'d SETS
1 Tracy McGrady .60 1.50
2 Tim Duncan 1.00 2.50
3 Shaquille O'Neal 1.50 4.00
4 Jason Kidd .60 1.50
5 Kobe Bryant 3.00 8.00
6 Kevin Garnett 1.00 2.50
7 Chris Webber .50 1.25
8 Dirk Nowitzki 1.00 2.50
9 Gary Payton .60 1.50
10 Allen Iverson 1.00 2.50
11 Ben Wallace .50 1.25
12 Jermaine O'Neal .30 .75
13 Dikembe Mutombo .60 1.50
14 Paul Pierce .60 1.50
15 Steve Nash .75 2.00
16 Pau Gasol .60 1.50
17 Jason Richardson .40 1.00
18 Tony Parker .60 1.50
19 Andrei Kirilenko .30 .75
20 Shane Battier .40 1.00
21 Jamaal Tinsley .25 .60
22 Richard Jefferson .30 .75
23 Joe Johnson .30 .75
24 Eddie Griffin .25 .60
25 Zeljko Rebraca .25 .60
26 Vladimir Radmanovic .25 .60
27 Damon Stoudamire .40 1.00
28 Eddie Jones .40 1.00
29 Tyson Chandler .40 1.00
30 Karl Malone .75 2.00
31 David Wesley .25 .60
32 Steve Francis .40 1.00
33 Hakeem Olajuwon .50 1.25
34 Baron Davis .40 1.00
35 Antonio McDyess .30 .75
36 Mike Bibby .40 1.00
37 Bonzi Wells .25 .60
38 Ray Allen .60 1.50
39 Doug Christie .25 .60
40 Richard Hamilton .50 1.25
41 Grant Hill .60 1.50
42 Elton Brand .30 .75
43 Gilbert Arenas .40 1.00
44 Vlade Divac .30 .75
45 Sam Cassell .30 .75
46 Jalen Rose .30 .75
47 Peja Stojakovic .30 .75
48 Glenn Robinson .40 1.00
49 Ricky Davis .30 .75
50 Antonio Daniels .25 .60
51 Tim Thomas .25 .60
52 Andre Miller .30 .75
53 Stephon Marbury .50 1.25
54 Robert Horry .40 1.00
55 Tony Delk .25 .60
56 David Robinson .75 2.00
57 Radoslav Nesterovic .25 .60
58 Lamond Murray .25 .60
59 Brent Barry .25 .60
60 Wally Szczerbiak .30 .75
61 Lee Nailon .25 .60
62 Rashard Lewis .30 .75
63 Kenyon Martin .40 1.00
64 Michael Finley .40 1.00
65 John Stockton .75 2.00
66 Allan Houston .40 1.00
67 Terrell Brandon .25 .60
68 Donyell Marshall .25 .60
69 Marcus Camby .30 .75
70 Cuttino Mobley .25 .60
71 Shawn Marion .40 1.00
72 Jason Williams .50 1.25
73 Rodney Rogers .25 .60
74 Scottie Pippen 1.00 2.50
75 Brian Grant .25 .60
76 Clifford Robinson .40 1.00
77 Antoine Walker .30 .75
78 Michael Dickerson .25 .60
79 Latrell Sprewell .40 1.00
80 Ron Artest .30 .75
81 Shareef Abdur-Rahim .40 1.00
82 Michael Jordan 4.00 10.00
83 Mike Miller .30 .75
84 Corey Maggette .30 .75
85 Antawn Jamison .30 .75
86 Rasheed Wallace .50 1.25
87 Alonzo Mourning .60 1.50
88 Eddy Curry .25 .60
89 Derrick Coleman .30 .75
90 Joe Smith .30 .75
91 Darius Miles .25 .60
92 Nick Van Exel .40 1.00
93 Derek Fisher .40 1.00
94 Nazr Mohammed .25 .60
95 Morris Peterson .30 .75
96 Jamal Mashburn .30 .75
97 Jerry Stackhouse .40 1.00
98 Kwame Brown .25 .60
99 Darrell Armstrong .25 .60
100 Reggie Miller .75 2.00
101 Desmond Mason .30 .75
102 Antonio Davis .30 .75
103 Elden Campbell .25 .60
104 Voshon Lenard .25 .60
105 Eric Snow .25 .60
106 Lamar Odom .40 1.00
107 Toni Kukoc .40 1.00
108 Vince Carter .75 2.00
109 Keith Van Horn .30 .75
110 Juwan Howard .30 .75
111 Jay Williams RC 1.25 3.00
112 Yao Ming RC 8.00 20.00
113 Mike Dunleavy RC 1.50 4.00
114 Drew Gooden RC 1.50 4.00
115 Nikoloz Tskitishvili RC 1.00 2.50
116 DaJuan Wagner RC 1.25 3.00
117 Nene Hilario RC 1.50 4.00
118 Chris Wilcox RC 1.25 3.00
119 Amare Stoudemire RC 4.00 10.00
120 Caron Butler RC 1.50 4.00
121 Melvin Ely RC 1.25 3.00
122 Marcus Haislip RC 1.00 2.50
123 Jared Jeffries RC 1.25 3.00
124 Fred Jones RC 1.25 3.00
125 Bostjan Nachbar RC 1.25 3.00
126 Jiri Welsch RC 1.25 3.00
127 Juan Dixon RC 1.25 3.00
128 Curtis Borchardt RC 1.00 2.50
129 Ryan Humphrey RC 1.25 3.00
130 Kareem Rush RC 1.25 3.00
131 Qyntel Woods RC 1.00 2.50
132 Casey Jacobsen RC 1.25 3.00
133 Tayshaun Prince RC 3.00 8.00
134 Carlos Boozer RC 1.50 4.00
135 Frank Williams RC 1.00 2.50
136 John Salmons RC 1.50 4.00
137 Chris Jefferies RC 1.00 2.50
138 Dan Dickau RC 1.00 2.50
139 Manu Ginobili RC 8.00 20.00
140 Roger Mason RC 1.25 3.00

2002-03 Fleer Premium Emerald

*STARS: 2.5X TO 6X BASE CARD HI
*RCs: 1X TO 2.5X BASE CARD HI
PRINT RUN 300 SER.#'d SETS
82 Michael Jordan 40.00 100.00

2002-03 Fleer Premium Star Rubies

*STARS: 5X TO 12X BASE CARD HI
*RCs: 1.5X TO 4X BASE CARD HI
PRINT RUN 100 SER.#'d SETS
5 Kobe Bryant 100.00 250.00
82 Michael Jordan 150.00 400.00
112 Yao Ming 60.00 150.00
139 Manu Ginobili 60.00 150.00

2002-03 Fleer Premium A Cut Above

STATED ODDS 1:120
*RUBY: .75X TO 2X A CUT ABOVE HI
RUBY PRINT RUN 100 SER.#'d SETS
1 Keith Van Horn 2.50 6.00
2 Vince Carter 6.00 15.00
3 Steve Francis/250 3.00 8.00
4 Grant Hill 5.00 12.00
5 DerMarr Johnson/250 2.00 5.00
6 Jamal Mashburn 2.50 6.00
7 Lamar Odom 3.00 8.00
8 Quentin Richardson 2.00 5.00
9 Richard Hamilton 4.00 10.00
10 Jason Terry 2.50 6.00

2002-03 Fleer Premium Court Collection

STATED ODDS 1:175
*RUBY: .75X TO 2X COURT COLL.HI
RUBY PRINT RUN 100 SER.#'d SETS
1 Shareef Abdur-Rahim 3.00 8.00
2 Keyon Dooling/250 2.00 5.00
3 Rashard Lewis 2.50 6.00
4 Shawn Marion 3.00 8.00
5 Tracy McGrady 5.00 12.00
6 Alonzo Mourning 5.00 12.00
7 John Stockton 6.00 15.00
8 Wally Szczerbiak/125 2.50 6.00
9 Desmond Mason 2.50 6.00
10 Corey Maggette 2.50 6.00

2002-03 Fleer Premium Gear

STATED ODDS 1:288
*RUBY: .75X TO 2X GEAR HI
RUBY PRINT RUN 100 SER.#'d SETS
1 Anfernee Hardaway 8.00 20.00
2 Vince Carter 6.00 15.00
3 Antawn Jamison 2.50 6.00
4 Karl Malone/125 6.00 15.00
5 Kenyon Martin 3.00 8.00
6 Andre Miller 2.50 6.00
7 Mike Miller 2.50 6.00
8 Dikembe Mutombo 5.00 12.00
9 Morris Peterson/50 2.50 6.00

2002-03 Fleer Premium Power

PRINT RUN 1000 SERIAL #'d SETS
1 Tim Duncan 4.00 10.00
2 Kobe Bryant 12.00 30.00
3 Ben Wallace 2.00 5.00
4 Michael Jordan 20.00 50.00
5 Shaquille O'Neal 6.00 15.00
6 Vince Carter 3.00 8.00
7 Kevin Garnett 4.00 10.00
8 Chris Webber 2.00 5.00
9 Karl Malone 3.00 8.00
10 Elton Brand 1.25 3.00

2002-03 Fleer Premium Power Ruby

*RUBY: 2X TO 5X POWER HI
PRINT RUN 100 SER.#'d SETS
4 Michael Jordan 125.00 300.00

2002-03 Fleer Premium Prime Time

COMPLETE SET (15) 12.00 30.00
PRINT RUN 1500 SERIAL #'d SETS
*RUBY: 2X TO 5X PRIME TIME HI
RUBY PRINT RUN 100 SER.#'d SETS
1 Dirk Nowitzki 3.00 8.00
2 Vince Carter 2.50 6.00
3 Allen Iverson 3.00 8.00
4 Ray Allen 2.00 5.00
5 Darius Miles .75 2.00
6 Chris Webber 1.50 4.00
7 Elton Brand 1.00 2.50
8 Jason Kidd 2.00 5.00
9 Paul Pierce 2.00 5.00
10 Baron Davis 1.25 3.00
11 Stephon Marbury 1.50 4.00
12 Jerry Stackhouse 1.25 3.00
13 David Robinson 2.50 6.00
14 Gary Payton 2.00 5.00
15 Antoine Walker 1.00 2.50

2002-03 Fleer Premium Prime Time Game Used

STATED ODDS 1:75
*RUBY: 2X TO 5X PT GAME USED HI
RUBY PRINT RUN 100 SER.#'d SETS
1 Vince Carter 6.00 15.00
2 Allen Iverson 8.00 20.00
3 Ray Allen 5.00 12.00
4 Darius Miles 2.00 5.00
5 Chris Webber 4.00 10.00
6 Elton Brand 2.50 6.00
7 Jason Kidd 5.00 12.00
8 Paul Pierce 5.00 12.00
9 Baron Davis 3.00 8.00
10 Stephon Marbury 4.00 10.00
11 Jerry Stackhouse 3.00 8.00
12 David Robinson 6.00 15.00
13 Gary Payton 5.00 12.00
14 Antoine Walker 2.50 6.00

2002-03 Fleer Premium Skylines

PRINT RUN 2500 SERIAL #'D SETS
1 Michael Jordan 12.00 30.00
2 Shaquille O'Neal 5.00 12.00
3 Vince Carter 2.50 6.00
4 Kevin Garnett 3.00 8.00
5 Allen Iverson 3.00 8.00
6 Dirk Nowitzki 3.00 8.00
7 Darius Miles .75 2.00
8 Tracy McGrady 2.00 5.00
9 Chris Webber 1.50 4.00
10 Steve Francis 1.25 3.00
11 Jason Kidd 2.00 5.00
12 Stephon Marbury 1.50 4.00
13 Paul Pierce 2.00 5.00
14 Ray Allen 2.00 5.00
15 Kobe Bryant 10.00 25.00
16 Jay Williams 1.00 2.50
17 DaJuan Wagner 1.00 2.50
18 Yao Ming 6.00 15.00
19 Jared Jeffries 1.00 2.50
20 Amare Stoudemire 3.00 8.00

2002-03 Fleer Premium Skylines Ruby

*RUBY: 4X TO 10X SKYLINES HI
PRINT RUN 100 SER.#'d SETS
1 Michael Jordan 150.00 400.00

2002-03 Fleer Premium Triple Threats

PRINT RUN 250 SERIAL #'D SETS
1 Allen Iverson 8.00 20.00
2 Tracy McGrady 5.00 12.00
3 Steve Francis 3.00 8.00
4 Ray Allen 5.00 12.00
5 Tim Duncan 8.00 20.00
6 Kobe Bryant 25.00 60.00
7 Michael Jordan 40.00 100.00
8 Shaquille O'Neal 12.00 30.00
9 Vince Carter 6.00 15.00
10 Kevin Garnett 8.00 20.00

2002-03 Fleer Premium Triple Threats Ruby

*RUBY: .6X TO 1.5X TRIPLE THREATS HI
PRINT RUN 100 SER.#'d SETS
7 Michael Jordan 75.00 200.00

2011-12 Fleer Retro

COMPLETE SET (83) 25.00 60.00
1 Michael Jordan 8.00 20.00
2 LeBron James 4.00 10.00
3 Walt Frazier .75 2.00
4 Larry Johnson .60 1.50
5 Hakeem Olajuwon 1.00 2.50
6 Candace Parker .75 2.00
7 Christian Laettner .50 1.25
8 Hal Greer .50 1.25
9 Jerry West 1.00 2.50
10 Dennis Rodman 1.25 3.00
11 Anfernee Hardaway 1.25 3.00
12 Gail Goodrich .50 1.25
13 George Gervin .75 2.00
14 Elgin Baylor .75 2.00
15 Bill Walton .75 2.00
16 Larry Bird 2.00 5.00
17 Rick Barry .60 1.50
18 James Worthy .75 2.00
19 Bill Laimbeer .50 1.25
20 Tim Hardaway .60 1.50
21 David Robinson 1.00 2.50
22 Adrian Dantley .40 1.00
23 Alonzo Mourning .75 2.00
24 Magic Johnson 2.00 5.00
25 Julius Erving 1.25 3.00
26 Mark Jackson .40 1.00
27 Bill Cartwright .40 1.00
28 Bill Russell 1.50 4.00
29 B.J. Armstrong .50 1.25
30 Bob McAdoo .60 1.50
31 Cazzie Russell .50 1.25
32 Brad Daugherty .40 1.00
33 Clyde Drexler .75 2.00
34 Danny Manning .40 1.00
35 John Havlicek 1.00 2.50
36 Grant Hill .75 2.00
37 Jim Jackson .40 1.00
38 David Thompson .50 1.25
39 Rudy Tomjanovich .50 1.25
40 Reggie Theus .40 1.00
41 Freddie Lewis .30 .75
42 Kenny Smith .40 1.00
43 Bill Sharman .50 1.25
44 Lonnie Shelton .30 .75
45 Toni Kukoc .60 1.50
46 Sam Cassell .40 1.00
47 Glen Rice .50 1.25
48 Darrell Griffith .50 1.25
49 Steve Nash 1.00 2.50
50 Chris Paul 1.00 2.50
51 Tristan Thompson RS .75 2.00
52 Jonas Valanciunas RS 1.00 2.50
53 Bismack Biyombo RS .60 1.50
54 Jimmer Fredette RS .75 2.00
55 Klay Thompson RS 15.00 40.00
56 Alec Burks RS .75 2.00
57 Markieff Morris RS .75 2.00
58 Marcus Morris RS .75 2.00
59 Kawhi Leonard RS 30.00 80.00
60 Nikola Vucevic RS .75 2.00
61 Chris Singleton RS .50 1.25
62 Tobias Harris RS 1.25 3.00
63 Scotty Hopson RS .50 1.25
64 Nolan Smith RS .50 1.25
65 Reggie Jackson RS .60 1.50
66 MarShon Brooks RS .60 1.50
67 JaJuan Johnson RS .50 1.25
68 Norris Cole RS .60 1.50
69 Cory Joseph RS .60 1.50
70 Justin Harper RS .50 1.25
71 Shelvin Mack RS .50 1.25
72 Tyler Honeycutt RS .50 1.25
73 Jordan Williams RS .50 1.25
74 Chandler Parsons RS .60 1.50
75 Jon Leuer RS .60 1.50
76 Malcolm Lee RS .60 1.50
77 Charles Jenkins RS .50 1.25
78 Travis Leslie RS .60 1.50
79 Keith Benson RS .60 1.50
80 Josh Selby RS .60 1.50
81 E'Twaun Moore RS 1.00 2.50
82 Demetri McCamey RS .60 1.50
83 Durrell Summers RS .50 1.25

2011-12 Fleer Retro 1961-62

STATED ODDS 1:100 PACKS
ALL BACKGROUND VARIATIONS SAME VALUE
BR1 Bill Russell 15.00 40.00
DR1 David Robinson 10.00 25.00
HO1 Hakeem Olajuwon 10.00 25.00
JE1 Julius Erving 15.00 40.00
JO1 Magic Johnson 40.00 100.00
JW1 Jerry West 10.00 25.00
LB1 Larry Bird 40.00 100.00
LJ1 LeBron James 200.00 500.00
MJ1 Michael Jordan 300.00 600.00
WO1 James Worthy 8.00 20.00

2011-12 Fleer Retro 1961-62 Autographs

ALL BACKGROUND VARIATIONS SAME VALUE
BR1 Bill Russell 600.00 1,200.00
DR1 David Robinson 250.00 500.00
HO1 Hakeem Olajuwon 100.00 250.00
JO1 Magic Johnson 250.00 500.00
LJ1 LeBron James EXCH 1,500.00 3,000.00
MJ1 Michael Jordan 2,000.00 4,000.00
WO1 James Worthy 75.00 200.00

2011-12 Fleer Retro 1986-87

COMPLETE SET (15) 20.00 50.00
STATED ODDS 1:20 PACKS
AD Adrian Dantley 2.00 5.00
AM Alonzo Mourning 4.00 10.00
BW Bill Walton 4.00 10.00
CD Clyde Drexler 4.00 10.00
CP Chris Paul 5.00 12.00
DM Danny Manning 2.00 5.00
DR Dennis Rodman 6.00 15.00
EB Elgin Baylor 4.00 10.00
GG George Gervin 4.00 10.00
GH Grant Hill 4.00 10.00
GO Gail Goodrich 2.50 6.00
JH John Havlicek 5.00 12.00
LJ Larry Johnson 3.00 8.00
SN Steve Nash 5.00 12.00
WF Walt Frazier 4.00 10.00

2011-12 Fleer Retro 1986-87 Autographs

AD Adrian Dantley 8.00 20.00
AM Alonzo Mourning 40.00 100.00
BW Bill Walton 40.00 100.00
CD Clyde Drexler 25.00 60.00
CP Chris Paul 40.00 100.00
DR Dennis Rodman 75.00 200.00
GG George Gervin 20.00 50.00
GH Grant Hill EXCH 75.00 200.00
GO Gail Goodrich 12.00 30.00
JH John Havlicek 75.00 200.00
LJ Larry Johnson 50.00 120.00

2011-12 Fleer Retro 1987-88

COMPLETE SET (20) 12.00 30.00
STATED ODDS 1:10 PACKS
AH Anfernee Hardaway 3.00 8.00
BA B.J. Armstrong 1.25 3.00
BL Bill Laimbeer 1.25 3.00
BM Bob McAdoo 1.50 4.00
BS Bill Sharman 1.25 3.00
CL Christian Laettner 1.25 3.00
CR Cazzie Russell 1.25 3.00
CW Chet Walker 1.00 2.50
DG Darrell Griffith 1.25 3.0
DT David Thompson 1.25 3.0
HG Hal Greer 1.25 3.0
JJ Jim Jackson 1.00 2.5
KS Kenny Smith 1.00 2.5
MJ Mark Jackson 1.00 2.5
FA Candace Parker 1.50 4.0
FB Rick Barry 1.50 4.0
FT Reggie Theus 1.00 2.5
SC Sam Cassell 1.00 2.5
TH Tim Hardaway 1.50 4.0
TD Rudy Tomjanovich 1.25 3.0

2011-12 Fleer Retro 1987-88 Autographs

AH Anfernee Hardaway 30.00 80.0
BA B.J. Armstrong 12.00 30.0
BL Bill Laimbeer 12.00 30.0
BM Bob McAdoo 20.00 50.0
CL Christian Laettner 15.00 40.0
CR Cazzie Russell 10.00 25.0
CW Chet Walker 10.00 25.0
DT David Thompson 12.00 30.0
JJ Jim Jackson 10.00 25.0
MJ Mark Jackson 10.00 25.0
PA Candace Parker 15.00 40.0
RT Reggie Theus 10.00 25.0
TH Tim Hardaway 15.00 40.0
TR Rudy Tomjanovich 10.00 25.0

2011-12 Fleer Retro 1988-89

COMPLETE SET (25) 15.00 40.00
STATED ODDS 1:5 PACKS
AB Alec Burks 1.00 2.50
BB Bismack Biyombo .75 2.00
BD Brad Daugherty .75 2.00
CJ Cory Joseph .75 2.00
CS Chris Singleton .60 1.50
FL Freddie Lewis .60 1.50
HA Tobias Harris 1.50 4.00
JF Jimmer Fredette 1.00 2.50
JH Justin Harper .60 1.50
JJ JaJuan Johnson .60 1.50
JV Jonas Valanciunas 1.25 3.00
KL Kawhi Leonard 20.00 50.00
KT Klay Thompson 20.00 50.00
LS Lonnie Shelton .60 1.50
MM Marcus Morris 1.00 2.50
MO Markieff Morris 1.00 2.50
MP MarShon Brooks .75 2.00
MF Micheal Ray Richardson .75 2.00
NS Nolan Smith .60 1.50
NV Nikola Vucevic 1.00 2.50
RH Robert Horry 1.00 2.50
RJ Reggie Jackson .75 2.00
TH Tyler Honeycutt .60 1.50
TK Toni Kukoc 1.25 3.00
TT Tristan Thompson 1.00 2.50

2011-12 Fleer Retro 1988-89 Autographs

AB Alec Burks 10.00 25.00
BB Bismack Biyombo 8.00 20.00
CJ Cory Joseph 8.00 20.00
CS Chris Singleton 6.00 15.00
FL Freddie Lewis 6.00 15.00
HA Tobias Harris 15.00 40.00
JF Jimmer Fredette 12.00 30.00
JH Justin Harper 6.00 15.00
JJ JaJuan Johnson 6.00 15.00
JV Jonas Valanciunas 20.00 50.00
KL Kawhi Leonard 150.00 400.00
KT Klay Thompson 150.00 400.00
LS Lonnie Shelton 6.00 15.00
NS Nolan Smith 6.00 15.00
RH Robert Horry 15.00 40.00
RJ Reggie Jackson 8.00 20.00
TH Tyler Honeycutt 6.00 15.00
TT Tristan Thompson 10.00 25.00

2011-12 Fleer Retro A Cut Above

STATED ODDS 1:144 PACKS
1 Jimmer Fredette 8.00 20.00
2 Grant Hill 15.00 40.00
3 George Gervin 12.00 30.00
4 Alonzo Mourning 12.00 30.00
5 Hakeem Olajuwon 30.00 80.00
6 Clyde Drexler 15.00 40.00
7 Larry Bird 75.00 200.00
8 Julius Erving 20.00 50.00
9 Elgin Baylor 12.00 30.00
10 Magic Johnson 75.00 200.00
11 David Robinson 25.00 60.00
12 Michael Jordan 600.00 1,200.00
13 James Worthy 15.00 40.00
14 Tim Hardaway 10.00 25.00
15 John Havlicek 15.00 40.00
16 Bill Russell 75.00 200.00
17 Steve Nash 40.00 100.00
18 Anfernee Hardaway 60.00 150.00
19 Dennis Rodman 40.00 100.00
20 LeBron James 400.00 800.00
21 Walt Frazier 15.00 40.00
22 Bill Walton 12.00 30.00
23 Larry Johnson 10.00 25.00
24 Chris Paul 20.00 50.00
25 Jerry West 15.00 40.00

2011-12 Fleer Retro Autographics 1996-97

AD Adrian Dantley 5.00 12.00
AJ Avery Johnson 6.00 15.00
AM Alonzo Mourning 40.00 80.00
BR Bill Russell 500.00 1,000.00
CC Cynthia Cooper 8.00 20.00
CD Clyde Drexler 15.00 40.00
CJ Cory Joseph 3.00 8.00
CR Cazzie Russell 4.00 10.00
CS Chris Singleton 2.50 6.00
CW Chet Walker 4.00 10.00
DA Dana Altman 10.00 25.00
DR David Robinson 20.00 50.00
DT David Thompson 8.00 20.00
GA Greg Anthony 8.00 20.00
GH Grant Hill EXCH 125.00 250.00
HG Hal Greer 5.00 12.00
HO Hakeem Olajuwon 30.00 80.00
JA LeBron James 1,000.00 2,000.00
JC Jim Calhoun 12.00 30.00

JE Julius Erving 30.00 60.00
JF Jimmer Fredette 6.00 15.00
JH John Havlicek 25.00 60.00
JO Michael Jordan 2,000.00 4,000.00
JS Jerry Sloan 10.00 25.00
JW James Worthy 25.00 60.00
LB Larry Bird 100.00 175.00
LJ Larry Johnson 12.00 30.00
LS Lonnie Shelton 3.00 8.00
MB Mike Brey 10.00 25.00
MF Mark Few 40.00 100.00
MJ Magic Johnson 125.00 300.00
PA Chris Paul 40.00 100.00
RH Robert Horry 12.00 30.00
RJ Reggie Jackson 3.00 8.00
RO Dennis Rodman 40.00 100.00
RT Reggie Theus 4.00 10.00
SA Steve Alford 5.00 12.00
SC Sam Cassell 4.00 10.00
TH Tim Hardaway 8.00 20.00
TM Thad Matta 12.00 30.00
TO Rudy Tomjanovich 4.00 10.00
WF Walt Frazier 10.00 25.00

2011-12 Fleer Retro Autographics 1997-98

AM Alonzo Mourning 50.00 125.00
BB Bismack Biyombo 3.00 8.00
BD Billy Donovan 40.00 100.00
BM Bob McAdoo 12.00 30.00
BR Bo Ryan 10.00 25.00
BW Bruce Weber 4.00 10.00
CC Cynthia Cooper 8.00 20.00
CP Chris Paul 40.00 100.00
CR Cazzie Russell 4.00 10.00
DM Demetri McCamey 3.00 8.00
DR David Robinson 40.00 100.00
DS Durrell Summers 2.50 6.00
DT David Thompson 6.00 15.00
FL Freddie Lewis 3.00 8.00
HG Hal Greer 5.00 12.00
JB Jim Boeheim 40.00 100.00
JC Jeff Capel III 4.00 10.00
JE Julius Erving 60.00 150.00
JF Jimmer Fredette 6.00 15.00
JH Justin Harper 2.50 6.00
JJ JaJuan Johnson 2.50 6.00
JS Jack Sikma 8.00 20.00
JW James Worthy 25.00 60.00
LA Larry Johnson 12.00 30.00
LB Larry Bird 100.00 175.00
LJ LeBron James 1,000.00 2,000.00
LS Lonnie Shelton 3.00 8.00
MH Matt Howard 4.00 10.00
MR Micheal Ray Richardson 3.00 8.00
NS Nolan Smith 2.50 6.00
RH Robert Horry 8.00 20.00
RO Dennis Rodman 50.00 125.00
RT Reggie Theus 4.00 10.00
RU Bill Russell 500.00 1,000.00
SC Sam Cassell 4.00 10.00
SF Steve Fisher 6.00 15.00
SL Jerry Sloan 10.00 25.00
TH Tobias Harris 6.00 15.00
TK Toni Kukoc 25.00 60.00
TO Rudy Tomjanovich 4.00 10.00
TP Terry Porter 6.00 15.00
TT Tristan Thompson 4.00 10.00
WF Walt Frazier 10.00 25.00

2011-12 Fleer Retro Autographics 1998-99

AD Adrian Dantley 6.00 15.00
AH Anfernee Hardaway 8.00 20.00
AJ Avery Johnson 4.00 10.00
AM Alonzo Mourning 40.00 100.00
BB Bismack Biyombo 2.50 6.00
BH Bob Huggins 20.00 50.00
BM Bob McAdoo 12.00 30.00
CC Cynthia Cooper 6.00 15.00
CP Chris Paul 40.00 100.00
CR Cazzie Russell 4.00 10.00
CW Chet Walker 3.00 8.00
DR David Robinson 30.00 80.00
DT David Thompson 8.00 20.00
GH Grant Hill EXCH 100.00 200.00
GW Gary Williams 10.00 25.00
HG Hal Greer 5.00 12.00
HO Ben Howland 3.00 8.00
JB John Beilein 4.00 10.00
JE Julius Erving 30.00 60.00
JF Jimmer Fredette 6.00 15.00
JH John Havlicek 25.00 60.00
JJ JaJuan Johnson 2.00 5.00
JO Magic Johnson 125.00 300.00
JS Jerry Sloan 25.00 60.00
JW James Worthy 25.00 60.00
LA Larry Johnson 15.00 40.00
LJ LeBron James 1,000.00 2,000.00
LS Lonnie Shelton 2.50 6.00
MB MarShon Brooks 8.00 20.00
MH Matt Howard 3.00 8.00
MJ Michael Jordan 2,000.00 4,000.00
MM Markieff Morris 3.00 8.00
MP Matt Painter 8.00 20.00
OL Hakeem Olajuwon 40.00 100.00
PA Candace Parker 15.00 40.00
RH Robert Horry 10.00 25.00
RT Reggie Theus 3.00 8.00
SM Sean Miller 4.00 10.00
ST John Starks 12.00 30.00
TH Tyler Honeycutt 2.00 5.00
TK Toni Kukoc 12.00 30.00
TO Rudy Tomjanovich 4.00 10.00
WE Jerry West 30.00 80.00
WF Walt Frazier 10.00 25.00

2011-12 Fleer Retro Autographics 1999-00

AD Adrian Dantley 5.00 12.00
AM Alonzo Mourning 30.00 80.00
BB Bismack Biyombo 2.50 6.00
BC Bobby Cremins 4.00 10.00
BR Bill Russell 500.00 1,000.00
BS Bill Self 12.00 30.00
CC Cynthia Cooper 5.00 12.00
CD Clyde Drexler 25.00 60.00
CP Chris Paul 40.00 100.00
CR Cazzie Russell 3.00 8.00
CS Chris Singleton 2.00 5.00
CW Chet Walker 3.00 8.00
DM Demetri McCamey 2.50 6.00
DT David Thompson 6.00 15.00
FL Freddie Lewis 3.00 8.00
GG George Gervin 6.00 15.00
GH Grant Hill 30.00 80.00
HD Homer Drew 4.00 10.00
HG Hal Greer 6.00 15.00
HO Hakeem Olajuwon 30.00 80.00
JE Julius Erving 40.00 100.00
JF Jimmer Fredette 12.00 30.00
JH Justin Harper 2.00 5.00
JO Magic Johnson 50.00 125.00
JS Jerry Sloan 10.00 25.00
JW Jay Wright 15.00 40.00
KB Keith Benson 2.50 6.00
LA Larry Johnson 30.00 80.00
LB Larry Bird 75.00 200.00
LJ LeBron James 1,000.00 2,000.00
LS Lonnie Shelton 2.50 6.00
MM Mike Montgomery 4.00 10.00
RH Robert Horry 6.00 15.00
RM Rick Majerus 6.00 15.00
RT Rudy Tomjanovich 5.00 12.00
SG Seth Greenberg 4.00 10.00
SH Scotty Hopson 2.00 5.00
TH Tobias Harris 5.00 12.00
TI Tim Hardaway 8.00 20.00
TP Terry Porter 6.00 15.00
WF Walt Frazier 10.00 25.00
WO James Worthy 25.00 60.00

2011-12 Fleer Retro Autographs

1 Michael Jordan 2,000.00 4,000.00
2 LeBron James 1,000.00 2,000.00
3 Walt Frazier 6.00 15.00
4 Larry Johnson 12.00 30.00
5 Hakeem Olajuwon 20.00 50.00
8 Hal Greer 8.00 20.00
9 Jerry West 30.00 80.00
10 Dennis Rodman 30.00 80.00
11 Anfernee Hardaway 100.00 250.00
12 Gail Goodrich 20.00 50.00
13 George Gervin 6.00 15.00
14 Elgin Baylor 15.00 40.00
15 Bill Walton 10.00 25.00
16 Larry Bird 50.00 125.00
17 Rick Barry 15.00 40.00
18 James Worthy 10.00 25.00
19 Bill Laimbeer 5.00 12.00
20 Tim Hardaway 6.00 15.00
21 David Robinson 25.00 60.00
22 Adrian Dantley 4.00 10.00
23 Alonzo Mourning 25.00 60.00
24 Magic Johnson 30.00 80.00
25 Julius Erving 30.00 80.00
26 Mark Jackson 4.00 10.00
28 Bill Russell 500.00 1,000.00
29 B.J. Armstrong 8.00 20.00
30 Bob McAdoo 6.00 15.00
31 Cazzie Russell 4.00 10.00
33 Clyde Drexler 20.00 50.00
34 Danny Manning 6.00 15.00
35 John Havlicek 15.00 40.00
36 Grant Hill 20.00 50.00
37 Jim Jackson 6.00 15.00
38 David Thompson 8.00 20.00
39 Rudy Tomjanovich 4.00 10.00
40 Reggie Theus 4.00 10.00
41 Freddie Lewis 4.00 10.00
42 Kenny Smith 4.00 10.00
43 Bill Sharman 10.00 25.00
44 Lonnie Shelton 4.00 10.00
45 Toni Kukoc 12.00 30.00
46 Sam Cassell 4.00 10.00
47 Glen Rice 10.00 25.00
48 Darrell Griffith 4.00 10.00
50 Chris Paul 40.00 100.00
51 Tristan Thompson RS 3.00 8.00
52 Jonas Valanciunas RS 3.00 8.00
53 Bismack Biyombo RS 2.50 6.00
54 Jimmer Fredette RS 6.00 15.00
55 Klay Thompson RS 125.00 300.00
56 Alec Burks RS 3.00 8.00
57 Markieff Morris RS 3.00 8.00
58 Marcus Morris RS 3.00 8.00
59 Kawhi Leonard RS 125.00 300.00
60 Nikola Vucevic RS 3.00 8.00
61 Chris Singleton RS 2.00 5.00
62 Tobias Harris RS 5.00 12.00
63 Scotty Hopson RS 2.00 5.00
64 Nolan Smith RS 2.00 5.00
65 Reggie Jackson RS 2.50 6.00
66 MarShon Brooks RS 2.50 6.00
67 JaJuan Johnson RS 2.00 5.00
68 Norris Cole RS 2.50 6.00
69 Cory Joseph RS 2.50 6.00
70 Justin Harper RS 2.00 5.00
71 Shelvin Mack RS 2.00 5.00
72 Tyler Honeycutt RS 2.00 5.00
73 Jordan Williams RS 2.00 5.00
74 Chandler Parsons RS 2.50 6.00
75 Jon Leuer RS 2.50 6.00
76 Malcolm Lee RS 2.50 6.00
77 Charles Jenkins RS 2.00 5.00
78 Travis Leslie RS 2.50 6.00
79 Keith Benson RS 2.50 6.00
80 Josh Selby RS 2.50 6.00
81 E'Twaun Moore RS 4.00 10.00
82 Demetri McCamey RS 2.00 5.00
83 Durrell Summers RS 2.00 5.00

2011-12 Fleer Retro Big Men on Court

STATED ODDS 1:180 PACKS
1 Michael Jordan 1,000.00 2,000.00
2 LeBron James 500.00 1,000.00
3 Magic Johnson 75.00 200.00
4 Larry Bird 75.00 200.00
5 Bill Russell 75.00 200.00
6 Julius Erving 40.00 100.00
7 David Robinson 20.00 50.00
8 Hakeem Olajuwon 20.00 50.00
9 Alonzo Mourning 20.00 50.00
10 Anfernee Hardaway 75.00 200.00
11 Chris Paul 20.00 50.00
12 Grant Hill 20.00 50.00
13 Walt Frazier 10.00 25.00
14 James Worthy 12.00 30.00
15 Steve Nash 30.00 80.00

2011-12 Fleer Retro Competitive Advantage

STATED ODDS 1:144 PACKS
1 Michael Jordan 200.00 400.00
2 Magic Johnson 8.00 20.00
3 LeBron James 150.00 400.00
4 Larry Bird 15.00 40.00
5 Bill Russell 12.00 30.00
6 Julius Erving 10.00 25.00
7 David Robinson 8.00 20.00
8 Jimmer Fredette 3.00 8.00
9 Anfernee Hardaway 10.00 25.00
10 George Gervin 6.00 15.00
11 Hakeem Olajuwon 8.00 20.00
12 Jerry West 6.00 15.00
13 David Thompson 5.00 12.00
14 Larry Johnson 5.00 12.00
15 Grant Hill 8.00 20.00
16 Chris Paul 8.00 20.00
17 Steve Nash 6.00 15.00
18 Clyde Drexler 6.00 15.00
19 James Worthy 6.00 15.00
20 Alonzo Mourning 6.00 15.00

2011-12 Fleer Retro Flair Showcase

STATED PRINT RUN 150 SER.#'d SETS
1 Michael Jordan 400.00 800.00
2 LeBron James 200.00 500.00
3 Alonzo Mourning 10.00 25.00
4 Bill Russell 75.00 200.00
5 Chris Paul 12.00 30.00
6 Clyde Drexler 10.00 25.00
7 David Robinson 12.00 30.00
8 Grant Hill 10.00 25.00
9 Hakeem Olajuwon 10.00 25.00
10 James Worthy 10.00 25.00
11 Jerry West 12.00 30.00
12 John Havlicek 12.00 30.00
13 Julius Erving 15.00 40.00
14 Larry Bird 75.00 200.00
15 Larry Johnson 8.00 20.00
16 Magic Johnson 75.00 200.00
17 Steve Nash 20.00 50.00
18 Walt Frazier 10.00 25.00
19 Bob McAdoo 8.00 20.00
20 Adrian Dantley 5.00 12.00
21 Cazzie Russell 6.00 15.00
22 Christian Laettner 8.00 20.00
23 Danny Manning 5.00 12.00
24 Darrell Griffith 6.00 15.00
25 Dennis Rodman 15.00 40.00
26 Elgin Baylor 6.00 15.00
27 Gail Goodrich 6.00 15.00
28 George Gervin 10.00 25.00
29 Anfernee Hardaway 15.00 40.00
30 Jim Jackson 5.00 12.00
31 Candace Parker 40.00 100.00
32 Rick Barry 8.00 20.00
33 Tim Hardaway 8.00 20.00
34 David Thompson 6.00 15.00
35 Bill Walton 10.00 25.00
36 Glen Rice 6.00 15.00
37 Toni Kukoc 8.00 20.00
38 Micheal Ray Richardson 5.00 12.00
39 Chet Walker 5.00 12.00
40 Terry Porter 5.00 12.00
41 Kawhi Leonard 125.00 300.00
42 Jimmer Fredette 6.00 15.00
43 Bill Cartwright 5.00 12.00
44 Bill Laimbeer 5.00 12.00
45 Bobby Hurley 6.00 15.00
46 Brad Daugherty 5.00 12.00
47 Hal Greer 6.00 15.00
48 Reggie Theus 5.00 12.00
49 Robert Horry 6.00 15.00
50 Sam Cassell 5.00 12.00
51 Dominique Wilkins 10.00 25.00
52 Karl Malone 12.00 30.00
53 Chandler Parsons 5.00 12.00
54 MarShon Brooks 5.00 12.00
55 Jon Leuer 5.00 12.00
56 Alec Burks 6.00 15.00
57 Tristan Thompson 6.00 15.00
58 Markieff Morris 6.00 15.00
59 Norris Cole 5.00 12.00
60 Klay Thompson 125.00 300.00

2011-12 Fleer Retro Golden Touch

STATED ODDS 1:180 PACKS
1 Michael Jordan 500.00 1,000.00
2 LeBron James 400.00 800.00
3 Magic Johnson 12.00 30.00
4 Julius Erving 8.00 20.00
5 Hakeem Olajuwon 6.00 15.00
6 David Robinson 6.00 15.00
7 Steve Nash 6.00 15.00
8 Chris Paul 6.00 15.00
9 Larry Bird 12.00 30.00
10 Bill Russell 6.00 15.00
11 Jerry West 6.00 15.00
12 Grant Hill 6.00 15.00
13 James Worthy 5.00 12.00
14 Anfernee Hardaway 8.00 20.00
15 Jimmer Fredette 3.00 8.00

2011-12 Fleer Retro Intimidation Nation

STATED ODDS 1:180 PACKS
1 Grant Hill 10.00 25.00
2 George Gervin 10.00 25.00
3 Alonzo Mourning 10.00 25.00
4 Clyde Drexler 10.00 25.00
5 Hakeem Olajuwon 20.00 50.00
6 Larry Bird 60.00 150.00
7 Darrell Griffith 6.00 15.00
8 Julius Erving 20.00 50.00
9 Magic Johnson 60.00 150.00
10 David Robinson 12.00 30.00
11 David Thompson 6.00 15.00
12 Michael Jordan 500.00 1,000.00
13 James Worthy 10.00 25.00
14 Jim Jackson 5.00 12.00
15 Bill Russell 60.00 150.00
16 Steve Nash 20.00 50.00
17 Elgin Baylor 10.00 25.00
18 Dennis Rodman 15.00 40.00
19 Walt Frazier 10.00 25.00
20 LeBron James 400.00 800.00
21 Bill Walton 10.00 25.00
22 Larry Johnson 8.00 20.00
23 Tim Hardaway 8.00 20.00
24 Chris Paul 20.00 50.00
25 Jerry West 12.00 30.00
26 Danny Manning 5.00 12.00
27 Bob McAdoo 8.00 20.00
28 Adrian Dantley 5.00 12.00
29 John Havlicek 12.00 30.00
30 Reggie Theus 5.00 12.00
31 Chet Walker 5.00 12.00
32 Bill Laimbeer 6.00 15.00
33 Jimmer Fredette 6.00 15.00
34 Kawhi Leonard 125.00 300.00
35 Anfernee Hardaway 15.00 40.00

2011-12 Fleer Retro Jambalaya

STATED ODDS 1:360 PACKS
1 Michael Jordan 3,000.00 6,000.00
2 LeBron James 600.00 1,200.00
3 Bill Russell 125.00 300.00
4 Chris Paul 80.00 200.00
5 Grant Hill 60.00 150.00
6 Dominique Wilkins 60.00 150.00
7 David Robinson 80.00 200.00
8 Hakeem Olajuwon 80.00 200.00
9 James Worthy 60.00 150.00
10 Julius Erving 100.00 250.00
11 Larry Bird 150.00 400.00
12 Magic Johnson 150.00 400.00
13 Anfernee Hardaway 100.00 250.00
14 Dennis Rodman 150.00 400.00
15 Larry Johnson 50.00 125.00
16 Clyde Drexler 60.00 150.00
17 Alonzo Mourning 60.00 150.00
18 Walt Frazier 60.00 150.00
19 John Havlicek 80.00 200.00
20 Karl Malone 80.00 200.00
21 Jerry West 80.00 200.00

2011-12 Fleer Retro Metal Championship Hardware

STATED ODDS 1:90 PACKS
1 Michael Jordan 200.00 500.00
2 LeBron James 150.00 400.00
3 Magic Johnson 20.00 50.00
4 Bill Walton 8.00 20.00
5 Danny Manning 4.00 10.00
6 David Thompson 5.00 12.00
7 Larry Johnson 6.00 15.00
8 James Worthy 8.00 20.00
9 Grant Hill 8.00 20.00
10 Bill Russell 15.00 40.00
11 Christian Laettner 5.00 12.00
12 Glen Rice 5.00 12.00
13 Darrell Griffith 5.00 12.00
14 Gail Goodrich 5.00 12.00
15 John Havlicek 10.00 25.00

2011-12 Fleer Retro Michael Jordan Buybacks

STATED PRINT RUN ONE SERIAL #'d SET

2011-12 Fleer Retro Noyz Boyz

STATED ODDS 1:144 PACKS
1 Bill Walton 12.00 30.00
2 Alonzo Mourning 15.00 40.00
3 Bill Russell 60.00 150.00
4 Chris Paul 25.00 60.00
5 Anfernee Hardaway 40.00 100.00
6 Clyde Drexler 20.00 50.00
7 David Robinson 30.00 80.00
8 David Thompson 12.00 30.00
9 Dennis Rodman 30.00 80.00
10 Grant Hill 15.00 40.00
11 Hakeem Olajuwon 30.00 80.00
12 James Worthy 15.00 40.00
13 Jerry West 25.00 60.00
14 Jim Jackson 10.00 25.00
15 Jimmer Fredette 10.00 25.00
16 Julius Erving 40.00 100.00
17 Kawhi Leonard 125.00 300.00
18 Larry Bird 60.00 150.00
19 Larry Johnson 15.00 40.00
20 LeBron James 600.00 1,200.00
21 Magic Johnson 60.00 150.00
22 Tim Hardaway 15.00 40.00
23 Michael Jordan 1,000.00 2,000.00
24 Steve Nash 30.00 80.00
25 Walt Frazier 10.00 25.00

2011-12 Fleer Retro Precious Metal Gems Red

STATED PRINT RUN 150 SER.#'d SETS
*BLUE/50: .75X TO 2X BASE HI
1 Michael Jordan 1,500.00 3,000.00
2 Mark Jackson 10.00 25.00
3 Hakeem Olajuwon 125.00 300.00
4 LeBron James 1,500.00 3,000.00
5 Clyde Drexler 60.00 150.00
6 David Robinson 25.00 60.00
7 Christian Laettner 25.00 60.00
8 Jim Jackson 10.00 25.00
9 Adrian Dantley 10.00 25.00
10 Reggie Theus 10.00 25.00
11 John Havlicek 60.00 150.00
12 Dennis Rodman 125.00 300.00
13 Gail Goodrich 30.00 80.00
14 Danny Manning 10.00 25.00
15 Bob McAdoo 15.00 40.00
16 Walt Frazier 30.00 80.00
17 Bill Laimbeer 12.00 30.00
18 Hal Greer 12.00 30.00
19 Bill Cartwright 10.00 25.00
20 Rudy Tomjanovich 10.00 25.00
21 Bill Russell 300.00 600.00
22 Tim Hardaway 15.00 40.00
23 Cazzie Russell 12.00 30.00
24 David Thompson 12.00 30.00
25 Darrell Griffith 12.00 30.00
26 Rick Barry 15.00 40.00
27 George Gervin 30.00 80.00
28 Elgin Baylor 20.00 50.00
29 Alonzo Mourning 60.00 150.00
30 Bill Walton 30.00 80.00
31 Larry Johnson 40.00 100.00
32 Magic Johnson 300.00 600.00
33 Julius Erving 30.00 80.00
34 Jimmer Fredette 12.00 30.00
35 John Starks 15.00 40.00
36 Bill Sharman 12.00 30.00
37 Larry Bird 300.00 600.00
38 Grant Hill 125.00 300.00
39 Steve Nash 125.00 300.00
40 James Worthy 40.00 100.00

2011-12 Fleer Retro Ultra Court Masters

STATED ODDS 1:90 PACKS
1 Michael Jordan 200.00 500.00
2 LeBron James 125.00 300.00
3 Larry Bird 15.00 40.00
4 Magic Johnson 15.00 40.00
5 Bill Russell 12.00 30.00
6 Julius Erving 10.00 25.00
7 David Robinson 8.00 20.00
8 Hakeem Olajuwon 8.00 20.00
9 Clyde Drexler 6.00 15.00
10 Grant Hill 6.00 15.00
11 Steve Nash 8.00 20.00
12 Chris Paul 8.00 20.00
13 Larry Johnson 5.00 12.00
14 Alonzo Mourning 6.00 15.00
15 James Worthy 6.00 15.00
16 David Thompson 4.00 10.00
17 Danny Manning 3.00 8.00
18 Jimmer Fredette 4.00 10.00
19 George Gervin 6.00 15.00
20 Anfernee Hardaway 10.00 25.00
21 Adrian Dantley 3.00 8.00
22 Walt Frazier 6.00 15.00
23 Bill Walton 6.00 15.00
24 Tim Hardaway 5.00 12.00
25 Jim Jackson 3.00 8.00

2011-12 Fleer Retro Ultra Stars

STATED ODDS 1:180 PACKS
1 Michael Jordan 400.00 800.00
2 LeBron James 300.00 600.00
3 Larry Bird 40.00 100.00
4 Magic Johnson 40.00 100.00
5 Bill Russell 40.00 100.00
6 Julius Erving 15.00 40.00
7 David Robinson 15.00 40.00
8 Hakeem Olajuwon 15.00 40.00
9 Jerry West 12.00 30.00
10 Grant Hill 15.00 40.00
11 Steve Nash 15.00 40.00
12 Chris Paul 12.00 30.00
13 Jimmer Fredette 5.00 12.00
14 John Havlicek 15.00 40.00
15 Alonzo Mourning 12.00 30.00
16 Clyde Drexler 12.00 30.00
17 Dennis Rodman 20.00 50.00
18 Larry Johnson 12.00 30.00
19 James Worthy 12.00 30.00
20 Tim Hardaway 10.00 25.00
21 Walt Frazier 10.00 25.00
22 Elgin Baylor 10.00 25.00
23 George Gervin 10.00 25.00
24 Anfernee Hardaway 60.00 150.00
25 Bill Walton 10.00 25.00

2012-13 Fleer Retro

STATED RS ODDS 1:3 HOBBY
1 Michael Jordan 8.00 20.00
2 LeBron James 4.00 10.00
3 Jason Kidd .75 2.00
4 Dominique Wilkins .60 1.50
5 Karl Malone .75 2.00
6 Bill Walton .75 2.00
7 Allen Iverson .75 2.00
8 Paul Pierce .75 2.00
9 Ray Allen .75 2.00
10 Grant Hill .75 2.00
11 Hakeem Olajuwon 1.00 2.50
12 Bernard King .60 1.50
13 Isiah Thomas 1.00 2.50
14 Dennis Rodman 1.25 3.00
15 Reggie Miller .75 2.00
16 Bill Russell 1.50 4.00
17 David Robinson .75 2.00
18 Jim Jackson .40 1.00
19 Larry Johnson .60 1.50
20 Nate Thurmond .50 1.25
21 Alonzo Mourning .75 2.00
22 Anfernee Hardaway 1.25 3.00
23 Glen Rice .40 1.00
24 Tim Hardaway .60 1.50
25 Walt Frazier .75 2.00
26 Larry Bird 1.50 4.00
27 John Havlicek 1.00 2.50
28 Nick Van Exel .50 1.25
29 Danny Manning .40 1.00
30 Spud Webb .40 1.00
31 Jamal Mashburn .40 1.00
32 David Thompson .50 1.25
33 Micheal Ray Richardson .40 1.00
34 Harold Miner .30 .75
35 Mark Price .50 1.25
36 Jeff Hornacek .40 1.00
37 Toni Kukoc .50 1.25
38 A.C. Green .50 1.25
39 Spencer Haywood .50 1.25
40 Sean Elliott .40 1.00
41 Allan Houston .40 1.00
42 Dave Cowens .75 2.00
43 Cheryl Miller .50 1.25
44 Christian Laettner .50 1.25
45 Magic Johnson 1.50 4.00
46 Mark A. Jackson .40 1.00
47 Vinny Del Negro .30 .75
48 Clyde Drexler .75 2.00
49 Gary Payton .60 1.50
50 Julius Erving 1.25 3.00
51 Meyers Leonard RS .60 1.50
52 Jeremy Lamb RS .75 2.00
53 Kendall Marshall RS .60 1.50
54 Moe Harkless RS .60 1.50
55 Tyler Zeller RS .50 1.25
56 Andrew Nicholson RS .50 1.25
57 Evan Fournier RS .75 2.00
58 Jared Cunningham RS .50 1.25
59 Miles Plumlee RS .50 1.25
60 Arnett Moultrie RS .50 1.25
61 Bernard James RS .50 1.25
62 Jae Crowder RS 1.00 2.50
63 Draymond Green RS 3.00 8.00
64 Quincy Acy RS .50 1.25
65 Khris Middleton RS 2.50 6.00
66 Will Barton RS 1.00 2.50
67 Tyshawn Taylor RS .50 1.25
68 Darius Miller RS .60 1.50
69 Kevin Murphy RS .50 1.25
70 Darius Johnson-Odom RS .50 1.25
71 Robbie Hummel RS .50 1.25
72 Robert Sacre RS .50 1.25
73 Wesley Witherspoon RS .50 1.25
74 William Buford RS .50 1.25
75 Ricardo Ratliffe RS .50 1.25
76 John Shurna RS .50 1.25
77 Tomas Satoransky RS .75 2.00
78 Justin Hamilton RS .50 1.25
79 JaMychal Green RS .60 1.50
80 Kris Joseph RS .50 1.25

2012-13 Fleer Retro 96-97 Flair Legacy Row 1

STATED PRINT RUN 150 SER.#'d SETS
96FL1 Julius Erving 20.00 50.00
96FL2 Michael Jordan 500.00 1,000.00
96FL3 Bob McAdoo 4.00 10.00
96FL4 Wilt Chamberlain 60.00 150.00
96FL5 Danny Manning 4.00 10.00
96FL6 Mark Price 5.00 12.00
96FL7 Magic Johnson 60.00 150.00
96FL8 Tony Gwynn 5.00 12.00
96FL9 Clyde Drexler 8.00 20.00
96FL10 Gary Payton 6.00 15.00
96FL11 LeBron James 400.00 800.00
96FL12 Shawn Bradley 3.00 8.00
96FL13 Elvin Hayes 6.00 15.00
96FL14 Allen Iverson 8.00 20.00
96FL15 Jamal Mashburn 4.00 10.00
96FL16 Nick Van Exel 5.00 12.00
96FL17 Allan Houston 4.00 10.00
96FL18 Antoine Walker 4.00 10.00
96FL19 Toni Kukoc 5.00 12.00
96FL20 David Robinson 20.00 50.00
96FL21 Larry Johnson 6.00 15.00
96FL22 Lou Hudson 4.00 10.00
96FL23 John Havlicek 10.00 25.00
96FL24 Grant Hill 8.00 20.00
96FL25 Isiah Thomas 10.00 25.00
96FL26 Bill Walton 8.00 20.00
96FL27 Reggie Miller 20.00 50.00
96FL28 Derrick Coleman 5.00 12.00
96FL29 Bill Laimbeer 6.00 15.00
96FL30 Sean Elliott 4.00 10.00
96FL31 Spud Webb 4.00 10.00
96FL32 Larry Bird 60.00 150.00
96FL33 Paul Pierce 8.00 20.00
96FL34 Bernard King 6.00 15.00
96FL35 Bill Russell 60.00 150.00
96FL36 Nate Thurmond 5.00 12.00
96FL37 Anfernee Hardaway 40.00 100.00
96FL38 Walt Frazier 8.00 20.00
96FL39 Jason Kidd 8.00 20.00
96FL40 Dennis Rodman 40.00 100.00
96FL41 Cheryl Miller 5.00 12.00
96FL42 Karl Malone 8.00 20.00
96FL43 Jeff Hornacek 4.00 10.00
96FL44 Alonzo Mourning 8.00 20.00
96FL45 Ray Allen 8.00 20.00
96FL46 Bobby Hurley 5.00 12.00
96FL47 Dominique Wilkins 6.00 15.00
96FL48 Hakeem Olajuwon 30.00 80.00
96FL49 A.C. Green 5.00 12.00
96FL50 Robert Horry 5.00 12.00

2012-13 Fleer Retro 96-97 Lucky 13

STATED ODDS 1:20 HOBBY
1 Meyers Leonard 2.00 5.00
2 Kendall Marshall 1.50 4.00
3 Tyler Zeller 1.50 4.00
4 Evan Fournier 2.50 6.00
5 Miles Plumlee 1.50 4.00
6 Tomas Satoransky 2.50 6.00
7 Bernard James 1.50 4.00
8 Draymond Green 10.00 25.00
9 Khris Middleton 8.00 20.00
10 Tyshawn Taylor 1.50 4.00
11 Kevin Murphy 1.50 4.00
12 Kris Joseph 1.50 4.00
13 Robbie Hummel 1.50 4.00

2012-13 Fleer Retro 96-97 Lucky 13 Autographs

OVERALL 96/97 L13 AU ODDS 1:240
EXCHANGE DEADLINE 5/31/2015
1 Meyers Leonard 4.00 10.00
2 Kendall Marshall 3.00 8.00
3 Tyler Zeller 3.00 8.00
4 Evan Fournier 5.00 12.00
5 Miles Plumlee 3.00 8.00
6 Tomas Satoransky 5.00 12.00
7 Bernard James 3.00 8.00
8 Draymond Green 20.00 50.00
9 Khris Middleton 15.00 40.00
10 Tyshawn Taylor EXCH 3.00 8.00
11 Kevin Murphy 3.00 8.00
12 Kris Joseph 3.00 8.00
13 Robbie Hummel 3.00 8.00

2012-13 Fleer Retro 96-97 Molten Metal

STATED ODDS 1:120 HOBBY
1 Magic Johnson 40.00 100.00
2 Gary Payton 12.00 30.00
3 LeBron James 200.00 500.00
4 Allen Iverson 40.00 100.00
5 Ray Allen 12.00 30.00
6 Dennis Rodman 40.00 100.00
7 Larry Johnson 12.00 30.00
8 Wilt Chamberlain 40.00 100.00
9 Karl Malone 12.00 30.00
10 Bill Russell 40.00 100.00
11 Grant Hill 30.00 80.00
12 Reggie Miller 15.00 40.00
13 Isiah Thomas 12.00 30.00
14 David Robinson 30.00 80.00
15 Hakeem Olajuwon 30.00 80.00
16 Paul Pierce 12.00 30.00
17 Julius Erving 20.00 50.00
18 Jason Kidd 12.00 30.00
19 Larry Bird 40.00 100.00
20 Michael Jordan 600.00 1,200.00

2012-13 Fleer Retro 96-97 Tradition Thrill Seekers

STATED ODDS 1:120 HOBBY
1 Isiah Thomas 12.00 30.00
2 Wilt Chamberlain 40.00 100.00
3 Reggie Miller 15.00 40.00
4 Larry Bird 40.00 100.00
5 Grant Hill 15.00 40.00
6 Allen Iverson 40.00 100.00
7 David Robinson 20.00 50.00
8 Larry Johnson 8.00 20.00
9 Paul Pierce 12.00 30.00
10 Bill Russell 40.00 100.00
11 Dominique Wilkins 8.00 20.00
12 Michael Jordan 400.00 800.00
13 Dennis Rodman 30.00 80.00
14 LeBron James 200.00 500.00
15 Magic Johnson 40.00 100.00
16 Gary Payton 8.00 20.00
17 Julius Erving 20.00 50.00
18 Anfernee Hardaway 30.00 80.00
19 Jason Kidd 10.00 25.00
20 Karl Malone 10.00 25.00

2012-13 Fleer Retro 97-98 EX 2001 Essential Credentials Future

PRINT RUNS B/WN 1-42 COPIES PER
EX1 Michael Jordan/42 2,000.00 4,000.00
EX2 Reggie Miller/41 40.00 100.00
EX3 A.C. Green/40 10.00 25.00
EX4 Mark Price/39 15.00 40.00
EX5 David Robinson/38 25.00 60.00
EX6 Clyde Drexler/37 50.00 120.00
EX7 Bernard King/36 12.00 30.00
EX8 Grant Hill/35 125.00 300.00
EX9 David Thompson/34 6.00 15.00
EX10 Elvin Hayes/33 8.00 20.00
EX11 Bill Walton/32 15.00 40.00
EX12 Allan Houston/31 15.00 40.00
EX13 Dennis Rodman/30 75.00 200.00
EX14 Tim Hardaway/29 12.00 30.00
EX15 Walt Frazier/28 10.00 25.00
EX16 Jason Kidd/27 20.00 50.00
EX17 Anfernee Hardaway/26 75.00 200.00
EX18 Spud Webb/25 15.00 40.00
EX19 Christian Laettner/24 15.00 40.00
EX20 John Havlicek/23 40.00 100.00
EX21 Mark A. Jackson/22 15.00 40.00
EX22 Karl Malone/21 40.00 100.00
EX23 Tony Gwynn/20 50.00 120.00

2012-13 Fleer Retro 97-98 EX 2001 Essential Credentials Now

PRINT RUNS B/WN 1-42 COPIES PER
NO PRICING ON QTY 19 OR LESS
EX20 John Havlicek/20 50.00 120.00
EX21 Mark A. Jackson/21 12.00 30.00
EX22 Karl Malone/22 50.00 120.00
EX23 Tony Gwynn/23 40.00 100.00
EX24 Julius Erving/24 75.00 200.00
EX25 Gary Payton/25 50.00 120.00
EX26 Ray Allen/26 50.00 120.00
EX27 Larry Johnson/27 30.00 80.00
EX28 Paul Pierce/28 40.00 100.00
EX29 Magic Johnson/29 125.00 300.00
EX30 Isiah Thomas/30 40.00 100.00
EX31 Derrick Coleman/31 30.00 80.00
EX32 Dominique Wilkins/32 40.00 100.00
EX33 Wilt Chamberlain/33 125.00 300.00
EX34 Allen Iverson/34 125.00 300.00
EX35 Danny Manning/35 12.00 30.00
EX36 Hakeem Olajuwon/36 150.00 400.00
EX37 Alonzo Mourning/37 40.00 100.00
EX38 Bill Russell/38 125.00 300.00
EX39 Antoine Walker/39 12.00 30.00
EX40 Jamal Mashburn/40 12.00 30.00
EX41 Larry Bird/41 125.00 300.00
EX42 LeBron James/42 1,000.00 2,000.00

2012-13 Fleer Retro 97-98 Flair Legacy Row 0

STATED PRINT RUN 100 SER.#'d SETS
97FL1 Dominique Wilkins 10.00 25.00
97FL2 Bill Russell 125.00 300.00
97FL3 Paul Pierce 12.00 30.00
97FL4 Grant Hill 15.00 40.00
97FL5 Isiah Thomas 15.00 40.00
97FL6 Dennis Rodman 125.00 300.00
97FL7 Walt Frazier 12.00 30.00
97FL8 Lou Hudson 6.00 15.00
97FL9 Julius Erving 25.00 60.00
97FL10 Anfernee Hardaway 40.00 100.00
97FL11 Nick Van Exel 8.00 20.00
97FL12 David Robinson 20.00 50.00
97FL13 Nate Thurmond 8.00 20.00
97FL14 Mark A. Jackson 6.00 15.00
97FL15 Clyde Drexler 15.00 40.00
97FL16 Bill Walton 12.00 30.00
97FL17 Tony Gwynn 25.00 60.00
97FL18 Ray Allen 40.00 100.00
97FL19 Tim Hardaway 8.00 20.00
97FL20 Robert Horry 8.00 20.00
97FL21 Cheryl Miller 8.00 20.00
97FL22 Allen Iverson 75.00 200.00
97FL23 Bernard King 6.00 15.00
97FL24 Eddie Jones 6.00 15.00
97FL25 Antoine Walker 6.00 15.00
97FL26 Danny Manning 6.00 15.00
97FL27 Jamal Mashburn 6.00 15.00
97FL28 Rod Strickland 4.00 10.00
97FL29 Gary Payton 15.00 40.00
97FL30 Muggsy Bogues 6.00 15.00
97FL31 Larry Johnson 10.00 25.00
97FL32 Magic Johnson 125.00 300.00
97FL33 Allan Houston 6.00 15.00
97FL34 Alonzo Mourning 15.00 40.00
97FL35 Jeff Hornacek 6.00 15.00
97FL36 Elvin Hayes 10.00 25.00
97FL37 Mark Price 8.00 20.00

97FL38 Karl Malone 15.00 40.00
97FL39 Hakeem Olajuwon 40.00 100.00
97FL40 Reggie Miller 40.00 100.00
97FL41 Harold Miner 5.00 12.00
97FL42 LeBron James 400.00 800.00
97FL43 Larry Bird 125.00 300.00
97FL44 Adrian Dantley 6.00 15.00
97FL45 Wilt Chamberlain 40.00 100.00
97FL46 A.C. Green 8.00 20.00
97FL47 Jason Kidd 15.00 40.00
97FL48 Michael Jordan 600.00 1,200.00
97FL49 Spud Webb 6.00 15.00
97FL50 Dave Cowens 12.00 30.00

2012-13 Fleer Retro 97-98 Fleer EX 2001

STATED ODDS 1:10 HOBBY
EX1 Michael Jordan 75.00 200.00
EX2 Reggie Miller 3.00 8.00
EX3 A.C. Green 2.00 5.00
EX4 Mark Price 2.00 5.00
EX5 David Robinson 3.00 8.00
EX6 Clyde Drexler 3.00 8.00
EX7 Bernard King 2.50 6.00
EX8 Grant Hill 3.00 8.00
EX9 David Thompson 2.00 5.00
EX10 Elvin Hayes 2.50 6.00
EX11 Bill Walton 3.00 8.00
EX12 Allan Houston 1.50 4.00
EX13 Dennis Rodman 8.00 20.00
EX14 Tim Hardaway 2.50 6.00
EX15 Walt Frazier 3.00 8.00
EX16 Jason Kidd 3.00 8.00
EX17 Anfernee Hardaway 5.00 12.00
EX18 Spud Webb 1.50 4.00
EX19 Christian Laettner 2.00 5.00
EX20 John Havlicek 4.00 10.00
EX21 Mark A. Jackson 1.50 4.00
EX22 Karl Malone 3.00 8.00
EX23 Tony Gwynn 2.00 5.00
EX24 Julius Erving 8.00 20.00
EX25 Gary Payton 2.50 6.00
EX26 Ray Allen 3.00 8.00
EX27 Larry Johnson 2.50 6.00
EX28 Paul Pierce 3.00 8.00
EX29 Magic Johnson 12.00 30.00
EX30 Isiah Thomas 4.00 10.00
EX31 Derrick Coleman 2.00 5.00
EX32 Dominique Wilkins 2.50 6.00
EX33 Wilt Chamberlain 12.00 30.00
EX34 Allen Iverson 12.00 30.00
EX35 Danny Manning 1.50 4.00
EX36 Hakeem Olajuwon 4.00 10.00
EX37 Alonzo Mourning 3.00 8.00
EX38 Bill Russell 12.00 30.00
EX39 Antoine Walker 1.50 4.00
EX40 Jamal Mashburn 1.50 4.00
EX41 Larry Bird 12.00 30.00
EX42 LeBron James 60.00 150.00

2012-13 Fleer Retro 97-98 Metal Universe Precious Metal Gems

STATED PRINT RUN 100 SER.#'d SETS
97PM1 Bernard King 12.00 30.00
97PM2 Bill Russell 150.00 400.00
97PM3 Mookie Blaylock 8.00 20.00
97PM4 Lou Hudson 8.00 20.00
97PM5 Magic Johnson 150.00 400.00
97PM6 Ray Allen 40.00 100.00
97PM7 Reggie Miller 60.00 150.00
97PM8 Spencer Haywood 10.00 25.00
97PM9 Walt Frazier 15.00 40.00
97PM10 Jeff Hornacek 8.00 20.00
97PM11 Spud Webb 8.00 20.00
97PM12 Alonzo Mourning 60.00 150.00
97PM13 Larry Bird 150.00 400.00
97PM14 Allan Houston 8.00 20.00
97PM15 Shawn Bradley 6.00 15.00
97PM16 Nate Thurmond 10.00 25.00
97PM17 Christian Laettner 10.00 25.00
97PM18 David Robinson 60.00 150.00
97PM19 Dennis Rodman 125.00 300.00
97PM20 Karl Malone 20.00 50.00
97PM21 Elvin Hayes 12.00 30.00
97PM22 Toni Kukoc 40.00 100.00
97PM23 Anfernee Hardaway 125.00 300.00
97PM24 Antoine Walker 10.00 25.00
97PM25 Mark Price 10.00 25.00
97PM26 Wilt Chamberlain 60.00 150.00
97PM27 Danny Manning 10.00 25.00
97PM28 Nick Van Exel 10.00 25.00
97PM29 Larry Johnson 15.00 40.00
97PM30 Dominique Wilkins 30.00 80.00
97PM31 Hakeem Olajuwon 60.00 150.00
97PM32 Dave Cowens 15.00 40.00
97PM33 Gary Payton 20.00 50.00
97PM34 Isiah Thomas 20.00 50.00
97PM35 LeBron James 1,000.00 2,000.00
97PM36 David Thompson 10.00 25.00
97PM37 Jason Kidd 30.00 80.00
97PM38 Paul Pierce 30.00 80.00
97PM39 Tim Hardaway 15.00 40.00
97PM40 A.C. Green 10.00 25.00
97PM41 John Havlicek 25.00 60.00
97PM42 Grant Hill 40.00 100.00
97PM43 Allen Iverson 150.00 400.00
97PM44 Mark A. Jackson 8.00 20.00
97PM45 Clyde Drexler 40.00 100.00
97PM46 Julius Erving 75.00 200.00
97PM47 Cheryl Miller 10.00 25.00
97PM48 Bill Walton 15.00 40.00
97PM49 Tony Gwynn 25.00 60.00
97PM50 Michael Jordan 1,000.00 2,000.00

2012-13 Fleer Retro 97-98 Ultra

STATED ODDS 1:5 HOBBY
ULT1 Ray Allen 1.25 3.00
ULT2 Reggie Miller 1.25 3.00
ULT3 Nick Van Exel .75 2.00
ULT4 Spud Webb .60 1.50
ULT5 Lou Hudson .60 1.50
ULT6 A.C. Green .75 2.00
ULT7 Antoine Walker .60 1.50
ULT8 Danny Manning .60 1.50
ULT9 Bill Walton 1.25 3.00
ULT10 Alonzo Mourning 1.25 3.00
ULT11 Anfernee Hardaway 2.00 5.00
ULT12 Larry Bird 2.50 6.00
ULT13 John Havlicek 1.50 4.00
ULT14 Derrick Coleman .75 2.00
ULT15 Hakeem Olajuwon 1.50 4.00
ULT16 Allan Houston .60 1.50
ULT17 David Robinson 1.25 3.00
ULT18 Muggsy Bogues .60 1.50
ULT19 Clyde Drexler 1.25 3.00
ULT20 Harold Miner .50 1.25
ULT21 Bernard King 1.00 2.50
ULT22 Bill Russell 2.50 6.00
ULT23 Magic Johnson 2.50 6.00
ULT24 Karl Malone 1.25 3.00
ULT25 David Thompson .75 2.00
ULT26 Larry Johnson 1.00 2.50
ULT27 Tony Gwynn .75 2.00
ULT28 Dennis Rodman 2.00 5.00
ULT29 Isiah Thomas 1.50 4.00
ULT30 Eddie Jones .60 1.50
ULT31 Cheryl Miller .75 2.00
ULT32 Gary Payton 1.00 2.50
ULT33 Allen Iverson 1.25 3.00
ULT34 Paul Pierce 1.25 3.00
ULT35 Christian Laettner .75 2.00
ULT36 Jason Kidd 1.25 3.00
ULT37 Walt Frazier 1.25 3.00
ULT38 Dominique Wilkins 1.25 3.00
ULT39 Michael Jordan 8.00 20.00
ULT40 Grant Hill 1.25 3.00
ULT41 LeBron James 8.00 20.00
ULT42 Julius Erving 2.00 5.00
ULT43 Micheal Ray Richardson .60 1.50
ULT44 Wilt Chamberlain 2.50 6.00
ULT45 Jamal Mashburn .60 1.50
ULT46 Meyers Leonard .60 1.50
ULT47 Jeremy Lamb .75 2.00
ULT48 Kendall Marshall .50 1.25
ULT49 Moe Harkless .60 1.50
ULT50 Tyler Zeller .50 1.25

2012-13 Fleer Retro 97-98 Ultra Court Masters

STATED ODDS 1:180 HOBBY
1 Magic Johnson 12.00 30.00
2 Bill Russell 12.00 30.00
3 Reggie Miller 12.00 30.00
4 Isiah Thomas 8.00 20.00
5 Michael Jordan 500.00 1,000.00
6 LeBron James 500.00 1,000.00
7 Wilt Chamberlain 12.00 30.00
8 Larry Bird 12.00 30.00
9 Allen Iverson 10.00 25.00
10 Anfernee Hardaway 10.00 25.00
11 Julius Erving 10.00 25.00
12 Ray Allen 6.00 15.00
13 Elvin Hayes 5.00 12.00
14 Grant Hill 12.00 30.00
15 David Robinson 6.00 15.00
16 Karl Malone 6.00 15.00
17 Dominique Wilkins 5.00 12.00
18 Jason Kidd 8.00 20.00
19 Walt Frazier 6.00 15.00
20 Paul Pierce 6.00 15.00
21 Hakeem Olajuwon 8.00 20.00

2012-13 Fleer Retro 97-98 Ultra Platinum Medallion

STATED PRINT RUN 100 SER.#'d SETS
ULT1 Ray Allen 8.00 20.00
ULT2 Reggie Miller 8.00 20.00
ULT3 Nick Van Exel 5.00 12.00
ULT4 Spud Webb 4.00 10.00
ULT5 Lou Hudson 4.00 10.00
ULT6 A.C. Green 5.00 12.00
ULT7 Antoine Walker 4.00 10.00
ULT8 Danny Manning 4.00 10.00
ULT9 Bill Walton 8.00 20.00
ULT10 Alonzo Mourning 8.00 20.00
ULT11 Anfernee Hardaway 12.00 30.00
ULT12 Larry Bird 20.00 50.00
ULT13 John Havlicek 10.00 25.00
ULT14 Derrick Coleman 6.00 15.00
ULT15 Hakeem Olajuwon 10.00 25.00
ULT16 Allan Houston 4.00 10.00
ULT17 David Robinson 8.00 20.00
ULT18 Muggsy Bogues 4.00 10.00
ULT19 Clyde Drexler 8.00 20.00
ULT20 Harold Miner 3.00 8.00
ULT21 Bernard King 6.00 15.00
ULT22 Bill Russell 15.00 40.00
ULT23 Magic Johnson 20.00 50.00
ULT24 Karl Malone 8.00 20.00
ULT25 David Thompson 5.00 12.00
ULT26 Larry Johnson 6.00 15.00
ULT27 Tony Gwynn 8.00 20.00
ULT28 Dennis Rodman 12.00 30.00
ULT29 Isiah Thomas 10.00 25.00
ULT30 Eddie Jones 4.00 10.00
ULT31 Cheryl Miller 5.00 12.00
ULT32 Gary Payton 6.00 15.00
ULT33 Allen Iverson 8.00 20.00
ULT34 Paul Pierce 8.00 20.00
ULT35 Christian Laettner 5.00 12.00
ULT36 Jason Kidd 6.00 15.00
ULT37 Walt Frazier 8.00 20.00
ULT38 Dominique Wilkins 6.00 15.00
ULT39 Michael Jordan 150.00 400.00
ULT40 Grant Hill 20.00 50.00
ULT41 LeBron James 150.00 400.00
ULT42 Julius Erving 12.00 30.00
ULT43 Micheal Ray Richardson 4.00 10.00
ULT44 Wilt Chamberlain 15.00 40.00
ULT45 Jamal Mashburn 4.00 10.00
ULT46 Meyers Leonard 4.00 10.00
ULT47 Jeremy Lamb 5.00 12.00
ULT48 Kendall Marshall 3.00 8.00
ULT49 Moe Harkless 4.00 10.00
ULT50 Tyler Zeller 3.00 8.00

2012-13 Fleer Retro 97-98 Ultra Starring Role

STATED ODDS 1:180 HOBBY
1 Larry Bird 10.00 25.00
2 Bill Russell 12.00 30.00
3 Dominique Wilkins 5.00 12.00
4 Anfernee Hardaway 10.00 25.00
5 Karl Malone 6.00 15.00
6 Magic Johnson 12.00 30.00
8 Wilt Chamberlain 12.00 30.00
9 Hakeem Olajuwon 8.00 20.00
10 Ray Allen 6.00 15.00
11 Reggie Miller 8.00 20.00
12 Paul Pierce 6.00 15.00
13 LeBron James 125.00 300.00
14 Grant Hill 10.00 25.00
15 Larry Johnson 5.00 12.00
16 David Robinson 8.00 20.00
17 Michael Jordan 150.00 400.00
18 Jason Kidd 6.00 15.00
19 Clyde Drexler 6.00 15.00
20 Allen Iverson 12.00 30.00
21 Julius Erving 10.00 25.00

2012-13 Fleer Retro 97-98 Z-Force Big Men on Court

STATED ODDS 1:120 HOBBY
1 BMOC Alonzo Mourning 10.00 25.00
2 BMOC David Robinson 10.00 25.00
3 BMOC Isiah Thomas 12.00 30.00
4 BMOC Larry Bird 20.00 50.00
5 BMOC Paul Pierce 10.00 25.00
6 BMOC Ray Allen 10.00 25.00
7 BMOC Grant Hill 10.00 25.00
8 BMOC Anfernee Hardaway 15.00 40.00
9 BMOC Magic Johnson 20.00 50.00
10 BMOC Larry Johnson 8.00 20.00
11 BMOC Bill Russell 20.00 50.00
12 BMOC Julius Erving 15.00 40.00
13 BMOC Allen Iverson 25.00 60.00
14 BMOC Karl Malone 10.00 25.00
15 BMOC Michael Jordan 400.00 800.00
16 BMOC LeBron James 300.00 600.00
17 BMOC Reggie Miller 10.00 25.00
18 BMOC Gary Payton 8.00 20.00
19 BMOC Jason Kidd 10.00 25.00
20 BMOC Wilt Chamberlain 20.00 50.00

2012-13 Fleer Retro 97-98 Z-Force Rave

STATED PRINT RUN 399 SER.#'d SETS
Z1 Isiah Thomas 4.00 10.00
Z2 Dennis Rodman 5.00 12.00
Z3 Larry Bird 6.00 15.00
Z4 John Havlicek 4.00 10.00
Z5 Dominique Wilkins 2.50 6.00
Z6 David Robinson 3.00 8.00
Z7 Muggsy Bogues 1.50 4.00
Z8 Mookie Blaylock 1.25 3.00
Z9 Larry Johnson 2.50 6.00
Z10 Danny Manning 1.50 4.00
Z11 Dave Cowens 3.00 8.00
Z12 Cheryl Miller 2.00 5.00
Z13 Allen Iverson 3.00 8.00
Z14 Nate Thurmond 2.00 5.00
Z15 Elvin Hayes 2.50 6.00
Z16 Lou Hudson 1.50 4.00
Z17 Antoine Walker 1.50 4.00
Z18 A.C. Green 2.00 5.00
Z19 Bill Walton 3.00 8.00
Z20 Magic Johnson 6.00 15.00
Z21 Ray Allen 3.00 8.00
Z22 Jamal Mashburn 1.50 4.00
Z23 Tony Gwynn 1.50 4.00
Z24 Jason Kidd 3.00 8.00
Z25 Hakeem Olajuwon 4.00 10.00
Z26 Hal Greer 2.50 6.00
Z27 Paul Pierce 3.00 8.00
Z28 Wilt Chamberlain 6.00 15.00
Z29 Shawn Bradley 1.25 3.00
Z30 Bill Laimbeer 2.50 6.00
Z31 Grant Hill 3.00 8.00
Z32 Karl Malone 3.00 8.00
Z33 Michael Jordan 150.00 400.00
Z34 Alonzo Mourning 3.00 8.00
Z35 Nick Van Exel 2.00 5.00
Z36 Clyde Drexler 3.00 8.00
Z37 Eddie Jones 1.50 4.00
Z38 Gary Payton 2.50 6.00
Z39 Allan Houston 1.50 4.00
Z40 Bill Russell 6.00 15.00
Z41 David Thompson 2.00 5.00
Z42 Julius Erving 5.00 12.00
Z43 Walt Frazier 3.00 8.00
Z44 Mark Price 2.00 5.00
Z45 Reggie Miller 3.00 8.00
Z46 Spencer Haywood 2.00 5.00
Z47 Harold Miner 1.25 3.00
Z48 Bernard King 2.50 6.00
Z49 Anfernee Hardaway 5.00 12.00
Z50 LeBron James 125.00 300.00

2012-13 Fleer Retro 97-98 Z-Force Super Rave

*SUPER RAVE: 1.2X TO 3X BASIC
STATED PRINT RUN 50 SER.#'d SETS
Z2 Dennis Rodman 15.00 40.00
Z6 David Robinson 15.00 40.00
Z13 Allen Iverson 15.00 40.00
Z31 Grant Hill 15.00 40.00
Z33 Michael Jordan 1,000.00 2,000.00
Z38 Gary Payton 10.00 25.00
Z45 Reggie Miller 15.00 40.00
Z50 LeBron James 800.00 1,500.00

2012-13 Fleer Retro 98-99 Lucky 13

STATED ODDS 1:40 HOBBY
1LT Jeremy Lamb 3.00 8.00
2LT Moe Harkless 2.50 6.00
3LT Andrew Nicholson 2.00 5.00
4LT Jared Cunningham 2.00 5.00
5LT Arnett Moultrie 2.00 5.00
6LT Jae Crowder 4.00 10.00
7LT Quincy Acy 2.00 5.00
8LT Will Barton 4.00 10.00
9LT Darius Miller 2.50 6.00
10LT Darius Johnson-Odom 2.00 5.00
11LT Justin Hamilton 2.00 5.00
12LT Robert Sacre 2.00 5.00
13LT William Buford 2.00 5.00

2012-13 Fleer Retro 98-99 Lucky 13 Autographs

OVERALL 98/99 L13 AU ODDS 1:240
EXCHANGE DEADLINE 5/31/2015
1LT Jeremy Lamb EXCH 5.00 12.00
2LT Moe Harkless 4.00 10.00
3LT Andrew Nicholson 3.00 8.00
4LT Jared Cunningham 3.00 8.00
5LT Arnett Moultrie 3.00 8.00
6LT Jae Crowder 6.00 15.00
7LT Quincy Acy 3.00 8.00
8LT Will Barton 6.00 15.00
9LT Darius Miller 6.00 15.00
10LT Darius Johnson-Odom 3.00 8.00
11LT Justin Hamilton 3.00 8.00
12LT Robert Sacre 3.00 8.00
13LT William Buford 3.00 8.00

2012-13 Fleer Retro 98-99 Metal Universe Precious Metal Gems

STATED PRINT RUN 50 SER.#'d SETS
98PM1 Elvin Hayes 8.00 20.00
98PM2 Mark Price 12.00 30.00
98PM3 Muggsy Bogues 10.00 25.00
98PM4 Dave Cowens 10.00 25.00
98PM5 Walt Frazier 10.00 25.00
98PM6 Alonzo Mourning 10.00 25.00
98PM7 Danny Manning 5.00 12.00
98PM8 Anfernee Hardaway 50.00 125.00
98PM9 Jason Kidd 20.00 50.00
98PM10 Spud Webb 5.00 12.00
98PM11 Larry Bird 15.00 40.00
98PM12 John Havlicek 12.00 30.00
98PM13 Nick Van Exel 6.00 15.00
98PM14 Robert Horry 6.00 15.00
98PM15 Reggie Miller 20.00 50.00
98PM16 Spencer Haywood 6.00 15.00
98PM17 Chet Walker 6.00 15.00
98PM18 Gary Payton 15.00 40.00
98PM19 Cheryl Miller 6.00 15.00
98PM20 Jeff Hornacek 5.00 12.00
98PM21 David Robinson 10.00 25.00
98PM22 Vinny Del Negro 4.00 10.00
98PM23 Michael Jordan 2,000.00 4,000.00
98PM24 Wilt Chamberlain 30.00 80.00
98PM25 Allan Houston 5.00 12.00
98PM26 Dominique Wilkins 8.00 20.00
98PM27 Micheal Ray Richardson 5.00 12.00
98PM28 Karl Malone 25.00 60.00
98PM29 Isiah Thomas 12.00 30.00
98PM30 Tim Hardaway 5.00 12.00
98PM31 Dennis Rodman 15.00 40.00
98PM32 Tony Gwynn 12.00 30.00
98PM33 Lou Hudson 5.00 12.00
98PM34 Bill Russell 10.00 25.00
98PM35 A.C. Green 6.00 15.00
98PM36 Grant Hill 12.00 30.00
98PM37 LeBron James 2,000.00 4,000.00
98PM38 Nate Thurmond 6.00 15.00
98PM39 Julius Erving 15.00 40.00
98PM40 Paul Pierce 12.00 30.00
98PM41 Allen Iverson 30.00 80.00
98PM42 Bill Walton 10.00 25.00
98PM43 Bernard King 8.00 20.00
98PM44 Antoine Walker 10.00 25.00
98PM45 Christian Laettner 15.00 40.00
98PM46 Hakeem Olajuwon 12.00 30.00
98PM47 Clyde Drexler 25.00 60.00
98PM48 Magic Johnson 12.00 30.00
98PM49 Ray Allen 20.00 50.00
98PM50 Larry Johnson 15.00 40.00

2012-13 Fleer Retro 98-99 Tradition Playmakers Theater

STATED PRINT RUN 100 SER.#'d SETS
1PT Jason Kidd 15.00 40.00
2PT Ray Allen 15.00 40.00
3PT Grant Hill 15.00 40.00
4PT Elvin Hayes 12.00 30.00
5PT Allen Iverson 15.00 40.00
6PT Isiah Thomas 20.00 50.00
7PT Larry Bird 60.00 150.00
8PT Paul Pierce 15.00 40.00
9PT Karl Malone 15.00 40.00
10PT Julius Erving 40.00 100.00
11PT Anfernee Hardaway 40.00 100.00
12PT Magic Johnson 60.00 150.00
13PT David Robinson 40.00 100.00
14PT Michael Jordan 1,500.00 3,000.00
15PT Wilt Chamberlain 30.00 80.00
16PT Bill Russell 40.00 100.00
17PT Walt Frazier 15.00 40.00
18PT LeBron James 1,000.00 2,000.00
19PT Bernard King 12.00 30.00
20PT Reggie Miller 15.00 40.00
21PT Hakeem Olajuwon 20.00 50.00

2012-13 Fleer Retro 99-00 Flair Showcase Fresh Ink

GROUP A ODDS 1:8975 HOBBY
GROUP B ODDS 1:1007 HOBBY
GROUP C ODDS 1:756 HOBBY
GROUP D ODDS 1:308 HOBBY
GROUP E ODDS 1:179 HOBBY
GROUP F ODDS 1:36 HOBBY
EXCHANGE DEADLINE 5/31/2015
SFIAD Adrian Dantley E 4.00 10.00
SFIAH Anfernee Hardaway B 40.00 100.00
SFIAI Allen Iverson B 40.00 100.00
SFIAM Alonzo Mourning C 15.00 40.00
SFIBD Brad Daugherty F 4.00 10.00
SFIBL Bill Laimbeer F 6.00 15.00
SFIBM Bob McAdoo F 6.00 15.00
SFIBR Bill Russell B 400.00 800.00
SFICD Clyde Drexler C 20.00 50.00
SFICM Cheryl Miller C 20.00 50.00
SFIDM Danny Manning D 6.00 15.00
SFIDR David Robinson B 25.00 60.00
SFIDW Dominique Wilkins B 12.00 30.00
SFIEJ Eddie Jones F 4.00 10.00
SFIFL Fat Lever F 4.00 10.00
SFIGH Grant Hill B 15.00 40.00
SFIHM Harold Miner F 3.00 8.00
SFIHO Allan Houston F 4.00 10.00
SFIIT Isiah Thomas C 12.00 30.00
SFIJA LeBron James B 1,250.00 2,500.00
SFIJC Jared Cunningham F 3.00 8.00
SFIJE Julius Erving B 40.00 100.00
SFIJJ Jim Jackson F 4.00 10.00
SFIJK Jason Kidd D 12.00 30.00
SFIJM Jamal Mashburn E 4.00 10.00
SFIKM Khris Middleton F 15.00 40.00
SFILB Larry Bird B 60.00 150.00
SFILJ Larry Johnson B 12.00 30.00
SFILS Lonnie Shelton F 5.00 12.00
SFIMA Karl Malone C 20.00 50.00
SFIMB Muggsy Bogues F 4.00 10.00
SFIMC Michael Cooper E 5.00 12.00
SFIMG Mike Glover F 3.00 8.00
SFIMJ Magic Johnson B 60.00 150.00
SFIML Meyers Leonard E 4.00 10.00
SFIMP Miles Plumlee F 3.00 8.00
SFINT Nate Thurmond D 5.00 12.00
SFIOC Olek Czyz F 4.00 10.00
SFIOL Hakeem Olajuwon C 40.00 100.00
SFIPP Paul Pierce D 12.00 30.00
SFIPR Mark Price F 5.00 12.00
SFIRA Ray Allen C 12.00 30.00
SFIRH Robbie Hummel F 3.00 8.00
SFIRO Robert Horry F 5.00 12.00
SFISH Spencer Haywood D 5.00 12.00
SFISW Spud Webb 4.00 10.00
SFITH Tim Hardaway E 6.00 15.00
SFIWB Will Barton F 6.00 15.00

2012-13 Fleer Retro 99-00 Focus Fresh Ink

GROUP A ODDS 1:10,770 HOBBY
GROUP B ODDS 1:798 HOBBY
GROUP C ODDS 1:453 HOBBY
GROUP D ODDS 1:308 HOBBY
GROUP E ODDS 1:33 HOBBY
EXCHANGE DEADLINE 5/31/2015
FFIAH Anfernee Hardaway C 15.00 40.00
FFIAI Allen Iverson B 40.00 80.00
FFIBJ Bernard James E 2.50 6.00
FFIBK Bernard King E 5.00 12.00
FFIBL Bill Laimbeer E 5.00 12.00
FFIBR Bill Russell B 300.00 600.00
FFICD Clyde Drexler B 15.00 40.00
FFICM Cheryl Miller C 4.00 10.00
FFIDC Dave Cowens C 6.00 15.00
FFIDM Danny Manning C 8.00 20.00
FFIDR David Robinson B 15.00 40.00
FFIDT David Thompson D 4.00 10.00
FFIDW Dominique Wilkins C 8.00 20.00
FFIEJ Eddie Jones C 6.00 15.00
FFIGH Grant Hill C 20.00 50.00
FFIGR Glen Rice E 3.00 8.00
FFIHM Harold Miner D 6.00 15.00
FFIIT Isiah Thomas B 6.00 15.00
FFIJC Jae Crowder E 5.00 12.00
FFIJE Julius Erving B 30.00 60.00
FFIJH Jeff Hornacek E 3.00 8.00
FFIJJ Jim Jackson E 3.00 8.00
FFIJM Jamal Mashburn E 3.00 8.00
FFIJO Magic Johnson B 50.00 120.00
FFIJS John Shurna E 2.50 6.00
FFIJW Jo Jo White E 3.00 8.00
FFIKJ Kris Joseph E 2.50 6.00
FFIKM Kevin Murphy E 2.50 6.00
FFILB Larry Bird B 40.00 80.00
FFILH Lou Hudson E 3.00 8.00
FFILJ LeBron James B 1,250.00 2,500.00
FFILS Lonnie Shelton E 4.00 10.00
FFIMA Karl Malone B 20.00 50.00
FFIMH Moe Harkless E 3.00 8.00
FFIMJ Michael Jordan A 800.00 1,500.00
FFIMR Micheal Ray Richardson E 3.00 8.00
FFINT Nate Thurmond E 4.00 10.00
FFIOC Olek Czyz E 3.00 8.00
FFIPP Paul Pierce D 10.00 25.00
FFIRA Ray Allen C 12.00 30.00
FFIRH Robert Horry E 4.00 10.00
FFIRM Reggie Miller B 75.00 200.00
FFIRO Dennis Rodman D 10.00 25.00
FFIRR Ricardo Ratliffe E 2.50 6.00
FFIRS Robert Sacre E 2.50 6.00
FFIRT Reggie Theus E 3.00 8.00
FFISE Sean Elliott C 3.00 8.00
FFISH Spencer Haywood A 4.00 10.00
FFITZ Tyler Zeller E 2.50 6.00
FFIWF Walt Frazier D 6.00 15.00

2012-13 Fleer Retro 99-00 Mystique Fresh Ink

GROUP A ODDS 1:8975 HOBBY
GROUP B ODDS 1:917 HOBBY
GROUP C ODDS 1:173 HOBBY
GROUP D ODDS 1:133 HOBBY
GROUP E ODDS 1:43 HOBBY
EXCHANGE DEADLINE 5/31/2015
MFIAD Adrian Dantley E 3.00 8.00
MFIAH Anfernee Hardaway C 40.00 100.00
MFIAI Allen Iverson B 50.00 120.00
MFIAM Arnett Moultrie E 2.50 6.00
MFIBK Bernard King D 5.00 12.00
MFIBM Bob McAdoo E 6.00 15.00
MFIBR Bill Russell B 400.00 800.00
MFICD Clyde Drexler C 12.00 30.00
MFICM Cheryl Miller C 4.00 10.00
MFICW Chet Walker E 4.00 10.00
MFIDR David Robinson B 15.00 40.00
MFIDT David Thompson C 4.00 10.00
MFIDW Dominique Wilkins C 8.00 20.00
MFIEF Evan Fournier E 4.00 10.00
MFIGH Grant Hill C 12.00 30.00
MFIHA Justin Hamilton E 2.50 6.00
MFIIT Isiah Thomas C 6.00 15.00
MFIJE Julius Erving B EXCH 50.00 120.00
MFIJG JaMychal Green E 3.00 8.00
MFIJH John Havlicek C EXCH 30.00 80.00
MFIJJ Jim Jackson D 3.00 8.00
MFIJL Jeremy Lamb C 4.00 10.00
MFIJO Michael Jordan A 1,000.00 2,000.00
MFIKM Karl Malone B 15.00 40.00
MFILB Larry Bird B 30.00 80.00
MFILJ LeBron James B 1,250.00 2,500.00
MFILS Lonnie Shelton D 4.00 10.00
MFIMA Mark A. Jackson B 4.00 10.00
MFIMJ Magic Johnson B 40.00 80.00
MFIMO Alonzo Mourning C 10.00 25.00
MFIMP Mark Price E 6.00 15.00
MFIMR Micheal Ray Richardson E 3.00 8.00
MFIMW Mark West D 2.50 6.00
MFINT Nate Thurmond D 4.00 10.00
MFINV Nick Van Exel E 4.00 10.00
MFIPP Paul Pierce C 12.00 30.00
MFIPR Pooh Richardson E 2.50 6.00
MFIQA Quincy Acy E 2.50 6.00
MFIRA Ray Allen C 20.00 50.00
MFIRE Bryant Reeves E 2.50 6.00
MFIRM Reggie Miller A 150.00 400.00
MFIRO Dennis Rodman C 10.00 25.00
MFISB Shawn Bradley D 2.50 6.00
MFISE Sean Elliott D 3.00 8.00
MFISN Swen Nater E 3.00 8.00
MFISW Spud Webb E 3.00 8.00
MFITT Tyshawn Taylor E 2.50 6.00
MFIWB William Buford E 2.50 6.00
MFIWF Walt Frazier D 6.00 15.00

2012-13 Fleer Retro 99-00 Mystique Raise the Roof

STATED PRINT RUN 100 SER.#'d SETS
1RR Dominique Wilkins 8.00 20.00
2RR Karl Malone 10.00 25.00
3RR Allen Iverson 40.00 100.00
4RR Michael Jordan 200.00 500.00
5RR LeBron James 200.00 500.00
6RR Paul Pierce 10.00 25.00
7RR Grant Hill 12.00 30.00
8RR David Robinson 10.00 25.00
9RR Magic Johnson 20.00 50.00
10RR Julius Erving 15.00 40.00
11RR Reggie Miller 10.00 25.00
12RR Isiah Thomas 12.00 30.00
13RR Ray Allen 10.00 25.00
14RR Jason Kidd 10.00 25.00
15RR Bill Russell 20.00 50.00
16RR Wilt Chamberlain 20.00 50.00
17RR Larry Bird 12.00 30.00
18RR Anfernee Hardaway 15.00 40.00
19RR Clyde Drexler 10.00 25.00
20RR Hakeem Olajuwon 12.00 30.00
21RR Jamal Mashburn 5.00 12.00

2012-13 Fleer Retro 99-00 Ultra Fresh Ink

GROUP A ODDS 1:11,967 HOBBY
GROUP B ODDS 1:3590 HOBBY
GROUP C ODDS 1:1026 HOBBY
GROUP D ODDS 1:359 HOBBY
GROUP E ODDS 1:116 HOBBY
GROUP F ODDS 1:35 HOBBY
EXCHANGE DEADLINE 5/31/2015
UFIAD Adrian Dantley F 4.00 10.00
UFIAG A.C. Green F 5.00 12.00
UFIAH Allan Houston F 12.00 30.00
UFIAI Allen Iverson C 60.00 150.00
UFIAM Alonzo Mourning D 6.00 15.00
UFIAN Andrew Nicholson F 3.00 8.00
UFIBD Brad Daugherty F 4.00 10.00
UFIBH Bobby Hurley F 10.00 25.00
UFIBL Bill Laimbeer F 6.00 15.00
UFIBM Bob McAdoo F 12.00 30.00
UFICD Clyde Drexler C 10.00 25.00
UFICH Connie Hawkins E 12.00 30.00
UFICW Chet Walker E 5.00 12.00
UFIDA Danny Manning D 5.00 12.00
UFIDG Draymond Green F 30.00 80.00
UFIDJ Darius Johnson-Odom F 3.00 8.00
UFIDM Darius Miller F 4.00 10.00
UFIDR David Robinson C 30.00 80.00
UFIGH Grant Hill D 30.00 80.00
UFIGS Garrett Stutz F 3.00 8.00
UFIHG Hal Greer F 20.00 50.00
UFIHM Harold Miner E 3.00 8.00
UFIHO Hakeem Olajuwon D 40.00 100.00
UFIIT Isiah Thomas D 20.00 50.00
UFIJA Mark A. Jackson E 4.00 10.00
UFIJE Julius Erving A 40.00 80.00
UFIJG JaMychal Green F 3.00 8.00
UFIJH John Havlicek B EXCH 40.00 100.00
UFIJM Jamal Mashburn F 4.00 10.00
UFIJO Magic Johnson C 60.00 150.00
UFIKM Kendall Marshall F 3.00 8.00
UFILA Larry Johnson B 12.00 30.00
UFILB Larry Bird C 60.00 150.00
UFILJ LeBron James C 1,250.00 2,500.00
UFILS Lonnie Shelton E 5.00 12.00
UFIMA Karl Malone C 20.00 50.00
UFIMC Michael Cooper F 5.00 12.00
UFIMP Mark Price E 5.00 12.00
UFIMW Maalik Wayns F 4.00 10.00
UFINV Nick Van Exel F 12.00 30.00
UFIPP Paul Pierce E 20.00 50.00
UFIRA Ray Allen D 20.00 50.00
UFIRM Reggie Miller B 75.00 200.00
UFIRT Reggie Theus E 4.00 10.00
UFITH Tim Hardaway E 12.00 30.00
UFITK Toni Kukoc F 15.00 40.00
UFITS Tomas Satoransky E 5.00 12.00
UFIVD Vinny Del Negro E 3.00 8.00
UFIWW Wesley Witherspoon F 3.00 8.00

2012-13 Fleer Retro Autographs

GROUP A ODDS 1:16,569 HOBBY
GROUP B ODDS 1:2595 HOBBY
GROUP C ODDS 1:206 HOBBY
GROUP D ODDS 1:176 HOBBY
GROUP E ODDS 1:77 HOBBY
GROUP A RS ODDS 1:194 HOBBY
GROUP B RS ODDS 1:9 HOBBY
EXCHANGE DEADLINE 5/31/2015
1 Michael Jordan C 1,500.00 3,000.00
2 LeBron James C 1,000.00 2,000.00
3 Jason Kidd B 15.00 40.00
4 Dominique Wilkins C 15.00 40.00
5 Karl Malone C 20.00 50.00
6 Bill Walton D 12.00 30.00
7 Allen Iverson C 75.00 200.00
8 Paul Pierce C 20.00 50.00
9 Ray Allen C 30.00 80.00
10 Grant Hill C 25.00 60.00
11 Hakeem Olajuwon C 40.00 100.00
12 Bernard King E 5.00 12.00
13 Isiah Thomas C 12.00 30.00
14 Dennis Rodman C 40.00 100.00
15 Reggie Miller A 125.00 300.00
16 Bill Russell C 400.00 800.00
17 David Robinson C 40.00 100.00
18 Jim Jackson D 3.00 8.00
19 Larry Johnson C 12.00 30.00
20 Nate Thurmond E 4.00 10.00
21 Alonzo Mourning C 20.00 50.00
22 Anfernee Hardaway C 40.00 100.00
23 Glen Rice D 3.00 8.00
24 Tim Hardaway E 12.00 30.00
25 Walt Frazier D 12.00 30.00
26 Larry Bird C 75.00 200.00
27 John Havlicek C EXCH 60.00 150.00
28 Nick Van Exel D 12.00 30.00
29 Danny Manning E 3.00 8.00
30 Spud Webb E 3.00 8.00
31 Jamal Mashburn E 3.00 8.00
32 David Thompson E 4.00 10.00
33 Micheal Ray Richardson E 3.00 8.00
34 Harold Miner E 2.50 6.00
35 Mark Price E 4.00 10.00
36 Jeff Hornacek E 3.00 8.00
37 Toni Kukoc E 12.00 30.00
38 A.C. Green E 4.00 10.00
39 Spencer Haywood D 4.00 10.00
40 Sean Elliott C 6.00 15.00
41 Allan Houston E 3.00 8.00
42 Dave Cowens D 6.00 15.00
43 Cheryl Miller E 12.00 30.00
44 Christian Laettner D 10.00 25.00
45 Magic Johnson C 75.00 200.00
46 Mark A. Jackson D 3.00 8.00
47 Vinny Del Negro E 2.50 6.00
48 Clyde Drexler C 20.00 50.00
50 Julius Erving B 40.00 100.00
51 Meyers Leonard RS B 3.00 8.00
52 Jeremy Lamb RS B 4.00 10.00
53 Kendall Marshall RS B 2.50 6.00
54 Moe Harkless RS B 3.00 8.00
55 Tyler Zeller RS B 2.50 6.00
56 Andrew Nicholson RS B 2.50 6.00
57 Evan Fournier RS B 4.00 10.00
58 Jared Cunningham RS B 2.50 6.00
59 Miles Plumlee RS B 2.50 6.00
60 Arnett Moultrie RS B 2.50 6.00
61 Bernard James RS B 2.50 6.00
62 Jae Crowder RS B 5.00 12.00
63 Draymond Green RS B 25.00 60.00
64 Quincy Acy RS B 2.50 6.00
65 Khris Middleton RS B 12.00 30.00
66 Will Barton RS B 5.00 12.00
67 Tyshawn Taylor RS B 2.50 6.00
68 Darius Miller RS B 3.00 8.00
69 Kevin Murphy RS B 2.50 6.00
70 Darius Johnson-Odom RS B 2.50 6.00
71 Robbie Hummel RS B 2.50 6.00
72 Robert Sacre RS B 2.50 6.00
73 Wesley Witherspoon RS B 2.50 6.00
74 William Buford RS B 2.50 6.00
75 Ricardo Ratliffe RS A 2.50 6.00
76 John Shurna RS B 2.50 6.00
77 Tomas Satoransky RS B 4.00 10.00
78 Justin Hamilton RS B 2.50 6.00
79 JaMychal Green RS B 3.00 8.00
80 Kris Joseph RS B 2.50 6.00

2013-14 Fleer Retro

COMPLETE SET (60) 6.00 15.00
1 Allen Iverson .75 2.00
2 Rajon Rondo .50 1.25
3 Glenn Robinson .30 .75
4 Dennis Rodman 1.00 2.50
5 Elvin Hayes .50 1.25
6 Donyell Marshall .25 .60
7 Calbert Cheaney .25 .60
8 Antoine Walker .30 .75
9 David Thompson .40 1.00
10 Kerry Kittles .25 .60
11 Grant Hill .60 1.50
12 Dominique Wilkins .60 1.50
13 Tim Hardaway .50 1.25
14 Alonzo Mourning .60 1.50
15 Anfernee Hardaway 1.00 2.50
16 Jason Kidd .60 1.50
17 Kenny Anderson .30 .75
18 Paul George .60 1.50
19 Isiah Thomas .60 1.50
20 Bill Walton .60 1.50
21 Danny Manning .30 .75
22 Jay Williams .25 .60
23 Larry Johnson .50 1.25
24 Jerry Lucas .40 1.00
25 Joe Smith .30 .75
26 James Harden .75 2.00
27 Otis Birdsong .30 .75
28 Derek Harper .30 .75
29 Sam Perkins .30 .75
30 Bill Russell 1.25 3.00
31 David Robinson .75 2.00
32 Reggie Miller .60 1.50
33 Hakeem Olajuwon .75 2.00
34 Larry Bird 1.50 4.00
35 Clyde Drexler .60 1.50
36 Julius Erving 1.00 2.50
37 Karl Malone .75 2.00
38 Christian Laettner .40 1.00
39 LeBron James 3.00 8.00
40 Michael Jordan 3.00 8.00
41 Mason Plumlee .40 1.00
42 Jamaal Franklin .30 .75
43 Shane Larkin .30 .75
44 Lucas Nogueira .30 .75
45 Isaiah Canaan .30 .75
46 Tim Hardaway Jr. .60 1.50
47 Giannis Antetokounmpo 40.00 100.00
48 Livio Jean-Charles .30 .75
49 Archie Goodwin .30 .75
50 Solomon Hill .40 1.00
51 Andre Roberson .40 1.00
52 Dennis Schroeder 1.00 2.50
53 Skylar Diggins 1.50 4.00
54 Grant Jerrett .30 .75
55 Rudy Gobert 1.25 3.00
56 Allen Crabbe .30 .75
57 Tony Snell .40 1.00
58 Reggie Bullock .40 1.00
59 Sergey Karasev .30 .75
60 Deshaun Thomas .30 .75

2013-14 Fleer Retro '92-93 Fleer Final Four Stars

STATED ODDS 1:36
1 Antoine Walker 2.00 5.00
2 Bill Laimbeer 2.50 6.00
3 Bill Russell 8.00 20.00
4 Bill Walton 4.00 10.00
5 Calbert Cheaney 1.50 4.00
6 Cheryl Miller 2.50 6.00

7 Christian Laettner 2.50 6.00
8 Corliss Williamson 1.50 4.00
9 Danny Manning 2.00 5.00
10 David Thompson 2.50 6.00
11 Elvin Hayes 3.00 8.00
12 Glen Rice 2.00 5.00
13 Grant Hill 4.00 10.00
14 Hakeem Olajuwon 5.00 12.00
15 Isiah Thomas 4.00 10.00
16 Jamal Mashburn 2.00 5.00
17 Jerry Lucas 2.50 6.00
18 Peyton Siva 1.50 4.00
19 Keith Smart 2.50 6.00
20 Larry Bird 10.00 25.00
21 Larry Johnson 3.00 8.00
22 Kendall Gill 2.50 6.00
23 Ron Mercer 1.50 4.00
24 Michael Jordan 15.00 40.00
25 Sean Elliott 2.50 6.00

2013-14 Fleer Retro '92-93 Fleer Final Four Stars Autographs

PRINT RUNS B/WN 15-25 COPIES PER
NO PRICING ON QTY 15
EXCHANGE DEADLINE 3/28/2016
5 Calbert Cheaney/25 12.00 30.00
13 Grant Hill/25 20.00 50.00
15 Isiah Thomas/25 15.00 40.00
17 Jerry Lucas/25 20.00 50.00
21 Larry Johnson/25 12.00 30.00
25 Sean Elliott/25 15.00 40.00

2013-14 Fleer Retro '92-93 Fleer Rookie Sensations Autographs

GROUP A ODDS 1:2448
GROUP B ODDS 1:429
GROUP C ODDS 1:233
GROUP D ODDS 1:147
EXCHANGE DEADLINE 3/28/2016
RS1 Mason Plumlee C 3.00 8.00
RS5 Tim Hardaway Jr. C 5.00 12.00
RS9 Reggie Bullock D 3.00 8.00
RS12 Grant Jerrett B 2.50 6.00
RS13 Ricardo Ledo A 2.50 6.00
RS15 Mike Muscala 4.00 10.00
RS18 Giannis Antetokounmpo B 200.00 500.00
RS22 Nemaja Nedovic 2.50 6.00

2013-14 Fleer Retro '92-93 Fleer Team Leaders

STATED ODDS 1:90
1 Grant Hill 3.00 8.00
2 Allen Iverson 4.00 10.00
3 Otis Birdsong 1.50 4.00
4 Hakeem Olajuwon 4.00 10.00
5 Isiah Thomas 3.00 8.00
6 Larry Bird 8.00 20.00
7 Danny Manning 1.50 4.00
8 Dominique Wilkins 3.00 8.00
9 Karl Malone 4.00 10.00
10 Julius Erving 5.00 12.00
11 Anfernee Hardaway 5.00 12.00
12 James Harden 4.00 10.00
13 David Robinson 4.00 10.00
14 David Thompson 2.00 5.00
15 Michael Jordan 75.00 200.00
16 Glenn Robinson 1.50 4.00
17 Dennis Rodman 5.00 12.00
18 LeBron James 30.00 80.00
19 Bill Walton 3.00 8.00
20 Larry Johnson 2.50 6.00

2013-14 Fleer Retro '92-93 Fleer Team Leaders Autographs

PRINT RUNS B/WN 15-25 COPIES PER
NO PRICING ON QTY 15 OR LESS
EXCHANGE DEADLINE 3/28/2016
1 Grant Hill/25 50.00 120.00
4 Hakeem Olajuwon/25 30.00 80.00
5 Isiah Thomas/25 20.00 50.00
9 Karl Malone/25 25.00 60.00
13 David Robinson/25 20.00 50.00
18 LeBron James/25 1,500.00 3,000.00
20 Larry Johnson/25 20.00 50.00

2013-14 Fleer Retro '92-93 Ultra Michael Jordan Career Highlights

COMMON CARD 10.00 25.00
STATED ODDS 1:60

2013-14 Fleer Retro '93-94 Ultra All Rookie Series Autographs

GROUP A ODDS 1:490
GROUP B ODDS 1:270
EXCHANGE DEADLINE 3/28/2016
ARS1 Tim Hardaway Jr. A 5.00 12.00
ARS2 Skylar Diggins B 12.00 30.00

2013-14 Fleer Retro '93-94 Ultra Power in the Key

STATED ODDS 1:60
1 Alonzo Mourning 15.00 40.00
2 Bill Russell 40.00 100.00
3 Buck Williams 5.00 12.00
4 Danny Manning 5.00 12.00
5 David Robinson 25.00 60.00
6 Dennis Rodman 25.00 60.00
7 Elvin Hayes 8.00 20.00
8 Hakeem Olajuwon 25.00 60.00
9 Jerry Lucas 6.00 15.00
10 Karl Malone 15.00 40.00
11 Larry Johnson 8.00 20.00
12 LeBron James 200.00 500.00
13 Michael Jordan 300.00 600.00
14 Antoine Walker 5.00 12.00
15 Bill Walton 10.00 25.00
16 Julius Erving 25.00 60.00
17 Corliss Williamson 4.00 10.00
18 Sam Perkins 5.00 12.00
19 Bill Laimbeer 6.00 15.00
20 Theo Ratliff 4.00 10.00

2013-14 Fleer Retro '93-94 Ultra Scoring Kings

STATED ODDS 1:60
1 Allan Houston 12.00 30.00
2 Allen Iverson 40.00 100.00
3 Bill Russell 40.00 100.00
4 Reggie Miller 40.00 100.00
5 Calbert Cheaney 4.00 10.00
6 Danny Manning 5.00 12.00
7 David Robinson 40.00 100.00
8 Dominique Wilkins 20.00 50.00
9 Elvin Hayes 8.00 20.00
10 Clyde Drexler 30.00 80.00
11 Hakeem Olajuwon 40.00 100.00
12 Julius Erving 40.00 100.00
13 Karl Malone 30.00 80.00
14 Larry Bird 60.00 150.00
15 Larry Johnson 15.00 40.00
16 LeBron James 600.00 1,200.00
17 Magic Johnson 60.00 150.00
18 Michael Jordan 1,000.00 2,000.00
19 Otis Birdsong 5.00 12.00
20 Grant Hill 40.00 100.00

2013-14 Fleer Retro '94-95 SkyBox Emotion N-Tense

STATED ODDS 1:120
1 Larry Johnson 12.00 30.00
2 Reggie Miller 40.00 100.00
3 Clyde Drexler 20.00 50.00
4 LeBron James 200.00 500.00
5 Bill Russell 40.00 100.00
6 Rajon Rondo 12.00 30.00
7 Michael Jordan 300.00 600.00
8 David Robinson 40.00 100.00
9 Magic Johnson 60.00 150.00
10 Anfernee Hardaway 40.00 100.00
11 Julius Erving 40.00 100.00
12 Karl Malone 20.00 50.00
13 Dominique Wilkins 15.00 40.00
14 Paul George 20.00 50.00
15 Larry Bird 60.00 150.00
16 James Harden 40.00 100.00
17 Hakeem Olajuwon 40.00 100.00
18 Alonzo Mourning 20.00 50.00
19 Allen Iverson 40.00 100.00
20 Grant Hill 25.00 60.00

2013-14 Fleer Retro '95-96 Metal Universe

STATED ODDS 1:10
221 Jason Kidd .60 1.50
222 Grant Hill .60 1.50
223 Jay Williams .25 .60
224 Allen Iverson .75 2.00
225 Alonzo Mourning .60 1.50
226 Kenny Anderson .30 .75
227 Hakeem Olajuwon .75 2.00
228 Jerry Stackhouse .30 .75
229 Paul George .60 1.50
230 Isiah Thomas .60 1.50
231 Larry Bird 1.50 4.00
232 Rajon Rondo .50 1.25
233 Karl Malone .75 2.00
234 Joe Smith .30 .75
235 Julius Erving 1.00 2.50
236 Anfernee Hardaway 1.00 2.50
237 Clyde Drexler .60 1.50
238 David Robinson .75 2.00
239 Dominique Wilkins .60 1.50
240 Michael Jordan 8.00 20.00
241 Jerry Lucas .40 1.00
242 John Havlicek 1.00 2.50
243 Glenn Robinson .30 .75
244 Bill Russell 1.25 3.00
245 James Harden .75 2.00
246 Dennis Rodman 1.00 2.50
247 LeBron James 3.00 8.00
248 Reggie Miller .60 1.50
249 Larry Johnson .50 1.25
250 Tim Hardaway .50 1.25

2013-14 Fleer Retro '95-96 Metal Universe Precious Metal Gems Blue

*PMG BLUE: 10X TO 25X BASIC
STATED PRINT RUN 50 SER.#'d SETS
221 Jason Kidd 25.00 60.00
222 Grant Hill 40.00 100.00
223 Jay Williams 12.00 30.00
224 Allen Iverson 600.00 1,200.00
225 Alonzo Mourning 60.00 150.00
227 Hakeem Olajuwon 200.00 500.00
228 Jerry Stackhouse 50.00 120.00
229 Paul George 150.00 400.00
230 Isiah Thomas 75.00 200.00
231 Larry Bird 400.00 800.00
232 Rajon Rondo 30.00 80.00
233 Karl Malone 150.00 400.00
235 Julius Erving 150.00 400.00
236 Anfernee Hardaway 200.00 500.00
237 Clyde Drexler 75.00 200.00
238 David Robinson 200.00 500.00
239 Dominique Wilkins 150.00 400.00
240 Michael Jordan 4,000.00 8,000.00
242 John Havlicek 150.00 400.00
244 Bill Russell 500.00 1,000.00
245 James Harden 400.00 800.00
246 Dennis Rodman 200.00 500.00
247 LeBron James 3,000.00 6,000.00
248 Reggie Miller 150.00 400.00
249 Larry Johnson 60.00 150.00
250 Tim Hardaway 40.00 100.00

2013-14 Fleer Retro '95-96 Metal Universe Precious Metal Gems Red

*PMG RED: 6X TO 15X BASIC
STATED PRINT RUN 150 SER.#'d SETS
221 Jason Kidd 15.00 40.00
222 Grant Hill 25.00 60.00
224 Allen Iverson 300.00 600.00
225 Alonzo Mourning 40.00 100.00
227 Hakeem Olajuwon 125.00 300.00
228 Jerry Stackhouse 25.00 60.00
229 Paul George 100.00 250.00
230 Isiah Thomas 50.00 120.00
231 Larry Bird 200.00 500.00
232 Rajon Rondo 20.00 50.00
233 Karl Malone 100.00 250.00
235 Julius Erving 100.00 250.00
236 Anfernee Hardaway 125.00 300.00
237 Clyde Drexler 50.00 120.00
238 David Robinson 125.00 300.00
239 Dominique Wilkins 100.00 250.00
240 Michael Jordan 2,500.00 5,000.00
242 John Havlicek 100.00 250.00
244 Bill Russell 300.00 600.00
245 James Harden 200.00 500.00
246 Dennis Rodman 125.00 300.00
247 LeBron James 2,000.00 4,000.00
248 Reggie Miller 100.00 250.00
249 Larry Johnson 40.00 100.00
250 Tim Hardaway 25.00 60.00

2013-14 Fleer Retro '95-96 Metal Universe Maximum Metal

STATED ODDS 1:60
1 Larry Johnson 3.00 8.00
2 Grant Hill 4.00 10.00
3 Allen Iverson 5.00 12.00
4 Hakeem Olajuwon 5.00 12.00
5 Larry Bird 10.00 25.00
6 Jason Kidd 4.00 10.00
7 Rajon Rondo 3.00 8.00
8 Karl Malone 5.00 12.00
9 Jerry Stackhouse 2.00 5.00
10 Julius Erving 6.00 15.00
11 Anfernee Hardaway 6.00 15.00
12 Magic Johnson 10.00 25.00
13 David Robinson 5.00 12.00
14 Michael Jordan 60.00 150.00
15 Clyde Drexler 4.00 10.00
16 Bill Russell 8.00 20.00
17 LeBron James 30.00 80.00
18 Reggie Miller 4.00 10.00
19 Paul George 4.00 10.00
20 James Harden 5.00 12.00

2013-14 Fleer Retro '95-96 SkyBox Premium Meltdown

STATED ODDS 1:60
M1 Jason Kidd 4.00 10.00
M2 Reggie Miller 4.00 10.00
M3 Clyde Drexler 4.00 10.00
M4 LeBron James 50.00 120.00
M5 Dennis Rodman 6.00 15.00
M6 Bill Russell 8.00 20.00
M7 Michael Jordan 75.00 200.00
M8 David Robinson 5.00 12.00
M9 Magic Johnson 10.00 25.00
M10 Julius Erving 6.00 15.00
M11 Karl Malone 5.00 12.00
M12 Rajon Rondo 3.00 8.00
M13 Jerry Stackhouse 2.00 5.00
M14 Larry Bird 10.00 25.00
M15 Hakeem Olajuwon 5.00 12.00
M16 James Harden 5.00 12.00
M17 Allen Iverson 5.00 12.00
M18 Grant Hill 4.00 10.00
M19 Paul George 4.00 10.00
M20 Tim Hardaway Jr. 3.00 8.00

2013-14 Fleer Retro '95-96 Ultra

STATED ODDS 1:6
161 Christian Laettner .40 1.00
162 Grant Hill .60 1.50
163 Allen Iverson .75 2.00
164 Alonzo Mourning .60 1.50
165 Hakeem Olajuwon .75 2.00
166 Isiah Thomas .60 1.50
167 Larry Bird 1.50 4.00
168 Ron Mercer .25 .60
169 Rajon Rondo .50 1.25
170 Karl Malone .75 2.00
171 Joe Smith .30 .75
172 Julius Erving 1.00 2.50
173 Anfernee Hardaway 1.00 2.50
174 Jerry Stackhouse .30 .75
175 David Robinson .75 2.00
176 Sam Perkins .30 .75
177 Michael Jordan 3.00 8.00
178 Dominique Wilkins .60 1.50
179 LaPhonso Ellis .25 .60
180 Jason Kidd .60 1.50
181 Jerry Lucas .40 1.00
182 Glenn Robinson .30 .75
183 James Harden .75 2.00
184 Bill Russell 1.25 3.00
185 Dennis Rodman 1.00 2.50
186 LeBron James 3.00 8.00
187 Reggie Miller .60 1.50
188 Larry Johnson .50 1.25
189 Paul George .60 1.50
190 Clyde Drexler .60 1.50
191 Grant Jerrett .25 .60
192 Nemanja Nedovic .25 .60
193 Mason Plumlee .30 .75
194 Jamaal Franklin .25 .60
195 Shane Larkin .25 .60
196 Isaiah Canaan .25 .60
197 Tim Hardaway Jr. .50 1.25
198 Livio Jean-Charles .25 .60
199 Archie Goodwin .25 .60
200 Skylar Diggins 1.25 3.00
201 Andre Roberson .30 .75
202 Sergey Karasev .25 .60
203 Erick Green .30 .75
204 Ryan Kelly .25 .60
205 Peyton Siva .25 .60
206 Solomon Hill .25 .60
207 Lucas Nogueira .25 .60
208 Giannis Antetokounmpo 40.00 100.00
209 Brandon Paul .25 .60
210 Allen Crabbe .25 .60
211 Will Clyburn .25 .60
212 Adonis Thomas .25 .60
213 Rudy Gobert 1.00 2.50
214 Pierre Jackson .25 .60
215 Reggie Bullock .30 .75
216 Tony Snell .30 .75
217 Deshaun Thomas .25 .60
218 Lorenzo Brown .25 .60
219 Phil Pressey .25 .60
220 Dennis Schroeder .75 2.00

2013-14 Fleer Retro '95-96 Ultra Autographs

GROUP A ODDS 1:1200
GROUP B ODDS 1:1262
GROUP C ODDS 1:203
EXCHANGE DEADLINE 3/28/2016
161 Christian Laettner C 8.00 20.00
162 Grant Hill B 25.00 60.00
165 Hakeem Olajuwon A 25.00 60.00
166 Isiah Thomas B 20.00 50.00
167 Larry Bird A 75.00 200.00
170 Karl Malone A 40.00 100.00
174 Jerry Stackhouse A 12.00 30.00
175 David Robinson A 25.00 60.00
177 Michael Jordan A 1,000.00 2,000.00
178 Dominique Wilkins B 20.00 50.00
181 Jerry Lucas C 8.00 20.00
183 James Harden B 40.00 100.00
184 Bill Russell A 200.00 500.00
185 Dennis Rodman A 40.00 100.00
186 LeBron James A 1,000.00 2,000.00
188 Larry Johnson A 12.00 30.00
189 Paul George A 20.00 50.00
197 Tim Hardaway Jr. C 5.00 12.00
200 Skylar Diggins C 8.00 20.00
208 Giannis Antetokounmpo C 400.00 800.00

2013-14 Fleer Retro '96-97 SkyBox Autographics

GROUP A ODDS 1:6800
GROUP B ODDS 1:621
GROUP C ODDS 1:378
EXCHANGE DEADLINE 3/28/2016
96AUAE Alex English D 6.00 15.00
96AUDC Dave Cowens D 5.00 12.00
96AUDM Donyell Marshall D 3.00 8.00
96AUEJ Eddie Jones B 4.00 10.00
96AUJH James Harden A 75.00 200.00
96AUJL Jerry Lucas C 12.00 30.00
96AUSA Stacey Augmon C 3.00 8.00
96AUWI Jay Williams B 3.00 8.00

2013-14 Fleer Retro '96-97 SkyBox Premium

STATED ODDS 1:3
61 Robert Horry .40 1.00
62 Jason Kidd .60 1.50
63 Corliss Williamson .25 .60
64 Shawn Bradley .25 .60
65 Donyell Marshall .25 .60
66 Bo Kimble .25 .60
67 Grant Hill .60 1.50
68 Jay Williams .25 .60
69 Dave Cowens .40 1.00
70 Allen Iverson .75 2.00
71 Alonzo Mourning .60 1.50
72 Kenny Anderson .30 .75
73 Elvin Hayes .50 1.25
74 Otis Birdsong .30 .75
75 Hakeem Olajuwon .75 2.00
76 Derek Harper .30 .75
77 Tim Hardaway .50 1.25
78 Calbert Cheaney .25 .60
79 Keith Smart .40 1.00
80 Isiah Thomas .60 1.50
81 Larry Bird 1.50 4.00
82 Danny Manning .30 .75
83 Dominique Wilkins .60 1.50
84 Rajon Rondo .50 1.25
85 Antoine Walker .30 .75
86 Karl Malone .75 2.00
87 Buck Williams .30 .75
88 Joe Smith .30 .75
89 Julius Erving 1.00 2.50
90 Anfernee Hardaway 1.00 2.50
91 Magic Johnson 1.50 4.00
92 Glen Rice .30 .75
93 Micheal Ray Richardson .30 .75
94 David Robinson .75 2.00
95 Spud Webb .40 1.00
96 David Thompson .40 1.00
97 Toni Kukoc .50 1.25
98 James Harden .75 2.00
99 Paul George .60 1.50
100 Sam Perkins .30 .75
101 Michael Jordan 3.00 8.00
102 John Havlicek 1.00 2.50
103 Jerry Lucas .40 1.00
104 Jerry Stackhouse .30 .75
105 Clyde Drexler .60 1.50
106 Bill Russell 1.25 3.00
107 Alex English .50 1.25
108 Dennis Rodman 1.00 2.50
109 LeBron James 3.00 8.00
110 Stacey Augmon .25 .60
111 Allan Houston .60 1.50
112 Bill Walton .60 1.50
113 Reggie Miller .60 1.50
114 Theo Ratliff .25 .60
115 Larry Johnson .50 1.25
116 Mason Plumlee .30 .75
117 Skylar Diggins 1.25 3.00
118 Shane Larkin .25 .60
119 Lucas Nogueira .25 .60
120 Tim Hardaway Jr. .50 1.25

2013-14 Fleer Retro '96-97 SkyBox Premium Star Rubies

*STAR RUBY: 6X TO 15X BASIC
STATED PRINT RUN 150 SER.#'d SETS
67 Grant Hill 20.00 50.00
70 Allen Iverson 40.00 100.00
71 Alonzo Mourning 20.00 50.00
75 Hakeem Olajuwon 40.00 100.00
80 Isiah Thomas 12.00 30.00
81 Larry Bird 40.00 100.00
86 Karl Malone 15.00 40.00
89 Julius Erving 20.00 50.00
90 Anfernee Hardaway 40.00 100.00
91 Magic Johnson 40.00 100.00
94 David Robinson 20.00 50.00
97 Toni Kukoc 12.00 30.00
98 James Harden 40.00 100.00
101 Michael Jordan 500.00 1,000.00
102 John Havlicek 20.00 50.00
105 Clyde Drexler 20.00 50.00
106 Bill Russell 40.00 100.00
108 Dennis Rodman 40.00 100.00
109 LeBron James 400.00 800.00
113 Reggie Miller 30.00 80.00

2013-14 Fleer Retro '96-97 SkyBox Premium Golden Touch

STATED ODDS 1:120
1 Grant Hill 30.00 80.00
2 Allen Iverson 75.00 200.00
3 Alonzo Mourning 20.00 50.00
4 Hakeem Olajuwon 40.00 100.00
5 Isiah Thomas 20.00 50.00
6 Larry Bird 75.00 200.00
7 Rajon Rondo 15.00 40.00
8 Karl Malone 30.00 80.00
9 Julius Erving 40.00 100.00
10 Anfernee Hardaway 40.00 100.00
11 Magic Johnson 75.00 200.00
12 Jason Kidd 20.00 50.00
13 David Robinson 40.00 100.00
14 Michael Jordan 500.00 1,000.00
15 Dominique Wilkins 20.00 50.00
16 Bill Russell 60.00 150.00
17 LeBron James 400.00 800.00
18 Clyde Drexler 20.00 50.00
19 Reggie Miller 40.00 100.00
20 James Harden 40.00 100.00

2013-14 Fleer Retro '97-98 Metal Universe

STATED ODDS 1:10
251 Skylar Diggins 2.00 5.00
252 Giannis Antetokounmpo 150.00 400.00
253 Lucas Nogueira .40 1.00
254 Dennis Schroeder 8.00 20.00
255 Shane Larkin .40 1.00
256 Sergey Karasev .40 1.00
257 Tony Snell .50 1.25
258 Mason Plumlee .50 1.25
259 Solomon Hill .50 1.25
260 Tim Hardaway Jr. .75 2.00
261 Reggie Bullock .50 1.25
262 Andre Roberson .50 1.25
263 Rudy Gobert 8.00 20.00
264 Livio Jean-Charles .40 1.00
265 Archie Goodwin .40 1.00
266 Nemanja Nedovic .40 1.00
267 Allen Crabbe .40 1.00
268 Isaiah Canaan .40 1.00
269 Grant Jerrett .40 1.00
270 Jamaal Franklin .40 1.00
271 Pierre Jackson .40 1.00
272 Ricardo Ledo .40 1.00
273 Mike Muscala .60 1.50
274 Erick Green .50 1.25
275 Ryan Kelly .40 1.00
276 Lorenzo Brown .40 1.00
277 Peyton Siva .40 1.00
278 Deshaun Thomas .40 1.00
279 C.J. Leslie .40 1.00
280 Seth Curry 1.00 2.50

2013-14 Fleer Retro '97-98 Metal Universe Precious Metal Gems Blue

*PMG BLUE: 6X TO 15X BASIC
STATED PRINT RUN 50 SER.#'d SETS
252 Giannis Antetokounmpo 6,000.00 12,000.00

2013-14 Fleer Retro '97-98 Metal Universe Precious Metal Gems Red

*PMG RED: 3X TO 8X BASIC
STATED PRINT RUN 150 SER.#'d SETS
252 Giannis Antetokounmpo 3,000.00 6,000.00
254 Dennis Schroeder 40.00 100.00
263 Rudy Gobert 60.00 150.00

2013-14 Fleer Retro '97-98 SkyBox Autographics

GROUP A ODDS 1:12,240
GROUP B ODDS 1:3060
GROUP C ODDS 1:2448
GROUP D ODDS 1:612
EXCHANGE DEADLINE 3/28/2016
97AUAH Allan Houston E 5.00 12.00
97AUAW Antoine Walker D 6.00 15.00
97AUEH Elvin Hayes E 6.00 15.00
97AUGH Grant Hill C 60.00 150.00
97AUHO Hakeem Olajuwon B 60.00 150.00
97AUKA Kenny Anderson E 4.00 10.00
97AUKM Karl Malone B 60.00 150.00

2013-14 Fleer Retro '97-98 SkyBox Premium

STATED ODDS 1:10
121 Grant Hill .60 1.50
122 Allen Iverson .75 2.00
123 Alonzo Mourning .60 1.50
124 Hakeem Olajuwon .75 2.00
125 Isiah Thomas .60 1.50
126 Larry Bird 1.50 4.00
127 Rajon Rondo .50 1.25
128 Karl Malone .75 2.00
129 Julius Erving 1.00 2.50
130 Anfernee Hardaway 1.00 2.50
131 Magic Johnson 1.50 4.00
132 David Robinson .75 2.00
133 Michael Jordan 3.00 8.00
134 Paul George .60 1.50
135 James Harden .75 2.00
136 Bill Russell 1.25 3.00
137 Dennis Rodman 1.00 2.50
138 LeBron James 3.00 8.00
139 Reggie Miller .60 1.50
140 Larry Johnson .50 1.25

2013-14 Fleer Retro '97-98 SkyBox Premium Star Rubies

*STAR RUBY: 4X TO 10X BASIC
STATED PRINT RUN 50 SER.#'d SETS
121 Grant Hill 20.00 50.00
122 Allen Iverson 40.00 100.00
123 Alonzo Mourning 20.00 50.00
124 Hakeem Olajuwon 25.00 60.00
125 Isiah Thomas 20.00 50.00
126 Larry Bird 40.00 100.00
127 Rajon Rondo 20.00 50.00
128 Karl Malone 20.00 50.00
129 Julius Erving 40.00 100.00
130 Anfernee Hardaway 40.00 100.00
131 Magic Johnson 40.00 100.00
132 David Robinson 40.00 100.00
133 Michael Jordan 500.00 1,000.00
134 Paul George 20.00 50.00
135 James Harden 40.00 100.00
136 Bill Russell 40.00 100.00
137 Dennis Rodman 25.00 60.00
138 LeBron James 400.00 800.00
139 Reggie Miller 25.00 60.00
140 Larry Johnson 12.00 30.00

2013-14 Fleer Retro '97-98 Ultra Star Power Supreme

STATED ODDS 1:216
1SPS Grant Hill 5.00 12.00
2SPS Allen Iverson 6.00 15.00
3SPS Alonzo Mourning 5.00 12.00
4SPS Dominique Wilkins 5.00 12.00
5SPS Paul George 5.00 12.00
6SPS Hakeem Olajuwon 6.00 15.00
7SPS Isiah Thomas 5.00 12.00
8SPS Larry Bird 12.00 30.00
9SPS James Harden 6.00 15.00
10SPS Antoine Walker 2.50 6.00
11SPS Julius Erving 8.00 20.00
12SPS Anfernee Hardaway 8.00 20.00
13SPS Clyde Drexler 5.00 12.00
14SPS Glen Rice 2.50 6.00
15SPS David Robinson 6.00 15.00
16SPS Michael Jordan 200.00 500.00
17SPS Bill Russell 10.00 25.00
18SPS LeBron James 150.00 400.00
19SPS Jerry Stackhouse 2.50 6.00
20SPS Larry Johnson 4.00 10.00
21SPS Jason Kidd 5.00 12.00

2013-14 Fleer Retro '98 Ultra Exclamation Points

STATED ODDS 1:216
1EP Allen Iverson 40.00 100.00
2EP Alonzo Mourning 15.00 40.00
3EP Anfernee Hardaway 40.00 100.00
4EP Bill Russell 40.00 100.00
5EP Dominique Wilkins 12.00 30.00
6EP James Harden 20.00 50.00
7EP David Robinson 20.00 50.00
8EP Reggie Miller 20.00 50.00
9EP Jason Kidd 12.00 30.00
10EP Paul George 20.00 50.00
11EP Grant Hill 20.00 50.00
12EP Hakeem Olajuwon 20.00 50.00
13EP Isiah Thomas 12.00 30.00
14EP Julius Erving 20.00 50.00
15EP Karl Malone 15.00 40.00
16EP Larry Bird 40.00 100.00
17EP Larry Johnson 10.00 25.00
18EP LeBron James 200.00 500.00
19EP Jerry Stackhouse 8.00 20.00
20EP Michael Jordan 300.00 600.00
21EP Rajon Rondo 3.00 8.00

2013-14 Fleer Retro '98-99 SkyBox Autographics

GROUP A ODDS 1:15,300
GROUP B ODDS 1:6120
GROUP C ODDS 1:2448
GROUP D ODDS 1:612
EXCHANGE DEADLINE 3/28/2016
98AUBL Bill Laimbeer E 5.00 12.00
98AUCC Calbert Cheaney E 3.00 8.00
98AUCL Christian Laettner D 5.00 12.00
98AUDM Danny Manning D 10.00 25.00
98AUPG Paul George B 50.00 120.00

2013-14 Fleer Retro '98-99 SkyBox Premium

STATED ODDS 1:10
141 Grant Hill .60 1.50
142 Allen Iverson .75 2.00
143 Alonzo Mourning .60 1.50
144 Hakeem Olajuwon .75 2.00
145 Isiah Thomas .60 1.50
146 Larry Bird 1.50 4.00
147 Rajon Rondo .50 1.25
148 Karl Malone .75 2.00
149 Julius Erving 1.00 2.50
150 Anfernee Hardaway 1.00 2.50
151 Magic Johnson 1.50 4.00
152 David Robinson .75 2.00
153 Michael Jordan 3.00 8.00
154 Paul George .60 1.50
155 James Harden .75 2.00
156 Bill Russell 1.25 3.00
158 LeBron James 3.00 8.00
159 Reggie Miller .60 1.50
160 Larry Johnson .50 1.25

2013-14 Fleer Retro '98-99 SkyBox Premium Star Rubies

*STAR RUBY: 4X TO 10X BASIC
STATED PRINT RUN 50 SER.#'d SETS
141 Grant Hill 20.00 50.00
142 Allen Iverson 40.00 100.00
143 Alonzo Mourning 20.00 50.00
144 Hakeem Olajuwon 25.00 60.00
145 Isiah Thomas 20.00 50.00
146 Larry Bird 40.00 100.00
147 Rajon Rondo 10.00 25.00
148 Karl Malone 25.00 60.00
149 Julius Erving 40.00 100.00
150 Anfernee Hardaway 40.00 100.00
151 Magic Johnson 40.00 100.00
152 David Robinson 25.00 60.00
153 Michael Jordan 500.00 1,000.00
154 Paul George 20.00 50.00
155 James Harden 40.00 100.00
156 Bill Russell 40.00 100.00
157 Dennis Rodman 25.00 60.00
158 LeBron James 400.00 800.00
159 Reggie Miller 25.00 60.00
160 Larry Johnson 12.00 30.00

2013-14 Fleer Retro '99-00 SkyBox Autographics

GROUP A ODDS 1:3060
GROUP B ODDS 1:2448
GROUP C ODDS 1:816
GROUP D ODDS 1:816
EXCHANGE DEADLINE 3/28/2016
99AUCM Cheryl Miller C 12.00 30.00
99AUDS Detlef Schrempf D 10.00 25.00
99AUHM Harold Miner D 10.00 25.00
99AUIT Isiah Thomas B 30.00 80.00
99AUKM Karl Malone A 60.00 150.00
99AURO Dennis Rodman A 60.00 150.00

2013-14 Fleer Retro '99-00 SkyBox Prime Time Autographs

PRINT RUNS B/WN 15-25 COPIES PER
NO PRICING ON QTY 15
EXCHANGE DEADLINE 3/28/2016
4PTV Alonzo Mourning/25 EXCH 50.00 120.00
5PTV Dominique Wilkins/25 25.00 60.00
6PTV Hakeem Olajuwon/25 50.00 120.00
7PTV Larry Bird/25 EXCH 125.00 300.00
10PTV Julius Erving/25 75.00 200.00
11PTV Anfernee Hardaway/25 75.00 200.00
13PTV David Robinson/25 50.00 120.00
16PTV James Harden/25 100.00 250.00
18PTV LeBron James/25 1,500.00 3,000.00

2013-14 Fleer Retro '99-00 SkyBox Prime Time Rookie Autographs

STATED PRINT RUN 60 SER.#'d SETS
EXCHANGE DEADLINE 3/28/2016
3PT Tim Hardaway Jr./45 8.00 20.00
4PT Ryan Kelly/60 4.00 10.00
5PT Andre Roberson/60 5.00 12.00
9PT Dennis Schroeder/60 12.00 30.00
10PT G.Antetokounmpo/60 2,000.00 4,000.00
15PT Allen Crabbe/99 4.00 10.00
16PT Skylar Diggins/60 20.00 50.00
17PT Jamaal Franklin/99 4.00 10.00

2013-14 Fleer Retro '00-01 Fleer Autographics

GROUP A ODDS 1:4080
GROUP B ODDS 1:600
GROUP C ODDS 1:360
GROUP D ODDS 1:188
GROUP E ODDS 1:60
GROUP F ODDS 1:34
EXCHANGE DEADLINE 3/28/2016
00AUAE Alex English E 6.00 15.00
00AUAM Alonzo Mourning C 12.00 30.00
00AUBJ B.J. Young F 3.00 8.00
00AUBK Bo Kimble F 3.00 8.00
00AUBP Brandon Paul 3.00 8.00
00AUBR Bill Russell A 400.00 800.00
00AUCC Calbert Cheaney F 3.00 8.00
00AUCM Cheryl Miller D 5.00 12.00
00AUDC Dave Cowens D 5.00 12.00
00AUDM Donyell Marshall F 3.00 8.00
00AUDR David Robinson B 12.00 30.00
00AUDS Dennis Schroeder E 10.00 25.00
00AUEH Elias Harris 3.00 8.00
00AUGH Grant Hill C 10.00 25.00
00AUHA Tim Hardaway E 6.00 15.00
00AUHM Harold Miner F 3.00 8.00
00AUHO Hakeem Olajuwon B 20.00 50.00
00AUIT Isiah Thomas C 12.00 30.00
00AUJA LeBron James A 1,000.00 2,000.00
00AUJL Jerry Lucas D 5.00 12.00
00AUJO Michael Jordan B 500.00 1,000.00
00AUJW Jay Williams D 3.00 8.00
00AUKK Kerry Kittles F 3.00 8.00
00AUKM Karl Malone B 15.00 40.00
00AULB Larry Bird B 40.00 80.00
00AULJ Larry Johnson C 15.00 40.00
00AUMJ Magic Johnson B 40.00 80.00
00AUMR Micheal Ray Richardson F 4.00 10.00
00AUOB Otis Birdsong B 4.00 10.00
00AUPS Peyton Siva F 3.00 8.00
00AURH Robert Horry E 5.00 12.00
00AURO Dennis Rodman C 12.00 30.00
00AURR Rajon Rondo C 12.00 30.00
00AUSA Stacey Augmon C 10.00 25.00
00AUSB Shawn Bradley F 3.00 8.00
00AUSD Skylar Diggins D 6.00 15.00
00AUSL Shane Larkin E 3.00 8.00
00AUTH Tim Hardaway Jr. E 6.00 15.00
00AUTK Toni Kukoc E 6.00 15.00
00AUTR Theo Ratliff F 3.00 8.00

2013-14 Fleer Retro Autographs

GROUP A ODDS 1:2720
GROUP B ODDS 1:862
GROUP C ODDS 1:480
GROUP D ODDS 1:272
GROUP E ODDS 1:77
GROUP F ODDS 1:58
GROUP G ODDS 1:26
EXCHANGE DEADLINE 3/28/2016
4 Dennis Rodman C 15.00 40.00
5 Elvin Hayes G 5.00 12.00
6 Donyell Marshall G 2.50 6.00
7 Calbert Cheaney G 2.50 6.00
8 Antoine Walker G 3.00 8.00
9 David Thompson E 12.00 30.00
10 Kerry Kittles G 2.50 6.00
11 Grant Hill D 15.00 40.00
12 Dominique Wilkins C 8.00 20.00
13 Tim Hardaway G 5.00 12.00
14 Alonzo Mourning C 8.00 20.00
17 Kenny Anderson E 3.00 8.00
18 Paul George B 25.00 60.00
19 Isiah Thomas C 12.00 30.00
21 Danny Manning E 3.00 8.00
22 Jay Williams G 2.50 6.00
23 Larry Johnson C 8.00 20.00
24 Jerry Lucas F 8.00 20.00
26 James Harden B EXCH 40.00 100.00
27 Otis Birdsong G 3.00 8.00
29 Sam Perkins B 12.00 30.00
30 Bill Russell A 400.00 800.00
31 David Robinson B 15.00 40.00
33 Hakeem Olajuwon B 20.00 50.00
34 Larry Bird A 40.00 100.00
37 Karl Malone B 12.00 30.00
38 Christian Laettner G 6.00 15.00
39 LeBron James A 1,000.00 2,000.00
40 Michael Jordan A 1,500.00 3,000.00
41 Mason Plumlee E 3.00 8.00
42 Jamaal Franklin G 2.50 6.00
43 Shane Larkin E 2.50 6.00
45 Isaiah Canaan F 2.50 6.00
46 Tim Hardaway Jr. E 2.50 6.00
47 Giannis Antetokounmpo F 400.00 800.00
48 Livio Jean-Charles F 2.50 6.00
49 Archie Goodwin E 2.50 6.00
50 Solomon Hill D 3.00 8.00
52 Dennis Schroeder D 8.00 20.00
53 Skylar Diggins D 8.00 20.00
54 Grant Jerrett F 2.50 6.00
58 Reggie Bullock F 3.00 8.00
60 Deshaun Thomas F 2.50 6.00

2001-02 Fleer Shoebox
COMP.SET w/o SP's (150) 10.00 25.00
151-180 PRINT RUN 2500 SERIAL #'d SETS
1 Tariq Abdul-Wahad .20 .50
2 Glen Rice .30 .75
3 Derek Anderson .20 .50
4 Desmond Mason .25 .60
5 Al Harrington .25 .60
6 Mitch Richmond .40 1.00
7 Felipe Lopez .20 .50
8 Andre Miller .25 .60
9 Jerry Stackhouse .30 .75
10 Jalen Rose .25 .60
11 Lindsey Hunter .20 .50
12 Tim Thomas .20 .50
13 Wally Szczerbiak .25 .60
14 Vince Carter .60 1.50
15 Nick Van Exel .30 .75
16 Jon Barry .20 .50
17 Aaron McKie .20 .50
18 Iakovos Tsakalidis .20 .50
19 Chris Webber .40 1.00
20 Karl Malone .60 1.50
21 Shareef Abdur-Rahim .25 .60
22 Baron Davis .30 .75
23 Michael Doleac .20 .50
24 Jermaine O'Neal .25 .60
25 Elton Brand .25 .60
26 Glenn Robinson .30 .75
27 Tracy McGrady .50 1.25
28 Allen Iverson .75 2.00
29 Anfernee Hardaway .75 2.00
30 Scot Pollard .20 .50
31 David Robinson .60 1.50
32 John Stockton .60 1.50
33 Jason Williams .50 1.25
34 Voshon Lenard .20 .50
35 Shaquille O'Neal 1.25 3.00
36 Grant Hill .50 1.25
37 Shawn Marion .30 .75
38 Vin Baker .25 .60
39 Raef LaFrentz .25 .60
40 Steve Francis .30 .75
41 Michael Dickerson .20 .50
42 Hedo Turkoglu .25 .60
43 Patrick Ewing .50 1.25
44 Dirk Nowitzki .75 2.00
45 Keyon Dooling .20 .50
46 Marcus Camby .25 .60
47 Bonzi Wells .20 .50
48 Tim Duncan .75 2.00
49 Jamaal Magloire .20 .50
50 Rick Fox .25 .60
51 Kendall Gill .20 .50
52 Michael Redd .30 .75
53 Keith Van Horn .25 .60
54 Eric Snow .20 .50
55 Theo Ratliff .20 .50
56 Clifford Robinson .30 .75
57 Moochie Norris .20 .50
58 Alonzo Mourning .50 1.25
59 Joe Smith .25 .60
60 Brent Barry .20 .50
61 Alvin Williams .20 .50
62 Antoine Walker .25 .60
63 Antonio McDyess .25 .60
64 Derek Fisher .25 .60
65 Ron Mercer .20 .50
66 Hakeem Olajuwon .60 1.50
67 Jamal Crawford .30 .75
68 Chris Mihm .20 .50
69 Ben Wallace .40 1.00
70 Brian Grant .20 .50
71 Kevin Garnett .75 2.00
72 Shandon Anderson .20 .50
73 Shawn Bradley .20 .50
74 Danny Fortson .20 .50
75 Jeff McInnis .20 .50
76 LaPhonso Ellis .25 .60
77 Sam Cassell .25 .60
78 Rasheed Wallace .40 1.00
79 Malik Rose .20 .50
80 Jahidi White .20 .50
81 Milt Palacio .20 .50
82 Tim Hardaway .40 1.00
83 Antonio Daniels .20 .50
84 Tyronn Lue .30 .75
85 Cuttino Mobley .25 .60
86 DerMarr Johnson .20 .50
87 Lamond Murray .20 .50
88 Larry Hughes .25 .60
89 Reggie Miller .60 1.50
90 Lorenzen Wright .20 .50
91 Eddie Jones .30 .75
92 Anthony Mason .30 .75
93 Todd MacCulloch .20 .50
94 Speedy Claxton .20 .50
95 Mateen Cleaves .20 .50
96 Gary Payton .50 1.25
97 Morris Peterson .25 .60
98 Mike Miller .25 .60
99 Hanno Mottola .20 .50
100 Steve Nash .60 1.50
101 Stromile Swift .25 .60
102 Ray Allen .50 1.25
103 Mark Jackson .25 .60
104 Stephon Marbury .40 1.00
105 Mike Bibby .30 .75
106 Rashard Lewis .25 .60
107 Jason Kidd .50 1.25
108 P.J. Brown .20 .50
109 Kobe Bryant 2.50 6.00
110 Tom Gugliotta .20 .50
111 Richard Hamilton .40 1.00
112 Antawn Jamison .25 .60
113 Lamar Odom .25 .60
114 Kurt Thomas .20 .50
115 Robert Horry .30 .75
116 Dikembe Mutombo .50 1.25
117 Tony Delk .20 .50
118 Peja Stojakovic .25 .60
119 Donyell Marshall .20 .50
120 Paul Pierce .50 1.25
121 Michael Finley .30 .75
122 Quentin Richardson .20 .50
123 Kenyon Martin .30 .75
124 Allan Houston .30 .75
125 Scottie Pippen .75 2.00
126 Steve Smith .25 .60
127 Bryon Russell .20 .50
128 James Posey .20 .50
129 Terrell Brandon .25 .60
130 Toni Kukoc .40 1.00
131 Stephen Jackson .25 .60
132 Marc Jackson .20 .50
133 Kelvin Cato .20 .50
134 Travis Best .20 .50
135 David Wesley .20 .50
136 Anthony Carter .20 .50
137 Michael Jordan 2.50 6.00
138 Darrell Armstrong .20 .50
139 Matt Harpring .20 .50
140 Antonio Davis .25 .60
141 Courtney Alexander .20 .50
142 Jamal Mashburn .25 .60
143 Jason Terry .30 .75
144 Marcus Fizer .20 .50
145 Juwan Howard .25 .60
146 Darius Miles .25 .60
147 Latrell Sprewell .40 1.00
148 Damon Stoudamire .30 .75
149 John Starks .20 .50
150 Jumaine Jones .20 .50
151 Kedrick Brown RC .50 1.25
152 Trenton Hassell RC .50 1.25
153 Kwame Brown RC .75 2.00
154 Terence Morris RC .50 1.25
155 Richard Jefferson RC 1.00 2.50
156 Vladimir Radmanovic RC .60 1.50
157 Brandon Armstrong RC .50 1.25
158 Kirk Haston RC .50 1.25
159 Eddie Griffin RC .60 1.50
160 Steven Hunter RC .50 1.25
161 Troy Murphy RC .60 1.50
162 Andrei Kirilenko RC 1.25 3.00
163 Jeryl Sasser RC .50 1.25
164 Michael Bradley RC .50 1.25
165 Rodney White RC .50 1.25
166 Loren Woods RC .50 1.25
167 Zach Randolph RC 1.50 4.00
168 Joe Johnson RC 1.25 3.00
169 Eddy Curry RC .75 2.00
170 Jason Richardson RC 1.25 3.00
171 DeSagana Diop RC .50 1.25
172 Jamaal Tinsley RC .60 1.50
173 Pau Gasol RC 3.00 8.00
174 Jason Collins RC .60 1.50
175 Zeljko Rebraca RC .75 2.00
176 Shane Battier RC 1.50 4.00
177 Gerald Wallace RC 1.00 2.50
178 Joseph Forte RC .50 1.25
179 Tyson Chandler RC 1.25 3.00
180 Tony Parker RC 3.00 8.00

2001-02 Fleer Shoebox Footprints
*FOOT.STARS: 5X TO 12X BASE CARD HI
*FOOT.RCs: 2X TO 5X BASE CARD HI
PRINT RUN 150 SERIAL #'d SETS
137 Michael Jordan 40.00 100.00

2001-02 Fleer Shoebox NBA Flight School
COMPLETE SET (20) 20.00 40.00
STATED ODDS 1:12
1 Richard Hamilton 1.00 2.50
2 Kobe Bryant 6.00 15.00
3 Michael Jordan 6.00 15.00
4 Desmond Mason .60 1.50
5 Antoine Walker .60 1.50
6 Baron Davis .75 2.00
7 Steve Francis .75 2.00
8 Elton Brand .60 1.50
9 Lamar Odom .60 1.50
10 Kevin Garnett 2.00 5.00
11 Latrell Sprewell 1.00 2.50
12 Tracy McGrady 1.25 3.00
13 Shawn Marion .75 2.00
14 Chris Webber 1.00 2.50
15 Vince Carter 1.50 4.00
16 Tim Duncan 2.00 5.00
17 Morris Peterson .50 1.25
18 Karl Malone 1.50 4.00
19 Jerry Stackhouse .75 2.00
20 Darius Miles .50 1.25

2001-02 Fleer Shoebox NBA Flight School Cadet
STATED ODDS 1:63
*CAPTAIN: 1.25X TO 3X CADET HI
CAPTAIN PRINT RUN 75 SER.#'d SETS
1 Richard Hamilton 4.00 10.00
2 Desmond Mason 2.50 6.00
3 Antoine Walker 2.50 6.00
4 Baron Davis 3.00 8.00
5 Steve Francis 3.00 8.00
6 Elton Brand 2.50 6.00
7 Lamar Odom 2.50 6.00
8 Tracy McGrady 5.00 12.00
9 Shawn Marion 3.00 8.00
10 Chris Webber 4.00 10.00
11 Vince Carter 6.00 15.00
12 Morris Peterson 2.00 5.00
13 Karl Malone 6.00 15.00
14 Jerry Stackhouse 3.00 8.00
15 Darius Miles 2.00 5.00

2001-02 Fleer Shoebox Sole of the Game
COMPLETE SET (15) 50.00 100.00
STATED ODDS 1:144
1 Karl Malone 4.00 10.00
2 Dirk Nowitzki 5.00 12.00
3 Ray Allen 3.00 8.00
4 Shaquille O'Neal 8.00 20.00
5 Antoine Walker 1.50 4.00
6 Grant Hill 3.00 8.00
7 Steve Francis 2.00 5.00
8 Kobe Bryant 15.00 40.00
9 Michael Jordan 20.00 50.00
10 Larry Bird 15.00 40.00
11 Darius Miles 1.25 3.00
12 Chris Webber 2.50 6.00
13 Allen Iverson 6.00 15.00
14 Rasheed Wallace 2.50 6.00
15 Vince Carter 4.00 10.00

2001-02 Fleer Shoebox Sole of the Game Ball
STATED PRINT RUN 300 SERIAL #'d SETS
1 Ray Allen 8.00 20.00
2 Vince Carter 10.00 25.00
3 Steve Francis 5.00 12.00
4 Grant Hill 8.00 20.00
5 Allen Iverson 12.00 30.00
6 Karl Malone 10.00 25.00
7 Darius Miles 3.00 8.00
8 Dirk Nowitzki 12.00 30.00
9 Antoine Walker 4.00 10.00
10 Rasheed Wallace 6.00 15.00
11 Chris Webber 6.00 15.00

2001-02 Fleer Shoebox Sole of the Game Jersey
STATED PRINT RUN 200 SERIAL #'d SETS
1 Ray Allen 6.00 15.00
2 Vince Carter 8.00 20.00
3 Steve Francis 4.00 10.00
4 Grant Hill 6.00 15.00
5 Allen Iverson 10.00 25.00
6 Karl Malone 8.00 20.00
7 Darius Miles 2.50 6.00
8 Dirk Nowitzki 10.00 25.00
9 Larry Bird 15.00 40.00
10 Antoine Walker 3.00 8.00
11 Rasheed Wallace 5.00 12.00

2001-02 Fleer Shoebox Sole of the Game Shoe
STATED PRINT RUN 100 SERIAL #'d SETS
1 Ray Allen 15.00 40.00
2 Larry Bird 15.00 40.00
3 Vince Carter 20.00 50.00
5 Grant Hill 15.00 40.00
6 Allen Iverson 25.00 60.00
7 Karl Malone 15.00 40.00
8 Darius Miles 6.00 15.00
9 Dirk Nowitzki 25.00 60.00
12 Rasheed Wallace 12.00 30.00
13 Chris Webber 12.00 30.00

2001-02 Fleer Shoebox Sole of the Game Triple
STATED PRINT RUN 50 SERIAL #'d SETS
1 Ray Allen 30.00 80.00
2 Vince Carter 40.00 100.00
3 Steve Francis 20.00 50.00
4 Grant Hill 30.00 80.00
5 Allen Iverson 50.00 120.00
6 Karl Malone 30.00 80.00
7 Darius Miles 12.00 30.00
8 Dirk Nowitzki 50.00 120.00

2001-02 Fleer Shoebox Tougher Than Leather
COMPLETE SET (20) 25.00 50.00
STATED ODDS 1:36
1 Alonzo Mourning 2.00 5.00
2 Antonio McDyess 1.00 2.50
3 Paul Pierce 2.00 5.00
4 Peja Stojakovic 1.00 2.50
5 Dirk Nowitzki 3.00 8.00
6 Allen Iverson 3.00 8.00
7 Marcus Camby 1.00 2.50
8 Tracy McGrady 2.00 5.00
9 Kenyon Martin 1.25 3.00
10 Dikembe Mutombo 2.00 5.00
11 Rasheed Wallace 1.50 4.00
12 David Robinson 2.50 6.00
13 Shareef Abdur-Rahim 1.00 2.50
14 Glenn Robinson 1.25 3.00
15 Vince Carter 2.50 6.00
16 Antoine Walker 1.00 2.50
17 Trajan Langdon .75 2.00
18 Scottie Pippen 3.00 8.00
19 Eddie Jones 1.25 3.00
20 Lamar Odom 1.00 2.50

2001-02 Fleer Shoebox Tougher Than Leather Shoes
STATED PRINT RUN 100 SERIAL #'d SETS
1 Alonzo Mourning 12.00 30.00
2 Antonio McDyess 6.00 15.00
3 Eddie Jones 8.00 20.00
5 Dirk Nowitzki 20.00 50.00
6 Marcus Camby 6.00 15.00
7 Tracy McGrady 12.00 30.00
8 Kenyon Martin 8.00 20.00
9 Dikembe Mutombo 12.00 30.00
10 Rasheed Wallace 10.00 25.00
11 David Robinson 15.00 40.00
12 Shareef Abdur-Rahim 6.00 15.00
13 Glenn Robinson 8.00 20.00
14 Vince Carter 15.00 40.00
14A Vince Carter AU 25.00 50.00
15 Antoine Walker 6.00 15.00
16 Allen Iverson 20.00 50.00
17 Scottie Pippen 20.00 50.00
18 Peja Stojakovic 6.00 15.00
19 Trajan Langdon 5.00 12.00
20 Lamar Odom 6.00 15.00

2000-01 Fleer Showcase
COMPLETE SET w/o RCs (90) 12.50 30.00
91-100/121: PRINT RUN 500 #'d SETS
101-110: PRINT RUN 1500 #'d SETS
111-121: PRINT RUN 2000 #'d SETS
1 Vince Carter .75 2.00
2 Lamar Odom .40 1.00
3 Larry Hughes .40 1.00
4 Brian Grant .30 .75
5 Bryon Russell .25 .60
6 Allan Houston .40 1.00
7 Juwan Howard .30 .75
8 Cuttino Mobley .30 .75
9 Keith Van Horn .30 .75
10 Mike Bibby .40 1.00
11 Jerome Williams .25 .60
12 Ray Allen .60 1.50
13 Antonio Davis .30 .75
14 Adrian Griffin .25 .60
15 Dan Majerle .40 1.00
16 Rasheed Wallace .50 1.25
17 Antonio McDyess .30 .75
18 Tim Thomas .25 .60
19 Theo Ratliff .25 .60
20 Charles Oakley .40 1.00
21 Nick Van Exel .40 1.00
22 Glenn Robinson .40 1.00
23 Cal Bowdler .25 .60
24 Raef LaFrentz .30 .75
25 Terrell Brandon .30 .75
26 Allen Iverson 1.00 2.50
27 Patrick Ewing .60 1.50
28 Ron Artest .40 1.00
29 Michael Olowokandi .25 .60
30 Derek Anderson .30 .75
31 Dirk Nowitzki 1.00 2.50
32 Wally Szczerbiak .30 .75
33 Gary Payton .60 1.50
34 Michael Finley .40 1.00
35 Chauncey Billups .50 1.25
36 Jason Kidd .60 1.50
37 Rashard Lewis .30 .75
38 Andre Miller .30 .75
39 Kevin Garnett 1.00 2.50
40 Tim Duncan 1.00 2.50
41 Jalen Rose .30 .75
42 Marcus Camby .30 .75
43 Richard Hamilton .50 1.25
44 Austin Croshere .25 .60
45 Latrell Sprewell .50 1.25
46 Shawn Marion .40 1.00
47 Jahidi White .25 .60
48 Elton Brand .40 1.00
49 Reggie Miller .75 2.00
50 David Robinson .75 2.00
51 Trajan Langdon .25 .60
52 Jonathan Bender .25 .60
53 Antonio Daniels .25 .60
54 Jason Terry .40 1.00
55 Eddie Jones .40 1.00
56 Mitch Richmond .50 1.25
57 Antoine Walker .40 1.00
58 Robert Horry .40 1.00
59 Tracy McGrady .75 2.00
60 Scottie Pippen 1.00 2.50
61 Jerry Stackhouse .40 1.00
62 Zydrunas Ilgauskas .30 .75
63 Toni Kukoc .30 .75
64 Karl Malone .75 2.00
65 Baron Davis .40 1.00
66 Shaquille O'Neal 1.50 4.00
67 Vlade Divac .40 1.00
68 Eddie Robinson .25 .60
69 Dion Glover .25 .60
70 Jason Williams .60 1.50
71 Steve Francis .40 1.00
72 Glen Rice .40 1.00
73 Clifford Robinson .40 1.00
74 Shareef Abdur-Rahim .40 1.00
75 Hakeem Olajuwon .75 2.00
76 Paul Pierce .60 1.50
77 Tim Hardaway .50 1.25
78 Darrell Armstrong .25 .60
79 Bonzi Wells .25 .60
80 Antawn Jamison .40 1.00
81 Stephon Marbury .50 1.25
82 Tony Delk .25 .60
83 Michael Dickerson .25 .60
84 Jamal Mashburn .30 .75
85 Kobe Bryant 10.00 25.00
86 Grant Hill .60 1.50
87 Chris Webber .50 1.25
88 Vonteego Cummings .25 .60
89 Jamie Feick .25 .60
90 John Stockton .75 2.00
91 Kenyon Martin RC 6.00 15.00
92 Stromile Swift RC 2.50 6.00
93 Darius Miles RC 3.00 8.00
94 Marcus Fizer RC 2.50 6.00
95 Mike Miller RC 5.00 12.00
96 DerMarr Johnson RC 2.00 5.00
97 Chris Mihm RC 2.00 5.00
98 Jamal Crawford RC 8.00 20.00
99 Joel Przybilla RC 2.50 6.00
100 Keyon Dooling RC 2.50 6.00
101 Jerome Moiso RC 1.25 3.00
102 Etan Thomas RC 1.50 4.00
103 Courtney Alexander RC 1.25 3.00
104 Mateen Cleaves RC 1.50 4.00
105 Jason Collier RC 2.00 5.00
106 Hedo Turkoglu RC 3.00 8.00
107 Desmond Mason RC 2.50 6.00
108 Quentin Richardson RC 1.50 4.00
109 Jamaal Magloire RC 2.00 5.00
110 Speedy Claxton RC 2.00 5.00
111 Morris Peterson RC 1.50 4.00
112 Donnell Harvey RC 1.25 3.00
113 DeShawn Stevenson RC 1.50 4.00
114 Dalibor Bagaric RC 1.25 3.00
115 Mamadou N'Diaye RC 1.00 2.50
116 Erick Barkley RC 1.00 2.50
117 Mark Madsen RC 1.50 4.00
118 Chris Porter RC 1.00 2.50
119 Brian Cardinal RC 1.00 2.50
120 Iakovos Tsakalidis RC 1.00 2.50
121 Marc Jackson RC 2.50 6.00

2000-01 Fleer Showcase Legacy Collection
*STARS: 15X TO 40X BASE CARD HI
*RCs 91-100/121: .75X TO 2X BASE HI
*RCs 101-110: 1.25X TO 3X BASE HI
*RCs 111-120: 1.5X TO 4X BASE HI
STATED PRINT RUN 50 SERIAL #'d SETS
26 Allen Iverson 60.00 150.00
27 Patrick Ewing 40.00 100.00
31 Dirk Nowitzki 75.00 200.00
39 Kevin Garnett 50.00 120.00
40 Tim Duncan 50.00 120.00
60 Scottie Pippen 40.00 100.00

2000-01 Fleer Showcase Avant Card
STATED PRINT RUN 201 SERIAL #'d SETS
1 Vince Carter 10.00 25.00
2 Lamar Odom 5.00 12.00
3 Kobe Bryant 40.00 100.00
4 Kevin Garnett 12.00 30.00
5 Steve Francis 5.00 12.00
6 Jason Williams 8.00 20.00
7 Eddie Jones 5.00 12.00
8 Grant Hill 8.00 20.00
9 Elton Brand 5.00 12.00
10 Shaquille O'Neal 20.00 50.00
11 Allen Iverson 12.00 30.00
12 Tim Duncan 12.00 30.00
13 Jason Kidd 8.00 20.00
14 Kenyon Martin 8.00 20.00
15 Stromile Swift 3.00 8.00
16 Darius Miles 4.00 10.00
17 Marcus Fizer 3.00 8.00
18 Mike Miller 6.00 15.00
19 Jamal Crawford 10.00 25.00
20 Mateen Cleaves 3.00 8.00

2000-01 Fleer Showcase Vince Carter Rookie Remnants
NNO Vince Carter FLR JSY/15 20.00 50.00
NNO Vince Carter FLR/100 12.50 30.00

2000-01 Fleer Showcase ELEMENTary
COMPLETE SET (10) 20.00 40.00
STATED ODDS 1:48
1 Vince Carter 2.50 6.00
2 Lamar Odom 1.25 3.00
3 Kevin Garnett 3.00 8.00
4 Steve Francis 1.25 3.00
5 Grant Hill 2.00 5.00
6 Eddie Jones 1.25 3.00
7 Jason Williams 2.00 5.00
8 Kobe Bryant 10.00 25.00
9 Allen Iverson 3.00 8.00
10 Shaquille O'Neal 5.00 12.00

2000-01 Fleer Showcase HIStory
COMPLETE SET (10) 12.50 25.00
STATED ODDS 1:24
1 Vince Carter 1.50 4.00
2 Lamar Odom .75 2.00
3 Kobe Bryant 6.00 15.00
4 Shaquille O'Neal 3.00 8.00
5 Kevin Garnett 2.00 5.00
6 Allen Iverson 2.00 5.00
7 Steve Francis .75 2.00
8 Eddie Jones .75 2.00
9 Jason Williams 1.25 3.00
10 Michael Finley .75 2.00

2000-01 Fleer Showcase In the Paint
STATED ODDS 1:110
1 Kenyon Martin 4.00 10.00
2 Stromile Swift 1.50 4.00
3 Darius Miles 2.00 5.00
4 Marcus Fizer 1.50 4.00
5 Mike Miller 3.00 8.00
6 DerMarr Johnson 1.25 3.00
7 Chris Mihm 1.25 3.00
8 Joel Przybilla 1.50 4.00
9 Keyon Dooling 1.50 4.00
10 Jerome Moiso 1.25 3.00
11 Etan Thomas 1.50 4.00
12 Courtney Alexander 1.25 3.00
13 Mateen Cleaves 1.50 4.00
14 Jason Collier 2.00 5.00
15 Hedo Turkoglu 3.00 8.00
16 Desmond Mason 2.50 6.00
17 Quentin Richardson 1.50 4.00
18 Jamaal Magloire 2.00 5.00
19 Speedy Claxton 2.00 5.00
20 Morris Peterson 2.00 5.00
21 Donnell Harvey 1.50 4.00
22 DeShawn Stevenson 2.00 5.00
23 Dalibor Bagaric 1.50 4.00
24 Mamadou N'Diaye 1.25 3.00
25 Erick Barkley 1.25 3.00
26 Mark Madsen 2.00 5.00

2000-01 Fleer Showcase Showstoppers
COMPLETE SET (20) 6.00 15.00
STATED ODDS 1:6
1 Vince Carter 1.00 2.50
2 Lamar Odom .50 1.25
3 Tracy McGrady 1.00 2.50
4 Karl Malone 1.00 2.50
5 Scottie Pippen 1.25 3.00
6 Antawn Jamison .50 1.25
7 Chris Webber .60 1.50
8 Allan Houston .50 1.25
9 Baron Davis .50 1.25
10 Rashard Lewis .40 1.00
11 Jerry Stackhouse .50 1.25
12 Ray Allen .75 2.00
13 Keith Van Horn .40 1.00
14 Tim Duncan 1.25 3.00
15 Shareef Abdur-Rahim .50 1.25
16 Jalen Rose .40 1.00
17 Gary Payton .75 2.00
18 Andre Miller .40 1.00
19 Paul Pierce .75 2.00
20 Antonio McDyess .40 1.00

2000-01 Fleer Showcase To Air is Human
COMPLETE SET (15) 6.00 15.00
STATED ODDS 1:12
1 Vince Carter 1.25 3.00
2 Lamar Odom .60 1.50
3 Grant Hill 1.00 2.50
4 Shareef Abdur-Rahim .60 1.50
5 Michael Finley .60 1.50
6 Larry Hughes .60 1.50
7 Latrell Sprewell .75 2.00
8 Tracy McGrady 1.25 3.00
9 Ray Allen 1.00 2.50
10 Desmond Mason .60 1.50
11 Kenyon Martin 1.25 3.00
12 Morris Peterson .60 1.50
13 Stromile Swift .50 1.25
14 DerMarr Johnson .40 1.00
15 Mike Miller 1.00 2.50

2001-02 Fleer Showcase
COMPLETE SET (123) 150.00 300.00
COMP.SET w/o SP's (86) 20.00 50.00
AVANT PRINT RUN 500 SER.#'d SETS
92-97 PRINT RUN 500 SER.#'d SETS
98-112 PRINT RUN 1000 SER.#'d SETS
113-122 PRINT RUN 1500 SER.#'d SETS
1 Grant Hill .60 1.50
2 Elton Brand .30 .75
3 Sam Cassell .30 .75
4 John Stockton .75 2.00
5 James Posey .25 .60
6 Eddie Jones .40 1.00
7 Damon Stoudamire .40 1.00
8 Nick Van Exel .40 1.00
9 Brian Grant .25 .60
10 Mike Miller .30 .75
11 Steve Smith .30 .75
12 Michael Finley .40 1.00
13 Peja Stojakovic .30 .75
14 DerMarr Johnson .25 .60
15 Reggie Miller .75 2.00
16 Quentin Richardson .25 .60
17 Latrell Sprewell .50 1.25
18 Richard Hamilton .50 1.25
19 Michael Doleac .25 .60
20 Derek Fisher .30 .75
21 Marcus Camby .30 .75
22 Stephon Marbury .50 1.25
23 Bryon Russell .25 .60
24 Jumaine Jones .25 .60
25 Anfernee Hardaway 1.00 2.50
26 P.J. Brown .25 .60
27 Marc Jackson .25 .60
28 Dikembe Mutombo .60 1.50
29 Andre Miller .30 .75
30 Robert Horry .40 1.00
31 Tom Gugliotta .25 .60
32 David Robinson .75 2.00
33 Ron Mercer .25 .60
34 Shawn Marion .40 1.00
35 Ron Artest .40 1.00
36 Jason Williams .60 1.50
37 Scottie Pippen 1.00 2.50
38 Jerry Stackhouse .40 1.00
39 Stromile Swift .25 .60
40 Rasheed Wallace .50 1.25
41 Alonzo Mourning .60 1.50
42 Eddie Robinson .25 .60
43 Shareef Abdur-Rahim .30 .75
44 Wally Szczerbiak .30 .75
45 Antonio Davis .30 .75
46 Glen Rice .40 1.00
47 Jason Kidd .60 1.50
48 Gary Payton .60 1.50
49 Steve Nash .75 2.00
50 Lamar Odom .30 .75
51 Glenn Robinson .40 1.00
52 Mike Bibby .40 1.00
53 Hakeem Olajuwon .75 2.00
54 Theo Ratliff .25 .60
55 Kenyon Martin .40 1.00
56 Jamal Mashburn .30 .75
57 Larry Hughes .30 .75
58 Speedy Claxton .25 .60
59 Rashard Lewis .30 .75
60 Raef LaFrentz .30 .75
61 Antonio Daniels .25 .60
62 Jason Terry .40 1.00
63 Jalen Rose .30 .75
64 Terrell Brandon .30 .75
65 Karl Malone .75 2.00
66 Antonio McDyess .30 .75
67 Anthony Carter .25 .60
68 Tim Hardaway .50 1.25
69 Antoine Walker .30 .75
70 Cuttino Mobley .30 .75
71 Allan Houston .40 1.00
72 Desmond Mason .25 .60
73 Kurt Thomas .25 .60
74 Juwan Howard .30 .75
75 Tim Thomas .25 .60
76 Tracy McGrady .60 1.50
77 Dirk Nowitzki 1.00 2.50
78 Tim Duncan 1.00 2.50
79 Chris Webber .50 1.25
80 Steve Francis .40 1.00
81 Paul Pierce .60 1.50
82 Darius Miles .40 1.00
83 Ray Allen .60 1.50
84 Baron Davis .40 1.00
85 Antawn Jamison .30 .75
86 Michael Jordan 4.00 10.00
87 Vince Carter AVANT 5.00 12.00
87A Vince Carter AU/150 60.00 150.00
88 Kobe Bryant AVANT 20.00 50.00
89 Allen Iverson AVANT 6.00 15.00
90 Kevin Garnett AVANT 6.00 15.00
91 Shaquille O'Neal AVANT 10.00 25.00
92 Kwame Brown AVANT RC 5.00 12.00
93 Eddie Griffin AVANT RC 4.00 10.00
94 Eddy Curry AVANT RC 5.00 12.00
95 Shane Battier AVANT RC 10.00 25.00
96 Joe Johnson AVANT RC 8.00 20.00
97 Tyson Chandler AVANT RC 8.00 20.00
98 Jason Richardson RC 2.00 5.00
99 Zach Randolph RC 2.50 6.00
100 Rodney White RC .60 1.50
101 Pau Gasol RC 5.00 12.00
102 Jamaal Tinsley RC 1.00 2.50
103 Troy Murphy RC 1.00 2.50
104 Richard Jefferson RC 1.50 4.00
105 DeSagana Diop RC .75 2.00
106 Joseph Forte RC .75 2.00
107 Gerald Wallace RC 1.50 4.00
108 Loren Woods RC .75 2.00
109 Jason Collins RC 1.00 2.50
110 Jeryl Sasser RC .75 2.00
111 Zeljko Rebraca RC 1.25 3.00
112 Kirk Haston RC .75 2.00
113 Kedrick Brown RC .75 2.00
114 Steven Hunter RC .75 2.00
115 Michael Bradley RC .75 2.00
116 Brandon Armstrong RC .75 2.00
117 Samuel Dalembert RC 1.25 3.00
118 Primoz Brezec RC 1.25 3.00
119 Andrei Kirilenko RC 2.00 5.00
120 Vladimir Radmanovic RC 1.00 2.50
121 Ratko Varda RC 1.25 3.00
122 Brendan Haywood RC 1.00 2.50
123 Wang Zhizhi AVANT 2.50 6.00

2001-02 Fleer Showcase Legacy
*STARS 1-86: 12X TO 30X BASE CARD HI
*AVANT STARS: 2X TO 5X BASE CARD HI
*AVANT RCs: .75X TO 2X BASE CARD HI
*RCs 97-122: 3X TO 8X BASE CARD HI
PRINT RUN 50 SER.#'d SETS
25 Anfernee Hardaway 30.00 80.00
86 Michael Jordan 150.00 400.00

2001-02 Fleer Showcase Beasts of the East
STATED ODDS 1:24
1 Vince Carter 6.00 15.00
1A Vince Carter AU/225 20.00 50.00
2 Allen Iverson 8.00 20.00
3 Alonzo Mourning 5.00 12.00
4 Paul Pierce 5.00 12.00
5 Tracy McGrady 5.00 12.00
6 Keith Van Horn 2.50 6.00
7 Antoine Walker 2.50 6.00
8 Richard Hamilton 4.00 10.00
9 Andre Miller 2.50 6.00
10 Dikembe Mutombo 5.00 12.00
11 Mike Miller 2.50 6.00
12 Kenyon Martin 3.00 8.00
13 Baron Davis 3.00 8.00
14 Ray Allen 5.00 12.00

2001-02 Fleer Showcase Best of the West
STATED ODDS 1:24
1 Terrell Brandon 2.50 6.00
2 Karl Malone 6.00 15.00
3 Lamar Odom 2.50 6.00
4 Darius Miles 2.00 5.00
5 David Robinson 6.00 15.00
6 Chris Webber 4.00 10.00
7 Gary Payton 5.00 12.00
8 Steve Francis 3.00 8.00
9 Desmond Mason 2.50 6.00
10 Elton Brand 2.50 6.00
11 Shawn Marion 3.00 8.00
12 John Stockton 6.00 15.00
13 Antawn Jamison 2.50 6.00
14 Antonio McDyess 2.50 6.00
15 Jason Williams 5.00 12.00

2001-02 Fleer Showcase Rival Revival
STATED PRINT RUN 100 SERIAL #'d SETS
1 V.Carter/T.McGrady 10.00 25.00
2 V.Carter/A.Jamison 8.00 20.00
3 V.Carter/A.Iverson 12.50 30.00
4 D.Robinson/D.Mutombo 10.00 25.00
5 D.Miles/K.Martin 8.00 20.00

2002-03 Fleer Showcase
COMP.SET w/o SP's (100) 12.50 30.00
113-118 PRINT RUN 1000 SER.#'d SETS
119-124 PRINT RUN 500 SER.#'d SETS
125-148 PRINT RUN 1500 SER.#'d SETS
1 Michael Jordan 4.00 10.00
2 Shareef Abdur-Rahim .40 1.00
3 Jalen Rose .30 .75
4 Antonio McDyess .30 .75
5 Malik Rose .25 .60
6 Juwan Howard .30 .75
7 Jason Williams .50 1.25
8 Darrell Armstrong .25 .60
9 Karl Malone .75 2.00
10 Jason Terry .30 .75
11 David Wesley .25 .60
12 David Robinson .75 2.00
13 Gary Payton .60 1.50
14 Quentin Richardson .25 .60
15 Allan Houston .40 1.00
16 Alvin Williams .25 .60
17 Jamal Mashburn .30 .75
18 Theo Ratliff .25 .60
19 Tyson Chandler .40 1.00
20 Gilbert Arenas .40 1.00
21 Dikembe Mutombo .60 1.50
22 Calbert Cheaney .25 .60
23 Rodney Rogers .25 .60
24 Shane Battier .40 1.00
25 Mike Miller .30 .75
26 John Stockton .75 2.00
27 Mengke Bateer .40 1.00
28 Andre Miller .30 .75
29 Sam Cassell .30 .75
30 Anfernee Hardaway 1.00 2.50
31 Keith Van Horn .30 .75
32 Tony Battie .25 .60
33 Derek Fisher .40 1.00
34 Grant Hill .60 1.50
35 Andrei Kirilenko .30 .75
36 Toni Kukoc .40 1.00
37 Jerry Stackhouse .40 1.00
38 Latrell Sprewell .40 1.00
39 Morris Peterson .30 .75
40 Darius Miles .25 .60
41 Eddie Jones .40 1.00
42 Stephon Marbury .50 1.25
43 Brent Barry .25 .60
44 DeShawn Stevenson .25 .60
45 Brian Grant .25 .60
46 Derrick Coleman .30 .75
47 Richard Hamilton .50 1.25
48 Jason Richardson .40 1.00
49 Kerry Kittles .25 .60
50 Desmond Mason .30 .75
51 Stromile Swift .25 .60
52 Richard Jefferson .30 .75
53 Vladimir Radmanovic .25 .60
54 Lamond Murray .25 .60
55 Troy Murphy .30 .75
56 Kenyon Martin .40 1.00
57 Vlade Divac .30 .75
58 Chris Mihm .25 .60
59 Eddie Griffin .25 .60
60 Marc Jackson .25 .60
61 Peja Stojakovic .30 .75
62 Vin Baker .30 .75
63 Cuttino Mobley .25 .60
64 Joe Smith .30 .75
65 Damon Stoudamire .40 1.00
66 Eddy Curry .25 .60
67 Alonzo Mourning .60 1.50
68 Aaron McKie .25 .60
69 Kwame Brown .25 .60
70 Raef LaFrentz .25 .60
71 Jermaine O'Neal .30 .75
72 Terrell Brandon .25 .60

73 Bonzi Wells .25 .60
74 Steve Nash .75 2.00
75 Jamaal Tinsley .25 .60
76 Wally Szczerbiak .30 .75
77 Scottie Pippen 1.00 2.50
78 Michael Finley .40 1.00
79 Reggie Miller .75 2.00
80 Glenn Robinson .40 1.00
81 Rasheed Wallace .50 1.25
82 Antoine Walker .30 .75
83 Robert Horry .40 1.00
84 Kurt Thomas .25 .60
85 Antonio Davis .30 .75
86 Nick Van Exel .40 1.00
87 Al Harrington .30 .75
88 Tony Delk .25 .60
89 Joe Johnson .30 .75
90 Chauncey Billups .40 1.00
91 P.J. Brown .25 .60
92 Tony Parker .60 1.50
93 Antawn Jamison .30 .75
94 Courtney Alexander .25 .60
95 Kenny Anderson .30 .75
96 Clifford Robinson .40 1.00
97 Lamar Odom .40 1.00
98 Anthony Carter .25 .60
99 Shawn Marion .40 1.00
100 Hedo Turkoglu .30 .75
101 Paul Pierce AVANT 1.50 4.00
102 Dirk Nowitzki AVANT 2.50 6.00
103 Ben Wallace AVANT 1.25 3.00
104 Steve Francis AVANT 1.25 3.00
105 Pau Gasol AVANT 1.50 4.00
106 Ray Allen AVANT 1.50 4.00
107 Kevin Garnett AVANT 2.50 6.00
108 Jason Kidd AVANT 1.50 4.00
109 Baron Davis AVANT 1.00 2.50
110 Mike Bibby AVANT 1.00 2.50
111 Chris Webber AVANT 1.25 3.00
112 Tim Duncan AVANT 2.50 6.00
113 Kobe Bryant AVANT 12.00 30.00
114 Shaquille O'Neal AVANT 6.00 15.00
115 Tracy McGrady AVANT 2.50 6.00
116 Allen Iverson AVANT 4.00 10.00
117 Vince Carter AVANT 3.00 8.00
118 Elton Brand AVANT 1.25 3.00
119 Jay Williams AVANT RC 2.00 5.00
120 Yao Ming AVANT RC 12.00 30.00
121 Mike Dunleavy AVANT RC 2.50 6.00
122 DaJuan Wagner AVANT RC 2.00 5.00
123 Caron Butler AVANT RC 2.50 6.00
124 Drew Gooden AVANT RC 2.50 6.00
125 Manu Ginobili RC 10.00 25.00
126 Mehmet Okur RC 2.00 5.00
127 Nene Hilario RC 2.00 5.00
128 Nikoloz Tskitishvili RC 1.25 3.00
129 Tayshaun Prince RC 4.00 10.00
130 Bostjan Nachbar RC 1.50 4.00
131 Fred Jones RC 1.50 4.00
132 Melvin Ely RC 1.50 4.00
133 Chris Wilcox RC 1.50 4.00
134 Kareem Rush RC 1.50 4.00
135 Marcus Haislip RC 1.25 3.00
136 Frank Williams RC 1.25 3.00
137 Ryan Humphrey RC 1.50 4.00
138 John Salmons RC 1.25 3.00
139 Casey Jacobsen RC 1.50 4.00
140 Amare Stoudemire RC 5.00 12.00
141 Qyntel Woods RC 1.25 3.00
142 Chris Jefferies RC 1.25 3.00
143 Juan Dixon RC 1.50 4.00
144 Jared Jeffries RC 1.50 4.00
145 Lonny Baxter RC 1.25 3.00
146 Dan Dickau RC 1.25 3.00
147 Carlos Boozer RC 2.00 5.00
148 Vincent Yarbrough RC 1.25 3.00

2002-03 Fleer Showcase Legacy

*1-100 STARS: 5X TO 12X BASE CARD HI
PRINT RUN 100 SERIAL #'d SETS
*101-112 AVANT: 3X TO 8X BASE AVANT HI
*113-118 AVANT: 2X TO 5X BASE HI
*119-124 AVANT RCs: 1.5X TO 4X BASE HI
101-124 PRINT RUN 50 SER.#'d SETS
*125-148 RCs: 1.25X TO 3X BASE CARD HI
125-148 PRINT RUN 100 SER.#'d SETS
12 David Robinson 15.00 40.00
30 Anfernee Hardaway 20.00 50.00
67 Alonzo Mourning 10.00 25.00
92 Tony Parker 8.00 20.00
112 Tim Duncan AVANT 25.00 60.00
125 Manu Ginobili 25.00 60.00

2002-03 Fleer Showcase Avant Card Materials

PRINT RUN 202 SERIAL #'d SETS
ACM1 Tracy McGrady 8.00 20.00
ACM2 Allen Iverson 12.00 30.00
ACM3 Vince Carter 10.00 25.00
ACM4 Elton Brand 4.00 10.00
ACM5 Yao Ming 25.00 60.00
ACM6 DaJuan Wagner 4.00 10.00
ACM7 Caron Butler 5.00 12.00
ACM8 Drew Gooden 5.00 12.00

2002-03 Fleer Showcase Avant Card SRO

*SRO: 1.25X TO 3X BASE HI 6.00 15.00
PRINT RUN 50 SERIAL #'d SETS
115 Tracy McGrady 15.00 40.00

2002-03 Fleer Showcase Basketball's Best

COMPLETE SET (30) 15.00 40.00
STATED ODDS 1:8
1 Vince Carter 1.25 3.00
2 Allen Iverson 1.50 4.00
3 Jason Kidd 1.00 2.50
4 Tracy McGrady 1.00 2.50
5 Ben Wallace .75 2.00
6 Baron Davis .60 1.50
7 Paul Pierce 1.00 2.50
8 Andre Miller .50 1.25
9 Jermaine O'Neal .50 1.25
10 Kevin Garnett 1.50 4.00
11 Pau Gasol 1.00 2.50
12 Dirk Nowitzki 1.50 4.00
13 Jason Terry .50 1.25
14 Tony Parker 1.00 2.50
15 Kobe Bryant 5.00 12.00
16 Mike Bibby .60 1.50
17 Steve Nash 1.25 3.00
18 Michael Jordan 6.00 15.00
19 Mike Miller .50 1.25
20 Kenyon Martin .60 1.50
21 Shareef Abdur-Rahim .60 1.50
22 Elton Brand .50 1.25
23 Grant Hill 1.00 2.50
24 Lamar Odom .60 1.50
25 Corey Maggette .50 1.25
26 Richard Jefferson .50 1.25
27 Keith Van Horn .50 1.25
28 Quentin Richardson .40 1.00
29 Andrei Kirilenko .50 1.25
30 Darius Miles .40 1.00

2002-03 Fleer Showcase Basketball's Best Memorabilia

STATED ODDS 1:10
*GOLD: .75X TO 2X HI
GOLD: STATED PRINT RUN 100 SER.#'d SETS
BBM1 Vince Carter JSY 6.00 15.00
BBM2 Allen Iverson JSY 8.00 20.00
BBM3 Jason Kidd JSY 5.00 12.00
BBM4 Tracy McGrady Short 5.00 12.00
BBM5 Ben Wallace JSY 4.00 10.00
BBM6 Paul Pierce JSY 5.00 12.00
BBM7 Andre Miller JSY 2.50 6.00
BBM8 Jermaine O'Neal JSY 2.50 6.00
BBM9 Kevin Garnett JSY 8.00 20.00
BBM10 Jason Terry JSY 2.50 6.00
BBM11 Steve Nash JSY 6.00 15.00
BBM12 Mike Miller Short 2.50 6.00
BBM13 Kenyon Martin WU 3.00 8.00
BBM14 Shareef Abdur-Rahim Short 3.00 8.00
BBM15 Elton Brand WU 2.50 6.00
BBM16 Grant Hill Short 5.00 12.00
BBM17 Lamar Odom WU 3.00 8.00
BBM18 Corey Maggette WU 2.50 6.00
BBM19 Richard Jefferson WU 2.50 6.00
BBM20 Keith Van Horn WU 2.50 6.00
BBM21 Quentin Richardson JSY 2.00 5.00
BBM22 Andrei Kirilenko JSY 2.50 6.00
BBM23 Darius Miles Short 2.00 5.00
BAS1 Vince Carter AU/400 12.00 30.00

2002-03 Fleer Showcase Vince Carter Legacy Collection

COMPLETE SET (15) 20.00 50.00
COMMON CARD (VCL1-VCL15) 2.50 6.00
PRINT RUN 1000 SERIAL #'d SETS

2002-03 Fleer Showcase Vince Carter Legacy Collection Game-Worn

STATED ODDS 1:48
VCG1 Vince Carter Warm 8.00 20.00
VCG2 Vince Carter JSY 10.00 25.00

2003-04 Fleer Showcase

COMP.SET w/o SP's (100) 15.00 40.00
101-130 PRINT RUN 1000 SER.#'d SETS
1 Jason Richardson .50 1.25
2 Andrei Kirilenko .50 1.25
3 Steve Francis .50 1.25
4 Shareef Abdur-Rahim .50 1.25
5 Ben Wallace .60 1.50
6 Predrag Drobnjak .30 .75
7 Jalen Rose .40 1.00
8 Rashard Lewis .40 1.00
9 Darius Miles .30 .75
10 Bobby Jackson .40 1.00
11 Steve Nash 1.00 2.50
12 Gilbert Arenas .50 1.25
13 Aaron McKie .30 .75
14 Reggie Miller 1.00 2.50
15 Elton Brand .40 1.00
16 Allan Houston .50 1.25
17 Pau Gasol .75 2.00
18 Jamaal Magloire .30 .75
19 Eddie Jones .50 1.25
20 Richard Jefferson .40 1.00
21 Wally Szczerbiak .40 1.00
22 Antonio McDyess .40 1.00
23 Michael Redd .50 1.25
24 Grant Hill .60 1.50
25 Jason Williams .75 2.00
26 Rasheed Wallace .60 1.50
27 Andre Miller .40 1.00
28 Peja Stojakovic .40 1.00
29 Cuttino Mobley .30 .75
30 David Robinson 1.00 2.50
31 Richard Hamilton .60 1.50
32 Morris Peterson .30 .75
33 Karl Malone 1.00 2.50
34 Zydrunas Ilgauskas .40 1.00
35 Jerry Stackhouse .50 1.25
36 Eddy Curry .30 .75
37 Sam Cassell .40 1.00
38 Troy Hudson .30 .75
39 Jason Terry .40 1.00
40 Kenyon Martin .50 1.25
41 Bonzi Wells .30 .75
42 Donnell Harvey .30 .75
43 Tracy McGrady .75 2.00
44 Allen Iverson 1.25 3.00
45 Jermaine O'Neal .50 1.25
46 Larry Hughes .40 1.00
47 Scottie Pippen 1.25 3.00
48 Antonio Davis .40 1.00
49 Chris Webber .60 1.50
50 Vladimir Radmanovic .30 .75
51 Glenn Robinson .40 1.00
52 Antoine Walker .50 1.25
53 Ricky Davis .40 1.00
54 Michael Finley .50 1.25
55 Nick Van Exel .50 1.25
56 Tayshaun Prince .50 1.25
57 Antawn Jamison .50 1.25
58 Jamal Mashburn .40 1.00
59 Jamaal Tinsley .30 .75
60 Kerry Kittles .40 1.00
61 Derek Fisher .50 1.25
62 Radoslav Nesterovic .50 1.25
63 Mike Miller .40 1.00
64 Gary Payton .75 2.00
65 Brian Grant .30 .75
66 Baron Davis .50 1.25
67 Shane Battier .40 1.00
68 Latrell Sprewell .60 1.50
69 Keith Van Horn .40 1.00
70 Eddie Griffin .30 .75
71 Stephon Marbury .60 1.50
72 Chauncey Billups .60 1.50
73 Shawn Marion .50 1.25
74 Juwan Howard .40 1.00
75 Mike Bibby .50 1.25
76 DaJuan Wagner .30 .75
77 Tony Parker .75 2.00
78 Tyson Chandler .40 1.00
79 Ray Allen .75 2.00
80 Matt Harpring .30 .75
81 Kwame Brown .30 .75
82 Troy Murphy .30 .75
83 Ron Artest .50 1.25
84 Corey Maggette .40 1.00
85 Tony Delk .40 1.00
86 Jamal Crawford .50 1.25
87 Vince Carter 1.00 2.50
88 Kevin Garnett 1.25 3.00
89 Jason Kidd .75 2.00
90 Paul Pierce .75 2.00
91 Nene SP 1.00 2.50
92 Drew Gooden SP 1.00 2.50
93 Caron Butler SP 1.00 2.50
94 Manu Ginobili SP 2.50 6.00
95 Dirk Nowitzki SP 3.00 8.00
96 Yao Ming SP 3.00 8.00
97 Amare Stoudemire SP 1.50 4.00
98 Kobe Bryant SP 10.00 25.00
99 Tim Duncan SP 3.00 8.00
100 Shaquille O'Neal SP 5.00 12.00
101 T.J. Ford RC 1.50 4.00
102 Chris Bosh RC 6.00 15.00
103 Boris Diaw RC 2.00 5.00
104 Luke Ridnour RC 2.00 5.00
105 Zoran Planinic RC 1.25 3.00
106 Josh Howard RC 2.00 5.00
107 Darko Milicic RC 1.50 4.00
108 Dahntay Jones RC 1.50 4.00
109 Mike Sweetney RC 1.25 3.00
110 Kirk Hinrich RC 2.00 5.00
111 Marcus Banks RC 1.25 3.00
112 Travis Outlaw RC 1.50 4.00
113 Brian Cook RC 1.25 3.00
114 Mario Austin RC 1.25 3.00
115 Dwyane Wade RC 15.00 40.00
116 Chris Kaman RC 2.00 5.00
117 Zarko Cabarkapa RC 1.25 3.00
118 Ndudi Ebi RC 1.25 3.00
119 Mickael Pietrus RC 1.50 4.00
120 Carmelo Anthony RC 10.00 25.00
121 Kendrick Perkins RC 1.50 4.00
122 Troy Bell RC 1.25 3.00
123 Maciej Lampe RC 1.25 3.00
124 Carlos Delfino RC 1.50 4.00
125 Leandro Barbosa RC 2.00 5.00
126 Sofoklis Schortsanitis RC 1.25 3.00
127 Reece Gaines RC 1.25 3.00
128 Nick Collison RC 1.50 4.00
129 David West RC 2.50 6.00
130 LeBron James RC 800.00 1,500.00

2003-04 Fleer Showcase Legacy

*LEGACY SINGLES: 2.5X TO 6X BASE HI
*LEGACY SPs: 1.25X TO 3X BASE HI
*LEGACY RCs: 1.25X TO 3X BASE HI
STATED PRINT RUN 125 SER.#'d SETS
98 Kobe Bryant 25.00 60.00
130 LeBron James 3,000.00 6,000.00

2003-04 Fleer Showcase Basketball's Best

COMPLETE SET (10) 8.00 20.00
STATED ODDS 1:24
1 Shaquille O'Neal 4.00 10.00
2 Amare Stoudemire 1.25 3.00
3 Jermaine O'Neal 1.00 2.50
4 Tim Duncan 2.50 6.00
5 Jason Richardson 1.00 2.50
6 Steve Francis 1.00 2.50
7 Ben Wallace 1.25 3.00
8 Chris Webber 1.25 3.00
9 DaJuan Wagner .60 1.50
10 Yao Ming 2.50 6.00

2003-04 Fleer Showcase Basketball's Best Memorabilia

STATED PRINT RUN 375 SER.#'d SETS
*GOLD: 1.25X TO 3X BEST MEM.HI
GOLD PRINT RUN 50 SER.#'d SETS
1 Yao Ming 6.00 15.00
2 Steve Francis 2.50 6.00
3 Amare Stoudemire 3.00 8.00
4 Elton Brand 2.00 5.00
5 Paul Pierce 4.00 10.00
6 Tracy McGrady 4.00 10.00
7 Allen Iverson 6.00 15.00
8 Dirk Nowitzki 6.00 15.00
9 Antawn Jamison 2.50 6.00
10 Drew Gooden 2.00 5.00
11 DaJuan Wagner 2.00 5.00
12 David Robinson 5.00 12.00
13 Jermaine O'Neal 2.50 6.00
14 Stephon Marbury 3.00 8.00
15 Kevin Garnett 6.00 15.00
16 Jason Kidd 4.00 10.00
17 Vince Carter 5.00 12.00
18 Karl Malone 5.00 12.00
19 Tony Parker 4.00 10.00
20 Peja Stojakovic 2.00 5.00
21 Reggie Miller 5.00 12.00
22 Jason Richardson 2.50 6.00
23 Ray Allen 4.00 10.00
24 Jerry Stackhouse 3.00 8.00
25 Latrell Sprewell 3.00 8.00

2003-04 Fleer Showcase Hot Hands

COMPLETE SET (10) 20.00 40.00
STATED ODDS 1:288
1 Tracy McGrady 4.00 10.00
2 Kobe Bryant 20.00 50.00
3 Allen Iverson 6.00 15.00
4 Dirk Nowitzki 6.00 15.00
5 Jason Kidd 4.00 10.00
6 Vince Carter 5.00 12.00
7 Steve Francis 2.50 6.00
8 Paul Pierce 4.00 10.00
9 Jason Richardson 2.50 6.00
10 Amare Stoudemire 3.00 8.00

2003-04 Fleer Showcase Hot Hands Game-Used

STATED PRINT RUN 375 SER.#'d SETS
1 Tracy McGrady 5.00 12.00
2 Allen Iverson 8.00 20.00
3 Dirk Nowitzki 8.00 20.00
4 Jason Kidd 5.00 12.00
5 Vince Carter 6.00 15.00
6 Jerry Stackhouse 4.00 10.00
7 Paul Pierce 5.00 12.00
8 Stephon Marbury 4.00 10.00
9 Steve Francis 3.00 8.00
10 Peja Stojakovic 2.50 6.00
11 Caron Butler 2.50 6.00
12 Reggie Miller 6.00 15.00
13 Jason Richardson 3.00 8.00
14 Ray Allen 5.00 12.00
15 Amare Stoudemire 4.00 10.00

2003-04 Fleer Showcase Sweet Sigs

PRINT RUNS LISTED BELOW
SGAM Amare Stoudemire/300 6.00 15.00
SGBC Brian Cook/800 2.50 6.00
SGCA Carmelo Anthony/400 12.00 30.00
SGEC Eddy Curry/540 2.50 6.00
SGJO J.O'Neal/760 6.00 15.00
SGKB Kwame Brown/390 4.00 10.00
SGKM Kenyon Martin/690 4.00 10.00
SGMG Manu Ginobili/555 10.00 25.00
SGMP Mickael Pietrus/800 3.00 8.00
SGMS Mike Sweetney/800 2.50 6.00
SGPS Peja Stojakovic/760 6.00 15.00
SGSA S.Abdur-Rahim/760 4.00 10.00
SGSF Steve Francis/760 6.00 15.00
SGTB Troy Bell/800 2.50 6.00
SGTJ Dahntay Jones/800 3.00 8.00
SGTM Tracy McGrady/380 12.50 30.00
SGTP Tayshaun Prince/760 4.00 10.00

2003-04 Fleer Showcase Sweet Stitch

COMPLETE SET (10) 6.00 15.00
STATED ODDS 1:12
1 Yao Ming 1.50 4.00
2 Kevin Garnett 1.50 4.00
3 Kobe Bryant 5.00 12.00
4 Elton Brand .50 1.25
5 DaJuan Wagner .40 1.00
6 Karl Malone 1.25 3.00
7 Antawn Jamison .60 1.50
8 Stephon Marbury .75 2.00
9 Michael Finley .60 1.50
10 Drew Gooden .50 1.25
11 David Robinson 1.25 3.00

2003-04 Fleer Showcase Sweet Stitch Game-Used

STATED ODDS 1:31
*PATCHES: 1.25X TO 3X GAME USE HI
PATCH PRINT RUN 50 SER.#'d SETS
1 Yao Ming 6.00 15.00
2 Kevin Garnett 6.00 15.00
3 Kobe Bryant 15.00 40.00
4 Elton Brand 2.00 5.00
5 DaJuan Wagner 2.00 5.00
6 Karl Malone 5.00 12.00
7 Antawn Jamison 2.50 6.00
8 Stephon Marbury 3.00 8.00
9 Michael Finley 2.50 6.00
10 Drew Gooden 2.00 5.00

2004-05 Fleer Showcase

COMP.SET w/o SP's (90) 25.00 60.00
1 Kirk Hinrich .30 .75
2 Shaquille O'Neal 1.25 3.00
3 Allen Iverson .75 2.00
4 Carlos Arroyo .20 .50
5 Darko Milicic .20 .50
6 Sam Cassell .25 .60
7 Peja Stojakovic .25 .60
8 Ben Wallace .40 1.00
9 T.J. Ford .20 .50
10 Chris Webber .40 1.00
11 LeBron James 25.00 60.00
12 Karl Malone .60 1.50
13 Glenn Robinson .25 .60
14 Jarvis Hayes .20 .50
15 Bob Sura .20 .50
16 Yao Ming .75 2.00
17 Baron Davis .30 .75
18 Rashard Lewis .25 .60
19 Carlos Boozer .25 .60
20 Pau Gasol .50 1.25
21 Tim Duncan .75 2.00
22 Gilbert Arenas .30 .75
23 Dajuan Wagner .20 .50
24 Bonzi Wells .20 .50
25 Dirk Nowitzki .75 2.00
26 Jason Williams .25 .60
27 Amare Stoudemire .30 .75
28 Gerald Wallace .25 .60
29 Corey Maggette .25 .60
30 Tim Thomas .20 .50
31 Andrei Kirilenko .25 .60
32 Steve Nash .60 1.50
33 Caron Butler .25 .60
34 Shawn Marion .30 .75
35 Michael Finley .30 .75
36 Dwyane Wade 1.25 3.00
37 Joe Johnson .25 .60
38 Carmelo Anthony .60 1.50
39 Lamar Odom .30 .75
40 Darius Miles .20 .50
41 Mike Dunleavy .20 .50
42 Jason Kidd .50 1.25
43 Manu Ginobili .60 1.50
44 Jason Richardson .30 .75
45 Latrell Sprewell .40 1.00
46 Willie Green .30 .75
47 Theron Smith .20 .50
48 Elton Brand .25 .60
49 Tracy McGrady .50 1.25
50 Matt Harpring .20 .50
51 Eddy Curry .20 .50
52 Chris Kaman .25 .60
53 Drew Gooden .20 .50
54 Stephen Jackson .25 .60
55 Mickael Pietrus .20 .50
56 Kenyon Martin .30 .75
57 Tony Parker .50 1.25
58 Paul Pierce .50 1.25
59 Cuttino Mobley .25 .60
60 Jamal Mashburn .25 .60
61 Luke Ridnour .25 .60
62 Jamal Crawford .30 .75
63 Kobe Bryant 6.00 15.00
64 Keith Bogans .20 .50
65 Jerry Stackhouse .30 .75
66 Ricky Davis .25 .60
67 Jermaine O'Neal .25 .60
68 Jamaal Magloire .20 .50
69 Vince Carter .60 1.50
70 Jason Kapono .20 .50
71 Ron Artest .30 .75
72 Allan Houston .30 .75
73 Chris Bosh .50 1.25
74 Rasheed Wallace .40 1.00
75 Kevin Garnett .75 2.00
76 Mike Bibby .30 .75
77 Jason Terry .25 .60
78 Steve Francis .30 .75
79 Richard Jefferson .25 .60
80 Ray Allen .50 1.25
81 Andre Miller .25 .60
82 Desmond Mason .25 .60
83 Zach Randolph .30 .75
84 Marcus Banks .20 .50
85 Reggie Miller .60 1.50
86 Stephon Marbury .40 1.00
87 Jalen Rose .25 .60
88 Nene .25 .60
89 Michael Redd .25 .60
90 Shareef Abdur-Rahim .30 .75
91 Emeka Okafor/199 RC 4.00 10.00
92 Jameer Nelson/199 RC 5.00 12.00
93 Dwight Howard/199 RC 15.00 40.00
94 Josh Smith/199 RC 5.00 12.00
95 Pavel Podkolzin/699 RC 1.25 3.00
96 Shaun Livingston/199 RC 5.00 12.00
97 Andre Iguodala/199 RC 8.00 20.00
98 Luol Deng/199 RC 5.00 12.00
99 Delonte West/699 RC 1.50 4.00
100 Andris Biedrins/699 RC 1.25 3.00
101 Sasha Vujacic/499 RC 2.00 5.00
102 Kris Humphries/499 RC 2.00 5.00
103 Ben Gordon/199 RC 5.00 12.00
104 Robert Swift/499 RC 1.50 4.00
105 Al Jefferson/499 RC 2.50 6.00
106 Sergei Monia/499 RC 1.50 4.00
107 Devin Harris/499 RC 2.00 5.00
108 Luke Jackson/499 RC 1.50 4.00
109 Anderson Varejao/499 RC 2.00 5.00
110 Sebastian Telfair/199 RC 4.00 10.00
111 Josh Childress/199 RC 3.00 8.00
112 J.R. Smith/499 RC 2.50 6.00
113 Viktor Khryapa/699 RC 1.25 3.00
114 Rafael Araujo/499 RC 1.50 4.00
115 Dorell Wright/499 RC 2.00 5.00
116 Ha Seung-Jin/699 RC 1.50 4.00
117 Tony Allen/699 RC 2.00 5.00
118 Kirk Snyder/699 RC 1.25 3.00
119 Chris Duhon/699 RC 1.50 4.00
120 Beno Udrih/699 RC 1.50 4.00

2004-05 Fleer Showcase Legacy

*LEGACY SINGLES: 4X TO 10X BASE HI
*RC/199: .3X TO .75X BASE CARD HI
*RC/499: .6X TO 1.5X BASE CARD HI
*RC/699: .75X TO 2X BASE CARD HI
PRINT RUN 125 SER.#'d SETS
2 Shaquille O'Neal 12.00 30.00
11 LeBron James 400.00 800.00
63 Kobe Bryant 75.00 200.00
85 Reggie Miller 12.00 30.00

2004-05 Fleer Showcase Feature Film

PRINT RUN 50 SER.#'d SETS
PATCH PRINT RUN 25 SER.#'d SETS
1 Allen Iverson 25.00 60.00
2 Kobe Bryant 200.00 500.00
3 Vince Carter 20.00 50.00
4 Kevin Garnett 25.00 60.00
5 LeBron James 400.00 800.00
6 Carmelo Anthony 20.00 50.00
7 Tracy McGrady 15.00 40.00
8 Shaquille O'Neal 40.00 100.00
9 Tim Duncan 25.00 60.00
10 Yao Ming 25.00 60.00
11 Jason Kidd 15.00 40.00
12 Karl Malone 20.00 50.00
13 Amare Stoudemire 10.00 25.00
14 Chris Bosh 15.00 40.00
15 Ray Allen 15.00 40.00

2004-05 Fleer Showcase Hot Hands

STATED ODDS 1:192 H, 1:480 R
*PATCH: .5X TO 1.25X BASE HI
PATCH PRINT RUN 50 SER.#'d SETS
1 Yao Ming 30.00 80.00
2 Shaquille O'Neal 60.00 150.00
3 LeBron James 800.00 1,500.00
4 Carmelo Anthony 25.00 60.00
5 Dwyane Wade 60.00 150.00
6 Vince Carter 40.00 100.00
7 Kobe Bryant 200.00 500.00
8 Tim Duncan 50.00 120.00
9 Baron Davis 12.00 30.00
10 Manu Ginobili 30.00 80.00
11 Ron Artest 12.00 30.00
12 Ben Wallace 15.00 40.00
13 Andrei Kirilenko 12.00 30.00
14 Mike Bibby 12.00 30.00
15 Allen Iverson 60.00 150.00

2004-05 Fleer Showcase Hot Hands Patches

CA Carmelo Anthony 60.00 150.00

2004-05 Fleer Showcase Playmakers

COMPLETE SET (20) 10.00 25.00
STATED ODDS 1:4 H, 1:8 R
1 Jermaine O'Neal .40 1.00
2 Gary Payton .75 2.00
3 Kenyon Martin .50 1.25
4 Tony Parker .75 2.00
5 Chris Bosh .75 2.00
6 Dwyane Wade 2.00 5.00
7 Ben Wallace .60 1.50
8 Jason Kidd .75 2.00
9 Tracy McGrady .75 2.00
10 Kevin Garnett 1.25 3.00
11 Kobe Bryant 4.00 10.00
12 LeBron James 4.00 10.00
13 Paul Pierce .75 2.00
14 Stephon Marbury .60 1.50
15 Manu Ginobili 1.00 2.50
16 Amare Stoudemire .50 1.25
17 Reggie Miller 1.00 2.50
18 Dirk Nowitzki 1.25 3.00
19 Jason Richardson .50 1.25
20 Steve Francis .50 1.25

2004-05 Fleer Showcase Playmakers Jerseys

STATED ODDS 1:96 H, 1:26 R
*JERSEY 300: .5X TO 1.25X BASE JSY HI
*JERSEY 100: .6X TO 1.5X BASE JSY HI
AS Amare Stoudemire 2.50 6.00
BW Ben Wallace 3.00 8.00
CB Chris Bosh 4.00 10.00
DN Dirk Nowitzki 6.00 15.00
DW Dwyane Wade 10.00 25.00
GP Gary Payton 4.00 10.00
JK Jason Kidd 4.00 10.00
JO Jermaine O'Neal 2.00 5.00
JR Jason Richardson 2.50 6.00
KG Kevin Garnett 6.00 15.00
KM Kenyon Martin 2.50 6.00
MG Manu Ginobili 5.00 12.00
PP Paul Pierce 4.00 10.00
RM Reggie Miller 5.00 12.00
SF Steve Francis 2.50 6.00
SM Stephon Marbury 3.00 8.00
TM Tracy McGrady 4.00 10.00
TP Tony Parker 4.00 10.00

2004-05 Fleer Showcase Playmakers Jerseys Nameplates

*NAMEPLATE: 1X TO 2.5X BASE JSY HI
PRINT RUN 50 SER.#'d SETS
RM Reggie Miller 10.00 25.00

2004-05 Fleer Showcase Playmakers Jerseys Numbers

STATED PRINT RUN ONE TO 41 SETS
AS Amare Stoudemire/32 15.00 40.00
DN Dirk Nowitzki/41 10.00 25.00
GP Gary Payton/20 10.00 25.00
JR Jason Richardson/23 10.00 25.00
MG Manu Ginobili/20 10.00 25.00
PP Paul Pierce/34 10.00 25.00
RM Reggie Miller/31 12.50 30.00

2004-05 Fleer Showcase Playmakers Jerseys Win Total

STATED PRINT RUN 21 TO 61 SETS
AS Amare Stoudemire/29 5.00 12.00
BW Ben Wallace/54 6.00 15.00
CB Chris Bosh/33 8.00 20.00
DN Dirk Nowitzki/52 12.00 30.00
DW Dwyane Wade/42 20.00 50.00
GP Gary Payton/56 8.00 20.00
JK Jason Kidd/47 8.00 20.00
JO Jermaine O'Neal/61 3.00 8.00
JR Jason Richardson/35 5.00 12.00
KG Kevin Garnett/58 12.00 30.00
KM Kenyon Martin/47 5.00 12.00
MG Manu Ginobili/57 10.00 25.00
PP Paul Pierce/36 8.00 20.00
RM Reggie Miller/61 10.00 25.00
SF Steve Francis/45 5.00 12.00
SM Stephon Marbury/39 6.00 15.00
TM Tracy McGrady/21 8.00 20.00
TP Tony Parker/57 8.00 20.00

2004-05 Fleer Showcase Signatures

PRINT RUN 71 TO 150 SER.#'d SETS
*BLUE: .5X TO 1.25X BASE SIG HI
BLUE PRINT RUN 75 TO 99 SETS
AM Andre Miller/150 3.00 8.00
AV Anderson Varejao/150 3.00 8.00
BG Ben Gordon/150 4.00 10.00
CA Carmelo Anthony/150 15.00 40.00
CB Carlos Boozer/150 3.00 8.00
CD Carlos Delfino/150 2.50 6.00
CD Chris Duhon/150 3.00 8.00
CM Corey Maggette/150 3.00 8.00
DH Devin Harris/150 3.00 8.00
DM Darius Miles/150 2.50 6.00
DW Dwyane Wade/150 30.00 80.00
DW2 Dorell Wright/150 3.00 8.00
DW3 David West/150 3.00 8.00
GP Gary Payton/112 10.00 25.00
HS Ha Seung-Jin/150 4.00 10.00
JC Josh Childress/150 2.50 6.00
JH Josh Howard/150 3.00 8.00
JK Jason Kidd/150 10.00 25.00
JN Jameer Nelson/150 4.00 10.00
JO Jermaine O'Neal/150 3.00 8.00
JS Jerry Stackhouse/150 3.00 8.00
JS Josh Smith/150 4.00 10.00
KB Kwame Brown/150 2.50 6.00
KH Kris Humphries/150 3.00 8.00
KS Kirk Snyder/150 2.50 6.00
LD Luol Deng/150 4.00 10.00
LJ Luke Jackson/150 2.50 6.00
LO Lamar Odom/150 3.00 8.00
MB Mike Bibby/150 4.00 10.00
PP Pavel Podkolzin/150 2.50 6.00
PS Peja Stojakovic/100 3.00 8.00
RA Rafael Araujo/150 2.50 6.00
SL Shaun Livingston/150 4.00 10.00
SM Shawn Marion/150 4.00 10.00
ST Sebastian Telfair/150 3.00 8.00
TB Troy Bell/150 4.00 10.00
TP Tony Parker/71 6.00 15.00
VC Vince Carter/150 12.00 30.00
CBO Chris Bosh/150 6.00 15.00
DJW Dajuan Wagner/150 2.50 6.00
JRS J.R. Smith/150 4.00 10.00

2004-05 Fleer Showcase Signatures Jerseys

PRINT RUNS LISTED BELOW
AS Amare Stoudemire/32 20.00 50.00
CA Carmelo Anthony/15 40.00 100.00
DM Darius Miles/23 10.00 25.00
GP Gary Payton/20 25.00 60.00
JS Jerry Stackhouse/42 10.00 25.00
SM Shawn Marion/31 12.00 30.00

2004-05 Fleer Showcase Supreme Showcase

COMPLETE SET (20) 10.00 25.00
STATED ODDS 1:16 H, 1:24 R
1 Carmelo Anthony 1.25 3.00
2 Yao Ming 1.50 4.00
3 Carlos Boozer .50 1.25
4 Vince Carter 1.25 3.00
5 Dwyane Wade 2.50 6.00
6 Dirk Nowitzki 1.50 4.00
7 Josh Howard .50 1.25
8 Steve Francis .60 1.50
9 Paul Pierce 1.00 2.50
10 Amare Stoudemire .60 1.50
11 Peja Stojakovic .50 1.25
12 Shaquille O'Neal 2.50 6.00
13 Tim Duncan 1.50 4.00
14 Kevin Garnett 1.50 4.00
15 Stephon Marbury .75 2.00
16 Tracy McGrady 1.00 2.50
17 Allen Iverson 1.50 4.00
18 Ray Allen 1.00 2.50
19 Ben Wallace .75 2.00
20 Jason Kidd 1.00 2.50

2004-05 Fleer Showcase Supreme Showcase Jerseys

PRINT RUN 300 SER.#'d SETS
*JERSEY 100: .5X TO 1.25X BASE JSY HI
*JERSEY ALL-STAR: .6X TO 1.5X BASE JSY HI
ALL-STAR PRINT RUN 45 SER.#'d SETS
*JERSEY POINTS: .6X TO 1.5X BASE HI
POINTS PRINT RUN 19 TO 62 SETS
AI Allen Iverson 6.00 15.00
AS Amare Stoudemire 2.50 6.00
BW Ben Wallace 3.00 8.00
CA Carmelo Anthony 5.00 12.00
CB Carlos Boozer 2.00 5.00
DN Dirk Nowitzki 6.00 15.00
DW Dwyane Wade 10.00 25.00
JH Josh Howard 2.00 5.00
JK Jason Kidd 4.00 10.00
KG Kevin Garnett 6.00 15.00
PP Paul Pierce 4.00 10.00
PS Peja Stojakovic 2.00 5.00
RA Ray Allen 4.00 10.00
SF Steve Francis 2.50 6.00
SM Stephon Marbury 3.00 8.00
SO Shaquille O'Neal 10.00 25.00
TD Tim Duncan 6.00 15.00
TM Tracy McGrady 4.00 10.00
VC Vince Carter 5.00 12.00
YM Yao Ming 6.00 15.00

2004-05 Fleer Showcase Supreme Showcase Jerseys Numbers

*NUMBER PATCH: 1X TO 2.5X BASE HI
STATED PRINT RUN ONE TO 41 SETS
AS Amare Stoudemire/32 6.00 15.00
DN Dirk Nowitzki/41 15.00 40.00
KG Kevin Garnett/21 15.00 40.00
PP Paul Pierce/34 10.00 25.00
RA Ray Allen/34 10.00 25.00
SO Shaquille O'Neal/32 25.00 60.00
VC Vince Carter/15 12.00 30.00

1996-97 Fleer Sprite

COMPLETE SET (40) 15.00 40.00
1 Dikembe Mutombo 1.00 2.50
2 Steve Smith .50 1.25
3 Antoine Walker 1.00 2.50
4 Anthony Mason .50 1.25
5 Toni Kukoc .60 1.50
6 Terrell Brandon .50 1.25
7 Jim Jackson .40 1.00
8 Jason Kidd 1.00 2.50
9 Oliver Miller .40 1.00
10 Antonio McDyess .60 1.50
11 Grant Hill 1.00 2.50
12 Joe Smith .50 1.25
13 Charles Barkley 1.50 4.00
14 Clyde Drexler 1.00 2.50
15 Reggie Miller 1.25 3.00
16 Brent Barry .50 1.25
17 Kobe Bryant 60.00 150.00
18 Nick Van Exel .60 1.50
19 Alonzo Mourning 1.00 2.50
20 Ray Allen 3.00 8.00
21 Vin Baker .50 1.25
22 Kevin Garnett 2.00 5.00
23 Stephon Marbury 2.00 5.00
24 Kerry Kittles .60 1.50
25 Patrick Ewing 1.00 2.50
26 Larry Johnson .75 2.00
27 Anfernee Hardaway 1.50 4.00
28 Allen Iverson 5.00 12.00
29 Arvydas Sabonis .60 1.50
30 Mitch Richmond .75 2.00
31 Vinny Del Negro .40 1.00
32 Gary Payton 1.00 2.50
33 Detlef Schrempf .60 1.50
34 Marcus Camby 1.00 2.50
35 Damon Stoudamire .60 1.50
36 Karl Malone 1.25 3.00
37 John Stockton 1.25 3.00
38 Shareef Abdur-Rahim 1.00 2.50
39 Juwan Howard .60 1.50
40 Chris Webber .75 2.00
NNO Grant Hill Checklist .40 1.00

1996-97 Fleer Sprite Grant Hill

COMPLETE SET (10) 4.00 10.00
COMMON CARD (1-10) .60 1.50

1996-97 Fleer Sprite Australian

COMPLETE SET (40) 40.00 80.00
1 Kenny Anderson 1.50 4.00
2 Chris Mills 1.25 3.00

3 Antonio McDyess 2.00 5.00
4 Joe Smith 1.50 4.00
5 Vin Baker 1.50 4.00
6 Ed O'Bannon 1.25 3.00
7 Anfernee Hardaway 5.00 12.00
8 Kevin Johnson 2.00 5.00
9 Mitch Richmond 2.50 6.00
10 Detlef Schrempf 2.00 5.00
11 John Stockton 4.00 10.00
12 Glen Rice 2.00 5.00
13 Clyde Drexler 3.00 8.00
14 Vlade Divac 2.00 5.00
15 Derek Harper 1.50 4.00
16 Charles Barkley 5.00 12.00
17 Hersey Hawkins 1.25 3.00
18 Karl Malone 4.00 10.00
19 Chris Webber 2.50 6.00
20 Alonzo Mourning 3.00 8.00
21 Clarence Weatherspoon 1.25 3.00
22 Dino Radja 1.25 3.00
23 Scottie Pippen 5.00 12.00
24 Jason Kidd 3.00 8.00
25 Grant Hill 3.00 8.00
26 Sam Cassell 1.50 4.00
27 Brian Williams 1.25 3.00
28 Tom Gugliotta 1.25 3.00
29 John Starks 2.00 5.00
30 Clifford Robinson 2.00 5.00
31 David Robinson 4.00 10.00
32 Damon Stoudamire 2.00 5.00
33 Greg Anthony 1.25 3.00
34 Toni Kukoc 2.00 5.00
35 Christian Laettner 2.00 5.00
36 Rik Smits 1.50 4.00
37 Tim Hardaway 2.50 6.00
38 Nick Anderson 1.25 3.00
39 Sean Elliott 2.00 5.00
40 Juwan Howard 2.00 5.00

2004-05 Fleer Sweet Sigs

COMP.SET w/o SP's (75) 15.00 40.00
76-100 RC PRINT RUN 999 SER.#'d SETS
1 Kirk Hinrich .30 .75
2 Ron Artest .30 .75
3 T.J. Ford .20 .50
4 Stephon Marbury .40 1.00
5 Antawn Jamison .25 .60
6 Jason Richardson .30 .75
7 Dwyane Wade 1.25 3.00
8 Shawn Marion .30 .75
9 Jermaine O'Neal .25 .60
10 Ricky Davis .25 .60
11 Richard Hamilton .40 1.00
12 Karl Malone .60 1.50
13 Jason Williams .25 .60
14 Lamar Odom .30 .75
15 Allan Houston .30 .75
16 Allen Iverson .75 2.00
17 Peja Stojakovic .25 .60
18 Jarvis Hayes .20 .50
19 Stephen Jackson .20 .50
20 Richard Jefferson .25 .60
21 Jahidi White .20 .50
22 Carmelo Anthony .60 1.50
23 Baron Davis .30 .75
24 Dajuan Wagner .20 .50
25 Nene .25 .60
26 Ben Wallace .40 1.00
27 Latrell Sprewell .40 1.00
28 Ray Allen .50 1.25
29 Andrei Kirilenko .25 .60
30 Antoine Walker .30 .75
31 Marcus Banks .20 .50
32 Pau Gasol .50 1.25
33 Tony Parker .50 1.25
34 Vince Carter .60 1.50
35 Mike Bibby .30 .75
36 Jim Jackson .25 .60
37 Shaquille O'Neal 1.25 3.00
38 Bonzi Wells .20 .50
39 Paul Pierce .50 1.25
40 Jason Kapono .20 .50
41 Reggie Miller .60 1.50
42 Drew Gooden .20 .50
43 Shareef Abdur-Rahim .30 .75
44 Chris Bosh .50 1.25
45 Steve Nash .60 1.50
46 Elton Brand .25 .60
47 Kevin Garnett .75 2.00
48 Kenyon Martin .30 .75
49 Jamal Crawford .30 .75
50 Dirk Nowitzki .75 2.00
51 Yao Ming .75 2.00
52 Jamaal Magloire .20 .50
53 Tim Duncan .75 2.00
54 Gilbert Arenas .30 .75
55 Steve Francis .30 .75
56 Corey Maggette .25 .60
57 Caron Butler .25 .60
58 Michael Redd .25 .60
59 Kyle Korver .30 .75
60 Amare Stoudemire .30 .75
61 Carlos Boozer .25 .60
62 Darko Milicic .20 .50
63 Kobe Bryant 2.50 6.00
64 Tracy McGrady .50 1.25
65 Zach Randolph .30 .75
66 Luke Ridnour .25 .60
67 Carlos Arroyo .20 .50
68 Michael Finley .30 .75
69 Mickael Pietrus .20 .50
70 Darius Miles .20 .50
71 Chris Webber .40 1.00
72 Eddy Curry .20 .50
73 Jason Kidd .50 1.25
74 Manu Ginobili .60 1.50
75 LeBron James 6.00 15.00
76 Emeka Okafor RC 1.25 3.00
77 Rafael Araujo RC 1.00 2.50
78 Andre Iguodala RC 2.50 6.00
79 Kris Humphries RC 1.25 3.00
80 Kevin Martin RC 2.00 5.00
81 Delonte West RC 1.25 3.00
82 Pavel Podkolzin RC 1.00 2.50
83 Al Jefferson RC 1.50 4.00
84 Shaun Livingston RC 1.50 4.00
85 Luke Jackson RC 1.00 2.50
86 Dorell Wright RC 1.25 3.00
87 Andris Biedrins RC 1.00 2.50
88 Sasha Vujacic RC 1.25 3.00
89 Jameer Nelson RC 1.50 4.00
90 Dwight Howard RC 5.00 12.00
91 Robert Swift RC 1.00 2.50
92 Josh Childress RC 1.00 2.50
93 Luol Deng RC 1.50 4.00
94 J.R. Smith RC 1.50 4.00
95 Kirk Snyder RC 1.00 2.50
96 Josh Smith RC 1.50 4.00
97 Devin Harris RC 1.25 3.00
98 Viktor Khryapa RC 1.00 2.50
99 Ben Gordon RC 1.50 4.00
100 Sebastian Telfair RC 1.25 3.00

2004-05 Fleer Sweet Sigs Parallel

*1-75 PAR.SINGLES: 2X TO 5X BASE HI
*76-100 PAR.RC's: 1X TO 2X BASE HI
PRINT RUN 99 SER.#'d SETS
POSITION PARALLEL SER.#'d
75 LeBron James 100.00 250.00

2004-05 Fleer Sweet Sigs Autographs

STATED PRINT RUN 50 TO 200 SETS
N Nene/200 4.00 10.00
AB Andris Biedrins/200 2.50 6.00
AJ Al Jefferson/200 15.00 40.00
AS Amare Stoudemire/200 8.00 20.00
AW Antoine Walker/50 10.00 25.00
BG Ben Gordon/200 15.00 30.00
CA Carmelo Anthony/150 20.00 50.00
CB Chris Bosh/150 8.00 20.00
DH Devin Harris/200 3.00 8.00
DW Dwyane Wade/150 30.00 80.00
EB Elton Brand/100 6.00 15.00
EC Eddy Curry/200 4.00 10.00
GA Gilbert Arenas/150 4.00 10.00
GP Gary Payton/50 12.50 30.00
JC Josh Childress/200 2.50 6.00
JH Josh Howard/200 4.00 10.00
JK Jason Kidd/50 15.00 40.00
JN Jameer Nelson/200 8.00 20.00
JS Jerry Stackhouse/150 6.00 15.00
KS Kirk Snyder/200 2.50 6.00
LD Luol Deng/150 10.00 25.00
LJ Luke Jackson/200 2.50 6.00
LO Lamar Odom/150 6.00 15.00
MB Mike Bibby/150 10.00 25.00
MD Mike Dunleavy/200 4.00 10.00
MS Mike Sweetney/200 4.00 10.00
PP Paul Pierce/50 15.00 40.00
RJ Richard Jefferson/200 4.00 10.00
RS Robert Swift/140 2.50 6.00
SF Steve Francis/50 8.00 20.00
SL Shaun Livingston/200 8.00 20.00
SM Stephon Marbury/50 8.00 20.00
ST Sebastian Telfair/200 3.00 8.00
TM Tracy McGrady/50 15.00 40.00
VC Vince Carter/150 12.50 30.00
YT Yuta Tabuse/149 4.00 10.00
ZR Zach Randolph/200 4.00 10.00
CAB Caron Butler/200 4.00 10.00
DAV David West/150 4.00 10.00
DEL Delonte West/150 6.00 15.00
DOR Dorell Wright/150 3.00 8.00
HSJ Ha Seung-Jin/99 4.00 10.00
JAS Jason Richardson/200 4.00 10.00
JON Jermaine O'Neal/100 10.00 25.00
JOS Josh Smith/200 8.00 20.00
JRS J.R. Smith/200 4.00 10.00
KEY Kenyon Martin/200 6.00 15.00
PAV Pavel Podkolzin/200 2.50 6.00
RAF Rafael Araujo/200 2.50 6.00
TAY Tayshaun Prince/200 6.00 15.00
TJF T.J. Ford/150 4.00 10.00

2004-05 Fleer Sweet Sigs Autographs Draft Pick

STATED PRINT RUN ONE TO 46 SETS
AJ Al Jefferson/15 40.00 100.00
JH Josh Howard/29 10.00 25.00
ZR Zach Randolph/19 10.00 25.00
DOR Dorell Wright/19 8.00 20.00
JOS Josh Smith/17 20.00 50.00
DEL Delonte West/24 15.00 40.00
JON Jermaine O'Neal/17 15.00 40.00
JRS J.R. Smith/18 20.00 50.00
HSJ Ha Seung-Jin/46 10.00 25.00

2004-05 Fleer Sweet Sigs Autographs Draft Year

STATED PRINT RUN ONE TO 99 SETS
AW Antoine Walker/96 8.00 20.00
EB Elton Brand/99 8.00 20.00
GP Gary Payton/90 12.00 30.00
JK Jason Kidd/94 12.00 30.00
JS Jerry Stackhouse/95 8.00 20.00
LO Lamar Odom/99 8.00 20.00
MB Mike Bibby/98 10.00 25.00
PP Paul Pierce/98 12.00 30.00
SF Steve Francis/99 8.00 20.00
SM Stephon Marbury/96 8.00 20.00
TM Tracy McGrady/97 12.00 30.00
VC Vince Carter/98 15.00 40.00
JON Jermaine O'Neal/96 8.00 20.00

2004-05 Fleer Sweet Sigs Hardcourt Heroics

COMPLETE SET (25) 10.00 25.00
STATED ODDS 1:6
1 Vince Carter .75 2.00
2 Kevin Garnett 1.00 2.50
3 Carmelo Anthony .75 2.00
4 Ben Wallace .50 1.25
5 Steve Francis .40 1.00
6 Richard Hamilton .40 1.00
7 Paul Pierce .60 1.50
8 Kobe Bryant 3.00 8.00
9 Chris Webber .50 1.25
10 Jason Richardson .40 1.00
11 Stephon Marbury .50 1.25
12 Jermaine O'Neal .30 .75
13 Shaquille O'Neal 1.50 4.00
14 Allen Iverson 1.00 2.50
15 Tony Parker .60 1.50
16 Dwyane Wade 1.50 4.00
17 Mike Bibby .40 1.00
18 Tracy McGrady .60 1.50
19 Pau Gasol .60 1.50
20 Dirk Nowitzki 1.00 2.50
21 Tim Duncan 1.00 2.50
22 Jason Kidd .60 1.50
23 Yao Ming 1.00 2.50
24 Amare Stoudemire .40 1.00
25 LeBron James 3.00 8.00

2004-05 Fleer Sweet Sigs Hardcourt Heroics Jerseys

PRINT RUNS LISTED IN CHECKLIST
AI Allen Iverson/250 6.00 15.00
BW Ben Wallace 3.00 8.00
CA Carmelo Anthony/184 5.00 12.00
DN Dirk Nowitzki/35 8.00 20.00
DW Dwyane Wade 10.00 25.00
JK Jason Kidd/215 4.00 10.00
JO Jermaine O'Neal/74 2.00 5.00
KG Kevin Garnett/223 6.00 15.00
MB Mike Bibby/55 2.50 6.00
PG Pau Gasol/110 4.00 10.00
PP Paul Pierce/250 4.00 10.00
SF Steve Francis/40 8.00 20.00
SM Stephon Marbury/175 3.00 8.00
SO Shaquille O'Neal/200 10.00 25.00
TD Tim Duncan/124 6.00 15.00
TM Tracy McGrady/235 4.00 10.00
VC Vince Carter 5.00 12.00
YM Yao Ming/35 10.00 25.00

2004-05 Fleer Sweet Sigs Hardcourt Heroics Jerseys Retail

*RETAIL: .4X TO 1X BASE HI 2.00 5.00

2004-05 Fleer Sweet Sigs Hardcourt Heroics Jerseys Dual

STATED PRINT RUN 2 TO 29 SETS
CP V.Carter/P.Pierce/29 20.00 50.00
FW S.Francis/D.Wade/18 20.00 50.00
GA K.Garnett/Carmelo/25 20.00 50.00
MK S.Marbury/J.Kidd/22 20.00 50.00

2004-05 Fleer Sweet Sigs Hardcourt Heroics Jerseys Quad

STATED PRINT RUN 9 TO 42 SETS
BPGA Bibby/Parker/KG/Melo/42 25.00 60.00
IMCP AI/T-Mac/Vince/Pierce/28 40.00 100.00
WNOG Webb/Dirk/J.O'Neal/Pau/33 40.00 100.00

2004-05 Fleer Sweet Sigs Hardcourt Heroics Patches

*PATCH: 1.25X TO 3X BASE HI
PRINT RUN 50 SER.#'d SETS
AI Allen Iverson 20.00 50.00
JO Jermaine O'Neal 6.00 15.00
YM Yao Ming 20.00 50.00

2004-05 Fleer Sweet Sigs Hardcourt Heroics Patches Black

PRINT RUNS LISTED IN CHECKLIST
BW Ben Wallace/35 10.00 25.00
CA Carmelo Anthony/15 15.00 40.00
DN Dirk Nowitzki/34 20.00 50.00
KG Kevin Garnett/21 20.00 50.00
TD Tim Duncan/21 20.00 50.00
TM Tracy McGrady/32 12.00 30.00

2004-05 Fleer Sweet Sigs Sweet Stitches Jerseys

PRINT RUN LISTED IN CHECKLIST
N Nene/19 4.00 10.00
AH Allan Houston/123 2.50 6.00
AS Amare Stoudemire/159 2.50 6.00
CB Chris Bosh/175 4.00 10.00
CW Chris Webber/129 3.00 8.00
DN Dirk Nowitzki/115 6.00 15.00
DW Dwyane Wade/137 10.00 25.00
EC Eddy Curry/113 1.50 4.00
GA Gilbert Arenas/89 2.50 6.00
JK Jason Kidd/136 4.00 10.00
JR Jason Richardson/64 2.50 6.00
JS Jerry Stackhouse/114 2.50 6.00
KG Kevin Garnett/95 6.00 15.00
KM Karl Malone/113 5.00 12.00
LS Latrell Sprewell/26 10.00 25.00
PG Pau Gasol/174 4.00 10.00
RH Richard Hamilton/103 3.00 8.00
RJ Richard Jefferson/143 2.00 5.00
SF Steve Francis/26 10.00 25.00
SM Stephon Marbury/101 3.00 8.00
SN Steve Nash/132 5.00 12.00
SO Shaquille O'Neal/151 10.00 25.00
TD Tim Duncan/163 6.00 15.00
TM Tracy McGrady/171 4.00 10.00
YM Yao Ming/152 6.00 15.00

2004-05 Fleer Sweet Sigs Sweet Stitches Jerseys Retail

N Nene SP 2.00 5.00
AH Allan Houston 2.50 6.00
AS Amare Stoudemire SP 2.50 6.00
BW Ben Wallace 3.00 8.00
CA Carmelo Anthony SP 5.00 12.00
CB Chris Bosh SP 4.00 10.00
CM Corey Maggette 2.00 5.00
CW Chris Webber 3.00 8.00
DN Dirk Nowitzki 6.00 15.00
DW Dwyane Wade 10.00 25.00
EC Eddy Curry 1.50 4.00
GA Gilbert Arenas 2.50 6.00
JK Jason Kidd 4.00 10.00
JR Jason Richardson SP 2.50 6.00
JS Jerry Stackhouse 2.50 6.00
KG Kevin Garnett 6.00 15.00
KM Karl Malone SP 5.00 12.00
LS Latrell Sprewell 3.00 8.00
MG Manu Ginobili 5.00 12.00
PG Pau Gasol SP 4.00 10.00
RH Richard Hamilton 3.00 8.00
RJ Richard Jefferson 2.00 5.00
SF Steve Francis SP 2.50 6.00
SM Stephon Marbury 3.00 8.00
SN Steve Nash 5.00 12.00
SO Shaquille O'Neal 10.00 25.00
TD Tim Duncan 6.00 15.00
TM Tracy McGrady 4.00 10.00
VC Vince Carter SP 5.00 12.00
YM Yao Ming SP 6.00 15.00

2004-05 Fleer Sweet Sigs Sweet Stitches Patches

*PATCH: 1X TO 2.5X BASE HI
PRINT RUN 50 SER.#'d SETS
N Nene 5.00 12.00
BW Ben Wallace 8.00 20.00
CA Carmelo Anthony 12.00 30.00
CM Corey Maggette 5.00 12.00
CW Chris Webber 10.00 25.00
LS Latrell Sprewell 8.00 20.00
MG Manu Ginobili 12.00 30.00
SF Steve Francis 6.00 15.00
VC Vince Carter 12.00 30.00

2004-05 Fleer Sweet Sigs Sweet Stitches Patches Black

PRINT RUNS LISTED IN CHECKLIST
N Nene/40 5.00 12.00
AS Amare Stoudemire/17 8.00 20.00
BW Ben Wallace/42 8.00 20.00
CA Carmelo Anthony/44 12.00 30.00
CB Chris Bosh/19 12.00 30.00
DN Dirk Nowitzki/28 20.00 50.00
GA Gilbert Arenas/40 6.00 15.00
JK Jason Kidd/33 10.00 25.00
JR Jason Richardson/36 6.00 15.00
JS Jerry Stackhouse/28 8.00 20.00
KG Kevin Garnett/35 15.00 40.00
KM Karl Malone/23 15.00 40.00
LS Latrell Sprewell/38 8.00 20.00
MG Manu Ginobili/41 12.00 30.00
PG Pau Gasol/27 12.00 30.00
RH Richard Hamilton/18 10.00 25.00
RJ Richard Jefferson/43 5.00 12.00
SF Steve Francis/36 6.00 15.00
SM Stephon Marbury/39 8.00 20.00
SO Shaquille O'Neal/31 30.00 80.00
TD Tim Duncan/23 20.00 50.00
TM Tracy McGrady/26 12.00 30.00
VC Vince Carter/15 15.00 40.00

2004-05 Fleer Sweet Sigs Sweet Stitches Jerseys Quad

PRINT RUNS LISTED BELOW
ANGS Melo/Nene/KG/Spree/30 40.00 80.00
BCAS Bosh/VC/Arenas/Stack/33 25.00 60.00
MFDG Yao/Francis/TD/Manu/18 40.00 80.00
MODG Malone/Shaq/TD/Manu/31 50.00 100.00
MSGA T-Mac/Amare/KG/Melo/25 20.00 50.00

2004-05 Fleer Sweet Sigs Sweet Stroke

COMPLETE SET (15) 8.00 20.00
STATED ODDS 1:12
1 Dwyane Wade 2.00 5.00
2 Allen Iverson 1.25 3.00
3 Peja Stojakovic .40 1.00
4 Tony Parker .75 2.00
5 Ray Allen .75 2.00
6 Reggie Miller 1.00 2.50
7 Kevin Garnett 1.25 3.00
8 Dirk Nowitzki 1.25 3.00
9 Tim Duncan 1.25 3.00
10 Kobe Bryant 4.00 10.00
11 Tracy McGrady .75 2.00
12 Michael Finley .50 1.25
13 LeBron James 4.00 10.00
14 Baron Davis .50 1.25
15 Steve Nash 1.00 2.50

2004-05 Fleer Sweet Sigs Sweet Stroke Jerseys

PRINT RUNS LISTED IN CHECKLIST
AI Allen Iverson/143 6.00 15.00
BD Baron Davis/224 2.50 6.00
DW Dwyane Wade/250 6.00 15.00
KG Kevin Garnett/197 6.00 15.00
MF Michael Finley/21 6.00 15.00
PS Peja Stojakovic/216 2.00 5.00
RA Ray Allen/238 4.00 10.00
RM Reggie Miller/163 5.00 12.00
SN Steve Nash/15 8.00 20.00
TD Tim Duncan/99 6.00 15.00
TM Tracy McGrady/200 4.00 10.00
TP Tony Parker/112 4.00 10.00

2004-05 Fleer Sweet Sigs Sweet Stroke Jerseys Retail

*RETAIL: .4X TO 1X BASE HI 2.00 5.00

2004-05 Fleer Sweet Sigs Sweet Stroke Jerseys Quad

PRINT RUNS LISTED IN CHECKLIST
MIGD T-Mac/AI/KG/B.Davis/35 40.00 100.00
WAMM Wade/T-Mac/Miller/Allen/29 30.00 80.00
WIMB Wade/AI/R.Miller/B.Davis/35 30.00 80.00

2004-05 Fleer Sweet Sigs Sweet Stroke Patches

*PATCH: 1X TO 2.5X BASE HI
PRINT RUN 50 SER.#'d SETS
DW Dwyane Wade 25.00 60.00
RM Reggie Miller 12.50 30.00

2004-05 Fleer Sweet Sigs Sweet Stroke Patches Black

PRINT RUNS LISTED IN CHECKLIST
AI Allen Iverson/37 20.00 50.00
BD Baron Davis/69 6.00 15.00
DW Dwyane Wade/19 30.00 80.00
KG Kevin Garnett/21 20.00 50.00
RA Ray Allen/59 10.00 25.00
RM Reggie Miller/31 12.50 30.00
TD Tim Duncan/32 20.00 50.00
TM Tracy McGrady/62 10.00 25.00
TP Tony Parker/29 12.00 30.00

2004-05 Fleer Throwbacks

COMP.SET w/o RC's (65) 15.00 40.00
66-76 RC PRINT RUN 50 SER.#'d SETS
77-100 JSY RC PRINT RUN 499 #'d SETS
1 Baron Davis .30 .75
2 Willie Green .30 .75
3 Allen Iverson .75 2.00
4 Jason Williams .25 .60
5 Kevin Garnett .75 2.00
6 Jason Richardson .30 .75
7 Lamar Odom .30 .75
8 Ben Wallace .40 1.00
9 Steve Nash .60 1.50
10 Kobe Bryant 2.50 6.00
11 Kenyon Martin .30 .75
12 Jermaine O'Neal .25 .60
13 Tracy McGrady .50 1.25
14 Darko Milicic .20 .50
15 Pau Gasol .50 1.25
16 Darius Miles .20 .50
17 Ray Allen .50 1.25
18 Michael Redd .25 .60
19 Chris Bosh .50 1.25
20 Peja Stojakovic .25 .60
21 Tim Duncan .75 2.00
22 Corey Maggette .25 .60
23 LeBron James 2.50 6.00
24 Antoine Walker .30 .75
25 Stephon Marbury .40 1.00
26 Carlos Boozer .25 .60
27 Jason Kapono .20 .50
28 Grant Hill .40 1.00
29 Mike Bibby .30 .75
30 Jamaal Magloire .20 .50
31 Rashard Lewis .25 .60
32 Jason Kidd .50 1.25
33 Al Harrington .25 .60
34 Steve Francis .30 .75
35 Kirk Hinrich .30 .75
36 Amare Stoudemire .30 .75
37 Gilbert Arenas .30 .75
38 Allan Houston .30 .75
39 Eddy Curry .20 .50
40 Latrell Sprewell .40 1.00
41 Mickael Pietrus .20 .50
42 Zach Randolph .30 .75
43 Shaquille O'Neal 1.25 3.00
44 Jason Terry .25 .60
45 Richard Hamilton .40 1.00
46 Karl Malone .60 1.50
47 Elton Brand .25 .60
48 Richard Jefferson .25 .60
49 Andrei Kirilenko .25 .60
50 Reggie Miller .60 1.50
51 Yao Ming .75 2.00
52 Gary Payton .50 1.25
53 Dirk Nowitzki .75 2.00
54 Dwyane Wade 1.25 3.00
55 Carmelo Anthony .60 1.50
56 Tony Parker .50 1.25
57 T.J. Ford .20 .50
58 Vince Carter .60 1.50
59 Paul Pierce .50 1.25
60 Drew Gooden .20 .50
61 Antawn Jamison .25 .60
62 Manu Ginobili .60 1.50
63 Chris Webber .40 1.00
64 Shawn Marion .30 .75
65 Jerry Stackhouse .30 .75
66 Andris Biedrins RC 2.00 5.00
67 Robert Swift RC 2.00 5.00
68 Pavel Podkolzin RC 2.00 5.00
69 Kevin Martin RC 4.00 10.00
70 Beno Udrih RC 2.50 6.00
71 David Harrison RC 2.00 5.00
72 Victor Khryapa RC 2.00 5.00
73 Jackson Vroman RC 2.00 5.00
74 Emeka Okafor RC 2.50 6.00
75 Andre Emmett RC 2.00 5.00
76 Andres Nocioni RC 3.00 8.00
77 Dwight Howard JSY RC 8.00 20.00
78 Ben Gordon JSY RC 2.50 6.00
79 Shaun Livingston JSY RC 2.50 6.00
80 Devin Harris JSY RC 2.00 5.00
81 Josh Childress JSY RC 1.50 4.00
82 Luol Deng JSY RC 2.50 6.00
83 Rafael Araujo JSY RC 1.50 4.00
84 Andre Iguodala JSY RC 4.00 10.00
85 Luke Jackson JSY RC 1.50 4.00
86 Sebastian Telfair JSY RC 2.00 5.00
87 Kris Humphries JSY RC 2.00 5.00
88 Al Jefferson JSY RC 2.50 6.00
89 Kirk Snyder JSY RC 1.50 4.00
90 Josh Smith JSY RC 2.50 6.00
91 J.R. Smith JSY RC 2.50 6.00
92 Dorell Wright JSY RC 2.00 5.00
93 Jameer Nelson JSY RC 2.50 6.00
94 Chris Duhon JSY RC 2.00 5.00
95 Delonte West JSY RC 2.00 5.00
96 Tony Allen JSY RC 2.50 6.00
97 Anderson Varejao JSY RC 2.00 5.00
98 Lionel Chalmers JSY RC 2.00 5.00
99 Bernard Robinson JSY RC 1.50 4.00
100 Trevor Ariza JSY RC 2.50 6.00

2004-05 Fleer Throwbacks 100

*1-65 SINGLES: 2X TO 5X BASE HI
STATED PRINT RUN 100 SER.#'d SETS
23 LeBron James 15.00 40.00

2004-05 Fleer Throwbacks 50

*1-65 SINGLES: 3X TO 8X BASE HI
STATED PRINT RUN 50 SER.#'d SETS
23 LeBron James 20.00 50.00

2004-05 Fleer Throwbacks 25

*1-65 SINGLES: 6X TO 15X BASE HI
*66-76 SINGLES: .75X TO 2X BASE
*77-100 SINGLES: 1X TO 2.5X BASE HI
STATED PRINT RUN 25 SER.#'d SETS
23 LeBron James 40.00 100.00

2004-05 Fleer Throwbacks Defining Authentic

COMPLETE SET (22) 12.50 30.00
STATED ODDS 1:15 H 1:24 R
1 Shaquille O'Neal 2.50 6.00
2 Tim Duncan 1.50 4.00
3 Tracy McGrady 1.00 2.50
4 Vince Carter 1.25 3.00
5 Yao Ming 1.50 4.00
6 Allen Iverson 1.50 4.00
7 Amare Stoudemire .60 1.50
8 Carmelo Anthony 1.25 3.00
9 Jason Kidd 1.00 2.50
10 Jermaine O'Neal .50 1.25
11 Jason Richardson .60 1.50
12 Kevin Garnett 1.50 4.00
13 Paul Pierce 1.00 2.50
14 Peja Stojakovic .50 1.25
15 Dirk Nowitzki 1.50 4.00
16 Kenyon Martin .60 1.50
17 Dwyane Wade 2.50 6.00
18 Steve Francis .60 1.50
19 Kobe Bryant 5.00 12.00
20 LeBron James 5.00 12.00

2004-05 Fleer Throwbacks Defining Authentic Jerseys

STATED ODDS 1:15 H, 1:29 R
*JERSEY 99: .5X TO 1.25X BASE HI
*JERSEY/PATCH: 1.25X TO 3X BASE HI
JERSEY/PATCH PRINT RUN 25 SETS
AI Allen Iverson 6.00 15.00
AS Amare Stoudemire 2.50 6.00
CA Carmelo Anthony 5.00 12.00
DN Dirk Nowitzki 6.00 15.00
DW Dwyane Wade 6.00 15.00
JK Jason Kidd 4.00 10.00
JO Jermaine O'Neal 2.00 5.00
JR Jason Richardson 2.50 6.00
KG Kevin Garnett 6.00 15.00
KM Kenyon Martin 2.50 6.00
PP Paul Pierce 4.00 10.00
PS Peja Stojakovic 2.00 5.00
SF Steve Francis 2.50 6.00
SM Stephon Marbury 3.00 8.00
SN Steve Nash 5.00 12.00
SO Shaquille O'Neal 10.00 25.00
TD Tim Duncan 6.00 15.00
TM Tracy McGrady 4.00 10.00
VC Vince Carter 5.00 12.00
YM Yao Ming 6.00 15.00

2004-05 Fleer Throwbacks Defining Authentic Jerseys Dual

PRINT RUN 99 SER.#'d SETS
1 Y.Ming/T.Duncan 8.00 20.00
2 T.McGrady/V.Carter 8.00 20.00
3 S.Marbury/A.Iverson 8.00 20.00
4 J.Kidd/P.Pierce 8.00 20.00
5 A.Iverson/V.Carter 10.00 25.00
7 D.Nowitzki/P.Stojakovic 8.00 20.00
8 A.Stoudemire/S.Nash 8.00 20.00
9 J.Kidd/K.Martin 6.00 15.00
10 T.McGrady/S.Francis 6.00 15.00
11 S.O'Neal/D.Wade 15.00 40.00
12 C.Anthony/K.Martin 6.00 15.00
13 T.McGrady/Y.Ming 8.00 20.00
14 C.Anthony/D.Wade 10.00 25.00
15 S.O'Neal/J.O'Neal 8.00 20.00

2004-05 Fleer Throwbacks Defining Authentic Jerseys and Patch Dual

PRINT RUN 25 SER.#'d SETS
AM C.Anthony/K.Martin 25.00 60.00
DG T.Duncan/K.Garnett 30.00 80.00
KM J.Kidd/K.Martin 25.00 60.00
KP J.Kidd/P.Pierce 25.00 60.00
MC T.McGrady/V.Carter 30.00 80.00
MD Y.Ming/T.Duncan 25.00 60.00
MF T.McGrady/S.Francis 25.00 60.00
MI S.Marbury/A.Iverson 25.00 60.00
MM T.McGrady/Y.Ming 25.00 60.00
NS D.Nowitzki/P.Stojakovic 30.00 80.00
OO S.O'Neal/J.O'Neal 30.00 80.00
OW S.O'Neal/D.Wade 40.00 100.00
SN A.Stoudemire/S.Nash 25.00 60.00

2004-05 Fleer Throwbacks Defining Authentic Jerseys Autographs

PRINT RUNS FROM 149 TO 449 #'d SETS
AJ Al Jefferson/149 5.00 12.00
BG Ben Gordon/249 5.00 12.00
CB Chauncey Billups/149 8.00 20.00
CD Chris Duhon/249 4.00 10.00
DH Devin Harris/149 4.00 10.00
DW2 Delonte West/149 4.00 10.00
EC Eddy Curry/249 3.00 8.00
GA Gilbert Arenas/199 5.00 12.00
JH Josh Howard/249 4.00 10.00
JS2 J.R. Smith/249 5.00 12.00
MD Marquis Daniels/249 3.00 8.00
NC Nick Collison/249 3.00 8.00
RA Rafael Araujo/449 3.00 8.00
TA Tony Allen/249 5.00 12.00
TF T.J. Ford/149 3.00 8.00
VC Vince Carter/249 10.00 25.00
YT Yuta Tabuse/449 5.00 12.00

2004-05 Fleer Throwbacks Defining Authentic Jerseys Autographs Numbers

PRINT RUNS LISTED IN CHECKLIST
CA Carmelo Anthony/15 40.00 100.00
DH Devin Harris/34 15.00 40.00
JS Josh Smith/42 25.00 60.00
JS2 J.R. Smith/23 20.00 50.00
LJ Luke Jackson/33 12.50 30.00
RA Rafael Araujo/55 10.00 25.00

2004-05 Fleer Throwbacks Defining Authentic Jerseys Autographs Silver

PRINT RUNS LISTED IN CHECKLIST
AJ Al Jefferson/50 10.00 25.00
BG Ben Gordon/50 10.00 25.00
CA Carmelo Anthony/50 25.00 60.00
CB Chauncey Billups/50 12.00 30.00
CD Chris Duhon/149 8.00 20.00
DH Devin Harris/50 8.00 20.00
DW Dwyane Wade/25 75.00 150.00
DW2 Delonte West/50 8.00 20.00
EC Eddy Curry/50 8.00 20.00
GA Gilbert Arenas/50 8.00 20.00
JH Josh Howard/149 8.00 20.00
JK Jason Kidd/25 20.00 50.00
JO Jermaine O'Neal/25 12.00 30.00
JS2 J.R. Smith/50 10.00 25.00
KM Kenyon Martin/25 20.00 50.00
LD Luol Deng/25 10.00 25.00
NC Nick Collison/149 8.00 20.00
RA Rafael Araujo/199 8.00 20.00
SL Shaun Livingston/50 10.00 25.00
SM Stephon Marbury/25 20.00 50.00
TA Tony Allen/199 10.00 25.00
TF T.J. Ford/50 8.00 20.00
VC Vince Carter/99 20.00 50.00
YT Yuta Tabuse/149 10.00 25.00

2004-05 Fleer Throwbacks Hardwood Classics

COMPLETE SET (15) 15.00 40.00
STATED ODDS 1:90 H, 1:288 R
1 Elton Brand 1.50 4.00
2 Lamar Odom 2.00 5.00
3 Carlos Boozer 1.50 4.00
4 Andrei Kirilenko 1.50 4.00
5 Zach Randolph 2.00 5.00
6 Darius Miles 1.25 3.00
7 Ben Wallace 2.50 6.00
8 Richard Hamilton 2.50 6.00
9 Pau Gasol 3.00 8.00
10 Chris Bosh 3.00 8.00
11 Baron Davis 2.00 5.00
12 Mike Bibby 2.00 5.00
13 Manu Ginobili 4.00 10.00
14 Tony Parker 3.00 8.00
15 Richard Jefferson 1.50 4.00

2004-05 Fleer Throwbacks Hardwood Classics Jerseys

PRINT RUN 99 SER.#'d SETS
AK Andrei Kirilenko 2.50 6.00
BD Baron Davis 3.00 8.00
BW Ben Wallace 4.00 10.00
CB Charles Barkley 50.00 120.00
CB Carlos Boozer 2.50 6.00
CB Chris Bosh 5.00 12.00
DM Darius Miles 2.00 5.00
DR David Robinson 15.00 40.00
IT Isiah Thomas 8.00 20.00
KA Kareem Abdul-Jabbar 10.00 25.00
LB Larry Bird 40.00 80.00
LE Lamar Odom 3.00 8.00
MB Mike Bibby 3.00 8.00
MG Manu Ginobili 6.00 15.00
PE Patrick Ewing 15.00 40.00
PG Pau Gasol 5.00 12.00
RH Richard Hamilton 4.00 10.00
RJ Richard Jefferson 2.50 6.00
WF Walt Frazier 10.00 25.00
ZR Zach Randolph 3.00 8.00

2004-05 Fleer Throwbacks Hardwood Classics Jerseys and Patch

PRINT RUNS LISTED IN CHECKLIST
1 Elton Brand/42 6.00 15.00
4 Andrei Kirilenko/47 6.00 15.00
5 Zach Randolph/50 8.00 20.00
6 Darius Miles/23 6.00 15.00
8 Richard Hamilton/32 10.00 25.00
9 Pau Gasol/16 12.00 30.00
16 Kareem Abdul-Jabbar/33 25.00 60.00
17 Charles Barkley/34 75.00 150.00
18 David Robinson/50 20.00 50.00
21 Larry Bird/33 30.00 80.00
22 Patrick Ewing/33 25.00 60.00
23 Scottie Pippen/33 30.00 80.00

2004-05 Fleer Throwbacks Hardwood Classics Jerseys Dual

PRINT RUN 50 SER.#'d SETS
*PATCH DUAL: .75X TO 2X BASE HI
PATCH DUAL PRINT RUN 25 SER.#'d SETS
BB C.Boozer/E.Brand 6.00 15.00
BK C.Boozer/A.Kirilenko 6.00 15.00
BO E.Brand/L.Odom 6.00 15.00
DB B.Davis/M.Bibby 6.00 15.00
GB P.Gasol/C.Bosh 8.00 20.00
GG P.Gasol/M.Ginobili 8.00 20.00
GP M.Ginobili/T.Parker 8.00 20.00
JH R.Jefferson/R.Hamilton 6.00 15.00
RM Z.Randolph/D.Miles 6.00 15.00
WH B.Wallace/R.Hamilton 8.00 20.00

2004-05 Fleer Throwbacks Hardwood Classics Jerseys Autographs

PRINT RUNS LISTED IN CHECKLIST
AB Andris Biedrins/249 6.00 15.00
AK Andrei Kirilenko/249 6.00 15.00
DW Dorell Wright/149 6.00 15.00
GG George Gervin 10.00 25.00
JC Josh Childress/249 6.00 15.00
KH Kris Humphries/249 6.00 15.00

2004-05 Fleer Throwbacks Hardwood Classics Jerseys Autographs Numbers

PRINT RUNS LISTED IN CHECKLIST
AB Andris Biedrins/15 12.50 30.00
AK Andrei Kirilenko/47 25.00 60.00
BW2 Bill Walton/32 15.00 40.00
DM Darius Miles/23 10.00 25.00
EB Elton Brand/42 10.00 25.00
GG George Gervin/44 15.00 40.00
KH Kris Humphries/43 10.00 25.00
RH Richard Hamilton/32 15.00 40.00

2004-05 Fleer Throwbacks Hardwood Classics Jerseys Autographs Silver

PRINT RUNS LISTED IN CHECKLIST
AK Andrei Kirilenko/149 8.00 20.00
BS Byron Scott/249 8.00 20.00
BW Bill Walton/249 8.00 20.00
CB Carlos Boozer/50 8.00 20.00
CB2 Chris Bosh/25 10.00 25.00
DW Dorell Wright/50 8.00 20.00
GG George Gervin/200 15.00 40.00
JC Josh Childress/50 8.00 20.00
KH Kris Humphries/199 8.00 20.00
MC Maurice Cheeks/249 8.00 20.00
RH Richard Hamilton/149 10.00 25.00
ZR Zach Randolph/149 10.00 25.00

2004-05 Fleer Throwbacks Hardwood Classics Jerseys Redemption

STATED ODDS 1:667
1 Dave Debusschere 20.00 50.00
2 Bill Russell 50.00 120.00
3 Bill Russell 50.00 120.00
4 George Gervin 40.00 100.00
5 Larry Bird 50.00 120.00
7 George Mikan 25.00 60.00
9 Magic Johnson 25.00 60.00
13 Bill Bradley 20.00 50.00
17 Jersey of Your Choice #1 100.00 200.00

2004-05 Fleer Throwbacks Nostalgia

COMPLETE SET (15) 15.00 40.00
PRINT RUNS FROM 1985 TO 2003 SETS
*GOLD/85-98: 1.25X TO 3X BASE HI
1 Allen Iverson/1996 2.50 6.00
2 Kobe Bryant/1996 8.00 20.00
3 Shaquille O'Neal/1992 4.00 10.00
4 Karl Malone/1985 2.00 5.00
5 Kevin Garnett/1995 2.50 6.00
6 LeBron James/2003 8.00 20.00
7 Carmelo Anthony/2003 2.00 5.00
8 Dwyane Wade/2003 4.00 10.00
9 Baron Davis/1999 1.00 2.50
10 Jason Kidd/1994 1.50 4.00
11 Tracy McGrady/1997 1.50 4.00
12 Paul Pierce/1998 1.50 4.00
13 Yao Ming/2002 2.50 6.00
14 Vince Carter/1998 2.00 5.00
15 Ben Wallace/1996 1.25 3.00

2002-03 Fleer Tradition

COMPLETE SET (300) 30.00 80.00
1 Shareef Abdur-Rahim .40 1.00
2 Dion Glover .25 .60
3 Theo Ratliff .25 .60
4 Nazr Mohammed .25 .60
5 Ira Newble .25 .60
6 Alan Henderson .25 .60
7 Vin Baker .30 .75
8 Tony Battie .25 .60
9 Eric Williams .25 .60
10 Shammond Williams .25 .60
11 Walter McCarty .25 .60
12 Bruno Sundov .25 .60
13 Donyell Marshall .25 .60
14 Marcus Fizer .25 .60
15 Eddie Robinson .25 .60
16 Trenton Hassell .25 .60
17 Ricky Davis .30 .75
18 Jumaine Jones .25 .60
19 Chris Mihm .25 .60
20 Zydrunas Ilgauskas .30 .75
21 Tyrone Hill .25 .60
22 Adrian Griffin .25 .60
23 Nick Van Exel .40 1.00
24 Raef LaFrentz .25 .60
25 Eduardo Najera .25 .60
26 Shawn Bradley .25 .60
27 Evan Eschmeyer .25 .60
28 Walt Williams .25 .60
29 Raja Bell .30 .75
30 Marcus Camby .30 .75
31 Donnell Harvey .25 .60
32 Kenny Satterfield .25 .60
33 Rodney White .25 .60
34 Chris Whitney .25 .60
35 Clifford Robinson .40 1.00
36 Zeljko Rebraca .25 .60
37 Corliss Williamson .25 .60
38 Chucky Atkins .25 .60
39 Jon Barry .25 .60
40 Michael Curry .25 .60
41 Erick Dampier .25 .60
42 Danny Fortson .25 .60
43 Adonal Foyle .25 .60
44 Troy Murphy .30 .75
45 Bob Sura .25 .60
46 Moochie Norris .25 .60
47 Kenny Thomas .25 .60
48 Terence Morris .25 .60
49 Glen Rice .30 .75
50 Maurice Taylor .25 .60
51 Erick Strickland .25 .60
52 Al Harrington .30 .75
53 Ron Artest .30 .75
54 Austin Croshere .25 .60
55 Ron Mercer .25 .60
56 Brad Miller .30 .75
57 Lamar Odom .40 1.00
58 Keyon Dooling .25 .60
59 Corey Maggette .30 .75
60 Michael Olowokandi .25 .60
61 Stanislav Medvedenko .25 .60
62 Rick Fox .25 .60
63 Derek Fisher .40 1.00
64 Samaki Walker .25 .60
65 Robert Horry .40 1.00
66 Mark Madsen .25 .60
67 Wesley Person .25 .60
68 Michael Dickerson .25 .60
69 Lorenzen Wright .25 .60
70 Brevin Knight .25 .60
71 Travis Best .25 .60
72 Brian Grant .25 .60
73 Eddie Jones .40 1.00
74 LaPhonso Ellis .25 .60
75 Anthony Carter .25 .60
76 Tim Thomas .25 .60
77 Toni Kukoc .40 1.00
78 Anthony Mason .30 .75
79 Ervin Johnson .25 .60
80 Joel Przybilla .25 .60
81 Rod Strickland .25 .60
82 Terrell Brandon .25 .60
83 Anthony Peeler .25 .60
84 Joe Smith .30 .75
85 Gary Trent .25 .60
86 Rasho Nesterovic .25 .60
87 Loren Woods .25 .60
88 Felipe Lopez .25 .60
89 Dikembe Mutombo .60 1.50
90 Rodney Rogers .25 .60
91 Jason Collins .25 .60
92 Kerry Kittles .25 .60
93 Lucious Harris .25 .60
94 Aaron Williams .25 .60
95 Jamal Mashburn .30 .75
96 David Wesley .25 .60
97 Elden Campbell .25 .60
98 Jerome Moiso .25 .60
99 P.J. Brown .25 .60
100 George Lynch .25 .60
101 Robert Traylor .25 .60
102 Antonio McDyess .30 .75
103 Kurt Thomas .25 .60
104 Clarence Weatherspoon .25 .60
105 Charlie Ward .25 .60
106 Lavor Postell .25 .60
107 Shandon Anderson .25 .60
108 Michael Doleac .25 .60
109 Othella Harrington .25 .60
110 Darrell Armstrong .25 .60
111 Steven Hunter .25 .60
112 Pat Garrity .25 .60
113 Horace Grant .30 .75
114 Jacque Vaughn .25 .60
115 Jeryl Sasser .25 .60
116 Todd MacCulloch .25 .60
117 Greg Buckner .25 .60
118 Eric Snow .25 .60
119 Samuel Dalembert .25 .60
120 Monty Williams .25 .60
121 Stephon Marbury .50 1.25
122 Anfernee Hardaway 1.00 2.50
123 Tom Gugliotta .25 .60
124 Iakovos Tsakalidis .25 .60
125 Bo Outlaw .25 .60
126 Damon Stoudamire .40 1.00
127 Jeff McInnis .25 .60
128 Derek Anderson .25 .60
129 Antonio Daniels .25 .60
130 Dale Davis .25 .60
131 Zach Randolph .30 .75
132 Bobby Jackson .25 .60
133 Chris Webber .50 1.25
134 Vlade Divac .30 .75
135 Keon Clark .25 .60
136 Doug Christie .25 .60
137 Scot Pollard .25 .60
138 Mengke Bateer .40 1.00
139 David Robinson .75 2.00
140 Steve Smith .30 .75
141 Malik Rose .25 .60
142 Speedy Claxton .25 .60
143 Danny Ferry .25 .60
144 Brent Barry .25 .60
145 Joseph Forte .25 .60
146 Vladimir Radmanovic .25 .60
147 Kenny Anderson .30 .75
148 Predrag Drobnjak .25 .60
149 Calvin Booth .25 .60
150 Ansu Sesay .25 .60
151 Voshon Lenard .25 .60
152 Lamond Murray .25 .60
153 Antonio Davis .30 .75
154 Lindsey Hunter .25 .60
155 Michael Bradley .25 .60
156 Jerome Williams .25 .60
157 Alvin Williams .25 .60
158 Mamadou N'Diaye .25 .60
159 Raul Lopez .40 1.00
160 John Stockton .75 2.00
161 Mark Jackson .25 .60
162 DeShawn Stevenson .25 .60
163 Calbert Cheaney .25 .60
164 Matt Harpring .25 .60
165 Jarron Collins .25 .60
166 Tyronn Lue .25 .60
167 Bryon Russell .25 .60
168 Larry Hughes .30 .75
169 Brendan Haywood .25 .60
170 Christian Laettner .30 .75
171 Glenn Robinson .40 1.00
172 Tony Delk .25 .60
173 Antoine Walker .30 .75
174 Jalen Rose .30 .75
175 Jamal Crawford .40 1.00
176 DeSagana Diop .25 .60
177 Michael Finley .40 1.00
178 Dirk Nowitzki 1.00 2.50
179 Juwan Howard .30 .75
180 Chauncey Billups .40 1.00
181 Richard Hamilton .50 1.25
182 Antawn Jamison .40 1.00
183 Steve Francis .40 1.00
184 Eddie Griffin .25 .60
185 Jonathan Bender .25 .60
186 Reggie Miller .75 2.00
187 Elton Brand .30 .75
188 Marco Jaric .40 1.00
189 Kobe Bryant 3.00 8.00
190 Shaquille O'Neal 1.50 4.00
191 Jason Williams .50 1.25
192 Stromile Swift .25 .60
193 Alonzo Mourning .60 1.50
194 Malik Allen .25 .60
195 Sam Cassell .30 .75
196 Ray Allen .60 1.50
197 Wally Szczerbiak .30 .75
197B Vince Carter Promo 1.00 2.50
198 Jason Kidd .60 1.50
199 Kenyon Martin .40 1.00
200 Courtney Alexander .25 .60
201 Baron Davis .40 1.00
202 Allan Houston .40 1.00
203 Grant Hill .60 1.50
204 Aaron McKie .30 .75
205 Keith Van Horn .30 .75
206 Shawn Marion .40 1.00
207 Joe Johnson .30 .75
208 Scottie Pippen 1.00 2.50
209 Rasheed Wallace .50 1.25
210 Peja Stojakovic .30 .75
211 Hedo Turkoglu .30 .75
212 Tony Parker .60 1.50
213 Tim Duncan 1.00 2.50
214 Gary Payton .60 1.50
215 Desmond Mason .30 .75
216 Vince Carter .75 2.00
217 Karl Malone .75 2.00
218 Andrei Kirilenko .30 .75
219 Jerry Stackhouse .30 .75
220 Michael Jordan 8.00 20.00
221 DerMarr Johnson .25 .60
222 Kedrick Brown .25 .60
223 Eddy Curry .25 .60
224 Tyson Chandler .40 1.00
225 Darius Miles .25 .60
226 Wang ZhiZhi .40 1.00
227 James Posey .25 .60
228 Ben Wallace .50 1.25
229 Jason Richardson .40 1.00
230 Gilbert Arenas .40 1.00
231 Eddie Griffin .25 .60
232 Jermaine O'Neal .30 .75
233 Quentin Richardson .25 .60
234 Devean George .25 .60
235 Shane Battier .40 1.00
236 Pau Gasol .60 1.50
237 Eddie House .25 .60
238 Michael Redd .30 .75
239 Troy Hudson .25 .60
240 Richard Jefferson .30 .75
241 Jamal Magloire .25 .60
242 Mike Miller .30 .75
243 Joe Johnson .30 .75
244 Ruben Patterson .25 .60
245 Gerald Wallace .30 .75
246 Tony Parker .60 1.50
247 Rashard Lewis .30 .75
248 Morris Peterson .30 .75
249 Andrei Kirilenko .30 .75
250 Kwame Brown .25 .60
251 Jason Terry .30 .75
252 Paul Pierce .60 1.50
253 Darius Miles .25 .60
254 Steve Nash .75 2.00
255 Cuttino Mobley .25 .60
256 Jamaal Tinsley .25 .60
257 Andre Miller .30 .75
258 Shaquille O'Neal 1.50 4.00
259 Kobe Bryant 3.00 8.00
260 Kevin Garnett 1.00 2.50
261 Kenyon Martin .40 1.00
262 Latrell Sprewell .40 1.00
263 Tracy McGrady .60 1.50
264 Allen Iverson 1.00 2.50
265 Shawn Marion .40 1.00
266 Bonzi Wells .25 .60
267 Mike Bibby .40 1.00
268 Tim Duncan 1.00 2.50
269 Vince Carter .75 2.00
270 Michael Jordan 4.00 10.00
271 Ming/Williams/Dunlvy RC 2.00 5.00
272 Ginobili/Prince/Giricek RC 2.00 5.00
273 Jeffries RC/Williams RC/Pargo RC .30 .75
274 Wilcox RC/Dixon RC/Baxter RC .30 .75
275 Wagnr RC/Dickau RC/Ginbili RC 2.00 5.00
276 Ely RC/Jefferies RC/Maddox RC .30 .75
277 Evans RC/Brmer RC/Williams RC .30 .75
278 Butler RC/Haislip RC/Hmphry RC .40 1.00
279 Archbld RC/Burke RC/Huffmn RC .25 .60
280 Goodn/Amare/Woods RC 1.00 2.50
281 Nachbr RC/Welsch RC/Savovic RC .30 .75
282 Borchrdt RC/Jacobsn RC/Gadzu RC .30 .75
283 Clancy RC/Okur RC/Sampson RC .40 1.00
284 Prince/Rush/Salmons RC .75 2.00
285 Ming/Tskitishvili/Hilario RC 2.00 5.00
286 Wagner RC/Woods RC/Slay RC .30 .75
287 Ely RC/Haislip RC/Jones RC .30 .75
288 Butler/Ginobili/Haislip RC 2.00 5.00
289 Mason RC/Yrbrogh RC/Dickau RC .30 .75
290 Murray RC/Owens RC/Parker RC .40 1.00
291 Butler RC/Pargo RC/Giricek RC .40 1.00
292 Goodn RC/Tskitsh RC/Wagnr RC .40 1.00
293 Hilario/Wilcox/Amare RC 1.00 2.50
294 Jay Will RC/Hmphry RC/Woods RC .30 .75
295 Ming/Stoudemire/Rush RC 2.00 5.00
296 Tskitshvili RC/Butler RC/Dixon RC .40 1.00
297 Wilcox RC/Jones RC/Nachbar RC .30 .75
298 Dunlvy RC/Hilario RC/Jacobsn RC .40 1.00
299 Jeffries RC/Dixon RC/Gooden RC .40 1.00
300 Boozer RC/Jay Will RC/Dunlvy RC .40 1.00
PROMO Caron Butler PROMO 1.00 2.50

2002-03 Fleer Tradition Crystal

*CRYSTAL: 3X TO 8X BASE CARD HI
PRINT RUN 199 SERIAL #'d SETS
189 Kobe Bryant 40.00 100.00
220 Michael Jordan 125.00 300.00
259 Kobe Bryant 40.00 100.00
270 Michael Jordan 125.00 300.00

2002-03 Fleer Tradition All-Stars

COMPLETE SET (10) 8.00 20.00
STATED ODDS 1:20
*SNEAK ED: 5X TO 12X ALL-STARS HI
SNEAK ED.PRINT RUN 50 SER.#'d SETS
1 Vince Carter 1.25 3.00
2 Tim Duncan 1.50 4.00
3 Tracy McGrady 1.00 2.50
4 Michael Jordan 6.00 15.00
5 Shaquille O'Neal 2.50 6.00
6 Pau Gasol 1.00 2.50
7 Kevin Garnett 1.50 4.00
8 Kobe Bryant 5.00 12.00
9 Jason Richardson .60 1.50
10 Dirk Nowitzki 1.50 4.00

2002-03 Fleer Tradition Heads Up

COMPLETE SET (10) 4.00 10.00
STATED ODDS 1:10
1 Baron Davis .60 1.50
2 Jason Terry .50 1.25
3 Ben Wallace .75 2.00
4 Paul Pierce 1.00 2.50
5 Bonzi Wells .40 1.00
6 Allen Iverson 1.50 4.00
7 Vince Carter 1.25 3.00
8 Quentin Richardson .40 1.00
9 Eddy Curry .40 1.00
10 Darius Miles .40 1.00

2002-03 Fleer Tradition Heads Up Game-Used

PRINT RUN UP TO 100 SETS/PLAYER
AI Allen Iverson 15.00 40.00
BW Bonzi Wells 4.00 10.00
BW Ben Wallace 8.00 20.00
DM Darius Miles 4.00 10.00
EC Eddy Curry 4.00 10.00
JT Jason Terry 5.00 12.00
PP Paul Pierce 10.00 25.00
QR Quentin Richardson 4.00 10.00

2002-03 Fleer Tradition Playground Rules

COMPLETE SET (30) 15.00 40.00
STATED ODDS 1:8
1 Yao Ming 3.00 8.00
2 Fred Jones .50 1.25
3 Ryan Humphrey .50 1.25
4 Drew Gooden .60 1.50
5 Nikoloz Tskitishvili .40 1.00
6 Caron Butler .60 1.50
7 DaJuan Wagner .50 1.25
8 Nene Hilario .60 1.50
9 Qyntel Woods .40 1.00
10 Jared Jeffries .50 1.25
11 Casey Jacobsen .50 1.25
12 Marcus Haislip .40 1.00
13 Kareem Rush .50 1.25
14 Melvin Ely .50 1.25
15 Steve Logan .60 1.50
16 Amare Stoudemire 1.50 4.00
17 John Salmons .60 1.50
18 Chris Jefferies .40 1.00
19 Juan Dixon .50 1.25
20 Carlos Boozer .60 1.50
21 Roger Mason .50 1.25
22 Manu Ginobili 3.00 8.00
23 Tayshaun Prince 1.25 3.00
24 Chris Wilcox .50 1.25
25 Bostjan Nachbar .50 1.25
26 Jiri Welsch .50 1.25
27 Dan Dickau .40 1.00
28 Jay Williams .50 1.25
29 Mike Dunleavy .60 1.50
30 Frank Williams .40 1.00

2002-03 Fleer Tradition Road to the NBA

COMPLETE SET (10) 8.00 20.00
STATED ODDS 1:40
1 Jerry Stackhouse 1.00 2.50
2 Rasheed Wallace 1.25 3.00
3 Allen Iverson 2.50 6.00
4 Kevin Garnett 2.50 6.00
5 Shawn Marion 1.00 2.50
6 Chris Webber 1.25 3.00
7 Glenn Robinson 1.00 2.50
8 Antawn Jamison .75 2.00
9 Dirk Nowitzki 2.50 6.00
10 Vince Carter 2.00 5.00

2002-03 Fleer Tradition Road to the NBA Game-Used

STATED ODDS 1:240
RTN1 Jerry Stackhouse 4.00 10.00
RTN3 Allen Iverson 10.00 25.00
RTN4 Kevin Garnett 10.00 25.00
RTN5 Shawn Marion 4.00 10.00
RTN6 Chris Webber 5.00 12.00
RTN7 Glenn Robinson 4.00 10.00
RTN8 Antawn Jamison 3.00 8.00
RTN9 Dirk Nowitzki 10.00 25.00
RTN10 Vince Carter 8.00 20.00

2002-03 Fleer Tradition School Ties

COMPLETE SET (10) 8.00 20.00
STATED ODDS 1:20
1 J.Stockton/D.Dickau 1.25 3.00
2 A.McDyess/L.Sprewell 1.25 3.00
3 M.Miller/J.Williams 1.00 2.50
4 K.Van Horn/A.Miller 1.00 2.50
5 J.Kidd/S.Abdur-Rahim 1.25 3.00
6 R.Jefferson/Terry/Bibby 1.00 2.50
7 Carter/Jordan/J.Stack 4.00 10.00
8 Rose/Howard/Webber 2.50 6.00
9 Mutmbo/Mourning/A.I. 1.25 3.00
10 Brand/G.Hill/S.Battier 1.00 2.50

2002-03 Fleer Tradition School Ties Game-Used Dual or Triple

CARDS LISTED W/BASE INSERT #SCHEME
PRINT RUN 100 SERIAL #'d SETS
ST1 Stocktn JSY/Dicku Shorts 10.00 25.00
ST3 Miller Shorts/Williams Jkt 6.00 15.00
ST4 V.Horn Pants/Miller Shorts 4.00 10.00
ST5 Kidd Shorts/A-Rahim JSY 8.00 20.00
ST6 Jeff.Jkt/Terry Jkt/Bibb Pnts 5.00 12.00
ST7 Carter Jkt/MJ/Stack Pants 15.00 40.00
ST8 Rose JSY/Hwrd/Web.Pants 6.00 15.00
ST9 Mtmbo.Jkt/Zo.JSY/AI.Shorts 12.00 30.00
ST10 Brnd Shts/Hill JSY/Bttier Jkt 8.00 20.00

2002-03 Fleer Tradition School Ties Game-Used Singles

CARDS LISTED W/BASE INSERT #SCHEME
STATED ODDS 1:23
ST1A Stockton JSY/Dickau 4.00 10.00
ST1B Stockton/Dickau Shorts 3.00 8.00
ST3A Miller Shorts/Williams 3.00 8.00
ST3B Miller/Williams Jacket 3.00 8.00
ST4A K.V.Horn Pants/A.Miller 3.00 8.00
ST4B K.V.Horn/A.Miller Shorts 3.00 8.00
ST5A Kidd Shorts/S.A-Rahim 5.00 12.00
ST5B Kidd/S.A-Rahim JSY 3.00 8.00
ST6A Jeffersn Jkt/Terry/Bibby 3.00 8.00
ST6B Jefferson/Terry Jkt/Bibby 3.00 8.00
ST6C Jefferson/Terry/Bibby Pnts 3.00 8.00
ST7A Carter Jacket/MJ/Stack 5.00 12.00
ST7B Carter/MJ/Stack Pants 4.00 10.00
ST8A Rose JSY/Howrd/Webb 3.00 8.00
ST8B Rose/Howrd/Webb Pnts 3.00 8.00
ST9A Mutombo Jkt/ZO/A.I. 3.00 8.00
ST9B Mutom./Mourn JSY/A.I. 4.00 10.00
ST9C Mutom./Mourn./A.I. Short 5.00 12.00
ST10A Brand Shorts/Hill/Battier 3.00 8.00
ST10B Brand/Hill JSY/Battier 4.00 10.00
ST10C Brand/Hill/Battier Jacket 3.00 8.00

2003-04 Fleer Tradition

COMP.SET w/o RC's (260) 15.00 40.00
221-260 SUBSETS SAME VALUE AS BASE
261-290 RC STATED ODDS 1:3
291-300 TRIPLE STATED ODDS 1:18
1 Shareef Abdur-Rahim .25 .60
2 Vince Carter .50 1.25
3 Kevin Garnett .60 1.50
4 Bobby Jackson .20 .50
5 Courtney Alexander .15 .40
6 Tracy McGrady .40 1.00
7 Paul Pierce .40 1.00
8 Sam Cassell .20 .50
9 Maurice Taylor .15 .40
10 Pat Garrity .15 .40
11 Casey Jacobsen .15 .40
12 Malik Allen .15 .40
13 Aaron McKie .15 .40
14 Tyson Chandler .20 .50
15 Scottie Pippen .60 1.50
16 Jason Terry .15 .40
17 Pau Gasol .40 1.00
18 Antawn Jamison .25 .60
19 Stanislav Medvedenko .15 .40
20 Ray Allen .40 1.00
21 James Posey .15 .40
22 Calbert Cheaney .15 .40
23 Devean George .15 .40
24 Tim Thomas .15 .40
25 Marko Jaric .15 .40
26 Ron Mercer .15 .40
27 Rafer Alston .15 .40
28 Tayshaun Prince .25 .60
29 Doug Christie .20 .50
30 Kendall Gill .25 .60
31 Kurt Thomas .15 .40
32 Richard Jefferson .20 .50
33 Darius Miles .20 .50
34 Kenny Anderson .20 .50
35 Keon Clark .15 .40
36 Vladimir Radmanovic .15 .40
37 Kenny Thomas .15 .40
38 Manu Ginobili .50 1.25
39 Jared Jeffries .15 .40
40 Brad Miller .20 .50
41 Derek Anderson .20 .50
42 Zach Randolph .25 .60
43 Speedy Claxton .15 .40
44 Jamaal Tinsley .15 .40
45 Gordan Giricek .15 .40
46 Joe Johnson .20 .50
47 Mike Miller .20 .50
48 Shandon Anderson .15 .40
49 Theo Ratliff .15 .40
50 Derrick Coleman .25 .60
51 Dion Glover .15 .40
52 Nikoloz Tskitishvili .15 .40
53 Jumaine Jones .15 .40
54 Gilbert Arenas .25 .60
55 Reggie Miller .50 1.25
56 Michael Redd .15 .40
57 Jason Collins .15 .40
58 Drew Gooden .20 .50
59 Hedo Turkoglu .20 .50
60 Eddie Jones .25 .60
61 Andre Miller .20 .50
62 Darrell Armstrong .15 .40
63 Glen Rice .15 .40
64 Jarron Collins .15 .40
65 Nick Van Exel .25 .60
66 Brian Grant .15 .40
67 Shawn Kemp .25 .60
68 Yao Ming .60 1.50
69 Ron Artest .25 .60
70 Jamal Crawford .25 .60
71 Jason Richardson .25 .60
72 Eddie Griffin .15 .40
73 Keith Van Horn .20 .50
74 Jason Kidd .40 1.00
75 Cuttino Mobley .15 .40
76 Brent Barry .15 .40
77 Eddy Curry .15 .40
78 Quentin Richardson .15 .40
79 Dajuan Wagner .15 .40
80 Tom Gugliotta .15 .40
81 Andrei Kirilenko .20 .50
82 Shane Battier .20 .50
83 Alonzo Mourning .30 .75
84 Clifford Robinson .15 .40
85 Erick Dampier .15 .40
86 Antoine Walker .25 .60
87 Marcus Haislip .15 .40
88 Kerry Kittles .20 .50
89 Lonny Baxter .15 .40
90 Troy Murphy .20 .50
91 Glenn Robinson .20 .50
92 Ricky Davis .20 .50
93 Richard Hamilton .20 .50
94 Ben Wallace .30 .75
95 Toni Kukoc .25 .60
96 Raja Bell .20 .50
97 Dikembe Mutombo .30 .75
98 Eddie Robinson .15 .40
99 Antonio Davis .15 .40
100 Anfernee Hardaway .60 1.50
101 Rasheed Wallace .30 .75
102 Christian Laettner .15 .40
103 Eduardo Najera .15 .40
104 Jonathan Bender .15 .40
105 Rodney Rogers .15 .40
106 Baron Davis .25 .60
107 Chris Webber .30 .75
108 Matt Harpring .15 .40
109 Raef LaFrentz .15 .40
110 Steve Nash .50 1.25
111 Travis Best .15 .40
112 Tony Delk .15 .40
113 Malik Rose .20 .50
114 Al Harrington .20 .50
115 Bonzi Wells .15 .40
116 Voshon Lenard .15 .40
117 Radoslav Nesterovic .15 .40
118 Mike Bibby .25 .60
119 Dan Dickau .15 .40
120 Jalen Rose .15 .40
121 Lucious Harris .15 .40
122 David Wesley .15 .40
123 Rashard Lewis .20 .50
124 Ira Newble .15 .40
125 Chauncey Billups .30 .75
126 Kareem Rush .15 .40
127 Michael Dickerson .15 .40
128 Walt Williams .15 .40
129 Donnell Harvey .15 .40
130 Tyronn Lue .15 .40
131 Carlos Boozer .20 .50
132 Moochie Norris .15 .40
133 John Salmons .20 .50
134 Vlade Divac .20 .50
135 Shammond Williams .15 .40
136 Brendan Haywood .15 .40
137 George Lynch .15 .40
138 Dirk Nowitzki .60 1.50
139 Bruce Bowen .20 .50
140 Brian Skinner .15 .40
141 Juan Dixon .15 .40
142 Eric Williams .15 .40
143 Grant Hill .30 .75
144 Corey Maggette .20 .50
145 Earl Boykins .15 .40
146 Lamar Odom .20 .50
147 Keyon Dooling .15 .40
148 Joe Smith .20 .50
149 Corliss Williamson .15 .40
150 Robert Horry .25 .60
151 Jamaal Magloire .15 .40
152 Mehmet Okur .20 .50
153 Elton Brand .20 .50
154 Steve Smith .20 .50
155 Predrag Drobnjak .15 .40
156 Allan Houston .25 .60
157 Jerome Williams .15 .40
158 Karl Malone .50 1.25
159 Michael Olowokandi .15 .40
160 Terrell Brandon .15 .40
161 Eric Snow .15 .40
162 Tim Duncan .60 1.50
163 Juwan Howard .20 .50
164 Jason Williams .40 1.00
165 Stephon Marbury .30 .75
166 J.R. Bremer .15 .40
167 Shaquille O'Neal 1.00 2.50
168 Mike Dunleavy .20 .50
169 Latrell Sprewell .30 .75
170 Troy Hudson .15 .40
171 Alvin Williams .15 .40
172 Shawn Marion .25 .60
173 Jermaine O'Neal .25 .60
174 P.J. Brown .15 .40
175 Howard Eisley .15 .40
176 Jerry Stackhouse .30 .75
177 Qyntel Woods .15 .40
178 Larry Hughes .20 .50
179 Donyell Marshall .15 .40
180 Greg Ostertag .15 .40
181 Kwame Brown .15 .40
182 Reggie Evans .15 .40
183 DeShawn Stevenson .15 .40
184 Lorenzen Wright .15 .40
185 Lindsey Hunter .15 .40
186 Kenyon Martin .25 .60
187 Kobe Bryant 2.00 5.00
188 Scott Padgett .15 .40
189 Michael Finley .25 .60
190 Peja Stojakovic .20 .50
191 Zydrunas Ilgauskas .20 .50
192 Vincent Yarbrough .15 .40
193 Jamal Mashburn .20 .50
194 Smush Parker .15 .40
195 Caron Butler .20 .50
196 Derek Fisher .25 .60
197 Damon Stoudamire .20 .50
198 Nene Hilario .20 .50
199 Allen Iverson .60 1.50
200 Anthony Mason .15 .40
201 Rasual Butler .15 .40
202 Tony Parker .40 1.00
203 Marcus Fizer .15 .40
204 Amare Stoudemire .30 .75
205 Marc Jackson .15 .40
206 Desmond Mason .15 .40
207 Marcus Camby .20 .50
208 Ruben Patterson .15 .40
209 Bob Sura .15 .40
210 Rick Fox .20 .50
211 Jim Jackson .15 .40
212 Walter McCarty .15 .40
213 Gary Payton .40 1.00
214 Elden Campbell .15 .40
215 Steve Francis .25 .60
216 Stromile Swift .15 .40
217 Stephen Jackson .20 .50
218 Antonio McDyess .20 .50
219 Morris Peterson .15 .40
220 Wally Szczerbiak .20 .50
221 Tim Duncan AW .60 1.50
222 Amare Stoudemire AW .30 .75
223 Bobby Jackson AW .20 .50
224 Ben Wallace AW .30 .75
225 Gilbert Arenas AW .25 .60
226 Tracy McGrady AW .40 1.00
227 Kobe Bryant AW 2.00 5.00
228 Kevin Garnett AW .60 1.50
229 Shaquille O'Neal AW 1.00 2.50
230 Yao Ming AW .60 1.50
231 Stephon Marbury BS .30 .75
232 Ron Artest BS .25 .60
233 Troy Hudson BS .15 .40
234 Ray Allen BS .40 1.00
235 Matt Harpring BS .15 .40
236 Jermaine O'Neal BS .25 .60
237 Jason Kidd BS .40 1.00
238 Jason Williams BS .40 1.00
239 Zydrunas Ilgauskas BS .20 .50
240 Jamal Mashburn BS .20 .50
241 Yao Ming BS .60 1.50
242 Peja Stojakovic BS .20 .50
243 Tony Parker BS .40 1.00
244 Caron Butler BS .20 .50
245 Amare Stoudemire BS .30 .75
246 Troy Murphy BS .15 .40
247 Nene Hilario BS .20 .50
248 Allen Iverson BS .60 1.50
249 Kobe Bryant BS 2.00 5.00
250 Tim Duncan BS .60 1.50
251 Tracy McGrady BS .40 1.00
252 Kevin Garnett BS .60 1.50
253 Drew Gooden BS .25 .60
254 Kenyon Martin BS .25 .60
255 Dirk Nowitzki BS .60 1.50
256 Paul Pierce BS .40 1.00
257 Steve Francis BS .25 .60
258 Steve Nash BS .50 1.25
259 Gary Payton BS .40 1.00
260 Chris Webber BS .30 .75
261 LeBron James RC 100.00 250.00
262 Darko Milicic RC .50 1.25
263 Carmelo Anthony RC 3.00 8.00
264 Chris Bosh RC 2.00 5.00
265 Dwyane Wade RC 5.00 12.00
266 Chris Kaman RC .60 1.50
267 Kirk Hinrich RC .60 1.50
268 T.J. Ford RC .50 1.25
269 Mike Sweetney RC .40 1.00
270 Mickael Pietrus RC .50 1.25
271 Jarvis Hayes RC .40 1.00
272 Nick Collison RC .50 1.25
273 Marcus Banks RC .40 1.00
274 Luke Ridnour RC .60 1.50
275 Reece Gaines RC .40 1.00
276 Troy Bell RC .40 1.00
277 Zarko Cabarkapa RC .40 1.00
278 David West RC .75 2.00
279 Luke Walton RC .60 1.50
280 Dahntay Jones RC .50 1.25
281 Boris Diaw RC .60 1.50
282 Zoran Planinic RC .40 1.00
283 Travis Outlaw RC .50 1.25
284 Brian Cook RC .40 1.00
285 Jason Kapono RC .40 1.00
286 Ndudi Ebi RC .40 1.00
287 Kendrick Perkins RC .50 1.25
288 Leandro Barbosa RC .60 1.50
289 Josh Howard RC .60 1.50
290 Maciej Lampe RC .40 1.00
291 James/Darko/Melo 75.00 200.00
292 Sweetney/Bosh/Hayes 1.50 4.00
293 Hinrich/Collison/Kaman 1.25 3.00
294 Sweetney/West/Cook 1.25 3.00
295 Kaman/Bosh/Darko 1.50 4.00
296 Ford/Wade/Hinrich 2.50 6.00
297 Pietrus/Jones/Gaines 1.25 3.00
298 Ford/Banks/Ridnour 1.25 3.00
299 Pietrus/Zarko/Hayes 1.25 3.00
300 LeBron/Melo/Wade 125.00 300.00

2003-04 Fleer Tradition Crystal

*CRYSTAL SINGLES: 6X TO 15X BASE HI
1-260 PRINT RUN 175 SERIAL #'d SETS
*CRYSTAL RC's: 3X TO 8X BASE CARD HI
261-290 PRINT RUN 125 SERIAL #'d SETS
*CRYSTAL TRIPLE: 4X TO 10X BASE HI
291-300 PRINT RUN 50 SERIAL #'d SETS
261 LeBron James 2,500.00 5,000.00
265 Dwyane Wade 300.00 600.00
300 James/Melo/Wade 5,000.00 10,000.00

2003-04 Fleer Tradition Draft Day Rookie

*261-290 DRAFT DAY: 1.5X TO 4X BASE HI
*291-300 DRAFT DAY: .75X TO 2X BASE HI
DRAFT DAY CARDS ARE #'s 261-300
STATED PRINT RUN 375 SERIAL #'d SETS
261 LeBron James 800.00 1,500.00
265 Dwyane Wade 125.00 300.00

2003-04 Fleer Tradition Heads Up

COMPLETE SET (10) 4.00 10.00
STATED ODDS 1:12
1 Kwame Brown .60 1.50
2 Scottie Pippen 2.50 6.00
3 Tim Thomas .60 1.50
4 Stephen Jackson .75 2.00
5 Allen Iverson 2.50 6.00
6 Richard Hamilton 1.25 3.00
7 Jermaine O'Neal 1.00 2.50
8 Elton Brand .75 2.00
9 Antoine Walker 1.00 2.50
10 Drew Gooden .75 2.00

2003-04 Fleer Tradition Heads Up Game Used

PRINT RUN LISTED IN CHECKLIST
HUCA Carmelo Anthony/50 40.00 100.00
HUCB Chris Bosh/55 25.00 60.00
HUDW Dwyane Wade/65 60.00 150.00
HUKB Kwame Brown/40 8.00 20.00
HULR Luke Ridnour/55 8.00 20.00
HUMB Marcus Banks/50 5.00 12.00
HUMP Mickael Pietrus/50 6.00 15.00
HURG Reece Gaines/55 5.00 12.00
HUTB Troy Bell 5.00 12.00
HUTT Tim Thomas/60 8.00 20.00

2003-04 Fleer Tradition Milestones

COMPLETE SET (10) 15.00 40.00
STATED ODDS 1:144
1 Karl Malone 3.00 8.00
2 Kobe Bryant 12.00 30.00
3 Paul Pierce 2.50 6.00
4 Tracy McGrady 2.50 6.00
5 Kevin Garnett 4.00 10.00
6 Allen Iverson 4.00 10.00
7 Tim Duncan 4.00 10.00
8 Shaquille O'Neal 6.00 15.00
9 Vince Carter 3.00 8.00
10 Chris Webber 2.00 5.00

2003-04 Fleer Tradition Playground Rules

COMPLETE SET (20) 15.00 40.00
STATED ODDS 1:6
1 LeBron James 30.00 80.00
2 Darko Milicic .50 1.25
3 Carmelo Anthony 3.00 8.00
4 Chris Bosh 2.00 5.00
5 Dwyane Wade 5.00 12.00
6 Chris Kaman .60 1.50
7 Kirk Hinrich .60 1.50
8 T.J. Ford .50 1.25
9 Mike Sweetney .40 1.00
10 Jarvis Hayes .40 1.00
11 Mickael Pietrus .50 1.25
12 Nick Collison .50 1.25
13 Marcus Banks .40 1.00
14 Luke Ridnour .60 1.50
15 Reece Gaines .40 1.00
16 Troy Bell .40 1.00
17 Zarko Cabarkapa .40 1.00
18 David West .75 2.00
19 Travis Outlaw .50 1.25
20 Dahntay Jones .50 1.25

2003-04 Fleer Tradition Rookie Hats Off

PRINT RUN 180 SER.#'d SETS
RHOCA Carmelo Anthony 25.00 60.00
RHOCB Chris Bosh 15.00 40.00
RHOCK Chris Kaman 5.00 12.00

RHODJ Dahntay Jones 4.00 10.00
RHODW Dwyane Wade 40.00 100.00
RHOJH Jarvis Hayes 3.00 8.00
RHOMJ Maciej Lampe 3.00 8.00
RHOMS Mike Sweetney 3.00 8.00
RHORG Reece Gaines 3.00 8.00
RHOSV Slavko Vranes 3.00 8.00
RHOZC Zarko Cabarkapa 3.00 8.00
RHOZP Zoran Planinic 3.00 8.00

2003-04 Fleer Tradition Throwback Threads

COMPLETE SET (10) 8.00 20.00
STATED ODDS 1:36
1 Carmelo Anthony 5.00 12.00
2 Luke Walton 1.00 2.50
3 Chris Kaman 1.00 2.50
4 Travis Outlaw .75 2.00
5 Kirk Hinrich 1.00 2.50
6 T.J. Ford .75 2.00
7 Brian Cook .60 1.50
8 Jarvis Hayes .60 1.50
9 Mickael Pietrus .75 2.00
10 Nick Collison .75 2.00

2003-04 Fleer Tradition Throwback Threads Event Worn

*COMBO: 1.25X TO 3X BASE JSY HI
COMBO PRINT RUN 150 SETS
BC Brian Cook 1.50 4.00
CA Carmelo Anthony 12.00 30.00
CK Chris Kaman 2.50 6.00
DW David West 3.00 8.00
JH Jarvis Hayes 1.50 4.00
LR Luke Ridnour 2.50 6.00
LW Luke Walton 2.50 6.00
MB Marcus Banks 1.50 4.00
MP Mickael Pietrus 2.00 5.00
MS Mike Sweetney 1.50 4.00
TO Travis Outlaw 2.00 5.00

2003-04 Fleer Tradition Throwback Threads Dual Event Worn

PRINT RUN 299 SERIAL #'d SETS
BCCK B.Cook/C.Kaman 5.00 12.00
CADW C.Anthony/D.West 8.00 20.00
LWTO L.Walton/T.Outlaw 5.00 12.00
MPJH M.Pietrus/J.Hayes 5.00 12.00
MSMB M.Sweetney/M.Banks 5.00 12.00

2003-04 Fleer Tradition All-Star Game

COMPLETE SET (13) 20.00 50.00
ANNCD PRINT RUN OF 2004 COPIES PER
1 Carmelo Anthony 8.00 20.00
2 Luke Walton 1.50 4.00
3 Jason Kidd 2.50 6.00
4 Allen Iverson 4.00 10.00
5 Tracy McGrady 2.50 6.00
6 Steve Francis 1.50 4.00
7 Kevin Garnett 4.00 10.00
8 Chris Kaman 1.50 4.00
9 Shaquille O'Neal 6.00 15.00
10 Dwyane Wade 12.00 30.00
11 Yao Ming 4.00 10.00
12 Amara Stoudemire 2.00 5.00
13 Vince Carter 3.00 8.00

2004-05 Fleer Tradition

COMP.SET w/o RC's (220) 20.00 50.00
RC STATED ODDS 1:4
TRIO STATED ODDS 1:18
*BLUE: .6X TO 1.5X BASE HI
*GREEN: .75X TO 2X BASE HI
1 Jonathan Bender .25 .60
2 Boris Diaw .30 .75
3 Eddie Robinson .25 .60
4 Jason Richardson .40 1.00
5 Bonzi Wells .25 .60
6 Elden Campbell .25 .60
7 P.J. Brown .25 .60
8 Ray Allen .60 1.50
9 Theron Smith .25 .60
10 Darko Milicic .25 .60
11 Bob Sura .25 .60
12 Sam Cassell .30 .75
13 Cuttino Mobley .30 .75
14 Andrei Kirilenko .30 .75
15 Raef LaFrentz .25 .60
16 Aleksandar Pavlovic .25 .60
17 Carmelo Anthony .75 2.00
18 Mickael Pietrus .25 .60
19 James Posey .30 .75
20 Nazr Mohammed .25 .60
21 Jalen Rose .30 .75
22 Jiri Welsch .25 .60
23 Drew Gooden .25 .60
24 Nene .30 .75
25 Troy Murphy .25 .60
26 Mike Miller .30 .75
27 T.J. Ford .25 .60
28 Allan Houston .40 1.00
29 Donyell Marshall .25 .60
30 Chris Crawford .25 .60
31 Eric Snow .25 .60
32 Marcus Camby .30 .75
33 Devean George .25 .60
34 Eric Williams .25 .60
35 Kurt Thomas .25 .60
36 Rashard Lewis .30 .75
37 Alvin Williams .25 .60
38 David West .30 .75
39 Shawn Marion .40 1.00
40 Mark Blount .25 .60
41 Dikembe Mutombo .40 1.00
42 Stephen Jackson .30 .75
43 Rasual Butler .25 .60
44 Michael Redd .30 .75
45 Jason Kidd .60 1.50
46 Malik Rose .25 .60
47 Chris Bosh .60 1.50
48 Antonio Daniels .25 .60
49 Doug Christie .30 .75
50 Stephon Marbury .50 1.25
51 Gary Payton .60 1.50
52 Michael Finley .40 1.00
53 Ben Wallace .50 1.25
54 Jason Williams .30 .75
55 Michael Olowokandi .25 .60
56 Steve Francis .40 1.00
57 Chris Webber .50 1.25
58 Tim Duncan 1.00 2.50
59 Carlos Arroyo .25 .60
60 Eddie House .25 .60
61 Mike Bibby .40 1.00
62 Tony Parker .60 1.50
63 Matt Harpring .25 .60
64 Richard Hamilton .50 1.25
65 Corey Maggette .30 .75
66 Damon Jones .25 .60
67 Keith Bogans .25 .60
68 Willie Green .40 1.00
69 Kirk Hinrich .40 1.00
70 Jerry Stackhouse .40 1.00
71 Chris Kaman .30 .75
72 Lamar Odom .40 1.00
73 Dwyane Wade 1.50 4.00
74 Kevin Garnett 1.00 2.50
75 Allen Iverson 1.00 2.50
76 Theo Ratliff .25 .60
77 Shareef Abdur-Rahim .40 1.00
78 Gilbert Arenas .40 1.00
79 Jamal Sampson .25 .60
80 Josh Howard .30 .75
81 Latrell Sprewell .50 1.25
82 Kyle Korver .30 .75
83 Brad Miller .30 .75
84 Rasho Nesterovic .25 .60
85 Larry Hughes .30 .75
86 Eddy Curry .25 .60
87 Rasheed Wallace .50 1.25
88 Chris Wilcox .25 .60
89 Mark Madsen .25 .60
90 Kenny Thomas .25 .60
91 Zach Randolph .40 1.00
92 Juan Dixon .25 .60
93 Tyson Chandler .30 .75
94 Stromile Swift .25 .60
95 Udonis Haslem .25 .60
96 Jason Collins .25 .60
97 Glenn Robinson .30 .75
98 Darius Miles .25 .60
99 Jared Jeffries .25 .60
100 Bobby Jackson .30 .75
101 Jahidi White .25 .60
102 Dirk Nowitzki 1.00 2.50
103 Wally Szczerbiak .30 .75
104 John Salmons .30 .75
105 Kwame Brown .25 .60
106 Jason Kapono .25 .60
107 Chauncey Billups .50 1.25
108 Shane Battier .30 .75
109 Samuel Dalembert .25 .60
110 Manu Ginobili .75 2.00
111 Anfernee Hardaway 1.00 2.50
112 Yao Ming 1.00 2.50
113 Eric Piatkowski .25 .60
114 Vlade Divac .40 1.00
115 Ron Mercer .25 .60
116 Quentin Richardson .25 .60
117 Derek Anderson .25 .60
118 Jarvis Hayes .25 .60
119 Antonio Davis .25 .60
120 Erick Dampier .25 .60
121 Antonio McDyess .30 .75
122 Fred Jones .25 .60
123 Damon Stoudamire .40 1.00
124 Jason Collier .25 .60
125 Frank Williams .25 .60
126 Kobe Bryant 3.00 8.00
127 Keith Van Horn .30 .75
128 Darrell Armstrong .25 .60
129 Steve Nash .75 2.00
130 Nick Collison .25 .60
131 Ricky Davis .30 .75
132 Tracy McGrady .60 1.50
133 Shaquille O'Neal 1.50 4.00
134 Desmond Mason .25 .60
135 Richard Jefferson .30 .75
136 Casey Jacobsen .25 .60
137 Ronald Murray .25 .60
138 Rafer Alston .25 .60
139 Tony Delk .25 .60
140 LeBron James 3.00 8.00
141 Earl Boykins .25 .60
142 Speedy Claxton .25 .60
143 Jamaal Tinsley .25 .60
144 Elton Brand .30 .75
145 Jamaal Magloire .25 .60
146 Jamal Crawford .40 1.00
147 Peja Stojakovic .30 .75
148 Bruce Bowen .30 .75
149 Paul Pierce .60 1.50
150 Jason Terry .30 .75
151 Kenyon Martin .40 1.00
152 Maurice Taylor .25 .60
153 Toni Kukoc .40 1.00
154 Aaron Williams .25 .60
155 Tony Battie .25 .60
156 Leandro Barbosa .30 .75
157 Carlos Boozer .30 .75
158 Brevin Knight .25 .60
159 Marquis Daniels .25 .60
160 Jim Jackson .30 .75
161 Caron Butler .30 .75
162 Troy Hudson .25 .60
163 DeShawn Stevenson .25 .60
164 Nick Van Exel .40 1.00
165 Antawn Jamison .40 1.00
166 Marcus Banks .25 .60
167 Derek Fisher .30 .75
168 Juwan Howard .30 .75
169 Reggie Miller .75 2.00
170 Joe Smith .25 .60
171 Alonzo Mourning .50 1.25
172 Mike Sweetney .25 .60
173 Mehmet Okur .30 .75
174 Brent Barry .25 .60
175 Al Harrington .30 .75
176 Dajuan Wagner .25 .60
177 Voshon Lenard .25 .60
178 Jermaine O'Neal .30 .75
179 Bobby Simmons .25 .60
180 Karl Malone .75 2.00
181 Dan Gadzuric .25 .60
182 David Wesley .25 .60
183 Tim Thomas .25 .60
184 Amare Stoudemire .40 1.00
185 Morris Peterson .25 .60
186 Fred Hoiberg .25 .60
187 Jeff McInnis .40 1.00
188 Andre Miller .30 .75
189 Mike Dunleavy .25 .60
190 Ron Artest .40 1.00
191 Kerry Kittles .30 .75
192 Baron Davis .40 1.00
193 Vince Carter .75 2.00
194 Gerald Wallace .30 .75
195 Tayshaun Prince .40 1.00
196 Marko Jaric .25 .60
197 Luke Walton .30 .75
198 Eddie Jones .40 1.00
199 Hedo Turkoglu .30 .75
200 Joe Johnson .30 .75
201 Vladimir Radmanovic .25 .60
202 Gordan Giricek .25 .60
203 Antoine Walker .40 1.00
204 Zydrunas Ilgauskas .30 .75
205 Clifford Robinson .25 .60
206 Pau Gasol .60 1.50
207 Jamal Mashburn .30 .75
208 Luke Ridnour .30 .75
209 Kevin Garnett AW 1.00 2.50
210 LeBron James AW 3.00 8.00
211 Jason Kidd AW .60 1.50
212 Kobe Bryant AW 3.00 8.00
213 Shaquille O'Neal AW 1.50 4.00
214 Tim Duncan AW 1.00 2.50
215 Ron Artest AW .40 1.00
216 Dwyane Wade AW 1.50 4.00
217 Kirk Hinrich AW .40 1.00
218 Chris Bosh AW .60 1.50
219 Carmelo Anthony AW .75 2.00
220 Antawn Jamison AW .30 .75
221 Dwight Howard RC 2.50 6.00
222 Emeka Okafor RC .60 1.50
223 Ben Gordon RC .75 2.00
224 Shaun Livingston RC .75 2.00
225 Devin Harris RC .60 1.50
226 Josh Childress RC .60 1.50
227 Luol Deng RC .75 2.00
228 Rafael Araujo RC .50 1.25
229 Andre Iguodala RC 1.25 3.00
230 Luke Jackson RC .50 1.25
231 Andris Biedrins RC .50 1.25
232 Robert Swift RC .50 1.25
233 Sebastian Telfair RC .60 1.50
234 Kris Humphries RC .60 1.50
235 Al Jefferson RC .75 2.00
236 Kirk Snyder RC .50 1.25
237 Josh Smith RC .75 2.00
238 J.R. Smith RC .75 2.00
239 Dorell Wright RC .60 1.50
240 Jameer Nelson RC .75 2.00
241 Pavel Podkolzine RC .50 1.25
242 Nenad Krstic RC .60 1.50
243 Andres Nocioni RC .75 2.00
244 Delonte West RC .60 1.50
245 Tony Allen RC .75 2.00
246 Kevin Martin RC 1.00 2.50
247 Sasha Vujacic RC .60 1.50
248 Beno Udrih RC .60 1.50
249 David Harrison RC .50 1.25
250 Anderson Varejao RC .60 1.50
251 Okafor/Gordon/Howard 3.00 8.00
252 Howard/Kasun RC/Nelson 3.00 8.00
253 Allen/Jefferson/West 1.00 2.50
254 Deng/Duhon/Gordon 1.00 2.50
255 Nocioni/Martin/Telfair 1.25 3.00
256 Childress/Ivey RC/Smith 1.00 2.50
257 Harris/Nelson/Telfair 1.00 2.50
258 Chlmrs RC/Burks RC/Emm RC .75 2.00
259 Deng/Duhon RC/Pickett RC 1.00 2.50
260 Childress/Jackson/Iguodala 1.50 4.00
261 Livingston/Howard/Swift 3.00 8.00
262 Smith/Jefferson/Telfair 1.00 2.50
263 Livingston/Wright/Smith 1.00 2.50
264 Reed RC/Vroman RC/Ramos RC .60 1.50
265 Podkolzin/Biedrins/Krstic .75 2.00
266 Vujacic/Tabuse RC/Udrih 1.00 2.50
267 Araujo/Humphries/Snyder .75 2.00
268 Robinson RC/Sow RC/Ariza RC 1.00 2.50

2004-05 Fleer Tradition Crystal

*CRYSTAL STARS: 2X TO 5X BASE HI
*CRYSTAL AW: 1.5X TO 4X BASE HI
PRINT RUN 150 SER.#'d SETS
*CRYSTAL RCs: 2X TO 5X BASE HI
*CRYSTAL TRIO: 3X TO 8X BASE HI
TRIO PRINT RUN 25 SETS
126 Kobe Bryant 12.00 30.00
140 LeBron James 125.00 300.00
210 LeBron James AW 100.00 250.00
212 Kobe Bryant AW 12.00 30.00

2004-05 Fleer Tradition Draft Day Rookies

*221-250 DRAFT: 1X TO 2.5X BASE HI
*251-268 DRAFT TRIO: .1X TO 2.5X BASE HI
PRINT RUN 375 SER.#'d SETS

2004-05 Fleer Tradition Classic Combinations

PRINT RUN 250 SER.#'d SETS
1 S.O'Neal/D.Wade 5.00 12.00
2 C.Anthony/K.Martin 2.50 6.00
3 K.Bryant/L.Odom 4.00 10.00
4 Y.Ming/T.McGrady 3.00 8.00
5 A.Houston/S.Marbury 1.50 4.00
6 S.Francis/D.Howard 4.00 10.00
7 K.Hinrich/B.Gordon 1.25 3.00
8 E.Brand/C.Maggette 1.00 2.50
9 P.Pierce/G.Payton 2.00 5.00
10 A.Iverson/A.Iguodala 3.00 8.00
11 L.James/L.Jackson 4.00 10.00
12 B.Davis/J.R.Smith 1.25 3.00
13 D.Nowitzki/D.Harris 3.00 8.00
14 A.Kirilenko/C.Boozer 1.00 2.50
15 B.Wallace/R.Wallace 1.50 4.00
16 R.Miller/J.O'Neal 2.50 6.00
17 A.Stoudemire/S.Nash 2.50 6.00
18 K.Garnett/L.Sprewell 3.00 8.00
19 J.Kidd/R.Jefferson 2.00 5.00
20 T.Duncan/M.Ginobili 3.00 8.00

2004-05 Fleer Tradition Hardcourt Tributes

COMPLETE SET (20) 12.50 30.00
STATED ODDS 1:6
1 Allen Iverson 1.50 4.00
2 Jason Kidd 1.00 2.50
3 Dwyane Wade 2.50 6.00
4 Kenyon Martin .60 1.50
5 Pau Gasol 1.00 2.50
6 Carmelo Anthony 1.25 3.00
7 Paul Pierce 1.00 2.50
8 Tracy McGrady 1.00 2.50
9 Shaquille O'Neal 2.50 6.00
10 Stephon Marbury .75 2.00
11 Steve Francis .60 1.50
12 Yao Ming 1.50 4.00
13 Peja Stojakovic .50 1.25
14 Kevin Garnett 1.50 4.00
15 Tim Duncan 1.50 4.00
16 Dirk Nowitzki 1.50 4.00
17 Vince Carter 1.25 3.00
18 Jason Richardson .60 1.50
19 Kobe Bryant 5.00 12.00
20 LeBron James 5.00 12.00

2004-05 Fleer Tradition Hardcourt Tributes Jerseys

STATED ODDS 1:102 H, 1:192 R
*PATCHES: 1X TO 2.5X BASE HI
PATCH PRINT RUN 50 SER.#'d SETS
1 Allen Iverson 6.00 15.00
2 Jason Kidd 4.00 10.00
3 Dwyane Wade 10.00 25.00
4 Kenyon Martin 2.50 6.00
5 Pau Gasol 4.00 10.00
6 Carmelo Anthony 5.00 12.00
7 Paul Pierce 4.00 10.00
8 Tracy McGrady 4.00 10.00
9 Shaquille O'Neal 10.00 25.00
10 Stephon Marbury 3.00 8.00
11 Steve Francis 3.00 8.00
12 Yao Ming 6.00 15.00
13 Peja Stojakovic 2.00 5.00
14 Kevin Garnett 6.00 15.00
15 Tim Duncan 6.00 15.00
16 Dirk Nowitzki 6.00 15.00
17 Vince Carter 5.00 12.00
18 Jason Richardson 2.50 6.00
19 Amare Stoudemire 2.50 6.00
20 Ben Wallace 3.00 8.00

2004-05 Fleer Tradition Rookie Hats Off

PRINT RUN 100 SER.#'d SETS
1 Dwight Howard 20.00 50.00
2 Ben Gordon 6.00 15.00
3 Shaun Livingston 6.00 15.00
4 Devin Harris 5.00 12.00
5 Josh Childress 4.00 10.00
6 Luol Deng 6.00 15.00
7 Rafael Araujo 4.00 10.00
8 Andre Iguodala 10.00 25.00
9 Andris Biedrins 4.00 10.00
10 Kirk Snyder 4.00 10.00
11 Josh Smith 6.00 15.00
12 Jameer Nelson 6.00 15.00
13 Pavel Podkolzin 4.00 10.00
14 Viktor Khryapa 4.00 10.00
15 Beno Udrih 5.00 12.00

2004-05 Fleer Tradition Rookie Throwback Threads Jerseys

STATED ODDS 1:112 H, 1:240 R
*BALL: .5X TO 1.25X BASE HI
BALL STATED ODDS 1:216 H 1:480 R
*HEADBAND: 1.25X TO 3X BASE HI
HEADBAND STATED ODDS 1:612 H, 1:960 R
*JERSEY/BALL: 1.5X TO 4X BASE HI
JERSEY/BALL PRINT RUN 50 SER.#'d SETS
*JSY/HEADBAND: 2X TO 5X BASE HI
JSY/HEADBAND PRINT RUN 25 SETS
1 Dwight Howard 8.00 20.00
2 Ben Gordon 2.50 6.00
3 Shaun Livingston 2.50 6.00
4 Devin Harris 2.00 5.00
5 Josh Childress 1.50 4.00
6 Luol Deng 2.50 6.00
7 Andre Iguodala 4.00 10.00
8 Rafael Araujo 1.50 4.00
9 Luke Jackson 1.50 4.00
10 Sebastian Telfair 2.00 5.00
11 Kris Humphries 2.00 5.00
12 Al Jefferson 2.50 6.00
13 Kirk Snyder 1.50 4.00
14 Josh Smith 2.50 6.00
15 J.R. Smith 2.50 6.00
16 Dorell Wright 2.00 5.00
17 Jameer Nelson 2.50 6.00
18 Delonte West 2.00 5.00
19 Tony Allen 2.50 6.00
20 Anderson Varejao 2.00 5.00
21 Lionel Chalmers 2.00 5.00
22 Chris Duhon 2.00 5.00
23 Bernard Robinson 1.50 4.00
24 Trevor Ariza 2.50 6.00

2004-05 Fleer Tradition Rookie Throwback Threads Dual

PRINT RUN 100 SER.#'d SETS
*PATCHES: .6X TO 1.5X BASE HI
PATCH PRINT RUN 75 SER.#'d SETS
1 B.Gordon/L.Deng 6.00 15.00
2 D.Howard/J.Nelson 8.00 20.00
3 J.Childress/J.Smith 6.00 15.00
4 A.Jefferson/T.Allen 5.00 12.00
5 S.Livingston/L.Chalmers 5.00 12.00
6 A.Iguodala/T.Ariza 8.00 20.00
7 K.Humphries/K.Snyder 5.00 12.00
8 D.Harris/C.Duhon 6.00 15.00
10 A.Varejao/B.Robinson 5.00 12.00
11 R.Araujo/L.Jackson 5.00 12.00
12 J.Nelson/D.West 5.00 12.00

2004-05 Fleer Tradition Signing Day

COMPLETE SET (15) 10.00 25.00
STATED ODDS 1:24 RETAIL
*CHROME: 1.25X TO 3X BASE HI
CHROME PRINT RUN 50 SER.#'d SETS
1 Dwight Howard 2.50 6.00
2 Emeka Okafor .60 1.50
3 Ben Gordon .75 2.00
4 Shaun Livingston .75 2.00
5 Devin Harris .60 1.50
6 Josh Childress .50 1.25
7 Luol Deng .75 2.00
8 Andre Iguodala 1.25 3.00
9 Luke Jackson .50 1.25
10 Andris Biedrins .50 1.25
11 Robert Swift .50 1.25
12 Sebastian Telfair .60 1.50
13 Josh Smith .75 2.00
14 J.R. Smith .75 2.00
15 Jameer Nelson .75 2.00

2004-05 Fleer Tradition USA Basketball

PRINT RUN 99 SER.#'d SETS
1 LeBron James 400.00 800.00
2 Carmelo Anthony 40.00 100.00
3 Tim Duncan 40.00 100.00
4 Shawn Marion 5.00 12.00
5 Allen Iverson 40.00 100.00
6 Dwyane Wade 40.00 100.00
7 Amare Stoudemire 5.00 12.00
8 Richard Jefferson 4.00 10.00
9 Stephon Marbury 15.00 40.00
10 Carlos Boozer 4.00 10.00
11 Lamar Odom 5.00 12.00
12 Emeka Okafor 4.00 10.00
13 Larry Brown 25.00 60.00

2000-01 Fleer Triple Crown

COMPLETE SET w/o RC (200) 15.00 40.00
RC SUBSET: STATED ODDS 1:4
1 Quentin Richardson RC .30 .75
2 Khalid El-Amin RC .25 .60
3 Courtney Alexander RC .25 .60
4 Mike Penberthy RC .40 1.00
5 DerMarr Johnson RC .25 .60
6 A.J. Guyton RC .25 .60
7 Erick Barkley RC .25 .60
8 Jamal Crawford RC 1.00 2.50
9 Hedo Turkoglu RC .60 1.50
10 Michael Redd RC 1.00 2.50
11 Stromile Swift RC .30 .75
12 Eddie House RC .30 .75
13 Keyon Dooling RC .30 .75
14 Lavor Postell RC .25 .60
15 Mateen Cleaves RC .30 .75
16 Morris Peterson RC .40 1.00
17 DeShawn Stevenson RC .40 1.00
18 Darius Miles RC .40 1.00
19 Hanno Mottola RC .25 .60
20 Jerome Moiso RC .25 .60
21 Desmond Mason RC .50 1.25
22 Jason Collier RC .40 1.00
23 Ruben Wolkowyski RC .25 .60
24 Eduardo Najera RC .40 1.00
25 Kenyon Martin RC .75 2.00
26 Marcus Fizer RC .30 .75
27 Etan Thomas RC .30 .75
28 Mark Madsen RC .40 1.00
29 Pepe Sanchez RC .30 .75
30 Brian Cardinal RC .25 .60
31 Chris Porter RC .25 .60
32 Dan Langhi RC .25 .60
33 Mike Miller RC .60 1.50
34 Chris Mihm RC .25 .60
35 Mamadou N'Diaye RC .25 .60
36 Dragan Tarlac RC .25 .60
37 Iakovos Tsakalidis RC .25 .60
38 Stephen Jackson RC .75 2.00
39 Jamaal Magloire RC .40 1.00
40 Joel Przybilla RC .30 .75
41 Adrian Griffin .25 .60
42 Allan Houston .40 1.00
43 Mahmoud Abdul-Rauf .25 .60
44 Avery Johnson .30 .75
45 Damon Stoudamire .40 1.00
46 Jim Jackson .30 .75
47 Jason Williams .60 1.50
48 Jason Kidd .60 1.50
49 Ray Allen .60 1.50
50 Baron Davis .40 1.00
51 Mark Jackson .30 .75
52 Darrick Martin .25 .60
53 Derek Fisher .40 1.00
54 Anthony Peeler .25 .60
55 Vince Carter .75 2.00
56 Tim Hardaway .50 1.25
57 Richard Hamilton .50 1.25
58 Malik Rose .25 .60
59 Antonio Daniels .25 .60
60 Lindsey Hunter .25 .60
61 William Avery .25 .60
62 Reggie Miller .75 2.00
63 Shareef Abdur-Rahim .40 1.00
64 Travis Best .25 .60
65 John Stockton .75 2.00
66 Kenny Anderson .30 .75
67 Trajan Langdon .25 .60
68 Sam Cassell .30 .75
69 Chucky Atkins .25 .60
70 Laron Profit .25 .60
71 Andre Miller .30 .75
72 Erick Strickland .25 .60
73 Ron Artest .40 1.00
74 Kobe Bryant 3.00 8.00
75 Ricky Davis .30 .75
76 Allen Iverson 1.00 2.50
77 Steve Smith .40 1.00
78 Alvin Williams .25 .60
79 Randy Brown .25 .60
80 Michael Dickerson .25 .60
81 Tyronn Lue .25 .60
82 Bonzi Wells .25 .60
83 Felipe Lopez .25 .60
84 Steve Francis .40 1.00
85 Jaren Jackson .25 .60
86 Anthony Carter .25 .60
87 Mitch Richmond .50 1.25
88 Sherman Douglas .25 .60
89 Cuttino Mobley .30 .75
90 Mario Elie .25 .60
91 Tariq Abdul-Wahad .25 .60
92 Ron Mercer .30 .75
93 Jalen Rose .30 .75
94 Mike Bibby .40 1.00
95 Voshon Lenard .25 .60
96 Derek Anderson .30 .75
97 Kendall Gill .40 1.00
98 Muggsy Bogues .40 1.00
99 Eddie Jones .40 1.00
100 Larry Hughes .40 1.00
101 Latrell Sprewell .50 1.25
102 Stephon Marbury .50 1.25
103 Eric Piatkowski .25 .60
104 Brevin Knight .25 .60
105 Isaiah Rider .30 .75
106 Wesley Person .25 .60
107 Nick Van Exel .40 1.00
108 Dell Curry .25 .60
109 Tony Delk .25 .60
110 Glen Rice .40 1.00
111 Bobby Jackson .30 .75
112 Kerry Kittles .30 .75
113 John Starks .40 1.00
114 Gary Payton .60 1.50
115 Mookie Blaylock .40 1.00
116 David Wesley .30 .75
117 Rod Strickland .25 .60
118 Terrell Brandon .30 .75
119 Steve Nash .60 1.50
120 Moochie Norris .25 .60
121 Eric Snow .25 .60
122 Chauncey Billups .50 1.25
123 Darrell Armstrong .25 .60
124 Ron Harper .40 1.00
125 Dion Glover .25 .60
126 Vin Baker .30 .75
127 Terry Mills .25 .60
128 Joe Smith .30 .75
129 Kurt Thomas .25 .60
130 Dirk Nowitzki 1.00 2.50
131 Sean Elliott .30 .75
132 Jerome Williams .25 .60
133 Larry Johnson .50 1.25
134 LaPhonso Ellis .30 .75
135 Pat Garrity .25 .60
136 Lawrence Funderburke .25 .60
137 Elton Brand .40 1.00
138 Rashard Lewis .30 .75
139 Shawn Kemp .60 1.50
140 Elden Campbell .25 .60
141 Christian Laettner .40 1.00
142 Al Harrington .30 .75
143 Billy Owens .25 .60
144 Wally Szczerbiak .30 .75
145 Jonathan Bender .25 .60
146 Karl Malone .75 2.00
147 Andrew DeClercq .25 .60
148 Danny Manning .25 .60
149 Antoine Walker .40 1.00
150 Jason Caffey .25 .60
151 P.J. Brown .25 .60
152 Matt Harpring .25 .60
153 Mark Strickland .25 .60
154 Theo Ratliff .25 .60
155 Ruben Patterson .25 .60
156 Tom Gugliotta .30 .75
157 Derrick Coleman .40 1.00
158 Lorenzen Wright .25 .60
159 Tracy McGrady .75 2.00
160 Quincy Lewis .25 .60
161 Tony Battie .25 .60
162 Keith Van Horn .30 .75
163 Paul Pierce .60 1.50
164 Glenn Robinson .25 .60
165 John Wallace .25 .60
166 Popeye Jones .25 .60
167 Kevin Garnett 1.00 2.50
168 Donyell Marshall .30 .75
169 Michael Finley .40 1.00
170 Nick Anderson .30 .75
171 Danny Fortson .30 .75
172 Keon Clark .30 .75
173 Juwan Howard .30 .75
174 Brian Grant .30 .75
175 Marcus Camby .30 .75
176 Scottie Pippen 1.00 2.50
177 Shawn Marion .40 1.00
178 Lamar Odom .40 1.00
179 Charles Oakley .40 1.00
180 Tim James .25 .60
181 Eric Williams .25 .60
182 Tim Duncan 1.00 2.50
183 Andrae Patterson .25 .60
184 Toni Kukoc .50 1.25
185 Chris Mullin .50 1.25
186 Alan Henderson .25 .60
187 Maurice Taylor .25 .60
188 Chris Webber .50 1.25
189 Jamal Mashburn .30 .75
190 Rodney Rogers .25 .60
191 Loy Vaught .25 .60
192 Carlos Rogers .25 .60
193 Grant Hill .60 1.50
194 George Lynch .25 .60
195 Antonio McDyess .30 .75
196 Tim Thomas .25 .60
197 Roshown McLeod .25 .60
198 Antawn Jamison .40 1.00
199 Clifford Robinson .40 1.00
200 Corey Maggette .30 .75
201 Horace Grant .40 1.00
202 David Benoit .25 .60
203 Cedric Ceballos .30 .75
204 Antonio Davis .25 .60
205 Lamond Murray .25 .60
206 Jerry Stackhouse .40 1.00
207 Jermaine O'Neal .30 .75
208 Anthony Mason .40 1.00
209 Cedric Henderson .25 .60
210 Corliss Williamson .25 .60
211 Austin Croshere .25 .60
212 Radoslav Nesterovic .25 .60
213 Hakeem Olajuwon .75 2.00
214 Nazr Mohammed .25 .60
215 David Robinson .75 2.00
216 Jeff McInnis .25 .60
217 Brad Miller .30 .75
218 Evan Eschmeyer .25 .60
219 Jelani McCoy .25 .60
220 Sean Rooks .25 .60
221 Dikembe Mutombo .60 1.50
222 Othella Harrington .25 .60
223 Jim Amaechi .25 .60
224 Erick Dampier .25 .60
225 Calvin Booth .25 .60
226 Adonal Foyle .25 .60
227 Michael Doleac .25 .60
228 Michael Olowokandi .25 .60
229 Matt Geiger .25 .60
230 Vlade Divac .40 1.00
231 Bryant Reeves .25 .60
232 Shaquille O'Neal 1.50 4.00
233 Todd Fuller .25 .60
234 Arvydas Sabonis .40 1.00
235 Jim McIlvaine .25 .60
236 Isaac Austin .25 .60
237 Raef LaFrentz .30 .75
238 Rasheed Wallace .50 1.25
239 Kelvin Cato .25 .60
240 Patrick Ewing .60 1.50
241 Marc Jackson RC .30 .75

2000-01 Fleer Triple Crown Vince Carter Rookie Remnants

NNO Vince Carter FLR/100 15.00 40.00
NNO Vince Carter FLR JSY/15 40.00 100.00

2000-01 Fleer Triple Crown Crown Jewels

COMPLETE SET (15) 75.00 200.00
STATED ODDS 1:84
1 Kevin Garnett 10.00 25.00
2 Lamar Odom 4.00 10.00
3 Allen Iverson 10.00 25.00
4 Marcus Fizer 3.00 8.00
5 Shaquille O'Neal 15.00 40.00
6 Steve Francis 4.00 10.00
7 Paul Pierce 6.00 15.00
8 Elton Brand 4.00 10.00
9 Chris Webber 5.00 12.00
10 Tim Duncan 10.00 25.00
11 Kobe Bryant 60.00 150.00
12 Grant Hill 6.00 15.00
13 Kenyon Martin 8.00 20.00
14 Darius Miles 4.00 10.00
15 Vince Carter 8.00 20.00

2000-01 Fleer Triple Crown Heir Force 01

COMPLETE SET (15) 10.00 20.00
STATED ODDS 1:10
1 Kenyon Martin 1.25 3.00
2 Stromile Swift .50 1.25
3 Darius Miles .60 1.50
4 Courtney Alexander .40 1.00
5 Marcus Fizer .50 1.25
6 Keyon Dooling .50 1.25
7 Steve Francis .60 1.50
8 Elton Brand .60 1.50
9 Lamar Odom .60 1.50
10 Wally Szczerbiak .50 1.25
11 Vince Carter 1.25 3.00
12 Anawn Jamison .60 1.50
13 Jason Williams 1.00 2.50
14 Tim Duncan 1.50 4.00
15 Kobe Bryant 5.00 12.00

2000-01 Fleer Triple Crown Scoring Kings

STATED PRINT RUN 100 SERIAL #'d SETS
1 Vince Carter 15.00 40.00
2 Shaquille O'Neal 75.00 200.00
3 Allen Iverson 40.00 100.00
4 Grant Hill 12.00 30.00
5 Chris Webber 10.00 25.00
6 Glenn Robinson 8.00 20.00
7 Lamar Odom 8.00 20.00
8 Gary Payton 12.00 30.00
9 Eddie Jones 8.00 20.00
10 Latrell Sprewell 10.00 25.00

2000-01 Fleer Triple Crown Scoring Menace

COMPLETE SET (10) 7.50 15.00
STATED ODDS 1:24
1 Vince Carter 1.50 4.00
2 Shaquille O'Neal 3.00 8.00
3 Allen Iverson 2.00 5.00
4 Grant Hill 1.25 3.00
5 Chris Webber 1.00 2.50
6 Glenn Robinson .75 2.00
7 Lamar Odom .75 2.00
8 Gary Payton 1.25 3.00
9 Eddie Jones .75 2.00
10 Latrell Sprewell 1.00 2.50

2000-01 Fleer Triple Crown Shoot Arounds

STATED ODDS 1:72
1 Vince Carter 6.00 15.00
2 Keyon Dooling 2.50 6.00
3 Grant Hill 5.00 12.00
4 Allen Iverson 8.00 20.00
5 Jason Kidd 5.00 12.00
6 Shawn Marion 3.00 8.00
7 Tracy McGrady 6.00 15.00
8 Chris Mihm 2.00 5.00
9 Darius Miles 3.00 8.00
10 Andre Miller 2.50 6.00
11 Mike Miller 5.00 12.00
12 Hanno Mottola 2.00 5.00
13 Lamar Odom 3.00 8.00
14 Quentin Richardson 2.50 6.00
15 John Stockton 6.00 15.00

2000-01 Fleer Triple Crown Triple Threats

COMPLETE SET (15) 5.00 12.00
STATED ODDS 1:5
1 Vince Carter 1.00 2.50
2 Jason Kidd .75 2.00
3 Gary Payton .75 2.00
4 Scottie Pippen 1.25 3.00
5 Hakeem Olajuwon 1.00 2.50
6 Kevin Garnett 1.25 3.00

7 Steve Francis .50 1.25
8 Antoine Walker .50 1.25
9 Andre Miller .40 1.00
10 Chris Webber .60 1.50
11 Lamar Odom .50 1.25
12 Tim Duncan 1.25 3.00
13 Grant Hill .75 2.00
14 David Robinson 1.00 2.50
15 Michael Finley .50 1.25

2000 Fleer Tuff Stuff Vince Carter

NNO Vince Carter 1.25 3.00

1996 Fleer USA

COMPLETE SET (52) 20.00 50.00
1 Anfernee Hardaway IB 1.00 2.50
2 Grant Hill IB 1.00 2.50
3 Karl Malone IB .75 2.00
4 Reggie Miller IB 1.00 2.50
5 Hakeem Olajuwon IB .75 2.00
6 Shaquille O'Neal IB 1.50 4.00
7 Scottie Pippen IB 1.00 2.50
8 David Robinson IB 1.00 2.50
9 Glenn Robinson IB .50 1.25
10 John Stockton IB .75 2.00
11 Anfernee Hardaway BN .50 1.25
12 Grant Hill BN .50 1.25
13 Karl Malone BN .40 1.00
14 Reggie Miller BN .50 1.25
15 Hakeem Olajuwon BN .40 1.00
16 Shaquille O'Neal BN .75 2.00
17 Scottie Pippen BN .50 1.25
18 David Robinson BN .50 1.25
19 Glenn Robinson BN .25 .60
20 John Stockton BN .40 1.00
21 Anfernee Hardaway DM 1.00 2.50
22 Grant Hill DM 1.00 2.50
23 Karl Malone DM .75 2.00
24 Reggie Miller DM 1.00 2.50
25 Hakeem Olajuwon DM .75 2.00
26 Shaquille O'Neal DM 1.50 4.00
27 Scottie Pippen DM 1.00 2.50
28 David Robinson DM 1.00 2.50
29 Glenn Robinson DM .50 1.25
30 John Stockton DM .75 2.00
31 Anfernee Hardaway MAS .50 1.25
32 Grant Hill MAS .50 1.25
33 Karl Malone MAS .40 1.00
34 Reggie Miller MAS .50 1.25
35 Hakeem Olajuwon MAS .40 1.00
36 Shaquille O'Neal MAS .75 2.00
37 Scottie Pippen MAS .50 1.25
38 David Robinson MAS .50 1.25
39 Glenn Robinson MAS .25 .60
40 John Stockton MAS .40 1.00
41 Anfernee Hardaway AW 1.00 2.50
42 Grant Hill AW 1.00 2.50
43 Karl Malone AW .75 2.00
44 Reggie Miller AW 1.00 2.50
45 Hakeem Olajuwon AW .75 2.00
46 Shaquille O'Neal AW 1.50 4.00
47 Scottie Pippen AW 1.00 2.50
48 David Robinson AW 1.00 2.50
49 Glenn Robinson AW .50 1.25
50 John Stockton AW .75 2.00
51 Team USA CL 51/52 1.25 3.00
52 Team USA CL 1.25 3.00

1996 Fleer USA Heroes

COMPLETE SET (10) 40.00 100.00
1 Anfernee Hardaway 8.00 20.00
2 Grant Hill 8.00 20.00
3 Karl Malone 6.00 15.00
4 Reggie Miller 8.00 20.00
5 Hakeem Olajuwon 6.00 15.00
6 Shaquille O'Neal 12.00 30.00
7 Scottie Pippen 8.00 20.00
8 David Robinson 8.00 20.00
9 Glenn Robinson 4.00 10.00
10 John Stockton 6.00 15.00

1996 Fleer USA Wrapper Exchange

COMPLETE SET (12) 4.00 10.00
M1 Charles Barkley ITB 1.00 2.50
M2 Mitch Richmond ITB .60 1.50
M3 Charles Barkley BTN .50 1.25
M4 Mitch Richmond BTN .30 .75
M5 Charles Barkley ATW 1.00 2.50
M6 Mitch Richmond ATW .60 1.50
M7 Charles Barkley MAS .50 1.25
M8 Mitch Richmond MAS .30 .75
M9 Charles Barkley DM 1.00 2.50
M10 Mitch Richmond DM .60 1.50
M11 Charles Barkley Heroes 1.50 4.00
M12 Mitch Richmond Heroes 1.00 2.50

2001 Fleer Viva Vince Carter

1 Vince Carter 1.50 4.00

2001 Fleer WNBA

COMP.SET w/o RC (165) 20.00 50.00
1 Lisa Leslie 1.50 4.00
2 Andrea Stinson .60 1.50
3 Tammy Jackson .30 .75
4 Nicky McCrimmon RC .60 1.50
5 Vickie Johnson .50 1.25
6 Maria Stepanova .30 .75
7 Michelle Edwards .60 1.50
8 Tausha Mills .30 .75
9 Edwina Brown .40 1.00
10 Jurgita Streimikyte .30 .75
11 Keitha Dickerson RC .30 .75
12 Taj McWilliams-Franklin .30 .75
13 DeMya Walker .30 .75
14 Adrienne Goodson .30 .75
15 Eva Nemcova .50 1.25
16 Danielle McCulley RC .30 .75
17 Shannon Johnson .30 .75
18 Margo Dydek .50 1.25
19 Mery Andrade .30 .75
20 Marlies Askamp .30 .75
21 Adrain Williams .30 .75
22 Sonja Henning .30 .75
23 Astou Ndiaye-Diatta .50 1.25
24 Latasha Byears .50 1.25
25 Kate Paye RC .30 .75
26 Yolanda Griffith 1.00 2.50
27 Kate Starbird .50 1.25
28 Jennifer Rizzotti .75 2.00
29 Umeki Webb .30 .75
30 Tari Phillips .30 .75
31 Tully Bevilaqua RC .50 1.25
32 Murriel Page .40 1.00
33 Tricia Bader Binford .30 .75
34 Sheryl Swoopes 2.00 5.00
35 Debbie Black .50 1.25
36 Teresa Weatherspoon 1.25 3.00
37 Alisa Burras .30 .75
38 Stacey Lovelace RC .75 2.00
39 Helen Darling .40 1.00
40 Tina Thompson 1.00 2.50
41 Katrina Colleton .30 .75
42 Tamika Whitmore .30 .75
43 Sylvia Crawley .30 .75
44 Jamie Redd RC .30 .75
45 Tracy Reid .50 1.25
46 Janeth Arcain .30 .75
47 Stacy Frese RC .50 1.25
48 Grace Daley .30 .75
49 Bridget Pettis .30 .75
50 Katy Steding .30 .75
51 Beth Cunningham .30 .75
52 Vicki Hall RC .30 .75
53 Amaya Valdemoro .40 1.00
54 Milena Flores .30 .75
55 Sue Wicks .50 1.25
56 Michelle Marciniak .50 1.25
57 Tracy Henderson .30 .75
58 Kisha Ford .30 .75
59 Jannon Roland .30 .75
60 Vanessa Nygaard RC .30 .75
61 Pollyanna Johns RC .30 .75
62 Gordana Grubin .30 .75
63 Shantia Owens .30 .75
64 Cintia Dos Santos .30 .75
65 Lynn Pride .30 .75
66 Robin Threatt RC .30 .75
67 Claudia Maria das Neves RC .30 .75
68 Chantel Tremitiere .30 .75
69 Betty Lennox 1.00 2.50
70 Ruthie Bolton-Holifield 1.00 2.50
71 Korie Hlede .50 1.25
72 Dominique Canty .50 1.25
73 Alicia Thompson .30 .75
74 Kristin Folkl .50 1.25
75 Elaine Powell .30 .75
76 Cindy Blodgett .50 1.25
77 Charlotte Smith .30 .75
78 Mwadi Mabika .30 .75
79 Marina Ferragut RC .50 1.25
80 Brandy Reed .50 1.25
81 Quacy Barnes .30 .75
82 Chamique Holdsclaw 2.00 5.00
83 Dawn Staley .75 2.00
84 Nekeshia Henderson RC .30 .75
85 Rhonda Mapp .40 1.00
86 Becky Hammon 6.00 15.00
87 Edna Campbell .40 1.00
88 Nikki McCray .75 2.00
89 Anna DeForge .30 .75
90 Rita Williams .40 1.00
91 Andrea Lloyd Curry .30 .75
92 Nykesha Sales .50 1.25
93 Stacy Clinesmith RC .50 1.25
94 LaTonya Johnson .30 .75
95 Markita Aldridge .30 .75
96 Shalonda Enis .30 .75
97 Wendy Palmer .75 2.00
98 Tamecka Dixon .50 1.25
99 Katie Smith 1.00 2.50
100 Tonya Edwards .30 .75
101 Lady Hardmon .30 .75
102 Dalma Ivanyi .30 .75
103 Tiffany Travis RC .50 1.25
104 Tiffani Johnson RC .30 .75
105 DeLisha Milton .30 .75
106 Rebecca Lobo 1.00 2.50
107 Michele Timms 1.00 2.50
108 Andrea Garner RC .30 .75
109 Andrea Nagy .50 1.25
110 Summer Erb .30 .75
111 Ukari Figgs .30 .75
112 Jennifer Gillom .75 2.00
113 Kedra Holland-Corn .30 .75
114 Natalie Williams .60 1.50
115 Clarisse Machanguana .30 .75
116 E.C. Hill RC .30 .75
117 Lisa Harrison .50 1.25
118 Tangela Smith .30 .75
119 Vicky Bullett .30 .75
120 Ann Wauters .40 1.00
121 Marla Brumfield RC .30 .75
122 Carla McGhee .30 .75
123 Sophia Witherspoon .50 1.25
124 Tamicha Jackson .30 .75
125 Kara Wolters .40 1.00
126 Maylana Martin .40 1.00
127 Tiffany McCain RC .50 1.25
128 Naomi Mulitauaopele .30 .75
129 Chasity Melvin .30 .75
130 Stephanie McCarty .60 1.50
131 Sheri Sam .30 .75
132 Adrienne Johnson .50 1.25
133 Jennifer Azzi 1.00 2.50
134 Allison Feaster .40 1.00
135 Elena Tornikidou RC .30 .75
136 Sonja Tate .30 .75
137 Michelle Brogan RC .30 .75
138 Ticha Penicheiro .75 2.00
139 Keisha Anderson .30 .75
140 Merlakia Jones .50 1.25
141 Monica Maxwell .30 .75
142 Kristen Rasmussen RC .50 1.25
143 Stacey Thomas .30 .75
144 Kamila Vodichkova .30 .75
145 Angie Braziel .50 1.25
146 Olympia Scott-Richardson .30 .75
147 Vedrana Grgin RC .30 .75
148 Shanele Stires .30 .75
149 Coquese Washington .30 .75
150 Crystal Robinson .50 1.25
151 Texlan Quinney .30 .75
152 Michelle Cleary RC .30 .75
153 La'Keshia Frett .30 .75
154 Jessie Hicks .30 .75
155 Katrina Hibbert .30 .75
156 Cass Bauer .50 1.25
157 Jessica Bibby .30 .75
158 Shea Mahoney RC .30 .75
159 Charmin Smith .50 1.25
160 Oksana Zakaluzhnaya .30 .75
161 Tonya Washington .40 1.00
162 Rushia Brown .30 .75
163 Amy Herrig RC .30 .75
164 Tara Williams .30 .75
165 Sandy Brondello .75 2.00
166 Tammy Sutton-Brown RC 5.00 12.00
167 Kelly Miller RC 5.00 12.00
168 Penny Taylor RC 8.00 20.00
169 Kelly Santos RC 5.00 12.00
170 Deanna Nolan RC 5.00 12.00
171 Jae Kingi RC 5.00 12.00
172 Amanda Lassiter RC 5.00 12.00
173 Trisha Stafford-Odom RC 5.00 12.00
174 Tynesha Lewis RC 5.00 12.00
175 Tamika Catchings RC 60.00 150.00
176 Kelly Schumacher RC 5.00 12.00
177 Niele Ivey RC 5.00 12.00
178 Nicole Levandusky RC 5.00 12.00
179 Wendy Willits RC 5.00 12.00
180 Ruth Riley RC 6.00 15.00
181 Levys Torres RC 5.00 12.00
182 Janell Burse RC 5.00 12.00
183 Svetlana Abrosimova RC 5.00 12.00
184 Erin Buescher RC 5.00 12.00
185 Georgia Schweitzer RC 5.00 12.00
186 Camille Cooper RC 5.00 12.00
187 Brooke Wyckoff RC 8.00 20.00
188 Jaclyn Johnson RC 5.00 12.00
189 Tawona Alehaleem RC 5.00 12.00
190 Katie Douglas RC 8.00 20.00
191 Jaynetta Saunders RC 5.00 12.00
192 Kristen Veal RC 5.00 12.00
193 Jenny Mowe RC 5.00 12.00
194 Jackie Stiles RC 50.00 20.00
195 LaQuanda Barksdale RC 5.00 12.00
196 Lauren Jackson RC 50.00 20.00
197 Semeka Randall RC 5.00 12.00
198 Michaela Pavlickova RC 5.00 12.00
199 Marie Ferdinand RC 5.00 12.00
200 Shea Ralph RC 5.00 12.00
201 Cara Consuegra RC 5.00 12.00
202 Tamara Stocks RC 5.00 12.00
203 Coco Miller RC 5.00 12.00
204 Helen Luz RC 5.00 12.00

2001 Fleer WNBA Autographics

COMPLETE SET (6) 60.00 120.00
STATED ODDS 1:144
EXTRA PRINT RUN 50 SER.#'d SETS
1 Jennifer Azzi 6.00 15.00
2 Betty Lennox 6.00 15.00
3 Lisa Leslie 30.00 80.00
4 Katie Smith 6.00 15.00
6 Sheryl Swoopes 30.00 80.00
5 Natalie Williams 10.00 25.00

2001 Fleer WNBA Autographics Extra

*EXTRA: .75X TO 2X AUTOGRAPHICS HI

2001 Fleer WNBA Award Winners

COMPLETE SET (10) 10.00 25.00
AW1 Sheryl Swoopes 4.00 10.00
AW2 Natalie Williams 1.25 3.00
AW3 Lisa Leslie 3.00 8.00
AW4 Ticha Penicheiro 1.50 4.00
AW5 Tina Thompson 2.00 5.00
AW6 Katie Smith 2.00 5.00
AW7 Yolanda Griffith 2.00 5.00
AW8 Teresa Weatherspoon 2.50 6.00
AW9 Betty Lennox 2.00 5.00
AW10 Tari Phillips .60 1.50

2001 Fleer WNBA Global Game

COMPLETE SET (20) 10.00 25.00
GG1 Janeth Arcain .50 1.25
GG2 Marlies Askamp .50 1.25
GG3 Mery Andrade .50 1.25
GG4 Tully Bevilaqua .75 2.00
GG5 Margo Dydek .75 2.00
GG6 Gordana Grubin .50 1.25
GG7 Mwadi Mabika .50 1.25
GG8 Andrea Nagy .75 2.00
GG9 Astou Ndiaye-Diatta .75 2.00
GG10 Eva Nemcova .75 2.00
GG11 Ticha Penicheiro 1.25 3.00
GG12 Maria Stepanova .75 2.00
GG13 Michele Timms 1.50 4.00
GG14 Kamila Vodichkova .50 1.25
GG15 Ann Wauters .60 1.50
GG16 Yolanda Griffith 1.50 4.00
GG17 Chamique Holdsclaw 3.00 8.00
GG18 Katie Smith 1.50 4.00
GG19 Nikki McCray 1.25 3.00
GG20 Natalie Williams 1.00 2.50

2001 Fleer WNBA Starting Five

COMPLETE SET (15) 12.50 30.00
SF1 Vicky Bullett .75 2.00
SF2 Andrea Stinson 1.00 2.50
SF3 Merlakia Jones .75 2.00
SF4 Eva Nemcova .75 2.00
SF5 Janeth Arcain .50 1.25
SF6 Sheryl Swoopes 3.00 8.00
SF7 Tina Thompson 1.50 4.00
SF8 Lisa Leslie 2.50 6.00
SF9 Mwadi Mabika .50 1.25
SF10 Rebecca Lobo 1.50 4.00
SF11 Sue Wicks .75 2.00
SF12 Teresa Weatherspoon 2.00 5.00
SF13 Michele Timms 1.50 4.00
SF14 Marlies Askamp .50 1.25
SF15 Ruthie Bolton-Holifield 1.50 4.00

2001 Fleer WNBA Supreme Court

COMPLETE SET (10) 12.50 30.00
SC1 Chamique Holdsclaw 3.00 8.00
SC2 Natalie Williams 1.00 2.50
SC3 Betty Lennox 1.50 4.00
SC4 Yolanda Griffith 1.50 4.00
SC5 Sheryl Swoopes 3.00 8.00
SC6 Tina Thompson 1.50 4.00
SC7 Lisa Leslie 2.50 6.00
SC8 Jennifer Gillom 1.25 3.00
SC9 Ticha Penicheiro 1.25 3.00
SC10 Michele Timms 1.50 4.00

2001 Fleer Hersey WNBA

COMPLETE SET (12) 6.00 15.00
1 Chamique Holdsclaw 2.00 5.00
2 Sonja Henning .30 .75
3 Wendy Palmer .60 1.50
4 Brandy Reed .30 .75
5 Teresa Weatherspoon 1.00 2.50
6 Shannon Johnson .30 .75
7 Natalie Williams .60 1.50
8 Sophia Witherspoon .30 .75
9 Lisa Leslie 1.25 3.00
10 Katie Smith 1.00 2.50
11 Andrea Stinson .60 1.50
12 Kara Wolters .30 .75

1996-97 Fleer/SkyBox Jerry Stackhouse Sample

1 Jerry Stackhouse 1.25 3.00
2 Grant Hill Jumbo 4.00 10.00

1999 Fleer/SkyBox Dunkography

NNO Vince Carter
Lamar Odom 8.00 20.00

1971-72 Floridians McDonald's

COMPLETE SET (10) 300.00 600.00
1 Warren Armstrong 40.00 80.00
2 Mack Calvin 40.00 80.00
3 Ron Franz 30.00 60.00
4 Ira Harge 30.00 60.00
5 Larry Jones 30.00 60.00
6 Willie Long 30.00 60.00
7 Sam Robinson 30.00 60.00
8 Al Tucker 30.00 60.00
9 George Tinsley 30.00 60.00
10 Lonnie Wright 30.00 60.00

1985 Fournier Ases del Baloncesto

COMPLETE SET (33) 30.00 80.00
1a Juan A. Corbalan 1.25 3.00
1b Fernando Martin 1.25 3.00
1c Fernando Romay 1.25 3.00
1d Lopez Iturriaga 1.25 3.00
2a Jordi Freixanet 1.25 3.00
2b Joaquin Costa 1.25 3.00
2c Miguel Angel Pou 1.25 3.00
2d Inaki Garayalde 1.25 3.00
3a Pedro Rodriguez 1.25 3.00
3b David Russell 4.00 10.00
3c Fco. Javier Lafuente 1.25 3.00
3d Alberto Ortega 1.25 3.00
4a Oscar Pena 1.25 3.00
4b Jose A. Alonso 1.25 3.00
4c Joaquin Salvo 1.25 3.00
4d Albert Illa 1.25 3.00
5a Francisco J. Zapata 1.25 3.00
5b Claude Riley 1.25 3.00
5c Jose Luis Diaz 1.25 3.00
5d Herminio San Epifanio 1.25 3.00
6a Manuel Sanchez 1.25 3.00
6b Jimmy Wright 2.50 6.00
6c Suso Fernandez 1.25 3.00
6d Pepe Collins 1.25 3.00
7a Jose Maria Margall 1.25 3.00
7b Jordi Villacampa 1.25 3.00
7c Jose A. Montero 1.25 3.00
7d Andres Jimenez 1.25 3.00
8a J.A. San Epifanio 1.25 3.00
8b Chico Sibilio 1.25 3.00
8c Ignacio Solozabal 1.25 3.00
8d Arturo S. Seara 1.25 3.00
NNO Title Card 2.00 5.00

1988 Fournier NBA Estrellas

COMPLETE SET (33) 75.00 200.00
1 Larry Bird 3.00 8.00
2 Robert Parish 1.25 3.00
3 Kevin McHale 1.25 3.00
4 Magic Johnson 3.00 8.00
5 Kareem Abdul-Jabbar 3.00 8.00
6 Byron Scott 1.00 2.50
7 Isiah Thomas 3.00 8.00
8 Adrian Dantley 1.00 2.50
9 Dominique Wilkins 3.00 8.00
10 Spud Webb 1.00 2.50
11 Clyde Drexler 3.00 8.00
12 Terry Porter 1.00 2.50
13 Mark Aguirre 1.00 2.50
14 Muggsy Bogues 1.00 2.50
15 Patrick Ewing 3.00 8.00
16 Karl Malone 3.00 8.00
17 Charles Barkley 3.00 8.00
18 Ron Harper 1.00 2.50
19 Alex English 2.00 5.00
20 Xavier McDaniel 1.00 2.50
21 Jeff Malone 1.00 2.50
22 Michael Jordan 20.00 50.00
23 Hakeem Olajuwon 3.00 8.00
24 Ralph Sampson 1.00 2.50
25 Buck Williams 1.00 2.50
26 Chuck Person 1.00 2.50
27 Alvin Robertson 1.00 2.50
28 Tom Chambers 1.00 2.50
29 Paul Pressey 1.00 2.50
30 Danny Manning 1.25 3.00
31 LaSalle Thompson 1.00 2.50
32 John Stockton 3.00 8.00
NNO Michael Jordan Rules 40.00 100.00

1988 Fournier NBA Estrellas Stickers

COMPLETE SET (10) 300.00 500.00
1 Kareem Abdul-Jabbar 40.00 100.00
2 Mark Aguirre 30.00 80.00
3 Larry Bird DP 20.00 50.00
4 Magic Johnson DP 20.00 50.00
5 Michael Jordan DP 150.00 400.00
6 Moses Malone 25.00 60.00
7 Kevin McHale 30.00 80.00
8 Robert Parish 30.00 80.00
9 Isiah Thomas 30.00 80.00
10 James Worthy 30.00 80.00

1998 GE David Robinson Phone Cards

COMPLETE SET (5) 40.00 100.00
1 David Robinson 30 units 4.00 10.00
2 David Robinson 60 units 8.00 20.00
3 David Robinson 75 units 10.00 25.00
4 David Robinson 90 units 12.50 30.00
5 David Robinson 120 units 15.00 40.00

1971-72 Globetrotters Cocoa Puffs 28

COMPLETE SET (28) 90.00 180.00
1 Geese Ausbie and Curly Neal 8.00 20.00
2 Neal and Meadowlark 5.00 12.00
3 Meadowlark is Safe 4.00 10.00
4 Meadowlark Lemon Curly Neal and Geese Ausbie 3.00 8.00
5 Mel Davis and Bill Meggett 2.00 5.00
6 Geese Ausbie Meadowlark Lemon and Curly Neal 3.00 8.00
7 Geese Ausbie Meadowlark Lemon and Curly Neal 3.00 8.00
8 Mel Davis and Curly Neal 2.50 6.00
9 Meadowlark Lemon Curly Neal and Geese Ausbie 3.00 8.00
10 Curly Neal Meadowlark Lemon and Mel Davis 3.00 8.00
11 Football Routine 2.00 5.00
12 1970-71 Highlights 2.00 5.00
13 Pabs Robertson 2.00 5.00
14 Bobby Joe Mason 2.00 5.00
15 Pabs Robertson 2.00 5.00
16 Clarence Smith 2.00 5.00
17 Clarence Smith 2.00 5.00
18 Hubert (Geese) Ausbie 2.50 6.00
19 Hubert (Geese) Ausbie (Two balls) 2.50 6.00
20 Bobby Hunter 2.00 5.00
21 Bobby Hunter (One leg up) 2.00 5.00
22 Meadowlark Lemon (Three balls) 3.00 8.00
23 Meadowlark Lemon 4.00 10.00
24 Freddie (Curly) Neal 3.00 8.00
25 Freddie (Curly) Neal (Three paint brushes) 3.00 8.00
26 Meadowlark Lemon (Palming two balls) 4.00 10.00
27 Mel Davis (Leaning over with ball) 2.00 5.00
28 Freddie Curly Neal 7.50 15.00

1971-72 Globetrotters 84

COMPLETE SET (85) 75.00 150.00
1 Bob Showboat Hall 5.00 12.00
2 Bob Showboat Hall (kicking ball) .75 2.00
3 Bob Showboat Hall (passing behind back) .75 2.00
4 Pabs Robertson .75 2.00
5 Pabs Robertson .75 2.00
6 Pabs Robertson .75 2.00
7 Pabs Robertson .75 2.00
8 Pabs Robertson .75 2.00
9 Meadowlark Lemon (kicking behind back) 2.50 6.00
10 Meadowlark Lemon (rolling ball on arm) 2.50 6.00
11 Meadowlark Lemon (palming two balls) 2.50 6.00
12 Meadowlark Lemon (ball on neck) 2.50 6.00
13 Meadowlark Lemon (three balls) 2.50 6.00
14 Meadowlark Lemon (three balls in front) 2.50 6.00
15 Meadowlark Lemon (three balls) 2.50 6.00
16 Meadowlark Lemon (dribbling two balls) 2.50 6.00
17 Meadowlark Lemon (with cap) 2.50 6.00
18 Curley Neal Meadowlark Lemon and Mel Davis 2.50 6.00
19 Football Play (Meadowlark centering) 2.50 6.00
20 Meadowlark Lemon (hooking) 2.50 6.00
21 Hubert Geese Ausbie (balls between legs) 1.00 2.50
22 Hubert Geese Ausbie (ball under arm) 1.00 2.50
23 Hubert Geese Ausbie (ball on finger) 1.00 2.50
24 Hubert Geese Ausbie (ball behind back) 1.00 2.50
25 Hubert Geese Ausbie (no ball) 1.00 2.50
26 Geese Ausbie and Curly Neal with confetti) 2.00 5.00
27 Freddie Curly Neal (artist) 2.50 6.00
28 Freddie Curly Neal (sitting on ball) 2.50 6.00
29 Freddie Curly Neal (two balls on head) 2.50 6.00
30 Mel Davis and Freddie Curly Neal 1.50 4.00
31 Freddie Curly Neall (smiling) 2.50 6.00
32 Freddie CurlyNeal (looking to side) 2.50 6.00
33 Mel Davis (looking down) .75 2.00
34 Mel Davis (ready to shoot) .75 2.00
35 Mel Davis (ball in hand) .75 2.00
36 Mel Davis (ball over head) .75 2.00
37 Mel Davis and Bill Meggett (leap frog) .75 2.00
38 Mel Davis (ball on knee) .75 2.00
39 Bobby Joe Mason (ball under arm) .75 2.00
40 Bobby Joe Mason (ball between legs) .75 2.00
41 Bobby Joe Mason (passing behind back) .75 2.00
42 Bobby Joe Mason and Frank Stephens .75 2.00
43 Bobby Joe Mason (ball to side) .75 2.00
44 Bobby Joe Mason (ready to shoot) .75 2.00
45 Clarence Smith (three balls between legs) .75 2.00
46 Clarence Smith (on bike) .75 2.00
47 Clarence Smith (ball at ear) .75 2.00
48 Clarence Smith (dribbling on side) .75 2.00
49 Jerry Venable .75 2.00
50 Frank Stephens (hands in front) .75 2.00
51 Frank Stephens (ball on finger) .75 2.00
52 Frank Stephens (waiting for ball) .75 2.00
53 Frank Stephens (ball in hand) .75 2.00
54 Theodis Ray Lee (ball on hip) .75 2.00
55 Theodis Ray Lee (ball between knees) .75 2.00
56 Jerry Venable (palming ball) .75 2.00
57 Doug Himes (ball in air) .75 2.00
58 Doug Himes (ball behind back) .75 2.00
59 Bill Meggett (dribbling two balls) .75 2.00
60 Bill Meggett (ready to shoot) .75 2.00
61 Vincent White (ball on hip) .75 2.00
62 Vincent White (kicking ball) .75 2.00
63 Pablo and Showboat .75 2.00
64 Meadowlark Lemon Curly Neal and Geese Ausbie balls behind back) 2.50 6.00
65 Curley Neal Quarterback 2.50 6.00
66 Ausbie, Meadowlark, and Neal (looking at ball) 2.50 6.00
67 Curly Neal Meadowlark Lemon 2.50 6.00
68 Football Routine 1.00 2.50
69 Meadowlark To Neal To Ausbie 2.50 6.00
70 Meadowlark Is Safe At The Plate 2.50 6.00
71 1970-71 Highlights (baseball act) 1.00 2.50
72 1970-71 Highlights (Lemon and Neal) 2.50 6.00
73 Bobby Hunter (ball on hip) .75 2.00
74 Bobby Hunter (ball in hand) .75 2.00
75 Bobby Hunter (ball on shoulder) .75 2.00
76 Bobby Hunter (ball in air) .75 2.00
77 Bobby Hunter (passing between legs) .75 2.00
78 Jackie Jackson (ball on hip) 1.00 2.50
79 Jackie Jackson (ball behind back) 1.00 2.50
80 Jackie Jackson (ball in air) 1.00 2.50
81 Jackie Jackson/ ball on finger) 1.00 2.50
82 The Globetrotters 1.00 2.50
83 The Globetrotters 1.00 2.50
84 Dallas Thornton 2.50 6.00
NNO Globetrotter Official Peel-off Team Emblem Sticker 1.50 4.00

1971-72 Globetrotters Phoenix Candy

COMPLETE SET (8) 175.00 350.00
1 J.C. Gipson 20.00 40.00
2 Bob Showboat Hall 20.00 40.00
3 Leon Hillard 20.00 40.00
4 Meadowlark Lemon 50.00 100.00
5 Freddie(Curly) Neal 40.00 80.00
6 Pablo Robertson 20.00 40.00
7 National Unit (Team picture) 25.00 50.00
8 International Unit (Team picture) 25.00 50.00

1980 Globetrotters

COMPLETE SET (6) 10.00 20.00
1 Geese Ausbie 1.50 4.00
2 Geese Ausbie Curly Neal Nate Branch 2.00 5.00
3 Nate Branch 1.25 3.00
4 Billy Ray Hobley 1.25 3.00
5 Curly Neal 2.50 6.00
6 Dallas Thornton Fred Neal Hubert Ausbie Nate Branch General Lee Holman Billy Ray Hobley Robert Paige Lionel Garrett Reggie Franklin Eddie Fields 1.50 4.00

1985 Globetrotters

COMPLETE SET (11) 8.00 20.00
12 Billy Ray Hobley .75 2.00
14 Larry Rivers .75 2.00
15 Clyde Austin .75 2.00
17 Ovie Dotson .75 2.00
18 Jimmy Blacklock .75 2.00
22 Fred Neal 2.50 6.00
26 Osborne Lockhart .75 2.00
29 Harold Hubbard .75 2.00
30 Robert Paige .75 2.00
35 Hubert Ausbie 1.25 3.00
41 Sweet Lou Dunbar 1.25 3.00

1992 Globetrotters Promos

COMPLETE SET (6) 6.00 15.00
P1 All-Time Greats Sixty-Fifth Anniversary 1.25 3.00
P2 Globetrotting Fred (Curly) Neal Alan Alda 1.50 4.00
P3 Famous Feats Fred (Curly) Neal 1.50 4.00
P4 Media Darlings Mickey Mouse Fred (Curly) Neal 2.00 5.00
P5 Honoraries Team Photo 1.25 3.00
P6 First City Goldie Hawn 2.00 5.00

1992 Globetrotters

COMPLETE SET (90) 5.00 12.00
1 Abe Saperstein .20 .50
2 In The Beginning .08 .25
3 Hinckley, Illinois .08 .25
4 What's In A Name .08 .25
5 Uniforms .08 .25
6 International Competition .08 .25
7 A Tie .08 .25
8 Hard Times .08 .25
9 Black and White .08 .25
10 Courting Success .08 .25
11 First Tournament .08 .25
12 World Champions .08 .25
13 Tricks and Treats Lynette Woodard) .20 .50
14 Individual Talents .08 .25
15 For The Boys .08 .25
16 Globetrotting .08 .25
17 The Big Screen .08 .25
18 The Small Screen .08 .25
19 Goodwill Ambassadors .08 .25
20 Leaving Their Mark .08 .25
21 Traveling Troubles .08 .25
22 Have Court Will Travel .08 .25
23 The NBA .08 .25
24 Magic Powers .08 .25
25 Almost Perfect .08 .25
26 The End Of An Era .08 .25
27 Celluloid Heroes .08 .25
28 Star Power .08 .25
29 Sweet Georgia Brown .08 .25
30 The Year Of The Woman Lynette Woodard .20 .50
31 Quotable Curly Fred (Curly) Neal .20 .50
32 Honorary Globie Speaks .08 .25
33 Whoopi For The Trotters .20 .50
34 Globie Recollections .08 .25
35 A B'Ball Oscar Bob Hope .20 .50
36 Singing Their Praises 8.00 .25
37 Hurray For Hollywood Geese Ausbie .08 .25
38 The Early Signs .08 .25
39 Fast Forward .08 .25
40 A Losing Streak .08 .25
41 Pioneering Prankster .08 .25
42 Changing Of The Guard .08 .25
43 Breaking In .08 .25
44 Trickster In Training Meadowlark Lemon .20 .50
45 Wearing Many Hats .08 .25
46 Beating The Odds Boid Buie .08 .25
47 Double Take Lance CudJoe Lawrence CudJoe .08 .25
48 Sweetwater .08 .25
49 Founding Father .08 .25
50 Fanciful First Inman Jackson .08 .25
51 Ernest Aughburns .08 .25
52 Clyde Austin .08 .25
53 J.B. Brown .08 .25
54 Michael Douglas .08 .25
55 Sherwin Durham .08 .25
56 Billy Ray Hobley .20 .50
57 Curley Johnson .08 .25
58 Jolette Law .08 .25
59 Derick Polk .08 .25
60 James(Twiggy) Sanders .08 .25
61 Donald(Clyde) Sinclair .08 .25
62 Antoine Scott .08 .25
63 Sweet Lou Dunbar .08 .25
64 Osbourne Lockhart .08 .25
65 Lifelong Dream Lynette Woodard .20 .50
66 A Real Show-Off Clyde Austin .08 .25
67 Competition Jimmy Blacklock .08 .25
68 A Blend Of Old And New Ovie Dotson .08 .25
69 Globie Spirit Harold Hubbard .08 .25
70 The Carrying The Torch Curly Neal .20 .50
71 Geese Ausbie .08 .25
72 Fred(Curly) Neal .20 .50
73 Go, Curly, Go .20 .50
74 Larry(Gator) Rivers .08 .25
75 Off Season .08 .25
76 Sore Losers Washington Generals (Team photo) .08 .25

77 Ovie Dotson .08 .25
78 Come On In .08 .25
79 Practice Makes Perfect .08 .25
80 Trotters' 1st Trip .08 .25
81 Winningest Team .08 .25
82 City Slickers .08 .25
83 You Win Some... .08 .25
84 From Russia, With Love .08 .25
85 Hold Your Fire .08 .25
86 What A Crowd .08 .25
87 Destined For Greatness .08 .25
88 A Fantastic First .08 .25
89 A Higher Calling
Gerald Ford .20 .50
NNO Checklist Card .08 .25

1996 Globetrotters Real Action

COMPLETE SET (11) 8.00 20.00
1 Arnold Bernard 1.25 3.00
2 Rodney English 1.50 4.00
3 Paul Gaffney 1.25 3.00
4 Barry Hardy 1.25 3.00
5 Curley Johnson 1.50 4.00
6 Reggie Perkins 1.25 3.00
7 Reggie Phillips 1.25 3.00
8 Trazel Silvers 1.25 3.00
9 Clyde Sinclair 1.25 3.00
10 Wun Versher 1.25 3.00
XX Display Card .25 .60

2001 Greats of the Game

COMPLETE SET (84) 20.00 50.00
1 Adolph Rupp .40 1.00
2 Alonzo Mourning .50 1.25
3 Antawn Jamison .30 .75
4 Antoine Walker .30 .75
5 Bill Walton .40 1.00
6 Bob Cousy .60 1.50
7 Bob Lanier .30 .75
8 Bobby Cremins .25 .60
9 Bobby Hurley .25 .60
10 Bobby Knight .60 1.50
11 Cazzie Russell .30 .75
12 Charlie Ward .25 .60
13 Christian Laettner .75 2.00
14 Clyde Drexler .50 1.25
15 Danny Ainge .40 1.00
16 Danny Ferry .75 2.00
17 Danny Manning .75 2.00
18 Darrell Griffith .25 .60
19 Dave Cowens .40 1.00
20 David Robinson .60 1.50
21 David Thompson .30 .75
22 Dean Smith .40 1.00
23 Don Haskins .40 1.00
24 Eddie Jones .30 .75
25 Elvin Hayes .40 1.00
26 Gene Keady .30 .75
27 George Mikan .75 2.00
28 Glen Rice .30 .75
29 Hakeem Olajuwon .50 1.25
30 Isiah Thomas .40 1.00
31 Jalen Rose .30 .75
32 Jamal Mashburn .30 .75
33 James Worthy .50 1.25
34 Jerry Stackhouse .30 .75
35 Jerry Lucas .40 1.00
36 Jerry Tarkanian .40 1.00
37 Jerry West .60 1.50
38 Jim Valvano .60 1.50
39 Joe Smith .30 .75
41 John Havlicek .50 1.25
42 John Wooden .50 1.25
43 John Lucas .30 .75
44 Kareem Abdul-Jabbar .60 1.50
45 Keith Van Horn .30 .75
46 Kent Benson .40 1.00
47 Kerry Kittles .25 .60
48 Lamar Odom .40 1.00
49 Larry Bird 1.00 2.50
50 Larry Johnson .40 1.00
51 Lefty Driesell .75 2.00
52 Lenny Wilkens .40 1.00
53 Lou Carnesecca .25 .60
54 Marques Johnson .30 .75
55 Mateen Cleaves .60 1.50
56 Mike Bibby .40 1.00
57 Mike Krzyzewski .60 1.50
58 Mychal Thompson .30 .75
59 Nate Archibald .30 .75
60 Pat Riley .50 1.25
61 Paul Arizin .40 1.00
62 Pete Maravich 1.00 2.50
63 Phil Ford .40 1.00
64 Ralph Sampson .30 .75
65 Ray Meyer .40 1.00
66 Rick Pitino .60 1.50
67 Rick Barry .30 .75
68 Rollie Massimino .25 .60
69 Sam Jones .40 1.00
70 Sidney Moncrief .25 .60
71 Spud Webb .30 .75
72 Steve Alford .40 1.00
73 Vince Carter .60 1.50
74 Walt Frazier .40 1.00
75 Wilt Chamberlain .75 2.00
76 Carol Blazejowski QC 1.00 2.50
77 Cynthia Cooper QC 1.00 2.50
78 Chamique Holdsclaw QC 1.00 2.50
79 Lisa Leslie QC 1.00 2.50
80 Nancy Lieberman QC 1.00 2.50
81 Rebecca Lobo QC 1.00 2.50
82 Cheryl Miller QC 1.00 2.50
83 Sheryl Swoopes QC 1.00 2.50
84 Marcus Camby .30 .75

2001 Greats of the Game All-American Collection

COMPLETE SET (14) 8.00 20.00
STATED ODDS 1:6
1 Hakeem Olajuwon .75 2.00
2 Vince Carter 1.00 2.50
3 James Worthy .75 2.00
4 David Thompson .50 1.25
5 Paul Arizin .60 1.50
6 George Mikan 1.25 3.00
7 Bob Cousy 1.00 2.50
8 Steve Alford .60 1.50
9 Kent Benson .60 1.50
10 Isiah Thomas .60 1.50
11 Wilt Chamberlain 1.25 3.00
12 Marques Johnson .50 1.25
13 Bill Walton .60 1.50
14 Jerry West 1.00 2.50

2001 Greats of the Game All-American Collection Autographs

STATED PRINT RUNS LISTED BELOW
AAC1 Hakeem Olajuwon/84 75.00 200.00
AAC2 Vince Carter/98 40.00 100.00
AAC3 James Worthy/82 60.00 150.00
AAC4 David Thompson/77 20.00 50.00
AAC5 Paul Arizin/50 20.00 50.00
AAC6 George Mikan/46 200.00 500.00
AAC7 Bob Cousy/50 30.00 80.00
AAC8 Steve Alford/87 20.00 50.00
AAC9 Kent Benson/77 20.00 50.00
AAC12 Marques Johnson/77 20.00 50.00
AAC13 Bill Walton/74 30.00 80.00

2001 Greats of the Game Autographs

STATED ODDS 1:12
1 Kareem Abdul-Jabbar 40.00 100.00
2 Danny Ainge 8.00 20.00
3 Steve Alford 12.00 30.00
4 Nate Archibald 10.00 25.00
5 Paul Arizin 12.00 30.00
6 Rick Barry 8.00 20.00
7 Kent Benson 8.00 20.00
8 Mike Bibby 8.00 20.00
9 Larry Bird/200 125.00 300.00
10 Carol Blazejowski 10.00 25.00
11 Vince Carter 20.00 50.00
12 Mateen Cleaves 6.00 15.00
13 Cynthia Cooper 8.00 20.00
14 Bob Cousy 40.00 100.00
15 Dave Cowens 6.00 15.00
16 Clyde Drexler 12.00 30.00
17 Danny Ferry 8.00 20.00
18 Phil Ford 8.00 20.00
19 Walt Frazier 8.00 20.00
20 Darrell Griffith 8.00 20.00
21 John Havlicek/200 50.00 120.00
22 Elvin Hayes 8.00 20.00
23 Chamique Holdsclaw 30.00 80.00
24 Bobby Hurley 12.00 30.00
25 Antawn Jamison 8.00 20.00
26 Larry Johnson 10.00 25.00
27 Marques Johnson 8.00 20.00
28 Eddie Jones 8.00 20.00
29 Sam Jones 10.00 25.00
30 Kerry Kittles 8.00 20.00
31 Bobby Knight 150.00 400.00
32 Christian Laettner 20.00 50.00
33 Bob Lanier 8.00 20.00
34 Lisa Leslie 8.00 20.00
35 Nancy Lieberman-Cline 8.00 20.00
36 Jerry Lucas 6.00 15.00
37 John Lucas 8.00 20.00
38 Danny Manning 12.00 30.00
39 Jamal Mashburn 8.00 20.00
40 George Mikan/300 100.00 250.00
41 Cheryl Miller 10.00 25.00
42 Sidney Moncrief 8.00 20.00
43 Alonzo Mourning 15.00 40.00
45 Hakeem Olajuwon 15.00 40.00
46 Rick Pitino 15.00 40.00
47 Glen Rice 6.00 15.00
48 Pat Riley/150 30.00 80.00
49 David Robinson 40.00 100.00
50 Jalen Rose 10.00 25.00
51 Cazzie Russell 8.00 20.00
52 Ralph Sampson 8.00 20.00
53 Joe Smith 6.00 15.00
54 Jerry Stackhouse 12.00 30.00
55 Sheryl Swoopes 15.00 30.00
56 Isiah Thomas/219 15.00 40.00
57 David Thompson 8.00 20.00
58 Mychal Thompson 8.00 20.00
59 Keith Van Horn 6.00 15.00
60 Antoine Walker 8.00 20.00
61 Bill Walton 10.00 25.00
62 Charlie Ward 8.00 20.00
63 Spud Webb 8.00 20.00
64 Jerry West 25.00 60.00
65 Lenny Wilkens 8.00 20.00
66 John Wooden/300 75.00 150.00
67 James Worthy 15.00 40.00

2001 Greats of the Game Coach's Corner

COMPLETE SET (16) 15.00 40.00
STATED ODDS 1:10
CC1 Lou Carnesecca 1.00 2.50
CC2 Bobby Cremins 1.00 2.50
CC3 Lefty Driesell 3.00 8.00
CC4 Don Haskins 1.00 2.50
CC5 Mike Krzyzewski 3.00 8.00
CC6 Rollie Massimino 1.00 2.50
CC7 Ray Meyer 1.00 2.50
CC8 Rick Pitino 2.50 6.00
CC9 Adolph Rupp 2.50 6.00
CC10 Dean Smith 2.50 6.00
CC11 Jerry Tarkanian 1.00 2.50
CC12 John Thompson 1.00 2.50
CC13 Bobby Knight 2.00 5.00
CC14 John Wooden 2.00 5.00
CC15 Jim Valvano 2.00 5.00
CC16 Gene Keady 1.00 2.50

2001 Greats of the Game Coach's Corner Autographs

STATED PRINT RUN 100 SERIAL #'d SETS
CC2 Bobby Cremins 15.00 40.00
CC3 Lefty Driesell 25.00 60.00
CC4 Don Haskins 15.00 40.00
CC5 Mike Krzyzewski 200.00 500.00
CC6 Rollie Massimino 20.00 50.00
CC7 Ray Meyer 15.00 40.00
CC8 Rick Pitino 20.00 50.00
CC10 Dean Smith 50.00 100.00
CC11 Jerry Tarkanian 20.00 50.00
CC12 John Thompson 60.00 150.00
CC13 Bobby Knight 150.00 400.00
CC14 John Wooden 100.00 200.00

2001 Greats of the Game Feel the Game Classics

STATED ODDS 1:24
1 Rick Barry 4.00 10.00
2 Larry Bird 12.00 30.00
3 Lou Carnasecca 4.00 10.00
4 Vince Carter JSY R 6.00 15.00
5 Vince Carter Shorts R 6.00 15.00
6 Vince Carter WU 6.00 15.00
7 Vince Carter Shirt 6.00 15.00
8 Vince Carter JSY H 6.00 15.00
9 Vince Carter Shorts H 6.00 15.00
10 V.Carter J-Short R/150 8.00 20.00
11 V.Carter J-Short H/150 8.00 20.00
12 V.Carter WU-Shirt/200 8.00 20.00
13 V.Carter J-Shor-Shir R/50 15.00 40.00
14 V.Carter J-Shor-Shir H/50 15.00 40.00
15 V.Carter J-Shor-WU R/75 12.00 30.00
16 V.Carter J-Shor-WU H/75 12.00 30.00
17 V.Carter J-Shor-Shir-WU H/15 20.00 50.00
18 V.Carter J-Shor-Shir-WU R/15 20.00 50.00
20 Larry Johnson 4.00 10.00
21 Bobby Knight Ball 10.00 25.00
22 Bobby Knight Shirt 10.00 25.00
23 Pete Maravich 30.00 80.00
24 Isaiah Rider 4.00 10.00
25 Bill Walton 4.00 10.00

2001 Greats of the Game Feel the Game Hardwood Classics

STATED ODDS 1:24
1 Steve Alford 3.00 8.00
2 Marcus Camby 3.00 8.00
4 Mateen Cleaves 3.00 8.00
6 Phil Ford SP 10.00 25.00
7 Antawn Jamison 3.00 8.00
8 Larry Johnson 3.00 8.00
9 Gene Keady 3.00 8.00
10 Bobby Knight 10.00 25.00
11 Mike Krzyzewski 6.00 15.00
13 Danny Manning 3.00 8.00
14 Glen Rice 3.00 8.00
15 Glenn Robinson 3.00 8.00
16 Jalen Rose 3.00 8.00
18 Sheryl Swoopes 3.00 8.00
19 Antoine Walker 3.00 8.00
20 Charlie Ward 3.00 8.00

2001 Greats of the Game Player of the Year

COMPLETE SET (10) 15.00 40.00
STATED ODDS 1:24
POY1 Christian Laettner 5.00 12.00
POY2 Elvin Hayes 1.50 4.00
POY3 Larry Bird 6.00 15.00
POY4 Joe Smith 1.50 4.00
POY5 Cazzie Russell 1.50 4.00
POY6 Antawn Jamison 1.50 4.00
POY7 Danny Manning 2.50 6.00
POY8 David Robinson 1.50 4.00
POY9 Jerry Lucas 1.50 4.00
POY10 Kareem Abdul-Jabbar 2.50 6.00

2001 Greats of the Game Player of the Year Autographs

STATED PRINT RUNS LISTED BELOW
POY1 Christian Laettner/91 30.00 80.00
POY2 Elvin Hayes/68 20.00 50.00
POY3 Larry Bird/79 100.00 200.00
POY4 Joe Smith/95 12.50 30.00
POY5 Cazzie Russell/66 40.00 100.00
POY6 Antawn Jamison/98 12.50 30.00
POY7 Danny Manning/88 12.50 30.00
POY8 David Robinson/87 40.00 100.00
POY10 Kareem Abdul-Jabbar/69 60.00 150.00

2005-06 Greats of the Game

COMP.SET w/o SP's (100) 15.00 40.00
101-169 PRINT RUN 99 SER.#'d SETS
1 Earl Monroe .75 2.00
2 World Free .50 1.25
3 James Worthy .75 2.00
4 Bob McAdoo .75 2.00
5 Connie Hawkins .75 2.00
6 John Starks .60 1.50
7 Byron Scott .60 1.50
8 Brad Daugherty .50 1.25
9 Chris Ford .60 1.50
10 Jamaal Wilkes .60 1.50
11 Julius Erving 1.25 3.00
12 Joe Carroll .60 1.50
13 Bill Laimbeer .60 1.50
14 Bill Walton .75 2.00
15 Brian Winters .60 1.50
16 David Robinson 1.25 3.00
17 Horace Grant .60 1.50
18 Bob Pettit .75 2.00
19 Dan Roundfield .60 1.50
20 Kenny Walker .40 1.00
21 Kenny Smith .50 1.25
22 Thurl Bailey .50 1.25
23 Cedric Maxwell .50 1.25
24 Joe Dumars .50 1.25
25 Adrian Dantley .60 1.50
26 Dale Ellis .50 1.25
27 John Stockton 1.25 3.00
28 Bob Lanier .75 2.00
29 Bernard King .75 2.00
30 Jerry Lucas .60 1.50
31 Bill Russell 2.00 5.00
32 Hal Greer .75 2.00
33 Billy Cunningham .60 1.50
34 Jack Sikma .60 1.50
35 Michael Cooper .60 1.50
36 David Thompson .50 1.25
37 Kareem Abdul-Jabbar 1.00 2.50
38 Bill Sharman .60 1.50
39 George Gervin .60 1.50
40 Kiki Vandeweghe .50 1.25
41 Calvin Murphy .50 1.25
42 Darryl Dawkins .60 1.50
43 Vern Mikkelsen .60 1.50
44 Dee Brown .50 1.25
45 Dennis Rodman 1.25 3.00
46 Bobby Jones .60 1.50
47 Hakeem Olajuwon 1.25 3.00
48 Alvin Robertson .50 1.25
49 Dennis Johnson .60 1.50
50 Clyde Drexler 1.00 2.50
51 Anthony Mason .50 1.25
52 Larry Bird 2.00 5.00
53 LeBron James 5.00 12.00
54 Magic Johnson 1.50 4.00
55 Manute Bol .60 1.50
56 Mookie Blaylock .40 1.00
57 Mark Eaton .60 1.50
58 Kevin McHale .75 2.00
59 Maurice Cheeks .50 1.25
60 Maurice Lucas .60 1.50
61 Michael Jordan 5.00 12.00
62 Michael Ray Richardson .50 1.25
63 B.J. Armstrong .60 1.50
64 ML Carr .60 1.50
65 Muggsy Bogues .60 1.50
66 Nate Archibald .60 1.50
67 Glen Rice .60 1.50
68 Nate Thurmond .60 1.50
69 Norm Nixon .50 1.25
70 Bob Love .60 1.50
71 Paul Arizin .60 1.50
72 Ralph Sampson .50 1.25
73 Rolando Blackman .50 1.25
74 Reggie Theus .50 1.25
75 Mitch Richmond .75 2.00
76 Robert Parish .75 2.00
77 Paul Westphal .60 1.50
78 Sam Perkins .50 1.25
79 Scottie Pippen 1.25 3.00
80 Sean Elliott .50 1.25
81 Spud Webb .60 1.50
82 Steve Kerr .60 1.50
83 Tom Chambers .60 1.50
84 Walt Bellamy .60 1.50
85 Walt Frazier .60 1.50
86 Jeff Hornacek .50 1.25
87 Danny Manning .50 1.25
88 Wes Unseld .75 2.00
89 Geoff Petrie .60 1.50
90 Xavier McDaniel .50 1.25
91 Chris Mullin .75 2.00
92 Buck Williams CC .50 1.25
93 Dave Bing CC .60 1.50
94 John Havlicek CC 1.00 2.50
95 Karl Malone CC 1.00 2.50
96 Artis Gilmore CC .75 2.00
97 Doug Moe CC .60 1.50
98 Doug Collins CC .60 1.50
99 Chuck Daly CC .60 1.50
100 Bob Knight CC 1.00 2.50
101 Alex Acker AU RC 5.00 12.00
102 Amir Johnson AU RC 8.00 20.00
103 Andray Blatche AU RC 8.00 20.00
104 Andrew Bogut AU RC 10.00 25.00
105 Andrew Bynum AU RC 6.00 15.00
106 Antoine Wright AU RC 6.00 15.00
107 Yaroslav Korolev AU RC 5.00 12.00
108 Bracey Wright AU RC 5.00 12.00
109 Brandon Bass AU RC 6.00 15.00
110 C.J. Miles AU RC 6.00 15.00
111 Channing Frye AU RC 6.00 15.00
112 Charlie Villanueva AU RC 6.00 15.00
113 Chris Paul AU RC 75.00 200.00
114 Chris Taft AU RC 5.00 12.00
115 Chuck Hayes AU RC 6.00 15.00
116 Daniel Ewing AU RC 8.00 20.00
117 Danny Granger AU RC 8.00 20.00
118 David Lee AU RC 8.00 20.00
119 Deron Williams AU RC 12.00 30.00
120 Dijon Thompson AU RC 5.00 12.00
121 Ersan Ilyasova AU RC 6.00 15.00
122 Francisco Garcia AU RC 5.00 12.00
123 Gerald Green AU RC 8.00 20.00
124 Hakim Warrick AU RC 6.00 15.00
125 Ike Diogu AU RC 5.00 12.00
126 Jarrett Jack AU RC 8.00 20.00
127 Jason Maxiell AU RC 6.00 15.00
128 Joey Graham AU RC 6.00 15.00
129 Johan Petro AU RC 5.00 12.00
130 Julius Hodge AU RC 5.00 12.00
131 Lawrence Roberts AU RC 5.00 12.00
132 Linas Kleiza AU RC 6.00 15.00
133 Louis Williams AU RC 20.00 50.00
134 Luther Head AU RC 5.00 12.00
135 Martell Webster AU RC 6.00 15.00
136 M.Andriuskevicius AU RC 5.00 12.00
137 Marvin Williams AU RC 8.00 20.00
138 Monta Ellis AU RC 10.00 25.00
139 Nate Robinson AU RC 8.00 20.00
140 Orien Greene AU RC 6.00 15.00
141 Rashad McCants AU RC 5.00 12.00
142 Raymond Felton AU RC 6.00 15.00
143 Robert Whaley AU RC 5.00 12.00
144 Ronny Turiaf AU RC 8.00 20.00
145 Ryan Gomes AU RC 6.00 15.00
146 Salim Stoudamire AU RC 6.00 15.00
147 Sarunas Jasikevicius AU RC 8.00 20.00
148 Sean May AU RC 5.00 12.00
149 Stephen Graham AU RC 6.00 15.00
150 Travis Diener AU RC 5.00 12.00
151 Von Wafer AU RC 5.00 12.00
152 Wayne Simien AU RC 5.00 12.00
153 Shavlik Randolph RC 2.00 5.00
154 Alan Anderson RC 2.00 5.00
155 Andre Owens RC 2.00 5.00
156 Anthony Roberson RC 2.50 6.00
157 Arvydas Macijauskas RC 2.00 5.00
158 Boniface N'Dong RC 3.00 8.00
159 Devin Green RC 3.00 8.00
160 Donell Taylor RC 2.00 5.00
161 Earl Barron RC 2.00 5.00
162 Esteban Batista RC 2.00 5.00
163 Fabricio Oberto RC 2.50 6.00
164 Rawle Marshall RC 2.00 5.00
165 James Singleton RC 2.00 5.00
166 Jose Calderon RC 3.00 8.00
167 Josh Powell RC 2.50 6.00
168 Kevin Burleson RC 3.00 8.00
169 Ronnie Price RC 2.50 6.00

2005-06 Greats of the Game Autographs

APPROXIMATELY TWO PER BOX
GGAD Adrian Dantley 8.00 20.00
GGAR Alvin Robertson 8.00 20.00
GGBA B.J. Armstrong 8.00 20.00
GGBD Brad Daugherty 5.00 12.00
GGBJ Bobby Jones 8.00 20.00
GGBK Bernard King/248* 12.00 30.00
GGBL Bill Laimbeer 12.00 30.00
GGBM Bob McAdoo 20.00 50.00
GGBO Muggsy Bogues/185* 15.00 40.00
GGBP Bob Pettit 12.00 30.00
GGBR Bill Russell/30* 1,000.00 2,000.00
GGBS Byron Scott/250* 6.00 15.00
GGBW Bill Walton/250* 15.00 40.00
GGCD Clyde Drexler/109* 50.00 120.00
GGCF Chris Ford 6.00 15.00
GGCH Connie Hawkins 15.00 40.00
GGCO Michael Cooper 12.00 30.00
GGDA Chuck Daly/84* 100.00 250.00
GGDB Dee Brown 4.00 10.00
GGDC Doug Collins 4.00 10.00
GGDD Darryl Dawkins 12.00 30.00
GGDE Dale Ellis 4.00 10.00
GGDJ Dennis Johnson/236* 50.00 120.00
GGDM Doug Moe 12.00 30.00
GGDR David Robinson/62* 75.00 200.00
GGDT David Thompson 10.00 25.00
GGFR Walt Frazier/63* 12.00 30.00
GGGG George Gervin/250* 15.00 40.00
GGHG Hal Greer 15.00 40.00
GGHO Hakeem Olajuwon/62* 100.00 250.00
GGJE Julius Erving/30* 100.00 250.00
GGJH Jeff Hornacek 12.00 30.00
GGJS John Starks/250* 20.00 50.00
GGJW Jamaal Wilkes 8.00 20.00
GGKA Kareem Abdul-Jabbar/30* 200.00 500.00
GGKV Kiki Vandeweghe 4.00 10.00
GGKW Kenny Walker 6.00 15.00
GGLB Larry Bird/40* 150.00 400.00
GGLJ LeBron James/30* 2,500.00 5,000.00
GGMA Magic Johnson/40* 150.00 400.00
GGMC Maurice Cheeks 6.00 15.00
GGME Mark Eaton 10.00 25.00
GGML Maurice Lucas 6.00 15.00
GGMR Michael Ray Richardson 6.00 15.00
GGMX Cedric Maxwell/250* 10.00 25.00
GGNA Nate Archibald/250* 12.00 30.00
GGNN Norm Nixon 5.00 12.00
GGNT Nate Thurmond 6.00 15.00
GGPA Paul Arizin 40.00 100.00
GGPW Paul Westphal/87* 15.00 40.00
GGRD Dennis Rodman/112* 75.00 200.00
GGRO Dan Roundfield 15.00 40.00
GGRS Ralph Sampson/230* 12.00 30.00
GGRT Reggie Theus 4.00 10.00
GGSE Sean Elliott/184* 15.00 40.00
GGSH Bill Sharman 20.00 50.00
GGSI Jack Sikma 8.00 20.00
GGSK Steve Kerr 20.00 50.00
GGSP Sam Perkins/184* 8.00 20.00
GGST John Stockton/40* 100.00 250.00
GGSW Spud Webb/234* 12.00 30.00
GGTC Tom Chambers 6.00 15.00
GGVM Vern Mikkelsen 25.00 60.00
GGWB Walt Bellamy/248* 12.00 30.00
GGWF World Free 6.00 15.00
GGWI Brian Winters 4.00 10.00
GGWU Wes Unseld 12.00 30.00
GGXM Xavier McDaniel 8.00 20.00

2005-06 Greats of the Game Gold

*1-100 GOLD: 1.25X TO 3X BASE HI
1-100 PRINT RUN 99 SER.#'d SETS
*101-152 GOLD AU: .6X TO 1.5X BASE HI
*153-169 GOLD: .75X TO 2X BASE HI
113 Chris Paul AU 300.00 600.00

2009-10 Greats of the Game

COMPLETE SET (163) 30.00 60.00
1 Mark Jackson .25 .60
2 Freddie Lewis .20 .50
3 Brad Daugherty .30 .75
4 John Stockton .50 1.25
5 Shareef Abdur-Rahim .25 .60
6 Michael Jordan 2.50 6.00
7 Larry Johnson .30 .75
8 B.J. Armstrong .30 .75
9 Hakeem Olajuwon .40 1.00
10 Sam Perkins .20 .50
11 Steve Kerr .30 .75
12 Julius Erving .75 2.00
13 John Havlicek .75 2.00
14 Clyde Lovellette .30 .75
15 Danny Manning .25 .60
16 Isiah Thomas .30 .75
17 Kevin Pittsnogle .20 .50
18 Clyde Drexler .50 1.25
19 Bill Cartwright .25 .60
20 Jerry West .50 1.25
21 Darrell Walker .30 .75
22 Pat Riley .30 .75
23 Cazzie Russell .30 .75
24 Lionel Hollins .20 .50
25 George Karl .30 .75
26 Terry Porter .20 .50
27 Jack Sikma .25 .60
28 Adrian Dantley .25 .60
29 Billy Donovan .40 1.00
30 Micheal Ray Richardson .25 .60
31 Hal Greer .40 1.00
32 Terry Cummings .25 .60
33 Rick Mahorn .20 .50
34 Larry Nance .25 .60
35 Oscar Robertson .40 1.00
36 James Harden RC 10.00 25.00
37 Horace Grant .30 .75
38 Steve Alford .30 .75
39 Magic Johnson 1.25 3.00
40 LeBron James 2.50 6.00
41 Yao Ming .75 2.00
42 Larry Bird 1.25 3.00
43 Tito Horford .30 .75
44 Ricky Rubio RC .40 1.00
45 George Gervin .40 1.00
46 Gail Goodrich .30 .75
47 Chet Walker .25 .60
48 Vlade Divac .30 .75
49 Thurl Bailey .20 .50
50 Dominique Wilkins .50 1.25
51 Bob Lanier .40 1.00
52 Bill Sharman .40 1.00
53 Don Nelson .30 .75
54 Ron Harper .30 .75
55 Bernard King .40 1.00
56 Robert Parish .40 1.00
57 Elgin Baylor .75 2.00
58 Dave Cowens .40 1.00
59 Dennis Rodman .60 1.50
60 Rod Hundley .30 .75
61 Bill Walton .50 1.25
62 David Thompson .25 .60
63 Bill Laimbeer .30 .75
64 Bob McAdoo .40 1.00
65 Kareem Abdul-Jabbar 1.00 2.50
66 Bill Russell 1.00 2.50
67 Alonzo Mourning .50 1.25
68 Jerry Sloan .40 1.00
69 Avery Johnson .25 .60
70 Bobby Hurley .30 .75
71 Moses Malone .50 1.25
72 Chris Mullin .40 1.00
73 Derrick Rose .50 1.25
74 Stacey Augmon .20 .50
75 Darrell Griffith .20 .50
76 Danny Ferry .20 .50
77 Michael Cooper .30 .75
78 Brandon Roy .40 1.00
79 Bob Pettit .40 1.00
80 David Robinson .60 1.50
81 Sam Cassell .25 .60
82 Glen Rice .25 .60
83 Calbert Cheaney .30 .75
84 Christian Laettner .25 .60
85 Mateen Cleaves .20 .50
86 Derrick Rose GD 1.00 2.50
87 Yao Ming GD 1.50 4.00
88 Brandon Roy GD .75 2.00
89 LeBron James GD 5.00 12.00
90 James Harden GD 4.00 10.00
91 Michael Jordan GD 5.00 12.00
92 Michael Cooper GD .60 1.50
93 Moses Malone GD 1.00 2.50
94 Kevin Pittsnogle GD .40 1.00
95 Chris Mullin GD .75 2.00
96 Alonzo Mourning GD 1.00 2.50
97 Horace Grant GD .60 1.50
98 Larry Nance GD .50 1.25
99 Larry Bird GD 2.50 6.00
100 Julius Erving GD 1.50 4.00
101 Tito Horford GD .60 1.50
102 George Gervin GD .75 2.00
103 Red Hundley GD .60 1.50
104 Mateen Cleaves GD .40 1.00
105 Calbert Cheaney GD .60 1.50
106 Brandon Roy BMC 1.00 2.50
107 Calbert Cheaney BMC .75 2.00
108 Bill Cartwright BMC .60 1.50
109 Danny Ferry BMC .50 1.25
110 Danny Manning BMC .60 1.50
111 Darrell Walker BMC .75 2.00
112 Bill Laimbeer BMC .75 2.00
113 LeBron James BMC 6.00 15.00
114 Derrick Rose BMC 1.25 3.00
115 Hakeem Olajuwon BMC 1.00 2.50
116 Horace Grant BMC .75 2.00
117 James Harden BMC 5.00 12.00
118 Bill Russell BMC 2.50 6.00
119 Larry Bird BMC 3.00 8.00
120 Larry Johnson BMC .75 2.00
121 Michael Jordan BMC 6.00 15.00
122 Bill Walton BMC 1.25 3.00
123 Shareef Abdur-Rahim BMC .60 1.50
124 Sam Perkins BMC .50 1.25
125 J.West/K.Pittsnogle 1.50 4.00
126 B.Walton/K.Abdul-Jabbar 3.00 8.00
127 L.Johnson/S.Augmon 1.00 2.50
128 D.Cowens/S.Cassell 1.25 3.00
129 D.Thompson/T.Bailey .75 2.00
130 M.Johnson/M.Cleaves 4.00 10.00
131 B.Cartwright/B.Russell 3.00 8.00
132 B.Hurley/D.Ferry 1.00 2.50
133 H.Grant/L.Nance 1.00 2.50
134 C.Laettner/D.Ferry .75 2.00
135 F.Lewis/L.Hollins .60 1.50
136 C.Russell/G.Rice 1.00 2.50
137 B.Armstrong/D.Nelson 1.00 2.50
138 A.Dantley/B.Laimbeer 1.00 2.50
139 C.Mullin/M.Jackson 1.25 3.00
140 B.McAdoo/G.Karl 1.25 3.00
141 C.Lovellette/D.Manning 1.00 2.50
142 C.Drexler/H.Olajuwon 1.50 4.00
143 Dave Cowens OS 1.00 2.50
144 Bernard King OS 1.00 2.50
145 Mark Jackson OS .60 1.50
146 Danny Ferry OS .50 1.25
147 Darrell Griffith OS .50 1.25
148 Cazzie Russell OS .75 2.00
149 George Karl OS .75 2.00
150 Sam Perkins OS .50 1.25
151 Julius Erving OS 2.00 5.00
152 Larry Bird OS 3.00 8.00
153 Isiah Thomas OS .75 2.00
154 Michael Jordan OS 6.00 15.00
155 Freddie Lewis OS .50 1.25
156 John Stockton OS 1.25 3.00
157 Pat Riley OS .75 2.00
158 Jack Sikma OS .60 1.50
159 Oscar Robertson OS 1.00 2.50
160 Chris Mullin OS 1.00 2.50
161 George Gervin OS 1.00 2.50
162 Bill Walton OS 1.25 3.00
163 Kareem Abdul-Jabbar OS 2.50 6.00

2009-10 Greats of the Game 199

*GREATS 199 1-85: 1.5X TO 4X BASE HI
*GREATS 199 86-105: .75X TO 2X BASE HI
*GREATS 199 106-124: .6X TO 1.5X BASE HI
*GREATS 199 125-142: .75X TO 2X BASE HI
*GREATS 199 143-163: .6X TO 1.5X BASE HI
STATED PRINT RUN 199 SER.#'d SETS

2009-10 Greats of the Game 50

*GREATS 50 1-85: 4X TO 10X BASE HI
*GREATS 50 86-105: 2X TO 5X BASE HI
*GREATS 50 106-124: 1.5X TO 4X BASE HI
*GREATS 50 125-142: 1.5X TO 4X BASE HI
*GREATS 50 143-163: 1.5X TO 4X BASE HI
PRINT RUN 50 SER.#'d SETS

2009-10 Greats of the Game Autographs

STATED ODDS 1:8
1 Mark Jackson 5.00 12.00
2 Freddie Lewis 4.00 10.00
3 Brad Daugherty SP 5.00 12.00
4 John Stockton 25.00 60.00
5 Shareef Abdur-Rahim 4.00 10.00
6 Michael Jordan 1,500.00 3,000.00
8 B.J. Armstrong 5.00 12.00
10 Sam Perkins SP 20.00 50.00
11 Steve Kerr 8.00 20.00
12 Julius Erving SP 100.00 250.00
13 John Havlicek 20.00 50.00
15 Danny Manning 8.00 20.00
17 Kevin Pittsnogle 4.00 10.00
19 Bill Cartwright 12.00 30.00
20 Jerry West 20.00 50.00
21 Darrell Walker 4.00 10.00
22 Pat Riley 20.00 50.00
25 George Karl SP 40.00 80.00
26 Terry Porter 8.00 20.00
27 Jack Sikma 4.00 10.00
28 Adrian Dantley 4.00 10.00
29 Bill Donovan 12.00 30.00
30 Michael Ray Richardson 4.00 10.00
31 Hal Greer 5.00 12.00
32 Terry Cummings 5.00 12.00
33 Rick Mahorn 5.00 12.00
34 Larry Nance 6.00 15.00
35 Oscar Robertson 50.00 120.00
36 James Harden 125.00 300.00
37 Horace Grant 12.00 30.00
38 Steve Alford 5.00 12.00
39 Magic Johnson SP 100.00 250.00
40 LeBron James 1,000.00 2,000.00
41 Yao Ming 200.00 500.00
42 Larry Bird 100.00 250.00
43 Tito Horford 4.00 10.00
44 Ricky Rubio 20.00 50.00
45 George Gervin 12.00 30.00
46 Gail Goodrich 8.00 20.00
47 Chet Walker 8.00 20.00
48 Vlade Divac 6.00 15.00
49 Thurl Bailey 5.00 12.00
50 Dominique Wilkins 12.00 30.00
51 Bob Lanier 8.00 20.00
52 Bill Sharman 15.00 40.00
53 Don Nelson 10.00 25.00
54 Ron Harper 8.00 20.00
55 Bernard King 5.00 12.00
57 Elgin Baylor 25.00 60.00
59 Dennis Rodman 20.00 50.00
60 Rod Hundley 15.00 40.00
61 Bill Walton 8.00 20.00
62 David Thompson 6.00 15.00
63 Bill Laimbeer 6.00 15.00
64 Bob McAdoo 15.00 40.00
66 Bill Russell SP 500.00 1,000.00
67 Alonzo Mourning 20.00 50.00
68 Jerry Sloan 15.00 40.00
69 Avery Johnson 4.00 10.00
70 Bobby Hurley 6.00 15.00
71 Moses Malone 10.00 25.00
72 Chris Mullin 15.00 40.00
73 Derrick Rose 25.00 60.00
75 Darrell Griffith 4.00 10.00
76 Danny Ferry 4.00 10.00
77 Michael Cooper 4.00 10.00
78 Brandon Roy 5.00 12.00
79 Bob Pettit SP 40.00 100.00
81 Sam Cassell 5.00 12.00
82 Glen Rice 8.00 20.00
83 Calbert Cheaney 4.00 10.00
84 Christian Laettner 12.00 30.00
85 Mateen Cleaves 4.00 10.00

2009-10 Greats of the Game Memorable Monikers

STATED PRINT RUN 15 SER.#'d SETS
MBD Billy Donovan 15.00 30.00
MBL Bill Laimbeer 10.00 25.00
MBR Brandon Roy 10.00 25.00
MCW Chet Walker 15.00 30.00
MGG George Gervin 10.00 25.00
MHA Ron Harper 25.00 50.00
MHU Rod Hundley 15.00 30.00
MJA LeBron James 1,500.00 3,000.00
MJE Julius Erving 40.00 100.00
MMR Micheal Ray Richardson 10.00 25.00
MSC Sam Cassell 15.00 30.00
MYM Yao Ming 30.00 80.00

2009-10 Greats of the Game Old School Swatches

STATED ODDS 1:16 PACKS
OS1 Adrian Dantley 2.00 5.00
OS2 Magic Johnson 10.00 25.00
OS3 Alonzo Mourning 4.00 10.00
OS4 Larry Bird 10.00 25.00
OS5 Bernard King 3.00 8.00
OS6 Bill Laimbeer 2.50 6.00
OS7 Bill Russell 8.00 20.00
OS8 Bill Walton 4.00 10.00
OS9 Michael Jordan 15.00 40.00
OS10 Walt Frazier 4.00 10.00
OS11 Clyde Drexler 4.00 10.00
OS12 Stacey Augmon 3.00 8.00
OS14 David Robinson 5.00 12.00
OS15 Dennis Rodman 5.00 12.00
OS16 George Gervin 3.00 8.00
OS17 Hakeem Olajuwon 3.00 8.00
OS18 Horace Grant 2.50 6.00
OS19 Isiah Thomas 3.00 8.00
OS20 LeBron James 8.00 20.00
OS21 Micheal Ray Richardson 2.00 5.00
OS22 Steve Francis 2.50 6.00
OS23 Michael Cooper 2.50 6.00
OS24 Jerry West 6.00 15.00
OS25 John Stockton 4.00 10.00
OS26 James Worthy SP 5.00 12.00
OS27 Julius Erving 6.00 15.00
OS28 Kareem Abdul-Jabbar 6.00 15.00
OS29 Vlade Divac 2.50 6.00
OS30 Steve Kerr 2.50 6.00
OS31 Moses Malone 4.00 10.00
OS32 Rick Fox 2.50 6.00

OS33 Oscar Robertson 5.00 12.00
OS34 Pat Riley 4.00 10.00
OS35 Robert Parish 3.00 8.00
OS36 Sam Cassell 2.00 5.00

1995-96 Grizzlies/Topps
COMPLETE SET (9) 3.00 8.00
10 Byron Scott UER Numbered 175 .50 1.25
11 Blue Edwards UER Numbered 177 .40 1.00
12 Antonio Harvey UER Numbered 236 .40 1.00
13 Kenny Gattison UER Numbered 180 .40 1.00
14 Gerald Wilkins UER Numbered 174 .40 1.00
15 Greg Anthony UER Numbered 178 .40 1.00
16 Lawrence Moten UER Numbered 231 .40 1.00
17 Bryant Reeves UER Numbered 202 1.25 3.00
18 Checklist .40 1.00

2001-02 Grizzlies Topps
COMPLETE SET (9) 1.50 4.00
VG1 Shareef Abdur-Rahim .40 1.00
VG3 Michael Dickerson .30 .75
VG4 Othella Harrington .30 .75
VG5 Bryant Reeves .30 .75
VG6 Damon Jones .30 .75
VG7 Isaac Austin .30 .75
VG8 Stromile Swift .30 .75
VG9 Tony Massenburg .30 .75
VG10 Grant Long .30 .75

2009-10 Hall of Fame
COMPLETE SET (149) 75.00 150.00
PRINT RUN 599 SER.#'d SETS
1 Kareem Abdul-Jabbar 5.00 12.00
2 Nate Archibald 2.00 5.00
3 Paul Arizin 1.50 4.00
4 Rick Barry 1.25 3.00
5 Elgin Baylor 4.00 10.00
6 John Beckman 1.50 4.00
7 Walt Bellamy 1.25 3.00
8 Dave Bing 2.00 5.00
9 Larry Bird 6.00 15.00
10 Carol Blazejowski 1.50 4.00
11 Al Cervi 1.50 4.00
12 Wilt Chamberlain 6.00 15.00
13 Cynthia Cooper 2.00 5.00
14 Bob Cousy 4.00 10.00
15 Dave Cowens 2.00 5.00
16 Billy Cunningham 1.50 4.00
17 Adrian Dantley 1.25 3.00
18 Bob Davies 1.50 4.00
19 Dave DeBusschere 1.50 4.00
20 Anne Donovan 1.50 4.00
21 Clyde Drexler 2.50 6.00
22 Joe Dumars 2.00 5.00
23 Alex English 2.00 5.00
24 Patrick Ewing 2.50 6.00
25 Walt Frazier 2.50 6.00
26 Joe Fulks 2.00 5.00
27 Harry Gallatin 1.50 4.00
28 Pop Gates 2.00 5.00
29 George Gervin 2.00 5.00
30 Tom Gola 1.50 4.00
31 Gail Goodrich 1.50 4.00
32 Hal Greer 2.00 5.00
33 Cliff Hagan 1.50 4.00
34 John Havlicek 4.00 10.00
35 Connie Hawkins 2.00 5.00
36 Elvin Hayes 2.50 6.00
37 Tom Heinsohn 1.50 4.00
38 Bailey Howell 1.50 4.00
39 Dan Issel 1.25 3.00
40 Buddy Jeannette 1.50 4.00
41 Dennis Johnson 1.25 3.00
42 Magic Johnson 6.00 15.00
43 Neil Johnston 1.50 4.00
44 K.C. Jones 1.50 4.00
45 Sam Jones 2.00 5.00
46 Bob Lanier 2.00 5.00
47 Nancy Lieberman 2.00 5.00
48 Clyde Lovellette 1.50 4.00
49 Jerry Lucas 1.50 4.00
50 Pete Maravich 5.00 12.00
51 Bob McAdoo 2.00 5.00
52 Kevin McHale 2.50 6.00
53 Ed Macauley 1.50 4.00
54 Karl Malone 2.00 5.00
55 Moses Malone 2.50 6.00
56 Slater Martin 1.50 4.00
57 Ann Meyers 1.50 4.00
58 George Mikan 5.00 12.00
59 Vern Mikkelsen 1.50 4.00
60 Cheryl Miller 1.50 4.00
61 Earl Monroe 2.00 5.00
62 Calvin Murphy 1.25 3.00
63 Hakeem Olajuwon 2.00 5.00
64 James Naismith 1.50 4.00
65 Robert Parish 2.00 5.00
66 Drazen Petrovic 3.00 8.00
67 Bob Pettit 2.00 5.00
68 Andy Phillip 2.00 5.00
69 Jim Pollard 2.00 5.00
70 Scottie Pippen 4.00 10.00
71 Frank Ramsey 1.50 4.00
72 Willis Reed 2.50 6.00
73 Arnie Risen 1.50 4.00
74 Oscar Robertson 2.50 6.00
75 David Robinson 3.00 8.00
76 Bill Russell 5.00 12.00
77 Dolph Schayes 1.50 4.00
78 Bill Sharman 2.00 5.00
79 John Stockton 2.50 6.00
80 Maurice Stokes 1.50 4.00
81 Isiah Thomas 1.50 4.00
82 David Thompson 1.25 3.00
83 Nate Thurmond 1.25 3.00
84 Jack Twyman 1.50 4.00
85 Wes Unseld 1.50 4.00
86 Bill Walton 2.50 6.00
87 Bobby Wanzer 1.00 2.50
88 Jerry West 2.50 6.00
89 Lenny Wilkens 1.50 4.00
90 Dominique Wilkins 2.50 6.00
91 Lynette Woodard 1.50 4.00
92 John Wooden 2.00 5.00
93 James Worthy 2.00 5.00
94 George Yardley 1.50 4.00
95 Phog Allen 1.50 4.00
96 Red Auerbach 2.00 5.00
97 Jim Boeheim 1.50 4.00
98 Larry Brown 1.50 4.00
99 Lou Carnesecca 1.50 4.00
100 Jody Conradt 2.00 5.00
101 Denny Crum 1.50 4.00
102 Chuck Daly 1.50 4.00
103 Ed Diddle 1.50 4.00
104 Clarence Gaines 1.50 4.00
105 Alex Hannum 1.50 4.00
106 Red Holzman 1.50 4.00
107 Hank Iba 1.50 4.00
108 Phil Jackson 2.00 5.00
109 Bob Knight 2.50 6.00
110 Mike Krzyzewski 2.00 5.00
111 John Kundla 1.50 4.00
112 Al McGuire 1.50 4.00
113 Ray Meyer 1.50 4.00
114 Jack Ramsay 1.50 4.00
116 Adolph Rupp 1.50 4.00
117 Jerry Sloan 2.00 5.00
118 Dean Smith 2.00 5.00
119 C. Vivian Stringer 1.50 4.00
120 Pat Summitt 12.00 30.00
122 Roy Williams 1.50 4.00
123 Meadowlark Lemon 1.50 4.00
124 Wilt Chamberlain 6.00 15.00
125 Lenny Wilkens 1.50 4.00
126 Marques Haynes 1.50 4.00
127 Oscar Robertson 2.00 5.00
128 Abe Saperstein 2.00 5.00
129 Harry Flournoy 1.50 4.00
130 Nevil Shed 1.50 4.00
131 David Lattin 2.00 5.00
132 Willie Worsley 1.50 4.00
133 Orsten Artis 1.50 4.00
134 Willie Cager 2.00 5.00
135 Don Haskins 2.00 5.00
136 Hubie Brown 1.50 4.00
137 Walter Brown 1.50 4.00
138 Jerry Colangelo 2.00 5.00
139 Chick Hearn 1.50 4.00
140 Pete Newell 1.50 4.00
141 Amos Alonzo Stagg 1.50 4.00
142 Chuck Taylor 1.50 4.00
143 Dick Vitale 2.00 5.00
144 Larry O'Brien 1.50 4.00
145 Nat Holman 2.00 5.00
146 Paul Endacott 1.50 4.00
147 Bud Foster 1.50 4.00
148 1960 USA Oly BK Team 2.00 5.00
149 1992 USA Oly BK Team 3.00 8.00
150 Bob Kurland 1.50 4.00

2009-10 Hall of Fame Black Border
*BLACK: .6X TO 1.5X BASE HI
BLACK PRINT RUN 199 SER.#'d SETS

2009-10 Hall of Fame Dream Team
COMPLETE SET (9) 25.00 50.00
PRINT RUN 349 SER.#'d SETS
*BLACK: .5X TO 1.25X BASE HI
BLACK PRINT RUN 199 SER.#'d SETS
1 Larry Bird 12.00 30.00
2 Magic Johnson 12.00 30.00
3 Clyde Drexler 5.00 12.00
4 Karl Malone 4.00 10.00
5 David Robinson 6.00 15.00
6 John Stockton 5.00 12.00
7 Patrick Ewing 5.00 12.00
8 Chris Mullin 4.00 10.00
9 Scottie Pippen 8.00 20.00

2009-10 Hall of Fame Dream Team Game Threads
STATED PRINT RUN 500 TO 1075 SETS
1 Larry Bird/975 10.00 25.00
2 Magic Johnson/750 12.00 30.00
3 Clyde Drexler/650 8.00 20.00
4 Karl Malone/1075 6.00 15.00
5 David Robinson/900 8.00 20.00
6 John Stockton/500 8.00 20.00
7 Patrick Ewing/975 8.00 20.00
8 Chris Mullin/600 6.00 15.00
9 Scottie Pippen/875 8.00 20.00

2009-10 Hall of Fame Dream Team Game Threads Prime
STATED PRINT RUN 99 SER.#'d SETS
1 Larry Bird 40.00 100.00
2 Magic Johnson 30.00 80.00
3 Clyde Drexler 30.00 80.00
4 Karl Malone 30.00 80.00
5 David Robinson 30.00 80.00
6 John Stockton 30.00 80.00
7 Patrick Ewing 30.00 80.00
8 Chris Mullin 30.00 80.00
9 Scottie Pippen 40.00 100.00

2009-10 Hall of Fame Dream Team Marks of Fame
STATED PRINT RUN 44 TO 49 SER.#'d SETS
1 Larry Bird/49 250.00 450.00
2 Magic Johnson/44 200.00 400.00
3 Clyde Drexler/49 125.00 250.00
6 John Stockton/49 125.00 250.00
8 Chris Mullin/49 75.00 150.00
9 Scottie Pippen/49 250.00 500.00

2009-10 Hall of Fame Famed Cuts
STATED PRINT RUN ONE TO 20 SER.#'d SETS
2 Clarence Gaines/20 60.00 150.00

2009-10 Hall of Fame Famed Fabrics
STATED PRINT RUN 20 TO 599 SER.#'d SETS
1 Alex English/325 4.00 10.00
2 Tom Heinsohn/99 3.00 8.00
3 Bob Lanier/399 4.00 10.00
4 Clyde Drexler/599 5.00 12.00
5 Larry Bird/20 25.00 50.00
6 Dave Cowens/149 5.00 12.00
7 Dominique Wilkins/549 5.00 12.00
9 Hakeem Olajuwon/399 4.00 10.00
10 Isiah Thomas/325 3.00 8.00
11 Joe Dumars/250 4.00 10.00
12 Dennis Johnson/325 4.00 10.00
13 Karl Malone/599 4.00 10.00
14 Kevin McHale/399 4.00 10.00
15 Magic Johnson/250 6.00 15.00
16 Patrick Ewing/599 5.00 12.00
17 John Stockton/99 6.00 15.00
18 George Mikan/99 12.00 30.00
19 Dan Issel/99 2.50 6.00
20 Robert Parish/549 4.00 10.00
21 Kareem Abdul-Jabbar/99 6.00 15.00
22 Scottie Pippen/599 6.00 15.00

2009-10 Hall of Fame Famed Signatures
STATED PRINT RUN 10 TO 899 SER.#'d SETS
1 Kareem Abdul-Jabbar/50 75.00 150.00
2 Nate Archibald/499 6.00 15.00
3 Rick Barry/489 6.00 15.00
4 Elgin Baylor/199 10.00 25.00
6 Carol Blazejowski/899 6.00 15.00
7 Cynthia Cooper/499 6.00 15.00
9 Dave Cowens/499 8.00 20.00
10 Adrian Dantley/499 6.00 15.00
11 Anne Donovan/899 6.00 15.00
12 Joe Dumars/399 6.00 15.00
13 Alex English/499 6.00 15.00
14 Walt Frazier/394 6.00 15.00
15 Harry Gallatin/699 6.00 15.00
16 George Gervin/398 8.00 20.00
17 Tom Gola/899 10.00 25.00
18 Gail Goodrich/499 6.00 15.00
19 Hal Greer/499 8.00 20.00
20 Cliff Hagan/499 6.00 15.00
21 John Havlicek/199 12.00 30.00
22 Connie Hawkins/599 6.00 15.00
23 Elvin Hayes/364 6.00 15.00
24 Bailey Howell/599 6.00 15.00
25 K.C. Jones/399 25.00 60.00
27 Bob Lanier/499 6.00 15.00
28 Nancy Lieberman/496 6.00 15.00
29 Bob McAdoo/391 8.00 20.00
30 Kevin McHale/100 40.00 100.00
33 Ann Meyers/499 8.00 20.00
35 Cheryl Miller/499 6.00 15.00
36 Earl Monroe/399 10.00 25.00
37 Hakeem Olajuwon/299 15.00 40.00
38 Robert Parish/499 8.00 20.00
39 Willis Reed/499 40.00 100.00
40 Oscar Robertson/99 50.00 120.00
42 Bill Russell/99 500.00 1,000.00
43 Bill Sharman/499 8.00 20.00
44 Isiah Thomas/499 10.00 25.00
45 David Thompson/599 6.00 15.00
46 Nate Thurmond/499 10.00 25.00
47 Wes Unseld/492 8.00 20.00
48 Bill Walton/249 10.00 25.00
49 Lenny Wilkens/499 6.00 15.00
50 Dominique Wilkins/199 10.00 25.00
51 James Worthy/249 15.00 40.00
58 Pat Summitt/599 50.00 120.00
60 Harry Flournoy/899 10.00 25.00
61 Nevil Shed/899 10.00 25.00
62 David Lattin/890 10.00 25.00
63 Orsten Artis/899 10.00 25.00
64 Willie Cager/899 10.00 25.00
65 Willie Worsley/850 10.00 25.00

2009-10 Hall of Fame High Class
COMPLETE SET (5) 10.00 25.00
STATED PRINT RUN 399 SER.#'d SETS
*BLACK: .6X TO 1.5X BASE HI
BLACK PRINT RUN 199 SER.#'d SETS
1 George Mikan 5.00 12.00
2 Bill Russell 5.00 12.00
3 Jerry West 2.50 6.00
4 Pete Maravich 5.00 12.00
5 Magic Johnson 6.00 15.00

2009-10 Hall of Fame High Praise
COMPLETE SET (9) 15.00 30.00
STATED PRINT RUN 399 SER.#'d SETS
1 Kareem Abdul-Jabbar 5.00 12.00
2 Oscar Robertson 2.00 5.00
3 Gail Goodrich 1.50 4.00
4 Bill Walton 2.50 6.00
5 Dominique Wilkins 2.50 6.00
6 Phil Jackson 2.00 5.00
7 David Robinson 3.00 8.00
8 Larry Bird 6.00 15.00
9 Wilt Chamberlain 6.00 15.00

2009-10 Hall of Fame Monikers
STATED PRINT RUN 10 TO 299 SER.#'d SETS
2 Walt Frazier/99 15.00 40.00
3 Nancy Lieberman/198 8.00 20.00
4 Dominique Wilkins/25 25.00 60.00
5 Bob Cousy/25 100.00 200.00
6 Elvin Hayes/99 15.00 40.00
7 George Gervin/199 15.00 40.00
8 Nate Archibald/299 8.00 20.00
9 Harry Gallatin/299 10.00 25.00
10 Connie Hawkins/199 8.00 20.00
11 Earl Monroe/199 10.00 25.00
12 Robert Parish/149 8.00 20.00
13 Jerry West/25 60.00 150.00
14 Hakeem Olajuwon/49 25.00 60.00
15 Oscar Robertson/25 100.00 225.00
16 John Havlicek/49 60.00 150.00
17 Nate Thurmond/199 12.50 30.00
18 Carol Blazejowski/299 8.00 20.00
19 Cynthia Cooper/294 8.00 20.00
20 Adrian Dantley/199 8.00 20.00
22 Clyde Drexler/99 15.00 40.00
23 Calvin Murphy/299 8.00 20.00
24 David Thompson/149 8.00 20.00
25 Isiah Thomas/99 10.00 25.00

2009-10 Hall of Fame Scoring Legends
COMPLETE SET (20) 20.00 40.00
STATED PRINT RUN 399 SER.#'d SETS
*BLACK: .6X TO 1.5X BASE HI
BLACK PRINT RUN 199 SER.#'d SETS
1 Kareem Abdul-Jabbar 5.00 12.00
2 Moses Malone 2.50 6.00
3 Dan Issel 1.25 3.00
4 Elvin Hayes 2.50 6.00
5 Oscar Robertson 2.00 5.00
6 Dominique Wilkins 2.50 6.00
7 George Gervin 2.00 5.00
8 John Havlicek 4.00 10.00
9 Rick Barry 1.25 3.00
10 Jerry West 2.50 6.00
11 Magic Johnson 6.00 15.00
12 Isiah Thomas 1.50 4.00
13 Lenny Wilkens 1.50 4.00
14 Bob Cousy 4.00 10.00
15 Nate Archibald 2.00 5.00
16 Bill Russell 5.00 12.00
17 Robert Parish 2.00 5.00
18 Nate Thurmond 1.25 3.00
19 Walt Bellamy 1.25 3.00
20 Wes Unseld 1.50 4.00

2009-10 Hall of Fame Scoring Legends Game Threads
STATED PRINT RUN 25 TO 249 SER.#'d SETS
1 Kareem Abdul-Jabbar/249 6.00 15.00
3 Dan Issel/249 2.50 6.00
6 Dominique Wilkins/249 5.00 12.00
8 John Havlicek/25 10.00 25.00
9 Rick Barry/49 2.50 6.00
11 Magic Johnson/249 6.00 15.00
12 Isiah Thomas/199 3.00 8.00
17 Robert Parish/249 4.00 10.00

2009-10 Hall of Fame Scoring Legends Game Threads Prime
STATED PRINT RUN 25 SER.#'d SETS
1 Kareem Abdul-Jabbar 8.00 20.00
3 Dan Issel 6.00 15.00
6 Dominique Wilkins 6.00 15.00
8 John Havlicek 12.00 30.00
9 Rick Barry 6.00 15.00
11 Magic Johnson 15.00 40.00
12 Isiah Thomas 15.00 40.00
17 Robert Parish 8.00 20.00

1968-74 Hall of Fame Bookmarks
COMPLETE SET (53) 150.00 300.00
1 Forrest C. Allen .60 1.50
2 Arnold J. Auerbach 1.25 3.00
3 Clair F. Bee .60 1.50
4 Bernhard Borgmann .20 .50
5 Walter A. Brown .20 .50
6 John W. Bunn .20 .50
7 Howard G. Cann .20 .50
8 H. Clifford Carlson .20 .50
9 Everett S. Dean .20 .50
10 Forrest S. DeBernardi .20 .50
11 Henry G. Dehnert .20 .50
12 Harold E. Foster .20 .50
13 Amory T. Gill .20 .50
14 Victor A. Hanson .20 .50
15 Edward J. Hickox .20 .50
16 Paul D. Hinkle .20 .50
17 Howard A. Hobson .20 .50
18 Nat Holman .75 2.00
19 Charles D. Hyatt .20 .50
20 Henry P. Iba .60 1.50
21 Edward S. Irish .25 .60
22 Alvin F. Julian .20 .50
23 Matthew P. Kennedy .20 .50
24 Robert A. Kurland .40 1.00
25 Ward L. Lambert .60 1.50
26 Joe Lapchick .40 1.00
27 Kenneth D. Loeffler .20 .50
28 Angelo Luisetti .50 1.25
29 Ed Macauley .50 1.25
30 Branch McCracken .25 .60
31 George Mikan 2.00 5.00
32 William G. Mokray .20 .50
33 Charles C. Murphy .60 1.50
34 James Naismith 1.25 3.00
35 Andy Phillip .40 1.00
36 John S. Roosma .20 .50
37 Adolph F. Rupp 1.50 4.00
38 John D. Russell .20 .50
39 Arthur A. Schabinger .20 .50
40 Amos Alonzo Stagg 1.25 3.00
41 Charles H. Taylor .20 .50
42 John A. Thompson .20 .50
43 David Tobey .20 .50
44 Oswald Tower .20 .50
45 David H. Walsh .20 .50
46 John R. Wooden 2.00 5.00
47 Bernard Carnevale 8.00 20.00
48 Bob Davies 12.00 30.00
49 Bob Cousy 25.00 60.00
50 Bob Pettit 15.00 40.00
51 Abraham M. Saperstein 20.00 50.00
52 Adolph Schayes 15.00 40.00
53 Bill Russell 40.00 100.00

2005 Hardwood Heroes NBA Medallions
COMPLETE SET (30) 25.00 60.00
1 Ray Allen 1.50 4.00
2 Carmelo Anthony 1.50 4.00
3 Elton Brand 1.25 3.00
4 Kobe Bryant 4.00 10.00
5 Vince Carter 1.50 4.00
6 Tim Duncan 1.50 4.00
7 Steve Francis 1.25 3.00
8 Kevin Garnett 2.00 5.00
9 Pau Gasol 1.25 3.00
10 Kirk Hinrich 1.25 3.00
11 Allen Iverson 1.50 4.00
12 LeBron James 5.00 12.00
13 Antawn Jamison 1.25 3.00
14 Jason Kidd 1.50 4.00
15 Andrei Kirilenko 1.25 3.00
16 Stephon Marbury 1.25 3.00
17 Tracy McGrady 1.50 4.00
18 Yao Ming 1.50 4.00
19 Steve Nash 1.50 4.00
20 Dirk Nowitzki 1.50 4.00
21 Jermaine O'Neal 1.25 3.00
22 Shaquille O'Neal 2.00 5.00
23 Emeka Okafor 1.25 3.00
24 Tony Parker 1.50 4.00
25 Paul Pierce 1.50 4.00
26 Jason Richardson 1.25 3.00
27 Peja Stojakovic 1.25 3.00
28 Amare Stoudemire 1.50 4.00
29 Dwyane Wade 1.50 4.00
30 Ben Wallace 1.25 3.00

1959-60 Hawks Busch Bavarian
COMPLETE SET (5) 400.00 800.00
1 Sihugo Green 100.00 200.00
2 Cliff Hagan 125.00 250.00
3 Clyde Lovellette 125.00 250.00
4 John McCarthy 75.00 150.00
5 Bob Pettit 250.00 450.00

1978-79 Hawks Coke/WPLO
COMPLETE SET (14) 25.00 50.00
1 Hubie Brown CO 5.00 12.00
2 Charlie Criss 2.00 5.00
3 John Drew 2.00 5.00
4 Mike Fratello CO 3.00 8.00
5 Jack Givens 3.00 8.00
6 Steve Hawes 1.25 3.00
7 Armond Hill 1.50 4.00
8 Eddie Johnson 2.00 5.00
9 Frank Layden CO 3.00 8.00
10 Butch Lee 1.25 3.00
11 Tom McMillen 2.50 6.00
12 Tree Rollins 2.50 6.00
13 Dan Roundfield 1.50 4.00
14 Rick Wilson 1.25 3.00

1961 Hawks Essex Meats
COMP.SET w/o SP (13) 200.00 400.00
1 Barney Cable 6.00 15.00
2 Al Ferrari 6.00 15.00
3 Larry Foust 6.00 15.00
4 Cliff Hagan 25.00 45.00
5 Sihugo Green SP 60.00 150.00
6 Vern Hatton 10.00 20.00
7 Cleo Hill 6.00 15.00
8 Fred LaCour 6.00 15.00
9 Fuzzy Levane CO 8.00 20.00
10 Clyde Lovellette 25.00 45.00
11 John McCarthy 6.00 15.00
12 Shellie McMillon 6.00 15.00
13 Bob Pettit 45.00 90.00
14 Bobby Sims 6.00 15.00

1979-80 Hawks Majik Market
COMPLETE SET (15) 25.00 50.00
1 Hubie Brown CO 3.00 8.00
2 John Brown 1.25 3.00
3 Charlie Criss 2.00 5.00
4 John Drew 2.00 5.00
5 Mike Fratello ACO 2.50 6.00
6 Jack Givens 2.50 6.00
7 Steve Hawes 1.50 4.00
8 Armond Hill 1.50 4.00
9 Eddie Johnson 2.00 5.00
10 Jimmy McElroy 1.25 3.00
11 Tom McMillen 2.50 6.00
12 Sam Pellom 1.25 3.00
13 Tree Rollins 2.50 6.00
14 Dan Roundfield 2.00 5.00
15 Brendan Suhr ACO 1.50 4.00

1986-87 Hawks Pizza Hut
COMPLETE SET (18) 15.00 40.00
1 Mike Fratello CO 1.25 3.00
2 Willis Reed ACO 1.50 4.00
3 Brendan Suhr ACO .40 1.00
4 Brian Hill ACO 1.00 2.50
5 Joe O'Toole TR .40 1.00
6 John Battle .60 1.50
7 Antoine Carr 1.00 2.50
8 Scott Hastings .75 2.00
9 Jon Koncak .75 2.00
10 Cliff Levingston .75 2.00
11 Mike McGee .75 2.00
12 Doc Rivers 2.50 6.00
13 Tree Rollins .75 2.00
14 Spud Webb 2.00 5.00
15 Dominique Wilkins 8.00 20.00
16 Gus Williams .75 2.00
17 Kevin Willis 2.50 6.00
18 Randy Wittman 1.25 3.00

1987-88 Hawks Pizza Hut
COMPLETE SET (17) 25.00 60.00
1 Mike Fratello CO 1.50 4.00
2 Brendan Suhr ASST .75 2.00
3 Brian Hill ASST 1.00 2.50
4 Don Chaney ASST .75 2.00
5 Joe O'Toole TR .40 1.00
6 John Battle .60 1.50
7 Antoine Carr 1.25 3.00
8 Scott Hastings .75 2.00
9 Jon Koncak .75 2.00
10 Cliff Levingston 1.00 2.50
11 Doc Rivers 3.00 8.00
12 Tree Rollins 1.00 2.50
13 Chris Washburn .75 2.00
14 Spud Webb 3.00 8.00
15 Dominique Wilkins 8.00 20.00
16 Kevin Willis 2.50 6.00
17 Randy Wittman 1.25 3.00

1968-69 Hawks Team Issue
COMPLETE SET (7) 20.00 40.00
1 Zelmo Beaty 5.00 10.00
2 Joe Caldwell 3.00 8.00
3 Jim Davis 2.50 6.00
4 Dennis Hamilton 2.50 6.00
5 Skip Harlicka 2.50 6.00
6 George Lehmann 3.00 8.00
7 Don Ohl 3.00 8.00

1969-70 Hawks Team Issue
COMPLETE SET (10) 30.00 60.00
1 Butch Beard 3.00 8.00
2 Bill Bridges 2.50 6.00
3 Joe Caldwell 2.50 6.00
4 Jim Davis 2.00 5.00
5 Gary Gregor 2.00 5.00
6 Richie Guerin CO 2.50 6.00
7 Walt Hazzard 5.00 10.00
8 Lou Hudson 6.00 12.00
9 Don Ohl 2.00 5.00
10 Grady O'Malley 2.00 5.00

1972-73 Hawks Team Issue
COMPLETE SET (9) 17.50 35.00
1 Don Adams 1.50 4.00
2 Walt Bellamy 3.00 8.00
3 Bob Christian 1.25 3.00
4 Herm Gilliam 1.25 3.00
5 Jeff Halliburton 1.25 3.00
6 Lou Hudson 3.00 8.00
7 Tom Payne 1.50 4.00
8 George Trapp 1.25 3.00
9 Jim Washington 1.25 3.00

1977-78 Hawks Team Issue
COMPLETE SET (12) 12.50 25.00
1 Hubie Brown HEAD CO 1.50 4.00
2 John Brown .75 2.00
3 Charles Criss 1.00 2.50
4 John Drew 1.00 2.50
5 Steve Hawes .75 2.00
6 Armond Hill 1.00 2.50
7 Eddie Johnson .75 2.00
8 Ollie Johnson .75 2.00
9 Tom McMillen 1.50 4.00
10 Tony Robertson .75 2.00
11 Wayne Rollins 1.00 2.50
12 Mike Fratello ACO Frank Layden ACO 1.50 4.00

1978-79 Hawks Team Issue
COMPLETE SET (11) 20.00 50.00
1 John Drew 2.50 6.00
2 Eddie Johnson 2.50 6.00
3 Dan Roundfield 3.00 8.00
4 Tree Rollins 3.00 8.00
5 Butch Lee 3.00 8.00
6 Jack Givens 3.00 8.00
7 Tom McMillen 3.00 8.00
8 Armond Hill 2.00 5.00
9 Steve Hawes 2.00 5.00
10 Charlie Criss 2.00 5.00
11 Rick Wilson 2.00 5.00

1993-94 Heat Bookmarks
COMPLETE SET (4) 1.60 4.00
1 Grant Long .40 1.00
2 Harold Miner .40 1.00
3 Rony Seikaly .40 1.00
4 Steve Smith .75 2.00

2001-02 Hawks Topps
COMPLETE SET (11) 2.00 5.00
AH2 Hanno Mottola .30 .75
AH4 Alan Henderson .30 .75
AH6 Anthony Johnson .30 .75
AH7 Chris Crawford .30 .75
AH9 Roshown McLeod .30 .75
AH10 DerMarr Johnson .30 .75
AH11 Cal Bowdler .30 .75
AH12 Lorenzen Wright .30 .75
AH13 Dion Glover .30 .75
AH14 Jason Terry .50 1.25
NNO Atlanta Hawks .25 .60

1989-90 Heat Publix
COMPLETE SET (15) 40.00 100.00
1 Terry Davis 2.00 5.00
2 Sherman Douglas 6.00 15.00
3 Kevin Edwards 3.00 8.00
4 Tony Fiorentino CO 2.00 5.00
5 Tellis Frank 2.00 5.00
6 Scott Haffner 2.00 5.00
7 Grant Long 6.00 15.00
8 Heat Mascot 1.50 4.00
9 Glen Rice 15.00 40.00
10 Ron Rothstein CO 5.00 12.00
11 Rony Seikaly 6.00 15.00
12 Rory Sparrow 2.50 6.00
13 Jon Sundvold 2.50 6.00
14 Billy Thompson 3.00 8.00
15 Dave Wohl CO 3.00 8.00

1990-91 Heat Publix
COMPLETE SET (16) 8.00 20.00
1 Keith Askins .60 1.50
2 Willie Burton .60 1.50
3 Bimbo Coles .75 2.00
4 Terry Davis .40 1.00
5 Sherman Douglas .75 2.00
6 Kevin Edwards .75 2.00
7 Alec Kessler .40 1.00
8 Grant Long 1.25 3.00
9 Alan Ogg .40 1.00
10 Glen Rice 3.00 8.00
11 Rony Seikaly 1.25 3.00
12 Jon Sundvold .40 1.00
13 Billy Thompson .75 2.00
14 Ron Rothstein CO 1.25 3.00
15 Dave Wohl CO 1.25 3.00
16 Tony Fiorentino CO .40 1.00

2008-09 Heat Upper Deck
COMPLETE SET (14) 2.50 6.00
1 Dwyane Wade .60 1.50
2 Shawn Marion .30 .75
3 Udonis Haslem .20 .50
4 Yakhouba Diawara .20 .50
5 Dorell Wright .20 .50
6 Daequan Cook .20 .50
7 Chris Quinn .20 .50
8 Mark Blount .20 .50
9 Marcus Banks .20 .50
10 Alonzo Mourning .40 1.00
11 Michael Beasley .30 .75
12 Mario Chalmers .30 .75
13 Erik Spoelstra CO .20 .50
14 Glen Rice .25 .60

1910 Helmar Premiums
COMPLETE SET 2,500.00 5,000.00
1 Card Stock 200.00 400.00
2 Individual Satin 400.00 800.00
3 Leather 1,000.00 2,000.00
4 Satin Pillow Top Eight Women shown including Basketball Girl 1,500.00 3,000.00

1997 Highland Mint Legends Mint-Cards
COMPLETE SET (7) 400.00 800.00
1 Kareem Abdul-Jabbar 95 S/1000 150.00 225.00
2 Kareem Abdul-Jabbar 95 B/5000 20.00 35.00
3 Larry Bird 95 G/500 250.00 450.00
4 Larry Bird 95 S/1000 150.00 225.00
5 Larry Bird 95 B/5000 20.00 35.00
6 Jerry West 95 S/500 150.00 225.00
7 Jerry West 95 B/2500 20.00 35.00

1997 Highland Mint Magnum Series Medallions
COMPLETE SET (2) 100.00 200.00
1 Michael Jordan Silver 750 175.00 250.00
2 Michael Jordan Bronze 3000 15.00 30.00

1997 Highland Mint Mini Mint-Cards
COMPLETE SET (4) 100.00 250.00
1 Grant Hill Jason Kidd Silver 1000 40.00 100.00
2 Grant Hill Jason Kidd Bronze 5000 15.00 30.00
3 Michael Jordan Michael Jordan Silver 1000 75.00 150.00
4 Michael Jordan Michael Jordan Bronze 5000 20.00 50.00

1997 Highland Mint Mint-Cards Fleer/Hoops/UD
COMPLETE SET (19) 1,200.00 2,000.00
1 Charles Barkley 86-87 S/1000 150.00 200.00
2 Charles Barkley 86-87 B/5000 12.50 30.00
3 Anfernee Hardaway 93-94UD S/500 150.00 200.00
4 Anfernee Hardaway 93-94UD B/2500 12.50 30.00
5 Anfernee Hardaway 93-94UDSE S/500 150.00 200.00
6 Anfernee Hardaway 93-94UDSE B/2500 10.00 25.00
7 Magic Johnson 90-91 S/1000 150.00 200.00
8 Magic Johnson 90-91 B/5000 20.00 35.00
9 Michael Jordan 91-92 G/500 250.00 450.00
10 Michael Jordan 91-92 S/1000 175.00 250.00
11 Michael Jordan 91-92 B/5000 20.00 50.00
12 Hakeem Olajuwon 86-87 S/250 150.00 200.00
13 Hakeem Olajuwon 86-87 B/1500 10.00 25.00
14 David Robinson 89-90 S/1000 150.00 200.00
15 David Robinson 89-90 B/5000 20.00 35.00
16 Jerry Stackhouse 95-96 S/500 150.00 200.00
17 Jerry Stackhouse 95-96 B/2500 10.00 25.00
18 Damon Stoudamire 95-96 S/500 150.00 200.00
19 Damon Stoudamire 95-96 B/2500 10.00 25.00

1997 Highland Mint Mint-Coins
COMPLETE SET (31) 900.00 1,500.00
1 Larry Bird Silver 7500 30.00 50.00
2 Chicago Bulls 70 Wins Silver 2500 30.00 50.00
3 Chicago Bulls Division Silver 5000 30.00 50.00
4 Chicago Bulls Conference Silver 5000 30.00 50.00
5 Chicago Bulls Finals Silver 7500 30.00 50.00
6 Chicago Bulls Finals Gold Signature 1500 35.00 60.00
7 Chicago Bulls Seattle SuperSonics Conference Silver 500 30.00 50.00
8 Kevin Garnett Silver 7500 30.00 50.00
9 Anfernee Hardaway Gold Signature 1500 30.00 50.00
10 Anfernee Hardaway Silver 7500 30.00 50.00
11 Anfernee Hardaway Bronze 25000 2.50 6.00
12 Allen Iverson Silver 3000 30.00 50.00
13 Larry Johnson Silver 7500 30.00 50.00
14 Michael Jordan Gold 100 400.00 800.00
15 Michael Jordan Gold Signature 1000 30.00 50.00
16 Michael Jordan Silver 7500 30.00 50.00
17 Michael Jordan Bronze 25000 5.00 12.00
18 Shawn Kemp Silver 7500 30.00 50.00
19 Orlando Magic Silver 5000 30.00 50.00
20 Orlando Magic Div. Silver 1000 30.00 50.00
21 Scottie Pippen Silver 7500 30.00 50.00
22 Mitch Richmond Gold Signature 1000 30.00 50.00
23 Dennis Rodman Red hair Silver 7500 30.00 50.00
24 Dennis Rodman Green hair Bronze 12500 2.50 6.00
25 Dennis Rodman Yellow hair

Bronze 12500 2.50 6.00
26 Dennis Rodman 3-coin set
Bronze 2500 20.00 40.00
27 San Antonio Spurs Div.
Silver 1000 30.00 50.00
28 Seattle Supersonics Div.
Silver 1000 30.00 50.00
29 Seattle Supersonics Conf.
Silver 5000 30.00 50.00
30 John Stockton
Silver 7500 30.00 50.00
31 Nick Van Exel
Silver 7500 30.00 50.00

1997 Highland Mint Sandblast Mint-Cards

COMPLETE SET (2) 100.00 175.00
1 Grant Hill 96
S/500 150.00 200.00
2 Grant Hill 96
B/2500 15.00 30.00

2001 Highland Mint Shaquille O'Neal Promo

NNO Shaquille O'Neal Jsy 30.00 65.00

1994-95 Hoop Magazine/Mother's Cookies

COMPLETE SET (27) 40.00 100.00
1 Mookie Blaylock 2.50 6.00
2 Dee Brown 2.00 5.00
3 Alonzo Mourning 4.00 10.00
4 B.J. Armstrong 2.50 6.00
5 Mark Price 2.50 6.00
6 Jason Kidd 5.00 12.00
7 Dikembe Mutombo 4.00 10.00
8 Joe Dumars 2.50 6.00
9 Latrell Sprewell 3.00 8.00
10 Hakeem Olajuwon 4.00 10.00
11 Reggie Miller 4.00 10.00
12 Loy Vaught 1.50 4.00
13 Vlade Divac 2.50 6.00
14 Glen Rice 2.50 6.00
15 Vin Baker 2.50 6.00
16 Isaiah Rider 2.50 6.00
17 Kenny Anderson 2.00 5.00
18 Patrick Ewing 4.00 10.00
19 Shaquille O'Neal 10.00 25.00
20 Clarence Weatherspoon 1.50 4.00
21 Charles Barkley 4.00 10.00
22 Clyde Drexler 5.00 12.00
23 Mitch Richmond 3.00 8.00
24 David Robinson 4.00 10.00
25 Gary Payton 4.00 10.00
26 John Stockton 4.00 10.00
27 Calbert Cheaney 2.00 5.00

1995-96 Hoop Magazine/Mother's Cookies

COMPLETE SET (29) 175.00 350.00
1 Craig Ehlo 1.50 4.00
2 Eric Montross 1.50 4.00
3 Larry Johnson 3.00 8.00
4 Michael Jordan 100.00 250.00
5 Terrell Brandon 2.00 5.00
6 Jim Jackson 2.00 5.00
7 Mahmoud Abdul-Rauf 2.00 5.00
8 Allan Houston 2.00 5.00
9 Tim Hardaway 3.00 8.00
10 Clyde Drexler 4.00 10.00
11 Rik Smits 2.00 5.00
12 Lamond Murray 1.50 4.00
13 Vlade Divac 2.50 6.00
14 Glen Rice 2.50 6.00
15 Glenn Robinson 2.50 6.00
16 Tom Gugliotta 1.50 4.00
17 Ed O'Bannon 2.00 5.00
18 Patrick Ewing 4.00 10.00
19 Anfernee Hardaway 6.00 15.00
20 Jerry Stackhouse 8.00 20.00
21 Kevin Johnson 2.50 6.00
22 Rod Strickland 1.50 4.00
23 Mitch Richmond 3.00 8.00
24 Avery Johnson 2.00 5.00
25 Detlef Schrempf 2.50 6.00
26 Damon Stoudamire 6.00 15.00
27 Karl Malone 5.00 12.00
28 Greg Anthony 1.50 4.00
29 Juwan Howard 2.50 6.00

1995-96 Hoop Magazine/Mother's Cookies Award Winners

COMPLETE SET (7) 10.00 25.00
1 David Robinson 5.00 12.00
2 Jason Kidd 4.00 10.00
3 Grant Hill 4.00 10.00
4 Dana Barros 2.00 5.00
5 Anthony Mason 1.50 4.00
6 Del Harris CO 1.50 4.00
7 Dikembe Mutombo 4.00 10.00

1989-90 Hoops

COMPLETE SET (352) 12.00 30.00
COMPLETE SERIES 1 (300) 10.00 25.00
COMPLETE SERIES 2 (52) 2.50 5.00
BEWARE ROBINSON 138 COUNTERFEIT
1 Joe Dumars .40 1.00
2 Tree Rollins .25 .60
3 Kenny Walker .25 .60
5 Alvin Robertson SP .75 2.00
7 Greg Anderson SP .75 2.00
8 Rod Strickland RC .60 1.50
9 Ed Pinckney .25 .60
10 Dale Ellis .30 .75
11 Chuck Daly CO RC 1.00 2.50
12 Eric Leckner .25 .60
13 Charles Davis .25 .60
14 Cotton Fitzsimmons CO .40 1.00
15 Byron Scott .40 1.00
16 Derrick Chievous .25 .60
18 Jim Paxson .30 .75
19 Tony Campbell RC .40 1.00
20 Rolando Blackman .30 .75
21 Michael Jordan AS 3.00 8.00
22 Cliff Levingston .30 .75
23 Roy Tarpley .25 .60
24 Harold Pressley UER .25 .60
25 Larry Nance .30 .75
26 Chris Morris RC .40 1.00
27 Bob Hansen UER .25 .60
28 Mark Price AS .40 1.00
29 Reggie Miller .75 2.00
30 Karl Malone .75 2.00
31 Sidney Lowe SP .75 2.00
32 Ron Anderson .25 .60
33 Mike Gminski .25 .60
34 Scott Brooks RC .50 1.25
35 Kevin Johnson RC 1.00 2.50
36 Mark Bryant RC .40 1.00
37 Rik Smits RC .60 1.50
38 Tim Perry RC .40 1.00
39 Ralph Sampson .40 1.00
40 Danny Manning UER RC .75 2.00
41 Kevin Edwards RC .40 1.00
42 Paul Mokeski .25 .60
43 Dale Ellis AS .30 .75
44 Walter Berry .25 .60
45 Chuck Person .30 .75
46 Rick Mahorn SP .75 2.00
47 Joe Kleine .25 .60
48 Brad Daugherty AS .30 .75
49 Mike Woodson .30 .75
50 Brad Daugherty .30 .75
51 Shelton Jones SP .75 2.00
52 Michael Adams .30 .75
53 Wes Unseld CO .40 1.00
54 Rex Chapman RC .60 1.50
55 Kelly Tripucka .30 .75
56 Rickey Green .25 .60
57 Frank Johnson SP .75 2.00
58 Johnny Newman RC .40 1.00
59 Billy Thompson .25 .60
60 Stu Jackson CO .30 .75
61 Walter Davis .30 .75
62 Brian Shaw SP UER RC .50 1.25
63 Gerald Wilkins .30 .75
64 Armon Gilliam .25 .60
65 Maurice Cheeks SP .75 2.00
66 Jack Sikma .40 1.00
68 Jim Lynam CO .30 .75
69 Clyde Drexler AS .60 1.50
70 Xavier McDaniel .40 1.00
71 Danny Young .25 .60
72 Fennis Dembo .25 .60
73 Mark Acres SP .75 2.00
74 Brad Lohaus SP RC .75 2.00
75 Manute Bol .40 1.00
76 Purvis Short .25 .60
77 Allen Leavell .25 .60
78 Johnny Dawkins SP .75 2.00
79 Paul Pressey .30 .75
80 Patrick Ewing .60 1.50
81 Bill Wennington RC .60 1.50
82 Danny Schayes .25 .60
83 Derek Smith .25 .60
84 Moses Malone AS .60 1.50
85 Jeff Malone .30 .75
86 Otis Smith SP RC .75 2.00
87 Trent Tucker .30 .75
88 Robert Reid .25 .60
89 John Paxson .40 1.00
90 Chris Mullin .60 1.50
91 Tom Garrick RC .30 .75
92 Willis Reed CO SP UER .75 2.00
93 Dave Corzine SP .75 2.00
94 Mark Alarie .25 .60
95 Mark Aguirre .30 .75
96 Charles Barkley AS 1.00 2.50
97 Sidney Green SP .75 2.00
98 Kevin Willis .30 .75
99 Dave Hoppen .25 .60
100 Terry Cummings SP .75 2.00
101 Dwayne Washington SP .75 2.00
102 Larry Brown CO .40 1.00
103 Kevin Duckworth .30 .75
104 Uwe Blab SP .75 2.00
105 Terry Porter .30 .75
106 Craig Ehlo RC .50 1.25
107 Don Casey CO .30 .75
108 Pat Riley CO .50 1.25
109 John Salley .30 .75
110 Charles Barkley 1.00 2.50
111 Sam Bowie SP .75 2.00
112 Earl Cureton .25 .60
113 Craig Hodges UER .30 .75
114 Benoit Benjamin .25 .60
115A S.Webb 9/27/89 ERR SP .75 2.00
115B S.Webb 9/26/85 COR .40 1.00
116 Karl Malone AS .75 2.00
117 Sleepy Floyd .30 .75
118 Hot Rod Williams .30 .75
119 Michael Holton .25 .60
120 Alex English .40 1.00
121 Dennis Johnson .40 1.00
122 Wayne Cooper SP .75 2.00
123A Don Chaney CO .30 .75
123B Don Chaney CO .30 .75
124 A.C. Green .30 .75
125 Adrian Dantley .40 1.00
126 Del Harris CO .30 .75
127 Dick Harter CO .25 .60
128 Reggie Williams RC .40 1.00
129 Bill Hanzlik .25 .60
130 Dominique Wilkins .60 1.50
131 Herb Williams .25 .60
132 Steve Johnson SP .75 2.00
133 Alex English AS .40 1.00
134 Darrell Walker .25 .60
135 Bill Laimbeer .40 1.00
136 Fred Roberts RC .30 .75
137 Hersey Hawkins RC .50 1.25
138 David Robinson SP RC 4.00 10.00
139 Brad Sellers SP .75 2.00
140 John Stockton .75 2.00
141 Grant Long RC .40 1.00
142 Marc Iavaroni SP .75 2.00
143 Steve Alford SP RC .75 2.00
144 Jeff Lamp SP .75 2.00
145 Buck Williams SP UER .75 2.00
146 Mark Jackson AS .30 .75
147 Jim Petersen .25 .60
148 Steve Stipanovich SP .75 2.00
149 Sam Vincent SP RC .75 2.00
150 Larry Bird 1.50 4.00
151 Jon Koncak RC .40 1.00
152 Olden Polynice RC .40 1.00
153 Randy Breuer .25 .60
154 John Battle RC .40 1.00
155 Mark Eaton .40 1.00
156 Kevin McHale AS UER .60 1.50
157 Jerry Sichting SP .75 2.00
158 Pat Cummings SP .75 2.00
159 Patrick Ewing AS .50 1.25
160 Mark Price .40 1.00
161 Jerry Reynolds CO .30 .75
162 Ken Norman RC .50 1.25
163 John Bagley SP UER .75 2.00
164 Christian Welp SP .75 2.00
165 Reggie Theus SP .75 2.00
166 Magic Johnson AS 1.50 4.00
168 Larry Smith SP .75 2.00
169 Charles Shackleford RC .40 1.00
170 Tom Chambers .40 1.00
171A John MacLeod CO SP ERR .30 .75
171B John MacLeod CO COR .30 .75
172 Ron Rothstein CO .30 .75
173 Joe Wolf .25 .60
174 Mark Eaton AS .40 1.00
175 Jon Sundvold .25 .60
176 Scott Hastings SP .75 2.00
177 Isiah Thomas AS .60 1.50
178 Hakeem Olajuwon AS .75 2.00
179 Mike Fratello CO .30 .75
180 Hakeem Olajuwon .75 2.00
181 Randolph Keys .25 .60
182 Richard Anderson UER .25 .60
183 Dan Majerle RC 1.00 2.50
184 Derek Harper .30 .75
185 Robert Parish .50 1.25
186 Ricky Berry SP .75 2.00
187 Michael Cooper .40 1.00
188 Vinnie Johnson .30 .75
189 James Donaldson .25 .60
190 Clyde Drexler UER .60 1.50
191 Jay Vincent SP .75 2.00
192 Nate McMillan .30 .75
193 Kevin Duckworth AS .30 .75
194 Ledell Eackles RC .40 1.00
195 Eddie Johnson .30 .75
196 Terry Teagle .30 .75
197 Tom Chambers AS .40 1.00
198 Joe Barry Carroll .25 .60
199 Dennis Hopson RC .40 1.00
200 Michael Jordan 3.00 8.00
201 Jerome Lane RC .40 1.00
202 Greg Kite RC .30 .75
203 David Rivers SP .75 2.00
204 Sylvester Gray .25 .60
205 Ron Harper .40 1.00
206 Frank Brickowski .25 .60
207 Rory Sparrow .25 .60
208 Gerald Henderson .25 .60
209 Rod Higgins UER .25 .60
210 James Worthy .60 1.50
211 Dennis Rodman 1.00 2.50
212 Ricky Pierce .30 .75
213 Charles Oakley .40 1.00
214 Steve Colter .25 .60
215 Danny Ainge .40 1.00
216 Lenny Wilkens CO UER .40 1.00
217 Larry Nance AS .30 .75
218 Muggsy Bogues .40 1.00
219 James Worthy AS .60 1.50
220 Lafayette Lever .40 1.00
221 Quintin Dailey SP .75 2.00
222 Lester Conner .25 .60
223 Jose Ortiz .25 .60
224 Micheal Williams SP UER RC .75 2.00
225 Wayman Tisdale .40 1.00
226 Mike Sanders SP .75 2.00
227 Jim Farmer SP .75 2.00
228 Mark West .25 .60
229 Jeff Hornacek RC .75 2.00
230 Chris Mullin AS .60 1.50
235 Willie Anderson RC .50 1.25
236 Keith Lee SP .75 2.00
237 Buck Johnson RC .40 1.00
238 Randy Wittman .25 .60
239 Terry Catledge SP .75 2.00
240 Bernard King .50 1.25
241 Darrell Griffith .30 .75
242 Horace Grant .40 1.00
243 Rony Seikaly RC .60 1.50
244 Scottie Pippen 1.00 2.50
245 Michael Cage UER .30 .75
246 Kurt Rambis .30 .75
247 Morlon Wiley SP RC .75 2.00
248 Ronnie Grandison .25 .60
249 Scott Skiles SP RC .75 2.00
250 Isiah Thomas .60 1.50
251 Thurl Bailey .30 .75
252 Doc Rivers .40 1.00
253 Stuart Gray SP .75 2.00
254 John Williams .25 .60
255 Bill Cartwright .30 .75
256 Terry Cummings AS .30 .75
257 Rodney McCray .30 .75
258 Larry Krystkowiak RC .40 1.00
259 Will Perdue RC .60 1.50
260 Mitch Richmond RC 1.25 3.00
261 Blair Rasmussen .25 .60
262 Charles Smith RC .50 1.25
263 Tyrone Corbin SP RC .75 2.00
264 Kelvin Upshaw .25 .60
265 Otis Thorpe .40 1.00
266 Phil Jackson CO 1.50 4.00
267 Jerry Sloan CO .40 1.00
268 John Shasky .25 .60
269A B.Bickerstaff CO SP ERR .75 2.00
269B B.Bickerstaff CO COR .30 .75
270 Magic Johnson 1.50 4.00
271 Vernon Maxwell RC .60 1.50
272 Tim McCormick .25 .60
273 Don Nelson CO .40 1.00
274 Gary Grant RC .50 1.25
275 Sidney Moncrief SP .75 2.00
276 Roy Hinson .25 .60
277 Jimmy Rodgers CO .30 .75
278 Antoine Carr .30 .75
279A Orlando Woolridge ERR .40 1.00
279B Orlando Woolridge COR .40 1.00
280 Kevin McHale .60 1.50
281 LaSalle Thompson .25 .60
282 Detlef Schrempf .30 .75
283 Doug Moe CO .30 .75
284A James Edwards .30 .75
284B James Edwards .30 .75
285 Jerome Kersey .30 .75
286 Sam Perkins .30 .75
287 Sedale Threatt .25 .60
288 Tim Kempton SP .75 2.00
289 Mark McNamara .25 .60
290 Moses Malone .60 1.50
291 Rick Adelman CO UER .30 .75
292 Dick Versace CO .30 .75
293 Alton Lister SP .75 2.00
294 Winston Garland .25 .60
295 Kiki Vandeweghe .30 .75
296 Brad Davis .25 .60
297 John Stockton AS .75 2.00
298 Jay Humphries .30 .75
299 Dell Curry .40 1.00
300 Mark Jackson .30 .75
301 Morlon Wiley .25 .60
302 Reggie Theus .30 .75
303 Otis Smith .25 .60
304 Tod Murphy RC .40 1.00
305 Sidney Green .25 .60
306 Shelton Jones .25 .60
307 Mark Acres .25 .60
308 Terry Catledge .25 .60
309 Larry Smith .25 .60
310 David Robinson IA .75 2.00
312 Terry Cummings .30 .75
313 Sidney Lowe .25 .60
314 Bill Musselman CO .30 .75
315 Buck Williams UER .40 1.00
316 Mel Turpin .25 .60
317 Scott Hastings .25 .60
318 Scott Skiles .40 1.00
319 Tyrone Corbin .30 .75
320 Maurice Cheeks .30 .75
321 Matt Guokas CO .30 .75
322 Jeff Turner .25 .60
323 David Wingate .30 .75
324 Steve Johnson .25 .60
325 Alton Lister .25 .60
326 Ken Bannister .25 .60
327 Bill Fitch CO UER .30 .75
328 Sam Vincent .25 .60
329 Larry Drew .25 .60
330 Rick Mahorn .30 .75
331 Christian Welp .25 .60
332 Brad Lohaus .25 .60
333 Frank Johnson .25 .60
334 Jim Farmer .25 .60
335 Wayne Cooper .25 .60
336 Mike Brown RC .40 1.00
337 Sam Bowie .30 .75
338 Kevin Gamble RC .40 1.00
339 Jerry Ice Reynolds RC .40 1.00
340 Mike Sanders .25 .60
341 Bill Jones UER .25 .60
342 Greg Anderson .25 .60
343 Dave Corzine .25 .60
344 Micheal Williams UER .25 .60
345 Jay Vincent .25 .60
346 David Rivers .25 .60
347 Caldwell Jones UER .25 .60
348 Brad Sellers .25 .60
349 Scott Roth .25 .60
350 Alvin Robertson .30 .75
351 Steve Kerr RC 2.00 5.00
352 Stuart Gray .25 .60
353A Pistons Champions SP 1.50 4.00
353B Pistons Champions UER .20 .50

1989-90 Hoops Checklists

COMPLETE SET (2) 1.60 4.00
COMMON CARD (1-2) .80 2.00

1990-91 Hoops

COMPLETE SET (440) 12.00 30.00
COMPLETE SERIES 1 (336) 8.00 20.00
COMPLETE SERIES 2 (104) 4.00 10.00
1 Charles Barkley AS SP 1.00 2.50
2 Larry Bird AS SP 1.50 4.00
3 Joe Dumars AS SP .50 1.25
4 Patrick Ewing AS SP UER .60 1.50
5 Michael Jordan AS SP UER 3.00 8.00
6 Kevin McHale AS SP .60 1.50
7 Reggie Miller AS SP .75 2.00
8 Robert Parish AS SP .50 1.25
9 Scottie Pippen AS SP 1.00 2.50
10 Dennis Rodman AS SP 1.00 2.50
11 Isiah Thomas AS SP .60 1.50
12 Dominique Wilkins AS SP .60 1.50
13A AS CL: ERR NNO SP 1.50 4.00
13B AS CL: COR SP .40 1.00
14 Rolando Blackman AS SP .30 .75
15 Tom Chambers AS SP .40 1.00
16 Clyde Drexler AS SP .60 1.50
17 A.C. Green AS SP .30 .75
18 Magic Johnson AS SP 1.50 4.00
19 Kevin Johnson AS SP .40 1.00
20 Lafayette Lever AS SP .30 .75
21 Karl Malone AS SP .75 2.00
22 Chris Mullin AS SP .50 1.25
23 Hakeem Olajuwon AS SP .75 2.00
24 David Robinson AS SP .75 2.00
25 John Stockton AS SP .75 2.00
26 James Worthy AS SP .60 1.50
27 John Battle .20 .50
28 Jon Koncak .20 .50
29 Cliff Levingston SP .25 .60
30 John Long SP .20 .50
31 Moses Malone .50 1.25
32 Doc Rivers .30 .75
33 Kenny Smith SP .25 .60
34 Alexander Volkov RC .20 .50
35 Spud Webb .30 .75
36 Dominique Wilkins .50 1.25
37 Kevin Willis .25 .60
38 John Bagley .20 .50
39 Larry Bird 1.25 3.00
40 Kevin Gamble .20 .50
41 Dennis Johnson SP .40 1.00
42 Joe Kleine .20 .50
43 Reggie Lewis .30 .75
44 Kevin McHale .50 1.25
45 Robert Parish .40 1.00
46 Jim Paxson SP .25 .60
47 Ed Pinckney .20 .50
48 Brian Shaw .25 .60
49 Richard Anderson SP .20 .50
50 Muggsy Bogues .30 .75
51 Rex Chapman .25 .60
52 Dell Curry .30 .75
53 Kenny Gattison RC .20 .50
54 Armon Gilliam .20 .50
55 Dave Hoppen .20 .50
56 Randolph Keys .20 .50
57 J.R. Reid RC .25 .60
58 Robert Reid SP .25 .60
59 Kelly Tripucka .25 .60
60 B.J. Armstrong RC .40 1.00
61 Bill Cartwright .25 .60
62 Charles Davis SP .20 .50
63 Horace Grant .30 .75
64 Craig Hodges .25 .60
65 Michael Jordan 2.50 6.00
66 Stacey King RC .30 .75
67 John Paxson .25 .60
68 Will Perdue .25 .60
69 Scottie Pippen .75 2.00
70 Winston Bennett .20 .50
71 Chucky Brown RC .20 .50
72 Derrick Chievous .20 .50
73 Brad Daugherty .30 .75
74 Craig Ehlo .25 .60
75 Steve Kerr .40 1.00
76 Paul Mokeski SP .20 .50
77 John Morton .20 .50
78 Larry Nance .30 .75
79 Mark Price .30 .75
80 Hot Rod Williams .25 .60
81 Steve Alford .25 .60
82 Rolando Blackman .25 .60
83 Adrian Dantley SP .30 .75
84 Brad Davis .20 .50
85 James Donaldson .20 .50
86 Derek Harper .30 .75
87 Sam Perkins SP .25 .60
88 Roy Tarpley .25 .60
89 Bill Wennington SP .25 .60
90 Herb Williams .25 .60
91 Michael Adams .25 .60
92 Joe Barry Carroll SP .20 .50
93 Walter Davis UER .25 .60
94 Alex English SP .40 1.00
95 Bill Hanzlik .20 .50
96 Jerome Lane .20 .50
97 Lafayette Lever SP .20 .50
98 Todd Lichti RC .20 .50
99 Blair Rasmussen .20 .50
100 Danny Schayes SP .20 .50
101 Mark Aguirre .25 .60
102 William Bedford RC .25 .60
103 Joe Dumars .40 1.00
104 James Edwards .20 .50
105 Scott Hastings .20 .50
106 Gerald Henderson SP .20 .50
107 Vinnie Johnson .25 .60
108 Bill Laimbeer .25 .60
109 Dennis Rodman .75 2.00
110 John Salley .20 .50
111 Isiah Thomas .50 1.25
112 Manute Bol SP .20 .50
113 Tim Hardaway RC .75 2.00
114 Rod Higgins .20 .50
115 Sarunas Marciulionis RC .50 1.25
116 Chris Mullin UER .40 1.00
117 Jim Petersen .20 .50
118 Mitch Richmond .40 1.00
119 Mike Smrek .20 .50
120 Terry Teagle SP .25 .60
121 Tom Tolbert RC .25 .60
122 Christian Welp SP .20 .50
123 Byron Dinkins SP .20 .50
124 Eric (Sleepy) Floyd .25 .60
125 Buck Johnson .20 .50
126 Vernon Maxwell .25 .60
127 Hakeem Olajuwon .60 1.50
128 Larry Smith .20 .50
129 Otis Thorpe .30 .75
130 Mitchell Wiggins SP .20 .50
131 Mike Woodson .25 .60
132 Greg Dreiling RC .20 .50
133 Vern Fleming .25 .60
134 Rickey Green SP .20 .50
135 Reggie Miller .60 1.50
136 Chuck Person .25 .60
137 Mike Sanders .20 .50
138 Detlef Schrempf .30 .75
139 Rik Smits .25 .60
140 LaSalle Thompson .20 .50
141 Randy Wittman .20 .50
142 Benoit Benjamin .20 .50
143 Winston Garland .20 .50
144 Tom Garrick .20 .50
145 Gary Grant .20 .50
146 Ron Harper .30 .75
147 Danny Manning .30 .75
148 Jeff Martin .20 .50
149 Ken Norman .20 .50
150 David Rivers SP .20 .50
151 Charles Smith .20 .50
152 Joe Wolf SP .20 .50
153 Michael Cooper SP .20 .50
154 Vlade Divac UER RC .50 1.25
155 Larry Drew .20 .50
156 A.C. Green .25 .60
157 Magic Johnson 1.25 3.00
158 Mark McNamara SP .20 .50
159 Byron Scott .30 .75
160 Mychal Thompson .25 .60
161 Jay Vincent SP .20 .50
162 Orlando Woolridge SP .25 .60
163 James Worthy .50 1.25
164 Sherman Douglas RC .25 .60
165 Kevin Edwards .20 .50
166 Tellis Frank SP .20 .50
167 Grant Long .20 .50
168 Glen Rice RC .40 1.00
169A Rony Seikaly Athens .25 .60
169B Rony Seikaly Beirut .25 .60
170 Rony Seikaly SP .20 .50
171A Jon Sundvold .20 .50
171B Billy Thompson .20 .50
172A Billy Thompson .20 .50
172B Jon Sundvold .20 .50
173 Greg Anderson .20 .50
174 Jeff Grayer RC .30 .75
175 Jay Humphries .25 .60
176 Frank Kornet .20 .50
177 Larry Krystkowiak .20 .50
178 Brad Lohaus .20 .50
179 Ricky Pierce .25 .60
180 Paul Pressey SP .25 .60
181 Fred Roberts .20 .50
182 Alvin Robertson .30 .75
183 Jack Sikma .40 1.00
184 Randy Breuer .20 .50
185 Tony Campbell .20 .50
186 Tyrone Corbin .20 .50
187 Sidney Lowe SP .20 .50
188 Sam Mitchell RC .30 .75
189 Tod Murphy .20 .50
190 Pooh Richardson RC .30 .75
191 Scott Roth SP .20 .50
192 Brad Sellers SP .20 .50
193 Mookie Blaylock RC .40 1.00
194 Sam Bowie .25 .60
195 Lester Conner .20 .50
196 Derrick Gervin .20 .50
197 Jack Haley RC .30 .75
198 Roy Hinson .25 .60
199 Dennis Hopson SP .20 .50
200 Chris Morris .20 .50
201 Purvis Short SP .20 .50
202 Maurice Cheeks .25 .60
203 Patrick Ewing .50 1.25
204 Stuart Gray .20 .50
205 M.Jackson Menendez bros 10.00 25.00
206 Johnny Newman SP .25 .60
207 Charles Oakley .25 .60
208 Trent Tucker .20 .50
209 Kiki Vandeweghe .25 .60
210 Kenny Walker .25 .60
211 Eddie Lee Wilkins .20 .50
212 Gerald Wilkins .25 .60
213 Mark Acres .20 .50
214 Nick Anderson RC .40 1.00
215 Michael Ansley UER .20 .50
216 Terry Catledge .20 .50
217 Dave Corzine SP .20 .50
218 Sidney Green SP .20 .50
219 Jerry Reynolds .20 .50
220 Scott Skiles .25 .60
221 Otis Smith .20 .50
222 Reggie Theus SP .25 .60
223A S.Vincent w/M.Jordan 2.50 6.00
223B Sam Vincent .20 .50
224 Ron Anderson .20 .50
225 Charles Barkley .75 2.00
226 Scott Brooks SP UER .20 .50
227 Johnny Dawkins .25 .60
228 Mike Gminski .20 .50
229 Hersey Hawkins .25 .60
230 Rick Mahorn .25 .60
231 Derek Smith SP .20 .50
232 Bob Thornton .20 .50
233 Kenny Battle RC .20 .50
234A Tom Chambers Forward .30 .75
234B Tom Chambers Guard .30 .75
235 Greg Grant SP RC .30 .75
236 Jeff Hornacek .25 .60
237 Eddie Johnson .20 .50
238A Kevin Johnson Guard .30 .75
238B Kevin Johnson Forward .30 .75
239 Dan Majerle .25 .60
240 Tim Perry .20 .50
241 Kurt Rambis .25 .60
242 Mark West .20 .50
243 Mark Bryant .20 .50
244 Wayne Cooper .20 .50
245 Clyde Drexler .50 1.25
246 Kevin Duckworth .25 .60
247 Jerome Kersey .25 .60
248 Drazen Petrovic RC .75 2.00
249A Terry Porter ERR .30 .75
249B Terry Porter COR .30 .75
250 Clifford Robinson RC .50 1.25
251 Buck Williams .30 .75
252 Danny Young .20 .50
253 Danny Ainge SP UER .30 .75
254 Randy Allen SP .20 .50
255 Antoine Carr .25 .60
256 Vinny Del Negro SP .25 .60
257 Pervis Ellison SP RC .40 1.00
258 Greg Kite SP .20 .50
259 Rodney McCray SP .25 .60
260 Harold Pressley SP .20 .50
261 Ralph Sampson .30 .75
262 Wayman Tisdale .30 .75
263 Willie Anderson .25 .60
264 Uwe Blab SP .20 .50
265 Frank Brickowski SP .20 .50
266 Terry Cummings .25 .60
267 Sean Elliott RC .40 1.00
268 Caldwell Jones SP .25 .60
269 Johnny Moore SP .25 .60
270 David Robinson .60 1.50
271 Rod Strickland .25 .60
272 Reggie Williams .20 .50
273 David Wingate SP .20 .50
274 Dana Barros UER RC .30 .75
275 Michael Cage UER .25 .60
276 Quintin Dailey .20 .50
277 Dale Ellis .25 .60
278 Steve Johnson SP .20 .50
279 Shawn Kemp RC 1.00 2.50
280 Xavier McDaniel .30 .75
281 Derrick McKey .25 .60
282 Nate McMillan .25 .60
283 Olden Polynice .20 .50
284 Sedale Threatt .20 .50
285 Thurl Bailey .25 .60
286 Mike Brown .20 .50
287 Mark Eaton UER .30 .75
288 Blue Edwards RC .30 .75
289 Darrell Griffith .30 .75
290 Bobby Hansen SP .20 .50
291 Eric Leckner SP .20 .50
292 Karl Malone .60 1.50
293 Delaney Rudd .20 .50
294 John Stockton .60 1.50
295 Mark Alarie .20 .50
296 Ledell Eackles SP .20 .50
297 Harvey Grant .25 .60
298A Tom Hammonds No Star RC 1.25 3.00
298B Tom Hammonds Star RC .30 .75
299 Charles Jones RC .20 .50
300 Bernard King .40 1.00
301 Jeff Malone SP .25 .60
302 Mel Turpin SP .20 .50
303 Darrell Walker .20 .50
304 John Williams .20 .50
305 Bob Weiss CO .30 .75
306 Chris Ford CO .30 .75
307 Gene Littles CO .30 .75
308 Phil Jackson CO .75 2.00
309 Lenny Wilkens CO .30 .75
310 Richie Adubato CO .30 .75
311 Doug Moe CO SP .30 .75
312 Chuck Daly CO .30 .75
313 Don Nelson CO .30 .75
314 Don Chaney CO .30 .75
315 Dick Versace CO .30 .75
316 Mike Schuler CO .30 .75
317 Pat Riley CO SP 1.00 2.50
318 Ron Rothstein CO .30 .75
319 Del Harris CO .30 .75
320 Bill Musselman CO .30 .75
321 Bill Fitch CO .30 .75
322 Stu Jackson CO .30 .75
323 Matt Guokas CO .30 .75
324 Jim Lynam CO .30 .75
325 Cotton Fitzsimmons CO .30 .75
326 Rick Adelman CO .30 .75
327 Dick Motta CO .30 .75
328 Larry Brown CO .30 .75
329 K.C. Jones CO .30 .75
330 Jerry Sloan CO .30 .75
331 Wes Unseld CO .30 .75
332 Checklist 1 SP .40 1.00
333 Checklist 2 SP .40 1.00
334 Checklist 3 SP .40 1.00
335 Checklist 4 SP .40 1.00
337 D.Rodman FIN .05 .15
338 D.Rodman/B.Williams FIN .05 .15
339 Joe Dumars FIN .05 .15
340 J.Kersey/I.Thomas FIN .02 .10
341A Pistons Win ERR w/o .02 .10
341B Pistons Win COR Sports .02 .10
342 Pistons Back to Back UER .02 .10
343 K.C. Jones CO .02 .10
344 Wes Unseld CO .02 .10
345 Don Nelson CO .02 .10
346 Bob Weiss CO .02 .10
347 Chris Ford CO .02 .10
348 Phil Jackson CO .05 .15
349 Lenny Wilkens CO .02 .10
350 Don Chaney CO .02 .10
351 Mike Dunleavy CO .02 .10
352 Matt Guokas CO .02 .10
353 Rick Adelman CO .02 .10
354 Jerry Sloan CO .02 .10
355 Dominique Wilkins TC .02 .10
356 Larry Bird TC .10 .30
357 Rex Chapman TC .02 .10
358 Michael Jordan TC .40 1.00
359 Mark Price TC .02 .10
360 Rolando Blackman TC .02 .10
361 Michael Adams TC UER .02 .10
362 Joe Dumars TC UER .02 .10
363 Chris Mullin TC .02 .10
364 Hakeem Olajuwon TC .05 .15
365 Reggie Miller TC .05 .15
366 Danny Manning TC .02 .10
367 Magic Johnson TC UER .08 .25
368 Rony Seikaly TC .02 .10
369 Alvin Robertson TC .02 .10
370 Pooh Richardson TC .02 .10
371 Chris Morris TC .02 .10
372 Patrick Ewing TC .02 .10
373 Nick Anderson TC .05 .15
374 Charles Barkley TC .05 .15
375 Kevin Johnson TC .02 .10
376 Clyde Drexler TC .02 .10
377 Wayman Tisdale TC .02 .10
378 David Robinson TC .08 .25
378B David Robinson TC half .10 .30
379 Xavier McDaniel TC .02 .10
380 Karl Malone TC .05 .15
381 Bernard King TC .02 .10
382 M.Jordan Playground .75 2.00
383 Karl Malone Lights .05 .15
384 V.Divac
Marciulionis .02 .10
385 M.Johnson
M.Jordan .40 1.00
386 Johnny Newman SIS .02 .10
387 Dell Curry SIS .02 .10
388 Patrick Ewing DFO .02 .10
389 Isiah Thomas DFO .02 .10
390 Derrick Coleman LS RC .10 .30
391 Gary Payton LS RC 2.00 5.00
392 Chris Jackson LS RC .02 .10
393 Dennis Scott LS RC .07 .20
394 Kendall Gill LS RC .10 .30
395 Felton Spencer LS RC .02 .10
396 Lionel Simmons LS RC .02 .10
397 Bo Kimble LS RC .02 .10
398 Willie Burton LS RC .02 .10
399 Rumeal Robinson LS RC .02 .10
400 Tyrone Hill LS RC .02 .10
401 Tim McCormick U .02 .10
402 Sidney Moncrief U .02 .10
403 Johnny Newman U .02 .10
404 Dennis Hopson U .02 .10
405 Cliff Levingston U .02 .10
406A Danny Ferry U ERR 1.50 4.00
406B Danny Ferry U COR .05 .15
407 Alex English U .02 .10
408 Lafayette Lever U .02 .10
409 Rodney McCray U .02 .10

410 Mike Dunleavy U CO .02 .10
411 Orlando Woolridge U .02 .10
412 Joe Wolf U .02 .10
413 Tree Rollins U .02 .10
414A Kenny Smith U ERR
(No position on front of card) 1.50 10.00
415 Sam Perkins U .02 .10
416 Terry Teagle U .02 .10
417 Frank Brickowski U .02 .10
418 Danny Schayes U .02 .10
419 Scott Brooks U .02 .10
420 Reggie Theus U .02 .10
421A Greg Grant U ERR
(No position on front of card) 1.50 4.00
422 Paul Westhead U CO .02 .10
423 Greg Kite U .02 .10
424 Manute Bol U .02 .10
425 Rickey Green U .02 .10
426 Ed Nealy U .02 .10
427 Danny Ainge U .02 .10
428 Bobby Hansen U .02 .10
429 Eric Leckner U .02 .10
430 Rory Sparrow U .02 .10
431 Bill Wennington U .02 .10
432 Paul Pressey U .02 .10
433 David Greenwood U .02 .10
434 Mark McNamara U .02 .10
435 Sidney Green U .02 .10
436 Dave Corzine U .02 .10
437 Jeff Malone U .02 .10
438A Pervis Ellison U ERR
(No position on front of card) 1.50 4.00
439 Checklist 5 .02 .10
440 Checklist 6 .02 .10
414B Kenny Smith U COR .20 .50
421B Greg Grant U COR .20 .50
438B Pervis Ellison U COR .20 .50
NNO D.Robinson/ART NoStats .50 1.25
NNO D.Robinson/ART Stats 2.50 6.00

1991-92 Hoops Prototypes

COMPLETE SET (10) 12.00 30.00
3 Sidney Moncrief 3.00 8.00
9 Larry Bird 6.00 15.00
18 Muggsy Bogues 1.50 4.00
120 Alvin Robertson 1.25 3.00
135 Chris Dudley 1.25 3.00
142 Charles Oakley 1.50 4.00
150 Jerry Reynolds 1.25 3.00
159 Armon Gilliam 1.25 3.00
204 Sedale Threatt 1.25 3.00
210 Jeff Malone 1.25 3.00

1991-92 Hoops Prototypes 00

COMPLETE SET (10) 60.00 150.00
1 Clyde Drexler 3.00 8.00
2 Patrick Ewing 3.00 8.00
3 Magic Johnson 4.00 10.00
4 Michael Jordan 40.00 100.00
4B Michael Jordan Metal 150.00 400.00
5 Karl Malone 3.00 8.00
6 Hakeem Olajuwon 3.00 8.00
7 Charles Barkley AS 6.00 15.00
8 Magic Johnson AS 8.00 20.00
9 Karl Malone AS 10.00 25.00
10 Dominique Wilkins AS 4.00 10.00

1991-92 Hoops

COMPLETE SET (590) 12.00 30.00
COMPLETE SERIES 1 (330) 5.00 12.00
COMPLETE SERIES 2 (260) 6.00 15.00
1 John Battle .20 .50
2 Moses Malone UER .50 1.25
3 Sidney Moncrief .30 .75
4 Doc Rivers .30 .75
5 Rumeal Robinson UER .20 .50
6 Spud Webb .30 .75
7 Dominique Wilkins .50 1.25
8 Kevin Willis .25 .60
9 Larry Bird 1.00 2.50
10 Dee Brown .25 .60
11 Kevin Gamble .20 .50
12 Joe Kleine .20 .50
13 Reggie Lewis .30 .75
14 Kevin McHale .50 1.25
15 Robert Parish .40 1.00
16 Ed Pinckney .25 .60
17 Brian Shaw .25 .60
18 Muggsy Bogues .30 .75
19 Rex Chapman .25 .60
20 Dell Curry .25 .60
21 Kendall Gill .30 .75
22 Mike Gminski .20 .50
23 Johnny Newman .20 .50
24 J.R. Reid .20 .50
25 Kelly Tripucka .25 .60
26 B.J. Armstrong UER .30 .75
27 Bill Cartwright .25 .60
28 Horace Grant .30 .75
29 Craig Hodges .25 .60
30 Michael Jordan 2.50 6.00
31 Stacey King .25 .60
32 Cliff Levingston .20 .50
33 John Paxson .25 .60
34 Scottie Pippen .75 2.00
35 Chucky Brown .20 .50
36 Brad Daugherty .30 .75
37 Craig Ehlo .20 .50
38 Danny Ferry .20 .50
39 Larry Nance .30 .75
40 Mark Price .30 .75
41 Darnell Valentine .20 .50
42 Hot Rod Williams .20 .50
43 Rolando Blackman .25 .60
44 Brad Davis .20 .50
45 James Donaldson .25 .60
46 Derek Harper .25 .60
47 Fat Lever .25 .60
48 Rodney McCray .25 .60
49 Roy Tarpley .25 .60
50 Herb Williams .25 .60
51 Michael Adams .25 .60
52 Chris Jackson UER .25 .60
53 Jerome Lane .20 .50
54 Todd Lichti .20 .50
55 Blair Rasmussen .20 .50
56 Reggie Williams .25 .60
57 Joe Wolf .20 .50
58 Orlando Woolridge .25 .60
59 Mark Aguirre .25 .60
60 Joe Dumars .40 1.00
61 James Edwards .25 .60
62 Vinnie Johnson .30 .75
63 Bill Laimbeer .30 .75
64 Dennis Rodman .60 1.50
65 John Salley .25 .60
66 Isiah Thomas .50 1.25
67 Tim Hardaway .40 1.00
68 Rod Higgins .20 .50
69 Tyrone Hill .25 .60
70 Alton Lister .20 .50
71 Sarunas Marciulionis .30 .75
72 Chris Mullin .40 1.00
73 Mitch Richmond .40 1.00
74 Tom Tolbert .20 .50
75 Eric(Sleepy) Floyd .25 .60
76 Buck Johnson .20 .50
77 Vernon Maxwell .25 .60
78 Hakeem Olajuwon .60 1.50
79 Kenny Smith .25 .60
80 Larry Smith .20 .50
81 Otis Thorpe .25 .60
82 David Wood RC .20 .50
83 Vern Fleming .20 .50
84 Reggie Miller .50 1.25
85 Chuck Person .25 .60
86 Mike Sanders .20 .50
87 Detlef Schrempf .25 .60
88 Rik Smits .25 .60
89 LaSalle Thompson .20 .50
90 Micheal Williams .20 .50
91 Winston Garland .20 .50
92 Gary Grant .20 .50
93 Ron Harper .30 .75
94 Danny Manning .25 .60
95 Jeff Martin .20 .50
96 Ken Norman .25 .60
97 Olden Polynice .20 .50
98 Charles Smith .25 .60
99 Vlade Divac .25 .60
100 A.C. Green .25 .60
101 Magic Johnson 1.00 2.50
102 Sam Perkins .25 .60
103 Byron Scott .30 .75
104 Terry Teagle .25 .60
105 Mychal Thompson .25 .60
106 James Worthy .40 1.00
107 Willie Burton .20 .50
108 Bimbo Coles .20 .50
109 Terry Davis .20 .50
110 Sherman Douglas .25 .60
111 Kevin Edwards .20 .50
112 Alec Kessler .20 .50
113 Glen Rice .30 .75
114 Rony Seikaly .25 .60
115 Frank Brickowski .20 .50
116 Dale Ellis .25 .60
117 Jay Humphries .25 .60
118 Brad Lohaus .20 .50
119 Fred Roberts .20 .50
120 Alvin Robertson .25 .60
121 Danny Schayes .20 .50
122 Jack Sikma .30 .75
123 Randy Breuer .20 .50
124 Tony Campbell .20 .50
125 Tyrone Corbin .20 .50
126 Gerald Glass .20 .50
127 Sam Mitchell .20 .50
128 Tod Murphy .20 .50
129 Pooh Richardson .25 .60
130 Felton Spencer .20 .50
131 Mookie Blaylock .30 .75
132 Sam Bowie .25 .60
133 Jud Buechler .25 .60
134 Derrick Coleman .30 .75
135 Chris Dudley .20 .50
136 Chris Morris .20 .50
137 Drazen Petrovic .40 1.00
138 Reggie Theus .25 .60
139 Maurice Cheeks .25 .60
140 Patrick Ewing .50 1.25
141 Mark Jackson .25 .60
142 Charles Oakley .25 .60
143 Trent Tucker .25 .60
144 Kiki Vandeweghe .25 .60
145 Kenny Walker .20 .50
146 Gerald Wilkins .25 .60
147 Nick Anderson .25 .60
148 Michael Ansley .20 .50
149 Terry Catledge .20 .50
150 Jerry Reynolds .20 .50
151 Dennis Scott .25 .60
152 Scott Skiles .25 .60
153 Otis Smith .20 .50
154 Sam Vincent .20 .50
155 Ron Anderson .20 .50
156 Charles Barkley .60 1.50
157 Manute Bol .30 .75
158 Johnny Dawkins .20 .50
159 Armon Gilliam .20 .50
160 Rickey Green .25 .60
161 Hersey Hawkins .25 .60
162 Rick Mahorn .20 .50
163 Tom Chambers .30 .75
164 Jeff Hornacek .25 .60
165 Kevin Johnson .30 .75
166 Andrew Lang .20 .50
167 Dan Majerle .30 .75
168 Xavier McDaniel .25 .60
169 Kurt Rambis .25 .60
170 Mark West .25 .60
171 Danny Ainge .25 .60
172 Mark Bryant .20 .50
173 Walter Davis .25 .60
174 Clyde Drexler .50 1.25
175 Kevin Duckworth .25 .60
176 Jerome Kersey .25 .60
177 Terry Porter .25 .60
178 Clifford Robinson .25 .60
179 Buck Williams .25 .60
180 Anthony Bonner .20 .50
181 Anthony Carr .25 .60
182 Duane Causwell .20 .50
183 Bobby Hansen .20 .50
184 Travis Mays .20 .50
185 Lionel Simmons .20 .50
186 Rory Sparrow .20 .50
187 Wayman Tisdale .25 .60
188 Willie Anderson .25 .60
189 Terry Cummings .30 .75
190 Sean Elliott .25 .60
191 Sidney Green .20 .50
192 David Greenwood .20 .50
193 Paul Pressey .25 .60
194 David Robinson .60 1.50
195 Dwayne Schintzius .20 .50
196 Rod Strickland .25 .60
197 Benoit Benjamin .20 .50
198 Michael Cage .25 .60
199 Eddie Johnson .20 .50
200 Shawn Kemp .50 1.25
201 Derrick McKey .20 .50
202 Gary Payton .50 1.25
203 Ricky Pierce .25 .60
204 Sedale Threatt .20 .50
205 Thurl Bailey .25 .60
206 Mike Brown .25 .60
207 Mark Eaton .30 .75
208 Blue Edwards UER .20 .50
209 Darrell Griffith .30 .75
210 Jeff Malone .25 .60
211 Karl Malone .60 1.50
212 John Stockton .60 1.50
213 Ledell Eackles .20 .50
214 Pervis Ellison .20 .50
215 A.J. English .20 .50
216 Harvey Grant .25 .60
217 Charles Jones .20 .50
218 Bernard King .40 1.00
219 Darrell Walker .20 .50
220 John Williams .20 .50
221 Bob Weiss CO .20 .50
222 Chris Ford CO .20 .50
223 Gene Littles CO .20 .50
224 Phil Jackson CO .40 1.00
225 Lenny Wilkens CO .30 .75
226 Richie Adubato CO .20 .50
227 Paul Westhead CO .20 .50
228 Chuck Daly CO .30 .75
229 Don Nelson CO .30 .75
230 Don Chaney CO .20 .50
231 Bob Hill CO UER RC .20 .50
232 Mike Schuler CO .20 .50
233 Mike Dunleavy CO .20 .50
234 Kevin Loughery CO .20 .50
235 Del Harris CO .20 .50
236 Jimmy Rodgers CO .20 .50
237 Bill Fitch CO .20 .50
238 Pat Riley CO .40 1.00
239 Matt Guokas CO .20 .50
240 Jim Lynam CO .20 .50
241 Cotton Fitzsimmons CO .20 .50
242 Rick Adelman CO .75 2.00
243 Dick Motta CO .20 .50
244 Larry Brown CO .30 .75
245 K.C. Jones CO .30 .75
246 Jerry Sloan CO .30 .75
247 Wes Unseld CO .30 .75
248 Charles Barkley AS .60 1.50
249 Brad Daugherty AS .30 .75
250 Joe Dumars AS .40 1.00
251 Patrick Ewing AS .50 1.25
252 Hersey Hawkins AS .25 .60
253 Michael Jordan AS 2.50 6.00
254 Bernard King AS .40 1.00
255 Kevin McHale AS .50 1.25
256 Robert Parish AS .40 1.00
257 Ricky Pierce AS .25 .60
258 Alvin Robertson AS .25 .60
259 Dominique Wilkins AS .50 1.25
260 Chris Ford CO AS .20 .50
261 Tom Chambers AS .30 .75
262 Clyde Drexler AS .50 1.25
263 Kevin Duckworth AS .20 .50
264 Tim Hardaway AS .40 1.00
265 Kevin Johnson AS .30 .75
266 Magic Johnson AS 1.00 2.50
267 Karl Malone AS .60 1.50
268 Chris Mullin AS .40 1.00
269 Terry Porter AS .25 .60
270 David Robinson AS .60 1.50
271 John Stockton AS .60 1.50
272 James Worthy AS .40 1.00
273 Rick Adelman CO AS .25 .60
274 Atlanta Hawks TC UER .20 .50
275 Boston Celtics TC UER .20 .50
276 Charlotte Hornets TC .20 .50
277 Chicago Bulls TC .20 .50
278 Cleveland Cavaliers TC .20 .50
279 Dallas Mavericks TC .20 .50
280 Denver Nuggets TC .20 .50
281 Detroit Pistons TC UER .20 .50
282 Golden State Warriors TC .20 .50
283 Houston Rockets TC .20 .50
284 Indiana Pacers TC .20 .50
285 Los Angeles Clippers TC .20 .50
286 Los Angeles Lakers TC .20 .50
287 Miami Heat TC .20 .50
288 Milwaukee Bucks TC .20 .50
289 Minnesota Timberwolves TC .20 .50
290 New Jersey Nets TC .20 .50
291 New York Knicks TC UER .20 .50
292 Orlando Magic TC .20 .50
293 Philadelphia 76ers TC .20 .50
294 Phoenix Suns TC .20 .50
295 Portland Trail Blazers TC .20 .50
296 Sacramento Kings TC .20 .50
297 San Antonio Spurs TC .20 .50
298 Seattle Supersonics TC .20 .50
299 Utah Jazz TC .20 .50
300 Washington Bullets TC .20 .50
301 Naismith CENT 1.00 2.50
302 Kevin Johnson IS .30 .75
303 Reggie Miller IS .50 1.25
304 Hakeem Olajuwon IS .60 1.50
305 Robert Parish IS .40 1.00
306 M.Jordan/K.Malone LL 2.50 6.00
307 3-Point FG Percent .25 .60
308 R.Miller/J.Malone LL .50 1.25
309 Olajuwon/D.Robinson LL .60 1.50
310 Steals League Leaders .60 1.50
311 D.Robinson/Rodman LL .60 1.50
312 J.Stockton/M.Johnson LL 1.00 2.50
313 Field Goal Percent .40 1.00
314 Larry Bird MS UER 1.00 2.50
315 A.English/M.Malone MS UER .50 1.25
316 Magic Johnson MS 1.00 2.50
317 Michael Jordan MS 2.50 6.00
318 Moses Malone MS .50 1.25
319 Larry Bird YB 1.00 2.50
320 Maurice Cheeks YB .25 .60
321 Magic Johnson YB 1.00 2.50
322 Bernard King YB .40 1.00
323 Moses Malone YB .50 1.25
324 Robert Parish YB .40 1.00
325 All-Star Jam 1.00 2.50
326 All-Star Jam 1.00 2.50
327 David Robinson DON'T .60 1.50
328 Checklist 1 .20 .50
329 Checklist 2 UER .20 .50
330 Checklist 3 UER .20 .50
331 Maurice Cheeks .25 .60
332 Duane Ferrell .20 .50
333 Jon Koncak .20 .50
334 Gary Leonard .20 .50
335 Travis Mays .20 .50
336 Blair Rasmussen .20 .50
337 Alexander Volkov .20 .50
338 John Bagley .20 .50
339 Rickey Green UER .25 .60
340 Derek Smith .20 .50
341 Stojko Vrankovic .20 .50
342 Anthony Frederick RC .20 .50
343 Kenny Gattison .20 .50
344 Eric Leckner .20 .50
345 Will Perdue .25 .60
346 Scott Williams RC .30 .75
347 John Battle .20 .50
348 Winston Bennett .20 .50
349 Henry James .20 .50
350 Steve Kerr .40 1.00
351 John Morton .20 .50
352 Terry Davis .20 .50
353 Randy White .20 .50
354 Greg Anderson .20 .50
355 Anthony Cook .20 .50
356 Walter Davis .25 .60
357 Winston Garland .20 .50
358 Scott Hastings .20 .50
359 Marcus Liberty .20 .50
360 William Bedford .20 .50
361 Lance Blanks .20 .50
362 Brad Sellers .20 .50
363 Darrell Walker .20 .50
364 Orlando Woolridge .25 .60
365 Vincent Askew RC .20 .50
366 Mario Elie RC .20 .50
367 Jim Petersen .20 .50
368 Matt Bullard RC .20 .50
369 Gerald Henderson .20 .50
370 Dave Jamerson .20 .50
371 Tree Rollins .20 .50
372 Greg Dreiling .20 .50
373 George McCloud .20 .50
374 Kenny Williams .20 .50
375 Randy Wittman .20 .50
376 Tony Brown .20 .50
377 Lanard Copeland .20 .50
378 James Edwards .25 .60
379 Bo Kimble .25 .60
380 Doc Rivers .30 .75
381 Loy Vaught .25 .60
382 Elden Campbell .25 .60
383 Jack Haley .20 .50
384 Tony Smith .20 .50
385 Sedale Threatt .20 .50
386 Keith Askins RC .20 .50
387 Grant Long .20 .50
388 Alan Ogg .20 .50
389 Jon Sundvold .20 .50
390 Lester Conner .20 .50
391 Jeff Grayer .20 .50
392 Steve Henson .20 .50
393 Larry Krystkowiak .20 .50
394 Moses Malone .50 1.25
395 Scott Brooks .20 .50
396 Tellis Frank .20 .50
397 Doug West .20 .50
398 Rafael Addison RC .20 .50
399 Dave Feitl RC .20 .50
400 Tate George .20 .50
401 Terry Mills RC .30 .75
402 Tim McCormick .20 .50
403 Xavier McDaniel .25 .60
404 Anthony Mason RC .40 1.00
405 Brian Quinnett .20 .50
406 John Starks RC 1.00 2.50
407 Mark Acres .20 .50
408 Greg Kite .20 .50
409 Jeff Turner .20 .50
410 Morlon Wiley .20 .50
411 Dave Hoppen .20 .50
412 Brian Oliver .20 .50
413 Kenny Payne .20 .50
414 Charles Shackleford .20 .50
415 Mitchell Wiggins .20 .50
416 Jayson Williams .20 .50
417 Cedric Ceballos .25 .60
418 Negele Knight .20 .50
419 Andrew Lang .20 .50
420 Jerrod Mustaf .20 .50
421 Ed Nealy .20 .50
422 Tim Perry .20 .50
423 Alaa Abdelnaby .20 .50
424 Wayne Cooper .20 .50
425 Danny Young .20 .50
426 Dennis Hopson .20 .50
427 Les Jepsen .20 .50
428 Jim Les RC .20 .50
429 Mitch Richmond .40 1.00
430 Dwayne Schintzius .20 .50
431 Spud Webb .30 .75
432 Jud Buechler .25 .60
433 Antoine Carr .20 .50
434 Tom Garrick .20 .50
435 Sean Higgins RC .20 .50
436 Avery Johnson .25 .60
437 Tony Massenburg .20 .50
438 Dana Barros .25 .60
439 Quintin Dailey .20 .50
440 Bart Kofoed RC .20 .50
441 Nate McMillan .25 .60
442 Delaney Rudd .20 .50
443 Michael Adams .25 .60
444 Mark Alarie .20 .50
445 Greg Foster .20 .50
446 Tom Hammonds .20 .50
447 Andre Turner .20 .50
448 David Wingate .20 .50
449 Dominique Wilkins SC .50 1.25
450 Kevin Willis SC .25 .60
451 Larry Bird SC 1.00 2.50
452 Robert Parish SC .40 1.00
453 Rex Chapman SC .25 .60
454 Kendall Gill SC .30 .75
455 Michael Jordan SC 2.50 6.00
456 Scottie Pippen SC .75 2.00
457 Brad Daugherty SC .30 .75
458 Larry Nance SC .30 .75
459 Rolando Blackman SC .25 .60
460 Derek Harper SC .25 .60
461 Chris Jackson SC .25 .60
462 Todd Lichti SC .20 .50
463 Joe Dumars SC .40 1.00
464 Isiah Thomas SC .50 1.25
465 Tim Hardaway SC .40 1.00
466 Chris Mullin SC .40 1.00
467 Hakeem Olajuwon SC .60 1.50
468 Otis Thorpe SC .25 .60
469 Reggie Miller SC .50 1.25
470 Detlef Schrempf SC .25 .60
471 Ron Harper SC .30 .75
472 Charles Smith SC .25 .60
473 Magic Johnson SC 1.00 2.50
474 James Worthy SC .40 1.00
475 Sherman Douglas SC .25 .60
476 Rony Seikaly SC .25 .60
477 Jay Humphries SC .25 .60
478 Alvin Robertson SC .25 .60
479 Tyrone Corbin SC .20 .50
480 Pooh Richardson SC .25 .60
481 Sam Bowie SC .25 .60
482 Derrick Coleman SC .30 .75
483 Patrick Ewing SC .50 1.25
484 Charles Oakley SC .25 .60
485 Dennis Scott SC .25 .60
486 Scott Skiles SC .25 .60
487 Charles Barkley SC .60 1.50
488 Hersey Hawkins SC .25 .60
489 Tom Chambers SC .30 .75
490 Kevin Johnson SC .30 .75
491 Clyde Drexler SC .50 1.25
492 Terry Porter SC .25 .60
493 Lionel Simmons SC .20 .50
494 Wayman Tisdale SC .25 .60
495 Terry Cummings SC .30 .75
496 David Robinson SC .60 1.50
497 Shawn Kemp SC .50 1.25
498 Ricky Pierce SC .25 .60
499 Karl Malone SC .60 1.50
500 John Stockton SC .60 1.50
501 Harvey Grant SC .20 .50
502 Bernard King SC .40 1.00
503 Travis Mays Art .20 .50
504 Kevin McHale Art .50 1.25
505 Muggsy Bogues Art .30 .75
506 Scottie Pippen Art .75 2.00
507 Brad Daugherty Art .30 .75
508 Derek Harper Art .25 .60
509 Chris Jackson Art .25 .60
510 Isiah Thomas Art .50 1.25
511 Tim Hardaway Art .40 1.00
512 Otis Thorpe Art .25 .60
513 Chuck Person Art .25 .60
514 Ron Harper Art .30 .75
515 James Worthy Art .40 1.00
516 Sherman Douglas Art .25 .60
517 Dale Ellis Art .25 .60
518 Tony Campbell Art .20 .50
519 Derrick Coleman Art .30 .75
520 Gerald Wilkins Art .25 .60
521 Scott Skiles Art .25 .60
522 Manute Bol Art .30 .75
523 Tom Chambers Art .30 .75
524 Terry Porter Art .25 .60
525 Lionel Simmons Art .20 .50
526 Sean Elliott Art .25 .60
527 Shawn Kemp Art .50 1.25
528 John Stockton Art .60 1.50
529 Harvey Grant Art .20 .50
530 Michael Adams AL .25 .60
531 Charles Barkley AL .60 1.50
532 Larry Bird AL 1.00 2.50
533 Maurice Cheeks AL .25 .60
534 Mark Eaton AL .30 .75
535 Magic Johnson AL 1.00 2.50
536 Michael Jordan AL 2.50 6.00
537 Moses Malone AL .50 1.25
538 Sam Perkins FIN .25 .60
539 S.Pippen/J.Worthy FIN .75 2.00
540 Vlade Divac FIN .25 .60
541 John Paxson FIN .25 .60
542 Michael Jordan FIN 2.50 6.00
543 Michael Jordan FIN 2.50 6.00
544 Otis Smith SIS .20 .50
545 Jeff Turner SIS .20 .50
546 Larry Johnson RC 1.00 2.50
547 Kenny Anderson RC .30 .75
548 Billy Owens RC .30 .75
549 Dikembe Mutombo RC 1.25 3.00
550 Steve Smith RC .50 1.25
551 Doug Smith RC .20 .50
552 Luc Longley RC .50 1.25
553 Mark Macon RC .30 .75
554 Stacey Augmon RC .30 .75
555 Brian Williams RC .30 .75
556 Terrell Brandon RC .25 .60
557 Walter Davis USA .25 .60
558 Vern Fleming USA .25 .60
559 Joe Kleine USA .25 .60
560 Jon Koncak USA .25 .60
561 Sam Perkins USA .25 .60
562 Alvin Robertson USA .25 .60
563 Wayman Tisdale USA .25 .60
564 Jeff Turner USA .20 .50
565 Willie Anderson USA .20 .50
566 Stacey Augmon USA .30 .75
567 Bimbo Coles USA .25 .60
568 Jeff Grayer USA .20 .50
569 Hersey Hawkins USA .25 .60
570 Dan Majerle USA .30 .75
571 Danny Manning USA .25 .60
572 J.R. Reid USA .20 .50
573 Mitch Richmond USA .40 1.00
574 Charles Smith USA .25 .60
575 Charles Barkley USA .60 1.50
576 Larry Bird USA 1.00 2.50
577 Patrick Ewing USA .50 1.25
578 Magic Johnson USA 1.00 2.50
579 Michael Jordan USA 4.00 10.00
580 Karl Malone USA .60 1.50
581 Chris Mullin USA .40 1.00
582 Scottie Pippen USA .75 2.00
583 David Robinson USA .60 1.50
584 John Stockton USA .60 1.50
585 Chuck Daly CO USA .30 .75
586 Lenny Wilkens CO USA .30 .75
587 P.J.Carlesimo CO USA RC 1.00 2.50
588 Mike Krzyzewski CO USA RC 3.00 8.00
589 Checklist Card 1 .20 .50
590 Checklist Card 2 .20 .50
CC1 Naismith Special .40 1.00
XX Head of the Class 8.00 20.00
NNO Centennial Sendaway Card 1.00 2.50
NNO Team USA Title Card 1.00 2.50

1991-92 Hoops All-Star MVP's

COMPLETE SET (6) 10.00 20.00
7 Isiah Thomas .75 2.00
8 Tom Chambers .30 .75
9 Michael Jordan 6.00 15.00
10 Karl Malone 1.00 2.50
11 Magic Johnson 1.50 4.00
12 Charles Barkley 1.00 2.50

1991-92 Hoops Slam Dunk

COMPLETE SET (6) 7.50 15.00
1 Larry Nance .40 1.00
2 Dominique Wilkins .75 2.00
3 Spud Webb .75 2.00
4 Michael Jordan 8.00 20.00
5 Kenny Walker .40 1.00
6 Dee Brown .40 1.00

1992-93 Hoops Prototypes

COMPLETE SET (7) 1.25 3.00
1 1992-93 Series I
(Advertisement) .40 1.00
2 Patrick Ewing Series 1 8.00 20.00
3 Magic Johnson Series 1 8.00 20.00
4 John Stockton Series 1 8.00 20.00
5 1992-93 Series II
Advertisement .40 1.00
6 Magic Johnson Series 2 8.00 20.00
7 David Robinson Series 2 8.00 20.00

1992-93 Hoops

COMPLETE SET (501) 20.00 50.00
COMPLETE SERIES 1 (350) 8.00 20.00
COMPLETE SERIES 2 (140) 12.00 30.00
AC1: SER.2 STATED ODDS 1:21
SU1: SER.2 STATED ODDS 1:92, 1:5,732 AU
TR1: SER.2 STATED ODDS 1:32
BAR.PLASTIC: SER.1 STATED ODDS 1:720
MAGIC AU: SER.1 STATED ODDS 1:14,400
EWING AU: SER.1 STATED ODDS: 1:14,400
1 Stacey Augmon .40 1.00
2 Maurice Cheeks .25 .60
3 Duane Ferrell .25 .60
4 Paul Graham .25 .60
5 Jon Koncak .25 .60
6 Blair Rasmussen .25 .60
7 Rumeal Robinson .25 .60
8 Dominique Wilkins .60 1.50
9 Kevin Willis .30 .75
10 Larry Bird 1.50 4.00
11 Dee Brown .30 .75
12 Sherman Douglas .30 .75
13 Rick Fox .40 1.00
14 Kevin Gamble .25 .60
15 Reggie Lewis .40 1.00
16 Kevin McHale .60 1.50
17 Robert Parish .50 1.25
18 Ed Pinckney UER .25 .60
19 Muggsy Bogues .40 1.00
20 Dell Curry .30 .75
21 Kenny Gattison .25 .60
22 Kendall Gill .30 .75
23 Mike Gminski .25 .60
24 Larry Johnson .50 1.25
25 Johnny Newman .25 .60
26 J.R. Reid .25 .60
27 B.J. Armstrong .40 1.00
28 Bill Cartwright .30 .75
29 Horace Grant .40 1.00
30 Michael Jordan 3.00 8.00
31 Stacey King .25 .60
32 John Paxson .30 .75
33 Will Perdue .25 .60
34 Scottie Pippen 1.00 2.50
35 Scott Williams .25 .60
36 John Battle .25 .60
37 Terrell Brandon .30 .75
38 Brad Daugherty .30 .75
39 Craig Ehlo .30 .75
40 Danny Ferry .30 .75
41 Henry James .25 .60
42 Larry Nance .30 .75
43 Mark Price .40 1.00
44 Hot Rod Williams .30 .75
45 Rolando Blackman .30 .75
46 Terry Davis .25 .60
47 Derek Harper .30 .75
48 Mike Iuzzolino .25 .60
49 Fat Lever .30 .75
50 Rodney McCray .25 .60
51 Doug Smith .25 .60
52 Randy White .25 .60
53 Herb Williams .30 .75
54 Greg Anderson .25 .60
55 Winston Garland .25 .60
56 Chris Jackson .30 .75
57 Marcus Liberty .25 .60
58 Todd Lichti .25 .60
59 Mark Macon .25 .60
60 Dikembe Mutombo .60 1.50
61 Reggie Williams .25 .60
62 Mark Aguirre .30 .75
63 William Bedford .25 .60
64 Joe Dumars .50 1.25
65 Bill Laimbeer .40 1.00
66 Dennis Rodman 1.00 2.50
67 John Salley .30 .75
68 Isiah Thomas .60 1.50
69 Darrell Walker .25 .60
70 Orlando Woolridge .40 1.00
71 Victor Alexander .25 .60
72 Mario Elie .30 .75
73 Chris Gatling .25 .60
74 Tim Hardaway .50 1.25
75 Tyrone Hill .25 .60
76 Alton Lister .25 .60
77 Sarunas Marciulionis .40 1.00
78 Chris Mullin .50 1.25
79 Billy Owens .30 .75
80 Matt Bullard .25 .60
81 Sleepy Floyd .30 .75
82 Avery Johnson .30 .75
83 Buck Johnson .25 .60
84 Vernon Maxwell .25 .60
85 Hakeem Olajuwon .75 2.00
86 Kenny Smith .30 .75
87 Larry Smith .25 .60
88 Otis Thorpe .30 .75
89 Dale Davis .25 .60
90 Vern Fleming .30 .75
91 George McCloud .25 .60
92 Reggie Miller .75 2.00
93 Chuck Person .30 .75
94 Detlef Schrempf .40 1.00
95 Rik Smits .30 .75
96 LaSalle Thompson .25 .60
97 Micheal Williams .25 .60
98 James Edwards .25 .60
99 Gary Grant .25 .60
100 Ron Harper .40 1.00
101 Danny Manning .30 .75
102 Ken Norman .25 .60
103 Olden Polynice .25 .60
104 Doc Rivers .40 1.00
105 Charles Smith .25 .60
106 Loy Vaught .25 .60
107 Elden Campbell .25 .60
108 Vlade Divac .40 1.00
109 A.C. Green .30 .75
110 Sam Perkins .30 .75
111 Byron Scott .40 1.00
112 Tony Smith .25 .60
113 Terry Teagle .25 .60
114 Sedale Threatt .25 .60
115 James Worthy .60 1.50
116 Willie Burton .25 .60
117 Bimbo Coles .25 .60
118 Kevin Edwards .25 .60
119 Alec Kessler .25 .60
120 Grant Long .25 .60
121 Glen Rice .40 1.00
122 Rony Seikaly .30 .75
123 Brian Shaw .25 .60
124 Steve Smith .40 1.00
125 Frank Brickowski .25 .60
126 Dale Ellis .30 .75
127 Jeff Grayer .25 .60
128 Jay Humphries .25 .60
129 Larry Krystkowiak .25 .60
130 Moses Malone .40 1.00
131 Fred Roberts .25 .60
132 Alvin Robertson .30 .75
133 Danny Schayes .25 .60
134 Thurl Bailey .25 .60
135 Scott Brooks .30 .75
136 Tony Campbell .25 .60
137 Gerald Glass .25 .60
138 Luc Longley .40 1.00
139 Sam Mitchell .25 .60
140 Pooh Richardson .25 .60
141 Felton Spencer .25 .60
142 Doug West .30 .75
143 Rafael Addison .25 .60
144 Kenny Anderson .30 .75
145 Mookie Blaylock .40 1.00
146 Sam Bowie .30 .75
147 Derrick Coleman .40 1.00
148 Chris Dudley .25 .60
149 Terry Mills .25 .60
150 Chris Morris .30 .75
151 Drazen Petrovic .50 1.25
152 Greg Anthony .30 .75
153 Patrick Ewing .60 1.50
154 Mark Jackson .40 1.00
155 Anthony Mason .30 .75
156 Xavier McDaniel .30 .75
157 Charles Oakley .40 1.00
158 John Starks .40 1.00
159 Gerald Wilkins .30 .75
160 Nick Anderson .30 .75
161 Terry Catledge .25 .60
162 Jerry Reynolds .25 .60
163 Stanley Roberts .25 .60
164 Dennis Scott .30 .75
165 Scott Skiles .30 .75
166 Jeff Turner .25 .60
167 Sam Vincent .25 .60
168 Brian Williams .30 .75
169 Ron Anderson .25 .60
170 Charles Barkley 1.00 2.50
171 Manute Bol .40 1.00
172 Johnny Dawkins .30 .75
173 Armon Gilliam .25 .60
174 Hersey Hawkins .30 .75
175 Brian Oliver .25 .60
176 Charles Shackleford .25 .60
177 Jayson Williams .25 .60
178 Cedric Ceballos .30 .75
179 Tom Chambers .40 1.00
180 Jeff Hornacek .30 .75
181 Kevin Johnson .40 1.00

182 Negele Knight .25 .60
183 Andrew Lang .25 .60
184 Dan Majerle .40 1.00
185 Tim Perry .25 .60
186 Mark West .30 .75
187 Alaa Abdelnaby .25 .60
188 Danny Ainge .40 1.00
189 Clyde Drexler .60 1.50
190 Kevin Duckworth .30 .75
191 Jerome Kersey .30 .75
192 Robert Pack .25 .60
193 Terry Porter .30 .75
194 Clifford Robinson .30 .75
195 Buck Williams .30 .75
196 Anthony Bonner .25 .60
197 Duane Causwell .25 .60
198 Pete Chilcutt .25 .60
199 Dennis Hopson .25 .60
200 Mitch Richmond .50 1.25
201 Lionel Simmons .25 .60
202 Wayman Tisdale .40 1.00
203 Spud Webb .40 1.00
204 Willie Anderson .30 .75
205 Antoine Carr .30 .75
206 Terry Cummings .30 .75
207 Sean Elliott .40 1.00
208 Sidney Green .25 .60
209 David Robinson .75 2.00
210 Rod Strickland .30 .75
211 Greg Sutton .25 .60
212 Dana Barros .25 .60
213 Benoit Benjamin .25 .60
214 Michael Cage .30 .75
215 Eddie Johnson .30 .75
216 Shawn Kemp .60 1.50
217 Derrick McKey .30 .75
218 Nate McMillan .30 .75
219 Gary Payton .60 1.50
220 Ricky Pierce .30 .75
221 David Benoit .25 .60
222 Mike Brown .25 .60
223 Tyrone Corbin .30 .75
224 Mark Eaton .40 1.00
225 Blue Edwards .30 .75
226 Jeff Malone .30 .75
227 Karl Malone .75 2.00
228 Eric Murdock .25 .60
229 John Stockton .75 2.00
230 Michael Adams .30 .75
231 Rex Chapman .30 .75
232 Ledell Eackles .25 .60
233 Pervis Ellison .25 .60
234 A.J. English .25 .60
235 Harvey Grant .30 .75
236 Charles Jones .25 .60
237 LaBradford Smith .25 .60
238 Larry Stewart .25 .60
239 Bob Weiss CO .25 .60
240 Chris Ford CO .25 .60
241 Allan Bristow CO .25 .60
242 Phil Jackson CO .60 1.50
243 Lenny Wilkens CO .40 1.00
244 Richie Adubato CO .25 .60
245 Dan Issel CO .50 1.25
246 Ron Rothstein CO .25 .60
247 Don Nelson CO .50 1.25
248 Rudy Tomjanovich CO .50 1.25
249 Bob Hill CO .25 .60
250 Larry Brown CO .40 1.00
251 Randy Pfund CO RC .25 .60
252 Kevin Loughery CO .25 .60
253 Mike Dunleavy CO .25 .60
254 Jimmy Rodgers CO .25 .60
255 Chuck Daly CO .50 1.25
256 Pat Riley CO .50 1.25
257 Matt Guokas CO .25 .60
258 Doug Moe CO .30 .75
259 Paul Westphal CO .40 1.00
260 Rick Adelman CO .30 .75
261 Garry St. Jean CO RC .25 .60
262 Jerry Tarkanian CO RC .40 1.00
263 George Karl CO .30 .75
264 Jerry Sloan CO .40 1.00
265 Wes Unseld CO .50 1.25
266 Atlanta Hawks TC .40 1.00
267 Boston Celtics TC .40 1.00
268 Charlotte Hornets TC .40 1.00
269 Chicago Bulls TC .40 1.00
270 Cleveland Cavaliers TC .40 1.00
271 Dallas Mavericks TC .40 1.00
272 Denver Nuggets TC .40 1.00
273 Detroit Pistons TC .40 1.00
274 Golden State Warriors TC .40 1.00
275 Houston Rockets TC .40 1.00
276 Indiana Pacers TC .40 1.00
277 Los Angeles Clippers TC .40 1.00
278 Los Angeles Lakers TC .40 1.00
279 Miami Heat TC .40 1.00
280 Milwaukee Bucks TC .40 1.00
281 Minnesota Timberwolves TC .40 1.00
282 New Jersey Nets TC .40 1.00
283 New York Knicks TC .40 1.00
284 Orlando Magic TC .40 1.00
285 Philadelphia 76ers TC .40 1.00
286 Phoenix Suns TC .40 1.00
287 Portland Trail Blazers TC .40 1.00
288 Sacramento Kings TC .40 1.00
289 San Antonio Spurs TC .40 1.00
290 Seattle Supersonics TC .40 1.00
291 Utah Jazz TC .40 1.00
292 Washington Bullets TC .40 1.00
293 Michael Adams AS .30 .75
294 Charles Barkley AS 1.00 2.50
295 Brad Daugherty AS .30 .75
296 Joe Dumars AS .50 1.25
297 Patrick Ewing AS .60 1.50
298 Michael Jordan AS 3.00 8.00
299 Reggie Lewis AS .40 1.00
300 Scottie Pippen AS 1.00 2.50
301 Mark Price AS .40 1.00
302 Dennis Rodman AS 1.00 2.50
303 Isiah Thomas AS .60 1.50
304 Kevin Willis AS .30 .75
305 Phil Jackson CO AS .60 1.50
306 Clyde Drexler AS .60 1.50
307 Tim Hardaway AS .50 1.25
308 Jeff Hornacek AS .30 .75
309 Magic Johnson AS 1.50 4.00
310 Dan Majerle AS .40 1.00
311 Karl Malone AS .75 2.00
312 Chris Mullin AS .50 1.25
313 Dikembe Mutombo AS .60 1.50
314 Hakeem Olajuwon AS .75 2.00
315 David Robinson AS .75 2.00
316 John Stockton AS .75 2.00
317 Otis Thorpe AS .30 .75
318 James Worthy AS .60 1.50
319 Don Nelson CO AS .50 1.25
320 M.Jordan/K.Malone LL 3.00 8.00
321 D.Barros/D.Petrovic LL .50 1.25
322 M.Price/L.Bird LL 1.50 4.00
323 D.Robinson/Olajuwon LL .75 2.00
324 J.Stockton/M.Williams LL .75 2.00
325 D.Rodman/K.Willis LL 1.00 2.50
326 J.Stockton/K.Johnson LL .75 2.00
327 B.Williams/O.Thorpe LL .30 .75
328 Magic Moments 1980 1.50 4.00
329 Magic Moments 1985 1.50 4.00
330 Magic Moments 87 and 88 1.50 4.00
331 Magic Numbers 1.50 4.00
332 Drazen Petrovic IS .50 1.25
333 Patrick Ewing IS .60 1.50
334 David Robinson STAY .75 2.00
335 Kevin Johnson STAY .40 1.00
336 Charles Barkley USA 1.00 2.50
337 Larry Bird USA 1.50 4.00
338 Clyde Drexler USA .60 1.50
339 Patrick Ewing USA .60 1.50
340 Magic Johnson USA 1.50 4.00
341 Michael Jordan USA 3.00 8.00
342 Christian Laettner USA RC 1.25 3.00
343 Karl Malone USA .75 2.00
344 Chris Mullin USA .50 1.25
345 Scottie Pippen USA 1.00 2.50
346 David Robinson USA .75 2.00
347 John Stockton USA .75 2.00
348 Checklist 1 .20 .50
349 Checklist 2 .20 .50
350 Checklist 3 .20 .50
351 Mookie Blaylock .40 1.00
352 Adam Keefe RC .25 .60
353 Travis Mays .25 .60
354 Morlon Wiley .25 .60
355 Joe Kleine .25 .60
356 Bart Kofoed .25 .60
357 Xavier McDaniel .30 .75
358 Tony Bennett RC .25 .60
359 Tom Hammonds .25 .60
360 Kevin Lynch .25 .60
361 Alonzo Mourning RC 2.00 5.00
362 Rodney McCray .25 .60
363 Trent Tucker .25 .60
364 Corey Williams RC .25 .60
365 Steve Kerr .30 .75
366 Jerome Lane .25 .60
367 Bobby Phills RC .30 .75
368 Mike Sanders .25 .60
369 Gerald Wilkins .30 .75
370 Donald Hodge .25 .60
371 Brian Howard RC .25 .60
372 Tracy Moore RC .25 .60
373 Sean Rooks RC .25 .60
374 Kevin Brooks .25 .60
375 LaPhonso Ellis RC .40 1.00
376 Scott Hastings .25 .60
377 Robert Pack .25 .60
378 Bryant Stith RC .30 .75
379 Robert Werdann RC .25 .60
380 Lance Blanks .25 .60
381 Terry Mills .25 .60
382 Isaiah Morris RC .30 .75
383 Olden Polynice .25 .60
384 Brad Sellers .30 .75
385 Jud Buechler .25 .60
386 Jeff Grayer .25 .60
387 Byron Houston RC .25 .60
388 Keith Jennings RC .25 .60
389 Latrell Sprewell RC 1.25 3.00
390 Scott Brooks .30 .75
391 Carl Herrera .25 .60
392 Robert Horry RC 1.00 2.50
393 Tree Rollins .30 .75
394 Kennard Winchester .25 .60
395 Greg Dreiling .25 .60
396 Sean Green .25 .60
397 Sam Mitchell .25 .60
398 Pooh Richardson .25 .60
399 Malik Sealy RC .30 .75
400 Kenny Williams .25 .60
401 Jaren Jackson RC .25 .60
402 Mark Jackson .40 1.00
403 Stanley Roberts .25 .60
404 Elmore Spencer RC .25 .60
405 Kiki Vandeweghe .30 .75
406 John Williams .25 .60
407 Randy Woods RC .25 .60
408 Alex Blackwell RC .25 .60
409 Duane Cooper RC .25 .60
410 Anthony Peeler RC .30 .75
411 Keith Askins .30 .75
412 Matt Geiger RC .30 .75
413 Harold Miner RC .50 1.25
414 John Salley .25 .60
415 Alaa Abdelnaby .25 .60
416 Todd Day RC .30 .75
417 Blue Edwards .25 .60
418 Brad Lohaus .25 .60
419 Lee Mayberry RC .25 .60
420 Eric Murdock .25 .60
421 Christian Laettner 1.25 3.00
422 Bob McCann RC .25 .60
423 Chuck Person .25 .60
424 Chris Smith RC .25 .60
425 Gundars Vetra RC .25 .60
426 Micheal Williams .25 .60
427 Chucky Brown .25 .60
428 Tate George .25 .60
429 Rick Mahorn .30 .75
430 Rumeal Robinson .25 .60
431 Jayson Williams .25 .60
432 Eric Anderson RC .25 .60
433 Rolando Blackman .30 .75
434 Tony Campbell .25 .60
435 Hubert Davis RC .30 .75
436 Bo Kimble .40 1.00
437 Doc Rivers .40 1.00
438 Charles Smith .30 .75
439 Anthony Bowie .25 .60
440 Litterial Green RC .25 .60
441 Greg Kite .25 .60
442 Shaquille O'Neal RC 3.00 8.00
443 Donald Royal .25 .60
444 Greg Grant .25 .60
445 Jeff Hornacek .30 .75
446 Andrew Lang .25 .60
447 Kenny Payne .25 .60
448 Tim Perry .25 .60
449 Clarence Weatherspoon RC .40 1.00
450 Danny Ainge .40 1.00
451 Charles Barkley 1.00 2.50
452 Tim Kempton .25 .60
453 Oliver Miller RC .30 .75
454 Mark Bryant .25 .60
455 Mario Elie .25 .60
456 Dave Jamerson RC .25 .60
457 Tracy Murray RC .30 .75
458 Rod Strickland .30 .75
459 Vincent Askew .25 .60
460 Randy Brown .25 .60
461 Marty Conlon .25 .60
462 Jim Les .25 .60
463 Walt Williams RC .40 1.00
464 William Bedford .25 .60
465 Lloyd Daniels RC .30 .75
466 Vinny Del Negro .30 .75
467 Dale Ellis .30 .75
468 Larry Smith .25 .60
469 David Wood .25 .60
470 Rich King .25 .60
471 Isaac Austin RC .25 .60
472 John Crotty RC .25 .60
473 Stephen Howard RC .25 .60
474 Jay Humphries .25 .60
475 Larry Krystkowiak .30 .75
476 Tom Gugliotta RC .40 1.00
477 Buck Johnson .25 .60
478 Don MacLean RC .30 .75
479 Doug Overton .30 .75
480 Brent Price RC .25 .60
481 David Robinson TRV .75 2.00
482 Magic Johnson TRV 1.50 4.00
483 John Stockton TRV .75 2.00
484 Patrick Ewing TRV .60 1.50
485 D.Rob/Ew/Stock/Mag TRV 1.50 4.00
486 John Stockton STAY .75 2.00
487 Ahmad Rashad .75 2.00
488 Rookie Checklist .20 .50
489 Checklist 1 .20 .50
490 Checklist 2 .20 .50
AC1 P.Ewing Art Card .75 2.00
SU1 J.Stockton Game AU 75.00 200.00
SU1 J.Stockton Game .75 2.00
TR1 M.Jordan/C.Drexler FIN 3.00 8.00
USA Team USA 3.00 8.00
NNO Team USA 2.00 5.00
NNO M.Johnson Comm 1.50 4.00
NNO M.Johnson Comm AU 125.00 300.00
NNO P.Ewing Game .60 1.50
NNO P.Ewing Game AU 60.00 150.00

1992-93 Hoops Draft Redemption

COMPLETE SET (10) 50.00 120.00
EXCH.CARD: SER.1 STATED ODDS 1:360
A Shaquille O'Neal 50.00 120.00
B Alonzo Mourning 4.00 10.00
C Christian Laettner 2.00 5.00
D LaPhonso Ellis .75 2.00
E Tom Gugliotta .75 2.00
F Walt Williams .75 2.00
G Todd Day .75 2.00
H Clarence Weatherspoon .75 2.00
I Adam Keefe .75 2.00
J Robert Horry 1.25 3.00
NNO Stamped Redemp.Card .40 1.00
NNO Unstamped Redemp.Card 1.25 3.00

1992-93 Hoops Magic's All-Rookies

COMPLETE SET (10) 25.00 60.00
SER.2 STATED ODDS 1:30
1 Shaquille O'Neal 20.00 50.00
2 Alonzo Mourning 5.00 12.00
3 Christian Laettner 2.00 5.00
4 LaPhonso Ellis 1.25 3.00
5 Tom Gugliotta 1.50 4.00
6 Walt Williams 1.25 3.00
7 Todd Day 1.25 3.00
8 Clarence Weatherspoon 1.25 3.00
9 Robert Horry 2.00 5.00
10 Harold Miner 1.25 3.00

1992-93 Hoops More Magic Moments

COMPLETE SET (3) 45.00 70.00
COMMON MAGIC (M1-M3) 15.00 25.00
SER.2 STATED ODDS 1:195

1992-93 Hoops Supreme Court

COMPLETE SET (10) 12.00 30.00
SER.2 STATED ODDS 1:11
SC1 Michael Jordan 4.00 10.00
SC2 Scottie Pippen 1.25 3.00
SC3 David Robinson 1.00 2.50
SC4 Patrick Ewing .75 2.00
SC5 Clyde Drexler .75 2.00
SC6 Karl Malone 1.00 2.50
SC7 Charles Barkley 1.25 3.00
SC8 John Stockton 1.00 2.50
SC9 Chris Mullin .60 1.50
SC10 Magic Johnson 2.00 5.00

1993-94 Hoops Promo Panel

NNO Hoops panel
Joe Dumars
Patrick Ewing
Tim Hardaway
Dan Majerle
Jeff Malone
Xavier McDaniel
Reggie Miller
David Robinson 2.00 5.00

1993-94 Hoops Prototypes

COMPLETE SET (7) 1.20 3.00
1 Jim Jackson .15 .40
2 Larry Johnson .30 .75
3 Karl Malone .40 1.00
4 Harold Miner .15 .40
5 Dikembe Mutombo .30 .75
6 Shaquille O'Neal 1.00 2.50
7 Cover Card .12 .30

1993-94 Hoops

COMPLETE SET (421) 15.00 40.00
COMPLETE SERIES 1 (300) 10.00 25.00
COMPLETE SERIES 2 (121) 6.00 15.00
SUBSET CARDS SAME VALUE AS BASE CARDS
DR1: SER.2 STATED ODDS 1:18
BOTH AUs: SER.2 STATED ODDS 1:13,886
BEWARE COUNTERFEIT BIRD/MAGIC AU
1 Stacey Augmon .30 .75
2 Mookie Blaylock .40 1.00
3 Duane Ferrell .25 .60
4 Paul Graham .25 .60
5 Adam Keefe .25 .60
6 Blair Rasmussen .25 .60
7 Dominique Wilkins .60 1.50
8 Kevin Willis .30 .75
9 Alaa Abdelnaby .25 .60
10 Dee Brown .30 .75
11 Sherman Douglas .25 .60
12 Rick Fox .30 .75
13 Kevin Gamble .25 .60
14 Joe Kleine .25 .60
15 Xavier McDaniel .40 1.00
16 Robert Parish .50 1.25
17 Tony Bennett .25 .60
18 Muggsy Bogues .40 1.00
19 Dell Curry .40 1.00
20 Kenny Gattison .25 .60
21 Kendall Gill .30 .75
22 Larry Johnson .50 1.25
23 Alonzo Mourning .60 1.50
24 Johnny Newman .25 .60
25 B.J. Armstrong .40 1.00
26 Bill Cartwright .25 .60
27 Horace Grant .40 1.00
28 Michael Jordan 4.00 10.00
29 Stacey King .25 .60
30 John Paxson .40 1.00
31 Will Perdue .25 .60
32 Scottie Pippen 1.00 2.50
33 Scott Williams .25 .60
34 Moses Malone .60 1.50
35 John Battle .25 .60
36 Terrell Brandon .30 .75
37 Brad Daugherty .30 .75
38 Craig Ehlo .25 .60
39 Danny Ferry .25 .60
40 Larry Nance .30 .75
41 Mark Price .40 1.00
42 Gerald Wilkins .30 .75
43 John Williams .30 .75
44 Terry Davis .25 .60
45 Derek Harper .30 .75
46 Donald Hodge .25 .60
47 Mike Iuzzolino .25 .60
48 Jim Jackson .30 .75
49 Sean Rooks .25 .60
50 Doug Smith .25 .60
51 Randy White .25 .60
52 Mahmoud Abdul-Rauf .30 .75
53 LaPhonso Ellis .30 .75
54 Marcus Liberty .25 .60
55 Mark Macon .25 .60
56 Dikembe Mutombo .60 1.50
57 Robert Pack .25 .60
58 Bryant Stith .25 .60
59 Reggie Williams .25 .60
60 Mark Aguirre .30 .75
61 Joe Dumars .50 1.25
62 Bill Laimbeer .40 1.00
63 Terry Mills .25 .60
64 Olden Polynice .25 .60
65 Alvin Robertson .30 .75
66 Dennis Rodman 1.00 2.50
67 Isiah Thomas .60 1.50
68 Victor Alexander .25 .60
69 Tim Hardaway .50 1.25
70 Tyrone Hill .25 .60
71 Byron Houston .25 .60
72 Sarunas Marciulionis .40 1.00
73 Chris Mullin .50 1.25
74 Billy Owens .30 .75
75 Latrell Sprewell .60 1.50
76 Scott Brooks .25 .60
77 Matt Bullard .25 .60
78 Carl Herrera .25 .60
79 Robert Horry .40 1.00
80 Vernon Maxwell .30 .75
81 Hakeem Olajuwon .75 2.00
82 Kenny Smith .30 .75
83 Otis Thorpe .40 1.00
84 Dale Davis .25 .60
85 Vern Fleming .25 .60
86 George McCloud .25 .60
87 Reggie Miller .75 2.00
88 Sam Mitchell .25 .60
89 Pooh Richardson .30 .75
90 Detlef Schrempf .40 1.00
91 Malik Sealy .25 .60
92 Rik Smits .30 .75
93 Gary Grant .25 .60
94 Ron Harper .40 1.00
95 Mark Jackson .30 .75
96 Danny Manning .30 .75
97 Ken Norman .25 .60
98 Stanley Roberts .25 .60
99 Elmore Spencer .25 .60
100 Loy Vaught .25 .60
101 John Williams .25 .60
102 Randy Woods .25 .60
103 Benoit Benjamin .25 .60
104 Elden Campbell .25 .60
105 Doug Christie UER .25 .60
106 Vlade Divac .40 1.00
107 Anthony Peeler .25 .60
108 Tony Smith .25 .60
109 Sedale Threatt .25 .60
110 James Worthy .50 1.25
111 Bimbo Coles .25 .60
112 Grant Long .25 .60
113 Harold Miner .30 .75
114 Glen Rice .40 1.00
115 John Salley .30 .75
116 Rony Seikaly .30 .75
117 Brian Shaw .25 .60
118 Steve Smith .30 .75
119 Anthony Avent .25 .60
120 Jon Barry .25 .60
121 Frank Brickowski .25 .60
122 Todd Day .25 .60
123 Blue Edwards .25 .60
124 Brad Lohaus .25 .60
125 Lee Mayberry .25 .60
126 Eric Murdock .25 .60
127 Derek Strong RC .30 .75
128 Thurl Bailey .25 .60
129 Christian Laettner .40 1.00
130 Luc Longley .30 .75
131 Marlon Maxey .25 .60
132 Chuck Person .30 .75
133 Chris Smith .25 .60
134 Doug West .25 .60
135 Micheal Williams .25 .60
136 Rafael Addison .25 .60
137 Kenny Anderson .30 .75
138 Sam Bowie .30 .75
139 Chucky Brown .25 .60
140 Derrick Coleman .40 1.00
141 Chris Morris .25 .60
142 Rumeal Robinson .25 .60
143 Greg Anthony .25 .60
144 Rolando Blackman .30 .75
145 Hubert Davis .25 .60
146 Patrick Ewing .60 1.50
147 Anthony Mason .30 .75
148 Charles Oakley .40 1.00
149 Doc Rivers .30 .75
150 Charles Smith .25 .60
151 John Starks .40 1.00
152 Nick Anderson .30 .75
153 Anthony Bowie .25 .60
154 Litterial Green .25 .60
155 Shaquille O'Neal 2.00 5.00
156 Donald Royal .25 .60
157 Dennis Scott .25 .60
158 Scott Skiles .25 .60
159 Tom Tolbert .25 .60
160 Jeff Turner .25 .60
161 Ron Anderson .25 .60
162 Johnny Dawkins .30 .75
163 Hersey Hawkins .30 .75
164 Jeff Hornacek .30 .75
165 Andrew Lang .25 .60
166 Tim Perry .25 .60
167 Clarence Weatherspoon .25 .60
168 Danny Ainge .40 1.00
169 Charles Barkley 1.00 2.50
170 Cedric Ceballos .30 .75
171 Richard Dumas .25 .60
172 Kevin Johnson .40 1.00
173 Dan Majerle .40 1.00
174 Oliver Miller .25 .60
175 Mark West .25 .60
176 Clyde Drexler .60 1.50
177 Kevin Duckworth .25 .60
178 Mario Elie .30 .75
179 Dave Johnson .25 .60
180 Jerome Kersey .30 .75
181 Tracy Murray .25 .60
182 Terry Porter .30 .75
183 Clifford Robinson .40 1.00
184 Rod Strickland .40 1.00
185 Buck Williams .30 .75
186 Anthony Bonner .25 .60
187 Randy Brown .25 .60
188 Duane Causwell .25 .60
189 Pete Chilcutt .25 .60
190 Mitch Richmond .50 1.25
191 Lionel Simmons .25 .60
192 Wayman Tisdale .30 .75
193 Spud Webb .30 .75
194 Walt Williams .40 1.00
195 Willie Anderson .25 .60
196 Antoine Carr .25 .60
197 Terry Cummings .30 .75
198 Lloyd Daniels .25 .60
199 Sean Elliott .40 1.00
200 Dale Ellis .25 .60
201 Avery Johnson .30 .75
202 J.R. Reid .30 .75
203 David Robinson .75 2.00
204 Dana Barros .25 .60
205 Michael Cage .30 .75
206 Eddie Johnson .25 .60
207 Shawn Kemp .60 1.50
208 Derrick McKey .30 .75
209 Nate McMillan .30 .75
210 Gary Payton .50 1.25
211 Sam Perkins .30 .75
212 Ricky Pierce .30 .75
213 David Benoit .25 .60
214 Tyrone Corbin .25 .60
215 Mark Eaton .40 1.00
216 Jay Humphries .30 .75
217 Jeff Malone .30 .75
218 Karl Malone .75 2.00
219 John Stockton .75 2.00
220 Michael Adams .30 .75
221 Rex Chapman .30 .75
222 Pervis Ellison .25 .60
223 Harvey Grant .25 .60
224 Tom Gugliotta .25 .60
225 Don MacLean .25 .60
226 Doug Overton .25 .60
227 Brent Price .25 .60
228 LaBradford Smith .25 .60
229 Larry Stewart .25 .60
230 Lenny Wilkens CO .40 1.00
231 Chris Ford CO .25 .60
232 Allan Bristow CO .25 .60
233 Phil Jackson CO .60 1.50
234 Mike Fratello CO .30 .75
235 Quinn Buckner CO .30 .75
236 Dan Issel CO .40 1.00
237 Don Chaney CO .30 .75
238 Don Nelson CO .40 1.00
239 Rudy Tomjanovich CO .40 1.00
240 Larry Brown CO .40 1.00
241 Bob Weiss CO .25 .60
242 Randy Pfund CO .25 .60
243 Kevin Loughery CO .25 .60
244 Mike Dunleavy CO .25 .60
245 Sidney Lowe CO .25 .60
246 Chuck Daly CO .40 1.00
247 Pat Riley CO .50 1.25
248 Brian Hill CO .25 .60
249 Fred Carter CO .25 .60
250 Paul Westphal CO .30 .75
251 Rick Adelman CO .25 .60
252 Garry St. Jean CO .25 .60
253 John Lucas CO .30 .75
254 George Karl CO .30 .75
255 Jerry Sloan CO .40 1.00
256 Wes Unseld CO .40 1.00
257 Michael Jordan AS 4.00 10.00
258 Isiah Thomas AS .60 1.50
259 Scottie Pippen AS 1.00 2.50
260 Larry Johnson AS .50 1.25
261 Dominique Wilkins AS .60 1.50
262 Joe Dumars AS .50 1.25
263 Mark Price AS .40 1.00
264 Shaquille O'Neal AS 2.00 5.00
265 Patrick Ewing AS .60 1.50
266 Larry Nance AS .30 .75
267 Detlef Schrempf AS .40 1.00
268 Brad Daugherty AS .30 .75
269 Charles Barkley AS 1.00 2.50
270 Clyde Drexler AS .60 1.50
271 Sean Elliott AS .40 1.00
272 Tim Hardaway AS .50 1.25
273 Shawn Kemp AS .60 1.50
274 Dan Majerle AS .40 1.00
275 Karl Malone AS .75 2.00
276 Danny Manning AS .30 .75
277 Hakeem Olajuwon AS .75 2.00
278 Terry Porter AS .30 .75
279 David Robinson AS .75 2.00
280 John Stockton AS .75 2.00
281 East Team Photo 4.00 10.00
282 West Team Photo 1.00 2.50
283 Jordan/Wilkins/Malone LL 4.00 10.00
284 Rodman/O'Neal/Mut LL 2.00 5.00
285 Ceballos/Daug/Davis LL .30 .75
286 Stock/Hardaway/Skiles L 2.00 5.00
287 Price/A-Rauf/L.Johnson L .50 1.25
288 Arm/Mullin/Smith LL .50 1.25
289 Jordan/Blaylock/Stock LL 4.00 10.00
290 Olajuwon/O'Neal/Mut LL 2.00 5.00
291 D.Robinson BOYS/GIRLS .75 2.00
292 B.J. Armstrong TRIB .40 1.00
293 Scottie Pippen TRIB 1.00 2.50
294 Kevin Johnson TRIB .40 1.00
295 Charles Barkley TRIB 1.00 2.50
296 Richard Dumas TRIB .25 .60
297 Horace Grant TRIB 1.00 2.50
298 David Robinson CL .75 2.00
299 David Robinson CL .75 2.00
300 David Robinson CL .75 2.00
301 Craig Ehlo .25 .60
302 Jon Koncak .25 .60
303 Andrew Lang .25 .60
304 Chris Corchiani .25 .60
305 Acie Earl RC .40 1.00
306 Dino Radja RC .40 1.00
307 Scott Burrell RC .40 1.00
308 Hersey Hawkins .30 .75
309 Eddie Johnson .25 .60
310 David Wingate .25 .60
311 Corie Blount RC .40 1.00
312 Steve Kerr .30 .75
313 Toni Kukoc RC 1.00 2.50
314 Pete Myers .25 .60
315 Jay Guidinger .25 .60
316 Tyrone Hill .25 .60
317 Gerald Madkins RC .40 1.00
318 Chris Mills RC .40 1.00
319 Bobby Phills .25 .60
320 Lucious Harris RC .40 1.00
321 Popeye Jones RC .40 1.00
322 Fat Lever .30 .75
323 Jamal Mashburn RC .75 2.00
324 Darren Morningstar RC .40 1.00
325 Kevin Brooks .25 .60
326 Tom Hammonds .25 .60
327 Darnell Mee RC .25 .60
328 Rodney Rogers RC .40 1.00
329 Brian Williams .25 .60
330 Greg Anderson .25 .60
331 Sean Elliott .40 1.00
332 Allan Houston RC .75 2.00
333 Lindsey Hunter RC .40 1.00
334 David Wood UER .25 .60
335 Jud Buechler .25 .60
336 Chris Gatling .25 .60
337 Josh Grant RC .30 .75
338 Jeff Grayer .25 .60
339 Keith Jennings .25 .60
340 Avery Johnson .25 .60
341 Chris Webber RC 2.00 5.00
342 Sam Cassell RC .75 2.00
343 Mario Elie .30 .75
344 Eric Riley RC .40 1.00
345 Antonio Davis RC .50 1.25
346 Scott Haskin RC .25 .60
347 Gerald Paddio .25 .60
348 LaSalle Thompson .25 .60
349 Ken Williams .25 .60
350 Mark Aguirre .30 .75
351 Terry Dehere RC .40 1.00
352 Henry James .25 .60
353 Sam Bowie .30 .75
354 George Lynch RC .40 1.00
355 Kurt Rambis .30 .75
356 Nick Van Exel RC 1.00 2.50
357 Trevor Wilson .25 .60
358 Keith Askins .25 .60
359 Manute Bol .25 .60
360 Willie Burton .25 .60
361 Matt Geiger .25 .60
362 Alec Kessler .25 .60
363 Vin Baker RC .60 1.50
364 Ken Norman .25 .60
365 Danny Schayes .25 .60
366 Mike Brown .25 .60
367 Isaiah Rider RC .60 1.50
368 Benoit Benjamin .25 .60
369 P.J. Brown RC .40 1.00
370 Kevin Edwards .25 .60
371 Armon Gilliam .25 .60
372 Rick Mahorn .30 .75
373 Dwayne Schintzius .25 .60
374 Rex Walters RC .30 .75
375 Jayson Williams .25 .60
376 Eric Anderson .25 .60
377 Anthony Bonner .25 .60
378 Tony Campbell .25 .60
379 Herb Williams .25 .60
380 Anfernee Hardaway RC 2.00 5.00
381 Greg Kite .25 .60
382 Larry Krystkowiak .25 .60
383 Todd Lichti .25 .60
384 Dana Barros .25 .60
385 Shawn Bradley RC .40 1.00
386 Greg Graham RC .25 .60
387 Warren Kidd RC .25 .60
388 Eric Leckner .25 .60
389 Moses Malone .60 1.50
390 A.C. Green .30 .75
391 Frank Johnson .25 .60
392 Joe Kleine .25 .60
393 Malcolm Mackey RC .25 .60
394 Jerrod Mustaf .25 .60
395 Mark Bryant .25 .60
396 Chris Dudley .25 .60
397 Harvey Grant .30 .75
398 James Robinson RC .40 1.00
399 Reggie Smith .25 .60
400 Randy Brown .25 .60
401 Bobby Hurley RC .40 1.00
402 Jim Les .25 .60
403 Vinny Del Negro .25 .60
404 Sleepy Floyd .30 .75
405 Dennis Rodman 1.00 2.50
406 Chris Whitney RC .30 .75
407 Vincent Askew .25 .60
408 Kendall Gill .30 .75
409 Ervin Johnson RC .40 1.00
410 Rich King .25 .60
411 Detlef Schrempf .40 1.00
412 Tom Chambers .40 1.00
413 John Crotty .25 .60
414 Felton Spencer .25 .60
415 Luther Wright RC .25 .60
416 Calbert Cheaney RC .40 1.00
417 Kevin Duckworth .30 .75
418 Gheorghe Muresan RC .40 1.00
419 David Robinson CL .75 2.00
420 David Robinson CL .75 2.00
421 David Robinson CL .75 2.00
DR1 D.Robinson Comm .75 2.00
MB1 Magic/Bird Comm 1.50 4.00
MB1A Magic/Bird Comm AU 150.00 400.00
NNO D.Robinson Comm AU 30.00 80.00
NNO D.Robinson Exp.Vouch. 4.00 10.00
NNO Magic/Bird Exp.Vouch. 15.00 30.00

1993-94 Hoops Fifth Anniversary Gold

COMPLETE SET (423) 30.00 60.00
COMPLETE SERIES 1 (301) 17.50 35.00
COMPLETE SERIES 2 (122) 12.50 25.00
*STARS: .75X TO 2X BASE CARD HI
*RCs: .75X TO 2X BASE HI

1993-94 Hoops Admiral's Choice

COMPLETE SET (5) 2.50 6.00
SER.2 STATED ODDS 1:12
AC1 Shawn Kemp .60 1.50
AC2 Derrick Coleman .40 1.00
AC3 Kenny Anderson .30 .75
AC4 Shaquille O'Neal 2.00 5.00
AC5 Chris Webber 2.00 5.00

1993-94 Hoops David's Best

COMPLETE SET (5) 2.50 6.00
COMMON CARD (DB1-DB5) .75 2.00
SER.1 STATED ODDS 1:10

1993-94 Hoops Draft Redemption

COMPLETE SET (11) 12.00 30.00
EXCH.CARD: SER.1 STATED ODDS 1:360
LP1 Chris Webber 5.00 12.00
LP2 Shawn Bradley .60 1.50
LP3 Anfernee Hardaway 5.00 12.00
LP4 Jamal Mashburn 1.25 3.00
LP5 Isaiah Rider 1.00 2.50
LP6 Calbert Cheaney .60 1.50
LP7 Bobby Hurley .60 1.50
LP8 Vin Baker 1.00 2.50
LP9 Rodney Rogers .60 1.50
LP10 Lindsey Hunter .60 1.50
LP11 Allan Houston 1.25 3.00
NNO Redeemed Draft Card .20 .50
NNO Unredeemed Draft Card 2.00 5.00

1993-94 Hoops Face to Face

COMPLETE SET (12) 6.00 15.00
SER.1 STATED ODDS 1:20
1 S.O'Neal/D.Robinson 2.00 5.00
2 A.Mourning/P.Ewing .60 1.50
3 C.Laettner/S.Kemp .60 1.50
4 J.Jackson/C.Drexler .60 1.50
5 L.Ellis/L.Johnson .50 1.25
6 C.Weatherspoon/C.Barkley 1.00 2.50
7 T.Gugliotta/K.Malone .75 2.00
8 W.Williams/M.Johnson .40 1.00
9 R.Horry/S.Pippen 1.00 2.50
10 H.Miner/M.Jordan 4.00 10.00
11 Todd Day/C.Mullin .50 1.25
12 R.Dumas/D.Wilkins .60 1.50

1993-94 Hoops Magic's All-Rookies

COMPLETE SET (10) 12.00 30.00
SER.2 STATED ODDS 1:30
1 Chris Webber 4.00 10.00
2 Shawn Bradley .75 2.00
3 Anfernee Hardaway 4.00 10.00

4 Jamal Mashburn 1.50 4.00
5 Isaiah Rider 1.25 3.00
6 Calbert Cheaney .75 2.00
7 Bobby Hurley .75 2.00
8 Vin Baker 1.25 3.00
9 Lindsey Hunter .75 2.00
10 Toni Kukoc 2.00 5.00

1993-94 Hoops Scoops
COMPLETE SET (28) 1.25 3.00
GOLD CARDS: .75X TO 2X HI COLUMN
HS1 Dominique Wilkins .60 1.50
HS2 Robert Parish .60 1.50
HS3 Alonzo Mourning .60 1.50
HS4 Scottie Pippen 1.00 2.50
HS5 Larry Nance .30 .75
HS6 Derek Harper .30 .75
HS7 Reggie Williams .25 .60
HS8 Bill Laimbeer .40 1.00
HS9 Tim Hardaway .50 1.25
HS10 Hakeem Olajuwon UER .75 2.00
HS11 LaSalle Thompson .25 .60
HS12 Danny Manning .30 .75
HS13 James Worthy .50 1.25
HS14 Grant Long .25 .60
HS15 Blue Edwards .25 .60
HS16 Christian Laettner .40 1.00
HS17 Derrick Coleman .40 1.00
HS18 Patrick Ewing .60 1.50
HS19 Nick Anderson .30 .75
HS20 Clarence Weatherspoon .25 .60
HS21 Charles Barkley 1.00 2.50
HS22 Clifford Robinson .40 1.00
HS23 Lionel Simmons .25 .60
HS24 David Robinson .75 2.00
HS25 Shawn Kemp .60 1.50
HS26 Karl Malone .75 2.00
HS27 Rex Chapman .25 .60
HS28 Answer Card .20 .50

1993-94 Hoops Supreme Court
COMPLETE SET (11) 6.00 15.00
SER.2 STATED ODDS 1:11
SC1 Charles Barkley 1.25 3.00
SC2 David Robinson 1.00 2.50
SC3 Patrick Ewing .75 2.00
SC4 Shaquille O'Neal 2.50 6.00
SC5 Larry Johnson .60 1.50
SC6 Karl Malone 1.00 2.50
SC7 Alonzo Mourning .75 2.00
SC8 John Stockton 1.00 2.50
SC9 Hakeem Olajuwon UER 1.00 2.50
SC10 Scottie Pippen 1.25 3.00
SC11 Michael Jordan 5.00 12.00

1994-95 Hoops Preview
NNO David Robinson .75 2.00

1994-95 Hoops Promo Sheet
COMPLETE SET (6) 1.00 2.50
1 Jason Kidd 1.00 2.50
2 Donyell Marshall .20 .50
3 Eric Montross
Rodney Rogers .15 .40
4 Alonzo Mourning .30 .75
5 John Starks .20 .50
6 Dennis Rodman .50 1.25

1994-95 Hoops Big Numbers
COMPLETE SET (12) 15.00 40.00
SER.1 STATED ODDS 1:30
*RAINBOW CARDS: EQUAL VALUE TO SILVER
ONE RAINBOW PER SER.1 RETAIL PACK
BN1 David Robinson 2.50 6.00
BN2 Jamal Mashburn 1.25 3.00
BN3 Hakeem Olajuwon 2.50 6.00
BN4 Patrick Ewing 2.00 5.00
BN5 Shaquille O'Neal 5.00 12.00
BN6 Latrell Sprewell 1.50 4.00
BN7 Chris Webber 2.50 6.00
BN8 Anfernee Hardaway 2.50 6.00
BN9 Scottie Pippen 3.00 8.00
BN10 Isaiah Rider 1.25 3.00
BN11 Alonzo Mourning 2.00 5.00
BN12 Charles Barkley 3.00 8.00

1994-95 Hoops Draft Redemption
COMPLETE SET (11) 8.00 20.00
EXCH.CARD: SER.1 STATED ODDS 1:360
1 Glenn Robinson 1.00 2.50
2 Jason Kidd 2.50 6.00
3 Grant Hill 2.50 6.00
4 Donyell Marshall .50 1.25
5 Juwan Howard .75 2.00
6 Sharone Wright .40 1.00
7 Lamond Murray .50 1.25
8 Brian Grant .75 2.00
9 Eric Montross .40 1.00
10 Eddie Jones 1.50 4.00
11 Carlos Rogers .40 1.00
NNO Expired Exch.Card .40 1.00

1994-95 Hoops Magic's All-Rookies
COMPLETE SET (10) 5.00 12.00
SER.2 STATED ODDS 1:12
*FOIL CARDS: 1.25X TO 3X HI COLUMN
FOIL SER.2 STATED ODDS 1:36
*JUMBO CARDS: .75X TO 2X HI COLUMN
JUMBO ONE PER SER.2 HOBBY BOX
AR1 Glenn Robinson .60 1.50
AR2 Jason Kidd 1.50 4.00
AR3 Grant Hill 1.50 4.00
AR4 Donyell Marshall .30 .75
AR5 Juwan Howard .50 1.25
AR6 Sharone Wright .25 .60
AR7 Brian Grant .50 1.25
AR8 Eddie Jones 1.00 2.50
AR9 Jalen Rose .75 2.00
AR10 Wesley Person .30 .75

1994-95 Hoops Power Ratings
COMPLETE SET (54) 3.00 8.00
ONE PER SERIES 2 PACK
PR1 Mookie Blaylock .20 .50
PR2 Stacey Augmon .15 .40
PR3 Dino Radja .12 .30
PR4 Dominique Wilkins .30 .75
PR5 Larry Johnson .25 .60
PR6 Alonzo Mourning .30 .75
PR7 Toni Kukoc .25 .60
PR8 Scottie Pippen .50 1.25
PR9 John Williams .12 .30
PR10 Mark Price .20 .50
PR11 Jim Jackson .15 .40
PR12 Jamal Mashburn .20 .50
PR13 Dale Ellis .12 .30
PR14 LaPhonso Ellis .12 .30
PR15 Joe Dumars .20 .50
PR16 Lindsey Hunter .12 .30
PR17 Latrell Sprewell .25 .60
PR18 Chris Mullin .25 .60
PR19 Vernon Maxwell .12 .30
PR20 Hakeem Olajuwon .40 1.00
PR21 Mark Jackson .15 .40
PR22 Reggie Miller .40 1.00
PR23 Pooh Richardson .12 .30
PR24 Loy Vaught .12 .30
PR25 Vlade Divac .20 .50
PR26 Nick Van Exel .20 .50
PR27 Glen Rice .20 .50
PR28 Billy Owens .12 .30
PR29 Vin Baker .20 .50
PR30 Eric Murdock .12 .30
PR31 Christian Laettner .15 .40
PR32 Isaiah Rider .12 .30
PR33 Kenny Anderson .15 .40
PR34 Derrick Coleman .20 .50
PR35 Patrick Ewing .30 .75
PR36 John Starks .20 .50
PR37 Nick Anderson .12 .30
PR38 Anfernee Hardaway .40 1.00
PR39 Shawn Bradley .12 .30
PR40 Clarence Weatherspoon .12 .30
PR41 Charles Barkley .50 1.25
PR42 Kevin Johnson .20 .50
PR43 Clyde Drexler .30 .75
PR44 Clifford Robinson .15 .40
PR45 Mitch Richmond .25 .60
PR46 Olden Polynice .12 .30
PR47 Sean Elliott .15 .40
PR48 Chuck Person .15 .40
PR49 Shawn Kemp .30 .75
PR50 Gary Payton .30 .75
PR51 Jeff Hornacek .15 .40
PR52 Karl Malone .40 1.00
PR53 Rex Chapman .12 .30
PR54 Don MacLean .12 .30

1994-95 Hoops Predators
COMPLETE SET (8) 1.25 3.00
SER.2 STATED ODDS 1:12
P1 Mahmoud Abdul-Rauf .20 .50
P2 Dikembe Mutombo .50 1.25
P3 Shaquille O'Neal 1.25 3.00
P4 Tracy Murray .20 .50
P5 David Robinson .60 1.50
P6 Dennis Rodman .75 2.00
P7 Nate McMillan .25 .60
P8 John Stockton .60 1.50
NNO David Robinson Jumbo .40 1.00

1994-95 Hoops Supreme Court
COMPLETE SET (50) 8.00 20.00
SER.1 STATED ODDS 1:4
SC1 Mookie Blaylock .25 .60
SC2 Danny Manning .20 .50
SC3 Dino Radja .15 .40
SC4 Larry Johnson .30 .75
SC5 Alonzo Mourning .40 1.00
SC6 B.J. Armstrong .25 .60
SC7 Horace Grant .25 .60
SC8 Toni Kukoc .30 .75
SC9 Brad Daugherty .20 .50
SC10 Mark Price .25 .60
SC11 Jim Jackson .20 .50
SC12 Jamal Mashburn .25 .60
SC13 Dikembe Mutombo .40 1.00
SC14 Joe Dumars .25 .60
SC15 Lindsey Hunter .15 .40
SC16 Tim Hardaway .30 .75
SC17 Chris Mullin .30 .75
SC18 Sam Cassell .25 .60
SC19 Hakeem Olajuwon .50 1.25
SC20 Reggie Miller .50 1.25
SC21 Dominique Wilkins .40 1.00
SC22 Nick Van Exel .25 .60
SC23 Harold Miner .15 .40
SC24 Steve Smith .20 .50
SC25 Vin Baker .25 .60
SC26 Christian Laettner .20 .50
SC27 Isaiah Rider .20 .50
SC28 Kenny Anderson .20 .50
SC29 Derrick Coleman .20 .50
SC30 Patrick Ewing .40 1.00
SC31 John Starks .25 .60
SC32 Anfernee Hardaway .50 1.25
SC33 Shaquille O'Neal 1.00 2.50
SC34 Shawn Bradley .15 .40
SC35 Clarence Weatherspoon .15 .40
SC36 Charles Barkley .60 1.50
SC37 Kevin Johnson .25 .60
SC38 Oliver Miller .15 .40
SC39 Clyde Drexler .40 1.00
SC40 Clifford Robinson .20 .50
SC41 Mitch Richmond .30 .75
SC42 Bobby Hurley .15 .40
SC43 David Robinson .50 1.25
SC44 Dennis Rodman .60 1.50
SC45 Gary Payton .40 1.00
SC46 Shawn Kemp .40 1.00
SC47 John Stockton .50 1.25
SC48 Karl Malone .50 1.25
SC49 Calbert Cheaney .20 .50
SC50 Tom Gugliotta .15 .40

1995-96 Hoops National Promos
COMPLETE SET (7) 1.25 3.00
1 Kenny Anderson .25 .60
2 Vin Baker .25 .60
3 A.C. Green .25 .60
4 Jason Kidd .50 1.25
5 Glen Rice .30 .75
6 Rony Seikaly .20 .50
7 Title Card .20 .50

1995-96 Hoops Promo Sheet 1
COMPLETE SET (6) 1.25 3.00
1 Eddie Jones .40 1.00
2 Detlef Schrempf .40 1.00
3 Dan Majerle .40 1.00
4 Juwan Howard .40 1.00
5 Larry Johnson .50 1.25
6 Scott Burrell .25 .60

1995-96 Hoops Promo Sheet 2
COMPLETE SET (6) 2.00 5.00
1 Anfernee Hardaway 1.00 2.50
2 John Stockton .75 2.00
3 Antonio McDyess .50 1.25
4 Charles Barkley 1.00 2.50
5 John Salley .25 .60
6 Glenn Robinson .40 1.00

1995-96 Hoops
COMPLETE SET (400) 15.00 40.00
COMPLETE SERIES 1 (250) 10.00 25.00
COMPLETE SERIES 2 (150) 6.00 15.00
SUBSET CARDS SAME VALUE AS BASE CARDS
HILL TRIB: SER.1 STATED ODDS 1:360
1 Stacey Augmon .12 .30
2 Mookie Blaylock .15 .40
3 Craig Ehlo .10 .25
4 Andrew Lang .10 .25
5 Grant Long .25 .60
6 Ken Norman .25 .60
7 Steve Smith .30 .75
8 Dee Brown .30 .75
9 Sherman Douglas .25 .60
10 Pervis Ellison .25 .60
11 Eric Montross .25 .60
12 Dino Radja .25 .60
13 Dominique Wilkins .60 1.50
14 Muggsy Bogues .40 1.00
15 Scott Burrell .25 .60
16 Dell Curry .40 1.00
17 Hersey Hawkins .30 .75
18 Larry Johnson .50 1.25
19 Alonzo Mourning .60 1.50
20 B.J. Armstrong .40 1.00
21 Michael Jordan 4.00 10.00
22 Toni Kukoc .50 1.25
23 Will Perdue .30 .75
24 Scottie Pippen 1.00 2.50
25 Dickey Simpkins .25 .60
26 Terrell Brandon .30 .75
27 Tyrone Hill .25 .60
28 Chris Mills .25 .60
29 Bobby Phills .30 .75
30 Mark Price .40 1.00
31 John Williams .25 .60
32 Tony Dumas .25 .60
33 Jim Jackson .30 .75
34 Popeye Jones .25 .60
35 Jason Kidd .60 1.50
36 Jamal Mashburn .40 1.00
37 Roy Tarpley .30 .75
38 Mahmoud Abdul-Rauf .30 .75
39 LaPhonso Ellis .30 .75
40 Dikembe Mutombo .60 1.50
41 Robert Pack .25 .60
42 Rodney Rogers .30 .75
43 Jalen Rose .50 1.25
44 Bryant Stith .25 .60
45 Joe Dumars .40 1.00
46 Grant Hill .60 1.50
47 Allan Houston .30 .75
48 Lindsey Hunter .25 .60
49 Oliver Miller .25 .60
50 Terry Mills .25 .60
51 Chris Gatling .25 .60
52 Tim Hardaway .50 1.25
53 Donyell Marshall .25 .60
54 Chris Mullin .40 1.00
55 Carlos Rogers .25 .60
56 Clifford Rozier .25 .60
57 Rony Seikaly .25 .60
58 Latrell Sprewell .40 1.00
59 Sam Cassell .40 1.00
60 Clyde Drexler .60 1.50
61 Robert Horry .40 1.00
62 Vernon Maxwell .25 .60
63 Hakeem Olajuwon .75 2.00
64 Kenny Smith .25 .60
65 Dale Davis .25 .60
66 Mark Jackson .30 .75
67 Derrick McKey .25 .60
68 Reggie Miller .75 2.00
69 Byron Scott .40 1.00
70 Rik Smits .30 .75
71 Terry Dehere .25 .60
72 Lamond Murray .25 .60
73 Eric Piatkowski .25 .60
74 Pooh Richardson .25 .60
75 Malik Sealy .25 .60
76 Loy Vaught .25 .60
77 Elden Campbell .25 .60
78 Cedric Ceballos .30 .75
79 Vlade Divac .40 1.00
80 Eddie Jones .40 1.00
81 Sedale Threatt .25 .60
82 Nick Van Exel .40 1.00
83 Bimbo Coles .25 .60
84 Harold Miner .25 .60
85 Billy Owens .25 .60
86 Khalid Reeves .25 .60
87 Glen Rice .40 1.00
88 Kevin Willis .25 .60
89 Vin Baker .30 .75
90 Marty Conlon .25 .60
91 Todd Day .25 .60
92 Eric Mobley .25 .60
93 Eric Murdock .25 .60
94 Glenn Robinson .40 1.00
95 Winston Garland .25 .60
96 Tom Gugliotta .25 .60
97 Christian Laettner .30 .75
98 Isaiah Rider .25 .60
99 Sean Rooks .25 .60
100 Doug West .25 .60
101 Kenny Anderson .30 .75
102 Benoit Benjamin .25 .60
103 Derrick Coleman .30 .75
104 Kevin Edwards .25 .60
105 Armon Gilliam .25 .60
106 Chris Morris .25 .60
107 Patrick Ewing .60 1.50
108 Derek Harper .30 .75
109 Anthony Mason .25 .60
110 Charles Oakley .25 .60
111 Charles Smith .25 .60
112 John Starks .40 1.00
113 Monty Williams .25 .60
114 Nick Anderson .30 .75
115 Horace Grant .30 .75
116 Anfernee Hardaway 1.00 2.50
117 Shaquille O'Neal 1.50 4.00
118 Dennis Scott .25 .60
119 Brian Shaw .25 .60
120 Dana Barros .30 .75
121 Shawn Bradley .25 .60
122 Willie Burton .30 .75
123 Jeff Malone .25 .60
124 Clarence Weatherspoon .25 .60
125 Sharone Wright .25 .60
126 Charles Barkley 1.00 2.50
127 A.C. Green .30 .75
128 Kevin Johnson .40 1.00
129 Dan Majerle .40 1.00
130 Danny Manning .30 .75
131 Elliot Perry .25 .60
132 Wesley Person .25 .60
133 Chris Dudley .25 .60
134 Clifford Robinson .40 1.00
135 James Robinson .25 .60
136 Rod Strickland .25 .60
137 Otis Thorpe .30 .75
138 Buck Williams .30 .75
139 Brian Grant .30 .75
140 Olden Polynice .25 .60
141 Mitch Richmond .50 1.25
142 Michael Smith .25 .60
143 Spud Webb .40 1.00
144 Walt Williams .25 .60
145 Vinny Del Negro .25 .60
146 Sean Elliott .30 .75
147 Avery Johnson .30 .75
148 Chuck Person .30 .75
149 David Robinson .75 2.00
150 Dennis Rodman .75 2.00
151 Kendall Gill .25 .60
152 Ervin Johnson .25 .60
153 Shawn Kemp .60 1.50
154 Nate McMillan .25 .60
155 Gary Payton .60 1.50
156 Detlef Schrempf .40 1.00
157 Dontonio Wingfield .25 .60
158 David Benoit .25 .60
159 Jeff Hornacek .30 .75
160 Karl Malone .75 2.00
161 Felton Spencer .25 .60
162 John Stockton .75 2.00
163 Jamie Watson .25 .60
164 Rex Chapman .25 .60
165 Calbert Cheaney .25 .60
166 Juwan Howard .40 1.00
167 Don MacLean .25 .60
168 Gheorghe Muresan .25 .60
169 Scott Skiles .25 .60
170 Chris Webber .50 1.25
171 Lenny Wilkens CO .40 1.00
172 Allan Bristow CO .25 .60
173 Phil Jackson CO .60 1.50
174 Mike Fratello CO .25 .60
175 Dick Motta CO .25 .60
176 Bernie Bickerstaff CO .25 .60
177 Doug Collins CO .30 .75
178 Rick Adelman CO .30 .75
179 Rudy Tomjanovich CO .40 1.00
180 Larry Brown CO .40 1.00
181 Bill Fitch CO .25 .60
182 Del Harris CO .25 .60
183 Mike Dunleavy CO .25 .60
184 Bill Blair CO .25 .60
185 Butch Beard CO .25 .60
186 Pat Riley CO .50 1.25
187 Brian Hill CO .25 .60
188 John Lucas CO .30 .75
189 Paul Westphal CO .30 .75
190 P.J. Carlesimo CO .30 .75
191 Garry St. Jean CO .25 .60
192 Bob Hill CO .25 .60
193 George Karl CO .30 .75
194 Brendan Malone CO .25 .60
195 Jerry Sloan CO .40 1.00
196 Kevin Pritchard CO .25 .60
197 Jim Lynam CO .25 .60
198 Brian Grant SS .30 .75
199 Grant Hill SS .60 1.50
200 Juwan Howard SS .40 1.00
201 Eddie Jones SS .40 1.00
202 Jason Kidd SS .60 1.50
203 Donyell Marshall SS .25 .60
204 Eric Montross SS .25 .60
205 Glenn Robinson SS .40 1.00
206 Jalen Rose SS .50 1.25
207 Sharone Wright SS .25 .60
208 Dana Barros MS .30 .75
209 Joe Dumars MS .40 1.00
210 A.C. Green MS .30 .75
211 Grant Hill MS .60 1.50
212 Karl Malone MS .75 2.00
213 Reggie Miller MS .75 2.00
214 Glen Rice MS .40 1.00
215 John Stockton MS .75 2.00
216 Lenny Wilkens MS .40 1.00
217 Dominique Wilkins MS .60 1.50
218 Kenny Anderson BB .30 .75
219 Mookie Blaylock BB .30 .75
220 Larry Johnson BB .50 1.25
221 Shawn Kemp BB .60 1.50
222 Toni Kukoc BB .50 1.25
223 Jamal Mashburn BB .40 1.00
224 Glen Rice BB .40 1.00
225 Mitch Richmond BB .50 1.25
226 Latrell Sprewell BB .40 1.00
227 Rod Strickland BB .25 .60
228 M.Adams/D.Martin PL .25 .60
229 C.Ehlo/J.Harmon PL .25 .60
230 M.Elie/G.McCloud PL .25 .60
231 A.Mason/C.Brown PL .25 .60
232 J.Starks/T.Legler PL .40 1.00
233 Muggsy Bogues CA .40 1.00
234 Joe Dumars CA .40 1.00
235 LaPhonso Ellis CA .30 .75
236 Patrick Ewing CA .60 1.50
237 Grant Hill CA .60 1.50
238 Kevin Johnson CA .40 1.00
239 Dan Majerle CA .40 1.00
240 Karl Malone CA .75 2.00
241 Hakeem Olajuwon CA .75 2.00
242 David Robinson CA .75 2.00
243 Dana Barros TT .30 .75
244 Scott Burrell TT .25 .60
245 Reggie Miller TT .75 2.00
246 Glen Rice TT .40 1.00
247 John Stockton TT .75 2.00
248 Checklist #1 .20 .50
249 Checklist #2 .20 .50
250 Checklist #3 .20 .50
251 Alan Henderson RC .40 1.00
252 Junior Burrough RC .40 1.00
253 Eric Williams RC .40 1.00
254 George Zidek RC .30 .75
255 Jason Caffey RC .40 1.00
256 Donny Marshall RC .40 1.00
257 Bob Sura RC .30 .75
258 Loren Meyer RC .25 .60
259 Cherokee Parks RC .30 .75
260 Antonio McDyess RC .50 1.25
261 Theo Ratliff RC .60 1.50
262 Lou Roe RC .40 1.00
263 Andrew DeClercq RC .40 1.00
264 Joe Smith RC .50 1.25
265 Travis Best RC .40 1.00
266 Brent Barry RC .60 1.50
267 Frankie King RC .40 1.00
268 Sasha Danilovic RC .40 1.00
269 Kurt Thomas RC .40 1.00
270 Shawn Respert RC .30 .75
271 Jerome Allen RC .40 1.00
272 Kevin Garnett RC 3.00 8.00
273 Ed O'Bannon RC .30 .75
274 David Vaughn RC .40 1.00
275 Jerry Stackhouse RC 1.25 3.00
276 Mario Bennett RC .30 .75
277 Michael Finley RC 1.00 2.50
278 Randolph Childress RC .30 .75
279 Arvydas Sabonis RC .75 2.00
280 Gary Trent RC .30 .75
281 Tyus Edney RC .40 1.00
282 Corliss Williamson RC .40 1.00
283 Cory Alexander RC .40 1.00
284 Sherrell Ford RC .30 .75
285 Jimmy King RC .40 1.00
286 Damon Stoudamire RC 1.00 2.50
287 Greg Ostertag RC .40 1.00
288 Lawrence Moten RC .40 1.00
289 Bryant Reeves RC .30 .75
290 Rasheed Wallace RC 1.25 3.00
291 Spud Webb .40 1.00
292 Dana Barros .25 .60
293 Rick Fox .25 .60
294 Kendall Gill .25 .60
295 Khalid Reeves .25 .60
296 Glen Rice .40 1.00
297 Luc Longley .30 .75
298 Dennis Rodman .75 2.00
299 Dan Majerle .40 1.00
300 Lorenzo Williams .25 .60
301 Dale Ellis .30 .75
302 Reggie Williams .25 .60
303 Otis Thorpe .30 .75
304 B.J. Armstrong .40 1.00
305 Pete Chilcutt .25 .60
306 Mario Elie .25 .60
307 Antonio Davis .25 .60
308 Ricky Pierce .25 .60
309 Rodney Rogers .30 .75
310 Brian Williams .25 .60
311 Corie Blount .25 .60
312 George Lynch .25 .60
313 Alonzo Mourning .60 1.50
314 Lee Mayberry .25 .60
315 Terry Porter .30 .75
316 P.J. Brown .25 .60
317 Hubert Davis .25 .60
318 Charlie Ward .30 .75
319 Jon Koncak .25 .60
320 Derrick Coleman .30 .75
321 Richard Dumas .25 .60
322 Vernon Maxwell .25 .60
323 Wayman Tisdale .25 .60
324 Dontonio Wingfield .25 .60
325 Tyrone Corbin .25 .60
326 Bobby Hurley .25 .60
327 Will Perdue .30 .75
328 J.R. Reid .25 .60
329 Hersey Hawkins .30 .75
330 Sam Perkins .30 .75
331 Adam Keefe .25 .60
332 Chris Morris .25 .60
333 Robert Pack .25 .60
334 M.L. Carr CO .10 .25
335 Pat Riley CO .15 .40
336 Don Nelson CO .12 .30
337 Brian Winters CO .10 .25
338 Willie Anderson ET .25 .60
339 Acie Earl ET .25 .60
340 Jimmy King ET .40 1.00
341 Oliver Miller ET .25 .60
342 Tracy Murray ET .25 .60
343 Ed Pinckney ET .25 .60
344 Alvin Robertson ET .25 .60
345 Carlos Rogers ET .25 .60
346 John Salley ET .25 .60
347 Damon Stoudamire ET 1.00 2.50
348 Zan Tabak ET .25 .60
349 Greg Anthony ET .25 .60
350 Blue Edwards ET .25 .60
351 Kenny Gattison ET .25 .60
352 Antonio Harvey ET .25 .60
353 Chris King ET .25 .60
354 Darrick Martin ET .25 .60
355 Lawrence Moten ET .40 1.00
356 Bryant Reeves ET .30 .75
357 Byron Scott ET .40 1.00
358 Michael Jordan ES 4.00 10.00
359 Dikembe Mutombo ES .60 1.50
360 Grant Hill ES .60 1.50
361 Robert Horry ES .40 1.00
362 Alonzo Mourning ES .60 1.50
363 Vin Baker ES .30 .75
364 Isaiah Rider ES .40 1.00
365 Charles Oakley ES .30 .75
366 Shaquille O'Neal ES 1.50 4.00
367 Jerry Stackhouse ES 1.25 3.00
368 Clarence Weatherspoon ES .25 .60
369 Charles Barkley ES 1.00 2.50
370 Sean Elliott ES .30 .75
371 Shawn Kemp ES .60 1.50
372 Chris Webber ES .50 1.25
373 Spud Webb RH .40 1.00
374 Muggsy Bogues RH .40 1.00
375 Toni Kukoc RH .50 1.25
376 Dennis Rodman RH .75 2.00
377 Jamal Mashburn RH .40 1.00
378 Jalen Rose RH .50 1.25
379 Clyde Drexler RH .60 1.50
380 Mark Jackson RH .30 .75
381 Cedric Ceballos RH .30 .75
382 Nick Van Exel RH .40 1.00
383 John Starks RH .40 1.00
384 Vernon Maxwell RH .25 .60
385 Shawn Kemp RH .60 1.50
386 Gary Payton RH .60 1.50
387 Karl Malone RH .75 2.00
388 Mookie Blaylock WD .40 1.00
389 Muggsy Bogues WD .40 1.00
390 Jason Kidd WD .60 1.50
391 Tim Hardaway WD .50 1.25
392 Nick Van Exel WD .40 1.00
393 Kenny Anderson WD .30 .75
394 Anfernee Hardaway WD 1.00 2.50
395 Rod Strickland WD .25 .60
396 Avery Johnson WD .30 .75
397 John Stockton WD .75 2.00
398 Grant Hill SPEC .60 1.50
399 Checklist (251-367) .20 .50
400 Checklist (368-400/Ins.) .20 .50
NNO G.Hill Co-ROY 6.00 15.00
NNO G.Hill Sweepstakes .30 .75
NNO G.Hill Tribute 10.00 25.00

1995-96 Hoops Block Party
COMPLETE SET (25) 3.00 8.00
SER.1 STATED ODDS 1:2 HOBBY/RETAIL
1 Oliver Miller .20 .50
2 Dennis Rodman .60 1.50
3 Scottie Pippen .75 2.00
4 Dikembe Mutombo .50 1.25
5 Vlade Divac .30 .75
6 Brian Grant .25 .60
7 Alonzo Mourning .50 1.25
8 Hakeem Olajuwon .60 1.50
9 Patrick Ewing .50 1.25
10 Shawn Kemp .50 1.25
11 Vin Baker .25 .60
12 Horace Grant .25 .60
13 Dale Davis .20 .50
14 Juwan Howard .30 .75
15 Eddie Jones .30 .75
16 Eric Montross .20 .50
17 Tyrone Hill .20 .50
18 Tom Gugliotta .20 .50
19 Shawn Bradley .20 .50
20 Dan Majerle .30 .75
21 Loy Vaught .20 .50
22 Donyell Marshall .20 .50
23 Chris Webber .40 1.00
24 Derrick Coleman .25 .60
25 Walt Williams .20 .50

1995-96 Hoops Grant Hill Dunks/Slams
COMPLETE SET (10) 10.00 20.00
COMPLETE DUNKS SET (5) 5.00 12.00
COMPLETE SLAMS SET (5) 5.00 12.00
COMMON DUNK/SLAM (D1-D5) 1.50 4.00
DUNK: SER.1 STATED ODDS 1:36 RETAIL
SLAM: SER.1 STATED ODDS 1:36 HOBBY

1995-96 Hoops Grant's All-Rookies
COMPLETE SET (10) 20.00 50.00
SER.2 STATED ODDS 1:64 HOBBY/RETAIL
AR1 Cherokee Parks .60 1.50
AR2 Antonio McDyess 1.00 2.50
AR3 Theo Ratliff 1.25 3.00
AR4 Joe Smith 1.00 2.50
AR5 Shawn Respert .60 1.50
AR6 Kevin Garnett 6.00 15.00
AR7 Ed O'Bannon .60 1.50
AR8 Jerry Stackhouse 2.50 6.00
AR9 Damon Stoudamire 2.00 5.00
AR10 Rasheed Wallace 2.50 6.00

1995-96 Hoops HoopStars
COMPLETE SET (12) 6.00 15.00
SER.2 STATED ODDS 1:16 HOBBY/RETAIL
HS1 Scottie Pippen 2.00 5.00
HS2 Jim Jackson .60 1.50
HS3 Antonio McDyess .50 1.25
HS4 Clyde Drexler 1.25 3.00
HS5 Alonzo Mourning 1.25 3.00
HS6 Glenn Robinson .75 2.00
HS7 Patrick Ewing 1.25 3.00
HS8 Anfernee Hardaway 2.00 5.00
HS9 Shawn Kemp 1.25 3.00
HS10 Karl Malone 1.50 4.00
HS11 Juwan Howard .75 2.00
HS12 Rasheed Wallace 1.25 3.00

1995-96 Hoops Hot List
COMPLETE SET (10) 60.00 150.00
SER.2 STATED ODDS 1:32 HOBBY
1 Michael Jordan 60.00 150.00
2 Jason Kidd 2.50 6.00
3 Jamal Mashburn 1.50 4.00
4 Grant Hill 2.50 6.00
5 Joe Smith 2.50 6.00
6 Hakeem Olajuwon 3.00 8.00
7 Glenn Robinson 1.50 4.00
8 Shaquille O'Neal 6.00 15.00
9 Jerry Stackhouse 5.00 12.00
10 David Robinson 3.00 8.00

1995-96 Hoops Number Crunchers
COMPLETE SET (25) 4.00 10.00
SER.1 STATED ODDS 1:2 HOBBY/RETAIL
1 Michael Jordan 2.00 5.00
2 Shaquille O'Neal .75 2.00
3 Grant Hill .30 .75
4 Detlef Schrempf .20 .50
5 Kenny Anderson .15 .40
6 Anfernee Hardaway .50 1.25
7 Latrell Sprewell .20 .50
8 Jamal Mashburn .20 .50
9 Nick Van Exel .20 .50
10 Charles Barkley .50 1.25
11 Mitch Richmond .25 .60
12 David Robinson .40 1.00
13 Gary Payton .30 .75
14 Rod Strickland .12 .30
15 Glenn Robinson .20 .50
16 Reggie Miller .40 1.00
17 Karl Malone .40 1.00
18 Jim Jackson .15 .40
19 Clyde Drexler .30 .75
20 Glen Rice .20 .50
21 Isaiah Rider .20 .50
22 Cedric Ceballos .15 .40
23 John Stockton .40 1.00
24 Jason Kidd .30 .75
25 Mookie Blaylock .20 .50

1995-96 Hoops Power Palette
COMPLETE SET (10) 15.00 40.00
SER.2 STATED ODDS 1:32 RETAIL
1 Michael Jordan 20.00 50.00
2 Jason Kidd 1.50 4.00
3 Grant Hill 1.50 4.00
4 Joe Smith 1.25 3.00
5 Hakeem Olajuwon 2.00 5.00
6 Glenn Robinson 1.00 2.50
7 Anfernee Hardaway 2.50 6.00
8 Shaquille O'Neal 4.00 10.00
9 Jerry Stackhouse 3.00 8.00
10 Charles Barkley 2.50 6.00

1995-96 Hoops SkyView
COMPLETE SET (10) 300.00 600.00
SER.2 STATED ODDS 1:480 HOBBY/RETAIL
SV1 Michael Jordan 200.00 500.00
SV2 Jason Kidd 8.00 20.00
SV3 Grant Hill 8.00 20.00
SV4 Joe Smith 6.00 15.00
SV5 Hakeem Olajuwon 10.00 25.00
SV6 Glenn Robinson 5.00 12.00
SV7 Anfernee Hardaway 12.00 30.00
SV8 Shaquille O'Neal 20.00 50.00
SV9 Jerry Stackhouse 15.00 40.00
SV10 Charles Barkley 12.00 30.00

1995-96 Hoops Slamland
COMPLETE SET (50) 3.00 8.00
ONE PER SER.2 PACK
SL1 Stacey Augmon .12 .30
SL2 Steve Smith .12 .30
SL3 Eric Montross .10 .25
SL4 Dino Radja .10 .25
SL5 Dell Curry .15 .40
SL6 Larry Johnson .20 .50
SL7 Scottie Pippen .40 1.00
SL8 Dennis Rodman .30 .75
SL9 Tyrone Hill .10 .25
SL10 Jim Jackson .12 .30
SL11 Jamal Mashburn .15 .40
SL12 Dikembe Mutombo .25 .60
SL13 Joe Dumars .15 .40
SL14 Grant Hill .25 .60
SL15 Allan Houston .12 .30
SL16 Donyell Marshall .10 .25
SL17 Latrell Sprewell .15 .40
SL18 Sam Cassell .15 .40
SL19 Hakeem Olajuwon .30 .75
SL20 Reggie Miller .30 .75
SL21 Loy Vaught .10 .25
SL22 Vlade Divac .15 .40
SL23 Eddie Jones .15 .40
SL24 Alonzo Mourning .25 .60
SL25 Kevin Willis .10 .25
SL26 Vin Baker .12 .30
SL27 Glenn Robinson .15 .40
SL28 Tom Gugliotta .10 .25
SL29 Kenny Anderson .12 .30
SL30 Derrick Coleman .12 .30
SL31 Patrick Ewing .25 .60
SL32 John Starks .15 .40
SL33 Dennis Scott .10 .25
SL34 Jerry Stackhouse .50 1.25
SL35 Charles Barkley .40 1.00
SL36 Kevin Johnson .15 .40
SL37 Danny Manning .12 .30
SL38 Clifford Robinson .15 .40
SL39 Brian Grant .12 .30
SL40 Mitch Richmond .20 .50
SL41 Walt Williams .10 .25
SL42 David Robinson .30 .75
SL43 Gary Payton .25 .60
SL44 Detlef Schrempf .15 .40
SL45 Damon Stoudamire .40 1.00
SL46 Karl Malone .30 .75
SL47 John Stockton .30 .75
SL48 Bryant Reeves .12 .30
SL49 Juwan Howard .15 .40
SL50 Chris Webber .20 .50

1995-96 Hoops Top Ten
COMPLETE SET (10) 10.00 25.00
SER.1 STATED ODDS 1:12 HOBBY/RETAIL
AR1 Shaquille O'Neal 3.00 8.00
AR2 Grant Hill 1.25 3.00
AR3 Chris Webber 1.00 2.50
AR4 Jamal Mashburn .75 2.00
AR5 Anfernee Hardaway 2.00 5.00
AR6 Alonzo Mourning 1.25 3.00
AR7 Michael Jordan 8.00 20.00
AR8 Charles Barkley 2.00 5.00
AR9 Glenn Robinson .75 2.00
AR10 Jason Kidd 1.25 3.00

1996-97 Hoops
COMPLETE SET (350) 25.00 60.00
COMPLETE SERIES 1 (200) 4.00 10.00
COMPLETE SERIES 2 (150) 20.00 50.00

HILL Z-F: SER.1 STATED ODDS 1:360 H/R
1 Stacey Augmon .25 .60
2 Mookie Blaylock .30 .75
3 Alan Henderson .20 .50
4 Christian Laettner .30 .75
5 Grant Long .20 .50
6 Steve Smith .25 .60
7 Dana Barros .20 .50
8 Todd Day .20 .50
9 Rick Fox .20 .50
10 Eric Montross .20 .50
11 Dino Radja .20 .50
12 Eric Williams .20 .50
13 Kenny Anderson .25 .60
14 Scott Burrell .20 .50
15 Dell Curry .30 .75
16 Matt Geiger .20 .50
17 Larry Johnson .40 1.00
18 Glen Rice .30 .75
19 Ron Harper .25 .60
20 Michael Jordan 3.00 8.00
21 Steve Kerr .25 .60
22 Toni Kukoc .30 .75
23 Luc Longley .25 .60
24 Scottie Pippen .75 2.00
25 Dennis Rodman .75 2.00
26 Terrell Brandon .25 .60
27 Danny Ferry .20 .50
28 Tyrone Hill .20 .50
29 Chris Mills .20 .50
30 Bobby Phills .20 .50
31 Bob Sura .20 .50
32 Tony Dumas .20 .50
33 Jim Jackson .20 .50
34 Popeye Jones .20 .50
35 Jason Kidd .50 1.25
36 Jamal Mashburn .30 .75
37 George McCloud .20 .50
38 Cherokee Parks .20 .50
39 Mahmoud Abdul-Rauf .25 .60
40 LaPhonso Ellis .20 .50
41 Antonio McDyess .30 .75
42 Dikembe Mutombo .50 1.25
43 Jalen Rose .25 .60
44 Bryant Stith .20 .50
45 Joe Dumars .40 1.00
46 Grant Hill .50 1.25
47 Allan Houston .30 .75
48 Lindsey Hunter .20 .50
49 Terry Mills .20 .50
50 Theo Ratliff .20 .50
51 Otis Thorpe .25 .60
52 B.J. Armstrong .25 .60
53 Donyell Marshall .20 .50
54 Chris Mullin .40 1.00
55 Joe Smith .25 .60
56 Rony Seikaly .25 .60
57 Latrell Sprewell .30 .75
58 Mark Bryant .20 .50
59 Sam Cassell .25 .60
60 Clyde Drexler .50 1.25
61 Mario Elie .20 .50
62 Robert Horry .30 .75
63 Hakeem Olajuwon .60 1.50
64 Travis Best .20 .50
65 Antonio Davis .20 .50
66 Mark Jackson .25 .60
67 Derrick McKey .20 .50
68 Reggie Miller .60 1.50
69 Rik Smits .25 .60
70 Brent Barry .25 .60
71 Terry Dehere .20 .50
72 Pooh Richardson .20 .50
73 Rodney Rogers .20 .50
74 Loy Vaught .20 .50
75 Brian Williams .20 .50
76 Elden Campbell .20 .50
77 Cedric Ceballos .25 .60
78 Vlade Divac .30 .75
79 Eddie Jones .30 .75
80 Anthony Peeler .20 .50
81 Nick Van Exel .30 .75
82 Sasha Danilovic .20 .50
83 Tim Hardaway .40 1.00
84 Alonzo Mourning .50 1.25
85 Kurt Thomas .20 .50
86 Walt Williams .20 .50
87 Vin Baker .25 .60
88 Sherman Douglas .20 .50
89 Johnny Newman .20 .50
90 Shawn Respert .20 .50
91 Glenn Robinson .30 .75
92 Kevin Garnett 1.00 2.50
93 Tom Gugliotta .20 .50
94 Andrew Lang .20 .50
95 Sam Mitchell .20 .50
96 Isaiah Rider .25 .60
97 Shawn Bradley .20 .50
98 P.J. Brown .20 .50
99 Chris Childs .20 .50
100 Armon Gilliam .20 .50
101 Ed O'Bannon .20 .50
102 Jayson Williams .20 .50
103 Hubert Davis .20 .50
104 Patrick Ewing .50 1.25
105 Anthony Mason .25 .60
106 Charles Oakley .30 .75
107 John Starks .30 .75
108 Charlie Ward .20 .50
109 Nick Anderson .20 .50
110 Horace Grant .30 .75
111 Anfernee Hardaway .75 2.00
112 Shaquille O'Neal 1.25 3.00
113 Dennis Scott .25 .60
114 Brian Shaw .20 .50
115 Derrick Coleman .25 .60
116 Vernon Maxwell .20 .50
117 Trevor Ruffin .20 .50
118 Jerry Stackhouse .40 1.00
119 Clarence Weatherspoon .20 .50
120 Charles Barkley .75 2.00
121 Michael Finley .30 .75
122 A.C. Green .25 .60
123 Kevin Johnson .30 .75
124 Danny Manning .25 .60
125 Wesley Person .20 .50
126 John Williams .20 .50
127 Harvey Grant .20 .50
128 Aaron McKie .20 .50
129 Clifford Robinson .30 .75
130 Arvydas Sabonis .30 .75
131 Rod Strickland .20 .50
132 Gary Trent .20 .50
133 Tyus Edney .20 .50
134 Brian Grant .25 .60
135 Billy Owens .20 .50
136 Olden Polynice .20 .50
137 Mitch Richmond .40 1.00
138 Corliss Williamson .20 .50
139 Vinny Del Negro .20 .50
140 Sean Elliott .30 .75
141 Avery Johnson .25 .60
142 Chuck Person .25 .60
143 David Robinson .60 1.50
144 Charles Smith .20 .50
145 Sherrell Ford .20 .50
146 Hersey Hawkins .20 .50
147 Shawn Kemp .50 1.25
148 Nate McMillan .20 .50
149 Gary Payton .50 1.25
150 Detlef Schrempf .30 .75
151 Oliver Miller .20 .50
152 Tracy Murray .20 .50
153 Carlos Rogers .20 .50
154 Damon Stoudamire .30 .75
155 Zan Tabak .20 .50
156 Sharone Wright .20 .50
157 Antoine Carr .20 .50
158 Jeff Hornacek .25 .60
159 Adam Keefe .20 .50
160 Karl Malone .60 1.50
161 Chris Morris .20 .50
162 John Stockton .60 1.50
163 Greg Anthony .20 .50
164 Blue Edwards .20 .50
165 Chris King .20 .50
166 Lawrence Moten .20 .50
167 Bryant Reeves .20 .50
168 Byron Scott .30 .75
169 Calbert Cheaney .20 .50
170 Juwan Howard .30 .75
171 Tim Legler .20 .50
172 Gheorghe Muresan .20 .50
173 Rasheed Wallace .40 1.00
174 Chris Webber .40 1.00
175 Steve Smith BF .25 .60
176 Michael Jordan BF 3.00 8.00
177 Scottie Pippen BF .75 2.00
178 Dennis Rodman BF .75 2.00
179 Allan Houston BF .30 .75
180 Hakeem Olajuwon BF .60 1.50
181 Patrick Ewing BF .50 1.25
182 Anfernee Hardaway BF .75 2.00
183 Shaquille O'Neal BF 1.25 3.00
184 Charles Barkley BF .75 2.00
185 Arvydas Sabonis BF .30 .75
186 David Robinson BF .60 1.50
187 Shawn Kemp BF .50 1.25
188 Gary Payton BF .50 1.25
189 Karl Malone BF .60 1.50
190 Kenny Anderson PLA .25 .60
191 Toni Kukoc PLA .30 .75
192 Brent Barry PLA .25 .60
193 Cedric Ceballos PLA .25 .60
194 Shawn Bradley PLA .20 .50
195 Charles Oakley PLA .30 .75
196 Dennis Scott PLA .25 .60
197 Clifford Robinson PLA .30 .75
198 Mitch Richmond PLA .40 1.00
199 Checklist .10 .25
200 Checklist .10 .25
201 Dikembe Mutombo .50 1.25
202 Dee Brown .20 .50
203 David Wesley .20 .50
204 Vlade Divac .30 .75
205 Anthony Mason .25 .60
206 Chris Gatling .20 .50
207 Eric Montross .20 .50
208 Ervin Johnson .20 .50
209 Stacey Augmon .25 .60
210 Joe Dumars .40 1.00
211 Grant Hill .50 1.25
212 Charles Barkley .75 2.00
213 Jalen Rose .25 .60
214 Lamond Murray .20 .50
215 Shaquille O'Neal 1.25 3.00
216 P.J. Brown .20 .50
217 Dan Majerle .30 .75
218 Armon Gilliam .20 .50
219 Andrew Lang .20 .50
220 Kevin Garnett 1.00 2.50
221 Tom Gugliotta .20 .50
222 Cherokee Parks .20 .50
223 Doug West .20 .50
224 Kendall Gill .30 .75
225 Robert Pack .20 .50
226 Allan Houston .30 .75
227 Larry Johnson .40 1.00
228 Rony Seikaly .25 .60
229 Gerald Wilkins .25 .60
230 Michael Cage .20 .50
231 Lucious Harris .20 .50
232 Sam Cassell .25 .60
233 Robert Horry .30 .75
234 Kenny Anderson .25 .60
235 Isaiah Rider .25 .60
236 Rasheed Wallace .40 1.00
237 Mahmoud Abdul-Rauf .25 .60
238 Vernon Maxwell .20 .50
239 Dominique Wilkins .50 1.25
240 Jim McIlvaine .20 .50
241 Hubert Davis .20 .50
242 Popeye Jones .20 .50
243 Walt Williams .20 .50
244 Karl Malone .60 1.50
245 John Stockton .60 1.50
246 Anthony Peeler .20 .50
247 Tracy Murray .20 .50
248 Rod Strickland .30 .75
249 Lenny Wilkens CO .75 2.00
250 M.L. Carr CO .50 .40
251 Dave Cowens CO .75 2.00
252 Phil Jackson CO .75 2.00
253 Mike Fratello CO .50 1.25
254 Jim Cleamons CO .40 1.00
255 Dick Motta CO .40 1.00
256 Doug Collins CO .75 2.00
257 Rick Adelman CO .75 2.00
258 Rudy Tomjanovich CO .75 2.00
259 Larry Brown CO .75 2.00
260 Bill Fitch CO .75 2.00
261 Del Harris CO .50 1.25
262 Pat Riley CO .75 2.00
263 Chris Ford CO .40 1.00
264 Flip Saunders CO .50 1.25
265 John Calipari CO 1.50 4.00
266 Jeff Van Gundy CO .75 2.00
267 Brian Hill CO .75 2.00
268 Johnny Davis CO .50 1.25
269 Danny Ainge CO .75 2.00
270 P.J. Carlesimo CO .75 .40
271 Garry St. Jean CO .40 1.00
272 Bob Hill CO .40 1.00
273 George Karl CO .75 2.00
274 Darrell Walker CO .75 2.00
275 Jerry Sloan CO .75 2.00
276 Brian Winters CO .75 2.00
277 Jim Lynam CO .40 1.00
278 Shareef Abdur-Rahim RC .50 1.25
279 Ray Allen RC 1.50 4.00
280 Shandon Anderson RC .25 .60
281 Kobe Bryant RC 15.00 40.00
282 Marcus Camby RC .50 1.25
283 Erick Dampier RC .30 .75
284 Emanual Davis RC .25 .60
285 Tony Delk RC .30 .75
286 Brian Evans RC .20 .50
287 Derek Fisher RC .40 1.00
288 Todd Fuller RC .20 .50
289 Dean Garrett RC .30 .75
290 Reggie Geary RC .30 .75
291 Darvin Ham RC .60 1.50
292 Othella Harrington RC .25 .60
293 Shane Heal RC .30 .75
294 Mark Hendrickson RC .30 .75
295 Allen Iverson RC 2.50 6.00
296 Dontae' Jones RC .25 .60
297 Kerry Kittles RC .30 .75
298 Priest Lauderdale RC .20 .50
299 Matt Maloney RC .25 .60
300 Stephon Marbury RC 1.00 2.50
301 Walter McCarty RC .30 .75
302 Jeff McInnis RC .30 .75
303 Martin Muursepp RC .20 .50
304 Steve Nash RC 2.00 5.00
305 Moochie Norris RC .30 .75
306 Jermaine O'Neal RC .50 1.25
307 Vitaly Potapenko RC .25 .60
308 Virginius Praskevicius RC .30 .75
309 Roy Rogers RC .25 .60
310 Malik Rose RC .40 1.00
311 James Scott RC .30 .75
312 Antoine Walker RC .50 1.25
313 Samaki Walker RC .25 .60
314 Ben Wallace RC 1.50 4.00
315 John Wallace RC .25 .60
316 Jerome Williams RC .25 .60
317 Lorenzen Wright RC .25 .60
318 Charles Barkley ST .75 2.00
319 Derrick Coleman ST .25 .60
320 Michael Finley ST .30 .75
321 Stephon Marbury ST 1.00 2.50
322 Reggie Miller ST .60 1.50
323 Alonzo Mourning ST .50 1.25
324 Shaquille O'Neal ST 1.25 3.00
325 Gary Payton ST .50 1.25
326 Dennis Rodman ST .75 2.00
327 Damon Stoudamire ST .30 .75
328 Vin Baker CBG .25 .60
329 Clyde Drexler CBG .50 1.25
330 Patrick Ewing CBG .50 1.25
331 Anfernee Hardaway CBG .75 2.00
332 Grant Hill CBG .50 1.25
333 Juwan Howard CBG .30 .75
334 Larry Johnson CBG .40 1.00
335 Michael Jordan CBG 3.00 8.00
336 Shawn Kemp CBG .50 1.25
337 Jason Kidd CBG .50 1.25
338 Karl Malone CBG .60 1.50
339 Reggie Miller CBG .60 1.50
340 Hakeem Olajuwon CBG .60 1.50
341 Scottie Pippen CBG .75 2.00
342 Mitch Richmond CBG .40 1.00
343 David Robinson CBG UER .60 1.50
344 Dennis Rodman CBG .75 2.00
345 Joe Smith CBG .25 .60
346 Jerry Stackhouse CBG .40 1.00
347 John Stockton CBG .60 1.50
348 Jerry Stackhouse BG .40 1.00
349 Checklist (201-350/inserts) .10 .25
350 Checklist (inserts) .10 .25
NNO G.Hill/J.Stackhouse Promo 2.00 5.00
NNO G.Hill Z-Force Preview 2.00 5.00

1996-97 Hoops Silver

COMPLETE SET (98) 15.00 40.00
*SILVER: 1.5X TO 4X BASE CARD HI
ONE PER SPECIAL SER.1 RETAIL PACK

1996-97 Hoops Fly With

COMPLETE SET (10) 10.00 25.00
SER.2 STATED ODDS 1:24 RETAIL
1 Charles Barkley 4.00 10.00
2 Juwan Howard 1.50 4.00
3 Jason Kidd 2.50 6.00
4 Alonzo Mourning 2.50 6.00
5 Gary Payton 2.50 6.00
6 David Robinson 3.00 8.00
7 Dennis Rodman 4.00 10.00
8 Joe Smith 1.25 3.00
9 Jerry Stackhouse 2.00 5.00
10 Damon Stoudamire 1.50 4.00

1996-97 Hoops Grant's All-Rookies

COMPLETE SET (11) 100.00 200.00
SER.2 STATED ODDS 1:360 HOBBY/RETAIL
STATED PRINT RUN 996 SETS
1 Shareef Abdur-Rahim 4.00 10.00
2 Ray Allen 12.00 30.00
3 Kobe Bryant 400.00 800.00
4 Marcus Camby 4.00 10.00
5 Grant Hill 4.00 10.00
6 Allen Iverson 15.00 40.00
7 Kerry Kittles 2.50 6.00
8 Stephon Marbury 8.00 20.00
9 Antoine Walker 4.00 10.00
10 Samaki Walker 2.00 5.00
11 Lorenzen Wright 2.00 5.00

1996-97 Hoops Head to Head

COMPLETE SET (10) 10.00 25.00
SER.1 STATED ODDS 1:24 HOBBY/RETAIL
HH1 L.Johnson/G.Rice 1.00 2.50
HH2 M.Jordan/S.Pippen 8.00 20.00
HH3 J.Kidd/G.Hill 1.25 3.00
HH4 C.Drexler/H.Olajuwon 1.50 4.00
HH5 V.Baker/G.Robinson .75 2.00
HH6 A.Hardaway/S.O'Neal 3.00 8.00
HH7 A.McDyess/Stackhouse 1.00 2.50
HH8 S.Elliott/D.Robinson 1.50 4.00
HH9 J.Smith/D.Stoudamire .75 2.00
HH10 K.Malone/J.Stockton 1.50 4.00

1996-97 Hoops HIPnotized

COMPLETE SET (20) 5.00 12.00
SER.1 STATED ODDS 1:4 HOBBY/RETAIL
H1 Steve Smith .40 1.00
H2 Dana Barros .30 .75
H3 Larry Johnson .60 1.50
H4 Dennis Rodman 1.25 3.00
H5 Terrell Brandon .40 1.00
H6 Jason Kidd .75 2.00
H7 Grant Hill .75 2.00
H8 Clyde Drexler .75 2.00
H9 Reggie Miller 1.00 2.50
H10 Alonzo Mourning .75 2.00
H11 Glenn Robinson .50 1.25
H12 Patrick Ewing .75 2.00
H13 Shaquille O'Neal 2.00 5.00
H14 Jerry Stackhouse .60 1.50
H15 Charles Barkley 1.25 3.00
H16 Clifford Robinson .50 1.25
H17 Mitch Richmond .60 1.50
H18 David Robinson 1.00 2.50
H19 Gary Payton .75 2.00
H20 Juwan Howard .50 1.25

1996-97 Hoops Hot List

COMPLETE SET (20) 75.00 150.00
SER.2 STATED ODDS 1:48 HOBBY
1 Vin Baker 2.50 6.00
2 Patrick Ewing 5.00 12.00
3 Michael Finley 3.00 8.00
4 Kevin Garnett 10.00 25.00
5 Anfernee Hardaway 8.00 20.00
6 Grant Hill 5.00 12.00
7 Allan Houston 3.00 8.00
8 Michael Jordan 125.00 300.00
9 Shawn Kemp 5.00 12.00
10 Christian Laettner 3.00 8.00
11 Karl Malone 6.00 15.00
12 Antonio McDyess 3.00 8.00
13 Reggie Miller 6.00 15.00
14 Hakeem Olajuwon 6.00 15.00
15 Shaquille O'Neal 12.00 30.00
16 Scottie Pippen 8.00 20.00
17 Mitch Richmond 4.00 10.00
18 Isaiah Rider 2.50 6.00
19 Rod Strickland 3.00 8.00
20 Chris Webber 4.00 10.00

1996-97 Hoops Rookie Headliners

COMPLETE SET (10) 15.00 40.00
SER.1 STATED ODDS 1:72 HOBBY
1 Antonio McDyess 2.50 6.00
2 Joe Smith 2.00 5.00
3 Brent Barry 2.00 5.00
4 Kevin Garnett 8.00 20.00
5 Jerry Stackhouse 3.00 8.00
6 Michael Finley 2.50 6.00
7 Arvydas Sabonis 2.50 6.00
8 Tyus Edney 1.50 4.00
9 Damon Stoudamire 2.50 6.00
10 Bryant Reeves 1.50 4.00

1996-97 Hoops Rookies

COMPLETE SET (30) 30.00 80.00
SER.2 STATED ODDS 1:6 HOBBY/RETAIL
1 Shareef Abdur-Rahim 1.00 2.50
2 Ray Allen 3.00 8.00
3 Kobe Bryant 75.00 200.00
4 Marcus Camby 1.00 2.50
5 Erick Dampier .60 1.50
6 Emanual Davis .50 1.25
7 Tony Delk .60 1.50
8 Brian Evans .40 1.00
9 Derek Fisher .75 2.00
10 Todd Fuller .40 1.00
11 Othella Harrington .50 1.25
12 Allen Iverson 5.00 12.00
13 Dontae' Jones .50 1.25
14 Kerry Kittles .60 1.50
15 Priest Lauderdale .40 1.00
16 Matt Maloney .50 1.25
17 Stephon Marbury 2.00 5.00
18 Walter McCarty .60 1.50
19 Jeff McInnis .60 1.50
20 Martin Muursepp .40 1.00
21 Steve Nash 4.00 10.00
22 Moochie Norris .60 1.50
23 Jermaine O'Neal 1.00 2.50
24 Vitaly Potapenko .50 1.25
25 Roy Rogers .50 1.25
26 Antoine Walker 1.00 2.50
27 Samaki Walker .50 1.25
28 John Wallace .50 1.25
29 Jerome Williams .50 1.25
30 Lorenzen Wright .50 1.25

1996-97 Hoops Starting Five

COMPLETE SET (29) 15.00 30.00
SER.2 STATED ODDS 1:12 HOBBY/RETAIL
1 Mookie Blaylock/Hawks 1.00 2.50
2 Dino Radja/Celtics .40 1.00
3 Glen Rice/Hornets .60 1.50
4 Michael Jordan/Bulls 6.00 15.00
5 Tyrone Hill/Cavs .50 1.25
6 Jason Kidd/Mavs 1.00 2.50
7 Antonio McDyess/Nuggets .60 1.50
8 Grant Hill/Pistons 1.00 2.50
9 Joe Smith/Warriors .75 2.00
10 Hakeem Olajuwon/Rockets 1.50 4.00
11 Reggie Miller/Pacers 1.25 3.00
12 Rodney Rogers/Clippers .40 1.00
13 Shaquille O'Neal/Lakers 2.50 6.00
14 Alonzo Mourning/Heat 1.00 2.50
15 Ray Allen/Bucks 1.50 4.00
16 Kevin Garnett/T'wolves 1.00 2.50
17 Jayson Williams/Nets .60 1.50
18 Patrick Ewing/Knicks 1.00 2.50
19 Anfernee Hardaway/Magic 1.50 4.00
20 Jerry Stackhouse/76ers 2.50 6.00
21 Danny Manning/Suns .60 1.50
22 Isaiah Rider/Blazers .75 2.00
23 Mitch Richmond/Kings .75 2.00
24 David Robinson/Spurs 1.25 3.00
25 Shawn Kemp/Sonics 1.00 2.50
26 D.Stoudamire/Raptors 1.00 2.50
27 Karl Malone/Jazz 1.25 3.00
28 Bryant Reeves/Grizzlies .50 1.25
29 Juwan Howard/Bullets .75 2.00

1996-97 Hoops Superfeats

COMPLETE SET (10) 25.00 60.00
SER.1 STATED ODDS 1:36 RETAIL
1 Michael Jordan 30.00 80.00
2 Jason Kidd 3.00 8.00
3 Grant Hill 3.00 8.00
4 Hakeem Olajuwon 4.00 10.00
5 Alonzo Mourning 3.00 8.00
6 Anthony Mason 1.50 4.00
7 Anfernee Hardaway 5.00 12.00
8 Jerry Stackhouse 2.50 6.00
9 Shawn Kemp 3.00 8.00
10 Damon Stoudamire 2.00 5.00

1997-98 Hoops

COMPLETE SET (330) 20.00 50.00
COMPLETE SERIES 1 (165) 8.00 20.00
COMPLETE SERIES 2 (165) 12.00 30.00
SUBSET CARDS HALF VALUE
1 Michael Jordan LL 4.00 10.00
2 Dennis Rodman LL 1.00 2.50
3 Mark Jackson LL .30 .75
4 Shawn Bradley LL .25 .60
5 Glen Rice LL .40 1.00
6 Mookie Blaylock LL .40 1.00
7 Gheorghe Muresan LL .25 .60
8 Mark Price LL .40 1.00
9 Tyrone Corbin .25 .60
10 Christian Laettner .40 1.00
11 Priest Lauderdale .25 .60
12 Dikembe Mutombo .60 1.50
13 Steve Smith .30 .75
14 Todd Day .25 .60
15 Rick Fox .30 .75
16 Brett Szabo .25 .60
17 Antoine Walker .40 1.00
18 David Wesley .30 .75
19 Muggsy Bogues .30 .75
20 Dell Curry .30 .75
21 Tony Delk .30 .75
22 Anthony Mason .30 .75
23 Glen Rice .40 1.00
24 Malik Rose .25 .60
25 Steve Kerr .50 1.25
26 Toni Kukoc .50 1.25
27 Luc Longley .40 1.00
28 Robert Parish .40 1.00
29 Scottie Pippen 1.00 2.50
30 Dennis Rodman 1.00 2.50
31 Terrell Brandon .30 .75
32 Danny Ferry .25 .60
33 Tyrone Hill .30 .75
34 Bobby Phills .30 .75
35 Vitaly Potapenko .25 .60
36 Shawn Bradley .25 .60
37 Sasha Danilovic .25 .60
38 Derek Harper .30 .75
39 Martin Muursepp .25 .60
40 Robert Pack .25 .60
41 Khalid Reeves .25 .60
42 Vincent Askew .25 .60
43 Dale Ellis .30 .75
44 LaPhonso Ellis .30 .75
45 Antonio McDyess .40 1.00
46 Bryant Stith .25 .60
47 Joe Dumars .50 1.25
48 Grant Hill .60 1.50
49 Lindsey Hunter .25 .60
50 Aaron McKie .25 .60
51 Theo Ratliff .30 .75
52 Scott Burrell .25 .60
53 Todd Fuller .25 .60
54 Chris Mullin .50 1.25
55 Mark Price .40 1.00
56 Joe Smith .30 .75
57 Latrell Sprewell .50 1.25
58 Clyde Drexler .60 1.50
59 Mario Elie .25 .60
60 Othella Harrington .25 .60
61 Matt Maloney .25 .60
62 Hakeem Olajuwon .75 2.00
63 Kevin Willis .30 .75
64 Travis Best .25 .60
65 Erick Dampier .30 .75
66 Antonio Davis .30 .75
67 Dale Davis .30 .75
68 Mark Jackson .30 .75
69 Reggie Miller .75 2.00
70 Brent Barry .30 .75
71 Darrick Martin .25 .60
72 Bo Outlaw .25 .60
73 Loy Vaught .30 .75
74 Lorenzen Wright .25 .60
75 Kobe Bryant 4.00 10.00
76 Derek Fisher .40 1.00
77 Robert Horry .40 1.00
78 Eddie Jones .40 1.00
79 Travis Knight .25 .60
80 George McCloud .25 .60
81 Shaquille O'Neal 1.25 3.00
82 P.J. Brown .25 .60
83 Tim Hardaway .50 1.25
84 Voshon Lenard .25 .60
85 Jamal Mashburn .30 .75
86 Alonzo Mourning .60 1.50
87 Ray Allen .75 2.00
88 Vin Baker .30 .75
89 Sherman Douglas .25 .60
90 Armon Gilliam .25 .60
91 Glenn Robinson .40 1.00
92 Kevin Garnett 1.00 2.50
93 Dean Garrett .25 .60
94 Tom Gugliotta .30 .75
95 Stephon Marbury .50 1.25
96 Doug West .25 .60
97 Chris Gatling .25 .60
98 Kendall Gill .30 .75
99 Kerry Kittles .30 .75
100 Jayson Williams .25 .60
101 Chris Childs .25 .60
102 Patrick Ewing .60 1.50
103 Allan Houston .40 1.00
104 Larry Johnson .50 1.25
105 Charles Oakley .30 .75
106 John Starks .40 1.00
107 John Wallace .25 .60
108 Nick Anderson .30 .75
109 Horace Grant .40 1.00
110 Anfernee Hardaway 1.00 2.50
111 Rony Seikaly .30 .75
112 Derek Strong .25 .60
113 Derrick Coleman .40 1.00
114 Allen Iverson 1.25 3.00
115 Doug Overton .25 .60
116 Jerry Stackhouse .40 1.00
117 Rex Walters .25 .60
118 Cedric Ceballos .30 .75
119 Kevin Johnson .40 1.00
120 Jason Kidd .60 1.50
121 Steve Nash 1.00 2.50
122 Wesley Person .30 .75
123 Kenny Anderson .30 .75
124 Jermaine O'Neal .30 .75
125 Isaiah Rider .30 .75
126 Arvydas Sabonis .50 1.25
127 Gary Trent .25 .60
128 Tyus Edney .25 .60
129 Brian Grant .30 .75
130 Olden Polynice .25 .60
131 Mitch Richmond .50 1.25
132 Corliss Williamson .25 .60
133 Vinny Del Negro .30 .75
134 Sean Elliott .30 .75
135 Avery Johnson .30 .75
136 Will Perdue .25 .60
137 Dominique Wilkins .50 1.25
138 Craig Ehlo .25 .60
139 Hersey Hawkins .30 .75
140 Shawn Kemp .60 1.50
141 Jim McIlvaine .25 .60
142 Sam Perkins .30 .75
143 Detlef Schrempf .40 1.00
144 Marcus Camby .40 1.00
145 Doug Christie .25 .60
146 Popeye Jones .25 .60
147 Damon Stoudamire .40 1.00
148 Walt Williams .30 .75
149 Jeff Hornacek .40 1.00
150 Karl Malone .75 2.00
151 Greg Ostertag .25 .60
152 Bryon Russell .25 .60
153 John Stockton .75 2.00
154 Shareef Abdur-Rahim .40 1.00
155 Greg Anthony .30 .75
156 Anthony Peeler .25 .60
157 Bryant Reeves .25 .60
158 Roy Rogers .25 .60
159 Calbert Cheaney .30 .75
160 Juwan Howard .30 .75
161 Gheorghe Muresan .25 .60
162 Rod Strickland .30 .75
163 Chris Webber .50 1.25
164 Checklist .20 .50
165 Checklist .20 .50
166 Tim Duncan RC 6.00 15.00
167 Chauncey Billups RC 1.25 3.00
168 Keith Van Horn RC .60 1.50
169 Tracy McGrady RC 3.00 8.00
170 John Thomas RC .25 .60
171 Tim Thomas RC .50 1.25
172 Ron Mercer RC .50 1.25
173 Scot Pollard RC .30 .75
174 Jason Lawson RC .40 1.00
175 Keith Booth RC .30 .75
176 Adonal Foyle RC .30 .75
177 Bubba Wells RC .25 .60
178 Derek Anderson RC .40 1.00
179 Rodrick Rhodes RC .30 .75
180 Kelvin Cato RC .30 .75
181 Serge Zwikker RC .30 .75
182 Ed Gray RC .40 1.00
183 Brevin Knight RC .40 1.00
184 Alvin Williams RC .40 1.00
185 Paul Grant RC .25 .60
186 Austin Croshere RC .30 .75
187 Chris Crawford RC .40 1.00
188 Anthony Johnson RC .40 1.00
189 James Cotton RC .40 1.00
190 James Collins RC .40 1.00
191 Tony Battie RC .40 1.00
192 Tariq Abdul-Wahad RC .30 .75
193 Danny Fortson RC .40 1.00
194 Maurice Taylor RC .30 .75
195 Bobby Jackson RC .50 1.25
196 Charles Smith RC .30 .75
197 Johnny Taylor RC .25 .60
198 Jerald Honeycutt RC .40 1.00
199 Marko Milic RC .40 1.00
200 Anthony Parker RC .40 1.00
201 Jacque Vaughn RC .30 .75
202 Antonio Daniels RC .40 1.00
203 Charles O'Bannon RC .30 .75
204 God Shammgod RC .40 1.00
205 Kebu Stewart RC .40 1.00
206 Mookie Blaylock .40 1.00
207 Chucky Brown .25 .60
208 Alan Henderson .25 .60
209 Dana Barros .25 .60
210 Tyus Edney .25 .60
211 Travis Knight .25 .60
212 Walter McCarty .25 .60
213 Vlade Divac .40 1.00
214 Matt Geiger .25 .60
215 Bobby Phills .30 .75
216 J.R. Reid .30 .75
217 David Wesley .30 .75
218 Scott Burrell .25 .60
219 Ron Harper .40 1.00
220 Michael Jordan 4.00 10.00
221 Bill Wennington .25 .60
222 Mitchell Butler .25 .60
223 Zydrunas Ilgauskas .40 1.00
224 Shawn Kemp .60 1.50
225 Wesley Person .30 .75
226 Shawnelle Scott RC .40 1.00
227 Bob Sura .25 .60
228 Hubert Davis .25 .60
229 Michael Finley .40 1.00
230 Dennis Scott .30 .75
231 Erick Strickland RC .25 .60
232 Samaki Walker .25 .60
233 Dean Garrett .25 .60
234 Priest Lauderdale .25 .60
235 Eric Williams .25 .60
236 Grant Long .25 .60
237 Malik Sealy .30 .75
238 Brian Williams .30 .75
239 Muggsy Bogues .30 .75
240 Bimbo Coles .25 .60
241 Brian Shaw .30 .75
242 Joe Smith .30 .75
243 Latrell Sprewell .50 1.25
244 Charles Barkley 1.00 2.50
245 Emanual Davis .25 .60
246 Brent Price .25 .60
247 Reggie Miller .75 2.00
248 Chris Mullin .50 1.25
249 Jalen Rose .30 .75
250 Rik Smits .30 .75
251 Mark West .25 .60
252 Lamond Murray .25 .60
253 Pooh Richardson .25 .60
254 Rodney Rogers .30 .75
255 Stojko Vrankovic .25 .60
256 Jon Barry .25 .60
257 Corie Blount .25 .60
258 Elden Campbell .25 .60
259 Rick Fox .30 .75
260 Nick Van Exel .40 1.00
261 Isaac Austin .25 .60
262 Dan Majerle .40 1.00
263 Terry Mills .25 .60
264 Mark Strickland RC .40 1.00
265 Terrell Brandon .30 .75
266 Tyrone Hill .30 .75
267 Ervin Johnson .25 .60
268 Andrew Lang .25 .60
269 Elliot Perry .25 .60
270 Chris Carr .25 .60
271 Reggie Jordan .25 .60
272 Sam Mitchell .25 .60
273 Stanley Roberts .25 .60
274 Michael Cage .25 .60
275 Sam Cassell .30 .75
276 Lucious Harris .25 .60
277 Kerry Kittles .30 .75
278 Don MacLean .25 .60
279 Chris Dudley .25 .60
280 Chris Mills .25 .60
281 Charlie Ward .30 .75
282 Buck Williams .25 .60
283 Herb Williams .25 .60
284 Derek Harper .30 .75
285 Mark Price .40 1.00
286 Gerald Wilkins .25 .60
287 Allen Iverson 1.25 3.00
288 Jim Jackson .30 .75
289 Eric Montross .25 .60
290 Jerry Stackhouse .40 1.00
291 Clarence Weatherspoon .25 .60
292 Tom Chambers .30 .75
293 Rex Chapman .25 .60
294 Danny Manning .30 .75
295 Antonio McDyess .40 1.00
296 Clifford Robinson .30 .75
297 Stacey Augmon .30 .75
298 Brian Grant .30 .75
299 Rasheed Wallace .50 1.25
300 Mahmoud Abdul-Rauf .25 .60
301 Terry Dehere .25 .60
302 Billy Owens .25 .60
303 Michael Smith .25 .60
304 Cory Alexander .25 .60
305 Chuck Person .30 .75
306 David Robinson .75 2.00
307 Charles Smith .25 .60
308 Monty Williams .30 .75
309 Vin Baker .30 .75
310 Jerome Kersey .25 .60
311 Nate McMillan .25 .60
312 Gary Payton .60 1.50
313 Eric Snow .25 .60
314 Carlos Rogers .25 .60
315 Zan Tabak .25 .60
316 John Wallace .25 .60
317 Sharone Wright .25 .60
318 Shandon Anderson .25 .60
319 Antoine Carr .25 .60
320 Howard Eisley .25 .60
321 Chris Morris .25 .60
322 Pete Chilcutt .25 .60
323 George Lynch .25 .60
324 Chris Robinson .40 1.00
325 Otis Thorpe .30 .75
326 Harvey Grant .25 .60
327 Darvin Ham .25 .60
328 Juwan Howard .30 .75
329 Ben Wallace .30 .75
330 Chris Webber .50 1.25
NNO Grant Hill Promo .60 1.50

1997-98 Hoops Chairman of the Boards

COMPLETE SET (10) 4.00 10.00
SER.2 STATED ODDS 1:9 HOBBY/RETAIL
CB1 Shaquille O'Neal 1.50 4.00
CB2 Dikembe Mutombo .75 2.00

CB3 Dennis Rodman 1.25 3.00
CB4 Patrick Ewing .75 2.00
CB5 Charles Barkley 1.25 3.00
CB6 Karl Malone 1.00 2.50
CB7 Rasheed Wallace .60 1.50
CB8 Chris Webber .60 1.50
CB9 Tim Duncan 1.50 4.00
CB10 Kevin Garnett 1.25 3.00

1997-98 Hoops Chill with Hill

COMPLETE SET (10) 4.00 10.00
COMMON HILL (1-10) .60 1.50
SER.1 STATED ODDS 1:10 HOB/RET

1997-98 Hoops Dish N Swish

COMPLETE SET (10) 12.00 30.00
SER.1 STATED ODDS 1:18 RETAIL
DS1 Mookie Blaylock 1.00 2.50
DS2 Terrell Brandon .75 2.00
DS3 Anfernee Hardaway 2.50 6.00
DS4 Allen Iverson 3.00 8.00
DS5 Michael Jordan 10.00 25.00
DS6 Jason Kidd 1.50 4.00
DS7 Stephon Marbury 1.25 3.00
DS8 Gary Payton 1.50 4.00
DS9 John Stockton 2.00 5.00
DS10 Damon Stoudamire 1.00 2.50

1997-98 Hoops Frequent Flyer Club

SER.1 STATED ODDS 1:36 HOBBY
*UPGRADE: 1.5X TO 4X BASE FREQ FLYER
UPGRADE: SER.1 STATED ODDS 1:360 HOB
FF1 Christian Laettner 2.00 5.00
FF2 Antoine Walker 2.00 5.00
FF3 Glen Rice 2.00 5.00
FF4 Michael Jordan 100.00 250.00
FF5 Dennis Rodman 5.00 12.00
FF6 Grant Hill 3.00 8.00
FF7 Latrell Sprewell 2.50 6.00
FF8 Charles Barkley 5.00 12.00
FF9 Kobe Bryant 40.00 100.00
FF10 Shaquille O'Neal 6.00 15.00
FF11 Ray Allen 4.00 10.00
FF12 Kevin Garnett 5.00 12.00
FF13 Kerry Kittles 1.50 4.00
FF14 Anfernee Hardaway 5.00 12.00
FF15 Jerry Stackhouse 2.00 5.00
FF16 Cedric Ceballos 1.50 4.00
FF17 Shawn Kemp 3.00 8.00
FF18 Marcus Camby 2.00 5.00
FF19 Juwan Howard 1.50 4.00
FF20 Chris Webber 2.50 6.00

1997-98 Hoops Great Shots

COMPLETE SET (30) 2.50 6.00
ONE PER SERIES 2 PACK
1 Dikembe Mutombo .15 .40
2 Antoine Walker .10 .25
3 Glen Rice .10 .25
4 Dennis Rodman .25 .60
5 D.Anderson/B.Knight .10 .25
6 Michael Finley .10 .25
7 Fortson/Battie/Jackson .12 .30
8 Grant Hill .15 .40
9 Joe Smith .07 .20
10 Charles Barkley .25 .60
11 Reggie Miller .20 .50
12 Lamond Murray .05 .15
13 Kobe Bryant 1.00 2.50
14 Alonzo Mourning .15 .40
15 Ray Allen .20 .50
16 Kevin Garnett .25 .60
17 Stephon Marbury .15 .40
18 Kerry Kittles .07 .20
19 Patrick Ewing .15 .40
20 Anfernee Hardaway .25 .60
21 Allen Iverson .30 .75
22 Jason Kidd .15 .40
23 Rasheed Wallace .12 .30
24 Mitch Richmond .12 .30
25 David Robinson .20 .50
26 Gary Payton .15 .40
27 Damon Stoudamire .10 .25
28 John Stockton .20 .50
29 Shareef Abdur-Rahim .20 .50
30 Chris Webber .12 .30

1997-98 Hoops High Voltage

SER.2 STATED ODDS 1:36 HOBBY
HV1 Kobe Bryant 200.00 500.00
HV2 Eddie Jones 5.00 12.00
HV3 Ray Allen 10.00 25.00
HV4 Anfernee Hardaway 15.00 40.00
HV5 Grant Hill 10.00 25.00
HV6 Shareef Abdur-Rahim 5.00 12.00
HV7 Marcus Camby 5.00 12.00
HV8 Allen Iverson 20.00 50.00
HV9 Kerry Kittles 4.00 10.00
HV10 Kevin Garnett 4.00 10.00
HV11 Stephon Marbury 6.00 15.00
HV12 Chris Webber 12.00 30.00
HV13 Antoine Walker 5.00 12.00
HV14 Michael Jordan 300.00 600.00
HV15 Tim Duncan 40.00 100.00
HV16 Dennis Rodman 25.00 60.00
HV17 Scottie Pippen 25.00 60.00
HV18 Shawn Kemp 12.00 30.00
HV19 Hakeem Olajuwon 12.00 30.00
HV20 Karl Malone 12.00 30.00

1997-98 Hoops High Voltage 500

*STARS: 4X TO 10X HI COLUMN
STATED PRINT RUN 500 SERIAL #'d SETS
HV1 Kobe Bryant 6,000.00 12,000.00
HV2 Eddie Jones 150.00 400.00
HV3 Ray Allen 150.00 400.00
HV4 Anfernee Hardaway 300.00 600.00
HV6 Shareef Abdur-Rahim 75.00 200.00
HV7 Marcus Camby 75.00 200.00
HV8 Allen Iverson 400.00 800.00
HV10 Kevin Garnett 200.00 500.00
HV11 Stephon Marbury 125.00 300.00
HV12 Chris Webber 150.00 400.00
HV13 Antoine Walker 75.00 200.00
HV14 Michael Jordan 10,000.00 20,000.00
HV15 Tim Duncan 600.00 1,200.00
HV16 Dennis Rodman 600.00 1,200.00
HV17 Scottie Pippen 600.00 1,200.00
HV18 Shawn Kemp 150.00 400.00
HV19 Hakeem Olajuwon 150.00 400.00

1997-98 Hoops HOOPerstars

COMPLETE SET (10) 75.00 150.00
SER.1 STATED ODDS 1:288 HOBBY/RETAIL
H1 Michael Jordan 150.00 400.00
H2 Grant Hill 6.00 15.00
H3 Shaquille O'Neal 12.00 30.00
H4 Ray Allen 8.00 20.00
H5 Stephon Marbury 5.00 12.00
H6 Anfernee Hardaway 12.00 30.00
H7 Allen Iverson 12.00 30.00
H8 Shawn Kemp 12.00 30.00
H9 Marcus Camby 4.00 10.00
H10 Shareef Abdur-Rahim 6.00 15.00

1997-98 Hoops 911

COMPLETE SET (10) 125.00 300.00
SER.2 STATED ODDS 1:288 HOB/RET
N1 Michael Jordan 150.00 400.00
N2 Grant Hill 8.00 20.00
N3 Shawn Kemp 8.00 20.00
N4 Stephon Marbury 8.00 20.00
N5 Damon Stoudamire 5.00 12.00
N6 Shaquille O'Neal 15.00 40.00
N7 Shareef Abdur-Rahim 5.00 12.00
N8 Allen Iverson 15.00 40.00
N9 Antoine Walker 5.00 12.00
N10 Anfernee Hardaway 12.00 30.00

1997-98 Hoops Rock the House

COMPLETE SET (10) 15.00 40.00
SER.2 STATED ODDS 1:18 RETAIL
RH1 Anfernee Hardaway 3.00 8.00
RH2 Stephon Marbury 1.50 4.00
RH3 Grant Hill 2.00 5.00
RH4 Shaquille O'Neal 4.00 10.00
RH5 Kerry Kittles 1.00 2.50
RH6 Michael Jordan 40.00 100.00
RH7 Ray Allen 2.50 6.00
RH8 Damon Stoudamire 1.25 3.00
RH9 Kevin Garnett 3.00 8.00
RH10 Shawn Kemp 1.25 3.00

1997-98 Hoops Rookie Headliners

COMPLETE SET (10) 15.00 30.00
SER.1 STATED ODDS 1:48 HOBBY/RETAIL
RH1 Antoine Walker 1.50 4.00
RH2 Matt Maloney 1.00 2.50
RH3 Kobe Bryant 15.00 40.00
RH4 Ray Allen 3.00 8.00
RH5 Stephon Marbury 2.00 5.00
RH6 Kerry Kittles 1.25 3.00
RH7 John Wallace 1.00 2.50
RH8 Allen Iverson 5.00 12.00
RH9 Marcus Camby 1.50 4.00
RH10 Shareef Abdur-Rahim 1.50 4.00

1997-98 Hoops Talkin' Hoops

COMPLETE SET (30) 4.00 10.00
ONE PER SER.1 PACK
1 Christian Laettner .20 .50
2 Antoine Walker .20 .50
3 Glen Rice .20 .50
4 Dennis Rodman .50 1.25
5 Scottie Pippen .50 1.25
6 Terrell Brandon .15 .40
7 Michael Finley .20 .50
8 Grant Hill .30 .75
9 Joe Smith .15 .40
10 Charles Barkley .50 1.25
11 Hakeem Olajuwon .40 1.00
12 Reggie Miller .40 1.00
13 Loy Vaught .15 .40
14 Shaquille O'Neal .60 1.50
15 Kobe Bryant 2.00 5.00
16 Kevin Garnett .50 1.25
17 Tom Gugliotta .15 .40
18 Kerry Kittles .15 .40
19 John Wallace .12 .30
20 Patrick Ewing .30 .75
21 Jerry Stackhouse .30 .75
22 David Robinson .40 1.00
23 Gary Payton .30 .75
24 Shawn Kemp .30 .75
25 Damon Stoudamire .20 .50
26 John Stockton .40 1.00
27 Karl Malone .40 1.00
28 Shareef Abdur-Rahim .20 .50
29 Juwan Howard .15 .40
30 Chris Webber .30 .75

1997-98 Hoops Top of the World

COMPLETE SET (15) 12.00 30.00
SER.2 STATED ODDS 1:48 HOB/RET
TW1 Tim Duncan 5.00 12.00
TW2 Tim Thomas 1.00 2.50
TW3 Tony Battie .75 2.00
TW4 Keith Van Horn 1.25 3.00
TW5 Antonio Daniels .75 2.00
TW6 Derek Anderson .75 2.00
TW7 Chauncey Billups 2.50 6.00
TW8 Tracy McGrady 4.00 10.00
TW9 Danny Fortson .75 2.00
TW10 Austin Croshere .60 1.50
TW11 Tariq Abdul-Wahad .60 1.50
TW12 Adonal Foyle .60 1.50
TW13 Rodrick Rhodes .60 1.50
TW14 Ron Mercer 1.00 2.50
TW15 Charles Smith .60 1.50

1998-99 Hoops Promo Sheet

1 Grant Hill .60 1.50
2 Kevin Garnett 1.00 2.50
3 Tim Duncan 1.00 2.50
4 Allen Iverson 1.00 2.50
5 Keith Van Horn .40 1.00
6 Shaquille O'Neal 1.50 4.00

1998-99 Hoops

COMPLETE SET (167) 12.00 30.00
1 Kobe Bryant 3.00 8.00
2 Glenn Robinson .40 1.00
3 Derek Anderson .30 .75
4 Terry Dehere .25 .60
5 Jalen Rose .30 .75
6 Zydrunas Ilgauskas .40 1.00
7 Scott Williams .25 .60
8 Toni Kukoc .40 1.00
9 John Stockton .75 2.00
10 Kevin Garnett 1.00 2.50
11 Jerome Williams .25 .60
12 Anthony Mason .30 .75
13 Harvey Grant .25 .60
14 Mookie Blaylock .30 .75
15 Tyrone Hill .25 .60
16 Dale Davis .25 .60
17 Eric Washington .25 .60
18 Aaron McKie .25 .60
19 Jermaine O'Neal .40 1.00
20 Anfernee Hardaway 1.00 2.50
21 Derrick Coleman .30 .75
22 Allan Houston .40 1.00
23 Michael Jordan 4.00 10.00
24 Jason Kidd .60 1.50
25 Tyrone Corbin .25 .60
26 Jacque Vaughn .25 .60
27 Bobby Jackson .30 .75
28 Chris Anstey .25 .60
29 Brent Barry .30 .75
30 Shareef Abdur-Rahim .40 1.00
31 Jeff Hornacek .30 .75
32 Ed Gray .25 .60
33 Grant Hill .60 1.50
34 Steve Smith .30 .75
35 Rony Seikaly .25 .60
36 Mark Jackson .30 .75
37 Shawn Bradley .25 .60
38 Corie Blount .25 .60
39 Erick Dampier .25 .60
40 Kerry Kittles .30 .75
41 David Wesley .25 .60
42 Horace Grant .40 1.00
43 Bobby Hurley .25 .60
44 Tariq Abdul-Wahad .25 .60
45 Brian Williams .25 .60
46 Ray Allen .60 1.50
47 Kenny Anderson .30 .75
48 Rodrick Rhodes .25 .60
49 Greg Foster .25 .60
50 Tim Duncan 1.00 2.50
51 Steve Nash .75 2.00
52 Kelvin Cato .25 .60
53 Donyell Marshall .25 .60
54 Marcus Camby .30 .75
55 Kevin Willis .25 .60
56 Michael Finley .40 1.00
57 Muggsy Bogues .30 .75
58 Mark Price .40 1.00
59 Larry Johnson .60 1.50
60 Karl Malone .75 2.00
61 Greg Ostertag .25 .60
62 Sean Elliott .40 1.00
63 Johnny Taylor .25 .60
64 Howard Eisley .25 .60
65 Chris Childs .25 .60
66 Walt Williams .25 .60
67 Tracy Murray .25 .60
68 Patrick Ewing .60 1.50
69 Olden Polynice .25 .60
70 Allen Iverson 1.00 2.50
71 David Robinson .75 2.00
72 Calbert Cheaney .25 .60
73 Lamond Murray .25 .60
74 Scot Pollard .25 .60
75 Alonzo Mourning .60 1.50
76 Tracy McGrady .60 1.50
77 Jim McIlvaine .25 .60
78 Bob Sura .25 .60
79 Anthony Peeler .25 .60
80 Keith Van Horn .40 1.00
81 Maurice Taylor .25 .60
82 Charles Smith .25 .60
83 Dikembe Mutombo .60 1.50
84 Nick Anderson .25 .60
85 Austin Croshere .25 .60
86 Armon Gilliam .25 .60
87 Eddie Jones .40 1.00
88 Glen Rice .40 1.00
89 Sam Cassell .30 .75
90 Stephon Marbury .50 1.25
91 Elliot Perry UER .25 .60
92 Jamal Mashburn .40 1.00
93 Adonal Foyle .25 .60
94 Avery Johnson .30 .75
95 Micheal Williams .25 .60
96 Danny Fortson .25 .60
97 Brevin Knight .25 .60
98 Ron Harper .40 1.00
99 Chauncey Billups .50 1.25
100 Shaquille O'Neal 1.50 4.00
101 Brent Price .25 .60
102 Tim Thomas .30 .75
103 Khalid Reeves .25 .60
104 Chris Gatling .25 .60
105 Terry Cummings .30 .75
106 Vin Baker .30 .75
107 Bryant Reeves .25 .60
108 John Starks .30 .75
109 Juwan Howard .30 .75
110 Antoine Walker .40 1.00
111 Rodney Rogers .25 .60
112 Nick Van Exel .40 1.00
113 Chris Whitney .25 .60
114 Bobby Phills .25 .60
115 Travis Knight .25 .60
116 Robert Horry .30 .75
117 Erick Strickland .25 .60
118 Dontae Jones .25 .60
119 Tony Battie .25 .60
120 Lindsey Hunter .25 .60
121 Reggie Miller .75 2.00
122 John Wallace .25 .60
123 Ron Mercer .30 .75
124 Antonio Daniels .25 .60
125 Paul Grant .25 .60
126 Voshon Lenard .25 .60
127 Shawn Kemp .60 1.50
128 Antonio Davis .25 .60
129 Hakeem Olajuwon .75 2.00
130 Danny Manning .30 .75
131 Bimbo Coles .25 .60
132 Tim Hardaway .50 1.25
133 Lorenzo Williams .25 .60
134 Dan Majerle .40 1.00
135 Bryant Stith .25 .60
136 Randy Brown .25 .60
137 Hubert Davis .25 .60
138 Gary Payton .60 1.50
139 Rasheed Wallace .50 1.25
140 Chris Robinson .25 .60
141 Doug Christie .30 .75
142 Brian Grant .25 .60
143 Isaiah Rider .30 .75
144 Kendall Gill .30 .75
145 Lorenzen Wright .25 .60
146 Ervin Johnson .25 .60
147 Monty Williams .30 .75
148 Keith Closs .25 .60
149 Tony Delk .25 .60
150 Hersey Hawkins .25 .60
151 Dean Garrett .25 .60
152 Cedric Henderson .25 .60
153 Detlef Schrempf .40 1.00
154 Dana Barros .25 .60
155 Dee Brown .25 .60
156 Jayson Williams SO .25 .60
157 Charles Barkley SO 1.00 2.50
158 Damon Stoudamire SO .40 1.00
159 Scottie Pippen SO 1.00 2.50
160 Joe Smith SO .30 .75
161 Antonio McDyess SO .30 .75
162 Jerry Stackhouse SO .40 1.00
163 Dennis Rodman SO 1.00 2.50
164 Shaquille O'Neal SO 1.50 4.00
165 Grant Hill SO .60 1.50
166 Checklist .20 .50
167 Checklist .20 .50

1998-99 Hoops Bams

STATED PRINT RUN 250 SERIAL #'d SETS
*SLAM BAMS/100: .75X TO 2X BAMS INSERT
1 Michael Jordan 10,000.00 20,000.00
2 Kobe Bryant 1,500.00 4,000.00
3 Allen Iverson 800.00 1,500.00
4 Shaquille O'Neal 800.00 1,500.00
5 Tim Duncan 800.00 1,500.00
6 Shareef Abdur-Rahim 125.00 300.00
7 Keith Van Horn 125.00 300.00
8 Grant Hill 400.00 800.00
9 Anfernee Hardaway 600.00 1,200.00
10 Kevin Garnett 600.00 1,200.00

1998-99 Hoops Freshman Flashback

COMPLETE SET (10) 40.00 100.00
STATED PRINT RUN 1000 SERIAL #'d SETS
1 Tim Duncan 25.00 60.00
2 Keith Van Horn 6.00 15.00
3 Tim Thomas 5.00 12.00
4 Antonio Daniels 4.00 10.00
5 Brevin Knight 4.00 10.00
6 Danny Fortson 4.00 10.00
7 Maurice Taylor 4.00 10.00
8 Chauncey Billups 8.00 20.00
9 Bobby Jackson 5.00 12.00
10 Derek Anderson 5.00 12.00

1998-99 Hoops Prime Twine

STATED PRINT RUN 500 SERIAL #'d SETS
1 Dennis Rodman 200.00 500.00
2 Allen Iverson 200.00 500.00
3 Karl Malone 100.00 250.00
4 Antonio McDyess 20.00 50.00
5 Damon Stoudamire 40.00 100.00
6 Eddie Jones 25.00 60.00
7 Scottie Pippen 200.00 500.00
8 Shawn Kemp 100.00 250.00
9 Antoine Walker 25.00 60.00
10 Stephon Marbury 30.00 80.00

1998-99 Hoops Pump Up The Jam

COMPLETE SET (10) 5.00 12.00
STATED ODDS 1:4 HOB/RET
1 Stephon Marbury .50 1.25
2 Allen Iverson 1.00 2.50
3 Grant Hill .60 1.50
4 Kobe Bryant 3.00 8.00
5 Michael Jordan 4.00 10.00
6 Antoine Walker .40 1.00
7 Shareef Abdur-Rahim .40 1.00
8 Shawn Kemp .60 1.50
9 Anfernee Hardaway 1.00 2.50
10 Antonio McDyess .30 .75

1998-99 Hoops Rejectors

COMPLETE SET (10) 30.00 60.00
STATED PRINT RUN 2500 SERIAL #'d SETS
1 Dikembe Mutombo 4.00 10.00
2 Marcus Camby 2.00 5.00
3 Shaquille O'Neal 10.00 25.00
4 Tim Duncan 6.00 15.00
5 Shawn Bradley 1.50 4.00
6 Chris Webber 3.00 8.00
7 Patrick Ewing 4.00 10.00
8 Kevin Garnett 6.00 15.00
9 David Robinson 5.00 12.00
10 Michael Stewart 1.50 4.00

1998-99 Hoops Shout Outs

COMPLETE SET (30) 8.00 20.00
STATED ODDS: ONE PER PACK
1 Shareef Abdur-Rahim .40 1.00
2 Chauncey Billups .50 1.25
3 Terrell Brandon UER .30 .75
4 Patrick Ewing .60 1.50
5 Michael Finley .60 1.50
6 Adonal Foyle .25 .60
7 Kevin Garnett 1.00 2.50
8 Anfernee Hardaway 1.00 2.50
9 Tim Hardaway .50 1.25
10 Grant Hill .60 1.50
11 Tim Thomas .30 .75
12 Bobby Jackson .30 .75
13 Michael Jordan 4.00 10.00
14 Shawn Kemp .60 1.50
15 Jason Kidd 1.00 2.50
16 Karl Malone .75 2.00
17 Stephon Marbury .50 1.25
18 Anthony Mason .30 .75
19 Reggie Miller .75 2.00
20 Dikembe Mutombo .60 1.50
21 Kobe Bryant 3.00 8.00
22 Hakeem Olajuwon .75 2.00
23 Gary Payton .60 1.50
24 Michael Stewart .25 .60
25 David Robinson .75 2.00
26 Maurice Taylor .25 .60
27 Keith Van Horn .40 1.00
28 Antoine Walker .40 1.00
29 Rasheed Wallace .50 1.25
30 Juwan Howard .30 .75

1999-00 Hoops

COMPLETE SET (185) 15.00 30.00
1 Paul Pierce .40 1.00
2 Ray Allen .30 .75
3 Jason Williams .30 .75
4 Sean Elliott .15 .40
5 Al Harrington .20 .50
6 Bobby Phills .12 .30
7 Tyronn Lue .12 .30
8 James Cotton .12 .30
9 Anthony Peeler .12 .30
10 LaPhonso Ellis .12 .30
11 Voshon Lenard .12 .30
12 Kornel David RC .12 .30
13 Michael Finley .20 .50
14 Danny Fortson .12 .30
15 Antawn Jamison .20 .50
16 Reggie Miller .40 1.00
17 Shaquille O'Neal .75 2.00
18 P.J. Brown .12 .30
19 Roshown McLeod .12 .30
20 Larry Johnson .20 .50
21 Rashard Lewis .15 .40
22 Tracy McGrady .30 .75
23 Peja Stojakovic .20 .50
24 Tracy Murray .12 .30
25 Gary Payton .30 .75
26 Ricky Davis .20 .50
27 Kobe Bryant 1.50 4.00
28 Avery Johnson .15 .40
29 Kevin Garnett .50 1.25
30 Charles Jones RC .12 .30
31 Brevin Knight .12 .30
32 Lindsey Hunter .12 .30
33 Felipe Lopez .12 .30
34 Rik Smits .15 .40
35 Maurice Taylor .12 .30
36 Corey Benjamin .12 .30
37 Ervin Johnson .12 .30
38 Steve Smith .15 .40
39 Austin Croshere .12 .30
40 Matt Geiger .12 .30
41 Tom Gugliotta .15 .40
42 Radoslav Nesterovic RC .20 .50
43 Juwan Howard .15 .40
44 Keon Clark .12 .30
45 Latrell Sprewell .25 .60
46 George Lynch .12 .30
47 Greg Ostertag .12 .30
48 J.R. Henderson .12 .30
49 Kerry Kittles .15 .40
50 Matt Harpring .20 .50
51 Duane Causwell .12 .30
52 Andrae Patterson .12 .30
53 Jerry Stackhouse .20 .50
54 Adonal Foyle .12 .30
55 Bryce Drew .12 .30
56 Chris Childs .12 .30
57 Charles Smith .12 .30
58 Rony Seikaly .12 .30
59 Chauncey Billups .20 .50
60 Grant Hill .30 .75
61 Marlon Garnett RC .20 .50
62 Tim Hardaway .25 .60
63 Vlade Divac .20 .50
64 Chris Gatling .12 .30
65 Glenn Robinson .15 .40
66 Michael Olowokandi .12 .30
67 Elliot Perry .12 .30
68 Howard Eisley .12 .30
69 Glen Rice .20 .50
70 Marcus Camby .15 .40
71 Theo Ratliff .15 .40
72 Brian Skinner .12 .30
73 Kenny Anderson .15 .40
74 Jamal Mashburn .15 .40
75 Vladimir Stepania .12 .30
76 Jayson Williams .12 .30
77 Brian Grant .12 .30
78 Raef LaFrentz .15 .40
79 John Starks .20 .50
80 Mike Bibby .20 .50
81 Stephon Marbury .25 .60
82 Armon Gilliam .12 .30
83 Sam Jacobson .12 .30
84 Derrick Coleman .15 .40
85 Allan Houston .15 .40
86 Miles Simon .12 .30
87 Allen Iverson .50 1.25
88 Derek Anderson .12 .30
89 Chris Anstey .12 .30
90 Larry Hughes .15 .40
91 Vitaly Potapenko .12 .30
92 Cherokee Parks .12 .30
93 Donyell Marshall .15 .40
94 Danny Manning .15 .40
95 Bryon Russell .12 .30
96 Randell Jackson .12 .30
97 Antoine Walker .20 .50
98 Dirk Nowitzki .60 1.50
99 Karl Malone .40 1.00
100 Vince Carter .50 1.25
101 Eddie Jones .20 .50
102 Bryant Stith .12 .30
103 Korleone Young .12 .30
104 Tim Duncan .50 1.25
105 Jerome Kersey .12 .30
106 Bonzi Wells .12 .30
107 Wesley Person .12 .30
108 Steve Nash .40 1.00
109 Tyrone Nesby RC .12 .30
110 Doug Christie .15 .40
111 David Robinson .40 1.00
112 Ruben Patterson .12 .30
113 Dikembe Mutombo .30 .75
114 Ron Mercer .15 .40
115 Elden Campbell .12 .30
116 Kevin Willis .12 .30
117 Hakeem Olajuwon .40 1.00
118 Shawn Kemp .30 .75
119 Eric Montross .12 .30
120 Shareef Abdur-Rahim .20 .50
121 Bob Sura .12 .30
122 James Robinson .12 .30
123 Shawn Bradley .12 .30
124 Robert Traylor .12 .30
125 Dean Garrett .12 .30
126 Keith Van Horn .15 .40
127 Patrick Ewing .25 .60
128 Isaac Austin .12 .30
129 Jason Kidd .30 .75
130 Isaiah Rider .15 .40
131 Jerome James RC .20 .50
132 John Stockton .30 .75
133 Jason Caffey .12 .30
134 Bryant Reeves .12 .30
135 Michael Dickerson .12 .30
136 Chris Mullin .20 .50
137 Rasheed Wallace .25 .60
138 Cuttino Mobley .12 .30
139 Antonio McDyess .15 .40
140 Chris Webber .25 .60
141 Jelani McCoy .12 .30
142 Damon Stoudamire .20 .50
143 Gerald Brown .20 .50
144 Cory Carr .12 .30
145 Brent Barry .15 .40
146 Alan Henderson .12 .30
147 Nazr Mohammed .12 .30
148 Bison Dele .12 .30
149 Scottie Pippen .50 1.25
150 Michael Doleac .12 .30
151 Nick Anderson .12 .30
152 Alonzo Mourning .30 .75
153 Jahidi White .12 .30
154 Jalen Rose .15 .40
155 Brad Miller .15 .40
156 Andrew DeClercq .12 .30
157 Erick Strickland .12 .30
158 Toni Kukoc .25 .60
159 Pat Garrity .12 .30
160 Bobby Jackson .15 .40
161 Steve Kerr .15 .40
162 Toby Bailey .12 .30
163 Charles Oakley .20 .50
164 Rod Strickland .15 .40
165 Rodrick Rhodes .12 .30
166 Ron Artest RC .50 1.25
167 William Avery RC .12 .30
168 Elton Brand RC .40 1.00
169 Baron Davis RC .50 1.25
170 John Celestand RC .12 .30
171 Jumaine Jones RC .12 .30
172 Andre Miller RC .40 1.00
173 Lee Nailon RC .20 .50
174 James Posey RC .20 .50
175 Jason Terry RC .30 .75
176 Kenny Thomas RC .20 .50
177 Steve Francis RC .40 1.00
178 Wally Szczerbiak RC .30 .75
179 Richard Hamilton RC .50 1.25
180 Jonathan Bender RC .20 .50
181 Shawn Marion RC .40 1.00
182 A.Radojevic RC .12 .30
183 Tim James RC .12 .30
184 Trajan Langdon RC .15 .40
185 Corey Maggette RC .25 .60

1999-00 Hoops Build Your Own Card

COMPLETE SET (10) 8.00 20.00
1 Tim Duncan 2.00 5.00
2 Keith Van Horn .60 1.50
3 Vince Carter 2.00 5.00
4 Grant Hill 1.25 3.00
5 Shaquille O'Neal 3.00 8.00
6 Kevin Garnett 2.00 5.00
7 Allen Iverson 2.00 5.00
8 Jason Williams 1.25 3.00
9 Kobe Bryant 6.00 15.00
10 Paul Pierce 1.50 4.00

1999-00 Hoops Build Your Own Card Redemptions

STATED PRINT RUN 250 SER.#'d SETS
ONLY ONE CARD IS LISTED PER PLAYER
1a T.Duncan Ball/Body 50.00 120.00
1b T.Duncan Ball/Head 50.00 120.00
1c T.Duncan Ball/Horiz 50.00 120.00
1d T.Duncan No Ball/Body 50.00 120.00
1e T.Duncan No Ball/Head 50.00 120.00
1f T.Duncan No Ball/Horiz 50.00 120.00
1g T.Duncan Shoot/Body 50.00 120.00
1h T.Duncan Shoot/Head 50.00 120.00
1i T.Duncan Shoot/Horiz 50.00 120.00
2a K.Van Horn Ball/Body 15.00 40.00
2b K.Van Horn Ball/Head 15.00 40.00
2c K.Van Horn Ball/Horiz 15.00 40.00
2d K.Van Horn No Ball/Body 15.00 40.00
2e K.Van Horn No Ball/Head 15.00 40.00
2f K.Van Horn No Ball/Horiz 15.00 40.00
2g K.Van Horn Shoot/Body 15.00 40.00
2h K.Van Horn Shoot/Head 15.00 40.00
2i K.Van Horn Shoot/Horiz 15.00 40.00
3a V.Carter Ball/Body 50.00 120.00
3b V.Carter Ball/Head 50.00 120.00
3c V.Carter Ball/Horiz 50.00 120.00
3d V.Carter No Ball/Body 50.00 120.00
3e V.Carter No Ball/Head 50.00 120.00
3f V.Carter No Ball/Horiz 50.00 120.00
3g V.Carter Shoot/Body 50.00 120.00
3h V.Carter Shoot/Head 50.00 120.00
3i V.Carter Shoot/Horiz 50.00 120.00
4a G.Hill Ball/Body 60.00 150.00
4b G.Hill Ball/Head 60.00 150.00
4c G.Hill Ball/Horiz 60.00 150.00
4d G.Hill No Ball/Body 60.00 150.00
4e G.Hill No Ball/Head 60.00 150.00
4f G.Hill No Ball/Horiz 60.00 150.00
4g G.Hill Shoot/Body 60.00 150.00
4h G.Hill Shoot/Head 60.00 150.00
4i G.Hill Shoot/Horiz 60.00 150.00
5a S.O'Neal Ball/Body 80.00 200.00
5b S.O'Neal Ball/Head 80.00 200.00
5c S.O'Neal Ball/Horiz 80.00 200.00
5d S.O'Neal No Ball/Body 80.00 200.00
5e S.O'Neal No Ball/Head 80.00 200.00
5f S.O'Neal No Ball/Horiz 80.00 200.00
5g S.O'Neal Shoot/Body 80.00 200.00
5h S.O'Neal Shoot/Head 80.00 200.00
5i S.O'Neal Shoot/Horiz 80.00 200.00
6a K.Garnett Ball/Body 50.00 120.00
6b K.Garnett Ball/Head 50.00 120.00
6c K.Garnett Ball/Horiz 50.00 120.00
6d K.Garnett No Ball/Body 50.00 120.00
6e K.Garnett No Ball/Head 50.00 120.00
6f K.Garnett No Ball/Horiz 50.00 120.00
6g K.Garnett Shoot/Body 50.00 120.00
6h K.Garnett Shoot/Head 50.00 120.00
6i K.Garnett Shoot/Horiz 50.00 120.00
7a A.Iverson Ball/Body 50.00 120.00
7b A.Iverson Ball/Head 50.00 120.00
7c A.Iverson Ball/Horiz 50.00 120.00
7d A.Iverson No Ball/Body 50.00 120.00
7e A.Iverson No Ball/Head 50.00 120.00
7f A.Iverson No Ball/Horiz 50.00 120.00
7g A.Iverson Shoot/Body 50.00 120.00
7h A.Iverson Shoot/Head 50.00 120.00
7i A.Iverson Shoot/Horiz 50.00 120.00
8a J.Williams Ball/Body 30.00 80.00
8b J.Williams Ball/Head 30.00 80.00
8c J.Williams Ball/Horiz 30.00 80.00
8d J.Williams No Ball/Body 30.00 80.00
8e J.Williams No Ball/Head 30.00 80.00
8f J.Williams No Ball/Horiz 30.00 80.00
8g J.Williams Shoot/Body 30.00 80.00
8h J.Williams Shoot/Head 30.00 80.00
8i J.Williams Shoot/Horiz 30.00 80.00
9a K.Bryant Ball/Body 150.00 400.00
9b K.Bryant Ball/Head 150.00 400.00
9c K.Bryant Ball/Horiz 150.00 400.00
9d K.Bryant No Ball/Body 150.00 400.00
9e K.Bryant No Ball/Head 150.00 400.00
9f K.Bryant No Ball/Horiz 150.00 400.00
9g K.Bryant Shoot/Body 150.00 400.00
9h K.Bryant Shoot/Head 150.00 400.00
9i K.Bryant Shoot/Horiz 150.00 400.00
10a P.Pierce Ball/Body 40.00 100.00
10b P.Pierce Ball/Head 40.00 100.00
10c P.Pierce Ball/Horiz 40.00 100.00
10d P.Pierce No Ball/Body 40.00 100.00
10e P.Pierce No Ball/Head 40.00 100.00
10f P.Pierce No Ball/Horiz 40.00 100.00
10g P.Pierce Shoot/Body 40.00 100.00
10h P.Pierce Shoot/Head 40.00 100.00
10i P.Pierce Shoot/Horiz 40.00 100.00

1999-00 Hoops Calling Card

COMPLETE SET (15) 5.00 12.00
STATED ODDS 1:8 HOB/RET
CC1 Kobe Bryant 4.00 10.00
CC2 Kevin Garnett 1.25 3.00
CC3 Tim Hardaway .60 1.50
CC4 Grant Hill .75 2.00
CC5 Allen Iverson 1.25 3.00
CC6 Karl Malone 1.00 2.50
CC7 Shawn Kemp .75 2.00
CC8 Stephon Marbury .60 1.50
CC9 Shaquille O'Neal 2.00 5.00
CC10 Hakeem Olajuwon 1.00 2.50
CC11 Ray Allen .75 2.00
CC12 Damon Stoudamire .50 1.25
CC13 Jason Williams .75 2.00
CC14 Keith Van Horn .40 1.00
CC15 Dikembe Mutombo .75 2.00

1999-00 Hoops Dunk Mob

COMPLETE SET (10) 40.00 100.00
STATED ODDS 1:144 HOB/RET
DM1 Shaquille O'Neal 20.00 50.00
DM2 Stephon Marbury 6.00 15.00
DM3 Paul Pierce 10.00 25.00
DM4 Antawn Jamison 5.00 12.00
DM5 Michael Olowokandi 3.00 8.00
DM6 Scottie Pippen 20.00 50.00
DM7 Antonio McDyess 4.00 10.00
DM8 Vince Carter 25.00 60.00
DM9 Ron Mercer 4.00 10.00
DM10 Shawn Kemp 8.00 20.00

1999-00 Hoops Name Plates

COMPLETE SET (10) 2.00 5.00
STATED ODDS 1:4 HOB/RET
NP1 Shareef Abdur-Rahim .25 .60
NP2 Allen Iverson .60 1.50
NP3 Karl Malone .50 1.25
NP4 Gary Payton .40 1.00
NP5 Hakeem Olajuwon .50 1.25
NP6 Glenn Robinson .20 .50
NP7 Kevin Garnett .60 1.50
NP8 Anfernee Hardaway .60 1.50
NP9 David Robinson .50 1.25
NP10 Shaquille O'Neal 1.00 2.50

1999-00 Hoops Pure Players

STATED PRINT RUN 500 SERIAL #'d SETS
PP1 Tim Duncan 30.00 80.00
PP2 Keith Van Horn 10.00 25.00
PP3 Stephon Marbury 15.00 40.00
PP4 Grant Hill 20.00 50.00
PP5 Kobe Bryant 100.00 250.00
PP6 Kevin Garnett 40.00 100.00
PP7 Allen Iverson 50.00 120.00
PP8 Antoine Walker 12.00 30.00
PP9 Shareef Abdur-Rahim 12.00 30.00
PP10 Anfernee Hardaway 50.00 120.00

1999-00 Hoops Pure Players 100%

*STARS: .75X TO 2X VALUE
STATED PRINT RUN 100 SERIAL #'d SETS
PP1 Tim Duncan 100.00 250.00
PP5 Kobe Bryant 300.00 600.00
PP10 Anfernee Hardaway 125.00 300.00

1999-00 Hoops Y2K Corps

COMPLETE SET (10) 3.00 8.00
STATED ODDS 1:16 HOB/RET
BB1 Michael Olowokandi .40 1.00
BB2 Mike Bibby .60 1.50
BB3 Jason Williams 1.00 2.50
BB4 Dirk Nowitzki 2.00 5.00
BB5 Vince Carter 1.50 4.00
BB6 Robert Traylor .40 1.00
BB7 Larry Hughes .50 1.25
BB8 Paul Pierce 1.25 3.00
BB9 Matt Harpring .40 1.00
BB10 Michael Dickerson .40 1.00

2004-05 Hoops

COMP.SET w/o SP's (165) 15.00 40.00
176-200 RC PRINT RUN 1750 SER.#'d SETS
CARDS 168-170 NOT RELEASED
1 Dwyane Wade 1.00 2.50
2 Vince Carter .50 1.25
3 Luke Walton .20 .50
4 Alonzo Mourning .30 .75
5 Antoine Walker .25 .60
6 Jerry Stackhouse .25 .60
7 Chris Wilcox .15 .40
8 Udonis Haslem .15 .40
9 Michael Redd .20 .50
10 Darius Miles .15 .40
11 Jarvis Hayes .15 .40
12 Kirk Hinrich .25 .60
13 Tayshaun Prince .25 .60
14 Caron Butler .20 .50
15 Sam Cassell .20 .50
16 Kurt Thomas .15 .40
17 Bruce Bowen .20 .50
18 Jared Jeffries .15 .40
19 Keith Bogans .15 .40
20 Chauncey Billups .30 .75
21 Lamar Odom .25 .60
22 Fred Hoiberg .15 .40
23 Cuttino Mobley .20 .50
24 Manu Ginobili .50 1.25
25 Juan Dixon .15 .40
26 Predrag Drobnjak .15 .40
27 Nene .20 .50
28 Elton Brand .20 .50
29 Rasual Butler .15 .40
30 Nick Van Exel .25 .60
31 Carlos Arroyo .15 .40
32 Zydrunas Ilgauskas .20 .50
33 Troy Murphy .15 .40
34 Jason Williams .20 .50
35 Jason Kidd .40 1.00
36 Samuel Dalembert .15 .40
37 Vladimir Radmanovic .15 .40
38 Kenny Anderson .20 .50
39 Kenyon Martin .25 .60
40 Jamaal Tinsley .15 .40
41 Damon Jones .15 .40
42 Shareef Abdur-Rahim .25 .60
43 Ricky Davis .20 .50
44 Earl Boykins .15 .40
45 Austin Croshere .15 .40
46 Keith Van Horn .20 .50
47 Theo Ratliff .15 .40
48 Mehmet Okur .20 .50
49 Paul Pierce .40 1.00
50 Marcus Camby .20 .50
51 Stephen Jackson .20 .50
52 Maurice Williams .20 .50
53 Brad Miller .20 .50
54 Carlos Boozer .20 .50
55 Dirk Nowitzki .60 1.50
56 Dikembe Mutombo .25 .60
57 James Posey .20 .50
58 Baron Davis .25 .60
59 Shawn Marion .25 .60
60 Ronald Murray .15 .40
61 Gary Payton .40 1.00
62 Andre Miller .20 .50
63 Reggie Miller .50 1.25
64 Zaza Pachulia .15 .40
65 Bobby Jackson .20 .50
66 Peja Stojakovic .20 .50
67 Jiri Welsch .15 .40
68 Darko Milicic .15 .40
69 Ron Artest .25 .60
70 T.J. Ford .15 .40
71 Andrei Kirilenko .20 .50
72 Jason Kapono .15 .40
73 Jermaine O'Neal .20 .50
74 Desmond Mason .20 .50
75 Chris Webber .30 .75
76 Morris Peterson .15 .40
77 Ben Wallace .30 .75
78 Antonio Davis .15 .40
79 Slava Medvedenko .15 .40
80 Brian Scalabrine .15 .40
81 Jamal Crawford .25 .60
82 Josh Howard .20 .50
83 Tyson Chandler .20 .50
84 Rasheed Wallace .30 .75
85 Chris Mihm .15 .40
86 Latrell Sprewell .30 .75
87 Mike Sweetney .15 .40
88 Robert Horry .20 .50
89 Michael Finley .25 .60
90 Bostjan Nachbar .15 .40
91 Allan Houston .25 .60
92 Joe Johnson .20 .50
93 Jalen Rose .20 .50
94 Marquis Daniels .15 .40
95 Tyronn Lue .15 .40
96 Stephon Marbury .30 .75
97 Quentin Richardson .15 .40
98 Chris Bosh .40 1.00
99 Dajuan Wagner .15 .40
100 Derek Fisher .20 .50
101 Devean George .15 .40
102 Zoran Planinic .15 .40
103 Corliss Williamson .15 .40
104 Brent Barry .15 .40
105 Drew Gooden .15 .40
106 Clifford Robinson .15 .40
107 Shane Battier .20 .50
108 P.J. Brown .15 .40
109 Willie Green .25 .60
110 Nick Collison .15 .40
111 Al Harrington .20 .50
112 Carmelo Anthony .50 1.25
113 Corey Maggette .20 .50
114 Eddie Jones .25 .60
115 Zach Randolph .25 .60
116 Raja Bell .20 .50
117 Jeff McInnis .15 .40
118 Yao Ming .60 1.50
119 Brian Cardinal .15 .40
120 Jamaal Magloire .15 .40
121 Kyle Korver .20 .50
122 Luke Ridnour .20 .50
123 Jason Terry .20 .50
124 Maurice Taylor .15 .40
125 Bonzi Wells .15 .40
126 David West .20 .50
127 Amare Stoudemire .25 .60
128 Ray Allen .40 1.00
129 Eddy Curry .15 .40
130 Richard Hamilton .30 .75
131 Kobe Bryant 2.00 5.00
132 Kevin Garnett .60 1.50
133 Steve Francis .25 .60
134 Tim Duncan .60 1.50
135 Larry Hughes .20 .50
136 LeBron James 2.00 5.00
137 Adonal Foyle .15 .40
138 Pau Gasol .40 1.00
139 Richard Jefferson .20 .50
140 Allen Iverson .60 1.50
141 Antonio Daniels .15 .40
142 Eric Williams .15 .40
143 Primoz Brezec .15 .40
144 Jason Richardson .25 .60
145 Chris Kaman .20 .50
146 Troy Hudson .15 .40
147 Hedo Turkoglu .20 .50
148 Tony Parker .40 1.00
149 Gilbert Arenas .25 .60
150 Eric Snow .15 .40
151 Tracy McGrady .40 1.00
152 Stromile Swift .15 .40
153 Dan Dickau .15 .40
154 Steve Nash .50 1.25
155 Rashard Lewis .20 .50
156 Gerald Wallace .20 .50
157 Mike Dunleavy .15 .40
158 Bobby Simmons .15 .40
159 Wally Szczerbiak .20 .50
160 Grant Hill .30 .75
161 Mike Bibby .25 .60
162 Antawn Jamison .20 .50
163 Antonio McDyess .20 .50
164 Shaquille O'Neal 1.00 2.50
165 Rafer Alston .15 .40
166 Charles Barkley HH 4.00 10.00
167 David Robinson HH 5.00 12.00
171 Larry Bird HH 10.00 25.00
172 Scottie Pippen HH 6.00 15.00
173 Isiah Thomas HH 4.00 10.00
174 Kevin McHale HH 3.00 8.00
175 Dominique Wilkins HH 3.00 8.00
176 Josh Childress RC 2.00 5.00
177 Josh Smith RC 1.25 3.00
178 Al Jefferson RC 1.25 3.00
179 Delonte West RC 1.00 2.50
180 Tony Allen RC 1.25 3.00
181 Emeka Okafor RC 1.00 2.50
182 Bernard Robinson RC .75 2.00
183 Ben Gordon RC 1.25 3.00
184 Luol Deng RC 1.25 3.00
185 Andres Nocioni RC 1.25 3.00
186 Luke Jackson RC .75 2.00
187 Devin Harris RC 1.00 2.50
188 Andris Biedrins RC .75 2.00
189 Shaun Livingston RC 1.25 3.00
190 Dorell Wright RC 1.00 2.50
191 J.R. Smith RC 1.25 3.00
192 Trevor Ariza RC 1.25 3.00
193 Dwight Howard RC 4.00 10.00
194 Jameer Nelson RC 1.25 3.00
195 Andre Iguodala RC 2.00 5.00
196 Sebastian Telfair RC 1.00 2.50
197 Kevin Martin RC 1.50 4.00
198 David Harrison RC .75 2.00
199 Rafael Araujo RC .75 2.00
200 Kirk Snyder RC .75 2.00

2004-05 Hoops 100

*1-165 SINGLES: 3X TO 8X BASE HI
*166-175 HH: .6X TO 1.5X BASE HI
*176-200 RC's: .75X TO 2X BASE HI
PRINT RUN 100 SER.#'d SETS

2004-05 Hoops Autographs

PRINT RUN 75 SER.#'d SETS
*AUTO 25: .6X TO 1.5X BASE HI
AB Andris Biedrins 3.00 8.00
BG Ben Gordon 5.00 12.00
CB2 Carlos Boozer 5.00 12.00
DH David Harrison 3.00 8.00
DW David West 6.00 15.00
KK Kyle Korver 10.00 25.00
LD Luol Deng 5.00 12.00
LJ Luke Jackson 3.00 8.00
LR Luke Ridnour 5.00 12.00
MD Marquis Daniels 5.00 12.00
PS Peja Stojakovic 12.00 30.00
RH Richard Hamilton 10.00 25.00
SB Shane Battier 5.00 12.00

2004-05 Hoops Great Shots

COMPLETE SET (10) 10.00 25.00
STATED ODDS 1:72
1 Kobe Bryant 6.00 15.00
2 LeBron James 6.00 15.00
3 Carmelo Anthony 1.50 4.00
4 Ben Wallace 1.00 2.50
5 Tim Duncan 2.00 5.00
6 Kevin Garnett 2.00 5.00
7 Jason Kidd 1.25 3.00
8 Yao Ming 2.00 5.00
9 Amare Stoudemire .75 2.00
10 Dwyane Wade 3.00 8.00

2004-05 Hoops Great Shots Jerseys

STATED ODDS 1:144
*GREEN: .4X TO 1X BASE JSY HI
*PATCH: 1X TO 2.5X BASE HI
PATCH PRINT RUN 25 SER.#'d SETS
AS Amare Stoudemire 2.50 6.00
BW Ben Wallace 3.00 8.00
CA Carmelo Anthony 5.00 12.00
DW Dwyane Wade 10.00 25.00
JK Jason Kidd 4.00 10.00
KG Kevin Garnett 6.00 15.00
TD Tim Duncan 6.00 15.00
YM Yao Ming 6.00 15.00

2004-05 Hoops Hot List

COMPLETE SET (15) 8.00 20.00
STATED ODDS 1:10
1 Dwyane Wade 2.00 5.00
2 LeBron James 4.00 10.00
3 Kobe Bryant 4.00 10.00
4 Shaquille O'Neal 2.00 5.00
5 Michael Redd .40 1.00
6 Tracy McGrady .75 2.00
7 Richard Hamilton .60 1.50
8 Tony Parker .75 2.00
9 Allen Iverson 1.25 3.00
10 Chris Webber .60 1.50
11 Paul Pierce .75 2.00
12 Jermaine O'Neal .40 1.00
13 Pau Gasol .75 2.00
14 Zach Randolph .50 1.25
15 Andrei Kirilenko .40 1.00

2004-05 Hoops Hot List Jerseys

STATED ODDS 1:144
AI Allen Iverson 6.00 15.00
AK Andrei Kirilenko 2.00 5.00
CW Chris Webber 3.00 8.00
DW Dwyane Wade 10.00 25.00
JO Jermaine O'Neal 2.00 5.00
MR Michael Redd 2.00 5.00
RH Richard Hamilton 3.00 8.00
SO Shaquille O'Neal 10.00 25.00
TM Tracy McGrady 4.00 10.00
ZR Zach Randolph 2.50 6.00

2004-05 Hoops Nameplates

PRINT RUNS LISTED IN CHECKLIST
AI Allen Iverson/49 15.00 40.00
AS Amare Stoudemire/43 6.00 15.00
CA Carmelo Anthony/48 12.00 30.00
CK Chris Kaman/40 5.00 12.00
KG Kevin Garnett/48 15.00 40.00
LD Luol Deng/26 8.00 20.00
MD Mike Dunleavy/48 4.00 10.00
MG Manu Ginobili/49 12.00 30.00
MS Mike Sweetney/47 5.00 12.00
RJ Richard Jefferson/50 5.00 12.00
SC Sam Cassell/28 6.00 15.00
VC Vince Carter/45 12.00 30.00

2004-05 Hoops Nameplates Dual

PRINT RUN 25 SER.#'d SETS
BD C.Boozer/L.Deng 15.00 40.00
DN B.Davis/J.Nelson 10.00 25.00
IG A.Iverson/K.Garnett 20.00 50.00
JM R.Jefferson/K.Martin 10.00 25.00
KL C.Kaman/S.Livingston 10.00 25.00
MS D.Milicic/P.Stojakovic 10.00 25.00
SG L.Sprewell/K.Garnett 12.00 30.00

2004-05 Hoops Nameplates Triple

PRINT RUN 13 SER.#'d SETS
GCS KG/Cassell/Sprewell 30.00 80.00
KSD Kaman/Stoj/Dunleavy 12.00 30.00

2004-05 Hoops Supreme Court

COMPLETE SET (20) 12.50 30.00
STATED ODDS 1:8
1 Kobe Bryant 4.00 10.00
2 LeBron James 4.00 10.00
3 Shaquille O'Neal 2.00 5.00
4 Ben Wallace .60 1.50
5 Yao Ming 1.25 3.00
6 Vince Carter 1.00 2.50
7 Tim Duncan 1.25 3.00
8 Kevin Garnett 1.25 3.00
9 Carmelo Anthony 1.00 2.50
10 Richard Jefferson .40 1.00
11 Dwyane Wade 2.00 5.00
12 Steve Francis .50 1.25
13 Dirk Nowitzki 1.25 3.00
14 Allen Iverson 1.25 3.00
15 Jermaine O'Neal .40 1.00
16 Corey Maggette .40 1.00
17 Paul Pierce .75 2.00
18 Baron Davis .50 1.25
19 Ray Allen .75 2.00
20 Jason Richardson .50 1.25

2004-05 Hoops Supreme Court Jerseys

STATED ODDS 1:72
*GREEN: .4X TO 1X BASE JSY HI
*PATCH: 1X TO 2.5X BASE HI
PATCH PRINT RUN 25 SER.#'d SETS
AI Allen Iverson 6.00 15.00
BW Ben Wallace 3.00 8.00
CA Carmelo Anthony 5.00 12.00
CM Corey Maggette 2.00 5.00
DN Dirk Nowitzki 6.00 15.00
DW Dwyane Wade 10.00 25.00
JR Jason Richardson 2.50 6.00
KG Kevin Garnett 6.00 15.00
PP Paul Pierce 4.00 10.00
RA Ray Allen 4.00 10.00
RJ Richard Jefferson 2.00 5.00
SO Shaquille O'Neal 10.00 25.00
TD Tim Duncan 6.00 15.00
VC Vince Carter 5.00 12.00
YM Yao Ming 6.00 15.00

2005-06 Hoops

COMPLETE SET (184) 30.00 80.00
1 Josh Childress .15 .40
2 Al Harrington .20 .50
3 Josh Smith .20 .50
4 Tony Delk .15 .40
5 Joe Johnson .20 .50
6 Al Jefferson .15 .40
7 Paul Pierce .40 1.00
8 Ricky Davis .20 .50
9 Tony Allen .15 .40
10 Dan Dickau .15 .40
11 Keith Bogans .15 .40
12 Emeka Okafor .20 .50
13 Kareem Rush .15 .40
14 Gerald Wallace .20 .50
15 Primoz Brezec .15 .40
16 Ben Gordon .20 .50
17 Luol Deng .20 .50
18 Kirk Hinrich .20 .50
19 Chris Duhon .15 .40
20 Michael Jordan 25.00 60.00
21 LeBron James 2.00 5.00
22 Larry Hughes .20 .50
23 Donyell Marshall .15 .40
24 Drew Gooden .15 .40
25 Zydrunas Ilgauskas .20 .50
26 Erick Dampier .15 .40
27 Jason Terry .20 .50
28 Josh Howard .20 .50
29 Dirk Nowitzki .60 1.50
30 Jerry Stackhouse .20 .50
31 Carmelo Anthony .40 1.00
32 Marcus Camby .20 .50
33 Nene .20 .50
34 Kenyon Martin .20 .50
35 Chauncey Billups .30 .75
36 Richard Hamilton .20 .50
37 Ben Wallace .30 .75
38 Rasheed Wallace .25 .60
39 Tayshaun Prince .25 .60
40 Baron Davis .25 .60
41 Mike Dunleavy .15 .40
42 Mickael Pietrus .15 .40
43 Jason Richardson .25 .60
44 Tracy McGrady .40 1.00
45 Yao Ming .50 1.25
46 Stromile Swift .15 .40
47 Bob Sura .15 .40
48 Jermaine O'Neal .20 .50
49 Ron Artest .20 .50
50 Fred Jones .15 .40
51 Stephen Jackson .20 .50
52 Corey Maggette .20 .50
53 Elton Brand .20 .50
54 Shaun Livingston .20 .50
55 Chris Wilcox .15 .40
56 Chris Kaman .20 .50
57 Kobe Bryant 2.00 5.00
58 Lamar Odom .20 .50
59 Kwame Brown .20 .50
60 Luke Walton .15 .40
61 Devean George .15 .40
62 Pau Gasol .40 1.00
63 Shane Battier .20 .50
64 Bobby Jackson .20 .50
65 Eddie Jones .20 .50
66 Lorenzen Wright .15 .40
67 Shaquille O'Neal .75 2.00
68 Dwyane Wade .50 1.25
69 Antoine Walker .25 .60
70 Jason Williams .40 1.00
71 James Posey .15 .40
72 T.J. Ford .15 .40
73 Dan Gadzuric .15 .40
74 Desmond Mason .15 .40
75 Michael Redd .20 .50
76 Kevin Garnett .60 1.50
77 Sam Cassell .20 .50
78 Eddie Griffin .15 .40
79 Wally Szczerbiak .20 .50
80 Michael Olowokandi .15 .40
81 Jeff McInnis .15 .40
82 Vince Carter .50 1.25
83 Jason Kidd .40 1.00
84 Richard Jefferson .20 .50
85 Clifford Robinson .15 .40
86 P.J. Brown .15 .40
87 Jamaal Magloire .15 .40
88 J.R. Smith .25 .60
89 Speedy Claxton .15 .40
90 Jamal Crawford .25 .60
91 Stephon Marbury .30 .75
92 Quentin Richardson .15 .40
93 Mike Sweetney .15 .40
94 Malik Rose .15 .40
95 Steve Francis .25 .60
96 Dwight Howard .30 .75
97 Keyon Dooling .15 .40
98 Grant Hill .40 1.00
99 Jameer Nelson .15 .40
100 Allen Iverson .50 1.25
101 Samuel Dalembert .15 .40
102 Chris Webber .30 .75
103 Andre Iguodala .25 .60
104 Kyle Korver .20 .50
105 Steve Nash .50 1.25
106 Shawn Marion .25 .60
107 Amare Stoudemire .25 .60
108 Kurt Thomas .15 .40
109 Darius Miles .15 .40
110 Zach Randolph .25 .60
111 Sebastian Telfair .20 .50
112 Ruben Patterson .15 .40
113 Joel Przybilla .15 .40
114 Mike Bibby .25 .60
115 Peja Stojakovic .20 .50
116 Brad Miller .20 .50
117 Bonzi Wells .15 .40
118 Tim Duncan .60 1.50
119 Manu Ginobili .50 1.25
120 Tony Parker .40 1.00
121 Robert Horry .25 .60
122 Bruce Bowen .20 .50
123 Ray Allen .40 1.00
124 Rashard Lewis .20 .50
125 Vladimir Radmanovic .15 .40
126 Luke Ridnour .20 .50
127 Reggie Evans .15 .40
128 Chris Bosh .30 .75
129 Morris Peterson .15 .40
130 Rafer Alston .20 .50
131 Rafael Araujo .15 .40
132 Jalen Rose .20 .50
133 Carlos Boozer .20 .50
134 Gordan Giricek .15 .40
135 Matt Harpring .15 .40
136 Andrei Kirilenko .20 .50
137 Mehmet Okur .15 .40
138 Gilbert Arenas .25 .60
139 Antawn Jamison .25 .60
140 Caron Butler .20 .50
141 Antonio Daniels .15 .40
142 Brendan Haywood .15 .40
143 Sarunas Jasikevicius RC .75 2.00
144 Ryan Gomes RC .60 1.50
145 Andray Blatche RC .75 2.00
146 Bracey Wright RC .50 1.25
147 Louis Williams RC 2.00 5.00
148 Martynas Andriuskevicius RC .50 1.25
149 Chris Taft RC .50 1.25
150 Monta Ellis RC 1.00 2.50
151 Travis Diener RC .50 1.25
152 Ersan Ilyasova RC .60 1.50
153 Yaroslav Korolev RC .50 1.25
154 C.J. Miles RC .50 1.25
155 Brandon Bass RC .60 1.50
156 Daniel Ewing RC .60 1.50
157 Salim Stoudamire RC .60 1.50
158 David Lee RC .75 2.00
159 Wayne Simien RC .50 1.25
160 Linas Kleiza RC .60 1.50
161 Jason Maxiell RC .60 1.50
162 Johan Petro RC .60 1.50
163 Luther Head RC .50 1.25
164 Francisco Garcia RC .50 1.25
165 Jarrett Jack RC .75 2.00
166 Nate Robinson RC .75 2.00
167 Julius Hodge RC .50 1.25
168 Hakim Warrick RC .60 1.50
169 Gerald Green RC .75 2.00
170 Danny Granger RC .75 2.00
171 Joey Graham RC .60 1.50
172 Antoine Wright RC .60 1.50
173 Rashad McCants RC .50 1.25
174 Sean May RC .50 1.25
175 Andrew Bynum RC .60 1.50
176 Ike Diogu RC .50 1.25
177 Channing Frye RC .60 1.50
178 Charlie Villanueva RC .60 1.50
179 Martell Webster RC .60 1.50
180 Raymond Felton RC .60 1.50
181 Chris Paul RC 4.00 10.00
182 Deron Williams RC 1.25 3.00
183 Marvin Williams RC .75 2.00
184 Andrew Bogut RC 1.00 2.50

2005-06 Hoops Genuine Coverage

GCAH Al Harrington 2.00 5.00
GCAK Andrei Kirilenko 2.00 5.00
GCAM Antonio McDyess 2.00 5.00
GCAS Amare Stoudemire SP 2.50 6.00
GCBD Baron Davis 2.50 6.00
GCCA Caron Butler 2.00 5.00
GCCB Carlos Boozer 2.00 5.00
GCCM Corey Maggette 2.00 5.00
GCCW Chris Webber 3.00 8.00
GCDA Darko Milicic 2.00 5.00
GCDF Derek Fisher 2.00 5.00
GCDG Devean George 2.00 5.00
GCDM Darius Miles 2.00 5.00
GCDN Dirk Nowitzki 6.00 15.00
GCDW David Wesley 2.00 5.00
GCJJ Joe Johnson 2.00 5.00
GCJT Jason Terry 2.00 5.00
GCKB Kwame Brown 2.00 5.00
GCKG Kevin Garnett SP 6.00 15.00
GCKT Kurt Thomas 2.00 5.00
GCLJ LeBron James SP 10.00 25.00
GCME Carmelo Anthony 4.00 10.00
GCMG Manu Ginobili 5.00 12.00
GCNE Nene 2.00 5.00
GCNK Nenad Krstic 2.00 5.00
GCQR Quentin Richardson 1.50 4.00
GCRA Rafael Araujo 2.00 5.00
GCRL Rashard Lewis 2.00 5.00
GCRW Rasheed Wallace 2.50 6.00
GCSA Shareef Abdur-Rahim 2.50 6.00
GCSB Shane Battier 2.00 5.00
GCSC Sam Cassell 2.00 5.00
GCSD Samuel Dalembert 2.00 5.00
GCSF Steve Francis 2.50 6.00
GCSM Shawn Marion 2.50 6.00
GCSS Stromile Swift 2.00 5.00
GCTC Tyson Chandler 2.00 5.00
GCTD Tim Duncan 6.00 15.00
GCTM Tracy McGrady 4.00 10.00
GCUH Udonis Haslem 1.50 4.00
GCWS Wally Szczerbiak 2.00 5.00

2005-06 Hoops HoopScripts

APPROXIMATELY ONE PER BOX
HSAA Alex Acker 2.50 6.00
HSAB Andray Blatche 4.00 10.00
HSAJ Amir Johnson 4.00 10.00
HSBB Brandon Bass 3.00 8.00
HSBW Bracey Wright 2.50 6.00
HSCM C.J. Miles 3.00 8.00
HSDH Dwight Howard SP 12.00 30.00
HSDL David Lee 4.00 10.00
HSDT Dijon Thompson 2.50 6.00
HSEI Ersan Ilyasova 3.00 8.00
HSFG Francisco Garcia 2.50 6.00
HSGG Gerald Green 4.00 10.00
HSID Ike Diogu 2.50 6.00
HSJG Joey Graham 3.00 8.00
HSJH Julius Hodge 2.50 6.00
HSJJ Jarrett Jack 4.00 10.00
HSJM Jason Maxiell 3.00 8.00
HSJP Johan Petro 2.50 6.00
HSJS James Singleton 2.50 6.00
HSLH Luther Head 2.50 6.00
HSLJ LeBron James SP 1,250.00 2,500.00
HSLK Linas Kleiza 3.00 8.00
HSLR Lawrence Roberts 2.50 6.00
HSLW Louis Williams 10.00 25.00
HSMA Martynas Andriuskevicius 2.50 6.00
HSMW Martell Webster 3.00 8.00
HSNR Nate Robinson 4.00 10.00
HSOG Orien Greene 3.00 8.00
HSRF Raymond Felton 3.00 8.00
HSRG Ryan Gomes 3.00 8.00
HSRM Rashad McCants 2.50 6.00
HSRW Robert Whaley 2.50 6.00
HSVW Von Wafer 2.50 6.00

2005-06 Hoops LBJ Profiles

COMPLETE SET (30) 15.00 40.00
COMMON CARD (LBJ1-LBJ30) 1.25 3.00
APPROXIMATELY EIGHT PER BOX

2005-06 Hoops MJ Profiles

COMPLETE SET (30) 20.00 50.00
COMMON CARD (MJ1-MJ30) 1.50 4.00
APPROXIMATELY EIGHT PER BOX

2011-12 Hoops

COMPLETE SET (278) 25.00 60.00
1 Jamal Crawford .30 .75
2 Kirk Hinrich .25 .60
3 Al Horford .30 .75
4 Joe Johnson .25 .60
5 Marvin Williams .20 .50
6 Josh Smith .25 .60
7 Ray Allen .50 1.25
8 Brandon Bass .20 .50
9 Glen Davis .20 .50
10 Kevin Garnett .75 2.00
11 Jeff Green .20 .50
12 Jermaine O'Neal .30 .75
13 Troy Murphy .20 .50
14 Paul Pierce .50 1.25
15 Rajon Rondo .40 1.00
16 D.J. Augustin .20 .50
17 Kwame Brown .20 .50
18 DeSagana Diop .20 .50
19 Eduardo Najera .20 .50
20 Tyrus Thomas .20 .50
21 Omer Asik .20 .50
22 Carlos Boozer .25 .60
23 Ronnie Brewer .20 .50
24 Rasual Butler .20 .50
25 Luol Deng .25 .60
26 Kyle Korver .25 .60
27 Joakim Noah .30 .75
28 Derrick Rose .50 1.25
29 Baron Davis .25 .60
30 Semih Erden .20 .50
31 Daniel Gibson .20 .50
32 Luke Harangody .20 .50
33 Antawn Jamison .25 .60
34 Anderson Varejao .20 .50
35 J.J. Barea .30 .75
36 Rodrigue Beaubois .20 .50
37 Caron Butler .25 .60
38 Brian Cardinal .20 .50
39 Tyson Chandler .25 .60
40 Rudy Fernandez .20 .50
41 Dominique Jones .20 .50
42 Jason Kidd .50 1.25
43 Ian Mahinmi .20 .50
44 Shawn Marion .30 .75
45 Dirk Nowitzki .75 2.00
46 DeShawn Stevenson .20 .50
47 Chris Andersen .25 .60
48 Danilo Gallinari .25 .60
49 Nene .25 .60
50 Ty Lawson .20 .50
51 Corey Brewer .20 .50
52 Andre Miller .25 .60
53 Timofey Mozgov .20 .50
54 Austin Daye .20 .50
55 Ben Gordon .25 .60
56 Richard Hamilton .40 1.00
57 Jonas Jerebko .20 .50
58 Tracy McGrady .60 1.50
59 Tayshaun Prince .30 .75
60 DaJuan Summers .20 .50
61 Charlie Villanueva .20 .50
62 Ben Wallace .40 1.00
63 Terrico White .20 .50
64 Stephen Curry 2.50 6.00
65 Monta Ellis .25 .60
66 David Lee .20 .50
67 Jeremy Lin .60 1.50
68 Andris Biedrins .20 .50
69 Ekpe Udoh .20 .50
70 Chase Budinger .20 .50
71 Goran Dragic .25 .60
72 Jordan Hill .20 .50
73 Kevin Martin .25 .60
74 Patrick Patterson .20 .50
75 Luis Scola .25 .60
76 Hasheem Thabeet .20 .50
77 Darren Collison .20 .50
78 Mike Dunleavy Jr. .20 .50
79 T.J. Ford .20 .50
80 Danny Granger .25 .60
81 Tyler Hansbrough .25 .60
82 George Hill .25 .60
83 Josh McRoberts .20 .50
84 Brandon Rush .20 .50
85 Lance Stephenson .25 .60
86 Al-Farouq Aminu .20 .50
87 Ike Diogu .20 .50
88 Randy Foye .20 .50
89 Eric Gordon .25 .60
90 Blake Griffin .30 .75
91 DeAndre Jordan .25 .60
92 Chris Kaman .25 .60
93 Ryan Gomes .25 .60
94 Mo Williams .25 .60
95 Metta World Peace .25 .60
96 Matt Barnes .20 .50
97 Steve Blake .20 .50
98 Kobe Bryant 2.50 6.00
99 Andrew Bynum .20 .50
100 Derrick Caracter .20 .50
101 Derek Fisher .30 .75
102 Pau Gasol .50 1.25
103 Lamar Odom .25 .60
104 Darrell Arthur .20 .50
105 Shane Battier .25 .60
106 Marc Gasol .30 .75
107 Rudy Gay .30 .75
108 O.J. Mayo .20 .50
109 Zach Randolph .25 .60
110 Ishmael Smith .20 .50
111 Greivis Vasquez .20 .50
112 Sam Young .20 .50
113 Joel Anthony .20 .50
114 Mike Bibby .30 .75
115 Chris Bosh .40 1.00
116 Mario Chalmers .25 .60
117 Juwan Howard .25 .60
118 Udonis Haslem .25 .60
119 LeBron James 2.50 6.00
120 Mike Miller .25 .60
121 Dexter Pittman .20 .50
122 Dwyane Wade .60 1.50
123 Jon Brockman .20 .50
124 Carlos Delfino .20 .50
125 Drew Gooden .25 .60
126 Ersan Ilyasova .20 .50
127 Stephen Jackson .25 .60
128 Brandon Jennings .25 .60
129 Luc Mbah a Moute .20 .50
130 Larry Sanders .20 .50
131 Beno Udrih .20 .50
132 Andrew Bogut .25 .60
133 Michael Beasley .20 .50
134 Wayne Ellington .20 .50
135 Lazar Hayward .20 .50
136 Kevin Love .30 .75
137 Darko Milicic .20 .50
138 Brad Miller .25 .60
139 Nikola Pekovic .20 .50
140 Luke Ridnour .25 .60
141 Ricky Rubio .30 .75
142 Martell Webster .25 .60
143 Jordan Farmar .20 .50
144 Sundiata Gaines .20 .50
145 Anthony Morrow .20 .50
146 Damion James .20 .50
147 Brook Lopez .30 .75
148 Brandan Wright .20 .50
149 Kris Humphries .20 .50
150 Johan Petro .20 .50
151 Deron Williams .25 .60
152 Trevor Ariza .20 .50
153 Carl Landry .20 .50
154 David West .25 .60
155 Jason Smith .20 .50
156 Jarrett Jack .20 .50
157 Emeka Okafor .25 .60
158 Chris Paul .60 1.50
159 Quincy Pondexter .20 .50
160 Carmelo Anthony .50 1.25
161 Chauncey Billups .40 1.00
162 Derrick Brown .20 .50
163 Anthony Carter .20 .50
164 Landry Fields .20 .50
165 Toney Douglas .20 .50
166 Amare Stoudemire .30 .75
167 Jerome Jordan RC .20 .50
168 Cole Aldrich .20 .50
169 Nick Collison .20 .50
170 Kevin Durant 1.25 3.00
171 James Harden .60 1.50
172 Serge Ibaka .25 .60
173 B.J. Mullens .20 .50
174 Eric Maynor .20 .50
175 Russell Westbrook .50 1.25
176 Ryan Anderson .20 .50
177 Chris Duhon .20 .50
178 Dwight Howard .40 1.00
179 Jameer Nelson .20 .50
180 J.J. Redick .30 .75
181 Jason Richardson .30 .75
182 Hedo Turkoglu .25 .60
183 Craig Brackins .20 .50
184 Elton Brand .30 .75
185 Andre Iguodala .30 .75
186 Jason Kapono .20 .50
187 Jodie Meeks .25 .60
188 Evan Turner .20 .50
189 Louis Williams .30 .75
190 Thaddeus Young .25 .60
191 Michael Redd .25 .60
192 Vince Carter .60 1.50
193 Channing Frye .20 .50
194 Grant Hill .50 1.25
195 Marcin Gortat .20 .50
196 Steve Nash .60 1.50
197 Hakim Warrick .20 .50
198 LaMarcus Aldridge .30 .75
199 Marcus Camby .25 .60
200 Raymond Felton .20 .50
201 Wesley Matthews .20 .50
202 Greg Oden .20 .50
203 Armon Johnson .20 .50
204 Gerald Wallace .25 .60
205 Elliot Williams .20 .50
206 DeMarcus Cousins .30 .75
207 Samuel Dalembert .20 .50
208 Tyreke Evans .25 .60
209 Francisco Garcia .20 .50
210 Donte Greene .20 .50
211 Jason Thompson .20 .50
212 Marcus Thornton .20 .50
213 Hassan Whiteside .25 .60
214 DeJuan Blair .20 .50
215 Da'Sean Butler .20 .50
216 Tim Duncan .75 2.00
217 Manu Ginobili .60 1.50
218 Richard Jefferson .25 .60
219 Matt Bonner .20 .50
220 Gary Neal .20 .50
221 Tony Parker .40 1.00
222 Tiago Splitter .20 .50
223 Solomon Alabi .20 .50
224 Leandro Barbosa .20 .50
225 Andrea Bargnani .20 .50
226 Jose Calderon .20 .50
227 Ed Davis .20 .50
228 DeMar DeRozan .40 1.00
229 Amir Johnson .20 .50
230 Raja Bell .25 .60
231 C.J. Miles .20 .50
232 Jeremy Evans .20 .50
233 Derrick Favors .25 .60
234 Devin Harris .20 .50
235 Gordon Hayward .30 .75
236 Al Jefferson .25 .60
237 Earl Watson .20 .50
238 Paul Millsap .25 .60
239 Mehmet Okur .20 .50
240 Andray Blatche .20 .50
241 Trevor Booker .20 .50
242 Jordan Crawford .20 .50
243 Josh Howard .20 .50
244 Ronny Turiaf .20 .50
245 Rashard Lewis .25 .60
246 JaVale McGee .25 .60
247 John Wall .40 1.00
248 Derrick Rose .50 1.25
249 Dwyane Wade .60 1.50
250 LeBron James 2.50 6.00

251 Chris Bosh .40 1.00
252 Amare Stoudemire .30 .75
253 Dwight Howard .40 1.00
254 Kevin Garnett .75 2.00
255 Paul Pierce .50 1.25
256 Rajon Rondo .40 1.00
257 Ray Allen .50 1.25
258 Kobe Bryant 2.50 6.00
259 Chris Paul .60 1.50
260 Carmelo Anthony .50 1.25
261 Dirk Nowitzki .75 2.00
262 Kevin Durant 1.25 3.00
263 Tim Duncan .75 2.00
264 Blake Griffin .30 .75
265 Pau Gasol .50 1.25
266 Deron Williams .25 .60
267 Manu Ginobili .60 1.50
268 Kobe Bryant 2.50 6.00
269 Blake Griffin .30 .75
270 Kevin Durant 1.25 3.00
271 Dirk Nowitzki .75 2.00
272 LeBron James 2.50 6.00
273 Derrick Rose .50 1.25
274 Chris Paul .60 1.50
275 Paul Pierce .50 1.25
276 Carmelo Anthony .50 1.25
277 Kevin Love .30 .75
278 Kobe Bryant 2.50 6.00
279 Dallas Mavericks SP 8.00 20.00
BG1 B.Griffin Blake Superior 50.00 120.00
KB1 K.Bryant Black Mamba 100.00 250.00

2011-12 Hoops Artist's Proofs

*ARTIST PROOF: 2.5X TO 6X BASE HI
67 Jeremy Lin 10.00 25.00

2011-12 Hoops Glossy

*GLOSSY: 1.5X TO 4X BASE HI

2011-12 Hoops 89-90 Buyback Autographs

70 Xavier McDaniel 20.00 50.00
120 Alex English 15.00 40.00
125 Adrian Dantley 20.00 50.00
310 David Robinson 125.00 225.00

2011-12 Hoops A Night to Remember

COMPLETE SET (20) 12.00 30.00
1 Wilt Chamberlain 2.00 5.00
2 Dwight Howard .75 2.00
3 Magic Johnson 2.50 6.00
4 Kobe Bryant 5.00 12.00
5 Bill Russell 2.00 5.00
6 Magic Johnson 2.50 6.00
7 Wilt Chamberlain 2.00 5.00
8 Wilt Chamberlain 2.00 5.00
9 Ray Allen 1.00 2.50
10 Elgin Baylor 1.00 2.50
11 John Stockton 1.25 3.00
12 Hakeem Olajuwon 1.25 3.00
13 Dwyane Wade 1.25 3.00
14 Ray Allen 1.00 2.50
15 Bob Cousy 1.00 2.50
16 Scott Skiles .50 1.25
17 Mark Eaton .60 1.50
18 Rick Barry .75 2.00
19 Jason Terry .50 1.25
20 Vince Carter 1.25 3.00

2011-12 Hoops Action Photos

COMPLETE SET (25) 10.00 25.00
1 Derrick Rose .75 2.00
2 JaVale McGee .40 1.00
3 Paul Pierce .75 2.00
4 LeBron James 4.00 10.00
5 Dwight Howard .60 1.50
6 Carmelo Anthony .75 2.00
7 Gary Neal .30 .75
8 Dirk Nowitzki 1.25 3.00
9 Kevin Love .50 1.25
10 Al Horford .50 1.25
11 Amare Stoudemire .50 1.25
12 Steve Nash 1.00 2.50
13 John Wall .60 1.50
14 Chris Paul 1.00 2.50
15 Kevin Durant 2.00 5.00
16 Pau Gasol .75 2.00
17 Tyson Chandler .40 1.00
18 Rajon Rondo .60 1.50
19 Nene .40 1.00
20 Deron Williams .40 1.00
21 Blake Griffin .50 1.25
22 Stephen Curry 4.00 10.00
23 Marc Gasol .50 1.25
24 Kobe Bryant 4.00 10.00
25 Dwyane Wade 1.00 2.50

2011-12 Hoops Autographs

4 Joe Johnson SP 6.00 15.00
11 Jeff Green SP 5.00 12.00
16 D.J. Augustin SP 5.00 12.00
18 DeSagana Diop 2.50 6.00
21 Omer Asik SP 8.00 20.00
22 Carlos Boozer SP 10.00 25.00
23 Ronnie Brewer SP 25.00 60.00
25 Luol Deng SP 20.00 50.00
27 Joakim Noah SP 12.00 30.00
28 Derrick Rose SP 75.00 200.00
30 Semih Erden 2.50 6.00
31 Daniel Gibson SP 15.00 40.00
32 Luke Harangody 2.50 6.00
33 Antawn Jamison SP 5.00 12.00
34 Anderson Varejao 2.50 6.00
35 J.J. Barea 6.00 15.00
36 Rodrigue Beaubois 2.50 6.00
37 Caron Butler SP 20.00 50.00
41 Dominique Jones 2.50 6.00
43 Ian Mahinmi 3.00 8.00
45 Dirk Nowitzki SP 75.00 200.00
47 Chris Andersen SP 15.00 40.00
48 Danilo Gallinari SP 5.00 12.00
53 Timofey Mozgov SP 5.00 12.00
54 Austin Daye SP 5.00 12.00
55 Ben Gordon SP 5.00 12.00
56 Richard Hamilton SP 10.00 25.00
57 Jonas Jerebko SP 5.00 12.00
58 Tracy McGrady SP 40.00 100.00
60 DaJuan Summers 2.50 6.00
61 Charlie Villanueva SP 5.00 12.00
63 Terrico White 2.50 6.00
64 Stephen Curry SP 300.00 600.00
65 Monta Ellis SP 12.00 30.00
66 David Lee SP 5.00 12.00
67 Jeremy Lin 30.00 80.00
69 Ekpe Udoh SP 5.00 12.00
70 Chase Budinger SP 6.00 15.00
71 Goran Dragic SP 15.00 40.00
72 Jordan Hill 2.50 6.00
73 Kevin Martin SP 10.00 25.00
74 Patrick Patterson 4.00 10.00
75 Luis Scola SP 5.00 12.00
76 Hasheem Thabeet 2.50 6.00
78 Mike Dunleavy Jr. SP 5.00 12.00
79 T.J. Ford SP 5.00 12.00
80 Danny Granger SP 12.00 30.00
81 Tyler Hansbrough SP 5.00 12.00
82 George Hill SP 8.00 20.00
85 Lance Stephenson 6.00 15.00
88 Randy Foye 2.50 6.00
90 Blake Griffin SP 40.00 100.00
92 Chris Kaman SP 5.00 12.00
93 Ryan Gomes SP 5.00 12.00
94 Mo Williams SP 5.00 12.00
98 Kobe Bryant SP 150.00 400.00
99 Andrew Bynum SP 12.00 30.00
100 Derrick Caracter 2.50 6.00
101 Derek Fisher SP 8.00 20.00
103 Lamar Odom SP 10.00 25.00
105 Shane Battier SP 8.00 20.00
107 Rudy Gay SP 60.00 150.00
108 O.J. Mayo SP 6.00 15.00
109 Zach Randolph SP 8.00 20.00
110 Ishmael Smith 2.50 6.00
111 Greivis Vasquez 2.50 6.00
112 Sam Young 2.50 6.00
114 Mike Bibby SP 5.00 12.00
115 Chris Bosh SP 25.00 60.00
121 Dexter Pittman SP 5.00 12.00
123 Jon Brockman 2.50 6.00
127 Stephen Jackson SP 40.00 80.00
130 Larry Sanders 2.50 6.00
131 Beno Udrih SP 5.00 12.00
132 Andrew Bogut SP 6.00 15.00
133 Michael Beasley SP 8.00 20.00
134 Wayne Ellington 2.50 6.00
135 Lazar Hayward SP 5.00 12.00
136 Kevin Love SP 40.00 100.00
137 Darko Milicic SP 6.00 15.00
139 Nikola Pekovic 10.00 25.00
140 Luke Ridnour SP 5.00 12.00
144 Sundiata Gaines SP 5.00 12.00
146 Damion James SP 5.00 12.00
147 Brook Lopez SP 12.00 30.00
149 Kris Humphries 4.00 10.00
151 Deron Williams SP 15.00 40.00
152 Trevor Ariza SP 5.00 12.00
153 Carl Landry 2.50 6.00
157 Emeka Okafor SP 5.00 12.00
158 Chris Paul SP 100.00 250.00
159 Quincy Pondexter SP 5.00 12.00
160 Carmelo Anthony SP 25.00 60.00
161 Chauncey Billups SP 15.00 40.00
162 Derrick Brown SP 5.00 12.00
164 Landry Fields SP 5.00 12.00
165 Toney Douglas SP 5.00 12.00
167 Jerome Jordan 2.50 6.00
168 Cole Aldrich 2.50 6.00
170 Kevin Durant SP 125.00 250.00
173 B.J. Mullens 2.50 6.00
175 Russell Westbrook SP 50.00 120.00
179 Jameer Nelson SP 5.00 12.00
180 J.J. Redick 5.00 12.00
182 Hedo Turkoglu SP 5.00 12.00
183 Craig Brackins SP 5.00 12.00
187 Jodie Meeks 3.00 8.00
189 Louis Williams SP 5.00 12.00
192 Vince Carter SP 25.00 60.00
193 Channing Frye SP 5.00 12.00
194 Grant Hill SP 75.00 150.00
196 Steve Nash SP 50.00 120.00
197 Hakim Warrick SP 5.00 12.00
198 LaMarcus Aldridge SP 10.00 25.00
199 Marcus Camby SP 8.00 20.00
200 Raymond Felton SP 8.00 20.00
201 Wesley Matthews SP 8.00 20.00
203 Armon Johnson 2.50 6.00
204 Gerald Wallace SP 6.00 15.00
205 Elliot Williams 2.50 6.00
206 DeMarcus Cousins SP 8.00 20.00
207 Samuel Dalembert 2.50 6.00
208 Tyreke Evans SP 20.00 50.00
210 Donte Greene 2.50 6.00
213 Hassan Whiteside 8.00 20.00
214 DeJuan Blair SP 8.00 20.00
215 Da'Sean Butler 2.50 6.00
220 Gary Neal SP 8.00 20.00
221 Tony Parker SP 15.00 40.00
222 Tiago Splitter SP 8.00 20.00
223 Solomon Alabi 2.50 6.00
225 Andrea Bargnani SP 8.00 20.00
226 Jose Calderon 2.50 6.00
227 Ed Davis 2.50 6.00
228 DeMar DeRozan SP 20.00 50.00
229 Amir Johnson 2.50 6.00
232 Jeremy Evans 2.50 6.00
233 Derrick Favors SP 5.00 12.00
234 Devin Harris SP 15.00 40.00
235 Gordon Hayward SP 12.00 30.00
236 Al Jefferson SP 5.00 12.00
238 Paul Millsap 2.50 6.00
241 Trevor Booker SP 5.00 12.00
242 Jordan Crawford SP 5.00 12.00
243 Josh Howard SP 5.00 12.00
246 JaVale McGee SP 10.00 25.00
248 Derrick Rose SP 30.00 80.00
251 Chris Bosh SP 25.00 60.00
258 Kobe Bryant SP 100.00 300.00
259 Chris Paul SP 75.00 200.00
261 Dirk Nowitzki SP 75.00 200.00
262 Kevin Durant SP 125.00 250.00
264 Blake Griffin SP 40.00 100.00
266 Deron Williams SP 12.00 30.00
268 Kobe Bryant SP 125.00 300.00
269 Blake Griffin SP 80.00 200.00
270 Kevin Durant SP 125.00 250.00
271 Dirk Nowitzki SP 75.00 200.00
273 Derrick Rose SP 30.00 80.00
274 Chris Paul SP 100.00 250.00
277 Kevin Love SP 40.00 100.00
278 Kobe Bryant SP 125.00 300.00

2011-12 Hoops BIGS

COMPLETE SET (15) 12.00 30.00
1 Dwight Howard 1.50 4.00
2 Tim Duncan 3.00 8.00
3 Andrew Bynum .75 2.00
4 Al Jefferson .75 2.00
5 Tyson Chandler 1.00 2.50
6 Kevin Love 1.25 3.00
7 Zach Randolph 1.00 2.50
8 Andrew Bogut 1.00 2.50
9 Nene 1.00 2.50
10 Brook Lopez 1.25 3.00
11 Joakim Noah 1.25 3.00
12 Amare Stoudemire 1.25 3.00
13 Andrea Bargnani .75 2.00
14 Al Horford 1.25 3.00
15 Samuel Dalembert .75 2.00

2011-12 Hoops Courtside

COMPLETE SET (15) 10.00 25.00
1 Kobe Bryant 4.00 10.00
2 LeBron James 4.00 10.00
3 Chris Paul 1.00 2.50
4 Dwight Howard .60 1.50
5 Kevin Durant 2.00 5.00
6 Blake Griffin .50 1.25
7 Carmelo Anthony .75 2.00
8 Kevin Love .50 1.25
9 Steve Nash 1.00 2.50
10 Dwyane Wade 1.00 2.50
11 Dirk Nowitzki 1.25 3.00
12 Derrick Rose .75 2.00
13 Tony Parker .60 1.50
14 Deron Williams .40 1.00
15 Paul Pierce .75 2.00

2011-12 Hoops Dreams

COMPLETE SET (9) 4.00 10.00
1 John Wall .60 1.50
2 DeMarcus Cousins .50 1.25
3 James Harden 1.00 2.50
4 Blake Griffin .50 1.25
5 Landry Fields .30 .75
6 Stephen Curry 4.00 10.00
7 Jordan Crawford .30 .75
8 Tyreke Evans .40 1.00
9 Darren Collison .30 .75

2011-12 Hoops Hall of Fame Heroes

COMPLETE SET (20) 12.00 30.00
1 Bill Russell 2.00 5.00
2 Jerry West 1.25 3.00
3 Oscar Robertson 1.25 3.00
4 Walt Bellamy .60 1.50
5 Nate Thurmond .75 2.00
6 Elgin Baylor 1.00 2.50
7 John Havlicek 1.25 3.00
8 Willis Reed 1.00 2.50
9 Magic Johnson 2.50 6.00
10 Bob Lanier .75 2.00
11 Wilt Chamberlain 2.00 5.00
12 Larry Bird 2.50 6.00
13 Karl Malone 1.25 3.00
14 David Robinson 1.25 3.00
15 Rick Barry .75 2.00
16 Dolph Schayes .60 1.50
17 Bill Walton 1.00 2.50
18 George Gervin 1.00 2.50
19 John Stockton 1.25 3.00
20 Pete Maravich 1.25 3.00

2011-12 Hoops Private Signings

STATED PRINT RUN 49 TO 299 SETS
1 Al Jefferson 10.00 25.00
2 Chauncey Billups 20.00 50.00
3 Zach Randolph 12.00 30.00
4 Lamar Odom 12.00 30.00
5 Louis Williams 12.00 30.00
6 Rudy Gay 10.00 25.00
7 Jose Calderon 10.00 25.00
8 George Hill 10.00 25.00
9 Stephen Jackson 10.00 25.00
10 Joe Johnson 10.00 25.00
11 Marcus Camby 10.00 25.00

2011-12 Hoops Slam Dunk Champion

COMPLETE SET (15) 8.00 20.00
1 Larry Nance .75 2.00
2 Dominique Wilkins 1.50 4.00
3 Spud Webb 1.00 2.50
4 Kenny Walker .60 1.50
5 Dominique Wilkins 1.50 4.00
6 Cedric Ceballos .75 2.00
7 Brent Barry .75 2.00
8 Kobe Bryant 8.00 20.00
9 Vince Carter 2.00 5.00
10 Jason Richardson 1.00 2.50
11 Josh Smith .60 1.50
12 Nate Robinson 1.00 2.50
13 Dwight Howard 1.25 3.00
14 Nate Robinson 1.00 2.50
15 Blake Griffin 1.00 2.50

2012-13 Hoops

COMPLETE SET (300) 40.00 100.00
*INTERNATIONAL: .5X TO 1.2X BASE HI
*ARTIST'S PROOFS: .75X TO 2X BASE HI
1 Avery Bradley .20 .50
2 Brandon Bass .20 .50
3 Kevin Garnett .75 2.00
4 Paul Pierce .50 1.25
5 Rajon Rondo .40 1.00
6 Ray Allen .50 1.25
7 Doc Rivers CO .30 .75
8 Deron Williams .25 .60
9 Brook Lopez .25 .60
10 Kris Humphries .20 .50
11 Anthony Morrow .20 .50
12 Jordan Farmar .20 .50
13 Gerald Wallace .25 .60
14 Avery Johnson CO .25 .60
15 Amare Stoudemire .30 .75
16 Carmelo Anthony .50 1.25
17 Landry Fields .20 .50
18 Tyson Chandler .25 .60
19 Jeremy Lin .50 1.25
20 Steve Novak .20 .50
21 Mike Woodson CO .30 .75
22 Andre Iguodala .30 .75
23 Jodie Meeks .20 .50
24 Jrue Holiday .40 1.00
25 Louis Williams .25 .60
26 Elton Brand .25 .60
27 Evan Turner .20 .50
28 Spencer Hawes .20 .50
29 Doug Collins CO .30 .75
30 Andrea Bargnani .30 .75
31 DeMar DeRozan .40 1.00
32 Gary Forbes .20 .50
33 Jose Calderon .20 .50
34 Linas Kleiza .20 .50
35 Ed Davis .20 .50
36 Dwane Casey CO .30 .75
37 Dirk Nowitzki .75 2.00
38 Rodrigue Beaubois .20 .50
39 Shawn Marion .30 .75
40 Jason Kidd .50 1.25
41 Jason Terry .25 .60
42 Vince Carter .60 1.50
43 Ian Mahinmi .20 .50
44 Rick Carlisle CO .30 .75
45 Kyle Lowry .30 .75
46 Kevin Martin .25 .60
47 Luis Scola .25 .60
48 Chase Budinger .20 .50
49 Patrick Patterson .20 .50
50 Goran Dragic .30 .75
51 Kevin McHale CO .40 1.00
52 Marc Gasol .30 .75
53 Mike Conley .25 .60
54 O.J. Mayo .20 .50
55 Rudy Gay .30 .75
56 Zach Randolph .30 .75
57 Lester Hudson .20 .50
58 Dante Cunningham .20 .50
59 Lionel Hollins CO .20 .50
60 Emeka Okafor .25 .60
61 Carl Landry .20 .50
62 Chris Kaman .25 .60
63 Eric Gordon .25 .60
64 Greivis Vasquez .20 .50
65 Trevor Ariza .20 .50
66 Monty Williams CO .30 .75
67 DeJuan Blair .20 .50
68 Boris Diaw .25 .60
69 Manu Ginobili .60 1.50
70 Tim Duncan .75 2.00
71 Tony Parker .50 1.25
72 Danny Green .25 .60
73 Gregg Popovich CO 4.00 10.00
74 Carlos Boozer .25 .60
75 Derrick Rose .50 1.25
76 Joakim Noah .25 .60
77 Luol Deng .25 .60
78 Richard Hamilton .30 .75
79 Taj Gibson .20 .50
80 Ronnie Brewer .20 .50
81 Tom Thibodeau CO .30 .75
82 Alonzo Gee .20 .50
83 Anderson Varejao .20 .50
84 Antawn Jamison .25 .60
85 Daniel Gibson .20 .50
86 Byron Scott CO .25 .60
87 Ben Gordon .25 .60
88 Greg Monroe .20 .50
89 Rodney Stuckey .20 .50
90 Tayshaun Prince .30 .75
91 Jonas Jerebko .20 .50
92 Lawrence Frank CO .30 .75
93 Danny Granger .20 .50
94 David West .25 .60
95 Paul George .50 1.25
96 Roy Hibbert .25 .60
97 Darren Collison .20 .50
98 George Hill .25 .60
99 A.J. Price .20 .50
100 Frank Vogel CO .30 .75
101 Brandon Jennings .20 .50
102 Drew Gooden .25 .60
103 Monta Ellis .25 .60
104 Ersan Ilyasova .20 .50
105 Mike Dunleavy .20 .50
106 Luc Mbah a Moute .20 .50
107 Scott Skiles CO .25 .60
108 Arron Afflalo .20 .50
109 Danilo Gallinari .20 .50
110 Ty Lawson .20 .50
111 Wilson Chandler .25 .60
112 JaVale McGee .25 .60
113 Andre Miller .25 .60
114 Timofey Mozgov .20 .50
115 George Karl CO .30 .75
116 Kevin Love .30 .75
117 Luke Ridnour .25 .60
118 Michael Beasley .20 .50
119 Nikola Pekovic .20 .50
120 Ricky Rubio .25 .60
121 Wesley Johnson .20 .50
122 J.J. Barea .25 .60
123 Rick Adelman CO .30 .75
124 LaMarcus Aldridge .30 .75
125 Nicolas Batum .25 .60
126 Wesley Matthews .20 .50
127 Jonny Flynn .20 .50
128 J.J. Hickson .20 .50
129 Jamal Crawford .30 .75
130 Raymond Felton .20 .50
131 Kaleb Canales CO .30 .75
132 Derek Fisher .25 .60
133 James Harden .60 1.50
134 Kendrick Perkins .20 .50
135 Kevin Durant 1.25 3.00
136 Russell Westbrook .50 1.25
137 Serge Ibaka .25 .60
138 Daequan Cook .20 .50
139 Nick Collison .20 .50
140 Scott Brooks CO .20 .50
141 Al Jefferson .20 .50
142 DeMarre Carroll .20 .50
143 Gordon Hayward .30 .75
144 Paul Millsap .25 .60
145 Derrick Favors .25 .60
146 Josh Howard .25 .60
147 Tyrone Corbin CO .30 .75
148 Al Horford .30 .75
149 Jeff Teague .20 .50
150 Joe Johnson .25 .60
151 Josh Smith .20 .50
152 Tracy McGrady .50 1.25
153 Marvin Williams .20 .50
154 Zaza Pachulia .20 .50
155 Larry Drew CO .30 .75
156 LeBron James 2.50 6.00
157 Dwyane Wade .60 1.50
158 Chris Bosh .40 1.00
159 Mario Chalmers .25 .60
160 Joel Anthony .20 .50
161 Udonis Haslem .25 .60
162 Shane Battier .25 .60
163 Erik Spoelstra CO .30 .75
164 Dwight Howard .40 1.00
165 Hedo Turkoglu .25 .60
166 J.J. Redick .30 .75
167 Jameer Nelson .20 .50
168 Jason Richardson .30 .75
169 Ryan Anderson .20 .50
170 Glen Davis .20 .50
171 Chris Duhon .20 .50
172 John Wall .40 1.00
173 Trevor Booker .20 .50
174 Jordan Crawford .20 .50
175 Nene .25 .60
176 Kevin Seraphin .20 .50
177 Rashard Lewis .30 .75
178 Randy Wittman CO .30 .75
179 Andrew Bogut .25 .60
180 Stephen Curry 2.50 6.00
181 David Lee .20 .50
182 Dorell Wright .20 .50
183 Nate Robinson .20 .50
184 Brandon Rush .20 .50
185 Richard Jefferson .25 .60
186 Mark Jackson CO .25 .60
187 Blake Griffin .30 .75
188 Chauncey Billups .40 1.00
189 Chris Paul .60 1.50
190 Mo Williams .25 .60
191 Nick Young .20 .50
192 Eric Bledsoe .25 .60
193 DeAndre Jordan .25 .60
194 Caron Butler .25 .60
195 Vinny Del Negro CO .20 .50
196 Ramon Sessions .20 .50
197 Andrew Bynum .20 .50
198 Kobe Bryant 2.50 6.00
199 Metta World Peace .25 .60
200 Pau Gasol .50 1.25
201 Matt Barnes .20 .50
202 Devin Ebanks .20 .50
203 Mike Brown CO .30 .75
204 Shannon Brown .30 .75
205 Marcin Gortat .20 .50
206 Grant Hill .50 1.25
207 Robin Lopez .20 .50
208 Steve Nash .60 1.50
209 Channing Frye .20 .50
210 Alvin Gentry CO .30 .75
211 Marcus Thornton .20 .50
212 DeMarcus Cousins .30 .75
213 Tyreke Evans .25 .60
214 Terrence Williams .20 .50
215 Jason Thompson .20 .50
216 John Salmons .25 .60
217 Keith Smart CO .30 .75
218 Gerald Henderson .30 .75
219 Corey Maggette .25 .60
220 D.J. Augustin .20 .50
221 Byron Mullens .20 .50
222 Mike Dunlap CO .30 .75
223 Kyrie Irving RC 4.00 10.00
224 Derrick Williams RC .40 1.00
225 Enes Kanter RC .60 1.50
226 Tristan Thompson RC .60 1.50
227 Jan Vesely RC .40 1.00
228 Bismack Biyombo RC .50 1.25
229 Brandon Knight RC .50 1.25
230 Kemba Walker RC 1.50 4.00
231 Jimmer Fredette RC .60 1.50
232 Klay Thompson RC 4.00 10.00
233 Alec Burks RC .60 1.50
234 Markieff Morris RC .60 1.50
235 Marcus Morris RC .60 1.50
236 Kawhi Leonard RC 5.00 12.00
237 Nikola Vucevic RC 1.50 4.00
238 Iman Shumpert RC .50 1.25
239 Chris Singleton RC .40 1.00
240 Tobias Harris RC 1.25 3.00
241 Nolan Smith RC .40 1.00
242 Kenneth Faried RC .50 1.25
243 Reggie Jackson RC .60 1.50
244 MarShon Brooks RC .40 1.00
245 Jordan Hamilton RC .40 1.00
246 JaJuan Johnson RC .40 1.00
247 Norris Cole RC .40 1.00
248 Cory Joseph RC .50 1.25
249 Jimmy Butler RC 4.00 10.00
250 Isaiah Thomas RC .75 2.00
251 Charles Jenkins RC .40 1.00
252 Chandler Parsons RC .50 1.25
253 Lavoy Allen RC .40 1.00
254 Jeremy Tyler RC .40 1.00
255 Jon Leuer RC .40 1.00
256 Jeremy Pargo RC .40 1.00
257 Greg Stiemsma RC .40 1.00
258 Andrew Goudelock RC .40 1.00
259 Josh Harrellson RC .40 1.00
260 Elliot Williams .20 .50
261 Vernon Macklin RC .40 1.00
262 Mickell Gladness RC .50 1.25
263 Jordan Williams RC .50 1.25
264 Terrel Harris RC .40 1.00
265 Josh Selby RC .40 1.00
266 DeAndre Liggins RC .40 1.00
267 Jerome Jordan .20 .50
268 Derrick Byars .20 .50
269 Tyler Honeycutt RC .40 1.00
270 Justin Harper RC .40 1.00
271 Shelvin Mack RC .50 1.25
272 Trey Thompkins RC .40 1.00
273 Julyan Stone RC .40 1.00
274 Walker Russell RC .50 1.25
275 Anthony Davis RC 5.00 12.00
276 Michael Kidd-Gilchrist RC .50 1.25
277 Bradley Beal RC 3.00 8.00
278 Dion Waiters RC .50 1.25
279 Thomas Robinson RC .40 1.00
280 Damian Lillard RC 4.00 10.00
281 Harrison Barnes RC .75 2.00
282 Terrence Ross RC 1.00 2.50
283 Andre Drummond RC 1.00 2.50
284 Austin Rivers RC .60 1.50
285 Meyers Leonard RC .50 1.25
286 Jeremy Lamb RC .60 1.50
287 John Henson RC .50 1.25
288 Moe Harkless RC .50 1.25
289 Tyler Zeller RC .40 1.00
290 Evan Fournier RC .60 1.50
291 Perry Jones RC .40 1.00
292 Bernard James RC .40 1.00
293 Quincy Acy RC .40 1.00
294 Quincy Miller RC .40 1.00
295 2012 West All-Stars .40 1.00
296 2012 East All-Stars .40 1.00
297 Serge Ibaka .25 .60
298 Rajon Rondo .40 1.00
299 Chris Paul .60 1.50
300 Dwight Howard .40 1.00
KD1 K.Durant Durantula 125.00 300.00
MH1 Miami Heat SP 12.00 30.00

2012-13 Hoops 89-90 Buyback Autographs

39 Ralph Sampson 20.00 50.00
178 Hakeem Olajuwon AS 50.00 125.00
183 Dan Majerle 35.00 70.00
244 Scottie Pippen 125.00 225.00
271 Vernon Maxwell 25.00 60.00

2012-13 Hoops Action Photos

COMPLETE SET (20) 8.00 20.00
1 Kobe Bryant 4.00 10.00
2 Kevin Durant 2.00 5.00
3 LeBron James 4.00 10.00
4 Dwyane Wade 1.00 2.50
5 Kevin Love .50 1.25
6 Dwight Howard .60 1.50
7 Derrick Rose .75 2.00
8 Chris Paul 1.00 2.50
9 Dirk Nowitzki 1.25 3.00
10 Russell Westbrook .75 2.00
11 Carmelo Anthony .75 2.00
12 Amare Stoudemire .50 1.25
13 Paul Pierce .75 2.00
14 Blake Griffin .50 1.25
15 LaMarcus Aldridge .50 1.25
16 Rajon Rondo .60 1.50
17 Serge Ibaka .40 1.00
18 Andrew Bynum .30 .75
19 James Harden 1.00 2.50
20 Chris Bosh .60 1.50

2012-13 Hoops Autographs

1 Avery Bradley SP 10.00 25.00
2 Brandon Bass 2.50 6.00
7 Doc Rivers CO 15.00 40.00
9 Brook Lopez SP 15.00 40.00
14 Avery Johnson CO 5.00 12.00
15 Amare Stoudemire SP 25.00 60.00
17 Landry Fields 2.50 6.00
19 Jeremy Lin SP 40.00 80.00
20 Steve Novak 2.50 6.00
24 Jrue Holiday SP 5.00 12.00
27 Evan Turner SP 5.00 12.00
30 Andrea Bargnani SP 5.00 12.00
32 Gary Forbes 2.50 6.00
33 Jose Calderon 2.50 6.00
42 Vince Carter SP 40.00 80.00
44 Rick Carlisle CO SP 20.00 50.00
45 Kyle Lowry 4.00 10.00
46 Kevin Martin SP 5.00 12.00
47 Luis Scola 3.00 8.00
48 Chase Budinger 2.50 6.00
49 Patrick Patterson 2.50 6.00
50 Goran Dragic 12.00 30.00
51 Kevin McHale CO SP 15.00 40.00
53 Mike Conley 4.00 10.00
56 Zach Randolph SP 20.00 50.00
57 Lester Hudson 2.50 6.00
58 Dante Cunningham 2.50 6.00
60 Emeka Okafor SP 5.00 12.00
63 Eric Gordon SP 10.00 25.00
67 DeJuan Blair 2.50 6.00
68 Boris Diaw 3.00 8.00
72 Danny Green 2.50 6.00
76 Joakim Noah SP 8.00 20.00
78 Richard Hamilton SP 10.00 25.00
79 Taj Gibson 2.50 6.00
80 Ronnie Brewer 2.50 6.00
84 Antawn Jamison SP 8.00 20.00
85 Daniel Gibson 2.50 6.00
86 Byron Scott CO SP 5.00 12.00
88 Greg Monroe 2.50 6.00
90 Tayshaun Prince SP 5.00 12.00
95 Paul George SP 15.00 40.00
98 George Hill 3.00 8.00
99 A.J. Price 2.50 6.00
103 Monta Ellis SP 5.00 12.00
104 Ersan Ilyasova 2.50 6.00
108 Arron Afflalo 2.50 6.00
109 Danilo Gallinari SP 5.00 12.00
111 Wilson Chandler 3.00 8.00
113 Andre Miller 3.00 8.00
116 Kevin Love SP 15.00 40.00
117 Luke Ridnour 2.50 6.00
120 Ricky Rubio SP 15.00 40.00
121 Wesley Johnson SP 5.00 12.00
127 Jonny Flynn 2.50 6.00
129 Jamal Crawford 5.00 12.00
134 Kendrick Perkins 5.00 12.00
135 Kevin Durant SP 100.00 250.00
136 Russell Westbrook SP 60.00 150.00
142 DeMarre Carroll 2.50 6.00
144 Paul Millsap 2.50 6.00
145 Derrick Favors SP 5.00 12.00
146 Josh Howard SP 5.00 12.00
148 Al Horford SP 8.00 20.00
149 Jeff Teague 2.50 6.00
161 Udonis Haslem 2.50 6.00
162 Shane Battier SP 10.00 25.00
173 Trevor Booker 2.50 6.00
174 Jordan Crawford SP 5.00 12.00
176 Kevin Seraphin 2.50 6.00
179 Andrew Bogut SP 20.00 50.00
180 Stephen Curry SP 500.00 1,000.00
187 Blake Griffin SP 20.00 50.00
188 Chauncey Billups SP 10.00 25.00
189 Chris Paul SP EXCH 50.00 120.00
190 Mo Williams SP 8.00 20.00
192 Eric Bledsoe 6.00 15.00
198 Kobe Bryant SP 400.00 800.00
202 Devin Ebanks SP 5.00 12.00
205 Marcin Gortat 8.00 20.00
207 Robin Lopez 2.50 6.00
208 Steve Nash SP 40.00 100.00
209 Channing Frye SP 5.00 12.00
212 DeMarcus Cousins SP 25.00 60.00
214 Terrence Williams 2.50 6.00
218 Gerald Henderson 2.50 6.00
223 Kyrie Irving 60.00 150.00
224 Derrick Williams 2.50 6.00
225 Enes Kanter 4.00 10.00
226 Tristan Thompson 4.00 10.00
227 Jan Vesely 2.50 6.00
228 Bismack Biyombo 3.00 8.00
229 Brandon Knight 3.00 8.00
230 Kemba Walker 8.00 20.00
231 Jimmer Fredette 4.00 10.00
232 Klay Thompson 100.00 250.00
233 Alec Burks 4.00 10.00
234 Markieff Morris 4.00 10.00
235 Marcus Morris 4.00 10.00
236 Kawhi Leonard 300.00 600.00
238 Iman Shumpert 3.00 8.00
239 Chris Singleton 2.50 6.00
240 Tobias Harris 8.00 20.00
241 Nolan Smith 2.50 6.00
242 Kenneth Faried 3.00 8.00
243 Reggie Jackson 4.00 10.00
244 MarShon Brooks 2.50 6.00
245 Jordan Hamilton 2.50 6.00
246 JaJuan Johnson 2.50 6.00
247 Norris Cole 2.50 6.00
248 Cory Joseph 3.00 8.00
249 Jimmy Butler 40.00 100.00
250 Isaiah Thomas 5.00 12.00
251 Charles Jenkins 2.50 6.00
252 Chandler Parsons 3.00 8.00
253 Lavoy Allen 2.50 6.00
254 Jeremy Tyler 2.50 6.00
255 Jon Leuer 2.50 6.00
257 Greg Stiemsma 2.50 6.00
258 Andrew Goudelock 2.50 6.00
259 Josh Harrellson 2.50 6.00
261 Vernon Macklin 2.50 6.00
263 Jordan Williams 3.00 8.00
265 Josh Selby 2.50 6.00
266 DeAndre Liggins 2.50 6.00
268 Derrick Byars 2.50 6.00
269 Tyler Honeycutt 2.50 6.00
271 Shelvin Mack 3.00 8.00
272 Trey Thompkins 2.50 6.00
275 Anthony Davis 150.00 400.00
276 Michael Kidd-Gilchrist 3.00 8.00
277 Bradley Beal 20.00 50.00
278 Dion Waiters 3.00 8.00
279 Thomas Robinson 2.50 6.00
281 Harrison Barnes 10.00 25.00
282 Terrence Ross 6.00 15.00
283 Andre Drummond 15.00 40.00
284 Austin Rivers 4.00 10.00
285 Meyers Leonard 3.00 8.00
286 Jeremy Lamb 4.00 10.00
287 John Henson 3.00 8.00
288 Moe Harkless 3.00 8.00
289 Tyler Zeller 2.50 6.00
290 Evan Fournier 4.00 10.00
291 Perry Jones 2.50 6.00
292 Bernard James 2.50 6.00
293 Quincy Acy 2.50 6.00
294 Quincy Miller 2.50 6.00
299 Chris Paul SP EXCH 50.00 120.00

2012-13 Hoops Board Members

COMPLETE SET (20) 6.00 15.00
1 Kevin Love .50 1.25
2 Dwight Howard .60 1.50
3 Andrew Bynum .30 .75
4 Kris Humphries .30 .75
5 Blake Griffin .50 1.25
6 DeMarcus Cousins .50 1.25
7 Pau Gasol .75 2.00
8 Marc Gasol .50 1.25
9 Marcin Gortat .30 .75
10 Tyson Chandler .40 1.00
11 Joakim Noah .40 1.00
12 Greg Monroe .30 .75
13 Josh Smith .30 .75
14 Al Jefferson .30 .75
15 David Lee .30 .75
16 Tim Duncan 1.25 3.00
17 Kevin Durant 2.00 5.00
18 LeBron James 4.00 10.00
19 DeAndre Jordan .40 1.00
20 LaMarcus Aldridge .50 1.25

2012-13 Hoops Courtside

COMPLETE SET (20) 12.00 30.00
1 Chris Paul 1.25 3.00
2 Tony Parker 1.00 2.50
3 Antawn Jamison .50 1.25
4 Derrick Rose 1.00 2.50
5 Rajon Rondo .75 2.00
6 Dwyane Wade 1.25 3.00
7 John Wall .75 2.00
8 Steve Nash 1.25 3.00
9 David Lee .40 1.00
10 Ricky Rubio .50 1.25
11 Kevin Love .60 1.50
12 Russell Westbrook 1.00 2.50
13 Deron Williams .50 1.25

14 LeBron James 5.00 12.00
15 Kobe Bryant 5.00 12.00
16 Kevin Durant 2.50 6.00
17 Blake Griffin .60 1.50
18 LaMarcus Aldridge .60 1.50
19 Dwight Howard .75 2.00
20 Dirk Nowitzki 1.50 4.00

2012-13 Hoops Draft Night

COMPLETE SET (20) 40.00 100.00
1 Anthony Davis 20.00 50.00
2 Michael Kidd-Gilchrist .75 2.00
3 Bradley Beal 5.00 12.00
4 Dion Waiters .75 2.00
5 Thomas Robinson .60 1.50
6 Damian Lillard 20.00 50.00
7 Harrison Barnes 1.25 3.00
8 Terrence Ross 1.50 4.00
9 Andre Drummond 1.50 4.00
10 Austin Rivers 1.00 2.50
11 Meyers Leonard .75 2.00
12 Jeremy Lamb 1.00 2.50
13 John Henson .75 2.00
14 Moe Harkless .75 2.00
15 Tyler Zeller .60 1.50
16 Evan Fournier 1.00 2.50
17 Perry Jones .60 1.50
18 Bernard James .60 1.50
19 Quincy Acy .60 1.50
20 Quincy Miller .60 1.50

2012-13 Hoops Draft Night Autographs

1 Anthony Davis 150.00 400.00
2 Michael Kidd-Gilchrist 4.00 10.00
3 Bradley Beal 50.00 120.00
4 Dion Waiters 4.00 10.00
5 Thomas Robinson 3.00 8.00
7 Harrison Barnes 6.00 15.00
8 Terrence Ross 8.00 20.00
9 Andre Drummond 15.00 40.00
10 Austin Rivers 5.00 12.00
11 Meyers Leonard 4.00 10.00
12 Jeremy Lamb 5.00 12.00
13 John Henson 4.00 10.00
14 Moe Harkless 4.00 10.00
15 Tyler Zeller 3.00 8.00
16 Evan Fournier 5.00 12.00
17 Perry Jones 3.00 8.00
18 Bernard James 3.00 8.00
19 Quincy Acy 3.00 8.00
20 Quincy Miller 3.00 8.00

2012-13 Hoops Franchise Greats

COMPLETE SET (20) 30.00 80.00
1 Magic Johnson 5.00 12.00
2 Kareem Abdul-Jabbar 5.00 12.00
3 Shaquille O'Neal 5.00 12.00
4 Wilt Chamberlain 5.00 12.00
5 Larry Bird 5.00 12.00
6 John Havlicek 3.00 8.00
7 Bill Russell 5.00 12.00
8 Patrick Ewing 2.50 6.00
9 Julius Erving 4.00 10.00
10 Scottie Pippen 4.00 10.00
11 John Stockton 3.00 8.00
12 Karl Malone 2.50 6.00
13 Dominique Wilkins 2.00 5.00
14 Isiah Thomas 3.00 8.00
15 Hakeem Olajuwon 3.00 8.00
16 Kobe Bryant 12.00 30.00
17 Dirk Nowitzki 4.00 10.00
18 Paul Pierce 2.50 6.00
19 Tim Duncan 4.00 10.00
20 Kevin Durant 6.00 15.00

2012-13 Hoops Kobe's All-Rookie Team

1 Isaiah Thomas 6.00 15.00
2 Kyrie Irving 30.00 80.00
3 Derrick Williams 3.00 8.00
4 Kemba Walker 12.00 30.00
5 Jimmer Fredette 5.00 12.00
6 Markieff Morris 5.00 12.00
7 Kenneth Faried 4.00 10.00
8 Brandon Knight 4.00 10.00
9 Kawhi Leonard 40.00 100.00
10 MarShon Brooks 3.00 8.00
11 Klay Thompson 30.00 80.00
12 Iman Shumpert 4.00 10.00
13 Chandler Parsons 4.00 10.00
14 Bismack Biyombo 4.00 10.00
15 Tristan Thompson 5.00 12.00
16 Ricky Rubio 4.00 10.00
17 Norris Cole 3.00 8.00
18 Alec Burks 5.00 12.00
19 Gustavo Ayon 3.00 8.00
20 Nikola Vucevic 12.00 30.00
21 Ivan Johnson 3.00 8.00
22 Enes Kanter 5.00 12.00
23 Lavoy Allen 3.00 8.00
24 Greg Stiemsma 3.00 8.00
25 Josh Harrellson 3.00 8.00
26 Darius Morris 4.00 10.00
27 Daniel Orton 3.00 8.00
28 E'Twaun Moore 4.00 10.00
29 Andrew Goudelock 3.00 8.00
30 Tobias Harris 10.00 25.00

2012-13 Hoops Rising Stars

COMPLETE SET (9) 8.00 20.00
1 Blake Griffin .75 2.00
2 Ricky Rubio .60 1.50
3 Russell Westbrook 1.25 3.00
4 John Wall 1.00 2.50
5 Jeremy Lin 1.25 3.00
6 Kevin Love .75 2.00
7 Derrick Rose 1.25 3.00
8 Avery Bradley .50 1.25
9 Tyreke Evans .60 1.50

2012-13 Hoops Rookie Impact

COMPLETE SET (28) 12.00 30.00
1 Kyrie Irving 3.00 8.00
2 Brandon Knight .40 1.00
3 MarShon Brooks .30 .75
4 Klay Thompson 3.00 8.00
5 Kemba Walker 1.25 3.00
6 Isaiah Thomas .60 1.50
7 Kenneth Faried .40 1.00
8 Chandler Parsons .40 1.00
9 Iman Shumpert .40 1.00
10 Derrick Williams .30 .75
11 Tristan Thompson .50 1.25
12 Kawhi Leonard 4.00 10.00
13 Jimmer Fredette .50 1.25
14 Markieff Morris .50 1.25
15 Alec Burks .50 1.25
16 Norris Cole .30 .75
17 Josh Harrellson .30 .75
18 Gustavo Ayon .30 .75
19 Charles Jenkins .30 .75
20 Bismack Biyombo .40 1.00
21 Jan Vesely .30 .75
22 Jimmy Butler 3.00 8.00
23 Enes Kanter .50 1.25
24 Jeremy Tyler .30 .75
25 Ricky Rubio .40 1.00
26 Tobias Harris 1.00 2.50
27 Andrew Goudelock .30 .75
28 Lavoy Allen .30 .75

2012-13 Hoops Rookie Impact Autographs

1 Kyrie Irving 75.00 200.00
2 Brandon Knight 4.00 10.00
3 MarShon Brooks 3.00 8.00
4 Klay Thompson 60.00 150.00
5 Kemba Walker 25.00 60.00
6 Isaiah Thomas 6.00 15.00
7 Kenneth Faried 4.00 10.00
8 Chandler Parsons 4.00 10.00
9 Iman Shumpert 4.00 10.00
10 Derrick Williams 3.00 8.00
11 Tristan Thompson 5.00 12.00
12 Kawhi Leonard 75.00 200.00
13 Jimmer Fredette 5.00 12.00
14 Markieff Morris 5.00 12.00
15 Alec Burks 5.00 12.00
16 Norris Cole 3.00 8.00
17 Josh Harrellson 3.00 8.00
18 Gustavo Ayon 3.00 8.00
19 Charles Jenkins 3.00 8.00
20 Bismack Biyombo 4.00 10.00
21 Jan Vesely 3.00 8.00
22 Jimmy Butler 40.00 100.00
23 Enes Kanter 5.00 12.00
24 Jeremy Tyler 3.00 8.00
26 Tobias Harris 10.00 25.00
27 Andrew Goudelock 3.00 8.00
28 Lavoy Allen 3.00 8.00

2012-13 Hoops Spark Plugs

COMPLETE SET (20) 6.00 15.00
1 James Harden 1.25 3.00
2 Jason Terry .50 1.25
3 Manu Ginobili 1.25 3.00
4 Joakim Noah .50 1.25
5 Tyson Chandler .50 1.25
6 Anderson Varejao .40 1.00
7 Steve Novak .40 1.00
8 Chase Budinger .40 1.00
9 Shane Battier .50 1.25
10 Mo Williams .50 1.25
11 Al Harrington .50 1.25
12 Louis Williams .50 1.25
13 J.R. Smith .60 1.50
14 Glen Davis .40 1.00
15 Tyler Hansbrough .40 1.00
16 Thaddeus Young .40 1.00
17 O.J. Mayo .40 1.00
18 George Hill .50 1.25
19 Jamal Crawford .60 1.50
20 Avery Bradley .40 1.00

2013-14 Hoops

COMPLETE SET (301) 75.00 200.00
1 Al Horford .30 .75
2 Steve Nash .60 1.50
3 Jrue Holiday .40 1.00
4 Pau Gasol .50 1.25
5 John Jenkins .20 .50
6 Spencer Hawes .20 .50
7 Steve Blake .20 .50
8 Lavoy Allen .20 .50
9 Kobe Bryant 2.50 6.00
10 DeMar DeRozan .40 1.00
11 Avery Bradley .20 .50
12 Darrell Arthur .20 .50
13 Evan Turner .20 .50
14 Jordan Hill .20 .50
15 Jason Terry .25 .60
16 Thaddeus Young .20 .50
17 Marc Gasol .30 .75
18 Glen Davis .20 .50
19 Jamal Crawford .30 .75
20 Amir Johnson .20 .50
21 Jeff Green .20 .50
22 Mike Conley .30 .75
23 Nikola Vucevic .40 1.00
24 Matt Barnes .20 .50
25 Jordan Crawford .20 .50
26 Jason Richardson .30 .75
27 Quincy Pondexter .20 .50
28 Tobias Harris .30 .75
29 Eric Bledsoe .25 .60
30 Kawhi Leonard 1.00 2.50
31 Brook Lopez .30 .75
32 Tayshaun Prince .30 .75
33 Serge Ibaka .25 .60
34 DeAndre Jordan .25 .60
35 Deron Williams .25 .60
36 Channing Frye .20 .50
37 Tony Wroten .20 .50
38 Thabo Sefolosha .20 .50
39 Caron Butler .25 .60
40 Gary Neal .20 .50
41 Kris Humphries .20 .50
42 Zach Randolph .25 .60
43 Jeremy Lamb .25 .60
44 Blake Griffin .30 .75
45 Tornike Shengelia .20 .50
46 Goran Dragic .25 .60
47 Chris Bosh .40 1.00
48 Arron Afflalo .20 .50
49 Roy Hibbert .20 .50
50 Cory Joseph .20 .50
51 Michael Kidd-Gilchrist .20 .50
52 Dwyane Wade .60 1.50
53 Jameer Nelson .20 .50
54 Louis Williams .25 .60
55 Kemba Walker .30 .75
56 Kendall Marshall .20 .50
57 Joel Anthony .20 .50
58 Maurice Harkless .20 .50
59 Paul George .50 1.25
60 Tony Parker .50 1.25
61 Ramon Sessions .20 .50
62 LeBron James 2.50 6.00
63 Reggie Jackson .25 .60
64 Orlando Johnson .20 .50
65 Kevin Garnett .75 2.00
66 Luis Scola .25 .60
67 Mike Miller .25 .60
68 Russell Westbrook .50 1.25
69 Lance Stephenson .25 .60
70 Tim Duncan .75 2.00
71 Jimmy Butler .60 1.50
72 Shane Battier .25 .60
73 Kevin Durant 1.00 2.50
74 George Hill .25 .60
75 Carlos Boozer .25 .60
76 Marcin Gortat .20 .50
77 Norris Cole .20 .50
78 Nick Collison .20 .50
79 Patrick Beverley .20 .50
80 Matt Bonner .20 .50
81 Joakim Noah .30 .75
82 Udonis Haslem .25 .60
83 Steve Novak .20 .50
84 Omer Asik .20 .50
85 Kirk Hinrich .25 .60
86 Marcus Morris .20 .50
87 Ray Allen .50 1.25
88 Kendrick Perkins .20 .50
89 Jeremy Lin .50 1.25
90 Danny Green .25 .60
91 Luol Deng .25 .60
92 Rashard Lewis .25 .60
93 Pablo Prigioni .20 .50
94 James Harden .60 1.50
95 Anderson Varejao .20 .50
96 Markieff Morris .20 .50
97 Mario Chalmers .25 .60
98 Raymond Felton .20 .50
99 Chandler Parsons .20 .50
100 Marcus Thornton .20 .50
101 C.J. Miles .20 .50
102 Ersan Ilyasova .20 .50
103 Iman Shumpert .20 .50
104 Carlos Delfino .20 .50
105 Kyrie Irving 1.00 2.50
106 Damian Lillard 1.00 2.50
107 John Henson .20 .50
108 Tyson Chandler .25 .60
109 Draymond Green .50 1.25
110 John Salmons .20 .50
111 Nene .25 .60
112 Luc Mbah a Moute .20 .50
113 Carmelo Anthony .50 1.25
114 David Lee .25 .60
115 Dirk Nowitzki .75 2.00
116 LaMarcus Aldridge .30 .75
117 Larry Sanders .25 .60
118 Marcus Camby .25 .60
119 Kent Bazemore .20 .50
120 Jimmer Fredette .30 .75
121 Jae Crowder .20 .50
122 Kevin Seraphin .20 .50
123 Amar'e Stoudemire .30 .75
124 Stephen Curry 2.50 6.00
125 Vince Carter .60 1.50
126 Nicolas Batum .25 .60
127 Derrick Williams .25 .60
128 Ryan Anderson .20 .50
129 Klay Thompson 1.00 2.50
130 Isaiah Thomas .25 .60
131 Danilo Gallinari .25 .60
132 J.J. Barea .25 .60
133 John Wall .40 1.00
134 Harrison Barnes .30 .75
135 Evan Fournier .25 .60
136 Victor Claver .20 .50
137 Kevin Love .30 .75
138 Robin Lopez .20 .50
139 Andrew Bogut .25 .60
140 DeMarcus Cousins .30 .75
141 JaVale McGee .25 .60
142 Andray Blatche .20 .50
143 Eric Gordon .25 .60
144 Rodney Stuckey .20 .50
145 Ty Lawson .25 .60
146 Wesley Matthews .20 .50
147 Jared Dudley .20 .50
148 Darius Miller .20 .50
149 Jonas Jerebko .20 .50
150 Will Barton .20 .50
151 Andre Drummond .30 .75
152 Ricky Rubio .30 .75
153 Brian Roberts .20 .50
154 Greg Monroe .25 .60
155 Wilson Chandler .20 .50
156 Trevor Booker .20 .50
157 Anthony Davis 1.00 2.50
158 Austin Rivers .25 .60
159 Brandon Knight .25 .60
160 Chuck Hayes .20 .50
161 Jonas Valanciunas .25 .60
162 Derrick Favors .20 .50
163 Bradley Beal .50 1.25
164 Kyle Lowry .25 .60
165 Alec Burks .25 .60
166 Terrence Ross .25 .60
167 Alexey Shved .20 .50
168 Gordon Hayward .25 .60
169 Rudy Gay .25 .60
170 Emeka Okafor .25 .60
171 Enes Kanter .20 .50
172 Landry Fields .20 .50
173 Greivis Vasquez .20 .50
174 Tristan Thompson .20 .50
175 Jan Vesely .20 .50
176 Quincy Acy .20 .50
177 Chris Andersen .25 .60
178 Jeff Teague .20 .50
179 Marco Belinelli .20 .50
180 Jeremy Evans .20 .50
181 Tyreke Evans .25 .60
182 Derrick Rose .50 1.25
183 Chris Copeland .20 .50
184 Andrei Kirilenko .30 .75
185 Chris Paul .60 1.50
186 Kenneth Faried .25 .60
187 J.R. Smith .30 .75
188 Nick Young .25 .60
189 Jarrett Jack .25 .60
190 Chauncey Billups .40 1.00
191 Tony Allen .25 .60
192 Richard Jefferson .20 .50
193 Elton Brand .25 .60
194 Dorell Wright .20 .50
195 Manu Ginobili .60 1.50
196 Shawn Marion .25 .60
197 Gerald Henderson .20 .50
198 Chris Kaman .25 .60
199 Ben Gordon .25 .60
200 Paul Pierce .50 1.25
201 Martell Webster .20 .50
202 Tiago Splitter .20 .50
203 Francisco Garcia .20 .50
204 Tyler Hansbrough .20 .50
205 Earl Clark .20 .50
206 J.J. Redick .30 .75
207 Nikola Pekovic .25 .60
208 Kevin Martin .25 .60
209 Andrew Nicholson .20 .50
210 DeJuan Blair .20 .50
211 Trevor Ariza .20 .50
212 Andris Biedrins .20 .50
213 David West .25 .60
214 Dwight Howard .40 1.00
215 Mike Dunleavy .20 .50
216 Chase Budinger .20 .50
217 Boris Diaw .25 .60
218 Gerald Wallace .25 .60
219 Brendan Haywood .20 .50
220 D.J. Augustin .20 .50
221 Al Jefferson .20 .50
222 J.J. Hickson .20 .50
223 Brandon Rush .20 .50
224 Andrea Bargnani .20 .50
225 Dion Waiters .20 .50
226 Monta Ellis .20 .50
227 Paul Millsap .25 .60
228 Arnett Moultrie .20 .50
229 Rajon Rondo .40 1.00
230 Samuel Dalembert .20 .50
231 Brandon Bass .20 .50
232 Danny Granger .20 .50
233 Kwame Brown .20 .50
234 Kenyon Martin .30 .75
235 Jason Smith .20 .50
236 Brandon Jennings .20 .50
237 Wesley Johnson .20 .50
238 Marvin Williams .20 .50
239 Courtney Lee .20 .50
240 Mo Williams .25 .60
241 Josh Smith .20 .50
242 Nate Robinson .20 .50
243 Kyle Korver .25 .60
244 Taj Gibson .20 .50
245 Byron Mullens .20 .50
246 Andre Iguodala .30 .75
247 Carl Landry .20 .50
248 Zaza Pachulia .20 .50
249 Devin Harris .20 .50
250 O.J. Mayo .20 .50
251 Corey Brewer .20 .50
252 Andrew Bynum .25 .60
253 Jerryd Bayless .20 .50
254 Metta World Peace .25 .60
255 Al-Farouq Aminu .20 .50
256 Darren Collison .20 .50
257 Randy Foye .20 .50
258 Jason Maxiell .20 .50
259 Brandan Wright .20 .50
260 Jose Calderon .20 .50
261 Anthony Bennett RC .40 1.00
262 Victor Oladipo RC 1.00 2.50
263 Otto Porter RC .60 1.50
264 Cody Zeller RC .50 1.25
265 Alex Len RC .50 1.25
266 Nerlens Noel RC .50 1.25
267 Ben McLemore RC .50 1.25
268 Kentavious Caldwell-Pope RC .60 1.50
269 Trey Burke RC .50 1.25
270 C.J. McCollum RC 1.50 4.00
271 M.Carter-Williams RC .50 1.25
272 Steven Adams RC 1.00 2.50
273 Kelly Olynyk RC .50 1.25
274 Shabazz Muhammad RC .40 1.00
275 G.Antetokounmpo RC 30.00 80.00
276 Ray McCallum RC .40 1.00
277 Dennis Schroeder RC 1.25 3.00
278 Shane Larkin RC .40 1.00
279 Sergey Karasev RC .40 1.00
280 Tony Snell RC .50 1.25
281 Gorgui Dieng RC .50 1.25
282 Mason Plumlee RC .50 1.25
283 Solomon Hill RC .50 1.25
284 Tim Hardaway Jr. RC .75 2.00
285 Reggie Bullock RC .50 1.25
286 Andre Roberson RC .50 1.25
287 Rudy Gobert RC 1.50 4.00
288 Archie Goodwin RC .40 1.00
289 Allen Crabbe RC .40 1.00
290 Carrick Felix RC .40 1.00
291 Isaiah Canaan RC .40 1.00
292 Glen Rice Jr. RC .40 1.00
293 Tony Mitchell RC .40 1.00
294 Grant Jerrett RC .40 1.00
295 Jeff Withey RC .40 1.00
296 Jamaal Franklin RC .40 1.00
297 Phil Pressey RC .40 1.00
298 Peyton Siva RC .40 1.00
299 Ryan Kelly RC .40 1.00
300 Erik Murphy RC .40 1.00
301 Miami Heat Champions 5.00 12.00

2013-14 Hoops Artist's Proofs

*AP VETS: 2X TO 5X BASE HI
*AP RCs: 1X TO 2.5X BASE HI

2013-14 Hoops Blue

*BLUE VETS: .75X TO 2X BASE HI
*BLUE RCs: .75X TO 2X BASE HI
275 Giannis Antetokounmpo 150.00 400.00

2013-14 Hoops Gold

*GOLD VETS: .6X TO 1.5X BASE HI
*GOLD RCs: .6X TO 1.5X BASE HI
275 Giannis Antetokounmpo 125.00 300.00

2013-14 Hoops Red

*RED VETS: 1X TO 2.5X BASE HI
*RED RCs: 1X TO 2.5X BASE HI
275 Giannis Antetokounmpo 150.00 400.00

2013-14 Hoops Red Backs

*RED BACK VETS: .6X TO 1.5X BASE HI
*RED BACK RCs: .6X TO 1.5X BASE HI

2013-14 Hoops Above the Rim

1 Kawhi Leonard 8.00 20.00
2 Anthony Davis 8.00 20.00
3 Andre Iguodala 2.50 6.00
4 Paul George 4.00 10.00
5 Dwyane Wade 5.00 12.00
6 JaVale McGee 2.00 5.00
7 Gerald Green 2.00 5.00
8 Zach Randolph 2.00 5.00
9 Tyson Chandler 2.00 5.00
10 Kevin Durant 8.00 20.00
11 LeBron James 20.00 50.00
12 Kenneth Faried 2.00 5.00
13 Russell Westbrook 4.00 10.00
14 Harrison Barnes 2.50 6.00
15 Carmelo Anthony 4.00 10.00
16 Kobe Bryant 20.00 50.00
17 Joakim Noah 2.50 6.00
18 Jeremy Evans 1.50 4.00
19 Bradley Beal 4.00 10.00
20 Michael Kidd-Gilchrist 1.50 4.00
21 Andre Drummond 2.50 6.00
22 Blake Griffin 2.50 6.00
23 J.R. Smith 2.50 6.00
24 Terrence Ross 2.00 5.00
25 Vince Carter 5.00 12.00

2013-14 Hoops Action Shots

COMPLETE SET (25) 5.00 12.00
1 Jrue Holiday .60 1.50
2 Dwyane Wade 1.00 2.50
3 Kevin Durant 1.50 4.00
4 Manu Ginobili 1.00 2.50
5 Ty Lawson .30 .75
6 Joe Johnson .40 1.00
7 Kevin Garnett 1.25 3.00
8 Harrison Barnes .50 1.25
9 Brandon Knight .40 1.00
10 Dirk Nowitzki 1.25 3.00
11 Tyreke Evans .40 1.00
12 Kobe Bryant 4.00 10.00
13 LeBron James 4.00 10.00
14 Iman Shumpert .30 .75
15 Kevin Love .50 1.25
16 Derrick Favors .30 .75
17 Joakim Noah .50 1.25
18 Mike Conley .50 1.25
19 Damian Lillard 1.50 4.00
20 Kemba Walker .50 1.25
21 Jimmy Butler 1.00 2.50
22 DeMar DeRozan .60 1.50
23 John Wall .60 1.50
24 Larry Sanders .30 .75
25 Paul George .75 2.00

2013-14 Hoops Authentics

PRIME PRINT RUNS B/WN 1-25 COPIES PER
NO PRIME PRICING ON QTY 20 OR LESS
1 Kobe Bryant 8.00 20.00
2 Al Jefferson 2.00 5.00
3 Blake Griffin 3.00 8.00
4 Carmelo Anthony 5.00 12.00
5 Danny Granger 2.00 5.00
6 David Lee 2.00 5.00
7 DeQuan Jones 2.00 5.00
8 Devin Harris 2.00 5.00
9 Ekpe Udoh 2.00 5.00
10 Glen Davis 2.00 5.00
11 Hedo Turkoglu 2.50 6.00
12 Tristan Thompson 2.00 5.00
13 Jeff Teague 2.00 5.00
14 Joe Johnson 2.50 6.00
15 John Wall 4.00 10.00
16 Kevin Garnett 8.00 20.00
17 Kyle Lowry 3.00 8.00
18 LeBron James 25.00 60.00
19 Luol Deng 2.50 6.00
20 Marcus Camby 2.50 6.00
21 Michael Beasley 2.00 5.00
22 Pablo Prigioni 2.00 5.00
23 Stephen Curry 6.00 15.00
24 Tim Duncan 8.00 20.00
25 Pau Gasol 5.00 12.00
26 Amar'e Stoudemire 3.00 8.00
27 Brandon Jennings 2.00 5.00
29 Danny Green 2.50 6.00
30 David West 2.50 6.00
31 Derrick Favors 2.00 5.00
32 Drew Gooden 2.50 6.00
33 Emeka Okafor 2.50 6.00
34 Goran Dragic 2.50 6.00
35 J.J. Barea 2.50 6.00
37 Jeremy Lin 5.00 12.00
38 Joel Anthony 2.00 5.00
39 Jonas Jerebko 2.00 5.00
40 Kevin Martin 2.50 6.00
41 Lamar Odom 2.50 6.00
42 Will Barton 2.00 5.00
43 Manu Ginobili 6.00 15.00
44 Bradley Beal 5.00 12.00
45 Monta Ellis 2.50 6.00
46 Paul Pierce 5.00 12.00
47 Steve Nash 6.00 15.00
48 Tony Parker 5.00 12.00
49 Kyrie Irving 10.00 25.00
50 Dirk Nowitzki 8.00 20.00
51 Andre Iguodala 3.00 8.00
52 Brook Lopez 3.00 8.00
53 Chris Bosh 4.00 10.00
54 Dante Cunningham 2.00 5.00
55 DeMar DeRozan 4.00 10.00
57 Dwight Howard 4.00 10.00
58 Evan Turner 2.00 5.00
59 Gordon Hayward 2.50 6.00
60 J.R. Smith 3.00 8.00
61 Jason Terry 5.00 12.00
62 Lavoy Allen 2.00 5.00
63 Joel Freeland 2.00 5.00
64 Kent Bazemore 5.00 12.00
65 Avery Bradley 2.00 5.00
66 LaMarcus Aldridge 3.00 8.00
68 Marc Gasol 3.00 8.00
69 Anthony Davis 10.00 25.00
70 Nene 2.50 6.00
71 Richard Hamilton 2.50 6.00
72 Brandon Knight 2.50 6.00
73 Viacheslav Kravtsov 2.00 5.00
74 Taj Gibson 2.00 5.00
75 Kevin Love 3.00 8.00
76 Andre Drummond 3.00 8.00
77 Carlos Delfino 2.00 5.00
78 Daniel Gibson 2.50 6.00
79 Tyreke Evans 2.50 6.00
80 DeMarcus Cousins 3.00 8.00
81 DeShawn Stevenson 2.00 5.00
82 Dwyane Wade 6.00 15.00
83 Gerald Wallace 2.50 6.00
86 JaVale McGee 2.50 6.00
89 Ty Lawson 2.00 5.00
90 Kris Humphries 2.00 5.00
91 Landry Fields 2.00 5.00
92 Luis Scola 2.50 6.00
93 Marcin Gortat 6.00 15.00
94 Austin Rivers 2.50 6.00
95 O.J. Mayo 2.00 5.00
96 Serge Ibaka 2.50 6.00
97 Al Horford 3.00 8.00
98 Kevin Durant 6.00 15.00
99 Darren Collison 2.00 5.00
100 Tyson Chandler 2.50 6.00

2013-14 Hoops Autographs

EXCHANGE DEADLINE 4/28/2015
2 Jeff Taylor 3.00 8.00
3 Brandon Knight 4.00 10.00
4 Derrick Williams 3.00 8.00
5 Maurice Harkless 3.00 8.00
6 Kim English 3.00 8.00
8 Donatas Motiejunas 3.00 8.00
9 Julyan Stone 3.00 8.00
10 James Anderson 3.00 8.00
11 Ekpe Udoh 3.00 8.00
12 Boris Diaw 3.00 8.00
13 Kyle Korver 3.00 8.00
15 Lance Stephenson 5.00 12.00
17 Xavier Henry 5.00 12.00
18 Andrei Kirilenko 5.00 12.00
20 Antawn Jamison 4.00 10.00
21 Carl Landry 3.00 8.00
22 Khris Middleton 8.00 20.00
23 Tyreke Evans 3.00 8.00
24 Kwame Brown 3.00 8.00
25 Dahntay Jones 3.00 8.00
26 C.J. Watson 4.00 10.00
27 Marcus Thornton 3.00 8.00
28 Joe Johnson 8.00 20.00
29 Jeff Green 4.00 10.00
30 Josh Smith 4.00 10.00
31 Patrick Patterson 4.00 10.00
32 John Salmons 3.00 8.00
33 Brandon Rush 3.00 8.00
34 Chris Wilcox 5.00 12.00
35 DeMarre Carroll 3.00 8.00
36 Chase Budinger 3.00 8.00
38 Marreese Speights 3.00 8.00
39 Lance Thomas 3.00 8.00
40 Mike Scott 3.00 8.00
41 Maalik Wayns 3.00 8.00
42 Jan Vesely 4.00 10.00
43 Tony Wroten 4.00 10.00
44 DeAndre Liggins 3.00 8.00
45 Jon Leuer 3.00 8.00
46 Patrick Beverley 3.00 8.00
47 Jordan Hamilton 3.00 8.00
48 Justin Holiday 3.00 8.00
50 Kyle O'Quinn 3.00 8.00
51 Dante Cunningham 3.00 8.00
52 Maurice Taylor 4.00 10.00
53 Travis Best 3.00 8.00
54 Terry Dehere 3.00 8.00
55 Todd Day 3.00 8.00
56 Marcus Liberty 3.00 8.00
57 Hot Rod Williams 3.00 8.00
58 James Robinson 3.00 8.00
59 John Wallace 5.00 12.00
60 Eric Murdock 3.00 8.00
61 Tracy Murray 3.00 8.00
62 Trent Tucker 5.00 12.00
63 Mahmoud Abdul-Rauf 10.00 25.00
64 Craig Hodges 3.00 8.00
65 Michael Bantom 3.00 8.00
66 Jerome Williams 4.00 10.00
67 Greg Minor 4.00 10.00
68 Greg Buckner 3.00 8.00
69 Ish Smith 3.00 8.00
70 Charlie Bell 3.00 8.00
71 Jared Jeffries 3.00 8.00
72 Jannero Pargo 3.00 8.00
73 Marquis Daniels 3.00 8.00
74 Chris Whitney 5.00 12.00
75 Elliot Williams 3.00 8.00
76 Viacheslav Kravtsov 3.00 8.00
77 Nando De Colo 4.00 10.00
78 Herb Williams 3.00 8.00
79 Rory Sparrow 3.00 8.00
80 Otis Birdsong 3.00 8.00
81 Dale Ellis 3.00 8.00
82 Chucky Brown 4.00 10.00
83 Mickael Pietrus 5.00 12.00
84 John Lucas III 3.00 8.00
85 Eric Maynor 5.00 12.00
86 P.J. Tucker 3.00 8.00
87 Greg Stiemsma 3.00 8.00
88 Keith Bogans 5.00 12.00
89 Sebastian Telfair 4.00 10.00
90 Diante Garrett 3.00 8.00
91 Josh Akognon 5.00 12.00
92 DeSagana Diop 3.00 8.00
93 C.J. Miles 3.00 8.00
94 Ronnie Price 3.00 8.00
95 Elgin Baylor 8.00 20.00
96 Kenny Smith 3.00 8.00
99 Gary Payton 8.00 20.00
100 Luis Scola 4.00 10.00
101 Tyson Chandler 5.00 12.00
103 Blake Griffin 12.00 30.00
105 Luke Ridnour 3.00 8.00
106 Allan Houston 5.00 12.00
108 Jason Kidd 6.00 15.00
109 Rajon Rondo 15.00 40.00
110 Kobe Bryant 400.00 800.00
111 Kevin Durant 50.00 120.00
112 Kyrie Irving 30.00 80.00
113 Juwan Howard 4.00 10.00
116 Alonzo Mourning 8.00 20.00
117 Mark Jackson 5.00 12.00
118 Isiah Thomas 12.00 30.00
119 Bob Lanier 8.00 20.00
120 Greg Ostertag 5.00 12.00
121 Sidney Moncrief 3.00 8.00
122 Harrison Barnes 4.00 10.00
124 Marcin Gortat 5.00 12.00
126 Goran Dragic 12.00 30.00
127 Jared Dudley 3.00 8.00
129 Jared Sullinger 4.00 10.00
130 Dominique Wilkins 10.00 25.00
131 James Johnson 3.00 8.00
132 David Robinson 20.00 50.00
133 Jordan Hill 5.00 12.00
134 Deron Williams 4.00 10.00
135 Chris Bosh 6.00 15.00
136 James Worthy 12.00 30.00
138 Andrea Bargnani 3.00 8.00
140 Kelly Tripucka 8.00 20.00
141 Rick Fox 5.00 12.00
142 Nate Thurmond 8.00 20.00
143 J.R. Smith 4.00 10.00
145 Dikembe Mutombo 5.00 12.00
146 David West 8.00 20.00
147 Andrew Bogut 8.00 20.00
148 Tiago Splitter 4.00 10.00
150 Ryan Anderson 3.00 8.00
151 Connie Hawkins 6.00 15.00
152 MarShon Brooks 4.00 10.00
153 Nicolas Batum 5.00 12.00
154 Byron Mullens 3.00 8.00
155 Corey Brewer 4.00 10.00
156 Michael Cooper 4.00 10.00
157 Jay Williams 6.00 15.00
158 Steve Kerr 6.00 15.00
159 Eric Gordon 4.00 10.00
160 Michael Finley 6.00 15.00
161 Kawhi Leonard 40.00 100.00
162 Lou Amundson 3.00 8.00
164 Ricky Davis 3.00 8.00
165 Marvin Williams 3.00 8.00
166 Ersan Ilyasova 3.00 8.00
167 Royce White 3.00 8.00
168 Tobias Harris 5.00 12.00
169 Kyle Lowry 3.00 8.00
170 Kenneth Faried 5.00 12.00
171 Jamaal Franklin 4.00 10.00
172 Giannis Antetokounmpo 200.00 500.00
173 Ian Clark 5.00 12.00
174 Ray McCallum 5.00 12.00
175 Dennis Schroeder 6.00 15.00
176 Peyton Siva 3.00 8.00
177 Erik Murphy 4.00 10.00
178 Grant Jerrett 4.00 10.00
179 Shane Larkin 3.00 8.00
180 Isaiah Canaan 3.00 8.00
181 Archie Goodwin 4.00 10.00
182 Trey Burke 5.00 12.00
183 Jeff Withey 4.00 10.00
184 Anthony Bennett 4.00 10.00
185 Victor Oladipo 8.00 20.00
186 Solomon Hill 5.00 12.00
187 Rudy Gobert 6.00 15.00
188 Ben McLemore 4.00 10.00
189 Otto Porter 12.00 30.00
190 Ryan Kelly 5.00 12.00
191 Nate Wolters 4.00 10.00
192 Allen Crabbe 3.00 8.00
193 Alex Len 4.00 10.00
194 Steven Adams 8.00 20.00
195 Mason Plumlee 5.00 12.00
196 Reggie Bullock 3.00 8.00
197 Michael Carter-Williams 5.00 12.00
198 Shabazz Muhammad 4.00 10.00
199 Cody Zeller 4.00 10.00
200 Nerlens Noel 5.00 12.00

2013-14 Hoops Autographs Blue

*RED p/r 99-100: .5X TO 1.2X BASIC
*RED p/r 49-50: .5X TO 1.2X BASIC
*RED p/r 25: .6X TO 1.5X BASIC
PRINT RUNS B/WN 10-100 COPIES PER
NO PRICING ON QTY 10
EXCHANGE DEADLINE 4/28/2015
110 Kobe Bryant/25 500.00 1,000.00
111 Kevin Durant/25 60.00 150.00
185 Victor Oladipo/49 30.00 80.00

2013-14 Hoops Autographs Red

*RED p/r 75-199: .5X TO 1.2X BASIC
*RED p/r 40-50: .5X TO 1.2X BASIC
*RED p/r 25: .6X TO 1.5X BASIC
PRINT RUNS B/WN 10-199 COPIES PER
NO PRICING ON QTY 10
EXCHANGE DEADLINE 4/28/2015
110 Kobe Bryant/25 500.00 1,000.00
111 Kevin Durant/25 60.00 150.00
185 Victor Oladipo/49 30.00 80.00

2013-14 Hoops Board Members

COMPLETE SET (25) 5.00 12.00
1 Joakim Noah .50 1.25
2 Kevin Love .50 1.25
3 DeMarcus Cousins .50 1.25
4 Al Horford .50 1.25
5 Dwight Howard .60 1.50
6 Marc Gasol .50 1.25

7 Blake Griffin .50 1.25
8 Tyson Chandler .40 1.00
9 Anderson Varejao .30 .75
10 Carlos Boozer .40 1.00
11 Reggie Evans .30 .75
12 Nikola Vucevic .60 1.50
13 Pau Gasol .75 2.00
14 Marcin Gortat .30 .75
15 Tristan Thompson .30 .75
16 Anthony Davis 1.50 4.00
17 Greg Monroe .30 .75
18 David Lee .30 .75
19 Omer Asik .30 .75
20 LeBron James 4.00 10.00
21 Tim Duncan 1.25 3.00
22 Roy Hibbert .30 .75
23 Andre Drummond .50 1.25
24 Larry Sanders .30 .75
25 Zach Randolph .40 1.00

2013-14 Hoops Class Action

COMPLETE SET (25) 6.00 15.00
1 Damian Lillard 1.50 4.00
2 Kyrie Irving 1.50 4.00
3 Paul George .75 2.00
4 Blake Griffin .50 1.25
5 Derrick Rose .75 2.00
6 Kevin Durant 1.50 4.00
7 LaMarcus Aldridge .50 1.25
8 Chris Paul 1.00 2.50
9 Dwight Howard .60 1.50
10 LeBron James 4.00 10.00
11 Amar'e Stoudemire .50 1.25
12 Tony Parker .75 2.00
13 Jamal Crawford .50 1.25
14 Shawn Marion .40 1.00
15 Dirk Nowitzki 1.25 3.00
16 Tim Duncan 1.25 3.00
17 Kobe Bryant 4.00 10.00
18 Kevin Garnett 1.25 3.00
19 Jason Kidd .75 2.00
20 Sam Cassell .40 1.00
21 Shaquille O'Neal 2.00 5.00
22 Larry Johnson .60 1.50
23 Gary Payton .75 2.00
24 Shawn Kemp .75 2.00
25 Mitch Richmond .60 1.50

2013-14 Hoops Courtside

COMPLETE SET (20) 5.00 12.00
1 Kobe Bryant 4.00 10.00
2 LeBron James 4.00 10.00
3 Kevin Durant 1.50 4.00
4 Blake Griffin .50 1.25
5 Dwyane Wade 1.00 2.50
6 Kyrie Irving 1.50 4.00
7 Russell Westbrook .75 2.00
8 Paul Pierce .75 2.00
9 Carmelo Anthony .75 2.00
10 Rajon Rondo .60 1.50
11 James Harden 1.00 2.50
12 Stephen Curry 4.00 10.00
13 Ricky Rubio .40 1.00
14 Brandon Jennings .30 .75
15 Klay Thompson 1.50 4.00
16 Paul George .75 2.00
17 Tony Parker .75 2.00
18 Marc Gasol .50 1.25
19 Kenneth Faried .40 1.00
20 Chris Paul 1.00 2.50
21 Deron Williams .40 1.00
22 Bradley Beal .75 2.00
23 Andre Drummond .50 1.25
24 Mike Conley .50 1.25
25 Jeremy Lin .75 2.00

2013-14 Hoops Dreams

COMPLETE SET (25) 6.00 15.00
1 Andrew Nicholson .40 1.00
2 Isaiah Thomas .50 1.25
3 Reggie Jackson .50 1.25
4 Larry Sanders .40 1.00
5 Greivis Vasquez .40 1.00
6 Jared Sullinger .40 1.00
7 Brandon Knight .50 1.25
8 Bradley Beal 1.00 2.50
9 Lance Stephenson .50 1.25
10 Eric Bledsoe .50 1.25
11 Nikola Vucevic .75 2.00
12 John Jenkins .40 1.00
13 Michael Kidd-Gilchrist .40 1.00
14 Marquis Teague .40 1.00
15 Jimmy Butler 1.25 3.00
16 Dion Waiters .40 1.00
17 Draymond Green 1.00 2.50
18 Harrison Barnes .60 1.50
19 Norris Cole .40 1.00
20 Malcolm Lee .40 1.00
21 Brian Roberts .40 1.00
22 Tobias Harris .60 1.50
23 Damian Lillard 2.00 5.00
24 Kawhi Leonard 2.00 5.00
25 Perry Jones .40 1.00

2013-14 Hoops Hall of Fame Heroes

COMPLETE SET (25) 8.00 20.00
1 Isiah Thomas 1.00 2.50
2 Bob McAdoo .75 2.00
3 Drazen Petrovic .75 2.00
4 Clyde Drexler 1.00 2.50
5 Hakeem Olajuwon 1.25 3.00
6 Bill Walton 1.00 2.50
7 Calvin Murphy .50 1.25
8 Julius Erving 1.50 4.00
9 Dave Cowens .60 1.50
10 Wes Unseld .75 2.00
11 Billy Cunningham .60 1.50
12 Sam Jones .60 1.50
13 Dave DeBusschere .60 1.50
14 Oscar Robertson 1.00 2.50
15 Wilt Chamberlain 2.00 5.00
16 Earl Monroe 1.00 2.50
17 Bernard King .75 2.00
18 Joe Dumars .75 2.00
19 Adrian Dantley .60 1.50
20 David Robinson 1.25 3.00
21 Gus Johnson .60 1.50
22 Scottie Pippen 1.50 4.00
23 Artis Gilmore .75 2.00
24 Jamaal Wilkes .50 1.25
25 Gary Payton 1.00 2.50

2013-14 Hoops Highlights

1 Kobe Bryant 75.00 200.00
2 Miami Heat 30.00 80.00
3 Kevin Garnett 20.00 50.00
4 Stephen Curry 40.00 100.00
5 Steve Nash 40.00 100.00

2013-14 Hoops Kobe All Rookie Team

1 Anthony Bennett 2.50 6.00
2 Victor Oladipo 6.00 15.00
3 Otto Porter 4.00 10.00
4 Cody Zeller 3.00 8.00
5 Alex Len 3.00 8.00
6 Nerlens Noel 3.00 8.00
7 Ben McLemore 3.00 8.00
8 Kentavious Caldwell-Pope 4.00 10.00
9 Trey Burke 3.00 8.00
10 C.J. McCollum 10.00 25.00
11 Michael Carter-Williams 3.00 8.00
12 Shabazz Muhammad 2.50 6.00
13 Tim Hardaway Jr. 5.00 12.00

2013-14 Hoops Spark Plugs

COMPLETE SET (24) 4.00 10.00
1 Jamal Crawford .50 1.25
2 Kevin Martin .40 1.00
3 Ryan Anderson .30 .75
4 Taj Gibson .30 .75
5 Nate Robinson .30 .75
6 Wilson Chandler .40 1.00
7 Alexey Shved .30 .75
8 Steve Novak .30 .75
9 Nick Young .30 .75
10 Jared Dudley .30 .75
11 Gerald Green .40 1.00
12 Jimmy Butler 1.00 2.50
13 Derrick Favors .30 .75
14 Terrence Ross .40 1.00
15 Manu Ginobili 1.00 2.50
16 Marcus Thornton .30 .75
17 Reggie Jackson .40 1.00
18 J.J. Barea .40 1.00
19 Norris Cole .30 .75
20 Quincy Pondexter .30 .75
21 MarShon Brooks .30 .75
22 Jason Terry .40 1.00
23 Louis Williams .40 1.00
24 Jarrett Jack .40 1.00

2014-15 Hoops

COMPLETE SET (300) 25.00 60.00
1 Al Horford .30 .75
2 Austin Rivers .25 .60
3 Deron Williams .25 .60
4 Nikola Vucevic .25 .60
5 Jimmy Butler .50 1.25
6 Markieff Morris .20 .50
7 JaVale McGee .25 .60
8 DeMarcus Cousins .25 .60
9 Stephen Curry 2.50 6.00
10 Jonas Valanciunas .25 .60
11 Dennis Schroder .30 .75
12 Tim Hardaway Jr. .25 .60
13 Marc Gasol .30 .75
14 Victor Oladipo .25 .60
15 Derrick Rose .60 1.50
16 Marcus Morris .20 .50
17 Kenneth Faried .25 .60
18 Carl Landry .20 .50
19 Andre Iguodala .30 .75
20 Tyler Hansbrough .20 .50
21 Jeff Teague .20 .50
22 Amar'e Stoudemire .30 .75
23 Mason Plumlee .20 .50
24 Arron Afflalo .20 .50
25 Taj Gibson .20 .50
26 Miles Plumlee .20 .50
27 Ty Lawson .20 .50
28 Derrick Williams .20 .50
29 Andrew Bogut .25 .60
30 Chuck Hayes .20 .50
31 Paul Millsap .25 .60
32 Tyson Chandler .30 .75
33 Paul Pierce .50 1.25
34 Maurice Harkless .20 .50
35 Joakim Noah .30 .75
36 Damian Lillard .75 2.00
37 Randy Foye .20 .50
38 Ray McCallum .20 .50
39 Klay Thompson .75 2.00
40 Steve Novak .20 .50
41 Kyle Korver .25 .60
42 J.R. Smith .30 .75
43 Joe Johnson .25 .60
44 Andrew Nicholson .20 .50
45 Mike Dunleavy .20 .50
46 LaMarcus Aldridge .30 .75
47 Wilson Chandler .20 .50
48 Tiago Splitter .20 .50
49 Harrison Barnes .25 .60
50 Enes Kanter .25 .60
51 Louis Williams .25 .60
52 Andrea Bargnani .20 .50
53 Andrei Kirilenko .20 .50
54 Nerlens Noel .25 .60
55 D.J. Augustin .20 .50
56 Nicolas Batum .25 .60
57 J.J. Hickson .20 .50
58 Tim Duncan .75 2.00
59 Kobe Bryant 2.50 6.00
60 Trey Burke .25 .60
61 Pero Antic .20 .50
62 Giannis Antetokounmpo 2.00 5.00
63 Mirza Teletovic .20 .50
64 Tony Wroten .20 .50
65 Kyrie Irving .60 1.50
66 C.J. McCollum .30 .75
67 Timofey Mozgov .20 .50
68 Tony Parker .50 1.25
69 Kevin Martin .25 .60
70 Derrick Favors .20 .50
71 Jared Sullinger .20 .50
72 Iman Shumpert .20 .50
73 Al Jefferson .20 .50
74 Michael Carter-Williams .20 .50
75 Tristan Thompson .20 .50
76 Wesley Matthews .20 .50
77 Josh Smith .20 .50
78 Kawhi Leonard .75 2.00
79 J.J. Barea .25 .60
80 Gordon Hayward .25 .60
81 Brandon Bass .20 .50
82 Nick Collison .25 .60
83 Kemba Walker .30 .75
84 Thaddeus Young .20 .50
85 Anthony Bennett .20 .50
86 Dorell Wright .20 .50
87 Brandon Jennings .20 .50
88 Manu Ginobili .60 1.50
89 Chase Budinger .20 .50
90 Alec Burks .25 .60
91 Kelly Olynyk .25 .60
92 Russell Westbrook .50 1.25
93 Gerald Henderson .20 .50
94 Jason Richardson .30 .75
95 Dion Waiters .20 .50
96 Dwight Howard .40 1.00
97 Andre Drummond .25 .60
98 Marco Belinelli .20 .50
99 Alexey Shved .20 .50
100 Jeremy Evans .20 .50
101 Shelvin Mack .20 .50
102 Robin Lopez .20 .50
103 Jae Crowder .20 .50
104 Terrence Jones .20 .50
105 Lance Stephenson .25 .60
106 Jamal Crawford .30 .75
107 Kosta Koufos .20 .50
108 Kevin Love .30 .75
109 Jason Smith .20 .50
110 Brandon Knight .20 .50
111 Kris Humphries .20 .50
112 Kyle Lowry .40 1.00
113 DeJuan Blair .20 .50
114 Mo Williams .25 .60
115 Evan Turner .20 .50
116 Blake Griffin .30 .75
117 LeBron James 2.50 6.00
118 Kevin Garnett .75 2.00
119 Carmelo Anthony .50 1.25
120 O.J. Mayo .20 .50
121 Shaun Livingston .20 .50
122 John Salmons .20 .50
123 Samuel Dalembert .20 .50
124 Donatas Motiejunas .20 .50
125 Danny Granger .20 .50
126 Chris Bosh .40 1.00
127 DeAndre Jordan .25 .60
128 Tayshaun Prince .30 .75
129 Shane Larkin .20 .50
130 Carlos Boozer .25 .60
131 Raymond Felton .25 .60
132 Richard Jefferson .20 .50
133 Devin Harris .20 .50
134 Roy Hibbert .25 .60
135 Jordan Hill .20 .50
136 Matt Barnes .25 .60
137 Dwyane Wade .60 1.50
138 Mike Conley .25 .60
139 Caron Butler .25 .60
140 Khris Middleton .40 1.00
141 Kirk Hinrich .25 .60
142 Marvin Williams .20 .50
143 Jordan Crawford .20 .50
144 David West .25 .60
145 Pau Gasol .50 1.25
146 Chris Paul .50 1.25
147 Francisco Garcia .30 .75
148 Zach Randolph .30 .75
149 Thabo Sefolosha .20 .50
150 John Henson .20 .50
151 Luol Deng .25 .60
152 Marcin Gortat .25 .60
153 Steve Blake .25 .60
154 George Hill .25 .60
155 Jodie Meeks .20 .50
156 J.J. Redick .30 .75
157 Mario Chalmers .25 .60
158 Courtney Lee .20 .50
159 Jameer Nelson .20 .50
160 Z. Pachulia/X.Henry .20 .50
161 Anderson Varejao .20 .50
162 Trevor Ariza .20 .50
163 Chandler Parsons .25 .60
164 Paul George .50 1.25
165 Chris Kaman .25 .60
166 Jared Dudley .20 .50
167 Udonis Haslem .25 .60
168 Tony Allen .20 .50
169 Kyle O'Quinn .20 .50
170 Ricky Rubio .25 .60
171 Spencer Hawes .20 .50
172 Draymond Green .40 1.00
173 Patrick Beverley .20 .50
174 Luis Scola .25 .60
175 Wesley Johnson .20 .50
176 Darren Collison .20 .50
177 Shawne Williams .20 .50
178 Henry Sims RC .20 .50
179 Norris Cole .20 .50
180 Corey Brewer .20 .50
181 Brandan Wright .20 .50
182 James Harden .60 1.50
183 C.J. Watson .20 .50
184 Omer Asik .20 .50
185 K.Marshall/C.Copeland .20 .50
186 Nate Wolters .25 .60
187 Nick Young .20 .50
188 Chris Andersen .20 .50
189 James Anderson .20 .50
190 Nikola Pekovic .20 .50
191 Jeremy Lin .60 1.50
192 Dirk Nowitzki .75 2.00
193 Omri Casspi .20 .50
194 Ian Mahinmi .20 .50
195 Mike Miller .25 .60
196 Steve Nash .60 1.50
197 Brandon Rush .20 .50
198 Ersan Ilyasova .20 .50
199 Hollis Thompson .20 .50
200 Gorgui Dieng .20 .50
201 Jeff Green .25 .60
202 Serge Ibaka .25 .60
203 Michael Kidd-Gilchrist .20 .50
204 Eric Bledsoe .25 .60
205 Tyler Zeller .20 .50
206 Thomas Robinson .20 .50
207 Kentavious Caldwell-Pope .25 .60
208 Boris Diaw .25 .60
209 Eric Gordon .25 .60
210 Bradley Beal .50 1.25
211 Rajon Rondo .40 1.00
212 Kevin Durant 1.00 2.50
213 Cody Zeller .20 .50
214 Alex Len .20 .50
215 Jarrett Jack .25 .60
216 Ben McLemore .25 .60
217 Greg Monroe .20 .50
218 Danny Green .25 .60
219 Al-Farouq Aminu .20 .50
220 Otto Porter .25 .60
221 Avery Bradley .20 .50
222 Steven Adams .40 1.00
223 Josh McRoberts .20 .50
224 Gerald Green .25 .60
225 Jose Calderon .20 .50
226 Rudy Gay .30 .75
227 Kyle Singler .20 .50
228 Patty Mills .30 .75
229 Jrue Holiday .40 1.00
230 John Wall .40 1.00
231 Gerald Wallace .25 .60
232 Kendrick Perkins .20 .50
233 Ramon Sessions .20 .50
234 Goran Dragic .30 .75
235 Vince Carter .60 1.50
236 Jason Thompson .20 .50
237 R.Stuckey/Lavoy Allen .20 .50
238 Amir Johnson .20 .50
239 Ryan Anderson .20 .50
240 Nene .25 .60
241 Joel Anthony .20 .50
242 Reggie Jackson .25 .60
243 Bismack Biyombo .20 .50
244 Archie Goodwin .20 .50
245 Monta Ellis .25 .60
246 Jason Terry .25 .60
247 Will Bynum .20 .50
248 DeMar DeRozan .40 1.00
249 Tyreke Evans .25 .60
250 Martell Webster .20 .50
251 Brook Lopez .30 .75
252 Tobias Harris .25 .60
253 Tony Snell .20 .50
254 Channing Frye .20 .50
255 Danilo Gallinari .25 .60
256 Isaiah Thomas .25 .60
257 David Lee .20 .50
258 Terrence Ross .25 .60
259 Anthony Davis .75 2.00
260 Trevor Booker .20 .50
261 Andrew Wiggins RC 2.00 5.00
262 Jabari Parker RC .50 1.25
263 Joel Embiid RC 4.00 10.00
264 Aaron Gordon RC 2.00 5.00
265 Dante Exum RC .60 1.50
266 Marcus Smart RC 1.50 4.00
267 Julius Randle RC 2.00 5.00
268 Nik Stauskas RC .40 1.00
269 Noah Vonleh RC .40 1.00
270 Elfrid Payton RC .60 1.50
271 Doug McDermott RC .60 1.50
272 Zach LaVine RC 2.50 6.00
273 T.J. Warren RC .60 1.50
274 Adreian Payne RC .40 1.00
275 James Young RC .40 1.00
276 Tyler Ennis RC .40 1.00
277 Gary Harris RC .60 1.50
278 Mitch McGary RC .40 1.00
279 Jordan Adams RC .40 1.00
280 Rodney Hood RC .50 1.25
281 Shabazz Napier RC .50 1.25
282 P.J. Hairston RC .40 1.00
283 C.J. Wilcox RC .40 1.00
284 Jusuf Nurkic RC 1.25 3.00
285 Kyle Anderson RC .60 1.50
286 K.J. McDaniels RC .40 1.00
287 Joe Harris RC .60 1.50
288 Cleanthony Early RC .40 1.00
289 Jarnell Stokes RC .40 1.00
290 Johnny O'Bryant RC .40 1.00
291 Cory Jefferson RC .40 1.00
292 Spencer Dinwiddie RC .60 1.50
293 Jerami Grant RC 2.00 5.00
294 Glenn Robinson III RC .50 1.25
295 Nick Johnson RC .40 1.00
296 Markel Brown RC .40 1.00
297 Bruno Caboclo RC .50 1.25
298 Cameron Bairstow RC .40 1.00
299 Alec Brown RC .40 1.00
300 Thanasis Antetokounmpo RC .60 1.50

2014-15 Hoops Artist's Proofs

*AP VETS/99: 2X TO 5X BASIC
*AP RC/99: 2X TO 5X BASIC
STATED PRINT RUN 99 SER.#'d SETS
117 LeBron James 15.00 40.00
261 Andrew Wiggins 30.00 80.00
262 Jabari Parker 2.50 6.00
263 Joel Embiid 12.00 30.00

2014-15 Hoops Blue

*BLUE VETS/349: 1X TO 2.5X BASIC
*BLUE RC/349: 1X TO 2.5X BASIC
STATED PRINT RUN 349 SER.#'d SETS

2014-15 Hoops Gold

*GOLD VETS: .6X TO 1.5X BASIC
*GOLD RC: .6X TO 1.5X BASIC

2014-15 Hoops Green

*GREEN VETS: .6X TO 1.5X BASIC
*GREEN RC: .6X TO 1.5X BASIC

2014-15 Hoops Red Backs

*RED BK VETS: .6X TO 1.5X BASIC
*RED BK RC: .6X TO 1.5X BASIC

2014-15 Hoops Silver

*SILVER VETS/399: 1X TO 2.5X BASIC
*SILVER RC/399: 1X TO 2.5X BASIC
STATED PRINT RUN 399 SER.#'d SETS

2014-15 Hoops Authentics

*PRIME/25: .75X TO 2X BASE HI
1 Luis Scola 2.50 6.00
2 Andrew Bogut 2.50 6.00
3 Austin Rivers 2.00 5.00
4 Dirk Nowitzki 8.00 20.00
5 Tim Duncan 6.00 15.00
6 Nick Young 2.00 5.00
7 O.J. Mayo 2.00 5.00
8 Monta Ellis 2.50 6.00
9 Pau Gasol 5.00 12.00
10 Kobe Bryant 8.00 20.00
11 Paul Pierce 5.00 12.00
12 Rajon Rondo 4.00 10.00
13 Randy Foye 2.00 5.00
14 Raymond Felton 2.00 5.00
15 Ryan Anderson 2.00 5.00
16 Shane Battier 2.50 6.00
17 Steve Nash 6.00 15.00
18 Tayshaun Prince 3.00 8.00
19 Tiago Splitter 2.00 5.00
20 Kevin Durant 6.00 15.00
21 Manu Ginobili 6.00 15.00
22 Tyler Hansbrough 2.00 5.00
23 Tyson Chandler 3.00 8.00
24 Wilson Chandler 2.00 5.00
25 Blake Griffin 4.00 10.00
26 Zach Randolph 3.00 8.00
27 Al Jefferson 2.00 5.00
28 Amar'e Stoudemire 3.00 8.00
29 Andre Drummond 2.50 6.00
30 Andre Iguodala 3.00 8.00

2014-15 Hoops Blast from the Past Memorabilia

*PRIME/17-25: .75X TO 2X BASIC
1 Andrea Bargnani 2.00 5.00
2 Andrew Bogut 2.50 6.00
3 Devin Harris 2.00 5.00
4 Dwight Howard 4.00 10.00
5 Elton Brand 3.00 8.00
6 Eric Bledsoe 2.50 6.00
7 Jermaine O'Neal 2.50 6.00
8 Joe Johnson 2.50 6.00
9 Kevin Martin 2.50 6.00
10 Luis Scola 2.50 6.00
11 Marcus Thornton 2.00 5.00
12 Mike Miller 2.50 6.00
13 Nene 2.50 6.00
14 Nick Young 2.00 5.00
15 Tayshaun Prince 3.00 8.00
16 Ray Allen 5.00 12.00
17 Tracy McGrady 5.00 12.00
18 Vince Carter 6.00 15.00
19 Aaron Brooks 2.00 5.00
20 Andray Blatche 2.00 5.00
21 Andre Miller 2.50 6.00
22 Beno Udrih 2.00 5.00
23 Boris Diaw 2.50 6.00
24 Brandon Jennings 2.00 5.00
25 Carl Landry 2.00 5.00
26 Carlos Boozer 2.50 6.00
27 Chris Bosh 4.00 10.00
28 Chris Kaman 2.50 6.00
29 Danilo Gallinari 2.00 5.00
30 Darren Collison 2.00 5.00
31 David West 2.50 6.00
32 Eric Gordon 2.50 6.00
33 Gerald Wallace 2.50 6.00
34 Greivis Vasquez 2.50 6.00
35 Hedo Turkoglu 2.50 6.00
36 J.J. Barea 2.50 6.00
37 Jason Richardson 3.00 8.00
38 JaVale McGee 2.50 6.00
39 Jose Calderon 2.00 5.00
40 Amar'e Stoudemire 3.00 8.00

2014-15 Hoops Champions

1 San Antonio Spurs 12.00 30.00
2 San Antonio Spurs 12.00 30.00

2014-15 Hoops Champions Trophy Portraits

STATED PRINT RUN 99 SER.#'d SETS
1 Kawhi Leonard 8.00 20.00
2 Marco Belinelli 12.00 30.00
3 Splttr/Gnbl/Diaw/Mills 15.00 40.00
4 Danny Green 8.00 20.00
5 Tim Duncan 8.00 20.00
6 Tony Parker 8.00 20.00
7 Matt Bonner 12.00 30.00
8 Parker/Duncan/Manu 12.00 30.00

2014-15 Hoops Class Action

COMPLETE SET (15) 6.00 15.00
*AP/99: 1.2X TO 3X BASE HI
1 Michael Carter-Williams .30 .75
2 Anthony Davis 1.25 3.00
3 Klay Thompson 1.25 3.00
4 John Wall .60 1.50
5 Kevin Love .50 1.25
6 Joakim Noah .50 1.25
7 Rajon Rondo .60 1.50
8 Deron Williams .40 1.00
9 Andre Iguodala .50 1.25
10 Carmelo Anthony .75 2.00
11 Yao Ming 1.25 3.00
12 Baron Davis .50 1.25
13 Vince Carter 1.00 2.50
14 Tracy McGrady .75 2.00
15 Allen Iverson 1.25 3.00

2014-15 Hoops Class Action Holo Green

*HOLO GREEN: 3X TO 8X BASE HI
STATED PRINT RUN 25 SER.#'d SETS
15 Allen Iverson 15.00 40.00

2014-15 Hoops Courtside

COMPLETE SET (20) 8.00 20.00
1 Manu Ginobili 1.00 2.50
2 Rajon Rondo .60 1.50
3 Dwyane Wade 1.00 2.50
4 Ricky Rubio .40 1.00
5 Tony Parker .75 2.00
6 Michael Carter-Williams .30 .75
7 John Wall .60 1.50
8 Blake Griffin .50 1.25
9 Kevin Durant 1.50 4.00
10 Chris Paul .75 2.00
11 Derrick Rose 1.00 2.50
12 Russell Westbrook .75 2.00
13 James Harden 1.00 2.50
14 Damian Lillard 1.25 3.00
15 Monta Ellis .40 1.00
16 Victor Oladipo .40 1.00
17 Kyrie Irving 1.00 2.50
18 DeMar DeRozan .60 1.50
19 Paul George .75 2.00
20 Stephen Curry 4.00 10.00

2014-15 Hoops Dreams

COMPLETE SET (10) 12.00 30.00
1 Jabari Parker .60 1.50
2 Dante Exum .75 2.00
3 Andrew Wiggins 2.50 6.00
4 Marcus Smart 2.00 5.00
5 Aaron Gordon 2.50 6.00
6 Joel Embiid 5.00 12.00
7 Julius Randle 2.50 6.00
8 Doug McDermott .75 2.00
9 Shabazz Napier .60 1.50
10 Thanasis Antetokounmpo .75 2.00

2014-15 Hoops End 2 End

COMPLETE SET (15) 8.00 20.00
1 Dwight Howard .60 1.50
2 Kevin Garnett 1.25 3.00
3 Blake Griffin .50 1.25
4 Kyrie Irving 1.00 2.50
5 Damian Lillard 1.25 3.00
6 LeBron James 4.00 10.00
7 Kevin Durant 1.50 4.00
8 Anthony Davis 1.25 3.00
9 Dirk Nowitzki 1.25 3.00
10 Tim Duncan 1.25 3.00
11 Kevin Love .50 1.25
12 Kobe Bryant 4.00 10.00
13 Chris Bosh .60 1.50
14 Paul Pierce .75 2.00
15 Dwyane Wade 1.00 2.50

2014-15 Hoops Faces of the Future

COMPLETE SET (20) 12.00 30.00
1 Anthony Davis 1.50 4.00
2 Victor Oladipo .50 1.25
3 Kyrie Irving 1.25 3.00
4 Michael Carter-Williams .40 1.00
5 Damian Lillard 1.50 4.00
6 Nerlens Noel .40 1.00
7 Klay Thompson 1.50 4.00
8 Giannis Antetokounmpo 4.00 10.00
9 Kawhi Leonard 1.50 4.00
10 Trey Burke .40 1.00
11 Andrew Wiggins 2.00 5.00
12 Jabari Parker .50 1.25
13 Joel Embiid 4.00 10.00
14 Aaron Gordon 2.00 5.00
15 Dante Exum .60 1.50
16 Julius Randle 2.00 5.00
17 Shabazz Napier .50 1.25
18 Marcus Smart 1.50 4.00
19 Noah Vonleh .40 1.00
20 Doug McDermott .60 1.50

2014-15 Hoops Fast Lane

COMPLETE SET (20) 8.00 20.00
1 John Wall .75 2.00
2 Jason Kidd 1.00 2.50
3 Kyrie Irving 1.25 3.00
4 Allen Iverson 1.50 4.00
5 Stephen Curry 5.00 12.00
6 Tony Parker 1.00 2.50
7 Kyle Lowry .75 2.00
8 Deron Williams .50 1.25
9 Damian Lillard 1.50 4.00
10 Kemba Walker .60 1.50
11 Derrick Rose 1.25 3.00
12 Magic Johnson 2.50 6.00
13 Isaiah Thomas .50 1.25
14 Isiah Thomas 1.00 2.50
15 Chris Paul 1.00 2.50
16 Ricky Rubio .50 1.25
17 Goran Dragic .60 1.50
18 Russell Westbrook 1.00 2.50
19 Mike Conley .50 1.25
20 John Stockton 1.25 3.00

2014-15 Hoops Finals MVP

STATED PRINT RUN 99 SER.#'d SETS
1 Kawhi Leonard 25.00 60.00

2014-15 Hoops Freshman Fabrics

*PRIME/25: .75X TO 2X BASE HI
1 Bruno Caboclo 2.50 6.00
2 Nik Stauskas 2.00 5.00
3 Rodney Hood 2.50 6.00
4 Doug McDermott 8.00 20.00
5 Kyle Anderson 3.00 8.00
6 Andrew Wiggins 10.00 25.00
7 Adreian Payne 2.00 5.00
8 Joel Embiid 20.00 50.00
9 Tyler Ennis 2.00 5.00
10 Marcus Smart 8.00 20.00
11 Mitch McGary 2.00 5.00
12 Noah Vonleh 2.00 5.00
13 Shabazz Napier 2.50 6.00
14 Zach LaVine 12.00 30.00
15 Cleanthony Early 2.00 5.00
16 Jabari Parker 2.50 6.00
17 James Young 2.00 5.00
18 Aaron Gordon 10.00 25.00
19 Gary Harris 3.00 8.00
20 Julius Randle 10.00 25.00
21 Jordan Adams 3.00 8.00
22 Elfrid Payton 3.00 8.00
23 P.J. Hairston 2.00 5.00
24 T.J. Warren 3.00 8.00
25 Glenn Robinson III 2.50 6.00

2014-15 Hoops Freshman Fabrics Prime

*PRIME: .75X TO 2X BASE HI
STATED PRINT RUN 25 SER.#'d SETS
16 Jabari Parker 5.00 12.00

2014-15 Hoops Great SIGnificance

1 Otto Porter 5.00 12.00
2 Kentavious Caldwell-Pope 5.00 12.00
3 Cody Zeller 4.00 10.00
4 Alex Len 4.00 10.00
7 Nerlens Noel 4.00 10.00
10 C.J. McCollum 6.00 15.00
11 Anthony Bennett 4.00 10.00
13 Gal Mekel 4.00 10.00
15 Ray McCallum 4.00 10.00
16 Phil Pressey 4.00 10.00
22 Thaddeus Young 4.00 10.00
27 Ryan Anderson 4.00 10.00
29 Jason Thompson 4.00 10.00
34 Allan Houston 6.00 15.00
40 Vinny Del Negro 8.00 20.00
41 George Gervin 8.00 20.00
47 Walt Bellamy 5.00 12.00
48 Ralph Sampson 8.00 20.00
49 Victor Oladipo 5.00 12.00
50 Dominique Wilkins 8.00 20.00
53 Steven Adams 8.00 20.00
55 Luigi Datome 4.00 10.00
57 Brandan Wright 4.00 10.00
58 Ryan Kelly 4.00 10.00
60 Bobby Jones 12.00 30.00
62 Carl Landry 4.00 10.00
63 Erik Murphy 4.00 10.00
66 Greg Buckner 4.00 10.00
71 Andrew Wiggins 50.00 120.00
72 Jabari Parker 5.00 12.00
73 Joel Embiid 40.00 100.00
74 Aaron Gordon 20.00 50.00
75 Dante Exum 6.00 15.00
76 Marcus Smart 15.00 40.00
77 Julius Randle 20.00 50.00
78 Nik Stauskas 4.00 10.00
79 Noah Vonleh 4.00 10.00
80 Elfrid Payton 6.00 15.00
81 Doug McDermott 6.00 15.00
82 Zach LaVine 15.00 40.00
83 T.J. Warren 6.00 15.00
84 Adreian Payne 4.00 10.00
85 James Young 4.00 10.00
86 Tyler Ennis 4.00 10.00
87 Gary Harris 6.00 15.00
88 Mitch McGary 4.00 10.00
89 Jordan Adams 4.00 10.00
90 Rodney Hood 5.00 12.00
91 Shabazz Napier 5.00 12.00
92 P.J. Hairston 4.00 10.00
93 C.J. Wilcox 4.00 10.00
94 Kyle Anderson 6.00 15.00
95 Joe Harris 6.00 15.00
96 Cleanthony Early 4.00 10.00
97 Glenn Robinson III 5.00 12.00
98 Spencer Dinwiddie 6.00 15.00
99 Markel Brown 4.00 10.00
100 Russ Smith 4.00 10.00

2014-15 Hoops High Honors

COMPLETE SET (25) 12.00 30.00
1 James Harden 1.25 3.00
2 Magic Johnson 2.00 5.00
3 Kareem Abdul-Jabbar 1.50 4.00
4 Kevin Durant 1.50 4.00
5 Derrick Rose 1.00 2.50
6 Goran Dragic .50 1.25
7 Dwight Howard .60 1.50
8 LeBron James 4.00 10.00
9 Dennis Rodman 1.25 3.00
10 Steve Nash 1.00 2.50
11 Shaquille O'Neal 2.00 5.00
12 Larry Bird 2.00 5.00
13 Wilt Chamberlain 1.50 4.00
14 Michael Carter-Williams .30 .75
15 Vince Carter 1.00 2.50
16 Jamal Crawford .50 1.25
17 Dikembe Mutombo .75 2.00
18 Kobe Bryant 4.00 10.00
19 Bill Walton .75 2.00
20 Tim Duncan 1.25 3.00
21 Oscar Robertson 1.00 2.50
22 Kyrie Irving 1.00 2.50
23 Dirk Nowitzki 1.25 3.00
24 Joakim Noah .50 1.25
25 Allen Iverson 1.25 3.00

2014-15 Hoops Highlights

1 Carmelo Anthony 6.00 15.00
2 Kevin Durant 5.00 12.00
3 Dirk Nowitzki 6.00 15.00

2014-15 Hoops Hot Signatures

*RED/25: .6X TO 1.5X BASIC
1 Otto Porter 4.00 10.00
2 Kentavious Caldwell-Pope 4.00 10.00
3 Cody Zeller 3.00 8.00
4 Alex Len 3.00 8.00
5 Shabazz Muhammad 3.00 8.00
6 Jason Terry 4.00 10.00
7 Nerlens Noel 3.00 8.00
8 Earl Monroe 8.00 20.00
9 Artis Gilmore 6.00 15.00
10 C.J. McCollum 5.00 12.00
11 Anthony Bennett 3.00 8.00
12 Peja Stojakovic 4.00 10.00
13 Michael Finley 5.00 12.00
14 Ben Gordon 4.00 10.00
15 Tayshaun Prince 5.00 12.00
16 Horace Grant 5.00 12.00
17 Dan Majerle 4.00 10.00
18 George Hill 4.00 10.00
19 Gal Mekel 3.00 8.00
20 Gorgui Dieng 3.00 8.00
21 Kevin Durant 75.00 200.00
22 Kurt Rambis 4.00 10.00
23 Brent Barry 3.00 8.00
24 Jason Thompson 3.00 8.00
25 Derrick Williams 3.00 8.00
26 Miroslav Raduljica 3.00 8.00
27 Brandon Knight 3.00 8.00
28 Carrick Felix 3.00 8.00
29 Pero Antic 3.00 8.00
30 Arnett Moultrie 3.00 8.00
31 Kyle O'Quinn 3.00 8.00
32 Ray McCallum 3.00 8.00

33 Nemanja Nedovic 3.00 8.00
34 Thabo Sefolosha 3.00 8.00
35 Phil Pressey 3.00 8.00
36 Danny Green 4.00 10.00
37 Mike Muscala 3.00 8.00
38 Terry Porter 3.00 8.00
39 Matthew Dellavedova 4.00 10.00
40 Ryan Kelly 3.00 8.00
41 Elvin Hayes 8.00 20.00
42 Bismack Biyombo 3.00 8.00
43 Allen Crabbe 3.00 8.00
44 Trey Burke 3.00 8.00
45 Allan Houston 5.00 12.00
46 Walt Frazier 8.00 20.00
47 Dwight Buycks 3.00 8.00
48 Danny Manning 4.00 10.00
49 Adrian Dantley 5.00 12.00
50 Caron Butler 4.00 10.00
51 Richard Jefferson 4.00 10.00
52 John Thompson 20.00 50.00
53 Bill Sharman 20.00 50.00
54 George McGinnis 3.00 8.00
55 Jon Leuer 3.00 8.00
56 Walt Bellamy 4.00 10.00
57 Steve Novak 3.00 8.00
58 Gerald Wallace 4.00 10.00
59 Ben McLemore 3.00 8.00
60 Michael Carter-Williams 3.00 8.00
61 Victor Oladipo 4.00 10.00
62 Kobe Bryant 600.00 1,200.00
64 Ryan Anderson 3.00 8.00
65 Dennis Schroder 5.00 12.00
66 Andrew Wiggins 15.00 40.00
67 Jabari Parker 4.00 10.00
68 Joel Embiid 75.00 200.00
69 Aaron Gordon 15.00 40.00
70 Dante Exum 5.00 12.00
71 Marcus Smart 12.00 30.00
72 Julius Randle 20.00 50.00
73 Nik Stauskas 3.00 8.00
74 Noah Vonleh 3.00 8.00
75 Elfrid Payton 5.00 12.00
76 Doug McDermott 5.00 12.00
77 Zach LaVine 20.00 50.00
78 T.J. Warren 5.00 12.00
79 Adreian Payne 3.00 8.00
80 James Young 3.00 8.00
81 Tyler Ennis 3.00 8.00
82 Gary Harris 5.00 12.00
83 Mitch McGary 3.00 8.00
84 Jordan Adams 3.00 8.00
85 Rodney Hood 4.00 10.00
86 Bruno Caboclo 4.00 10.00
87 Shabazz Napier 4.00 10.00
88 P.J. Hairston 3.00 8.00
89 C.J. Wilcox 3.00 8.00
90 Kyle Anderson 5.00 12.00
91 Joe Harris 5.00 12.00
92 Cleanthony Early 5.00 12.00
93 Jarnell Stokes 3.00 8.00
94 Spencer Dinwiddie 5.00 12.00
95 Glenn Robinson III 4.00 10.00
96 Markel Brown 3.00 8.00
97 Russ Smith 3.00 8.00
98 Xavier Thames 3.00 8.00
99 Cory Jefferson 3.00 8.00
100 Alec Brown 3.00 8.00

2014-15 Hoops Kobe's All Rookie Team

1 Andrew Wiggins 15.00 40.00
2 Jabari Parker 4.00 10.00
3 Aaron Gordon 15.00 40.00
4 Dante Exum 5.00 12.00
5 Marcus Smart 12.00 30.00
6 Julius Randle 15.00 40.00
7 Nik Stauskas 3.00 8.00
8 Noah Vonleh 3.00 8.00
9 Elfrid Payton 5.00 12.00
10 Doug McDermott 5.00 12.00
11 Tyler Ennis 3.00 8.00
12 Shabazz Napier 4.00 10.00

2014-15 Hoops Lights Camera Action

COMPLETE SET (46) 20.00 50.00
1 Chris Paul .75 2.00
2 Dirk Nowitzki 1.25 3.00
3 Joe Johnson .40 1.00
4 Klay Thompson 1.25 3.00
5 Michael Carter-Williams .30 .75
6 Stephen Curry 4.00 10.00
7 Vince Carter 1.00 2.50
8 LaMarcus Aldridge .50 1.25
9 Rajon Rondo .60 1.50
10 Kenneth Faried .30 .75
11 Jeff Teague .30 .75
12 Derrick Rose 1.00 2.50
13 Brandon Jennings .30 .75
14 Al Horford .50 1.25
15 DeAndre Jordan .40 1.00
16 Goran Dragic .50 1.25
17 Kevin Garnett 1.25 3.00
18 Paul George .75 2.00
19 Tony Parker .75 2.00
20 Anthony Davis 1.25 3.00
21 DeMar DeRozan .60 1.50
22 Dwight Howard .60 1.50
23 Bradley Beal .75 2.00
24 John Wall .60 1.50
25 Kyrie Irving 1.00 2.50
26 Manu Ginobili 1.00 2.50
27 Pau Gasol .75 2.00
28 Russell Westbrook .75 2.00
29 Victor Oladipo .40 1.00
30 Tim Duncan 1.25 3.00
31 Ricky Rubio .40 1.00
32 Paul Pierce .75 2.00
33 Monta Ellis .40 1.00
34 LeBron James 4.00 10.00
35 Kobe Bryant 4.00 10.00
36 Kevin Love .50 1.25
36 Carmelo Anthony .75 2.00
37 Blake Griffin .50 1.25
38 Chris Bosh .60 1.50
39 Damian Lillard 1.25 3.00
40 DeMarcus Cousins .40 1.00
41 Dwyane Wade 1.00 2.50
42 James Harden 1.00 2.50
43 Joakim Noah .50 1.25
44 Kemba Walker .50 1.25
45 Kevin Durant 1.50 4.00

2014-15 Hoops Matchups

1 K.Bryant/L.James 8.00 20.00
2 D.Nowitzki/T.Duncan 1.25 3.00
3 D.Williams/C.Paul .75 2.00
4 B.Griffin/Z.Randolph .50 1.25
5 K.Bryant/T.McGrady 4.00 10.00
6 D.DeRozan/D.Williams .60 1.50
7 R.Westbrook/T.Parker .75 2.00
8 K.Durant/L.James 4.00 10.00
9 C.Anthony/D.Wade 1.00 2.50
10 R.Rubio/S.Nash 1.00 2.50
11 M.Carter-Williams/V.Oladipo .40 1.00
12 S.Curry/C.Paul 4.00 10.00
13 K.Bryant/K.Durant 4.00 10.00
14 K.Irving/S.Curry 4.00 10.00
15 A.Iverson/J.Kidd 1.25 3.00
16 S.O'Neal/H.Olajuwon 2.00 5.00
17 D.Wilkins/L.Bird 2.00 5.00
18 B.Russell/W.Chamberlain 1.50 4.00
19 L.Bird/M.Johnson 2.00 5.00
20 K.Malone/S.Pippen 1.25 3.00

2014-15 Hoops Matchups Holo Artist's Proof

*HOLO AP: 1.2X TO 3X BASE HI
STATED PRINT RUN 99 SER.#'d SETS
8 K.Durant/L.James 8.00 20.00

2014-15 Hoops Matchups Holo Green

*HOLO GREEN: 2.5X TO 6X BASE HI
STATED PRINT RUN 25 SER.#'d SETS

2014-15 Hoops Moments of Greatness

COMPLETE SET (25) 12.00 30.00
1 Al Jefferson .40 1.00
2 Elgin Baylor 1.25 3.00
3 Dwight Howard .75 2.00
4 Latrell Sprewell .75 2.00
5 LeBron James 5.00 12.00
6 DeAndre Jordan .50 1.25
7 Anthony Davis 1.50 4.00
8 Spud Webb .60 1.50
9 Terrence Ross .50 1.25
10 Andre Drummond .50 1.25
11 LaMarcus Aldridge .60 1.50
12 Magic Johnson 2.50 6.00
13 Rajon Rondo .75 2.00
14 Kendall Gill .60 1.50
15 Kevin Love .60 1.50
16 Victor Oladipo .60 1.50
17 Chris Paul 1.00 2.50
18 Kobe Bryant 5.00 12.00
19 Corey Brewer .40 1.00
20 Bill Russell 2.00 5.00
21 Timofey Mozgov .40 1.00
22 Damian Lillard 1.50 4.00
23 Michael Carter-Williams .40 1.00
24 Kevin Garnett 1.50 4.00
25 Kevin Durant 2.00 5.00

2014-15 Hoops Picture Perfect

COMPLETE SET (30) 8.00 20.00
1 Stephen Curry 4.00 10.00
2 Kevin Garnett 1.25 3.00
3 Dwight Howard .60 1.50
4 Russell Westbrook .75 2.00
5 Blake Griffin .60 1.50
7 Kevin Durant 1.50 4.00
8 Kobe Bryant 4.00 10.00
9 Manu Ginobili 1.00 2.50
10 Dirk Nowitzki 1.25 3.00
11 Tony Parker .75 2.00
12 Rajon Rondo .60 1.50
13 Damian Lillard 1.25 3.00
14 Anthony Davis 1.25 3.00
15 LaMarcus Aldridge .50 1.25
16 John Wall .60 1.50
17 Tim Duncan 1.25 3.00
18 Joakim Noah .50 1.25
19 Dwyane Wade 1.00 2.50
20 Kevin Love .50 1.25
21 Chris Bosh .60 1.50
22 Pau Gasol .75 2.00
23 LeBron James 4.00 10.00
24 Kyrie Irving 1.00 2.50
25 Carmelo Anthony .75 2.00
26 Paul George .75 2.00
27 Chris Paul .75 2.00
28 Michael Carter-Williams .30 .75
29 Vince Carter 1.00 2.50
30 Derrick Rose 1.00 2.50

2014-15 Hoops Picture Perfect Holo Artist's Proof

*HOLO AP: 1.2X TO 3X BASE HI
STATED PRINT RUN 99 SER.#'d SETS
23 LeBron James 8.00 20.00

2014-15 Hoops Picture Perfect Holo Green

*HOLO GREEN: 3X TO 8X BASE HI
STATED PRINT RUN 25 SER.#'d SETS
23 LeBron James 20.00 50.00

2014-15 Hoops Rise and Shine Memorabilia

*PRIME/25: .75X TO 2X BASE HI
1 Andrew Wiggins 10.00 25.00
2 Jabari Parker 2.50 6.00
3 Joel Embiid 20.00 50.00
4 Aaron Gordon 10.00 25.00
6 Marcus Smart 8.00 20.00
7 Julius Randle 10.00 25.00
8 Nik Stauskas 2.00 5.00
9 Noah Vonleh 2.00 5.00
10 Elfrid Payton 3.00 8.00
11 Doug McDermott 3.00 8.00
12 Zach LaVine 12.00 30.00
13 T.J. Warren 3.00 8.00
14 Adreian Payne 2.00 5.00
15 James Young 2.00 5.00
16 Tyler Ennis 2.00 5.00
17 Gary Harris 3.00 8.00
18 Mitch McGary 2.00 5.00
19 Jordan Adams 2.00 5.00
20 Rodney Hood 2.50 6.00
21 Shabazz Napier 2.50 6.00
22 Russ Smith 2.00 5.00
23 P.J. Hairston 2.00 5.00
24 C.J. Wilcox 2.00 5.00
25 Bruno Caboclo 2.50 6.00
26 Kyle Anderson 3.00 8.00
27 K.J. McDaniels 2.00 5.00
28 Cleanthony Early 2.00 5.00
29 Glenn Robinson III 2.50 6.00
30 Jarnell Stokes 2.00 5.00

2014-15 Hoops Road to the Finals

1-50 PRINT RUN 2014 SER.#'d SETS
51-72 PRINT RUN 999 SER.#'d SETS
73-84 PRINT RUN 299 SER.#'d SETS
1 Joe Johnson R1 .60 1.50
2 DeMar DeRozan R1 1.00 2.50
3 Joe Johnson R1 .60 1.50
4 Kyle Lowry R1 1.00 2.50
5 Kyle Lowry R1 1.00 2.50
6 Deron Williams R1 .60 1.50
7 Paul Pierce R1 1.25 3.00
8 Jeff Teague R1 .50 1.25
9 Paul George R1 1.25 3.00
10 Kyle Korver R1 .60 1.50
11 Paul George R1 1.25 3.00
12 Mike Scott R1 .50 1.25
13 David West R1 .60 1.50
14 Paul George R1 1.25 3.00
15 Dwyane Wade R1 1.50 4.00
16 LeBron James R1 6.00 15.00
17 LeBron James R1 6.00 15.00
18 LeBron James R1 6.00 15.00
19 Nene R1 .60 1.50
20 Bradley Beal R1 1.25 3.00
21 Mike Dunleavy R1 .50 1.25
22 Trevor Ariza R1 .50 1.25
23 John Wall R1 1.00 2.50
24 Klay Thompson R1 2.00 5.00
25 Blake Griffin R1 .75 2.00
26 DeAndre Jordan R1 .60 1.50
27 Stephen Curry R1 6.00 15.00
28 DeAndre Jordan R1 .60 1.50
29 Stephen Curry R1 6.00 15.00
30 Chris Paul R1 1.25 3.00
31 Kevin Durant R1 2.50 6.00
32 Zach Randolph R1 .75 2.00
33 Mike Conley R1 .60 1.50
34 Reggie Jackson R1 .60 1.50
35 Mike Miller R1 .60 1.50
36 Kevin Durant R1 2.50 6.00
37 Russell Westbrook R1 1.25 3.00
38 Tim Duncan R1 2.00 5.00
39 Shawn Marion R1 .60 1.50
40 Vince Carter R1 1.50 4.00
41 Boris Diaw R1 .60 1.50
42 Tony Parker R1 1.25 3.00
43 Monta Ellis R1 .60 1.50
44 Tony Parker R1 1.25 3.00
45 LaMarcus Aldridge R1 .75 2.00
46 LaMarcus Aldridge R1 .75 2.00
47 Troy Daniels R1 .50 1.25
48 LaMarcus Aldridge R1 .75 2.00
49 Dwight Howard R1 1.00 2.50
50 Damian Lillard R1 2.00 5.00
51 Ray Allen R2 1.50 4.00
52 LeBron James R2 8.00 20.00
53 Joe Johnson R2 .75 2.00
54 LeBron James R2 8.00 20.00
55 Ray Allen R2 1.50 4.00
56 Tony Parker R2 1.50 4.00
57 Kawhi Leonard R2 2.50 6.00
58 Tony Parker R2 1.50 4.00
59 Nicolas Batum R2 .75 2.00
60 Patty Mills R2 1.00 2.50
61 Trevor Ariza R2 .60 1.50
62 Roy Hibbert R2 .75 2.00
63 David West R2 .75 2.00
64 Paul George R2 1.50 4.00
65 Marcin Gortat R2 .60 1.50
66 David West R2 .75 2.00
67 Chris Paul R2 1.50 4.00
68 Kevin Durant R2 3.00 8.00
69 Russell Westbrook R2 1.50 4.00
70 Darren Collison R2 .60 1.50
71 Russell Westbrook R2 1.50 4.00
72 Kevin Durant R2 3.00 8.00
73 Paul George CF 2.00 5.00
74 Dwyane Wade CF 2.50 6.00
75 Ray Allen CF 2.00 5.00
76 LeBron James CF 10.00 25.00
77 Paul George CF 2.00 5.00
78 Chris Bosh CF 1.50 4.00
79 Manu Ginobili CF 2.50 6.00
80 Danny Green CF 1.00 2.50
81 Serge Ibaka CF 1.00 2.50
82 Russell Westbrook CF 2.00 5.00
83 Tim Duncan CF 6.00 15.00
84 Kawhi Leonard CF 3.00 8.00

2014-15 Hoops Road to the Finals NBA Championship

STATED PRINT RUN 199 SER.#'d SETS
1 Tim Duncan 10.00 25.00
2 LeBron James 15.00 40.00
3 Kawhi Leonard 12.00 30.00
4 Kawhi Leonard 12.00 30.00
5 Manu Ginobili 4.00 10.00

2014-15 Hoops Rookie Remembrance Memorabilia

*PRIME/25: .75X TO 2X BASE HI
1 Harrison Barnes 2.50 6.00
2 Anthony Davis 8.00 20.00
3 Klay Thompson 8.00 20.00
4 Jonas Valanciunas 2.50 6.00
5 Kyrie Irving 6.00 15.00
6 Dion Waiters 2.00 5.00
7 Tristan Thompson 2.00 5.00
8 Markieff Morris 2.00 5.00
9 Kawhi Leonard 8.00 20.00
10 Reggie Jackson 2.50 6.00
11 Nikola Vucevic 2.50 6.00
12 Enes Kanter 2.50 6.00
13 Kemba Walker 3.00 8.00
14 Jared Sullinger 2.00 5.00
15 Michael Kidd-Gilchrist 2.00 5.00
16 Isaiah Thomas 2.50 6.00
17 Kenneth Faried 2.00 5.00
18 Andre Drummond 2.50 6.00
19 Bradley Beal 5.00 12.00
20 Ben McLemore 2.00 5.00
21 Kelly Olynyk 2.00 5.00
22 Giannis Antetokounmpo 20.00 50.00
23 Michael Carter-Williams 2.00 5.00
24 Trey Burke 2.00 5.00
25 Victor Oladipo 2.50 6.00

2014-15 Hoops Shining Stars

COMPLETE SET (20) 8.00 20.00
*HOLO AP/99: 2X TO 5X BASE HI
*HOLO GREEN/25: 4X TO 10X BASE HI
1 Kevin Durant 1.50 4.00
2 Rajon Rondo .60 1.50
3 Russell Westbrook .75 2.00
4 Paul George .75 2.00
5 Dwyane Wade 1.00 2.50
6 Derrick Rose 1.00 2.50
7 LeBron James 4.00 10.00
8 Anthony Davis 1.25 3.00
9 Dirk Nowitzki 1.25 3.00
10 Stephen Curry 4.00 10.00
11 Blake Griffin .50 1.25
12 Kyrie Irving 1.00 2.50
13 Chris Paul .75 2.00
14 Kevin Love .50 1.25
15 Tim Duncan 1.25 3.00
16 Damian Lillard 1.25 3.00
17 Tony Parker .75 2.00
18 James Harden 1.00 2.50
19 Kobe Bryant 4.00 10.00
20 Dwight Howard .60 1.50

2014-15 Hoops Trading Places

COMPLETE SET (20) 6.00 15.00
1 D.Rodman/W.Perdue 1.25 3.00
2 J.Mashburn/E.Jones .50 1.25
3 A.Iverson/A.Miller 1.25 3.00
4 J.Starks/L.Sprewell .60 1.50
5 G.Payton/R.Allen .75 2.00
6 C.Paul/E.Gordon .75 2.00
7 A.Dantley/M.Aguirre .50 1.25
8 K.Bryant/V.Divac 4.00 10.00
9 J.Redick/E.Bledsoe .50 1.25
10 N.Noel/J.Holiday .60 1.50
11 T.McGrady/S.Francis .75 2.00
12 R.Horry/C.Ceballos .50 1.25
13 P.Gasol/M.Gasol .75 2.00
14 G.Green/L.Scola .40 1.00
15 J.Kidd/M.Finley .75 2.00
16 S.Marion/S.O'Neal 2.00 5.00
17 A.Jamison/V.Carter 1.00 2.50
18 A.Mourning/G.Rice .75 2.00
19 R.Gay/G.Vasquez .50 1.25
20 B.Jennings/B.Knight .30 .75

2015-16 Hoops

COMPLETE SET (300) 25.00 60.00
1 Ersan Ilyasova .20 .50
2 Josh Smith .20 .50
3 James Harden .60 1.50
4 Langston Galloway .20 .50
5 Aaron Brooks .20 .50
6 Mike Dunleavy .20 .50
7 Bradley Beal .40 1.00
8 Quincy Pondexter .20 .50
9 Dante Exum .25 .60
10 Taj Gibson .25 .60
11 Evan Fournier .25 .60
12 Jrue Holiday .40 1.00
13 Jared Dudley .20 .50
14 LeBron James 2.50 6.00
15 Aaron Gordon .30 .75
16 Mike Muscala .20 .50
17 Brandon Bass .20 .50
18 Rajon Rondo .40 1.00
19 Darren Collison .20 .50
20 Terrence Jones .20 .50
21 Evan Turner .20 .50
22 Julius Randle .40 1.00
23 Jared Sullinger .20 .50
24 Lou Williams .25 .60
25 Al-Farouq Aminu .20 .50
26 Tim Hardaway Jr. .25 .60
27 Brandon Jennings .20 .50
28 Randy Foye .20 .50
29 Shane Larkin .20 .50
30 Terrence Ross .25 .60
31 Gary Harris .25 .60
32 Jusuf Nurkic .25 .60
33 Jarrett Jack .25 .60
34 Isaiah Canaan .20 .50
35 Al Horford .30 .75
36 Mirza Teletovic .20 .50
37 Brandon Knight .20 .50
38 Archie Goodwin .20 .50
39 David West .25 .60
40 Thabo Sefolosha .20 .50
41 George Hill .25 .60
42 Kawhi Leonard 1.00 2.50
43 Jason Smith .20 .50
44 Luis Scola .25 .60
45 Al Jefferson .25 .60
46 Monta Ellis .25 .60
47 Brian Roberts .20 .50
48 Raymond Felton .20 .50
49 DeAndre Jordan .25 .60
50 Thaddeus Young .20 .50
51 Gerald Green .25 .60
52 Kemba Walker .30 .75
53 Jason Terry .25 .60
54 Luol Deng .25 .60
55 Alan Anderson .20 .50
56 Nene .25 .60
57 Brook Lopez .30 .75
58 Reggie Jackson .25 .60
59 DeMar DeRozan .40 1.00
60 Tim Duncan .75 2.00
61 Gerald Henderson .20 .50
62 Kenneth Faried .25 .60
63 Jeff Green .20 .50
64 Manu Ginobili .60 1.50
65 Alec Burks .20 .50
66 Nerlens Noel .20 .50
67 C.J. McCollum .30 .75
68 Ricky Rubio .25 .60
69 DeMarcus Cousins .30 .75
70 Timofey Mozgov .20 .50
71 Giannis Antetokounmpo 1.50 4.00
72 Kent Bazemore .20 .50
73 Jeff Teague .20 .50
74 Marc Gasol .30 .75
75 Alex Len .20 .50
76 Nick Collison .20 .50
77 Quincy Acy .20 .50
78 Robert Covington .25 .60
79 DeMarre Carroll .20 .50
80 T.J. Warren .30 .75
81 Goran Dragic .30 .75
82 Kentavious Caldwell-Pope .25 .60
83 Jerami Grant .30 .75
84 Marcin Gortat .20 .50
85 Alexis Ajinca .20 .50
86 Nick Young .20 .50
87 Cleanthony Early .20 .50
88 Robin Lopez .20 .50
89 Dennis Schroder .30 .75
90 Tobias Harris .25 .60
91 Gordon Hayward .30 .75
92 Kevin Durant 1.25 3.00
93 Jeremy Evans .20 .50
94 Marco Belinelli .20 .50
95 Amir Johnson .20 .50
96 Nicolas Batum .20 .50
97 Carmelo Anthony .50 1.25
98 Rodney Hood .25 .60
99 Deron Williams .25 .60
100 Tony Allen .20 .50
101 Gorgui Dieng .20 .50
102 Kevin Garnett .75 2.00
103 Jeremy Lamb .20 .50
104 Marcus Morris .20 .50
105 Anderson Varejao .20 .50
106 Nikola Mirotic .20 .50
107 Chandler Parsons .20 .50
108 Rodney Stuckey .20 .50
109 Derrick Favors .25 .60
110 Tony Parker .50 1.25
111 Greg Monroe .25 .60
112 Kevin Love .30 .75
113 Jimmy Butler .60 1.50
114 Marcus Smart .40 1.00
115 Andre Drummond .30 .75
116 Nikola Vucevic .25 .60
117 Channing Frye .20 .50
118 Roy Hibbert .25 .60
119 Derrick Rose .50 1.25
120 Tony Wroten .20 .50
121 Greivis Vasquez .20 .50
122 Kevin Martin .25 .60
123 J.J. Hickson .20 .50
124 Mario Chalmers .25 .60
125 Andre Iguodala .30 .75
126 Noah Vonleh .20 .50
127 Chase Budinger .20 .50
128 Rudy Gay .30 .75
129 Derrick Williams .20 .50
130 Trevor Ariza .20 .50
131 Harrison Barnes .25 .60
132 Kevin Seraphin .20 .50
133 J.J. Redick .30 .75
134 Markieff Morris .20 .50
135 Andre Roberson .20 .50
136 Norris Cole .20 .50
137 Chris Andersen .25 .60
138 Rudy Gobert .40 1.00
139 Devin Harris .20 .50
140 Trevor Booker .20 .50
141 Hassan Whiteside .25 .60
142 Khris Middleton .40 1.00
143 Joakim Noah .20 .50
144 Marreese Speights .20 .50
145 Andrew Bogut .25 .60
146 O.J. Mayo .20 .50
147 Chris Bosh .40 1.00
148 Russell Westbrook .50 1.25
149 Dion Waiters .20 .50
150 Trey Burke .20 .50
151 Sergey Karasev .25 .60
152 Kirk Hinrich .20 .50
153 Jodie Meeks .20 .50
154 Martell Webster .20 .50
155 Andrew Wiggins .40 1.00
156 Omer Asik .20 .50
157 Chris Kaman .25 .60
158 Ryan Anderson .20 .50
159 Dirk Nowitzki .75 2.00
160 Tristan Thompson .20 .50
161 Henry Sims .20 .50
162 Klay Thompson .75 2.00
163 Joe Ingles .25 .60
164 Marvin Williams .20 .50
165 Anthony Davis .75 2.00
166 Omri Casspi .20 .50
167 Chris Paul .60 1.50
168 Serge Ibaka .25 .60
169 Donald Sloan .20 .50
170 Ty Lawson .20 .50
171 Hollis Thompson .20 .50
172 Kobe Bryant 2.50 6.00
173 Joe Johnson .25 .60
174 Mason Plumlee .20 .50
175 Thomas Robinson .20 .50
176 Otto Porter .25 .60
177 C.J. Miles .20 .50
178 Shabazz Muhammad .20 .50
179 Draymond Green .40 1.00
180 Tyler Zeller .20 .50
181 Ian Mahinmi .20 .50
182 Kosta Koufos .20 .50
183 JaKarr Sampson .20 .50
184 Matt Barnes .20 .50
185 Arron Afflalo .20 .50
186 Patrick Beverley .20 .50
187 Cody Zeller .20 .50
188 Shabazz Napier .20 .50
189 Dwight Howard .40 1.00
190 Tyreke Evans .25 .60
191 Iman Shumpert .20 .50
192 Josh McRoberts .20 .50
193 John Henson .20 .50
194 Matt Bonner .20 .50
195 Austin Rivers .25 .60
196 Patrick Patterson .20 .50
197 Corey Brewer .20 .50
198 Shaun Livingston .20 .50
199 Dwight Powell .20 .50
200 Tyson Chandler .25 .60
201 Isaiah Thomas .25 .60
202 Kyle Korver .25 .60
203 John Wall .40 1.00
204 Matthew Dellavedova .25 .60
205 Avery Bradley .20 .50
206 Patty Mills .30 .75
207 Cory Joseph .20 .50
208 Shelvin Mack .20 .50
209 Dwyane Wade .60 1.50
210 Victor Oladipo .25 .60
211 J.J. Barea .25 .60
212 Kyle Lowry .30 .75
213 Jonas Valanciunas .25 .60
214 Will Barton .20 .50
215 Ben McLemore .20 .50
216 Pau Gasol .50 1.25
217 Courtney Lee .20 .50
218 Solomon Hill .20 .50
219 Ed Davis .20 .50
220 Vince Carter .60 1.50
221 J.R. Smith .30 .75
222 Kyrie Irving .60 1.50
223 Jordan Clarkson .30 .75
224 Meyers Leonard .20 .50
225 Bismack Biyombo .20 .50
226 Paul George .50 1.25
227 Damian Lillard .75 2.00
228 Spencer Dinwiddie .25 .60
229 Elfrid Payton .25 .60
230 Wesley Matthews .20 .50
231 Jabari Parker .20 .50
232 LaMarcus Aldridge .30 .75
233 Wesley Johnson .20 .50
234 Michael Carter-Williams .20 .50
235 Blake Griffin .30 .75
236 Paul Millsap .25 .60
237 Danilo Gallinari .25 .60
238 Spencer Hawes .20 .50
239 Enes Kanter .20 .50
240 Wilson Chandler .25 .60
241 Jamal Crawford .30 .75
242 Lance Stephenson .25 .60
243 Jose Calderon .20 .50
244 Michael Kidd-Gilchrist .20 .50
245 Bojan Bogdanovic .25 .60
246 Paul Pierce .50 1.25
247 Danny Green .25 .60
248 Stephen Curry 2.50 6.00
249 Eric Bledsoe .25 .60
250 Zach LaVine .75 2.00
251 Jameer Nelson .20 .50
252 Lance Thomas .20 .50
253 Leandro Barbosa .20 .50
254 Mike Conley .30 .75
255 Boris Diaw .25 .60
256 P.J. Tucker .20 .50
257 Dante Cunningham .20 .50
258 Steven Adams .25 .60
259 Eric Gordon .25 .60
260 Zach Randolph .30 .75
261 Kristaps Porzingis RC 2.50 6.00
262 Walter Tavares RC .40 1.00
263 Trey Lyles RC .50 1.25
264 Pierre Jackson RC .40 1.00
265 D'Angelo Russell RC 1.50 4.00
266 Jarell Martin RC .40 1.00
267 Stanley Johnson RC .50 1.25
268 Devin Booker RC 5.00 12.00
269 Rashad Vaughn RC .40 1.00
270 Kevon Looney RC 1.25 3.00
271 R.J. Hunter RC .40 1.00
272 Myles Turner RC 1.50 4.00
273 Pat Connaughton RC .60 1.50
274 Terry Rozier RC 1.50 4.00
275 Bobby Portis RC 1.00 2.50
276 Willie Cauley-Stein RC .50 1.25
277 Jordan Mickey RC .40 1.00
278 Montrezl Harrell RC 1.25 3.00
279 Andrew Harrison RC .50 1.25
280 Jahlil Okafor RC .50 1.25
281 Frank Kaminsky RC .50 1.25
282 Dakari Johnson RC .40 1.00
283 Kelly Oubre Jr. RC 1.25 3.00
284 Nemanja Bjelica RC .60 1.50
285 Mario Hezonja RC .50 1.25
286 Chris McCullough RC .40 1.00
287 Jerian Grant RC .40 1.00
288 Cameron Payne RC .60 1.50
289 Karl-Anthony Towns RC 5.00 12.00
290 Justin Anderson RC .40 1.00
291 Larry Nance Jr. RC .75 2.00
292 Delon Wright RC .50 1.25
293 Tyus Jones RC .50 1.25
294 Emmanuel Mudiay RC .50 1.25
295 Anthony Brown RC .40 1.00
296 Sam Dekker RC .40 1.00
297 Darrun Hilliard RC .40 1.00
298 Rakeem Christmas RC .40 1.00
299 Rondae Hollis-Jefferson RC .50 1.25
300 Justise Winslow RC .60 1.50

2015-16 Hoops Artist Proof

*AP: 2X TO 5X BASIC
*AP RC: 2X TO 5X BASIC
STATED PRINT RUN 99 SER.#'d SETS
261 Kristaps Porzingis 20.00 50.00
289 Karl-Anthony Towns 30.00 80.00

2015-16 Hoops Gold

*GOLD: .75X TO 2X BASIC
*GOLD RC: .75X TO 2X BASIC

2015-16 Hoops Green

*GREEN: 1X TO 2.5X BASIC
*GREEN RC: 1X TO 2.5X BASIC
289 Karl-Anthony Towns 10.00 25.00

2015-16 Hoops Red

*RED: 1.5X TO 4X BASIC
*RED RC: 1.5X TO 4X BASIC
STATED PRINT RUN 299 SER.#'d SETS

2015-16 Hoops Red Backs

*RED BACK: .6X TO 1.5X BASIC
*RED BACK RC: .6X TO 1.5X BASIC

2015-16 Hoops Silver

*SILVER: 1.5X TO 4X BASIC
*SILVER RC: 1.5X TO 4X BASIC
STATED PRINT RUN 299 SER.#'d SETS
268 Devin Booker 100.00 250.00

2015-16 Hoops Action Shots

1 Andrew Wiggins .75 2.00
2 James Harden 1.25 3.00
3 Chris Paul 1.25 3.00
4 Damian Lillard 1.50 4.00
5 Blake Griffin .60 1.50
6 Stephen Curry 5.00 12.00
7 Russell Westbrook 1.00 2.50
8 Carmelo Anthony 1.00 2.50
9 Kobe Bryant 5.00 12.00
10 Derrick Rose 1.00 2.50
11 Kevin Durant 2.50 6.00
12 LeBron James 5.00 12.00
13 Anthony Davis 1.50 4.00
14 Kyrie Irving 1.25 3.00
15 Tony Parker 1.00 2.50
16 John Wall .75 2.00
17 Klay Thompson 1.50 4.00

2015-16 Hoops Birds Eye View

*AP/99: .6X TO 1.5X BASIC
1 John Wall .75 2.00
2 Carmelo Anthony 1.00 2.50
3 DeMarcus Cousins .60 1.50
4 Derrick Rose 1.00 2.50
5 Jimmy Butler 1.25 3.00
6 James Harden 1.25 3.00
7 Bradley Beal .75 2.00
8 LeBron James 5.00 12.00
9 Dirk Nowitzki 1.50 4.00
10 Chris Paul 1.25 3.00
11 Kyrie Irving 1.25 3.00
12 Stephen Curry 5.00 12.00
13 DeMar DeRozan .75 2.00
14 Russell Westbrook 1.00 2.50
15 Klay Thompson 1.50 4.00
16 Kobe Bryant 5.00 12.00
17 Andrew Wiggins .75 2.00
18 Kevin Durant 2.50 6.00
19 Damian Lillard 1.50 4.00
20 Anthony Davis 1.50 4.00
21 Dwyane Wade 1.25 3.00
22 Blake Griffin .60 1.50
23 Kawhi Leonard 2.00 5.00
24 Tony Parker 1.00 2.50
25 DeAndre Jordan .50 1.25

2015-16 Hoops Birds Eye View Holo Green

*HOLO GREEN: .75X TO 2X BASIC
STATED PRINT RUN 25 SER.#'d SETS
8 LeBron James 12.00 30.00
16 Kobe Bryant 12.00 30.00

2015-16 Hoops Champions

83 Golden State Warriors 6.00 15.00
84 Golden State Warriors 6.00 15.00

2015-16 Hoops Champions Trophy Portraits

STATED PRINT RUN 99 SER.#'d SETS
85 Stephen Curry 20.00 50.00
86 Klay Thompson 20.00 50.00
87 Andre Iguodala 10.00 25.00
88 Draymond Green 12.00 30.00
89 Harrison Barnes 8.00 20.00
90 Shaun Livingston 6.00 15.00
91 Leandro Barbosa 6.00 15.00
92 David Lee 6.00 15.00
93 Andrew Bogut 8.00 20.00
94 Steve Kerr 10.00 25.00
95 Thompson/Curry 20.00 50.00
96 Iguodala/Green 20.00 50.00
97 Dell Curry
Stephen Curry 30.00 80.00
98 Marreese Speights 6.00 15.00
99 Iguodala/Russell 30.00 80.00
100 Stephen Curry 20.00 50.00

2015-16 Hoops Courtside

1 Kevin Durant 2.50 6.00
2 LeBron James 5.00 12.00
3 Anthony Davis 1.50 4.00
4 Kyrie Irving 1.25 3.00
5 Kawhi Leonard 2.00 5.00
6 John Wall .75 2.00
7 Russell Westbrook 1.00 2.50
8 Derrick Rose 1.00 2.50
9 Kobe Bryant 5.00 12.00
10 James Harden 1.25 3.00
11 Damian Lillard 1.50 4.00
12 Chris Paul 1.25 3.00
13 Blake Griffin .60 1.50
14 Stephen Curry 5.00 12.00
15 Tony Parker 1.00 2.50
16 Carmelo Anthony 1.00 2.50
17 Klay Thompson 1.50 4.00
18 Jimmy Butler 1.25 3.00
19 Andrew Wiggins .75 2.00
20 Bradley Beal .75 2.00

2015-16 Hoops Courtside Holo Green

*HOLO GREEN: .75X TO 2X BASIC
STATED PRINT RUN 25 SER.#'d SETS
2 LeBron James 12.00 30.00
9 Kobe Bryant 12.00 30.00

2015-16 Hoops Double Trouble

1 B.Beal/J.Wall .75 2.00
2 L.James/K.Irving 5.00 12.00
3 K.Durant/R.Westbrook 2.50 6.00
4 T.Duncan/T.Parker 1.50 4.00
5 P.Gasol/D.Rose 1.00 2.50
6 K.Thompson/S.Curry 5.00 12.00
7 B.Griffin/C.Paul 1.25 3.00

8 C.Bosh/D.Wade 1.25 3.00
9 J.Harden/D.Howard 1.25 3.00
10 A.Wiggins/Z.LaVine 1.50 4.00

2015-16 Hoops Dreams
1 D'Angelo Russell 2.00 5.00
2 Emmanuel Mudiay .60 1.50
3 Mario Hezonja .60 1.50
4 Willie Cauley-Stein .60 1.50
5 Frank Kaminsky .60 1.50
6 Karl-Anthony Towns 3.00 8.00
7 Jahlil Okafor .60 1.50
8 Kristaps Porzingis 3.00 8.00
9 Justise Winslow .75 2.00
10 Jerian Grant .50 1.25

2015-16 Hoops Dreams Holo Artist Proof
*AP: 1.2X TO 3X BASIC
STATED PRINT RUN 99 SER.#'d SETS
6 Karl-Anthony Towns 20.00 50.00
7 Jahlil Okafor 8.00 20.00

2015-16 Hoops Dreams Holo Green
*HOLO GREEN: 5X TO 12X BASIC
STATED PRINT RUN 25 SER.#'d SETS

2015-16 Hoops End 2 End
1 Kyrie Irving 1.25 3.00
2 Stephen Curry 5.00 12.00
3 Russell Westbrook 1.00 2.50
4 Klay Thompson 1.50 4.00
5 Kobe Bryant 5.00 12.00
6 Bradley Beal .75 2.00
7 Kevin Durant 2.50 6.00
8 Damian Lillard 1.50 4.00
9 LeBron James 5.00 12.00
10 Chris Paul 1.25 3.00
11 John Wall .75 2.00
12 Tony Parker 1.00 2.50
13 Derrick Rose 1.00 2.50
14 Andrew Wiggins .75 2.00
15 James Harden 1.25 3.00

2015-16 Hoops Faces of the Future
1 Mario Hezonja .50 1.25
2 Willie Cauley-Stein .50 1.25
3 Frank Kaminsky .50 1.25
4 Myles Turner 1.50 4.00
5 Karl-Anthony Towns 2.50 6.00
6 Cameron Payne .60 1.50
7 D'Angelo Russell 1.50 4.00
8 Sam Dekker .40 1.00
9 Emmanuel Mudiay .50 1.25
10 Rondae Hollis-Jefferson .50 1.25
11 Devin Booker 5.00 12.00
12 Justise Winslow .60 1.50
13 Trey Lyles .50 1.25
14 Delon Wright .50 1.25
15 Jahlil Okafor .50 1.25
16 Tyus Jones .50 1.25
17 Kristaps Porzingis 2.50 6.00
18 Kelly Oubre Jr. 1.25 3.00
19 Jerian Grant .40 1.00
20 Justin Anderson .40 1.00

2015-16 Hoops Finals MVP
STATED PRINT RUN 99 SER.#'d SETS
82 Andre Iguodala 10.00 25.00

2015-16 Hoops Ginormous Signatures
TWO AUTOS PER HOBBY BOX
EXCHANGE DEADLINE 4/14/2017
2 David Robinson 20.00 50.00
9 Thomas Robinson 6.00 15.00
14 Markieff Morris 6.00 15.00

2015-16 Hoops Great SIGnificance
EXCHANGE DEADLINE 4/14/2017
1 Julius Randle 8.00 20.00
2 Jerami Grant 4.00 10.00
3 Michael Carter-Williams 2.50 6.00
4 Alex Len 2.50 6.00
6 C.J. McCollum 4.00 10.00
7 Dwight Powell 2.50 6.00
8 Cody Zeller 2.50 6.00
10 Lorenzo Brown 2.50 6.00
12 Jerry West 15.00 40.00
14 Allen Iverson 50.00 120.00
15 Otto Porter 3.00 8.00
16 Cameron Bairstow 2.50 6.00
17 Robert Covington 3.00 8.00
18 Dante Exum 3.00 8.00
20 Isaiah Canaan 2.50 6.00
23 Mike Muscala 2.50 6.00
24 Anthony Bennett 2.50 6.00
25 Cleanthony Early 2.50 6.00
26 Carl Landry 2.50 6.00
27 Scott Skiles 3.00 8.00
28 Devyn Marble 2.50 6.00
30 James Ennis 2.50 6.00
32 Jordan Clarkson 4.00 10.00
33 Billy Paultz 4.00 10.00
34 Anthony Davis 25.00 60.00
35 Phil Pressey 2.50 6.00
37 Shabazz Muhammad 2.50 6.00
38 Erick Green 2.50 6.00
39 Mark Landsberger 2.50 6.00
40 James Michael McAdoo 2.50 6.00
42 Josh Huestis 2.50 6.00
45 Ray McCallum 2.50 6.00
46 Charles Oakley 6.00 15.00
48 Glenn Robinson III 4.00 10.00
49 Trey Burke 2.50 6.00
51 Matthew Dellavedova 3.00 8.00
52 Julius Erving 30.00 60.00
53 Noah Vonleh 2.50 6.00
55 Ricky Pierce 2.50 6.00
56 Chucky Brown 2.50 6.00
57 Steve Novak 2.50 6.00
58 Grant Jerrett 2.50 6.00
59 Victor Oladipo 3.00 8.00
60 Jeff Withey 2.50 6.00
61 Karl-Anthony Towns 100.00 250.00
62 D'Angelo Russell 20.00 50.00
63 Jahlil Okafor 15.00 40.00
64 Emmanuel Mudiay 3.00 8.00
65 Kristaps Porzingis 60.00 150.00
67 Justise Winslow 10.00 25.00
68 Willie Cauley-Stein 15.00 40.00
69 Stanley Johnson 8.00 20.00
70 Frank Kaminsky 8.00 20.00
71 Devin Booker 200.00 500.00
72 Myles Turner 8.00 20.00
73 Jerian Grant 2.50 6.00
74 Trey Lyles 3.00 8.00
75 Cameron Payne 4.00 10.00
76 Delon Wright 3.00 8.00
77 Rashad Vaughn 2.50 6.00
78 Kelly Oubre Jr. 8.00 20.00
79 Sam Dekker 2.50 6.00
80 Terry Rozier 10.00 25.00
81 Rondae Hollis-Jefferson 3.00 8.00
82 Bobby Portis 6.00 15.00
83 Justin Anderson 2.50 6.00
84 Jarell Martin 2.50 6.00
85 R.J. Hunter 2.50 6.00
86 Anthony Brown 2.50 6.00
87 Tyus Jones 3.00 8.00
88 Chris McCullough 2.50 6.00
89 Jordan Mickey 2.50 6.00
90 Larry Nance Jr. 5.00 12.00
91 Montrezl Harrell 8.00 20.00
92 Dakari Johnson 2.50 6.00
94 Pat Connaughton 4.00 10.00
95 Rakeem Christmas 2.50 6.00
96 Richaun Holmes 4.00 10.00
97 Seth Curry 12.00 30.00
99 Lamar Patterson 2.50 6.00
100 Joe Young 2.50 6.00

2015-16 Hoops High Flyers
*AP/99: .6X TO 1.5X BASIC
1 LeBron James 5.00 12.00
2 Tracy McGrady 1.00 2.50
3 Spud Webb .50 1.25
4 Anfernee Hardaway 1.50 4.00
5 Julius Erving 1.50 4.00
6 Dwyane Wade 1.25 3.00
7 Shawn Kemp 1.00 2.50
8 Scottie Pippen 1.50 4.00
9 Kobe Bryant 5.00 12.00
10 Zach LaVine 1.50 4.00
11 Dwight Howard .75 2.00
12 Shaquille O'Neal 2.00 5.00
13 Blake Griffin .60 1.50
14 Grant Hill 1.00 2.50
15 Dominique Wilkins 1.00 2.50

2015-16 Hoops High Flyers Holo Green
*HOLO GREEN: .75X TO 2X BASIC
STATED PRINT RUN 25 SER.#'d SETS
1 LeBron James 12.00 30.00
9 Kobe Bryant 12.00 30.00

2015-16 Hoops Highlights
1 LeBron James 10.00 25.00
2 Kobe Bryant 10.00 25.00
3 Klay Thompson 3.00 8.00
4 Kyrie Irving 2.50 6.00
5 Stephen Curry 10.00 25.00

2015-16 Hoops Hot Signatures
TWO AUTOS PER HOBBY BOX
*RED HOT/25: .6X TO 1.5X BASIC
EXCHANGE DEADLINE 4/14/2017
1 Kyrie Irving EXCH 20.00 50.00
2 Gary Payton 10.00 25.00
3 Nerlens Noel 2.50 6.00
4 Jerry West 20.00 50.00
5 Ricky Pierce 2.50 6.00
6 Alex Len 2.50 6.00
7 Dwyane Wade 25.00 60.00
8 Blake Griffin 12.00 30.00
9 Julius Erving 25.00 60.00
10 Clyde Drexler 10.00 25.00
11 Matthew Dellavedova 3.00 8.00
12 Hakeem Olajuwon 10.00 25.00
13 Noah Vonleh 2.50 6.00
14 Joel Embiid 25.00 60.00
15 Ricky Rubio 8.00 20.00
16 Allen Iverson 50.00 120.00
17 Tarik Black 2.50 6.00
18 C.J. McCollum 6.00 15.00
19 Julius Randle 5.00 12.00
20 Cody Zeller 2.50 6.00
21 Michael Carter-Williams 2.50 6.00
22 Lorenzo Brown 2.50 6.00
23 Oscar Robertson 25.00 60.00
24 John Stockton 15.00 40.00
25 Dwight Powell 2.50 6.00
26 Andrew Wiggins 12.00 30.00
27 Quincy Acy 2.50 6.00
28 Cameron Bairstow 2.50 6.00
29 Kentavious Caldwell-Pope 3.00 8.00
30 Dante Exum 3.00 8.00
31 Michael Kidd-Gilchrist 2.50 6.00
32 James Ennis 2.50 6.00
33 Otto Porter 3.00 8.00
34 John Wall 20.00 50.00
35 Robert Covington 3.00 8.00
36 Anthony Bennett 2.50 6.00
37 Ray McCallum 2.50 6.00
38 Carl Landry 2.50 6.00
39 Kevin Durant 50.00 120.00
40 David Robinson 15.00 40.00
41 Mike Muscala 2.50 6.00
42 James Michael McAdoo 2.50 6.00
43 Pau Gasol 8.00 20.00
44 Jordan Clarkson 4.00 10.00
45 Shabazz Muhammad 2.50 6.00
46 Anthony Davis 50.00 120.00
47 Trey Burke 2.50 6.00
48 Carmelo Anthony 10.00 25.00
49 Kevin McHale 10.00 25.00
50 Dennis Rodman 15.00 40.00
51 Mason Plumlee 2.50 6.00
52 James Worthy 10.00 25.00
53 Phil Pressey 2.50 6.00
54 Josh Huestis 2.50 6.00
55 Shaquille O'Neal 40.00 100.00
56 Ben McLemore 2.50 6.00
57 Victor Oladipo 6.00 15.00
58 Chris Webber 50.00 120.00
59 Kobe Bryant 400.00 800.00
60 Erick Green 2.50 6.00
61 Karl-Anthony Towns 30.00 80.00
62 D'Angelo Russell 8.00 20.00
63 Jahlil Okafor 3.00 8.00
64 Emmanuel Mudiay 3.00 8.00
65 Kristaps Porzingis 30.00 80.00
67 Justise Winslow 4.00 10.00
68 Willie Cauley-Stein 3.00 8.00
69 Stanley Johnson 3.00 8.00
70 Frank Kaminsky 3.00 8.00
71 Devin Booker 300.00 600.00
72 Myles Turner 10.00 25.00
73 Jerian Grant 2.50 6.00
74 Trey Lyles 3.00 8.00
75 Cameron Payne 4.00 10.00
76 Delon Wright 3.00 8.00
77 Rashad Vaughn 2.50 6.00
78 Kelly Oubre Jr. 8.00 20.00
79 Sam Dekker 2.50 6.00
80 Terry Rozier 10.00 25.00
81 Rondae Hollis-Jefferson 3.00 8.00
82 Bobby Portis 6.00 15.00
83 Justin Anderson 2.50 6.00
84 Jarell Martin 2.50 6.00
85 R.J. Hunter 2.50 6.00
86 Anthony Brown 2.50 6.00
87 Branden Dawson 2.50 6.00
88 Chris McCullough 2.50 6.00
89 Jordan Mickey 2.50 6.00
90 Larry Nance Jr. 5.00 12.00
91 Montrezl Harrell 8.00 20.00
92 Dakari Johnson 2.50 6.00
93 Darrun Hilliard 2.50 6.00
94 Pat Connaughton 4.00 10.00
95 Rakeem Christmas 2.50 6.00
97 Seth Curry 4.00 10.00
99 Tyus Jones 3.00 8.00
100 Lamar Patterson 2.50 6.00

2015-16 Hoops Kobe's All Rookie Team
1 Emmanuel Mudiay 5.00 12.00
2 Jerian Grant 5.00 12.00
3 Mario Hezonja 5.00 12.00
4 Devin Booker 150.00 400.00
5 Frank Kaminsky 5.00 12.00
6 Trey Lyles 5.00 12.00
7 Karl-Anthony Towns 60.00 150.00
8 Jahlil Okafor 5.00 12.00
9 D'Angelo Russell 15.00 40.00
10 Kristaps Porzingis 25.00 60.00
11 Willie Cauley-Stein 5.00 12.00
12 Justise Winslow 6.00 15.00

2015-16 Hoops Lights Camera Action
1 Jimmy Butler 1.25 3.00
2 Jabari Parker .40 1.00
3 Dirk Nowitzki 1.50 4.00
4 Victor Oladipo .50 1.25
5 DeMar DeRozan .75 2.00
6 Magic Johnson 2.50 6.00
7 Andrew Wiggins .75 2.00
8 Dwyane Wade 1.25 3.00
9 John Wall .75 2.00
10 DeAndre Jordan .50 1.25
11 James Harden 1.25 3.00
12 Elfrid Payton .50 1.25
13 Chris Paul 1.25 3.00
14 Kyle Lowry .60 1.50
15 Russell Westbrook 1.00 2.50
16 Shaquille O'Neal 2.00 5.00
17 Kevin Durant 2.50 6.00
18 Blake Griffin .60 1.50
19 Carmelo Anthony 1.00 2.50
20 Eric Bledsoe .50 1.25
21 Bradley Beal .75 2.00
22 Gordon Hayward .60 1.50
23 Kyrie Irving 1.25 3.00
24 Allen Iverson 1.50 4.00
25 Klay Thompson 1.50 4.00
26 Chris Webber .75 2.00
27 Damian Lillard 1.50 4.00
28 Kawhi Leonard 2.00 5.00
29 DeMarcus Cousins .60 1.50
30 Jeff Teague .40 1.00
31 LeBron James 5.00 12.00
32 Nikola Vucevic .50 1.25
33 Stephen Curry 5.00 12.00
34 Larry Bird 2.50 6.00
35 Kobe Bryant 5.00 12.00
36 Latrell Sprewell .50 1.25
37 Anthony Davis 1.50 4.00
38 Tony Parker 1.00 2.50
39 Derrick Rose 1.00 2.50
40 Michael Carter-Williams .40 1.00

2015-16 Hoops Picture Perfect
1 Blake Griffin .60 1.50
2 Kawhi Leonard 2.00 5.00
3 Tony Parker 1.00 2.50
4 Russell Westbrook 1.00 2.50
5 Klay Thompson 1.50 4.00
6 Kobe Bryant 5.00 12.00
7 Andrew Wiggins .75 2.00
8 Kevin Durant 2.50 6.00
9 Damian Lillard 1.50 4.00
10 Anthony Davis 1.50 4.00
11 Stephen Curry 5.00 12.00
12 John Wall .75 2.00
13 Carmelo Anthony 1.00 2.50
14 Derrick Rose 1.00 2.50
15 Giannis Antetokounmpo 3.00 8.00
16 James Harden 1.25 3.00
17 Jabari Parker .40 1.00
18 LeBron James 5.00 12.00
19 Chris Paul 1.25 3.00
20 Kyrie Irving 1.25 3.00

2015-16 Hoops Rise N Shine Memorabilia
*PRIME/25: .75X TO 2X BASE HI
1 Anthony Brown 2.00 5.00
2 Emmanuel Mudiay 2.50 6.00
3 Kristaps Porzingis 10.00 25.00
4 Chris McCullough 2.00 5.00
5 Jerian Grant 2.00 5.00
6 Devin Booker 25.00 60.00
7 Bobby Portis 5.00 12.00
8 Justise Winslow 3.00 8.00
9 Terry Rozier 8.00 20.00
10 Karl-Anthony Towns 6.00 15.00
11 Jarell Martin 2.00 5.00
12 Stanley Johnson 2.50 6.00
13 Montrezl Harrell 6.00 15.00
14 Tyler Harvey 2.00 5.00
15 Cameron Payne 3.00 8.00
17 Myles Turner 8.00 20.00
18 D'Angelo Russell 6.00 15.00
19 Dakari Johnson 2.00 5.00
20 Joe Young 2.00 5.00
21 Frank Kaminsky 2.50 6.00
22 Jordan Mickey 2.00 5.00
23 Willie Cauley-Stein 2.50 6.00
24 Justin Anderson 2.00 5.00
25 Kelly Oubre Jr. 6.00 15.00
26 Tyus Jones 2.50 6.00
27 Trey Lyles 2.50 6.00
28 Sam Dekker 2.00 5.00
29 Jahlil Okafor 5.00 12.00
30 R.J. Hunter 2.00 5.00
31 Josh Huestis 2.00 5.00
33 Richaun Holmes 3.00 8.00
34 Pat Connaughton 3.00 8.00
35 Walter Tavares 2.00 5.00

2015-16 Hoops Road to the Finals
1-41 PRINT RUN 2015 SER.#'d SETS
42-66 PRINT RUN 999 SER.#'d SETS
67-75 PRINT RUN 499 SER.#'d SETS
76-81 PRINT RUN 199 SER.#'d SETS
1 Paul Pierce R1 1.25 3.00
2 Stephen Curry R1 6.00 15.00
3 Derrick Rose R1 1.25 3.00
4 James Harden R1 1.50 4.00
5 Kyrie Irving R1 1.50 4.00
6 Kyle Korver R1 .60 1.50
7 Beno Udrih R1 .50 1.25
8 Blake Griffin R1 .75 2.00
9 Joakim Noah R1 .50 1.25
10 Klay Thompson R1 2.00 5.00
11 Josh Smith R1 .50 1.25
12 LeBron James R1 6.00 15.00
13 John Wall R1 1.00 2.50
14 Al Horford R1 .75 2.00
15 Mike Conley R1 .75 2.00
16 Tim Duncan R1 2.00 5.00
17 LeBron James R1 6.00 15.00
18 Derrick Rose R1 1.25 3.00
19 Stephen Curry R1 6.00 15.00
20 James Harden R1 1.50 4.00
21 John Wall R1 1.00 2.50
22 Kawhi Leonard R1 2.50 6.00
23 Brook Lopez R1 .75 2.00
24 Jerryd Bayless R1 .50 1.25
25 Stephen Curry R1 6.00 15.00
26 Marc Gasol R1 .75 2.00
27 Monta Ellis R1 .60 1.50
28 LeBron James R1 6.00 15.00
29 Blake Griffin R1 .75 2.00
30 Marcin Gortat R1 .50 1.25
31 Deron Williams R1 .60 1.50
32 Michael Carter-Williams R1 .50 1.25
33 Damian Lillard R1 2.00 5.00
34 Dwight Howard R1 1.00 2.50
35 Tim Duncan R1 2.00 5.00
36 Al Horford R1 .75 2.00
37 Marc Gasol R1 .75 2.00
38 Mike Dunleavy R1 .50 1.25
39 Blake Griffin R1 .75 2.00
40 Paul Millsap R1 .60 1.50
41 Chris Paul R1 1.50 4.00
42 Bradley Beal R2 1.25 3.00
43 Stephen Curry R2 8.00 20.00
44 Pau Gasol R2 1.50 4.00
45 Blake Griffin R2 1.00 2.50
46 DeMarre Carroll R2 .60 1.50
47 Mike Conley R2 1.00 2.50
48 LeBron James R2 8.00 20.00
49 James Harden R2 2.00 5.00
50 Derrick Rose R2 1.50 4.00
51 Austin Rivers R2 .75 2.00
52 Paul Pierce R2 1.50 4.00
53 Marc Gasol R2 1.00 2.50
54 LeBron James R2 8.00 20.00
55 DeAndre Jordan R2 .75 2.00
56 Jeff Teague R2 .60 1.50
57 Stephen Curry R2 8.00 20.00
58 LeBron James R2 8.00 20.00
59 James Harden R2 2.00 5.00
60 Al Horford R2 1.00 2.50
61 Klay Thompson R2 2.50 6.00
62 Josh Smith R2 .60 1.50
63 Matthew Dellavedova R2 .75 2.00
64 DeMarre Carroll R2 .60 1.50
65 Stephen Curry R2 8.00 20.00
66 James Harden R2 2.00 5.00
67 Stephen Curry CF 12.00 30.00
68 J.R. Smith CF 1.50 4.00
69 Stephen Curry CF 12.00 30.00
70 LeBron James CF 12.00 30.00
71 Stephen Curry CF 12.00 30.00
72 LeBron James CF 12.00 30.00
73 James Harden CF 3.00 8.00
74 Kyrie Irving CF 3.00 8.00
75 Klay Thompson CF 4.00 10.00
76 Stephen Curry F 15.00 40.00
77 LeBron James F 15.00 40.00
78 LeBron James F 15.00 40.00
79 Andre Iguodala F 2.00 5.00
80 Stephen Curry F 15.00 40.00
81 Draymond Green F 2.50 6.00

2015-16 Hoops Rookie Remembrance Memorabilia
*PRIME/25: .75X TO 2X BASE HI
1 Alec Burks 2.00 5.00
2 Alex Len 2.00 5.00
3 Andre Drummond 3.00 8.00
4 Anthony Bennett 2.00 5.00
5 Archie Goodwin 2.00 5.00
6 Ben McLemore 2.00 5.00
7 Bradley Beal 4.00 10.00
8 C.J. McCollum 3.00 8.00
9 Cody Zeller 2.00 5.00
10 Dennis Schroder 3.00 8.00
11 Dion Waiters 2.00 5.00
12 Draymond Green 4.00 10.00
13 Enes Kanter 2.00 5.00
14 Evan Fournier 2.50 6.00
15 Giannis Antetokounmpo 10.00 25.00
16 Gorgui Dieng 2.00 5.00
17 Harrison Barnes 2.50 6.00
18 Iman Shumpert 2.00 5.00
19 Isaiah Thomas 2.50 6.00
20 Jared Sullinger 2.00 5.00
21 Jimmy Butler 6.00 15.00
22 John Henson 2.00 5.00
23 Jonas Valanciunas 2.50 6.00
24 Kawhi Leonard 10.00 25.00
25 Kelly Olynyk 2.00 5.00
26 Kemba Walker 3.00 8.00
27 Kenneth Faried 2.50 6.00
28 Kentavious Caldwell-Pope 2.50 6.00
29 Khris Middleton 4.00 10.00
30 Klay Thompson 8.00 20.00
31 Kyrie Irving 6.00 15.00
32 Marcus Morris 2.00 5.00
33 Markieff Morris 2.00 5.00
34 Mason Plumlee 2.00 5.00
35 Maurice Harkless 2.00 5.00
36 Michael Carter-Williams 2.00 5.00
37 Michael Kidd-Gilchrist 2.00 5.00
38 Nerlens Noel 2.00 5.00
39 Norris Cole 2.00 5.00
40 Otto Porter 2.50 6.00
41 Reggie Jackson 2.50 6.00
42 Terrence Jones 2.00 5.00
43 Terrence Ross 2.50 6.00
44 Thomas Robinson 2.00 5.00
45 Tim Hardaway Jr. 2.50 6.00
46 Tobias Harris 2.50 6.00
47 Tony Wroten 2.00 5.00
48 Trey Burke 2.00 5.00
49 Tristan Thompson 2.00 5.00
50 Victor Oladipo 2.50 6.00

2015-16 Hoops Swat Team
1 Anthony Davis 1.50 4.00
2 Rudy Gobert .75 2.00
3 DeAndre Jordan .50 1.25
4 Serge Ibaka .50 1.25
5 Andre Drummond .60 1.50
6 Tim Duncan 1.50 4.00
7 Pau Gasol 1.00 2.50
8 Nerlens Noel .40 1.00
9 Marc Gasol .60 1.50
10 Gorgui Dieng .40 1.00
11 Hakeem Olajuwon 1.25 3.00
12 Dikembe Mutombo 1.00 2.50
13 Kareem Abdul-Jabbar 2.00 5.00
14 David Robinson 1.25 3.00
15 Shaquille O'Neal 2.00 5.00

2015-16 Hoops Team Leaders
*AP/99: .6X TO 1.5X BASIC
1 Andrew Wiggins .75 2.00
2 Nikola Vucevic .50 1.25
3 Khris Middleton .75 2.00
4 Kawhi Leonard 2.00 5.00
5 DeMar DeRozan .75 2.00
6 Stephen Curry 5.00 12.00
7 Nerlens Noel .40 1.00
8 DeMarcus Cousins .60 1.50
9 Russell Westbrook 1.00 2.50
10 John Wall .75 2.00
11 LeBron James 5.00 12.00
12 James Harden 1.25 3.00
13 George Hill .50 1.25
14 Chandler Parsons .40 1.00
15 Marcus Smart .75 2.00
16 DeAndre Jordan .50 1.25
17 Carmelo Anthony 1.00 2.50
18 Kobe Bryant 5.00 12.00
19 Rudy Gobert .75 2.00
20 Dwyane Wade 1.25 3.00
21 Pau Gasol 1.00 2.50
22 Zach Randolph .60 1.50
23 Andre Drummond .60 1.50
24 Anthony Davis 1.50 4.00
25 Brook Lopez .60 1.50
26 Eric Bledsoe .50 1.25
27 Damian Lillard 1.50 4.00
28 Jeff Teague .40 1.00
29 Kenneth Faried .50 1.25
30 Klay Thompson 1.50 4.00

2015-16 Hoops Team Leaders Holo Green
*HOLO GREEN: .75X TO 2X BASIC
STATED PRINT RUN 25 SER.#'d SETS
11 LeBron James 12.00 30.00
18 Kobe Bryant 12.00 30.00

2015-16 Hoops Triple Double
1 Chris Paul 1.25 3.00
2 Rajon Rondo .75 2.00
3 Kyle Lowry .60 1.50
4 Michael Carter-Williams .40 1.00
5 Kobe Bryant 5.00 12.00
6 Tim Duncan 1.50 4.00
7 Rajon Rondo .75 2.00
8 Eric Bledsoe .50 1.25
9 Rajon Rondo .75 2.00
10 Michael Carter-Williams .40 1.00
11 James Harden 1.25 3.00
12 Eric Bledsoe .50 1.25
13 Kobe Bryant 5.00 12.00
14 Draymond Green .75 2.00
15 Al Horford .60 1.50
16 Russell Westbrook 1.00 2.50
17 Hassan Whiteside .50 1.25
18 Michael Carter-Williams .40 1.00
19 Russell Westbrook 1.00 2.50
20 Tyreke Evans .50 1.25
21 James Harden 1.25 3.00
22 Russell Westbrook 1.00 2.50
23 Evan Turner .40 1.00
24 Russell Westbrook 1.00 2.50
25 George Hill .50 1.25
26 Russell Westbrook 1.00 2.50
27 Ricky Rubio .50 1.25
28 Russell Westbrook 1.00 2.50
29 James Harden 1.25 3.00
30 Russell Westbrook 1.00 2.50
31 Russell Westbrook 1.00 2.50
32 Kyle Lowry .60 1.50
33 Reggie Jackson .50 1.25
34 Elfrid Payton .50 1.25
35 Elfrid Payton .50 1.25
36 Russell Westbrook 1.00 2.50
37 Evan Turner .40 1.00
38 Reggie Jackson .50 1.25
39 Evan Turner .40 1.00
40 DeMarcus Cousins .60 1.50
41 Russell Westbrook 1.00 2.50
42 DeMarcus Cousins .60 1.50
43 LeBron James 5.00 12.00
44 Russell Westbrook 1.00 2.50
45 LeBron James 5.00 12.00
46 James Harden 1.25 3.00

2016-17 Hoops
COMPLETE SET (300) 25.00 60.00
*BLUE: .75X TO 2X BASIC
*TEAL EXP: 1X TO 2.5X BASIC
*GREEN/149: 1.2X TO 3X BASIC
*SILVER/99: 2X TO 5X BASIC
*BLUE CHECK/75: 2.5X TO 6X BASIC
*ORANGE EXP/75: 2.5X TO 6X BASIC
*RED/49: 3X TO 8X BASIC
*TEAL/49: 3X TO 8X BASIC
*ARTIST PROOF/25: 5X TO 12X BASIC
*ORANGE/25: 5X TO 12X BASIC
*RED CHECK/15: 6X TO 15X BASIC
1 Jahlil Okafor .20 .50
2 Nerlens Noel .20 .50
3 Robert Covington .25 .60
4 Joel Embiid .75 2.00
5 Ish Smith .20 .50
6 Giannis Antetokounmpo 1.50 4.00
7 Jabari Parker .20 .50
8 Khris Middleton .30 .75
9 Greg Monroe .20 .50
10 Tyler Ennis .20 .50
11 Derrick Rose .50 1.25
12 Jimmy Butler .60 1.50
13 Bobby Portis .30 .75
14 Nikola Mirotic .20 .50
15 Doug McDermott .25 .60
16 Pau Gasol .50 1.25
17 LeBron James 2.50 6.00
18 Kyrie Irving .60 1.50
19 Kevin Love .30 .75
20 Mike Dunleavy .20 .50
21 Matthew Dellavedova .25 .60
22 Tristan Thompson .25 .60
23 Isaiah Thomas .25 .60
24 Avery Bradley .20 .50
25 Jae Crowder .20 .50
26 Marcus Smart .40 1.00
27 Evan Turner .20 .50
28 Jared Sullinger .20 .50
29 Chris Paul .50 1.25
30 Blake Griffin .30 .75
31 DeAndre Jordan .25 .60
32 J.J. Redick .30 .75
33 Jamal Crawford .30 .75
34 Jeff Green .20 .50
35 Mike Conley .25 .60
36 Marc Gasol .30 .75
37 Zach Randolph .30 .75
38 Matt Barnes .20 .50
39 Brandan Wright .20 .50
40 Paul Millsap .25 .60
41 Dennis Schroder .30 .75
42 Kent Bazemore .20 .50
43 Al Horford .30 .75
44 Kyle Korver .25 .60
45 Dwyane Wade .60 1.50
46 Chris Bosh .40 1.00
47 Luol Deng .25 .60
48 Goran Dragic .30 .75
49 Hassan Whiteside .25 .60
50 Jeremy Lin .60 1.50
51 Kemba Walker .25 .60
52 Frank Kaminsky .20 .50
53 Nicolas Batum .25 .60
54 Al Jefferson .20 .50
55 Gordon Hayward .30 .75
56 Rudy Gobert .40 1.00
57 Rodney Hood .25 .60
58 Derrick Favors .20 .50
59 Alec Burks .25 .60
60 DeMarcus Cousins .25 .60
61 Rajon Rondo .40 1.00
62 Rudy Gay .30 .75
63 Willie Cauley-Stein .25 .60
64 Darren Collison .20 .50
65 Carmelo Anthony .50 1.25
66 Kristaps Porzingis .50 1.25
67 Jerian Grant .20 .50
68 Arron Afflalo .20 .50
69 Derrick Williams .20 .50
70 D'Angelo Russell .40 1.00
71 Jordan Clarkson .30 .75
72 Julius Randle .40 1.00
73 Larry Nance Jr. .20 .50
74 Brandon Bass .20 .50
75 Victor Oladipo .25 .60
76 Mario Hezonja .20 .50
77 Aaron Gordon .30 .75
78 Nikola Vucevic .30 .75
79 Elfrid Payton .25 .60
80 Dirk Nowitzki .75 2.00
81 Justin Anderson .20 .50
82 Deron Williams .25 .60
83 Chandler Parsons .20 .50
84 Zaza Pachulia .20 .50
85 Brook Lopez .25 .60
86 Thaddeus Young .20 .50
87 Rondae Hollis-Jefferson .20 .50
88 Bojan Bogdanovic .25 .60
89 Jarrett Jack .25 .60
90 Emmanuel Mudiay .20 .50
91 Danilo Gallinari .25 .60
92 Kenneth Faried .25 .60
93 Nikola Jokic 1.50 4.00
94 Will Barton .20 .50
95 Paul George .50 1.25
96 Myles Turner .30 .75
97 Monta Ellis .25 .60
98 George Hill .25 .60
99 Ian Mahinmi .20 .50
100 Anthony Davis 1.00 2.50
101 Ryan Anderson .20 .50
102 Jrue Holiday .40 1.00
103 Tyreke Evans .25 .60
104 Eric Gordon .25 .60
105 Jeff Withey .20 .50
106 Reggie Jackson .25 .60
107 Stanley Johnson .20 .50
108 Tobias Harris .30 .75
109 Kentavious Caldwell-Pope .25 .60
110 Kyle Lowry .30 .75
111 DeMar DeRozan .40 1.00
112 Jonas Valanciunas .25 .60
113 DeMarre Carroll .20 .50
114 Bismack Biyombo .20 .50
115 Cory Joseph .20 .50
116 James Harden .60 1.50
117 Dwight Howard .40 1.00
118 Sam Dekker .20 .50
119 Trevor Ariza .20 .50
120 Clint Capela .25 .60
121 Kawhi Leonard .75 2.00
122 LaMarcus Aldridge .30 .75
123 Tony Parker .50 1.25
124 Kyle Anderson .20 .50
125 Manu Ginobili .60 1.50
126 Devin Booker 1.25 3.00
127 Eric Bledsoe .25 .60
128 Brandon Knight .25 .60
129 Alex Len .20 .50
130 Tyson Chandler .25 .60
131 Russell Westbrook .50 1.25
132 Steven Adams .25 .60
133 Enes Kanter .20 .50
134 Serge Ibaka .25 .60
135 Cameron Payne .30 .75
136 Dion Waiters .20 .50
137 Karl-Anthony Towns .60 1.50
138 Andrew Wiggins .40 1.00
139 Kevin Garnett .75 2.00
140 Zach LaVine .60 1.50
141 Ricky Rubio .25 .60
142 Shabazz Muhammad .20 .50
143 Damian Lillard .75 2.00
144 C.J. McCollum .30 .75
145 Al-Farouq Aminu .20 .50
146 Mason Plumlee .20 .50
147 Ed Davis .20 .50
148 Stephen Curry 2.50 6.00
149 Klay Thompson .75 2.00
150 Draymond Green .40 1.00
151 Andre Drummond .30 .75
152 Harrison Barnes .25 .60
153 Andrew Bogut .30 .75
154 John Wall .40 1.00
155 Markieff Morris .20 .50
156 Bradley Beal .40 1.00
157 Marcin Gortat .20 .50
158 Kelly Oubre Jr. .40 1.00
159 Justise Winslow .25 .60
160 Trey Lyles .25 .60
161 Nik Stauskas .20 .50
162 Jerami Grant .30 .75
163 Isaiah Canaan .20 .50
164 John Henson .20 .50
165 Rashad Vaughn .20 .50
166 Michael Carter-Williams .20 .50
167 Cristiano Felicio .20 .50
168 E'Twaun Moore .20 .50
169 Aaron Brooks .20 .50
170 Channing Frye .20 .50
171 Iman Shumpert .20 .50
172 Richard Jefferson .25 .60
173 Mo Williams .25 .60
174 Kelly Olynyk .20 .50
175 Terry Rozier .30 .75
176 Jordan Mickey .20 .50
177 Tyler Zeller .20 .50
178 Paul Pierce .50 1.25
179 Austin Rivers .25 .60
180 Cole Aldrich .20 .50
181 Luc Mbah a Moute .20 .50
182 Vince Carter .60 1.50
183 Chris Andersen .25 .60
184 Tony Allen .20 .50
185 Thabo Sefolosha .20 .50
186 Walter Tavares .20 .50
187 Kirk Hinrich .25 .60
188 Tyler Johnson .20 .50
189 Josh Richardson .25 .60
190 Gerald Green .25 .60
191 Michael Kidd-Gilchrist .20 .50
192 Courtney Lee .20 .50
193 Marvin Williams .20 .50
194 Trey Burke .20 .50
195 Dante Exum .25 .60
196 Joe Ingles .25 .60
197 Seth Curry .25 .60
198 Marco Belinelli .20 .50
199 Ben McLemore .20 .50
200 Lance Thomas .20 .50
201 Jose Calderon .20 .50
202 Robin Lopez .20 .50
203 Marcelo Huertas .20 .50
204 Lou Williams .30 .75
205 Tarik Black .20 .50
206 Evan Fournier .25 .60
207 Brandon Jennings .20 .50
208 Ersan Ilyasova .20 .50
209 J.J. Barea .25 .60
210 Salah Mejri .20 .50
211 Wesley Matthews .20 .50
212 Greivis Vasquez .20 .50
213 Chris McCullough .20 .50
214 Trevor Booker .20 .50
215 Jusuf Nurkic .25 .60
216 Wilson Chandler .25 .60
217 D.J. Augustin .20 .50
218 Joe Young .20 .50
219 Jordan Hill .20 .50
220 Rodney Stuckey .20 .50
221 Terrence Jones .20 .50
222 Omer Asik .20 .50
223 Langston Galloway .20 .50

224 Marcus Morris .20 .50
225 Jodie Meeks .20 .50
226 Joel Anthony .20 .50
227 Patrick Patterson .20 .50
228 Norman Powell .30 .75
229 Delon Wright .25 .60
230 Michael Beasley .20 .50
231 Jason Terry .25 .60
232 Corey Brewer .20 .50
233 Boban Marjanovic .25 .60
234 David Lee .20 .50
235 Danny Green .25 .60
236 David West .25 .60
237 Archie Goodwin .20 .50
238 T.J. Warren .25 .60
239 P.J. Tucker .20 .50
240 Kevin Durant 1.25 3.00
241 Andre Roberson .20 .50
242 Anthony Morrow .20 .50
243 Randy Foye .20 .50
244 Tyus Jones .20 .50
245 Gorgui Dieng .20 .50
246 Adreian Payne .20 .50
247 Brandon Rush .20 .50
248 Allen Crabbe .20 .50
249 Meyers Leonard .20 .50
250 Gerald Henderson .20 .50
251 Shaun Livingston .20 .50
252 Leandro Barbosa .20 .50
253 Marreese Speights .20 .50
254 Festus Ezeli .20 .50
255 Otto Porter .25 .60
256 Nene .20 .50
257 Jared Dudley .20 .50
258 Ramon Sessions .20 .50
259 Udonis Haslem .25 .60
260 Jason Smith .20 .50
261 Ben Simmons RC 1.25 3.00
262 Brandon Ingram RC 1.50 4.00
263 Jaylen Brown RC 6.00 15.00
264 Dragan Bender RC .40 1.00
265 Kris Dunn RC .60 1.50
266 Buddy Hield RC 1.25 3.00
267 Jamal Murray RC 3.00 8.00
268 Marquese Chriss RC .50 1.25
269 Jakob Poeltl RC .75 2.00
270 Thon Maker RC .50 1.25
271 Domantas Sabonis RC 2.50 6.00
272 Taurean Prince RC .50 1.25
273 Denzel Valentine RC .40 1.00
274 Wade Baldwin IV RC .40 1.00
275 Henry Ellenson RC .40 1.00
276 Malik Beasley RC .75 2.00
277 Caris LeVert RC 1.00 2.50
278 DeAndre' Bembry RC .60 1.50
279 Malachi Richardson RC .40 1.00
280 T. Luwawu-Cabarrot RC .60 1.50
281 Tomas Satoransky RC .60 1.50
282 Brice Johnson RC .40 1.00
283 Pascal Siakam RC 2.50 6.00
284 Skal Labissiere RC .40 1.00
285 Dejounte Murray RC 2.00 5.00
286 Damian Jones RC .40 1.00
287 Deyonta Davis RC .40 1.00
288 Ivica Zubac RC 1.00 2.50
289 Cheick Diallo RC .40 1.00
290 Tyler Ulis RC .50 1.25
291 Malcolm Brogdon RC 1.25 3.00
292 Chinanu Onuaku RC .40 1.00
293 Patrick McCaw RC .40 1.00
294 Diamond Stone RC .40 1.00
295 Isaiah Whitehead RC .40 1.00
296 Demetrius Jackson RC .40 1.00
297 A.J. Hammons RC .40 1.00
298 Michael Gbinije RC .40 1.00
299 Dario Saric RC .60 1.50
300 Kay Felder RC .40 1.00

2016-17 Hoops Artist Proof
*ARTIST PROOF: 5X TO 12X BASIC
*ARTIST PROOF RC: 5X TO 12X BASIC
STATED PRINT RUN 25 SER.#'d SETS

2016-17 Hoops Orange
*ORANGE: 5X TO 12X BASIC
*ORANGE RC: 5X TO 12X BASIC
STATED PRINT RUN 25 SER.#'d SETS

2016-17 Hoops Red
*RED: 3X TO 8X BASIC
*RED RC: 3X TO 8X BASIC
STATED PRINT RUN 49 SER.#'d SETS

2016-17 Hoops Red Backs
*RED BACK: .6X TO 1.5X BASIC
*RED BACK RC: .6X TO 1.5X BASIC

2016-17 Hoops Teal
*TEAL: 3X TO 8X BASIC
*TEAL RC: 3X TO 8X BASIC
STATED PRINT RUN 49 SER.#'d SETS

2016-17 Hoops Action Shots
1 Stephen Curry 4.00 10.00
2 John Wall .60 1.50
3 Brandon Knight .40 1.00
4 James Harden 1.00 2.50
5 Jonas Valanciunas .40 1.00
6 Andre Drummond .50 1.25
7 DeMarcus Cousins .40 1.00
8 Chris Paul .75 2.00
9 Alec Burks .40 1.00
10 Jamal Crawford .50 1.25
11 Zach LaVine 1.00 2.50
12 Kevin Love .50 1.25
13 Marc Gasol .50 1.25
14 Hassan Whiteside .40 1.00
15 Kemba Walker .40 1.00
16 Julius Randle .60 1.50
17 Jabari Parker .30 .75
18 Jimmy Butler 1.00 2.50
19 Avery Bradley .30 .75
20 Elfrid Payton .40 1.00

2016-17 Hoops Birds Eye View
1 LeBron James 4.00 10.00
2 Andrew Wiggins .60 1.50
3 Zach LaVine 1.00 2.50
4 Aaron Gordon .50 1.25
5 DeAndre Jordan .40 1.00
6 Blake Griffin .50 1.25
7 Giannis Antetokounmpo 2.50 6.00
8 John Wall .60 1.50
9 Andre Iguodala .50 1.25
10 Russell Westbrook .75 2.00
11 Norman Powell .50 1.25
12 Kenneth Faried .40 1.00
13 Justise Winslow .40 1.00
14 Kristaps Porzingis .75 2.00
15 Andre Drummond .50 1.25
16 Kawhi Leonard 1.25 3.00
17 Rudy Gay .50 1.25
18 Jordan Clarkson .50 1.25
19 Paul Millsap .40 1.00
20 Jimmy Butler 1.00 2.50
21 Hassan Whiteside .40 1.00
22 Paul George .75 2.00
23 Anthony Davis 1.50 4.00
24 Justin Anderson .30 .75
25 Rodney Hood .40 1.00

2016-17 Hoops Birds Eye View Artist Proof
*ARTIST PROOF: 1.2X TO 3X BASIC
STATED PRINT RUN 25 SER.#'d SETS
1 LeBron James 12.00 30.00

2016-17 Hoops Champions
1 Cleveland Cavaliers 12.00 30.00

2016-17 Hoops Champions Trophy Portraits
STATED PRINT RUN 99 SER.#'d SETS
1 Kobe Bryant 40.00 100.00
2 Stephen Curry 30.00 80.00
3 LeBron James 100.00 250.00
4 David Robinson 15.00 40.00
5 Dirk Nowitzki 30.00 80.00
6 Shaquille O'Neal 25.00 60.00
7 Kevin Garnett 30.00 80.00
8 Tony Parker 20.00 50.00
9 Dwyane Wade 20.00 50.00
10 Magic Johnson 25.00 60.00
11 Larry Bird 25.00 60.00

2016-17 Hoops Courtside
1 John Wall .60 1.50
2 Draymond Green .60 1.50
3 Damian Lillard 1.25 3.00
4 Karl-Anthony Towns 1.00 2.50
5 Russell Westbrook .75 2.00
6 Kawhi Leonard 1.25 3.00
7 James Harden 1.00 2.50
8 Kyle Lowry .50 1.25
9 Andre Drummond .50 1.25
10 Anthony Davis 1.50 4.00
11 Paul George .75 2.00
12 Dirk Nowitzki 1.25 3.00
13 Jimmy Butler 1.00 2.50
14 Kristaps Porzingis .75 2.00
15 DeMarcus Cousins .40 1.00
16 Kemba Walker .40 1.00
17 Devin Booker 2.00 5.00
18 Blake Griffin .50 1.25
19 LeBron James 4.00 10.00
20 Giannis Antetokounmpo 2.50 6.00

2016-17 Hoops Courtside Artist Proof
*ARTIST PROOF: 1.2X TO 3X BASIC
STATED PRINT RUN 25 SER.#'d SETS
19 LeBron James 25.00 60.00

2016-17 Hoops Double Trouble
1 C.Anthony/K.Porzingis .75 2.00
2 M.Ellis/P.George .75 2.00
3 A.Drummond/R.Jackson .50 1.25
4 C.McCollum/D.Lillard 1.25 3.00
5 K.Thompson/S.Curry 4.00 10.00
6 D.Booker/E.Bledsoe 2.00 5.00
7 N.Jokic/E.Mudiay 2.50 6.00
8 A.Wiggins/K.Towns 1.00 2.50
9 B.Griffin/C.Paul .75 2.00
10 L.James/K.Irving 4.00 10.00

2016-17 Hoops Dreams
*ARTIST PROOF/25: 1.2X TO 3X BASIC
1 Kyrie Irving 1.00 2.50
2 Stephen Curry 4.00 10.00
3 Karl-Anthony Towns 1.00 2.50
4 Giannis Antetokounmpo 2.50 6.00
5 John Wall .60 1.50
6 Damian Lillard 1.25 3.00
7 Anthony Davis 1.50 4.00
8 Devin Booker 2.00 5.00
9 Kristaps Porzingis .75 2.00
10 D'Angelo Russell .60 1.50

2016-17 Hoops End 2 End
1 Blake Griffin .50 1.25
2 Rudy Gay .50 1.25
3 Kyrie Irving 1.00 2.50
4 Jimmy Butler 1.00 2.50
5 Marcus Smart .60 1.50
6 Jeremy Lin 1.00 2.50
7 Dennis Schroder .50 1.25
8 Jordan Clarkson .50 1.25
9 Aaron Gordon .50 1.25
10 Jrue Holiday .60 1.50
11 Reggie Jackson .40 1.00
12 Russell Westbrook .75 2.00
13 Draymond Green .60 1.50
14 John Wall .60 1.50
15 Dwyane Wade .60 1.50

2016-17 Hoops Faces of the Future
1 Karl-Anthony Towns 1.00 2.50
2 Kristaps Porzingis .75 2.00
3 Jahlil Okafor .30 .75
4 Devin Booker 2.00 5.00
5 Justise Winslow .40 1.00
6 D'Angelo Russell .60 1.50
7 Andrew Wiggins .60 1.50
8 Jabari Parker .30 .75
9 Joel Embiid 1.25 3.00
10 Aaron Gordon .50 1.25
11 Julius Randle .60 1.50
12 Nikola Jokic 2.50 6.00
13 Victor Oladipo .40 1.00
14 Kentavious Caldwell-Pope .40 1.00
15 C.J. McCollum .50 1.25
16 Steven Adams .40 1.00
17 Giannis Antetokounmpo 2.50 6.00
18 Dennis Schroder .50 1.25
19 Rudy Gobert .60 1.50
20 Myles Turner .50 1.25

2016-17 Hoops Finals MVP
1 LeBron James 75.00 200.00

2016-17 Hoops Great SIGnificance
EXCHANGE DEADLINE 4/12/2018
1 Cody Zeller 3.00 8.00
2 Dwight Powell 3.00 8.00
3 Aaron Harrison 3.00 8.00
4 Walter Tavares 3.00 8.00
5 Allen Crabbe 3.00 8.00
6 Alex Len 3.00 8.00
7 Jonas Valanciunas 4.00 10.00
8 Rashad Vaughn 3.00 8.00
9 Matthew Dellavedova 4.00 10.00
10 Kelly Olynyk 3.00 8.00
11 Bobby Portis 5.00 12.00
12 Festus Ezeli 3.00 8.00
13 Jason Terry 4.00 10.00
14 Michael Kidd-Gilchrist 3.00 8.00
15 Deron Williams 4.00 10.00
16 Jonathon Simmons 3.00 8.00
17 Michael Carter-Williams 3.00 8.00
18 Dennis Schroder 5.00 12.00
19 Donatas Motiejunas 3.00 8.00
20 Kent Bazemore 3.00 8.00
21 Raul Neto 3.00 8.00
22 Cristiano Felicio 3.00 8.00
23 Clint Capela 4.00 10.00
24 Gorgui Dieng 3.00 8.00
25 Draymond Green 6.00 15.00
26 Ed Davis 3.00 8.00
27 Nikola Jokic 100.00 250.00
28 Paul Millsap 4.00 10.00
29 DeMarre Carroll 3.00 8.00
30 Andrew Bogut 5.00 12.00
31 Zaza Pachulia 3.00 8.00
32 Sam Dekker 3.00 8.00
33 Goran Dragic 5.00 12.00
34 Carmelo Anthony 12.00 30.00
35 Jusuf Nurkic 4.00 10.00
36 Norman Powell 5.00 12.00
37 Larry Nance Jr. 3.00 8.00
38 Shabazz Muhammad 3.00 8.00
39 Khris Middleton 5.00 12.00
40 Marcelo Huertas 3.00 8.00
41 Avery Bradley 3.00 8.00
42 C.J. McCollum 5.00 12.00
43 Montrezl Harrell 5.00 12.00
44 Devin Harris 3.00 8.00
45 Gary Harris 4.00 10.00
46 Jarell Martin 3.00 8.00
47 T.J. McConnell 4.00 10.00
48 Seth Curry 8.00 20.00
49 Gerald Henderson 3.00 8.00
50 Otto Porter 4.00 10.00
51 Jerami Grant 5.00 12.00
52 Sasha Kaun 3.00 8.00
53 Spencer Hawes 3.00 8.00
54 Tony Allen 3.00 8.00
55 R.J. Hunter 3.00 8.00
57 Anthony Davis 25.00 60.00
58 Pau Gasol 8.00 20.00
59 Tyus Jones 3.00 8.00
60 Timofey Mozgov 3.00 8.00
64 Lamar Patterson 3.00 8.00
65 Ian Clark 3.00 8.00
66 E'Twaun Moore 3.00 8.00
67 Reggie Bullock 3.00 8.00
68 James Ennis 3.00 8.00
69 Josh Huestis 3.00 8.00
70 Ray McCallum 3.00 8.00
71 JaKarr Sampson 3.00 8.00
72 Jeff Withey 3.00 8.00
73 Jason Thompson 3.00 8.00
74 Jason Smith 3.00 8.00
75 Tyler Ennis 3.00 8.00
76 James Johnson 3.00 8.00
77 Terrence Jones 3.00 8.00
78 Robert Covington 4.00 10.00
79 Dante Exum 4.00 10.00
80 Salah Mejri 3.00 8.00
81 James Young 3.00 8.00
82 Richaun Holmes 4.00 10.00
83 Kris Humphries 3.00 8.00
84 Joel Embiid 60.00 150.00
85 Brandon Bass 3.00 8.00
86 Amir Johnson 3.00 8.00
87 Chris McCullough 3.00 8.00
88 James Michael McAdoo 3.00 8.00
89 Lance Thomas 3.00 8.00
90 Willie Cauley-Stein 4.00 10.00
91 Shabazz Napier 3.00 8.00
92 Jordan Clarkson 5.00 12.00
93 Wilson Chandler 4.00 10.00
94 Norris Cole 3.00 8.00
95 Kyle Singler 3.00 8.00
96 Mo Williams 4.00 10.00
97 Nick Young 3.00 8.00
98 Trey Burke 3.00 8.00
99 Tobias Harris 5.00 12.00
100 Isaiah Canaan 3.00 8.00

2016-17 Hoops High Flyers
*ARTIST PROOF/25: 1.2X TO 3X BASIC
1 DeMarcus Cousins .40 1.00
2 Zach LaVine 1.00 2.50
3 Aaron Gordon .50 1.25
4 Jabari Parker .30 .75
5 Julius Randle .60 1.50
6 Andrew Wiggins .60 1.50
7 DeMar DeRozan .60 1.50
8 Will Barton .30 .75
9 Eric Bledsoe .40 1.00
10 Mason Plumlee .30 .75
11 James Harden 1.00 2.50
12 Kentavious Caldwell-Pope .40 1.00
13 Blake Griffin .50 1.25
14 Jahlil Okafor .30 .75
15 Marcus Smart .60 1.50

2016-17 Hoops Highlights
1 Tim Duncan 1.25 3.00
2 Stephen Curry 5.00 12.00
3 Kobe Bryant 15.00 40.00
4 Russell Westbrook 1.00 2.50
5 Dwyane Wade 1.25 3.00
6 Andre Drummond .60 1.50
7 Anthony Davis 2.00 5.00
8 Stephen Curry 5.00 12.00
9 Hassan Whiteside .50 1.25
10 Rajon Rondo .75 2.00
11 Aaron Gordon .60 1.50
12 LeBron James 5.00 12.00
13 Klay Thompson 1.50 4.00
14 DeMarcus Cousins .50 1.25
15 Dirk Nowitzki 1.50 4.00
16 Emmanuel Mudiay .40 1.00
17 Kristaps Porzingis 1.00 2.50
18 Karl-Anthony Towns 1.25 3.00
19 D'Angelo Russell .75 2.00
20 Devin Booker 2.50 6.00

2016-17 Hoops Hot Signatures
EXCHANGE DEADLINE 4/12/2018
*RED/25: .75X TO 2X BASIC
1 Cody Zeller 3.00 8.00
2 Dwight Powell 3.00 8.00
3 T.J. McConnell 4.00 10.00
4 Aaron Harrison 3.00 8.00
5 Walter Tavares 3.00 8.00
6 Allen Crabbe 3.00 8.00
7 Alex Len 3.00 8.00
8 Jonas Valanciunas 4.00 10.00
9 Robert Covington 4.00 10.00
10 Rashad Vaughn 3.00 8.00
11 Matthew Dellavedova 4.00 10.00
12 Kelly Olynyk 3.00 8.00
13 Seth Curry 4.00 10.00
14 Bobby Portis 5.00 12.00
15 Festus Ezeli 3.00 8.00
16 Jason Terry 4.00 10.00
17 Michael Kidd-Gilchrist 3.00 8.00
18 Deron Williams 4.00 10.00
19 Jarell Martin 3.00 8.00
20 Jonathon Simmons 3.00 8.00
21 Michael Carter-Williams 3.00 8.00
22 Devin Harris 3.00 8.00
23 Gary Harris 4.00 10.00
24 Dennis Schroder 5.00 12.00
25 Donatas Motiejunas 3.00 8.00
26 Kent Bazemore 3.00 8.00
27 Raul Neto 3.00 8.00
28 Cristiano Felicio 3.00 8.00
30 C.J. McCollum 5.00 12.00
31 Gorgui Dieng 3.00 8.00
32 Tyler Ennis 3.00 8.00
33 Marcelo Huertas 3.00 8.00
34 Ed Davis 3.00 8.00
35 Avery Bradley 3.00 8.00
36 Shabazz Muhammad 3.00 8.00
37 Larry Nance Jr. 3.00 8.00
38 Norman Powell 5.00 12.00
39 Gerald Henderson 3.00 8.00
40 Khris Middleton 5.00 12.00
41 Luis Scola 4.00 10.00
42 Paul Millsap 4.00 10.00
43 Nikola Jokic 100.00 250.00
44 Otto Porter 4.00 10.00
45 DeMarre Carroll 3.00 8.00
46 Jerami Grant 5.00 12.00
47 Andrew Bogut 5.00 12.00
48 Zaza Pachulia 3.00 8.00
49 Goran Dragic 5.00 12.00
50 Sam Dekker 3.00 8.00
51 Salah Mejri 3.00 8.00
52 Boban Marjanovic 4.00 10.00
54 Ian Clark 3.00 8.00
55 Eric Bledsoe 4.00 10.00
56 Emmanuel Mudiay 3.00 8.00
57 Anthony Davis 30.00 80.00
58 Kyrie Irving EXCH 25.00 60.00
59 Kevin Durant 60.00 150.00
60 Andrew Wiggins 6.00 15.00

2016-17 Hoops Hot Signatures Rookies
EXCHANGE DEADLINE 4/12/2018
*RED/25: .6X TO 1.5X BASIC
1 Brandon Ingram 25.00 60.00
2 Jaylen Brown 75.00 200.00
3 Dragan Bender 3.00 8.00
4 Kris Dunn 5.00 12.00
5 Buddy Hield 12.00 30.00
6 Jamal Murray 20.00 50.00
7 Marquese Chriss 4.00 10.00
8 Jakob Poeltl 6.00 15.00
9 Thon Maker 4.00 10.00
10 Domantas Sabonis 20.00 50.00
11 Taurean Prince 4.00 10.00
12 Denzel Valentine 3.00 8.00
13 Wade Baldwin IV 3.00 8.00
14 Henry Ellenson 3.00 8.00
15 Malik Beasley 6.00 15.00
16 DeAndre' Bembry 5.00 12.00
17 Malachi Richardson 3.00 8.00
18 T. Luwawu-Cabarrot 5.00 12.00
19 Brice Johnson 3.00 8.00
20 Pascal Siakam 12.00 30.00
21 Skal Labissiere 3.00 8.00
22 Damian Jones 3.00 8.00
23 Deyonta Davis 3.00 8.00
24 Cheick Diallo 3.00 8.00
25 Tyler Ulis 4.00 10.00
26 Patrick McCaw 3.00 8.00
28 Demetrius Jackson 3.00 8.00
29 Kay Felder 3.00 8.00
30 Ivica Zubac 8.00 20.00
31 Malcolm Brogdon 10.00 25.00
32 A.J. Hammons 3.00 8.00
33 Diamond Stone 3.00 8.00
34 Gary Payton II 8.00 20.00
35 Caris LeVert 8.00 20.00
37 Ron Baker 3.00 8.00
39 Ben Bentil 3.00 8.00
40 Anthony Barber 3.00 8.00

2016-17 Hoops Kobe 2K Hoops
1 Kobe Bryant 4.00 10.00
2 Kobe Bryant 4.00 10.00
3 Kobe Bryant 4.00 10.00
4 Kobe Bryant 4.00 10.00
5 Kobe Bryant 4.00 10.00
6 Kobe Bryant 4.00 10.00
7 Kobe Bryant 4.00 10.00
8 Kobe Bryant 4.00 10.00
9 Kobe Bryant 4.00 10.00
10 Kobe Bryant 4.00 10.00
11 Kobe Bryant 4.00 10.00
12 Kobe Bryant 4.00 10.00
13 Kobe Bryant 4.00 10.00
14 Kobe Bryant 4.00 10.00
15 Kobe Bryant 4.00 10.00
16 Kobe Bryant 4.00 10.00
17 Kobe Bryant 4.00 10.00
18 Kobe Bryant 4.00 10.00
19 Kobe Bryant 4.00 10.00
20 Kobe Bryant 4.00 10.00

2016-17 Hoops Kobe Bryant Tribute
1 Kobe Bryant 15.00 40.00

2016-17 Hoops Lights Camera Action
1 Giannis Antetokounmpo 2.50 6.00
2 Khris Middleton .50 1.25
3 Jimmy Butler 1.00 2.50
4 Kevin Love .50 1.25
5 Kyrie Irving 1.00 2.50
6 Isaiah Thomas .40 1.00
7 Marcus Smart .60 1.50
8 Chris Paul .75 2.00
9 DeAndre Jordan .40 1.00
10 Marc Gasol .50 1.25
11 Kristaps Porzingis .75 2.00
12 Dennis Schroder .50 1.25
13 Paul Millsap .40 1.00
14 Carmelo Anthony .75 2.00
15 Goran Dragic .50 1.25
16 Chris Bosh .60 1.50
17 Reggie Jackson .40 1.00
18 Gordon Hayward .50 1.25
19 DeMarcus Cousins .40 1.00
20 D'Angelo Russell .60 1.50
21 Aaron Gordon .50 1.25
22 Dirk Nowitzki 1.25 3.00
23 Brook Lopez .40 1.00
24 Emmanuel Mudiay .30 .75
25 Paul George .75 2.00
26 Jrue Holiday .60 1.50
27 Kentavious Caldwell-Pope .40 1.00
28 Jonas Valanciunas .40 1.00
29 Kyle Lowry .50 1.25
30 James Harden 1.00 2.50
31 Kawhi Leonard 1.25 3.00
32 Tony Parker .75 2.00
33 Devin Booker 2.00 5.00
34 Steven Adams .40 1.00
35 Russell Westbrook .75 2.00
36 Andrew Wiggins .60 1.50
37 Damian Lillard 1.25 3.00
38 Klay Thompson 1.25 3.00
39 Draymond Green .60 1.50
40 John Wall .60 1.50

2016-17 Hoops One on One
1 C.Anthony/L.James 4.00 10.00
2 D.Lillard/J.Wall 1.25 3.00
3 K.Towns/A.Davis 1.50 4.00
4 A.Wiggins/J.Parker .60 1.50
5 M.Turner/P.Millsap .50 1.25
6 K.Leonard/J.Harden 1.25 3.00
7 R.Jackson/R.Westbrook .75 2.00
8 D.Nowitzki/K.Porzingis 1.25 3.00
9 S.Curry/B.Griffin 4.00 10.00
10 L.James/D.Green 4.00 10.00

2016-17 Hoops Picture Perfect
1 DeAndre Jordan .40 1.00
2 Carmelo Anthony .75 2.00
3 Kyrie Irving 1.00 2.50
4 Rudy Gay .50 1.25
5 Jahlil Okafor .30 .75
6 Jabari Parker .30 .75
7 Jordan Clarkson .50 1.25
8 Derrick Rose .75 2.00
9 Isaiah Thomas .40 1.00
10 Gordon Hayward .50 1.25
11 Monta Ellis .40 1.00
12 LaMarcus Aldridge .50 1.25
13 Devin Booker 2.00 5.00
14 Klay Thompson 1.25 3.00
15 Zach LaVine 1.00 2.50
16 Kevin Durant 2.00 5.00
17 C.J. McCollum .50 1.25
18 Dennis Schroder .50 1.25
19 Kenneth Faried .40 1.00
20 Jeremy Lin 1.00 2.50

2016-17 Hoops Rise N Shine Memorabilia
*PRIME/25: .75X TO 2X BASIC
2 Brandon Ingram 6.00 15.00
3 Jaylen Brown 5.00 12.00
4 Dragan Bender 2.00 5.00
5 Kris Dunn 3.00 8.00
6 Buddy Hield 6.00 15.00
7 Jamal Murray 8.00 20.00
8 Marquese Chriss 2.50 6.00
9 Jakob Poeltl 4.00 10.00
10 Thon Maker 2.50 6.00
11 Taurean Prince 2.50 6.00
12 Georgios Papagiannis 2.00 5.00
13 Denzel Valentine 2.00 5.00
14 Juan Hernangomez 4.00 10.00
15 Wade Baldwin IV 2.00 5.00
16 Henry Ellenson 2.00 5.00
17 Malik Beasley 4.00 10.00
18 Caris LeVert 5.00 12.00
19 DeAndre' Bembry 3.00 8.00
20 Malachi Richardson 2.00 5.00
21 T. Luwawu-Cabarrot 3.00 8.00
22 Brice Johnson 2.00 5.00
23 Pascal Siakam 12.00 30.00
24 Skal Labissiere 2.00 5.00
25 Dejounte Murray 10.00 25.00
26 Damian Jones 2.00 5.00
27 Deyonta Davis 2.00 5.00
28 Cheick Diallo 2.00 5.00
29 Tyler Ulis 2.50 6.00
30 Patrick McCaw 2.00 5.00
31 Malcolm Brogdon 4.00 10.00
32 Isaiah Whitehead 2.00 5.00
33 Demetrius Jackson 2.00 5.00
34 Kay Felder 2.00 5.00
35 Gary Payton II 5.00 12.00
36 Diamond Stone 2.00 5.00
37 Ivica Zubac 5.00 12.00
38 Chinanu Onuaku 2.00 5.00
39 Stephen Zimmerman 2.00 5.00
40 A.J. Hammons 2.00 5.00

2016-17 Hoops Road to the Finals
1-44 PRINT RUN 2016 SER.#'d SETS
45-66 PRINT RUN 999 SER.#'d SETS
67-79 PRINT RUN 499 SER.#'d SETS
80-86 PRINT RUN 199 SER.#'d SETS
1 Kyrie Irving R1 1.25 3.00
2 LeBron James R1 5.00 12.00
3 Kevin Love R1 .60 1.50
4 J.R. Smith R1 .60 1.50
5 Al Horford R1 .60 1.50
6 Kyle Korver R1 .50 1.25
7 Isaiah Thomas R1 .50 1.25
8 Marcus Smart R1 .75 2.00
9 Jeff Teague R1 .40 1.00
10 Paul Millsap R1 .50 1.25
11 Luol Deng R1 .50 1.25
12 Dwyane Wade R1 1.25 3.00
13 Jeremy Lin R1 1.25 3.00
14 Kemba Walker R1 .50 1.25
15 Marvin Williams R1 .40 1.00
16 Goran Dragic R1 .60 1.50
17 Hassan Whiteside R1 .50 1.25
18 Paul George R1 1.00 2.50
19 Jonas Valanciunas R1 .50 1.25
20 Kyle Lowry R1 .60 1.50
21 Ian Mahinmi R1 .40 1.00
22 DeMar DeRozan R1 .75 2.00
23 Myles Turner R1 .60 1.50
24 DeMar DeRozan R1 .75 2.00
25 Stephen Curry R1 5.00 12.00
26 Klay Thompson R1 1.50 4.00
27 James Harden R1 1.25 3.00
28 Draymond Green R1 .75 2.00
29 Shaun Livingston R1 .40 1.00
30 Chris Paul R1 1.00 2.50
31 DeAndre Jordan R1 .50 1.25
32 Damian Lillard R1 1.50 4.00
33 Al-Farouq Aminu R1 .40 1.00
34 C.J. McCollum R1 .60 1.50
35 Mason Plumlee R1 .40 1.00
36 Russell Westbrook R1 1.00 2.50
37 Raymond Felton R1 .40 1.00
38 Russell Westbrook R1 1.00 2.50
39 Enes Kanter R1 .40 1.00
40 Steven Adams R1 .50 1.25
41 Kawhi Leonard R1 1.50 4.00
42 Patty Mills R1 .60 1.50
43 LaMarcus Aldridge R1 .60 1.50
44 Tony Parker R1 1.00 2.50
45 LeBron James R2 6.00 15.00
46 J.R. Smith R2 .75 2.00
47 Channing Frye R2 .50 1.25
48 Kevin Love R2 .75 2.00
49 Goran Dragic R2 .75 2.00
50 Kyle Lowry R2 .75 2.00
51 Jonas Valanciunas R2 .60 1.50
52 Dwyane Wade R2 1.50 4.00
53 DeMar DeRozan R2 1.00 2.50
54 Goran Dragic R2 .75 2.00
55 Kyle Lowry R2 .75 2.00
56 Klay Thompson R2 2.00 5.00
57 Draymond Green R2 1.00 2.50
58 Damian Lillard R2 2.00 5.00
59 Stephen Curry R2 6.00 15.00
60 Harrison Barnes R2 .60 1.50
61 LaMarcus Aldridge R2 .75 2.00
62 Russell Westbrook R2 1.25 3.00
63 Kawhi Leonard R2 2.00 5.00
64 Kevin Durant R2 3.00 8.00
65 Steven Adams R2 .60 1.50
66 Kevin Durant R2 3.00 8.00
67 LeBron James CF 8.00 20.00
68 Kyrie Irving CF 2.00 5.00
69 DeMar DeRozan CF 1.25 3.00
70 Kyle Lowry CF 1.00 2.50
71 Kevin Love CF 1.00 2.50
72 LeBron James CF 8.00 20.00
73 Kevin Durant CF 4.00 10.00
74 Stephen Curry CF 8.00 20.00
75 Russell Westbrook CF 1.50 4.00
76 Serge Ibaka CF .75 2.00
77 Klay Thompson CF 2.50 6.00
78 Draymond Green CF 1.25 3.00
79 Stephen Curry CF 8.00 20.00
80 Shaun Livingston F 20.00 50.00
81 Draymond Green F 8.00 20.00
82 LeBron James F 30.00 80.00
83 Stephen Curry F 10.00 25.00
84 Kyrie Irving F 20.00 50.00
85 LeBron James F 30.00 80.00
86 LeBron James F 30.00 80.00

2016-17 Hoops Rookie Remembrance Memorabilia
*PRIME/25: .75X TO 2X BASIC
1 Brandon Knight 2.50 6.00
2 Gorgui Dieng 2.00 5.00
3 Jerami Grant 3.00 8.00
4 Jeff Withey 2.00 5.00
5 Allen Crabbe 2.00 5.00
6 Tyler Zeller 2.00 5.00
7 Derrick Williams 2.00 5.00
8 Isaiah Canaan 2.00 5.00
9 Ryan Kelly 2.00 5.00
10 Dennis Schroder 3.00 8.00
11 E'Twaun Moore 2.00 5.00
12 Andre Roberson 2.00 5.00
13 Shabazz Muhammad 2.00 5.00
14 K.J. McDaniels 2.00 5.00
15 James Young 2.00 5.00
16 Tyler Ennis 2.00 5.00
17 Cody Zeller 2.00 5.00
18 Shane Larkin 2.00 5.00
19 Cleanthony Early 2.00 5.00
20 Kentavious Caldwell-Pope 2.50 6.00
21 Noah Vonleh 2.00 5.00
22 Alex Len 2.00 5.00
23 Nerlens Noel 2.00 5.00
24 T.J. Warren 2.50 6.00
25 Mitch McGary 2.00 5.00
26 C.J. McCollum 3.00 8.00
27 Alec Burks 2.50 6.00
28 Gary Harris 2.50 6.00
29 Julius Randle 4.00 10.00
30 Shabazz Napier 2.00 5.00
31 Otto Porter 2.50 6.00
32 Will Barton 2.00 5.00
33 Joel Embiid 8.00 20.00
34 Tony Snell 2.00 5.00
35 Mason Plumlee 2.00 5.00
36 Doug McDermott 2.50 6.00
37 Nik Stauskas 2.00 5.00
38 Rodney Hood 2.50 6.00
39 Steven Adams 2.50 6.00
40 Aaron Gordon 3.00 8.00
41 Trey Burke 2.00 5.00
42 Ben McLemore 2.00 5.00
43 Jabari Parker 2.00 5.00
44 Michael Carter-Williams 2.00 5.00
45 Victor Oladipo 2.50 6.00
46 Marcus Smart 4.00 10.00
47 Archie Goodwin 2.00 5.00
48 Giannis Antetokounmpo 15.00 40.00
49 Zach LaVine 6.00 15.00
50 Andrew Wiggins 4.00 10.00
51 Aaron Harrison 2.00 5.00
52 Andre Drummond 3.00 8.00
53 Dante Exum 2.50 6.00
54 Elfrid Payton 2.50 6.00
55 Glenn Robinson III 2.00 5.00
56 James Ennis 2.00 5.00
57 Jerian Grant 2.00 5.00
58 Kelly Olynyk 2.00 5.00
59 Kyle Anderson 2.00 5.00
60 Trey Lyles 2.50 6.00

2016-17 Hoops Sparkplugs
1 Jamal Crawford .50 1.25
2 Will Barton .30 .75
3 Ryan Anderson .30 .75
4 Enes Kanter .30 .75
5 Dennis Schroder .50 1.25
6 Evan Turner .30 .75
7 Jeremy Lamb .30 .75
8 Aaron Brooks .30 .75
9 Dwight Powell .30 .75
10 Stanley Johnson .30 .75
11 Andre Iguodala .50 1.25
12 Justise Winslow .40 1.00
13 Victor Oladipo .40 1.00
14 Allen Crabbe .30 .75
15 Cory Joseph .30 .75

2016-17 Hoops Swat Team
1 Myles Turner .50 1.25
2 Hassan Whiteside .40 1.00
3 DeAndre Jordan .40 1.00
4 Nerlens Noel .30 .75
5 Paul Millsap .40 1.00
6 Karl-Anthony Towns 1.00 2.50
7 Rudy Gobert .60 1.50
8 Kristaps Porzingis .75 2.00
9 DeMarcus Cousins .40 1.00
10 Robin Lopez .30 .75
11 Jerami Grant .50 1.25
12 Anthony Davis 1.50 4.00
13 John Henson .30 .75
14 Brook Lopez .40 1.00
15 Andrew Bogut .50 1.25

2016-17 Hoops Team Leaders
*ARTIST PROOF/25: 1.2X TO 3X BASIC
1 Jahlil Okafor .30 .75
2 Jimmy Butler 1.00 2.50
3 Khris Middleton .50 1.25
4 LeBron James 4.00 10.00
5 Isaiah Thomas .40 1.00
6 DeAndre Jordan .40 1.00
7 Zach Randolph .50 1.25
8 Paul Millsap .40 1.00
9 Hassan Whiteside .40 1.00
10 Kemba Walker .40 1.00
11 Rudy Gobert .60 1.50
12 DeMarcus Cousins .40 1.00
13 Kristaps Porzingis .75 2.00
14 Julius Randle .60 1.50
15 Elfrid Payton .40 1.00
16 Dirk Nowitzki 1.25 3.00
17 Brook Lopez .40 1.00
18 Emmanuel Mudiay .30 .75
19 Paul George .75 2.00
20 Anthony Davis 1.50 4.00
21 Andre Drummond .50 1.25
22 Kyle Lowry .50 1.25
23 James Harden 1.00 2.50
24 LaMarcus Aldridge .50 1.25
25 Eric Bledsoe .40 1.00
26 Russell Westbrook .75 2.00
27 Karl-Anthony Towns 1.00 2.50
28 Damian Lillard 1.25 3.00
29 Stephen Curry 4.00 10.00
30 John Wall .60 1.50

2016-17 Hoops Tip Off
1 Warriors/Cavaliers 1.25 3.00
2 Warriors/Thunder .75 2.00
3 Cavaliers/Raptors .75 2.00
4 Thunder/Spurs .75 2.00
5 Warriors/Trail Blazers .75 2.00
6 Cavaliers/Hawks .75 2.00
7 Pacers/Raptors .75 2.00
8 Celtics/Hawks .75 2.00
9 Grizzlies/Spurs .75 2.00
10 K.Bryant/L.James 50.00 120.00
11 Clippers/Bucks .75 2.00
12 Pacers/Heat .75 2.00
13 Nuggets/Timberwolves .75 2.00
14 Pacers/Raptors .75 2.00
15 Lakers/Pacers .75 2.00

2017-18 Hoops
COMPLETE SET (300) 30.00 80.00
COMMON KOBE (291-300) 3.00 8.00
*BLUE: .75X TO 2X BASIC

*RED BACK: .75X TO 2X BASIC
*TEAL EXP: 1.5X TO 4X BASIC
1 Joel Embiid .60 1.50
2 Ben Simmons .30 .75
3 Dario Saric .25 .60
4 Robert Covington .20 .50
5 Timothe Luwawu-Cabarrot .20 .50
6 Richaun Holmes .20 .50
7 Jahlil Okafor .20 .50
8 Nik Stauskas .20 .50
9 Giannis Antetokounmpo 1.50 4.00
10 Jabari Parker .20 .50
11 Matthew Dellavedova .25 .60
12 Malcolm Brogdon .25 .60
13 Thon Maker .25 .60
14 Khris Middleton .40 1.00
15 John Henson .20 .50
16 Michael Beasley .20 .50
17 Dwyane Wade .60 1.50
18 Jimmy Butler .50 1.25
19 Michael Carter-Williams .20 .50
20 Jerian Grant .20 .50
21 Denzel Valentine .20 .50
22 Robin Lopez .20 .50
23 Paul Zipser .20 .50
24 Bobby Portis .20 .50
25 LeBron James 2.50 6.00
26 Kyrie Irving .60 1.50
27 Kevin Love .30 .75
28 J.R. Smith .25 .60
29 Tristan Thompson .20 .50
30 Iman Shumpert .20 .50
31 Kay Felder .20 .50
32 Kyle Korver .25 .60
33 Isaiah Thomas .25 .60
34 Al Horford .30 .75
35 Jaylen Brown .75 2.00
36 Jae Crowder .20 .50
37 Avery Bradley .20 .50
38 Marcus Smart .30 .75
39 Kelly Olynyk .20 .50
40 Demetrius Jackson .20 .50
41 Blake Griffin .30 .75
42 Chris Paul .50 1.25
43 Austin Rivers .25 .60
44 DeAndre Jordan .25 .60
45 JJ Redick .30 .75
46 Jamal Crawford .30 .75
47 Marreese Speights .20 .50
48 Luc Mbah a Moute .20 .50
49 Marc Gasol .30 .75
50 Mike Conley .25 .60
51 Zach Randolph .30 .75
52 Vince Carter .60 1.50
53 Chandler Parsons .20 .50
54 Wade Baldwin IV .20 .50
55 Brandan Wright .20 .50
56 Wayne Selden Jr. RC .40 1.00
57 Dwight Howard .40 1.00
58 Paul Millsap .25 .60
59 Dennis Schroder .25 .60
60 Tim Hardaway Jr. .25 .60
61 Taurean Prince .20 .50
62 Kent Bazemore .20 .50
63 Malcolm Delaney .20 .50
64 DeAndre' Bembry .20 .50
65 Hassan Whiteside .25 .60
66 Dion Waiters .20 .50
67 Goran Dragic .25 .60
68 Tyler Johnson .20 .50
69 James Johnson .20 .50
70 Justise Winslow .20 .50
71 Josh Richardson .25 .60
72 Udonis Haslem .20 .50
73 Kemba Walker .25 .60
74 Nicolas Batum .20 .50
75 Frank Kaminsky .20 .50
76 Michael Kidd-Gilchrist .20 .50
77 Cody Zeller .20 .50
78 Marvin Williams .20 .50
79 Jeremy Lamb .20 .50
80 Marco Belinelli .20 .50
81 Gordon Hayward .25 .60
82 Rudy Gobert .40 1.00
83 George Hill .25 .60
84 Derrick Favors .25 .60
85 Dante Exum .20 .50
86 Rodney Hood .20 .50
87 Alec Burks .20 .50
88 Trey Lyles .20 .50
89 Skal Labissiere .20 .50
90 Darren Collison .20 .50
91 Willie Cauley-Stein .20 .50
92 Tomas Satoransky .25 .60
93 Buddy Hield .30 .75
94 Georgios Papagiannis .20 .50
95 Tyreke Evans .20 .50
96 Malachi Richardson .20 .50
97 Arron Afflalo .20 .50
98 Derrick Rose .50 1.25
99 Carmelo Anthony .50 1.25
100 Kristaps Porzingis .40 1.00
101 Joakim Noah .20 .50
102 Ron Baker .20 .50
103 Willy Hernangomez .20 .50
104 Mindaugas Kuzminskas .20 .50
105 Courtney Lee .20 .50
106 Lance Thomas .20 .50
107 D'Angelo Russell .25 .60
108 Brandon Ingram .40 1.00
109 Jordan Clarkson .20 .50
110 Nick Young .20 .50
111 Ivica Zubac .30 .75
112 Julius Randle .30 .75
113 Thomas Bryant .30 .75
114 Larry Nance Jr. .25 .60
115 Elfrid Payton .20 .50
116 Aaron Gordon .30 .75
117 Nikola Vucevic .25 .60
118 Evan Fournier .25 .60
119 Bismack Biyombo .20 .50
120 Jeff Green .20 .50
121 Terrence Ross .25 .60
122 D.J. Augustin .20 .50
123 Dirk Nowitzki .75 2.00
124 Seth Curry .30 .75
125 Harrison Barnes .25 .60
126 Yogi Ferrell .20 .50
127 J.J. Barea .25 .60
128 Wesley Matthews .20 .50
129 Nerlens Noel .20 .50
130 Salah Mejri .20 .50
131 Devin Harris .20 .50
132 Jeremy Lin .50 1.25
133 Brook Lopez .25 .60
134 Sean Kilpatrick .20 .50
135 Caris LeVert .30 .75
136 Joe Harris .25 .60
137 Rondae Hollis-Jefferson .20 .50
138 Trevor Booker .20 .50
139 Isaiah Whitehead .20 .50
140 Nikola Jokic 2.00 5.00
141 Danilo Gallinari .25 .60
142 Kenneth Faried .25 .60
143 Emmanuel Mudiay .20 .50
144 Jamal Murray .50 1.25
145 Wilson Chandler .25 .60
146 Gary Harris .25 .60
147 Will Barton .20 .50
148 Juan Hernangomez .30 .75
149 Paul George .50 1.25
150 Lance Stephenson .20 .50
151 Jeff Teague .25 .60
152 Myles Turner .30 .75
153 Ike Anigbogu RC .40 1.00
154 Al Jefferson .25 .60
155 Thaddeus Young .20 .50
156 C.J. Miles .20 .50
157 Rodney Stuckey .20 .50
158 Anthony Davis .75 2.00
159 Jrue Holiday .40 1.00
160 DeMarcus Cousins .25 .60
161 Tim Frazier .20 .50
162 Omer Asik .20 .50
163 Solomon Hill .20 .50
164 E'Twaun Moore .20 .50
165 Cheick Diallo .20 .50
166 Andre Drummond .25 .60
167 Reggie Jackson .25 .60
168 Boban Marjanovic .25 .60
169 Kentavious Caldwell-Pope .25 .60
170 Stanley Johnson .20 .50
171 Tobias Harris .25 .60
172 Marcus Morris .20 .50
173 Aron Baynes .20 .50
174 Henry Ellenson .20 .50
175 DeMar DeRozan .40 1.00
176 Kyle Lowry .30 .75
177 Jonas Valanciunas .25 .60
178 Serge Ibaka .25 .60
179 DeMarre Carroll .20 .50
180 Pascal Siakam .60 1.50
181 Lucas Nogueira .20 .50
182 Jakob Poeltl .25 .60
183 Patrick Patterson .20 .50
184 James Harden .60 1.50
185 Nene .25 .60
186 Eric Gordon .25 .60
187 Ryan Anderson .20 .50
188 Trevor Ariza .20 .50
189 Clint Capela .25 .60
190 Patrick Beverley .20 .50
191 Lou Williams .25 .60
192 Kawhi Leonard .75 2.00
193 Manu Ginobili .60 1.50
194 Pau Gasol .50 1.25
195 LaMarcus Aldridge .30 .75
196 Tony Parker .50 1.25
197 Danny Green .25 .60
198 Jonathon Simmons .20 .50
199 Dejounte Murray .30 .75
200 Devin Booker .75 2.00
201 Eric Bledsoe .25 .60
202 Marquese Chriss .20 .50
203 Tyler Ulis .20 .50
204 Tyson Chandler .25 .60
205 Dragan Bender .20 .50
206 T.J. Warren .25 .60
207 Alan Williams .20 .50
208 Russell Westbrook .50 1.25
209 Steven Adams .25 .60
210 Victor Oladipo .25 .60
211 Enes Kanter .25 .60
212 Domantas Sabonis .60 1.50
213 Andre Roberson .20 .50
214 Alex Abrines .20 .50
215 Taj Gibson .20 .50
216 Doug McDermott .20 .50
217 Karl-Anthony Towns .50 1.25
218 Ricky Rubio .25 .60
219 Andrew Wiggins .40 1.00
220 Zach LaVine .50 1.25
221 Kris Dunn .20 .50
222 Gorgui Dieng .20 .50
223 Tyus Jones .20 .50
224 Cole Aldrich .20 .50
225 Nemanja Bjelica .20 .50
226 Damian Lillard .75 2.00
227 C.J. McCollum .30 .75
228 Jusuf Nurkic .20 .50
229 Shabazz Napier .20 .50
230 Allen Crabbe .20 .50
231 Evan Turner .20 .50
232 Al-Farouq Aminu .20 .50
233 Maurice Harkless .20 .50
234 Ed Davis .20 .50
235 Noah Vonleh .20 .50
236 Stephen Curry 2.50 6.00
237 Kevin Durant 1.25 3.00
238 Klay Thompson .75 2.00
239 Draymond Green .40 1.00
240 Andre Iguodala .30 .75
241 Patrick McCaw .25 .60
242 Zaza Pachulia .20 .50
243 Shaun Livingston .25 .60
244 John Wall .40 1.00
245 Bradley Beal .40 1.00
246 Marcin Gortat .20 .50
247 Markieff Morris .20 .50
248 Kelly Oubre Jr. .30 .75
249 Otto Porter .25 .60
250 Sindarius Thornwell RC .40 1.00
251 Markelle Fultz RC 1.00 2.50
252 Lonzo Ball RC 1.50 4.00
253 Jayson Tatum RC 10.00 25.00
254 Josh Jackson RC .50 1.25
255 De'Aaron Fox RC 3.00 8.00
256 Jonathan Isaac RC 1.00 2.50
257 Lauri Markkanen RC 2.50 6.00
258 Frank Ntilikina RC .50 1.25
259 Dennis Smith Jr. RC .50 1.25
260 Zach Collins RC .60 1.50
261 Malik Monk RC 1.50 4.00
262 Luke Kennard RC .75 2.00
263 Donovan Mitchell RC 4.00 10.00
264 Bam Adebayo RC 2.50 6.00
265 Justin Jackson RC .40 1.00
266 Justin Patton RC .40 1.00
267 D.J. Wilson RC .40 1.00
268 T.J. Leaf RC .40 1.00
269 John Collins RC 1.00 2.50
270 Harry Giles RC .40 1.00
271 Terrance Ferguson RC .40 1.00
272 Jarrett Allen RC 1.00 2.50
273 OG Anunoby RC 2.00 5.00
274 Tyler Lydon RC .40 1.00
275 Tyler Dorsey RC .40 1.00
276 Caleb Swanigan RC .40 1.00
277 Kyle Kuzma RC 1.50 4.00
278 Tony Bradley RC .40 1.00
279 Derrick White RC 1.50 4.00
280 Josh Hart RC 1.00 2.50
281 Frank Jackson RC .40 1.00
282 Davon Reed RC .40 1.00
283 Wesley Iwundu RC .40 1.00
284 Frank Mason III RC .40 1.00
285 Ivan Rabb RC .40 1.00
286 Sterling Brown RC .40 1.00
287 Semi Ojeleye RC .50 1.25
288 Jordan Bell RC .40 1.00
289 Jawun Evans RC .40 1.00
290 Dwayne Bacon RC .40 1.00
291 Kobe Bryant CT 3.00 8.00
292 Kobe Bryant CT 3.00 8.00
293 Kobe Bryant CT 3.00 8.00
294 Kobe Bryant CT 3.00 8.00
295 Kobe Bryant CT 3.00 8.00
296 Kobe Bryant CT 3.00 8.00
297 Kobe Bryant CT 3.00 8.00
298 Kobe Bryant CT 3.00 8.00
299 Kobe Bryant CT 3.00 8.00
300 Kobe Bryant CT 3.00 8.00

2017-18 Hoops Artist Proof

*ARTST PRF: 4X TO 10X BASIC
*ARTST PRF KOBE: 4X TO 10X BASIC
*ARTIST PRF RC: 4X TO 10X BASIC
STATED PRINT RUN 25 SER.#'d SETS
252 Lonzo Ball 60.00 150.00
253 Jayson Tatum 200.00 500.00
257 Lauri Markkanen 40.00 100.00
258 Frank Ntilikina 30.00 80.00
263 Donovan Mitchell 60.00 150.00
264 Bam Adebayo 125.00 300.00

2017-18 Hoops Blue Checkerboard

*BLUE CHK: 2.5X TO 6X BASIC
*BLUE CHK.KOBE: 2.5X TO 6X BASIC
*BLUE CHK.RC: 2.5X TO 6X BASIC
STATED PRINT RUN 75 SER.#'d SETS
253 Jayson Tatum 125.00 300.00

2017-18 Hoops Green

*GREEN: 2X TO 5X BASIC
*GREEN KOBE: 2X TO 5X BASIC
*GREEN RC: 2X TO 5X BASIC
STATED PRINT RUN 99 SER.#'d SETS
253 Jayson Tatum 100.00 250.00

2017-18 Hoops Orange

*ORANGE: 4X TO 10X BASIC
*ORANGE KOBE: 4X TO 10X BASIC
*ORANGE RC: 4X TO 10X BASIC
STATED PRINT RUN 25 SER.#'d SETS
253 Jayson Tatum 200.00 500.00
257 Lauri Markkanen 40.00 100.00
258 Frank Ntilikina 30.00 80.00
263 Donovan Mitchell 60.00 150.00
264 Bam Adebayo 125.00 300.00

2017-18 Hoops Orange Explosion

*ORANGE: 2.5X TO 6X BASIC
*ORANGE KOBE: 2.5X TO 6X BASIC
*ORANGE RC: 2.5X TO 6X BASIC
STATED PRINT RUN 75 SER.#'d SETS
253 Jayson Tatum 125.00 300.00

2017-18 Hoops Premium

*PREMIUM: 1.5X TO 4X BASIC
*PREM.KOBE: 1.5X TO 4X BASIC
*PREMIUM RC: 1.5X TO 4X BASIC
STATED PRINT RUN 199 SER.#'d SETS
253 Jayson Tatum 75.00 200.00

2017-18 Hoops Red

*RED: 3X TO 8X BASIC
*RED KOBE: 3X TO 8X BASIC
*RED RC: 3X TO 8X BASIC
STATED PRINT RUN 49 SER.#'d SETS
253 Jayson Tatum 150.00 400.00

2017-18 Hoops Silver

*SILVER: 1.5X TO 4X BASIC
*SILVER.KOBE: 1.5X TO 4X BASIC
*SILVER RC: 1.5X TO 4X BASIC
STATED PRINT RUN 199 SER.#'d SETS
253 Jayson Tatum 75.00 200.00

2017-18 Hoops Teal

*TEAL: 2X TO 5X BASIC
*TEAL KOBE: 2X TO 5X BASIC
*TEAL RC: 2X TO 5X BASIC
STATED PRINT RUN 125 SER.#'d SETS
253 Jayson Tatum 100.00 250.00

2017-18 Hoops Action Shots

1 Dario Saric .40 1.00
2 Dwyane Wade 1.00 2.50
3 Jabari Parker .30 .75
4 Kyrie Irving 1.00 2.50
5 Marcus Smart .50 1.25
6 Justise Winslow .30 .75
7 Michael Kidd-Gilchrist .30 .75
8 Alec Burks .30 .75
9 Buddy Hield .50 1.25
10 Willy Hernangomez .30 .75
11 Jordan Clarkson .50 1.25
12 Yogi Ferrell .30 .75
13 Emmanuel Mudiay .30 .75
14 Myles Turner .50 1.25
15 Anthony Davis 1.25 3.00
16 James Harden 1.00 2.50
17 Damian Lillard 1.25 3.00
18 Kevin Durant 2.00 5.00
19 John Wall .60 1.50
20 Klay Thompson 1.25 3.00

2017-18 Hoops Backstage Pass

1 LeBron James 4.00 10.00
2 Kevin Durant 2.00 5.00
3 DeMar DeRozan .60 1.50
4 Gary Harris .40 1.00
5 Delon Wright .30 .75
6 Giannis Antetokounmpo 2.50 6.00
7 Marc Gasol .50 1.25
8 Joel Embiid 1.00 2.50
9 Kristaps Porzingis .60 1.50
10 Marcus Smart .50 1.25

2017-18 Hoops Backstage Pass Artist Proof

*ARTIST PROOF: 1.2X TO 3X BASIC
STATED PRINT RUN 25 SER.#'d SETS
1 LeBron James 12.00 30.00

2017-18 Hoops Championship Moments

STATED PRINT RUN 99 SER.#'d SETS
1 Durant/Curry 80.00 200.00
2 Russell/Durant/Curry 80.00 200.00
3 Russell/Durant 20.00 50.00
4 Stephen Curry 80.00 200.00
5 Zaza Pachulia 6.00 15.00
6 Draymond Green 25.00 60.00
7 Green/Thompson 25.00 60.00
8 Damian Jones 12.00 30.00
9 Patrick McCaw 6.00 15.00
10 Andre Iguodala 20.00 50.00
11 Shaun Livingston 20.00 50.00
12 David West 12.00 30.00
13 Matt Barnes 12.00 30.00
14 JaVale McGee 8.00 20.00
15 Ian Clark 12.00 30.00
16 Kevon Looney 20.00 50.00
17 James Michael McAdoo 8.00 20.00
18 West/Durant 40.00 100.00
19 Klay Thompson 25.00 60.00

2017-18 Hoops Class of 2017

1 Markelle Fultz 1.00 2.50
2 Lonzo Ball 1.50 4.00
3 Jayson Tatum 5.00 12.00
4 Josh Jackson .50 1.25
5 De'Aaron Fox 3.00 8.00
6 Jonathan Isaac 1.00 2.50
7 Lauri Markkanen 2.50 6.00
8 Frank Ntilikina .50 1.25
9 Dennis Smith Jr. .50 1.25
10 Zach Collins .60 1.50
11 Malik Monk 1.50 4.00
12 Luke Kennard .75 2.00
13 Donovan Mitchell 4.00 10.00
14 Bam Adebayo 2.50 6.00
15 Justin Jackson .40 1.00

2017-18 Hoops Courtside

*AP/99: 1.2X TO 3X BASIC
1 Kevin Durant 2.00 5.00
2 Kyrie Irving 1.00 2.50
3 Joel Embiid 1.00 2.50
4 Dwyane Wade 1.00 2.50
5 Isaiah Thomas .40 1.00
6 Mike Conley .40 1.00
7 Kemba Walker .40 1.00
8 Buddy Hield .50 1.25
9 Dirk Nowitzki 1.25 3.00
10 Anthony Davis 1.25 3.00
11 James Harden 1.00 2.50
12 John Wall .60 1.50
13 Damian Lillard 1.25 3.00
14 Andrew Wiggins .60 1.50
15 Kawhi Leonard 1.25 3.00
16 Devin Booker 1.25 3.00
17 Goran Dragic .40 1.00
18 Nikola Jokic 3.00 8.00
19 Harrison Barnes .40 1.00
20 Brandon Ingram .60 1.50

2017-18 Hoops Faces of the Future

1 Markelle Fultz 1.00 2.50
2 Lonzo Ball 1.50 4.00
3 Josh Jackson .50 1.25
4 Jayson Tatum 5.00 12.00
5 De'Aaron Fox 3.00 8.00
6 Jonathan Isaac 1.00 2.50
7 Lauri Markkanen 2.50 6.00
8 Frank Ntilikina .50 1.25
9 Dennis Smith Jr. .50 1.25
10 Terrance Ferguson .40 1.00
11 Malik Monk 1.50 4.00
12 Luke Kennard .75 2.00
13 Ivan Rabb .40 1.00
14 Frank Jackson .40 1.00
15 OG Anunoby 2.00 5.00
16 Justin Patton .40 1.00
17 D.J. Wilson .40 1.00
18 T.J. Leaf .40 1.00
19 John Collins 1.00 2.50
20 Harry Giles .40 1.00

2017-18 Hoops Finals MVP

STATED PRINT RUN 99 SER.#'d SETS
1 Kevin Durant 60.00 150.00

2017-18 Hoops Great SIGnificance Autographs

1 Mike Muscala 3.00 8.00
2 Semaj Christon 3.00 8.00
3 Dwight Powell 3.00 8.00
4 Marcus Smart 5.00 12.00
5 Jeff Withey 3.00 8.00
6 Chris McCullough 3.00 8.00
7 James Ennis 3.00 8.00
8 Jon Leuer 3.00 8.00
9 Frank Kaminsky 3.00 8.00
10 Yogi Ferrell 3.00 8.00
11 Cody Zeller 3.00 8.00
12 E'Twaun Moore 3.00 8.00
13 Chinanu Onuaku 3.00 8.00
14 Harvey Grant 3.00 8.00
15 Joel Bolomboy 3.00 8.00
16 Trey Lyles 3.00 8.00
17 Justin Anderson 3.00 8.00
18 Sean Kilpatrick 3.00 8.00
19 Troy Daniels 3.00 8.00
20 Taurean Prince 3.00 8.00
21 Josh Huestis 3.00 8.00
22 Kyle Wiltjer 3.00 8.00
23 Bill Willoughby 3.00 8.00
24 Ian Clark 3.00 8.00
25 Willy Hernangomez 3.00 8.00
26 C.J. Watson 3.00 8.00
27 Cheick Diallo 3.00 8.00
28 Mario Hezonja 3.00 8.00
29 James Johnson 3.00 8.00
30 JaKarr Sampson 3.00 8.00
31 Larry Nance Jr. 4.00 10.00
32 Nemanja Bjelica 3.00 8.00
33 Jusuf Nurkic 4.00 10.00
34 Pat Connaughton 3.00 8.00
35 Jason Terry 4.00 10.00
36 Demetrius Jackson 3.00 8.00
37 Mindaugas Kuzminskas 3.00 8.00
38 DeMarre Carroll 3.00 8.00
39 Malcolm Delaney 3.00 8.00
40 Luke Kennard 8.00 20.00
41 Malik Monk 20.00 50.00
42 Zach Collins 5.00 12.00
43 Dennis Smith Jr. 4.00 10.00
44 Frank Ntilikina 25.00 60.00
45 Lauri Markkanen 30.00 80.00
46 Jonathan Isaac 12.00 30.00
47 De'Aaron Fox 50.00 120.00
48 Jayson Tatum 100.00 250.00
49 Lonzo Ball 30.00 80.00
50 Markelle Fultz 30.00 80.00
51 Bam Adebayo 20.00 50.00
52 Caleb Swanigan 3.00 8.00
53 D.J. Wilson 3.00 8.00
54 Derrick White 12.00 30.00
55 Donovan Mitchell 50.00 120.00
56 Harry Giles 3.00 8.00
57 Jarrett Allen 8.00 20.00
58 John Collins 8.00 20.00
59 Josh Hart 8.00 20.00
61 Justin Jackson 3.00 8.00
62 Justin Patton 3.00 8.00
63 Kyle Kuzma 12.00 30.00
64 OG Anunoby 15.00 40.00
65 T.J. Leaf 3.00 8.00
66 Terrance Ferguson 3.00 8.00
67 Tony Bradley 3.00 8.00
68 Tyler Lydon 3.00 8.00
69 Robin Lopez 3.00 8.00
70 DeAndre' Bembry 3.00 8.00
71 Langston Galloway 3.00 8.00
72 Georgios Papagiannis 3.00 8.00
73 Larry Brown 6.00 15.00
74 Kenny Anderson 4.00 10.00
75 Jake Layman 4.00 10.00
76 Kenny Sky Walker 3.00 8.00
77 Rodney McGruder 3.00 8.00
78 Richaun Holmes 3.00 8.00
79 Kay Felder 3.00 8.00
80 Rex Chapman 5.00 12.00
81 Frank Ramsey 10.00 25.00
82 Jonas Valanciunas 4.00 10.00
83 Evan Turner 3.00 8.00
84 Bob Dandridge 5.00 12.00
85 Reggie Bullock 3.00 8.00
86 Cazzie Russell 5.00 12.00
87 Alan Williams 3.00 8.00
88 Kent Bazemore 3.00 8.00
89 Michael Cooper 4.00 10.00
90 Tony Delk 3.00 8.00
91 Bill Cartwright 4.00 10.00
92 Rony Seikaly 3.00 8.00
93 Gary Payton II 8.00 20.00
94 Dorian Finney-Smith 3.00 8.00
95 Noah Vonleh 3.00 8.00
96 Andrei Kirilenko 4.00 10.00
97 Gary Trent 3.00 8.00
98 Dakari Johnson 3.00 8.00
99 Sarunas Marciulionis 3.00 8.00
100 Lindsey Hunter 3.00 8.00

2017-18 Hoops Highlights

1 Devin Booker 1.25 3.00
2 James Harden 1.00 2.50
3 Russell Westbrook .75 2.00
4 Anthony Davis 1.25 3.00
5 Damian Lillard 1.25 3.00
6 Klay Thompson 1.25 3.00
7 Karl-Anthony Towns .75 2.00
8 John Wall .60 1.50
9 LeBron James 4.00 10.00
10 Kevin Durant 2.00 5.00
11 Kyrie Irving 1.00 2.50
12 Isaiah Thomas .40 1.00
13 Rudy Gobert .60 1.50
14 Giannis Antetokounmpo 2.50 6.00
15 Kawhi Leonard 1.25 3.00
16 Tim Duncan 1.25 3.00
17 Dion Waiters .30 .75
18 Anthony Davis 1.25 3.00
19 Stephen Curry 4.00 10.00
20 Kyrie Irving 1.00 2.50

2017-18 Hoops Hot Signatures

*RED/25: .5X TO 1.2X BASIC
1 Yogi Ferrell 3.00 8.00
2 Willy Hernangomez 3.00 8.00
3 Marcus Smart 5.00 12.00
4 Frank Kaminsky 3.00 8.00
5 Cody Zeller 3.00 8.00
6 Trey Lyles 3.00 8.00
7 James Johnson 3.00 8.00
8 C.J. McCollum 6.00 15.00
9 Jusuf Nurkic 4.00 10.00
10 Julius Randle 10.00 25.00
11 Nikola Jokic 125.00 300.00
12 Jabari Parker 3.00 8.00
13 Rondae Hollis-Jefferson 3.00 8.00
14 Gordon Hayward 4.00 10.00
15 Alec Burks 3.00 8.00
16 D'Angelo Russell 4.00 10.00
17 Khris Middleton 15.00 40.00
18 Juan Hernangomez 12.00 30.00
19 JJ Redick 5.00 12.00
20 Kyrie Irving 30.00 80.00
21 Buddy Hield 5.00 12.00
22 Robert Covington 3.00 8.00
23 Victor Oladipo 4.00 10.00
24 J.J. Barea 6.00 15.00
25 George Hill 4.00 10.00
26 Michael Kidd-Gilchrist 3.00 8.00
28 Ricky Rubio 8.00 20.00
29 Domantas Sabonis 10.00 25.00
30 Kevin Durant 100.00 250.00
31 Carmelo Anthony 30.00 80.00
32 Dwyane Wade 20.00 50.00
33 Damian Lillard 30.00 80.00
34 Dirk Nowitzki 60.00 150.00
35 John Wall 15.00 40.00
36 Joel Embiid 75.00 200.00
37 Malcolm Brogdon 4.00 10.00
38 Stephen Curry 600.00 1,200.00
39 Giannis Antetokounmpo 125.00 300.00
40 Vince Carter 30.00 80.00
41 Karl-Anthony Towns 30.00 80.00
42 Patrick McCaw 3.00 8.00
43 Aaron Gordon 5.00 12.00
44 Gary Harris 4.00 10.00
45 Marquese Chriss 3.00 8.00
46 Magic Johnson 60.00 150.00
47 Kobe Bryant 1,000.00 2,000.00
48 Jason Kidd 30.00 80.00
49 Damon Stoudamire 5.00 12.00
50 Danny Manning 4.00 10.00

2017-18 Hoops Hot Signatures Rookies

1 Markelle Fultz 15.00 40.00
2 Lonzo Ball 25.00 60.00
3 Jayson Tatum 150.00 400.00
4 Luke Kennard 6.00 15.00
5 Justin Jackson 3.00 8.00
6 Jarrett Allen 12.00 30.00
7 Dwayne Bacon 3.00 8.00
8 De'Aaron Fox 30.00 80.00
9 Jonathan Isaac 8.00 20.00
10 Lauri Markkanen 20.00 50.00
11 Frank Ntilikina 4.00 10.00
12 Dennis Smith Jr. 4.00 10.00
13 Zach Collins 5.00 12.00
14 Malik Monk 15.00 40.00
15 Donovan Mitchell 75.00 200.00
16 Bam Adebayo 20.00 50.00
17 Justin Patton 3.00 8.00
18 D.J. Wilson 3.00 8.00
19 T.J. Leaf 3.00 8.00
20 John Collins 8.00 20.00
21 Harry Giles 3.00 8.00
22 Terrance Ferguson 3.00 8.00
23 OG Anunoby 15.00 40.00
24 Tyler Lydon 3.00 8.00
25 Kyle Kuzma 12.00 30.00
26 Frank Jackson 3.00 8.00
27 Frank Mason III 3.00 8.00
28 Tyler Dorsey 3.00 8.00
29 Jordan Bell 3.00 8.00
30 Wesley Iwundu 3.00 8.00
31 Josh Jackson 4.00 10.00
32 Derrick White 8.00 20.00
33 Monte Morris 12.00 30.00
34 Jawun Evans 3.00 8.00
35 Caleb Swanigan 3.00 8.00
36 Sterling Brown 3.00 8.00
37 Josh Hart 8.00 20.00
38 Ike Anigbogu 3.00 8.00
39 Sindarius Thornwell 3.00 8.00
40 Tony Bradley 3.00 8.00

2017-18 Hoops Hot Signatures Rookies Red

*RED: .6X TO 1.5X BASIC
STATED PRINT RUN 25 SER.#'d SETS
3 Jayson Tatum 400.00 800.00
15 Donovan Mitchell 200.00 500.00
33 Monte Morris 40.00 100.00

2017-18 Hoops Ink

*RED/25: .5X TO 1.2X BASIC
1 Bill Willoughby 3.00 8.00
2 C.J. Wilcox 3.00 8.00
3 Chinanu Onuaku 3.00 8.00
4 Chris McCullough 3.00 8.00
5 Dakari Johnson 3.00 8.00
6 Damian Jones 3.00 8.00
7 Daniel Hamilton 3.00 8.00
8 Darren Collison 3.00 8.00
9 Demetrius Jackson 3.00 8.00
10 Dwight Powell 3.00 8.00
11 E'Twaun Moore 3.00 8.00
12 Gary Payton II 12.00 30.00
13 JaKarr Sampson 3.00 8.00
14 James Ennis 3.00 8.00
15 James Posey 3.00 8.00
16 Jeff Withey 3.00 8.00
17 Joel Bolomboy 3.00 8.00
18 Jon Leuer 3.00 8.00
19 Josh Huestis 3.00 8.00
20 Justin Anderson 3.00 8.00
21 Kyle Wiltjer 3.00 8.00
22 LaMarcus Aldridge 10.00 25.00
23 Lorenzo Brown 3.00 8.00
24 Luis Montero 3.00 8.00
25 Marcus Paige 3.00 8.00
26 Maurice Harkless 3.00 8.00
27 Michael Cage 4.00 10.00
28 Mike Muscala 3.00 8.00
29 Semaj Christon 3.00 8.00
30 Stephen Zimmerman 3.00 8.00
31 Treveon Graham 4.00 10.00
32 Troy Daniels 3.00 8.00
33 Magic Johnson 60.00 150.00
34 Marcus Smart 5.00 12.00
35 Jason Kidd 30.00 80.00
36 Kobe Bryant 1,000.00 2,000.00
37 Reggie Miller 75.00 200.00
38 Dwyane Wade 20.00 50.00
39 Carmelo Anthony 30.00 80.00
40 Kyrie Irving 30.00 80.00
41 Chris Paul 30.00 80.00
42 Damian Lillard 40.00 100.00
43 Karl Malone 25.00 60.00
44 Julius Erving 30.00 80.00
45 John Stockton 30.00 80.00
46 Anthony Davis 40.00 100.00
47 Kareem Abdul-Jabbar 75.00 200.00
48 Oscar Robertson 60.00 150.00
49 Jerry West 30.00 80.00
50 Pau Gasol 12.00 30.00

2017-18 Hoops Legends of the Ball

1 Larry Bird 2.00 5.00
2 Magic Johnson 2.00 5.00
3 Shaquille O'Neal 1.50 4.00
4 Kobe Bryant 4.00 10.00
5 Bill Russell 1.50 4.00
6 Wilt Chamberlain 1.50 4.00
7 Kareem Abdul-Jabbar 1.50 4.00
8 Hakeem Olajuwon 1.00 2.50
9 Tim Duncan 1.25 3.00
10 Oscar Robertson 1.00 2.50
11 Jerry West 1.00 2.50
12 Julius Erving 1.25 3.00
13 Karl Malone 1.00 2.50
14 Scottie Pippen 1.25 3.00
15 John Stockton 1.00 2.50
16 Allen Iverson 1.25 3.00
17 David Robinson 1.00 2.50
18 Patrick Ewing .75 2.00
19 Pete Maravich 1.25 3.00
20 Reggie Miller 1.00 2.50

2017-18 Hoops Lights Camera Action

1 Joel Embiid 1.00 2.50
2 Giannis Antetokounmpo 2.50 6.00
3 Dwyane Wade 1.00 2.50
4 LeBron James 4.00 10.00
5 Kyrie Irving 1.00 2.50
6 Isaiah Thomas .40 1.00
7 Al Horford .50 1.25
8 DeAndre Jordan .40 1.00
9 Mike Conley .40 1.00
10 Dennis Schroder .40 1.00
11 Hassan Whiteside .40 1.00
12 Kemba Walker .40 1.00
13 Rodney Hood .30 .75
14 Buddy Hield .50 1.25
15 Kristaps Porzingis .60 1.50
16 Brandon Ingram .60 1.50
17 Elfrid Payton .30 .75
18 Seth Curry .50 1.25
19 Harrison Barnes .40 1.00
20 Jeremy Lin .75 2.00
21 Nikola Jokic 3.00 8.00
22 Myles Turner .50 1.25
23 Anthony Davis 1.25 3.00
24 DeMarcus Cousins .40 1.00
25 Reggie Jackson .40 1.00
26 DeMar DeRozan .60 1.50
27 James Harden 1.00 2.50
28 Kawhi Leonard 1.25 3.00
29 Devin Booker 1.25 3.00
30 John Wall .60 1.50
31 Bradley Beal .60 1.50
32 Stephen Curry 4.00 10.00
33 Kevin Durant 2.00 5.00
34 Damian Lillard 1.25 3.00
35 C.J. McCollum .50 1.25
36 Andrew Wiggins .60 1.50
37 Russell Westbrook .75 2.00
38 Karl-Anthony Towns .75 2.00
39 Eric Gordon .40 1.00
40 Jamal Murray .75 2.00

2017-18 Hoops Picture Perfect

1 Robert Covington .30 .75
2 Khris Middleton .60 1.50
3 Isaiah Thomas .40 1.00
4 Blake Griffin .50 1.25
5 Mike Conley .40 1.00
6 Goran Dragic .40 1.00
7 Nicolas Batum .30 .75
8 Kyrie Irving 1.00 2.50
9 Willie Cauley-Stein .30 .75
10 Kristaps Porzingis .60 1.50
11 Brandon Ingram .60 1.50
12 Nikola Vucevic .40 1.00
13 Harrison Barnes .40 1.00
14 Nikola Jokic 3.00 8.00
15 Jrue Holiday .60 1.50
16 Stephen Curry 4.00 10.00
17 Trevor Ariza .30 .75
18 LaMarcus Aldridge .50 1.25
19 Devin Booker 1.25 3.00
20 Andrew Wiggins .60 1.50

2017-18 Hoops Rise N Shine Memorabilia

*PRIME/25: .75X TO 2X BASIC
1 Markelle Fultz 5.00 12.00
2 Lonzo Ball 8.00 20.00
3 Jayson Tatum 25.00 60.00
4 Josh Jackson 2.50 6.00
5 De'Aaron Fox 6.00 15.00
6 Jonathan Isaac 5.00 12.00
7 Dwayne Bacon 2.00 5.00
8 Frank Ntilikina 2.50 6.00
9 Dennis Smith Jr. 3.00 8.00
10 Zach Collins 3.00 8.00
11 Malik Monk 8.00 20.00
12 Luke Kennard 4.00 10.00
13 Donovan Mitchell 20.00 50.00
14 Bam Adebayo 12.00 30.00
15 D.J. Wilson 2.00 5.00
17 T.J. Leaf 2.00 5.00
18 John Collins 5.00 12.00
19 Harry Giles 2.00 5.00
20 Terrance Ferguson 2.00 5.00
21 Jarrett Allen 5.00 12.00
22 OG Anunoby 10.00 25.00
23 Tyler Lydon 2.00 5.00
24 Caleb Swanigan 2.00 5.00

25 Kyle Kuzma 8.00 20.00
26 Tony Bradley 2.00 5.00
27 Derrick White 8.00 20.00
28 Josh Hart 5.00 12.00
29 Frank Jackson 2.00 5.00
30 Davon Reed 2.00 5.00
31 Wesley Iwundu 2.00 5.00
33 Ivan Rabb 2.00 5.00
34 Semi Ojeleye 2.50 6.00
35 Jordan Bell 2.00 5.00
36 Jawun Evans 2.00 5.00
37 Tyler Dorsey 2.00 5.00
38 Sindarius Thornwell 2.00 5.00
39 Ante Zizic 2.50 6.00
40 Sterling Brown 2.00 5.00

2017-18 Hoops Road to the Finals

1-44 PRINT RUN 2017 SER.#'d SETS
45-65 PRINT RUN 999 SER.#'d SETS
66-74 PRINT RUN 499 SER.#'d SETS
74-79 PRINT RUN 199 SER.#'d SETS
1 Jimmy Butler R1/2017 1.00 2.50
2 Rajon Rondo R1/2017 .75 2.00
3 Al Horford R1/2017 .60 1.50
4 Isaiah Thomas R1/2017 .50 1.25
5 Avery Bradley R1/2017 .40 1.00
6 Gerald Green R1/2017 .50 1.25
7 John Wall R1/2017 .75 2.00
8 Bradley Beal R1/2017 .75 2.00
9 Paul Millsap R1/2017 .50 1.25
10 Dwight Howard R1/2017 .75 2.00
11 Otto Porter R1/2017 .50 1.25
12 John Wall R1/2017 .75 2.00
13 Giannis Antetokounmpo R1/2017 3.00 8.00
14 Kyle Lowry R1/2017 .60 1.50
15 Khris Middleton R1/2017 .75 2.00
16 DeMar DeRozan R1/2017 .75 2.00
17 Norman Powell R1/2017 .60 1.50
18 Serge Ibaka R1/2017 .50 1.25
19 LeBron James R1/2017 5.00 12.00
20 Kyrie Irving R1/2017 1.25 3.00
21 LeBron James R1/2017 5.00 12.00
22 Deron Williams R1/2017 .50 1.25
23 Kevin Durant R1/2017 2.50 6.00
24 Stephen Curry R1/2017 5.00 12.00
25 Klay Thompson R1/2017 1.50 4.00
26 Draymond Green R1/2017 .75 2.00
27 Joe Johnson R1/2017 .50 1.25
28 Blake Griffin R1/2017 .60 1.50
29 Chris Paul R1/2017 1.00 2.50
30 Rudy Gobert R1/2017 .75 2.00
31 Gordon Hayward R1/2017 .50 1.25
32 DeAndre Jordan R1/2017 .50 1.25
33 George Hill R1/2017 .50 1.25
34 James Harden R1/2017 1.25 3.00
35 Eric Gordon R1/2017 .50 1.25
36 Russell Westbrook R1/2017 1.00 2.50
37 Nene R1/2017 .50 1.25
38 Lou Williams R1/2017 .50 1.25
39 Kawhi Leonard R1/2017 1.50 4.00
40 Tony Parker R1/2017 1.00 2.50
41 Mike Conley R1/2017 .50 1.25
42 Marc Gasol R1/2017 .60 1.50
43 Patty Mills R1/2017 .60 1.50
44 LaMarcus Aldridge R1/2017 .60 1.50
45 Isaiah Thomas R2/999 .60 1.50
46 Isaiah Thomas R2/999 .60 1.50
47 John Wall R2/999 1.00 2.50
48 Bradley Beal R2/999 1.00 2.50
49 Avery Bradley R2/999 .50 1.25
50 Markieff Morris R2/999 .50 1.25
51 Kelly Olynyk R2/999 .50 1.25
52 Kyrie Irving R2/999 1.50 4.00
53 LeBron James R2/999 6.00 15.00
54 Kevin Love R2/999 .75 2.00
55 Kyle Korver R2/999 .60 1.50
56 Draymond Green R2/999 1.00 2.50
57 Stephen Curry R2/999 6.00 15.00
58 Kevin Durant R2/999 3.00 8.00
59 Draymond Green R2/999 1.00 2.50
60 Trevor Ariza R2/999 .50 1.25
61 Kawhi Leonard R2/999 2.00 5.00
62 LaMarcus Aldridge R2/999 .75 2.00
63 James Harden R2/999 1.50 4.00
64 Manu Ginobili R2/999 1.50 4.00
65 LaMarcus Aldridge R2/999 .75 2.00
66 LeBron James CF/499 8.00 20.00
67 Kevin Love CF/499 1.00 2.50
68 Marcus Smart CF/499 1.00 2.50
69 Kyrie Irving CF/499 2.00 5.00
70 LeBron James CF/499 8.00 20.00
71 Kevin Durant CF/499 4.00 10.00
72 Stephen Curry CF/499 8.00 20.00
73 Kevin Durant CF/499 4.00 10.00
74 Stephen Curry CF/499 8.00 20.00
75 Kevin Durant F/199 25.00 60.00
76 Stephen Curry F/199 50.00 120.00
77 Klay Thompson F/199 20.00 50.00
78 LeBron James F/199 40.00 100.00
79 Andre Iguodala F/199 20.00 50.00

2017-18 Hoops Rookie Autographs

1 Markelle Fultz 8.00 20.00
2 Ike Anigbogu 3.00 8.00
3 Lonzo Ball 12.00 30.00
4 Josh Hart 8.00 20.00
5 Luke Kennard 6.00 15.00
6 Abdel Nader 4.00 10.00
7 Semi Ojeleye 4.00 10.00
8 Damyean Dotson 4.00 10.00
9 Tony Bradley 3.00 8.00
10 Edmond Sumner 5.00 12.00
11 De'Aaron Fox 40.00 100.00
12 Jarrett Allen 8.00 20.00
13 Lauri Markkanen 30.00 80.00
14 Justin Jackson 3.00 8.00
15 Malik Monk 12.00 30.00
16 Alec Peters 3.00 8.00
17 Sindarius Thornwell 3.00 8.00
18 Davon Reed 3.00 8.00
19 Tyler Dorsey 3.00 8.00
20 Frank Jackson 3.00 8.00
21 Dennis Smith Jr. 4.00 10.00
22 Jawun Evans 3.00 8.00
23 Jayson Tatum 75.00 200.00
24 Justin Patton 3.00 8.00
25 Monte Morris 12.00 30.00
26 Bam Adebayo 20.00 50.00
27 Sterling Brown 3.00 8.00
28 Derrick White 12.00 30.00
29 Tyler Lydon 3.00 8.00
30 Frank Mason III 3.00 8.00
31 Frank Ntilikina 4.00 10.00
32 John Collins 10.00 25.00
33 Jonathan Isaac 12.00 30.00
34 Ivan Rabb 3.00 8.00
35 Johnathan Motley 3.00 8.00
36 Cameron Oliver 3.00 8.00
37 T.J. Leaf 3.00 8.00
38 Donovan Mitchell 75.00 200.00
39 Wesley Iwundu 3.00 8.00
40 Guerschon Yabusele 3.00 8.00
41 Josh Jackson 4.00 10.00
42 Jordan Bell 3.00 8.00
43 Zach Collins 5.00 12.00
44 Kyle Kuzma 12.00 30.00
45 OG Anunoby 15.00 40.00
46 D.J. Wilson 4.00 10.00
47 Terrance Ferguson 3.00 8.00
48 Dwayne Bacon 3.00 8.00
49 Zhou Qi 12.00 30.00
50 Harry Giles 3.00 8.00

2017-18 Hoops Rookie Autographs Red

*RED: .6X TO 1.5X BASIC
STATED PRINT 25 SER.#'d SETS
13 Lauri Markkanen 100.00 250.00
23 Jayson Tatum 150.00 400.00
25 Monte Morris 40.00 100.00
38 Donovan Mitchell 150.00 400.00

2017-18 Hoops Rookie Remembrance Memorabilia

*PRIME/25: .75X TO 2X BASIC
1 AJ Hammons 2.00 5.00
2 Andrew Harrison 2.00 5.00
3 Andrew Wiggins 4.00 10.00
4 Bobby Portis 2.00 5.00
5 Brice Johnson 2.50 6.00
6 Buddy Hield 3.00 8.00
7 Cameron Payne 2.00 5.00
8 Caris LeVert 3.00 8.00
9 Cheick Diallo 2.00 5.00
10 Chinanu Onuaku 2.00 5.00
11 Chris McCullough 2.00 5.00
12 Cristiano Felicio 2.00 5.00
13 Damian Jones 2.00 5.00
14 Dante Exum 2.00 5.00
15 Dejounte Murray 3.00 8.00
16 Delon Wright 2.00 5.00
17 Demetrius Jackson 2.00 5.00
18 Denzel Valentine 2.00 5.00
19 Devin Booker 8.00 20.00
20 Deyonta Davis 2.00 5.00
21 Diamond Stone 2.00 5.00
22 Domantas Sabonis 6.00 15.00
23 Dragan Bender 2.00 5.00
24 Emmanuel Mudiay 2.00 5.00
25 Frank Kaminsky 2.00 5.00
26 Georges Niang 2.00 5.00
27 Georgios Papagiannis 2.00 5.00
28 Henry Ellenson 2.00 5.00
29 Isaiah Whitehead 2.00 5.00
30 Ivica Zubac 2.50 6.00
31 Jahlil Okafor 2.00 5.00
32 Jake Layman 2.50 6.00
33 Jakob Poeltl 2.50 6.00
34 Jamal Murray 5.00 12.00
35 Jarell Martin 2.00 5.00
36 Jaylen Brown 8.00 20.00
37 Jerian Grant 2.00 5.00
38 Joe Young 2.00 5.00
39 Joel Bolomboy 2.00 5.00
40 Jordan Mickey 2.00 5.00
41 Josh Huestis 2.00 5.00
42 Josh Richardson 2.50 6.00
43 Juan Hernangomez 3.00 8.00
44 Justin Anderson 2.00 5.00
45 Justise Winslow 2.00 5.00
46 Kay Felder 2.00 5.00
47 Kelly Oubre Jr. 3.00 8.00
48 Kevon Looney 2.00 5.00
49 Kris Dunn 2.00 5.00
50 Larry Nance Jr. 2.50 6.00
51 Malachi Richardson 2.00 5.00
52 Malcolm Brogdon 2.50 6.00
53 Malik Beasley 2.50 6.00
54 Mario Hezonja 2.00 5.00
55 Marquese Chriss 2.00 5.00
56 Paul Zipser 2.00 5.00
57 Patrick McCaw 2.50 6.00
58 Mindaugas Kuzminskas 2.00 5.00
59 Montrezl Harrell 3.00 8.00
60 Richaun Holmes 2.00 5.00

2017-18 Hoops Shaquille O'Neal NBA 2K

16 Shaquille O'Neal 1.00 2.50
17 Shaquille O'Neal 1.00 2.50
18 Shaquille O'Neal 1.00 2.50
19 Shaquille O'Neal 1.00 2.50
20 Shaquille O'Neal 1.00 2.50
21 Shaquille O'Neal 1.00 2.50
22 Shaquille O'Neal 1.00 2.50
23 Shaquille O'Neal 1.00 2.50
24 Shaquille O'Neal 1.00 2.50
25 Shaquille O'Neal 1.00 2.50
NNO Shaquille O'Neal FOIL Heat 1.50 4.00

2017-18 Hoops Special Delivery

1 Aaron Gordon .50 1.25
2 James Harden 1.00 2.50
3 Andrew Wiggins .60 1.50
4 Larry Nance Jr. .40 1.00
5 Jaylen Brown 1.25 3.00
6 Blake Griffin .60 1.50
7 LeBron James 4.00 10.00
8 DeMar DeRozan .60 1.50
9 Russell Westbrook .75 2.00
10 Giannis Antetokounmpo 2.50 6.00
11 Terrence Ross .40 1.00
12 Kobe Bryant 4.00 10.00
13 Dominique Wilkins .75 2.00
14 Clyde Drexler .75 2.00
15 Julius Erving 1.25 3.00

2017-18 Hoops Special Delivery Artist Proof

*ARTIST PROOF: 1.2X TO 3X BASIC
STATED PRINT RUN 25 SER.#'d SETS
7 LeBron James 10.00 25.00

2017-18 Hoops Swat Team

1 Rudy Gobert .60 1.50
2 Anthony Davis 1.25 3.00
3 Myles Turner .50 1.25
4 Hassan Whiteside .40 1.00
5 Kristaps Porzingis .60 1.50
6 Giannis Antetokounmpo 2.50 6.00
7 DeAndre Jordan .40 1.00
8 LeBron James 4.00 10.00
9 Kevin Durant 2.00 5.00
10 Serge Ibaka .40 1.00
11 Draymond Green .60 1.50
12 Marc Gasol .50 1.25
13 LaMarcus Aldridge .50 1.25
14 Alex Len .30 .75
15 Andre Drummond .40 1.00

2017-18 Hoops Team Leaders

1 Russell Westbrook .75 2.00
2 LeBron James 4.00 10.00
3 Kevin Durant 2.00 5.00
4 James Harden 1.00 2.50
5 Isaiah Thomas .40 1.00
6 Anthony Davis 1.25 3.00
7 DeMar DeRozan .60 1.50
8 Damian Lillard 1.25 3.00
9 Trevor Booker .30 .75
10 Kristaps Porzingis .60 1.50
11 Robert Covington .30 .75
12 Dwyane Wade 1.00 2.50
13 Tobias Harris .40 1.00
14 Myles Turner .50 1.25
15 Giannis Antetokounmpo 2.50 6.00
16 Dennis Schroder .40 1.00
17 Kemba Walker .40 1.00
18 Goran Dragic .40 1.00
19 Evan Fournier .40 1.00
20 John Wall .60 1.50
21 DeAndre Jordan .40 1.00
22 Julius Randle .50 1.25
23 Devin Booker 1.25 3.00
24 Buddy Hield .50 1.25
25 Harrison Barnes .40 1.00
26 Mike Conley .40 1.00
27 Kawhi Leonard 1.25 3.00
28 Nikola Jokic 3.00 8.00
29 Karl-Anthony Towns .75 2.00
30 Rudy Gobert .60 1.50

2017-18 Hoops Team Leaders Artist Proof

*ARTIST PROOF: 1.2X TO 3X BASIC
STATED PRINT RUN 25 SER.#'d SETS
2 LeBron James 10.00 25.00

2017-18 Hoops Tip Off

1 Embiid/Thompson 1.00 2.50
2 JOrdan/Porzingis .60 1.50
3 Gasol/Maker .50 1.25
4 DeAndre Jordan
Hassan Whiteside .40 1.00
5 Nowitzki/Chandler 1.25 3.00
6 Myles Turner
Zaza Pachulia .50 1.25
7 Davis/James 4.00 10.00
8 Andre Drummond
Jonas Valanciunas .40 1.00
9 Clint Capela
Pau Gasol .75 2.00
10 Towns/Prozingis .75 2.00
11 Durant/Gasol 2.00 5.00
12 Tristan Thompson
Zaza Pachulia .30 .75
13 Jahlil Okafor
Steven Adams .40 1.00
14 Davis/Chandler 1.25 3.00
15 Davis/Gortat 1.25 3.00

2017-18 Hoops Triple Double

1 Oscar Robertson 1.00 2.50
2 Magic Johnson 2.00 5.00
3 Jason Kidd .75 2.00
4 Russell Westbrook .75 2.00
5 Wilt Chamberlain 1.50 4.00

2017-18 Hoops We Got Next

1 Markelle Fultz 1.00 2.50
2 Lonzo Ball 1.50 4.00
3 Jayson Tatum 5.00 12.00
4 Josh Jackson .50 1.25
5 De'Aaron Fox 3.00 8.00
6 Jonathan Isaac 1.00 2.50
7 Lauri Markkanen 2.50 6.00
8 Frank Ntilikina .50 1.25
9 Dennis Smith Jr. .50 1.25
10 Zach Collins .60 1.50
11 Malik Monk 1.50 4.00
12 Luke Kennard .75 2.00
13 Donovan Mitchell 4.00 10.00
14 Bam Adebayo 2.50 6.00
15 Justin Jackson .40 1.00
16 Justin Patton .40 1.00
17 D.J. Wilson .40 1.00
18 T.J. Leaf .40 1.00
19 John Collins 1.00 2.50
20 Harry Giles .40 1.00
21 Terrance Ferguson .40 1.00
22 Jarrett Allen 1.00 2.50
23 OG Anunoby 2.00 5.00
24 Tyler Lydon .40 1.00
25 Kyle Kuzma 1.50 4.00

2017-18 Hoops We Got Next Artist Proof

*ARTIST PROOF: 1.2X TO 3X BASIC
STATED PRINT RUN 25 SER.#'d SETS
2 Lonzo Ball 25.00 60.00

2017-18 Hoops Zero Gravity

1 Terrence Ross .40 1.00
2 Jaylen Brown 1.25 3.00
3 Aaron Gordon .50 1.25
4 Will Barton .30 .75
5 DeMar DeRozan .60 1.50
6 Larry Nance Jr. .40 1.00
7 LeBron James 4.00 10.00
8 Russell Westbrook .75 2.00
9 Kawhi Leonard 1.25 3.00
10 Derrick Jones Jr. .30 .75

2018-19 Hoops

COMPLETE SET (300) 25.00 60.00
1 Dennis Schroder .25 .60
2 Nikola Jokic 1.50 4.00
3 LaMarcus Aldridge .30 .75
4 Giannis Antetokounmpo 1.50 4.00
5 Kevin Durant 1.25 3.00
6 DeMar DeRozan .40 1.00
7 Zach Randolph .25 .60
8 Kristaps Porzingis .40 1.00
9 Bradley Beal .40 1.00
10 Paul George .50 1.25
11 Taurean Prince .20 .50
12 Gary Harris .25 .60
13 Kawhi Leonard .75 2.00
14 Khris Middleton .30 .75
15 Stephen Curry 2.50 6.00
16 Kyle Lowry .30 .75
17 Buddy Hield .30 .75
18 Tim Hardaway Jr. .20 .50
19 John Wall .40 1.00
20 Carmelo Anthony .50 1.25
21 Kent Bazemore .20 .50
22 Jamal Murray .60 1.50
23 Rudy Gay .30 .75
24 Eric Bledsoe .25 .60
25 Draymond Green .40 1.00
26 Jonas Valanciunas .30 .75
27 Willie Cauley-Stein .20 .50
28 Enes Kanter .25 .60
29 Otto Porter Jr. .25 .60
30 Russell Westbrook .50 1.25
31 John Collins .30 .75
32 Will Barton .20 .50
33 Pau Gasol .50 1.25
34 Malcolm Brogdon .30 .75
35 Klay Thompson .75 2.00
36 Serge Ibaka .25 .60
37 Bogdan Bogdanovic .30 .75
38 Michael Beasley .20 .50
39 Kelly Oubre Jr. .30 .75
40 Steven Adams .25 .60
41 Dewayne Dedmon .20 .50
42 Paul Millsap .25 .60
43 Patty Mills .30 .75
44 Jabari Parker .20 .50
45 Andre Iguodala .25 .60
46 C.J. Miles .20 .50
47 De'Aaron Fox .60 1.50
48 Courtney Lee .20 .50
49 Markieff Morris .20 .50
50 Jerami Grant .30 .75
51 Mike Muscala .20 .50
52 Wilson Chandler .20 .50
53 Manu Ginobili .60 1.50
54 Thon Maker .20 .50
55 Jonas Jerebko .20 .50
56 Pascal Siakam .50 1.25
57 Skal Labissiere .20 .50
58 Damyean Dotson .20 .50
59 Marcin Gortat .20 .50
60 Raymond Felton .20 .50
61 Malcolm Delaney .20 .50
62 Mason Plumlee .20 .50
63 Tony Parker .50 1.25
64 Tony Snell .20 .50
65 Shaun Livingston .25 .60
66 Jakob Poeltl .25 .60
67 Justin Jackson .20 .50
68 Frank Ntilikina .20 .50
69 Tomas Satoransky .20 .50
70 Patrick Patterson .20 .50
71 Tyler Dorsey .20 .50
72 Trey Lyles .20 .50
73 Dejounte Murray .40 1.00
74 John Henson .20 .50
75 Zaza Pachulia .20 .50
76 OG Anunoby .30 .75
77 Vince Carter .60 1.50
78 Kyle O'Quinn .20 .50
79 Mike Scott .20 .50
80 Terrance Ferguson .20 .50
81 James Harden .60 1.50
82 LeBron James 2.50 6.00
83 Harrison Barnes .25 .60
84 Blake Griffin .30 .75
85 Lou Williams .25 .60
86 Gordon Hayward .30 .75
87 Devin Booker .75 2.00
88 Jeremy Lin .50 1.25
89 Kemba Walker .25 .60
90 Donovan Mitchell 1.00 2.50
91 Chris Paul .60 1.50
92 JR Smith .30 .75
93 Dennis Smith Jr. .20 .50
94 Andre Drummond .25 .60
95 Tobias Harris .25 .60
96 Kyrie Irving .75 2.00
97 TJ Warren .20 .50
98 D'Angelo Russell .30 .75
99 Dwight Howard .40 1.00
100 Rudy Gobert .40 1.00
101 Eric Gordon .25 .60
102 Kevin Love .25 .60
103 Wesley Matthews .20 .50
104 Anthony Tolliver .20 .50
105 Danilo Gallinari .25 .60
106 Jaylen Brown .50 1.25
107 Josh Jackson .20 .50
108 Rondae Hollis-Jefferson .20 .50
109 Jeremy Lamb .20 .50
110 Ricky Rubio .25 .60
111 Clint Capela .25 .60
112 George Hill .25 .60
113 Dirk Nowitzki .75 2.00
114 Reggie Jackson .25 .60
115 Austin Rivers .25 .60
116 Jayson Tatum 1.25 3.00
117 Elfrid Payton .25 .60
118 DeMarre Carroll .20 .50
119 Nicolas Batum .20 .50
120 Derrick Favors .20 .50
121 Gerald Green .25 .60
122 Rodney Hood .25 .60
123 J.J. Barea .30 .75
124 Luke Kennard .25 .60
125 Patrick Beverley .20 .50
126 Marcus Morris .20 .50
127 Dragan Bender .20 .50
128 Allen Crabbe .20 .50
129 Frank Kaminsky .20 .50
130 Joe Ingles .25 .60
131 Trevor Ariza .20 .50
132 Tristan Thompson .20 .50
133 Yogi Ferrell .20 .50
134 Reggie Bullock .20 .50
135 DeAndre Jordan .25 .60
136 Al Horford .30 .75
137 Troy Daniels .20 .50
138 Spencer Dinwiddie .25 .60
139 Marvin Williams .20 .50
140 Dante Exum .25 .60
141 Ryan Anderson .20 .50
142 Kyle Korver .25 .60
143 Dwight Powell .20 .50
144 Ish Smith .20 .50
145 Milos Teodosic .20 .50
146 Terry Rozier .25 .60
147 Marquese Chriss .20 .50
148 Caris LeVert .30 .75
149 Michael Kidd-Gilchrist .20 .50
150 Jae Crowder .20 .50
151 P.J. Tucker .20 .50
152 Jeff Green .20 .50
153 Maxi Kleber .25 .60
154 Stanley Johnson .20 .50
155 Wesley Johnson .20 .50
156 Aron Baynes .20 .50
157 Tyson Chandler .25 .60
158 Joe Harris .25 .60
159 Malik Monk .30 .75
160 Royce O'Neale .20 .50
161 Anthony Davis .75 2.00
162 Victor Oladipo .25 .60
163 MarShon Brooks .20 .50
164 Zach LaVine .50 1.25
165 Lonzo Ball .30 .75
166 Joel Embiid .75 2.00
167 Goran Dragic .25 .60
168 Damian Lillard .75 2.00
169 Evan Fournier .25 .60
170 Jimmy Butler .50 1.25
171 DeMarcus Cousins .25 .60
172 Bojan Bogdanovic .25 .60
173 Tyreke Evans .20 .50
174 Lauri Markkanen .50 1.25
175 Kyle Kuzma .30 .75
176 JJ Redick .30 .75
177 Dion Waiters .20 .50
178 CJ McCollum .30 .75
179 Aaron Gordon .30 .75
180 Andrew Wiggins .40 1.00
181 Jrue Holiday .40 1.00
182 Myles Turner .30 .75
183 Marc Gasol .30 .75
184 Kris Dunn .20 .50
185 Brandon Ingram .30 .75
186 Ben Simmons .30 .75
187 Hassan Whiteside .25 .60
188 Jusuf Nurkic .25 .60
189 Nikola Vucevic .25 .60
190 Karl-Anthony Towns .50 1.25
191 E'Twaun Moore .20 .50
192 Darren Collison .20 .50
193 Mike Conley .25 .60
194 Bobby Portis .30 .75
195 Isaiah Thomas .25 .60
196 Dario Saric .25 .60
197 Josh Richardson .25 .60
198 Al-Farouq Aminu .20 .50
199 Jonathon Simmons .20 .50
200 Taj Gibson .20 .50
201 Nikola Mirotic .20 .50
202 Thaddeus Young .20 .50
203 Dillon Brooks .30 .75
204 Justin Holiday .20 .50
205 Julius Randle .30 .75
206 Robert Covington .25 .60
207 Dwyane Wade .60 1.50
208 Evan Turner .20 .50
209 D.J. Augustin .20 .50
210 Jeff Teague .20 .50
211 Rajon Rondo .40 1.00
212 Domantas Sabonis .40 1.00
213 JaMychal Green .20 .50
214 Robin Lopez .20 .50
215 Kentavious Caldwell-Pope .20 .50
216 Markelle Fultz .25 .60
217 Tyler Johnson .20 .50
218 Shabazz Napier .20 .50
219 Mario Hezonja .20 .50
220 Jamal Crawford .30 .75
221 Darius Miller .20 .50
222 Cory Joseph .20 .50
223 Chandler Parsons .20 .50
224 Denzel Valentine .20 .50
225 Brook Lopez .25 .60
226 T.J. McConnell .20 .50
227 Kelly Olynyk .20 .50
228 Maurice Harkless .20 .50
229 Terrence Ross .25 .60
230 Tyus Jones .20 .50
231 Ian Clark .20 .50
232 Lance Stephenson .25 .60
233 Svi Mykhailiuk RC .25 .60
234 Jerian Grant .20 .50
235 Josh Hart .25 .60
236 Amir Johnson .20 .50
237 Bam Adebayo .50 1.25
238 Zach Collins .25 .60
239 Jonathan Isaac .30 .75
240 Derrick Rose .60 1.50
241 Dzanan Musa RC .40 1.00
242 Kevin Knox RC .50 1.25
243 Jalen Brunson RC 3.00 8.00
244 Jerome Robinson RC .40 1.00
245 Keita Bates-Diop RC .50 1.25
246 Donte DiVincenzo RC 1.00 2.50
247 Grayson Allen RC .75 2.00
248 Deandre Ayton RC 1.25 3.00
249 Moritz Wagner RC .75 2.00
250 Trae Young RC 3.00 8.00
251 Omari Spellman RC .40 1.00
252 Mikal Bridges RC 2.00 5.00
253 Devonte' Graham RC .60 1.50
254 Michael Porter Jr. RC 1.50 4.00
255 Bruce Brown RC .75 2.00
256 Lonnie Walker IV RC .75 2.00
257 Chandler Hutchison RC .50 1.25
258 Marvin Bagley III RC .60 1.50
259 Landry Shamet RC .60 1.50
260 Mo Bamba RC .60 1.50
261 Elie Okobo RC .40 1.00
262 Shai Gilgeous-Alexander RC 8.00 20.00
263 Gary Trent Jr. RC .75 2.00
264 Troy Brown Jr. RC .50 1.25
265 De'Anthony Melton RC .75 2.00
266 Kevin Huerter RC .75 2.00
267 Aaron Holiday RC .60 1.50
268 Luka Doncic RC 15.00 40.00
269 Robert Williams III RC .75 2.00
270 Wendell Carter Jr. RC 1.00 2.50
271 Jevon Carter RC .60 1.50
272 Miles Bridges RC 1.00 2.50
273 Jarred Vanderbilt RC .75 2.00
274 Zhaire Smith RC .40 1.00
275 Hamidou Diallo RC .60 1.50
276 Josh Okogie RC .60 1.50
277 Anfernee Simons RC 2.00 5.00
278 Jaren Jackson Jr. RC 3.00 8.00
279 Jacob Evans III RC .40 1.00
280 Collin Sexton RC 1.25 3.00
281 Stephen Curry HT 2.50 6.00
282 Dwyane Wade HT .60 1.50
283 Magic Johnson HT 1.25 3.00
284 Damian Lillard HT .75 2.00
285 Dirk Nowitzki HT .75 2.00
286 Charles Barkley HT .60 1.50
287 Julius Erving HT .75 2.00
288 Bill Russell HT 1.00 2.50
289 Oscar Robertson HT .60 1.50
290 Reggie Miller HT .60 1.50
291 Larry Bird HT 1.25 3.00
292 Kyrie Irving HT .75 2.00
293 Kevin Durant HT 1.25 3.00
294 Karl Malone HT .60 1.50
295 John Stockton HT .60 1.50
296 Kobe Bryant HT 2.50 6.00
297 Kareem Abdul-Jabbar HT 1.00 2.50
298 Shaquille O'Neal HT 1.00 2.50
299 Giannis Antetokounmpo HT 1.50 4.00
300 Allen Iverson HT .75 2.00

2018-19 Hoops Artist Proof

*ARTST PRF: 4X TO 10X BASIC
*ARTST PRF RC: 4X TO 10X BASIC
STATED PRINT RUN 25 SER.#'d SETS
243 Jalen Brunson 60.00 150.00
262 Shai Gilgeous-Alexander 125.00 300.00
268 Luka Doncic 600.00 1,200.00

2018-19 Hoops Blue

*BLUE: .75X TO 2X BASIC
*BLUE RC: .75X TO 2X BASIC
262 Shai Gilgeous-Alexander 12.00 30.00
268 Luka Doncic 75.00 200.00

2018-19 Hoops Blue Checkerboard

*BLUE CHK: 2X TO 5X BASIC
*BLUE CHK.RC: 2X TO 5X BASIC
STATED PRINT RUN 75 SER.#'d SETS
243 Jalen Brunson 30.00 80.00
262 Shai Gilgeous-Alexander 60.00 150.00
268 Luka Doncic 300.00 600.00

2018-19 Hoops Green

*GREEN: 1.5X TO 4X BASIC
*GREEN RC: 1.5X TO 4X BASIC
STATED PRINT RUN 99 SER.#'d SETS
243 Jalen Brunson 25.00 60.00
262 Shai Gilgeous-Alexander 50.00 120.00
268 Luka Doncic 200.00 500.00

2018-19 Hoops Orange

*ORANGE: 3X TO 8X BASIC
*ORANGE RC: 3X TO 8X BASIC
STATED PRINT RUN 25 SER.#'d SETS
243 Jalen Brunson 60.00 150.00
262 Shai Gilgeous-Alexander 125.00 300.00
268 Luka Doncic 600.00 1,200.00

2018-19 Hoops Orange Explosion

*ORNGE EXPLSN: 4X TO 10X BASIC
*ORNGE EXPLSN RC: 4X TO 10X BASIC
STATED PRINT RUN 25 SER.#'d SETS
243 Jalen Brunson 60.00 150.00
262 Shai Gilgeous-Alexander 125.00 300.00
268 Luka Doncic 600.00 1,200.00

2018-19 Hoops Picture Perfect

1 Karl-Anthony Towns .60 1.50
2 Chris Paul .75 2.00
3 Russell Westbrook .60 1.50
4 Devin Booker 1.00 2.50
5 Jimmy Butler .60 1.50
6 Donovan Mitchell 1.25 3.00
7 Kyrie Irving 1.00 2.50
8 Blake Griffin .40 1.00
9 John Wall .50 1.25
10 Anthony Davis 1.00 2.50
11 Andre Drummond .30 .75
12 Giannis Antetokounmpo 2.00 5.00
13 Jayson Tatum 1.50 4.00
14 Lonzo Ball .40 1.00
15 LeBron James 3.00 8.00
16 Ben Simmons .40 1.00
17 Joel Embiid 1.00 2.50
18 Klay Thompson 1.00 2.50
19 Damian Lillard 1.00 2.50
20 Stephen Curry 3.00 8.00
21 Kevin Durant 1.50 4.00
22 Kristaps Porzingis .50 1.25
23 James Harden .75 2.00
24 Andrew Wiggins .50 1.25
25 DeMar DeRozan .50 1.25

2018-19 Hoops Premium Box Set

*PREMIUM: 1.2X TO 3X BASIC
*PREMIUM RC: 1.2X TO 3X BASIC
STATED PRINT RUN 199 SER.#'d SETS
243 Jalen Brunson 20.00 50.00
250 Trae Young 125.00 300.00
262 Shai Gilgeous-Alexander 40.00 100.00
268 Luka Doncic 150.00 400.00

2018-19 Hoops Purple

*PURPLE: .75X TO 2X BASIC
*PURPLE RC: .75X TO 2X BASIC
262 Shai Gilgeous-Alexander 12.00 30.00
268 Luka Doncic 60.00 150.00

2018-19 Hoops Purple Winter

262 Shai Gilgeous-Alexander 12.00 30.00
268 Luka Doncic 75.00 200.00

2018-19 Hoops Red

*RED: 2.5X TO 6X BASIC
*RED RC: 2.5X TO 6X BASIC
STATED PRINT RUN 49 SER.#'d SETS
243 Jalen Brunson 40.00 100.00
262 Shai Gilgeous-Alexander 75.00 200.00
268 Luka Doncic 400.00 800.00

2018-19 Hoops Red Backs

*RED BACK: .6X TO 1.5X BASIC
*RED BACK KOBE: .6X TO 1.5X BASIC
262 Shai Gilgeous-Alexander 12.00 30.00
268 Luka Doncic 75.00 200.00

2018-19 Hoops Silver

*SILVER: 1.2X TO 3X BASIC
*SILVER RC: 1.2X TO 3X BASIC
STATED PRINT RUN 199 SER.#'d SETS
243 Jalen Brunson 20.00 50.00
262 Shai Gilgeous-Alexander 40.00 100.00
268 Luka Doncic 150.00 400.00

2018-19 Hoops Teal

*TEAL: 2X TO 5X BASIC
*TEAL RC: 2X TO 5X BASIC
STATED PRINT RUN 49 SER.#'d SETS
243 Jalen Brunson 40.00 100.00
262 Shai Gilgeous-Alexander 75.00 200.00
268 Luka Doncic 400.00 800.00

2018-19 Hoops Teal Explosion

*TEAL EXP: 1.5X TO 4X BASIC
*TEAL EXP RC: 1.5X TO 4X BASIC
243 Jalen Brunson 15.00 40.00
262 Shai Gilgeous-Alexander 30.00 80.00
268 Luka Doncic 125.00 300.00

2018-19 Hoops Winter

*WINTER: .5X TO 1.2X BASIC
*WINTER RC: .5X TO 1.2X BASIC

2018-19 Hoops Yellow

*YELLOW: .75X TO 2X BASIC
262 Shai Gilgeous-Alexander 12.00 30.00
268 Luka Doncic 75.00 200.00

2018-19 Hoops Action Shots

1 Donovan Mitchell 1.25 3.00
2 Ben Simmons .40 1.00
3 Blake Griffin .40 1.00
4 Klay Thompson 1.00 2.50
5 Anthony Davis 1.00 2.50
6 Stephen Curry 4.00 10.00
7 Chris Paul .75 2.00
8 Giannis Antetokounmpo 2.00 5.00
9 Kemba Walker .30 .75
10 Kristaps Porzingis .50 1.25
11 Devin Booker 1.00 2.50
12 Lonzo Ball .40 1.00
13 Andrew Wiggins .50 1.25
14 Jimmy Butler .60 1.50
15 Nikola Jokic 2.00 5.00
16 LeBron James 3.00 8.00
17 DeMar DeRozan .50 1.25
18 Kyrie Irving 1.00 2.50
19 Victor Oladipo .30 .75
20 Joel Embiid 1.00 2.50
21 John Wall .50 1.25
22 Damian Lillard 1.00 2.50
23 Kyle Kuzma .40 1.00
24 Karl-Anthony Towns .60 1.50
25 Andre Drummond .30 .75
26 Kevin Durant 1.50 4.00
27 LaMarcus Aldridge .40 1.00
28 Russell Westbrook .60 1.50
29 Jayson Tatum 1.50 4.00
30 James Harden .75 2.00

2018-19 Hoops Amplifiers

1 Damian Lillard 1.00 2.50
2 Stephen Curry 3.00 8.00
3 Russell Westbrook .60 1.50
4 Kyrie Irving 1.00 2.50
5 Victor Oladipo .30 .75
6 Lou Williams .30 .75
7 CJ McCollum .40 1.00
8 Kemba Walker .30 .75
9 Chris Paul .75 2.00
10 Donovan Mitchell 1.25 3.00

2018-19 Hoops ARCeologists

*AP/25: 2.5X TO 6X BASIC
1 Paul George .60 1.50
2 Ray Allen .50 1.25
3 Kemba Walker .30 .75
4 Larry Bird 1.50 4.00
5 Damian Lillard 1.00 2.50
6 Mark Price .40 1.00
7 CJ McCollum .40 1.00
8 Donovan Mitchell 1.25 3.00
9 James Harden .75 2.00
10 Reggie Miller .75 2.00
11 Kyle Lowry .40 1.00
12 Steve Kerr .50 1.25
13 Klay Thompson 1.00 2.50
14 Dirk Nowitzki 1.00 2.50
15 Stephen Curry 3.00 8.00

2018-19 Hoops Backstage Pass

*AP/25: 2.5X TO 6X BASIC
1 Stephen Curry 3.00 8.00
2 Kevin Durant 1.50 4.00
3 Giannis Antetokounmpo 2.00 5.00
4 Kyrie Irving 1.00 2.50
5 Russell Westbrook .60 1.50
6 Donovan Mitchell 1.25 3.00

7 Anthony Davis 1.00 2.50
8 James Harden .75 2.00
9 Jayson Tatum 1.50 4.00
10 Chris Paul .75 2.00

2018-19 Hoops Class of 2018

*HOLO: .5X TO 1.2X BASIC
*WINTER: .5X TO 1.2X BASIC
1 Deandre Ayton .75 2.00
2 Marvin Bagley III .40 1.00
3 Luka Doncic 20.00 50.00
4 Jaren Jackson Jr. 2.00 5.00
5 Trae Young 8.00 20.00
6 Mo Bamba .40 1.00
7 Wendell Carter Jr. .60 1.50
8 Collin Sexton .75 2.00
9 Kevin Knox .30 .75
10 Mikal Bridges 1.25 3.00
11 Shai Gilgeous-Alexander 2.50 6.00
12 Miles Bridges .60 1.50
13 Jerome Robinson .25 .60
14 Michael Porter Jr. 1.00 2.50
15 Donte DiVincenzo .60 1.50

2018-19 Hoops Courtside

*AP/25: 2.5X TO 6X BASIC
1 Russell Westbrook .60 1.50
2 Damian Lillard 1.00 2.50
3 Kyrie Irving 1.00 2.50
4 Kevin Durant 1.50 4.00
5 Andre Drummond .30 .75
6 James Harden .75 2.00
7 Jayson Tatum 1.50 4.00
8 Dirk Nowitzki 1.00 2.50
9 Karl-Anthony Towns .60 1.50
10 Joel Embiid 1.00 2.50
11 Donovan Mitchell 1.25 3.00
12 Stephen Curry 3.00 8.00
13 Anthony Davis 1.00 2.50
14 Kristaps Porzingis .50 1.25
15 Giannis Antetokounmpo 2.00 5.00
16 Andrew Wiggins .50 1.25
17 Lonzo Ball .40 1.00
18 Ben Simmons .40 1.00
19 Chris Paul .75 2.00
20 Klay Thompson 1.00 2.50

2018-19 Hoops Faces of the Future

*HOLO: .5X TO 1.2X BASIC
*WINTER: .5X TO 1.2X BASIC
1 Deandre Ayton .75 2.00
2 Marvin Bagley III .40 1.00
3 Luka Doncic 15.00 40.00
4 Jaren Jackson Jr. 2.00 5.00
5 Trae Young 8.00 20.00
6 Mo Bamba .40 1.00
7 Wendell Carter Jr. .60 1.50
8 Collin Sexton .75 2.00
9 Kevin Knox .30 .75
10 Mikal Bridges 1.25 3.00
11 Shai Gilgeous-Alexander 2.50 6.00
12 Miles Bridges .60 1.50
13 Jerome Robinson .25 .60
14 Michael Porter Jr. 1.00 2.50
15 Troy Brown Jr. .30 .75
16 Zhaire Smith .25 .60
17 Donte DiVincenzo .60 1.50
18 Lonnie Walker IV .50 1.25
19 Kevin Huerter .50 1.25
20 Josh Okogie .40 1.00

2018-19 Hoops Get Out The Way

*HOLO: .5X TO 1.2X BASIC
*WINTER: .5X TO 1.2X BASIC
1 Russell Westbrook .60 1.50
2 James Harden .75 2.00
3 LeBron James 3.00 8.00
4 John Wall .50 1.25
5 Jayson Tatum 1.50 4.00
6 Rajon Rondo .50 1.25
7 Kevin Durant 1.50 4.00
8 Donovan Mitchell 1.25 3.00
9 Giannis Antetokounmpo 2.00 5.00
10 Tony Parker .60 1.50
11 Kyrie Irving 1.00 2.50
12 Paul George .60 1.50
13 Jimmy Butler .60 1.50
14 DeMar DeRozan .50 1.25
15 Kyle Lowry .40 1.00
16 Goran Dragic .30 .75
17 Manu Ginobili .75 2.00
18 Jeremy Lin .60 1.50
19 Andre Iguodala .30 .75
20 Victor Oladipo .30 .75

2018-19 Hoops Great SIGnificance Autographs

EXCHANGE DEADLINE 4/24/2020
1 Antoine Carr 3.00 8.00
2 Charlie Bell 3.00 8.00
3 Chris Ford 5.00 12.00
4 Daequan Cook 3.00 8.00
5 Dale Ellis 3.00 8.00
6 Freddie Lewis 3.00 8.00
7 Henry Bibby 3.00 8.00
8 James Posey 3.00 8.00
9 James Robinson 3.00 8.00
10 Jeff Malone 3.00 8.00
11 Jerome Williams 3.00 8.00
12 Jim Jackson 4.00 10.00
13 John Hot Rod Williams 3.00 8.00
14 John Salley 4.00 10.00
15 Johnny Newman 3.00 8.00
16 Kiki Vandeweghe 4.00 10.00
17 Kurt Rambis 4.00 10.00
18 Michael Cage 3.00 8.00
19 Nazr Mohammed 3.00 8.00
20 Paul Westphal 5.00 12.00
21 Raef LaFrentz 3.00 8.00
22 Rory Sparrow 3.00 8.00
23 Rudy Tomjanovich 4.00 10.00
24 Alan Williams 3.00 8.00
25 Cheick Diallo 3.00 8.00
26 Cristiano Felicio 3.00 8.00
27 Deyonta Davis 3.00 8.00
28 Domantas Sabonis 6.00 15.00
29 Dragan Bender 3.00 8.00
30 Cherokee Parks 3.00 8.00
31 Henry Ellenson 3.00 8.00
32 Ish Smith 3.00 8.00
34 Justin Holiday 3.00 8.00
35 Yante Maten 8.00 20.00
36 Luke Kornet 3.00 8.00
37 Raul Neto 3.00 8.00
38 Solomon Hill 3.00 8.00
39 Tomas Satoransky 3.00 8.00
40 Tony Snell 3.00 8.00
41 Theo Pinson 3.00 8.00
42 Udonis Haslem 3.00 8.00
43 Willy Hernangomez 3.00 8.00
44 Craig Hodges 4.00 10.00
45 Wade Baldwin IV 3.00 8.00
46 Mangok Mathiang 6.00 15.00
47 TJ Warren 3.00 8.00
48 Jairus Lyles 10.00 25.00
49 Angel Delgado 8.00 20.00
50 Terry Rozier 4.00 10.00
51 Deandre Ayton 60.00 150.00
52 Marvin Bagley III 5.00 12.00
53 Luka Doncic 500.00 1,000.00
54 Jaren Jackson Jr. 40.00 100.00
55 Trae Young 50.00 120.00
56 Mo Bamba 15.00 40.00
57 Wendell Carter Jr. 15.00 40.00
58 Collin Sexton 12.00 30.00
59 Kevin Knox 4.00 10.00
60 Mikal Bridges 6.00 15.00
61 Shai Gilgeous-Alexander 300.00 600.00
62 J.P. Macura 4.00 10.00
64 Michael Porter Jr. 15.00 40.00
65 Troy Brown Jr. 4.00 10.00
66 Zhaire Smith 3.00 8.00
67 Donte DiVincenzo 12.00 30.00
68 Lonnie Walker IV 10.00 25.00
69 Kevin Huerter 6.00 15.00
70 Josh Okogie 10.00 25.00
71 Chandler Hutchison 4.00 10.00
72 Aaron Holiday 5.00 12.00
73 Anfernee Simons 15.00 40.00
74 Moritz Wagner 6.00 15.00
75 Landry Shamet 6.00 15.00
76 Jacob Evans III 3.00 8.00
77 Dzanan Musa 3.00 8.00
78 Omari Spellman 3.00 8.00
79 Elie Okobo 3.00 8.00
82 Hamidou Diallo 5.00 12.00
83 Melvin Frazier Jr. 3.00 8.00
85 Khyri Thomas 3.00 8.00
86 Isaac Bonga 15.00 40.00
88 Svi Mykhailiuk 4.00 10.00
89 Chimezie Metu 4.00 10.00
90 Alize Johnson 15.00 40.00
91 Ray Spalding 6.00 15.00
93 Duncan Robinson 60.00 150.00
95 Kevin Hervey 3.00 8.00
97 Kostas Antetokounmpo 8.00 20.00
98 Robert Williams III 6.00 15.00
100 Jalen Brunson 25.00 60.00

2018-19 Hoops Highlights

1 Kobe Bryant 3.00 8.00
2 James Harden .75 2.00
3 LeBron James 3.00 8.00
4 Karl-Anthony Towns .60 1.50
5 Stephen Curry 3.00 8.00

2018-19 Hoops Hoops Ink

EXCHANGE DEADLINE 4/24/2020
*RED/25: .5X TO 1.2X BASIC
1 Andrei Kirilenko 4.00 10.00
2 Kobe Bryant 300.00 600.00
3 Dino Radja 3.00 8.00
4 Julius Erving 40.00 100.00
5 Ish Smith 3.00 8.00
6 David Robinson 8.00 20.00
7 Kevin Johnson 8.00 20.00
8 Dennis Rodman 15.00 40.00
9 Paul Silas 5.00 12.00
10 Kristaps Porzingis 10.00 25.00
11 Henry Ellenson 3.00 8.00
12 Charles Barkley 100.00 250.00
13 Doug Collins 5.00 12.00
14 Oscar Robertson 20.00 50.00
15 Arvydas Sabonis 5.00 12.00
16 Paul Pierce 15.00 40.00
17 Maurice Harkless 3.00 8.00
18 Anfernee Hardaway 12.00 30.00
19 Ron Mercer 3.00 8.00
20 De'Aaron Fox 10.00 25.00
21 Channing Frye 3.00 8.00
22 Shaquille O'Neal 40.00 100.00
23 Erick Dampier 3.00 8.00
24 Jerry West 15.00 40.00
25 Walter Berry 3.00 8.00
26 Tracy McGrady 12.00 30.00
27 Nazr Mohammed 3.00 8.00
28 Tony Parker 6.00 15.00
29 Rony Seikaly 3.00 8.00
30 Lonzo Ball 20.00 50.00
31 Damon Stoudamire 5.00 12.00
HI-KDR Kevin Durant 100.00 250.00
33 Frank Kaminsky 3.00 8.00
34 Alonzo Mourning 12.00 30.00
35 Jonas Jerebko 3.00 8.00
36 Kevin McHale 8.00 20.00
37 Shareef Abdur-Rahim 4.00 10.00
38 Jeremy Lin 10.00 25.00
39 Sam Perkins 4.00 10.00
40 Gordon Hayward 10.00 25.00
41 Dee Brown 4.00 10.00
42 Magic Johnson 20.00 50.00
43 Hersey Hawkins 3.00 8.00
44 Karl-Anthony Towns 12.00 30.00
45 Felipe Lopez 3.00 8.00
46 Jason Kidd 6.00 15.00
47 Otis Birdsong 4.00 10.00
48 James Worthy 8.00 20.00
49 Stephen Jackson 4.00 10.00
50 Allen Crabbe 3.00 8.00

2018-19 Hoops Hot Signatures

EXCHANGE DEADLINE 4/24/2020
1 Oscar Robertson 20.00 50.00
2 Eddie Jones 4.00 10.00
3 Tracy McGrady 12.00 30.00
4 Sam Bowie 3.00 8.00
5 Jeremy Lin 10.00 25.00
6 Ed Pinckney 3.00 8.00
7 A.C. Green 5.00 12.00
8 Detlef Schrempf 5.00 12.00
9 Kobe Bryant 300.00 600.00
10 Jacque Vaughn 3.00 8.00
11 Jerry West 15.00 40.00
12 Bryant Reeves 3.00 8.00
13 Kevin McHale 8.00 20.00
14 Spencer Dinwiddie 4.00 10.00
15 James Worthy 8.00 20.00
16 Bam Adebayo 20.00 50.00
17 Alvan Adams 4.00 10.00
18 Domantas Sabonis 6.00 15.00
19 Charles Barkley 100.00 250.00
20 Jeff Hornacek 4.00 10.00
21 Alonzo Mourning 12.00 30.00
22 Charles Oakley 4.00 10.00
23 Jason Kidd 6.00 15.00
24 Spencer Haywood 5.00 12.00
25 Kristaps Porzingis 10.00 25.00
26 Gerald Henderson Sr. 3.00 8.00
27 Bismack Biyombo 3.00 8.00
28 Elden Campbell 3.00 8.00
29 Shaquille O'Neal 40.00 100.00
30 Joe Smith 4.00 10.00
31 Karl-Anthony Towns 12.00 30.00
32 Patrick Beverley 3.00 8.00
33 Dennis Rodman 15.00 40.00
34 Brad Daugherty 4.00 10.00
35 De'Aaron Fox 10.00 25.00
36 Stacey Augmon 3.00 8.00
37 Caris LeVert 5.00 12.00
38 Ernie DiGregorio 10.00 25.00
39 Kevin Durant 50.00 120.00
40 Kelly Oubre Jr. 5.00 12.00
41 David Robinson 8.00 20.00
42 Rafer Alston 4.00 10.00
43 Anfernee Hardaway 12.00 30.00
44 Jamal Mashburn 4.00 10.00
45 Lonzo Ball 20.00 50.00
46 Marquese Chriss 3.00 8.00
47 Craig Hodges 4.00 10.00
48 James Johnson 3.00 8.00
49 Stephen Curry 400.00 800.00
50 Kerry Kittles 3.00 8.00
51 Paul Pierce 15.00 40.00
52 Rik Smits 4.00 10.00
53 Tony Parker 6.00 15.00
54 Jack Sikma 4.00 10.00
55 Gordon Hayward 10.00 25.00
56 MarShon Brooks 3.00 8.00
58 Isaiah Rider 4.00 10.00
59 Kyrie Irving 30.00 80.00
60 Langston Galloway 3.00 8.00

2018-19 Hoops Hot Signatures Red

*RED: .5X TO 1.2X BASIC
STATED PRINT RUN 25 SER.#'d SETS
EXCHANGE DEADLINE 4/24/2020
57 Rondae Hollis-Jefferson 4.00 10.00

2018-19 Hoops Hot Signatures Rookies

EXCHANGE DEADLINE 4/24/2020
*RED/25: .6X TO 1.5X BASIC
1 Deandre Ayton 10.00 25.00
2 Marvin Bagley III 5.00 12.00
3 Luka Doncic 500.00 1,000.00
4 Jaren Jackson Jr. 40.00 100.00
5 Trae Young 125.00 300.00
6 Mo Bamba 12.00 30.00
7 Wendell Carter Jr. 12.00 30.00
8 Collin Sexton 12.00 30.00
9 Kevin Knox 4.00 10.00
10 Mikal Bridges 15.00 40.00
11 Shai Gilgeous-Alexander 200.00 500.00
12 J.P. Macura 4.00 10.00
13 Jerome Robinson 3.00 8.00
14 Michael Porter Jr. 15.00 40.00
15 Troy Brown Jr. 4.00 10.00
16 Zhaire Smith 3.00 8.00
17 Donte DiVincenzo 8.00 20.00
18 Lonnie Walker IV 10.00 25.00
19 Kevin Huerter 6.00 15.00
20 Josh Okogie 5.00 12.00
21 Grayson Allen 6.00 15.00
22 Chandler Hutchison 4.00 10.00
23 Aaron Holiday 5.00 12.00
24 Anfernee Simons 15.00 40.00
25 Moritz Wagner 6.00 15.00
26 Landry Shamet 6.00 15.00
27 Robert Williams III 6.00 15.00
28 Jacob Evans III 3.00 8.00
29 Dzanan Musa 3.00 8.00
30 Omari Spellman 3.00 8.00
31 Elie Okobo 3.00 8.00
32 Jevon Carter 5.00 12.00
33 Jalen Brunson 25.00 60.00
34 Devonte' Graham 5.00 12.00
35 Gary Trent Jr. 6.00 15.00
36 Allonzo Trier 3.00 8.00
37 Keita Bates-Diop 4.00 10.00
38 Bruce Brown 6.00 15.00
39 De'Anthony Melton 6.00 15.00
40 Hamidou Diallo 5.00 12.00

2018-19 Hoops Legends of the Ball

1 Dominique Wilkins 1.25 3.00
2 David Robinson 1.50 4.00
3 Julius Erving 2.00 5.00
4 Magic Johnson 3.00 8.00
5 Ray Allen 1.00 2.50
6 Charles Barkley 1.50 4.00
7 Clyde Drexler 1.25 3.00
8 Reggie Miller 1.50 4.00
9 Patrick Ewing 1.25 3.00
10 John Stockton 1.50 4.00
11 Allen Iverson 2.00 5.00
12 Hakeem Olajuwon 1.00 2.50
13 Kareem Abdul-Jabbar 2.50 6.00
14 Gary Payton 1.00 2.50
15 Jason Kidd 1.25 3.00
16 Kobe Bryant 12.00 30.00
17 Steve Nash 1.50 4.00
18 Karl Malone 1.50 4.00
19 Scottie Pippen 2.00 5.00
20 Shaquille O'Neal 2.50 6.00

2018-19 Hoops Lights Camera Action

*HOLO: .5X TO 1.2X BASIC
*WINTER: .5X TO 1.2X BASIC
1 Stephen Curry 3.00 8.00
2 LeBron James 3.00 8.00
3 Kevin Durant 1.50 4.00
4 Giannis Antetokounmpo 2.00 5.00
5 Kyrie Irving 1.00 2.50
6 Russell Westbrook .60 1.50
7 Kristaps Porzingis .50 1.25
8 Joel Embiid 1.00 2.50
9 James Harden .75 2.00
10 Ben Simmons .40 1.00
11 Lonzo Ball .40 1.00
12 Damian Lillard 1.00 2.50
13 Klay Thompson 1.00 2.50
14 Jimmy Butler .60 1.50
15 Karl-Anthony Towns .60 1.50
16 Anthony Davis 1.00 2.50
17 Nikola Jokic 2.00 5.00
18 Andre Drummond .30 .75
19 Chris Paul .75 2.00
20 DeMar DeRozan .50 1.25
21 LaMarcus Aldridge .40 1.00
22 Kemba Walker .30 .75
23 Victor Oladipo .30 .75
24 Jayson Tatum 1.50 4.00
25 Donovan Mitchell 1.25 3.00
26 Devin Booker 1.00 2.50
27 John Wall .50 1.25
28 Blake Griffin .60 1.50
29 Andrew Wiggins .50 1.25
30 Kyle Kuzma .40 1.00

2018-19 Hoops NBA City

*AP/25: 2.5X TO 6X BASIC
1 Kevin Love .30 .75
2 Stephen Curry 3.00 8.00
3 Russell Westbrook .60 1.50
4 Goran Dragic .30 .75
5 John Wall .50 1.25
6 Anthony Davis 1.00 2.50
7 Giannis Antetokounmpo 2.00 5.00
8 James Harden .75 2.00
9 Blake Griffin .40 1.00
10 Tobias Harris .30 .75
11 Damian Lillard 1.00 2.50
12 Kemba Walker .30 .75
13 Kyle Lowry .40 1.00
14 Karl-Anthony Towns .60 1.50
15 Kyrie Irving 1.00 2.50
16 LaMarcus Aldridge .40 1.00
17 Marc Gasol .40 1.00
18 Nikola Jokic 2.00 5.00
19 Donovan Mitchell 1.25 3.00
20 Kristaps Porzingis .50 1.25
21 Lonzo Ball .40 1.00
22 Ben Simmons .40 1.00
23 Taurean Prince .25 .60
24 De'Aaron Fox .75 2.00
25 Aaron Gordon .40 1.00
26 D'Angelo Russell .40 1.00
27 Victor Oladipo .30 .75
28 Josh Jackson .25 .60
29 Zach LaVine .60 1.50
30 Dennis Smith Jr. .25 .60

2018-19 Hoops Rise N Shine Memorabilia

*WINTER: .5X TO 1.2X BASIC
*PRIME/25: 1X TO 2.5X BASIC
1 Deandre Ayton 10.00 25.00
2 Marvin Bagley III 4.00 10.00
3 Luka Doncic 40.00 100.00
4 Jaren Jackson Jr. 4.00 10.00
5 Trae Young 12.00 30.00
6 Mo Bamba 2.50 6.00
7 Wendell Carter Jr. 4.00 10.00
8 Collin Sexton 4.00 10.00
9 Kevin Knox 2.00 5.00
10 Mikal Bridges 8.00 20.00
11 Shai Gilgeous-Alexander 15.00 40.00
12 Svi Mykhailiuk 2.00 5.00
13 Jerome Robinson 1.50 4.00
14 Michael Porter Jr. 6.00 15.00
15 Troy Brown Jr. 2.00 5.00
16 Zhaire Smith 1.50 4.00
17 Donte DiVincenzo 4.00 10.00
18 Lonnie Walker IV 3.00 8.00
19 Kevin Huerter 3.00 8.00
20 Josh Okogie 2.50 6.00
21 Grayson Allen 4.00 10.00
22 Chandler Hutchison 2.00 5.00
23 Aaron Holiday 2.50 6.00
24 Anfernee Simons 8.00 20.00
25 Moritz Wagner 3.00 8.00
26 Landry Shamet 3.00 8.00
27 Robert Williams III 3.00 8.00
28 Jacob Evans III 1.50 4.00
29 Dzanan Musa 1.50 4.00
30 Omari Spellman 1.50 4.00
31 Elie Okobo 1.50 4.00
32 Jevon Carter 2.50 6.00
33 Jalen Brunson 12.00 30.00
34 Devonte' Graham 2.50 6.00
35 Gary Trent Jr. 3.00 8.00
36 Jarred Vanderbilt 3.00 8.00
37 Keita Bates-Diop 2.00 5.00
RNS-BB Bruce Brown 3.00 8.00
39 De'Anthony Melton 3.00 8.00
40 Hamidou Diallo 3.00 8.00

2018-19 Hoops Road to the Finals

1-45 PRINT RUN 2018 SER.#'d SETS
46-64 PRINT RUN 999 SER.#'d SETS
65-82 PRINT RUN 499 SER.#'d SETS
83-100 PRINT RUN 199 SER.#'d SETS
83-100 PRINT RUN 99 SER.#'d SETS
1 Klay Thompson R1 1.50 4.00
2 Serge Ibaka R1 .50 1.25
3 Ben Simmons R1 .60 1.50
4 Anthony Davis R1 1.50 4.00
5 Terry Rozier R1 .50 1.25
6 Victor Oladipo R1 .50 1.25
7 Paul George R1 1.00 2.50
8 James Harden R1 1.25 3.00
9 Dwyane Wade R1 1.25 3.00
10 Kevin Durant R1 2.50 6.00
11 DeMar DeRozan R1 .75 2.00
12 Jaylen Brown R1 1.00 2.50
13 Jrue Holiday R1 .75 2.00
14 LeBron James R1 5.00 12.00
15 Donovan Mitchell R1 2.00 5.00
16 Chris Paul R1 1.25 3.00
17 Joel Embiid R1 1.50 4.00
18 Nikola Mirotic R1 .40 1.00
19 Kevin Durant R1 2.50 6.00
20 Bojan Bogdanovic R1 .50 1.25
21 John Wall R1 .75 2.00
22 Khris Middleton R1 .60 1.50
23 Ben Simmons R1 .60 1.50
24 Anthony Davis R1 1.50 4.00
25 Jimmy Butler R1 1.00 2.50
26 Ricky Rubio R1 .50 1.25
27 Giannis Antetokounmpo R1 3.00 8.00
28 LaMarcus Aldridge R1 .60 1.50
29 Bradley Beal R1 .75 2.00
30 LeBron James R1 5.00 12.00
31 James Harden R1 1.25 3.00
32 Donovan Mitchell R1 2.00 5.00
33 Al Horford R1 .60 1.50
34 JJ Redick R1 .60 1.50
35 Draymond Green R1 .75 2.00
36 DeMar DeRozan R1 .75 2.00
37 LeBron James R1 5.00 12.00
38 Clint Capela R1 .50 1.25
39 Russell Westbrook R1 1.00 2.50
40 Giannis Antetokounmpo R1 3.00 8.00
41 Kyle Lowry R1 .60 1.50
42 Victor Oladipo R1 .50 1.25
43 Donovan Mitchell R1 2.00 5.00
44 Terry Rozier R1 .50 1.25
45 LeBron James R1 5.00 12.00
46 Kevin Durant R2 3.00 8.00
47 James Harden R2 1.50 4.00
48 Jayson Tatum R2 3.00 8.00
49 LeBron James R2 6.00 15.00
50 Stephen Curry R2 6.00 15.00
51 Joe Ingles R2 .60 1.50
52 Jayson Tatum R2 3.00 8.00
53 LeBron James R2 6.00 15.00
54 Rajon Rondo R2 1.00 2.50
55 James Harden R2 1.50 4.00
56 Jayson Tatum R2 3.00 8.00
57 LeBron James R2 6.00 15.00
58 Kevin Durant R2 3.00 8.00
59 Chris Paul R2 1.50 4.00
60 Ben Simmons R2 .75 2.00
61 LeBron James R2 6.00 15.00
62 Chris Paul R2 1.50 4.00
63 Draymond Green R2 1.00 2.50
64 Jaylen Brown R2 1.25 3.00
65 Marcus Morris CF .60 1.50
66 Kevin Durant CF 4.00 10.00
67 Jaylen Brown CF 1.50 4.00
68 James Harden CF 2.00 5.00
69 LeBron James CF 8.00 20.00
70 Stephen Curry CF 8.00 20.00
71 LeBron James CF 8.00 20.00
72 James Harden CF 2.00 5.00
73 Jayson Tatum CF 4.00 10.00
74 Chris Paul CF 2.00 5.00
75 LeBron James CF 8.00 20.00
76 Klay Thompson CF 2.50 6.00
77 LeBron James CF 8.00 20.00
78 Stephen Curry CF 8.00 20.00
79 Kevin Durant F 5.00 12.00
80 Stephen Curry F 10.00 25.00
81 Kevin Durant F 5.00 12.00
82 Stephen Curry F 10.00 25.00
83 Kevin Durant F MVP 60.00 150.00
84 Warriors Champs 20.00 50.00
85 Kevin Durant CM 60.00 150.00
86 Jordan Bell CM 10.00 25.00
87 Stephen Curry CM 120.00 300.00
88 Steve Kerr CM 30.00 80.00
89 Andre Iguodala CM 25.00 60.00
90 Draymond Green CM 20.00 50.00
91 Klay Thompson CM 40.00 100.00
92 Quinn Cook CM 12.00 30.00
93 Damian Jones CM 10.00 25.00
94 JaVale McGee CM 12.00 30.00
95 David West CM 12.00 30.00
96 Patrick McCaw CM 10.00 25.00
97 Zaza Pachulia CM 10.00 25.00
98 Kevon Looney CM 12.00 30.00
99 Kevin Durant CM 60.00 150.00
100 Stephen Curry CM 120.00 300.00

2018-19 Hoops Rookie Ink

EXCHANGE DEADLINE 4/24/2020
1 Deandre Ayton 20.00 50.00
2 Marvin Bagley III 5.00 12.00
3 Luka Doncic 500.00 1,000.00
4 Jaren Jackson Jr. 40.00 100.00
5 Trae Young 125.00 300.00
6 Mo Bamba 15.00 40.00
7 Wendell Carter Jr. 15.00 40.00
8 Collin Sexton 12.00 30.00
9 Kevin Knox 4.00 10.00
10 Mikal Bridges 6.00 15.00
11 Shai Gilgeous-Alexander 200.00 500.00
12 Billy Preston 3.00 8.00
13 Jerome Robinson 3.00 8.00
14 Michael Porter Jr. 15.00 40.00
15 Troy Brown Jr. 4.00 10.00
16 Zhaire Smith 3.00 8.00
17 Donte DiVincenzo 8.00 20.00
18 Lonnie Walker IV 6.00 15.00
19 Kevin Huerter 6.00 15.00
20 Josh Okogie 5.00 12.00
22 Chandler Hutchison 4.00 10.00
23 Aaron Holiday 5.00 12.00
24 Anfernee Simons 15.00 40.00
25 Moritz Wagner 6.00 15.00
26 Landry Shamet 6.00 15.00
27 Robert Williams III 6.00 15.00
28 Jacob Evans III 3.00 8.00
29 Dzanan Musa 3.00 8.00
30 Omari Spellman 3.00 8.00
31 Elie Okobo 3.00 8.00
32 Jevon Carter 5.00 12.00
33 Jalen Brunson 25.00 60.00
34 Devonte' Graham 5.00 12.00
35 Gary Trent Jr. 6.00 15.00
36 Chimezie Metu 4.00 10.00
37 Keita Bates-Diop 4.00 10.00
38 Bruce Brown 6.00 15.00
39 De'Anthony Melton 6.00 15.00
40 Hamidou Diallo 5.00 12.00
41 Khyri Thomas 3.00 8.00
42 Svi Mykhailiuk 4.00 10.00
43 Vincent Edwards 3.00 8.00
44 Rodions Kurucs 8.00 20.00
45 Kevin Hervey 3.00 8.00
46 Kostas Antetokounmpo 8.00 20.00
48 Melvin Frazier Jr. 3.00 8.00
50 George King 3.00 8.00

2018-19 Hoops Rookie Ink Red

*RED: .6X TO 1.5X BASIC
STATED PRINT RUN 25 SER.#'d SETS
EXCHANGE DEADLINE 4/24/2020
21 Grayson Allen 20.00 50.00
47 Yante Maten 5.00 12.00

2018-19 Hoops Rookie Remembrance Relics

*WINTER: .5X TO 1.2X BASIC
*PRIME/25: 1X TO 2.5X BASIC
1 Davon Reed 1.50 4.00
2 Dejounte Murray 3.00 8.00
3 Semi Ojeleye 1.50 4.00
4 Derrick White 2.50 6.00
5 Josh Hart 2.00 5.00
6 Buddy Hield 2.50 6.00
7 Ivan Rabb 1.50 4.00
8 Denzel Valentine 1.50 4.00
9 Jarell Martin 1.50 4.00
10 Kelly Oubre Jr. 2.50 6.00
11 Malcolm Brogdon 2.50 6.00
12 Jaylen Brown 4.00 10.00
13 Dragan Bender 1.50 4.00
14 Milos Teodosic 1.50 4.00
15 Sindarius Thornwell 1.50 4.00
16 Dillon Brooks 2.50 6.00
17 Luke Kennard 2.00 5.00
18 TJ Leaf 1.50 4.00
19 Donovan Mitchell 8.00 20.00
20 Bam Adebayo 4.00 10.00
21 Dante Exum 2.00 5.00
22 Brandon Ingram 2.50 6.00
23 Josh Jackson 1.50 4.00
24 OG Anunoby 2.50 6.00
25 Kyle Kuzma 2.50 6.00
26 Justin Jackson 1.50 4.00
27 Jonathan Isaac 2.50 6.00
28 Frank Jackson 2.00 5.00
29 Andrew Wiggins 3.00 8.00
30 Willie Cauley-Stein 1.50 4.00
31 Jawun Evans 1.50 4.00
32 Frank Mason III 1.50 4.00
33 Bobby Portis 2.50 6.00
34 Thon Maker 1.50 4.00
35 Malik Monk 2.50 6.00
36 Markelle Fultz 2.00 5.00
37 Bogdan Bogdanovic 2.50 6.00
38 Dwayne Bacon 1.50 4.00
39 Kris Dunn 1.50 4.00
40 Stanley Johnson 1.50 4.00
41 Dennis Smith Jr. 1.50 4.00
42 Frank Kaminsky 1.50 4.00
43 Tyler Dorsey 1.50 4.00
44 Frank Ntilikina 1.50 4.00
45 Jarrett Allen 2.50 6.00
46 Terrance Ferguson 1.50 4.00
47 De'Aaron Fox 5.00 12.00
48 Terry Rozier 2.00 5.00
49 Josh Richardson 2.00 5.00
50 Jamal Murray 5.00 12.00
51 Sterling Brown 1.50 4.00
52 Tyler Lydon 1.50 4.00
53 Lonzo Ball 2.50 6.00
54 Pascal Siakam 4.00 10.00
55 Wes Iwundu 1.50 4.00
56 Jordan Bell 1.50 4.00
57 Lauri Markkanen 4.00 10.00
58 John Collins 2.50 6.00
59 Caris LeVert 2.50 6.00
60 Devin Booker 4.00 10.00

2018-19 Hoops The Pulse

*HOLO: .5X TO 1.2X BASIC
*WINTER: .5X TO 1.2X BASIC
1 Stephen Curry 3.00 8.00
2 Blake Griffin .40 1.00
3 Isaiah Thomas .30 .75
4 Joel Embiid 1.00 2.50
5 CJ McCollum .40 1.00
6 Jimmy Butler .60 1.50
7 James Harden .75 2.00
8 Kyle Lowry .40 1.00
9 Ben Simmons .40 1.00
10 Rudy Gobert .50 1.25
11 DeAndre Jordan .30 .75
12 Draymond Green .50 1.25
13 Hassan Whiteside .30 .75
14 Dirk Nowitzki 1.00 2.50
15 Kyle Kuzma .40 1.00

2018-19 Hoops Tip Off

1 Capela/Towns .60 1.50
2 Andre Drummond
Marc Gasol .40 1.00
3 DeAndre Jordan
Clint Capela .30 .75
4 Andre Drummond
Steven Adams .30 .75
5 Marc Gasol
Pau Gasol .60 1.50
6 Porzingis/Kleber .50 1.25
7 Julius Randle
Steven Adams .40 1.00
8 Embiid/Towns 1.00 2.50
9 Clint Capela
Marc Gasol .40 1.00
10 Davis/Durant 1.50 4.00

2018-19 Hoops We Got Next

1 Deandre Ayton .75 2.00
2 Marvin Bagley III .40 1.00
3 Luka Doncic 25.00 60.00
4 Jaren Jackson Jr. 2.00 5.00
5 Trae Young 8.00 20.00
6 Mo Bamba .40 1.00
7 Wendell Carter Jr. .60 1.50
8 Collin Sexton .75 2.00
9 Kevin Knox .30 .75
10 Mikal Bridges 1.25 3.00
11 Shai Gilgeous-Alexander 2.50 6.00
12 Miles Bridges .60 1.50
13 Jerome Robinson .25 .60
14 Michael Porter Jr. 1.00 2.50
15 Troy Brown Jr. .30 .75
16 Landry Shamet .40 1.00
17 Donte DiVincenzo .60 1.50
18 Lonnie Walker IV .50 1.25
19 Kevin Huerter .50 1.25
20 Josh Okogie .40 1.00
21 Grayson Allen .50 1.25
22 Chandler Hutchison .30 .75
23 Aaron Holiday .40 1.00
24 Anfernee Simons 1.25 3.00
25 Jacob Evans III .25 .60

2018-19 Hoops We Got Next Artist Proof

*AP: 2.5X TO 6X BASIC
STATED PRINT RUN 25 SER.#'d SETS
3 Luka Doncic 200.00 500.00

2019-20 Hoops

COMPLETE SET (300) 20.00 50.00
*WINTER: .5X TO 1.2X BASIC
*RED BACKS: .75X TO 2X BASIC
*BLUE: 1X TO 2.5X BASIC
*PURPLE: 1X TO 2.5X BASIC
*YELLOW: 1X TO 2.5X BASIC
*PRPLE WIN: 1.25X TO 3X BASIC
*NEON GREEN: 1.5X TO 4X BASIC
*TEAL EXP: 1.5X TO 4X BASIC
*PREMIUM BOX SET/199: 1.5X TO 4X BASIC
1 Trae Young .75 2.00
2 John Collins .30 .75
3 Kevin Huerter .30 .75
4 Kent Bazemore .20 .50
5 Allen Crabbe .20 .50
6 Jayson Tatum 1.25 3.00
7 Jaylen Brown .50 1.25
8 Marcus Smart .25 .60
9 Gordon Hayward .25 .60
10 Terry Rozier .25 .60
11 Kyrie Irving .60 1.50
12 Jarrett Allen .30 .75
13 Spencer Dinwiddie .25 .60
14 Joe Harris .25 .60
15 Caris LeVert .25 .60
16 Taurean Prince .20 .50
17 Rodions Kurucs .30 .75
18 D'Angelo Russell .25 .60
19 Kemba Walker .25 .60
20 Miles Bridges .30 .75
21 Michael Kidd-Gilchrist .20 .50
22 Nicolas Batum .20 .50
23 Bismack Biyombo .20 .50
24 Dwayne Bacon .20 .50
25 Zach LaVine .50 1.25
26 Kris Dunn .20 .50
27 Lauri Markkanen .40 1.00
28 Otto Porter Jr. .20 .50
29 Wendell Carter Jr. .30 .75
30 Denzel Valentine .20 .50
31 Robin Lopez .20 .50
32 Kevin Love .30 .75
33 Jordan Clarkson .30 .75
34 Matthew Dellavedova .25 .60
35 John Henson .20 .50
36 Tristan Thompson .20 .50
37 Larry Nance Jr. .25 .60
38 Collin Sexton .40 1.00
39 Luka Doncic 2.00 5.00
40 Kristaps Porzingis .40 1.00
41 Tim Hardaway Jr. .20 .50
42 Jalen Brunson .75 2.00
43 Courtney Lee .20 .50
44 Justin Jackson .20 .50
45 Dwight Powell .20 .50
46 Jamal Murray .50 1.25
47 Nikola Jokic 1.50 4.00
48 Will Barton .20 .50
49 Malik Beasley .25 .60
50 Torrey Craig RC .30 .75
51 Michael Porter Jr. .50 1.25
52 Gary Harris .25 .60
53 Blake Griffin .30 .75
54 Andre Drummond .25 .60
55 Luke Kennard .25 .60
56 Langston Galloway .20 .50
57 Reggie Jackson .25 .60
58 Thon Maker .20 .50
59 Stephen Curry 2.50 6.00
60 Klay Thompson .75 2.00
61 Kevin Durant 1.00 2.50
62 Draymond Green .40 1.00
63 Andre Iguodala .25 .60
64 DeMarcus Cousins .25 .60
65 Kevon Looney .20 .50
66 James Harden .60 1.50
67 Chris Paul .60 1.50
68 Eric Gordon .25 .60
69 Clint Capela .25 .60
70 P.J. Tucker .25 .60
71 Gerald Green .25 .60
72 Austin Rivers .20 .50
73 Victor Oladipo .25 .60
74 Aaron Holiday .25 .60
75 Wesley Matthews .20 .50
76 Domantas Sabonis .40 1.00
77 Myles Turner .30 .75
78 Thaddeus Young .20 .50
79 Bojan Bogdanovic .25 .60
80 Shai Gilgeous-Alexander 1.50 4.00
81 Danilo Gallinari .25 .60
82 Montrezl Harrell .25 .60
83 Landry Shamet .25 .60
84 Lou Williams .30 .75
85 Ivica Zubac .25 .60
86 Wilson Chandler .20 .50

87 LeBron James 2.50 6.00
88 Kyle Kuzma .40 1.00
89 Anthony Davis .75 2.00
90 Jaren Jackson Jr. .50 1.25
91 Avery Bradley .20 .50
92 Jae Crowder .20 .50
93 George Hill .25 .60
94 Chandler Parsons .20 .50
95 Bam Adebayo .50 1.25
96 Goran Dragic .25 .60
97 Kelly Olynyk .20 .50
98 Josh Richardson .20 .50
99 Dion Waiters .20 .50
100 Justise Winslow .20 .50
101 Derrick Jones Jr. .20 .50
102 Giannis Antetokounmpo 1.50 4.00
103 Eric Bledsoe .25 .60
104 Malcolm Brogdon .25 .60
105 Pau Gasol .50 1.25
106 Brook Lopez .25 .60
107 Khris Middleton .30 .75
108 Nerlens Noel .20 .50
109 Ersan Ilyasova .20 .50
110 Andrew Wiggins .40 1.00
111 Karl-Anthony Towns .50 1.25
112 Gorgui Dieng .20 .50
113 Josh Okogie .25 .60
114 Derrick Rose .60 1.50
115 Jeff Teague .20 .50
116 Lonzo Ball .30 .75
117 Josh Hart .25 .60
118 Jrue Holiday .40 1.00
119 Brandon Ingram .30 .75
120 Jahlil Okafor .20 .50
121 Julius Randle .40 1.00
122 DeAndre Jordan .25 .60
123 Kevin Knox II .20 .50
124 Emmanuel Mudiay .20 .50
125 Frank Ntilikina .20 .50
126 Mitchell Robinson .30 .75
127 Dennis Smith Jr. .20 .50
128 Allonzo Trier .20 .50
129 Russell Westbrook .50 1.25
130 Steven Adams .25 .60
131 Hamidou Diallo .25 .60
132 Paul George .50 1.25
133 Dennis Schroder .25 .60
134 Andre Roberson .20 .50
135 Terrance Ferguson .20 .50
136 Markieff Morris .20 .50
137 Aaron Gordon .30 .75
138 Mo Bamba .25 .60
139 Evan Fournier .25 .60
140 Markelle Fultz .25 .60
141 Jonathan Isaac .30 .75
142 Nikola Vucevic .25 .60
143 Terrence Ross .30 .75
144 Ben Simmons .30 .75
145 Joel Embiid .60 1.50
146 Jimmy Butler .60 1.50
147 Tobias Harris .25 .60
148 JJ Redick .30 .75
149 Devin Booker .07 .20
150 Deandre Ayton .30 .75
151 Josh Jackson .20 .50
152 T.J. Warren .25 .60
153 Mikal Bridges .50 1.25
154 Isaiah Thomas .25 .60
155 Tyler Johnson .20 .50
156 Kelly Oubre Jr. .25 .60
157 Damian Lillard .75 2.00
158 CJ McCollum .30 .75
159 Zach Collins .20 .50
160 Seth Curry .25 .60
161 Meyers Leonard .20 .50
162 Jusuf Nurkic .25 .60
163 Evan Turner .20 .50
164 Enes Kanter .20 .50
165 De'Aaron Fox .50 1.25
166 Marvin Bagley III .25 .60
167 Buddy Hield .25 .60
168 Bogdan Bogdanovic .30 .75
169 Willie Cauley-Stein .20 .50
170 Harry Giles .20 .50
171 LaMarcus Aldridge .30 .75
172 DeMar DeRozan .40 1.00
173 Rudy Gay .25 .60
174 Dejounte Murray .30 .75
175 Lonnie Walker IV .25 .60
176 Derrick White .30 .75
177 Kawhi Leonard .75 2.00
178 Marc Gasol .30 .75
179 Danny Green .25 .60
180 Serge Ibaka .25 .60
181 Kyle Lowry .30 .75
182 Pascal Siakam .50 1.25
183 Fred VanVleet .40 1.00
184 Norman Powell .25 .60
185 Donovan Mitchell .60 1.50
186 Mike Conley .25 .60
187 Rudy Gobert .40 1.00
188 Joe Ingles .25 .60
189 Ricky Rubio .25 .60
190 Derrick Favors .20 .50
191 John Wall .40 1.00
192 Bradley Beal .40 1.00
193 Thomas Bryant .25 .60
194 Troy Brown Jr. .20 .50
195 Jabari Parker .20 .50
196 Hassan Whiteside .20 .50
197 Trevor Ariza .20 .50
198 Jeff Green .20 .50
199 Vince Carter .60 1.50
200 Alex Len .20 .50
201 RJ Barrett RC 1.25 3.00
202 De'Andre Hunter RC 1.25 3.00
203 Jarrett Culver RC .30 .75
204 Coby White RC 1.00 2.50
205 Jaxson Hayes RC .50 1.25
206 Rui Hachimura RC 1.25 3.00
207 Cam Reddish RC .50 1.25
208 Cameron Johnson RC .75 2.00
209 PJ Washington Jr. RC 1.00 2.50
210 Tyler Herro RC 1.50 4.00
211 Romeo Langford RC .30 .75
212 Sekou Doumbouya RC .30 .75
213 Chuma Okeke RC .50 1.25
214 Nickeil Alexander-Walker RC .50 1.25
215 Goga Bitadze RC .50 1.25
216 Luka Samanic RC .40 1.00
217 Brandon Clarke RC .60 1.50
218 Grant Williams RC .50 1.25
219 Ty Jerome RC .60 1.50
220 Nassir Little RC .50 1.25
221 Dylan Windler RC .40 1.00
222 Mfiondu Kabengele RC .40 1.00
223 Jordan Poole RC 1.25 3.00
224 Keldon Johnson RC 1.00 2.50
225 Kevin Porter Jr. RC .60 1.50
226 KZ Okpala RC .40 1.00
227 Carsen Edwards RC .40 1.00
228 Bruno Fernando RC .40 1.00
229 Cody Martin RC .50 1.25
230 Eric Paschall RC .40 1.00
231 Admiral Schofield RC .40 1.00
232 Jaylen Nowell RC .40 1.00
233 Bol Bol RC .75 2.00
234 Isaiah Roby RC .40 1.00
235 Ignas Brazdeikis RC .40 1.00
236 Quinndary Weatherspoon RC .30 .75
237 Tremont Waters RC .40 1.00
238 Kyle Guy RC .40 1.00
239 Matisse Thybulle RC .60 1.50
240 Jordan Bone RC .30 .75
241 Nicolas Claxton RC .60 1.50
242 Jaylen Hands RC .30 .75
243 Daniel Gafford RC .60 1.50
244 Justin James RC .30 .75
245 Terance Mann RC .60 1.50
246 Jalen McDaniels RC .75 2.00
247 Alen Smailagic RC .30 .75
248 Talen Horton-Tucker RC .50 1.25
249 Darius Bazley RC .30 .75
250 Marcos Louzada Silva RC .30 .75
251 Darius Garland RC 1.25 3.00
252 Marial Shayok RC .30 .75
253 Josh Reaves RC .30 .75
254 Dewan Hernandez RC .30 .75
255 Jarrell Brantley RC .30 .75
256 Justin Wright-Foreman RC .30 .75
257 Miye Oni RC .30 .75
258 Zion Williamson RC 2.50 6.00
259 Ja Morant RC 3.00 8.00
260 Al Horford .30 .75
261 Marcus Morris .20 .50
262 DeMarre Carroll .20 .50
263 Jeremy Lamb .20 .50
264 Malik Monk .30 .75
265 JR Smith .25 .60
266 Paul Millsap .25 .60
267 Quinn Cook .25 .60
268 Anfernee Simons .50 1.25
269 Alfonzo McKinnie .20 .50
270 Iman Shumpert .20 .50
271 Patrick Beverley .25 .60
272 Kentavious Caldwell-Pope .25 .60
273 Rajon Rondo .40 1.00
274 Jonas Valanciunas .25 .60
275 Kyle Anderson .20 .50
276 Moritz Wagner .20 .50
277 Robert Covington .20 .50
278 Dewayne Dedmon .20 .50
279 Mike Scott .20 .50
280 Harrison Barnes .25 .60
281 Charles Barkley .60 1.50
282 Kobe Bryant 2.50 6.00
283 Shaquille O'Neal 1.25 3.00
284 Kevin Durant 1.00 2.50
285 Allen Iverson .75 2.00
286 Karl Malone .60 1.50
287 Dwyane Wade .60 1.50
288 Chris Paul .60 1.50
289 Larry Bird 1.25 3.00
290 Kyrie Irving .60 1.50
291 Damian Lillard .75 2.00
292 John Stockton .60 1.50
293 Julius Erving .75 2.00
294 Anthony Davis .75 2.00
295 Coby White 1.00 2.50
296 Zion Williamson 2.50 6.00
297 Ja Morant 3.00 8.00
298 RJ Barrett 1.25 3.00
299 De'Andre Hunter 1.25 3.00
300 Rui Hachimura 1.25 3.00

2019-20 Hoops Artist Proof

*ARTIST PRF: 5X TO 12X BASIC
STATED PRINT RUN 25 SER.#'d SETS
258 Zion Williamson 100.00 250.00
259 Ja Morant 100.00 250.00

2019-20 Hoops Blue Explosion

*BLUE EXPLSN: 4X TO 10X BASIC
STATED PRINT RUN 49 SER.#'d SETS
258 Zion Williamson 60.00 150.00
259 Ja Morant 60.00 150.00

2019-20 Hoops Green

*GREEN: 2.5X TO 6X BASIC
STATED PRINT RUN 99 SER.#'d SETS
258 Zion Williamson 40.00 100.00
259 Ja Morant 40.00 100.00

2019-20 Hoops Orange

*ORNG: 5X TO 12X BASIC
STATED PRINT RUN 25 SER.#'d SETS
258 Zion Williamson 100.00 250.00
259 Ja Morant 100.00 250.00

2019-20 Hoops Orange Explosion

*ORNG EXPLSN: 5X TO 12X BASIC
STATED PRINT RUN 25 SER.#'d SETS
258 Zion Williamson 100.00 250.00
259 Ja Morant 100.00 250.00

2019-20 Hoops Red

*RED: 3X TO 8X BASIC
STATED PRINT RUN 75 SER.#'d SETS
258 Zion Williamson 50.00 120.00
259 Ja Morant 50.00 120.00

2019-20 Hoops Silver

*SILVER: 1.2X TO 3X BASIC
*SILVER RC: 1.2X TO 3X BASIC
STATED PRINT RUN 199 SER.#'d SETS
87 LeBron James 20.00 50.00
295 Coby White 3.00 8.00
296 Zion Williamson 40.00 100.00
297 Ja Morant 20.00 50.00
298 RJ Barrett 8.00 20.00
300 Rui Hachimura 8.00 20.00

2019-20 Hoops Teal

*TEAL: 4X TO 10X BASIC
STATED PRINT RUN 49 SER.#'d SETS
87 LeBron James 25.00 60.00
258 Zion Williamson 60.00 150.00
259 Ja Morant 60.00 150.00

2019-20 Hoops Action Shots

1 D'Angelo Russell .30 .75
2 Kyrie Irving .75 2.00
3 Russell Westbrook .60 1.50
4 LeBron James 3.00 8.00
5 Devin Booker .10 .25
6 Jaren Jackson Jr. .60 1.50
7 Jayson Tatum 1.50 4.00
8 Kemba Walker .30 .75
9 Paul George .60 1.50
10 Marvin Bagley III .30 .75
11 Damian Lillard 1.00 2.50
12 Nikola Jokic 2.00 5.00
13 Joel Embiid .75 2.00
14 Luka Doncic 2.50 6.00
15 De'Aaron Fox .60 1.50
16 Trae Young 1.00 2.50
17 Anthony Davis 1.00 2.50
18 Steven Adams .30 .75
19 Rudy Gobert .50 1.25
20 Kevin Durant 1.25 3.00
21 Kawhi Leonard 1.00 2.50
22 Ben Simmons .40 1.00
23 Klay Thompson 1.00 2.50
24 Pascal Siakam .60 1.50
25 Giannis Antetokounmpo 2.00 5.00
26 Donovan Mitchell .75 2.00
27 James Harden .75 2.00
28 Bradley Beal .50 1.25
29 Stephen Curry 3.00 8.00
30 Deandre Ayton .40 1.00

2019-20 Hoops Arriving Now

*WINTER: .4X TO 1X BASIC
*HOLO: .75X TO 2X BASIC
1 PJ Washington Jr. .75 2.00
2 Zion Williamson 2.00 5.00
3 Matisse Thybulle .50 1.25
4 RJ Barrett 1.00 2.50
5 Romeo Langford .25 .60
6 Jarrett Culver .25 .60
7 Chuma Okeke .40 1.00
8 Jaxson Hayes .40 1.00
9 Goga Bitadze .40 1.00
10 Cam Reddish .40 1.00
11 Darius Garland 1.00 2.50
12 Ja Morant 2.50 6.00
13 Tyler Herro 1.25 3.00
14 De'Andre Hunter 1.00 2.50
15 Sekou Doumbouya .25 .60
16 Coby White .75 2.00
17 Nickeil Alexander-Walker .40 1.00
18 Rui Hachimura 1.00 2.50
19 Luka Samanic .30 .75
20 Cameron Johnson .60 1.50

2019-20 Hoops Backstage Pass

*HOLO: 1.25X TO 3X BASIC
*AP/25: 4X TO 10X BASIC
1 Draymond Green .50 1.25
2 Chris Paul .75 2.00
3 Luka Doncic 2.50 6.00
4 Nikola Jokic 2.00 5.00
5 Russell Westbrook .60 1.50
6 Jaren Jackson Jr. .60 1.50
7 LeBron James 3.00 8.00
8 Kawhi Leonard 1.00 2.50
9 Giannis Antetokounmpo 2.00 5.00
10 Gary Harris .30 .75

2019-20 Hoops Class of 2019

*WINTER: .4X TO 1X BASIC
*HOLO: .75X TO 2X BASIC
1 RJ Barrett 1.00 2.50
2 Darius Garland 1.00 2.50
3 Jarrett Culver .25 .60
4 Romeo Langford .25 .60
5 Jaxson Hayes .40 1.00
6 Cam Reddish .40 1.00
7 Zion Williamson 2.00 5.00
8 Cameron Johnson .60 1.50
9 Ja Morant 2.50 6.00
10 PJ Washington Jr. .75 2.00
11 De'Andre Hunter 1.00 2.50
12 Tyler Herro 1.25 3.00
13 Coby White .75 2.00
14 Sekou Doumbouya .25 .60
15 Rui Hachimura 1.00 2.50

2019-20 Hoops Courtside

*HOLO: 1.25X TO 3X BASIC
*AP/25: 4X TO 10X BASIC
1 LeBron James 3.00 8.00
2 Stephen Curry 3.00 8.00
3 Russell Westbrook .60 1.50
4 Donovan Mitchell .75 2.00
5 Paul George .60 1.50
6 Damian Lillard 1.00 2.50
7 James Harden .75 2.00
8 Karl-Anthony Towns .60 1.50
9 John Wall .50 1.25
10 Blake Griffin .40 1.00
11 Giannis Antetokounmpo 2.00 5.00
12 Joel Embiid .75 2.00
13 Ben Simmons .40 1.00
14 Luka Doncic 2.50 6.00
15 Trae Young 1.00 2.50

2019-20 Hoops Frequent Flyers

*WINTER: .4X TO 1X BASIC
*HOLO: 1.25X TO 3X BASIC
1 Kevin Durant 1.25 3.00
2 Anthony Davis 1.00 2.50
3 Giannis Antetokounmpo 2.00 5.00
4 Jayson Tatum 1.50 4.00
5 Miles Bridges .40 1.00
6 Aaron Gordon .40 1.00
7 Zach LaVine .60 1.50
8 Kawhi Leonard 1.00 2.50
9 Russell Westbrook .60 1.50
10 Ben Simmons .40 1.00
11 Derrick Jones Jr. .25 .60
12 Paul George .60 1.50
13 James Harden .75 2.00
14 DeMar DeRozan .50 1.25
15 LeBron James 3.00 8.00

2019-20 Hoops Get Out the Way

*WINTER: .4X TO 1X BASIC
*HOLO: 1.25X TO 3X BASIC
1 Luka Doncic 2.50 6.00
2 Aaron Gordon .40 1.00
3 Karl-Anthony Towns .60 1.50
4 Derrick Jones Jr. .25 .60
5 Miles Bridges .40 1.00
6 Donovan Mitchell .75 2.00
7 Dennis Smith Jr. .25 .60
8 John Collins .40 1.00
9 Kevin Durant 1.25 3.00
10 Joel Embiid .75 2.00
11 Hamidou Diallo .30 .75
12 Clint Capela .30 .75
13 De'Aaron Fox .60 1.50
14 Giannis Antetokounmpo 2.00 5.00
15 Jarrett Allen .40 1.00
16 Marvin Bagley III .30 .75
17 Allonzo Trier .25 .60
18 Domantas Sabonis .50 1.25
19 Terrence Ross .25 .60
20 Kevin Knox II .25 .60

2019-20 Hoops Great SIGnificance

EXCHANGE DEADLINE 05/06/2021
1 RJ Barrett 40.00 100.00
2 Edmond Sumner 3.00 8.00
3 De'Andre Hunter 12.00 30.00
4 Kenrich Williams 4.00 10.00
5 Damian Lillard 20.00 50.00
7 Zion Williamson 500.00 1,000.00
8 Jakob Poeltl 3.00 8.00
9 Ja Morant 300.00 600.00
10 Royce O'Neale 3.00 8.00
11 Kevin Porter Jr. 6.00 15.00
12 Danny Green 4.00 10.00
13 KZ Okpala 4.00 10.00
14 Lauri Markkanen 6.00 15.00
15 Kobe Bryant 500.00 1,000.00
16 John Stockton 12.00 30.00
17 Alen Smailagic 3.00 8.00
18 Khyri Thomas 3.00 8.00
19 Keldon Johnson 10.00 25.00
20 Dario Saric 4.00 10.00
21 Jaxson Hayes 5.00 12.00
22 Isaac Bonga 4.00 10.00
23 Rui Hachimura 60.00 150.00
24 Thon Maker 3.00 8.00
25 Jared Harper 4.00 10.00
27 Jarrett Culver 3.00 8.00
28 Cedi Osman 4.00 10.00
29 Coby White 40.00 100.00
30 Chandler Hutchison 3.00 8.00
31 Cody Martin 5.00 12.00
32 Al-Farouq Aminu 3.00 8.00
33 Eric Paschall 4.00 10.00
34 Daniel Theis 3.00 8.00
37 Carsen Edwards 4.00 10.00
38 Shake Milton 3.00 8.00
39 Bruno Fernando 4.00 10.00
40 Theo Pinson 3.00 8.00
41 PJ Washington Jr. 10.00 25.00
42 Dewayne Dedmon 3.00 8.00
43 Tyler Herro 40.00 100.00
44 DeAndre' Bembry 3.00 8.00
45 Ky Bowman 4.00 10.00
46 Jordan Bone 3.00 8.00
47 Cam Reddish 5.00 12.00
48 Montrezl Harrell 4.00 10.00
49 Cameron Johnson 8.00 20.00
50 Duncan Robinson 30.00 80.00
51 Bol Bol 8.00 20.00
52 Monte Morris 5.00 12.00
53 Isaiah Roby 4.00 10.00
54 Jon Leuer 3.00 8.00
55 Karl Malone 15.00 40.00
56 Kareem Abdul-Jabbar 75.00 200.00
57 Admiral Schofield 4.00 10.00
58 Otto Porter Jr. 3.00 8.00
59 Jaylen Nowell 4.00 10.00
60 Aron Baynes 3.00 8.00
61 Chuma Okeke 5.00 12.00
62 Malcolm Brogdon 4.00 10.00
63 Nickeil Alexander-Walker 5.00 12.00
64 Cristiano Felicio 3.00 8.00
65 Dwyane Wade 12.00 30.00
66 Justin Jackson 3.00 8.00
67 Justin James 3.00 8.00
68 Chimezie Metu 3.00 8.00
69 Talen Horton-Tucker 5.00 12.00
70 De'Anthony Melton 3.00 8.00
71 Darius Bazley 3.00 8.00
72 Thaddeus Young 3.00 8.00
73 Kyle Guy 4.00 10.00
74 Nikola Vucevic 4.00 10.00
75 Chris Paul 25.00 60.00
76 Tyrone Wallace 3.00 8.00
77 Daniel Gafford 6.00 15.00
78 Ryan Broekhoff 5.00 12.00
79 Jaylen Hoard 3.00 8.00
80 Semi Ojeleye 3.00 8.00
81 Brandon Clarke 6.00 15.00
82 Tomas Satoransky 3.00 8.00
83 Grant Williams 5.00 12.00
84 Andrew Wiggins 6.00 15.00
86 Gary Clark 3.00 8.00
87 Goga Bitadze 5.00 12.00
88 Jarred Vanderbilt 3.00 8.00
89 Luka Samanic 4.00 10.00
90 Ray Spalding 3.00 8.00
91 Dylan Windler 4.00 10.00
92 Ersan Ilyasova 3.00 8.00
93 Mfiondu Kabengele 4.00 10.00
94 Malik Beasley 4.00 10.00
95 Kyrie Irving 10.00 25.00
96 Alize Johnson 3.00 8.00
97 Ty Jerome 6.00 15.00
98 Jonah Bolden 5.00 12.00
99 Nassir Little 5.00 12.00
100 Terrence Ross 5.00 12.00

2019-20 Hoops High Voltage

1 Kawhi Leonard 2.50 6.00
2 LeBron James 8.00 20.00
3 Kevin Durant 3.00 8.00
4 Andrew Wiggins 1.25 3.00
5 Victor Oladipo .75 2.00
6 Paul George 1.50 4.00
7 Anthony Davis 2.50 6.00
8 Donovan Mitchell 2.00 5.00
9 Luka Doncic 6.00 15.00
10 Stephen Curry 8.00 20.00
11 Giannis Antetokounmpo 5.00 12.00
12 Montrezl Harrell .75 2.00
13 Jimmy Butler 2.00 5.00
14 Blake Griffin 1.00 2.50
15 Draymond Green 1.25 3.00
16 Pascal Siakam 1.50 4.00
17 Joel Embiid 2.00 5.00
18 Devin Booker .25 .60
19 DeMar DeRozan 1.25 3.00
20 James Harden 2.00 5.00
21 Zach LaVine 1.50 4.00
22 Nikola Jokic 5.00 12.00
23 Julius Randle 1.25 3.00
24 Patrick Beverley .75 2.00
25 Jayson Tatum 4.00 10.00

2019-20 Hoops Highlights

1 James Harden .75 2.00
2 Russell Westbrook .60 1.50
3 Dirk Nowitzki 1.00 2.50
4 Dwyane Wade .75 2.00
5 Derrick Rose .75 2.00

2019-20 Hoops Hoops Art Signatures

EXCHANGE DEADLINE 05/06/2021
HAZWL Zion Williamson 1,500.00 3,000.00
HAJMT Ja Morant 1,500.00 3,000.00
HARJB RJ Barrett 150.00 400.00
HAZJ Morant/Zion 2,000.00 4,000.00
HAZR Barrett/Zion 800.00 1,500.00
6 Barrett/Morant 800.00 1,500.00
HAKBR Kobe Bryant 1,500.00 3,000.00
HAKZ Zion/Kobe 3,000.00 6,000.00
HAKJ Morant/Kobe 3,000.00 6,000.00
HAKR Barrett/Bryant 1,000.00 2,000.00

2019-20 Hoops Hoops Ink

1 Alex English 6.00 15.00
2 Damian Lillard 12.00 30.00
3 Dana Barros 3.00 8.00
4 Kobe Bryant 300.00 600.00
5 Jalen Rose 4.00 10.00
6 Robert Covington 3.00 8.00
7 Luc Longley 4.00 10.00
8 Nemanja Bjelica 3.00 8.00
9 Quentin Richardson 3.00 8.00
10 World B. Free 4.00 10.00
11 Antoine Walker 4.00 10.00
12 Anthony Davis EXCH 15.00 40.00
13 Dennis Rodman 25.00 60.00
14 Cedi Osman 4.00 10.00
15 Keith Van Horn 4.00 10.00
16 Noah Vonleh 3.00 8.00
17 Magic Johnson 15.00 40.00
18 Courtney Lee 3.00 8.00
19 Raef LaFrentz 3.00 8.00
20 Kevin Durant EXCH 25.00 60.00
21 Calvin Murphy 5.00 12.00
22 Karl-Anthony Towns 10.00 25.00
23 Devean George 4.00 10.00
24 Royce O'Neale 3.00 8.00
25 Kenny Sky Walker 4.00 10.00
26 Ersan Ilyasova 3.00 8.00
27 Mark Price 5.00 12.00
28 Maxi Kleber 3.00 8.00
29 Ricky Davis 4.00 10.00
30 Dwyane Wade 12.00 30.00
31 Caron Butler 4.00 10.00
32 Andrew Wiggins 6.00 15.00
33 Fat Lever 4.00 10.00
34 Dario Saric 4.00 10.00
35 Kurt Thomas 3.00 8.00
36 Jarrett Allen 5.00 12.00
37 Michael Cooper 5.00 12.00
38 Spencer Dinwiddie 4.00 10.00
39 Stromile Swift 3.00 8.00
40 Chris Paul 25.00 60.00
41 Chris Bosh 6.00 15.00
42 Charles Barkley EXCH 50.00 120.00
43 Hakeem Olajuwon 10.00 25.00
44 Aron Baynes 3.00 8.00
45 Lenny Wilkens 6.00 15.00
46 Seth Curry 4.00 10.00
47 Nate McMillan 4.00 10.00
48 Luke Kennard 4.00 10.00
49 Toni Kukoc 6.00 15.00
50 Kyrie Irving 10.00 25.00

2019-20 Hoops Hot Signatures

1 Craig Hodges 4.00 10.00
2 Quinn Cook 4.00 10.00
3 Jerry West 12.00 30.00
4 Jared Dudley 3.00 8.00
5 Mahmoud Abdul-Rauf 4.00 10.00
6 Joe Harris 4.00 10.00
7 Sam Cassell 4.00 10.00
8 Damian Lillard 12.00 30.00
9 A.C. Green 5.00 12.00
10 Justin Jackson 3.00 8.00
11 Darius Miles 5.00 12.00
12 Daniel Theis 5.00 12.00
13 Kelly Tripucka 4.00 10.00
14 Ivica Zubac 4.00 10.00
15 Maurice Cheeks 4.00 10.00
16 Jose Calderon 3.00 8.00
17 Tom Chambers 5.00 12.00
18 Anthony Davis EXCH 15.00 40.00
19 Alvan Adams 3.00 8.00
20 Antonio Blakeney 3.00 8.00
21 Derek Fisher 5.00 12.00
22 Jon Leuer 3.00 8.00
23 Keyon Dooling 3.00 8.00
24 TJ Leaf 3.00 8.00
25 Micheal Ray Richardson 5.00 12.00
26 Tyus Jones 3.00 8.00
27 Kevin Durant EXCH 25.00 60.00
28 Karl-Anthony Towns 10.00 25.00
29 Allen Iverson 30.00 80.00
30 James Ennis 3.00 8.00
31 Don Chaney 5.00 12.00
32 Cristiano Felicio 3.00 8.00
33 Latrell Sprewell 6.00 15.00
34 Yuta Watanabe 5.00 12.00
35 Otis Birdsong 5.00 12.00
36 Kelly Olynyk 3.00 8.00
37 Dwyane Wade 12.00 30.00
38 Andrew Wiggins 6.00 15.00
39 Carlos Boozer 4.00 10.00
40 Jakob Poeltl 3.00 8.00
41 Fred Hoiberg 3.00 8.00
42 Malik Beasley 4.00 10.00
43 Lionel Hollins 3.00 8.00
44 Reggie Bullock 3.00 8.00
45 Quinn Buckner 3.00 8.00
46 Wayne Ellington 3.00 8.00
47 Chris Paul 25.00 60.00
48 Charles Barkley EXCH 50.00 120.00
49 Cazzie Russell 4.00 10.00
50 Dewayne Dedmon 3.00 8.00
51 Jack Marin 3.00 8.00
52 Kyle O'Quinn 3.00 8.00
53 M.L. Carr 5.00 12.00
54 Mike Scott 3.00 8.00
55 Raja Bell 4.00 10.00
56 Udonis Haslem 3.00 8.00
57 Antonio Daniels 3.00 8.00
58 Kobe Bryant 300.00 600.00
59 Cedric Maxwell 4.00 10.00
60 Justin Holiday 3.00 8.00

2019-20 Hoops Hot Signatures Red

50 Dewayne Dedmon 5.00 12.00

2019-20 Hoops Hot Signatures Rookies

1 Zion Williamson 200.00 500.00
2 Jordan Poole 12.00 30.00
3 Jarrett Culver 3.00 8.00
4 Carsen Edwards 4.00 10.00
5 Cam Reddish 5.00 12.00
6 Admiral Schofield 4.00 10.00
7 Romeo Langford 3.00 8.00
8 Ignas Brazdeikis 4.00 10.00
9 Goga Bitadze 5.00 12.00
10 Ty Jerome 6.00 15.00
11 Ja Morant 75.00 200.00
12 Keldon Johnson 10.00 25.00
13 Coby White 15.00 40.00
14 Bruno Fernando 3.00 8.00
15 Cameron Johnson 8.00 20.00
16 Jaylen Nowell 4.00 10.00
17 Sekou Doumbouya 3.00 8.00
18 Quinndary Weatherspoon 3.00 8.00
19 Luka Samanic 4.00 10.00
20 Nassir Little 5.00 12.00
21 RJ Barrett 40.00 100.00
22 Kevin Porter Jr. 6.00 15.00
23 Jaxson Hayes 5.00 12.00
24 Cody Martin 5.00 12.00
25 PJ Washington Jr. 10.00 25.00
26 Bol Bol 8.00 20.00
27 Chuma Okeke 5.00 12.00
28 Tremont Waters 4.00 10.00
29 Brandon Clarke 6.00 15.00
30 Dylan Windler 4.00 10.00
31 De'Andre Hunter 12.00 30.00
32 KZ Okpala 4.00 10.00
33 Rui Hachimura 60.00 150.00
34 Eric Paschall 4.00 10.00
35 Tyler Herro 15.00 40.00
36 Isaiah Roby 4.00 10.00
37 Nickeil Alexander-Walker 5.00 12.00
38 Kyle Guy 4.00 10.00
39 Grant Williams 5.00 12.00
40 Mfiondu Kabengele 4.00 10.00

2019-20 Hoops Legends of the Ball

1 Alonzo Mourning .60 1.50
2 Bill Russell 1.25 3.00
3 Charles Barkley .75 2.00
4 Dirk Nowitzki 1.00 2.50
5 Dwyane Wade .75 2.00
6 Jerry West .60 1.50
7 John Stockton .75 2.00
8 Kareem Abdul-Jabbar 1.25 3.00
9 Kevin Garnett 1.00 2.50
10 Kobe Bryant 3.00 8.00
11 Nate Archibald .40 1.00
12 Oscar Robertson 1.00 2.50
13 Reggie Miller .60 1.50
14 Shaquille O'Neal 1.50 4.00
15 Walt Frazier .60 1.50

2019-20 Hoops Lights Camera Action

*WINTER: .4X TO 1X BASIC
*HOLO: 1.25X TO 3X BASIC
1 Kevin Durant 1.25 3.00
2 Stephen Curry 3.00 8.00
3 De'Aaron Fox .60 1.50
4 Deandre Ayton .40 1.00
5 Paul George .60 1.50
6 Ben Simmons .40 1.00
7 Victor Oladipo .30 .75
8 Damian Lillard 1.00 2.50
9 Donovan Mitchell .75 2.00
10 Andre Drummond .30 .75
11 Bradley Beal .50 1.25
12 Karl-Anthony Towns .60 1.50
13 Russell Westbrook .60 1.50
14 Kemba Walker .30 .75
15 Luka Doncic 2.50 6.00
16 Kevin Love .40 1.00
17 Kawhi Leonard 1.00 2.50
18 Zach LaVine .60 1.50
19 Giannis Antetokounmpo 2.00 5.00
20 LeBron James 3.00 8.00
21 Rudy Gobert .50 1.25
22 Trae Young 1.00 2.50
23 Kyrie Irving .75 2.00
24 Jayson Tatum 1.50 4.00
25 Devin Booker .10 .25
26 Kyle Lowry .40 1.00
27 Joel Embiid .75 2.00
28 Nikola Jokic 2.00 5.00
29 James Harden .75 2.00
30 Julius Randle .50 1.25

2019-20 Hoops NBA City

*HOLO: 1.25X TO 3X BASIC
*AP/25: 4X TO 10X BASIC
1 Goran Dragic .30 .75
2 Stephen Curry 3.00 8.00
3 Steven Adams .30 .75
4 Kyle Lowry .40 1.00
5 Giannis Antetokounmpo 2.00 5.00
6 Damian Lillard 1.00 2.50
7 John Wall .50 1.25
8 Blake Griffin .40 1.00
9 James Harden .75 2.00
10 Jaren Jackson Jr. .60 1.50
11 Jayson Tatum 1.50 4.00
12 Kevin Knox II .25 .60
13 Kevin Love .40 1.00
14 Karl-Anthony Towns .60 1.50
15 DeMar DeRozan .50 1.25
16 Miles Bridges .40 1.00
17 Jarrett Allen .40 1.00
18 Nikola Jokic 2.00 5.00
19 Lou Williams .40 1.00
20 Jrue Holiday .50 1.25
21 Aaron Gordon .40 1.00
22 Donovan Mitchell .75 2.00
23 Zach LaVine .60 1.50
24 Victor Oladipo .30 .75
25 Joel Embiid .75 2.00
26 Devin Booker .10 .25
27 LeBron James 3.00 8.00
28 Trae Young 1.00 2.50
29 De'Aaron Fox .60 1.50
30 Luka Doncic 2.50 6.00

2019-20 Hoops Rise N Shine Memorabilia

*WINTER: .5X TO 1.2X BASIC
*PRIME/25: 1X TO 2.5X BASIC
1 Goga Bitadze 2.50 6.00
2 Ty Jerome 3.00 8.00
3 Zion Williamson 25.00 60.00
4 Jordan Poole 6.00 15.00
5 Jarrett Culver 1.50 4.00
6 Carsen Edwards 2.00 5.00
7 Cam Reddish 2.50 6.00
8 Admiral Schofield 2.00 5.00
9 Romeo Langford 1.50 4.00
10 Ignas Brazdeikis 2.00 5.00
11 Luka Samanic 2.00 5.00
12 Nassir Little 3.00 8.00
13 Ja Morant 8.00 20.00
14 Keldon Johnson 5.00 12.00
15 Coby White 5.00 12.00
16 Bruno Fernando 2.00 5.00
17 Cameron Johnson 4.00 10.00
18 Jaylen Nowell 2.00 5.00
19 Sekou Doumbouya 1.50 4.00
20 Quinndary Weatherspoon 1.50 4.00
21 Brandon Clarke 3.00 8.00
22 Dylan Windler 2.00 5.00
23 RJ Barrett 6.00 15.00
24 Kevin Porter Jr. 3.00 8.00
25 Jaxson Hayes 2.50 6.00
26 Cody Martin 2.50 6.00
27 PJ Washington Jr. 5.00 12.00
28 Bol Bol 3.00 8.00
29 Chuma Okeke 2.50 6.00
30 Tremont Waters 2.00 5.00
31 Grant Williams 2.50 6.00
32 Mfiondu Kabengele 2.00 5.00
33 De'Andre Hunter 3.00 8.00
34 KZ Okpala 2.00 5.00
36 Eric Paschall 2.00 5.00
37 Tyler Herro 4.00 10.00
38 Isaiah Roby 2.00 5.00
39 Nickeil Alexander-Walker 2.50 6.00
40 Kyle Guy 2.00 5.00

2019-20 Hoops Road to the Finals

1-41 PRINT RUN 2019 SER.#'d SETS
42-66 PRINT RUN 999 SER.#'d SETS
67-76 PRINT RUN 499 SER.#'d SETS
83-96 PRINT RUN 99 SER.#'d SETS
77-82 PRINT RUN 199 SER.#'d SETS
1 D.J. Augustin R1 .40 1.00
2 D'Angelo Russell R1 .50 1.25
3 Stephen Curry R1 5.00 12.00
4 DeMar DeRozan R1 .75 2.00
5 Giannis Antetokounmpo R1 3.00 8.00
6 Kyrie Irving R1 1.25 3.00
7 Damian Lillard R1 1.50 4.00
8 James Harden R1 1.25 3.00
9 Ben Simmons R1 .60 1.50
10 Lou Williams R1 .60 1.50
11 Kawhi Leonard R1 1.50 4.00
12 Nikola Jokic R1 3.00 8.00
13 CJ McCollum R1 .60 1.50
14 Kyrie Irving R1 1.25 3.00
15 James Harden R1 1.25 3.00
16 Giannis Antetokounmpo R1 3.00 8.00
17 Tobias Harris R1 .50 1.25
18 Kevin Durant R1 2.00 5.00
19 Derrick White R1 .60 1.50
20 Jaylen Brown R1 1.00 2.50
21 Russell Westbrook R1 1.00 2.50
22 Pascal Siakam R1 1.00 2.50
23 Khris Middleton R1 .60 1.50
24 James Harden R1 1.25 3.00
25 Nikola Jokic R1 3.00 8.00
26 Joel Embiid R1 1.25 3.00
27 Gordon Hayward R1 .50 1.25
28 Klay Thompson R1 1.50 4.00
29 CJ McCollum R1 .60 1.50
30 Kawhi Leonard R1 1.50 4.00
31 Giannis Antetokounmpo R1 3.00 8.00
32 Donovan Mitchell R1 1.25 3.00
33 Jamal Murray R1 1.00 2.50
34 Joel Embiid R1 1.25 3.00
35 Damian Lillard R1 1.50 4.00
36 Kawhi Leonard R1 1.50 4.00

37 Lou Williams R1 .60 1.50
38 James Harden R1 1.25 3.00
39 LaMarcus Aldridge R1 .60 1.50
40 Kevin Durant R1 2.00 5.00
41 Nikola Jokic R1 3.00 8.00
42 Kawhi Leonard R2 2.00 5.00
43 Kevin Durant R2 2.50 6.00
44 Kyrie Irving R2 1.50 4.00
45 Nikola Jokic R2 4.00 10.00
46 Jimmy Butler R2 1.50 4.00
47 Kevin Durant R2 2.50 6.00
48 Giannis Antetokounmpo R2 4.00 10.00
49 CJ McCollum R2 .75 2.00
50 Joel Embiid R2 1.50 4.00
51 Giannis Antetokounmpo R2 4.00 10.00
52 CJ McCollum R2 .75 2.00
53 James Harden R2 1.50 4.00
54 Kawhi Leonard R2 2.00 5.00
55 Nikola Jokic R2 4.00 10.00
56 Giannis Antetokounmpo R2 4.00 10.00
57 James Harden R2 1.50 4.00
58 Nikola Jokic R2 4.00 10.00
59 Pascal Siakam R2 1.25 3.00
60 Stephen Curry R2 6.00 15.00
61 Giannis Antetokounmpo R2 4.00 10.00
62 Joel Embiid R2 1.50 4.00
63 Damian Lillard R2 2.00 5.00
64 Stephen Curry R2 6.00 15.00
65 CJ McCollum R2 .75 2.00
66 Kawhi Leonard R2 2.00 5.00
67 Stephen Curry CF 8.00 20.00
68 Brook Lopez CF .75 2.00
69 Stephen Curry CF 8.00 20.00
70 Giannis Antetokounmpo CF 5.00 12.00
71 Draymond Green CF 1.25 3.00
72 Kawhi Leonard CF 2.50 6.00
73 Stephen Curry CF 8.00 20.00
74 Kyle Lowry CF 1.00 2.50
75 Kawhi Leonard CF 2.50 6.00
76 Kawhi Leonard CF 2.50 6.00
77 Pascal Siakam F 1.50 4.00
78 Draymond Green F 1.25 3.00
79 Kawhi Leonard F 2.50 6.00
80 Kawhi Leonard F 2.50 6.00
81 Stephen Curry F 8.00 20.00
82 Kyle Lowry F 1.00 2.50
83 Jeremy Lin CM 15.00 40.00
84 Serge Ibaka CM 12.00 30.00
85 Malcolm Miller CM 10.00 25.00
86 Danny Green CM 12.00 30.00
87 Norman Powell CM 12.00 30.00
88 Pascal Siakam CM 25.00 60.00
89 Marc Gasol CM 15.00 40.00
90 Kawhi Leonard CM 40.00 100.00
91 Fred VanVleet CM 20.00 50.00
92 Kyle Lowry CM 15.00 40.00
93 Jodie Meeks CM 10.00 25.00
94 Leonard/Lowry CM 40.00 100.00
95 Russell/Lowry CM 50.00 120.00
96 Leonard/Russell CM 50.00 120.00
97 Kawhi Leonard MVP 10.00 25.00
98 Toronto Raptors CHAMPS 25.00 60.00

2019-20 Hoops Rookie Ink

1 Nicolas Claxton 6.00 15.00
2 Jaylen Nowell 4.00 10.00
3 Luguentz Dort 12.00 30.00
4 RJ Barrett 40.00 100.00
5 Bol Bol 8.00 20.00
6 Zion Williamson 200.00 500.00
7 De'Andre Hunter 12.00 30.00
8 Admiral Schofield 4.00 10.00
9 Isaiah Roby 4.00 10.00
10 Ja Morant 75.00 200.00
11 Daniel Gafford 6.00 15.00
12 Sekou Doumbouya 3.00 8.00
13 Josh Reaves 3.00 8.00
14 Kevin Porter Jr. 6.00 15.00
15 Chuma Okeke 5.00 12.00
16 Jordan Poole 12.00 30.00
17 KZ Okpala 4.00 10.00
18 Romeo Langford 3.00 8.00
19 Nickeil Alexander-Walker 5.00 12.00
20 Keldon Johnson 10.00 25.00
21 Louis King 4.00 10.00
22 Quinndary Weatherspoon 3.00 8.00
23 Jalen Lecque 3.00 8.00
24 Jaxson Hayes 5.00 12.00
25 Tremont Waters 4.00 10.00
26 Jarrett Culver 3.00 8.00
27 Rui Hachimura 60.00 150.00
28 Ignas Brazdeikis 4.00 10.00
29 Kyle Guy 4.00 10.00
30 Coby White 15.00 40.00
31 Zach Norvell Jr. 4.00 10.00
32 Luka Samanic 4.00 10.00
34 Cody Martin 5.00 12.00
35 Brandon Clarke 6.00 15.00
36 Carsen Edwards 4.00 10.00
37 Eric Paschall 4.00 10.00
38 Goga Bitadze 5.00 12.00
39 Grant Williams 5.00 12.00
40 Bruno Fernando 4.00 10.00
41 Max Strus 15.00 40.00
42 Nassir Little 5.00 12.00
43 Jaylen Hands 3.00 8.00
44 PJ Washington Jr. 10.00 25.00
45 Dylan Windler 4.00 10.00
46 Cam Reddish 5.00 12.00
47 Tyler Herro 15.00 40.00
48 Ty Jerome 6.00 15.00
49 Mfiondu Kabengele 4.00 10.00
50 Cameron Johnson 8.00 20.00

2019-20 Hoops Rookie Ink Red

14 Kevin Porter Jr. 10.00 25.00
41 Max Strus 50.00 120.00
47 Tyler Herro 50.00 120.00

2019-20 Hoops Rookie Remembrance Jerseys

*WINTER: .5X TO 1.2X BASIC
*PRIME/25: 1X TO 2.5X BASIC
1 Dennis Smith Jr. 1.50 4.00
2 Kyle Kuzma 3.00 8.00
3 Donovan Mitchell 6.00 15.00
4 Frank Ntilikina 1.50 4.00
5 Josh Jackson 1.50 4.00
6 John Collins 2.50 6.00
7 Malik Monk 2.50 6.00
8 Jarrett Allen 2.50 6.00
9 Markelle Fultz 2.00 5.00
10 Bam Adebayo 4.00 10.00
11 Jayson Tatum 10.00 25.00
12 Lonzo Ball 2.50 6.00
13 Bogdan Bogdanovic 2.50 6.00
14 De'Aaron Fox 4.00 10.00
15 Montrezl Harrell 2.00 5.00
16 Lauri Markkanen 3.00 8.00
17 Harry Giles 1.50 4.00
18 Domantas Sabonis 3.00 8.00
19 Andrew Wiggins 3.00 8.00
20 Kris Dunn 1.50 4.00
21 Josh Richardson 1.50 4.00
22 Caris LeVert 2.00 5.00
23 Dante Exum 1.50 4.00
24 Kostas Antetokounmpo 2.00 5.00
25 Dragan Bender 1.50 4.00
26 Bobby Portis 1.50 4.00
27 Mitchell Robinson 2.50 6.00
28 Pascal Siakam 4.00 10.00
29 Collin Sexton 3.00 8.00
30 Allonzo Trier 1.50 4.00
31 Buddy Hield 2.00 5.00
32 Emmanuel Mudiay 1.50 4.00
33 Jakob Poeltl 1.50 4.00
34 Josh Okogie 2.00 5.00
35 Luka Doncic 40.00 100.00
36 Rondae Hollis-Jefferson 1.50 4.00
37 Lonnie Walker IV 2.00 5.00
38 Troy Brown Jr. 1.50 4.00
39 Donte DiVincenzo 2.00 5.00
40 Mo Bamba 2.00 5.00
41 Hamidou Diallo 2.00 5.00
42 Wendell Carter Jr. 2.50 6.00
43 Michael Porter Jr. 4.00 10.00
44 Terry Rozier 2.00 5.00
45 Deandre Ayton 2.50 6.00
46 Trae Young 6.00 15.00
47 Kevin Knox II 1.50 4.00
48 Justise Winslow 1.50 4.00
49 Marvin Bagley III 2.00 5.00
50 Devin Booker 8.00 20.00
51 Taurean Prince 1.50 4.00
52 Dejounte Murray 2.50 6.00
53 Jamal Murray 4.00 10.00
54 Jaylen Brown 4.00 10.00
55 Klay Thompson 6.00 15.00
56 Kawhi Leonard 4.00 10.00
57 Jimmy Butler 5.00 12.00
58 Al-Farouq Aminu 1.50 4.00
59 Khris Middleton 2.50 6.00
60 Norman Powell 2.00 5.00

2019-20 Hoops Rookie Special

SPEC1 Zion Williamson 50.00 120.00
2 Ja Morant 30.00 80.00

2019-20 Hoops Rookie Sweaters

1 Matisse Thybulle 8.00 20.00
2 Coby White 10.00 25.00
3 Kevin Porter Jr. 6.00 15.00
4 Dylan Windler 4.00 10.00
5 Carsen Edwards 4.00 10.00
6 Grant Williams 5.00 12.00
7 Romeo Langford 3.00 8.00
8 Tremont Waters 4.00 10.00
9 Mfiondu Kabengele 4.00 10.00
10 Isaiah Roby 4.00 10.00
11 Brandon Clarke 6.00 15.00
12 Ja Morant 30.00 80.00
13 Cam Reddish 5.00 12.00
14 De'Andre Hunter 12.00 30.00
15 Bruno Fernando 4.00 10.00
16 KZ Okpala 4.00 10.00
17 Tyler Herro 15.00 40.00
18 Cody Martin 5.00 12.00
19 PJ Washington Jr. 10.00 25.00
20 Kyle Guy 4.00 10.00
21 Ignas Brazdeikis 4.00 10.00
22 RJ Barrett 12.00 30.00
23 Chuma Okeke 5.00 12.00
24 Bol Bol 8.00 20.00
25 Goga Bitadze 5.00 12.00
26 Jaxson Hayes 5.00 12.00
27 Nickeil Alexander-Walker 5.00 12.00
28 Zion Williamson 25.00 60.00
29 Sekou Doumbouya 3.00 8.00
30 Keldon Johnson 10.00 25.00
31 Luka Samanic 4.00 10.00
32 Quinndary Weatherspoon 3.00 8.00
33 Cameron Johnson 8.00 20.00
34 Ty Jerome 6.00 15.00
35 Jarrett Culver 3.00 8.00
36 Jaylen Nowell 4.00 10.00
37 Nassir Little 5.00 12.00
38 Eric Paschall 8.00 20.00
39 Jordan Poole 12.00 30.00
40 Admiral Schofield 4.00 10.00
41 Darius Bazley 3.00 8.00

2019-20 Hoops Rookie Sweaters Dual

1 Barrett/Williamson 40.00 100.00
2 Morant/Williamson 40.00 100.00
4 Brazdeikis/Barrett 12.00 30.00
5 Reddish/Barrett 12.00 30.00
6 Morant/Clarke 20.00 50.00
7 White/Morant 20.00 50.00
8 Reddish/Hunter 12.00 30.00
9 Jerome/Hunter 12.00 30.00
10 Culver/Hayes 5.00 12.00
11 Johnson/White 10.00 25.00
12 Bol/Doumbouya 8.00 20.00
13 Washington Jr./Herro 15.00 40.00
15 Hayes/Alexander-Walker 5.00 12.00
16 Johnson/Herro 15.00 40.00
17 Brazdeikis/Poole 12.00 30.00
18 Guy/Jerome 12.00 30.00

2019-20 Hoops Spark Plugs

1 Stephen Curry 3.00 8.00
2 Trae Young 1.00 2.50
3 D'Angelo Russell .30 .75
4 James Harden .75 2.00
5 Russell Westbrook .60 1.50
6 Damian Lillard 1.00 2.50
7 Bradley Beal .50 1.25
8 Kemba Walker .30 .75
9 De'Aaron Fox .60 1.50
10 Kyrie Irving .75 2.00
11 Collin Sexton .50 1.25
12 Ben Simmons .40 1.00
13 Marcus Smart .30 .75
14 Jamal Murray .60 1.50
15 Devin Booker .10 .25

2019-20 Hoops Tip-Off

1 Durant/Gasol 1.25 3.00
2 Myles Turner
Nikola Vucevic .40 1.00
3 Barkley/Robinson .75 2.00
4 Dwight Powell
Nikola Vucevic .30 .75
5 Andre Drummond
Brook Lopez .30 .75
6 Bryant/James 25.00 60.00
7 Murray/Harden .75 2.00
8 Poeltl/Jokic 2.00 5.00
9 Embiid/Vucevic .75 2.00
10 Gasol/Duncan 1.00 2.50

2019-20 Hoops We Got Next

*HOLO: .75X TO 2X BASIC
*AP/25: 4X TO 10X BASIC
1 RJ Barrett 1.00 2.50
2 Nickeil Alexander-Walker .40 1.00
3 Coby White .75 2.00
4 Brandon Clarke .50 1.25
5 Cam Reddish .40 1.00
6 Nassir Little .40 1.00
7 Matisse Thybulle .50 1.25
8 Tyler Herro 1.25 3.00
9 Zion Williamson 2.00 5.00
10 Sekou Doumbouya .25 .60
11 De'Andre Hunter 1.00 2.50
12 Goga Bitadze .40 1.00
13 Jaxson Hayes .40 1.00
14 Grant Williams .40 1.00
15 Cameron Johnson .60 1.50
16 Darius Bazley .25 .60
17 PJ Washington Jr. .75 2.00
18 Romeo Langford .25 .60
19 Ja Morant 2.50 6.00
20 Chuma Okeke .40 1.00
21 Jarrett Culver .25 .60
22 Luka Samanic .30 .75
23 Rui Hachimura 1.00 2.50
24 Ty Jerome .50 1.25
25 Darius Garland 1.00 2.50

2019-20 Hoops Zero Gravity

*HOLO: 1.25X TO 3X BASIC
*AP/25: 4X TO 10X BASIC
1 Hamidou Diallo .30 .75
2 Blake Griffin .40 1.00
3 Terrence Ross .40 1.00
4 DeMar DeRozan .50 1.25
5 Ben Simmons .40 1.00
6 Giannis Antetokounmpo 2.00 5.00
7 John Wall .50 1.25
8 Donovan Mitchell .75 2.00
9 Kevin Durant 1.25 3.00
10 Aaron Gordon .40 1.00
11 De'Aaron Fox .60 1.50
12 Anthony Davis 1.00 2.50
13 Jaylen Brown .60 1.50
14 Victor Oladipo .30 .75
15 DeAndre Jordan .30 .75
16 Zach LaVine .60 1.50
17 Karl-Anthony Towns .60 1.50
18 LeBron James 3.00 8.00
19 Joel Embiid .75 2.00
20 Russell Westbrook .60 1.50

2020-21 Hoops

COMPLETE SET (270)
1 Miles Bridges .40 1.00
2 Torrey Craig .30 .75
3 Zach Collins .30 .75
4 Danny Green .30 .75
5 Ricky Rubio .40 1.00
6 Brook Lopez .30 .75
7 Collin Sexton .40 1.00
8 T.J. Warren .30 .75
9 Landry Shamet .30 .75
10 Marcus Morris Sr. .25 .60
11 Kelly Oubre Jr. .40 1.00
12 Josh Okogie .30 .75
13 Buddy Hield .40 1.00
14 Malik Beasley .30 .75
15 Lonzo Ball .50 1.25
16 Juancho Hernangomez .30 .75
17 Bojan Bogdanovic .30 .75
18 Darius Bazley .25 .60
19 Dwayne Bacon .25 .60
20 Aron Baynes .25 .60
21 Reggie Jackson .30 .75
22 Andre Drummond .40 1.00
23 Kyle Kuzma .50 1.25
24 Eric Bledsoe .30 .75
25 Christian Wood .30 .75
26 Andre Iguodala .30 .75
27 Troy Brown Jr. .30 .75
28 Wendell Carter Jr. .30 .75
29 Jonas Valanciunas .30 .75
30 Coby White .50 1.25
31 Derrick White .40 1.00
32 Devin Booker 1.00 2.50
33 Kyrie Irving .75 2.00
34 Tim Hardaway Jr. .25 .60
35 Thon Maker .25 .60
36 Karl-Anthony Towns .60 1.50
37 Jarrett Culver .25 .60
38 Dwight Howard .50 1.25
39 Steven Adams .40 1.00
40 Dwight Powell .25 .60
41 Michael Porter Jr. .50 1.25
42 Bradley Beal .50 1.25
43 Jaylen Brown .60 1.50
44 Seth Curry .40 1.00
45 Marquese Chriss .25 .60
46 Trae Young 1.00 2.50
47 Kevin Knox II .25 .60
48 Otto Porter Jr. .25 .60
49 Ben Simmons .40 1.00
50 Serge Ibaka .30 .75
51 Spencer Dinwiddie .30 .75
52 Kevin Love .40 1.00
53 Kendrick Nunn .30 .75
54 Danilo Gallinari .30 .75
55 PJ Washington Jr. .40 1.00
56 Joe Ingles .30 .75
57 Markelle Fultz .30 .75
58 Kevin Huerter .30 .75
59 Bam Adebayo .60 1.50
60 Russell Westbrook .75 2.00
61 Kyle Lowry .50 1.25
62 Kris Dunn .25 .60
63 Mitchell Robinson .40 1.00
64 Brandon Clarke .40 1.00
65 Dennis Schroder .40 1.00
66 Jaxson Hayes .30 .75
67 Josh Richardson .30 .75
68 Eric Paschall .30 .75
69 Evan Fournier .30 .75
70 Thaddeus Young .25 .60
71 Donovan Mitchell .75 2.00
72 Jaren Jackson Jr. .60 1.50
73 JJ Redick .40 1.00
74 Kentavious Caldwell-Pope .30 .75
75 Andrew Wiggins .50 1.25
76 John Wall .50 1.25
77 Klay Thompson 1.00 2.50
78 Robert Covington .30 .75
79 Luke Kennard .30 .75
80 Nikola Vucevic .40 1.00
81 Matthew Dellavedova .30 .75
82 Brandon Ingram .50 1.25
83 De'Andre Hunter .40 1.00
84 Nicolas Batum .25 .60
85 Jimmy Butler .75 2.00
86 Taurean Prince .25 .60
87 Tristan Thompson .25 .60
88 Al Horford .40 1.00
89 De'Aaron Fox .60 1.50
90 RJ Barrett .60 1.50
91 Fred VanVleet .60 1.50
92 Draymond Green .50 1.25
93 Darius Garland .60 1.50
94 Marcus Smart .40 1.00
95 Patrick Beverley .25 .60
96 Victor Oladipo .30 .75
97 Paul George .60 1.50
98 Jeremy Lamb .25 .60
99 Matisse Thybulle .50 1.25
100 Domantas Sabonis .50 1.25
101 Damian Lillard 1.00 2.50
102 Jonathan Isaac .40 1.00
103 Kevon Looney .30 .75
104 Daniel Theis .30 .75
105 Sekou Doumbouya .25 .60
106 Aaron Gordon .40 1.00
107 Clint Capela .40 1.00
108 Dillon Brooks .30 .75
109 Danuel House Jr. .30 .75
110 Tyler Herro .75 2.00
111 LaMarcus Aldridge .40 1.00
112 Patty Mills .40 1.00
113 Wesley Matthews .25 .60
114 Blake Griffin .40 1.00
115 John Collins .40 1.00
116 Jayson Tatum 1.50 4.00
117 Kawhi Leonard 1.00 2.50
118 George Hill .30 .75
119 Tobias Harris .40 1.00
120 Ja Morant 1.25 3.00
121 Rudy Gay .40 1.00
122 DeMar DeRozan .50 1.25
123 OG Anunoby .40 1.00
124 Davis Bertans .30 .75
125 Marc Gasol .40 1.00
126 Anthony Davis 1.00 2.50
127 Eric Gordon .30 .75
128 Jeff Teague .25 .60
129 Will Barton .25 .60
130 Stephen Curry 3.00 8.00
131 Terry Rozier .40 1.00
132 Bogdan Bogdanovic .40 1.00
133 CJ McCollum .40 1.00
134 Shai Gilgeous-Alexander 2.00 5.00
135 Derrick Favors .30 .75
136 Kristaps Porzingis .50 1.25
137 Jrue Holiday .40 1.00
138 Joel Embiid 1.00 2.50
139 Elfrid Payton .30 .75
140 Cam Reddish .50 1.25
141 Harrison Barnes .40 1.00
142 Marvin Bagley III .30 .75
143 Jamal Murray .60 1.50
144 Terence Davis II .40 1.00
145 DeAndre Jordan .30 .75
146 LeBron James 3.00 8.00
147 Austin Rivers .30 .75
148 Cameron Johnson .50 1.25
149 Lou Williams .40 1.00
150 Luka Doncic 2.50 6.00
151 Carmelo Anthony .60 1.50
152 Gordon Hayward .40 1.00
153 Jordan Clarkson .40 1.00
154 Mo Bamba .40 1.00
155 Pascal Siakam .60 1.50
156 Gary Harris .30 .75
157 Frank Ntilikina .25 .60
158 Malik Monk .40 1.00
159 Julius Randle .40 1.00
160 Cody Zeller .25 .60
161 Lauri Markkanen .50 1.25
162 Chris Paul .75 2.00
163 Zion Williamson 1.25 3.00
164 Malcolm Brogdon .40 1.00
165 Goran Dragic .40 1.00
166 Giannis Antetokounmpo 2.00 5.00
167 Lonnie Walker IV .40 1.00
168 Anfernee Simons .50 1.25
169 Paul Millsap .30 .75
170 Romeo Langford .25 .60
171 Markieff Morris .25 .60
172 Dejounte Murray .40 1.00
173 Kemba Walker .40 1.00
174 Derrick Rose .60 1.50
175 Jarrett Allen .40 1.00
176 Khris Middleton .50 1.25
177 Daniel Gafford .30 .75
178 James Harden .75 2.00
179 Donte DiVincenzo .40 1.00
180 Duncan Robinson .40 1.00
181 Harry Giles III .25 .60
182 Rudy Gobert .50 1.25
183 Montrezl Harrell .40 1.00
184 Mike Conley .30 .75
185 Willie Cauley-Stein .25 .60
186 Alex Caruso .40 1.00
187 Hassan Whiteside .30 .75
188 D'Angelo Russell .40 1.00
189 Kevin Durant 1.50 4.00
190 Devonte' Graham .30 .75
191 Nikola Jokic 2.00 5.00
192 Thomas Bryant .30 .75
193 Caris LeVert .40 1.00
194 Josh Jackson .25 .60
195 Shake Milton .30 .75
196 Zach LaVine .60 1.50
197 Rui Hachimura .50 1.25
198 Deandre Ayton .40 1.00
199 Myles Turner .40 1.00
200 Kevin Porter Jr. .30 .75
201 Deni Avdija RC 1.25 3.00
202 Aaron Nesmith RC 1.00 2.50
203 Daniel Oturu RC .50 1.25
204 Payton Pritchard RC 1.50 4.00
205 James Wiseman RC .60 1.50
206 Saben Lee RC .60 1.50
207 Tyrese Maxey RC 4.00 10.00
208 Tre Jones RC .75 2.00
209 Devin Vassell RC 1.50 4.00
210 Precious Achiuwa RC 1.00 2.50
211 Jordan Nwora RC .60 1.50
212 Josh Green RC 1.00 2.50
213 Udoka Azubuike RC .60 1.50
214 Vernon Carey Jr. RC .50 1.25
215 Cassius Stanley RC .50 1.25
216 Anthony Edwards RC 5.00 12.00
217 Grant Riller RC .50 1.25
218 Tyrell Terry RC .40 1.00
219 Aleksej Pokusevski RC .60 1.50
220 Tyler Bey RC .50 1.25
221 Xavier Tillman RC .50 1.25
222 Nick Richards RC .60 1.50
223 LaMelo Ball RC 4.00 10.00
224 Elijah Hughes RC .50 1.25
225 Onyeka Okongwu RC 1.00 2.50
226 Obi Toppin RC 1.00 2.50
227 Cassius Winston RC .50 1.25
228 Patrick Williams RC 1.25 3.00
229 Kira Lewis Jr. RC .50 1.25
230 Theo Maledon RC .50 1.25
231 Robert Woodard II RC .50 1.25
232 Kenyon Martin Jr. RC .75 2.00
233 Isaiah Stewart RC 1.00 2.50
234 Cole Anthony RC 1.25 3.00
235 Zeke Nnaji RC .60 1.50
236 Jahmi'us Ramsey RC .50 1.25
237 Saddiq Bey RC 1.00 2.50
238 Tyrese Haliburton RC 4.00 10.00
239 RJ Hampton RC .50 1.25
240 Jalen Smith RC 1.00 2.50
241 Killian Hayes RC .50 1.25
242 Malachi Flynn RC .50 1.25
243 Skylar Mays RC .50 1.25
244 Isaac Okoro RC .75 2.00
245 Jaden McDaniels RC 1.50 4.00
246 Desmond Bane RC 1.50 4.00
247 Leandro Bolmaro RC .50 1.25
248 Nico Mannion RC .50 1.25
249 Immanuel Quickley RC 1.25 3.00
250 CJ Elleby RC .50 1.25
251 Zion Williamson 4.00 10.00
252 Stephen Curry 10.00 25.00
253 Charles Barkley 3.00 8.00
254 Giannis Antetokounmpo 6.00 15.00
255 Kevin Garnett 3.00 8.00
256 Rui Hachimura 1.50 4.00
257 Kareem Abdul-Jabbar 4.00 10.00
258 Trae Young 3.00 8.00
259 Larry Bird 5.00 12.00
260 Oscar Robertson 3.00 8.00
261 Anthony Davis 3.00 8.00
262 Julius Erving 3.00 8.00
263 Karl Malone 2.50 6.00
264 Dwyane Wade 2.50 6.00
265 RJ Barrett 2.00 5.00
266 Allen Iverson 3.00 8.00
267 Bill Russell 4.00 10.00
268 Kevin Durant 5.00 12.00
269 Shaquille O'Neal 5.00 12.00
270 Ja Morant 4.00 10.00

2020-21 Hoops Artist Proof

STATED PRINT RUN 25 SER.#'d SETS
146 LeBron James 75.00 200.00
216 Anthony Edwards 150.00 400.00
223 LaMelo Ball 100.00 250.00

2020-21 Hoops Blue Explosion

STATED PRINT RUN 59 SER.#'d SETS
216 Anthony Edwards 100.00 250.00
223 LaMelo Ball 60.00 150.00

2020-21 Hoops Green

STATED PRINT RUN 99 SER.#'d SETS
216 Anthony Edwards 60.00 150.00
223 LaMelo Ball 50.00 120.00

2020-21 Hoops Green Explosion

STATED PRINT RUN 89 SER.#'d SETS
216 Anthony Edwards 60.00 150.00
223 LaMelo Ball 50.00 120.00

2020-21 Hoops Hyper Green

STATED PRINT RUN 25 SER.#'d SETS
216 Anthony Edwards 150.00 400.00
223 LaMelo Ball 100.00 250.00

2020-21 Hoops Hyper Red

STATED PRINT RUN 99 SER.#'d SETS
216 Anthony Edwards 60.00 150.00
223 LaMelo Ball 50.00 120.00

2020-21 Hoops Orange

STATED PRINT RUN 25 SER.#'d SETS
216 Anthony Edwards 150.00 400.00
223 LaMelo Ball 100.00 250.00

2020-21 Hoops Orange Explosion

STATED PRINT RUN 25 SER.#'d SETS
216 Anthony Edwards 150.00 400.00
223 LaMelo Ball 100.00 250.00

2020-21 Hoops Purple Explosion

120 Ja Morant 10.00 25.00
216 Anthony Edwards 40.00 100.00
223 LaMelo Ball 60.00 150.00
238 Tyrese Haliburton 30.00 80.00

2020-21 Hoops Red

*RED: 2.5X TO 6X BASIC
STATED PRINT RUN 75 SER.#'d SETS
216 Anthony Edwards 75.00 200.00
223 LaMelo Ball 50.00 120.00

2020-21 Hoops Silver

STATED PRINT RUN 199 SER.#'d SETS
216 Anthony Edwards 50.00 120.00
223 LaMelo Ball 40.00 100.00

2020-21 Hoops Teal

STATED PRINT RUN 49 SER.#'d SETS
46 Trae Young 20.00 50.00
120 Ja Morant 20.00 50.00
130 Stephen Curry 20.00 50.00
146 LeBron James 50.00 120.00
150 Luka Doncic 40.00 100.00
163 Zion Williamson 40.00 100.00
201 Deni Avdija 20.00 50.00
202 Aaron Nesmith 15.00 40.00
204 Payton Pritchard 25.00 60.00
207 Tyrese Maxey 30.00 80.00
209 Devin Vassell 20.00 50.00
210 Precious Achiuwa 20.00 50.00
216 Anthony Edwards 100.00 250.00
223 LaMelo Ball 300.00 600.00
226 Obi Toppin 20.00 50.00
228 Patrick Williams 30.00 80.00
230 Theo Maledon 15.00 40.00
234 Cole Anthony 30.00 80.00
238 Tyrese Haliburton 60.00 150.00
241 Killian Hayes 25.00 60.00
244 Isaac Okoro 25.00 60.00
245 Jaden McDaniels 30.00 80.00
246 Desmond Bane 20.00 50.00
249 Immanuel Quickley 25.00 60.00

2020-21 Hoops Teal Explosion

216 Anthony Edwards 40.00 100.00

2020-21 Hoops Arriving Now

1 Killian Hayes .50 1.25
2 Immanuel Quickley 1.25 3.00
3 Patrick Williams 1.25 3.00
4 Payton Pritchard 1.50 4.00
5 Precious Achiuwa 1.00 2.50
6 James Wiseman .60 1.50
7 Josh Green 1.00 2.50
8 Aaron Nesmith 1.00 2.50
9 RJ Hampton .50 1.25
10 Kira Lewis Jr. .50 1.25
11 Aleksej Pokusevski .60 1.50
12 Devin Vassell 1.50 4.00
13 Saddiq Bey 1.00 2.50
14 Tyrese Haliburton 4.00 10.00
15 LaMelo Ball 4.00 10.00
16 Isaiah Stewart 1.00 2.50
17 Tyrese Maxey 4.00 10.00
18 Obi Toppin 1.00 2.50
19 Anthony Edwards 5.00 12.00
20 Deni Avdija 1.25 3.00
21 Cole Anthony 1.25 3.00
22 Desmond Bane 1.50 4.00
23 Onyeka Okongwu 1.00 2.50
24 Isaac Okoro .75 2.00
25 Jalen Smith 1.00 2.50

2020-21 Hoops Back Stage Pass

*HYPER RED/99: 2X TO 5X BASIC
*ARTIST PRF/25: 4X TO 10X BASIC
*HYPER GREEN/25: 4X TO 10X BASIC
1 Luka Doncic 4.00 10.00
2 Giannis Antetokounmpo 3.00 8.00
3 Anthony Davis 1.50 4.00
4 Jimmy Butler 1.25 3.00
5 Ja Morant 2.00 5.00
6 Kawhi Leonard 1.50 4.00
7 James Harden 1.25 3.00
8 LeBron James 5.00 12.00
9 Jamal Murray 1.00 2.50
10 Zion Williamson 2.00 5.00

2020-21 Hoops Back Stage Pass Hyper Red

STATED PRINT RUN 99 SER.#'d SETS

2020-21 Hoops City Edition

*HYPER RED/99: 2X TO 5X BASIC
*ARTIST PRF/25: 4X TO 10X BASIC
*HYPER GREEN/25: 4X TO 10X BASIC
1 Trae Young 1.50 4.00
2 Jayson Tatum 2.50 6.00
3 Kyrie Irving 1.25 3.00
4 Devonte' Graham .50 1.25
5 Zach LaVine 1.00 2.50
6 Kevin Love .60 1.50
7 Luka Doncic 4.00 10.00
8 Nikola Jokic 3.00 8.00
9 Derrick Rose 1.00 2.50
10 Draymond Green .75 2.00
11 James Harden 1.25 3.00
12 Victor Oladipo .50 1.25
13 Kawhi Leonard 1.50 4.00
14 LeBron James 5.00 12.00
15 Ja Morant 2.00 5.00
16 Jimmy Butler 1.25 3.00
17 Giannis Antetokounmpo 3.00 8.00
18 Karl-Anthony Towns 1.00 2.50
19 Zion Williamson 2.00 5.00
20 RJ Barrett 1.00 2.50
21 Chris Paul 1.25 3.00
22 Nikola Vucevic .60 1.50
23 Ben Simmons .60 1.50
24 Devin Booker 1.50 4.00
25 Damian Lillard 1.50 4.00
26 De'Aaron Fox 1.00 2.50
27 DeMar DeRozan .75 2.00
28 Pascal Siakam 1.00 2.50
29 Donovan Mitchell 1.25 3.00
30 Bradley Beal .75 2.00

2020-21 Hoops Class of 2020

1 Patrick Williams 1.25 3.00
2 Anthony Edwards 5.00 12.00
3 James Wiseman .60 1.50
4 Cole Anthony 1.25 3.00
5 Aaron Nesmith 1.00 2.50
6 LaMelo Ball 4.00 10.00
7 Devin Vassell 1.50 4.00
8 Obi Toppin 1.00 2.50
9 Kira Lewis Jr. .50 1.25
10 Tyrese Maxey 4.00 10.00
11 Deni Avdija 1.25 3.00
12 Tyrese Haliburton 4.00 10.00
13 Killian Hayes .50 1.25
14 Isaac Okoro .75 2.00
15 Onyeka Okongwu 1.00 2.50

2020-21 Hoops Courtside

*HYPER RED/99: 2X TO 5X BASIC
*ARTIST PRF/25: 4X TO 10X BASIC
*HYPER GREEN/25: 4X TO 10X BASIC
1 Kawhi Leonard 1.50 4.00
2 Ja Morant 2.00 5.00
3 James Harden 1.25 3.00
4 Luka Doncic 4.00 10.00
5 Donovan Mitchell 1.25 3.00
6 Stephen Curry 5.00 12.00
7 LeBron James 5.00 12.00
8 Jayson Tatum 2.50 6.00
9 Russell Westbrook 1.25 3.00
10 Damian Lillard 1.50 4.00
11 Trae Young 1.50 4.00
12 Paul George 1.00 2.50
13 Zion Williamson 2.00 5.00
14 Giannis Antetokounmpo 3.00 8.00
15 Anthony Davis 1.50 4.00

2020-21 Hoops Courtside Artist Proof

STATED PRINT RUN 25 SER.#'d SETS

2020-21 Hoops Courtside Holo

*HOLO: 1.25X TO 3X BASIC
4 Luka Doncic 25.00 60.00
7 LeBron James 25.00 60.00
13 Zion Williamson 30.00 80.00

2020-21 Hoops Frequent Flyers

1 Aaron Gordon .60 1.50
2 Derrick Jones Jr. .50 1.25
3 LeBron James 5.00 12.00
4 Zion Williamson 2.00 5.00
5 Anthony Davis 1.50 4.00
6 Paul George 1.00 2.50
7 Ja Morant 2.00 5.00
8 Donovan Mitchell 1.25 3.00
9 Giannis Antetokounmpo 3.00 8.00
10 Ben Simmons .60 1.50
11 Russell Westbrook 1.25 3.00
12 Zach LaVine 1.00 2.50
13 Kawhi Leonard 1.50 4.00
14 Damian Lillard 1.50 4.00
15 Joel Embiid 1.50 4.00

2020-21 Hoops Frequent Flyers Green Explosion

STATED PRINT RUN 89 SER.#'d SETS

2020-21 Hoops Future Legends of the Game

STATED PRINT RUN 999 SER.#'d SETS
1 Devin Booker 4.00 10.00
2 Shai Gilgeous-Alexander 8.00 20.00
3 Jayson Tatum 6.00 15.00
4 Zion Williamson 5.00 12.00
5 Bam Adebayo 2.50 6.00
6 Rui Hachimura 2.00 5.00
7 Jamal Murray 2.50 6.00
8 Tyler Herro 3.00 8.00
9 Domantas Sabonis 2.00 5.00
10 Luka Doncic 10.00 25.00
11 D'Angelo Russell 1.50 4.00
12 Deandre Ayton 1.50 4.00
13 De'Aaron Fox 2.50 6.00
14 Ja Morant 5.00 12.00
15 Buddy Hield 1.50 4.00
16 Coby White 2.00 5.00
17 Brandon Ingram 2.00 5.00
18 Trae Young 4.00 10.00
19 Karl-Anthony Towns 2.50 6.00
20 Collin Sexton 1.50 4.00
21 Kristaps Porzingis 2.00 5.00
22 Donovan Mitchell 3.00 8.00
23 John Collins 1.50 4.00
24 RJ Barrett 2.50 6.00
25 Ben Simmons 1.50 4.00

2020-21 Hoops Future Legends of the Game Artist Proof

STATED PRINT RUN 25 SER.#'d SETS

2020-21 Hoops Future Legends of the Game Silver

STATED PRINT RUN 199 SER.#'d SETS

2020-21 Hoops Great SIGnificance

EXCHANGE DEADLINE 08/03/2022
1 Jaylen Hoard 3.00 8.00
2 Monte Morris 3.00 8.00
3 Isaiah Hartenstein 3.00 8.00
4 Isaac Bonga 3.00 8.00
5 Dale Ellis 4.00 10.00
6 Alen Smailagic 3.00 8.00
7 Ben McLemore 3.00 8.00
8 Langston Galloway 3.00 8.00
9 Damian Jones 3.00 8.00
10 Devonte' Graham 4.00 10.00
11 Dennis Rodman 40.00 100.00
12 Mikal Bridges 6.00 15.00
13 Malcolm Brogdon 5.00 12.00
14 Tyronn Lue 12.00 30.00
15 Rolando Blackman 4.00 10.00
16 Keita Bates-Diop 3.00 8.00
17 Jason Terry 4.00 10.00
18 Ricky Pierce 3.00 8.00
19 Jalen Brunson 8.00 20.00
20 Xavier McDaniel 4.00 10.00
21 Jack Sikma 5.00 12.00
22 Danny Granger 3.00 8.00
23 Kurt Rambis 4.00 10.00
24 Zhaire Smith 3.00 8.00

25 Anderson Varejao 3.00 8.00
26 Terrence Ross 4.00 10.00
27 Eric Gordon 4.00 10.00
28 Doug McDermott 4.00 10.00
29 David Thompson 12.00 30.00
30 Sam Cassell 4.00 10.00
31 Kendall Gill 8.00 20.00
33 Garrison Mathews 3.00 8.00
35 Bobby Portis 5.00 12.00
36 Kevin Huerter 4.00 10.00
37 Kris Humphries 3.00 8.00
38 Charles Oakley 5.00 12.00
39 Grayson Allen 5.00 12.00
40 Vin Baker 4.00 10.00
41 Marial Shayok 3.00 8.00
42 Jerry West 30.00 80.00
43 Ersan Ilyasova 3.00 8.00
44 Mario Hezonja 3.00 8.00
45 Kent Benson 3.00 8.00
46 Charles Barkley 50.00 120.00
48 Rod Strickland 4.00 10.00
49 Boban Marjanovic 4.00 10.00
51 Saben Lee 4.00 10.00
52 Vernon Carey Jr. 4.00 10.00
53 Immanuel Quickley 50.00 120.00
54 Onyeka Okongwu 8.00 20.00
58 Jordan Nwora 8.00 20.00
59 Saddiq Bey 40.00 100.00
60 Jalen Smith 8.00 20.00
61 Terry Porter 4.00 10.00
62 Jalen Lecque 3.00 8.00
63 Nico Mannion 4.00 10.00
64 Malachi Flynn 4.00 10.00
65 Tyrese Maxey 40.00 100.00
66 CJ Elleby 4.00 10.00
67 Tre Jones 6.00 15.00
68 Jahmi'us Ramsey 4.00 10.00
69 RJ Hampton 4.00 10.00
70 Isaiah Stewart 8.00 20.00
71 Nick Richards 5.00 12.00
72 Leandro Bolmaro 4.00 10.00
73 Udoka Azubuike 5.00 12.00
74 Robert Woodard II 4.00 10.00
75 Daniel Oturu 4.00 10.00
77 Cassius Stanley 12.00 30.00
79 Kira Lewis Jr. 30.00 80.00
80 Zeke Nnaji 10.00 25.00
81 Desmond Bane 20.00 50.00
83 Josh Green 8.00 20.00
83 Deni Avdija 40.00 100.00
84 Theo Maledon 12.00 30.00
85 Aleksej Pokusevski 5.00 12.00
86 Tyler Bey 4.00 10.00
87 Killian Hayes 30.00 80.00
89 Anthony Edwards 150.00 400.00
91 Grant Riller 4.00 10.00
92 Elijah Hughes 4.00 10.00
93 Precious Achiuwa 8.00 20.00
94 Xavier Tillman 12.00 30.00
95 Jaden McDaniels 20.00 50.00
96 Cole Anthony 40.00 100.00
97 Skylar Mays 4.00 10.00
98 Devin Vassell 12.00 30.00
100 Tyrell Terry 3.00 8.00

2020-21 Hoops High Voltage

1 Paul George 3.00 8.00
2 Stephen Curry 12.00 30.00
3 Joel Embiid 5.00 12.00
4 Anthony Davis 5.00 12.00
5 Ja Morant 12.00 30.00
6 Giannis Antetokounmpo 10.00 25.00
7 Kevin Durant 8.00 20.00
8 Zion Williamson 12.00 30.00
9 Devin Booker 5.00 12.00
10 Donovan Mitchell 4.00 10.00
11 Russell Westbrook 4.00 10.00
12 Ben Simmons 2.00 5.00
13 Kyrie Irving 4.00 10.00
14 Jimmy Butler 4.00 10.00
15 LeBron James 30.00 80.00
16 RJ Barrett 3.00 8.00
17 DeMar DeRozan 2.50 6.00
18 Luka Doncic 15.00 40.00
19 Pascal Siakam 3.00 8.00
20 Bam Adebayo 3.00 8.00
21 James Harden 4.00 10.00
22 Nikola Jokic 10.00 25.00
23 Trae Young 5.00 12.00
24 Jayson Tatum 8.00 20.00
25 Kawhi Leonard 5.00 12.00

2020-21 Hoops Highlights

1 Anthony Davis 5.00 12.00
2 Damian Lillard 5.00 12.00
3 Derrick Jones Jr. 2.00 5.00
4 Kawhi Leonard 5.00 12.00
5 Zion Williamson 8.00 20.00

2020-21 Hoops HIPnotized

1 Kyrie Irving 1.25 3.00
2 Anthony Davis 1.50 4.00
3 Paul George 1.00 2.50
4 Zion Williamson 10.00 25.00
5 James Harden 1.25 3.00
6 LeBron James 15.00 40.00
7 Russell Westbrook 1.25 3.00
8 Nikola Jokic 3.00 8.00
9 Ja Morant 6.00 15.00
10 Donovan Mitchell 1.25 3.00
11 Kawhi Leonard 1.50 4.00
12 Trae Young 6.00 15.00
13 Ben Simmons .60 1.50
14 Stephen Curry 8.00 20.00
15 Kevin Durant 6.00 15.00
16 Jimmy Butler 1.25 3.00
17 Jayson Tatum 2.50 6.00
18 Brandon Ingram .75 2.00
19 Giannis Antetokounmpo 6.00 15.00
20 Luka Doncic 15.00 40.00

2020-21 Hoops Hoops Art Signatures

3 LaMelo Ball 1,500.00 3,000.00
5 Anthony Edwards
Stephen Curry 4,000.00 8,000.00
6 James Wiseman
Stephen Curry 1,000.00 2,000.00
7 LaMelo Ball
Stephen Curry 4,000.00 8,000.00
8 Anthony Edwards
James Wiseman 500.00 1,000.00
10 James Wiseman
LaMelo Ball 150.00 400.00

2020-21 Hoops Hoops Ink

EXCHANGE DEADLINE 08/03/2022
1 Malcolm Brogdon 5.00 12.00
2 Mikal Bridges 10.00 25.00
3 Dale Ellis 4.00 10.00
4 Damian Jones 3.00 8.00
5 Alen Smailagic 3.00 8.00
6 Langston Galloway 3.00 8.00
7 Ricky Davis 4.00 10.00
8 Micheal Ray Richardson 3.00 8.00
9 Dick Barnett 4.00 10.00
10 Otis Birdsong 4.00 10.00
11 Jonas Valanciunas 4.00 10.00
12 Hamidou Diallo 4.00 10.00
13 Magic Johnson 60.00 150.00
14 Tony Delk 4.00 10.00
15 De'Andre Hunter 5.00 12.00
16 Quentin Richardson 3.00 8.00
17 Tony Snell 3.00 8.00
18 Dave Bing 6.00 15.00
19 John Collins 5.00 12.00
20 Cam Reddish 6.00 15.00
21 Bonzi Wells 4.00 10.00
22 Daniel Theis 4.00 10.00
23 Moritz Wagner 3.00 8.00
24 Jerry West 10.00 25.00
25 Jarrett Culver 3.00 8.00
26 T.J. Ford 3.00 8.00
27 Austin Rivers 4.00 10.00
28 Derrick Coleman 5.00 12.00
29 Dennis Rodman 30.00 80.00
30 Andre Miller 4.00 10.00
31 Jason Richardson 5.00 12.00
32 Ernie DiGregorio 4.00 10.00
33 B.J. Armstrong 4.00 10.00
34 Troy Brown Jr. 4.00 10.00
35 Keita Bates-Diop 3.00 8.00
36 DeShawn Stevenson 3.00 8.00
37 Josh Richardson 4.00 10.00
38 Naz Reid 6.00 15.00
39 Jerry Lucas 6.00 15.00
40 Joe Dumars 6.00 15.00
41 Jason Kidd 8.00 20.00
42 Cherokee Parks 3.00 8.00
43 Terence Davis II 5.00 12.00
44 Delon Wright 3.00 8.00
45 Tim Hardaway 3.00 8.00
46 Hedo Turkoglu 4.00 10.00
47 Charles Barkley 50.00 120.00
49 Larry Bird 60.00 150.00
50 Kristaps Porzingis 6.00 15.00

2020-21 Hoops Hoops Ink Red

STATED PRINT RUN 25 SER.#'d SETS
EXCHANGE DEADLINE 08/03/2022
18 Dave Bing 25.00 60.00
20 Cam Reddish 15.00 40.00

2020-21 Hoops Hot Signatures

EXCHANGE DEADLINE 08/03/2022
1 Monte Morris 3.00 8.00
2 Isaac Bonga 3.00 8.00
3 Ben McLemore 3.00 8.00
4 Devonte' Graham 4.00 10.00
5 RJ Barrett 20.00 50.00
6 Larry Nance Jr. 4.00 10.00
7 Brian Scalabrine 3.00 8.00
8 Jordan Bone 3.00 8.00
9 Alex Caruso 30.00 80.00
10 Kevon Looney 4.00 10.00
11 Bob Love 5.00 12.00
12 Desmond Mason 4.00 10.00
13 Magic Johnson 60.00 150.00
14 Danuel House Jr. 4.00 10.00
15 Shawn Kemp 50.00 120.00
16 Darius Miles 3.00 8.00
17 Terry Cummings 5.00 12.00
18 Craig Ehlo 4.00 10.00
19 Jarrett Allen 5.00 12.00
20 Dorian Finney-Smith 4.00 10.00
21 Quinn Cook 3.00 8.00
22 Ron Harper 5.00 12.00
23 Fat Lever 5.00 12.00
24 Boban Marjanovic 4.00 10.00
25 Matt Bonner 3.00 8.00
26 Stephon Marbury 8.00 20.00
27 Kenyon Martin 5.00 12.00
28 Jerry West 40.00 100.00
29 Robin Lopez 3.00 8.00
30 Al Harrington 3.00 8.00
31 Dennis Rodman 30.00 80.00
32 Spud Webb 8.00 20.00
34 Malik Beasley 4.00 10.00
35 Ky Bowman 3.00 8.00
36 Torrey Craig 4.00 10.00
37 Isaiah Hartenstein 3.00 8.00
38 Isaiah Rider 4.00 10.00
39 Brandon Clarke 5.00 12.00
40 Vlade Divac 4.00 10.00
41 Gheorghe Muresan 4.00 10.00
42 Allen Iverson 75.00 200.00
43 Zion Williamson 400.00 800.00
44 Kirk Hinrich 4.00 10.00
45 Spencer Haywood 5.00 12.00
46 Mason Plumlee 3.00 8.00
47 Mike Miller 4.00 10.00
48 Jack Sikma 5.00 12.00
49 Stephen Curry 400.00 800.00
50 Dino Radja 4.00 10.00

2020-21 Hoops Hot Signatures Red

*RED: 1X TO 2.5X BASIC
STATED PRINT RUN 25 SER.#'d SETS
EXCHANGE DEADLINE 08/03/2022
26 Stephon Marbury 30.00 80.00

2020-21 Hoops Hot Signatures Rookies

EXCHANGE DEADLINE 08/03/2022
1 Xavier Tillman 5.00 12.00
2 Leandro Bolmaro 4.00 10.00
3 Tyrese Haliburton 150.00 400.00
4 Nick Richards 5.00 12.00
5 Isaac Okoro 40.00 100.00
6 Theo Maledon 4.00 10.00
7 Immanuel Quickley 75.00 200.00
8 CJ Elleby 4.00 10.00
9 Daniel Oturu 4.00 10.00
10 Cassius Stanley 15.00 40.00
11 Anthony Edwards 150.00 400.00
12 Elijah Hughes 4.00 10.00
13 Cassius Winston 4.00 10.00
14 Tyrese Maxey 40.00 100.00
15 Precious Achiuwa 25.00 60.00
16 Jahmi'us Ramsey 4.00 10.00
17 Zeke Nnaji 5.00 12.00
18 Grant Riller 4.00 10.00
19 Nico Mannion 4.00 10.00
20 Udoka Azubuike 5.00 12.00
21 Aleksej Pokusevski 5.00 12.00
22 RJ Hampton 4.00 10.00
23 Saddiq Bey 40.00 100.00
24 James Wiseman 5.00 12.00
25 Tyrell Terry 3.00 8.00
26 Jalen Smith 8.00 20.00
27 Josh Green 12.00 30.00
28 Onyeka Okongwu 25.00 60.00
29 Tyler Bey 4.00 10.00
30 LaMelo Ball 800.00 1,500.00
31 Killian Hayes 30.00 80.00
32 Saben Lee 15.00 40.00
33 Robert Woodard II 4.00 10.00
34 Malachi Flynn 4.00 10.00
35 Aaron Nesmith 20.00 50.00
36 Skylar Mays 4.00 10.00
37 Obi Toppin 75.00 200.00
38 Deni Avdija 50.00 120.00
39 Patrick Williams 125.00 300.00
40 Jordan Nwora 12.00 30.00
41 Vernon Carey Jr. 12.00 30.00
42 Devin Vassell 20.00 50.00
43 Jaden McDaniels 20.00 50.00
44 Kenyon Martin Jr. 12.00 30.00
45 Isaiah Stewart 8.00 20.00
46 Kira Lewis Jr. 20.00 50.00
47 Desmond Bane 20.00 50.00
48 Payton Pritchard 50.00 120.00
49 Cole Anthony 40.00 100.00
50 Tre Jones 6.00 15.00

2020-21 Hoops Hot Signatures Rookies Red

STATED PRINT RUN 25 SER.#'d SETS
EXCHANGE DEADLINE 08/03/2022

2020-21 Hoops Jersey Swap

1 P.Washington/T.Herro 1.25 3.00
2 R.Hachimura/Y.Watanabe .75 2.00
3 J.Morant/T.Young 2.00 5.00
4 A.Holiday/Jr.Holiday/Ju.Holiday .60 1.50
5 C.Reddish/M.Bamba .75 2.00
6 A.Davis/Jr.Holiday 1.50 4.00
7 J.Morant/L.Doncic 4.00 10.00
8 B.Adebayo/D.Mitchell 1.25 3.00
9 Giannis/Kostas/Thanasis 3.00 8.00
10 J.Morant/Z.Williamson 2.00 5.00

2020-21 Hoops Jersey Swap Green Explosion

STATED PRINT RUN 89 SER.#'d SETS
7 Ja Morant
Luka Doncic 40.00 100.00
10 Ja Morant
Zion Williamson 40.00 100.00

2020-21 Hoops Legends of the Ball

1 Scottie Pippen 4.00 10.00
2 Wilt Chamberlain 6.00 15.00
3 Magic Johnson 8.00 20.00
4 Dwyane Wade 4.00 10.00
5 Shaquille O'Neal 8.00 20.00
6 Anfernee Hardaway 5.00 12.00
7 Clyde Drexler 3.00 8.00
8 Julius Erving 5.00 12.00
9 David Robinson 4.00 10.00
10 Shawn Kemp 3.00 8.00
11 Dennis Rodman 5.00 12.00
12 Kevin Garnett 5.00 12.00
13 Jerry West 4.00 10.00
14 Larry Bird 8.00 20.00
15 Bill Russell 6.00 15.00

2020-21 Hoops Legends of the Game

STATED PRINT RUN 699 SER.#'d SETS
1 LeBron James 25.00 60.00
2 Chris Mullin 3.00 8.00
3 Ray Allen 4.00 10.00
4 Dennis Johnson 2.50 6.00
5 Steve Nash 5.00 12.00
6 Gary Payton 4.00 10.00
7 Jason Kidd 4.00 10.00
8 Adrian Dantley 2.50 6.00
9 Kareem Abdul-Jabbar 8.00 20.00
10 Billy Cunningham 2.50 6.00
11 Magic Johnson 10.00 25.00
12 Chris Paul 5.00 12.00
13 Rick Barry 3.00 8.00
14 Dennis Rodman 6.00 15.00
15 Tim Duncan 6.00 15.00
16 George Gervin 4.00 10.00
17 Jerry Lucas 3.00 8.00
18 Alex English 2.50 6.00
19 Karl Malone 5.00 12.00
20 Bob Cousy 3.00 8.00
21 Moses Malone 3.00 8.00
22 Chris Webber 3.00 8.00
23 Robert Parish 3.00 8.00
24 Dikembe Mutombo 4.00 10.00
25 Tony Parker 4.00 10.00
26 George Mikan 4.00 10.00
27 Jerry West 5.00 12.00
28 Allen Iverson 6.00 15.00
29 Kevin Durant 10.00 25.00
30 Bob Lanier 2.50 6.00
31 Nate Archibald 3.00 8.00
32 Clyde Drexler 4.00 10.00
33 Russell Westbrook 5.00 12.00
34 Dirk Nowitzki 6.00 15.00
35 Tracy McGrady 4.00 10.00
36 Grant Hill 4.00 10.00
37 Joe Dumars 3.00 8.00
38 Alonzo Mourning 3.00 8.00
39 Kevin Garnett 6.00 15.00
40 Bob McAdoo 2.50 6.00
41 Oscar Robertson 6.00 15.00
42 Dan Issel 3.00 8.00
43 Sam Jones 2.50 6.00
44 Dominique Wilkins 4.00 10.00
45 Vince Carter 5.00 12.00
46 Hakeem Olajuwon 5.00 12.00
47 John Havlicek 5.00 12.00
48 Artis Gilmore 3.00 8.00
49 Kevin McHale 3.00 8.00
50 Bob Pettit 3.00 8.00
51 Patrick Ewing 3.00 8.00
52 Bill Walton 4.00 10.00
53 Scottie Pippen 5.00 12.00
54 Dwyane Wade 5.00 12.00
55 Walt Frazier 4.00 10.00
56 Isiah Thomas 4.00 10.00
57 John Stockton 5.00 12.00
58 Bernard King 3.00 8.00
59 Kobe Bryant 40.00 100.00
60 Carmelo Anthony 4.00 10.00
61 Paul Pierce 4.00 10.00
62 Dave Cowens 3.00 8.00
63 Shaquille O'Neal 10.00 25.00
64 Elgin Baylor 3.00 8.00
65 Wilt Chamberlain 8.00 20.00
66 James Harden 5.00 12.00
67 Julius Erving 6.00 15.00
68 Bill Russell 8.00 20.00
69 Larry Bird 10.00 25.00
70 Charles Barkley 6.00 15.00
71 Pete Maravich 6.00 15.00
72 David Robinson 5.00 12.00
73 Stephen Curry 20.00 50.00
74 Elvin Hayes 3.00 8.00
75 Yao Ming 4.00 10.00

2020-21 Hoops Legends of the Game Artist Proof

STATED PRINT RUN 25 SER.#'d SETS
1 LeBron James 150.00 400.00
20 Bob Cousy 15.00 40.00
28 Allen Iverson 20.00 50.00
59 Kobe Bryant 200.00 500.00
73 Stephen Curry 50.00 120.00
75 Yao Ming 50.00 120.00

2020-21 Hoops Legends of the Game Silver

STATED PRINT RUN 199 SER.#'d SETS
1 LeBron James 75.00 200.00
59 Kobe Bryant 100.00 250.00
73 Stephen Curry 25.00 60.00
75 Yao Ming 25.00 60.00

2020-21 Hoops Lights Camera Action

1 Donovan Mitchell 1.25 3.00
2 Paul George 1.00 2.50
3 Bam Adebayo 1.00 2.50
4 Chris Paul 1.25 3.00
5 Bradley Beal .75 2.00
6 Jayson Tatum 2.50 6.00
7 Devin Booker 1.50 4.00
8 Trae Young 1.50 4.00
9 Karl-Anthony Towns 1.00 2.50
10 Kemba Walker .60 1.50
11 Ben Simmons .60 1.50
12 Joel Embiid 1.50 4.00
13 Russell Westbrook 1.25 3.00
14 Pascal Siakam 1.00 2.50
15 Jimmy Butler 1.25 3.00
16 Nikola Jokic 3.00 8.00
17 Damian Lillard 1.50 4.00
18 Luka Doncic 4.00 10.00
19 Kawhi Leonard 1.50 4.00
20 Anthony Davis 1.50 4.00
21 James Harden 1.25 3.00
22 LeBron James 5.00 12.00
23 Giannis Antetokounmpo 3.00 8.00
24 Zion Williamson 2.00 5.00
25 Kyrie Irving 1.25 3.00
26 Stephen Curry 5.00 12.00
27 Klay Thompson 1.50 4.00
28 Victor Oladipo .50 1.25
29 Kevin Durant 2.50 6.00
30 Ja Morant 2.00 5.00

2020-21 Hoops Lights Camera Action Green Explosion

STATED PRINT RUN 89 SER.#'d SETS
18 Luka Doncic 50.00 120.00
22 LeBron James 50.00 120.00
24 Zion Williamson 40.00 100.00
30 Ja Morant 30.00 80.00

2020-21 Hoops Now Playing

1 Vernon Carey Jr. .50 1.25
2 James Wiseman .60 1.50
3 Jalen Smith 1.00 2.50
4 Zeke Nnaji .60 1.50
5 Josh Green 1.00 2.50
6 Anthony Edwards 5.00 12.00
7 Theo Maledon .50 1.25
8 RJ Hampton .50 1.25
9 Leandro Bolmaro .50 1.25
10 Kira Lewis Jr. .50 1.25
11 Isaac Okoro .75 2.00
12 Deni Avdija 1.25 3.00
13 Killian Hayes .50 1.25
14 Devin Vassell 1.50 4.00
15 Aleksej Pokusevski .60 1.50
16 Desmond Bane 1.50 4.00
17 Patrick Williams 1.25 3.00
18 Malachi Flynn .50 1.25
19 Obi Toppin 1.00 2.50
20 Onyeka Okongwu 1.00 2.50
21 Tyrese Haliburton 4.00 10.00
22 Tyrese Maxey 4.00 10.00
23 Tyrell Terry .40 1.00
24 Cole Anthony 1.25 3.00
25 Precious Achiuwa 1.00 2.50
26 Saddiq Bey 1.00 2.50
27 Immanuel Quickley 1.25 3.00
28 Aaron Nesmith 1.00 2.50
29 Cassius Winston .50 1.25
30 Payton Pritchard 1.50 4.00
31 LaMelo Ball 4.00 10.00
32 Isaiah Stewart 1.00 2.50
33 Jaden McDaniels 1.50 4.00

2020-21 Hoops Now Playing Holo

17 Patrick Williams 10.00 25.00
31 LaMelo Ball 75.00 200.00

2020-21 Hoops Prime Twine

1 LeBron James 12.00 30.00
2 Kawhi Leonard 1.50 4.00
3 Stephen Curry 5.00 12.00
4 Giannis Antetokounmpo 5.00 12.00
5 Anthony Davis 1.50 4.00
6 James Harden 1.25 3.00
7 Joel Embiid 1.50 4.00
8 Paul George 1.00 2.50
9 Damian Lillard 1.50 4.00
10 Nikola Jokic 3.00 8.00
11 Devin Booker 1.50 4.00
12 Bradley Beal .75 2.00
13 Jimmy Butler 1.25 3.00
14 Kyrie Irving 1.25 3.00
15 Kemba Walker .60 1.50
16 Russell Westbrook 1.25 3.00
17 Ben Simmons .60 1.50
18 Luka Doncic 12.00 30.00
19 Trae Young 1.50 4.00
20 Jayson Tatum 2.50 6.00
21 Donovan Mitchell 1.25 3.00
22 Pascal Siakam 1.00 2.50
23 Zion Williamson 12.00 30.00
24 Ja Morant 6.00 15.00
25 Karl-Anthony Towns 1.00 2.50

2020-21 Hoops Prime Twine Artist Proof

STATED PRINT RUN 25 SER.#'d SETS
1 LeBron James 300.00 600.00
3 Stephen Curry 60.00 150.00
18 Luka Doncic 300.00 600.00
23 Zion Williamson 200.00 500.00
24 Ja Morant 125.00 300.00

2020-21 Hoops Prime Twine Hyper Green

STATED PRINT RUN 25 SER.#'d SETS
1 LeBron James 300.00 600.00
3 Stephen Curry 60.00 150.00
18 Luka Doncic 300.00 600.00
23 Zion Williamson 200.00 500.00
24 Ja Morant 125.00 300.00

2020-21 Hoops Prime Twine Hyper Red

STATED PRINT RUN 99 SER.#'d SETS

2020-21 Hoops Rise N Shine Memorabilia

1 Jalen Smith 3.00 8.00
2 Aleksej Pokusevski 2.00 5.00
3 Nico Mannion 1.50 4.00
4 RJ Hampton 1.50 4.00
5 Malachi Flynn 1.50 4.00
6 Daniel Oturu 1.50 4.00
7 Killian Hayes 1.50 4.00
8 James Wiseman 2.00 5.00
9 Isaac Okoro 2.50 6.00
10 Tyrese Maxey 12.00 30.00
11 Udoka Azubuike 2.00 5.00
12 Anthony Edwards 15.00 40.00
13 Saddiq Bey 3.00 8.00
14 Devin Vassell 5.00 12.00
15 Obi Toppin 3.00 8.00
16 Payton Pritchard 5.00 12.00
17 Robert Woodard II 1.50 4.00
18 Xavier Tillman 2.00 5.00
19 Jaden McDaniels 5.00 12.00
21 Theo Maledon 1.50 4.00
22 Immanuel Quickley 4.00 10.00
23 Precious Achiuwa 3.00 8.00
24 Tyrese Haliburton 12.00 30.00
25 Tyrell Terry 1.25 3.00
26 Josh Green 3.00 8.00
27 Deni Avdija 4.00 10.00
28 Zeke Nnaji 2.00 5.00
29 Cole Anthony 4.00 10.00
30 Onyeka Okongwu 3.00 8.00
31 Aaron Nesmith 3.00 8.00
32 Isaiah Stewart 3.00 8.00
33 Desmond Bane 5.00 12.00
34 Patrick Williams 4.00 10.00
35 Jordan Nwora 2.00 5.00
36 Vernon Carey Jr. 1.50 4.00
37 Tyler Bey 1.50 4.00
38 LaMelo Ball 12.00 30.00
39 Kira Lewis Jr. 1.50 4.00
40 Tre Jones 2.50 6.00

2020-21 Hoops Rookie Ink

EXCHANGE DEADLINE 08/03/2022
1 Tre Jones 6.00 15.00
2 Kira Lewis Jr. 20.00 50.00
3 Aaron Nesmith 20.00 50.00
4 Saben Lee 15.00 40.00
5 Saddiq Bey 40.00 100.00
6 Josh Green 12.00 30.00
7 Tyler Bey 4.00 10.00
8 Deni Avdija 50.00 120.00
9 Vernon Carey Jr. 12.00 30.00
10 Jaden McDaniels 20.00 50.00
11 Kenyon Martin Jr. 12.00 30.00
12 Killian Hayes 30.00 80.00
13 Jahmi'us Ramsey 8.00 20.00
14 Tyrese Maxey 40.00 100.00
15 Isaac Okoro 40.00 100.00
16 CJ Elleby 4.00 10.00
17 Immanuel Quickley 75.00 200.00
18 Nico Mannion 4.00 10.00
19 Xavier Tillman 5.00 12.00
20 Theo Maledon 12.00 30.00
21 Anthony Edwards 150.00 400.00
22 Daniel Oturu 4.00 10.00
23 RJ Hampton 4.00 10.00
24 Onyeka Okongwu 25.00 60.00
25 Robert Woodard II 4.00 10.00
26 Isaiah Stewart 8.00 20.00
27 Cole Anthony 40.00 100.00
28 Tyrese Haliburton 150.00 400.00
29 Cassius Stanley 15.00 40.00
30 Udoka Azubuike 5.00 12.00
31 Precious Achiuwa 25.00 60.00
32 Grant Riller 4.00 10.00
33 LaMelo Ball 800.00 1,500.00
34 Skylar Mays 4.00 10.00
35 Patrick Williams 125.00 300.00
36 Nick Richards 5.00 12.00
37 Elijah Hughes 4.00 10.00
38 Zeke Nnaji 5.00 12.00
39 Malachi Flynn 4.00 10.00
40 Devin Vassell 20.00 50.00
41 Jordan Nwora 12.00 30.00
42 Leandro Bolmaro 4.00 10.00
43 Cassius Winston 4.00 10.00
44 Aleksej Pokusevski 5.00 12.00
45 James Wiseman 5.00 12.00
46 Jalen Smith 8.00 20.00
47 Obi Toppin 75.00 200.00
48 Desmond Bane 20.00 50.00
49 Tyrell Terry 3.00 8.00
50 Payton Pritchard 50.00 120.00

2020-21 Hoops Rookie Ink Red

STATED PRINT RUN 25 SER.#'d SETS
EXCHANGE DEADLINE 08/03/2022
2 Kira Lewis Jr. 75.00 200.00
3 Aaron Nesmith 40.00 100.00
8 Deni Avdija 150.00 400.00
10 Jaden McDaniels 125.00 300.00
12 Killian Hayes 75.00 200.00
17 Immanuel Quickley 400.00 800.00
21 Anthony Edwards 400.00 800.00
28 Tyrese Haliburton 400.00 800.00
33 LaMelo Ball 2,000.00 4,000.00
35 Patrick Williams 400.00 800.00
50 Payton Pritchard 125.00 300.00

2020-21 Hoops Rookie Remembrance Jerseys

*PRIME/25: 1.25X TO 3X BASIC
1 Zion Williamson 8.00 20.00
2 Ja Morant 8.00 20.00
3 Rui Hachimura 3.00 8.00
4 Tyler Herro 5.00 12.00
5 PJ Washington Jr. 2.50 6.00
6 Kendrick Nunn 2.00 5.00
7 Cam Reddish 3.00 8.00
8 Coby White 3.00 8.00
9 Brandon Clarke 2.50 6.00
10 Michael Porter Jr. 3.00 8.00
11 Matisse Thybulle 2.00 5.00
12 Jaxson Hayes 2.00 5.00
13 Eric Paschall 2.00 5.00
14 Kevin Porter Jr. 2.00 5.00
15 De'Andre Hunter 2.50 6.00
16 RJ Barrett 4.00 10.00
17 Jarrett Culver 1.50 4.00
18 Bol Bol 2.50 6.00
19 Keldon Johnson 4.00 10.00
20 Sekou Doumbouya 1.50 4.00

2020-21 Hoops Rookie Special

1 Anthony Edwards 8.00 20.00
2 LaMelo Ball 6.00 15.00

2020-21 Hoops Rookie Special Holo

1 Anthony Edwards 15.00 40.00
2 LaMelo Ball 12.00 30.00

2020-21 Hoops Rookie Sweaters

COMMON CARD 1.25 3.00
SEMISTARS 1.50 4.00
UNLISTED STARS 2.00 5.00
1 Tyrese Maxey 12.00 30.00
2 CJ Elleby 1.50 4.00
3 Jordan Nwora 2.00 5.00
4 Patrick Williams 4.00 10.00
5 Isaac Okoro 2.50 6.00
6 Payton Pritchard 5.00 12.00
7 Aaron Nesmith 3.00 8.00
8 Daniel Oturu 1.50 4.00
9 Desmond Bane 5.00 12.00
10 Xavier Tillman 2.00 5.00
11 Skylar Mays 1.50 4.00
12 Onyeka Okongwu 3.00 8.00
13 Precious Achiuwa 3.00 8.00
14 Udoka Azubuike 2.00 5.00
15 Tyrese Haliburton 12.00 30.00
16 Robert Woodard II 1.50 4.00
17 Obi Toppin 3.00 8.00
18 Immanuel Quickley 4.00 10.00
19 Cole Anthony 4.00 10.00
20 Josh Green 3.00 8.00
21 Tyrell Terry 1.25 3.00
22 RJ Hampton 1.50 4.00
23 Zeke Nnaji 2.00 5.00
24 Saddiq Bey 3.00 8.00
25 Killian Hayes 1.50 4.00
26 Malachi Flynn 1.50 4.00
27 Tre Jones 2.50 6.00
28 Devin Vassell 5.00 12.00
29 Jalen Smith 3.00 8.00
30 Theo Maledon 1.50 4.00
31 Aleksej Pokusevski 2.00 5.00
32 Nico Mannion 1.50 4.00
33 James Wiseman 2.00 5.00
34 Deni Avdija 4.00 10.00
35 Jaden McDaniels 5.00 12.00
36 Anthony Edwards 20.00 50.00

2020-21 Hoops SLAM

1 Allen Iverson 4.00 10.00
2 LeBron James 12.00 30.00
3 Carmelo Anthony 2.50 6.00
4 Stephen Curry 12.00 30.00
5 Luka Doncic 10.00 25.00
6 Trae Young 4.00 10.00
7 Jason Williams 2.50 6.00
8 Tim Duncan 4.00 10.00
9 Shaquille O'Neal 6.00 15.00
10 Kawhi Leonard 4.00 10.00
11 Kevin Garnett 4.00 10.00
12 Dirk Nowitzki 4.00 10.00
13 Kevin Durant 6.00 15.00
14 Vince Carter 3.00 8.00
15 Anthony Davis 4.00 10.00
16 Damian Lillard 4.00 10.00
17 Zion Williamson 5.00 12.00
18 Ja Morant 5.00 12.00
19 Kobe Bryant 12.00 30.00
20 Tracy McGrady 2.50 6.00

2020-21 Hoops SLAM Green Explosion

STATED PRINT RUN 89 SER.#'d SETS
1 Allen Iverson 200.00 500.00
2 LeBron James 500.00 1,000.00
3 Carmelo Anthony 125.00 300.00
4 Stephen Curry 500.00 1,000.00
5 Luka Doncic 400.00 800.00
6 Trae Young 150.00 400.00
7 Jason Williams 150.00 400.00
8 Tim Duncan 150.00 400.00
9 Shaquille O'Neal 150.00 400.00
10 Kawhi Leonard 150.00 400.00
11 Kevin Garnett 150.00 400.00
12 Dirk Nowitzki 150.00 400.00
13 Kevin Durant 150.00 400.00
14 Vince Carter 150.00 400.00
15 Anthony Davis 150.00 400.00
16 Damian Lillard 125.00 300.00
17 Zion Williamson 200.00 500.00
18 Ja Morant 200.00 500.00
19 Kobe Bryant 600.00 1,200.00
20 Tracy McGrady 125.00 300.00

2020-21 Hoops SLAM Holo

1 Allen Iverson 12.00 30.00
2 LeBron James 40.00 100.00
3 Carmelo Anthony 8.00 20.00
4 Stephen Curry 40.00 100.00
5 Luka Doncic 30.00 80.00
6 Trae Young 12.00 30.00
7 Jason Williams 8.00 20.00
8 Tim Duncan 12.00 30.00
9 Shaquille O'Neal 20.00 50.00
10 Kawhi Leonard 12.00 30.00
11 Kevin Garnett 12.00 30.00
12 Dirk Nowitzki 12.00 30.00
13 Kevin Durant 20.00 50.00
14 Vince Carter 10.00 25.00
15 Anthony Davis 12.00 30.00
16 Damian Lillard 12.00 30.00
17 Zion Williamson 15.00 40.00
18 Ja Morant 15.00 40.00
19 Kobe Bryant 40.00 100.00
20 Tracy McGrady 8.00 20.00

2020-21 Hoops SLAM Purple Explosion

1 Allen Iverson 12.00 30.00
2 LeBron James 40.00 100.00
3 Carmelo Anthony 8.00 20.00
4 Stephen Curry 40.00 100.00
5 Luka Doncic 30.00 80.00
6 Trae Young 12.00 30.00
7 Jason Williams 8.00 20.00
8 Tim Duncan 12.00 30.00
9 Shaquille O'Neal 20.00 50.00
10 Kawhi Leonard 12.00 30.00
11 Kevin Garnett 12.00 30.00
12 Dirk Nowitzki 12.00 30.00
13 Kevin Durant 20.00 50.00
14 Vince Carter 10.00 25.00
15 Anthony Davis 12.00 30.00
16 Damian Lillard 12.00 30.00
17 Zion Williamson 15.00 40.00
18 Ja Morant 15.00 40.00
19 Kobe Bryant 40.00 100.00
20 Tracy McGrady 8.00 20.00

2020-21 Hoops SLAM Winter Holo

*WINTER HOLO: 1.25X TO 3X BASIC

2020-21 Hoops Spark Plugs

1 De'Aaron Fox 2.50 6.00
2 Ja Morant 15.00 40.00
3 Marcus Smart 1.50 4.00
4 Bradley Beal 2.00 5.00
5 Stephen Curry 12.00 30.00
6 RJ Barrett 2.50 6.00
7 Damian Lillard 4.00 10.00
8 Kyrie Irving 3.00 8.00
9 Tyler Herro 3.00 8.00
10 Derrick Rose 2.50 6.00
11 Kendrick Nunn 1.25 3.00
12 Devin Booker 4.00 10.00
13 James Harden 3.00 8.00
14 Russell Westbrook 3.00 8.00
15 Patrick Beverley 1.00 2.50

2020-21 Hoops Vanity Plates

1 Zion Williamson 1.25 3.00
2 Ja Morant 1.25 3.00
3 LeBron James 3.00 8.00
4 Kawhi Leonard 1.00 2.50
5 James Harden .75 2.00
6 Russell Westbrook .75 2.00
7 Anthony Davis 1.00 2.50
8 Paul George .60 1.50
9 Giannis Antetokounmpo 2.00 5.00
10 Luka Doncic 2.50 6.00
11 Kyrie Irving .75 2.00
12 Damian Lillard 1.00 2.50
13 Donovan Mitchell .75 2.00
14 Kevin Durant 1.50 4.00
15 Devin Booker 1.00 2.50
16 Stephen Curry 3.00 8.00
17 Nikola Jokic 2.00 5.00
18 Kemba Walker .40 1.00
19 Brandon Ingram .50 1.25
20 Ben Simmons .40 1.00
21 Pascal Siakam .60 1.50
22 Jayson Tatum 1.50 4.00
23 Trae Young 1.00 2.50
24 Rui Hachimura .50 1.25
25 RJ Barrett .60 1.50

2020-21 Hoops We Got Next

*HOLO: 1.25X TO 3X BASIC
1 Anthony Edwards 5.00 12.00
2 James Wiseman .60 1.50
3 LaMelo Ball 4.00 10.00
4 Patrick Williams 1.25 3.00
5 Isaac Okoro .75 2.00
6 Onyeka Okongwu 1.00 2.50
7 Killian Hayes .50 1.25
8 Obi Toppin 1.00 2.50
9 Deni Avdija 1.25 3.00

10 Jalen Smith 1.00 2.50
11 Devin Vassell 1.50 4.00
12 Tyrese Haliburton 4.00 10.00
13 Kira Lewis Jr. .50 1.25
14 Aaron Nesmith 1.00 2.50
15 Cole Anthony 1.25 3.00
16 Isaiah Stewart 1.00 2.50
17 Aleksej Pokusevski .60 1.50
18 Josh Green 1.00 2.50
19 Saddiq Bey 1.00 2.50
20 Precious Achiuwa 1.00 2.50
21 Tyrese Maxey 4.00 10.00
22 Zeke Nnaji .60 1.50
23 Malachi Flynn .50 1.25
24 RJ Hampton .50 1.25
25 Immanuel Quickley 1.25 3.00

2020-21 Hoops Zero Gravity

*HOLO: 1.25X TO 3X BASIC
1 Zach LaVine 1.50 4.00
2 Julius Erving 2.50 6.00
3 Vince Carter 2.00 5.00
4 Derrick Jones Jr. .75 2.00
5 Dwyane Wade 2.00 5.00
6 Anthony Davis 2.50 6.00
7 Donovan Mitchell 2.00 5.00
8 Scottie Pippen 2.00 5.00
9 Kevin Garnett 2.50 6.00
10 LeBron James 8.00 20.00
11 Ja Morant 3.00 8.00
12 Anfernee Hardaway 2.50 6.00
13 Russell Westbrook 2.00 5.00
14 Shawn Kemp 1.50 4.00
15 Aaron Gordon 1.00 2.50
16 Paul George 1.50 4.00
17 Tracy McGrady 1.50 4.00
18 Giannis Antetokounmpo 5.00 12.00
19 Dwight Howard 1.25 3.00
20 Zion Williamson 3.00 8.00

2020-21 Hoops Zero Gravity Artist Proof

STATED PRINT RUN 25 SER.#'d SETS
1 Zach LaVine 15.00 40.00
5 Dwyane Wade 20.00 50.00
8 Scottie Pippen 20.00 50.00
9 Kevin Garnett 20.00 50.00
10 LeBron James 200.00 500.00
11 Ja Morant 60.00 150.00
17 Tracy McGrady 20.00 50.00
18 Giannis Antetokounmpo 40.00 100.00
20 Zion Williamson 150.00 400.00

2020-21 Hoops Zero Gravity Hyper Green

STATED PRINT RUN 25 SER.#'d SETS
8 Scottie Pippen 20.00 50.00
9 Kevin Garnett 20.00 50.00
10 LeBron James 100.00 250.00
11 Ja Morant 75.00 200.00

2020-21 Hoops Zero Gravity Hyper Red

STATED PRINT RUN 99 SER.#'d SETS
1 Zach LaVine 15.00 40.00
10 LeBron James 50.00 120.00
11 Ja Morant 40.00 100.00

2021-22 Hoops

COMPLETE SET (270)
*WINTER: .4X TO 1X BASIC
*BLUE: .75X TO 2X BASIC
*HYPER BLUE: .75X TO 2X BASIC
*PURPLE: .75X TO 2X BASIC
*PURPLE WINTER: .75X TO 2X BASIC
*RED BACKS: .75X TO 2X BASIC
*YELLOW: .75X TO 2X BASIC
*NEON GREEN: 1.25X TO 3X BASIC
*TEAL EXPLOSION: 1.5X TO 4X BASIC
*ANNV ED: 2.5X TO 6X BASIC
*GREEN ICE: 2.5X TO 6X BASIC
*PREM BOX SET/199: 2.5X TO 6X BASIC
*SILVER/199: 2.5X TO 6X BASIC
*GREEN/99: 3X TO 8X BASIC
*HYPER RED/99: 3X TO 8X BASIC
*NBA 75 ANNV/75: 3X TO 8X BASIC
*RED/75: 3X TO 8X BASIC
*BLUE EXPLOSION/59: 4X TO 10X BASIC
*ARTIST PROOF/25: 6X TO 15X BASIC
*HYPER GREEN/25: 6X TO 15X BASIC
*ORANGE EXPLOSION/25: 6X TO 15X BASIC
1 Jamal Murray .50 1.25
2 Terrence Ross .25 .60
3 Shai Gilgeous-Alexander 1.50 4.00
4 DeMar DeRozan .40 1.00
5 T.J. Warren .20 .50
6 Devin Booker .75 2.00
7 Tobias Harris .25 .60
8 Klay Thompson .75 2.00
9 Jaylen Brown .50 1.25
10 Jimmy Butler .50 1.25
11 Nikola Jokic 1.50 4.00
12 Cole Anthony .40 1.00
13 Aleksej Pokusevski .25 .60
14 Dejounte Murray .30 .75
15 Zach LaVine .50 1.25
16 Mikal Bridges .40 1.00
17 Ben Simmons .30 .75
18 Stephen Curry 2.00 5.00
19 Marcus Smart .30 .75
20 Bam Adebayo .50 1.25
21 Michael Porter Jr. .40 1.00
22 RJ Hampton .20 .50
23 Darius Bazley .20 .50
24 Derrick White .30 .75
25 Nikola Vucevic .30 .75
26 Chris Paul .60 1.50
27 Joel Embiid .75 2.00
28 Draymond Green .40 1.00
29 Kemba Walker .30 .75
30 Duncan Robinson .25 .60
31 Will Barton .20 .50
32 Markelle Fultz .20 .50
33 Luguentz Dort .30 .75
34 Keldon Johnson .40 1.00
35 Coby White .30 .75
36 Deandre Ayton .30 .75
37 Seth Curry .25 .60
38 Andrew Wiggins .40 1.00
39 Evan Fournier .25 .60
40 Tyler Herro .50 1.25
41 Paul Millsap .25 .60
42 Wendell Carter Jr. .25 .60
43 Al Horford .30 .75
44 Jakob Poeltl .25 .60
45 Patrick Williams .30 .75
46 Jae Crowder .20 .50
47 Danny Green .25 .60
48 Kelly Oubre Jr. .30 .75
49 Tristan Thompson .20 .50
50 Goran Dragic .25 .60
51 Monte Morris .25 .60
52 Gary Harris .25 .60
53 Kenrich Williams .20 .50
54 Lonnie Walker IV .25 .60
55 Lauri Markkanen .40 1.00
56 Cameron Johnson .30 .75
57 Tyrese Maxey .75 2.00
58 James Wiseman .25 .60
59 Payton Pritchard .30 .75
60 Kendrick Nunn .25 .60
61 Damian Lillard .75 2.00
62 Luka Doncic 2.00 5.00
63 Theo Maledon .25 .60
64 Devin Vassell .50 1.25
65 Thaddeus Young .20 .50
66 Jalen Smith .30 .75
67 James Harden .60 1.50
68 Otto Porter Jr. .20 .50
69 Fred VanVleet .40 1.00
70 Victor Oladipo .25 .60
71 Norman Powell .25 .60
72 Dorian Finney-Smith .20 .50
73 Brook Lopez .20 .50
74 Brandon Ingram .40 1.00
75 Tomas Satoransky .20 .50
76 Kawhi Leonard .75 2.00
77 Kyrie Irving .60 1.50
78 Harrison Barnes .25 .60
79 Pascal Siakam .50 1.25
80 Deni Avdija .30 .75
81 CJ McCollum .25 .60
82 Kristaps Porzingis .40 1.00
83 Khris Middleton .30 .75
84 Zion Williamson .75 2.00
85 Collin Sexton .30 .75
86 Paul George .50 1.25
87 Kevin Durant 1.00 2.50
88 De'Aaron Fox .50 1.25
89 Kyle Lowry .30 .75
90 Russell Westbrook .50 1.25
91 Robert Covington .20 .50
92 Josh Richardson .25 .60
93 Donte DiVincenzo .30 .75
94 Lonzo Ball .30 .75
95 Darius Garland .50 1.25
96 Nicolas Batum .25 .60
97 Joe Harris .25 .60
98 Buddy Hield .25 .60
99 OG Anunoby .25 .60
100 Bradley Beal .40 1.00
101 Carmelo Anthony .50 1.25
102 Tim Hardaway Jr. .25 .60
103 Giannis Antetokounmpo 1.50 4.00
104 Eric Bledsoe .25 .60
105 Isaac Okoro .25 .60
106 Marcus Morris Sr. .20 .50
107 DeAndre Jordan .20 .50
108 Tyrese Haliburton .60 1.50
109 Gary Trent Jr. .25 .60
110 Rui Hachimura .30 .75
111 Enes Freedom .25 .60
112 Maxi Kleber .25 .60
113 Jrue Holiday .40 1.00
114 Steven Adams .25 .60
115 Jarrett Allen .30 .75
116 Luke Kennard .25 .60
117 Jeff Green .25 .60
118 Richaun Holmes .20 .50
119 Aron Baynes .20 .50
120 Thomas Bryant .20 .50
121 Jusuf Nurkic .25 .60
122 Boban Marjanovic .30 .75
123 Bobby Portis .25 .60
124 Kira Lewis Jr. .20 .50
125 Kevin Love .30 .75
126 Patrick Beverley .20 .50
127 Julius Randle .40 1.00
128 Marvin Bagley III .25 .60
129 Chris Boucher .30 .75
130 Davis Bertans .25 .60
131 Derrick Jones Jr. .20 .50
132 Ja Morant 1.00 2.50
133 P.J. Tucker .25 .60
134 Christian Wood .25 .60
135 Cedi Osman .25 .60
136 LeBron James 2.50 6.00
137 RJ Barrett .50 1.25
138 Trae Young .75 2.00
139 Donovan Mitchell .60 1.50
140 LaMelo Ball .75 2.00
141 Karl-Anthony Towns .50 1.25
142 Dillon Brooks .30 .75
143 Domantas Sabonis .40 1.00
144 John Wall .40 1.00
145 Jerami Grant .30 .75
146 Anthony Davis .75 2.00
147 Reggie Bullock .20 .50
148 Kevin Huerter .25 .60
149 Royce O'Neale .25 .60
150 Terry Rozier .25 .60
151 Anthony Edwards 1.50 4.00
152 Jonas Valanciunas .25 .60
153 Malcolm Brogdon .25 .60
154 Kevin Porter Jr. .25 .60
155 Saddiq Bey .25 .60
156 Dennis Schroder .30 .75
157 Mitchell Robinson .30 .75
158 Clint Capela .30 .75
159 Bojan Bogdanovic .25 .60
160 Gordon Hayward .25 .60
161 D'Angelo Russell .30 .75
162 Kyle Anderson .20 .50
163 Caris LeVert .25 .60
164 Eric Gordon .25 .60
165 Mason Plumlee .20 .50
166 Kyle Kuzma .40 1.00
167 Derrick Rose .50 1.25
168 Bogdan Bogdanovic .30 .75
169 Rudy Gobert .40 1.00
170 PJ Washington Jr. .30 .75
171 Ricky Rubio .30 .75
172 Jaren Jackson Jr. .50 1.25
173 Myles Turner .30 .75
174 Jae'Sean Tate .30 .75
175 Killian Hayes .30 .75
176 Kentavious Caldwell-Pope .20 .50
177 Obi Toppin .30 .75
178 John Collins .30 .75
179 Mike Conley .25 .60
180 Devonte' Graham .25 .60
181 Malik Beasley .25 .60
182 Brandon Clarke .30 .75
183 Justin Holiday .20 .50
184 Kelly Olynyk .20 .50
185 Josh Jackson .20 .50
186 Andre Drummond .25 .60
187 Immanuel Quickley .30 .75
188 De'Andre Hunter .30 .75
189 Joe Ingles .25 .60
190 Miles Bridges .25 .60
191 Jaden McDaniels .30 .75
192 Desmond Bane .60 1.50
193 Doug McDermott .25 .60
194 Kenyon Martin Jr. .30 .75
195 Isaiah Stewart .30 .75
196 Montrezl Harrell .25 .60
197 Jayson Tatum 1.25 3.00
198 Onyeka Okongwu .30 .75
199 Jordan Clarkson .30 .75
200 Spencer Dinwiddie .25 .60
201 Cade Cunningham RC 4.00 10.00
202 Josh Giddey RC 2.00 5.00
203 James Bouknight RC .50 1.25
204 Alperen Sengun RC 2.00 5.00
205 Keon Johnson RC .60 1.50
206 Quentin Grimes RC 1.25 3.00
207 Santi Aldama RC .75 2.00
208 Isaiah Livers RC .60 1.50
209 Scottie Lewis RC .50 1.25
210 Jalen Suggs RC 1.50 4.00
211 Ziaire Williams RC .75 2.00
212 Corey Kispert RC .75 2.00
213 Jalen Johnson RC 2.00 5.00
214 Josh Christopher RC .50 1.25
215 Day'Ron Sharpe RC .60 1.50
216 Jared Butler RC .60 1.50
217 Charles Bassey RC .60 1.50
218 Jalen Green RC 3.00 8.00
219 Jonathan Kuminga RC 2.00 5.00
220 Joshua Primo RC .50 1.25
221 Trey Murphy III RC 2.00 5.00
222 David Johnson RC .50 1.25
223 Isaiah Jackson RC .60 1.50
224 Bones Hyland RC .75 2.00
225 Jeremiah Robinson-Earl RC .60 1.50
226 Greg Brown III RC .50 1.25
227 Scottie Barnes RC 2.00 5.00
228 Davion Mitchell RC .60 1.50
229 Moses Moody RC 1.25 3.00
230 Kai Jones RC .50 1.25
231 Cameron Thomas RC 1.25 3.00
232 Miles McBride RC 1.00 2.50
233 Brandon Boston Jr. RC .60 1.50
234 Evan Mobley RC 2.50 6.00
235 Franz Wagner RC 2.00 5.00
236 Chris Duarte RC .50 1.25
237 Tre Mann RC 1.00 2.50
238 Usman Garuba RC .50 1.25
239 Jaden Springer RC .60 1.50
240 Ayo Dosunmu RC 1.25 3.00
241 Isaiah Todd RC .50 1.25
242 Jason Preston RC .50 1.25
243 Herbert Jones RC .75 2.00
244 JT Thor RC .60 1.50
245 Joe Wieskamp RC .60 1.50
246 Kessler Edwards RC .60 1.50
247 Aaron Wiggins RC .75 2.00
248 Juan Toscano-Anderson RC .60 1.50
249 Sharife Cooper RC .50 1.25
250 Luka Garza RC .60 1.50
251 Luka Doncic 2.00 5.00
252 Shaquille O'Neal 1.00 2.50
253 Bill Russell 1.00 2.50
254 Anthony Davis .75 2.00
255 Allen Iverson .75 2.00
256 Karl Malone .60 1.50
257 Larry Bird 1.00 2.50
258 John Stockton .60 1.50
259 Ja Morant 1.00 2.50
260 Oscar Robertson .60 1.50
261 Kareem Abdul-Jabbar 1.00 2.50
262 Anthony Edwards 1.50 4.00
263 Trae Young .75 2.00
264 CJ McCollum .25 .60
265 Jamal Murray .50 1.25
266 Magic Johnson 1.00 2.50
267 Rasheed Wallace .40 1.00
268 Karl-Anthony Towns .50 1.25
269 Stephen Curry 2.00 5.00
270 Dirk Nowitzki .75 2.00

2021-22 Hoops Silver

*SILVER: 2.5X TO 6X BASIC
STATED PRINT RUN 199 COPIES PER

2021-22 Hoops Arriving Now

COMMON CARD .40 1.00
SEMISTARS .50 1.25
UNLISTED STARS .60 1.50
*WINTER: .4X TO 1X BASIC
*HOLO: .75X TO 2X BASIC
*WINTER HOLO: .75X TO 2X BASIC
1 Cade Cunningham 4.00 10.00
2 Evan Mobley 2.50 6.00
3 Jalen Suggs 1.50 4.00
4 Jonathan Kuminga 2.00 5.00
5 Davion Mitchell .60 1.50
6 James Bouknight .50 1.25
7 Chris Duarte .50 1.25
8 Corey Kispert .75 2.00
9 Trey Murphy III 2.00 5.00
10 Kai Jones .50 1.25
11 Keon Johnson .60 1.50
12 Usman Garuba .50 1.25
13 Quentin Grimes 1.25 3.00
14 Jalen Green 3.00 8.00
15 Scottie Barnes 2.00 5.00
16 Josh Giddey 2.00 5.00
17 Franz Wagner 2.00 5.00
18 Ziaire Williams .75 2.00
19 Joshua Primo .50 1.25
20 Moses Moody 1.25 3.00
21 Alperen Sengun 2.00 5.00
22 Tre Mann 1.00 2.50
23 Jalen Johnson 2.00 5.00
24 Isaiah Jackson .60 1.50
25 Josh Christopher .50 1.25

2021-22 Hoops City Edition

COMMON CARD .40 1.00
SEMISTARS .50 1.25
UNLISTED STARS .60 1.50
*HOLO: 1.25X TO 3X BASIC
*HYPER RED/99: 2X TO 5X BASIC
*HOLO ARTIST PROOF/25: 4X TO 10X BASIC
*HYPER GREEN/25: 4X TO 10X BASIC
1 Stephen Curry 4.00 10.00
2 Kevin Durant 2.00 5.00
3 Ben Simmons .60 1.50
4 Paul George 1.00 2.50
5 LeBron James 5.00 12.00
6 Donovan Mitchell 1.25 3.00
7 Giannis Antetokounmpo 3.00 8.00
8 Jimmy Butler 1.00 2.50
9 Zion Williamson 1.50 4.00
10 Jayson Tatum 2.50 6.00
11 Ja Morant 2.00 5.00
12 Damian Lillard 1.50 4.00
13 John Wall .75 2.00
14 Bradley Beal .75 2.00
15 Anthony Edwards 3.00 8.00
16 Domantas Sabonis .75 2.00
17 Collin Sexton .60 1.50
18 Nikola Jokic 3.00 8.00
19 Dejounte Murray .60 1.50
20 Pascal Siakam 1.00 2.50
21 Zach LaVine 1.00 2.50
22 Devin Booker 1.50 4.00
23 Luka Doncic 4.00 10.00
24 Cole Anthony .75 2.00
25 Trae Young 1.50 4.00
26 Jerami Grant .60 1.50
27 LaMelo Ball 1.50 4.00
28 De'Aaron Fox 1.00 2.50
29 Julius Randle .75 2.00
30 Shai Gilgeous-Alexander 3.00 8.00

2021-22 Hoops Class of 2021

COMMON CARD .40 1.00
SEMISTARS .50 1.25
UNLISTED STARS .60 1.50
*WINTER: .4X TO 1X BASIC
*HOLO: .75X TO 2X BASIC
*WINTER HOLO: .75X TO 2X BASIC
1 Cade Cunningham 4.00 10.00
2 Evan Mobley 2.50 6.00
3 Jalen Suggs 1.50 4.00
4 Jonathan Kuminga 2.00 5.00
5 Davion Mitchell .60 1.50
6 James Bouknight .50 1.25
7 Chris Duarte .50 1.25
8 Corey Kispert .75 2.00
9 Trey Murphy III 2.00 5.00
10 Kai Jones .50 1.25
11 Keon Johnson .60 1.50
12 Usman Garuba .50 1.25
13 Quentin Grimes 1.25 3.00
14 Jalen Green 3.00 8.00
15 Scottie Barnes 2.00 5.00
16 Josh Giddey 2.00 5.00
17 Franz Wagner 2.00 5.00
18 Ziaire Williams .75 2.00
19 Joshua Primo .50 1.25
20 Moses Moody 1.25 3.00
21 Alperen Sengun 2.00 5.00
22 Tre Mann 1.00 2.50
23 Jalen Johnson 2.00 5.00
24 Isaiah Jackson .60 1.50
25 Josh Christopher .50 1.25

2021-22 Hoops Frequent Flyers

COMMON CARD .25 .60
SEMISTARS .30 .75
UNLISTED STARS .40 1.00
*WINTER: .4X TO 1X BASIC
*HOLO: .75X TO 2X BASIC
*WINTER HOLO: .75X TO 2X BASIC
*GREEN ICE: 1X TO 2.5X BASIC
1 Zion Williamson 1.00 2.50
2 Giannis Antetokounmpo 2.00 5.00
3 Rudy Gobert .50 1.25
4 Bam Adebayo .60 1.50
5 Ben Simmons .40 1.00
6 Michael Porter Jr. .50 1.25
7 Anthony Edwards 2.00 5.00
8 Kawhi Leonard 1.00 2.50
9 Jayson Tatum 1.50 4.00
10 Anthony Davis 1.00 2.50
11 Zach LaVine .60 1.50
12 Derrick Jones Jr. .25 .60
13 LeBron James 3.00 8.00
14 Ja Morant 1.25 3.00
15 Kevin Durant 1.25 3.00

2021-22 Hoops Great SIGnificance

COMMON CARD 4.00 10.00
SEMISTARS 5.00 12.00
UNLISTED STARS 6.00 15.00
EXCHANGE DEADLINE 07/07/2023
1 Will Perdue 5.00 12.00
2 Kurt Thomas 5.00 12.00
3 Theo Ratliff 5.00 12.00
4 Herb Williams 4.00 10.00
5 Walter Davis 5.00 12.00
6 Darrell Griffith 6.00 15.00
7 Tree Rollins 5.00 12.00
8 Bryon Russell 4.00 10.00
9 Kiki Vandeweghe 5.00 12.00
10 Kenny Anderson 6.00 15.00
11 Felipe Lopez 5.00 12.00
12 Rashard Lewis 6.00 15.00
13 Mychal Thompson 5.00 12.00
14 Scott Skiles 5.00 12.00
15 Fred Hoiberg 4.00 10.00
16 Doug Christie 5.00 12.00
17 Stacey Augmon 5.00 12.00
18 Sean Elliott 6.00 15.00
19 Mel Davis 5.00 12.00
20 Aaron McKie 4.00 10.00
21 Ricky Davis 5.00 12.00
22 Tracy Murray 4.00 10.00
23 Corey Maggette 5.00 12.00
24 Nick Anderson 5.00 12.00
25 Brad Davis 4.00 10.00
26 Marques Johnson 5.00 12.00
27 Antonio McDyess 5.00 12.00
28 Terrell Brandon 5.00 12.00
29 Doug Collins 5.00 12.00
30 Joe Smith 5.00 12.00
31 Walt Williams 5.00 12.00
34 Allen Iverson 75.00 200.00
36 Oscar Robertson 40.00 100.00
38 Larry Bird 100.00 250.00
40 Kareem Abdul-Jabbar 100.00 250.00
42 Mario Chalmers 5.00 12.00
43 Kent Benson 4.00 10.00
44 Elmore Smith 6.00 15.00
45 Alvin Robertson 5.00 12.00
46 Josh Howard 5.00 12.00
47 Harold Miner 6.00 15.00
48 Andrea Bargnani 4.00 10.00
49 Carlos Boozer 5.00 12.00
50 Mark Eaton 6.00 15.00
51 Cade Cunningham 200.00 500.00
52 James Bouknight 5.00 12.00
53 Keon Johnson 6.00 15.00
54 Jeremiah Robinson-Earl 6.00 15.00
55 Jason Preston 20.00 50.00
56 Jalen Suggs 125.00 300.00
57 Corey Kispert 20.00 50.00
58 Quentin Grimes 15.00 40.00
59 Isaiah Livers 10.00 25.00
60 Kessler Edwards 15.00 40.00
61 Jalen Green 200.00 500.00
62 Joshua Primo 5.00 12.00
63 Isaiah Jackson 12.00 30.00
64 Miles McBride 25.00 60.00
65 Herbert Jones 40.00 100.00
66 Scottie Barnes 150.00 400.00
67 Moses Moody 50.00 120.00
68 Josh Christopher 25.00 60.00
69 Jared Butler 6.00 15.00
70 Joe Wieskamp 20.00 50.00
71 Evan Mobley 200.00 500.00
72 Chris Duarte 40.00 100.00
73 Usman Garuba 5.00 12.00
74 Ayo Dosunmu 150.00 400.00
75 JT Thor 12.00 30.00
76 Marcus Zegarowski 5.00 12.00
77 Luka Garza 25.00 60.00
78 Jaden Springer 6.00 15.00
79 Tre Mann 25.00 60.00
80 Franz Wagner 125.00 300.00
81 David Johnson 5.00 12.00
82 Charles Bassey 6.00 15.00
83 Day'Ron Sharpe 12.00 30.00
84 Kai Jones 12.00 30.00
85 Davion Mitchell 40.00 100.00
86 Neemias Queta 6.00 15.00
87 Brandon Boston Jr. 40.00 100.00
88 Cameron Thomas 40.00 100.00
89 Trey Murphy III 20.00 50.00
90 Jonathan Kuminga 200.00 500.00
91 Sandro Mamukelashvili 12.00 30.00
92 Scottie Lewis 5.00 12.00
93 Santi Aldama 8.00 20.00
94 Jalen Johnson 20.00 50.00
95 Ziaire Williams 40.00 100.00
96 Aaron Wiggins 8.00 20.00
97 Greg Brown III 15.00 40.00
98 Bones Hyland 50.00 120.00
99 Alperen Sengun 60.00 150.00
100 Josh Giddey 150.00 400.00

2021-22 Hoops High Court

COMMON CARD .40 1.00
SEMISTARS .50 1.25
UNLISTED STARS .60 1.50
*HOLO: .75X TO 2X BASIC
*HYPER RED/99: 1.5X TO 4X BASIC
*HOLO ARTIST PROOF/25: 3X TO 8X BASIC
*HYPER GREEN/25: 3X TO 8X BASIC
1 Stephen Curry 4.00 10.00
2 Kawhi Leonard 1.50 4.00
3 Jayson Tatum 2.50 6.00
4 Trae Young 1.50 4.00
5 Anthony Davis 1.50 4.00
6 Joel Embiid 1.50 4.00
7 Giannis Antetokounmpo 3.00 8.00
8 Nikola Jokic 3.00 8.00
9 Kevin Durant 2.00 5.00
10 Zion Williamson 1.50 4.00
11 James Harden 1.25 3.00
12 Ja Morant 2.00 5.00
13 Donovan Mitchell 1.25 3.00
14 Luka Doncic 4.00 10.00
15 LeBron James 5.00 12.00

2021-22 Hoops High Voltage

COMMON CARD .75 2.00
SEMISTARS 1.00 2.50
UNLISTED STARS 1.25 3.00
1 LeBron James 10.00 25.00
2 Bradley Beal 1.50 4.00
3 Kyrie Irving 2.50 6.00
4 Devin Booker 3.00 8.00
5 Stephen Curry 8.00 20.00
6 Nikola Jokic 6.00 15.00
7 Kawhi Leonard 3.00 8.00
8 Jayson Tatum 5.00 12.00
9 CJ McCollum 1.00 2.50
10 Trae Young 3.00 8.00
11 Anthony Davis 3.00 8.00
12 Russell Westbrook 2.00 5.00
13 Paul George 2.00 5.00
14 Joel Embiid 3.00 8.00
15 Karl-Anthony Towns 2.00 5.00
16 Zion Williamson 3.00 8.00
17 Kevin Durant 4.00 10.00
18 Giannis Antetokounmpo 6.00 15.00
19 Zach LaVine 2.00 5.00
20 James Harden 2.50 6.00
21 LaMelo Ball 3.00 8.00
22 Ja Morant 4.00 10.00
23 Donovan Mitchell 2.50 6.00
24 De'Aaron Fox 2.00 5.00
25 Luka Doncic 8.00 20.00

2021-22 Hoops Highlights

COMMON CARD .50 1.25
SEMISTARS .60 1.50
UNLISTED STARS .75 2.00
1 Stephen Curry 5.00 12.00
2 Russell Westbrook 1.25 3.00
3 Enes Freedom .60 1.50
4 T.J. McConnell .60 1.50
5 Clint Capela .75 2.00

2021-22 Hoops HIPnotized

COMMON CARD .60 1.50
SEMISTARS .75 2.00
UNLISTED STARS 1.00 2.50
1 Giannis Antetokounmpo 5.00 12.00
2 LaMelo Ball 2.50 6.00
3 Paul George 1.50 4.00
4 Zion Williamson 2.50 6.00
5 Stephen Curry 6.00 15.00
6 James Harden 2.00 5.00
7 Luka Doncic 6.00 15.00
8 Russell Westbrook 1.50 4.00
9 Kevin Durant 3.00 8.00
10 LeBron James 8.00 20.00
11 Trae Young 2.50 6.00
12 Kyrie Irving 2.50 6.00
13 Ja Morant 3.00 8.00
14 Donovan Mitchell 2.00 5.00
15 Kawhi Leonard 2.50 6.00
16 Zach LaVine 1.50 4.00
17 Anthony Davis 2.50 6.00
18 Joel Embiid 2.50 6.00
19 Nikola Jokic 5.00 12.00
20 Jayson Tatum 4.00 10.00

2021-22 Hoops Hoopla

*HOLO: .75X TO 2X BASIC
*HYPER RED/99: 1.5X TO 4X BASIC
*HOLO ARTIST PROOF/25: 5X TO 12X BASIC
*HYPER GREEN/25: 5X TO 12X BASIC
1 Kawhi Leonard 1.00 2.50
2 LeBron James 3.00 8.00
3 Anthony Davis 1.00 2.50
4 Kevin Durant 1.25 3.00
5 Luka Doncic 2.50 6.00
6 Giannis Antetokounmpo 2.00 5.00
7 Joel Embiid 1.00 2.50
8 Stephen Curry 2.50 6.00
9 Nikola Jokic 2.00 5.00
10 James Harden .75 2.00

2021-22 Hoops Hoops Ink

COMMON CARD 4.00 10.00
SEMISTARS 5.00 12.00
UNLISTED STARS 6.00 15.00
EXCHANGE DEADLINE 07/07/2023
*HYPER GOLD: .4X TO 1X BASIC
1 Jason Kidd 15.00 40.00
2 Louie Dampier 6.00 15.00
3 Jamal Murray 25.00 60.00
4 Andrea Bargnani 4.00 10.00
5 Jrue Holiday 8.00 20.00
6 Kent Benson 4.00 10.00
7 Walt Frazier 12.00 30.00
8 Kevin Johnson 6.00 15.00
9 Anthony Davis 40.00 100.00
10 Elvin Hayes 8.00 20.00
11 Trae Young 75.00 200.00
12 Wang Zhi-zhi 20.00 50.00
13 Lonzo Ball 20.00 50.00
15 Buddy Hield 5.00 12.00
17 Eric Gordon 5.00 12.00
19 Larry Bird 75.00 200.00
20 Bill Walton 10.00 25.00
21 Clyde Drexler 20.00 50.00
22 Darius Bazley 4.00 10.00
23 Khris Middleton 6.00 15.00
24 Harold Miner 6.00 15.00
25 Al Horford 6.00 15.00
26 Tom Gugliotta 5.00 12.00
29 Ja Morant 150.00 400.00
30 Clint Capela 6.00 15.00
31 Pat Riley 12.00 30.00
32 Glen Rice 6.00 15.00
33 De'Andre Hunter 6.00 15.00
34 Alvin Robertson 5.00 12.00
35 Isiah Thomas 20.00 50.00
36 Slick Watts 6.00 15.00
37 Chris Mullin 8.00 20.00
38 Rick Fox 6.00 15.00
39 Kareem Abdul-Jabbar 75.00 200.00
40 David Lee 5.00 12.00
42 Lamar Odom 6.00 15.00
44 Elmore Smith 6.00 15.00
46 Reggie Theus 5.00 12.00
47 Jason Williams 30.00 80.00
48 Brandon Clarke 6.00 15.00
50 Joakim Noah 5.00 12.00

2021-22 Hoops Hoops Ink Red

*RED: .75X TO 2X BASIC
STATED PRINT RUN 25 COPIES PER
EXCHANGE DEADLINE 07/07/2023
45 Cam Reddish 12.00 30.00

2021-22 Hoops Hot Signatures

COMMON CARD 4.00 10.00
SEMISTARS 5.00 12.00
UNLISTED STARS 6.00 15.00
EXCHANGE DEADLINE 07/07/2023
*HYPER GOLD: .4X TO 1X BASIC
1 Shawn Kemp 30.00 80.00
2 Andre Drummond 5.00 12.00
3 Mark Eaton 6.00 15.00
4 Danilo Gallinari 5.00 12.00
5 JJ Redick 6.00 15.00
6 Luka Doncic 400.00 800.00
7 Calvin Murphy 6.00 15.00
8 Anthony Edwards 125.00 300.00
9 Juwan Howard 5.00 12.00
10 Vince Carter 40.00 100.00
11 B.J. Armstrong 6.00 15.00
12 Julius Randle 8.00 20.00
13 Mario Chalmers 5.00 12.00
14 Duncan Robinson 12.00 30.00
15 Michael Porter Jr. 8.00 20.00
16 Zion Williamson 200.00 500.00
17 Avery Bradley 4.00 10.00
18 Magic Johnson 75.00 200.00
19 Mark Jackson 5.00 12.00
20 CJ McCollum 5.00 12.00
21 Doug McDermott 5.00 12.00
22 Jarrett Culver 4.00 10.00
23 Thanasis Antetokounmpo 6.00 15.00
24 Richard Hamilton 8.00 20.00
25 Myles Turner 6.00 15.00
26 Allen Iverson 75.00 200.00
27 Chauncey Billups 8.00 20.00
28 David Robinson 25.00 60.00
29 Carlos Boozer 5.00 12.00
30 Tony Parker 15.00 40.00
31 Josh Howard 5.00 12.00
32 Ben Wallace 20.00 50.00
33 Tomas Satoransky 4.00 10.00
34 Bernard King 8.00 20.00
35 Ralph Sampson 6.00 15.00
36 John Stockton 30.00 80.00
37 Danny Manning 5.00 12.00
38 Anfernee Hardaway 40.00 100.00
39 George McGinnis 6.00 15.00
40 Steve Kerr 15.00 40.00
41 Benoit Benjamin 4.00 10.00
42 Artis Gilmore 8.00 20.00
43 Rod Strickland 5.00 12.00
45 T.J. Warren 4.00 10.00
46 Oscar Robertson 30.00 80.00
47 Ivica Zubac 6.00 15.00
48 Nikola Jokic 75.00 200.00
50 James Worthy 10.00 25.00

2021-22 Hoops Hot Signatures Rookies

COMMON CARD 4.00 10.00
SEMISTARS 5.00 12.00
UNLISTED STARS 6.00 15.00
EXCHANGE DEADLINE 07/07/2023
*GREEN: .5X TO 1.2X BASIC
*HYPER GOLD: .5X TO 1.2X BASIC
*RED/25: .75X TO 2X BASIC
1 Cade Cunningham 75.00 200.00
2 James Bouknight 5.00 12.00
3 Keon Johnson 6.00 15.00
4 Jeremiah Robinson-Earl 6.00 15.00
5 Jason Preston 5.00 12.00
6 Jalen Suggs 15.00 40.00
7 Corey Kispert 8.00 20.00
8 Quentin Grimes 12.00 30.00
9 Isaiah Livers 6.00 15.00
10 Kessler Edwards 6.00 15.00
11 Jalen Green 40.00 100.00
12 Joshua Primo 5.00 12.00
13 Isaiah Jackson 6.00 15.00
14 Miles McBride 10.00 25.00
15 Herbert Jones 8.00 20.00
16 Scottie Barnes 20.00 50.00
17 Moses Moody 12.00 30.00
18 Josh Christopher 5.00 12.00
19 Jared Butler 6.00 15.00
20 Joe Wieskamp 5.00 12.00
21 Evan Mobley 40.00 100.00
22 Chris Duarte 5.00 12.00
24 Ayo Dosunmu 12.00 30.00
25 JT Thor 6.00 15.00
26 Marcus Zegarowski 5.00 12.00
27 Luka Garza 6.00 15.00
28 Jaden Springer 6.00 15.00
29 Tre Mann 10.00 25.00
30 Franz Wagner 20.00 50.00
31 David Johnson 5.00 12.00
32 Charles Bassey 6.00 15.00
33 Day'Ron Sharpe 6.00 15.00
34 Kai Jones 5.00 12.00
35 Davion Mitchell 6.00 15.00
36 Neemias Queta 6.00 15.00
37 Brandon Boston Jr. 6.00 15.00
38 Cameron Thomas 12.00 30.00
39 Trey Murphy III 20.00 50.00
40 Jonathan Kuminga 20.00 50.00
41 Sandro Mamukelashvili 8.00 20.00
42 Scottie Lewis 5.00 12.00
43 Santi Aldama 8.00 20.00
44 Jalen Johnson 20.00 50.00
45 Ziaire Williams 8.00 20.00
46 Aaron Wiggins 8.00 20.00
47 Greg Brown III 5.00 12.00
48 Bones Hyland 8.00 20.00
49 Alperen Sengun 20.00 50.00
50 Josh Giddey 20.00 50.00

2021-22 Hoops Hot Signatures Rookies Red

*RED: .75X TO 2X BASIC
STATED PRINT RUN 25 COPIES PER
EXCHANGE DEADLINE 07/07/2023
40 Jonathan Kuminga 40.00 100.00
50 Josh Giddey 40.00 100.00

2021-22 Hoops JAM-tastic

1 Giannis Antetokounmpo 5.00 12.00
2 Bam Adebayo 1.50 4.00
3 Zion Williamson 2.50 6.00
4 John Collins 1.00 2.50
5 Ben Simmons 1.00 2.50
6 James Wiseman .75 2.00
7 Anthony Edwards 5.00 12.00
8 Kawhi Leonard 2.50 6.00
9 Jayson Tatum 4.00 10.00
10 Zach LaVine 1.50 4.00
11 Jason Richardson 1.00 2.50
12 Shawn Kemp 1.50 4.00
13 Dominique Wilkins 1.50 4.00
14 LeBron James 8.00 20.00
15 Vince Carter 2.00 5.00

2021-22 Hoops Legends of the Ball
1 Kareem Abdul-Jabbar 2.50 6.00
2 Bill Russell 2.50 6.00
3 Larry Bird 2.50 6.00
4 Bob Cousy 1.25 3.00
5 Patrick Ewing 1.25 3.00
6 Oscar Robertson 1.50 4.00
7 John Havlicek 1.50 4.00
8 George Mikan 1.50 4.00
9 Pete Maravich 2.00 5.00
10 Wilt Chamberlain 2.50 6.00
11 Magic Johnson 2.50 6.00
12 Bob Pettit 1.00 2.50
13 Charles Barkley 2.00 5.00
14 Jerry West 1.50 4.00
15 Hakeem Olajuwon 1.50 4.00

2021-22 Hoops Lights Camera Action
COMMON CARD .25 .60
SEMISTARS .30 .75
UNLISTED STARS .40 1.00
*WINTER: .4X TO 1X BASIC
*HOLO: .75X TO 2X BASIC
*WINTER HOLO: .75X TO 2X BASIC
*GREEN ICE: 1X TO 2.5X BASIC
1 Kyrie Irving .75 2.00
2 Trae Young 1.00 2.50
3 Donovan Mitchell .75 2.00
4 Bradley Beal .50 1.25
5 Karl-Anthony Towns .60 1.50
6 Ja Morant 1.25 3.00
7 Zach LaVine .60 1.50
8 Kawhi Leonard 1.00 2.50
9 Joel Embiid 1.00 2.50
10 Anthony Davis 1.00 2.50
11 Jayson Tatum 1.50 4.00
12 Jimmy Butler .60 1.50
13 Nikola Jokic 2.00 5.00
14 LaMelo Ball 1.00 2.50
15 Giannis Antetokounmpo 2.00 5.00
16 Zion Williamson 1.00 2.50
17 Collin Sexton .40 1.00
18 Paul George .60 1.50
19 James Harden .75 2.00
20 Stephen Curry 2.50 6.00
21 Pascal Siakam .60 1.50
22 Russell Westbrook .60 1.50
23 CJ McCollum .30 .75
24 Luka Doncic 2.50 6.00
25 Domantas Sabonis .50 1.25
26 John Wall .50 1.25
27 Devin Booker 1.00 2.50
28 LeBron James 3.00 8.00
29 Kevin Durant 1.25 3.00
30 De'Aaron Fox .60 1.50

2021-22 Hoops Now Playing
*HOLO: .75X TO 2X BASIC
1 Cade Cunningham 4.00 10.00
2 Jalen Green 3.00 8.00
3 Evan Mobley 2.50 6.00
4 Scottie Barnes 2.00 5.00
5 Jalen Suggs 1.50 4.00
6 Josh Giddey 2.00 5.00
7 Jonathan Kuminga 2.00 5.00
8 Franz Wagner 2.00 5.00
9 Davion Mitchell .60 1.50
10 Ziaire Williams .75 2.00
11 James Bouknight .50 1.25
12 Joshua Primo .50 1.25
13 Chris Duarte .50 1.25
14 Moses Moody 1.25 3.00
15 Corey Kispert .75 2.00
16 Alperen Sengun 2.00 5.00
17 Trey Murphy III 2.00 5.00
18 Tre Mann 1.00 2.50
19 Kai Jones .50 1.25
20 Jalen Johnson 2.00 5.00
21 Keon Johnson .60 1.50
22 Isaiah Jackson .60 1.50
23 Usman Garuba .50 1.25

2021-22 Hoops Prime Twine
COMMON CARD .40 1.00
SEMISTARS .50 1.25
UNLISTED STARS .60 1.50
*HOLO: .75X TO 2X BASIC
*HYPER RED/99: 1.5X TO 4X BASIC
*ARTIST PROOF/25: 4X TO 10X BASIC
*HYPER GREEN/25: 4X TO 10X BASIC
1 Kevin Durant 1.25 3.00
2 Stephen Curry 2.50 6.00
3 James Harden .75 2.00
4 Jayson Tatum 1.50 4.00
5 Donovan Mitchell .75 2.00
6 Anthony Davis 1.00 2.50
7 Paul George .60 1.50
8 LeBron James 3.00 8.00
9 Karl-Anthony Towns .60 1.50
10 Kyrie Irving .75 2.00
11 Giannis Antetokounmpo 2.00 5.00
12 Nikola Jokic 2.00 5.00
13 LaMelo Ball 1.00 2.50
14 CJ McCollum .30 .75
15 De'Aaron Fox .60 1.50
16 Russell Westbrook .60 1.50
17 Joel Embiid 1.00 2.50
18 Bradley Beal .50 1.25
19 Zion Williamson 1.00 2.50
20 Devin Booker 1.00 2.50
21 Zach LaVine .60 1.50
22 Kawhi Leonard 1.00 2.50
23 Ja Morant 1.25 3.00
24 Trae Young 1.00 2.50
25 Luka Doncic 2.50 6.00

2021-22 Hoops Pure Players
COMMON CARD .30 .75
SEMISTARS .40 1.00
UNLISTED STARS .50 1.25
*WINTER: .4X TO 1X BASIC
*HOLO: .6X TO 1.5X BASIC
*WINTER HOLO: .6X TO 1.5X BASIC
*GREEN ICE: .75X TO 2X BASIC
1 LaMelo Ball 1.25 3.00
2 Zion Williamson 1.25 3.00
3 Donovan Mitchell 1.00 2.50
4 LeBron James 4.00 10.00
5 Giannis Antetokounmpo 2.50 6.00
6 Trae Young 1.25 3.00
7 Ja Morant 1.50 4.00
8 Stephen Curry 3.00 8.00
9 Luka Doncic 3.00 8.00
10 Kevin Durant 1.50 4.00

2021-22 Hoops Rise N Shine Memorabilia
COMMON CARD 1.25 3.00
SEMISTARS 1.50 4.00
UNLISTED STARS 2.00 5.00
*WINTER: .4X TO 1X BASIC
*PRIME/25: 1.5X TO 4X BASIC
1 Ziaire Williams 2.50 6.00
2 James Bouknight 1.50 4.00
3 Joshua Primo 1.50 4.00
4 Chris Duarte 1.50 4.00
5 Moses Moody 4.00 10.00
6 Corey Kispert 2.50 6.00
7 Alperen Sengun 6.00 15.00
8 Trey Murphy III 6.00 15.00
9 Tre Mann 3.00 8.00
10 Kai Jones 1.50 4.00
11 Jalen Johnson 6.00 15.00
12 Keon Johnson 2.00 5.00
13 Isaiah Jackson 2.00 5.00
14 Usman Garuba 1.50 4.00
15 Josh Christopher 1.50 4.00
16 Quentin Grimes 4.00 10.00
17 Cade Cunningham 12.00 30.00
18 Jalen Green 10.00 25.00
19 Evan Mobley 8.00 20.00
20 Scottie Barnes 6.00 15.00
21 Jalen Suggs 5.00 12.00
22 Josh Giddey 6.00 15.00
23 Jonathan Kuminga 6.00 15.00
24 Franz Wagner 6.00 15.00
25 Davion Mitchell 2.00 5.00
26 Bones Hyland 2.50 6.00
27 Cameron Thomas 4.00 10.00
28 Jaden Springer 2.00 5.00
29 Day'Ron Sharpe 2.00 5.00
30 Santi Aldama 2.50 6.00
31 Jeremiah Robinson-Earl 2.00 5.00
32 Miles McBride 3.00 8.00
33 Ayo Dosunmu 4.00 10.00
34 Jared Butler 2.00 5.00
35 Isaiah Livers 2.00 5.00

2021-22 Hoops Rookie Ink
COMMON CARD 4.00 10.00
SEMISTARS 5.00 12.00
UNLISTED STARS 6.00 15.00
EXCHANGE DEADLINE 07/07/2023
*GREEN: .5X TO 1.2X BASIC
*HYPER GOLD: .5X TO 1.2X BASIC
1 Cade Cunningham 75.00 200.00
2 Josh Giddey 20.00 50.00
3 James Bouknight 5.00 12.00
4 Alperen Sengun 20.00 50.00
5 Keon Johnson 6.00 15.00
6 Bones Hyland 8.00 20.00
7 Jeremiah Robinson-Earl 6.00 15.00
8 Greg Brown III 5.00 12.00
9 Jason Preston 5.00 12.00
10 Aaron Wiggins 8.00 20.00
11 Jalen Suggs 15.00 40.00
12 Ziaire Williams 8.00 20.00
13 Corey Kispert 8.00 20.00
14 Jalen Johnson 20.00 50.00
15 Quentin Grimes 12.00 30.00
16 Santi Aldama 8.00 20.00
17 Isaiah Livers 6.00 15.00
18 Scottie Lewis 5.00 12.00
19 Kessler Edwards 6.00 15.00
20 Sandro Mamukelashvili 8.00 20.00
21 Jalen Green 40.00 100.00
22 Jonathan Kuminga 20.00 50.00
23 Joshua Primo 5.00 12.00
24 Trey Murphy III 20.00 50.00
25 Isaiah Jackson 6.00 15.00
26 Cameron Thomas 12.00 30.00
27 Miles McBride 10.00 25.00
28 Brandon Boston Jr. 6.00 15.00
29 Herbert Jones 8.00 20.00
30 Neemias Queta 6.00 15.00
31 Scottie Barnes 20.00 50.00
32 Davion Mitchell 6.00 15.00
33 Moses Moody 12.00 30.00
34 Kai Jones 5.00 12.00
35 Josh Christopher 5.00 12.00
36 Day'Ron Sharpe 5.00 12.00
37 Jared Butler 6.00 15.00
38 Charles Bassey 6.00 15.00
39 Joe Wieskamp 5.00 12.00
40 David Johnson 5.00 12.00
41 Evan Mobley 40.00 100.00
42 Franz Wagner 20.00 50.00
43 Chris Duarte 5.00 12.00
44 Tre Mann 10.00 25.00
46 Jaden Springer 6.00 15.00
47 Ayo Dosunmu 12.00 30.00
48 Luka Garza 6.00 15.00
49 JT Thor 6.00 15.00
50 Marcus Zegarowski 5.00 12.00

2021-22 Hoops Rookie Ink Red
*RED: .75X TO 2X BASIC
STATED PRINT RUN 25 COPIES PER
EXCHANGE DEADLINE 07/07/2023

2021-22 Hoops Rookie Remembrance
*WINTER: .4X TO 1X BASIC
*PRIME/25: 1.5X TO 4X BASIC
1 Zion Williamson 6.00 15.00
2 Jayson Tatum 10.00 25.00
3 Anthony Edwards 12.00 30.00
4 Tyrese Haliburton 5.00 12.00
5 Lonzo Ball 2.50 6.00
6 Donovan Mitchell 5.00 12.00
7 Luka Doncic 15.00 40.00
8 Pascal Siakam 4.00 10.00
9 Trae Young 6.00 15.00
10 Ja Morant 8.00 20.00
11 RJ Barrett 4.00 10.00
12 Collin Sexton 2.50 6.00
13 Bam Adebayo 4.00 10.00
14 LaMelo Ball 6.00 15.00
15 Shai Gilgeous-Alexander 12.00 30.00

2021-22 Hoops Rookie Special
*HOLO: 1.25X TO 3X BASIC
1 Cade Cunningham 4.00 10.00
2 Jalen Green 3.00 8.00

2021-22 Hoops Rookie Sweaters
1 Kai Jones 1.25 3.00
2 Jalen Johnson 5.00 12.00
3 Keon Johnson 1.50 4.00
4 Isaiah Jackson 1.50 4.00
5 Usman Garuba 1.25 3.00
6 Josh Christopher 1.25 3.00
7 Quentin Grimes 3.00 8.00
8 Cade Cunningham 10.00 25.00
9 Jalen Green 8.00 20.00
10 Evan Mobley 6.00 15.00
11 Scottie Barnes 5.00 12.00
12 Jalen Suggs 4.00 10.00
13 Josh Giddey 5.00 12.00
14 Jonathan Kuminga 5.00 12.00
15 Franz Wagner 5.00 12.00
16 Davion Mitchell 1.50 4.00
17 Bones Hyland 2.00 5.00
18 Cameron Thomas 3.00 8.00
19 Jaden Springer 1.50 4.00
20 Day'Ron Sharpe 1.50 4.00
21 Santi Aldama 2.00 5.00
22 Jeremiah Robinson-Earl 1.50 4.00
23 Miles McBride 2.50 6.00
24 Ayo Dosunmu 3.00 8.00
25 Ziaire Williams 2.00 5.00
26 James Bouknight 1.25 3.00
27 Joshua Primo 1.25 3.00
28 Chris Duarte 1.25 3.00
29 Moses Moody 3.00 8.00
30 Corey Kispert 2.00 5.00
31 Alperen Sengun 5.00 12.00
32 Trey Murphy III 5.00 12.00
33 Tre Mann 2.50 6.00

2021-22 Hoops Skyview
*WINTER: .4X TO 1X BASIC
*HOLO: .75X TO 2X BASIC
*WINTER HOLO: .75X TO 2X BASIC
*GREEN ICE: 1.25X TO 3X BASIC
1 CJ McCollum .30 .75
2 Zach LaVine .60 1.50
3 LeBron James 3.00 8.00
4 Anthony Davis 1.00 2.50
5 LaMelo Ball 1.00 2.50
6 Kyrie Irving .75 2.00
7 Paul George .60 1.50
8 Donovan Mitchell .75 2.00
9 Stephen Curry 2.50 6.00
10 Karl-Anthony Towns .60 1.50
11 Luka Doncic 2.50 6.00
12 Kawhi Leonard 1.00 2.50
13 Kevin Durant 1.25 3.00
14 Jayson Tatum 1.50 4.00
15 Giannis Antetokounmpo 2.00 5.00
16 Trae Young 1.00 2.50
17 James Harden .75 2.00
18 Bradley Beal .50 1.25
19 Russell Westbrook .60 1.50
20 Ja Morant 1.25 3.00
21 Devin Booker 1.00 2.50
22 Joel Embiid 1.00 2.50
23 De'Aaron Fox .60 1.50
24 Nikola Jokic 2.00 5.00
25 Zion Williamson 1.00 2.50

2021-22 Hoops We Got Next
*HOLO: .75X TO 2X BASIC
1 Cade Cunningham 4.00 10.00
2 Jalen Green 3.00 8.00
3 Evan Mobley 2.50 6.00
4 Scottie Barnes 2.00 5.00
5 Jalen Suggs 1.50 4.00
6 Josh Giddey 2.00 5.00
7 Jonathan Kuminga 2.00 5.00
8 Franz Wagner 2.00 5.00
9 Davion Mitchell .60 1.50
10 Ziaire Williams .75 2.00
11 James Bouknight .50 1.25
12 Joshua Primo .50 1.25
13 Chris Duarte .50 1.25
14 Moses Moody 1.25 3.00
15 Corey Kispert .75 2.00
16 Alperen Sengun 2.00 5.00
17 Trey Murphy III 2.00 5.00
18 Tre Mann 1.00 2.50
19 Kai Jones .50 1.25
20 Jalen Johnson 2.00 5.00
21 Keon Johnson .60 1.50
22 Isaiah Jackson .60 1.50
23 Usman Garuba .50 1.25
24 Josh Christopher .50 1.25
25 Quentin Grimes 1.25 3.00

2021-22 Hoops Zero Gravity
*HOLO: .75X TO 2X BASIC
*HYPER RED/99: 4X TO 10X BASIC
*HOLO ARTIST PRF/25: 8X TO 20X BASIC
*HYPER GREEN: 8X TO 20X BASIC
1 Kevin Durant 1.25 3.00
2 Ben Simmons .40 1.00
3 Dominique Wilkins .60 1.50
4 Anthony Edwards 2.00 5.00
5 Shaquille O'Neal 1.25 3.00
6 Jayson Tatum 1.50 4.00
7 Zach LaVine .60 1.50
8 Zion Williamson 1.00 2.50
9 LeBron James 3.00 8.00
10 Rudy Gobert .50 1.25
11 Vince Carter .75 2.00
12 Michael Porter Jr. .50 1.25
13 Tracy McGrady .60 1.50
14 Kawhi Leonard 1.00 2.50
15 Harold Miner .40 1.00
16 Anthony Davis 1.00 2.50
17 Derrick Jones Jr. .25 .60
18 Giannis Antetokounmpo 2.00 5.00
19 Ja Morant 1.25 3.00
20 Bam Adebayo .60 1.50

2022-23 Hoops
COMPLETE SET (300)
*WINTER: .5X TO 1.2X BASIC
*YELLOW: .75X TO 2X BASIC
*BLUE: 1X TO 2.5X BASIC
*HYPER BLUE: 1X TO 2.5X BASIC
*PURPLE: 1X TO 2.5X BASIC
*PURPLE WINTER: 1.2X TO 3X BASIC
*RED BACKS: 1.5X TO 4X BASIC
*TEAL EXPLOSION: 1.5X TO 4X BASIC
*PRM BOX SET/199: 2X TO 5X BASIC
*SILVER/199: 2X TO 5X BASIC
*IMPULSE: 2.5X TO 6X BASIC
*GREEN/99: 2.5X TO 6X BASIC
*HYPER RED/99: 2.5X TO 6X BASIC
*GRAVITY/75: 2.5X TO 6X BASIC
1 Jayson Tatum 1.25 3.00
2 Jaylen Brown .60 1.50
3 Robert Williams III .25 .60
4 Marcus Smart .40 1.00
5 Al Horford .30 .75
6 Derrick White .30 .75
7 Payton Pritchard .30 .75
8 Grant Williams .25 .60
9 Kyrie Irving .60 1.50
10 Kevin Durant 1.00 2.50
11 Ben Simmons .30 .75
12 Seth Curry .25 .60
13 Blake Griffin .30 .75
14 Cameron Thomas .50 1.25
15 Joe Harris .25 .60
16 Kessler Edwards .25 .60
17 Day'Ron Sharpe .25 .60
18 RJ Barrett .50 1.25
19 Evan Fournier .25 .60
20 Julius Randle .40 1.00
21 Obi Toppin .30 .75
22 Kemba Walker .30 .75
23 Quentin Grimes .25 .60
24 Derrick Rose .60 1.50
25 Cam Reddish .25 .60
26 Alec Burks .25 .60
27 Miles McBride .30 .75
28 Immanuel Quickley .30 .75
29 James Harden .60 1.50
30 Joel Embiid .50 1.25
31 Tyrese Maxey .60 1.50
32 Tobias Harris .25 .60
33 Matisse Thybulle .25 .60
34 Danny Green .25 .60
35 DeAndre Jordan .25 .60
36 OG Anunoby .40 1.00
37 Scottie Barnes .50 1.25
38 Fred VanVleet .40 1.00
39 Gary Trent Jr. .30 .75
40 Pascal Siakam .50 1.25
41 Precious Achiuwa .30 .75
42 Chris Boucher .25 .60
43 Dalano Banton .20 .50
44 Giannis Antetokounmpo 1.50 4.00
45 Khris Middleton .40 1.00
46 Jrue Holiday .40 1.00
47 Grayson Allen .30 .75
48 Bobby Portis .30 .75
49 Pat Connaughton .25 .60
50 George Hill .25 .60
51 Tyrese Haliburton .60 1.50
52 Buddy Hield .30 .75
53 Myles Turner .30 .75
54 Malcolm Brogdon .25 .60
55 Chris Duarte .25 .60
56 Aaron Nesmith .30 .75
57 Oshae Brissett .25 .60
58 Isaiah Jackson .30 .75
59 Cade Cunningham 1.00 2.50
60 Jerami Grant .40 1.00
61 Marvin Bagley III .25 .60
62 Saddiq Bey .25 .60
63 Isaiah Stewart .25 .60
64 Killian Hayes .20 .50
65 Isaiah Livers .25 .60
66 Darius Garland .50 1.25
67 Evan Mobley .75 2.00
68 Jarrett Allen .30 .75
69 Lauri Markkanen .50 1.25
70 Caris LeVert .25 .60
71 Isaac Okoro .25 .60
72 Kevin Love .30 .75
73 Collin Sexton .40 1.00
74 Zach LaVine .60 1.50
75 DeMar DeRozan .60 1.50
76 Lonzo Ball .30 .75
77 Nikola Vucevic .30 .75
78 Alex Caruso .30 .75
79 Ayo Dosunmu .40 1.00
80 Trae Young .75 2.00
81 John Collins .30 .75
82 De'Andre Hunter .30 .75
83 Kevin Huerter .30 .75
84 Bogdan Bogdanovic .30 .75
85 Clint Capela .30 .75
86 Jalen Johnson .40 1.00
87 Onyeka Okongwu .30 .75
88 Kai Jones .25 .60
89 Terry Rozier III .40 1.00
90 LaMelo Ball .75 2.00
91 Gordon Hayward .25 .60
92 PJ Washington Jr. .30 .75
93 Kelly Oubre Jr. .30 .75
94 Cody Martin .25 .60
95 James Bouknight .20 .50
96 Tyler Herro .50 1.25
97 Kyle Lowry .40 1.00
98 Duncan Robinson .30 .75
99 Jimmy Butler .60 1.50
100 Bam Adebayo .50 1.25
101 P.J. Tucker .25 .60
102 Max Strus .30 .75
103 Gabe Vincent .30 .75
104 Caleb Martin .30 .75
105 Cole Anthony .30 .75
106 Franz Wagner .75 2.00
107 Wendell Carter Jr. .30 .75
108 Gary Harris .25 .60
109 Jalen Suggs .40 1.00
110 Mo Bamba .25 .60
111 Terrence Ross .30 .75
112 Bradley Beal .40 1.00
113 Kyle Kuzma .40 1.00
114 Kentavious Caldwell-Pope .25 .60
115 Kristaps Porzingis .40 1.00
116 Corey Kispert .30 .75
117 Rui Hachimura .30 .75
118 Deni Avdija .30 .75
119 Luka Doncic 2.00 5.00
120 Dorian Finney-Smith .25 .60
121 Jalen Brunson .60 1.50
122 Spencer Dinwiddie .25 .60
123 Tim Hardaway Jr. .25 .60
124 Maxi Kleber .25 .60
125 Davis Bertans .20 .50
126 Jalen Green 1.00 2.50
127 Kevin Porter Jr. .25 .60
128 Christian Wood .20 .50
129 Jae'Sean Tate .20 .50
130 Eric Gordon .25 .60
131 Alperen Sengun .40 1.00
132 Josh Christopher .20 .50
133 Ja Morant 1.00 2.50
134 Desmond Bane .40 1.00
135 Dillon Brooks .30 .75
136 Jaren Jackson Jr. .50 1.25
137 De'Anthony Melton .25 .60
138 Ziaire Williams .25 .60
139 Brandon Clarke .25 .60
140 Santi Aldama .25 .60
141 Brandon Ingram .40 1.00
142 CJ McCollum .30 .75
143 Jonas Valanciunas .25 .60
144 Herbert Jones .30 .75
145 Devonte' Graham .25 .60
146 Jaxson Hayes .20 .50
147 Zion Williamson .75 2.00
148 Jose Alvarado .30 .75
149 Trey Murphy III .40 1.00
150 Dejounte Murray .40 1.00
151 Keldon Johnson .40 1.00
152 Devin Vassell .40 1.00
153 Lonnie Walker IV .25 .60
154 Joshua Primo .20 .50
155 Doug McDermott .20 .50
156 Joe Wieskamp .25 .60
157 De'Aaron Fox .60 1.50
158 Harrison Barnes .25 .60
159 Domantas Sabonis .40 1.00
160 Davion Mitchell .25 .60
161 Justin Holiday .20 .50
162 Malik Monk .30 .75
163 Mikal Bridges .40 1.00
164 Devin Booker .75 2.00
165 Chris Paul .60 1.50
166 Deandre Ayton .30 .75
167 Cameron Johnson .25 .60
168 Landry Shamet .20 .50
169 Jae Crowder .20 .50
170 LeBron James 2.50 6.00
171 Anthony Davis .75 2.00
172 Russell Westbrook .50 1.25
173 Juan Toscano-Anderson .20 .50
174 Carmelo Anthony .50 1.25
175 Talen Horton-Tucker .25 .60
176 Austin Reaves .75 2.00
177 Paul George .50 1.25
178 Kawhi Leonard .75 2.00
179 Reggie Jackson .25 .60
180 Marcus Morris Sr. .20 .50
181 Terance Mann .25 .60
182 Norman Powell .30 .75
183 Luke Kennard .25 .60
184 Robert Covington .20 .50
185 Brandon Boston Jr. .20 .50
186 Jamal Murray .50 1.25
187 Nikola Jokic 1.50 4.00
188 Will Barton .20 .50
189 Aaron Gordon .30 .75
190 Monte Morris .20 .50
191 Michael Porter Jr. .40 1.00
192 Bones Hyland .25 .60
193 Jeff Green .20 .50
194 Anthony Edwards 1.50 4.00
195 Karl-Anthony Towns .50 1.25
196 D'Angelo Russell .25 .60
197 Malik Beasley .25 .60
198 Jarred Vanderbilt .25 .60
199 Jaden McDaniels .30 .75
200 Patrick Beverley .25 .60
201 Shai Gilgeous-Alexander 1.50 4.00
202 Luguentz Dort .30 .75
203 Josh Giddey .50 1.25
204 Darius Bazley .20 .50
205 Tre Mann .25 .60
206 Aaron Wiggins .25 .60
207 Jeremiah Robinson-Earl .25 .60
208 Damian Lillard .75 2.00
209 Josh Hart .30 .75
210 Anfernee Simons .40 1.00
211 Gary Payton II .25 .60
212 Drew Eubanks .20 .50
213 Keon Johnson .20 .50
214 Greg Brown III .20 .50
215 Donovan Mitchell .60 1.50
216 Rudy Gobert .40 1.00
217 Bojan Bogdanovic .30 .75
218 Mike Conley .30 .75
219 Jordan Clarkson .30 .75
220 Rudy Gay .30 .75
221 Royce O'Neale .25 .60
222 Jared Butler .50 1.25
223 Stephen Curry 2.50 6.00
224 Klay Thompson .75 2.00
225 Draymond Green .40 1.00
226 Jordan Poole .50 1.25
227 Andrew Wiggins .40 1.00
228 James Wiseman .25 .60
229 Jonathan Kuminga .75 2.00
230 Moses Moody .40 1.00
231 Paolo Banchero RC 4.00 10.00
232 Chet Holmgren RC 3.00 8.00
233 Jabari Smith Jr. RC 2.00 5.00
234 Keegan Murray RC 1.50 4.00
235 Jaden Ivey RC 2.00 5.00
236 Bennedict Mathurin RC 2.00 5.00
237 Shaedon Sharpe RC 2.50 6.00
238 Dyson Daniels RC 1.50 4.00
239 Jeremy Sochan RC 2.00 5.00
240 Johnny Davis RC .60 1.50
241 Ousmane Dieng RC .75 2.00
242 Jalen Williams RC 3.00 8.00
243 Jalen Duren RC 2.00 5.00
244 Ochai Agbaji RC .75 2.00
245 Mark Williams RC 1.25 3.00
246 AJ Griffin RC .50 1.25
247 Tari Eason RC 1.50 4.00
248 Dalen Terry RC .60 1.50
249 Jake LaRavia RC .60 1.50
250 Malaki Branham RC .60 1.50
251 Christian Braun RC 1.50 4.00
252 Walker Kessler RC 1.25 3.00
253 David Roddy RC .75 2.00
254 MarJon Beauchamp RC .60 1.50
255 Blake Wesley RC .60 1.50
256 Nikola Jovic RC 1.25 3.00
257 Patrick Baldwin Jr. RC .60 1.50
258 TyTy Washington Jr. RC .60 1.50
259 Andrew Nembhard RC 1.25 3.00
260 Caleb Houstan RC .60 1.50
261 Christian Koloko RC .60 1.50
262 Max Christie RC 1.50 4.00
263 Jaden Hardy RC 1.00 2.50
264 Kennedy Chandler RC .60 1.50
265 Moussa Diabate RC .60 1.50
266 E.J. Liddell RC .60 1.50
267 Trevor Keels RC .50 1.25
268 Isaiah Mobley RC .60 1.50
269 Jaylin Williams RC .75 2.00
270 Vince Williams Jr. RC .75 2.00
271 Kenneth Lofton Jr. RC .75 2.00
272 Luke Travers RC .50 1.25
273 Jabari Walker RC .50 1.25
274 Wendell Moore Jr. RC .60 1.50
275 Peyton Watson RC 1.00 2.50
276 Bryce McGowens RC .60 1.50
277 Ryan Rollins RC .60 1.50
278 Josh Minott RC .60 1.50
279 Kendall Brown RC .50 1.25
280 Tyrese Martin RC .50 1.25
281 Paolo Banchero 4.00 10.00
282 Chet Holmgren 3.00 8.00
283 Jabari Smith Jr. 2.00 5.00
284 Keegan Murray 1.50 4.00
285 Jaden Ivey 2.00 5.00
286 Jayson Tatum 1.25 3.00
287 Nikola Jokic 1.50 4.00
288 Chris Paul .60 1.50
289 Ja Morant 1.00 2.50
290 Anthony Davis .75 2.00
291 Trae Young .75 2.00
292 Anthony Edwards 1.50 4.00
293 Luka Doncic 2.00 5.00
294 Stephen Curry 2.50 6.00
295 Bradley Beal .40 1.00
296 Zion Williamson .75 2.00
297 Allen Iverson .75 2.00
298 Dwyane Wade .60 1.50
299 Kevin Garnett .75 2.00
300 Vince Carter .60 1.50

2022-23 Hoops Artist Proof
*ARTIST PROOF: 5X TO 12X BASIC
STATED PRINT RUN 25 SER.#'d SETS
231 Paolo Banchero 100.00 250.00
232 Chet Holmgren 100.00 250.00
281 Paolo Banchero 100.00 250.00
282 Chet Holmgren 100.00 250.00

2022-23 Hoops Blue Explosion
*BLUE EXPLOSION: 3X TO 8X BASIC
STATED PRINT RUN 59 SER.#'d SETS
231 Paolo Banchero 60.00 150.00
232 Chet Holmgren 60.00 150.00
281 Paolo Banchero 60.00 150.00
282 Chet Holmgren 60.00 150.00

2022-23 Hoops Hyper Green
*HYPER GREEN: 5X TO 12X BASIC
STATED PRINT RUN 25 SER.#'d SETS
231 Paolo Banchero 100.00 250.00
232 Chet Holmgren 100.00 250.00
281 Paolo Banchero 100.00 250.00
282 Chet Holmgren 100.00 250.00

2022-23 Hoops Orange Explosion
*ORANGE EXPLOSION: 5X TO 12X BASIC
STATED PRINT RUN 25 SER.#'d SETS
231 Paolo Banchero 100.00 250.00
232 Chet Holmgren 100.00 250.00
281 Paolo Banchero 100.00 250.00
282 Chet Holmgren 100.00 250.00

2022-23 Hoops Premium Box Set
*PREMIUM BOX SET: 2X TO 5X BASIC
STATED PRINT RUN 199 COPIES PER

2022-23 Hoops Red
*RED: 2.5X TO 6X BASIC
STATED PRINT RUN 75 SER.#'d SETS
231 Paolo Banchero 75.00 200.00
236 Bennedict Mathurin 50.00 120.00
281 Paolo Banchero 75.00 200.00

2022-23 Hoops Arriving Now
COMMON CARD .50 1.25
SEMISTARS .60 1.50
UNLISTED STARS .75 2.00
*WINTER: .4X TO 1X BASIC
*HOLO: 1.25X TO 3X BASIC
*WINTER HOLO: 1.25X TO 3X BASIC
1 Paolo Banchero 5.00 12.00
2 Chet Holmgren 4.00 10.00
3 Jabari Smith Jr. 2.50 6.00
4 Keegan Murray 2.00 5.00
5 Jaden Ivey 2.50 6.00
6 Bennedict Mathurin 2.50 6.00
7 Shaedon Sharpe 3.00 8.00
8 Dyson Daniels 2.00 5.00
9 Jeremy Sochan 2.50 6.00
10 Johnny Davis .75 2.00
11 Ousmane Dieng 1.00 2.50
12 Jalen Williams 4.00 10.00
13 Jalen Duren 2.50 6.00
14 Ochai Agbaji 1.00 2.50
15 Mark Williams 1.50 4.00
16 AJ Griffin .60 1.50
17 Tari Eason 2.00 5.00
18 Dalen Terry .75 2.00
19 Jake LaRavia .75 2.00
20 Malaki Branham .75 2.00
21 Christian Braun 2.00 5.00
22 Walker Kessler 1.50 4.00
23 David Roddy 1.00 2.50
24 MarJon Beauchamp .75 2.00
25 Blake Wesley .75 2.00
26 Wendell Moore Jr. .75 2.00
27 Nikola Jovic 1.50 4.00
28 Patrick Baldwin Jr. .75 2.00
29 TyTy Washington Jr. .75 2.00
30 Peyton Watson 1.25 3.00

2022-23 Hoops City Edition
COMMON CARD .40 1.00
SEMISTARS .50 1.25
UNLISTED STARS .60 1.50
*HOLO: 1.25X TO 3X BASIC
*HYPER RED/99: 2X TO 5X BASIC
*HOLO ARTIST PROOF/25: 4X TO 10X BASIC
*HYPER GREEN/25: 4X TO 10X BASIC
1 Jayson Tatum 2.50 6.00
2 Kevin Durant 2.00 5.00
3 RJ Barrett 1.00 2.50
4 James Harden 1.25 3.00
5 Scottie Barnes 1.00 2.50
6 Nikola Jokic 3.00 8.00
7 Anthony Edwards 3.00 8.00
8 Josh Giddey 1.00 2.50
9 Damian Lillard 1.50 4.00
10 Evan Mobley 1.50 4.00
11 Zach LaVine 1.25 3.00
12 Mike Conley .50 1.25
13 Cade Cunningham 2.00 5.00
14 Tyrese Haliburton 1.25 3.00
15 Giannis Antetokounmpo 3.00 8.00
16 Stephen Curry 5.00 12.00
17 Kawhi Leonard 1.50 4.00
18 LeBron James 5.00 12.00
19 Devin Booker 1.50 4.00
20 De'Aaron Fox 1.25 3.00
21 Trae Young 1.50 4.00
22 LaMelo Ball 1.50 4.00
23 Jimmy Butler 1.25 3.00
24 Jalen Suggs .75 2.00
25 Bradley Beal .75 2.00
26 Luka Doncic 4.00 10.00
27 Jalen Green 2.00 5.00
28 Ja Morant 2.00 5.00
29 Zion Williamson 1.50 4.00
30 Joshua Primo .40 1.00

2022-23 Hoops Class Action
COMMON CARD .50 1.25
SEMISTARS .60 1.50
UNLISTED STARS .75 2.00
*HOLO: 1.25X TO 3X BASIC
1 Paolo Banchero 5.00 12.00
2 Chet Holmgren 4.00 10.00
3 Jabari Smith Jr. 2.50 6.00
4 Keegan Murray 2.00 5.00
5 Jaden Ivey 2.50 6.00
6 Bennedict Mathurin 2.50 6.00
7 Shaedon Sharpe 3.00 8.00
8 Dyson Daniels 2.00 5.00
9 Jeremy Sochan 2.50 6.00
10 Johnny Davis .75 2.00
11 Ousmane Dieng 1.00 2.50
12 Jalen Williams 4.00 10.00
13 AJ Griffin .60 1.50
14 Tari Eason 2.00 5.00
15 Dalen Terry .75 2.00
16 Jake LaRavia .75 2.00
17 Malaki Branham .75 2.00
18 Christian Braun 2.00 5.00
19 Walker Kessler 1.50 4.00
20 David Roddy 1.00 2.50
21 Blake Wesley .75 2.00
22 Wendell Moore Jr. .75 2.00
23 Nikola Jovic 1.50 4.00
24 Patrick Baldwin Jr. .75 2.00
25 TyTy Washington Jr. .75 2.00
26 Peyton Watson 1.25 3.00
27 Andrew Nembhard 1.50 4.00
28 Christian Koloko .75 2.00
29 Max Christie 2.00 5.00
30 Jaden Hardy 1.25 3.00

2022-23 Hoops Frequent Flyers
COMMON CARD .40 1.00
SEMISTARS .50 1.25
UNLISTED STARS .60 1.50
*WINTER: .4X TO 1X BASIC
*HOLO: 1.25X TO 3X BASIC
*WINTER HOLO: 1.25X TO 3X BASIC
1 Anthony Edwards 3.00 8.00
2 Zach LaVine 1.25 3.00
3 Zion Williamson 1.50 4.00
4 Giannis Antetokounmpo 3.00 8.00
5 Ja Morant 2.00 5.00
6 LeBron James 5.00 12.00
7 Jayson Tatum 2.50 6.00
8 Jalen Green 2.00 5.00
9 Cade Cunningham 2.00 5.00
10 Joel Embiid 1.00 2.50
11 Bam Adebayo 1.00 2.50
12 Kawhi Leonard 1.50 4.00
13 Kevin Durant 2.00 5.00
14 Donovan Mitchell 1.25 3.00
15 Darius Garland 1.00 2.50

2022-23 Hoops Great SIGnificance
COMMON CARD 4.00 10.00
SEMISTARS 5.00 12.00
UNLISTED STARS 6.00 15.00
1 Joe Ingles 5.00 12.00
2 Jordan Nwora 6.00 15.00
3 Keldon Johnson 8.00 20.00
4 Gabe Vincent 6.00 15.00
5 Nicolas Claxton 6.00 15.00
6 Georges Niang 5.00 12.00
7 Christian Wood 4.00 10.00
8 Royce O'Neale 5.00 12.00
9 Cameron Thomas 10.00 25.00
10 Will Barton 4.00 10.00
11 Dwight Powell 4.00 10.00

12 Chuma Okeke 6.00 15.00
13 Xavier Tillman 6.00 15.00
14 Keon Johnson 4.00 10.00
15 Jarrett Culver 4.00 10.00
16 Grant Williams 5.00 12.00
17 Evan Fournier 5.00 12.00
18 Justin Holiday 4.00 10.00
19 Daniel Theis 5.00 12.00
20 Hedo Turkoglu 6.00 15.00
21 Jonathan Kuminga 15.00 40.00
22 Nassir Little 6.00 15.00
23 Robin Lopez 5.00 12.00
24 Grayson Allen 6.00 15.00
25 Onyeka Okongwu 6.00 15.00
26 Luke Kennard 5.00 12.00
27 Robert Williams III 5.00 12.00
28 Jeff Green 4.00 10.00
29 Luka Doncic 400.00 800.00
30 Vernon Carey Jr. 6.00 15.00
31 Carlos Boozer 5.00 12.00
32 Ty Jerome 5.00 12.00
34 Larry Johnson 12.00 30.00
35 Nerlens Noel 4.00 10.00
36 Rajon Rondo 12.00 30.00
37 Jordan Clarkson 20.00 50.00
38 Jaylen Nowell 6.00 15.00
39 Reggie Jackson 5.00 12.00
40 Kevin Willis 5.00 12.00
41 Jerry West 25.00 60.00
42 Landry Shamet 4.00 10.00
43 John Stockton 25.00 60.00
44 Isiah Thomas 15.00 40.00
45 Grant Hill 15.00 40.00
46 Jack Sikma 8.00 20.00
48 Gail Goodrich 6.00 15.00
49 Dale Ellis 6.00 15.00
50 Bob McAdoo 8.00 20.00
51 Paolo Banchero 125.00 300.00
52 Chet Holmgren 125.00 300.00
53 Jabari Smith Jr. 20.00 50.00
54 Keegan Murray 15.00 40.00
55 Jaden Ivey 20.00 50.00
56 Bennedict Mathurin 20.00 50.00
57 Shaedon Sharpe 60.00 150.00
58 Dyson Daniels 15.00 40.00
59 Jeremy Sochan 20.00 50.00
60 Johnny Davis 6.00 15.00
61 Ousmane Dieng 8.00 20.00
62 Jalen Williams 30.00 80.00
63 Jalen Duren 20.00 50.00
64 Ochai Agbaji 8.00 20.00
65 Mark Williams 12.00 30.00
66 AJ Griffin 5.00 12.00
67 Tari Eason 15.00 40.00
68 Dalen Terry 6.00 15.00
69 Jake LaRavia 6.00 15.00
70 Malaki Branham 6.00 15.00
71 Christian Braun 15.00 40.00
72 Walker Kessler 12.00 30.00
73 David Roddy 8.00 20.00
74 MarJon Beauchamp 6.00 15.00
75 Blake Wesley 6.00 15.00
76 TyTy Washington Jr. 6.00 15.00
77 Wendell Moore Jr. 6.00 15.00
78 Nikola Jovic 12.00 30.00
79 Patrick Baldwin Jr. 6.00 15.00
80 Peyton Watson 10.00 25.00
81 Andrew Nembhard 12.00 30.00
82 Caleb Houstan 6.00 15.00
83 Christian Koloko 6.00 15.00
84 Max Christie 15.00 40.00
85 Jaden Hardy 10.00 25.00
86 Kennedy Chandler 6.00 15.00
87 Moussa Diabate 6.00 15.00
88 E.J. Liddell 6.00 15.00
89 Trevor Keels 5.00 12.00
90 Isaiah Mobley 6.00 15.00
91 Collin Gillespie 6.00 15.00
92 Jaylin Williams 8.00 20.00
93 Kendall Brown 5.00 12.00
94 Bryce McGowens 6.00 15.00
95 Vince Williams Jr. 8.00 20.00
96 Justin Lewis 6.00 15.00
97 Luke Travers 5.00 12.00
98 Jabari Walker 5.00 12.00
99 Scotty Pippen Jr. 8.00 20.00
100 Ryan Rollins 6.00 15.00

2022-23 Hoops HIPnotized

1 Jalen Green 2.00 5.00
2 LaMelo Ball 1.50 4.00
3 Anthony Edwards 3.00 8.00
4 LeBron James 5.00 12.00
5 Giannis Antetokounmpo 3.00 8.00
6 Zion Williamson 1.50 4.00
7 Stephen Curry 5.00 12.00
8 Luka Doncic 4.00 10.00
9 Kevin Durant 2.00 5.00
10 Trae Young 1.50 4.00
11 Ja Morant 2.00 5.00
12 Kawhi Leonard 1.50 4.00
13 Jayson Tatum 2.50 6.00
14 Zach LaVine 1.25 3.00
15 Nikola Jokic 3.00 8.00
16 Donovan Mitchell 1.25 3.00
17 Devin Booker 1.50 4.00
18 Joel Embiid 1.00 2.50
19 Cade Cunningham 2.00 5.00
20 Evan Mobley 1.50 4.00

2022-23 Hoops Hoopla

COMMON CARD .40 1.00
SEMISTARS .50 1.25
UNLISTED STARS .60 1.50
*HOLO: 1.25X TO 3X BASIC
*HYPER RED/99: 2X TO 5X BASIC
*HOLO ARTIST PROOF/25: 4X TO 10X BASIC
*HYPER GREEN/25: 4X TO 10X BASIC
1 Nikola Jokic 3.00 8.00
2 Stephen Curry 5.00 12.00
3 LeBron James 5.00 12.00
4 Giannis Antetokounmpo 3.00 8.00
5 Jayson Tatum 2.50 6.00
6 Luka Doncic 4.00 10.00
7 Kevin Durant 2.00 5.00
8 Joel Embiid 1.00 2.50
9 Ja Morant 2.00 5.00
10 Anthony Edwards 3.00 8.00
11 LaMelo Ball 1.50 4.00
12 Trae Young 1.50 4.00
13 Devin Booker 1.50 4.00
14 James Harden 1.25 3.00
15 Kawhi Leonard 1.50 4.00

2022-23 Hoops Hoops Art Signatures

1 Paolo Banchero 2,000.00 4,000.00
2 Chet Holmgren 1,000.00 2,000.00
3 Jabari Smith Jr. 400.00 800.00
4 Keegan Murray 500.00 1,000.00
5 Jaden Ivey 500.00 1,000.00

2022-23 Hoops Hoops Art Signatures Horizontal

6 Ja Morant
Paolo Banchero 2,500.00 5,000.00
7 Chet Holmgren
Ja Morant 1,500.00 3,000.00
8 Ja Morant
Jabari Smith Jr. 800.00 1,500.00
9 Ja Morant
Keegan Murray 1,000.00 2,000.00
10 Ja Morant
Jaden Ivey 1,000.00 2,000.00

2022-23 Hoops Hoops Ink

COMMON CARD 4.00 10.00
SEMISTARS 5.00 12.00
UNLISTED STARS 6.00 15.00
*RED/25: .75X TO 2X BASIC
1 Cade Cunningham 75.00 200.00
2 RJ Barrett 15.00 40.00
3 Jonathan Kuminga 25.00 60.00
4 Amar'e Stoudemire 6.00 15.00
5 Christian Wood 4.00 10.00
6 Karl-Anthony Towns 15.00 40.00
7 Onyeka Okongwu 6.00 15.00
8 Victor Oladipo 5.00 12.00
9 Rajon Rondo 12.00 30.00
10 Reggie Jackson 5.00 12.00
11 Dejounte Murray 20.00 50.00
12 Danny Green 5.00 12.00
13 Kevin Porter Jr. 5.00 12.00
14 RJ Hampton 5.00 12.00
15 Jason Williams 25.00 60.00
16 Rudy Gobert 12.00 30.00
17 Tobias Harris 5.00 12.00
18 Luguentz Dort 6.00 15.00
19 Pau Gasol 50.00 120.00
20 Robert Williams III 5.00 12.00
21 Spencer Dinwiddie 5.00 12.00
22 Josh Giddey 10.00 25.00
23 Sam Cassell 6.00 15.00
24 Jayson Tatum 200.00 500.00
25 T.J. Warren 5.00 12.00
26 John Collins 6.00 15.00
27 Davion Mitchell 5.00 12.00
28 Patrick Williams 6.00 15.00
29 CJ McCollum 6.00 15.00
30 Artis Gilmore 8.00 20.00
31 Bob McAdoo 8.00 20.00
32 Adrian Dantley 6.00 15.00
33 Isaac Okoro 5.00 12.00
34 Steve Francis 6.00 15.00
35 Jordan Clarkson 20.00 50.00
36 Jerry Stackhouse 8.00 20.00
37 Dominique Wilkins 12.00 30.00
38 Larry Bird 75.00 200.00
39 Dwyane Wade 40.00 100.00
40 Ja Morant 200.00 500.00
41 Desmond Bane 8.00 20.00
42 Robert Parish 8.00 20.00
43 Moses Moody 8.00 20.00
44 Jonas Valanciunas 5.00 12.00
45 Alperen Sengun 30.00 80.00
46 Mitch Richmond 8.00 20.00
47 Bradley Beal 8.00 20.00
48 Elton Brand 6.00 15.00
49 Zion Williamson 150.00 400.00
50 Isiah Thomas 6.00 15.00

2022-23 Hoops Hoops Throwback

COMMON CARD .50 1.25
SEMISTARS .60 1.50
UNLISTED STARS .75 2.00
1 Donovan Mitchell 1.50 4.00
2 DeMar DeRozan 1.00 2.50
3 RJ Barrett 1.25 3.00
4 Damian Lillard 2.00 5.00
5 CJ McCollum .75 2.00
6 Darius Garland 1.25 3.00
7 Joel Embiid 1.25 3.00
8 LaMelo Ball 2.00 5.00
9 Anthony Edwards 4.00 10.00
10 Klay Thompson 2.00 5.00
11 Paul George 1.25 3.00
12 Carmelo Anthony 1.25 3.00
13 Chris Paul 1.50 4.00
14 Ja Morant 2.50 6.00
15 Zion Williamson 2.00 5.00
16 Kawhi Leonard 2.00 5.00
17 Trae Young 2.00 5.00
18 Bradley Beal 1.00 2.50
19 Jayson Tatum 3.00 8.00
20 Luka Doncic 5.00 12.00
21 Giannis Antetokounmpo 4.00 10.00
22 Stephen Curry 6.00 15.00
23 Kyrie Irving 1.50 4.00
24 Kevin Durant 2.50 6.00
25 LeBron James 6.00 15.00

2022-23 Hoops Hot Signatures

COMPLETE SET (49)
*RED/25: .75X TO 2X BASIC
1 Luka Doncic 400.00 800.00
2 Anthony Davis 40.00 100.00
3 Bradley Beal 8.00 20.00
4 Stephen Curry 500.00 1,000.00
5 Jaren Jackson Jr. 30.00 80.00
6 Michael Porter Jr. 8.00 20.00
7 Anfernee Simons 12.00 30.00
8 Shawn Kemp 25.00 60.00
9 Nickeil Alexander-Walker 5.00 12.00
10 Jonathan Kuminga 15.00 40.00
11 Duncan Robinson 6.00 15.00
12 Trae Young 200.00 500.00
14 Jalen Brunson 15.00 40.00
15 Chris Duarte 5.00 12.00
16 Herbert Jones 6.00 15.00
17 RJ Barrett 15.00 40.00
18 Ayo Dosunmu 8.00 20.00
19 Obi Toppin 6.00 15.00
20 Shai Gilgeous-Alexander 300.00 600.00
21 Danilo Gallinari 5.00 12.00
22 Jamal Murray 20.00 50.00
23 Avery Johnson 5.00 12.00
24 Tyrese Haliburton 40.00 100.00
25 JJ Redick 6.00 15.00
26 Wendell Carter Jr. 6.00 15.00
27 Jerry West 30.00 80.00
28 Kevin Garnett 75.00 200.00
29 Grant Hill 20.00 50.00
30 Vince Carter 50.00 120.00
31 Julius Randle 8.00 20.00
32 Anthony Edwards 75.00 200.00
33 Tony Parker 20.00 50.00
34 Myles Turner 6.00 15.00
35 Collin Sexton 8.00 20.00
36 Alex Caruso 15.00 40.00
37 Franz Wagner 30.00 80.00
38 Calvin Murphy 6.00 15.00
39 Latrell Sprewell 8.00 20.00
40 Joe Dumars 8.00 20.00
41 B.J. Armstrong 6.00 15.00
42 Antawn Jamison 6.00 15.00
43 Bernard King 8.00 20.00
44 Jamaal Wilkes 6.00 15.00
45 Jalen Green 60.00 150.00
46 Tim Hardaway 8.00 20.00
47 Kevin Huerter 6.00 15.00
48 Scottie Barnes 40.00 100.00
49 Bobby Portis 6.00 15.00
50 Jason Richardson 6.00 15.00

2022-23 Hoops Hot Signatures Rookies

COMMON CARD 4.00 10.00
SEMISTARS 5.00 12.00
UNLISTED STARS 6.00 15.00
*GREEN: .4X TO 1X BASIC
*HYPER GOLD: .4X TO 1X BASIC
*RED/25: .75X TO 2X BASIC
1 Paolo Banchero 300.00 800.00
2 Chet Holmgren 150.00 400.00
3 Jabari Smith Jr. 75.00 200.00
4 Keegan Murray 100.00 250.00
5 Jaden Ivey 100.00 250.00
6 Bennedict Mathurin 125.00 300.00
7 Shaedon Sharpe 60.00 150.00
8 Dyson Daniels 25.00 60.00
9 Jeremy Sochan 75.00 200.00
10 Johnny Davis 6.00 15.00
11 Ousmane Dieng 8.00 20.00
12 Jalen Williams 75.00 200.00
13 Jalen Duren 50.00 120.00
14 Ochai Agbaji 20.00 50.00
15 Mark Williams 12.00 30.00
16 AJ Griffin 5.00 12.00
17 Tari Eason 30.00 80.00
18 Dalen Terry 6.00 15.00
19 Jake LaRavia 6.00 15.00
20 Malaki Branham 20.00 50.00
21 Christian Braun 20.00 50.00
22 Walker Kessler 40.00 100.00
23 David Roddy 8.00 20.00
24 MarJon Beauchamp 6.00 15.00
25 Blake Wesley 6.00 15.00
26 Wendell Moore Jr. 6.00 15.00
27 Nikola Jovic 20.00 50.00
28 Patrick Baldwin Jr. 6.00 15.00
29 TyTy Washington Jr. 6.00 15.00
30 Peyton Watson 10.00 25.00
31 Andrew Nembhard 25.00 60.00
32 Caleb Houstan 6.00 15.00
33 Christian Koloko 6.00 15.00
34 Max Christie 15.00 40.00
35 Jaden Hardy 50.00 120.00
36 Kennedy Chandler 6.00 15.00
37 Moussa Diabate 6.00 15.00
38 E.J. Liddell 6.00 15.00
39 Trevor Keels 5.00 12.00
40 Isaiah Mobley 6.00 15.00
41 Jaylin Williams 8.00 20.00
42 Kendall Brown 5.00 12.00
43 Bryce McGowens 6.00 15.00
44 Vince Williams Jr. 8.00 20.00
45 Josh Minott 6.00 15.00
46 Vlatko Cancar 8.00 20.00
47 Collin Gillespie 6.00 15.00
48 Johnny Juzang 8.00 20.00
49 Scotty Pippen Jr. 8.00 20.00
50 Mac McClung 125.00 300.00

2022-23 Hoops JAM-tastic

COMMON CARD .50 1.25
SEMISTARS .60 1.50
UNLISTED STARS .75 2.00
1 Zion Williamson 2.00 5.00
2 Kawhi Leonard 2.00 5.00
3 Dwyane Wade 1.50 4.00
4 Cade Cunningham 2.50 6.00
5 Anthony Edwards 4.00 10.00
6 LeBron James 6.00 15.00
7 Kevin Durant 2.50 6.00
8 Zach LaVine 1.50 4.00
9 Jayson Tatum 3.00 8.00
10 Jaylen Brown 1.50 4.00
11 Donovan Mitchell 1.50 4.00
12 Ja Morant 2.50 6.00
13 Bam Adebayo 1.25 3.00
14 Jalen Green 2.50 6.00
15 Paul George 1.25 3.00
16 Giannis Antetokounmpo 4.00 10.00
17 Anthony Davis 2.00 5.00
18 Damian Lillard 2.00 5.00
19 Joel Embiid 1.25 3.00
20 John Collins .75 2.00
21 Dominique Wilkins 1.25 3.00
22 Andrew Wiggins 1.00 2.50
23 Shawn Kemp 1.25 3.00
24 Vince Carter 1.50 4.00
25 Scottie Barnes 1.25 3.00

2022-23 Hoops Now Playing

COMMON CARD .50 1.25
SEMISTARS .60 1.50
UNLISTED STARS .75 2.00
*HOLO: 1.25X TO 3X BASIC
1 Paolo Banchero 5.00 12.00
2 Chet Holmgren 4.00 10.00
3 Jabari Smith Jr. 2.50 6.00
4 Keegan Murray 2.00 5.00
5 Jaden Ivey 2.50 6.00
6 Bennedict Mathurin 2.50 6.00
7 Shaedon Sharpe 3.00 8.00
8 Dyson Daniels 2.00 5.00
9 Jeremy Sochan 2.50 6.00
10 Johnny Davis .75 2.00
11 Ousmane Dieng 1.00 2.50
12 Jalen Williams 4.00 10.00
13 AJ Griffin .60 1.50
14 Tari Eason 2.00 5.00
15 Dalen Terry .75 2.00
16 Jake LaRavia .75 2.00
17 Malaki Branham .75 2.00
18 Christian Braun 2.00 5.00
19 Walker Kessler 1.50 4.00
20 David Roddy 1.00 2.50
21 MarJon Beauchamp .75 2.00
22 Blake Wesley .75 2.00
23 Wendell Moore Jr. .75 2.00
24 Nikola Jovic 1.50 4.00
25 Patrick Baldwin Jr. .75 2.00
26 TyTy Washington Jr. .75 2.00
27 Peyton Watson 1.25 3.00
28 Andrew Nembhard 1.50 4.00
29 Caleb Houstan .75 2.00
30 Christian Koloko .75 2.00
31 Max Christie 2.00 5.00

2022-23 Hoops Panini Presents

COMMON CARD .40 1.00
SEMISTARS .50 1.25
UNLISTED STARS .60 1.50
*HOLO: 1.25X TO 3X BASIC
*HYPER RED/99: 2X TO 5X BASIC
*HOLO ARTIST PROOF/25: 6X TO 12X BASIC
*HYPER GREEN/25: 6X TO 12X BASIC
1 Ja Morant 2.00 5.00
2 Ja Morant 2.00 5.00
3 Ja Morant 2.00 5.00
4 Ja Morant 2.00 5.00
5 Ja Morant 2.00 5.00
6 Ja Morant 2.00 5.00
7 Ja Morant 2.00 5.00
8 Ja Morant 2.00 5.00
9 Ja Morant 2.00 5.00
10 Ja Morant 2.00 5.00

2022-23 Hoops Prime Twine

COMMON CARD .40 1.00
SEMISTARS .50 1.25
UNLISTED STARS .60 1.50
*HOLO: 1.25X TO 3X BASIC
*HYPER RED/99: 2X TO 5X BASIC
*HOLO ARTIST PROOF/25: 6X TO 12X BASIC
*HYPER GREEN/25: 6X TO 12X BASIC
1 Stephen Curry 5.00 12.00
2 Jayson Tatum 2.50 6.00
3 Luka Doncic 4.00 10.00
4 Giannis Antetokounmpo 3.00 8.00
5 Devin Booker 1.50 4.00
6 LeBron James 5.00 12.00
7 Donovan Mitchell 1.25 3.00
8 Kawhi Leonard 1.50 4.00
9 Anthony Edwards 3.00 8.00
10 LaMelo Ball 1.50 4.00
11 Nikola Jokic 3.00 8.00
12 Brandon Ingram .75 2.00
13 Bradley Beal .75 2.00
14 Zach LaVine 1.25 3.00
15 Trae Young 1.50 4.00
16 Ja Morant 2.00 5.00
17 Jalen Green 2.00 5.00
18 Evan Mobley 1.50 4.00
19 Cade Cunningham 2.00 5.00
20 Scottie Barnes 1.00 2.50
21 Zion Williamson 1.50 4.00
22 Paul George 1.00 2.50
23 Joel Embiid 1.00 2.50
24 Kyrie Irving 1.25 3.00
25 James Harden 1.25 3.00

2022-23 Hoops Rise N Shine Memorabilia

COMMON CARD 1.25 3.00
SEMISTARS 1.50 4.00
UNLISTED STARS 2.00 5.00
*WINTER: .4X TO 1X BASIC
*PRIME/25: 1.25X TO 3X BASIC
1 Jaden Hardy 3.00 8.00
2 Max Christie 5.00 12.00
3 Christian Koloko 2.00 5.00
4 Andrew Nembhard 4.00 10.00
5 TyTy Washington Jr. 2.00 5.00
6 Patrick Baldwin Jr. 2.00 5.00
7 Nikola Jovic 4.00 10.00
8 Wendell Moore Jr. 2.00 5.00
9 Blake Wesley 2.00 5.00
10 MarJon Beauchamp 2.00 5.00
11 David Roddy 2.50 6.00
12 Walker Kessler 4.00 10.00
13 Christian Braun 5.00 12.00
14 Malaki Branham 2.00 5.00
15 Jake LaRavia 2.00 5.00
16 Dalen Terry 2.00 5.00
17 AJ Griffin 1.50 4.00
18 Mark Williams 4.00 10.00
19 Ochai Agbaji 2.50 6.00
20 Jalen Duren 6.00 15.00
21 Jalen Williams 10.00 25.00
22 Ousmane Dieng 2.50 6.00
23 Johnny Davis 2.00 5.00
24 Jeremy Sochan 6.00 15.00
25 Dyson Daniels 5.00 12.00
26 Shaedon Sharpe 8.00 20.00
27 Bennedict Mathurin 6.00 15.00
28 Jaden Ivey 6.00 15.00
29 Keegan Murray 5.00 12.00
30 Jabari Smith Jr. 6.00 15.00
31 Chet Holmgren 10.00 25.00
32 Paolo Banchero 12.00 30.00
33 Tari Eason 5.00 12.00
34 E.J. Liddell 2.00 5.00
35 Kennedy Chandler 2.00 5.00

2022-23 Hoops Rookie Greetings

COMMON CARD .50 1.25
SEMISTARS .60 1.50
UNLISTED STARS .75 2.00
*WINTER: .4X TO 1X BASIC
*HOLO: 1.25X TO 3X BASIC
*WINTER HOLO: 1.25X TO 3X BASIC
1 Paolo Banchero 5.00 12.00
2 Chet Holmgren 4.00 10.00
3 Jabari Smith Jr. 2.50 6.00
4 Keegan Murray 2.00 5.00
5 Jaden Ivey 2.50 6.00
6 Bennedict Mathurin 2.50 6.00
7 Shaedon Sharpe 3.00 8.00
8 Dyson Daniels 2.00 5.00
9 Jeremy Sochan 2.50 6.00
10 Johnny Davis .75 2.00
11 Ousmane Dieng 1.00 2.50
12 Jalen Williams 4.00 10.00
13 Jalen Duren 2.50 6.00
14 Ochai Agbaji 1.00 2.50
15 Mark Williams 1.50 4.00
16 AJ Griffin .60 1.50
17 Tari Eason 2.00 5.00
18 Dalen Terry .75 2.00
19 Jake LaRavia .75 2.00
20 Malaki Branham .75 2.00

2022-23 Hoops Rookie Ink

COMMON CARD 4.00 10.00
SEMISTARS 5.00 12.00
UNLISTED STARS 6.00 15.00
*GREEN: .4X TO 1X BASIC
*HYPER GOLD: .4X TO 1X BASIC
*RED/25: .75X TO 2X BASIC
1 Paolo Banchero 150.00 400.00
2 Chet Holmgren 150.00 400.00
3 Jabari Smith Jr. 40.00 100.00
4 Keegan Murray 40.00 100.00
5 Jaden Ivey 40.00 100.00
6 Bennedict Mathurin 40.00 100.00
7 Shaedon Sharpe 60.00 150.00
8 Dyson Daniels 15.00 40.00
9 Jeremy Sochan 20.00 50.00
10 Johnny Davis 6.00 15.00
11 Ousmane Dieng 8.00 20.00
12 Jalen Williams 40.00 100.00
13 Jalen Duren 20.00 50.00
14 Ochai Agbaji 8.00 20.00
15 Mark Williams 12.00 30.00
16 AJ Griffin 5.00 12.00
17 Tari Eason 15.00 40.00
18 Dalen Terry 6.00 15.00
19 Jake LaRavia 6.00 15.00
20 Malaki Branham 6.00 15.00
21 Christian Braun 15.00 40.00
22 Walker Kessler 12.00 30.00
23 David Roddy 8.00 20.00
24 MarJon Beauchamp 6.00 15.00
25 Blake Wesley 6.00 15.00
26 Wendell Moore Jr. 6.00 15.00
27 Nikola Jovic 12.00 30.00
28 Patrick Baldwin Jr. 6.00 15.00
29 TyTy Washington Jr. 6.00 15.00
30 Peyton Watson 10.00 25.00
31 Andrew Nembhard 12.00 30.00
32 Caleb Houstan 6.00 15.00
33 Christian Koloko 6.00 15.00
34 Max Christie 15.00 40.00
35 Jaden Hardy 10.00 25.00
36 Kennedy Chandler 6.00 15.00
37 Moussa Diabate 6.00 15.00
38 E.J. Liddell 6.00 15.00
39 Trevor Keels 5.00 12.00
40 Isaiah Mobley 6.00 15.00
41 Jaylin Williams 8.00 20.00
42 Kendall Brown 5.00 12.00
43 Bryce McGowens 6.00 15.00
44 Vince Williams Jr. 8.00 20.00
45 Justin Lewis 6.00 15.00
46 Alondes Williams 6.00 15.00
47 Collin Gillespie 6.00 15.00
48 Jabari Walker 5.00 12.00
49 Scotty Pippen Jr. 8.00 20.00
50 Ryan Rollins 6.00 15.00

2022-23 Hoops Rookie Remembrance

COMMON CARD 1.25 3.00
SEMISTARS 1.50 4.00
UNLISTED STARS 2.00 5.00
*WINTER: .5X TO 1.2X BASIC
*PRIME/25: 1.5X TO 4X BASIC
1 Zion Williamson 5.00 12.00
2 Ja Morant 6.00 15.00
3 Anthony Edwards 10.00 25.00
4 Jayson Tatum 8.00 20.00
5 Donovan Mitchell 4.00 10.00
6 Andrew Wiggins 2.50 6.00
7 LaMelo Ball 5.00 12.00
8 Cade Cunningham 6.00 15.00
9 Jalen Green 6.00 15.00
10 Jordan Poole 3.00 8.00
11 Tyrese Maxey 4.00 10.00
12 Josh Giddey 3.00 8.00
13 Evan Mobley 5.00 12.00
14 Tyler Herro 3.00 8.00
15 RJ Barrett 3.00 8.00

2022-23 Hoops Rookie Special

*HOLO: 1.25X TO 3X BASIC
1 Paolo Banchero 12.00 30.00
2 Chet Holmgren 6.00 15.00
3 Jabari Smith Jr. 5.00 12.00
4 Jaden Ivey 5.00 12.00

2022-23 Hoops Rookie Sweaters

COMMON CARD 2.00 5.00
SEMISTARS 2.50 6.00
UNLISTED STARS 3.00 8.00
1 Paolo Banchero 25.00 60.00
2 Chet Holmgren 15.00 40.00
3 Jabari Smith Jr. 10.00 25.00
4 Keegan Murray 8.00 20.00
5 Jaden Ivey 10.00 25.00
6 Bennedict Mathurin 10.00 25.00
7 Shaedon Sharpe 12.00 30.00
8 Dyson Daniels 8.00 20.00
9 Jeremy Sochan 10.00 25.00
10 Johnny Davis 3.00 8.00
11 Ousmane Dieng 4.00 10.00
12 Jalen Williams 15.00 40.00
13 Jalen Duren 10.00 25.00
14 Ochai Agbaji 4.00 10.00
15 Mark Williams 6.00 15.00
16 AJ Griffin 2.50 6.00
17 Tari Eason 8.00 20.00
18 Dalen Terry 3.00 8.00
19 Jake LaRavia 3.00 8.00
20 Malaki Branham 3.00 8.00
21 Christian Braun 8.00 20.00
22 Walker Kessler 6.00 15.00
23 David Roddy 4.00 10.00
24 MarJon Beauchamp 3.00 8.00
25 Blake Wesley 3.00 8.00
26 Wendell Moore Jr. 3.00 8.00
27 Nikola Jovic 6.00 15.00
28 Patrick Baldwin Jr. 3.00 8.00
29 TyTy Washington Jr. 3.00 8.00
30 Peyton Watson 5.00 12.00
31 Andrew Nembhard 6.00 15.00
32 Caleb Houstan 3.00 8.00
33 Christian Koloko 3.00 8.00

2022-23 Hoops Spark Plugs

COMMON CARD .40 1.00
SEMISTARS .50 1.25
UNLISTED STARS .60 1.50
1 Kyrie Irving 1.25 3.00
2 LeBron James 5.00 12.00
3 Giannis Antetokounmpo 3.00 8.00
4 Stephen Curry 5.00 12.00
5 Jayson Tatum 2.50 6.00
6 Trae Young 1.50 4.00
7 Bradley Beal .75 2.00
8 Paul George 1.00 2.50
9 Devin Booker 1.50 4.00
10 Zion Williamson 1.50 4.00
11 Kevin Durant 2.00 5.00
12 Zach LaVine 1.25 3.00
13 James Harden 1.25 3.00
14 LaMelo Ball 1.50 4.00
15 Ja Morant 2.00 5.00
16 Anthony Edwards 3.00 8.00
17 Jalen Green 2.00 5.00
18 Luka Doncic 4.00 10.00
19 Donovan Mitchell 1.25 3.00
20 Tyrese Maxey 1.25 3.00
21 Jordan Poole 1.00 2.50
22 Joel Embiid 1.00 2.50
23 DeMar DeRozan .75 2.00
24 Shai Gilgeous-Alexander 3.00 8.00
25 Jaylen Brown 1.25 3.00

2022-23 Hoops We Got Next

COMMON CARD .50 1.25
SEMISTARS .60 1.50
UNLISTED STARS .75 2.00
*HOLO: 1.25X TO 3X BASIC
1 Paolo Banchero 5.00 12.00
2 Chet Holmgren 4.00 10.00
3 Jabari Smith Jr. 2.50 6.00
4 Keegan Murray 2.00 5.00
5 Jaden Ivey 2.50 6.00
6 Bennedict Mathurin 2.50 6.00
7 Shaedon Sharpe 3.00 8.00
8 Dyson Daniels 2.00 5.00
9 Jeremy Sochan 2.50 6.00
10 Johnny Davis .75 2.00
11 Ousmane Dieng 1.00 2.50
12 Jalen Williams 4.00 10.00
13 AJ Griffin .60 1.50
14 Tari Eason 2.00 5.00
15 Dalen Terry .75 2.00
16 Jake LaRavia .75 2.00
17 Malaki Branham .75 2.00
18 Christian Braun 2.00 5.00
19 Walker Kessler 1.50 4.00
20 David Roddy 1.00 2.50
21 MarJon Beauchamp .75 2.00
22 Blake Wesley .75 2.00
23 Wendell Moore Jr. .75 2.00
24 Nikola Jovic 1.50 4.00
25 Patrick Baldwin Jr. .75 2.00
26 TyTy Washington Jr. .75 2.00
27 Peyton Watson 1.25 3.00
28 Andrew Nembhard 1.50 4.00
29 Caleb Houstan .75 2.00
30 Christian Koloko .75 2.00
31 Max Christie 2.00 5.00
32 Jaden Hardy 1.25 3.00
33 Kennedy Chandler .75 2.00
34 Moussa Diabate .75 2.00
35 E.J. Liddell .75 2.00

2022-23 Hoops Zero Gravity

COMMON CARD .40 1.00
SEMISTARS .50 1.25
UNLISTED STARS .60 1.50
*HOLO: 1.25X TO 3X BASIC
*HYPER RED/99: 2X TO 5X BASIC
*HOLO ARTIST PROOF/25: 6X TO 12X BASIC
*HYPER GREEN/25: 6X TO 12X BASIC
1 Ja Morant 2.00 5.00
2 Anthony Edwards 3.00 8.00
3 Kevin Durant 2.00 5.00
4 Zach LaVine 1.25 3.00
5 Zion Williamson 1.50 4.00
6 Jayson Tatum 2.50 6.00
7 Jaylen Brown 1.25 3.00
8 Giannis Antetokounmpo 3.00 8.00
9 Andrew Wiggins .75 2.00
10 LeBron James 5.00 12.00
11 Donovan Mitchell 1.25 3.00
12 Paul George 1.00 2.50
13 Joel Embiid 1.00 2.50
14 Bam Adebayo 1.00 2.50
15 Jalen Green 2.00 5.00
16 Cade Cunningham 2.00 5.00
17 Dwyane Wade 1.25 3.00
18 Tracy McGrady 1.00 2.50
19 Dominique Wilkins 1.00 2.50
20 Vince Carter 1.25 3.00

2023-24 Hoops

COMPLETE SET (300)
*WINTER: .4X TO 1X BASIC
*BLUE: 1X TO 2.5X BASIC
1 Joe Harris .30 .75
2 Jalen McDaniels .30 .75
3 Dorian Finney-Smith .30 .75
4 Jalen Suggs .50 1.25
5 Andrew Wiggins .50 1.25
6 CJ McCollum .40 1.00
7 Derrick White .50 1.25
8 Jonathan Kuminga 1.00 2.50
9 Markelle Fultz .30 .75
10 Tobias Harris .40 1.00
11 Wendell Carter Jr. .40 1.00
12 Ayo Dosunmu .40 1.00
13 Walker Kessler .40 1.00
14 Josh Hart .40 1.00
15 Zion Williamson 1.00 2.50
16 Collin Sexton .50 1.25
17 Keldon Johnson .50 1.25
18 Klay Thompson 1.00 2.50
19 Karl-Anthony Towns .60 1.50
20 Trey Murphy III .50 1.25
21 Damian Lillard 1.00 2.50
22 Talen Horton-Tucker .30 .75
23 Ja Morant 1.25 3.00
24 Chet Holmgren 1.00 2.50
25 MarJon Beauchamp .30 .75
26 Zach LaVine .60 1.50
27 Julius Randle .50 1.25
28 PJ Washington Jr. .40 1.00
29 De'Andre Hunter .40 1.00
30 Tyrese Haliburton .75 2.00
31 Bennedict Mathurin .60 1.50
32 Gordon Hayward .40 1.00
33 Shake Milton .30 .75
34 Jimmy Butler .60 1.50
35 Stephen Curry 3.00 8.00
36 Kyle Lowry .50 1.25
37 OG Anunoby .50 1.25
38 Kai Jones .30 .75
39 Jalen Williams .75 2.00
40 Malik Monk .50 1.25
41 Austin Reaves 1.00 2.50
42 Keegan Murray .50 1.25
43 Malcolm Brogdon .40 1.00
44 Dyson Daniels .50 1.25
45 Jaden Hardy .50 1.25
46 Mark Williams .50 1.25
47 Josh Minott .40 1.00
48 Mac McClung .50 1.25
49 Gabe Vincent .40 1.00
50 Jae Crowder .30 .75
51 Kentavious Caldwell-Pope .30 .75
52 LeBron James 3.00 8.00
53 Isaiah Mobley .25 .60
54 Jeremy Sochan .50 1.25
55 Max Christie .40 1.00
56 Myles Turner .40 1.00
57 Cameron Johnson .40 1.00
58 Norman Powell .40 1.00
59 Shai Gilgeous-Alexander 2.00 5.00
60 Jaylen Brown .75 2.00
61 Kevin Durant 1.25 3.00
62 Ivica Zubac .40 1.00
63 Gary Trent Jr. .40 1.00
64 Cameron Thomas .50 1.25
65 Jalen Brunson .75 2.00
66 Tyrese Maxey .75 2.00
67 Joel Embiid 1.00 2.50
68 Josh Green .30 .75
69 Mason Plumlee .30 .75
70 RJ Barrett .60 1.50
71 Darius Garland .60 1.50
72 AJ Griffin .30 .75
73 Ousmane Dieng .40 1.00
74 Nikola Vucevic .40 1.00
75 Kenneth Lofton Jr. .40 1.00
76 Paolo Banchero 1.00 2.50
77 Dennis Schroder .40 1.00
78 John Collins .40 1.00
79 Rui Hachimura .40 1.00
80 Max Strus .40 1.00
81 Alex Caruso .40 1.00
82 Bones Hyland .30 .75
83 Quentin Grimes .40 1.00
84 Jamal Murray .75 2.00
85 Coby White .40 1.00
86 Jae'Sean Tate .30 .75
87 LaMelo Ball 1.00 2.50
88 Danny Green .30 .75
89 Jabari Walker .25 .60
90 Robert Williams III .40 1.00
91 Peyton Watson .40 1.00
92 Jalen Green .50 1.25
93 Eric Gordon .30 .75
94 Jalen Johnson .50 1.25
95 Mikal Bridges .50 1.25
96 Caleb Martin .30 .75
97 Deandre Ayton .40 1.00
98 Victor Oladipo .30 .75
99 Patrick Williams .30 .75
100 Jarred Vanderbilt .30 .75
101 Bogdan Bogdanovic .40 1.00
102 Chris Paul .75 2.00
103 Desmond Bane .50 1.25
104 Isaac Okoro .30 .75
105 Marvin Bagley III .30 .75
106 DeMar DeRozan .60 1.50
107 Buddy Hield .40 1.00
108 Caris LeVert .40 1.00
109 Jonas Valanciunas .30 .75
110 Lonnie Walker IV .40 1.00
111 Marcus Smart .50 1.25
112 Khris Middleton .40 1.00
113 Scottie Barnes .50 1.25
114 Kelly Oubre Jr. .40 1.00
115 Kevin Love .40 1.00
116 Moses Moody .50 1.25
117 Trae Young .75 2.00
118 Herbert Jones .40 1.00
119 James Harden .75 2.00
120 Derrick Rose .60 1.50

121 Mitchell Robinson .40 1.00
122 Franz Wagner .60 1.50
123 Royce O'Neale .30 .75
124 Jaxson Hayes .30 .75
125 Robert Covington .30 .75
126 Aaron Wiggins .30 .75
127 Luke Kennard .30 .75
128 Deni Avdija .40 1.00
129 Russell Westbrook .60 1.50
130 Terance Mann .30 .75
131 Patrick Beverley .30 .75
132 De'Anthony Melton .40 1.00
133 Payton Pritchard .40 1.00
134 Kristaps Porzingis .50 1.25
135 James Wiseman .30 .75
136 Saddiq Bey .40 1.00
137 Jordan Poole .60 1.50
138 Evan Mobley .60 1.50
139 Anfernee Simons .50 1.25
140 D'Angelo Russell .40 1.00
141 Dejounte Murray .50 1.25
142 Cam Reddish .30 .75
143 Clint Capela .30 .75
144 Simone Fontecchio .40 1.00
145 Draymond Green .50 1.25
146 David Roddy .30 .75
147 Giannis Antetokounmpo 2.00 5.00
148 Naz Reid .40 1.00
149 Donovan Mitchell .75 2.00
150 Jaden Ivey .50 1.25
151 Gary Payton II .30 .75
152 Mo Bamba .30 .75
153 Rudy Gobert .50 1.25
154 Christian Braun .40 1.00
155 Matisse Thybulle .30 .75
156 Nikola Jovic .40 1.00
157 Cameron Payne .30 .75
158 Luka Doncic 2.50 6.00
159 Mike Conley .30 .75
160 Immanuel Quickley .40 1.00
161 Spencer Dinwiddie .30 .75
162 Lauri Markkanen .60 1.50
163 Richaun Holmes .25 .60
164 Evan Fournier .30 .75
165 Onyeka Okongwu .30 .75
166 Shaedon Sharpe .75 2.00
167 Kevin Huerter .30 .75
168 Tre Jones .40 1.00
169 Johnny Davis .30 .75
170 Jaden McDaniels .40 1.00
171 Kyle Kuzma .50 1.25
172 Alperen Sengun .60 1.50
173 Tim Hardaway Jr. .30 .75
174 De'Aaron Fox .75 2.00
175 Brook Lopez .30 .75
176 Jordan Clarkson .40 1.00
177 Devin Vassell .50 1.25
178 Kyrie Irving .75 2.00
179 Aaron Gordon .40 1.00
180 Nikola Jokic 2.00 5.00
181 Andrew Nembhard .40 1.00
182 Davion Mitchell .30 .75
183 Jayson Tatum 1.50 4.00
184 Ben Simmons .40 1.00
185 Pascal Siakam .60 1.50
186 Obi Toppin .40 1.00
187 Dillon Brooks .40 1.00
188 Cade Cunningham 1.00 2.50
189 Anthony Edwards 2.00 5.00
190 Jaren Jackson Jr. .60 1.50
191 Devin Booker 1.00 2.50
192 Tari Eason .50 1.25
193 Bojan Bogdanovic .40 1.00
194 Jaylin Williams .40 1.00
195 Bam Adebayo .60 1.50
196 Al Horford .40 1.00
197 DeAndre Jordan .30 .75
198 Reggie Bullock .25 .60
199 Kawhi Leonard 1.00 2.50
200 Jrue Holiday .50 1.25
201 Kenyon Martin Jr. .40 1.00
202 Bobby Portis .50 1.25
203 Jerami Grant .50 1.25
204 Bruce Brown .40 1.00
205 Jabari Smith Jr. .60 1.50
206 Paul George .60 1.50
207 Jarrett Allen .40 1.00
208 Malik Beasley .40 1.00
209 Jose Alvarado .40 1.00
210 Wendell Moore Jr. .30 .75
211 Domantas Sabonis .60 1.50
212 Jake LaRavia .30 .75
213 Michael Porter Jr. .50 1.25
214 Brandon Ingram .50 1.25
215 Luguentz Dort .40 1.00
216 Seth Curry .40 1.00
217 Anthony Davis 1.00 2.50
218 Terry Rozier III .50 1.25
219 Devonte' Graham .30 .75
220 Boban Marjanovic .40 1.00
221 Tyler Herro .60 1.50
222 Fred VanVleet .60 1.50
223 Harrison Barnes .30 .75
224 Grant Williams .30 .75
225 Bradley Beal .50 1.25
226 Jalen Green .60 1.50
227 Duncan Robinson .40 1.00
228 Ochai Agbaji .40 1.00
229 Josh Giddey .50 1.25
230 Cole Anthony .40 1.00
231 Toumani Camara RC 1.50 4.00
232 Scoot Henderson RC 2.50 6.00
233 Mouhamed Gueye RC .75 2.00
234 Brice Sensabaugh RC 1.25 3.00
235 Nick Smith Jr. RC 1.00 2.50
236 Taylor Hendricks RC .75 2.00
237 Leonard Miller RC .75 2.00
238 Jalen Hood-Schifino RC .75 2.00
239 Maxwell Lewis RC .60 1.50
240 James Nnaji RC .60 1.50
241 Dereck Lively II RC 1.50 4.00
242 Amen Thompson RC 4.00 10.00
243 Gradey Dick RC 1.50 4.00
244 Seth Lundy RC .60 1.50
245 Olivier-Maxence Prosper RC .75 2.00
246 Kobe Bufkin RC 1.00 2.50
247 Jordan Walsh RC .75 2.00
248 Jett Howard RC 1.00 2.50
249 Jaime Jaquez Jr. RC 1.25 3.00
250 Julian Strawther RC 1.00 2.50
251 Jarace Walker RC 1.50 4.00
252 Cason Wallace RC 1.50 4.00
253 Kobe Brown RC .75 2.00
254 Tristan Vukcevic RC .75 2.00
255 Ausar Thompson RC 2.00 5.00
256 Julian Phillips RC .75 2.00
257 Anthony Black RC 1.50 4.00
258 Jalen Wilson RC .75 2.00
259 Hunter Tyson RC .75 2.00
260 Marcus Sasser RC 1.25 3.00
261 Ben Sheppard RC .75 2.00
262 Kris Murray RC .75 2.00
263 Keyontae Johnson RC .75 2.00
264 Brandin Podziemski RC 2.50 6.00
265 Cam Whitmore RC 2.00 5.00
266 Emoni Bates RC 1.00 2.50
267 Amari Bailey RC .75 2.00
268 Andre Jackson Jr. RC 1.25 3.00
269 Jordan Hawkins RC 1.25 3.00
270 Colby Jones RC .75 2.00
271 Keyonte George RC 2.50 6.00
272 Brandon Miller RC 3.00 8.00
273 Rayan Rupert RC .75 2.00
274 Dariq Whitehead RC 1.00 2.50
275 GG Jackson II RC 1.50 4.00
276 Bilal Coulibaly RC 2.00 5.00
277 Victor Wembanyama RC 6.00 15.00
278 Jalen Pickett RC .60 1.50
279 Jalen Slawson RC .75 2.00
280 Noah Clowney RC 1.00 2.50
281 Ja Morant 1.25 3.00
282 Kevin Durant 1.25 3.00
283 Kevin Garnett 1.00 2.50
284 Brandon Miller 3.00 8.00
285 Giannis Antetokounmpo 2.00 5.00
286 Anthony Edwards 2.00 5.00
287 Jayson Tatum 1.50 4.00
288 Trae Young .75 2.00
289 Shaquille O'Neal 1.25 3.00
290 LeBron James 3.00 8.00
291 Nikola Jokic 2.00 5.00
292 Stephen Curry 3.00 8.00
293 Ausar Thompson 2.00 5.00
294 Vince Carter .75 2.00
295 Luka Doncic 2.50 6.00
296 Allen Iverson 1.00 2.50
297 Scoot Henderson 2.50 6.00
298 Victor Wembanyama 6.00 15.00
299 Dwyane Wade .75 2.00
300 Amen Thompson 4.00 10.00

2023-24 Hoops Artist Proof
*ARTIST PROOF: 5X TO 12X BASIC
STATED PRINT RUN 25 SER.#'d SETS
232 Scoot Henderson 100.00 250.00
277 Victor Wembanyama 1,250.00 2,500.00
297 Scoot Henderson 100.00 250.00
298 Victor Wembanyama 1,250.00 2,500.00

2023-24 Hoops Blue Explosion
*BLUE EXPLOSION: 3X TO 8X BASIC
STATED PRINT RUN 59 SER.#'d SETS
232 Scoot Henderson 50.00 120.00
277 Victor Wembanyama 500.00 1,000.00
297 Scoot Henderson 50.00 120.00
298 Victor Wembanyama 500.00 1,000.00

2023-24 Hoops Gravity
*GRAVITY: 3X TO 8X BASIC
STATED PRINT RUN 75 SER.#'d SETS
232 Scoot Henderson 50.00 120.00
277 Victor Wembanyama 400.00 800.00
297 Scoot Henderson 50.00 120.00
298 Victor Wembanyama 400.00 800.00

2023-24 Hoops Green
*GREEN: 2.5X TO 6X BASIC
STATED PRINT RUN 99 SER.#'d SETS
232 Scoot Henderson 40.00 100.00
277 Victor Wembanyama 350.00 700.00
297 Scoot Henderson 40.00 100.00
298 Victor Wembanyama 350.00 700.00

2023-24 Hoops Hyper Blue
*HYPER BLUE: 1X TO 2.5X BASIC
277 Victor Wembanyama 50.00 120.00
298 Victor Wembanyama 50.00 120.00

2023-24 Hoops Hyper Green
*HYPER GREEN: 5X TO 12X BASIC
STATED PRINT RUN 25 SER.#'d SETS
232 Scoot Henderson 100.00 250.00
277 Victor Wembanyama 1,250.00 2,500.00
297 Scoot Henderson 100.00 250.00
298 Victor Wembanyama 1,250.00 2,500.00

2023-24 Hoops Hyper Red
*HYPER RED: 2.5X TO 6X BASIC
STATED PRINT RUN 99 SER.#'d SETS
232 Scoot Henderson 40.00 100.00
277 Victor Wembanyama 350.00 700.00
297 Scoot Henderson 40.00 100.00
298 Victor Wembanyama 350.00 700.00

2023-24 Hoops Impulse
*IMPULSE: 3X TO 8X BASIC
232 Scoot Henderson 50.00 120.00
277 Victor Wembanyama 400.00 800.00
297 Scoot Henderson 50.00 120.00
298 Victor Wembanyama 400.00 800.00

2023-24 Hoops Orange Explosion
*ORANGE EXPLOSION: 5X TO 12X BASIC
STATED PRINT RUN 25 SER.#'d SETS
232 Scoot Henderson 100.00 250.00
277 Victor Wembanyama 1,250.00 2,500.00
297 Scoot Henderson 100.00 250.00
298 Victor Wembanyama 1,250.00 2,500.00

2023-24 Hoops Premium Box Set
*PREMIUM BOX SET: 2X TO 5X BASIC
STATED PRINT RUN 199 COPIES PER
232 Scoot Henderson 30.00 80.00
277 Victor Wembanyama 300.00 600.00
297 Scoot Henderson 30.00 80.00
298 Victor Wembanyama 300.00 600.00

2023-24 Hoops Purple
*PURPLE: 1X TO 2.5X BASIC
277 Victor Wembanyama 40.00 100.00
298 Victor Wembanyama 40.00 100.00

2023-24 Hoops Purple Winter
*PURPLE WINTER: 1X TO 2.5X BASIC
277 Victor Wembanyama 40.00 100.00
298 Victor Wembanyama 40.00 100.00

2023-24 Hoops Red
*RED: 2.5X TO 6X BASIC
STATED PRINT RUN 75 SER.#'d SETS
232 Scoot Henderson 40.00 100.00
277 Victor Wembanyama 350.00 700.00
297 Scoot Henderson 40.00 100.00
298 Victor Wembanyama 350.00 700.00

2023-24 Hoops Red Backs
*RED BACKS: 1.25X TO 3X BASIC
277 Victor Wembanyama 60.00 150.00
298 Victor Wembanyama 60.00 150.00

2023-24 Hoops Silver
*SILVER: 2X TO 5X BASIC
STATED PRINT RUN 199 COPIES PER
232 Scoot Henderson 30.00 80.00
277 Victor Wembanyama 300.00 600.00
297 Scoot Henderson 30.00 80.00
298 Victor Wembanyama 300.00 600.00

2023-24 Hoops Teal Explosion
*TEAL EXPLOSION: 1.2X TO 3X BASIC
277 Victor Wembanyama 40.00 100.00
298 Victor Wembanyama 40.00 100.00

2023-24 Hoops Yellow
*YELLOW: 1X TO 2.5X BASIC
277 Victor Wembanyama 60.00 150.00
298 Victor Wembanyama 60.00 150.00

2023-24 Hoops Anti Gravity
*HOLO: .75X TO 2X BASIC
1 Ja Morant 1.50 4.00
2 Anthony Edwards 2.50 6.00
3 Zach LaVine .75 2.00
4 Zion Williamson 1.25 3.00
5 LeBron James 4.00 10.00
6 Cade Cunningham 1.25 3.00
7 Jaylen Brown 1.00 2.50
8 Giannis Antetokounmpo 2.50 6.00
9 Donovan Mitchell 1.00 2.50
10 De'Aaron Fox 1.00 2.50
11 Scoot Henderson 1.50 4.00
12 Jordan Hawkins .75 2.00
13 Keyonte George 1.50 4.00
14 Brandon Miller 2.50 6.00
15 Victor Wembanyama 4.00 10.00
16 Anthony Black 1.00 2.50
17 Amen Thompson 2.50 6.00
18 Ausar Thompson 1.25 3.00
19 Jett Howard .60 1.50
20 Taylor Hendricks .50 1.25

2023-24 Hoops Anti Gravity Holo Artist Proof
*HOLO ARTIST PROOF: 6X TO 15X BASIC
STATED PRINT RUN 25 SER.#'d SETS
15 Victor Wembanyama 400.00 800.00

2023-24 Hoops Anti Gravity Hyper Green
*HYPER GREEN: 6X TO 15X BASIC
STATED PRINT RUN 25 SER.#'d SETS
15 Victor Wembanyama 400.00 800.00

2023-24 Hoops Anti Gravity Hyper Red
*HYPER RED: 3X TO 8X BASIC
STATED PRINT RUN 99 SER.#'d SETS
15 Victor Wembanyama 150.00 400.00

2023-24 Hoops Arriving Now
*WINTER: .4X TO 1X BASIC
*HOLO: .75X TO 2X BASIC
*WINTER HOLO: .75X TO 2X BASIC
1 Jordan Hawkins 1.00 2.50
2 Gradey Dick 1.25 3.00
3 Jarace Walker 1.25 3.00
4 Scoot Henderson 2.00 5.00
5 Toumani Camara 1.25 3.00
6 Keyonte George 2.00 5.00
7 Jett Howard .75 2.00
8 Colby Jones .60 1.50
9 Rayan Rupert .60 1.50
10 Jalen Hood-Schifino .60 1.50
11 GG Jackson II 1.25 3.00
12 Brice Sensabaugh 1.00 2.50
13 Brandon Miller 2.50 6.00
14 Maxwell Lewis .50 1.25
15 Brandin Podziemski 2.00 5.00
16 Amen Thompson 3.00 8.00
17 Dariq Whitehead .75 2.00
18 Bilal Coulibaly 1.50 4.00
19 Dereck Lively II 1.25 3.00
20 Nick Smith Jr. .75 2.00
21 Ausar Thompson 1.50 4.00
22 Cam Whitmore 1.50 4.00
23 Kobe Bufkin .75 2.00
24 Anthony Black 1.25 3.00
25 Kris Murray .75 2.00
26 Victor Wembanyama 5.00 12.00
27 Taylor Hendricks .60 1.50
28 Jalen Wilson .60 1.50
29 Cason Wallace 1.25 3.00
30 Jaime Jaquez Jr. 1.00 2.50

2023-24 Hoops Attack the Rack
*HOLO: .75X TO 2X BASIC
1 Victor Wembanyama 3.00 8.00
2 Amen Thompson 2.00 5.00
3 Ausar Thompson 1.00 2.50
4 Scoot Henderson 1.25 3.00
5 Brandon Miller 1.50 4.00
6 LeBron James 3.00 8.00
7 Ja Morant 1.25 3.00
8 Giannis Antetokounmpo 2.00 5.00
9 Anthony Edwards 2.00 5.00
10 Donovan Mitchell .75 2.00

2023-24 Hoops Attack the Rack Holo Artist Proof
*HOLO ARTIST PROOF: 8X TO 20X BASIC
STATED PRINT RUN 25 SER.#'d SETS
1 Victor Wembanyama 400.00 800.00

2023-24 Hoops Attack the Rack Hyper Green
*HYPER GREEN: 8X TO 20X BASIC
STATED PRINT RUN 25 SER.#'d SETS
1 Victor Wembanyama 400.00 800.00

2023-24 Hoops Attack the Rack Hyper Red
*HYPER RED: 4X TO 10X BASIC
STATED PRINT RUN 99 SER.#'d SETS
1 Victor Wembanyama 150.00 400.00

2023-24 Hoops Championship Moments
STATED PRINT RUN 99 SER.#'d SETS
1 Christian Braun 60.00 150.00
2 Aaron Gordon 75.00 200.00
3 Nikola Jokic 125.00 300.00
4 Jamal Murray 100.00 250.00
5 Bruce Brown 50.00 120.00
6 Michael Porter Jr. 60.00 150.00
7 Kentavious Caldwell-Pope 50.00 120.00
8 Jeff Green 50.00 120.00
9 DeAndre Jordan 40.00 100.00
10 Michael Malone 40.00 100.00

2023-24 Hoops City Edition
*HOLO: 1.25X TO 3X BASIC
1 LaMelo Ball 1.50 4.00
2 Tyrese Haliburton 1.25 3.00
3 Anthony Edwards 3.00 8.00
4 Cade Cunningham 1.50 4.00
5 LeBron James 5.00 12.00
6 Giannis Antetokounmpo 3.00 8.00
7 Mikal Bridges .75 2.00
8 Luka Doncic 4.00 10.00
9 Jayson Tatum 2.50 6.00
10 Damian Lillard 1.50 4.00
11 Nikola Jokic 3.00 8.00
12 Joel Embiid 1.50 4.00
13 Shai Gilgeous-Alexander 3.00 8.00
14 De'Aaron Fox 1.25 3.00
15 Donovan Mitchell 1.25 3.00
16 Stephen Curry 5.00 12.00
17 Lauri Markkanen 1.00 2.50
18 Ja Morant 2.00 5.00
19 Pascal Siakam 1.00 2.50
20 Trae Young 1.25 3.00
21 Jalen Brunson 1.25 3.00
22 Jimmy Butler 1.00 2.50
23 Devin Booker 1.50 4.00
24 Paolo Banchero 1.50 4.00
25 Kyle Kuzma .75 2.00
26 Kawhi Leonard 1.50 4.00
27 Zach LaVine 1.00 2.50
28 Amen Thompson 3.00 8.00
29 Zion Williamson 1.50 4.00
30 Victor Wembanyama 5.00 12.00

2023-24 Hoops City Edition Holo Artist Proof
*HOLO ARTIST PROOF: 4X TO 10X BASIC
STATED PRINT RUN 25 SER.#'d SETS
30 Victor Wembanyama 300.00 600.00

2023-24 Hoops City Edition Hyper Green
*HYPER GREEN: 4X TO 10X BASIC
STATED PRINT RUN 25 SER.#'d SETS
30 Victor Wembanyama 300.00 600.00

2023-24 Hoops City Edition Hyper Red
*HYPER RED: 2X TO 5X BASIC
STATED PRINT RUN 99 SER.#'d SETS
30 Victor Wembanyama 125.00 300.00

2023-24 Hoops Dynamos
*WINTER: .4X TO 1X BASIC
*HOLO: 1.25X TO 3X BASIC
*WINTER HOLO: 1.25X TO 3X BASIC
1 De'Aaron Fox 1.00 2.50
2 LeBron James 4.00 10.00
3 Nikola Jokic 2.50 6.00
4 Damian Lillard 1.25 3.00
5 Luka Doncic 3.00 8.00
6 Shai Gilgeous-Alexander 2.50 6.00
7 Kevin Durant 1.50 4.00
8 Jayson Tatum 2.00 5.00
9 Stephen Curry 4.00 10.00
10 Devin Booker 1.25 3.00
11 Anthony Edwards 2.50 6.00
12 Ja Morant 1.50 4.00
13 Kyrie Irving 1.00 2.50
14 Giannis Antetokounmpo 2.50 6.00
15 Joel Embiid 1.25 3.00

2023-24 Hoops Extreme Team
1 Victor Wembanyama 8.00 20.00
2 Amen Thompson 5.00 12.00
3 Ausar Thompson 2.50 6.00
4 Anthony Black 2.00 5.00
5 Cam Whitmore 2.00 5.00
6 Scoot Henderson 3.00 8.00
7 Jaime Jaquez Jr. 1.50 4.00
8 Stephen Curry 8.00 20.00
9 Giannis Antetokounmpo 5.00 12.00
10 LeBron James 8.00 20.00
11 Ja Morant 3.00 8.00
12 Jayson Tatum 4.00 10.00
13 Luka Doncic 6.00 15.00
14 Donovan Mitchell 2.00 5.00
15 Kyrie Irving 2.00 5.00

2023-24 Hoops Finals MVP
1 Nikola Jokic 6.00 15.00

2023-24 Hoops Great SIGnificance
COMPLETE SET (92)
1 Jalen Pickett 5.00 12.00
2 Adama Sanogo 6.00 15.00
3 Rod Strickland 6.00 15.00
4 Joey Hauser 5.00 12.00
5 Brice Sensabaugh 10.00 25.00
6 Tristan Vukcevic 6.00 15.00
7 Julian Champagnie 6.00 15.00
8 Leaky Black 5.00 12.00
9 Evan Fournier 5.00 12.00
10 Kenyon Martin Jr. 6.00 15.00
11 Cameron Payne 5.00 12.00
12 Jose Alvarado 6.00 15.00
13 Leonard Miller 6.00 15.00
14 Rashard Lewis 5.00 12.00
15 Tony Allen 4.00 10.00
16 Bilal Coulibaly 30.00 80.00
18 Mouhamed Gueye 6.00 15.00
19 Kevin Huerter 5.00 12.00
20 Rayan Rupert 6.00 15.00
21 Amen Thompson 40.00 100.00
22 Jordan Goodwin 5.00 12.00
23 Colby Jones 6.00 15.00
24 Cason Wallace 30.00 80.00
25 Hunter Tyson 6.00 15.00
26 Ricky Council IV 8.00 20.00
27 Dariq Whitehead 8.00 20.00
29 Mike Miller 5.00 12.00
30 Nick Richards 5.00 12.00
31 Noah Clowney 8.00 20.00
32 Bryce McGowens 6.00 15.00
33 Moussa Diabate 5.00 12.00
34 Ben Sheppard 6.00 15.00
35 Jalen Slawson 6.00 15.00
36 Gary Harris 5.00 12.00
37 Ausar Thompson 40.00 100.00
38 Brandin Podziemski 30.00 80.00
39 James Nnaji 5.00 12.00
40 Monte Morris 6.00 15.00
41 Jordan Walsh 15.00 40.00
42 Kobe Bufkin 8.00 20.00
43 Collin Gillespie 6.00 15.00
44 Keyontae Johnson 6.00 15.00
45 Seth Lundy 5.00 12.00
46 Scotty Pippen Jr. 6.00 15.00
47 Isaiah Wong 6.00 15.00
48 Markquis Nowell 6.00 15.00
49 Maxwell Lewis 5.00 12.00
50 Dennis Scott 5.00 12.00
51 Ivica Zubac 6.00 15.00
52 Sidy Cissoko 6.00 15.00
53 Theo Ratliff 5.00 12.00
54 Julian Strawther 8.00 20.00
56 Dorian Finney-Smith 5.00 12.00
57 Colin Castleton 5.00 12.00
58 Julian Phillips 6.00 15.00
59 Craig Hodges 5.00 12.00
60 Juan Toscano-Anderson 5.00 12.00
61 Isaiah Rider 6.00 15.00
62 Azuolas Tubelis 5.00 12.00
63 Andre Jackson Jr. 10.00 25.00
64 Simone Fontecchio 6.00 15.00
65 Toumani Camara 12.00 30.00
66 Tyrese Martin 5.00 12.00
67 Mark Williams 6.00 15.00
68 Tre Rollins 5.00 12.00
70 Dereck Lively II 12.00 30.00
72 James Donaldson 5.00 12.00
73 Jaylen Clark 6.00 15.00
76 Dale Ellis 6.00 15.00
77 Ayo Dosunmu 6.00 15.00
78 Nick Anderson 6.00 15.00
79 Olivier-Maxence Prosper 6.00 15.00
80 Grayson Allen 6.00 15.00
81 Kobe Brown 6.00 15.00
82 Willie Green 6.00 15.00
84 Jalen Wilson 6.00 15.00
85 Marcus Sasser 10.00 25.00
86 Jabari Walker 4.00 10.00
87 Josh Minott 6.00 15.00
88 GG Jackson II 12.00 30.00
89 Trayce Jackson-Davis 8.00 20.00
90 Kris Murray 6.00 15.00
91 Herbert Jones 6.00 15.00
92 Max Christie 6.00 15.00
93 Ryan Rollins 6.00 15.00
94 Jalen McDaniels 5.00 12.00
95 Cole Swider 5.00 12.00
96 Malik Monk 8.00 20.00
97 Keyonte George 40.00 100.00
98 Walter McCarty 5.00 12.00
99 Mark Price 5.00 12.00
100 Derek Harper 5.00 12.00

2023-24 Hoops High Voltage
1 Anthony Edwards 3.00 8.00
2 Domantas Sabonis 1.00 2.50
3 Paul George 1.00 2.50
4 Jamal Murray 1.25 3.00
5 Anthony Davis 1.50 4.00
6 Luka Doncic 4.00 10.00
7 LeBron James 5.00 12.00
8 Brandon Ingram .75 2.00
9 Cade Cunningham 1.50 4.00
10 Donovan Mitchell 1.25 3.00
11 Jalen Green 1.00 2.50
12 Stephen Curry 5.00 12.00
13 Giannis Antetokounmpo 3.00 8.00
14 Tyrese Maxey 1.25 3.00
15 Zion Williamson 1.50 4.00
16 Jalen Brunson 1.25 3.00
17 Kevin Durant 2.00 5.00
18 Jayson Tatum 2.50 6.00
19 Bam Adebayo 1.00 2.50
20 Russell Westbrook 1.00 2.50
21 Ja Morant 2.00 5.00
22 Zach LaVine 1.00 2.50
23 Lauri Markkanen 1.00 2.50
24 Devin Booker 1.50 4.00
25 Jaylen Brown 1.25 3.00

2023-24 Hoops Highlights
1 LeBron James 20.00 50.00
2 Donovan Mitchell 2.50 6.00
3 Luka Doncic 8.00 20.00
4 James Harden 2.50 6.00
5 Nikola Jokic 6.00 15.00

2023-24 Hoops HIPnotized
1 LaMelo Ball 2.00 5.00
2 Tyrese Haliburton 1.50 4.00
3 Luka Doncic 5.00 12.00
4 Stephen Curry 6.00 15.00
5 Ja Morant 2.50 6.00
6 LeBron James 6.00 15.00
7 Trae Young 1.50 4.00
8 Nikola Jokic 4.00 10.00
9 James Harden 1.50 4.00
10 Anthony Edwards 4.00 10.00
11 Darius Garland 1.25 3.00
12 Josh Giddey 1.00 2.50
13 De'Aaron Fox 1.50 4.00
14 Damian Lillard 2.00 5.00
15 Shai Gilgeous-Alexander 4.00 10.00
16 Tyrese Maxey 1.50 4.00
17 Cade Cunningham 2.00 5.00
18 Kevin Durant 2.50 6.00
19 Jayson Tatum 3.00 8.00
20 Kyrie Irving 1.50 4.00

2023-24 Hoops Hoopla
*HOLO: .75X TO 2X BASIC
*HYPER RED/99: 2X TO 5X BASIC
*HOLO ARTIST PROOF/25: 4X TO 10X BASIC
*HYPER GREEN/25: 4X TO 10X BASIC
1 Nikola Jokic 2.00 5.00
2 Kevin Durant 1.25 3.00
3 Luka Doncic 2.50 6.00
4 Stephen Curry 3.00 8.00
5 Damian Lillard 1.00 2.50
6 Jayson Tatum 1.50 4.00
7 Shai Gilgeous-Alexander 2.00 5.00
8 Trae Young .75 2.00
9 LeBron James 3.00 8.00
10 Giannis Antetokounmpo 2.00 5.00
11 Kyrie Irving .75 2.00
12 Joel Embiid 1.00 2.50
13 LaMelo Ball 1.00 2.50
14 De'Aaron Fox .75 2.00
15 Paul George .60 1.50

2023-24 Hoops Hoops Ink
*HYPER GOLD: .4X TO 1X BASIC
*RED/25: .75X TO 2X BASIC
1 Dale Ellis 5.00 12.00
2 Kevin Garnett 75.00 200.00
3 Anthony Edwards 75.00 200.00
4 Steve Kerr 6.00 15.00
5 Kevin Huerter 4.00 10.00
6 Bradley Beal 6.00 15.00
7 Nikola Jokic 75.00 200.00
8 Bob McAdoo 6.00 15.00
9 Dennis Rodman 40.00 100.00
10 Jaylin Williams 5.00 12.00
11 Joakim Noah 5.00 12.00
12 Cole Anthony 5.00 12.00
13 Jalen Duren 6.00 15.00
14 Chris Mullin 6.00 15.00
15 Jason Williams 12.00 30.00
16 Saddiq Bey 5.00 12.00
17 Christian Braun 5.00 12.00
18 Johnny Davis 4.00 10.00
19 Marcus Smart 6.00 15.00
20 Steve Francis 5.00 12.00
21 Tari Eason 6.00 15.00
22 Dyson Daniels 6.00 15.00
23 Lauri Markkanen 8.00 20.00
24 Markelle Fultz 4.00 10.00
25 Jalen Williams 40.00 100.00
26 Ben Wallace 12.00 30.00
27 Ochai Agbaji 5.00 12.00
28 Zach Randolph 5.00 12.00
29 Ja Morant 100.00 250.00
30 Bobby Portis 6.00 15.00
31 Shaedon Sharpe 30.00 80.00
32 Ralph Sampson 5.00 12.00
33 Austin Reaves 40.00 100.00
34 AJ Griffin 4.00 10.00
35 Tyrese Haliburton 40.00 100.00
36 Nikola Vucevic 5.00 12.00
37 Nick Van Exel 5.00 12.00
38 Shawn Kemp 12.00 30.00
39 Ivica Zubac 5.00 12.00
40 Larry Johnson 12.00 30.00
41 Keldon Johnson 6.00 15.00
42 Jaden Ivey 12.00 30.00
44 Tim Hardaway Jr. 4.00 10.00
45 Chet Holmgren 100.00 250.00
46 Jonathan Kuminga 12.00 30.00
47 Max Strus 5.00 12.00
48 Seth Curry 5.00 12.00
49 Bennedict Mathurin 8.00 20.00
50 Josh Giddey 6.00 15.00

2023-24 Hoops Hoops Throwback
1 Klay Thompson 2.50 6.00
2 Darius Garland 1.50 4.00
3 Anthony Edwards 5.00 12.00
4 Jalen Brunson 2.00 5.00
5 Kawhi Leonard 2.50 6.00
6 LeBron James 8.00 20.00
7 Giannis Antetokounmpo 5.00 12.00
8 Stephen Curry 8.00 20.00
9 Trae Young 2.00 5.00
10 Damian Lillard 2.50 6.00
11 Luka Doncic 6.00 15.00
12 Kevin Durant 3.00 8.00
13 DeMar DeRozan 1.50 4.00
14 Zion Williamson 2.50 6.00
15 Jayson Tatum 4.00 10.00
16 Bradley Beal 1.25 3.00
17 Ja Morant 3.00 8.00
18 Devin Booker 2.50 6.00
19 Joel Embiid 2.50 6.00
20 James Harden 2.00 5.00
21 LaMelo Ball 2.50 6.00
22 Jimmy Butler 1.50 4.00
23 De'Aaron Fox 2.00 5.00
24 Shai Gilgeous-Alexander 5.00 12.00
25 Nikola Jokic 5.00 12.00

2023-24 Hoops Hot Signatures
*HYPER GOLD: .4X TO 1X BASIC
*RED/15-25: .75X TO 2X BASIC
1 Shaedon Sharpe 30.00 80.00
2 Peja Stojakovic 5.00 12.00
4 Walker Kessler 5.00 12.00
5 Bennedict Mathurin 8.00 20.00
6 Nikola Jovic 5.00 12.00
7 Jeremy Sochan 12.00 30.00
8 Austin Reaves 40.00 100.00
9 Jason Williams 12.00 30.00
10 Jabari Smith Jr. 8.00 20.00
11 Alperen Sengun 20.00 50.00
12 Antawn Jamison 5.00 12.00
13 Richard Hamilton 6.00 15.00
14 Harold Miner 5.00 12.00
15 Jaden Hardy 6.00 15.00
16 Jordan Clarkson 12.00 30.00
17 David Thompson 6.00 15.00
18 Deandre Ayton 5.00 12.00
19 Caron Butler 4.00 10.00
20 Ayo Dosunmu 5.00 12.00
21 Bojan Bogdanovic 5.00 12.00
22 Jonathan Kuminga 12.00 30.00
24 Ralph Sampson 5.00 12.00
25 Amar'e Stoudemire 6.00 15.00
26 Ben Wallace 12.00 30.00
27 RJ Barrett 8.00 20.00
28 Keegan Murray 12.00 30.00
29 James Wiseman 4.00 10.00
30 Bruce Brown 5.00 12.00
31 Max Christie 5.00 12.00
32 Paolo Banchero 60.00 150.00
33 Russell Westbrook 40.00 100.00
34 Anthony Edwards 75.00 200.00
35 Pau Gasol 20.00 50.00
36 Artis Gilmore 6.00 15.00
37 Carlos Boozer 4.00 10.00
38 Jordan Poole 8.00 20.00
39 Dale Ellis 5.00 12.00
40 Tony Parker 12.00 30.00
41 Ousmane Dieng 5.00 12.00
42 Shawn Kemp 12.00 30.00
43 Jalen Suggs 6.00 15.00
44 Nikola Jokic 75.00 200.00
45 Bobby Portis 6.00 15.00
46 Jalen Williams 12.00 30.00
47 Dick Van Arsdale 5.00 12.00
48 Gary Trent Jr. 5.00 12.00
49 Rick Fox 5.00 12.00
50 Brandon Ingram 12.00 30.00

2023-24 Hoops Hot Signatures Rookies
*HYPER GOLD: .4X TO 1X BASIC
*GREEN: .4X TO 1X BASIC
*RED/25: .75X TO 2X BASIC
1 Isaiah Wong 6.00 15.00
2 Jordan Miller 8.00 20.00
3 Tristan Vukcevic 6.00 15.00
4 Ricky Council IV 8.00 20.00
5 Ben Sheppard 6.00 15.00
6 GG Jackson II 12.00 30.00
7 Jalen Pickett 5.00 12.00
8 Jordan Walsh 6.00 15.00
9 Jalen Wilson 6.00 15.00
10 Olivier-Maxence Prosper 6.00 15.00
11 Keyonte George 20.00 50.00
12 Kobe Brown 6.00 15.00
13 Dereck Lively II 12.00 30.00
14 Noah Clowney 8.00 20.00
15 Hunter Tyson 6.00 15.00
16 Oscar Tshiebwe 8.00 20.00
17 Jalen Slawson 6.00 15.00
18 Leonard Miller 6.00 15.00
19 Andre Jackson Jr. 10.00 25.00
20 Colin Castleton 5.00 12.00
21 Colby Jones 6.00 15.00
22 Filip Petrusev 6.00 15.00
24 Seth Lundy 5.00 12.00
25 Joey Hauser 5.00 12.00
26 Julian Strawther 8.00 20.00
27 Kobe Bufkin 8.00 20.00
28 James Nnaji 5.00 12.00
29 Omari Moore 5.00 12.00
30 Maxwell Lewis 5.00 12.00
31 Julian Phillips 6.00 15.00
32 Markquis Nowell 6.00 15.00
33 Keyontae Johnson 6.00 15.00
34 Brice Sensabaugh 10.00 25.00
35 Bilal Coulibaly 15.00 40.00
36 Kris Murray 6.00 15.00
37 Toumani Camara 12.00 30.00
38 Ausar Thompson 15.00 40.00
39 Brandin Podziemski 20.00 50.00
40 Marcus Sasser 10.00 25.00
41 Adama Sanogo 6.00 15.00
42 Trayce Jackson-Davis 8.00 20.00
43 D'Moi Hodge 5.00 12.00
44 Sidy Cissoko 6.00 15.00
45 Rayan Rupert 6.00 15.00
46 Amen Thompson 30.00 80.00
47 Dariq Whitehead 8.00 20.00
48 Jaylen Clark 6.00 15.00
49 Cason Wallace 12.00 30.00
50 Leaky Black 5.00 12.00

2023-24 Hoops Ignition
*HOLO: .75X TO 2X BASIC
1 LeBron James 3.00 8.00
2 Luka Doncic 2.50 6.00
3 Ja Morant 1.25 3.00
4 Stephen Curry 3.00 8.00
5 Jayson Tatum 1.50 4.00
6 Nikola Jokic 2.00 5.00
7 Giannis Antetokounmpo 2.00 5.00
8 Kyrie Irving .75 2.00
9 Kevin Durant 1.25 3.00
10 Shai Gilgeous-Alexander 2.00 5.00
11 Dereck Lively II .75 2.00
12 Gradey Dick .75 2.00
13 Jordan Hawkins .60 1.50
14 Kobe Bufkin .50 1.25
15 Keyonte George 1.25 3.00
16 Jalen Hood-Schifino .40 1.00
17 Jaime Jaquez Jr. .60 1.50
18 Brandin Podziemski 1.25 3.00
19 Cam Whitmore 1.00 2.50
20 Victor Wembanyama 15.00 40.00
21 Brandon Miller 1.50 4.00
22 Scoot Henderson 1.25 3.00
23 Amen Thompson 2.00 5.00
24 Ausar Thompson 1.00 2.50
25 Bilal Coulibaly 1.00 2.50
26 Anthony Black .75 2.00
27 Jarace Walker .75 2.00
28 Taylor Hendricks .40 1.00
29 Cason Wallace .75 2.00
30 Jett Howard .50 1.25

2023-24 Hoops JAM-tastic
1 Jalen Green 2.00 5.00
2 Zion Williamson 3.00 8.00
3 Bam Adebayo 2.00 5.00
4 Paul George 2.00 5.00

LeBron James 10.00 25.00
Giannis Antetokounmpo 6.00 15.00
Anthony Edwards 6.00 15.00
Zach LaVine 2.00 5.00
Kevin Durant 4.00 10.00
0 Joel Embiid 3.00 8.00
1 Ja Morant 4.00 10.00
2 Jayson Tatum 5.00 12.00
3 Julius Erving 3.00 8.00
4 Jimmy Butler 2.00 5.00
5 Nikola Jokic 6.00 15.00
6 De'Aaron Fox 2.50 6.00
7 DeMar DeRozan 2.00 5.00
8 Jamal Murray 2.50 6.00
9 Jaylen Brown 2.50 6.00
20 Dwyane Wade 2.50 6.00
21 Shaquille O'Neal 4.00 10.00
22 Vince Carter 2.50 6.00
23 Dominique Wilkins 2.00 5.00
24 Tracy McGrady 2.00 5.00
25 Shawn Kemp 2.00 5.00

2023-24 Hoops Now Playing

*HOLO: 1.25X TO 3X BASIC
1 Keyonte George 2.50 6.00
2 Nick Smith Jr. 1.00 2.50
3 Brandin Podziemski 2.50 6.00
4 Gradey Dick 1.50 4.00
5 Bilal Coulibaly 2.00 5.00
6 Jett Howard 1.00 2.50
7 Anthony Black 1.50 4.00
8 Kobe Brown .75 2.00
9 Cam Whitmore 2.00 5.00
10 Cason Wallace 1.50 4.00
11 Dariq Whitehead 1.00 2.50
12 Brice Sensabaugh 1.25 3.00
13 Jalen Hood-Schifino .75 2.00
14 Dereck Lively II 1.50 4.00
15 Scoot Henderson 2.50 6.00
16 Brandon Miller 3.00 8.00
17 Taylor Hendricks .75 2.00
18 Amen Thompson 4.00 10.00
19 Kobe Bufkin 1.00 2.50
20 Ausar Thompson 2.00 5.00
21 James Nnaji .60 1.50
22 Julian Strawther 1.00 2.50
23 Jordan Hawkins 1.25 3.00
24 Ben Sheppard .75 2.00
25 Jarace Walker 1.50 4.00
26 Victor Wembanyama 25.00 60.00
27 Noah Clowney 1.00 2.50
28 Kris Murray .75 2.00
29 Marcus Sasser 1.25 3.00
30 Jaime Jaquez Jr. 1.25 3.00
31 Olivier-Maxence Prosper .75 2.00

2023-24 Hoops Presentations

1 Jimmy Butler 15.00 40.00
2 Stephen Curry 50.00 120.00
3 LeBron James 50.00 120.00
4 Jayson Tatum 25.00 60.00
5 Ja Morant 25.00 60.00
6 Giannis Antetokounmpo 30.00 80.00
7 Luka Doncic 40.00 100.00
8 Trae Young 15.00 40.00
9 Kevin Durant 20.00 50.00
10 Damian Lillard 15.00 40.00
11 Keyonte George 25.00 60.00
12 Dariq Whitehead 10.00 25.00
13 Cason Wallace 20.00 50.00
14 Jalen Hood-Schifino 8.00 20.00
15 Kris Murray 10.00 25.00
16 Brandon Miller 25.00 60.00
17 Ausar Thompson 15.00 40.00
18 Amen Thompson 25.00 60.00
19 Scoot Henderson 25.00 60.00
20 Victor Wembanyama 150.00 400.00

2023-24 Hoops Pure Players

*WINTER: .4X TO 1X BASIC
*HOLO: 1.25X TO 3X BASIC
*WINTER HOLO: 1.25X TO 3X BASIC
1 Luka Doncic 2.50 6.00
2 Ja Morant 1.25 3.00
3 Giannis Antetokounmpo 2.00 5.00
4 LeBron James 3.00 8.00
5 Jayson Tatum 1.50 4.00
6 Nikola Jokic 2.00 5.00
7 Damian Lillard 1.00 2.50
8 Donovan Mitchell .75 2.00
9 Stephen Curry 3.00 8.00
10 Trae Young .75 2.00

2023-24 Hoops Rise N Shine Memorabilia

*WINTER: .4X TO 1X BASIC
*PRIME/25: 1.25X TO 3X BASIC
1 Brandon Miller 8.00 20.00
2 James Nnaji 1.50 4.00
3 Jett Howard 2.50 6.00
4 Leonard Miller 2.00 5.00
5 Jarace Walker 4.00 10.00
6 Cason Wallace 4.00 10.00
7 Nick Smith Jr. 2.50 6.00
8 Ben Sheppard 2.00 5.00
9 Anthony Black 4.00 10.00
10 Gradey Dick 4.00 10.00
11 Amen Thompson 10.00 25.00
12 Noah Clowney 2.50 6.00
13 Bilal Coulibaly 5.00 12.00
14 Kris Murray 2.00 5.00
15 Dariq Whitehead 2.50 6.00
16 Colby Jones 2.00 5.00
17 Kobe Bufkin 2.50 6.00
18 Jordan Hawkins 3.00 8.00
19 Victor Wembanyama 15.00 40.00
20 Ausar Thompson 5.00 12.00
21 Olivier-Maxence Prosper 2.00 5.00
22 Julian Phillips 2.00 5.00
23 Keyonte George 6.00 15.00
24 Marcus Sasser 3.00 8.00
25 Julian Strawther 2.50 6.00
26 Jaime Jaquez Jr. 3.00 8.00
27 Dereck Lively II 4.00 10.00
28 Cam Whitmore 5.00 12.00
29 Brandin Podziemski 6.00 15.00
30 Kobe Brown 2.00 5.00
31 Scoot Henderson 6.00 15.00
32 Brice Sensabaugh 3.00 8.00
33 Jalen Pickett 1.50 4.00
34 Jalen Hood-Schifino 2.00 5.00
35 Taylor Hendricks 2.00 5.00

2023-24 Hoops Rookie Greetings

*WINTER: .4X TO 1X BASIC
*HOLO: 1.25X TO 3X BASIC
*WINTER HOLO: 1.25X TO 3X BASIC
1 Victor Wembanyama 12.00 30.00
2 Jaime Jaquez Jr. 1.25 3.00
3 Scoot Henderson 2.50 6.00
4 Jordan Hawkins 1.25 3.00
5 Kris Murray .75 2.00
6 Jalen Hood-Schifino .75 2.00
7 Nick Smith Jr. 1.00 2.50
8 Amen Thompson 4.00 10.00
9 Bilal Coulibaly 2.00 5.00
10 Cason Wallace 1.50 4.00
11 Gradey Dick 1.50 4.00
12 Jarace Walker 1.50 4.00
13 Ausar Thompson 2.00 5.00
14 Keyonte George 2.50 6.00
15 Taylor Hendricks .75 2.00
16 Jett Howard 1.00 2.50
17 Dariq Whitehead 1.00 2.50
18 Brandon Miller 3.00 8.00
19 Cam Whitmore 2.00 5.00
20 Anthony Black 1.50 4.00

2023-24 Hoops Rookie Ink

*GREEN: .4X TO 1X BASIC
*HYPER GOLD: .4X TO 1X BASIC
*RED/25: .75X TO 2X BASIC
1 Julian Phillips 6.00 15.00
2 Keyontae Johnson 6.00 15.00
3 GG Jackson II 12.00 30.00
4 Sir'Jabari Rice 5.00 12.00
5 Cason Wallace 30.00 80.00
6 Noah Clowney 8.00 20.00
7 Ricky Council IV 8.00 20.00
8 Jordan Walsh 15.00 40.00
9 Bilal Coulibaly 30.00 80.00
10 Jalen Slawson 6.00 15.00
11 Markquis Nowell 6.00 15.00
12 Julian Strawther 8.00 20.00
14 Kobe Bufkin 8.00 20.00
15 Joey Hauser 5.00 12.00
16 Mouhamed Gueye 6.00 15.00
17 Colby Jones 6.00 15.00
18 Adama Sanogo 6.00 15.00
19 Filip Petrusev 6.00 15.00
21 Keyonte George 40.00 100.00
22 Maxwell Lewis 5.00 12.00
23 Dariq Whitehead 8.00 20.00
24 Kobe Brown 6.00 15.00
25 Hunter Tyson 6.00 15.00
26 Trayce Jackson-Davis 8.00 20.00
27 Jalen Wilson 6.00 15.00
28 Kris Murray 6.00 15.00
29 Marcus Sasser 10.00 25.00
30 Tristan Vukcevic 6.00 15.00
31 Jaylen Clark 6.00 15.00
32 Ausar Thompson 40.00 100.00
33 Isaiah Wong 6.00 15.00
34 Leonard Miller 6.00 15.00
35 Dereck Lively II 12.00 30.00
36 Jalen Pickett 5.00 12.00
37 Sidy Cissoko 6.00 15.00
38 Brice Sensabaugh 10.00 25.00
39 Seth Lundy 5.00 12.00
40 D'Moi Hodge 5.00 12.00
41 Ben Sheppard 6.00 15.00
42 Amen Thompson 40.00 100.00
43 Rayan Rupert 6.00 15.00
44 Colin Castleton 5.00 12.00
45 Brandin Podziemski 30.00 80.00
46 James Nnaji 5.00 12.00
47 Olivier-Maxence Prosper 6.00 15.00
48 Toumani Camara 12.00 30.00
49 Andre Jackson Jr. 10.00 25.00
50 Mike Miles Jr. 5.00 12.00

2023-24 Hoops Rookie Remembrance

*WINTER: .5X TO 1.2X BASIC
*PRIME/25: 1.5X TO 4X BASIC
1 Paolo Banchero 5.00 12.00
2 Jalen Williams 4.00 10.00
3 Bennedict Mathurin 3.00 8.00
4 Cade Cunningham 5.00 12.00
5 Jalen Green 3.00 8.00
6 Evan Mobley 3.00 8.00
7 LaMelo Ball 5.00 12.00
8 Anthony Edwards 10.00 25.00
9 Tyrese Haliburton 4.00 10.00
10 Zion Williamson 5.00 12.00
11 Ja Morant 6.00 15.00
12 Jayson Tatum 8.00 20.00
13 Donovan Mitchell 4.00 10.00
14 Bam Adebayo 3.00 8.00
15 Tyler Herro 3.00 8.00

2023-24 Hoops Rookie Special

*HOLO: 1.25X TO 3X BASIC
1 Amen Thompson 5.00 12.00
2 Ausar Thompson 2.50 6.00
3 Victor Wembanyama 50.00 120.00
4 Scoot Henderson 10.00 25.00

2023-24 Hoops Sheesh

*HOLO: .75X TO 2X BASIC
*HYPER RED/99: 2X TO 5X BASIC
*HOLO ARTIST PROOF/25: 4X TO 10X BASIC
*HYPER GREEN/25: 4X TO 10X BASIC
1 Luka Doncic 3.00 8.00
2 Giannis Antetokounmpo 2.50 6.00
3 Stephen Curry 4.00 10.00
4 Jamal Murray 1.00 2.50
5 Nikola Jokic 2.50 6.00
6 LeBron James 4.00 10.00
7 Ja Morant 1.50 4.00
8 Jayson Tatum 2.00 5.00
9 Kevin Durant 1.50 4.00
10 Kyrie Irving 1.00 2.50
11 Scoot Henderson 1.50 4.00
12 Nick Smith Jr. .60 1.50
13 Dereck Lively II 1.00 2.50
14 Ausar Thompson 1.25 3.00
15 Kobe Bufkin .60 1.50
16 Amen Thompson 2.50 6.00
17 Brandin Podziemski 1.50 4.00
18 Dariq Whitehead .60 1.50
19 Bilal Coulibaly 1.25 3.00
20 Jarace Walker 1.00 2.50
21 Jalen Hood-Schifino .50 1.25
22 Gradey Dick 1.00 2.50
23 Victor Wembanyama 4.00 10.00
24 Cason Wallace 1.00 2.50
25 Cam Whitmore 1.25 3.00

2023-24 Hoops Skyview

*WINTER: .4X TO 1X BASIC
*HOLO: 1.25X TO 3X BASIC
*WINTER HOLO: 1.25X TO 3X BASIC
1 Kevin Durant 1.25 3.00
2 Donovan Mitchell .75 2.00
3 James Harden .75 2.00
4 Jamal Murray .75 2.00
5 Jimmy Butler .60 1.50
6 Kyrie Irving .75 2.00
7 LeBron James 3.00 8.00
8 Kawhi Leonard 1.00 2.50
9 Anthony Edwards 2.00 5.00
10 Stephen Curry 3.00 8.00
11 Shai Gilgeous-Alexander 2.00 5.00
12 Jayson Tatum 1.50 4.00
13 Ja Morant 1.25 3.00
14 LaMelo Ball 1.00 2.50
15 De'Aaron Fox .75 2.00
16 Giannis Antetokounmpo 2.00 5.00
17 Joel Embiid 1.00 2.50
18 Zach LaVine .60 1.50
19 Nikola Jokic 2.00 5.00
20 Trae Young .75 2.00
21 Paul George .60 1.50
22 Luka Doncic 2.50 6.00
23 Damian Lillard 1.00 2.50
24 Devin Booker 1.00 2.50
25 Zion Williamson 1.00 2.50

2023-24 Hoops We Got Next

*HOLO: 1.25X TO 3X BASIC
1 Kobe Bufkin .75 2.00
2 Jaime Jaquez Jr. 1.00 2.50
3 Keyontae Johnson .60 1.50
4 Olivier-Maxence Prosper .60 1.50
5 Maxwell Lewis .50 1.25
6 Kris Murray .60 1.50
7 Taylor Hendricks .60 1.50
8 Jordan Hawkins 1.00 2.50
9 Keyonte George 2.00 5.00
10 Ausar Thompson 1.50 4.00
11 Andre Jackson Jr. 1.00 2.50
12 Ben Sheppard .60 1.50
13 Marcus Sasser 1.00 2.50
14 Noah Clowney .75 2.00
15 Dariq Whitehead .75 2.00
16 Kobe Brown .60 1.50
17 Jett Howard .75 2.00
18 Julian Phillips .60 1.50
19 Gradey Dick 1.25 3.00
20 Brandon Miller 2.50 6.00
21 Cason Wallace 1.25 3.00
22 Nick Smith Jr. .75 2.00
23 Jalen Hood-Schifino .60 1.50
24 Brice Sensabaugh 1.00 2.50
25 Jarace Walker 1.25 3.00
26 Rayan Rupert .60 1.50
27 Cam Whitmore 1.50 4.00
28 Anthony Black 1.25 3.00
29 Dereck Lively II 1.25 3.00
30 Scoot Henderson 2.00 5.00
31 Julian Strawther .75 2.00
32 Bilal Coulibaly 1.50 4.00
33 Victor Wembanyama 5.00 12.00
34 Brandin Podziemski 2.00 5.00
35 Amen Thompson 3.00 8.00

2024-25 Hoops

*WINTER: .4X TO 1X BASIC
*BLUE: 1X TO 2.5X BASIC
*PREMIUM: 1X TO 2.5X BASIC
*PURPLE: 1X TO 2.5X BASIC
*PURPLE WINTER: 1X TO 2.5X BASIC
*TEXTURE: 1X TO 2.5X BASIC
*PREMIUM GREEN: 1.25X TO 3X BASIC
*PREMIUM SILVER: 1.25X TO 3X BASIC
*PREMIUM WINTER: 1.25X TO 3X BASIC
*PREMIUM PRPL WINTER: 1.25X TO 3X BASIC
*RED BACKS: 1.25X TO 3X BASIC
*TEAL EXPLOSION: 1.25X TO 3X BASIC
*PREMIUM CHECKERBOARD: 2X TO 5X BASIC
*STORM/299: 2.5X TO 6X BASIC
*PREMIUM PRPL/249: 2.5X TO 6X BASIC
*PREMIUM BOX SET/199: 2.5X TO 6X BASIC
*PREMIUM ORANGE/199: 2.5X TO 6X BASIC
*PREMIUM RED PULSAR/199: 2.5X TO 6X BASIC
*SILVER/199: 2.5X TO 6X BASIC
*TEAL/175: 3X TO 8X BASIC
*LIME GREEN/149: 3X TO 8X BASIC
*ORANGE/149: 3X TO 8X BASIC
*WHITE EXPLOSION/149: 3X TO 8X BASIC
*PRPL EXPLOSION/110: 3X TO 8X BASIC
*BLUE SCOPE/99: 4X TO 10X BASIC
*GREEN/99: 4X TO 10X BASIC
*GREEN EXPLOSION/99: 4X TO 10X BASIC
*PREMIUM BLUE PULSAR/99: 4X TO 10X BASIC
*PREMIUM BLUE SCOPE/99: 4X TO 10X BASIC
*PREMIUM BLUE WAVE/99: 4X TO 10X BASIC
*PREMIUM RED LAZER/99: 4X TO 10X BASIC
*RED/99: 4X TO 10X BASIC
*BLUE WINTER HOLO/88: 4X TO 10X BASIC
*PREMIUM WINTER BLIZZARD/88: 4X TO 10X BASIC
*DRAGON YEAR/75: 5X TO 12X BASIC
*RED/75: 5X TO 12X BASIC
*BLUE EXPLOSION/59: 6X TO 15X BASIC
*PREMIUM BLUE/49: 6X TO 15X BASIC
*PREMIUM BLUE LAZER/49: 6X TO 15X BASIC
*PREMIUM RED SCOPE/49: 6X TO 15X BASIC
*RED SCOPE/49: 6X TO 15X BASIC
*ARTIST PROOF/25: 10X TO 25X BASIC
*PREMIUM GREEN LAZER/25: 10X TO 25X BASIC
*PREMIUM GREEN PULSAR/25: 10X TO 25X BASIC
*PREMIUM GREEN SCOPE/25: 10X TO 25X BASIC
*PREMIUM GREEN WAVE/25: 10X TO 25X BASIC
*MOJO/25: 10X TO 25X BASIC
*ORANGE/25: 10X TO 25X BASIC
1 Devin Booker .75 2.00
2 Jordan Clarkson .30 .75
3 Klay Thompson .75 2.00
4 Caris LeVert .25 .60
5 Karl-Anthony Towns .50 1.25
6 Jaden McDaniels .30 .75
7 Taurean Prince .20 .50
8 Jarrett Allen .25 .60
9 Kristaps Porzingis .40 1.00
10 Wendell Carter Jr. .25 .60
11 Aaron Nesmith .25 .60
12 Nikola Jokic 1.50 4.00
13 Scoot Henderson .40 1.00
14 Herbert Jones .25 .60
15 Ayo Dosunmu .25 .60
16 Simone Fontecchio .25 .60
17 Kyle Kuzma .25 .60
18 LeBron James 2.50 6.00
19 Isaiah Joe .25 .60
20 Scotty Pippen Jr. .30 .75
21 D'Angelo Russell .25 .60
22 Khris Middleton .30 .75
23 Bobby Portis .25 .60
24 John Collins .25 .60
25 Dyson Daniels .40 1.00
26 Jalen Green .60 1.50
27 Dejounte Murray .30 .75
28 Buddy Hield .25 .60
29 Myles Turner .25 .60
30 Vince Williams Jr. .25 .60
31 Cam Whitmore .30 .75
32 Draymond Green .40 1.00
33 Ben Simmons .30 .75
34 Zion Williamson .75 2.00
35 Collin Sexton .30 .75
36 Cameron Thomas .30 .75
37 Derrick Rose .75 2.00
38 Tyler Herro .50 1.25
39 P.J. Washington Jr. .25 .60
40 Clint Capela .25 .60
41 Bruce Brown .25 .60
42 Gradey Dick .40 1.00
43 Coby White .30 .75
44 Kyle Anderson .20 .50
45 Kentavious Caldwell-Pope .20 .50
46 Nicolas Claxton .25 .60
47 Kelly Olynyk .20 .50
48 Harrison Barnes .25 .60
49 T.J. McConnell .25 .60
50 Keyonte George .40 1.00
51 Donte DiVincenzo .30 .75
52 Andrew Nembhard .25 .60
53 Reggie Jackson .20 .50
54 Saddiq Bey .25 .60
55 Jamal Murray .50 1.25
56 Bennedict Mathurin .40 1.00
57 Zach Collins .20 .50
58 Tobias Harris .25 .60
59 Andrew Wiggins .40 1.00
60 Dennis Schroder .30 .75
61 Damian Lillard .75 2.00
62 RJ Barrett .40 1.00
63 Trayce Jackson-Davis .30 .75
64 Ivica Zubac .30 .75
65 Desmond Bane .30 .75
66 CJ McCollum .25 .60
67 Tari Eason .25 .60
68 Cason Wallace .40 1.00
69 Jusuf Nurkic .25 .60
70 Brandin Podziemski .40 1.00
71 Pascal Siakam .40 1.00
72 Taylor Hendricks .30 .75
73 Peyton Watson .25 .60
74 Norman Powell .30 .75
75 Caleb Martin .20 .50
76 Kyle Lowry .30 .75
77 Derrick White .30 .75
78 Robert Williams III .25 .60
79 Malaki Branham .25 .60
80 DeMar DeRozan .40 1.00
81 Paul George .50 1.25
82 Evan Mobley .50 1.25
83 Tre Jones .25 .60
84 Tyrese Maxey .60 1.50
85 Trae Young .60 1.50
86 Marvin Bagley III .20 .50
87 Kobe Bufkin .25 .60
88 Alex Caruso .30 .75
89 Julius Randle .30 .75
90 Cameron Johnson .25 .60
91 De'Andre Hunter .30 .75
92 Cam Reddish .20 .50
93 Jrue Holiday .40 1.00
94 Franz Wagner .50 1.25
95 Bradley Beal .40 1.00
96 Bilal Coulibaly .40 1.00
97 Precious Achiuwa .25 .60
98 Grant Williams .20 .50
99 Jaden Ivey .40 1.00
100 Patrick Williams .25 .60
101 Scottie Barnes .40 1.00
102 Jose Alvarado .25 .60
103 Brook Lopez .25 .60
104 Tyrese Haliburton .60 1.50
105 Moritz Wagner .25 .60
106 GG Jackson II .30 .75
107 Isaiah Stewart .25 .60
108 Kyrie Irving .75 2.00
109 Jordan Hawkins .25 .60
110 Mark Williams .25 .60
111 De'Aaron Fox .60 1.50
112 Kelly Oubre Jr. .25 .60
113 Jaren Jackson Jr. .50 1.25
114 Russell Westbrook .50 1.25
115 Luka Doncic 2.00 5.00
116 Fred VanVleet .30 .75
117 Rui Hachimura .30 .75
118 Gary Trent Jr. .25 .60
119 Nikola Vucevic .25 .60
120 Spencer Dinwiddie .20 .50
121 Lauri Markkanen .30 .75
122 Jaylen Brown .50 1.25
123 Immanuel Quickley .25 .60
124 OG Anunoby .25 .60
125 Marcus Sasser .25 .60
126 Shai Gilgeous-Alexander 1.50 4.00
127 Anfernee Simons .30 .75
128 Jaime Jaquez Jr. .30 .75
129 Malcolm Brogdon .20 .50
130 Jae Crowder .20 .50
131 Joel Embiid .50 1.25
132 Al Horford .30 .75
133 Daniel Gafford .25 .60
134 Andre Drummond .25 .60
135 Tim Hardaway Jr. .20 .50
136 Jerami Grant .25 .60
137 Ausar Thompson .50 1.25
138 Austin Reaves .40 1.00
139 Isaiah Hartenstein .25 .60
140 Keldon Johnson .25 .60
141 Stephen Curry 2.50 6.00
142 Corey Kispert .25 .60
143 Chris Paul .50 1.25
144 Andre Jackson Jr. .25 .60
145 Malik Beasley .25 .60
146 Tyus Jones .25 .60
147 Bogdan Bogdanovic .25 .60
148 Trey Murphy III .40 1.00
149 Miles Bridges .25 .60
150 Max Strus .25 .60
151 Amen Thompson .75 2.00
152 Bam Adebayo .40 1.00
153 Malik Monk .30 .75
154 Grayson Allen .25 .60
155 Zach LaVine .50 1.25
156 Rudy Gobert .30 .75
157 Derrick Jones Jr. .20 .50
158 Nicolas Batum .20 .50
159 Anthony Black .40 1.00
160 Jaden Hardy .30 .75
161 Jonathan Kuminga .40 1.00
162 Darius Garland .40 1.00
163 Jalen Suggs .30 .75
164 Paolo Banchero .75 2.00
165 Victor Wembanyama 2.50 6.00
166 Giannis Antetokounmpo 1.25 3.00
167 Jeremy Sochan .30 .75
168 Ja Morant 1.00 2.50
169 Deandre Ayton .25 .60
170 Jabari Smith Jr. .30 .75
171 Tre Mann .25 .60
172 Jayson Tatum 1.00 2.50
173 Kevin Durant 1.00 2.50
174 Julian Strawther .30 .75
175 Chet Holmgren .50 1.25
176 Terry Rozier III .25 .60
177 Jalen Duren .30 .75
178 Cole Anthony .30 .75
179 Payton Pritchard .30 .75
180 Vasilije Micic .25 .60
181 Anthony Edwards 1.50 4.00
182 LaMelo Ball .60 1.50
183 Deni Avdija .30 .75
184 Shaedon Sharpe .40 1.00
185 Jakob Poeltl .25 .60
186 Jalen Brunson .60 1.50
187 Michael Porter Jr. .30 .75
188 Marcus Smart .30 .75
189 Terance Mann .20 .50
190 Jordan Poole .30 .75
191 Mike Conley .25 .60
192 Aaron Wiggins .25 .60
193 Obi Toppin .25 .60
194 Cade Cunningham .75 2.00
195 Devin Vassell .40 1.00
196 Toumani Camara .30 .75
197 Bol Bol .20 .50
198 Nickeil Alexander-Walker .20 .50
199 Brandon Ingram .30 .75
200 Kris Murray .25 .60
201 Jalen Williams .60 1.50
202 James Harden .60 1.50
203 Mikal Bridges .30 .75
204 Dorian Finney-Smith .20 .50
205 Jalen Johnson .40 1.00
206 Isaac Okoro .20 .50
207 Josh Hart .25 .60
208 Mitchell Robinson .25 .60
209 Domantas Sabonis .50 1.25
210 Alperen Sengun .50 1.25
211 Donovan Mitchell .60 1.50
212 Brice Sensabaugh .25 .60
213 Aaron Gordon .30 .75
214 Jimmy Butler .50 1.25
215 Nick Smith Jr. .25 .60
216 Anthony Davis .75 2.00
217 Josh Giddey .40 1.00
218 Julian Champagnie .25 .60
219 Luguentz Dort .25 .60
220 Markelle Fultz .20 .50
221 Eric Gordon .20 .50
222 Duncan Robinson .25 .60
223 Naz Reid .30 .75
224 Brandon Miller .50 1.25
225 Kevin Huerter .25 .60
226 Kawhi Leonard .60 1.50
227 Dillon Brooks .25 .60
228 Dereck Lively II .30 .75
229 Jonas Valanciunas .25 .60
230 Keegan Murray .25 .60
231 Zaccharie Risacher RC 2.00 5.00
232 Alexandre Sarr RC 2.00 5.00
233 Reed Sheppard RC 2.00 5.00
234 Stephon Castle RC 4.00 10.00
235 Ron Holland II RC 1.25 3.00
236 Tidjane Salaun RC .60 1.50
237 Donovan Clingan RC 1.50 4.00
238 Rob Dillingham RC 1.50 4.00
239 Zach Edey RC 2.00 5.00
240 Cody Williams RC .75 2.00
241 Matas Buzelis RC 3.00 8.00
242 Nikola Topic RC 2.00 5.00
243 Devin Carter RC .75 2.00
244 Bub Carrington RC 1.50 4.00
245 Kel'el Ware RC 1.50 4.00
246 Jared McCain RC 2.50 6.00
247 Dalton Knecht RC 2.00 5.00
248 Tristan da Silva RC 1.50 4.00
249 Ja'Kobe Walter RC .75 2.00
250 Jaylon Tyson RC .60 1.50
251 Yves Missi RC 1.50 4.00
252 DaRon Holmes II RC .75 2.00
253 AJ Johnson RC 1.25 3.00
254 Kyshawn George RC 1.00 2.50
255 Pacome Dadiet RC .75 2.00
256 Dillon Jones RC .60 1.50
257 Terrence Shannon Jr. RC 1.25 3.00
258 Ryan Dunn RC .75 2.00
259 Isaiah Collier RC 1.25 3.00
260 Baylor Scheierman RC .75 2.00
261 Jonathan Mogbo RC 1.00 2.50
262 Kyle Filipowski RC 1.50 4.00
263 Tyler Smith RC .75 2.00
264 Tyler Kolek RC 1.00 2.50
265 Johnny Furphy RC 1.00 2.50
266 Juan Nunez RC .60 1.50
267 Bobi Klintman RC .75 2.00
268 Ajay Mitchell RC 1.00 2.50
269 Jaylen Wells RC 2.00 5.00
270 Oso Ighodaro RC .75 2.00
271 Adem Bona RC .75 2.00
272 KJ Simpson Jr. RC .60 1.50
273 Nikola Durisic RC .75 2.00
274 Pelle Larsson RC .75 2.00
275 Jamal Shead RC .75 2.00
276 Cam Christie RC .75 2.00
277 Antonio Reeves RC .60 1.50
278 Harrison Ingram RC .60 1.50
279 Tristen Newton RC .60 1.50
280 Bronny James Jr. RC 2.00 5.00
281 Luka Doncic 2.00 5.00
282 Stephen Curry 2.50 6.00
283 Shai Gilgeous-Alexander 1.50 4.00
284 Nikola Jokic 1.50 4.00
285 Giannis Antetokounmpo 1.25 3.00
286 Anthony Edwards 1.50 4.00
287 Trae Young .60 1.50
288 Ja Morant 1.00 2.50
289 Chet Holmgren .50 1.25
290 Zion Williamson .75 2.00
291 Reed Sheppard 2.00 5.00
292 Tidjane Salaun .60 1.50
293 Donovan Clingan 1.50 4.00
294 Dalton Knecht 2.00 5.00
295 Matas Buzelis 3.00 8.00
296 Shaquille O'Neal .75 2.00
297 Tim Duncan .75 2.00
298 Yao Ming .60 1.50
299 Larry Bird 1.00 2.50
300 Julius Erving .75 2.00

2024-25 Hoops Anti Gravity

*HOLO: .75X TO 2X BASIC
*HOLO ARTIST PROOF/25: 10X TO 25X BASIC
1 Giannis Antetokounmpo 2.00 5.00
2 Joel Embiid .75 2.00
3 Tidjane Salaun .50 1.25
4 Dalton Knecht 1.50 4.00
5 Anthony Edwards 2.50 6.00
6 Donovan Mitchell 1.00 2.50
7 Ja Morant 1.50 4.00
8 Paolo Banchero 1.25 3.00
9 Luka Doncic 3.00 8.00
10 Zaccharie Risacher 1.25 3.00
11 Kevin Durant 1.50 4.00
12 Alexandre Sarr 1.50 4.00
13 Stephen Curry 4.00 10.00
14 Donovan Clingan 1.25 3.00
15 Victor Wembanyama 4.00 10.00
16 Jaylen Brown .75 2.00
17 LeBron James 4.00 10.00
18 Zion Williamson 1.25 3.00
19 Anthony Davis 1.25 3.00
20 Jayson Tatum 1.50 4.00

2024-25 Hoops Arriving Now

*WINTER: .4X TO 1X BASIC
*HOLO: .75X TO 2X BASIC
*WINTER HOLO: .75X TO 2X BASIC
1 Devin Carter .75 2.00
2 Johnny Furphy 1.00 2.50
3 Tidjane Salaun .60 1.50
4 Matas Buzelis 3.00 8.00
5 Dillon Jones .60 1.50
6 Zach Edey 2.00 5.00
7 Yves Missi 1.50 4.00
8 Stephon Castle 3.00 8.00
9 Jared McCain 2.50 6.00
10 Zaccharie Risacher 1.50 4.00
11 Kel'el Ware 1.50 4.00
12 Bronny James Jr. 2.50 6.00
13 Tyler Kolek 1.00 2.50
14 Ron Holland II 1.25 3.00
15 Pacome Dadiet .75 2.00
16 Tristan da Silva 1.50 4.00
17 Kyle Filipowski 1.50 4.00
18 Kyshawn George 1.00 2.50
19 AJ Johnson 1.00 2.50
20 Ja'Kobe Walter .75 2.00
21 Bub Carrington 1.50 4.00
22 Donovan Clingan 1.50 4.00
23 Alexandre Sarr 2.00 5.00
24 Rob Dillingham 1.50 4.00
25 Reed Sheppard 2.00 5.00
26 Dalton Knecht 2.00 5.00
27 Jaylon Tyson .75 2.00
28 Nikola Topic 2.00 5.00
29 Cody Williams .75 2.00
30 DaRon Holmes II .75 2.00

2024-25 Hoops Champions

1 Boston Celtics 75.00 200.00

2024-25 Hoops Championship Moments

STATED PRINT RUN 99 SER.#'d SETS
1 Jayson Tatum 75.00 200.00
2 Jaylen Brown 75.00 200.00
3 Jrue Holiday 75.00 200.00
4 Kristaps Porzingis 75.00 200.00
5 Derrick White 75.00 200.00
6 Al Horford 75.00 200.00
7 Payton Pritchard 75.00 200.00
8 Sam Hauser 20.00 50.00
9 Xavier Tillman 30.00 80.00
10 Joe Mazzulla 60.00 150.00

2024-25 Hoops City Edition

*HOLO: .75X TO 2X BASIC
*HOLO ARTIST PROOF/25: 10X TO 25X BASIC
1 Paolo Banchero 1.25 3.00
2 Victor Wembanyama 4.00 10.00
3 Giannis Antetokounmpo 2.00 5.00
4 De'Aaron Fox 1.00 2.50
5 Jalen Brunson 1.00 2.50
6 Trae Young 1.00 2.50
7 Jayson Tatum 1.50 4.00
8 LeBron James 4.00 10.00
9 Kawhi Leonard 1.00 2.50
10 Ja Morant 1.50 4.00
11 Tyrese Maxey 1.00 2.50
12 Luka Doncic 3.00 8.00
13 Lauri Markkanen .50 1.25
14 Zach LaVine .75 2.00
15 Stephen Curry 4.00 10.00
16 Shai Gilgeous-Alexander 2.00 5.00
17 Kevin Durant 1.50 4.00
18 Jordan Poole .50 1.25
19 Scottie Barnes .60 1.50
20 Anthony Edwards 2.50 6.00
21 Donovan Mitchell 1.00 2.50
22 LaMelo Ball 1.00 2.50
23 Deandre Ayton .40 1.00
24 Cameron Thomas .50 1.25
25 Zion Williamson 1.25 3.00
26 Cade Cunningham 1.25 3.00
27 Alperen Sengun .75 2.00
28 Jimmy Butler .75 2.00
29 Nikola Jokic 2.50 6.00
30 Tyrese Haliburton 1.00 2.50

2024-25 Hoops Dreamcatchers

1 Giannis Antetokounmpo 50.00 120.00
2 Nikola Jokic 50.00 120.00
3 LeBron James 75.00 200.00
4 Victor Wembanyama 125.00 300.00
5 Trae Young 25.00 60.00
6 Reed Sheppard 50.00 120.00
7 Alexandre Sarr 40.00 100.00
8 Luka Doncic 60.00 150.00
9 Anthony Edwards 60.00 150.00
10 Kevin Durant 50.00 120.00
11 Stephen Curry 60.00 150.00
12 Jayson Tatum 50.00 120.00
13 Zaccharie Risacher 50.00 120.00
14 Ja Morant 50.00 120.00
15 Shai Gilgeous-Alexander 75.00 200.00

2024-25 Hoops Finals MVP

1 Jaylen Brown 75.00 200.00

2024-25 Hoops Frequent Flyers

*WINTER: .4X TO 1X BASIC
*HOLO: .75X TO 2X BASIC
*WINTER HOLO: .75X TO 2X BASIC
1 Damian Lillard 1.25 3.00
2 Jayson Tatum 1.50 4.00
3 Luka Doncic 3.00 8.00
4 Reed Sheppard 1.50 4.00
5 Jalen Brunson 1.00 2.50
6 Stephen Curry 4.00 10.00
7 Tyrese Haliburton 1.00 2.50
8 Nikola Jokic 2.50 6.00
9 Zaccharie Risacher 1.25 3.00
10 Victor Wembanyama 4.00 10.00
11 Shai Gilgeous-Alexander 2.00 5.00
12 Trae Young 1.00 2.50
13 LeBron James 4.00 10.00
14 Alexandre Sarr 1.50 4.00
15 Kyrie Irving 1.25 3.00

2024-25 Hoops Funkadelic

1 Shai Gilgeous-Alexander 3.00 8.00
2 Zaccharie Risacher 2.00 5.00
3 LeBron James 6.00 15.00
4 Stephon Castle 4.00 10.00
5 Giannis Antetokounmpo 3.00 8.00
6 Luka Doncic 5.00 12.00
7 Jalen Brunson 1.50 4.00
8 Donovan Clingan 2.00 5.00
9 Jayson Tatum 2.50 6.00
10 Anthony Edwards 4.00 10.00
11 Victor Wembanyama 6.00 15.00
12 Alexandre Sarr 2.50 6.00
13 Ron Holland II 1.50 4.00
14 Dalton Knecht 2.50 6.00
15 Bronny James Jr. 3.00 8.00
16 Tidjane Salaun .75 2.00
17 Jared McCain 3.00 8.00
18 Trae Young 1.50 4.00
19 Kevin Durant 2.50 6.00
20 Zion Williamson 2.00 5.00
21 Nikola Jokic 4.00 10.00
22 Stephen Curry 6.00 15.00
23 Reed Sheppard 2.50 6.00
24 Ja Morant 2.50 6.00
25 Tyrese Haliburton 1.50 4.00

2024-25 Hoops Great SIGnificance

1 Matt Ryan 4.00 10.00
2 Bruno Fernando 3.00 8.00
3 Adam Flagler 5.00 12.00
4 Johnny Juzang 4.00 10.00
5 Jeremiah Robinson-Earl 4.00 10.00
6 Cole Swider 4.00 10.00
7 Pete Nance 3.00 8.00
8 Jason Preston 3.00 8.00
9 Collin Gillespie 4.00 10.00
10 Duane Washington 4.00 10.00
11 Terquavion Smith 4.00 10.00
12 Jaden Hardy 5.00 12.00
13 Wendell Moore Jr. 4.00 10.00
14 Trevelin Queen 4.00 10.00
15 Charles Bassey 4.00 10.00
16 Keon Ellis 4.00 10.00
17 Eugene Omoruyi 4.00 10.00
18 Trendon Watford 4.00 10.00
19 Kendall Brown 4.00 10.00
20 Greg Brown III 3.00 8.00
21 Kessler Edwards 4.00 10.00
22 Garrett Temple 4.00 10.00
23 Chimezie Metu 4.00 10.00
24 Dalano Banton 5.00 12.00
25 Julian Champagnie 4.00 10.00
26 Ryan Rollins 5.00 12.00
27 Cason Wallace 6.00 15.00
28 Alondes Williams 4.00 10.00
29 Cade Cunningham 50.00 120.00

30 E.J. Liddell 4.00 10.00
31 Vit Krejci 4.00 10.00
32 Justin Champagnie 5.00 12.00
33 Jay Huff 4.00 10.00
34 RaiQuan Gray 4.00 10.00
35 Buddy Boeheim 4.00 10.00
36 Jared Butler 4.00 10.00
37 Jules Bernard 4.00 10.00
38 Jalen Duren 5.00 12.00
39 Orlando Robinson 3.00 8.00
40 Ruben Patterson 4.00 10.00
41 Malik Rose 4.00 10.00
42 Don Buse 4.00 10.00
43 Walter McCarty 3.00 8.00
44 Jerome Williams 4.00 10.00
45 Sam Mitchell 4.00 10.00
46 John Lucas 4.00 10.00
47 Otis Thorpe 5.00 12.00
48 John Drew 4.00 10.00
49 Morris Peterson 4.00 10.00
50 Jay Humphries 4.00 10.00
51 Reed Sheppard 60.00 150.00
52 Jared McCain 60.00 150.00
53 Matas Buzelis 60.00 150.00
54 Dalton Knecht 60.00 150.00
55 Tristan da Silva 20.00 50.00
56 Jaylon Tyson 6.00 15.00
57 Tidjane Salaun 5.00 12.00
58 Pacome Dadiet 6.00 15.00
59 AJ Johnson 8.00 20.00
60 Devin Carter 6.00 15.00
61 Ja'Kobe Walter 6.00 15.00
62 Baylor Scheierman 6.00 15.00
63 Yves Missi 12.00 30.00
64 Donovan Clingan 25.00 60.00
65 Jonathan Mogbo 8.00 20.00
66 Kyshawn George 8.00 20.00
67 Dillon Jones 5.00 12.00
68 Tyler Kolek 8.00 20.00
69 Bub Carrington 25.00 60.00
70 Johnny Furphy 8.00 20.00
71 Terrence Shannon Jr. 25.00 60.00
72 DaRon Holmes II 6.00 15.00
73 Zach Edey 30.00 80.00
74 Bobi Klintman 6.00 15.00
75 Ajay Mitchell 8.00 20.00
76 KJ Simpson Jr. 5.00 12.00
77 Adem Bona 6.00 15.00
78 Oso Ighodaro 6.00 15.00
79 Cam Christie 6.00 15.00
80 Tristen Newton 5.00 12.00
81 Jamal Shead 6.00 15.00
82 Jaylen Wells 40.00 100.00
83 Pelle Larsson 5.00 12.00
84 Melvin Ajinca 4.00 10.00
85 Harrison Ingram 5.00 12.00
86 Cam Spencer 5.00 12.00
87 Kevin McCullar Jr. 5.00 12.00
88 Ulrich Chomche 4.00 10.00
89 Ariel Hukporti 4.00 10.00
90 PJ Hall 4.00 10.00
91 Keshad Johnson 4.00 10.00
92 Jalen Bridges 4.00 10.00
93 Trey Alexander 4.00 10.00
95 Armando Bacot 4.00 10.00
96 Quinten Post 25.00 60.00
97 Anton Watson 4.00 10.00
98 Enrique Freeman 4.00 10.00
99 Antonio Reeves 5.00 12.00
100 Judah Mintz 4.00 10.00

2024-25 Hoops High Voltage
1 Magic Johnson 3.00 8.00
2 Ron Holland II 1.50 4.00
3 Ja Morant 2.50 6.00
4 Anthony Edwards 4.00 10.00
5 Luka Doncic 5.00 12.00
6 Alexandre Sarr 2.50 6.00
7 Stephon Castle 4.00 10.00
8 Donovan Mitchell 1.50 4.00
9 Charles Barkley 2.00 5.00
10 Tracy McGrady 1.50 4.00
11 Tim Duncan 2.00 5.00
12 Zaccharie Risacher 2.50 6.00
13 Trae Young 1.50 4.00
14 Larry Bird 3.00 8.00
15 Victor Wembanyama 6.00 15.00
16 Karl Malone 1.50 4.00
17 Jayson Tatum 2.50 6.00
18 Carmelo Anthony 1.25 3.00
19 Reed Sheppard 2.50 6.00
20 Shai Gilgeous-Alexander 3.00 8.00
21 Stephen Curry 6.00 15.00
22 Yao Ming 1.50 4.00
23 Julius Erving 2.00 5.00
24 Shaquille O'Neal 3.00 8.00
25 LeBron James 6.00 15.00

2024-25 Hoops Highlights
1 Luka Doncic 4.00 10.00
2 Victor Wembanyama 5.00 12.00
3 LeBron James 5.00 12.00
4 Nikola Jokic 3.00 8.00
5 Damian Lillard 1.50 4.00

2024-25 Hoops HIPnotized
1 James Harden 1.50 4.00
2 Anthony Davis 2.00 5.00
3 Luka Doncic 5.00 12.00
4 Zach Edey 2.50 6.00
5 Zaccharie Risacher 2.00 5.00
6 Jaylen Brown 1.25 3.00
7 Joel Embiid 1.25 3.00
8 Shai Gilgeous-Alexander 3.00 8.00
9 Victor Wembanyama 6.00 15.00
10 Alexandre Sarr 2.50 6.00
11 Stephen Curry 6.00 15.00
12 Anthony Edwards 4.00 10.00
13 LeBron James 6.00 15.00
14 Jayson Tatum 2.50 6.00
15 Kevin Durant 2.50 6.00
16 Nikola Jokic 4.00 10.00
17 Kyrie Irving 2.00 5.00
18 Cody Williams 1.00 2.50
19 Damian Lillard 2.00 5.00
20 Reed Sheppard 2.00 5.00

2024-25 Hoops Hoopla
*HOLO: .75X TO 2X BASIC
*HOLO ARTIST PROOF/25: 10X TO 25X BASIC
1 Trae Young 1.00 2.50
2 Nikola Jokic 2.50 6.00
3 LeBron James 4.00 10.00
4 Stephon Castle 2.50 6.00
5 Zaccharie Risacher 1.25 3.00
6 Reed Sheppard 1.50 4.00
7 Anthony Edwards 2.50 6.00
8 Shai Gilgeous-Alexander 2.00 5.00
9 Stephen Curry 4.00 10.00
10 Ja Morant 1.50 4.00
11 Alexandre Sarr 1.50 4.00
12 Victor Wembanyama 4.00 10.00
13 Luka Doncic 3.00 8.00
14 Jayson Tatum 1.50 4.00
15 Ron Holland II 1.00 2.50

2024-25 Hoops Hoops Art Signatures Horizontal
1 Anthony Edwards
Donovan Clingan 600.00 1,200.00
2 Anthony Edwards
Matas Buzelis 800.00 1,500.00
3 Anthony Edwards
Reed Sheppard 800.00 1,500.00
4 Anthony Edwards
Tidjane Salaun 600.00 1,200.00
5 Anthony Edwards
Dalton Knecht 800.00 1,500.00

2024-25 Hoops Hoops Art Signatures Vertical
1 Donovan Clingan 300.00 600.00
2 Matas Buzelis 300.00 600.00
3 Reed Sheppard 300.00 600.00
4 Tidjane Salaun 200.00 500.00
5 Dalton Knecht 300.00 600.00

2024-25 Hoops Hoops Hopeful Memorabilia
*WINTER: .4X TO 1X BASIC
*PRIME/25: 1.25X TO 3X BASIC
1 Cody Williams 2.50 6.00
2 Yves Missi 5.00 12.00
3 Rob Dillingham 5.00 12.00
4 Devin Carter 2.50 6.00
5 Donovan Clingan 5.00 12.00
6 DaRon Holmes II 2.50 6.00
7 Pacome Dadiet 2.50 6.00
8 Zach Edey 6.00 15.00
9 Dalton Knecht 6.00 15.00
10 Terrence Shannon Jr. 4.00 10.00
11 Alexandre Sarr 6.00 15.00
12 Tidjane Salaun 2.00 5.00
13 Ron Holland II 4.00 10.00
14 Stephon Castle 10.00 25.00
15 Isaiah Collier 4.00 10.00
16 Jared McCain 8.00 20.00
17 Matas Buzelis 10.00 25.00
18 Kyshawn George 3.00 8.00
19 Jonathan Mogbo 3.00 8.00
20 Tristan da Silva 5.00 12.00
21 Bub Carrington 5.00 12.00
22 Zaccharie Risacher 5.00 12.00
23 Bronny James Jr. 8.00 20.00
24 Kyle Filipowski 5.00 12.00
25 Reed Sheppard 6.00 15.00
26 Johnny Furphy 3.00 8.00
27 Antonio Reeves 2.00 5.00
28 Baylor Scheierman 2.50 6.00
29 Jaylon Tyson 2.50 6.00
30 Nikola Topic 6.00 15.00
31 Ryan Dunn 2.50 6.00
32 Ja'Kobe Walter 2.50 6.00
33 Kel'el Ware 5.00 12.00
34 Dillon Jones 2.00 5.00
35 AJ Johnson 3.00 8.00

2024-25 Hoops Hoops Ink
*RED/25: .75X TO 2X BASIC
1 Stephen Curry 400.00 800.00
2 Cade Cunningham 50.00 120.00
3 Jalen Duren 5.00 12.00
4 Cason Wallace 6.00 15.00
5 Max Christie 5.00 12.00
6 Shawn Kemp 15.00 40.00
8 Christian Braun 6.00 15.00
9 Miles McBride 4.00 10.00
10 Chet Holmgren 40.00 100.00
11 Jaden Hardy 5.00 12.00
12 Amen Thompson 40.00 100.00
13 Nikola Vucevic 4.00 10.00
14 Jabari Smith Jr. 5.00 12.00
15 Ausar Thompson 8.00 20.00
16 Anfernee Hardaway 40.00 100.00
17 Jalen Suggs 5.00 12.00
18 Jake LaRavia 4.00 10.00
19 Shaedon Sharpe 6.00 15.00
20 Ousmane Dieng 4.00 10.00
21 Walker Kessler 4.00 10.00
22 Aaron Gordon 5.00 12.00
23 Larry Nance 3.00 8.00
24 Jeff Hornacek 4.00 10.00
25 Harold Miner 4.00 10.00
26 Russell Westbrook 60.00 150.00
29 Yuta Watanabe 5.00 12.00
30 Paolo Banchero 50.00 120.00
31 Brad Daugherty 4.00 10.00
32 Caris LeVert 4.00 10.00
33 Dorian Finney-Smith 3.00 8.00
35 Magic Johnson 50.00 120.00
36 Gabe Vincent 3.00 8.00
37 Daniel Gafford 4.00 10.00
38 Jaden Ivey 6.00 15.00
39 Chris Mullin 6.00 15.00
40 Jabari Walker 3.00 8.00
41 Dominique Wilkins 8.00 20.00
42 Nickeil Alexander-Walker 3.00 8.00
43 Nicolas Batum 3.00 8.00
44 Shai Gilgeous-Alexander 200.00 500.00
45 GG Jackson II 10.00 25.00
46 Alex Caruso 5.00 12.00
47 MarJon Beauchamp 4.00 10.00
48 Brook Lopez 4.00 10.00
49 Terry Cummings 5.00 12.00
50 Moses Moody 5.00 12.00

2024-25 Hoops Hoops Throwback
1 Zion Williamson 2.00 5.00
2 Victor Wembanyama 6.00 15.00
3 Ja Morant 2.50 6.00
4 Luka Doncic 5.00 12.00
5 Shai Gilgeous-Alexander 3.00 8.00
6 Jayson Tatum 2.50 6.00
7 Jaylen Brown 1.25 3.00
8 Stephen Curry 6.00 15.00
9 Kawhi Leonard 1.50 4.00
10 Giannis Antetokounmpo 3.00 8.00
11 Tyrese Haliburton 1.50 4.00
12 Joel Embiid 1.25 3.00
13 Jimmy Butler 1.25 3.00
14 LeBron James 6.00 15.00
15 Donovan Mitchell 1.50 4.00
16 Paolo Banchero 2.00 5.00
17 Anthony Edwards 4.00 10.00
18 Nikola Jokic 4.00 10.00
19 Jalen Brunson 1.50 4.00
20 Damian Lillard 2.00 5.00
21 Devin Booker 2.00 5.00
22 De'Aaron Fox 1.50 4.00
23 Trae Young 1.50 4.00
24 Kevin Durant 2.50 6.00
25 Tyrese Maxey 1.50 4.00

2024-25 Hoops Hot Signatures
*RED/25: .75X TO 2X BASIC
1 Trae Young 40.00 100.00
2 Johnny Davis 4.00 10.00
3 Ja Morant 100.00 250.00
4 Ben Simmons 5.00 12.00
6 Cole Anthony 5.00 12.00
7 Tyler Herro 20.00 50.00
8 Jarrett Allen 4.00 10.00
9 Jaylin Williams 4.00 10.00
10 Lance Stephenson 4.00 10.00
11 Jalen Suggs 5.00 12.00
12 Jusuf Nurkic 4.00 10.00
13 Dyson Daniels 6.00 15.00
14 Jalen Green 10.00 25.00
15 Amen Thompson 40.00 100.00
16 Andrew Nembhard 4.00 10.00
17 Shaedon Sharpe 6.00 15.00
18 Jeremy Sochan 5.00 12.00
19 Jabari Smith Jr. 5.00 12.00
20 Mark Williams 4.00 10.00
21 George McGinnis 5.00 12.00
22 Christian Laettner 5.00 12.00
23 P.J. Washington Jr. 4.00 10.00
24 Rik Smits 4.00 10.00
25 Max Christie 5.00 12.00
26 Evan Mobley 6.00 15.00
27 Paolo Banchero 12.00 30.00
29 Jeff Green 4.00 10.00
30 Shawn Kemp 15.00 40.00
31 Evan Fournier 4.00 10.00
32 Sun Yue 12.00 30.00
33 Trey Murphy III 6.00 15.00
34 Thanasis Antetokounmpo 4.00 10.00
35 Quentin Richardson 4.00 10.00
37 Max Strus 4.00 10.00
38 Dell Curry 5.00 12.00
39 Jaden Ivey 6.00 15.00
40 Norman Powell 5.00 12.00
41 Luke Kennard 4.00 10.00
42 Tom Van Arsdale 5.00 12.00
43 Cade Cunningham 50.00 120.00
44 Royce O'Neale 4.00 10.00
45 Jalen Duren 5.00 12.00
46 Cameron Thomas 5.00 12.00
47 Jeff Hornacek 4.00 10.00
48 Jaden Hardy 5.00 12.00
49 Carlos Boozer 4.00 10.00
50 Cason Wallace 6.00 15.00

2024-25 Hoops Hot Signatures Rookies
*RED/25: .75X TO 2X BASIC
1 Reed Sheppard 60.00 150.00
2 Jared McCain 60.00 150.00
3 Matas Buzelis 60.00 150.00
4 Dalton Knecht 60.00 150.00
5 Tristan da Silva 20.00 50.00
6 Jaylon Tyson 6.00 15.00
7 Tidjane Salaun 5.00 12.00
8 Pacome Dadiet 6.00 15.00
9 AJ Johnson 8.00 20.00
10 Devin Carter 6.00 15.00
11 Ja'Kobe Walter 6.00 15.00
12 Baylor Scheierman 6.00 15.00
13 Yves Missi 12.00 30.00
14 Donovan Clingan 25.00 60.00
15 Jonathan Mogbo 8.00 20.00
16 Kyshawn George 8.00 20.00
17 Dillon Jones 5.00 12.00
18 Tyler Kolek 8.00 20.00
19 Bub Carrington 25.00 60.00
20 Johnny Furphy 8.00 20.00
21 Terrence Shannon Jr. 25.00 60.00
22 DaRon Holmes II 6.00 15.00
23 Zach Edey 30.00 80.00
24 Bobi Klintman 6.00 15.00
25 Ajay Mitchell 8.00 20.00
26 KJ Simpson Jr. 5.00 12.00
27 Adem Bona 6.00 15.00
28 Oso Ighodaro 6.00 15.00
29 Cam Christie 6.00 15.00
30 Tristen Newton 5.00 12.00
31 Jamal Shead 6.00 15.00
32 Jaylen Wells 40.00 100.00
33 Pelle Larsson 5.00 12.00
34 Melvin Ajinca 4.00 10.00
35 Harrison Ingram 5.00 12.00
36 Cam Spencer 5.00 12.00
37 Kevin McCullar Jr. 4.00 10.00
38 Ulrich Chomche 4.00 10.00
39 Ariel Hukporti 4.00 10.00
40 PJ Hall 4.00 10.00
41 Keshad Johnson 4.00 10.00
42 Jalen Bridges 4.00 10.00
43 Trey Alexander 4.00 10.00
44 Trentyn Flowers 4.00 10.00
45 Armando Bacot 4.00 10.00
46 Quinten Post 25.00 60.00
47 Anton Watson 4.00 10.00
48 Enrique Freeman 4.00 10.00
49 Antonio Reeves 5.00 12.00
50 Judah Mintz 4.00 10.00

2024-25 Hoops Ignition
*HOLO: .75X TO 2X BASIC
1 Dalton Knecht 1.50 4.00
2 Kevin Durant 1.50 4.00
3 Stephen Curry 4.00 10.00
4 Zaccharie Risacher 1.25 3.00
5 Stephon Castle 2.50 6.00
6 Paolo Banchero 1.25 3.00
7 Jaylen Brown .75 2.00
8 Bronny James Jr. 2.00 5.00
9 Tyrese Haliburton 1.00 2.50
10 Anthony Edwards 2.50 6.00
11 Shai Gilgeous-Alexander 2.00 5.00
12 Reed Sheppard 1.50 4.00
13 Jayson Tatum 1.50 4.00
14 Rob Dillingham 1.25 3.00
15 Damian Lillard 1.25 3.00
16 Ja Morant 1.50 4.00
17 Nikola Jokic 2.50 6.00
18 Victor Wembanyama 4.00 10.00
19 Anthony Davis 1.25 3.00
20 Luka Doncic 3.00 8.00
21 Jalen Brunson 1.00 2.50
22 Giannis Antetokounmpo 2.00 5.00
23 Ron Holland II 1.00 2.50
24 Zion Williamson 1.25 3.00
25 Donovan Clingan 1.25 3.00
26 Tyrese Maxey 1.00 2.50
27 LeBron James 4.00 10.00
28 Alexandre Sarr 1.50 4.00
29 Jared McCain 2.00 5.00
30 Trae Young 1.00 2.50

2024-25 Hoops Nobility
*HOLO: .75X TO 2X BASIC
*HOLO ARTIST PROOF/25: 8X TO 20X BASIC
1 Anthony Edwards 2.50 6.00
2 Nikola Jokic 2.50 6.00
3 Damian Lillard 1.25 3.00
4 LeBron James 4.00 10.00
5 Tyrese Haliburton 1.00 2.50
6 Ja Morant 1.50 4.00
7 Jayson Tatum 1.50 4.00
8 Zion Williamson 1.25 3.00
9 Stephen Curry 4.00 10.00
10 Jalen Brunson 1.00 2.50
11 Kevin Durant 1.50 4.00
12 Shai Gilgeous-Alexander 2.00 5.00
13 Victor Wembanyama 4.00 10.00
14 Trae Young 1.00 2.50
15 Luka Doncic 3.00 8.00

2024-25 Hoops Now Playing
*HOLO: .75X TO 2X BASIC
1 Matas Buzelis 3.00 8.00
2 Dalton Knecht 2.50 6.00
3 Johnny Furphy 1.00 2.50
4 Bub Carrington 1.50 4.00
5 AJ Johnson 1.00 2.50
6 Rob Dillingham 1.50 4.00
7 Ja'Kobe Walter .75 2.00
8 Jared McCain 2.50 6.00
9 Jamal Shead .75 2.00
10 Nikola Topic 2.00 5.00
11 Cody Williams .75 2.00
12 Yves Missi 1.50 4.00
13 Bronny James Jr. 2.50 6.00
14 Kyshawn George 1.00 2.50
15 Antonio Reeves .60 1.50
16 Stephon Castle 3.00 8.00
17 Ron Holland II 1.25 3.00
18 Tidjane Salaun .60 1.50
19 Reed Sheppard 2.00 5.00
20 Donovan Clingan 1.50 4.00
21 Kel'el Ware 1.50 4.00
22 Zach Edey 2.00 5.00
23 Tyler Smith .75 2.00
24 Tristan da Silva 1.50 4.00
25 DaRon Holmes II .75 2.00
26 Jaylon Tyson .75 2.00
27 Alexandre Sarr 2.00 5.00
28 Tyler Kolek 1.00 2.50
29 Pacome Dadiet .75 2.00
30 Devin Carter .75 2.00
31 Zaccharie Risacher 1.50 4.00

2024-25 Hoops Parade
1 Boston Celtics 8.00 20.00

2024-25 Hoops Presentations
1 Luka Doncic 60.00 150.00
2 LeBron James 80.00 200.00
3 Stephen Curry 80.00 200.00
4 Jayson Tatum 30.00 80.00
5 Ja Morant 30.00 80.00
6 Shai Gilgeous-Alexander 40.00 100.00
7 Anthony Edwards 50.00 125.00
8 Nikola Jokic 50.00 125.00
9 Zion Williamson 25.00 60.00
10 Victor Wembanyama 80.00 200.00
11 Zaccharie Risacher 25.00 60.00
12 Alexandre Sarr 30.00 80.00
13 Reed Sheppard 30.00 80.00
14 Stephon Castle 50.00 125.00
15 Ron Holland II 20.00 50.00
16 Rob Dillingham 25.00 60.00
17 Donovan Clingan 25.00 60.00
18 Matas Buzelis 50.00 120.00
19 Dalton Knecht 30.00 80.00
20 Bronny James Jr. 40.00 100.00

2024-25 Hoops Pure Players
*WINTER: .4X TO 1X BASIC
*HOLO: .75X TO 2X BASIC
*WINTER HOLO: .75X TO 2X BASIC
1 Stephen Curry 4.00 10.00
2 Jayson Tatum 1.50 4.00
3 Nikola Jokic 2.50 6.00
4 Anthony Edwards 2.50 6.00
5 Ja Morant 1.50 4.00
6 Shai Gilgeous-Alexander 2.00 5.00
7 Giannis Antetokounmpo 2.00 5.00
8 LeBron James 4.00 10.00
9 Victor Wembanyama 4.00 10.00
10 Luka Doncic 3.00 8.00

2024-25 Hoops Rise N Shine Dual Memorabilia
*WINTER: .4X TO 1X BASIC
*PRIME/25: 1.25X TO 3X BASIC
1 Alexandre Sarr
Zaccharie Risacher 8.00 20.00
2 Reed Sheppard
Rob Dillingham 8.00 20.00
3 Donovan Clingan
Stephon Castle 12.00 30.00
4 Donovan Clingan
Zach Edey 8.00 20.00
5 Tidjane Salaun
Zaccharie Risacher 6.00 15.00
6 Cody Williams
Tristan da Silva 6.00 15.00
7 Reed Sheppard
Stephon Castle 12.00 30.00
8 Nikola Topic
Tidjane Salaun 8.00 20.00
9 Bronny James Jr.
Isaiah Collier 10.00 25.00
10 Jared McCain
Kyle Filipowski 10.00 25.00
11 Rob Dillingham
Terrence Shannon Jr. 6.00 15.00
12 Alexandre Sarr
Bub Carrington 8.00 20.00
13 Ja'Kobe Walter
Yves Missi 6.00 15.00
14 Matas Buzelis
Ron Holland II 12.00 30.00
15 Bronny James Jr.
Dalton Knecht 15.00 40.00

2024-25 Hoops Rise N Shine Memorabilia
*WINTER: .4X TO 1X BASIC
*PRIME/25: 1.25X TO 3X BASIC
1 Dalton Knecht 6.00 15.00
2 Reed Sheppard 6.00 15.00
3 Tyler Kolek 3.00 8.00
4 Bub Carrington 5.00 12.00
5 DaRon Holmes II 2.50 6.00
6 Kyshawn George 3.00 8.00
7 Ron Holland II 4.00 10.00
8 Nikola Topic 6.00 15.00
9 Ryan Dunn 2.50 6.00
10 Zaccharie Risacher 6.00 15.00
11 Cody Williams 2.50 6.00
12 Devin Carter 2.50 6.00
13 Baylor Scheierman 2.50 6.00
14 Kel'el Ware 5.00 12.00
15 Pacome Dadiet 2.50 6.00
16 Terrence Shannon Jr. 2.50 6.00
17 Stephon Castle 6.00 15.00
18 AJ Johnson 3.00 8.00
19 Dillon Jones 2.00 5.00
20 Bronny James Jr. 10.00 25.00
21 Matas Buzelis 10.00 25.00
22 Donovan Clingan 5.00 12.00
23 Yves Missi 5.00 12.00
24 Alexandre Sarr 6.00 15.00
25 Jaylon Tyson 2.50 6.00
26 Jared McCain 8.00 20.00
27 Tyler Smith 2.50 6.00
28 Johnny Furphy 3.00 8.00
29 Ja'Kobe Walter 2.50 6.00
30 Tristan da Silva 5.00 12.00
31 Zach Edey 6.00 15.00
32 Kyle Filipowski 5.00 12.00
33 Rob Dillingham 5.00 12.00
34 Isaiah Collier 4.00 10.00
35 Tidjane Salaun 2.00 5.00

2024-25 Hoops Road to the Finals Conference Finals
STATED PRINT RUN 499 SER.#'d SETS
1 Luka Doncic 15.00 40.00
2 Kyrie Irving 6.00 15.00
3 P.J. Washington Jr. 2.00 5.00
4 Dereck Lively II 2.50 6.00
5 Anthony Edwards 12.00 30.00
6 Karl-Anthony Towns 4.00 10.00
7 Jayson Tatum 8.00 20.00
8 Jaylen Brown 4.00 10.00
9 Derrick White 2.50 6.00
10 Jrue Holiday 3.00 8.00
11 Tyrese Haliburton 5.00 12.00
12 Pascal Siakam 3.00 8.00

2024-25 Hoops Road to the Finals First Round Recap
1 Shai Gilgeous-Alexander 3.00 8.00
2 Luka Doncic 5.00 12.00
3 Anthony Edwards 4.00 10.00
4 Nikola Jokic 4.00 10.00
5 Jayson Tatum 2.50 6.00
6 Donovan Mitchell 1.50 4.00
7 Tyrese Haliburton 1.50 4.00
8 Jalen Brunson 1.50 4.00

2024-25 Hoops Road to the Finals NBA Championship
STATED PRINT RUN 199 SER.#'d SETS
1 Jayson Tatum 15.00 40.00
2 Jaylen Brown 8.00 20.00
3 Derrick White 5.00 12.00
4 Jrue Holiday 6.00 15.00
5 Luka Doncic 30.00 80.00
6 Kyrie Irving 12.00 30.00

2024-25 Hoops Road to the Finals Second Round
STATED PRINT RUN 999 SER.#'d SETS
1 Shai Gilgeous-Alexander 5.00 12.00
2 Chet Holmgren 2.00 5.00
3 Jalen Williams 2.50 6.00
4 Luka Doncic 8.00 20.00
5 Kyrie Irving 3.00 8.00
6 P.J. Washington Jr. 1.00 2.50
7 Dereck Lively II 1.25 3.00
8 Nikola Jokic 6.00 15.00
9 Jamal Murray 2.00 5.00
10 Michael Porter Jr. 1.25 3.00
11 Anthony Edwards 6.00 15.00
12 Karl-Anthony Towns 2.00 5.00
13 Jaden McDaniels 1.25 3.00
14 Jayson Tatum 4.00 10.00
15 Jaylen Brown 2.00 5.00
16 Derrick White 1.25 3.00
17 Jrue Holiday 1.50 4.00
18 Donovan Mitchell 2.50 6.00
19 Evan Mobley 1.50 4.00
20 Caris LeVert 1.00 2.50
21 Tyrese Haliburton 2.50 6.00
22 Pascal Siakam 1.50 4.00
23 Myles Turner 1.00 2.50
24 Jalen Brunson 2.50 6.00
25 Donte DiVincenzo 1.25 3.00
26 Josh Hart 1.00 2.50

2024-25 Hoops Rookie Greetings
*WINTER: .4X TO 1X BASIC
*HOLO: .75X TO 2X BASIC
*WINTER HOLO: .75X TO 2X BASIC
1 Reed Sheppard 2.00 5.00
2 Kel'el Ware 1.50 4.00
3 Ron Holland II 1.25 3.00
4 Zach Edey 2.00 5.00
5 Donovan Clingan 1.50 4.00
6 Bronny James Jr. 2.50 6.00
7 Tidjane Salaun .60 1.50
8 Ja'Kobe Walter .75 2.00
9 Jared McCain 2.50 6.00
10 Rob Dillingham 1.50 4.00
11 Bub Carrington 1.50 4.00
12 Cody Williams .75 2.00
13 Stephon Castle 3.00 8.00
14 Devin Carter .75 2.00
15 Zaccharie Risacher 1.50 4.00
16 Matas Buzelis 3.00 8.00
17 Alexandre Sarr 2.00 5.00
18 Tristan da Silva 1.50 4.00
19 Dalton Knecht 2.00 5.00
20 Nikola Topic 2.00 5.00

2024-25 Hoops Rookie Ink
*RED/25: .75X TO 2X BASIC
1 Ariel Hukporti 4.00 10.00
2 Baylor Scheierman 6.00 15.00
3 Donovan Clingan 25.00 60.00
4 Jaylen Wells 40.00 100.00
5 Adem Bona 6.00 15.00
6 Reed Sheppard 60.00 150.00
7 Oso Ighodaro 6.00 15.00
8 KJ Simpson Jr. 5.00 12.00
9 Ulrich Chomche 4.00 10.00
10 Trey Alexander 4.00 10.00
11 Dillon Jones 5.00 12.00
12 Tyler Kolek 8.00 20.00
13 Jaylon Tyson 6.00 15.00
14 Tristen Newton 5.00 12.00
15 Tidjane Salaun 5.00 12.00
16 Terrence Shannon Jr. 25.00 60.00
17 Yves Missi 12.00 30.00
18 Pelle Larsson 5.00 12.00
19 AJ Johnson 8.00 20.00
20 Harrison Ingram 5.00 12.00
21 Kevin McCullar Jr. 5.00 12.00
22 DaRon Holmes II 6.00 15.00
23 Jonathan Mogbo 8.00 20.00
24 Kyshawn George 8.00 20.00
25 Melvin Ajinca 4.00 10.00
26 Devin Carter 6.00 15.00
27 Keshad Johnson 4.00 10.00
28 Cam Christie 6.00 15.00
29 Dalton Knecht 60.00 150.00
30 Ajay Mitchell 8.00 20.00
31 Johnny Furphy 8.00 20.00
32 Matas Buzelis 60.00 150.00
33 Jared McCain 60.00 150.00
34 Armando Bacot 4.00 10.00
35 Pacome Dadiet 6.00 15.00
36 Jalen Bridges 4.00 10.00
37 Ja'Kobe Walter 6.00 15.00
38 Jamal Shead 6.00 15.00
39 PJ Hall 4.00 10.00
40 Zach Edey 30.00 80.00
41 Bub Carrington 25.00 60.00
42 Tristan da Silva 20.00 50.00
43 Cam Spencer 5.00 12.00
44 Trentyn Flowers 4.00 10.00
45 Bobi Klintman 6.00 15.00
46 Quinten Post 25.00 60.00
47 Anton Watson 4.00 10.00
48 Enrique Freeman 4.00 10.00
49 Antonio Reeves 5.00 12.00
50 Judah Mintz 4.00 10.00

2024-25 Hoops Rookie Remembrance Memorabilia
*WINTER: .4X TO 1X BASIC
*PRIME/25: 1.25X TO 3X BASIC
1 Ja Morant 6.00 15.00
2 Zion Williamson 5.00 12.00
3 Tyrese Haliburton 4.00 10.00
4 Anthony Edwards 10.00 25.00
5 Cade Cunningham 5.00 12.00
6 Paolo Banchero 5.00 12.00
7 Chet Holmgren 3.00 8.00
8 Tyrese Maxey 4.00 10.00
9 Donovan Mitchell 4.00 10.00
10 Jayson Tatum 6.00 15.00
11 Alperen Sengun 3.00 8.00
12 Scottie Barnes 2.50 6.00
13 Victor Wembanyama 15.00 40.00
14 Brandon Miller 3.00 8.00
15 Scoot Henderson 2.50 6.00

2024-25 Hoops Rookie Special
*HOLO: .75X TO 2X BASIC
1 Reed Sheppard 2.50 6.00
2 Tidjane Salaun .75 2.00
3 Donovan Clingan 2.00 5.00
4 Dalton Knecht 2.50 6.00

2024-25 Hoops Rookie Sweaters
1 Zaccharie Risacher 8.00 20.00
2 Alexandre Sarr 10.00 25.00
3 Reed Sheppard 10.00 25.00
4 Stephon Castle 15.00 40.00
5 Ron Holland II 6.00 15.00
6 Tidjane Salaun 3.00 8.00
7 Donovan Clingan 8.00 20.00
8 Rob Dillingham 8.00 20.00
9 Zach Edey 10.00 25.00
10 Cody Williams 4.00 10.00
11 Matas Buzelis 15.00 40.00
12 Nikola Topic 10.00 25.00
13 Devin Carter 4.00 10.00
14 Bub Carrington 8.00 20.00
15 Kel'el Ware 8.00 20.00
16 Jared McCain 12.00 30.00
17 Dalton Knecht 10.00 25.00
18 Tristan da Silva 8.00 20.00
19 Ja'Kobe Walter 4.00 10.00
20 Jaylon Tyson 4.00 10.00
21 Yves Missi 8.00 20.00
22 DaRon Holmes II 4.00 10.00
23 AJ Johnson 5.00 12.00
24 Kyshawn George 5.00 12.00
25 Pacome Dadiet 4.00 10.00
26 Dillon Jones 3.00 8.00
28 Jonathan Mogbo 5.00 12.00
29 Johnny Furphy 5.00 12.00
30 Bobi Klintman 4.00 10.00
31 Tyler Kolek 5.00 12.00
32 Bronny James Jr. 12.00 30.00
33 Antonio Reeves 3.00 8.00

2024-25 Hoops Sheesh
*HOLO: .75X TO 2X BASIC
*HOLO ARTIST PROOF/25: 8X TO 20X BASIC
1 De'Aaron Fox 1.00 2.50
2 Zaccharie Risacher 1.25 3.00
3 Cody Williams .60 1.50
4 Kawhi Leonard 1.00 2.50
5 Matas Buzelis 2.50 6.00
6 Shai Gilgeous-Alexander 2.00 5.00
7 Jayson Tatum 1.50 4.00
8 Damian Lillard 1.25 3.00
9 Nikola Jokic 2.50 6.00
10 Stephen Curry 4.00 10.00
11 LeBron James 4.00 10.00
12 Luka Doncic 3.00 8.00
13 Anthony Edwards 2.50 6.00
14 Kyrie Irving 1.25 3.00
15 Alexandre Sarr 1.50 4.00
16 Giannis Antetokounmpo 2.00 5.00
17 Reed Sheppard 1.50 4.00
18 Tyrese Maxey 1.00 2.50
19 Victor Wembanyama 4.00 10.00
20 Devin Booker 1.25 3.00

2024-25 Hoops Skyview
*WINTER: .4X TO 1X BASIC
*HOLO: .75X TO 2X BASIC
*WINTER HOLO: .75X TO 2X BASIC
1 Jaylen Brown .75 2.00
2 Donovan Mitchell 1.00 2.50
3 Stephon Castle 2.50 6.00
4 Dalton Knecht 1.50 4.00
5 Cody Williams .60 1.50
6 Zion Williamson 1.25 3.00
7 Giannis Antetokounmpo 2.00 5.00
8 Alexandre Sarr 1.50 4.00
9 Ron Holland II 1.00 2.50
10 Stephen Curry 4.00 10.00
11 Anthony Edwards 2.50 6.00
12 Anthony Davis 1.25 3.00
13 Reed Sheppard 1.50 4.00
14 Zach Edey 1.50 4.00
15 Chet Holmgren .75 2.00
16 Victor Wembanyama 4.00 10.00
17 LeBron James 4.00 10.00
18 Donovan Clingan 1.25 3.00
19 Luka Doncic 3.00 8.00
20 Paolo Banchero 1.25 3.00
21 Bronny James Jr. 2.00 5.00
22 Joel Embiid .75 2.00
23 Zaccharie Risacher 1.25 3.00
24 Jayson Tatum 1.50 4.00
25 Ja Morant 1.50 4.00

2024-25 Hoops We Got Next
*HOLO: .75X TO 2X BASIC
1 AJ Johnson 1.00 2.50
2 Zaccharie Risacher 1.50 4.00
3 Bobi Klintman .75 2.00
4 Isaiah Collier 1.25 3.00
5 Rob Dillingham 1.50 4.00
6 Reed Sheppard 2.00 5.00
7 Devin Carter .75 2.00
8 Ja'Kobe Walter .75 2.00
9 Kyle Filipowski 1.50 4.00
10 Tyler Kolek 1.00 2.50
11 Dillon Jones .60 1.50
12 Tidjane Salaun .60 1.50
13 Ron Holland II 1.25 3.00
14 Donovan Clingan 1.50 4.00
15 Bronny James Jr. 2.50 6.00
16 Matas Buzelis 3.00 8.00
17 Alexandre Sarr 2.00 5.00
18 Cam Christie .75 2.00
19 Yves Missi 1.50 4.00
20 Johnny Furphy 1.00 2.50
21 Jared McCain 2.50 6.00
22 Terrence Shannon Jr. 1.25 3.00
23 DaRon Holmes II .75 2.00
24 Tristan da Silva 1.50 4.00
25 Jaylon Tyson .75 2.00
26 Nikola Topic 2.00 5.00
27 Kyshawn George 1.00 2.50
28 Bub Carrington 1.50 4.00
29 Stephon Castle 3.00 8.00
30 Dalton Knecht 2.00 5.00
31 Zach Edey 2.00 5.00
32 Cody Williams .75 2.00
33 Ryan Dunn .75 2.00
34 Kel'el Ware 1.50 4.00
35 Pacome Dadiet .75 2.00

1990 Hoops 100 Superstars
COMP.FACT SET (100) 6.00 15.00
1 Doc Rivers .20 .50
2 Dominique Wilkins .40 1.00
3 Spud Webb .20 .50
4 Moses Malone .20 .50
5 Reggie Lewis .20 .50
6 Larry Bird .75 2.00
7 Kevin McHale .40 1.00
8 Robert Parish .20 .50
9 Muggsy Bogues .30 .75
10 Rex Chapman .20 .50
11 Kelly Tripucka .07 .10
12 Michael Jordan 2.00 5.00

13 Scottie Pippen .75 2.00
14 John Paxson .15 .40
15 Bill Cartwright .15 .40
16 Mark Price .30 .75
17 Larry Nance .20 .50
18 Hot Rod Williams .07 .10
19 Brad Daugherty .07 .20
20 Derek Harper .20 .50
21 Rolando Blackman .20 .50
22 Sam Perkins .20 .50
23 James Donaldson .07 .10
24 Michael Adams .07 .10
25 Lafayette Lever .07 .10
26 Alex English .07 .20
27 Isiah Thomas .40 1.00
28 Joe Dumars .40 1.00
29 Bill Laimbeer .30 .75
30 Dennis Rodman .50 1.25
31 Mitch Richmond .60 1.50
32 Chris Mullin .30 .75
33 Manute Bol .07 .20
34 Rod Higgins .07 .10
35 Sleepy Floyd .07 .10
36 Otis Thorpe .07 .20
37 Buck Johnson .07 .10
38 Hakeem Olajuwon .40 1.00
39 Vern Fleming .07 .10
40 Reggie Miller .40 1.00
41 Chuck Person .07 .20
42 Rik Smits .30 .75
43 Benoit Benjamin .07 .10
44 Charles Smith .08 .25
45 Gary Grant .07 .10
46 Danny Manning .50 1.25
47 Magic Johnson .60 1.50
48 Byron Scott .20 .50
49 A.C. Green .20 .50
50 James Worthy .30 .75
51 Kevin Edwards .07 .10
52 Rory Sparrow .07 .10
53 Rony Seikaly .07 .20
54 Jay Humphries .07 .10
55 Alvin Robertson .07 .20
56 Ricky Pierce .07 .20
57 Jack Sikma .07 .20
58 Tyrone Corbin .07 .10
59 Sidney Lowe .07 .10
60 Steve Johnson .07 .10
61 Dennis Hopson .07 .10
62 Chris Morris .07 .10
63 Roy Hinson .07 .10
64 Mark Jackson .30 .75
65 Gerald Wilkins .07 .10
66 Charles Oakley .07 .20
67 Patrick Ewing .40 1.00
68 Reggie Theus .20 .50
69 Sam Vincent .07 .10
70 Terry Catledge .07 .10
71 Hersey Hawkins .30 .75
72 Johnny Dawkins .07 .10
73 Charles Barkley .40 1.00
74 Mike Gminski .07 .20
75 Kevin Johnson .40 1.00
76 Jeff Hornacek .40 1.00
77 Tom Chambers .20 .50
78 Eddie Johnson .07 .20
79 Terry Porter .20 .50
80 Clyde Drexler .40 1.00
81 Jerome Kersey .07 .10
82 Kevin Duckworth .07 .10
83 Danny Ainge .30 .75
84 Rodney McCray .07 .10
85 Wayman Tisdale .20 .50
86 Willie Anderson .07 .20
87 Terry Cummings .15 .40
88 David Robinson .75 2.00
89 Dale Ellis .07 .20
90 Derrick McKey .07 .20
91 Xavier McDaniel .07 .10
92 Michael Cage .07 .10
93 John Stockton .60 1.50
94 Karl Malone .60 1.50
95 Thurl Bailey .07 .20
96 Mark Eaton .07 .20
97 Jeff Malone .07 .10
98 Darrell Walker .07 .10
99 Bernard King .20 .50
100 John Williams .07 .20

1991 Hoops 100 Superstars
COMP.FACT SET (100) 25.00 60.00
1 Moses Malone .40 1.00
2 Doc Rivers .40 1.00
3 Spud Webb .25 .60
4 Dominique Wilkins 1.25 3.00
5 Larry Bird 2.50 6.00
6 Reggie Lewis .40 1.00
7 Kevin McHale .50 1.25
8 Robert Parish .40 1.00
9 Brian Shaw .25 .60
10 Muggsy Bogues .40 1.00
11 Johnny Newman .15 .40
12 Horace Grant .40 1.00
13 Michael Jordan 10.00 25.00
14 Scottie Pippen 2.00 5.00
15 Brad Daugherty .15 .40
16 Craig Ehlo .15 .40
17 Larry Nance .40 1.00
18 Mark Price .60 1.50
19 Hot Rod Williams .15 .40
20 Rolando Blackman .15 .40
21 James Donaldson .15 .40
22 Derek Harper .40 1.00
23 Fat Lever .15 .40
24 Roy Tarpley .15 .40
25 Michael Adams .15 .40
26 Orlando Woolridge .15 .40
27 Joe Dumars .75 2.00
28 Bill Laimbeer .75 2.00
29 Vinnie Johnson .40 1.00
30 Dennis Rodman 1.25 3.00
31 Isiah Thomas 1.25 3.00
32 Chris Mullin .75 2.00
33 Tim Hardaway .75 2.00
34 Mitch Richmond .75 2.00
35 Sleepy Floyd .15 .40
36 Hakeem Olajuwon 1.00 2.50
37 Kenny Smith .40 1.00
38 Otis Thorpe .25 .60
39 Reggie Miller 1.25 3.00
40 Chuck Person .15 .40
41 Detlef Schrempf .30 .75
42 Danny Manning .30 .75
43 Ken Norman .15 .40
44 Ron Harper .40 1.00
45 Charles Smith .15 .40
46 Vlade Divac .40 1.00
47 A.C. Green .40 1.00
48 Magic Johnson 2.00 5.00
49 Byron Scott .60 1.50
50 James Worthy .75 2.00
51 Sam Perkins .30 .75
52 Rony Seikaly .40 1.00
53 Sherman Douglas .15 .40
54 Glen Rice .75 2.00
55 Jay Humphries .15 .40
56 Alvin Robertson .15 .40
57 Jack Sikma .15 .40
58 Tony Campbell .15 .40
59 Tyrone Corbin .15 .40
60 Pooh Richardson .15 .40
61 Roy Hinson .15 .40
62 Chris Morris .15 .40
63 Reggie Theus .30 .75
64 Maurice Cheeks .30 .75
65 Patrick Ewing 1.00 2.50
66 Mark Jackson 8.00 20.00
67 Charles Oakley .25 .60
68 Nick Anderson .25 .60
69 Terry Catledge .15 .40
70 Scott Skiles .30 .75
71 Charles Barkley 1.50 4.00
72 Johnny Dawkins .25 .60
73 Hersey Hawkins .25 .60
74 Rick Mahorn .15 .40
75 Tom Chambers .25 .60
76 Jeff Hornacek .40 1.00
77 Kevin Johnson .40 1.00
78 Dan Majerle .40 1.00
79 Mark West .15 .40
80 Clyde Drexler 1.25 3.00
81 Terry Porter .20 .50
82 Jerome Kersey .15 .40
83 Buck Williams .30 .75
84 Antoine Carr .15 .40
85 Wayman Tisdale .15 .40
86 Willie Anderson .15 .40
87 Terry Cummings .25 .60
88 Paul Pressey .15 .40
89 David Robinson 2.00 5.00
90 Rod Strickland .25 .60
91 Michael Cage .15 .40
92 Shawn Kemp .75 2.00
93 Derrick McKey .15 .40
94 Thurl Bailey .15 .40
95 Jeff Malone .15 .40
96 Karl Malone 1.50 4.00
97 John Stockton 2.00 5.00
98 Harvey Grant .15 .40
99 Bernard King .30 .75
100 Darrell Walker .15 .40

1992 Hoops 100 Superstars
COMP.FACT SET (100) 60.00 150.00
1 Rumeal Robinson .25 .60
2 Dominique Wilkins 2.50 6.00
3 Kevin Willis .50 1.25
4 Larry Bird 6.00 15.00
5 Dee Brown .25 .60
6 Kevin Gamble .25 .60
7 Kevin McHale 1.50 4.00
8 Robert Parish 1.00 2.50
9 Dell Curry .25 .60
10 Muggsy Bogues 1.00 2.50
11 Kendall Gill .50 1.25
12 Johnny Newman .25 .60
13 Horace Grant 1.00 2.50
14 Michael Jordan 30.00 80.00
15 John Paxson 1.00 2.50
16 Scottie Pippen 4.00 10.00
17 Brad Daugherty .25 .60
18 Larry Nance .60 1.50
19 Mark Price 1.00 2.50
20 Hot Rod Williams .25 .60
21 Rolando Blackman .75 2.00
22 Derek Harper .75 2.00
23 Rodney McCray .25 .60
24 Chris Jackson .25 .60
25 Todd Lichti .25 .60
26 Orlando Woolridge .25 .60
27 Joe Dumars 1.25 3.00
28 Bill Laimbeer 1.00 2.50
29 Dennis Rodman 3.00 8.00
30 Isiah Thomas 2.50 6.00
31 Tim Hardaway 1.50 4.00
32 Sarunas Marciulionis .50 1.25
33 Chris Mullin 1.25 3.00
34 Hakeem Olajuwon 2.00 5.00
35 Kenny Smith .50 1.25
36 Otis Thorpe .50 1.25
37 Reggie Miller 2.00 5.00
38 Chuck Person .25 .60
39 Detlef Schrempf .50 1.25
40 Ron Harper .75 2.00
41 Danny Manning .75 2.00
42 Ken Norman .25 .60
43 Charles Smith .25 .60
44 Vlade Divac .75 2.00
45 A.C. Green .75 2.00
46 Magic Johnson 5.00 12.00
47 Sam Perkins .75 2.00
48 Byron Scott .75 2.00
49 James Worthy 1.50 4.00
50 Kevin Edwards .25 .60
51 Glen Rice 1.00 2.50
52 Rony Seikaly .25 .60
53 Dale Ellis .25 .60
54 Jay Humphries .25 .60
55 Moses Malone .75 2.00
56 Alvin Robertson .25 .60
57 Tony Campbell .25 .60
58 Sam Mitchell .25 .60
59 Pooh Richardson .25 .60
60 Felton Spencer .25 .60
61 Mookie Blaylock .50 1.25
62 Sam Bowie .50 1.25
63 Derrick Coleman .50 1.25
64 Patrick Ewing 2.00 5.00
65 Xavier McDaniel .25 .60
66 Charles Oakley .50 1.25
67 Kiki Vandeweghe .75 2.00
68 Gerald Wilkins .40 1.00
69 Terry Catledge .25 .60
70 Dennis Scott .40 1.00
71 Scott Skiles .50 1.25
72 Charles Barkley 4.00 0.00
73 Johnny Dawkins .25 .60
74 Armon Gilliam .25 .60
75 Hersey Hawkins .50 1.25
76 Tom Chambers .75 2.00
77 Jeff Hornacek .75 2.00
78 Kevin Johnson 1.00 2.50
79 Clyde Drexler 2.50 6.00
80 Jerome Kersey .50 1.25
81 Terry Porter .40 1.00
82 Mitch Richmond 1.25 3.00
83 Lionel Simmons .25 .60
84 Wayman Tisdale .25 .60
85 Spud Webb .75 2.00
86 Antoine Carr .25 .60
87 Sean Elliott 1.00 2.50
88 David Robinson 4.00 10.00
89 Rod Strickland .25 .60
90 Shawn Kemp 2.00 5.00
91 Gary Payton 2.00 5.00
92 Ricky Pierce .25 .60
93 Blue Edwards .25 .60
94 Jeff Malone .25 .60
95 Karl Malone 5.00 12.00
96 John Stockton 6.00 15.00
97 Michael Adams .25 .60
98 Pervis Ellison .25 .60
99 Harvey Grant .25 .60
100 Bernard King .75 2.00

1990 Hoops Action Photos
COMPLETE SET (160) 30.00 75.00
1 Michael Adams .50 1.25
2 Danny Ainge .50 1.25
3 Willie Anderson .50 1.25
4 Michael Ansley .50 1.25
5 Thurl Bailey .50 1.25
6 Charles Barkley .75 2.00
7 Charles Barkley .75 2.00
8 John Battle .50 1.25
9 Larry Bird 1.50 4.00
10 Larry Bird 1.50 4.00
11 Rolando Blackman .50 1.25
12 Muggsy Bogues .50 1.25
13 Manute Bol .50 1.25
14 Mark Bryant .50 1.25
15 Michael Cage .50 1.25
16 Tony Campbell .50 1.25
17 Bill Cartwright .50 1.25
18 Terry Catledge .50 1.25
19 Tom Chambers .50 1.25
20 Tom Chambers .50 1.25
21 Rex Chapman .50 1.25
22 Maurice Cheeks .50 1.25
23 Lester Conner .50 1.25
24 Michael Cooper .50 1.25
25 Tyrone Corbin .50 1.25
26 Dave Corzine .50 1.25
27 Terry Cummings .50 1.25
28 Dell Curry .50 1.25
29 Brad Daugherty .50 1.25
30 Brad Davis .50 1.25
31 Johnny Dawkins .50 1.25
32 James Donaldson .50 1.25
33 Sherman Douglas .50 1.25
34 Clyde Drexler .75 2.00
35 Clyde Drexler .75 2.00
36 Kevin Duckworth .50 1.25
37 Joe Dumars .50 1.25
38 Joe Dumars .50 1.25
39 Mark Eaton .50 1.25
40 Kevin Edwards .50 1.25
40 Scottie Pippen 1.50 4.00
41 Blue Edwards .50 1.25
42 Craig Ehlo .50 1.25
43 Sean Elliott .75 2.00
44 Dale Ellis .50 1.25
45 Dale Ellis .50 1.25
46 Alex English .50 1.25
47 Alex English .50 1.25
48 Patrick Ewing .75 2.00
49 Patrick Ewing .75 2.00
50 Vern Fleming .50 1.25
51 Mike Gminski .50 1.25
52 Gary Grant .50 1.25
53 A.C. Green .50 1.25
54 Sidney Green .50 1.25
55 Tim Hardaway 1.25 3.00
56 Derek Harper .50 1.25
57 Ron Harper .50 1.25
58 Hersey Hawkins .50 1.25
59 Rod Higgins .50 1.25
60 Roy Hinson .50 1.25
61 Dennis Hopson .50 1.25
62 Jeff Hornacek .50 1.25
63 Jay Humphries .50 1.25
64 Mark Jackson .50 1.25
65 Mark Jackson .50 1.25
66 Buck Johnson .50 1.25
67 Dennis Johnson .50 1.25
68 Eddie Johnson .50 1.25
69 Kevin Johnson .50 1.25
70 Magic Johnson 1.25 3.00
71 Magic Johnson 1.25 3.00
72 Charles Jones .50 1.25
73 Michael Jordan
white jsy 3.00 8.00
74 Michael Jordan
red jsy 3.00 8.00
75 Jerome Kersey .50 1.25
76 Bernard King .50 1.25
77 Stacey King .50 1.25
78 Bill Laimbeer .50 1.25
79 Fat Lever .50 1.25
80 Reggie Lewis .50 1.25
81 Grant Long .50 1.25
82 Sidney Lowe .50 1.25
83 John Lucas .50 1.25
84 Rick Mahorn .50 1.25
85 Jeff Malone .50 1.25
86 Karl Malone .75 2.00
87 Karl Malone .75 2.00
88 Moses Malone .50 1.25
89 Moses Malone .50 1.25
90 Danny Manning .50 1.25
91 Rodney McCray .50 1.25
92 Xavier McDaniel .50 1.25
93 Kevin McHale .50 1.25
94 Kevin McHale .50 1.25
95 Derrick McKey .50 1.25
96 Nate McMillan .50 1.25
97 Reggie Miller .75 2.00
98 Sam Mitchell .50 1.25
99 Chris Morris .50 1.25
100 Chris Mullin .50 1.25
101 Chris Mullin .50 1.25
102 Larry Nance .50 1.25
103 Johnny Newman .50 1.25
104 Ken Norman .50 1.25
105 Charles Oakley .50 1.25
106 Hakeem Olajuwon .75 2.00
107 Hakeem Olajuwon .75 2.00
108 Robert Parish .50 1.25
109 John Paxson .50 1.25
110 Sam Perkins .50 1.25
111 Chuck Person .50 1.25
112 Ricky Pierce .50 1.25
114 Terry Porter .50 1.25
115 Paul Pressey .50 1.25
116 Harold Pressley .50 1.25
117 Mark Price .50 1.25
118 Mark Price .50 1.25
119 Blair Rasmussen .50 1.25
120 J.R. Reid .50 1.25
121 Jerry Reynolds .50 1.25
122 Pooh Richardson .50 1.25
123 Mitch Richmond .50 1.25
124 Doc Rivers .50 1.25
125 Alvin Robertson .50 1.25
126 David Robinson 1.25 3.00
127 David Robinson 1.25 3.00
128 Dennis Rodman 1.25 3.00
129 John Salley .50 1.25
130 Danny Schayes .50 1.25
131 Byron Scott .50 1.25
132 Rony Seikaly .50 1.25
133 Charles Shackleford .50 1.25
134 Jack Sikma .50 1.25
135 Charles Smith .50 1.25
136 Kenny Smith .50 1.25
137 Rik Smits .50 1.25
138 Rory Sparrow .50 1.25
139 John Stockton .75 2.00
140 John Stockton .75 2.00
141 Reggie Theus .50 1.25
142 Isiah Thomas .50 1.25
143 Isiah Thomas .50 1.25
144 LaSalle Thompson .50 1.25
145 Otis Thorpe .50 1.25
146 Wayman Tisdale .50 1.25
147 Kelly Tripucka .50 1.25
148 Sam Vincent .50 1.25
149 Darrell Walker .50 1.25
150 Spud Webb .50 1.25
151 Mark West .50 1.25
152 Mitchell Wiggins .50 1.25
153 Dominique Wilkins .50 1.25
154 Dominique Wilkins .50 1.25
155 Gerald Wilkins .50 1.25
156 John Williams .50 1.25
157 John Williams .50 1.25
158 James Worthy .50 1.25
159 James Worthy .50 1.25

2011 Hoops All-Star Game
COMPLETE SET (4) 10.00 20.00
AS-BG Blake Griffin 5.00 12.00
AS-JW John Wall 6.00 15.00
AS-KB Kobe Bryant 5.00 12.00
AS-KD Kevin Durant 2.00 5.00

1989-90 Hoops All-Star Panels
COMPLETE SET (4) 8.00 20.00
1 Panel 1 3.00 8.00
2 Panel 2 3.00 8.00
3 Panel 3 3.00 8.00
4 Panel 4 4.00 10.00

1990-91 Hoops All-Star Panels
COMPLETE SET (5) 10.00 25.00
1 Panel 1 2.50 6.00
2 Panel 2 3.00 8.00
3 Panel 3 1.50 4.00
4 Panel 4 2.50 6.00
5 Panel 5 3.00 8.00

1989-90 Hoops Announcers
COMP.SET w/o BARRY (40) 50.00 120.00
1 Al Albert 2.00 5.00
2 Marv Albert 8.00 20.00
3 Steve Albert 3.00 8.00
4 John Andariese 2.00 5.00
5 Jim Barnett 4.00 10.00
6B Rick Barry AU 75.00 200.00
7 Ron Boone 2.50 6.00
8 Hubie Brown 6.00 15.00
9 James Brown 5.00 12.00
10 Larry Burnett 2.00 5.00
11 Kevin Calabro 6.00 15.00
12 Jim Durham 3.00 8.00
13 Kevin Harlan 2.00 5.00
14 Bill Hazen 2.50 6.00
15 Chick Hearn 8.00 20.00
16 Steve Holman 2.00 5.00
17 Rod Hundley 8.00 20.00
18 Jim Irwin 2.00 5.00
19 Dan Issel 4.00 10.00
20 Steve Jones 2.00 5.00
21 Clark Kellogg 6.00 15.00
22 John Kerr 4.00 10.00
23 Pat Lafferty 2.00 5.00
24 Stu Lantz 2.00 5.00
25 Steve Martin 2.50 6.00
26 Al McCoy 5.00 12.00
27 John McGlocklin 3.00 8.00
28 Gil McGregor 2.00 5.00
29 Brent Musburger 2.00 5.00
30 Pat O'Brien 2.00 5.00
31 Greg Papa 5.00 12.00
32 Jim Paschke 2.00 5.00
33 Steve Physioc 2.00 5.00
34A Bill Raftery 6.00 15.00
34B Bill Raftery
CBS Sports 2.00 5.00
35 Eric Reid 2.00 5.00
36 Sam Smith 2.00 5.00
37 Dick Stockton 2.00 5.00
38 Ron Thulin 3.00 8.00
39 Dick Van Arsdale 2.50 6.00
40 Lesley Visser 6.00 15.00

1990-91 Hoops Announcers
COMPLETE SET (58) 900.00 1,800.00
1 Marv Albert 15.00 40.00
2 Steve Albert 12.00 30.00
3 John Andariese 12.00 30.00
4 Jerry Baker 12.00 30.00
5 Jim Barnett 12.00 30.00
6 Jim Barniak 12.00 30.00
7 Rick Barry 60.00 150.00
8 Ron Boone 12.00 30.00
9 Mark Boyle 12.00 30.00
10 Hubie Brown 20.00 50.00
11 Kevin Calabro 12.00 30.00
12 Harry Caray III 12.00 30.00
13 Skip Caray 20.00 50.00
14 Doug Collins 20.00 50.00
15 Chet Coppock 12.00 30.00
16 Bob Costas 40.00 100.00
17 Jim Durham 12.00 30.00
18 Dick Enberg 25.00 60.00
19 Jim Foley 12.00 30.00
20 Mike Fratello 20.00 50.00
21 Gary Gerould 12.00 30.00
22 Jack Givens 15.00 40.00
23 Mike Gorman 12.00 30.00
24 Tom Hanneman 12.00 30.00
25 Kevin Harlan 12.00 30.00
26 Dick Harter 12.00 30.00
27 Fred Hickman 15.00 40.00
28 Steve Holman 12.00 30.00
29 Jay Howard 12.00 30.00
30 Jim Irwin 12.00 30.00
31 Dan Issel 40.00 100.00
32 Ernie Johnson Jr. 25.00 60.00
33 Steve Jones 15.00 40.00
34 Johnny (Red) Kerr 24.00 60.00
35 Jeff Kingery 15.00 40.00
36 Ralph Lawler 15.00 40.00
37 Joe McConnell 12.00 30.00
38 L. Allen McCoy 12.00 30.00
39 Jonathan Miller 12.00 30.00
40 Bob Neal 12.00 30.00
41 Glenn Ordway 20.00 50.00
42 M. John Proctor 12.00 30.00
43 Ed Randall 12.00 30.00
44 Mike Rice 12.00 30.00
45 Pat Riley 50.00 120.00
46 Andrew Rosenberg 12.00 30.00
47 Tommy Roy 12.00 30.00
48 Tim James Roye 12.00 30.00
49 Craig Sager
(Play-by-play) 40.00 100.00
50 Craig Sager
(Biography) 40.00 100.00
51 Bill Schonely 12.00 30.00
52 Charles Slowes 12.00 30.00
53 David Steele 12.00 30.00
54 Hannah Storm 20.00 50.00
55 Ron Thulin 12.00 30.00
56 Gerry Vaillancourt 12.00 30.00
57 Pete Van Wieren 12.00 30.00
58 William Worrell 12.00 30.00

1990-91 Hoops CollectABooks
COMPLETE SET (48) 6.00 15.00
1 Sam Bowie .05 .15
2 Tom Chambers .10 .30
3 Clyde Drexler .40 1.00
4 Michael Jordan 2.00 5.00
5 Karl Malone .60 1.50
6 Kevin McHale .20 .50
7 Reggie Miller .40 1.00
8 Mark Price .20 .50
9 Mitch Richmond .40 1.00
10 Doc Rivers .10 .30
11 Rony Seikaly .10 .30
12 Wayman Tisdale .05 .15
13 Charles Barkley .40 1.00
14 Terry Cummings .10 .30
15 Patrick Ewing .40 1.00
16 Terry Porter .10 .30
17 Danny Manning .10 .30
18 Larry Nance .10 .30
19 Robert Parish .10 .30
20 Chuck Person .10 .30
21 Ricky Pierce .05 .15
22 John Stockton .60 1.50
23 Isiah Thomas .20 .50
24 Spud Webb .10 .30
25 Michael Adams .05 .15
26 Muggsy Bogues .10 .30
27 Joe Dumars .20 .50
28 Hersey Hawkins .10 .30
29 Magic Johnson .50 1.25
30 Bernard King .20 .50
31 Chris Mullin .20 .50
32 Charles Oakley .10 .30
33 Alvin Robertson .05 .15
34 David Robinson .50 1.25
35 Dominique Wilkins .30 .75
36 Buck Williams .10 .30
37 Larry Bird .75 2.00
38 Rolando Blackman .05 .15
39 Mark Eaton .10 .30
40 Kevin Johnson .20 .50
41 J.R. Reid .05 .15
42 Xavier McDaniel .05 .15
43 Hakeem Olajuwon .40 1.00
44 Scottie Pippen .60 1.50
45 Pooh Richardson .05 .15
46 Dennis Rodman .50 1.25
47 Charles Smith .05 .15
48 James Worthy .20 .50
XX Detroit Pistons .20 .50

1999-00 Hoops Decade
COMPLETE SET (180) 20.00 40.00
1 David Robinson .40 1.00
2 Mookie Blaylock .12 .30
3 Jaren Jackson .12 .30
4 Andre Miller RC .40 1.00
5 Michael Olowokandi .12 .30
6 Glenn Robinson .15 .40
7 Steve Smith .15 .40
8 Eric Snow .12 .30
9 Antoine Walker .20 .50
10 Nick Anderson .12 .30
11 Jonathan Bender RC .20 .50
12 Sean Elliott .15 .40
13 Danny Fortson .12 .30
14 Adonal Foyle .12 .30
15 Richard Hamilton RC .50 1.25
16 Shawn Kemp .30 .75
17 Christian Laettner .15 .40
18 Rashard Lewis .15 .40
19 Danny Manning .15 .40
20 Mitch Richmond .25 .60
21 Shawn Bradley .12 .30
22 Tim Duncan .50 1.25
23 Tim Hardaway .25 .60
24 Antawn Jamison .20 .50
25 Jeff Hornacek .15 .40
26 Jumaine Jones RC .12 .30
27 Corey Maggette RC .25 .60
28 Vitaly Potapenko .12 .30
29 Jerry Stackhouse .20 .50
30 Jason Terry RC .30 .75
31 Baron Davis RC .50 1.25
32 Matt Harpring .12 .30
33 Glen Rice .20 .50
34 Vladimir Stepania .12 .30
35 Jayson Williams .12 .30
36 Wally Szczerbiak RC .30 .75
37 Michael Doleac .12 .30
38 Hersey Hawkins .12 .30
39 Allan Houston .15 .40
40 Hakeem Olajuwon .40 1.00
41 Damon Stoudamire .12 .30
42 Jelani McCoy .12 .30
43 A.Radojevic RC .12 .30
44 Cal Bowdler RC .12 .30
45 Tyronn Lue .12 .30
46 Andrae Patterson .12 .30
47 Karl Malone .40 1.00
48 Alonzo Mourning .30 .75
49 Vince Carter .50 1.25
50 Darrell Armstrong .12 .30
51 Terrell Brandon .12 .30
52 John Celestand RC .12 .30
53 Grant Hill .30 .75
54 Stephon Marbury .25 .60
55 Tracy McGrady .30 .75
56 Reggie Miller .40 1.00
57 Clifford Robinson .15 .40
58 Arvydas Sabonis .15 .40
59 William Avery RC .12 .30
60 Calbert Cheaney .12 .30
61 Jermaine Jackson RC .12 .30
62 Allen Iverson .50 1.25
63 Larry Johnson .20 .50
64 Toni Kukoc .25 .60
65 Rael LaFrentz .15 .40
66 Isaiah Rider .15 .40
67 Jeff Foster RC .20 .50
68 Juwan Howard .15 .40
69 Kerry Kittles .15 .40
70 Brevin Knight .12 .30
71 Voshon Lenard .12 .30
72 Latrell Sprewell .25 .60
73 Maurice Taylor .12 .30
74 Chris Webber .25 .60
75 Jerome Williams .12 .30
76 Scott Padgett RC .15 .40
77 Vin Baker .15 .40
78 Chris Childs .12 .30
79 Erick Dampier .12 .30
80 Anfernee Hardaway .50 1.25
81 Jamal Mashburn .15 .40
82 Todd Fuller .12 .30
83 Eric Piatkowski .12 .30
84 Gary Trent .12 .30
85 Kevin Garnett .50 1.25
86 Chris Mullin .25 .60
87 Charles Oakley .12 .30
88 Detlef Schrempf .15 .40
89 Elton Brand RC .40 1.00
90 Patrick Ewing .25 .60
91 Devean George RC .15 .40
92 Brian Grant .12 .30
93 Larry Hughes .15 .40
94 Dan Majerle .20 .50
95 Shawn Marion RC .40 1.00
96 Cuttino Mobley .12 .30
97 Paul Pierce .40 1.00
98 Bryant Reeves .12 .30
99 Keith Van Horn .15 .40
100 Corliss Williamson .12 .30
101 Tariq Abdul-Wahad .12 .30
102 Brent Barry .12 .30
103 Elden Campbell .15 .40
104 Mark Jackson .12 .30
105 Lamond Murray .12 .30
106 Bryon Russell .12 .30
107 Jason Williams .30 .75
108 Ray Allen .30 .75
109 Ron Artest RC .50 1.25
110 Charles Barkley .50 1.25
111 Cedric Ceballos .12 .30
112 Jason Kidd .30 .75
113 Donyell Marshall .15 .40
114 John Stockton .30 .75
115 Mike Bibby .30 .75
116 Ricky Davis .20 .50
117 Steve Francis RC .40 1.00
118 Tom Gugliotta .15 .40
119 Lamond Profit RC .12 .30
120 Joe Smith .15 .40
121 Doug Christie .15 .40
122 Kenny Anderson .15 .40
123 Michael Dickerson .12 .30
124 Zydrunas Ilgauskas .15 .40
125 Bobby Jackson .15 .40
126 Quincy Lewis RC .12 .30
127 Shandon Anderson .12 .30
128 Bo Outlaw .12 .30
129 Scottie Pippen .50 1.25
130 Rodney Rogers .12 .30
131 Rik Smits .15 .40
132 Chauncey Billups .20 .50
133 Chris Crawford .12 .30
134 Kornel David RC .12 .30
135 Tony Delk .12 .30
136 Kendall Gill .20 .50
137 Trajan Langdon RC .15 .40
138 Ron Mercer .15 .40
139 Othella Harrington .12 .30
140 Gheorghe Muresan .12 .30
141 Isaac Austin .12 .30
142 Dion Glover RC .12 .30
143 Avery Johnson .15 .40
144 Antonio McDyess .15 .40
145 Steve Nash .40 1.00
146 Tyrone Nesby RC .12 .30
147 Shaquille O'Neal .75 2.00
148 James Posey RC .20 .50
149 Rod Strickland .15 .40
150 Kobe Bryant 1.50 4.00
151 Michael Finley .20 .50
152 Anthony Mason .20 .50
153 Dikembe Mutombo .30 .75
154 John Starks .20 .50
155 Kenny Thomas RC .20 .50
156 Matt Geiger .12 .30
157 Tim James RC .12 .30
158 Eddie Jones .20 .50
159 Lamar Odom RC .40 1.00
160 Nick Van Exel .15 .40
161 Sam Cassell .15 .40
162 Vonteego Cummings RC .12 .30
163 Lindsey Hunter .12 .30
164 Dirk Nowitzki .60 1.50
165 Gary Payton .30 .75
166 Shareef Abdur-Rahim .20 .50
167 Jalen Rose .15 .40
168 Robert Traylor .12 .30
169 Derek Anderson .12 .30
170 Corey Benjamin .12 .30
171 Marcus Camby .15 .40
172 Vlade Divac .20 .50
173 Mario Elie .12 .30
174 Felipe Lopez .12 .30
175 Rafer Alston RC .25 .60
176 Antonio Davis .12 .30
177 Howard Eisley .12 .30
178 Theo Ratliff .15 .40
179 Tim Thomas .15 .40
180 Rasheed Wallace .25 .60

1999-00 Hoops Decade Hoopla
*HOOPLA: 1.25X TO 3X BASE CARD HI
STATED ODDS 1:3

1999-00 Hoops Decade Hoopla Plus
*PLUS: 8X TO 20X BASE CARD HI
STATED ODDS 1:30

1999-00 Hoops Decade Draft Day Dominance
COMPLETE SET (10) 8.00 20.00
STATED ODDS 1:32
*PARALLEL: .75X TO 2X HI COLUMN
PARALLEL: PRINT RUN 1989 SERIAL #'d SETS
DD1 David Robinson 2.00 5.00
DD2 Gary Payton 1.50 4.00
DD3 Dikembe Mutombo 1.50 4.00
DD4 Shaquille O'Neal 4.00 10.00
DD5 Anfernee Hardaway 2.50 6.00
DD6 Grant Hill 1.50 4.00
DD7 Antonio McDyess .75 2.00
DD8 Kobe Bryant 8.00 20.00
DD9 Keith Van Horn .75 2.00
DD10 Vince Carter 2.50 6.00

1999-00 Hoops Decade Genuine Coverage
STATED ODDS 1:893
1 Shareef Abdur-Rahim 10.00 25.00
2 Ray Allen 15.00 40.00
3 Patrick Ewing 12.00 30.00
4 Grant Hill 15.00 40.00
5 Juwan Howard 8.00 20.00
6 Antonio McDyess 8.00 20.00
7 Hakeem Olajuwon 20.00 50.00
8 David Robinson 20.00 50.00
9 Keith Van Horn 8.00 20.00
10 Antoine Walker 10.00 25.00

1999-00 Hoops Decade New Style
COMPLETE SET (15) 4.00 10.00
STATED ODDS 1:18
*PARALLEL: 1X TO 2.5X HI COLUMN
PARALLEL: PRINT RUN 1989 SERIAL #'d SETS
NS1 Steve Francis .60 1.50
NS2 Lamar Odom .60 1.50
NS3 Wally Szczerbiak .50 1.25
NS4 Elton Brand .60 1.50
NS5 Baron Davis .75 2.00
NS6 Corey Maggette .40 1.00
NS7 Trajan Langdon .25 .60
NS8 Cal Bowdler .20 .50
NS9 Richard Hamilton .75 2.00
NS10 Ron Artest .75 2.00
NS11 Jason Terry .50 1.25
NS12 Jonathan Bender .30 .75
NS13 Andre Miller .60 1.50
NS14 Shawn Marion .60 1.50
NS15 William Avery .20 .50

1999-00 Hoops Decade Retrospection Collection
COMPLETE SET (10) 60.00 150.00
STATED ODDS 1:108
PARALLEL: PRINT RUN 89 SER.#'d SETS
RC1 Kevin Garnett 8.00 20.00
RC2 Kobe Bryant 25.00 60.00
RC3 Allen Iverson 8.00 20.00
RC4 Vince Carter 8.00 20.00

RC5 Jason Williams 5.00 12.00
RC6 Ron Mercer 2.50 6.00
RC7 Tim Duncan 8.00 20.00
RC8 Anfernee Hardaway 8.00 20.00
RC9 Scottie Pippen 8.00 20.00
RC10 Shaquille O'Neal 12.00 30.00

1999-00 Hoops Decade Up Tempo

COMPLETE SET (15) 5.00 12.00
STATED ODDS 1:9
*PARALLEL: 2X TO 5X HI COLUMN
PARALLEL: PRINT RUN 1989 SERIAL #'d SETS
UT1 Allen Iverson 1.00 2.50
UT2 Kevin Garnett 1.00 2.50
UT3 Shaquille O'Neal 1.50 4.00
UT4 Tim Duncan 1.00 2.50
UT5 Stephon Marbury .50 1.25
UT6 Keith Van Horn .30 .75
UT7 Paul Pierce .75 2.00
UT8 Vince Carter 1.00 2.50
UT9 Antawn Jamison .40 1.00
UT10 Larry Hughes .30 .75
UT11 Jason Williams .60 1.50
UT12 Antoine Walker .40 1.00
UT13 Grant Hill .60 1.50
UT14 Steve Francis .75 2.00
UT15 Lamar Odom .75 2.00

2014 Hoops Draft

NNO Andrew Wiggins 10.00 25.00
NNO Dante Exum 5.00 12.00
NNO Doug McDermott 8.00 20.00
NNO Jabari Parker 8.00 20.00
JE Joel Embiid 5.00 12.00
NNO Julius Randle 6.00 15.00

2013 Hoops Franchise Greats All-Star Game

COMPLETE SET (6) 10.00 25.00
1 Kobe Bryant 8.00 20.00
2 Blake Griffin 3.00 8.00
3 Kevin Durant 5.00 12.00
4 Deron Williams 1.25 3.00
5 James Harden 3.00 8.00
6 Hakeem Olajuwon 2.00 5.00

1993-94 Hoops Gold Medal Bread

COMPLETE SET (49) 40.00 100.00
1 B.J. Armstrong 1.50 4.00
2 Thurl Bailey 1.00 2.50
3 Rolando Blackman 1.00 2.50
4 Mookie Blaylock 1.50 4.00
5 Muggsy Bogues 1.50 4.00
6 Anthony Bowie 1.00 2.50
7 Chucky Brown 1.00 2.50
8 Dee Brown 1.25 3.00
9 Duane Causwell 1.00 2.50
10 Cedric Ceballos 1.25 3.00
11 Rex Chapman 1.00 2.50
12 Bimbo Coles 1.00 2.50
13 Tyrone Corbin 1.00 2.50
14 Terry Cummings 1.25 3.00
15 Todd Day 1.00 2.50
16 Joe Dumars 2.00 5.00
17 Mark Eaton 1.50 4.00
18 Vern Fleming 1.25 3.00
19 Kevin Gamble 1.00 2.50
20 Kendall Gill 1.25 3.00
21 Tom Gugliotta 1.25 3.00
22 Derek Harper 1.25 3.00
23 Ron Harper 1.50 4.00
24 Hersey Hawkins 1.25 3.00
25 Tyrone Hill 1.00 2.50
26 Adam Keefe 1.00 2.50
27 Shawn Kemp 2.50 6.00
28 Jerome Kersey 1.25 3.00
29 Stacey King 1.00 2.50
30 Luc Longley 1.25 3.00
31 Moses Malone 2.50 6.00
32 Anthony Mason 1.25 3.00
33 Vernon Maxwell 1.25 3.00
34 Xavier McDaniel 1.50 4.00
35 Oliver Miller 1.00 2.50
36 Sam Mitchell 1.00 2.50
37 Chris Morris 1.00 2.50
38 Dikembe Mutombo 2.50 6.00
39 Billy Owens 1.25 3.00
40 Robert Parish 2.00 5.00
41 Sam Perkins 1.25 3.00
42 Olden Polynice 1.00 2.50
43 Terry Porter 1.25 3.00
44 J.R. Reid 1.25 3.00
45 Rony Seikaly 1.25 3.00
46 Lionel Simmons 1.00 2.50
47 Scott Skiles 1.00 2.50
48 Sedale Threatt 1.00 2.50
49 Loy Vaught 1.00 2.50

2023-24 Hoops Haunted Hoops

*ORANGE: .75X TO 2X BASIC
*SLIME: .75X TO 2X BASIC
1 Nikola Jokic 1.50 4.00
2 Kristaps Porzingis .40 1.00
3 Caris LeVert .30 .75
4 Brook Lopez .25 .60
5 Jalen Green .50 1.25
6 Patrick Beverley .25 .60
7 Ivica Zubac .30 .75
8 Corey Kispert .25 .60
9 Luka Doncic 2.00 5.00
10 Toumani Camara RC 1.00 2.50
11 Deandre Ayton .30 .75
12 D'Angelo Russell .30 .75
13 Oscar Tshiebwe RC .60 1.50
14 Lauri Markkanen .50 1.25
15 Brandin Podziemski RC 1.50 4.00
16 Nikola Vucevic .30 .75
17 Saddiq Bey .30 .75
18 Jordan Walsh RC .50 1.25
19 Jalen Hood-Schifino RC .50 1.25
20 Paul George .50 1.25
21 Vince Williams Jr. .30 .75
22 Jerami Grant .40 1.00
23 Giannis Antetokounmpo 1.50 4.00
24 Rui Hachimura .30 .75
25 Clint Capela .25 .60
26 Talen Horton-Tucker .25 .60
27 Mouhamed Gueye RC .50 1.25
28 Gary Harris .25 .60
29 Hunter Tyson RC .50 1.25
30 Nicolas Batum .20 .50
31 Nick Smith Jr. RC .60 1.50
32 Jamal Murray .60 1.50
33 Andre Drummond .25 .60
34 Jeremy Sochan .40 1.00
35 Bradley Beal .40 1.00
36 Donovan Mitchell .60 1.50
37 Bol Bol .30 .75
38 Chet Holmgren .75 2.00
39 Jaden Ivey .40 1.00
40 Jusuf Nurkic .30 .75
41 Mark Williams .30 .75
42 Julius Randle .40 1.00
43 GG Jackson II RC 1.00 2.50
44 Kelly Olynyk .20 .50
45 Marcus Sasser RC .75 2.00
46 Obi Toppin .30 .75
47 Adama Sanogo RC .50 1.25
48 Bobby Portis .40 1.00
49 Colby Jones RC .50 1.25
50 Terquavion Smith RC .50 1.25
51 Jaime Jaquez Jr. RC .75 2.00
52 Rudy Gobert .40 1.00
53 Tre Mann .30 .75
54 Reggie Jackson .20 .50
55 Kobe Brown RC .50 1.25
56 Maxwell Lewis RC .40 1.00
57 Markquis Nowell RC .50 1.25
58 Jalen Slawson RC .50 1.25
59 Jrue Holiday .40 1.00
60 Damian Lillard .75 2.00
61 Julian Phillips RC .50 1.25
62 Ochai Agbaji .30 .75
63 Moritz Wagner .30 .75
64 Isaiah Joe .30 .75
65 Craig Porter Jr. RC .60 1.50
66 Bam Adebayo .50 1.25
67 Andre Jackson Jr. RC .75 2.00
68 Trayce Jackson-Davis RC .60 1.50
69 Stanley Umude RC .40 1.00
70 Josh Giddey .40 1.00
71 Jabari Smith Jr. .50 1.25
72 Derrick Rose .50 1.25
73 Khris Middleton .30 .75
74 Emoni Bates RC .60 1.50
75 Vasilije Micic RC .50 1.25
76 Cason Wallace RC 1.00 2.50
77 James Harden .60 1.50
78 Draymond Green .40 1.00
79 Anfernee Simons .40 1.00
80 Leonard Miller RC .50 1.25
81 Jaylen Brown .60 1.50
82 Trae Young .60 1.50
83 Kyle Lowry .40 1.00
84 Terance Mann .25 .60
85 Franz Wagner .50 1.25
86 Amen Thompson RC 2.50 6.00
87 Anthony Edwards 1.50 4.00
88 Anthony Black RC 1.00 2.50
89 Kentavious Caldwell-Pope .25 .60
90 Kelly Oubre Jr. .30 .75
91 Mike Conley .25 .60
92 Mitchell Robinson .30 .75
93 Cameron Johnson .30 .75
94 Dorian Finney-Smith .25 .60
95 Marvin Bagley III .25 .60
96 Devin Booker .75 2.00
97 John Collins .30 .75
98 Keyonte George RC 1.50 4.00
99 Chris Livingston RC .50 1.25
100 Ausar Thompson RC 1.25 3.00
101 Taurean Prince .20 .50
102 Ja Morant 1.00 2.50
103 Olivier-Maxence Prosper RC .50 1.25
104 Jarrett Allen .30 .75
105 Immanuel Quickley .30 .75
106 Kevon Looney .30 .75
107 Jarace Walker RC 1.00 2.50
108 Victor Wembanyama RC 4.00 10.00
109 Cam Whitmore RC 1.25 3.00
110 Jalen Suggs .40 1.00
111 Duop Reath RC .50 1.25
112 Jonas Valanciunas .25 .60
113 Michael Porter Jr. .40 1.00
114 Kawhi Leonard .75 2.00
115 Evan Mobley .50 1.25
116 Alex Caruso .30 .75
117 Jalen Williams .60 1.50
118 Keldon Johnson .40 1.00
119 Jalen Johnson .40 1.00
120 Austin Reaves .75 2.00
121 PJ Washington Jr. .30 .75
122 Jakob Poeltl .25 .60
123 Malik Monk .40 1.00
124 Jaren Jackson Jr. .50 1.25
125 Jordan Hawkins RC .75 2.00
126 Tyler Herro .50 1.25
127 Spencer Dinwiddie .25 .60
128 Jalen McDaniels .25 .60
129 Jett Howard RC .60 1.50
130 Cameron Thomas .40 1.00
131 Collin Sexton .40 1.00
132 Aaron Gordon .30 .75
133 Tosan Evbuomwan RC .40 1.00
134 Chris Paul .60 1.50
135 Darius Garland .50 1.25
136 Tim Hardaway Jr. .25 .60
137 Scoot Henderson RC 1.50 4.00
138 De'Anthony Melton .30 .75
139 Isaiah Wong RC .50 1.25
140 Andrew Wiggins .40 1.00
141 Desmond Bane .40 1.00
142 Max Christie .30 .75
143 Sidy Cissoko RC .50 1.25
144 Tyrese Maxey .60 1.50
145 Donte DiVincenzo .50 1.25
146 MarJon Beauchamp .25 .60
147 Shai Gilgeous-Alexander 1.50 4.00
148 Kobe Bufkin RC .60 1.50
149 LeBron James 2.50 6.00
150 Terry Rozier III .30 .75
151 Alperen Sengun .40 1.00
152 Markelle Fultz .25 .60
153 Dennis Schroder .30 .75
154 Domantas Sabonis .50 1.25
155 Rayan Rupert RC .50 1.25
156 Kevin Love .30 .75
157 Sasha Vezenkov RC .40 1.00
158 RJ Barrett .50 1.25
159 Derrick White .40 1.00
160 De'Andre Hunter .30 .75
161 Isaiah Stewart .30 .75
162 Kyle Kuzma .40 1.00
163 Dejounte Murray .40 1.00
164 Duncan Robinson .30 .75
165 Tre Jones .30 .75
166 Andrew Nembhard .30 .75
167 Daniel Gafford .30 .75
168 Ricky Council IV RC .60 1.50
169 Jimmy Butler .50 1.25
170 Keyontae Johnson RC .50 1.25
171 Keegan Murray .40 1.00
172 CJ McCollum .30 .75
173 Walker Kessler .30 .75
174 Wendell Carter Jr. .30 .75
175 Bilal Coulibaly RC 1.25 3.00
176 Precious Achiuwa .25 .60
177 Anthony Davis .75 2.00
178 Eric Gordon .25 .60
179 Jalen Pickett RC .40 1.00
180 Mikal Bridges .40 1.00
181 Payton Pritchard .30 .75
182 Paolo Banchero .75 2.00
183 Myles Turner .30 .75
184 Pascal Siakam .50 1.25
185 Ben Simmons .30 .75
186 Jordan Clarkson .30 .75
187 Caleb Martin .25 .60
188 Buddy Hield .30 .75
189 Jaylen Clark RC .50 1.25
190 Grayson Allen .30 .75
191 Brandon Ingram .40 1.00
192 Stephen Curry 2.50 6.00
193 Luguentz Dort .30 .75
194 Evan Fournier .25 .60
195 Zach LaVine .50 1.25
196 Harrison Barnes .25 .60
197 Herbert Jones .30 .75
199 De'Aaron Fox .60 1.50
200 Gary Trent Jr. .30 .75
201 Tyrese Haliburton .60 1.50
202 Bruce Brown .30 .75
203 Norman Powell .30 .75
204 Bones Hyland .25 .60
205 Ayo Dosunmu .30 .75
206 Seth Lundy RC .40 1.00
207 Trey Murphy III .40 1.00
208 Bojan Bogdanovic .30 .75
209 Kevin Durant 1.00 2.50
210 Jose Alvarado .30 .75
211 Russell Westbrook .50 1.25
212 Tobias Harris .30 .75
213 Julian Strawther RC .60 1.50
214 Shaedon Sharpe .60 1.50
215 Jalen Wilson RC .50 1.25
216 Quentin Grimes .30 .75
217 Marcus Smart .40 1.00
218 Bogdan Bogdanovic .30 .75
219 Ben Sheppard RC .50 1.25
220 Malcolm Brogdon .30 .75
221 Naz Reid .30 .75
222 Taylor Hendricks RC .50 1.25
223 OG Anunoby .40 1.00
224 Dyson Daniels .30 .75
225 Brice Sensabaugh RC .75 2.00
226 Deni Avdija .30 .75
227 Jaden Hardy .40 1.00
228 Tyus Jones .25 .60
229 Miles Bridges .30 .75
230 Al Horford .30 .75
231 Jonathan Kuminga .75 2.00
232 Devin Vassell .40 1.00
233 Sam Merrill .30 .75
234 Max Strus .30 .75
235 Malaki Branham .25 .60
236 Amari Bailey RC .50 1.25
237 Jordan Miller RC .60 1.50
238 Dariq Whitehead RC .60 1.50
239 Malik Beasley .30 .75
240 LaMelo Ball .75 2.00
241 Zach Collins .25 .60
242 Jalen Brunson .60 1.50
243 Noah Clowney RC .60 1.50
244 Onyeka Okongwu .25 .60
245 Brandon Miller RC 2.00 5.00
246 Tari Eason .40 1.00
247 Kyle Anderson .25 .60
248 Leaky Black RC .40 1.00
249 Fred VanVleet .50 1.25
250 Josh Green .25 .60
251 Gradey Dick RC 1.00 2.50
252 Grant Williams .25 .60
253 Dereck Lively II RC 1.00 2.50
254 Bennedict Mathurin .50 1.25
255 Klay Thompson .60 1.50
256 Kyrie Irving .60 1.50
257 Scottie Barnes .75 2.00
258 Cade Cunningham .75 2.00
259 Nicolas Claxton .30 .75
260 Ziaire Williams .30 .75
261 Jaden Springer .25 .60
262 Josh Hart .30 .75
263 Gordon Hayward .30 .75
264 Dillon Brooks .30 .75
265 Jayson Tatum 1.25 3.00
266 Peyton Watson .30 .75
267 Nikola Jovic .30 .75
268 Cole Anthony .30 .75
269 DeMar DeRozan .50 1.25
270 Zion Williamson .75 2.00
271 Joel Embiid .75 2.00
272 Cam Reddish .25 .60
273 Patrick Williams .25 .60
274 Jalen Duren .40 1.00
275 Karl-Anthony Towns .50 1.25
276 Isaac Okoro .25 .60
277 Jordan Poole .50 1.25
278 Coby White .30 .75
279 Kris Murray RC .50 1.25
280 Scoot Henderson RS 1.50 4.00
281 Cason Wallace RS 1.00 2.50
282 Victor Wembanyama RS 4.00 10.00
283 Keyonte George RS 1.50 4.00
284 Jaden Ivey RS .40 1.00
285 Jabari Smith Jr. RS .50 1.25
286 Bennedict Mathurin RS .50 1.25
287 Bilal Coulibaly RS 1.25 3.00
288 Jordan Hawkins RS .75 2.00
289 Keegan Murray RS .40 1.00
290 Jalen Williams RS .60 1.50
291 Dereck Lively II RS 1.00 2.50
292 Vince Williams Jr. RS .30 .75
293 Chet Holmgren RS .75 2.00
294 Jaime Jaquez Jr. RS .75 2.00
295 Paolo Banchero RS .75 2.00
296 Jeremy Sochan RS .40 1.00
297 Brandin Podziemski RS 1.50 4.00
298 Brandon Miller RS 2.00 5.00
299 Jalen Duren RS .40 1.00
300 Walker Kessler RS .30 .75

2023-24 Hoops Haunted Hoops Holo Candy

*HOLO CANDY: 4X TO 10X BASIC
108 Victor Wembanyama 200.00 500.00
282 Victor Wembanyama RS 150.00 400.00

2023-24 Hoops Haunted Hoops Holo Webs

*HOLO WEBS: 2.5X TO 6X BASIC
108 Victor Wembanyama 60.00 150.00
282 Victor Wembanyama RS 40.00 100.00

2024-25 Hoops Haunted Hoops

*ORANGE: .6X TO 1.6X BASIC
*SLIME: .6X TO 1.5X BASIC
*HOLO WEBS: 2.5X TO 6X BASIC
*HOLO BATS/399: 2.5X TO 6X BASIC
*HOLO TICK OR TREAT/99: 5X TO 12X BASIC
*HOLO SKY/31: 8X TO 20X BASIC
1 Anthony Davis .75 2.00
2 Franz Wagner .50 1.25
3 Ja Morant 1.00 2.50
4 Naz Reid .30 .75
5 Myles Turner .25 .60
6 Buddy Hield .25 .60
7 Giannis Antetokounmpo 1.25 3.00
8 Jaden Ivey .40 1.00
9 Jimmy Butler III .40 1.00
10 Brice Sensabaugh .30 .75
11 Jose Alvarado .25 .60
12 Cole Anthony .25 .60
13 LaMelo Ball .60 1.50
14 Coby White .30 .75
15 Grayson Allen .25 .60
16 Daniel Gafford .25 .60
17 Grant Williams .20 .50
18 Patrick Williams .25 .60
19 Dorian Finney-Smith .20 .50
20 Kevin Durant 1.00 2.50
21 Tari Eason .30 .75
22 Stephen Curry 2.50 6.00
23 Tre Jones .25 .60
24 Aaron Gordon .30 .75
25 Scottie Barnes .40 1.00
26 Jusuf Nurkic .25 .60
27 Gary Trent Jr. .25 .60
28 Zach LaVine .50 1.25
29 Onyeka Okongwu .30 .75
30 Ty Jerome .30 .75
31 Dennis Schroder .30 .75
32 Cameron Johnson .30 .75
33 Donte DiVincenzo .30 .75
34 Bobby Portis .25 .60
35 Joel Embiid .50 1.25
36 Kelly Oubre Jr. .25 .60
37 Cameron Thomas .30 .75
38 Kyrie Irving .75 2.00
39 Evan Mobley .50 1.25
40 Paul George .50 1.25
41 Vince Williams Jr. .25 .60
42 Marcus Sasser .25 .60
43 Deni Avdija .25 .60
44 Christian Braun .40 1.00
45 Anfernee Simons .30 .75
46 Simone Fontecchio .25 .60
47 Nicolas Claxton .25 .60
48 Jrue Holiday .40 1.00
49 Saddiq Bey .25 .60
50 Mikal Bridges .30 .75
51 Bradley Beal .40 1.00
52 Kyle Anderson .25 .60
53 Isaiah Hartenstein .25 .60
54 OG Anunoby .25 .60
55 Rudy Gobert .30 .75
56 Zach Collins .20 .50
57 Dejounte Murray .30 .75
58 Malik Monk .30 .75
59 DeMar DeRozan .40 1.00
60 Josh Hart .25 .60
61 Jalen Duren .30 .75
62 Corey Kispert .25 .60
63 Max Strus .25 .60
64 T.J. McConnell .25 .60
65 Draymond Green .40 1.00
66 Jalen Williams .60 1.50
67 Payton Pritchard .30 .75
68 Tim Hardaway Jr. .25 .60
69 Jakob Poeltl .25 .60
70 Victor Wembanyama 2.50 6.00
71 Nikola Jokic 1.50 4.00
72 Tobias Harris .25 .60
73 Ben Simmons .30 .75
74 Jalen Brunson .60 1.50
75 Dereck Lively II .30 .75
76 Immanuel Quickley .25 .60
77 Fred VanVleet .30 .75
78 Nick Smith Jr. .30 .75
79 Nikola Vucevic .25 .60
80 Precious Achiuwa .25 .60
81 Brandin Podziemski .40 1.00
82 Bennedict Mathurin .40 1.00
83 Tyus Jones .20 .50
84 Khris Middleton .30 .75
85 Klay Thompson .75 2.00
86 Jonathan Kuminga .40 1.00
87 Taylor Hendricks .30 .75
88 Donovan Mitchell .60 1.50
89 Peyton Watson .25 .60
90 Devin Booker .75 2.00
91 Derrick White .30 .75
92 Paolo Banchero .75 2.00
93 Cam Reddish .20 .50
94 Austin Reaves .40 1.00
95 Taurean Prince .20 .50
96 Marcus Smart .30 .75
97 Jaime Jaquez Jr. .30 .75
98 Jeremy Sochan .30 .75
99 Clint Capela .25 .60
100 Tyler Herro .50 1.25
101 Nicolas Batum .20 .50
102 Shaedon Sharpe .40 1.00
103 Keldon Johnson .25 .60
104 Aaron Nesmith .25 .60
105 Max Christie .30 .75
106 Trae Young .60 1.50
107 Michael Porter Jr. .30 .75
108 Trayce Jackson-Davis .30 .75
109 De'Andre Hunter .30 .75
110 Zion Williamson .75 2.00
111 Amen Thompson .75 2.00
112 Ochai Agbaji .25 .60
113 Jarrett Allen .25 .60
114 Jayson Tatum 1.00 2.50
115 Jaren Jackson Jr. .50 1.25
116 Julius Randle .30 .75
117 Brandon Ingram .30 .75
118 Josh Giddey .40 1.00
119 D'Angelo Russell .25 .60
120 Malik Beasley .25 .60
121 Miles Bridges .25 .60
122 Cason Wallace .40 1.00
123 Deandre Ayton .25 .60
124 Andrew Wiggins .40 1.00
125 Anthony Black .30 .75
126 Andre Jackson Jr. .25 .60
127 Ivica Zubac .30 .75
128 Andre Drummond .25 .60
129 Isaiah Joe .25 .60
130 Jabari Smith Jr. .30 .75
131 Brook Lopez .25 .60
132 Brandon Miller .50 1.25
133 Jalen Suggs .30 .75
134 Luka Doncic 2.00 5.00
135 Bam Adebayo .40 1.00
136 Scotty Pippen Jr. .30 .75
137 Anthony Edwards 1.50 4.00
138 Kevin Huerter .25 .60
139 Lonzo Ball .30 .75
140 Bogdan Bogdanovic .25 .60
141 Collin Sexton .30 .75
142 Al Horford .30 .75
143 Jerami Grant .25 .60
144 Kyle Kuzma .25 .60
145 Bruce Brown .25 .60
146 Alperen Sengun .50 1.25
147 De'Aaron Fox .60 1.50
148 Shai Gilgeous-Alexander 1.50 4.00
149 Moritz Wagner .25 .60
150 Tyrese Haliburton .60 1.50
151 Andrew Nembhard .25 .60
152 Jonas Valanciunas .25 .60
153 James Harden .60 1.50
154 Dillon Brooks .25 .60
155 Caris LeVert .25 .60
156 Gradey Dick .40 1.00
157 Mike Conley .25 .60
158 Jaden McDaniels .30 .75
159 Nickeil Alexander-Walker .20 .50
160 GG Jackson II .25 .60
161 Kris Murray .30 .75
162 Marvin Bagley III .20 .50
163 Jaden Hardy .30 .75
164 Bilal Coulibaly .40 1.00
165 Rui Hachimura .30 .75
166 Domantas Sabonis .50 1.25
167 Keyonte George .40 1.00
168 Aaron Wiggins .25 .60
169 Isaiah Stewart .25 .60
170 P.J. Washington Jr. .25 .60
171 Ayo Dosunmu .30 .75
172 Trey Murphy III .40 1.00
173 Jordan Clarkson .30 .75
174 John Collins .25 .60
175 Desmond Bane .30 .75
176 Mark Williams .25 .60
177 Ausar Thompson .50 1.25
178 Alex Caruso .30 .75
179 Quentin Grimes .25 .60
180 Julian Strawther .30 .75
181 Kelly Olynyk .20 .50
182 Herbert Jones .30 .75
183 Kyle Lowry .30 .75
184 Kobe Bufkin .30 .75
185 Chet Holmgren .50 1.25
186 Cam Whitmore .30 .75
187 Terance Mann .25 .60
188 Julian Champagnie .25 .60
189 Damian Lillard .75 2.00
190 Vasilije Micic .25 .60
191 Dyson Daniels .40 1.00
192 Terry Rozier III .25 .60
193 LeBron James 2.50 6.00
194 Kawhi Leonard .60 1.50
195 Tyrese Maxey .60 1.50
196 CJ McCollum .25 .60
197 Harrison Barnes .25 .60
198 Jalen Green .60 1.50
199 Norman Powell .25 .60
200 Jamal Murray .60 1.50
201 Russell Westbrook .50 1.25
202 Naji Marshall .30 .75
203 Duncan Robinson .25 .60
204 Luguentz Dort .25 .60
205 Scoot Henderson .40 1.00
206 Keegan Murray .25 .60
207 Toumani Camara .30 .75
208 Caleb Martin .25 .60
209 Cade Cunningham .75 2.00
210 Wendell Carter Jr. .30 .75
211 Tre Mann .25 .60
212 Obi Toppin .25 .60
213 Kristaps Porzingis .40 1.00
214 Darius Garland .40 1.00
215 Kentavious Caldwell-Pope .20 .50
216 Devin Vassell .40 1.00
217 Eric Gordon .25 .60
218 Jordan Poole .30 .75
219 Pascal Siakam .40 1.00
220 Lauri Markkanen .30 .75
221 RJ Barrett .40 1.00
222 Spencer Dinwiddie .20 .50
223 Derrick Jones Jr. .20 .50
224 Jordan Hawkins .25 .60
225 Malaki Branham .25 .60
226 Isaac Okoro .20 .50
227 Jaylen Brown .50 1.25
228 Jalen Johnson .40 1.00
229 Robert Williams III .25 .60
230 Karl-Anthony Towns .50 1.25
231 Kel'el Ware RC 1.25 3.00
232 Alexandre Sarr RC 1.50 4.00
233 KJ Simpson Jr. RC .50 1.25
234 Pacome Dadiet RC .60 1.50
235 Tidjane Salaun RC .60 1.50
236 Jonathan Mogbo RC .75 2.00
237 Matas Buzelis RC 2.50 6.00
238 Cody Williams RC .60 1.50
239 Devin Carter RC .60 1.50
240 Tyler Kolek RC .75 2.00
241 Jaylon Tyson RC .50 1.25
242 AJ Johnson RC 1.00 2.50
243 Dillon Jones RC .50 1.25
244 Oso Ighodaro RC .60 1.50
245 Zaccharie Risacher RC 1.50 4.00
246 DaRon Holmes II RC .60 1.50
247 Antonio Reeves RC .50 1.25
248 Cam Christie RC .60 1.50
249 Baylor Scheierman RC .60 1.50
250 Stephon Castle RC 3.00 8.00
251 Jamal Shead RC .60 1.50
252 Cam Spencer RC .50 1.25
253 Yongxi "Jacky" Cui RC 1.00 2.50
254 Isaiah Collier RC 1.00 2.50
255 Ja'Kobe Walter RC .60 1.50
256 Zach Edey RC 1.50 4.00
257 Rob Dillingham RC 1.25 3.00
258 Ryan Dunn RC .60 1.50
259 Pelle Larsson RC .60 1.50
260 Ron Holland II RC 1.00 2.50
261 Donovan Clingan RC 1.25 3.00
262 Bobi Klintman RC .60 1.50
263 Jared McCain RC 2.00 5.00
264 Dalton Knecht RC 1.50 4.00
265 Johnny Furphy RC .75 2.00
266 Terrence Shannon Jr. RC 1.00 2.50
267 Nikola Topic RC 1.50 4.00
268 Quinten Post RC 1.00 2.50
269 Yves Missi RC 1.25 3.00
270 Kyle Filipowski RC 1.25 3.00
271 Reed Sheppard RC 1.50 4.00
272 Jaylen Wells RC 1.50 4.00
273 Ajay Mitchell RC .75 2.00
274 Kyshawn George RC .75 2.00
275 Yuki Kawamura RC .60 1.50
276 Tristan da Silva RC 1.25 3.00
277 Bub Carrington RC 1.25 3.00
278 Harrison Ingram RC .50 1.25
279 Bronny James Jr. RC 1.50 4.00
280 Adem Bona RC .60 1.50
281 Luka Doncic 2.00 5.00
282 LeBron James 2.50 6.00
283 Stephen Curry 2.50 6.00
284 Jayson Tatum 1.00 2.50
285 Victor Wembanyama 2.50 6.00
286 Ja Morant 1.00 2.50
287 Shai Gilgeous-Alexander 1.50 4.00
288 Giannis Antetokounmpo 1.25 3.00
289 Nikola Jokic 1.50 4.00
290 Anthony Edwards 1.50 4.00
291 Zaccharie Risacher 1.50 4.00
292 Alexandre Sarr 1.50 4.00
293 Reed Sheppard 1.50 4.00
294 Stephon Castle 3.00 8.00
295 Zach Edey 1.50 4.00
296 Jared McCain 2.00 5.00
297 Dalton Knecht 1.50 4.00
298 Jaylen Wells 1.50 4.00
299 Matas Buzelis 2.50 6.00
300 Kel'el Ware 1.25 3.00

2024-25 Hoops Haunted Hoops Extended

1 VJ Edgecombe 3.00 8.00
2 Tre Johnson 1.50 4.00
3 Jeremiah Fears 1.50 4.00
4 Asa Newell 1.25 3.00
5 Derik Queen 1.50 4.00
6 Carter Bryant 1.00 2.50
7 Maxime Raynaud 1.00 2.50
8 Johni Broome .75 2.00
9 Khaman Maluach 1.25 3.00
10 Nique Clifford 1.00 2.50
11 Cedric Coward .75 2.00
12 Ryan Kalkbrenner .75 2.00
13 Will Riley 1.00 2.50
14 Dink Pate 1.00 2.50
15 Ryan Nembhard .75 2.00
16 Koby Brea 1.00 2.50
17 Vlad Goldin .75 2.00
18 Kam Jones .75 2.00
19 Chaz Lanier .75 2.00
20 Sion James .75 2.00
21 Izan Almansa .60 1.50
22 Rasheer Fleming .75 2.00
23 Walter Clayton Jr. 1.25 3.00
24 Hansen Yang 2.50 6.00
25 Rocco Zikarsky 2.00 5.00

2000-01 Hoops Hot Prospects

COMPLETE SET w/o RC (120) 15.00 40.00
RCs: PRINT RUN 1000 SERIAL #'d SETS
1 Vince Carter .75 2.00
2 Wesley Person .25 .60
3 Juwan Howard .30 .75
4 Rodney Rogers .25 .60
5 Tim Duncan 1.00 2.50
6 Rasheed Wallace .50 1.25
7 Anthony Peeler .25 .60
8 John Amaechi .25 .60
9 Tim Hardaway .50 1.25
10 Mark Jackson .30 .75
11 Latrell Sprewell .50 1.25
12 Kevin Garnett 1.00 2.50
13 Alonzo Mourning .60 1.50
14 Jerome Williams .25 .60
15 Anfernee Hardaway .60 1.50
16 Clifford Robinson .40 1.00
17 Mike Bibby .40 1.00
18 Allen Iverson 1.00 2.50
19 Terrell Brandon .30 .75
20 Jerry Stackhouse .40 1.00
21 Brian Grant .30 .75
22 Lamond Murray .25 .60
23 Nick Anderson .30 .75
24 Alan Henderson .25 .60
25 Bryon Russell .25 .60
26 Elton Brand .40 1.00
27 Antawn Jamison .40 1.00
28 Mitch Richmond .50 1.25
29 Marcus Camby .30 .75
30 Raef LaFrentz .30 .75
31 Damon Stoudamire .40 1.00
32 Vin Baker .30 .75
33 Allan Houston .40 1.00
34 Doug Christie .30 .75
35 Stephon Marbury .50 1.25
36 Tim Thomas .25 .60
37 Tracy McGrady .75 2.00
38 Shareef Abdur-Rahim .40 1.00
39 Eddie Jones .40 1.00
40 Glenn Robinson .40 1.00
41 Sam Cassell .30 .75
42 Dan Majerle .40 1.00
43 Maurice Taylor .25 .60
44 Anthony Mason .40 1.00
45 Dirk Nowitzki 1.00 2.50
46 Kobe Bryant 3.00 8.00
47 Kerry Kittles .30 .75
48 Derrick Coleman .40 1.00
49 Cuttino Mobley .30 .75
50 Nick Van Exel .40 1.00
51 LaPhonso Ellis .30 .75
52 Kendall Gill .40 1.00
53 Hakeem Olajuwon .75 2.00
54 Rashard Lewis .30 .75
55 Dale Davis .30 .75
56 Keith Van Horn .30 .75
57 Michael Finley .40 1.00
58 Othella Harrington .25 .60
59 Gary Payton .60 1.50
60 Michael Dickerson .25 .60
61 Voshon Lenard .25 .60
62 Patrick Ewing .60 1.50
63 Ron Mercer .30 .75
64 Kenny Anderson .30 .75
65 Shaquille O'Neal 1.50 4.00
66 Tariq Abdul-Wahad .25 .60
67 Antonio Davis .30 .75
68 Rick Fox .30 .75
69 Lamar Odom .40 1.00
70 Derek Anderson .30 .75
71 Vitaly Potapenko .25 .60
72 Karl Malone .75 2.00
73 Wally Szczerbiak .30 .75
74 Jason Williams .60 1.50
75 Steve Francis .40 1.00
76 John Starks .40 1.00
77 Ron Artest .40 1.00
78 Grant Hill .60 1.50
79 Theo Ratliff .25 .60
80 Antonio McDyess .30 .75
81 Antoine Walker .40 1.00
82 Sean Elliott .30 .75
83 Ruben Patterson .25 .60
84 Ray Allen .60 1.50
85 Tom Gugliotta .30 .75
86 Scottie Pippen 1.00 2.50
87 Jim Jackson .30 .75
88 Joe Smith .30 .75
89 Reggie Miller .75 2.00
90 Richard Hamilton .50 1.25
91 Paul Pierce .60 1.50
92 Mookie Blaylock .30 .75
93 Glen Rice .40 1.00
94 P.J. Brown .25 .60
95 Avery Johnson .30 .75
96 John Stockton .75 2.00
97 Tyrone Hill .25 .60
98 Tracy Murray .25 .60
99 Darrell Armstrong .25 .60
100 Steve Smith .40 1.00
101 Shawn Kemp .60 1.50
102 Jalen Rose .40 1.00
103 Vonteego Cummings .25 .60
104 Larry Hughes .40 1.00
105 Charles Oakley .40 1.00
106 Rod Strickland .25 .60
107 Christian Laettner .40 1.00
108 Baron Davis .40 1.00
109 Jamal Mashburn .30 .75
110 Lindsey Hunter .25 .60
111 Toni Kukoc .50 1.25
112 Austin Croshere .25 .60
113 Chris Webber .50 1.25
114 Vlade Divac .40 1.00
115 Andre Miller .30 .75
116 Larry Johnson .50 1.25
117 Jason Kidd .60 1.50
118 David Robinson .75 2.00
119 Donyell Marshall .30 .75
120 Jason Terry .60 1.50
121 Kenyon Martin JSY RC 4.00 10.00
122 Stromile Swift JSY RC 1.50 4.00
123 Chris Mihm JSY RC 1.25 3.00
124 Marcus Fizer JSY RC 1.50 4.00
125 Courtney Alexander JSY RC 1.25 3.00
126 Darius Miles JSY RC 2.00 5.00
127 Jerome Moiso JSY RC 1.25 3.00
128 Joel Przybilla JSY RC 1.50 4.00
129 DerMarr Johnson JSY RC 1.25 3.00
130 Mike Miller JSY RC 3.00 8.00
131 Quentin Richardson JSY RC 1.50 4.00
132 Morris Peterson JSY RC 2.00 5.00
133 Speedy Claxton JSY RC 2.00 5.00
134 Keyon Dooling JSY RC 1.50 4.00
135 Mark Madsen JSY RC 2.00 5.00
136 Mateen Cleaves JSY RC 1.50 4.00

137 Etan Thomas JSY RC 1.50 4.00
138 Jason Collier JSY RC 2.00 5.00
139 Erick Barkley JSY RC 1.25 3.00
140 Desmond Mason JSY RC 2.50 6.00
141 Mamadou N'Diaye JSY RC 1.25 3.00
142 DeShawn Stevenson JSY RC 2.00 5.00
143 Donnell Harvey JSY RC 1.50 4.00
144 Jamaal Magloire JSY RC 2.00 5.00
145 Hedo Turkoglu JSY RC 3.00 8.00

2000-01 Hoops Hot Prospects A'la Carter

COMPLETE SET (20) 12.00 30.00
COMMON CARD (AC1-AC20) .75 2.00
STATED ODDS 1:5 RETAIL
AC17 Vince Carter .75 2.00
AC19 Vince Carter .75 2.00

2000-01 Hoops Hot Prospects Vince Carter First In Flight

1 V.Carter JSY/250 15.00 40.00
3 V.Carter Shirt/750 12.50 30.00
5 V.Carter WU/1000 10.00 25.00

2000-01 Hoops Hot Prospects Vince Carter Rookie Remnants

NNO Vince Carter FLR/100 12.50 30.00
NNO Vince Carter FLR JSY/15 20.00 50.00

2000-01 Hoops Hot Prospects Determined

COMPLETE SET (10) 4.00 10.00
STATED ODDS 1:12 HOB, 1:20 RET
D1 Vince Carter .75 2.00
D2 Lamar Odom .40 1.00
D3 Steve Francis .40 1.00
D4 Kobe Bryant 3.00 8.00
D5 Jason Williams .60 1.50
D6 Karl Malone .75 2.00
D7 Allen Iverson 1.00 2.50
D8 Elton Brand .40 1.00
D9 Tim Duncan 1.00 2.50
D10 Kevin Garnett 1.00 2.50

2000-01 Hoops Hot Prospects Genuine Coverage

STATED ODDS 1:96 RETAIL
GC1 Lamar Odom 5.00 12.00
GC2 Antoine Walker 5.00 12.00
GC3 Shaquille O'Neal 15.00 40.00
GC4 Darrell Armstrong 3.00 8.00
GC5 Larry Hughes 5.00 12.00
GC6 Marcus Camby 4.00 10.00
GC7 Nick Van Exel 5.00 12.00
GC8 Michael Dickerson 3.00 8.00
GC9 Baron Davis 5.00 12.00
GC10 Vince Carter 10.00 25.00
GC11 Mike Bibby 5.00 12.00
GC12 Wally Szczerbiak 4.00 10.00
GC13 Jerry Stackhouse 5.00 12.00
GC14 Eddie Jones 5.00 12.00
GC15 Shawn Kemp 8.00 20.00
GC16 Rick Fox 4.00 10.00
GC17 Jamal Mashburn 4.00 10.00

2000-01 Hoops Hot Prospects Originals

COMPLETE SET (10) 10.00 25.00
STATED ODDS 1:24 HOB, 1:48 RET
H1 Vince Carter 2.00 5.00
H2 Tim Duncan 2.50 6.00
H3 Kevin Garnett 2.50 6.00
H4 Kobe Bryant 8.00 20.00
H5 Lamar Odom 1.00 2.50
H6 Steve Francis 1.00 2.50
H7 Shaquille O'Neal 4.00 10.00
H8 David Robinson 2.00 5.00
H9 Grant Hill 1.50 4.00
H10 Allen Iverson 2.50 6.00

2000-01 Hoops Hot Prospects Rookie Headliners

COMPLETE SET (15) 3.00 8.00
STATED ODDS 1:8 HOB, 1:16 RET
1 Kenyon Martin .60 1.50
2 Stromile Swift .25 .60
3 Darius Miles .30 .75
4 Jerome Moiso .20 .50
5 Chris Mihm .20 .50
6 Marcus Fizer .25 .60
7 Courtney Alexander .20 .50
8 DerMarr Johnson .20 .50
9 Mike Miller .50 1.25
10 Quentin Richardson .25 .60
11 Morris Peterson .30 .75
12 Keyon Dooling .25 .60
13 Mateen Cleaves .25 .60
14 Etan Thomas .25 .60
15 Jamal Crawford .75 2.00

2001-02 Hoops Hot Prospects

COMP.SET w/o SP's (80) 15.00 40.00
RC PRINT RUN 300 OR 1000 SERIAL #'d SETS
1 Vince Carter .75 2.00
2 John Stockton .75 2.00
3 Steve Smith .30 .75
4 Kevin Garnett 1.00 2.50
5 Larry Hughes .30 .75
6 Ron Mercer .25 .60
7 Marcus Fizer .25 .60
8 Rashard Lewis .30 .75
9 Mike Miller .30 .75
10 Darius Miles .25 .60
11 Michael Finley .40 1.00
12 Marcus Camby .30 .75
13 Morris Peterson .25 .60
14 Shawn Marion .40 1.00
15 Alonzo Mourning .60 1.50
16 Jamal Mashburn .30 .75
17 Michael Jordan 3.00 8.00
18 Jason Williams .60 1.50
19 Latrell Sprewell .50 1.25
20 Reggie Miller .75 2.00
21 Glenn Robinson .40 1.00
22 Steve Francis .40 1.00
23 Antoine Walker .30 .75
24 Stromile Swift .25 .60
25 Damon Stoudamire .40 1.00
26 Allan Houston .40 1.00
27 Kobe Bryant 3.00 8.00
28 Dirk Nowitzki 1.00 2.50
29 Iakovos Tsakalidis .25 .60
30 Gary Payton .60 1.50
31 Allen Iverson 1.00 2.50
32 Eddie Jones .40 1.00
33 Mateen Cleaves .25 .60
34 Nick Van Exel .40 1.00
35 Terrell Brandon .30 .75
36 Wally Szczerbiak .30 .75
37 Jalen Rose .30 .75
38 Elton Brand .30 .75
39 DerMarr Johnson .25 .60
40 Peja Stojakovic .30 .75
41 Jason Kidd .60 1.50
42 Sam Cassell .30 .75
43 Cuttino Mobley .30 .75
44 Toni Kukoc .50 1.25
45 DeShawn Stevenson .25 .60
46 David Robinson .75 2.00
47 Grant Hill .60 1.50
48 Shaquille O'Neal 1.50 4.00
49 Andre Miller .30 .75
50 Corey Maggette .30 .75
51 Jason Terry .40 1.00
52 Aaron McKie .25 .60
53 Eddie House .25 .60
54 Steve Nash .75 2.00
55 Clifford Robinson .40 1.00
56 Chris Webber .50 1.25
57 Kenyon Martin .40 1.00
58 Jermaine O'Neal .30 .75
59 Baron Davis .40 1.00
60 Mitch Richmond .50 1.25
61 Antawn Jamison .30 .75
62 Paul Pierce .60 1.50
63 Shareef Abdur-Rahim .30 .75
64 Rasheed Wallace .50 1.25
65 Ray Allen .60 1.50
66 Lamar Odom .30 .75
67 Chris Mihm .25 .60
68 Raef LaFrentz .25 .60
69 Patrick Ewing .60 1.50
70 Tracy McGrady .60 1.50
71 Derek Fisher .30 .75
72 Jerry Stackhouse .40 1.00
73 Antonio McDyess .30 .75
74 Karl Malone .75 2.00
75 Dikembe Mutombo .60 1.50
76 Hakeem Olajuwon .75 2.00
77 David Wesley .25 .60
78 Courtney Alexander .25 .60
79 Tim Duncan 1.00 2.50
80 Stephon Marbury .50 1.25
81 Kwame Brown JSY RC 3.00 8.00
82 Tyson Chandler JSY RC 5.00 12.00
83 Pau Gasol JSY RC 12.00 30.00
84 Eddy Curry JSY RC 3.00 8.00
85 J.Richardson JSY/300 RC 8.00 20.00
86 Shane Battier JSY RC 6.00 15.00
87 Eddie Griffin JSY/300 RC 4.00 10.00
88 DeSagana Diop JSY RC 2.00 5.00
89 Rodney White JSY RC 2.00 5.00
90 Joe Johnson JSY/300 RC 8.00 20.00
91 Kedrick Brown JSY/300 RC 3.00 8.00
92 V.Radmanovic JSY RC 2.50 6.00
93 Richard Jefferson JSY RC 4.00 10.00
94 Troy Murphy JSY RC 2.50 6.00
95 Steven Hunter JSY RC 2.00 5.00
96 Kirk Haston JSY RC 2.00 5.00
97 Michael Bradley JSY RC 2.00 5.00
98 Jason Collins JSY RC 2.50 6.00
99 Zach Randolph JSY RC 6.00 15.00
100 Brendan Haywood JSY RC 2.50 6.00
101 Joseph Forte JSY RC 2.00 5.00
102 Jeryl Sasser JSY RC 2.00 5.00
103 B.Armstrong JSY/300 RC 3.00 8.00
104 Andrei Kirilenko JSY RC 5.00 12.00
105 Primos Brezec JSY RC 3.00 8.00
106 S.Dalembert JSY/300 RC 5.00 12.00
107 Jamaal Tinsley JSY RC 2.50 6.00
108 Tony Parker JSY RC 10.00 25.00

2001-02 Hoops Hot Prospects Rookie Autographs

PRINT RUN 100 SERIAL #'d SETS
81 Kwame Brown JSY AU 10.00 25.00
84 Eddy Curry JSY AU 10.00 25.00
90 Joe Johnson JSY AU 15.00 40.00
91 Kedrick Brown JSY AU 6.00 15.00
97 Michael Bradley JSY AU 6.00 15.00

2001-02 Hoops Hot Prospects Certified Cuts

STATED ODDS 1:64
1 Kwame Brown 5.00 12.00
2 Eddy Curry 5.00 12.00
3 Kedrick Brown 3.00 8.00
4 Joe Johnson 8.00 20.00
5 Michael Bradley 3.00 8.00
6 Richard Jefferson 6.00 15.00
7 Brendan Haywood 4.00 10.00
8 Kirk Haston 3.00 8.00
9 Omar Cook 5.00 12.00
10 Vince Carter 20.00 50.00
11 Larry Bird 100.00 200.00

2001-02 Hoops Hot Prospects Hot Materials

STATED ODDS 1:8
1 Vince Carter 6.00 15.00
2 Darius Miles 2.00 5.00
3 Stephon Marbury 4.00 10.00
4 John Stockton 6.00 15.00
5 Steve Francis 3.00 8.00
6 Tracy McGrady 5.00 12.00
7 Lamar Odom 2.50 6.00
8 Corey Maggette 2.50 6.00
9 Stromile Swift 2.00 5.00
10 Morris Peterson 2.00 5.00
11 Jason Kidd 5.00 12.00
12 Karl Malone 6.00 15.00
13 Baron Davis 3.00 8.00
14 Gary Payton 5.00 12.00
15 Paul Pierce 5.00 12.00
16 Desmond Mason 2.50 6.00
17 Dikembe Mutombo 2.50 6.00
18 Mike Miller 2.50 6.00
19 Craig Claxton 2.00 5.00
20 Antoine Walker 2.50 6.00
21 Allen Iverson 8.00 20.00
22 Reggie Miller 4.00 10.00
23 Chris Webber 4.00 10.00
24 Shawn Marion 3.00 8.00
25 Allan Houston 3.00 8.00
26 Kenyon Martin 3.00 8.00
27 Alonzo Mourning 5.00 12.00
28 Grant Hill 5.00 12.00
29 Kwame Brown 2.00 5.00
30 Tyson Chandler 3.00 8.00
31 Eddy Curry 2.00 5.00
32 Shane Battier 4.00 10.00
33 Eddie Griffin 1.50 4.00
34 Rodney White 1.25 3.00
35 Pau Gasol 8.00 20.00
36 Vladimir Radmanovic 1.50 4.00
37 Richard Jefferson 2.50 6.00
38 Steven Hunter 1.25 3.00
39 Kirk Haston 1.25 3.00
40 Michael Bradley 1.25 3.00
41 Jason Collins 1.50 4.00
42 Zach Randolph 4.00 10.00
43 Brendan Haywood 1.50 4.00

2001-02 Hoops Hot Prospects Hot Tandems

PRINT RUN 100 SERIAL #'d SETS
1 V.Carter/T.McGrady 10.00 25.00
2 K.Brown/E.Curry 6.00 15.00
3 K.Malone/J.Stockton 6.00 15.00
4 D.Diop/S.Swift 6.00 15.00
5 S.Battier/S.Swift 6.00 15.00
6 P.Pierce/A.Walker 8.00 20.00
7 E.Griffin/J.Kidd 6.00 15.00
8 R.White/S.Francis 6.00 15.00
9 M.Miller/M.Bradley 6.00 15.00
10 T.Chandler/D.Miles 8.00 20.00
11 S.Marbury/J.Kidd 10.00 25.00
12 A.Iverson/V.Carter 10.00 25.00
13 A.Iverson/D.Miles 8.00 20.00
14 R.Miller/B.Davis 8.00 20.00
15 C.Webber/K.Malone 8.00 20.00
16 A.Mourning/D.Mutombo 10.00 25.00
17 K.Martin/L.Odom 6.00 15.00
18 A.Houston/R.Miller 6.00 15.00
19 G.Hill/T.McGrady 6.00 15.00
20 P.Gasol/C.Webber 10.00 25.00
21 D.Mutombo/S.Claxton 6.00 15.00
22 G.Hill/S.Francis 10.00 25.00
23 G.Payton/S.Marbury 6.00 15.00
24 V.Radmanovic/D.Mason 6.00 15.00
25 S.Marion/D.Mason 6.00 15.00
26 R.Jefferson/K.Martin 6.00 15.00
27 K.Haston/B.Davis 6.00 15.00
28 V.Carter/M.Peterson 10.00 25.00
29 V.Carter/L.Odom 10.00 25.00
30 V.Carter/D.Miles 10.00 25.00
31 V.Carter/K.Brown 8.00 20.00
32 V.Carter/C.Webber 10.00 25.00
33 A.Iverson/J.Kidd 10.00 25.00
34 E.Griffin/D.Miles 6.00 15.00
35 E.Curry/E.Griffin 6.00 15.00
36 E.Griffin/K.Brown 6.00 15.00
37 A.Iverson/S.Claxton 10.00 25.00
38 T.Chandler/E.Curry 6.00 15.00
39 T.Chandler/K.Brown 6.00 15.00
40 S.Battier/T.Chandler 8.00 20.00
41 S.Battier/P.Gasol 8.00 20.00
42 G.Hill/R.Miller 10.00 25.00
43 C.Webber/D.Miles 8.00 20.00

2001-02 Hoops Hot Prospects Inside Vince Carter

PRINT RUNS LISTED BELOW
1 V.Carter JSY H/1000 6.00 15.00
2 V.Carter JSY R/900 6.00 15.00
3 V.Carter WARM/800 6.00 15.00
4 V.Carter SHIRT/700 6.00 15.00
5 V.Carter HS FLOOR/600 8.00 20.00
6 V.Carter UNC JSY/500 10.00 25.00
7 V.Carter BALL/400 8.00 20.00
8 V.Carter USA JSY/300 10.00 25.00
9 V.Carter FLOOR/200 12.00 30.00
10 V.Carter SHOE/100 25.00 60.00

2001-02 Hoops Hot Prospects Inside Vince Carter Autographs

PRINT RUN 15 SERIAL #'d SETS
1 V.Carter JSY H 75.00 150.00
2 V.Carter JSY R 75.00 150.00
3 V.Carter WARM 75.00 150.00
4 V.Carter SHIRT 75.00 150.00
5 V.Carter HS FLOOR 75.00 150.00
6 V.Carter UNC JSY 100.00 200.00
7 V.Carter FLOOR 100.00 200.00
8 V.Carter USA JSY 75.00 150.00
9 V.Carter FLOOR 75.00 150.00
10 V.Carter SHOE 100.00 200.00

2002-03 Hoops Hot Prospects

COMP.SET w/o SP's (80) 20.00 50.00
81-108 PRINT RUN 500 SER.#'d SETS
109-114 PRINT RUN 900 SER.#'d SETS
115-120 PRINT RUN 1500 SER.#'d SETS
1 Vince Carter .75 2.00
2 Chris Webber .50 1.25
3 Latrell Sprewell .40 1.00
4 Brian Grant .25 .60
5 Jerry Stackhouse .40 1.00
6 Joe Smith .30 .75
7 Jason Terry .30 .75
8 Shawn Marion .40 1.00
9 Wally Szczerbiak .30 .75
10 Reggie Miller .75 2.00
11 Steve Nash .75 2.00
12 Karl Malone .75 2.00
13 Damon Stoudamire .40 1.00
14 Jamal Mashburn .30 .75
15 Kobe Bryant 3.00 8.00
16 Paul Pierce .60 1.50
17 Tony Parker .60 1.50
18 Mike Miller .30 .75
19 Sam Cassell .30 .75
20 Eddie Griffin .25 .60
21 Jason Williams .50 1.25
22 Jason Richardson .40 1.00
23 Antoine Walker .30 .75
24 Tim Duncan 1.00 2.50
25 Baron Davis .40 1.00
26 Glenn Robinson .40 1.00
27 Darius Miles .25 .60
28 Dirk Nowitzki 1.00 2.50
29 John Stockton .75 2.00
30 Allen Iverson 1.00 2.50
31 Richard Jefferson .30 .75
32 Rick Fox .25 .60
33 Ben Wallace .50 1.25
34 Michael Jordan 4.00 10.00
35 Rasheed Wallace .50 1.25
36 Alonzo Mourning .60 1.50
37 Steve Francis .40 1.00
38 Jalen Rose .30 .75
39 Rashard Lewis .30 .75
40 Tracy McGrady .60 1.50
41 David Wesley .25 .60
42 Pau Gasol .60 1.50
43 Antawn Jamison .30 .75
44 Shareef Abdur-Rahim .40 1.00
45 Mike Bibby .40 1.00
46 Dikembe Mutombo .60 1.50
47 Kevin Garnett 1.00 2.50
48 Elton Brand .30 .75
49 Lamond Murray .25 .60
50 Morris Peterson .30 .75
51 Joe Johnson .30 .75
52 Kenyon Martin .40 1.00
53 Shaquille O'Neal 1.50 4.00
54 Antonio McDyess .30 .75
55 Vin Baker .30 .75
56 Marcus Camby .30 .75
57 Ray Allen .60 1.50
58 Jermaine O'Neal .30 .75
59 Eddy Curry .25 .60
60 David Robinson .75 2.00
61 Clifford Robinson .40 1.00
62 Rodney Rogers .25 .60
63 Peja Stojakovic .30 .75
64 Allan Houston .40 1.00
65 Shane Battier .40 1.00
66 Jamal Tinsley .25 .60
67 Michael Finley .40 1.00
68 Kenny Anderson .30 .75
69 Stephon Marbury .50 1.25
70 Terrell Brandon .25 .60
71 Lamar Odom .40 1.00
72 Raef LaFrentz .25 .60
73 Jamaal Magloire .25 .60
74 Bonzi Wells .25 .60
75 Jason Kidd .60 1.50
76 Cuttino Mobley .25 .60
77 Tyson Chandler .40 1.00
78 Gary Payton .60 1.50
79 Grant Hill .60 1.50
80 Eddie Jones .40 1.00
81 Yao Ming JSY RC 20.00 50.00
82 Fred Jones JSY RC 3.00 8.00
83 Ryan Humphrey JSY RC 3.00 8.00
84 Drew Gooden JSY RC 4.00 10.00
85 Nikoloz Tskitishvili JSY RC 2.50 6.00
86 Caron Butler JSY RC 4.00 10.00
87 Vincent Yarbrough JSY RC 2.50 6.00
88 DaJuan Wagner JSY RC 3.00 8.00
89 Nene Hilario JSY RC 4.00 10.00
90 Qyntel Woods JSY RC 2.50 6.00
91 Jared Jeffries JSY RC 3.00 8.00
92 Casey Jacobsen JSY RC 3.00 8.00
93 Marcus Haislip JSY RC 2.50 6.00
94 Kareem Rush JSY RC 3.00 8.00
95 Predrag Savovic JSY RC 3.00 8.00
96 Melvin Ely JSY RC 3.00 8.00
97 Steve Logan JSY RC 4.00 10.00
98 Amare Stoudemire JSY RC 5.00 12.00
99 John Salmons JSY RC 3.00 8.00
100 Chris Jefferies JSY RC 2.50 6.00
101 Juan Dixon JSY RC 3.00 8.00
102 Carlos Boozer JSY RC 4.00 10.00
103 Roger Mason JSY RC 3.00 8.00
104 Rod Grizzard JSY RC 2.50 6.00
105 Tayshaun Prince JSY RC 8.00 20.00
106 Chris Wilcox JSY RC 3.00 8.00
107 Sam Clancy JSY RC 3.00 8.00
108 Dan Gadzuric JSY RC 3.00 8.00
109 Dan Dickau/900 RC 1.25 3.00
110 Jay Williams/900 RC 1.50 4.00
111 Mike Dunleavy/900 RC 2.00 5.00
112 Robert Archibald/900 RC 1.25 3.00
113 Curtis Borchardt/900 RC 1.25 3.00
114 Bostjan Nachbar/900 RC 1.50 4.00
115 Jiri Welsch/1500 RC 1.50 4.00
116 Frank Williams/1500 RC 1.25 3.00
117 Rasual Butler/1500 RC 1.50 4.00
118 Tamar Slay/1500 RC 1.25 3.00
119 Ronald Murray/1500 RC 2.00 5.00
120 Corsley Edwards/1500 RC 1.50 4.00

2002-03 Hoops Hot Prospects Certified Cuts

STATED ODDS 1:142
1 Vince Carter 12.00 30.00
2 Shareef Abdur-Rahim 8.00 20.00
4 Kwame Brown 8.00 20.00
5 Joe Johnson 12.00 30.00
6 Michael Bradley 8.00 20.00
7 Eddy Curry 10.00 25.00
9 Cuttino Mobley 8.00 20.00
10 Matt Harpring 8.00 20.00
11 Brian Grant 8.00 20.00
12 Tracy McGrady 40.00 80.00
13 Antonio McDyess 10.00 25.00
14 Larry Hughes 10.00 25.00

2002-03 Hoops Hot Prospects Class Of

STATED ODDS 1:15
1 K.Martin/D.Miles 1.50 4.00
2 K.Van Horn/T.McGrady 2.00 5.00
3 S.Francis/B.Davis 1.50 4.00
4 A.Iverson/S.Marbury 2.00 5.00
5 J.Tinsley/P.Gasol 1.50 4.00
6 G.Robinson/J.Kidd 2.00 5.00
7 H.Turkoglu/Q.Richardson 1.50 4.00
8 D.Robinson/R.Miller 2.00 5.00
9 D.Nowitzki/V.Carter 3.00 8.00
10 R.Allen/A.Walker 1.50 4.00
11 M.Miller/S.Claxton 1.50 4.00
12 J.Jeffries/D.Wagner 1.50 4.00
13 J.Richardson/T.Parker 2.00 5.00
14 L.Odom/A.Kirilenko 1.50 4.00
15 W.Szczerbiak/E.Brand 1.50 4.00
16 A.Stoudemire/D.Gooden 2.00 5.00
17 S.Marion/J.Terry 1.50 4.00
18 S.Nash/P.Stojakovic 2.00 5.00
19 P.Pierce/V.Carter 2.50 6.00
20 C.Butler/Y.Ming 2.50 6.00

2002-03 Hoops Hot Prospects Class Of Jerseys

PRINT RUN 375 SERIAL #'d SETS
1 K.Martin/D.Miles 5.00 12.00
2 K.Van Horn/T.McGrady 8.00 20.00
3 S.Francis/B.Davis 6.00 15.00
4 A.Iverson/S.Marbury 8.00 20.00
5 J.Tinsley/P.Gasol 5.00 12.00
6 G.Robinson/J.Kidd 6.00 15.00
7 H.Turkoglu/Q.Richardson 5.00 12.00
8 D.Robinson/R.Miller 10.00 25.00
9 D.Nowitzki/V.Carter 12.00 30.00
10 R.Allen/A.Walker 5.00 12.00
11 M.Miller/S.Claxton 5.00 12.00
12 J.Jeffries/D.Wagner 5.00 12.00
13 J.Richardson/T.Parker 6.00 15.00
14 L.Odom/A.Kirilenko 5.00 12.00
15 W.Szczerbiak/E.Brand 5.00 12.00
16 A.Stoudemire/D.Gooden 6.00 15.00
17 S.Marion/J.Terry 5.00 12.00
18 S.Nash/P.Stojakovic 5.00 12.00
19 P.Pierce/V.Carter 10.00 25.00
20 C.Butler/Y.Ming 8.00 20.00

2002-03 Hoops Hot Prospects Hot Materials

STATED ODDS 1:8
*RED HOT: 1X TO 2.5X HOT MAT.HI
RED HOT PRINT RUN 50 SER.#'d SETS
1 Vince Carter 5.00 12.00
2 Steve Francis 2.50 6.00
3 Hedo Turkoglu 2.00 5.00
4 Baron Davis 2.50 6.00
5 Dikembe Mutombo 4.00 10.00
6 Allen Iverson 6.00 15.00
7 Pau Gasol 4.00 10.00
8 Keith Van Horn 2.00 5.00
9 Lamar Odom 2.50 6.00
10 Jason Kidd 4.00 10.00
11 Paul Pierce 4.00 10.00
12 Speedy Claxton 1.50 4.00
13 Steve Nash 5.00 12.00
14 Alonzo Mourning 4.00 10.00
15 Elton Brand 2.00 5.00
16 Corey Maggette 2.00 5.00
17 Jason Richardson 2.50 6.00
18 Desmond Mason 2.00 5.00
19 Antoine Walker 2.00 5.00
20 Cuttino Mobley 1.50 4.00
21 Richard Jefferson 2.00 5.00
22 Darius Miles 1.50 4.00
23 Tracy McGrady 4.00 10.00
24 Peja Stojakovic 2.00 5.00
25 Gary Payton 4.00 10.00
26 Mike Miller 2.00 5.00
27 Tony Parker 4.00 10.00
28 Kenyon Martin 2.50 6.00
29 Yao Ming 12.00 30.00
30 Amare Stoudemire 6.00 15.00
31 Dan Dickau 1.50 4.00
32 Drew Gooden 2.50 6.00
33 Nikoloz Tskitishvili 1.50 4.00
34 Caron Butler 2.50 6.00
35 Fred Jones 2.00 5.00
36 DaJuan Wagner 2.00 5.00
37 Nene Hilario 2.50 6.00
38 Qyntel Woods 1.50 4.00
39 Jared Jeffries 2.00 5.00
40 Tayshaun Prince 5.00 12.00
41 Marcus Haislip 1.50 4.00
42 Kareem Rush 2.00 5.00
43 Ryan Humphrey 2.00 5.00
44 Melvin Ely 2.00 5.00
45 Carlos Boozer 2.50 6.00

2002-03 Hoops Hot Prospects Hot Tandems

PRINT RUN 100 SERIAL #'d SETS
ASTERISK NEVER INSERTED IN PACKS
1 V.Carter/S.Francis 10.00 25.00
2 V.Carter/Y.Ming 12.50 30.00
3 V.Carter/T.McGrady 10.00 25.00
4 V.Carter/D.Wagner 6.00 15.00
5 V.Carter/P.Pierce 10.00 25.00
6 H.Turkoglu/P.Stojakovic 6.00 15.00
7 T.McGrady/A.Iverson 10.00 25.00
8 B.Davis/C.Mobley 6.00 15.00
9 D.Mutombo/N.Hilario 6.00 15.00
10 A.Iverson/Y.Ming 8.00 20.00
11 P.Gasol/R.Humphrey 6.00 15.00
13 L.Odom/D.Miles 8.00 20.00
14 R.Jefferson/J.Kidd 8.00 20.00
15 C.Mobley/S.Francis 6.00 15.00
16 G.Payton/T.Parker 8.00 20.00
17 M.Miller/K.Martin 6.00 15.00
18 D.Gooden/C.Boozer 8.00 20.00
19 M.Ely/M.Haislip 6.00 15.00
20 Q.Woods/A.Stoudemire 8.00 20.00
21 C.Butler/F.Jones 6.00 15.00
22 J.Jeffries/N.Hilario 6.00 15.00
23 A.Stoudemire/M.Miles 8.00 20.00
24 R.Jefferson/C.Butler 6.00 15.00
25 D.Wagner/K.Rush 6.00 15.00
26 T.Parker/J.Kidd 8.00 20.00
27 P.Gasol/D.Nowitzki 8.00 20.00
28 B.Davis/K.Rush 6.00 15.00
29 S.Nash/D.Nowitzki 10.00 25.00
30 C.Boozer/E.Brand 6.00 15.00
31 A.Mourning/D.Mutombo 8.00 20.00
32 M.Ely/E.Brand 6.00 15.00
34 K.Van Horn/K.Martin 6.00 15.00
35 R.Humphrey/P.Stojakovic 6.00 15.00
36 L.Odom/C.Maggette 6.00 15.00
37 H.Turkoglu/N.Tskitishvili 6.00 15.00
38 J.Richardson/P.Pierce 6.00 15.00
39 J.Richardson/D.Gooden 6.00 15.00
40 M.Haislip/D.Woods 6.00 15.00
41 F.Jones/A.Walker 6.00 15.00
42 A.Walker/G.Payton 6.00 15.00
43 M.Miller/C.Jacobsen 6.00 15.00

2002-03 Hoops Hot Prospects Stat Tracker

PRINT RUNS LISTED BELOW
1 Vince Carter/57 10.00 25.00
2 Michael Jordan/60 125.00 300.00
3 Kobe Bryant/80 40.00 100.00
4 Shaquille O'Neal/67 20.00 50.00
5 Kevin Garnett/79 12.00 30.00
6 Allen Iverson 12.00 30.00
7 Tracy McGrady/74 8.00 20.00
8 Tim Duncan/82 12.00 30.00
10 Dirk Nowitzki/76 12.00 30.00

2002-03 Hoops Hot Prospects Supreme Court

COMPLETE SET (15) 12.50 30.00
STATED ODDS 1:7
1 Melvin Ely .75 2.00
2 Jay Williams .75 2.00
3 Mike Dunleavy 1.00 2.50
4 Drew Gooden 1.00 2.50
5 Nikoloz Tskitishvili .60 1.50
6 Caron Butler 1.00 2.50
7 Chris Wilcox .75 2.00
8 DaJuan Wagner .75 2.00
9 Nene Hilario 1.00 2.50
10 Qyntel Woods .60 1.50
11 Jared Jeffries .75 2.00
12 Juan Dixon .75 2.00
13 Amare Stoudemire 2.50 6.00
14 Kareem Rush .75 2.00
15 Bostjan Nachbar .75 2.00

2002-03 Hoops Hot Prospects Triple Patch

PRINT RUN 75 SERIAL #'d SETS
1 Kidd/Francis/McGrady 25.00 60.00
2 Iverson/Carter/Pierce 40.00 100.00
3 Richardson/Jefferson/Miles 15.00 40.00
4 Davis/Gasol/Odom 15.00 40.00
5 Nash/Mourning/Brand 15.00 40.00
6 Walker/Stojakovic/Payton 25.00 60.00
7 Parker/Martin/Turkoglu 20.00 50.00
8 Mutombo/Van Horn/Claxton 15.00 40.00
9 Maggette/Mason/Mobley 15.00 40.00
10 Miller/Ming/Wagner 20.00 50.00
11 Stoudemire/Dickau/Gooden 20.00 50.00
12 Butler/Woods/Jeffries 15.00 40.00
13 Rush/Ely/Tskitishvili 15.00 40.00
14 Jones/Hilario/Prince 15.00 40.00
15 Haislip/Humphrey/Boozer 15.00 40.00

2003-04 Hoops Hot Prospects

COMP.SET w/o SP's 15.00 40.00
AU RC PRINT RUN 600 SER.#'d SETS
JSY RC PRINT RUN 500 SER.#'d SETS
JSY AU RC PRINT RUN 400 SER.#'d SETS
112-117 RC PRINT RUN 1000 SER.#'d SETS
1 Shareef Abdur-Rahim .40 1.00
2 Mike Bibby .40 1.00
3 Allan Houston .40 1.00
4 Pau Gasol .60 1.50
5 Tayshaun Prince .40 1.00
6 Darius Miles .25 .60
7 Ray Allen .60 1.50
8 Amare Stoudemire .50 1.25
9 Latrell Sprewell .50 1.25
10 Jamaal Tinsley .25 .60
11 Nene .30 .75
12 Matt Harpring .25 .60
13 Bonzi Wells .25 .60
14 Alonzo Mourning .50 1.25
15 Elton Brand .30 .75
16 Paul Pierce .60 1.50
17 Tony Parker .60 1.50
18 Glenn Robinson .30 .75
19 Marcus Haislip .25 .60
20 Eddie Griffin .25 .60
21 Jamaal Magloire .25 .60
22 Gilbert Arenas .40 1.00
23 Antoine Walker .40 1.00
24 Manu Ginobili .75 2.00
25 Jamal Mashburn .30 .75
26 Michael Redd .40 1.00
27 Ron Artest .40 1.00
28 Steve Nash .75 2.00
29 Andrei Kirilenko .30 .75
30 Stephon Marbury .50 1.25
31 Richard Jefferson .30 .75
32 Kobe Bryant 3.00 8.00
33 Cuttino Mobley .25 .60
34 Juan Dixon .25 .60
35 Rasheed Wallace .50 1.25
36 Eddie Jones .40 1.00
37 Steve Francis .40 1.00
38 Dajuan Wagner .25 .60
39 Vladimir Radmanovic .25 .60
40 Drew Gooden .30 .75
41 Baron Davis .40 1.00
42 Mike Miller .30 .75
43 Jason Richardson .40 1.00
44 Dan Dickau .25 .60
45 Chris Webber .50 1.25
46 Kenny Thomas .25 .60
47 Kevin Garnett 1.00 2.50
48 Reggie Miller .75 2.00
49 Dirk Nowitzki 1.00 2.50
50 Vince Carter .75 2.00
51 Zach Randolph .40 1.00
52 Jason Kidd .60 1.50
53 Shaquille O'Neal 1.50 4.00
54 Nikoloz Tskitishvili .25 .60
55 Jerry Stackhouse .50 1.25
56 Tracy McGrady .60 1.50
57 Desmond Mason .30 .75
58 Yao Ming 1.00 2.50
59 Jalen Rose .30 .75
60 Tim Duncan 1.00 2.50
61 Ben Wallace .50 1.25
62 Mike Dunleavy .30 .75
63 Peja Stojakovic .30 .75
64 Keith Van Horn .30 .75
65 Karl Malone .75 2.00
66 Jermaine O'Neal .40 1.00
67 Michael Finley .40 1.00
68 Morris Peterson .25 .60
69 Shawn Marion .40 1.00
70 John Salmons .30 .75
71 Chris Wilcox .25 .60
72 Rodney White .25 .60
73 Kwame Brown .25 .60
74 Bobby Jackson .30 .75
75 Kenyon Martin .40 1.00
76 Antawn Jamison .40 1.00
77 Eddy Curry .25 .60
78 Bruce Bowen .30 .75
79 Allen Iverson 1.00 2.50
80 Caron Butler .30 .75
81 Boris Diaw AU RC 4.00 10.00
82 Quinton Ross AU RC 3.00 8.00
83 Matt Carroll AU RC 2.50 6.00
84 Travis Hansen AU RC 2.50 6.00
85 Zaur Pachulia AU RC 4.00 10.00
86 Zarko Cabarkapa AU RC 2.50 6.00
87 Maciej Lampe AU RC 2.50 6.00
88 Ndudi Ebi JSY RC 3.00 8.00
89 Jarvis Hayes JSY RC 3.00 8.00
90 Steve Blake JSY RC 4.00 10.00
91 Keith Bogans JSY RC 3.00 8.00
92 Reece Gaines JSY RC 3.00 8.00
93 Chris Kaman JSY RC 5.00 12.00
94 Slavko Vranes JSY RC 3.00 8.00
95 C.Anthony JSY AU RC 50.00 100.00
96 Troy Bell JSY AU RC 4.00 10.00
97 Travis Outlaw JSY AU RC 5.00 12.00
98 M.Sweetney JSY AU RC 4.00 10.00
99 Dahntay Jones JSY AU RC 5.00 12.00
100 Chris Bosh JSY AU RC 15.00 40.00
101 Brian Cook JSY AU RC 4.00 10.00
102 Luke Ridnour JSY AU RC 6.00 15.00
103 David West JSY AU RC 8.00 20.00
104 M.Banks JSY AU RC 4.00 10.00
105 K.Perkins JSY AU RC 5.00 12.00
106 L.Barbosa JSY AU RC 6.00 15.00
107 M.Pietrus JSY AU RC 5.00 12.00
108 D.Wade JSY AU RC 100.00 250.00
109 Josh Howard JSY AU RC 6.00 15.00
110 J.Kapono JSY AU RC 4.00 10.00
111 Luke Walton JSY AU RC 6.00 15.00
112 LeBron James RC 150.00 400.00
113 T.J. Ford RC 1.50 4.00
114 Zoran Planinic RC 1.25 3.00
115 Darko Milicic RC 1.50 4.00
116 Kirk Hinrich RC 2.00 5.00
117 Nick Collison RC 1.50 4.00

2003-04 Hoops Hot Prospects Cream of the Crop

COMPLETE SET (15) 15.00 40.00
STATED ODDS 1:5
1 LeBron James 60.00 150.00
2 Mike Sweetney .50 1.25
3 Chris Bosh 2.50 6.00
4 Darko Milicic .60 1.50
5 Nick Collison .60 1.50
6 Luke Ridnour .75 2.00
7 Kirk Hinrich .75 2.00
8 Carmelo Anthony 4.00 10.00
9 Chris Kaman .75 2.00
10 Mickael Pietrus .60 1.50
11 Jarvis Hayes .50 1.25
12 Reece Gaines .50 1.25
13 Dwyane Wade 8.00 20.00
14 Marcus Banks .50 1.25
15 T.J. Ford .60 1.50

2003-04 Hoops Hot Prospects Hot Materials

PRINT RUN 500 SER.#'d SETS
*RED SINGLES: .75X TO 2X HI COLUMN
RED PRINT RUN 50 SER.#'d SETS
1 Carmelo Anthony 12.00 30.00
2 Dwyane Wade 40.00 100.00
3 Mickael Pietrus 2.00 5.00
4 Mike Sweetney 1.50 4.00
5 Chris Bosh 8.00 20.00
6 Chris Kaman 2.50 6.00
7 Tayshaun Prince 2.50 6.00
8 Amare Stoudemire 3.00 8.00
9 Paul Pierce 4.00 10.00
10 Tony Parker 4.00 10.00
11 Manu Ginobili 5.00 12.00
12 Steve Nash 5.00 12.00
13 Steve Francis 2.50 6.00
14 Jason Richardson 2.50 6.00
15 Kevin Garnett 6.00 15.00
16 Dirk Nowitzki 6.00 15.00
17 Vince Carter 5.00 12.00
18 Jason Kidd 4.00 10.00
19 Tracy McGrady 4.00 10.00
20 Yao Ming 6.00 15.00
21 Ben Wallace 3.00 8.00
22 Kenyon Martin 2.50 6.00
23 Allen Iverson 6.00 15.00
24 Caron Butler 2.00 5.00
25 Shaquille O'Neal 10.00 25.00
26 Baron Davis 2.50 6.00
27 Drew Gooden 2.00 5.00
28 Michael Redd 2.50 6.00
29 Bonzi Wells 2.00 5.00
30 Mike Dunleavy 2.00 5.00

2003-04 Hoops Hot Prospects Hot Tandems

PRINT RUN 100 SER.#'d SETS
1 C.Anthony/D.Wade 75.00 200.00
2 M.Pietrus/M.Sweetney 5.00 12.00
3 C.Bosh/C.Kaman 8.00 20.00
4 Amare/Y.Ming 12.50 30.00
5 T.Prince/B.Wallace 5.00 12.00
6 J.Rich/M.Dunleavy 5.00 12.00
7 K.Garnett/D.Nowitzki 8.00 20.00
8 M.Redd/B.Wells 5.00 12.00
9 T.Parker/M.Ginobili 8.00 20.00
10 T.McGrady/D.Gooden 6.00 15.00
11 B.Davis/S.Francis 5.00 12.00
12 V.Carter/A.Iverson 10.00 25.00
13 S.Nash/J.Kidd 8.00 20.00
14 K.Martin/S.O'Neal 8.00 20.00
15 P.Pierce/C.Butler 6.00 15.00
16 C.Anthony/T.McGrady 20.00 40.00
17 C.Bosh/V.Carter 10.00 25.00
18 Amare/K.Garnett 8.00 20.00
19 Y.Ming/A.Iverson 10.00 25.00

20 D.Nowitzki/K.Martin 6.00 15.00
21 B.Wallace/S.O'Neal 15.00 30.00
22 J.Rich/M.Pietrus 5.00 12.00
23 T.Parker/S.Nash 6.00 15.00
24 J.Kidd/B.Davis 6.00 15.00
25 T.Prince/D.Gooden 5.00 12.00

2003-04 Hoops Hot Prospects Player Graphs

PN Nene 8.00 20.00
PVC Vince Carter 15.00 40.00

2003-04 Hoops Hot Prospects Sweet Selections

COMPLETE SET (10) 10.00 25.00
STATED ODDS 1:15
1 Y.Ming/A.Iverson 2.50 6.00
2 J.Richardson/R.Allen 1.50 4.00
3 P.Gasol/B.Davis 1.50 4.00
4 Amare/S.Marion 2.00 5.00
5 S.O'Neal/T.Duncan 2.50 6.00
6 T.Chandler/S.Francis 1.50 4.00
7 V.Carter/K.Garnett 2.50 6.00
8 J.Kidd/G.Payton 2.00 5.00
9 D.Miles/S.Abdur-Rahim 1.50 4.00
10 D.Nowitzki/T.McGrady 2.00 5.00

2003-04 Hoops Hot Prospects Sweet Selections Game Used

PRINT RUN 375 SER.#'d SETS
1 Y.Ming/A.Iverson 8.00 20.00
2 J.Richardson/R.Allen 4.00 10.00
3 P.Gasol/B.Davis 4.00 10.00
4 Amare/S.Marion 5.00 12.00
5 S.O'Neal/T.Duncan 10.00 25.00
6 T.Chandler/S.Francis 4.00 10.00
7 V.Carter/K.Garnett 8.00 20.00
8 J.Kidd/G.Payton 6.00 15.00
9 D.Miles/S.Abdur-Rahim 4.00 10.00
10 D.Nowitzki/T.McGrady 6.00 15.00

2003-04 Hoops Hot Prospects Triple Patches

PRINT RUN 50 SER.#'d SETS
1 Melo/Wade/Pietrus 75.00 200.00
2 Sweetney/Bosh/Kaman 30.00 80.00
3 Amare/Ming/Prince 30.00 80.00
4 Manu/Nash/Francis 30.00 80.00
5 KG/Nowitzki/Vince 30.00 80.00
6 T-Mac/K-Mart/Iverson 40.00 100.00
7 Pierce/Parker/J-Rich 30.00 80.00
8 Wallace/Butler/Shaq 30.00 80.00
9 Wells/Dunleavy/Gooden 25.00 60.00
10 Kidd/B.Davis/Redd 30.00 80.00
11 Melo/Vince/T-Mac 40.00 100.00
12 Amare/KG/Nowitzki 30.00 80.00
13 Iverson/Pierce/J-Rich 30.00 80.00
14 Ming/Wallace/Kaman 25.00 60.00
15 Nash/Francis/Kidd 25.00 60.00

2003 Hoops Hot Prospects All-Star Game

COMPLETE SET (6) 15.00 40.00
1 Yao Ming 8.00 20.00
2 Drew Gooden 2.50 6.00
3 Caron Butler 2.50 6.00
4 Amare Stoudemire 6.00 15.00
5 Nene Hilario 2.00 5.00
6 DaJuan Wagner 1.50 4.00

2004-05 Hoops Hot Prospects

COMP.SET w/o SP's (70) 15.00 40.00
71-90 PRINT RUNS LISTED IN CHECKLIST
91-99 PRINT RUN 350 SER.#'d SETS
100-110 PRINT RUN 1000 SER.#'d SETS
1 Dwyane Wade 1.50 4.00
2 Chris Bosh .60 1.50
3 Peja Stojakovic .30 .75
4 Darius Miles .25 .60
5 Drew Gooden .25 .60
6 Latrell Sprewell .50 1.25
7 Caron Butler .30 .75
8 Shaquille O'Neal 1.50 4.00
9 Reggie Miller .75 2.00
10 Corey Maggette .30 .75
11 Tracy McGrady .60 1.50
12 Ben Wallace .50 1.25
13 Steve Nash .75 2.00
14 Paul Pierce .60 1.50
15 Jarvis Hayes .25 .60
16 Ray Allen .60 1.50
17 Chris Webber .50 1.25
18 Amare Stoudemire .40 1.00
19 Pau Gasol .60 1.50
20 Jermaine O'Neal .30 .75
21 Yao Ming 1.00 2.50
22 Richard Hamilton .50 1.25
23 Kirk Hinrich .40 1.00
24 Antoine Walker .40 1.00
25 Carlos Arroyo .25 .60
26 Luke Ridnour .30 .75
27 Mike Bibby .40 1.00
28 Tim Duncan 1.00 2.50
29 Shareef Abdur-Rahim .40 1.00
30 Willie Green .40 1.00
31 Jamaal Magloire .25 .60
32 Stephen Jackson .30 .75
33 Karl Malone .75 2.00
34 Elton Brand .30 .75
35 Jason Richardson .40 1.00
36 Steve Francis .40 1.00
37 Jason Kidd .60 1.50
38 Kevin Garnett 1.00 2.50
39 Jason Williams .30 .75
40 Ron Artest .40 1.00
41 Darko Milicic .25 .60
42 Carmelo Anthony .75 2.00
43 Carlos Boozer .30 .75
44 Michael Finley .40 1.00
45 Marcus Fizer .25 .60
46 Ricky Davis .30 .75
47 Andrei Kirilenko .30 .75
48 Tony Parker .60 1.50
49 Shawn Marion .40 1.00
50 Allan Houston .40 1.00
51 Kenyon Martin .40 1.00
52 T.J. Ford .25 .60
53 Nene .30 .75
54 LeBron James 3.00 8.00
55 Eddy Curry .25 .60
56 Jason Terry .30 .75
57 Vince Carter .75 2.00
58 Zach Randolph .40 1.00
59 Allen Iverson 1.00 2.50
60 Stephon Marbury .50 1.25
61 Richard Jefferson .30 .75
62 Baron Davis .40 1.00
63 Michael Redd .30 .75
64 Lamar Odom .40 1.00
65 Kobe Bryant 3.00 8.00
66 Mickael Pietrus .25 .60
67 Dirk Nowitzki 1.00 2.50
68 Dajuan Wagner .25 .60
69 Jason Kapono .25 .60
70 Antawn Jamison .30 .75
71 B.Gordon JSY AU/350 RC 6.00 15.00
72 S.Livingston JSY AU/350 RC 6.00 20.00
73 Devin Harris JSY AU/150 RC 5.00 12.00
74 J.Childress JSY AU/150 RC 4.00 10.00
75 Luol Deng JSY AU/150 RC 12.00 30.00
76 R.Araujo JSY AU/150 RC 4.00 10.00
77 L.Jackson JSY AU/150 RC 4.00 10.00
78 Andris Biedrins JSY AU RC 4.00 10.00
79 Y.Tabuse JSY AU/350 RC 6.00 15.00
80 S.Telfair JSY AU/350 RC 5.00 12.00
81 K.Humphries JSY AU/350 RC 5.00 12.00
82 Kirk Snyder JSY AU/150 RC 4.00 10.00
83 Josh Smith JSY AU/150 RC 6.00 15.00
84 J.R. Smith JSY AU/350 RC 6.00 15.00
85 D.Wright JSY AU/350 RC 5.00 12.00
86 J.Nelson JSY AU/350 RC 6.00 15.00
87 D.West JSY AU/350 RC 5.00 12.00
88 Tony Allen JSY AU/350 RC 6.00 15.00
89 Seung-Jin JSY AU/350 RC 6.00 15.00
90 Al Jefferson JSY AU/150 RC 6.00 15.00
91 Dwight Howard JSY RC 15.00 40.00
92 Andre Iguodala JSY RC 8.00 20.00
93 Jackson Vroman JSY RC 3.00 8.00
94 Lionel Chalmers JSY RC 4.00 10.00
95 Kevin Martin JSY RC 6.00 15.00
96 Sasha Vujacic JSY RC 4.00 10.00
97 Andre Emmett JSY RC 3.00 8.00
98 David Harrison JSY RC 3.00 8.00
99 Anderson Varejao JSY RC 4.00 10.00
100 Chris Duhon JSY RC 4.00 10.00
101 Emeka Okafor RC 1.50 4.00
102 Viktor Khryapa RC 1.25 3.00
103 Peter John Ramos RC 1.25 3.00
104 Sergei Monia RC 1.25 3.00
105 Beno Udrih RC 1.50 4.00
106 Pavel Podkolzin RC 1.25 3.00
107 Trevor Ariza RC 2.00 5.00
108 Royal Ivey RC 1.25 3.00
109 Bernard Robinson RC 1.25 3.00
110 Robert Swift RC 1.25 3.00

2004-05 Hoops Hot Prospects Red Hot

*1-70 RED: 2X TO 5X BASE HI
*71-90 RED: 1X TO 2.5X BASE HI
*91-100 RED: .6X TO 1.5X BASE HI
*101-110 RED: .75X TO 2X BASE HI
PRINT RUN 50 SER.#'d SETS
54 LeBron James 20.00 50.00
65 Kobe Bryant 12.00 30.00

2004-05 Hoops Hot Prospects Alumni Ink

PRINT RUN 50 SER.#'d SETS
CJ V.Carter/A.Jamison 30.00 60.00
KA J.Kidd/S.Abdur-Rahim 25.00 60.00
MB S.Marbury/C.Bosh 15.00 40.00
RR Z.Randolph/J.Richardson 15.00 40.00
WN D.West/J.Nelson 15.00 40.00
WP A.Walker/T.Prince 15.00 40.00

2004-05 Hoops Hot Prospects Double Team

COMPLETE SET (13) 12.50 30.00
STATED ODDS 1:45 H, 1:96 R
AI Allen Iverson 2.00 5.00
AS Amare Stoudemire .75 2.00
CA Carmelo Anthony 1.50 4.00
CB Carlos Boozer .60 1.50
DW Dwyane Wade 3.00 8.00
EO Emeka Okafor .60 1.50
LB Larry Brown 2.50 6.00
LJ LeBron James 6.00 15.00
LO Lamar Odom .75 2.00
RJ Richard Jefferson .60 1.50
SM Stephon Marbury 1.00 2.50
SM Shawn Marion .75 2.00
TD Tim Duncan 2.00 5.00

2004-05 Hoops Hot Prospects Double Team Jerseys

PRINT RUN 100 SER.#'d SETS
*RED HOT: .6X TO 1.5X BASE HI
RED HOT PRINT RUN 25 SER.#'d SETS
*PATCH SINGLES: 1.25X TO 3X BASE JSY HI
PATCH PRINT RUN 50 SER.#'d SETS
AI Allen Iverson 8.00 20.00
AS Amare Stoudemire 3.00 8.00
CA Carmelo Anthony 6.00 15.00
CB Carlos Boozer 2.50 6.00
DW Dwyane Wade 12.00 30.00
LO Lamar Odom 3.00 8.00
RJ Richard Jefferson 2.50 6.00
SM Stephon Marbury 3.00 8.00
SM Shawn Marion 3.00 8.00
TD Tim Duncan 6.00 15.00

2004-05 Hoops Hot Prospects Double Team Patches Autographs

PRINT RUN 25 SER.#'d SETS
CA Carmelo Anthony 75.00 200.00
RJ Richard Jefferson 15.00 40.00
SM Stephon Marbury 40.00 100.00

2004-05 Hoops Hot Prospects Draft Rewind

COMPLETE SET (30) 10.00 25.00
STATED ODDS 1:5
1 Dwyane Wade 1.50 4.00
2 Lamar Odom .40 1.00
3 Peja Stojakovic .30 .75
4 Shaquille O'Neal 1.50 4.00
5 Reggie Miller .75 2.00
6 Tracy McGrady .60 1.50
7 Steve Nash .75 2.00
8 Paul Pierce .60 1.50
9 Ray Allen .60 1.50
10 Dirk Nowitzki 1.00 2.50
11 Amare Stoudemire .40 1.00
12 Pau Gasol .60 1.50
13 Jermaine O'Neal .30 .75
14 Yao Ming 1.00 2.50
15 Kirk Hinrich .40 1.00
16 Tim Duncan 1.00 2.50
17 Karl Malone .75 2.00
18 Mike Bibby .40 1.00
19 Steve Francis .40 1.00
20 Jason Kidd .60 1.50
21 Kevin Garnett 1.00 2.50
22 Darko Milicic .25 .60
23 Carmelo Anthony .75 2.00
24 Tony Parker .60 1.50
25 Kenyon Martin .40 1.00
26 LeBron James 3.00 8.00
27 Vince Carter .75 2.00
28 Allen Iverson 1.00 2.50
29 Stephon Marbury .50 1.25
30 Kobe Bryant 3.00 8.00

2004-05 Hoops Hot Prospects Draft Rewind Jerseys

STATED PRINT RUN 101 TO 117 SETS
AI Allen Iverson/101 8.00 20.00
AS Amare Stoudemire/109 3.00 8.00
CA Carmelo Anthony/103 6.00 15.00
DM Darko Milicic/102 2.00 5.00
DN Dirk Nowitzki/109 8.00 20.00
DW Dwyane Wade/105 12.00 30.00
JK Jason Kidd/102 5.00 12.00
JO Jermaine O'Neal/117 2.50 6.00
KG Kevin Garnett/105 8.00 20.00
KH Kirk Hinrich/107 3.00 8.00
KM Karl Malone/103 6.00 15.00
KM Kenyon Martin/101 3.00 8.00
LO Lamar Odom/104 3.00 8.00
MB Mike Bibby/102 3.00 8.00
PG Pau Gasol/103 5.00 12.00
PP Paul Pierce/110 5.00 12.00
PS Peja Stojakovic/114 2.50 6.00
RA Ray Allen/105 5.00 12.00
RM Reggie Miller/111 6.00 15.00
SF Steve Francis/102 3.00 8.00
SM Stephon Marbury/104 4.00 10.00
SN Steve Nash/115 6.00 15.00
SO Shaquille O'Neal/101 12.00 30.00
TD Tim Duncan/101 8.00 20.00
TM Tracy McGrady/109 5.00 12.00
TP Tony Parker/128 5.00 12.00
VC Vince Carter/105 6.00 15.00
YM Yao Ming/101 8.00 20.00

2004-05 Hoops Hot Prospects Draft Rewind Patches

PRINT RUNS LISTED IN CHECKLIST
AS Amare Stoudemire/19 8.00 20.00
CA Carmelo Anthony/13 15.00 40.00
DN Dirk Nowitzki/19 20.00 50.00
DW Dwyane Wade/15 15.00 40.00
JO Jermaine O'Neal/27 6.00 15.00
LO Lamar Odom/14 8.00 20.00
PG Pau Gasol/13 12.00 30.00
PP Paul Pierce/20 12.00 30.00
PS Peja Stojakovic/24 6.00 15.00
SM Stephon Marbury/14 8.00 20.00
TM Tracy McGrady/19 12.00 30.00
TP Tony Parker/38 12.00 30.00
VC Vince Carter/15 15.00 40.00

2004-05 Hoops Hot Prospects Hot Materials

PRINT RUN 500 SER.#'d SETS
*RED SINGLES: .6X TO 1.5X BASE JSY HI
RED HOT PRINT RUN 50 SER.#'d SETS
AI Allen Iverson 6.00 15.00
AS Amare Stoudemire 2.50 6.00
BD Baron Davis 2.50 6.00
BG Ben Gordon 2.50 6.00
BW Ben Wallace 3.00 8.00
CA Carmelo Anthony 5.00 12.00
CB Chris Bosh 4.00 10.00
DH Devin Harris 2.00 5.00
DH2 Dwight Howard 8.00 20.00
DM Darko Milicic 2.00 5.00
DN Dirk Nowitzki 6.00 15.00
DW Dwyane Wade 6.00 15.00
JC Josh Childress 1.50 4.00
JK Jason Kidd 4.00 10.00
JO Jermaine O'Neal 2.00 5.00
JR Jason Richardson 2.50 6.00
KG Kevin Garnett 6.00 15.00
KH Kirk Hinrich 2.50 6.00
LD Luol Deng 2.50 6.00
LO Lamar Odom 2.50 6.00
MB Mike Bibby 2.50 6.00
PG Pau Gasol 4.00 10.00
PP Paul Pierce 4.00 10.00
PS Peja Stojakovic 2.00 5.00
RA Ray Allen 4.00 10.00
RJ Richard Jefferson 2.00 5.00
SF Steve Francis 2.50 6.00
SL Shaun Livingston 2.50 6.00
SM Stephon Marbury 3.00 8.00
SM2 Shawn Marion 2.50 6.00
SO Shaquille O'Neal 10.00 25.00
TD Tim Duncan 6.00 15.00
TM Tracy McGrady 4.00 10.00
VC Vince Carter 5.00 12.00
YM Yao Ming 6.00 15.00

2004-05 Hoops Hot Prospects Notable Newcomers

COMPLETE SET (15) 12.00 30.00
STATED ODDS 1:15
1 Dwight Howard 2.50 6.00
2 Emeka Okafor .60 1.50
3 Ben Gordon .75 2.00
4 Shaun Livingston .75 2.00
5 Devin Harris .60 1.50
6 Josh Childress .50 1.25
7 Luol Deng .75 2.00
8 Andre Iguodala 1.25 3.00
9 Luke Jackson .50 1.25
10 Sebastian Telfair .60 1.50
11 Kris Humphries .60 1.50
12 Al Jefferson .75 2.00
13 LeBron James 6.00 15.00
14 Carmelo Anthony 1.50 4.00
15 Dwyane Wade 3.00 8.00

2004-05 Hoops Hot Prospects Notable Notations

PRINT RUN 50 SER.#'d SETS
AJ Al Jefferson 8.00 20.00
BG Ben Gordon 8.00 20.00
CA Carmelo Anthony 20.00 50.00
DH Devin Harris 6.00 15.00
JC Josh Childress 5.00 12.00
KH Kris Humphries 6.00 15.00
LJ Luke Jackson 5.00 12.00
SL Shaun Livingston 8.00 20.00
ST Sebastian Telfair 6.00 15.00

1991 Hoops Larry Bird Video

NNO Larry Bird 10.00 25.00

1991-92 Hoops McDonald's

COMPLETE SET (70) 12.00 30.00
COMPLETE NAT.SET (62) 8.00 20.00
COMPLETE BULLS SET (8) 2.50 6.00
1 Dominique Wilkins .50 1.25
2 Larry Bird 1.00 2.50
3 Kevin McHale .50 1.25
4 Robert Parish .40 1.00
5 Michael Jordan 2.50 6.00
6 John Paxson .25 .60
7 Scottie Pippen .75 2.00
8 Brad Daugherty .30 .75
9 Rolando Blackman .25 .60
10 Derek Harper .25 .60
11 Joe Dumars .40 1.00
12 Bill Laimbeer .30 .75
13 Isiah Thomas .50 1.25
14 Tim Hardaway .40 1.00
15 Chris Mullin .40 1.00
16 Hakeem Olajuwon .60 1.50
17 Reggie Miller .50 1.25
18 Chuck Person .25 .60
19 Charles Smith .25 .60
20 Vlade Divac .25 .60
21 James Worthy .40 1.00
22 Rony Seikaly .25 .60
23 Alvin Robertson .25 .60
24 Pooh Richardson .25 .60
25 Derrick Coleman .30 .75
26 Patrick Ewing .50 1.25
27 Xavier McDaniel .25 .60
28 Dennis Scott .25 .60
29 Scott Skiles .25 .60
30 Charles Barkley .60 1.50
31 Hersey Hawkins .25 .60
32 Tom Chambers .30 .75
33 Kevin Johnson .30 .75
34 Clyde Drexler .50 1.25
35 Terry Porter .25 .60
36 Buck Williams .25 .60
37 Mitch Richmond .40 1.00
38 Lionel Simmons .20 .50
39 Terry Cummings .30 .75
40 Sean Elliott .25 .60
41 David Robinson .60 1.50
42 Shawn Kemp .50 1.25
43 Ricky Pierce .25 .60
44 Karl Malone .60 1.50
45 John Stockton .60 1.50
46 Bernard King .40 1.00
47 Larry Johnson 1.00 2.50
48 Dikembe Mutombo 1.25 3.00
49A Billy Owens ERR .30 .75
49B Billy Owens COR .30 .75
50 Kenny Anderson .30 .75
51 Charles Barkley USA .60 1.50
52 Larry Bird USA 1.00 2.50
53 Patrick Ewing USA .50 1.25
54 Magic Johnson USA 1.00 2.50
55 Michael Jordan USA 2.50 6.00
56 Karl Malone USA .60 1.50
57 Chris Mullin USA .40 1.00
58 Scottie Pippen USA .75 2.00
59 David Robinson USA .60 1.50
60 John Stockton USA .60 1.50
61 Chuck Daly CO USA .30 .75
62 USAB Team .40 1.00
63 B.J. Armstrong .30 .75
64 Bill Cartwright .25 .60
65 Horace Grant .30 .75
66 Craig Hodges .25 .60
67 Stacey King .25 .60
68 Cliff Levingston .25 .60
69 Will Perdue .25 .60
70 Scott Williams .30 .75

1994-95 Hoops NSCC Sheet

NNO Hoops panel
Dino Radja
Scott Burrell
Anfernee Hardaway
Latrell Sprewell
Jim Jackson
Hakeem Olajuwon
Vin Baker
Gheorghe Muresan 2.00 5.00

2019-20 Hoops Premium Stock

*GREEN .6X TO 1.5X BASIC
*PULSAR: .6X TO 1.5X BASIC
*SILVER LASER: .6X TO 1.5X BASIC
*BLUE CRACKED ICE: .75X TO 2X BASIC
*PURPLE DISCO: .75X TO 2X BASIC
*RED CRACKED ICE: .75X TO 2X BASIC
*BLUE: 1.25X TO 3X BASIC
*SILVER SCOPE: 1.25X TO 3X BASIC
*GREEN PULSAR: 1.5X TO 4X BASIC
*TEAL: 1.5X TO 4X BASIC
*BLUE LASER/99: 2.5X TO 6X BASIC
*BLUE MOJO/99: 2.5X TO 6X BASIC
*BLUE FLASH/49: 3X TO 8X BASIC
*PURPLE FLASH/35: 4X TO 10X BASIC
*PINK FLASH/25: 5X TO 12X BASIC
*PURPLE CRACKED ICE/25: 5X TO 12X BASIC
1 Trae Young 1.00 2.50
2 John Collins .40 1.00
3 Kevin Huerter .40 1.00
4 Kent Bazemore .25 .60
5 Alex Caruso .40 1.00
6 Jayson Tatum 1.50 4.00
7 Jaylen Brown .60 1.50
8 Marcus Smart .30 .75
9 Gordon Hayward .30 .75
10 Terry Rozier .30 .75
11 Kyrie Irving .75 2.00
12 Jarrett Allen .40 1.00
13 Spencer Dinwiddie .30 .75
14 Joe Harris .30 .75
15 Caris LeVert .30 .75
16 Taurean Prince .25 .60
17 Rodions Kurucs .40 1.00
18 D'Angelo Russell .30 .75
19 Kemba Walker .30 .75
20 Miles Bridges .40 1.00
21 Michael Kidd-Gilchrist .25 .60
22 Nicolas Batum .25 .60
23 Bismack Biyombo .25 .60
24 Dwayne Bacon .25 .60
25 Zach LaVine .60 1.50
26 Kris Dunn .25 .60
27 Lauri Markkanen .50 1.25
28 Otto Porter Jr. .25 .60
29 Wendell Carter Jr. .40 1.00
30 Denzel Valentine .25 .60
31 Robin Lopez .25 .60
32 Kevin Love .40 1.00
33 Jordan Clarkson .40 1.00
34 Matthew Dellavedova .30 .75
35 John Henson .25 .60
36 Tristan Thompson .25 .60
37 Larry Nance Jr. .30 .75
38 Collin Sexton .50 1.25
39 Luka Doncic 2.50 6.00
40 Kristaps Porzingis .50 1.25
41 Tim Hardaway Jr. .25 .60
42 Jalen Brunson 1.00 2.50
43 Courtney Lee .25 .60
44 Justin Jackson .25 .60
45 Dwight Powell .25 .60
46 Jamal Murray .60 1.50
47 Nikola Jokic 2.00 5.00
48 Will Barton .25 .60
49 Malik Beasley .30 .75
50 Torrey Craig RC .30 .75
51 Michael Porter Jr. .60 1.50
52 Gary Harris .30 .75
53 Blake Griffin .40 1.00
54 Andre Drummond .30 .75
55 Luke Kennard .30 .75
56 Langston Galloway .25 .60
57 Reggie Jackson .30 .75
58 Thon Maker .25 .60
59 Stephen Curry 3.00 8.00
60 Klay Thompson 1.00 2.50
61 Kevin Durant 1.25 3.00
62 Draymond Green .50 1.25
63 Andre Iguodala .30 .75
64 Christian Wood .30 .75
65 Kevon Looney .25 .60
66 James Harden .75 2.00
67 Chris Paul .75 2.00
68 Eric Gordon .30 .75
69 Danuel House Jr. .25 .60
70 P.J. Tucker .30 .75
71 Davis Bertans .25 .60
72 Austin Rivers .25 .60
73 Victor Oladipo .30 .75
74 Aaron Holiday .30 .75
75 Wesley Matthews .25 .60
76 Domantas Sabonis .50 1.25
77 Myles Turner .40 1.00
78 Thaddeus Young .25 .60
79 Bojan Bogdanovic .30 .75
80 Shai Gilgeous-Alexander 2.00 5.00
81 Danilo Gallinari .30 .75
82 Montrezl Harrell .30 .75
83 Landry Shamet .30 .75
84 Lou Williams .40 1.00
85 Ivica Zubac .30 .75
86 Wilson Chandler .25 .60
87 LeBron James 3.00 8.00
88 Kyle Kuzma .50 1.25
89 Anthony Davis 1.00 2.50
90 Jaren Jackson Jr. .60 1.50
91 Avery Bradley .25 .60
92 Jae Crowder .25 .60
93 George Hill .30 .75
94 Maxi Kleber .25 .60
95 Bam Adebayo .60 1.50
96 Goran Dragic .30 .75
97 Kelly Olynyk .25 .60
98 Josh Richardson .25 .60
99 Dion Waiters .25 .60
100 Justise Winslow .25 .60
101 Derrick Jones Jr. .25 .60
102 Giannis Antetokounmpo 2.00 5.00
103 Eric Bledsoe .30 .75
104 Malcolm Brogdon .30 .75
105 Carmelo Anthony .60 1.50
106 Brook Lopez .30 .75
107 Khris Middleton .40 1.00
108 Nerlens Noel .25 .60
109 Ersan Ilyasova .25 .60
110 Andrew Wiggins .50 1.25
111 Karl-Anthony Towns .60 1.50
112 Gorgui Dieng .25 .60
113 Josh Okogie .30 .75
114 Derrick Rose .75 2.00
115 Jeff Teague .25 .60
116 Lonzo Ball .40 1.00
117 Josh Hart .30 .75
118 Jrue Holiday .50 1.25
119 Brandon Ingram .40 1.00
120 Jahlil Okafor .25 .60
121 Julius Randle .50 1.25
122 DeAndre Jordan .30 .75
123 Kevin Knox II .25 .60
124 Emmanuel Mudiay .25 .60
125 Frank Ntilikina .25 .60
126 Mitchell Robinson .40 1.00
127 Dennis Smith Jr. .25 .60
128 Aron Baynes .25 .60
129 Russell Westbrook .60 1.50
130 Steven Adams .30 .75
131 Hamidou Diallo .30 .75
132 Paul George .60 1.50
133 Dennis Schroder .30 .75
134 Andre Roberson .25 .60
135 Terrance Ferguson .25 .60
136 Markieff Morris .25 .60
137 Aaron Gordon .40 1.00
138 Mo Bamba .30 .75
139 Evan Fournier .30 .75
140 Markelle Fultz .30 .75
141 Jonathan Isaac .40 1.00
142 Nikola Vucevic .30 .75
143 Terrence Ross .40 1.00
144 Ben Simmons .40 1.00
145 Joel Embiid .75 2.00
146 Jimmy Butler .75 2.00
147 Tobias Harris .30 .75
148 JJ Redick .40 1.00
149 Devin Booker .10 .25
150 Deandre Ayton .40 1.00
151 Josh Jackson .25 .60
152 T.J. Warren .30 .75
153 Mikal Bridges .60 1.50
154 Dillon Brooks .30 .75
155 Tyler Johnson .25 .60
156 Kelly Oubre Jr. .30 .75
157 Damian Lillard 1.00 2.50
158 CJ McCollum .40 1.00
159 Zach Collins .25 .60
160 Seth Curry .30 .75
161 Meyers Leonard .25 .60
162 Jusuf Nurkic .30 .75
163 Juancho Hernangomez .40 1.00
164 Enes Kanter .25 .60
165 De'Aaron Fox .60 1.50
166 Marvin Bagley III .30 .75
167 Buddy Hield .30 .75
168 Bogdan Bogdanovic .40 1.00
169 Willie Cauley-Stein .25 .60
170 Harry Giles III .25 .60
171 LaMarcus Aldridge .40 1.00
172 DeMar DeRozan .50 1.25
173 Rudy Gay .30 .75
174 Dejounte Murray .40 1.00
175 Lonnie Walker IV .30 .75
176 Derrick White .40 1.00
177 Kawhi Leonard 1.00 2.50
178 Marc Gasol .40 1.00
179 Danny Green .30 .75
180 Serge Ibaka .30 .75
181 Kyle Lowry .40 1.00
182 Pascal Siakam .60 1.50
183 Fred VanVleet .50 1.25
184 Norman Powell .30 .75
185 Donovan Mitchell .75 2.00
186 Mike Conley .30 .75
187 Rudy Gobert .50 1.25
188 Joe Ingles .30 .75
189 Ricky Rubio .30 .75
190 Derrick Favors .25 .60
191 John Wall .50 1.25
192 Bradley Beal .50 1.25
193 Thomas Bryant .30 .75
194 Troy Brown Jr. .25 .60
195 Jabari Parker .25 .60
196 Hassan Whiteside .25 .60
197 Trevor Ariza .25 .60
198 Jeff Green .25 .60
199 Vince Carter .75 2.00
200 Jerami Grant .40 1.00
201 RJ Barrett RC 2.00 5.00
202 De'Andre Hunter RC 2.00 5.00
203 Jarrett Culver RC .50 1.25
204 Coby White RC 1.50 4.00
205 Jaxson Hayes RC .75 2.00
206 Rui Hachimura RC 2.00 5.00
207 Cam Reddish RC .75 2.00
208 Cameron Johnson RC 1.25 3.00
209 PJ Washington Jr. RC 1.50 4.00
210 Tyler Herro RC 2.50 6.00
211 Romeo Langford RC .50 1.25
212 Sekou Doumbouya RC .50 1.25
213 Luguentz Dort RC 2.00 5.00
214 Nickeil Alexander-Walker RC .75 2.00
215 Goga Bitadze RC .75 2.00
216 Luka Samanic RC .60 1.50
217 Brandon Clarke RC 1.00 2.50
218 Grant Williams RC .75 2.00
219 Ty Jerome RC 1.00 2.50
220 Nassir Little RC .75 2.00
221 Dylan Windler RC .60 1.50
222 Mfiondu Kabengele RC .60 1.50
223 Jordan Poole RC 2.00 5.00
224 Keldon Johnson RC 1.50 4.00
225 Kevin Porter Jr. RC 1.00 2.50
226 KZ Okpala RC .60 1.50
227 Carsen Edwards RC .60 1.50
228 Bruno Fernando RC .60 1.50
229 Cody Martin RC .75 2.00
230 Eric Paschall RC .60 1.50
231 Admiral Schofield RC .60 1.50
232 Jaylen Nowell RC .60 1.50
233 Bol Bol RC 1.25 3.00
234 Isaiah Roby RC .60 1.50
235 Ignas Brazdeikis RC .60 1.50
236 Quinndary Weatherspoon RC .50 1.25
237 Tremont Waters RC .60 1.50
238 Kyle Guy RC .60 1.50
239 Matisse Thybulle RC 1.00 2.50
240 Tacko Fall RC .60 1.50
241 Nicolas Claxton RC 1.00 2.50
242 Nicolo Melli RC .60 1.50
243 Daniel Gafford RC 1.00 2.50
244 Justin James RC .50 1.25
245 Terance Mann RC 1.00 2.50
246 Jalen McDaniels RC 1.25 3.00
247 Alen Smailagic RC .50 1.25
248 Talen Horton-Tucker RC .75 2.00
249 Darius Bazley RC .50 1.25
250 Kendrick Nunn RC .75 2.00
251 Darius Garland RC 2.00 5.00
252 Marial Shayok RC .50 1.25
253 Naz Reid RC 2.00 5.00
254 Jalen Lecque RC .50 1.25
255 Jordan McLaughlin RC 2.00 5.00
256 Dean Wade RC .60 1.50
257 Terence Davis II RC .75 2.00
258 Zion Williamson RC 4.00 10.00
259 Ja Morant RC 5.00 12.00
260 Al Horford .40 1.00
261 Marcus Morris Sr. .25 .60
262 Duncan Robinson .60 1.50
263 Jeremy Lamb .25 .60
264 Malik Monk .40 1.00
265 JR Smith .30 .75
266 Paul Millsap .30 .75
267 Quinn Cook .30 .75
268 Anfernee Simons .60 1.50
269 Alfonzo McKinnie .25 .60
270 Bryn Forbes .30 .75
271 Patrick Beverley .30 .75
272 Kentavious Caldwell-Pope .30 .75
273 Rajon Rondo .50 1.25
274 Jonas Valanciunas .30 .75
275 Kyle Anderson .25 .60
276 Moritz Wagner .25 .60
277 Robert Covington .25 .60
278 Dewayne Dedmon .25 .60
279 Mike Scott .25 .60
280 Harrison Barnes .30 .75
281 Charles Barkley .75 2.00
282 Dirk Nowitzki 1.00 2.50
283 Shaquille O'Neal 1.50 4.00
284 Kevin Durant 1.25 3.00
285 Allen Iverson 1.00 2.50
286 Karl Malone .75 2.00
287 Dwyane Wade .75 2.00
288 Chris Paul .75 2.00
289 Larry Bird 1.50 4.00
290 Kyrie Irving .75 2.00
291 Damian Lillard 1.00 2.50
292 John Stockton .75 2.00
293 Julius Erving 1.00 2.50
294 Anthony Davis 1.00 2.50
295 Coby White 1.50 4.00
296 Zion Williamson 4.00 10.00
297 Ja Morant 5.00 12.00
298 RJ Barrett 2.00 5.00
299 De'Andre Hunter 2.00 5.00
300 Rui Hachimura 2.00 5.00

2019-20 Hoops Premium Stock Prizms Black Pulsar

*BLACK PULSAR: 2.5X TO 6X BASIC
39 Luka Doncic 125.00 300.00
59 Stephen Curry 60.00 150.00
87 LeBron James 125.00 300.00
102 Giannis Antetokounmpo 60.00 150.00
223 Jordan Poole 75.00 200.00
233 Bol Bol 30.00 80.00
258 Zion Williamson 200.00 500.00
259 Ja Morant 150.00 400.00

2019-20 Hoops Premium Stock Prizms Gold Pulsar

*GOLD PULSAR: 2.5X TO 6X BASIC
39 Luka Doncic 125.00 300.00
59 Stephen Curry 40.00 100.00
87 LeBron James 125.00 300.00
102 Giannis Antetokounmpo 40.00 100.00
223 Jordan Poole 75.00 200.00
233 Bol Bol 30.00 80.00
258 Zion Williamson 200.00 500.00
259 Ja Morant 150.00 400.00

2019-20 Hoops Premium Stock Arriving Now

*HOLO: .75X TO 2X BASIC
*ORANGE: .75X TO 2X BASIC
*PURPLE: .75X TO 2X BASIC
1 PJ Washington Jr. 1.25 3.00
2 Zion Williamson 3.00 8.00
3 Matisse Thybulle .75 2.00
4 RJ Barrett 1.50 4.00
5 Romeo Langford .40 1.00
6 Jarrett Culver .40 1.00
7 Kendrick Nunn .60 1.50
8 Jaxson Hayes .60 1.50
9 Goga Bitadze .60 1.50
10 Cam Reddish .60 1.50
11 Darius Garland 1.50 4.00
12 Ja Morant 4.00 10.00
13 Tyler Herro 2.00 5.00
14 De'Andre Hunter 1.50 4.00
15 Sekou Doumbouya .40 1.00
16 Coby White 1.25 3.00
17 Nickeil Alexander-Walker .60 1.50
18 Rui Hachimura 1.50 4.00
19 Luka Samanic .50 1.25
20 Cameron Johnson 1.00 2.50

2019-20 Hoops Premium Stock Back Stage Pass

*BLUE: .75X TO 2X BASIC
*HOLO: .75X TO 2X BASIC
*RED: .75X TO 2X BASIC
1 Draymond Green .50 1.25
2 Chris Paul .75 2.00
3 Luka Doncic 2.50 6.00
4 Nikola Jokic 2.00 5.00
5 Russell Westbrook .60 1.50
6 Jaren Jackson Jr. .60 1.50
7 LeBron James 3.00 8.00
8 Kawhi Leonard 1.00 2.50
9 Giannis Antetokounmpo 2.00 5.00
10 Gary Harris .30 .75

2019-20 Hoops Premium Stock Class of 2019

*HOLO: .75X TO 2X BASIC
*ORANGE: .75X TO 2X BASIC
*PURPLE: .75X TO 2X BASIC
1 RJ Barrett 1.50 4.00
2 Darius Garland 1.50 4.00
3 Jarrett Culver .40 1.00
4 Romeo Langford .40 1.00
5 Jaxson Hayes .60 1.50
6 Cam Reddish .60 1.50
7 Zion Williamson 3.00 8.00
8 Cameron Johnson 1.00 2.50
9 Ja Morant 4.00 10.00
10 PJ Washington Jr. 1.25 3.00
11 De'Andre Hunter 1.50 4.00
12 Tyler Herro 2.00 5.00
13 Coby White 1.25 3.00

14 Sekou Doumbouya .40 1.00
15 Rui Hachimura 1.50 4.00

2019-20 Hoops Premium Stock Courtside

*BLUE: .75X TO 2X BASIC
*HOLO: .75X TO 2X BASIC
*RED: .75X TO 2X BASIC
1 LeBron James 3.00 8.00
2 Stephen Curry 3.00 8.00
3 Russell Westbrook .60 1.50
4 Donovan Mitchell .75 2.00
5 Paul George .60 1.50
6 Damian Lillard 1.00 2.50
7 James Harden .75 2.00
8 Karl-Anthony Towns .60 1.50
9 John Wall .50 1.25
10 Blake Griffin .40 1.00
11 Giannis Antetokounmpo 2.00 5.00
12 Joel Embiid .75 2.00
13 Ben Simmons .40 1.00
14 Luka Doncic 2.50 6.00
15 Trae Young 1.00 2.50

2019-20 Hoops Premium Stock Frequent Flyers

*HOLO: .75X TO 2X BASIC
*ORANGE: .75X TO 2X BASIC
*PURPLE: .75X TO 2X BASIC
1 Kevin Durant 1.25 3.00
2 Anthony Davis 1.00 2.50
3 Giannis Antetokounmpo 2.00 5.00
4 Jayson Tatum 1.50 4.00
5 Miles Bridges .40 1.00
6 Aaron Gordon .40 1.00
7 Zach LaVine .60 1.50
8 Kawhi Leonard 1.00 2.50
9 Russell Westbrook .60 1.50
10 Ben Simmons .40 1.00
11 Derrick Jones Jr. .25 .60
12 Paul George .60 1.50
13 James Harden .75 2.00
14 DeMar DeRozan .50 1.25
15 LeBron James 3.00 8.00

2019-20 Hoops Premium Stock Get Out the Way

*HOLO: .75X TO 2X BASIC
*ORANGE: .75X TO 2X BASIC
*PURPLE: .75X TO 2X BASIC
1 Luka Doncic 2.50 6.00
2 Aaron Gordon .40 1.00
3 Karl-Anthony Towns .60 1.50
4 Derrick Jones Jr. .25 .60
5 Miles Bridges .40 1.00
6 Donovan Mitchell .75 2.00
7 Dennis Smith Jr. .25 .60
8 John Collins .40 1.00
9 Kevin Durant 1.25 3.00
10 Joel Embiid .75 2.00
11 Hamidou Diallo .30 .75
12 Ja Morant 2.50 6.00
13 De'Aaron Fox .60 1.50
14 Giannis Antetokounmpo 2.00 5.00
15 Jarrett Allen .40 1.00
16 Marvin Bagley III .30 .75
17 Zion Williamson 2.00 5.00
18 Domantas Sabonis .50 1.25
19 Terrence Ross .40 1.00
20 Kevin Knox II .25 .60

2019-20 Hoops Premium Stock High Voltage

1 Kawhi Leonard 3.00 8.00
2 LeBron James 10.00 25.00
3 Kevin Durant 4.00 10.00
4 Andrew Wiggins 1.50 4.00
5 Victor Oladipo 1.00 2.50
6 Paul George 2.00 5.00
7 Anthony Davis 3.00 8.00
8 Donovan Mitchell 2.50 6.00
9 Luka Doncic 8.00 20.00
10 Stephen Curry 10.00 25.00
11 Giannis Antetokounmpo 6.00 15.00
12 Jimmy Butler 2.50 6.00
13 Blake Griffin 1.25 3.00
14 Draymond Green 1.50 4.00
15 Pascal Siakam 2.00 5.00
16 Joel Embiid 2.50 6.00
17 Devin Booker .30 .75
18 DeMar DeRozan 1.50 4.00
19 James Harden 2.50 6.00
20 Zach LaVine 2.00 5.00
21 Nikola Jokic 6.00 15.00
22 Julius Randle 1.50 4.00
23 Jayson Tatum 5.00 12.00

2019-20 Hoops Premium Stock Hoops Ink

EXCHANGE DEADLINE 5/27/2022
*FLASH: .5X TO 1.2X BASIC
*SHIMMER: .5X TO 1.2X BASIC
1 Torrey Craig 4.00 10.00
2 De'Anthony Melton 4.00 10.00
3 Jack Sikma 6.00 15.00
4 Chris Boucher 6.00 15.00
5 Jayson Tatum 125.00 300.00
6 Charles Barkley 75.00 200.00
7 Mason Plumlee 4.00 10.00
8 Ish Smith 4.00 10.00
9 Karl Malone 40.00 100.00
10 Ray Allen 40.00 100.00
11 Kelly Oubre Jr. 5.00 12.00
12 Frank Jackson 4.00 10.00
13 Monte Morris 6.00 15.00
14 James Johnson 4.00 10.00
15 Jerry West 25.00 60.00
16 Derrick White 6.00 15.00
17 Bruce Brown 6.00 15.00
18 Justin Holiday 4.00 10.00
19 Dwyane Wade 50.00 120.00
20 T.J. Ford 5.00 12.00
21 Kevin Durant 75.00 200.00
22 Raef LaFrentz 4.00 10.00
23 Magic Johnson 50.00 120.00
24 Noah Vonleh 4.00 10.00
25 Dennis Rodman 40.00 100.00
26 Cedi Osman 5.00 12.00
27 Dennis Rodman 40.00 100.00
28 Anthony Davis 40.00 100.00
29 Tobias Harris 5.00 12.00
30 Markelle Fultz 5.00 12.00
32 Josh Jackson 4.00 10.00
33 Damian Lillard 40.00 100.00
34 Keita Bates-Diop 4.00 10.00
35 TJ Leaf 4.00 10.00
36 Elton Brand 5.00 12.00
37 Langston Galloway 4.00 10.00
38 Brian Scalabrine 4.00 10.00
39 Meyers Leonard 4.00 10.00
40 Donovan Mitchell 30.00 80.00

2019-20 Hoops Premium Stock Hot Signatures Rookies

EXCHANGE DEADLINE 5/27/2022
1 Amir Coffey 6.00 15.00
2 Justin James 4.00 10.00
3 Jaylen Hoard 4.00 10.00
4 Kendrick Nunn 6.00 15.00
5 Terence Davis II 6.00 15.00
6 Louis King 5.00 12.00
7 Ky Bowman 5.00 12.00
8 Dewan Hernandez 4.00 10.00
9 Justin Wright-Foreman 4.00 10.00
10 Miye Oni 4.00 10.00
11 RJ Barrett 50.00 120.00
12 Alen Smailagic 4.00 10.00
13 Brian Bowen II 4.00 10.00
14 Josh Reaves 4.00 10.00
17 Dean Wade 5.00 12.00
19 Zion Williamson 400.00 800.00
20 Ja Morant 300.00 600.00
25 Nicolo Melli 5.00 12.00
26 Jarrell Brantley 4.00 10.00
27 Oshae Brissett 12.00 30.00
29 Terance Mann 8.00 20.00
30 DaQuan Jeffries 4.00 10.00

2019-20 Hoops Premium Stock Hot Signatures Rookies Flash

EXCHANGE DEADLINE 5/27/2022
15 Chris Clemons 8.00 20.00
16 Naz Reid 30.00 80.00
21 Tyler Herro 125.00 300.00
28 Jalen Lecque 8.00 20.00

2019-20 Hoops Premium Stock Hot Signatures Rookies Shimmer

*SHIMMER: .75X TO 2X BASIC
EXCHANGE DEADLINE 5/27/2022
16 Naz Reid 30.00 80.00
21 Tyler Herro 125.00 300.00
28 Jalen Lecque 8.00 20.00

2019-20 Hoops Premium Stock Lights Camera Action

*HOLO: .75X TO 2X BASIC
*ORANGE: .75X TO 2X BASIC
*PURPLE: .75X TO 2X BASIC
1 Kevin Durant 1.25 3.00
2 Stephen Curry 3.00 8.00
3 De'Aaron Fox .60 1.50
4 Deandre Ayton .40 1.00
5 Paul George .60 1.50
6 Ben Simmons .40 1.00
7 Victor Oladipo .30 .75
8 Damian Lillard 1.00 2.50
9 Donovan Mitchell .75 2.00
10 Zion Williamson 2.00 5.00
11 Bradley Beal .50 1.25
12 Karl-Anthony Towns .60 1.50
13 Russell Westbrook .60 1.50
14 Kemba Walker .30 .75
15 Luka Doncic 2.50 6.00
16 Kevin Love .40 1.00
17 Kawhi Leonard 1.00 2.50
18 Zach LaVine .60 1.50
19 Giannis Antetokounmpo 2.00 5.00
20 LeBron James 3.00 8.00
21 Rudy Gobert .50 1.25
22 Trae Young 1.00 2.50
23 Kyrie Irving .75 2.00
24 Jayson Tatum 1.50 4.00
25 Devin Booker .10 .25
26 Kyle Lowry .40 1.00
27 Joel Embiid .75 2.00
28 Nikola Jokic 2.00 5.00
29 James Harden .75 2.00
30 Julius Randle .50 1.25

2019-20 Hoops Premium Stock NBA City

*BLUE: .75X TO 2X BASIC
*HOLO: .75X TO 2X BASIC
*RED: .75X TO 2X BASIC
1 Goran Dragic .30 .75
2 Stephen Curry 3.00 8.00
3 Steven Adams .30 .75
4 Kyle Lowry .40 1.00
5 Giannis Antetokounmpo 2.00 5.00
6 Damian Lillard 1.00 2.50
7 John Wall .50 1.25
8 Blake Griffin .40 1.00
9 James Harden .75 2.00
10 Jaren Jackson Jr. .60 1.50
11 Jayson Tatum 1.50 4.00
12 Kevin Knox II .25 .60
13 Kevin Love .40 1.00
14 Karl-Anthony Towns .60 1.50
15 DeMar DeRozan .50 1.25
16 Miles Bridges .40 1.00
17 Jarrett Allen .40 1.00
18 Nikola Jokic 2.00 5.00
19 Lou Williams .40 1.00
20 Jrue Holiday .50 1.25
21 Aaron Gordon .40 1.00
22 Donovan Mitchell .75 2.00
23 Zach LaVine .60 1.50
24 Victor Oladipo .30 .75
25 Joel Embiid .75 2.00
26 Devin Booker .10 .25
27 LeBron James 3.00 8.00
28 Trae Young 1.00 2.50
29 De'Aaron Fox .60 1.50
30 Luka Doncic 2.50 6.00

2019-20 Hoops Premium Stock Rookie Ink

EXCHANGE DEADLINE 5/27/2022
1 Nicolas Claxton 8.00 20.00
4 RJ Barrett 15.00 40.00
5 Bol Bol 10.00 25.00
6 Zion Williamson 300.00 600.00
7 De'Andre Hunter 15.00 40.00
8 Admiral Schofield 5.00 12.00
9 Isaiah Roby 5.00 12.00
10 Ja Morant 300.00 600.00
11 Daniel Gafford 8.00 20.00
12 Alen Smailagic 4.00 10.00
13 Josh Reaves 4.00 10.00
15 Chuma Okeke 6.00 15.00
16 Carsen Edwards 5.00 12.00
20 Bruno Fernando 5.00 12.00
21 Louis King 5.00 12.00
26 Jarrett Culver 4.00 10.00
27 Rui Hachimura 40.00 100.00
30 Coby White 12.00 30.00

2019-20 Hoops Premium Stock Rookie Ink Flash

EXCHANGE DEADLINE 5/27/2022

2019-20 Hoops Premium Stock Rookie Special

1 Zion Williamson 8.00 20.00
2 Ja Morant 10.00 25.00

2019-20 Hoops Premium Stock Rookie Special Flash

*FLASH: .75X TO 2X BASIC
1 Zion Williamson 15.00 40.00
2 Ja Morant 20.00 50.00

2019-20 Hoops Premium Stock Rookie Variations

*FLASH: .75X TO 2X BASIC
*SHIMMER: .75X TO 2X BASIC
201 RJ Barrett 2.00 5.00
202 De'Andre Hunter 2.00 5.00
203 Jarrett Culver .50 1.25
204 Coby White 1.50 4.00
206 Rui Hachimura 2.00 5.00
207 Cam Reddish .75 2.00
209 PJ Washington Jr. 1.50 4.00
210 Tyler Herro 2.50 6.00
212 Sekou Doumbouya .50 1.25
217 Brandon Clarke 1.00 2.50
230 Eric Paschall .60 1.50
250 Kendrick Nunn .75 2.00
251 Darius Garland 2.00 5.00
258 Zion Williamson 4.00 10.00
259 Ja Morant 5.00 12.00

2019-20 Hoops Premium Stock We Got Next

*BLUE: .75X TO 2X BASIC
*HOLO: .75X TO 2X BASIC
*RED: .75X TO 2X BASIC
1 RJ Barrett 1.50 4.00
2 Nickeil Alexander-Walker .60 1.50
3 Coby White 1.25 3.00
4 Brandon Clarke .75 2.00
5 Cam Reddish .60 1.50
6 Nassir Little .60 1.50
7 Matisse Thybulle .75 2.00
8 Tyler Herro 2.00 5.00
9 Zion Williamson 3.00 8.00
10 Sekou Doumbouya .40 1.00
11 De'Andre Hunter 1.50 4.00
12 Goga Bitadze .60 1.50
13 Jaxson Hayes .60 1.50
14 Grant Williams .60 1.50
15 Cameron Johnson 1.00 2.50
16 Darius Bazley .40 1.00
17 PJ Washington Jr. 1.25 3.00
18 Romeo Langford .40 1.00
19 Ja Morant 4.00 10.00
20 Kendrick Nunn .60 1.50
21 Jarrett Culver .40 1.00
22 Luka Samanic .50 1.25
23 Rui Hachimura 1.50 4.00
24 Ty Jerome .75 2.00
25 Darius Garland 1.50 4.00

2019-20 Hoops Premium Stock Zero Gravity

*BLUE: .75X TO 2X BASIC
*HOLO: .75X TO 2X BASIC
*RED: .75X TO 2X BASIC
1 Hamidou Diallo .30 .75
2 Blake Griffin .40 1.00
3 Terrence Ross .40 1.00
4 DeMar DeRozan .50 1.25
5 Ben Simmons .40 1.00
6 Giannis Antetokounmpo 2.00 5.00
7 John Wall .50 1.25
8 Donovan Mitchell .75 2.00
9 Kevin Durant 1.25 3.00
10 Aaron Gordon .40 1.00
11 De'Aaron Fox .60 1.50
12 Anthony Davis 1.00 2.50
13 Jaylen Brown .60 1.50
14 Victor Oladipo .30 .75
15 DeAndre Jordan .30 .75
16 Zach LaVine .60 1.50
17 Karl-Anthony Towns .60 1.50
18 LeBron James 3.00 8.00
19 Joel Embiid .75 2.00
20 Russell Westbrook .60 1.50

2023-24 Hoops Premium Stock

1 Nikola Jokic 2.00 5.00
2 Kristaps Porzingis .50 1.25
3 Caris LeVert .40 1.00
4 Brook Lopez .30 .75
5 Jalen Green .60 1.50
6 Patrick Beverley .30 .75
7 Ivica Zubac .40 1.00
8 Corey Kispert .30 .75
9 Luka Doncic 2.50 6.00
10 Toumani Camara RC 1.50 4.00
11 Deandre Ayton .40 1.00
12 D'Angelo Russell .40 1.00
13 Oscar Tshiebwe RC 1.00 2.50
14 Lauri Markkanen .60 1.50
15 Brandin Podziemski RC 2.50 6.00
16 Nikola Vucevic .40 1.00
17 Saddiq Bey .40 1.00
18 Jordan Walsh RC .75 2.00
19 Jalen Hood-Schifino RC .75 2.00
20 Paul George .60 1.50
21 Vince Williams Jr. .40 1.00
22 Jerami Grant .50 1.25
23 Giannis Antetokounmpo 2.00 5.00
24 Rui Hachimura .40 1.00
25 Clint Capela .40 1.00
26 Talen Horton-Tucker .30 .75
27 Mouhamed Gueye .40 1.00
28 Gary Harris .30 .75
29 Hunter Tyson RC .75 2.00
30 Nicolas Batum .25 .60
31 Nick Smith Jr. RC .75 2.00
32 Jamal Murray .75 2.00
33 Andre Drummond .30 .75
34 Jeremy Sochan .50 1.25
35 Bradley Beal .50 1.25
36 Donovan Mitchell .75 2.00
37 Bol Bol .40 1.00
38 Chet Holmgren 1.00 2.50
39 Jaden Ivey .50 1.25
40 Jusuf Nurkic .40 1.00
41 Mark Williams .40 1.00
42 Julius Randle .50 1.25
43 GG Jackson II RC 1.50 4.00
44 Kelly Olynyk .25 .60
45 Marcus Sasser RC 1.25 3.00
46 Obi Toppin .40 1.00
47 Adama Sanogo RC .75 2.00
48 Bobby Portis .50 1.25
49 Colby Jones RC .75 2.00
50 Terquavion Smith RC .75 2.00
51 Jaime Jaquez Jr. RC 1.25 3.00
52 Rudy Gobert .50 1.25
53 Tre Mann .40 1.00
54 Reggie Jackson .25 .60
55 Kobe Brown RC .75 2.00
56 Maxwell Lewis RC .60 1.50
57 Markquis Nowell .40 1.00
58 Jalen Slawson RC .75 2.00
59 Jrue Holiday .50 1.25
60 Damian Lillard 1.00 2.50
61 Julian Phillips RC .75 2.00
62 Ochai Agbaji .40 1.00
63 Moritz Wagner .40 1.00
64 Isaiah Joe .40 1.00
65 Craig Porter Jr. RC 1.00 2.50
66 Bam Adebayo .60 1.50
67 Andre Jackson Jr. RC 1.25 3.00
68 Trayce Jackson-Davis RC 1.00 2.50
69 Stanley Umude RC .60 1.50
70 Josh Giddey .50 1.25
71 Jabari Smith Jr. .60 1.50
72 Derrick Rose .60 1.50
73 Khris Middleton .40 1.00
74 Emoni Bates RC 1.00 2.50
75 Vasilije Micic RC 1.00 2.50
76 Cason Wallace RC 1.50 4.00
77 James Harden .75 2.00
78 Draymond Green .50 1.25
79 Anfernee Simons .50 1.25
80 Leonard Miller RC .75 2.00
81 Jaylen Brown .75 2.00
82 Trae Young .75 2.00
83 Kyle Lowry .50 1.25
84 Terance Mann .30 .75
85 Franz Wagner .60 1.50
86 Amen Thompson RC 4.00 10.00
87 Anthony Edwards 2.00 5.00
88 Anthony Black RC 1.50 4.00
89 Kentavious Caldwell-Pope .30 .75
90 Kelly Oubre Jr. .40 1.00
91 Mike Conley .30 .75
92 Mitchell Robinson .40 1.00
93 Cameron Johnson .40 1.00
94 Dorian Finney-Smith .30 .75
95 Marvin Bagley III .30 .75
96 Devin Booker 1.00 2.50
97 John Collins .40 1.00
98 Keyonte George RC 2.50 6.00
99 Chris Livingston RC .75 2.00
100 Ausar Thompson RC 2.00 5.00
101 Taurean Prince .25 .60
102 Ja Morant 1.25 3.00
103 Olivier-Maxence Prosper RC .75 2.00
104 Jarrett Allen .40 1.00
105 Immanuel Quickley .40 1.00
106 Kevon Looney .40 1.00
107 Jarace Walker RC 1.50 4.00
108 Victor Wembanyama RC 6.00 15.00
109 Cam Whitmore RC 2.00 5.00
110 Jalen Suggs .50 1.25
111 Duop Reath RC .75 2.00
112 Jonas Valanciunas .40 1.00
113 Michael Porter Jr. .50 1.25
114 Kawhi Leonard 1.00 2.50
115 Evan Mobley .60 1.50
116 Alex Caruso .40 1.00
117 Jalen Williams .60 1.50
118 Keldon Johnson .50 1.25
119 Jalen Johnson .50 1.25
120 Austin Reaves 1.00 2.50
121 P.J. Washington Jr. .40 1.00
122 Jakob Poeltl .30 .75
123 Malik Monk .50 1.25
124 Jaren Jackson Jr. .50 1.25
125 Jordan Hawkins RC 1.25 3.00
126 Tyler Herro .60 1.50
127 Spencer Dinwiddie .30 .75
128 Jaden McDaniels .40 1.00
129 Jett Howard RC 1.00 2.50
130 Cameron Thomas .50 1.25
131 Collin Sexton .50 1.25
132 Aaron Gordon .40 1.00
133 Tosan Evbuomwan RC .60 1.50
134 Chris Paul .75 2.00
135 Darius Garland .60 1.50
136 Tim Hardaway Jr. .30 .75
137 Scoot Henderson RC 2.50 6.00
138 De'Anthony Melton .40 1.00
139 Isaiah Wong RC .75 2.00
140 Andrew Wiggins .50 1.25
141 Desmond Bane .50 1.25
142 Max Christie .40 1.00
143 Sidy Cissoko RC .75 2.00
144 Tyrese Maxey .75 2.00
145 Donte DiVincenzo .40 1.00
146 MarJon Beauchamp .30 .75
147 Shai Gilgeous-Alexander 1.25 3.00
148 Kobe Bufkin RC 1.00 2.50
149 LeBron James 3.00 8.00
150 Terry Rozier III .50 1.25
151 Alperen Sengun .60 1.50
152 Markelle Fultz .40 1.00
153 Dennis Schroder .40 1.00
154 Domantas Sabonis .60 1.50
155 Rayan Rupert RC .75 2.00
156 Kevin Love .40 1.00
157 Sasha Vezenkov RC .75 2.00
158 RJ Barrett .60 1.50
159 Derrick White .50 1.25
160 De'Andre Hunter .40 1.00
161 Isaiah Stewart .40 1.00
162 Kyle Kuzma .50 1.25
163 Dejounte Murray .50 1.25
164 Duncan Robinson .40 1.00
165 Tre Jones .40 1.00
166 Andrew Nembhard .40 1.00
167 Daniel Gafford .40 1.00
168 Ricky Council IV RC 1.00 2.50
169 Jimmy Butler .75 2.00
170 Keyontae Johnson RC .75 2.00
171 Keegan Murray .60 1.50
172 CJ McCollum .40 1.00
173 Walker Kessler .40 1.00
174 Wendell Carter Jr. .40 1.00
175 Bilal Coulibaly RC 2.00 5.00
176 Precious Achiuwa .30 .75
177 Anthony Davis 1.00 2.50
178 Eric Gordon .30 .75
179 Jalen Pickett RC .60 1.50
180 Mikal Bridges .60 1.50
181 Payton Pritchard .40 1.00
182 Paolo Banchero 1.00 2.50
183 Myles Turner .40 1.00
184 Pascal Siakam .60 1.50
185 Ben Simmons .40 1.00
186 Jordan Clarkson .40 1.00
187 Caleb Martin .40 1.00
188 Buddy Hield .40 1.00
189 Jaylen Clark RC .75 2.00
190 Grayson Allen .40 1.00
191 Brandon Ingram .50 1.25
192 Stephen Curry 3.00 8.00
193 Luguentz Dort .40 1.00
194 Evan Fournier .30 .75
195 Zach LaVine .60 1.50
196 Harrison Barnes .30 .75
197 Herbert Jones .40 1.00
198 Kevin Huerter .40 1.00
199 De'Aaron Fox .75 2.00
200 Gary Trent Jr. .40 1.00
201 Tyrese Haliburton .75 2.00
202 Bruce Brown .40 1.00
203 Norman Powell .40 1.00
204 Bones Hyland .30 .75
205 Ayo Dosunmu .40 1.00
206 Seth Lundy RC .75 2.00
207 Trey Murphy III .50 1.25
208 Bojan Bogdanovic .40 1.00
209 Kevin Durant 1.25 3.00
210 Jose Alvarado .40 1.00
211 Russell Westbrook .60 1.50
212 Tobias Harris .40 1.00
213 Julian Strawther RC 1.00 2.50
214 Shaedon Sharpe .75 2.00
215 Jalen Wilson RC .75 2.00
216 Quentin Grimes .40 1.00
217 Marcus Smart .50 1.25
218 Bogdan Bogdanovic .40 1.00
219 Ben Sheppard RC .75 2.00
220 Malcolm Brogdon .40 1.00
221 Naz Reid .40 1.00
222 Taylor Hendricks RC .75 2.00
223 OG Anunoby .50 1.25
224 Dyson Daniels .50 1.25
225 Brice Sensabaugh RC 1.25 3.00
226 Deni Avdija .40 1.00
227 Jaden Hardy .50 1.25
228 Tyus Jones .30 .75
229 Miles Bridges .40 1.00
230 Al Horford .40 1.00
231 Jonathan Kuminga 1.00 2.50
232 Devin Vassell .50 1.25
233 Sam Merrill .40 1.00
234 Max Strus .40 1.00
235 Malaki Branham .30 .75
236 Amari Bailey RC .75 2.00
237 Jordan Miller RC 1.00 2.50
238 Dariq Whitehead RC 1.00 2.50
239 Malik Beasley .40 1.00
240 LaMelo Ball 1.00 2.50
241 Zach Collins .30 .75
242 Jalen Brunson .75 2.00
243 Noah Clowney RC 1.00 2.50
244 Onyeka Okongwu .40 1.00
245 Brandon Miller RC 3.00 8.00
246 Tari Eason .50 1.25
247 Kyle Anderson .30 .75
248 Leaky Black RC .60 1.50
249 Fred VanVleet .60 1.50
250 Josh Green .30 .75
251 Gradey Dick RC 1.50 4.00
252 Grant Williams .30 .75
253 Dereck Lively II RC 1.50 4.00
254 Bennedict Mathurin .40 1.00
255 Klay Thompson 1.00 2.50
256 Kyrie Irving .75 2.00
257 Scottie Barnes .60 1.50
258 Cade Cunningham 1.00 2.50
259 Nicolas Claxton .40 1.00
260 Zaire Williams .40 1.00
261 Jaden Springer .30 .75
262 Josh Hart .40 1.00
263 Gordon Hayward .40 1.00
264 Dillon Brooks .40 1.00
265 Jayson Tatum 1.50 4.00
266 Peyton Watson .40 1.00
267 Nikola Jovic .40 1.00
268 Cole Anthony .40 1.00
269 DeMar DeRozan .60 1.50
270 Zion Williamson 1.00 2.50
271 Joel Embiid 1.00 2.50
272 Cam Reddish .30 .75
273 Patrick Williams .30 .75
274 Jalen Duren .50 1.25
275 Karl-Anthony Towns .60 1.50
276 Isaac Okoro .30 .75
277 Jordan Poole .60 1.50
278 Coby White .40 1.00
279 Kris Murray RC .75 2.00
280 Scoot Henderson 2.50 6.00
281 Cason Wallace 1.50 4.00
282 Victor Wembanyama 6.00 15.00
283 Keyonte George 2.50 6.00
284 Jaden Ivey .50 1.25
285 Jabari Smith Jr. .60 1.50
286 Bennedict Mathurin .60 1.50
287 Bilal Coulibaly 2.00 5.00
288 Jordan Hawkins 1.25 3.00
289 Keegan Murray .50 1.25
290 Jalen Williams .75 2.00
291 Dereck Lively II 1.50 4.00
292 Vince Williams Jr. .40 1.00
293 Chet Holmgren 1.00 2.50
294 Jaime Jaquez Jr. 1.25 3.00
295 Paolo Banchero 1.00 2.50
296 Jeremy Sochan .50 1.25
297 Brandin Podziemski 2.50 6.00
298 Brandon Miller 3.00 8.00
299 Jalen Duren .50 1.25
300 Walker Kessler .40 1.00

2023-24 Hoops Premium Stock Blue Disco Prizm

*BLUE DISCO: 2.5X TO 6X BASIC
STATED PRINT RUN 99 SER.#'d SETS
108 Victor Wembanyama 150.00 400.00
282 Victor Wembanyama 100.00 250.00

2023-24 Hoops Premium Stock Blue Ice Prizm

*BLUE ICE: 2.5X TO 6X BASIC
STATED PRINT RUN 99 SER.#'d SETS
108 Victor Wembanyama 150.00 400.00
282 Victor Wembanyama 100.00 250.00

2023-24 Hoops Premium Stock Blue Prizm

*BLUE: 2X TO 5X BASIC
STATED PRINT RUN 120 SER.#'d SETS
108 Victor Wembanyama 125.00 300.00
282 Victor Wembanyama 75.00 200.00

2023-24 Hoops Premium Stock Blue Pulsar

*BLUE PULSAR: 3X TO 8X BASIC
STATED PRINT RUN 75 SER.#'d SETS
108 Victor Wembanyama 200.00 500.00
282 Victor Wembanyama 125.00 300.00

2023-24 Hoops Premium Stock Blue Seismic Prizm

*BLUE SEISMIC: 2.5X TO 6X BASIC
STATED PRINT RUN 99 SER.#'d SETS
108 Victor Wembanyama 150.00 400.00
282 Victor Wembanyama 100.00 250.00

2023-24 Hoops Premium Stock Disco Prizm

*DISCO: .75X TO 2X BASIC
108 Victor Wembanyama 30.00 80.00
282 Victor Wembanyama 20.00 50.00

2023-24 Hoops Premium Stock Green Prizm

*GREEN: 3X TO 8X BASIC
STATED PRINT RUN 75 SER.#'d SETS
108 Victor Wembanyama 200.00 500.00
282 Victor Wembanyama 125.00 300.00

2023-24 Hoops Premium Stock Ice Prizm

*ICE: .75X TO 2X BASIC
108 Victor Wembanyama 30.00 80.00
282 Victor Wembanyama 20.00 50.00

2023-24 Hoops Premium Stock Orange Ice Prizm

*ORANGE ICE: 2X TO 5X BASIC
STATED PRINT RUN 125 SER.#'d SETS
108 Victor Wembanyama 125.00 300.00
282 Victor Wembanyama 75.00 200.00

2023-24 Hoops Premium Stock Orange Prizm

*ORANGE: 1.25X TO 3X BASIC
STATED PRINT RUN 299 SER.#'d SETS
108 Victor Wembanyama 75.00 200.00
282 Victor Wembanyama 50.00 120.00

2023-24 Hoops Premium Stock Pink Ice Prizm

*PINK ICE: 5X TO 12X BASIC
STATED PRINT RUN 35 SER.#'d SETS
108 Victor Wembanyama 400.00 800.00
282 Victor Wembanyama 150.00 400.00

2023-24 Hoops Premium Stock Premium

*PREMIUM: .75X TO 2X BASIC
108 Victor Wembanyama 30.00 80.00
282 Victor Wembanyama 20.00 50.00

2023-24 Hoops Premium Stock Premium Blue Prizm

*PREMIUM BLUE: 6X TO 15X BASIC
STATED PRINT RUN 25 SER.#'d SETS
108 Victor Wembanyama 500.00 1,000.00
282 Victor Wembanyama 300.00 600.00

2023-24 Hoops Premium Stock Premium Red Prizm

*PREMIUM RED: 2.5X TO 6X BASIC
STATED PRINT RUN 88 SER.#'d SETS
108 Victor Wembanyama 150.00 400.00
282 Victor Wembanyama 100.00 250.00

2023-24 Hoops Premium Stock Pulsar

*PULSAR: .75X TO 2X BASIC
108 Victor Wembanyama 30.00 80.00
282 Victor Wembanyama 20.00 50.00

2023-24 Hoops Premium Stock Purple Ice Prizm

*PURPLE ICE: 1.5X TO 4X BASIC
STATED PRINT RUN 149 SER.#'d SETS
108 Victor Wembanyama 100.00 250.00
282 Victor Wembanyama 60.00 150.00

2023-24 Hoops Premium Stock Red Disco Prizm

*RED DISCO: 1.5X TO 4X BASIC
STATED PRINT RUN 149 SER.#'d SETS
108 Victor Wembanyama 100.00 250.00
282 Victor Wembanyama 60.00 150.00

2023-24 Hoops Premium Stock Red Ice Prizm

*RED ICE: 2.5X TO 6X BASIC
STATED PRINT RUN 99 SER.#'d SETS
108 Victor Wembanyama 150.00 400.00
282 Victor Wembanyama 100.00 250.00

2023-24 Hoops Premium Stock Red Prizm

*RED: 1.25X TO 3X BASIC
STATED PRINT RUN 275 SER.#'d SETS
108 Victor Wembanyama 75.00 200.00
282 Victor Wembanyama 50.00 120.00

2023-24 Hoops Premium Stock Red Pulsar

*RED PULSAR: 1X TO 2.5X BASIC
108 Victor Wembanyama 40.00 100.00
282 Victor Wembanyama 25.00 60.00

2023-24 Hoops Premium Stock Red Seismic Prizm

*RED SEISMIC: 1.5X TO 4X BASIC
STATED PRINT RUN 199 SER.#'d SETS
108 Victor Wembanyama 100.00 250.00
282 Victor Wembanyama 60.00 150.00

2023-24 Hoops Premium Stock Seismic Prizm

*SEISMIC: .75X TO 2X BASIC
108 Victor Wembanyama 30.00 80.00
282 Victor Wembanyama 20.00 50.00

2023-24 Hoops Premium Stock Silver Prizm

*SILVER: .75X TO 2X BASIC
108 Victor Wembanyama 30.00 80.00
282 Victor Wembanyama 20.00 50.00

2023-24 Hoops Premium Stock White Ice Prizm

*WHITE ICE: 6X TO 15X BASIC
STATED PRINT RUN 25 SER.#'d SETS
108 Victor Wembanyama 500.00 1,000.00
282 Victor Wembanyama 300.00 600.00

2023-24 Hoops Premium Stock White Seismic Prizm

*WHITE SEISMIC: 3X TO 8X BASIC
STATED PRINT RUN 75 SER.#'d SETS
108 Victor Wembanyama 200.00 500.00
282 Victor Wembanyama 125.00 300.00

2023-24 Hoops Premium Stock Anti Gravity

*DISCO: .75X TO 2X BASIC
*SILVER: .75X TO 2X BASIC
1 Zion Williamson 1.25 3.00
2 LeBron James 4.00 10.00
3 Stephen Curry 4.00 10.00
4 Luka Doncic 3.00 8.00
5 Victor Wembanyama 8.00 20.00
6 Jayson Tatum 2.00 5.00
7 Joel Embiid 1.25 3.00
8 Ausar Thompson 1.25 3.00
9 Scoot Henderson 1.50 4.00
10 Donovan Mitchell 1.00 2.50
11 Brandon Miller 2.00 5.00
12 Giannis Antetokounmpo 2.50 6.00
13 Brandin Podziemski 1.50 4.00
14 Anthony Edwards 2.50 6.00
15 Keyonte George 1.50 4.00
16 Amen Thompson 2.50 6.00
17 Nikola Jokic 2.50 6.00
18 Anthony Davis 1.25 3.00
19 Ja Morant 1.50 4.00
20 Jaime Jaquez Jr. .75 2.00

2023-24 Hoops Premium Stock Anti Gravity Blue Ice

*BLUE ICE: 2X TO 5X BASIC
STATED PRINT RUN 99 SER.#'d SETS
5 Victor Wembanyama 75.00 200.00

2023-24 Hoops Premium Stock Anti Gravity Blue Seismic Prizm

5 Victor Wembanyama 75.00 200.00

2023-24 Hoops Premium Stock Anti Gravity Premium

*PREMIUM: 1.25X TO 3X BASIC
5 Victor Wembanyama 40.00 100.00

2023-24 Hoops Premium Stock Anti Gravity Premium Blue Prizm

*PREMIUM BLUE: 5X TO 12X BASIC
STATED PRINT RUN 25 SER.#'d SETS
5 Victor Wembanyama 200.00 500.00

2023-24 Hoops Premium Stock Anti Gravity Premium Red Prizm

*PREMIUM RED: 2X TO 5X BASIC
STATED PRINT RUN 88 SER.#'d SETS
5 Victor Wembanyama 75.00 200.00

2023-24 Hoops Premium Stock Anti Gravity Red Disco Prizm

*RED DISCO: 2X TO 5X BASIC
STATED PRINT RUN 99 SER.#'d SETS
5 Victor Wembanyama 75.00 200.00

2023-24 Hoops Premium Stock Anti Gravity Red Ice

*RED ICE: 2X TO 5X BASIC
STATED PRINT RUN 99 SER.#'d SETS
5 Victor Wembanyama 75.00 200.00

2023-24 Hoops Premium Stock Anti Gravity Red Seismic Prizm

*RED SEISMIC: 1.5X TO 4X BASIC
STATED PRINT RUN 199 SER.#'d SETS
5 Victor Wembanyama 60.00 150.00

2023-24 Hoops Premium Stock Attack the Rack
*DISCO: .75X TO 2X BASIC
*SILVER: .75X TO 2X BASIC
1 Jaime Jaquez Jr. .75 2.00
2 Giannis Antetokounmpo 2.50 6.00
3 Victor Wembanyama 6.00 15.00
4 LeBron James 4.00 10.00
5 Ausar Thompson 1.25 3.00
6 Scoot Henderson 1.50 4.00
7 Anthony Edwards 2.50 6.00
8 Zion Williamson 1.25 3.00
9 Amen Thompson 2.50 6.00
10 Brandon Miller 2.00 5.00

2023-24 Hoops Premium Stock Attack the Rack Blue Ice
*BLUE ICE: 2X TO 5X BASIC
STATED PRINT RUN 99 SER.#'d SETS
3 Victor Wembanyama 75.00 200.00

2023-24 Hoops Premium Stock Attack the Rack Blue Seismic Prizm
*BLUE SEISMIC: 2X TO 5X BASIC
STATED PRINT RUN 99 SER.#'d SETS
3 Victor Wembanyama 75.00 200.00

2023-24 Hoops Premium Stock Attack the Rack Premium
*PREMIUM: 1.25X TO 3X BASIC
3 Victor Wembanyama 40.00 100.00

2023-24 Hoops Premium Stock Attack the Rack Premium Blue Prizm
*PREMIUM BLUE: 5X TO 12X BASIC
STATED PRINT RUN 25 SER.#'d SETS
3 Victor Wembanyama 200.00 500.00

2023-24 Hoops Premium Stock Attack the Rack Premium Red Prizm
*PREMIUM RED: 2X TO 5X BASIC
STATED PRINT RUN 88 SER.#'d SETS
3 Victor Wembanyama 75.00 200.00

2023-24 Hoops Premium Stock Attack the Rack Red Disco Prizm
*RED DISCO: 2X TO 5X BASIC
STATED PRINT RUN 99 SER.#'d SETS
3 Victor Wembanyama 75.00 200.00

2023-24 Hoops Premium Stock Attack the Rack Red Ice
*RED ICE: 2X TO 5X BASIC
STATED PRINT RUN 99 SER.#'d SETS
3 Victor Wembanyama 75.00 200.00

2023-24 Hoops Premium Stock Attack the Rack Red Seismic Prizm
*RED SEISMIC: 1.5X TO 4X BASIC
STATED PRINT RUN 199 SER.#'d SETS
3 Victor Wembanyama 60.00 150.00

2023-24 Hoops Premium Stock Box Topper
*SILVER: .75X TO 2X BASIC
1 Jordan Hawkins 1.50 4.00
2 Shai Gilgeous-Alexander 3.00 8.00
3 Scoot Henderson 3.00 8.00
4 Giannis Antetokounmpo 5.00 12.00
5 Kevin Durant 3.00 8.00
6 Ausar Thompson 2.50 6.00
7 Ja Morant 3.00 8.00
8 Damian Lillard 2.50 6.00
9 Jayson Tatum 4.00 10.00
10 Chet Holmgren 2.50 6.00
11 Brandon Miller 4.00 10.00
12 Bilal Coulibaly 2.50 6.00
13 Trae Young 2.00 5.00
14 Stephen Curry 8.00 20.00
15 Jaime Jaquez Jr. 1.50 4.00
16 LeBron James 8.00 20.00
17 Luka Doncic 6.00 15.00
18 Tyrese Haliburton 2.00 5.00
19 Victor Wembanyama 25.00 60.00
20 Keyonte George 3.00 8.00
21 Amen Thompson 5.00 12.00
22 Anthony Edwards 5.00 12.00
23 Brandin Podziemski 3.00 8.00
24 Nikola Jokic 5.00 12.00
25 Paolo Banchero 2.50 6.00

2023-24 Hoops Premium Stock City Edition
*DISCO: .75X TO 2X BASIC
*SILVER: .75X TO 2X BASIC
1 Jaylen Brown 1.00 2.50
2 Dereck Lively II 1.50 4.00
3 Jayson Tatum 2.00 5.00
4 Anthony Edwards 2.50 6.00
5 Scoot Henderson 1.50 4.00
6 Gradey Dick 1.00 2.50
7 Jordan Hawkins .75 2.00
8 Tyrese Haliburton 1.00 2.50
9 Chet Holmgren 1.25 3.00
10 Paolo Banchero 1.25 3.00
11 Ausar Thompson 1.25 3.00
12 Brandon Miller 2.00 5.00
13 Nikola Jokic 2.50 6.00
14 Amen Thompson 2.50 6.00
15 LeBron James 4.00 10.00
16 Keyonte George 1.50 4.00
17 Zach LaVine .75 2.00
18 Tyrese Maxey 1.00 2.50
19 Giannis Antetokounmpo 2.50 6.00
20 James Harden 1.00 2.50
21 Jalen Brunson 1.00 2.50
22 Jaime Jaquez Jr. .75 2.00
23 Luka Doncic 3.00 8.00
24 De'Aaron Fox 1.00 2.50
25 Victor Wembanyama 6.00 15.00
26 Shai Gilgeous-Alexander 1.50 4.00
27 Kawhi Leonard 1.25 3.00
28 Trae Young 1.00 2.50
29 Cade Cunningham 1.25 3.00
30 Stephen Curry 4.00 10.00

2023-24 Hoops Premium Stock City Edition Blue Ice
*BLUE ICE: 2X TO 5X BASIC
STATED PRINT RUN 99 SER.#'d SETS
25 Victor Wembanyama 75.00 200.00

2023-24 Hoops Premium Stock City Edition Blue Seismic Prizm
*BLUE SEISMIC: 2X TO 5X BASIC
STATED PRINT RUN 99 SER.#'d SETS
25 Victor Wembanyama 75.00 200.00

2023-24 Hoops Premium Stock City Edition Premium
*PREMIUM: 1.25X TO 3X BASIC
25 Victor Wembanyama 40.00 100.00

2023-24 Hoops Premium Stock City Edition Premium Blue Prizm
*PREMIUM BLUE: 5X TO 12X BASIC
STATED PRINT RUN 25 SER.#'d SETS
25 Victor Wembanyama 200.00 500.00

2023-24 Hoops Premium Stock City Edition Premium Red Prizm
*PREMIUM RED: 2X TO 5X BASIC
STATED PRINT RUN 88 SER.#'d SETS
25 Victor Wembanyama 75.00 200.00

2023-24 Hoops Premium Stock City Edition Red Disco Prizm
*RED DISCO: 2X TO 5X BASIC
STATED PRINT RUN 99 SER.#'d SETS
25 Victor Wembanyama 75.00 200.00

2023-24 Hoops Premium Stock City Edition Red Ice
*RED ICE: 2X TO 5X BASIC
STATED PRINT RUN 99 SER.#'d SETS
25 Victor Wembanyama 75.00 200.00

2023-24 Hoops Premium Stock City Edition Red Seismic Prizm
*RED SEISMIC: 1.5X TO 4X BASIC
STATED PRINT RUN 199 SER.#'d SETS
25 Victor Wembanyama 60.00 150.00

2023-24 Hoops Premium Stock High Voltage Premium
1 Scoot Henderson 20.00 50.00
2 Tyrese Haliburton 12.00 30.00
3 Amen Thompson 30.00 80.00
4 Damian Lillard 15.00 40.00
5 Stephen Curry 50.00 125.00
6 LeBron James 50.00 125.00
7 Giannis Antetokounmpo 30.00 80.00
8 Ausar Thompson 15.00 40.00
9 Paolo Banchero 15.00 40.00
10 Victor Wembanyama 200.00 500.00
11 Nikola Jokic 30.00 80.00
12 Brandon Miller 25.00 60.00
13 Jayson Tatum 25.00 60.00
14 Luka Doncic 40.00 100.00
15 Shai Gilgeous-Alexander 20.00 50.00
16 Jimmy Butler 12.00 30.00
17 Brandin Podziemski 20.00 50.00
18 Kyrie Irving 12.00 30.00
19 Paul George 10.00 25.00
20 Anthony Edwards 30.00 80.00

2023-24 Hoops Premium Stock HIPnotized Premium
1 Nikola Jokic 30.00 80.00
2 Shai Gilgeous-Alexander 20.00 50.00
3 Victor Wembanyama 200.00 500.00
4 Scoot Henderson 20.00 50.00
5 Devin Booker 15.00 40.00
6 Jayson Tatum 25.00 60.00
7 Brandon Miller 25.00 60.00
8 LeBron James 50.00 125.00
9 Luka Doncic 40.00 100.00
10 Tyrese Haliburton 12.00 30.00
11 Zion Williamson 15.00 40.00
12 Giannis Antetokounmpo 30.00 80.00
13 Anthony Edwards 30.00 80.00
14 Stephen Curry 50.00 125.00
15 Trae Young 12.00 30.00

2023-24 Hoops Premium Stock Hoopla
*DISCO: .75X TO 2X BASIC
*SILVER: .75X TO 2X BASIC
1 Kevin Durant 1.50 4.00
2 Damian Lillard 1.25 3.00
3 Brandon Miller 2.00 5.00
4 Shai Gilgeous-Alexander 1.50 4.00
5 Victor Wembanyama 6.00 15.00
6 Nikola Jokic 2.50 6.00
7 Luka Doncic 3.00 8.00
8 Stephen Curry 4.00 10.00
9 Giannis Antetokounmpo 2.50 6.00
10 LeBron James 4.00 10.00
11 Tyrese Haliburton 1.00 2.50
12 Jayson Tatum 2.00 5.00
13 Scoot Henderson 1.50 4.00
14 Chet Holmgren 1.25 3.00
15 Trae Young 1.00 2.50

2023-24 Hoops Premium Stock Hoopla Blue Ice
*BLUE ICE: 2X TO 5X BASIC
STATED PRINT RUN 99 SER.#'d SETS
5 Victor Wembanyama 75.00 200.00

2023-24 Hoops Premium Stock Hoopla Blue Seismic Prizm
*BLUE SEISMIC: 2X TO 5X BASIC
STATED PRINT RUN 99 SER.#'d SETS
5 Victor Wembanyama 75.00 200.00

2023-24 Hoops Premium Stock Hoopla Premium
*PREMIUM: 1.25X TO 3X BASIC
5 Victor Wembanyama 40.00 100.00

2023-24 Hoops Premium Stock Hoopla Premium Blue Prizm
*PREMIUM BLUE: 5X TO 12X BASIC
STATED PRINT RUN 25 SER.#'d SETS
5 Victor Wembanyama 200.00 500.00

2023-24 Hoops Premium Stock Hoopla Premium Red Prizm
*PREMIUM RED: 2X TO 5X BASIC
STATED PRINT RUN 88 SER.#'d SETS
5 Victor Wembanyama 75.00 200.00

2023-24 Hoops Premium Stock Hoopla Red Disco Prizm
*RED DISCO: 2X TO 5X BASIC
STATED PRINT RUN 99 SER.#'d SETS
5 Victor Wembanyama 75.00 200.00

2023-24 Hoops Premium Stock Hoopla Red Ice
*RED ICE: 2X TO 5X BASIC
STATED PRINT RUN 99 SER.#'d SETS
5 Victor Wembanyama 75.00 200.00

2023-24 Hoops Premium Stock Hoopla Red Seismic Prizm
*RED SEISMIC: 1.5X TO 4X BASIC
STATED PRINT RUN 199 SER.#'d SETS
5 Victor Wembanyama 60.00 150.00

2023-24 Hoops Premium Stock Hoops Ink
*DISCO: .5X TO 1.25X BASIC
*ICE: .5X TO 1.25X BASIC
*PREMIUM/75: .6X TO 1.5X BASIC
1 Jonathan Isaac 4.00 10.00
2 Johnny Davis 4.00 10.00
3 Blake Wesley 3.00 8.00
4 Rolando Blackman 4.00 10.00
5 Tari Eason 6.00 15.00
6 De'Anthony Melton 5.00 12.00
7 Corey Kispert 4.00 10.00
8 Tony Delk 4.00 10.00
9 Ricky Pierce 4.00 10.00
10 Harold Miner 5.00 12.00
11 Sam Hauser 5.00 12.00
12 Vit Krejci 6.00 15.00
13 Jaden Springer 4.00 10.00
14 Trendon Watford 5.00 12.00
15 Cazzie Russell 5.00 12.00
16 Jermaine O'Neal 5.00 12.00
17 Usman Garuba 4.00 10.00
18 Eddy Curry 3.00 8.00
19 Jalen Duren 5.00 12.00
20 Vince Williams Jr. 5.00 12.00
21 Nikola Jovic 5.00 12.00
22 Jaylin Williams 5.00 12.00
23 Marvin Bagley III 4.00 10.00
24 Grant Williams 4.00 10.00
25 Dante Exum 4.00 10.00
26 Evan Fournier 4.00 10.00
27 Kiki Vandeweghe 4.00 10.00
28 Jarred Vanderbilt 5.00 12.00
29 Josh Green 4.00 10.00
30 Talen Horton-Tucker 4.00 10.00
31 Patty Mills 5.00 12.00
32 Charles Oakley 5.00 12.00
33 Gabe Vincent 5.00 12.00
34 Quentin Grimes 5.00 12.00
35 T.J. McConnell 5.00 12.00
36 Sidy Cissoko 5.00 12.00
37 Jalen Slawson 5.00 12.00
38 Chris Livingston 5.00 12.00
39 Keyontae Johnson 5.00 12.00
40 Kerry Kittles 4.00 10.00

2023-24 Hoops Premium Stock Hot Signatures
*DISCO: .5X TO 1.25X BASIC
*ICE: .5X TO 1.25X BASIC
*PREMIUM/75: .6X TO 1.5X BASIC
1 Jaden Hardy 6.00 15.00
2 Julius Randle 6.00 15.00
3 Ben Simmons 5.00 12.00
4 Aaron Wiggins 4.00 10.00
5 Jakob Poeltl 4.00 10.00
6 Damian Jones 4.00 10.00
7 Jalen Green 12.00 30.00
8 Chet Holmgren 40.00 100.00
9 Ish Smith 4.00 10.00
10 Nick Richards 4.00 10.00
11 Tree Rollins 4.00 10.00
12 Drew Eubanks 3.00 8.00
13 Monte Morris 5.00 12.00
14 Jeremy Sochan 6.00 15.00
15 Johnny Juzang 3.00 8.00
16 Max Christie 5.00 12.00
17 Devonte' Graham 4.00 10.00
18 MarJon Beauchamp 4.00 10.00
19 Ousmane Dieng 5.00 12.00
20 Garrison Mathews 5.00 12.00
21 Deandre Ayton 5.00 12.00
22 Larry Nance Jr. 3.00 8.00
23 Isaiah Hartenstein 5.00 12.00
24 Dalano Banton 4.00 10.00
25 Justin Holiday 4.00 10.00
26 Carlos Boozer 4.00 10.00
27 Day'Ron Sharpe 4.00 10.00
28 JT Thor 4.00 10.00
29 Paolo Banchero 40.00 100.00
30 Norman Powell 5.00 12.00

2023-24 Hoops Premium Stock Presentations Premium
1 Jimmy Butler 20.00 50.00
2 Stephen Curry 80.00 200.00
3 LeBron James 80.00 200.00
4 Jayson Tatum 40.00 100.00
5 Ja Morant 30.00 80.00
6 Giannis Antetokounmpo 50.00 125.00
7 Luka Doncic 60.00 150.00
8 Trae Young 20.00 50.00
9 Kevin Durant 30.00 80.00
10 Damian Lillard 25.00 60.00
11 Keyonte George 30.00 80.00
12 Dariq Whitehead 12.00 30.00
13 Cason Wallace 20.00 50.00
14 Jalen Hood-Schifino 10.00 25.00
15 Kris Murray 12.00 30.00
16 Brandon Miller 40.00 100.00
17 Ausar Thompson 25.00 60.00
18 Amen Thompson 50.00 120.00
19 Scoot Henderson 30.00 80.00
20 Victor Wembanyama 300.00 600.00

2023-24 Hoops Premium Stock Retro Net Marvels Premium
1 Tyrese Haliburton 30.00 80.00
2 LeBron James 125.00 300.00
3 Joel Embiid 40.00 100.00
4 Kevin Durant 50.00 125.00
5 Jayson Tatum 60.00 150.00
6 Trae Young 30.00 80.00
7 Jaime Jaquez Jr. 25.00 60.00
8 Stephen Curry 125.00 300.00
9 Zion Williamson 40.00 100.00
10 Brandin Podziemski 50.00 125.00
11 Nikola Jokic 80.00 200.00
12 Dereck Lively II 50.00 125.00
13 Paolo Banchero 40.00 100.00
14 Scoot Henderson 50.00 125.00
15 Anthony Davis 40.00 100.00
16 Luka Doncic 100.00 250.00
17 Victor Wembanyama 500.00 1,000.00
18 Shai Gilgeous-Alexander 50.00 125.00
19 Ja Morant 50.00 125.00
20 Chet Holmgren 40.00 100.00
21 Ausar Thompson 40.00 100.00
22 Cason Wallace 30.00 80.00
23 LaMelo Ball 40.00 100.00
24 Amen Thompson 80.00 200.00
25 Donovan Mitchell 30.00 80.00
26 Keyonte George 50.00 125.00
27 Anthony Edwards 80.00 200.00
28 Giannis Antetokounmpo 80.00 200.00
29 Brandon Miller 60.00 150.00
30 Damian Lillard 40.00 100.00

2023-24 Hoops Premium Stock Rookie Ink
*DISCO: .5X TO 1.25X BASIC
*ICE: .5X TO 1.25X BASIC
*PREMIUM/75: .6X TO 1.5X BASIC
1 Amen Thompson 25.00 60.00
2 Dereck Lively II 12.00 30.00
3 Keyonte George 15.00 40.00
4 Vasilije Micic 6.00 15.00
5 Ausar Thompson 12.00 30.00
6 Cason Wallace 10.00 25.00
7 Marcus Sasser 8.00 20.00
8 Brandin Podziemski 15.00 40.00
9 Toumani Camara 8.00 20.00
10 Bilal Coulibaly 12.00 30.00
11 Kris Murray 6.00 15.00
12 GG Jackson II 12.00 30.00
13 Trayce Jackson-Davis 6.00 15.00
14 Sasha Vezenkov 5.00 12.00
15 Dariq Whitehead 6.00 15.00
16 Jalen Wilson 5.00 12.00
17 Julian Strawther 6.00 15.00
18 Noah Clowney 6.00 15.00
19 Ben Sheppard 5.00 12.00
20 Brice Sensabaugh 8.00 20.00
21 Andre Jackson Jr. 8.00 20.00
22 Jordan Walsh 5.00 12.00
23 Maxwell Lewis 4.00 10.00
24 Duop Reath 5.00 12.00
25 Hunter Tyson 5.00 12.00
26 Julian Phillips 5.00 12.00
27 Rayan Rupert 5.00 12.00
28 Kobe Bufkin 6.00 15.00
29 Olivier-Maxence Prosper 5.00 12.00
30 Kobe Brown 5.00 12.00

2023-24 Hoops Premium Stock Sheesh
*DISCO: .75X TO 2X BASIC
*SILVER: .75X TO 2X BASIC
1 Kevin Durant 1.50 4.00
2 Anthony Black 1.00 2.50
3 Cason Wallace 1.00 2.50
4 Amen Thompson 2.50 6.00
5 Stephen Curry 4.00 10.00
6 Damian Lillard 1.25 3.00
7 Devin Booker 1.25 3.00
8 Keyonte George 1.50 4.00
9 Tyrese Haliburton 1.00 2.50
10 Nikola Jokic 2.50 6.00
11 Giannis Antetokounmpo 2.50 6.00
12 Victor Wembanyama 8.00 20.00
13 Dereck Lively II 1.50 4.00
14 Bilal Coulibaly 1.25 3.00
15 Shai Gilgeous-Alexander 1.50 4.00
16 Luka Doncic 3.00 8.00
17 LeBron James 4.00 10.00
18 Kyrie Irving 1.00 2.50
19 Anthony Edwards 2.50 6.00
20 Jaime Jaquez Jr. .75 2.00
21 Brandin Podziemski 1.50 4.00
22 Jayson Tatum 2.00 5.00
23 Scoot Henderson 1.50 4.00
24 Ausar Thompson 1.25 3.00
25 Brandon Miller 2.00 5.00

2023-24 Hoops Premium Stock Sheesh Blue Ice
*BLUE ICE: 2X TO 5X BASIC
STATED PRINT RUN 99 SER.#'d SETS
12 Victor Wembanyama 75.00 200.00

2023-24 Hoops Premium Stock Sheesh Blue Seismic Prizm
*BLUE SEISMIC: 2X TO 5X BASIC
STATED PRINT RUN 99 SER.#'d SETS
12 Victor Wembanyama 75.00 200.00

2023-24 Hoops Premium Stock Sheesh Premium
*PREMIUM: 1.25X TO 3X BASIC
12 Victor Wembanyama 40.00 100.00

2023-24 Hoops Premium Stock Sheesh Premium Blue Prizm
*PREMIUM BLUE: 5X TO 12X BASIC
STATED PRINT RUN 25 SER.#'d SETS
12 Victor Wembanyama 200.00 500.00

2023-24 Hoops Premium Stock Sheesh Premium Red Prizm
*PREMIUM RED: 2X TO 5X BASIC
STATED PRINT RUN 88 SER.#'d SETS
12 Victor Wembanyama 75.00 200.00

2023-24 Hoops Premium Stock Sheesh Red Disco Prizm
*RED DISCO: 2X TO 5X BASIC
STATED PRINT RUN 99 SER.#'d SETS
12 Victor Wembanyama 75.00 200.00

2023-24 Hoops Premium Stock Sheesh Red Seismic Prizm
*RED SEISMIC: 1.5X TO 4X BASIC
STATED PRINT RUN 199 SER.#'d SETS
12 Victor Wembanyama 60.00 150.00

2023-24 Hoops Premium Stock Trophy Case Premium
1 Ja Morant 30.00 80.00
2 Giannis Antetokounmpo 50.00 125.00
3 Tim Duncan 25.00 60.00
4 Luka Doncic 60.00 150.00
5 LeBron James 80.00 200.00
6 Kevin Garnett 25.00 60.00
7 Stephen Curry 80.00 200.00
8 Paolo Banchero 25.00 60.00
9 Nikola Jokic 50.00 125.00
10 Dirk Nowitzki 25.00 60.00
11 Damian Lillard 25.00 60.00
12 Shaquille O'Neal 30.00 80.00
13 Kawhi Leonard 25.00 60.00
14 Joel Embiid 25.00 60.00
15 Kevin Durant 30.00 80.00

1994-95 Hoops Schick
COMPLETE SET (30) 12.00 30.00
1 Sergei Bazarevich .75 2.00
2 Bill Curley .50 1.25
3 Tony Dumas .60 1.50
4 Brian Grant 1.25 3.00
5 Darrin Hancock .60 1.50
6 Grant Hill 4.00 10.00
7 Eddie Jones 2.50 6.00
8 Jason Kidd 4.00 10.00
9 Aaron McKie .75 2.00
10 Donyell Marshall .75 2.00
11 Anthony Miller .75 2.00
12 Greg Minor .75 2.00
13 Eric Mobley .50 1.25
14 Eric Montross .60 1.50
15 Lamond Murray .75 2.00
16 Eric Piatkowski .75 2.00
17 Wesley Person .75 2.00
18 Khalid Reeves .60 1.50
19 Glenn Robinson 1.50 4.00
20 Carlos Rogers .60 1.50
21 Jalen Rose 2.00 5.00
22 Clifford Rozier .50 1.25
23 Dickey Simpkins .60 1.50
24 Brooks Thompson .60 1.50
25 Anthony Tucker .50 1.25
26 B.J. Tyler .50 1.25
27 Charlie Ward .75 2.00
28 Monty Williams 1.00 2.50
29 Sharone Wright .60 1.50
30 Donyell Marshall CL
Shaving) .75 2.00

1993-94 Hoops Sheets
COMPLETE SET (6) 12.00 30.00
1 B.J. Armstrong
Bill Cartwright
Horace Grant
Phil Jackson
Stacy King
John Paxson
Will Perdue
Scottie Pippen
Scott Williams 4.00 10.00
2 Greg Anderson
Don Chaney CO
Joe Dumars
Sean Elliott
Allan Houston
Lindsey Hunter
Terry Mills
Olden Polynice
Isiah Thomas
David Wood 2.50 6.00
3 Kenny Anderson
Derrick Coleman
Chris Morris
Chuck Daly CO
Rick Mahorn
Jayson Williams
Kevin Edwards
Armon Gilliam
Dwayne Schintzius
Chucky Brown
Benoit Benjamin
Rex Walters 2.50 6.00
4 Greg Anthony
Patrick Ewing
Charles Oakley
Charles Smith
John Starks 2.50 6.00
5 Danny Ainge
Charles Barkley
Cedric Ceballos
A.C. Green
Kevin Johnson
Dan Majerle
Oliver Miller
Mark West
Paul Westphal CO 3.00 8.00
6 Nick Anderson
Anthony Bowie
Shaquille O'Neal
Donald Royal
Scott Skiles
Jeff Turner 4.00 10.00

1994-95 Hoops Sheets
COMPLETE SET (18) 30.00 80.00
1 Stacey Augmon
Mookie Blaylock
Tyrone Corbin
Craig Ehlo
Jon Koncak
Andrew Lang
Ken Norman
Steve Smith
Lenny Wilkens CO 2.50 6.00
2 Michael Adams
Tony Bennett
Muggsy Bogues
Scott Burrell
Dell Curry
Kenny Gattison
Darrin Hancock
Hersey Hawkins
Larry Johnson
Alonzo Mourning
Robert Parish
David Wingate 2.50 6.00
3 Muggsy Bogues
Dell Curry
Hersey Hawkins
Larry Johnson
Alonzo Mourning 2.50 6.00
4 Michael Adams
Tony Bennett
Muggsy Bogues
Scott Burrell
Dell Curry
Kenny Gattison
Hersey Hawkins
Larry Johnson
Alonzo Mourning
Robert Parish
David Wingate 2.50 6.00
5 B.J. Armstrong
Corie Blount
Phil Jackson
Steve Kerr
Toni Kukoc
Luc Longley
Scottie Pippen
Bill Wennington 3.00 8.00
6 Terry Davis
Tony Dumas
Lucious Harris
Jim Jackson
Popeye Jones
Jason Kidd
Jamal Mashburn
Dick Motta CO 3.00 8.00
7 Mahmoud Abdul-Rauf
LaPhonso Ellis
Dan Issel CO
Dikembe Mutombo
Robert Pack
Rodney Rogers
Bryant Stith
Brian Williams
Reggie Williams 2.50 6.00
8 Don Chaney CO
Bill Curley
Joe Dumars
Grant Hill
Allan Houston
Lindsey Hunter
Mark Macon
Oliver Miller
Terry Mills
Mark West 5.00 12.00
9 Bill Blair CO
Mike Brown
Stacey King
Christian Laettner
Donyell Marshall
Isaiah Rider
Doug West
Michael Williams 2.50 6.00
10 Greg Anthony
Anthony Bonner
Hubert Davis
Patrick Ewing
Derek Harper
Anthony Mason
Charles Oakley
Charles Smith
John Starks
Herb Williams 3.00 8.00
11 Nick Anderson
Anthony Bowie
Horace Grant
Anfernee Hardaway
Shaquille O'Neal
Tree Rollins
Donald Royal
Dennis Scott
Brian Shaw
Brooks Thompson
Jeff Turner 5.00 12.00
12 Danny Ainge
Charles Barkley
A.C. Green
Kevin Johnson
Joe Kleine
Dan Majerle
Danny Manning
Elliot Perry
Wesley Person
Wayman Tisdale 4.00 10.00
13 P.J. Carlesimo CO
Clyde Drexler
Chris Dudley
Harvey Grant
Jerome Kersey
Tracy Murray
Terry Porter
Clifford Robinson
James Robinson 4.00 10.00
14 Vincent Askew
Bill Cartwright
Ervin Johnson
George Karl CO
Shawn Kemp
Sarunas Marciulionis
Nate McMillan
Gary Payton
Sam Perkins
Detlef Schrempf
Dontonio Wingfield 3.00 8.00
15 David Benoit
Tom Chambers
John Crotty
Jeff Hornacek
Karl Malone
Byron Russell
Jerry Sloan CO
Felton Spencer
John Stockton 2.50 6.00
16 Mitchell Butler
Rex Chapman
Calbert Cheaney
Don MacLean
Gheorghe Muresan
Scott Skiles
Chris Webber
Team Card 2.50 6.00
17 Mitchell Butler
Rex Chapman
Calbert Cheaney
Kevin Duckworth
Juwan Howard
Don MacLean
Jim McIlvaine
Gheorghe Muresan
Scott Skiles
Kenny Walker
Chris Webber 4.00 10.00
18 Mitchell Butler
Rex Chapman
Calbert Cheaney
Kevin Duckworth
Juwan Howard
Don MacLean
Jim McIlvaine
Gheorghe Muresan
Scott Skiles
Kenny Walker
Chris Webber 4.00 10.00

1995-96 Hoops Sheets
COMPLETE SET (13) 15.00 40.00
1 Lenny Wilkens CO
Stacey Augmon
Mookie Blaylock
Craig Ehlo
Alan Henderson
Andrew Lang
Grant Long
Ken Norman
Steve Smith
Spud Webb 2.00 5.00
2 Muggsy Bogues
Kendall Gill
Glen Rice
Scott Burrell
Larry Johnson
Dell Curry
George Zidek
Khalid Reeves 2.00 5.00
3 Phil Jackson CO
Jason Caffey
Michael Jordan
Toni Kukoc
Luc Longley
Scottie Pippen
Dennis Rodman
Dickey Simpkins 4.00 10.00
4 Grant Hill
Joe Dumars
Terry Mills
Allan Houston
Lindsey Hunter
Theo Ratliff
Otis Thorpe
Doug Collins CO 2.50 6.00
5 Sedale Threatt
Frankie King
Nick Van Exel
Vlade Divac
Cedric Ceballos
Eddie Jones
George Lynch
Elden Campbell
Corie Blount
Del Harris CO 2.50 6.00
6 Shawn Bradley
Kevin Edwards
Rick Mahorn
Kendall Gill
P.J. Brown
Butch Beard CO
Armon Gilliam
Ed O'Bannon
Chris Childs
Yinka Dare
Jayson Williams 2.00 5.00
7 Patrick Ewing
Charles Oakley
John Starks
Anthony Mason
Don Nelson CO
Derek Harper
Charles Smith
Herb Williams
Hubert Davis 2.00 5.00
8 Nick Anderson
Anthony Bowie
Horace Grant
Anfernee Hardaway
Jon Koncak
Shaquille O'Neal
Donald Royal
Dennis Scott
Brian Shaw
Jeff Turner
David Vaughn 2.50 6.00
9 Elliot Perry
A.C. Green
Wayman Tisdale
Mario Bennett
Charles Barkley
Danny Manning
Wesley Person
Michael Finley
Kevin Johnson 2.00 5.00
10 Clifford Robinson
Rod Strickland
Chris Dudley
Arvydas Sabonis
Buck Williams
James Robinson
P.J. Carlesimo CO
Randolph Childress
Gary Trent
Dontonio Wingfield 2.00 5.00
11 Mitch Richmond
Olden Polynice
Brian Grant
Michael Smith
Tyus Edney
Bobby Hurley

Corliss Williamson
Garry St. Jean CO 2.00 5.00
12 David Benoit
Jeff Hornacek
Karl Malone
Felton Spencer
John Stockton
Adam Keefe
Jerry Sloan CO 3.00 8.00
13 Mitchell Butler
Calbert Cheaney
Juwan Howard
Tim Legler
Jim McIlvaine
Gheorghe Muresan
Robert Pack
Brent Price
Mark Price
Rasheed Wallace
Chris Webber 2.50 6.00

1996-97 Hoops Sheets

COMPLETE SET (2) 12.00 30.00
1A Byron Scott
Nick Van Exel
Shaquille O'Neal
Del Harris
Derek Fisher
Kobe Bryant
Robert Horry
Sean Rooks
Eddie Jones
Jerome Kersey
Elden Campbell 12.00 30.00
1B Byron Scott LA .40 1.00
1C Nick Van Exel LA .40 1.00
1D Shaquille O'Neal LA .75 2.00
1E Del Harris LA .40 1.00
1F Derek Fisher LA .75 2.00
1G Robert Horry LA .40 1.00
1H Kobe Bryant LA 25.00 60.00
1I Sean Rooks LA .40 1.00
1J Eddie Jones LA .40 1.00
1K Jerome Kersey LA .40 1.00
1L Elden Campbell LA .40 1.00
2A Wesley Person
John Williams
Danny Manning
Kevin Johnson 1.50 4.00
2B Wesley Person SUNS .40 1.00
2C John Williams SUNS .40 1.00
2D Danny Manning SUNS .40 1.00
2E Kevin Johnson SUNS .40 1.00

2002-03 Hoops Stars

COMP.SET w/o RC's (170) 12.50 30.00
1 Tracy McGrady .50 1.25
2 Kevin Garnett .75 2.00
3 Allen Iverson .75 2.00
4 Keith Van Horn .25 .60
5 Kwame Brown .20 .50
6 Alan Henderson .20 .50
7 Kenny Anderson .25 .60
8 Antoine Walker .25 .60
9 Tony Delk .20 .50
10 Tony Battie .20 .50
11 Wally Szczerbiak .25 .60
12 Paul Pierce .50 1.25
13 Glenn Robinson .30 .75
14 Tim Thomas .20 .50
15 Vince Carter .60 1.50
16 Pau Gasol .50 1.25
17 Eddy Curry .20 .50
18 Darrell Armstrong .20 .50
19 Sam Cassell .25 .60
20 Darius Miles .25 .60
21 Jason Richardson .30 .75
22 Elton Brand .30 .75
23 Michael Jordan 3.00 8.00
24 Andre Miller .25 .60
25 Anfernee Hardaway .75 2.00
26 Steve Nash .60 1.50
27 Ron Artest .25 .60
28 Raef LaFrentz .20 .50
29 Troy Hudson .20 .50
30 Rasheed Wallace .40 1.00
31 Ricky Davis .25 .60
32 Juwan Howard .25 .60
33 Steve Francis .30 .75
34 Shaquille O'Neal 1.25 3.00
35 James Posey .20 .50
36 DeShawn Stevenson .20 .50
37 Clifford Robinson .30 .75
38 Jerry Stackhouse .30 .75
39 Chauncey Billups .30 .75
40 Mike Bibby .30 .75
41 Dirk Nowitzki .75 2.00
42 Corliss Williamson .20 .50
43 Antawn Jamison .25 .60
44 Jamal Mashburn .25 .60
45 Danny Fortson .20 .50
46 Reggie Miller .60 1.50
47 Scottie Pippen .75 2.00
48 Donnell Harvey .20 .50
49 Moochie Norris .20 .50
50 Corey Maggette .25 .60
51 Eddie Griffin .20 .50
52 Karl Malone .60 1.50
53 Maurice Taylor .20 .50
54 Al Harrington .25 .60
55 Kenyon Martin .30 .75
56 Nick Van Exel .30 .75
57 Jermaine O'Neal .25 .60
58 Anthony Mason .25 .60
59 Jamaal Tinsley .20 .50
60 Chris Mihm .20 .50
61 Lamar Odom .30 .75
62 Cuttino Mobley .25 .60
63 Michael Olowokandi .20 .50
64 Michael Finley .30 .75
65 Anthony Peeler .20 .50
66 Mengke Bateer .30 .75
67 Rick Fox .25 .60
68 Steve Smith .25 .60
69 Robert Horry .30 .75
70 Devean George .20 .50
71 Jason Williams .40 1.00
72 Stromile Swift .20 .50
73 Marcus Fizer .20 .50
74 Michael Dickerson .20 .50
75 Shane Battier .30 .75
76 Larry Hughes .25 .60
77 Brian Skinner .20 .50
78 Eddie Jones .30 .75
79 Malik Allen .20 .50
80 Ray Allen .50 1.25
81 Jumaine Jones .20 .50
82 Donyell Marshall .20 .50
83 Toni Kukoc .30 .75
84 Michael Redd .25 .60
85 Ron Mercer .20 .50
86 Terrell Brandon .20 .50
87 Latrell Sprewell .30 .75
88 Kobe Bryant 2.50 6.00
89 Kurt Thomas .20 .50
90 Rasho Nesterovic .20 .50
91 Shareef Abdur-Rahim .30 .75
92 Eduardo Najera .20 .50
93 Jamaal Magloire .20 .50
94 Antonio Davis .25 .60
95 Rodney Rogers .20 .50
96 Jason Collins .20 .50
97 Marcus Camby .25 .60
98 Joe Smith .25 .60
99 Richard Jefferson .25 .60
100 Gilbert Arenas .30 .75
101 Courtney Alexander .20 .50
102 David Wesley .20 .50
103 Baron Davis .30 .75
104 Eiden Campbell .20 .50
105 Jason Kidd .50 1.25
106 P.J. Brown .20 .50
107 Rashard Lewis .25 .60
108 Alvin Williams .20 .50
109 Kerry Kittles .20 .50
110 Charlie Ward .20 .50
111 Kedrick Brown .20 .50
112 Shandon Anderson .20 .50
113 Grant Hill .50 1.25
114 Tyson Chandler .30 .75
115 Brent Barry .20 .50
116 Travis Best .20 .50
117 Mike Miller .25 .60
118 Aaron McKie .20 .50
119 Theo Ratliff .20 .50
120 Todd MacCulloch .20 .50
121 Trenton Hassell .20 .50
122 Vin Baker .25 .60
123 Dion Glover .20 .50
124 Stephon Marbury .40 1.00
125 Ben Wallace .40 1.00
126 Glen Rice .25 .60
127 Joe Johnson .25 .60
128 Chris Webber .40 1.00
129 Damon Stoudamire .30 .75
130 Voshon Lenard .20 .50
131 Troy Murphy .25 .60
132 Desmond Mason .25 .60
133 Ruben Patterson .20 .50
134 John Stockton .60 1.50
135 Bobby Jackson .20 .50
136 Shawn Marion .30 .75
137 Jarron Collins .20 .50
138 Tom Gugliotta .20 .50
139 Doug Christie .20 .50
140 Zeljko Rebraca .20 .50
141 Tim Duncan .75 2.00
142 David Robinson .60 1.50
143 Tony Parker .50 1.25
144 Derek Fisher .30 .75
145 Speedy Claxton .20 .50
146 Eric Snow .20 .50
147 Gary Payton .50 1.25
148 Pat Garrity .20 .50
149 Joseph Forte .20 .50
150 Derek Anderson .20 .50
151 Vladimir Radmanovic .20 .50
152 Samuel Dalembert .20 .50
153 Allan Houston .30 .75
154 Jalen Rose .25 .60
155 Dikembe Mutombo .50 1.25
156 Jerome Williams .20 .50
157 Antonio McDyess .25 .60
158 Morris Peterson .25 .60
159 Bonzi Wells .20 .50
160 Hedo Turkoglu .20 .50
161 Gerald Wallace .20 .50
162 Andrei Kirilenko .25 .60
163 Matt Harpring .25 .60
164 Peja Stojakovic .25 .60
165 Zydrunas Ilgauskas .25 .60
166 Richard Hamilton .40 1.00
167 Brian Grant .20 .50
168 Christian Laettner .25 .60
169 Jason Terry .25 .60
170 Alonzo Mourning .50 1.25
171 Yao Ming RC 5.00 12.00
172 Jay Williams RC .75 2.00
173 Mike Dunleavy RC 1.00 2.50
174 Chris Wilcox RC .75 2.00
175 Amare Stoudemire RC 2.50 6.00
176 Fred Jones RC .75 2.00
177 Caron Butler RC 1.00 2.50
178 Melvin Ely RC .75 2.00
179 Drew Gooden RC 1.00 2.50
180 DaJuan Wagner RC .75 2.00
181 Jared Jeffries RC .75 2.00
182 Nikoloz Tskitishvili RC .60 1.50
183 Nene Hilario RC 1.00 2.50
184 Dan Dickau RC .60 1.50
185 Marcus Haislip RC .60 1.50
186 Gordan Giricek RC 1.00 2.50
187 Jiri Welsch RC .75 2.00
188 Juan Dixon RC .75 2.00
189 Curtis Borchardt RC .60 1.50
190 Ryan Humphrey RC .75 2.00
191 Kareem Rush RC .75 2.00
192 Qyntel Woods RC .60 1.50
193 Casey Jacobsen RC .75 2.00
194 Tayshaun Prince RC 2.00 5.00
195 Frank Williams RC .60 1.50
196 Pat Burke RC .60 1.50
197 Chris Jefferies RC .60 1.50
198 Carlos Boozer RC 1.00 2.50
199 Manu Ginobili RC 5.00 12.00
200 Vincent Yarbrough RC .60 1.50

2002-03 Hoops Stars Five-Star

*STARS: 2.5X TO 6X BASE CARD HI
*RCs: .6X TO 1.5X BASE CARD HI
PRINT RUN 299 SERIAL #'d SETS

2002-03 Hoops Stars Platinum

*STARS: 4X TO 10X BASE CARD HI
*RC's: 1.25X TO 3X BASE CARD HI
INSERTED INTO SUPERSTARS PACKS
PRINT RUN 100 SERIAL #'d SETS
SKIP-NUMBERED SET
23 Michael Jordan 30.00 80.00
34 Shaquille O'Neal 12.00 30.00
88 Kobe Bryant 25.00 60.00
141 Tim Duncan 8.00 20.00
172 Jay Williams 2.50 6.00
173 Mike Dunleavy 3.00 8.00

2002-03 Hoops Stars Red

*STARS: 1.25X TO 3X BASE CARD HI
*RCs: .4X TO 1X BASE CARD HI
INSERTED INTO SUPERSTAR PACKS
SKIP-NUMBERED SET
1 Tracy McGrady 1.50 4.00
2 Kevin Garnett 2.50 6.00
3 Allen Iverson 2.50 6.00
12 Paul Pierce 1.50 4.00
15 Vince Carter 2.00 5.00
16 Pau Gasol 1.50 4.00
20 Darius Miles .60 1.50
21 Jason Richardson 1.00 2.50
23 Michael Jordan 25.00 50.00
33 Steve Francis 1.00 2.50
34 Shaquille O'Neal 4.00 10.00
40 Mike Bibby 1.00 2.50
41 Dirk Nowitzki 2.50 6.00
52 Karl Malone 2.00 5.00
88 Kobe Bryant 8.00 20.00
103 Baron Davis 1.00 2.50
105 Jason Kidd 1.50 4.00
141 Tim Duncan 2.50 6.00
171 Yao Ming 5.00 12.00
172 Jay Williams .75 2.00
173 Mike Dunleavy 1.00 2.50
177 Caron Butler 1.00 2.50
179 Drew Gooden 1.00 2.50
180 DaJuan Wagner .75 2.00

2002-03 Hoops Stars Future Stars

COMPLETE SET (15) 10.00 25.00
STATED ODDS 1:10
*BLUE: .6X TO 1.5X FUTURE STAR HI
FS1 Yao Ming 4.00 10.00
FS2 Jay Williams .60 1.50
FS3 Mike Dunleavy .75 2.00
FS4 Chris Wilcox .60 1.50
FS5 Amare Stoudemire 2.00 5.00
FS6 Fred Jones .60 1.50
FS7 Caron Butler .75 2.00
FS8 Melvin Ely .60 1.50
FS9 Drew Gooden .75 2.00
FS10 DaJuan Wagner .60 1.50
FS11 Jared Jeffries .60 1.50
FS12 Nikoloz Tskitishvili .50 1.25
FS13 Nene Hilario .75 2.00
FS14 Dan Dickau .50 1.25
FS15 Juan Dixon .60 1.50

2002-03 Hoops Stars Future Stars Game-Used

STATED ODDS 1:52
FSGU1 Chris Wilcox 2.00 5.00
FSGU2 Amare Stoudemire 6.00 15.00
FSGU3 Fred Jones 2.00 5.00
FSGU4 Caron Butler 2.50 6.00
FSGU5 Melvin Ely 2.00 5.00
FSGU6 Drew Gooden 2.50 6.00
FSGU7 DaJuan Wagner 2.00 5.00
FSGU8 Jared Jeffries 2.00 5.00
FSGU9 Nene Hilario 2.50 6.00
FSGU11 Juan Dixon 2.00 5.00

2002-03 Hoops Stars Raising Up

COMPLETE SET (25) 15.00 40.00
STATED ODDS 1:5
*BLUE: .6X TO 1.5X RAISING UP HI
RU1 Jason Kidd 1.00 2.50
RU2 Kevin Garnett 1.50 4.00
RU3 Vince Carter 1.25 3.00
RU4 Baron Davis .60 1.50
RU5 Paul Pierce 1.00 2.50
RU6 Dirk Nowitzki 1.50 4.00
RU7 Shaquille O'Neal 2.50 6.00
RU8 Michael Jordan 6.00 15.00
RU9 Tim Duncan 1.50 4.00
RU10 Allen Iverson 1.50 4.00
RU11 Jason Richardson .60 1.50
RU12 Pau Gasol 1.00 2.50
RU13 Steve Francis .60 1.50
RU14 Kobe Bryant 5.00 12.00
RU15 Mike Bibby .60 1.50
RU16 Grant Hill .60 1.50
RU17 Tracy McGrady 1.00 2.50
RU18 Karl Malone 1.25 3.00
RU19 Darius Miles .40 1.00
RU20 Jay Williams .50 1.25
RU21 Mike Dunleavy .60 1.50
RU22 Drew Gooden .60 1.50
RU23 DaJuan Wagner .50 1.25
RU24 Caron Butler .60 1.50
RU25 Yao Ming 3.00 8.00

2002-03 Hoops Stars Raising Up Game-Used

STATED PRINT RUN 250 SERIAL #'d SETS
RUGU1 Jason Kidd Pants 5.00 12.00
RUGU2 Kevin Garnett Jacket 8.00 20.00
RUGU3 Vince Carter JSY 6.00 15.00
RUGU4 Paul Pierce Pants 5.00 12.00
RUGU5 Allen Iverson JSY 6.00 15.00
RUGU6 Pau Gasol Jacket 5.00 12.00
RUGU7 Steve Francis Shorts 3.00 8.00
RUGU8 Grant Hill JSY 5.00 12.00
RUGU9 Tracy McGrady JSY 5.00 12.00
RUGU10 Karl Malone Pants 6.00 15.00
RUGU11 Darius Miles JSY 2.00 5.00
RUGU12 Drew Gooden Shorts 3.00 8.00
RUGU13 DaJuan Wagner Shorts 2.50 6.00
RUGU14 Caron Butler Shorts 3.00 8.00
RUGU15 Yao Ming JSY 15.00 40.00

2002-03 Hoops Stars Rare Air

COMPLETE SET (20) 20.00 50.00
STATED ODDS 1:30
*BLUE: .6X TO 1.5X RARE AIR HI
RA1 Jason Kidd 2.00 5.00
RA2 Kevin Garnett 3.00 8.00
RA3 Vince Carter 2.50 6.00
RA4 Baron Davis 1.25 3.00
RA5 Paul Pierce 2.00 5.00
RA6 Dirk Nowitzki 3.00 8.00
RA7 Shaquille O'Neal 5.00 12.00
RA8 Michael Jordan 12.00 30.00
RA9 Tim Duncan 3.00 8.00
RA10 Allen Iverson 3.00 8.00
RA11 Jason Richardson 1.25 3.00
RA12 Pau Gasol 2.00 5.00
RA13 Steve Francis 1.25 3.00
RA14 Kobe Bryant 10.00 25.00
RA15 Mike Bibby 1.25 3.00
RA16 Grant Hill 2.00 5.00
RA17 Tracy McGrady 2.00 5.00
RA18 Karl Malone 2.50 6.00
RA19 Darius Miles .75 2.00
RA20 Latrell Sprewell 1.25 3.00

2002-03 Hoops Stars Rare Air Game-Used

STATED ODDS 1:52
RAGU1 Jason Kidd Jacket 5.00 12.00
RAGU2 Kevin Garnett JSY 8.00 20.00
RAGU3 Vince Carter JSY 6.00 15.00
RAGU4 Paul Pierce Jacket 5.00 12.00
RAGU5 Dirk Nowitzki JSY 8.00 20.00
RAGU6 Allen Iverson Pants 8.00 20.00
RAGU7 Pau Gasol Pants 5.00 12.00
RAGU8 Grant Hill Pants 5.00 12.00
RAGU9 Tracy McGrady Pants 5.00 12.00
RAGU10 Karl Malone JSY 6.00 15.00

2002-03 Hoops Stars Star Gazing

COMPLETE SET (25) 20.00 50.00
STATED ODDS 1:20
*BLUE: .6X TO 1.5X STAR GAZE HI
SG1 Jason Kidd 1.50 4.00
SG2 Kevin Garnett 2.50 6.00
SG3 Vince Carter 2.00 5.00
SG4 Baron Davis 1.00 2.50
SG5 Paul Pierce 1.50 4.00
SG6 Dirk Nowitzki 2.50 6.00
SG7 Shaquille O'Neal 4.00 10.00
SG8 Michael Jordan 10.00 25.00
SG9 Tim Duncan 2.50 6.00
SG10 Allen Iverson 2.50 6.00
SG11 Jason Richardson 1.00 2.50
SG12 Pau Gasol 1.50 4.00
SG13 Steve Francis 1.00 2.50
SG14 Kobe Bryant 8.00 20.00
SG15 Mike Bibby 1.00 2.50
SG16 Grant Hill 1.50 4.00
SG17 Tracy McGrady 1.50 4.00
SG18 Karl Malone 2.00 5.00
SG19 Darius Miles .60 1.50
SG20 Jay Williams .75 2.00
SG21 Mike Dunleavy 1.00 2.50
SG22 Drew Gooden 1.00 2.50
SG23 DaJuan Wagner .75 2.00
SG24 Caron Butler 1.00 2.50
SG25 Yao Ming 5.00 12.00

2002-03 Hoops Stars Star Gazing Game-Used

PRINT RUN 50 SERIAL #'d SETS
AI Allen Iverson JSY 15.00 40.00
CB Caron Butler JSY 6.00 15.00
DG Drew Gooden Shorts 6.00 15.00
DN Dirk Nowitzki JSY 15.00 40.00
DW DaJuan Wagner Shorts 5.00 12.00
JK Jason Kidd Shorts 10.00 25.00
KG Kevin Garnett JSY 15.00 40.00
MB Mike Bibby JSY 6.00 15.00
PG Pau Gasol Jacket 10.00 25.00
PP Paul Pierce JSY 10.00 25.00
TM Tracy McGrady JSY 10.00 25.00
VC Vince Carter JSY 12.00 30.00

2002-03 Hoops Stars Superstars Game-Used

INSERTED INTO SUPERSTAR PACKS
AI Allen Iverson JSY 8.00 20.00
BD Baron Davis Pants 3.00 8.00
CB Caron Butler Shirt 3.00 8.00
DG Drew Gooden Shirt 3.00 8.00
DM Darius Miles Jacket 2.00 5.00
DN Dirk Nowitzki JSY 8.00 20.00
DW DaJuan Wagner Shirt 2.50 6.00
GH Grant Hill Jacket 5.00 12.00
JK Jason Kidd Jacket 5.00 12.00
JR Jason Richardson Pants 3.00 8.00
KG Kevin Garnett JSY 8.00 20.00
KM Karl Malone Pants 6.00 15.00
MB Mike Bibby Jacket 3.00 8.00
PG Pau Gasol Jacket 5.00 12.00
PP Paul Pierce Jacket 5.00 12.00
SF Steve Francis JSY 3.00 8.00
TM Tracy McGrady Pants 5.00 12.00
VC Vince Carter JSY 6.00 15.00
YM Yao Ming JSY 15.00 40.00

2012-13 Hoops Taco Bell

1 Avery Bradley .75 2.00
2 Kevin Garnett 3.00 8.00
3 Paul Pierce 2.00 5.00
4 Rajon Rondo 1.50 4.00
5 Jared Sullinger .75 2.00
6 Deron Williams 1.00 2.50
7 Brook Lopez 1.00 2.50
8 Kris Humphries .75 2.00
9 Joe Johnson 1.00 2.50
10 Gerald Wallace 1.00 2.50
11 Amare Stoudemire 1.25 3.00
12 Carmelo Anthony 2.00 5.00
13 Iman Shumpert 1.00 2.50
14 Tyson Chandler 1.00 2.50
15 Jason Kidd 2.00 5.00
16 Andrew Bynum .75 2.00
17 Jrue Holiday 1.50 4.00
18 Thaddeus Young .75 2.00
19 Evan Turner .75 2.00
20 Spencer Hawes .75 2.00
21 Andrea Bargnani .75 2.00
22 DeMar DeRozan 1.50 4.00
23 Landry Fields .75 2.00
24 Jose Calderon .75 2.00
25 Linas Kleiza .75 2.00
26 Dirk Nowitzki 3.00 8.00
27 Rodrigue Beaubois .75 2.00
28 Shawn Marion 1.25 3.00
29 Vince Carter 2.50 6.00
30 Delonte West .75 2.00
31 Jeremy Lamb 1.25 3.00
32 Kevin Martin 1.00 2.50
33 Terrence Jones .75 2.00
34 Jeremy Lin 2.00 5.00
35 Earl Boykins .75 2.00
36 Marc Gasol 1.25 3.00
37 Mike Conley 1.00 2.50
38 Rudy Gay 1.25 3.00
39 Zach Randolph 1.25 3.00
40 Lester Hudson .75 2.00
41 Anthony Davis 25.00 60.00
42 Lance Thomas .75 2.00
43 Austin Rivers 1.25 3.00
44 Eric Gordon 1.00 2.50
45 Greivis Vasquez .75 2.00
46 DeJuan Blair .75 2.00
47 Boris Diaw 1.00 2.50
48 Manu Ginobili 2.50 6.00
49 Tim Duncan 3.00 8.00
50 Tony Parker 2.00 5.00
51 Carlos Boozer 1.00 2.50
52 Derrick Rose 2.00 5.00
53 Joakim Noah 1.00 2.50
54 Luol Deng 1.00 2.50
55 Richard Hamilton 1.25 3.00
56 Kyrie Irving 12.00 30.00
57 Anderson Varejao .75 2.00
58 Dion Waiters 1.00 2.50
59 Daniel Gibson .75 2.00
60 Omri Casspi .75 2.00
61 Andre Drummond 2.00 5.00
62 Greg Monroe .75 2.00
63 Rodney Stuckey .75 2.00
64 Tayshaun Prince 1.25 3.00
65 Brandon Knight 1.00 2.50
66 Danny Granger .75 2.00
67 David West 1.00 2.50
68 Paul George 2.00 5.00
69 Roy Hibbert 1.00 2.50
70 George Hill 1.00 2.50
71 Brandon Jennings .75 2.00
72 Drew Gooden 1.00 2.50
73 Monta Ellis 1.00 2.50
74 Ersan Ilyasova .75 2.00
75 Mike Dunleavy .75 2.00
76 Danilo Gallinari .75 2.00
77 Ty Lawson .75 2.00
78 Andre Iguodala 1.25 3.00
79 JaVale McGee 1.00 2.50
80 Andre Miller 1.00 2.50
81 Kevin Love 1.25 3.00
82 Luke Ridnour 1.00 2.50
83 Ricky Rubio 1.00 2.50
84 Wesley Johnson .75 2.00
85 J.J. Barea 1.00 2.50
86 LaMarcus Aldridge 1.25 3.00
87 Nicolas Batum 1.00 2.50
88 Wesley Matthews .75 2.00
89 Jonny Flynn .75 2.00
90 J.J. Hickson .75 2.00
91 James Harden 2.50 6.00
92 Kendrick Perkins .75 2.00
93 Kevin Durant 5.00 12.00
94 Russell Westbrook 2.00 5.00
95 Serge Ibaka 1.00 2.50
96 Al Jefferson .75 2.00
97 DeMarre Carroll .75 2.00
98 Gordon Hayward 1.25 3.00
99 Paul Millsap 1.00 2.50
100 Derrick Favors 1.00 2.50
101 Al Horford 1.25 3.00
102 Jeff Teague .75 2.00
103 John Jenkins .75 2.00
104 Josh Smith .75 2.00
105 Erick Dampier .75 2.00
106 LeBron James 20.00 50.00
107 Dwyane Wade 2.50 6.00
108 Chris Bosh 1.50 4.00
109 Mario Chalmers 1.00 2.50
110 Ray Allen 2.00 5.00
111 Andrew Nicholson .75 2.00
112 Hedo Turkoglu 1.00 2.50
113 J.J. Redick 1.25 3.00
114 Jameer Nelson .75 2.00
115 Glen Davis .75 2.00
116 John Wall 1.50 4.00
117 Trevor Booker .75 2.00
118 Jordan Crawford .75 2.00
119 Nene 1.00 2.50
120 Kevin Seraphin .75 2.00
121 Andrew Bogut 1.00 2.50
122 Stephen Curry 15.00 40.00
123 David Lee .75 2.00
124 Harrison Barnes 1.50 4.00
125 Festus Ezeli .75 2.00
126 Blake Griffin 1.25 3.00
127 Chauncey Billups 1.50 4.00
128 Chris Paul 2.50 6.00
129 Eric Bledsoe 1.00 2.50
130 DeAndre Jordan 1.00 2.50
131 Steve Nash 2.50 6.00
132 Dwight Howard 1.50 4.00
133 Kobe Bryant 15.00 40.00
134 Metta World Peace 1.00 2.50
135 Pau Gasol 2.00 5.00
136 Shannon Brown .75 2.00
137 Marcin Gortat .75 2.00
138 Markieff Morris 1.25 3.00
139 Kendall Marshall .75 2.00
140 Channing Frye .75 2.00
141 Jimmer Fredette 1.25 3.00
142 Marcus Thornton .75 2.00
143 DeMarcus Cousins 1.25 3.00
144 Tyreke Evans 1.00 2.50
145 Thomas Robinson .75 2.00
146 Gerald Henderson .75 2.00
147 Michael Kidd-Gilchrist 1.00 2.50
148 Byron Mullens .75 2.00
149 Bismack Biyombo 1.00 2.50
150 Kemba Walker 3.00 8.00

1990-91 Hoops Team Night Sheets

COMPLETE SET (26) 80.00 200.00
1 John Battle
Jon Koncak
Moses Malone
Tim McCormick
Sidney Moncrief
Doc Rivers
Rumeal Robinson
Spud Webb
Dominique Wilkins
Kevin Willis 2.50 6.00
2 Larry Bird
Chris Ford CO
Kevin Gamble
Joe Kleine
Reggie Lewis
Kevin McHale
Robert Parish
Ed Pinckney
Brian Shaw 4.00 10.00
3 Muggsy Bogues
Rex Chapman
Dell Curry
Kenny Gattison
Mike Gminski *
Randolph Keys
Gene Littles CO
Johnny Newman
Robert Reid
Kelly Tripucka 2.50 6.00
4 B.J. Armstrong
Bill Cartwright
Horace Grant
H.Grant
S.Pippen *
Dennis Hopson
Michael Jordan
Stacey King
Cliff Levingston
John Paxson
Will Perdue
Scottie Pippen 5.00 12.00
5 Winston Bennett
Chucky Brown
Brad Daugherty
Craig Ehlo
Danny Ferry
Steve Kerr
Larry Nance
Mark Price
Len Wilkens CO
Hot Rod Williams 2.50 6.00
6 Richie Adubato CO
Alex English
Rolando Blackman
Brad Davis
James Donaldson
Derek Harper
Fat Lever
Rodney McCray
Roy Tarpley
Randy White *
Herb Williams 2.50 6.00
7 Michael Adams
Walter Davis
Bill Hanzlik
Chris Jackson
Jerome Lane
Todd Lichti
Blair Rasmussen
Paul Westhead CO
Joe Wolf
Orlando Woolridge 2.50 6.00
8 Mark Aguirre
William Bedford
Chuck Daly CO
Joe Dumars
James Edwards
Scott Hastings
Vinnie Johnson
Bill Laimbeer
Dennis Rodman
John Salley
Isiah Thomas 3.00 8.00
9 Tim Hardaway
Rod Higgins
Tyrone Hill
Sarunas Marciulionis
Chris Mullin
Don Nelson CO
Jim Petersen
Mitch Richmond
Mike Smrek
Tom Tolbert 4.00 10.00
10 Don Chaney CO
Sleepy Floyd
Buck Johnson
Vernon Maxwell
Hakeem Olajuwon
Kenny Smith
Larry Smith
Otis Thorpe 4.00 10.00
11 Greg Dreiling *
Vern Fleming *
George McCloud *
Reggie Miller *
Chuck Person *
Mike Sanders *
Detlef Schrempf *
Rik Smits *
LaSalle Thompson *
Randy Wittman * 2.50 6.00
12 Benoit Benjamin
Winston Garland
Tom Garrick
Gary Grant
Ron Harper
Bo Kimble
Danny Manning
Jeff Martin
Ken Norman
Mike Schuler CO
Charles Smith 2.50 6.00
13 Vlade Divac S2
Mike Dunleavy CO S3
A.C. Green S2
Magic Johnson S3
Sam Perkins S2
Byron Scott S1
Terry Teagle S1 *
Mychal Thompson S3
James Worthy S1 3.00 8.00
14 Willie Burton
Sherman Douglas
Kevin Edwards
Grant Long
Glen Rice
Ron Rothstein CO
Rony Seikaly
Jon Sundvold
Billy Thompson 2.50 6.00
15 Greg Anderson
Frank Brickowski
Jeff Grayer
Del Harris CO
Jay Humphries
Frank Kornet
Brad Lohaus
Ricky Pierce
Fred Roberts
Alvin Robertson
Dan Schayes
Jack Sikma 2.50 6.00
16 Randy Breuer S3
Scott Brooks S4
Tony Campbell S3
Tyrone Corbin S4
Sam Mitchell S2
Tod Murphy S2
Bill Musselman CO S1
Pooh Richardson S1 2.50 6.00
17 Charles Chips
Mookie Blaylock
Sam Bowie
Derrick Coleman
Lester Conner
Bill Fitch CO
Derrick Gervin
Jack Haley
Roy Hinson
Chris Morris
Reggie Theus 2.50 6.00
18A Maurice Cheeks
Patrick Ewing
Stuart Gray
Mark Jackson
Charles Oakley
Trent Tucker
Kiki Vandeweghe
Kenny Walker
Eddie Lee Wilkins
Gerald Wilkins 10.00 25.00
18B Maurice Cheeks
Patrick Ewing
Mark Jackson
Charles Oakley
Brian Quinnett
John Starks
Trent Tucker
Kiki Vandeweghe
Kenny Walker
Eddie Lee Wilkins
Gerald Wilkins 5.00 12.00
19 Mark Acres
Nick Anderson
Michael Ansley
Terry Catledge
Matt Guokas CO
Greg Kite
Jerry Reynolds
Dennis Scott
Scott Skiles
Otis Smith
Sam Vincent 2.50 6.00
20 Ron Anderson
Charles Barkley
Manute Bol
Johnny Dawkins
Armon Gilliam *
Hersey Hawkins
Jim Lynam CO
Rick Mahorn 3.00 8.00
21 Ken Battle
Tom Chambers
Cotton Fitzsimmons CO
Jeff Hornacek
Kevin Johnson
Dan Majerle
Ed Nealy
Tim Perry
Kurt Rambis
Mark West 8.00 20.00
22 Rick Adelman CO
Danny Ainge
Mark Bryant
Wayne Cooper
Clyde Drexler
Kevin Duckworth
Jerome Kersey
Drazen Petrovic
Terry Porter
Cliff Robinson
Buck Williams
Danny Young 10.00 25.00
23 Willie Anderson
Larry Brown CO
Terry Cummings
Sean Elliott
David Greenwood
Paul Pressey
David Robinson
Rod Strickland
The Coyote (Mascot)

Brad Townsend
Buck Harvey/89-90
Midwest Div.Champs 5.00 12.00
24A Dana Barros
Michael Cage
Quintin Dailey
Dale Ellis
Eddie Johnson *
Shawn Kemp
Derrick McKey
Nate McMillan
Gary Payton
Olden Polynice
Sedale Threatt 4.00 10.00
24B Combos
Dana Barros
Michael Cage
Quintin Dailey
Dale Ellis
Eddie Johnson *
Shawn Kemp
Derrick McKey
Nate McMillan
Gary Payton
Olden Polynice
Sedale Threatt 4.00 10.00
24C Dana Barros
Benoit Benjamin
Michael Cage
Quintin Dailey
Eddie Johnson *
Shawn Kemp
Derrick McKey
Nate McMillan
Gary Payton
Ricky Pierce
Sedale Threatt 4.00 10.00
24D Dana Barros
Benoit Benjamin
Michael Cage
Quintin Dailey
Eddie Johnson *
Shawn Kemp
Derrick McKey
Nate McMillan
Gary Payton
Ricky Pierce
Sedale Threatt 4.00 10.00
25 Thurl Bailey
Mike Brown
Mark Eaton
Blue Edwards
Darrell Griffith
Jeff Malone
Karl Malone
Delaney Rudd
Jerry Sloan CO
John Stockton 5.00 12.00
26 Mark Alarie
Pervis Ellison
Harvey Grant
Tom Hammonds
Charles Jones
Bernard King
Wes Unseld CO
Darrell Walker
John Williams 2.50 6.00

1991-92 Hoops Team Night Sheets

COMPLETE SET (27) 60.00 150.00
1 Stacey Augmon
Maurice Cheeks
Jon Koncak
Blair Rasmussen
Rumeal Robinson
Alexander Volkov
Bob Weiss CO
Dominique Wilkins
Kevin Willis 3.00 8.00
2 John Bagley
Larry Bird
Dee Brown
Kevin Gamble
Joe Kleine
Reggie Lewis
Kevin McHale
Robert Parish
Ed Pinckney 4.00 10.00
3 Muggsy Bogues
Rex Chapman
Dell Curry
Kenny Gattison
Kendall Gill
Mike Gminski
Hugo (Mascot)
Larry Johnson
Eric Leckner
Johnny Newman
J.R. Reid 3.00 8.00
4A B.J. Armstrong
Bill Cartwright
Horace Grant
Bobby Hansen
Craig Hodges
Michael Jordan
Stacey King
Cliff Levingston
John Paxson
Will Perdue
Scottie Pippen
Scott Williams 5.00 12.00
4B B.J. Armstrong
Bill Cartwright
Horace Grant
Bobby Hansen
Craig Hodges
Michael Jordan
Stacey King
Cliff Levingston
John Paxson
Will Perdue
Scottie Pippen
Mark Randall 5.00 12.00
5 John Battle
Winston Bennett
Terrell Brandon
Brad Daugherty
Craig Ehlo
Danny Ferry
Henry James
Steve Kerr
Larry Nance
Mark Price
Lenny Wilkens CO
John Williams 3.00 8.00
6 Richie Adubato CO
Rolando Blackman
Brad Davis
Terry Davis
James Donaldson
Derek Harper
Fat Lever
Rodney McCray
Doug Smith
Randy White
Herb Williams 2.50 6.00
7 Cadillac Anderson
Walter Davis
Winston Garland
Chris Jackson
Marcus Liberty
Todd Lichti
Mark Macon
Dikembe Mutombo
Paul Westhead CO
Reggie Williams 2.50 6.00
8 Mark Aguirre
William Bedford
Chuck Daly CO
Joe Dumars
Bill Laimbeer
Dennis Rodman
John Salley
Brad Sellers
Isiah Thomas
Darrell Walker
Orlando Woolridge 3.00 8.00
9 Vincent Askew
Mario Elie
Tim Hardaway
Rod Higgins
Tyrone Hill
Alton Lister
Sarunas Marciulionis
Chris Mullin
Don Nelson CO
Jim Petersen
Tom Tolbert 2.50 6.00
10 Don Chaney CO
Eric Floyd
Dave Jamerson
Buck Johnson
Vernon Maxwell
Hakeem Olajuwon
Kenny Smith
Larry Smith
Otis Thorpe 3.00 8.00
11 Greg Dreiling
Vern Fleming
George McCloud
Reggie Miller
Chuck Person
Detlef Schrempf
Rik Smits
LaSalle Thompson
Micheal Williams
Randy Wittman 2.50 6.00
12 James Edwards
Gary Grant
Ron Harper
Bo Kimble
Danny Manning
Ken Norman
Olden Polynice
Doc Rivers
Mike Schuler CO
Charles Smith
Loy Vaught 2.50 6.00
13 Elden Campbell
Vlade Divac
A.C. Green
Jack Haley
Sam Perkins
Byron Scott
Tony Smith
Sedale Threatt
James Worthy 2.50 6.00
14 Keith Askins
Willie Burton
Bimbo Coles
Kevin Edwards
Alec Kessler
Grant Long
Glen Rice
Rony Seikaly
Brian Shaw
Steve Smith 2.50 6.00
15 Frank Brickowski
Dale Ellis
Jeff Grayer
Jay Humphries
Larry Krystkowiak
Brad Lohaus
Moses Malone
Fred Roberts
Alvin Robertson
Dan Schayes
Snickers USA Olympic
Team 1992 with
Steve Henson and
Lester Conner 3.00 8.00
16 Randy Breuer
Scott Brooks
Tony Campbell
Luc Longley
Sam Mitchell
Pooh Richardson
Felton Spencer
Doug West 2.50 6.00
17 Rafael Addison
Kenny Anderson
Mookie Blaylock
Sam Bowie
Derrick Coleman
Chris Dudley
Tate George
Terry Mills
Chris Morris
Drazen Petrovic 2.50 6.00
18 Greg Anthony
Anthony Mason
Patrick Ewing
Mark Jackson
Tim McCormick
Xavier McDaniel
Charles Oakley
Brian Quinnett
John Starks
Kiki Vandeweghe
Gerald Wilkins 3.00 8.00
19 Mark Acres
Nick Anderson
Terry Catledge
Greg Kite
Jerry Reynolds
Dennis Scott
Scott Skiles
Otis Smith
Jeff Turner
Sam Vincent
Brian Williams 2.50 6.00
20 Ron Anderson
Charles Barkley
Manute Bol
Johnny Dawkins
Armon Gilliam
Hersey Hawkins
Jim Lynam CO
Charles Shackleford 2.50 6.00
21 Cedric Ceballos
Tom Chambers
Cotton Fitzsimmons CO
Jeff Hornacek
Kevin Johnson
Negele Knight
Andrew Lang
Dan Majerle
Tim Perry 2.50 6.00
22 Alaa Abdelnaby
Danny Ainge
Mark Bryant
Wayne Cooper
Clyde Drexler
Kevin Duckworth
Jerome Kersey
Terry Porter
Cliff Robinson
Buck Williams
Danny Young 3.00 8.00
23 Anthony Bonner
Randy Brown
Duane Causwell
Pete Chilcutt
Dennis Hopson
Les Jepsen
Jim Les
Mitch Richmond
Dwayne Schintzius
Lionel Simmons
Wayman Tisdale
Spud Webb 2.50 6.00
24 Willie Anderson
Antoine Carr
Terry Cummings
Coby Dietrick and
with Dave Barnett ANN
Sean Elliott
Sidney Green
Paul Pressey
David Robinson
David Robinson (Portrait)
Rod Strickland
Greg Sutton 3.00 8.00
25 Dana Barros
Benoit Benjamin
Michael Cage
Marty Conlon
Eddie Johnson
Shawn Kemp
Rich King
Derrick McKey
Nate McMillan
Gary Payton
Ricky Pierce 3.00 8.00
26 David Benoit
Mike Brown
Tyrone Corbin
Mark Eaton
Blue Edwards
Jeff Malone
Karl Malone
Eric Murdock
Delaney Rudd
Jerry Sloan CO
John Stockton 4.00 10.00
27 Michael Adams
Mark Alarie
Ledell Eackles
Pervis Ellison
A.J. English
Greg Foster
Harvey Grant
Tom Hammonds
Charles Jones
Bernard King
Wes Unseld CO 2.50 6.00

1999 Hoops WNBA

COMPLETE SET (110) 6.00 15.00
1 Cynthia Cooper PR .60 1.50
2 Houston vs. Phoenix PR .20 .50
3 Houston vs. Phoenix PR .20 .50
4 Houston vs. Phoenix PR .20 .50
5 Houston vs. Charlotte PR .20 .50
6 Phoenix vs. Cleveland PR .20 .50
7 Cynthia Cooper
Jennifer Gillom
Nikki McCray
Lisa Leslie .60 1.50
8 Lisa Leslie
Cindy Brown
Jennifer Gillom
Margo Dydek .50 1.25
9 Isabelle Fijalkowski
Janice Braxton
Michelle Griffiths
Razija Mujanovic .10 .25
10 Eva Nemcova
Cynthia Cooper
Penny Toler
Suzie McConnell Serio .60 1.50
11 Sandy Brondello
Eva Nemcova
Bridget Pettis
Cynthia Cooper .60 1.50
12 Ticha Penicheiro
Suzie McConnell Serio
Teresa Weatherspoon
Michele Timms .50 1.25
13 Teresa Weatherspoon
Kim Perrot
Sheryl Swoopes
Ticha Penicheiro .60 1.50
14 Margo Dydek
Lisa Leslie
Tangela Smith
Vicky Bullett .50 1.25
15 Andrea Kuklova .20 .50
16 Christy Smith .20 .50
17 Penny Moore .30 .75
18 Octavia Blue RC .20 .50
19 Vickie Johnson .30 .75
20 Latasha Byears .30 .75
21 Vicky Bullett .30 .75
22 Franthea Price RC .20 .50
23 Tina Thompson .75 2.00
24 Teresa Weatherspoon .75 2.00
25 Maria Stepanova RC .20 .50
26 Merlakia Jones .30 .75
27 Razija Mujanovic RC .20 .50
28 Rhonda Mapp .25 .60
29 Kristi Harrower RC .30 .75
30 Penny Toler .30 .75
31 Margo Dydek RC .75 2.00
32 Kim Perrot .60 1.50
33 Cindy Brown .40 1.00
34 Eva Nemcova .30 .75
35 Quacy Barnes .20 .50
36 Tracy Reid RC .40 1.00
37 Chantel Tremitiere .20 .50
38 Lady Hardmon .20 .50
39 Michelle Griffiths RC .40 1.00
40 Sheryl Swoopes 1.25 3.00
41 Sandy Brondello RC .75 2.00
42 Andrea Stinson .40 1.00
43 Marlies Askamp RC .30 .75
44 Rachael Sporn RC .30 .75
45 Nikki McCray .60 1.50
46 Andrea Congreaves .30 .75
47 Toni Foster .30 .75
48 Kim Williams .30 .75
49 Carla Porter RC .30 .75
50 Jamila Wideman .30 .75
51 Isabelle Fijalkowski .30 .75
52 Korie Hlede RC .60 1.50
53 Tora Suber .30 .75
54 Sue Wicks .30 .75
55 Coquese Washington RC .40 1.00
56 Sharon Manning .20 .50
57 Tammy Jackson .20 .50
58 Tangela Smith .20 .50
59 Suzie McConnell-Serio .50 1.25
60 Lisa Leslie 1.00 2.50
61 Wendy Palmer .50 1.25
62 Adia Barnes RC .30 .75
63 La'Shawn Brown RC .30 .75
64 Janeth Arcain .20 .50
65 Ruthie Bolton-Holifield .60 1.50
66 Bridget Pettis .20 .50
67 Pamela McGee .30 .75
68 Rebecca Lobo .60 1.50
69 Cindy Blodgett RC .60 1.50
70 Rita Williams .25 .60
71 Mwadi Mabika .20 .50
72 Sophia Witherspoon .30 .75
73 Janice Braxton .20 .50
74 Cynthia Cooper 1.25 3.00
75 Tammi Reiss .30 .75
76 Umeki Webb .20 .50
77 Kym Hampton .30 .75
78 LaTonya Johnson RC .30 .75
79 Michele Timms .60 1.50
80 Kisha Ford .20 .50
81 Monica Lamb RC .30 .75
82 Keri Chaconas RC .30 .75
83 Elena Baranova .50 1.25
84 Linda Burgess .20 .50
85 Tamecka Dixon .30 .75
86 Heidi Burge .20 .50
87 Michelle Edwards .40 1.00
88 Yolanda Moore RC .20 .50
89 Ticha Penicheiro RC 1.00 2.50
90 A.Santos de Oliveira RC .30 .75
91 Rushia Brown .20 .50
92 Lynette Woodard .40 1.00
93 Katrina Colleton RC .20 .50
94 Bridgette Gordon .20 .50
95 Jennifer Gillom .50 1.25
96 Murriel Page .30 .75
97 Olympia Scott-Richardson .30 .75
98 Adrienne Johnson RC .60 1.50
99 Gergana Branzova FP RC .30 .75
100 Allison Feaster FP RC .50 1.25
101 Brandy Reed FP RC .60 1.50
102 Katie Smith FP RC .75 2.00
103 Natalie Williams FP RC .60 1.50
104 Jennifer Azzi FP RC .75 2.00
105 Chamique Holdsclaw FP RC 1.25 3.00
106 Dawn Staley FP RC 1.25 3.00
107 Nykesha Sales FP RC .60 1.50
108 Kristin Folkl FP RC .50 1.25
109 Checklist .20 .50
110 Checklist .20 .50

1999 Hoops WNBA Autographics

STATED ODDS 1:144
*BLUE CENTURY MARKS: 1.25X TO 3X HI
BLUE: PRINT RUN 50 SERIAL #'d SETS
1 Cynthia Cooper 30.00 80.00
2 Kristin Folkl 12.00 30.00
3 Bridgette Gordon 5.00 12.00
4 Lisa Leslie 25.00 60.00
5 Suzie McConnell-Serio 12.00 30.00
6 Nikki McCray 15.00 40.00
7 Nykesha Sales 10.00 25.00
8 Dawn Staley 50.00 120.00
9 Andrea Stinson 10.00 25.00
10 Sheryl Swoopes 30.00 80.00
11 Michele Timms 15.00 40.00
12 Penny Toler 8.00 20.00
13 Teresa Weatherspoon 20.00 50.00

1999 Hoops WNBA Award Winners

COMPLETE SET (10) 20.00 50.00
1 Tina Thompson 4.00 10.00
2 Sheryl Swoopes 6.00 15.00
3 Jennifer Gillom 2.50 6.00
4 Cynthia Cooper 6.00 15.00
5 Suzie McConnell-Serio 2.50 6.00
6 Cindy Brown 2.00 5.00
7 Eva Nemcova 1.50 4.00
8 Lisa Leslie 5.00 12.00
9 Andrea Stinson 2.00 5.00
10 Teresa Weatherspoon 4.00 10.00

1999 Hoops WNBA Building Blocks

COMPLETE SET (8) 3.00 8.00
1 Dawn Staley 1.50 4.00
2 Rebecca Lobo .75 2.00
3 Tracy Reid .50 1.25
4 Korie Hlede .75 2.00
5 Ticha Penicheiro 1.25 3.00
6 Tammi Reiss .40 1.00
7 Nikki McCray .75 2.00
8 Jennifer Gillom .60 1.50

1999 Hoops WNBA Talk of the Town

COMPLETE SET (12) 10.00 25.00
1 Cynthia Cooper 3.00 8.00
2 Michele Timms 1.50 4.00
3 Suzie McConnell-Serio 1.25 3.00
4 Lisa Leslie 2.50 6.00
5 Andrea Stinson 1.00 2.50
6 Elena Baranova 1.25 3.00
7 Cindy Brown 1.00 2.50
8 Teresa Weatherspoon 2.00 5.00
9 Nikki McCray 1.50 4.00
10 Ruthie Bolton-Holifield 1.50 4.00
11 Nykesha Sales 1.50 4.00
12 Kristin Folkl 1.25 3.00

1992-93 Hornets Hive Five

COMPLETE SET (11) 6.00 15.00
1 Larry Johnson 1.50 4.00
2 Kendall Gill 1.25 3.00
3 Muggsy Bogues 1.25 3.00
4 Dell Curry .75 2.00
5 Alonzo Mourning 3.00 8.00
NNO Hugo the Hornet .20 .50
NNO Kim Bailey .20 .50
NNO Paris Floyd .20 .50
NNO Michelle Lee .20 .50
NNO Angela Pooser .20 .50
NNO Tara Wood .20 .50

1992-93 Hornets Standups

COMPLETE SET (12) 20.00 50.00
1 Tony Bennett 1.50 4.00
2 Dell Curry 2.00 5.00
3 Alonzo Mourning 6.00 15.00
4 Muggsy Bogues 3.00 8.00
5 Mike Gminski 1.50 4.00
6 Johnny Newman 1.50 4.00
7 Kenny Gattison 1.50 4.00
8 Kendall Gill 2.50 6.00
9 David Wingate 1.50 4.00
10 Sidney Green 1.50 4.00
11 Larry Johnson 3.00 8.00
12 Kevin Lynch 1.50 4.00

2008-09 Hot Prospects

COMP.SET w/o SPs (90) 10.00 25.00
DRAFT PRINT RUN 499 SER.#'d SETS
111-136 PRINT RUN 399 SER.#'d SETS
137-142 PRINT RUN 199 SER.#'d SETS
143-162 PRINT RUN 199 SER.#'d SETS
1 LaMarcus Aldridge .40 1.00
2 Ray Allen .60 1.50
3 Carmelo Anthony .50 1.25
4 Gilbert Arenas .50 1.25
5 Ron Artest .40 1.00
6 Mike Bibby .40 1.00
7 Chauncey Billups .50 1.25
8 Andrew Bogut .30 .75
9 Carlos Boozer .30 .75
10 Chris Bosh .50 1.25
11 Elton Brand .30 .75
12 Corey Brewer .30 .75
13 Kobe Bryant 3.00 8.00
14 Caron Butler .30 .75
15 Jose Calderon .25 .60
16 Marcus Camby .30 .75
17 Vince Carter .75 2.00
18 Mike Conley Jr. .30 .75
19 Daequan Cook .25 .60
20 Jamal Crawford .40 1.00
21 Baron Davis .40 1.00
22 Luol Deng .30 .75
23 Tim Duncan 1.00 2.50
24 Mike Dunleavy .25 .60
25 Kevin Durant 1.50 4.00
26 Francisco Garcia .25 .60
27 Kevin Garnett 1.00 2.50
28 Pau Gasol .50 1.25
29 Rudy Gay .40 1.00
30 Daniel Gibson .25 .60
31 Manu Ginobili .75 2.00
32 Ben Gordon .30 .75
33 Danny Granger .30 .75
34 Jeff Green .30 .75
35 Richard Hamilton .40 1.00
36 Al Harrington .30 .75
37 Al Horford .40 1.00
38 Dwight Howard .50 1.25
39 Josh Howard .30 .75
40 Andre Iguodala .30 .75
41 Allen Iverson .75 2.00
42 Stephen Jackson .30 .75
43 LeBron James 3.00 8.00
44 Antawn Jamison .30 .75
45 Al Jefferson .25 .60
46 Richard Jefferson .30 .75
47 Yi Jianlian .50 1.25
48 Joe Johnson .40 1.00
49 Chris Kaman .25 .60
50 Jason Kidd .60 1.50
51 Kyle Korver .30 .75
52 Rashard Lewis .30 .75
53 Corey Maggette .30 .75
54 Stephon Marbury .40 1.00
55 Shawn Marion .40 1.00
56 Kevin Martin .30 .75
57 Rashad McCants .25 .60
58 Tracy McGrady .60 1.50
59 Andre Miller .30 .75
60 Yao Ming 1.00 2.50
61 Jamario Moon .25 .60
62 Steve Nash .75 2.00
63 Joakim Noah .25 .60
64 Andres Nocioni .25 .60
65 Dirk Nowitzki 1.00 2.50
66 Jermaine O'Neal .40 1.00
67 Shaquille O'Neal 1.25 3.00
68 Greg Oden .25 .60
69 Emeka Okafor .25 .60
70 Tony Parker .50 1.25
71 Chris Paul .75 2.00
72 Paul Pierce .60 1.50
73 Zach Randolph .40 1.00
74 Michael Redd .30 .75
75 Jason Richardson .40 1.00
76 Brandon Roy .30 .75
77 Luis Scola .30 .75
78 Peja Stojakovic .30 .75
79 Amare Stoudemire .40 1.00
80 Hedo Turkoglu .30 .75
81 Dwyane Wade .75 2.00
82 Ben Wallace .50 1.25
83 Gerald Wallace .30 .75
84 Rasheed Wallace .50 1.25
85 Luke Walton .30 .75
86 David West .30 .75
87 Chris Wilcox .25 .60
88 Deron Williams .30 .75
89 Sean Williams .25 .60
90 Thaddeus Young .30 .75
91 Ray Allen 1.25 3.00
92 Carmelo Anthony 1.00 2.50
93 Chauncey Billups 1.00 2.50
94 Kobe Bryant 6.00 15.00
95 Vince Carter 1.50 4.00
96 Baron Davis .75 2.00
97 Tim Duncan 2.00 5.00
98 Kevin Garnett 2.00 5.00
99 Pau Gasol 1.00 2.50
100 Dwight Howard 1.00 2.50
101 Allen Iverson 1.50 4.00
102 LeBron James 6.00 15.00
103 Michael Jordan 6.00 15.00
104 Tracy McGrady 1.25 3.00
105 Yao Ming 2.00 5.00
106 Steve Nash 1.50 4.00
107 Joakim Noah .50 1.25
108 Dirk Nowitzki 2.00 5.00
109 Shaquille O'Neal 2.50 6.00
110 Dwyane Wade 1.50 4.00
111 Kyle Weaver JSY AU RC 4.00 10.00
112 Joe Alexander JSY AU RC 4.00 10.00
113 D.J. Augustin JSY AU RC 6.00 15.00
114 Brook Lopez JSY AU RC 4.00 10.00
115 Jerryd Bayless JSY AU RC 5.00 12.00
116 Jason Thompson JSY AU RC 4.00 10.00
117 Brandon Rush JSY AU RC 4.00 10.00
118 Anthony Randolph JSY AU RC 4.00 10.00
119 Robin Lopez JSY AU RC 5.00 12.00
120 Marreese Speights JSY AU RC 5.00 12.00
121 Roy Hibbert JSY AU RC 5.00 12.00
122 Javale McGee JSY AU RC 6.00 15.00
123 J.J. Hickson JSY AU RC 4.00 10.00
124 Ryan Anderson JSY AU RC 5.00 12.00
125 Courtney Lee JSY AU RC 5.00 12.00
126 Kosta Koufos JSY AU RC 4.00 10.00
127 George Hill JSY AU RC 6.00 15.00
128 Darrell Arthur JSY AU RC 5.00 12.00
129 Donte Greene JSY AU RC 4.00 10.00
130 Sonny Weems JSY AU RC 4.00 10.00
131 J.R. Giddens JSY AU RC 4.00 10.00
132 Walter Sharpe JSY AU RC 4.00 10.00
133 Joey Dorsey JSY AU RC 4.00 10.00
134 Mario Chalmers JSY AU RC 6.00 15.00
135 DeAndre Jordan JSY AU RC 8.00 20.00
136 Patrick Ewing Jr JSY AU RC 4.00 10.00
137 Derrick Rose JSY AU RC 25.00 60.00
138 M.Beasley JSY AU RC 12.00 30.00
139 O.J. Mayo JSY AU RC 10.00 25.00
140 R.Westbrook JSY AU RC 200.00 500.00
141 Kevin Love JSY AU RC 30.00 80.00
142 Eric Gordon JSY AU RC 10.00 25.00
143 Luc Richard Mbah A Moute AU RC 4.00 10.00
144 James Mays AU RC 5.00 12.00
145 Sonny Weems AU 3.00 8.00
146 Chris Douglas-Roberts AU RC 3.00 8.00
147 Deron Washington AU RC 3.00 8.00
148 David Padgett AU RC 5.00 12.00
149 Bill Walker AU RC 3.00 8.00
150 Malik Hairston AU RC 3.00 8.00
151 Richard Hendrix AU RC 3.00 8.00
152 DeVon Hardin AU RC 3.00 8.00
153 Darnell Jackson AU RC 3.00 8.00
154 Maarty Leunen AU RC 3.00 8.00
155 Mike Taylor AU RC 3.00 8.00
156 James Gist AU RC 3.00 8.00
157 Sean Singletary AU RC 3.00 8.00
158 Joe Crawford RC 3.00 8.00
159 Trent Plaisted RC 3.00 8.00
160 Shan Foster RC 3.00 8.00
161 Juan Palacios RC 5.00 12.00
162 Jaycee Carroll RC 5.00 12.00

2008-09 Hot Prospects Blue

*1-110 BLUE: .5X TO 1.25X BASE HI
111 Kyle Weaver 1.00 2.50
112 Joe Alexander 1.00 2.50
113 D.J. Augustin 1.50 4.00
115 Jerryd Bayless 1.25 3.00
116 Jason Thompson 1.00 2.50
117 Brandon Rush 1.00 2.50
118 Anthony Randolph 1.00 2.50
119 Robin Lopez 1.25 3.00
120 Marreese Speights 1.25 3.00
121 Roy Hibbert 1.25 3.00
122 Javale McGee 1.50 4.00
123 J.J. Hickson 1.00 2.50
124 Ryan Anderson 1.25 3.00
125 Courtney Lee 1.25 3.00
126 Kosta Koufos 1.00 2.50
127 George Hill 1.50 4.00
128 Darrell Arthur 1.25 3.00
129 Donte Greene 1.00 2.50
130 Sonny Weems 1.00 2.50
131 J.R. Giddens 1.00 2.50
132 Walter Sharpe 1.00 2.50
133 Joey Dorsey 1.00 2.50
134 Mario Chalmers 1.50 4.00
135 DeAndre Jordan 2.00 5.00
136 Patrick Ewing Jr. 1.00 2.50
137 Derrick Rose 6.00 15.00
138 Michael Beasley 1.50 4.00
139 O.J. Mayo 1.25 3.00
140 Russell Westbrook 15.00 40.00
141 Kevin Love 3.00 8.00
142 Eric Gordon 2.50 6.00
143 Luc Richard Mbah A Moute .75 2.00
144 James Mays 1.00 2.50
145 Sonny Weems .60 1.50
146 Chris Douglas-Roberts .60 1.50
147 Deron Washington .60 1.50
148 David Padgett 1.00 2.50
149 Bill Walker .60 1.50
150 Malik Hairston .60 1.50
151 Richard Hendrix .60 1.50
152 DeVon Hardin .60 1.50
153 Darnell Jackson .60 1.50
154 Maarty Leunen .60 1.50
155 Mike Taylor .60 1.50
156 James Gist .60 1.50
157 Sean Singletary .60 1.50
158 Joe Crawford .60 1.50
159 Trent Plaisted .60 1.50
160 Shan Foster .60 1.50
161 Juan Palacios 1.00 2.50
162 Jaycee Carroll 1.00 2.50

2008-09 Hot Prospects Red

*1-90 RED: 3X TO 8X BASE HI
*91-110 RED: 1.5X TO 4X BASE HI
*111-162 RED: .75X TO 2X BASE HI
RED PRINT RUN 25 SER.#'d SETS
13 Kobe Bryant 20.00 50.00
43 LeBron James 25.00 60.00
103 Michael Jordan 60.00 150.00

2008-09 Hot Prospects Alumni Mates

COMPLETE SET (20) 10.00 25.00
APPROXIMATE ODDS 1:6
AM1 G.Arenas/R.Jefferson 1.50 4.00
AM2 J.Kidd/S.Abdur-Rahim 1.50 4.00
AM3 S.Battier/C.Boozer 1.50 4.00
AM4 D.Majerle/C.Kaman 1.50 4.00
AM5 A.Horford/J.Noah 1.50 4.00
AM6 D.Mutombo/A.Mourning 3.00 8.00
AM7 W.Bellamy/E.Gordon 1.50 4.00
AM8 M.Beasley/R.Blackman 2.00 5.00
AM9 S.O'Neal/G.Davis 3.00 8.00
AM10 D.Rose/S.Williams 2.50 6.00
AM11 J.Richardson/Z.Randolph 1.50 4.00
AM12 V.Carter/A.Jamison 2.50 6.00
AM13 A.Dantley/B.Laimbeer 1.50 4.00
AM14 M.Conley/G.Oden 1.50 4.00
AM15 K.Durant/L.Aldridge 2.00 5.00
AM16 R.Allen/R.Hamilton 1.50 4.00
AM17 J.Erving/M.Camby 2.00 5.00
AM18 K.Abdul-Jabbar/B.Walton 2.00 5.00
AM19 B.Sharman/O.Mayo 1.50 4.00
AM20 D.West/J.Posey 1.50 4.00

2008-09 Hot Prospects Cream of the Crop

COMPLETE SET (30) 12.00 30.00
APPROXIMATE ODDS 1:6
CC1 Brandon Roy .60 1.50
CC2 Chris Paul 1.50 4.00
CC3 LeBron James 6.00 15.00
CC4 Amare Stoudemire .75 2.00
CC5 Joe Johnson .75 2.00
CC6 Tony Parker 1.00 2.50
CC7 Gilbert Arenas .75 2.00
CC8 Michael Redd .60 1.50
CC9 Richard Hamilton .75 2.00
CC10 Shawn Marion .75 2.00
CC11 Manu Ginobili 1.50 4.00
CC12 Dirk Nowitzki 2.00 5.00
CC13 Paul Pierce 1.25 3.00
CC14 Tracy McGrady 1.25 3.00
CC15 Kobe Bryant 6.00 15.00
CC16 Steve Nash 1.50 4.00
CC17 Rasheed Wallace 1.00 2.50
CC18 Larry Johnson .75 2.00
CC19 Detlef Schrempf .75 2.00
CC20 Vlade Divac .75 2.00
CC21 Mitch Richmond .75 2.00
CC22 Scottie Pippen 1.25 3.00
CC23 David Robinson 1.50 4.00
CC24 Chris Mullin .75 2.00
CC25 Karl Malone 1.00 2.50
CC26 Isiah Thomas 1.25 3.00
CC27 Kevin McHale 1.00 2.50
CC28 Larry Bird 2.50 6.00
CC29 Oscar Robertson .75 2.00
CC30 Wilt Chamberlain 2.50 6.00

2008-09 Hot Prospects Draft Day Postmarks

STATED PRINT RUN 50 SER.#'d SETS
DDAA Alexis Ajinca 5.00 12.00
DDAD Darrell Arthur 6.00 15.00

DDAR Anthony Randolph 5.00 12.00
DDBL Brook Lopez 10.00 25.00
DDBR Brandon Rush 5.00 12.00
DDCD Chris Douglas-Roberts 5.00 12.00
DDDA D.J. Augustin 8.00 20.00
DDDG Danilo Gallinari 12.00 30.00
DDDR Derrick Rose 30.00 80.00
DDDW D.J. White 5.00 12.00
DDEG Eric Gordon 12.00 30.00
DDGR Donte Greene 5.00 12.00
DDJA Joe Alexander 5.00 12.00
DDJB Jerryd Bayless 6.00 15.00
DDJD Joey Dorsey 5.00 12.00
DDJG J.R. Giddens 5.00 12.00
DDJH J.J. Hickson 5.00 12.00
DDJM Javale McGee 8.00 20.00
DDJT Jason Thompson 5.00 12.00
DDKK Kosta Koufos 5.00 12.00
DDKL Kevin Love 15.00 40.00
DDLM Luc Richard Mbah A Moute 6.00 15.00
DDMB Michael Beasley 8.00 20.00
DDMC Mario Chalmers 8.00 20.00
DDOJ O.J. Mayo 6.00 15.00
DDPE Patrick Ewing Jr 5.00 12.00
DDRA Ryan Anderson 6.00 15.00
DDRH Roy Hibbert 6.00 15.00
DDRL Robin Lopez 6.00 15.00
DDRW Russell Westbrook 200.00 500.00

2008-09 Hot Prospects Hot Materials

COMBINED AU/MEM ODDS 1:9
*RED: .75X TO 2X BASE HI
RED PRINT RUN 25 SER.#'d SETS
HMAB Andrew Bogut 2.00 5.00
HMAI Allen Iverson 5.00 12.00
HMAS Amare Stoudemire 2.50 6.00
HMBR Brandon Roy 2.00 5.00
HMCA Carmelo Anthony 3.00 8.00
HMCB Caron Butler 2.00 5.00
HMDG Danny Granger 2.00 5.00
HMDH Dwight Howard 3.00 8.00
HMDN Dirk Nowitzki 6.00 15.00
HMEO Emeka Okafor 1.50 4.00
HMJJ Joe Johnson 2.50 6.00
HMJK Jason Kidd 4.00 10.00
HMKB Kobe Bryant 40.00 100.00
HMKD Kevin Durant 10.00 25.00
HMKG Kevin Garnett 6.00 15.00
HMLJ LeBron James 12.00 30.00
HMMB Mike Bibby 2.50 6.00
HMPG Pau Gasol 3.00 8.00
HMRA Ray Allen 4.00 10.00
HMRH Richard Hamilton 2.50 6.00
HMRJ Richard Jefferson 2.00 5.00
HMRW Rasheed Wallace 3.00 8.00
HMSB Shane Battier 2.00 5.00
HMSM Shawn Marion 2.50 6.00
HMSN Steve Nash 5.00 12.00
HMSO Shaquille O'Neal 8.00 20.00
HMTD Tim Duncan 6.00 15.00
HMTP Tayshaun Prince 2.50 6.00
HMVC Vince Carter 5.00 12.00
HMYM Yao Ming 6.00 15.00

2008-09 Hot Prospects Hot Tandems

COMPLETE SET (20) 8.00 20.00
APPROXIMATE ODDS 1:6
HT1 L.Bird/P.Pierce 2.00 5.00
HT2 M.Jordan/S.Pippen 4.00 10.00
HT3 A.Iverson/C.Anthony 1.50 4.00
HT4 I.Thomas/J.Dumars 1.25 3.00
HT5 C.Billups/R.Hamilton 1.25 3.00
HT6 J.Kidd/D.Nowitzki 1.25 3.00
HT7 T.McGrady/Y.Ming 1.50 4.00
HT8 C.Drexler/H.Olajuwon 2.00 5.00
HT9 M.Johnson/K.Bryant 3.00 8.00
HT10 M.Redd/R.Jefferson 1.25 3.00
HT11 C.Paul/D.West 2.00 5.00
HT12 P.Ewing/W.Reed 1.50 4.00
HT13 P.Jackson/B.Bradley 1.25 3.00
HT14 J.Erving/W.Chamberlain 3.00 8.00
HT15 S.Nash/A.Stoudemire 2.00 5.00
HT16 B.Roy/G.Oden 1.25 3.00
HT17 G.Gervin/D.Robinson 2.00 5.00
HT18 K.Durant/J.Green 1.50 4.00
HT19 J.Stockton/K.Malone 2.00 5.00
HT20 G.Arenas/A.Jamison 1.25 3.00

2008-09 Hot Prospects NBA Game Issue Jerseys

PRINT RUN 149 SER.#'d SETS
*RED: .75X TO 2X BASE HI
RED PRINT RUN 25 SER.#'d SETS
NBAAB Andrew Bynum 1.50 4.00
NBAAI Allen Iverson 5.00 12.00
NBAAS Amare Stoudemire 2.50 6.00
NBABA Andrea Bargnani 2.00 5.00
NBABD Baron Davis 2.50 6.00
NBABR Brandon Roy 2.00 5.00
NBABU Caron Butler 2.00 5.00
NBACA Carmelo Anthony 3.00 8.00
NBACB Carlos Boozer 2.00 5.00
NBADH Dwight Howard 3.00 8.00
NBADN Dirk Nowitzki 6.00 15.00
NBADW Deron Williams 2.00 5.00
NBAGA Gilbert Arenas 2.50 6.00
NBAJH Josh Howard 2.00 5.00
NBAJJ Joe Johnson 2.50 6.00
NBAJK Jason Kidd 4.00 10.00
NBAJR Jason Richardson 2.50 6.00
NBAKB Kobe Bryant 50.00 120.00
NBAKG Kevin Garnett 6.00 15.00
NBALJ LeBron James 8.00 20.00
NBAMB Mike Bibby 2.50 6.00
NBAMJ Michael Jordan 20.00 50.00
NBAPG Pau Gasol 3.00 8.00
NBARG Rudy Gay 2.50 6.00
NBASM Shawn Marion 2.50 6.00
NBASN Steve Nash 5.00 12.00
NBASO Shaquille O'Neal 6.00 15.00
NBATD Tim Duncan 6.00 15.00
NBATP Tony Parker 3.00 8.00
NBAYM Yao Ming 6.00 15.00

2008-09 Hot Prospects Numbers Game Autographs Jerseys

CARDS #'d TO PLAYER JSY #
NGAB Andrew Bynum/17 15.00 40.00
NGAH Al Horford/15 20.00 40.00
NGBW Bill Walton/32 10.00 25.00
NGCA Carmelo Anthony/15 20.00 40.00
NGCK Chris Kaman/35 6.00 15.00
NGDG Danny Granger/33 12.00 30.00
NGDH Dwight Howard/12 40.00 70.00
NGDM Desmond Mason/24 10.00 25.00
NGDR David Robinson/50 40.00 100.00
NGEO Emeka Okafor/50 6.00 15.00
NGJS John Stockton/12 75.00 200.00
NGKB Kobe Bryant/24 600.00 1,200.00
NGKD Kevin Durant/35 75.00 200.00
NGLJ LeBron James/23 1,500.00 3,000.00
NGMA Donyell Marshall/42 6.00 15.00
NGMG Corey Maggette/50 6.00 15.00
NGRF Raymond Felton/20 8.00 20.00
NGRJ Richard Jefferson/24 8.00 20.00
NGSB Shane Battier/31 6.00 15.00
NGTP Tayshaun Prince/22 8.00 20.00
NGTT Tyrus Thomas/24 8.00 20.00
NGVC Vince Carter/15 20.00 50.00
NGYM Yao Ming/11 30.00 80.00

2008-09 Hot Prospects Property of Jerseys

STATED PRINT RUN 199 SER.#'d SETS
*RED: .75X TO 2X BASE HI
RED PRINT RUN 25 SER.#'d SETS
POAB Andrew Bogut 2.00 5.00
POAI Andre Iguodala 2.00 5.00
POAJ Antawn Jamison 2.00 5.00
POBO Chris Bosh 3.00 8.00
POBW Ben Wallace 3.00 8.00
POCB Chauncey Billups 3.00 8.00
POCK Chris Kaman 1.50 4.00
POCM Corey Maggette 2.00 5.00
POCP Chris Paul 5.00 12.00
PODG Daniel Gibson 1.50 4.00
PODW Dwyane Wade 5.00 12.00
POEB Elton Brand 2.00 5.00
POGR Danny Granger 2.00 5.00
POGW Gerald Wallace 2.00 5.00
POJC Jose Calderon 6.00 15.00
POJJ Joe Johnson 2.50 6.00
POJR Jason Richardson 2.50 6.00
POKD Kevin Durant 10.00 25.00
POKG Kevin Garnett 6.00 15.00
POKM Kevin Martin 2.00 5.00
POLJ LeBron James 8.00 20.00
POMB Mike Bibby 2.50 6.00
POMG Manu Ginobili 5.00 12.00
POPG Pau Gasol 3.00 8.00
PORJ Richard Jefferson 2.00 5.00
PORL Rashard Lewis 2.00 5.00
PORW Rasheed Wallace 3.00 8.00
POSB Shane Battier 2.00 5.00
POSM Shawn Marion 2.50 6.00
POWI Deron Williams 2.00 5.00

2008-09 Hot Prospects Rookie Materials Autographs Patches

COMBINED AU/MEM ODDS 1:9
RMAD Darrell Arthur 6.00 15.00
RMAR Anthony Randolph 5.00 12.00
RMBL Brook Lopez 10.00 25.00
RMBR Brandon Rush 5.00 12.00
RMBW Bill Walker 5.00 12.00
RMCD Chris Douglas-Roberts 5.00 12.00
RMDA Darnell Jackson 5.00 12.00
RMDG Danilo Gallinari 12.00 30.00
RMDJ D.J. Augustin 8.00 20.00
RMDR Derrick Rose 75.00 150.00
RMDW D.J. White 5.00 12.00
RMEG Eric Gordon 12.00 30.00
RMGH George Hill 8.00 20.00
RMGR Donte Greene 5.00 12.00
RMJA Joe Alexander 5.00 12.00
RMJB Jerryd Bayless 6.00 15.00
RMJC Joe Crawford 5.00 12.00
RMJD Joey Dorsey 5.00 12.00
RMJG J.R. Giddens 5.00 12.00
RMJH J.J. Hickson 5.00 12.00
RMJM JaVale McGee 8.00 20.00
RMJO DeAndre Jordan 15.00 40.00
RMJT Jason Thompson 5.00 12.00
RMKK Kosta Koufos 5.00 12.00
RMKL Kevin Love 15.00 40.00
RMKW Kyle Weaver 5.00 12.00
RMLM Luc Richard Mbah A Moute 6.00 15.00
RMMB Michael Beasley 8.00 20.00
RMMC Mario Chalmers 8.00 20.00
RMMH Malik Hairston 5.00 12.00
RMMS Marreese Speights 6.00 15.00
RMOM O.J. Mayo 6.00 15.00
RMPE Patrick Ewing Jr 5.00 12.00
RMRA Ryan Anderson 6.00 15.00
RMRH Roy Hibbert 6.00 15.00
RMRL Robin Lopez 6.00 15.00
RMSS Sean Singletary 5.00 12.00
RMSW Sonny Weems 5.00 12.00
RMWA Deron Washington 5.00 12.00
RMWS Walter Sharpe 5.00 12.00

2008-09 Hot Prospects Supreme Court

COMPLETE SET (20) 10.00 25.00
APPROXIMATE ODDS 1:6
SC1 Mike Bibby .75 2.00
SC2 Ray Allen 1.25 3.00
SC3 Michael Jordan 8.00 20.00
SC4 LeBron James 6.00 15.00
SC5 Jason Kidd 1.25 3.00
SC6 Chauncey Billups 1.00 2.50
SC7 Shane Battier .60 1.50
SC8 Tracy McGrady 1.25 3.00
SC9 Elton Brand .60 1.50
SC10 Kobe Bryant 6.00 15.00
SC11 Derek Fisher .60 1.50
SC12 Dwyane Wade 1.50 4.00
SC13 Dwight Howard 1.00 2.50
SC14 Andre Miller .60 1.50
SC15 Steve Nash 1.50 4.00
SC16 Greg Oden .50 1.25
SC17 Tony Parker 1.00 2.50
SC18 Jeff Green .60 1.50
SC19 Chris Bosh 1.00 2.50
SC20 Antawn Jamison .60 1.50

2008-09 Hot Prospects Sweet Selections Autographs

STATED PRINT RUN 25 SER.#'d SETS
SSAJ Antawn Jamison 8.00 20.00
SSAM Alonzo Mourning 30.00 80.00
SSBW Bill Walton 15.00 30.00
SSCB Chauncey Billups 8.00 20.00
SSCP Chris Paul 75.00 200.00
SSDG Darrell Griffith 8.00 20.00
SSDH Dwight Howard 12.00 30.00
SSDR David Robinson 30.00 80.00
SSDT David Thompson 8.00 20.00
SSDW Dominique Wilkins 25.00 50.00
SSHO Hakeem Olajuwon 20.00 50.00
SSJA LeBron James 1,250.00 2,500.00
SSJK Jason Kidd 15.00 40.00
SSKD Kevin Durant 75.00 150.00
SSLJ Larry Johnson 12.00 30.00
SSMO Sidney Moncrief 8.00 20.00
SSRR Micheal Ray Richardson 8.00 20.00
SSYM Yao Ming 15.00 30.00

1980-81 Hustle Chicago/La-Z-Boy Team Issue

1 B.Caldwell
B.Candler
S.Digitale
R.Easterling
J.Fincher
D.Gells
B.Gleason CO
P.Hodgson
P.Kilday
L.Matthews
P.Mayo
C.McWhorter
I.Nissen
C.Steele TR
E.White 12.50 25.00

1972-73 Icee Bear

COMPLETE SET (20) 300.00 600.00
1 Kareem Abdul-Jabbar 60.00 150.00
2 Dennis Awtrey 1.25 3.00
3 Tom Boerwinkle 2.00 5.00
4 Austin Carr SP 6.00 5.00
5 Wilt Chamberlain 60.00 140.00
6 Archie Clark SP 15.00 40.00
7 Dave DeBusschere 3.00 8.00
8 Walt Frazier SP 12.00 30.00
9 John Havlicek 12.00 30.00
10 Connie Hawkins 6.00 15.00
11 Bob Love 2.00 5.00
12 Jerry Lucas 5.00 12.00
13 Pete Maravich SP 30.00 30.00
14 Calvin Murphy 2.00 5.00
15 Oscar Robertson 30.00 30.00
16 Jerry Sloan 3.00 8.00
17 Wes Unseld 2.50 6.00
18 Dick Van Arsdale 8.00 20.00
19 Jerry West 30.00 80.00
20 Sidney Wicks 3.00 8.00

2000 IMAX Michael Jordan Postcards

COMPLETE SET (2) 4.00 10.00

2012-13 Immaculate Collection

1-100 PRINT RUN 99 SER.#'d SETS
101-200 STATED PRINT RUN 99 SER.#'d SETS
PREMIUM PATCHES MAY SELL FOR MORE
EXCHANGE DEADLINE 5/4/2015
1 Al Horford 3.00 8.00
2 Louis Williams 2.50 6.00
3 Dominique Wilkins 4.00 10.00
4 Paul Pierce 5.00 12.00
5 Kevin Garnett 8.00 20.00
6 Rajon Rondo 4.00 10.00
7 Larry Bird 10.00 25.00
8 Reggie Lewis 3.00 8.00
9 Deron Williams 2.50 6.00
10 Joe Johnson 2.50 6.00
11 Gerald Henderson 2.00 5.00
12 Ben Gordon 2.00 5.00
13 Ramon Sessions 2.00 5.00
14 Derrick Rose 5.00 12.00
15 Joakim Noah 2.50 6.00
16 Scottie Pippen 8.00 20.00
17 Dennis Rodman 8.00 20.00
18 Anderson Varejao 2.00 5.00
19 Wayne Ellington 2.00 5.00
20 Dirk Nowitzki 8.00 20.00
21 Vince Carter 6.00 15.00
22 O.J. Mayo 2.00 5.00
23 Shawn Marion 3.00 8.00
24 Andre Iguodala 3.00 8.00
25 Ty Lawson 2.00 5.00
26 Alex English 4.00 10.00
27 Greg Monroe 2.00 5.00
28 Isiah Thomas 6.00 15.00
29 Joe Dumars 4.00 10.00
30 Stephen Curry 25.00 60.00
31 David Lee 2.00 5.00
32 Chris Mullin 4.00 10.00
33 Tim Hardaway 4.00 10.00
34 James Harden 6.00 15.00
35 Jeremy Lin 5.00 12.00
36 Hakeem Olajuwon 6.00 15.00
37 Yao Ming 6.00 15.00
38 David West 2.50 6.00
39 Paul George 5.00 12.00
40 Tyler Hansbrough 2.00 5.00
41 Chris Paul 6.00 15.00
42 Blake Griffin 3.00 8.00
43 Grant Hill 5.00 12.00
44 Kobe Bryant 200.00 500.00
45 Steve Nash 6.00 15.00
46 Dwight Howard 4.00 10.00
47 George Mikan 10.00 25.00
48 Wilt Chamberlain 10.00 25.00
49 Shaquille O'Neal 10.00 25.00
50 Zach Randolph 3.00 8.00
51 Marc Gasol 3.00 8.00
52 Mike Conley 2.50 6.00
53 LeBron James 125.00 300.00
54 Dwyane Wade 6.00 15.00
55 Chris Bosh 4.00 10.00
56 Chris Andersen 2.50 6.00
57 Brandon Jennings 2.00 5.00
58 Monta Ellis 2.50 6.00
59 Eric Gordon 2.50 6.00
60 Ryan Anderson 2.00 5.00
61 Greivis Vasquez 2.00 5.00
62 Kevin Love 3.00 8.00
63 Andrei Kirilenko 2.50 6.00
64 Ricky Rubio 2.50 6.00
65 Carmelo Anthony 5.00 12.00
66 Jason Kidd 5.00 12.00
67 Tyson Chandler 2.50 6.00
68 Amar'e Stoudemire 3.00 8.00
69 Kevin Martin 2.50 6.00
70 Kevin Durant 12.00 30.00
71 Russell Westbrook 5.00 12.00
72 Arron Afflalo 2.00 5.00
73 Serge Ibaka 2.50 6.00
74 Jameer Nelson 2.00 5.00
75 Jrue Holiday 4.00 10.00
76 Evan Turner 2.00 5.00
77 Julius Erving 8.00 20.00
78 Moses Malone 5.00 12.00
79 Allen Iverson 6.00 15.00
80 Anfernee Hardaway 8.00 20.00
81 Goran Dragic 3.00 8.00
82 Luis Scola 2.50 6.00
83 Kevin Johnson 3.00 8.00
84 LaMarcus Aldridge 3.00 8.00
85 J.J. Hickson 2.00 5.00
86 DeMarcus Cousins 3.00 8.00
87 Tyreke Evans 2.50 6.00
88 Tim Duncan 8.00 20.00
89 Tony Parker 6.00 15.00
90 Manu Ginobili 6.00 15.00
91 David Robinson 5.00 12.00
92 Sean Elliott 2.50 6.00
93 Rudy Gay 3.00 8.00
94 DeMar DeRozan 4.00 10.00
95 Al Jefferson 2.00 5.00
96 Pete Maravich 6.00 15.00
97 John Stockton 6.00 15.00
98 John Wall 4.00 10.00
99 Martell Webster 2.00 5.00
100 Nene 2.50 6.00
101 K.Irving JSY AU RC 600.00 1,200.00
102 Derrick Williams JSY AU RC 6.00 15.00
103 Enes Kanter JSY AU RC 12.00 30.00
104 T. Thompson JSY AU RC 10.00 25.00
105 J.Valanciunas JSY AU RC 12.00 30.00
106 Jan Vesely JSY AU RC 6.00 15.00
107 B. Biyombo JSY AU RC 8.00 20.00
108 B.Knight JSY AU RC 8.00 20.00
109 K.Walker JSY AU RC 75.00 200.00
110 Jimmer Fredette JSY AU RC 10.00 25.00
111 Alec Burks JSY AU RC 10.00 25.00
112 K.Leonard JSY AU RC 1,500.00 3,000.00
113 N.Vucevic JSY AU RC 50.00 120.00
114 Iman Shumpert JSY AU RC 8.00 20.00
115 Chris Singleton JSY AU RC 6.00 15.00
116 T.Harris JSY AU RC 40.00 100.00
117 Donatas Motiejunas JSY AU RC 8.00 20.00
118 Nolan Smith JSY AU RC 6.00 15.00
119 K.Faried JSY AU RC 8.00 20.00
120 R.Jackson JSY AU RC 15.00 40.00
121 MarShon Brooks JSY AU RC 6.00 15.00
122 Jordan Hamilton JSY AU RC 6.00 15.00
123 N.Cole JSY AU RC 6.00 15.00
124 Cory Joseph JSY AU RC EXCH 8.00 20.00
125 J.Butler JSY AU RC 600.00 1,200.00
126 Kyle Singler JSY AU RC 6.00 15.00
127 C.Parsons JSY AU RC 8.00 20.00
128 Darius Morris JSY AU RC 8.00 20.00
129 Malcolm Lee JSY AU RC 6.00 15.00
130 D.Lillard JSY AU 1,000.00 2,000.00
131 Lavoy Allen JSY AU RC 6.00 15.00
132 E'Twaun Moore JSY AU RC 8.00 20.00
133 I.Thomas JSY AU RC 12.00 30.00
134 A.Davis JSY AU RC 1,500.00 3,000.00
135 Kidd-Gilchrist JSY AU RC 8.00 20.00
136 B.Beal JSY AU RC 125.00 300.00
137 D.Waiters JSY AU RC EXCH 8.00 20.00
138 Thomas Robinson JSY AU RC 10.00 25.00
139 H.Barnes JSY AU RC 25.00 60.00
140 Terrence Ross JSY AU RC 10.00 25.00
141 A.Drummond JSY AU RC 40.00 100.00
142 A.Rivers JSY AU RC 10.00 25.00
143 Meyers Leonard JSY AU RC 8.00 20.00
144 J.Lamb JSY AU RC 10.00 25.00
145 Kendall Marshall JSY AU RC 6.00 15.00
146 J.Henson JSY AU RC EXCH 8.00 20.00
147 M.Harkless JSY AU RC 8.00 20.00
148 Royce White JSY AU RC 6.00 15.00
149 Tyler Zeller JSY AU RC 6.00 15.00
150 T.Jones JSY AU RC EXCH 6.00 15.00
151 Andrew Nicholson JSY AU RC 6.00 15.00
152 Evan Fournier JSY AU RC 25.00 60.00
153 J.Sullinger JSY AU RC EXCH 6.00 15.00
154 Fab Melo JSY AU RC 6.00 15.00
155 Jared Cunningham JSY AU RC 6.00 15.00
156 Miles Plumlee JSY AU RC 6.00 15.00
157 Arnett Moultrie JSY AU RC 6.00 15.00
158 Marquis Teague JSY AU RC 6.00 15.00
159 Bernard James JSY AU RC 6.00 15.00
160 Jae Crowder JSY AU RC 15.00 40.00
161 D.Green JSY AU RC 800.00 1,500.00
162 O.Johnson JSY AU RC 6.00 15.00
163 Quincy Acy JSY AU RC 6.00 15.00
164 Khris Middleton JSY AU RC 100.00 250.00
165 Will Barton JSY AU RC 12.00 30.00
166 Doron Lamb JSY AU RC 6.00 15.00
167 Kim English JSY AU RC 6.00 15.00
168 Tyshawn Taylor JSY AU RC EXCH 6.00 15.00
169 Kevin Murphy JSY AU RC 6.00 15.00
170 Kyle O'Quinn JSY AU RC 8.00 20.00
171 Tornike Shengelia JSY AU RC 6.00 15.00
172 Robert Sacre JSY AU RC 6.00 15.00
173 Lance Thomas JSY AU RC 6.00 15.00
174 Gustavo Ayon JSY AU RC 6.00 15.00
175 Greg Stiemsma JSY AU RC 6.00 15.00
176 DeQuan Jones JSY AU RC 6.00 15.00
177 Chris Copeland JSY AU RC 6.00 15.00
178 Brian Roberts JSY AU RC 6.00 15.00
179 Victor Claver JSY AU RC 6.00 15.00
180 K.Thompson JSY AU RC 1,500.00 3,000.00
181 Mirza Teletovic JSY AU RC 8.00 20.00
182 Kent Bazemore JSY AU RC 10.00 25.00
183 Pablo Prigioni JSY RC 3.00 8.00
184 Markieff Morris JSY RC 5.00 12.00
185 Marcus Morris JSY RC 5.00 12.00
186 Ivan Johnson JSY RC 3.00 8.00
187 D.Lillard JSY RC 75.00 200.00
188 John Jenkins JSY RC 3.00 8.00
189 Tony Wroten JSY RC 3.00 8.00
190 Perry Jones JSY RC 3.00 8.00
191 Quincy Miller JSY RC 3.00 8.00
192 Mike Scott JSY RC 4.00 10.00
193 Darius Miller JSY RC 4.00 10.00
194 Alexey Shved AU RC 3.00 8.00
195 Julyan Stone AU RC 3.00 8.00
196 Nando De Colo AU RC 3.00 8.00
197 Jon Leuer AU RC 3.00 8.00
198 Jeff Taylor AU RC 3.00 8.00
199 DeAndre Liggins AU RC 3.00 8.00
200 Viacheslav Kravtsov AU RC EXCH 3.00 8.00

2012-13 Immaculate Collection Gold

*GOLD: .75X TO 2X BASIC
STATED PRINT RUN 25 SER.#'d SETS
53 LeBron James 40.00 100.00
70 Kevin Durant 40.00 80.00

2012-13 Immaculate Collection Numbers Parallel

*NUM.101-182 p/r 40-100: .4X TO 1X BASIC
*NUM.101-182 p/r 15-35: .6X TO 1.5X BASIC
*NUM.183-193 p/r 44-100: .4X TO 1X BASIC
*NUM.183-193 p/r 15-32: .6X TO 1.5X BASIC
*NUM.194-200 p/r 44-55: .4X TO 1X BASIC
*NUM.194-200 p/r 22-30: .6X TO 1.5X BASIC
PRINT RUNS B/WN 1-100 COPIES PER
NO PRICING ON QTY 15 OR LESS
PREMIUM PATCHES MAY SELL FOR MORE
EXCHANGE DEADLINE 5/4/2015
3 Dominique Wilkins/21 20.00 50.00
4 Paul Pierce/34 15.00 40.00
7 Larry Bird/33 30.00 80.00
8 Reggie Lewis/35 15.00 40.00
16 Scottie Pippen/33 60.00 150.00
17 Dennis Rodman/91 25.00 60.00
18 Anderson Varejao/17 6.00 15.00
19 Wayne Ellington/21 6.00 15.00
20 Dirk Nowitzki/41 25.00 60.00
21 Vince Carter/25 25.00 60.00
22 O.J. Mayo/32 6.00 15.00
23 Shawn Marion/30 10.00 25.00
30 Stephen Curry/30 60.00 150.00
32 Chris Mullin/17 25.00 60.00
36 Hakeem Olajuwon/34 20.00 50.00
38 David West/21 8.00 20.00
39 Paul George/24 40.00 100.00
40 Tyler Hansbrough/50 6.00 15.00
42 Blake Griffin/32 6.00 15.00
43 Grant Hill/33 20.00 50.00
44 Kobe Bryant/24 800.00 1,500.00
49 Shaquille O'Neal/34 30.00 80.00
50 Zach Randolph/50 10.00 25.00
51 Marc Gasol/33 10.00 25.00
60 Ryan Anderson/33 6.00 15.00
61 Greivis Vasquez/21 30.00 80.00
62 Kevin Love/42 15.00 40.00
63 Andrei Kirilenko/47 8.00 20.00
69 Kevin Martin/23 8.00 20.00
70 Kevin Durant/35 50.00 120.00
71 Russell Westbrook/100 15.00 40.00
85 J.J. Hickson/21 6.00 15.00
88 Tim Duncan/21 30.00 80.00
90 Manu Ginobili/20 25.00 60.00
91 David Robinson/50 25.00 60.00
92 Sean Elliott/32 15.00 40.00
93 Rudy Gay/22 12.00 30.00
95 Al Jefferson/25 6.00 15.00
96 Pete Maravich/44 60.00 150.00
100 Nene/42 8.00 20.00
164 Khris Middleton JSY AU/32 150.00 400.00
185 Marcus Morris JSY/15 8.00 20.00
186 Ivan Johnson JSY/44 6.00 15.00

2012-13 Immaculate Collection All Star Lineage Autographs

PRINT RUNS B/WN 1-19 COPIES PER
NO PRICING ON QTY 15 OR LESS
EXCHANGE DEADLINE 5/4/2015
KA Kareem Abdul-Jabbar/19 500.00 1,000.00

2012-13 Immaculate Collection Caps

PRINT RUNS B/WN 9-60 COPIES PER
NO PRICING ON QTY 12 OR LESS
AD Anthony Davis/42 150.00 400.00
AM Arnett Moultrie/60 6.00 15.00
AN Andrew Nicholson/31 6.00 15.00
AR Austin Rivers/24 10.00 25.00
BB Bradley Beal/30 30.00 80.00
BJ Bernard James/30 6.00 15.00
BK Brandon Knight/40 15.00 40.00
DD Andre Drummond/19 15.00 40.00
DW Derrick Williams/60 6.00 15.00
DW Dion Waiters/17 8.00 20.00
EF Evan Fournier/18 8.00 20.00
FM Fab Melo/30 6.00 15.00
HB Harrison Barnes/60 15.00 40.00
JC Jae Crowder/30 15.00 40.00
JC Jared Cunningham/30 8.00 20.00
JH John Henson/30 8.00 20.00
JL Jeremy Lamb/60 10.00 25.00
JS Jared Sullinger/27 6.00 15.00
JV Jonas Valanciunas/51 12.00 30.00
KF Kenneth Faried/25 8.00 20.00
KI Kyrie Irving/24 125.00 300.00
KM Kendall Marshall/18 6.00 15.00
KT Klay Thompson/30 125.00 300.00
LE Kawhi Leonard/29 150.00 400.00
MH Maurice Harkless/30 6.00 15.00
MK Michael Kidd-Gilchrist/29 8.00 20.00
ML Meyers Leonard/36 8.00 20.00
MP Miles Plumlee/60 10.00 25.00
MT Marquis Teague/32 6.00 15.00
NC Norris Cole/31 6.00 15.00
PJ Perry Jones/18 6.00 15.00
RS Robert Sacre/45 6.00 15.00
TH Tobias Harris/30 20.00 50.00
TJ Terrence Jones/32 6.00 15.00
TR Thomas Robinson/31 6.00 15.00
TR Terrence Ross/41 20.00 50.00
TT Tristan Thompson/18 12.00 30.00

2012-13 Immaculate Collection Inscriptions

PRINT RUNS B/WN 5-99 COPIES PER
NO PRICING ON QTY 25 OR LESS
EXCHANGE DEADLINE 5/4/2015
AB Alec Burks/99 6.00 15.00
AD Anthony Davis/25 800.00 1,500.00
AE Alex English/99 8.00 20.00
AH Anfernee Hardaway/99 60.00 150.00
AM Arnett Moultrie/99 4.00 10.00
AN Andrew Nicholson/99 4.00 10.00
AR Austin Rivers/99 6.00 15.00
AS Alexey Shved/99 4.00 10.00
BB Bradley Beal/99 60.00 150.00
BG Blake Griffin/25 40.00 100.00
BK Bernard King/99 8.00 20.00
BK Brandon Knight/99 5.00 12.00
BL Bill Laimbeer/99 8.00 20.00
BR Brian Roberts/99 4.00 10.00
BR Brandon Rush/99 4.00 10.00
BS Byron Scott/99 5.00 12.00
CC Chris Copeland/99 4.00 10.00
CD Clyde Drexler/25 60.00 150.00
CJ Cory Joseph/99 5.00 12.00
CO Charles Oakley/99 6.00 15.00
CP Chandler Parsons/99 5.00 12.00
CS Chris Singleton/99 4.00 10.00
DD Andre Drummond/99 12.00 30.00
DD Darryl Dawkins/99 4.00 10.00
DW Derrick Williams/99 4.00 10.00
DW Dion Waiters/99 5.00 12.00
DW Dominique Wilkins/25 40.00 100.00
EC Earl Clark/99 4.00 10.00
GG George Gervin/99 12.00 30.00
GH Grant Hill/25 40.00 100.00
GR Glen Rice/99 5.00 12.00
GS Greg Stiemsma/99 4.00 10.00
HB Harrison Barnes/99 12.00 30.00
HO Hakeem Olajuwon/25 75.00 200.00
IS Iman Shumpert/99 5.00 12.00
IT Isaiah Thomas/99 20.00 50.00
JC Jae Crowder/99 12.00 30.00
JC Jordan Crawford/99 4.00 10.00
JE Julius Erving/25 100.00 250.00
JF Jimmer Fredette/99 6.00 15.00
JH James Harden/99 150.00 400.00
JJ Jim Jackson/99 5.00 12.00
JR Jalen Rose/99 5.00 12.00
JS John Starks/99 5.00 12.00
JS John Stockton/25 75.00 200.00
JS Julyan Stone/99 4.00 10.00
JV Jonas Valanciunas/99 8.00 20.00
JW Jerry West/25 75.00 200.00
KA Kenny Anderson/99 5.00 12.00
KA Kareem Abdul-Jabbar/25 150.00 400.00
KB Kobe Bryant/99 2,500.00 5,000.00
KB Kent Bazemore/99 6.00 15.00
KD Kevin Durant/99 600.00 1,200.00
KI Kyrie Irving/99 600.00 1,200.00
KM Kevin Murphy/99 4.00 10.00
KS Kyle Singler/99 5.00 12.00
KW Kemba Walker/99 25.00 60.00
LB Larry Bird/99 125.00 300.00
LE Kawhi Leonard/99 800.00 1,500.00
LJ Larry Johnson/99 8.00 20.00
LN Larry Nance/99 5.00 12.00
LT Lance Thomas/99 4.00 10.00
MB Muggsy Bogues/99 8.00 20.00
MB MarShon Brooks/99 4.00 10.00
MC Mario Chalmers/99 5.00 12.00
MC Michael Cooper/99 6.00 15.00
MC Maurice Cheeks/99 5.00 12.00
MJ Magic Johnson/25 EXCH 125.00 300.00
MK Michael Kidd-Gilchrist/99 5.00 12.00
MP Miles Plumlee/99 4.00 10.00
MP Mark Price/99 8.00 20.00
MR Micheal Ray Richardson/99 5.00 12.00
MR Mitch Richmond/99 6.00 15.00
MT Marquis Teague/99 5.00 12.00
MT Mirza Teletovic/99 5.00 12.00
NB Nicolas Batum/99 5.00 12.00
NC Norris Cole/99 4.00 10.00
ND Nando De Colo/99 4.00 10.00
NV Nikola Vucevic/99 15.00 40.00
QA Quincy Acy/99 4.00 10.00
RJ Reggie Jackson/99 8.00 20.00
RS Robert Sacre/99 4.00 10.00
RW Royce White/99 4.00 10.00
SC Stephen Curry/99 1,000.00 2,000.00
SE Sean Elliott/99 6.00 15.00
SW Spud Webb/99 5.00 12.00
TH Tim Hardaway/99 12.00 30.00
TK Toni Kukoc/99 12.00 30.00
TP Terry Porter/99 5.00 12.00
TR Terrence Ross/99 8.00 20.00
TR Thomas Robinson/25 4.00 10.00
TS Tornike Shengelia/99 4.00 10.00
TT Tristan Thompson/99 6.00 15.00
VC Victor Claver/99 4.00 10.00
VC Vince Carter/50 100.00 250.00
VK Viacheslav Kravtsov/99 EXCH 4.00 10.00
WB Will Barton/99 8.00 20.00

2012-13 Immaculate Collection Logos

PRINT RUNS B/WN 6-38 COPIES PER
NO PRICING ON QTY 15 OR LESS
PREMIUM PATCHES MAY SELL FOR MORE
AB Andrew Bogut/20 20.00 50.00
AS Amar'e Stoudemire/16 50.00 120.00
CA Carmelo Anthony/21 100.00 250.00
CP Chris Paul/26 125.00 300.00
CP Chandler Parsons/24 20.00 50.00
DD DeMar DeRozan/28 30.00 80.00
DG Danny Green/16 25.00 60.00
DW David West/36 20.00 50.00
EK Enes Kanter/23 20.00 50.00
GH Grant Hill/24 60.00 150.00
HB Harrison Barnes/20 30.00 80.00
IS Iman Shumpert/18 20.00 50.00
IT Isaiah Thomas/28 30.00 80.00
JB Jimmy Butler/17 125.00 300.00
JF Jimmer Fredette/25 25.00 60.00
JN Joakim Noah/17 20.00 50.00
KD Kevin Durant/19 200.00 500.00
KF Kenneth Faried/21 25.00 60.00
KG Kevin Garnett/21 125.00 300.00
KH Kirk Hinrich/26 40.00 100.00
KI Kyrie Irving/21 150.00 400.00
KM Karl Malone/38 50.00 120.00
KT Klay Thompson/19 150.00 400.00
LD Luol Deng/18 20.00 50.00
MB MarShon Brooks/21 20.00 50.00
MT Marquis Teague/25 20.00 50.00
OM O.J. Mayo/20 20.00 50.00
PE Patrick Ewing/16 100.00 250.00
PJ Perry Jones/17 20.00 50.00
RA Ray Allen/26 75.00 200.00
RG Rudy Gay/19 30.00 80.00
RH Roy Hibbert/21 20.00 50.00
RR Rajon Rondo/16 60.00 150.00
RR Ricky Rubio/24 50.00 120.00
RS Robert Sacre/20 15.00 40.00
RW Russell Westbrook/17 150.00 400.00
SO Shaquille O'Neal/36 300.00 600.00
TC Tyson Chandler/16 20.00 50.00
TR Terrence Ross/28 20.00 50.00
TZ Tyler Zeller/16 20.00 50.00
VC Vince Carter/38 200.00 500.00

2012-13 Immaculate Collection Numbers Patches

PRINT RUNS B/WN 4-36 COPIES PER
NO PRICING ON QTY 15 OR LESS
PREMIUM PATCHES MAY SELL FOR MORE
BR Brian Roberts/21 10.00 25.00
AD Anthony Davis/23 200.00 500.00
AJ Amir Johnson/16 10.00 25.00
AM Arnett Moultrie/24 10.00 25.00
AN Andrew Nicholson/20 10.00 25.00
AR Austin Rivers/20 15.00 40.00
BG Blake Griffin/23 75.00 150.00
BL Bill Laimbeer/16 20.00 50.00
CA Chris Andersen/18 12.00 30.00
CP Chandler Parsons/31 12.00 30.00
DD DeMar DeRozan/18 40.00 100.00
DG Danny Green/18 12.00 30.00
DH Dwight Howard/17 30.00 80.00
DN Dirk Nowitzki/19 60.00 150.00
DW Deron Williams/19 12.00 30.00
DW David West/34 12.00 30.00
DY Dwyane Wade/19 100.00 200.00
EF Evan Fournier/23 12.00 30.00
EK Enes Kanter/18 15.00 40.00
GH Gordon Hayward/31 20.00 50.00
GH Grant Hill/28 60.00 150.00
HB Harrison Barnes/16 30.00 80.00
IS Iman Shumpert/30 12.00 30.00
IT Isaiah Thomas/36 20.00 50.00
JB Jimmy Butler/31 50.00 120.00
JD Joe Dumars/23 25.00 60.00
JF Jimmer Fredette/36 15.00 40.00
JH Jrue Holiday/18 20.00 50.00
JH John Henson/20 12.00 30.00
JJ Joe Johnson/15 12.00 30.00
JK Jason Kidd/21 75.00 150.00
JN Jameer Nelson/18 10.00 25.00
JN Joakim Noah/32 12.00 30.00
JS Jared Sullinger/17 12.00 30.00
JV Jonas Valanciunas/20 20.00 50.00
KB Kobe Bryant/32 400.00 800.00
KD Kevin Durant/35 150.00 300.00
KF Kenneth Faried/21 12.00 30.00
KG Kevin Garnett/18 100.00 250.00
KH Kirk Hinrich/23 25.00 60.00
KM Karl Malone/23 25.00 60.00
KS Kyle Singler/29 10.00 25.00
LD Luol Deng/30 12.00 30.00
LE Kawhi Leonard/25 150.00 400.00
ME Monta Ellis/18 12.00 30.00
MG Manu Ginobili/36 50.00 100.00
MH Maurice Harkless/18 20.00 50.00
MK Michael Kidd-Gilchrist/19 12.00 30.00
MT Marquis Teague/35 15.00 40.00
NC Norris Cole/28 10.00 25.00
OM O.J. Mayo/24 10.00 25.00
PE Patrick Ewing/36 60.00 150.00
PP Paul Pierce/34 40.00 100.00
RA Ray Allen/25 50.00 120.00
RG Rudy Gay/29 15.00 40.00
RH Roy Hibbert/21 12.00 30.00
RR Rajon Rondo/21 50.00 120.00
SN Steve Nash/32 25.00 60.00
SO Shaquille O'Neal/32 125.00 300.00
TC Tyson Chandler/18 20.00 50.00
TD Tim Duncan/33 100.00 200.00
TL Ty Lawson/19 10.00 25.00
TP Tony Parker/21 60.00 150.00
TR Terrence Ross/18 25.00 60.00
TS Tiago Splitter/34 10.00 25.00
TT Tristan Thompson/19 15.00 40.00
TZ Tyler Zeller/25 10.00 25.00
VC Vince Carter/21 75.00 200.00
ZR Zach Randolph/18 15.00 40.00

2012-13 Immaculate Collection Patch Autographs

PRINT RUNS B/WN 50-100 COPIES PER
EXCHANGE DEADLINE 5/4/2015
PREMIUM PATCHES MAY SELL FOR MORE
AB Alec Burks/100 10.00 25.00
AD Anthony Davis/100 1,000.00 2,000.00
AE Alex English/100 8.00 20.00
AI Andre Iguodala/100 12.00 30.00
AM Arnett Moultrie/100 6.00 15.00
AM Alonzo Mourning/75 40.00 100.00
AN Andrew Nicholson/100 8.00 20.00
AR Austin Rivers/100 12.00 30.00
BB Bradley Beal/100 125.00 300.00
BG Blake Griffin/100 50.00 120.00
BK Brandon Knight/100 10.00 25.00
BL Brook Lopez/100 8.00 20.00
BR Brian Roberts/100 8.00 20.00
CC Chris Copeland/100 6.00 15.00
CD Clyde Drexler/75 30.00 80.00
CM Chris Mullin/100 20.00 50.00
CP Chandler Parsons/100 10.00 25.00
CS Chris Singleton/100 6.00 15.00
DD Andre Drummond/100 20.00 50.00

DW Dominique Wilkins/80 40.00 80.00
DW Derrick Williams/100 10.00 25.00
EF Evan Fournier/100 10.00 25.00
FE Festus Ezeli/100 8.00 20.00
FM Fab Melo/100 6.00 15.00
GH Grant Hill/100 20.00 50.00
GM Greg Monroe/100 6.00 15.00
HB Harrison Barnes/100 25.00 60.00
HO Hakeem Olajuwon/100 40.00 100.00
IS Iman Shumpert/100 10.00 25.00
IT Isaiah Thomas/100 20.00 50.00
JE Julius Erving/100 60.00 150.00
JF Jimmer Fredette/100 8.00 20.00
JH Jordan Hamilton/100 6.00 15.00
JH James Harden/100 125.00 300.00
JJ Joe Johnson/100 15.00 40.00
JJ Jim Jackson/100 10.00 25.00
JK Jason Kidd/100 25.00 60.00
JN Joakim Noah/100 6.00 15.00
JN Jameer Nelson/100 6.00 15.00
JS John Stockton/50 50.00 120.00
JS Jared Sullinger/100 EXCH 6.00 15.00
JV Jonas Valanciunas/100 15.00 40.00
KA Kenny Anderson/100 6.00 15.00
KA Kareem Abdul-Jabbar/50 50.00 120.00
KB Kobe Bryant/100 2,000.00 4,000.00
KD Kevin Durant/100 100.00 250.00
KE Kim English/100 6.00 15.00
KF Kenneth Faried/100 12.00 30.00
KI Kyrie Irving/100 250.00 500.00
KL Kyle Lowry/100 20.00 50.00
KL Kevin Love/75 25.00 60.00
KM Kevin Martin/100 6.00 15.00
KM Kendall Marshall/100 6.00 15.00
KM Khris Middleton/100 25.00 60.00
KM Kevin Murphy/100 6.00 15.00
KS Kyle Singler/100 8.00 20.00
KT Klay Thompson/100 1,500.00 3,000.00
KW Kemba Walker/100 60.00 150.00
LA LaMarcus Aldridge/100 15.00 40.00
LB Larry Bird/50 75.00 150.00
LE Kawhi Leonard/100 800.00 1,500.00
LN Larry Nance/100 10.00 25.00
LT Lance Thomas/100 6.00 15.00
MA Mark Aguirre/100 6.00 15.00
MB MarShon Brooks/100 8.00 20.00
MH Maurice Harkless/100 12.00 30.00
MJ Magic Johnson/50 EXCH 60.00 150.00
MK Michael Kidd-Gilchrist/100 8.00 20.00
ML Meyers Leonard/100 8.00 20.00
MP Miles Plumlee/100 10.00 25.00
MP Mark Price/100 20.00 50.00
MR Mitch Richmond/100 20.00 50.00
MT Marquis Teague/100 8.00 20.00
NC Norris Cole/100 10.00 25.00
NV Nikola Vucevic/100 20.00 50.00
PJ Perry Jones/100 10.00 25.00
QA Quincy Acy/100 6.00 15.00
RA Ryan Anderson/100 6.00 15.00
RJ Reggie Jackson/100 10.00 25.00
RS Robert Sacre/100 6.00 15.00
RW Royce White/100 6.00 15.00
SC Stephen Curry/100 3,000.00 6,000.00
SE Sean Elliott/100 12.00 30.00
SN Steve Nash/50 30.00 80.00
TC Tyson Chandler/100 10.00 25.00
TG Taj Gibson/100 8.00 20.00
TH Tobias Harris/100 25.00 60.00
TH Tim Hardaway/100 12.00 30.00
TJ Terrence Jones/100 6.00 15.00
TL Ty Lawson/100 6.00 15.00
TR Thomas Robinson/100 6.00 15.00
TR Terrence Ross/100 20.00 50.00
TT Tristan Thompson/100 EXCH 12.00 30.00
TZ Tyler Zeller/100 8.00 20.00
VC Vince Carter/100 20.00 50.00

2012-13 Immaculate Collection Patch Autographs Red

*RED: .5X TO 1.2X BASIC
PRINT RUNS B/WN 2-25 COPIES PER
EXCHANGE DEADLINE 5/4/2015
PREMIUM PATCHES MAY SELL FOR MORE
AD Anthony Davis/25 2,000.00 4,000.00
KB Kobe Bryant/25 3,000.00 6,000.00
LE Kawhi Leonard/25 2,000.00 4,000.00

2012-13 Immaculate Collection Jumbo Patch Autographs

PRINT RUNS B/WN 15-75 COPIES PER
NO PRICING ON QTY 15
EXCHANGE DEADLINE 5/4/2015
PREMIUM PATCHES MAY SELL FOR MORE
*RED: .5X TO 1.2X BASIC
AB Alec Burks/75 25.00 60.00
AB Andrew Bogut/75 20.00 50.00
AD Anthony Davis/75 1,000.00 2,000.00
AI Andre Iguodala/75 20.00 50.00
AM Andre Miller/75 10.00 25.00
AM Arnett Moultrie/75 10.00 25.00
AN Andrew Nicholson/75 10.00 25.00
AR Austin Rivers/75 25.00 60.00
BB Bismack Biyombo/75 10.00 25.00
BB Bradley Beal/75 200.00 500.00
BG Blake Griffin/50 100.00 250.00
BJ Bernard James/75 10.00 25.00
BK Brandon Knight/75 30.00 80.00
BR Brian Roberts/55 10.00 25.00
CA Chris Andersen/25 100.00 200.00
CB Chris Bosh/75 30.00 80.00
CM Chris Mullin/75 30.00 80.00
CP Chandler Parsons/75 20.00 50.00
CS Chris Singleton/75 10.00 25.00
DD Andre Drummond/75 75.00 200.00
DH Dwight Howard/75 40.00 100.00
DL Doron Lamb/75 10.00 25.00
DR Dennis Rodman/50 60.00 150.00
DW Derrick Williams/75 10.00 25.00
DW Dion Waiters/75 EXCH 50.00 120.00
DY Dwyane Wade/25 125.00 300.00
DY Draymond Green/75 200.00 500.00
EF Evan Fournier/75 50.00 120.00
EK Enes Kanter/75 15.00 40.00
FM Fab Melo/75 10.00 25.00
GH George Hill/50 20.00 50.00
GH Gordon Hayward/75 30.00 80.00
GR Glen Rice/35 30.00 80.00
HB Harrison Barnes/75 60.00 150.00
IS Iman Shumpert/75 15.00 40.00
IH Isaiah Thomas/75 40.00 100.00
JB Jimmy Butler/75 200.00 400.00
JC Jared Cunningham/75 10.00 20.00
JC Jae Crowder/75 15.00 40.00
JF Jimmer Fredette/75 15.00 40.00
JH J.J. Hickson/75 10.00 25.00
JH Jordan Hamilton/75 10.00 25.00
JJ Joe Johnson/55 20.00 50.00
JK Jason Kidd/75 100.00 200.00
JN Jameer Nelson/75 10.00 25.00
JR J.J. Redick/75 40.00 100.00
JV Jan Vesely/75 10.00 25.00
JV Jonas Valanciunas/75 20.00 50.00
KA Kenny Anderson/65 15.00 40.00
KA Kareem Abdul-Jabbar/30 250.00 400.00
KB Kobe Bryant/75 5,000.00 10,000.00
KD Kevin Durant/75 800.00 1,500.00
KF Kenneth Faried/75 25.00 60.00
KI Kyrie Irving/75 500.00 1,000.00
KL Kevin Love/75 40.00 100.00
KM Kendall Marshall/75 12.00 30.00
KM Khris Middleton/75 50.00 120.00
KM Kevin Murphy/75 10.00 25.00
KO Kyle O'Quinn/75 10.00 25.00
KS Kyle Singler/75 10.00 25.00
KT Klay Thompson/75 1,500.00 3,000.00
KW Kemba Walker/75 125.00 300.00
LA Lavoy Allen/75 10.00 25.00
LA LaMarcus Aldridge/75 40.00 100.00
LE Kawhi Leonard/75 2,000.00 4,000.00
LP Miles Plumlee/75 12.00 30.00
LT Lance Thomas/75 10.00 25.00
MB MarShon Brooks/75 12.00 30.00
MC Mike Conley/25 25.00 60.00
MH Maurice Harkless/75 15.00 40.00
MK Michael Kidd-Gilchrist/75 30.00 80.00
ML Meyers Leonard/75 12.00 30.00
MP Mark Price/35 100.00 250.00
MT Marquis Teague/75 10.00 25.00
NC Norris Cole/75 12.00 30.00
NV Nikola Vucevic/75 20.00 50.00
OJ Orlando Johnson/75 10.00 25.00
QA Quincy Acy/75 10.00 25.00
RJ Reggie Jackson/75 40.00 100.00
RS Robert Sacre/75 12.00 30.00
RW Royce White/75 10.00 25.00
SC Stephen Curry/75 4,000.00 8,000.00
SN Steve Nash/75 300.00 600.00
TC Tyson Chandler/75 10.00 25.00
TH Tobias Harris/75 15.00 40.00
TR Terrence Ross/75 25.00 60.00
TR Thomas Robinson/75 15.00 40.00
TS Tiago Splitter/75 12.00 30.00
TT Tristan Thompson/75 20.00 50.00
TZ Tyler Zeller/75 10.00 25.00
VC Vince Carter/75 75.00 150.00
WB Will Barton/75 25.00 60.00

2012-13 Immaculate Collection Quads

PRINT RUNS B/WN 10-50 COPIES PER
NO PRICING QTY ON 10
1 Lopez/Williams/Wallace/Johnson 2.50 6.00
2 Kobe/Gasol/Peace/How 75.00 200.00
3 Garn/Pierce/Rondo/Brad 8.00 20.00
4 Durant/Ibaka/Martin/Jack 12.00 30.00
5 Robins/Butler/Booz/Noah 20.00 50.00
6 Fredette/Cousins/Evans/Thomas 4.00 10.00
7 Jennings/Ellis/Ilyasova/Henson 2.50 6.00
8 Leon/Ginob/Dunc/Parker 25.00 60.00
9 Law/Faried/McGee/Iguod 3.00 8.00
10 Holiday/Turner/Allen/Young 4.00 10.00
11 Anthony Davis 100.00 250.00
12 Kyrie Irving 12.00 30.00
13 Bradley Beal 15.00 40.00
14 Kawhi Leonard 100.00 250.00
15 Kenneth Faried 2.50 6.00
16 Dion Waiters 2.50 6.00
17 Andre Drummond 5.00 12.00
18 Damian Lillard 100.00 250.00
19 Harrison Barnes 4.00 10.00
20 Tristan Thompson 3.00 8.00
21 Davis/Beal/Kidd-Gil/Waiters 25.00 60.00
22 Irving/Willi/Kant/Thomp 10.00 25.00
23 Paul/Willi/Felt/Robin 6.00 15.00
24 Hens/Barnes/Marsh/Zel 4.00 10.00
25 Durant/Ald/Thomp/Brad 8.00 20.00
26 Battier/Boozer/Deng/Hill 10.00 25.00
27 Mann/Pierce/Robin/Mor 10.00 25.00
28 Wall/Rub/Westb/Will 5.00 12.00
29 Nowitz/Dunc/Garn/Gasol 8.00 20.00
30 Thom/Stock/Jack/Kidd 8.00 20.00
31 Irving/Lillard 20.00 50.00
32 Kidd/Hill 10.00 25.00
33 Durant/Bryant 125.00 300.00
34 Nowitzki/Garnett 40.00 100.00
35 Irving/Knight 40.00 100.00
36 Drex/Bird/Mullin/Pip 20.00 50.00
37 Ewing/Malone/Robin/Shaq 25.00 60.00
38 George/Hill/James/Wade 75.00 200.00
39 Dunc/Park/Rand/Conley 8.00 20.00
40 James/Bosh/Dunc/Ginob 75.00 200.00

2012-13 Immaculate Collection Veteran Patch Autographs

PRINT RUNS B/WN 5-99 COPIES PER
NO PRICING ON QTY 15 OR LESS
EXCHANGE DEADLINE 5/4/2015
PREMIUM PATCHES MAY SELL FOR MORE
AB Andrew Bogut/25 12.00 30.00
AH Anfernee Hardaway/25 100.00 250.00
BG Blake Griffin/25 100.00 250.00
BK Bernard King/25 12.00 30.00
187 Brandon Knight/25 25.00 60.00
BL Brook Lopez/25 15.00 40.00
CB Chris Bosh/25 75.00 200.00
CD Clyde Drexler/25 75.00 200.00
CM Chris Mullin/25 30.00 80.00
DG Danilo Gallinari/25 12.00 30.00
DH Dwight Howard/25 40.00 100.00
DL Damian Lillard/99 1,000.00 2,000.00
DM Danny Manning/25 12.00 30.00
DR Dennis Rodman/25 200.00 500.00
DR David Robinson/25 125.00 300.00
DW Deron Williams/25 30.00 80.00
DW Dominique Wilkins/25 75.00 200.00
GG George Gervin/25 40.00 100.00
GH Grant Hill/25 75.00 200.00
GP Gary Payton/25 75.00 200.00
HO Hakeem Olajuwon/25 150.00 400.00
IT Isiah Thomas/25 125.00 300.00
JD Joe Dumars/25 30.00 80.00
JE Julius Erving/25 400.00 800.00
JF Jimmer Fredette/25 15.00 40.00
JH Jrue Holiday/25 40.00 100.00
JK Jason Kidd/25 75.00 200.00
JS John Stockton/25 60.00 150.00
JS John Starks/25 25.00 60.00
JW James Worthy/25 100.00 250.00
KB Kobe Bryant/25 5,000.00 10,000.00
KD Kevin Durant/25 800.00 1,200.00
KI Kyrie Irving/25 1,000.00 2,000.00
KL Kevin Love/25 40.00 100.00
KW Kemba Walker/25 50.00 120.00
LE Kawhi Leonard/25 2,000.00 4,000.00
LJ Larry Johnson/25 75.00 200.00
MB MarShon Brooks/25 12.00 30.00
MJ Magic Johnson/25 500.00 1,000.00
MR Mitch Richmond/25 60.00 150.00
NC Norris Cole/25 12.00 30.00
PG Paul George/25 200.00 500.00
RP Robert Parish/25 12.00 30.00
SN Steve Nash/25 200.00 500.00
SP Scottie Pippen/25 300.00 600.00
TH Tim Hardaway/25 25.00 60.00
TL Ty Lawson/25 20.00 50.00
VC Vince Carter/25 500.00 1,000.00
YM Yao Ming/25 1,000.00 2,000.00

2012-13 Immaculate Collection Rookie Red

*RED 101-182: .6X TO 1.5X BASIC
*RED 183-200: .5X TO 1.2X BASIC
PRINT RUNS B/WN 12-25 COPIES PER
NO COPELAND PRICING AVAILABLE
EXCHANGE DEADLINE 5/4/2015
112 Kawhi Leonard/25 2,500.00 5,000.00
187 Damian Lillard/25 200.00 500.00

2012-13 Immaculate Collection Multisport Patch Autographs

PRINT RUN B/WN 5-25 COPIES PER
NO PRICING ON QTY 10 OR LESS
EXCHANGE DEADLINE 5/4/2015
134D Martin Brodeur/25 75.00 150.00
134H Dwight Gooden/25 20.00 50.00
134K Brett Hull/25 30.00 80.00
134N Patrick Kane/25 40.00 100.00
134O Henrik Lundqvist/25 20.00 50.00
134R Alex Ovechkin/25 125.00 250.00
134S Jonathan Quick/25 30.00 80.00
134U Cal Ripken Jr./25 75.00 150.00
134V Patrick Roy/25 75.00 150.00
134W Nolan Ryan/25 100.00 200.00
134ZB Ozzie Smith/25 60.00 120.00
134ZC Jonathan Toews/25 75.00 150.00

2012-13 Immaculate Collection The Immaculate Collection Standard

PRINT RUNS B/WN 5-75 COPIES PER
NO PRICING ON QTY 15 OR LESS
AA Arron Afflalo/75 2.50 6.00
AD Anthony Davis/75 125.00 300.00
AH Anfernee Hardaway/75 25.00 60.00
AM Alonzo Mourning/75 6.00 15.00
AR Austin Rivers/75 4.00 10.00
AS Amar'e Stoudemire/75 4.00 10.00
BB Bradley Beal/75 20.00 50.00
BG Blake Griffin/75 4.00 10.00
BJ Brandon Jennings/75 2.50 6.00
BK Brandon Knight/75 3.00 8.00
BL Brook Lopez/75 3.00 8.00
CA Chris Andersen/75 10.00 25.00
CA Carmelo Anthony/75 15.00 40.00
CB Chris Bosh/75 5.00 12.00
CD Clyde Drexler/75 10.00 25.00
CP Chris Paul/75 25.00 60.00
DC DeMarcus Cousins/75 4.00 10.00
DD DeMar DeRozan/75 5.00 12.00
DD Andre Drummond/75 6.00 15.00
DH Dwight Howard/75 5.00 12.00
DJ DeAndre Jordan/75 3.00 8.00
DL David Lee/75 2.50 6.00
DL Damian Lillard/75 125.00 300.00
DM Danny Manning/75 3.00 8.00
DN Dirk Nowitzki/75 40.00 100.00
DR Derrick Rose/65 12.00 30.00
DR Dennis Rodman/60 20.00 50.00
DW Derrick Williams/75 2.50 6.00
DW Dion Waiters/75 3.00 8.00
DY Dwyane Wade/75 15.00 40.00
GG George Gervin/75 12.00 30.00
GH Grant Hill/75 6.00 15.00
GM George Mikan/50 75.00 200.00
HB Harrison Barnes/75 6.00 15.00
HO Hakeem Olajuwon/75 40.00 100.00
IS Iman Shumpert/75 3.00 8.00
IT Isaiah Thomas/75 5.00 12.00
JB Jimmy Butler/75 10.00 25.00
JC Jose Calderon/75 2.50 6.00
JF Jimmer Fredette/75 4.00 10.00
JH Jrue Holiday/75 4.00 10.00
JH James Harden/75 40.00 100.00
JJ Joe Johnson/75 3.00 8.00
JK Jason Kidd/75 8.00 20.00
JL Jeremy Lin/75 12.00 30.00
JL Jeremy Lamb/75 4.00 10.00
JR J.J. Redick/75 4.00 10.00
JS Josh Smith/75 2.50 6.00
JS Jared Sullinger/75 2.50 6.00
JV Jonas Valanciunas/75 3.00 8.00
JW John Wall/75 10.00 25.00
KB Kobe Bryant/75 125.00 300.00
KD Kevin Durant/75 75.00 200.00
KF Kenneth Faried/75 3.00 8.00
KG Kevin Garnett/75 40.00 100.00
KI Kyrie Irving/75 75.00 200.00
KL Kevin Love/75 4.00 10.00
KM Karl Malone/75 6.00 15.00
KT Klay Thompson/75 75.00 200.00
KW Kemba Walker/75 10.00 25.00
LA LaMarcus Aldridge/75 4.00 10.00
LB Larry Bird/75 40.00 100.00
LB LeBron James/75 125.00 300.00
LE Kawhi Leonard/75 125.00 300.00
MG Manu Ginobili/75 12.00 30.00
MG Marc Gasol/75 4.00 10.00
MK Michael Kidd-Gilchrist/75 3.00 8.00
MM Markieff Morris/75 2.50 6.00
OM O.J. Mayo/75 2.50 6.00
PE Patrick Ewing/75 10.00 25.00
PG Pau Gasol/75 8.00 20.00
PP Paul Pierce/75 6.00 15.00
RA Ray Allen/75 12.00 30.00
RG Rudy Gay/75 4.00 10.00
RL Reggie Lewis/75 12.00 30.00
RR Ricky Rubio/75 3.00 8.00
RR Rajon Rondo/75 5.00 12.00
RW Russell Westbrook/75 6.00 15.00
SC Stephen Curry/75 75.00 200.00
SE Sean Elliott/75 3.00 8.00
SI Serge Ibaka/75 3.00 8.00
SO Shaquille O'Neal/75 40.00 100.00
SP Scottie Pippen/50 15.00 40.00
TC Tyson Chandler/75 3.00 8.00
TD Tim Duncan/75 15.00 40.00
TJ Terrence Jones/75 6.00 15.00
TL Ty Lawson/75 2.50 6.00
TP Tony Parker/75 8.00 20.00
TR Terrence Ross/75 6.00 15.00
TR Thomas Robinson/75 2.50 6.00
TT Tristan Thompson/75 4.00 10.00
TZ Tyler Zeller/75 2.50 6.00
VC Vince Carter/75 15.00 40.00

2012-13 Immaculate Collection Trios

PRINT RUNS B/WN 10-99 COPIES PER
NO PRICING ON QTY 15 OR LESS
1 Laimbeer/Lanier/Cartwright/99 5.00 12.00
2 Griffin/Paul/Jordan/99 15.00 40.00
3 Anthony/Smith/Amare/99 6.00 15.00
4 Dunc/Parker/Gino/99 40.00 100.00
5 Wade/Bosh/James/99 75.00 200.00
6 Olaj/Mourning/Shaq/99 20.00 50.00
7 Durant/Westb/Sefo/99 20.00 50.00
8 Bryant/Gasol/How/99 75.00 200.00
9 Lillard/Davis/Kidd-Gil/99 20.00 50.00
10 Irving/Thom/Faried/99 60.00 150.00
11 Pierce/Rondo/Garn/99 30.00 80.00
12 Rose/Noah/Robin/99 10.00 25.00
13 Bryant/James/Paul/99 125.00 300.00
14 Carter/Carter/Carter/99 40.00 100.00
15 Gasol/Randolph/Allen/99 4.00 10.00
17 Wade/Will/Rondo/99 8.00 20.00
18 Westb/Paul/Harden/99 6.00 15.00
19 Griffin/Curry/Harden/99 30.00 80.00
20 Bird/McHale/Parish/99 12.00 30.00
21 Kareem/Malone/Bryant/25 50.00 120.00
22 Muto/Ewing/Hibbert/99 6.00 15.00
23 Valanciunas/Ilgauskas/Motiejunas/99 5.00 12.00
24 Batum/Parker/Fournier/99 6.00 15.00
25 Nene/Splitter/Varejao/99 3.00 8.00
26 Ginobili/Prigioni/Scola/99 8.00 20.00
27 Biyombo/Ibaka/Muto/25 20.00 50.00
28 Conley/Sulling/Turner/99 3.00 8.00
29 Green/Richardson/Smith/99 15.00 40.00
30 Anthony/Durant/Bryant/99 40.00 100.00
31 Holiday/Love/Collison/99 5.00 12.00
32 Allen/Butler/Drum/99 6.00 15.00
33 Kareem/Wilk/Allen/50 8.00 20.00
35 Lee/Noah/Beal/99 20.00 50.00
36 Pierce/Gooden/Morris/99 6.00 15.00
37 Davis/Cous/Kidd-Gil/99 10.00 25.00
38 Evans/Rose/Hard/99 12.00 30.00
39 Felton/Anth/Chandler/99 6.00 15.00
40 Williams/Johnson/Lopez/99 3.00 8.00
41 Rose/Griffin/Wall/99 12.00 30.00
42 Irving/Williams/Kanter/99 6.00 15.00
43 Davis/Kidd-Gil/Beal/99 30.00 80.00
44 Robin/Richard/Griffin/99 4.00 10.00
45 Nowitzki/Pierce/Irving/99 25.00 60.00
46 Murphy/Olaju/Drexler/75 10.00 25.00
47 Robin/Pip/Stockton/99 10.00 25.00
48 Johnson/Drexler/Mullin/35 12.00 30.00
49 Bird/Malone/Ewing/99 10.00 25.00
50 Cole/Shumpert/Butler/99 25.00 60.00
51 Ewing/Shaq/Robin/99 8.00 20.00
52 Bosh/Gasol/Duncan/99 10.00 25.00
53 Dikembe Mutombo 6.00 15.00
54 Teague/Jack/Wrot/99 4.00 10.00
55 Drum/Henson/Sull/99 6.00 15.00
56 Lee/Curry/Thomp/99 25.00 60.00
57 Waiters/Beal/Rivers/99 20.00 50.00
58 Irving/Thomp/Butler/99 15.00 40.00
59 Dragic/Collison/Jennings/99 4.00 10.00
60 Leon/Barnes/Ross/99 6.00 15.00

2013-14 Immaculate Collection

1-100 PRINT RUN 99 SER.#'d SETS
101-150 PRINT RUN 99 SER.#'d SETS
151-200 PRINT RUN 75 SER.#'d SETS
PREMIUM PATCHES MAY SELL FOR MORE
EXCHANGE DEADLINE 3/3/2016
1 Paul George 4.00 10.00
2 Jeremy Lin 4.00 10.00
3 Dion Waiters 1.50 4.00
4 Anfernee Hardaway 6.00 15.00
5 DeMar DeRozan 3.00 8.00
6 David Lee 1.50 4.00
7 Rajon Rondo 3.00 8.00
8 LeBron James 125.00 300.00
9 Nicolas Batum 2.00 5.00
10 Gerald Henderson 1.50 4.00
11 Roy Hibbert 1.50 4.00
12 Dirk Nowitzki 6.00 15.00
13 Luol Deng 2.00 5.00
14 Allen Iverson 5.00 12.00
15 Kyle Lowry 2.50 6.00
16 Goran Dragic 2.00 5.00
17 Jared Sullinger 1.50 4.00
18 Dwyane Wade 5.00 12.00
19 Kenneth Faried 2.00 5.00
20 Kemba Walker 2.50 6.00
21 Lance Stephenson 2.00 5.00
22 Monta Ellis 2.00 5.00
23 Brandon Knight 2.00 5.00
24 Shaquille O'Neal 10.00 25.00
25 Terrence Ross 2.00 5.00
26 Gerald Green 2.00 5.00
27 Evan Turner 1.50 4.00
28 Chris Bosh 3.00 8.00
29 Ty Lawson 1.50 4.00
30 Arron Afflalo 1.50 4.00
31 Joakim Noah 2.50 6.00
32 Vince Carter 5.00 12.00
33 John Henson 1.50 4.00
34 David Robinson 5.00 12.00
35 Kevin Garnett 6.00 15.00
36 Channing Frye 1.50 4.00
37 Thaddeus Young 1.50 4.00
38 Paul Millsap 2.00 5.00
39 Nate Robinson 1.50 4.00
40 Jameer Nelson 1.50 4.00
41 Carlos Boozer 2.00 5.00
42 Zach Randolph 2.00 5.00
43 O.J. Mayo 1.50 4.00
44 Dennis Rodman 6.00 15.00
45 Paul Pierce 4.00 10.00
46 Kobe Bryant 100.00 250.00
47 Spencer Hawes 1.50 4.00
48 Al Horford 2.50 6.00
49 Kevin Love 2.50 6.00
50 Nikola Vucevic 3.00 8.00
51 Derrick Rose 4.00 10.00
52 Mike Conley 2.50 6.00
53 Blake Griffin 2.50 6.00
54 Wilt Chamberlain 8.00 20.00
55 Deron Williams 2.00 5.00
56 Pau Gasol 4.00 10.00
57 Kevin Durant 25.00 60.00
58 Kyle Korver 2.00 5.00
59 Kevin Martin 2.00 5.00
60 Tony Parker 4.00 10.00
61 Brandon Jennings 1.50 4.00
62 Marc Gasol 2.50 6.00
63 Chris Paul 5.00 12.00
64 Tracy McGrady 4.00 10.00
65 Iman Shumpert 1.50 4.00
66 Steve Nash 5.00 12.00
67 Serge Ibaka 2.00 5.00
68 John Wall 3.00 8.00
69 Ricky Rubio 2.00 5.00
70 Tim Duncan 6.00 15.00
71 Greg Monroe 1.50 4.00
72 Anthony Davis 8.00 20.00
73 J.J. Redick 2.50 6.00
74 Larry Bird 10.00 25.00
75 Carmelo Anthony 4.00 10.00
76 Rudy Gay 2.00 5.00
77 Russell Westbrook 4.00 10.00
78 Bradley Beal 4.00 10.00
79 Richard Jefferson 2.00 5.00
80 Manu Ginobili 5.00 12.00
81 Andre Drummond 2.50 6.00
82 Ryan Anderson 1.50 4.00
83 Stephen Curry 6.00 15.00
84 Magic Johnson 10.00 25.00
85 Tyson Chandler 2.00 5.00
86 Isaiah Thomas 2.00 5.00
87 LaMarcus Aldridge 2.50 6.00
88 Marcin Gortat 1.50 4.00
89 Gordon Hayward 2.00 5.00
90 James Harden 5.00 12.00
91 Kyrie Irving 8.00 20.00
92 Jrue Holiday 3.00 8.00
93 Klay Thompson 8.00 20.00
94 Julius Erving 4.00 10.00
95 Jeff Green 1.50 4.00
96 DeMarcus Cousins 2.50 6.00
97 Damian Lillard 8.00 20.00
98 Al Jefferson 1.50 4.00
99 Enes Kanter 2.00 5.00
100 Dwight Howard 3.00 8.00
101 D.Schroder JSY AU RC 20.00 50.00
102 Ricky Ledo JSY AU RC 5.00 12.00
103 Glen Rice Jr. JSY AU RC 5.00 12.00
104 Shane Larkin JSY AU RC 8.00 20.00
105 Kelly Olynyk JSY AU RC 12.00 30.00
106 Tony Mitchell JSY AU RC 6.00 15.00
107 Alex Len JSY AU RC EXCH 8.00 20.00
108 M.Dellavedova JSY AU RC 20.00 50.00
109 Archie Goodwin JSY AU RC 8.00 20.00
110 Otto Porter JSY AU RC 10.00 25.00
111 Erik Murphy JSY AU RC 6.00 15.00
112 Rudy Gobert JSY AU RC 200.00 500.00
113 Isaiah Canaan JSY AU RC 6.00 15.00
114 Solomon Hill JSY AU RC 6.00 15.00
115 Caldwell-Pope JSY AU RC 10.00 25.00
116 Tony Snell JSY AU RC 8.00 20.00
117 Allen Crabbe JSY AU RC 6.00 15.00
118 MCW JSY AU RC 8.00 20.00
119 Ben McLemore JSY AU RC 8.00 20.00
120 Peyton Siva JSY AU RC 6.00 15.00
121 Gal Mekel JSY AU RC 6.00 15.00
122 Ryan Kelly JSY AU RC 6.00 15.00
123 Jamaal Franklin JSY AU RC 6.00 15.00
124 Steven Adams JSY AU RC 40.00 100.00
125 Luigi Datome JSY AU RC 6.00 15.00
126 Trey Burke JSY AU RC 8.00 20.00
127 Andre Roberson JSY AU RC 8.00 20.00
128 Nate Wolters JSY AU RC 6.00 15.00
129 C.J. McCollum JSY AU RC 125.00 300.00
130 Ray McCallum JSY AU RC 6.00 15.00
131 Antetokounmpo JSY AU RC 15,000.00 30,000.00
132 S.Muhammad JSY AU RC 6.00 15.00
133 Gorgui Dieng JSY AU RC 8.00 20.00
134 T.Hardaway Jr. JSY AU RC 12.00 30.00
135 Mason Plumlee JSY AU RC 8.00 20.00
136 Victor Oladipo JSY AU RC 125.00 300.00
137 A.Bennett JSY AU RC 6.00 15.00
138 Nerlens Noel JSY AU RC 8.00 20.00
139 Cody Zeller JSY AU RC 8.00 20.00
140 Reggie Bullock JSY AU RC 8.00 20.00
141 Pero Antic AU RC 4.00 10.00
142 Sergey Karasev AU RC 4.00 10.00
143 Jeff Withey AU RC 4.00 10.00
144 Dwight Buycks AU RC 4.00 10.00
145 Ian Clark AU RC 5.00 12.00
146 Nemanja Nedovic AU RC 4.00 10.00
147 Raduljica AU RC EXCH 5.00 12.00
148 Phil Pressey AU RC 5.00 12.00
149 Carrick Felix AU RC 4.00 10.00
150 Vitor Faverani AU RC 4.00 10.00
151 Enes Kanter JSY AU/75 8.00 20.00
152 C.Anthony JSY AU/75 40.00 100.00
153 Isiah Thomas JSY AU/75 20.00 50.00
154 S.Curry JSY AU/75 EXCH 1,000.00 2,000.00
155 A.Mourning JSY AU/75 EX 40.00 100.00
156 Abdul-Jabbar JSY AU/75 EX 125.00 300.00
157 Bill Laimbeer JSY AU/75 10.00 25.00
158 Kevin Love JSY AU/75 20.00 50.00
159 David Robinson JSY AU/75 50.00 120.00
160 LaMarcus Aldridge JSY AU/75 10.00 25.00
161 Robert Parish JSY AU/75 12.00 30.00
162 Gary Payton JSY AU/75 30.00 80.00
163 Jared Sullinger JSY AU/75 EXCH 6.00 15.00
164 Tony Parker JSY AU/75 30.00 80.00
165 A. Drummond JSY AU/75 30.00 80.00
166 Karl Malone JSY AU/75 50.00 120.00
167 Bradley Beal JSY AU/75 30.00 80.00
168 K. McHale JSY AU/75 EXCH 15.00 40.00
169 Deron Williams JSY AU/75 12.00 30.00
170 Larry Bird JSY AU/75 200.00 500.00
171 Goran Dragic JSY AU/75 25.00 60.00
172 Ryan Anderson JSY AU/75 20.00 50.00
173 Jerry Lucas JSY AU/75 15.00 40.00
174 Tracy McGrady JSY AU/75 40.00 100.00
175 Andre Iguodala JSY AU/75 12.00 30.00
176 Kelly Tripucka JSY AU/75 8.00 20.00
177 Chris Andersen JSY AU/75 20.00 50.00
178 Chris Mullin JSY AU/75 15.00 40.00
179 Dikembe Mutombo JSY AU/75 15.00 40.00
180 Larry Johnson JSY AU/75 15.00 40.00
181 Greg Monroe JSY AU/75 6.00 15.00
182 Scottie Pippen JSY AU/75 75.00 200.00
183 Anthony Davis JSY AU/75 100.00 250.00
184 Tyson Chandler JSY AU/75 10.00 25.00
185 A. Hardaway JSY AU/75 50.00 120.00
186 Kenneth Faried JSY AU/75 10.00 25.00
187 Manu Ginobili JSY AU/75 60.00 150.00
188 Kobe Bryant JSY AU/75 1,500.00 3,000.00
189 D. Wilkins JSY AU/75 15.00 40.00
190 Magic Johnson JSY AU/75 200.00 500.00
191 Olajuwon JSY AU/75 50.00 120.00
192 S. O'Neal JSY AU/75 125.00 300.00
193 John Starks JSY AU/75 40.00 100.00
194 Sidney Moncrief JSY AU/75 10.00 25.00
195 Bernard King JSY AU/75 12.00 30.00
196 Kevin Durant JSY AU/75 200.00 500.00
197 Darrell Griffith JSY AU/75 8.00 20.00
198 Kyrie Irving JSY AU/75 100.00 250.00
199 Elgin Baylor JSY AU/75 40.00 100.00
200 Dwight Howard JSY AU/75 20.00 50.00

2013-14 Immaculate Collection Autographs Jersey Number

*JSY NUM p/r 26-55: .6X TO 1.5X BASIC
*JSY NUM p/r 15-25: .75X TO 2X BASIC
PRINT RUNS B/WN 1-55 COPIES PER
NO PRICING ON QTY 14 OR LESS
EXCHANGE DEADLINE 3/3/2016
154 Stephen Curry JSY AU/30 2,000.00 4,000.00
155 A. Mourning JSY AU/33 150.00 400.00
156 Abdul-Jabbar JSY AU/33 500.00 1,000.00
157 Bill Laimbeer JSY AU/40 20.00 50.00
158 Kevin Love JSY AU/42 20.00 50.00
162 Gary Payton JSY AU/20 150.00 300.00
168 Kevin McHale JSY AU/32 40.00 100.00
170 Larry Bird JSY AU/33 400.00 800.00
173 Jerry Lucas JSY AU/32 30.00 80.00
178 Chris Mullin JSY AU/17 40.00 100.00
182 Scottie Pippen JSY AU/33 500.00 1,000.00
183 Anthony Davis JSY AU/23 400.00 800.00
187 Manu Ginobili JSY AU/20 800.00 1,500.00
188 Kobe Bryant JSY AU/24 4,000.00 8,000.00
190 M. Johnson JSY AU/32 400.00 800.00
191 Olajuwon JSY AU/34 400.00 800.00
192 S. O'Neal JSY AU/34 500.00 1,000.00

2013-14 Immaculate Collection Christmas Day Materials

STATED PRINT RUN 85 SER.#'d SETS
1 James Harden 10.00 25.00
2 Dwyane Wade 6.00 15.00
3 Tim Duncan 12.00 30.00
4 Jodie Meeks 3.00 8.00
5 Joakim Noah 5.00 12.00
6 Kevin Durant 12.00 30.00
7 Kevin Garnett 6.00 15.00
8 J.R. Smith 5.00 12.00
9 Chris Paul 6.00 15.00
10 Klay Thompson 15.00 40.00
11 Dwight Howard 6.00 15.00
12 LeBron James 20.00 50.00
13 Tony Parker 6.00 15.00
14 Pau Gasol 8.00 20.00
15 Jimmy Butler 10.00 25.00
16 Russell Westbrook 6.00 15.00
17 Deron Williams 4.00 10.00
18 Tyson Chandler 4.00 10.00
19 DeAndre Jordan 4.00 10.00
20 David Lee 3.00 8.00
21 Jeremy Lin 8.00 20.00
22 Chris Bosh 8.00 20.00
23 Kawhi Leonard 10.00 25.00
24 Nick Young 3.00 8.00
25 Carlos Boozer 4.00 10.00
26 Serge Ibaka 6.00 15.00
27 Paul Pierce 8.00 20.00
28 Tim Hardaway Jr. 6.00 15.00
29 Jamal Crawford 5.00 12.00
30 Andrew Bogut 4.00 10.00
31 Chandler Parsons 3.00 8.00
32 Ray Allen 6.00 15.00
33 Manu Ginobili 6.00 15.00
34 Xavier Henry 3.00 8.00
35 Kirk Hinrich 4.00 10.00
36 Reggie Jackson 4.00 10.00
37 Reggie Evans 3.00 8.00
38 Amar'e Stoudemire 5.00 12.00
39 Blake Griffin 6.00 15.00
40 Harrison Barnes 5.00 12.00
41 Terrence Jones 3.00 8.00
42 Mario Chalmers 4.00 10.00
43 Darren Collison 3.00 8.00
44 Stephen Curry 25.00 60.00
45 D.J. Augustin 3.00 8.00
46 Jeremy Lamb 3.00 8.00
47 Mirza Teletovic 3.00 8.00
48 Iman Shumpert 3.00 8.00
49 Jordan Hill 3.00 8.00
50 Andre Iguodala 5.00 12.00

2013-14 Immaculate Collection Elite Scorers Club Signatures

PRINT RUNS B/WN 49-60 COPIES PER
EXCHANGE DEADLINE 3/3/2016
1 Jerry West/49 25.00 60.00
2 Dan Issel/60 8.00 20.00
3 Kobe Bryant/49 2,500.00 5,000.00
4 Carmelo Anthony/60 25.00 60.00
5 Shaquille O'Neal/49 100.00 250.00
6 David Robinson/49 25.00 60.00
7 Larry Bird/49 40.00 100.00
8 Vince Carter/49 15.00 40.00
9 Allen Iverson/49 100.00 250.00
10 John Havlicek/49 30.00 80.00
11 Karl Malone/49 30.00 80.00
12 Oscar Robertson/49 40.00 100.00
13 Julius Erving/49 40.00 100.00
14 Kevin Durant/49 60.00 150.00
15 Adrian Dantley/60 6.00 15.00

2013-14 Immaculate Collection HOF Heroes Signatures

PRINT RUNS B/WN 49-60 COPIES PER
EXCHANGE DEADLINE 3/3/2016
1 David Thompson/60 12.00 30.00
2 David Robinson/49 50.00 120.00
3 Kareem Abdul-Jabbar/49 75.00 200.00
4 Dominique Wilkins/49 15.00 40.00
5 Walt Frazier/60 15.00 40.00
6 Gary Payton/49 25.00 60.00
7 Robert Parish/60 15.00 40.00
8 Artis Gilmore/60 12.00 30.00
9 Kevin McHale/49 20.00 50.00
10 Dennis Rodman/49 60.00 150.00
11 Dan Issel/60 8.00 20.00
12 Hakeem Olajuwon/49 50.00 120.00
13 Bill Walton/60 15.00 40.00
14 Joe Dumars/60 8.00 20.00
15 Elgin Baylor/49 30.00 80.00
16 Bernard King/60 12.00 30.00
17 Magic Johnson/49 75.00 200.00
18 Arvydas Sabonis/60 15.00 40.00
19 Larry Bird/49 75.00 200.00
20 Scottie Pippen/49 75.00 200.00
21 Gail Goodrich/60 8.00 20.00
22 Adrian Dantley/60 6.00 15.00
23 James Worthy/49 15.00 40.00
24 Julius Erving/49 40.00 100.00
25 Jerry West/49 30.00 80.00
26 Isiah Thomas/60 25.00 60.00
27 Jamaal Wilkes/60 10.00 25.00
28 Chris Mullin/60 12.00 30.00
29 Oscar Robertson/49 40.00 100.00
30 Karl Malone/49 40.00 100.00

2013-14 Immaculate Collection Immaculate Standard Materials

PRINT RUNS B/WN 5-75 COPIES PER
NO PRICING ON QTY 10 OR LESS
1 Hakeem Olajuwon/49 20.00 50.00
2 Reggie Jackson/75 4.00 10.00
4 Zydrunas Ilgauskas/65 4.00 10.00
5 Kobe Bryant/75 100.00 250.00
6 Dwight Howard/49 6.00 15.00
7 Shaquille O'Neal/49 40.00 100.00
8 Andray Blatche/75 3.00 8.00
9 John Wall/75 6.00 15.00
10 Dikembe Mutombo/75 8.00 20.00
11 Kevin McHale/25 10.00 25.00
12 Thabo Sefolosha/75 4.00 10.00
14 Walter Berry/75 3.00 8.00
15 Pau Gasol/75 8.00 20.00
16 Chris Kaman/75 4.00 10.00
17 Shaquille O'Neal/49 40.00 100.00
18 Anfernee Hardaway/49 25.00 60.00
19 Michael Beasley/75 3.00 8.00
20 Jimmy Butler/75 12.00 30.00
21 Magic Johnson/25 25.00 60.00
22 Nate Thurmond/25 20.00 50.00
23 Jeremy Lin/75 12.00 30.00
24 Sean Elliott/75 5.00 12.00
25 Kevin Love/75 5.00 12.00
26 Tracy McGrady/49 15.00 40.00
27 Clyde Drexler/75 12.00 30.00
28 Brandon Bass/75 3.00 8.00
29 Andrew Bynum/75 3.00 8.00
30 Jodie Meeks/75 3.00 8.00
31 Larry Bird/75 25.00 60.00
32 Chris Morris/75 3.00 8.00
33 Fat Lever/49 4.00 10.00
34 Kenneth Faried/49 4.00 10.00
35 Norris Cole/75 3.00 8.00
36 Greg Monroe/75 3.00 8.00
37 Ray Allen/75 10.00 25.00
38 Carlos Boozer/75 4.00 10.00
39 DeMar DeRozan/75 6.00 15.00
40 Jordan Hill/75 3.00 8.00
41 Robert Parish/25 10.00 25.00
42 Hal Greer/49 10.00 25.00
43 Tyson Chandler/75 4.00 10.00
44 Omer Asik/75 3.00 8.00
45 Derek Fisher/75 4.00 10.00
46 Grant Hill/75 8.00 20.00
47 Carmelo Anthony/49 12.00 30.00
48 Chandler Parsons/75 3.00 8.00
49 Karl Malone/40 12.00 30.00
50 Kendrick Perkins/75 3.00 8.00
51 Larry Johnson/49 12.00 30.00
52 Lou Hudson/49 3.00 8.00
53 Raymond Felton/75 3.00 8.00
54 Serge Ibaka/49 4.00 10.00
55 Joe Johnson/75 4.00 10.00
56 James Jones/75 3.00 8.00
57 Kevin Durant/49 40.00 100.00
58 DeAndre Jordan/75 4.00 10.00
59 John Stockton/25 12.00 30.00
60 Kirk Hinrich/75 4.00 10.00
61 Larry Johnson/75 12.00 30.00
64 Shane Battier/75 6.00 15.00
65 Dirk Nowitzki/75 12.00 30.00
66 Joe Dumars/75 6.00 15.00
67 Kevin Garnett/75 12.00 30.00
68 Donatas Motiejunas/75 4.00 10.00
69 Udonis Haslem/75 4.00 10.00
70 Luol Deng/75 4.00 10.00

71 Bill Cartwright/49 4.00 10.00
72 Bob Lanier/49 6.00 15.00
73 Jermaine O'Neal/75 4.00 10.00
74 Steve Nash/25 40.00 100.00
75 Shaquille O'Neal/49 20.00 50.00
76 Greivis Vasquez/75 3.00 8.00
77 Paul Pierce/75 8.00 20.00
78 JaVale McGee/75 4.00 10.00
79 David Robinson/49 25.00 60.00
80 Mario Chalmers/75 4.00 10.00
81 Kareem Abdul-Jabbar/25 30.00 80.00
82 Brad Daugherty/75 5.00 12.00
83 Gail Goodrich/75 5.00 12.00
84 Tracy McGrady/49 15.00 40.00
85 Chris Bosh/75 6.00 15.00
86 Jared Sullinger/75 3.00 8.00
87 Dwyane Wade/75 15.00 40.00
88 Jason Kidd/75 8.00 20.00
90 Matt Barnes/75 3.00 8.00
91 John Havlicek/49 15.00 40.00
92 Gus Williams/75 3.00 8.00
93 Iman Shumpert/75 3.00 8.00
94 Moses Malone/49 8.00 20.00
95 Scottie Pippen/75 20.00 50.00
96 Alex English/49 6.00 15.00
97 Al Horford/75 5.00 12.00
98 Jeremy Lamb/75 3.00 8.00
99 Julius Erving/25 20.00 50.00
100 Nick Collison/75 3.00 8.00

2013-14 Immaculate Collection Ink

PRINT RUNS B/WN 60-99 COPIES PER
EXCHANGE DEADLINE 3/3/2016
1 John Wall/60 40.00 100.00
2 Phil Jackson/60 40.00 100.00
3 Joe Johnson/75 4.00 10.00
4 Thaddeus Young/99 3.00 8.00
5 Michael Finley/75 5.00 12.00
6 Alexey Shved/99 3.00 8.00
7 George Karl/75 8.00 20.00
8 John Lucas/99 4.00 10.00
9 Clark Kellogg/99 5.00 12.00
10 Earl Monroe/60 12.00 30.00
11 Luis Scola/99 4.00 10.00
12 Jonas Valanciunas/99 4.00 10.00
13 Derrick Williams/75 3.00 8.00
14 Theo Ratliff/99 3.00 8.00
15 Peja Stojakovic/75 4.00 10.00
16 Darrell Griffith/99 4.00 10.00
17 Kenny Smith/75 4.00 10.00
18 Jimmer Fredette/99 5.00 12.00
19 Eddie Jones/99 6.00 15.00
20 Thabo Sefolosha/99 4.00 10.00
21 Jason Kidd/60 12.00 30.00
22 Al-Farouq Aminu/99 3.00 8.00
23 Christian Laettner/75 5.00 12.00
24 Vin Baker/99 3.00 8.00
25 Walt Bellamy/99 5.00 12.00
26 Bruce Bowen/99 4.00 10.00
27 Andrei Kirilenko/75 5.00 12.00
28 Arvydas Sabonis/99 8.00 20.00
29 Chet Walker/99 4.00 10.00
30 Danny Green/99 4.00 10.00
31 Elgin Baylor/60 20.00 50.00
32 Amir Johnson/99 3.00 8.00
33 Al Horford/75 10.00 25.00
34 Marvin Williams/99 3.00 8.00
35 Brandon Knight/75 4.00 10.00
36 Buck Williams/99 4.00 10.00
37 Don Nelson/75 10.00 25.00
38 Rodney Stuckey/99 3.00 8.00
39 Dwight Howard/60 6.00 15.00
40 Horace Grant/99 8.00 20.00
41 Clyde Drexler/60 12.00 30.00
42 Adrian Smith/99 3.00 8.00
43 Willis Reed/75 40.00 100.00
44 Luc Longley/99 4.00 10.00
45 Gail Goodrich/75 6.00 15.00
46 Bill Laimbeer/99 5.00 12.00
47 Bill Sharman/99 12.00 30.00
48 Connie Hawkins/99 6.00 15.00
49 Scott Skiles/99 4.00 10.00
50 Greg Anthony/99 3.00 8.00
51 John Havlicek/60 60.00 150.00
52 Dave Cowens/60 10.00 25.00
53 Artis Gilmore/75 10.00 25.00
54 Cedric Ceballos/99 6.00 15.00
55 Danny Manning/75 4.00 10.00
56 Antoine Walker/99 4.00 10.00
57 Devin Harris/75 3.00 8.00
58 Bailey Howell/99 8.00 20.00
59 Jared Dudley/99 3.00 8.00
60 Jo Jo White/99 4.00 10.00
61 Ray Allen/60 20.00 50.00
62 Dan Issel/99 6.00 15.00
63 Bernard King/75 6.00 15.00
65 Avery Johnson/75 4.00 10.00
66 Dale Davis/99 4.00 10.00
67 Luol Deng/75 4.00 10.00
68 Billy Paultz/99 5.00 12.00
69 Dirk Nowitzki/60 40.00 100.00
70 Kurt Rambis/99 5.00 12.00
71 Kevin Love/60 15.00 40.00
72 Maurice Harkless/99 3.00 8.00
73 Chris Mullin/75 12.00 30.00
74 Dick Van Arsdale/99 5.00 12.00
75 John Thompson/75 30.00 80.00
76 David Robinson/60 25.00 60.00
77 Steve Francis/75 4.00 10.00
78 Kenneth Faried/75 4.00 10.00
79 John Stockton/60 25.00 60.00
80 Chase Budinger/99 3.00 8.00
81 Tony Parker/75 15.00 40.00
82 Brandan Wright/99 3.00 8.00
83 Walt Frazier/75 12.00 30.00
84 Tom Van Arsdale/99 5.00 12.00
85 Jerry Lucas/75 5.00 12.00
86 Bradley Beal/75 20.00 50.00
87 Mike Conley/99 5.00 12.00
88 Shane Battier/75 4.00 10.00
89 Anthony Davis/60 75.00 200.00
90 Wayne Embry/99 8.00 20.00

2013-14 Immaculate Collection Patches

PRINT RUNS B/WN 1-50 COPIES PER
NO PRICING ON QTY 13 OR LESS
4 Anthony Davis/23 125.00 300.00
5 Dirk Nowitzki/41 125.00 300.00
7 Stephen Curry/30 500.00 1,000.00
8 Tim Duncan/21 150.00 400.00
10 Larry Bird/33 150.00 400.00
13 Paul Pierce/34 100.00 250.00
19 Paul George/24 75.00 200.00
20 Magic Johnson/32 150.00 400.00
22 Karl Malone/32 100.00 250.00
24 Kevin Durant/35 200.00 500.00
27 Harrison Barnes/40 15.00 40.00
29 Blake Griffin/32 25.00 60.00
30 Kevin McHale/32 40.00 100.00
31 Kevin Love/42 10.00 25.00
33 Kemba Walker/15 10.00 25.00
36 DeMarcus Cousins/15 20.00 50.00
40 Kareem Abdul-Jabbar/33 150.00 400.00
42 David Robinson/50 125.00 300.00
46 Isaiah Thomas/22 8.00 20.00
49 Kobe Bryant/24 800.00 1,500.00
50 Dominique Wilkins/21 75.00 200.00

2013-14 Immaculate Collection Player Caps

PRINT RUNS B/WN 45-99 COPIES PER
PREMIUM PATCHES MAY SELL FOR MORE
1 Shabazz Muhammad/99 2.50 6.00
2 Kentavious Caldwell-Pope/84 4.00 10.00
3 Tim Hardaway Jr./80 5.00 12.00
4 Alex Len/73 3.00 8.00
5 Mason Plumlee/75 3.00 8.00
6 Archie Goodwin/45 2.50 6.00
7 Nerlens Noel/79 3.00 8.00
8 Cody Zeller/75 3.00 8.00
9 Reggie Bullock/70 3.00 8.00
10 Isaiah Canaan/70 2.50 6.00
11 Solomon Hill/72 3.00 8.00
12 C.J. McCollum/79 10.00 25.00
13 Trey Burke/99 3.00 8.00
14 Andre Roberson/74 3.00 8.00
15 M.Carter-Williams/60 3.00 8.00
16 Ben McLemore/75 3.00 8.00
17 Otto Porter/90 4.00 10.00
18 G.Antetokounmpo/99 125.00 300.00
19 Ryan Kelly/69 2.50 6.00
20 Kelly Olynyk/60 3.00 8.00
21 Steven Adams/75 12.00 30.00
22 Glen Rice Jr./60 2.50 6.00
23 Victor Oladipo/75 6.00 15.00
24 Anthony Bennett/73 2.50 6.00
25 Jeff Withey/78 2.50 6.00

2013-14 Immaculate Collection Premium Autograph Patches

STATED PRINT RUN 25 SER.#'d SETS
EXCHANGE DEADLINE 3/3/2016
PREMIUM PATCHES MAY SELL FOR MORE
1 Anthony Bennett 12.00 30.00
2 Ben McLemore 15.00 40.00
3 Alonzo Mourning 100.00 250.00
4 Bradley Beal 100.00 250.00
5 C.J. McCollum 150.00 400.00
6 Isiah Thomas 30.00 80.00
7 Andre Iguodala 30.00 80.00
8 Greg Monroe 12.00 30.00
9 Kiki Vandeweghe 15.00 40.00
10 Thaddeus Young 12.00 30.00
11 Shaquille O'Neal 150.00 400.00
12 Chandler Parsons 12.00 30.00
13 Giannis Antetokounmpo 3,000.00 4,000.00
14 Stephen Curry 1,000.00 2,000.00
15 Dee Brown 20.00 50.00
16 Jimmer Fredette 30.00 80.00
17 Jamal Mashburn 15.00 40.00
18 Tony Parker 100.00 200.00
19 Kelly Olynyk 15.00 40.00
20 Mason Plumlee 15.00 40.00
21 Sidney Moncrief 25.00 60.00
22 Dikembe Mutombo 40.00 100.00
23 Anthony Mason 15.00 40.00
24 Al Horford 20.00 50.00
25 Dennis Rodman 50.00 120.00
26 Enes Kanter 15.00 40.00
27 Michael Carter-Williams 15.00 40.00
28 Iman Shumpert 12.00 30.00
29 Larry Johnson 50.00 120.00
30 Nate Wolters 12.00 30.00
31 Tracy McGrady 100.00 200.00
32 Nerlens Noel 75.00 200.00
33 Fred Brown 15.00 40.00
34 LaMarcus Aldridge 60.00 150.00
35 Dominique Wilkins 60.00 120.00
36 Kawhi Leonard 400.00 800.00
37 Jerry Lucas 30.00 80.00
38 Nikola Vucevic 25.00 60.00
39 Larry Nance 15.00 40.00
40 Jared Sullinger 12.00 30.00
41 Vince Carter 50.00 120.00
43 Avery Johnson 15.00 40.00
44 Otto Porter 50.00 120.00
45 Harrison Barnes 75.00 200.00
46 Steve Nash 100.00 250.00
47 Nick Young 40.00 100.00
48 John Stockton 100.00 250.00
49 Monta Ellis 15.00 40.00
50 Tayshaun Prince 20.00 50.00
51 Kobe Bryant 4,000.00 8,000.00
52 Jason Terry 15.00 40.00
53 Paul George 100.00 250.00
54 Bernard King 25.00 60.00
55 Gail Goodrich 20.00 50.00
56 Isaiah Thomas 15.00 40.00
57 Kareem Abdul-Jabbar 150.00 300.00
58 Kevin Durant 350.00 700.00
59 Steven Adams 30.00 80.00
60 Allen Iverson 600.00 900.00
61 Kenneth Faried 30.00 80.00
62 Joakim Noah 20.00 50.00
63 Bill Laimbeer 20.00 50.00
64 Baron Davis 15.00 40.00
65 Gary Payton 50.00 120.00
66 Deron Williams 30.00 80.00
67 Karl Malone 100.00 200.00
68 Chris Andersen 200.00 300.00
69 Dwight Howard 75.00 150.00
70 Anderson Varejao 12.00 30.00
71 Blake Griffin 60.00 150.00
72 John Starks 50.00 120.00
73 Andre Drummond 20.00 50.00
74 Tim Hardaway Jr. 125.00 300.00
75 Grant Hill 50.00 120.00
76 Tyson Chandler 25.00 60.00
77 Kelly Tripucka 15.00 40.00
78 Ryan Anderson 12.00 30.00
79 Tony Snell 15.00 40.00
80 Bill Cartwright 12.00 30.00
81 Kyrie Irving 200.00 400.00
82 Norm Nixon 15.00 40.00
84 Derrick Favors 12.00 30.00
85 Jeff Green 12.00 30.00
87 Kevin McHale 30.00 80.00
88 Spencer Hawes 12.00 30.00
89 Robert Parish 30.00 80.00
90 Kevin Love 250.00 350.00
91 Brandon Bass 12.00 30.00
92 Steve Mix 12.00 30.00
93 Darrell Griffith 15.00 40.00
94 Hakeem Olajuwon 100.00 250.00
95 Gordon Hayward 40.00 100.00
96 Maurice Harkless 25.00 60.00
97 Kevin Willis 20.00 50.00
98 Trey Burke 15.00 40.00
99 Victor Oladipo 150.00 400.00
100 Terry Cummings 15.00 40.00

2013-14 Immaculate Collection Quad Materials

PRINT RUNS B/WN 10-25 COPIES PER
NO PRICING ON QTY 10
1 Hrfrd/Krvr/Millsp/Tg/25 5.00 12.00
2 Walker/Kidd-Gilchrist
Jefferson/Henderson/25 5.00 12.00
3 Crtr/Nwtzk/Cldrn/Ells/25 12.00 30.00
4 Jennings/Monroe
Drummond/Smith/25 5.00 12.00
5 Brns/Thmpsn/Igul/Crry/25 12.00 30.00
6 Prsns/Hwrd/Hrdn/Ln/25 12.00 30.00
7 Stphnsn/Grg/Wst/Hibbrt/25 10.00 25.00
8 Wd/Jms/Alln/Bsh/25 125.00 300.00
9 Anthn/Fltn/Chndlr/Stdmr/25 8.00 20.00
10 Jcksn/Wstbrk/Ibk/Drnt/25 12.00 30.00
11 Lnrd/Gnbl/Prkr/Dncn/25 25.00 60.00
12 DRzn/Vlcns/Lwry/Rss/25 8.00 20.00
13 Dvs/Wtrs/Kdd-Glchrst/Bl/25 8.00 20.00
14 Vlncns/Kntr/Irvng/Thmpsn/25 15.00 40.00
15 Csns/Fvrs/Wll/Grg/25 8.00 20.00
16 Hrdn/Rb/Grffn/Evns/25 6.00 15.00
17 Afflll/Hlld/Lv/Wstbrk/25 6.00 15.00
18 Bzr/Hll/Irvng/Bttr/25 12.00 30.00
19 Brdly/Thmpsn/Drnt/Aldrdg/25 8.00 20.00
20 Cldrn/Gsl/Gsl/Rb/25 8.00 20.00
21 Pl/Mln/Grffn/Stcktn/25 12.00 30.00
22 Hwrd/Hrdn/Brnt/O'Nl/25 100.00 250.00
23 Pytn/Drnt/Wstbrk/Kmp/25 25.00 60.00
24 Rc/Rc Jr./Hrdwy/Hrdwy Jr./25 10.00 25.00
26 Bl/Brdl/Smpsn/Mng/25 12.00 30.00
27 Brynt/Abdl-Jbbr/Jhnsn/O'Nl/25 500.00 1000.00
28 Crtwght/Okly/Wlkr/Ewng/25 12.00 30.00
29 Rbnsn/Rdmn/Rvrs/Jhnsn/25 20.00 50.00
30 Jhnsn/Jffrsn/Mrnng/Hndrsn/25 25.00 60.00
31 Bnntt/Oldpo/Zllr/Prtr/25 6.00 15.00
32 McLmr/Nl/Ln/Cldwll-Pp/25 6.00 15.00
33 McClln/Crtr-Wllms/Adms/Brk/25 6.00 15.00
34 Anttknmp/Olnk/Schrdr/Mhmmd/25 50.00 125.00
35 Wthy/Nl/Gdwn/McLmr/25 6.00 15.00
36 Dng/Brk/Sy/Hrdwy/25 6.00 15.00
37 Schrdr/Gbrt/Anttknmp/Adms/25 50.00 125.00
38 Hrdwy/Brk/Crtr-Wllms/Oldp/25 8.00 20.00
39 Oldp/Olnk/Prtr/Brk/25 8.00 20.00
40 Schrdr/Crtr-Wllms/Wltrs/Brk/25 10.00 25.00

2013-14 Immaculate Collection Scorers Club Autographs

PRINT RUNS B/WN 49-60 COPIES PER
EXCHANGE DEADLINE 3/3/2016
1 Vince Carter/49 20.00 50.00
2 Oscar Robertson/49 40.00 100.00
3 Gary Payton/49 15.00 40.00
4 Paul George/49 25.00 60.00
5 Kareem Abdul-Jabbar/49 30.00 80.00
6 Kevin Durant/49 100.00 200.00
7 Jerry West/49 25.00 60.00
8 Robert Parish/60 10.00 25.00
9 Kobe Bryant/49 3,000.00 6,000.00
10 Clyde Drexler/49 15.00 40.00
11 Shaquille O'Neal/49 60.00 150.00
12 Dominique Wilkins/49 25.00 60.00
13 Larry Bird/49 50.00 120.00
14 Allen Iverson/49 125.00 250.00
15 Bernard King/60 8.00 20.00
16 Karl Malone/49 30.00 80.00
17 Artis Gilmore/60 8.00 20.00
18 Julius Erving/49 40.00 100.00
19 Adrian Dantley/60 6.00 15.00
20 Baron Davis/60 5.00 12.00
21 Tracy McGrady/49 50.00 120.00
22 George Gervin/60 15.00 40.00
23 Rick Barry/49 20.00 50.00
24 David Robinson/49 25.00 60.00
25 Tom Chambers/60 6.00 15.00

2013-14 Immaculate Collection Sole of the Game

PRINT RUNS B/WN 4-55 COPIES PER
NO PRICING ON QTY 10 OR LESS
1 Deron Williams/30 25.00 60.00
2 M.Carter-Williams/35 25.00 60.00
3 David Robinson/45 75.00 200.00
4 Scottie Pippen/45 150.00 400.00
5 John Stockton/25 75.00 200.00
6 Kyrie Irving/40 150.00 400.00
8 Kevin Durant/50 200.00 500.00
9 Anfernee Hardaway/40 50.00 120.00
10 LeBron James/45 1,000.00 2,000.00
11 Kevin Garnett/15 150.00 400.00
12 Victor Oladipo/35 40.00 100.00
13 Carmelo Anthony/25 75.00 200.00
14 Trey Burke/35 25.00 60.00
15 Alonzo Mourning/45 60.00 150.00
16 Blake Griffin/25 40.00 100.00
17 Shaquille O'Neal/55 150.00 400.00
18 Dirk Nowitzki/40 125.00 300.00
19 Patrick Ewing/30 75.00 200.00
20 Anthony Davis/45 75.00 200.00
21 Shawn Marion/30 20.00 50.00
22 Stephen Curry/30 400.00 800.00
23 Kobe Bryant/40 1,000.00 2,000.00
24 Michael Kidd-Gilchrist/35 20.00 50.00
25 Larry Johnson/30 50.00 120.00
27 Grant Hill/35 40.00 100.00
28 Derrick Rose/33 75.00 200.00

2013-14 Immaculate Collection Team Logos

PRINT RUNS B/WN 1-40 COPIES PER
NO PRICING ON QTY 10 OR LESS
5 Al Jefferson/18 30.00 80.00
7 David Lee/22 10.00 25.00
8 Anthony Bennett/16 10.00 25.00
18 Victor Oladipo/21 50.00 120.00
20 Steven Adams/40 25.00 60.00
28 Shabazz Muhammad/36 10.00 25.00
30 Kelly Olynyk/33 12.00 30.00
38 Cody Zeller/15 12.00 30.00
40 G.Antetokounmpo/17 1,500.00 3,000.00
41 Patrick Ewing/15 100.00 250.00
44 Luis Scola/18 12.00 30.00
46 Russell Westbrook/18 100.00 250.00
48 Alex Len/20 12.00 30.00
50 Dennis Schroder/36 75.00 200.00
54 Luol Deng/28 12.00 30.00
58 Nerlens Noel/23 12.00 30.00
60 Gorgui Dieng/40 12.00 30.00
66 Terrence Ross/15 25.00 60.00
68 Ben McLemore/40 12.00 30.00
78 Kentavious Caldwell-Pope/40 15.00 40.00
80 Tim Hardaway Jr./37 20.00 50.00
90 Archie Goodwin/28 10.00 25.00
95 Danny Granger/35 10.00 25.00
98 C.J. McCollum/39 150.00 400.00
100 Nate Wolters/40 10.00 25.00

2013-14 Immaculate Collection Team Logos Numbers

PRINT RUNS B/WN 1-50 COPIES PER
NO PRICING ON QTY 14 OR LESS
2 James Harden/18 150.00 400.00
5 Al Jefferson/24 10.00 25.00
6 Pau Gasol/15 40.00 100.00
8 Anthony Bennett/50 10.00 25.00
10 M.Carter-Williams/50 12.00 30.00
12 Jason Collins/23 10.00 25.00
18 Victor Oladipo/50 25.00 60.00
20 Steven Adams/50 25.00 60.00
22 Jimmy Butler/21 75.00 200.00
28 Shabazz Muhammad/50 10.00 25.00
30 Kelly Olynyk/50 12.00 30.00
35 Blake Griffin/21 60.00 150.00
37 Derrick Favors/28 10.00 25.00
38 Cody Zeller/50 12.00 30.00
39 Shaquille O'Neal/23 200.00 500.00
40 G.Antetokounmpo/50 1,500.00 3,000.00
48 Alex Len/50 12.00 30.00
50 Dennis Schroder/50 60.00 150.00
54 Luol Deng/50 12.00 30.00
58 Nerlens Noel/50 12.00 30.00
60 Gorgui Dieng/50 12.00 30.00
63 John Stockton/18 100.00 250.00
64 Manu Ginobili/38 100.00 250.00
66 Terrence Ross/23 12.00 30.00
68 Ben McLemore/50 12.00 30.00
72 Mason Plumlee/50 12.00 30.00
74 Marc Gasol/28 30.00 80.00
76 Tim Duncan/42 150.00 400.00
78 Kentavious Caldwell-Pope/50 15.00 40.00
80 Tim Hardaway Jr./50 20.00 50.00
84 Michael Kidd-Gilchrist/19 10.00 25.00
88 Trey Burke/50 12.00 30.00
90 Archie Goodwin/50 10.00 25.00
95 Danny Granger/27 10.00 25.00
96 Zach Randolph/18 12.00 30.00
98 C.J. McCollum/50 125.00 300.00
100 Nate Wolters/50 10.00 25.00

2013-14 Immaculate Collection The Greatest Autographs

PRINT RUNS B/WN 49-60 COPIES PER
EXCHANGE DEADLINE 3/3/2016
1 George Gervin/60 15.00 40.00
2 James Worthy/49 EXCH 25.00 60.00
3 Karl Malone/49 40.00 100.00
4 Shaquille O'Neal/49 200.00 500.00
5 Nate Thurmond/60 8.00 20.00
6 Bill Russell/49 1,000.00 2,000.00
7 Kareem Abdul-Jabbar/49 200.00 500.00
8 Larry Bird/49 125.00 300.00
9 Wes Unseld/49 20.00 50.00
10 John Havlicek/49 100.00 250.00
11 Allen Iverson/49 125.00 300.00
12 Kevin McHale/49 25.00 60.00
13 Oscar Robertson/49 75.00 200.00
14 Robert Parish/60 40.00 100.00
15 Dolph Schayes/60 8.00 20.00
16 Nate Archibald/60 12.00 30.00
17 Bill Walton/60 20.00 50.00
18 Magic Johnson/49 125.00 300.00
19 Dwyane Wade/60 125.00 300.00
20 Scottie Pippen/49 125.00 300.00
21 Rick Barry/49 20.00 50.00
22 Isiah Thomas/49 40.00 100.00
23 Julius Erving/49 100.00 250.00
24 Jerry West/49 75.00 200.00
25 Jerry Lucas/60 20.00 50.00
26 Hakeem Olajuwon/49 100.00 250.00
27 David Robinson/49 100.00 250.00
28 Elgin Baylor/49 40.00 100.00
29 John Stockton/49 40.00 100.00
30 Walt Frazier/49 25.00 60.00

2013-14 Immaculate Collection Trios Materials

PRINT RUNS B/WN 10-49 COPIES PER
NO PRICING ON QTY 10
1 Teague/Horford/Korver/49 5.00 12.00
2 Rnd/Brdly/Grn/49 6.00 15.00
3 Wllms/Prc/Grntt/49 8.00 20.00
4 Walker/Jefferson/Kidd-Gilchrist/49 5.00 12.00
5 Butler/Noah/Gibson/49 8.00 20.00
6 Irvng/Wtrs/Thmpsn/49 15.00 40.00
7 Nowitzki/Ellis/Carter/49 12.00 30.00
8 Lawson/McGee/Faried/49 4.00 10.00
9 Drmmnd/Jnnngs/Smth/49 5.00 12.00
10 Igdl/Brns/Crry/49 15.00 40.00
11 Harden/Lin/Howard/49 10.00 25.00
12 Hill/George/Hibbert/49 8.00 20.00
13 Griffin/Paul/Redick/49 10.00 25.00
14 Bryant/Gasol/Nash/49 40.00 100.00
15 Conley/Randolph/Gasol/49 5.00 12.00
16 Wade/Bosh/James/49 60.00 150.00
17 Knight/Sanders/Mayo/49 4.00 10.00
18 Love/Rubio/Brewer/49 5.00 12.00
19 Davis/Evans/Holiday/49 15.00 40.00
20 Fltn/Anthony/Chndlr/49 8.00 20.00
21 Drnt/Wstbrk/Ibk/49 12.00 30.00
22 Aldridge/Batum/Lillard/49 15.00 40.00
23 Cousins/Gay/Thomas/49 5.00 12.00
24 Prkr/Lnrd/Dncn/49 20.00 50.00
25 DeRozan/Lowry/Ross/49 6.00 15.00
26 Fvrs/Kntr/Hywrd/49 4.00 10.00
27 Wall/Beal/Ariza/49 8.00 20.00
28 Horford/Brewer/Noah/49 5.00 12.00
29 Nwtzk/Prc/Crtr/49 12.00 30.00
30 Paul/Williams/Felton/49 6.00 15.00
31 Dvs/Kdd-Glchrst/Jns/49 15.00 40.00
32 Frd/Irvng/Wkr/49 15.00 40.00
33 Wd/Btlr/Mtthws/49 8.00 20.00
34 Jnnngs/Anthn/Smth/49 8.00 20.00
35 Griffin/Harden/Curry/49 15.00 40.00
36 Felton/Barnes/Lawson/49 5.00 12.00
37 Fye/Lee/Hill/49 3.00 8.00
38 Ginobili/Smith/Harden/49 10.00 25.00
39 Griffin/Irving/Lillard/49 15.00 40.00
40 Teague/Duncan/Paul/49 8.00 20.00
41 Schrdr/Giannis/Adms/49 75.00 200.00
42 Plumlee/Bullock/Kelly/49 4.00 10.00
43 Crtr-Wllms/Brk/Oldp/49 6.00 15.00
44 Giannis/Crtr-Wllms/Olnk/49 40.00 100.00
45 Oladipo/Bennett/Porter/49 6.00 15.00
46 Garnett/Plumlee/Morris/49 6.00 15.00
47 Gibson/Snell/Pippen/49 12.00 30.00
48 Englsh/Lrkn/Nwtzk/49 12.00 30.00
49 Irving/Price/Bennett/49 15.00 40.00
50 King/Wall/Porter/25 6.00 15.00
51 Mln/McGrd/Wlkns/49 10.00 25.00
52 Brd/McHl/Prsh/49 15.00 40.00
53 Mrnng/Trpck/Jhnsn/49 10.00 25.00
54 Prsh/Glmr/Prd/25 8.00 20.00
55 English/Lever/Vandeweghe/49 6.00 15.00
56 Thms/Jhnsn/Dmrs/20 10.00 25.00
57 Barry/Free/Lucas/20 6.00 15.00
58 Mkn/Abdl-Jbbr/Chmbrln/20 100.00 250.00
59 Oljwn/Drxlr/Hrry/49 12.00 30.00

2014-15 Immaculate Collection

STATED PRINT RUN 99 SER.#'d SETS
1 Blake Griffin 2.00 5.00
2 Dwyane Wade 4.00 10.00
3 Al Horford 2.00 5.00
4 Ty Lawson 1.25 3.00
5 Carlos Boozer 1.50 4.00
6 Nerlens Noel 1.25 3.00
7 Rajon Rondo 2.50 6.00
8 Larry Sanders 1.25 3.00
9 Serge Ibaka 1.50 4.00
10 Monta Ellis 1.50 4.00
11 Anthony Davis 5.00 12.00
12 Enes Kanter 1.50 4.00
13 Kevin Garnett 5.00 12.00
14 Tim Duncan 5.00 12.00
15 Brandon Jennings 1.25 3.00
16 Damian Lillard 5.00 12.00
17 Pau Gasol 3.00 8.00
18 Victor Oladipo 1.50 4.00
19 Luis Scola 1.50 4.00
20 Isaiah Thomas 1.50 4.00
21 Paul Millsap 1.50 4.00
22 Jonas Valanciunas 1.50 4.00
23 Andrew Bogut 1.50 4.00
24 Bradley Beal 3.00 8.00
25 LeBron James 75.00 200.00
26 Kevin Durant 6.00 15.00
27 Chris Paul 3.00 8.00
28 Channing Frye 1.25 3.00
29 Al Jefferson 1.25 3.00
30 Kobe Bryant 75.00 200.00
31 LaMarcus Aldridge 2.00 5.00
32 Dirk Nowitzki 5.00 12.00
33 Trey Burke 1.25 3.00
34 Roy Hibbert 1.50 4.00
35 Eric Bledsoe 1.50 4.00
36 Kelly Olynyk 1.50 4.00
37 Chris Bosh 2.50 6.00
38 Kawhi Leonard 5.00 12.00
39 Marc Gasol 2.00 5.00
40 Nikola Vucevic 1.50 4.00
41 Joakim Noah 2.00 5.00
42 DeMarcus Cousins 1.50 4.00
43 Kenneth Faried 1.25 3.00
44 Ricky Rubio 1.50 4.00
45 Goran Dragic 2.00 5.00
46 Jeff Teague 1.50 4.00
47 Tim Hardaway Jr. 1.25 3.00
48 James Harden 4.00 10.00
49 Gordon Hayward 1.50 4.00
50 Kyrie Irving 4.00 10.00
51 Michael Carter-Williams 1.25 3.00
52 Josh Smith 1.25 3.00
53 Luol Deng 1.25 3.00
54 Tony Parker 3.00 8.00
55 Joe Johnson 1.50 4.00
56 Jrue Holiday 2.50 6.00
57 Paul George 3.00 8.00
58 DeMar DeRozan 2.50 6.00
59 Chandler Parsons 1.25 3.00
60 Zach Randolph 2.00 5.00
61 Nicolas Batum 1.50 4.00
62 Lance Stephenson 1.50 4.00
63 Jeremy Lin 4.00 10.00
64 Carmelo Anthony 3.00 8.00
65 Arron Afflalo 1.25 3.00
66 Brandon Knight 1.25 3.00
67 John Wall 2.50 6.00
68 Jared Sullinger 1.25 3.00
69 Ben McLemore 1.25 3.00
70 Stephen Curry 30.00 80.00
71 Thaddeus Young 1.25 3.00
72 Tony Wroten 1.25 3.00
73 Kevin Love 2.00 5.00
74 Mike Conley 1.50 4.00
75 Omer Asik 1.25 3.00
76 Kemba Walker 2.00 5.00
77 Russell Westbrook 3.00 8.00
78 Trevor Ariza 1.25 3.00
79 Rudy Gay 2.00 5.00
80 Derrick Rose 4.00 10.00
81 Iman Shumpert 1.25 3.00
82 Dwight Howard 2.50 6.00
83 Ersan Ilyasova 1.25 3.00
84 Paul Pierce 3.00 8.00
85 Deron Williams 1.50 4.00
86 Nikola Pekovic 1.25 3.00
87 DeAndre Jordan 1.50 4.00
88 Kyle Lowry 2.50 6.00
89 Andre Drummond 1.50 4.00
90 Klay Thompson 5.00 12.00
91 Wilt Chamberlain 6.00 15.00
92 Hakeem Olajuwon 4.00 10.00
93 Larry Bird 8.00 20.00
94 Karl Malone 4.00 10.00
95 Bill Russell 6.00 15.00
96 Kareem Abdul-Jabbar 6.00 15.00
97 Shaquille O'Neal 8.00 20.00
98 David Robinson 4.00 10.00
99 Julius Erving 5.00 12.00
100 Magic Johnson 8.00 20.00
101 A. Wiggins JSY AU RC 150.00 400.00
102 Jabari Parker JSY AU RC 8.00 20.00
103 Julius Randle JSY AU RC 300.00 600.00
104 Joel Embiid JSY AU RC 1,500.00 3,000.00
105 Dante Exum JSY AU RC 10.00 25.00
107 Marcus Smart JSY AU RC 30.00 80.00
108 Cleanthony Early JSY AU RC 6.00 15.00
110 Aaron Gordon JSY AU RC 100.00 250.00
111 Elfrid Payton JSY AU RC 30.00 80.00
112 Bruno Caboclo JSY AU RC 8.00 20.00
113 James Ennis JSY AU RC 6.00 15.00
114 Gary Harris JSY AU RC 10.00 25.00
115 Glenn Robinson III JSY AU RC 8.00 20.00
116 Cory Jefferson JSY AU RC 6.00 15.00
118 Russ Smith JSY AU RC 6.00 15.00
119 Zach LaVine JSY AU RC 1,500.00 3,000.00
120 Spencer Dinwiddie JSY AU RC 40.00 100.00
121 Rodney Hood JSY AU RC 8.00 20.00
122 T.J. Warren JSY AU RC 75.00 200.00
123 Tyler Ennis JSY AU RC 6.00 15.00
124 Jordan Adams JSY AU RC 6.00 15.00
125 D. McDermott JSY AU RC 10.00 25.00
126 Adreian Payne JSY AU RC 6.00 15.00
127 K.J. McDaniels JSY AU RC 6.00 15.00
128 Nik Stauskas JSY AU RC 6.00 15.00
129 Noah Vonleh JSY AU RC 6.00 15.00
131 Johnny O'Bryant JSY AU RC 6.00 15.00
132 Jarnell Stokes JSY AU RC 6.00 15.00
133 Damien Inglis JSY AU RC 6.00 15.00
134 Markel Brown JSY AU RC 6.00 15.00
136 C.J. Wilcox JSY AU RC 6.00 15.00
137 P.J. Hairston JSY AU RC 6.00 15.00
138 Joe Harris JSY AU RC 20.00 50.00
139 Zoran Dragic AU RC 6.00 15.00
140 Damjan Rudez AU RC 6.00 15.00
141 Jordan Clarkson AU RC 30.00 80.00
143 Lucas Nogueira AU RC 6.00 15.00
145 Erick Green AU RC 6.00 15.00
146 Nikola Mirotic AU RC 10.00 25.00
147 Devyn Marble AU RC 6.00 15.00

2014-15 Immaculate Collection Red

*RED: .6X TO 1.5X BASE HI
STATED PRINT RUN 25 SER.#'d SETS
97 Shaquille O'Neal 8.00 20.00

2014-15 Immaculate Collection Rookie Autographs Jersey Number

STATED PRINT RUN B/WN 6-92 COPIES PER
NO PRICING ON QTY 11 OR LESS
142 Cameron Bairstow/41 20.00 50.00
143 Lucas Nogueira/92 8.00 20.00
146 Nikola Mirotic/44 40.00 100.00

2014-15 Immaculate Collection Rookie Patch Autographs Jersey Number

*JSY NUMBER: 1.5X TO 4X BASE HI
STATED PRINT RUN B/WN 1-36 COPIES PER
NO PRICING ON QTY 14 OR LESS

2014-15 Immaculate Collection Dual Autographs

STATED PRINT RUN 49 SER.#'d SETS
DAAA A.Wiggins/A.Bennett 30.00 80.00
DAAJ A.Davis/J.Wall 150.00 400.00
DAAS A.Iguodala/S.Curry 400.00 800.00
DABJ B.Beal/J.Wall 100.00 250.00
DADT D.Exum/T.Burke 15.00 40.00
DAGI G.Dragic/I.Thomas 15.00 40.00
DAGJ Antetokounmpo/J.Parker 300.00 600.00
DAIJ I.Thomas/J.Dumars 60.00 150.00
DAJK J.Randle/K.Bryant 1,500.00 3,000.00
DAJK J.Stockton/K.Malone 400.00 800.00
DAMM M.Morris/M.Morris 10.00 25.00
DATD D.Green/T.Parker 40.00 100.00
DAVZ V.Carter/Z.Randolph 60.00 150.00

2014-15 Immaculate Collection Dual Memorabilia

STATED PRINT RUN B/WN 25-99 COPIES PER
DMAG Aaron Gordon/99 10.00 25.00
DMAH Anfernee Hardaway/49 8.00 20.00
DMAW Andrew Wiggins/99 10.00 25.00
DMBG Blake Griffin/49 3.00 8.00
DMBK Brandon Knight/49 2.00 5.00
DMCA Carmelo Anthony/99 5.00 12.00
DMCB Chris Bosh/99 4.00 10.00
DMCD Clyde Drexler/25 5.00 12.00
DMCP Chris Paul/49 5.00 12.00
DMDC DeMarcus Cousins/99 2.50 6.00
DMDD DeMar DeRozan/99 4.00 10.00
DMDE Dante Exum/99 3.00 8.00
DMDM Dikembe Mutombo/49 5.00 12.00
DMDN Dirk Nowitzki/99 12.00 30.00
DMDW Dwyane Wade/99 12.00 30.00
DMEB Eric Bledsoe/99 2.50 6.00
DMEP Elfrid Payton/99 3.00 8.00
DMGD Goran Dragic/99 3.00 8.00
DMGH Grant Hill/25 12.00 30.00
DMGM Greg Monroe/99 2.00 5.00
DMGP Gary Payton/99 6.00 15.00
DMHO Hakeem Olajuwon/25 8.00 20.00
DMJB Jimmy Butler/49 6.00 15.00
DMJE Joel Embiid/99 75.00 200.00
DMJH James Harden/99 10.00 25.00
DMJP Jabari Parker/99 2.50 6.00
DMJR Julius Randle/99 10.00 25.00
DMJS Jared Sullinger/99 2.00 5.00
DMJT Jeff Teague/99 2.00 5.00
DMJW John Wall/99 4.00 10.00
DMJY James Young/99 2.00 5.00
DMKA Kareem Abdul-Jabbar/25 50.00 120.00
DMKB Kobe Bryant/99 150.00 400.00
DMKD Kevin Durant/99 15.00 40.00
DMKF Kenneth Faried/99 2.00 5.00
DMKG Kevin Garnett/99 8.00 20.00
DMKI Kyrie Irving/99 6.00 15.00
DMKL Kawhi Leonard/99 8.00 20.00
DMKL Kevin Love/49 3.00 8.00
DMKM K.J. McDaniels/99 2.00 5.00
DMKM Karl Malone/25 6.00 15.00
DMKT Klay Thompson/99 8.00 20.00
DMLB Larry Bird/25 12.00 30.00
DMLJ Larry Johnson/99 4.00 10.00
DMMS Marcus Smart/99 8.00 20.00
DMNB Nicolas Batum/99 2.50 6.00
DMNN Nerlens Noel/99 2.00 5.00
DMPE Patrick Ewing/25 5.00 12.00
DMRR Ricky Rubio/99 2.50 6.00
DMRW Russell Westbrook/99 5.00 12.00
DMSC Stephen Curry/99 125.00 300.00
DMSN Shabazz Napier/99 2.50 6.00
DMSO Shaquille O'Neal/25 20.00 50.00
DMTD Tim Duncan/49 12.00 30.00
DMTE Tyreke Evans/99 2.50 6.00
DMVO Victor Oladipo/99 2.50 6.00
DMZL Zach LaVine/99 12.00 30.00
DMZR Zach Randolph/99 3.00 8.00
DMDMC Doug McDermott/99 3.00 8.00
DMLBJ LeBron James/99 150.00 400.00
DMMCW M.Carter-Williams/99 2.00 5.00
DMMKG Michael Kidd-Gilchrist/99 2.00 5.00

2014-15 Immaculate Collection HOF Heroes Signatures

STATED PRINT RUN 75 SER.#'d SETS
1 Gary Payton 15.00 40.00
2 Alonzo Mourning 15.00 40.00
4 Larry Bird 75.00 200.00
5 George Gervin 15.00 40.00
6 Hakeem Olajuwon 40.00 100.00
7 Dennis Rodman 40.00 100.00
8 Walt Frazier 15.00 40.00
9 Jerry West 30.00 80.00
10 Julius Erving 40.00 100.00
11 Clyde Drexler 15.00 40.00
12 John Stockton 30.00 80.00
13 James Worthy 15.00 40.00
15 Willis Reed 75.00 200.00
17 Robert Parish 12.00 30.00
18 Ralph Sampson 10.00 25.00
19 Rick Barry 12.00 30.00
20 Kareem Abdul-Jabbar 75.00 200.00
21 Dan Issel 12.00 30.00
22 David Thompson 10.00 25.00
23 Joe Dumars 12.00 30.00
24 Earl Monroe 15.00 40.00
25 Magic Johnson 75.00 200.00

2014-15 Immaculate Collection Immaculate Standard Materials

STATED PRINT RUN B/WN 25-99 COPIES PER
1 LeBron James/50 125.00 300.00
2 Dion Waiters/75 2.50 6.00
3 Pau Gasol/75 6.00 15.00
4 Goran Dragic/50 4.00 10.00
5 Aaron Gordon/75 12.00 30.00
6 T.J. Warren/75 4.00 10.00
7 Jeff Green/75 3.00 8.00
8 Ben McLemore/50 2.50 6.00
9 Karl Malone/50 8.00 20.00
10 Chris Bosh/75 5.00 12.00
11 Luc Longley/50 3.00 8.00
12 Dirk Nowitzki/50 10.00 25.00
13 Ricky Rubio/75 3.00 8.00
14 Grant Hill/50 6.00 15.00
15 Terrence Ross/50 3.00 8.00
16 Al Horford/75 4.00 10.00
17 Jeremy Lin/75 8.00 20.00
18 Bernard King/25 5.00 12.00
19 Kenneth Faried/75 2.50 6.00
20 Marcus Smart/75 10.00 25.00
21 Chris Mullin/25 8.00 20.00
22 Dominique Wilkins/25 10.00 25.00
23 Greg Monroe/75 2.50 6.00
24 Robert Parish/25 5.00 12.00
25 Tim Hardaway Jr./75 3.00 8.00
26 Alex English/25 5.00 12.00
27 Joe Harris/75 4.00 10.00
28 Bill Laimbeer/25 4.00 10.00
29 Kevin Duckworth/75 2.50 6.00
30 Cleanthony Early/75 2.50 6.00
31 Moses Malone/25 10.00 25.00
32 Doug McDermott/75 4.00 10.00
33 Rodney Hood/75 3.00 8.00
34 Hakeem Olajuwon/25 10.00 25.00
35 Tristan Thompson/75 2.50 6.00
36 Alex Len/75 2.50 6.00
37 Joel Embiid/75 25.00 60.00
38 Blake Griffin/25 4.00 10.00
39 Kevin Garnett/75 12.00 30.00
40 Clifford Robinson/75 4.00 10.00
41 Nik Stauskas/75 2.50 6.00
42 Dwyane Wade/75 12.00 30.00
43 Rudy Gay/50 4.00 10.00
45 Tyler Ennis/75 2.50 6.00
46 Allen Iverson/25 25.00 60.00
47 John Starks/25 8.00 20.00
48 Brandon Knight/75 2.50 6.00
49 Kevin Love/25 4.00 10.00
50 Clyde Drexler/25 12.00 30.00
51 Noah Vonleh/75 2.50 6.00
52 Elfrid Payton/75 4.00 10.00
53 Scottie Pippen/25 15.00 40.00
54 Jabari Parker/75 3.00 8.00

55 Tyson Chandler/75 4.00 10.00
56 Alonzo Mourning/75 6.00 15.00
57 John Wall/75 5.00 12.00
58 Brook Lopez/75 4.00 10.00
59 Kevin McHale/25 10.00 25.00
60 Clyde Drexler/25 10.00 25.00
61 Norris Cole/75 2.50 6.00
62 Gary Harris/75 4.00 10.00
63 Shabazz Napier/75 3.00 8.00
64 James Worthy/25 6.00 15.00
65 Walter Davis/75 3.00 8.00
66 Amar'e Stoudemire/75 4.00 10.00
68 Bruno Caboclo/75 3.00 8.00
69 Kobe Bryant/75 125.00 300.00
70 Cody Zeller/75 2.50 6.00
71 Otto Porter/75 3.00 8.00
72 Gary Payton/25 10.00 25.00
73 Shaquille O'Neal/25 30.00 80.00
74 James Young/75 2.50 6.00
75 Zach LaVine/75 20.00 50.00
76 Anderson Varejao/75 2.50 6.00
77 Julius Randle/75 12.00 30.00
78 Larry Bird/25 15.00 40.00
79 Byron Scott/25 4.00 10.00
80 Dante Exum/75 4.00 10.00
81 P.J. Hairston/75 2.50 6.00
83 Shaquille O'Neal/75 30.00 80.00
84 Jared Sullinger/75 2.50 6.00
86 Andrew Wiggins/75 12.00 30.00
87 K.J. McDaniels/75 2.50 6.00
88 Cedric Maxwell/75 3.00 8.00
89 Larry Johnson/50 5.00 12.00
90 David Robinson/25 12.00 30.00
91 Patrick Ewing/50 10.00 25.00
92 Glenn Robinson III/75 3.00 8.00
93 Shaquille O'Neal/25 30.00 80.00
94 Jason Kidd/25 8.00 20.00
96 Anfernee Hardaway/25 15.00 40.00
97 Kareem Abdul-Jabbar/25 30.00 80.00
98 Chris Andersen/75 3.00 8.00
99 Larry Johnson/25 12.00 30.00
100 Dikembe Mutombo/75 6.00 15.00

2014-15 Immaculate Collection Ink

STATED PRINT RUN B/WN 49-99 COPIES PER
1 Paul George/99 15.00 40.00
2 Carmelo Anthony/49 25.00 60.00
3 Steve Nash/49 40.00 100.00
4 Ray Allen/49 15.00 40.00
5 Michael Kidd-Gilchrist/49 4.00 10.00
6 Zach Randolph/75 6.00 15.00
7 Bradley Beal/75 10.00 25.00
8 Ben McLemore/75 4.00 10.00
9 Michael Carter-Williams/75 4.00 10.00
10 Brandon Knight/75 4.00 10.00
11 John Stockton/49 40.00 100.00
12 Julius Erving/49 75.00 200.00
13 Jerry West/49 40.00 100.00
14 David Robinson/49 75.00 200.00
15 Pat Riley/49 20.00 50.00
16 Earl Monroe/49 12.00 30.00
17 Kevin McHale/49 25.00 60.00
18 Hakeem Olajuwon/49 75.00 200.00
19 Clyde Drexler/49 40.00 100.00
20 Dennis Rodman/49 75.00 200.00
21 John Havlicek/49 75.00 200.00
22 Elgin Baylor/49 75.00 200.00
23 Gary Payton/49 10.00 25.00
24 James Worthy/49 20.00 50.00
25 Dominique Wilkins/49 12.00 30.00
26 Rick Barry/75 8.00 20.00
27 Sam Jones/75 15.00 40.00
28 Willis Reed/75 40.00 100.00
29 Chris Mullin/75 8.00 20.00
30 Artis Gilmore/75 8.00 20.00
31 Walt Frazier/75 20.00 50.00
32 Don Nelson/75 15.00 40.00
33 George Gervin/75 15.00 40.00
34 Gail Goodrich/75 6.00 15.00
35 Joe Dumars/75 8.00 20.00
36 Dick Vitale/75 10.00 25.00
37 Hal Greer/75 6.00 15.00
38 Nate Thurmond/75 8.00 20.00
39 Robert Parish/75 15.00 40.00
40 Dolph Schayes/75 6.00 15.00
41 Glen Rice/99 6.00 15.00
42 Chet Walker/99 5.00 12.00
43 Dale Ellis/99 5.00 12.00
44 Bonzi Wells/99 4.00 10.00
45 Bob Lanier/75 8.00 20.00
46 Bryon Russell/99 4.00 10.00
47 Earl Lloyd/99 6.00 15.00
48 Connie Hawkins/99 12.00 30.00
49 Marques Johnson/99 5.00 12.00
50 Steve Kerr/75 20.00 50.00
51 Shaquille O'Neal/49 125.00 300.00
52 Yao Ming/49 125.00 300.00
53 Tracy McGrady/49 40.00 100.00
54 Anfernee Hardaway/49 40.00 100.00
55 Grant Hill/49 15.00 40.00
56 Christian Laettner/75 8.00 20.00
57 Baron Davis/75 6.00 15.00
58 Brent Barry/75 4.00 10.00
59 Byron Scott/75 8.00 20.00
60 Bill Walton/75 10.00 25.00
61 Latrell Sprewell/75 15.00 40.00
62 Dave Bing/75 15.00 40.00
63 Vinny Del Negro/75 5.00 12.00
64 Kenny Smith/75 5.00 12.00
65 Dikembe Mutombo/99 10.00 25.00
66 Chuck Person/99 6.00 15.00
67 Tim Hardaway/99 12.00 30.00
68 Allan Houston/99 6.00 15.00
69 Toni Kukoc/99 8.00 20.00
70 Kurt Rambis/99 6.00 15.00
71 Adrian Smith/99 5.00 12.00
72 Horace Grant/99 6.00 15.00
73 Scott Brooks/99 4.00 10.00
74 George Karl/99 6.00 15.00
75 Vlade Divac/99 6.00 15.00
76 Chris Paul/49 50.00 120.00
77 Nate Archibald/49 8.00 20.00
78 Goran Dragic/49 4.00 10.00
79 Michael Cooper/49 4.00 10.00
80 Marcin Gortat/49 4.00 10.00
81 Wes Unseld/99 20.00 50.00
82 Elvin Hayes/75 10.00 25.00
83 Karl Malone/49 20.00 50.00
84 Wesley Matthews/99 4.00 10.00
85 Jrue Holiday/49 10.00 25.00
86 Brook Lopez/49 6.00 15.00
87 Bailey Howell/49 8.00 20.00
88 Derrick Favors/75 4.00 10.00
89 Alonzo Mourning/49 40.00 100.00
90 Manu Ginobili/49 75.00 200.00

2014-15 Immaculate Collection Ink Red

*RED: .6X TO 1.5X BASE HI
STATED PRINT RUN 25 SER.#'d SETS

2014-15 Immaculate Collection NBA Champions Autographs

STATED PRINT RUN 75 SER.#'d SETS
1 Mychal Thompson 8.00 20.00
2 B.J. Armstrong 8.00 20.00
3 Tony Parker 20.00 50.00
5 Clyde Drexler 40.00 100.00
6 Kobe Bryant 2,500.00 5,000.00
7 Shaquille O'Neal 150.00 400.00
8 Larry Bird 125.00 300.00
9 Robert Horry 15.00 40.00
10 Jason Terry 6.00 15.00
11 Toni Kukoc 12.00 30.00
12 Dennis Rodman 100.00 250.00
13 Bill Walton 20.00 50.00
14 David Robinson 100.00 250.00
16 Hakeem Olajuwon 100.00 250.00
17 Tiago Splitter 5.00 12.00
18 A.C. Green 8.00 20.00
19 Ray Allen 40.00 100.00
20 Magic Johnson 125.00 300.00

2014-15 Immaculate Collection Patches

STATED PRINT RUN B/WN 1-55 COPIES PER
NO PRICING ON QTY 17 OR LESS
PAD Anthony Davis/23 25.00 60.00
PAJ Al Jefferson/25 5.00 12.00
PAM Alonzo Mourning/33 25.00 60.00
PBK Bernard King/30 12.00 30.00
PCZ Cody Zeller/40 5.00 12.00
PDG Draymond Green/23 30.00 80.00
PDM Dikembe Mutombo/55 12.00 30.00
PDN Dirk Nowitzki/41 20.00 50.00
PDR David Robinson/50 20.00 50.00
PGP Gary Payton/20 20.00 50.00
PHO Hakeem Olajuwon/34 20.00 50.00
PJB Jimmy Butler/21 20.00 50.00
PJG Jeff Green/32 6.00 15.00
PJK Jason Kidd/32 20.00 50.00
PKA Kareem Abdul-Jabbar/33 20.00 50.00
PKF Kenneth Faried/35 5.00 12.00
PKK Kyle Korver/26 6.00 15.00
PLB Larry Bird/33 30.00 80.00
PLN Larry Nance/22 6.00 15.00
PNE Nene/42 6.00 15.00
PPE Patrick Ewing/33 15.00 40.00
PPP Paul Pierce/34 15.00 40.00
PRH Roy Hibbert/55 6.00 15.00
PSM Shawn Marion/31 6.00 15.00
PSO Shaquille O'Neal/32 30.00 80.00
PTD Tim Duncan/21 20.00 50.00
PTR Terrence Ross/31 6.00 15.00
PDWE David West/21 6.00 15.00
PDWI Dominique Wilkins/21 12.00 30.00
PGHI Grant Hill/33 12.00 30.00
PKMA Karl Malone/32 15.00 40.00
PKMC Kevin McHale/32 12.00 30.00
PLBJ LeBron James/23 150.00 400.00

2014-15 Immaculate Collection Patches Autographs

STATED PRINT RUN B/WN 60-75 COPIES PER
16 Jeff Teague/75 6.00 15.00
PAAL Al Horford/75 8.00 20.00
PABG Blake Griffin/75 40.00 100.00
PABS Byron Scott/75 6.00 15.00
PACA Carmelo Anthony/75 75.00 200.00
PACL Carl Landry/75 6.00 15.00
PADF Derrick Favors/75 6.00 15.00
PADR David Robinson/75 75.00 200.00
PAGD Goran Dragic/75 10.00 25.00
PAIS Iman Shumpert/75 6.00 15.00
PAIT Isaiah Thomas/75 40.00 100.00
PAJJ Jim Jackson/75 8.00 20.00
PAJK Jason Kidd/75 30.00 80.00
PAJW James Worthy/75 25.00 60.00
PAKB Kobe Bryant/75 3,000.00 6,000.00
PAKD Kevin Durant/75 400.00 800.00
PAKI Kyrie Irving/75 125.00 300.00
PAKL Kevin Love/75 20.00 50.00
PAKL Kawhi Leonard/75 200.00 500.00
PAKW Kemba Walker/75 15.00 40.00
PALB Larry Bird/75 125.00 300.00
PALS Lance Stephenson/75 8.00 20.00
PAMK Michael Kidd-Gilchrist/75 6.00 15.00
PAMP Mason Plumlee/75 6.00 15.00
PARH Robert Horry/75 10.00 25.00
PARP Robert Parish/75 12.00 30.00
PASO Shaquille O'Neal/75 300.00 600.00
PATB Trey Burke/75 6.00 15.00
PATH Tim Hardaway/75 20.00 50.00
PATM Tracy McGrady/60 100.00 250.00
PATO Tobias Harris/75 8.00 20.00
PAWP Will Perdue/75 6.00 15.00
PAYM Yao Ming/75 500.00 1,000.00
PAZI Zydrunas Ilgauskas/60 12.00 30.00
PAAHA Anfernee Hardaway/75 75.00 200.00
PAAHO Allan Houston/75 10.00 25.00
PABLA Bill Laimbeer/75 20.00 50.00
PABLO Brook Lopez/75 10.00 25.00
PADMA Danny Manning/75 8.00 20.00
PADMU Dikembe Mutombo/75 20.00 50.00
PAJWA John Wall/75 40.00 100.00
PAMCW M.Carter-Williams/75 6.00 15.00

2014-15 Immaculate Collection Patches Autographs Jersey Number

*JSY NUMBER: .8X TO 2X BASE HI
STATED PRINT RUN B/WN 1-55 COPIES PER
NO PRICING ON QTY 17 OR LESS
PADR David Robinson/50 150.00 400.00
PAJW James Worthy/42 60.00 150.00
PAKB Kobe Bryant/24 3,000.00 6,000.00

2014-15 Immaculate Collection Player Caps

STATED PRINT RUN B/WN 31-39 COPIES PER
PCAG Aaron Gordon/38 12.00 30.00
PCBC Bruno Caboclo/37 5.00 12.00
PCCE Cleanthony Early/39 4.00 10.00
PCDI Damien Inglis/38 4.00 10.00
PCDM Doug McDermott/38 6.00 15.00
PCEP Elfrid Payton/38 6.00 15.00
PCGH Gary Harris/39 6.00 15.00
PCGR Glenn Robinson III/39 5.00 12.00
PCJA Jordan Adams/37 4.00 10.00
PCJE Joel Embiid/35 100.00 250.00
PCJG Jerami Grant/35 20.00 50.00
PCJH Joe Harris/31 6.00 15.00
PCJP Jabari Parker/38 5.00 12.00
PCJR Julius Randle/35 50.00 120.00
PCJY James Young/37 4.00 10.00
PCKM K.J. McDaniels/35 4.00 10.00
PCMM Mitch McGary/38 4.00 10.00
PCMS Marcus Smart/37 15.00 40.00
PCNV Noah Vonleh/37 4.00 10.00
PCPH P.J. Hairston/37 4.00 10.00
PCRH Rodney Hood/37 5.00 12.00
PCSN Shabazz Napier/38 5.00 12.00
PCTE Tyler Ennis/35 4.00 10.00
PCTW T.J. Warren/35 6.00 15.00
PCZL Zach LaVine/39 50.00 120.00

2014-15 Immaculate Collection Premium Autograph Patches

STATED PRINT RUN B/WN 5-25 COPIES PER
NO PRICING ON QTY 18 OR LESS
1 Kobe Bryant/20 6,000.00 10,000.00
2 Kyrie Irving/25 200.00 500.00
3 Kevin Durant/25 1,000.00 2,000.00
5 Kareem Abdul-Jabbar/25 200.00 500.00
6 Goran Dragic/25 15.00 40.00
7 Bernard King/25 25.00 60.00
8 Isiah Thomas/25 40.00 100.00
9 Gary Payton/25 60.00 150.00
10 James Worthy/25 50.00 120.00
11 Eddie Jones/25 50.00 120.00
12 Jim Jackson/25 25.00 60.00
14 Andre Drummond/25 40.00 100.00
15 Trey Burke/25 10.00 25.00
16 Gordon Hayward/25 30.00 80.00
17 Carl Landry/25 10.00 25.00
18 Reggie Jackson/25 50.00 120.00
19 Marcin Gortat/25 25.00 60.00
20 Jason Terry/25 12.00 30.00
21 Magic Johnson/25 200.00 500.00
22 Grant Hill/25 125.00 300.00
23 Clifford Robinson/25 15.00 40.00
24 Dikembe Mutombo/25 75.00 200.00
25 Robert Horry/25 25.00 60.00
26 Byron Scott/25 75.00 150.00
27 Chris Mullin/25 40.00 100.00
28 Anfernee Hardaway/25 125.00 300.00
29 Antoine Walker/25 25.00 60.00
30 Nick Van Exel/25 60.00 150.00
31 Clyde Drexler/25 75.00 200.00
32 Marques Johnson/25 12.00 30.00
33 Tim Hardaway/25 25.00 60.00
36 Jared Sullinger/25 12.00 30.00
37 Shaquille O'Neal/25 300.00 600.00
38 John Stockton/25 75.00 150.00
39 Karl Malone/25 75.00 200.00
41 Larry Bird/25 200.00 500.00
42 Tristan Thompson/25 15.00 40.00
43 Tyreke Evans/25 12.00 30.00
44 Klay Thompson/25 200.00 500.00
47 Hakeem Olajuwon/25 75.00 200.00
48 Michael Kidd-Gilchrist/25 10.00 25.00
49 Eric Gordon/25 10.00 25.00
50 Bradley Beal/25 100.00 250.00
51 John Wall/25 60.00 150.00
52 Stephen Curry/25 1,500.00 3,000.00
56 Joe Dumars/25 25.00 60.00
57 David Robinson/25 75.00 200.00
58 Al Horford/25 15.00 40.00
59 Walter Davis/25 40.00 100.00
60 Kevin Love/25 25.00 60.00
64 Mike Conley/25 20.00 50.00
65 Anthony Davis/25 300.00 600.00
67 Danny Green/25 40.00 100.00
69 Enes Kanter/25 20.00 50.00
71 Tyson Chandler/25 15.00 40.00
72 Ben McLemore/25 10.00 25.00
73 M.Carter-Williams/25 10.00 25.00
74 Jeff Green/25 12.00 30.00
75 Nikola Vucevic/25 12.00 30.00
76 Mason Plumlee/25 10.00 25.00
77 Steven Adams/25 20.00 50.00
78 Brook Lopez/25 15.00 40.00
79 Archie Goodwin/25 10.00 25.00
80 Tyler Zeller/25 10.00 25.00
81 Andrew Wiggins/25 150.00 400.00
82 Jabari Parker/25 12.00 30.00
83 Tyler Ennis/25 10.00 25.00
84 T.J. Warren/25 15.00 40.00
85 Elfrid Payton/25 15.00 40.00
86 Aaron Gordon/25 50.00 120.00
87 Doug McDermott/25 15.00 40.00
88 Marcus Smart/25 75.00 200.00
89 Julius Randle/25 150.00 400.00
90 Cleanthony Early/25 10.00 25.00
91 Zach LaVine/25 300.00 600.00
92 Gary Harris/25 15.00 40.00
93 Adreian Payne/25 15.00 40.00
94 Bruno Caboclo/25 12.00 30.00
95 Joe Harris/25 15.00 40.00
98 Dante Exum/25 15.00 40.00
99 Rodney Hood/25 12.00 30.00
100 Jordan Adams/25 10.00 25.00

2014-15 Immaculate Collection Quad Materials

STATED PRINT RUN B/WN 25-49 COPIES PER
31 Anthony/Drmt/Lve/Jms/35 12.00 30.00
32 Pl/Wl/Rbo/Crry/35 50.00 120.00
37 Grdn/Pytn/Vnllt/Npr/49 20.00 50.00
QATL Hrfrd/Tge/Krvr/Millsp/49 6.00 15.00
QBOS Mxl/Jhn/McHl/Brd/25 25.00 60.00
QBRK Lpz/Wllms/Jhnsn/Plmle/35 15.00 40.00
QCED McDrmtt/Prkr/Hrrs/Drwdde/49 8.00 20.00
QCHA Jffrsn/Hndrsn/Wlkr/Glchrst/35 6.00 15.00
QCHI Rse/Btlr/Nh/Gbsn/49 10.00 25.00
QCLE Lve/Irvng/Jms/Mrn/49 50.00 120.00
QDAL Prsns/Nwtzki/Ells/Chndlr/49 15.00 40.00
QDEN Afflo/Frd/Lwsn/Chndlr/49 4.00 10.00
QDET Drmmnd/Jnnngs/Mnre/Ppe/35 5.00 12.00
QGSW Bgt/Grn/Thmpsn/Crry/49 25.00 60.00
QHOU Motjns/Hwrd/Hrdn/Arza/35 12.00 30.00
QIND Wst/Scla/Hbbrt/Hill/35 5.00 12.00
QLAC Grffn/Pl/Jrdn/Rdck/35 20.00 50.00
QLAL Jbbr/Brynt/Jhnsn/ONl/25 50.00 120.00
QMEM Gsl/Cnly/Alln/Rndlph/35 15.00 40.00
QMIA And/Bsh/Wde/Chlm/49 12.00 30.00
QMIN Dng/Pkvc/Rbo/Yng/49 8.00 20.00
QNOP Dvs/Grdn/Hldy/Evns/35 15.00 40.00
QNYK Anthony/Cldrn/Lrkn/Hrdwy/49 6.00 15.00
QOKC Drnt/Wstbrk/Ibka/Adms/35 20.00 50.00
QPAD Wlcx/Rndle/Stsks/Wrrn/49 5.00 12.00
QPHI Ivrsn/Grr/Ervng/Mlne/25 20.00 50.00
QPHX Ln/Bldse/Drgc/Mrrs/35 5.00 12.00
QPOR Rbn/Dlx/Dckw/Pppn/49 15.00 40.00
QREB Drmmnd/Jrdn/Hwrd/Chndlr/35 20.00 50.00
QRSG Wggns/Exm/Pytn/LVne/49 12.00 30.00
QSAC McLmre/Cllsn/Csns/Gy/35 6.00 15.00
QSAN Lnrd/Gnbli/Dncn/Prkr/35 20.00 50.00
QTOR DRzn/Vlncns/Lwry/Rss/35 8.00 20.00
QWAS Bl/Wll/Grtt/Nne/35 10.00 25.00
QKUUK Wggns/Yng/Embd/Rndle/49 15.00 40.00
QMSMU Hrrs/Rbnsn/McGry/Stsks/49 6.00 15.00

2014-15 Immaculate Collection Rookie Jerseys

STATED PRINT RUN 99 SER.#'d SETS
1 Shabazz Napier 3.00 8.00
2 Jabari Parker 3.00 8.00
3 Glenn Robinson III 3.00 8.00
4 K.J. McDaniels 2.50 6.00
5 James Ennis 2.50 6.00
6 Markel Brown 2.50 6.00
7 Elfrid Payton 4.00 10.00
8 C.J. Wilcox 2.50 6.00
9 Bruno Caboclo 3.00 8.00
10 Johnny O'Bryant 2.50 6.00
11 Julius Randle 12.00 30.00
12 Rodney Hood 3.00 8.00
13 James Young 2.50 6.00
14 Zach LaVine 15.00 40.00
15 Aaron Gordon 12.00 30.00
16 Andrew Wiggins 12.00 30.00
17 Cleanthony Early 2.50 6.00
18 Noah Vonleh 2.50 6.00
19 Cory Jefferson 2.50 6.00
20 Gary Harris 4.00 10.00
21 Damien Inglis 2.50 6.00
22 Marcus Smart 10.00 25.00
23 Jerami Grant 12.00 30.00
24 Jarnell Stokes 2.50 6.00
25 P.J. Hairston 2.50 6.00
26 Jordan Adams 2.50 6.00
27 Adreian Payne 2.50 6.00
28 Joe Harris 4.00 10.00
29 Joel Embiid 25.00 60.00
30 Russ Smith 2.50 6.00
31 Doug McDermott 4.00 10.00
32 Kyle Anderson 4.00 10.00
33 Mitch McGary 2.50 6.00
34 Tyler Ennis 2.50 6.00
35 Nik Stauskas 2.50 6.00
36 Dante Exum 4.00 10.00
37 Spencer Dinwiddie 4.00 10.00
38 T.J. Warren 4.00 10.00

2014-15 Immaculate Collection Rookie Jerseys Prime

*PRIME: 1.2X TO 3X BASE HI
STATED PRINT RUN 20 SER.#'d SETS

2014-15 Immaculate Collection Shadowbox Signatures

STATED PRINT RUN B/WN 35-60 COPIES PER
SHAD Anthony Davis/35 100.00 200.00
SHAD Adrian Dantley/49 6.00 15.00
SHAE Alex English/49 6.00 15.00
SHAG Artis Gilmore/49 6.00 15.00
SHAH Anfernee Hardaway/49 40.00 100.00
SHAH Al Horford/49 6.00 15.00
SHAW Andrew Wiggins/35 75.00 200.00
SHAW Antoine Walker/60 5.00 12.00
SHBB Bradley Beal/49 15.00 40.00
SHBR Bill Russell/35 1,000.00 2,000.00
SHBW Bill Walton/49 8.00 20.00
SHCD Clyde Drexler/35 25.00 60.00
SHCM Chris Mullin/49 8.00 20.00
SHDE Dante Exum/49 6.00 15.00
SHDI Dan Issel/49 6.00 15.00
SHDM Doug McDermott/49 6.00 15.00
SHDR David Robinson/35 20.00 50.00
SHDR Dennis Rodman/35 50.00 120.00
SHEJ Eddie Jones/60 6.00 15.00
SHGG George Gervin/49 10.00 25.00
SHGH Grant Hill/49 25.00 60.00
SHGP Gary Payton/35 30.00 80.00
SHHO Hakeem Olajuwon/35 15.00 40.00
SHIT Isaiah Thomas/49 10.00 25.00
SHJE Julius Erving/35 40.00 100.00
SHJK Jason Kidd/35 25.00 60.00
SHJP Jabari Parker/35 5.00 12.00
SHJR Julius Randle/49 75.00 200.00
SHJS John Starks/49 6.00 15.00
SHJS John Stockton/35 30.00 80.00
SHJW James Worthy/49 20.00 50.00
SHJW Jerry West/35 30.00 80.00
SHJW John Wall/35 25.00 60.00
SHJY James Young/49 4.00 10.00
SHKB Kobe Bryant/35 2,000.00 4,000.00
SHKD Kevin Durant/35 100.00 250.00
SHKI Kyrie Irving/35 60.00 150.00
SHKL Kevin Love/35 15.00 40.00
SHKM Karl Malone/35 40.00 100.00
SHKR Kurt Rambis/49 5.00 12.00
SHLB Larry Bird/35 125.00 300.00
SHMB Muggsy Bogues/60 10.00 25.00
SHMJ Magic Johnson/35 125.00 300.00
SHMP Mark Price/60 6.00 15.00
SHMS Marcus Smart/49 10.00 25.00
SHNS Nik Stauskas/49 4.00 10.00
SHRB Rick Barry/49 6.00 15.00
SHRF Rick Fox/49 5.00 12.00
SHRH Rodney Hood/60 5.00 12.00
SHRH Robert Horry/49 10.00 25.00
SHSC Stephen Curry/49 500.00 1,000.00
SHSN Steve Nash/35 40.00 100.00
SHSN Shabazz Napier/60 5.00 12.00
SHSO Shaquille O'Neal/35 75.00 200.00
SHSW Spud Webb/60 6.00 15.00
SHTC Tom Chambers/49 6.00 15.00
SHTH Tim Hardaway/60 10.00 25.00
SHTK Toni Kukoc/49 8.00 20.00
SHTL Ty Lawson/49 4.00 10.00
SHTM Tracy McGrady/35 40.00 100.00
SHTP Tony Parker/49 30.00 80.00
SHTW T.J. Warren/49 6.00 15.00
SHTY Thaddeus Young/60 6.00 15.00
SHVC Vince Carter/35 40.00 100.00
SHVD Vlade Divac/60 6.00 15.00
SHVO Victor Oladipo/49 5.00 12.00
SHWF Walt Frazier/49 10.00 25.00
SHZI Zydrunas Ilgauskas/60 5.00 12.00
SHZL Zach LaVine/49 75.00 200.00
SHZR Zach Randolph/49 10.00 25.00
SHMCW M.Carter-Williams/49 4.00 10.00

2014-15 Immaculate Collection Sole of the Game

STATED PRINT RUN B/WN 11-30 COPIES PER
NO PRICING ON QTY 19 OR LESS
SGAI Allen Iverson/23 100.00 250.00
SGAW Andrew Wiggins/23 60.00 150.00
SGDW Dominique Wilkins/26 30.00 80.00
SGHO Hakeem Olajuwon/30 40.00 100.00
SGKM Karl Malone/30 30.00 80.00
SGMJ Magic Johnson/26 75.00 200.00
SGMM Moses Malone/20 30.00 80.00
SGRS Ralph Sampson/30 30.00 80.00

2014-15 Immaculate Collection Special Event Jumbo Jerseys

STATED PRINT RUN B/WN 4-39 COPIES PER
10 Steven Adams/25 40.00 100.00
12 Donatas Motiejunas/34 15.00 40.00
13 Tarik Black/24 20.00 50.00
15 Jason Terry/26 12.00 30.00
16 Kostas Papanikolaou/32 10.00 25.00
17 Serge Ibaka/20 12.00 30.00
18 Reggie Jackson/24 12.00 30.00
33 Mo Williams/39 12.00 30.00
35 Thaddeus Young/36 10.00 25.00
36 Kevin Martin/36 10.00 25.00
37 Zach LaVine/22 100.00 200.00
38 Nikola Pekovic/37 10.00 25.00
39 Gorgui Dieng/28 10.00 25.00
41 Nick Young/21 15.00 40.00
51 Manu Ginobili/31 40.00 100.00
59 Tiago Splitter/35 10.00 25.00

2014-15 Immaculate Collection Sports Variations Autographs

STATED PRINT RUN 25 SER.#'d SETS
SVAJM Joe Montana 100.00 200.00
SVATB T.Bradshaw EXCH 30.00 80.00
SVAMF Marshall Faulk 20.00 50.00
SVAMD M.Ditka EXCH 30.00 80.00
SVACR Cristiano Ronaldo 1,000.00 2,000.00
SVARH R.Henderson EXCH 50.00 120.00
SVAFR F.Robinson EXCH 75.00 200.00
SVAMM M.McGwire EXCH 50.00 120.00
SVABB B.Bonds EXCH 125.00 300.00

2014-15 Immaculate Collection Statistical Standouts Signatures

STATED PRINT RUN 49 SER.#'d SETS
1 Joakim Noah 10.00 25.00
2 Kevin Durant 400.00 800.00
3 Michael Carter-Williams 6.00 15.00
4 Shaquille O'Neal 400.00 800.00
5 Kyle Korver 8.00 20.00
6 Willis Reed 60.00 150.00
7 Dikembe Mutombo 75.00 200.00
8 Alonzo Mourning 125.00 300.00
9 Magic Johnson 200.00 500.00
10 Stephen Curry 800.00 1,500.00
11 John Wall 60.00 150.00
12 Bernard King 30.00 80.00
13 Charlie Scott 10.00 25.00
14 Blake Griffin 30.00 80.00
15 Tracy McGrady 300.00 600.00
16 Kareem Abdul-Jabbar 300.00 600.00
17 Jason Kidd 40.00 100.00
18 Carmelo Anthony 125.00 300.00
19 Kobe Bryant 3,000.00 6,000.00
20 Karl Malone 150.00 400.00

2014-15 Immaculate Collection Team Logos

STATED PRINT RUN 1-28 COPIES PER
NO PRICING ON QTY 18 OR LESS
64 Rudy Gay/24 15.00 40.00
98 Tyler Ennis/28 10.00 25.00

2014-15 Immaculate Collection Team Numbers

STATED PRINT RUN B/WN 1-50 COPIES PER
NO PRICING ON QTY 18 OR LESS
3 Zach Randolph/23 10.00 25.00
4 Marc Gasol/22 10.00 25.00
6 Grant Hill/24 30.00 80.00
8 Rudy Gobert/24 15.00 40.00
13 Kenneth Faried/21 6.00 15.00
18 Pau Gasol/25 20.00 50.00
23 Chandler Parsons/23 25.00 60.00
33 Kobe Bryant/25 200.00 500.00
36 Al Jefferson/39 20.00 50.00
37 Anthony Davis/20 100.00 200.00
38 Jrue Holiday/21 10.00 25.00
42 Nicolas Batum/21 20.00 50.00
43 Derrick Favors/23 6.00 15.00
44 Gordon Hayward/29 8.00 20.00
48 Al Horford/21 20.00 50.00
50 Thabo Sefolosha/27 6.00 15.00
54 DeMarcus Cousins/21 25.00 60.00
55 Ben McLemore/25 6.00 15.00
56 Vince Carter/22 50.00 120.00
57 Blake Griffin/22 20.00 50.00
63 LeBron James/32 300.00 600.00
64 Rudy Gay/26 10.00 25.00
71 Aaron Gordon/32 40.00 100.00
72 Adreian Payne/40 6.00 15.00
73 Andrew Wiggins/23 40.00 100.00
74 Bruno Caboclo/30 8.00 20.00
75 Cleanthony Early/44 6.00 15.00
76 Damien Inglis/26 6.00 15.00
77 Dante Exum/20 10.00 25.00
78 Doug McDermott/50 10.00 25.00
79 Elfrid Payton/32 10.00 25.00
80 Gary Harris/30 10.00 25.00
81 Glenn Robinson III/28 8.00 20.00
82 Jabari Parker/32 8.00 20.00
83 James Ennis/36 6.00 15.00
84 James Young/42 6.00 15.00
85 Jerami Grant/44 40.00 100.00
86 Joe Harris/40 20.00 50.00
87 Joel Embiid/46 125.00 300.00
88 Julius Randle/46 60.00 150.00
89 K.J. McDaniels/44 6.00 15.00
90 Kyle Anderson/50 10.00 25.00
91 Marcus Smart/50 25.00 60.00
92 Mitch McGary/32 6.00 15.00
93 Nik Stauskas/42 6.00 15.00
94 Noah Vonleh/26 6.00 15.00
95 P.J. Hairston/26 6.00 15.00
96 Rodney Hood/42 8.00 20.00
97 Shabazz Napier/38 10.00 25.00
98 Tyler Ennis/28 6.00 15.00
99 T.J. Warren/32 10.00 25.00
100 Zach LaVine/30 30.00 80.00

2014-15 Immaculate Collection Trio Autographs

STATED PRINT RUN 25 SER.#'d SETS
1 Wiggins/Bennett/LaVine 60.00 150.00
2 Davis/Durant/Bryant 8,000.00 12,000.00
3 Mullin/Richmond/Hardaway 150.00 400.00
4 Wiggins/Parker/Randle 100.00 250.00
5 Robinson III/McGary/Stauskas 40.00 100.00
6 Iguodala/Thompson/Curry 1,500.00 3,000.00

2014-15 Immaculate Collection Trios Materials

STATED PRINT RUN B/WN 10-99 COPIES PER
NO PRICING ON QTY 10 OR LESS
2 McHale/Bird/Parish/49 15.00 40.00
7 Love/Irving/James/75 30.00 80.00
8 Dantley/English/Aguirre/49 5.00 12.00
10 Gallinari/Faried/Lawson/75 2.50 6.00
11 English/Mutombo/Lever/49 8.00 20.00
12 Drummond/Monroe
Caldwell-Pope/75 3.00 8.00
13 Laimbeer/Thomas/Dumars/49 6.00 15.00
14 Jefferson/Walker/Kidd-Gilchrist/75 4.00 10.00
15 Green/Thompson/Curry/75 25.00 60.00
20 Jones/Bryant/O'Neal/75 30.00 80.00
23 Andersen/Bosh/Wade/75 8.00 20.00
25 Jason Terry 10.00 25.00
26 Davis/Holiday/Evans/75 10.00 25.00
28 Starks/Johnson/Ewing/49 12.00 30.00
34 Majerle/Chambers/McDaniel/49 4.00 10.00
36 Robinson/Drexler/Duckworth/49 6.00 15.00
37 McCollum/Aldridge/Batum/75 4.00 10.00
38 McLemore/Cousins/Gay/75 4.00 10.00
39 Robinson/Horry/Duncan/49 12.00 30.00
43 Stockton/Malone/Eaton/49 12.00 30.00
44 Beal/Wall/Porter/75 6.00 15.00
45 Wiggins/Robinson III/LaVine/99 15.00 40.00
48 Caboclo/Inglis/Exum/99 4.00 10.00
52 Harris/Robinson III/Stauskas/99 4.00 10.00
57 McDermott/Parker/Harris/99 4.00 10.00
TADG Wiggins/Exum/Robinson III/99 12.00 30.00
TAES Gordon/Payton/Napier/99 12.00 30.00
TAJJ Wiggins/Embiid/Randle/99 25.00 60.00
TAJM Wiggins/Embiid/Smart/99 25.00 60.00
TATL Horford/Wilkins/Teague/75 6.00 15.00
TBRK Williams/Johnson/Plumlee/75 3.00 8.00
TCDE Early/McDermott/Payton/99 3.00 8.00
TCHI Rose/Butler/Noah/75 8.00 20.00
TGSW Iguodala/Bogut/Lee/75 4.00 10.00
THOU Drexler/Olajuwon/Horry/49 15.00 40.00
TJBK Caboclo/Embiid/McDaniels/99 25.00 60.00
TJJC Early/Young/Randle/99 3.00 8.00
TJNG Robinson III/Randle/Stauskas/99 3.00 8.00
TJPR Parker/Hairston/Hood/99 3.00 8.00
TLAC Griffin/Paul/Jordan/75 6.00 15.00
TLAL Wrthy/Abdl-Jbbr/Jhnsn/49 15.00 40.00
TMCJ Early/Young/Smart/99 3.00 8.00
TMIL Knight/Henson/Mayo/75 2.50 6.00
TMIN Dieng/Pekovic/Rubio/75 3.00 8.00
TMMZ Gasol/Conley/Randolph/75 4.00 10.00
TNYK Anthony/Cldrn/Hrdwy Jr./75 3.00 8.00
TOKC Durant/Westbrook/Ibaka/75 10.00 25.00
TORL Vucevic/Harris/Oladipo/75 3.00 8.00
TORL Hardaway/Scott/O'Neal/49 15.00 40.00
TPHI Collins/Erving/Malone/49 12.00 30.00
TRJK Harris/McDaniels/Hood/99 4.00 10.00
TSEA Schrempf/Payton/Kemp/49 25.00 60.00
TSNP Vonleh/Hairston/Napier/99 3.00 8.00
TTOR DeRozan/Valanciunas/Ross/75 5.00 12.00
TCHH2 Mrnng/Trpcka/Jhnsn/49 12.00 30.00
TDAL2 Nowitzki/Kidd/Finley/49 8.00 20.00
THOU2 Mtjns/Hwrd/Hrdn/75 8.00 20.00
TNYK3 King/Cartwright/Walker/49 15.00 40.00
TPHO2 Len/Bledsoe/Dragic/75 4.00 10.00
TSAS2 Ginobili/Duncan/Parker/75 12.00 30.00

2015-16 Immaculate Collection

STATED PRINT RUN 99 SER.#'d SETS
EXCHANGE DEADLINE 3/14/2018
1 Nerlens Noel 1.25 3.00
2 Robert Covington 1.50 4.00
3 Ish Smith 1.25 3.00
4 Jabari Parker 1.25 3.00
5 Khris Middleton 2.50 6.00
6 Michael Carter-Williams 1.25 3.00
7 Jimmy Butler 4.00 10.00
8 Pau Gasol 3.00 8.00
9 Derrick Rose 3.00 8.00
10 Doug McDermott 1.50 4.00
11 LeBron James 125.00 300.00
12 Kevin Love 2.00 5.00
13 Kyrie Irving 4.00 10.00
14 J.R. Smith 2.00 5.00
15 Marcus Smart 2.50 6.00
16 Jared Sullinger 1.25 3.00
17 Isaiah Thomas 1.50 4.00
18 Jae Crowder 1.25 3.00
19 Chris Paul 4.00 10.00
20 J.J. Redick 2.00 5.00
21 Blake Griffin 2.00 5.00
22 DeAndre Jordan 1.50 4.00
23 Marc Gasol 2.00 5.00
24 Mike Conley 2.00 5.00
25 Mario Chalmers 1.50 4.00
26 Paul Millsap 1.50 4.00
27 Al Horford 2.00 5.00
28 Dennis Schroder 2.00 5.00
29 Dwyane Wade 4.00 10.00
30 Hassan Whiteside 1.50 4.00
31 Chris Bosh 2.50 6.00
32 Joe Johnson 1.50 4.00
33 Jeremy Lin 4.00 10.00
34 Kemba Walker 2.00 5.00
35 Al Jefferson 1.25 3.00
36 Derrick Favors 1.50 4.00
37 Rodney Hood 1.50 4.00
38 Gordon Hayward 2.00 5.00
39 DeMarcus Cousins 2.00 5.00
40 Rudy Gay 2.00 5.00
41 Rajon Rondo 2.50 6.00
42 Carmelo Anthony 3.00 8.00
43 Arron Afflalo 1.25 3.00
44 Derrick Williams 1.25 3.00
45 Kobe Bryant 75.00 200.00
46 Jordan Clarkson 2.00 5.00
47 Julius Randle 2.50 6.00
48 Victor Oladipo 1.50 4.00
49 Elfrid Payton 1.50 4.00
50 Nikola Vucevic 1.50 4.00
51 Dirk Nowitzki 5.00 12.00
52 Chandler Parsons 1.25 3.00
53 Wesley Matthews 1.25 3.00
54 Brook Lopez 2.00 5.00
55 Thaddeus Young 1.25 3.00
56 Bojan Bogdanovic 1.50 4.00
57 Kenneth Faried 1.50 4.00
58 Will Barton 1.25 3.00
59 Gary Harris 1.50 4.00
60 Paul George 3.00 8.00
61 George Hill 1.50 4.00
62 Jordan Hill 1.25 3.00
63 Anthony Davis 5.00 12.00
64 Tyreke Evans 1.50 4.00
65 Eric Gordon 1.50 4.00
66 Tobias Harris 1.50 4.00
67 Reggie Jackson 1.50 4.00
68 Andre Drummond 2.00 5.00
69 DeMarre Carroll 1.25 3.00
70 Jonas Valanciunas 1.50 4.00
71 DeMar DeRozan 2.50 6.00
72 Kyle Lowry 2.00 5.00
73 Trevor Ariza 1.25 3.00
74 James Harden 4.00 10.00
75 Jason Terry 1.50 4.00
76 Dwight Howard 2.50 6.00
77 Kawhi Leonard 6.00 15.00
78 Tony Parker 3.00 8.00
79 Manu Ginobili 4.00 10.00
80 Tim Duncan 5.00 12.00
81 T.J. Warren 2.00 5.00
82 Eric Bledsoe 1.50 4.00
83 Brandon Knight 1.25 3.00
84 Serge Ibaka 1.50 4.00
85 Russell Westbrook 3.00 8.00
86 Kevin Durant 8.00 20.00
87 Enes Kanter 1.25 3.00
88 Andrew Wiggins 2.50 6.00
89 Kevin Garnett 5.00 12.00
90 Zach LaVine 5.00 12.00
91 C.J. McCollum 2.00 5.00
92 Gerald Henderson 1.25 3.00
93 Damian Lillard 5.00 12.00
94 Harrison Barnes 1.50 4.00
95 Klay Thompson 5.00 12.00
96 Stephen Curry 15.00 40.00
97 Draymond Green 2.50 6.00
98 John Wall 2.50 6.00
99 Marcin Gortat 1.25 3.00
100 Bradley Beal 2.50 6.00
101 Towns JSY AU/99 RC 300.00 600.00
102 Jerian Grant JSY AU/99 RC 6.00 15.00
103 Kaminsky JSY AU/99 RC 12.00 30.00
104 Russell JSY AU/99 RC 150.00 400.00
105 Cauley-Stein JSY AU/99 RC 25.00 60.00
106 Jarell Martin JSY AU/99 RC EXCH 6.00 15.00
107 Joe Young JSY AU/99 RC 6.00 15.00
108 Jones JSY AU/99 RC 15.00 40.00
109 Sasha Kaun JSY AU/99 RC 6.00 15.00
110 Okafor JSY AU/99 RC 15.00 40.00
111 Richardson JSY AU/99 RC 25.00 60.00
112 Lyles JSY AU/99 RC 8.00 20.00
113 Cristiano Felicio JSY AU/99 RC 8.00 20.00
114 Anderson JSY AU/99 RC 6.00 15.00
115 Rozier JSY AU/99 RC 60.00 150.00
116 Marcelo Huertas JSY
AU/99 RC EXCH 6.00 15.00
117 Mudiay JSY AU/99 RC 20.00 50.00
118 Winslow JSY AU/99 RC 30.00 80.00
119 Johnson JSY AU/99 RC 15.00 40.00
120 Raul Neto JSY AU/99 RC EXCH 6.00 15.00
121 Booker JSY AU/99 RC 1,000.00 2,000.00
122 Hollis-Jefferson JSY AU/99 RC 15.00 40.00
123 Dekker JSY AU/99 RC 20.00 50.00
124 Simmons JSY AU/99 RC 8.00 20.00
125 Delon Wright JSY AU/99 RC 8.00 20.00
126 Oubre Jr. JSY AU/99 RC 100.00 250.00
127 Luis Montero JSY AU/99 RC 6.00 15.00
128 Nemanja Bjelica JSY AU/95 RC 10.00 25.00
129 Jordan Mickey JSY AU/99 RC 6.00 15.00
130 Salah Mejri JSY AU/99 RC 6.00 15.00
131 Looney JSY AU/99 RC 20.00 50.00
132 Holmes JSY AU/99 RC 10.00 25.00
133 Jokic JSY AU/99 RC 5,000.00 10,000.00
134 Chris McCullough JSY AU/99 RC 6.00 15.00
135 Porzingis JSY AU/99 RC 200.00 500.00
136 Rakeem Christmas JSY AU/99 RC 6.00 15.00
137 Powell JSY AU/82 RC 40.00 100.00
138 Payne JSY AU/99 RC 10.00 25.00
139 Nance Jr. JSY AU/99 RC 30.00 80.00
140 R.J. Hunter JSY AU/99 RC 6.00 15.00
141 Cliff Alexander JSY AU/99 RC 6.00 15.00
142 Portis JSY AU/99 RC 15.00 40.00
143 Hznja JSY AU/99 RC EXCH 8.00 20.00
144 Pat Connaughton JSY AU/99 RC 10.00 25.00
145 Walter Tavares JSY AU/99 RC 6.00 15.00
146 Anthony Brown JSY AU/99 RC 6.00 15.00

147 Montrezl Harrell JSY AU/99 RC 40.00 100.00
148 Turner JSY AU/99 RC 50.00 120.00
149 Huestis JSY AU/99 RC 6.00 15.00
150 T.J. McConnell JSY AU/99 RC 50.00 120.00

2015-16 Immaculate Collection Bronze

*BRONZE: .6X TO 1.5X BASIC
STATED PRINT RUN 49 SER.#'d SETS

2015-16 Immaculate Collection Autographs

PRINT RUNS B/WN 32-99 COPIES PER
EXCHANGE DEADLINE 3/14/2018
*BRONZE p/r 30-75: .4X TO 1X BASIC
*BRONZE p/r 25-26: .5X TO 1.2X BASIC
*RED/25: .5X TO 1.2X BASIC
1 Zaza Pachulia/99 4.00 10.00
2 Matthew Dellavedova/99 5.00 12.00
3 Jonas Valanciunas/99 5.00 12.00
4 Draymond Green/99 40.00 100.00
5 Khris Middleton/99 10.00 25.00
6 DeMarre Carroll/99 4.00 10.00
7 Goran Dragic/99 6.00 15.00
8 Eric Bledsoe/99 5.00 12.00
9 Andrew Wiggins/35 20.00 50.00
10 Dirk Nowitzki/35 100.00 250.00
11 Avery Bradley/99 4.00 10.00
12 Dennis Schroder/99 6.00 15.00
13 Gerald Henderson/99 4.00 10.00
14 Anthony Davis/35 50.00 120.00
15 Pau Gasol/35 25.00 60.00
16 Jordan Clarkson/99 15.00 40.00
17 Giannis Antetokounmpo/99 300.00 600.00
18 Al Horford/99 6.00 15.00
19 Nerlens Noel/70 4.00 10.00
20 Gordon Hayward/85 6.00 15.00
21 Nicolas Batum/99 4.00 10.00
22 C.J. McCollum/99 6.00 15.00
23 Gorgui Dieng/99 4.00 10.00
24 Jason Terry/99 5.00 12.00
25 Andrew Bogut/99 10.00 25.00
26 Bobby Portis/99 10.00 25.00
27 Nikola Jokic/99 600.00 1,200.00
28 Boban Marjanovic/99 12.00 30.00
29 Rondae Hollis-Jefferson/99 5.00 12.00
30 Devin Booker/99 200.00 500.00
31 Jahlil Okafor/49 5.00 12.00
32 Artis Gilmore/99 8.00 20.00
33 James Worthy/35 12.00 30.00
34 John Starks/99 6.00 15.00
35 Charles Oakley/99 5.00 12.00
36 Vinny Del Negro/99 5.00 12.00
37 Peja Stojakovic/99 5.00 12.00
38 Ralph Sampson/45 5.00 12.00
39 Shaquille O'Neal/32 75.00 200.00
40 Allen Iverson/35 75.00 200.00
41 Dikembe Mutombo/99 15.00 40.00
42 David Robinson/35 20.00 50.00
43 Chauncey Billups/99 15.00 40.00
44 Isiah Thomas/99 15.00 40.00
45 Bernard King/99 8.00 20.00
46 Oscar Robertson/35 40.00 100.00
47 George Gervin/99 10.00 25.00
48 Ray Allen/99 30.00 80.00
49 John Stockton/35 40.00 100.00
50 Danny Manning/80 5.00 12.00

2015-16 Immaculate Collection Christmas Day Materials

PRINT RUNS B/WN 1-74 COPIES PER
NO PRICING ON QTY 17 OR LESS
PRICING FOR BASIC PATCHES
1 Pau Gasol/61 10.00 25.00
2 Doug McDermott/35 6.00 15.00
4 Eric Gordon/49 6.00 15.00
5 Tyreke Evans/49 6.00 15.00
6 Ryan Anderson/58 5.00 12.00
7 Goran Dragic/39 8.00 20.00
8 Luol Deng/44 10.00 25.00
9 Jonathon Simmons/48 6.00 15.00
10 Jordan Clarkson/40 15.00 40.00
11 Marcelo Huertas/44 5.00 12.00
19 James Harden/20 50.00 120.00
20 Dwight Howard/20 20.00 50.00
21 Clint Capela/74 10.00 25.00
29 Serge Ibaka/42 8.00 20.00
32 Steven Adams/65 25.00 60.00
36 Danny Green/45 15.00 40.00
45 Trevor Ariza/52 8.00 20.00
46 Enes Kanter/43 8.00 20.00
47 Gerald Green/51 8.00 20.00
51 Alonzo Gee/65 5.00 12.00
52 Andre Roberson/67 5.00 12.00
53 Anthony Morrow/43 5.00 12.00
55 Brandon Bass/43 5.00 12.00
56 Corey Brewer/56 5.00 12.00
58 D.J. Augustin/53 5.00 12.00
59 Donatas Motiejunas/46 5.00 12.00
63 Nick Collison/43 5.00 12.00
64 Norris Cole/53 5.00 12.00
65 Omer Asik/55 5.00 12.00
67 Patrick Beverley/64 5.00 12.00
68 Roy Hibbert/57 6.00 15.00
69 Tony Snell/58 5.00 12.00
70 Terrence Jones/40 5.00 12.00
71 Udonis Haslem/59 5.00 12.00
73 Ty Lawson/42 5.00 12.00
74 Jason Terry/50 12.00 30.00

2015-16 Immaculate Collection Dual Autographs

PRINT RUNS B/WN 25-49 COPIES PER
EXCHANGE DEADLINE 3/14/2018
1 Russell/Towns/49 75.00 200.00
2 Okafor/Towns/49 75.00 200.00
3 Cly-Stn/Towns/49 75.00 200.00
4 J.Parker/R.Vaughn/49 12.00 30.00
5 D.Booker/B.Knight/49 200.00 500.00
6 D.Wade/S.O'Neal/25 500.00 1,000.00
7 C.Paul/B.Griffin/25 150.00 400.00
8 A.Davis/K.Durant/25 150.00 400.00
9 Dekker/Kaminsky/49 40.00 100.00
10 E.Mudiay/K.Faried/49 15.00 40.00
11 K.Porzingis/J.Grant/49 75.00 200.00
12 J.Young/M.Turner/49 50.00 125.00
13 M.Harrell/T.Rozier/49 40.00 100.00
14 J.Grant/P.Connaughton/49 15.00 40.00
15 D.Wade/C.Bosh/49 1,000.00 2,000.00
16 N.Powell/D.Wright/49 25.00 60.00
17 D.Exum/A.Bogut/49 25.00 60.00
18 D.Exum/J.Ingles/49 30.00 80.00
19 Finley/Nash/49 EXCH 75.00 200.00
20 K.Durant/K.Bryant/49 3,000.00 6,000.00
21 K.Love/K.Irving/49 100.00 250.00
22 Russell/Kobe/49 EXCH 2,000.00 4,000.00
23 Clrksn/Rssll/49 EXCH 50.00 120.00
24 R.Gay/D.Cousins/49 30.00 80.00
25 E.Payton/M.Hezonja/49 15.00 40.00
26 McGrady/Carter/25 1,500.00 3,000.00
27 L.Bird/M.Johnson/25 3,000.00 6,000.00
28 Abdul-Jabbar/Magic/25 150.00 400.00
29 K.Bryant/A.Iverson/25 8,000.00 12,000.00
30 Bryant/Anthony/25 5,000.00 10,000.00
31 E.Hayes/W.Unseld/49 25.00 60.00
32 I.Thomas/M.Smart/49 25.00 60.00
33 Melo/Porzingis/49 125.00 300.00
34 J.Erving/A.Iverson/25 300.00 600.00
35 Shaq/Hardaway/25 1,500.00 3,000.00
36 Hlis-Jffrsn/Jhnsn/49 15.00 40.00
37 J.Winslow/J.Okafor/49 20.00 50.00
38 Gay/Cauley-Stein/49 20.00 50.00
39 Drexler/Olajuwon/49 400.00 800.00
40 M.Hezonja/T.Kukoc/49 40.00 100.00
41 Kobe/Shaq/25 6,000.00 12,000.00
42 Sprewell/Jackson/49 30.00 80.00
43 B.Knight/T.Warren/49 20.00 50.00
44 M.Jackson/J.Rose/49 15.00 40.00
45 Z.Randolph/M.Conley/49 20.00 50.00
46 A.Horford/D.Schroder/49 EXCH 20.00 50.00
47 N.Bjelica/V.Divac/49 20.00 50.00
48 Porzingis/Towns/49 200.00 500.00
49 McConnell/Okafor/49 50.00 120.00
50 N.Bjelica/N.Jokic/49 800.00 1,500.00
51 Mudiay/Russell/49 20.00 50.00
52 Stdmre/Stckhse/49 40.00 100.00
53 Robinson/Shaq/25 400.00 800.00
54 Robinson/Elliott/49 125.00 300.00
55 Parker/Robinson/49 200.00 500.00
56 R.Barry/J.Wilkes/49 40.00 100.00
57 D.Cowens/D.Nelson/49 40.00 100.00
58 Stdmre/McGrady/49 150.00 400.00
59 L.Wilkens/C.Hagan/49 40.00 100.00
60 E.Jones/N.Van Exel/49 40.00 100.00

2015-16 Immaculate Collection Dual Memorabilia

PRINT RUNS B/WN 25-75 COPIES PER
*PRIME/25: 1X TO 2.5X BASIC
1 Derrick Rose/75 5.00 12.00
2 DeAndre Jordan/75 2.50 6.00
3 Paul Millsap/75 2.50 6.00
4 Tony Parker/75 5.00 12.00
5 Al Horford/75 3.00 8.00
6 Rodney Hood/75 2.50 6.00
7 Kyle Korver/75 2.50 6.00
8 Blake Griffin/75 3.00 8.00
9 Kyle Lowry/75 3.00 8.00
10 Chandler Parsons/75 2.00 5.00
11 Kobe Bryant/75 75.00 200.00
12 Isaiah Thomas/75 5.00 12.00
13 Victor Oladipo/75 2.50 6.00
14 Kemba Walker/75 3.00 8.00
15 Pau Gasol/75 5.00 12.00
16 Al Jefferson/75 2.00 5.00
17 Jeremy Lamb/75 2.00 5.00
18 LeBron James/75 25.00 60.00
19 Shaquille O'Neal/75 10.00 25.00
20 Kyrie Irving/75 6.00 15.00
21 Kevin Love/75 3.00 8.00
22 DeMarre Carroll/75 2.00 5.00
23 Rudy Gobert/75 4.00 10.00
24 Kevin Durant/75 12.00 30.00
25 Tim Duncan/75 8.00 20.00
26 Russell Westbrook/75 10.00 25.00
27 Serge Ibaka/75 2.50 6.00
28 Deron Williams/75 2.50 6.00
29 Jimmy Butler/75 6.00 15.00
30 Reggie Jackson/75 2.50 6.00
31 Damian Lillard/75 8.00 20.00
32 Andre Drummond/75 3.00 8.00
33 Marcus Morris/75 2.00 5.00
34 Elfrid Payton/75 2.50 6.00
35 Nikola Vucevic/75 2.50 6.00
36 DeMar DeRozan/75 4.00 10.00
37 Trey Burke/75 2.00 5.00
38 Gordon Hayward/25 3.00 8.00
39 Josh Smith/75 2.00 5.00
40 Lance Stephenson/75 2.50 6.00
41 Dirk Nowitzki/75 8.00 20.00
42 Manu Ginobili/75 5.00 12.00
43 Michael Beasley/75 2.50 6.00
44 George Hill/75 2.50 6.00
45 Mason Plumlee/75 2.00 5.00
46 Draymond Green/75 4.00 10.00
47 Paul George/75 5.00 12.00
48 Tristan Thompson/75 5.00 12.00
49 Tyler Zeller/75 2.00 5.00

2015-16 Immaculate Collection Dual Patch Autographs

PRINT RUNS B/WN 28-75 COPIES PER
EXCHANGE DEADLINE 3/14/2018
DPAABU Alec Burks/50 6.00 15.00
DPAADA Anthony Davis/50 60.00 150.00
DPAAHO Al Horford/50 10.00 25.00
DPAAWI Andrew Wiggins/50 60.00 150.00
DPABBE Bradley Beal/50 20.00 50.00
DPABKN Brandon Knight/50 6.00 15.00
DPABPO Bobby Portis/75 30.00 80.00
DPACPA Cameron Payne/75 10.00 25.00
DPADMU Dikembe Mutombo/35 30.00 80.00
DPADRO Dennis Rodman/35 60.00 150.00
DPAEKA Enes Kanter/50 8.00 20.00
DPAGHA Gordon Hayward/50 12.00 30.00
DPAITH Isiah Thomas/35 25.00 50.00
DPAJCR Jae Crowder/35 12.00 30.00
DPAJRA Julius Randle/50 15.00 40.00
DPAJST John Starks/35 12.00 30.00
DPAJWA John Wall/50 20.00 50.00
DPAJWO James Worthy/31 30.00 80.00
DPAKDU Kevin Durant/50 75.00 200.00
DPAKIR Kyrie Irving/50 60.00 150.00
DPAKOU Kelly Oubre Jr./75 12.00 30.00
DPALBI Larry Bird/35 50.00 120.00
DPAMCW Michael Carter-Williams/50 6.00 15.00
DPAMDE M. Dellavedova/50 8.00 20.00
DPAMJO Magic Johnson/35 50.00 120.00
DPAMTU Myles Turner/75 30.00 80.00
DPANBA Nicolas Batum/50 6.00 15.00
DPARHO Robert Horry/28 10.00 25.00
DPARSA Ralph Sampson/35 8.00 20.00
DPASBA Shane Battier/35 10.00 25.00
DPATHA Tobias Harris/50 8.00 20.00
DPATLY Trey Lyles/75 15.00 40.00
DPATTH Tristan Thompson/50 12.00 30.00
DPAVOL Victor Oladipo/50 12.00 30.00
DPAZLA Zach LaVine/50 30.00 80.00

2015-16 Immaculate Collection Dual Patch Autographs Jersey Number

*JSY NUM p/r 20-91: .75X TO 2X BASIC
PRINT RUNS B/WN 2-91 COPIES PER
NO PRICING ON QTY 15 OR LESS
EXCHANGE DEADLINE 3/14/2018
DPADRO Dennis Rodman/91 40.00 100.00

2015-16 Immaculate Collection Ink

PRINT RUNS B/WN 50-99 COPIES PER
EXCHANGE DEADLINE 3/14/2018
*RED/25: .5X TO 1.2X BASIC
IKABO Andrew Bogut/99 5.00 12.00
IKABR Avery Bradley/99 4.00 10.00
IKADR Andre Drummond/99 6.00 15.00
IKAHO Allan Houston/99 5.00 12.00
IKAWI Andrew Wiggins/60 15.00 40.00
IKBGR Blake Griffin/60 15.00 40.00
IKBKN Brandon Knight/99 4.00 10.00
IKBPO Bobby Portis/99 10.00 25.00
IKBWA Bill Walton/99 40.00 100.00
IKDBO Devin Booker/99 300.00 600.00
IKDMA Dan Majerle/99 6.00 15.00
IKDMO Donatas Motiejunas/99 4.00 10.00
IKDMU Dikembe Mutombo/50 10.00 25.00
IKDRO Dennis Rodman/60 20.00 50.00
IKDRU D'Angelo Russell/60 15.00 40.00
IKEBL Eric Bledsoe/99 5.00 12.00
IKEFO Evan Fournier/99 5.00 12.00
IKEMU Emmanuel Mudiay/60 5.00 12.00
IKETU Evan Turner/99 4.00 10.00
IKGGE George Gervin/99 10.00 25.00
IKGOH Gordon Hayward/99 8.00 20.00
IKGHA Gary Harris/99 5.00 12.00
IKGHI Grant Hill/60 15.00 40.00
IKJCR Jae Crowder/99 4.00 10.00
IKJIN Joe Ingles/99 5.00 12.00
IKJOK Jahlil Okafor/60 5.00 12.00
IKJRA Julius Randle/99 8.00 20.00
IKJRO Jalen Rose/99 5.00 12.00
IKJTE Jason Terry/99 5.00 12.00
IKJVA Jonas Valanciunas/99 5.00 12.00
IKJWA John Wall/60 15.00 40.00
IKJWI Justise Winslow/99 8.00 20.00
IKKBA Kent Bazemore/99 4.00 10.00
IKKBR Kobe Bryant/60 2,000.00 4,000.00
IKKDU Kevin Durant/60 50.00 120.00
IKKFA Kenneth Faried/99 5.00 12.00
IKKIR Kyrie Irving/60 40.00 100.00
IKKLO Kevin Love/60 6.00 15.00
IKKOU Kelly Oubre Jr./99 8.00 20.00
IKKPO Kristaps Porzingis/99 40.00 100.00
IKKTO Karl-Anthony Towns/60 50.00 120.00
IKMGA Marc Gasol/60 20.00 50.00
IKMRI Mitch Richmond/99 10.00 25.00
IKMTU Myles Turner/99 12.00 30.00
IKNBA Nicolas Batum/99 4.00 10.00
IKNVE Nick Van Exel/99 8.00 20.00
IKRAL Ray Allen/60 20.00 50.00
IKRGA Rudy Gay/99 6.00 15.00
IKRHO Robert Horry/99 5.00 12.00
IKRNE Raul Neto/99 4.00 10.00
IKSNA Steve Nash/60 60.00 150.00
IKSON Shaquille O'Neal/60 40.00 100.00
IKTHA Tim Hardaway Jr./99 5.00 12.00
IKTLY Trey Lyles/99 5.00 12.00
IKTMC T.J. McConnell/99 25.00 60.00
IKTMA Tracy McGrady/60 20.00 50.00
IKTRO Terry Rozier/99 15.00 40.00
IKTWA T.J. Warren/99 6.00 15.00
IKWCS Willie Cauley-Stein/99 5.00 12.00
IKZLA Zach LaVine/99 12.00 30.00

2015-16 Immaculate Collection Jumbo Patches Jersey Numbers

PRINT RUNS B/WN 8-25 COPIES PER
NO PRICING ON QTY 18 OR LESS
10 Timofey Mozgov/23 8.00 20.00
16 Dante Cunningham/21 5.00 12.00
19 LeBron James/24 150.00 400.00
27 R.J. Hunter/25 5.00 12.00
40 Reggie Evans/25 8.00 20.00
54 Jerian Grant/22 10.00 25.00
57 Marcus Morris/25 8.00 20.00
59 Joakim Noah/25 8.00 20.00
68 Joe Smith/21 10.00 25.00
70 Walter Tavares/23 8.00 20.00
71 Cole Aldrich/20 8.00 20.00
73 Ben McLemore/25 8.00 20.00
76 Mike Scott/25 8.00 20.00
80 Jonas Jerebko/20 20.00 50.00
84 Mo Williams/23 6.00 15.00
90 Nemanja Bjelica/20 8.00 20.00
99 Jordan Mickey/25 8.00 20.00

2015-16 Immaculate Collection Jumbo Patches Team Logos

PRINT RUNS B/WN 6-22 COPIES PER
NO PRICING ON QTY 14 OR LESS
45 Tyson Chandler/22 8.00 20.00

2015-16 Immaculate Collection Memorabilia

STATED PRINT RUN 99 SER.#'d SETS
*RED/25: 1X TO 2.5X BASIC
1 Nerlens Noel 2.50 6.00
2 Robert Covington 2.50 6.00
3 Jabari Parker 2.00 5.00
4 Michael Carter-Williams 2.00 5.00
5 Derrick Rose 5.00 12.00
6 LeBron James 25.00 60.00
7 Kevin Love 3.00 8.00
8 Kyrie Irving 6.00 15.00
9 Marcus Smart 4.00 10.00
10 Jared Sullinger 2.00 5.00
11 J.J. Redick 3.00 8.00
12 Blake Griffin 3.00 8.00
13 Marc Gasol 3.00 8.00
14 Al Horford 3.00 8.00
15 Dwyane Wade 6.00 15.00
16 Hassan Whiteside 2.50 6.00
17 Kemba Walker 3.00 8.00
18 Al Jefferson 2.00 5.00
19 Derrick Favors 2.50 6.00
20 Rajon Rondo 4.00 10.00
21 Carmelo Anthony 5.00 12.00
22 Arron Afflalo 2.00 5.00
23 Derrick Williams 2.00 5.00
24 Kobe Bryant 25.00 60.00
25 Victor Oladipo 2.50 6.00
26 Chandler Parsons 2.00 5.00
27 Kenneth Faried 2.50 6.00
28 Will Barton 2.00 5.00
29 Gary Harris 2.50 6.00
30 Paul George 5.00 12.00
31 George Hill 2.50 6.00
32 Anthony Davis 8.00 20.00
33 Tyreke Evans 2.50 6.00
34 Reggie Jackson 2.50 6.00
35 Andre Drummond 3.00 8.00
36 DeMar DeRozan 4.00 10.00
37 Kyle Lowry 3.00 8.00
38 James Harden 6.00 15.00
39 Dwight Howard 4.00 10.00
40 Kawhi Leonard 10.00 25.00
41 Tony Parker 5.00 12.00
42 Tim Duncan 8.00 20.00
43 Eric Bledsoe 2.50 6.00
44 Brandon Knight 2.00 5.00
45 Serge Ibaka 2.50 6.00
46 Russell Westbrook 5.00 12.00
47 Andrew Wiggins 4.00 10.00
48 Gerald Henderson 2.00 5.00
49 Damian Lillard 8.00 20.00
50 Stephen Curry 25.00 60.00

2015-16 Immaculate Collection Milestones Autographs

PRINT RUNS B/WN 25-50 COPIES PER
EXCHANGE DEADLINE 3/14/2018
1 Kobe Bryant/25 6,000.00 10,000.00
2 Klay Thompson/25 500.00 800.00
3 Stephen Curry/25 1,500.00 3,000.00
4 Dwyane Wade/25 600.00 900.00
5 Dikembe Mutombo/50 75.00 200.00
6 Andre Drummond/25 EXCH 150.00 300.00
7 Draymond Green/25 250.00 500.00
8 DeMarcus Cousins/25 EXCH 250.00 400.00
9 Jimmy Butler/25 200.00 400.00
10 Anthony Davis/50 150.00 400.00
11 Hassan Whiteside/50 75.00 200.00
12 Steve Kerr/50 EXCH 125.00 300.00
13 Devin Booker/50 500.00 1,000.00
14 Zach LaVine/50 200.00 500.00
15 Aaron Gordon/50 150.00 300.00

2015-16 Immaculate Collection Patch Autographs

PRINT RUNS B/WN 14-99 COPIES PER
NO PRICING ON QTY 19 OR LESS
EXCHANGE DEADLINE 3/14/2018
PAN Nene/60 8.00 20.00
PAAAM Al-Farouq Aminu/60 6.00 15.00
PAADA Anthony Davis/60 100.00 250.00
PAAGI Artis Gilmore/60 15.00 40.00
PAAHO Al Horford/60 10.00 25.00
PAAIV Allen Iverson/40 200.00 500.00
PABBO Bojan Bogdanovic/60 10.00 25.00
PABGR Blake Griffin/60 40.00 100.00
PABKN Brandon Knight/60 6.00 15.00
PACAN Carmelo Anthony/60 75.00 200.00
PACBO Chris Bosh/60 60.00 150.00
PACDR Clyde Drexler/60 40.00 100.00
PACPA Chris Paul/60 200.00 500.00
PADMC Doug McDermott/60 8.00 20.00
PADRO Dennis Rodman/40 100.00 250.00
PADSC Dennis Schroder/60 12.00 30.00
PADWA Dwyane Wade/60 200.00 500.00
PAEBL Eric Bledsoe/60 8.00 20.00
PAEDA Ed Davis/50 6.00 15.00
PAEFO Evan Fournier/60 8.00 20.00
PAEGO Eric Gordon/60 8.00 20.00
PAEKA Enes Kanter/60 6.00 15.00
PAETU Evan Turner/60 6.00 15.00
PAFEZ Festus Ezeli/44 6.00 15.00
PAGHE Gerald Henderson/60 6.00 15.00
PAGHI Grant Hill/60 20.00 50.00
PAHOL Hakeem Olajuwon/60 125.00 300.00
PAJCR Jae Crowder/60 10.00 25.00
PAJER Julius Erving/40 200.00 500.00
PAJHO Jrue Holiday/60 12.00 30.00
PAJRO Jalen Rose/35 8.00 20.00
PAJSM J.R. Smith/51 25.00 60.00
PAJST John Stockton/40 30.00 80.00
PAJTE Jeff Teague/60 6.00 15.00
PAJVA Jonas Valanciunas/60 8.00 20.00
PAJWA John Wall/60 75.00 200.00
PAJWE Jerry West/50 200.00 500.00
PAKBR Kobe Bryant/60 4,000.00 8,000.00
PAKDU Kevin Durant/60 400.00 800.00
PAKIR Kyrie Irving/60 125.00 300.00
PAKLO Kevin Love/60 20.00 50.00
PAKMA Karl Malone/40 75.00 200.00
PALBI Larry Bird/26 125.00 300.00
PAMBR Markel Brown/60 6.00 15.00
PAMCO Mike Conley/60 10.00 25.00
PAMGO Marcin Gortat/60 6.00 15.00
PAMJO Magic Johnson/40 125.00 300.00
PANBA Nicolas Batum/60 6.00 15.00
PANYO Nick Young/60 8.00 20.00
PAOPO Otto Porter/60 8.00 20.00
PAPGE Paul George/60 75.00 200.00
PARGA Rudy Gay/60 30.00 80.00
PARHO Robert Horry/40 40.00 100.00
PARLO Robin Lopez/60 6.00 15.00
PARPA Robert Parish/60 12.00 30.00
PASBA Shane Battier/60 8.00 20.00
PASCU Stephen Curry/60 3,000.00 6,000.00
PASNA Steve Nash/60 75.00 200.00
PASON Shaquille O'Neal/40 400.00 800.00
PATAL Tony Allen/60 6.00 15.00
PATWA T.J. Warren/60 10.00 25.00
PAVOL Victor Oladipo/60 20.00 50.00

2015-16 Immaculate Collection Patch Autographs Jersey Number

*JSY NUM p/r 22-91: .5X TO 1.2X BASIC
PRINT RUNS B/WN 1-91 COPIES PER
NO PRICING ON QTY 17 OR LESS
EXCHANGE DEADLINE 3/14/2018
PAADA Anthony Davis/23 150.00 300.00
PABGR Blake Griffin/32 50.00 120.00
PACDR Clyde Drexler/22 50.00 120.00
PAGHI Grant Hill/33 40.00 100.00
PAJVA Jonas Valanciunas/58 20.00 50.00
PAKBR Kobe Bryant/24 2,500.00 5,000.00
PAKDU Kevin Durant/35 150.00 400.00
PAKMA Karl Malone/32 75.00 200.00
PAMJO Magic Johnson/32 125.00 300.00
PASCU Stephen Curry/30 4,000.00 8,000.00
PASON Shaquille O'Neal/32 200.00 400.00

2015-16 Immaculate Collection Patches Jersey Number

PRINT RUNS B/WN 1-50 COPIES PER
NO PRICING ON QTY 15 OR LESS
PJAD Anthony Davis/23 75.00 200.00
PJAJ Al Jefferson/25 4.00 10.00
PJAW Andrew Wiggins/22 60.00 150.00
PJCP Chandler Parsons/25 4.00 10.00
PJDW Derrick Williams/23 4.00 10.00
PJGA Giannis Antetokounmpo/34 300.00 600.00
PJGR Glen Rice/41 5.00 12.00
PJJB Jimmy Butler/21 30.00 80.00
PJKF Kenneth Faried/35 5.00 12.00
PJKM Khris Middleton/22 20.00 50.00
PJLJ LeBron James/23 400.00 800.00
PJMG Marc Gasol/33 6.00 15.00
PJMS Marcus Smart/36 8.00 20.00
PJPP Paul Pierce/34 10.00 25.00
PJRC Robert Covington/33 8.00 20.00
PJRG Rudy Gobert/27 15.00 40.00
PJSC Stephen Curry/30 150.00 400.00
PJTD Tim Duncan/21 75.00 200.00
PJTY Thaddeus Young/30 4.00 10.00
PJZR Zach Randolph/50 6.00 15.00

2015-16 Immaculate Collection Premium Autograph Patches

PRINT RUNS B/WN 16-25 COPIES PER
NO PRICING ON QTY 19 OR LESS
EXCHANGE DEADLINE 3/14/2018
PPAN Nene/25 15.00 40.00
PPAABO A. Bogut/25 EXCH 40.00 100.00
PPAABR Avery Bradley/24 20.00 50.00
PPAABR Anthony Brown/25 25.00 60.00
PPAABU Alec Burks/25 6.00 15.00
PPAAHO Al Horford/25 12.00 30.00
PPAAWI Andrew Wiggins/25 75.00 200.00
PPABGR Blake Griffin/25 75.00 200.00
PPABKN Brandon Knight/25 12.00 30.00
PPABPO Bobby Portis/25 75.00 200.00
PPACAN Carmelo Anthony/25 60.00 150.00
PPACBO Chris Bosh/25 15.00 40.00
PPACDR Clyde Drexler/25 100.00 250.00
PPACMC Chris McCullough/25 15.00 40.00
PPACPA Cameron Payne/25 30.00 80.00
PPACWA C.J. Watson/25 6.00 15.00
PPADBO Devin Booker/25 1,500.00 3,000.00
PPADGA Danilo Gallinari/25 20.00 50.00
PPADGR Draymond Green/25 75.00 200.00
PPADMO D. Motiejunas/25 12.00 30.00
PPADRO Dennis Rodman/25 75.00 200.00
PPADRO David Robinson/25 50.00 120.00
PPADRU D'Angelo Russell/25 150.00 400.00
PPADSC Dennis Schroder/25 40.00 100.00
PPADWA Dwyane Wade/25 150.00 400.00
PPAEBL Eric Bledsoe/25 20.00 50.00
PPAEFO Evan Fournier/25 12.00 30.00
PPAEMU E. Mudiay/25 30.00 80.00
PPAEPA Elfrid Payton/25 15.00 40.00
PPAETU Evan Turner/25 6.00 15.00
PPAFKA Frank Kaminsky/25 25.00 60.00
PPAGDR Goran Dragic/25 12.00 30.00
PPAGHA Gary Harris/25 8.00 20.00
PPAGHA Gordon Hayward/25 25.00 60.00
PPAGHE Gerald Henderson/25 8.00 20.00
PPAGHI Grant Hill/25 50.00 120.00
PPAHOL Hakeem Olajuwon/25 30.00 80.00
PPAJDU Joe Dumars/25 12.00 30.00
PPAJKI Jason Kidd/25 50.00 120.00
PPAJMA Jamal Mashburn/25 30.00 80.00
PPAJMI Jordan Mickey/25 10.00 25.00
PPAJOK Jahlil Okafor/25 50.00 120.00
PPAJPA Jabari Parker/25 50.00 120.00
PPAJRA Julius Randle/25 20.00 50.00
PPAJRI Josh Richardson/25 30.00 80.00
PPAJSM J.R. Smith/25 40.00 100.00
PPAJST John Stockton/25 40.00 100.00
PPAJTE Jeff Teague/25 6.00 15.00
PPAJVA Jonas Valanciunas/25 10.00 25.00
PPAJWA John Wall/25 40.00 100.00
PPAJWI Justise Winslow/25 100.00 250.00
PPAJYO Joe Young/25 15.00 40.00
PPAKBR Kobe Bryant/25 6,000.00 10,000.00
PPAKDU Kevin Durant/25 250.00 500.00
PPAKFA Kenneth Faried/25 15.00 40.00
PPAKIR Kyrie Irving/25 125.00 250.00
PPAKLO Kevon Looney/25 20.00 50.00
PPAKMA Karl Malone/25 60.00 150.00
PPAKOU Kelly Oubre Jr./25 50.00 120.00
PPAKTH Klay Thompson/25 125.00 300.00
PPAKVH Keith Van Horn/25 15.00 40.00
PPALGA Langston Galloway/25 6.00 15.00
PPAMAG Mark Aguirre/23 8.00 20.00
PPAMCO Mike Conley/25 12.00 30.00
PPAMCW M. Carter-Williams/25 12.00 30.00
PPAMDE M. Dellavedova/25 15.00 40.00
PPAMGA Marc Gasol/25 40.00 100.00
PPAMGO Marcin Gortat/25 10.00 25.00
PPAMHA M. Harkless/25 EXCH 15.00 40.00
PPAMHE Mario Hezonja/25 40.00 100.00
PPAMHU M. Huertas/25 EXCH 20.00 50.00
PPAMPR Mark Price/25 20.00 50.00
PPAMSM Marcus Smart/25 20.00 50.00
PPAMTU Myles Turner/25 150.00 300.00
PPANBA Nicolas Batum/25 15.00 40.00
PPANCO Norris Cole/25 6.00 15.00
PPANVU Nikola Vucevic/25 15.00 40.00
PPANYO Nick Young/22 10.00 25.00
PPARGA Rudy Gay/25 20.00 50.00
PPARHJ R. Hollis-Jefferson/25 40.00 100.00
PPARLO Robin Lopez/25 10.00 25.00
PPASBA Shane Battier/25 20.00 50.00
PPASCU Stephen Curry/25 3,000.00 6,000.00
PPASKA Sasha Kaun/25 8.00 20.00
PPASON S. O'Neal/25 EXCH 150.00 300.00
PPATLY Trey Lyles/25 50.00 120.00
PPATMC T.J. McConnell/25 60.00 150.00
PPATMO Timofey Mozgov/25 6.00 15.00
PPATRO Terry Rozier/25 75.00 200.00
PPATTH Tristan Thompson/25 20.00 50.00
PPATYO Thaddeus Young/25 8.00 20.00
PPAVOL Victor Oladipo/25 20.00 50.00
PPAWMA Wesley Matthews/25 15.00 40.00
PPAZPA Zaza Pachulia/19 15.00 40.00
PPAZRA Z. Randolph/25 EXCH 15.00 40.00

2015-16 Immaculate Collection Quad Materials

STATED PRINT RUN 49 SER.#'d SETS
QMCHI Rose/Gsl/Btlr/Mrtc 8.00 20.00
QMLAC Grffn/Paul/Jrdn/Prce 8.00 20.00
QMLAL West/Chmbrln/Bmt/O'Nl 60.00 150.00
QMMIN Wggns/Twns/Grntt/LVne 10.00 25.00
QMOKC Wstbrk/Adms/Drnt/Ibka 15.00 40.00
QMORL Fournier/Oladipo
Gordon/Payton 4.00 10.00
QMPOR Drxlr/Lllrd/Dckwrth/Rbnsn 10.00 25.00
QMSAS Dmpr/Rbnsn/Grvn/Dncn 10.00 25.00
QMUTA Favors/Hayward/Hood/Burke 4.00 10.00

2015-16 Immaculate Collection Rookie Patch Autographs Jersey Number

*JSY NUM p/r 20-55: .6X TO 1.5X BASIC
PRINT RUNS B/WN 1-55 COPIES PER
NO PRICING ON QTY 17 OR LESS
EXCHANGE DEADLINE 3/14/2018
101 Karl-Anthony Towns/32 1,000.00 3,000.00
103 Frank Kaminsky/44 25.00 60.00
112 Trey Lyles/41 50.00 120.00
124 R. Hollis-Jefferson/24 100.00 250.00
147 Montrezl Harrell/35 60.00 150.00
148 Myles Turner/33 400.00 600.00

2015-16 Immaculate Collection Rookie Patch Autographs Red

*RED: .5X TO 1.2X BASIC
STATED PRINT RUN 25 SER.#'d SETS
EXCHANGE DEADLINE 3/14/2018
121 Devin Booker 2,000.00 4,000.00
147 Montrezl Harrell 125.00 300.00

2015-16 Immaculate Collection Shadowbox Signatures

PRINT RUNS B/WN 60-99 COPIES PER
EXCHANGE DEADLINE 3/14/2018
SSN Nene/99 5.00 12.00
SSAB Avery Bradley/99 4.00 10.00
SSAC Antoine Carr/99 4.00 10.00
SSAD Anthony Davis/60 100.00 250.00
SSAD Adrian Dantley/99 6.00 15.00
SSAE Alex English/99 8.00 20.00
SSAG A.C. Green/99 6.00 15.00
SSAW Andrew Wiggins/60 12.00 30.00
SSBG Blake Griffin/60 12.00 30.00
SSBK Brandon Knight/99 4.00 10.00
SSBM Bob McAdoo/99 12.00 30.00
SSBP Bobby Portis/99 10.00 25.00
SSCB Chris Bosh/60 15.00 40.00
SSCM Calvin Murphy/99 5.00 12.00
SSCP Cameron Payne/99 6.00 15.00
SSDB Devin Booker/99 500.00 1,000.00
SSDC Dave Cowens/99 8.00 20.00
SSDG Danilo Gallinari/99 5.00 12.00
SSDR D'Angelo Russell/60 40.00 100.00
SSDS Dennis Schroder/99 6.00 15.00
SSDT David Thompson/99 8.00 20.00
SSDW Dwyane Wade/60 100.00 250.00
SSEG Eric Gordon/99 5.00 12.00
SSEM Emmanuel Mudiay/60 6.00 15.00
SSET Evan Turner/99 4.00 10.00
SSGG George Gervin/99 15.00 40.00
SSGH Gary Harris/99 5.00 12.00
SSGH Gordon Hayward/99 8.00 20.00
SSGH Grant Hill/60 20.00 50.00
SSGH Gerald Henderson/99 4.00 10.00
SSHG Horace Grant/99 12.00 30.00
SSJC Jae Crowder/99 4.00 10.00
SSJD Joe Dumars/99 12.00 30.00
SSJE Julius Erving/60 75.00 200.00
SSJG Jerian Grant/99 6.00 15.00
SSJH Jrue Holiday/99 5.00 12.00
SSJK Jason Kidd/60 15.00 40.00
SSJO Jahlil Okafor/60 5.00 12.00
SSJS Jerry Stackhouse/99 10.00 25.00
SSJS Jonathon Simmons/99 5.00 12.00
SSJS John Stockton/60 40.00 100.00
SSJT Jeff Teague/99 4.00 10.00
SSJW John Wall/60 25.00 60.00
SSJY Joe Young/99 4.00 10.00
SSKB Kent Bazemore/99 4.00 10.00
SSKB Kobe Bryant/60 2,500.00 5,000.00
SSKD Kevin Durant/60 125.00 300.00
SSKF Kenneth Faried/99 5.00 12.00
SSKI Kyrie Irving/60 60.00 150.00
SSKL Kevon Looney/99 8.00 20.00
SSKM Karl Malone/60 40.00 100.00
SSKO Kelly Oubre Jr./99 12.00 30.00
SSKP Kristaps Porzingis/99 75.00 200.00
SSKT Karl-Anthony Towns/60 125.00 300.00
SSLN Larry Nance Jr./99 8.00 20.00
SSMA Mark Aguirre/99 5.00 12.00
SSMF Michael Finley/99 6.00 15.00
SSMG Marcin Gortat/99 4.00 10.00
SSMJ Mark Jackson/99 5.00 12.00
SSMJ Magic Johnson/60 100.00 250.00
SSMJ Marques Johnson/99 5.00 12.00
SSMP Mason Plumlee/99 4.00 10.00
SSMT Myles Turner/99 20.00 50.00
SSNB Nicolas Batum/99 4.00 10.00
SSNJ Nikola Jokic/99 1,500.00 3,000.00
SSNP Norman Powell/99 8.00 20.00
SSOR Oscar Robertson/60 75.00 200.00
SSPG Paul George/60 60.00 150.00
SSRF Rick Fox/99 15.00 40.00
SSRH Rondae Hollis-Jefferson/99 5.00 12.00
SSRH Robert Horry/99 15.00 40.00
SSRH Ron Harper/99 6.00 15.00
SSRN Raul Neto/99 4.00 10.00
SSRP Robert Parish/99 8.00 20.00
SSSB Shane Battier/99 8.00 20.00
SSSO Shaquille O'Neal/60 100.00 250.00
SSSW Spud Webb/99 5.00 12.00
SSTH Tim Hardaway/99 12.00 30.00
SSTK Toni Kukoc/99 15.00 40.00
SSTM T.J. McConnell/99 15.00 40.00
SSTM Tracy McGrady/99 75.00 200.00
SSTW T.J. Warren/99 6.00 15.00
SSWF Walt Frazier/99 15.00 40.00
SSZI Zydrunas Ilgauskas/99 5.00 12.00

2015-16 Immaculate Collection Signatures

PRINT RUNS B/WN 40-99 COPIES PER
EXCHANGE DEADLINE 3/14/2018
*RED/25: .5X TO 1.2X BASIC
SAA Alvan Adams/99 4.00 10.00
SAB Avery Bradley/99 4.00 10.00
SAB Andrew Bogut/99 5.00 12.00
SAD Anthony Davis/60 30.00 80.00
SAD Andre Drummond/99 8.00 20.00
SAW Andrew Wiggins/60 25.00 60.00
SBG Blake Griffin/60 15.00 40.00
SBR Bill Russell/40 800.00 1,500.00
SCA Carmelo Anthony/60 20.00 50.00
SDC Dave Cowens/99 8.00 20.00
SDG Draymond Green/99 12.00 30.00
SDR Dennis Rodman/60 20.00 50.00
SDR David Robinson/60 20.00 50.00
SDT David Thompson/99 8.00 20.00
SDW Dwyane Wade/60 30.00 80.00
SEF Evan Fournier/99 5.00 12.00
SEP Elfrid Payton/99 5.00 12.00
SET Evan Turner/99 4.00 10.00
SGD Goran Dragic/99 6.00 15.00
SGG George Gervin/99 10.00 25.00
SGH Grant Hill/60 15.00 40.00
SGH Gordon Hayward/99 6.00 15.00
SHW Hassan Whiteside/99 12.00 30.00
SJC Jae Crowder/99 4.00 10.00
SJE Julius Erving/60 30.00 80.00
SJI Joe Ingles/99 5.00 12.00
SJP Jabari Parker/60 12.00 30.00
SKB Kobe Bryant/60 800.00 1,500.00
SKD Kevin Durant/60 50.00 120.00
SKI Kyrie Irving/60 30.00 80.00
SKT Klay Thompson/60 25.00 60.00
SMC Michael Carter-Williams/99 4.00 10.00
SPG Pau Gasol/60 10.00 25.00
SRG Rudy Gay/99 6.00 15.00
SSB Sam Bowie/99 4.00 10.00
SSM Sidney Moncrief/99 4.00 10.00
STK Toni Kukoc/99 6.00 15.00
SVO Victor Oladipo/60 5.00 12.00
SWM Wesley Matthews/99 6.00 15.00
SZL Zach LaVine/99 12.00 30.00

2015-16 Immaculate Collection Sneaker Swatches

PRINT RUNS B/WN 1-60 COPIES PER
NO PRICING ON QTY 17 OR LESS
3 Carmelo Anthony/60 10.00 25.00
4 Grant Hill/60 15.00 40.00
5 Karl-Anthony Towns/38 20.00 50.00
6 Andrew Wiggins/60 6.00 15.00
7 John Wall/26 10.00 25.00
8 Andre Drummond/60 5.00 12.00
9 Dennis Rodman/32 30.00 80.00
10 Dominique Wilkins/44 12.00 30.00
11 Dwight Howard/60 6.00 15.00
14 Paul Pierce/42 10.00 25.00
15 Ray Allen/52 10.00 25.00
16 Eric Bledsoe/26 4.00 10.00
19 John Stockton/38 10.00 25.00
20 Derrick Rose/60 12.00 30.00
21 Shaquille O'Neal/60 15.00 40.00
22 Dante Exum/56 8.00 20.00
23 Karl Malone/60 10.00 25.00
24 Anfernee Hardaway/44 20.00 50.00
27 Kevin Durant/32 20.00 50.00
29 Robert Horry/27 5.00 12.00
30 Emmanuel Mudiay/56 4.00 10.00

2015-16 Immaculate Collection Sole of the Game

PRINT RUNS B/WN 8-25 COPIES PER
NO PRICING ON QTY 18 OR LESS
1 Anthony Davis/25 60.00 150.00
2 Draymond Green/22 30.00 80.00
3 Carmelo Anthony/25 40.00 100.00
4 Grant Hill/25 50.00 120.00
5 Karl-Anthony Towns/20 75.00 200.00
6 Andrew Wiggins/25 30.00 80.00
7 John Wall/25 40.00 100.00
9 Dennis Rodman/25 60.00 150.00
11 Dwight Howard/25 30.00 80.00
12 LaMarcus Aldridge/25 25.00 60.00
13 Magic Johnson/24 100.00 250.00
16 Eric Bledsoe/20 20.00 50.00
18 Spud Webb/22 50.00 120.00
19 John Stockton/25 50.00 120.00
20 Derrick Rose/25 40.00 100.00
22 Dante Exum/25 20.00 50.00
26 D'Angelo Russell/25 60.00 150.00
27 Kevin Durant/25 100.00 250.00
30 Emmanuel Mudiay/25 20.00 50.00

2015-16 Immaculate Collection Standard Materials

PRINT RUNS B/WN 13-75 COPIES PER
NO PRICING ON QTY 13
STABR Avery Bradley/75 2.50 6.00
STADA Anthony Davis/75 6.00 15.00
STADR Andre Drummond/75 4.00 10.00
STAHA Anfernee Hardaway/75 8.00 20.00
STAIG Andre Iguodala/75 4.00 10.00
STAMO Alonzo Mourning/75 6.00 15.00
STAWI Andrew Wiggins/75 5.00 12.00
STBGR Blake Griffin/75 4.00 10.00
STBKN Brandon Knight/75 2.50 6.00
STBLO Brook Lopez/75 4.00 10.00
STBPO Bobby Portis/75 6.00 15.00
STCAN Carmelo Anthony/75 6.00 15.00
STCBO Chris Bosh/75 6.00 15.00

STCCA Clint Capela/75 3.00 8.00
STCDR Clyde Drexler/75 6.00 15.00
STCMC C.J. McCollum/75 4.00 10.00
STCPA Chris Paul/75 8.00 20.00
STCPA Chandler Parsons/75 2.50 6.00
STCWE Chris Webber/75 6.00 15.00
STDBO Devin Booker/75 8.00 20.00
STDCA DeMarre Carroll/75 2.50 6.00
STDCO DeMarcus Cousins/75 4.00 10.00
STDDE DeMar DeRozan/75 5.00 12.00
STDGA Danilo Gallinari/75 3.00 8.00
STDGR Draymond Green/75 5.00 12.00
STDHO Dwight Howard/75 5.00 12.00
STDLI Damian Lillard/75 6.00 15.00
STDNO Dirk Nowitzki/75 10.00 25.00
STDRO Derrick Rose/75 6.00 15.00
STDRP David Robinson/75 8.00 20.00
STDWA Dwyane Wade/75 6.00 15.00
STDWI Dominique Wilkins/52 6.00 15.00
STDWI Deron Williams/75 3.00 8.00
STEBL Eric Bledsoe/75 3.00 8.00
STEGO Eric Gordon/75 3.00 8.00
STEMU Emmanuel Mudiay/75 3.00 8.00
STEPA Elfrid Payton/75 3.00 8.00
STFKA Frank Kaminsky/75 3.00 8.00
STGAN G. Antetokounmpo/75 20.00 50.00
STGHA Gordon Hayward/75 4.00 10.00
STITH Isaiah Thomas/75 3.00 8.00
STJBU Jimmy Butler/75 8.00 20.00
STJER Julius Erving/75 10.00 25.00
STJGR Jerian Grant/75 2.50 6.00
STJHA James Harden/75 10.00 25.00
STJHO Jrue Holiday/75 5.00 12.00
STJKI Jason Kidd/75 6.00 15.00
STJOK Jahlil Okafor/75 3.00 8.00
STJPA Jabari Parker/75 2.50 6.00
STJRA Julius Randle/75 5.00 12.00
STJTE Jeff Teague/75 2.50 6.00
STJWA John Wall/75 5.00 12.00
STJWI Justise Winslow/75 4.00 10.00
STKBR Kobe Bryant/75 40.00 100.00
STKCP Kentavious Caldwell-Pope/75 3.00 8.00
STKDU Kevin Durant/75 8.00 20.00
STKFA Kenneth Faried/75 3.00 8.00
STKGA Kevin Garnett/75 10.00 25.00
STKIR Kyrie Irving/75 6.00 15.00
STKLE Kawhi Leonard/75 12.00 30.00
STKLO Kevin Love/75 4.00 10.00
STKLO Kyle Lowry/75 4.00 10.00
STKMC Kevin McHale/75 6.00 15.00
STKMI Khris Middleton/75 5.00 12.00
STKOU Kelly Oubre Jr./75 8.00 20.00
STKTH Klay Thompson/75 10.00 25.00
STKWA Kemba Walker/75 4.00 10.00
STLAL LaMarcus Aldridge/75 4.00 10.00
STLBI Larry Bird/75 8.00 20.00
STLJA LeBron James/75 30.00 80.00
STMCO Mike Conley/75 4.00 10.00
STMEL Monta Ellis/75 3.00 8.00
STMGA Marc Gasol/75 4.00 10.00
STMHE Mario Hezonja/75 3.00 8.00
STNBA Nicolas Batum/75 2.50 6.00
STNNO Nerlens Noel/75 2.50 6.00
STNVU Nikola Vucevic/75 3.00 8.00
STPEW Patrick Ewing/75 6.00 15.00
STPGE Paul George/75 6.00 15.00
STPMI Paul Millsap/75 3.00 8.00
STPPI Paul Pierce/75 6.00 15.00
STRAL Ray Allen/75 5.00 12.00
STRGA Rudy Gay/75 4.00 10.00
STRGO Rudy Gobert/75 5.00 12.00
STRWE Russell Westbrook/75 6.00 15.00
STSCU Stephen Curry/75 30.00 80.00
STSIB Serge Ibaka/75 3.00 8.00
STSJO Stanley Johnson/75 3.00 8.00
STSPI Scottie Pippen/75 10.00 25.00
STTDU Tim Duncan/75 10.00 25.00
STTJO Tyus Jones/75 3.00 8.00
STTLY Trey Lyles/75 3.00 8.00
STTYO Thaddeus Young/75 2.50 6.00
STVOL Victor Oladipo/75 3.00 8.00
STWCH Wilt Chamberlain/75 40.00 100.00
STWCS Willie Cauley-Stein/75 3.00 8.00
STZRA Zach Randolph/75 3.00 8.00

2015-16 Immaculate Collection Trio Autographs

PRINT RUNS B/WN 15-25 COPIES PER
NO PRICING ON QTY 15
EXCHANGE DEADLINE 3/14/2018
1 Towns/Jones/Bjelica/25 125.00 300.00
2 Twns/Lyls/Cly-Stn/25 125.00 300.00
3 Smth/Dlvdva/Mzgv/25 40.00 100.00
4 Gnns/Crtr-Wllms/Prkr/25 EXCH 75.00 200.00
5 Grant/Grant/Grant/25 40.00 100.00
6 Kaminsky/Dukan/Dekker/25 EXCH 30.00 80.00
7 Oldpo/Pytn/Hznja/25 25.00 60.00
9 Lnrd/Prkr/Aldrdge/25 300.00 600.00
12 Lanier/Johnson/Moncrief/25 40.00 100.00
13 Dandridge/Hayes/Unseld/25 60.00 150.00
14 Lanier/Drummond/Laimbeer/25 50.00 120.00
15 Bryant/Shaq/Horry/25 3,000.00 6,000.00
16 Motiejunas/Ilgauskas
Valanciunas/25 EXCH 30.00 80.00
17 Jcksn/Hstn/Sprwll/25 125.00 300.00
19 Mshbrn/Kidd/Jcksn/25 150.00 400.00
22 Cwns/Nlsn/White/25 50.00 120.00
23 Frazier/Reed/Monroe/25 EXCH 300.00 600.00
25 Brd/Magic/Erving/25 500.00 1,000.00

2015-16 Immaculate Collection Trio Materials

STATED PRINT RUN 49 SER.#'d SETS
TMATL Korver/Millsap/Horford 4.00 10.00
TMBOS Brdly/Thms/Crwdr 12.00 30.00
TMCHA Walker/Jefferson/Lamb 4.00 10.00
TMCHI Rose/Butler/Gasol 8.00 20.00
TMCLE Irving/Lve/Jms 30.00 80.00
TMDAL Jackson/Mashburn/Kidd 6.00 15.00
TMDAL Prsns/Wllms/Nwtzki 10.00 25.00
TMDET Drummond/Morris/Jackson 4.00 10.00
TMHOU Dnlr/Oljwn/Horry 8.00 20.00
TMLAC Griffin/Paul/Jordan 8.00 20.00
TMLAL Clrksn/Wrld Pce/Brnt 40.00 100.00
TMOKC Wstbrk/Ibka/Drnt 8.00 20.00
TMORL Payton/Vucevic/Oladipo 3.00 8.00
TMORL Hrdwy/Andrsn/O'Neal 12.00 30.00
TMPOR McClim/Lllrd/Plmle 6.00 15.00
TMSAS Gnbli/Prkr/Dncn 10.00 25.00
TMTOR DeRozan/Carroll/Lowry 5.00 12.00
TMUTA Hood/Burke/Gobert 5.00 12.00
TMWAS Beal/Porter/Wall 5.00 12.00

2016-17 Immaculate Collection

1-100 PRINT RUN 99 SER.#'d SETS
JSY AU PRINT RUN B/WN 81-99 COPIES PER
EXCHANGE DEADLINE 4/4/2019
1 Aaron Gordon 1.50 4.00
2 Al Horford 1.50 4.00
3 Allen Iverson 2.50 6.00
4 Andre Drummond 1.50 4.00
5 Andrew Wiggins 2.00 5.00
6 Anthony Davis 5.00 12.00
7 Avery Bradley 1.00 2.50
8 Ben Simmons RC 3.00 8.00
9 Blake Griffin 1.50 4.00
10 Bradley Beal 2.00 5.00
11 Brook Lopez 1.25 3.00
12 C.J. McCollum 1.50 4.00
13 Carmelo Anthony 2.50 6.00
14 Chris Paul 2.50 6.00
15 Damian Lillard 4.00 10.00
16 D'Angelo Russell 2.50 6.00
17 Darren Collison 1.00 2.50
18 David Robinson 3.00 8.00
19 DeAndre Jordan 1.25 3.00
20 DeMar DeRozan 2.00 5.00
21 DeMarcus Cousins 1.25 3.00
22 Dennis Schroder 1.50 4.00
23 Derrick Rose 2.50 6.00
24 Devin Booker 6.00 15.00
25 Dion Waiters 1.00 2.50
26 Dirk Nowitzki 4.00 10.00
27 Draymond Green 2.00 5.00
28 Dwight Howard 2.00 5.00
29 Dwyane Wade 3.00 8.00
30 Emmanuel Mudiay 1.00 2.50
31 Eric Bledsoe 1.25 3.00
32 Eric Gordon 1.25 3.00
33 Evan Fournier 1.25 3.00
34 Giannis Antetokounmpo 8.00 20.00
35 Goran Dragic 1.50 4.00
36 Gordon Hayward 1.50 4.00
37 Greg Monroe 1.00 2.50
38 Harrison Barnes 1.25 3.00
39 Hassan Whiteside 1.25 3.00
40 Isaiah Thomas 1.25 3.00
41 Jabari Parker 1.00 2.50
42 Jahlil Okafor 1.00 2.50
43 James Harden 3.00 8.00
44 Jeff Teague 1.00 2.50
45 Jeremy Lin 3.00 8.00
46 Jimmy Butler 3.00 8.00
47 Joel Embiid 4.00 10.00
48 John Wall 2.00 5.00
49 Jonas Valanciunas 1.25 3.00
50 Jordan Clarkson 1.50 4.00
51 Jrue Holiday 2.00 5.00
52 Julius Randle 2.00 5.00
53 Jusuf Nurkic 1.25 3.00
54 Karl Malone 2.50 6.00
55 Karl-Anthony Towns 3.00 8.00
56 Kawhi Leonard 4.00 10.00
57 Kemba Walker 1.25 3.00
58 Kenneth Faried 1.25 3.00
59 Kentavious Caldwell-Pope 1.25 3.00
60 Kevin Durant 6.00 15.00
61 Kevin Love 1.50 4.00
62 Klay Thompson 4.00 10.00
63 Kobe Bryant 125.00 300.00
64 Kristaps Porzingis 2.50 6.00
65 Kyle Lowry 1.50 4.00
66 Kyrie Irving 3.00 8.00
67 LaMarcus Aldridge 1.50 4.00
68 LeBron James 15.00 40.00
69 Lou Williams 1.50 4.00
70 Marc Gasol 1.50 4.00
71 Markieff Morris 1.00 2.50
72 Michael Kidd-Gilchrist 1.00 2.50
73 Mike Conley 1.25 3.00
74 Myles Turner 1.50 4.00
75 Nicolas Batum 1.25 3.00
76 Nikola Jokic 8.00 20.00
77 Nikola Mirotic 1.00 2.50
78 Nikola Vucevic 1.50 4.00
79 Paul George 2.50 6.00
80 Paul Millsap 1.25 3.00
81 Reggie Jackson 1.25 3.00
82 Reggie Miller 2.50 6.00
83 Robert Covington 1.25 3.00
84 Rodney Hood 1.25 3.00
85 Rudy Gay 1.50 4.00
86 Rudy Gobert 2.00 5.00
87 Russell Westbrook 2.50 6.00
88 Scottie Pippen 3.00 8.00
89 Seth Curry 1.25 3.00
90 Shaquille O'Neal 5.00 12.00
91 Stephen Curry 12.00 30.00
92 Steven Adams 1.25 3.00
93 T.J. Warren 1.25 3.00
94 Taj Gibson 1.00 2.50
95 Tony Parker 2.50 6.00
96 Trevor Booker 1.00 2.50
97 Tristan Thompson 1.50 4.00
98 Willie Cauley-Stein 1.25 3.00
99 Zach LaVine 3.00 8.00
100 Zach Randolph 1.50 4.00
101 Paul Zipser JSY AU/99 RC 5.00 12.00
102 Tomas Satoransky JSY AU/99 RC 8.00 20.00
103 Stephen Zimmerman JSY AU/99 RC 5.00 12.00
104 Kay Felder JSY AU/99 RC 5.00 12.00
105 D.Murray JSY AU/99 RC 200.00 500.00
106 Jake Layman JSY AU/99 RC 6.00 15.00
107 Georgios Papagiannis
JSY AU/99 RC 5.00 12.00
108 Skal Labissiere JSY AU/99 RC 5.00 12.00
109 M.Brogdon JSY AU/99 RC 40.00 100.00
110 Juan Hernangomez JSY AU/99 RC 25.00 60.00
111 Patrick McCaw JSY AU/99 RC 5.00 12.00
112 Caris LeVert JSY AU/99 RC 12.00 30.00
113 Willy Hernangomez JSY AU/99 RC 6.00 15.00
114 Chinanu Onuaku JSY AU/99 RC 5.00 12.00
115 Cheick Diallo JSY AU/99 RC 5.00 12.00
116 Marquese Chriss JSY AU/81 RC 6.00 15.00
117 Henry Ellenson JSY AU/99 RC 5.00 12.00
118 Ivica Zubac JSY AU/99 RC 8.00 20.00
119 D.Sabonis JSY AU/99 RC 25.00 60.00
120 Malachi Richardson JSY AU/99 RC 5.00 12.00
121 Timothe Luwawu-Cabarrot
JSY AU/99 RC 8.00 20.00
122 Malik Beasley JSY AU/99 RC 10.00 25.00
123 Deyonta Davis JSY AU/99 RC 5.00 12.00
124 Pascal Siakam JSY AU/99 RC 75.00 200.00
125 Marshall Plumlee JSY AU/99 RC 5.00 12.00
126 Buddy Hield JSY AU/99 RC 50.00 120.00
127 Dragan Bender JSY AU/99 RC 5.00 12.00
128 Demetrius Jackson JSY AU/99 RC 5.00 12.00
129 Jakob Poeltl JSY AU/99 RC 10.00 25.00
130 B.Ingram JSY AU/99 RC 125.00 300.00
131 Thon Maker JSY AU/99 RC 6.00 15.00
132 Mindaugas Kuzminskas
JSY AU/99 RC 5.00 12.00
133 Wade Baldwin IV JSY AU/99 RC 5.00 12.00
134 Kris Dunn JSY AU/85 RC 8.00 20.00
135 Jamal Murray JSY AU/99 RC 200.00 500.00
136 Tyler Ulis JSY AU/99 RC 6.00 15.00
137 Georges Niang JSY AU/99 RC 8.00 20.00
139 Isaiah Whitehead JSY AU/99 RC 5.00 12.00
140 Denzel Valentine JSY AU/99 RC 5.00 12.00

2016-17 Immaculate Collection Blue

*BLUE: .6X TO 1.5X BASIC
STATED PRINT RUN 35 SER.#'d SETS

2016-17 Immaculate Collection Red

*RED: .6X TO 1.5X BASIC
STATED PRINT RUN 25 SER.#'d SETS

2016-17 Immaculate Collection All Time Greats Autographs

PRINT RUNS B/WN 35-75 COPIES PER
EXCHANGE DEADLINE 4/4/2019
1 Shaquille O'Neal/35 400.00 800.00
2 Gail Goodrich/75 12.00 30.00
3 Artis Gilmore/75 12.00 30.00
4 Dominique Wilkins/35 40.00 100.00
5 Kareem Abdul-Jabbar/35 300.00 600.00
6 Alex English/75 12.00 30.00
7 Alonzo Mourning/35 75.00 200.00
8 James Worthy/35 75.00 200.00
9 Hakeem Olajuwon/35 100.00 250.00
10 Dennis Rodman/35 125.00 300.00
11 Bernard King/75 12.00 30.00
12 David Thompson/75 12.00 30.00
13 Oscar Robertson/35 125.00 300.00
14 Magic Johnson/35 125.00 300.00
15 Dan Issel/75 12.00 30.00
16 Jerry West/35 75.00 200.00
17 George Gervin/75 15.00 40.00
18 Allen Iverson/35 300.00 600.00
19 Bill Russell/35 1,000.00 2,000.00
20 Bob McAdoo/75 20.00 50.00
21 Lenny Wilkens/75 12.00 30.00
22 Glen Rice/75 12.00 30.00
23 Anfernee Hardaway/35 300.00 5,600.00
24 Mark Aguirre/75 4.00 10.00
25 Kobe Bryant/35 4,000.00 8,000.00

2016-17 Immaculate Collection Celebration Signatures

PRINT RUNS B/WN 40-99 COPIES PER
EXCHANGE DEADLINE 4/4/2019
1 Andrew Wiggins/40 40.00 100.00
2 Anthony Davis/40 75.00 200.00
3 Brandon Ingram/40 125.00 300.00
4 Buddy Hield/40 20.00 50.00
5 C.J. McCollum/75 20.00 50.00
6 Dario Saric/99 15.00 40.00
7 Darren Collison/99 3.00 8.00
8 Goran Dragic/99 12.00 30.00
9 Gordon Hayward/75 12.00 30.00
10 Isaiah Thomas/75 15.00 40.00
11 Jae Crowder/99 15.00 40.00
12 Jason Terry/99 8.00 20.00
13 John Wall/40 60.00 150.00
14 Jonas Valanciunas/99 12.00 30.00
15 Jordan Clarkson/99 20.00 50.00
16 Jrue Holiday/99 8.00 20.00
17 Juan Hernangomez/99 40.00 100.00
18 Justin Anderson/99 3.00 8.00
19 Karl-Anthony Towns/40 60.00 150.00
20 Kenneth Faried/99 4.00 10.00
21 Kevin Durant/40 300.00 600.00
22 Kristaps Porzingis/75 40.00 100.00
23 Kyrie Irving/40 75.00 200.00
24 Malcolm Brogdon/99 30.00 80.00
25 Marcin Gortat/99 3.00 8.00
26 Michael Kidd-Gilchrist/99 3.00 8.00
27 Paul Millsap/75 4.00 10.00
28 Stephen Curry/40 1,000.00 2,000.00
29 Tim Hardaway Jr./99 8.00 20.00
30 Vince Carter/40 150.00 400.00

2016-17 Immaculate Collection Dual Autographs

STATED PRINT RUN 49 SER.#'d SETS
EXCHANGE DEADLINE 4/4/2019
1 Curry/Durant 4,000.00 8,000.00
2 Davis/Towns 200.00 500.00
3 Towns/Dunn 40.00 100.00
4 Ingram/Brown 300.00 600.00
5 Wade/Butler 500.00 1,000.00
6 Saric/Embiid 150.00 400.00
7 Bender/Saric 20.00 50.00
8 Dunn/Ingram 100.00 250.00
9 Stoudamire/Camby 40.00 100.00
10 Valentine/Zipser 8.00 20.00
11 Gasol/Gasol 125.00 300.00
12 Houston/Camby 25.00 60.00
13 Brown/Thomas 150.00 400.00
14 Sabonis/Sabonis 100.00 250.00
15 Brogdon/Anderson 25.00 60.00
16 Love/Walton 50.00 120.00
17 Booker/Murray 500.00 1,000.00
18 Carter/Kidd 300.00 600.00
19 Hill/Stackhouse 100.00 250.00
20 Ingram/Deng 75.00 200.00
21 Kareem/Bryant 5,000.00 10,000.00
22 Irving/Wall 125.00 300.00
23 Hield/Murray 125.00 300.00
24 Walton/Kareem 300.00 600.00
25 Murray/Hrnngmz 75.00 200.00
26 Billups/Hamilton 150.00 400.00
27 Kareem/Robertson 200.00 500.00
28 Bembry/Prince 10.00 25.00
29 Wallace/Billups 125.00 300.00
30 Ulis/Chriss 10.00 25.00
31 Bird/Johnson 1,000.00 2,000.00
32 Anthony/King 75.00 200.00
33 Ellenson/Gbinije 8.00 20.00
34 Papagiannis/Giannis 200.00 500.00
35 Holiday/Holiday 15.00 40.00
36 Webb/Richmond 60.00 150.00
37 Wilkins/Webb 100.00 250.00
38 Payton/Allen 125.00 300.00
39 Hardaway/O'Neal 1,000.00 2,000.00
41 Curry/Kerr 4,000.00 8,000.00
42 Maxwell/Archibald 12.00 30.00
43 Fitch/Bird 125.00 300.00
44 Fitch/Olajuwon 100.00 250.00
45 Dampier/Issel 40.00 100.00
46 Sabonis/Ilgauskas 60.00 150.00
47 Grant/Kukoc 50.00 120.00
48 Mashburn/Jackson 50.00 120.00
49 English/Vandeweghe 25.00 60.00
50 Lanier/Laimbeer 75.00 200.00
51 O'Neal/Ming 1,500.00 3,000.00
52 West/Kareem 300.00 600.00
53 Stockton/Hill 40.00 100.00
55 Whitehead Baldwin IV 8.00 20.00
56 Wiggins/Embiid 300.00 600.00
57 Iverson/Camby 150.00 400.00
58 Sampson/Olajuwon 100.00 250.00
59 Giannis/Brogdon 200.00 500.00
60 Jackson/Brown 125.00 300.00
61 Crabbe/McCollum 40.00 100.00
62 Murray/English 150.00 400.00
63 Gervin/Parker 125.00 300.00
65 Giannis/Kidd 400.00 800.00

2016-17 Immaculate Collection Dual Materials

STATED PRINT RUN 99 SER.#'d SETS
1 AJ Hammons 2.50 6.00
2 Brandon Ingram 6.00 15.00
3 Dejounte Murray 4.00 10.00
4 Denzel Valentine 2.50 6.00
5 Deyonta Davis 2.50 6.00
6 Domantas Sabonis 15.00 40.00
7 Georges Niang 4.00 10.00
8 Georgios Papagiannis 2.50 6.00
9 Ivica Zubac 6.00 15.00
10 Jaylen Brown 6.00 15.00
11 Michael Gbinije 2.50 6.00
12 Paul Zipser 2.50 6.00
13 Skal Labissiere 2.50 6.00
14 Stephen Zimmerman 2.50 6.00
16 Tomas Satoransky 4.00 10.00
17 Wade Baldwin IV 2.50 6.00
18 Willy Hernangomez 3.00 8.00
19 Brice Johnson 2.50 6.00
20 Buddy Hield 4.00 10.00
21 Damian Jones 2.50 6.00
22 Demetrius Jackson 2.50 6.00
23 Diamond Stone 2.50 6.00
24 Jamal Murray 40.00 100.00
25 Isaiah Whitehead 2.50 6.00
26 Joel Bolomboy 2.50 6.00
28 Malachi Richardson 2.50 6.00
29 Malcolm Brogdon 8.00 20.00
30 Thon Maker 5.00 12.00
31 Malik Beasley 5.00 12.00
32 Marquese Chriss 3.00 8.00

2016-17 Immaculate Collection Dual Materials Red

*RED: .75X TO 2X BASIC
STATED PRINT RUN 25 SER.#'d SETS
27 Juan Hernangomez 10.00 25.00

2016-17 Immaculate Collection Dual Patches

PRINT RUNS B/WN 5-35 COPIES PER
NO PRICING ON QTY 18 OR LESS
2 Alec Burks/35 4.00 10.00
3 Bobby Portis/35 5.00 12.00
4 Brook Lopez/35 6.00 15.00
7 DeAndre Jordan/35 4.00 10.00
9 Devin Harris/35 3.00 8.00
11 Dwight Powell/35 3.00 8.00
14 J.J. Barea/35 12.00 30.00
15 JJ Redick/35 5.00 12.00

2016-17 Immaculate Collection Grand Memorabilia

STATED PRINT RUN 50 SER.#'d SETS
1 Zach LaVine 10.00 25.00
2 Brandon Ingram 6.00 15.00
3 Dejounte Murray 6.00 15.00
4 Demetrius Jackson 3.00 8.00
5 Domantas Sabonis 20.00 50.00
6 Denzel Valentine 3.00 8.00
7 Georges Niang 5.00 12.00
8 Georgios Papagiannis 3.00 8.00
9 Ivica Zubac 8.00 20.00
10 Jaylen Brown 8.00 20.00
11 Kay Felder 3.00 8.00
12 Malachi Richardson 3.00 8.00
14 Tomas Satoransky 5.00 12.00
15 Wade Baldwin IV 3.00 8.00
16 Willy Hernangomez 4.00 10.00
17 Zach Randolph 5.00 12.00
18 Tyson Chandler 4.00 10.00
19 Trevor Ariza 3.00 8.00
20 Steven Adams 4.00 10.00
21 Stanley Johnson 3.00 8.00
23 Rudy Gay 5.00 12.00
25 Ricky Rubio 4.00 10.00

2016-17 Immaculate Collection Heralded Signatures

STATED PRINT RUN 99 SER.#'d SETS
EXCHANGE DEADLINE 4/4/2019
1 James Posey 4.00 10.00
2 Bill Willoughby 5.00 12.00
3 Frank Ramsey 8.00 20.00
4 Willis Reed 50.00 120.00
6 Nate Thurmond 12.00 30.00
7 Kenny Anderson 5.00 12.00
8 Kenny Sky Walker 4.00 10.00
9 Tony Delk 4.00 10.00
10 Damon Stoudamire 12.00 30.00
11 Vin Baker 5.00 12.00
12 Allan Houston 5.00 12.00
13 Kelly Tripucka 4.00 10.00
14 Jim Chones 4.00 10.00
15 Gail Goodrich 12.00 30.00
16 Dell Curry 15.00 40.00
17 Sidney Moncrief 5.00 12.00
18 Anfernee Hardaway 125.00 300.00
19 Dennis Rodman 75.00 200.00
20 Tom Gugliotta 4.00 10.00
21 Grant Hill 40.00 100.00
22 Dominique Wilkins 40.00 100.00
23 Bonzi Wells 5.00 12.00
24 Jamal Mashburn 5.00 12.00
25 Spud Webb 15.00 40.00
26 Joe Dumars 15.00 40.00
27 Vernon Maxwell 4.00 10.00
28 Mark Aguirre 5.00 12.00
29 Shawn Marion 12.00 30.00
30 Sean Elliott 12.00 30.00
31 Ben Wallace 20.00 50.00
32 Detlef Schrempf 12.00 30.00
33 Kurt Thomas 4.00 10.00
34 Dan Issel 12.00 30.00
35 Terry Cummings 5.00 12.00
36 Robert Parish 8.00 20.00
37 Dan Majerle 5.00 12.00
38 James Worthy 40.00 100.00
39 Kendall Gill 15.00 40.00
40 Dave Cowens 12.00 30.00

2016-17 Immaculate Collection Heralded Signatures Red

*RED: .6X TO 1.5X BASIC
STATED PRINT RUN 25 SER.#'d SETS
EXCHANGE DEADLINE 4/4/2019
5 Magic Johnson 30.00 80.00

2016-17 Immaculate Collection Historical Significance Autographs

STATED PRINT RUN 99 SER.#'d SETS
EXCHANGE DEADLINE 4/4/2019
1 Adrian Dantley 6.00 15.00
2 Alex English 5.00 12.00
3 Antoine Carr 3.00 8.00
4 Arvydas Sabonis 8.00 20.00
5 Bernard King 6.00 15.00
6 Bill Laimbeer 5.00 12.00
7 Bob Dandridge 5.00 12.00
8 Calvin Murphy 5.00 12.00
9 Cedric Ceballos 5.00 12.00
10 Dan Majerle 6.00 15.00
11 Dell Curry 5.00 12.00
12 Dennis Scott 3.00 8.00
13 Detlef Schrempf 8.00 20.00
14 Eddie Jones 6.00 15.00
15 George Gervin 6.00 15.00
16 Glen Rice 5.00 12.00
17 Horace Grant 8.00 20.00
18 Jamal Mashburn 6.00 15.00
19 Jerry West 20.00 50.00
20 Kenny Sky Walker 3.00 8.00
21 Kurt Rambis 5.00 12.00
22 Latrell Sprewell 10.00 25.00
23 Mark Aguirre 4.00 10.00
24 Rick Barry 6.00 15.00
25 Sean Elliott 5.00 12.00
26 Shawn Kemp 30.00 80.00
27 Spud Webb 5.00 12.00
28 Tim Hardaway 8.00 20.00
29 Vlade Divac 8.00 20.00
30 Walter Berry 6.00 15.00

2016-17 Immaculate Collection Jumbo Patches Jersey Numbers

PRINT RUNS B/WN 2-42 COPIES PER
NO PRICING ON QTY 11 OR LESS
1 Adreian Payne/33 3.00 8.00
4 Andre Miller/24 8.00 20.00
5 Andre Roberson/21 12.00 30.00
7 Andrew Wiggins/22 20.00 50.00
13 Devin Harris/20 12.00 30.00
28 Lance Thomas/42 3.00 8.00
29 LeBron James/23 150.00 400.00
31 Michael Redd/22 40.00 100.00
36 Rondae Hollis-Jefferson/24 12.00 30.00
49 Trevor Booker/35 10.00 25.00

2016-17 Immaculate Collection Jumbo Patches Team Logos

PRINT RUNS B/WN 1-34 COPIES PER
NO PRICING ON QTY 18 OR LESS
6 Andrew Bogut/21 40.00 100.00
9 Brook Lopez/27 12.00 30.00
13 Devin Harris/34 15.00 40.00
41 Zach LaVine/21 25.00 60.00

2016-17 Immaculate Collection Marks of Greatness Autographs

PRINT RUNS B/WN 35-75 COPIES PER
EXCHANGE DEADLINE 4/4/2019
1 Karl-Anthony Towns/35 50.00 120.00
2 D'Angelo Russell/35 20.00 50.00
3 DeMarre Carroll/75 5.00 12.00
4 Marc Gasol/35 12.00 30.00
5 Gordon Hayward/75 12.00 30.00
6 Doug McDermott/75 4.00 10.00
7 Ryan Anderson/75 3.00 8.00
8 Eric Gordon/75 8.00 20.00
9 Will Barton/75 3.00 8.00
10 Zach LaVine/75 75.00 200.00
11 Patty Mills/75 20.00 50.00
12 Jordan Clarkson/75 12.00 30.00
13 Joel Embiid/50 200.00 500.00
14 Julius Randle/50 12.00 30.00
15 George Hill/75 4.00 10.00
16 Jrue Holiday/75 12.00 30.00
17 C.J. McCollum/50 20.00 50.00
18 Kristaps Porzingis/50 25.00 60.00
19 Devin Booker/75 150.00 400.00
20 Elfrid Payton/75 4.00 10.00
21 Jimmy Butler/35 75.00 200.00
22 Stephen Curry/35 1,000.00 2,000.00
23 Kevin Durant/35 200.00 500.00
24 Kyrie Irving/35 75.00 200.00
25 James Harden/75 75.00 200.00

2016-17 Immaculate Collection Milestones Autographs

STATED PRINT RUN 25 SER.#'d SETS
EXCHANGE DEADLINE 4/4/2019
1 Kyrie Irving 125.00 300.00
2 Stephen Curry 1,000.00 2,000.00
3 Shaquille O'Neal 400.00 800.00
4 Chris Paul 125.00 300.00
5 Dirk Nowitzki 400.00 800.00
6 David Robinson 75.00 200.00
8 Kareem Abdul-Jabbar 200.00 500.00
9 Louie Dampier 15.00 40.00
10 Magic Johnson 150.00 400.00

2016-17 Immaculate Collection Modern Marks Autographs

STATED PRINT RUN 99 SER.#'d SETS
EXCHANGE DEADLINE 4/4/2019
1 Andre Drummond 5.00 12.00
2 Marcus Smart 6.00 15.00
3 Tristan Thompson 4.00 10.00
4 Jrue Holiday 6.00 15.00
5 Gary Harris 4.00 10.00
6 James Johnson 3.00 8.00
7 C.J. McCollum 5.00 12.00
8 Jusuf Nurkic 4.00 10.00
9 Jason Terry 4.00 10.00
10 Steven Adams 4.00 10.00
11 DeMarre Carroll 3.00 8.00
12 Emmanuel Mudiay 3.00 8.00
13 Julius Randle 6.00 15.00
14 Nikola Jokic 125.00 300.00
15 Alec Burks 4.00 10.00
16 Tim Hardaway Jr. 4.00 10.00
17 Reggie Jackson 4.00 10.00
18 D'Angelo Russell 6.00 15.00
19 Khris Middleton 5.00 12.00
20 Thaddeus Young 3.00 8.00
21 JJ Redick 5.00 12.00
22 Jordan Clarkson 5.00 12.00
23 Robert Covington 4.00 10.00
24 Harrison Barnes 4.00 10.00
25 Aaron Gordon 5.00 12.00
26 Frank Kaminsky 3.00 8.00
27 Eric Gordon 4.00 10.00
28 Joel Embiid 125.00 300.00
30 Norman Powell 5.00 12.00
31 Kristaps Porzingis 8.00 20.00
32 Doug McDermott 4.00 10.00
33 Bojan Bogdanovic 4.00 10.00
34 Matthew Dellavedova 4.00 10.00
35 Jeff Teague 3.00 8.00
37 Zach LaVine 20.00 50.00
39 Paul Millsap 4.00 10.00
40 Evan Turner 3.00 8.00

2016-17 Immaculate Collection Modern Marks Autographs Red

*RED: .6X TO 1.5X BASIC
STATED PRINT RUN 25 SER.#'d SETS
EXCHANGE DEADLINE 4/4/2019
29 Damian Lillard 40.00 100.00
36 John Wall 20.00 50.00
38 Dwyane Wade 40.00 100.00

2016-17 Immaculate Collection Moments Autographs

PRINT RUNS B/WN 10-50 COPIES PER
NO PRICING ON QTY 10
EXCHANGE DEADLINE 4/4/2019
2 Yogi Ferrell/50 12.00 30.00
3 Isaiah Thomas/50 12.00 30.00
4 Devin Booker/50 200.00 500.00
5 Nikola Jokic/50 300.00 600.00
6 Giannis Antetokounmpo/50 125.00 300.00
7 Marc Gasol/25 15.00 40.00
8 T.J. McConnell/50 12.00 30.00
11 Isaiah Thomas/50 12.00 30.00
12 Eric Bledsoe/50 12.00 30.00
13 Jimmy Butler/25 60.00 150.00
14 Juan Hernangomez/50 20.00 50.00
15 Andrew Wiggins/25 40.00 100.00
16 Malcolm Brogdon/50 30.00 80.00
17 Jamal Murray/50 75.00 200.00
18 Dejounte Murray/50 100.00 250.00
20 Buddy Hield/50 30.00 80.00
21 James Harden/50 200.00 400.00
22 Tracy McGrady/25 400.00 800.00
24 Robert Horry/50 25.00 60.00
28 Jeremy Lin/50 100.00 250.00
29 Ray Allen/25 400.00 800.00

2016-17 Immaculate Collection Patch Autographs

PRINT RUNS B/WN 19-40 COPIES PER
NO PRICING ON QTY 19
EXCHANGE DEADLINE 4/4/2019
*JSY NUM 40-50: .4X TO 1X BASE
*JSY NUM 30-35: .5X TO 1.2X BASE
*JSY NUM 20-25: .6X TO 1.5X BASE
1 Vince Carter/40 60.00 150.00
2 Devin Harris/40 5.00 12.00
3 Rudy Gay/40 8.00 20.00
4 Evan Fournier/40 6.00 15.00
5 Julius Randle/40 10.00 25.00
6 J.J. Barea/40 12.00 30.00
7 Marc Gasol/40 8.00 20.00
8 Zach Randolph/40 8.00 20.00
9 Nik Stauskas/40 5.00 12.00
10 George Hill/40 6.00 15.00
11 Pau Gasol/40 15.00 40.00
12 Nicolas Batum/40 6.00 15.00
13 Shaquille O'Neal/40 100.00 250.00
14 Jordan Clarkson/40 8.00 20.00
15 Kemba Walker/40 8.00 20.00
16 Rashard Lewis/40 6.00 15.00
18 James Johnson/40 5.00 12.00
19 Kristaps Porzingis/40 12.00 30.00
20 Gordon Hayward/40 12.00 30.00
22 Tobias Harris/40 8.00 20.00
23 Justin Holiday/40 6.00 15.00
24 Langston Galloway/40 5.00 12.00
25 Doug McDermott/40 6.00 15.00
26 Dwyane Wade/40 40.00 100.00
27 Isaiah Canaan/40 5.00 12.00
28 Kenneth Faried/40 6.00 15.00
29 Nikola Vucevic/40 8.00 20.00
30 Tim Hardaway Jr./40 6.00 15.00
31 Darren Collison/40 5.00 12.00
32 Danilo Gallinari/40 6.00 15.00
33 Bojan Bogdanovic/40 6.00 15.00
34 Joel Embiid/40 150.00 400.00
35 D'Angelo Russell/40 10.00 25.00
37 Ricky Rubio/40 10.00 25.00
38 Allen Iverson/40 100.00 250.00
39 Andrei Kirilenko/40 6.00 15.00
40 Myles Turner/40 8.00 20.00
41 John Wall/40 20.00 50.00
42 Elfrid Payton/40 6.00 15.00
44 Marcus Camby/40 6.00 15.00
45 Zach LaVine/40 40.00 100.00
46 C.J. McCollum/40 12.00 30.00
47 Karl-Anthony Towns/40 20.00 50.00
48 Udonis Haslem/40 6.00 15.00
49 Tony Snell/40 5.00 12.00
50 Luol Deng/40 6.00 15.00
51 Solomon Hill/40 5.00 12.00
52 Goran Dragic/40 8.00 20.00
53 Nikola Mirotic/40 5.00 12.00
54 Jason Terry/40 6.00 15.00
55 Mario Hezonja/40 5.00 12.00
56 Tristan Thompson/40 6.00 15.00
57 Kyrie Irving/40 40.00 100.00
58 David Robinson/40 25.00 60.00
59 Kevin Durant/40 125.00 300.00
60 Grant Hill/40 25.00 60.00

2016-17 Immaculate Collection Patch Autographs Red

*RED: .5X TO 1.2X BASIC
STATED PRINT RUN 25 SER.#'d SETS
EXCHANGE DEADLINE 4/4/2019
15 Paul Millsap 8.00 20.00

2016-17 Immaculate Collection Premium Patch Autographs

PRINT RUNS B/WN 27-35 COPIES PER
EXCHANGE DEADLINE 4/4/2019
1 Grant Hill/35 30.00 80.00
3 Kevin Durant/35 100.00 250.00
4 Shaquille O'Neal/33 75.00 200.00
5 Allen Iverson/35 250.00 500.00
6 Kyrie Irving/35 50.00 120.00
7 Pau Gasol/35 20.00 50.00
9 Karl-Anthony Towns/35 25.00 60.00
10 Tony Parker/35 20.00 50.00
12 Marc Gasol/35 10.00 25.00
13 Ricky Rubio/35 12.00 30.00
14 David Robinson/35 25.00 60.00
15 Vince Carter/35 30.00 80.00
16 D'Angelo Russell/35 12.00 30.00
17 Joel Embiid/35 125.00 300.00
18 Julius Randle/27 12.00 30.00
19 Zach Randolph/35 10.00 25.00
20 C.J. McCollum/35 15.00 40.00
22 Gordon Hayward/35 15.00 40.00
23 Anthony Davis/35 75.00 200.00
24 Danilo Gallinari/35 8.00 20.00
26 Zach LaVine/35 12.00 30.00
28 Devin Harris/35 6.00 15.00
29 George Hill/35 8.00 20.00
30 Jordan Clarkson/35 10.00 25.00
31 Tobias Harris/35 10.00 25.00
32 Dwyane Wade/35 25.00 60.00
33 Kenneth Faried/35 8.00 20.00
34 Nikola Vucevic/35 10.00 25.00
35 Elfrid Payton/32 6.00 15.00
36 Nikola Mirotic/35 6.00 15.00
37 Jason Terry/35 8.00 20.00
38 Tristan Thompson/35 8.00 20.00
40 Nicolas Batum/29 8.00 20.00
42 Giannis Antetokounmpo/35 125.00 300.00
43 Luol Deng/35 8.00 20.00
44 Mario Hezonja/35 6.00 15.00
46 Udonis Haslem/35 8.00 20.00
47 Evan Fournier/35 8.00 20.00
48 J.J. Barea/35 15.00 40.00
49 Rashard Lewis/35 8.00 20.00
50 James Johnson/35 6.00 15.00
51 Langston Galloway/35 6.00 15.00
52 Tim Hardaway Jr./35 8.00 20.00
53 Bojan Bogdanovic/35 8.00 20.00
54 Andrei Kirilenko/35 8.00 20.00
55 Marcus Camby/35 8.00 20.00
57 Patty Mills/35 20.00 50.00
58 Isaiah Canaan/35 6.00 15.00
59 Tony Snell/35 6.00 15.00
60 Solomon Hill/35 6.00 15.00
61 Kristaps Porzingis/35 50.00 120.00
64 Deron Williams/35 8.00 20.00
66 Jimmy Butler/35 40.00 100.00
69 Ray Allen/35 50.00 120.00
71 Patrick McCaw/31 6.00 15.00
72 Caris LeVert/35 15.00 40.00
73 Willy Hernangomez/35 8.00 20.00
74 Dejounte Murray/35 200.00 500.00
75 Georgios Papagiannis/35 6.00 15.00
76 Skal Labissiere/35 6.00 15.00
77 Malcolm Brogdon/35 20.00 50.00
78 Juan Hernangomez/35 12.00 30.00
79 Domantas Sabonis/35 25.00 60.00
80 Malachi Richardson/35 6.00 15.00
81 Timothe Luwawu-Cabarrot/35 10.00 25.00
82 Malik Beasley/35 12.00 30.00
83 Deyonta Davis/35 6.00 15.00
84 Pascal Siakam/35 40.00 100.00
86 Michael Gbinije/35 6.00 15.00
88 Demetrius Jackson/35 6.00 15.00
89 Jakob Poeltl/35 15.00 40.00
90 Brandon Ingram/35 125.00 300.00
91 Thon Maker/27 8.00 20.00
92 Mindaugas Kuzminskas/35 6.00 15.00
93 Henry Ellenson/35 6.00 15.00
94 Kay Felder/35 6.00 15.00
95 Jamal Murray/35 300.00 600.00
96 Tyler Ulis/35 8.00 20.00
97 Damian Jones/35 6.00 15.00
99 Isaiah Whitehead/35 6.00 15.00
100 Denzel Valentine/35 6.00 15.00

2016-17 Immaculate Collection Premium Patch Autographs Red

*RED: .5X TO 1.2X BASIC
STATED PRINT RUN 25 SER.#'d SETS
EXCHANGE DEADLINE 4/4/2019
2 Stephen Curry/25 1,500.00 3,000.00
21 Paul Millsap/25 10.00 25.00

65 Andre Drummond/25 12.00 30.00
67 Jrue Holiday/25 15.00 40.00
68 Kevin Love/25 20.00 50.00
70 E'Twaun Moore/25 8.00 20.00

2016-17 Immaculate Collection Prime Jersey Number

PRINT RUNS B/WN 1-44 COPIES PER
NO PRICING ON QTY 12 OR LESS
3 Al Horford/42 5.00 12.00
5 Alonzo Mourning/33 15.00 40.00
7 Andre Miller/24 8.00 20.00
8 Andrew Wiggins/22 10.00 25.00
10 Blake Griffin/32 5.00 12.00
14 Christian Laettner/32 10.00 25.00
15 Cody Zeller/40 3.00 8.00
19 Danny Ainge/44 5.00 12.00
20 Danny Manning/25 6.00 15.00
21 Darko Milicic/31 3.00 8.00
23 Derrick Rose/25 12.00 30.00
24 Dirk Nowitzki/41 12.00 30.00
26 Frank Kaminsky/44 3.00 8.00
28 Gordon Hayward/20 8.00 20.00
29 Hassan Whiteside/21 8.00 20.00
33 Jimmy Butler/21 15.00 40.00
34 Joel Embiid/21 20.00 50.00
37 Karl-Anthony Towns/32 25.00 60.00
39 Kevin Durant/35 20.00 50.00
41 LeBron James/23 100.00 250.00
44 Rudy Gobert/27 10.00 25.00
48 Tim Duncan/21 50.00 120.00

2016-17 Immaculate Collection Remarkable Memorabilia

PRINT RUNS B/WN 74-99 COPIES PER
1 John Wall/99 5.00 12.00
2 Brandon Ingram/99 6.00 15.00
3 Dejounte Murray/99 5.00 121.00
4 Demetrius Jackson/99 2.50 6.00
5 Domantas Sabonis/99 15.00 40.00
6 Denzel Valentine/99 2.50 6.00
7 Georges Niang/99 4.00 10.00
8 Georgios Papagiannis/99 2.50 6.00
9 Ivica Zubac/99 6.00 15.00
10 Jaylen Brown/99 6.00 15.00
11 Kay Felder/99 2.50 6.00
12 Malachi Richardson/99 2.50 6.00
14 Tomas Satoransky/99 4.00 10.00
15 Wade Baldwin IV/99 2.50 6.00
16 Willy Hernangomez/99 3.00 8.00
17 Zach Randolph/99 4.00 10.00
18 Kawhi Leonard/99 5.00 12.00
19 Trevor Ariza/99 2.50 6.00
20 Steven Adams/99 3.00 8.00
21 Kelly Oubre Jr./99 5.00 12.00
22 Russell Westbrook/74 6.00 15.00
23 Justise Winslow/99 3.00 8.00
25 Ricky Rubio/99 3.00 8.00
26 Rajon Rondo/99 5.00 12.00
27 Paul George/99 6.00 15.00
29 Markieff Morris/99 2.50 6.00
30 Marcus Smart/99 5.00 12.00
31 Manu Ginobili/99 8.00 20.00
32 LeBron James/99 30.00 80.00
33 LaMarcus Aldridge/99 4.00 10.00
34 Kevin Love/99 4.00 10.00
35 Kemba Walker/99 3.00 8.00

2016-17 Immaculate Collection Rookie Patch Autographs Jersey Number

*JSY NUM p/r 91: .4X TO 1X BASE
*JSY NUM p/r 27-45: .5X TO 1.2X BASE
*JSY NUM p/r 20-25: .6X TO 1.5X BASE
PRINT RUNS B/WN 1-91 COPIES PER
NO PRICING ON QTY 16 OR LESS
EXCHANGE DEADLINE 4/4/2019
124 Pascal Siakam/43 125.00 300.00

2016-17 Immaculate Collection Rookie Patch Autographs Red

*RED: .6X TO 1.5X BASE
STATED PRINT RUN 25 SER.#'d SETS
EXCHANGE DEADLINE 4/4/2019

2016-17 Immaculate Collection Scripts

STATED PRINT RUN 99 SER.#'d SETS
EXCHANGE DEADLINE 4/4/2019
*RED/25: .6X TO 1.5X BASIC
1 Yogi Ferrell 4.00 10.00
2 Rodney McGruder 4.00 10.00
3 Taurean Prince 4.00 10.00
4 Willy Hernangomez 4.00 10.00
5 Mindaugas Kuzminskas 3.00 8.00
6 Juan Hernangomez 20.00 50.00
7 Kay Felder 3.00 8.00
8 Malcolm Brogdon 10.00 25.00
9 Domantas Sabonis 20.00 50.00
10 Brandon Ingram 25.00 60.00
11 Thon Maker 4.00 10.00
13 Buddy Hield 10.00 25.00
14 Marquese Chriss 4.00 10.00
15 Jamal Murray 75.00 200.00
16 Tomas Satoransky 5.00 12.00
17 Paul Zipser 3.00 8.00
18 Timothe Luwawu-Cabarrot 5.00 12.00
19 Damian Jones 3.00 8.00
20 Patrick McCaw 3.00 8.00

2016-17 Immaculate Collection Shadowbox Signatures

PRINT RUNS B/WN 35-75 COPIES PER
EXCHANGE DEADLINE 4/4/2019
1 Karl-Anthony Towns/35 40.00 100.00
2 D'Angelo Russell/35 8.00 20.00
3 DeMarre Carroll/75 3.00 8.00
4 Marc Gasol/35 10.00 25.00
5 Gordon Hayward/75 10.00 25.00
6 Doug McDermott/75 4.00 10.00
7 Ryan Anderson/75 3.00 8.00
8 Eric Gordon/75 4.00 10.00
9 Will Barton/75 3.00 8.00
10 Zach LaVine/75 40.00 100.00
11 Jordan Clarkson/75 25.00 60.00
12 Joel Embiid/50 150.00 400.00
13 Julius Randle/50 50.00 120.00
14 George Hill/75 4.00 10.00
15 Jrue Holiday/75 6.00 15.00
16 Myles Turner/75 10.00 25.00
17 Tobias Harris/75 5.00 12.00
18 C.J. McCollum/75 8.00 20.00
19 Anthony Davis/35 75.00 200.00
20 Tim Hardaway Jr./75 4.00 10.00
21 Kristaps Porzingis/50 25.00 60.00
22 Devin Booker/75 150.00 400.00
23 Dwyane Wade/35 75.00 200.00
24 Elfrid Payton/75 4.00 10.00
25 Kevin Durant/35 300.00 600.00
26 Allen Crabbe/75 3.00 8.00
27 Clint Capela/75 15.00 40.00
28 Michael Kidd-Gilchrist/75 3.00 8.00
29 Jimmy Butler/35 40.00 100.00
30 Jae Crowder/75 3.00 8.00
31 James Harden/75 75.00 200.00
32 Zach Randolph/75 5.00 12.00
33 Marcin Gortat/75 3.00 8.00
34 Vince Carter/35 75.00 200.00
35 Stephen Curry/35 500.00 1,000.00
36 Ricky Rubio/35 15.00 40.00
37 Kyrie Irving/35 75.00 200.00
38 John Wall/35 40.00 100.00
39 Nikola Mirotic/75 3.00 8.00
40 Dan Issel/75 6.00 15.00
41 George Gervin/75 15.00 40.00
42 Allen Iverson/35 200.00 500.00
43 Bill Russell/35 1,000.00 2,000.00
44 Adrian Dantley/75 5.00 12.00
45 Nick Van Exel/75 15.00 40.00
46 Rashard Lewis/75 4.00 10.00
47 Jo Jo White/75 10.00 25.00
48 Dennis Scott/75 3.00 8.00
49 Dell Curry/75 12.00 30.00
50 Latrell Sprewell/35 15.00 40.00

2016-17 Immaculate Collection Sneaker Swatch Signatures

PRINT RUNS B/WN 15-50 COPIES PER
NO PRICING ON QTY 18 OR LESS
EXCHANGE DEADLINE 4/4/2019
1 Aaron Gordon/50 12.00 30.00
2 Andrew Wiggins/25 75.00 200.00
3 Anthony Davis/25 125.00 300.00
4 Brandon Ingram/22 125.00 300.00
5 Chris Paul/25 150.00 400.00
6 D'Angelo Russell/25 40.00 100.00
7 Dejounte Murray/15 200.00 500.00
16 Hakeem Olajuwon/25 125.00 300.00
17 Henry Ellenson/50 5.00 12.00
20 Jakob Poeltl/50 12.00 30.00
24 John Stockton/25 75.00 200.00
25 John Wall/25 40.00 100.00
27 Julius Randle/25 40.00 100.00
29 Karl Malone/25 125.00 300.00
30 Karl-Anthony Towns/25 40.00 100.00
33 Kris Dunn/25 12.00 30.00
35 Larry Bird/25 150.00 400.00
38 Nikola Vucevic/32 20.00 50.00
39 Pascal Siakam/30 75.00 200.00
40 Patrick McCaw/25 8.00 20.00
41 Pau Gasol/25 75.00 200.00
42 Shaquille O'Neal/25 400.00 800.00
43 Stephen Curry/25 2,000.00 4,000.00
44 Stephen Zimmerman/42 5.00 12.00
45 Taurean Prince/31 8.00 20.00
46 Thon Maker/50 6.00 15.00
47 Timothe Luwawu-Cabarrot/33 10.00 25.00
49 Victor Oladipo/25 15.00 40.00

2016-17 Immaculate Collection Sneaker Swatch Signatures Red

*RED/25: .6X TO 1.5X p/r 42-50
*RED/25: .5X TO 1.2X p/r 30-33
PRINT RUNS B/WN 5-25 COPIES PER
NO PRICING ON QTY 15 OR LESS
EXCHANGE DEADLINE 4/4/2019
26 Juan Hernangomez/25 30.00 80.00
37 Malcolm Brogdon/22 25.00 60.00

2016-17 Immaculate Collection Sneaker Swatches

PRINT RUNS B/WN 11-25 COPIES PER
NO PRICING ON QTY 18 OR LESS
1 Aaron Gordon/25 8.00 20.00
2 Andrew Wiggins/25 15.00 40.00
3 Anthony Davis/25 25.00 60.00
4 Carmelo Anthony/25 12.00 30.00
5 D'Angelo Russell/25 10.00 25.00
6 Emmanuel Mudiay/25 10.00 25.00
7 Frank Kaminsky/25 5.00 12.00
8 Gordon Hayward/25 8.00 20.00
9 Joe Johnson/25 10.00 25.00
10 Julius Randle/25 8.00 20.00
12 Karl-Anthony Towns/25 15.00 40.00
13 Marc Gasol/25 8.00 20.00
14 Paul George/25 12.00 30.00
16 Scottie Pippen/25 40.00 100.00
17 Shaquille O'Neal/25 30.00 80.00
21 Bismack Biyombo/25 5.00 12.00
22 Detlef Schrempf/24 30.00 80.00
25 Jahlil Okafor/24 5.00 12.00

2016-17 Immaculate Collection Special Event Materials

PRINT RUNS B/WN 3-99 COPIES PER
NO PRICING ON QTY 18 OR LESS
2 Amar'e Stoudemire/99 3.00 8.00
6 Tyson Chandler/99 3.00 8.00
9 Chandler Parsons/99 2.50 6.00
12 Cory Joseph/99 2.50 6.00
13 David Lee/99 2.50 6.00
14 David West/28 4.00 10.00
15 Demetrius Jackson/99 2.50 6.00
17 Dion Waiters/99 2.50 6.00
20 Isaiah Canaan/82 2.50 6.00
21 Jabari Parker/99 2.50 6.00
25 Julius Randle/99 5.00 12.00
26 Kelly Olynyk/99 2.50 6.00
27 Shaun Livingston/99 2.50 6.00
29 Luol Deng/99 3.00 8.00
31 Michael Beasley/99 2.50 6.00
32 Mike Dunleavy/99 2.50 6.00
33 Mike Miller/99 3.00 8.00
35 Aaron Gordon/99 4.00 10.00
36 Nik Stauskas/99 2.50 6.00
41 Robert Covington/99 3.00 8.00
43 Roy Hibbert/20 6.00 15.00
47 Tiago Splitter/20 5.00 12.00
48 Tim Duncan/31 50.00 120.00
49 Trevor Ariza/99 2.50 6.00
50 Trevor Booker/99 2.50 6.00
52 Tony Parker/99 6.00 15.00
53 Tim Duncan/99 8.00 20.00
54 Amar'e Stoudemire/99 3.00 8.00
55 Derrick Rose/85 6.00 15.00
56 Chris Bosh/99 5.00 12.00
57 Iman Shumpert/99 2.50 6.00
58 Jeremy Lamb/99 2.50 6.00
59 Jeremy Lin/99 8.00 20.00
62 Paul Pierce/99 6.00 15.00
63 Pau Gasol/99 6.00 15.00
64 Ray Allen/99 6.00 15.00

2016-17 Immaculate Collection Standout Materials

PRINT RUNS B/WN 81-99 COPIES PER
*RED/25: .75X TO 2X BASIC
1 Brandon Ingram/99 6.00 15.00
2 Dejounte Murray/99 5.00 12.00
3 Domantas Sabonis/99 15.00 40.00
4 Jaylen Brown/99 6.00 15.00
5 Demetrius Jackson/99 2.50 6.00
6 Denzel Valentine/99 2.50 6.00
7 Deyonta Davis/99 2.50 6.00
8 Georges Niang/99 4.00 10.00
9 Ivica Zubac/99 6.00 15.00
10 Kay Felder/99 2.50 6.00
11 Pascal Siakam/99 15.00 40.00
12 Paul Zipser/99 2.50 6.00
14 Wade Baldwin IV/99 2.50 6.00
15 Willy Hernangomez/99 3.00 8.00
16 Georgios Papagiannis/99 2.50 6.00
17 Stephen Zimmerman/99 2.50 6.00
18 Tomas Satoransky/99 4.00 10.00
19 Andre Roberson/99 2.50 6.00
20 Zach Randolph/99 4.00 10.00
21 Vince Carter/99 8.00 20.00
22 Tyson Chandler/99 3.00 8.00
23 Tony Parker/99 6.00 15.00
24 Russell Westbrook/81 6.00 15.00
25 Rudy Gobert/99 5.00 12.00
26 Rudy Gay/99 4.00 10.00
27 Rodney Hood/99 3.00 8.00
29 Reggie Jackson/99 3.00 8.00
30 Rajon Rondo/99 5.00 12.00
31 Otto Porter/99 3.00 8.00
32 Nikola Vucevic/99 4.00 10.00
33 Myles Turner/99 4.00 10.00
34 Monta Ellis/99 3.00 8.00
35 Markieff Morris/99 2.50 6.00
36 Manu Ginobili/99 8.00 20.00
37 Kawhi Leonard/99 5.00 12.00
38 Jimmy Butler/99 8.00 20.00
40 Giannis Antetokounmpo/99 20.00 50.00

2016-17 Immaculate Collection The Standard Relics

PRINT RUNS B/WN 11-99 COPIES PER
NO PRICING ON QTY 18 OR LESS
1 Zach LaVine/99 8.00 20.00
2 Aaron Gordon/99 4.00 10.00
3 Adreian Payne/99 2.50 6.00
4 Al Horford/99 4.00 10.00
5 Al Jefferson/99 2.50 6.00
6 Alec Burks/99 3.00 8.00
7 Al-Farouq Aminu/99 2.50 6.00
8 Allen Iverson/28 10.00 25.00
9 Amar'e Stoudemire/99 3.00 8.00
10 Andre Drummond/99 4.00 10.00
11 Andre Iguodala/99 4.00 10.00
12 Andrei Kirilenko/99 3.00 8.00
13 Andrew Wiggins/99 5.00 12.00
14 Anfernee Hardaway/99 8.00 20.00
15 Anthony Davis/99 6.00 15.00
16 Avery Bradley/99 2.50 6.00
17 Ben McLemore/99 2.50 6.00
18 Ben Wallace/99 5.00 12.00
19 Blake Griffin/99 4.00 10.00
20 Bojan Bogdanovic/99 3.00 8.00
21 Boris Diaw/99 3.00 8.00
22 Bradley Beal/99 5.00 12.00
23 Brandon Jennings/99 2.50 6.00
24 Brandon Knight/99 3.00 8.00
25 Brent Barry/99 2.50 6.00
26 Brook Lopez/99 3.00 8.00
27 C.J. McCollum/99 4.00 10.00
28 Carmelo Anthony/99 6.00 15.00
29 Chandler Parsons/99 2.50 6.00
30 Channing Frye/99 2.50 6.00
31 Chauncey Billups/99 5.00 12.00
32 Kristaps Porzingis/99 5.00 12.00
33 Chris Mullin/28 5.00 12.00
34 Chris Paul/99 5.00 12.00
35 Chris Webber/99 4.00 10.00
36 Christian Laettner/99 4.00 10.00
37 Clyde Drexler/99 6.00 15.00
38 Cody Zeller/99 2.50 6.00
39 Cole Aldrich/99 2.00 5.00
40 D.J. Augustin/99 2.50 6.00
41 Damian Lillard/99 5.00 12.00
42 D'Angelo Russell/33 6.00 15.00
43 Danilo Gallinari/99 3.00 8.00
44 Danny Green/99 3.00 8.00
45 Dante Cunningham/99 2.50 6.00
46 David Lee/99 2.50 6.00
47 David Robinson/28 10.00 25.00
48 David West/99 3.00 8.00
49 DeAndre Jordan/99 3.00 8.00
50 DeMar DeRozan/99 5.00 12.00
51 DeMarcus Cousins/99 3.00 8.00
52 Dennis Schroder/99 4.00 10.00
53 Derrick Rose/99 6.00 15.00
54 Devin Booker/46 6.00 15.00
55 Devin Harris/99 2.50 6.00
56 Dirk Nowitzki/99 10.00 25.00
57 Draymond Green/99 5.00 12.00
58 Dwight Howard/99 5.00 12.00
59 Dwyane Wade/99 8.00 20.00
60 Elfrid Payton/79 3.00 8.00
61 Enes Kanter/99 2.50 6.00
62 Evan Turner/99 2.50 6.00
63 Frank Kaminsky/99 2.50 6.00
64 George Hill/99 3.00 8.00
65 Gerald Henderson/99 2.50 6.00
66 Giannis Antetokounmpo/28 25.00 60.00
67 Greg Monroe/99 2.50 6.00
68 Harrison Barnes/99 3.00 8.00
69 Iman Shumpert/99 2.50 6.00
70 Isaiah Whitehead/99 2.50 6.00
71 J.J. Barea/99 3.00 8.00
72 J.R. Smith/99 4.00 10.00
73 Jabari Parker/99 2.50 6.00
74 Jameer Nelson/99 2.50 6.00
75 James Harden/99 5.00 12.00
76 Jason Kidd/99 6.00 15.00
77 Jason Terry/99 3.00 8.00
78 Jeff Foster/99 3.00 8.00
79 Jeff Teague/99 2.50 6.00
80 Jeremy Lin/99 8.00 20.00
81 Jimmy Butler/99 8.00 20.00
82 John Wall/99 5.00 12.00
83 Karl-Anthony Towns/99 5.00 12.00
85 Kevin Durant/99 8.00 20.00
86 Klay Thompson/99 10.00 25.00
87 Kobe Bryant/99 125.00 300.00
88 Kyrie Irving/99 6.00 15.00
89 LeBron James/99 125.00 300.00
90 Marc Gasol/88 4.00 10.00
91 Pau Gasol/99 6.00 15.00
92 Rajon Rondo/28 6.00 15.00
93 Ricky Rubio/99 3.00 8.00
94 Russell Westbrook/99 6.00 15.00
96 Stephen Curry/99 12.00 30.00
98 Vince Carter/99 8.00 20.00
99 Yao Ming/99 10.00 25.00
100 Zach Randolph/99 4.00 10.00

2016-17 Immaculate Collection Triple Autographs

STATED PRINT RUN 25 SER.#'d SETS
EXCHANGE DEADLINE 4/4/2019
1 Love/Thompson/Irving 50.00 125.00
2 Parker/Robinson/Gervin 125.00 300.00
3 Ingram/Randle/Clarkson 75.00 200.00
4 Fournier/Batum/Parker 40.00 100.00
5 Sabonis/Kuzminskas/Valanciunas 25.00 60.00
6 Houston King Harris 30.00 80.00
7 Starks/Sprewell/Ewing 150.00 400.00
8 Hill/Winslow/Deng 125.00 300.00
10 Hill/Stackhouse/Dumars 200.00 500.00
13 Ingram/Hield/Brown 400.00 800.00
14 Murray/Ingram/Dunn 125.00 300.00
15 Drexler/Olajuwon/Ming 1,000.00 2,000.00
16 LeVert/Whitehead/Lin 125.00 300.00
17 Davis/Towns/Porzingis 250.00 500.00
18 Davis/Durant/Irving 500.00 1,000.00
19 King/Porzingis/Ewing 300.00 600.00
21 Anderson/Kidd/Brown 200.00 500.00
22 Paul/Griffin/Redick 150.00 400.00
23 Butler/Mirotic/Wade 100.00 250.00
24 Billups/Wallace/Hamilton 500.00 1,000.00
25 Davis/Rbisn/Oljwn 300.00 600.00
26 Payton/Allen/Kemp 800.00 1,500.00
28 Ingram/Bryant/Johnson 3,000.00 6,000.00
29 DRzn/Carroll/Vlncns 40.00 100.00
30 Saric/Embd/Lwwu-Cbrrt 125.00 300.00
31 Hrnngmz/Bsly/Mrry 125.00 300.00
32 Bender/Chriss/Ulis 20.00 50.00

2016-17 Immaculate Collection Triple Materials

STATED PRINT RUN 99 SER.#'d SETS
*RED/25: .75X TO 2X BASIC
1 Aaron Gordon 4.00 10.00
2 Alec Burks 3.00 8.00
3 Bojan Bogdanovic 3.00 8.00
4 Carmelo Anthony 6.00 15.00
5 Jaylen Brown 6.00 15.00
6 Damian Lillard 5.00 12.00
7 DeMarre Carroll 2.50 6.00
8 Dion Waiters 2.50 6.00
9 Dirk Nowitzki 10.00 25.00
11 Kevin Love 4.00 10.00
12 LeBron James 20.00 50.00
13 LaMarcus Aldridge 4.00 10.00
14 Myles Turner 4.00 10.00
15 Jeff Teague 2.50 6.00
16 Otto Porter 3.00 8.00
18 Russell Westbrook 6.00 15.00
19 Trevor Ariza 2.50 6.00
20 Dejounte Murray 5.00 12.00
21 Trey Burke 2.50 6.00
22 Victor Oladipo 3.00 8.00
23 Zach LaVine 8.00 20.00
24 Zach Randolph 4.00 10.00
25 Domantas Sabonis 15.00 40.00
26 Brandon Ingram 6.00 15.00
27 Jeremy Lin 8.00 20.00
28 Jimmy Butler 8.00 20.00

2017-18 Immaculate Collection

1-100 PRINT RUN 75 SER.#'d SETS
JSY AU PRINT RUN 99 SER.#'d SETS
EXCHANGE DEADLINE 4/17/2020
1 Ben Simmons 1.50 4.00
2 Dario Saric 1.25 3.00
3 Joel Embiid 3.00 8.00
4 Markelle Fultz RC 4.00 10.00
5 Eric Bledsoe 1.25 3.00
6 Khris Middleton 2.00 5.00
7 Giannis Antetokounmpo 30.00 80.00
8 Kris Dunn 1.00 2.50
9 Lauri Markkanen RC 10.00 25.00
10 Zach LaVine 2.50 6.00
11 George Hill 1.25 3.00
12 Kevin Love 1.50 4.00
13 Larry Nance Jr. 1.25 3.00
14 LeBron James 150.00 400.00
15 Al Horford 1.50 4.00
16 Gordon Hayward 1.25 3.00
17 Jayson Tatum RC 125.00 300.00
18 Kyrie Irving 3.00 8.00
19 Avery Bradley 1.00 2.50
20 DeAndre Jordan 1.25 3.00
21 Lou Williams 1.25 3.00
22 Marc Gasol 1.50 4.00
23 Dillon Brooks 3.00 8.00
24 Mike Conley 1.25 3.00
25 Dennis Schroder 1.25 3.00
26 Kent Bazemore 1.00 2.50
27 Taurean Prince 1.00 2.50
28 Dwyane Wade 3.00 8.00
29 Goran Dragic 1.25 3.00
30 Hassan Whiteside 1.25 3.00
31 Dwight Howard 2.00 5.00
32 Kemba Walker 1.25 3.00
33 Nicolas Batum 1.00 2.50
34 Derrick Favors 1.00 2.50
35 Donovan Mitchell RC 125.00 300.00
36 Ricky Rubio 1.25 3.00
37 Rudy Gobert 2.00 5.00
38 Buddy Hield 1.50 4.00
39 De'Aaron Fox RC 20.00 50.00
40 Frank Mason III RC 1.50 4.00
41 Enes Kanter 1.25 3.00
42 Kristaps Porzingis 2.00 5.00
43 Frank Ntilikina RC 2.00 5.00
44 Brandon Ingram 2.00 5.00
45 Julius Randle 1.50 4.00
46 Kyle Kuzma RC 6.00 15.00
47 Lonzo Ball RC 6.00 15.00
48 Aaron Gordon 1.50 4.00
49 Evan Fournier 1.25 3.00
50 Nikola Vucevic 1.25 3.00
51 Dennis Smith Jr. RC 2.00 5.00
52 Dirk Nowitzki 4.00 10.00
53 Harrison Barnes 1.25 3.00
54 Wesley Matthews 1.00 2.50
55 D'Angelo Russell 1.25 3.00
56 Rondae Hollis-Jefferson 1.00 2.50
57 Jeremy Lin 2.50 6.00
58 Jamal Murray 2.50 6.00
59 Nikola Jokic 10.00 25.00
60 Paul Millsap 1.25 3.00
61 Myles Turner 1.50 4.00
62 Darren Collison 1.00 2.50
63 Victor Oladipo 1.25 3.00
64 Anthony Davis 4.00 10.00
65 DeMarcus Cousins 1.25 3.00
66 Jrue Holiday 2.00 5.00
67 Andre Drummond 1.25 3.00
68 Blake Griffin 1.50 4.00
69 Reggie Jackson 1.25 3.00
70 DeMar DeRozan 2.00 5.00
71 Jonas Valanciunas 1.25 3.00
72 Kyle Lowry 1.50 4.00
73 Chris Paul 2.50 6.00
74 Clint Capela 1.25 3.00
75 Eric Gordon 1.25 3.00
76 James Harden 3.00 8.00
77 Kawhi Leonard 4.00 10.00
78 LaMarcus Aldridge 1.50 4.00
79 Pau Gasol 2.50 6.00
80 Rudy Gay 1.25 3.00
81 Devin Booker 4.00 10.00
82 TJ Warren 1.25 3.00
83 Tyson Chandler 1.25 3.00
84 Carmelo Anthony 2.50 6.00
85 Paul George 2.50 6.00
86 Russell Westbrook 2.50 6.00
87 Andrew Wiggins 2.00 5.00
88 Derrick Rose 2.50 6.00
89 Jimmy Butler 2.50 6.00
90 Karl-Anthony Towns 2.50 6.00
91 CJ McCollum 1.50 4.00
92 Damian Lillard 4.00 10.00
93 Jusuf Nurkic 1.25 3.00
94 Draymond Green 2.00 5.00
95 Kevin Durant 6.00 15.00
96 Klay Thompson 4.00 10.00
97 Stephen Curry 10.00 25.00
98 Bradley Beal 2.00 5.00
99 John Wall 2.00 5.00
100 Otto Porter Jr. 1.25 3.00
101 Frank Mason III JSY AU 5.00 12.00
102 Donovan Mitchell JSY AU 1,000.00 2,000.00
103 Jawun Evans JSY AU RC 5.00 12.00
104 D.J. Wilson JSY AU RC 5.00 12.00
105 Terrance Ferguson JSY AU RC 5.00 12.00
106 Markelle Fultz JSY AU 30.00 80.00
107 Caleb Swanigan JSY AU RC 5.00 12.00
108 De'Aaron Fox JSY AU 300.00 600.00
109 Josh Hart JSY AU RC 50.00 120.00
110 Dennis Smith Jr. JSY AU EXCH 6.00 15.00
112 Bam Adebayo JSY AU RC 200.00 500.00
113 Dwayne Bacon JSY AU RC 5.00 12.00
114 TJ Leaf JSY AU RC 5.00 12.00
115 Jarrett Allen JSY AU RC 15.00 40.00
116 Lonzo Ball JSY AU 300.00 600.00
117 Kyle Kuzma JSY AU 20.00 50.00
118 Jonathan Isaac JSY AU RC 50.00 120.00
119 Frank Jackson JSY AU RC 12.00 30.00
120 Zach Collins JSY AU RC 12.00 30.00
121 Semi Ojeleye JSY AU RC 6.00 15.00
122 Justin Jackson JSY AU RC 5.00 12.00
123 Tyler Dorsey JSY AU RC 5.00 12.00
124 John Collins JSY AU RC 200.00 500.00
125 OG Anunoby JSY AU RC 200.00 500.00
126 Jayson Tatum JSY AU EXCH 2,000.00 4,000.00
127 Tony Bradley JSY AU RC 5.00 12.00
128 Lauri Markkanen JSY AU 100.00 250.00
129 Davon Reed JSY AU RC 5.00 12.00
130 Malik Monk JSY AU RC 125.00 300.00
131 Jordan Bell JSY AU RC 5.00 12.00
132 Justin Patton JSY AU RC 5.00 12.00
133 Sterling Brown JSY AU RC 5.00 12.00
134 Harry Giles JSY AU RC 5.00 12.00
135 Tyler Lydon JSY AU RC 5.00 12.00
136 Josh Jackson JSY AU RC 6.00 15.00
137 Derrick White JSY AU RC 30.00 80.00
138 Frank Ntilikina JSY AU 12.00 30.00
139 Wes Iwundu JSY AU RC 5.00 12.00
140 Luke Kennard JSY AU RC 15.00 40.00

2017-18 Immaculate Collection Red

*RED: .6X TO 1.5X BASIC
*RED: .8X TO 2X BASIC RC
*RED: .6X TO 1.5X JSY AU
1-100 PRINT RUN 35 SER.#'d SETS
JSY AU PRINT RUN 25 SER.#'d SETS
EXCHANGE DEADLINE 4/17/2020
102 Donovan Mitchell JSY AU 1,500.00 3,000.00
106 Markelle Fultz JSY AU 60.00 150.00
109 Josh Hart JSY AU 75.00 200.00
118 Jonathan Isaac JSY AU 100.00 250.00
130 Malik Monk JSY AU 50.00 120.00

2017-18 Immaculate Collection All Time Greats Signatures

PRINT RUNS B/WN 25-75 COPIES PER
EXCHANGE DEADLINE 4/17/2020
1 Alex English/75 10.00 25.00
2 Paul Silas/75 8.00 20.00
3 John Starks/75 6.00 15.00
4 Gary Payton/49 20.00 50.00
5 Elvin Hayes/75 10.00 25.00
6 Charles Barkley/49 150.00 400.00
7 Jermaine O'Neal/75 8.00 20.00
8 Reggie Miller/25 75.00 200.00
9 Antawn Jamison/75 6.00 15.00
10 Jerry West/25 20.00 50.00
11 Sam Cassell/75 6.00 15.00
12 Tracy McGrady/49 20.00 50.00
13 Tom Gugliotta/75 5.00 12.00
14 James Worthy/49 12.00 30.00
15 Dave Cowens/75 12.00 30.00
16 Shaquille O'Neal/25 50.00 120.00
17 Robert Horry/75 8.00 20.00
18 John Stockton/25 30.00 80.00
19 David Thompson/75 10.00 25.00
20 Hakeem Olajuwon/49 20.00 50.00
21 Tom Chambers/75 8.00 20.00
22 Dennis Rodman/49 40.00 100.00
23 George Gervin/75 12.00 30.00
24 Bernard King/75 10.00 25.00
25 Joe Dumars/75 10.00 25.00

2017-18 Immaculate Collection Dual Autographs

PRINT RUNS B/WN 25-49 COPIES PER
EXCHANGE DEADLINE 4/17/2020
1 Lauri Markkanen
Zach LaVine/49 150.00 400.00
2 Nate Archibald
Tim Hardaway/49 20.00 50.00
3 Dirk Nowitzki
Giannis Antetokounmpo/25 400.00 800.00
4 Bill Walton
Kareem Abdul-Jabbar/25 50.00 120.00
5 Jason Kidd
Lonzo Ball/49 60.00 150.00
6 Clyde Drexler
Dominique Wilkins/49 25.00 60.00
7 Derek Harper
Rolando Blackman/49 12.00 30.00
8 Kareem Abdul-Jabbar
Shaquille O'Neal/25 300.00 600.00
9 Kristaps Porzingis
Frank Ntilikina/49 EXCH 20.00 50.00
10 Kevin McHale
Robert Parish/49 30.00 80.00
11 Reggie Jackson
Luke Kennard/49 20.00 50.00
13 Alonzo Mourning
Anthony Davis/25 50.00 120.00
15 Lonzo Ball
Reggie Miller/25 75.00 200.00
16 Bill Russell
Larry Bird/25 1,500.00 3,000.00
17 Gordon Hayward
Kyrie Irving/25 60.00 150.00
18 Walt Frazier
Willis Reed/49 200.00 500.00
19 Kyrie Irving
Jayson Tatum/25 500.00 1,000.00
20 Grant Hill
Jason Kidd/49 60.00 150.00
21 Dennis Smith Jr.
Jason Kidd/49 25.00 60.00
22 Ben Wallace
Jerry Stackhouse/49 EXCH 20.00 50.00
23 Kevin Durant
Kobe Bryant/25 2,000.00 4,000.00
24 Cliff Hagan
Louie Dampier/49 20.00 50.00
25 Markelle Fultz
Lonzo Ball/49 75.00 200.00
26 Alex English
David Thompson/49 15.00 40.00
27 Avery Bradley
Reggie Jackson/49 12.00 30.00
28 Dennis Rodman
Karl Malone/25 150.00 400.00
29 Devin Booker
Josh Jackson/49 150.00 400.00
30 Mark Aguirre
Joe Dumars/49 20.00 50.00
31 Dwayne Bacon
Jonathan Isaac/49 25.00 60.00
32 Louie Dampier
George Gervin/49 25.00 60.00
33 Kobe Bryant
Stephen Curry/25 5,000.00 10,000.00
34 Kyle Kuzma
Lonzo Ball/25 EXCH 75.00 200.00
36 Ben Wallace
Richard Hamilton/49 20.00 50.00
37 Stacey Augmon
Isaiah Rider/49 12.00 30.00
39 Aaron Gordon
Jonathan Isaac/49 25.00 60.00
40 George Gervin
Rick Barry/49 25.00 60.00
41 Josh Jackson
Frank Mason III/49 12.00 30.00
42 Latrell Sprewell
Robert Horry/49 20.00 50.00
43 Reggie Miller
Allen Iverson/25 200.00 500.00
44 Lonzo Ball
Magic Johnson/25 100.00 250.00
45 Joel Embiid
Markelle Fultz/49 100.00 250.00

2017-18 Immaculate Collection Dual Patches Jersey Number

PRINT RUNS B/WN 1-23 COPIES PER
NO PRICING ON QTY 17 OR LESS
3 Andrew Wiggins
Khris Middleton/22 10.00 25.00
11 Josh Jackson
Markelle Fultz/20 12.00 30.00
13 Otto Porter Jr.
Rudy Gay/22 6.00 15.00
21 Hassan Whiteside
Joel Embiid/21 15.00 40.00
23 Anthony Davis
LeBron James/23 300.00 600.00

2017-18 Immaculate Collection Heralded Signatures

PRINT RUNS B/WN 49-99 COPIES PER
EXCHANGE DEADLINE 4/17/2020
*RED: .5X TO 1.5X BASIC p/r 99
*RED: .5X TO 1.2X BASIC p/r 49-57
1 Gail Goodrich/99 5.00 12.00
2 Isaiah Rider/99 4.00 10.00
3 Avery Johnson/99 4.00 10.00
4 Kenny ""Sky"" Walker/99 3.00 8.00
5 Shaquille O'Neal/49 30.00 80.00
6 Ronny Turiaf/99 3.00 8.00
7 David Robinson/99 12.00 30.00
8 John Starks/99 4.00 10.00
9 Sam Jones/99 12.00 30.00
10 Jack Sikma/99 5.00 12.00
11 Jermaine O'Neal/99 5.00 12.00
12 Ed Pinckney/99 3.00 8.00
13 Freddie Lewis/99 3.00 8.00
14 Kurt Rambis/99 4.00 10.00
15 John Stockton/49 15.00 40.00
16 Kevin Willis/99 3.00 8.00
17 Dennis Rodman/99 20.00 50.00
18 Dan Issel/99 6.00 15.00
19 Christian Laettner/99 5.00 12.00
20 Jason Williams/99 8.00 20.00
21 Kelly Tripucka/99 4.00 10.00
22 Elden Campbell/99 3.00 8.00
23 George McGinnis/99 3.00 8.00
24 Sam Cassell/99 4.00 10.00
25 Jerry West/99 15.00 40.00
26 Mark Aguirre/99 4.00 10.00
27 Anfernee Hardaway/57 15.00 40.00
28 Tom Meschery/99 3.00 8.00
29 Calvin Murphy/99 5.00 12.00
30 Jeff Hornacek/99 4.00 10.00
31 Rick Fox/99 4.00 10.00
32 Chris Herren/99 4.00 10.00
33 Dale Ellis/99 3.00 8.00
34 Marques Johnson/99 4.00 10.00
35 Oscar Robertson/49 15.00 40.00
36 Damon Stoudamire/99 5.00 12.00
37 Grant Hill/99 10.00 25.00
38 Doug Collins/99 5.00 12.00
39 Lenny Wilkens/99 6.00 15.00
40 P.J. Brown/99 3.00 8.00

2017-18 Immaculate Collection Heralded Signatures Red

*RED: .6X TO 1.5X BASIC p/r 99
*RED: .5X TO 1.2X BASIC p/r 49-57
STATED PRINT RUN 25 SER.#'d SETS
EXCHANGE DEADLINE 4/17/2020
35 Oscar Robertson 30.00 80.00

2017-18 Immaculate Collection Immaculate Inductions Autographs

PRINT RUNS B/WN 25-49 COPIES PER
EXCHANGE DEADLINE 4/17/2020
1 Robert Parish/49 10.00 25.00
2 Dave Cowens/49 12.00 30.00
3 Bill Walton/49 10.00 25.00
4 John Stockton/25 25.00 60.00
5 Joe Dumars/49 10.00 25.00
6 Ralph Sampson/49 8.00 20.00
7 Alex English/49 10.00 25.00
8 Nate Archibald/49 10.00 25.00
9 Bob McAdoo/49 10.00 25.00
10 Lenny Wilkens/49 10.00 25.00
11 Jamaal Wilkes/49 8.00 20.00
12 Adrian Dantley/49 8.00 20.00
13 Larry Bird/25 60.00 150.00
14 Magic Johnson/25 40.00 100.00
15 Cliff Hagan/49 10.00 25.00
16 Jerry West/25 20.00 50.00
17 Elvin Hayes/49 10.00 25.00
18 Calvin Murphy/49 8.00 20.00
19 Dennis Rodman/49 40.00 100.00
20 James Worthy/49 12.00 30.00
21 Hakeem Olajuwon/49 20.00 50.00
22 Alonzo Mourning/49 15.00 40.00
23 George Gervin/49 12.00 30.00
24 Artis Gilmore/49 10.00 25.00
25 Bernard King/49 10.00 25.00
26 Shaquille O'Neal/25 75.00 200.00
27 David Robinson/49 25.00 60.00
28 Allen Iverson/25 50.00 120.00
29 Reggie Miller/25 60.00 150.00
30 Charles Barkley/49 150.00 400.00

2017-18 Immaculate Collection Immaculate Ink

STATED PRINT RUN 99 SER.#'d SETS
EXCHANGE DEADLINE 4/17/2020
*RED: .6X TO 1.5X BASIC
1 Lou Williams 4.00 10.00
2 Mario Hezonja 3.00 8.00
3 Aaron McKie 3.00 8.00
4 George Gervin 8.00 20.00
5 Detlef Schrempf 5.00 12.00
6 Stephen Jackson 4.00 10.00
7 Thaddeus Young 3.00 8.00
8 Magic Johnson 20.00 50.00
9 D.J. Augustin 3.00 8.00
10 James Worthy 6.00 15.00
11 Bob Lanier 6.00 15.00
12 Victor Oladipo 4.00 10.00
13 Dwight Powell 3.00 8.00
14 Kyle Korver 4.00 10.00
15 Gerald Henderson Sr. 3.00 8.00
16 Paul Silas 5.00 12.00
17 Willie Cauley-Stein 3.00 8.00
18 Earl Monroe 5.00 12.00
19 Jerian Grant 3.00 8.00
20 Al Horford 5.00 12.00

2017-18 Immaculate Collection Immaculate Introductions Autographs

STATED PRINT RUN 75 SER.#'d SETS
EXCHANGE DEADLINE 4/17/2020
1 Semi Ojeleye 8.00 20.00
2 Josh Jackson 8.00 20.00

3 Malik Monk 25.00 60.00
4 Frank Ntilikina 8.00 20.00
5 Josh Hart 15.00 40.00
6 Markelle Fultz 25.00 60.00
7 Luke Kennard 12.00 30.00
8 Donovan Mitchell 100.00 250.00
9 Sindarius Thornwell 6.00 15.00
10 Dillon Brooks 20.00 50.00
11 Justin Jackson 6.00 15.00
12 De'Aaron Fox 100.00 250.00
13 Zhou Qi 40.00 100.00
14 John Collins 20.00 50.00
15 Bam Adebayo 40.00 100.00
16 Jayson Tatum 125.00 300.00
17 Jarrett Allen 15.00 40.00
18 Lonzo Ball 25.00 60.00
19 Frank Mason III 6.00 15.00
20 Bogdan Bogdanovic 15.00 40.00
21 Jonathan Isaac 12.00 30.00
22 OG Anunoby 30.00 80.00
24 Maxi Kleber 10.00 25.00
25 Jawun Evans 6.00 15.00
26 Kyle Kuzma 25.00 60.00
27 Daniel Theis 12.00 30.00
28 Lauri Markkanen 100.00 250.00
29 Jordan Bell 6.00 15.00
30 Dennis Smith Jr. 8.00 20.00

2017-18 Immaculate Collection Immaculate Milestones Autographs

STATED PRINT RUN 25 SER.#'d SETS
EXCHANGE DEADLINE 4/17/2020
1 Kevin Durant 250.00 600.00
3 Anthony Davis 125.00 300.00
4 Stephen Curry 1,500.00 3,000.00
5 Kobe Bryant 6,000.00 10,000.00
6 Kobe Bryant 6,000.00 10,000.00
7 Lauri Markkanen 125.00 300.00
8 Steve Kerr 100.00 250.00
9 Kemba Walker 60.00 150.00
10 Markelle Fultz 60.00 150.00

2017-18 Immaculate Collection Immaculate Moments Autographs

PRINT RUNS B/WN 25-75 COPIES PER
EXCHANGE DEADLINE 4/17/2020
2 Andre Drummond/75 10.00 25.00
3 Lonzo Ball/75 30.00 80.00
4 Dennis Smith Jr./75 10.00 25.00
5 Stephen Curry/25 1,500.00 3,000.00
6 Gerald Green/75 10.00 25.00
7 Lou Williams/75 10.00 25.00
8 Donovan Mitchell/75 80.00 200.00
10 Joel Embiid/49 40.00 100.00
11 Kevin Durant/25 125.00 300.00
12 CJ McCollum/75 12.00 30.00
13 Nikola Jokic/25 300.00 600.00
14 Giannis Antetokounmpo/49 125.00 300.00
15 Brandon Ingram/49 20.00 50.00
16 Ricky Rubio/34 25.00 60.00
17 Tyson Chandler/75 10.00 25.00
18 Al Horford/75 12.00 30.00
19 De'Aaron Fox/75 60.00 150.00
20 Harrison Barnes/75 10.00 25.00
21 Lou Williams/75 10.00 25.00
22 Bogdan Bogdanovic/75 15.00 40.00
23 Nikola Jokic/75 400.00 800.00
24 Donovan Mitchell/75 80.00 200.00
25 Spencer Dinwiddie/75 10.00 25.00
26 Bogdan Bogdanovic/75 15.00 40.00
28 Dwyane Wade/25 100.00 250.00
29 Karl-Anthony Towns/49 25.00 60.00
30 Donovan Mitchell/75 80.00 200.00

2017-18 Immaculate Collection Jumbo Patches Jersey Number

PRINT RUNS B/WN 3-75 COPIES PER
NO PRICING ON QTY 19 OR LESS
*TEAM LOGO/25: .6X TO 1.5X BASIC p/r 75
*TEAM LOGO/25: .5X TO 1.2X BASIC p/r 50
51 John Collins/75 8.00 20.00
52 Tyler Dorsey/75 3.00 8.00
53 Jarrett Allen/75 8.00 20.00
54 Jayson Tatum/50 200.00 500.00
55 Ante Zizic/50 5.00 12.00
56 Semi Ojeleye/75 4.00 10.00
57 Malik Monk/75 12.00 30.00
58 Dwayne Bacon/75 3.00 8.00
59 Dennis Smith Jr./50 5.00 12.00
60 Tyler Lydon/75 3.00 8.00
61 Luke Kennard/75 6.00 15.00
62 Jordan Bell/50 4.00 10.00
63 TJ Leaf/50 4.00 10.00
64 Sindarius Thornwell/75 3.00 8.00
66 Lonzo Ball/75 12.00 30.00
67 Kyle Kuzma/75 12.00 30.00
68 Josh Hart/75 8.00 20.00
69 Ivan Rabb/75 3.00 8.00
70 Bam Adebayo/50 40.00 100.00
71 Sterling Brown/75 3.00 8.00
73 Justin Patton/75 3.00 8.00
75 Frank Ntilikina/75 4.00 10.00
76 Terrance Ferguson/75 3.00 8.00
77 Jonathan Isaac/75 8.00 20.00
78 Wes Iwundu/75 3.00 8.00
79 Markelle Fultz/50 15.00 40.00
80 Josh Jackson/75 4.00 10.00
81 Davon Reed/75 3.00 8.00
82 Zach Collins/75 5.00 12.00
83 Caleb Swanigan/75 3.00 8.00
84 De'Aaron Fox/75 30.00 80.00
85 Harry Giles/75 3.00 8.00
86 Frank Mason III/75 3.00 8.00
87 Bogdan Bogdanovic/75 8.00 20.00
88 Justin Jackson/75 3.00 8.00
89 Derrick White/75 12.00 30.00
91 Donovan Mitchell/50 75.00 200.00
92 Tony Bradley/75 3.00 8.00

2017-18 Immaculate Collection Jumbo Patches Team Logo

*TEAM LOGO/25: .5X TO 1.2X BASIC p/r 50
*TEAM LOGO/25: .6X TO 1.5X BASIC p/r 75
PRINT RUNS B/WN 2-25 COPIES PER
NO PRICING ON QTY 16 OR LESS
54 Jayson Tatum/25 60.00 150.00
67 Kyle Kuzma/25 20.00 50.00
91 Donovan Mitchell/25 60.00 150.00

2017-18 Immaculate Collection Marks of Greatness Autographs

PRINT RUNS B/WN 25-99 COPIES PER
EXCHANGE DEADLINE 4/17/2020
1 Nate Archibald/99 8.00 20.00
2 Allen Iverson/25 60.00 150.00
3 Lenny Wilkens/99 8.00 20.00
4 Alonzo Mourning/49 20.00 50.00
5 Ralph Sampson/99 6.00 15.00
6 Ray Allen/49 12.00 30.00
7 Adrian Dantley/99 6.00 15.00
8 Grant Hill/75 12.00 30.00
9 Rolando Blackman/99 5.00 12.00
10 Sam Jones/75 20.00 50.00
11 Robert Parish/99 8.00 20.00
12 Karl Malone/25 30.00 80.00
13 Rick Fox/99 5.00 12.00
14 David Robinson/49 25.00 60.00
15 Stephen Jackson/99 5.00 12.00
16 Anfernee Hardaway/49 40.00 100.00
17 Jerry Stackhouse/99 5.00 12.00
18 Rick Barry/75 10.00 25.00
19 Damon Stoudamire/99 6.00 15.00
20 Artis Gilmore/99 8.00 20.00
21 Chauncey Billups/99 8.00 20.00
22 Magic Johnson/25 50.00 120.00
23 B.J. Armstrong/99 6.00 15.00
24 Clyde Drexler/49 25.00 60.00
25 Mark Aguirre/99 5.00 12.00

2017-18 Immaculate Collection Massive Memorabilia

STATED PRINT RUN 25 SER.#'d SETS
1 Sterling Brown 3.00 8.00
2 Bam Adebayo 6.00 15.00
3 Josh Jackson 4.00 10.00
4 Lonzo Ball 20.00 50.00
5 Semi Ojeleye 4.00 10.00
6 Frank Mason III 3.00 8.00
7 John Collins 20.00 50.00
8 Terrance Ferguson 3.00 8.00
9 Jayson Tatum 40.00 100.00
10 Caleb Swanigan 3.00 8.00
11 Harry Giles 3.00 8.00
12 Dwayne Bacon 3.00 8.00
13 Derrick White 12.00 30.00
14 Jonathan Isaac 15.00 40.00
15 Tyler Dorsey 3.00 8.00
16 Donovan Mitchell 40.00 100.00
17 OG Anunoby 15.00 40.00
18 Markelle Fultz 15.00 40.00
19 Lauri Markkanen 20.00 50.00
20 Dennis Smith Jr. 4.00 10.00
21 Tyler Lydon 3.00 8.00
22 Jarrett Allen 10.00 25.00
23 Frank Ntilikina 4.00 10.00
24 Zach Collins 5.00 12.00
25 Wes Iwundu 3.00 8.00

2017-18 Immaculate Collection Modern Marks Autographs

PRINT RUNS B/WN 49-99 COPIES PER
EXCHANGE DEADLINE 4/17/2020
*RED: .6X TO 1.5X BASIC p/r 99
*RED: .5X TO 1.2X BASIC p/r 49
1 Frank Kaminsky/99 3.00 8.00
2 Damian Lillard/49 20.00 50.00
3 Marvin Williams/99 3.00 8.00
4 Kristaps Porzingis/49 10.00 25.00
5 Allen Crabbe/99 3.00 8.00
6 Michael Carter-Williams/99 3.00 8.00
7 Trey Lyles/99 3.00 8.00
8 Jrue Holiday/99 6.00 15.00
9 Caris LeVert/99 5.00 12.00
10 JJ Redick/99 5.00 12.00
11 Nick Young/99 3.00 8.00
12 Carmelo Anthony/49 12.00 30.00
13 Doug McDermott/99 3.00 8.00
14 Marcus Smart/99 5.00 12.00
15 J.J. Barea/99 4.00 10.00
16 Derrick Favors/99 3.00 8.00
17 Robin Lopez/99 3.00 8.00
18 Trevor Ariza/99 3.00 8.00
19 Skal Labissiere/99 3.00 8.00
20 Jakob Poeltl/99 4.00 10.00
21 Meyers Leonard/99 3.00 8.00
22 Pau Gasol/99 8.00 20.00
23 Domantas Sabonis/99 10.00 25.00
24 Kentavious Caldwell-Pope/99 4.00 10.00
25 Gary Harris/99 4.00 10.00
26 Marquese Chriss/99 3.00 8.00
27 Denzel Valentine/99 3.00 8.00
28 Channing Frye/99 3.00 8.00
29 Kelly Oubre Jr./99 5.00 12.00
30 Malcolm Brogdon/99 4.00 10.00
31 Rondae Hollis-Jefferson/99 3.00 8.00
32 Jeremy Lin/99 8.00 20.00
33 Myles Turner/99 3.00 8.00
34 Aaron Gordon/99 5.00 12.00
35 Udonis Haslem/99 3.00 8.00
36 Nerlens Noel/99 3.00 8.00
37 John Henson/99 3.00 8.00
38 Jose Calderon/99 3.00 8.00
39 Courtney Lee/99 3.00 8.00
40 Elfrid Payton/99 3.00 8.00

2017-18 Immaculate Collection Modern Marks Autographs Red

*RED: .6X TO 1.5X BASIC p/r 99
*RED: .5X TO 1.2X BASIC p/r 49
STATED PRINT RUN 25 SER.#'d SETS
EXCHANGE DEADLINE 4/17/2020
32 Jeremy Lin 15.00 40.00

2017-18 Immaculate Collection Patch Autographs

PRINT RUNS B/WN 15-25 COPIES PER
NO PRICING ON QTY 15 OR LESS
EXCHANGE DEADLINE 4/17/2020
*JSY NUM/20-30: .4X TO 1X BASIC p/r 25
1 Vince Carter/25 40.00 100.00
2 Thaddeus Young/25 8.00 20.00
3 Gordon Hayward/25 10.00 25.00
5 Rudy Gobert/25 15.00 40.00
6 J.J. Barea/25 10.00 25.00
7 Rondae Hollis-Jefferson/25 8.00 20.00
8 Derrick Favors/25 8.00 20.00
9 Harrison Barnes/25 10.00 25.00
10 Stephen Jackson/25 10.00 25.00
11 Giannis Antetokounmpo/25 150.00 400.00
12 Myles Turner/25 12.00 30.00
13 Seth Curry/25 12.00 30.00
14 Caris LeVert/25 12.00 30.00
15 Courtney Lee/25 8.00 20.00
17 Blake Griffin/25 20.00 50.00
18 Aaron Gordon/25 12.00 30.00
19 David Robinson/25 25.00 60.00
20 Jrue Holiday/25 15.00 40.00
22 Serge Ibaka/25 10.00 25.00
23 Brandon Ingram/25 EXCH 25.00 60.00
24 Khris Middleton/25 25.00 60.00
25 Nikola Jokic/25 500.00 1,000.00
26 Rodney Hood/25 8.00 20.00
28 Gary Harris/25 10.00 25.00
30 Kevin Love/25 12.00 30.00
31 CJ McCollum/25 12.00 30.00
32 Elfrid Payton/25 8.00 20.00
34 Kemba Walker/25 10.00 25.00
35 Charlie Scott/25 12.00 30.00
36 Kenny Smith/25 10.00 25.00
38 Grant Hill/25 25.00 60.00
40 B.J. Armstrong/25 12.00 30.00
41 Dan Issel/25 15.00 40.00
44 James Worthy/25 15.00 40.00
46 Sam Perkins/25 10.00 25.00
47 Kristaps Porzingis/25 15.00 40.00
49 Dominique Wilkins/25 20.00 50.00
50 Detlef Schrempf/25 12.00 30.00
51 Louie Dampier/25 12.00 30.00
52 Doug Collins/25 12.00 30.00
53 Hakeem Olajuwon/25 25.00 60.00
55 Kobe Bryant/15 3,000.00 6,000.00
59 World B. Free/25 10.00 25.00
60 Artis Gilmore/25 15.00 40.00

2017-18 Immaculate Collection Patches Jersey Number

PRINT RUNS B/WN 1-23 COPIES PER
NO PRICING ON QTY 17 OR LESS
1 Khris Middleton/22 20.00 50.00
4 Joel Embiid/21 20.00 50.00
6 Anthony Davis/23 20.00 50.00
7 Markelle Fultz/20 12.00 30.00
8 Rudy Gay/22 6.00 15.00
14 Hassan Whiteside/21 6.00 15.00
17 Josh Jackson/20 6.00 15.00
44 LeBron James/23 100.00 250.00
47 Otto Porter Jr./22 6.00 15.00
49 Andrew Wiggins/22 10.00 25.00

2017-18 Immaculate Collection Premium Patch Autographs

PRINT RUNS B/WN 2-25 COPIES PER
NO PRICING ON QTY 18 OR LESS
EXCHANGE DEADLINE 4/17/2020
56 Wayne Selden/25 8.00 20.00
57 Dillon Brooks/25 15.00 40.00
58 Sindarius Thornwell/25 8.00 20.00
59 Sterling Brown/25 8.00 20.00
60 Tyler Dorsey/25 8.00 20.00
61 Davon Reed/25 8.00 20.00
62 Dwayne Bacon/25 8.00 20.00
63 Frank Jackson/25 8.00 20.00
64 Frank Mason III/25 8.00 20.00
66 Jawun Evans/25 8.00 20.00
68 Semi Ojeleye/25 10.00 25.00
69 Wes Iwundu/25 8.00 20.00
70 Derrick White/25 40.00 100.00
71 Josh Hart/25 75.00 200.00
73 Tony Bradley/25 8.00 20.00
75 Jarrett Allen/25 20.00 50.00
76 OG Anunoby/25 15.00 40.00
77 Terrance Ferguson/25 8.00 20.00
78 Tyler Lydon/25 8.00 20.00
80 John Collins/25 75.00 200.00
81 TJ Leaf/25 8.00 20.00
82 Ante Zizic/25 10.00 25.00
83 D.J. Wilson/25 25.00 60.00
84 Justin Patton/25 8.00 20.00
85 Bam Adebayo/25 125.00 300.00
86 Donovan Mitchell/25 200.00 500.00
87 Luke Kennard/25 15.00 40.00
88 Malik Monk/22 40.00 100.00
89 Zach Collins/25 12.00 30.00
90 Dennis Smith Jr./21 10.00 25.00
91 Caleb Swanigan/25 8.00 20.00
92 Frank Ntilikina/25 10.00 25.00
93 Lauri Markkanen/25 100.00 250.00
95 De'Aaron Fox/25 125.00 300.00
96 Jonathan Isaac/25 50.00 120.00
98 Lonzo Ball/25 75.00 200.00
99 Josh Jackson/25 10.00 25.00
100 Markelle Fultz/25 125.00 300.00

2017-18 Immaculate Collection Remarkable Memorabilia

*RED/25: .5X TO 1.2X BASIC
PRINT RUNS B/WN 25-49 COPIES PER
1 Denzel Valentine/49 2.50 6.00
2 Dwight Powell/49 2.50 6.00
3 Tony Parker/49 6.00 15.00
4 Jaylen Brown/49 10.00 25.00
5 Jusuf Nurkic/49 3.00 8.00
6 John Henson/49 2.50 6.00
7 Skal Labissiere/49 2.50 6.00
8 Jakob Poeltl/49 3.00 8.00
9 Mark Price/49 4.00 10.00
10 Doug Collins/49 4.00 10.00
11 Zach LaVine/49 6.00 15.00
12 Jarell Martin/49 2.50 6.00
13 Kelly Tripucka/49 3.00 8.00
14 Julius Randle/49 4.00 10.00
15 Marcus Smart/49 4.00 10.00
16 Kevin Johnson/49 4.00 10.00
17 Jason Kidd/49 6.00 15.00
18 John Stockton/49 8.00 20.00
19 Udonis Haslem/49 2.50 6.00
20 James Worthy/49 5.00 12.00
21 J.J. Barea/49 3.00 8.00
22 Jrue Holiday/49 5.00 12.00
23 Marvin Williams/49 2.50 6.00
24 Manu Ginobili/49 8.00 20.00
25 Ben Simmons/49 4.00 10.00
26 Al Horford/49 4.00 10.00
27 Taurean Prince/49 2.50 6.00
28 Kobe Bryant/49 60.00 150.00
29 Wesley Matthews/49 2.50 6.00
30 Jordan Clarkson/49 4.00 10.00
31 Alonzo Mourning/49 6.00 15.00
32 LeBron James/49 20.00 50.00
33 Wilt Chamberlain/25 40.00 100.00
34 B.J. Armstrong/49 4.00 10.00
35 Rajon Rondo/49 5.00 12.00
36 Maurice Harkless/49 2.50 6.00
37 JJ Redick/49 4.00 10.00
38 Allen Crabbe/49 2.50 6.00
39 Brook Lopez/49 3.00 8.00
40 LaMarcus Aldridge/49 4.00 10.00
41 DeAndre Jordan/49 3.00 8.00
42 Andrei Kirilenko/49 3.00 8.00
43 Ray Allen/49 6.00 15.00
44 Patrick Ewing/49 6.00 15.00
45 Sam Perkins/49 3.00 8.00
46 Charlie Scott/49 4.00 10.00
47 Terry Rozier/49 3.00 8.00
48 Nick Young/49 2.50 6.00
49 Willie Cauley-Stein/49 2.50 6.00
50 Andre Drummond/49 3.00 8.00
51 Gerald Green/49 3.00 8.00
52 Pascal Siakam/49 8.00 20.00
53 Caris LeVert/49 4.00 10.00
54 Darrell Griffith/49 3.00 8.00
55 Dennis Schroder/49 3.00 8.00
56 Rondae Hollis-Jefferson/49 2.50 6.00
57 Tim Hardaway Jr./49 3.00 8.00
58 Chris Paul/49 6.00 15.00
59 Reggie Lewis/49 5.00 12.00
60 Nicolas Batum/49 2.50 6.00
61 Joe Ingles/49 3.00 8.00
62 Cody Zeller/49 2.50 6.00
63 Shaquille O'Neal/49 12.00 30.00
64 Gerald Henderson/49 2.50 6.00
65 Serge Ibaka/49 3.00 8.00
66 Derrick Favors/49 2.50 6.00
67 Kelly Oubre Jr./49 4.00 10.00
68 Ryan Anderson/49 2.50 6.00
69 Wilson Chandler/49 3.00 8.00
70 Clyde Drexler/49 6.00 15.00
71 Thon Maker/49 2.50 6.00
72 Eric Gordon/49 3.00 8.00
73 Rodney Hood/49 2.50 6.00
74 Jerami Grant/49 3.00 8.00
75 Herb Williams/49 2.50 6.00

2017-18 Immaculate Collection Remarkable Memorabilia Red

*RED/22-25: .5X TO 1.2X BASIC p/r 49
PRINT RUNS B/WN 5-25 COPIES PER
NO PRICING ON QTY 17 OR LESS
32 LeBron James/25 40.00 100.00

2017-18 Immaculate Collection Rookie Patch Autographs Jersey Number

*JSY NUM: .6X TO 1.5X BASE
PRINT RUNS B/WN 1-50 COPIES PER
NO PRICING ON QTY 15 OR LESS
EXCHANGE DEADLINE 4/17/2020
102 Donovan Mitchell JSY AU/45 500.00 100.00
105 Terrance Ferguson JSY AU/23 8.00 20.00
106 Markelle Fultz JSY AU/20 125.00 300.00
114 TJ Leaf JSY AU/22 15.00 40.00
115 Jarrett Allen JSY AU/31 60.00 150.00
124 John Collins JSY AU/20 200.00 500.00
128 Lauri Markkanen JSY AU/24 300.00 600.00

2017-18 Immaculate Collection Shadowbox Signatures

PRINT RUNS B/WN 25-99 COPIES PER
EXCHANGE DEADLINE 4/17/2020
2 Mike Conley/99 6.00 15.00
3 Bill Russell/25 1,500.00 3,000.00
4 Al Horford/99 20.00 50.00
5 JJ Redick/99 8.00 20.00
6 Dwyane Wade/25 125.00 300.00
7 Justise Winslow/99 5.00 12.00
8 Brandon Ingram/49 100.00 250.00
9 Emmanuel Mudiay/99 5.00 12.00
10 Jeremy Lin/49 75.00 200.00
11 Kobe Bryant/25 6,000.00 10,000.00
12 Dion Waiters/99 5.00 12.00
13 Julius Erving/25 150.00 400.00
14 Nikola Jokic/99 400.00 800.00
15 Myles Turner/99 8.00 20.00
16 Damian Lillard/25 150.00 400.00
17 Reggie Jackson/99 6.00 15.00
18 Vince Carter/49 150.00 400.00
20 Kristaps Porzingis/49 40.00 100.00
21 Magic Johnson/25 150.00 400.00
22 Rodney Hood/99 5.00 12.00
23 Kyrie Irving/25 125.00 300.00
24 Eric Bledsoe/99 6.00 15.00
25 Trevor Ariza/99 5.00 12.00
26 Blake Griffin/25 20.00 50.00
27 Clint Capela/99 6.00 15.00
29 Shaun Livingston/99 6.00 15.00
30 Tracy McGrady/49 150.00 400.00
31 Larry Bird/25 150.00 400.00
32 Kentavious Caldwell-Pope/99 6.00 15.00
33 John Stockton/25 100.00 250.00
34 Derrick Favors/99 5.00 12.00
35 Jrue Holiday/99 30.00 80.00
36 Giannis Antetokounmpo/25 500.00 1,000.00
37 Serge Ibaka/99 6.00 15.00
38 Tony Parker/99 12.00 30.00
39 Kevin Durant/25 300.00 600.00
40 Gordon Hayward/99 15.00 40.00
41 Kareem Abdul-Jabbar/25 200.00 500.00
42 Tyson Chandler/99 6.00 15.00
43 Karl Malone/25 150.00 400.00
44 Avery Bradley/99 5.00 12.00
45 Elfrid Payton/99 5.00 12.00
46 Karl-Anthony Towns/49 60.00 150.00
47 Michael Kidd-Gilchrist/99 5.00 12.00
48 Isaiah Thomas/49 8.00 20.00
49 Stephen Curry/25 2,000.00 4,000.00
50 Kemba Walker/99 15.00 40.00

2017-18 Immaculate Collection Sneaker Swatches Signatures

PRINT RUNS B/WN 5-25 COPIES PER
NO PRICING ON QTY 15 OR LESS
EXCHANGE DEADLINE 4/17/2020
6 Andrew Wiggins/25 15.00 40.00
8 Blake Griffin/25 15.00 40.00
12 Karl-Anthony Towns/25 20.00 50.00
22 Rick Fox/25 6.00 15.00
26 Andre Drummond/25 10.00 25.00
28 Derrick Favors/25 8.00 20.00
32 Gordon Hayward/25 10.00 25.00
34 Sterling Brown/20 8.00 20.00
38 Karl Malone/25 30.00 80.00
40 Brandon Ingram/25 EXCH 40.00 100.00
42 Ante Zizic/25 10.00 25.00
48 Rodney Hood/25 EXCH 8.00 20.00

2017-18 Immaculate Collection Sole of the Game

PRINT RUNS B/WN 10-25 COPIES PER
NO PRICING ON QTY 18 OR LESS
4 Andre Drummond/25 20.00 50.00
5 Blake Griffin/25 25.00 60.00
6 Karl Malone/25 50.00 120.00
7 Hakeem Olajuwon/25 50.00 125.00
8 Andrew Wiggins/25 40.00 100.00
9 Karl-Anthony Towns/25 40.00 100.00
10 Shaquille O'Neal/25 80.00 200.00
11 Dikembe Mutombo/25 30.00 80.00
12 Scottie Pippen/25 60.00 150.00
13 Aaron Gordon/25 25.00 60.00
14 Chris Paul/25 40.00 100.00
15 John Wall/25 30.00 80.00
16 Anthony Davis/25 60.00 150.00
17 Paul George/25 40.00 100.00
18 Dominique Wilkins/25 40.00 100.00
19 Kevin McHale/25 40.00 100.00
20 Larry Bird/25 75.00 200.00
24 Markelle Fultz/24 60.00 150.00

2017-18 Immaculate Collection Special Event Materials

STATED PRINT RUN 99 SER.#'d SETS
*RED/25: .5X TO 1.2X BASIC
1 Trevor Ariza 2.50 6.00
2 Corey Brewer 2.50 6.00
3 Clint Capela 3.00 8.00
4 Nene 3.00 8.00
5 JaMychal Green 2.50 6.00
6 Chandler Parsons 2.50 6.00
7 Jabari Parker 2.50 6.00
8 Larry Bird 12.00 30.00
9 Andrew Wiggins 5.00 12.00
10 Carmelo Anthony 6.00 15.00
11 Draymond Green 6.00 15.00
12 Dwyane Wade 8.00 20.00
13 Isaiah Thomas 3.00 8.00
14 Jimmy Butler 6.00 15.00
15 Karl-Anthony Towns 6.00 15.00
16 Kawhi Leonard 10.00 25.00
17 Kevin Durant 15.00 40.00
18 Klay Thompson 10.00 25.00
19 Kristaps Porzingis 5.00 12.00
20 Kyrie Irving 8.00 20.00
21 LeBron James 30.00 80.00
22 Pau Gasol 6.00 15.00
23 Russell Westbrook 6.00 15.00
24 Brandon Ingram 5.00 12.00
25 Derrick Rose 6.00 15.00

2017-18 Immaculate Collection Special Event Materials Red

*RED/25: .5X TO 1.2X BASIC
PRINT RUNS B/WN 7-25 COPIES PER
NO PRICING ON QTY 15 OR LESS
21 LeBron James/25 25.00 60.00

2017-18 Immaculate Collection Standout Memorabilia

PRINT RUNS B/WN 35-49 COPIES PER
*RED/25: .5X TO 1.2X BASIC
1 Damian Lillard/49 10.00 25.00
2 Kevin Durant/49 15.00 40.00
3 Tree Rollins/49 2.50 6.00
4 Paul George/49 6.00 15.00
5 Gary Harris/49 3.00 8.00
6 Dominique Wilkins/35 6.00 15.00
7 Danny Green/49 3.00 8.00
8 Khris Middleton/49 3.00 8.00
9 Lance Stephenson/49 3.00 8.00
10 Artis Gilmore/49 5.00 12.00
11 Avery Bradley/49 2.50 6.00
12 Larry Bird/35 15.00 40.00
13 Myles Turner/49 4.00 10.00
14 Paul Pierce/49 6.00 15.00
15 Mychal Thompson/49 2.50 6.00
16 Kristaps Porzingis/49 5.00 12.00
17 Terrence Ross/49 3.00 8.00
18 Harrison Barnes/49 3.00 8.00
19 Nikola Vucevic/49 3.00 8.00
20 Caron Butler/49 3.00 8.00
21 Ron Harper/49 4.00 10.00
22 Magic Johnson/49 15.00 40.00
23 Kyle Korver/49 3.00 8.00
24 Grant Hill/49 6.00 15.00
25 Darren Collison/49 2.50 6.00
26 Stephen Curry/49 30.00 80.00
27 Karl Malone/49 8.00 20.00
28 Jamal Murray/49 6.00 15.00
29 Noah Vonleh/49 2.50 6.00
30 Tyson Chandler/49 3.00 8.00

2017-18 Immaculate Collection Swatches

PRINT RUNS B/WN 35-49 COPIES PER
*RED/25: .5X TO 1.2X BASIC
1 Buddy Hield/49 4.00 10.00
2 Nikola Mirotic/49 2.50 6.00
3 Dan Issel/49 5.00 12.00
4 Scottie Pippen/49 10.00 25.00
5 Draymond Green/49 5.00 12.00
6 Tom Chambers/49 4.00 10.00
7 Jeff Teague/49 2.50 6.00
8 Kawhi Leonard/49 10.00 25.00
9 Aaron Gordon/49 4.00 10.00
10 Kyrie Irving/49 8.00 20.00
11 Chandler Parsons/49 2.50 6.00
12 Paul Millsap/49 3.00 8.00
13 Dario Saric/49 3.00 8.00
14 Shaun Livingston/49 3.00 8.00
15 Giannis Antetokounmpo/49 20.00 50.00
16 Tyreke Evans/49 2.50 6.00
17 Joe Johnson/49 3.00 8.00
18 Kenny Anderson/49 3.00 8.00
19 Allen Iverson/49 10.00 25.00
20 Larry Nance Jr./49 3.00 8.00
21 CJ McCollum/49 4.00 10.00
22 Robert Parish/49 5.00 12.00
23 DeMar DeRozan/49 5.00 12.00
24 Steven Adams/49 3.00 8.00
25 Isiah Thomas/35 6.00 15.00
26 Walter Davis/49 2.50 6.00
27 John Wall/49 5.00 12.00
28 Kevin Love/49 4.00 10.00
29 Anthony Davis/49 8.00 20.00
30 Marc Gasol/49 4.00 10.00
31 Courtney Lee/49 2.50 6.00
32 Rudy Gay/49 3.00 8.00
33 Derrick Rose/49 6.00 15.00
34 Thaddeus Young/49 2.50 6.00
35 Jamaal Wilkes/35 4.00 10.00
36 Xavier McDaniel/49 2.50 6.00
37 Julius Erving/49 10.00 25.00
38 Kris Dunn/49 2.50 6.00
39 Bobby Portis/49 2.50 6.00
40 Nerlens Noel/49 2.50 6.00

2017-18 Immaculate Collection Swatches Red

*RED: .5X TO 1.2X BASIC p/r 35-49
STATED PRINT RUN 25 SER.#'d SETS
4 Scottie Pippen 15.00 40.00
15 Giannis Antetokounmpo 30.00 80.00

2017-18 Immaculate Collection The Standard Relics

PRINT RUNS B/WN 10-25 COPIES PER
NO PRICING ON QTY 10 OR LESS
ST5 Pete Maravich/25 40.00 100.00
ST11 Larry Bird/49 15.00 40.00
ST12 Karl Malone/25 8.00 20.00
ST13 Kobe Bryant/49 75.00 200.00
ST14 Tim Duncan/49 10.00 25.00
ST15 Allen Iverson/49 10.00 25.00
ST16 Kareem Abdul-Jabbar/25 12.00 30.00
ST17 Patrick Ewing/49 6.00 15.00
ST18 Andrew Wiggins/49 5.00 12.00
ST19 Karl-Anthony Towns/49 6.00 15.00
ST20 Dirk Nowitzki/49 10.00 25.00
ST21 Zach LaVine/49 6.00 15.00
ST22 Rudy Gobert/49 5.00 12.00
ST23 Kevin Garnett/49 10.00 25.00
ST24 Kevin Love/49 4.00 10.00
ST25 Rondae Hollis-Jefferson/49 2.50 6.00
ST26 Nicolas Batum/49 2.50 6.00
ST27 Scottie Pippen/49 10.00 25.00
ST28 Shawn Marion/49 3.00 8.00
ST29 Grant Hill/49 6.00 15.00
ST30 Trevor Ariza/49 2.50 6.00
ST31 Hakeem Olajuwon/49 8.00 20.00
ST32 Danny Granger/49 2.50 6.00
ST33 DeAndre Jordan/49 3.00 8.00
ST34 Blake Griffin/49 4.00 10.00
ST35 Shaquille O'Neal/49 12.00 30.00
ST36 Marc Gasol/49 4.00 10.00
ST37 Ricky Rubio/49 3.00 8.00
ST38 Kris Dunn/49 2.50 6.00
ST39 Steven Adams/49 3.00 8.00
ST40 Nikola Vucevic/49 3.00 8.00
ST41 Shaquille O'Neal/49 12.00 30.00
ST42 CJ McCollum/49 4.00 10.00
ST43 Damian Lillard/49 10.00 25.00
ST44 Willie Cauley-Stein/49 2.50 6.00
ST45 David Robinson/49 8.00 20.00
ST46 Pau Gasol/49 6.00 15.00
ST47 Paul Silas/49 4.00 10.00
ST49 Jonas Valanciunas/49 3.00 8.00
ST50 Rodney Hood/49 2.50 6.00
ST51 John Wall/49 5.00 12.00
ST52 Bradley Beal/49 5.00 12.00
ST53 Marcin Gortat/49 2.50 6.00
ST54 Yao Ming/49 8.00 20.00
ST55 Tracy McGrady/49 6.00 15.00
ST56 Michael Finley/49 4.00 10.00
ST57 Steve Francis/49 3.00 8.00
ST58 Rafer Alston/49 2.50 6.00
ST59 Chris Webber/49 6.00 15.00
ST60 LaMarcus Aldridge/49 4.00 10.00
ST61 Sindarius Thornwell/49 2.50 6.00
ST62 Derrick White/49 10.00 25.00
ST63 Josh Hart/49 6.00 15.00
ST64 D.J. Wilson/49 2.50 6.00
ST65 John Collins/49 6.00 15.00
ST66 Terrance Ferguson/49 2.50 6.00
ST67 Semi Ojeleye/49 3.00 8.00
ST68 Josh Jackson/49 3.00 8.00
ST69 Tyler Lydon/49 2.50 6.00
ST70 De'Aaron Fox/49 20.00 50.00
ST71 Jawun Evans/49 2.50 6.00
ST72 OG Anunoby/49 12.00 30.00
ST73 Ivan Rabb/49 2.50 6.00
ST74 Justin Patton/49 2.50 6.00
ST75 Tyler Dorsey/49 2.50 6.00
ST76 Jonathan Isaac/49 6.00 15.00
ST77 Malik Monk/49 10.00 25.00
ST78 Davon Reed/49 2.50 6.00
ST79 Luke Kennard/49 5.00 12.00
ST80 Harry Giles/49 2.50 6.00
ST81 Lonzo Ball/49 10.00 25.00
ST82 Tony Bradley/49 2.50 6.00
ST83 Bam Adebayo/49 15.00 40.00
ST84 Frank Jackson/49 2.50 6.00
ST85 Jarrett Allen/49 6.00 15.00
ST86 Wes Iwundu/49 2.50 6.00
ST87 Dwayne Bacon/49 2.50 6.00
ST88 Zach Collins/49 4.00 10.00
ST89 Jordan Bell/49 2.50 6.00
ST90 Frank Mason III/49 2.50 6.00
ST91 Kyle Kuzma/49 10.00 25.00
ST92 Donovan Mitchell/49 25.00 60.00
ST93 Sterling Brown/49 2.50 6.00
ST94 Frank Ntilikina/49 3.00 8.00
ST96 Markelle Fultz/49 6.00 15.00
ST97 Dennis Smith Jr./49 3.00 8.00
ST98 Caleb Swanigan/49 2.50 6.00
ST99 TJ Leaf/49 2.50 6.00
ST100 Bogdan Bogdanovic/49 6.00 15.00

2017-18 Immaculate Collection Triple Autographs

PRINT RUNS B/WN 10-25 COPIES PER
NO PRICING ON QTY 10 OR LESS
EXCHANGE DEADLINE 4/17/2020
2 Andre Drummond
Reggie Jackson
Avery Bradley/25 EXCH 20.00 50.00
3 CJ McCollum
Damian Lillard
Evan Turner/25 60.00 150.00
4 Jayson Tatum
Lonzo Ball
Markelle Fultz/25 300.00 600.00
5 Tom Heinsohn
Bill Russell
Frank Ramsey/25 1,500.00 3,000.00
6 Steve Kerr
Dennis Rodman
Toni Kukoc/25 200.00 500.00
7 D'Angelo Russell
DeMarre Carroll
Rondae Hollis-Jefferson/25 30.00 80.00
9 Isaiah Thomas
Kevin Love
Tristan Thompson/25 25.00 60.00
10 Jamaal Wilkes
Kareem Abdul-Jabbar
Gail Goodrich/25 60.00 150.00
13 Rudy Gay
LaMarcus Aldridge
Tony Parker/25 50.00 120.00
14 Jonathan Isaac
De'Aaron Fox
Josh Jackson/25 125.00 300.00
15 Harry Giles
Jayson Tatum
Luke Kennard/25 200.00 500.00

2018-19 Immaculate Collection

STATED PRINT RUN 99 SER.#'d SETS
EXCHANGE DEADLINE 4/4/2021
1 Bradley Beal 2.00 5.00
2 John Wall 2.00 5.00
3 Thomas Bryant 1.25 3.00
4 Donovan Mitchell 5.00 12.00
5 Rudy Gobert 2.00 5.00
6 Ricky Rubio 1.25 3.00
7 Kyle Lowry 1.50 4.00
8 Kawhi Leonard 4.00 10.00
9 Marc Gasol 1.50 4.00
10 Pascal Siakam 2.50 6.00
11 DeMar DeRozan 2.00 5.00
12 Rudy Gay 1.50 4.00
13 LaMarcus Aldridge 1.50 4.00
14 Dejounte Murray 2.00 5.00
15 De'Aaron Fox 3.00 8.00
16 Buddy Hield 1.50 4.00
17 Harrison Barnes 1.25 3.00
18 Damian Lillard 4.00 10.00
19 CJ McCollum 1.50 4.00
20 Jusuf Nurkic 1.25 3.00
21 Devin Booker 4.00 10.00
22 T.J. Warren 1.25 3.00
23 Jamal Crawford 1.50 4.00
24 Ben Simmons 1.50 4.00
25 Joel Embiid 4.00 10.00
26 Jimmy Butler 2.50 6.00
27 Tobias Harris 1.25 3.00
28 Nikola Vucevic 1.25 3.00
29 Gary Harris 1.25 3.00
30 Aaron Gordon 1.50 4.00
31 Jonathan Isaac 1.50 4.00
32 Russell Westbrook 2.50 6.00
33 Paul George 2.50 6.00
34 Steven Adams 1.25 3.00
35 Dennis Schroder 1.25 3.00
36 Dennis Smith Jr. 1.00 2.50
37 Frank Ntilikina 1.00 2.50
38 DeAndre Jordan 1.25 3.00
39 Julius Randle 1.50 4.00
40 Anthony Davis 4.00 10.00
41 Elfrid Payton 1.25 3.00
42 Andrew Wiggins 2.00 5.00
43 Karl-Anthony Towns 2.50 6.00
44 Derrick Rose 3.00 8.00
45 Giannis Antetokounmpo 12.00 30.00
46 Khris Middleton 1.50 4.00
47 Eric Bledsoe 1.25 3.00
48 Malcolm Brogdon 1.50 4.00
49 Dwyane Wade 3.00 8.00
50 Hassan Whiteside 1.25 3.00
51 Goran Dragic 1.25 3.00
52 Mike Conley 1.25 3.00
53 Jonas Valanciunas 1.50 4.00
54 Avery Bradley 1.00 2.50
55 LeBron James 75.00 200.00
56 Lonzo Ball 1.50 4.00
57 Kyle Kuzma 1.50 4.00
58 Brandon Ingram 1.50 4.00
59 Lou Williams 1.25 3.00
60 Danilo Gallinari 1.25 3.00
61 Patrick Beverley 1.00 2.50
62 Myles Turner 1.50 4.00
63 Victor Oladipo 1.25 3.00
64 Thaddeus Young 1.00 2.50
65 James Harden 3.00 8.00
66 Chris Paul 3.00 8.00
67 Clint Capela 1.25 3.00
68 Stephen Curry 12.00 30.00
69 Klay Thompson 4.00 10.00
70 Kevin Durant 6.00 15.00
71 Draymond Green 2.00 5.00
72 DeMarcus Cousins 1.25 3.00
73 Blake Griffin 1.50 4.00
74 Andre Drummond 1.25 3.00
75 Luke Kennard 1.25 3.00
76 Reggie Jackson 1.25 3.00
77 Nikola Jokic 8.00 20.00
78 Jamal Murray 3.00 8.00
79 Dirk Nowitzki 4.00 10.00
80 Kristaps Porzingis 2.00 5.00
81 Tim Hardaway Jr. 1.00 2.50
82 Kevin Love 1.25 3.00
83 Jordan Clarkson 1.50 4.00
84 Zach LaVine 2.50 6.00

85 Lauri Markkanen 2.50 6.00
86 Otto Porter Jr. 1.25 3.00
87 Kemba Walker 1.25 3.00
88 Miles Bridges RC 10.00 25.00
89 Malik Monk 1.50 4.00
90 D'Angelo Russell 1.50 4.00
91 Jarrett Allen 1.50 4.00
92 Caris LeVert 1.50 4.00
93 Kyrie Irving 4.00 10.00
94 Jayson Tatum 6.00 15.00
95 Jaylen Brown 2.50 6.00
96 Gordon Hayward 1.50 4.00
97 Al Horford 1.50 4.00
98 John Collins 1.50 4.00
99 Vince Carter 3.00 8.00
100 Andre Iguodala 1.25 3.00
101 Aaron Holiday JSY AU RC 10.00 25.00
102 Allonzo Trier JSY AU RC 6.00 15.00
103 Anfernee Simons JSY AU RC 100.00 250.00
104 Chandler Hutchison JSY AU RC 8.00 20.00
105 Collin Sexton JSY AU RC 30.00 80.00
106 Deandre Ayton JSY AU RC 20.00 50.00
107 Donte DiVincenzo JSY AU RC 15.00 40.00
108 Dzanan Musa JSY AU RC 6.00 15.00
109 Elie Okobo JSY AU RC 6.00 15.00
110 Grayson Allen JSY AU RC 12.00 30.00
111 Hamidou Diallo JSY AU RC 10.00 25.00
112 Jacob Evans III JSY AU RC 6.00 15.00
113 Jaren Jackson Jr. JSY AU RC 500.00 1,000.00
114 Jarred Vanderbilt JSY AU RC 12.00 30.00
115 Jerome Robinson JSY AU RC 6.00 15.00
116 Jevon Carter JSY AU RC 10.00 25.00
117 Josh Okogie JSY AU RC 10.00 25.00
118 Keita Bates-Diop JSY AU RC 8.00 20.00
119 Kevin Huerter JSY AU RC 20.00 50.00
120 Kevin Knox II JSY AU RC 8.00 20.00
121 Khyri Thomas JSY AU RC 6.00 15.00
122 Landry Shamet JSY AU RC 10.00 25.00
123 Lonnie Walker IV JSY AU RC 12.00 30.00
124 Luka Doncic JSY
AU RC EXCH 4,000.00 8,000.00
125 Marvin Bagley III JSY AU RC 10.00 25.00
126 Melvin Frazier Jr. JSY AU RC 6.00 15.00
128 Mikal Bridges JSY AU RC 150.00 400.00
129 Mo Bamba JSY AU RC 10.00 25.00
130 Moritz Wagner JSY AU RC 12.00 30.00
131 Omari Spellman JSY AU RC 6.00 15.00
132 Robert Williams III JSY AU RC 12.00 30.00
134 Shai Gilgeous-Alexander
JSY AU RC 2,500.00 5,000.00
135 Svi Mykhailiuk JSY AU RC 8.00 20.00
136 Trae Young JSY AU RC 1,500.00 3,000.00
137 Troy Brown Jr. JSY AU RC 8.00 20.00
138 Wendell Carter Jr. JSY AU RC 15.00 40.00
139 Yuta Watanabe JSY AU RC 25.00 60.00
140 Zhaire Smith JSY AU RC 6.00 15.00

2018-19 Immaculate Collection Red

*RED: .6X TO 1.5X BASIC
*RED: .6X TO 1.5X JSY AU
1-100 PRINT RUN 35 SER.#'d SETS
JSY AU PRINT RUN 25 SER.#'d SETS
EXCHANGE DEADLINE 4/4/2021

2018-19 Immaculate Collection All-Time Greats Signatures

PRINT RUNS B/WN 25-99 COPIES PER
EXCHANGE DEADLINE 4/4/2021
1 Larry Bird/25 60.00 150.00
2 Bob Lanier/99 6.00 15.00
3 Kareem Abdul-Jabbar/25 40.00 100.00
4 George Gervin/99 8.00 20.00
5 Alonzo Mourning/49 15.00 40.00
6 Grant Hill/49 15.00 40.00
7 Charles Barkley/75 75.00 200.00
8 Jason Kidd/49 12.00 30.00
9 Shaquille O'Neal/25 75.00 200.00
10 Dominique Wilkins/49 10.00 25.00
11 Julius Erving/25 30.00 80.00
12 Artis Gilmore/99 6.00 15.00
13 Oscar Robertson/25 30.00 80.00
14 Elvin Hayes/99 6.00 15.00
15 Hakeem Olajuwon/49 12.00 30.00
16 Clyde Drexler/49 15.00 40.00
17 Kobe Bryant/99 1,500.00 3,000.00
18 Ray Allen/49 20.00 50.00
19 Reggie Miller/25 60.00 150.00
20 Sam Jones/99 12.00 30.00
21 Kevin Garnett/49 125.00 300.00
22 Walt Frazier/99 8.00 20.00
23 Jerry West/25 25.00 60.00
24 Robert Parish/99 8.00 20.00
25 David Robinson/49 20.00 50.00

2018-19 Immaculate Collection Dual Autographs

PRINT RUNS B/WN 10-49 COPIES PER
NO PRICING ON QTY 15 OR LESS
EXCHANGE DEADLINE 4/4/2021
1 Kyle Kuzma
Lonzo Ball/49 25.00 60.00
3 Deandre Ayton
Mikal Bridges/49 25.00 60.00
4 Muggsy Bogues
Dell Curry/49 12.00 30.00
5 Wendell Carter Jr.
Marvin Bagley III/49 12.00 30.00
6 Hamidou Diallo
Kevin Knox II/49 8.00 20.00
7 Kevin Huerter
Trae Young/49 200.00 500.00
8 Jaren Jackson Jr.
Luka Doncic/49 EXCH 1,500.00 3,000.00
9 Collin Sexton
Kevin Love/49 15.00 40.00
10 Antoine Walker
Paul Pierce/49 30.00 80.00
13 De'Aaron Fox
Marvin Bagley III/49 60.00 150.00
14 Dennis Rodman
Toni Kukoc/49 60.00 150.00
15 Grayson Allen
Wendell Carter Jr./49 12.00 30.00
16 Donte DiVincenzo
Mikal Bridges/49 25.00 60.00
18 Jaren Jackson Jr.
Trae Young/49 800.00 1,500.00
19 Dirk Nowitzki
Luka Doncic/25 3,000.00 6,000.00
20 Ralph Sampson
Hakeem Olajuwon/49 25.00 60.00
21 Giannis Antetokounmpo
Donte DiVincenzo/49 EXCH 300.00 600.00
23 LaMarcus Aldridge
Lonnie Walker IV/49 25.00 60.00
24 Latrell Sprewell
Sam Cassell/49 10.00 25.00
25 Grayson Allen
Marvin Bagley III/49 10.00 25.00
26 Marvin Bagley III
Deandre Ayton/49 15.00 40.00
28 Deandre Ayton
Luka Doncic/49 EXCH 1,500.00 3,000.00
29 Nikola Jokic
Michael Porter Jr./49 400.00 800.00
31 Allonzo Trier
Kevin Knox II/49 6.00 15.00
33 Grayson Allen
Donovan Mitchell/49 EXCH 75.00 200.00
34 Allan Houston
Charlie Ward/49 12.00 30.00
35 Shai Gilgeous-Alexander
Kevin Knox II/49 500.00 1,000.00
36 Luka Doncic
Marvin Bagley III/49 EXCH 1,000.00 2,000.00
37 Lauri Markkanen
Wendell Carter Jr./49 12.00 30.00
38 Luka Doncic
Trae Young/49 EXCH 3,000.00 6,000.00
39 Landry Shamet
Shai Gilgeous-Alexander/49 500.00 1,000.00
41 Mo Bamba
Nikola Vucevic/49 8.00 20.00
42 Vlade Divac
Jason Williams/49 60.00 150.00
43 Deandre Ayton
Allonzo Trier/49 25.00 60.00
45 Hamidou Diallo
Shai Gilgeous-Alexander/49 500.00 1,000.00

2018-19 Immaculate Collection Dual Patches Jersey Number

PRINT RUNS B/WN 1-25 COPIES PER
NO PRICING ON QTY 15 OR LESS
2 John Collins
Josh Jackson/20 8.00 20.00
4 Khris Middleton
Andrew Wiggins/22 10.00 25.00
6 Blake Griffin
Draymond Green/23 10.00 25.00
12 Gordon Hayward
Justise Winslow/20 8.00 20.00
14 Caris LeVert
Rudy Gay/22 8.00 20.00
16 Ben Simmons
Derrick Rose/25 20.00 50.00
22 Dwight Howard
Joel Embiid/21 20.00 50.00
24 Anthony Davis
LeBron James/23 150.00 400.00

2018-19 Immaculate Collection Heralded Signatures

PRINT RUNS B/WN 25-99 COPIES PER
EXCHANGE DEADLINE 4/4/2021
*BLUE/49: .5X TO 1.2X p/r 99
*BLUE/49: .4X TO 1X p/r 42-49
1 Latrell Sprewell/99 6.00 15.00
2 John Stockton/25 40.00 100.00
3 Mark Aguirre/99 4.00 10.00
4 Clyde Drexler/49 20.00 50.00
5 Marques Johnson/99 4.00 10.00
6 Derek Fisher/99 4.00 10.00
7 Darius Miles/99 3.00 8.00
8 Stromile Swift/99 3.00 8.00
9 Rashard Lewis/99 4.00 10.00
10 Avery Johnson/99 4.00 10.00
11 World B. Free/99 4.00 10.00
12 Alonzo Mourning/49 30.00 80.00
13 John Starks/99 4.00 10.00
14 Jason Kidd/49 20.00 50.00
15 Cedric Maxwell/99 4.00 10.00
16 Tyronn Lue/99 4.00 10.00
17 Isaiah Rider/99 4.00 10.00
18 Devean George/99 4.00 10.00
19 Don Chaney/99 4.00 10.00
20 Doc Rivers/99 5.00 12.00
21 Michael Cooper/99 5.00 12.00
22 Magic Johnson/49 60.00 150.00
23 Kurt Rambis/99 4.00 10.00
24 Ray Allen/49 40.00 100.00
25 Glen Rice/99 5.00 12.00
26 Nate McMillan/99 4.00 10.00
27 Lionel Hollins/99 4.00 10.00
28 Kenyon Martin/99 4.00 10.00
29 M.L. Carr/99 5.00 12.00
30 Jalen Rose/42 5.00 12.00
31 Shane Battier/99 4.00 10.00
33 Calvin Murphy/99 4.00 10.00
34 Grant Hill/49 15.00 40.00
35 Dino Radja/99 3.00 8.00
36 Quinn Buckner/99 3.00 8.00
37 Sam Perkins/99 4.00 10.00
38 Robert Parish/99 10.00 25.00
39 Quentin Richardson/99 4.00 10.00
40 Rick Fox/99 4.00 10.00

2018-19 Immaculate Collection Heralded Signatures Red

*RED/25: .6X TO 1.5X p/r 99
*RED/25: .5X TO 1.2X p/r 42-49
*RED/25: .4X TO 1X p/r 25
STATED PRINT RUN 25 SER.#'d SETS
EXCHANGE DEADLINE 4/4/2021
32 Tracy McGrady 60.00 150.00

2018-19 Immaculate Collection Immaculate Inductions Autographs

PRINT RUNS B/WN 25-99 COPIES PER
EXCHANGE DEADLINE 4/4/2021
1 Jerry Lucas/99 12.00 30.00
2 Shaquille O'Neal/25 150.00 400.00
3 Walt Frazier/99 15.00 40.00
4 Julius Erving/25 75.00 200.00
5 Elvin Hayes/99 12.00 30.00
6 Oscar Robertson/25 75.00 200.00
7 Gail Goodrich/99 12.00 30.00
8 Hakeem Olajuwon/49 75.00 200.00
9 George McGinnis/99 10.00 25.00
10 Dominique Wilkins/49 40.00 100.00
11 Bob Lanier/99 12.00 30.00
12 Reggie Miller/25 75.00 200.00
13 George Gervin/99 15.00 40.00
14 John Stockton/25 40.00 100.00
15 Robert Parish/99 12.00 30.00
16 Jerry West/49 40.00 100.00
17 Bill Walton/99 40.00 100.00
18 David Robinson/49 75.00 200.00
19 Tom Satch Sanders/99 5.00 12.00
20 Rick Barry/99 12.00 30.00
21 Artis Gilmore/99 12.00 30.00
22 Larry Bird/25 150.00 400.00
23 Nate Archibald/99 6.00 15.00
24 Kareem Abdul-Jabbar/25 150.00 400.00
25 Joe Dumars/99 12.00 30.00
26 Alonzo Mourning/49 60.00 150.00
27 Louie Dampier/99 5.00 12.00
28 Clyde Drexler/49 40.00 100.00
29 Charles Barkley/75 125.00 300.00
30 Sam Jones/99 60.00 150.00

2018-19 Immaculate Collection Immaculate Ink

PRINT RUNS B/WN 25-99 COPIES PER
1 Kenny Sky Walker/99 3.00 8.00
2 Karl Malone/25 15.00 40.00
3 Larry Bird/25 40.00 100.00
4 Julius Erving/25 20.00 50.00
5 Dan Issel/99 6.00 15.00
6 Arvydas Sabonis/99 5.00 12.00
7 Antoine Walker/99 4.00 10.00
8 Hakeem Olajuwon/49 12.00 30.00
9 David Robinson/49 12.00 30.00
10 Dominique Wilkins/99 8.00 20.00
11 Rick Barry/99 6.00 15.00
12 Sam Jones/99 12.00 30.00
13 Bob Lanier/99 6.00 15.00
14 Artis Gilmore/99 6.00 15.00
16 George Gervin/99 8.00 20.00
17 Nate Archibald/99 6.00 15.00
18 Lenny Wilkens/99 6.00 15.00
19 Adrian Dantley/99 4.00 10.00
20 Alex English/99 5.00 12.00

2018-19 Immaculate Collection Immaculate Ink Blue

*BLUE/49: .5X TO 1.2X p/r 99
*BLUE/49: .4X TO 1X p/r 49
STATED PRINT RUN 49 SER.#'d SETS
EXCHANGE DEADLINE 4/4/2021
15 Walt Frazier 10.00 25.00

2018-19 Immaculate Collection Immaculate Ink Red

*RED/25: .6X TO 1.5X p/r 99
*RED/25: .5X TO 1.2X p/r 49
*RED/25: .4X TO 1X p/r 25
STATED PRINT RUN 25 SER.#'d SETS
EXCHANGE DEADLINE 4/4/2021
15 Walt Frazier 12.00 30.00

2018-19 Immaculate Collection Immaculate Introductions Autographs

PRINT RUNS B/WN 25-99 COPIES PER
EXCHANGE DEADLINE 4/4/2021
1 Deandre Ayton/99 30.00 80.00
2 Marvin Bagley III/99 5.00 12.00
3 Luka Doncic/99 EXCH 2,000.00 4,000.00
4 Jaren Jackson Jr./25 150.00 400.00
5 Trae Young/99 500.00 1,000.00
6 Mo Bamba/99 6.00 15.00
7 Wendell Carter Jr./99 6.00 15.00
8 Collin Sexton/25 25.00 60.00
9 Kevin Knox II/25 6.00 15.00
10 Mikal Bridges/99 15.00 40.00
11 Shai Gilgeous-Alexander/25 1,500.00 3,000.00
12 Jerome Robinson/99 3.00 8.00
14 Troy Brown Jr./99 4.00 10.00
15 Zhaire Smith/99 3.00 8.00
16 Donte DiVincenzo/99 8.00 20.00
17 Lonnie Walker IV/25 40.00 100.00
18 Kevin Huerter/25 10.00 25.00
19 Mitchell Robinson/99 8.00 20.00
20 Grayson Allen/25 6.00 15.00
21 Chandler Hutchison/99 4.00 10.00
22 Aaron Holiday/99 5.00 12.00
23 Anfernee Simons/99 20.00 50.00
24 Moritz Wagner/99 5.00 12.00
25 Landry Shamet/99 6.00 15.00
26 Robert Williams III/99 5.00 12.00
27 Jacob Evans III/99 3.00 8.00
28 Dzanan Musa/99 3.00 8.00
29 Omari Spellman/99 3.00 8.00
30 Jalen Brunson/99 25.00 60.00

2018-19 Immaculate Collection Immaculate Milestones Autographs

PRINT RUNS B/WN 10-25 COPIES PER
NO PRICING ON QTY 15 OR LESS
EXCHANGE DEADLINE 4/4/2021
4 Vince Carter/25 400.00 800.00
5 Vince Carter/25 400.00 800.00
6 Stephen Curry/25 1,500.00 3,000.00
7 Stephen Curry/25 1,500.00 3,000.00
8 Tony Parker/25 125.00 300.00
9 Luka Doncic/25 EXCH 10,000.00 15,000.00
10 Luka Doncic/25 EXCH 10,000.00 15,000.00

2018-19 Immaculate Collection Immaculate Moments Autographs

PRINT RUNS B/WN 25-99 COPIES PER
EXCHANGE DEADLINE 4/4/2021
1 Trae Young/49 800.00 1,500.00
2 D'Angelo Russell/99 40.00 100.00
3 Kevin Knox II/25 6.00 15.00
5 Kawhi Leonard/49 600.00 1,200.00
6 Mike Conley/99 4.00 10.00
8 Kelly Olynyk/99 3.00 8.00
9 Luka Doncic/99 EXCH 2,500.00 5,000.00
10 Pascal Siakam/99 60.00 150.00
11 Trae Young/49 800.00 1,500.00
12 Lauri Markkanen/49 75.00 200.00
13 Giannis Antetokounmpo/49 800.00 1,500.00
14 Donovan Mitchell/49 125.00 300.00
15 Kawhi Leonard/49 600.00 1,200.00
16 Dwyane Wade/25 800.00 1,200.00
19 Luka Doncic/99 EXCH 2,500.00 5,000.00
20 Rudy Gay/99 12.00 30.00
21 Trae Young/49 800.00 1,500.00
22 Anthony Davis/25 150.00 400.00
23 Giannis Antetokounmpo/49 800.00 1,500.00
24 Donovan Mitchell/49 125.00 300.00
26 Stephen Curry/25 1,500.00 3,000.00
27 Luka Doncic/99 EXCH 2,500.00 5,000.00
28 Danny Green/99 12.00 30.00
29 Luka Doncic/99 EXCH 2,500.00 5,000.00

2018-19 Immaculate Collection Jumbo Patches Jersey Number

PRINT RUNS B/WN 3-50 COPIES PER
NO PRICING ON QTY 15 OR LESS
6 Wendell Carter Jr./34 12.00 30.00
7 Enes Kanter/16 6.00 15.00
10 Kevin Huerter/17 10.00 25.00
21 Nemanja Bjelica/50 5.00 12.00
26 Moritz Wagner/50 12.00 30.00
32 Devonte' Graham/50 8.00 20.00
36 Jevon Carter/29 8.00 20.00
39 Kris Dunn/18 10.00 25.00
40 Chandler Hutchison/50 6.00 15.00
43 Roy Hibbert/50 6.00 15.00
46 Jarred Vanderbilt/50 10.00 25.00
52 Bruce Brown/50 10.00 25.00
67 Jimmy Butler/16 15.00 40.00
72 De'Anthony Melton/42 10.00 25.00
79 Malik Beasley/20 10.00 25.00
80 Robert Williams III/50 10.00 25.00
82 Svi Mykhailiuk/50 6.00 15.00
83 Devin Harris/50 5.00 12.00
84 Damyean Dotson/22 5.00 12.00
92 Keita Bates-Diop/44 6.00 15.00
94 Danny Granger/50 5.00 12.00
95 Dwight Powell/32 5.00 12.00

2018-19 Immaculate Collection Jumbo Patches Team Logo

PRINT RUNS B/WN 1-25 COPIES PER
NO PRICING ON QTY 15 OR LESS
53 Tyus Jones/17 15.00 40.00
83 Devin Harris/25 8.00 20.00
90 Jacob Evans III/25 25.00 60.00

2018-19 Immaculate Collection Marks of Greatness Autographs

PRINT RUNS B/WN 25-99 COPIES PER
EXCHANGE DEADLINE 4/4/2021
1 Charles Barkley/75 75.00 200.00
2 Jason Kidd/49 12.00 30.00
3 Karl Malone/25 30.00 80.00
4 Sam Jones/99 12.00 30.00
5 Kevin Garnett/49 150.00 400.00
6 Walt Frazier/99 8.00 20.00
7 Jerry West/25 25.00 60.00
8 Horace Grant/99 8.00 20.00
9 Hakeem Olajuwon/49 12.00 30.00
10 Grant Hill/49 15.00 40.00
11 Kobe Bryant/99 3,000.00 6,000.00
12 Ray Allen/49 20.00 50.00
13 Larry Bird/25 60.00 150.00
14 Bob Lanier/99 6.00 15.00
15 Kareem Abdul-Jabbar/25 40.00 100.00
16 Latrell Sprewell/99 8.00 20.00
17 Alonzo Mourning/49 15.00 40.00
18 Allan Houston/99 5.00 12.00
19 David Robinson/49 20.00 50.00
20 Clyde Drexler/49 15.00 40.00
21 Reggie Miller/25 60.00 150.00
22 Dominique Wilkins/49 10.00 25.00
23 Julius Erving/25 30.00 80.00
24 Artis Gilmore/99 6.00 15.00
25 Oscar Robertson/25 30.00 80.00

2018-19 Immaculate Collection Massive Memorabilia

PRINT RUNS B/WN 5-25 COPIES PER
NO PRICING ON QTY 15 OR LESS
1 Lonnie Walker IV/25 6.00 15.00
2 Trae Young/25 40.00 100.00
3 Grayson Allen/25 6.00 15.00
4 Collin Sexton/25 10.00 25.00
5 Anfernee Simons/25 15.00 40.00
6 Shai Gilgeous-Alexander/25 20.00 50.00
7 Michael Porter Jr./25 12.00 30.00
8 Deandre Ayton/25 10.00 25.00
9 Zhaire Smith/25 3.00 8.00
11 Kevin Huerter/25 6.00 15.00
12 Mo Bamba/25 5.00 12.00
13 Chandler Hutchison/25 4.00 10.00
14 Kevin Knox II/25 4.00 10.00
15 Moritz Wagner/25 6.00 15.00
16 Jerome Robinson/25 3.00 8.00
17 Troy Brown Jr./25 4.00 10.00
18 Marvin Bagley III/25 5.00 12.00
20 Jaren Jackson Jr./25 25.00 60.00
21 Josh Okogie/25 5.00 12.00
22 Wendell Carter Jr./25 8.00 20.00
23 Aaron Holiday/25 5.00 12.00
24 Mikal Bridges/25 15.00 40.00
25 Robert Williams III/25 6.00 15.00

2018-19 Immaculate Collection Materials

PRINT RUNS B/WN 49-99 COPIES PER
1 Joe Harris/99 2.50 6.00
2 Nemanja Bjelica/99 2.00 5.00
3 Nerlens Noel/99 2.00 5.00
4 Paul Pierce/99 5.00 12.00
5 Ben Simmons/99 3.00 8.00
6 Markieff Morris/99 2.00 5.00
7 Brandon Knight/99 2.00 5.00
8 Lauri Markkanen/99 5.00 12.00
9 Myles Turner/99 3.00 8.00
10 Josh Jackson/49 2.50 6.00
11 Taj Gibson/99 2.00 5.00
12 DeMar DeRozan/99 4.00 10.00
13 Josh Richardson/99 2.50 6.00
14 Harrison Barnes/99 2.50 6.00
15 Roy Hibbert/99 2.50 6.00
16 Jrue Holiday/49 2.50 6.00
17 Terrance Ferguson/49 2.50 6.00
18 Bogdan Bogdanovic/49 4.00 10.00
19 Harry Giles/49 2.50 6.00
20 Jonathan Isaac/49 4.00 10.00
21 Giannis Antetokounmpo/49 20.00 50.00
22 Jamal Murray/99 6.00 15.00
23 Eric Gordon/99 2.50 6.00
24 Gary Payton/49 5.00 12.00
25 Klay Thompson/99 10.00 25.00
26 OG Anunoby/49 4.00 10.00
27 Stephen Curry/49 30.00 80.00
28 Al-Farouq Aminu/99 2.00 5.00
29 Lonzo Ball/49 4.00 10.00
30 Rashard Lewis/99 2.50 6.00
31 John Wall/99 4.00 10.00
32 Andre Drummond/99 2.50 6.00
33 Dwyane Wade/99 6.00 15.00
34 Reggie Miller/49 8.00 20.00
35 Stephon Marbury/99 4.00 10.00
36 Khris Middleton/99 3.00 8.00
37 J.J. Barea/99 3.00 8.00
38 Tim Hardaway Jr./49 2.50 6.00
39 Seth Curry/49 3.00 8.00
40 M.L. Carr/49 4.00 10.00

2018-19 Immaculate Collection Materials Red

*RED/25: .6X TO 1.5X p/r 99
*RED/25: .5X TO 1.2X p/r 49
STATED PRINT RUN 25 SER.#'d SETS
21 Giannis Antetokounmpo 40.00 100.00

2018-19 Immaculate Collection Modern Marks Autographs

PRINT RUNS B/WN 25-99 COPIES PER
EXCHANGE DEADLINE 4/4/2021
*BLUE/49: .5X TO 1.2X p/r 99
*BLUE/49: .4X TO 1X p/r 49
1 Anthony Davis/25 20.00 50.00
2 Willie Cauley-Stein/99 3.00 8.00
3 Kevin Love/99 4.00 10.00
4 Cody Zeller/99 3.00 8.00
5 LaMarcus Aldridge/99 5.00 12.00
6 Fred VanVleet/99 15.00 40.00
8 JJ Redick/99 5.00 12.00
9 Dwyane Wade/25 20.00 50.00
10 Malcolm Brogdon/99 5.00 12.00
11 Karl-Anthony Towns/25 15.00 40.00
12 JR Smith/99 5.00 12.00
13 Kristaps Porzingis/99 8.00 20.00
14 Al-Farouq Aminu/99 3.00 8.00
15 Jeremy Lin/99 10.00 25.00
16 J.J. Barea/99 5.00 12.00
17 Tyson Chandler/99 4.00 10.00
18 Nikola Vucevic/99 4.00 10.00
20 Rudy Gay/99 5.00 12.00
21 Jayson Tatum/49 75.00 200.00
22 Danny Green/99 4.00 10.00
23 Isaiah Thomas/99 4.00 10.00
24 Montrezl Harrell/99 5.00 12.00
25 Lauri Markkanen/99 8.00 20.00
26 Thaddeus Young/99 3.00 8.00
27 Kyle Kuzma/99 8.00 20.00
28 Reggie Jackson/99 4.00 10.00
29 Damian Lillard/25 25.00 60.00
30 Pascal Siakam/99 15.00 40.00
31 Donovan Mitchell/49 EXCH 20.00 50.00
32 Enes Kanter/99 4.00 10.00
33 Lonzo Ball/99 20.00 50.00
34 Nene/99 4.00 10.00
36 Nemanja Bjelica/99 3.00 8.00
37 Danilo Gallinari/99 4.00 10.00
38 Gary Harris/99 4.00 10.00
39 Kyrie Irving/25 20.00 50.00
40 Elfrid Payton/99 4.00 10.00

2018-19 Immaculate Collection Modern Marks Autographs Red

*RED/25: .6X TO 1.5X p/r 99
*RED/25: .5X TO 1.2X p/r 49
*RED/25: .4X TO 1X p/r 25
STATED PRINT RUN 25 SER.#'d SETS
EXCHANGE DEADLINE 4/4/2021
35 Nikola Jokic 150.00 400.00

2018-19 Immaculate Collection Patch Autographs

PRINT RUNS B/WN 25-60 COPIES PER
EXCHANGE DEADLINE 4/4/2021
2 Kyrie Irving/25 EXCH 30.00 80.00
3 Elfrid Payton/60 8.00 20.00
5 Isaiah Rider/60 8.00 20.00
7 Charles Barkley/25 125.00 300.00
8 John Wall/25 15.00 40.00
9 Kristaps Porzingis/35 40.00 100.00
10 De'Aaron Fox/35 25.00 60.00
11 Danny Manning/60 8.00 20.00
14 World B. Free/40 8.00 20.00
15 Kevin Love/35 8.00 20.00
16 CJ McCollum/35 10.00 25.00
17 Dikembe Mutombo/60 15.00 40.00
19 Buddy Hield/60 10.00 25.00
20 Isaiah Thomas/35 8.00 20.00
21 Jarrett Allen/60 10.00 25.00
22 Dwyane Wade/25 40.00 100.00
23 Chris Mullin/60 12.00 30.00
24 Tim Hardaway Jr./60 6.00 15.00
25 LaMarcus Aldridge/35 10.00 25.00
27 Donovan Mitchell/33 50.00 120.00
28 Mike Conley/35 8.00 20.00
31 Malcolm Brogdon/60 10.00 25.00
32 Kyle Kuzma/60 10.00 25.00
33 Don Chaney/60 8.00 20.00
34 Jayson Tatum/35 40.00 100.00
35 Khris Middleton/60 10.00 25.00
36 Karl-Anthony Towns/25 25.00 60.00
38 Otto Porter Jr./60 8.00 20.00
40 Giannis Antetokounmpo/35 200.00 500.00
41 Clyde Drexler/35 20.00 50.00
42 Tony Parker/35 15.00 40.00
43 Fred VanVleet/60 12.00 30.00
44 Lonzo Ball/35 15.00 40.00
45 Chris Paul/25 200.00 500.00
47 Anthony Davis/25 75.00 200.00
48 Josh Jackson/35 6.00 15.00
49 Paul Pierce/35 40.00 100.00
50 Stephen Curry/25 1,000.00 2,000.00
51 Dirk Nowitzki/25 75.00 200.00
52 D'Angelo Russell/60 EXCH 10.00 25.00
53 Rondae Hollis-Jefferson/60 6.00 15.00
54 Zach LaVine/60 20.00 50.00
55 Enes Kanter/60 8.00 20.00
57 Lauri Markkanen/35 15.00 40.00
60 Kevin Durant/25 500.00 1,000.00

2018-19 Immaculate Collection Patch Autographs Premium Edition

*PREM/20: .5X TO 1.2X p/r 33-60
PRINT RUNS B/WN 14-20 COPIES PER
NO PRICING ON QTY 17 OR LESS
EXCHANGE DEADLINE 4/4/2021
27 Donovan Mitchell/20 125.00 300.00
32 Kyle Kuzma/20 20.00 50.00
34 Jayson Tatum/20 60.00 150.00
37 Nikola Jokic/20 300.00 600.00

2018-19 Immaculate Collection Patch Autographs Red

*RED/25: .5X TO 1.2X p/r 33-60
PRINT RUNS B/WN 15-25 COPIES PER
NO PRICING ON QTY 15 OR LESS
EXCHANGE DEADLINE 4/4/2021
32 Kyle Kuzma/25 20.00 50.00
34 Jayson Tatum/25 60.00 150.00

2018-19 Immaculate Collection Premium Patch Autographs

PRINT RUNS B/WN 10-50 COPIES PER
NO PRICING ON QTY 15 OR LESS
EXCHANGE DEADLINE 4/4/2021
1 Kevin Huerter/20 60.00 150.00
2 Karl-Anthony Towns/25 40.00 100.00
3 Khyri Thomas/50 6.00 15.00
4 Ernie DiGregorio/25 20.00 50.00
5 Otto Porter Jr./25 10.00 25.00
9 Rondae Hollis-Jefferson/25 8.00 20.00
10 J.J. Barea/25 15.00 40.00
13 Landry Shamet/50 30.00 80.00
14 Khris Middleton/25 30.00 80.00
18 Giannis Antetokounmpo
25 EXCH 1,500.00 3,000.00
19 Jerome Robinson/50 6.00 15.00
20 CJ McCollum/25 40.00 100.00
21 Aaron Holiday/50 25.00 60.00
22 Deandre Ayton/50 150.00 400.00
23 Omari Spellman/50 6.00 15.00
24 Luka Doncic/25 20,000.00 40,000.00
25 Malcolm Brogdon/25 12.00 30.00
28 Derek Fisher/25 20.00 50.00
29 Yuta Watanabe/50 25.00 60.00
31 Anfernee Simons/50 100.00 250.00
33 Elie Okobo/50 6.00 15.00
34 Buddy Hield/25 20.00 50.00
35 Elfrid Payton/17 10.00 25.00
37 Fred VanVleet/22 40.00 100.00
41 Chandler Hutchison/50 8.00 20.00
42 Carlos Boozer/25 12.00 30.00
43 Jevon Carter/50 10.00 25.00
44 Zach LaVine/25 40.00 100.00
48 Isaiah Thomas/25 10.00 25.00
49 Jarrett Allen/25 12.00 30.00
50 Josh Jackson/25 8.00 20.00
51 Keita Bates-Diop/50 8.00 20.00
52 Lauri Markkanen/25 25.00 60.00
53 Melvin Frazier Jr./50 6.00 15.00
54 Kyle Kuzma/25 20.00 50.00
55 Allonzo Trier/25 15.00 40.00
57 Mikal Bridges/50 200.00 500.00
59 Donte DiVincenzo/50 25.00 60.00
60 Mike Conley/25 20.00 50.00
61 Moritz Wagner/50 12.00 30.00
62 Marvin Bagley III/50 10.00 25.00
65 Mo Bamba/50 25.00 60.00
67 Shai Gilgeous-Alexander/50 1,500.00 3,000.00
68 Jayson Tatum/25 200.00 500.00
69 Troy Brown Jr./50 25.00 60.00
70 Tony Parker/25 50.00 120.00
73 Hamidou Diallo/50 10.00 25.00
75 Enes Kanter/25 10.00 25.00
77 Tim Hardaway Jr./25 15.00 40.00
79 Zhaire Smith/50 6.00 15.00
80 Gordon Hayward/25 15.00 40.00
81 Dzanan Musa/49 6.00 15.00
82 Rashard Lewis/25 10.00 25.00
83 Jarred Vanderbilt/50 15.00 40.00
85 Wendell Carter Jr./50 30.00 80.00
88 Brandon Ingram/25 EXCH 40.00 100.00
89 Grayson Allen/50 12.00 30.00
90 Lonzo Ball/25 75.00 200.00
91 Jacob Evans III/50 6.00 15.00
92 Caris LeVert/25 12.00 30.00
93 Svi Mykhailiuk/50 6.00 15.00
97 Harry Giles/25 8.00 20.00
100 Trae Young/50 2,000.00 4,000.00

2018-19 Immaculate Collection Premium Patch Autographs Red

*RED/25: .5X TO 1.2X p/r 49-50
PRINT RUNS B/WN 5-25 COPIES PER
NO PRICING ON QTY 15 OR LESS
EXCHANGE DEADLINE 4/4/2021
19 Jerome Robinson/25 15.00 40.00
62 Marvin Bagley III/25 12.00 30.00
67 Shai Gilgeous-Alexander/25 2,000.00 4,000.00

2018-19 Immaculate Collection Remarkable Memorabilia

PRINT RUNS B/WN 49-99 COPIES PER
1 Enes Kanter/99 2.50 6.00
2 Vince Carter/49 8.00 20.00
3 Danny Granger/99 2.00 5.00
4 Tim Duncan/99 8.00 20.00
5 Derrick Favors/99 2.00 5.00
6 LeBron James/49 30.00 80.00
7 Paul George/49 6.00 15.00
8 Rondae Hollis-Jefferson/49 2.50 6.00
9 Steven Adams/99 2.50 6.00
10 Dirk Nowitzki/49 10.00 25.00
11 Rudy Gobert/99 4.00 10.00
12 Kevin Garnett/49 8.00 20.00
13 Markelle Fultz/49 3.00 8.00
14 Dwight Powell/99 2.00 5.00
15 Wesley Matthews/99 2.00 5.00
16 Jimmy Butler/49 6.00 15.00
17 Russell Westbrook/49 6.00 15.00
18 Charles Barkley/49 12.00 30.00
19 Aaron Gordon/99 3.00 8.00
20 Pau Gasol/49 6.00 15.00
21 Lou Williams/49 3.00 8.00
22 Andrew Wiggins/49 5.00 12.00
23 Paul Pierce/99 5.00 12.00
24 Hassan Whiteside/99 2.50 6.00
25 Julius Randle/49 4.00 10.00
26 Otto Porter Jr./99 2.50 6.00
27 Ben Simmons/49 4.00 10.00
28 Dennis Schroder/49 3.00 8.00
29 Joel Embiid/49 10.00 25.00
30 Myles Turner/49 4.00 10.00
31 Dante Exum/49 3.00 8.00
32 Josh Jackson/49 2.50 6.00
33 Taj Gibson/99 2.00 5.00
34 Blake Griffin/49 4.00 10.00
35 Josh Richardson/49 3.00 8.00
36 DeMar DeRozan/49 5.00 12.00
37 Marc Gasol/49 4.00 10.00
38 Justise Winslow/99 2.50 6.00
39 Harrison Barnes/49 3.00 8.00
40 Jabari Parker/49 2.50 6.00
41 Bogdan Bogdanovic/49 4.00 10.00
42 Jrue Holiday/49 5.00 12.00
43 Harry Giles/49 2.50 6.00
44 Roy Hibbert/49 2.50 6.00
45 Devin Booker/49 10.00 25.00
46 Tobias Harris/49 3.00 8.00
47 Jonathan Isaac/49 4.00 10.00
48 Trevor Ariza/49 2.50 6.00
49 Dennis Smith Jr./49 2.50 6.00
50 Giannis Antetokounmpo/49 20.00 50.00
51 Kawhi Leonard/49 10.00 25.00
52 Gary Payton/49 4.00 10.00
53 Domantas Sabonis/49 5.00 12.00
54 Dillon Brooks/49 4.00 10.00
55 Dragan Bender/99 2.00 5.00
56 Karl-Anthony Towns/49 6.00 15.00
57 Kemba Walker/49 3.00 8.00
58 Lonzo Ball/49 4.00 10.00
59 Kyle Kuzma/49 4.00 10.00
60 Frank Ntilikina/49 2.50 6.00
61 Avery Bradley/49 2.50 6.00
62 Andre Drummond/49 3.00 8.00
63 Bam Adebayo/49 6.00 15.00
64 Alvin Robertson/65 2.50 6.00
65 Al Horford/99 3.00 8.00

2018-19 Immaculate Collection Remarkable Memorabilia Red

*RED/24-25: .5X TO 1.5X p/r 65-99
*RED/24-25: .5X TO 1.2X p/r 49
PRINT RUNS B/WN 24-25 COPIES PER
6 LeBron James 60.00 150.00
10 Dirk Nowitzki 12.00 30.00
50 Giannis Antetokounmpo 40.00 100.00

2018-19 Immaculate Collection Remarkable Rookie Jerseys

PRINT RUNS B/WN 41-99 COPIES PER
1 Jarred Vanderbilt/99 4.00 10.00
2 Chandler Hutchison/99 2.50 6.00
3 Zhaire Smith/99 2.00 5.00
4 Hamidou Diallo/99 3.00 8.00
5 Devonte' Graham/99 3.00 8.00
6 Bruce Brown/99 4.00 10.00
7 Landry Shamet/99 3.00 8.00
8 Svi Mykhailiuk/99 2.50 6.00
9 Robert Williams III/99 4.00 10.00
10 Jevon Carter/99 3.00 8.00
11 Moritz Wagner/99 4.00 10.00
12 Gary Trent Jr./99 4.00 10.00
13 Keita Bates-Diop/99 2.50 6.00
14 Mo Bamba/99 3.00 8.00
15 De'Anthony Melton/99 4.00 10.00
16 Wendell Carter Jr./99 5.00 12.00
17 Melvin Frazier Jr./99 2.00 5.00
18 Shai Gilgeous-Alexander/99 6.00 15.00
19 Mitchell Robinson/99 5.00 12.00
20 Marvin Bagley III/99 3.00 8.00
21 Lonnie Walker IV/99 4.00 10.00
22 Omari Spellman/99 2.00 5.00
23 Elie Okobo/99 2.00 5.00
24 Jacob Evans III/99 2.00 5.00
25 Yuta Watanabe/99 3.00 8.00
26 Mikal Bridges/99 10.00 25.00
27 Anfernee Simons/99 10.00 25.00
28 Kevin Huerter/99 4.00 10.00
29 Jalen Brunson/99 15.00 40.00
30 Allonzo Trier/99 2.00 5.00
31 Jaren Jackson Jr./41 20.00 50.00
32 Deandre Ayton/99 6.00 15.00
33 Luka Doncic/99 150.00 400.00
34 Trae Young/99 75.00 200.00
35 Kevin Knox II/99 2.50 6.00

2018-19 Immaculate Collection Remarkable Rookie Jerseys Red

*RED/24-25: .6X TO 1.5X p/r 99
*RED/24-25: .5X TO 1.2X p/r 41
PRINT RUNS B/WN 24-25 COPIES PER
18 Shai Gilgeous-Alexander/25 25.00 60.00

2018-19 Immaculate Collection Rookie Patch Autographs Jersey Number

*JSY NUM: .6X TO 1.5X JSY AU
PRINT RUNS B/WN 1-77 COPIES PER
NO PRICING ON QTY 15 OR LESS
EXCHANGE DEADLINE 4/4/2021

2018-19 Immaculate Collection Rookie Patch Autographs Premium Edition

*PREM: .6X TO 1.5X JSY AU
STATED PRINT RUN 24 SER.#'d SETS
EXCHANGE DEADLINE 4/4/2021

2018-19 Immaculate Collection Shadowbox Signatures

PRINT RUNS B/WN 25-99 COPIES PER
EXCHANGE DEADLINE 4/4/2021
1 Grant Hill/49 15.00 40.00
2 Shane Battier/99 4.00 10.00
3 Lauri Markkanen/49 10.00 25.00
4 Montrezl Harrell/99 5.00 12.00
5 Doc Rivers/99 5.00 12.00
6 CJ McCollum/49 10.00 25.00
7 World E. Free/99 4.00 10.00
8 Elfrid Payton/99 4.00 10.00
9 Kyrie Irving/25 EXCH 20.00 50.00
10 Enes Kanter/99 4.00 10.00
11 Jason Kidd/49 12.00 30.00

12 Allan Houston/99 5.00 12.00
13 Josh Jackson/49 4.00 10.00
15 Jalen Rose/99 4.00 10.00
16 Fred VanVleet/99 6.00 15.00
17 Reggie Jackson/99 4.00 10.00
18 Willie Cauley-Stein/99 3.00 8.00
19 Reggie Miller/25 60.00 150.00
20 Danny Green/99 4.00 10.00
21 Kobe Bryant/99 2,500.00 5,000.00
22 Juwan Howard/99 4.00 10.00
23 Steve Kerr/99 8.00 20.00
24 Bam Adebayo/99 25.00 60.00
25 Robert Horry/99 5.00 12.00
26 Kevin Willis/99 4.00 10.00
28 Rudy Gay/99 5.00 12.00
29 Anthony Davis/25 60.00 150.00
30 J.J. Barea/99 5.00 12.00
31 Kevin Garnett/49 125.00 300.00
34 Thon Maker/99 3.00 8.00
35 Latrell Sprewell/99 8.00 20.00
36 John Wall/49 12.00 30.00
38 Pascal Siakam/99 8.00 20.00
39 Chris Paul/49 150.00 400.00
40 Horace Grant/99 8.00 20.00
41 Donovan Mitchell/49 30.00 80.00
43 JJ Redick/99 5.00 12.00
45 Gary Harris/99 4.00 10.00
46 Mark Aguirre/99 4.00 10.00
47 Malcolm Brogdon/99 5.00 12.00
48 Kristaps Porzingis/49 15.00 40.00
49 D'Angelo Russell/99 5.00 12.00
50 Michael Cooper/99 5.00 12.00

2018-19 Immaculate Collection Sneaker Swatches Signatures

PRINT RUNS B/WN 6-49 COPIES PER
NO PRICING ON QTY 15 OR LESS
EXCHANGE DEADLINE 4/4/2021
1 Buddy Hield/49 10.00 25.00
3 Elfrid Payton/49 8.00 20.00
5 B.J. Armstrong/49 10.00 25.00
7 Bill Cartwright/49 8.00 20.00
8 Hakeem Olajuwon/25 30.00 80.00
9 Sam Perkins/36 8.00 20.00
10 Grant Hill/25 60.00 150.00
11 Dennis Rodman/49 30.00 80.00
13 Ralph Sampson/49 10.00 25.00
15 Horace Grant/49 10.00 25.00
17 Jerry Stackhouse/49 15.00 40.00
20 Kevin McHale/25 20.00 50.00
23 Robert Parish/49 15.00 40.00
25 Thon Maker/44 6.00 15.00
27 Nate McMillan/49 8.00 20.00
28 Brandon Ingram/25 EXCH 12.00 30.00
29 Troy Brown Jr./48 8.00 20.00
30 Tony Parker/25 20.00 50.00
31 Chris Mullin/36 12.00 30.00
33 Dikembe Mutombo/40 15.00 40.00
36 Alonzo Mourning/25 30.00 80.00
37 Mikal Bridges/49 30.00 80.00
38 Chris Bosh/25 12.00 30.00
40 Dominique Wilkins/25 25.00 60.00
43 Allan Houston/34 10.00 25.00
45 Kevin Knox II/35 8.00 20.00
47 Ersan Ilyasova/49 10.00 25.00
48 Jason Kidd/25 30.00 80.00
49 Anfernee Simons/48 125.00 300.00
50 Gordon Hayward/49 12.00 30.00

2018-19 Immaculate Collection Sneaker Swatches Signatures Red

*RED/21-25: .5X TO 1.2X p/r 34-49
PRINT RUNS B/WN 5-25 COPIES PER
NO PRICING ON QTY 15 OR LESS
EXCHANGE DEADLINE 4/4/2021
49 Anfernee Simons/25 150.00 400.00

2018-19 Immaculate Collection Sole of the Game

PRINT RUNS B/WN 7-25 COPIES PER
NO PRICING ON QTY 15 OR LESS
1 Chris Paul/24 25.00 60.00
2 Nikola Vucevic/25 10.00 25.00
3 Manute Bol/20 75.00 200.00
4 Shawn Kemp/24 75.00 200.00
5 Kevin McHale/25 15.00 40.00
6 Robert Parish/24 20.00 50.00
7 Charles Barkley/25 50.00 120.00
8 Reggie Miller/25 50.00 120.00
9 Dwyane Wade/16 75.00 200.00
11 Kevin Garnett/24 75.00 200.00
12 Horace Grant/25 12.00 30.00
13 Scottie Pippen/25 60.00 150.00
14 Draymond Green/16 15.00 40.00
15 Karl Malone/25 25.00 60.00
16 Chris Webber/16 75.00 200.00
17 John Stockton/25 30.00 80.00
18 Jamal Mashburn/25 10.00 25.00
23 Isiah Thomas/25 20.00 50.00

2018-19 Immaculate Collection Standout Memorabilia

PRINT RUNS B/WN 49-99 COPIES PER
1 Enes Kanter/49 3.00 8.00
2 Vince Carter/49 8.00 20.00
3 Danny Granger/99 2.00 5.00
4 Tim Duncan/99 8.00 20.00
5 Derrick Favors/49 2.50 6.00
6 LeBron James/49 30.00 80.00
7 Paul George/49 6.00 15.00
8 Rondae Hollis-Jefferson/49 2.50 6.00
9 Derrick Rose/49 8.00 20.00
10 Steven Adams/49 3.00 8.00
11 Dirk Nowitzki/49 10.00 25.00
12 Tyus Jones/49 2.50 6.00
13 Rudy Gobert/99 4.00 10.00
14 Kevin Garnett/49 10.00 25.00
15 Markelle Fultz/49 3.00 8.00
16 Wesley Matthews/99 2.00 5.00
17 Jimmy Butler/49 6.00 15.00
18 Russell Westbrook/49 6.00 15.00
19 Charles Barkley/49 12.00 30.00
20 Aaron Gordon/99 3.00 8.00

2018-19 Immaculate Collection Standout Memorabilia Red

*RED/25: .6X TO 1.5X p/r 99
*RED/25: .5X TO 1.2X p/r 49
STATED PRINT RUN 25 SER.#'d SETS
6 LeBron James 150.00 400.00
11 Dirk Nowitzki 12.00 30.00
19 Charles Barkley 40.00 100.00

2018-19 Immaculate Collection Swatches

PRINT RUNS B/WN 49-99 COPIES PER
*RED/21-25: .5X TO 1.5X p/r 99
*RED/21-25: .5X TO 1.2X p/r 49
1 Pau Gasol/49 6.00 15.00
2 Lou Williams/49 3.00 8.00
3 Andrew Wiggins/49 5.00 12.00
4 George Hill/49 3.00 8.00
5 Otto Porter Jr./99 2.50 6.00
6 Hassan Whiteside/99 2.50 6.00
7 DeMarre Carroll/99 2.00 5.00
8 Julius Randle/49 4.00 10.00
9 Dennis Schroder/49 3.00 8.00
10 Joel Embiid/99 8.00 20.00
11 Blake Griffin/49 4.00 10.00
12 Jamal Crawford/99 3.00 8.00
13 Gordon Hayward/99 3.00 8.00
14 Marc Gasol/99 3.00 8.00
15 Ersan Ilyasova/99 2.00 5.00
16 Justise Winslow/99 2.50 6.00
17 Jabari Parker/49 2.50 6.00
18 Tobias Harris/49 3.00 8.00
19 Dennis Smith Jr./49 2.50 6.00
20 Devin Booker/49 10.00 25.00
21 John Stockton/99 6.00 15.00
22 Kawhi Leonard/99 8.00 20.00
23 DeAndre' Bembry/99 2.00 5.00
24 Michael Kidd-Gilchrist/99 2.00 5.00
25 Domantas Sabonis/99 4.00 10.00
26 Karl-Anthony Towns/99 5.00 12.00
27 Dillon Brooks/99 3.00 8.00
28 Kemba Walker/49 3.00 8.00
29 Patrick Ewing/99 5.00 12.00
30 Kyle Kuzma/49 4.00 10.00
31 Frank Ntilikina/99 2.00 5.00
32 Kyrie Irving/99 8.00 20.00
33 Avery Bradley/49 2.50 6.00
34 Larry Bird/99 12.00 30.00
35 Vinnie Johnson/99 3.00 8.00
36 Kevin Durant/99 12.00 30.00
37 Christian Laettner/99 3.00 8.00
38 Steve Francis/49 3.00 8.00
39 Ricky Rubio/99 2.50 6.00
40 Jarrett Allen/99 3.00 8.00

2018-19 Immaculate Collection The Standard Relics

PRINT RUNS B/WN 5-99 COPIES PER
NO PRICING ON QTY 15 OR LESS
1 Dan Issel/99 4.00 10.00
2 Manute Bol/25 8.00 20.00
3 Kevin Love/99 2.50 6.00
4 Joel Embiid/49 10.00 25.00
5 Karl Malone/49 8.00 20.00
6 Tim Duncan/99 8.00 20.00
8 Dennis Rodman/25 25.00 60.00
9 Charles Barkley/25 20.00 50.00
10 Karl-Anthony Towns/99 5.00 12.00
11 Charlie Scott/25 5.00 12.00
12 Tracy McGrady/25 8.00 20.00
14 Clint Capela/99 2.50 6.00
15 Earl Monroe/25 10.00 25.00
16 M.L. Carr/25 5.00 12.00
17 Jason Kidd/49 6.00 15.00
18 Alex English/99 3.00 8.00
19 Mitch Kupchak/25 5.00 12.00
20 Grant Hill/99 5.00 12.00
22 Kevin McHale/25 8.00 20.00
23 Shawn Bradley/99 2.00 5.00
24 Paul Westphal/25 5.00 12.00
28 Patrick Ewing/49 6.00 15.00
29 Bernard King/25 5.00 12.00
31 CJ McCollum/99 3.00 8.00
33 Danny Ainge/25 5.00 12.00
34 Brandon Ingram/99 4.00 10.00
35 Shaquille O'Neal/49 12.00 30.00
37 Reggie Miller/99 6.00 15.00
38 Walter Davis/99 3.00 8.00
39 Larry Bird/25 20.00 50.00
40 Kobe Bryant/99 75.00 200.00
41 Doug Collins/99 3.00 8.00
42 Allen Iverson/49 8.00 20.00
43 Dirk Nowitzki/99 8.00 20.00
44 Steve Kerr/25 6.00 15.00
45 Magic Johnson/49 15.00 40.00
46 James Harden/49 8.00 20.00
48 Mark Jackson/25 4.00 10.00
49 Damian Lillard/99 8.00 20.00
50 Julius Erving/49 10.00 25.00
51 James Worthy/25 8.00 20.00
52 Aaron Gordon/99 3.00 8.00
53 David Thompson/25 6.00 15.00
54 Dennis Johnson/25 5.00 12.00
55 Chris Mullin/25 6.00 15.00
56 Nikola Jokic/99 15.00 40.00
57 Andrew Wiggins/99 4.00 10.00
59 Mike Bibby/49 4.00 10.00
60 Deandre Ayton/99 6.00 15.00
61 Marvin Bagley III/99 3.00 8.00
62 Luka Doncic/99 30.00 80.00
63 Jaren Jackson Jr./99 15.00 40.00
64 Trae Young/99 12.00 30.00
65 Mo Bamba/99 3.00 8.00
66 Wendell Carter Jr./99 5.00 12.00
67 Collin Sexton/99 6.00 15.00
68 Kevin Knox II/99 2.50 6.00
69 Mikal Bridges/99 10.00 25.00
70 Shai Gilgeous-Alexander/99 6.00 15.00
71 Jerome Robinson/99 2.00 5.00
72 Michael Porter Jr./99 8.00 20.00
73 Troy Brown Jr./99 2.50 6.00
74 Zhaire Smith/99 2.00 5.00
75 Donte DiVincenzo/99 5.00 12.00
76 Lonnie Walker IV/99 4.00 10.00
77 Kevin Huerter/99 6.00 15.00
78 Josh Okogie/99 3.00 8.00
79 Grayson Allen/99 4.00 10.00
80 Chandler Hutchison/99 2.50 6.00
81 Aaron Holiday/49 4.00 10.00
82 Anfernee Simons/99 10.00 25.00
83 Moritz Wagner/49 5.00 12.00
84 Landry Shamet/99 3.00 8.00
85 Robert Williams III/49 5.00 12.00
86 Jacob Evans III/49 2.50 6.00
87 Dzanan Musa/49 2.50 6.00
88 Omari Spellman/49 2.50 6.00
89 Elie Okobo/49 2.50 6.00
90 Jevon Carter/49 4.00 10.00
91 Jalen Brunson/49 20.00 50.00
92 Devonte' Graham/49 4.00 10.00
93 Hamidou Diallo/49 4.00 10.00
94 Mitchell Robinson/99 5.00 12.00
95 Allonzo Trier/99 2.00 5.00
96 Rodions Kurucs/49 3.00 8.00
97 Kostas Antetokounmpo/99 2.50 6.00
98 De'Anthony Melton/49 5.00 12.00
99 Bruce Brown/49 5.00 12.00
100 Keita Bates-Diop/49 3.00 8.00

2018-19 Immaculate Collection Triple Autographs

PRINT RUNS B/WN 10-25 COPIES PER
NO PRICING ON QTY 15 OR LESS
EXCHANGE DEADLINE 4/4/2021
1 Trae Young
Kevin Huerter
Omari Spellman/25 200.00 500.00
2 Shai Gilgeous-Alexander
Jerome Robinson
Landry Shamet/25 300.00 600.00
3 De'Anthony Melton
Deandre Ayton
Mikal Bridges/25 30.00 80.00
4 Deandre Ayton
Marvin Bagley III
Luka Doncic/25 1,000.00 2,000.00
5 Allonzo Trier
Kevin Knox II
Mitchell Robinson/25 100.00 250.00
6 Doc Rivers
Kevin Willis
Dominique Wilkins/25 30.00 80.00
9 Nick Anderson
Scott Skiles
Dennis Scott/25 40.00 100.00
10 Alvan Adams
Larry Nance
Walter Davis/25 20.00 50.00
11 Peja Stojakovic
Vlade Divac
Jason Williams/25 EXCH 200.00 500.00
13 David Robinson
Sean Elliott
Bruce Bowen/25 75.00 200.00
14 Hamidou Diallo
Kevin Knox II
Shai Gilgeous-Alexander/25 500.00 1,000.00
15 Marvin Bagley III
Grayson Allen
Wendell Carter Jr./25 15.00 40.00

2022-23 Immaculate Collection

STATED PRINT RUN 99 SER.#'d SETS
*RED/49 (1-100): .5X TO 1.2X BASIC
*RED/49 (101-140): .5X TO 1.2X BASIC
*BLUE/25 (1-100): .75X TO 2X BASIC
1 LaMelo Ball 8.00 20.00
2 Trae Young 8.00 20.00
3 Malcolm Brogdon 2.50 6.00
4 Julius Randle 4.00 10.00
5 Paolo Banchero 20.00 50.00
6 Joel Embiid 5.00 12.00
7 Zach LaVine 6.00 15.00
8 Franz Wagner 8.00 20.00
9 Jaylen Brown 6.00 15.00
10 Cade Cunningham 10.00 25.00
11 Giannis Antetokounmpo 15.00 40.00
12 Fred VanVleet 4.00 10.00
13 Damian Lillard 8.00 20.00
14 Jabari Smith Jr. 10.00 25.00
15 Klay Thompson 8.00 20.00
16 Darius Garland 5.00 12.00
17 LeBron James 25.00 60.00
18 Bam Adebayo 5.00 12.00
19 Kevin Durant 10.00 25.00
20 Michael Porter Jr. 4.00 10.00
21 Ja Morant 10.00 25.00
22 Bennedict Mathurin 10.00 25.00
23 Nikola Jokic 15.00 40.00
24 Kawhi Leonard 8.00 20.00
25 Cameron Johnson 2.50 6.00
26 Keegan Murray 8.00 20.00
27 Josh Giddey 5.00 12.00
28 Jayson Tatum 12.00 30.00
29 Russell Westbrook 5.00 12.00
30 Karl-Anthony Towns 5.00 12.00
31 Dejounte Murray 4.00 10.00
32 Jordan Clarkson 3.00 8.00
33 Austin Reaves 8.00 20.00
34 Tyler Herro 5.00 12.00
35 D'Angelo Russell 2.50 6.00
36 Tyrese Haliburton 6.00 15.00
37 Dillon Brooks 3.00 8.00
38 Immanuel Quickley 3.00 8.00
39 Devin Booker 8.00 20.00
40 Bojan Bogdanovic 3.00 8.00
41 Jaden Ivey 10.00 25.00
42 Andrew Wiggins 4.00 10.00
43 Rudy Gobert 4.00 10.00
44 Kristaps Porzingis 4.00 10.00
45 RJ Barrett 5.00 12.00
46 Kevin Porter Jr. 2.50 6.00
47 Jeremy Sochan 10.00 25.00
48 Caris LeVert 2.50 6.00
49 Zion Williamson 8.00 20.00
50 Tyrese Maxey 6.00 15.00
51 DeMar DeRozan 4.00 10.00
52 Jerami Grant 4.00 10.00
53 PJ Washington Jr. 3.00 8.00
54 Paul George 5.00 12.00
55 Chet Holmgren 15.00 40.00
56 Luka Doncic 20.00 50.00
57 Pascal Siakam 5.00 12.00
58 Alperen Sengun 4.00 10.00
59 Jalen Brunson 6.00 15.00
60 Brandon Ingram 4.00 10.00
61 Walker Kessler 6.00 15.00
62 Stephen Curry 25.00 60.00
63 Jaren Jackson Jr. 5.00 12.00
64 James Harden 6.00 15.00
65 Mark Williams 6.00 15.00
66 Anthony Davis 8.00 20.00
67 Mikal Bridges 4.00 10.00
68 Tobias Harris 2.50 6.00
69 Shai Gilgeous-Alexander 15.00 40.00
70 Evan Mobley 8.00 20.00
71 Malik Monk 3.00 8.00
72 Shaedon Sharpe 12.00 30.00
73 Keldon Johnson 4.00 10.00
74 Domantas Sabonis 4.00 10.00
75 Bradley Beal 4.00 10.00
76 Cameron Thomas 5.00 12.00
77 Jaden Hardy 5.00 12.00
78 Lauri Markkanen 5.00 12.00
79 Donovan Mitchell 6.00 15.00
80 De'Aaron Fox 6.00 15.00
81 Jimmy Butler 6.00 15.00
82 Desmond Bane 4.00 10.00
83 Jamal Murray 5.00 12.00
84 Scottie Barnes 5.00 12.00
85 Khris Middleton 4.00 10.00
86 Kyrie Irving 6.00 15.00
87 Jalen Duren 10.00 25.00
88 Quentin Grimes 2.50 6.00
89 Buddy Hield 3.00 8.00
90 Chris Paul 6.00 15.00
91 Kyle Kuzma 4.00 10.00
92 Anfernee Simons 4.00 10.00
93 Anthony Edwards 15.00 40.00
94 Terry Rozier III 4.00 10.00
95 Jalen Williams 15.00 40.00
96 CJ McCollum 3.00 8.00
97 Jalen Green 10.00 25.00
98 Jrue Holiday 4.00 10.00
99 Jordan Poole 5.00 12.00
100 Jalen Suggs 6.00 15.00
101 Kennedy Chandler JSY AU RC 15.00 40.00
102 Max Christie JSY AU RC 75.00 200.00
103 Jalen Duren JSY AU RC 75.00 200.00
104 Jaylin Williams JSY AU RC 20.00 50.00
105 Paolo Banchero JSY AU RC 500.00 1,000.00
106 Simone Fontecchio JSY AU RC 15.00 40.00
107 Christian Koloko JSY AU RC 15.00 40.00
108 Patrick Baldwin Jr. JSY AU RC 15.00 40.00
109 Jake LaRavia JSY AU RC 15.00 40.00
110 Peyton Watson JSY AU RC 25.00 60.00
111 MarJon Beauchamp JSY AU RC 15.00 40.00
112 Shaedon Sharpe JSY AU RC 125.00 300.00
113 Nikola Jovic JSY AU RC 60.00 150.00
114 Malaki Branham JSY AU RC 15.00 40.00
115 Mac McClung JSY AU RC 60.00 150.00
116 Caleb Houstan JSY AU RC 15.00 40.00
117 Johnny Davis JSY AU RC 15.00 40.00
118 Mark Williams JSY AU RC 30.00 80.00
119 Jaden Hardy JSY AU RC 60.00 150.00
120 David Roddy JSY AU RC 20.00 50.00
121 Dyson Daniels JSY AU RC 40.00 100.00
122 Andrew Nembhard JSY AU RC 30.00 80.00
123 Chet Holmgren JSY AU RC 600.00 1,200.00
124 Ousmane Dieng JSY AU RC 20.00 50.00
125 Moussa Diabate JSY AU RC 15.00 40.00
126 Blake Wesley JSY AU RC 15.00 40.00
127 Wendell Moore Jr. JSY AU RC 15.00 40.00
128 Bennedict Mathurin JSY AU RC 125.00 300.00
129 Keegan Murray JSY AU RC 125.00 300.00
130 Jeremy Sochan JSY AU RC 100.00 250.00
131 Jalen Williams JSY AU RC 400.00 800.00
132 Christian Braun JSY AU RC 40.00 100.00
133 Dalen Terry JSY AU RC 15.00 40.00
134 Ochai Agbaji JSY AU RC 20.00 50.00
135 Jaden Ivey JSY AU RC 125.00 300.00
136 Jordan Goodwin JSY AU RC 12.00 30.00
137 AJ Griffin JSY AU RC 12.00 30.00
138 Walker Kessler JSY AU RC 30.00 80.00
139 Jabari Smith Jr. JSY AU RC 125.00 300.00
140 Tari Eason JSY AU RC 40.00 100.00

2022-23 Immaculate Collection Clutch Time Signatures

STATED PRINT RUN 15-99 SER.#'d SETS
2 Ray Allen/49 125.00 300.00
3 Derek Fisher/75 40.00 100.00
4 Bob Cousy/25 125.00 300.00
5 Cole Anthony/49 25.00 60.00
6 Nikola Jokic/25 500.00 1,000.00
7 Deandre Ayton/25 40.00 100.00
8 Mark Price/99 25.00 60.00
9 Bill Laimbeer/75 25.00 60.00
10 Peja Stojakovic/49 30.00 80.00
11 Anfernee Hardaway/25 150.00 400.00
12 Robert Horry/49 40.00 100.00
13 Kareem Abdul-Jabbar/25 150.00 400.00
14 Allen Iverson/15 150.00 400.00
15 Isiah Thomas/49 40.00 100.00
16 Paul Pierce/25 125.00 300.00
17 Bradley Beal/25 75.00 200.00
18 Stephen Curry/15 1,000.00 2,000.00
19 Magic Johnson/25 150.00 400.00
20 John Stockton/25 125.00 300.00
21 Larry Bird/15 150.00 400.00
22 Luka Doncic/25 800.00 1,500.00
23 Sam Cassell/75 20.00 50.00
24 Steve Kerr/49 40.00 100.00
25 Tyrese Haliburton/25 300.00 600.00

2022-23 Immaculate Collection Dual Autographs

STATED PRINT RUN 10-49 SER.#'d SETS
2 Gary Payton
Anfernee Hardaway/25 200.00 500.00
4 Robert Horry
Derek Fisher/49 75.00 200.00
6 Jaden Ivey
Jalen Duren/49 300.00 600.00
8 Bill Walton
Robert Parish/49 75.00 200.00
15 Walker Kessler
Ochai Agbaji/49 60.00 150.00
16 Alex English
Fat Lever/49 40.00 100.00
17 Lenny Wilkens
Bill Walton/49 75.00 200.00
18 Ochai Agbaji
Christian Braun/49 60.00 150.00
20 Jason Kidd
Paul Pierce/25 150.00 400.00
21 Khris Middleton
Jrue Holiday/25 60.00 150.00
24 John Stockton
Mark Price/25 100.00 250.00
26 Jaden Hardy
MarJon Beauchamp/49 40.00 100.00
27 Jordan Clarkson
Walker Kessler/25 60.00 150.00
32 Shawn Kemp
Gary Payton/25 60.00 150.00
33 Ralph Sampson
Bill Walton/49 75.00 200.00
36 Caron Butler
Antawn Jamison/49 30.00 80.00
43 Shawn Kemp
Dominique Wilkins/25 100.00 250.00

2022-23 Immaculate Collection Heralded Signatures

STATED PRINT RUN 25-99 SER.#'d SETS
*RED/15-25: .5X TO 1.2X BASIC
1 Bobby Portis/99 6.00 15.00
2 Udonis Haslem/99 5.00 12.00
3 Michael Cooper/99 6.00 15.00
4 Nate Archibald/99 8.00 20.00
5 Carmelo Anthony/49 75.00 200.00
6 De'Aaron Fox/49 40.00 100.00
7 Oscar Robertson/49 30.00 80.00
8 Boban Marjanovic/99 6.00 15.00
9 Herbert Jones/99 6.00 15.00
10 Bob Pettit/75 8.00 20.00
11 Elvin Hayes/99 8.00 20.00
13 Swen Nater/99 6.00 15.00
14 Brad Daugherty/99 5.00 12.00
15 James Worthy/49 10.00 25.00
16 Rudy Gobert/99 8.00 20.00
17 Jamaal Wilkes/99 6.00 15.00
18 James Harden/49 100.00 250.00
19 Karl Malone/49 40.00 100.00
20 Calvin Murphy/99 6.00 15.00
21 Shawn Kemp/99 15.00 40.00
22 Antawn Jamison/99 6.00 15.00
23 Patty Mills/99 6.00 15.00
24 Isaiah Rider/99 6.00 15.00
25 Ivica Zubac/99 6.00 15.00
26 Christian Laettner/99 6.00 15.00
27 Clyde Drexler/25 30.00 80.00
28 Dennis Rodman/75 75.00 200.00
29 Zach Randolph/75 6.00 15.00
31 Steve Nash/49 60.00 150.00
32 Metta World Peace/75 6.00 15.00
33 Patrick Ewing/75 100.00 250.00
34 Austin Reaves/99 40.00 100.00
35 Lauri Markkanen/99 20.00 50.00
36 Luguentz Dort/99 6.00 15.00
37 Charles Barkley/25 75.00 200.00
38 Manu Ginobili/49 40.00 100.00
39 Kenny "Sky" Walker/99 5.00 12.00
40 Jonathan Kuminga/99 20.00 50.00

2022-23 Immaculate Collection Immaculate Award Winners Autographs

1 Stephen Curry/25 1,000.00 2,000.00
2 Larry Bird/49 125.00 300.00
3 Karl Malone/49 125.00 300.00
4 Ja Morant/25 600.00 1,200.00
5 Hakeem Olajuwon/49 125.00 300.00
6 Allen Iverson/49 200.00 500.00
7 Kareem Abdul-Jabbar/49 125.00 300.00
8 Charles Barkley/25 150.00 400.00
9 Paolo Banchero /99 400.00 800.00

2022-23 Immaculate Collection Immaculate Championship Runs Autographs

1 Bob Cousy/75 150.00 400.00
2 Hakeem Olajuwon/75 75.00 200.00
3 Rasheed Wallace/75 100.00 250.00
4 David Robinson/49 75.00 200.00
5 Toni Kukoc/99 40.00 100.00
6 Kareem Abdul-Jabbar/49 125.00 300.00
7 Dwyane Wade/25 300.00 600.00
8 Stephen Curry/25 1,000.00 2,000.00
9 Steve Kerr/99 40.00 100.00
10 Pat Riley/75 75.00 200.00

2022-23 Immaculate Collection Immaculate Ink

*RED/25: .5X TO 1.2X BASIC
1 Jaren Jackson Jr./49 25.00 60.00
2 Bill Walton/99 20.00 50.00
3 Metta World Peace/99 10.00 25.00
4 Jordan Poole/49 15.00 40.00
7 Jason Williams/99 60.00 150.00
8 Ralph Sampson/99 8.00 20.00
9 Lauri Markkanen/99 15.00 40.00
10 Franz Wagner/99 25.00 60.00
12 Jalen Suggs/99 20.00 50.00
13 George McGinnis/99 10.00 25.00
14 Steve Kerr/99 12.00 30.00
15 Jonathan Kuminga/99 25.00 60.00
16 RJ Barrett/75 15.00 40.00
17 Mo Bamba/99 6.00 15.00
18 Tim Hardaway Jr./99 8.00 20.00
19 Antoine Walker/99 10.00 25.00
20 Alex English/99 12.00 30.00
21 Magic Johnson/75 75.00 200.00
22 Shai Gilgeous-Alexander/49 500.00 1,000.00
23 Robert Parish/99 15.00 40.00
24 Seth Curry/99 8.00 20.00
25 Nate Archibald/99 12.00 30.00
26 Isaac Okoro/99 8.00 20.00
27 Bill Laimbeer/99 10.00 25.00
28 Khris Middleton/99 12.00 30.00
29 Jason Kidd/75 30.00 80.00
30 Dorian Finney-Smith/99 8.00 20.00
32 Hakeem Olajuwon/75 40.00 100.00
33 Saddiq Bey/99 8.00 20.00
34 Cole Anthony/99 10.00 25.00
35 Richard Hamilton/99 12.00 30.00
36 Mike Miller/99 8.00 20.00
37 Tom Chambers/99 10.00 25.00
38 Mark Aguirre/99 10.00 25.00
39 Carlos Boozer/99 8.00 20.00
40 Bobby Portis/99 10.00 25.00

2022-23 Immaculate Collection Immaculate Legends Autographs

1 Gary Payton/75 40.00 100.00
2 Isiah Thomas/75 40.00 100.00
3 Larry Bird/49 125.00 300.00
4 Tim Hardaway/99 30.00 80.00
5 Nate Archibald/75 15.00 40.00
6 Allen Iverson/49 150.00 400.00
7 Kevin Garnett/25 125.00 300.00
8 Nick Van Exel/99 30.00 80.00
9 Robert Parish/75 15.00 40.00
10 Bob Cousy/49 125.00 300.00
11 Kareem Abdul-Jabbar/49 125.00 300.00
12 Steve Kerr/49 40.00 100.00
13 Hakeem Olajuwon/49 75.00 200.00
14 Karl Malone/49 75.00 200.00
15 Robert Horry/99 30.00 80.00
16 Bob McAdoo/99 15.00 40.00
18 Tom Chambers/99 12.00 30.00
19 Larry Johnson/99 60.00 150.00
20 Magic Johnson/49 125.00 300.00

2022-23 Immaculate Collection Immaculate Milestones Autographs

1 Luka Doncic/25 1,000.00 2,000.00
2 Nikola Jokic/25 600.00 1,200.00
3 Josh Giddey/75 100.00 250.00
4 Walker Kessler/99 60.00 150.00
5 Chris Paul/25 150.00 400.00
6 Nikola Jokic/25 600.00 1,200.00
8 Paul Pierce/49 125.00 300.00
9 Paolo Banchero /49 400.00 800.00

2022-23 Immaculate Collection Immaculate Rookie Introductions Autographs

1 Paolo Banchero /99 350.00 700.00
2 Ochai Agbaji/99 12.00 30.00
3 Christian Koloko/99 10.00 25.00
4 Max Christie/99 75.00 200.00
5 Walker Kessler/99 20.00 50.00
6 Christian Braun/99 25.00 60.00
7 Keegan Murray/99 125.00 300.00
8 Bennedict Mathurin/99 125.00 300.00
9 David Roddy/99 12.00 30.00
10 Mark Williams/99 20.00 50.00
11 Shaedon Sharpe/99 125.00 300.00
12 Andrew Nembhard/99 20.00 50.00
13 Tari Eason/99 25.00 60.00
14 Jordan Goodwin/99 8.00 20.00
15 Jaden Ivey/99 100.00 250.00
16 AJ Griffin/99 8.00 20.00
17 Jeremy Sochan/99 100.00 250.00
18 Simone Fontecchio/99 10.00 25.00
19 Jaden Hardy/99 40.00 100.00
20 Dalen Terry/99 10.00 25.00
21 Jalen Williams/99 200.00 500.00
22 Blake Wesley/99 10.00 25.00
23 Jabari Smith Jr./99 125.00 300.00
24 Jake LaRavia/99 10.00 25.00
25 Moussa Diabate/99 10.00 25.00
26 Jalen Duren/99 75.00 200.00
27 Nikola Jovic/99 40.00 100.00
28 Jaylin Williams/99 12.00 30.00
30 Chet Holmgren/99 400.00 800.00

2022-23 Immaculate Collection Immaculate Signature Moves

1 Kevin Garnett/99 300.00 600.00
2 Larry Johnson/99 75.00 200.00
3 Stephen Curry/25 3,000.00 6,000.00
4 Deandre Ayton/99 75.00 200.00
5 Jordan Poole/49 75.00 200.00
6 Anthony Edwards/25 1,000.00 2,000.00
7 Brandon Ingram/25 125.00 300.00
8 Ja Morant/25 1,000.00 2,000.00
9 Jason Kidd/99 125.00 300.00
10 Josh Giddey/99 100.00 250.00
11 Richard Hamilton/99 75.00 200.00
12 Paolo Banchero /49 500.00 1,000.00
13 Anfernee Hardaway/25 200.00 500.00
14 Jordan Clarkson/99 60.00 150.00
15 Jalen Green/49 150.00 400.00
16 Clyde Drexler/49 75.00 200.00
17 Shai Gilgeous-Alexander/49 2,000.00 4,000.00
18 Paul Pierce/49 125.00 300.00
19 Luka Doncic/49 1,500.00 3,000.00
20 Jaden Ivey/49 200.00 500.00

2022-23 Immaculate Collection Immaculate Signatures

STATED PRINT RUN 49-99 SER.#'d SETS
*RED/15-25: .5X TO 1.2X BASIC
1 Manu Ginobili/99 30.00 80.00
2 Bill Laimbeer/99 6.00 15.00
3 Bob Pettit/49 8.00 20.00
4 Pau Gasol/75 30.00 80.00
5 Steve Nash/49 60.00 150.00
6 Patrick Ewing/49 100.00 250.00
7 Bernard King/99 8.00 20.00
8 Rick Mahorn/99 5.00 12.00
9 Dan Majerle/99 6.00 15.00
10 Jerry Stackhouse/99 8.00 20.00
11 Cuttino Mobley/99 5.00 12.00
12 Oscar Robertson/49 30.00 80.00
13 John Starks/99 6.00 15.00
14 Kevin Garnett/75 75.00 200.00
15 Robert Parish/99 8.00 20.00
16 Carmelo Anthony/49 40.00 100.00
17 Pat Riley/75 25.00 60.00
18 Kareem Abdul-Jabbar/75 75.00 200.00
19 Rasheed Wallace/75 40.00 100.00
20 Toni Kukoc/99 8.00 20.00

2022-23 Immaculate Collection Massive Memorabilia

1 Isaiah Mobley 10.00 25.00
2 Johnny Davis 10.00 25.00
3 Jalen Duren 30.00 80.00
5 Jaden Ivey 30.00 80.00
6 Christian Koloko 10.00 25.00
7 Patrick Baldwin Jr. 10.00 25.00
9 Christian Braun 25.00 60.00
10 Jabari Walker 8.00 20.00
11 Caleb Houstan 10.00 25.00
12 Shaedon Sharpe 40.00 100.00
13 Keegan Murray 25.00 60.00
14 Malaki Branham 10.00 25.00
15 David Roddy 12.00 30.00
16 AJ Griffin 8.00 20.00
17 Jaylin Williams 12.00 30.00
18 Wendell Moore Jr. 10.00 25.00
19 Jalen Williams 50.00 125.00
20 Kenneth Lofton Jr. 12.00 30.00
21 Jeremy Sochan 30.00 80.00
23 Moussa Diabate 10.00 25.00
24 Paolo Banchero 75.00 200.00
26 Mark Williams 20.00 50.00
27 Walker Kessler 20.00 50.00
28 A.J. Green 12.00 30.00
29 Peyton Watson 15.00 40.00
30 Chet Holmgren 75.00 200.00
32 Bryce McGowens 10.00 25.00
33 Andrew Nembhard 20.00 50.00
34 Tyrese Martin 8.00 20.00
35 Blake Wesley 10.00 25.00
36 Mac McClung 25.00 60.00
37 Nikola Jovic 20.00 50.00
38 Dyson Daniels 25.00 60.00
39 Ochai Agbaji 12.00 30.00
40 Dalen Terry 10.00 25.00
41 Max Christie 25.00 60.00
42 Ryan Rollins 10.00 25.00
43 Jake LaRavia 10.00 25.00
44 Kevon Harris 8.00 20.00
47 Ousmane Dieng 12.00 30.00
48 Jaden Hardy 15.00 40.00
49 MarJon Beauchamp 10.00 25.00
50 Josh Minott 10.00 25.00

2022-23 Immaculate Collection Materials

*RED/10-25: .75X TO 2X BASIC
1 Rui Hachimura/99 6.00 15.00
2 Russell Westbrook/99 10.00 25.00
3 LeBron James/99 60.00 150.00
4 Stephen Curry/99 50.00 125.00
5 Steven Adams/99 6.00 15.00
6 Talen Horton-Tucker/99 5.00 12.00
7 Tobias Harris/99 5.00 12.00
8 Trae Young/99 15.00 40.00
9 Tre Mann/99 5.00 12.00
10 Paul George/99 10.00 25.00
11 Klay Thompson/99 15.00 40.00
12 Al Horford/99 6.00 15.00
13 Anthony Davis/99 15.00 40.00
14 Cam Reddish/99 5.00 12.00
15 Cameron Thomas/99 10.00 25.00
16 Cole Anthony/99 6.00 15.00
17 Bam Adebayo/99 10.00 25.00
18 De'Andre Hunter/99 6.00 15.00
19 Ja Morant/99 20.00 50.00
20 Deandre Ayton/99 6.00 15.00
21 Dorian Finney-Smith/99 5.00 12.00
22 Devin Booker/99 15.00 40.00
23 Jarrett Allen/99 6.00 15.00
24 Giannis Antetokounmpo/99 30.00 80.00
25 Jerami Grant/99 8.00 20.00
26 Jimmy Butler/99 12.00 30.00
27 Joe Ingles/99 5.00 12.00
28 Josh Okogie/99 6.00 15.00
29 Kevin Durant/99 20.00 50.00
30 Kenyon Martin Jr./49 6.00 15.00
31 LaMelo Ball/99 15.00 40.00
32 Kevin Huerter/99 6.00 15.00
33 Kevon Looney/99 6.00 15.00
34 Khris Middleton/99 8.00 20.00
35 Killian Hayes/49 4.00 10.00
36 Julius Randle/99 8.00 20.00
37 Luka Doncic/99 40.00 100.00
38 Joel Embiid/99 10.00 25.00
39 Jaylen Brown/99 12.00 30.00
40 Dejounte Murray/99 8.00 20.00

2022-23 Immaculate Collection Modern Marks

*RED/15-25: .6X TO 1.5X BASIC
1 Patty Mills/99 6.00 15.00
2 Lauri Markkanen/99 20.00 50.00
3 Brandon Ingram/75 20.00 50.00
4 Jalen Suggs/99 8.00 20.00
6 Dejounte Murray/75 8.00 20.00
7 Larry Nance Jr./99 6.00 15.00
8 Udonis Haslem/99 5.00 12.00
9 Jordan Clarkson/99 20.00 50.00
10 RJ Barrett/99 10.00 25.00
11 Kevon Looney/99 6.00 15.00
12 Gabe Vincent/99 6.00 15.00
13 Franz Wagner/99 25.00 60.00
14 Ayo Dosunmu/99 8.00 20.00
16 Davion Mitchell/99 5.00 12.00
17 Alperen Sengun/99 20.00 50.00
18 Cameron Payne/99 5.00 12.00
19 Josh Giddey/75 15.00 40.00
20 Jose Alvarado/99 6.00 15.00
21 Doug McDermott/99 4.00 10.00
22 Isaac Okoro/99 5.00 12.00
23 Tim Hardaway Jr./99 5.00 12.00
24 Grayson Allen/99 6.00 15.00
25 Evan Fournier/99 5.00 12.00
26 Georges Niang/99 5.00 12.00
27 Jarred Vanderbilt/99 5.00 12.00
28 Nicolas Claxton/99 6.00 15.00
29 De'Aaron Fox/49 40.00 100.00
30 Bones Hyland/99 5.00 12.00
31 Devonte' Graham/99 5.00 12.00
32 Herbert Jones/99 6.00 15.00
33 Brook Lopez/99 6.00 15.00
34 Devin Vassell/49 12.00 30.00
35 Kevin Huerter/99 6.00 15.00
36 Isaiah Stewart/99 5.00 12.00
37 Evan Mobley/99 15.00 40.00
38 Austin Reaves/99 40.00 100.00
39 Goran Dragic/99 5.00 12.00
40 Jock Landale/99 6.00 15.00

2022-23 Immaculate Collection Remarkable Jerseys

*RED/10-25: 1.25X TO 3X BASIC
1 Giannis Antetokounmpo 25.00 60.00
2 Nikola Jokic 25.00 60.00
3 Julius Randle 6.00 15.00
4 Jimmy Butler 10.00 25.00
5 Josh Giddey 8.00 20.00
6 LeBron James 40.00 100.00
7 Brandon Ingram 6.00 15.00

8 Jrue Holiday 6.00 15.00
9 Ja Morant 15.00 40.00
10 DeMar DeRozan 6.00 15.00
11 RJ Barrett 8.00 20.00
12 Dejounte Murray 6.00 15.00
13 Jayson Tatum 20.00 50.00
14 Joel Embiid 8.00 20.00
15 Tyrese Maxey 10.00 25.00
16 Shai Gilgeous-Alexander 25.00 60.00
17 Bam Adebayo 8.00 20.00
18 Marcus Smart 6.00 15.00
19 Fred VanVleet 6.00 15.00
20 D'Angelo Russell 4.00 10.00
21 Zach LaVine 10.00 25.00
22 Rudy Gobert 6.00 15.00
23 Jamal Murray 8.00 20.00
24 Franz Wagner 12.00 30.00
25 James Harden 10.00 25.00

2022-23 Immaculate Collection Remarkable Rookie Jerseys

*RED/25: 1.25X TO 3X BASIC
1 Malaki Branham 4.00 10.00
2 Nikola Jovic 8.00 20.00
3 Dalen Terry 4.00 10.00
4 Tari Eason 10.00 25.00
5 Wendell Moore Jr. 4.00 10.00
6 AJ Griffin 3.00 8.00
7 MarJon Beauchamp 4.00 10.00
8 Mark Williams 8.00 20.00
9 TyTy Washington Jr. 4.00 10.00
10 Bennedict Mathurin 12.00 30.00
11 Dyson Daniels 10.00 25.00
12 Peyton Watson 6.00 15.00
13 Keegan Murray 10.00 25.00
14 David Roddy 5.00 12.00
15 Ousmane Dieng 5.00 12.00
16 Jabari Smith Jr. 12.00 30.00
17 Johnny Davis 4.00 10.00
18 Kenneth Lofton Jr. 5.00 12.00
19 Jaden Ivey 12.00 30.00
20 Moussa Diabate 4.00 10.00
21 Chet Holmgren 20.00 50.00
22 Jaylin Williams 5.00 12.00
23 Kennedy Chandler 4.00 10.00
24 Jeremy Sochan 12.00 30.00
25 Bryce McGowens 4.00 10.00
26 Patrick Baldwin Jr. 4.00 10.00
27 Ochai Agbaji 5.00 12.00
28 Walker Kessler 8.00 20.00
29 Andrew Nembhard 8.00 20.00
30 Christian Koloko 4.00 10.00
31 Jake LaRavia 4.00 10.00
32 Jalen Duren 12.00 30.00
33 Shaedon Sharpe 15.00 40.00
34 Max Christie 10.00 25.00
35 Caleb Houstan 4.00 10.00
36 Jaden Hardy 6.00 15.00
37 Blake Wesley 4.00 10.00
38 Christian Braun 10.00 25.00
39 Paolo Banchero 25.00 60.00
40 Jalen Williams 20.00 50.00

2022-23 Immaculate Collection Remarkable Rookie Jerseys Dual

*RED/25: 1.25X TO 3X BASIC
1 Jalen Williams
Chet Holmgren 20.00 50.00
2 Jalen Duren
Walker Kessler 12.00 30.00
3 Jalen Williams
Shaedon Sharpe 20.00 50.00
4 Paolo Banchero
Jaden Ivey 25.00 60.00
5 Jeremy Sochan
Malaki Branham 12.00 30.00
6 Jaden Ivey
Jalen Duren 12.00 30.00
7 Jabari Smith Jr.
Keegan Murray 12.00 30.00
8 Paolo Banchero
Bennedict Mathurin 25.00 60.00
9 Ochai Agbaji
AJ Griffin 5.00 12.00
10 Dyson Daniels
Jeremy Sochan 12.00 30.00
11 Jaden Hardy
Johnny Davis 6.00 15.00
12 Mark Williams
Walker Kessler 8.00 20.00
13 Bennedict Mathurin
Andrew Nembhard 12.00 30.00
14 Keegan Murray
Shaedon Sharpe 15.00 40.00
15 Jabari Smith Jr.
Tari Eason 12.00 30.00

2022-23 Immaculate Collection Remarkable Rookie Jerseys Quad

*RED/10: 1.25X TO 3X BASIC
1 Keegan Murray
Chet Holmgren
Jabari Smith Jr.
Paolo Banchero 30.00 80.00
2 Bennedict Mathurin
Jalen Williams
Jaden Ivey
Shaedon Sharpe 25.00 60.00
3 Johnny Davis
Dyson Daniels
Tari Eason
Jeremy Sochan 15.00 40.00
4 Chet Holmgren
Ousmane Dieng
Jalen Williams
Jaylin Williams 25.00 60.00
5 Bennedict Mathurin
Keegan Murray
Paolo Banchero
Jalen Williams 30.00 80.00
6 Jalen Duren
Andrew Nembhard
Bennedict Mathurin
Jaden Ivey 15.00 40.00
7 Malaki Branham
Jabari Smith Jr.
Tari Eason
Jeremy Sochan 15.00 40.00
8 Mark Williams
Paolo Banchero
Wendell Moore Jr.
AJ Griffin 30.00 80.00
9 Dyson Daniels
Ousmane Dieng
Jaden Hardy
MarJon Beauchamp 12.00 30.00
10 Kenneth Lofton Jr.
David Roddy
Kennedy Chandler
Jake LaRavia 6.00 15.00

2022-23 Immaculate Collection Remarkable Rookie Jerseys Triple

*RED/25: 1.25X TO 3X BASIC
1 Jabari Smith Jr.
Tari Eason
TyTy Washington Jr. 12.00 30.00
2 Ousmane Dieng
Chet Holmgren
Jalen Williams 20.00 50.00
3 Blake Wesley
Malaki Branham
Jeremy Sochan 12.00 30.00
4 Chet Holmgren
Jabari Smith Jr.
Paolo Banchero 25.00 60.00
5 Jalen Williams
Paolo Banchero
Bennedict Mathurin 25.00 60.00
6 Mark Williams
Walker Kessler
Jalen Duren 12.00 30.00
7 AJ Griffin
Ochai Agbaji
Keegan Murray 10.00 25.00
8 Jaden Hardy
Jaden Ivey
Bennedict Mathurin 12.00 30.00
9 Tari Eason
Dyson Daniels
Jeremy Sochan 12.00 30.00
10 Keegan Murray
Shaedon Sharpe
Chet Holmgren 20.00 50.00

2022-23 Immaculate Collection Scorers Club Signatures

STATED PRINT RUN 25-99 SER.#'d SETS
1 Karl Malone/49 60.00 150.00
2 Paul Pierce/25 125.00 300.00
3 Bradley Beal/25 20.00 50.00
4 Dirk Nowitzki/25 150.00 400.00
5 Kareem Abdul-Jabbar/49 125.00 300.00
6 Alex English/75 12.00 30.00
7 Larry Bird/25 125.00 300.00
8 Stephen Curry/25 1,000.00 2,000.00
9 Kevin Garnett/25 125.00 300.00
10 Ray Allen/25 100.00 250.00
11 Charles Barkley/25 125.00 300.00
12 Ja Morant/25 350.00 700.00
13 Clyde Drexler/49 50.00 120.00
14 Dwyane Wade/25 125.00 300.00
15 Magic Johnson/25 125.00 300.00
16 James Harden/25 200.00 500.00
18 Hakeem Olajuwon/49 60.00 150.00
19 David Robinson/49 60.00 150.00
20 Tom Chambers/75 10.00 25.00
21 Gary Payton/49 40.00 100.00
22 Mitch Richmond/99 20.00 50.00
23 Pau Gasol/25 75.00 200.00
24 Luka Doncic/25 800.00 1,500.00
25 Allen Iverson/25 150.00 400.00

2022-23 Immaculate Collection Shadowbox Signatures

1 Chris Mullin/49 15.00 40.00
2 Hakeem Olajuwon/25 60.00 150.00
3 Bradley Beal/25 20.00 50.00
4 Maurice Cheeks/99 12.00 30.00
5 Jordan Clarkson/99 20.00 50.00
6 Shawn Kemp/99 40.00 100.00
7 Ja Morant/25 350.00 700.00
9 Antawn Jamison/75 12.00 30.00
10 Saddiq Bey/75 10.00 25.00
11 Dorian Finney-Smith/99 10.00 25.00
12 Bojan Bogdanovic/99 12.00 30.00
13 Luka Doncic/25 1,000.00 2,000.00
14 Tom Chambers/75 12.00 30.00
15 Antoine Walker/99 12.00 30.00
16 Bobby Portis/75 12.00 30.00
17 Seth Curry/99 12.00 30.00
18 Austin Reaves/99 75.00 200.00
19 Wally Szczerbiak/99 10.00 25.00
20 Malik Monk/99 10.00 25.00
21 Kevin Garnett/25 125.00 300.00
22 RJ Barrett/49 20.00 50.00
23 James Harden/25 200.00 500.00
24 Richard Hamilton/75 15.00 40.00
25 Dan Issel/99 15.00 40.00
26 Gary Payton/25 40.00 100.00
27 Brandon Ingram/25 40.00 100.00
28 Artis Gilmore/99 15.00 40.00
29 Charles Barkley/25 30.00 80.00
30 Nikola Vucevic/75 12.00 30.00
31 Rashard Lewis/99 10.00 25.00
32 Cole Anthony/49 20.00 50.00
33 Kareem Abdul-Jabbar/25 150.00 400.00
34 Larry Johnson/49 50.00 120.00
35 Marcus Smart/49 15.00 40.00
36 Juwan Howard/99 12.00 30.00
37 Carlos Boozer/99 12.00 30.00
38 Robert Horry/49 12.00 30.00
39 Jaren Jackson Jr./49 75.00 200.00
40 Allen Iverson/25 150.00 400.00
41 Steve Kerr/25 30.00 80.00
42 Nick Van Exel/99 20.00 50.00
43 Jrue Holiday/49 15.00 40.00
45 Magic Johnson/25 125.00 300.00
47 Tim Hardaway Jr./75 10.00 25.00
48 Ivica Zubac/99 12.00 30.00
49 Ayo Dosunmu/75 15.00 40.00

2022-23 Immaculate Collection Sneaker Swatches Signatures

*RED/5-25: .5X TO 1.25X BASIC
1 Chet Holmgren/25 800.00 1,500.00
2 Kevin Garnett/25 100.00 250.00
3 Allen Iverson/15 200.00 500.00
4 Johnny Davis/49 15.00 40.00
5 Jalen Williams/49 150.00 400.00
6 Clyde Drexler/25 125.00 300.00
7 Ochai Agbaji/49 20.00 50.00
8 AJ Griffin/49 12.00 30.00
9 Larry Johnson/25 125.00 300.00
11 Shawn Kemp/25 100.00 250.00
12 Andrew Nembhard/49 30.00 80.00
13 Charles Barkley/15 125.00 300.00
14 Shaedon Sharpe/49 125.00 300.00
15 Carmelo Anthony/15 125.00 300.00
16 Jalen Duren/49 75.00 200.00
17 Hakeem Olajuwon/25 100.00 250.00
18 John Stockton/15 125.00 300.00
19 Dyson Daniels/25 40.00 100.00
20 Max Christie/49 75.00 200.00
21 Paolo Banchero /49 500.00 1,000.00
22 James Harden/10 1,000.00 2,000.00
23 Jabari Smith Jr./40 150.00 400.00
24 David Roddy/49 20.00 50.00
25 Antoine Carr/49 12.00 30.00
26 Malaki Branham/49 15.00 40.00
27 Paul George/15 150.00 400.00
28 Chris Paul/15 125.00 300.00
29 Bennedict Mathurin/49 125.00 300.00
30 Jake LaRavia/49 15.00 40.00
31 RJ Barrett/25 75.00 200.00
32 Jeremy Sochan/25 125.00 300.00
33 Ralph Sampson/15 12.00 30.00
34 Walker Kessler/49 30.00 80.00
35 Pau Gasol/15 75.00 200.00
36 Christian Braun/49 40.00 100.00
37 Dalen Terry/49 15.00 40.00
38 Tari Eason/49 40.00 100.00
39 Dwyane Wade/15 150.00 400.00
40 Jaden Hardy/49 40.00 100.00
41 Nikola Jovic/49 40.00 100.00
42 Keegan Murray/40 100.00 250.00
43 Glen Rice/25 15.00 40.00
44 Amar'e Stoudemire/25 15.00 40.00
45 Blake Wesley/49 15.00 40.00
46 Dominique Wilkins/25 75.00 200.00
47 Ousmane Dieng/49 20.00 50.00
48 Karl Malone/15 100.00 250.00
49 MarJon Beauchamp/49 15.00 40.00
50 Jaden Ivey/49 100.00 250.00

2022-23 Immaculate Collection Sole of the Game

2 Bennedict Mathurin/11 150.00 400.00
3 Zach LaVine/8 100.00 250.00
7 Paolo Banchero /8 200.00 500.00
8 D'Angelo Russell/25 25.00 60.00
15 Chet Holmgren/25 200.00 500.00
16 Jaden Ivey/25 60.00 150.00
17 Shaedon Sharpe/18 75.00 200.00
18 Paul George/4 125.00 300.00
19 Anthony Davis/25 50.00 120.00
20 Blake Griffin/25 50.00 120.00
21 Jabari Smith Jr./25 75.00 200.00
23 Keegan Murray/12 75.00 200.00
24 Tom Chambers/6 40.00 100.00
25 Karl Malone/9 75.00 200.00

2022-23 Immaculate Collection Sophisticated Signatures

*RED/25: .5X TO 1.2X BASIC
1 Nikola Jokic/49 150.00 400.00
2 Chris Mullin/99 12.00 30.00
3 Zach Randolph/99 10.00 25.00
4 Anthony Edwards/49 200.00 500.00
5 Cade Cunningham/99 75.00 200.00
6 Bob Dandridge/99 10.00 25.00
7 Bradley Beal/75 20.00 50.00
8 Stephen Jackson/99 10.00 25.00
9 Nikola Vucevic/99 10.00 25.00
12 Fat Lever/99 8.00 20.00
13 RJ Barrett/99 20.00 50.00
14 Alperen Sengun/99 75.00 200.00
15 Nick Van Exel/99 20.00 50.00
16 Ray Allen/99 75.00 200.00
17 Dominique Wilkins/99 25.00 60.00
19 Adrian Dantley/99 10.00 25.00
22 Dell Curry/99 10.00 25.00
23 Tony Allen/99 6.00 15.00
24 David Thompson/99 12.00 30.00
25 Precious Achiuwa/99 10.00 25.00
26 Dirk Nowitzki/49 100.00 250.00
27 Bob McAdoo/99 12.00 30.00
28 Bernard King/99 12.00 30.00
29 Manu Ginobili/75 40.00 100.00
30 Pau Gasol/75 40.00 100.00

2022-23 Immaculate Collection Standout Memorabilia

*RED/10-25: 1.25X TO 3X BASIC
1 Nikola Jokic 25.00 60.00
2 Christian Wood 3.00 8.00
3 Cameron Johnson 4.00 10.00
4 Andrew Wiggins 6.00 15.00
5 Bones Hyland 4.00 10.00
6 RJ Barrett 8.00 20.00
7 Saddiq Bey 4.00 10.00
8 Scottie Barnes 8.00 20.00
9 Spencer Dinwiddie 4.00 10.00
10 Zion Williamson 12.00 30.00
11 Tyrese Maxey 10.00 25.00
12 Zach LaVine 10.00 25.00
13 DeMar DeRozan 6.00 15.00
14 LeBron James 40.00 100.00
15 Giannis Antetokounmpo 25.00 60.00
16 Luka Doncic 30.00 80.00
17 Ja Morant 15.00 40.00
18 Julius Randle 6.00 15.00
19 Pascal Siakam 8.00 20.00
20 Josh Giddey 8.00 20.00

2022-23 Immaculate Collection Swatches

*RED/10-25: 1.25X TO 3X BASIC
1 Jayson Tatum 20.00 50.00
2 LeBron James 40.00 100.00
3 Julius Randle 6.00 15.00
4 Luka Doncic 30.00 80.00
5 Nikola Jokic 25.00 60.00
6 Zach LaVine 10.00 25.00
7 RJ Barrett 8.00 20.00
8 Shai Gilgeous-Alexander 25.00 60.00
9 Jamal Murray 8.00 20.00
10 Joel Embiid 8.00 20.00
11 Gordon Hayward 4.00 10.00
12 Immanuel Quickley 5.00 12.00
13 Jaden McDaniels 5.00 12.00
14 Jae Crowder 3.00 8.00
15 Jalen Brunson 10.00 25.00
16 James Bouknight 3.00 8.00
17 Jaren Jackson Jr. 8.00 20.00
18 John Collins 5.00 12.00
19 John Wall 6.00 15.00
20 Jonathan Isaac 5.00 12.00
21 Paul George 8.00 20.00
22 PJ Washington Jr. 5.00 12.00
23 Miles McBride 5.00 12.00
24 Royce O'Neale 4.00 10.00
25 T.J. Warren 4.00 10.00
26 Terance Mann 4.00 10.00
27 Terrence Ross 5.00 12.00
28 Alperen Sengun 6.00 15.00
29 Bojan Bogdanovic 5.00 12.00
30 Bruce Brown 5.00 12.00
31 Dennis Schroder 5.00 12.00
32 Derrick Rose 10.00 25.00
33 Derrick White 5.00 12.00
34 Desmond Bane 6.00 15.00
35 Dillon Brooks 5.00 12.00
36 Domantas Sabonis 6.00 15.00
37 Draymond Green 6.00 15.00
38 Georges Niang 4.00 10.00
39 Isaiah Stewart 4.00 10.00
40 Jakob Poeltl 4.00 10.00

2022-23 Immaculate Collection The Standard

STATED PRINT RUN 99 SER.#'d SETS
1 Trae Young 12.00 30.00
2 Robert Williams III 4.00 10.00
3 Kevin Durant 15.00 40.00
4 Kyrie Irving 10.00 25.00
5 Ben Simmons 5.00 12.00
6 T.J. Warren 4.00 10.00
7 LaMelo Ball 12.00 30.00
8 James Bouknight 3.00 8.00
9 Gordon Hayward 4.00 10.00
10 Terry Rozier III 6.00 15.00
11 Alex Caruso 5.00 12.00
12 DeMar DeRozan 6.00 15.00
13 Zach LaVine 10.00 25.00
14 Darius Garland 8.00 20.00
15 Caris LeVert 4.00 10.00
16 Kevin Love 5.00 12.00
17 Ricky Rubio 5.00 12.00
18 Luka Doncic 30.00 80.00
19 Jamal Murray 8.00 20.00
20 Michael Porter Jr. 6.00 15.00
21 Stephen Curry 40.00 100.00
22 Draymond Green 6.00 15.00
23 Klay Thompson 12.00 30.00
24 Andrew Wiggins 6.00 15.00
25 Jalen Green 15.00 40.00
26 Myles Turner 5.00 12.00
27 Reggie Jackson 4.00 10.00
28 Kawhi Leonard 12.00 30.00
29 Norman Powell 5.00 12.00
30 John Wall 6.00 15.00
31 Anthony Davis 12.00 30.00
32 LeBron James 40.00 100.00
33 Lonnie Walker IV 4.00 10.00
34 Russell Westbrook 8.00 20.00
35 Ja Morant 15.00 40.00
36 Bam Adebayo 8.00 20.00
37 Jimmy Butler 10.00 25.00
38 Tyler Herro 8.00 20.00
39 Kyle Lowry 6.00 15.00
40 Victor Oladipo 4.00 10.00
41 Giannis Antetokounmpo 25.00 60.00
42 Jrue Holiday 6.00 15.00
43 Rudy Gobert 6.00 15.00
44 D'Angelo Russell 4.00 10.00
45 CJ McCollum 5.00 12.00
46 Zion Williamson 12.00 30.00
47 RJ Barrett 8.00 20.00
48 Cam Reddish 4.00 10.00
49 Joel Embiid 8.00 20.00
50 James Harden 10.00 25.00
51 Tyrese Maxey 10.00 25.00
52 P.J. Tucker 4.00 10.00
53 Devin Booker 12.00 30.00
54 Mikal Bridges 6.00 15.00
55 Cameron Johnson 4.00 10.00
56 Chris Paul 10.00 25.00
57 Jerami Grant 6.00 15.00
58 Josh Hart 5.00 12.00
59 Anfernee Simons 6.00 15.00
60 De'Aaron Fox 10.00 25.00
61 Davion Mitchell 4.00 10.00
62 Domantas Sabonis 6.00 15.00
63 Keldon Johnson 6.00 15.00
64 Devin Vassell 6.00 15.00
65 OG Anunoby 6.00 15.00
66 Scottie Barnes 8.00 20.00
67 Pascal Siakam 8.00 20.00
68 Fred VanVleet 6.00 15.00
69 Jordan Clarkson 5.00 12.00
70 Mike Conley 4.00 10.00
71 Georges Niang 4.00 10.00
72 Bradley Beal 6.00 15.00
73 Kyle Kuzma 6.00 15.00
74 Kristaps Porzingis 6.00 15.00
75 Jayson Tatum 20.00 50.00
76 Jaylen Brown 10.00 25.00
77 Immanuel Quickley 5.00 12.00
78 Tobias Harris 4.00 10.00
79 Jarrett Allen 5.00 12.00
80 Dejounte Murray 6.00 15.00
81 Donovan Mitchell 10.00 25.00
83 Markelle Fultz 4.00 10.00
84 Karl-Anthony Towns 8.00 20.00
85 Shai Gilgeous-Alexander 25.00 60.00
86 Josh Giddey 8.00 20.00
87 Damian Lillard 12.00 30.00
88 Tyrese Haliburton 10.00 25.00
89 Luke Kennard 4.00 10.00
90 Tyus Jones 4.00 10.00
91 Marcus Smart 6.00 15.00
92 Mitchell Robinson 5.00 12.00
93 Santi Aldama 5.00 12.00
94 Tre Mann 4.00 10.00
95 Onyeka Okongwu 5.00 12.00
96 Cameron Thomas 8.00 20.00
97 Quentin Grimes 4.00 10.00
98 John Collins 5.00 12.00
99 Malcolm Brogdon 4.00 10.00
100 Dorian Finney-Smith 4.00 10.00

1991 Impel U.S. Olympic Hall of Fame

COMPLETE SET (90) 6.00 15.00
55 Bill Bradley .20 .50
56 Lucious Jackson .12 .30
57 1964 U.S. Basketball Team
Soviet player .12 .30
58 Bill Bradley .20 .50
59 1964 U.S. Basketball Team Photo .12 .30
60 Lucious Jackson
Bill Bradley .20 .50
61 Henry Iba CO .12 .30
74 Henry Iba .10 .25

1992 Impel U.S. Olympic Hopefuls

COMPLETE SET (110) 8.00 20.00
7 U.S. Olympic Baseball Team .20 .50
8 Charles Barkley BK .75 2.00
9 Larry Bird BK .75 2.00
10 Patrick Ewing BK .40 1.00
11 Magic Johnson BK .60 1.50
12 Michael Jordan BK 2.00 5.00
13 Karl Malone BK .40 1.00
14 Chris Mullin BK .20 .50
15 Scottie Pippen BK .75 2.00
16 David Robinson BK .50 1.25
17 John Stockton BK .40 1.00
18 U.S. Olympic Basketball Team 1.00 2.50
19 Teresa Edwards BK .10 .25
20 Bridgette Gordon BK .10 .25
21 Andrea Lloyd BK .10 .25
22 Katrina McClain BK .10 .25

1994-95 Imprinted Pins

COMPLETE SET (29) 20.00 50.00
1 Atlanta Hawks .75 2.00
2 Boston Celtics 1.25 3.00
3 Charlotte Hornets .75 2.00
4 Chicago Bulls 1.25 3.00
5 Cleveland Cavaliers .75 2.00
6 Dallas Mavericks .75 2.00
7 Denver Nuggets .75 2.00
8 Detroit Pistons .75 2.00
9 Golden State Warriors .75 2.00
10 Houston Rockets .75 2.00
11 Indiana Pacers .75 2.00
12 Los Angeles Clippers .75 2.00
13 Los Angeles Lakers 1.25 3.00
14 Miami Heat .75 2.00
15 Milwaukee Bucks .75 2.00
16 Minnesota Timberwolves .75 2.00
17 New Jersey Nets .75 2.00
18 New York Knicks 1.25 3.00
19 Orlando Magic 1.25 3.00
20 Philadelphia 76ers .75 2.00
21 Phoenix Suns .75 2.00
22 Portland Trail Blazers .75 2.00
23 Sacramento Kings .75 2.00
24 San Antonio Spurs .75 2.00
25 Seattle Supersonics .75 2.00
26 Toronto Raptors .75 2.00
27 Utah Jazz .75 2.00
28 Vancouver Grizzlies .75 2.00
29 Washington Bullets .75 2.00

2012-13 Innovation

101-175 PRINT RUN 349 SER.#'d SETS
176-200 PRINT RUN 349 SER.#'d SETS
1 Serge Ibaka .60 1.50
2 Tony Parker 1.25 3.00
3 Shawn Marion .75 2.00
4 Jameer Nelson .50 1.25
5 Chris Bosh 1.00 2.50
6 Taj Gibson .50 1.25
7 Dwight Howard 1.00 2.50
8 Tyson Chandler .60 1.50
9 Grant Hill 1.25 3.00
10 James Harden 1.50 4.00
11 Nene .60 1.50
12 Kevin Love .75 2.00
13 Dirk Nowitzki 2.00 5.00
14 Raymond Felton .50 1.25
15 O.J. Mayo .50 1.25
16 Jason Kidd 1.25 3.00
17 Gerald Henderson .50 1.25
18 Russell Westbrook 1.25 3.00
19 LaMarcus Aldridge .75 2.00
20 Ray Allen 1.25 3.00
21 Jeremy Lin 1.25 3.00
22 Larry Sanders .50 1.25
23 LeBron James 6.00 15.00
24 Joakim Noah .60 1.50
25 Ersan Ilyasova .50 1.25
26 Steve Novak .50 1.25
27 Andrew Bogut .60 1.50
28 Jrue Holiday 1.00 2.50
29 Paul George 1.25 3.00
30 Marc Gasol .75 2.00
31 Manu Ginobili 1.50 4.00
32 Eric Gordon .60 1.50
33 Anderson Varejao .50 1.25
34 Vince Carter 1.50 4.00
35 JaVale McGee .60 1.50
36 Roy Hibbert .60 1.50
37 DeMarcus Cousins .75 2.00
38 Andre Miller .60 1.50
39 Blake Griffin .75 2.00
40 Nicolas Batum .60 1.50
41 John Wall 1.00 2.50
42 Metta World Peace .60 1.50
43 Tim Duncan 2.00 5.00
44 Stephen Curry 6.00 15.00
45 Brandon Jennings .50 1.25
46 Kevin Martin .60 1.50
47 Goran Dragic .75 2.00
48 Ricky Rubio .60 1.50
49 Tyreke Evans .60 1.50
50 Derrick Rose 1.25 3.00
51 Greivis Vasquez .50 1.25
52 Jose Calderon .50 1.25
53 Kobe Bryant 6.00 15.00
54 Marcin Gortat .50 1.25
55 Josh Smith .50 1.25
56 Jeff Teague .50 1.25
57 Rudy Gay .75 2.00
58 Ty Lawson .50 1.25
59 Chris Paul 1.50 4.00
60 David West .60 1.50
61 Paul Pierce 1.25 3.00
62 Joe Johnson .60 1.50
63 Andre Iguodala .75 2.00
64 Brook Lopez .60 1.50
65 Al Jefferson .50 1.25
66 Dwyane Wade 1.50 4.00
67 Carmelo Anthony 1.25 3.00
68 Ben Gordon .60 1.50
69 Jamal Crawford .75 2.00
70 Deron Williams .60 1.50
71 Greg Monroe .50 1.25
72 Al Horford .75 2.00
73 Rajon Rondo 1.00 2.50
74 Chauncey Billups 1.00 2.50
75 Nick Young .50 1.25
76 J.J. Redick .75 2.00
77 Kevin Garnett 2.00 5.00
78 Luol Deng .60 1.50
79 Kyle Lowry .75 2.00
80 Kevin Durant 3.00 8.00
81 Evan Turner .50 1.25
82 David Lee .50 1.25
83 Steve Nash 1.50 4.00
84 Gordon Hayward .75 2.00
85 Zach Randolph .75 2.00
86 Dominique Wilkins 1.00 2.50
87 Magic Johnson 2.50 6.00
88 Yao Ming 1.50 4.00
89 Shaquille O'Neal 2.50 6.00
90 Scottie Pippen 2.00 5.00
91 Pete Maravich 1.50 4.00
92 Bill Walton 1.25 3.00
93 David Robinson 1.25 3.00
94 Dennis Rodman 2.00 5.00
95 Hakeem Olajuwon 1.50 4.00
96 Jerry West 1.50 4.00
97 Larry Bird 2.50 6.00
98 Kareem Abdul-Jabbar 2.50 6.00
99 Julius Erving 2.00 5.00
100 Nate Archibald 1.00 2.50
101 Tyler Zeller RC 1.25 3.00
102 Jimmy Butler RC 40.00 100.00
103 Tristan Thompson RC 2.00 5.00
104 Nikola Vucevic RC 5.00 12.00
105 Mirza Teletovic RC 1.50 4.00
106 E'Twaun Moore RC 1.50 4.00
107 Harrison Barnes RC 2.50 6.00
108 DeAndre Liggins RC 1.25 3.00
109 Kenneth Faried RC 1.50 4.00
110 Enes Kanter RC 2.00 5.00
111 Brian Roberts RC 1.25 3.00
112 Kent Bazemore RC 2.00 5.00
113 Kawhi Leonard RC 75.00 200.00
114 Chandler Parsons RC 1.50 4.00
115 Gustavo Ayon RC 1.25 3.00
116 Jeff Taylor RC 1.25 3.00
117 Klay Thompson RC 12.00 30.00
118 Pablo Prigioni RC 1.25 3.00
119 Nolan Smith RC 1.25 3.00
120 Kim English RC 1.25 3.00
121 Derrick Williams RC 1.25 3.00
122 Miles Plumlee RC 1.25 3.00
123 Michael Kidd-Gilchrist RC 1.50 4.00
124 Kyle Singler RC 1.25 3.00
125 Darius Miller RC 1.50 4.00
126 Isaiah Thomas RC 2.50 6.00
127 Alexey Shved RC 1.25 3.00
128 Jonas Valanciunas RC 2.50 6.00
129 Darius Morris RC 1.50 4.00
130 Alec Burks RC 2.00 5.00
131 Julyan Stone RC 1.25 3.00
132 Kemba Walker RC 8.00 20.00
133 Jae Crowder RC 2.50 6.00
134 Terrence Jones RC 1.25 3.00
135 Evan Fournier RC 2.00 5.00
136 Meyers Leonard RC 1.50 4.00
137 Markieff Morris RC 2.00 5.00
138 Victor Claver RC 1.25 3.00
139 Jeremy Lamb RC 2.00 5.00
140 Jeremy Pargo RC 1.25 3.00
141 Jimmer Fredette RC 2.00 5.00
142 Damian Lillard RC 50.00 120.00
143 Festus Ezeli RC 1.25 3.00
144 Jan Vesely RC 1.25 3.00
145 Iman Shumpert RC 1.50 4.00
146 Tobias Harris RC 4.00 10.00
147 Austin Rivers RC 2.00 5.00
148 Reggie Jackson RC 2.00 5.00
149 Greg Stiemsma RC 1.25 3.00
150 Chris Copeland RC 1.25 3.00
151 Will Barton RC 2.50 6.00
152 Andre Drummond RC 3.00 8.00
153 Anthony Davis RC 75.00 200.00
154 John Henson RC 1.50 4.00
155 Orlando Johnson RC 1.25 3.00
156 Brandon Knight RC 1.50 4.00
157 Andrew Nicholson RC 1.25 3.00
158 Draymond Green RC 8.00 20.00
159 Terrence Ross RC 3.00 8.00
160 MarShon Brooks RC 1.25 3.00
161 Kyrie Irving RC 20.00 50.00
162 Marcus Morris RC 2.00 5.00
163 Lavoy Allen RC 1.25 3.00
164 Thomas Robinson RC 1.25 3.00
165 Jared Cunningham RC 1.25 3.00
166 Jared Sullinger RC 1.25 3.00
167 Nando De Colo RC 1.25 3.00
168 Bradley Beal RC 15.00 40.00
169 Tornike Shengelia RC 1.25 3.00
170 Lance Thomas RC 1.25 3.00
171 Norris Cole RC 1.25 3.00
172 Jordan Hamilton RC 1.25 3.00
173 Kendall Marshall RC 1.25 3.00
174 Dion Waiters RC 1.50 4.00
175 John Jenkins RC 1.25 3.00
176 Kobe Bryant/349 12.00 30.00
177 Tyson Chandler/349 1.25 3.00
178 Ricky Rubio/349 1.25 3.00
179 Deron Williams/349 1.25 3.00
180 John Wall/349 2.00 5.00
181 Chris Paul/349 3.00 8.00
182 Carmelo Anthony/349 2.50 6.00
183 Paul George/349 2.50 6.00
184 Derrick Rose/349 2.50 6.00
185 Kevin Durant/349 6.00 15.00
186 Steve Nash/349 3.00 8.00
187 Dwyane Wade/349 3.00 8.00
188 Kevin Garnett/349 4.00 10.00
189 Joakim Noah/349 1.25 3.00
190 Russell Westbrook/349 2.50 6.00
191 Dirk Nowitzki/349 4.00 10.00
192 LeBron James/349 12.00 30.00
193 Paul Pierce/349 2.50 6.00
194 Andre Iguodala/349 1.50 4.00
195 James Harden/349 3.00 8.00
196 Vince Carter/349 3.00 8.00
197 Kevin Love/349 1.50 4.00
198 Rajon Rondo/349 2.00 5.00
199 Stephen Curry/349 12.00 30.00
200 Blake Griffin/349 1.50 4.00

2012-13 Innovation Red

*RED 101-175: 1.2X TO 3X BASIC
*RED 175-200: 1.5X TO 4X BASIC
STATED PRINT RUN 25 SER.#'d SETS
113 Kawhi Leonard 500.00 1,000.00
153 Anthony Davis 400.00 800.00
176 Kobe Bryant 60.00 150.00
192 LeBron James 100.00 250.00
199 Stephen Curry 40.00 100.00

2012-13 Innovation All Rookies

1 Kyrie Irving 15.00 40.00
2 Bradley Beal 12.00 30.00
3 Andre Drummond 4.00 10.00
4 Anthony Davis 20.00 50.00
5 Kenneth Faried 2.00 5.00
6 Harrison Barnes 3.00 8.00
7 Damian Lillard 40.00 100.00
8 Kemba Walker 6.00 15.00
9 Chandler Parsons 2.00 5.00
10 Dion Waiters 2.00 5.00

2012-13 Innovation Efficiency

1 Joakim Noah 1.25 3.00
2 James Harden 3.00 8.00
3 David Lee 1.00 2.50
4 Blake Griffin 1.50 4.00
5 Carmelo Anthony 2.50 6.00
6 Chris Paul 3.00 8.00
7 LaMarcus Aldridge 1.50 4.00
8 Kevin Love 1.50 4.00
9 Nikola Vucevic 4.00 10.00
10 Rajon Rondo 2.00 5.00
11 Tony Parker 2.50 6.00
12 LeBron James 12.00 30.00
13 Deron Williams 1.25 3.00
14 Russell Westbrook 2.50 6.00
15 Tim Duncan 4.00 10.00

2012-13 Innovation Fine Print Autographs

EXCHANGE DEADLINE 03/04/2015
1 Nikola Pekovic 3.00 8.00
2 Mark Price 5.00 12.00
3 Kevin Durant 125.00 300.00
4 Mario Chalmers 4.00 10.00
5 Jarrett Jack 4.00 10.00
6 Danilo Gallinari 3.00 8.00
7 Ryan Anderson 3.00 8.00
8 Kobe Bryant 800.00 1,500.00
9 Walt Frazier 15.00 40.00
10 Antawn Jamison 4.00 10.00
11 Cedric Ceballos 4.00 10.00
12 Antoine Walker 4.00 10.00
13 Elvin Hayes 6.00 15.00
14 James Worthy 12.00 30.00
15 Jason Terry 4.00 10.00
16 Jeff Green 3.00 8.00
17 Ed Davis 3.00 8.00
18 Alan Anderson 3.00 8.00
19 Tim Hardaway 10.00 25.00
20 Joel Anthony 3.00 8.00
21 Blake Griffin 12.00 30.00
22 George Gervin 12.00 30.00
23 Nick Anderson 4.00 10.00
24 Arnie Risen 15.00 40.00
25 George McGinnis 5.00 12.00
26 Jerry West 30.00 80.00
27 Patrick Beverley 8.00 20.00
28 Tom Chambers 5.00 12.00
29 Hakeem Olajuwon 30.00 80.00
30 Jim Jackson 4.00 10.00
31 Randy Foye 3.00 8.00
32 Clyde Drexler 20.00 50.00
33 Alex English 6.00 15.00
34 Doug Christie 3.00 8.00
35 Kevin Martin 4.00 10.00
36 Nick Collison 3.00 8.00
37 Greg Monroe 3.00 8.00
38 Wesley Matthews 3.00 8.00
39 Serge Ibaka 4.00 10.00
40 Rick Mahorn 3.00 8.00
41 DeMarcus Cousins 5.00 12.00
42 Nate Archibald 6.00 15.00
43 David Robinson 30.00 80.00
44 Jerryd Bayless 3.00 8.00
45 Anfernee Hardaway 30.00 80.00
46 Jay Williams 3.00 8.00
47 Roy Hibbert 4.00 10.00
48 Chris Bosh 6.00 15.00
49 Tyson Chandler 4.00 10.00
50 J.J. Redick 5.00 12.00
51 Damian Lillard 150.00 400.00

2012-13 Innovation Innovative Ink

EXCHANGE DEADLINE 03/04/2015
1 Chris Bosh 20.00 50.00
2 Steve Nash 40.00 100.00
3 Josh Smith 3.00 8.00
4 Blake Griffin 12.00 30.00
5 Kobe Bryant 600.00 1,200.00
6 Ryan Anderson 3.00 8.00
7 George Hill 4.00 10.00
8 J.J. Redick 5.00 12.00
9 Antawn Jamison 4.00 10.00
10 Jarrett Jack 4.00 10.00

11 Gordon Hayward 5.00 12.00
12 Grant Hill 20.00 50.00
13 Andre Iguodala 5.00 12.00
14 Stephen Curry 600.00 1,200.00
15 Anderson Varejao 3.00 8.00
16 Andre Miller 4.00 10.00
17 Nick Young 3.00 8.00
18 Larry Bird 75.00 200.00
19 Magic Johnson 75.00 200.00
20 Bill Russell 600.00 1,200.00
21 Chris Mullin 6.00 15.00
22 Bernard King 6.00 15.00
23 Greg Monroe 3.00 8.00
24 Taj Gibson 3.00 8.00
25 Kevin Durant 125.00 300.00
26 Tom Chambers 5.00 12.00
27 Rashard Lewis 5.00 12.00
28 Earl Clark 3.00 8.00
29 Courtney Lee 3.00 8.00
30 Marcus Camby 5.00 12.00
31 Jamaal Wilkes 5.00 12.00
32 Kyle Korver 4.00 10.00
33 Kyle Lowry 10.00 25.00
34 Dan Issel 5.00 12.00
35 Sean Elliott 4.00 10.00
36 Dorell Wright 3.00 8.00
37 Ronnie Brewer 3.00 8.00
38 Tim Hardaway 12.00 30.00
39 Anfernee Hardaway 75.00 200.00
40 Udonis Haslem 4.00 10.00

2012-13 Innovation Innovators

1 Dominique Wilkins 2.00 5.00
2 Kareem Abdul-Jabbar 5.00 12.00
3 Gary Payton 2.00 5.00
4 Shaquille O'Neal 5.00 12.00
5 Allen Iverson 2.50 6.00
6 Bill Russell 5.00 12.00
7 Hakeem Olajuwon 3.00 8.00
8 Bernard King 2.00 5.00
9 David Robinson 2.50 6.00
10 Dennis Rodman 4.00 10.00
11 Ray Allen 2.50 6.00
12 Kevin Garnett 4.00 10.00
13 Kyrie Irving 10.00 25.00
14 Kevin Durant 6.00 15.00
15 Dwyane Wade 3.00 8.00
16 Tim Duncan 4.00 10.00
17 Carmelo Anthony 2.50 6.00
18 LeBron James 12.00 30.00
19 Dirk Nowitzki 4.00 10.00
20 Kobe Bryant 12.00 30.00

2012-13 Innovation Jerseys

PRINT RUNS B/WN 49-199 COPIES PER
1 Joakim Noah/49 3.00 8.00
2 Emeka Okafor/49 3.00 8.00
3 Tony Parker/49 6.00 15.00
4 Goran Dragic/99 4.00 10.00
5 Kevin Durant/99 15.00 40.00
6 Eric Gordon/99 3.00 8.00
7 Ray Allen/49 6.00 15.00
8 Kobe Bryant/99 30.00 80.00
9 James Harden/99 8.00 20.00
10 Dirk Nowitzki/99 10.00 25.00
11 Deron Williams/49 3.00 8.00
12 Al Horford/199 4.00 10.00
13 Mo Williams/99 3.00 8.00
14 Tim Duncan/199 10.00 25.00
15 Jameer Nelson/199 2.50 6.00
16 Tyson Chandler/99 3.00 8.00
17 Ricky Rubio/199 3.00 8.00
18 LeBron James/99 30.00 80.00
19 Dwight Howard/199 5.00 12.00
20 Carl Landry/49 2.50 6.00
21 O.J. Mayo/199 2.50 6.00
22 Brandon Bass/99 2.50 6.00
24 Derrick Favors/99 3.00 8.00
25 Tyreke Evans/99 3.00 8.00
26 Glen Davis/99 2.50 6.00
27 Marcus Camby/49 4.00 10.00
28 Kevin Love/199 4.00 10.00
29 Dwyane Wade/99 5.00 12.00
30 Jamal Crawford/99 4.00 10.00
31 Stephen Curry/199 10.00 25.00
32 Anderson Varejao/99 2.50 6.00
33 Paul Pierce/99 6.00 15.00
34 Devin Harris/99 2.50 6.00
35 Al Jefferson/99 2.50 6.00
36 DeMarcus Cousins/99 4.00 10.00
37 Arron Afflalo/99 2.50 6.00
38 Kurt Thomas/199 2.50 6.00
39 Andrei Kirilenko/99 3.00 8.00
40 Zach Randolph/199 4.00 10.00
41 DeAndre Jordan/49 3.00 8.00
42 David Lee/99 2.50 6.00
43 Ben Gordon/199 2.50 6.00
44 Kevin Garnett/49 10.00 25.00
45 Nene/149 3.00 8.00
46 Rudy Gay/199 4.00 10.00
47 LaMarcus Aldridge/99 4.00 10.00
48 Serge Ibaka/199 3.00 8.00
49 Jason Kidd/199 6.00 15.00
51 Tayshaun Prince/199 4.00 10.00
52 Blake Griffin/99 4.00 10.00
53 Greg Monroe/49 2.50 6.00
54 Joe Johnson/99 3.00 8.00
55 Rajon Rondo/99 5.00 12.00
56 Derrick Rose/49 6.00 15.00
57 DeMar DeRozan/199 5.00 12.00
59 Russell Westbrook/149 6.00 15.00
60 Carmelo Anthony/99 6.00 15.00
61 Drew Gooden/199 3.00 8.00
62 Marc Gasol/49 4.00 10.00
63 Paul George/99 10.00 25.00
65 Brook Lopez/99 3.00 8.00
66 John Wall/199 5.00 12.00
67 Josh Smith/199 2.50 6.00
68 Andrea Bargnani/199 2.50 6.00
69 Luis Scola/99 3.00 8.00
70 Kevin Martin/99 3.00 8.00
71 Amare Stoudemire/199 4.00 10.00
72 Brandon Jennings/199 2.50 6.00
73 Steve Nash/99 8.00 20.00
74 Jeremy Lin/99 6.00 15.00
75 Elton Brand/99 3.00 8.00

2012-13 Innovation Laser Cut

1 Kevin Love 4.00 10.00
2 Tony Parker 6.00 15.00
3 Chris Bosh 5.00 12.00
4 Dwight Howard 5.00 12.00
5 Tyson Chandler 3.00 8.00
6 Grant Hill 6.00 15.00
7 Paul George 6.00 15.00
8 James Harden 8.00 20.00
9 Dirk Nowitzki 10.00 25.00
10 Russell Westbrook 6.00 15.00
11 Marc Gasol 4.00 10.00
12 Ersan Ilyasova 2.50 6.00
13 Eric Gordon 3.00 8.00
14 Jrue Holiday 5.00 12.00
15 LaMarcus Aldridge 4.00 10.00
16 Ray Allen 6.00 15.00
17 Jeremy Lin 6.00 15.00
18 LeBron James 40.00 100.00
19 Joakim Noah 3.00 8.00
20 Vince Carter 8.00 20.00
21 Jonas Valanciunas 5.00 12.00
22 Kemba Walker 10.00 25.00
23 Jimmer Fredette 4.00 10.00
24 Damian Lillard 25.00 60.00
25 Andre Iguodala 4.00 10.00
26 Al Jefferson 2.50 6.00
27 Dwyane Wade 8.00 20.00
28 Andre Drummond 6.00 15.00
29 Harrison Barnes 5.00 12.00
30 DeMarcus Cousins 4.00 10.00
31 Blake Griffin 4.00 10.00
32 Tyreke Evans 3.00 8.00
33 John Wall 5.00 12.00
34 Tim Duncan 10.00 25.00
35 Stephen Curry 40.00 100.00
36 Brandon Jennings 2.50 6.00
37 Carmelo Anthony 6.00 15.00
38 Goran Dragic 4.00 10.00
39 Ricky Rubio 3.00 8.00
40 Kobe Bryant 30.00 80.00
41 Derrick Rose 6.00 15.00
42 David West 3.00 8.00
43 Chris Paul 8.00 20.00
44 Marcin Gortat 2.50 6.00
45 Josh Smith 2.50 6.00
46 Rudy Gay 4.00 10.00
47 Paul Pierce 6.00 15.00
48 Kyrie Irving 25.00 60.00
49 Andrew Nicholson 2.50 6.00
50 Michael Kidd-Gilchrist 3.00 8.00
51 Gordon Hayward 4.00 10.00
52 Zach Randolph 4.00 10.00
53 Dominique Wilkins 5.00 12.00
54 Magic Johnson 12.00 30.00
55 Shaquille O'Neal 12.00 30.00
56 David Robinson 6.00 15.00
57 Anfernee Hardaway 10.00 25.00
58 Larry Bird 15.00 40.00
59 Julius Erving 10.00 25.00
60 Kenneth Faried 3.00 8.00
61 Bradley Beal 20.00 50.00
62 Anthony Davis 30.00 80.00
63 Deron Williams 3.00 8.00
64 Kawhi Leonard 60.00 150.00
65 Chandler Parsons 3.00 8.00
66 Rajon Rondo 5.00 12.00
67 Klay Thompson 30.00 80.00
68 Greg Monroe 2.50 6.00
69 Nikola Vucevic 10.00 25.00
70 Brandon Knight 3.00 8.00
71 Dion Waiters 3.00 8.00
72 Kevin Garnett 10.00 25.00
73 Kevin Durant 20.00 50.00
74 David Lee 2.50 6.00
75 Steve Nash 8.00 20.00

2012-13 Innovation Laser Cut Accomplishments

1 Steve Nash 15.00 40.00
4 Grant Hill 15.00 40.00
9 Rajon Rondo 12.00 30.00
10 Tracy McGrady 50.00 120.00
12 Derrick Rose 12.00 30.00
17 Chris Bosh 5.00 12.00
19 Kyrie Irving 60.00 150.00
22 Blake Griffin 15.00 40.00
24 Tony Parker 6.00 15.00

2012-13 Innovation Passing Grade

1 Steve Nash 2.50 6.00
2 Jason Kidd 2.00 5.00
3 Damian Lillard 15.00 40.00
4 Ricky Rubio 1.00 2.50
5 Jrue Holiday 1.50 4.00
6 Rajon Rondo 1.50 4.00
7 Chris Paul 2.50 6.00
8 Tony Parker 2.00 5.00
9 Deron Williams 1.00 2.50
10 Greivis Vasquez .75 2.00

2012-13 Innovation Pride of the NBA

1 LeBron James 15.00 40.00
2 Kobe Bryant 15.00 40.00
3 Anthony Davis 15.00 40.00
4 Kyrie Irving 12.00 30.00
5 Paul Pierce 3.00 8.00
6 Tim Duncan 5.00 12.00
7 Derrick Rose 3.00 8.00
8 Kevin Durant 8.00 20.00
9 Steve Nash 4.00 10.00
10 Rajon Rondo 2.50 6.00

2012-13 Innovation Producers

1 Stephen Curry 12.00 30.00
2 Anderson Varejao 1.00 2.50
3 Steve Nash 3.00 8.00
4 Kevin Durant 6.00 15.00
5 Greivis Vasquez 1.00 2.50
6 Kobe Bryant 12.00 30.00
7 James Harden 3.00 8.00
8 Zach Randolph 1.50 4.00
9 LeBron James 12.00 30.00
10 Russell Westbrook 2.50 6.00
11 David Lee 1.00 2.50
12 Josh Smith 1.00 2.50
13 LaMarcus Aldridge 1.50 4.00
14 Kevin Love 1.50 4.00
15 Carmelo Anthony 2.50 6.00
16 Chris Paul 3.00 8.00
17 Deron Williams 1.25 3.00
18 Greg Monroe 1.00 2.50
19 Blake Griffin 1.50 4.00
20 Tyson Chandler 1.25 3.00

2012-13 Innovation Rookie Autographs

EXCHANGE DEADLINE 03/04/2015
1 Andre Drummond 8.00 20.00
2 Alexey Shved 3.00 8.00
3 Draymond Green 20.00 50.00
4 Enes Kanter 5.00 12.00
5 Jimmer Fredette 5.00 12.00
6 John Henson 4.00 10.00
7 Klay Thompson 125.00 300.00
8 Kyle Singler 3.00 8.00
9 Nolan Smith 3.00 8.00
10 Orlando Johnson 3.00 8.00
11 Will Barton 6.00 15.00
12 Andrew Nicholson 3.00 8.00
13 DeQuan Jones 3.00 8.00
14 E'Twaun Moore 4.00 10.00
15 Jeremy Pargo 3.00 8.00
16 Jonas Valanciunas 6.00 15.00
17 Kevin Murphy 3.00 8.00
18 Kyrie Irving EXCH 125.00 300.00
19 Nikola Vucevic 12.00 30.00
20 Reggie Jackson 8.00 20.00
21 Khris Middleton 15.00 40.00
22 Alec Burks 5.00 12.00
23 Darius Morris 4.00 10.00
24 Greg Stiemsma 3.00 8.00
25 Jeff Taylor 3.00 8.00
26 Julyan Stone 3.00 8.00
27 Kevin Jones EXCH 3.00 8.00
28 Malcolm Lee 3.00 8.00
29 Kim English 3.00 8.00
30 Robert Sacre 3.00 8.00
31 Tristan Thompson 5.00 12.00
32 Anthony Davis 150.00 400.00
33 Chandler Parsons 4.00 10.00
34 Gustavo Ayon 3.00 8.00
35 Jared Sullinger 3.00 8.00
36 Kemba Walker EXCH 12.00 30.00
37 Kent Bazemore 5.00 12.00
38 MarShon Brooks 3.00 8.00
39 Miles Plumlee 3.00 8.00
40 Terrence Jones 3.00 8.00
41 Tornike Shengelia 3.00 8.00
42 Bradley Beal 12.00 30.00
43 Brandon Knight 4.00 10.00
44 Harrison Barnes 5.00 12.00
45 Mike Scott 4.00 10.00
46 Kendall Marshall 3.00 8.00
47 Kenneth Faried 4.00 10.00
48 Marquis Teague 3.00 8.00
49 Meyers Leonard 4.00 10.00
50 Terrence Ross 8.00 20.00
51 Damian Lillard 150.00 400.00

2012-13 Innovation Rookie Basketballs

PRINT RUNS B/WN 49-199 COPIES PER
1 Lavoy Allen/49 2.50 6.00
2 Bernard James/49 2.50 6.00
3 Terrence Jones/49 2.50 6.00
4 Bismack Biyombo/99 3.00 8.00
5 Terrence Ross/99 6.00 15.00
6 Fab Melo/49 2.50 6.00
7 Festus Ezeli/49 2.50 6.00
8 Kenneth Faried/99 3.00 8.00
9 Kendall Marshall/49 2.50 6.00
10 Marcus Morris/99 4.00 10.00
11 Austin Rivers/99 4.00 10.00
12 Thomas Robinson/99 2.50 6.00
13 Markieff Morris/99 4.00 10.00
14 Robert Sacre/49 2.50 6.00
15 Royce White/49 2.50 6.00
16 Bradley Beal/199 20.00 50.00
17 Tobias Harris/99 8.00 20.00
19 Brandon Knight/99 3.00 8.00
20 Evan Fournier/99 6.00 15.00
21 Harrison Barnes/199 6.00 15.00
22 Kemba Walker/199 10.00 25.00
23 Khris Middleton/49 12.00 30.00
24 Will Barton/49 5.00 12.00
25 John Henson/199 3.00 8.00
26 Jimmer Fredette/99 4.00 10.00
27 Darius Morris/49 3.00 8.00
28 Nolan Smith/49 2.50 6.00
29 Darius Miller/49 3.00 8.00
30 Miles Plumlee/49 2.50 6.00
31 Lance Thomas/49 2.50 6.00
32 John Jenkins/49 2.50 6.00
33 Enes Kanter/99 4.00 10.00
34 Iman Shumpert/199 3.00 8.00
35 Kawhi Leonard/199 75.00 200.00
36 Kim English/99 2.50 6.00
37 Jared Sullinger/99 2.50 6.00
38 Anthony Davis/199 40.00 100.00
39 Chandler Parsons/199 3.00 8.00
40 Marquis Teague/99 2.50 6.00
41 Reggie Jackson/99 4.00 10.00
42 Tony Wroten/49 2.50 6.00
43 Quincy Miller/49 2.50 6.00
44 Tristan Thompson/99 4.00 10.00
45 Andre Drummond/199 6.00 15.00
46 Draymond Green/99 15.00 40.00
47 Isaiah Thomas/99 5.00 12.00
48 Julyan Stone/49 2.50 6.00
49 Klay Thompson/199 25.00 60.00
50 MarShon Brooks/99 2.50 6.00
51 Andrew Nicholson/49 2.50 6.00
52 Chris Singleton/49 2.50 6.00
53 Doron Lamb/49 2.50 6.00
54 Jae Crowder/49 5.00 12.00
55 Jordan Hamilton/99 2.00 5.00
56 Kyle Singler/99 2.00 5.00
57 Meyers Leonard/49 2.50 6.00
58 Cory Joseph/99 2.50 6.00
59 Dion Waiters/99 2.50 6.00
60 Jared Cunningham/49 2.00 5.00
61 Jonas Valanciunas/99 4.00 10.00
62 Kyrie Irving/199 12.00 30.00
63 Michael Kidd-Gilchrist/199 2.50 6.00
64 Norris Cole/49 2.00 5.00
65 Jeremy Lamb/99 3.00 8.00
66 Derrick Williams/199 2.00 5.00
67 Quincy Acy/99 2.00 5.00
68 Charles Jenkins/49 2.00 5.00
69 Tyler Zeller/99 2.00 5.00
70 Alec Burks/49 3.00 8.00

2012-13 Innovation Rookie Innovative Ink

EXCHANGE DEADLINE 03/04/2015
1 Austin Rivers 5.00 12.00
2 Thomas Robinson 3.00 8.00
3 Terrence Jones 3.00 8.00
4 Kevin Jones 3.00 8.00
5 Bradley Beal 10.00 25.00
6 Tobias Harris 10.00 25.00
7 Terrence Ross 8.00 20.00
8 Kenneth Faried 4.00 10.00
9 Kendall Marshall 3.00 8.00
10 Brandon Knight 4.00 10.00
11 Malcolm Lee 3.00 8.00
12 Harrison Barnes 6.00 15.00
13 Kemba Walker 12.00 30.00
14 Will Barton 6.00 15.00
15 John Henson 4.00 10.00
16 Jimmer Fredette 5.00 12.00
17 Darius Morris 4.00 10.00
18 Mike Scott 4.00 10.00
19 Lance Thomas 3.00 8.00
20 Kevin Murphy 3.00 8.00
21 E'Twaun Moore 4.00 10.00
22 Iman Shumpert 4.00 10.00
23 Kawhi Leonard 150.00 400.00
24 Jared Sullinger 3.00 8.00
25 Anthony Davis 150.00 400.00
26 Chandler Parsons 4.00 10.00
27 Marquis Teague 3.00 8.00
28 Reggie Jackson 5.00 12.00
29 Tristan Thompson 5.00 12.00
30 Andre Drummond 8.00 20.00
31 Khris Middleton 15.00 40.00
32 Isaiah Thomas 6.00 15.00
33 Julyan Stone 3.00 8.00
34 MarShon Brooks 3.00 8.00
35 Andrew Nicholson 3.00 8.00
36 Orlando Johnson 3.00 8.00
37 Alec Burks 5.00 12.00
38 Jae Crowder 6.00 15.00
39 Jordan Hamilton 3.00 8.00
40 Kyle Singler 3.00 8.00
41 Meyers Leonard 4.00 10.00
42 Dion Waiters 4.00 10.00
43 Jeff Taylor 3.00 8.00
44 Kyrie Irving 40.00 100.00
45 Michael Kidd-Gilchrist 4.00 10.00
46 DeQuan Jones 3.00 8.00
47 Greg Stiemsma 3.00 8.00
48 Derrick Williams 3.00 8.00
49 Victor Claver 3.00 8.00
50 Tyler Zeller 3.00 8.00
51 Ben Hansbrough 3.00 8.00
52 Brian Roberts 3.00 8.00
53 Chris Copeland 3.00 8.00
54 Kent Bazemore 5.00 12.00
55 Kim English 3.00 8.00
56 Jonas Valanciunas 6.00 15.00
57 Gustavo Ayon 3.00 8.00
58 Mirza Teletovic 4.00 10.00
59 Nando De Colo 3.00 8.00
60 Alexey Shved 3.00 8.00

2012-13 Innovation Rookie Innovative Ink Gold

*GOLD: .6X TO 1.5X BASIC
STATED PRINT RUN 25 SER.#'d SETS
EXCHANGE DEADLINE 03/04/2015
5 Bradley Beal 30.00 80.00
44 Kyrie Irving 75.00 200.00

2012-13 Innovation Rookie Jumbo Jerseys

PRINT RUNS B/WN 99-199 COPIES PER
2 Terrence Ross/99 6.00 15.00
3 Kenneth Faried/99 3.00 8.00
4 Kendall Marshall/99 2.50 6.00
5 Harrison Barnes/199 5.00 12.00
6 Austin Rivers/199 4.00 10.00
7 Thomas Robinson/199 2.50 6.00
8 Markieff Morris/99 4.00 10.00
9 Bradley Beal/199 20.00 50.00
10 Kemba Walker/99 10.00 25.00
11 Jared Sullinger/199 2.50 6.00
12 Chandler Parsons/199 3.00 8.00
13 Reggie Jackson/99 4.00 10.00
14 Tyler Zeller/99 2.50 6.00
15 Jimmer Fredette/99 4.00 10.00
16 Derrick Williams/99 2.50 6.00
17 Enes Kanter/99 4.00 10.00
18 Iman Shumpert/99 3.00 8.00
19 Kawhi Leonard/199 75.00 200.00
20 Andre Drummond/199 6.00 15.00
21 Kyrie Irving/199 10.00 25.00
22 Klay Thompson/199 12.00 30.00
23 Tristan Thompson/99 4.00 10.00
24 Anthony Davis/199 40.00 100.00
25 Isaiah Thomas/99 5.00 12.00
26 Jonas Valanciunas/99 5.00 12.00
27 Dion Waiters/199 3.00 8.00
28 Meyers Leonard/99 3.00 8.00
29 Michael Kidd-Gilchrist/199 3.00 8.00
30 Andrew Nicholson/99 2.50 6.00

2012-13 Innovation Stained Glass

1 Vince Carter 6.00 15.00
2 Dwight Howard 4.00 10.00
3 Chauncey Billups 4.00 10.00
4 Ray Allen 5.00 12.00
5 Jeff Green 2.00 5.00
6 Chandler Parsons 2.50 6.00
7 Alexey Shved 2.50 6.00
8 Kevin Durant 12.00 30.00
9 Anthony Davis 20.00 50.00
10 Paul George 5.00 12.00
11 Kevin Martin 2.50 6.00
12 Stephen Curry 25.00 60.00
13 Andre Iguodala 3.00 8.00
14 Derrick Rose 5.00 12.00
15 Kevin Garnett 8.00 20.00
16 Rudy Gay 3.00 8.00
17 J.J. Hickson 2.00 5.00
18 Russell Westbrook 5.00 12.00
19 Steve Nash 6.00 15.00
20 Kirk Hinrich 2.50 6.00
21 Jimmy Butler 40.00 100.00
22 Klay Thompson 60.00 150.00
23 Shawn Marion 3.00 8.00
24 Michael Kidd-Gilchrist 2.50 6.00
25 Avery Bradley 2.00 5.00
26 Jonas Valanciunas 4.00 10.00
27 LaMarcus Aldridge 3.00 8.00
28 Kevin Love 3.00 8.00
29 Pau Gasol 5.00 12.00
30 George Hill 2.50 6.00
31 Jared Sullinger 2.00 5.00
32 David Lee 2.00 5.00
33 O.J. Mayo 2.00 5.00
34 Kemba Walker 8.00 20.00
35 Josh Smith 2.00 5.00
36 DeMar DeRozan 4.00 10.00
37 Damian Lillard 150.00 400.00
38 Ricky Rubio 2.50 6.00
39 Zach Randolph 3.00 8.00
40 Roy Hibbert 2.50 6.00
41 Serge Ibaka 2.50 6.00
42 Greg Monroe 2.50 6.00
43 Dirk Nowitzki 8.00 20.00
44 Ben Gordon 2.50 6.00
45 Al Horford 3.00 8.00
46 Tony Parker 5.00 12.00
47 Marcin Gortat 2.00 5.00
48 Blake Griffin 3.00 8.00
49 Mike Conley 2.50 6.00
50 Andrei Kirilenko 2.50 6.00
51 Chris Paul 6.00 15.00
52 Brandon Knight 2.50 6.00
53 Tristan Thompson 3.00 8.00
54 Brook Lopez 2.50 6.00
55 Nene 2.50 6.00
56 Tim Duncan 8.00 20.00
57 Goran Dragic 3.00 8.00
58 Tyson Chandler 2.50 6.00
59 Brandon Jennings 2.00 5.00
60 Hedo Turkoglu 2.50 6.00
61 Kobe Bryant 200.00 500.00
62 Andre Drummond 5.00 12.00
63 Kyrie Irving 50.00 120.00
64 Joe Johnson 2.50 6.00
65 John Wall 4.00 10.00
66 Manu Ginobili 6.00 15.00
67 Evan Turner 2.00 5.00
68 Austin Rivers 3.00 8.00
69 Monta Ellis 2.50 6.00
70 Jose Calderon 2.00 5.00
71 Danny Granger 2.00 5.00
72 Ty Lawson 2.00 5.00
73 Dion Waiters 2.50 6.00
74 Deron Williams 2.50 6.00
75 Bradley Beal 15.00 40.00
76 Tyreke Evans 2.50 6.00
77 Jrue Holiday 4.00 10.00
78 Amare Stoudemire 3.00 8.00
79 Chris Bosh 4.00 10.00
80 Harrison Barnes 4.00 10.00
81 Jeremy Lin 5.00 12.00
82 Kenneth Faried 2.50 6.00
83 Anderson Varejao 2.00 5.00
84 Rajon Rondo 4.00 10.00
85 Gordon Hayward 3.00 8.00
86 Isaiah Thomas 4.00 10.00
87 Tobias Harris 6.00 15.00
88 Carmelo Anthony 5.00 12.00
89 Dwyane Wade 8.00 20.00
90 Luis Scola 2.50 6.00
91 James Harden 40.00 100.00
92 Andre Miller 2.50 6.00
93 Joakim Noah 2.50 6.00
94 Paul Pierce 5.00 12.00
95 Enes Kanter 3.00 8.00
96 DeMarcus Cousins 3.00 8.00
97 Jameer Nelson 2.00 5.00
98 Jason Kidd 5.00 12.00
99 LeBron James 400.00 800.00
100 Kawhi Leonard 400.00 800.00

2012-13 Innovation Stained Glass Purple

*PURPLE: .6X TO 1.5X BASIC
12 Stephen Curry 30.00 80.00

2012-13 Innovation Stat Line Jerseys

PRINT RUNS B/WN 99-199 COPIES PER
1 Russell Westbrook/199 5.00 12.00
2 Carmelo Anthony/199 5.00 12.00
3 O.J. Mayo/199 2.00 5.00
4 Vince Carter/99 6.00 15.00
5 Marcin Gortat/199 2.00 5.00
6 Kenneth Faried/199 2.00 5.00
7 Kevin Durant/99 12.00 30.00
8 Kyrie Irving/199 15.00 40.00
9 George Hill/199 2.50 6.00
10 Al Horford/199 2.00 5.00
11 Blake Griffin/99 3.00 8.00
12 DeAndre Jordan/199 2.50 6.00
13 Anderson Varejao/149 2.00 5.00
14 Dwight Howard/199 4.00 10.00
15 Josh Smith/199 2.00 5.00
16 J.R. Smith/199 2.00 5.00
17 Kobe Bryant/99 25.00 60.00
18 Kyle Lowry/149 3.00 8.00
19 LaMarcus Aldridge/149 3.00 8.00
20 Al Jefferson/199 2.00 5.00
21 Chris Paul/199 6.00 15.00
22 Damian Lillard/199 12.00 30.00
23 Anthony Davis/199 12.00 30.00
24 Tyson Chandler/99 2.50 6.00
25 Goran Dragic/149 3.00 8.00

2012-13 Innovation Stat Line Jerseys Prime

*PRIME: 2X TO 5X BASIC
PRINT RUNS B/WN 10-25 COPIES PER
NO PRICING ON QTY 15 OR LESS

2012-13 Innovation Swat Team

1 Serge Ibaka 1.50 4.00
2 Anthony Davis 20.00 50.00
3 Larry Sanders 1.25 3.00
4 Josh Smith 1.25 3.00
5 Tim Duncan 5.00 12.00
6 Dwight Howard 2.50 6.00
7 JaVale McGee 1.50 4.00
8 Chris Andersen 1.50 4.00
9 Marcus Camby 2.00 5.00
10 Andrei Kirilenko 1.50 4.00
11 Dikembe Mutombo 3.00 8.00
12 Alonzo Mourning 3.00 8.00
13 David Robinson 3.00 8.00
14 Hakeem Olajuwon 4.00 10.00
15 Manute Bol 2.00 5.00

2013-14 Innovation

STATED PRINT RUN 199 SER.#'d SETS
1 Brook Lopez 2.00 5.00
2 Luol Deng 1.50 4.00
3 Andre Iguodala 2.00 5.00
4 Kobe Bryant 15.00 40.00
5 Kevin Love 2.00 5.00
6 Serge Ibaka 1.50 4.00
7 DeMarcus Cousins 2.00 5.00
8 Tim Duncan 5.00 12.00
9 Eric Bledsoe 1.50 4.00
10 Eric Gordon 1.50 4.00
11 Steve Nash 4.00 10.00
12 Jeremy Lin 3.00 8.00
13 Kenneth Faried 1.50 4.00
14 Derrick Rose 3.00 8.00
15 Brandon Bass 1.25 3.00
16 Dirk Nowitzki 5.00 12.00
17 Paul George 3.00 8.00
18 Mike Conley 2.00 5.00
19 Ricky Rubio 1.50 4.00
20 Kevin Durant 6.00 15.00
21 Evan Turner 1.25 3.00
22 Greivis Vasquez 1.25 3.00
23 Enes Kanter 1.50 4.00
24 Damian Lillard 6.00 15.00
25 Iman Shumpert 1.25 3.00
26 Chris Bosh 2.50 6.00
27 Chris Paul 4.00 10.00
28 Andre Drummond 2.00 5.00
29 Kemba Walker 2.00 5.00
30 Al Horford 2.00 5.00
31 Tristan Thompson 1.25 3.00
32 Stephen Curry 15.00 40.00
33 Roy Hibbert 1.25 3.00
34 Marc Gasol 2.00 5.00
35 Anthony Davis 6.00 15.00
36 Nikola Vucevic 2.50 6.00
37 Isaiah Thomas 1.50 4.00
38 Rudy Gay 1.50 4.00
39 Zaza Pachulia 1.25 3.00
40 Paul Pierce 3.00 8.00
41 Bradley Beal 3.00 8.00
42 DeMar DeRozan 2.50 6.00
43 Tiago Splitter 1.25 3.00
44 J.J. Redick 2.00 5.00
45 James Harden 4.00 10.00
46 Ty Lawson 1.25 3.00
47 Jeff Green 1.25 3.00
48 John Wall 2.50 6.00
49 Kyle Lowry 2.00 5.00
50 LaMarcus Aldridge 2.00 5.00
51 Spencer Hawes 1.25 3.00
52 Russell Westbrook 3.00 8.00
53 Kevin Martin 1.50 4.00
54 Dwyane Wade 4.00 10.00
55 Pau Gasol 3.00 8.00
56 Lance Stephenson 1.50 4.00
57 Klay Thompson 6.00 15.00
58 Monta Ellis 1.50 4.00
59 Anderson Varejao 1.25 3.00
60 Michael Kidd-Gilchrist 1.25 3.00
61 Paul Millsap 1.50 4.00
62 Gordon Hayward 1.50 4.00
63 Tony Parker 3.00 8.00
64 Gerald Green 1.50 4.00
65 Arron Afflalo 1.25 3.00
66 Carmelo Anthony 3.00 8.00
67 John Henson 1.25 3.00
68 LeBron James 15.00 40.00
69 Blake Griffin 2.00 5.00
70 Dwight Howard 2.50 6.00
71 Greg Monroe 1.25 3.00
72 Kyrie Irving 6.00 15.00
73 Carlos Boozer 1.50 4.00
74 Joe Johnson 1.50 4.00
75 Jordan Crawford 1.25 3.00
76 C.J. McCollum RC 5.00 12.00
77 Vitor Faverani RC 1.25 3.00
78 Gal Mekel RC 1.25 3.00
79 Otto Porter RC 2.00 5.00
80 Nerlens Noel RC 1.50 4.00
81 Rudy Gobert RC 5.00 12.00
82 G.Antetokounmpo RC 150.00 400.00
83 Steven Adams RC 10.00 25.00
84 Kentavious Caldwell-Pope RC 2.00 5.00
85 Tim Hardaway Jr. RC 2.50 6.00
86 Dennis Schroder RC 4.00 10.00
87 Anthony Bennett RC 1.25 3.00
88 Cody Zeller RC 1.50 4.00
89 Glen Rice Jr. RC 1.25 3.00
90 Alex Len RC 1.50 4.00
91 Mason Plumlee RC 1.50 4.00
92 Ben McLemore RC 1.50 4.00
93 Reggie Bullock RC 1.50 4.00
94 Tony Snell RC 1.50 4.00
95 Shabazz Muhammad RC 1.50 4.00
96 M.Carter-Williams RC 1.50 4.00
97 Victor Oladipo RC 3.00 8.00
98 Trey Burke RC 1.50 4.00
99 Kelly Olynyk RC 1.50 4.00
100 Nate Wolters RC 1.25 3.00

2013-14 Innovation Blue

*BLUE VET: 1X TO 2.5X BASIC
*BLUE RC: 1X TO 2.5X BASIC RC
STATED PRINT RUN 25 SER.#'d SETS
4 Kobe Bryant 75.00 200.00
32 Stephen Curry 60.00 150.00
68 LeBron James 75.00 200.00
82 Giannis Antetokounmpo 1,000.00 2,000.00

2013-14 Innovation Purple

*PURPLE VET: .75X TO 2X BASIC
*PURPLE RC: .75X TO 2X BASIC RC
ANNCD PRINT RUN OF 60
82 Giannis Antetokounmpo 500.00 1,000.00

2013-14 Innovation All Rookies

1 Ben McLemore 1.25 3.00
2 Archie Goodwin 1.00 2.50
3 Kentavious Caldwell-Pope 1.50 4.00
4 Tim Hardaway Jr. 2.00 5.00
5 Trey Burke 1.25 3.00
6 Anthony Bennett 1.00 2.50
7 C.J. McCollum 4.00 10.00
8 Victor Oladipo 2.50 6.00
9 Michael Carter-Williams 1.25 3.00
10 Otto Porter 1.50 4.00
11 Kelly Olynyk 1.25 3.00
12 Cody Zeller 1.25 3.00
13 Giannis Antetokounmpo 75.00 200.00
14 Alex Len 1.25 3.00
15 Dennis Schroder 3.00 8.00

2013-14 Innovation Digs and Sigs

PRINT RUNS B/WN 15-199 COPIES PER
EXCHANGE DEADLINE 12/11/2015
*PRIME: .5X TO 1.2X BASIC
1 Kevin Durant/25 125.00 300.00
2 Dee Brown/199 5.00 12.00
3 Lavoy Allen/199 4.00 10.00
6 Ray Allen/25 40.00 100.00
7 Goran Dragic/15 5.00 12.00
8 Ty Lawson/15 4.00 10.00
9 Deron Williams/25 5.00 12.00
11 Vince Carter/25 60.00 150.00
12 Chris Bosh/25 15.00 40.00
13 Kevin Love/25 20.00 50.00
14 Anderson Varejao/15 4.00 10.00
15 LaMarcus Aldridge/15 15.00 40.00
16 Draymond Green/199 25.00 60.00
18 Dwight Howard/25 15.00 40.00
20 Jared Sullinger/15 4.00 10.00
21 Greg Smith/199 4.00 10.00
23 Jordan Hill/15 4.00 10.00
24 Raymond Felton/15 4.00 10.00
25 Andre Drummond/25 6.00 15.00
27 Dirk Nowitzki/25 125.00 300.00
28 Jose Calderon/15 4.00 10.00
29 Kyle Singler/199 4.00 10.00
30 Kobe Bryant/25 1,000.00 2,000.00
31 Anthony Davis/25 75.00 200.00
32 Jamal Mashburn/50 8.00 20.00
33 Steve Blake/199 4.00 10.00
34 Karl Malone/25 50.00 120.00
35 Scottie Pippen/25 75.00 200.00
37 Larry Bird/25 125.00 300.00
40 Harrison Barnes/25 6.00 15.00
41 Danny Manning/15 5.00 12.00
42 Stephen Curry/25 500.00 1,000.00
43 Kenny Sky Walker/15 4.00 10.00
44 John Wall/15 25.00 60.00
46 Kendrick Perkins/15 4.00 10.00
47 Marreese Speights/199 4.00 10.00
48 Bradley Beal/25 20.00 50.00
49 Kareem Abdul-Jabbar/25 125.00 300.00
50 Danny Green/15 5.00 12.00

2013-14 Innovation Digs and Sigs Prime

*PRIME: .6X TO 1.5X BASIC
PRINT RUNS B/WN 10-25 COPIES PER
NO PRICING ON QTY 10
EXCHANGE DEADLINE 12/11/2015

2013-14 Innovation Foundations Ink

PRINT RUNS B/WN 10-199 COPIES PER
NO PRICING ON QTY 10
EXCHANGE DEADLINE 12/11/2015
*PRIME: .6X TO 1.5X BASIC
6 Charlie Bell/199 3.00 8.00
7 Nick Collison/49 3.00 8.00
8 Tim Hardaway/199 6.00 15.00
9 Kenny Anderson/199 4.00 10.00
10 P.J. Tucker/199 5.00 12.00
11 Jeff Malone/199 4.00 10.00
12 Michael Cooper/199 5.00 12.00
14 Cazzie Russell/199 4.00 10.00
19 Magic Johnson/25 75.00 200.00
24 Dorell Wright/99 3.00 8.00
25 Corey Brewer/125 3.00 8.00
26 Mark Aguirre/199 4.00 10.00
27 Mateen Cleaves/199 3.00 8.00
28 Leonard Truck Robinson/199 3.00 8.00
29 Jordan Hamilton/199 3.00 8.00
30 Arnett Moultrie/199 3.00 8.00
31 Dale Davis/199 8.00 20.00
32 Dan Issel/99 6.00 15.00
38 Kobe Bryant/35 1,000.00 2,000.00
39 Karl Malone/25 50.00 120.00
46 Steve Blake/199 3.00 8.00
47 Jerome Williams/199 3.00 8.00
48 Travis Best/199 3.00 8.00
49 Kevin Durant/35 75.00 200.00
58 Bob Dandridge/199 4.00 10.00
59 Jeff Hornacek/99 4.00 10.00
60 Bobby Jones/199 6.00 15.00
61 Len Elmore/199 4.00 10.00
62 Rex Chapman/199 5.00 12.00
63 Nando De Colo/199 3.00 8.00
64 Larry Bird/25 75.00 200.00
65 Kyrie Irving/40 60.00 150.00
75 Jonas Jerebko/199 3.00 8.00
76 Eddie Johnson/199 3.00 8.00
77 Gary Trent/199 3.00 8.00
78 Raef LaFrentz/199 3.00 8.00
79 Anthony Mason/199 4.00 10.00
80 Cedric Maxwell/199 4.00 10.00
81 Kyle Singler/199 3.00 8.00
82 Travis Outlaw/199 3.00 8.00
92 Udonis Haslem/49 4.00 10.00
93 Marreese Speights/199 3.00 8.00
94 Bill Laimbeer/199 5.00 12.00
95 Lindsey Hunter/199 3.00 8.00
96 Sleepy Floyd/199 4.00 10.00
97 Antonio Davis/199 4.00 10.00

98 Vernon Maxwell/149 4.00 10.00
99 Festus Ezeli/199 3.00 8.00
100 Robert Sacre/199 3.00 8.00

2013-14 Innovation Game Jerseys Autographs

PRINT RUNS B/WN 15-199 COPIES PER
NO PRICING ON QTY 15
EXCHANGE DEADLINE 12/11/2015
1 Kevin Willis/35 5.00 12.00
2 Cazzie Russell/99 5.00 12.00
3 Steve Smith/199 5.00 12.00
4 Kevin Durant/35 150.00 400.00
5 Fat Lever/199 5.00 12.00
6 Sean Elliott/199 6.00 15.00
8 Kyrie Irving/35 60.00 150.00
11 Kiki Vandeweghe/199 EXCH 5.00 12.00
13 Scott Wedman/199 5.00 12.00
17 David Robinson/35 60.00 150.00
21 Fred Brown/199 5.00 12.00
22 Anthony Mason/199 5.00 12.00
23 Spencer Hawes/199 4.00 10.00
25 Rory Sparrow/199 4.00 10.00
26 Kobe Bryant/35 1,000.00 2,000.00
28 Kevin Love/25 12.00 30.00
29 Ricky Pierce/199 5.00 12.00
31 C.J. Watson/199 4.00 10.00
32 Jeff Malone/199 5.00 12.00
33 Larry Nance/199 5.00 12.00
35 Julius Erving/35 75.00 200.00
36 Larry Bird/35 125.00 300.00
37 Vince Carter/25 75.00 200.00
41 Bill Laimbeer/199 12.00 30.00
42 Jodie Meeks/199 4.00 10.00
43 Eddie Johnson/199 4.00 10.00
44 Brad Daugherty/199 6.00 15.00
45 Magic Johnson/35 125.00 300.00
47 Steve Nash/25 75.00 200.00
48 Anfernee Hardaway/25 75.00 200.00

2013-14 Innovation Game Jerseys Autographs Prime

*PRIME: .6X TO 1.5X BASIC
PRINT RUNS B/WN 10-25 COPIES PER
NO PRICING ON QTY 10
EXCHANGE DEADLINE 12/11/2015
15 Cedric Maxwell/25 12.00 30.00

2013-14 Innovation Juggernauts

1 Brook Lopez 1.50 4.00
2 Marc Gasol 1.50 4.00
3 Serge Ibaka 1.25 3.00
4 Kevin Love 1.50 4.00
5 Kevin Garnett 4.00 10.00
6 Derrick Rose 2.50 6.00
7 Rajon Rondo 2.00 5.00
8 James Harden 3.00 8.00
9 Paul George 2.50 6.00
10 Carmelo Anthony 2.50 6.00
11 Deron Williams 1.25 3.00
12 Kobe Bryant 12.00 30.00
13 Roy Hibbert 1.00 2.50
14 Dwyane Wade 3.00 8.00
15 Al Horford 1.50 4.00
16 Dwight Howard 2.00 5.00
17 Joakim Noah 1.50 4.00
18 Tim Duncan 4.00 10.00
19 Kyrie Irving 5.00 12.00
20 Russell Westbrook 2.50 6.00
21 Blake Griffin 1.50 4.00
22 Chris Paul 3.00 8.00
23 LaMarcus Aldridge 1.50 4.00
24 Tony Parker 2.50 6.00
25 Chris Bosh 2.00 5.00
26 Kevin Durant 5.00 12.00
27 Dirk Nowitzki 4.00 10.00
28 LeBron James 12.00 30.00
29 Stephen Curry 12.00 30.00
30 Anthony Davis 5.00 12.00

2013-14 Innovation Kaboom

1 Rajon Rondo 150.00 400.00
2 Derrick Rose 200.00 500.00
3 Russell Westbrook 125.00 300.00
4 Dirk Nowitzki 300.00 600.00
5 Stephen Curry 1,500.00 3,000.00
6 Dwight Howard 125.00 300.00
7 Tim Duncan 300.00 600.00
8 Dwyane Wade 300.00 600.00
9 Kobe Bryant 1,500.00 3,000.00
10 James Harden 200.00 500.00
11 Anthony Davis 150.00 400.00
12 John Wall 75.00 200.00
13 Blake Griffin 125.00 300.00
14 Kevin Durant 500.00 1,000.00
15 Carmelo Anthony 150.00 400.00
16 Kyrie Irving 150.00 400.00
17 Chris Paul 200.00 500.00
18 LeBron James 2,000.00 4,000.00
19 Damian Lillard 300.00 600.00
20 Paul Pierce 125.00 300.00

2013-14 Innovation Main Exhibit Signatures

PRINT RUNS B/WN 10-199 COPIES PER
NO PRICING ON QTY 15 OR LESS
EXCHANGE DEADLINE 12/11/2015
1 Ron Harper/75 8.00 20.00
2 Spud Webb/75 5.00 12.00
4 Evan Fournier/199 4.00 10.00
6 Alexey Shved/199 3.00 8.00
8 Jason Smith/199 3.00 8.00
9 E'Twaun Moore/199 3.00 8.00
11 Kyrie Irving/49 60.00 150.00
12 Ramon Sessions/199 3.00 8.00
14 John Salmons/75 4.00 10.00
15 Kobe Bryant/25 1,000.00 2,000.00
18 Kevin Durant/25 125.00 300.00
20 Julius Erving/25 60.00 150.00
22 C.J. Watson/199 3.00 8.00
24 Darrell Griffith/199 4.00 10.00
26 Chris Mullin/25 12.00 30.00
27 Andray Blatche/75 EXCH 3.00 8.00
28 Elgin Baylor/25 50.00 120.00
31 Zydrunas Ilgauskas/125 4.00 10.00
33 Marcin Gortat/149 3.00 8.00
35 Darryl Dawkins/75 4.00 10.00
36 Isiah Thomas/25 25.00 60.00
40 J.R. Smith/25 12.00 30.00
43 Scottie Pippen/35 75.00 200.00
46 Jack Sikma/199 5.00 12.00
47 Vernon Maxwell/199 4.00 10.00
48 Michael Curry/199 3.00 8.00
49 Lance Stephenson/149 4.00 10.00
51 Rory Sparrow/199 3.00 8.00
53 Rashard Lewis/75 4.00 10.00
55 Luc Longley/199 4.00 10.00

2013-14 Innovation Memorable Memorabilia

PRINT RUNS B/WN 75-299 COPIES PER
*PRIME: .8X TO 2X BASIC
1 Tim Duncan/299 10.00 25.00
2 Rudy Gay/175 3.00 8.00
3 John Henson/149 2.50 6.00
4 Raymond Felton/299 2.50 6.00
5 Rajon Rondo/175 5.00 12.00
6 Andre Drummond/175 4.00 10.00
7 Kevin Garnett/299 10.00 25.00
8 Enes Kanter/175 3.00 8.00
9 Andre Iguodala/125 4.00 10.00
10 Eric Bledsoe/299 3.00 8.00
11 Kevin Durant/299 12.00 30.00
12 Dwight Howard/299 5.00 12.00
13 Tyson Chandler/299 3.00 8.00
14 Damian Lillard/175 12.00 30.00
15 Evan Turner/99 2.50 6.00
16 Brandon Jennings/99 2.50 6.00
17 Deron Williams/175 3.00 8.00
18 Kevin Love/299 4.00 10.00
19 David Lee/99 2.50 6.00
20 Kobe Bryant/299 30.00 80.00
21 Monta Ellis/175 3.00 8.00
22 Paul George/299 6.00 15.00
23 Kyrie Irving/99 12.00 30.00
24 O.J. Mayo/299 2.50 6.00
25 Dwyane Wade/299 8.00 20.00
26 Josh Smith/175 2.50 6.00
27 Paul Pierce/299 6.00 15.00
28 Ricky Rubio/99 3.00 8.00
29 LaMarcus Aldridge/149 4.00 10.00
30 DeMarcus Cousins/175 4.00 10.00
31 Kenneth Faried/299 3.00 8.00
32 James Harden/175 8.00 20.00
33 LeBron James/299 30.00 80.00
34 Dirk Nowitzki/199 10.00 25.00
35 Kemba Walker/99 4.00 10.00
36 Blake Griffin/299 4.00 10.00
37 Derrick Favors/99 2.50 6.00
38 Harrison Barnes/199 4.00 10.00
39 Carmelo Anthony/299 6.00 15.00
40 Anthony Davis/175 12.00 30.00
41 Marc Gasol/125 4.00 10.00
42 Jrue Holiday/99 5.00 12.00
43 Al Jefferson/299 2.50 6.00
44 Zach Randolph/250 3.00 8.00
45 John Wall/299 5.00 12.00
46 Chris Paul/75 8.00 20.00
47 Gordon Hayward/99 3.00 8.00
48 Stephen Curry/175 30.00 80.00
49 Bradley Beal/175 6.00 15.00
50 Goran Dragic/175 3.00 8.00

2013-14 Innovation Rookie Jumbo Jerseys

STATED PRINT RUN 199 SER.#'d SETS
*PRIME: 1.2X TO 3X BASIC
1 Nate Wolters 2.50 6.00
2 Ben McLemore 3.00 8.00
3 Michael Carter-Williams 3.00 8.00
4 Glen Rice Jr. 2.50 6.00
5 Steven Adams 6.00 15.00
6 Isaiah Canaan 2.50 6.00
7 C.J. McCollum 10.00 25.00
8 Solomon Hill 3.00 8.00
9 Kentavious Caldwell-Pope 4.00 10.00
10 Victor Oladipo 6.00 15.00
11 Cody Zeller 3.00 8.00
12 Anthony Bennett 2.50 6.00
13 Trey Burke 3.00 8.00
14 Alex Len 3.00 8.00
15 Shabazz Muhammad 2.50 6.00
16 Giannis Antetokounmpo 125.00 300.00
17 Kelly Olynyk 3.00 8.00
18 Andre Roberson 3.00 8.00
19 Tim Hardaway Jr. 5.00 12.00
20 Shane Larkin 2.50 6.00
21 Mason Plumlee 3.00 8.00
22 Nerlens Noel 3.00 8.00
23 Archie Goodwin 2.50 6.00
24 Otto Porter 4.00 10.00
25 Dennis Schroder 8.00 20.00

2013-14 Innovation Rookie Stained Glass

*GOLD: .6X TO 1.5X BASIC
1 Otto Porter 3.00 8.00
2 Tim Hardaway Jr. 4.00 10.00
3 Mason Plumlee 2.50 6.00
4 Victor Oladipo 5.00 12.00
5 Gal Mekel 2.00 5.00
6 Kentavious Caldwell-Pope 3.00 8.00
7 Cody Zeller 2.50 6.00
8 Ben McLemore 2.50 6.00
9 Michael Carter-Williams 2.50 6.00
10 Nate Wolters 2.00 5.00
11 Rudy Gobert 75.00 200.00
12 Anthony Bennett 2.00 5.00
13 Reggie Bullock 2.50 6.00
14 Kelly Olynyk 2.50 6.00
15 Nerlens Noel 2.50 6.00
16 Dennis Schroder 6.00 15.00
17 Alex Len 2.50 6.00
18 Tony Snell 2.50 6.00
19 Trey Burke 2.50 6.00
20 Vitor Faverani 2.00 5.00
21 Steven Adams 10.00 25.00
22 Glen Rice Jr. 2.00 5.00
23 Shabazz Muhammad 2.00 5.00
24 C.J. McCollum 25.00 60.00
25 Giannis Antetokounmpo 1,000.00 2,000.00

2013-14 Innovation Rookies Main Exhibit Signatures

PRINT RUNS B/WN 75-299 COPIES PER
EXCHANGE DEADLINE 12/11/2015
1 Vitor Faverani/299 3.00 8.00
2 Carrick Felix/299 3.00 8.00
3 Solomon Hill/299 4.00 10.00
4 Trey Burke/125 4.00 10.00
5 Sergey Karasev/299 3.00 8.00
6 Toure Murry/299 3.00 8.00
7 Gal Mekel/299 3.00 8.00
8 Mason Plumlee/299 4.00 10.00
9 Shabazz Muhammad/75 3.00 8.00
10 Cody Zeller/75 4.00 10.00
11 Luigi Datome/299 3.00 8.00
12 Ian Clark/299 4.00 10.00
13 Tim Hardaway Jr./299 6.00 15.00
14 Victor Oladipo/75 8.00 20.00
15 Nemanja Nedovic/299 3.00 8.00
16 Gorgui Dieng/299 4.00 10.00
17 Archie Goodwin/299 3.00 8.00
18 G.Antetokounmpo/299 1,000.00 2,000.00
19 Ben McLemore/75 4.00 10.00
20 C.J. McCollum/75 40.00 100.00
21 Robert Covington/299 5.00 12.00
22 Shane Larkin/299 3.00 8.00
23 Dennis Schroder/199 10.00 25.00
24 Alex Len/75 4.00 10.00
25 Dwight Buycks/299 3.00 8.00
26 Phil Pressey/299 3.00 8.00
27 Andre Roberson/299 4.00 10.00
28 Kelly Olynyk/299 4.00 10.00
29 Otto Porter/75 5.00 12.00
30 Ray McCallum/299 3.00 8.00
31 Nate Wolters/299 3.00 8.00
32 Glen Rice Jr./199 3.00 8.00
33 Anthony Bennett/75 3.00 8.00
34 Lorenzo Brown/299 3.00 8.00
35 Tony Snell/299 4.00 10.00
36 Isaiah Canaan/299 3.00 8.00
37 Steven Adams/199 8.00 20.00
38 Nerlens Noel/75 4.00 10.00
39 Rudy Gobert/299 40.00 100.00
40 Erik Murphy/299 3.00 8.00
41 M.Carter-Williams/125 4.00 10.00
42 Kentavious Caldwell-Pope/75 5.00 12.00
43 Pero Antic/299 3.00 8.00
44 Miroslav Raduljica/299 3.00 8.00
45 Matthew Dellavedova/299 5.00 12.00

2013-14 Innovation Stained Glass

*GOLD: .75X TO 2X BASIC
1 Luol Deng 4.00 10.00
2 Mike Conley 5.00 12.00
3 LaMarcus Aldridge 5.00 12.00
4 Marc Gasol 5.00 12.00
5 Carmelo Anthony 30.00 80.00
6 DeMarcus Cousins 5.00 12.00
7 Evan Turner 3.00 8.00
8 Anthony Davis 40.00 100.00
9 Kyle Lowry 15.00 40.00
10 Tony Parker 15.00 40.00
11 Kobe Bryant 300.00 600.00
12 Kevin Durant 125.00 300.00
13 Nikola Vucevic 6.00 15.00
14 Russell Westbrook 30.00 80.00
15 LeBron James 300.00 600.00
16 Eric Bledsoe 4.00 10.00
17 Enes Kanter 4.00 10.00
18 Isaiah Thomas 4.00 10.00
19 Spencer Hawes 3.00 8.00
20 Arron Afflalo 3.00 8.00
21 Serge Ibaka 4.00 10.00
22 Greivis Vasquez 3.00 8.00
23 Rudy Gay 4.00 10.00
24 Dwyane Wade 40.00 100.00
25 Dwight Howard 6.00 15.00
26 Steve Nash 40.00 100.00
27 Iman Shumpert 3.00 8.00
28 Zaza Pachulia 3.00 8.00
29 Kevin Martin 4.00 10.00
30 John Henson 3.00 8.00
31 Tim Duncan 50.00 120.00
32 Damian Lillard 40.00 100.00
33 Paul Pierce 30.00 80.00
34 Lance Stephenson 4.00 10.00
35 Kyrie Irving 60.00 150.00
36 Kenneth Faried 4.00 10.00
37 Chris Paul 40.00 100.00
38 Bradley Beal 8.00 20.00
39 Pau Gasol 8.00 20.00
40 Blake Griffin 5.00 12.00
41 Eric Gordon 4.00 10.00
42 Chris Bosh 6.00 15.00
43 DeMar DeRozan 20.00 50.00
44 Monta Ellis 4.00 10.00
45 Joe Johnson 4.00 10.00
46 Brandon Bass 3.00 8.00
47 Kemba Walker 5.00 12.00
48 Tiago Splitter 3.00 8.00
49 Klay Thompson 75.00 200.00
50 Greg Monroe 3.00 8.00
51 Jeremy Lin 40.00 100.00
52 Andre Drummond 5.00 12.00
53 J.J. Redick 5.00 12.00
54 Michael Kidd-Gilchrist 3.00 8.00
55 Brook Lopez 5.00 12.00
56 Paul George 30.00 80.00
57 Tristan Thompson 3.00 8.00
58 James Harden 40.00 100.00
59 Anderson Varejao 3.00 8.00
60 Carlos Boozer 4.00 10.00
61 Al Horford 5.00 12.00
62 Derrick Rose 40.00 100.00
63 Ty Lawson 3.00 8.00
64 Gordon Hayward 4.00 10.00
65 Andre Iguodala 5.00 12.00
66 Ricky Rubio 4.00 10.00
67 Roy Hibbert 3.00 8.00
68 Jeff Green 3.00 8.00
69 Paul Millsap 4.00 10.00
70 Jordan Crawford 3.00 8.00
71 Dirk Nowitzki 12.00 30.00
72 Stephen Curry 200.00 500.00
73 John Wall 6.00 15.00
74 Gerald Green 4.00 10.00
75 Kevin Love 5.00 12.00

2013-14 Innovation Starters

1 76ers 2.50 6.00
2 Celtics 2.50 6.00
3 Amir Johnson
DeMar DeRozan
Jonas Valanciunas
Kyle Lowry
Terrence Ross 2.50 6.00
4 Knicks 3.00 8.00
5 Nets 5.00 12.00
6 Pacers 3.00 8.00
7 Bulls 6.00 15.00
8 Cavaliers 6.00 15.00
9 Andre Drummond
Brandon Jennings
Greg Monroe
Josh Smith
Kyle Singler 2.00 5.00
10 Brandon Knight
Ersan Ilyasova
Khris Middleton
Larry Sanders
Nate Wolters 4.00 10.00
11 Heat 5.00 12.00
12 Al Horford
DeMarre Carroll
Jeff Teague
Kyle Korver
Paul Millsap 2.00 5.00
13 Al Jefferson
Gerald Henderson
Josh McRoberts
Kemba Walker
Michael Kidd-Gilchrist 2.00 5.00
14 Magic 3.00 8.00
15 Wizards 3.00 8.00
16 Trail Blazers 6.00 15.00
17 Timberwolves 2.00 5.00
18 Thunder 6.00 15.00
19 J.J. Hickson
Kenneth Faried
Randy Foye
Ty Lawson
Wilson Chandler 1.50 4.00
20 Jazz 1.50 4.00
21 Warriors 15.00 40.00
22 Clippers 4.00 10.00
23 Channing Frye
Eric Bledsoe
Goran Dragic
Miles Plumlee
P.J. Tucker 2.00 5.00
24 Lakers 15.00 40.00
25 Kings 2.00 5.00
26 Spurs 12.00 30.00
27 Mavericks 5.00 12.00
28 Rockets 4.00 10.00
29 Courtney Lee
Marc Gasol
Mike Conley
Tayshaun Prince
Zach Randolph 2.00 5.00
30 Pelicans 6.00 15.00

2013-14 Innovation Starters Legends

1 00s Lakers 6.00 15.00
2 Spurs 10.00 25.00
3 Rockets 8.00 20.00
4 Pistons 6.00 15.00
5 80s Lakers 15.00 40.00
6 80s Celtics 15.00 40.00
7 70s Celtics 10.00 25.00
8 Heat 6.00 15.00
9 76ers 5.00 12.00
10 60s Celtics 12.00 30.00

2013-14 Innovation Stat Line Jerseys

PRINT RUNS B/WN 49-299 COPIES PER
*PRIME/20-25: 1X TO 2.5X BASIC
1 John Wall/125 5.00 12.00
2 Carmelo Anthony/125 6.00 15.00
3 Jrue Holiday/149 5.00 12.00
4 Serge Ibaka/299 3.00 8.00
5 Kevin Durant/299 12.00 30.00
6 Al Jefferson/299 2.50 6.00
7 Stephen Curry/299 30.00 80.00
8 Deron Williams/175 3.00 8.00
9 Kemba Walker/125 4.00 10.00
10 Dirk Nowitzki/175 10.00 25.00
11 Kevin Love/125 4.00 10.00
12 Dwyane Wade/299 8.00 20.00
13 LaMarcus Aldridge/299 4.00 10.00
14 Russell Westbrook/199 6.00 15.00
15 Monta Ellis/125 3.00 8.00
16 Glen Davis/125 2.50 6.00
17 LeBron James/125 30.00 80.00
18 Ricky Rubio/125 3.00 8.00
19 Damian Lillard/199 12.00 30.00
20 Dion Waiters/199 2.50 6.00
21 DeMarcus Cousins/299 4.00 10.00
22 Josh Smith/125 2.50 6.00
23 Tony Parker/49 6.00 15.00
24 Kevin Garnett/199 10.00 25.00
25 Anthony Davis/175 12.00 30.00

2013-14 Innovation Swat Team

1 Anthony Davis 5.00 12.00
2 Larry Sanders 1.00 2.50
3 Serge Ibaka 1.25 3.00
4 Roy Hibbert 1.00 2.50
5 DeAndre Jordan 1.25 3.00
6 Tyson Chandler 1.25 3.00
7 Josh Smith 1.00 2.50
8 Dwight Howard 2.00 5.00
9 Kevin Garnett 4.00 10.00
10 Tim Duncan 4.00 10.00
11 Bill Russell 5.00 12.00
12 Hakeem Olajuwon 3.00 8.00
13 Kareem Abdul-Jabbar 5.00 12.00
14 Dikembe Mutombo 2.50 6.00
15 Manute Bol 1.50 4.00

2013-14 Innovation Top Notch Autographs

PRINT RUNS B/WN 10-325 COPIES PER
NO PRICING ON QTY 15 OR LESS
EXCHANGE DEADLINE 12/11/2015
1 Theo Ratliff/325 3.00 8.00
5 Vlade Divac/325 5.00 12.00
6 Adrian Smith/199 3.00 8.00
7 Anfernee Hardaway/25 60.00 150.00
8 Kevin Durant/25 125.00 300.00
10 Spencer Hawes/225 3.00 8.00
11 Vin Baker/325 3.00 8.00
12 Amir Johnson/199 3.00 8.00
13 Larry Nance/325 4.00 10.00
16 Mark Aguirre/325 4.00 10.00
18 Anthony Davis/25 50.00 120.00
21 Kenny Anderson/325 4.00 10.00
24 Kyle Singler/325 3.00 8.00
25 Tom Van Arsdale/325 5.00 12.00
26 Mike Conley/325 5.00 12.00
27 Shaquille O'Neal/25 125.00 300.00
30 Kobe Bryant/25 1,000.00 2,000.00
31 Steve Smith/325 4.00 10.00
33 Gus Williams/325 3.00 8.00
35 Dick Van Arsdale/325 5.00 12.00
38 Jerry West/25 30.00 80.00
40 Kyrie Irving/25 75.00 200.00
46 Mahmoud Abdul-Rauf/325 3.00 8.00
51 Darryl Dawkins/199 8.00 20.00
52 Khris Middleton/225 10.00 25.00
53 Clifford Robinson/325 8.00 20.00
55 Rory Sparrow/325 3.00 8.00
56 Jodie Meeks/325 3.00 8.00
57 Grant Hill/25 15.00 40.00
59 Magic Johnson/25 125.00 300.00
61 Jack Sikma/325 5.00 12.00
63 Cazzie Russell/325 4.00 10.00
64 Scott Wedman/325 4.00 10.00
66 Thurl Bailey/325 3.00 8.00
70 Vince Carter/25 75.00 200.00
71 Buck Williams/325 4.00 10.00
74 Bradley Beal/25 8.00 20.00
75 Rod Strickland/325 4.00 10.00
76 Greg Oden/325 3.00 8.00
81 Luc Longley/325 4.00 10.00
83 Darrell Griffith/325 4.00 10.00
88 DeMarre Carroll/325 3.00 8.00
91 Eddie Johnson/325 3.00 8.00
94 John Starks/325 5.00 12.00
97 Larry Bird/25 125.00 300.00
98 Kenyon Martin/325 5.00 12.00

2013-14 Innovation Top Notch Autographs Gold

*GOLD: .6X TO 1.5X BASIC
PRINT RUNS B/WN 5-25 COPIES PER
NO PRICING ON QTY 10 OR LESS
EXCHANGE DEADLINE 12/11/2015

1950-70 J.D. McCarthy Postcards

COMPLETE SET (15)

1993-94 Jam Session

COMPLETE SET (240) 20.00 50.00
1 Stacey Augmon .30 .75
2 Mookie Blaylock .40 1.00
3 Doug Edwards RC .40 1.00
4 Duane Ferrell .25 .60
5 Paul Graham .25 .60
6 Adam Keefe .25 .60
7 Jon Koncak .25 .60
8 Dominique Wilkins .60 1.50
9 Kevin Willis .30 .75
10 Alaa Abdelnaby .25 .60
11 Dee Brown .30 .75
12 Sherman Douglas .25 .60
13 Rick Fox .30 .75
14 Kevin Gamble .25 .60
15 Xavier McDaniel .40 1.00
16 Robert Parish .50 1.25
17 Muggsy Bogues .40 1.00
18 Scott Burrell RC .40 1.00
19 Dell Curry .40 1.00
20 Kenny Gattison .25 .60
21 Hersey Hawkins .30 .75
22 Eddie Johnson .25 .60
23 Larry Johnson .50 1.25
24 Alonzo Mourning .60 1.50
25 Johnny Newman .25 .60
26 David Wingate .25 .60
27 B.J. Armstrong .40 1.00
28 Corie Blount RC .40 1.00
29 Bill Cartwright .30 .75
30 Horace Grant .40 1.00
31 Stacey King .25 .60
32 John Paxson .40 1.00
33 Michael Jordan 4.00 10.00
34 Scottie Pippen 1.00 2.50
35 Scott Williams .25 .60
36 Terrell Brandon .30 .75
37 Brad Daugherty .30 .75
38 Danny Ferry .25 .60
39 Tyrone Hill .25 .60
40 Chris Mills RC .40 1.00
41 Larry Nance .30 .75
42 Mark Price .40 1.00
43 Gerald Wilkins .30 .75
44 John Williams .25 .60
45 Terry Davis .25 .60
46 Derek Harper .30 .75
47 Donald Hodge .25 .60
48 Jim Jackson .30 .75
49 Jamal Mashburn RC .75 2.00
50 Sean Rooks .25 .60
51 Doug Smith .25 .60
52 Mahmoud Abdul-Rauf .30 .75
53 Kevin Brooks .25 .60
54 LaPhonso Ellis .30 .75
55 Mark Macon .25 .60
56 Dikembe Mutombo .60 1.50
57 Rodney Rogers RC .40 1.00
58 Bryant Stith .25 .60
59 Reggie Williams .25 .60
60 Joe Dumars .50 1.25
61 Sean Elliott .40 1.00
62 Bill Laimbeer .40 1.00
63 Terry Mills .25 .60
64 Olden Polynice .25 .60
65 Alvin Robertson .30 .75
66 Isiah Thomas .60 1.50
67 Victor Alexander .25 .60
68 Chris Gatling .25 .60
69 Tim Hardaway .50 1.25
70 Byron Houston .25 .60
71 Sarunas Marciulionis .40 1.00
72 Chris Mullin .50 1.25
73 Billy Owens .30 .75
74 Latrell Sprewell .60 1.50
75 Chris Webber RC 2.00 5.00
76 Scott Brooks .25 .60
77 Matt Bullard .25 .60
78 Sam Cassell RC .75 2.00
79 Mario Elie .30 .75
80 Carl Herrera .25 .60
81 Robert Horry .40 1.00
82 Vernon Maxwell .30 .75
83 Hakeem Olajuwon .75 2.00
84 Kenny Smith .30 .75
85 Otis Thorpe .40 1.00
86 Dale Davis .30 .75
87 Vern Fleming .30 .75
88 Scott Haskin RC .25 .60
89 Reggie Miller .75 2.00
90 Sam Mitchell .25 .60
91 Pooh Richardson .30 .75
92 Detlef Schrempf .40 1.00
93 Malik Sealy .25 .60
94 Rik Smits .30 .75
95 Terry Dehere RC .40 1.00
96 Ron Harper .40 1.00
97 Mark Jackson .30 .75
98 Danny Manning .30 .75
99 Stanley Roberts .25 .60
100 Loy Vaught .25 .60
101 John Williams .25 .60
102 Sam Bowie .30 .75
103 Elden Campbell .25 .60
104 Doug Christie .30 .75
105 Vlade Divac .40 1.00
106 James Edwards .25 .60
107 George Lynch RC .40 1.00
108 Anthony Peeler .25 .60
109 Sedale Threatt .25 .60
110 James Worthy .50 1.25
111 Bimbo Coles .25 .60
112 Grant Long .25 .60
113 Harold Miner .30 .75
114 Glen Rice .40 1.00
115 John Salley .30 .75
116 Rony Seikaly .30 .75
117 Brian Shaw .25 .60
118 Steve Smith .30 .75
119 Anthony Avent .25 .60
120 Vin Baker RC .60 1.50
121 Jon Barry .25 .60
122 Frank Brickowski .25 .60
123 Todd Day .25 .60
124 Blue Edwards .25 .60
125 Brad Lohaus .25 .60
126 Lee Mayberry .25 .60
127 Eric Murdock .25 .60
128 Ken Norman .25 .60
129 Thurl Bailey .25 .60
130 Mike Brown .25 .60
131 Christian Laettner .40 1.00
132 Luc Longley .30 .75
133 Chuck Person .30 .75
134 Chris Smith .25 .60
135 Doug West .25 .60
136 Micheal Williams .25 .60
137 Kenny Anderson .30 .75
138 Benoit Benjamin .25 .60
139 Derrick Coleman .40 1.00
140 Armon Gilliam .25 .60
141 Rick Mahorn .30 .75
142 Chris Morris .25 .60
143 Rumeal Robinson .25 .60
144 Rex Walters RC .30 .75
145 Greg Anthony .25 .60
146 Rolando Blackman .30 .75
147 Tony Campbell .25 .60
148 Hubert Davis .30 .75
149 Patrick Ewing .60 1.50
150 Anthony Mason .30 .75
151 Charles Oakley .40 1.00
152 Doc Rivers .30 .75
153 Charles Smith .25 .60
154 John Starks .40 1.00
155 Herb Williams .25 .60
156 Nick Anderson .30 .75
157 Anthony Bowie .25 .60
158 Litterial Green .25 .60
159 Anfernee Hardaway RC 2.00 5.00
160 Shaquille O'Neal 2.00 5.00
161 Donald Royal .25 .60
162 Dennis Scott .25 .60
163 Scott Skiles .25 .60
164 Jeff Turner .25 .60
165 Dana Barros .25 .60
166 Shawn Bradley RC .40 1.00
167 Johnny Dawkins .30 .75
168 Greg Graham RC .25 .60
169 Jeff Hornacek .30 .75
170 Moses Malone .60 1.50
171 Tim Perry .25 .60
172 Clarence Weatherspoon .25 .60
173 Danny Ainge .40 1.00
174 Charles Barkley 1.00 2.50
175 Cedric Ceballos .30 .75
176 A.C. Green .30 .75
177 Frank Johnson .25 .60
178 Kevin Johnson .40 1.00
179 Negele Knight .25 .60
180 Malcolm Mackey RC .25 .60
181 Dan Majerle .40 1.00
182 Oliver Miller .25 .60
183 Mark West .25 .60
184 Clyde Drexler .60 1.50
185 Chris Dudley .25 .60
186 Harvey Grant .30 .75
187 Jerome Kersey .30 .75
188 Terry Porter .30 .75
189 Clifford Robinson .40 1.00
190 James Robinson RC .40 1.00
191 Rod Strickland .30 .75
192 Buck Williams .30 .75
193 Randy Brown .25 .60
194 Duane Causwell .25 .60
195 Bobby Hurley RC .40 1.00
196 Mitch Richmond .50 1.25
197 Lionel Simmons .25 .60
198 Wayman Tisdale .30 .75
199 Spud Webb .30 .75
200 Walt Williams .40 1.00
201 Willie Anderson .25 .60
202 Antoine Carr .25 .60
203 Terry Cummings .30 .75
204 Lloyd Daniels .25 .60
205 Vinny Del Negro .25 .60
206 Sleepy Floyd .30 .75
207 Avery Johnson .30 .75
208 J.R. Reid .30 .75
209 David Robinson .75 2.00
210 Dennis Rodman 1.00 2.50
211 Michael Cage .30 .75
212 Kendall Gill .30 .75
213 Ervin Johnson RC .40 1.00
214 Shawn Kemp .60 1.50
215 Derrick McKey .30 .75
216 Nate McMillan .30 .75
217 Gary Payton .50 1.25
218 Sam Perkins .30 .75
219 Ricky Pierce .30 .75
220 Isaac Austin .25 .60
221 David Benoit .25 .60
222 Tom Chambers .40 1.00
223 Tyrone Corbin .25 .60
224 Mark Eaton .40 1.00
225 Jay Humphries .30 .75
226 Jeff Malone .30 .75
227 Karl Malone .75 2.00
228 John Stockton .75 2.00
229 Luther Wright RC .25 .60
230 Michael Adams .30 .75
231 Calbert Cheaney RC .40 1.00
232 Kevin Duckworth .30 .75
233 Pervis Ellison .25 .60
234 Tom Gugliotta .30 .75
235 Buck Johnson .25 .60
236 Doug Overton .25 .60
237 LaBradford Smith .25 .60
238 Larry Stewart .25 .60
239 Checklist .20 .50
240 Checklist .20 .50

1993-94 Jam Session Gamebreakers

COMPLETE SET (8) 3.00 8.00
1 Charles Barkley 1.25 3.00
2 Tim Hardaway .60 1.50
3 Kevin Johnson .50 1.25
4 Dan Majerle .50 1.25
5 Scottie Pippen 1.25 3.00
6 Mark Price .50 1.25
7 John Starks .50 1.25
8 Dominique Wilkins .75 2.00

1993-94 Jam Session Rookie Standouts

COMPLETE SET (8) 5.00 12.00
1 Vin Baker .75 2.00
2 Shawn Bradley .50 1.25
3 Calbert Cheaney .50 1.25
4 Anfernee Hardaway UER 2.50 6.00
5 Bobby Hurley .50 1.25
6 Jamal Mashburn 1.00 2.50
7 Rodney Rogers .50 1.25
8 Chris Webber 2.50 6.00

1993-94 Jam Session Second Year Stars

COMPLETE SET (8) 3.00 8.00
1 Tom Gugliotta .40 1.00
2 Jim Jackson .40 1.00
3 Christian Laettner .50 1.25
4 Oliver Miller .30 .75
5 Harold Miner .40 1.00
6 Alonzo Mourning .75 2.00
7 Shaquille O'Neal 2.50 6.00
8 Walt Williams .50 1.25

1993-94 Jam Session Slam Dunk Heroes

COMPLETE SET (8) 4.00 10.00
1 Patrick Ewing .75 2.00
2 Larry Johnson .60 1.50
3 Shawn Kemp .75 2.00
4 Karl Malone 1.00 2.50
5 Alonzo Mourning .75 2.00
6 Hakeem Olajuwon 1.00 2.50
7 Shaquille O'Neal 2.50 6.00
8 David Robinson 1.00 2.50

1993-94 Jam Session Team Night Sheets

COMPLETE SET (9) 12.00 30.00
1 Alaa Abdelnaby
Dee Brown
Sherman Douglas
Rick Fox
Kevin Gamble
Xavier McDaniel
Robert Parish 00
Sony (Ad card) 2.00 5.00
2 Quinn Buckner CO
Terry Davis
Lucious Harris
Donald Hodge
Jim Jackson
Popeye Jones
Tom Legler
Fat Lever
Jamal Mashburn
Sean Rooks
Doug Smith
Doritos (Ad Card) 2.50 6.00
3 B.J. Armstrong
Corie Blount
Bill Cartwright
Horace Grant
Phil Jackson CO
Stacey King
Toni Kukoc
John Paxson
Will Perdue
Scottie Pippen
Scott Williams
Rust-oleum (Ad Card) 2.50 6.00
4 Joe Dumars
Sean Elliott
Bill Laimbeer
Terry Mills
Olden Polynice

Isiah Thomas
Pistons Logo
LCI International (Ad card) 2.00 5.00
5 Larry Brown CO
Antonio Davis
Dale Davis
Vern Fleming
Scott Haskin
Derrick McKey
Reggie Miller
Sam Mitchell
Pooh Richardson
Malik Sealy
Rik Smits
Combos Snacks (Ad card) 2.00 5.00
6 Mark Aguirre
Terry Dehere
Gary Grant
Ron Harper
Mark Jackson
Danny Manning
Stanley Roberts
Elmore Spencer
Tom Tolbert
Loy Vaught
Bob Weiss CO
Snickers
Kudos (Ad card) 2.00 5.00
7 Sam Bowie
Elden Campbell
Doug Christie
Vlade Divac
James Edwards
George Lynch
Anthony Peeler
Tony Smith
Sedale Threatt
Nick Van Exel
Team Logo 2.00 5.00
8 Vin Baker
Jon Barry
Frank Brickowski
Todd Day
Blue Edwards
Brad Lohaus
Lee Mayberry
Eric Murdock
Ken Norman
Danny Schayes
Derek Strong
Usinger's (Ad card) 2.50 6.00
9 Greg Anthony
Rolando Blackman
Hubert Davis
Patrick Ewing
Derek Harper
Anthony Mason
Charles Oakley
Charles Smith
John Starks
Herb Williams
WIZ (Two ad cards) 2.00 5.00

1993-94 Jam Session Ticket Stubs

COMPLETE SET (4) 6.00 15.00
1 Charles Barkley 3.00 8.00
2 David Robinson 2.50 6.00
3 Shaquille O'Neal 6.00 15.00
4 Scottie Pippen 3.00 8.00

1994-95 Jam Session

COMPLETE SET (200) 10.00 25.00
1 Stacey Augmon .20 .50
2 Mookie Blaylock .25 .60
3 Tyrone Corbin .15 .40
4 Craig Ehlo .15 .40
5 Ken Norman .15 .40
6 Kevin Willis .20 .50
7 Dee Brown .20 .50
8 Sherman Douglas .15 .40
9 Acie Earl .15 .40
10 Blue Edwards .15 .40
11 Pervis Ellison .15 .40
12 Rick Fox .15 .40
13 Xavier McDaniel .15 .40
14 Eric Montross RC .20 .50
15 Dino Radja .15 .40
16 Dominique Wilkins .40 1.00
17 Michael Adams .15 .40
18 Muggsy Bogues .20 .50
19 Dell Curry .15 .40
20 Kenny Gattison .15 .40
21 Hersey Hawkins .15 .40
22 Larry Johnson .30 .75
23 Alonzo Mourning .40 1.00
24 Robert Parish .25 .60
25 B.J. Armstrong .25 .60
26 Ron Harper .20 .50
27 Steve Kerr .20 .50
28 Toni Kukoc .30 .75
29 Pete Myers .15 .40
30 Will Perdue .15 .40
31 Scottie Pippen .60 1.50
32 Terrell Brandon .15 .40
33 Michael Cage .15 .40
34 Brad Daugherty .20 .50
35 Chris Mills .20 .50
36 Bobby Phills .15 .40
37 Mark Price .25 .60
38 Gerald Wilkins .20 .50
39 John Williams .15 .40
40 Jim Jackson .20 .50
41 Jason Kidd RC 1.25 3.00
42 Jamal Mashburn .25 .60
43 Sean Rooks .15 .40
44 Doug Smith .15 .40
45 Mahmoud Abdul-Rauf .15 .40
46 LaPhonso Ellis .15 .40
47 Dikembe Mutombo .40 1.00
48 Robert Pack .20 .50
49 Rodney Rogers .15 .40
50 Jalen Rose RC .60 1.50
51 Bryant Stith .15 .40
52 Reggie Williams .15 .40
53 Bill Curley RC .15 .40
54 Joe Dumars .25 .60
55 Grant Hill RC 1.25 3.00
56 Allan Houston .25 .60
57 Lindsey Hunter .15 .40
58 Oliver Miller .15 .40
59 Terry Mills .15 .40
60 Mark West .15 .40
61 Chris Gatling .15 .40
62 Tim Hardaway .30 .75
63 Chris Mullin .30 .75
64 Billy Owens .15 .40
65 Ricky Pierce .15 .40
66 Latrell Sprewell .30 .75
67 Chris Webber .50 1.25
68 Sam Cassell .25 .60
69 Mario Elie .15 .40
70 Carl Herrera .15 .40
71 Robert Horry .25 .60
72 Vernon Maxwell .15 .40
73 Hakeem Olajuwon .50 1.25
74 Kenny Smith .20 .50
75 Otis Thorpe .15 .40
76 Antonio Davis .20 .50
77 Dale Davis .15 .40
78 Mark Jackson .20 .50
79 Derrick McKey .15 .40
80 Reggie Miller .50 1.25
81 Byron Scott .20 .50
82 Rik Smits .20 .50
83 Haywoode Workman .15 .40
84 Gary Grant .15 .40
85 Pooh Richardson .15 .40
86 Stanley Roberts .15 .40
87 Elmore Spencer .15 .40
88 Loy Vaught .15 .40
89 Elden Campbell .15 .40
90 Cedric Ceballos .20 .50
91 Doug Christie .20 .50
92 Vlade Divac .25 .60
93 Eddie Jones RC .75 2.00
94 George Lynch .15 .40
95 Anthony Peeler .15 .40
96 Nick Van Exel .25 .60
97 James Worthy .30 .75
98 Grant Long .15 .40
99 Harold Miner .15 .40
100 Glen Rice .25 .60
101 John Salley .15 .40
102 Rony Seikaly .15 .40
103 Steve Smith .20 .50
104 Kevin Willis .25 .60
105 Jon Barry .15 .40
106 Todd Day .15 .40
107 Lee Mayberry .15 .40
108 Eric Murdock .15 .40
109 Stacey King .15 .40
110 Christian Laettner .20 .50
111 Donyell Marshall RC .25 .60
112 Isaiah Rider .25 .60
113 Doug West .15 .40
114 Micheal Williams .15 .40
115 Kenny Anderson .20 .50
116 P.J. Brown .15 .40
117 Derrick Coleman .25 .60
118 Yinka Dare RC .15 .40
119 Kevin Edwards .15 .40
120 Armon Gilliam .15 .40
121 Chris Morris .15 .40
122 Anthony Bonner .15 .40
123 Hubert Davis .15 .40
124 Patrick Ewing .40 1.00
125 Derek Harper .20 .50
126 Anthony Mason .20 .50
127 Charles Oakley .25 .60
128 Doc Rivers .20 .50
129 Charles Smith .15 .40
130 John Starks .25 .60
131 Charlie Ward RC .25 .60
132 Nick Anderson .15 .40
133 Anthony Bowie .15 .40
134 Horace Grant .25 .60
135 Anfernee Hardaway .50 1.25
136 Shaquille O'Neal 1.00 2.50
137 Dennis Scott .20 .50
138 Jeff Turner .15 .40
139 Dana Barros .15 .40
140 Shawn Bradley .15 .40
141 Johnny Dawkins .15 .40
142 Jeff Malone .15 .40
143 Tim Perry .15 .40
144 Clarence Weatherspoon .15 .40
145 Scott Williams .15 .40
146 Danny Ainge .25 .60
147 Charles Barkley .60 1.50
148 A.C. Green .20 .50
149 Kevin Johnson .25 .60
150 Joe Kleine .15 .40
151 Antonio Lang .25 .60
152 Dan Majerle .25 .60
153 Danny Manning .20 .50
154 Wayman Tisdale .15 .40
155 Clyde Drexler .40 1.00
156 Harvey Grant .15 .40
157 Tracy Murray .15 .40
158 Terry Porter .15 .40
159 Clifford Robinson .20 .50
160 Rod Strickland .15 .40
161 Buck Williams .15 .40
162 Bobby Hurley .15 .40
163 Olden Polynice .15 .40
164 Mitch Richmond .30 .75
165 Lionel Simmons .15 .40
166 Spud Webb .20 .50
167 Walt Williams .15 .40
168 Willie Anderson .15 .40
169 Terry Cummings .20 .50
170 Vinny Del Negro .15 .40
171 Sean Elliott .20 .50
172 Avery Johnson .20 .50
173 Chuck Person .20 .50
174 J.R. Reid .15 .40
175 David Robinson .50 1.25
176 Dennis Rodman .60 1.50
177 Bill Cartwright .20 .50
178 Kendall Gill .15 .40
179 Shawn Kemp .40 1.00
180 Nate McMillan .20 .50
181 Gary Payton .40 1.00
182 Sam Perkins .15 .40
183 Detlef Schrempf .25 .60
184 David Benoit .15 .40
185 Jeff Hornacek .20 .50
186 Jay Humphries .15 .40
187 Karl Malone .50 1.25
188 Bryon Russell .15 .40
189 Felton Spencer .15 .40
190 John Stockton .50 1.25
191 Mitchell Butler .15 .40
192 Rex Chapman .15 .40
193 Calbert Cheaney .20 .50
194 Tom Gugliotta .15 .40
195 Don MacLean .15 .40
196 Gheorghe Muresan .15 .40
197 Scott Skiles .15 .40
198 Checklist .15 .40
199 Checklist .15 .40
200 Checklist .15 .40

1994-95 Jam Session Flashing Stars

COMPLETE SET (8) 2.00 5.00
1 Anfernee Hardaway 1.00 2.50
2 Robert Horry .50 1.25
3 Dan Majerle .50 1.25
4 Reggie Miller 1.00 2.50
5 Mitch Richmond .60 1.50
6 Isaiah Rider .50 1.25
7 Latrell Sprewell .60 1.50
8 Dominique Wilkins .75 2.00

1994-95 Jam Session Gamebreakers

COMPLETE SET (8) 3.00 8.00
1 Charles Barkley 1.25 3.00
2 Patrick Ewing .75 2.00
3 Karl Malone 1.00 2.50
4 Alonzo Mourning .75 2.00
5 Hakeem Olajuwon 1.00 2.50
6 Shaquille O'Neal 2.00 5.00
7 Scottie Pippen 1.25 3.00
8 David Robinson 1.00 2.50

1994-95 Jam Session Rookie Standouts

COMPLETE SET (20) 5.00 12.00
1 Brian Grant .40 1.00
2 Grant Hill 1.25 3.00
3 Juwan Howard .40 1.00
4 Eddie Jones .75 2.00
5 Jason Kidd 1.25 3.00
6 Donyell Marshall .25 .60
7 Eric Montross .20 .50
8 Lamond Murray .25 .60
9 Wesley Person .25 .60
10 Khalid Reeves .20 .50
11 Glenn Robinson .50 1.25
12 Carlos Rogers .20 .50
13 Jalen Rose .60 1.50
14 Clifford Rozier .15 .40
15 Dickey Simpkins .20 .50
16 Michael Smith .15 .40
17 Anthony Tucker .15 .40
18 Charlie Ward .25 .60
19 Monty Williams .30 .75
20 Sharone Wright .20 .50

1994-95 Jam Session Second Year Stars

COMPLETE SET (8) 2.00 5.00
1 Vin Baker .50 1.25
2 Anfernee Hardaway 1.00 2.50
3 Lindsey Hunter .30 .75
4 Toni Kukoc .60 1.50
5 Jamal Mashburn .50 1.25
6 Dino Radja .30 .75
7 Isaiah Rider .50 1.25
8 Chris Webber 1.00 2.50

1994-95 Jam Session Slam Dunk Heroes

COMPLETE SET (8) 25.00 60.00
1 Charles Barkley 8.00 20.00
2 Larry Johnson 4.00 10.00
3 Shawn Kemp 5.00 12.00
4 Jamal Mashburn 3.00 8.00
5 Dikembe Mutombo 5.00 12.00
6 Hakeem Olajuwon 6.00 15.00
7 Shaquille O'Neal 12.00 30.00
8 Chris Webber 6.00 15.00

1995-96 Jam Session

COMPLETE SET (120) 10.00 25.00
1 Stacey Augmon CC .20 .50
2 Mookie Blaylock .25 .60
3 Grant Long .15 .40
4 Steve Smith .20 .50
5 Dee Brown CC .20 .50
6 Sherman Douglas .15 .40
7 Eric Montross .15 .40
8 Dino Radja .15 .40
9 Muggsy Bogues CC .25 .60
10 Scott Burrell .15 .40
11 Larry Johnson CC .30 .75
12 Alonzo Mourning .40 1.00
13 Michael Jordan CC 2.50 6.00
14 Steve Kerr .25 .60
15 Toni Kukoc CC .30 .75
16 Scottie Pippen .60 1.50
17 Terrell Brandon .20 .50
18 Tyrone Hill .15 .40
19 Mark Price CC .25 .60
20 John Williams .15 .40
21 Jim Jackson .20 .50
22 Popeye Jones CC .15 .40
23 Jason Kidd CC .40 1.00
24 Jamal Mashburn .25 .60
25 Mahmoud Abdul-Rauf .20 .50
26 Dikembe Mutombo CC .40 1.00
27 Robert Pack CC .20 .50
28 Jalen Rose .30 .75
29 Joe Dumars CC .25 .60
30 Grant Hill CC .40 1.00
31 Allan Houston .20 .50
32 Terry Mills .15 .40
33 Chris Gatling .15 .40
34 Tim Hardaway CC .30 .75
35 Donyell Marshall .15 .40
36 Chris Mullin CC .25 .60
37 Latrell Sprewell .25 .60
38 Sam Cassell .25 .60
39 Clyde Drexler CC .40 1.00
40 Robert Horry .25 .60
41 Hakeem Olajuwon CC .50 1.25
42 Kenny Smith .20 .50
43 Dale Davis .15 .40
44 Mark Jackson .20 .50
45 Reggie Miller CC .50 1.25
46 Rik Smits .20 .50
47 Lamond Murray .15 .40
48 Pooh Richardson CC .15 .40
49 Malik Sealy .15 .40
50 Loy Vaught .15 .40
51 Cedric Ceballos .20 .50
52 Vlade Divac .25 .60
53 Eddie Jones .25 .60
54 Nick Van Exel .25 .60
55 Billy Owens .15 .40
56 Khalid Reeves .15 .40
57 Glen Rice CC .25 .60
58 Kevin Willis .15 .40
59 Vin Baker .20 .50
60 Todd Day .15 .40
61 Eric Murdock .15 .40
62 Glenn Robinson CC .25 .60
63 Tom Gugliotta .15 .40
64 Christian Laettner CC .20 .50
65 Isaiah Rider CC .25 .60
66 Doug West .15 .40
67 Kenny Anderson .20 .50
68 P.J. Brown .15 .40
69 Derrick Coleman .20 .50
70 Armon Gilliam .15 .40
71 Patrick Ewing CC .40 1.00
72 Derek Harper .20 .50
73 Charles Oakley .20 .50
74 John Starks CC .25 .60
75 Horace Grant CC .20 .50
76 Anfernee Hardaway CC .60 1.50
77 Shaquille O'Neal CC 1.00 2.50
78 Dennis Scott .15 .40
79 Dana Barros CC .20 .50
80 Shawn Bradley .15 .40
81 Clarence Weatherspoon .15 .40
82 Sharone Wright .15 .40
83 Charles Barkley CC .60 1.50
84 Kevin Johnson CC .25 .60
85 Dan Majerle CC .25 .60
86 Wesley Person CC .25 .60
87 Harvey Grant .15 .40
88 Clifford Robinson .25 .60
89 Rod Strickland .15 .40
90 Buck Williams .15 .40
91 Brian Grant .20 .50
92 Olden Polynice .15 .40
93 Mitch Richmond .30 .75
94 Walt Williams .15 .40
95 Sean Elliott .20 .50
96 Avery Johnson .20 .50
97 David Robinson CC .50 1.25
98 Dennis Rodman .50 1.25
99 Shawn Kemp CC .40 1.00
100 Nate McMillan .15 .40
101 Gary Payton .40 1.00
102 Detlef Schrempf .25 .60
103 Willie Anderson .15 .40
104 Jerome Kersey .15 .40
105 Oliver Miller .15 .40
106 Ed Pinckney CC .15 .40
107 David Benoit .15 .40
108 Jeff Hornacek CC .20 .50
109 Karl Malone CC .50 1.25
110 John Stockton .50 1.25
111 Greg Anthony .15 .40
112 Benoit Benjamin .15 .40
113 Blue Edwards .15 .40
114 Kenny Gattison .15 .40
115 Calbert Cheaney .15 .40
116 Juwan Howard .25 .60
117 Gheorghe Muresan CC .15 .40
118 Chris Webber CC .30 .75
119 Checklist .15 .40
120 Checklist .15 .40
NNO Grant Hill
Foil Tribute 12.50 30.00

1995-96 Jam Session Die Cuts

COMPLETE SET (120) 25.00 60.00
*DIE CUTS: .75X TO 2X HI COLUMN
D13 Michael Jordan CC 12.00 30.00

1995-96 Jam Session Fuel Injectors

COMPLETE SET (9) 40.00 80.00
1 Grant Hill 6.00 15.00
2 Larry Johnson 5.00 12.00
3 Eddie Jones 4.00 10.00
4 Jason Kidd 6.00 15.00
5 Hakeem Olajuwon 8.00 20.00
6 Shaquille O'Neal 15.00 40.00
7 Scottie Pippen 10.00 25.00
8 Glenn Robinson 4.00 10.00
9 Latrell Sprewell 4.00 10.00

1995-96 Jam Session Pop-Ups

COMPLETE SET (25) 4.00 10.00
1 Kenny Anderson .25 .60
2 Charles Barkley .75 2.00
3 Mookie Blaylock .30 .75
4 Muggsy Bogues .30 .75
5 Shawn Bradley .20 .50
6 Sam Cassell .30 .75
7 Clyde Drexler .50 1.25
8 Brian Grant .25 .60
9 Horace Grant .25 .60
10 Tim Hardaway .40 1.00
11 Grant Hill .50 1.25
12 Jim Jackson .25 .60
13 Shawn Kemp .50 1.25
14 Christian Laettner .25 .60
15 Dan Majerle .30 .75
16 Eric Montross .20 .50
17 Alonzo Mourning .50 1.25
18 Gheorghe Muresan .20 .50
19 Lamond Murray .20 .50
20 Dikembe Mutombo .50 1.25
21 Charles Oakley .25 .60
22 Scottie Pippen .75 2.00
23 Mark Price .30 .75
24 Glen Rice .30 .75
25 Clifford Robinson .30 .75

1995-96 Jam Session Pop-Ups Bonus

COMPLETE SET (5) 8.00 20.00
1 Patrick Ewing 4.00 10.00
2 Grant Hill 4.00 10.00
3 Glenn Robinson 2.50 6.00
4 Jason Kidd 4.00 10.00
5 Jerry Stackhouse 4.00 10.00

1995-96 Jam Session Rookies

COMPLETE SET (10) 5.00 12.00
1 Joe Smith .60 1.50
2 Antonio McDyess .60 1.50
3 Jerry Stackhouse 1.50 4.00
4 Rasheed Wallace 1.50 4.00
5 Bryant Reeves .40 1.00
6 Shawn Respert .40 1.00
7 Cherokee Parks .40 1.00
8 Alan Henderson .50 1.25
9 George Zidek .40 1.00
10 Sherrell Ford .40 1.00

1995-96 Jam Session Show Stoppers

COMPLETE SET (9) 150.00 400.00
1 Anfernee Hardaway 15.00 40.00
2 Grant Hill 12.00 30.00
3 Michael Jordan 125.00 300.00
4 Karl Malone 15.00 40.00
5 Jamal Mashburn 8.00 20.00
6 Reggie Miller 12.00 30.00
7 David Robinson 15.00 40.00
8 John Stockton 15.00 40.00
9 Chris Webber 10.00 25.00

1995 Jam Session Game Test Samples

COMPLETE SET (14) 350.00 650.00
P1 Michael Jordan 75.00 150.00
P2 Scottie Pippen 25.00 60.00
P3 Anfernee Hardaway 20.00 40.00
P4 Larry Johnson 15.00 30.00
P5 Shaquille O'Neal 40.00 80.00
P6 Alonzo Mourning 20.00 40.00
P7 Grant Hill 20.00 40.00
P8 John Stockton 40.00 80.00
P9 Karl Malone 40.00 80.00
P10 Kevin Johnson 15.00 30.00
P11 Charles Barkley 35.00 70.00
P12 David Robinson 35.00 70.00
P13 Shawn Kemp 20.00 40.00
P14 Jason Kidd 30.00 60.00

1992-93 Jazz Chevron

COMPLETE SET (5) 9.00 18.00
1 Tyrone Corbin .75 2.00
2 John Stockton 3.00 8.00
3 Jeff Malone .75 2.00
4 Tom Chambers 1.25 3.00
5 Karl Malone 3.00 8.00

1989 Jazz Old Home

COMPLETE SET (13) 40.00 80.00
1 Thurl Bailey 2.00 5.00
2 Mike Brown 1.00 2.50
3 Mark Eaton 2.00 5.00
4 Darrell Griffith 2.00 5.00
5 Bobby Hansen 1.50 4.00
6 Marc Iavaroni 1.50 4.00
7 Frank Layden CO 2.50 6.00
8 Eric Leckner 1.25 3.00
9 Jim Les 1.25 3.00
10 Karl Malone 12.50 30.00
11 Jose Ortiz 1.50 4.00
12 Scott Roth 1.25 3.00
13 John Stockton 15.00 40.00

1993-94 Jazz Old Home

COMPLETE SET (11) 15.00 35.00
1 David Benoit .40 1.00
2 Tom Chambers 1.25 3.00
3 Ty Corbin .40 1.00
4 Mark Eaton .40 1.00
5 Jay Humphries .40 1.00
6 Jeff Malone .40 1.00
7 Karl Malone 6.00 15.00
8 Jerry Sloan CO 2.00 5.00
9 Felton Spencer .40 1.00
10 John Stockton 6.00 15.00
11 Logo Card DP .40 1.00

1988-89 Jazz Smokey

COMPLETE SET (8) 45.00 85.00
1 Thurl Bailey 3.00 8.00
2 Mark Eaton 3.00 8.00
3 Bobby Hansen 3.00 8.00
4 Frank Layden CO 3.00 8.00
5 Karl Malone 12.00 30.00
6 Marc Iavaroni 4.00 10.00
7 John Stockton 15.00 40.00
8 Smokey Bear 1.25 3.00

1990-91 Jazz Star

COMPLETE SET (12) 1.50 4.00
1 Karl Malone .75 2.00
2 John Stockton .75 2.00
3 Mark Eaton .20 .50
4 Blue Edwards .20 .50
5 Thurl Bailey .20 .50
6 Mike Brown .08 .25
7 Jeff Malone .20 .50
8 Andy Toolson .08 .25
9 Darrell Griffith .20 .50
10 Delaney Rudd .08 .25
11 Walter Palmer .08 .25
12 Jerry Sloan CO .20 .50

1975-76 Jazz Team Issue

COMPLETE SET (9) 12.50 25.00
1 Ron Behagen 1.25 3.00
2 Fred Boyd 1.25 3.00
3 E.C. Coleman 1.25 3.00
4 Aaron James 1.25 3.00
5 Rich Kelley 1.25 3.00
6 Jim McElroy 1.25 3.00
7 Louie Nelson 1.25 3.00
8 Bud Stallworth 1.25 3.00
9 Nate Williams 1.25 3.00

1973-74 Jets Allentown CBA

COMPLETE SET (8) 15.00 40.00
1 Tony Johnson 2.00 5.00
2 Allie McGuire 3.00 8.00
3 Frank Card 2.00 5.00
4 George Lehmann 2.50 6.00
5 Dennis Bell 2.00 5.00
6 Ken Wilburn 2.00 5.00
7 George Bruns 2.00 5.00
8 Ed Mast 2.50 6.00

1973 Jewish Sports Champions

COMPLETE SET (16) 65.00 125.00
1 Arnold (Red) Auerbach BK 15.00 30.00

1985-86 JMS Game

COMPLETE SET (27) 50.00 120.00
1 Maurice Cheeks 2.00 5.00
2 Moses Malone 2.50 6.00
3 Bobby Jones 2.00 5.00
4 Charles Barkley 10.00 25.00
5 Julius Erving 8.00 20.00
6 Clint Richardson .75 2.00
7 Andrew Toney 1.25 3.00
8 Sedale Threatt .75 2.00
9 Clem Johnson .75 2.00
10 Bill Walton 3.00 8.00
11 Danny Ainge 2.50 6.00
12 Robert Parish 2.50 6.00
13 Kevin McHale 3.00 8.00
14 Larry Bird 10.00 25.00
15 Dennis Johnson 2.00 5.00
16 Ray Williams .75 2.00
17 Scott Wedman .75 2.00
18 Greg Kite .75 2.00
19 Michael Cooper 1.50 4.00
20 Kareem Abdul-Jabbar 5.00 12.00
21 Jamaal Wilkes 1.50 4.00
22 Bob McAdoo 2.00 5.00
23 James Worthy 3.00 8.00
24 Magic Johnson 8.00 20.00
25 Michael McGee .75 2.00
26 Kurt Rambis 1.50 4.00
27 Byron Scott 2.00 5.00

1957-58 Kahn's

COMPLETE SET (11) 2,000.00 3,000.00
1 Richard Duckett 75.00 150.00
2 George King 75.00 150.00
3 Clyde Lovellette 300.00 550.00
4 Tom Marshall 75.00 150.00
5 Jim Paxson UER 150.00 275.00
6 Dave Piontek 75.00 150.00
7 Richard Regan 75.00 150.00
8 Dick Ricketts 175.00 275.00
9 Maurice Stokes 300.00 600.00
10 Jack Twyman 300.00 500.00
11 Bobby Wanzer 150.00 275.00

1958-59 Kahn's

COMPLETE SET (10) 1,000.00 1,500.00
1 Arlen Bockhorn 60.00 125.00
2 Archie Dees 60.00 125.00
3 Sihugo Green 100.00 175.00
4 Vern Hatton 80.00 160.00
5 Tom Marshall 60.00 125.00
6 Jack Parr 80.00 160.00
7 Jim Palmer
Card lists him as George,
his middle name 60.00 125.00
8 Jim Palmer 60.00 125.00
9 Dave Piontek 60.00 125.00
10 Jack Twyman 200.00 325.00

1959-60 Kahn's

COMPLETE SET (10) 500.00 900.00
1 Arlen Bockhorn 50.00 100.00
2 Wayne Embry 75.00 150.00
3 Tom Marshall 50.00 100.00
4 Med Park 60.00 120.00
5 Dave Piontek 50.00 100.00
6 Hub Reed 50.00 100.00
7 Phil Rollins 50.00 100.00
8 Larry Staverman 50.00 100.00
9 Jack Twyman 100.00 225.00
10 Win Wilfong 50.00 100.00

1960-61 Kahn's

COMPLETE SET (12) 2,000.00 3,200.00
1 Arlen Bockhorn 30.00 60.00
2 Bob Boozer 45.00 90.00
3 Ralph E. Davis 25.00 60.00
4 Wayne Embry 50.00 100.00
5 Mike Farmer 25.00 60.00
6 Phil Jordan 30.00 60.00
7 Hub Reed 25.00 60.00
8 Oscar Robertson 700.00 1,300.00
9 Larry Staverman 25.00 60.00
10 Jack Twyman 75.00 150.00
11 Jerry West 900.00 1,500.00
12 Win Wilfong 25.00 60.00

1961-62 Kahn's

COMPLETE SET (13) 1,100.00 1,600.00
1 Arlen Bockhorn 20.00 50.00
2 Bob Boozer 35.00 75.00
3 Joe Buckhalter 25.00 50.00
4 Wayne Embry 30.00 60.00
5 Bob Nordmann 25.00 50.00
6 Hub Reed 25.00 50.00
7 Oscar Robertson 300.00 600.00
8 Adrian Smith 35.00 75.00
9 Jack Twyman 65.00 125.00
10 Bob Wiesenhahn 25.00 50.00
11 Jerry West 400.00 800.00
12 Charley Wolf CO 20.00 50.00
13 Dave Zeller 25.00 50.00

1962-63 Kahn's

COMPLETE SET (11) 500.00 1,000.00
1 Arlen Bockhorn HOR 15.00 40.00
2 Bob Boozer HOR 25.00 50.00
3 Wayne Embry 30.00 55.00
4 Tom Hawkins 30.00 65.00
5 Bud Olsen 15.00 40.00
6 Hub Reed HOR 15.00 40.00
7 Oscar Robertson 150.00 300.00
8 Adrian Smith 25.00 50.00
9 Jack Twyman HOR 40.00 80.00
10 Jerry West 200.00 400.00
11 Charley Wolf CO 15.00 40.00

1963-64 Kahn's

COMPLETE SET (13) 400.00 800.00
1 Jay Arnette 15.00 30.00
2 Arlen Bockhorn 15.00 30.00
3 Bob Boozer HOR 20.00 45.00
4 Wayne Embry 20.00 45.00
5 Tom Hawkins 35.00 55.00
6 Jerry Lucas 60.00 120.00
7 Jack McMahon CO 15.00 30.00
8 Bud Olsen 15.00 30.00
9 Oscar Robertson 100.00 200.00
10 Adrian Smith 15.00 40.00
11 Tom Thacker 15.00 30.00
12 Jack Twyman HOR 30.00 65.00
13 Jerry West 125.00 250.00

1964-65 Kahn's

COMPLETE SET (14) 325.00 650.00
1 Happy Hairston 35.00 70.00
2 Jack McMahon CO 15.00 40.00
3 George Wilson 15.00 30.00
4 Jay Arnette 15.00 30.00
5 Arlen Bockhorn 15.00 30.00
6 Wayne Embry 20.00 45.00
7 Tom Hawkins 20.00 50.00
8A Jerry Lucas 40.00 80.00
8B Jerry Lucas 40.00 80.00
9 Bud Olsen 15.00 30.00
10A Oscar Robertson 75.00 150.00
10B Oscar Robertson 75.00 150.00
11 Adrian Smith 15.00 40.00
12 Jack Twyman 30.00 60.00

1965-66 Kahn's

COMPLETE SET (4) 150.00 300.00
1 Wayne Embry 20.00 40.00
2 Jerry Lucas 40.00 80.00
3 Oscar Robertson 75.00 150.00
4 Jack Twyman 30.00 60.00

1991-92 Kellogg's College Greats

COMPLETE SET (18) 4.00 10.00
1 Kenny Anderson .30 .75
2 Clyde Drexler .50 1.25
3 Wayman Tisdale .25 .60
4 Horace Grant .30 .75
5 Kevin Johnson .30 .75
6 Karl Malone .60 1.50
7 Larry Bird 1.00 2.50
8 John Stockton .60 1.50
9 Doug Smith .20 .50
10 Mark Price .30 .75
11 Hakeem Olajuwon .60 1.50
12 Charles Smith .25 .60
13 Bernard King .40 1.00
14 Tim Hardaway .40 1.00
15 Spud Webb .30 .75
16 Mark Macon .30 .75
17 Scottie Pippen .75 2.00
18 Gary Payton .50 1.25
xx Album Holder .60 1.50

1993 Kellogg's College Greats Postercards

COMPLETE SET (10) 3.00 8.00
1 Kareem Abdul-Jabbar 1.00 2.50
2 Teresa Edwards 1.00 2.50
3 Christian Laettner .30 .75
4 Danny Manning .30 .75
5 Cheryl Miller 1.00 2.50
6 Harold Miner .20 .50
7 Chris Mullin .30 .75
8 Scottie Pippen 1.25 3.00
9 David Robinson .75 2.00
10 Isiah Thomas .30 .75

1998-99 Kellogg's NBA/WNBA

COMPLETE SET (56) 3.00 8.00
*SILVER: .4 TO 1X BASE HI
1 Grant Hill .15 .40
2 Dikembe Mutombo .15 .40
3 Mookie Blaylock .07 .20
4 Antoine Walker .15 .40
5 Chauncey Billups .12 .30
6 Glen Rice .10 .25
7 Vlade Divac .10 .25
8 Scott Burrell .05 .15
9 Ron Harper .10 .25
10 Luc Longley .07 .20
11 Samaki Walker .05 .15
12 Michael Finley .10 .25
13 Tony Battie .05 .15
14 Joe Dumars .10 .25
15 Jerry Stackhouse .10 .25
16 Joe Smith .07 .20
17 Hakeem Olajuwon .20 .50
18 Chris Mullin .12 .30
19 Brent Barry .07 .20
20 Eddie Jones .10 .25
21 Kobe Bryant .75 2.00
22 Tim Hardaway .12 .30
23 Terrell Brandon .07 .20
24 Keith Van Horn .10 .25
25 Sam Cassell .07 .20
26 Charlie Ward .05 .15
27 Horace Grant .10 .25
28 Jason Kidd .15 .40
29 Antonio McDyess .07 .20
30 Jermaine O'Neal .10 .25
31 Mitch Richmond .12 .30
32 David Robinson .12 .30
33 Tim Duncan .25 .60
34 Vin Baker .07 .20
35 Marcus Camby .07 .20
36 Damon Stoudamire .10 .25
37 Karl Malone .20 .50
38 John Stockton .20 .50
39 Shareef Abdur-Rahim .10 .25
40 Juwan Howard .07 .20
41 Sheryl Swoopes .20 .50
42 Cynthia Cooper .20 .50
43 Vicky Bullett .05 .15
44 Andrea Stinson .05 .15
45 Michelle Edwards .12 .30
46 Eva Nemcova .05 .15
47 Lisa Leslie .20 .50
48 Tamecka Dixon .05 .15

49 Rebecca Lobo .15 .40
50 Teresa Weatherspoon .12 .30
51 Michele Timms .10 .25
52 Bridget Pettis .05 .15
53 Ruthie Bolton-Holifield .10 .25
54 Bridgette Gordon .05 .15
55 Tammi Reiss .05 .15
56 Wendy Palmer .05 .15

1996 Kellogg's Raptors Stoudamire

COMPLETE SET (3) 4.00 10.00
COMMON CARD (1-3) 1.50 4.00

1992 Kellogg's Team USA Posters

COMPLETE SET (5) 10.00 25.00
1 Larry Bird
Larry Legend 5.00 12.00
2 Karl Malone
Mailman 3.00 8.00
3 Chris Mullin
Court Warrior 2.00 5.00
4 David Robinson
Admiral 3.00 8.00
5 John Stockton
Playmaker 4.00 9.00

1988 Kenner Starting Lineup Cards

1 Kareem Abdul-Jabbar 2.00 5.00
2 Michael Adams .75 2.00
3 Mark Aguirre 1.25 3.00
4 Danny Ainge 1.25 3.00
5 Thurl Bailey 5.00 12.00
6 Charles Barkley 2.50 6.00
7 Walter Berry .75 2.00
8 Larry Bird 3.00 8.00
9 Rolando Blackman 1.50 4.00
10 Michael Cage .75 2.00
11 Joe Barry Carroll .75 2.00
12 Tom Chambers .75 2.00
13 Maurice Cheeks .75 2.00
14 Michael Cooper 2.00 5.00
15 Terry Cummings .75 2.00
16 Adrian Dantley 2.00 5.00
17 Brad Daugherty 1.50 4.00
18 Johnny Dawkins .75 2.00
19 Clyde Drexler 1.50 4.00
20 Mark Eaton 5.00 12.00
21 Dale Ellis 1.25 3.00
22 Alex English 1.25 3.00
23 Patrick Ewing 1.50 4.00
24 Sleepy Floyd 1.25 3.00
25 Winston Garland .75 2.00
26 Armon Gilliam .75 2.00
27 Mike Gminski .75 2.00
28 David Greenwood .75 2.00
29 Derek Harper 1.25 3.00
30 Ron Harper 3.00 8.00
31 Rod Higgins .75 2.00
32 Dennis Hopson .75 2.00
33 Jeff Hornacek 1.25 3.00
34 Mark Jackson 1.00 2.50
35 Dennis Johnson 1.00 2.50
36 Eddie Johnson .75 2.00
37 Magic Johnson 2.50 6.00
38 Steve Johnson .75 2.00
39 Vinnie Johnson 1.50 4.00
40 Michael Jordan 30.00 80.00
41 Bernard King .75 2.00
42 Bill Laimbeer 2.00 5.00
43 Lafayette Lever .75 2.00
44 Jeff Malone .75 2.00
45 Karl Malone 10.00 25.00
46 Moses Malone 2.00 5.00
47 Danny Manning 1.00 2.50
48 Rodney McCray 1.50 4.00
49 Xavier McDaniel .75 2.00
50 Kevin McHale 1.00 2.50
51 Derrick McKey .75 2.00
52 Reggie Miller 6.00 15.00
53 Sidney Moncrief 1.50 4.00
54 Chris Mullin 1.50 4.00
55 Hakeem Olajuwon 1.50 4.00
56 Robert Parish 2.00 5.00
57 John Paxon .75 2.00
58 Sam Perkins 1.50 4.00
59 Chuck Person .75 2.00
60 Scottie Pippen 4.00 10.00
61 Terry Porter .75 2.00
62 Paul Pressey .75 2.00
63 Mark Price 4.00 10.00
64 Doc Rivers 1.00 2.50
65 Alvin Robertson .75 2.00
66 Cliff Robinson .75 2.00
67 Ralph Sampson .75 2.00
68 Danny Schayes 1.50 4.00
69 Jack Sikma 1.25 3.00
70 Kenny Smith .75 2.00
71 Steve Stipanovich 1.25 3.00
72 John Stockton 10.00 25.00
73 Isiah Thomas 1.25 3.00
74 Lasalle Thompson .75 2.00
75 Otis Thorpe .75 2.00
76 Wayman Tisdale .75 2.00
77 Kiki Vandeweghe .75 2.00
78 Spud Webb 1.00 2.50
79 Dominique Wilkins 1.50 4.00
80 Gerald Wilkins .75 2.00
81 Buck Williams .75 2.00
82 John Williams 2.00 5.00
83 Reggie Williams .75 2.00
84 Kevin Willis .75 2.00
85 James Worthy 1.50 4.00

1988 Kenner Starting Lineup Unissued Cards

COMPLETE SET (5) 20.00 50.00
1 Muggsy Bogues 6.00 15.00
2 Walter Davis 2.00 5.00
3 Charles Oakley 6.00 15.00
4 Reggie Theus 4.00 10.00
5 Orlando Woolridge 2.00 5.00

1989 Kenner Starting Lineup Cards

1 Rex Chapman 2.50 6.00
2 Dell Curry 2.50 6.00
3 Ron Harper 2.50 6.00
4 Larry Nance 2.50 6.00
5 Kelly Tripucka 2.50 6.00

1989 Kenner Starting Lineup Legends Collection Cards

1 Julius Erving 3.00 8.00
2 Wilt Chamberlain 2.50 6.00
3 John Havlicek 1.50 4.00
4 Oscar Robertson 2.00 5.00

1989 Kenner Starting Lineup One On One Cards

1 Charles Barkley 3.00 8.00
2 Larry Bird 5.00 12.00
3 Patrick Ewing 2.50 6.00
4 Magic Johnson 4.00 10.00
5 Michael Jordan 10.00 25.00
6 Kevin McHale 2.50 6.00
7 Isiah Thomas 2.50 6.00
8 Dominique Wilkins 2.50 6.00

1990 Kenner Starting Lineup Cards

1 Charles Barkley RY 2.00 5.00
1b Charles Barkley 2.00 5.00
2 Larry Bird RY 3.00 8.00
2b Larry Bird 3.00 8.00
3 Tom Chambers RY .75 2.00
3b Tom Chambers .75 2.00
4 Clyde Drexler RY 1.50 4.00
4b Clyde Drexler 1.50 4.00
5 Joe Dumars RY 1.25 3.00
5b Joe Dumars 1.25 3.00
6 Patrick Ewing RY 1.50 4.00
6b Patrick Ewing 1.50 4.00
7 Magic Johnson RY 2.50 6.00
7b Magic Johnson 2.50 6.00
8 Michael Jordan RY 15.00 40.00
8b Michael Jordan 15.00 40.00
9 Karl Malone RY 1.50 4.00
9b Karl Malone 1.50 4.00
10 Chris Mullin RY 1.25 3.00
10b Chris Mullin 1.25 3.00
11 David Robinson RY 2.00 5.00
11b David Robinson 2.00 5.00
12 Byron Scott RY .75 2.00
12b Byron Scott .75 2.00
13 John Stockton RY 1.50 4.00
13b John Stockton 1.50 4.00
14 Isiah Thomas RY 1.25 3.00
14b Isiah Thomas 1.25 3.00
15 Spud Webb RY 1.00 2.50
15b Spud Webb 1.00 2.50
16 Dominique Wilkins RY 1.25 3.00
16b Dominique Wilkins 1.25 3.00
17 James Worthy RY 1.25 3.00
17b James Worthy 1.25 3.00

1991 Kenner Starting Lineup Cards

1 Charles Barkley 1.50 4.00
2 Clyde Drexler 1.25 3.00
3 David Robinson 1.50 4.00
4 Dennis Rodman 2.00 5.00
5 Derrick Coleman 1.00 2.50
6 Dominique Wilkins 1.25 3.00
7 Isiah Thomas 1.00 2.50
8 Joe Dumars 1.00 2.50
9 Kevin Johnson 1.00 2.50
10 Larry Bird 2.50 6.00
11 Magic Johnson 2.00 5.00
12 Michael Jordan Dunk 4.00 10.00
13 Michael Jordan Dribbling 4.00 10.00
14 Patrick Ewing 1.25 3.00
15 Reggie Lewis 1.00 2.50
16 Spud Webb 1.00 2.50

1992 Kenner Starting Lineup Cards

NNO Charles Barkley 1.50 4.00
NNO Larry Bird 2.50 6.00
NNO Manute Bol .75 2.00
NNO Dee Brown .75 2.00
NNO Derrick Coleman .75 2.00
NNO Vlade Divac .75 2.00
NNO Clyde Drexler 1.25 3.00
NNO Joe Dumars 1.00 2.50
NNO Patrick Ewing 1.25 3.00
NNO Tim Hardaway 1.00 2.50
NNO Kevin Johnson 1.00 2.50
NNO Larry Johnson 1.50 4.00
NNO Magic Johnson 2.00 5.00
NNO Michael Jordan
White Jersey 20.00 50.00
NNO Michael Jordan
Red Jersey 20.00 50.00
NNO Dan Majerle .75 2.00
NNO Karl Malone 1.25 3.00
NNO Reggie Miller 1.25 3.00
NNO Chris Mullin 1.00 2.50
NNO Dikembe Mutombo 1.25 3.00
NNO Hakeem Olajuwon 1.25 3.00
NNO John Paxson .75 2.00
NNO Scottie Pippen 2.00 5.00
NNO Mark Price 1.00 2.50
NNO David Robinson 1.50 4.00
NNO Dennis Rodman 2.00 5.00
NNO John Stockton 1.25 3.00
NNO Isiah Thomas 1.00 2.50

1993 Kenner Starting Lineup Cards

1 Kenny Anderson TSC 1.00 2.50
1b Kenny Anderson Topps .75 2.00
2 Stacey Augmon TSC 1.00 2.50
2b Stacey Augmon Topps .75 2.00
3 Charles Barkley TSC 2.00 5.00
3b Charles Barkley Topps 1.50 4.00
4 Brad Daugherty TSC 1.00 2.50
4b Brad Daugherty Topps .75 2.00
5 Todd Day TSC 1.00 2.50
5b Todd Day Topps .75 2.00
6 Clyde Drexler TSC 1.50 4.00
6b Clyde Drexler Topps 1.25 3.00
7 Sean Elliott TSC 1.25 3.00
7b Sean Elliott Topps 1.00 2.50
8 Patrick Ewing TSC 1.50 4.00
8b Patrick Ewing Topps 1.25 3.00
9 Horace Grant TSC 1.00 2.50
9b Horace Grant Topps .75 2.00
10 Tom Gugliotta TSC 1.00 2.50
10b Tom Gugliotta Topps .75 2.00
11 Tim Hardaway TSC 1.25 3.00
11b Tim Hardaway Topps 1.00 2.50
12 Larry Johnson TSC 1.25 3.00
12b Larry Johnson Topps 1.00 2.50
13 Michael Jordan TSC 25.00 60.00
58SL Michael Jordan Topps 25.00 60.00
14 Shawn Kemp TSC 1.25 3.00
14b Shawn Kemp Topps 1.00 2.50
15 Christian Laettner TSC 1.25 3.00
15b Christian Laettner Topps 1.00 2.50
16 Dan Majerle TSC 1.00 2.50
16b Dan Majerle Topps .75 2.00
17 Karl Malone TSC 1.50 4.00
17b Karl Malone Topps 1.25 3.00
18 Alonzo Mourning TSC 2.00 5.00
18b Alonzo Mourning Topps 1.50 4.00
19 Dikembe Mutombo TSC 1.25 3.00
19b Dikembe Mutombo Topps 1.00 2.50
20 Shaquille O'Neal TSC 5.00 12.00
20b Shaquille O'Neal Topps 4.00 10.00
21 Scottie Pippen TSC 2.50 6.00
21b Scottie Pippen Topps 2.00 5.00
22 Terry Porter TSC 1.00 2.50
22b Terry Porter Topps .75 2.00
23 Mark Price TSC 1.25 3.00
23b Mark Price Topps 1.00 2.50
24 Glen Rice TSC 1.25 3.00
24b Glen Rice Topps 1.00 2.50
25 Mitch Richmond TSC 1.25 3.00
25b Mitch Richmond Topps 1.00 2.50
26 David Robinson TSC 2.00 5.00
26b David Robinson Topps 1.50 4.00
27 Detlef Schrempf TSC 1.25 3.00
27b Detlef Schrempf Topps 1.00 2.50
28 John Stockton TSC 1.50 4.00
28b John Stockton Topps 1.25 3.00
29 Dominique Wilkins TSC 1.50 4.00
29b Dominique Wilkins Topps 1.25 3.00

1994 Kenner Starting Lineup Cards

1 B.J. Armstrong .75 2.00
2 Stacey Augmon .75 2.00
3 Charles Barkley 1.50 4.00
4 Shawn Bradley 1.00 2.50
5 Calbert Cheaney 1.00 2.50
6 Derrick Coleman .75 2.00
7 Sean Elliott 1.00 2.50
8 LaPhonso Ellis 1.00 2.50
9 Patrick Ewing 1.25 3.00
10 Anfernee Hardaway 3.00 8.00
11 Jim Jackson 1.00 2.50
12 Larry Johnson 1.00 2.50
13 Shawn Kemp 1.25 3.00
14 Karl Malone 1.25 3.00
15 Jamal Mashburn 1.25 3.00
16 Harold Miner .75 2.00
17 Alonzo Mourning 1.25 3.00
18 Chris Mullin 1.00 2.50
19 Hakeem Olajuwon 1.25 3.00
20 Shaquille O'Neal 2.50 6.00
21 Scottie Pippen 2.00 5.00
22 David Robinson 1.50 4.00
23 Dennis Rodman 2.00 5.00
24 Latrell Sprewell 1.50 4.00
25 Chris Webber 2.50 6.00
26 Dominique Wilkins 1.25 3.00

1995 Kenner Starting Lineup Cards

1 Charles Barkley 1.50 4.00
2 Muggsy Bogues 1.00 2.50
3 Patrick Ewing 1.25 3.00
4 Horace Grant .75 2.00
5 Anfernee Hardaway 1.50 4.00
6 Grant Hill 3.00 8.00
7 Jeff Hornacek .75 2.00
8 Jim Jackson .75 2.00
9 Shawn Kemp 1.00 2.50
10 Jason Kidd 3.00 8.00
11 Toni Kukoc .75 2.00
12 Dan Majerle .75 2.00
13 Karl Malone 1.25 3.00
14 Reggie Miller 1.25 3.00
15 Eric Montross .75 2.00
16 Alonzo Mourning 1.25 3.00
17 Hakeem Olajuwon 1.25 3.00
18 Shaquille O'Neal 2.50 6.00
19 Robert Pack .75 2.00
20 Scottie Pippen 2.00 5.00
21 Mark Price .75 2.00
22 Cliff Robinson .75 2.00
23 David Robinson 1.50 4.00
24 Glenn Robinson 1.25 3.00
25 Steve Smith 1.00 2.50
26 Latrell Sprewell 1.00 2.50
27 John Starks 1.00 2.50
28 Nick Van Exel 1.00 2.50
29 Clarence Weatherspoon .75 2.00
30 Chris Webber 1.25 3.00
31 Dominique Wilkins 1.25 3.00

1995 Kenner Starting Lineup Timeless Legends Cards

1 Kareem Abdul-Jabbar 1.50 4.00
2 Wilt Chamberlain 2.00 5.00

1996 Kenner Starting Lineup Cards

1 Vin Baker 1.00 2.50
2 Charles Barkley 1.50 4.00
3 Clyde Drexler 1.25 3.00
4 Sean Elliott 1.00 2.50
5 Patrick Ewing 1.25 3.00
6 Kevin Garnett 4.00 10.00
7 Anfernee Hardaway 1.50 4.00
8 Grant Hill 1.50 4.00
9 Tyrone Hill .75 2.00
10 Juwan Howard 1.00 2.50
11 Larry Johnson 1.00 2.50
12 Eddie Jones 1.25 3.00
13 Jason Kidd 1.50 4.00
14 Karl Malone 1.25 3.00
15 Jamal Mashburn 1.00 2.50
16 Antonio McDyess 1.00 2.50
17 Reggie Miller 1.25 3.00
18 Alonzo Mourning 1.25 3.00
19 Hakeem Olajuwon 1.25 3.00
20 Shaquille O'Neal 2.50 6.00
21 Gary Payton 1.00 2.50
22 Scottie Pippen 2.00 5.00
23 Dino Radja .75 2.00
24 Bryant Reeves .75 2.00
25 Pooh Richardson .75 2.00
26 Mitch Richmond 1.00 2.50
27 Cliff Robinson .75 2.00
28 David Robinson 1.50 4.00
29 Glenn Robinson 1.00 2.50
30 Dennis Rodman 2.00 5.00
31 Joe Smith 1.00 2.50
32 Rik Smits .75 2.00
33 Jerry Stackhouse 1.25 3.00
34 Damon Stoudamire 1.25 3.00
NNO Grant Hill
Kmart Special 1.50 4.00
NNO Grant Hill
Detroit Pistons Exclusive 1.50 4.00

1996 Kenner Starting Lineup Extended Series Cards

1 Charles Barkley 1.50 4.00
2 Kobe Bryant 150.00 400.00
3 Grant Hill 1.50 4.00
4 Allen Iverson 4.00 10.00
5 Larry Johnson 1.00 2.50
6 Dikembe Mutombo 1.00 2.50
7 Shaquille O'Neal 2.50 6.00
8 Damon Stoudamire 1.00 2.50

1997 Kenner Starting Lineup Anaheim Convention Cards

1 Jason Kidd
w/Traded To Phoenix Line 1.50 4.00
2 Shaquille O'Neal 2.50 6.00

1997 Kenner Starting Lineup Atlanta Convention Cards

1 Christian Laettner 1.00 2.50
2 Glen Rice 1.00 2.50

1997 Kenner Starting Lineup Cards

1 Shareef Abdur-Rahim 1.25 3.00
2 Ray Allen 2.50 6.00
3 Kenny Anderson .75 2.00
4 Vin Baker .75 2.00
5 Charles Barkley 1.50 4.00
6 Terrell Brandon .75 2.00
7 Marcus Camby 1.25 3.00
8 Vlade Divac .75 2.00
9 Patrick Ewing 1.25 3.00
10 Michael Finley 1.00 2.50
11 Kevin Garnett 2.00 5.00
12 Horace Grant .75 2.00
14 Grant Hill 1.50 4.00
15 Allan Houston 1.00 2.50
16 Juwan Howard .75 2.00
171 Allen Iverson 1.50 4.00
18 Shawn Kemp 1.00 2.50
19 Jason Kidd 1.50 4.00
20 Kerry Kittles .75 2.00
21 Stephon Marbury 1.00 2.50
22 Reggie Miller 1.25 3.00
23 Alonzo Mourning 1.25 3.00
24 Hakeem Olajuwon 1.25 3.00
25 Shaquille O'Neal 2.50 6.00
26 Gary Payton 1.00 2.50
27 Scottie Pippen 2.00 5.00
28 Mitch Richmond 1.00 2.50
29 David Robinson 1.50 4.00
30 Dennis Rodman 2.00 5.00
31 Bill Russell Dunking 2.00 5.00
32 Bill Russell Dribbling 2.00 5.00
33 Steve Smith 1.00 2.50
34 Latrell Sprewell 1.00 2.50
35 John Stockton 1.25 3.00
36 Damon Stoudamire 1.00 2.50
37 Nick Van Exel .75 2.00
38 Loy Vaught .75 2.00
39 Antoine Walker 1.00 2.50
40 Chris Webber 1.25 3.00

1997 Kenner Starting Lineup Classic Doubles Cards

1 Kareem Abdul-Jabbar 1.50 4.00
2 Wilt Chamberlain 2.00 5.00
3 Joe Dumars 1.00 2.50
4 Patrick Ewing 1.25 3.00
5 Karl Malone 1.25 3.00
6 Kevin McHale 1.00 2.50
7 Hakeem Olajuwon 1.25 3.00
8 Willis Reed 1.00 2.50
9 John Stockton 1.25 3.00

1997 Kenner Starting Lineup Edison Convention Cards

1 Larry Johnson 1.00 2.50
2 Jerry Stackhouse 1.00 2.50

1997 Kenner Starting Lineup Timeless Legends Cards

1 Walt Frazier 1.00 2.50
2 Bill Walton 1.00 2.50

1998 Kenner Starting Lineup Cards

1 Vin Baker 1.00 2.50
2 Terrell Brandon .75 2.00
3 Kobe Bryant 4.00 10.00
4 Patrick Ewing 1.25 3.00
5 Kevin Garnett 1.50 4.00
6 Grant Hill 1.50 4.00
7 Allen Iverson 1.50 4.00
8 Magic Johnson 2.00 5.00
9 Shawn Kemp 1.00 2.50
10 Jason Kidd 1.25 3.00
11 Karl Malone 1.25 3.00
12 Stephon Marbury 1.00 2.50
13 Alonzo Mourning 1.25 3.00
14 Shaquille O'Neal 2.50 6.00
15 Dennis Rodman 2.00 5.00
16 Rik Smits .75 2.00

1985-86 Kings Big League

COMPLETE SET (18) 10.00 25.00
2 Bill Jones
Frank Hamblen .40 1.00
3 Joe Axelson .40 1.00
9 Joe Meriweather .40 1.00
10 Eddie Nealy .40 1.00
11 Mark Olberding .40 1.00
13 LaSalle Thompson .40 1.00
16 Mike Woodson .40 1.00
17 Don Buse .75 2.00
18 Larry Drew .40 1.00
19 Rick Benner
Bob Whitsitt
Sondra Kasserman .40 1.00
22 Phil Johnson .40 1.00
23 Kings Team Photo .75 2.00
24 Sacramento Arena .40 1.00
25 Eddie Johnson .75 2.00
26 Mark McNamara .40 1.00
30 Reggie Theus 2.00 5.00
32 Otis Thorpe 2.00 5.00
33 Peter Verhoeven .40 1.00

1988-89 Kings Carl's Jr.

COMPLETE SET (12) 4.00 10.00
2 Michael Jackson .20 .50
7 Danny Ainge 1.25 3.00
15 Vinny Del Negro 1.00 2.50
21 Harold Pressley .20 .50
22 Rodney McCray .40 1.00
23 Wayman Tisdale .60 1.50
30 Kenny Smith 1.25 3.00
34 Ricky Berry .20 .50
43 Jim Petersen .20 .50
50 Ben Gillery .20 .50
54 Brad Lohaus .20 .50
NNO Jerry Reynolds CO .20 .50

1989-90 Kings Carl's Jr.

COMPLETE SET (12) 4.00 10.00
2 Michael Jackson .20 .50
7 Danny Ainge 1.25 3.00
15 Vinny Del Negro .60 1.50
21 Harold Pressley .20 .50
22 Rodney McCray .40 1.00
23 Wayman Tisdale .40 1.00
30 Kenny Smith 1.00 2.50
32 Greg Kite .20 .50
40 Randy Allen .20 .50
42 Pervis Ellison .60 1.50
50 Ralph Sampson .40 1.00
NNO Jerry Reynolds CO .20 .50

1973-74 Kings Linnett

COMPLETE SET (9) 20.00 40.00
1 Nate Archibald 7.50 15.00
2 Ron Behagen 1.00 2.50
3 John Block 2.00 5.00
4 Mike D'Antoni 2.00 5.00
5 Ken Durrett 1.00 2.50
6 Sam Lacey 3.00 8.00
7 Larry McNeill 1.00 2.50
8 Jimmy Walker 3.00 8.00
9 Nate Williams 1.00 2.50

1990-91 Kings Safeway

COMPLETE SET (12) 4.00 8.00
1 Anthony Bonner .30 .75
2 Antoine Carr .40 1.00
3 Duane Causwell .40 1.00
4 Steve Colter .30 .75
5 Bobby Hansen .40 1.00
6 Eric Leckner .30 .75
7 Travis Mays .30 .75
8 Dick Motta CO .40 1.00
9 Lionel Simmons .40 1.00
10 Rory Sparrow .30 .75
11 Wayman Tisdale .60 1.50
12 Bill Wennington .40 1.00

1985-86 Kings Smokey

COMPLETE SET (16) 10.00 25.00
1 Smokey Emblem .75 2.00
2 Phil Johnson CO .75 2.00
3 Frank Hamblen ACO
Jerry Reynolds ACO
Bill Jones TR .75 2.00
4 Smokey Bear .75 2.00
5 Michael Adams 1.25 3.00
6 Larry Drew 1.00 2.50
7 Carl Henry 1.00 2.50
8 Eddie Johnson 2.00 5.00
9 Rich Kelley .75 2.00
10 Joe Kleine 1.25 3.00
11 Mark Olberding .75 2.00
12 Reggie Theus 2.50 6.00
13 LaSalle Thompson .75 2.00
14 Otis Thorpe 2.50 6.00
15 Terry Tyler .75 2.00
16 Mike Woodson 1.25 3.00

1986-87 Kings Smokey

COMPLETE SET (15) 10.00 25.00
1 Don Buse ACO .75 2.00
2 Franklin Edwards 10 .75 2.00
3 Eddie Johnson 8 2.00 5.00
4 Bill Jones TR .75 2.00
5 Joe Kleine 35 1.00 2.50
6 Mark Olberding 53 .75 2.00
7 Harold Pressley 21 .75 2.00
8 Jerry Reynolds CO .75 2.00
9 Johnny Rogers 32 .75 2.00
10 Derek Smith 18 1.25 3.00
11 Reggie Theus 24 2.00 5.00
12 LaSalle Thompson 41 .75 2.00
13 Otis Thorpe 33 2.00 5.00
14 Terry Tyler 40 .75 2.00
15 Othell Wilson 2 .75 2.00

1975-76 Kings Team Issue

COMPLETE SET (10) 12.50 25.00
1 Bob Bigelow 1.25 3.00
2 Glenn Hansen 1.25 3.00
3 Ollie Johnson 1.25 3.00
4 Larry McNeill 1.25 3.00
5 Bill Robinzine 1.25 3.00
6 Jimmy Walker 1.50 4.00
7 Lee Winfield 1.25 3.00
8 Richard Washington 1.25 3.00
9 Dan Sparks ACO 1.25 3.00
10 Phil Johnson CO 1.25 3.00

1993-94 Knicks Alamo

COMPLETE SET (5) 1.50 4.00
1 Greg Anthony .40 1.00
2 Anthony Mason .40 1.00
3 Charles Oakley .40 1.00
4 Pat Riley CO 1.25 3.00
5 John Starks .75 2.00

1988-89 Knicks Frito Lay

COMPLETE SET (15) 20.00 50.00
1 Greg Butler .40 1.00
2 Patrick Ewing 8.00 20.00
3 Sidney Green .40 1.00
4 Mark Jackson 4.00 10.00
5 Pete Myers .75 2.00
6 Johnny Newman .75 2.00
7 Charles Oakley 1.50 4.00
8 Rick Pitino CO 2.50 6.00
9 Rod Strickland 1.50 4.00
10 Trent Tucker .75 2.00
11 Kiki Vandeweghe 2.00 5.00
12 Kenny Walker .75 2.00
13 Eddie Lee Wilkins .40 1.00
14 Gerald Wilkins 1.25 3.00
15 Frito Lay
Manufacturer's Coupon .40 1.00

1984-85 Knicks Getty Photos

COMPLETE SET (11) 20.00 50.00
1 James Bailey 1.25 3.00
2 Ken Bannister 1.25 3.00
3 Hubie Brown CO 4.00 9.00
4 Butch Carter 2.00 5.00
5 Pat Cummings 1.50 4.00
6 Ernie Grunfeld 3.00 8.00
7 Bernard King 5.00 12.00
8 Louis Orr 1.50 4.00
9 Rory Sparrow 2.00 5.00
10 Trent Tucker 2.00 5.00
11 Darrell Walker 3.00 8.00

1989-90 Knicks Marine Midland

COMPLETE SET (14) 15.00 40.00
1 Greg Butler .50 1.25
2 Patrick Ewing 6.00 15.00
3 Mark Jackson 2.50 6.00
4 Stu Jackson CO .75 2.00
5 Charles Oakley 1.50 4.00
6 Pete Myers .60 1.50
7 Johnny Newman .60 1.50
8 Brian Quinnett .50 1.25
9 Rod Strickland 1.25 3.00
10 Trent Tucker .60 1.50
11 Kiki Vandeweghe 1.50 4.00
12 Kenny Walker .75 2.00
13 Gerald Wilkins .75 2.00
14 Eddie Lee Wilkins .50 1.25

1970-71 Knicks Photos

COMPLETE SET (6) 75.00 150.00
1 Dick Barnett 5.00 10.00
2 Bill Bradley 12.00 30.00
3 Dave DeBusschere 15.00 30.00
4 Walt Frazier 20.00 40.00
5 Willis Reed 15.00 40.00
6 Danny Whelan TR 5.00 10.00

1962-63 Knicks Photos

COMPLETE SET (6) 75.00 150.00
1 Dave Budd 10.00 20.00
2 Donnis Butcher 10.00 20.00
3 Knicks Team Photo 20.00 40.00
4 Whitey Martin 10.00 20.00
5 Willie Naulls 25.00 50.00

1972-73 Knicks Photos

COMPLETE SET (2) 12.50 25.00
1 Dick Barnett
Henry Bibby
Bill Bradley
Dave DeBusschere
Walt Frazier
John Gianelli
Phil Jackson 7.50 15.00
2 Jerry Lucas
Dean Meminger
Earl Monroe
Willis Reed
Tom Riker
Red Holzman CO 6.00 15.00

1970-71 Knicks Portraits

COMPLETE SET (8) 75.00 150.00
1 Dick Barnett 5.00 10.00
2 Dave DeBusschere 12.50 25.00
3 Walt Frazier 20.00 40.00
4 Red Holzman CO 10.00 20.00
5 Willis Reed 15.00 40.00
6 Mike Riordan 5.00 10.00
7 Cazzie Russell 10.00 20.00
8 Dave Stallworth 5.00 10.00

1986-87 Knicks Tickets

COMPLETE SET (24) 25.00 60.00
1 Dick McGuire
Joe Lapchick
Carl Braun 1.25 3.00
2 N.Y. Knicks Team Photo 1.50 4.00
3 Hubie Brown 1.50 4.00
4 Rory Sparrow .75 2.00
5 Dave Stallworth .75 2.00
6 Bill Bradley 3.00 8.00
7 Jerry Lucas 1.50 4.00
8 Trent Tucker .75 2.00
9 Walt Frazier 2.50 6.00
10 Willis Reed 2.00 5.00
11 Red Holzman CO 1.50 4.00
12 Mike Riordan .75 2.00
13 Harry Gallatin .75 2.00
14 Johnny Green .75 2.00
15 Kenny Walker .75 2.00
16 Bill Cartwright 1.25 3.00
17 Butch Beard .75 2.00
18 Dean Meminger .75 2.00
19 Mel Hutchins .75 2.00
20 Phil Jackson 2.50 6.00
21 Pat Cummings .75 2.00
22 Kenny Sears 1.25 3.00
23 Bernard King 1.50 4.00
24 Howard Komives .75 2.00

2008-09 Knicks Upper Deck

COMPLETE SET (14) 2.50 6.00
1 Jamal Crawford .30 .75
2 Stephon Marbury .30 .75
3 Zach Randolph .30 .75
4 David Lee .20 .50
5 Quentin Richardson .20 .50
6 Nate Robinson .20 .50
7 Eddy Curry .20 .50
8 Wilson Chandler .25 .60
9 Jared Jeffries .20 .50
10 Mardy Collins .20 .50
11 Chris Duhon .20 .50
12 Danilo Gallinari .50 1.25
13 Mike D'Antoni CO .20 .50
14 Patrick Ewing .50 1.25

1996 Kraft Space Jam

COMPLETE SET (15) 6.00 15.00
1 Bugs Bunny .20 .50
2 Daffy Duck .20 .50
3 Lola Bunny .20 .50
4 Marvin the Martian .20 .50
5 Michael Jordan
Green background 2.00 5.00
6 Michael Jordan
Red background 2.00 5.00
7 Michael Jordan
Blue background 2.00 5.00
8 Monster Bang .20 .50
9 Monster Pound .20 .50
10 Nerdluck Bang .20 .50
11 Nerdluck Pound .20 .50
12 Slyvester and Tweety .20 .50
13 Space Jam Logo .20 .50
14 Swackhammer .20 .50
15 Tasmanian Devil .20 .50

2001-02 Lakers American Express

COMPLETE SET (6) 8.00 20.00
1 John Kundla CO 1.25 3.00
2 Clyde Lovellette 1.25 3.00
3 Slater Martin 1.25 3.00
4 George Mikan 3.00 8.00
5 Vern Mikkelsen 1.25 3.00
6 Jim Pollard 1.25 3.00

1982-83 Lakers BASF

COMPLETE SET (13) 8.00 20.00
1 Kareem Abdul-Jabbar 2.00 5.00
2 Michael Cooper 1.00 2.50
3 Clay Johnson .60 1.50
4 Magic Johnson 2.50 6.00
5 Eddie Jordan .75 2.00
6 Mark Landsberger .60 1.50
7 Bob McAdoo 1.25 3.00
8 Mike McGee .60 1.50
9 Norm Nixon 1.00 2.50
10 Kurt Rambis 1.50 4.00
11 Jamaal Wilkes 1.00 2.50
12 James Worthy 3.00 8.00
13 Team Card 1.00 2.50

1983-84 Lakers BASF

COMPLETE SET (14) 10.00 25.00
1 Kareem Abdul-Jabbar 2.00 5.00
2 Michael Cooper 1.00 2.50
3 Calvin Garrett .60 1.50
4 Magic Johnson 3.00 8.00
5 Mitch Kupchak .75 2.00
6 Bob McAdoo 1.25 3.00
7 Mike McGee .60 1.50
8 Swen Nater .60 1.50
9 Kurt Rambis 1.25 3.00
10 Byron Scott 1.50 4.00
11 Larry Spriggs .60 1.50
12 Jamaal Wilkes 1.00 2.50
13 James Worthy 1.50 4.00
14 Team Photo
(Team roster on back) 1.25 3.00

1984-85 Lakers BASF

COMPLETE SET (12) 12.00 30.00
1 Kareem Abdul-Jabbar 2.50 6.00
2 Michael Cooper 1.25 3.00
3 Magic Johnson 3.00 8.00
4 Mitch Kupchak 1.00 2.50
5 Ronnie Lester 1.25 3.00
6 Bob McAdoo 1.50 4.00
7 Mike McGee .60 1.50
8 Kurt Rambis 1.25 3.00
9 Byron Scott 1.25 3.00
10 Larry Spriggs .75 2.00
10A Jamaal Wilkes 1.50 4.00
11 James Worthy 2.00 5.00
12 Team Photo
(Team roster on back) 2.00 5.00

1960-61 Lakers Bell Brand

NNO Frank Selvy 400.00 700.00

1961-62 Lakers Bell Brand

COMPLETE SET (10) 5,000.00 8,000.00
1 Elgin Baylor 1,500.00 2,500.00
2 Ray Felix 200.00 400.00
3 Tom Hawkins 300.00 600.00
4 Rod Hundley 400.00 800.00
5 Howard Jolliff 175.00 350.00
6 Rudy LaRusso 250.00 500.00
7 Fred Schaus CO 200.00 600.00
8 Frank Selvy 225.00 450.00
9 Jerry West 2,400.00 3,000.00
10 Wayne Yates 150.00 300.00

1992 Lakers Chevron Pins

COMPLETE SET (5) 8.00 20.00
1 Elgin Baylor 2.00 5.00
2 Gail Goodrich 1.25 3.00
3 Rod Hundley .75 2.00
4 Jerry West 2.50 6.00
5 Jamaal Wilkes 1.25 3.00

1974-75 Lakers Datsun

COMPLETE SET (16) 25.00 50.00
1 B.Sharman/J.Barnhill 2.00 5.00
2 P.Newell/L.Creger 1.25 3.00
3 C.Hearn/L.Shackelford 3.00 8.00
4 Lucius Allen 1.25 3.00
5 Zelmo Beaty 1.25 3.00
6 Corky Calhoun 1.25 3.00
7 Gail Goodrich 2.00 5.00
8 Happy Hairston 1.25 3.00
9 Connie Hawkins 2.00 5.00
10 Stu Lantz 1.25 3.00
11 Stan Love 1.25 3.00
12 Pat Riley 3.00 8.00
13 Cazzie Russell 1.50 4.00

14 Elmore Smith 1.25 3.00
15 Kermit Washington 1.25 3.00
16 Brian Winters 1.25 3.00

1985-86 Lakers Denny's Coins

COMPLETE SET (9) 15.00 40.00
1 Kareem Abdul-Jabbar 4.00 10.00
2 Michael Cooper 1.25 3.00
3 Magic Johnson 6.00 15.00
4 Bob McAdoo 1.25 3.00
5 Mike McGee .60 1.50
6 Kurt Rambis 1.25 3.00
7 Byron Scott 1.25 3.00
8 Jamaal Wilkes 1.25 3.00
9 James Worthy 2.50 6.00

1972-73 Lakers Lunch Bags

COMPLETE SET (5) 25.00 50.00
1 Wilt Chamberlain 10.00 20.00
2 Happy Hairston 3.00 8.00
3 Gail Goodrich 5.00 10.00
4 Jim McMillian 2.50 6.00
5 Jerry West 6.00 12.00

1950-51 Lakers Scott's

COMPLETE SET (13) 14,000.00 21,000.00
1 Bobby Doll 300.00 600.00
2 Arnie Ferrin 400.00 800.00
3 Bud Grant 2,000.00 2,500.00
4 Bob Harrison 400.00 800.00
5 Joey Hutton 300.00 600.00
6 Tony Jaros 300.00 600.00
7 John Kundla CO 400.00 800.00
8 Slater Martin 900.00 1,400.00
9 George Mikan 6,000.00 12,000.00
10 Vern Mikkelsen 1,000.00 1,600.00
11 Kevin O'Shea 300.00 600.00
12 Jim Pollard 1,000.00 1,600.00
13 Herm Schaefer 300.00 600.00

1969-70 Lakers Tickets

COMPLETE SET 40.00 80.00
1 Elgin Baylor 12.50 25.00
2 Wilt Chamberlain 15.00 30.00
3 Keith Erickson 5.00 10.00
4 Jerry West 15.00 30.00

2008-09 Lakers Upper Deck

COMPLETE SET (14) 2.50 6.00
1 Kobe Bryant 2.50 6.00
2 Lamar Odom .25 .60
3 Pau Gasol .40 1.00
4 Andrew Bynum .20 .50
5 Derek Fisher .25 .60
6 Luke Walton .25 .60
7 Vladimir Radmanovic .20 .50
8 Jordan Farmar .20 .50
9 Sasha Vujacic .20 .50
10 Trevor Ariza .20 .50
11 Chris Mihm .20 .50
12 Sun Yue .40 1.00
13 Phil Jackson CO .30 .75
14 Magic Johnson 1.00 2.50

1979-80 Lakers/Kings Alta-Dena

COMPLETE SET (8) 10.00 20.00
1 Adrian Dantley 1.25 3.00
2 Don Ford .40 1.00
3 Kareem Abdul-Jabbar 5.00 12.00
4 Norm Nixon .75 2.00

1999-00 Las Vegas Silver Bandits

COMPLETE SET (21) 2.50 6.00
1 Team CL .08 .25
2 Bandit MASCOT .08 .25
3 Silver Bandit Dancers .08 .25
4 Radio Crew .08 .25
5 Patrick Ballinger TR .08 .25
6 Isaac Burton .20 .50
7 Harold Ellis .40 1.00
8 Michael J. Frog .20 .50
9 Barry Hecker CO .40 1.00
10 J.R. Henderson .30 .75
11 Deeandre Hulett .20 .50
12 Michael Johnson .20 .50
13 Doug Lee .20 .50
14 Marcus Liberty .30 .75
15 Jeff Martin .30 .75
16 Tim Neverett ANN .20 .50
17 Eric Schraeder .20 .50
18 Rolland Todd CO .20 .50
19 Doug Swenson .20 .50
20 Mark Wade .20 .50
21 Rocky Walls .20 .50

2012-13 Leaf

COMPLETE SET (100) 15.00 40.00
AG1 Artis Gilmore .75 2.00
AM1 Arnett Moultrie .40 1.00
AN1 Andrew Nicholson .40 1.00
AY1 Alex Young .50 1.25
BB1 Bradley Beal 3.00 8.00
BHS Bob Hurley Sr. .60 1.50
BJ1 Bernard James .40 1.00
BR1 Bill Russell 2.00 5.00
CB1 Carol Blazejowski .60 1.50
CD1 Clyde Drexler 1.00 2.50
CH1 Cliff Hagan .50 1.25
CH2 Connie Hawkins .60 1.50
CM1 Chris Mullin .75 2.00
DC1 Dave Cowens 1.00 2.50
DC2 Dusan Cantekin .50 1.25
DG1 Draymond Green 2.50 6.00
DG2 Drew Gordon .50 1.25
DI1 Dan Issel .60 1.50
DJO Darius Johnson-Odom .40 1.00
DL1 Damian Lillard 6.00 15.00
DL2 Doron Lamb .40 1.00
DR1 Dennis Rodman 1.50 4.00
DS1 Dolph Schayes .75 2.00
DW1 Dominique Wilkins .75 2.00
DW2 Dion Waiters .50 1.25
EB1 Elgin Baylor 1.50 4.00
EH1 Elvin Hayes .75 2.00
EL1 Earl Lloyd .60 1.50
EU1 Edwin Ubiles .60 1.50
FA1 Furkan Aldemir .50 1.25
FE1 Festus Ezeli .40 1.00
FM1 Fab Melo .40 1.00
GG1 Gail Goodrich .50 1.25
GP1 Gary Payton .75 2.00
HG1 Hal Greer .75 2.00
HG2 Harry Gallatin .60 1.50
HP1 Herb Pope .50 1.25
IK1 Ilkan Karaman .50 1.25
JC1 Jae Crowder .75 2.00
JC2 Jared Cunningham .40 1.00
JC3 Jim Calhoun .60 1.50
JCB J'Covan Brown .50 1.25
JG1 Jorge Gutierrez .50 1.25
JJ1 John Jenkins .40 1.00
JK1 John Kundla .60 1.50
JL1 Jeremy Lamb .60 1.50
JS1 Jerry Sloan .60 1.50
JS2 John Shurna .40 1.00
JT1 Jordan Taylor .40 1.00
JT2 Jeffery Taylor .40 1.00
JW1 James Worthy 1.00 2.50
KE1 Kim English .40 1.00
KM1 Karl Malone 1.00 2.50
KM2 Kendall Marshall .40 1.00
KM3 Kevin Murphy .40 1.00
KM4 Khris Middleton 2.00 5.00
KOQ Kyle O'Quinn .50 1.25
LR1 Leon Radosevic .50 1.25
MD1 Marcus Denmon .50 1.25
MH1 Marques Haynes .50 1.25
MH2 Moe Harkless .50 1.25
MJ1 Magic Johnson 2.00 5.00
ML1 Meyers Leonard .50 1.25
MM1 Moses Malone 1.00 2.50
MP1 Miles Plumlee .40 1.00
MS1 Mike Scott .50 1.25
MSB MarShon Brooks .40 1.00
MT1 Marquis Teague .40 1.00
NA1 Nate Archibald .75 2.00
ND1 Nihad Djedovic .50 1.25
NN1 Nemanja Nedovic .50 1.25
NO1 Nnemkadi Ogwumike .60 1.50
NT1 Nate Thurmond .60 1.50
OC1 Olek Czyz .50 1.25
OJ1 Orlando Johnson .40 1.00
PJ3 Perry Jones .40 1.00
RB1 Rick Barry .50 1.25
RH1 Robbie Hummel .40 1.00
RR1 Ricky Rubio .50 1.25
RS1 Robert Sacre .40 1.00
RW1 Royce White .40 1.00
SM1 Scott Machado .40 1.00
SP1 Scottie Pippen 1.50 4.00
SS1 Sertac Sanli .50 1.25
TH1 Tu Holloway .50 1.25
TJ1 Terrence Jones .40 1.00
TM1 Tony Mitchell .50 1.25
TP1 The Professor .50 1.25
TR1 Terrence Ross 1.00 2.50
TS1 Tornike Shengelia .40 1.00
TT1 Tristan Thompson .60 1.50
TT2 Tyshawn Taylor .40 1.00
TW1 Tony Wroten .40 1.00
TZ1 Tomislav Zubcic .50 1.25
TZ2 Tyler Zeller .40 1.00
WB1 Will Barton .75 2.00
WB2 William Buford .40 1.00
XG1 Xavier Gibson .50 1.25
YG1 Yancy Gates .50 1.25
CW11 Chet Walker .60 1.50

2012-13 Leaf Autographs

AG1 Artis Gilmore 4.00 10.00
AM1 Arnett Moultrie 2.00 5.00
AN1 Andrew Nicholson 2.00 5.00
AY1 Alex Young 2.50 6.00
BB1 Bradley Beal 15.00 40.00
BJ1 Bernard James 2.00 5.00
CH1 Cliff Hagan 2.50 6.00
CH2 Connie Hawkins 3.00 8.00
DC1 Dave Cowens 4.00 10.00
DG1 Draymond Green 10.00 25.00
DG2 Drew Gordon 2.50 6.00
DJO Darius Johnson-Odom 6.00 15.00
DL1 Damian Lillard 50.00 120.00
DL2 Doron Lamb 6.00 15.00
DR1 Dennis Rodman 6.00 15.00
DW1 Dominique Wilkins 10.00 25.00
DW2 Dion Waiters 10.00 25.00
EH1 Elvin Hayes 4.00 10.00
EU1 Edwin Ubiles 3.00 8.00
FE1 Festus Ezeli 2.00 5.00
FM1 Fab Melo 10.00 25.00
GG1 Gail Goodrich 2.50 6.00
HG1 Hal Greer 4.00 10.00
HP1 Herb Pope 2.50 6.00
JC1 Jae Crowder 4.00 10.00
JC2 Jared Cunningham 2.00 5.00
JC3 Jim Calhoun 10.00 25.00
JCB J'Covan Brown 2.50 6.00
JG1 Jorge Gutierrez 2.50 6.00
JJ1 John Jenkins 2.00 5.00
JL1 Jeremy Lamb 3.00 8.00
JS2 John Shurna 2.00 5.00
JT1 Jordan Taylor 3.00 8.00
JT2 Jeffery Taylor 2.00 5.00
JW1 James Worthy 8.00 20.00
KE1 Kim English 2.00 5.00
KM2 Kendall Marshall 8.00 20.00
KM3 Kevin Murphy 2.00 5.00
KM4 Khris Middleton 10.00 25.00
KOQ Kyle O'Quinn 2.50 6.00
MD1 Marcus Denmon 2.50 6.00
MH2 Moe Harkless 2.50 6.00
ML1 Meyers Leonard 15.00 40.00
MP1 Miles Plumlee 2.00 5.00
MS1 Mike Scott 2.50 6.00
MT1 Marquis Teague 2.00 5.00
NA1 Nate Archibald 4.00 10.00
NO1 Nnemkadi Ogwumike 6.00 15.00
OC1 Olek Czyz 5.00 12.00
OJ1 Orlando Johnson 2.00 5.00
PJ3 Perry Jones 2.00 5.00
RH1 Robbie Hummel 5.00 12.00
RS1 Robert Sacre 2.00 5.00
SM1 Scott Machado 2.00 5.00
TH1 Tu Holloway 2.50 6.00
TJ1 Terrence Jones 2.00 5.00
TR1 Terrence Ross 5.00 12.00
TS1 Tornike Shengelia 2.00 5.00
TT2 Tyshawn Taylor 2.00 5.00
TW1 Tony Wroten 2.00 5.00
TZ1 Tomislav Zubcic 2.50 6.00
TZ2 Tyler Zeller 2.00 5.00
WB1 Will Barton 4.00 10.00
WB2 William Buford 2.00 5.00
YG1 Yancy Gates 2.50 6.00

2011-12 Leaf Best of Basketball Autographs

ONE PER PACK
AG1 Artis Gilmore 5.00 12.00
BH1 Bailey Howell 5.00 12.00
BH2 Bob Hurley Sr. 10.00 25.00
BR1 Bill Russell 300.00 600.00
CB1 Carol Blazejowski 5.00 12.00
CH1 Cliff Hagan 5.00 12.00
DI1 Dan Issel 5.00 12.00
DR1 Dennis Rodman 15.00 40.00
DS1 Dolph Schayes 5.00 12.00
EH1 Elvin Hayes 5.00 12.00
EL1 Earl Lloyd 10.00 25.00
HG1 Harry Gallatin 5.00 12.00
JK1 John Kundla 10.00 25.00
JS1 Jerry Sloan 6.00 15.00
MB1 MarShon Brooks 6.00 15.00
MG1 Marques Haynes 6.00 15.00
MJ1 Magic Johnson 30.00 80.00
ML1 Meadowlark Lemon 15.00 40.00
MM1 Moses Malone 8.00 20.00
NT1 Nate Thurmond 5.00 12.00
OR1 Oscar Robertson 25.00 60.00
RB1 Rick Barry 6.00 15.00
RR1 Ricky Rubio 6.00 15.00
TP1 The Professor 6.00 15.00
TT1 Tristan Thompson 8.00 20.00
SP1A Scottie Pippen 100.00 200.00

2011-12 Leaf Best of Basketball Autographs Green

*GREEN: .5X TO 1.25X HI COLUMN
STATED PRINT RUN 5 TO 25 SER.#'d SETS
EL1 Earl Lloyd/25 15.00 40.00
MB1 MarShon Brooks/25 15.00 40.00
RR1 Ricky Rubio/25 15.00 40.00
TP1 The Professor/25 15.00 40.00
TT1 Tristan Thompson/25 15.00 40.00

2012-13 Leaf Best of Basketball

AG1 Artis Gilmore 5.00 12.00
AM1 Ann Meyers 5.00 12.00
AS1 Arvydas Sabonis 40.00 100.00
BM1 Bob McAdoo 6.00 15.00
BW1 Bill Walton 12.00 30.00
CB1 Carol Blazejowski 5.00 12.00
CD1 Clyde Drexler 12.00 30.00
CL1 Clyde Lovellette 5.00 12.00
CW1 Chet Walker 5.00 12.00
DC1 Denise Curry 5.00 12.00
DC2 Denny Crum 5.00 12.00
DL1 Damian Lillard 75.00 200.00
DR1 David Robinson 12.00 30.00
DR2 Dennis Rodman 10.00 25.00
DS1 Dolph Schayes 5.00 12.00
DW1 Dominique Wilkins 8.00 20.00
EH1 Elvin Hayes 5.00 12.00
EL1 Earl Lloyd 12.00 30.00
GG1 Gail Goodrich 5.00 12.00
GG2 George Gervin 5.00 12.00
GP1 Gary Payton 12.50 30.00
HG1 Hal Greer 5.00 12.00
HG3 Horace Grant 8.00 20.00
HO1 Hakeem Olajuwon 12.00 30.00
JC1 Jim Calhoun 5.00 12.00
JW1 Jamaal Wilkes 5.00 12.00
LB1 Larry Bird 40.00 100.00
LW1 Lenny Wilkens 5.00 12.00
LW2 Lynette Woodard 5.00 12.00
MJ1 Magic Johnson 30.00 60.00
NA1 Nate Archibald 5.00 12.00
NL1 Nancy Lieberman 5.00 12.00
PR1 Pat Riley 10.00 25.00
RB1 Rick Barry 5.00 12.00
RP1 Robert Parish 5.00 12.00
SP1 Scottie Pippen 20.00 50.00
SS1 Sheryl Swoopes 5.00 12.00
SW1 Spud Webb 5.00 12.00
TK1 Toni Kukoc 6.00 15.00

2012-13 Leaf Best of Basketball Green

*GREEN: .5X TO 1.25X HI COLUMN
STATED PRINT RUN 25 SER.#'d SETS
DL1 Damian Lillard 150.00 400.00

2016-17 Leaf Best of Basketball Career Achievement

COMMON CARD 3.00 8.00

2023-24 Leaf Ink

*BLUE: .5X TO 1.2X BASIC
*GOLD: .5X TO 1.25X BASIC
BAAB1 Armando Bacot 4.00 10.00
BAAB2 Alex Barcello 2.00 5.00
BAAF1 Alex Fudge 2.00 5.00
BAAJG A.J. Griffin 2.50 6.00
BAAK1 Arthur Kaluma 2.50 6.00
BAAM1 Aminu Mohammed 2.00 5.00
BAAM2 Arterio Morris 2.00 5.00
BAAN1 Andrew Nembhard 3.00 8.00
BABM1 Bennedict Mathurin 5.00 12.00
BABM2 Brandon Miller 12.00 30.00
BABW1 Blake Wesley 2.00 5.00
BACB1 Chris Bell 2.00 5.00
BACH1 Caleb Houstan 3.00 8.00
BACJ1 Colby Jones 4.00 10.00
BACL1 Caleb Love 4.00 10.00
BACRF Camâ•Ron Fletcher 2.00 5.00
BADC1 Devan Cambridge 2.00 5.00
BADD1 Darius Days 2.00 5.00
BADH1 Destanni Henderson 5.00 12.00
BADL1 Dereck Lively 6.00 15.00
BADT1 Dalen Terry 3.00 8.00
BAEB1 Enoch Boakye 2.00 5.00
BAEE1 Emily Engstler 2.50 6.00
BAEJL E.J. Liddell 2.50 6.00
BAGB1 Gabe Brown 2.50 6.00
BAGGJ GG Jackson 6.00 15.00
BAHD1 Hunter Dickinson 5.00 12.00
BAIB1 Izaiah Brockington 2.00 5.00
BAIM1 Iverson Molinar 2.50 6.00
BAJB1 Jamaree Bouyea 2.50 6.00
BAJC1 Jalen Cook 2.00 5.00
BAJH1 Jordan Hawkins 5.00 12.00
BAJH2 Jett Howard 4.00 10.00
BAJHS Jalen Hood-Schifino 3.00 8.00
BAJJ1 Johnny Juzang 2.00 5.00
BAJK1 Jaxon Kohler 2.00 5.00
BAJL1 Jake Laravia 2.50 6.00
BAJL2 Justin Lewis 2.50 6.00
BAJM1 Jean Montero 2.00 5.00
BAJM2 Justin Moore 2.00 5.00
BAJP1 Julian Phillips 3.00 8.00
BAJS1 Jermaine Samuels 2.50 6.00
BAJS2 Jeremy Sochan 4.00 10.00
BAJW1 Jabari Walker 2.00 5.00
BAJW2 Jalen Wilson 3.00 8.00
BAKB1 Kendall Brown 2.00 5.00
BAKC1 Kennedy Chandler 2.00 5.00
BAKC2 Kofi Cockburn 2.00 5.00
BAKE1 Keon Ellis 2.00 5.00
BAKF1 Kyle Filipowski 5.00 12.00
BAKL1 Kamari Lands 2.00 5.00
BAKM1 Keegan Murray 6.00 15.00
BAKM2 Kris Murray 3.00 8.00
BAKMC Kevin McCullar 2.50 6.00
BAKMG Kameron McGusty 2.00 5.00
BAKW1 Keldâ•el Ware 3.00 8.00
BAMC1 Max Christie 4.00 10.00
BAMF1 Matthew Filipowski 2.50 6.00
BAMF2 Mike Foster 2.00 5.00
BAMG1 Mouhamed Gueye 3.00 8.00
BAMM1 Mike Miles 2.50 6.00
BAMW1 Mark Williams 3.00 8.00
BANJ1 Nikola Jovic 4.00 10.00
BANS1 NaLyssa Smith 3.00 8.00
BANSJ Nick Smith Jr. 4.00 10.00
BAOD1 Ousmane Dieng 3.00 8.00
BAPBJ Patrick Baldwin Jr. 2.50 6.00
BAPN1 Pete Nance 2.50 6.00
BAPW1 Peyton Watson 3.00 8.00
BARGJ Roddy Gayle Jr. 2.00 5.00
BARH1 Rhyne Howard 4.00 10.00
BARHJ Ron Harper Jr. 2.50 6.00
BARR1 Ryan Rollins 3.00 8.00
BASC1 Skyy Clark 2.00 5.00
BASH1 Scott Henderson 10.00 25.00
BASS1 Shaedon Sharpe 6.00 15.00
BATB1 Tevin Brown 2.00 5.00
BATE1 Tari Eason 4.00 10.00
BATJD Trayce Jackson-Davis 4.00 10.00
BATK1 Trevor Keels 2.00 5.00
BATN1 Tyler Nickel 2.00 5.00
BATVO Talia Von Oelhoffen 2.00 5.00
BATW1 Trevion Williams 2.00 5.00
BATWJ TyTy Washington Jr. 2.50 6.00
BAVB1 Veronica Burton 2.50 6.00
BAVWJ Vince Williams Jr. 4.00 10.00
BAWM1 Wendell Moore 2.50 6.00
BAYT1 Yohan Traore 2.00 5.00
BAZE1 Zach Edey 8.00 20.00

2012 Leaf Legends of Sport Remembering the Games Autographs

RTGSS1 Sheryl Swoopes 6.00 15.00

2012-13 Leaf Metal

BAAD2 Adrian Dantley 4.00 10.00
BAAD3 Anne Donovan 4.00 10.00
BAAG1 Artis Gilmore 4.00 10.00
BAAM3 Ann Meyers 4.00 10.00
BABA1 B.J. Armstrong 8.00 20.00
BABC1 Bob Cousy 30.00 80.00
BABH1 Bailey Howell 5.00 12.00
BABH2 Bob Houbregs 5.00 12.00
BABM1 Billie Moore 5.00 12.00
BABM1 Bob McAdoo 8.00 20.00
BABR1 Bill Russell 300.00 600.00
BABW1 Bill Walton 10.00 25.00
BACB1 Carol Blazejowski 4.00 10.00
BACH1 Cliff Hagan 4.00 10.00
BACL2 Clyde Lovellette 5.00 12.00
BACM1 Chris Mullin 6.00 15.00
BACO1 Charles Oakley 4.00 10.00
BACW1 Chet Walker 4.00 10.00
BACW2 Charlie Ward 4.00 10.00
BADB1 Dave Bing 12.00 30.00
BADC1 Denny Crum 5.00 12.00
BADD1 Darryl Dawkins 4.00 10.00
BADI1 Dan Issel 4.00 10.00
BADL1 Damian Lillard 50.00 120.00
BADN1 Don Nelson 6.00 15.00
BADR2 Dennis Rodman 15.00 40.00
BADR3 David Robinson 15.00 40.00
BADS1 Dolph Schayes 5.00 12.00
BADW1 Dominique Wilkins 6.00 15.00
BAEH1 Elvin Hayes 5.00 12.00
BAEL1 Earl Lloyd 20.00 50.00
BAGA1 Geno Auriemma 10.00 25.00
BAGG1 George Gervin 6.00 15.00
BAGG2 Gail Goodrich 5.00 12.00
BAHG1 Hal Greer 8.00 20.00
BAHG3 Horace Grant 12.00 30.00
BAJC2 Joan Crawford 4.00 10.00
BAJC3 Jody Conradt 4.00 10.00
BAJC4 John Chaney 5.00 12.00
BAJH2 John Havlicek 10.00 25.00
BAJS2 John Salley 4.00 10.00
BAJS4 John Stockton 20.00 50.00
BAJW1 James Worthy 6.00 15.00
BAJW2 Jamaal Wilkes 8.00 20.00
BAKA1 Kenny Anderson 4.00 10.00
BAKM1 Karl Malone 15.00 40.00
BALB1 Larry Bird 25.00 60.00
BALB2 Leon Barmore 4.00 10.00
BALC1 Lou Carnesecca 5.00 12.00
BALJ1 Larry Johnson 8.00 20.00
BALO1 Lute Olson 15.00 40.00
BALW1 Lenny Wilkens 5.00 12.00
BALW1 Lynette Woodard 4.00 10.00
BAMD3 Mel Daniels 5.00 12.00
BAMH1 Marques Haynes 12.00 30.00
BAMJ1 Magic Johnson 20.00 50.00
BANA1 Nate Archibald 5.00 12.00
BAOB1 Otis Birdsong 4.00 10.00
BAPK1 Phil Knight 8.00 20.00
BAPR1 Pat Riley 8.00 20.00
BARB1 Rick Barry 4.00 10.00
BARH1 Robert Horry 4.00 10.00
BARP1 Robert Parish 6.00 15.00
BARR1 Ricky Rubio 12.00 30.00
BARW2 Roy Williams 10.00 25.00
BASJ1 Sam Jones 6.00 15.00
BASK1 Shawn Kemp 12.00 30.00
BASO1 Shaquille O'Neal 30.00 80.00
BASP1 Scottie Pippen 25.00 60.00
BASS1 Sheryl Swoopes 4.00 10.00
BASS3 Satch Sanders 4.00 10.00
BASW1 Spud Webb 4.00 10.00
BATH2 Tom Heinsohn 10.00 25.00
BATK1 Toni Kukoc 5.00 12.00
BAVC1 Van Chancellor 4.00 10.00
BAXM1 Xavier McDaniel 4.00 10.00

2012-13 Leaf Metal Holo

*HOLO: .5X TO 1.2X BASIC
STATED PRINT RUN 50 SER.#'d SETS
BABK1 Bobby Knight 40.00 100.00

2012-13 Leaf Metal Holo Blue

*HOLO BLUE: .6X TO 1.5X BASIC
PRINT RUNS B/WN 15-25 COPIES PER
NO PRICING ON QTY 15

2012-13 Leaf Metal Patrick Ewing Patch Autograph

STATED PRINT RUN 99 SER.#'d SETS
PE2 Patrick Ewing 150.00 400.00

2012-13 Leaf Metal 1960

1 Bill Russell 2.00 5.00
2 Bradley Beal 3.00 8.00
4 Damian Lillard 6.00 15.00
5 Dion Waiters .50 1.25
6 Gary Payton .75 2.00
7 Larry Bird 2.00 5.00
8 Magic Johnson 2.00 5.00
9 Moe Harkless .50 1.25
10 Ricky Rubio .50 1.25
11 Shaquille O'Neal 2.00 5.00
12 Tyler Zeller .40 1.00

2012-13 Leaf Metal 1960 Green

*GREEN: 1X TO 2.5X BASIC
STATED PRINT RUN 25 SER.#'d SETS
4 Damian Lillard 20.00 50.00

2012-13 Leaf Metal Faces of the Game Holo

STATED PRINT RUN 50 SER.#'d SETS
FGBR1 Bill Russell 200.00 500.00
FGCM1 Chris Mullin 10.00 25.00
FGDL1 Damian Lillard 75.00 200.00
FGDR1 David Robinson 20.00 50.00
FGDR2 Dennis Rodman 15.00 40.00
FGGG1 George Gervin 15.00 40.00
FGJS4 John Stockton 25.00 60.00
FGKM1 Karl Malone 20.00 50.00
FGLB1 Larry Bird 30.00 80.00
FGMJ1 Magic Johnson 25.00 60.00
FGRR1 Ricky Rubio 20.00 50.00
FGSJ1 Sam Jones 8.00 20.00
FGSK1 Shawn Kemp 15.00 40.00
FGSO1 Shaquille O'Neal 40.00 100.00
FGSP1 Scottie Pippen 30.00 80.00
FGSS1 Sheryl Swoopes 4.00 10.00

2012-13 Leaf Metal Faces of the Game Holo Blue

*HOLO BLUE: .5X TO 1.2X BASIC
STATED PRINT RUN 25 SER.#'d SETS

2012-13 Leaf Metal Hoop Matrix

HMBB1 Bradley Beal 3.00 8.00
HMBC1 Bob Cousy 1.00 2.50
HMBR1 Bill Russell 2.00 5.00
HMDL1 Damian Lillard 10.00 25.00
HMDL2 Damian Lillard 10.00 25.00
HMDL3 Damian Lillard 10.00 25.00
HMDR1 David Robinson 1.00 2.50
HMDR2 Dennis Rodman 1.50 4.00
HMDW1 Dion Waiters .50 1.25
HMGP1 Gary Payton .75 2.00
HMJH1 John Havlicek 1.25 3.00
HMJL1 Jeremy Lamb .60 1.50
HMJS1 John Stockton 1.25 3.00
HMKM1 Karl Malone 1.00 2.50
HMKM2 Kendall Marshall .40 1.00
HMLB1 Larry Bird 2.00 5.00
HMMH1 Moe Harkless .50 1.25
HMMJ1 Magic Johnson 2.00 5.00
HMPR1 Pat Riley .60 1.50
HMRR1 Ricky Rubio .50 1.25
HMSK1 Shawn Kemp 1.00 2.50
HMSO1 Shaquille O'Neal 2.00 5.00
HMSP1 Scottie Pippen 1.50 4.00
HMTR1 Terrence Ross 1.00 2.50
HMTZ1 Tyler Zeller .40 1.00

2012-13 Leaf Metal Hoop Matrix Green

*GREEN: .6X TO 1.5X BASIC
STATED PRINT RUN 99 SER.#'d SETS

2012-13 Leaf Metal Hoop Matrix Pink

*PINK: 1.5X TO 4X BASIC
STATED PRINT RUN 25 SER.#'d SETS

2012-13 Leaf Metal Inductions Holo

STATED PRINT RUN 50 SER.#'d SETS
IBH1 Bailey Howell 5.00 12.00
IBR1 Bill Russell 300.00 600.00
IBW1 Bill Walton 12.00 30.00
ICM1 Chris Mullin 10.00 25.00
IDI1 Dan Issel 5.00 12.00
IDR1 David Robinson 20.00 50.00
IDW1 Dominique Wilkins 8.00 20.00
IGG2 Gail Goodrich 8.00 20.00
IJW1 James Worthy 10.00 25.00
IKM1 Karl Malone 25.00 60.00
ILB1 Larry Bird 25.00 60.00
IMH1 Marques Haynes 6.00 15.00
IMJ1 Magic Johnson 25.00 60.00
IRB1 Rick Barry 5.00 12.00
ISJ1 Sam Jones 6.00 15.00
ISP1 Scottie Pippen 40.00 100.00

2012-13 Leaf Metal Inductions Holo Blue

*HOLO BLUE: .5X TO 1.2X BASIC
STATED PRINT RUN 25 SER.#'d SETS

2012-13 Leaf Metal Nicknames Holo

STATED PRINT RUN 50 SER.#'d SETS
NNDR1 David Robinson 20.00 50.00
NNDR2 Dennis Rodman 25.00 60.00
NNDW1 Dominique Wilkins 15.00 40.00
NNKM1 Karl Malone 30.00 80.00
NNLB1 Larry Bird 40.00 100.00
NNLJ1 Larry Johnson 12.00 30.00

2012-13 Leaf Metal Nicknames Holo Blue

*HOLO BLUE: .5X TO 1.2X BASIC
STATED PRINT RUN 25 SER.#'d SETS

2012-13 Leaf Metal Unsung Heroes Holo

STATED PRINT RUN 50 SER.#'d SETS
UHBA1 B.J. Armstrong 5.00 12.00
UHDD1 Darryl Dawkins 5.00 12.00
UHKA1 Kenny Anderson 5.00 12.00
UHLJ1 Larry Johnson 8.00 20.00
UHRH1 Robert Horry 8.00 20.00
UHSK1 Shawn Kemp 20.00 50.00
UHTK1 Toni Kukoc 6.00 15.00

2012-13 Leaf Metal Unsung Heroes Holo Blue

*HOLO BLUE: .5X TO 1.2X BASIC
STATED PRINT RUN 25 SER.#'d SETS

2014 Leaf National Convention Andrew Wiggins

COMPLETE SET (5) 4.00 10.00
COMMON WIGGINS 1.00 2.50
ANNOUNCED PRINT RUN 2000

2014 Leaf National Convention Andrew Wiggins Autographs

COMMON WIGGINS AU 60.00 120.00
ANNOUNCED PRINT RUN 20

2012-13 Leaf Signature

AM1 Arnett Moultrie 2.50 6.00
AN1 Andrew Nicholson 2.50 6.00
AY1 Alex Young 3.00 8.00
BB1 Bradley Beal 20.00 50.00
CD1 Clyde Drexler 10.00 25.00
DG1 Draymond Green 12.00 30.00
DG2 Drew Gordon 3.00 8.00
DL1 Damian Lillard 60.00 150.00
DL2 Doron Lamb 2.50 6.00
DR1 Dennis Rodman 8.00 20.00
DW1 Dominique Wilkins 12.00 30.00
DW2 Dion Waiters 6.00 15.00
EU1 Edwin Ubiles 4.00 10.00
FE1 Festus Ezeli 2.50 6.00
FM1 Fab Melo 2.50 6.00
HP1 Herb Pope 3.00 8.00
JC1 Jae Crowder 5.00 12.00
JC2 Jared Cunningham 2.50 6.00
JCB J'Covan Brown 2.50 6.00
JJ1 John Jenkins 2.50 6.00
JL1 Jeremy Lamb 4.00 10.00
JT2 Jeffery Taylor 2.50 6.00
KE1 Kim English 2.50 6.00
KM1 Karl Malone 15.00 40.00
KM2 Kendall Marshall 2.50 6.00
KM4 Khris Middleton 12.00 30.00
MD1 Marcus Denmon 3.00 8.00
MH1 Marques Haynes 6.00 15.00
MH2 Moe Harkless 3.00 8.00
ML1 Meyers Leonard 3.00 8.00
MS1 Mike Scott 3.00 8.00
MT1 Marquis Teague 2.50 6.00
NO1 Nnemkadi Ogwumike 3.00 8.00
OJ1 Orlando Johnson 2.50 6.00
PJ3 Perry Jones 2.50 6.00
RS1 Robert Sacre 2.50 6.00
RW1 Royce White 2.50 6.00
SM1 Scott Machado 2.50 6.00
SP1 Scottie Pippen 40.00 100.00
TH1 Tu Holloway 3.00 8.00
TJ1 Terrence Jones 2.50 6.00
TR1 Terrence Ross 6.00 15.00
TT2 Tyshawn Taylor 2.50 6.00
TW1 Tony Wroten 2.50 6.00
TZ2 Tyler Zeller 2.50 6.00
WB1 Will Barton 5.00 12.00
XG1 Xavier Gibson 3.00 8.00
YG1 Yancy Gates 3.00 8.00

2012-13 Leaf Signature Gold

*GOLD: .6X TO 1.5X BASE HI
STATED PRINT RUN 10 TO 25 SETS
BB1 Bradley Beal 30.00 80.00
FM1 Fab Melo 12.00 30.00
JJ1 John Jenkins 10.00 25.00
NO1 Nnemkadi Ogwumike 8.00 20.00
PJ3 Perry Jones 15.00 40.00
RW1 Royce White 15.00 40.00

2012-13 Leaf Signature Silver

*SILVER: .5X TO 1.25X BASE HI
STATED PRINT RUN 25 TO 99 SETS
BB1 Bradley Beal/99 25.00 60.00
JJ1 John Jenkins/50 10.00 25.00
TT2 Tyshawn Taylor/99 6.00 15.00

2012-13 Leaf Signature All-American Gold

*GOLD: .6X TO 1.5X SILVER
STATED PRINT RUN 25 SER.#'d SETS
NO1 Nnemkadi Ogwumike 6.00 15.00

2012-13 Leaf Signature All-American Silver

STATED PRINT RUN 75 TO 99 SER.#'d SETS
AM1 Arnett Moultrie/99 2.50 6.00
BB1 Bradley Beal/99 20.00 50.00
DL1 Damian Lillard/99 75.00 200.00
DL2 Doron Lamb/99 2.50 6.00
DW2 Dion Waiters/99 3.00 8.00
FM1 Fab Melo/99 2.50 6.00
JL1 Jeremy Lamb/99 4.00 10.00
JT2 Jeffery Taylor/99 2.50 6.00
KM2 Kendall Marshall/99 2.50 6.00
MH2 Moe Harkless/99 3.00 8.00
ML1 Meyers Leonard/99 3.00 8.00
NO1 Nnemkadi Ogwumike/99 4.00 10.00
PJ3 Perry Jones/99 2.50 6.00
TJ1 Terrence Jones/99 2.50 6.00
TR1 Terrence Ross/99 6.00 15.00
TW1 Tony Wroten/99 2.50 6.00
TZ2 Tyler Zeller/75 2.50 6.00

2012-13 Leaf Signature Black and White

BB1 Bradley Beal 25.00 60.00
CD1 Clyde Drexler 15.00 40.00
DL1 Damian Lillard 75.00 200.00
DL2 Doron Lamb 3.00 8.00
DR1 Dennis Rodman 15.00 40.00
KM1 Karl Malone 40.00 100.00
KM2 Kendall Marshall 3.00 8.00
PJ3 Perry Jones 3.00 8.00
SP1 Scottie Pippen 100.00 200.00
TJ1 Terrence Jones 3.00 8.00

2012-13 Leaf Signature Droppin' Dimes Gold

*GOLD: .5X TO 1.25X SILVER
STATED PRINT RUN 25 SER.#'d SETS

2012-13 Leaf Signature Droppin' Dimes Silver

STATED PRINT RUN 40 TO 99 SETS
DL1 Damian Lillard/75 75.00 200.00
KM2 Kendall Marshall/99 3.00 8.00
MT1 Marquis Teague/99 3.00 8.00
SM1 Scott Machado/49 3.00 8.00
TT2 Tyshawn Taylor/99 3.00 8.00
TW1 Tony Wroten/99 3.00 8.00

2012-13 Leaf Signature Scottie Pippen Patch Autographs

STATED PRINT RUN ONE TO 99 SETS
SP1 Scottie Pippen/99 40.00 100.00
SP2 Scottie Pippen Blue/25 100.00 200.00

2012-13 Leaf Signature So Money! Gold

*GOLD: .5X TO 1.25X SILVER
STATED PRINT RUN 25 SER.#'d SETS
NO1 Nnemkadi Ogwumike 8.00 20.00

2012-13 Leaf Signature So Money! Silver

STATED PRINT RUN 40 TO 99 SETS
BB1 Bradley Beal/99 25.00 60.00
DL1 Damian Lillard/99 75.00 200.00
DL2 Doron Lamb/99 3.00 8.00
JJ1 John Jenkins/99 8.00 20.00
JL1 Jeremy Lamb/99 5.00 12.00
KM1 Karl Malone/40 25.00 60.00
MH2 Moe Harkless/99 4.00 10.00
MT1 Marquis Teague/99 3.00 8.00
NO1 Nnemkadi Ogwumike/99 4.00 10.00
PJ3 Perry Jones/75 3.00 8.00
TR1 Terrence Ross/99 8.00 20.00
TZ2 Tyler Zeller/75 3.00 8.00

2012-13 Leaf Signature Takin' it to the Hole Gold

*GOLD: .5X TO 1.25X SILVER
STATED PRINT RUN 25 SER.#'d SETS
BB1 Bradley Beal 75.00 200.00
DG1 Draymond Green 25.00 60.00
DL1 Damian Lillard 150.00 400.00
NO1 Nnemkadi Ogwumike 8.00 20.00

2012-13 Leaf Signature Takin' it to the Hole Silver

STATED PRINT RUN 99 SER.#'d SETS
AM1 Arnett Moultrie/99 3.00 8.00
AN1 Andrew Nicholson/99 3.00 8.00
BB1 Bradley Beal/99 50.00 120.00
DG1 Draymond Green/49 20.00 50.00
DL1 Damian Lillard/75 100.00 250.00
DW2 Dion Waiters/49 4.00 10.00
JT2 Jeffery Taylor/49 3.00 8.00
MH2 Moe Harkless/49 4.00 10.00
NO1 Nnemkadi Ogwumike/99 4.00 10.00
RW1 Royce White/99 3.00 8.00
TJ1 Terrence Jones/49 3.00 8.00
TR1 Terrence Ross/99 8.00 20.00
WB1 Will Barton/99 6.00 15.00

2013 Leaf Sports Heroes Going for the Gold Autographs

*SILVER/25: .5X TO 1.2X BASIC CARDS
GGDR2 David Robinson 20.00 50.00
GGDW2 Dominique Wilkins 8.00 20.00

2013 Leaf Sports Heroes Going for the Gold Autographs Silver

*SILVER: .5X TO 1.2X BASIC CARDS
STATED PRINT RUN 25 SER.#'d SETS

2013 Leaf Sports Heroes Inscriptions Autographs

STATED PRINT RUN 60 SER. #'d SETS
IDL1 Damian Lillard 40.00 80.00

2013 Leaf Sports Heroes Inscriptions Autographs Silver

*SILVER: .5X TO 1.2X BASIC CARDS
STATED PRINT RUN 25 SER.#'d SETS

2013 Leaf Sports Heroes Pink Ribbon Inscription Autographs

STATED PRINT RUN 60 SER. #'d SETS
DL1 Damian Lillard 50.00 100.00

2013 Leaf Sports Heroes Pink Ribbon Inscription Autographs Silver

*SILVER: .5X TO 1.2X BASIC CARDS
STATED PRINT RUN 25 SER.#'d SETS

2013 Leaf Sports Heroes Springfield's Finest Autographs

SFAM2 Ann Meyers 4.00 10.00
SFAS1 Arvydas Sabonis 15.00 40.00
SFBW1 Bill Walton 8.00 20.00
SFCC1 Cynthia Cooper 4.00 10.00
SFCD1 Clyde Drexler/17* 8.00 20.00
SFCH1 Cliff Hagan 4.00 10.00
SFDR1 Dennis Rodman 10.00 25.00
SFDW2 Dominique Wilkins 10.00 25.00
SFGG1 George Gervin 6.00 15.00
SFGG2 Gail Goodrich 6.00 15.00
SFGP1 Gary Payton 5.00 12.00
SFJC2 Jim Calhoun 5.00 12.00

SFRB1 Rick Barry 5.00 12.00
SFRP1 Robert Parish 6.00 15.00

2013 Leaf Sports Heroes Springfield's Finest Autographs Silver

*SILVER: .5X TO 1.2X BASIC CARDS
STATED PRINT RUN 25 SER.#'d SETS

2013 Leaf Sports Heroes Valiant Damian Lillard Autographs

BADL1 Damian Lillard 20.00 50.00
ROYDL1 Damian Lillard 20.00 50.00

2013 Leaf Sports Heroes Valiant Damian Lillard Autographs Orange

*ORANGE: .5X TO 1.2X BASIC CARDS
STATED PRINT RUN 50 SER.#'d SETS

2013 Leaf Sports Heroes Valiant Damian Lillard Autographs Purple

*PURPLE: .6X TO 1.5X BASIC CARDS
STATED PRINT RUN 25 SER. #'d SETS

2012-13 Leaf Ultimate

AN1 Andrew Nicholson 2.00 5.00
BB1 Bradley Beal 20.00 50.00
BJ1 Bernard James 2.00 5.00
CD1 Clyde Drexler 12.00 30.00
DG1 Draymond Green 12.00 30.00
DL1 Damian Lillard 75.00 200.00
DL2 Doron Lamb 2.00 5.00
DR1 Dennis Rodman 12.00 30.00
DW1 Dominique Wilkins 10.00 25.00
DW2 Dion Waiters 2.50 6.00
EL1 Earl Lloyd 15.00 40.00
FE1 Festus Ezeli 2.00 5.00
FM1 Fab Melo 2.00 5.00
HP1 Herb Pope 2.50 6.00
JC1 Jae Crowder 4.00 10.00
JC2 Jared Cunningham 2.00 5.00
JJ1 John Jenkins 2.00 5.00
JL1 Jeremy Lamb 3.00 8.00
JT2 Jeffery Taylor 2.00 5.00
JW1 James Worthy 10.00 25.00
KE1 Kim English 2.00 5.00
KM1 Karl Malone 20.00 50.00
KM2 Kendall Marshall 2.00 5.00
KM4 Khris Middleton 10.00 25.00
KOQ Kyle O'Quinn 2.50 6.00
MH1 Marques Haynes 10.00 25.00
MH2 Moe Harkless 2.50 6.00
ML1 Meyers Leonard 2.50 6.00
MP1 Miles Plumlee 2.00 5.00
MS1 Mike Scott 2.50 6.00
MT1 Marquis Teague 2.00 5.00
NO1 Nnemkadi Ogwumike 2.00 5.00
OJ1 Orlando Johnson 2.00 5.00
PJ3 Perry Jones 2.00 5.00
RH1 Robbie Hummel 2.00 5.00
RS1 Robert Sacre 2.00 5.00
RW1 Royce White 2.00 5.00
SM1 Scott Machado 2.00 5.00
SP1 Scottie Pippen 30.00 80.00
TJ1 Terrence Jones 2.00 5.00
TR1 Terrence Ross 5.00 12.00
TS1 Tornike Shengelia 2.00 5.00
TT2 Tyshawn Taylor 2.00 5.00
TW1 Tony Wroten 2.00 5.00
TZ2 Tyler Zeller 2.00 5.00
WB1 Will Barton 4.00 10.00

2012-13 Leaf Ultimate Silver

*SILVER: .75X TO 2X BASE HI
STATED PRINT RUN 25 SER.#'d SETS

2012-13 Leaf Ultimate Inscriptions

STATED PRINT RUN 25 SER.#'d SETS
DL1 Damian Lillard 125.00 300.00
DR1 Dennis Rodman 40.00 100.00
EL1 Earl Lloyd 12.00 30.00
KM1 Karl Malone 50.00 100.00
MH1 Marques Haynes 8.00 20.00

2012-13 Leaf Ultimate Karl Malone Patch Autographs

PRINT RUNS LISTED BELOW
KM1 Karl Malone/99 25.00 60.00
KM2 Karl Malone Blue/25 60.00 120.00

2012-13 Leaf Ultimate Numeration

STATED PRINT RUN 4 TO 91 SETS
AN1 Andrew Nicholson/44 6.00 15.00
BB1 Bradley Beal/23 75.00 200.00
DG1 Draymond Green/23 12.00 30.00
DL2 Doron Lamb/20 6.00 15.00
DR1 Dennis Rodman/91 25.00 60.00
DW1 Dominique Wilkins/21 20.00 50.00
FM1 Fab Melo/51 6.00 15.00
JJ1 John Jenkins/23 6.00 15.00
JT2 Jeffery Taylor/44 6.00 15.00
JW1 James Worthy/42 15.00 40.00
KM1 Karl Malone/32 25.00 60.00
MT1 Marquis Teague/25 6.00 15.00
NO1 Nnemkadi Ogwumike/30 6.00 15.00
RW1 Royce White/30 6.00 15.00
SP1 Scottie Pippen/33 60.00 150.00
TR1 Terrence Ross/31 8.00 20.00

2012-13 Leaf Ultimate Rim Rockers

AN1 Andrew Nicholson 2.00 5.00
DW1 Dominique Wilkins 8.00 20.00
FM1 Fab Melo 2.00 5.00
JT2 Jeffery Taylor 2.00 5.00
ML1 Meyers Leonard 2.50 6.00
PJ3 Perry Jones 2.00 5.00
TJ1 Terrence Jones 2.00 5.00
TZ2 Tyler Zeller 2.00 5.00

2012-13 Leaf Ultimate Rim Rockers Silver

*SILVER: .75X TO 2X BASE HI
STATED PRINT RUN 25 SER.#'d SETS

2012-13 Leaf Ultimate State Pride

BB1 Bradley Beal 20.00 50.00
DG1 Draymond Green 15.00 40.00
DL1 Damian Lillard 100.00 250.00
DL2 Doron Lamb 2.50 6.00
DW2 Dion Waiters 3.00 8.00
JL1 Jeremy Lamb 4.00 10.00
KM2 Kendall Marshall 2.50 6.00
ML1 Meyers Leonard 3.00 8.00
MT1 Marquis Teague 2.50 6.00
NO1 Nnemkadi Ogwumike 4.00 10.00
PJ3 Perry Jones 2.50 6.00
TJ1 Terrence Jones 2.50 6.00
TR1 Terrence Ross 6.00 15.00
TT2 Tyshawn Taylor 2.50 6.00
TW1 Tony Wroten 2.50 6.00
TZ2 Tyler Zeller 2.50 6.00

2012-13 Leaf Ultimate State Pride Silver

*SILVER: .6X TO 1.5X BASE HI
STATED PRINT RUN 25 SER.#'d SETS
DL1 Damian Lillard 150.00 400.00

2012 Leaf Valiant Stars Damian Lillard Autographs

*ORANGE/50: .6X TO 1.5X
*PURPLE/25: .75X TO 2X BASIC
SDL1 Damian Lillard 12.00 30.00

1992 Lime Rock Larry Bird

COMPLETE SET (3) 1.50 4.00
COMMON CARD (1-3) .60 1.50

2009-10 Limited

1-100 PRINT RUN 199 SER.#'d SETS
101-150 PRINT RUN 99 SER.#'d SETS
151-180 PRINT RUN 299 SER.#'d SETS
1 Andre Iguodala 1.50 4.00
2 Elton Brand 1.25 3.00
3 Samuel Dalembert 1.00 2.50
4 Chris Duhon 1.00 2.50
5 David Lee 1.00 2.50
6 Wilson Chandler 1.25 3.00
7 Kevin Garnett 4.00 10.00
8 Paul Pierce 2.50 6.00
9 Rasheed Wallace 2.00 5.00
10 Ray Allen 2.50 6.00
11 Brook Lopez 1.50 4.00
12 Courtney Lee 1.00 2.50
13 Devin Harris 1.00 2.50
14 Andrea Bargnani 1.00 2.50
15 Chris Bosh 2.00 5.00
16 Hedo Turkoglu 1.25 3.00
17 Ben Wallace 2.00 5.00
18 Richard Hamilton 1.50 4.00
19 Rodney Stuckey 1.00 2.50
20 Tayshaun Prince 1.50 4.00
21 Derrick Rose 2.50 6.00
22 Luol Deng 1.25 3.00
23 Tyrus Thomas 1.00 2.50
24 Daniel Gibson 1.00 2.50
25 LeBron James 12.00 30.00
26 Mo Williams 1.25 3.00
27 Shaquille O'Neal 5.00 12.00
28 Danny Granger 1.00 2.50
29 Jeff Foster 1.00 2.50
30 T.J. Ford 1.00 2.50
31 Andrew Bogut 1.25 3.00
32 Kurt Thomas 1.00 2.50
33 Michael Redd 1.25 3.00
34 Dwight Howard 2.00 5.00
35 Jameer Nelson 1.00 2.50
36 Rashard Lewis 1.25 3.00
37 Vince Carter 3.00 8.00
38 Joe Johnson 1.25 3.00
39 Marvin Williams 1.00 2.50
40 Mike Bibby 1.50 4.00
41 Antawn Jamison 1.25 3.00
42 Caron Butler 1.25 3.00
43 Gilbert Arenas 1.25 3.00
44 Gerald Wallace 1.25 3.00
45 Raymond Felton 1.00 2.50
46 Tyson Chandler 1.25 3.00
47 Dwyane Wade 3.00 8.00
48 Jermaine O'Neal 1.50 4.00
49 Mario Chalmers 1.25 3.00
50 Michael Beasley 1.00 2.50
51 Aaron Brooks 1.25 3.00
52 Shane Battier 1.50 4.00
53 Trevor Ariza 1.00 2.50
54 O.J. Mayo 1.00 2.50
55 Rudy Gay 1.50 4.00
56 Zach Randolph 1.50 4.00
57 Chris Paul 3.00 8.00
58 David West 1.25 3.00
59 Emeka Okafor 1.25 3.00
60 James Posey 1.00 2.50
61 Dirk Nowitzki 4.00 10.00
62 Jason Kidd 2.50 6.00
63 Jason Terry 1.25 3.00
64 Josh Howard 1.25 3.00
65 Antonio McDyess 1.25 3.00
66 Tim Duncan 4.00 10.00
67 Tony Parker 2.50 6.00
68 Brandon Roy 2.00 5.00
69 Greg Oden 1.00 2.50
70 LaMarcus Aldridge 1.50 4.00
71 Rudy Fernandez 1.00 2.50
72 Corey Brewer 1.00 2.50
73 Kevin Love 1.50 4.00
74 Ramon Sessions 1.00 2.50
75 Andrei Kirilenko 1.25 3.00
76 Carlos Boozer 1.25 3.00
77 Deron Williams 1.25 3.00
78 Jeff Green 1.25 3.00
79 Kevin Durant 6.00 15.00
80 Russell Westbrook 3.00 8.00
81 Carmelo Anthony 2.50 6.00
82 Chauncey Billups 2.00 5.00
83 Kenyon Martin 1.25 3.00
84 Derek Fisher 1.50 4.00
85 Kobe Bryant 12.00 30.00
86 Lamar Odom 1.25 3.00
87 Pau Gasol 2.50 6.00
88 Ron Artest 1.50 4.00
89 Andris Biedrins 1.00 2.50
90 Anthony Randolph 1.00 2.50
91 Stephen Jackson 1.25 3.00
92 Amare Stoudemire 1.25 3.00
93 Channing Frye 1.00 2.50
94 Steve Nash 3.00 8.00
95 Baron Davis 1.25 3.00
96 Eric Gordon 1.25 3.00
97 Marcus Camby 1.25 3.00
98 Andres Nocioni 1.00 2.50
99 Kenyon Martin 1.25 3.00
100 Spencer Hawes 1.00 2.50
101 Magic Johnson 8.00 20.00
102 Glen Rice 1.50 4.00
103 Wilt Chamberlain 8.00 20.00
104 World B. Free 1.50 4.00
105 Julius Erving 5.00 12.00
106 Alex English 2.50 6.00
107 Al Cervi 2.00 5.00
108 John Salley 1.50 4.00
109 Al Attles 1.50 4.00
110 Maurice Cheeks 1.50 4.00
111 Bob Cousy 5.00 12.00
112 Cazzie Russell 2.00 5.00
113 Dave Bing 2.50 6.00
114 Bob McAdoo 2.50 6.00
115 Albert King 1.50 4.00
116 Alonzo Mourning 3.00 8.00
117 Sleepy Floyd 1.50 4.00
118 John Havlicek 5.00 12.00
119 Gheorghe Muresan 1.25 3.00
120 Sidney Moncrief 1.50 4.00
121 Jamal Mashburn 1.50 4.00
122 Kevin McHale 3.00 8.00
123 Larry Bird 8.00 20.00
124 Vlade Divac 2.00 5.00
125 Sean Elliott 1.50 4.00
126 Chris Ford 1.50 4.00
127 Campy Russell 1.50 4.00
128 Muggsy Bogues 2.00 5.00
129 Elgin Baylor 5.00 12.00
130 Bill Walton 3.00 8.00
131 Rickey Green 2.00 5.00
132 Hal Greer 2.50 6.00
133 Norm Nixon 2.00 5.00
134 Jerry Sloan 2.50 6.00
135 David Robinson 4.00 10.00
136 Darryl Dawkins 2.00 5.00
137 Cliff Hagan 2.00 5.00
138 Clyde Drexler 3.00 8.00
139 Dikembe Mutombo 3.00 8.00
140 Jo Jo White 2.00 5.00
141 LaSalle Thompson 1.50 4.00
142 Michael Cooper 2.00 5.00
143 Shawn Bradley 1.25 3.00
144 Walt Frazier 3.00 8.00
145 Harry Gallatin 2.00 5.00
146 Connie Hawkins 2.50 6.00
147 Moses Malone 3.00 8.00
148 Walt Bellamy 1.50 4.00
149 Pete Maravich 6.00 15.00
150 Bill Russell 6.00 15.00
151 Blake Griffin JSY AU RC 25.00 60.00
152 Hasheem Thabeet JSY AU RC 4.00 10.00
153 James Harden JSY AU RC 75.00 200.00
154 Tyreke Evans JSY AU RC 5.00 12.00
155 Jonny Flynn JSY AU RC 4.00 10.00
156 Stephen Curry JSY AU RC 1,000.00 2,000.00
157 Jordan Hill JSY AU RC 4.00 10.00
158 Brandon Jennings JSY AU RC 6.00 15.00
159 Terrence Williams JSY AU RC 4.00 10.00
160 Gerald Henderson JSY AU RC 4.00 10.00
161 Tyler Hansbrough JSY AU RC 5.00 12.00
162 Earl Clark JSY AU RC 4.00 10.00
163 Austin Daye JSY AU RC 4.00 10.00
164 James Johnson JSY AU RC 5.00 12.00
165 Jrue Holiday JSY AU RC 20.00 50.00
166 Ty Lawson JSY AU RC 5.00 12.00
167 Jeff Teague JSY AU RC 25.00 60.00
168 Eric Maynor JSY AU RC 4.00 10.00
169 Darren Collison JSY AU RC 6.00 15.00
170 Omri Casspi JSY AU RC 4.00 10.00
171 B.J. Mullens JSY AU RC 4.00 10.00
172 R.Beaubois JSY AU RC 4.00 10.00
173 Taj Gibson JSY AU RC 5.00 12.00
174 DeMarre Carroll JSY AU RC 5.00 12.00
175 Wayne Ellington JSY AU RC 5.00 12.00
176 Toney Douglas JSY AU RC 4.00 10.00
177 DeJuan Blair JSY AU RC 5.00 12.00
178 Chase Budinger JSY AU RC 5.00 12.00
179 Sam Young JSY AU RC 4.00 10.00
180 Jodie Meeks JSY AU RC 4.00 10.00

2009-10 Limited Silver Spotlight

*1-100 SILVER: 1X TO 2.5X BASE HI
*101-150 SILVER: .75X TO 2X BASE HI
*151-180 SILVER: .75X TO 2X BASE HI
SILVER PRINT RUN 25 SER.#'d SETS
153 James Harden JSY AU 200.00 500.00
154 Tyreke Evans JSY AU 40.00 100.00
156 Stephen Curry JSY AU 2,000.00 4,000.00

2009-10 Limited Banner Season

COMPLETE SET (20) 25.00 50.00
PRINT RUN 99 SER.#'d SETS
*SILVER: .75X TO 2X BASE HI
SILVER PRINT RUN 25 SER.#'d SETS
1 Al Jefferson 1.00 2.50
2 Brandon Roy 2.00 5.00
3 Joe Johnson 1.50 4.00
4 Kevin Martin 1.25 3.00
5 Dirk Nowitzki 4.00 10.00
6 Danny Granger 1.00 2.50
7 Tony Parker 2.50 6.00
8 Kobe Bryant 12.00 30.00
9 Dwyane Wade 3.00 8.00
10 LeBron James 12.00 30.00
11 Stephen Jackson 1.25 3.00
12 Dwight Howard 3.00 8.00
13 Chris Paul 3.00 8.00
14 Carmelo Anthony 2.50 6.00
15 Deron Williams 1.25 3.00
16 Kevin Durant 6.00 15.00
17 Chris Bosh 2.00 5.00
18 Devin Harris 1.00 2.50
19 Paul Pierce 2.50 6.00
20 Michael Redd 1.25 3.00

2009-10 Limited Banner Season Materials

STATED PRINT RUN 5 TO 99 SER.#'d SETS
*PRIME: .75X TO 2X BASE HI
PRIME PRINT RUN ONE TO 25 SER.#'d SETS
1 Al Jefferson/99 2.00 5.00
2 Brandon Roy/99 4.00 10.00
3 Joe Johnson/99 3.00 8.00
5 Dirk Nowitzki/99 6.00 15.00
8 Kobe Bryant/99 8.00 20.00
9 Dwyane Wade/49 6.00 15.00
10 LeBron James/49 10.00 25.00
11 Stephen Jackson/99 2.50 6.00
12 Dwight Howard/99 4.00 10.00
13 Chris Paul/99 4.00 10.00
14 Carmelo Anthony/49 5.00 12.00
15 Deron Williams/49 2.50 6.00
17 Chris Bosh/99 4.00 10.00
19 Paul Pierce/49 5.00 12.00
20 Michael Redd/49 2.50 6.00

2009-10 Limited Banner Season Materials Signatures

STATED PRINT RUN 5 TO 49 SER.#'d SETS
8 Kobe Bryant/49 500.00 1,000.00

2009-10 Limited Decade Dominance

COMPLETE SET (20) 30.00 60.00
PRINT RUN 99 SER.#'d SETS
*SILVER: .6X TO 1.5X BASE HI
SILVER PRINT RUN 25 SER.#'d SETS
1 Jerry West 3.00 8.00
2 Oscar Robertson 2.50 6.00
3 Wilt Chamberlain 8.00 20.00
4 Bill Russell 6.00 15.00
5 Bill Sharman 2.50 6.00
6 Bill Walton 3.00 8.00
7 Willis Reed 3.00 8.00
8 Walt Frazier 3.00 8.00
9 John Havlicek 5.00 12.00
10 Alex English 2.50 6.00
11 Elvin Hayes 3.00 8.00
12 Larry Bird 10.00 25.00
13 Magic Johnson 8.00 20.00
14 Isiah Thomas 2.00 5.00
15 Kareem Abdul-Jabbar 6.00 15.00
16 Dennis Rodman 4.00 10.00
17 Dell Curry 2.00 5.00
18 Kobe Bryant 12.00 30.00
19 LeBron James 12.00 30.00
20 Dirk Nowitzki 4.00 10.00

2009-10 Limited Decade Dominance Materials Signatures

STATED PRINT RUN 10 TO 49 SER.#'d SETS
1 Jerry West/25 50.00 120.00
9 John Havlicek/25 75.00 200.00
10 Alex English/20 15.00 40.00
18 Kobe Bryant/49 2,000.00 4,000.00

2009-10 Limited Decade Dominance Signatures

STATED PRINT RUN 5 TO 49 SER.#'d SETS
1 Jerry West/25 40.00 100.00
2 Oscar Robertson/49 50.00 120.00
5 Bill Sharman/49 8.00 20.00
6 Bill Walton/49 8.00 20.00
9 John Havlicek/49 75.00 200.00
10 Alex English/15 10.00 25.00
17 Dell Curry/49 8.00 20.00
18 Kobe Bryant/25 3,000.00 6,000.00
20 Dirk Nowitzki/25 125.00 300.00

2009-10 Limited Freshmen Jumbo

STATED PRINT RUN 99 SER.#'d SETS
*NUMBERS: .4X TO 1X JUMBO
NUMBERS PRINT RUN 99 SER.#'d SETS
1 Blake Griffin 10.00 25.00
2 Hasheem Thabeet 1.50 4.00
3 James Harden 40.00 100.00
4 Tyreke Evans 2.00 5.00
5 DeMar DeRozan 12.00 30.00
6 Jonny Flynn 1.50 4.00
7 Stephen Curry 150.00 400.00
8 Jordan Hill 1.50 4.00
9 Brandon Jennings 2.50 6.00
10 Terrence Williams 1.50 4.00
11 Gerald Henderson 1.50 4.00
12 Tyler Hansbrough 2.00 5.00
13 Earl Clark 1.50 4.00
14 Austin Daye 1.50 4.00
15 James Johnson 2.00 5.00
16 Jrue Holiday 8.00 20.00
17 Ty Lawson 2.00 5.00
18 Jeff Teague 2.00 5.00
19 Eric Maynor 1.50 4.00
20 Darren Collison 2.50 6.00
21 Omri Casspi 1.50 4.00
22 B.J. Mullens 1.50 4.00
23 Rodrigue Beaubois 1.50 4.00
24 Taj Gibson 2.00 5.00
25 DeMarre Carroll 2.00 5.00
26 Wayne Ellington 2.00 5.00
27 Toney Douglas 1.50 4.00
28 DeJuan Blair 2.00 5.00
29 Chase Budinger 1.50 4.00
30 Sam Young 1.50 4.00

2009-10 Limited Freshmen Jumbo Jersey Numbers Signatures

STATED PRINT RUN 49 SER.#'d SETS
JUMBO SIGS: .4X TO 1X BASE HI
JUMBO SIGS PRINT RUN 49 SER.#'d SETS
1 Blake Griffin 60.00 150.00
2 Hasheem Thabeet 4.00 10.00
4 Tyreke Evans 12.00 30.00
6 Jonny Flynn 4.00 10.00
7 Stephen Curry 1,500.00 3,000.00
8 Jordan Hill 4.00 10.00
9 Brandon Jennings 6.00 15.00
10 Terrence Williams 4.00 10.00
11 Gerald Henderson 4.00 10.00
12 Tyler Hansbrough 5.00 12.00
13 Earl Clark 4.00 10.00
14 Austin Daye 4.00 10.00
15 James Johnson 5.00 12.00
16 Jrue Holiday 20.00 50.00
17 Ty Lawson 5.00 12.00
18 Jeff Teague 5.00 12.00
20 Darren Collison 6.00 15.00
21 Omri Casspi 4.00 10.00
22 B.J. Mullens 4.00 10.00
23 Rodrigue Beaubois 4.00 10.00
24 Taj Gibson 5.00 12.00
25 DeMarre Carroll 5.00 12.00
27 Toney Douglas 4.00 10.00
28 DeJuan Blair 5.00 12.00
29 Chase Budinger 5.00 12.00
30 Sam Young 4.00 10.00

2009-10 Limited Glass Cleaners

COMPLETE SET (20) 30.00 60.00
PRINT RUN 99 SER.#'d SETS
*SILVER: .75X TO 2X BASE HI
SILVER PRINT RUN 25 SER.#'d SETS
1 Kareem Abdul-Jabbar 5.00 12.00
2 Shaquille O'Neal 5.00 12.00
3 Bill Russell 5.00 12.00
4 Dennis Rodman 3.00 8.00
5 Elvin Hayes 2.50 6.00
6 Kobe Bryant 12.00 30.00
7 Elton Brand 1.25 3.00
8 Dirk Nowitzki 4.00 10.00
9 Tim Duncan 4.00 10.00
10 Nate Thurmond 1.25 3.00
11 Hakeem Olajuwon 2.00 5.00
12 Wes Unseld 1.50 4.00
13 Jermaine O'Neal 1.50 4.00
14 Chris Bosh 2.00 5.00
15 Robert Parish 2.00 5.00
16 Artis Gilmore 2.00 5.00
17 David Robinson 3.00 8.00
18 Pau Gasol 2.50 6.00
19 Dikembe Mutombo 2.50 6.00
20 Moses Malone 2.50 6.00

2009-10 Limited Glass Cleaners Materials

STATED PRINT RUN 49 TO 99 SER.#'d SETS
*PRIME: .75X TO 2X BASE HI
PRIME PRINT RUN ONE TO 25 SER.#'d SETS
1 Kareem Abdul-Jabbar/49 12.00 30.00
6 Kobe Bryant/99 10.00 25.00
7 Elton Brand/49 2.50 6.00
8 Dirk Nowitzki/99 8.00 20.00
9 Tim Duncan/99 8.00 20.00
11 Hakeem Olajuwon/99 5.00 12.00
13 Jermaine O'Neal/49 3.00 8.00
14 Chris Bosh/99 4.00 10.00
15 Robert Parish/99 5.00 12.00
18 Pau Gasol/99 5.00 12.00
20 Moses Malone/99 6.00 15.00

2009-10 Limited Glass Cleaners Materials Signatures

STATED PRINT RUN 10 TO 49 SER.#'d SETS
6 Kobe Bryant/49 500.00 1,000.00
15 Robert Parish/25 8.00 20.00

2009-10 Limited Glass Cleaners Signatures

STATED PRINT RUN 49 SER.#'d SETS
1 Kareem Abdul-Jabbar 40.00 80.00
3 Bill Russell 600.00 1,200.00
4 Dennis Rodman 30.00 80.00
5 Elvin Hayes 8.00 20.00
6 Kobe Bryant 500.00 1,000.00
7 Elton Brand 8.00 20.00
10 Nate Thurmond 10.00 25.00
12 Wes Unseld 8.00 20.00
13 Jermaine O'Neal 8.00 20.00
14 Chris Bosh 8.00 20.00
15 Robert Parish 10.00 25.00
16 Artis Gilmore 10.00 25.00
18 Pau Gasol 25.00 50.00

2009-10 Limited Jumbo Jersey Numbers Signatures

STATED PRINT RUN 10 TO 49 SER.#'d SETS
NUM.PRIME SIG. PRINT RUN ONE TO 5 SETS
13 Andre Iguodala/49 6.00 15.00
14 Kobe Bryant/25 800.00 1,500.00
15 Carlos Boozer/25 6.00 15.00

2009-10 Limited Jumbo Signatures

PRINT RUN 10 TO 25 SER.#'d SETS
14 Kobe Bryant/25 800.00 1,500.00
15 Carlos Boozer/25 6.00 15.00

2009-10 Limited Monikers Gold

STATED PRINT RUN ONE TO 25 SER.#'d SETS
13 Devin Harris/25 10.00 25.00
28 Danny Granger/25 6.00 15.00
40 Mike Bibby/25 8.00 20.00
50 Michael Beasley/25 10.00 25.00
52 Shane Battier/25 6.00 15.00
73 Kevin Love/25 10.00 25.00
76 Carlos Boozer/25 6.00 15.00
85 Kobe Bryant/25 800.00 1,500.00
107 Al Cervi/25 6.00 15.00
109 Al Attles/15 8.00 20.00
111 Bob Cousy/25 25.00 60.00
112 Cazzie Russell/25 8.00 20.00
114 Bob McAdoo/25 20.00 40.00
117 Sleepy Floyd/25 8.00 20.00
120 Sidney Moncrief/25 8.00 20.00
125 Sean Elliott/25 15.00 40.00
127 Campy Russell/25 8.00 20.00
130 Bill Walton/25 8.00 20.00
132 Hal Greer/25 6.00 15.00
138 Clyde Drexler/25 30.00 60.00
145 Harry Gallatin/25 6.00 15.00

2009-10 Limited Monikers Materials

STATED PRINT RUN 10 TO 25 SER.#'d SETS
2 Andre Iguodala/25 8.00 20.00
7 Carlos Boozer/25 8.00 20.00
10 Chris Bosh/25 12.00 30.00
14 David Lee/25 8.00 20.00
15 Deron Williams/25 12.00 30.00
18 Elton Brand/25 8.00 20.00
20 Jason Kidd/25 15.00 30.00
21 Jermaine O'Neal/25 8.00 15.00
23 Kobe Bryant/25 800.00 1,500.00
25 Michael Beasley/25 15.00 30.00
26 Mike Bibby/25 8.00 20.00
27 Rajon Rondo/25 20.00 50.00
28 Ray Allen/25 30.00 60.00
32 Shane Battier/25 8.00 20.00
36 Alex English/20 8.00 20.00
37 Artis Gilmore/25 12.00 30.00
38 Dikembe Mutombo/25 30.00 75.00
40 Kareem Abdul-Jabbar/25 30.00 60.00
43 Larry Bird/25 40.00 100.00
47 Robert Parish/25 8.00 20.00
48 Dan Issel/25 10.00 25.00

2009-10 Limited Monikers Materials Prime

STATED PRINT RUN ONE TO 25 SER.#'d SETS
37 Artis Gilmore/25 20.00 40.00
48 Dan Issel/25 15.00 30.00

2009-10 Limited Retired Numbers

COMPLETE SET (20) 25.00 50.00
STATED PRINT RUN 99 SER.#'d SETS
*SILVER: .6X TO 1.5X BASE HI
SILVER PRINT RUN 25 SER.#'d SETS
1 Bill Russell 6.00 15.00
2 Larry Bird 8.00 20.00
3 Bob Love 2.00 5.00
4 Larry Nance 1.50 4.00
5 Alex English 2.50 6.00
6 Isiah Thomas 2.00 5.00
7 Rick Barry 1.50 4.00
8 Clyde Drexler 3.00 8.00
9 Magic Johnson 8.00 20.00
10 Kareem Abdul-Jabbar 6.00 15.00
11 Jerry West 3.00 8.00
12 Oscar Robertson 2.50 6.00
13 Willis Reed 3.00 8.00
14 Julius Erving 5.00 12.00
15 Bill Walton 3.00 8.00
16 Mitch Richmond 2.00 5.00
17 David Robinson 4.00 10.00
18 John Stockton 3.00 8.00
19 Elvin Hayes 3.00 8.00
20 Wes Unseld 2.00 5.00

2009-10 Limited Retired Numbers Materials

STATED PRINT RUN 99 SER.#'d SETS
2 Larry Bird 10.00 25.00
5 Alex English 5.00 12.00
6 Isiah Thomas 4.00 10.00
8 Clyde Drexler 6.00 15.00
9 Magic Johnson 8.00 20.00
10 Kareem Abdul-Jabbar 8.00 20.00
11 Jerry West 8.00 20.00
14 Julius Erving 10.00 25.00
16 Mitch Richmond 4.00 10.00
18 John Stockton 6.00 15.00

2009-10 Limited Retired Numbers Materials Signatures

STATED PRINT RUN 10 TO 49 SER.#'d SETS
5 Alex English/25 10.00 25.00
8 Clyde Drexler/49 12.00 30.00
11 Jerry West/25 40.00 80.00

2009-10 Limited Retired Numbers Signatures

STATED PRINT RUN ONE TO 25 SER.#'d SETS
5 Alex English/15 10.00 25.00
7 Rick Barry/25 10.00 25.00
8 Clyde Drexler/25 25.00 50.00
11 Jerry West/25 25.00 50.00
12 Oscar Robertson/25 30.00 80.00
13 Willis Reed/25 40.00 100.00
20 Wes Unseld/25 10.00 25.00

2009-10 Limited Team Trademarks

COMPLETE SET (20) 15.00 30.00
STATED PRINT RUN 99 SER.#'d SETS
*SILVER: 1.25X TO 3X BASE HI
SILVER PRINT RUN 25 SER.#'d SETS
1 Tony Parker 1.50 4.00
2 Kobe Bryant 8.00 20.00
3 Dirk Nowitzki 2.50 6.00
4 Chris Bosh 1.25 3.00
5 Paul Pierce 1.50 4.00
6 Richard Hamilton 1.00 2.50
7 Yao Ming 2.50 6.00
8 Chris Paul 2.00 5.00
9 Dwight Howard 1.25 3.00
10 Amare Stoudemire .75 2.00
11 Brandon Roy 1.25 3.00
12 Kevin Love 1.00 2.50
13 Dwyane Wade 2.00 5.00
14 Gilbert Arenas .75 2.00
15 Deron Williams .75 2.00
16 Andre Iguodala 1.00 2.50
17 Devin Harris .60 1.50
18 Andrew Bogut .75 2.00
19 Carmelo Anthony 1.50 4.00
20 LeBron James 8.00 20.00

2009-10 Limited Team Trademarks Materials

STATED PRINT RUN 10 TO 99 SER.#'d SETS
*PRIME: .75X TO 2X BASE HI
PRIME PRINT RUN ONE TO 25 SETS
2 Kobe Bryant/49 12.00 30.00
3 Dirk Nowitzki/99 8.00 20.00
4 Chris Bosh/99 4.00 10.00
5 Paul Pierce/49 5.00 12.00
6 Richard Hamilton/99 3.00 8.00
7 Yao Ming/99 8.00 20.00
8 Chris Paul/99 6.00 15.00
9 Dwight Howard/99 4.00 10.00
10 Amare Stoudemire/99 2.50 6.00
11 Brandon Roy/99 4.00 10.00
12 Kevin Love/99 2.50 6.00
13 Dwyane Wade/49 6.00 15.00
14 Gilbert Arenas/99 2.50 6.00
15 Deron Williams/49 2.50 6.00
16 Andre Iguodala/99 3.00 8.00
18 Andrew Bogut/99 3.00 8.00
19 Carmelo Anthony/99 5.00 12.00
20 LeBron James/49 10.00 25.00

2009-10 Limited Team Trademarks Materials Prime Signatures

STATED PRINT RUN ONE TO 25 SER.#'d SETS
16 Andre Iguodala/25 8.00 20.00

2009-10 Limited Team Trademarks Materials Signatures

STATED PRINT RUN 5 TO 25 SER.#'d SETS
2 Kobe Bryant/25 800.00 1,500.00
12 Kevin Love/25 15.00 40.00

2009-10 Limited Threads Prime

STATED PRINT RUN ONE TO 25 SER.#'d SETS
1 Andre Iguodala/25 6.00 15.00
4 Chris Duhon/25 4.00 10.00
5 David Lee/25 4.00 10.00
7 Kevin Garnett/25 15.00 40.00
18 Richard Hamilton/25 6.00 15.00
25 LeBron James/25 25.00 50.00
29 Jeff Foster/25 4.00 10.00
36 Rashard Lewis/25 5.00 12.00
41 Antawn Jamison/25 5.00 12.00
44 Gerald Wallace/25 5.00 12.00
51 Aaron Brooks/25 4.00 10.00
58 David West/25 5.00 12.00
63 Jason Terry/25 5.00 12.00
64 Josh Howard/25 5.00 12.00
66 Tim Duncan/25 15.00 40.00
68 Brandon Roy/25 8.00 20.00
69 Greg Oden/25 4.00 10.00
70 LaMarcus Aldridge/25 6.00 15.00
73 Kevin Love/25 6.00 15.00
75 Andrei Kirilenko/25 5.00 12.00
76 Carlos Boozer/25 5.00 12.00
85 Kobe Bryant/25 25.00 60.00
98 Andres Nocioni/25 4.00 10.00
101 Magic Johnson/25 15.00 30.00
106 Alex English/25 8.00 20.00
122 Kevin McHale/25 8.00 20.00
138 Clyde Drexler/25 15.00 30.00
139 Dikembe Mutombo/25 15.00 30.00

2009-10 Limited Trios

COMPLETE SET (15) 25.00 50.00
STATED PRINT RUN 99 SER.#'d SETS
*SILVER: .75X TO 2X BASE HI
SILVER PRINT RUN 25 SER.#'d SETS
1 Bryant/Wade/James 12.00 30.00
2 Howard/Robinson/O'Neal 5.00 12.00
3 Paul/Kidd/Nash 3.00 8.00
4 Griffin/Thabeet/Harden 10.00 25.00
5 Evans/Flynn/Curry 125.00 300.00
6 Garnett/Pierce/Allen 4.00 10.00
7 Bird/McHale/Parish 6.00 15.00
8 Artest/Boozer/Brand 1.50 4.00
9 Johnson/Kareem/Cooper 6.00 15.00
10 Granger/Odom/Battier 1.50 4.00
11 Parker/Bibby/Ford 2.50 6.00
12 Frazier/Goodrich/Wilkens 2.50 6.00
13 Russell/Reed/Schayes 5.00 12.00
14 Hayes/Gilmore/Unseld 2.50 6.00
15 West/Robertson/Cousy 4.00 10.00

2009-10 Limited Trios Materials

STATED PRINT RUN 10 TO 49 SER.#'d SETS
1 Bryant/Wade/James 20.00 50.00
4 Griffin/Thabeet/Harden 12.00 30.00
5 Evans/Flynn/Curry 125.00 300.00
6 Garnett/Pierce/Allen 10.00 25.00
7 Bird/McHale/Parish 20.00 40.00

2009-10 Limited Trios Signatures

STATED PRINT RUN 10 TO 49 SER.#'d SETS
4 Griffin/Thabeet/Harden/49 75.00 200.00
5 Evans/Flynn/Curry/25 500.00 1,000.00

2010-11 Limited

COMP.SET w/o RCs (150) 125.00 250.00
1-150 STATED PRINT RUN 199 SETS
151-190 RC JSY AU PRINT RUN 249 SETS
EXCH EXPIRATION 5/3/2012
1 Nate Robinson 1.25 3.00
2 Paul Pierce 2.50 6.00
3 Rajon Rondo 2.00 5.00
4 Shaquille O'Neal 6.00 15.00
5 Brook Lopez 1.25 3.00
6 Devin Harris 1.00 2.50
7 Travis Outlaw 1.00 2.50
8 Amare Stoudemire 1.50 4.00
9 Danilo Gallinari 1.25 3.00
10 Raymond Felton 1.00 2.50
11 Toney Douglas 1.00 2.50
12 Andre Iguodala 1.50 4.00
13 Elton Brand 1.25 3.00
14 Jrue Holiday 2.00 5.00
15 Louis Williams 1.25 3.00
16 Andrea Bargnani 1.00 2.50
17 DeMar DeRozan 2.50 6.00
18 Jose Calderon 1.00 2.50
19 Carlos Boozer 1.25 3.00
20 Derrick Rose 3.00 8.00
21 Joakim Noah 1.50 4.00
22 Anderson Varejao 1.00 2.50
23 Antawn Jamison 1.25 3.00
24 Mo Williams 1.25 3.00
25 Ben Wallace 2.00 5.00
26 Richard Hamilton 2.00 5.00
27 Rodney Stuckey 1.00 2.50
28 Tracy McGrady 2.50 6.00
29 Danny Granger 1.00 2.50
30 T.J. Ford 1.00 2.50
31 Tyler Hansbrough 1.00 2.50
32 Andrew Bogut 1.25 3.00
33 Brandon Jennings 1.00 2.50
34 Corey Maggette 1.25 3.00
35 Michael Redd 1.25 3.00
36 Al Horford 1.50 4.00
37 Joe Johnson 1.50 4.00
38 Josh Smith 1.00 2.50
39 Gerald Wallace 1.25 3.00
40 Stephen Jackson 1.25 3.00
41 Tyrus Thomas 1.00 2.50
42 Chris Bosh 2.00 5.00
43 Dwyane Wade 3.00 8.00
44 LeBron James 12.00 30.00
45 Mike Miller 1.25 3.00
46 Dwight Howard 2.00 5.00
47 J.J. Redick 1.50 4.00
48 Jason Williams 1.25 3.00
49 Rashard Lewis 1.25 3.00
50 JaVale McGee 1.25 3.00
51 Kirk Hinrich 1.25 3.00
52 Yi Jianlian 1.50 4.00
53 Caron Butler 1.25 3.00
54 Dirk Nowitzki 4.00 10.00
55 Jason Kidd 2.50 6.00
56 Tyson Chandler 1.25 3.00
57 Aaron Brooks 1.00 2.50
58 Kevin Martin 1.25 3.00
59 Shane Battier 1.25 3.00
60 Yao Ming 3.00 8.00
61 Marc Gasol 1.50 4.00
62 O.J. Mayo 1.00 2.50
63 Rudy Gay 1.50 4.00
64 Zach Randolph 1.50 4.00

65 Chris Paul 3.00 8.00
66 Marcus Thornton 1.00 2.50
67 Trevor Ariza 1.00 2.50
68 Manu Ginobili 3.00 8.00
69 Tim Duncan 4.00 10.00
70 Tony Parker 2.50 6.00
71 Carmelo Anthony 2.50 6.00
72 Chauncey Billups 2.00 5.00
73 Chris Andersen 1.50 4.00
74 Jonny Flynn 1.00 2.50
75 Kevin Love 1.50 4.00
76 Michael Beasley 1.00 2.50
77 Brandon Roy 2.00 5.00
78 LaMarcus Aldridge 1.50 4.00
79 Marcus Camby 1.25 3.00
80 James Harden 4.00 10.00
81 Kevin Durant 6.00 15.00
82 Russell Westbrook 2.50 6.00
83 Al Jefferson 1.00 2.50
84 Deron Williams 1.25 3.00
85 Raja Bell 1.25 3.00
86 David Lee 1.00 2.50
87 Monta Ellis 1.25 3.00
88 Stephen Curry 12.00 30.00
89 Baron Davis 1.50 4.00
90 Blake Griffin 1.50 4.00
91 Chris Kaman 1.00 2.50
92 Derek Fisher 1.50 4.00
93 Kobe Bryant 12.00 30.00
94 Pau Gasol 2.50 6.00
95 Grant Hill 2.50 6.00
96 Jason Richardson 1.50 4.00
97 Steve Nash 3.00 8.00
98 Carl Landry 1.00 2.50
99 Samuel Dalembert 1.00 2.50
100 Tyreke Evans 1.25 3.00
101 Alex English 1.25 3.00
102 Alvan Adams 1.00 2.50
103 Artis Gilmore 2.00 5.00
104 Bernard King 2.00 5.00
105 Bill Laimbeer 1.25 3.00
106 Bill Russell 5.00 12.00
107 Bill Sharman 1.50 4.00
108 Bill Walton 2.50 6.00
109 Bob Lanier 2.50 6.00
110 Bob McAdoo 2.50 6.00
111 Bob Pettit 1.50 4.00
112 Calvin Murphy 1.25 3.00
113 Cazzie Russell 1.25 3.00
114 Cedric Maxwell 1.50 4.00
115 Cliff Hagan 1.50 4.00
116 Connie Hawkins 2.00 5.00
117 Darrell Griffith 1.00 2.50
118 Dominique Wilkins 2.50 6.00
119 Elgin Baylor 3.00 8.00
120 Elvin Hayes 2.50 6.00
121 Gail Goodrich 1.50 4.00
122 Gary Payton 2.50 6.00
123 George Gervin 2.50 6.00
124 George Mikan 5.00 12.00
125 Hakeem Olajuwon 3.00 8.00
126 James Worthy 2.00 5.00
127 Jeff Hornacek 1.25 3.00
128 Jerry Lucas 1.50 4.00
129 Jerry Sloan 1.50 4.00
130 Jerry West 3.00 8.00
131 Kareem Abdul-Jabbar 5.00 12.00
132 Karl Malone 3.00 8.00
133 K.C. Jones 1.50 4.00
134 Kelly Tripucka 1.00 2.50
135 Larry Bird 6.00 15.00
136 Lenny Wilkens 1.50 4.00
137 Magic Johnson 6.00 15.00
138 Mark Aguirre 1.25 3.00
139 Nate Archibald 1.50 4.00
140 Nate Thurmond 2.00 5.00
141 Robert Parish 2.50 6.00
142 Walt Frazier 2.50 6.00
143 Wes Unseld 2.00 5.00
144 Willis Reed 2.50 6.00
145 Adrian Dantley 1.50 4.00
146 Bailey Howell 1.50 4.00
147 Chris Mullin 2.00 5.00
148 Clyde Drexler 2.50 6.00
149 Hal Greer 1.25 3.00
150 Harry Gallatin 1.50 4.00
151 Al-Farouq Aminu JSY AU RC 4.00 10.00
152 Andy Rautins JSY AU RC 3.00 8.00
153 Avery Bradley JSY AU RC 5.00 12.00
154 Cole Aldrich JSY AU RC 3.00 8.00
155 Craig Brackins JSY AU RC 3.00 8.00
156 Damion James JSY AU RC 3.00 8.00
157 Daniel Orton JSY AU RC 3.00 8.00
158 Da'Sean Butler JSY AU RC 4.00 10.00
159 D.Cousins JSY AU RC 10.00 25.00
160 Derrick Favors JSY AU RC 5.00 12.00
161 Devin Ebanks JSY AU RC 3.00 8.00
162 Dexter Pittman JSY AU RC 3.00 8.00
163 Dominique Jones JSY AU RC 3.00 8.00
164 Ed Davis JSY AU RC 4.00 10.00
165 Ekpe Udoh JSY AU RC 3.00 8.00
166 Elliot Williams JSY AU RC 3.00 8.00
167 Eric Bledsoe JSY AU RC 6.00 15.00
168 Evan Turner JSY AU RC 4.00 10.00
169 Gani Lawal JSY AU RC 3.00 8.00
170 Gordon Hayward JSY AU RC 12.00 30.00
171 Greg Monroe JSY AU RC 4.00 10.00
172 Greivis Vasquez JSY AU RC 3.00 8.00
173 Hassan Whiteside JSY AU RC 6.00 15.00
174 James Anderson JSY AU RC 3.00 8.00
175 John Wall JSY AU RC 25.00 60.00
176 Jordan Crawford JSY AU RC 3.00 8.00
177 L.Stephenson JSY AU RC 8.00 20.00
178 Larry Sanders JSY AU RC 3.00 8.00
179 Lazar Hayward JSY AU RC 3.00 8.00
180 Luke Babbitt JSY AU RC 3.00 8.00
181 L.Harangody JSY AU RC 3.00 8.00
182 Patrick Patterson JSY AU RC 4.00 10.00
183 Paul George JSY AU RC 50.00 120.00
184 Quincy Pondexter JSY AU RC 3.00 8.00
185 Terrico White JSY AU RC 3.00 8.00
186 Keith Gallon JSY AU RC 3.00 8.00
187 Trevor Booker JSY AU RC 3.00 8.00
188 Wesley Johnson JSY AU RC 3.00 8.00
189 Willie Warren JSY AU RC 3.00 8.00
190 Xavier Henry JSY AU RC 3.00 8.00

2010-11 Limited Gold Spotlight

*1-150 GOLD: .6X TO 1.5X BASE HI
1-150 PRINT RUN 49 SER.#'d SETS
151-190 PRINT RUN 10 SER.#'d SETS

2010-11 Limited Silver Spotlight

*1-150 SILVER: .5X TO 1.25X BASE HI
1-150 PRINT RUN 149 SER.#'d SETS
*151-190 SILVER: 1X TO 2.5X BASE HI
151-190 PRINT RUN 25 SER.#'d SETS

2010-11 Limited Banner Season

COMPLETE SET (20) 20.00 50.00
STATED PRINT RUN 149 SER.#'d SETS
*GOLD: .75X TO 2X BASE HI
GOLD PRINT RUN 24 SER.#'d SETS
*SILVER: .6X TO 1.5X BASE HI
SILVER PRINT RUN 49 SER.#'d SETS
1 Kevin Durant 5.00 12.00
2 LeBron James 10.00 25.00
3 Carmelo Anthony 2.00 5.00
4 Kobe Bryant 10.00 25.00
5 Dwyane Wade 2.50 6.00
6 Monta Ellis 1.00 2.50
7 Dirk Nowitzki 3.00 8.00
8 Danny Granger .75 2.00
9 Chris Bosh 1.50 4.00
10 Amare Stoudemire 1.25 3.00
11 Brandon Jennings .75 2.00
12 Joe Johnson 1.25 3.00
13 Derrick Rose 2.50 6.00
14 Zach Randolph 1.25 3.00
15 Kevin Martin 1.00 2.50
16 David Lee .75 2.00
17 Tyreke Evans 1.00 2.50
18 Brook Lopez 1.00 2.50
19 Deron Williams 1.00 2.50
20 Paul Pierce 2.00 5.00

2010-11 Limited Banner Season Materials

STATED PRINT RUN 25 TO 99 SER.#'d SETS
*PRIME: .75X TO 2X HI
PRIME: PRINT RUN 5 TO 25 SER.#'d SETS
1 Kevin Durant/99 12.00 30.00
2 LeBron James/49 8.00 20.00
3 Carmelo Anthony/99 5.00 12.00
4 Kobe Bryant/99 8.00 20.00
5 Dwyane Wade/99 6.00 15.00
7 Dirk Nowitzki/99 8.00 20.00
8 Danny Granger/25 2.00 5.00
9 Chris Bosh/99 4.00 10.00
10 Amare Stoudemire/99 3.00 8.00
11 Brandon Jennings/99 2.00 5.00
12 Joe Johnson/99 3.00 8.00
13 Derrick Rose/49 6.00 15.00
16 David Lee/49 2.00 5.00
17 Tyreke Evans/25 2.50 6.00
18 Brook Lopez/49 2.50 6.00
19 Deron Williams/99 2.50 6.00
20 Paul Pierce/99 5.00 12.00

2010-11 Limited Banner Season Materials Signatures

STATED PRINT RUN 5 TO 49 SER.#'d SETS
PRIME SIG.PRINT RUN ONE TO 10 SETS
4 Kobe Bryant/25 1,500.00 3,000.00
11 Brandon Jennings/49 4.00 10.00

2010-11 Limited Decade Dominance

COMPLETE SET (20) 25.00 50.00
STATED PRINT RUN 149 SER.#'d SETS
*GOLD: 1X TO 2.5X BASE HI
GOLD PRINT RUN 24 SER.#'d SETS
*SILVER: .6X TO 1.5X BASE HI
SILVER PRINT RUN 49 SER.#'d SETS
1 Bob Pettit 1.50 4.00
2 Elgin Baylor 3.00 8.00
3 Lenny Wilkens 1.50 4.00
4 Gail Goodrich 1.50 4.00
5 Earl Monroe 1.50 4.00
6 George Gervin 2.50 6.00
7 David Thompson 1.50 4.00
8 Sidney Moncrief 1.00 2.50
9 Hakeem Olajuwon 3.00 8.00
10 Bernard King 2.00 5.00
11 Isiah Thomas 2.50 6.00
12 Darryl Dawkins 1.50 4.00
13 Patrick Ewing 2.50 6.00
14 Scottie Pippen 4.00 10.00
15 Karl Malone 3.00 8.00
16 Clyde Drexler 2.50 6.00
17 John Stockton 2.50 6.00
18 Kobe Bryant 12.00 30.00
19 Tim Duncan 4.00 10.00
20 Dwyane Wade 3.00 8.00

2010-11 Limited Decade Dominance Materials

STATED PRINT RUN 99 SER.#'d SETS
MAT.PRIME PRINT RUN 5 TO 10 SER.#'d SETS
PRIME SIG.PRINT RUN ONE TO 5 SER.#'d SETS
9 Hakeem Olajuwon/99 6.00 15.00
10 Bernard King/99 4.00 10.00
13 Patrick Ewing/99 6.00 15.00
14 Scottie Pippen/99 10.00 25.00
15 Karl Malone/99 6.00 15.00
16 Clyde Drexler/99 5.00 12.00
17 John Stockton/99 5.00 12.00
18 Kobe Bryant/99 8.00 20.00
19 Tim Duncan/99 8.00 20.00
20 Dwyane Wade/99 6.00 15.00

2010-11 Limited Decade Dominance Materials Signatures

STATED PRINT RUN ONE TO 25 SER.#'d SETS
9 Hakeem Olajuwon/25 30.00 80.00
14 Scottie Pippen/25 125.00 300.00
17 John Stockton/25 40.00 100.00
18 Kobe Bryant/25 1,500.00 3,000.00

2010-11 Limited Decade Dominance Signatures

STATED PRINT RUN 25 TO 99 SER.#'d SETS
1 Bob Pettit/99 6.00 15.00
2 Elgin Baylor/99 EXCH 6.00 15.00
3 Lenny Wilkens/99 6.00 15.00
4 Gail Goodrich/99 6.00 15.00
5 Earl Monroe/99 10.00 25.00
6 George Gervin/99 8.00 20.00
7 David Thompson/99 6.00 15.00
8 Sidney Moncrief/99 6.00 15.00
9 Hakeem Olajuwon/99 20.00 50.00
10 Bernard King/99 6.00 15.00
11 Isiah Thomas/99 EXCH 8.00 20.00
12 Darryl Dawkins/99 8.00 20.00
14 Scottie Pippen/99 60.00 150.00
16 Clyde Drexler/99 15.00 40.00
17 John Stockton/99 25.00 60.00
18 Kobe Bryant/25 1,500.00 3,000.00

2010-11 Limited Freshmen Jumbo

STATED PRINT RUN 99 SER.#'d SETS
*NUMBERS: .4X TO 1X BASE HI
NUMBERS PRINT RUN 99 SER.#'d SETS
1 John Wall 8.00 20.00
2 Evan Turner 2.00 5.00
3 Derrick Favors 2.50 6.00
4 Wesley Johnson 1.50 4.00
5 DeMarcus Cousins 5.00 12.00
6 Ekpe Udoh 1.50 4.00
7 Greg Monroe 2.00 5.00
8 Al-Farouq Aminu 2.00 5.00
9 Gordon Hayward 6.00 15.00
10 Paul George 15.00 40.00
11 Cole Aldrich 1.50 4.00
12 Xavier Henry 1.50 4.00
13 Ed Davis 2.00 5.00
14 Patrick Patterson 2.00 5.00
15 Larry Sanders 1.50 4.00
16 Luke Babbitt 1.50 4.00
17 Kevin Seraphin 1.50 4.00
18 Eric Bledsoe 3.00 8.00
19 Avery Bradley 2.50 6.00
20 James Anderson 1.50 4.00
21 Craig Brackins 1.50 4.00
22 Elliot Williams 1.50 4.00
23 Trevor Booker 1.50 4.00
24 Damion James 1.50 4.00
25 Dominique Jones 1.50 4.00
26 Quincy Pondexter 1.50 4.00
27 Jordan Crawford 1.50 4.00
28 Greivis Vasquez 1.50 4.00
29 Daniel Orton 1.50 4.00
30 Lazar Hayward 1.50 4.00

2010-11 Limited Freshmen Jumbo Prime

*PRIME: 1X TO 2.5X BASE HI
STATED PRINT RUN 25 SER.#'d SETS
*NUMBERS: .4X TO 1X BASE HI
NUMBERS: PRINT RUN 10 TO 25 SETS
1 John Wall 20.00 50.00
2 Evan Turner 5.00 12.00
3 Derrick Favors 6.00 15.00
4 Wesley Johnson 4.00 10.00
5 DeMarcus Cousins 12.00 30.00
6 Ekpe Udoh 4.00 10.00
7 Greg Monroe 5.00 12.00
8 Al-Farouq Aminu 5.00 12.00
9 Gordon Hayward 15.00 40.00
10 Paul George 30.00 80.00
11 Cole Aldrich 4.00 10.00
12 Xavier Henry 4.00 10.00
13 Ed Davis 5.00 12.00
14 Patrick Patterson 5.00 12.00
15 Larry Sanders 4.00 10.00
16 Luke Babbitt 4.00 10.00
17 Kevin Seraphin 4.00 10.00
18 Eric Bledsoe 8.00 20.00
19 Avery Bradley 6.00 15.00
20 James Anderson 4.00 10.00
21 Craig Brackins 4.00 10.00
22 Elliot Williams 4.00 10.00
23 Trevor Booker 4.00 10.00
24 Damion James 4.00 10.00
25 Dominique Jones 4.00 10.00
26 Quincy Pondexter 4.00 10.00
27 Jordan Crawford 4.00 10.00
28 Greivis Vasquez 4.00 10.00
29 Daniel Orton 4.00 10.00
30 Lazar Hayward 4.00 10.00

2010-11 Limited Freshmen Jumbo Signatures

STATED PRINT RUN 99 SER.#'d SETS
*NUMBERS: .4X TO 1X BASE HI
NUMBERS PRINT RUN 99 SER.#'d SETS
1 John Wall 40.00 100.00
2 Evan Turner 5.00 12.00
3 Derrick Favors 6.00 15.00
4 Wesley Johnson 4.00 10.00
5 DeMarcus Cousins 12.00 30.00
6 Ekpe Udoh 4.00 10.00
7 Greg Monroe 6.00 15.00
8 Al-Farouq Aminu 5.00 12.00
9 Gordon Hayward 15.00 40.00
10 Paul George 50.00 120.00
11 Cole Aldrich 4.00 10.00
12 Xavier Henry 4.00 10.00
13 Ed Davis 5.00 12.00
14 Patrick Patterson 5.00 12.00
15 Larry Sanders 4.00 10.00
16 Luke Babbitt 4.00 10.00
17 Kevin Seraphin 4.00 10.00
18 Eric Bledsoe 8.00 20.00
19 Avery Bradley 6.00 15.00
20 James Anderson 4.00 10.00
21 Craig Brackins 4.00 10.00
22 Elliot Williams 4.00 10.00
23 Trevor Booker 4.00 10.00
24 Damion James 4.00 10.00
25 Dominique Jones 4.00 10.00
26 Quincy Pondexter 4.00 10.00
27 Jordan Crawford 4.00 10.00
28 Greivis Vasquez 4.00 10.00
29 Daniel Orton 4.00 10.00
30 Lazar Hayward 4.00 10.00

2010-11 Limited Glass Cleaners

COMPLETE SET (20) 20.00 40.00
STATED PRINT RUN 149 SER.#'d SETS
*GOLD: 1X TO 2.5X BASE HI
GOLD PRINT RUN 24 SER.#'d SETS
*SILVER: .6X TO 1.5X BASE HI
SILVER PRINT RUN 49 SER.#'d SETS
1 Shaquille O'Neal 5.00 12.00
2 David Lee .75 2.00
3 Chris Bosh 1.50 4.00
4 Carlos Boozer 1.00 2.50
5 Kevin Love 1.25 3.00
6 Lamar Odom 1.00 2.50
7 Jason Kidd 2.00 5.00
8 Elgin Baylor 2.50 6.00
9 Oscar Robertson 3.00 8.00
10 Kevin McHale 2.00 5.00
11 Bill Walton 2.00 5.00
12 Troy Murphy .75 2.00
13 Dave Cowens 2.00 5.00
14 Mark Eaton 1.25 3.00
15 Alonzo Mourning 2.00 5.00
16 Elvin Hayes 1.50 4.00
17 Kareem Abdul-Jabbar 4.00 10.00
18 Bill Russell 4.00 10.00
19 Artis Gilmore 1.50 4.00
20 Kobe Bryant 10.00 25.00

2010-11 Limited Glass Cleaners Materials

STATED PRINT RUN 49 TO 99 SER.#'d SETS
PRIME PRINT RUN 5 TO 25 SER.#'d SETS
2 David Lee/49 2.00 5.00
3 Chris Bosh/49 4.00 10.00
4 Carlos Boozer/49 2.50 6.00
5 Kevin Love/99 3.00 8.00
6 Lamar Odom/99 2.50 6.00
7 Jason Kidd/49 4.00 10.00
10 Kevin McHale/99 5.00 12.00
13 Dave Cowens/99 5.00 12.00
14 Mark Eaton/99 3.00 8.00
15 Alonzo Mourning/99 6.00 15.00
19 Artis Gilmore/99 4.00 10.00
20 Kobe Bryant/99 8.00 20.00

2010-11 Limited Glass Cleaners Materials Signatures

STATED PRINT RUN 5 TO 49 SER.#'d SETS
PRIME SIG.PRINT RUN ONE TO FIVE SETS
5 Kevin Love/49 15.00 40.00
6 Lamar Odom/49 10.00 25.00
10 Kevin McHale/49 20.00 50.00
13 Dave Cowens/25 10.00 25.00
19 Artis Gilmore/49 10.00 25.00
20 Kobe Bryant/25 1,500.00 3,000.00

2010-11 Limited Glass Cleaners Signatures

STATED PRINT RUN 25 TO 99 SER.#'d SETS
2 David Lee/99 EXCH 5.00 12.00
3 Chris Bosh/49 8.00 20.00
4 Carlos Boozer/49 EXCH 6.00 15.00
5 Kevin Love/99 15.00 40.00
6 Lamar Odom/49 8.00 20.00
7 Jason Kidd/49 12.00 30.00
8 Elgin Baylor/49 EXCH 6.00 15.00
9 Oscar Robertson/49 30.00 80.00
10 Kevin McHale/49 20.00 50.00
11 Bill Walton/49 20.00 50.00
13 Dave Cowens/49 6.00 15.00
15 Alonzo Mourning/49 20.00 50.00
16 Elvin Hayes/49 5.00 12.00
17 Kareem Abdul-Jabbar/49 30.00 80.00
18 Bill Russell/25 1,000.00 2,000.00
19 Artis Gilmore/99 6.00 15.00
20 Kobe Bryant/25 1,500.00 3,000.00

2010-11 Limited Jumbo

STATED PRINT RUN 25 TO 99 SER.#'d SETS
*NUMBERS: .4X TO 1X BASE HI
NUMBERS PRINT RUN 25 TO 99 SETS
PRIME PRINT RUN 5 TO 10 SER.#'d SETS
NUMBERS PRIME PRINT RUN 5 TO 10 SETS
1 Chris Paul/99 6.00 15.00
2 Dwyane Wade/99 5.00 12.00
3 LeBron James/99 12.00 30.00
4 Kobe Bryant/99 10.00 25.00
5 Kevin Durant/99 12.00 30.00
6 Allen Iverson/49 6.00 15.00
7 Andrew Bogut/99 2.50 6.00
8 Ben Gordon/99 2.50 6.00
9 Carmelo Anthony/99 5.00 12.00
10 Chris Bosh/99 4.00 10.00
11 Deron Williams/99 2.50 6.00
12 Tyreke Evans/25 2.50 6.00
13 Dwight Howard/99 4.00 10.00
14 Tim Duncan/99 8.00 20.00
15 Kevin Garnett/99 8.00 20.00
16 Luol Deng/49 2.50 6.00
17 Gerald Wallace/99 2.50 6.00
18 Alex English/25 2.50 6.00
19 Dominique Wilkins/49 5.00 12.00
20 Patrick Ewing/99 6.00 15.00

2010-11 Limited Jumbo Jersey Numbers Signatures

STATED PRINT RUN 5 TO 25 SER.#'d SETS
PRIME SIG.PRINT RUN ONE TO 5 SER.#'d SETS
4 Kobe Bryant/25 1,500.00 3,000.00
19 Dominique Wilkins/25 20.00 50.00

2010-11 Limited Jumbo Signatures

STATED PRINT RUN 5 TO 25 SER.#'d SETS
NUMBERS PRINT RUN 5 TO 25 SER.#'d SETS
PRIME SIG.PRINT RUN ONE TO 5 SER.#'d SETS
NUMBERS PR.SIG PRINT RUN ONE TO 5 SETS
4 Kobe Bryant/25 1,500.00 3,000.00
19 Dominique Wilkins/25 8.00 20.00

2010-11 Limited Monikers Gold

STATED PRINT RUN 5 TO 99 SER.#'d SETS
6 Devin Harris/49 5.00 12.00
8 Amare Stoudemire/15 25.00 60.00
11 Toney Douglas/99 5.00 12.00
12 Andre Iguodala/99 6.00 15.00
14 Jrue Holiday/99 6.00 15.00
17 DeMar DeRozan/99 12.00 30.00
26 Richard Hamilton/99 6.00 15.00
31 Tyler Hansbrough/99 5.00 12.00
33 Brandon Jennings/25 10.00 25.00
57 Aaron Brooks/99 5.00 12.00
59 Shane Battier/99 5.00 12.00
66 Marcus Thornton/99 5.00 12.00
74 Jonny Flynn/99 5.00 12.00
77 Brandon Roy/49 5.00 12.00
80 James Harden/99 50.00 120.00
83 Al Jefferson/99 5.00 12.00
89 Baron Davis/49 6.00 15.00
90 Blake Griffin/99 30.00 80.00
93 Kobe Bryant/25 1,500.00 3,000.00
98 Carl Landry/99 5.00 12.00
100 Tyreke Evans/99 5.00 12.00
101 Alex English/25 6.00 15.00
102 Alvan Adams/49 6.00 15.00
103 Artis Gilmore/49 8.00 20.00
106 Bill Russell/25 500.00 1,000.00
109 Bob Lanier/49 5.00 12.00
110 Bob McAdoo/49 12.00 30.00
111 Bob Pettit/49 12.00 30.00
113 Cazzie Russell/49 6.00 15.00
115 Cliff Hagan/25 5.00 12.00
118 Dominique Wilkins/49 12.00 30.00
120 Elvin Hayes/49 5.00 12.00
121 Gail Goodrich/49 5.00 12.00
122 Gary Payton/25 20.00 50.00
123 George Gervin/25 8.00 20.00
125 Hakeem Olajuwon/25 15.00 40.00
127 Jeff Hornacek/25 8.00 20.00
133 K.C. Jones/25 10.00 25.00
135 Larry Bird/24 50.00 125.00
136 Lenny Wilkens/49 6.00 15.00
139 Nate Archibald/99 6.00 15.00
140 Nate Thurmond/99 5.00 12.00
141 Robert Parish/25 8.00 20.00
144 Willis Reed/49 40.00 100.00
145 Adrian Dantley/25 6.00 15.00
149 Hal Greer/99 5.00 12.00

2010-11 Limited Monikers Materials

STATED PRINT RUN 5 TO 99 SER.#'d SETS
3 Brandon Jennings/49 6.00 15.00
4 Brandon Roy/49 6.00 15.00
5 Carlos Boozer/25 8.00 20.00
8 Chris Andersen/49 12.00 30.00
10 Chris Kaman/49 6.00 15.00
11 Chris Mullin/25 12.00 30.00
14 Danny Manning/25 12.00 30.00
16 Derek Fisher/49 12.00 30.00
17 Detlef Schrempf/99 6.00 15.00
19 Gary Payton/25 15.00 40.00
20 Glen Rice/99 6.00 15.00
21 Jalen Rose/25 10.00 25.00
23 Jeff Hornacek/25 8.00 20.00
24 Jermaine O'Neal/25 10.00 25.00
25 Joe Dumars/25 10.00 25.00
26 Kareem Abdul-Jabbar/25 50.00 120.00
27 Kelly Tripucka/99 6.00 15.00
28 Kevin Johnson/99 10.00 25.00
29 Kevin Love/99 20.00 50.00
30 Kobe Bryant/25 1,500.00 3,000.00
31 Lamar Odom/49 6.00 15.00
32 Larry Johnson/99 10.00 25.00
33 Magic Johnson/25 30.00 80.00
34 Maurice Cheeks/49 6.00 15.00
35 Michael Cage/99 6.00 15.00
36 Pau Gasol/25 12.00 30.00
37 Ray Allen/49 25.00 60.00
38 Robert Parish/25 6.00 15.00
39 Ron Artest/99 10.00 25.00
40 Russell Westbrook/99 30.00 80.00
41 Rudy Fernandez/99 EXCH 6.00 15.00
42 Sam Perkins/25 8.00 20.00
43 Scottie Pippen/25 75.00 200.00
44 Shane Battier/99 8.00 20.00
45 Shawn Bradley/99 6.00 15.00
46 Stephen Curry/99 800.00 1,500.00
47 Steve Nash/21 25.00 60.00
48 Tony Parker/25 15.00 40.00
49 Tyreke Evans/25 6.00 15.00
50 Vince Carter/25 20.00 50.00

2010-11 Limited Monikers Materials Prime

STATED PRINT RUN ONE TO 25 SER.#'d SETS
4 Brandon Roy/25 10.00 25.00
20 Glen Rice/25 15.00 40.00
27 Kelly Tripucka/25 10.00 25.00
28 Kevin Johnson/25 40.00 100.00
29 Kevin Love/25 30.00 80.00
32 Larry Johnson/25 20.00 50.00
34 Maurice Cheeks/25 10.00 25.00
35 Michael Cage/25 10.00 25.00
37 Ray Allen/25 30.00 80.00
39 Ron Artest/25 20.00 50.00
40 Russell Westbrook/25 75.00 200.00
41 Rudy Fernandez/25 EXCH 12.00 30.00
44 Shane Battier/25 12.00 30.00
45 Shawn Bradley/25 10.00 25.00
46 Stephen Curry/25 1,500.00 3,000.00

2010-11 Limited Next Day Autographs

STATED PRINT RUN 90 TO 99 SER.#'d SETS
1 Ekpe Udoh/99 4.00 10.00
2 Gordon Hayward/99 25.00 60.00
3 Lance Stephenson/99 6.00 15.00
4 Trevor Booker/99 4.00 10.00
5 Jeremy Lin/99 150.00 400.00
6 Paul George/99 300.00 600.00
7 Greg Monroe/90 5.00 12.00
8 Derrick Favors/99 6.00 15.00
9 Gani Lawal/93 4.00 10.00
10 Craig Brackins/99 4.00 10.00
11 Cole Aldrich/99 4.00 10.00
12 Xavier Henry/99 4.00 10.00
13 John Wall/99 100.00 250.00
14 DeMarcus Cousins/99 60.00 150.00
15 Patrick Patterson/99 5.00 12.00
16 Eric Bledsoe/99 20.00 50.00
17 Daniel Orton/99 4.00 10.00
18 Lazar Hayward/99 4.00 10.00
19 Hassan Whiteside/95 8.00 20.00
20 Greivis Vasquez/99 4.00 10.00
21 Elliot Williams/99 4.00 10.00
22 Luke Babbitt/99 4.00 10.00
23 Ed Davis/99 5.00 12.00
24 Luke Harangody/98 4.00 10.00
25 Evan Turner/99 5.00 12.00
26 Willie Warren/99 4.00 10.00
27 Keith Gallon/99 4.00 10.00
28 James Anderson/99 4.00 10.00
29 Dominique Jones/99 4.00 10.00
30 Wesley Johnson/99 4.00 10.00
31 Terrico White/96 4.00 10.00
32 Avery Bradley/99 15.00 40.00
33 Dexter Pittman/97 4.00 10.00
34 Damion James/99 4.00 10.00
35 Larry Sanders/99 4.00 10.00
36 Al-Farouq Aminu/99 5.00 12.00
37 Quincy Pondexter/97 4.00 10.00
38 Da'Sean Butler/99 5.00 12.00
39 Devin Ebanks/99 4.00 10.00
40 Jordan Crawford/99 4.00 10.00

2010-11 Limited Retired Numbers

COMPLETE SET (20) 20.00 40.00
STATED PRINT RUN 149 SER.#'d SETS
*GOLD: 1X TO 2.5X BASE HI
GOLD PRINT RUN 24 SER.#'d SETS
*SILVER: .6X TO 1.5X BASE HI
SILVER PRINT RUN 49 SER.#'d SETS
1 Bob Pettit 1.50 4.00
2 Mark Price 1.50 4.00
3 Rolando Blackman 1.25 3.00
4 Elgin Baylor 3.00 8.00
5 Nate Archibald 1.50 4.00
6 Darrell Griffith 1.00 2.50
7 Dan Issel 2.00 5.00
8 Al Attles 1.50 4.00
9 Sidney Moncrief 1.00 2.50
10 Earl Monroe 1.50 4.00
11 Mark Eaton 1.50 4.00
12 Tom Heinsohn 1.50 4.00
13 Hakeem Olajuwon 3.00 8.00
14 Gail Goodrich 1.50 4.00
15 George Gervin 2.50 6.00
16 Nate Thurmond 2.00 5.00
17 Joe Dumars 1.50 4.00
18 Calvin Murphy 1.25 3.00
19 Dave Cowens 2.50 6.00
20 Alvan Adams 1.00 2.50

2010-11 Limited Retired Numbers Materials

STATED PRINT RUN 99 SER.#'d SETS
PRIME PRINT RUN 5 TO 10 SER.#'d SETS
2 Mark Price 5.00 12.00
3 Rolando Blackman 2.50 6.00
6 Darrell Griffith 2.00 5.00
7 Dan Issel 4.00 10.00
11 Mark Eaton 3.00 8.00
13 Hakeem Olajuwon 6.00 15.00
17 Joe Dumars 3.00 8.00
19 Dave Cowens 5.00 12.00
20 Alvan Adams 2.00 5.00

2010-11 Limited Retired Numbers Materials Signatures

STATED PRINT RUN ONE TO 49 SER.#'d SETS
PRIME SIG.PRINT RUN ONE TO 5 SER.#'d SETS
2 Mark Price/49 8.00 20.00
3 Rolando Blackman/49 8.00 20.00
7 Dan Issel/49 8.00 20.00
13 Hakeem Olajuwon/25 15.00 40.00
19 Dave Cowens/25 8.00 20.00
20 Alvan Adams/49 8.00 20.00

2010-11 Limited Retired Numbers Signatures

STATED PRINT RUN 49 TO 99 SER.#'d SETS
1 Bob Pettit/99 12.00 30.00
2 Mark Price/99 EXCH 10.00 25.00
3 Rolando Blackman/99 5.00 12.00
4 Elgin Baylor/99 EXCH 5.00 12.00
5 Nate Archibald/99 6.00 15.00
7 Dan Issel/99 8.00 20.00
8 Al Attles/39 EXCH 5.00 12.00
9 Sidney Moncrief/99 5.00 12.00
10 Earl Monroe/99 8.00 20.00
12 Tom Heinsohn/49 EXCH 10.00 25.00
13 Hakeem Olajuwon/99 12.00 30.00
14 Gail Goodrich/99 8.00 20.00
15 George Gervin/99 6.00 15.00
16 Nate Thurmond/99 5.00 12.00
17 Joe Dumars/99 10.00 25.00
18 Calvin Murphy/49 5.00 12.00
19 Dave Cowens/49 5.00 12.00
20 Alvan Adams/99 5.00 12.00

2010-11 Limited Team Trademarks

COMPLETE SET (20) 15.00 30.00
STATED PRINT RUN 149 SER.#'d SETS
*GOLD: 1.5X TO 4X BASE HI
GOLD PRINT RUN 24 SER.#'d SETS
*SILVER: 1X TO 2.5X BASE HI
SILVER PRINT RUN 49 SER.#'d SETS
1 Al Jefferson .50 1.25
2 Brandon Jennings .50 1.25
3 Brook Lopez .60 1.50
4 David Lee .50 1.25
5 David West .60 1.50
6 Deron Williams .60 1.50
7 Derrick Rose 1.50 4.00
8 Elton Brand .60 1.50
9 Gerald Wallace .60 1.50
10 Jason Kidd 1.25 3.00
11 Joe Johnson .75 2.00
12 Kevin Durant 3.00 8.00
13 Kevin Martin .60 1.50
14 Kobe Bryant 6.00 15.00
15 LeBron James 6.00 15.00
16 Marc Gasol .75 2.00
17 Monta Ellis .60 1.50
18 Rajon Rondo 1.00 2.50
19 Steve Nash 1.50 4.00
20 Vince Carter 1.50 4.00

2010-11 Limited Team Trademarks Materials

STATED PRINT RUN 49 TO 99 SER.#'d SETS
PRIME PRINT RUN 5 TO 25 SER.#'d SETS
1 Al Jefferson 2.00 5.00
2 Brandon Jennings 2.00 5.00
3 Brook Lopez 2.50 6.00
4 David Lee 2.00 5.00
5 David West 2.50 6.00
6 Deron Williams 2.50 6.00
7 Derrick Rose 6.00 15.00
8 Elton Brand 2.50 6.00
9 Gerald Wallace 2.50 6.00
10 Jason Kidd 5.00 12.00
11 Joe Johnson 3.00 8.00
12 Kevin Durant 8.00 20.00
14 Kobe Bryant 10.00 25.00
15 LeBron James 12.00 30.00
16 Marc Gasol 3.00 8.00
18 Rajon Rondo 4.00 10.00
19 Steve Nash 6.00 15.00
20 Vince Carter 6.00 15.00

2010-11 Limited Team Trademarks Materials Prime Signatures

STATED PRINT RUN ONE TO 25 SER.#'d SETS
16 Marc Gasol/25 40.00 100.00

2010-11 Limited Team Trademarks Materials Signatures

STATED PRINT RUN 5 TO 49 SER.#'d SETS
2 Brandon Jennings/49 12.50 30.00
14 Kobe Bryant/25 1,500.00 3,000.00
16 Marc Gasol/49 30.00 80.00
18 Rajon Rondo/49 10.00 25.00
19 Steve Nash/25 20.00 50.00
20 Vince Carter/25 20.00 50.00

2010-11 Limited Threads

STATED PRINT RUN 10 TO 199 SER.#'d SETS
2 Paul Pierce/99 5.00 12.00
3 Rajon Rondo/199 4.00 10.00
5 Brook Lopez/99 2.50 6.00
6 Devin Harris/199 2.00 5.00
8 Amare Stoudemire/199 3.00 8.00
11 Toney Douglas/199 2.00 5.00
12 Andre Iguodala/199 3.00 8.00
13 Elton Brand/199 2.50 6.00
14 Jrue Holiday/199 4.00 10.00
16 Andrea Bargnani/199 2.00 5.00
17 DeMar DeRozan/199 5.00 12.00
18 Jose Calderon/199 2.00 5.00
19 Carlos Boozer/199 2.50 6.00
20 Derrick Rose/49 6.00 15.00
21 Joakim Noah/199 3.00 8.00
26 Richard Hamilton/199 4.00 10.00
27 Rodney Stuckey/199 2.00 5.00
29 Danny Granger/25 2.00 5.00
30 T.J. Ford/199 2.00 5.00
31 Tyler Hansbrough/199 2.00 5.00
32 Andrew Bogut/199 2.50 6.00
33 Brandon Jennings/199 2.00 5.00
35 Michael Redd/199 2.50 6.00
36 Al Horford/199 3.00 8.00
37 Joe Johnson/199 3.00 8.00
38 Josh Smith/199 3.00 8.00
39 Gerald Wallace/199 2.50 6.00
42 Chris Bosh/199 4.00 10.00
43 Dwyane Wade/199 6.00 15.00
44 LeBron James/99 10.00 25.00
46 Dwight Howard/199 4.00 10.00
47 J.J. Redick/199 3.00 8.00
48 Jason Williams/199 4.00 10.00
49 Rashard Lewis/199 2.50 6.00
53 Caron Butler/199 2.50 6.00
54 Dirk Nowitzki/199 8.00 20.00
55 Jason Kidd/49 5.00 12.00
59 Shane Battier/199 2.50 6.00
61 Marc Gasol/199 3.00 8.00
62 O.J. Mayo/199 2.00 5.00
63 Rudy Gay/199 3.00 8.00
65 Chris Paul/199 6.00 15.00
68 Manu Ginobili/199 6.00 15.00
69 Tim Duncan/99 8.00 20.00
70 Tony Parker/199 5.00 12.00
71 Carmelo Anthony/199 5.00 12.00
72 Chauncey Billups/199 4.00 10.00
73 Chris Andersen/199 3.00 8.00
74 Jonny Flynn/199 2.00 5.00
75 Kevin Love/199 3.00 8.00
77 Brandon Roy/199 4.00 10.00
78 LaMarcus Aldridge/199 3.00 8.00
79 Marcus Camby/199 2.50 6.00
80 James Harden/199 8.00 20.00
82 Russell Westbrook/199 5.00 12.00
83 Al Jefferson/199 2.00 5.00
84 Deron Williams/199 2.50 6.00
86 David Lee/99 2.00 5.00
88 Stephen Curry/199 25.00 60.00
89 Baron Davis/199 3.00 8.00
90 Blake Griffin/199 6.00 15.00
91 Chris Kaman/199 2.00 5.00
92 Derek Fisher/199 3.00 8.00
93 Kobe Bryant/199 25.00 60.00
94 Pau Gasol/199 5.00 12.00
95 Grant Hill/199 5.00 12.00
96 Jason Richardson/199 3.00 8.00
97 Steve Nash/199 6.00 15.00
101 Alex English/99 2.50 6.00
102 Alvan Adams/199 2.00 5.00
104 Bernard King/199 4.00 10.00
109 Bob Lanier/199 5.00 12.00
117 Darrell Griffith/199 2.00 5.00
118 Dominique Wilkins/99 5.00 12.00
124 George Mikan/99 12.00 30.00
125 Hakeem Olajuwon/199 6.00 15.00
127 Jeff Hornacek/99 2.50 6.00
132 Karl Malone/199 6.00 15.00
137 Magic Johnson/199 6.00 15.00
141 Robert Parish/199 5.00 12.00
147 Chris Mullin/199 4.00 10.00
148 Clyde Drexler/199 5.00 12.00

2010-11 Limited Threads Prime

*PRIME: .75X TO 2X BASE HI
STATED PRINT RUN 5 TO 25 SER.#'d SETS
17 DeMar DeRozan/25 12.00 30.00
48 Jason Williams/25 10.00 25.00
71 Carmelo Anthony/25 12.00 30.00
81 Kevin Durant/25 25.00 60.00
95 Grant Hill/25 12.50 30.00
97 Steve Nash/25 12.00 30.00
104 Bernard King/25 10.00 25.00
118 Dominique Wilkins/25 10.00 25.00
125 Hakeem Olajuwon/25 10.00 25.00
131 Kareem Abdul-Jabbar/25 12.50 30.00
132 Karl Malone/25 12.50 30.00
147 Chris Mullin/25 8.00 20.00

2010-11 Limited Trios

COMPLETE SET (10) 20.00 40.00
STATED PRINT RUN 149 SER.#'d SETS
*GOLD: .75X TO 2X BASE HI
GOLD PRINT RUN 24 SER.#'d SETS
*SILVER: .6X TO 1.5X BASE HI
SILVER PRINT RUN 99 SER.#'d SETS
1 Bryant/Odom/Gasol 4.00 10.00

2 Jennings/Curry/Evans 20.00 50.00
3 Anthony/Billups/Andersen 1.50 4.00
4 Iverson/Kidd/Nash 3.00 8.00
5 Durant/Bryant/James 6.00 15.00
6 Mikan/Maravich/Chamberlain 5.00 12.00
7 Baylor/Bellamy/Unseld 1.50 4.00
8 Drexler/Thomas/Stockton 5.00 12.00
9 Kareem/Bird/Magic 6.00 15.00
10 Russell/West/Robertson 4.00 10.00

2010-11 Limited Trios Materials

STATED PRINT RUN 49 SER.#'d SETS
1 Bryant/Odom/Gasol 10.00 25.00
2 Jennings/Curry/Evans 40.00 100.00
3 Anthony/Billups/Andersen 5.00 12.00
4 Iverson/Kidd/Nash 8.00 20.00
5 Durant/Bryant/James 25.00 60.00
8 Drexler/Thomas/Stockton 10.00 25.00

2010-11 Limited Trios Signatures

STATED PRINT RUN 5 TO 49 SER.#'d SETS
1 Bryant/Odom/Gasol/49 800.00 1,500.00
2 Jennings/Curry/Evans/49 500.00 1,000.00

2011-12 Limited

STATED PRINT RUN 299 SER.#'d SETS
1 Kobe Bryant 15.00 40.00
2 Metta World Peace 1.50 4.00
3 Pau Gasol 3.00 8.00
4 Andrew Bynum 1.25 3.00
5 Derek Fisher 2.00 5.00
6 Chris Bosh 2.50 6.00
7 Dwyane Wade 4.00 10.00
8 LeBron James 15.00 40.00
9 Mario Chalmers 1.50 4.00
10 Shane Battier 1.50 4.00
11 Dirk Nowitzki 5.00 12.00
12 Delonte West 1.25 3.00
13 Jason Kidd 3.00 8.00
14 Jason Terry 1.50 4.00
15 Lamar Odom 1.50 4.00
16 Vince Carter 4.00 10.00
17 Blake Griffin 2.00 5.00
18 Chauncey Billups 2.50 6.00
19 Chris Paul 4.00 10.00
20 Eric Bledsoe 2.00 5.00
21 Caron Butler 1.50 4.00
22 DeAndre Jordan 1.50 4.00
23 Grant Hill 3.00 8.00
24 Hakim Warrick 1.25 3.00
25 Steve Nash 4.00 10.00
26 Marcin Gortat 1.25 3.00
27 David Lee 1.25 3.00
28 Monta Ellis 1.50 4.00
29 Nate Robinson 2.00 5.00
30 Stephen Curry 15.00 40.00
31 James Harden 4.00 10.00
32 Kevin Durant 8.00 20.00
33 Russell Westbrook 3.00 8.00
34 Serge Ibaka 1.50 4.00
35 Nick Collison 1.25 3.00
36 Dwight Howard 2.50 6.00
37 J.J. Redick 2.00 5.00
38 Jason Richardson 2.00 5.00
39 Hedo Turkoglu 1.50 4.00
40 John Wall 2.50 6.00
41 Nick Young 1.25 3.00
42 Andray Blatche 1.25 3.00
43 Kevin Garnett 5.00 12.00
44 Paul Pierce 3.00 8.00
45 Rajon Rondo 2.50 6.00
46 Ray Allen 3.00 8.00
47 Brook Lopez 2.00 5.00
48 Deron Williams 1.50 4.00
49 Kris Humphries 1.25 3.00
50 Mehmet Okur 1.25 3.00
51 J.J. Barea 2.00 5.00
52 Kevin Love 2.00 5.00
53 Ricky Rubio 2.00 5.00
54 Michael Beasley 1.25 3.00
55 DeMarcus Cousins 2.00 5.00
56 Marcus Thornton 1.25 3.00
57 Francisco Garcia 1.25 3.00
58 Tyreke Evans 1.50 4.00
59 Emeka Okafor 1.50 4.00
60 Eric Gordon 1.50 4.00
61 Jarrett Jack 1.50 4.00
62 Chris Kaman 1.50 4.00
63 Jeff Teague 1.25 3.00
64 Joe Johnson 1.50 4.00
65 Josh Smith 1.25 3.00
66 Jerry Stackhouse 1.50 4.00
67 Tracy McGrady 4.00 10.00
68 Mike Conley 1.50 4.00
69 Rudy Gay 2.00 5.00
70 Marc Gasol 2.00 5.00
71 Zach Randolph 1.50 4.00
72 Danny Granger 1.50 4.00
73 Darren Collison 1.25 3.00
74 Roy Hibbert 1.50 4.00
75 George Hill 1.50 4.00
76 Tyler Hansbrough 1.25 3.00
77 Amare Stoudemire 2.00 5.00
78 Jeremy Lin 6.00 15.00
79 Carmelo Anthony 3.00 8.00
80 Tyson Chandler 1.50 4.00
81 LaMarcus Aldridge 2.00 5.00
82 Raymond Felton 1.25 3.00
83 Wesley Matthews 1.25 3.00
84 Andre Iguodala 2.00 5.00
85 Evan Turner 1.25 3.00
86 Jrue Holiday 2.50 6.00
87 Spencer Hawes 1.25 3.00
88 Al Jefferson 1.25 3.00
89 Gordon Hayward 2.00 5.00
90 Paul Millsap 1.50 4.00
91 Raja Bell 1.50 4.00
92 DeJuan Blair 1.25 3.00
93 Manu Ginobili 4.00 10.00
94 Tim Duncan 5.00 12.00
95 Tony Parker 2.50 6.00
96 Carlos Boozer 1.50 4.00
97 Derrick Rose 3.00 8.00
98 Joakim Noah 2.00 5.00
99 Luol Deng 1.50 4.00
100 Chris Andersen 1.50 4.00
101 Danilo Gallinari 1.50 4.00
102 Nene 1.50 4.00
103 Ty Lawson 1.25 3.00
104 Andrea Bargnani 1.25 3.00
105 DeMar DeRozan 2.50 6.00
106 Jose Calderon 1.25 3.00
107 Ed Davis 1.25 3.00
108 Anderson Varejao 1.25 3.00
109 Antawn Jamison 1.50 4.00
110 Daniel Gibson 1.25 3.00
111 Andrew Bogut 1.50 4.00
112 Brandon Jennings 1.25 3.00
113 Stephen Jackson 1.50 4.00
114 Ersan Ilyasova 1.25 3.00
115 Boris Diaw 1.50 4.00
116 D.J. Augustin 1.25 3.00
117 Tyrus Thomas 1.25 3.00
118 Chase Budinger 1.25 3.00
119 Kevin Martin 1.50 4.00
120 Kyle Lowry 2.00 5.00
121 Luis Scola 1.50 4.00
122 Ben Gordon 1.50 4.00
123 Greg Monroe 1.25 3.00
124 Rodney Stuckey 1.25 3.00
125 Tayshaun Prince 2.00 5.00
126 Jerry West 4.00 10.00
127 Pete Maravich 4.00 10.00
128 Scottie Pippen 5.00 12.00
129 Hakeem Olajuwon 4.00 10.00
130 Adrian Dantley 1.50 4.00
131 Tom Chambers 2.00 5.00
132 Larry Bird 8.00 20.00
133 Bernard King 2.50 6.00
134 Moses Malone 3.00 8.00
135 Robert Parish 2.50 6.00
136 Bill Cartwright 1.50 4.00
137 Rolando Blackman 1.50 4.00
138 Bob Lanier 2.50 6.00
139 Walt Frazier 3.00 8.00
140 Elvin Hayes 2.00 5.00
141 Elgin Baylor 3.00 8.00
142 Dave Cowens 2.50 6.00
143 Kareem Abdul-Jabbar 6.00 15.00
144 Nate Thurmond 2.50 6.00
145 Oscar Robertson 4.00 10.00
146 Bill Russell 6.00 15.00
147 Wilt Chamberlain 6.00 15.00
148 Karl Malone 4.00 10.00
149 Magic Johnson 8.00 20.00
150 Isiah Thomas 3.00 8.00
151 George Gervin 3.00 8.00
152 Dikembe Mutombo 2.50 6.00
153 Kevin Willis 1.50 4.00
154 Dennis Rodman 5.00 12.00
155 John Stockton 4.00 10.00
156 Gary Payton 2.50 6.00
157 Anfernee Hardaway 5.00 12.00
158 John Starks 2.00 5.00
159 Wes Unseld 3.00 8.00
160 Rick Mahorn 1.50 4.00
161 Charles Oakley 2.00 5.00
162 Spud Webb 2.00 5.00
163 Larry Johnson 2.50 6.00
164 Julius Erving 5.00 12.00
165 Joe Dumars 2.00 5.00
166 Shawn Kemp 6.00 15.00
167 Nick Van Exel 2.00 5.00
168 Mitch Richmond 2.50 6.00
169 Jeff Hornacek 1.50 4.00
170 David Robinson 4.00 10.00
171 Patrick Ewing 3.00 8.00
172 Clyde Drexler 3.00 8.00
173 Xavier McDaniel 1.25 3.00
174 Alonzo Mourning 3.00 8.00
175 Dominique Wilkins 3.00 8.00
176 James Worthy 3.00 8.00
177 Steve Kerr 2.50 6.00
178 Connie Hawkins 2.00 5.00
179 Darryl Dawkins 2.00 5.00
180 Mark Jackson 1.50 4.00
181 Kurt Rambis 1.25 3.00
182 Earl Monroe 3.00 8.00
183 Maurice Cheeks 1.50 4.00
184 Ernie DiGregorio 1.25 3.00
185 Detlef Schrempf 2.00 5.00
186 Bill Walton 3.00 8.00
187 Artis Gilmore 2.50 6.00
188 Nate Archibald 2.50 6.00
189 David Thompson 2.00 5.00
190 John Havlicek 4.00 10.00
191 Dan Majerle 2.00 5.00
192 Muggsy Bogues 2.00 5.00
193 Tim Hardaway 2.50 6.00
194 Jalen Rose 1.50 4.00
195 Shaquille O'Neal 8.00 20.00
196 Scott Brooks 1.25 3.00
197 Mike Dunleavy Sr. 2.00 5.00
198 Pat Riley 2.00 5.00
199 Kenny Smith 1.50 4.00
200 Alonzo Mourning 3.00 8.00

2011-12 Limited Gold Spotlight

*GOLD STARS: 1.5X TO 4X BASE HI
*GOLD LEGENDS: 1.25X TO 3X HI
STATED PRINT RUN 25 SER.#'d SETS
1 Kobe Bryant 100.00 250.00
8 LeBron James 100.00 250.00
30 Stephen Curry 100.00 250.00

2011-12 Limited Silver Spotlight

*SILVER: .6X TO 1.5X BASE HI
STATED PRINT RUN 49 SER.#'d SETS
154 Dennis Rodman 6.00 15.00
166 Shawn Kemp 15.00 40.00
174 Alonzo Mourning 8.00 20.00
195 Shaquille O'Neal 6.00 15.00
200 Alonzo Mourning 8.00 20.00

2011-12 Limited 2011 Draft Pick Redemptions Autographs

1 Kyrie Irving 60.00 150.00
XRCA Isaiah Thomas 10.00 25.00
XRCB Shelvin Mack 2.50 6.00
XRCC Alec Burks 4.00 10.00
XRCD Lavoy Allen 3.00 8.00
XRCE MarShon Brooks 3.00 8.00
XRCF Josh Harrellson 2.50 6.00
XRCG Klay Thompson 60.00 150.00
XRCH Brandon Knight 3.00 8.00
XRCI Kemba Walker 6.00 15.00
XRCJ Chris Singleton 2.50 6.00
XRCK Markieff Morris 4.00 10.00
XRCL Marcus Morris 4.00 10.00
XRCM Gustavo Ayon 2.50 6.00
XRCN Kawhi Leonard 75.00 200.00
XRCP Justin Harper 2.50 6.00
XRCQ JaJuan Johnson 2.50 6.00
XRCR Jan Vesely 2.50 6.00
XRCS Kenneth Faried 4.00 10.00
XRCT Norris Cole 3.00 8.00
XRCU Jeremy Tyler 2.50 6.00
XRCV Charles Jenkins 2.50 6.00
XRCW Enes Kanter 4.00 10.00
XRCX Nolan Smith 2.50 6.00
XRCY Jimmy Butler 40.00 100.00
XRCZ Chandler Parsons 3.00 8.00
XRCAA Cory Joseph 3.00 8.00
XRCBB Bismack Biyombo 3.00 8.00
XRCCC Tristan Thompson 4.00 10.00
XRCDD Tobias Harris 6.00 15.00
XRCEE Reggie Jackson 3.00 8.00
XRCFF Iman Shumpert 4.00 10.00
XRCGG Derrick Williams 2.50 6.00
XRCHH Jimmer Fredette 4.00 10.00
XRCII Jordan Hamilton 2.50 6.00

2011-12 Limited 2012 Draft Pick Redemptions

1 Anthony Davis 50.00 125.00
2 Michael Kidd-Gilchrist 6.00 15.00
3 Bradley Beal 12.00 30.00
4 Dion Waiters 6.00 15.00
5 Thomas Robinson 4.00 10.00
6 Damian Lillard 40.00 100.00
7 Harrison Barnes 12.00 30.00
8 Terrence Ross 6.00 15.00
9 Andre Drummond 20.00 50.00
10 Austin Rivers 8.00 20.00
11 Meyers Leonard 5.00 12.00
12 Jeremy Lamb 6.00 15.00
13 Kendall Marshall 4.00 10.00
14 John Henson 6.00 15.00
15 Maurice Harkless 6.00 15.00
16 Royce White 4.00 10.00
17 Tyler Zeller 5.00 12.00
18 Terrence Jones 5.00 12.00
19 Andrew Nicholson 4.00 10.00
20 Evan Fournier 6.00 15.00

2011-12 Limited Decade Dominance Materials

STATED PRINT RUN 5 TO 99 SER.#'d SETS
1 Larry Bird/99 12.00 30.00
2 Robert Parish/99 4.00 10.00
3 Artis Gilmore/99 4.00 10.00
4 Dennis Johnson/99 4.00 10.00
5 David Robinson/99 6.00 15.00
6 Alex English/99 4.00 10.00
8 James Worthy/49 5.00 12.00
9 Dennis Rodman/99 8.00 20.00
10 Kevin Johnson/99 3.00 8.00
11 Shaquille O'Neal/99 12.00 30.00
12 Patrick Ewing/99 5.00 12.00
13 Ray Allen/99 5.00 12.00
14 Karl Malone/99 6.00 15.00
15 Clyde Drexler/99 5.00 12.00
16 LeBron James/99 40.00 100.00
17 Dwyane Wade/99 6.00 15.00
18 Kevin Garnett/49 8.00 20.00
19 Tim Duncan/99 8.00 20.00
20 Allen Iverson/25 6.00 15.00

2011-12 Limited Decade Dominance Materials Prime

*PRIME: 1.25X TO 3X BASE HI
STATED PRINT RUN ONE TO 25 SETS

2011-12 Limited Decade Dominance Materials Signatures

STATED PRINT RUN 10 TO 49 SER.#'d SETS
3 Robert Parish/49 12.00 30.00
4 Kevin McHale/49 15.00 40.00
5 Joe Dumars/49 12.00 30.00
6 Isiah Thomas/49 20.00 50.00
7 Spencer Haywood/49 10.00 25.00
9 Alex English/49 12.00 30.00
15 Kobe Bryant/49 800.00 1,500.00
20 Dikembe Mutombo/49 15.00 40.00

2011-12 Limited Decade Dominance Signatures

STATED PRINT RUN 10 TO 99 SER.#'d SETS
1 Wes Unseld/99 10.00 25.00
2 Dave Cowens/99 8.00 20.00
3 Walt Frazier/99 10.00 25.00
4 John Havlicek/25 100.00 250.00
5 Bob McAdoo/99 12.00 30.00
6 Bob Dandridge/99 6.00 15.00
7 Nate Archibald/99 8.00 20.00
8 Bill Walton/99 12.00 30.00
10 George Gervin/99 12.00 30.00
11 Grant Hill/50 75.00 200.00
13 Hakeem Olajuwon/50 75.00 200.00
17 Kobe Bryant/99 800.00 1,500.00

2011-12 Limited Glass Cleaners Materials

STATED PRINT RUN 49 TO 99 SER.#'d SETS
1 Kobe Bryant/99 75.00 200.00
2 Blake Griffin/99 4.00 10.00
3 Kevin Durant/99 15.00 40.00
4 Joakim Noah/99 4.00 10.00
5 Kevin Love/99 4.00 10.00
6 Marc Gasol/99 4.00 10.00
7 LaMarcus Aldridge/99 4.00 10.00
8 Dwight Howard/99 5.00 12.00
9 Shaquille O'Neal/99 20.00 50.00
10 Moses Malone/49 6.00 15.00
11 Robert Parish/99 10.00 25.00
12 Dennis Rodman/99 10.00 25.00
13 Hakeem Olajuwon/60 8.00 20.00
14 Dikembe Mutombo/99 5.00 12.00
15 Yao Ming/99 8.00 20.00
16 Karl Malone/99 8.00 20.00
17 DeAndre Jordan/99 3.00 8.00
18 Amare Stoudemire/99 4.00 10.00
19 Tyson Chandler/99 3.00 8.00
20 LeBron James/99 75.00 200.00

2011-12 Limited Glass Cleaners Materials Prime

*PRIME: 1.25X TO 3X BASE HI
STATED PRINT RUN 5 TO 25 SER.#'d SETS

2011-12 Limited Glass Cleaners Materials Signatures

STATED PRINT RUN 25 TO 49 SER.#'d SETS
1 Kobe Bryant/49 800.00 1,500.00
2 Blake Griffin/49 30.00 80.00
3 Kevin Durant/49 125.00 300.00
4 Joakim Noah/49 8.00 20.00
5 Kevin Love/49 20.00 50.00
6 Marc Gasol/49 EXCH 12.00 30.00
7 Marcin Gortat/49 6.00 15.00
8 Dirk Nowitzki/25 150.00 400.00
9 Serge Ibaka/49 12.00 30.00
10 A.Varejao/49 6.00 15.00
11 Robert Parish/25 15.00 40.00
12 Dennis Rodman/25 75.00 200.00
13 Hakeem Olajuwon/25 60.00 150.00
14 Dikembe Mutombo/25 30.00 80.00
15 Artis Gilmore/25 12.00 30.00
16 Nate Thurmond/25 10.00 25.00
17 David Robinson/25 60.00 150.00
18 DeMarcus Cousins/49 8.00 20.00
19 Josh Smith/49 5.00 12.00
20 Andrew Bynum/25 5.00 12.00

2011-12 Limited Glass Cleaners Materials Signatures Prime

STATED PRINT RUN 5 TO 25 SER.#'d SETS
4 Joakim Noah/25 12.00 30.00
6 Marc Gasol/15 EXCH 20.00 50.00
7 Marcin Gortat/25 10.00 25.00
9 Serge Ibaka/25 20.00 50.00
10 A.Varejao/25 EXCH 10.00 25.00
18 DeMarcus Cousins/25 15.00 40.00
19 Josh Smith/15 8.00 20.00
20 Andrew Bynum/15 8.00 20.00

2011-12 Limited Glass Cleaners Signatures

STATED PRINT RUN 25 TO 99 SER.#'d SETS
1 Kobe Bryant/50 800.00 1,500.00
2 Blake Griffin/99 15.00 40.00
3 Kevin Durant/25 125.00 300.00
4 Joakim Noah/99 6.00 15.00
5 Kevin Love/25 15.00 40.00
6 Marc Gasol/99 EXCH 8.00 20.00
7 Marcin Gortat/99 6.00 15.00
8 K.Humphries/99 EXCH 6.00 15.00
9 Serge Ibaka/99 EXCH 10.00 25.00
10 A.Varejao/99 EXCH 6.00 15.00
11 Robert Parish/99 8.00 20.00
12 Dennis Rodman/25 40.00 100.00
13 Hakeem Olajuwon/25 40.00 100.00
14 Dikembe Mutombo/99 12.00 30.00
15 Artis Gilmore/99 8.00 20.00
16 Nate Thurmond/99 8.00 20.00
17 David Robinson/25 40.00 100.00
18 DeMarcus Cousins/99 12.00 30.00
19 Josh Smith/99 6.00 15.00
20 Andrew Bynum/99 6.00 15.00

2011-12 Limited Jumbo

STATED PRINT RUN 49 TO 99 SER.#'d SETS
1 LeBron James/49 60.00 150.00
2 Dwyane Wade/49 10.00 25.00
3 Dwight Howard/49 6.00 15.00
4 Kevin Garnett/49 12.00 30.00
5 David Lee/99 3.00 8.00
6 Grant Hill/49 8.00 20.00
7 David West/99 4.00 10.00
8 Manu Ginobili/49 10.00 25.00
9 Jason Terry/49 4.00 10.00
10 O.J. Mayo/99 3.00 8.00
11 Ben Gordon/99 4.00 10.00
12 Joe Johnson/99 4.00 10.00
13 Jrue Holiday/99 6.00 15.00
14 Ryan Anderson/99 3.00 8.00
15 Nick Young/99 3.00 8.00
16 Mo Williams/49 4.00 10.00
17 Pau Gasol/99 8.00 20.00
18 DeMarcus Cousins/99 5.00 12.00
19 Luis Scola/99 3.00 8.00
20 Marcus Thornton/99 3.00 8.00
21 Emeka Okafor/99 4.00 10.00
22 Tim Duncan/49 12.00 30.00
23 Chris Andersen/99 4.00 10.00
24 Michael Beasley/99 3.00 8.00
25 Serge Ibaka/99 4.00 10.00
26 Gerald Wallace/99 4.00 10.00
27 Marcus Camby/99 4.00 10.00
28 Chauncey Billups/99 6.00 15.00
29 Tyson Chandler/99 4.00 10.00
30 Tyler Hansbrough/99 3.00 8.00

2011-12 Limited Jumbo Signatures

STATED PRINT RUN 10 TO 99 SER.#'d SETS
1 Blake Griffin/15 20.00 50.00
2 Deron Williams/15 12.00 30.00
3 Stephen Curry/24 600.00 1,200.00
4 James Harden/24 EXCH 100.00 250.00
5 Kobe Bryant/24 800.00 1,500.00
7 Marcus Thornton/99 6.00 15.00
8 Eric Gordon/24 10.00 25.00
9 Ray Allen/15 EXCH 40.00 100.00
10 Jrue Holiday/49 40.00 100.00
11 Joakim Noah/24 8.00 20.00
12 Jeff Teague/99 6.00 15.00
13 Shane Battier/49 10.00 25.00
14 J.J. Redick/49 10.00 25.00
15 Nene/24 EXCH 6.00 15.00
16 Raymond Felton/24 6.00 15.00
17 Gordon Hayward/99 10.00 25.00
18 Rudy Gay/49 EXCH 10.00 25.00
19 DeMar DeRozan/24 40.00 100.00
20 Serge Ibaka/99 EXCH 10.00 25.00

2011-12 Limited Jumbo Signatures Prime

STATED PRINT RUN 5 TO 15 SER.#'d SETS
7 Marcus Thornton/15 12.00 30.00
11 Joakim Noah/15 20.00 50.00
13 Shane Battier/15 15.00 40.00
14 J.J. Redick/15 20.00 50.00
15 Nene/15 EXCH 12.00 30.00
17 Gordon Hayward/15 20.00 50.00

2011-12 Limited Jumbo Jersey Numbers

STATED PRINT RUN 49 TO 99 SER.#'d SETS
1 Dwight Howard/49 5.00 12.00
2 Carmelo Anthony/49 6.00 15.00
3 Boris Diaw/99 3.00 8.00
4 Shawn Marion/99 4.00 10.00
5 Vince Carter/99 8.00 20.00
6 LeBron James/49 30.00 80.00
7 Tim Duncan/49 10.00 25.00
8 Kevin Garnett/99 10.00 25.00
9 Dwyane Wade/99 8.00 20.00
10 DeAndre Jordan/99 3.00 8.00
11 Darren Collison/99 2.50 6.00
12 Danilo Gallinari/99 3.00 8.00
13 Pau Gasol/99 6.00 15.00
14 Nick Young/99 2.50 6.00
15 Devin Harris/99 2.50 6.00
16 Kyle Lowry/99 4.00 10.00
17 Metta World Peace/99 3.00 8.00
18 Mario Chalmers/99 3.00 8.00
19 LaMarcus Aldridge/99 4.00 10.00
20 Lamar Odom/99 3.00 8.00

2011-12 Limited Jumbo Jersey Numbers Prime

*PRIME: 1.5X TO 4X BASE HI
STATED PRINT RUN 14 TO 25 SER.#'d SETS
5 Vince Carter/15 25.00 60.00
7 Tim Duncan/15 60.00 150.00
17 Metta World Peace/15 20.00 50.00

2011-12 Limited Jumbo Jersey Numbers Signatures

STATED PRINT RUN 5 TO 99 SER.#'d SETS
3 Andre Miller/99 5.00 12.00
4 Andrea Bargnani/49 4.00 10.00
5 James Harden/49 100.00 250.00
6 Blake Griffin/25 20.00 50.00
7 Tyson Chandler/25 5.00 12.00
8 Tyreke Evans/25 5.00 12.00
10 Anderson Varejao/49 4.00 10.00
11 Andrew Bogut/99 5.00 12.00
12 Greg Monroe/99 4.00 10.00
13 Paul George/99 100.00 250.00
14 Kevin Love/25 20.00 50.00
16 Trevor Booker/99 4.00 10.00
17 Wesley Matthews/99 4.00 10.00
18 Derrick Favors/49 5.00 12.00
19 Patrick Patterson/99 4.00 10.00
20 Marc Gasol/25 EXCH 25.00 60.00

2011-12 Limited Jumbo Jersey Numbers Signatures Prime

STATED PRINT RUN 5 TO 25 SER.#'d SETS
3 Andre Miller/25 10.00 25.00
4 Andrea Bargnani/25 10.00 25.00
5 James Harden/25 150.00 400.00
7 Tyson Chandler/25 8.00 20.00
8 Tyreke Evans/25 8.00 20.00
10 Anderson Varejao/25 8.00 20.00
11 Andrew Bogut/25 12.00 30.00
12 Greg Monroe/25 6.00 15.00
16 Trevor Booker/25 6.00 15.00
17 Wesley Matthews/25 6.00 15.00
18 Derrick Favors/25 8.00 20.00
20 Marc Gasol/25 EXCH 40.00 100.00

2011-12 Limited Masterful Marks Signatures

STATED PRINT RUN 10 TO 50 SER.#'d SETS
1 Adrian Dantley/50 5.00 12.00
2 Andre Iguodala/50 5.00 12.00
3 Andre Miller/50 4.00 10.00
4 Anfernee Hardaway/25 60.00 150.00
5 Arron Afflalo/50 4.00 10.00
6 Bill Walton/50 12.00 30.00
7 Blake Griffin/25 20.00 50.00
8 Brook Lopez/50 12.00 30.00
9 Carlos Boozer/50 8.00 20.00
10 Charlie Villanueva/50 4.00 10.00
11 Chase Budinger/50 4.00 10.00
12 Chris Andersen/25 12.00 30.00
13 Chris Paul/25 EXCH 75.00 200.00
14 Daniel Gibson/50 4.00 10.00
15 Danny Manning/50 4.00 10.00
16 Darren Collison/50 6.00 15.00
17 DeAndre Jordan/50 EXCH 6.00 15.00
18 Derek Fisher/50 8.00 20.00
19 Derrick Rose/25 EXCH 75.00 200.00
20 Gordon Hayward/50 8.00 20.00
21 Ian Mahinmi/50 EXCH 4.00 10.00
22 J.J. Barea/50 EXCH 10.00 25.00
23 Roy Hibbert/50 4.00 10.00
24 James Harden/50 75.00 200.00
25 Jason Kidd/25 20.00 50.00
26 Jeremy Lin/50 60.00 150.00
27 Joe Johnson/25 8.00 20.00
28 John Starks/50 12.00 30.00
29 Jordan Crawford/50 4.00 10.00
30 Jordan Farmar/50 EXCH 4.00 10.00
31 Jose Calderon/50 4.00 10.00
32 Kendrick Perkins/50 8.00 20.00
33 Kevin Durant/10 150.00 400.00
34 Kevin Martin/50 6.00 15.00
35 Kobe Bryant/50 500.00 1,000.00
36 LaMarcus Aldridge/50 10.00 25.00
37 Luol Deng/50 4.00 10.00
38 Marcin Gortat/50 5.00 12.00
39 Michael Finley/50 6.00 15.00
40 Monta Ellis/50 8.00 20.00
41 Nene/50 EXCH 5.00 12.00
42 Pau Gasol/50 20.00 50.00
43 Deron Williams/50 8.00 20.00
44 Rajon Rondo/25 12.00 30.00
45 Richard Hamilton/25 10.00 25.00
46 Rodrigue Beaubois/50 4.00 10.00
47 Russell Westbrook/25 60.00 150.00
48 Serge Ibaka/50 EXCH 6.00 15.00
49 Stephen Curry/50 600.00 1,200.00
50 Zach Randolph/50 6.00 15.00

2011-12 Limited Monikers Materials

STATED PRINT RUN 10 TO 49 SER.#'d SETS
1 Kobe Bryant/25 1,000.00 2,000.00
4 Brandon Jennings/25 EXCH 8.00 20.00
5 Kevin Love/25 20.00 50.00
6 Russell Westbrook/49 100.00 250.00
7 Andre Iguodala/49 12.00 30.00
8 Greg Monroe/49 8.00 20.00
10 Tyson Chandler/49 10.00 25.00
11 Paul Millsap/49 8.00 20.00
12 Tony Parker/25 40.00 100.00
13 LaMarcus Aldridge/25 12.00 30.00
16 Marc Gasol/49 EXCH 12.00 30.00
17 Danny Granger/15 8.00 20.00
19 Danilo Gallinari/25 8.00 20.00
20 Andrea Bargnani/25 8.00 20.00

2011-12 Limited Potential Signatures

STATED PRINT RUN 25 TO 99 SER.#'d SETS
1 DeMar DeRozan/50 20.00 50.00
2 Greg Monroe/99 3.00 8.00
3 Chase Budinger/99 3.00 8.00
4 Jonas Jerebko/99 3.00 8.00
6 Ed Davis/99 3.00 8.00
7 Eric Bledsoe/99 5.00 12.00
8 Al-Farouq Aminu/99 3.00 8.00
9 Landry Fields/99 3.00 8.00
10 James Harden/50 60.00 150.00
11 Derrick Favors/50 4.00 10.00
12 Evan Turner/25 3.00 8.00
13 Wesley Matthews/99 3.00 8.00
14 Timofey Mozgov/99 3.00 8.00
15 DeMarcus Cousins/50 5.00 12.00
16 Serge Ibaka/99 4.00 10.00
17 Jeremy Lin/99 EXCH 60.00 150.00
18 D.J. Augustin/50 3.00 8.00
19 Trevor Booker/99 3.00 8.00
20 Darren Collison/99 EXCH 3.00 8.00
21 Jrue Holiday/99 8.00 20.00
22 Tyreke Evans/25 4.00 10.00
23 John Wall/25 30.00 80.00
24 Brandon Jennings/25 3.00 8.00
25 Eric Gordon/99 4.00 10.00
26 Ekpe Udoh/99 3.00 8.00
27 Tyler Hansbrough/50 3.00 8.00
28 Jordan Crawford/99 3.00 8.00
29 George Hill/99 4.00 10.00
30 JaVale McGee/99 4.00 10.00
31 Paul George/99 40.00 100.00
32 Gordon Hayward/99 8.00 20.00
33 Tiago Splitter/99 3.00 8.00
34 Gary Neal/99 EXCH 3.00 8.00
35 Ty Lawson/99 3.00 8.00
36 Marcus Thornton/99 3.00 8.00
37 Blake Griffin/25 20.00 50.00
38 Russell Westbrook/50 60.00 150.00
39 Patrick Patterson/99 3.00 8.00
40 Austin Daye/99 3.00 8.00
41 Marc Gasol/99 EXCH 12.00 30.00
42 Jason Thompson/99 3.00 8.00
43 Greivis Vasquez/99 3.00 8.00
44 Stephen Curry/50 600.00 1,200.00
45 DeJuan Blair/99 3.00 8.00
46 Gerald Henderson/99 3.00 8.00
47 Terrence Williams/99 3.00 8.00
48 Jodie Meeks/99 4.00 10.00
49 Jeff Teague/99 3.00 8.00
50 Nikola Pekovic/99 3.00 8.00

2011-12 Limited Retired Numbers Materials

STATED PRINT RUN 5 TO 99 SER.#'d SETS
1 Magic Johnson/25 20.00 50.00
2 Kareem Abdul-Jabbar/99 15.00 40.00
5 Patrick Ewing/99 8.00 20.00
6 Hakeem Olajuwon/49 10.00 25.00
7 John Stockton/99 10.00 25.00
8 Alonzo Mourning/99 8.00 20.00
9 Chris Mullin/99 6.00 15.00
10 David Robinson/99 10.00 25.00
11 Mitch Richmond/99 6.00 15.00
12 Julius Erving/99 12.00 30.00
13 Alex English/99 6.00 15.00
14 Dennis Johnson/99 6.00 15.00
15 Kevin McHale/99 8.00 20.00
16 Larry Bird/49 20.00 50.00
17 Sam Jones/99 6.00 15.00
18 Bill Laimbeer/99 5.00 12.00
19 Darrell Griffith/99 5.00 12.00
20 Karl Malone/99 10.00 25.00

2011-12 Limited Retired Numbers Materials Prime

*PRIME: 1X TO 2.5X BASE HI
STATED PRINT RUN ONE TO 25 SER.#'d SETS

2011-12 Limited Retired Numbers Materials Signatures

STATED PRINT RUN 5 TO 49 SER.#'d SETS
2 Chris Mullin/49 12.00 30.00
3 Clyde Drexler/25 15.00 40.00
4 Kevin McHale/25 15.00 40.00
5 Robert Parish/49 12.00 30.00
6 Sam Jones/25 12.00 30.00
7 Isiah Thomas/49 15.00 40.00
9 Joe Dumars/49 10.00 25.00
10 Dominique Wilkins/25 15.00 40.00
11 Scottie Pippen/25 25.00 60.00
12 Magic Johnson/25 40.00 100.00
13 James Worthy/25 15.00 40.00
14 John Stockton/25 20.00 50.00
15 Mark Eaton/49 10.00 25.00
16 Tom Chambers/49 10.00 25.00
17 George Gervin/49 15.00 40.00
19 Dan Issel/49 10.00 25.00
20 Alex English/49 12.00 30.00

2011-12 Limited Retired Numbers Materials Signatures Prime

STATED PRINT RUN ONE TO 25 SER.#'d SETS
2 Chris Mullin/15 20.00 50.00
9 Joe Dumars/25 8.00 20.00
14 John Stockton/15 80.00 160.00
15 Mark Eaton/15 6.00 15.00
16 Tom Chambers/15 8.00 20.00
17 George Gervin/25 12.00 30.00
18 Mark Price/15 75.00 150.00
19 Dan Issel/15 8.00 20.00
20 Alex English/25 8.00 20.00

2011-12 Limited Retired Numbers Signatures

STATED PRINT RUN 25 TO 99 SER.#'d SETS
1 Dave Cowens/50 15.00 40.00
2 Bill Walton/50 20.00 50.00
3 Terry Porter/99 10.00 25.00
4 Rolando Blackman/99 10.00 25.00
5 Joe Dumars/50 12.00 30.00
6 Bob Love/99 12.00 30.00
7 George McGinnis/99 12.00 30.00
8 Bob Pettit/50 15.00 40.00
9 Gail Goodrich/50 12.00 30.00
10 Dominique Wilkins/50 20.00 50.00
11 Earl Monroe/25 20.00 50.00
12 Walt Frazier/50 20.00 50.00
13 K.C. Jones/50 12.00 30.00
14 Wes Unseld/50 20.00 50.00
15 Dan Majerle/99 12.00 30.00
16 Jeff Hornacek/99 10.00 25.00
17 Vlade Divac/99 12.00 30.00
18 George Gervin/50 20.00 50.00
19 Sean Elliott/99 10.00 25.00
20 Lenny Wilkens/50 12.00 30.00

2011-12 Limited Signatures

STATED PRINT RUN 10 TO 99 SER.#'d SETS
1 Blake Griffin/15 10.00 25.00
2 Rajon Rondo/25 12.00 30.00
3 Deron Williams/25 8.00 20.00
4 Tyson Chandler/25 8.00 20.00
5 Stephen Jackson/49 8.00 20.00
6 Andrea Bargnani/49 6.00 15.00
7 Monta Ellis/49 8.00 20.00
8 Kobe Bryant/49 600.00 1,200.00
9 Chris Paul/15 EXCH 75.00 200.00
10 Tyreke Evans/25 8.00 20.00
11 Derrick Rose/15 75.00 200.00
12 Antawn Jamison/49 8.00 20.00
13 Steve Nash/15 75.00 200.00
14 Danny Granger/25 8.00 20.00
15 Ben Gordon/25 8.00 20.00
16 Andre Iguodala/25 10.00 25.00
18 Kevin Martin/49 8.00 20.00
19 Rudy Gay/49 EXCH 10.00 25.00
20 Eric Gordon/49 8.00 20.00
21 Tony Parker/25 20.00 50.00
22 Josh Smith/49 EXCH 6.00 15.00
23 D.J. Augustin/49 6.00 15.00
24 Chris Bosh/15 12.00 30.00
25 Jeremy Lin/25 75.00 200.00
27 Nene/49 EXCH 8.00 20.00
28 Kevin Love/25 10.00 25.00
30 LaMarcus Aldridge/49 10.00 25.00
31 Al Jefferson/25 EXCH 6.00 15.00
32 Bailey Howell/49 12.00 30.00
33 Darryl Dawkins/99 10.00 25.00
34 Nate Archibald/49 12.00 30.00
35 Cedric Maxwell/99 10.00 25.00
36 Chris Mullin/49 12.00 30.00
37 Kurt Rambis/99 6.00 15.00
38 Robert Parish/25 12.00 30.00
39 George Gervin/49 15.00 40.00
40 Detlef Schrempf/99 10.00 25.00
41 Kenny Smith/49 8.00 20.00
42 Bill Walton/25 15.00 40.00
43 Isiah Thomas/25 15.00 40.00
44 Vlade Divac/99 10.00 25.00
45 Tom Chambers/49 10.00 25.00
46 David Robinson/15 30.00 80.00
47 Jeff Hornacek/99 8.00 20.00
48 Joe Dumars/25 10.00 25.00
50 Tim Hardaway/99 12.00 30.00

2011-12 Limited Signatures Gold Spotlight

STATED PRINT RUN 3 TO 24 SER.#'d SETS
5 Stephen Jackson/24 6.00 15.00
6 Andrea Bargnani/15 6.00 15.00
12 Antawn Jamison/24 6.00 15.00
18 Kevin Martin/24 8.00 20.00
19 Rudy Gay/24 EXCH 8.00 20.00
32 Bailey Howell/24 8.00 20.00
33 Darryl Dawkins/24 6.00 15.00
35 Cedric Maxwell/24 6.00 15.00
36 Chris Mullin/24 12.00 30.00
37 Kurt Rambis/24 8.00 20.00
40 Detlef Schrempf/24 10.00 25.00
44 Vlade Divac/24 10.00 25.00
45 Tom Chambers/24 6.00 15.00
47 Jeff Hornacek/24 6.00 15.00
50 Tim Hardaway/24 15.00 40.00

2011-12 Limited Signatures Silver Spotlight

STATED PRINT RUN 5 TO 49 SER.#'d SETS
3 Deron Williams/15 8.00 20.00
5 Stephen Jackson/49 5.00 12.00
6 Andrea Bargnani/25 5.00 12.00
7 Monta Ellis/25 10.00 25.00
8 Kobe Bryant/25 100.00 200.00
12 Antawn Jamison/49 5.00 12.00
18 Kevin Martin/49 5.00 12.00
19 Rudy Gay/49 EXCH 6.00 15.00
20 Eric Gordon/25 8.00 20.00
22 Josh Smith/25 8.00 20.00
23 D.J. Augustin/25 5.00 12.00
25 Jeremy Lin/15 60.00 120.00
27 Nene/25 EXCH 8.00 20.00
30 LaMarcus Aldridge/25 12.00 30.00
32 Bailey Howell/49 5.00 12.00
33 Darryl Dawkins/49 5.00 12.00
34 Nate Archibald/25 6.00 15.00
35 Cedric Maxwell/49 5.00 12.00
36 Chris Mullin/49 10.00 25.00
37 Kurt Rambis/49 10.00 25.00
39 George Gervin/25 8.00 20.00
40 Detlef Schrempf/49 5.00 12.00
41 Kenny Smith/25 5.00 12.00
44 Vlade Divac/49 8.00 20.00
45 Tom Chambers/49 5.00 12.00
47 Jeff Hornacek/49 5.00 12.00
48 Joe Dumars/25 12.00 30.00
50 Tim Hardaway/49 8.00 20.00

2011-12 Limited Team Trademarks Materials

STATED PRINT RUN 75 TO 99 SER.#'d SETS
*PRIME: 1X TO 2.5X HI COLUMN
PRIME PRINT RUN 5 TO 25 SETS
1 Kobe Bryant/75 20.00 50.00
2 Blake Griffin/99 2.50 6.00
3 Carlos Boozer/99 2.00 5.00
4 Rajon Rondo/99 3.00 8.00
5 Carmelo Anthony/99 4.00 10.00

6 Tyreke Evans/99 2.00 5.00
7 Dwyane Wade/99 5.00 12.00
8 Dirk Nowitzki/99 6.00 15.00
9 Danny Granger/99 2.00 5.00
10 David Lee/99 1.50 4.00
11 Tony Parker/99 3.00 8.00
12 Dwight Howard/99 3.00 8.00
13 Al Horford/99 2.50 6.00
14 Kevin Durant/99 10.00 25.00
15 LeBron James/99 20.00 50.00
16 Stephen Jackson/99 2.00 5.00
17 Paul Millsap/99 2.00 5.00
18 Kevin Love/99 2.50 6.00
19 Kevin Garnett/99 6.00 15.00
20 LaMarcus Aldridge/99 2.50 6.00

2011-12 Limited Team Trademarks Materials Signatures

STATED PRINT RUN 25 TO 99 SER.#'d SETS
1 Kobe Bryant/25 100.00 200.00
2 Rudy Gay/99 EXCH 10.00 25.00
3 Ty Lawson/99 EXCH 8.00 20.00
4 Roy Hibbert/99 8.00 20.00
5 James Harden/49 25.00 60.00
6 Tyreke Evans/49 10.00 25.00
7 Deron Williams/49 12.00 30.00
8 Greg Monroe/99 6.00 15.00
9 Stephen Curry/49 500.00 1,000.00
10 Kevin Love/25 15.00 40.00
11 Serge Ibaka/99 6.00 15.00
12 Kevin Durant/25 125.00 225.00
13 LaMarcus Aldridge/49 10.00 25.00
14 Josh Smith/49 6.00 15.00
15 Blake Griffin/25 25.00 60.00
16 Brandon Jennings/25 EXCH 10.00 25.00
17 Andre Iguodala/49 6.00 15.00
18 DeMarcus Cousins/49 15.00 40.00
19 Kevin Martin/49 6.00 15.00
20 Gordon Hayward/99 6.00 15.00

2011-12 Limited Team Trademarks Materials Signatures Prime

STATED PRINT RUN 5 TO 25 SER.#'d SETS

2011-12 Limited Team Trademarks Signatures

STATED PRINT RUN 10 TO 49 SER.#'d SETS
2 Tyreke Evans/25 12.00 30.00
3 Luol Deng/49 8.00 20.00
4 Al Jefferson/25 8.00 20.00
8 Kobe Bryant/49 75.00 150.00
9 Monta Ellis/49 8.00 20.00
10 Kevin Love/15 25.00 60.00
11 Rajon Rondo/25 12.00 30.00
12 Russell Westbrook/25 40.00 100.00
13 LaMarcus Aldridge/49 10.00 25.00
17 Eric Gordon/49 6.00 15.00
18 Danny Granger/25 8.00 20.00
19 Kevin Martin/49 6.00 15.00
20 Danilo Gallinari/49 EXCH 6.00 15.00

2011-12 Limited Threads

STATED PRINT RUN 49 TO 99 SER.#'d SETS
1 Derrick Rose/99 5.00 12.00
2 Ray Allen/99 5.00 12.00
3 Chris Paul/99 6.00 15.00
4 Dwight Howard/99 4.00 10.00
5 Jason Kidd/99 5.00 12.00
6 Deron Williams/99 2.50 6.00
7 Evan Turner/99 2.00 5.00
8 Kobe Bryant/99 60.00 150.00
9 Amare Stoudemire/99 3.00 8.00
10 Elton Brand/99 3.00 8.00
11 Jose Calderon/99 2.00 5.00
12 Stephen Curry/99 60.00 150.00
13 Steve Nash/99 6.00 15.00
14 Andrew Bynum/99 2.00 5.00
15 DeMarcus Cousins/99 2.50 6.00
16 Joakim Noah/99 3.00 8.00
17 Anderson Varejao/99 2.00 5.00
18 Greg Monroe/99 2.00 5.00
19 Tyler Hansbrough/99 2.00 5.00
20 Manu Ginobili/99 6.00 15.00
21 Tim Duncan/99 8.00 20.00
22 Luis Scola/99 2.50 6.00
23 LeBron James/99 60.00 150.00
24 Dwyane Wade/99 6.00 15.00
25 John Wall/99 4.00 10.00
26 Brandon Jennings/99 2.00 5.00
27 Joe Johnson/99 2.50 6.00
28 D.J. Augustin/99 2.00 5.00
29 Zach Randolph/99 2.50 6.00
30 Emeka Okafor/99 2.50 6.00
31 Jason Terry/99 2.50 6.00
32 Ricky Rubio/99 3.00 8.00
33 Ty Lawson/99 2.00 5.00
34 Paul Pierce/99 5.00 12.00
35 Kevin Durant/99 12.00 30.00
36 James Harden/99 6.00 15.00
37 Kevin Love/99 3.00 8.00
38 LaMarcus Aldridge/99 3.00 8.00
39 Tyreke Evans/99 2.50 6.00
40 Carlos Boozer/99 2.50 6.00
41 Dirk Nowitzki/99 8.00 20.00
42 Paul Millsap/99 2.50 6.00
43 Alonzo Mourning/99 5.00 12.00
44 Derrick Coleman/49 3.00 8.00
45 Clyde Drexler/99 5.00 12.00
46 Dennis Scott/99 2.00 5.00
47 Chuck Person/99 2.50 6.00
48 Glen Rice/99 3.00 8.00
49 Jalen Rose/99 2.50 6.00
50 Karl Malone/99 6.00 15.00

2011-12 Limited Threads Prime

*PRIME: 1.25X TO 3X BASE HI
STATED PRINT RUN 5 TO 25 SER.#'d SETS

2011-12 Limited Trios Materials

STATED PRINT RUN 25 TO 49 SER.#'d SETS
1 Rose/Kobe/Wade/25 50.00 120.00
2 BG/Aldridge/Love/49 8.00 20.00
3 Marion/Nash/Amare/49 10.00 25.00
4 LeBron/Dirk/Durant/25 50.00 120.00
5 Howard/Barg/Bogut/49 8.00 20.00
6 KG/Carmelo/Bosh/49 15.00 40.00
7 Paul/Rondo/Ellis/49 10.00 25.00
8 Wstbrk/Deron/Parker/49 12.00 30.00
9 Hill/Kidd/Allen/25 15.00 40.00
10 Zo/Rice/Shaq/25 20.00 50.00

2011-12 Limited Trios Materials Prime

*PRIME: 1X TO 2.5X HI COLUMN
STATED PRINT RUN 5 TO 15 SER.#'d SETS

2011-12 Limited Trophy Case Materials

STATED PRINT RUN 25 TO 99 SER.#'d SETS
1 Derrick Rose/75 5.00 12.00
2 Kobe Bryant/49 60.00 150.00
3 Steve Nash/75 6.00 15.00
4 David Robinson/75 6.00 15.00
5 Hakeem Olajuwon/49 6.00 15.00
6 Blake Griffin/75 3.00 8.00
7 Josh Smith/99 2.00 5.00
8 Vince Carter/99 6.00 15.00
9 Daequan Cook/99 2.00 5.00
10 Glen Rice/99 3.00 8.00
11 Jason Kidd/99 5.00 12.00
12 Deron Williams/99 2.50 6.00
13 Stephen Curry/99 50.00 120.00
14 Kevin Love/99 3.00 8.00
15 Danny Granger/99 2.50 6.00
16 Hedo Turkoglu/99 2.50 6.00
17 Monta Ellis/99 2.50 6.00
18 Tyreke Evans/99 2.50 6.00
19 Isiah Thomas/99 5.00 12.00
20 Tom Chambers/99 3.00 8.00
21 Zydrunas Ilgauskas/99 2.00 5.00
22 Andre Iguodala/99 3.00 8.00
23 David Lee/99 2.00 5.00
24 Daniel Gibson/99 2.00 5.00
25 Kevin Durant/49 12.00 30.00
26 John Wall/99 4.00 10.00
27 Rajon Rondo/99 4.00 10.00
28 Tony Parker/99 4.00 10.00
29 Derek Fisher/99 4.00 10.00
30 Robert Parish/49 4.00 10.00
31 Michael Cooper/49 2.50 6.00
32 Pau Gasol/99 5.00 12.00
33 Joe Dumars/75 3.00 8.00
34 Kevin McHale/75 5.00 12.00
35 Kareem Abdul-Jabbar/25 10.00 25.00
36 Dennis Rodman/75 8.00 20.00
37 Scottie Pippen/75 8.00 20.00
38 Allen Iverson/75 6.00 15.00
39 Eddie Jones/99 3.00 8.00
40 Manu Ginobili/99 6.00 15.00
41 Peja Stojakovic/99 2.50 6.00
42 Quentin Richardson/99 2.00 5.00
43 Dwight Howard/99 4.00 10.00
44 Nate Robinson/99 3.00 8.00
45 Karl Malone/99 6.00 15.00
46 Shaquille O'Neal/49 12.00 30.00
47 Allen Iverson/25 6.00 15.00
48 Kevin Garnett/49 8.00 20.00
49 Dirk Nowitzki/99 8.00 20.00
50 LeBron James/49 60.00 150.00

2011-12 Limited Trophy Case Materials Prime

*PRIME: 1.25X TO 3X BASE HI
STATED PRINT RUN ONE TO 25 SER.#'d SETS
38 Allen Iverson/15 20.00 50.00

2011-12 Limited Trophy Case Materials Signatures

STATED PRINT RUN 15 TO 49 SER.#'d SETS
1 Derrick Rose/25 100.00 200.00
2 Kobe Bryant/25 1,000.00 2,000.00
3 Steve Nash/15 20.00 50.00
4 David Robinson/15 25.00 60.00
5 Hakeem Olajuwon/15 25.00 60.00
6 Blake Griffin/25 30.00 80.00
7 Josh Smith/49 6.00 15.00
8 Vince Carter/15 40.00 100.00
9 Daequan Cook/49 6.00 15.00
10 Glen Rice/49 6.00 15.00
11 Jason Kidd/15 20.00 50.00
12 Deron Williams/15 12.00 30.00
13 Stephen Curry/49 500.00 1,000.00
14 Kevin Love/15 30.00 80.00
15 Danny Granger/15 6.00 15.00
16 Hedo Turkoglu/49 6.00 15.00
17 Monta Ellis/49 8.00 20.00
18 Tyreke Evans/15 15.00 40.00
19 Isiah Thomas/25 15.00 40.00
20 Tom Chambers/25 6.00 15.00
21 Zydrunas Ilgauskas/49 8.00 20.00
22 Andre Iguodala/49 6.00 15.00
23 David Lee/49 6.00 15.00
24 Daniel Gibson/49 6.00 15.00
25 Kevin Durant/25 150.00 400.00
26 John Wall/15 40.00 100.00
28 Tony Parker/15 25.00 60.00
29 Derek Fisher/49 8.00 20.00
30 Robert Parish/25 10.00 25.00
31 Michael Cooper/49 12.00 30.00
32 Pau Gasol/15 15.00 40.00
33 Joe Dumars/25 6.00 15.00
34 Sam Jones/25 15.00 40.00
35 Bailey Howell/15 15.00 40.00
36 Earl Monroe/15 15.00 40.00
37 Amare Stoudemire/49 12.00 30.00
38 Clyde Drexler/25 20.00 50.00
39 Bill Laimbeer/25 10.00 25.00
40 Dennis Rodman/25 40.00 100.00
41 Ron Harper/49 12.00 30.00
42 Dominique Wilkins/25 12.00 30.00
43 Dikembe Mutombo/25 25.00 60.00
44 Gary Payton/25 15.00 40.00
45 Mark Eaton/49 6.00 15.00
46 Chris Paul/25 EXCH 60.00 150.00
47 Tyreke Evans/25 10.00 25.00
48 Mitch Richmond/25 30.00 80.00
49 Larry Bird/25 50.00 125.00
50 Julius Erving/25 50.00 125.00

2011-12 Limited Trophy Case Materials Signatures Prime

STATED PRINT RUN ONE TO 25 SER.#'d SETS
1 Derrick Rose/15 175.00 350.00
2 Kobe Bryant/15 1,500.00 3,000.00
4 David Robinson/15 75.00 150.00
5 Hakeem Olajuwon/15 30.00 80.00
6 Blake Griffin/15 100.00 200.00
7 Josh Smith/25 12.00 30.00
9 Daequan Cook/25 10.00 25.00
10 Glen Rice/25 12.00 30.00
11 Jason Kidd/15 30.00 80.00
13 Stephen Curry/25 800.00 1,500.00
19 Isiah Thomas/25 15.00 40.00
20 Tom Chambers/15 12.00 30.00
21 Zydrunas Ilgauskas/25 15.00 40.00
22 Andre Iguodala/25 10.00 25.00
23 David Lee/25 10.00 25.00
24 Daniel Gibson/25 10.00 25.00
25 Kevin Durant/15 300.00 600.00
26 John Wall/25 50.00 125.00
29 Derek Fisher/25 15.00 40.00
30 Robert Parish/15 12.00 30.00
31 Michael Cooper/25 15.00 40.00
33 Joe Dumars/15 15.00 40.00
34 Sam Jones/15 30.00 80.00
37 Amare Stoudemire/25 15.00 40.00
38 Clyde Drexler/25 40.00 70.00
40 Dennis Rodman/15 75.00 200.00
41 Ron Harper/25 30.00 80.00
42 Dominique Wilkins/15 30.00 80.00
43 Dikembe Mutombo/15 50.00 125.00
44 Gary Payton/25 40.00 100.00
45 Mark Eaton/25 10.00 25.00
47 Tyreke Evans/15 20.00 50.00
48 Mitch Richmond/25 40.00 100.00
50 Julius Erving/15 100.00 175.00

2011-12 Limited Trophy Case Signatures

STATED PRINT RUN 25 TO 49 SER.#'d SETS
1 Derrick Rose/25 EXCH 75.00 200.00
2 Kobe Bryant/25 800.00 1,500.00
3 Steve Nash/25 40.00 100.00
4 David Robinson/25 30.00 80.00
5 Hakeem Olajuwon/25 30.00 80.00
6 Blake Griffin/25 20.00 50.00
7 Josh Smith/49 6.00 15.00
8 Vince Carter/25 40.00 100.00
9 Daequan Cook/49 6.00 15.00
10 Glen Rice/49 6.00 15.00
11 Jason Kidd/25 10.00 25.00
12 Deron Williams/25 6.00 15.00
13 Stephen Curry/49 500.00 1,000.00
14 Kevin Love/25 12.00 30.00
15 Danny Granger/25 6.00 15.00
16 Hedo Turkoglu/49 6.00 15.00
17 Monta Ellis/49 8.00 20.00
18 Tyreke Evans/25 6.00 15.00
19 Isiah Thomas/49 12.00 30.00
20 Tom Chambers/49 6.00 15.00
21 Zydrunas Ilgauskas/49 6.00 15.00
22 Andre Iguodala/25 8.00 20.00
23 David Lee/49 6.00 15.00
24 Daniel Gibson/49 6.00 15.00
25 Kevin Durant/25 125.00 300.00
26 John Wall/25 25.00 60.00
27 Rajon Rondo/25 EXCH 12.00 30.00
28 Tony Parker/25 15.00 40.00
29 Derek Fisher/49 8.00 20.00
30 Robert Parish/49 10.00 25.00
31 Michael Cooper/49 8.00 20.00
32 Pau Gasol/25 40.00 100.00
33 Joe Dumars/49 8.00 20.00
34 Anfernee Hardaway/25 100.00 250.00
35 Ralph Sampson/49 6.00 15.00
36 George Gervin/49 12.00 30.00
37 David Thompson/49 8.00 20.00
38 Lenny Wilkens/49 8.00 20.00
39 Hal Greer/49 12.00 30.00
40 Bill Sharman/49 12.00 30.00
41 Aaron Brooks/49 6.00 15.00
42 Dale Ellis/49 6.00 15.00
43 Mark Price/49 8.00 20.00
44 Jeff Hornacek/49 6.00 15.00
45 Bill Walton/49 12.00 30.00
46 Dave Cowens/49 10.00 25.00
47 Bob McAdoo/49 12.00 30.00
48 Mitch Richmond/49 10.00 25.00
49 Larry Bird/25 75.00 200.00
50 Julius Erving/25 50.00 125.00

2012-13 Limited

COMP.SET w/o RCs (150) 25.00 60.00
AU RC PRINT RUN 199 TO 399 SETS
1 Paul Pierce 1.25 3.00
2 Kevin Garnett 2.00 5.00
3 Rajon Rondo 1.00 2.50
4 Brandon Bass .50 1.25
5 Jason Terry .50 1.25
6 Avery Bradley .50 1.25
7 Brook Lopez .60 1.50
8 Deron Williams .60 1.50
9 Gerald Wallace .60 1.50
10 Joe Johnson .60 1.50
11 Kris Humphries .50 1.25
12 Amare Stoudemire .75 2.00
13 Carmelo Anthony 1.25 3.00
14 J.R. Smith .75 2.00
15 Jason Kidd 1.25 3.00
16 Marcus Camby .75 2.00
17 Raymond Felton .50 1.25
18 Tyson Chandler .60 1.50
19 Andre Iguodala .75 2.00
20 Evan Turner .50 1.25
21 Jrue Holiday 1.00 2.50
22 Thaddeus Young .50 1.25
23 Andrea Bargnani .50 1.25
24 DeMar DeRozan 1.00 2.50
25 Jose Calderon .50 1.25
26 Kyle Lowry .75 2.00
27 Landry Fields .50 1.25
28 Carlos Boozer .60 1.50
29 Derrick Rose 1.25 3.00
30 Joakim Noah .60 1.50
31 John Lucas III .50 1.25
32 Kirk Hinrich .60 1.50
33 Luol Deng .60 1.50
34 Anderson Varejao .50 1.25
35 Daniel Gibson .50 1.25
36 Omri Casspi .50 1.25
37 Corey Maggette .60 1.50
38 Greg Monroe .60 1.50
39 Jason Maxiell .50 1.25
40 Rodney Stuckey .50 1.25
41 Tayshaun Prince .75 2.00
42 D.J. Augustin .50 1.25
43 Danny Granger .50 1.25
44 George Hill .60 1.50
45 Paul George 1.25 3.00
46 Roy Hibbert .60 1.50
47 Brandon Jennings .50 1.25
48 Ersan Ilyasova .50 1.25
49 Monta Ellis .60 1.50
50 Samuel Dalembert .50 1.25
51 Al Horford .75 2.00
52 Jeff Teague .60 1.50
53 Josh Smith .50 1.25
54 Louis Williams .60 1.50
55 Zaza Pachulia .50 1.25
56 Ben Gordon .60 1.50
57 Brendan Haywood .50 1.25
58 Ramon Sessions .50 1.25
59 Tyrus Thomas .50 1.25
60 Chris Bosh 1.00 2.50
61 Dwyane Wade 1.50 4.00
62 LeBron James 6.00 15.00
63 Mario Chalmers .60 1.50
64 Ray Allen 1.25 3.00
65 Shane Battier .60 1.50
66 Dwight Howard 1.00 2.50
67 Glen Davis .50 1.25
68 J.J. Redick .75 2.00
69 Jameer Nelson .50 1.25
70 Emeka Okafor .60 1.50
71 John Wall 1.00 2.50
72 Jordan Crawford .50 1.25
73 Nene .60 1.50
74 Trevor Ariza .50 1.25
75 Chris Kaman .60 1.50
76 Darren Collison .60 1.50
77 Dirk Nowitzki 2.00 5.00
78 Elton Brand .60 1.50
79 O.J. Mayo .60 1.50
80 Gary Forbes .50 1.25
81 Jeremy Lin 1.25 3.00
82 Kevin Martin .60 1.50
83 Omer Asik .60 1.50
84 Patrick Patterson .50 1.25
85 Marc Gasol .75 2.00
86 Mike Conley .60 1.50
87 Rudy Gay .75 2.00
88 Tony Allen .60 1.50
89 Zach Randolph .75 2.00
90 Carl Landry .60 1.50
91 Eric Gordon .60 1.50
92 Greivis Vasquez .50 1.25
93 Ryan Anderson .60 1.50
94 Danny Green .60 1.50
95 Gary Neal .50 1.25
96 Manu Ginobili 1.50 4.00
97 Stephen Jackson .60 1.50
98 Tim Duncan 2.00 5.00
99 Tony Parker 1.25 3.00
100 Arron Afflalo .50 1.25
101 Corey Brewer .50 1.25
102 JaVale McGee .60 1.50
103 Ty Lawson .60 1.50
104 Andrei Kirilenko .60 1.50
105 Brandon Roy .60 1.50
106 J.J. Barea .60 1.50
107 Kevin Love .75 2.00
108 Ricky Rubio .60 1.50
109 Jonny Flynn .50 1.25
110 LaMarcus Aldridge .75 2.00
111 Nicolas Batum .60 1.50
112 Wesley Matthews .50 1.25
113 James Harden 1.50 4.00
114 Kendrick Perkins .50 1.25
115 Kevin Durant 3.00 8.00
116 Nick Collison .50 1.25
117 Russell Westbrook 1.25 3.00
118 Serge Ibaka .60 1.50
119 Al Jefferson .50 1.25
120 Gordon Hayward .75 2.00
121 Marvin Williams .50 1.25
122 Mo Williams .60 1.50
123 Paul Millsap .60 1.50
124 Andrew Bogut .60 1.50
125 Brandon Rush .50 1.25
126 David Lee .50 1.25
127 Stephen Curry 6.00 15.00
128 Jarrett Jack .60 1.50
129 Blake Griffin .75 2.00
130 Chris Paul 1.50 4.00
131 Eric Bledsoe .60 1.50
132 Grant Hill 1.25 3.00
133 Jamal Crawford .75 2.00
134 Lamar Odom .60 1.50
135 Andrew Bynum .50 1.25
136 Antawn Jamison .60 1.50
137 Kobe Bryant 6.00 15.00
138 Metta World Peace .60 1.50
139 Pau Gasol 1.25 3.00
140 Steve Nash 1.50 4.00
141 Wesley Johnson .50 1.25
142 Goran Dragic .75 2.00
143 Luis Scola .60 1.50
144 Marcin Gortat .50 1.25
145 Michael Beasley .60 1.50
146 Aaron Brooks .50 1.25
147 DeMarcus Cousins .75 2.00
148 James Johnson .50 1.25
149 Marcus Thornton .50 1.25
150 Tyreke Evans .60 1.50
151 Thomas Robinson AU/199 RC 3.00 8.00
152 Harrison Barnes AU/199 RC 6.00 15.00
153 Jimmy Butler AU/349 RC 30.00 80.00
154 Norris Cole AU/349 RC 3.00 8.00
155 K.Irving AU/199 RC 60.00 150.00
156 Anthony Davis AU/199 RC 100.00 250.00
157 Bismack Biyombo AU/349 RC 4.00 10.00
158 M.Kidd-Gilchrist AU/199 RC 4.00 10.00
159 Bradley Beal AU/199 RC 25.00 60.00
160 MarShon Brooks AU/349 RC 3.00 8.00
161 Kenneth Faried AU/349 RC 4.00 10.00
162 Dion Waiters AU/299 RC 4.00 10.00
163 Terrence Ross AU/299 RC 8.00 20.00
164 Jimmer Fredette AU/299 RC 5.00 12.00
165 Jordan Hamilton AU/399 RC 3.00 8.00
166 Andre Drummond AU/199 RC 8.00 20.00
167 Austin Rivers AU/199 RC 5.00 12.00
168 Tobias Harris AU/349 RC 10.00 25.00
169 Reggie Jackson AU/349 RC 5.00 12.00
170 Meyers Leonard AU/299 RC 4.00 10.00
171 Jeremy Lamb AU/299 RC 5.00 12.00
172 Enes Kanter AU/306 RC 5.00 12.00
173 Brandon Knight AU/299 RC 4.00 10.00
174 K.Leonard AU/349 RC 100.00 250.00
175 Kendall Marshall AU/349 RC 3.00 8.00
176 John Henson AU/299 RC 4.00 10.00
177 Marc.Morris AU/349 RC EXCH 5.00 12.00
178 Markieff Morris AU/349 RC 5.00 12.00
180 Royce White AU/399 RC EXCH 3.00 8.00
181 Chandler Parsons AU/349 RC 4.00 10.00
182 Iman Shumpert AU/349 RC 4.00 10.00
183 Tyler Zeller AU/349 RC 3.00 8.00
184 Terrence Jones AU/349 RC 3.00 8.00
185 Chris Singleton AU/349 RC 3.00 8.00
186 Nolan Smith AU/349 RC 3.00 8.00
187 A.Nicholson AU/399 RC 3.00 8.00
188 E.Fournier AU/349 RC 5.00 12.00
189 Isaiah Thomas AU/399 RC 6.00 15.00
190 K.Thompson AU/299 RC 75.00 200.00
191 Jared Sullinger AU/199 RC 3.00 8.00
192 Fab Melo AU/349 RC 3.00 8.00
193 Tristan Thompson AU/299 RC 5.00 12.00
194 Jan Vesely AU/349 RC 3.00 8.00
195 John Jenkins AU/349 RC 3.00 8.00
196 J.Cunningham AU/349 RC 3.00 8.00
197 Kemba Walker AU/278 RC 12.00 30.00
198 Derrick Williams AU/199 RC 3.00 8.00
199 Tony Wroten AU/349 RC 3.00 8.00
200 Miles Plumlee AU/399 RC 3.00 8.00
201 Cory Joseph AU/399 RC 4.00 10.00
202 JaJuan Johnson AU/349 RC EXCH 3.00 8.00
203 Arnett Moultrie AU/349 RC 3.00 8.00
204 Perry Jones AU/349 RC EXCH 3.00 8.00
205 Justin Harper AU/399 RC 3.00 8.00
206 Shelvin Mack AU/399 RC 4.00 10.00
207 Marquis Teague AU/349 RC 3.00 8.00
208 Festus Ezeli AU/349 RC 3.00 8.00
209 Gustavo Ayon AU/349 RC 3.00 8.00
210 Charles Jenkins AU/399 RC 3.00 8.00
211 Jeremy Tyler AU/399 RC 3.00 8.00
212 J.Harrellson AU/399 RC 3.00 8.00
213 Jeff Taylor AU/399 RC 3.00 8.00
214 Bernard James AU/399 RC 3.00 8.00
215 Jae Crowder AU/399 RC 6.00 15.00
216 Draymond Green AU/399 RC 25.00 60.00
217 Lavoy Allen AU/399 RC 3.00 8.00
218 Alec Burks AU/349 RC 5.00 12.00
219 Nikola Vucevic AU/349 RC 12.00 30.00
220 Tyler Honeycutt AU/399 RC 3.00 8.00
221 Trey Thompkins AU/399 RC 3.00 8.00
222 Jon Leuer AU/349 RC 3.00 8.00
223 Orlando Johnson AU/399 RC 3.00 8.00
224 Quincy Acy AU/399 RC 3.00 8.00
225 Quincy Miller AU/399 RC 3.00 8.00
226 Darius Morris AU/399 RC 4.00 10.00
227 Malcolm Lee AU/399 RC 3.00 8.00
228 Travis Leslie AU/399 RC 3.00 8.00
229 Khris Middleton AU/399 RC 15.00 40.00
230 Will Barton AU/399 RC 6.00 15.00
231 Tyshawn Taylor AU/399 RC 3.00 8.00
232 Josh Selby AU/399 RC 3.00 8.00
233 Ivan Johnson AU/349 RC EXCH 3.00 8.00
234 Greg Stiemsma AU/399 RC 3.00 8.00
235 Courtney Fortson AU/399 RC 3.00 8.00
236 E'Twaun Moore AU/349 RC 4.00 10.00
237 Doron Lamb AU/399 RC 3.00 8.00
238 Mike Scott AU/380 RC 4.00 10.00
239 Kim English AU/399 RC 3.00 8.00
240 Kyle Singler AU/399 RC 3.00 8.00
241 Darius Miller AU/399 RC 4.00 10.00
242 Kevin Murphy AU/399 RC 3.00 8.00
243 Kyle O'Quinn AU/399 RC 4.00 10.00
244 Kris Joseph AU/399 RC 3.00 8.00
245 D.Jnsn-Odom AU/399 RC 3.00 8.00
246 DeAndre Liggins AU/356 RC 3.00 8.00
247 A.Goudelock AU/399 RC EXCH 3.00 8.00
248 R.Sacre AU/399 RC EXCH 3.00 8.00
249 Tornike Shengelia AU/399 RC EXCH 3.00 8.00
250 Lance Thomas AU/399 RC 3.00 8.00

2012-13 Limited Gold Spotlight

*GOLD: 2.5X TO 6X BASE HI
STATED PRINT RUN 25 SER.#'d SETS
106 J.J. Barea 8.00 20.00
132 Grant Hill 8.00 20.00

2012-13 Limited Silver Spotlight

*SILVER: 1.5X TO 4X BASE HI
STATED PRINT RUN 49 SER.#'d SETS
132 Grant Hill 5.00 12.00

2012-13 Limited Center Stage Materials

STATED PRINT RUN 49 TO 99 SER.#'d SETS
1 Kevin Durant/199 12.00 30.00
2 Dwight Howard/199 4.00 10.00
3 Tim Duncan/199 8.00 20.00
4 LeBron James/49 25.00 60.00
5 Kyrie Irving/49 20.00 50.00
6 Tristan Thompson/49 3.00 8.00
7 Amare Stoudemire/199 3.00 8.00
8 Tony Parker/199 5.00 12.00
9 Paul Pierce/49 5.00 12.00
10 Derrick Rose/199 5.00 12.00
11 Rudy Gay/66 3.00 8.00
12 Chris Bosh/199 4.00 10.00
13 Pau Gasol/199 5.00 12.00
14 Dirk Nowitzki/199 8.00 20.00
15 Blake Griffin/199 3.00 8.00
16 Chris Paul/49 6.00 15.00
17 LaMarcus Aldridge/49 3.00 8.00
18 Kevin Love/199 3.00 8.00
19 Deron Williams/199 2.50 6.00
20 David Lee/49 2.00 5.00
21 Brandon Jennings/199 2.00 5.00
22 Josh Smith/49 2.00 5.00
23 Danny Granger/199 2.00 5.00
24 Tyreke Evans/199 2.50 6.00
25 John Wall/49 4.00 10.00
26 Brandon Knight/199 2.50 6.00
27 Tayshaun Prince/49 3.00 8.00
28 DeMar DeRozan/199 4.00 10.00
29 Gordon Hayward/49 3.00 8.00
30 Chandler Parsons/49 10.00 25.00
31 Evan Turner/199 2.00 5.00
32 Marc Gasol/199 3.00 8.00
33 Metta World Peace/199 2.50 6.00
34 Al Horford/199 3.00 8.00
35 Ty Lawson/49 3.00 8.00
36 Jameer Nelson/199 2.00 5.00
37 Joakim Noah/125 2.50 6.00
38 Carmelo Anthony/49 5.00 12.00
39 Carlos Boozer/49 2.50 6.00
40 Rajon Rondo/199 4.00 10.00
41 Andre Iguodala/199 3.00 8.00
42 Stephen Curry/199 8.00 20.00
43 Kawhi Leonard/49 25.00 60.00
44 Greg Monroe/49 2.00 5.00
45 Kevin Garnett/199 8.00 20.00
46 Brook Lopez/99 2.50 6.00
47 Al Jefferson/199 2.00 5.00
48 Wesley Matthews/199 2.00 5.00
49 Jrue Holiday/49 4.00 10.00
50 Jeff Teague/199 2.00 5.00

2012-13 Limited Curtain Call Materials

STATED PRINT RUN 3 TO 199 SER.#'d SETS
1 Larry Bird/199 10.00 25.00
2 Scottie Pippen/199 8.00 20.00
3 Shaquille O'Neal/199 8.00 20.00
4 Kareem Abdul-Jabbar/25 6.00 15.00
5 Karl Malone/199 5.00 12.00
6 Danny Ainge/199 3.00 8.00
7 Robert Parish/49 5.00 12.00
8 John Stockton/25 10.00 25.00
9 Dennis Rodman/199 8.00 20.00
11 Hakeem Olajuwon/199 6.00 15.00
12 Ron Harper/199 3.00 8.00
14 Patrick Ewing/199 8.00 20.00
15 Derek Fisher/199 2.50 6.00
16 Kobe Bryant/199 8.00 20.00
17 Tim Duncan/199 8.00 20.00
18 Kevin Durant/199 5.00 12.00
19 Tony Parker/199 5.00 12.00
20 Manu Ginobili/199 6.00 15.00
21 Ben Wallace/199 2.50 6.00
22 Paul Pierce/199 8.00 20.00
23 Dirk Nowitzki/199 8.00 20.00
25 Tayshaun Prince/199 3.00 8.00
26 LeBron James/99 25.00 60.00
27 Dwyane Wade/199 6.00 15.00
28 Pau Gasol/199 5.00 12.00
29 David Robinson/199 5.00 12.00
30 Jeff Hornacek/199 2.50 6.00
31 Julius Erving/49 8.00 20.00
32 Clyde Drexler/199 5.00 12.00
34 Mark Jackson/199 2.50 6.00
36 Michael Cooper/49 3.00 8.00
37 Bill Cartwright/49 2.50 6.00
38 Bill Laimbeer/199 4.00 10.00
39 Joe Dumars/49 4.00 10.00
40 Dikembe Mutombo/199 5.00 12.00
41 Toni Kukoc/49 5.00 12.00
42 John Starks/49 6.00 15.00
43 Alonzo Mourning/199 8.00 20.00
44 Steve Smith/199 2.50 6.00
45 Jason Kidd/199 5.00 12.00
46 Udonis Haslem/199 2.50 6.00
47 Steve Nash/199 4.00 10.00
48 Ray Allen/199 5.00 12.00
49 Kenyon Martin/199 3.00 8.00
50 Hedo Turkoglu/199 2.50 6.00

2012-13 Limited Glass Cleaners Materials

STATED PRINT RUN 10 TO 99 SER.#'d SETS
1 Dwight Howard/99 4.00 10.00
2 Kareem Abdul-Jabbar/99 10.00 25.00
3 Kevin Garnett/99 8.00 20.00
4 LeBron James/99 25.00 60.00
5 Marc Gasol/99 3.00 8.00
6 DeMarcus Cousins/99 3.00 8.00
7 Tim Duncan/99 8.00 20.00
8 JaVale McGee/99 2.50 6.00
10 Shawn Marion/99 3.00 8.00
11 Amare Stoudemire/99 3.00 8.00
12 Tristan Thompson/99 3.00 8.00
13 DeAndre Jordan/99 2.50 6.00
14 Derrick Favors/99 2.50 6.00
15 Udonis Haslem/99 2.50 6.00
16 Ed Davis/99 2.50 6.00
17 Patrick Ewing/99 5.00 12.00
18 Karl Malone/99 5.00 12.00
19 Dikembe Mutombo/99 5.00 12.00
20 Shawn Kemp/99 10.00 25.00
21 Shaquille O'Neal/99 8.00 20.00
22 Dennis Rodman/99 8.00 20.00
23 Charles Oakley/99 3.00 8.00
24 Chris Kaman/99 2.50 6.00
25 David West/99 2.50 6.00

2012-13 Limited Glass Cleaners Materials Signatures

STATED PRINT RUN 25 TO 49 SER.#'d SETS
1 Charles Oakley/25 15.00 40.00
2 Kevin Durant/25 75.00 150.00
3 Kobe Bryant/49 500.00 1,000.00
4 Blake Griffin/25 20.00 50.00
5 Alonzo Mourning/25 30.00 60.00
6 Kareem Abdul-Jabbar/25 30.00 80.00
7 Hakeem Olajuwon/49 15.00 40.00
8 David Robinson/25 20.00 50.00
9 Emeka Okafor/49 6.00 15.00
10 Kenneth Faried/49 6.00 15.00
11 Toni Kukoc/49 10.00 25.00
12 Anderson Varejao/49 6.00 15.00
13 Kawhi Leonard/49 40.00 100.00
14 Pau Gasol/25 EXCH 20.00 50.00
15 Zach Randolph/49 6.00 15.00
16 LaMarcus Aldridge/49 8.00 20.00
17 Tristan Thompson/49 10.00 25.00
18 Brook Lopez/49 6.00 15.00
19 Derrick Favors/49 6.00 15.00
20 Charlie Villanueva/49 6.00 15.00
21 Al Jefferson/49 8.00 20.00
22 Joakim Noah/49 12.00 30.00
23 Robert Parish/49 8.00 20.00
25 Anthony Davis/49 200.00 500.00

2012-13 Limited Glass Cleaners Signatures

STATED PRINT RUN 25 TO 199 SER.#'d SETS
1 Kevin Durant/49 50.00 120.00
2 Kevin Love/49 12.00 30.00
3 Andrew Bynum/49 8.00 20.00
4 DeMarcus Cousins/49 12.00 30.00
5 Kris Humphries/199 5.00 12.00
6 Blake Griffin/49 15.00 40.00
7 Pau Gasol/25 EXCH 10.00 25.00
8 Marcin Gortat/199 10.00 25.00
10 Joakim Noah/49 10.00 25.00
11 Greg Monroe/199 5.00 12.00
12 Al Jefferson/49 5.00 12.00
13 Josh Smith/49 5.00 12.00
14 David Lee/99 EXCH 5.00 12.00
15 Marcus Camby/199 5.00 12.00
16 DeAndre Jordan/199 5.00 12.00
17 Chris Bosh/25 30.00 60.00
18 Ersan Ilyasova/199 5.00 12.00
19 Roy Hibbert/199 5.00 12.00
20 Drew Gooden/99 EXCH 5.00 12.00
21 Udonis Haslem/99 5.00 12.00
22 Yao Ming/25 30.00 80.00
23 Dikembe Mutombo/199 6.00 15.00
24 Elgin Baylor/25 10.00 25.00
25 Dave Cowens/49 6.00 15.00

2012-13 Limited Home and Away Materials

STATED PRINT RUN 49 TO 99 SER.#'d SETS
1 Kobe Bryant/99 25.00 60.00
2 Tim Duncan/99 8.00 20.00
3 Blake Griffin/99 3.00 8.00
4 Tony Parker/99 5.00 12.00
5 LeBron James/99 15.00 40.00
6 Kevin Durant/99 12.00 30.00
7 Dirk Nowitzki/99 8.00 20.00
8 Derrick Rose/99 5.00 12.00
9 Paul Pierce/99 5.00 12.00
10 Tyson Chandler/99 2.50 6.00
11 Chris Paul/99 6.00 15.00
12 Shaquille O'Neal/99 10.00 25.00
13 Russell Westbrook/49 5.00 12.00
14 Kevin Love/99 3.00 8.00
15 Vince Carter/99 6.00 15.00
16 Stephen Curry/99 12.00 30.00
17 Andrea Bargnani/99 2.00 5.00
18 Dwyane Wade/99 6.00 15.00
19 Tyreke Evans/99 2.50 6.00
20 Brandon Jennings/99 2.00 5.00
21 LaMarcus Aldridge/99 3.00 8.00
22 Zach Randolph/99 3.00 8.00
23 Kevin Martin/99 2.50 6.00
24 John Wall/99 4.00 10.00
25 Kyrie Irving/49 20.00 50.00

2012-13 Limited Lights Out Materials

STATED PRINT RUN 49 TO 199 SER.#'d SETS
1 Dirk Nowitzki/199 10.00 25.00
2 LeBron James/99 10.00 25.00
3 Kevin Durant/199 5.00 12.00
4 Kobe Bryant/99 8.00 20.00
5 Paul Pierce/199 8.00 20.00
6 Carmelo Anthony/199 6.00 15.00
7 Dwyane Wade/199 8.00 20.00
8 Stephen Curry/199 30.00 80.00
9 Manu Ginobili/199 8.00 20.00
10 Ben Gordon/199 3.00 8.00
11 Deron Williams/199 3.00 8.00
12 Joe Johnson/199 3.00 8.00
13 Brandon Jennings/199 2.50 6.00
14 Kevin Love/199 4.00 10.00
15 James Harden/199 8.00 20.00
16 Jason Richardson/199 4.00 10.00
17 Danny Granger/199 2.50 6.00
18 Russell Westbrook/199 6.00 15.00
19 Tony Parker/49 6.00 15.00
20 J.J. Redick/199 8.00 20.00
21 Steve Nash/199 8.00 20.00
22 Ray Allen/199 6.00 15.00
23 Caron Butler/199 3.00 8.00
24 Kyrie Irving/49 20.00 50.00
25 Klay Thompson/49 4.00 10.00
26 Brandon Knight/49 2.50 6.00
27 Derrick Rose/199 6.00 15.00
28 Ryan Anderson/64 2.50 6.00
29 Blake Griffin/199 4.00 10.00
30 Chris Paul/49 8.00 20.00
31 Rudy Gay/199 4.00 10.00
32 Andre Iguodala/199 4.00 10.00
33 Chauncey Billups/199 5.00 12.00
35 Richard Hamilton/90 4.00 10.00
36 Wesley Matthews/199 2.50 6.00
37 Randy Foye/199 2.50 6.00
38 Al Harrington/199 3.00 8.00
39 Dorell Wright/199 2.50 6.00
40 Hedo Turkoglu/199 3.00 8.00
41 Nick Young/199 2.50 6.00
42 Ty Lawson/199 2.50 6.00
43 Shane Battier/199 3.00 8.00
44 Kevin Martin/199 3.00 8.00
45 Jimmer Fredette/199 3.00 8.00
46 D.J. Augustin/199 2.50 6.00
47 Eric Gordon/199 3.00 8.00
48 Brandon Roy/199 3.00 8.00
49 Jameer Nelson/199 2.50 6.00
50 Raymond Felton/199 2.50 6.00

2012-13 Limited Masterful Marks Signatures

STATED PRINT RUN 25 TO 199 SER.#'d SETS
2 Deron Williams/25 4.00 10.00
3 Jason Kidd/25 12.00 30.00
4 Kobe Bryant/99 400.00 800.00
5 Brandon Roy/25 4.00 10.00
6 Raymond Felton/99 3.00 8.00
7 Nick Collison/99 3.00 8.00
8 Al Horford/99 5.00 12.00
9 Grant Hill/49 15.00 40.00
10 Darren Collison/99 3.00 8.00
11 Andre Iguodala/99 5.00 12.00
12 LaMarcus Aldridge/49 5.00 12.00
13 James Harden/99 EXCH 20.00 50.00
14 David Lee/99 EXCH 3.00 8.00
15 Ersan Ilyasova/199 3.00 8.00
16 Vlade Divac/199 5.00 12.00
17 Gordon Hayward/199 5.00 12.00
18 Stephen Curry/99 400.00 800.00
19 Marcus Thornton/199 3.00 8.00

20 Antoine Walker/199 4.00 10.00
21 Jordan Crawford/99 3.00 8.00
22 Charles Oakley/99 5.00 12.00
23 Anderson Varejao/99 3.00 8.00
24 O.J. Mayo/49 3.00 8.00
25 Al-Farouq Aminu/99 3.00 8.00
26 Kevin Durant/49 60.00 150.00
27 Joakim Noah/49 4.00 10.00
28 Tony Parker/49 12.00 30.00
29 Kevin Love/49 10.00 25.00
30 Joe Johnson/49 4.00 10.00
31 Brandon Jennings/49 3.00 8.00
32 Derrick Favors/99 4.00 10.00
33 Brook Lopez/99 4.00 10.00
34 Isiah Thomas/99 8.00 20.00
35 Eric Gordon/99 4.00 10.00
36 Ty Lawson/99 3.00 8.00
37 Serge Ibaka/199 4.00 10.00
38 Kevin Martin/99 4.00 10.00
39 Jrue Holiday/99 6.00 15.00
40 Blake Griffin/49 15.00 40.00
41 Mitch Richmond/199 5.00 12.00
42 Dan Majerle/199 4.00 10.00
43 JaVale McGee/99 4.00 10.00
44 Mark Jackson/199 4.00 10.00
45 Jerry West/25 20.00 50.00
46 Antawn Jamison/49 4.00 10.00
47 Delonte West/99 3.00 8.00
48 Steve Novak/99 3.00 8.00
49 Andrew Bogut/99 EXCH 4.00 10.00
50 Drew Gooden/99 EXCH 4.00 10.00

2012-13 Limited Monikers Materials

STATED PRINT RUN 25 TO 99 SER.#'d SETS
1 John Stockton/25 25.00 60.00
2 Amare Stoudemire/49 12.00 30.00
3 Tony Parker/25 15.00 40.00
4 Robert Parish/99 6.00 15.00
5 Tayshaun Prince/99 6.00 15.00
6 Jason Richardson/99 6.00 15.00
7 David Robinson/25 15.00 40.00
8 Kevin Martin/99 4.00 10.00
9 Kevin McHale/25 6.00 15.00
10 Al Jefferson/49 6.00 15.00
11 Kevin Durant/25 75.00 150.00
12 Jalen Rose/99 EXCH 6.00 15.00
13 Joe Dumars/49 6.00 15.00
14 Brandon Knight/99 4.00 10.00
15 LaMarcus Aldridge/49 10.00 25.00
16 Jameer Nelson/49 6.00 15.00
17 Kareem Abdul-Jabbar/49 40.00 100.00
18 Markieff Morris/99 5.00 12.00
19 Derrick Williams/99 3.00 8.00
20 Carlos Boozer/49 6.00 15.00
21 Zach Randolph/49 10.00 25.00
22 David Lee/99 EXCH 8.00 20.00
23 Mark Jackson/99 EXCH 6.00 15.00
24 J.J. Redick/49 8.00 20.00
25 Jimmer Fredette/99 5.00 12.00
26 Blake Griffin/49 30.00 80.00
27 Brook Lopez/49 6.00 15.00
28 Kobe Bryant/99 800.00 1,500.00
29 Ivan Johnson/99 3.00 8.00
30 Gary Payton/49 12.00 30.00
31 Chandler Parsons/99 4.00 10.00
32 Jeff Teague/99 6.00 15.00
33 Anternee Hardaway/49 15.00 40.00
34 Luke Ridnour/49 6.00 15.00
35 Beno Udrih/99 3.00 8.00
36 Anthony Mason/99 6.00 15.00
37 Danny Granger/49 6.00 15.00
38 Andre Iguodala/49 8.00 20.00
39 Metta World Peace/49 6.00 15.00
40 Al Horford/49 6.00 15.00
41 Chris Bosh/25 12.00 30.00
42 Toni Kukoc/99 15.00 40.00
43 Luol Deng/49 6.00 15.00
45 Mark Price/99 5.00 12.00
46 Andre Miller/99 6.00 15.00
47 Caron Butler/49 6.00 15.00
48 Ty Lawson/99 3.00 8.00
49 Jerry West/25 25.00 60.00
50 Andrew Bynum/49 10.00 25.00

2012-13 Limited Monikers Materials Prime

*PRIME: .75X TO 2X BASE HI
STATED PRINT RUN 5 TO 25 SER.#'d SETS
4 Robert Parish/25 15.00 40.00

2012-13 Limited Performers Materials

STATED PRINT RUN ONE TO 199 SER.#'d SETS
1 Kevin Martin/199 2.50 6.00
2 J.J. Redick/99 6.00 15.00
3 Tyrus Thomas/199 2.00 5.00
4 Grant Hill/199 6.00 15.00
5 Elton Brand/199 2.50 6.00
7 Zach Randolph/199 3.00 8.00
8 Caron Butler/199 2.50 6.00
9 Kevin Garnett/199 8.00 20.00
10 Marc Gasol/199 3.00 8.00
11 LeBron James/199 25.00 60.00
12 Tim Duncan/199 8.00 20.00
13 Dwyane Wade/199 6.00 15.00
14 Dwight Howard/199 4.00 10.00
15 David West/199 2.50 6.00
16 Kirk Hinrich/199 2.50 6.00
17 Shawn Marion/199 3.00 8.00
18 Thaddeus Young/199 2.00 5.00
19 Linas Kleiza/199 2.00 5.00
20 Carmelo Anthony/199 5.00 12.00
21 Amare Stoudemire/199 3.00 8.00
22 Rajon Rondo/199 4.00 10.00
23 Paul Pierce/199 5.00 12.00
24 John Wall/199 4.00 10.00
25 Derrick Rose/199 5.00 12.00
26 Manu Ginobili/199 6.00 15.00
27 Raymond Felton/199 2.00 5.00
28 Kemba Walker/99 6.00 15.00
29 J.J. Barea/199 2.50 6.00
30 DeMar DeRozan/199 4.00 10.00
31 Nick Collison/109 2.00 5.00
32 Glen Davis/199 2.00 5.00
33 George Hill/199 2.50 6.00
34 Josh Smith/199 2.00 5.00
36 Carlos Delfino/199 2.00 5.00
37 Tiago Splitter/199 2.00 5.00
38 Channing Frye/199 2.00 5.00
39 Tyler Hansbrough/199 2.00 5.00
40 Spencer Hawes/199 2.00 5.00
41 Tobias Harris/199 5.00 12.00
42 John Salmons/199 2.50 6.00
44 Tristan Thompson/199 2.50 6.00
45 MarShon Brooks/199 1.50 4.00
46 Udonis Haslem/199 2.50 6.00
47 Wesley Matthews/199 2.00 5.00
48 Ed Davis/199 2.00 5.00
50 Kenneth Faried/25 2.00 5.00

2012-13 Limited Private Signings

1 Alex English 6.00 15.00
2 Christian Laettner 15.00 40.00
3 Hakeem Olajuwon 75.00 200.00
4 Rajon Rondo 20.00 50.00

2012-13 Limited Spotlight Signatures

STATED PRINT RUN 10 TO 99 SER.#'d SETS
1 Glen Rice/99 8.00 20.00
2 Magic Johnson/25 40.00 100.00
3 Dirk Nowitzki/15 100.00 200.00
4 Kobe Bryant/49 500.00 1,000.00
5 Ralph Sampson/99 4.00 10.00
6 Bailey Howell/99 6.00 15.00
7 Blake Griffin/25 15.00 40.00
10 Luis Scola/99 4.00 10.00
12 Chris Kaman/99 4.00 10.00
13 Andrew Bynum/25 3.00 8.00
14 Kevin Durant/25 100.00 200.00
15 Chauncey Billups/25 EXCH 5.00 12.00
16 Delonte West/99 3.00 8.00
17 Greg Monroe/49 4.00 10.00
18 Muggsy Bogues/99 4.00 10.00
19 Marcus Camby/49 4.00 10.00
20 Andrew Bogut/49 4.00 10.00
21 Mario Chalmers/99 EXCH 4.00 10.00
22 DeAndre Jordan/99 5.00 12.00
23 Marcin Gortat/99 4.00 10.00
24 Eric Bledsoe/99 4.00 10.00
25 Avery Bradley/99 4.00 10.00
26 Gerald Wallace/99 4.00 10.00
27 Tayshaun Prince/99 4.00 10.00
28 Steve Nash/25 15.00 40.00
29 Al Jefferson/49 4.00 10.00
30 Zach Randolph/49 4.00 10.00
31 Derek Fisher/49 4.00 10.00
32 Jose Calderon/49 3.00 8.00
33 Stephen Jackson/99 4.00 10.00
35 Julius Erving/25 30.00 80.00
36 Byron Scott/49 4.00 10.00
37 Bill Cartwright/49 4.00 10.00
38 Kevin Willis/99 4.00 10.00
39 Bob Pettit/25 EXCH 6.00 15.00
40 Anfernee Hardaway/49 20.00 50.00
41 Will Bynum/99 3.00 8.00
42 Elgin Baylor/49 8.00 20.00
43 Gary Payton/25 10.00 25.00
44 Bob Lanier/49 4.00 10.00
45 Earl Monroe/25 10.00 25.00
46 Vince Carter/25 30.00 80.00
47 Artis Gilmore/49 4.00 10.00
48 Robert Horry/49 4.00 10.00
49 Chris Bosh/25 12.00 30.00
50 Monta Ellis/49 4.00 10.00

2012-13 Limited Unlimited Potential Signatures

STATED PRINT RUN 49 TO 199 SER.#'d SETS
1 Derrick Favors/99 3.00 8.00
2 Kyrie Irving/199 60.00 150.00
3 MarShon Brooks/199 2.50 6.00
4 Anthony Davis/99 150.00 400.00
5 Brandon Knight/199 3.00 8.00
6 Klay Thompson/99 75.00 200.00
7 Quincy Acy/199 2.50 6.00
8 Isaiah Thomas/199 5.00 12.00
9 Markieff Morris/99 4.00 10.00
10 Ivan Johnson/199 2.50 6.00
11 Thomas Robinson/199 2.50 6.00
12 Kendall Marshall/199 2.50 6.00
13 Chandler Parsons/99 3.00 8.00
14 Michael Kidd-Gilchrist/199 3.00 8.00
15 Tyler Zeller/199 2.50 6.00
16 Andrew Goudelock/199 EXCH 2.50 6.00
17 Dion Waiters/199 EXCH 3.00 8.00
18 Austin Rivers/199 4.00 10.00
19 Andre Drummond/199 8.00 20.00
20 Iman Shumpert/199 3.00 8.00
21 Jeremy Lamb/199 4.00 10.00
22 Kenneth Faried/199 3.00 8.00
23 Meyers Leonard/99 3.00 8.00
24 John Henson/199 3.00 8.00
25 Jonas Valanciunas/199 5.00 12.00
26 Bradley Beal/199 20.00 50.00
27 Tristan Thompson/199 4.00 10.00
28 Jimmer Fredette/199 4.00 10.00
29 Alec Burks/199 4.00 10.00
30 Norris Cole/199 2.50 6.00
31 Enes Kanter/199 4.00 10.00
32 Gustavo Ayon/199 2.50 6.00
33 Royce White/199 2.50 6.00
34 Terrence Ross/199 6.00 15.00
35 Andrew Nicholson/199 2.50 6.00
36 Evan Fournier/199 4.00 10.00
37 Jared Sullinger/199 2.50 6.00
38 Fab Melo/199 2.50 6.00
39 John Jenkins/49 2.50 6.00
40 Jared Cunningham/199 2.50 6.00
41 Tony Wroten/199 2.50 6.00
42 Miles Plumlee/199 2.50 6.00
43 Arnett Moultrie/199 2.50 6.00
44 Perry Jones/199 2.50 6.00
45 Marquis Teague/99 2.50 6.00
46 Festus Ezeli/199 2.50 6.00
47 Bernard James/199 2.50 6.00
48 Draymond Green/199 10.00 25.00
49 Jeff Taylor/199 2.50 6.00
50 Jae Crowder/199 5.00 12.00

2015-16 Limited

STATED PRINT RUN 80 SER.#'d SETS
1 Paul Millsap .60 1.50
2 Gordon Hayward .75 2.00
3 John Wall 1.00 2.50
4 Danilo Gallinari .60 1.50
5 Marc Gasol .75 2.00
6 Jimmy Butler 1.50 4.00
7 Stephen Curry 6.00 15.00
8 DeMar DeRozan 1.00 2.50
9 Rajon Rondo 1.00 2.50
10 Joe Johnson .60 1.50
11 Al Horford .75 2.00
12 Derrick Favors .60 1.50
13 Otto Porter .60 1.50
14 Will Barton .50 1.25
15 Mike Conley .60 1.50
16 Derrick Rose 1.25 3.00
17 Draymond Green 1.00 2.50
18 Kyle Lowry .75 2.00
19 Rudy Gay .75 2.00
20 Brook Lopez .75 2.00
21 Kyle Korver .60 1.50
22 Alec Burks .50 1.25
23 Bradley Beal 1.00 2.50
24 Kenneth Faried .60 1.50
25 Zach Randolph .75 2.00
26 Pau Gasol 1.25 3.00
27 Klay Thompson 2.00 5.00
28 DeMarre Carroll .50 1.25
29 DeMarcus Cousins .75 2.00
30 Thaddeus Young .50 1.25
31 Jeff Teague .50 1.25
32 Rodney Hood .60 1.50
33 Marcin Gortat .50 1.25
34 Gary Harris .60 1.50
35 Tony Allen .60 1.50
36 Nikola Mirotic .50 1.25
37 Andre Iguodala .75 2.00
38 Jonas Valanciunas .60 1.50
39 Ben McLemore .50 1.25
40 Jarrett Jack .60 1.50
41 Dennis Schroder .75 2.00
42 Rudy Gobert 1.00 2.50
43 Nene .60 1.50
44 Jameer Nelson .50 1.25
45 Vince Carter 1.50 4.00
46 Joakim Noah .60 1.50
47 Harrison Barnes .60 1.50
48 Luis Scola .60 1.50
49 Omri Casspi .50 1.25
50 Bojan Bogdanovic .60 1.50
51 Chris Bosh 1.00 2.50
52 Andrew Wiggins 1.00 2.50
53 Kawhi Leonard 2.50 6.00
54 LeBron James 6.00 15.00
55 James Harden 1.50 4.00
56 Kentavious Caldwell-Pope .60 1.50
57 Blake Griffin .75 2.00
58 Isaiah Thomas .60 1.50
59 Jordan Clarkson .75 2.00
60 Hollis Thompson .50 1.25
61 Goran Dragic .75 2.00
62 Zach LaVine 2.00 5.00
63 Tony Parker 1.25 3.00
64 Kevin Love .75 2.00
65 Trevor Ariza .50 1.25
66 Marcus Morris .50 1.25
67 Chris Paul 1.50 4.00
68 Jae Crowder .50 1.25
69 Kobe Bryant 6.00 15.00
70 Jerami Grant .50 1.25
71 Hassan Whiteside .60 1.50
72 Kevin Martin .50 1.25
73 LaMarcus Aldridge .75 2.00
74 Kyrie Irving 1.50 4.00
75 Ty Lawson .50 1.25
76 Andre Drummond .75 2.00
77 DeAndre Jordan .60 1.50
78 Avery Bradley .50 1.25
79 Julius Randle 1.00 2.50
80 Isaiah Canaan .50 1.25
81 Dwyane Wade 1.50 4.00
82 Ricky Rubio .60 1.50
83 Tim Duncan 2.00 5.00
84 J.R. Smith .75 2.00
85 Dwight Howard 1.00 2.50
86 Reggie Jackson .60 1.50
87 J.J. Redick .75 2.00
88 Jared Sullinger .50 1.25
89 Roy Hibbert .60 1.50
90 Nerlens Noel .50 1.25
91 Gerald Green .60 1.50
92 Kevin Garnett 2.00 5.00
93 Manu Ginobili 1.50 4.00
94 Mo Williams .50 1.25
95 Corey Brewer .50 1.25
96 Ersan Ilyasova .50 1.25
97 Paul Pierce 1.25 3.00
98 Marcus Smart 1.00 2.50
99 Lou Williams .60 1.50
100 Robert Covington .60 1.50
101 Evan Fournier .60 1.50
102 Damian Lillard 2.00 5.00
103 Deron Williams .60 1.50
104 Paul George 1.25 3.00
105 Eric Gordon .60 1.50
106 Khris Middleton 1.00 2.50
107 Tyson Chandler .60 1.50
108 Carmelo Anthony 1.25 3.00
109 Nicolas Batum .60 1.50
110 Russell Westbrook 1.25 3.00
111 Tobias Harris .60 1.50
112 C.J. McCollum .75 2.00
113 Zaza Pachulia .60 1.50
114 Monta Ellis .60 1.50
115 Ryan Anderson .60 1.50
116 Giannis Antetokounmpo 4.00 10.00
117 Brandon Knight .60 1.50
118 Jose Calderon .50 1.25
119 Kemba Walker .75 2.00
120 Serge Ibaka .60 1.50
121 Elfrid Payton .60 1.50
122 Al-Farouq Aminu .50 1.25
123 Dirk Nowitzki 2.00 5.00
124 George Hill .50 1.25
125 Anthony Davis 2.00 5.00
126 Greg Monroe .60 1.50
127 Eric Bledsoe .60 1.50
128 Langston Galloway .50 1.25
129 Marvin Williams .50 1.25
130 Dion Waiters .50 1.25
131 Victor Oladipo .60 1.50
132 Mason Plumlee .50 1.25
133 Wesley Matthews .50 1.25
134 C.J. Miles .50 1.25
135 Jrue Holiday 1.00 2.50
136 Michael Carter-Williams .50 1.25
137 T.J. Warren .75 2.00
138 Robin Lopez .50 1.25
139 Jeremy Lin 1.50 4.00
140 Kevin Durant 3.00 8.00
141 Nikola Vucevic .60 1.50
142 Ed Davis .50 1.25
143 Chandler Parsons .50 1.25
144 Ian Mahinmi .50 1.25
145 Tyreke Evans .60 1.50
146 Jabari Parker .50 1.25
147 Markieff Morris .50 1.25
148 Arron Afflalo .50 1.25
149 Al Jefferson .50 1.25
150 Enes Kanter .50 1.25
151 Frank Kaminsky RC 1.25 3.00
152 Rondae Hollis-Jefferson RC 1.25 3.00
153 Aaron Harrison RC 1.00 2.50
154 Cristiano Felicio RC 1.25 3.00
155 Rashad Vaughn RC 1.00 2.50
156 Richaun Holmes RC 1.50 4.00
157 Jerian Grant RC 1.00 2.50
158 Josh Richardson RC 1.50 4.00
159 D'Angelo Russell RC 5.00 12.00
160 Cliff Alexander RC 1.00 2.50
161 Raul Neto RC 1.00 2.50
162 Delon Wright RC 1.25 3.00
163 Trey Lyles RC 1.25 3.00
164 Tyus Jones RC 1.25 3.00
165 Montrezl Harrell RC 3.00 8.00
166 Jarell Eddie RC 1.50 4.00
167 Stanley Johnson RC 1.25 3.00
168 Norman Powell RC 2.00 5.00
169 Karl-Anthony Towns RC 8.00 20.00
170 Pat Connaughton RC 1.50 4.00
171 Jahlil Okafor RC 1.25 3.00
172 Anthony Brown RC 1.00 2.50
173 Nemanja Bjelica RC 1.50 4.00
174 Luis Montero RC 1.00 2.50
175 R.J. Hunter RC 1.00 2.50
176 Marcelo Huertas RC 1.00 2.50
177 Kristaps Porzingis RC 10.00 25.00
178 Jonathon Simmons RC 1.25 3.00
179 Willie Cauley-Stein RC 1.25 3.00
180 Darrun Hilliard RC 1.00 2.50
181 Justise Winslow RC 1.50 4.00
182 Sam Dekker RC 1.25 3.00
183 Larry Nance Jr. RC 2.00 5.00
184 Jarell Martin RC 1.00 2.50
185 Terry Rozier RC 4.00 10.00
186 Boban Marjanovic RC 5.00 12.00
187 T.J. McConnell RC 4.00 10.00
188 Myles Turner RC 4.00 10.00
189 Mario Hezonja RC 1.25 3.00
190 Sasha Kaun RC 1.00 2.50
191 Devin Booker RC 6.00 15.00
192 Bobby Portis RC 2.50 6.00
193 Justin Anderson RC 1.00 2.50
194 Chris McCullough RC 1.00 2.50
195 Kelly Oubre Jr. RC 3.00 8.00
196 Cameron Payne RC 1.50 4.00
197 Emmanuel Mudiay RC 1.25 3.00
198 Joe Young RC 1.00 2.50
199 Nikola Jokic RC 200.00 500.00
200 Salah Mejri RC 4.00 10.00

2015-16 Limited Gold Spotlight

*GOLD 1-150: 1.5X TO 4X BASIC
*GOLD 151-200: .75X TO 2X BASIC
STATED PRINT RUN 25 SER.#'d SETS

2015-16 Limited Silver Spotlight

*SILVER 1-150: .6X TO 1.5X BASIC
*SILVER 151-200: .5X TO 1.2X BASIC
STATED PRINT RUN 49 SER.#'d SETS

2015-16 Limited All Star Shorts

PRINT RUNS B/WN 146-149 COPIES PER
*PRIME/25: 1.5X TO 4X BASIC
1 LaMarcus Aldridge 3.00 8.00
2 Kyle Korver 2.50 6.00
3 Damian Lillard 5.00 12.00
4 DeMarcus Cousins 3.00 8.00
5 Jeff Teague 2.00 5.00
6 Al Horford 3.00 8.00
7 John Wall 4.00 10.00
8 Paul Millsap 2.50 6.00

2015-16 Limited Decade Dominance Materials

PRINT RUNS B/WN 49-149 COPIES PER
*PRIME/25: .75X TO 2X BASIC
1 David Robinson/149 6.00 15.00
2 Kevin Durant/49 6.00 15.00
3 John Stockton/149 6.00 15.00
4 Scottie Pippen/149 8.00 20.00
5 Calvin Murphy/99 2.50 6.00
6 Ben Wallace/149 2.50 6.00
7 Clyde Drexler/149 5.00 12.00
8 Kevin Garnett/149 8.00 20.00
9 Larry Bird/149 6.00 15.00
10 Tim Duncan/149 6.00 15.00
11 Dennis Rodman/149 8.00 20.00
12 LeBron James/149 12.00 30.00
13 Karl Malone/149 5.00 12.00
14 Shaquille O'Neal/149 10.00 25.00
15 Louie Dampier/149 3.00 8.00
16 Dirk Nowitzki/149 8.00 20.00
17 Isiah Thomas/149 3.00 8.00
18 Kobe Bryant/149 10.00 25.00
19 Moses Malone/149 5.00 12.00
20 Tony Parker/149 3.00 8.00
21 Hakeem Olajuwon/149 6.00 15.00
22 Stephen Curry/99 25.00 60.00
23 Patrick Ewing/149 5.00 12.00
24 Allen Iverson/149 8.00 20.00
25 Alex English/149 4.00 10.00
26 Dwyane Wade/149 6.00 15.00
27 Kareem Abdul-Jabbar/149 10.00 25.00
28 Paul Pierce/149 5.00 12.00
29 Clifford Robinson/149 3.00 8.00
30 James Harden/149 6.00 15.00

2015-16 Limited Duos Signatures

PRINT RUNS B/WN 10-49 COPIES PER
NO PRICING ON QTY 10
*SILVER/25: .5X TO 1.2X BASIC
1 R.Hunter/T.Rozier/49 15.00 40.00
2 C.McCullough/R.Hollis-Jefferson/49 5.00 12.00
3 M.Harrell/S.Dekker/49 12.00 30.00
4 Russell/Nance Jr./49 25.00 60.00
5 Winslow/Richardson/49 25.00 60.00
6 Jones/Towns/49 75.00 200.00
7 Porzingis/Grant/49 30.00 80.00
8 C.Payne/J.Huestis/49 6.00 15.00
9 Okafor/Noel/49 5.00 12.00
10 Jhnsn/Hlls-Jffrsn/49 5.00 12.00
11 Booker/Lyles/49 75.00 200.00
12 M.Harrell/T.Rozier/49 15.00 40.00
13 J.Grant/P.Connaughton/49 6.00 15.00
14 A.Brown/J.Huestis/49 4.00 10.00
15 R.Christmas/C.McCullough/49 4.00 10.00
16 Dekker/Kaminsky/49 15.00 40.00
17 J.Nurkic/W.Chandler/49 5.00 12.00
18 Drummond/Caldwell-Pope/49 10.00 25.00
19 Paul/Griffin/25 125.00 300.00
21 Nowitzki/Porzingis/25 150.00 300.00
22 M.Price/B.Daugherty/49 6.00 15.00
23 Hamilton/Prince/49 8.00 20.00
24 Ramsey/Sanders/49 12.00 30.00
26 van Arsdale/van Arsdale/49 12.00 30.00
27 L.Nance Jr./L.Nance/49 8.00 20.00
28 D.Manning/R.LaFrentz/49 5.00 12.00
29 Hagan/Ramsey/49 10.00 25.00
30 B.Scott/K.Rambis/49 10.00 25.00
31 Kerr/Johnson/49 12.00 30.00
32 Porter/Drexler/49 15.00 40.00
33 Payton/Hawkins/49 12.00 30.00
34 Johnson/Houston/49 8.00 20.00

2015-16 Limited Glass Cleaners Materials

STATED PRINT RUN 149 COPIES PER
*PRIME/25: .75X TO 2X BASIC
1 Tim Duncan 4.00 10.00
2 DeMarcus Cousins 3.00 8.00
3 Andre Drummond 3.00 8.00
4 Zaza Pachulia 2.00 5.00
5 Kevin Love 3.00 8.00
6 Rudy Gobert 4.00 10.00
7 Anthony Davis 5.00 12.00
8 Tristan Thompson 2.00 5.00
9 Pau Gasol 5.00 12.00
10 LaMarcus Aldridge 3.00 8.00
11 Marc Gasol 3.00 8.00
12 Greg Monroe 2.50 6.00
13 Karl-Anthony Towns 8.00 20.00
14 Kristaps Porzingis 6.00 15.00
15 Chris Bosh 4.00 10.00
16 Tyson Chandler 2.50 6.00
17 Zach Randolph 3.00 8.00
18 Derrick Favors 2.50 6.00
19 Blake Griffin 4.00 10.00
20 Julius Randle 4.00 10.00
21 Serge Ibaka 2.50 6.00
22 Nerlens Noel 2.00 5.00
23 Kenneth Faried 2.50 6.00
24 DeAndre Jordan 2.50 6.00
25 Paul Millsap 2.50 6.00
26 Joakim Noah 2.50 6.00
27 Draymond Green 4.00 10.00
28 Mason Plumlee 2.00 5.00
29 Brook Lopez 3.00 8.00
30 Jahlil Okafor 4.00 10.00

2015-16 Limited Material Monikers

STATED PRINT RUN 149 COPIES PER
*PRIME/25: 1X TO 2.5X BASIC
1 Carmelo Anthony/149 6.00 15.00
3 Giannis Antetokounmpo/45 20.00 50.00
4 Paul George/49 6.00 15.00
5 Derrick Rose/49 6.00 15.00
6 Paul Pierce/99 6.00 15.00
7 Dirk Nowitzki/149 10.00 25.00
9 Kobe Bryant/49 20.00 50.00
10 Kevin Garnett/149 10.00 25.00
11 Shaquille O'Neal/99 10.00 25.00
12 DeMarcus Cousins/149 4.00 10.00
14 Al Jefferson/99 2.50 6.00
16 Ben Wallace/149 3.00 8.00
17 James Harden/99 8.00 20.00
18 Roy Hibbert/99 2.50 6.00
19 Anthony Davis/99 6.00 15.00
20 Iman Shumpert/99 2.50 6.00
22 Hakeem Olajuwon/99 6.00 15.00
23 Goran Dragic/149 4.00 10.00
24 Jeremy Lin/99 10.00 25.00
25 LeBron James/49 20.00 50.00
26 Steven Adams/99 3.00 8.00
27 Chris Paul/99 6.00 15.00
28 Kawhi Leonard/99 6.00 15.00
29 Dwyane Wade/149 8.00 20.00
30 Deron Williams/99 3.00 8.00
31 Dwight Howard/99 5.00 12.00
32 Clyde Drexler/99 5.00 12.00

2015-16 Limited Phenoms

1 Kobe Bryant 10.00 25.00
2 Kevin Durant 5.00 12.00
3 LeBron James 10.00 25.00
4 Anthony Davis 3.00 8.00
5 Carmelo Anthony 2.00 5.00
6 Chris Paul 2.50 6.00
7 Dwyane Wade 2.50 6.00
8 James Harden 2.50 6.00
9 Stephen Curry 8.00 20.00
10 Russell Westbrook 2.00 5.00
11 Blake Griffin 2.00 5.00
12 Andrew Wiggins 1.50 4.00
13 Damian Lillard 2.00 5.00
14 John Wall 1.50 4.00
15 Tim Duncan 3.00 8.00

2015-16 Limited Rookie Jersey Autographs

STATED PRINT RUN 99 SER.#'d SETS
1 Karl-Anthony Towns 40.00 100.00
2 D'Angelo Russell 15.00 40.00
3 Jahlil Okafor 5.00 12.00
4 Kristaps Porzingis 30.00 80.00
5 Mario Hezonja 5.00 12.00
6 Willie Cauley-Stein 5.00 12.00
7 Emmanuel Mudiay 5.00 12.00
8 Stanley Johnson 5.00 12.00
9 Frank Kaminsky 5.00 12.00
10 Justise Winslow 6.00 15.00
11 Myles Turner 15.00 40.00
12 Trey Lyles 5.00 12.00
13 Devin Booker 200.00 500.00
14 Cameron Payne 6.00 15.00
15 Kelly Oubre Jr. 12.00 30.00
16 Terry Rozier 15.00 40.00
17 Nikola Jokic 800.00 1,500.00
18 Salah Mejri 4.00 10.00
19 Jerian Grant 4.00 10.00
20 Delon Wright 5.00 12.00
21 Justin Anderson 4.00 10.00
22 Bobby Portis 10.00 25.00
23 Rondae Hollis-Jefferson 5.00 12.00
24 Tyus Jones 5.00 12.00
25 Jarell Martin 4.00 10.00
26 R.J. Hunter 4.00 10.00
27 Chris McCullough 4.00 10.00
28 Montrezl Harrell 12.00 30.00
29 Jordan Mickey 4.00 10.00
30 Anthony Brown 4.00 10.00
31 Rakeem Christmas 4.00 10.00
32 Richaun Holmes 6.00 15.00
33 Pat Connaughton 6.00 15.00
35 Nemanja Bjelica 6.00 15.00
36 Kevon Looney 12.00 30.00
37 Josh Richardson 6.00 15.00
38 Josh Huestis 4.00 10.00

2015-16 Limited Rookie Jersey Autographs Gold Spotlight

*GOLD: .75X TO 2X BASIC
STATED PRINT RUN 25 SER.#'d SETS
34 Joe Young 8.00 20.00

2015-16 Limited Rookie Jersey Autographs Silver Spotlight

*SILVER: .5X TO 1.2X BASIC
STATED PRINT RUN 49 SER.#'d SETS
34 Joe Young 5.00 12.00

2015-16 Limited Rookie Phenoms

1 Karl-Anthony Towns 8.00 20.00
2 D'Angelo Russell 5.00 12.00
3 Jahlil Okafor 1.50 4.00
4 Kristaps Porzingis 8.00 20.00
5 Mario Hezonja 1.50 4.00
6 Willie Cauley-Stein 1.50 4.00
7 Emmanuel Mudiay 1.50 4.00
8 Stanley Johnson 1.50 4.00
9 Frank Kaminsky 1.50 4.00
10 Justise Winslow 2.00 5.00
11 Myles Turner 5.00 12.00
12 Trey Lyles 1.50 4.00
13 Devin Booker 15.00 40.00
14 Cameron Payne 2.00 5.00
15 Kelly Oubre Jr. 4.00 10.00

2015-16 Limited Signatures

PRINT RUNS B/WN 15-99 COPIES PER
NO PRICING ON QTY 15
*SILVER/25: .5X TO 1.2X BASIC
3 Kyrie Irving/35 25.00 60.00
4 Anthony Davis/35 40.00 100.00
5 Chris Paul/35 40.00 100.00
6 Allen Iverson/35 50.00 120.00
7 Chris Webber/99 40.00 100.00
8 Kareem Abdul-Jabbar/35 20.00 50.00
9 Tracy McGrady/99 12.00 30.00
10 Elgin Baylor/99 6.00 15.00
11 James Worthy/99 6.00 15.00
12 Gary Payton/75 10.00 25.00
13 Harrison Barnes/99 4.00 10.00
14 Julius Randle/99 6.00 15.00
15 Bob Lanier/99 6.00 15.00
16 Ben McLemore/99 3.00 8.00
17 Artis Gilmore/99 6.00 15.00
18 Wes Unseld/99 6.00 15.00
19 Walt Frazier/99 8.00 20.00
20 Trey Burke/99 3.00 8.00
21 Brandon Knight/99 3.00 8.00
22 Hal Greer/99 6.00 15.00
23 Dolph Schayes/99 5.00 12.00
24 Lenny Wilkens/99 5.00 12.00
25 Ralph Sampson/99 5.00 12.00
26 Nikola Mirotic/99 3.00 8.00
27 T.J. Warren/99 5.00 12.00
28 Jrue Holiday/99 6.00 15.00
29 Bob McAdoo/99 3.00 8.00
30 Bernard King/99 6.00 15.00
31 Sonny Weems/99 3.00 8.00
32 Jason Smith/99 3.00 8.00
33 Jeff Malone/99 3.00 8.00
34 Kevin Willis/99 3.00 8.00
35 Sam Bowie/99 3.00 8.00
36 Antoine Carr/99 3.00 8.00
37 Cuttino Mobley/99 3.00 8.00
38 Eddie Jones/99 5.00 12.00
39 Rafer Alston/99 3.00 8.00
40 Avery Johnson/99 4.00 10.00
41 Hersey Hawkins/99 3.00 8.00
42 Doug Collins/99 5.00 12.00
43 Spencer Haywood/99 5.00 12.00
44 Jerome Williams/99 3.00 8.00
45 Maurice Cheeks/99 4.00 10.00
46 Harry Gallatin/99 5.00 12.00
47 Jordan Clarkson/99 5.00 12.00
48 T.J. McConnell/99 15.00 40.00
49 Darrun Hilliard/99 3.00 8.00
50 Nemanja Bjelica/99 5.00 12.00
51 Nikola Jokic/99 600.00 1,200.00
52 Larry Nance Jr./99 6.00 15.00
53 Raul Neto/99 3.00 8.00

2015-16 Limited Team Trademarks

STATED PRINT RUN 45-149 COPIES PER
*PRIME/25: .75X TO 2X BASIC
1 Paul Millsap/99 3.00 8.00
2 Isaiah Thomas/99 2.50 6.00
3 Brook Lopez/149 4.00 10.00
4 Nicolas Batum/149 2.50 6.00
5 Derrick Rose/99 6.00 15.00
6 LeBron James/49 25.00 60.00
7 Dirk Nowitzki/149 10.00 25.00
8 Kenneth Faried/149 3.00 8.00
9 Andre Drummond/149 4.00 10.00
10 Stephen Curry/49 25.00 60.00
11 James Harden/99 8.00 20.00
12 Paul George/49 6.00 15.00
13 Chris Paul/149 8.00 20.00
14 Kobe Bryant/149 12.00 30.00
15 Marc Gasol/99 4.00 10.00
16 Dwyane Wade/149 6.00 15.00
17 Giannis Antetokounmpo/45 25.00 60.00
18 Andrew Wiggins/149 5.00 12.00
19 Anthony Davis/149 8.00 20.00
20 Kristaps Porzingis/99 8.00 20.00
21 Kevin Durant/49 8.00 20.00
22 Evan Fournier/149 3.00 8.00
23 Jahlil Okafor/149 3.00 8.00
24 Eric Bledsoe/149 3.00 8.00
25 Damian Lillard/99 6.00 15.00
26 DeMarcus Cousins/149 4.00 10.00
27 Kawhi Leonard/149 12.00 30.00
28 DeMar DeRozan/149 5.00 12.00
29 Rudy Gobert/99 5.00 12.00
30 John Wall/99 5.00 12.00

2015-16 Limited Trios Signatures

PRINT RUNS B/WN 10-49 COPIES PER
NO PRICING ON QTY 10
*SILVER/25: .5X TO 1.2X BASIC
1 Mickey/Hunter/Rozier/49 15.00 40.00
3 Cauley-Stein/Towns/Booker/49 150.00 400.00
4 Jones/Okafor/Winslow/49 20.00 50.00
5 Russell/Okafor/Towns/49 60.00 150.00
6 Havlicek/Maxwell/White/49 30.00 80.00
7 Laimbeer/Salley/Mahorn/49 12.00 30.00
9 Jackson/Oakley/Newman/49 8.00 20.00
11 Grant/Grant/Grant/49 10.00 25.00
12 Carter-Williams/Grant/Ennis/49 12.00 30.00
13 Okafor/Holmes/McConnell/49 25.00 60.00

2015-16 Limited Trophy Case Materials

STATED PRINT RUN 49-149 COPIES PER
*PRIME/25: .75X TO 2X BASIC
1 Kobe Bryant/149 25.00 60.00
2 Dirk Nowitzki/149 8.00 20.00
3 Andre Iguodala/149 3.00 8.00
4 Karl Malone/149 5.00 12.00
5 Bobby Jackson/149 2.00 5.00
6 Andrew Wiggins/149 4.00 10.00
7 Damian Lillard/149 5.00 12.00
8 Stephen Curry/149 25.00 60.00
9 Ben Wallace/149 2.50 6.00
10 LeBron James/99 25.00 60.00
11 Tony Parker/149 5.00 12.00
12 Grant Hill/149 5.00 12.00
13 Tim Duncan/149 8.00 20.00
14 Kevin Garnett/149 8.00 20.00
15 Tyreke Evans/149 2.50 6.00
16 Michael Carter-Williams/149 2.00 5.00
17 Kawhi Leonard/149 10.00 25.00
18 Kevin Durant/49 6.00 15.00
19 Manu Ginobili/149 6.00 15.00
20 Derrick Rose/149 5.00 12.00

2015-16 Limited Unlimited Potential Materials

PRINT RUNS B/WN 99-149 COPIES PER
*PRIME/25: 1.2X TO 3X BASIC
1 Aaron Gordon/149 3.00 8.00
2 Terry Rozier/149 8.00 20.00
3 Noah Vonleh/149 2.00 5.00
4 Justin Anderson/149 2.00 5.00
5 R.J. Hunter/149 2.00 5.00
6 Karl-Anthony Towns/149 10.00 25.00
7 Rakeem Christmas/149 2.00 5.00
8 Willie Cauley-Stein/149 2.50 6.00
9 Nemanja Bjelica/149 3.00 8.00
10 Myles Turner/149 8.00 20.00
11 Doug McDermott/149 2.50 6.00
12 Rodney Hood/149 2.50 6.00
13 Zach LaVine/149 8.00 20.00
14 Bobby Portis/149 5.00 12.00
15 Chris McCullough/149 2.00 5.00
16 D'Angelo Russell/149 6.00 15.00
17 Richaun Holmes/149 3.00 8.00
18 Emmanuel Mudiay/149 2.50 6.00
19 Marcelo Huertas/149 2.00 5.00
20 Trey Lyles/149 2.50 6.00
21 Dante Exum/149 2.50 6.00
22 Salah Mejri/149 2.00 5.00
23 T.J. Warren/149 3.00 8.00
24 Rondae Hollis-Jefferson/149 2.50 6.00
25 Montrezl Harrell/149 6.00 15.00
26 Jahlil Okafor/149 5.00 12.00
27 Pat Connaughton/149 3.00 8.00
28 Stanley Johnson/149 2.50 6.00
29 Andrew Wiggins/149 4.00 10.00
30 Devin Booker/149 6.00 15.00
31 Marcus Smart/149 4.00 10.00
32 Jerian Grant/149 2.00 5.00
33 Jordan Clarkson/149 3.00 8.00
34 Tyus Jones/149 2.50 6.00
35 Jordan Mickey/149 2.00 5.00
36 Kristaps Porzingis/99 10.00 25.00
37 Joe Young/149 2.00 5.00
38 Frank Kaminsky/149 2.50 6.00
39 Jabari Parker/149 2.00 5.00
40 Cameron Payne/149 3.00 8.00
41 Julius Randle/99 4.00 10.00
42 Delon Wright/149 2.50 6.00
43 Langston Galloway/149 2.00 5.00
44 Jarell Martin/149 2.00 5.00
45 Anthony Brown/149 2.00 5.00
46 Mario Hezonja/149 2.50 6.00
47 Raul Neto/149 2.00 5.00
48 Justise Winslow/149 3.00 8.00
49 Elfrid Payton/149 2.50 6.00
50 Kelly Oubre Jr./149 6.00 15.00

2016-17 Limited

101-140 PRINT RUN 99 SER.#'d SETS
1 C.J. McCollum .60 1.50
2 Draymond Green .75 2.00
3 Kyle Lowry .60 1.50
4 Chris Paul 1.00 2.50
5 Justise Winslow .50 1.25
6 Dwight Howard .75 2.00
7 Jrue Holiday .75 2.00

8 Nicolas Batum .50 1.25
9 Nikola Vucevic .60 1.50
10 Harrison Barnes .50 1.25
11 Al-Farouq Aminu .40 1.00
12 Kentavious Caldwell-Pope .50 1.25
13 DeMar DeRozan .75 2.00
14 Blake Griffin .60 1.50
15 Goran Dragic .60 1.50
16 Paul Millsap .50 1.25
17 Tyreke Evans .50 1.25
18 Kemba Walker .50 1.25
19 Mario Hezonja .40 1.00
20 Emmanuel Mudiay .40 1.00
21 DeMarcus Cousins .50 1.25
22 Patrick Beverley .40 1.00
23 Jonas Valanciunas .50 1.25
24 DeAndre Jordan .50 1.25
25 Hassan Whiteside .50 1.25
26 Kyle Korver .50 1.25
27 Anthony Davis 2.00 5.00
28 Rajon Rondo .75 2.00
29 Evan Fournier .50 1.25
30 Jusuf Nurkic .50 1.25
31 Willie Cauley-Stein .50 1.25
32 Trevor Ariza .40 1.00
33 Derrick Favors .40 1.00
34 D'Angelo Russell .75 2.00
35 Jabari Parker .40 1.00
36 Al Horford .60 1.50
37 Brandon Jennings .40 1.00
38 Dwyane Wade 1.25 3.00
39 Nerlens Noel .40 1.00
40 Nikola Jokic 3.00 8.00
41 Rudy Gay .60 1.50
42 Ryan Anderson .40 1.00
43 Gordon Hayward .60 1.50
44 Jordan Clarkson .60 1.50
45 Giannis Antetokounmpo 3.00 8.00
46 Isaiah Thomas .50 1.25
47 Carmelo Anthony 1.00 2.50
48 Jimmy Butler 1.25 3.00
49 Jahlil Okafor .40 1.00
50 Reggie Jackson .50 1.25
51 Arron Afflalo .40 1.00
52 Jeff Teague .40 1.00
53 Rudy Gobert .75 2.00
54 Julius Randle .75 2.00
55 Michael Carter-Williams .40 1.00
56 Jae Crowder .40 1.00
57 Kristaps Porzingis 1.00 2.50
58 Kyrie Irving 1.25 3.00
59 Joel Embiid 1.50 4.00
60 Tobias Harris .60 1.50
61 Kawhi Leonard 1.50 4.00
62 Monta Ellis .50 1.25
63 John Wall .75 2.00
64 Luol Deng .50 1.25
65 Ricky Rubio .50 1.25
66 Brook Lopez .50 1.25
67 Joakim Noah .40 1.00
68 Tristan Thompson .50 1.25
69 Tyson Chandler .40 1.00
70 Andre Drummond .60 1.50
71 Pau Gasol 1.00 2.50
72 Paul George 1.00 2.50
73 Bradley Beal .75 2.00
74 Mike Conley .50 1.25
75 Zach LaVine 1.25 3.00
76 Jeremy Lin 1.25 3.00
77 Enes Kanter .40 1.00
78 Kevin Love .60 1.50
79 Devin Booker 2.50 6.00
80 Stephen Curry 5.00 12.00
81 LaMarcus Aldridge .60 1.50
82 Myles Turner .60 1.50
83 Otto Porter .50 1.25
84 Marc Gasol .60 1.50
85 Andrew Wiggins .75 2.00
86 Bojan Bogdanovic .50 1.25
87 Victor Oladipo .50 1.25
88 Dirk Nowitzki 1.50 4.00
89 Eric Bledsoe .50 1.25
90 Kevin Durant 2.50 6.00
91 Tony Parker 1.00 2.50
92 Paul Pierce 1.00 2.50
93 Marcin Gortat .40 1.00
94 Chandler Parsons .40 1.00
95 Karl-Anthony Towns 1.25 3.00
96 Roy Hibbert .50 1.25
97 Steven Adams .50 1.25
98 Deron Williams .50 1.25
99 Damian Lillard 1.50 4.00
100 Klay Thompson 1.50 4.00
101 Taurean Prince JSY AU RC 4.00 10.00
102 DeAndre' Bembry JSY AU RC 5.00 12.00
103 Jaylen Brown JSY AU RC 125.00 300.00
104 Demetrius Jackson JSY AU RC 3.00 8.00
105 Isaiah Whitehead JSY AU RC 3.00 8.00
106 Caris LeVert JSY AU RC 8.00 20.00
107 D.Valentine JSY AU RC 3.00 8.00
108 Kay Felder JSY AU RC 3.00 8.00
109 A.J. Hammons JSY AU RC 3.00 8.00
110 Jamal Murray JSY AU RC 100.00 250.00
111 Malik Beasley JSY AU RC 6.00 15.00
112 Juan Hernangomez JSY AU RC 12.00 30.00
113 Henry Ellenson JSY AU RC 3.00 8.00
114 Damian Jones JSY AU RC 3.00 8.00
115 P.McCaw JSY AU RC 3.00 8.00
116 Georges Niang JSY AU RC 5.00 12.00
117 Chinanu Onuaku JSY AU RC 3.00 8.00
118 Brice Johnson JSY AU RC 3.00 8.00
119 Diamond Stone JSY AU RC 3.00 8.00
120 B.Ingram JSY AU RC 100.00 250.00
121 Ivica Zubac JSY AU RC 8.00 20.00
122 Wade Baldwin IV JSY AU RC 3.00 8.00
123 Deyonta Davis JSY AU RC 3.00 8.00
124 Thon Maker JSY AU RC 4.00 10.00
125 Kris Dunn JSY AU RC 5.00 12.00
126 Buddy Hield JSY AU RC 12.00 30.00
127 Cheick Diallo JSY AU RC 3.00 8.00
128 D.Sabonis JSY AU RC 20.00 50.00
129 Stephen Zimmerman JSY AU RC 3.00 8.00
130 Lwwu-Cabarrot JSY AU RC 5.00 12.00
131 Dario Saric JSY AU RC 5.00 12.00
132 Dragan Bender JSY AU RC 3.00 8.00
133 M.Chriss JSY AU RC 4.00 10.00
134 Tyler Ulis JSY AU RC 4.00 10.00
135 Georgios Papagiannis JSY AU RC 3.00 8.00
136 Malachi Richardson JSY AU RC 3.00 8.00
137 Labissiere JSY AU RC 3.00 8.00
139 Jakob Poeltl JSY AU RC 6.00 15.00
140 Pascal Siakam JSY AU RC 20.00 50.00
141 LeBron James SP 12.00 30.00
142 James Harden SP 3.00 8.00
143 Derrick Rose SP 2.50 6.00
144 Russell Westbrook SP 2.50 6.00
145 Ben Simmons SP RC 3.00 8.00
146 Malcolm Brogdon SP RC 3.00 8.00
147 Georgios Papagiannis SP RC 1.00 2.50
148 Willy Hernangomez SP RC 1.25 3.00
149 Ron Baker SP RC 1.00 2.50
150 Alex Abrines SP RC 1.25 3.00

2016-17 Limited Gold Spotlight

*GLD SPOTLGHT 1-100: 1.2X TO 3X BASIC
*GLD SPTLGHT 101-140: .6X TO 1.5X BASIC
PRINT RUNS B/WN 10-25 COPIES PER
NO PRICING ON QTY 10

2016-17 Limited Red Spotlight

*RED SPOTLIGHT: .6X TO 1.5X BASIC
STATED PRINT RUN 99 SER.#'d SETS

2016-17 Limited Silver Spotlight

*SLVR SPTLGHT 1-100: .75X TO 2X BASIC
*SLVR SPTLGHT 101-140: .5X TO 1.2X BASIC
STATED PRINT RUN 49 SER.#'d SETS

2016-17 Limited Counterparts

1 Iverson/Bryant 10.00 25.00
2 Anthony/James 10.00 25.00
3 Olajuwon/O'Neal 4.00 10.00
4 Harden/Paul 2.50 6.00
5 Bird/Johnson 5.00 12.00
6 James/Curry 6.00 15.00
7 Olajuwon/Ewing 2.50 6.00
8 DeRozan/Irving 2.50 6.00
9 Johnson/Erving 5.00 12.00
10 Lillard/Curry 10.00 25.00
11 Kidd/Nash 2.00 5.00
12 Durant/James 10.00 25.00
13 Nash/Parker 2.00 5.00
14 Westbrook/Durant 5.00 12.00
15 Russell/Chamberlain 4.00 10.00
16 Westbrook/Curry 10.00 25.00
17 Robinson/Olajuwon 2.50 6.00
18 Westbrook/Leonard 3.00 8.00
19 Malone/Kemp 2.00 5.00
20 McGrady/Bryant 10.00 25.00

2016-17 Limited Decade Dominance Materials

STATED PRINT RUN 99 SER. #'d SETS
1 LeBron James 10.00 25.00
2 Russell Westbrook 4.00 10.00
3 Kobe Bryant 8.00 20.00
4 Allen Iverson 5.00 12.00
5 Shaquille O'Neal 6.00 15.00
6 Magic Johnson 6.00 15.00
7 Stephen Curry 10.00 25.00
8 James Harden 4.00 10.00
9 Kevin Garnett 8.00 20.00
10 Scottie Pippen 8.00 20.00
11 Dan Issel 4.00 10.00
12 Rick Barry 4.00 10.00
13 Anthony Davis 10.00 25.00
14 Dennis Rodman 6.00 15.00
15 Larry Bird 12.00 30.00
16 Andre Drummond 3.00 8.00
17 DeMarcus Cousins 2.50 6.00
18 Alex English 2.50 6.00
19 Anfernee Hardaway 6.00 15.00
20 Paul Pierce 5.00 12.00

2016-17 Limited Limited Jersey Signatures

PRINT RUNS B/WN 25-99 COPIES PER
1 Victor Oladipo/99 4.00 10.00
2 Brandon Knight/49 4.00 10.00
4 Kevin Durant/25 75.00 200.00
6 Alex Len/99 3.00 8.00
7 Clyde Drexler/49 10.00 25.00
10 Nikola Mirotic/99 3.00 8.00
11 Maurice Harkless/99 3.00 8.00
12 Chauncey Billups/99 6.00 15.00
13 Justise Winslow/99 4.00 10.00
14 Carmelo Anthony/25 20.00 50.00
17 Kevin McHale/49 10.00 25.00
18 Frank Kaminsky/99 3.00 8.00
19 Damjan Rudez/99 3.00 8.00
20 Tristan Thompson/99 4.00 10.00
21 P.J. Tucker/99 3.00 8.00
22 Danilo Gallinari/89 4.00 10.00
23 Kenneth Faried/99 4.00 10.00
24 Chris Paul/25 40.00 100.00
25 Ralph Sampson/99 4.00 10.00
26 Bobby Portis/99 5.00 12.00
27 Jason Smith/99 3.00 8.00
28 Gary Harris/99 4.00 10.00
29 Brian Roberts/99 3.00 8.00
30 Tyson Chandler/80 4.00 10.00
31 Norman Powell/99 5.00 12.00
32 Danny Manning/99 4.00 10.00
33 Khris Middleton/99 5.00 12.00
34 Dwyane Wade/25 25.00 60.00
35 Robert Parish/99 6.00 15.00
36 Cody Zeller/99 3.00 8.00
37 Terrence Jones/99 3.00 8.00
38 Hassan Whiteside/99 4.00 10.00
39 Tony Snell/99 3.00 8.00
40 Kobe Bryant/25 500.00 1,000.00
41 Archie Goodwin/99 3.00 8.00
42 Eric Bledsoe/49 4.00 10.00
43 LaMarcus Aldridge/49 5.00 12.00
44 Dirk Nowitzki/99 50.00 120.00
45 Tobias Harris/99 5.00 12.00
46 Dante Exum/49 4.00 10.00
47 Dwight Powell/99 3.00 8.00
48 Jonas Valanciunas/99 4.00 10.00
49 Kyle Anderson/99 3.00 8.00
50 Artis Gilmore/49 6.00 15.00
51 T.J. McConnell/99 5.00 12.00
52 Goran Dragic/49 5.00 12.00
54 Anthony Davis/25 25.00 60.00
55 Hakeem Olajuwon/49 15.00 40.00
56 Derrick Williams/40 3.00 8.00
57 Kelly Olynyk/99 3.00 8.00
58 Jordan Clarkson/99 5.00 12.00
59 Mario Hezonja/99 3.00 8.00
60 Bernard King/49 6.00 15.00

2016-17 Limited Limited Jersey Signatures Gold Spotlight

*GOLD p/r 25: .5X TO 1.2X BASIC p/r 40-99
PRINT RUNS B/WN 5-25 COPIES PER
NO PRICING ON QTY 10 OR LESS
9 Adreian Payne/25 4.00 10.00

2016-17 Limited Limited Jersey Signatures Silver Spotlight

*SILVER p/r 49: .4X TO 1X BASIC p/r 40-99
*SILVER p/r 25: .5X TO 1.2X BASIC p/r 40-99
PRINT RUNS B/WN 10-49 COPIES PER
9 Adreian Payne/49 3.00 8.00
16 Andrew Nicholson/49 3.00 8.00

2016-17 Limited Limited Legends Jersey Autographs

STATED PRINT RUN 25 SER. #'d SETS
1 Scottie Pippen 50.00 120.00
2 Karl Malone 25.00 60.00
3 Patrick Ewing 75.00 150.00
4 David Robinson 15.00 40.00
5 Hakeem Olajuwon 20.00 50.00
6 Clyde Drexler 12.00 30.00
7 Kevin McHale 12.00 30.00
8 Dennis Rodman 15.00 40.00
9 Kobe Bryant 500.00 1,000.00
10 Yao Ming 30.00 80.00

2016-17 Limited Limited Rookies

1 Malik Beasley 1.50 4.00
2 Kris Dunn 1.25 3.00
3 Dario Saric 1.25 3.00
4 Marquese Chriss 1.00 2.50
5 Pascal Siakam 5.00 12.00
6 Taurean Prince 1.00 2.50
7 Denzel Valentine .75 2.00
8 Ben Simmons 2.50 6.00
9 Wade Baldwin IV .75 2.00
10 Jaylen Brown 12.00 30.00
11 Caris LeVert 2.00 5.00
12 Buddy Hield 2.50 6.00
13 DeAndre' Bembry 1.25 3.00
14 Jakob Poeltl 1.50 4.00
15 Skal Labissiere .75 2.00
16 Georgios Papagiannis .75 2.00
17 Juan Hernangomez 1.50 4.00
18 Brandon Ingram 3.00 8.00
19 Henry Ellenson .75 2.00
20 Dragan Bender .75 2.00
21 Malachi Richardson .75 2.00
22 Jamal Murray 12.00 30.00
23 Brice Johnson .75 2.00
24 Thon Maker 1.00 2.50
25 Dejounte Murray 6.00 15.00

2016-17 Limited No Limit

STATED ODDS 1:12 HOBBY
1 Carmelo Anthony 2.00 5.00
2 Klay Thompson 6.00 15.00
3 Kawhi Leonard 6.00 15.00
4 Karl-Anthony Towns 5.00 12.00
5 Jimmy Butler 5.00 12.00
6 Stephen Curry 20.00 50.00
7 Andrew Wiggins 3.00 8.00
8 Kevin Durant 10.00 25.00
9 Kristaps Porzingis 4.00 10.00
10 James Harden 5.00 12.00
11 Devin Booker 10.00 25.00
12 Kyrie Irving 5.00 12.00
13 Anthony Davis 8.00 20.00
14 LeBron James 20.00 50.00
15 Russell Westbrook 4.00 10.00

2016-17 Limited Phenoms Jersey Autographs

PRINT RUNS B/WN 25-99 COPIES PER
1 Bill Laimbeer/99 5.00 12.00
3 Kevin Durant/25 75.00 200.00
4 Tyson Chandler/49 4.00 10.00
5 Anthony Davis/25 25.00 60.00
7 Andrew Wiggins/49 15.00 40.00
8 Vince Carter/49 12.00 30.00
9 Jason Kidd/49 12.00 30.00
10 Dante Exum/49 4.00 10.00
11 Zydrunas Ilgauskas/99 4.00 10.00
12 Jonas Valanciunas/99 4.00 10.00
13 Carmelo Anthony/25 20.00 50.00
14 Kobe Bryant/25 1,000.00 2,000.00
17 Karl-Anthony Towns/49 50.00 120.00
18 Alex Len/99 3.00 8.00
19 Rashard Lewis/99 4.00 10.00
21 Mark Price/99 5.00 12.00
22 Jordan Clarkson/99 5.00 12.00
23 Chris Paul/25 25.00 60.00
24 Jason Smith/99 3.00 8.00
25 Dwight Howard/25 8.00 20.00
26 Damjan Rudez/99 3.00 8.00
27 D'Angelo Russell/49 6.00 15.00
29 Glen Rice/99 5.00 12.00
31 Dennis Scott/99 3.00 8.00
32 Nikola Mirotic/99 3.00 8.00
33 Dwyane Wade/25 25.00 60.00
34 Terrence Jones/99 3.00 8.00
36 Brian Roberts/99 3.00 8.00
37 Kevin Love/49 15.00 40.00
38 Bobby Portis/99 5.00 12.00
39 Dikembe Mutombo/99 8.00 20.00
40 Frank Kaminsky/99 3.00 8.00
42 Tristan Thompson/99 4.00 10.00
43 Dirk Nowitzki/25 60.00 150.00
47 Deron Williams/99 4.00 10.00
48 Cody Zeller/49 3.00 8.00
49 Shawn Kemp/99 50.00 120.00
50 Gary Harris/99 4.00 10.00

2016-17 Limited Phenoms Jersey Autographs Prime

*PRIME/20-39: .5X TO 1.2X BASIC p/r 49-99
PRINT RUNS B/WN 5-39 COPIES PER
NO PRICING ON QTY 10 OR LESS
16 Adreian Payne/39 4.00 10.00
28 Andrew Nicholson/39 4.00 10.00

2016-17 Limited Preparation Jerseys

STATED ODDS 1:24 HOBBY
STATED PRINT RUN 99 SER. #'d SETS
*PRIME/22-29: .75X TO 2X BASIC
1 Stephen Curry 10.00 25.00
2 LeBron James 10.00 25.00
3 Karl-Anthony Towns 5.00 12.00
4 Kenneth Faried 2.50 6.00
5 Kobe Bryant 8.00 20.00
6 Emmanuel Mudiay 2.00 5.00
7 Kyrie Irving 5.00 12.00
8 Andrew Wiggins 4.00 10.00
9 Larry Bird 12.00 30.00
10 Shaquille O'Neal 6.00 15.00

2016-17 Limited Rookie Phenoms Jersey Autographs

STATED PRINT RUN 99 SER. #'d SETS
1 Marquese Chriss 4.00 10.00
2 Henry Ellenson 3.00 8.00
3 Skal Labissiere 3.00 8.00
4 Chinanu Onuaku 3.00 8.00
5 Ivica Zubac 8.00 20.00
6 Taurean Prince 4.00 10.00
7 Kris Dunn 5.00 12.00
8 Isaiah Whitehead 3.00 8.00
9 Stephen Zimmerman 3.00 8.00
10 A.J. Hammons 3.00 8.00
11 Tyler Ulis 4.00 10.00
12 Damian Jones 3.00 8.00
13 Dejounte Murray 40.00 100.00
14 Brice Johnson 3.00 8.00
15 Wade Baldwin IV 3.00 8.00
16 DeAndre' Bembry 5.00 12.00
17 Buddy Hield 10.00 25.00
18 Caris LeVert 8.00 20.00
19 Timothe Luwawu-Cabarrot 5.00 12.00
20 Jamal Murray 60.00 150.00
21 Georgios Papagiannis 3.00 8.00
22 Patrick McCaw 3.00 8.00
23 Jakob Poeltl 6.00 15.00
24 Diamond Stone 3.00 8.00
25 Deyonta Davis 3.00 8.00
26 Jaylen Brown 125.00 300.00
27 Cheick Diallo 3.00 8.00
28 Denzel Valentine 3.00 8.00
29 Dario Saric 5.00 12.00
30 Malik Beasley 6.00 15.00
31 Malachi Richardson 3.00 8.00
32 Georges Niang 5.00 12.00
33 Pascal Siakam 20.00 50.00
34 Brandon Ingram 20.00 50.00
35 Thon Maker 4.00 10.00
36 Demetrius Jackson 3.00 8.00
37 Domantas Sabonis 20.00 50.00
38 Kay Felder 3.00 8.00
39 Dragan Bender 3.00 8.00
40 Juan Hernangomez 6.00 15.00

2016-17 Limited Rookie Phenoms Jersey Autographs Prime

*PRIME/20-25: .5X TO 1.2X BASIC
PRINT RUNS B/WN 10-39 COPIES PER
NO PRICING ON QTY 10 OR LESS
13 Dejounte Murray/39 60.00 150.00
20 Jamal Murray/39 75.00 200.00
26 Jaylen Brown/39 200.00 500.00

2016-17 Limited Star Factor

1 Draymond Green 1.50 4.00
2 Anthony Davis 4.00 10.00
3 Andre Drummond 1.25 3.00
4 Carmelo Anthony 2.00 5.00
5 DeAndre Jordan 1.00 2.50
6 Paul George 2.00 5.00
7 John Wall 1.50 4.00
8 Andrew Wiggins 1.50 4.00
9 Isaiah Thomas 1.00 2.50
10 James Harden 2.50 6.00
11 Ricky Rubio 1.00 2.50
12 LeBron James 10.00 25.00
13 Hassan Whiteside 1.00 2.50
14 Klay Thompson 3.00 8.00
15 Chris Paul 2.00 5.00
16 Jimmy Butler 2.50 6.00
17 DeMarcus Cousins 1.00 2.50
18 Kevin Durant 5.00 12.00
19 Kyle Lowry 1.25 3.00
20 Devin Booker 5.00 12.00
21 Karl-Anthony Towns 2.50 6.00
22 Russell Westbrook 2.00 5.00
23 Giannis Antetokounmpo 6.00 15.00
24 Kawhi Leonard 3.00 8.00
25 Blake Griffin 1.25 3.00
26 Stephen Curry 10.00 25.00
27 Damian Lillard 3.00 8.00
28 Kristaps Porzingis 2.00 5.00
29 Dwight Howard 1.50 4.00
30 Kyrie Irving 2.50 6.00

2016-17 Limited Team Trademarks Jerseys

STATED PRINT RUN 99 SER. #'d SETS
*PRIME/23-25: 1X TO 2.5X BASIC
1 Kyle Korver 2.50 6.00
2 Isaiah Thomas 8.00 20.00
3 Brook Lopez 2.50 6.00
4 Nicolas Batum 2.50 6.00
5 Taj Gibson 2.00 5.00
6 Kyrie Irving 5.00 12.00
7 Dirk Nowitzki 8.00 20.00
8 Andre Drummond 3.00 8.00
9 Kenneth Faried 2.50 6.00
10 Andre Iguodala 3.00 8.00
11 James Harden 4.00 10.00
12 Monta Ellis 2.50 6.00
13 Blake Griffin 3.00 8.00
14 Jordan Clarkson 3.00 8.00
15 Zach Randolph 3.00 8.00
16 Udonis Haslem 2.50 6.00
17 Greg Monroe 2.00 5.00
18 Karl-Anthony Towns 5.00 12.00
19 Tyreke Evans 2.50 6.00
20 Carmelo Anthony 5.00 12.00
21 Russell Westbrook 4.00 10.00
22 Mario Hezonja 2.00 5.00
23 Nerlens Noel 2.00 5.00
24 Eric Bledsoe 2.50 6.00
25 Damian Lillard 4.00 10.00
26 DeMarcus Cousins 2.50 6.00
27 Kawhi Leonard 4.00 10.00
28 Kyle Lowry 3.00 8.00
29 Rodney Hood 2.50 6.00
30 John Wall 4.00 10.00

2016-17 Limited Unlimited Potential Materials

STATED PRINT RUN 99 SER. #'d SETS
*PRIME/20-39: .75X TO 2X BASIC
1 Buddy Hield 6.00 15.00
2 Georgios Papagiannis 2.00 5.00
3 Marquese Chriss 2.50 6.00
4 Deyonta Davis 2.00 5.00
5 Ivica Zubac 5.00 12.00
6 Dario Saric 3.00 8.00
7 Stephen Zimmerman 2.00 5.00
8 Pascal Siakam 12.00 30.00
9 Dejounte Murray 10.00 25.00
10 Domantas Sabonis 12.00 30.00
11 Caris LeVert 5.00 12.00
12 Patrick McCaw 2.00 5.00
13 Henry Ellenson 2.00 5.00
14 Jaylen Brown 4.00 10.00
15 Taurean Prince 2.50 6.00
16 Malik Beasley 4.00 10.00
17 A.J. Hammons 2.00 5.00
18 Brandon Ingram 6.00 15.00
19 Brice Johnson 2.00 5.00
20 Kay Felder 2.00 5.00
21 Timothe Luwawu-Cabarrot 3.00 8.00
22 Jakob Poeltl 4.00 10.00
23 Skal Labissiere 2.00 5.00
24 Cheick Diallo 2.00 5.00
25 Kris Dunn 3.00 8.00
26 Malachi Richardson 2.00 5.00
27 Tyler Ulis 2.50 6.00
28 Thon Maker 2.50 6.00
29 Wade Baldwin IV 2.00 5.00
30 Dragan Bender 2.00 5.00
31 Jamal Murray 4.00 10.00
32 Diamond Stone 2.00 5.00
33 Chinanu Onuaku 2.00 5.00
34 Denzel Valentine 2.00 5.00
35 Isaiah Whitehead 2.00 5.00
37 Damian Jones 2.00 5.00
38 Demetrius Jackson 2.00 5.00
39 DeAndre' Bembry 3.00 8.00
40 Juan Hernangomez 4.00 10.00

2017-18 Limited Silver

STATED PRINT RUN 249 SER.#'d SETS
376 Lauri Markkanen 5.00 12.00
377 OG Anunoby 4.00 10.00
378 Markelle Fultz 2.00 5.00
379 Harry Giles .75 2.00
380 De'Aaron Fox 6.00 15.00
381 Tony Bradley .75 2.00
382 Frank Ntilikina 1.00 2.50
383 Derrick White 3.00 8.00
384 Jonathan Isaac 2.00 5.00
385 John Collins 2.00 5.00
386 Lonzo Ball 3.00 8.00
387 Terrance Ferguson .75 2.00
388 Bogdan Bogdanovic 2.00 5.00
389 Jordan Bell .75 2.00
390 Dennis Smith Jr. 1.00 2.50
391 Bam Adebayo 5.00 12.00
392 Jayson Tatum 10.00 25.00
393 Frank Mason III .75 2.00
394 Josh Jackson 1.00 2.50
395 Justin Patton .75 2.00
396 Malik Monk 3.00 8.00
397 Zach Collins 1.25 3.00
398 Donovan Mitchell 8.00 20.00
399 Kyle Kuzma 3.00 8.00
400 Semi Ojeleye 1.00 2.50

2017-18 Limited Blue

*BLUE: .5X TO 1.2X BASIC
STATED PRINT RUN 149 SER.#'d SETS

1973-74 Linnett Portraits

COMPLETE SET (112) 350.00 700.00
1 Walt Bellamy 2.50 6.00
2 Steve Bracey 2.00 5.00
3 John Brown 2.00 5.00
4 Bob Christian 2.00 5.00
5 Herm Gilliam 2.00 5.00
6 Lou Hudson 2.50 6.00
7 Dwight Jones 2.00 5.00
8 Pete Maravich 12.50 25.00
9 Dale Schlueter 2.00 5.00
10 Jim Washington 2.00 5.00
11 Don Chaney 2.50 6.00
12 Dave Cowens 5.00 10.00
13 Steve Downing 2.00 5.00
14 Hank Finkel 2.00 5.00
15 Phil Hankinson 2.00 5.00
16 John Havlicek 7.50 15.00
17 Steve Kuberski 2.00 5.00
18 Don Nelson 3.00 8.00
19 Paul Silas 2.50 6.00
20 Paul Westphal 5.00 10.00
21 Jo Jo White 2.50 6.00
22 Art Williams 2.00 5.00
23 Ken Charles 2.00 5.00
24 Ernie DiGregorio (Wearing a turtle neck) 3.00 8.00
25 Ernie DiGregorio (Wearing a t-shirt) 3.00 8.00
26 Garfield Heard 2.50 6.00
27 Bob Kauffman 2.00 5.00
28 Mike Macaluso 2.00 5.00
29 Bob McAdoo 6.00 12.00
30 Jim McMillian 2.50 6.00
31 Paul Ruffner 2.00 5.00
32 Randy Smith 2.50 6.00
33 Dave Wohl 2.00 5.00
34 Archie Clark 2.50 6.00
35 Elvin Hayes 6.00 12.00
36 Howard Porter 2.50 6.00
37 Dennis Awtrey 2.00 5.00
38 Tom Boerwinkle 2.50 6.00
39 Bob Love 2.50 6.00
40 Jerry Sloan 3.00 8.00
41 Norm Van Lier 2.50 6.00
42 Chet Walker 2.50 6.00
43 Bob Weiss 2.50 6.00
44 Austin Carr 2.50 6.00
45 Lenny Wilkens 3.00 8.00
46 Bob Lanier 5.00 10.00
47 Jim Barnett 2.00 5.00
48 Rick Barry 5.00 10.00
49 Butch Beard 2.50 6.00
50 Derrek Dickey 2.50 6.00
51 Charlie Johnson 2.00 5.00
52 Clyde Lee 2.00 5.00
53 Jeff Mullins 2.50 6.00
54 Clifford Ray 2.00 5.00
55 Cazzie Russell 2.50 6.00
56 Nate Thurmond 3.00 8.00
57 Kevin Kunnert 2.00 5.00
58 Calvin Murphy 3.00 8.00
59 Jimmy Walker 2.50 6.00
60 Nate Archibald 3.00 8.00
61 Ron Behagen 2.00 5.00
62 John Block 2.00 5.00
63 Mike D'Antoni 2.00 5.00
64 Ken Durrett 2.00 5.00
65 Sam Lacey 2.00 5.00
66 Larry McNeill 2.00 5.00
67 Nate Williams 2.00 5.00
68 Bill Bridges 2.00 5.00
69 Mel Counts 2.00 5.00
70 Keith Erickson 2.00 5.00
71 Gail Goodrich 3.00 8.00
72 Happy Hairston 2.50 6.00
73 Jim Price 2.00 5.00
74 Pat Riley 6.00 12.00
75 Elmore Smith 2.00 5.00
76 Jerry West 6.00 12.00
77 Kareem Abdul-Jabbar 10.00 20.00
78 Lucius Allen 2.00 5.00
79 Bob Dandridge 2.50 6.00
80 Mickey Davis 2.00 5.00
81 Terry Driscoll 2.00 5.00
82 Russell Lee 2.00 5.00
83 Jon McGlocklin 2.00 5.00
84 Curtis Perry 2.00 5.00
85 Oscar Robertson 5.00 10.00
86 Henry Bibby 2.50 6.00
87 Bill Bradley 6.00 12.00
88 Dave DeBusschere 3.00 8.00
89 Walt Frazier 5.00 10.00
90 John Gianelli 2.00 5.00
91 Phil Jackson 5.00 10.00
92 Jerry Lucas 3.00 8.00
93 Dean Meminger 2.00 5.00
94 Earl Monroe 3.00 8.00
95 Willis Reed 6.00 15.00
96 Harthorne Wingo 2.00 5.00
97 Tom Van Arsdale 2.50 6.00
98 Mike Bantom 2.00 5.00
99 Corky Calhoun 2.00 5.00
100 Lamar Green 2.00 5.00
101 Clem Haskins 2.00 5.00
102 Connie Hawkins 5.00 10.00
103 Charlie Scott 2.50 6.00
104 Dick Van Arsdale 2.50 6.00
105 Neal Walk 2.00 5.00
106 Geoff Petrie 2.50 6.00
107 Sidney Wicks 3.00 8.00
108 Spencer Haywood 3.00 8.00
109 Geese Ausbie 2.50 6.00
110 Marques Haynes 3.00 8.00
111 Meadowlark Lemon 3.00 8.00
112 Curly Neal 3.00 8.00

1991 Little Basketball Big Leaguers

COMPLETE SET (45) 12.00 30.00
1 Danny Ainge .20 .50
2 Charles Barkley .75 2.00
3 Larry Bird 2.00 5.00
4 Rolando Blackman .10 .30
5 Muggsy Bogues .20 .50
6 Sam Bowie .10 .30
7 Brad Daugherty .10 .30
8 Johnny Dawkins .10 .30
9 James Donaldson .10 .30
10 Kevin Duckworth .10 .30
11 Chris Dudley .10 .30
12 A.J. English .10 .30
13 Harvey Grant
Horace Grant .20 .50
14 Jeff Hornacek .20 .50
15 Chris Jackson .10 .30
16 Mark Jackson .20 .50
17 Magic Johnson 1.50 4.00
18 Kevin Johnson .30 .75
19 Michael Jordan 8.00 20.00
20 Greg Kite .10 .30
21 Reggie Lewis .20 .50
22 Kevin McHale .40 1.00
23 Reggie Miller .60 1.50
24 Johnny Newman .10 .30
25 Robert Parish .30 .75
26 John Paxson .10 .30
27 Chuck Person .10 .30
28 Terry Porter .10 .30
29 Mark Price .10 .30
30 J.R. Reid .10 .30
31 Glen Rice .60 1.50
32 Doc Rivers .20 .50
33 Fred Roberts .10 .30
34 Byron Scott .20 .50
35 Jack Sikma .10 .30
36 Kenny Smith .10 .30
37 John Stockton 1.00 2.50
38 Wayman Tisdale .10 .30
39 Kiki Vandeweghe .10 .30
40 Spud Webb .20 .50
41 Dominique Wilkins .40 1.00
42 John Williams .10 .30
43 David Wood .10 .30
44 Orlando Woolridge .10 .30
45 James Worthy .40 1.00

1997 Little Sun Tim Duncan

1 Tim Duncan 5.00 12.00

1989-90 Magic Pepsi

COMPLETE SET (8) 15.00 40.00
1 Nick Anderson 6.00 15.00
2 Michael Ansley 2.00 5.00
3 Terry Catledge 2.00 5.00
4 Dave Corzine 2.00 5.00
5 Sidney Green 2.00 5.00
6 Otis Smith 2.00 5.00
7 Sam Vincent 2.00 5.00
8 Stuff the Magic Dragon 2.50 6.00

2001-02 Magic Topps

COMPLETE SET (7) 1.25 3.00
OM2 Darrell Armstrong .30 .75
OM3 Michael Doleac .30 .75
OM4 Pat Garrity .30 .75
OM5 Andrew DeClercq .30 .75
OM8 Bo Outlaw .30 .75
OM9 Doc Rivers CO .40 1.00
OM10 John Amaechi .30 .75

2006-07 Magic Upper Deck

COMPLETE SET (15) 5.00 12.00
1 Trevor Ariza .40 1.00
2 Carlos Arroyo .40 1.00
3 James Augustine .40 1.00
4 Tony Battie .40 1.00
5 Keith Bogans .40 1.00
6 Travis Diener .40 1.00
7 Keyon Dooling .40 1.00
8 Pat Garrity .40 1.00
9 Grant Hill 1.00 2.50
10 Dwight Howard 2.00 5.00
11 Darko Milicic .40 1.00
12 Jameer Nelson .60 1.50
13 Bo Outlaw .40 1.00
14 J.J. Redick 1.00 2.50
15 Hedo Turkoglu .40 1.00

2007-08 Magic Upper Deck

COMPLETE SET (15) 5.00 12.00
1 Trevor Ariza .40 1.00
2 Carlos Arroyo .40 1.00
3 James Augustine .40 1.00
4 Tony Battie .40 1.00
5 Keith Bogans .40 1.00
6 Keyon Dooling .40 1.00
7 Pat Garrity .40 1.00
8 Dwight Howard 1.50 4.00
9 Rashard Lewis .60 1.50
10 Jameer Nelson .60 1.50
11 J.J. Redick .40 1.00
12 Hedo Turkoglu .40 1.00
13 Marcin Gortat .40 1.00
14 Adonal Foyle .40 1.00
15 Mascot .40 1.00

2008-09 Magic Upper Deck 20th Anniversary

COMPLETE SET (20) 8.00 20.00
1 Nick Anderson .50 1.25
2 Scott Skiles .50 1.25
3 Otis Smith .50 1.25
4 Anthony Bowie .50 1.25
5 Jeff Turner .50 1.25
6 Donald Royal .50 1.25
7 Shaquille O'Neal 1.50 4.00
8 Dennis Scott .50 1.25
9 Danny Schayes .50 1.25
10 Darrell Armstrong .50 1.25
11 Bo Outlaw .50 1.25
12 Mike Miller .50 1.25
13 Pat Garrity .50 1.25
14 Tracy McGrady 1.00 2.50
15 Grant Hill 1.00 2.50
16 Jameer Nelson .60 1.50
17 Hedo Turkoglu .50 1.25
18 Dwight Howard 1.50 4.00
19 Rashard Lewis .60 1.50
20 Courtney Lee .75 2.00

1989 Magnetables

COMPLETE SET (35) 45.00 90.00
1 Mark Aguirre 1.25 3.00
2 Willie Anderson .75 2.00
3 Charles Barkley 2.50 6.00
4 Larry Bird 3.00 8.00
5 Rolando Blackman 1.25 3.00
6 Tom Chambers 1.25 3.00
7 Clyde Drexler 2.00 5.00
8 Joe Dumars 1.25 3.00
9 Dale Ellis .75 2.00
10 Alex English 1.25 3.00
11 Patrick Ewing 1.50 4.00
12 Roy Hinson .75 2.00
13 Kevin Johnson 1.25 3.00
14 Magic Johnson 3.00 8.00
15 Vinnie Johnson .75 2.00
16 Michael Jordan 8.00 20.00
17 Bernard King 1.25 3.00
18 Bill Laimbeer 1.25 3.00
19 Dan Majerle 1.50 4.00
20 Karl Malone 2.50 6.00
21 Moses Malone 1.25 3.00
22 Kevin McHale 1.50 4.00
23 Chris Mullin 1.50 4.00
24 Ken Norman .75 2.00
25 Hakeem Olajuwon 2.00 5.00
26 Chuck Person .75 2.00
27 Mark Price 1.25 3.00
28 Mitch Richmond 2.50 6.00
29 Dennis Rodman 2.00 5.00
30 Kenny Smith .75 2.00
31 Jon Sundvold .75 2.00
32 Isiah Thomas 1.50 4.00
33 Kelly Tripucka .75 2.00
34 Dominique Wilkins 2.50 6.00
35 James Worthy 1.50 4.00

1994-95 Mavericks Bookmarks

COMPLETE SET (6) 5.00 12.00
1 Jim Jackson 1.25 3.00
2 Jamal Mashburn 1.25 3.00
3 Jason Kidd 2.50 6.00
4 Popeye Jones .40 1.00
5 Tony Dumas .40 1.00
6 Terry Davis .40 1.00

1988-89 Mavericks Bud Light BLC

COMPLETE SET (14) 10.00 25.00
12 Derek Harper 1.50 4.00
15 Brad Davis .50 1.25
20 Morlon Wiley .25 .60
22 Rolando Blackman 1.50 4.00

23 Bill Wennington .50 1.50
24 Mark Aguirre 1.50 4.00
32 Detlef Schrempf 3.00 8.00
33 Uwe Blab .25 .60
40 James Donaldson .25 .60
41 Terry Tyler .25 .60
42 Roy Tarpley 1.00 2.50
44 Sam Perkins 1.50 4.00
NNO Richie Adubato ACO
Garfield Heard ACO .50 1.25
NNO John MacLeod CO .50 1.25

1988-89 Mavericks Bud Light Card Night

COMPLETE SET (13) 6.00 15.00
4 Adrian Dantley 1.25 3.00
12 Derek Harper 1.25 3.00
15 Brad Davis .40 1.00
20 Morton Wiley .20 .50
21 Anthony Jones .20 .50
22 Rolando Blackman 1.25 3.00
23 Bill Wennington .40 1.00
32 Herb Williams .40 1.00
33 Uwe Blab .20 .50
40 James Donaldson .20 .50
41 Terry Tyler .20 .50
44 Sam Perkins 1.25 3.00
NNO John MacLeod CO .20 .50

1989-90 Mavericks Dr. Pepper

COMPLETE SET (13) 8.00 20.00
1 Richie Adubato CO .40 1.00
2 Steve Alford 1.25 3.00
3 Rolando Blackman 1.50 4.00
4 Adrian Dantley 1.50 4.00
5 Brad Davis 1.25 3.00
6 James Donaldson .40 1.00
7 Derek Harper 1.50 4.00
8 Anthony Jones .40 1.00
9 Sam Perkins 1.50 4.00
10 Roy Tarpley .40 1.00
11 Bill Wennington .40 1.00
12 Randy White .40 1.00
13 Herb Williams .60 1.50

1987-88 Mavericks Miller Lite

COMPLETE SET (5) 6.00 15.00
1 Mark Aguirre 1.50 4.00
2 Rolando Blackman 1.50 4.00
3 James Donaldson .75 2.00
4 Derek Harper 1.50 4.00
5 Sam Perkins 1.50 4.00

2010-11 Mavericks Panini NBA Champions

COMPLETE SET (36) 12.50 25.00
1 Dirk Nowitzki 2.00 5.00
2 Jason Kidd 1.25 3.00
3 Jason Terry .60 1.50
4 Tyson Chandler .60 1.50
5 Shawn Marion .75 2.00
6 J.J. Barea .60 1.50
7 DeShawn Stevenson .50 1.25
8 Brendan Haywood .50 1.25
9 Brian Cardinal .50 1.25
10 Caron Butler .60 1.50
11 Peja Stojakovic .60 1.50
12 Ian Mahinmi .75 2.00
13 Corey Brewer .50 1.25
14 Dominique Jones .50 1.25
15 Rodrigue Beaubois .50 1.25
16 Alexis Ajinca .50 1.25
17 Sasha Pavlovic .50 1.25
18 Steve Novak .50 1.25
19 Rick Carlisle CO .50 1.25
20 Playoff Win 1 .50 1.25
21 Playoff Win 2 .50 1.25
22 Playoff Win 3 .50 1.25
23 Playoff Win 4 .50 1.25
24 Playoff Win 5 .50 1.25
25 Playoff Win 6 .50 1.25
26 Playoff Win 7 .50 1.25
27 Playoff Win 8 .50 1.25
28 Playoff Win 9 .50 1.25
29 Playoff Win 10 .50 1.25
30 Playoff Win 11 .50 1.25
31 Playoff Win 12 .50 1.25
32 Playoff Win 13 .50 1.25
33 Playoff Win 14 .50 1.25
34 Playoff Win 15 .50 1.25
35 Playoff Win 16 .50 1.25
36 Dirk Nowitzki MVP 2.00 5.00

2000 Mavericks Rolando Blackman Retirement Sheet

1 Rolando Blackman 1.25 3.00

1995-96 Mavericks Taco Bell

COMPLETE SET (4) 2.50 6.00
1 Jim Jackson .40 1.00
2 Jason Kidd
(NBA Rookie of the Year) 1.25 3.00
3 Jason Kidd 1.25 3.00
4 Jamal Mashburn .40 1.00
NNO Triple J Ad Card 2.50 6.00

1981-82 Mavericks Team Issue

COMPLETE SET (5) 8.00 20.00
1 Mark Aguirre 2.50 6.00
2 Brad Davis 2.00 5.00
3 Jim Spanarkel 1.50 4.00
4 Tom LaGarde 1.25 3.00
5 Oliver Mack 1.25 3.00

2001-02 Mavericks Topps

COMPLETE SET (15) 5.00 12.00
DMAG Adrian Griffin .40 1.00
DMDH Donnell Harvey .40 1.00
DMDN Dirk Nowitzki 1.25 3.00
DMDAN Don Nelson CO .40 1.00
DMDRM Danny Manning .50 1.25
DMEE Evan Eschmeyer .40 1.00
DMEN Eduardo Najera .40 1.00
DMGB Greg Buckner .40 1.00
DMJH Juwan Howard .50 1.25
DMJN Johnny Newman .40 1.00
DMMF Michael Finley .60 1.50
DMSB Shawn Bradley .40 1.00
DMSN Steve Nash 1.25 3.00
DMTH Tim Hardaway .75 2.00
DMWZ Wang Zhizhi .60 1.50

2018-19 Mavericks Hoops

COMPLETE SET (6)
DAL1 Luka Doncic 75.00 200.00
DAL2 Harrison Barnes 1.00 2.50
DAL3 Dennis Smith Jr. .75 2.00
DAL4 DeAndre Jordan 1.00 2.50
DAL5 Wesley Matthews .75 2.00
DAL6 Maxi Kleber 1.00 2.50

1990-91 McDonald's Jordan Joyner-Kersee

COMPLETE SET (16) 6.00 15.00
COMMON MJ 1.00 2.50
COMMON JJK .75 2.00

1993-94 McDonald's Lakers Magnets

COMPLETE SET (3) 6.00 15.00
1 Nick Van Exel 3.00 8.00
2 Doug Christie 1.50 4.00
3 George Lynch 1.50 4.00

1995 McDonald's Looney Tunes All-Star Showdown Cups

COMPLETE SET (6) 5.00 12.00
1 Larry Bird
Sylvester 1.25 3.00
2 Charles Barkley
Tasmanian Devil 1.25 3.00
3 Shawn Kemp
Daffy Duck .60 1.50
4 Michael Jordan
Bugs Bunny 3.00 8.00
5 Larry Johnson
Wile E. Coyote .60 1.50
6 Reggie Miller
Road Runner 1.25 3.00

1994 McDonald's Nothing But Net MVP Cups

COMPLETE SET (6) 7.00 14.00
1 Michael Jordan 2.50 6.00
2 Julius Erving 1.25 3.00
3 Larry Bird 1.25 3.00
4 Moses Malone .75 2.00
5 Charles Barkley 1.00 2.50
6 Bill Walton .75 2.00

1994 McDonald's Nothing But Net MVP Fry Boxes

COMPLETE SET (6) 8.00 20.00
1 Charles Barkley 1993 MVP 1.50 4.00
2 Larry Bird 1984 MVP 1.50 4.00
3 Julius Erving 1981 MVP 1.50 4.00
4 Michael Jordan
1988, 1991, 1992 MVP 2.50 6.00
5 Moses Malone
1979, 1982, 1983 MVP 1.00 2.50
6 Bill Walton 1978 MVP 1.00 2.50

1992 McDonald's USA Dream Team Cups

COMPLETE SET (10) 10.00 25.00
1 Charles Barkley 1.25 3.00
2 Larry Bird 1.50 4.00
3 Patrick Ewing .75 2.00
4 Magic Johnson 1.50 4.00
5 Michael Jordan 3.00 8.00
6 Karl Malone 1.25 3.00
7 Chris Mullin .75 2.00
8 Scottie Pippen 1.25 3.00
9 David Robinson 1.25 3.00
10 John Stockton 1.50 4.00
NNO Christian Laettner 1.50 4.00
NNO Clyde Drexler 2.50 6.00

1994 McDonald's USA Dream Team 2 Cups

COMPLETE SET (13) 6.00 15.00
1 Isiah Thomas .60 1.50
2 Larry Johnson .60 1.50
3 Shawn Kemp .60 1.50
4 Dan Majerle .60 1.50
5 Dominique Wilkins .75 2.00
6 Derrick Coleman .40 1.00
7 Alonzo Mourning .60 1.50
8 Steve Smith .60 1.50
9 Joe Dumars .60 1.50
10 Mark Price .60 1.50
11 Shaquille O'Neal 2.00 5.00
12 Reggie Miller .75 2.00
13 Tim Hardaway .60 1.50

1994 McDonald's USA Dream Team 2 Fry Boxes

COMPLETE SET (11) 8.00 20.00
1 Derrick Coleman .75 2.00
2 Joe Dumars .75 2.00
3 Tim Hardaway .75 2.00
4 Larry Johnson .75 2.00
5 Shawn Kemp .75 2.00
6 Dan Majerle .75 2.00
7 Reggie Miller 1.50 4.00
8 Alonzo Mourning 1.25 3.00
9 Steve Smith .75 2.00
10 Isiah Thomas .75 2.00
11 Dominique Wilkins 1.50 4.00

1993 McDonald's/Footlocker Patrick Ewing

1 Patrick Ewing 8.00 20.00

1995-96 Metal

COMPLETE SET (220) 50.00 120.00
COMPLETE SERIES 1 (120) 25.00 60.00
COMPLETE SERIES 2 (100) 25.00 60.00
1 Stacey Augmon .30 .75
2 Mookie Blaylock .40 1.00
3 Grant Long .25 .60
4 Steve Smith .30 .75
5 Dee Brown .30 .75
6 Sherman Douglas .25 .60
7 Eric Montross .25 .60
8 Dino Radja .25 .60
9 Muggsy Bogues .40 1.00
10 Scott Burrell .25 .60
11 Larry Johnson .50 1.25
12 Alonzo Mourning .60 1.50
13 Michael Jordan 15.00 40.00
14 Toni Kukoc .50 1.25
15 Scottie Pippen 1.00 2.50
16 Terrell Brandon .30 .75
17 Tyrone Hill .25 .60
18 Mark Price .40 1.00
19 John Williams .25 .60
20 Jim Jackson .30 .75
21 Popeye Jones .25 .60
22 Jason Kidd .60 1.50
23 Jamal Mashburn .40 1.00
24 Mahmoud Abdul-Rauf .30 .75
25 Dikembe Mutombo .60 1.50
26 Robert Pack .25 .60
27 Jalen Rose .50 1.25
28 Joe Dumars .40 1.00
29 Grant Hill .60 1.50
30 Lindsey Hunter .25 .60
31 Terry Mills .25 .60
32 Tim Hardaway .50 1.25
33 Donyell Marshall .25 .60
34 Chris Mullin .40 1.00
35 Clifford Rozier .25 .60
36 Latrell Sprewell .40 1.00
37 Sam Cassell .40 1.00
38 Clyde Drexler .60 1.50
39 Robert Horry .40 1.00
40 Hakeem Olajuwon .75 2.00
41 Kenny Smith .30 .75
42 Dale Davis .25 .60
43 Mark Jackson .30 .75
44 Derrick McKey .25 .60
45 Reggie Miller .75 2.00
46 Rik Smits .30 .75
47 Lamond Murray .25 .60
48 Pooh Richardson .25 .60
49 Malik Sealy .25 .60
50 Loy Vaught .25 .60
51 Elden Campbell .25 .60
52 Cedric Ceballos .30 .75
53 Vlade Divac .40 1.00
54 Eddie Jones .40 1.00
55 Nick Van Exel .40 1.00
56 Bimbo Coles .25 .60
57 Billy Owens .25 .60
58 Khalid Reeves .25 .60
59 Glen Rice .40 1.00
60 Kevin Willis .25 .60
61 Vin Baker .30 .75
62 Todd Day .25 .60
63 Eric Murdock .25 .60
64 Glenn Robinson .40 1.00
65 Tom Gugliotta .25 .60
66 Christian Laettner .30 .75
67 Isaiah Rider .40 1.00
68 Kenny Anderson .30 .75
69 P.J. Brown .25 .60
70 Derrick Coleman .30 .75
71 Patrick Ewing .60 1.50
72 Anthony Mason .25 .60
73 Charles Oakley .30 .75
74 John Starks .40 1.00
75 Nick Anderson .30 .75
76 Horace Grant .30 .75
77 Anfernee Hardaway 1.00 2.50
78 Shaquille O'Neal 1.50 4.00
79 Dennis Scott .25 .60
80 Dana Barros .30 .75
81 Shawn Bradley .25 .60
82 Clarence Weatherspoon .25 .60
83 Sharone Wright .25 .60
84 Charles Barkley 1.00 2.50
85 Kevin Johnson .40 1.00
86 Dan Majerle .40 1.00
87 Danny Manning .30 .75
88 Wesley Person .25 .60
89 Clifford Robinson .40 1.00
90 Rod Strickland .25 .60
91 Otis Thorpe .30 .75
92 Buck Williams .25 .60
93 Brian Grant .30 .75
94 Olden Polynice .25 .60
95 Mitch Richmond .50 1.25
96 Walt Williams .25 .60
97 Sean Elliott .30 .75
98 Avery Johnson .25 .60
99 David Robinson .75 2.00
100 Dennis Rodman .75 2.00
101 Shawn Kemp .60 1.50
102 Nate McMillan .25 .60
103 Gary Payton .60 1.50
104 Detlef Schrempf .40 1.00
105 B.J. Armstrong .40 1.00
106 Oliver Miller .25 .60
107 John Salley .25 .60
108 David Benoit .25 .60
109 Jeff Hornacek .30 .75
110 Karl Malone .75 2.00
111 John Stockton .75 2.00
112 Greg Anthony .25 .60
113 Benoit Benjamin .25 .60
114 Byron Scott .40 1.00
115 Calbert Cheaney .25 .60
116 Juwan Howard .40 1.00
117 Gheorghe Muresan .25 .60
118 Chris Webber .50 1.25
119 Checklist .15 .40
120 Checklist .15 .40
121 Stacey Augmon .30 .75
122 Mookie Blaylock .40 1.00
123 Alan Henderson RC .40 1.00
124 Andrew Lang .25 .60
125 Ken Norman .25 .60
126 Steve Smith .30 .75
127 Dana Barros .30 .75
128 Rick Fox .25 .60
129 Eric Williams RC .40 1.00
130 Kendall Gill .25 .60
131 Khalid Reeves .25 .60
132 Glen Rice .40 1.00
133 George Zidek RC .30 .75
134 Dennis Rodman .75 2.00
135 Danny Ferry .25 .60
136 Dan Majerle .40 1.00
137 Chris Mills .25 .60
138 Bobby Phills .30 .75
139 Bob Sura RC .30 .75
140 Tony Dumas .25 .60
141 Dale Ellis .30 .75
142 Don MacLean .25 .60
143 Antonio McDyess RC .50 1.25
144 Bryant Stith .25 .60
145 Allan Houston .30 .75
146 Theo Ratliff RC .60 1.50
147 Otis Thorpe .30 .75
148 B.J. Armstrong .40 1.00
149 Rony Seikaly .25 .60
150 Joe Smith RC .50 1.25
151 Sam Cassell .40 1.00
152 Clyde Drexler .60 1.50
153 Robert Horry .40 1.00
154 Hakeem Olajuwon .75 2.00
155 Antonio Davis .25 .60
156 Ricky Pierce .25 .60
157 Brent Barry RC .60 1.50
158 Terry Dehere .25 .60
159 Rodney Rogers .30 .75
160 Brian Williams .25 .60
161 Magic Johnson 1.25 3.00
162 Sasha Danilovic RC .40 1.00
163 Alonzo Mourning .60 1.50
164 Kurt Thomas RC .40 1.00
165 Sherman Douglas .25 .60
166 Shawn Respert RC .30 .75
167 Kevin Garnett RC 6.00 15.00
168 Terry Porter .25 .60
169 Shawn Bradley .25 .60
170 Kevin Edwards .25 .60
171 Ed O'Bannon RC .30 .75
172 Jayson Williams .25 .60
173 Derek Harper .30 .75
174 Charles Smith .25 .60
175 Brian Shaw .25 .60
176 Derrick Coleman .30 .75
177 Vernon Maxwell .25 .60
178 Trevor Ruffin .25 .60
179 Jerry Stackhouse RC 1.25 3.00
180 Michael Finley RC 1.00 2.50
181 A.C. Green .30 .75
182 John Williams .25 .60
183 Aaron McKie .25 .60
184 Arvydas Sabonis RC .75 2.00
185 Gary Trent RC .30 .75
186 Tyus Edney RC .40 1.00
187 Sarunas Marciulionis .40 1.00
188 Michael Smith .25 .60
189 Corliss Williamson RC .40 1.00
190 Vinny Del Negro .25 .60
191 Hersey Hawkins .30 .75
192 Shawn Kemp .60 1.50
193 Gary Payton .60 1.50
194 Sam Perkins .30 .75
195 Detlef Schrempf .40 1.00
196 Willie Anderson .25 .60
197 Oliver Miller .25 .60
198 Tracy Murray .25 .60
199 Alvin Robertson .25 .60
200 Damon Stoudamire RC 1.00 2.50
201 Chris Morris .25 .60
202 Greg Anthony .25 .60
203 Blue Edwards .25 .60
204 Eric Murdock .25 .60
205 Bryant Reeves RC .30 .75
206 Byron Scott .40 1.00
207 Robert Pack .25 .60
208 Rasheed Wallace RC 1.25 3.00
209 Anfernee Hardaway NB 1.00 2.50
210 Grant Hill NB .60 1.50
211 Larry Johnson NB .50 1.25
212 Michael Jordan NB 15.00 40.00
213 Jason Kidd NB .60 1.50
214 Karl Malone NB .75 2.00
215 Shaquille O'Neal NB 1.50 4.00
216 Scottie Pippen NB 1.00 2.50
217 David Robinson NB .75 2.00
218 Glenn Robinson NB .40 1.00
219 Checklist .15 .40
220 Checklist .15 .40

1995-96 Metal Silver Spotlight

COMPLETE SET (120) 25.00 60.00
*STARS: 1X TO 2.5X BASE CARD HI
ONE PER SERIES 1 PACK

1995-96 Metal Maximum Metal

COMPLETE SET (10) 50.00 120.00
SER.1 STATED ODDS 1:36 HOBBY/RETAIL
1 Charles Barkley 4.00 10.00
2 Patrick Ewing 2.50 6.00
3 Grant Hill 2.50 6.00
4 Michael Jordan 40.00 100.00
5 Shawn Kemp 2.50 6.00
6 Karl Malone 3.00 8.00
7 Hakeem Olajuwon 3.00 8.00
8 Shaquille O'Neal 6.00 15.00
9 Mitch Richmond 2.00 5.00
10 David Robinson 3.00 8.00

1995-96 Metal Metal Force

COMPLETE SET (15) 75.00 150.00
SER.2 STATED ODDS 1:54 RETAIL
1 Vin Baker 3.00 8.00
2 Charles Barkley 10.00 25.00
3 Cedric Ceballos 3.00 8.00
4 Grant Hill 6.00 15.00
5 Larry Johnson 5.00 12.00
6 Magic Johnson 12.00 30.00
7 Shawn Kemp 6.00 15.00
8 Karl Malone 8.00 20.00
9 Jamal Mashburn 4.00 10.00
10 Scottie Pippen 8.00 20.00
11 Glenn Robinson 4.00 10.00
12 Dennis Rodman 8.00 20.00
13 Joe Smith 2.50 6.00
14 Jerry Stackhouse 6.00 15.00
15 Chris Webber 5.00 12.00

1995-96 Metal Molten Metal

COMPLETE SET (10) 40.00 100.00
SER.1 STATED ODDS 1:72 HOBBY/RETAIL
1 Anfernee Hardaway 10.00 25.00
2 Grant Hill 6.00 15.00
3 Robert Horry 4.00 10.00
4 Eddie Jones 4.00 10.00
5 Toni Kukoc 5.00 12.00
6 Jamal Mashburn 4.00 10.00
7 Alonzo Mourning 6.00 15.00
8 Glenn Robinson 4.00 10.00
9 Latrell Sprewell 4.00 10.00
10 Chris Webber 5.00 12.00

1995-96 Metal Rookie Roll Call

COMPLETE SET (10) 2.00 5.00
*SILV.SPOTLIGHT: 1X TO 2.5X HI COLUMN
R1 Brent Barry .50 1.25
R2 Antonio McDyess .40 1.00
R3 Ed O'Bannon .25 .60
R4 Cherokee Parks .25 .60
R5 Bryant Reeves .25 .60
R6 Shawn Respert .25 .60
R7 Joe Smith .40 1.00
R8 Jerry Stackhouse 1.00 2.50
R9 Gary Trent .25 .60
R10 Rasheed Wallace 1.00 2.50

1995-96 Metal Scoring Magnets

COMPLETE SET (8) 150.00 400.00
SER.2 STATED ODDS 1:54 HOBBY
1 Anfernee Hardaway 10.00 25.00
2 Grant Hill 6.00 15.00
3 Magic Johnson 12.00 30.00
4 Michael Jordan 150.00 400.00
5 Jason Kidd 6.00 15.00
6 Hakeem Olajuwon 8.00 20.00
7 Shaquille O'Neal 20.00 50.00
8 David Robinson 8.00 20.00

1995-96 Metal Slick Silver

COMPLETE SET (10) 60.00 150.00
SER.1 STATED ODDS 1:7 HOBBY/RETAIL
1 Kenny Anderson 1.50 4.00
2 Anfernee Hardaway 5.00 12.00
3 Michael Jordan 100.00 250.00
4 Jason Kidd 3.00 8.00
5 Reggie Miller 4.00 10.00
6 Gary Payton 3.00 8.00
7 Mitch Richmond 2.50 6.00
8 Latrell Sprewell 2.00 5.00
9 John Stockton 4.00 10.00
10 Nick Van Exel 2.00 5.00

1995-96 Metal Stackhouse's Scrapbook

COMPLETE SET (2) 3.00 8.00
STATED ODDS 1:24
S7 J.Stackhouse w/Jordan 2.50 6.00
S8 Jerry Stackhouse 1.25 3.00

1995-96 Metal Steel Towers

COMPLETE SET (10) 5.00 12.00
SER.1 STATED ODDS 1:4 RETAIL
1 Shawn Bradley .60 1.50
2 Vlade Divac 1.00 2.50
3 Patrick Ewing 1.50 4.00
4 Alonzo Mourning 1.50 4.00
5 Dikembe Mutombo 1.50 4.00
6 Hakeem Olajuwon 2.00 5.00
7 Shaquille O'Neal 4.00 10.00
8 David Robinson 2.00 5.00
9 Rik Smits .75 2.00
10 Kevin Willis .60 1.50

1995-96 Metal Tempered Steel

COMPLETE SET (12) 15.00 30.00
SER.2 STATED ODDS 1:12 HOBBY/RETAIL
1 Sasha Danilovic .75 2.00
2 Tyus Edney .75 2.00
3 Michael Finley 2.00 5.00
4 Kevin Garnett 6.00 15.00
5 Antonio McDyess 1.00 2.50
6 Bryant Reeves .60 1.50
7 Arvydas Sabonis 1.50 4.00
8 Joe Smith 1.00 2.50
9 Jerry Stackhouse 2.50 6.00
10 Damon Stoudamire 2.00 5.00
11 Rasheed Wallace 2.50 6.00
12 Eric Williams .75 2.00

1996-97 Metal

COMPLETE SET (250) 100.00 250.00
COMPLETE SERIES 1 (150) 40.00 100.00
COMPLETE SERIES 2 (100) 60.00 150.00
1 Mookie Blaylock .40 1.00
2 Christian Laettner .40 1.00
3 Steve Smith .30 .75
4 Dana Barros .25 .60
5 Rick Fox .25 .60
6 Dino Radja .25 .60
7 Eric Williams .25 .60
8 Dell Curry .40 1.00
9 Matt Geiger .25 .60
10 Glen Rice .40 1.00
11 Michael Jordan 4.00 10.00
12 Toni Kukoc .40 1.00
13 Luc Longley .30 .75
14 Scottie Pippen 1.00 2.50
15 Dennis Rodman 1.00 2.50
16 Terrell Brandon .30 .75
17 Danny Ferry .25 .60
18 Chris Mills .25 .60
19 Bobby Phills .25 .60
20 Bob Sura .25 .60
21 Jim Jackson .25 .60
22 Jason Kidd .60 1.50
23 Jamal Mashburn .40 1.00
24 George McCloud .25 .60
25 LaPhonso Ellis .25 .60
26 Antonio McDyess .40 1.00
27 Bryant Stith .25 .60
28 Joe Dumars .50 1.25
29 Grant Hill .60 1.50
30 Theo Ratliff .25 .60
31 Otis Thorpe .30 .75
32 Chris Mullin .50 1.25
33 Joe Smith .30 .75
34 Latrell Sprewell .40 1.00
35 Sam Cassell .30 .75
36 Clyde Drexler .60 1.50
37 Robert Horry .40 1.00
38 Hakeem Olajuwon .75 2.00
39 Antonio Davis .25 .60
40 Dale Davis .25 .60
41 Derrick McKey .25 .60
42 Reggie Miller .75 2.00
43 Rik Smits .30 .75
44 Brent Barry .30 .75
45 Malik Sealy .25 .60
46 Loy Vaught .25 .60
47 Elden Campbell .25 .60
48 Cedric Ceballos .30 .75
49 Eddie Jones .40 1.00
50 Nick Van Exel .40 1.00
51 Sasha Danilovic .25 .60
52 Tim Hardaway .50 1.25
53 Alonzo Mourning .60 1.50
54 Kurt Thomas .25 .60
55 Vin Baker .30 .75
56 Sherman Douglas .25 .60
57 Glenn Robinson .40 1.00
58 Kevin Garnett 1.25 3.00
59 Tom Gugliotta .25 .60
60 Doug West .25 .60
61 Shawn Bradley .25 .60
62 Ed O'Bannon .25 .60
63 Jayson Williams .25 .60
64 Patrick Ewing .60 1.50
65 Charles Oakley .40 1.00
66 John Starks .40 1.00
67 Nick Anderson .25 .60
68 Horace Grant .40 1.00
69 Anfernee Hardaway 1.00 2.50
70 Dennis Scott .30 .75
71 Brian Shaw .25 .60
72 Derrick Coleman .30 .75
73 Jerry Stackhouse .50 1.25
74 Clarence Weatherspoon .25 .60
75 Charles Barkley 1.00 2.50
76 Michael Finley .40 1.00
77 Kevin Johnson .40 1.00
78 Wesley Person .25 .60
79 Aaron McKie .25 .60
80 Clifford Robinson .40 1.00
81 Arvydas Sabonis .40 1.00
82 Gary Trent .25 .60
83 Tyus Edney .25 .60
84 Brian Grant .30 .75
85 Billy Owens .25 .60
86 Olden Polynice .25 .60
87 Mitch Richmond .50 1.25
88 Vinny Del Negro .25 .60
89 Sean Elliott .40 1.00
90 Avery Johnson .30 .75
91 David Robinson .75 2.00
92 Hersey Hawkins .25 .60
93 Shawn Kemp .60 1.50
94 Gary Payton .60 1.50
95 Sam Perkins .30 .75
96 Detlef Schrempf .40 1.00
97 Doug Christie .25 .60
98 Damon Stoudamire .40 1.00
99 Sharone Wright .25 .60
100 Jeff Hornacek .30 .75
101 Karl Malone .75 2.00
102 John Stockton .75 2.00
103 Greg Anthony .25 .60
104 Blue Edwards .25 .60
105 Bryant Reeves .25 .60
106 Juwan Howard .40 1.00
107 Gheorghe Muresan .25 .60
108 Chris Webber .50 1.25
109 Kenny Anderson OTM .30 .75
110 Stacey Augmon OTM .30 .75
111 Chris Childs OTM .25 .60
112 Vlade Divac OTM .40 1.00
113 Allan Houston OTM .40 1.00
114 Mark Jackson OTM .30 .75
115 Larry Johnson OTM .50 1.25
116 Grant Long OTM .25 .60
117 Anthony Mason OTM .30 .75
118 Dikembe Mutombo OTM .60 1.50
119 Shaquille O'Neal OTM 1.50 4.00
120 Isaiah Rider OTM .30 .75
121 Rod Strickland OTM .40 1.00
122 Rasheed Wallace OTM .50 1.25
123 Jalen Rose OTM .30 .75
124 Anfernee Hardaway MET 1.00 2.50
125 Tim Hardaway MET .50 1.25
126 Allan Houston MET .40 1.00
127 Eddie Jones MET .40 1.00
128 Michael Jordan MET 4.00 10.00
129 Reggie Miller MET .75 2.00
130 Glen Rice MET .40 1.00
131 Mitch Richmond MET .50 1.25
132 Steve Smith MET .30 .75
133 John Stockton MET .75 2.00
134 Stephon Marbury FF RC 1.25 3.00
135 Shareef Abdur-Rahim FF RC .60 1.50
136 Ray Allen FF RC 2.00 5.00
137 Kobe Bryant FF RC 20.00 50.00
138 Steve Nash FF RC 2.50 6.00
139 Grant Hill MS .60 1.50
140 Jason Kidd MS .60 1.50
141 Karl Malone MS .75 2.00
142 Hakeem Olajuwon MS .75 2.00
143 Shaquille O'Neal MS 1.50 4.00
144 Gary Payton MS .60 1.50
145 Scottie Pippen MS 1.00 2.50
146 Jerry Stackhouse MS .50 1.25
147 Damon Stoudamire MS .40 1.00
148 Rod Strickland MS .40 1.00
149 Checklist (1-102) .15 .40
150 Checklist (103-150/inserts) .15 .40
151 Tyrone Corbin .25 .60
152 Dikembe Mutombo .60 1.50
153 Antoine Walker RC .60 1.50
154 David Wesley .25 .60
155 Vlade Divac .40 1.00
156 Anthony Mason .30 .75
157 Ron Harper .30 .75
158 Steve Kerr .30 .75
159 Robert Parish .50 1.25
160 Tyrone Hill .25 .60
161 Vitaly Potapenko RC .30 .75
162 Sam Cassell .30 .75
163 Chris Gatling .25 .60
164 Samaki Walker RC .30 .75
165 Dale Ellis .30 .75
166 Mark Jackson .30 .75
167 Ervin Johnson .25 .60
168 Grant Hill .60 1.50
169 Lindsey Hunter .25 .60
170 Todd Fuller RC .25 .60
171 Mark Price .40 1.00
172 Charles Barkley 1.00 2.50
173 Othella Harrington RC .30 .75
174 Matt Maloney RC .30 .75
175 Kevin Willis .30 .75
176 Travis Best .25 .60
177 Erick Dampier RC .40 1.00
178 Jalen Rose .30 .75
179 Rodney Rogers .25 .60
180 Lorenzen Wright RC .30 .75
181 Kobe Bryant 25.00 60.00
182 Robert Horry .40 1.00
183 Shaquille O'Neal 1.50 4.00
184 P.J. Brown .25 .60
185 Dan Majerle .40 1.00
186 Ray Allen 2.00 5.00
187 Armon Gilliam .25 .60
188 Andrew Lang .25 .60
189 Stephon Marbury 1.25 3.00
190 Stojko Vrankovic .25 .60
191 Kendall Gill .40 1.00
192 Kerry Kittles RC .40 1.00
193 Robert Pack .25 .60
194 Chris Childs .25 .60
195 Allan Houston .40 1.00
196 Larry Johnson .50 1.25
197 John Wallace RC .30 .75
198 Rony Seikaly .30 .75
199 Gerald Wilkins .30 .75
200 Lucious Harris .25 .60
201 Allen Iverson RC 3.00 8.00
202 Cedric Ceballos .30 .75
203 Jason Kidd .60 1.50
204 Danny Manning .30 .75
205 Steve Nash 2.50 6.00
206 Kenny Anderson .30 .75
207 Isaiah Rider .30 .75
208 Rasheed Wallace .50 1.25
209 Mahmoud Abdul-Rauf .30 .75
210 Corliss Williamson .25 .60
211 Vernon Maxwell .25 .60
212 Dominique Wilkins .60 1.50
213 Craig Ehlo .25 .60
214 Jim McIlvaine .25 .60
215 Marcus Camby RC .60 1.50
216 Hubert Davis .25 .60
217 Walt Williams .25 .60
218 Shandon Anderson RC .30 .75
219 Bryon Russell .25 .60
220 Shareef Abdur-Rahim .60 1.50
221 Roy Rogers RC .30 .75
222 Tracy Murray .25 .60
223 Rod Strickland .40 1.00
224 Kevin Garnett MET 1.25 3.00
225 Karl Malone MET .75 2.00
226 Alonzo Mourning MET .60 1.50
227 Hakeem Olajuwon MET .75 2.00
228 Gary Payton MET .60 1.50
229 Scottie Pippen MET 1.00 2.50
230 David Robinson MET .75 2.00
231 Dennis Rodman MET 1.00 2.50
232 Latrell Sprewell MET .40 1.00
233 Jerry Stackhouse MET .50 1.25
234 Marcus Camby FF .60 1.50
235 Todd Fuller FF .25 .60
236 Allen Iverson FF 3.00 8.00
237 Kerry Kittles FF .40 1.00
238 Roy Rogers FF .30 .75
239 Anfernee Hardaway MS 1.00 2.50
240 Juwan Howard MS .40 1.00
241 Michael Jordan MS 12.00 30.00
242 Shawn Kemp MS .60 1.50
243 Gary Payton MS .60 1.50
244 Mitch Richmond MS .50 1.25
245 Glenn Robinson MS .40 1.00
246 John Stockton MS .75 2.00
247 Damon Stoudamire MS .40 1.00
248 Chris Webber MS .50 1.25
249 Checklist .15 .40
250 Checklist .15 .40

1996-97 Metal Precious Metal

*STARS: 10X TO 25X HI COLUMN
*ROOKIES: 5X TO 12X HI
*ROOKIE FF SUBSET: 5X TO 12X HI
SER.2 STATED ODDS 1:36 HOBBY
181 Kobe Bryant 1,500.00 3,000.00
201 Allen Iverson 100.00 250.00
205 Steve Nash 75.00 200.00
236 Allen Iverson FF 75.00 200.00
241 Michael Jordan MS 600.00 1,200.00

1996-97 Metal Cyber-Metal

COMPLETE SET (20) 125.00 300.00
SER.2 STATED ODDS 1:6 HOBBY/RETAIL
1 Shareef Abdur-Rahim 2.00 5.00
2 Ray Allen 6.00 15.00
3 Vin Baker 1.00 2.50
4 Charles Barkley 3.00 8.00
5 Kobe Bryant 50.00 120.00
6 Patrick Ewing 2.00 5.00
7 Jason Kidd 2.00 5.00
8 Karl Malone 2.50 6.00
9 Stephon Marbury 4.00 10.00
10 Reggie Miller 2.50 6.00
11 Alonzo Mourning 2.00 5.00
12 Hakeem Olajuwon 2.50 6.00
13 Gary Payton 2.50 6.00
14 Scottie Pippen 3.00 8.00
15 Mitch Richmond 1.50 4.00
16 David Robinson 2.50 6.00
17 Joe Smith 1.00 2.50
18 Latrell Sprewell 1.25 3.00
19 John Stockton 2.50 6.00
20 Chris Webber 1.50 4.00

1996-97 Metal Decade of Excellence

COMPLETE SET (10) 15.00 40.00
SER.1 STATED ODDS 1:100 HOBBY/RETAIL
M1 Clyde Drexler 2.50 6.00
M2 Joe Dumars 2.00 5.00
M3 Derek Harper 1.25 3.00
M4 Michael Jordan 40.00 100.00
M5 Karl Malone 3.00 8.00
M6 Chris Mullin 2.00 5.00
M7 Charles Oakley 1.50 4.00
M8 Sam Perkins 1.25 3.00
M9 Ricky Pierce 1.25 3.00
M10 Buck Williams 1.50 4.00

1996-97 Metal Freshly Forged
COMPLETE SET (15) 30.00 80.00
SER.2 STATED ODDS 1:24 HOBBY/RETAIL
1 Shareef Abdur-Rahim 2.00 5.00
2 Ray Allen 6.00 15.00
3 Kobe Bryant 60.00 150.00
4 Marcus Camby 2.00 5.00
5 Kevin Garnett 4.00 10.00
6 Anfernee Hardaway 3.00 8.00
7 Grant Hill 2.00 5.00
8 Allen Iverson 10.00 25.00
9 Jason Kidd 2.00 5.00
10 Stephon Marbury 4.00 10.00
11 Glenn Robinson 1.25 3.00
12 Joe Smith 1.00 2.50
13 Jerry Stackhouse 1.50 4.00
14 Damon Stoudamire 1.25 3.00
15 Antoine Walker 1.25 3.00

1996-97 Metal Maximum Metal
COMPLETE SET (20) 190.00 375.00
COMPLETE SERIES 1 (10) 150.00 300.00
COMPLETE SERIES 2 (10) 40.00 75.00
1-10: SER.1 STATED ODDS 1:180 HOBBY
11-20: SER.2 STATED ODDS 1:120 RETAIL
1 Charles Barkley 25.00 60.00
2 Anfernee Hardaway 25.00 60.00
3 Grant Hill 15.00 40.00
4 Michael Jordan 600.00 1,200.00
5 Jason Kidd 15.00 40.00
6 Karl Malone 20.00 50.00
7 Hakeem Olajuwon 20.00 50.00
8 Gary Payton 15.00 40.00
9 David Robinson 20.00 50.00
10 Damon Stoudamire 10.00 25.00
11 Juwan Howard 10.00 25.00
12 Shawn Kemp 15.00 40.00
13 Kerry Kittles 10.00 25.00
14 Stephon Marbury 30.00 80.00
15 Dennis Rodman 40.00 100.00
16 Joe Smith 8.00 20.00
17 Jerry Stackhouse 12.00 30.00
18 John Stockton 20.00 50.00
19 Antoine Walker 15.00 40.00
20 Chris Webber 12.00 30.00

1996-97 Metal Metal Edge
COMPLETE SET (15) 35.00 70.00
SER.1 STATED ODDS 1:36 HOBBY/RETAIL
1 Charles Barkley 6.00 15.00
2 Jamal Mashburn 2.50 6.00
3 Alonzo Mourning 4.00 10.00
4 Gary Payton 4.00 10.00
5 Scottie Pippen 6.00 15.00
6 Steve Smith 2.00 5.00
7 Latrell Sprewell 2.50 6.00
8 John Stockton 5.00 12.00
9 Nick Van Exel 2.50 6.00
10 Chris Webber 3.00 8.00
11 Stephon Marbury 4.00 10.00
12 Shareef Abdur-Rahim 2.00 5.00
13 Ray Allen 6.00 15.00
14 Antoine Walker 2.00 5.00
15 Kobe Bryant 75.00 200.00

1996-97 Metal Minted Metal
COMP.BRONZE SET (2) 40.00 80.00
SER.2 STATED ODDS 1:720 HOBBY FOR ANY
1 Grant Hill Bronze 15.00 30.00
2 Jerry Stackhouse Bronze 12.50 25.00
3 Grant Hill Silver 40.00 100.00
4 Jerry Stackhouse Silver 30.00 80.00

1996-97 Metal Molten Metal
COMPLETE SET (30) 200.00 400.00
COMPLETE SERIES 1 (10) 75.00 150.00
COMPLETE SERIES 2 (20) 125.00 250.00
1-10: SER.1 STATED ODDS 1:180 RETAIL
11-30: SER.2 STATED ODDS 1:72 HOBBY
1 Michael Finley 10.00 25.00
2 Kevin Garnett 30.00 80.00
3 Anfernee Hardaway 25.00 60.00
4 Grant Hill 15.00 40.00
5 Juwan Howard 10.00 25.00
6 Jason Kidd 15.00 40.00
7 Antonio McDyess 10.00 25.00
8 Joe Smith 8.00 20.00
9 Jerry Stackhouse 12.00 30.00
10 Damon Stoudamire 10.00 25.00
11 Shareef Abdur-Rahim 12.00 30.00
12 Ray Allen 12.00 30.00
13 Charles Barkley 12.00 30.00
14 Terrell Brandon 4.00 10.00
15 Marcus Camby 4.00 10.00
16 Tom Gugliotta 3.00 8.00
17 Allen Iverson 20.00 50.00
18 Michael Jordan 400.00 800.00
19 Kerry Kittles 2.50 6.00
20 Karl Malone 10.00 25.00
21 Hakeem Olajuwon 10.00 25.00
22 Shaquille O'Neal 20.00 50.00
23 Gary Payton 8.00 20.00
24 Scottie Pippen 12.00 30.00
25 David Robinson 10.00 25.00
26 Glenn Robinson 5.00 12.00
27 Joe Smith 4.00 10.00
28 Latrell Sprewell 5.00 12.00
29 Antoine Walker 4.00 10.00
30 Chris Webber 6.00 15.00

1996-97 Metal Net-Rageous
COMPLETE SET (10) 300.00 600.00
SER.2 STATED ODDS 1:288 HOBBY/RETAIL
1 Kevin Garnett 75.00 200.00
2 Anfernee Hardaway 75.00 200.00
3 Grant Hill 40.00 100.00
4 Juwan Howard 12.00 30.00
5 Michael Jordan 1,000.00 2,000.00
6 Shawn Kemp 40.00 100.00
7 Shaquille O'Neal 125.00 300.00
8 Dennis Rodman 75.00 200.00
9 Jerry Stackhouse 25.00 60.00
10 Damon Stoudamire 15.00 40.00

1996-97 Metal Platinum Portraits
COMPLETE SET (10) 200.00 500.00
SER.2 STATED ODDS 1:96 HOBBY/RETAIL
1 Charles Barkley 12.00 30.00
2 Kevin Garnett 15.00 40.00
3 Anfernee Hardaway 12.00 30.00
4 Grant Hill 8.00 20.00
5 Michael Jordan 150.00 400.00
6 Shawn Kemp 8.00 20.00
7 Karl Malone 10.00 25.00
8 Shaquille O'Neal 20.00 50.00
9 Hakeem Olajuwon 10.00 25.00
10 Damon Stoudamire 5.00 12.00

1996-97 Metal Power Tools
COMPLETE SET (10) 10.00 20.00
SER.1 STATED ODDS 1:18 HOBBY/RETAIL
1 Vin Baker 1.50 4.00
2 Charles Barkley 5.00 12.00
3 Horace Grant 2.00 5.00
4 Juwan Howard 2.00 5.00
5 Larry Johnson 2.50 6.00
6 Shawn Kemp 3.00 8.00
7 Karl Malone 4.00 10.00
8 Antonio McDyess 2.00 5.00
9 Dennis Rodman 5.00 12.00
10 Joe Smith 1.50 4.00

1996-97 Metal Steel Slammin'
COMPLETE SET (10) 125.00 300.00
SER.1 STATED ODDS 1:72 HOBBY/RETAIL
1 Brent Barry 3.00 8.00
2 Clyde Drexler 6.00 15.00
3 Michael Finley 4.00 10.00
4 Kevin Garnett 12.00 30.00
5 Eddie Jones 4.00 10.00
6 Michael Jordan 150.00 400.00
7 Shawn Kemp 6.00 15.00
8 Shaquille O'Neal 15.00 40.00
9 Joe Smith 3.00 8.00
10 Jerry Stackhouse 5.00 12.00

1999-00 Metal
COMPLETE SET (180) 20.00 50.00
151-180 STATED ODDS 1:2
1 Vince Carter 1.00 2.50
2 Stephon Marbury .50 1.25
3 David Robinson .75 2.00
4 Ray Allen .60 1.50
5 P.J. Brown .30 .75
6 Shawn Kemp .60 1.50
7 Cedric Ceballos .25 .60
8 Dale Davis .25 .60
9 Rodney Rogers .25 .60
10 Chris Gatling .25 .60
11 Bryant Reeves .25 .60
12 Al Harrington .40 1.00
13 Brent Barry .30 .75
14 Brevin Knight .25 .60
15 Radoslav Nesterovic RC .40 1.00
16 Tom Gugliotta .30 .75
17 Charles Barkley 1.00 2.50
18 Cuttino Mobley .25 .60
19 Corliss Williamson .25 .60
20 Hersey Hawkins .25 .60
21 Mike Bibby .40 1.00
22 Pat Garrity .25 .60
23 Kelvin Cato .25 .60
24 Alan Henderson .25 .60
25 Alvin Williams .25 .60
26 Antonio McDyess .30 .75
27 Damon Stoudamire .40 1.00
28 Kerry Kittles .30 .75
29 Michael Olowokandi .25 .60
30 Brent Price .25 .60
31 Fred Hoiberg .25 .60
32 Glenn Robinson .30 .75
33 Hakeem Olajuwon .75 2.00
34 Monty Williams .30 .75
35 Terry Porter .25 .60
36 Allen Iverson 1.00 2.50
37 Juwan Howard .30 .75
38 Mario Elie .25 .60
39 Mookie Blaylock .25 .60
40 Sam Cassell .30 .75
41 Toni Kukoc .50 1.25
42 Anthony Mason .40 1.00
43 George Lynch .25 .60
44 John Starks .40 1.00
45 Malik Rose .25 .60
46 Rod Strickland .30 .75
47 Tim Thomas .30 .75
48 Howard Eisley .25 .60
49 Kenny Anderson .30 .75
50 Kurt Thomas .25 .60
51 Lindsey Hunter .25 .60
52 Rick Fox .25 .60
53 Vlade Divac .40 1.00
54 Avery Johnson .30 .75
55 Dale Ellis .25 .60
56 Donyell Marshall .30 .75
57 Elden Campbell .25 .60
58 Larry Hughes .30 .75
59 Mitch Richmond .50 1.25
60 Chris Mills .25 .60
61 David Wesley .25 .60
62 Gary Payton .60 1.50
63 Isaac Austin .25 .60
64 Robert Traylor .25 .60
65 Theo Ratliff .30 .75
66 Antawn Jamison .40 1.00
67 Eddie Jones .40 1.00
68 Kevin Garnett 1.00 2.50
69 Matt Geiger .25 .60
70 Vernon Maxwell .25 .60
71 Antonio Davis .25 .60
72 Dirk Nowitzki 1.25 3.00
73 Johnny Newman .25 .60
74 Maurice Taylor .25 .60
75 Steve Smith .30 .75
76 Derek Anderson .30 .75
77 Doug Christie .30 .75
78 Erick Strickland .25 .60
79 Keith Van Horn .30 .75
80 Luc Longley .30 .75
81 Alonzo Mourning .60 1.50
82 Christian Laettner .30 .75
83 Jamal Mashburn .30 .75
84 Jon Barry .25 .60
85 Patrick Ewing .50 1.25
86 Shareef Abdur-Rahim .50 1.25
87 Vitaly Potapenko .25 .60
88 Darrell Armstrong .25 .60
89 Eric Williams .25 .60
90 Jerome Williams .25 .60
91 Nick Anderson .25 .60
92 Othella Harrington .25 .60
93 Tim Hardaway .50 1.25
94 Eric Piatkowski .25 .60
95 Isaiah Rider .30 .75
96 Kendall Gill .40 1.00
97 Rasheed Wallace .50 1.25
98 Robert Pack .25 .60
99 Tracy McGrady .60 1.50
100 Allan Houston .30 .75
101 Brian Grant .25 .60
102 Dikembe Mutombo .60 1.50
103 Karl Malone .75 2.00
104 Nick Van Exel .30 .75
105 Shaquille O'Neal 1.50 4.00
106 Chris Anstey .25 .60
107 Michael Dickerson .25 .60
108 Shandon Anderson .25 .60
109 Tariq Abdul-Wahad .25 .60
110 Tim Duncan 1.00 2.50
111 Voshon Lenard .25 .60
112 Bimbo Coles .25 .60
113 Detlef Schrempf .30 .75
114 John Stockton .60 1.50
115 Kobe Bryant 3.00 8.00
116 Latrell Sprewell .50 1.25
117 Raef LaFrentz .30 .75
118 Antoine Walker .40 1.00
119 Bryon Russell .25 .60
120 Derek Fisher .30 .75
121 Jason Williams .60 1.50
122 Jerry Stackhouse .40 1.00
123 Larry Johnson .40 1.00
124 Clifford Robinson .30 .75
125 Horace Grant .30 .75
126 Malik Sealy .25 .60
127 Michael Finley .40 1.00
128 Rik Smits .30 .75
129 Dell Curry .25 .60
130 Jim Jackson .25 .60
131 Ron Mercer .30 .75
132 Scott Burrell .25 .60
133 Scottie Pippen 1.00 2.50
134 Troy Hudson .40 1.00
135 Anfernee Hardaway 1.00 2.50
136 Anthony Peeler .25 .60
137 Jalen Rose .30 .75
138 Lamond Murray .25 .60
139 Ruben Patterson .25 .60
140 Chris Webber .50 1.25
141 Glen Rice .40 1.00
142 Grant Hill .60 1.50
143 Jeff Hornacek .30 .75
144 Marcus Camby .30 .75
145 Paul Pierce .75 2.00
146 Bob Sura .25 .60
147 Jason Kidd .60 1.50
148 Reggie Miller .75 2.00
149 Terrell Brandon .25 .60
150 Vin Baker .30 .75
151 Lamar Odom RC .75 2.00
152 Steve Francis RC .75 2.00
153 Elton Brand RC .75 2.00
154 Wally Szczerbiak RC .60 1.50
155 Adrian Griffin RC .30 .75
156 Andre Miller RC .75 2.00
157 Jason Terry RC .60 1.50
158 Richard Hamilton RC 1.00 2.50
159 Ron Artest RC 1.00 2.50
160 Shawn Marion RC .75 2.00
161 James Posey RC .40 1.00
162 Greg Buckner RC .40 1.00
163 Chucky Atkins RC .30 .75
164 Corey Maggette RC .50 1.25
165 Todd MacCulloch RC .25 .60
166 Baron Davis RC 1.00 2.50
167 Trajan Langdon RC .30 .75
168 Bruno Sundov RC .40 1.00
169 Scott Padgett RC .30 .75
170 Vonteego Cummings RC .25 .60
171 Ryan Bowen RC .30 .75
172 Jonathan Bender RC .40 1.00
173 Jermaine Jackson RC .40 1.00
174 Devean George RC .40 1.00
175 Chris Herren RC .40 1.00
176 Rodney Buford RC .40 1.00
177 Laron Profit RC .40 1.00
178 Mirsad Turkcan RC .40 1.00
179 Eddie Robinson RC .40 1.00
180 Anthony Carter RC .30 .75

1999-00 Metal Emeralds
*STARS: 1.2X TO 3X BASE CARD HI
*RCs: .5X TO 1.25X BASE HI
STARS: STATED ODDS 1:4
RCs: STATED ODDS 1:8

1999-00 Metal Vince Carter Scrapbook
COMPLETE SET (10) 12.50 25.00
COMMON CARD (VC1-VC10) 1.50 4.00
STATED ODDS 1:8

1999-00 Metal Genuine Coverage
STATED ODDS 1:288
1 Vince Carter 15.00 40.00
2 Karl Malone 12.00 30.00
3 Shaquille O'Neal 25.00 60.00
4 Paul Pierce 12.00 30.00
5 John Stockton 10.00 25.00
6 Antoine Walker 6.00 15.00

1999-00 Metal Heavy Metal
COMPLETE SET (10) 8.00 20.00
STATED ODDS 1:20
HM1 Kobe Bryant 15.00 40.00
HM2 Vince Carter 2.00 5.00
HM3 Lamar Odom 1.50 4.00
HM4 Kevin Garnett 2.00 5.00
HM5 Shawn Kemp 1.25 3.00
HM6 Shareef Abdur-Rahim .75 2.00
HM7 Antonio McDyess .60 1.50
HM8 Tim Duncan 2.00 5.00
HM9 Keith Van Horn .60 1.50
HM10 Shaquille O'Neal 3.00 8.00

1999-00 Metal Platinum Portraits
COMPLETE SET (15) 6.00 15.00
STATED ODDS 1:4
PP1 Elton Brand .75 2.00
PP2 Lamar Odom .75 2.00
PP3 Steve Francis .75 2.00
PP4 Richard Hamilton 1.00 2.50
PP5 Baron Davis 1.00 2.50
PP6 Vonteego Cummings .25 .60
PP7 Corey Maggette .50 1.25
PP8 James Posey .40 1.00
PP9 Shawn Marion .75 2.00
PP10 Wally Szczerbiak .60 1.50
PP11 Jason Terry .60 1.50
PP12 Andre Miller .75 2.00
PP13 Scott Padgett .30 .75
PP14 Trajan Langdon .30 .75
PP15 Jonathan Bender .40 1.00

1999-00 Metal Rivalries
COMPLETE SET (15) 6.00 15.00
STATED ODDS 1:4
R1 A.Iverson/S.Marbury .75 2.00
R2 J.Kidd/G.Payton .50 1.25
R3 M.Bibby/J.Williams .50 1.25
R4 P.Ewing/A.Mourning .50 1.25
R5 T.Duncan/K.Garnett .75 2.00
R6 A.Hardaway/K.Bryant 2.50 6.00
R7 C.Barkley/K.Malone .75 2.00
R8 A.McDyess/S.Abdur-Rahim .30 .75
R9 V.Carter/G.Hill .75 2.00
R10 A.Walker/K.Van Horn .30 .75
R11 S.Kemp/E.Brand .60 1.50
R12 S.O'Neal/D.Robinson 1.25 3.00
R13 R.LaFrentz/D.Nowitzki 1.00 2.50
R14 S.Francis/J.Stockton .60 1.50
R15 L.Odom/S.Pippen .75 2.00

1999-00 Metal Scoring Magnets
COMPLETE SET (10) 6.00 15.00
STATED ODDS 1:20
SM1 Grant Hill 1.25 3.00
SM2 Stephon Marbury 1.00 2.50
SM3 Allen Iverson 2.00 5.00
SM4 Ray Allen 1.25 3.00
SM5 Steve Francis 1.50 4.00
SM6 Ron Mercer .60 1.50
SM7 Paul Pierce 1.50 4.00
SM8 Latrell Sprewell 1.00 2.50
SM9 Glenn Robinson .60 1.50
SM10 Eddie Jones .75 2.00

1997-98 Metal Universe
COMPLETE SET (125) 200.00 500.00
1 Charles Barkley 1.50 4.00
2 Dell Curry .50 1.25
3 Derek Fisher .60 1.50
4 Derek Harper .50 1.25
5 Avery Johnson .50 1.25
6 Steve Smith .50 1.25
7 Alonzo Mourning 1.00 2.50
8 Rod Strickland .50 1.25
9 Chris Mullin .75 2.00
10 Rony Seikaly .50 1.25
11 Vin Baker .50 1.25
12 Austin Croshere RC .50 1.25
13 Vinny Del Negro .50 1.25
14 Sherman Douglas .40 1.00
15 Priest Lauderdale .40 1.00
16 Cedric Ceballos .40 1.00
17 LaPhonso Ellis .50 1.25
18 Luc Longley .60 1.50
19 Brian Grant .50 1.25
20 Allen Iverson 2.00 5.00
21 Anthony Mason .50 1.25
22 Bryant Reeves .40 1.00
23 Michael Jordan 40.00 100.00
24 Dale Ellis .50 1.25
25 Terrell Brandon .50 1.25
26 Patrick Ewing 1.00 2.50
27 Allan Houston .60 1.50
28 Damon Stoudamire .60 1.50
29 Loy Vaught .50 1.25
30 Walt Williams .50 1.25
31 Shareef Abdur-Rahim .60 1.50
32 Mario Elie .40 1.00
33 Juwan Howard .50 1.25
34 Tom Gugliotta .50 1.25
35 Glen Rice .60 1.50
36 Isaiah Rider .50 1.25
37 Arvydas Sabonis .75 2.00
38 Derrick Coleman .60 1.50
39 Kevin Willis .50 1.25
40 Kendall Gill .50 1.25
41 John Wallace .40 1.00
42 Tracy McGrady RC 3.00 8.00
43 Travis Best .40 1.00
44 Malik Rose .40 1.00
45 Anfernee Hardaway 1.50 4.00
46 Roy Rogers .50 1.25
47 Kerry Kittles .50 1.25
48 Matt Maloney .40 1.00
49 Antonio McDyess .50 1.25
50 Shaquille O'Neal 2.00 5.00
51 George McCloud .40 1.00
52 Wesley Person .50 1.25
53 Shawn Bradley .40 1.00
54 Antonio Davis .50 1.25
55 P.J. Brown .40 1.00
56 Joe Dumars .75 2.00
57 Horace Grant .60 1.50
58 Steve Kerr .75 2.00
59 Hakeem Olajuwon 1.25 3.00
60 Tim Hardaway .75 2.00
61 Toni Kukoc .75 2.00
62 Ron Mercer RC .75 2.00
63 Gary Payton 1.00 2.50
64 Grant Hill 1.00 2.50
65 Detlef Schrempf .60 1.50
66 Tim Duncan RC 12.00 30.00
67 Shawn Kemp 1.00 2.50
68 Voshon Lenard .40 1.00
69 Othella Harrington .40 1.00
70 Hersey Hawkins .50 1.25
71 Lindsey Hunter .40 1.00
72 Antoine Walker .60 1.50
73 Jamal Mashburn .50 1.25
74 Kenny Anderson .50 1.25
75 Todd Day .40 1.00
76 Todd Fuller .40 1.00
77 Jermaine O'Neal .50 1.25
78 David Robinson 1.25 3.00
79 Erick Dampier .50 1.25
80 Keith Van Horn RC 1.00 2.50
81 Kobe Bryant 30.00 80.00
82 Chris Childs .40 1.00
83 Scottie Pippen 1.50 4.00
84 Marcus Camby .60 1.50
85 Danny Ferry .40 1.00
86 Jeff Hornacek .60 1.50
87 Bo Outlaw .40 1.00
88 Larry Johnson .75 2.00
89 Tony Delk .50 1.25
90 Stephon Marbury .75 2.00
91 Robert Pack .40 1.00
92 Chris Webber .75 2.00
93 Clyde Drexler 1.00 2.50
94 Eddie Jones .60 1.50
95 Jerry Stackhouse .60 1.50
96 Tyrone Hill .50 1.25
97 Karl Malone 1.25 3.00
98 Reggie Miller 1.25 3.00
99 Bryon Russell .40 1.00
100 Dale Davis .50 1.25
101 Steve Nash 1.50 4.00
102 Vitaly Potapenko .40 1.00
103 Nick Anderson .50 1.25
104 Ray Allen 1.25 3.00
105 Sean Elliott .50 1.25
106 Dikembe Mutombo 1.00 2.50
107 Dennis Rodman 1.50 4.00
108 Lorenzen Wright .40 1.00
109 Kevin Garnett 1.50 4.00
110 Christian Laettner .60 1.50
111 Mitch Richmond .75 2.00
112 Joe Smith .50 1.25
113 Jason Kidd 1.00 2.50
114 Glenn Robinson .60 1.50
115 Mark Price .60 1.50
116 Mark Jackson .50 1.25
117 Bobby Phills .50 1.25
118 John Starks .60 1.50
119 John Stockton 1.25 3.00
120 Mookie Blaylock .60 1.50
121 Dean Garrett .40 1.00
122 Olden Polynice .40 1.00
123 Latrell Sprewell .75 2.00
124 Checklist .15 .40
125 Checklist .15 .40

1997-98 Metal Universe Precious Metal Gems
*STARS: 200X TO 500X BASE CARD HI
*RCs: 200X TO 500X BASE HI
PRINT RUN 100 TOTAL SERIAL #'d SETS
1 Charles Barkley 4,000.00 8,000.00
2 Dell Curry 600.00 1,200.00
3 Derek Fisher 1,500.00 3,000.00
6 Steve Smith 300.00 600.00
7 Alonzo Mourning 1,000.00 2,000.00
9 Chris Mullin 150.00 400.00
11 Vin Baker 600.00 1,200.00
12 Austin Croshere 500.00 1,000.00
13 Vinny Del Negro 200.00 500.00
14 Sherman Douglas 500.00 1,000.00
15 Priest Lauderdale 200.00 500.00
16 Cedric Ceballos 300.00 600.00
17 LaPhonso Ellis 300.00 600.00
18 Luc Longley 400.00 800.00
19 Brian Grant 500.00 1,000.00
20 Allen Iverson 3,000.00 6,000.00
22 Bryant Reeves 125.00 300.00
23 Michael Jordan 150,000.00200,000.00
25 Terrell Brandon 300.00 600.00
26 Patrick Ewing 3,000.00 6,000.00
27 Allan Houston 2,000.00 4,000.00
28 Damon Stoudamire 125.00 300.00
30 Walt Williams 300.00 600.00
31 Shareef Abdur-Rahim 500.00 1,000.00
32 Mario Elie 500.00 1,000.00
33 Juwan Howard 300.00 600.00
34 Tom Gugliotta 125.00 300.00
36 Isaiah Rider 300.00 600.00
37 Arvydas Sabonis 2,000.00 4,000.00
38 Derrick Coleman 600.00 1,200.00
42 Tracy McGrady 10,000.00 15,000.00
50 Shaquille O'Neal 10,000.00 20,000.00
54 Antonio Davis 150.00 400.00
55 P.J. Brown 300.00 600.00
56 Joe Dumars 200.00 500.00
57 Horace Grant 500.00 1,000.00
58 Steve Kerr 600.00 1,200.00
59 Hakeem Olajuwon 4,000.00 8,000.00
61 Toni Kukoc 2,000.00 4,000.00
62 Ron Mercer 150.00 400.00
63 Gary Payton 3,000.00 6,000.00
64 Grant Hill 3,000.00 6,000.00
65 Detlef Schrempf 500.00 1,000.00
66 Tim Duncan 15,000.00 30,000.00
67 Shawn Kemp 3,000.00 6,000.00
68 Voshon Lenard 300.00 600.00
73 Jamal Mashburn 1,000.00 2,000.00
77 Jermaine O'Neal 1,000.00 2,000.00
78 David Robinson 3,000.00 6,000.00
80 Keith Van Horn 1,000.00 2,000.00
81 Kobe Bryant 60,000.00100,000.00
83 Scottie Pippen 4,000.00 8,000.00
86 Jeff Hornacek 400.00 800.00
88 Larry Johnson 2,000.00 4,000.00
89 Tony Delk 500.00 1,000.00
91 Robert Pack 300.00 600.00
92 Chris Webber 2,500.00 5,000.00
93 Clyde Drexler 2,000.00 4,000.00
94 Eddie Jones 300.00 600.00
95 Jerry Stackhouse 300.00 600.00
97 Karl Malone 1,500.00 3,000.00
98 Reggie Miller 3,000.00 6,000.00
99 Bryon Russell 600.00 1,200.00
100 Dale Davis 500.00 1,000.00
101 Steve Nash 2,000.00 4,000.00
102 Vitaly Potapenko 800.00 1,500.00
104 Ray Allen 600.00 1,200.00
105 Sean Elliott 300.00 600.00
106 Dikembe Mutombo 2,500.00 5,000.00
107 Dennis Rodman 5,000.00 10,000.00
109 Kevin Garnett 1,000.00 3,000.00
110 Christian Laettner 300.00 600.00
111 Mitch Richmond 1,500.00 3,000.00
112 Joe Smith 200.00 500.00
113 Jason Kidd 2,000.00 4,000.00
114 Glenn Robinson 600.00 1,200.00
115 Mark Price 400.00 800.00
116 Mark Jackson 300.00 600.00
117 Bobby Phills 300.00 600.00
118 John Starks 300.00 600.00
119 John Stockton 1,000.00 3,000.00
120 Mookie Blaylock 200.00 500.00
121 Dean Garrett 300.00 600.00
122 Olden Polynice 300.00 600.00
123 Latrell Sprewell 1,000.00 2,000.00

1997-98 Metal Universe Gold Universe
COMPLETE SET (10) 50.00 120.00
STATED ODDS 1:120 RETAIL
1 Damon Stoudamire 8.00 20.00
2 Shawn Kemp 12.00 30.00
3 John Stockton 15.00 40.00
4 Jerry Stackhouse 8.00 20.00
5 John Wallace 5.00 12.00
6 Juwan Howard 6.00 15.00
7 David Robinson 15.00 40.00
8 Gary Payton 12.00 30.00
9 Joe Smith 6.00 15.00
10 Charles Barkley 20.00 50.00

1997-98 Metal Universe Planet Metal
COMPLETE SET (15) 600.00 1,200.00
STATED ODDS 1:24 HOBBY/RETAIL
1 Michael Jordan 400.00 800.00
2 Allen Iverson 40.00 100.00
3 Kobe Bryant 125.00 300.00
4 Shaquille O'Neal 30.00 80.00
5 Stephon Marbury 12.00 30.00
6 Marcus Camby 10.00 25.00
7 Anfernee Hardaway 25.00 60.00
8 Kevin Garnett 25.00 60.00
9 Shareef Abdur-Rahim 10.00 25.00
10 Dennis Rodman 25.00 60.00
11 Grant Hill 15.00 40.00
12 Hakeem Olajuwon 20.00 50.00
13 David Robinson 20.00 50.00
14 Charles Barkley 25.00 60.00
15 Gary Payton 15.00 40.00

1997-98 Metal Universe Platinum Portraits
STATED ODDS 1:288 HOBBY/RETAIL
1 Michael Jordan 4,000.00 8,000.00
2 Allen Iverson 300.00 600.00
3 Kobe Bryant 2,000.00 4,000.00
4 Shaquille O'Neal 400.00 800.00
5 Stephon Marbury 125.00 300.00
6 Marcus Camby 60.00 150.00
7 Anfernee Hardaway 200.00 500.00
8 Kevin Garnett 200.00 500.00
9 Shareef Abdur-Rahim 60.00 150.00
10 Dennis Rodman 300.00 600.00
11 Ray Allen 150.00 400.00
12 Grant Hill 150.00 400.00
13 Kerry Kittles 60.00 150.00
14 Antoine Walker 60.00 150.00
15 Scottie Pippen 300.00 600.00

1997-98 Metal Universe Reebok Chase Bronze
COMPLETE SET (15) 2.00 5.00
*GOLD: 1.25X TO 3X BRONZE
*SILVER: .5X TO 1.25X BRONZE
ONE PER SER.1 PACK
5 Avery Johnson .30 .75
6 Steve Smith .30 .75
13 Vinny Del Negro .30 .75
16 Cedric Ceballos .30 .75
20 Allen Iverson 1.25 3.00
32 Mario Elie .25 .60
50 Shaquille O'Neal 1.25 3.00
67 Shawn Kemp .60 1.50
68 Voshon Lenard .25 .60
74 Kenny Anderson .30 .75
91 Robert Pack .25 .60
93 Clyde Drexler .60 1.50
96 Tyrone Hill .30 .75
114 Glenn Robinson .40 1.00
116 Mark Jackson .30 .75

1997-98 Metal Universe Silver Slams
COMPLETE SET (20) 15.00 40.00
STATED ODDS 1:6 HOBBY/RETAIL
1 Ray Allen 2.50 6.00
2 Kerry Kittles 1.00 2.50
3 Antoine Walker 1.25 3.00
4 Scottie Pippen 3.00 8.00
5 Damon Stoudamire 1.25 3.00
6 Shawn Kemp 2.00 5.00
7 Jerry Stackhouse 1.25 3.00
8 John Wallace .75 2.00
9 Juwan Howard 1.00 2.50
10 Gary Payton 2.00 5.00
11 Joe Smith 1.00 2.50
12 Terrell Brandon 1.00 2.50
13 Hakeem Olajuwon 2.50 6.00
14 Tom Gugliotta 1.00 2.50
15 Glen Rice 1.25 3.00
16 Charles Barkley 3.00 8.00
17 David Robinson 2.50 6.00
18 Patrick Ewing 2.00 5.00
19 Christian Laettner 1.25 3.00
20 Chris Webber 1.50 4.00

1997-98 Metal Universe Titanium
COMPLETE SET (20) 1,500.00 3,000.00
STATED ODDS 1:72 HOBBY
1 Michael Jordan 1,500.00 3,000.00
2 Allen Iverson 125.00 300.00
3 Kobe Bryant 600.00 1,200.00
4 Shaquille O'Neal 150.00 400.00
5 Stephon Marbury 30.00 80.00
6 Marcus Camby 15.00 40.00
7 Anfernee Hardaway 200.00 500.00
8 Kevin Garnett 75.00 200.00
9 Shareef Abdur-Rahim 20.00 50.00
10 Dennis Rodman 75.00 200.00
11 Ray Allen 60.00 150.00
12 Grant Hill 60.00 150.00
13 Kerry Kittles 15.00 40.00
14 Antoine Walker 20.00 50.00
15 Scottie Pippen 75.00 200.00
16 Damon Stoudamire 20.00 50.00
17 Shawn Kemp 60.00 150.00
18 Hakeem Olajuwon 60.00 150.00
19 Jerry Stackhouse 20.00 50.00
20 Juwan Howard 10.00 25.00

1998-99 Metal Universe
COMPLETE SET (125) 25.00 60.00
1 Michael Jordan 12.00 30.00
2 Mario Elie .30 .75
3 Voshon Lenard .30 .75
4 John Starks .50 1.25
5 Juwan Howard .40 1.00
6 Michael Finley .50 1.25
7 Bobby Jackson .40 1.00
8 Glenn Robinson .50 1.25
9 Antonio McDyess .40 1.00
10 Marcus Camby .40 1.00
11 Zydrunas Ilgauskas .50 1.25
12 LaPhonso Ellis .30 .75
13 Terrell Brandon .40 1.00
14 Rex Chapman .40 1.00
15 Rod Strickland .40 1.00
16 Dennis Rodman 1.25 3.00
17 Clarence Weatherspoon .30 .75
18 P.J. Brown .30 .75
19 Anfernee Hardaway 1.25 3.00
20 Dikembe Mutombo .75 2.00
21 Gary Trent .30 .75
22 Patrick Ewing .75 2.00
23 Sam Mack .30 .75
24 Scottie Pippen 1.25 3.00
25 Shaquille O'Neal 2.00 5.00
26 Donyell Marshall .30 .75
27 Bo Outlaw .30 .75
28 Isaiah Rider .40 1.00
29 Detlef Schrempf .50 1.25
30 Mark Price .50 1.25
31 Jim Jackson .30 .75
32 Eddie Jones .50 1.25
33 Allen Iverson 1.25 3.00
34 Corliss Williamson .30 .75
35 Tim Duncan 1.25 3.00
36 Ron Harper .50 1.25
37 Tony Delk .30 .75
38 Derek Fisher .40 1.00
39 Kendall Gill .40 1.00
40 Theo Ratliff .40 1.00
41 Kelvin Cato .30 .75
42 Antoine Walker .50 1.25
43 Lamond Murray .30 .75
44 Avery Johnson .40 1.00
45 John Stockton 1.00 2.50
46 David Wesley .30 .75
47 Brian Williams .30 .75
48 Elden Campbell .30 .75
49 Sam Cassell .40 1.00
50 Grant Hill .75 2.00
51 Tracy McGrady .75 2.00
52 Glen Rice .50 1.25
53 Kobe Bryant 4.00 10.00
54 Cherokee Parks .30 .75
55 John Wallace .30 .75
56 Bobby Phills .30 .75
57 Jerry Stackhouse .50 1.25
58 Lorenzen Wright .30 .75
59 Stephon Marbury .60 1.50
60 Shandon Anderson .30 .75
61 Jeff Hornacek .40 1.00
62 Joe Dumars .50 1.25
63 Tom Gugliotta .40 1.00
64 Johnny Newman .30 .75
65 Kevin Garnett 1.25 3.00
66 Clifford Robinson .30 .75
67 Dennis Scott .30 .75
68 Anthony Mason .40 1.00
69 Rodney Rogers .30 .75
70 Bryon Russell .30 .75
71 Maurice Taylor .30 .75
72 Mookie Blaylock .40 1.00
73 Shawn Bradley .30 .75
74 Matt Maloney .30 .75
75 Karl Malone 1.00 2.50
76 Larry Johnson .75 2.00
77 Calbert Cheaney .30 .75
78 Steve Smith .40 1.00
79 Toni Kukoc .50 1.25
80 Reggie Miller 1.00 2.50
81 Jayson Williams .30 .75
82 Gary Payton .75 2.00
83 George Lynch .30 .75
84 Wesley Person .30 .75
85 Charles Barkley 1.25 3.00
86 Tim Hardaway .60 1.50
87 Darrell Armstrong .30 .75
88 Rasheed Wallace .60 1.50
89 Tariq Abdul-Wahad .30 .75
90 Kenny Anderson .40 1.00
91 Chris Mullin .60 1.50
92 Keith Van Horn .50 1.25
93 Hersey Hawkins .30 .75
94 Billy Owens .30 .75
95 Ron Mercer .40 1.00
96 Rik Smits .40 1.00
97 David Robinson 1.00 2.50
98 Derek Anderson .40 1.00
99 Danny Fortson .30 .75
100 Jason Kidd .75 2.00
101 Sean Elliott .50 1.25
102 Chauncey Billups .60 1.50
103 Tyrone Hill .30 .75
104 Alan Henderson .30 .75
105 Chris Anstey .30 .75
106 Hakeem Olajuwon 1.00 2.50
107 Allan Houston .50 1.25
108 Bryant Reeves .30 .75
109 Anthony Johnson .30 .75
110 Shawn Kemp .75 2.00
111 Brevin Knight .30 .75
112 A.C. Green .40 1.00
113 Ray Allen .75 2.00
114 Tim Thomas .40 1.00

115 Walter McCarty .30 .75
116 Jalen Rose .40 1.00
117 Kerry Kittles .40 1.00
118 Vin Baker .40 1.00
119 Shareef Abdur-Rahim .50 1.25
120 Alonzo Mourning .75 2.00
121 Joe Smith .40 1.00
122 Tracy Murray .30 .75
123 Damon Stoudamire .50 1.25
124 Checklist .20 .50
125 Checklist .20 .50
NNO Grant Hill SAMPLE 1.00 2.50

1998-99 Metal Universe Precious Metal Gems

*STARS: 125X TO 300X BASE CARD HI
STATED PRINT RUN 50 SERIAL #'d SETS
1 Michael Jordan 60,000.00 100,000.00
16 Dennis Rodman 2,500.00 5,000.00
19 Anfernee Hardaway 2,500.00 5,000.00
20 Dikembe Mutombo 1,500.00 3,000.00
22 Patrick Ewing 1,500.00 3,000.00
24 Scottie Pippen 2,500.00 5,000.00
25 Shaquille O'Neal 2,500.00 5,000.00
33 Allen Iverson 2,500.00 5,000.00
35 Tim Duncan 2,500.00 5,000.00
45 John Stockton 2,500.00 5,000.00
50 Grant Hill 1,500.00 3,000.00
51 Tracy McGrady 1,500.00 3,000.00
53 Kobe Bryant 30,000.00 60,000.00
65 Kevin Garnett 2,500.00 5,000.00
75 Karl Malone 2,500.00 5,000.00
80 Reggie Miller 2,500.00 5,000.00
82 Gary Payton 1,500.00 3,000.00
85 Charles Barkley 2,500.00 5,000.00
97 David Robinson 2,500.00 5,000.00
100 Jason Kidd 1,500.00 3,000.00
106 Hakeem Olajuwon 2,500.00 5,000.00
110 Shawn Kemp 1,500.00 3,000.00
113 Ray Allen 1,500.00 3,000.00
120 Alonzo Mourning 1,500.00 3,000.00

1998-99 Metal Universe Grant Hill Blowup

1 Grant Hill 3.00 8.00

1998-99 Metal Universe Big Ups

COMPLETE SET (15) 12.00 30.00
STATED ODDS 1:18
1 Stephon Marbury 1.50 4.00
2 Shareef Abdur-Rahim 1.25 3.00
3 Scottie Pippen 3.00 8.00
4 Marcus Camby 1.00 2.50
5 Ray Allen 2.00 5.00
6 Allen Iverson 3.00 8.00
7 Kerry Kittles 1.00 2.50
8 Dennis Rodman 3.00 8.00
9 Damon Stoudamire 1.25 3.00
10 Antoine Walker 1.25 3.00
11 Anfernee Hardaway 3.00 8.00
12 Shawn Kemp 2.00 5.00
13 Juwan Howard 1.00 2.50
14 Gary Payton 2.00 5.00
15 Tim Duncan 3.00 8.00

1998-99 Metal Universe Linchpins

COMPLETE SET (10)
STATED ODDS 1:360
1 Shaquille O'Neal 300.00 600.00
2 Kobe Bryant 1,250.00 2,500.00
3 Kevin Garnett 125.00 300.00
4 Grant Hill 75.00 200.00
5 Shawn Kemp 60.00 150.00
6 Keith Van Horn 25.00 60.00
7 Antoine Walker 30.00 80.00
8 Michael Jordan 2,500.00 5,000.00
9 Gary Payton 75.00 200.00
10 Tim Duncan 125.00 300.00

1998-99 Metal Universe Neophytes

COMPLETE SET (15) 3.00 8.00
STATED ODDS 1:6
1 Antonio Daniels .30 .75
2 Bobby Jackson .40 1.00
3 Brevin Knight .30 .75
4 Chauncey Billups .60 1.50
5 Danny Fortson .30 .75
6 Derek Anderson .40 1.00
7 Jacque Vaughn .30 .75
8 Keith Van Horn .50 1.25
9 Maurice Taylor .30 .75
10 Michael Stewart .30 .75
11 Ron Mercer .40 1.00
12 Tim Thomas .40 1.00
13 Tim Duncan 1.25 3.00
14 Tracy McGrady .75 2.00
15 Zydrunas Ilgauskas .50 1.25

1998-99 Metal Universe Planet Metal

COMPLETE SET (15) 800.00 1,500.00
STATED ODDS 1:36
1 Michael Jordan 600.00 1,200.00
2 Antoine Walker 12.00 30.00
3 Scottie Pippen 30.00 80.00
4 Grant Hill 20.00 50.00
5 Dennis Rodman 50.00 120.00
6 Kobe Bryant 150.00 400.00
7 Kevin Garnett 25.00 60.00
8 Shaquille O'Neal 50.00 120.00
9 Stephon Marbury 12.00 30.00
10 Kerry Kittles 12.00 30.00
11 Anfernee Hardaway 30.00 80.00
12 Allen Iverson 40.00 100.00
13 Damon Stoudamire 12.00 30.00
14 Marcus Camby 12.00 30.00
15 Shareef Abdur-Rahim 12.00 30.00

1998-99 Metal Universe Two for Me, Zero for You

COMPLETE SET (15) 400.00 800.00
STATED ODDS 1:96
1 Kobe Bryant 80.00 200.00
2 Anfernee Hardaway 25.00 60.00
3 Allen Iverson 25.00 60.00
4 Michael Jordan 300.00 600.00
5 Stephon Marbury 12.00 30.00
6 Ron Mercer 8.00 20.00
7 Shareef Abdur-Rahim 10.00 25.00
8 Marcus Camby 8.00 20.00
9 Damon Stoudamire 10.00 25.00
10 Kevin Garnett 25.00 60.00
11 Grant Hill 15.00 40.00
12 Scottie Pippen 25.00 60.00
13 Keith Van Horn 10.00 25.00
14 Dennis Rodman 25.00 60.00
15 Shaquille O'Neal 40.00 100.00

1997-98 Metal Universe Championship Promo Sheet

1 Grant Hill
Kobe Bryant
Allen Iverson
Keith Van Horn
Kevin Garnett
Tim Duncan 1.25 3.00

1997-98 Metal Universe Championship

COMPLETE SET (100) 75.00 200.00
1 Shaquille O'Neal 1.25 3.00
2 Chris Mills .25 .60
3 Tariq Abdul-Wahad RC .30 .75
4 Adonal Foyle RC .30 .75
5 Kendall Gill .30 .75
6 Vin Baker .30 .75
7 Chauncey Billups RC 1.25 3.00
8 Bobby Jackson RC .50 1.25
9 Keith Van Horn RC .60 1.50
10 Avery Johnson .30 .75
11 Juwan Howard .30 .75
12 Steve Smith .30 .75
13 Alonzo Mourning .60 1.50
14 Anfernee Hardaway 1.00 2.50
15 Sean Elliott .30 .75
16 Danny Fortson RC .40 1.00
17 John Stockton .75 2.00
18 John Thomas RC .25 .60
19 Lorenzen Wright .25 .60
20 Mark Price .40 1.00
21 Rasheed Wallace .50 1.25
22 Ray Allen .75 2.00
23 Michael Jordan 40.00 100.00
24 John Wallace .25 .60
25 Bryant Reeves .25 .60
26 Allen Iverson 1.25 3.00
27 Antoine Walker .40 1.00
28 Terrell Brandon .30 .75
29 Damon Stoudamire .40 1.00
30 Antonio Daniels RC .40 1.00
31 Corey Beck .40 1.00
32 Tyrone Hill .30 .75
33 Grant Hill .60 1.50
34 Tim Thomas RC .50 1.25
35 Clifford Robinson .30 .75
36 Tracy McGrady RC 2.00 5.00
37 Chris Webber .50 1.25
38 Austin Croshere RC .30 .75
39 Reggie Miller .75 2.00
40 Derek Anderson RC .40 1.00
41 Kevin Garnett 1.00 2.50
42 Kevin Johnson .40 1.00
43 Antonio McDyess .40 1.00
44 Brevin Knight RC .40 1.00
45 Charles Barkley 1.00 2.50
46 Tom Gugliotta .30 .75
47 Jason Kidd .60 1.50
48 Marcus Camby .40 1.00
49 God Shammgod RC .40 1.00
50 Wesley Person .30 .75
51 Clyde Drexler .60 1.50
52 Paul Grant RC .25 .60
53 Rod Strickland .30 .75
54 Tony Delk .30 .75
55 Stephon Marbury .50 1.25
56 Detlef Schrempf .30 .75
57 Joe Smith .30 .75
58 Sam Cassell .30 .75
59 Gary Payton .60 1.50
60 Chris Crawford RC .40 1.00
61 Hakeem Olajuwon .75 2.00
62 Dennis Rodman 1.00 2.50
63 Eddie Jones .40 1.00
64 Mitch Richmond .40 1.00
65 David Wesley .30 .75
66 Tony Battie RC .40 1.00
67 Isaac Austin .25 .60
68 Isaiah Rider .30 .75
69 Jacque Vaughn RC .30 .75
70 Tim Hardaway .50 1.25
71 Darrell Armstrong .25 .60
72 Tim Duncan RC 2.50 6.00
73 Glen Rice .40 1.00
74 Bubba Wells RC .25 .60
75 Maurice Taylor RC .30 .75
76 Kelvin Cato RC .30 .75
77 Shareef Abdur-Rahim .50 1.25
78 Shawn Kemp .60 1.50
79 Michael Finley .40 1.00
80 Chris Mullin .50 1.25
81 Ron Mercer RC .50 1.25
82 Brian Williams .30 .75
83 Kerry Kittles .30 .75
84 David Robinson .75 2.00
85 Scottie Pippen 1.00 2.50
86 Kobe Bryant 4.00 10.00
87 Anthony Johnson RC .40 1.00
88 Karl Malone .75 2.00
89 Mookie Blaylock .40 1.00
90 Joe Dumars .60 1.50
91 Patrick Ewing .60 1.50
92 Bobby Phills .30 .75
93 Dennis Scott .30 .75
94 Rodney Rogers .30 .75
95 Jim Jackson .30 .75
96 Kenny Anderson .30 .75
97 Jerry Stackhouse .40 1.00
98 Larry Johnson .50 1.25
99 Checklist .15 .40
100 Checklist .15 .40

1997-98 Metal Universe Championship Precious Metal Gems

*STARS:60X TO 150X BASE CARD HI
*RCs: 30X TO 80X BASE HI
STATED PRINT RUN 50 SERIAL #'d SETS
1 Shaquille O'Neal 500.00 1,000.00
9 Keith Van Horn 75.00 200.00
12 Steve Smith 200.00 500.00
13 Alonzo Mourning 400.00 800.00
14 Anfernee Hardaway 800.00 1,500.00
17 John Stockton 150.00 400.00
21 Rasheed Wallace 200.00 500.00
22 Ray Allen 200.00 500.00
23 Michael Jordan 60,000.00 100,000.00
26 Allen Iverson 2,000.00 4,000.00
29 Damon Stoudamire 200.00 500.00
33 Grant Hill 1,000.00 3,000.00
36 Tracy McGrady 1,000.00 2,000.00
37 Chris Webber 125.00 300.00
39 Reggie Miller 500.00 1,000.00
41 Kevin Garnett 500.00 1,000.00
42 Kevin Johnson 150.00 400.00
45 Charles Barkley 1,000.00 3,000.00
47 Jason Kidd 100.00 250.00
51 Clyde Drexler 150.00 400.00
56 Detlef Schrempf 125.00 300.00
61 Hakeem Olajuwon 500.00 1,000.00
62 Dennis Rodman 500.00 1,000.00
70 Tim Hardaway 150.00 400.00
72 Tim Duncan 5,000.00 8,000.00
78 Shawn Kemp 150.00 400.00
79 Michael Finley 150.00 400.00
80 Chris Mullin 100.00 250.00
84 David Robinson 1,500.00 3,000.00
85 Scottie Pippen 1,500.00 3,000.00
86 Kobe Bryant 15,000.00 25,000.00
88 Karl Malone 300.00 600.00
90 Joe Dumars 150.00 400.00
91 Patrick Ewing 400.00 800.00
97 Jerry Stackhouse 150.00 400.00

1997-98 Metal Universe Championship All-Millenium Team

COMPLETE SET (20) 30.00 80.00
STATED ODDS 1:6
1 Stephon Marbury 1.00 2.50
2 Shareef Abdur-Rahim .75 2.00
3 Karl Malone 1.50 4.00
4 Scottie Pippen 2.00 5.00
5 Michael Jordan 30.00 80.00
6 Marcus Camby .75 2.00
7 Kobe Bryant 15.00 40.00
8 Allen Iverson 2.50 6.00
9 Kerry Kittles .60 1.50
10 Ray Allen 1.50 4.00
11 Dennis Rodman 2.00 5.00
12 Damon Stoudamire .75 2.00
13 Antoine Walker .75 2.00
14 Anfernee Hardaway 2.00 5.00
15 Hakeem Olajuwon 1.50 4.00
16 Shawn Kemp 1.25 3.00
17 Antonio Daniels .75 2.00
18 Juwan Howard .60 1.50
19 Gary Payton 1.25 3.00
20 Tim Duncan 5.00 12.00

1997-98 Metal Universe Championship Championship Galaxy

COMPLETE SET (15) 1,000.00 2,000.00
STATED ODDS 1:192
1 Michael Jordan 1,500.00 3,000.00
2 Allen Iverson 125.00 300.00
3 Kobe Bryant UER 1,000.00 2,000.00
4 Shaquille O'Neal 125.00 300.00
5 Stephon Marbury 20.00 50.00
6 Marcus Camby 15.00 40.00
7 Anfernee Hardaway 125.00 300.00
8 Kevin Garnett 100.00 250.00
9 Shareef Abdur-Rahim 20.00 50.00
10 Dennis Rodman 100.00 250.00
11 Grant Hill 75.00 200.00
12 Kerry Kittles 15.00 40.00
13 Antoine Walker 15.00 40.00
14 Scottie Pippen 100.00 250.00
15 Damon Stoudamire 15.00 40.00

1997-98 Metal Universe Championship Future Champions

COMPLETE SET (15) 10.00 25.00
STATED ODDS 1:18
1 Tim Duncan 4.00 10.00
2 Tony Battie .60 1.50
3 Keith Van Horn 1.00 2.50
4 Antonio Daniels .60 1.50
5 Chauncey Billups 2.00 5.00
6 Ron Mercer .75 2.00
7 Tracy McGrady 3.00 8.00
8 Danny Fortson .60 1.50
9 Brevin Knight .60 1.50
10 Derek Anderson .60 1.50
11 Bobby Jackson .75 2.00
12 Jacque Vaughn .50 1.25
13 Tim Thomas .75 2.00
14 Austin Croshere .50 1.25
15 Kelvin Cato .50 1.25

1997-98 Metal Universe Championship Hardware

COMPLETE SET (15) 1,000.00 3,000.00
STATED ODDS 1:360
1 Stephon Marbury 15.00 40.00
2 Shareef Abdur-Rahim 30.00 80.00
3 Shaquille O'Neal 60.00 150.00
4 Scottie Pippen 60.00 150.00
5 Michael Jordan 1,500.00 3,000.00
6 Marcus Camby 10.00 25.00
7 Kobe Bryant 500.00 1,000.00
8 Kevin Garnett 60.00 150.00
9 Kerry Kittles 8.00 20.00
10 Grant Hill 30.00 80.00
11 Dennis Rodman 75.00 200.00
12 Tim Duncan 60.00 150.00
13 Antonio Daniels 6.00 15.00
14 Anfernee Hardaway 60.00 150.00
15 Allen Iverson 60.00 150.00

1997-98 Metal Universe Championship Trophy Case

COMPLETE SET (10) 40.00 100.00
STATED ODDS 1:96
1 Kevin Garnett 10.00 25.00
2 Grant Hill 6.00 15.00
3 Damon Stoudamire 4.00 10.00
4 Shaquille O'Neal 12.00 30.00
5 Ray Allen 8.00 20.00
6 Gary Payton 6.00 15.00
7 Shawn Kemp 6.00 15.00
8 Hakeem Olajuwon 8.00 20.00
9 John Stockton 8.00 20.00
10 Antoine Walker 4.00 10.00

1994 Metallic Impressions

COMPLETE SET (20) 15.00 40.00
1 Hakeem Olajuwon 1.00 2.50
2 Hakeem Olajuwon 1.00 2.50
3 Hakeem Olajuwon 1.00 2.50
4 Hakeem Olajuwon 1.00 2.50
5 Patrick Ewing 1.00 2.50
6 Patrick Ewing 1.00 2.50
7 Patrick Ewing 1.00 2.50
8 Patrick Ewing 1.00 2.50
9 Alonzo Mourning 1.00 2.50
10 Alonzo Mourning 1.00 2.50
11 Alonzo Mourning 1.00 2.50
12 Alonzo Mourning 1.00 2.50
13 Dikembe Mutombo .75 2.00
14 Dikembe Mutombo .75 2.00
15 Dikembe Mutombo .75 2.00
16 Dikembe Mutombo .75 2.00
17 Shaquille O'Neal 2.50 6.00
18 Shaquille O'Neal 2.50 6.00
19 Shaquille O'Neal 2.50 6.00
20 Shaquille O'Neal 2.50 6.00

1997 Mexico Wonder Bread

COMPLETE SET (40) 125.00 250.00
1 Dikembe Mutombo 4.00 10.00
2 Mookie Blaylock 3.00 8.00
3 Dino Radja 2.50 6.00
4 Glen Rice 4.00 10.00
5 Toni Kukoc 4.00 10.00
6 Luc Longley 2.50 6.00
7 Terrell Brandon 2.50 6.00
8 A.C. Green 3.00 8.00
9 Antonio McDyess 3.00 8.00
10 Otis Thorpe 2.50 6.00
11 Joe Dumars 4.00 10.00
12 Chris Mullin 4.00 10.00
13 Hakeem Olajuwon 8.00 20.00
14 Charles Barkley 6.00 15.00
15 Rik Smits 3.00 8.00
16 Brent Barry 3.00 8.00
17 Eddie Jones 4.00 10.00
18 Elden Campbell 2.50 6.00
19 Alonzo Mourning 6.00 15.00
20 Tim Hardaway 4.00 10.00
21 Vin Baker 3.00 8.00
22 Tom Gugliotta 2.50 6.00
23 Kevin Garnett 8.00 20.00
24 Jayson Williams 2.50 6.00
25 Allan Houston 3.00 8.00
26 Anfernee Hardaway 10.00 25.00
27 Jerry Stackhouse 4.00 10.00
28 Allen Iverson 10.00 25.00
29 Cedric Ceballos 2.50 6.00
30 Arvydas Sabonis 3.00 8.00
31 Mitch Richmond 5.00 12.00
32 David Robinson 8.00 20.00
33 Avery Johnson 3.00 8.00
34 Gary Payton 6.00 15.00
35 Shawn Kemp 6.00 15.00
36 Damon Stoudamire 5.00 12.00
37 Marcus Camby 4.00 10.00
38 Karl Malone 8.00 20.00
39 Shareef Abdur-Rahim 4.00 10.00
40 Chris Webber 4.00 10.00

1984-85 Miller Lite/NBA All-Star Charity Classic

COMPLETE SET (6) 10.00 25.00
1 Connie Hawkins 2.50 6.00
2 Pete Maravich 8.00 20.00
3 Calvin Murphy 1.50 4.00
4 Nate Thurmond 1.50 4.00
5 Paul Westphal 1.50 4.00
6 Jo Jo White 1.50 4.00

2012-13 Momentum

1 Devin Harris .75 2.00
2 Al Horford 1.25 3.00
3 Kyle Korver 1.00 2.50
4 Josh Smith .75 2.00
5 Jeff Teague .75 2.00
6 John Jenkins RC 1.00 2.50
7 Mike Scott RC 1.25 3.00
8 Pete Maravich 2.50 6.00
9 Dominique Wilkins 1.50 4.00
10 Kevin Garnett 3.00 8.00
11 Jeff Green .75 2.00
12 Paul Pierce 2.00 5.00
13 Rajon Rondo 1.50 4.00
14 Brandon Bass .75 2.00
15 Jason Terry 1.00 2.50
16 Jared Sullinger RC 1.00 2.50
17 Larry Bird 4.00 10.00
18 John Havlicek 2.50 6.00
19 Bill Russell 4.00 10.00
20 Deron Williams 1.00 2.50
21 Joe Johnson 1.00 2.50
22 Brook Lopez 1.00 2.50
23 MarShon Brooks RC 1.00 2.50
24 Gerald Wallace 1.00 2.50
25 Kris Humphries .75 2.00
26 Mirza Teletovic RC 1.25 3.00
27 Tyshawn Taylor RC 1.00 2.50
28 Drazen Petrovic 1.25 3.00
29 Gerald Henderson .75 2.00
30 Michael Kidd-Gilchrist RC 1.25 3.00
31 Kemba Walker RC 4.00 10.00
32 Byron Mullens .75 2.00
33 Ramon Sessions .75 2.00
34 Bismack Biyombo RC 1.25 3.00
35 Carlos Boozer 1.00 2.50
36 Luol Deng 1.00 2.50
37 Joakim Noah 1.00 2.50
38 Derrick Rose 2.00 5.00
39 Richard Hamilton 1.25 3.00
40 Marquis Teague RC 1.00 2.50
41 Jimmy Butler RC 10.00 25.00
42 Jerry Sloan 1.25 3.00
43 Scottie Pippen 3.00 8.00
44 Reggie Theus 1.00 2.50
45 Kyrie Irving RC 10.00 25.00
46 Anderson Varejao .75 2.00
47 Alonzo Gee .75 2.00
48 C.J. Miles .75 2.00
49 Tristan Thompson RC 1.50 4.00
50 Dion Waiters RC 1.25 3.00
51 Tyler Zeller RC 1.00 2.50
52 Mark Price 1.25 3.00
53 Vince Carter 2.50 6.00
54 Chris Kaman 1.00 2.50
55 O.J. Mayo .75 2.00
56 Dirk Nowitzki 3.00 8.00
57 Darren Collison .75 2.00
58 Bernard James RC 1.00 2.50
59 Jae Crowder RC 2.00 5.00
60 Shawn Marion 1.25 3.00
61 Rolando Blackman 1.00 2.50
62 Michael Finley 1.25 3.00
63 Danilo Gallinari .75 2.00
64 Andre Iguodala 1.25 3.00
65 Ty Lawson .75 2.00
66 Kenneth Faried RC 1.25 3.00
67 Kosta Koufos .75 2.00
68 Evan Fournier RC 1.50 4.00
69 Quincy Miller RC 1.00 2.50
70 Corey Brewer .75 2.00
71 Fat Lever 1.00 2.50
72 Dan Issel 1.25 3.00
73 Tayshaun Prince 1.25 3.00
74 Brandon Knight RC 1.25 3.00
75 Greg Monroe .75 2.00
76 Jason Maxiell .75 2.00
77 Andre Drummond RC 2.50 6.00
78 Kim English RC 1.00 2.50
79 Kyle Singler RC 1.00 2.50
80 Vinnie Johnson 1.25 3.00
81 Dave Bing 1.25 3.00
82 Isiah Thomas 2.50 6.00
83 Stephen Curry 10.00 25.00
84 Klay Thompson RC 10.00 25.00
85 David Lee .75 2.00
86 Jarrett Jack 1.00 2.50
87 Harrison Barnes RC 2.00 5.00
88 Festus Ezeli RC 1.00 2.50
89 Draymond Green RC 6.00 15.00
90 Chris Mullin 1.50 4.00
91 Tim Hardaway 1.50 4.00
92 Sleepy Floyd .75 2.00
93 Jeremy Lin 2.00 5.00
94 James Harden 2.50 6.00
95 Chandler Parsons RC 1.25 3.00
96 Patrick Patterson .75 2.00
97 Omer Asik .75 2.00
98 Terrence Jones RC 1.00 2.50
99 Marcus Morris RC 1.50 4.00
100 Clyde Drexler 2.00 5.00
101 Hakeem Olajuwon 2.50 6.00
102 Paul George 2.00 5.00
103 Roy Hibbert 1.00 2.50
104 George Hill 1.00 2.50
105 David West 1.00 2.50
106 Tyler Hansbrough .75 2.00
107 Ben Hansbrough RC 1.00 2.50
108 Miles Plumlee RC 1.00 2.50
109 Lance Stephenson 1.00 2.50
110 Detlef Schrempf 1.25 3.00
111 Clark Kellogg 1.25 3.00
112 Blake Griffin 2.50 6.00
113 Chris Paul 2.50 6.00
114 DeAndre Jordan 1.00 2.50
115 Jamal Crawford 1.25 3.00
116 Eric Bledsoe 1.00 2.50
117 Caron Butler 1.00 2.50
118 Grant Hill 2.00 5.00
119 Chauncey Billups 1.50 4.00
120 Danny Manning 1.00 2.50
121 Bob McAdoo 1.00 2.50
122 Kobe Bryant 10.00 25.00
123 Steve Nash 2.50 6.00
124 Dwight Howard 1.50 4.00
125 Pau Gasol 2.00 5.00
126 Antawn Jamison 1.00 2.50
127 Darius Johnson-Odom RC 1.00 2.50
128 Robert Sacre RC 1.00 2.50
129 Jerry West 2.50 6.00
130 Elgin Baylor 3.00 8.00
131 A.C. Green 1.25 3.00
132 Gail Goodrich 1.00 2.50
133 Kareem Abdul-Jabbar 4.00 10.00
134 Magic Johnson 4.00 10.00
135 Wilt Chamberlain 4.00 10.00
136 Tony Allen .75 2.00
137 Mike Conley 1.00 2.50
138 Marc Gasol 1.25 3.00
139 Rudy Gay 1.25 3.00
140 Zach Randolph 1.25 3.00
141 Quincy Pondexter .75 2.00
142 Marreese Speights .75 2.00
143 Darrell Arthur .75 2.00
144 Tony Wroten RC 1.00 2.50
145 LeBron James 10.00 25.00
146 Dwyane Wade 2.50 6.00
147 Chris Bosh 1.50 4.00
148 Ray Allen 2.00 5.00
149 Shane Battier 1.00 2.50
150 Mario Chalmers 1.00 2.50
151 Rashard Lewis 1.25 3.00
152 Norris Cole RC 1.00 2.50
153 Udonis Haslem 1.00 2.50
154 Mike Miller 1.00 2.50
155 Alonzo Mourning 2.00 5.00
156 Mike Dunleavy .75 2.00
157 Monta Ellis 1.00 2.50
158 Brandon Jennings .75 2.00
159 Ersan Ilyasova .75 2.00
160 Ekpe Udoh .75 2.00
161 John Henson RC 1.25 3.00
162 Doron Lamb RC 1.00 2.50
163 Quinn Buckner .75 2.00
164 Bob Lanier 1.00 2.50
165 Oscar Robertson 2.50 6.00
166 Kevin Love 1.25 3.00
167 Ricky Rubio 1.00 2.50
168 Andrei Kirilenko 1.00 2.50
169 Nikola Pekovic .75 2.00
170 Luke Ridnour 1.00 2.50
171 Chase Budinger .75 2.00
172 Derrick Williams RC 1.00 2.50
173 Alexey Shved RC 1.00 2.50
174 Malcolm Lee RC 1.00 2.50
175 Al-Farouq Aminu .75 2.00
176 Ryan Anderson .75 2.00
177 Anthony Davis RC 12.00 30.00
178 Austin Rivers RC 1.50 4.00
179 Brian Roberts RC 1.00 2.50
180 Darius Miller RC 1.25 3.00
181 Eric Gordon 1.00 2.50
182 Greivis Vasquez .75 2.00
183 Robin Lopez .75 2.00
184 Dell Curry .75 2.00
185 Carmelo Anthony 2.00 5.00
186 Amar'e Stoudemire 1.25 3.00
187 Tyson Chandler 1.00 2.50
188 Raymond Felton .75 2.00
189 J.R. Smith 1.25 3.00
190 Jason Kidd 2.00 5.00
191 Steve Novak .75 2.00
192 Chris Copeland RC 1.00 2.50
193 Pablo Prigioni RC 1.00 2.50
194 Dave DeBusschere 1.25 3.00
195 Patrick Ewing 2.00 5.00
196 Walt Frazier 2.00 5.00
197 Allan Houston 1.00 2.50
198 Phil Jackson 1.50 4.00
199 Willis Reed 2.00 5.00
200 Kevin Durant 5.00 12.00
201 Russell Westbrook 2.00 5.00
202 Serge Ibaka 1.00 2.50
203 Kevin Martin 1.00 2.50
204 Kendrick Perkins .75 2.00
205 Thabo Sefolosha .75 2.00
206 Nick Collison .75 2.00
207 Jeremy Lamb RC 1.50 4.00
208 Perry Jones RC 1.00 2.50
209 Shawn Kemp 2.00 5.00
210 Gary Payton 1.50 4.00
211 Jameer Nelson .75 2.00
212 J.J. Redick 1.25 3.00
213 E'Twaun Moore RC 1.25 3.00
214 Nikola Vucevic RC 4.00 10.00
215 Maurice Harkless RC 1.25 3.00
216 Andrew Nicholson RC 1.00 2.50
217 DeQuan Jones RC 1.00 2.50
218 Kyle O'Quinn RC 1.25 3.00
219 Arron Afflalo .75 2.00
220 Anfernee Hardaway 3.00 8.00
221 Jrue Holiday 1.50 4.00
222 Jason Richardson 1.25 3.00
223 Evan Turner .75 2.00
224 Thaddeus Young .75 2.00
225 Andrew Bynum .75 2.00
226 Arnett Moultrie RC 1.00 2.50
227 Maalik Wayns RC 1.25 3.00
228 Hal Greer 1.50 4.00
229 Allen Iverson 2.00 5.00
230 Moses Malone 2.00 5.00
231 Julius Erving 3.00 8.00
232 Goran Dragic 1.25 3.00
233 Shannon Brown .75 2.00
234 Luis Scola 1.00 2.50
235 Marcin Gortat .75 2.00
236 Jared Dudley .75 2.00
237 Michael Beasley .75 2.00
238 Markieff Morris RC 1.50 4.00
239 Kendall Marshall RC 1.00 2.50
240 Luke Zeller RC 1.00 2.50
241 Kevin Johnson 1.25 3.00
242 Dan Majerle 1.00 2.50
243 LaMarcus Aldridge 1.25 3.00
244 Nicolas Batum 1.00 2.50
245 Wesley Matthews .75 2.00
246 J.J. Hickson .75 2.00
247 Damian Lillard RC 8.00 20.00
248 Meyers Leonard RC 1.25 3.00
249 Will Barton RC 2.00 5.00
250 Joel Freeland .75 2.00
251 Victor Claver RC 1.00 2.50
252 Bill Walton 2.00 5.00
253 DeMarcus Cousins 1.00 2.50
254 Tyreke Evans 1.00 2.50
255 Isaiah Thomas RC 2.00 5.00
256 Marcus Thornton .75 2.00
257 Jason Thompson .75 2.00
258 Jimmer Fredette RC 1.50 4.00
259 Thomas Robinson RC 1.00 2.50
260 Nate Archibald 1.50 4.00
261 Tim Duncan 3.00 8.00
262 Tony Parker 2.00 5.00
263 Manu Ginobili 2.50 6.00
264 Gary Neal .75 2.00
265 Kawhi Leonard RC 12.00 30.00
266 Danny Green 1.00 2.50
267 Tiago Splitter .75 2.00
268 DeJuan Blair .75 2.00
269 Stephen Jackson 1.00 2.50
270 Cory Joseph RC 1.25 3.00
271 Nando De Colo RC 1.00 2.50
272 George Gervin 2.00 5.00
273 David Robinson 2.00 5.00
274 Andrea Bargnani .75 2.00
275 Jose Calderon .75 2.00
276 DeMar DeRozan 1.50 4.00
277 Kyle Lowry 1.25 3.00
278 Landry Fields .75 2.00
279 Jonas Valanciunas RC 2.00 5.00
280 Terrence Ross RC 2.50 6.00
281 Quincy Acy RC 1.00 2.50
282 Ed Davis .75 2.00
283 Al Jefferson .75 2.00
284 Paul Millsap 1.00 2.50
285 Mo Williams 1.00 2.50
286 Gordon Hayward 1.25 3.00
287 Randy Foye .75 2.00
288 Derrick Favors 1.00 2.50
289 Enes Kanter RC 1.50 4.00
290 Alec Burks RC 1.50 4.00
291 Karl Malone 2.00 5.00
292 John Stockton 2.50 6.00
293 John Wall 1.50 4.00
294 Wes Unseld 1.50 4.00
295 Jordan Crawford .75 2.00
296 Trevor Ariza .75 2.00
297 Chris Singleton RC 1.00 2.50
298 Bradley Beal RC 8.00 20.00
299 Nene 1.00 2.50
300 Elvin Hayes 1.50 4.00

2012-13 Momentum Drive

*DRIVE VET: 1X TO 2.5X BASIC VET
*DRIVE RC: .75X TO 2X BASIC RC
STATED PRINT RUN 49 SER.#'d SETS

2012-13 Momentum Force

*FORCE VET: 1.2X TO 3X BASIC VET
*FORCE RC: 1X TO 2.5X BASIC RC
STATED PRINT RUN 25 SER.#'d SETS
8 Pete Maravich 15.00 40.00
247 Damian Lillard 30.00 80.00
265 Kawhi Leonard 75.00 200.00

2012-13 Momentum Autographs

PRINT RUNS B/WN 15-199 COPIES PER
NO PRICING ON QTY 15 OR LESS
EXCHANGE DEADLINE 11/15/2014
1 Kevin Durant/149 125.00 300.00
5 Cedric Maxwell/199 3.00 8.00
6 Kenny Anderson/199 4.00 10.00
9 Mark Price/199 10.00 25.00
10 Eddie Johnson/199 3.00 8.00
11 James Worthy/25 20.00 50.00
13 Rashard Lewis/199 5.00 12.00
14 Tiago Splitter/99 3.00 8.00
15 Greivis Vasquez/199 3.00 8.00
16 Larry Johnson/199 12.00 30.00
18 Dominique Wilkins/35 12.00 30.00
20 Steve Smith/199 4.00 10.00
22 Alonzo Mourning/25 40.00 100.00
27 Chris Mullin/25 10.00 25.00
28 Courtney Lee/199 3.00 8.00
29 Jamaal Tinsley/199 3.00 8.00
31 Kobe Bryant/49 1,000.00 2,000.00
33 Dikembe Mutombo/35 10.00 25.00
34 David Robinson/49 40.00 100.00
35 Jeremy Lamb/25 12.00 30.00
39 Ed Davis/199 3.00 8.00
41 Blake Griffin/99 EXCH 5.00 12.00
42 Larry Bird/49 125.00 300.00
43 Marcus Camby/199 8.00 20.00
49 Rick Mahorn/199 3.00 8.00
51 John Paxson/199 4.00 10.00
55 Dwyane Wade/35 50.00 120.00
56 Muggsy Bogues/199 10.00 25.00
60 Hakeem Olajuwon/35 40.00 100.00
61 Jim Jackson/199 4.00 10.00
62 David Thompson/25 5.00 12.00
63 Ersan Ilyasova/199 3.00 8.00
65 Dennis Scott/199 3.00 8.00
66 Kareem Abdul-Jabbar/99 125.00 300.00
68 Deron Williams/35 10.00 25.00
70 Grant Hill/49 20.00 50.00
71 Cazzie Russell/199 4.00 10.00
77 Julius Erving/49 60.00 150.00
78 Anthony Mason/199 8.00 20.00
81 Vince Carter/25 50.00 120.00
82 Scottie Pippen/25 75.00 200.00
84 J.J. Hickson/149 3.00 8.00
85 Michael Cooper/199 5.00 12.00
88 Gordon Hayward/99 5.00 12.00
89 Brandon Rush/199 3.00 8.00
91 Magic Johnson/49 125.00 300.00
93 Byron Mullens/99 3.00 8.00
96 Lance Stephenson/199 4.00 10.00
98 Steve Francis/25 6.00 15.00
100 Bruce Bowen/199 4.00 10.00

2012-13 Momentum Autographs Drive

*DRIVE 49: .5X TO 1.2X BASIC AUTO
*DRIVE 25: .6X TO 1.5X BASIC AUTO
PRINT RUNS B/WN 10-49 COPIES PER
NO PRICING ON QTY 15 OR LESS
EXCHANGE DEADLINE 11/15/2014

2012-13 Momentum Autographs Force

*FORCE: .6X TO 1.5X BASIC AUTO
PRINT RUNS B/WN 5-25 COPIES PER
NO PRICING ON QTY 10 OR LESS
EXCHANGE DEADLINE 11/15/2014

2012-13 Momentum Momentous Rookies Autographs

EXCHANGE DEADLINE 11/15/2014
1 Kawhi Leonard 125.00 300.00
2 Jimmer Fredette 5.00 12.00
3 MarShon Brooks 3.00 8.00
4 Alec Burks 5.00 12.00
5 E'Twaun Moore 4.00 10.00
6 Bradley Beal 25.00 60.00
7 Kyle Singler 3.00 8.00
8 Darius Morris 4.00 10.00
9 Jae Crowder 6.00 15.00
10 Nolan Smith 3.00 8.00
11 Trey Thompkins 3.00 8.00
12 Terrence Jones 3.00 8.00
13 Kemba Walker 12.00 30.00
14 Jimmy Butler 40.00 100.00
15 Meyers Leonard 4.00 10.00
16 Andre Drummond 8.00 20.00
17 Evan Fournier 5.00 12.00
18 Brandon Knight 4.00 10.00
19 Kyrie Irving 50.00 120.00
20 DeAndre Liggins 3.00 8.00
21 Jan Vesely 3.00 8.00
22 Norris Cole 3.00 8.00
23 Tristan Thompson 5.00 12.00
24 Terrence Ross 8.00 20.00
25 Kendall Marshall 3.00 8.00
26 John Henson 4.00 10.00
27 Michael Kidd-Gilchrist 4.00 10.00
28 Andrew Nicholson 4.00 10.00
29 Festus Ezeli 3.00 8.00
30 Chandler Parsons EXCH 4.00 10.00
31 Lance Thomas 3.00 8.00
32 DeQuan Jones 3.00 8.00
33 Jared Cunningham 3.00 8.00
34 Orlando Johnson 3.00 8.00
35 Ivan Johnson 3.00 8.00
36 Thomas Robinson EXCH 3.00 8.00
37 Kenneth Faried 4.00 10.00
38 John Jenkins 3.00 8.00
39 Jon Leuer 3.00 8.00

40 Anthony Davis 125.00 300.00
41 Greg Stiemsma 3.00 8.00
42 Charles Jenkins 3.00 8.00
43 Lavoy Allen 3.00 8.00
44 Derrick Williams 3.00 8.00
45 Jared Sullinger 3.00 8.00
46 Kevin Jones 3.00 8.00
47 Tyler Zeller 3.00 8.00
48 Tobias Harris 10.00 25.00
49 Marquis Teague 3.00 8.00
50 Darius Miller 4.00 10.00
51 Miles Plumlee 3.00 8.00
52 Arnett Moultrie 3.00 8.00
53 Harrison Barnes 6.00 15.00
54 Chris Copeland 3.00 8.00
55 Malcolm Lee 3.00 8.00
56 Dion Waiters 4.00 10.00
57 Jeff Taylor 3.00 8.00
58 Quincy Acy 3.00 8.00
59 Tyshawn Taylor 3.00 8.00
60 Jeremy Tyler 3.00 8.00
61 Nikola Vucevic 12.00 30.00
62 Jonas Valanciunas 6.00 15.00
63 Maurice Harkless 4.00 10.00
64 Austin Rivers 5.00 12.00
65 Iman Shumpert 4.00 10.00
66 Chris Singleton 3.00 8.00
67 Marcus Morris 5.00 12.00
68 Doron Lamb 3.00 8.00
69 Kent Bazemore 5.00 12.00
70 Reggie Jackson 5.00 12.00
71 Will Barton 6.00 15.00
72 Tornike Shengelia 3.00 8.00
73 Bismack Biyombo 4.00 10.00
74 Ben Hansbrough 3.00 8.00
75 Nando De Colo 3.00 8.00
76 Bernard James 3.00 8.00
77 Isaiah Thomas 6.00 15.00
78 Cory Joseph 4.00 10.00
79 Markieff Morris 5.00 12.00
80 Draymond Green 25.00 60.00
81 Jeremy Pargo 3.00 8.00
82 Robert Sacre 3.00 8.00
83 Jordan Hamilton 3.00 8.00
84 Enes Kanter 5.00 12.00
85 Josh Selby 3.00 8.00

2012-13 Momentum Momentous Rookies Autographs Blue

*BLUE: .5X TO 1.2X BASIC
PRINT RUNS B/WN 48-49 COPIES PER
EXCHANGE DEADLINE 11/15/2014

2012-13 Momentum Monumental Marks

PRINT RUNS B/WN 15-149 COPIES PER
NO PRICING ON QTY 15 OR LESS
EXCHANGE DEADLINE 11/15/2014
3 C.J. Watson/49 3.00 8.00
4 Jerryd Bayless/25 3.00 8.00
5 Luc Longley/99 12.00 30.00
7 Marcus Thornton/25 3.00 8.00
9 Hedo Turkoglu/25 4.00 10.00
11 Courtney Lee/25 3.00 8.00
12 John Salmons/25 4.00 10.00
15 Tiago Splitter/99 3.00 8.00
16 Jamaal Tinsley/25 3.00 8.00
17 Charles Oakley/149 5.00 12.00
18 Ronnie Brewer/99 3.00 8.00
19 Alex English/35 6.00 15.00
21 Anthony Morrow/99 3.00 8.00
23 Jeff Teague/25 3.00 8.00
25 Andrew Bogut/25 4.00 10.00
26 Taj Gibson/25 3.00 8.00
27 Satch Sanders/25 8.00 20.00
29 Tom Chambers/25 5.00 12.00
30 Mario Chalmers/25 4.00 10.00
32 Muggsy Bogues/149 10.00 25.00
33 J.J. Hickson/25 3.00 8.00
34 Spencer Haywood/99 5.00 12.00
35 A.C. Green/25 15.00 40.00
36 Larry Johnson/99 10.00 25.00
38 Lance Stephenson/149 4.00 10.00
39 Fat Lever/99 4.00 10.00
40 Jared Dudley/25 3.00 8.00
41 Zydrunas Ilgauskas/99 4.00 10.00
42 Bob Love/49 5.00 12.00
43 Greg Ostertag/49 12.00 30.00
44 Len Elmore/49 12.00 30.00
45 Tyronn Lue/99 10.00 25.00
46 Walt Williams/25 3.00 8.00
47 Scot Pollard/49 3.00 8.00
48 Rod Strickland/99 3.00 8.00
49 Jamaal Wilkes/25 5.00 12.00
50 Ronny Turiaf/25 3.00 8.00
51 Danny Ferry/49 3.00 8.00
52 Sam Perkins/25 4.00 10.00
54 Timofey Mozgov/149 3.00 8.00
55 Bruce Bowen/49 4.00 10.00
56 Mario Elie/49 3.00 8.00
57 Johan Petro/129 3.00 8.00
58 Jordan Crawford/149 3.00 8.00
59 Keith Erickson/25 5.00 12.00
60 Kwame Brown/49 3.00 8.00
61 Alonzo Gee/129 3.00 8.00
62 Rex Chapman/49 4.00 10.00
63 JaVale McGee/25 4.00 10.00
64 Larry Nance/49 4.00 10.00
65 Stacey Augmon/49 3.00 8.00
66 Brian Grant/99 3.00 8.00
68 Landry Fields/25 3.00 8.00
69 Arron Afflalo/25 3.00 8.00
70 Rodney Stuckey/25 3.00 8.00
72 Jason Kidd/25 15.00 40.00
73 Thabo Sefolosha/25 3.00 8.00
74 Ekpe Udoh/79 3.00 8.00
75 Gordon Hayward/25 15.00 40.00
76 Slick Watts/25 3.00 8.00
77 Danny Green/129 4.00 10.00
79 Glen Rice/25 8.00 20.00
82 Antonio Davis/25 3.00 8.00
83 Elliot Williams/99 3.00 8.00
84 Antoine Walker/99 4.00 10.00
85 Dwyane Wade/35 50.00 120.00
86 Jason Thompson/25 3.00 8.00
87 Corey Brewer/149 3.00 8.00
88 Jeremy Evans/25 3.00 8.00
91 Austin Daye/149 3.00 8.00
93 Marcus Camby/25 5.00 12.00
94 Al-Farouq Aminu/25 3.00 8.00
96 Bill Cartwright/25 8.00 20.00
98 Will Bynum/99 3.00 8.00
100 Tree Rollins/49 3.00 8.00
101 Bonzi Wells/99 3.00 8.00
102 Jerome Williams/99 3.00 8.00
103 Lamond Murray/49 3.00 8.00
104 Isaiah Rider/99 4.00 10.00
105 Darrell Armstrong/49 3.00 8.00
106 Damon Jones/49 3.00 8.00
107 Brandon Bass/25 3.00 8.00
108 Darryl Dawkins/99 6.00 15.00
109 Bernard King/25 6.00 15.00
111 Michael Bantom/99 3.00 8.00
112 Jonathan Bender/49 3.00 8.00
113 Bo Kimble/149 3.00 8.00
114 Tony Campbell/49 3.00 8.00
115 Dick Barnett/99 4.00 10.00
116 Charlie Ward/49 3.00 8.00
118 Jim Jackson/99 4.00 10.00
119 Alan Anderson/99 3.00 8.00
120 Chris Wilcox/99 3.00 8.00
121 Robert Horry/25 12.00 30.00
124 Anthony Mason/99 4.00 10.00
126 Greivis Vasquez/129 3.00 8.00
127 Ersan Ilyasova/49 3.00 8.00
129 Xavier Henry/99 3.00 8.00
131 Nick Anderson/99 4.00 10.00
132 Kurt Rambis/25 10.00 25.00
133 Bobby Jackson/99 3.00 8.00
134 Kevin Willis/25 3.00 8.00
135 Boris Diaw/25 4.00 10.00
136 Morlon Wiley/25 3.00 8.00
137 Mitch Richmond/25 12.00 30.00
138 Tom Gugliotta/99 3.00 8.00
140 Bryant Reeves/49 3.00 8.00
141 Dee Brown/99 3.00 8.00
142 Jonas Jerebko/49 3.00 8.00
143 Kevin Love/25 12.00 30.00
144 Chase Budinger/25 3.00 8.00
145 Rick Mahorn/25 3.00 8.00
146 Trevor Booker/25 3.00 8.00
147 Jason Richardson/25 6.00 15.00
148 J.J. Redick/25 5.00 12.00
152 Brandon Rush/99 3.00 8.00
154 Earl Lloyd/25 10.00 25.00
155 Cedric Ceballos/99 4.00 10.00
156 Adrian Dantley/25 4.00 10.00
161 Mel Davis/99 3.00 8.00
162 Daequan Cook/25 3.00 8.00
164 B.J. Armstrong/25 10.00 25.00
166 Kobe Bryant/149 1,000.00 2,000.00
167 Blake Griffin/99 EXCH 5.00 12.00
168 Kevin Durant/99 125.00 300.00
171 Vince Carter/35 50.00 120.00
172 Steve Smith/99 4.00 10.00
174 Reggie Theus/49 4.00 10.00
176 Carl Landry/25 3.00 8.00
177 Andray Blatche/25 3.00 8.00
180 Bailey Howell/25 10.00 25.00
181 Gary Payton/25 15.00 40.00
183 Tariq Abdul-Wahad/49 3.00 8.00
186 Otis Birdsong/49 4.00 10.00
187 Craig Hodges/99 8.00 20.00
188 Truck Robinson/99 3.00 8.00
189 Johnny Newman/99 3.00 8.00
190 Cazzie Russell/99 3.00 8.00
191 Henry Bibby/99 3.00 8.00
192 Aaron Brooks/25 3.00 8.00
193 Klay Thompson/25 125.00 300.00
194 James Johnson/25 3.00 8.00
195 Herb Williams/99 3.00 8.00
196 Victor Claver/149 3.00 8.00
197 Eddie Johnson/99 3.00 8.00
198 Allan Houston/25 4.00 10.00
199 Jason Smith/99 3.00 8.00
200 DeMarre Carroll/149 3.00 8.00
202 Dahntay Jones/49 3.00 8.00
203 Andre Miller/25 4.00 10.00
204 Dan Issel/149 5.00 12.00
206 Larry Bird/25 125.00 300.00
207 Larry Sanders/25 3.00 8.00
208 Antawn Jamison/25 4.00 10.00
209 Cazzie Russell/99 4.00 10.00
210 Buck Williams/99 3.00 8.00
211 Bryon Russell/49 3.00 8.00
212 Bob Sura/49 3.00 8.00
213 Michael Cooper/99 5.00 12.00
214 Campy Russell/99 3.00 8.00
215 George Hill/25 4.00 10.00
216 Vin Baker/49 3.00 8.00
217 Chris Ford/25 5.00 12.00
218 Chris Mullin/25 10.00 25.00
220 Detlef Schrempf/49 8.00 20.00
222 Reggie Evans/25 3.00 8.00
223 Ed Davis/49 3.00 8.00
224 Sean Elliott/25 4.00 10.00
225 Tom Heinsohn/25 20.00 50.00
226 Toni Kukoc/25 15.00 40.00
227 Brad Daugherty/99 4.00 10.00
228 Vernon Maxwell/99 3.00 8.00
229 Jayson Williams/99 3.00 8.00
230 John Salley/99 3.00 8.00
233 Zaza Pachulia/99 3.00 8.00
234 Walter Berry/79 3.00 8.00
237 David West/25 4.00 10.00
239 John Havlicek/25 75.00 200.00
240 Udonis Haslem/99 4.00 10.00
241 Gerald Henderson/25 3.00 8.00
244 Bobby Jones/49 6.00 15.00
246 Jerry West/25 50.00 120.00
247 Beno Udrih/149 3.00 8.00
248 Kyle Lowry/25 20.00 50.00
249 Earl Clark/49 3.00 8.00
250 Marreese Speights/25 3.00 8.00
252 Roy Hibbert/25 4.00 10.00
254 David Robinson/25 50.00 120.00
255 Richard Jefferson/25 3.00 8.00
256 Marco Belinelli/49 3.00 8.00
257 Stephen Jackson/25 4.00 10.00
258 Maurice Cheeks/49 4.00 10.00
260 Bob McAdoo/25 15.00 40.00
261 Marcin Gortat/25 3.00 8.00
264 Xavier McDaniel/49 3.00 8.00
265 M.L. Carr/49 5.00 12.00
266 Kendrick Perkins/25 3.00 8.00
268 Mark Price/49 10.00 25.00
271 Juwan Howard/25 10.00 25.00
273 Wesley Matthews/149 3.00 8.00
274 Luke Ridnour/25 4.00 10.00
275 Jason Maxiell/129 3.00 8.00
276 Joel Anthony/129 3.00 8.00
277 Sidney Moncrief/99 3.00 8.00
278 Harry Gallatin/25 5.00 12.00
279 Steve Novak/25 3.00 8.00
280 Cedric Maxwell/99 3.00 8.00
281 Derek Anderson/99 3.00 8.00
282 Ricky Pierce/49 3.00 8.00
283 Al Attles/49 4.00 10.00
284 Gus Williams/99 3.00 8.00
285 Louis Williams/99 4.00 10.00
286 Ryan Anderson/99 3.00 8.00
287 Jeff Green/25 3.00 8.00
288 Dave Stallworth/99 3.00 8.00
289 Patrick Patterson/79 3.00 8.00
290 Nikola Pekovic/49 3.00 8.00
291 Marvin Williams/149 3.00 8.00
292 George McGinnis/25 8.00 20.00
293 Mark Eaton/49 10.00 25.00
297 Sleepy Floyd/99 3.00 8.00
299 Leandro Barbosa/25 4.00 10.00

2012-13 Momentum Monumental Marks Blue

*BLUE 49: .5X TO 1.2X BASIC AUTO
*BLUE 25: .6X TO 1.5X BASIC AUTO
PRINT RUNS B/WN 10-49 COPIES PER
NO PRICING ON QTY 10 OR LESS
EXCHANGE DEADLINE 11/15/2014

2012-13 Momentum Monumental Marks Red

*RED 25: .6X TO 1.5X BASIC
PRINT RUNS B/WN 5-25 COPIES PER
EXCHANGE DEADLINE 11/15/2014

2017-18 Momentum

326 Justin Patton .60 1.50
327 Lauri Markkanen 4.00 10.00
328 Sindarius Thornwell .60 1.50
329 Markelle Fultz 1.50 4.00
330 Derrick White 2.50 6.00
331 Caleb Swanigan .60 1.50
332 Frank Mason III .60 1.50
333 Frank Ntilikina .75 2.00
334 John Collins 1.50 4.00
335 Jonathan Isaac 1.50 4.00
336 Luke Kennard 1.25 3.00
337 Lonzo Ball 2.50 6.00
338 Terrance Ferguson .60 1.50
339 Bam Adebayo 4.00 10.00
340 Dwayne Bacon .60 1.50
341 Dennis Smith Jr. .75 2.00
342 Ivan Rabb .60 1.50
343 Jayson Tatum 20.00 50.00
344 Josh Hart 1.50 4.00
345 Josh Jackson .75 2.00
346 OG Anunoby 3.00 8.00
347 Malik Monk 2.50 6.00
348 Tyler Dorsey .60 1.50
349 De'Aaron Fox 5.00 12.00
350 Zach Collins 1.00 2.50

2017-18 Momentum Blue

*BLUE: .5X TO 1.2X BASIC
STATED PRINT RUN 199 SER.#'d SETS

2017-18 Momentum Red

*RED: .5X TO 1.2X BASIC
STATED PRINT RUN 249 SER.#'d SETS

2017-18 Momentum Silver

*SILVER: .6X TO 1.5X BASIC
STATED PRINT RUN 99 SER.#'d SETS

1976-77 MSA Drinking Cups

1 Kareem Abdul-Jabbar 25.00 50.00
2 Alvan Adams 10.00 20.00
3 Nate Archibald 15.00 30.00
4 Dennis Awtrey 10.00 20.00
5 Rick Barry 15.00 30.00
6 Otis Birdsong 10.00 20.00
7 Mike Bratz 10.00 20.00
8 Allan Bristow 10.00 20.00
9 Fred Brown 10.00 20.00
10 Louis Dampier 10.00 20.00
11 Adrian Dantley 15.00 30.00
12 Walter Davis 10.00 20.00
13 John Drew 10.00 20.00
14 Julius Erving 25.00 50.00
15 Walt Frazier 15.00 30.00
16 George Gervin 20.00 40.00
17 Artis Gilmore 15.00 30.00
18 Bob Gross 10.00 20.00
19 John Havlicek 20.00 40.00
20 Elvin Hayes 20.00 40.00
21 Spencer Haywood 15.00 30.00
22 Garfield Heard 10.00 20.00
23 Lionel Hollins 10.00 20.00
24 Dan Issel 15.00 30.00
25 Marques Johnson 10.00 20.00
26 Bernard King 15.00 30.00
27 Billy Knight 10.00 20.00
28 Bob Lanier 15.00 30.00
29 Ron Lee 10.00 20.00
30 Maurice Lucas 10.00 20.00
31 Pete Maravich 30.00 60.00
32 Bob McAdoo 15.00 30.00
33 Earl Monroe 15.00 30.00
34 Calvin Murphy 15.00 30.00
35 Mark Olberding 10.00 20.00
36 Curtis Perry 10.00 20.00
37 Charlie Scott 10.00 20.00
38 Phil Smith 10.00 20.00
39 Ricky Sobers 10.00 20.00
40 David Thompson 15.00 30.00
41 Rudy Tomjanovich 15.00 30.00
42 Dave Twardzik 10.00 20.00
43 Norm Van Lier 10.00 20.00
44 Bill Walton 15.00 30.00
45 Marvin Webster 10.00 20.00
46 Paul Westphal 10.00 20.00

1997 Nabisco/Post Penny Hardaway Posters

COMPLETE SET (4) 2.50 6.00
COMMON POSTER (1-4) .75 2.00

2001 NBA All-Star Game

COMPLETE SET (3) 5.00 12.00
1 Vince Carter Fleer 2.50 6.00
2 Shaquille O'Neal Topps 1.50 4.00
3 Kobe Bryant Upper Deck 3.00 8.00

1973-74 NBA Players Association

COMPLETE SET (40) 300.00 600.00
1 Lucius Allen 1.50 4.00
2 Dave Bing SP 8.00 20.00
3 Bill Bradley 4.00 10.00
4 Fred Carter SP 7.50 15.00
5 Austin Carr 1.50 4.00
6 Dave Cowens 5.00 10.00
7 Dave DeBusschere 5.00 10.00
8 Ernie DiGregorio 2.50 6.00
9 Gail Goodrich 5.00 10.00
10 Hal Greer 3.00 8.00
11 John Havlicek 7.50 15.00
12 Connie Hawkins 5.00 10.00
13 Spencer Haywood 2.00 5.00
14 Lou Hudson 2.00 5.00
15 Bob Kauffman 1.25 3.00
16 Bob Lanier 4.00 10.00
17 Bob Love 3.00 8.00
18 Jack Marin 2.00 5.00
19 Jim McMillian 2.00 5.00
20 Earl Monroe SP 12.50 25.00
21 Calvin Murphy 3.00 8.00
22 Mike Newlin SP 50.00 100.00
23 Geoff Petrie 2.50 6.00
24 Willis Reed SP 15.00 40.00
25 Rich Rinaldi 1.50 4.00
26 Mike Riordan SP 7.50 15.00
27 Oscar Robertson SP 20.00 40.00
28 Cazzie Russell 2.00 5.00
29 Paul Silas SP 50.00 100.00
30 Jerry Sloan 3.00 8.00
31 Elmore Smith 1.50 4.00
32 Dick Snyder 1.50 4.00
33 Nate Thurmond 3.00 8.00
34 Rudy Tomjanovich 4.00 10.00
35 Wes Unseld 5.00 10.00
36 Dick Van Arsdale SP 10.00 20.00
37 Tom Van Arsdale 1.50 4.00
38 Chet Walker SP 10.00 25.00
39 Jo Jo White 2.50 6.00
40 Len Wilkens 5.00 10.00

1973-74 NBA Players Association 8x10

COMPLETE SET (10) 100.00 200.00
A Dave DeBusschere 10.00 20.00
B John Havlicek 20.00 40.00
C Willis Reed 12.00 30.00
D Ernie DiGregorio 5.00 10.00
E Dave Cowens 10.00 20.00
F Oscar Robertson 20.00 40.00
G Bill Bradley 12.50 25.00
H Jo Jo White 5.00 10.00
I Nate Thurmond 7.50 15.00
J Gail Goodrich 10.00 20.00

2002-03 NBA Showdown

1 Shareef Abdur-Rahim STAR .75 2.00
2 Emanual Davis .20 .50
3 Alan Henderson .20 .50
4 Dermarr Johnson .20 .50
5 Toni Kukoc .30 .75
6 Theo Ratliff .20 .50
7 Jason Terry .25 .60
8 Jacque Vaughn .20 .50
9 Kenny Anderson .25 .60
10 Mark Blount .20 .50
11 Randy Brown .20 .50
12 Milt Palacio .20 .50
13 Paul Pierce STAR 1.25 3.00
14 Vitaly Potapenko .20 .50
15 Antoine Walker .25 .60
16 Eric Williams .20 .50
17 P.J. Brown .20 .50
18 Elden Campbell .20 .50
19 Baron Davis STAR .75 2.00
20 Bryce Drew .20 .50
21 George Lynch .20 .50
22 Jamaal Magloire .20 .50
23 Jamal Mashburn STAR .60 1.50
24 Jerome Moiso .20 .50
25 Robert Traylor .20 .50
26 David Wesley .20 .50
27 Ron Artest .25 .60
28 Marcus Fizer .20 .50
29 A.J. Guyton .20 .50
30 Fred Hoiberg .20 .50
31 Ron Mercer STAR .50 1.25
32 Brad Miller .25 .60
33 Charles Oakley .20 .50
34 Kevin Ollie .20 .50
35 Eddie Robinson .20 .50
36 Michael Doleac .20 .50
37 Tyrone Hill .20 .50
38 Chris Mihm .20 .50
39 Andre Miller .25 .60
40 Lamond Murray .20 .50
41 Bryant Stith .20 .50
42 Shawn Bradley .20 .50
43 Greg Buckner .20 .50
44 Evan Eschmeyer .20 .50
45 Michael Finley STAR .75 2.00
46 Tim Hardaway .30 .75
47 Juwan Howard .25 .60
48 Danny Manning .25 .60
50 Steve Nash .60 1.50
51 Dirk Nowitzki STAR 2.00 5.00
52 Avery Johnson .25 .60
53 Raef Lafrentz .20 .50
54 Voshon Lenard .20 .50
55 George McCloud .20 .50
56 Antonio McDyess STAR .60 1.50
57 James Posey .25 .60
58 Isaiah Rider .25 .60
59 Nick Van Exel STAR .75 2.00
60 Scott Williams .20 .50
61 Chucky Atkins .20 .50
62 Jon Barry .20 .50
63 Michael Curry .20 .50
64 Mikki Moore .20 .50
65 Clifford Robinson .30 .75
66 Jerry Stackhouse STAR .75 2.00
67 Corliss Williamson .20 .50
68 Mookie Blaylock .20 .50
69 Danny Fortson STAR .50 1.25
70 Adonal Foyle .20 .50
71 Larry Hughes .25 .60
72 Marc Jackson .20 .50
73 Antawn Jamison STAR .60 1.50
74 Bob Sura .20 .50
75 Steve Francis STAR .75 2.00
76 Cuttino Mobley STAR .50 1.25
77 Moochie Norris .20 .50
78 Glen Rice .25 .60
79 Maurice Taylor .20 .50
80 Kenny Thomas .20 .50
81 Walt Williams .20 .50
82 Travis Best .20 .50
83 Austin Croshere .20 .50
84 Al Harrington .25 .60
85 Reggie Miller STAR 1.50 4.00
86 Jermaine O'Neal .25 .60
87 Jalen Rose STAR .60 1.50
88 Elton Brand STAR .60 1.50
89 Corey Maggette .25 .60
90 Jeff McInnis .20 .50
91 Darius Miles .20 .50
92 Lamar Odom STAR .75 2.00
93 Michael Olowokandi .20 .50
94 Eric Piatkowski .20 .50
95 Quentin Richardson .20 .50
97 Kobe Bryant STAR 6.00 15.00
98 Derek Fisher .30 .75
99 Rick Fox .20 .50
100 Robert Horry .30 .75
101 Lindsey Hunter .20 .50
102 Shaquille O'Neal STAR 3.00 8.00
103 Mitch Richmond .30 .75
104 Brian Shaw .20 .50
105 Isaac Austin .20 .50
106 Michael Dickerson .20 .50
107 Brevin Knight .20 .50
108 Grant Long .20 .50
109 Bryant Reeves .20 .50
110 Stromile Swift .20 .50
111 Jason Williams .40 1.00
112 Lorenzen Wright STAR .50 1.25
113 Anthony Carter .20 .50
114 Laphonso Ellis .25 .60
115 Kendall Gill .20 .50
116 Brian Grant .20 .50
117 Eddie House .20 .50
118 Eddie Jones STAR .75 2.00
119 Alonzo Mourning STAR 1.25 3.00
120 Ray Allen STAR 1.25 3.00
121 Jason Caffey .20 .50
122 Sam Cassell .25 .60
123 Darvin Ham .25 .60
124 Ervin Johnson .20 .50
125 Anthony Mason .25 .60
126 Glenn Robinson STAR .75 2.00
127 Tim Thomas .20 .50
128 Chauncey Billups .30 .75
129 Terrell Brandon STAR .50 1.25
130 Kevin Garnett STAR 2.00 5.00
131 Dean Garrett .20 .50
132 Felipe Lopez .20 .50
133 Radoslav Nesterovic .20 .50
134 Anthony Peeler .20 .50
135 Joe Smith .25 .60
136 Wally Szczerbiak .25 .60
137 Lucious Harris .20 .50
138 Jason Kidd STAR 1.25 3.00
139 Todd MacCulloch .20 .50
140 Kenyon Martin .30 .75
141 Keith Van Horn STAR .60 1.50
142 Aaron Williams .20 .50
144 Marcus Camby STAR .60 1.50
146 Allan Houston .30 .75
147 Mark Jackson .25 .60
148 Latrell Sprewell .30 .75
152 Darrell Armstrong .20 .50
153 Andrew Declercq .20 .50
154 Patrick Ewing .40 1.00
155 Pat Garrity .20 .50
156 Horace Grant .25 .60
157 Grant Hill STAR 1.25 3.00
158 Tracy Mcgrady STAR 1.25 3.00
159 Mike Miller .25 .60
160 Monty Williams .20 .50
161 Derrick Coleman .25 .60
162 Vonteego Cummings .20 .50
163 Matt Geiger .20 .50
164 Matt Harpring .20 .50
165 Allen Iverson STAR 2.00 5.00
166 Aaron McKie .20 .50
167 Dikembe Mutombo STAR 1.25 3.00
168 Eric Snow .20 .50
169 Tony Delk .20 .50
170 Tom Gugliotta .20 .50
171 Anfernee Hardaway .75 2.00
172 Dan Majerle .30 .75
173 Stephon Marbury STAR 1.00 2.50
174 Shawn Marion STAR .75 2.00
175 Bo Outlaw .20 .50
176 Rodney Rogers .20 .50
177 Iakovos Tsakalidis .20 .50
178 Derek Anderson .20 .50
179 Dale Davis .20 .50
180 Shawn Kemp .30 .75
181 Ruben Patterson .20 .50
182 Scottie Pippen .75 2.00
183 Damon Stoudamire .30 .75
184 Rasheed Wallace STAR 1.00 2.50
185 Bonzi Wells STAR .50 1.25
186 Mike Bibby .30 .75
187 Doug Christie .20 .50
188 Vlade Divac .25 .60
189 Bobby Jackson .20 .50
190 Scot Pollard .20 .50
191 Peja Stojakovic STAR .60 1.50
192 Hedo Turkoglu .25 .60
193 Chris Webber STAR 1.00 2.50
194 Bruce Bowen .20 .50
195 Antonio Daniels .20 .50
196 Tim Duncan STAR 2.00 5.00
197 Danny Ferry .20 .50
198 Terry Porter .20 .50
199 David Robinson STAR 1.50 4.00
203 Brent Barry .20 .50
204 Calvin Booth .20 .50
205 Rashard Lewis STAR .60 1.50
206 Desmond Mason .25 .60
207 Gary Payton STAR 1.25 3.00
208 Vince Carter STAR 1.50 4.00
209 Chris Childs .20 .50
210 Keon Clark .20 .50
211 Dell Curry .20 .50
212 Antonio Davis STAR .60 1.50
213 Hakeem Olajuwon .40 1.00
214 Morris Peterson .25 .60
215 Alvin Williams .20 .50
216 Jerome Williams .20 .50
217 Karl Malone STAR 1.50 4.00
218 Donyell Marshall .20 .50
219 Greg Ostertag .20 .50
220 Bryon Russell .20 .50
221 John Starks .60 1.50
222 John Stockton STAR 1.50 4.00
223 Hubert Davis .20 .50
224 Richard Hamilton STAR 1.00 2.50
225 Christian Laettner .25 .60
226 Tyrone Nesby .20 .50
227 Jahidi White .20 .50
228 Chris Whitney .20 .50

2002-03 NBA Showdown Strategy

S01 3-pointer
Jerry Stackhouse .25 .60
S02 Aggressive Play
Kevin Garnett STAR .60 1.50
S03 Alley-Oop
Desmond Mason STAR .20 .50
S04 And One!
Chris Mihm
Grant Hill .40 1.00
S05 Blink and You'll Miss Him
Allen Iverson .60 1.50
S06 Brute Force
Shaquille O'Neal STAR 1.00 2.50
S07 Clean the Glass
Tim Duncan .60 1.50
S08 Clutch Shot
Jalen Rose STAR .20 .50
S09 Double-Foul
Karl Malone
Gary Payton STAR .50 1.25
S10 Drive the Lane
John Starks STAR .20 .50
S11 Find the Open Man
Karl Malone STAR .50 1.25
S12 From Way Downtown!
Reggie Miller STAR .50 1.25
S13 Half-Court Set
Gary Payton .40 1.00
S14 He's Healing Up!
Allen Iverson .60 1.50
S15 Hot Hand
Rasheed Wallace
Damon Stoudamire STAR .30 .75
S16 It's My Job - It's What I Do
John Stockton
Wally Szczerbiak STAR .50 1.25
S17 Jumper
Allen Iverson .60 1.50
S18 Killer Crossover
Steve Francis STAR .25 .60
S19 Layup
Jerome Moiso .15 .40
S20 Outside Pick
Karl Malone
John Stockton .50 1.25
S21 Power Move
Vince Carter
Tim Thomas .50 1.25
S22 Rimshaker
Vince Carter STAR .50 1.25
S23 Run'N Gun
Richard Hamilton .30 .75
S24 Scrapping in the Paint
Kurt Thomas .15 .40
S25 Slam Dunk
Derek Anderson .15 .40
S26 Starting the Fast Break
Grant Hill STAR .40 1.00
S27 Take Two
Shaquille O'Neal 1.00 2.50
S28 Time-Out
Steve Francis
Cuttino Mobley .25 .60
S29 Tomahawk Dunk
Kobe Bryant STAR 2.00 5.00
S30 Wham Bam Slam!
Shaquille O'Neal STAR 1.00 2.50
S31 All over the Place
Scottie Pippen STAR .60 1.50
S32 Anticipate the Pass
Steve Francis STAR .25 .60
S33 Boxing Out
Steve Francis
Kelvin Cato .25 .60
S34 Change in Strategy
Karl Malone
John Stockton .50 1.25
S35 De-fense! De-fense!
Jumaine Jones
Dikembe Mutombo
Eric Snow
Jason Terry .40 1.00
S36 Defensive Stopper
Dikembe Mutombo .40 1.00
S37 Get the Crowd Into It!
Paul Pierce STAR .40 1.00
S38 Good D!
Kobe Bryant
Scottie Pippen
Wallace .60 1.50
S39 Good Position
Kenyon Martin .25 .60
S40 Guard the Paint
Anthony Mason
Tracy McGrady STAR .40 1.00
S41 Pick His Pocket
Steve Francis .25 .60
S42 Play 'Em Tight
Gary Payton
Terrell Brandon STAR .40 1.00
S43 Quick Feet
John Stockton .50 1.25
S44 Raising the Bar
John Starks
Anthony Peeler STAR .20 .50
S45 Rejected!
Tim Duncan .60 1.50
S46 Switching Strategies
Brian Grant
Anthony Carter .15 .40
S47 Taking the Charge
Antonio Daniels STAR .15 .40
S48 This is My House!
Alonzo Mourning
Joe Smith STAR .40 1.00
S49 Tough Shot
Kenyon Martin
Lamond Murray .25 .60
S50 Turnover
Fred Hoiberg
Jon Barry STAR .15 .40

2008-09 NBA Starting Five

1 LeBron James AU
Upper Deck 750.00 2,000.00
1 LeBron James Black 8.00 20.00
LJ LeBron James White 8.00 20.00
DR Derrick Rose 4.00 10.00
MJ Michael Jordan 8.00 20.00
NNO Magic Johnson 3.00 8.00
NNO Magic Johnson AU 100.00 200.00
NNO Greg Oden .60 1.50
NNO Dwyane Wade 2.00 5.00
AUDR Derrick Rose AU 200.00 400.00
AUMJ Michael Jordan AU 300.00 500.00

2010-11 NBA Starting Five

COMPLETE SET (6) 4.00 10.00
DC DeMarcus Cousins AU
Playoff Preferred 10.00 25.00
DF Derrick Favors AU
Playoff Preferred 8.00 20.00
DH Dwight Howard .50 1.25
DW Dwyane Wade .75 2.00
ET Evan Turner AU
Playoff Preferred 6.00 15.00
JW John Wall 1.25 3.00
KB Kobe Bryant 3.00 8.00
KD Kevin Durant 1.50 4.00
LJ LeBron James 3.00 8.00
SC Stephen Curry AU
Playoff Preferred 500.00 1,000.00
WJ Wesley Johnson AU
Playoff Preferred 6.00 15.00

2012-13 NBA Starting Five

COMPLETE SET (12)
1 Kobe Bryant 3.00 8.00
2 Blake Griffin .40 1.00
3 Kevin Durant 1.50 4.00
4 Kyrie Irving 5.00 12.00
5 Anthony Davis 6.00 15.00
6 Michael Kidd-Gilchrist .60 1.50
7 Thomas Robinson .50 1.25
8 Harrison Barnes 1.00 2.50
9 Derrick Williams .50 1.25
10 Kenneth Faried .60 1.50
11 Austin Rivers .75 2.00
12 Jared Sullinger .50 1.25

2012-13 NBA Starting Five Panini Authentic

1 Kobe Bryant 5.00 12.00
2 Blake Griffin .60 1.50
3 Kevin Durant 2.50 6.00
4 Kyrie Irving 4.00 10.00

2012-13 NBA Starting Five Playmakers

1 Anthony Davis 10.00 25.00
2 Michael Kidd-Gilchrist 1.00 2.50

1971-72 NBA Stickers

1 Team Logos 2.00 5.00

1998 NBA Wrapper Rebound Shaquille O'Neal

COMPLETE SET (4) 12.00 30.00
1 Shaquille O'Neal Fleer 4.00 10.00
2 Shaquille O'Neal SkyBox 4.00 10.00
3 Shaquille O'Neal Topps 4.00 10.00
4 Shaquille O'Neal Upper Deck 4.00 10.00
NNO Uncut NBA Sheet 15.00 40.00
NNO Shaquille O'Neal Poster 4.00 10.00

2007 NBA Valentines

NNO LeBron James .75 2.00
NNO Allen Iverson .40 1.00
NNO Dirk Nowitzki .40 1.00
NNO Tim Duncan .40 1.00
NNO Tracy McGrady .40 1.00
NNO Steve Nash .40 1.00
NNO Tim Duncan
Allen Iverson
LeBron James
Tracy McGrady
Steve Nash
Dirk Nowitzki
Dwyane Wade
Poster .75 2.00
NNO Tattoos .20 .50
NNO Dwyane Wade .60 1.50

1969 NBAP Members

COMPLETE SET (20) 3,500.00 5,000.00
1 Kareem Abdul-Jabbar 300.00 600.00
2 Elgin Baylor 200.00 400.00
3 Zelmo Beaty 75.00 150.00
4 Bob Boozer 75.00 150.00
5 Bill Bradley 100.00 200.00
6 Wilt Chamberlain 400.00 800.00
7 John Havlicek 200.00 500.00
8 Don Kojis 75.00 150.00
9 Jerry Lucas 100.00 200.00

10 Eddie Miles 75.00 150.00
11 Jeff Mullins 75.00 150.00
12 Willis Reed 100.00 200.00
13 Oscar Robertson 250.00 500.00
14 Bill Russell 400.00 800.00
15 Wes Unseld 100.00 200.00
16 Dick Van Arsdale 75.00 150.00
17 Chet Walker 75.00 150.00
18 Jerry West 400.00 800.00
19 Len Wilkens 100.00 200.00
20 NBAP Logo 75.00 150.00

1984-85 Nets Getty

COMPLETE SET (12) 15.00 40.00
1 Stan Albeck CO 1.25 3.00
2 Otis Birdsong 2.00 5.00
3 Darwin Cook 1.25 3.00
4 Darryl Dawkins 3.00 8.00
5 Mike Gminski 2.00 5.00
6 Albert King 1.50 4.00
7 Mike O'Koren 1.50 4.00
8 Kelvin Ransey 1.25 3.00
9 M.Ray Richardson 1.50 4.00
10 Jeff Turner 2.00 5.00
11 Buck Williams 3.00 8.00
12 Duncan (Mascot) 1.25 3.00

1990-91 Nets Kayo/Breyers

COMPLETE SET (14) 3.00 8.00
1 Mookie Blaylock .75 2.00
2 Sam Bowie .60 1.50
3 Jud Buechler .40 1.00
4 Derrick Coleman .75 2.00
5 Lester Conner .30 .75
6 Chris Dudley .40 1.00
7 Tate George .30 .75
8 Derrick Gervin .30 .75
9 Jack Haley .30 .75
10 Kirk Lee .30 .75
11 Chris Morris .40 1.00
12 Reggie Theus 1.00 2.50
13 Bill Fitch CO .30 .75
14 Nets Home Schedule .30 .75

1986 Nets Lifebuoy/Star

COMPLETE SET (14) 5.00 12.00
1 Dave Wohl CO .75 2.00
2 Otis Birdsong .60 1.50
3 Bobby Cattage .40 1.00
4 Darwin Cook .40 1.00
5 Darryl Dawkins 1.50 4.00
6 Mike Gminski .60 1.50
7 Mickey Johnson .40 1.00
8 Albert King .50 1.25
9 Mike O'Koren .50 1.25
10 Kelvin Ransey .40 1.00
11 Micheal Ray Richardson .50 1.25
12 Jeff Turner .75 2.00
13 Buck Williams 1.50 4.00
14 Title Card/
Checklist on back) .40 1.00

1971-72 Nets New York Team Issue

COMPLETE SET (2) 12.50 25.00
1 Jim Ard
Rick Barry
Jeff Congdon
Joe Depre
Sonny Dove
Jarrett Durham
Manny Leaks
Bill Melchionni 7.50 15.00
2 Roy Boe PRES
Lou Carnesecca CO
Billy Paultz
John Roche
Ollie Taylor
Tom Washington 5.00 10.00

2001-02 Nets Topps

COMPLETE SET (10) 2.00 5.00
NN1 Stephon Marbury .60 1.50
NN2 Keith Van Horn .40 1.00
NN3 Kendall Gill .30 .75
NN4 Jamie Feick .30 .75
NN5 Stephen Jackson .40 1.00
NN6 Byron Scott .40 1.00
NN7 Johnny Newman .30 .75
NN8 Aaron Williams .30 .75
NN9 Lucious Harris .30 .75
NN10 Kenyon Martin .50 1.25

1991 Nike Michael Jordan/Spike Lee

COMPLETE SET (6) 6.00 15.00
1 Earth/Mars 1988 1.25 3.00
2 High Flying 1989 1.00 2.50
3 Do You Know 1990 1.00 2.50
4 Stay in School 1991 1.00 2.50
5 Genie 1991
With Little Richard 1.00 2.50
6 Michael Jordan Flight 1.25 3.00

1993 Nike/Warner Michael Jordan

COMPLETE SET (12) 5.00 12.00
1 Martian
(With basketball) .40 1.00
2 Martian
(The Best on Earth,
The Best on Mars) .40 1.00
3 Martian and his dog
(Hanging from
pulverized planetoid) .40 1.00
4 Michael Jordan
(Palming Martian
by helmet crest) .75 2.00
5 Michael Jordan
(Riding in Bugs'
flying saucer) .75 2.00
6 Porky Pig
(Piloting flying saucer) .40 1.00
7 Aerospace
(Michael Jordan slam
dunking in space) .75 2.00
8 J-J-Just Do It
(Porky Pig in Nikes) .40 1.00
9 Nice Shoes Indeed
(Martian with his dog,
holding a Nike) .40 1.00
10 The Scream Team
(Michael Jordan with Bugs) .75 2.00
11 Warning:
(Martian and
warning message) .40 1.00
12 What's Up Jock
(Bugs slam dunking
in space) .40 1.00

1996 No Fear

COMPLETE SET (8) 5.00 12.00
7 Chris Mills BK .40 1.00

1977-78 Nuggets Iron-On

COMPLETE SET (6) 20.00 40.00
1 Dan Issel 5.00 10.00
2 Brian Taylor 2.00 5.00
3 Bobby Wilkerson 2.00 5.00
4 Bobby Jones 5.00 10.00
5 Larry Brown CO 3.00 8.00
6 David Thompson 5.00 10.00

1975-76 Nuggets Pepsi Cans

COMPLETE SET (15) 80.00 160.00
1 Byron Beck 5.00 10.00
2 Larry Brown CO 7.50 15.00
3 Jimmy Foster 3.00 8.00
4 Gus Gerard 3.00 8.00
5 George Irvine 3.00 8.00
6 Dan Issel 12.50 25.00
7 Bobby Jones 10.00 20.00
8 Doug Moe ACO 7.50 15.00
9 Carl Scheer GM 3.00 8.00
10 Ralph Simpson 5.00 10.00
11 Claude Terry 3.00 8.00
12 David Thompson 12.50 25.00
13 Monte Towe 5.00 10.00
14 Marvin Webster 3.00 8.00
15 Chuck Williams 3.00 8.00

1976-77 Nuggets Pepsi Cans

COMPLETE SET (17) 60.00 120.00
1 Byron Beck 3.00 8.00
2 Larry Brown CO 5.00 10.00
3 Mack Calvin 3.00 8.00
4 Frank Hamblen ACO 2.00 5.00
5 George Irvine ACO 2.00 5.00
6 Dan Issel 10.00 20.00
7 Bobby Jones 7.50 15.00
8 Ted McClain 2.00 5.00
9 Jim Price 2.00 5.00
10 Carl Scheer GM 2.00 5.00
11 Paul Silas 3.00 8.00
12 Roland Taylor 2.00 5.00
13 David Thompson 10.00 20.00
14 Monte Towe 3.00 8.00
15 Bob Travaglini TR 2.00 5.00
16 Marvin Webster 2.00 5.00
17 Willie Wise 3.00 8.00

1982-83 Nuggets Police

COMPLETE SET (14) 4.00 8.00
2 Alex English 1.25 3.00
7 Billy McKinney .30 .75
21 Rob Williams .30 .75
22 Glen Gondrezick .30 .75
23 T.R. Dunn .30 .75
24 Bill Hanzlik .30 .75
25 Dave Robisch .30 .75
43 James Ray .30 .75
44 Dan Issel 1.00 2.50
53 Rich Kelley .30 .75
55 Kiki Vandeweghe .75 2.00
NNO Carl Scheer Pres/GM .30 .75
NNO Doug Moe CO .40 1.00
NNO Bill Ficke ACO
Bob Travaglini TR .30 .75

1983-84 Nuggets Police

COMPLETE SET (14) 4.00 8.00
2 Alex English 1.00 2.50
5 Mike Evans .30 .75
21 Rob Williams .30 .75
23 T.R. Dunn .30 .75
24 Bill Hanzlik .30 .75
32 Howard Carter .30 .75
33 Ken Dennard .30 .75
34 Danny Schayes .40 1.00
35 Richard Anderson .30 .75
44 Dan Issel .75 2.00
55 Kiki Vandeweghe .50 1.25
NNO Carl Scheer Pres GM .30 .75
NNO Bill Ficke ACO .30 .75
NNO Doug Moe CO .40 1.00

1985-86 Nuggets Police/Wendy's

COMPLETE SET (12) 3.00 8.00
1 Alex English .75 2.00
2 Mike Evans .30 .75
3 Bill Hanzlik .30 .75
4 Pete Williams .30 .75
5 Danny Schayes .30 .75
6 Wayne Cooper .30 .75
7 Blair Rasmussen .30 .75
8 Elston Turner 1.25 3.00
9 Lafayette Lever .40 1.00
10 T.R. Dunn .30 .75
11 Willie White .30 .75
12 Calvin Natt .30 .75

1988-89 Nuggets Police/Pepsi

COMPLETE SET (12) 3.00 7.00
2A Alex English
(If someone is hurt
in an accident ...) .75 2.00
2B Alex English
(You should never
run around ...) .75 2.00
6 Walter Davis .60 1.50
12A Fat Lever
(Always wear a helmet
when you're ...) .20 .50
12B Fat Lever
(If you're ever in
danger& the most ...) .20 .50
14 Michael Adams .40 1.00
20 Elston Turner .20 .50
24 Bill Hanzlik .20 .50
34 Danny Schayes .30 .75
35 Jerome Lane .20 .50
41 Blair Rasmussen .20 .50
42 Wayne Cooper .20 .50

1988-89 Nuggets Portraits

COMPLETE SET (6) 9.00 18.00
1 Wayne Cooper 1.25 3.00
2 T.R. Dunn 1.25 3.00
3 Alex English 2.50 6.00
4 Fat Lever 1.50 4.00
5 Calvin Natt 1.25 3.00
6 Elston Turner
Mike Evans
Bill Hanzlik 1.25 3.00

1989-90 Nuggets Police/Pepsi

COMPLETE SET (12) 3.00 8.00
1 Michael Adams .25 .60
2 Walter Davis .60 1.50
3 T.R. Dunn .20 .50
4 Alex English .75 2.00
5 Bill Hanzlik .20 .50
6 Eddie Hughes .20 .50
7 Tim Kempton .20 .50
8 Jerome Lane .20 .50
9 Lafayette Lever .30 .75
10 Todd Lichti .20 .50
11 Blair Rasmussen .20 .50
12 Danny Schayes .30 .75

2002-03 Nuggets Team Issue

COMPLETE SET (11) 6.00 15.00
1 Chris Anderson 1.25 3.00
2 Ryan Bowen .75 2.00
3 Marcus Camby 1.25 3.00
4 Junior Harrington .75 2.00
5 Donnell Harvey .75 2.00
6 Nene Hilario 1.00 2.50
7 Juwan Howard 1.00 2.50
8 Predrag Savovic .75 2.00
9 Nikoloz Tskitishvili .75 2.00
10 Rodney White .75 2.00
11 Vincent Yarbrough .75 2.00

1999 Omni CBA

7 Wang ZhiZhi .30 .75
32 Yao Ming 1.50 4.00
36 Mengke Bateer .30 .75

1993-94 Oklahoma City Cavalry CBA

COMPLETE SET (14) 1.50 4.00
1 Isaac Austin .40 1.00
2 Mike Bell .15 .40
3 Henry Bibby CO .60 1.50
4 Mike Bell .15 .40
5 Terry Faggins .15 .40
6 Kermit Holmes .15 .40
7 Steffond Johnson .15 .40
8 Sebastian Neal .15 .40
9 Keith Owens .15 .40
10 Kelsey Weems .15 .40
11 Corey Williams .15 .40
12 Byron Wilson .15 .40
13 Cheerleaders .15 .40
14 Checklist .15 .40

1994 Hakeem Olajuwon Fan Club

COMPLETE SET (2) 3.00 8.00

1991-92 Outlaws Wichita GBA

COMPLETE SET (11) 3.00 8.00
1 Rick Shore .40 1.00
2 Jeff Cummings .40 1.00
3 Brent Dabbs .50 1.25
4 Melvon Foster .50 1.25
5 Paul Guffrovich .40 1.00
6 Tyrone Powell .40 1.00
7 Omar Roland .40 1.00
8 Ricky Ross .40 1.00
9 Robert Spellman .40 1.00
10 Cody Walters .40 1.00
NNO Checklist Card .40 1.00

1971-72 Pacers Volpe Tumblers

COMPLETE SET (6) 50.00 100.00
1 Mel Daniels 10.00 25.00
2 Bill Keller 6.00 15.00
3 Art Becker 6.00 15.00
4 Bob Netolicky 8.00 20.00
5 Roger Brown 10.00 25.00
6 Rick Mount 8.00 20.00

1971-72 Pacers Volpe Marathon Oil

COMPLETE SET (12) 40.00 80.00
1 Warren Armstrong 2.50 6.00
2 John Barnhill 2.00 5.00
3 Art Becker 3.00 8.00
4 Roger Brown 3.00 8.00
5A Mel Daniels
Releasing ball from both hands 5.00 12.00
5B Mel Daniels
Releasing ball from right hand 5.00 12.00
6 Earle Higgins 2.00 5.00
7 Bill Keller 4.00 10.00
8 Bob Leonard CO 4.00 10.00
9 Freddie Lewis 3.00 8.00
10 Rick Mount 6.00 15.00
11 Bob Netolicky 3.00 8.00

1971-72 Pacers Team Issue

COMPLETE SET (2) 12.50 25.00
1 Roger Brown
Wayne Chapman
Mel Daniels
Earle Higgins
Darnell Hillman
Bill Keller
Freddie Lewis
George McGinnis 8.00 20.00
2 Bob Hooper ACO
Bob Leonard CO
Rick Mount
Bob Netolicky
Don Sidle
John Weissert GM
Marv Winkler 5.00 12.00

1988-89 Pacers Team Issue

COMPLETE SET (12) 15.00 40.00
1 Greg Dreiling .75 2.00
2 Vern Fleming 2.00 5.00
3 Anthony Frederick .75 2.00
4 Stuart Gray .75 2.00
5 John Long
with Julius Erving 2.00 5.00
6 Reggie Miller 8.00 20.00
7 Chuck Person 2.50 6.00
8 Scott Skiles 2.50 6.00
9 Everette Stephens .75 2.00
10 Steve Stipanovich .75 2.00
11 Wayman Tisdale 2.50 6.00
12 Herb Williams 2.00 5.00

2009-10 Panini

COMPLETE SET (400) 50.00 120.00
ALL RC VERSIONS SAME VALUE
1 Eddie House .20 .50
2 Glen Davis .20 .50
3 Kendrick Perkins .20 .50
4 Kevin Garnett .75 2.00
5 Leon Powe .20 .50
6 Paul Pierce .50 1.25
7 Rajon Rondo .40 1.00
8 Rasheed Wallace .40 1.00
9 Ray Allen .50 1.25
10 Stephon Marbury .40 1.00
11 Tony Allen .20 .50
12 Bobby Simmons .20 .50
13 Brook Lopez .30 .75
14 Chris Douglas-Roberts .20 .50
15 Courtney Lee .20 .50
16 Devin Harris .20 .50
17 Jarvis Hayes .20 .50
18 Josh Boone .20 .50
19 Keyon Dooling .20 .50
20 Rafer Alston .20 .50
21 Tony Battie .20 .50
22 Yi Jianlian .40 1.00
23 Al Harrington .25 .60
24 Chris Duhon .20 .50
25 Danilo Gallinari .25 .60
26 Darko Milicic .20 .50
27 David Lee .20 .50
28 Jared Jeffries .20 .50
29 Larry Hughes .25 .60
30 Nate Robinson .25 .60
31 Wilson Chandler .25 .60
32 Andre Iguodala .30 .75
33 Donyell Marshall .20 .50
34 Elton Brand .25 .60
35 Jason Kapono .20 .50
36 Louis Williams .30 .75
37 Marreese Speights .25 .60
38 Samuel Dalembert .20 .50
39 Thaddeus Young .20 .50
40 Willie Green .20 .50
41 Andrea Bargnani .20 .50
42 Chris Bosh .40 1.00
43 Hedo Turkoglu .25 .60
44 Joey Graham .20 .50
45 Jose Calderon .20 .50
46 Pops Mensah-Bonsu .20 .50
47 Quincy Douby .20 .50
48 Reggie Evans .20 .50
49 Devean George .20 .50
50 Antoine Wright .20 .50
51 Jarrett Jack .25 .60
52 Aaron Gray .20 .50
53 Brad Miller .25 .60
54 Derrick Rose .50 1.25
55 Joakim Noah .20 .50
56 John Salmons .25 .60
57 Kirk Hinrich .25 .60
58 Luol Deng .25 .60
59 Tyrus Thomas .20 .50
60 Anderson Varejao .20 .50
61 Daniel Gibson .20 .50
62 Delonte West .20 .50
63 Joe Smith .25 .60
64 LeBron James 2.50 6.00
65 Mo Williams .25 .60
66 Shaquille O'Neal 1.00 2.50
67 Wally Szczerbiak .25 .60
68 Zydrunas Ilgauskas .25 .60
69 Anthony Parker .20 .50
70 Jamario Moon .20 .50
71 Allen Iverson .60 1.50
72 Ben Gordon .25 .60
73 Charlie Villanueva .20 .50
74 Fabricio Oberto .20 .50
75 Jason Maxiell .20 .50
76 Kwame Brown .20 .50
77 Chris Wilcox .20 .50
78 Richard Hamilton .30 .75
79 Rodney Stuckey .20 .50
80 Tayshaun Prince .30 .75
81 Will Bynum .20 .50
82 Brandon Rush .20 .50
83 Danny Granger .20 .50
84 Jeff Foster .20 .50
85 Marquis Daniels .20 .50
86 Mike Dunleavy .20 .50
87 Rasho Nesterovic .20 .50
88 Roy Hibbert .25 .60
89 Stephen Graham .20 .50
90 T.J. Ford .20 .50
91 Travis Diener .20 .50
92 Troy Murphy .20 .50
93 Dahntay Jones .20 .50
94 Earl Watson .20 .50
95 Andrew Bogut .25 .60
96 Bruce Bowen .25 .60
97 Joe Alexander .20 .50
98 Keith Bogans .20 .50
99 Kurt Thomas .20 .50
100 Luc Mbah a Moute .20 .50
101 Luke Ridnour .25 .60
102 Michael Redd .25 .60
103 Ramon Sessions .20 .50
104 Al Horford .30 .75
105 Joe Johnson .30 .75
106 Josh Smith .20 .50
107 Marvin Williams .20 .50
108 Maurice Evans .20 .50
109 Mike Bibby .30 .75
110 Ronald Murray .20 .50
111 Solomon Jones .20 .50
112 Jamal Crawford .30 .75
113 Zaza Pachulia .20 .50
114 Boris Diaw .25 .60
115 D.J. Augustin .20 .50
116 DeSagana Diop .20 .50
117 Dontell Jefferson RC .30 .75
118 Gerald Wallace .25 .60
119 Juwan Howard .25 .60
120 Nazr Mohammed .20 .50
121 Raja Bell .25 .60
122 Raymond Felton .20 .50
123 Vladimir Radmanovic .20 .50
124 Tyson Chandler .25 .60
125 Chris Quinn .20 .50
126 Daequan Cook .20 .50
127 Dwyane Wade .60 1.50
128 James Jones .30 .75
129 Jermaine O'Neal .30 .75
130 Luther Head .20 .50
131 Mario Chalmers .25 .60
132 Michael Beasley .20 .50
133 Udonis Haslem .20 .50
134 Anthony Johnson .20 .50
135 Dwight Howard .40 1.00
136 J.J. Redick .30 .75
137 Jameer Nelson .20 .50
138 Mickael Pietrus .20 .50
139 Rashard Lewis .20 .50
140 Vince Carter .60 1.50
141 Brandon Bass .20 .50
142 Matt Barnes .20 .50
143 Andray Blatche .20 .50
144 Antawn Jamison .20 .50
145 Brendan Haywood .20 .50
146 Caron Butler .20 .50
147 DeShawn Stevenson .20 .50
148 Gilbert Arenas .25 .60
149 Mike James .20 .50
150 Mike Miller .25 .60
151 Nick Young .20 .50
152 Randy Foye .20 .50
153 Tim Thomas .20 .50
154 Dirk Nowitzki .75 2.00
155 Erick Dampier .20 .50
156 Gerald Green .25 .60
157 James Singleton .20 .50
158 Jason Kidd .50 1.25
159 Jason Terry .25 .60
160 Greg Buckner .20 .50
161 Shawn Marion .30 .75
162 Jose Barea .30 .75
163 Josh Howard .25 .60
164 Aaron Brooks .20 .50
165 Brent Barry .20 .50
166 Carl Landry .20 .50
167 Dikembe Mutombo .50 1.25
168 Luis Scola .25 .60
169 Shane Battier .30 .75
170 Tracy McGrady .60 1.50
171 Trevor Ariza .20 .50
172 Von Wafer .20 .50
173 Yao Ming .75 2.00
174 Darius Miles .20 .50
175 Darrell Arthur .20 .50
176 Hakim Warrick .20 .50
177 Marc Gasol .30 .75
178 Mike Conley Jr. .25 .60
179 O.J. Mayo .20 .50
180 Jerry Stackhouse .25 .60
181 Zach Randolph .30 .75
182 Rudy Gay .30 .75
183 Chris Paul .60 1.50
184 Emeka Okafor .25 .60
185 David West .25 .60
186 Devin Brown .20 .50
187 James Posey .20 .50
188 Julian Wright .20 .50
189 Morris Peterson .20 .50
190 Peja Stojakovic .25 .60
191 Rasual Butler .20 .50
192 Drew Gooden .25 .60
193 Manu Ginobili .60 1.50
194 Matt Bonner .20 .50
195 Michael Finley .30 .75
196 Richard Jefferson .25 .60
197 Roger Mason .20 .50
198 Tim Duncan .75 2.00
199 Antonio McDyess .25 .60
200 Tony Parker .50 1.25
201 Anthony Carter .20 .50
202 Carmelo Anthony .50 1.25
203 Chauncey Billups .40 1.00
204 Chris Andersen .30 .75
205 J.R. Smith .30 .75
206 Kenyon Martin .25 .60
207 Linas Kleiza .20 .50
208 Arron Afflalo .20 .50
209 Nene .25 .60
210 Al Jefferson .20 .50
211 Bobby Brown .20 .50
212 Corey Brewer .20 .50
213 Darius Songaila .20 .50
214 Kevin Love .30 .75
215 Rodney Carney .20 .50
216 Quentin Richardson .20 .50
217 Ryan Gomes .20 .50
218 Brandon Roy .40 1.00
219 Greg Oden .20 .50
220 Jerryd Bayless .20 .50
221 Joel Przybilla .20 .50
222 LaMarcus Aldridge .30 .75
223 Nicolas Batum .25 .60
224 Rudy Fernandez .20 .50
225 Steve Blake .20 .50
226 Travis Outlaw .20 .50
227 Andre Miller .30 .75
228 D.J. White .20 .50
229 Desmond Mason .20 .50
230 Jeff Green .25 .60
231 Kevin Durant 1.25 3.00
232 Nenad Krstic .20 .50
233 Nick Collison .20 .50
234 Russell Westbrook .60 1.50
235 Thabo Sefolosha .20 .50
236 Andrei Kirilenko .25 .60
237 C.J. Miles .20 .50
238 Carlos Boozer .25 .60
239 Deron Williams .25 .60
240 Kosta Koufos .20 .50
241 Kyle Korver .25 .60
242 Matt Harpring .20 .50
243 Mehmet Okur .20 .50
244 Paul Millsap .25 .60
245 Ronnie Brewer .20 .50
246 Andris Biedrins .20 .50
247 Anthony Morrow .20 .50
248 Anthony Randolph .20 .50
249 Brandan Wright .20 .50
250 C.J. Watson .20 .50
251 Corey Maggette .25 .60
252 Kelenna Azubuike .20 .50
253 Marco Belinelli .20 .50
254 Monta Ellis .25 .60
255 Acie Law .20 .50
256 Ronny Turiaf .20 .50
257 Stephen Jackson .25 .60
258 Al Thornton .20 .50
259 Baron Davis .25 .60
260 Chris Kaman .25 .60
261 Eric Gordon .25 .60
262 Fred Jones .20 .50
263 Marcus Camby .25 .60
264 Ricky Davis .25 .60
265 Steve Novak .20 .50
266 Sebastian Telfair .20 .50
267 Craig Smith .20 .50
268 Adam Morrison .20 .50
269 Andrew Bynum .20 .50
270 Derek Fisher .30 .75
271 Jordan Farmar .20 .50
272 Josh Powell .20 .50
273 Kobe Bryant 2.50 6.00
274 Lamar Odom .25 .60
275 Luke Walton .25 .60
276 Pau Gasol .50 1.25
277 Ron Artest .30 .75
278 Sasha Vujacic .20 .50
279 Alando Tucker .20 .50
280 Sasha Pavlovic .20 .50
281 Amare Stoudemire .25 .60
282 Ben Wallace .40 1.00
283 Goran Dragic RC 6.00 15.00
284 Grant Hill .50 1.25
285 Jared Dudley .20 .50
286 Jason Richardson .30 .75
287 Leandro Barbosa .25 .60
288 Channing Frye .20 .50
289 Steve Nash .60 1.50
290 Andres Nocioni .20 .50
291 Bobby Udrih .20 .50
292 Bobby Jackson .20 .50
293 Francisco Garcia .20 .50
294 Ike Diogu .20 .50
295 Jason Thompson .20 .50
296 Kevin Martin .25 .60
297 Rashad McCants .20 .50
298 Sergio Rodriguez .20 .50
299 Sean May .20 .50
300 Spencer Hawes .20 .50
301 Blake Griffin RC 2.50 6.00
302 Hasheem Thabeet RC .40 1.00
303 James Harden RC 20.00 50.00
304 Tyreke Evans RC .50 1.25
305 Hasheem Thabeet RC .40 1.00
306 Jonny Flynn RC .40 1.00
307 Stephen Curry RC 100.00 250.00
308 Jordan Hill RC .40 1.00
309 DeMar DeRozan RC 6.00 15.00
310 Brandon Jennings RC .60 1.50
311 Terrence Williams RC .40 1.00
312 Gerald Henderson RC .40 1.00
313 Tyler Hansbrough RC .50 1.25
314 Earl Clark RC .40 1.00
315 Austin Daye RC .40 1.00
316 James Johnson RC .50 1.25
317 Jrue Holiday RC 2.00 5.00
318 Ty Lawson RC .50 1.25
319 Jeff Teague RC .50 1.25
320 Eric Maynor RC .40 1.00
321 Darren Collison RC .60 1.50
322 Blake Griffin RC 2.50 6.00
323 Omri Casspi RC .40 1.00
324 B.J. Mullens RC .40 1.00
325 Rodrigue Beaubois RC .40 1.00
326 Taj Gibson RC .50 1.25
327 DeMarre Carroll RC .50 1.25
328 Wayne Ellington RC .50 1.25
329 Toney Douglas RC .40 1.00
330 Tyreke Evans RC .50 1.25
331 Jeff Pendergraph RC .40 1.00
332 Jermaine Taylor RC .40 1.00
333 Dante Cunningham RC .40 1.00
334 DaJuan Summers RC .40 1.00
335 Sam Young RC .40 1.00
336 DeJuan Blair RC .50 1.25
337 Jon Brockman RC .40 1.00
338 Derrick Brown RC .40 1.00
339 Jodie Meeks RC .40 1.00
340 Patrick Beverley RC .60 1.50
341 Marcus Thornton RC .50 1.25
342 Chase Budinger RC .40 1.00
343 Jack McClinton RC .40 1.00
344 Danny Green RC .60 1.50
345 Taylor Griffin RC .40 1.00
346 A.J. Price RC .40 1.00
347 Jonas Jerebko RC .50 1.25
348 Lester Hudson RC .40 1.00
349 Goran Suton RC .40 1.00
350 Ty Lawson RC .50 1.25
351 Blake Griffin RC 2.50 6.00
352 Hasheem Thabeet RC .40 1.00
353 James Harden RC 20.00 50.00
354 Tyreke Evans RC .50 1.25
355 Jordan Hill RC .40 1.00
356 Jonny Flynn RC .40 1.00
357 Stephen Curry RC 100.00 250.00
358 Jordan Hill RC .40 1.00
359 DeMar DeRozan RC 6.00 15.00
360 Brandon Jennings RC .60 1.50
361 Terrence Williams RC .40 1.00
362 Gerald Henderson RC .40 1.00
363 Tyler Hansbrough RC .50 1.25
364 Earl Clark RC .40 1.00
365 Austin Daye RC .40 1.00
366 James Johnson RC .50 1.25
367 Jrue Holiday RC 2.00 5.00
368 Ty Lawson RC .50 1.25
369 Jeff Teague RC .50 1.25
370 Eric Maynor RC .40 1.00
371 Darren Collison RC .60 1.50
372 Stephen Curry RC 100.00 250.00
373 Omri Casspi RC .40 1.00
374 B.J. Mullens RC .40 1.00
375 Rodrigue Beaubois RC .40 1.00
376 Taj Gibson RC .50 1.25
377 DeMarre Carroll RC .50 1.25
378 Wayne Ellington RC .50 1.25
379 Toney Douglas RC .40 1.00
380 Tyler Hansbrough RC .50 1.25
381 Jeff Pendergraph RC .40 1.00
382 Jermaine Taylor RC .40 1.00
383 Dante Cunningham RC .40 1.00
384 DaJuan Summers RC .40 1.00
385 Sam Young RC .40 1.00
386 DeJuan Blair RC .50 1.25
387 Jon Brockman RC .40 1.00
388 Derrick Brown RC .40 1.00
389 Jodie Meeks RC .40 1.00
390 Patrick Beverley RC .60 1.50
391 Marcus Thornton RC .50 1.25
392 Chase Budinger RC .40 1.00
393 Jack McClinton RC .40 1.00
394 Danny Green RC .60 1.50
395 Taylor Griffin RC .40 1.00
396 A.J. Price RC .40 1.00
397 Jonas Jerebko RC .50 1.25
398 Lester Hudson RC .40 1.00
399 Goran Suton RC .40 1.00
400 James Harden RC 20.00 50.00

2009-10 Panini Artists Proof

*AP 1-300: 1.25X TO 3X BASE HI
*AP 301-400: 1X TO 2.5X BASE HI
STATED PRINT RUN 199 SER.#'d SETS
303 James Harden 25.00 60.00
307 Stephen Curry 150.00 400.00
353 James Harden 25.00 60.00
400 James Harden 25.00 60.00

2009-10 Panini Glossy

*GLOSSY: 1-300: .75X TO 2X BASE HI
*GLOSSY: 301-400: .6X TO 1.5X BASE HI

2009-10 Panini All-Pro Team

COMPLETE SET (20) 8.00 20.00
*AP: .75X TO 2X BASE HI
AP PRINT RUN 199 SER.#'d SETS
*GLOSSY: .6X TO 1.5X BASE HI
1 LeBron James 4.00 10.00
2 Dirk Nowitzki 1.25 3.00
3 Dwight Howard .60 1.50
4 Kobe Bryant 4.00 10.00
5 Dwyane Wade 1.00 2.50
6 Tim Duncan 1.25 3.00
7 Paul Pierce .75 2.00
8 Yao Ming 1.25 3.00
9 Brandon Roy .60 1.50
10 Chris Paul 1.00 2.50
11 Carmelo Anthony .75 2.00
12 Pau Gasol .75 2.00
13 Shaquille O'Neal 1.50 4.00
14 Chauncey Billups .60 1.50
15 Tony Parker .75 2.00
16 Deron Williams .40 1.00
17 Kevin Garnett 1.25 3.00
18 Chris Bosh .60 1.50
19 Joe Johnson .50 1.25
20 Kevin Durant 2.00 5.00

2019-20 Panini Black

STATED PRINT RUN 149 SER.#'d SETS
*SILVER/65: .75X TO 2X BASIC
*COPPER/49: 1X TO 2.5X BASIC
*GOLD/25: 1.25X TO 3X BASIC
1 Trae Young 5.00 12.00
2 John Collins 2.00 5.00
3 Kemba Walker 1.50 4.00
4 Jayson Tatum 8.00 20.00
5 Kyrie Irving 4.00 10.00
6 Kevin Durant 6.00 15.00
7 Devonte' Graham 1.50 4.00
8 Miles Bridges 2.00 5.00
9 Zach LaVine 3.00 8.00
10 Lauri Markkanen 2.50 6.00
11 Collin Sexton 2.50 6.00
12 Andre Drummond 1.50 4.00
13 Luka Doncic 12.00 30.00
14 Kristaps Porzingis 2.50 6.00
15 Nikola Jokic 10.00 25.00
16 Jamal Murray 3.00 8.00
17 Derrick Rose 4.00 10.00
18 Blake Griffin 2.00 5.00
19 Stephen Curry 15.00 40.00
20 Andrew Wiggins 2.50 6.00
21 James Harden 4.00 10.00
22 Russell Westbrook 3.00 8.00
23 Domantas Sabonis 2.50 6.00
24 Malcolm Brogdon 1.50 4.00
25 Kawhi Leonard 5.00 12.00
26 Paul George 3.00 8.00
27 LeBron James 15.00 40.00
28 Anthony Davis 5.00 12.00
29 Kyle Kuzma 2.50 6.00
30 Jaren Jackson Jr. 3.00 8.00
31 Dillon Brooks 1.50 4.00
32 Jimmy Butler 4.00 10.00
33 Bam Adebayo 3.00 8.00
34 Giannis Antetokounmpo 10.00 25.00
35 Khris Middleton 2.00 5.00
36 Karl-Anthony Towns 3.00 8.00
37 D'Angelo Russell 1.50 4.00
38 Brandon Ingram 2.00 5.00
39 Lonzo Ball 2.00 5.00
40 Jrue Holiday 2.50 6.00
41 Julius Randle 2.50 6.00
42 Elfrid Payton 1.25 3.00
43 Chris Paul 4.00 10.00
44 Shai Gilgeous-Alexander 10.00 25.00
45 Dennis Schroder 1.50 4.00
46 Nikola Vucevic 1.50 4.00
47 Aaron Gordon 2.00 5.00
48 Joel Embiid 4.00 10.00
49 Ben Simmons 2.00 5.00
50 Devin Booker .50 1.25
51 Deandre Ayton 2.00 5.00

52 Damian Lillard 5.00 12.00
53 CJ McCollum 2.00 5.00
54 Buddy Hield 1.50 4.00
55 De'Aaron Fox 3.00 8.00
56 DeMar DeRozan 2.50 6.00
57 LaMarcus Aldridge 2.00 5.00
58 Pascal Siakam 3.00 8.00
59 Kyle Lowry 2.00 5.00
60 Fred VanVleet 2.50 6.00
61 Donovan Mitchell 4.00 10.00
62 Bojan Bogdanovic 1.50 4.00
63 Rudy Gobert 2.50 6.00
64 Bradley Beal 2.50 6.00
65 John Wall 2.50 6.00
66 Zion Williamson RC 20.00 50.00
67 Ja Morant RC 20.00 50.00
68 RJ Barrett RC 5.00 12.00
69 Rui Hachimura RC 5.00 12.00
70 Tyler Herro RC 6.00 15.00
71 Kendrick Nunn RC 2.00 5.00
72 Coby White RC 4.00 10.00
73 Eric Paschall RC 1.50 4.00
74 Darius Garland RC 5.00 12.00
75 De'Andre Hunter RC 5.00 12.00
76 PJ Washington Jr. RC 4.00 10.00
77 Jarrett Culver RC 1.25 3.00
78 Cam Reddish RC 2.00 5.00
79 Terence Davis RC 2.00 5.00
80 Jaxson Hayes RC 2.00 5.00
81 Kevin Porter Jr. RC 2.50 6.00
82 Jordan Poole RC 5.00 12.00
83 Cameron Johnson RC 3.00 8.00
84 Darius Bazley RC 1.25 3.00
85 Matisse Thybulle RC 2.50 6.00
86 Nickeil Alexander-Walker RC 2.00 5.00
87 Sekou Doumbouya RC 1.25 3.00
88 Grant Williams RC 2.00 5.00
89 Bruno Fernando RC 1.50 4.00
90 Keldon Johnson RC 4.00 10.00
91 Nassir Little RC 2.00 5.00
92 Goga Bitadze RC 2.00 5.00
93 Ty Jerome RC 2.50 6.00
94 Carsen Edwards RC 1.50 4.00
95 Luka Samanic RC 1.50 4.00

2019-20 Panini Black Rookie Memorabilia Autographs

STATED PRINT RUN 49-99 SER.#'d SETS
*SILVER/25-49: .5X TO 1.2X BASIC
*COPPER/15-25: .6X TO 1.5X BASIC
NO PRICING ON QTY 15
1 Zion Williamson 300.00 600.00
2 Ja Morant 300.00 600.00
3 RJ Barrett 25.00 60.00
4 Tyler Herro 30.00 80.00
5 Rui Hachimura 25.00 60.00
6 Cam Reddish 10.00 25.00
7 PJ Washington Jr. 20.00 50.00
8 Coby White 20.00 50.00
9 Carsen Edwards 8.00 20.00
10 Jarrett Culver 6.00 15.00
11 Jaxson Hayes 10.00 25.00
12 De'Andre Hunter 25.00 60.00
13 Keldon Johnson 20.00 50.00
14 Sekou Doumbouya 6.00 15.00
15 KZ Okpala 8.00 20.00
16 Brandon Clarke 12.00 30.00
17 Bol Bol 15.00 40.00
18 Nassir Little 10.00 25.00
19 Kendrick Nunn 10.00 25.00
20 Eric Paschall 8.00 20.00
21 Luka Samanic 8.00 20.00
22 Kevin Porter Jr. 12.00 30.00
23 Matisse Thybulle 12.00 30.00
24 Nickeil Alexander-Walker 10.00 25.00
25 Romeo Langford 6.00 15.00
26 Cameron Johnson 15.00 40.00
27 Grant Williams 10.00 25.00
28 Bruno Fernando 8.00 20.00
29 Dylan Windler 8.00 20.00
30 Quinndary Weatherspoon 6.00 15.00
31 Ty Jerome 12.00 30.00
32 Cody Martin 10.00 25.00
33 Goga Bitadze 10.00 25.00
34 Jordan Poole 25.00 60.00
35 Admiral Schofield 8.00 20.00
36 Jaylen Nowell 8.00 20.00
37 Tremont Waters 8.00 20.00
38 Darius Bazley 6.00 15.00
39 Nicolo Melli 8.00 20.00
40 Terence Davis 10.00 25.00

2019-20 Panini Black Rookie Variation

STATED PRINT RUN 99 SER.#'d SETS
*RC VAR SILVER/49: .5X TO 1.2X BASIC
*RC VAR COPPER/25: .75X TO 2X BASIC
66 Zion Williamson 30.00 80.00
67 Ja Morant 30.00 80.00
68 RJ Barrett 8.00 20.00
69 Rui Hachimura 8.00 20.00
70 Tyler Herro 10.00 25.00

2019-20 Panini Black Rookie Variation Memorabilia Autographs

STATED PRINT RUN 49 SER.#'d SETS
*SILVER/25: .5X TO 1.2X BASIC
1 Zion Williamson 300.00 600.00
2 Ja Morant 300.00 600.00
3 RJ Barrett 25.00 60.00
4 Tyler Herro 30.00 80.00
5 Rui Hachimura 25.00 60.00
6 Cam Reddish 10.00 25.00
7 PJ Washington Jr. 20.00 50.00
8 Coby White 20.00 50.00
9 Carsen Edwards 8.00 20.00
10 Kendrick Nunn 10.00 25.00

2021-22 Panini Black

COMPLETE SET (95)
STATED PRINT RUN 149 SER.#'d SETS
*SILVER/75: .75X TO 2X BASIC
*COPPER/49: 1.25X TO 3X BASIC
*GOLD/25: 2X TO 5X BASIC
1 Jimmy Butler 2.00 5.00
2 Tyler Herro 2.00 5.00
3 DeMar DeRozan 1.50 4.00
4 Lonzo Ball 1.25 3.00
5 Zach LaVine 2.00 5.00
6 Joel Embiid 3.00 8.00
7 James Harden 2.50 6.00
8 Darius Garland 2.00 5.00
9 Collin Sexton 1.25 3.00
10 Giannis Antetokounmpo 6.00 15.00
11 Khris Middleton 1.25 3.00
12 Jayson Tatum 5.00 12.00
13 Jaylen Brown 2.00 5.00
14 Fred VanVleet 1.50 4.00
15 Pascal Siakam 1.50 4.00
16 Kevin Durant 4.00 10.00
17 Ben Simmons 1.25 3.00
18 Kyrie Irving 2.50 6.00
19 LaMelo Ball 3.00 8.00
20 Miles Bridges 1.00 2.50
21 Trae Young 3.00 8.00
22 De'Andre Hunter 1.25 3.00
23 Kristaps Porzingis 1.50 4.00
24 Bradley Beal 1.50 4.00
25 RJ Barrett 2.00 5.00
26 Julius Randle 1.50 4.00
27 Tyrese Haliburton 2.50 6.00
28 Malcolm Brogdon 1.00 2.50
29 Jerami Grant 1.25 3.00
30 Marvin Bagley III 1.00 2.50
31 Cole Anthony 1.50 4.00
32 Wendell Carter Jr. 1.25 3.00
33 Deandre Ayton 1.25 3.00
34 Devin Booker 3.00 8.00
35 Chris Paul 2.50 6.00
36 Stephen Curry 8.00 20.00
37 Klay Thompson 3.00 8.00
38 Draymond Green 1.50 4.00
39 Ja Morant 4.00 10.00
40 Desmond Bane 2.50 6.00
41 Donovan Mitchell 2.50 6.00
42 Rudy Gobert 1.50 4.00
43 Luka Doncic 8.00 20.00
44 Spencer Dinwiddie 1.00 2.50
45 Nikola Jokic 6.00 15.00
46 Aaron Gordon 1.25 3.00
47 Anthony Edwards 6.00 15.00
48 Karl-Anthony Towns 2.00 5.00
49 Kawhi Leonard 3.00 8.00
50 Paul George 2.00 5.00
51 LeBron James 10.00 25.00
52 Russell Westbrook 2.00 5.00
53 Anthony Davis 3.00 8.00
54 Damian Lillard 3.00 8.00
55 Anfernee Simons 2.00 5.00
56 Dejounte Murray 1.25 3.00
57 Keldon Johnson 1.50 4.00
58 CJ McCollum 1.00 2.50
59 Zion Williamson 3.00 8.00
60 De'Aaron Fox 2.00 5.00
61 Domantas Sabonis 1.50 4.00
62 Luguentz Dort 1.25 3.00
63 Shai Gilgeous-Alexander 6.00 15.00
64 Christian Wood 1.00 2.50
65 Kevin Porter Jr. 1.00 2.50
66 Josh Giddey RC 6.00 15.00
67 Jalen Green RC 10.00 25.00
68 Jalen Suggs RC 5.00 12.00
69 Scottie Barnes RC 6.00 15.00
70 Evan Mobley RC 8.00 20.00
71 Cade Cunningham RC 12.00 30.00
72 Franz Wagner RC 6.00 15.00
73 Herbert Jones RC 2.50 6.00
74 Chris Duarte RC 1.50 4.00
75 Ayo Dosunmu RC 4.00 10.00
76 Davion Mitchell RC 2.00 5.00
77 Corey Kispert RC 2.50 6.00
78 Josh Christopher RC 1.50 4.00
79 Cameron Thomas RC 4.00 10.00
80 Jonathan Kuminga RC 6.00 15.00
81 Alperen Sengun RC 6.00 15.00
82 Bones Hyland RC 2.50 6.00
83 Joshua Primo RC 1.50 4.00
84 Moses Moody RC 4.00 10.00
85 Tre Mann RC 3.00 8.00
86 Brandon Boston Jr. RC 2.00 5.00
87 Trey Murphy III RC 6.00 15.00
88 Jeremiah Robinson-Earl RC 2.00 5.00
89 Ziaire Williams RC 2.50 6.00
90 Quentin Grimes RC 4.00 10.00
91 Austin Reaves RC 10.00 25.00
92 Aaron Wiggins RC 2.50 6.00
93 Day'Ron Sharpe RC 2.00 5.00
94 Luka Garza RC 2.00 5.00
95 James Bouknight RC 1.50 4.00

2021-22 Panini Black Rookie Jumbo Memorabilia Autographs

COMPLETE SET (20)
STATED PRINT RUN 25 SER.#'d SETS
1 Scottie Barnes 125.00 300.00
2 Austin Reaves 200.00 500.00
3 Franz Wagner 100.00 250.00
4 Cade Cunningham 300.00 600.00
5 Kessler Edwards 15.00 40.00
6 Chris Duarte 12.00 30.00
7 Ayo Dosunmu 30.00 80.00
8 Jeremiah Robinson-Earl 15.00 40.00
9 Joshua Primo 12.00 30.00
10 Jonathan Kuminga 100.00 250.00
11 Herbert Jones 20.00 50.00
12 Moses Moody 30.00 80.00
13 Cameron Thomas 30.00 80.00
14 Josh Giddey 125.00 300.00
15 Davion Mitchell 15.00 40.00
16 Day'Ron Sharpe 15.00 40.00
17 Tre Mann 25.00 60.00
18 Bones Hyland 20.00 50.00
19 Joe Wieskamp 12.00 30.00
20 Jalen Green 150.00 400.00

2021-22 Panini Black Rookie Memorabilia Autographs

COMPLETE SET (40)
STATED PRINT RUN 49 SER.#'d SETS
*SILVER/25: .5X TO 1.25X BASIC
1 Aaron Wiggins 12.00 30.00
2 Austin Reaves 125.00 300.00
3 Ayo Dosunmu 20.00 50.00
4 Bones Hyland 12.00 30.00
5 Brandon Boston Jr. 10.00 25.00
6 Cade Cunningham 150.00 400.00
7 Cameron Thomas 20.00 50.00
8 Charles Bassey 10.00 25.00
9 Chris Duarte 8.00 20.00
10 Corey Kispert 12.00 30.00
11 Davion Mitchell 10.00 25.00
12 Day'Ron Sharpe 10.00 25.00
13 Evan Mobley 75.00 200.00
14 Franz Wagner 60.00 150.00
15 Greg Brown III 8.00 20.00
16 Herbert Jones 12.00 30.00
17 Isaiah Jackson 10.00 25.00
18 Jaden Springer 10.00 25.00
19 Jalen Green 100.00 250.00
20 Jalen Johnson 30.00 80.00
21 Jalen Suggs 25.00 60.00
22 James Bouknight 8.00 20.00
23 Jared Butler 10.00 25.00
24 Jeremiah Robinson-Earl 10.00 25.00
25 Jonathan Kuminga 60.00 150.00
26 Josh Giddey 75.00 200.00
27 Joshua Primo 8.00 20.00
28 JT Thor 10.00 25.00
29 Jason Preston 8.00 20.00
30 Keon Johnson 8.00 20.00
31 Kessler Edwards 10.00 25.00
32 Sandro Mamukelashvili 12.00 30.00
33 Moses Moody 20.00 50.00
34 Quentin Grimes 20.00 50.00
35 Santi Aldama 12.00 30.00
36 Scottie Barnes 75.00 200.00
37 Scottie Lewis 8.00 20.00
38 Tre Mann 15.00 40.00
39 Isaiah Todd 8.00 20.00
40 Ziaire Williams 12.00 30.00

2021-22 Panini Black Smoke Show Signatures

COMPLETE SET (40)
STATED PRINT RUN 25 SER.#'d SETS
1 Ziaire Williams 12.00 30.00
2 Sandro Mamukelashvili 12.00 30.00
3 Tre Mann 15.00 40.00
4 Scottie Lewis 8.00 20.00
5 Scottie Barnes 30.00 80.00
6 Santi Aldama 12.00 30.00
7 Quentin Grimes 20.00 50.00
8 Moses Moody 20.00 50.00
9 Jose Alvarado 25.00 60.00
10 Kessler Edwards 10.00 25.00
11 Keon Johnson 10.00 25.00
12 David Johnson 8.00 20.00
13 Joe Wieskamp 8.00 20.00
14 Joshua Primo 8.00 20.00
15 Josh Giddey 30.00 80.00
16 Alperen Sengun 50.00 120.00
17 Jeremiah Robinson-Earl 10.00 25.00
18 Jared Butler 10.00 25.00
19 Isaiah Todd 8.00 20.00
20 Jalen Suggs 25.00 60.00
21 Jalen Johnson 30.00 80.00
22 Jalen Green 50.00 120.00
23 Jaden Springer 10.00 25.00
24 Isaiah Jackson 10.00 25.00
25 Herbert Jones 12.00 30.00
26 Greg Brown III 8.00 20.00
27 Franz Wagner 30.00 80.00
28 Evan Mobley 40.00 100.00
29 Day'Ron Sharpe 10.00 25.00
30 Davion Mitchell 10.00 25.00
31 Corey Kispert 12.00 30.00
32 Chris Duarte 8.00 20.00
33 Charles Bassey 10.00 25.00
34 Cameron Thomas 20.00 50.00
35 Cade Cunningham 125.00 300.00
36 Brandon Boston Jr. 10.00 25.00
37 Bones Hyland 12.00 30.00
38 Ayo Dosunmu 20.00 50.00
39 Austin Reaves 100.00 250.00
40 Aaron Wiggins 12.00 30.00

2021-22 Panini Black White Night

COMPLETE SET (5)
1 Giannis Antetokounmpo 500.00 1,000.00
2 Luka Doncic 500.00 1,000.00
3 Stephen Curry 600.00 1,200.00
4 LeBron James 600.00 1,200.00
5 Cade Cunningham 400.00 800.00

2009-10 Panini Block Party

COMPLETE SET (10) 5.00 12.00
*AP: 1X TO 2.5X BASE HI
AP PRINT RUN 199 SER.#'d SETS
*GLOSSY: .6X TO 1.5X BASE HI
1 Dwight Howard 1.00 2.50
2 Chris Andersen .75 2.00
3 Jermaine O'Neal .75 2.00
4 Yao Ming 2.00 5.00
5 Chris Kaman .60 1.50
6 Joakim Noah .50 1.25
7 Kevin Garnett 2.00 5.00
8 Pau Gasol 1.25 3.00
9 Amare Stoudemire .60 1.50
10 Dikembe Mutombo 1.25 3.00

2021-22 Panini Chronicles Draft Picks

*BRONZE: .5X TO 1.2X BASIC
*GREEN: .5X TO 1.2X BASIC
*ORANGE: .5X TO 1.2X BASIC
*PINK: .5X TO 1.2X BASIC
*HOLO: .75X TO 2X BASIC
*PULSAR: .75X TO 2X BASIC
*SILVER: 1.25X TO 3X BASIC
*RED/149: 1.5X TO 4X BASIC
*BLACK: 2X TO 5X BASIC
*BLUE/99: 2X TO 5X BASIC
1 Cade Cunningham 2.00 5.00
2 Evan Mobley 1.25 3.00
3 Jalen Suggs .75 2.00
4 Jalen Green 1.50 4.00
5 Jonathan Kuminga 1.00 2.50
6 Keon Johnson .30 .75
7 Scottie Barnes 1.00 2.50
8 Corey Kispert .40 1.00
9 Franz Wagner 1.00 2.50
10 Davion Mitchell .30 .75
11 Moses Moody .60 1.50
12 Kai Jones .25 .60
13 Jalen Johnson 1.00 2.50
14 Greg Brown III .25 .60
15 Cameron Thomas .60 1.50
16 Ziaire Williams .40 1.00
17 Isaiah Jackson .30 .75
18 Chris Duarte .25 .60
19 Ayo Dosunmu .60 1.50
20 Jaden Springer .30 .75
21 Tre Mann .50 1.25
22 Josh Christopher .25 .60
23 Charles Bassey .30 .75
24 Jared Butler .30 .75
25 Brandon Boston Jr. .30 .75
26 Cade Cunningham Donruss 4.00 10.00
27 Evan Mobley Donruss 2.50 6.00
28 Jalen Suggs Donruss 1.50 4.00
29 Jalen Green Donruss 3.00 8.00
30 Jonathan Kuminga Donruss 2.00 5.00
31 Keon Johnson Donruss .60 1.50
32 Scottie Barnes Donruss 2.00 5.00
33 Corey Kispert Donruss .75 2.00
34 Franz Wagner Donruss 2.00 5.00
35 Davion Mitchell Donruss .60 1.50
36 Moses Moody Donruss 1.25 3.00
37 Kai Jones Donruss .50 1.25
38 Jalen Johnson Donruss 2.00 5.00
39 Greg Brown III Donruss .50 1.25
40 Cameron Thomas Donruss 1.25 3.00
41 Ziaire Williams Donruss .75 2.00
42 Isaiah Jackson Donruss .60 1.50
43 Chris Duarte Donruss .50 1.25
44 Ayo Dosunmu Donruss 1.25 3.00
45 Jaden Springer Donruss .60 1.50
46 Tre Mann Donruss 1.00 2.50
47 Josh Christopher Donruss .50 1.25
48 Charles Bassey Donruss .60 1.50
49 Jared Butler Donruss .60 1.50
50 Brandon Boston Jr. Donruss .60 1.50
51 Cade Cunningham Hoops Retro 4.00 10.00
52 Evan Mobley Hoops Retro 2.50 6.00
53 Jalen Suggs Hoops Retro 1.50 4.00
54 Jalen Green Hoops Retro 3.00 8.00
55 Jonathan Kuminga Hoops Retro 2.00 5.00
56 Keon Johnson Hoops Retro .60 1.50
57 Scottie Barnes Hoops Retro 2.00 5.00
58 Corey Kispert Hoops Retro .75 2.00
59 Franz Wagner Hoops Retro 2.00 5.00
60 Davion Mitchell Hoops Retro .60 1.50
61 Moses Moody Hoops Retro 1.25 3.00
62 Kai Jones Hoops Retro .50 1.25
63 Jalen Johnson Hoops Retro 2.00 5.00
64 Greg Brown III Hoops Retro .50 1.25
65 Cameron Thomas Hoops Retro 1.25 3.00
66 Ziaire Williams Hoops Retro .75 2.00
67 Isaiah Jackson Hoops Retro .60 1.50
68 Chris Duarte Hoops Retro .50 1.25
69 Ayo Dosunmu Hoops Retro 1.25 3.00
70 Jaden Springer Hoops Retro .60 1.50
71 Tre Mann Hoops Retro 1.00 2.50
72 Josh Christopher Hoops Retro .50 1.25
73 Charles Bassey Hoops Retro .60 1.50
74 Jared Butler Hoops Retro .60 1.50
75 Brandon Boston Jr. Hoops Retro .60 1.50
76 Cade Cunningham Luminance 4.00 10.00
77 Evan Mobley Luminance 2.50 6.00
78 Jalen Suggs Luminance 1.50 4.00
79 Jalen Green Luminance 3.00 8.00
80 Jonathan Kuminga Luminance 2.00 5.00
81 Keon Johnson Luminance .60 1.50
82 Scottie Barnes Luminance 2.00 5.00
83 Corey Kispert Luminance .75 2.00
84 Franz Wagner Luminance 2.00 5.00
85 Davion Mitchell Luminance .60 1.50
86 Moses Moody Luminance 1.25 3.00
87 Kai Jones Luminance .50 1.25
88 Jalen Johnson Luminance 2.00 5.00
89 Neemias Queta Luminance .60 1.50
90 Cameron Thomas Luminance 1.25 3.00
91 Ziaire Williams Luminance .75 2.00
92 Isaiah Jackson Luminance .60 1.50
93 Joel Ayayi Luminance .50 1.25
94 Ayo Dosunmu Luminance 1.25 3.00
95 Jaden Springer Luminance .60 1.50
96 Day'Ron Sharpe Luminance .60 1.50
97 Herbert Jones Luminance .75 2.00
98 Luka Garza Luminance .60 1.50
99 Matt Hurt Luminance .60 1.50
100 RaiQuan Gray Luminance .50 1.25
101 Cade Cunningham Essentials 4.00 10.00
102 Evan Mobley Essentials 2.50 6.00
103 Jalen Suggs Essentials 1.50 4.00
104 Jalen Green Essentials 3.00 8.00
105 Jonathan Kuminga Essentials 2.00 5.00
106 Keon Johnson Essentials .60 1.50
107 Scottie Barnes Essentials 2.00 5.00
108 Corey Kispert Essentials .75 2.00
109 Franz Wagner Essentials 2.00 5.00
110 Davion Mitchell Essentials .60 1.50
111 Moses Moody Essentials 1.25 3.00
112 Kai Jones Essentials .50 1.25
113 Jalen Johnson Essentials 2.00 5.00
114 Tre Mann Essentials 1.00 2.50
115 Cameron Thomas Essentials 1.25 3.00
116 Ziaire Williams Essentials .75 2.00
117 Isaiah Jackson Essentials .60 1.50
118 Josh Christopher Essentials .50 1.25
119 Ayo Dosunmu Essentials 1.25 3.00
120 Jaden Springer Essentials .60 1.50
121 Cade Cunningham Recon 4.00 10.00
122 Evan Mobley Recon 2.50 6.00
123 Jalen Suggs Recon 1.50 4.00
124 Jalen Green Recon 3.00 8.00
125 Jonathan Kuminga Recon 2.00 5.00
126 Keon Johnson Recon .60 1.50
127 Scottie Barnes Recon 2.00 5.00
128 Corey Kispert Recon .75 2.00
129 Franz Wagner Recon 2.00 5.00
130 Davion Mitchell Recon .60 1.50
131 Moses Moody Recon 1.25 3.00
132 Kai Jones Recon .50 1.25
133 Jalen Johnson Recon 2.00 5.00
134 Tre Mann Recon 1.00 2.50
135 Cameron Thomas Recon 1.25 3.00
136 Ziaire Williams Recon .75 2.00
137 Isaiah Jackson Recon .60 1.50
138 Josh Christopher Recon .50 1.25
139 Ayo Dosunmu Recon 1.25 3.00
140 Jaden Springer Recon .60 1.50
141 Cade Cunningham Marquee 4.00 10.00
142 Evan Mobley Marquee 2.50 6.00
143 Jalen Suggs Marquee 1.50 4.00
144 Jalen Green Marquee 3.00 8.00
145 Jonathan Kuminga Marquee 2.00 5.00
146 Keon Johnson Marquee .60 1.50
147 Scottie Barnes Marquee 2.00 5.00
148 Corey Kispert Marquee .75 2.00
149 Franz Wagner Marquee 2.00 5.00
150 Davion Mitchell Marquee .60 1.50
151 Moses Moody Marquee 1.25 3.00
152 Kai Jones Marquee .50 1.25
153 Jalen Johnson Marquee 2.00 5.00
154 Tre Mann Marquee 1.00 2.50
155 Cameron Thomas Marquee 1.25 3.00
156 Ziaire Williams Marquee .75 2.00
157 Isaiah Jackson Marquee .60 1.50
158 Josh Christopher Marquee .50 1.25
159 Ayo Dosunmu Marquee 1.25 3.00
160 Jaden Springer Marquee .60 1.50
161 Cade Cunningham XR 4.00 10.00
162 Evan Mobley XR 2.50 6.00
163 Jalen Suggs XR 1.50 4.00
164 Jalen Green XR 3.00 8.00
165 Jonathan Kuminga XR 2.00 5.00
166 Keon Johnson XR .60 1.50
167 Scottie Barnes XR 2.00 5.00
168 Corey Kispert XR .75 2.00
169 Franz Wagner XR 2.00 5.00
170 Davion Mitchell XR .60 1.50
171 Moses Moody XR 1.25 3.00
172 Kai Jones XR .50 1.25
173 Jalen Johnson XR 2.00 5.00
174 Tre Mann XR 1.00 2.50
175 Cameron Thomas XR 1.25 3.00
176 Ziaire Williams XR .75 2.00
177 Isaiah Jackson XR .60 1.50
178 Josh Christopher XR .50 1.25
179 Ayo Dosunmu XR 1.25 3.00
180 Jaden Springer XR .60 1.50
181 Cade Cunningham Gala 5.00 12.00
182 Evan Mobley Gala 3.00 8.00
183 Jalen Suggs Gala 2.00 5.00
184 Jalen Green Gala 4.00 10.00
185 Jonathan Kuminga Gala 2.50 6.00
186 Keon Johnson Gala .75 2.00
187 Scottie Barnes Gala 2.50 6.00
188 Corey Kispert Gala 1.00 2.50
189 Franz Wagner Gala 2.50 6.00
190 Davion Mitchell Gala .75 2.00
191 Moses Moody Gala 1.50 4.00
192 Kai Jones Gala .60 1.50
193 Jalen Johnson Gala 2.50 6.00
194 Tre Mann Gala 1.25 3.00
195 Cameron Thomas Gala 1.50 4.00
196 Ziaire Williams Gala 1.00 2.50
197 Isaiah Jackson Gala .75 2.00
198 Josh Christopher Gala .60 1.50
199 Ayo Dosunmu Gala 1.50 4.00
200 Jaden Springer Gala .75 2.00
201 Cade Cunningham Donruss Optic 5.00 12.00
202 Evan Mobley Donruss Optic 3.00 8.00
203 Jalen Suggs Donruss Optic 2.00 5.00
204 Jalen Green Donruss Optic 4.00 10.00
205 Jonathan Kuminga Donruss Optic 2.50 6.00
206 Keon Johnson Donruss Optic .75 2.00
207 Scottie Barnes Donruss Optic 2.50 6.00
208 Corey Kispert Donruss Optic 1.00 2.50
209 Franz Wagner Donruss Optic 2.50 6.00
210 Davion Mitchell Donruss Optic .75 2.00
211 Moses Moody Donruss Optic 1.50 4.00
212 Kai Jones Donruss Optic .60 1.50
213 Jalen Johnson Donruss Optic 2.50 6.00
215 Cameron Thomas Donruss Optic 1.50 4.00
216 Ziaire Williams Donruss Optic 1.00 2.50
217 Isaiah Jackson Donruss Optic .75 2.00
219 Ayo Dosunmu Donruss Optic 1.50 4.00
220 Jaden Springer Donruss Optic .75 2.00
221 Tre Mann Donruss Optic 1.25 3.00
222 Josh Christopher Donruss Optic .60 1.50
223 Charles Bassey Donruss Optic .75 2.00
224 Jared Butler Donruss Optic .75 2.00
225 Brandon Boston Jr. Donruss Optic .75 2.00
226 Cade Cunningham Flux 5.00 12.00
226 Greg Brown III Donruss Optic .60 1.50
227 Evan Mobley Flux 3.00 8.00
228 Jalen Suggs Flux 2.00 5.00
229A Jalen Green Flux 4.00 10.00
229B Chris Duarte Donruss Optic .60 1.50
230 Jonathan Kuminga Flux 2.50 6.00
231 Keon Johnson Flux .75 2.00
232 Scottie Barnes Flux 2.50 6.00
233 Corey Kispert Flux 1.00 2.50
234 Franz Wagner Flux 2.50 6.00
235 Davion Mitchell Flux .75 2.00
236 Moses Moody Flux 1.50 4.00
237 Kai Jones Flux .60 1.50
238 Jalen Johnson Flux 2.50 6.00
239 Greg Brown III Flux .60 1.50
240 Cameron Thomas Flux 1.50 4.00
241 Ziaire Williams Flux 1.00 2.50
242 Isaiah Jackson Flux .75 2.00
243 Chris Duarte Flux .60 1.50
244 Ayo Dosunmu Flux 1.50 4.00
245 Jaden Springer Flux .75 2.00
246 Tre Mann Flux 1.25 3.00
247 Josh Christopher Flux .60 1.50
248 Charles Bassey Flux .75 2.00
249 Jared Butler Flux .75 2.00
250 Brandon Boston Jr. Flux .75 2.00
251 Cade Cunningham Mosaic 5.00 12.00
252 Evan Mobley Mosaic 3.00 8.00
253 Jalen Suggs Mosaic 2.00 5.00
254 Jalen Green Mosaic 4.00 10.00
255 Jonathan Kuminga Mosaic 2.50 6.00
256 Keon Johnson Mosaic .75 2.00
257 Scottie Barnes Mosaic 2.50 6.00
258 Corey Kispert Mosaic 1.00 2.50
259 Franz Wagner Mosaic 2.50 6.00
260 Davion Mitchell Mosaic .75 2.00
261 Moses Moody Mosaic 1.50 4.00
262 Kai Jones Mosaic .60 1.50
263 Jalen Johnson Mosaic 2.50 6.00
264 Greg Brown III Mosaic .60 1.50
265 Cameron Thomas Mosaic 1.50 4.00
266 Ziaire Williams Mosaic 1.00 2.50
267 Isaiah Jackson Mosaic .75 2.00
268 Chris Duarte Mosaic .60 1.50
269 Ayo Dosunmu Mosaic 1.50 4.00
270 Jaden Springer Mosaic .75 2.00
271 Tre Mann

Mosaic 1.25 3.00
272 Josh Christopher Mosaic .60 1.50
273 Charles Bassey Mosaic .75 2.00
274 Jared Butler Mosaic .75 2.00
275 Brandon Boston Jr. Mosaic .75 2.00
276 Cade Cunningham Select 5.00 12.00
277 Evan Mobley Select 3.00 8.00
278 Jalen Suggs Select 2.00 5.00
279 Jalen Green Select 4.00 10.00
280 Jonathan Kuminga Select 2.50 6.00
281 Keon Johnson Select .75 2.00
282 Scottie Barnes Select 2.50 6.00
283 Corey Kispert Select 1.00 2.50
284 Franz Wagner Select 2.50 6.00
285 Davion Mitchell Select .75 2.00
286 Moses Moody Select 1.50 4.00
287 Kai Jones Select .60 1.50
288 Jalen Johnson Select 2.50 6.00
289 Neemias Queta Select .75 2.00
290 Cameron Thomas Select 1.50 4.00
291 Ziaire Williams Select 1.00 2.50
292 Isaiah Jackson Select .75 2.00
293 Joel Ayayi Select .60 1.50
294 Ayo Dosunmu Select 1.50 4.00
295 Jaden Springer Select .75 2.00
296 Day'Ron Sharpe Select .75 2.00
297 Herbert Jones Select 1.00 2.50
298 Luka Garza Select .75 2.00
299 Matt Hurt Select .75 2.00
300 RaiQuan Gray Select .60 1.50
301 Cade Cunningham Rookies and Stars 4.00 10.00
302 Evan Mobley Rookies and Stars 2.50 6.00
303 Jalen Suggs Rookies and Stars 1.50 4.00
304 Jalen Green Rookies and Stars 3.00 8.00
305 Jonathan Kuminga Rookies and Stars 2.00 5.00
306 Keon Johnson Rookies and Stars .60 1.50
307 Scottie Barnes Rookies and Stars 2.00 5.00
308 Corey Kispert Rookies and Stars .75 2.00
309 Franz Wagner Rookies and Stars 2.00 5.00
310 Davion Mitchell Rookies and Stars .60 1.50
311 Moses Moody Rookies and Stars 1.25 3.00
312 Kai Jones Rookies and Stars .50 1.25
313 Jalen Johnson Rookies and Stars 2.00 5.00
315 Cameron Thomas Rookies and Stars 1.25 3.00
316 Ziaire Williams Rookies and Stars .75 2.00
317 Isaiah Jackson Rookies and Stars .60 1.50
318 Cade Cunningham Playbook 4.00 10.00
319A Evan Mobley Playbook 2.50 6.00
319B Ayo Dosunmu Rookies and Stars 1.25 3.00
320 Jalen Suggs Playbook 1.50 4.00
321 Jalen Green Playbook 3.00 8.00
322 Jonathan Kuminga Playbook 2.00 5.00
323 Keon Johnson Playbook .60 1.50
324 Scottie Barnes Playbook 2.00 5.00
325 Corey Kispert Playbook .75 2.00
326 Franz Wagner Playbook 2.00 5.00
327 Davion Mitchell Playbook .60 1.50
328 Moses Moody Playbook 1.25 3.00
329 Kai Jones Playbook .50 1.25
330 Jalen Johnson Playbook 2.00 5.00
331 Ayo Dosunmu Playbook 1.25 3.00
332 Cameron Thomas Playbook 1.25 3.00
333 Ziaire Williams Playbook .75 2.00
334 Isaiah Jackson Playbook .60 1.50
335 Cade Cunningham Legacy 4.00 10.00
336 Evan Mobley Legacy 2.50 6.00
337 Jalen Suggs Legacy 1.50 4.00
338 Jalen Green Legacy 3.00 8.00
339 Jonathan Kuminga Legacy 2.00 5.00
340 Keon Johnson Legacy .60 1.50
341 Scottie Barnes Legacy 2.00 5.00
342 Corey Kispert Legacy .75 2.00
343 Franz Wagner Legacy 2.00 5.00
344 Davion Mitchell Legacy .60 1.50
345 Moses Moody Legacy 1.25 3.00
346 Kai Jones Legacy .50 1.25
347 Jalen Johnson Legacy 2.00 5.00
348 Ayo Dosunmu Legacy 1.25 3.00
349 Cameron Thomas Legacy 1.25 3.00
350 Ziaire Williams Legacy .75 2.00
351 Isaiah Jackson Legacy .60 1.50
352 Cade Cunningham Playoff 4.00 10.00
353 Evan Mobley Playoff 2.50 6.00
354 Jalen Suggs Playoff 1.50 4.00
355 Jalen Green Playoff 3.00 8.00
356 Jonathan Kuminga Playoff 2.00 5.00
357 Keon Johnson Playoff .60 1.50
358 Scottie Barnes Playoff 2.00 5.00
359 Corey Kispert Playoff .75 2.00
360 Franz Wagner Playoff 2.00 5.00
361 Davion Mitchell Playoff .60 1.50
362 Moses Moody Playoff 1.25 3.00
363 Kai Jones Playoff .50 1.25
364 Jalen Johnson Playoff 2.00 5.00
365 Ayo Dosunmu Playoff 1.25 3.00
366 Cameron Thomas Playoff 1.25 3.00
367 Ziaire Williams Playoff .75 2.00
368 Isaiah Jackson Playoff .60 1.50
369 Cade Cunningham Prestige 4.00 10.00
370 Evan Mobley Prestige 2.50 6.00
371 Jalen Suggs Prestige 1.50 4.00
372 Jalen Green Prestige 3.00 8.00
373 Jonathan Kuminga Prestige 2.00 5.00
374 Keon Johnson Prestige .60 1.50
375 Scottie Barnes Prestige 2.00 5.00
376 Corey Kispert Prestige .75 2.00
377 Franz Wagner Prestige 2.00 5.00
378 Davion Mitchell Prestige .60 1.50
379 Moses Moody Prestige 1.25 3.00
380 Kai Jones Prestige .50 1.25
381 Jalen Johnson Prestige 2.00 5.00
382 Isaiah Jackson Prestige .60 1.50
383 Cameron Thomas Prestige 1.25 3.00
384 Ziaire Williams Prestige .75 2.00
385 Cade Cunningham Score 4.00 10.00
386 Evan Mobley Score 2.50 6.00
387 Jalen Suggs Score 1.50 4.00
388 Jalen Green Score 3.00 8.00
389 Jonathan Kuminga Score 2.00 5.00
390 Keon Johnson Score .60 1.50
391 Scottie Barnes Score 2.00 5.00
392 Corey Kispert Score .75 2.00
393 Franz Wagner Score 2.00 5.00
394 Davion Mitchell Score .60 1.50
395 Moses Moody Score 1.25 3.00
396 Kai Jones Score .50 1.25
397 Jalen Johnson Score 2.00 5.00
398 Isaiah Jackson Score .60 1.50
399 Cameron Thomas Score 1.25 3.00
400 Ziaire Williams Score .75 2.00

2021-22 Panini Chronicles Draft Picks Pink

*PINK: .5X TO 1.2X BASIC

2021-22 Panini Chronicles Draft Picks Absolute Tools of the Trade

*GREEN: .4X TO 1X BASIC
*RED/199: .5X TO 1.2X BASIC
*BLUE/99: .6X TO 1.5X BASIC
1 Cade Cunningham 12.00 30.00
2 Evan Mobley 8.00 20.00
3 Jalen Suggs 5.00 12.00
4 Jalen Green 10.00 25.00
5 Jonathan Kuminga 6.00 15.00
6 Scottie Barnes 6.00 15.00
7 Keon Johnson 2.00 5.00
8 Corey Kispert 2.50 6.00
9 Franz Wagner 6.00 15.00
10 Jalen Johnson 6.00 15.00
12 James Bouknight 1.50 4.00
13 Davion Mitchell 2.00 5.00
14 Kai Jones 1.50 4.00
15 Ziaire Williams 2.50 6.00
16 Isaiah Jackson 2.00 5.00
17 Josh Giddey 6.00 15.00
18 Cameron Thomas 4.00 10.00
19 Trendon Watford 2.50 6.00
20 Ayo Dosunmu 4.00 10.00
21 Tre Mann 3.00 8.00
22 Josh Christopher 1.50 4.00
23 Chris Duarte 1.50 4.00
24 Brandon Boston Jr. 2.00 5.00
25 Day'Ron Sharpe 2.00 5.00
27 Greg Brown III 1.50 4.00
29 Joel Ayayi 1.50 4.00
30 Jared Butler 2.00 5.00
32 Miles McBride 3.00 8.00
33 Herbert Jones 2.50 6.00
34 Matt Hurt 2.00 5.00
38 David Johnson 1.50 4.00
40 Neemias Queta 2.00 5.00

2021-22 Panini Chronicles Draft Picks Certified Freshman Fabric Signatures

EXCHANGE DEADLINE 3/29/2023
1 Cade Cunningham 60.00 150.00
2 Evan Mobley 30.00 80.00
3 Jalen Suggs 20.00 50.00
4 Jalen Green 50.00 120.00
5 Jonathan Kuminga 25.00 60.00
6 Scottie Barnes 25.00 60.00
7 Keon Johnson 8.00 20.00
8 Corey Kispert 10.00 25.00
9 Franz Wagner 25.00 60.00
10 Jalen Johnson 25.00 60.00
12 James Bouknight 6.00 15.00
13 Davion Mitchell 8.00 20.00
14 Kai Jones 6.00 15.00
15 Ziaire Williams 10.00 25.00
16 Isaiah Jackson 8.00 20.00
17 Josh Giddey 25.00 60.00
18 Cameron Thomas 15.00 40.00
20 Ayo Dosunmu 15.00 40.00
21 Tre Mann 12.00 30.00
22 Josh Christopher 6.00 15.00
23 Chris Duarte 6.00 15.00
24 Brandon Boston Jr. 8.00 20.00
25 Day'Ron Sharpe 8.00 20.00
29 Joel Ayayi 6.00 15.00

2021-22 Panini Chronicles Draft Picks Chronicles Rookie Signatures

EXCHANGE DEADLINE 3/29/2023
*BLACK: .5X TO 1.2X BASIC
*BRONZE: .5X TO 1.2X BASIC
*GREEN: .5X TO 1.2X BASIC
*ORANGE: .5X TO 1.2X BASIC
*PINK: .5X TO 1.2X BASIC
1 Aamir Simms 3.00 8.00
3 AJ Lawson 4.00 10.00
4 Amar Sylla 3.00 8.00
5 Balsa Koprivica 3.00 8.00
7 Brandon Rachal 3.00 8.00
9 Dejon Jarreau 3.00 8.00
10 D.J. Funderburk 3.00 8.00
11 DJ Stewart Jr. 3.00 8.00
12 Derek Culver 3.00 8.00
13 Derrick Alston Jr. 3.00 8.00
14 Ethan Thompson 3.00 8.00
15 Elyjah Goss 3.00 8.00
16 Feron Hunt 3.00 8.00
17 Haowen Guo 4.00 10.00
18 Isaiah Miller 3.00 8.00
19 Jay Huff 4.00 10.00
21 Jalen Crutcher 3.00 8.00
22 Johnny Wang 3.00 8.00
23 Anthony Tarke 3.00 8.00
25 Joshua Langford 3.00 8.00
28 Loren Cristian Jackson 3.00 8.00
29 Luka Garza 5.00 12.00
30 MaCio Teague 3.00 8.00
31 Marcus Garrett 4.00 10.00
32 Justin Champagnie 4.00 10.00
33 Jordan Burns 3.00 8.00
34 Matt Coleman III 3.00 8.00
35 Matt Mitchell 3.00 8.00
36 Jordan Schakel 3.00 8.00
37 MJ Walker 4.00 10.00
38 RaiQuan Gray 4.00 10.00
40 Sam Hauser 12.00 30.00
43 Tahj Eaddy 3.00 8.00
44 Jose Alvarado 12.00 30.00
45 Justin Gorham 3.00 8.00
46 Troy Baxter Jr. 3.00 8.00
47 Juwan Durham 3.00 8.00
48 Marcus Burk 3.00 8.00
49 Marcus Zegarowski 4.00 10.00
50 Mitch Ballock 4.00 10.00
51 Romello White 4.00 10.00
52 Moses Wright 4.00 10.00
53 Terrell Gomez 3.00 8.00
54 Tom Digbeu 4.00 10.00
55 Vrenz Bleijenbergh 3.00 8.00
57 Micah Potter 3.00 8.00

2021-22 Panini Chronicles Draft Picks Contenders Optic College Tickets

STATED PRINT RUN 99 SER.#'d SETS
EXCHANGE DEADLINE 3/29/2023
*BLACK: .4X TO 1X BASIC
*BRONZE: .4X TO 1X BASIC
*GREEN: .4X TO 1X BASIC
*ORANGE: .4X TO 1X BASIC
*PINK: .4X TO 1X BASIC
*BLUE/49: .5X TO 1.2X BASIC
*PURPLE/25: .6X TO 1.5X BASIC
1 Cade Cunningham 50.00 125.00
2 Jalen Green 40.00 100.00
3 Scottie Barnes 25.00 60.00
4 Davion Mitchell 8.00 20.00
5 Moses Moody 15.00 40.00
6 James Bouknight 6.00 15.00
7 Corey Kispert 10.00 25.00
8 Ziaire Williams 10.00 25.00
9 Josh Giddey 25.00 60.00
10 Josh Christopher 6.00 15.00
11 Isaiah Jackson 8.00 20.00
12 Tre Mann 12.00 30.00
13 Neemias Queta 8.00 20.00
14 Brandon Boston Jr. 8.00 20.00
17 Miles McBride 12.00 30.00
18 Day'Ron Sharpe 8.00 20.00
19 Herbert Jones 10.00 25.00
20 Matt Hurt 8.00 20.00
21 Scottie Lewis 6.00 15.00
22 Luka Garza 8.00 20.00
25 Bones Hyland 10.00 25.00
27 Austin Reaves 40.00 100.00
28 David Duke Jr. 8.00 20.00
30 RaiQuan Gray 6.00 15.00

2021-22 Panini Chronicles Draft Picks Donruss Rated Rookie Autographs

STATED PRINT RUN 199 SER.#'d SETS
EXCHANGE DEADLINE 3/29/2023
*BLACK: .4X TO 1X BASIC
*BRONZE: .4X TO 1X BASIC
*GREEN: .4X TO 1X BASIC
*ORANGE: .4X TO 1X BASIC
*PINK: .4X TO 1X BASIC
*RED/99: .5X TO 1.2X BASIC
*BLUE/75: .5X TO 1.2X BASIC
*PURPLE/49: .6X TO 1.5X BASIC
1 Sandro Mamukelashvili 8.00 20.00
2 DJ Steward 5.00 12.00
4 Dikembe Andre 5.00 12.00
5 Ibou Dianko Badji 5.00 12.00
6 John Petty Jr. 5.00 12.00
7 Yves Pons 5.00 12.00
10 Mac McClung 12.00 30.00
11 Justin Smith 5.00 12.00
12 Mark Vital 4.00 10.00
13 Mike Smith 4.00 10.00
15 Jay Huff 5.00 12.00
16 DJ Carton 5.00 12.00
17 Cameron Krutwig 5.00 12.00
18 Eugene Omoruyi 5.00 12.00
21 Manny Camper 5.00 12.00
24 Jalen Tate 4.00 10.00
28 Javion Hamlet 4.00 10.00
30 Romeo Weems 4.00 10.00
31 Anthony Tarke 4.00 10.00
32 Chudier Bile 4.00 10.00

2021-22 Panini Chronicles Draft Picks Encased Substantial Rookie Swatches

*GREEN: .4X TO 1X BASIC
*RED/199: .5X TO 1.2X BASIC
*BLUE/99: .6X TO 1.5X BASIC
1 Cade Cunningham 12.00 30.00
2 Evan Mobley 8.00 20.00
3 Jalen Suggs 5.00 12.00
4 Jalen Green 10.00 25.00
5 Jonathan Kuminga 6.00 15.00
6 Scottie Barnes 6.00 15.00
7 Keon Johnson 2.00 5.00
8 Corey Kispert 2.50 6.00
9 Franz Wagner 6.00 15.00
10 Jalen Johnson 6.00 15.00
12 James Bouknight 1.50 4.00
13 Davion Mitchell 2.00 5.00
14 Kai Jones 1.50 4.00
15 Ziaire Williams 2.50 6.00
16 Isaiah Jackson 2.00 5.00
17 Josh Giddey 6.00 15.00
18 Cameron Thomas 4.00 10.00
19 Trendon Watford 2.50 6.00
20 Ayo Dosunmu 4.00 10.00
21 Tre Mann 3.00 8.00
22 Josh Christopher 1.50 4.00
23 Chris Duarte 1.50 4.00
24 Brandon Boston Jr. 2.00 5.00
25 Day'Ron Sharpe 2.00 5.00
27 Greg Brown III 1.50 4.00
29 Joel Ayayi 1.50 4.00
30 Jared Butler 2.00 5.00
32 Miles McBride 3.00 8.00
33 Herbert Jones 2.50 6.00
34 Matt Hurt 2.00 5.00
38 David Johnson 1.50 4.00
40 Neemias Queta 2.00 5.00

2021-22 Panini Chronicles Draft Picks Flux Rookie Autographs

STATED PRINT RUN 99 SER.#'d SETS
EXCHANGE DEADLINE 3/29/2023
*BLACK: .4X TO 1X BASIC
*BRONZE: .4X TO 1X BASIC
*GREEN: .4X TO 1X BASIC
*ORANGE: .4X TO 1X BASIC
*PINK: .4X TO 1X BASIC
*BLUE/49: .5X TO 1.2X BASIC
*PURPLE/25: .6X TO 1.5X BASIC
1 Jalen Suggs 20.00 50.00
2 Evan Mobley 30.00 80.00
3 Jonathan Kuminga 25.00 60.00
4 Keon Johnson 8.00 20.00
5 Jalen Johnson 25.00 60.00
6 Kai Jones 6.00 15.00
7 Chris Duarte 6.00 15.00
8 Franz Wagner 25.00 60.00
9 Charles Bassey 8.00 20.00
10 Cameron Thomas 15.00 40.00
11 Jaden Springer 8.00 20.00
13 Ayo Dosunmu 15.00 40.00
14 Greg Brown III 6.00 15.00
15 Jared Butler 8.00 20.00
18 Joel Ayayi 6.00 15.00
20 Quentin Grimes 15.00 40.00
21 John Petty Jr. 6.00 15.00
22 Alperen Sengun 25.00 60.00
23 Usman Garuba 6.00 15.00
26 Trendon Watford 10.00 25.00
28 Isaiah Livers 8.00 20.00
29 Jeremiah Robinson-Earl 8.00 20.00

2021-22 Panini Chronicles Draft Picks Gold Standard Rookie Jersey Autograph

STATED PRINT RUN 99 SER.#'d SETS
EXCHANGE DEADLINE 3/29/2023
1 Cade Cunningham 50.00 125.00
2 Evan Mobley 30.00 80.00
3 Jalen Suggs 20.00 50.00
4 Jalen Green 40.00 100.00
5 Jonathan Kuminga 25.00 60.00
6 Scottie Barnes 25.00 60.00
7 Keon Johnson 8.00 20.00
8 Corey Kispert 10.00 25.00
9 Franz Wagner 25.00 60.00
10 Jalen Johnson 25.00 60.00
12 James Bouknight 6.00 15.00
13 Davion Mitchell 8.00 20.00
14 Kai Jones 6.00 15.00
15 Ziaire Williams 10.00 25.00
16 Isaiah Jackson 8.00 20.00
17 Josh Giddey 25.00 60.00
18 Cameron Thomas 15.00 40.00
20 Ayo Dosunmu 15.00 40.00
21 Tre Mann 12.00 30.00
22 Josh Christopher 6.00 15.00
23 Chris Duarte 6.00 15.00
24 Brandon Boston Jr. 8.00 20.00
25 Day'Ron Sharpe 8.00 20.00
27 Greg Brown III 6.00 15.00
29 Joel Ayayi 6.00 15.00

2021-22 Panini Chronicles Draft Picks Hoops Retro Autographs

STATED PRINT RUN 199 SER.#'d SETS
EXCHANGE DEADLINE 3/29/2023
*BLACK: .4X TO 1X BASIC
*BRONZE: .4X TO 1X BASIC
*GREEN: .4X TO 1X BASIC
*ORANGE: .4X TO 1X BASIC
*PINK: .4X TO 1X BASIC
*RED/99: .5X TO 1.2X BASIC
*BLUE/75: .5X TO 1.2X BASIC
*PURPLE/49: .6X TO 1.5X BASIC
2 Cameron Krutwig 4.00 10.00
4 Trey Murphy III 15.00 40.00
5 Jalen Tate 3.00 8.00
7 Romeo Weems 3.00 8.00
9 Ibou Dianko Badji 4.00 10.00
10 Aaron Henry 3.00 8.00
11 Dejon Jarreau 3.00 8.00
13 Eugene Omoruyi 4.00 10.00
15 Javion Hamlet 3.00 8.00
17 Justin Champagnie 4.00 10.00
23 Justin Smith 4.00 10.00
24 JaQuori McLaughlin 3.00 8.00
25 Justin Turner 3.00 8.00
26 Chandler Vaudrin 3.00 8.00
28 LJ Figueroa 3.00 8.00
29 Jordan Burns 3.00 8.00
30 Nojel Eastern 3.00 8.00
31 Aleem Ford 3.00 8.00
32 Giorgi Bezhanishvili 3.00 8.00
33 Damien Jefferson 3.00 8.00

2021-22 Panini Chronicles Draft Picks Illusions First Impressions Jersey Autograph

STATED PRINT RUN 99 SER.#'d SETS
EXCHANGE DEADLINE 3/29/2023
1 Cade Cunningham 50.00 125.00
2 Evan Mobley 30.00 80.00
3 Jalen Suggs 20.00 50.00
4 Jalen Green 40.00 100.00
5 Jonathan Kuminga 25.00 60.00
6 Scottie Barnes 25.00 60.00
7 Keon Johnson 8.00 20.00
8 Corey Kispert 10.00 25.00
9 Franz Wagner 25.00 60.00
10 Jalen Johnson 25.00 60.00
29 Joel Ayayi 6.00 15.00
30 Jared Butler 8.00 20.00
31 DJ Steward 6.00 15.00
32 Miles McBride 12.00 30.00
33 Herbert Jones 10.00 25.00
34 Matt Hurt 8.00 20.00
38 David Johnson 6.00 15.00
40 Neemias Queta 8.00 20.00
41 Isaiah Livers 8.00 20.00
42 Jeremiah Robinson-Earl 8.00 20.00
43 RaiQuan Gray 6.00 15.00
44 Trendon Watford 10.00 25.00

2021-22 Panini Chronicles Draft Picks In Flight Signatures

STATED PRINT RUN 99 SER.#'d SETS
EXCHANGE DEADLINE 3/29/2023
*BLACK: .4X TO 1X BASIC
*BRONZE: .4X TO 1X BASIC
*GREEN: .4X TO 1X BASIC
*ORANGE: .4X TO 1X BASIC
*PINK: .4X TO 1X BASIC
*BLUE/49: .5X TO 1.2X BASIC
*PURPLE/25: .6X TO 1.5X BASIC
1 Jalen Suggs 15.00 40.00
2 Evan Mobley 25.00 60.00
3 Jonathan Kuminga 20.00 50.00
4 Keon Johnson 6.00 15.00
5 Jalen Johnson 20.00 50.00
6 Kai Jones 5.00 12.00
7 Chris Duarte 5.00 12.00
8 Franz Wagner 20.00 50.00
9 Charles Bassey 6.00 15.00
10 Cameron Thomas 12.00 30.00
11 Jaden Springer 6.00 15.00
13 Ayo Dosunmu 12.00 30.00
14 Greg Brown III 5.00 12.00
15 Jared Butler 6.00 15.00
18 Joel Ayayi 5.00 12.00
20 Quentin Grimes 12.00 30.00
21 John Petty Jr. 5.00 12.00
22 Alperen Sengun 20.00 50.00
23 Usman Garuba 5.00 12.00
26 Trendon Watford 8.00 20.00
28 Isaiah Livers 6.00 15.00
29 Jeremiah Robinson-Earl 6.00 15.00

2021-22 Panini Chronicles Draft Picks Limited Rookie Jersey Autograph

STATED PRINT RUN 99 SER.#'d SETS
1 Cade Cunningham 50.00 125.00
2 Evan Mobley 30.00 80.00
3 Jalen Suggs 20.00 50.00
4 Jalen Green 40.00 100.00
5 Jonathan Kuminga 25.00 60.00
6 Scottie Barnes 25.00 60.00
7 Keon Johnson 8.00 20.00
8 Corey Kispert 10.00 25.00
9 Franz Wagner 25.00 60.00
10 Jalen Johnson 25.00 60.00
29 Joel Ayayi 6.00 15.00
30 Jared Butler 8.00 20.00
31 DJ Steward 6.00 15.00
32 Miles McBride 12.00 30.00
33 Herbert Jones 10.00 25.00
34 Matt Hurt 8.00 20.00
38 David Johnson 6.00 15.00
40 Neemias Queta 8.00 20.00
41 Isaiah Livers 8.00 20.00
42 Jeremiah Robinson-Earl 8.00 20.00
43 RaiQuan Gray 6.00 15.00
44 Trendon Watford 10.00 25.00

2021-22 Panini Chronicles Draft Picks Mosaic Scripts Autographs

STATED PRINT RUN 99 SER.#'d SETS
*BLACK: .4X TO 1X BASIC
*BRONZE: .4X TO 1X BASIC
*GREEN: .4X TO 1X BASIC
*ORANGE: .4X TO 1X BASIC
*PINK: .4X TO 1X BASIC
*BLUE/49: .5X TO 1.2X BASIC
*PURPLE/25: .6X TO 1.5X BASIC
1 Cade Cunningham 40.00 100.00
2 Jalen Green 30.00 80.00
3 Scottie Barnes 20.00 50.00
4 Davion Mitchell 6.00 15.00
5 Moses Moody 12.00 30.00
6 James Bouknight 5.00 12.00
7 Corey Kispert 8.00 20.00
8 Ziaire Williams 8.00 20.00
9 Josh Giddey 20.00 50.00
10 Josh Christopher 5.00 12.00
11 Isaiah Jackson 6.00 15.00
12 Tre Mann 10.00 25.00
13 Neemias Queta 6.00 15.00
14 Brandon Boston Jr. 6.00 15.00
17 Miles McBride 10.00 25.00
18 Day'Ron Sharpe 6.00 15.00
19 Herbert Jones 8.00 20.00
20 Matt Hurt 6.00 15.00
21 Scottie Lewis 5.00 12.00
22 Luka Garza 6.00 15.00
25 Bones Hyland 8.00 20.00
27 Austin Reaves 30.00 80.00
28 David Duke Jr. 6.00 15.00
30 RaiQuan Gray 5.00 12.00

2021-22 Panini Chronicles Draft Picks Origins Rookie Autographs

STATED PRINT RUN 199 SER.#'d SETS
EXCHANGE DEADLINE 3/29/2023
*BLACK: .4X TO 1X BASIC
*BRONZE: .4X TO 1X BASIC
*GREEN: .4X TO 1X BASIC
*ORANGE: .4X TO 1X BASIC
*PINK: .4X TO 1X BASIC
*RED/99: .5X TO 1.2X BASIC
*BLUE/75: .5X TO 1.2X BASIC
*PURPLE/49: .6X TO 1.5X BASIC
1 JaQuori McLaughlin 3.00 8.00
2 Dejon Jarreau 3.00 8.00
3 Trendon Watford 6.00 15.00
4 Terrell Gomez 3.00 8.00
5 LJ Figueroa 3.00 8.00
7 Nojel Eastern 3.00 8.00
8 Aleem Ford 3.00 8.00
9 Giorgi Bezhanishvili 3.00 8.00
10 Damien Jefferson 3.00 8.00
11 Jordan Schakel 3.00 8.00
12 Romello White 4.00 10.00
13 Marcus Burk 3.00 8.00
14 Brandon Rachal 3.00 8.00
15 Isaiah Miller 3.00 8.00
16 Juwan Durham 3.00 8.00
17 Jalen Crutcher 3.00 8.00
18 Justin Gorham 3.00 8.00
19 Ariel Hukporti 3.00 8.00
20 D.J. Funderburk 3.00 8.00
21 Vrenz Bleijenbergh 3.00 8.00
22 Derrick Alston Jr. 3.00 8.00
23 Johnny Wang 3.00 8.00
24 Elyjah Goss 3.00 8.00
25 Balsa Koprivica 3.00 8.00
26 Amar Sylla 3.00 8.00

2021-22 Panini Chronicles Draft Picks Prestige Bonus Shots Signatures

EXCHANGE DEADLINE 3/29/2023
*BLACK: .5X TO 1.2X BASIC
*BRONZE: .5X TO 1.2X BASIC
*GREEN: .5X TO 1.2X BASIC
*ORANGE: .5X TO 1.2X BASIC
*PINK: .5X TO 1.2X BASIC
1 Anthony Tarke 2.50 6.00
2 D'Mitrik Trice 2.50 6.00
3 Ariel Hukporti 2.50 6.00
4 Chudier Bile 2.50 6.00
5 Cameron Krutwig 3.00 8.00
7 Dikembe Andre 3.00 8.00
10 DJ Steward 3.00 8.00
11 DJ Carton 3.00 8.00
13 Aamir Simms 2.50 6.00
14 Eugene Omoruyi 3.00 8.00
16 Ibou Dianko Badji 3.00 8.00
17 Jalen Tate 2.50 6.00
18 Javion Hamlet 2.50 6.00
22 John Petty Jr. 3.00 8.00
23 DJ Stewart Jr. 2.50 6.00
24 Ethan Thompson 2.50 6.00
25 Joshua Langford 2.50 6.00
26 Kessler Edwards 4.00 10.00
27 Justin Turner 2.50 6.00
29 Mac McClung 8.00 20.00
30 Manny Camper 3.00 8.00
31 Loren Cristian Jackson 2.50 6.00
32 Mark Vital 2.50 6.00
36 Mike Smith 2.50 6.00
37 Neemias Queta 4.00 10.00
40 Sandro Mamukelashvili 5.00 12.00
44 Trendon Watford 5.00 12.00
45 Trey Murphy III 12.00 30.00
46 Yves Pons 3.00 8.00
47 Chandler Vaudrin 2.50 6.00
48 MaCio Teague 2.50 6.00
49 Marcus Garrett 3.00 8.00
50 Matt Coleman III 2.50 6.00
51 Matt Mitchell 2.50 6.00
52 MJ Walker 3.00 8.00
53 Sam Hauser 10.00 25.00
54 Tahj Eaddy 2.50 6.00
55 Troy Baxter Jr. 2.50 6.00
57 Micah Potter 2.50 6.00
58 Romeo Weems 2.50 6.00

2021-22 Panini Chronicles Draft Picks Score Rookie Autographs

STATED PRINT RUN 199 SER.#'d SETS
EXCHANGE DEADLINE 3/29/2023
*BLACK: .4X TO 1X BASIC
*BRONZE: .4X TO 1X BASIC
*GREEN: .4X TO 1X BASIC
*ORANGE: .4X TO 1X BASIC
*PINK: .4X TO 1X BASIC
*RED/99: .5X TO 1.2X BASIC
*BLUE/75: .5X TO 1.2X BASIC
*PURPLE/49: .6X TO 1.5X BASIC
1 JaQuori McLaughlin 3.00 8.00
2 Justin Turner 3.00 8.00
3 Chandler Vaudrin 3.00 8.00
4 Terrell Gomez 3.00 8.00
5 LJ Figueroa 3.00 8.00
6 Jordan Burns 3.00 8.00
7 Nojel Eastern 3.00 8.00
8 Aleem Ford 3.00 8.00
9 Giorgi Bezhanishvili 3.00 8.00
10 Damien Jefferson 3.00 8.00
11 Jordan Schakel 3.00 8.00
12 Romello White 4.00 10.00
13 Marcus Burk 3.00 8.00
14 Brandon Rachal 3.00 8.00
15 Isaiah Miller 3.00 8.00
16 Juwan Durham 3.00 8.00
17 Jalen Crutcher 3.00 8.00
18 Justin Gorham 3.00 8.00
19 Ariel Hukporti 3.00 8.00
20 D.J. Funderburk 3.00 8.00
21 Vrenz Bleijenbergh 3.00 8.00
22 Derrick Alston Jr. 3.00 8.00
23 Johnny Wang 3.00 8.00
24 Elyjah Goss 3.00 8.00
25 Balsa Koprivica 3.00 8.00

2021-22 Panini Chronicles Draft Picks Threads Rookie Memorabilia

*GREEN: .4X TO 1X BASIC
*RED/199: .5X TO 1.2X BASIC
*BLUE/99: .6X TO 1.5X BASIC
1 Cade Cunningham 12.00 30.00
2 Evan Mobley 8.00 20.00
3 Jalen Suggs 5.00 12.00
4 Jalen Green 10.00 25.00
5 Jonathan Kuminga 6.00 15.00
6 Scottie Barnes 6.00 15.00
7 Keon Johnson 2.00 5.00
8 Corey Kispert 2.50 6.00
9 Franz Wagner 6.00 15.00
10 Jalen Johnson 6.00 15.00
13 Davion Mitchell 2.00 5.00
14 Kai Jones 1.50 4.00
15 Ziaire Williams 2.50 6.00
16 Isaiah Jackson 2.00 5.00
17 Josh Giddey 6.00 15.00
18 Cameron Thomas 4.00 10.00
20 Ayo Dosunmu 4.00 10.00
21 Tre Mann 3.00 8.00
22 Josh Christopher 1.50 4.00
23 Chris Duarte 1.50 4.00
24 Brandon Boston Jr. 2.00 5.00
25 Day'Ron Sharpe 2.00 5.00
26 Sharife Cooper 1.50 4.00
27 Greg Brown III 1.50 4.00
29 Joel Ayayi 1.50 4.00
30 Jared Butler 2.00 5.00
32 Miles McBride 3.00 8.00
33 Herbert Jones 2.50 6.00
34 Matt Hurt 2.00 5.00
38 David Johnson 1.50 4.00

2009-10 Panini Decals

COMPLETE SET (31) 15.00 30.00
1 Josh Smith .40 1.00
2 Paul Pierce 1.00 2.50
3 Gerald Wallace .50 1.25
4 Derrick Rose 1.00 2.50
5 LeBron James 5.00 12.00
6 Dirk Nowitzki 1.50 4.00
7 Carmelo Anthony 1.00 2.50
8 Richard Hamilton .60 1.50
9 Stephen Jackson .60 1.50

10 Yao Ming 1.50 4.00
11 Danny Granger .40 1.00
12 Zach Randolph .60 1.50
13 Kobe Bryant 5.00 12.00
14 O.J. Mayo .40 1.00
15 Dwyane Wade 1.25 3.00
16 Michael Redd .50 1.25
17 Al Jefferson .40 1.00
18 Devin Harris .40 1.00
19 Chris Paul 1.25 3.00
20 Al Harrington .60 1.50
21 Kevin Durant 2.50 6.00
22 Dwight Howard .75 2.00
23 Andre Iguodala .60 1.50
24 Steve Nash 1.25 3.00
25 Brandon Roy .75 2.00
26 Kevin Martin .50 1.25
27 Tony Parker 1.00 2.50
28 Chris Bosh .75 2.00
29 Deron Williams .50 1.25
30 Gilbert Arenas .50 1.25
32 Blake Griffin 2.50 6.00

2009-10 Panini Future Stars

COMPLETE SET (20) 4.00 10.00
*AP: 1.25X TO 3X BASE HI
AP PRINT RUN 199 SER.#'d SETS
*GLOSSY: .75X TO 2X BASE HI
1 Al Thornton .30 .75
2 Andrew Bynum .30 .75
3 Charlie Villanueva .30 .75
4 David Lee .30 .75
5 J.J. Redick .50 1.25
6 Jarrett Jack .40 1.00
7 Jeff Green .40 1.00
8 Kelenna Azubuike .30 .75
9 LaMarcus Aldridge .50 1.25
10 Linas Kleiza .30 .75
11 Luis Scola .40 1.00
12 Monta Ellis .40 1.00
13 Nate Robinson .40 1.00
14 Nick Young .30 .75
15 Paul Millsap .40 1.00
16 Rajon Rondo .60 1.50
17 Ronnie Brewer .30 .75
18 Rudy Gay .50 1.25
19 Ryan Gomes .30 .75
20 Randy Foye .30 .75

2009-10 Panini Glow in the Dark Stickers

COMPLETE SET (30) 3.00 8.00
1 Atlanta Hawks .20 .50
2 Boston Celtics .60 1.50
3 Charlotte Bobcats .20 .50
4 Chicago Bulls .40 1.00
5 Cleveland Cavaliers .40 1.00
6 Dallas Mavericks .20 .50
7 Denver Nuggets .20 .50
8 Detroit Pistons .30 .75
9 Golden State Warriors .20 .50
10 Houston Rockets .20 .50
11 Indiana Pacers .20 .50
12 Los Angeles Clippers .20 .50
13 Los Angeles Lakers .60 1.50
14 Memphis Grizzlies .20 .50
15 Miami Heat .20 .50
16 Milwaukee Bucks .20 .50
17 Minnesota Timberwolves .20 .50
18 New Jersey Nets .20 .50
19 New Orleans Hornets .20 .50
20 New York Knicks .40 1.00
21 Oklahoma City Thunder .20 .50
22 Orlando Magic .20 .50
23 Philadelphia 76ers .20 .50
24 Phoenix Suns .20 .50
25 Portland Trail Blazers .20 .50
26 Sacramento Kings .20 .50
27 San Antonio Spurs .30 .75
28 Toronto Raptors .20 .50
29 Utah Jazz .20 .50
30 Washington Wizards .20 .50

2009-10 Panini Headliners

COMPLETE SET (10) 6.00 15.00
*AP: 1X TO 2.5X BASE HI
AP PRINT RUN 199 SER.#'d SETS
*GLOSSY: .6X TO 1.5X BASE HI
1 Chauncey Billups .75 2.00
2 Nate Robinson .50 1.25
3 Jason Kidd 1.00 2.50
4 LeBron James 5.00 12.00
5 Derrick Rose 1.00 2.50
6 Dwight Howard .75 2.00
7 LeBron James 5.00 12.00
8 Kobe Bryant 5.00 12.00
9 Pat Riley .60 1.50
10 Blake Griffin 2.50 6.00
8a Kobe Bryant AU/30 500.00 1,000.00

2009-10 Panini Inscriptions

109 Mike Bibby 5.00 12.00
169 Shane Battier 5.00 12.00
301 Blake Griffin 40.00 100.00
303 James Harden 40.00 100.00
304 Tyreke Evans 4.00 10.00
307 Stephen Curry 1,000.00 2,000.00
308 Jordan Hill 3.00 8.00
310 Brandon Jennings 5.00 12.00
311 Terrence Williams 3.00 8.00
312 Gerald Henderson 3.00 8.00
313 Tyler Hansbrough 10.00 25.00
314 Earl Clark 3.00 8.00
315 Austin Daye 3.00 8.00
316 James Johnson 4.00 10.00
317 Jrue Holiday 15.00 40.00
319 Jeff Teague 4.00 10.00
321 Darren Collison 5.00 12.00
322 Blake Griffin 75.00 200.00
323 Omri Casspi 3.00 8.00
324 B.J. Mullens 3.00 8.00
325 Rodrigue Beaubois 3.00 8.00
326 Taj Gibson 4.00 10.00
327 DeMarre Carroll 4.00 10.00
329 Toney Douglas 3.00 8.00
330 Tyreke Evans 4.00 10.00
331 Jeff Pendergraph 3.00 8.00
332 Jermaine Taylor 3.00 8.00
333 Dante Cunningham 3.00 8.00
334 DaJuan Summers 3.00 8.00
336 DeJuan Blair 4.00 10.00
337 Jon Brockman 3.00 8.00
338 Derrick Brown 3.00 8.00
339 Jodie Meeks 3.00 8.00
341 Marcus Thornton 4.00 10.00
342 Chase Budinger 3.00 8.00
343 Jack McClinton 3.00 8.00
344 Danny Green 5.00 12.00
345 Taylor Griffin 3.00 8.00
346 A.J. Price 3.00 8.00
348 Lester Hudson 3.00 8.00
349 Goran Suton 3.00 8.00
351 Blake Griffin 75.00 200.00
354 Tyreke Evans 4.00 10.00
355 Jordan Hill 3.00 8.00
357 Stephen Curry 1,000.00 2,000.00
358 Jordan Hill 3.00 8.00
360 Brandon Jennings 5.00 12.00
361 Terrence Williams 3.00 8.00
362 Gerald Henderson 3.00 8.00
363 Tyler Hansbrough 10.00 25.00
364 Earl Clark 3.00 8.00
365 Austin Daye 3.00 8.00
366 James Johnson 4.00 10.00
367 Jrue Holiday 15.00 40.00
369 Jeff Teague 4.00 10.00
371 Darren Collison 5.00 12.00
372 Stephen Curry 1,000.00 2,000.00
373 Omri Casspi 3.00 8.00
374 B.J. Mullens 3.00 8.00
375 Rodrigue Beaubois 3.00 8.00
376 Taj Gibson 4.00 10.00
377 DeMarre Carroll 4.00 10.00
379 Toney Douglas 3.00 8.00
380 Tyler Hansbrough 10.00 25.00
381 Jeff Pendergraph 3.00 8.00
382 Jermaine Taylor 3.00 8.00
383 Dante Cunningham 3.00 8.00
384 DaJuan Summers 3.00 8.00
386 DeJuan Blair 4.00 10.00
387 Jon Brockman 3.00 8.00
388 Derrick Brown 3.00 8.00
389 Jodie Meeks 3.00 8.00
391 Marcus Thornton 4.00 10.00
392 Chase Budinger 3.00 8.00
393 Jack McClinton 3.00 8.00
394 Danny Green 5.00 12.00
395 Taylor Griffin 3.00 8.00
396 A.J. Price 3.00 8.00
398 Lester Hudson 3.00 8.00
399 Goran Suton 3.00 8.00

2009-10 Panini Jam Masters

COMPLETE SET (10) 6.00 15.00
*AP: 1X TO 2.5X BASE HI
AP PRINT RUN 199 SER.#'d SETS
*GLOSSY: .6X TO 1.5X BASE HI
1 Tim Duncan 2.00 5.00
2 Shaquille O'Neal 2.50 6.00
3 Dwyane Wade 1.50 4.00
4 LeBron James 6.00 15.00
5 Kobe Bryant 6.00 15.00
6 Danny Granger .50 1.25
7 Nate Robinson .60 1.50
8 Chris Bosh 1.00 2.50
9 Kevin Durant 3.00 8.00
10 Chris Paul 1.50 4.00

2009-10 Panini Legends of the Game

COMPLETE SET (10) 4.00 10.00
*AP: .75X TO 2X BASE HI
AP PRINT RUN 199 SER.#'d SETS
*GLOSSY: .6X TO 1.5X BASE HI
1 Jerry West 1.50 4.00
2 John Havlicek 2.50 6.00
3 Bernard King 1.25 3.00
4 Glen Rice .75 2.00
5 Willis Reed 1.50 4.00
6 Detlef Schrempf 1.00 2.50
7 Dennis Rodman 2.00 5.00
8 Lenny Wilkens 1.00 2.50
9 Bob Cousy 2.50 6.00
10 Sleepy Floyd .75 2.00

2009-10 Panini Legends of the Game Signatures

1 Jerry West 20.00 40.00
5 Willis Reed 40.00 100.00
8 Lenny Wilkens 6.00 15.00
10 Sleepy Floyd 6.00 15.00

2009-10 Panini Next Day Signatures

1 Austin Daye 20.00 50.00
2 B.J. Mullens 20.00 50.00
3 Blake Griffin 125.00 300.00
4 Brandon Jennings 30.00 80.00
5 Chase Budinger 20.00 50.00
6 DaJuan Summers 20.00 50.00
7 Darren Collison 30.00 80.00
8 DeJuan Blair 25.00 60.00
9 DeMarre Carroll 25.00 60.00
10 Earl Clark 20.00 50.00
11 Eric Maynor 20.00 50.00
12 Gerald Henderson 20.00 50.00
13 Hasheem Thabeet 20.00 50.00
14 James Harden 1,000.00 2,000.00
15 James Johnson 25.00 60.00
16 Jeff Pendergraph 20.00 50.00
17 Jeff Teague 25.00 60.00
18 Jermaine Taylor 20.00 50.00
19 Jodie Meeks 20.00 50.00
20 Jonny Flynn 20.00 50.00
21 Jordan Hill 20.00 50.00
22 Jrue Holiday 100.00 250.00
23 Omri Casspi 20.00 50.00
24 Rodrigue Beaubois 20.00 50.00
25 Sam Young 20.00 50.00
26 Stephen Curry 3,000.00 6,000.00
27 Taj Gibson 25.00 60.00
28 Taylor Griffin 20.00 50.00
29 Terrence Williams 20.00 50.00
30 Toney Douglas 20.00 50.00
31 Ty Lawson 25.00 60.00
32 Tyler Hansbrough 25.00 60.00
33 Tyreke Evans 25.00 60.00
34 Wayne Ellington 25.00 60.00

2009-10 Panini The Franchise

COMPLETE SET (20) 10.00 25.00
*AP: .75X TO 2X BASE HI
AP PRINT RUN 199 SER.#'d SETS
*GLOSSY: .6X TO 1.5X BASE HI
1 Andre Iguodala .75 2.00
2 Carmelo Anthony 1.25 3.00
3 Chris Paul 1.50 4.00
4 Derrick Rose 1.25 3.00
5 Dirk Nowitzki 2.00 5.00
6 Dwight Howard 1.00 2.50
7 Dwyane Wade 1.50 4.00
8 Gerald Wallace .60 1.50
9 Josh Smith .50 1.25
10 Kevin Durant 3.00 8.00
11 Kevin Garnett 2.00 5.00
12 Kevin Martin .60 1.50
13 Kobe Bryant 6.00 15.00
14 LeBron James 6.00 15.00
15 Richard Hamilton .75 2.00
16 Rudy Gay .75 2.00
17 Stephen Jackson .60 1.50
18 Steve Nash 1.50 4.00
19 Tony Parker 1.25 3.00
20 Yao Ming 2.00 5.00

2012-13 Panini

COMPLETE SET (300) 15.00 40.00
1 Al Horford .40 1.00
2 Al Jefferson .25 .60
3 Amare Stoudemire .40 1.00
4 Anderson Varejao .25 .60
5 Andray Blatche .25 .60
6 Andre Iguodala .40 1.00
7 Andre Miller .30 .75
8 Andrea Bargnani .25 .60
9 Andrei Kirilenko .30 .75
10 Andrew Bogut .30 .75
11 Andrew Bynum .25 .60
12 Antawn Jamison .30 .75
13 Anthony Morrow .25 .60
14 Anthony Randolph .30 .75
15 Alonzo Gee .25 .60
16 Arron Afflalo .25 .60
17 Ben Gordon .30 .75
18 Beno Udrih .25 .60
19 Blake Griffin .40 1.00
20 Boris Diaw .30 .75
21 Brandon Bass .25 .60
22 Brandon Rush .25 .60
23 Brandon Jennings .25 .60
24 Brandon Roy .30 .75
25 Brook Lopez .30 .75
26 Carl Landry .25 .60
27 Carlos Boozer .30 .75
28 Carmelo Anthony .60 1.50
29 Caron Butler .30 .75
30 Channing Frye .25 .60
31 Chauncey Billups .50 1.25
32 Chris Bosh .50 1.25
33 Chris Kaman .30 .75
34 Chris Paul .75 2.00
35 Corey Brewer .25 .60
36 Courtney Lee .25 .60
37 Daniel Gibson .25 .60
38 Danilo Gallinari .25 .60
39 Danny Granger .25 .60
40 Darren Collison .25 .60
41 David Lee .25 .60
42 David West .30 .75
43 DeAndre Jordan .30 .75
44 DeJuan Blair .25 .60
45 DeMar DeRozan .50 1.25
46 DeMarcus Cousins .40 1.00
47 Deron Williams .30 .75
48 Derrick Favors .30 .75
49 Derrick Rose .60 1.50
50 Marco Belinelli .25 .60
51 Devin Harris .25 .60
52 Dirk Nowitzki 1.00 2.50
53 Drew Gooden .30 .75
54 Dwight Howard .50 1.25
55 Dwyane Wade .75 2.00
56 Elton Brand .30 .75
57 Emeka Okafor .30 .75
58 Eric Bledsoe .30 .75
59 Eric Gordon .30 .75
60 Eric Maynor .25 .60
61 Ersan Ilyasova .25 .60
62 Evan Turner .25 .60
63 Gerald Wallace .30 .75
64 Gerald Henderson .25 .60
65 Glen Davis .25 .60
66 Goran Dragic .40 1.00
67 Gordon Hayward .40 1.00
68 Grant Hill .60 1.50
69 Greg Monroe .25 .60
70 Greivis Vasquez .25 .60
71 Hedo Turkoglu .30 .75
72 Jameer Nelson .25 .60
73 James Harden .75 2.00
74 Jason Kidd .60 1.50
75 Jason Richardson .40 1.00
76 Jason Terry .25 .60
77 Jason Thompson .25 .60
78 JaVale McGee .30 .75
79 Jeff Green .25 .60
80 Jeff Teague .25 .60
81 Jeremy Lin .60 1.50
82 Joakim Noah .30 .75
83 Joe Johnson .30 .75
84 John Salmons .30 .75
85 John Wall .50 1.25
86 Jonas Jerebko .25 .60
87 Jose Calderon .25 .60
88 Josh Smith .25 .60
89 J.R. Smith .40 1.00
90 Jrue Holiday .50 1.25
91 Kendrick Perkins .25 .60
92 Kevin Garnett 1.00 2.50
93 Kirk Hinrich .30 .75
94 Kevin Love .40 1.00
95 Kevin Martin .30 .75
96 Kevin Durant 1.50 4.00
97 Kobe Bryant 3.00 8.00
98 Kris Humphries .25 .60
99 Kyle Korver .30 .75
100 Kyle Lowry .40 1.00
101 Lamar Odom .30 .75
102 LaMarcus Aldridge .40 1.00
103 Landry Fields .25 .60
104 LeBron James 3.00 8.00
105 Louis Williams .30 .75
106 Luc Mbah a Moute .25 .60
107 Luis Scola .30 .75
108 Luol Deng .30 .75
109 Manu Ginobili .75 2.00
110 Marc Gasol .40 1.00
111 Marcin Gortat .25 .60
112 Marcus Camby .40 1.00
113 Marcus Thornton .25 .60
114 Mario Chalmers .30 .75
115 Marreese Speights .25 .60
116 Martell Webster .25 .60
117 Marvin Williams .25 .60
118 Metta World Peace .30 .75
119 Michael Beasley .25 .60
120 Mike Conley .30 .75
121 Mike Miller .30 .75
122 Mike Dunleavy .25 .60
123 Mo Williams .30 .75
124 Monta Ellis .30 .75
125 Nate Robinson .25 .60
126 Nene .30 .75
127 Nick Collison .25 .60
128 Nick Young .25 .60
129 Nicolas Batum .30 .75
130 Nikola Pekovic .25 .60
131 O.J. Mayo .25 .60
132 Patrick Patterson .25 .60
133 Pau Gasol .60 1.50
134 Paul Pierce .60 1.50
135 Paul George .60 1.50
136 Paul Millsap .30 .75
137 Rajon Rondo .50 1.25
138 Ramon Sessions .25 .60
139 Ray Allen .60 1.50
140 Raymond Felton .25 .60
141 Richard Hamilton .40 1.00
142 Richard Jefferson .30 .75
143 Ricky Rubio .30 .75
144 Robin Lopez .25 .60
145 Rodney Stuckey .25 .60
146 Roy Hibbert .30 .75
147 Rudy Gay .40 1.00
148 Russell Westbrook .60 1.50
149 Ryan Anderson .25 .60
150 Serge Ibaka .30 .75
151 Shane Battier .30 .75
152 Shannon Brown .25 .60
153 Shawn Marion .40 1.00
154 Spencer Hawes .25 .60
155 Stephen Curry 3.00 8.00
156 Stephen Jackson .30 .75
157 Steve Nash .75 2.00
158 Steve Novak .25 .60
159 Steve Blake .25 .60
160 Taj Gibson .25 .60
161 Tayshaun Prince .40 1.00
162 Tim Duncan 1.00 2.50
163 Tony Allen .25 .60
164 Tony Parker .60 1.50
165 Trevor Ariza .25 .60
166 Ty Lawson .25 .60
167 Tyler Hansbrough .25 .60
168 Tyreke Evans .30 .75
169 Tyrus Thomas .25 .60
170 Tyson Chandler .30 .75
171 Vince Carter .75 2.00
172 Wayne Ellington .25 .60
173 Wesley Matthews .30 .75
174 Wilson Chandler .30 .75
175 Zach Randolph .40 1.00
176 Adrian Dantley .30 .75
177 Allen Iverson .60 1.50
178 Bill Laimbeer .50 1.25
179 Chris Webber .40 1.00
180 Connie Hawkins .40 1.00
181 David Robinson .60 1.50
182 Earl Monroe .50 1.25
183 Elgin Baylor 1.00 2.50
184 Gary Payton .50 1.25
185 George Gervin .60 1.50
186 George Mikan 1.25 3.00
187 James Worthy .60 1.50
188 Joe Dumars .50 1.25
189 Karl Malone .60 1.50
190 Larry Bird 1.25 3.00
191 Mark Jackson .30 .75
192 Nate Thurmond .40 1.00
193 Oscar Robertson .75 2.00
194 Pete Maravich .75 2.00
195 Shaquille O'Neal 1.25 3.00
196 Steve Kerr .40 1.00
197 Tim Hardaway .50 1.25
198 Tom Chambers .40 1.00
199 Wes Unseld .50 1.25
200 Willis Reed .60 1.50
201 Alec Burks RC .40 1.00
202 Brandon Knight RC .75 2.00
203 Dion Waiters RC .30 .75
204 Iman Shumpert RC .30 .75
205 Jeremy Tyler RC .25 .60
206 Josh Selby RC .25 .60
207 Klay Thompson RC 5.00 12.00
208 Meyers Leonard RC .60 1.50
209 Perry Jones RC .50 1.25
210 Tristan Thompson RC .75 2.00
211 Andre Drummond RC 1.25 3.00
212 Chandler Parsons RC .60 1.50
213 Doron Lamb RC .50 1.25
214 Isaiah Thomas RC 1.00 2.50
215 Jimmer Fredette RC .75 2.00
216 Kawhi Leonard RC 6.00 15.00
217 Kyle O'Quinn RC .60 1.50
218 Michael Kidd-Gilchrist RC .60 1.50
219 Quincy Acy RC .50 1.25
220 Tyler Honeycutt RC .50 1.25
221 Andrew Nicholson RC .50 1.25
222 Charles Jenkins RC .50 1.25
223 Draymond Green RC 3.00 8.00
224 Ivan Johnson RC .50 1.25
225 Jimmy Butler RC 5.00 12.00
226 Kemba Walker RC 2.00 5.00
227 Kyrie Irving RC 5.00 12.00
228 Mike Scott RC .60 1.50
229 Reggie Jackson RC .75 2.00
230 Tyler Zeller RC .50 1.25
231 Darius Miller RC .60 1.50
232 Chris Copeland RC .50 1.25
233 Enes Kanter RC .75 2.00
234 Jae Crowder RC 1.00 2.50
235 John Henson RC .60 1.50
236 Kendall Marshall RC .50 1.25
237 Lance Thomas RC .50 1.25
238 Miles Plumlee RC .50 1.25
239 Robert Sacre RC .50 1.25
240 Tyshawn Taylor RC .50 1.25
241 Anthony Davis RC 6.00 15.00
242 Chris Singleton RC .50 1.25
243 E'Twaun Moore RC .60 1.50
244 Jan Vesely RC .50 1.25
245 John Jenkins RC .50 1.25
246 Kenneth Faried RC .60 1.50
247 Lavoy Allen RC .50 1.25
248 Maurice Harkless RC .60 1.50
249 Royce White RC .50 1.25
250 Nando De Colo RC .50 1.25
251 Arnett Moultrie RC .50 1.25
252 Cory Joseph RC .60 1.50
253 Evan Fournier RC .75 2.00
254 Jared Cunningham RC .50 1.25
255 Jon Leuer RC .50 1.25
256 Kent Bazemore RC .75 2.00
257 Marcus Morris RC .75 2.00
258 Nikola Vucevic RC 2.00 5.00
259 Terrence Jones RC .50 1.25
260 Harrison Barnes RC 1.00 2.50
261 Austin Rivers RC .75 2.00
262 Damian Lillard RC 5.00 12.00
263 Festus Ezeli RC .50 1.25
264 Jared Sullinger RC .50 1.25
265 Jonas Valanciunas RC 1.00 2.50
266 Kevin Murphy RC .50 1.25
267 Markieff Morris RC .75 2.00
268 Nolan Smith RC .50 1.25
269 Terrence Ross RC 1.25 3.00
270 Will Barton RC 1.00 2.50
271 Bernard James RC .50 1.25
272 Darius Johnson-Odom RC .50 1.25
273 Greg Stiemsma RC .50 1.25
274 Jeff Taylor RC .50 1.25
275 Jordan Hamilton RC .50 1.25
276 Khris Middleton RC 2.50 6.00
277 Marquis Teague RC .50 1.25
278 Norris Cole RC .50 1.25
279 Thomas Robinson RC .50 1.25
280 Mirza Teletovic RC .60 1.50
281 Bismack Biyombo RC .60 1.50
282 Darius Morris RC .60 1.50
283 Gustavo Ayon RC .50 1.25
284 Jeremy Lamb RC .75 2.00
285 Josh Harrellson RC .50 1.25
286 Kim English RC .50 1.25
287 MarShon Brooks RC .50 1.25
288 Orlando Johnson RC .50 1.25
289 Tobias Harris RC 1.50 4.00
290 Tony Wroten RC .50 1.25
291 Bradley Beal RC 4.00 10.00
292 Derrick Williams RC .50 1.25
293 Tornike Shengelia RC .50 1.25
294 Brian Roberts RC .50 1.25
295 Pablo Prigioni RC .50 1.25
296 DeQuan Jones RC .50 1.25
297 Alexey Shved RC .50 1.25
298 Luke Zeller RC .50 1.25
299 Ben Hansbrough RC .50 1.25
300 Maalik Wayns RC .60 1.50

2012-13 Panini Gold Knight

*GOLD VET: 1.2X TO 3X BASIC
*GOLD RC: .75X TO 2X BASIC

2012-13 Panini All-Panini

*GOLD: 1.5X TO 4X BASIC
GOLD PRINT RUN 25 SER.#'d SETS
1 Kobe Bryant 8.00 20.00
2 Kevin Durant 4.00 10.00
3 Blake Griffin 1.00 2.50
4 Kyrie Irving 6.00 15.00
5 Anthony Davis 8.00 20.00
6 Kevin Love 1.00 2.50
7 LeBron James 8.00 20.00
8 Rajon Rondo 1.25 3.00
9 Carmelo Anthony 1.50 4.00
10 Deron Williams .75 2.00
11 Chris Paul 2.00 5.00
12 Dirk Nowitzki 2.50 6.00
13 Russell Westbrook 2.50 6.00
14 Paul Pierce 1.50 4.00
15 Derrick Rose 1.50 4.00
16 Jason Kidd 1.50 4.00
17 Dwight Howard 1.25 3.00
18 Grant Hill 1.50 4.00
19 Joe Johnson .75 2.00
20 Damian Lillard 6.00 15.00
21 Kevin Garnett 2.50 6.00
22 Vince Carter 2.00 5.00
23 Josh Smith .60 1.50
24 Steve Nash 2.00 5.00
25 Dwyane Wade 2.00 5.00
26 James Harden 2.00 5.00
27 O.J. Mayo .60 1.50
28 LaMarcus Aldridge 1.00 2.50
29 Chris Bosh 1.00 2.50
30 Rudy Gay 1.00 2.50
31 Brook Lopez .75 2.00
32 Tim Duncan 2.50 6.00
33 Jrue Holiday 1.25 3.00
34 Stephen Curry 8.00 20.00
35 Tony Parker 1.50 4.00
36 Ricky Rubio .75 2.00
37 Marc Gasol 1.00 2.50
38 Kevin Martin .75 2.00
39 Al Horford 1.00 2.50
40 Greg Monroe .60 1.50
41 Roy Hibbert .60 1.50
42 Al Jefferson .60 1.50
43 Nicolas Batum .75 2.00
44 Zach Randolph 1.00 2.50
45 Luol Deng .75 2.00
46 Chandler Parsons .75 2.00
47 Brandon Jennings .60 1.50
48 Goran Dragic 1.00 2.50
49 Andrea Bargnani .60 1.50
50 Andre Iguodala 1.00 2.50
51 Kenneth Faried .75 2.00
52 Kawhi Leonard 8.00 20.00
53 Manu Ginobili 2.00 5.00
54 Ray Allen 1.50 4.00
55 Andrei Kirilenko .75 2.00
56 Serge Ibaka .75 2.00
57 Dion Waiters .75 2.00
58 Joakim Noah .75 2.00
59 Brandon Knight .75 2.00
60 Ty Lawson .60 1.50
61 Pau Gasol 1.50 4.00
62 Tyson Chandler .75 2.00
63 Jeremy Lin 1.50 4.00
64 Michael Kidd-Gilchrist .75 2.00
65 Harrison Barnes 1.25 3.00
66 Bradley Beal 5.00 12.00
67 John Wall 1.25 3.00
68 Chauncey Billups 1.25 3.00
69 Amare Stoudemire 1.00 2.50
70 Klay Thompson 6.00 15.00
71 Tyreke Evans .75 2.00
72 Richard Hamilton 1.00 2.50
73 Anderson Varejao .60 1.50
74 Thaddeus Young .60 1.50
75 Raymond Felton .60 1.50
76 Metta World Peace .75 2.00
77 Paul George 1.50 4.00
78 Jamal Crawford 1.00 2.50
79 Kemba Walker 2.50 6.00
80 David Lee .60 1.50
81 Wesley Matthews .60 1.50
82 Mike Conley .75 2.00
83 Gordon Hayward 1.00 2.50
84 J.J. Hickson .60 1.50
85 Jameer Nelson .60 1.50
86 Jonas Valanciunas 1.25 3.00
87 Jason Terry .75 2.00
88 Shawn Marion 1.00 2.50
89 DeMarcus Cousins 1.00 2.50
90 Pete Maravich 2.00 5.00
91 Wilt Chamberlain 3.00 8.00
92 Karl Malone 1.50 4.00
93 Jerry West 2.00 5.00
94 Bill Russell 3.00 8.00
95 George Mikan 3.00 8.00
96 Kareem Abdul-Jabbar 3.00 8.00
97 Magic Johnson 3.00 8.00
98 Oscar Robertson 2.00 5.00
99 Shaquille O'Neal 3.00 8.00
100 Julius Erving 2.50 6.00

2012-13 Panini Dress Code Jumbo Jerseys

1 Manu Ginobili 5.00 12.00
2 Jonas Valanciunas 3.00 8.00
3 Tim Duncan 6.00 15.00
4 Al Jefferson 1.50 4.00
5 Bradley Beal 12.00 30.00
6 DeMar DeRozan 3.00 8.00
7 Chris Paul 5.00 12.00
8 John Wall 3.00 8.00
9 Derrick Favors 3.00 8.00
10 Tony Parker 4.00 10.00
11 Andrea Bargnani 1.50 4.00
12 DeMarcus Cousins 2.50 6.00
13 Paul Pierce 4.00 10.00
14 Thomas Robinson 1.50 4.00
15 Dwight Howard 3.00 8.00
17 Tyreke Evans 2.00 5.00
18 Rajon Rondo 3.00 8.00
19 Deron Williams 2.00 5.00
20 LaMarcus Aldridge 2.50 6.00
22 Jameer Nelson 1.50 4.00
23 Dirk Nowitzki 6.00 15.00
24 Steve Nash 5.00 12.00
25 Evan Turner 1.50 4.00
26 Glen Davis 1.50 4.00
27 Channing Frye 1.50 4.00
28 Kevin Durant 10.00 25.00
29 Dwyane Wade 5.00 12.00
30 Carmelo Anthony 4.00 10.00
31 O.J. Mayo 1.50 4.00
32 Kyrie Irving 15.00 40.00
33 Brandon Jennings 1.50 4.00
34 Derrick Rose 4.00 10.00
35 Ricky Rubio 2.00 5.00
36 Monta Ellis 2.00 5.00
37 Austin Rivers 2.50 6.00
38 LeBron James 20.00 50.00
39 Russell Westbrook 4.00 10.00
40 Ray Allen 4.00 10.00
41 Rudy Gay 2.50 6.00
42 Joakim Noah 2.50 6.00
43 Kobe Bryant 20.00 50.00
44 Damian Lillard 30.00 80.00
45 Jrue Holiday 3.00 8.00
46 Blake Griffin 2.50 6.00
47 Gordon Hayward 2.50 6.00
48 Grant Hill 4.00 10.00
49 Michael Kidd-Gilchrist 2.00 5.00

2012-13 Panini Game Jerseys

1 Chris Paul 6.00 15.00
2 John Wall 4.00 10.00
3 George Hill 2.50 6.00
4 Evan Turner 2.50 6.00
5 Dwyane Wade 6.00 15.00
6 Dirk Nowitzki 8.00 20.00
7 Derrick Rose 5.00 12.00
8 Derrick Favors 2.50 6.00
9 Chris Bosh 4.00 10.00
10 Channing Frye 2.50 6.00
11 Carlos Boozer 2.50 6.00
12 Anderson Varejao 2.00 5.00
13 Amare Stoudemire 3.00 8.00
14 Al Jefferson 2.00 5.00
15 Al Horford 3.00 8.00
16 Zach Randolph 3.00 8.00
17 Tyrus Thomas 2.00 5.00
18 Tyreke Evans 2.50 6.00
19 Ty Lawson 2.00 5.00
20 Tayshaun Prince 3.00 8.00
21 Taj Gibson 2.00 5.00
22 Spencer Hawes 2.00 5.00
23 Raymond Felton 2.00 5.00
24 Rajon Rondo 4.00 10.00
25 Pau Gasol 5.00 12.00
26 Mike Conley 2.50 6.00
27 Marc Gasol 3.00 8.00
28 Manu Ginobili 6.00 15.00
29 Luol Deng 2.50 6.00
30 Kirk Hinrich 2.50 6.00
31 Kevin Love 3.00 8.00
32 Kevin Garnett 8.00 20.00
33 Josh Smith 2.00 5.00
34 Glen Davis 2.00 5.00
35 J.J. Redick 3.00 8.00
36 Derrick Williams 2.00 5.00
37 DeMar DeRozan 4.00 10.00
38 David Lee 2.00 5.00
39 Caron Butler 2.50 6.00
40 Brandon Jennings 2.00 5.00
41 Tony Parker 5.00 12.00
42 Tim Duncan 8.00 20.00
43 Andrea Bargnani 2.00 5.00
44 Thaddeus Young 2.00 5.00
45 Hedo Turkoglu 2.50 6.00
46 Jeff Teague 2.00 5.00
47 Jordan Hamilton 2.00 5.00
48 Tyson Chandler 2.50 6.00
49 Danny Granger 2.00 5.00
50 DeMarcus Cousins 3.00 8.00

2012-13 Panini Hall of Fame Signatures

LACK OF PRICING DUE TO MARKET INFO
3 Chris Mullin/99 8.00 20.00
6 Connie Hawkins/99 4.00 10.00
10 Bill Sharman/99 10.00 25.00
11 Larry Bird/25 60.00 120.00
16 Isiah Thomas/99 10.00 25.00
18 Bill Walton/99 15.00 40.00
19 Julius Erving/25 30.00 80.00

2012-13 Panini Heroes of the Hall

COMPLETE SET (25) 12.00 30.00
1 Hakeem Olajuwon 1.50 4.00
2 John Stockton 1.50 4.00
3 Moses Malone 1.25 3.00
4 Bob McAdoo .60 1.50
5 Lenny Wilkens 1.00 2.50
6 Walt Frazier 1.25 3.00
7 Dave Cowens 1.25 3.00
8 Nate Archibald 1.00 2.50
9 Bob Lanier .60 1.50
10 Wilt Chamberlain 2.50 6.00
11 Bob Pettit .75 2.00
12 Gail Goodrich .60 1.50
13 Larry Bird 2.50 6.00
14 Calvin Murphy .60 1.50
15 Bill Sharman 1.00 2.50
16 Bob Cousy 1.25 3.00
17 Dolph Schayes 1.00 2.50
18 Robert Parish 1.25 3.00
19 Patrick Ewing 1.25 3.00
20 Dennis Johnson .60 1.50
21 Artis Gilmore 1.00 2.50
22 Drazen Petrovic .75 2.00
23 Kevin McHale 1.00 2.50
24 Chris Mullin 1.00 2.50
25 Magic Johnson 2.50 6.00

2012-13 Panini Knights of the Round

COMMON CARD 3.00 8.00
SEMISTARS 4.00 10.00
UNLISTED STARS 5.00 12.00
1 LeBron James 125.00 300.00
2 Chris Paul 40.00 100.00
3 Ricky Rubio 8.00 20.00
4 Carmelo Anthony 15.00 40.00
5 Steve Nash 15.00 40.00
6 Dwyane Wade 15.00 40.00
7 Anthony Davis 100.00 250.00
8 Kevin Durant 75.00 200.00
9 John Wall 12.00 30.00
10 Kobe Bryant 100.00 250.00
11 Russell Westbrook 15.00 40.00
12 Rajon Rondo 10.00 25.00
13 Blake Griffin 5.00 12.00
14 Kevin Love 5.00 12.00
15 Derrick Rose 12.00 30.00
16 Tyreke Evans 4.00 10.00
17 Jrue Holiday 6.00 15.00
18 James Harden 10.00 25.00
19 Kyrie Irving 100.00 250.00
20 Dirk Nowitzki 12.00 30.00

2012-13 Panini Matching Numbers

1 B.Griffin/E.Davis .75 2.00
2 Monta Ellis/Jrue Holiday 1.00 2.50
3 Eric Gordon/DeMar DeRozan 1.00 2.50
4 K.Durant/K.Faried 3.00 8.00
5 J.Teague/R.Westbrook 1.25 3.00
6 M.Brooks/T.Parker 1.25 3.00
7 D.Howard/L.Aldridge 1.00 2.50
8 J.Harden/T.Evans 1.50 4.00
9 R.Rubio/R.Rondo 1.00 2.50
10 M.Beasley/T.Robinson .50 1.25
11 K.Leonard/T.Setolosha 6.00 15.00
12 D.Cousins/D.Favors .75 2.00
13 Gordon Hayward/Manu Ginobili 1.50 4.00
14 Rudy Gay/Anthony Morrow .75 2.00
15 Chris Bosh/Amare Stoudemire 1.00 2.50
16 D.Wade/B.Beal 4.00 10.00
17 A.Davis/M.Camby 3.00 8.00
18 K.Bryant/P.George 6.00 15.00
19 N.Cole/S.Curry 6.00 15.00
20 D.Rose/G.Dragic 1.25 3.00
21 C.Paul/B.Jennings 1.50 4.00
22 J.Redick/J.Fredette .75 2.00
23 C.Anthony/J.Lin 1.25 3.00
24 J.Smith/K.Garnett 2.00 5.00
25 J.Wall/K.Irving 3.00 8.00

2012-13 Panini Player of the Year

UNLISTED STARS 2.50 6.00
1 Steve Nash 5.00 12.00

2 Dirk Nowitzki 6.00 15.00
3 Kobe Bryant 20.00 50.00
4 Derrick Rose 4.00 10.00
5 LeBron James 20.00 50.00

2012-13 Panini Rated Rookie Signatures

PRINT RUNS B/WN 25-50 COPIES PER
NO PRICING ON MOST DUE TO LACK OF INFO
EXCHANGE DEADLINE 9/06/2014
1 Anthony Davis/50 150.00 400.00
2 Michael Kidd-Gilchrist/50 4.00 10.00
3 Bradley Beal/50 20.00 50.00
4 Dion Waiters/50 4.00 10.00
5 Thomas Robinson/50 3.00 8.00
6 Harrison Barnes/48 6.00 15.00
7 Terrence Ross/50 8.00 20.00
8 Andre Drummond/50 8.00 20.00
9 Austin Rivers/50 5.00 12.00
10 Meyers Leonard/50 4.00 10.00
11 John Henson/50 4.00 10.00
12 Maurice Harkless/50 4.00 10.00
14 Tyler Zeller/50 3.00 8.00
15 Jeremy Lamb/49 5.00 12.00
16 Kendall Marshall/50 3.00 8.00
19 Evan Fournier/50 5.00 12.00
20 Jared Sullinger/50 3.00 8.00
21 John Jenkins/50 3.00 8.00
22 Fab Melo/50 3.00 8.00
23 Jared Cunningham/50 3.00 8.00
24 Tony Wroten/50 3.00 8.00
25 Miles Plumlee/50 3.00 8.00
26 Arnett Moultrie/50 3.00 8.00
27 Perry Jones/50 3.00 8.00
28 Marquis Teague/50 3.00 8.00
30 Jeff Taylor/50 3.00 8.00
31 Bernard James/50 3.00 8.00
32 Jae Crowder/50 6.00 15.00
33 Draymond Green/50 12.00 30.00
34 Quincy Acy/50 3.00 8.00
36 Khris Middleton/50 20.00 50.00
37 Doron Lamb/50 3.00 8.00
40 Darius Miller/50 4.00 10.00
41 Kyle O'Quinn/49 4.00 10.00
42 Darius Johnson-Odom/50 3.00 8.00
43 Robert Sacre/50 3.00 8.00
44 Jonas Valanciunas/25 6.00 15.00
45 Kyle Singler/25 3.00 8.00
46 Derrick Williams/50 3.00 8.00
47 Enes Kanter/50 5.00 12.00
48 Tristan Thompson/50 8.00 20.00
49 Bismack Biyombo/50 4.00 10.00
50 Kemba Walker/50 40.00 100.00
51 Klay Thompson/50 60.00 150.00
52 Jimmer Fredette/50 5.00 12.00
53 Alec Burks/50 5.00 12.00
54 Markieff Morris/50 8.00 20.00
55 Marcus Morris/50 8.00 20.00
56 Kawhi Leonard/50 150.00 400.00
57 Iman Shumpert/50 4.00 10.00
58 Chris Singleton/50 3.00 8.00
59 Tobias Harris/50 10.00 25.00
61 Kenneth Faried/50 4.00 10.00
62 Reggie Jackson/50 5.00 12.00
63 MarShon Brooks/50 3.00 8.00
64 Jordan Hamilton/50 3.00 8.00
65 JaJuan Johnson/50 3.00 8.00
66 Norris Cole/50 3.00 8.00
67 Cory Joseph/50 4.00 10.00
68 Jimmy Butler/50 60.00 150.00
69 Shelvin Mack/50 4.00 10.00
71 Kyrie Irving/49 60.00 150.00
72 Trey Thompkins/50 3.00 8.00
73 Chandler Parsons/50 4.00 10.00
74 Jeremy Tyler/50 3.00 8.00
76 Darius Morris/50 4.00 10.00
77 Malcolm Lee/50 3.00 8.00
78 Nikola Vucevic/50 12.00 30.00
79 Josh Selby/50 3.00 8.00
80 Isaiah Thomas/50 8.00 20.00
82 Ivan Johnson/50 3.00 8.00
83 Lance Thomas/50 3.00 8.00
84 Travis Leslie/50 3.00 8.00

2012-13 Panini Rookie Signatures

EXCHANGE DEADLINE 9/06/2014
1 Kyrie Irving 30.00 80.00
2 Iman Shumpert 3.00 8.00
3 MarShon Brooks 2.50 6.00
4 Kyle Singler 2.50 6.00
5 Chandler Parsons 3.00 8.00
6 Malcolm Lee 2.50 6.00
7 Anthony Davis 150.00 400.00
8 Harrison Barnes 6.00 15.00
9 Jeremy Lamb 4.00 10.00
10 Miles Plumlee 2.50 6.00
11 Quincy Acy 2.50 6.00
12 Tyshawn Taylor 2.50 6.00
13 Draymond Green 10.00 25.00
14 Bernard James 2.50 6.00
15 Perry Jones 2.50 6.00
16 Tyler Zeller 2.50 6.00
17 Jared Sullinger 2.50 6.00
18 Royce White 2.50 6.00
19 Austin Rivers 4.00 10.00
20 Terrence Ross 6.00 15.00
21 Dion Waiters 3.00 8.00
22 Lavoy Allen 2.50 6.00
23 Josh Harrellson 2.50 6.00
24 Jon Leuer 2.50 6.00
25 Jimmy Butler 15.00 40.00
26 Norris Cole 2.50 6.00
27 Kawhi Leonard 100.00 250.00
28 Markieff Morris 4.00 10.00
29 Jimmer Fredette 4.00 10.00
30 Brandon Knight 3.00 8.00
31 Jan Vesely 2.50 6.00
32 Derrick Williams 2.50 6.00
33 Tristan Thompson 4.00 10.00
34 Kemba Walker 10.00 25.00
35 Marcus Morris 4.00 10.00
36 Kenneth Faried 3.00 8.00
37 Cory Joseph 3.00 8.00
38 Darius Morris 3.00 8.00
39 Brian Roberts 2.50 6.00
40 Isaiah Thomas 8.00 20.00
41 Michael Kidd-Gilchrist 3.00 8.00
42 Meyers Leonard 3.00 8.00
43 Jae Crowder 5.00 12.00
44 Quincy Miller 2.50 6.00
45 Doron Lamb 2.50 6.00
46 Darius Miller 3.00 8.00
47 Kris Joseph 2.50 6.00
48 Will Barton 5.00 12.00
49 Andre Drummond 10.00 25.00
50 Lance Thomas 2.50 6.00
51 DeAndre Liggins 2.50 6.00
52 Klay Thompson 30.00 80.00
53 Jonas Valanciunas 5.00 12.00
54 Enes Kanter 4.00 10.00
55 Nikola Vucevic 10.00 25.00
56 Tyler Honeycutt 2.50 6.00
57 Bradley Beal 20.00 50.00
58 Thomas Robinson 2.50 6.00
59 Kendall Marshall 2.50 6.00
60 Marquis Teague 2.50 6.00

2012-13 Panini Signature Inserts

EXCHANGE DEADLINE 9/06/2014
1 Roy Hibbert 3.00 8.00
2 Marcin Gortat 2.50 6.00
3 Jrue Holiday 6.00 15.00
4 Leandro Barbosa 3.00 8.00
5 Kevin Martin 3.00 8.00
7 Darren Collison EXCH 2.50 6.00
8 Antawn Jamison 3.00 8.00
9 DeAndre Jordan EXCH 3.00 8.00
10 Serge Ibaka 12.00 30.00
11 Kevin Love 4.00 10.00
13 Anderson Varejao 2.50 6.00
14 Ryan Anderson EXCH 2.50 6.00
15 Andrei Kirilenko 3.00 8.00
16 George Hill 3.00 8.00
18 Kendrick Perkins 2.50 6.00
19 Zach Randolph 4.00 10.00
20 Andre Iguodala 6.00 15.00

2012-13 Panini Spirit of the Game

COMPLETE SET (25) 12.00 30.00
1 Chris Paul 1.50 4.00
2 Jeremy Lin 1.25 3.00
3 Russell Westbrook 1.50 4.00
4 Rajon Rondo 1.00 2.50
5 Kyle Lowry .75 2.00
6 Kenneth Faried .60 1.50
7 Jrue Holiday 1.00 2.50
8 Kevin Love .75 2.00
9 Kawhi Leonard 6.00 15.00
10 LaMarcus Aldridge .75 2.00
11 Josh Smith .50 1.25
12 JaVale McGee .60 1.50
13 Blake Griffin .75 2.00
14 Serge Ibaka .60 1.50
15 Roy Hibbert .60 1.50
16 Louis Williams .60 1.50
17 Derrick Favors .60 1.50
18 DeAndre Jordan .60 1.50
19 Derrick Rose 1.25 3.00
20 Deron Williams .60 1.50
21 Ricky Rubio .60 1.50
22 Michael Beasley .50 1.25
23 Stephen Curry 6.00 15.00
24 Joe Johnson .60 1.50
25 Kemba Walker 2.00 5.00

2013-14 Panini

1 Gerald Wallace .15 .40
2 Brook Lopez .20 .50
3 Carlos Boozer .15 .40
4 Jose Calderon .12 .30
5 Rodney Stuckey .12 .30
6 Dwight Howard .25 .60
7 Jamal Crawford .20 .50
9 Chris Bosh .25 .60
10 Kevin Martin .15 .40
11 Amare Stoudemire .20 .50
12 Serge Ibaka .15 .40
13 Markieff Morris .12 .30
14 LaMarcus Aldridge .20 .50
15 Danny Green .15 .40
16 Gordon Hayward .15 .40
17 DeMarcus Cousins .20 .50
18 Eric Bledsoe .15 .40
19 Thabo Sefolosha .15 .40
20 Eric Gordon .15 .40
21 Michael Beasley .12 .30
22 Chris Kaman .15 .40
23 Lance Stephenson .15 .40
24 Andrew Bogut .15 .40
25 J.J. Hickson .12 .30
26 Kyrie Irving .60 1.50
27 Ben Gordon .15 .40
28 Deron Williams .15 .40
29 Al Horford .20 .50
30 Kemba Walker .20 .50
31 Dion Waiters .12 .30
32 JaVale McGee .15 .40
33 Klay Thompson .60 1.50
34 Jeremy Lin .30 .75
35 Chris Paul .40 1.00
36 Mike Conley .20 .50
37 Mario Chalmers .15 .40
38 Ricky Rubio .15 .40
39 Tyson Chandler .15 .40
40 Glen Davis .12 .30
41 Marcus Morris .15 .40
42 Isaiah Thomas .15 .40
43 Tim Duncan .50 1.25
44 Marvin Williams .12 .30
45 Martell Webster .12 .30
46 Jeff Teague .12 .30
47 Kris Humphries .12 .30
48 Paul Pierce .30 .75
49 Joakim Noah .20 .50
50 Shawn Marion .15 .40
51 Josh Smith .15 .40
52 Harrison Barnes .20 .50
53 George Hill .15 .40
54 Blake Griffin .20 .50
55 John Henson .12 .30
56 Tyreke Evans .12 .30
57 Thaddeus Young .12 .30
58 Wesley Matthews .12 .30
59 Jonas Valanciunas .15 .40
60 Trevor Ariza .12 .30
61 Joe Johnson .15 .40
62 Monta Ellis .15 .40
63 Chandler Parsons .12 .30
64 Nick Young .12 .30
65 Ersan Ilyasova .12 .30
66 Kendrick Perkins .12 .30
67 Terrence Jones .12 .30
68 Tiago Splitter .12 .30
69 Jan Vesely .12 .30
70 Marcus Thornton .12 .30
71 Nikola Vucevic .25 .60
72 Anthony Davis .60 1.50
73 Dwyane Wade .40 1.00
74 Roy Hibbert .12 .30
75 Brandon Jennings .12 .30
76 Anderson Varejao .12 .30
77 Andray Blatche .12 .30
78 Jeff Green .12 .30
79 Luol Deng .15 .40
80 Kenneth Faried .15 .40
81 James Harden .40 1.00
82 J.J. Redick .20 .50
83 Zach Randolph .15 .40
84 Larry Sanders .12 .30
85 Jrue Holiday .25 .60
86 Arron Afflalo .12 .30
87 Damian Lillard .60 1.50
88 Tony Parker .30 .75
89 Derrick Favors .15 .40
90 Paul Millsap .15 .40
91 Al Jefferson .15 .40
92 Andrei Kirilenko .20 .50
93 Derrick Rose .30 .75
94 Dirk Nowitzki .50 1.25
95 Andre Iguodala .20 .50
96 Danny Granger .12 .30
97 Jordan Hill .12 .30
98 Shane Battier .15 .40
99 Kobe Bryant 1.50 4.00
100 Nikola Pekovic .12 .30
101 Carmelo Anthony .30 .75
102 Evan Turner .12 .30
103 Thomas Robinson .12 .30
104 DeMar DeRozan .25 .60
105 Marcin Gortat .12 .30
106 Danilo Gallinari .15 .40
107 Steve Nash .40 1.00
108 J.J. Barea .15 .40
109 Russell Westbrook .30 .75
110 Jimmer Fredette .20 .50
111 Enes Kanter .15 .40
112 Goran Dragic .15 .40
113 Al-Farouq Aminu .12 .30
114 LeBron James 1.50 4.00
115 Paul George .30 .75
116 Vince Carter .40 1.00
117 Gerald Henderson .12 .30
118 Kyle Lowry .20 .50
119 Jason Richardson .20 .50
120 Iman Shumpert .12 .30
121 O.J. Mayo .12 .30
122 Tayshaun Prince .20 .50
123 David West .15 .40
124 Andre Drummond .20 .50
125 Kirk Hinrich .15 .40
126 Brandon Bass .12 .30
127 Kyle Korver .15 .40
128 Manu Ginobili .40 1.00
129 Rajon Rondo .25 .60
130 Andrew Bynum .12 .30
131 David Lee .12 .30
132 Marc Gasol .20 .50
133 Nicolas Batum .15 .40
134 John Wall .25 .60
135 Kevin Garnett .50 1.25
136 Ty Lawson .12 .30
137 Luis Scola .15 .40
138 Raymond Felton .12 .30
139 Rudy Gay .15 .40
140 Avery Bradley .15 .40
141 Bradley Beal .30 .75
142 Michael Kidd-Gilchrist .12 .30
143 Richard Jefferson .12 .30
144 Taj Gibson .12 .30
145 Tyler Hansbrough .12 .30
146 Tristan Thompson .12 .30
147 Kawhi Leonard .60 1.50
148 Gerald Green .15 .40
149 Greivis Vasquez .12 .30
150 Greg Monroe .12 .30
151 Spencer Hawes .12 .30
152 Stephen Curry 1.50 4.00
153 Jameer Nelson .12 .30
154 Brandon Knight .12 .30
155 J.R. Smith .12 .30
156 Pau Gasol .30 .75
157 Kevin Durant .60 1.50
158 Kevin Love .30 .75
159 Ray Allen .30 .75
160 DeAndre Jordan .15 .40
161 Kelly Olynyk RC .30 .75
162 Tony Snell RC .30 .75
163 Kentavious Caldwell-Pope RC .40 1.00
164 Solomon Hill RC .30 .75
165 Nate Wolters RC .25 .60
166 Andre Roberson RC .30 .75
167 Nerlens Noel RC .30 .75
168 C.J. McCollum RC 1.00 2.50
169 Otto Porter RC .40 1.00
170 Gal Mekel RC .25 .60
171 Mason Plumlee RC .30 .75
172 Anthony Bennett RC .25 .60
173 Peyton Siva RC .25 .60
174 Reggie Bullock RC .30 .75
175 Shabazz Muhammad RC .25 .60
176 Steven Adams RC .60 1.50
177 Alex Len RC .30 .75
178 Ben McLemore RC .30 .75
179 Vitor Faverani RC .25 .60
180 Luigi Datome RC .25 .60
181 Cody Zeller RC .30 .75
182 Ricky Ledo RC .25 .60
183 Tony Mitchell RC .25 .60
184 Jamaal Franklin RC .25 .60
185 Jeff Withey RC .25 .60
186 Victor Oladipo RC .60 1.50
187 Archie Goodwin RC .25 .60
188 Trey Burke RC .30 .75
189 Pero Antic RC .25 .60
190 Rudy Gobert RC 1.00 2.50
191 Erik Murphy RC .25 .60
192 Shane Larkin RC .25 .60
193 Isaiah Canaan RC .25 .60
194 G.Antetokounmpo RC 75.00 200.00
195 Tim Hardaway Jr. RC .50 1.25
196 M.Carter-Williams RC .30 .75
197 Allen Crabbe RC .25 .60
198 Glen Rice Jr. RC .25 .60
199 Phil Pressey RC .25 .60
200 Nemanja Nedovic RC .25 .60

2013-14 Panini Gold Knights

*GOLD VET: 1.2X TO 3X BASIC
*GOLD RC: .75X TO 2X BASIC
194 Giannis Antetokounmpo 400.00 800.00

2013-14 Panini All-Panini

*GOLD: .6X TO 1.5X BASIC
1 Carlos Boozer 1.25 3.00
2 Eric Gordon 1.25 3.00
3 Chris Paul 3.00 8.00
4 Josh Smith 1.00 2.50
5 Dwyane Wade 3.00 8.00
6 Arron Afflalo 1.00 2.50
7 Evan Turner 1.00 2.50
8 Kyle Lowry 1.50 4.00
9 John Wall 2.00 5.00
10 Greivis Vasquez 1.00 2.50
11 Dwight Howard 2.00 5.00
12 Lance Stephenson 1.25 3.00
13 Mike Conley 1.50 4.00
14 Harrison Barnes 1.50 4.00
15 Roy Hibbert 1.00 2.50
16 Damian Lillard 5.00 12.00
17 DeMar DeRozan 2.00 5.00
18 Iman Shumpert 1.00 2.50
19 Ty Lawson 1.00 2.50
20 Greg Monroe 1.00 2.50
21 Chris Bosh 2.00 5.00
22 Andrew Bogut 1.25 3.00
23 Ricky Rubio 1.25 3.00
24 George Hill 1.25 3.00
25 Brandon Jennings 1.25 3.00
26 Tony Parker 2.50 6.00
27 Steve Nash 3.00 8.00
28 O.J. Mayo 1.00 2.50
29 Raymond Felton 1.00 2.50
30 Spencer Hawes 1.00 2.50
31 Kevin Martin 1.25 3.00
32 Kyrie Irving 5.00 12.00
33 Tyson Chandler 1.25 3.00
34 Blake Griffin 1.50 4.00
35 Jeff Green 1.25 3.00
36 Al Jefferson 1.00 2.50
37 J.J. Barea 1.25 3.00
38 Andre Drummond 1.50 4.00
39 Rudy Gay 1.25 3.00
40 Stephen Curry 12.00 30.00
41 Amare Stoudemire 1.50 4.00
42 Deron Williams 1.25 3.00
43 Glen Davis 1.00 2.50
44 Joe Johnson 1.25 3.00
45 Luol Deng 1.25 3.00
46 Andrei Kirilenko 1.50 4.00
47 Russell Westbrook 2.50 6.00
48 Kirk Hinrich 1.25 3.00
49 Bradley Beal 2.50 6.00
50 Jameer Nelson 1.00 2.50
51 Serge Ibaka 1.25 3.00
52 Al Horford 1.50 4.00
53 Tim Duncan 4.00 10.00
54 Monta Ellis 1.25 3.00
55 Kenneth Faried 1.25 3.00
56 Derrick Rose 2.50 6.00
57 Enes Kanter 1.25 3.00
58 Manu Ginobili 3.00 8.00
59 Michael Kidd-Gilchrist 1.00 2.50
60 J.R. Smith 1.50 4.00
61 LaMarcus Aldridge 1.50 4.00
62 Kemba Walker 1.50 4.00
63 Jeff Teague 1.00 2.50
64 Chandler Parsons 1.00 2.50
65 Dirk Nowitzki 4.00 10.00
66 James Harden 3.00 8.00
67 Goran Dragic 1.25 3.00
68 Rajon Rondo 2.00 5.00
69 Taj Gibson 1.25 3.00
70 Pau Gasol 2.50 6.00
71 Gordon Hayward 1.25 3.00
72 JaVale McGee 1.25 3.00
73 Paul Pierce 2.50 6.00
74 Tiago Splitter 1.00 2.50
75 J.J. Redick 1.50 4.00
76 Andre Iguodala 1.50 4.00
77 LeBron James 10.00 25.00
78 David Lee 1.00 2.50
79 Tristan Thompson 1.00 2.50
80 Kevin Durant 5.00 12.00
81 DeMarcus Cousins 1.50 4.00
82 Klay Thompson 5.00 12.00
83 Joakim Noah 1.50 4.00
84 Nikola Vucevic 2.00 5.00
85 Zach Randolph 1.25 3.00
86 Kobe Bryant 10.00 25.00
87 Paul George 2.50 6.00
88 Marc Gasol 1.50 4.00
89 Kawhi Leonard 5.00 12.00
90 Kevin Love 1.50 4.00
91 Eric Bledsoe 1.25 3.00
92 Jeremy Lin 2.50 6.00
93 Shawn Marion 1.25 3.00
94 Anthony Davis 5.00 12.00
95 Carmelo Anthony 2.50 6.00
96 Jrue Holiday 2.00 5.00
97 Vince Carter 3.00 8.00
98 Nicolas Batum 1.25 3.00
99 Gerald Green 1.25 3.00
100 Ray Allen 2.50 6.00

2013-14 Panini Bird's Eye View

1 Derrick Rose .50 1.25
2 Victor Oladipo .50 1.25
3 Paul George .50 1.25
4 Pau Gasol .50 1.25
5 Eric Gordon .25 .60
6 Tim Duncan .75 2.00
7 Blake Griffin .30 .75
8 Kobe Bryant 2.50 6.00
9 Michael Carter-Williams .25 .60
10 Chris Paul .60 1.50

2013-14 Panini Energizers Ink

EXCHANGE DEADLINE 10/09/2015
1 Jared Sullinger 5.00 12.00
2 Vince Carter 25.00 60.00
3 Andrew Nicholson 5.00 12.00
4 Xavier Henry 5.00 12.00
5 Steve Kerr 12.00 30.00
6 J.R. Smith 8.00 20.00
7 Harrison Barnes 8.00 20.00
8 Andray Blatche 5.00 12.00
9 Courtney Lee 5.00 12.00
11 Marvin Williams 5.00 12.00
12 Tony Wroten 5.00 12.00
13 Michael Cooper 8.00 20.00
14 Ramon Sessions 5.00 12.00
15 Ricky Pierce 6.00 15.00

2013-14 Panini Family Business

1 B.Barry/R.Barry 1.00 2.50
2 D.Curry/S.Curry 6.00 15.00
3 M.Thompson/K.Thompson 2.50 6.00
4 A.Rivers/D.Rivers .60 1.50
5 T.Hardaway/T.Hardaway Jr. 1.00 2.50
6 G.Rice/G.Rice Jr. .40 1.00
7 L.Walton/B.Walton 1.25 3.00
8 J.Bryant/K.Bryant 6.00 15.00

2013-14 Panini Favorites

1 James Harden 6.00 15.00
2 LeBron James 20.00 50.00
3 Victor Oladipo 5.00 12.00
4 Ricky Rubio 2.50 6.00
5 Kobe Bryant 25.00 60.00
6 Anthony Davis 10.00 25.00
7 Rajon Rondo 4.00 10.00
8 Carmelo Anthony 5.00 12.00
9 Derrick Rose 5.00 12.00
10 Kevin Durant 10.00 25.00
11 Kyrie Irving 10.00 25.00
12 Michael Carter-Williams 2.50 6.00
13 Dirk Nowitzki 8.00 20.00
14 Damian Lillard 8.00 20.00
15 Stephen Curry 25.00 60.00

2013-14 Panini First Impressions Autographs

EXCHANGE DEADLINE 10/09/2015
1 Kelly Olynyk 4.00 10.00
2 Erik Murphy 3.00 8.00
3 Gal Mekel 3.00 8.00
4 Isaiah Canaan 3.00 8.00
5 Cody Zeller 4.00 10.00
6 Shabazz Muhammad 3.00 8.00
7 Michael Carter-Williams 4.00 10.00
8 Alex Len 4.00 10.00
9 Ben McLemore 4.00 10.00
10 Otto Porter 5.00 12.00
11 Phil Pressey 3.00 8.00
12 Tony Snell 4.00 10.00
13 Tony Mitchell 3.00 8.00
15 Anthony Bennett 3.00 8.00
16 Victor Oladipo 8.00 20.00
17 Nerlens Noel 4.00 10.00
18 C.J. McCollum 12.00 30.00
19 Trey Burke 4.00 10.00
20 Dennis Schroder 10.00 25.00
21 Mason Plumlee 4.00 10.00
24 Ryan Kelly 3.00 8.00
25 Kentavious Caldwell-Pope 5.00 12.00

2013-14 Panini Hall of Fame Signatures

EXCHANGE DEADLINE 10/09/2015
1 Walt Bellamy 5.00 12.00
2 Wes Unseld 10.00 25.00
4 Dominique Wilkins 8.00 20.00
5 Chris Mullin 10.00 25.00
6 David Robinson 20.00 50.00
10 Nate Thurmond 5.00 12.00
11 Isiah Thomas 8.00 20.00
12 James Worthy 15.00 40.00
16 Dennis Rodman 25.00 60.00
18 David Thompson 5.00 12.00
20 Robert Parish 10.00 25.00
21 Walt Frazier 8.00 20.00
22 Elgin Baylor 12.00 30.00
24 Artis Gilmore 6.00 15.00
25 Bill Sharman 15.00 40.00
26 Bob McAdoo 6.00 15.00
28 Hal Greer 4.00 10.00
29 Nate Archibald 10.00 25.00
30 Gail Goodrich 5.00 12.00

2013-14 Panini Insert Signatures

EXCHANGE DEADLINE 10/09/2015
3 Michael Finley 12.00 30.00
4 Charlie Bell 3.00 8.00
5 Gary Trent 3.00 8.00
8 Chris Whitney 3.00 8.00
10 Steve Blake 8.00 20.00
14 Lindsey Hunter 3.00 8.00
15 James Posey 3.00 8.00
16 Greg Buckner 3.00 8.00
17 Bill Willoughby 5.00 12.00
20 Kenyon Martin 5.00 12.00
23 Bernard King 10.00 25.00
24 Dale Davis 5.00 12.00
25 Dennis Rodman 20.00 50.00
26 Vlade Divac 5.00 12.00
27 Pearl Washington 3.00 8.00
29 Travis Outlaw 3.00 8.00
30 Darrell Griffith 4.00 10.00
32 Peja Stojakovic 8.00 20.00
33 Tracy McGrady 8.00 20.00
36 Walter Berry 3.00 8.00
39 Greg Stiemsma 3.00 8.00
40 Vernon Maxwell 4.00 10.00
41 Kyle Korver 4.00 10.00
44 Chucky Brown 3.00 8.00
45 Kevin Love 15.00 40.00
46 Fred Jones 3.00 8.00
47 Chet Walker 4.00 10.00
48 Ramon Sessions 3.00 8.00
49 Theo Ratliff 3.00 8.00
50 James Jones 3.00 8.00
55 World B. Free 4.00 10.00

2013-14 Panini Knight School

1 Kevin Love .40 1.00
2 Klay Thompson 1.25 3.00
3 Michael Carter-Williams .30 .75
4 Damian Lillard 1.25 3.00
5 Kenneth Faried .30 .75
6 Kyrie Irving 1.25 3.00
7 Paul George .60 1.50
8 Blake Griffin .40 1.00
9 Rajon Rondo .50 1.25
10 Derrick Rose .60 1.50
11 Russell Westbrook .60 1.50
12 James Harden .75 2.00
13 Victor Oladipo .60 1.50
14 Stephen Curry 3.00 8.00
15 Kevin Durant 1.25 3.00

2013-14 Panini Knights of the Round

1 Paul George 10.00 25.00
2 Ricky Rubio 5.00 12.00
3 Dwyane Wade 12.00 30.00
4 John Wall 8.00 20.00
5 Rajon Rondo 8.00 20.00
6 Klay Thompson 60.00 150.00
7 Kevin Love 6.00 15.00
8 James Harden 12.00 30.00
9 Dirk Nowitzki 15.00 40.00
10 LeBron James 200.00 500.00
11 Tony Parker 10.00 25.00
12 Carmelo Anthony 10.00 25.00
13 Anthony Davis 20.00 50.00
14 Kobe Bryant 200.00 500.00
15 Blake Griffin 6.00 15.00
16 Derrick Rose 10.00 25.00
17 Damian Lillard 20.00 50.00
18 Kyrie Irving 20.00 50.00
19 DeMar DeRozan 15.00 40.00
20 Chris Paul 20.00 50.00
21 Monta Ellis 5.00 12.00
22 Kevin Durant 20.00 50.00
23 Stephen Curry 125.00 300.00
24 Russell Westbrook 10.00 25.00

2013-14 Panini Preparation

1 Monta Ellis .50 1.25
2 Chandler Parsons .40 1.00
3 Evan Turner .40 1.00
4 John Wall .75 2.00
5 LeBron James 12.00 30.00
6 Jrue Holiday .75 2.00
7 Mario Chalmers .50 1.25
8 Kevin Durant 2.00 5.00
9 George Hill .50 1.25
10 Dwyane Wade 1.25 3.00
11 Paul George 1.00 2.50
12 Kevin Garnett 1.50 4.00
13 Daniel Gibson .50 1.25
14 Deron Williams .50 1.25
15 Kyrie Irving 2.00 5.00
16 Jeremy Lin 1.00 2.50
17 Chris Paul 1.25 3.00
18 James Harden 1.25 3.00

2013-14 Panini Rated Rookie Signatures

EXCHANGE DEADLINE 10/09/2015
1 Solomon Hill 5.00 12.00
2 Giannis Antetokounmpo 500.00 1,000.00
3 Tim Hardaway Jr. 8.00 20.00
4 Michael Carter-Williams 5.00 12.00
5 Allen Crabbe 5.00 12.00
6 Trey Burke 5.00 12.00
7 Kelly Olynyk 5.00 12.00
8 Erik Murphy 4.00 10.00
9 Ricky Ledo 4.00 10.00
10 Peyton Siva 4.00 10.00
11 Reggie Bullock 5.00 12.00
12 Nate Wolters 4.00 10.00
13 Andre Roberson 5.00 12.00
14 Nerlens Noel 5.00 12.00
15 C.J. McCollum 15.00 40.00
16 Glen Rice Jr. 4.00 10.00
17 Mason Plumlee 5.00 12.00
18 Tony Snell 5.00 12.00
19 Shane Larkin 4.00 10.00
20 Tony Mitchell 4.00 10.00
21 Ryan Kelly 4.00 10.00
22 Shabazz Muhammad 4.00 10.00
23 Steven Adams 10.00 25.00
24 Alex Len 5.00 12.00
25 Ben McLemore 5.00 12.00
26 Otto Porter 6.00 15.00
27 Cody Zeller 5.00 12.00
28 Anthony Bennett 4.00 10.00
29 Kentavious Caldwell-Pope 6.00 15.00
30 Isaiah Canaan 4.00 10.00
31 Jamaal Franklin 4.00 10.00
32 Jeff Withey 4.00 10.00
33 Victor Oladipo 10.00 25.00
34 Archie Goodwin 4.00 10.00

2013-14 Panini Rising Tide Autographs

EXCHANGE DEADLINE 10/09/2015
1 Jon Leuer 3.00 8.00
3 Tyshawn Taylor 3.00 8.00
4 Nick Young 3.00 8.00
5 Jeff Withey 3.00 8.00
6 Michael Carter-Williams 4.00 10.00
7 Allen Crabbe 3.00 8.00
8 Jonas Jerebko 3.00 8.00
9 Pero Antic 3.00 8.00
11 Quincy Acy 3.00 8.00
12 Toure Murry 3.00 8.00
14 Kawhi Leonard 40.00 100.00
15 Jamaal Franklin 3.00 8.00
16 Tim Hardaway Jr. 6.00 15.00
17 Dwight Buycks 3.00 8.00
18 Daniel Orton 3.00 8.00
19 Carrick Felix 3.00 8.00
20 Gordon Hayward 4.00 10.00
21 Andre Drummond 5.00 12.00
22 Ricky Ledo 3.00 8.00
23 Jared Cunningham 3.00 8.00
24 Goran Dragic 8.00 20.00
25 Giannis Antetokounmpo 150.00 400.00
26 Andre Roberson 4.00 10.00
27 Rudy Gobert 12.00 30.00
28 Elliot Williams 3.00 8.00
29 Serge Ibaka 4.00 10.00
30 Nando De Colo 3.00 8.00
31 Greg Monroe 3.00 8.00
32 Matthew Dellavedova 10.00 25.00
33 Jason Smith 3.00 8.00
34 Jared Sullinger 3.00 8.00
35 Nate Wolters 3.00 8.00
36 Steven Adams 8.00 20.00
37 Glen Rice Jr. 3.00 8.00
38 Ty Lawson 3.00 8.00
39 Derrick Williams 3.00 8.00
40 Evan Fournier 4.00 10.00
41 Jrue Holiday 6.00 15.00
42 DeMarre Carroll 3.00 8.00
43 Lorenzo Brown 3.00 8.00
44 Jordan Hill 3.00 8.00
45 Gorgui Dieng 4.00 10.00
46 Archie Goodwin 3.00 8.00
47 Hollis Thompson 3.00 8.00
48 Luigi Datome 3.00 8.00
49 Stephen Curry 400.00 800.00
50 Arnett Moultrie 3.00 8.00

2013-14 Panini Rookie Jerseys

MOST NOT PRICED DUE TO LACK OF INFO
1 Isaiah Canaan 2.00 5.00
2 Andre Roberson 2.50 6.00
3 Jamaal Franklin 2.00 5.00
4 Nerlens Noel 2.50 6.00
5 Jeff Withey 2.00 5.00
6 C.J. McCollum 8.00 20.00
7 Victor Oladipo 5.00 12.00
8 Glen Rice Jr. 2.00 5.00
9 Archie Goodwin 2.00 5.00
10 Mason Plumlee 2.50 6.00
11 Solomon Hill 2.50 6.00
12 Tony Snell 2.50 6.00
13 Giannis Antetokounmpo 12.00 30.00
14 Shane Larkin 2.00 5.00
15 Tim Hardaway Jr. 4.00 10.00
16 Tony Mitchell 2.00 5.00
17 Michael Carter-Williams 2.50 6.00
18 Ryan Kelly 2.00 5.00
19 Allen Crabbe 2.00 5.00
20 Shabazz Muhammad 2.00 5.00
21 Trey Burke 2.50 6.00
22 Steven Adams 5.00 12.00
23 Kelly Olynyk 2.50 6.00
24 Alex Len 2.50 6.00
25 Erik Murphy 2.00 5.00
26 Ben McLemore 2.50 6.00
27 Ricky Ledo 2.00 5.00
28 Otto Porter 3.00 8.00
29 Peyton Siva 2.00 5.00
30 Cody Zeller 2.50 6.00
31 Reggie Bullock 2.50 6.00
32 Anthony Bennett 2.00 5.00
33 Nate Wolters 2.00 5.00
34 Kentavious Caldwell-Pope 3.00 8.00

2013-14 Panini Rookie Top 10

1 Michael Carter-Williams .50 1.25
2 Vitor Faverani .40 1.00
3 Nate Wolters .40 1.00
4 Ben McLemore .50 1.25
5 Victor Oladipo 1.00 2.50
6 Kelly Olynyk .50 1.25
7 Steven Adams 1.00 2.50
8 Anthony Bennett .40 1.00
9 Cody Zeller .50 1.25
10 Alex Len .50 1.25

2013-14 Panini Superstar Signatures

EXCHANGE DEADLINE 10/09/2015
1 Kobe Bryant 400.00 800.00
2 Kevin Durant EXCH 40.00 100.00
3 Kyrie Irving 25.00 60.00
4 Blake Griffin 20.00 50.00
5 Anthony Davis 25.00 60.00
7 Steve Nash 50.00 120.00
9 Jason Kidd 10.00 25.00
10 Tracy McGrady 10.00 25.00

2017-18 Panini

276 Frank Ntilikina .40 1.00
277 Kyle Kuzma 1.25 3.00
278 Josh Jackson .40 1.00
279 Tony Bradley .30 .75
280 Malik Monk 1.25 3.00
281 Mike James .30 .75
282 Bogdan Bogdanovic .75 2.00
283 Dwayne Bacon .30 .75
284 De'Aaron Fox 2.50 6.00
285 Jawun Evans .30 .75
286 Jayson Tatum 4.00 10.00
287 OG Anunoby 1.50 4.00
288 Lauri Markkanen 2.00 5.00
289 Wesley Iwundu .30 .75
290 Markelle Fultz .75 2.00
291 Daniel Theis .60 1.50
292 Davon Reed .30 .75
293 Harry Giles .30 .75
294 Dennis Smith Jr. .40 1.00
295 Josh Hart .75 2.00
296 Jonathan Isaac 1.25 3.00
297 Sterling Brown .30 .75
298 Lonzo Ball 1.25 3.00
299 Cedi Osman .60 1.50
300 Zhou Qi .60 1.50

2017-18 Panini Artist Proof Blue

*AP BLUE: .5X TO 1.2X BASIC
STATED PRINT RUN 199 SER.#'d SETS

2017-18 Panini Artist Proof Red

*AP RED: .5X TO 1.2X BASIC
STATED PRINT RUN 249 SER.#'d SETS

2017-18 Panini Artist Proof Silver

*AP SILVER: .6X TO 1.5X BASIC
STATED PRINT RUN 99 SER.#'d SETS

2010 Panini All-Star Game

COMPLETE SET (14) 20.00 40.00
BG Blake Griffin 8.00 20.00

BJ Brandon Jennings 3.00 8.00
CP Chris Paul 1.00 2.50
DH Dwight Howard 1.00 2.50
DN Dirk Nowitzki 1.00 2.50
DW Dwyane Wade 1.25 3.00
KB Kobe Bryant 3.00 8.00
KD Kevin Durant 2.00 5.00
KG Kevin Garnett 1.00 2.50
LJ LeBron James 3.00 8.00
SN Steve Nash 1.00 2.50
TD Tim Duncan 1.00 2.50
TE Tyreke Evans 4.00 10.00
YM Yao Ming 1.00 2.50

2013 Panini All-Star Game Patches

COMPLETE SET (9)
AD Anthony Davis 25.00 60.00
KD Kevin Durant 12.00 30.00
KB1 Kobe Bryant Yellow Jersey 20.00 50.00
KB2 Kobe Bryant White Jersey 20.00 50.00

2016-17 Panini Aficionado

COMPLETE SET (150) 30.00 80.00
COMP.SET w/o SP (100) 12.00 30.00
1 Jimmy Butler 1.00 2.50
2 Anthony Davis 1.50 4.00
3 Elfrid Payton .40 1.00
4 LaMarcus Aldridge .50 1.25
5 Bradley Beal .60 1.50
6 Dwight Howard .60 1.50
7 Henry Ellenson RC .50 1.25
8 Denzel Valentine RC .50 1.25
9 Zach LaVine 1.00 2.50
10 Chandler Parsons .30 .75
11 Kenneth Faried .40 1.00
12 Tyreke Evans .40 1.00
13 Jahlil Okafor .30 .75
14 Darren Collison .30 .75
15 Dario Saric RC .75 2.00
16 Dennis Schroder .50 1.25
17 Marquese Chriss RC .60 1.50
18 Karl-Anthony Towns 1.00 2.50
19 Nikola Jokic 2.50 6.00
20 Mike Conley .40 1.00
21 Andre Drummond .50 1.25
22 Kristaps Porzingis .75 2.00
23 Nerlens Noel .30 .75
24 Kawhi Leonard 1.25 3.00
25 Brandon Ingram RC 2.00 5.00
26 Al Horford .50 1.25
27 Dragan Bender RC .50 1.25
28 Emmanuel Mudiay .30 .75
29 Andrew Wiggins .60 1.50
30 Julius Randle .60 1.50
31 Tobias Harris .50 1.25
32 Carmelo Anthony .75 2.00
33 Eric Bledsoe .40 1.00
34 Tony Parker .75 2.00
35 Ben Simmons RC 1.50 4.00
36 Isaiah Thomas .40 1.00
37 Malachi Richardson RC .50 1.25
38 Khris Middleton .50 1.25
39 Deron Williams .40 1.00
40 D'Angelo Russell .60 1.50
41 Reggie Jackson .40 1.00
42 Derrick Rose .75 2.00
43 Devin Booker 2.00 5.00
44 Kyle Lowry .50 1.25
45 Jaylen Brown RC 4.00 10.00
46 Avery Bradley .30 .75
47 Diamond Stone RC .50 1.25
48 Jabari Parker .30 .75
49 Dirk Nowitzki 1.25 3.00
50 Jordan Clarkson .50 1.25
51 Kevin Durant 2.00 5.00
52 Russell Westbrook .75 2.00
53 Brandon Knight .40 1.00
54 DeMar DeRozan .60 1.50
55 Domantas Sabonis RC 3.00 8.00
56 Brook Lopez .40 1.00
57 Kris Dunn RC .75 2.00
58 LeBron James 4.00 10.00
59 Giannis Antetokounmpo 2.50 6.00
60 Jamal Crawford .50 1.25
61 Stephen Curry 4.00 10.00
62 Steven Adams .40 1.00
63 Damian Lillard 1.25 3.00
64 Gordon Hayward .50 1.25
65 Buddy Hield RC 1.50 4.00
66 Jeremy Lin 1.00 2.50
67 Demetrius Jackson RC .50 1.25
68 Kyrie Irving 1.00 2.50
69 Goran Dragic .50 1.25
70 Blake Griffin .50 1.25
71 Klay Thompson 1.25 3.00
72 Cameron Payne .50 1.25
73 C.J. McCollum .50 1.25
74 Rodney Hood .40 1.00
75 Jamal Murray RC 6.00 15.00
76 Nicolas Batum .50 1.25
77 A.J. Hammons RC .50 1.25
78 Justise Winslow .50 1.25
79 Kevin Love .50 1.25
80 Chris Paul .75 2.00
81 James Harden 1.00 2.50
82 Evan Fournier .40 1.00
83 Allen Crabbe .30 .75
84 Rudy Gobert .60 1.50
85 Taurean Prince .40 1.00
86 Kemba Walker .60 1.50
87 Thon Maker RC .60 1.50
88 Hassan Whiteside .60 1.50
89 Rajon Rondo .60 1.50
90 Myles Turner .50 1.25
91 Trevor Ariza .30 .75
92 Aaron Gordon .50 1.25
93 DeMarcus Cousins .60 1.50
94 John Wall .60 1.50
95 Jakob Poeltl RC 1.00 2.50
96 Michael Kidd-Gilchrist .30 .75
97 Pascal Siakam RC 3.00 8.00
98 Dwyane Wade 1.00 2.50
99 Marc Gasol .50 1.25
100 Paul George .75 2.00
101 Manu Ginobili GR 3.00 8.00
102 Danilo Gallinari GR 1.25 3.00
103 Dirk Nowitzki GR 4.00 10.00
104 Kristaps Porzingis GR 2.50 6.00
105 Boban Marjanovic GR 1.25 3.00
106 Clint Capela GR 1.25 3.00
107 Jordan Clarkson GR 1.50 4.00
108 Marc Gasol GR 1.50 4.00
109 Pau Gasol GR 2.50 6.00
110 Andrew Wiggins GR 2.00 5.00
111 Mario Hezonja GR 1.00 2.50
112 Emmanuel Mudiay GR 1.00 2.50
113 Nicolas Batum GR 1.25 3.00
114 Nikola Mirotic GR 1.00 2.50
115 Ersan Ilyasova GR 1.00 2.50
116 Giannis Antetokounmpo GR 8.00 20.00
117 Ben Simmons GR 3.00 8.00
118 Buddy Hield GR 3.00 8.00
119 Dragan Bender GR 1.00 2.50
120 Juan Hernangomez GR RC 1.00 2.50
121 Timofey Mozgov GR 1.00 2.50
122 Bojan Bogdanovic GR 1.25 3.00
123 Zaza Pachulia GR 1.00 2.50
124 Jusuf Nurkic GR 1.25 3.00
125 Jonas Valanciunas GR 1.25 3.00
126 Jonas Jerebko GR 1.00 2.50
127 Nik Stauskas GR 1.00 2.50
128 Patty Mills GR 1.50 4.00
129 Mirza Teletovic GR 1.00 2.50
130 Tiago Splitter GR 1.00 2.50
131 Matthew Dellavedova GR 1.25 3.00
132 Joel Embiid GR 4.00 10.00
133 Ricky Rubio GR 1.25 3.00
134 Thabo Sefolosha GR 1.00 2.50
135 Thon Maker GR 1.25 3.00
136 Steven Adams GR 1.25 3.00
137 Marco Belinelli GR 1.00 2.50
138 Omri Casspi GR 1.00 2.50
139 Dennis Schroder GR 1.50 4.00
140 Al Horford GR 1.50 4.00
141 Shaquille O'Neal IN 5.00 12.00
142 Allen Iverson IN 2.50 6.00
143 David Robinson IN 3.00 8.00
144 Scottie Pippen IN 3.00 8.00
145 Wilt Chamberlain IN 5.00 12.00
146 Pete Maravich IN 2.50 6.00
147 Karl Malone IN 2.50 6.00
148 Yao Ming IN 4.00 10.00
149 Patrick Ewing IN 2.00 5.00
150 Bill Russell IN 5.00 12.00

2016-17 Panini Aficionado Artist's Proof

*AP: .75X TO 2X BASIC
*AP RC: .5X TO 1.2X BASIC
*AP 101-150: .5X TO 1.2X BASIC

2016-17 Panini Aficionado Artist's Proof Purple

*AP RED: 1.5X TO 4X BASIC
*AP RED RC: 1X TO 2.5X BASIC
*AP RED 101-150: .6X TO 1.5X BASIC
STATED PRINT RUN 99 SER.#'d SETS

2016-17 Panini Aficionado Authentics

PRINT RUNS B/WN 93-175 COPIES PER
*PRIME/25: .75X TO 2X BASIC
1 Blake Griffin/175 2.50 6.00
2 Derrick Rose/175 4.00 10.00
3 Giannis Antetokounmpo/175 12.00 30.00
4 Russell Westbrook/175 4.00 10.00
5 Tim Hardaway Jr./175 2.00 5.00
6 Deron Williams/175 2.00 5.00
7 Damian Lillard/175 6.00 15.00
8 Kentavious Caldwell-Pope/175 2.00 5.00
9 LaMarcus Aldridge/175 2.50 6.00
10 Kyrie Irving/175 5.00 12.00
11 Danilo Gallinari/175 2.00 5.00
12 Terry Rozier/131 2.50 6.00
13 Bojan Bogdanovic/175 2.00 5.00
14 Karl-Anthony Towns/175 5.00 12.00
16 Brook Lopez/175 2.00 5.00
17 Derrick Favors/175 1.50 4.00
18 Kevin Love/175 2.50 6.00
19 Kristaps Porzingis/175 4.00 10.00
20 Monta Ellis/175 2.00 5.00
21 Vince Carter/175 5.00 12.00
22 Terrence Ross/175 2.00 5.00
23 Jeremy Lamb/175 1.50 4.00
24 Ryan Anderson/175 1.50 4.00
25 Dwyane Wade/175 5.00 12.00
26 Noah Vonleh/175 1.50 4.00
27 Jrue Holiday/175 3.00 8.00
28 James Harden/175 5.00 12.00
29 Jimmy Butler/175 5.00 12.00
30 Tony Parker/175 4.00 10.00
31 Cory Joseph/175 1.50 4.00
32 Greg Monroe/175 1.50 4.00
33 Nik Stauskas/175 1.50 4.00
34 Jahlil Okafor/175 1.50 4.00
35 Frank Kaminsky/175 1.50 4.00
36 Jeremy Lin/175 5.00 12.00
37 Nicolas Batum/175 2.00 5.00
38 J.J. Redick/175 2.50 6.00
39 Dirk Nowitzki/175 6.00 15.00
40 Julius Randle/175 2.50 6.00
41 T.J. Warren/175 2.00 5.00
42 Roy Hibbert/175 2.00 5.00
43 Aaron Gordon/175 2.50 6.00
44 Rodney Stuckey/175 1.50 4.00
45 Rodney Hood/175 2.00 5.00
46 Zach Randolph/175 2.50 6.00
47 Norman Powell/175 2.50 6.00
48 George Hill/175 2.00 5.00
49 Carmelo Anthony/175 4.00 10.00
50 Rajon Rondo/175 3.00 8.00
51 Enes Kanter/175 1.50 4.00
52 Tim Frazier/175 1.50 4.00
53 Kawhi Leonard/175 6.00 15.00
54 Kobe Bryant/175 60.00 150.00
55 John Wall/175 3.00 8.00
56 Rudy Gay/175 2.50 6.00
57 Ricky Rubio/175 2.00 5.00
58 Goran Dragic/175 2.50 6.00
59 Andre Iguodala/175 2.50 6.00
60 Jusuf Nurkic/175 2.00 5.00
61 Tyler Zeller/93 1.50 4.00
62 LeBron James/175 15.00 40.00
63 Brandon Knight/175 2.00 5.00
64 Brandon Jennings/175 1.50 4.00
65 Bismack Biyombo/175 1.50 4.00

2016-17 Panini Aficionado Craftwork

1 Jimmy Butler 1.50 4.00
2 LeBron James 6.00 15.00
3 Dennis Schroder .75 2.00
4 Kenneth Faried .60 1.50
5 Kevin Durant 3.00 8.00
6 James Harden 1.50 4.00
7 Blake Griffin .75 2.00
8 Julius Randle 1.00 2.50
9 Giannis Antetokounmpo 4.00 10.00
10 Brook Lopez .60 1.50
11 Andrew Wiggins 1.00 2.50
12 Anthony Davis 2.50 6.00
13 Derrick Rose 1.25 3.00
14 Russell Westbrook 1.25 3.00
15 Joel Embiid 2.00 5.00
16 T.J. Warren .60 1.50
17 DeMarcus Cousins .60 1.50
18 Tony Parker 1.25 3.00
19 Kyle Lowry .75 2.00
20 Rudy Gobert 1.00 2.50
21 Dwyane Wade 1.50 4.00
22 Dirk Nowitzki 2.00 5.00
23 Dwight Howard 1.00 2.50
24 Andre Drummond .75 2.00
25 Klay Thompson 2.00 5.00
26 Jeff Teague .50 1.25
27 Chris Paul 1.25 3.00
28 Marc Gasol .75 2.00
29 Josh Richardson .60 1.50
30 Jeremy Lin 1.50 4.00
31 Karl-Anthony Towns 1.50 4.00
32 Jrue Holiday 1.00 2.50
33 Kristaps Porzingis 1.25 3.00
34 Elfrid Payton .60 1.50
35 Sergio Rodriguez .50 1.25
36 C.J. McCollum .75 2.00
37 Rudy Gay .75 2.00
38 DeMar DeRozan 1.00 2.50
39 Terrence Ross .60 1.50
40 Bradley Beal 1.00 2.50
41 Kevin Love .75 2.00
42 Harrison Barnes .60 1.50
43 Isaiah Thomas .60 1.50
44 Reggie Jackson .60 1.50
45 Stephen Curry 6.00 15.00
46 Myles Turner .75 2.00
47 J.J. Redick .75 2.00
48 Mike Conley .60 1.50
49 Jabari Parker .60 1.50
50 Kemba Walker .60 1.50
51 Zach LaVine 1.50 4.00
52 Carmelo Anthony 1.25 3.00
53 Enes Kanter .50 1.25
54 Evan Fournier .60 1.50
55 Devin Booker 3.00 8.00
56 Damian Lillard 2.00 5.00
57 Kawhi Leonard 2.00 5.00
58 Jonas Valanciunas .60 1.50
59 Rodney Hood .60 1.50
60 John Wall 1.00 2.50
61 Kyrie Irving 1.50 4.00
62 Emmanuel Mudiay .50 1.25
63 Jae Crowder .50 1.25
64 Draymond Green 1.00 2.50
65 Ryan Anderson .50 1.25
66 Paul George 1.25 3.00
67 D'Angelo Russell 1.00 2.50
68 Goran Dragic .75 2.00
69 Matthew Dellavedova .60 1.50
70 Nicolas Batum .60 1.50

2016-17 Panini Aficionado Dual Authentics Memorabilia

PRINT RUNS B/WN 5-299 COPIES PER
NO PRICING ON QTY 5
*PRIME/25: .75X TO 2X BASIC
1 Korver/Sefolosha/299 2.50 6.00
2 Leonard/Aldridge/299 8.00 20.00
3 Wstbrk/Adams/299 5.00 12.00
4 Lopez/Bogdanovic/299 2.50 6.00
8 Hrdwy/O'Neal/299 10.00 25.00
9 Anthny/Przngs/299 5.00 12.00
10 Cousins/Cauley-Stein/299 2.50 6.00
11 Gasol/Randolph/299 3.00 8.00
12 Wstbrk/Harden/299 6.00 15.00
13 Dirk/Porzingis/299 8.00 20.00
14 Bryant/O'Neal/299 60.00 150.00
15 Wiggins/Towns/299 6.00 15.00
16 Giannis/Parker/299 15.00 40.00
17 Butler/Gibson/299 6.00 15.00
18 Kaminsky/Walker/299 2.50 6.00
19 Redick/Crawford/299 3.00 8.00
20 Irving/James/299 15.00 40.00
21 Hill/Irving/299 6.00 15.00
22 Oubre/Porter/299 4.00 10.00
23 Stcktn/Mlne/299 5.00 12.00
24 McClim/Lillard/299 8.00 20.00
25 Davis/Wstbrk/299 10.00 25.00
26 Curry/Thmpsn/299 15.00 40.00
27 Williams/Dirk/299 8.00 20.00
28 Bledsoe/Warren/299 2.50 6.00
29 Mudiay/Faried/299 2.50 6.00
30 Okafor/Towns/299 6.00 15.00
31 O'Neal/Mrnng/60 10.00 25.00
32 Oljwn/Drexler/299 6.00 15.00
33 Richmond/Strickland/299 3.00 8.00
35 Hrdwy Jr./Hrdwy/299 4.00 10.00

2016-17 Panini Aficionado Endorsments

PRINT RUNS B/WN 53-199 COPIES PER
1 Michael Carter-Williams/149 2.50 6.00
2 Langston Galloway/199 2.50 6.00
3 James Ennis/199 2.50 6.00
4 T.J. McConnell/199 3.00 8.00
5 Allen Crabbe/199 2.50 6.00
6 Jordan Clarkson/99 5.00 12.00
7 Will Barton/175 2.50 6.00
9 Dirk Nowitzki/65 50.00 120.00
11 Justise Winslow/199 3.00 8.00
17 Karl-Anthony Towns/99 30.00 80.00
18 Vince Carter/65 10.00 25.00
19 Matthew Dellavedova/199 3.00 8.00
20 Joel Embiid/53 150.00 400.00
22 Victor Oladipo/149 3.00 8.00
23 Tyler Johnson/199 5.00 12.00
24 Julius Randle/99 5.00 12.00
26 Elfrid Payton/99 3.00 8.00
27 Tim Hardaway/149 6.00 15.00
29 Scottie Pippen/65 25.00 60.00
30 Dan Issel/199 5.00 12.00
31 Adrian Dantley/199 4.00 10.00
32 Calvin Murphy/149 4.00 10.00
33 Rick Barry/65 5.00 12.00
34 Tom Heinsohn/199 12.00 30.00
35 Artis Gilmore/149 5.00 12.00
36 Elvin Hayes/149 5.00 12.00
38 Tom Sanders/199 6.00 15.00
39 Bob Lanier/145 5.00 12.00
41 David Robinson/60 12.00 30.00
44 Hakeem Olajuwon/60 10.00 25.00
45 Junior Bridgeman/199 3.00 8.00
46 Jim Jackson/199 10.00 25.00
47 Dan Majerle/199 3.00 8.00
48 Jamal Mashburn/199 6.00 15.00
49 Yao Ming/70 30.00 80.00

2016-17 Panini Aficionado Endorsments Artist's Proof Bronze

*PROOF BRONZE: .5X TO 1.2X BASIC
STATED PRINT RUN 49 SER.#'d SETS
21 Alan Williams 5.00 12.00

2016-17 Panini Aficionado First Impressions Autographs

PRINT RUNS B/WN 199-249 COPIES PER
1 Jaylen Brown/199 75.00 200.00
2 Dragan Bender/199 2.50 6.00
3 Marquese Chriss/199 3.00 8.00
4 Jakob Poeltl/249 5.00 12.00
5 Thon Maker/249 3.00 8.00
6 Domantas Sabonis/249 15.00 40.00
7 Georgios Papagiannis/249 2.50 6.00
8 Kris Dunn/199 4.00 10.00
9 Denzel Valentine/249 2.50 6.00
10 Demetrius Jackson/249 2.50 6.00
11 Damian Jones/249 2.50 6.00
12 Henry Ellenson/249 2.50 6.00
13 Wade Baldwin IV/249 2.50 6.00
14 Jamal Murray/199 125.00 300.00
15 Willy Hernangomez/249 3.00 8.00
16 Malik Beasley/249 5.00 12.00
17 Kay Felder/249 2.50 6.00
18 Brice Johnson/249 2.50 6.00
19 Pascal Siakam/249 15.00 40.00
20 Juan Hernangomez/249 12.00 30.00
21 Ivica Zubac/249 6.00 15.00
22 Brandon Ingram/199 30.00 80.00
23 Jake Layman/249 3.00 8.00
24 Georges Niang/249 4.00 10.00

2016-17 Panini Aficionado First Impressions Autographs Artist's Proof Bronze

*PROOF BRONZE: .5X TO 1.2X BASIC
STATED PRINT RUN 49 SER.#'d SETS

2016-17 Panini Aficionado Innovators

1 Chris Paul 4.00 10.00
2 Carmelo Anthony 4.00 10.00
3 LeBron James 20.00 50.00
4 Stephen Curry 20.00 50.00
5 Russell Westbrook 4.00 10.00
6 Anthony Davis 8.00 20.00
7 Dwyane Wade 5.00 12.00
8 Pete Maravich 4.00 10.00
9 Magic Johnson 10.00 25.00
10 Larry Bird 10.00 25.00

2016-17 Panini Aficionado International Ink

PRINT RUNS B/WN 59-249 COPIES PER
1 Dirk Nowitzki/60 125.00 300.00
2 Yao Ming/60 75.00 200.00
3 Pau Gasol/59 20.00 50.00
4 Andrew Wiggins/60 25.00 60.00
5 Tony Parker/70 15.00 40.00
6 Dragan Bender/199 2.50 6.00
7 Jamal Murray/199 40.00 100.00
8 Tristan Thompson/149 6.00 15.00
11 Jakob Poeltl/199 5.00 12.00
12 Nikola Mirotic/199 2.50 6.00
13 Thon Maker/199 3.00 8.00
14 Toni Kukoc/199 12.00 30.00
15 Dario Saric/199 8.00 20.00
16 Zydrunas Ilgauskas/199 3.00 8.00
17 Kristaps Porzingis/199 10.00 25.00
18 Boban Marjanovic/99 3.00 8.00
19 Juan Hernangomez/249 12.00 30.00
20 T. Luwawu-Cabarrot/249 4.00 10.00
21 Mindaugas Kuzminskas/249 2.50 6.00
22 Pascal Siakam/249 15.00 40.00
23 Willy Hernangomez/249 3.00 8.00
24 Ivica Zubac/249 6.00 15.00
25 Paul Zipser/249 2.50 6.00

2016-17 Panini Aficionado International Ink Artist's Proof Bronze

*PROOF BRONZE: .5X TO 1.2X BASIC
STATED PRINT RUN 49 SER.#'d SETS
9 Jonas Valanciunas 4.00 10.00
10 Dikembe Mutombo 20.00 50.00

2016-17 Panini Aficionado Magic Numbers

PROOF: .75X TO 2X BASIC
PROOF RED/99: 1.2X TO 3X BASIC
1 John Wall 1.00 2.50
2 LeBron James 6.00 15.00
3 Karl-Anthony Towns 1.50 4.00
4 Stephen Curry 6.00 15.00
5 Dwyane Wade 1.50 4.00
6 Carmelo Anthony 1.25 3.00
7 Dirk Nowitzki 2.00 5.00
8 Damian Lillard 2.00 5.00
9 Reggie Jackson .60 1.50
10 Paul George 1.25 3.00
11 Isaiah Thomas .60 1.50
12 Kyle Lowry .75 2.00

2016-17 Panini Aficionado Meteor

1 Stephen Curry 15.00 40.00
2 Dirk Nowitzki 5.00 12.00
3 LeBron James 20.00 50.00
4 Kawhi Leonard 5.00 12.00
5 Karl-Anthony Towns 4.00 10.00
6 James Harden 4.00 10.00
7 John Wall 2.50 6.00
8 Isaiah Thomas 1.50 4.00
9 D'Angelo Russell 2.50 6.00
10 Jimmy Butler 4.00 10.00
11 Kevin Durant 8.00 20.00
12 Russell Westbrook 3.00 8.00
13 Kyrie Irving 15.00 40.00
14 Devin Booker 8.00 20.00
15 Myles Turner 2.00 5.00
16 Andrew Wiggins 2.50 6.00
17 Damian Lillard 5.00 12.00
18 Chris Paul 3.00 8.00
19 Justise Winslow 1.50 4.00
20 DeMarcus Cousins 1.50 4.00

2016-17 Panini Aficionado Opening Night Preview

*OPENING NIGHT: 2.5X TO 6X BASIC
*OPNG NGHT RC: 1.5X TO 4X BASIC RC
45 Jaylen Brown 75.00 200.00

2016-17 Panini Aficionado Power Surge

PROOF: .75X TO 2X BASIC
PROOF RED/99: 1.2X TO 3X BASIC
1 Kevin Durant 3.00 8.00
2 Devin Booker 3.00 8.00
3 D'Angelo Russell 1.00 2.50
4 Emmanuel Mudiay .50 1.25
5 James Harden 1.50 4.00
6 Anthony Davis 2.50 6.00
7 DeMar DeRozan 1.00 2.50
8 Aaron Gordon .75 2.00
9 Zach LaVine 1.50 4.00
10 Jimmy Butler 1.50 4.00
11 Russell Westbrook 1.25 3.00
12 Tracy McGrady 1.25 3.00
13 Kobe Bryant 40.00 100.00
14 Shawn Kemp 1.25 3.00
15 Blake Griffin .75 2.00
16 Dee Brown .50 1.25
17 Spud Webb .75 2.00
18 Dominique Wilkins 1.00 2.50

2016-17 Panini Aficionado Signatures

2 Kevin Durant 75.00 200.00
3 Kyrie Irving 40.00 100.00
4 Karl-Anthony Towns 40.00 100.00
6 Chris Paul 40.00 100.00
7 Anthony Davis 30.00 80.00
10 Andrew Wiggins 12.00 30.00
11 Bill Russell 600.00 1,200.00
12 Yao Ming 30.00 80.00
13 Karl Malone 25.00 60.00
14 Julius Erving 25.00 60.00
15 Shaquille O'Neal 40.00 100.00
16 Brandon Ingram 30.00 80.00
18 Buddy Hield 12.00 30.00
19 Jamal Murray 75.00 200.00
20 Jaylen Brown 75.00 200.00

2016-17 Panini Aficionado Slick Picks

PROOF: .6X TO 1.5X BASIC
1 Ben Simmons 1.50 4.00
2 Brandon Ingram 2.00 5.00
3 Jaylen Brown 4.00 10.00
4 Dragan Bender .50 1.25
5 Kris Dunn .75 2.00
6 Buddy Hield 1.50 4.00
7 Jamal Murray 6.00 15.00
8 Marquese Chriss .60 1.50
9 Jakob Poeltl 1.00 2.50
10 Thon Maker .60 1.50
11 Domantas Sabonis 3.00 8.00
12 Taurean Prince .60 1.50
13 Georgios Papagiannis .50 1.25
14 Denzel Valentine .50 1.25
15 Juan Hernangomez 1.00 2.50
16 Wade Baldwin IV .50 1.25
17 Henry Ellenson .50 1.25
18 Malik Beasley 1.00 2.50
19 Caris LeVert 1.25 3.00
20 DeAndre' Bembry .75 2.00

2016-17 Panini Aficionado Slick Picks Artist's Proof Purple

*ARTIST PROOF RED: 1X TO 2.5X BASIC
STATED PRINT RUN 99 SER.#'d SETS

2016-17 Panini Aficionado Tip-Off

*TIPOFF: 2.5X TO 6X BASIC
*TIPOFF RC: 1.5X TO 4X BASIC RC

2017-18 Panini Ascension

COMP.BASE SET (100) 15.00 40.00
1 Giannis Antetokounmpo 1.50 4.00
2 Draymond Green .40 1.00
3 Kawhi Leonard .75 2.00
4 Buddy Hield .30 .75
5 Dennis Schroder .25 .60
6 Nikola Jokic 2.00 5.00
7 Stephen Curry 2.50 6.00
8 Karl-Anthony Towns .50 1.25
9 Blake Griffin .30 .75
10 Malcolm Brogdon .25 .60
11 Doug McDermott .20 .50
12 Reggie Jackson .25 .60
13 Tony Parker .50 1.25
14 C.J. McCollum .30 .75
15 Jaylen Brown .75 2.00
16 Kevin Love .30 .75
17 Bobby Portis .20 .50
18 Rudy Gobert .40 1.00
19 Norman Powell .30 .75
20 Jrue Holiday .40 1.00
21 Paul George .50 1.25
22 Devin Harris .20 .50
23 DeMar DeRozan .40 1.00
24 Damian Lillard .75 2.00
25 D'Angelo Russell .25 .60
26 Kyrie Irving .60 1.50
27 Klay Thompson .30 .75
28 Myles Turner .30 .75
29 Kelly Oubre Jr. .30 .75
30 DeMarcus Cousins .25 .60
31 Kenneth Faried .25 .60
32 Zach LaVine .50 1.25
33 Rodney Hood .20 .50
34 Eric Bledsoe .25 .60
35 Jimmy Butler .50 1.25
36 Dirk Nowitzki .75 2.00
37 Evan Fournier .25 .60
38 Victor Oladipo .25 .60
39 DeAndre Jordan .25 .60
40 Kristaps Porzingis .40 1.00
41 Jabari Parker .20 .50
42 DeMarre Carroll .20 .50
43 Ricky Rubio .20 .50
44 Devin Booker .75 2.00
45 Gordon Hayward .25 .60
46 Jamal Murray .50 1.25
47 Brandon Ingram .40 1.00
48 Jusuf Nurkic .25 .60
49 Chandler Parsons .20 .50
50 Willy Hernangomez .20 .50
51 Larry Nance Jr. .25 .60
52 Taurean Prince .20 .50
53 John Wall .40 1.00
54 Ben Simmons .30 .75
55 Kemba Walker .25 .60
56 J.R. Smith .20 .50
57 Julius Randle .30 .75
58 Cory Joseph .20 .50
59 Nikola Vucevic .20 .50
60 Russell Westbrook .50 1.25
61 Patrick Beverley .20 .50
62 Marcus Smart .30 .75
63 Otto Porter Jr. .25 .60
64 Joel Embiid .60 1.50
65 Nicolas Batum .20 .50
66 Stanley Johnson .20 .50
67 Marc Gasol .30 .75
68 Andrew Wiggins .40 1.00
69 Tyler Ulis .25 .60
70 Enes Kanter .25 .60
71 Ryan Anderson .20 .50
72 DeAndre' Bembry .20 .50
73 Bradley Beal .40 1.00
74 Dario Saric .25 .60
75 Kent Bazemore .20 .50
76 Andre Drummond .25 .60
77 Mike Conley .25 .60
78 Hassan Whiteside .25 .60
79 Willie Cauley-Stein .25 .60
80 Aaron Gordon .30 .75
81A Chris Paul HOU .50 1.25
81B Chris Paul NOH 1.00 2.50
82A Dion Waiters MIA .20 .50
82B Dion Waiters CLE .40 1.00
83A Jeff Teague MIN .20 .50
83B Jeff Teague ATL .40 1.00
84A Harrison Barnes DAL .25 .60
84B Harrison Barnes GSW .50 1.25
85A Eric Gordon HOU .25 .60
85B Eric Gordon LAC .50 1.25
86A Vince Carter SAC .60 1.50
86B Vince Carter TOR 1.25 3.00
87A LeBron James CLE 2.50 6.00
87B LeBron James MIA 5.00 12.00
88A Carmelo Anthony OKC .50 1.25
88B Carmelo Anthony DEN 1.00 2.50
89A Isaiah Thomas CLE .25 .60
89B Isaiah Thomas SAC .50 1.25
90A James Harden HOU .60 1.50
90B James Harden OKC 1.25 3.00
91A Dwyane Wade CLE .60 1.50
91B Dwyane Wade MIA 1.25 3.00
92A Paul Millsap DEN .25 .60
92B Paul Millsap UTA .50 1.25
93A Pau Gasol SAN .50 1.25
93B Pau Gasol MEM 1.00 2.50
94A Dwight Howard CHA .40 1.00
94B Dwight Howard ORL .75 2.00
95A Kevin Durant GSW 1.25 3.00
95B Kevin Durant SEA 2.50 6.00
96A Anthony Davis NOP .75 2.00
96B Anthony Davis NOH 1.50 4.00
97A Kyle Lowry TOR .30 .75
97B Kyle Lowry MEM .60 1.50
98A Goran Dragic MIA .25 .60
98B Goran Dragic HOU .50 1.25
99A Jeremy Lin BKY .50 1.25
99B Jeremy Lin NYK 1.00 2.50
100A Joe Johnson UTA .25 .60
100B Joe Johnson PHO .50 1.25
101A Markelle Fultz RC 2.00 5.00
101B Markelle Fultz RC 2.00 5.00
102A John Collins RC 2.00 5.00
102B John Collins RC 2.00 5.00
103A Lauri Markkanen RC 5.00 12.00
103B Lauri Markkanen RC 5.00 12.00
104A Tyler Lydon RC .75 2.00
104B Tyler Lydon RC .75 2.00
105A Kyle Kuzma RC 3.00 8.00
105B Kyle Kuzma RC 3.00 8.00
106A Justin Patton RC .75 2.00
106B Justin Patton RC .75 2.00
107A Malik Monk RC 3.00 8.00
107B Malik Monk RC 3.00 8.00
108A Frank Ntilikina RC 1.00 2.50
108B Frank Ntilikina RC 1.00 2.50
109A D.J. Wilson RC .75 2.00
109B D.J. Wilson RC .75 2.00
110A Frank Mason III RC .75 2.00
110B Frank Mason III RC .75 2.00
111A Justin Jackson RC .75 2.00
111B Justin Jackson RC .75 2.00
112A Frank Jackson RC .75 2.00
112B Frank Jackson RC .75 2.00
113A Dennis Smith Jr. RC 1.00 2.50
113B Dennis Smith Jr. RC 1.00 2.50
114A Dwayne Bacon RC .75 2.00
114B Dwayne Bacon RC .75 2.00
115A Josh Jackson RC 1.00 2.50
115B Josh Jackson RC 1.00 2.50
116A Luke Kennard RC 1.50 4.00
116B Luke Kennard RC 1.50 4.00
117A Sindarius Thornwell RC .75 2.00
117B Sindarius Thornwell RC .75 2.00
118A Josh Hart RC 2.00 5.00
118B Josh Hart RC 2.00 5.00
119A Bam Adebayo RC 5.00 12.00
119B Bam Adebayo RC 5.00 12.00
120A Caleb Swanigan RC .75 2.00
120B Caleb Swanigan RC .75 2.00
121A Tony Bradley RC .75 2.00
121B Tony Bradley RC .75 2.00
122A Derrick White RC 3.00 8.00
122B Derrick White RC 3.00 8.00
123A Semi Ojeleye RC 1.00 2.50
123B Semi Ojeleye RC 1.00 2.50
124A Ivan Rabb RC .75 2.00
124B Ivan Rabb RC .75 2.00
125A Terrance Ferguson RC .75 2.00
125B Terrance Ferguson RC .75 2.00
126A De'Aaron Fox RC 6.00 15.00
126B De'Aaron Fox RC 6.00 15.00
127A Zach Collins RC 1.25 3.00
127B Zach Collins RC 1.25 3.00
128A Jordan Bell RC .75 2.00
128B Jordan Bell RC .75 2.00
129A Jarrett Allen RC 2.00 5.00
129B Jarrett Allen RC 2.00 5.00
130A Jayson Tatum RC 10.00 25.00
130B Jayson Tatum RC 10.00 25.00
131A Jawun Evans RC .75 2.00
131B Jawun Evans RC .75 2.00
132A Wesley Iwundu RC .75 2.00
132B Wesley Iwundu RC .75 2.00
133A T.J. Leaf RC .75 2.00
133B T.J. Leaf RC .75 2.00
134A Tyler Dorsey RC .75 2.00
134B Tyler Dorsey RC .75 2.00
135A Harry Giles RC .75 2.00
135B Harry Giles RC .75 2.00
136A Donovan Mitchell RC 8.00 20.00
136B Donovan Mitchell RC 8.00 20.00
137A OG Anunoby RC 4.00 10.00
137B OG Anunoby RC 4.00 10.00
138A Jonathan Isaac RC 2.00 5.00
138B Jonathan Isaac RC 2.00 5.00
139A Sterling Brown RC .75 2.00
139B Sterling Brown RC .75 2.00
140A Lonzo Ball RC 3.00 8.00
140B Lonzo Ball RC 3.00 8.00

2017-18 Panini Ascension Blue

*BLUE 1-100: 1.5X TO 4X BASIC
*BLUE 101-140: .6X TO 1.5X BASIC
1-100 PRINT RUN 125 SER.#'d SETS
101-140 PRINT RUN 129 SER.#'d SETS
136A Donovan Mitchell 20.00 50.00
136B Donovan Mitchell 20.00 50.00

2017-18 Panini Ascension Green

*GREEN 1-100: 3X TO 8X BASIC
*GREEN 101-140: 1.5X TO 4X BASIC
STATED PRINT RUN 25 SER.#'d SETS
136A Donovan Mitchell 75.00 200.00
136B Donovan Mitchell 75.00 200.00

2017-18 Panini Ascension Purple

*PURPLE 101-140: 1.2X TO 3X BASIC
STATED PRINT RUN 50 SER.#'d SETS
136A Donovan Mitchell 40.00 100.00
136B Donovan Mitchell 40.00 100.00

2017-18 Panini Ascension Red

*RED 1-100: 2.5X TO 6X BASIC
*RED 101-140: 1X TO 2.5X BASIC
STATED PRINT RUN 75 SER.#'d SETS
136A Donovan Mitchell 30.00 80.00
136B Donovan Mitchell 30.00 80.00

2017-18 Panini Ascension Autographs

PRINT RUNS B/WN 5-199 COPIES PER
NO PRICING ON QTY 17 OR LESS
EXCHANGE DEADLINE 5/22/2019
*GREEN/25: .5X TO 1.2X p/r 50-199
*GREEN/25: .4X TO 1X p/r 20-44
1 Giannis Antetokounmpo/144 75.00 200.00
2 Draymond Green/30 12.00 30.00
3 Kawhi Leonard/100 60.00 150.00
4 Buddy Hield/87 6.00 15.00
5 Dennis Schroder/28 10.00 25.00
6 Nikola Jokic/75 125.00 300.00
8 Karl-Anthony Towns/100 20.00 50.00
10 Malcolm Brogdon/75 3.00 8.00
11 Doug McDermott/71 2.50 6.00
12 Reggie Jackson/199 3.00 8.00
14 C.J. McCollum/149 5.00 12.00
19 Norman Powell/142 4.00 10.00
20 Jrue Holiday/199 5.00 12.00
22 Devin Harris/199 2.50 6.00
24 Damian Lillard/50 25.00 60.00
25 D'Angelo Russell/100 12.00 30.00
26 Kyrie Irving/50 25.00 60.00
29 Kelly Oubre Jr./199 4.00 10.00
32 Zach LaVine/199 5.00 12.00
34 Eric Bledsoe/68 3.00 8.00
36 Dirk Nowitzki/25 50.00 120.00
38 Victor Oladipo/199 6.00 15.00
40 Kristaps Porzingis/75 25.00 60.00
41 Jabari Parker/77 2.50 6.00
42 DeMarre Carroll/199 2.50 6.00
43 Ricky Rubio/125 6.00 15.00
44 Devin Booker/199 100.00 250.00
45 Gordon Hayward/99 3.00 8.00
47 Brandon Ingram/75 5.00 12.00
48 Jusuf Nurkic/149 3.00 8.00
50 Willy Hernangomez/75 2.50 6.00
51 Larry Nance Jr./178 3.00 8.00
52 Taurean Prince/199 2.50 6.00
53 John Wall/30 12.00 30.00
57 Julius Randle/99 8.00 20.00
62 Marcus Smart/199 5.00 12.00
64 Joel Embiid/60 25.00 60.00
65 Nicolas Batum/26 8.00 20.00

67 Marc Gasol/125 4.00 10.00
68 Andrew Wiggins/75 10.00 25.00
71 Ryan Anderson/53 2.50 6.00
72 DeAndre' Bembry/199 2.50 6.00
75 Kent Bazemore/111 2.50 6.00
76 Andre Drummond/149 6.00 15.00
80 Aaron Gordon/106 10.00 25.00
84 Harrison Barnes/199 3.00 8.00
85 Eric Gordon/180 3.00 8.00
86 Vince Carter/100 20.00 50.00
92 Paul Millsap/44 10.00 25.00
95 Kevin Durant/100 30.00 80.00
96 Anthony Davis/100 12.00 30.00
98 Goran Dragic/99 6.00 15.00

2017-18 Panini Ascension Composure

1 Russell Westbrook 1.00 2.50
2 Stephen Curry 5.00 12.00
3 Kyrie Irving 1.25 3.00
4 Kyle Lowry .60 1.50
5 Isaiah Thomas .50 1.25
6 Damian Lillard 1.50 4.00
7 James Harden 1.25 3.00
8 Kemba Walker .50 1.25
9 John Wall .75 2.00
10 Mike Conley .50 1.25
11 Goran Dragic .50 1.25
12 Dennis Schroder .50 1.25
13 Jeremy Lin 1.00 2.50
14 Dwyane Wade 1.25 3.00
15 Chauncey Billups .75 2.00
16 Nate Archibald .75 2.00
17 Oscar Robertson 1.25 3.00
18 John Stockton 1.25 3.00
19 Jason Kidd 1.00 2.50
20 Steve Nash 1.00 2.50

2017-18 Panini Ascension Golden Era

1 Bill Russell 2.00 5.00
2 Oscar Robertson 1.25 3.00
3 Wilt Chamberlain 2.00 5.00
4 Elgin Baylor 1.00 2.50
5 Jerry Lucas .60 1.50
6 Bob Pettit .60 1.50
7 Bob Cousy 1.00 2.50
8 Jerry West 1.25 3.00
9 Willis Reed 1.00 2.50
10 Nate Thurmond .60 1.50

2017-18 Panini Ascension Making History

1 Stephen Curry 5.00 12.00
2 Kevin Durant 2.50 6.00
3 Draymond Green .75 2.00
4 Russell Westbrook 1.00 2.50
5 LeBron James 5.00 12.00
6 James Harden 1.25 3.00
7 Giannis Antetokounmpo 3.00 8.00
8 Carmelo Anthony 1.00 2.50
9 Isaiah Thomas .50 1.25
10 Karl-Anthony Towns 1.00 2.50
11 Dwyane Wade 1.25 3.00
12 Blake Griffin .60 1.50
13 Rudy Gobert .75 2.00
14 Kawhi Leonard 1.50 4.00
15 Dirk Nowitzki 1.50 4.00
16 Hassan Whiteside .50 1.25
17 Anthony Davis 1.50 4.00
18 Damian Lillard 1.50 4.00
19 John Wall .75 2.00
20 Joel Embiid 1.25 3.00
21 Kemba Walker .50 1.25
22 Andre Drummond .50 1.25
23 Devin Booker 1.50 4.00
24 Kyrie Irving 1.25 3.00
25 Yao Ming 1.25 3.00
26 Jerry West 1.25 3.00
27 Hakeem Olajuwon 1.25 3.00
28 David Robinson 1.25 3.00
29 Shaquille O'Neal 2.00 5.00
30 Alonzo Mourning 1.00 2.50
31 Gary Payton 1.00 2.50
32 Magic Johnson 2.50 6.00
33 Tim Duncan 1.50 4.00
34 Kobe Bryant 5.00 12.00
35 Allen Iverson 1.50 4.00
36 Reggie Miller 1.25 3.00
37 Larry Bird 2.50 6.00
38 Dennis Rodman 1.50 4.00
39 Scottie Pippen 1.50 4.00
40 Oscar Robertson 1.25 3.00

2017-18 Panini Ascension New Frontiers Die Cuts

1 Lonzo Ball 12.00 30.00
2 Dennis Smith Jr. 1.50 4.00
3 D.J. Wilson 1.25 3.00
4 Jonathan Isaac 3.00 8.00
5 Josh Jackson 1.50 4.00
6 Frank Ntilikina 1.50 4.00
7 OG Anunoby 6.00 15.00
8 Luke Kennard 2.50 6.00
9 Malik Monk 5.00 12.00
10 Donovan Mitchell 12.00 30.00
11 Bam Adebayo 8.00 20.00
12 Kyle Kuzma 5.00 12.00
13 Harry Giles 6.00 15.00
14 Terrance Ferguson 1.25 3.00
15 John Collins 3.00 8.00
16 Jayson Tatum 20.00 50.00
17 De'Aaron Fox 10.00 25.00
18 Markelle Fultz 3.00 8.00
19 Jordan Bell 8.00 20.00
20 Zach Collins 2.00 5.00

2017-18 Panini Ascension Overdrive Die Cuts

1 James Harden 12.00 30.00
2 Russell Westbrook 8.00 20.00
3 Isaiah Thomas 4.00 10.00
4 Steve Nash 25.00 60.00
5 Stephen Curry 25.00 60.00
6 Allen Iverson 20.00 50.00
7 Devin Booker 25.00 60.00
8 Kobe Bryant 25.00 60.00
9 Blake Griffin 5.00 12.00
10 Tim Duncan 20.00 50.00
11 John Wall 6.00 15.00
12 Ray Allen 10.00 25.00
13 Joel Embiid 10.00 25.00
14 Tracy McGrady 10.00 25.00
15 Kawhi Leonard 20.00 50.00
16 Anthony Davis 12.00 30.00
17 Andrew Wiggins 6.00 15.00
18 Kristaps Porzingis 15.00 40.00
19 Kevin Durant 15.00 40.00
20 Damian Lillard 12.00 30.00

2017-18 Panini Ascension Reaching New Heights

1 Blake Griffin .60 1.50
2 Aaron Gordon .60 1.50
3 DeMar DeRozan .75 2.00
4 Kawhi Leonard 1.50 4.00
5 Kevin Durant 2.50 6.00
6 Anthony Davis 1.50 4.00
7 Brandon Ingram .75 2.00
8 Karl-Anthony Towns 1.00 2.50
9 Russell Westbrook 1.00 2.50
10 James Harden 1.25 3.00

2017-18 Panini Ascension Rookie Ascent Autographs

STATED PRINT RUN 299 SER.#'d SETS
EXCHANGE DEADLINE 5/22/2019
*RED/75: .5X TO 1.2X BASIC
*PURPLE/50: .5X TO 1.2X BASIC
*GREEN/25: .75X TO 2X BASIC
1 Markelle Fultz 10.00 25.00
2 Lonzo Ball 20.00 50.00
3 Jayson Tatum 40.00 100.00
4 Josh Jackson 3.00 8.00
5 De'Aaron Fox 25.00 60.00
6 Jonathan Isaac 6.00 15.00
7 Lauri Markkanen 15.00 40.00
8 Dennis Smith Jr. 3.00 8.00
9 Luke Kennard 6.00 15.00
10 Malik Monk 10.00 25.00
11 Donovan Mitchell 40.00 100.00
12 Bam Adebayo 12.00 30.00
13 Justin Jackson 2.50 6.00
14 Justin Patton 2.50 6.00
15 D.J. Wilson 2.50 6.00
16 T.J. Leaf 2.50 6.00
17 John Collins 8.00 20.00
18 Zach Collins 4.00 10.00
19 Harry Giles 2.50 6.00
20 Jarrett Allen 6.00 15.00
21 OG Anunoby 12.00 30.00
22 Tyler Lydon 2.50 6.00
23 Caleb Swanigan 2.50 6.00
24 Jordan Bell 2.50 6.00
25 Kyle Kuzma 10.00 25.00
26 Derrick White 10.00 25.00
27 Frank Jackson 2.50 6.00
28 Jawun Evans 2.50 6.00
29 Dwayne Bacon 2.50 6.00
30 Josh Hart 6.00 15.00
31 Edmond Sumner 4.00 10.00
32 Dillon Brooks 8.00 20.00
33 Jaron Blossomgame 2.50 6.00

2017-18 Panini Ascension Thrill of Victory

1 Stephen Curry 5.00 12.00
2 Kevin Durant 2.50 6.00
3 Devin Booker 1.50 4.00
4 James Harden 1.25 3.00
5 John Wall .75 2.00
6 Dirk Nowitzki 1.50 4.00
7 Draymond Green .75 2.00
8 Kevin Love .60 1.50
9 Manu Ginobili 1.25 3.00
10 Norman Powell .60 1.50
11 Russell Westbrook 1.00 2.50
12 Damian Lillard 1.50 4.00
13 Kemba Walker .50 1.25
14 Bradley Beal .75 2.00
15 Karl-Anthony Towns 1.00 2.50
16 Kobe Bryant 5.00 12.00
17 Shaquille O'Neal 2.00 5.00
18 Reggie Miller 1.25 3.00
19 Scottie Pippen 1.50 4.00
20 Hakeem Olajuwon 1.25 3.00

2022-23 Panini Black

COMPLETE SET (95)
*SILVER/75: 2.5X TO 6X BASIC
*COPPER/35: 4X TO 10X BASIC
*GOLD/25: 5X TO 12X BASIC
1 Stephen Curry 3.00 8.00
2 Desmond Bane .50 1.25
3 Paul George .60 1.50
4 Domantas Sabonis .50 1.25
5 DeMar DeRozan .50 1.25
6 Zion Williamson 1.00 2.50
7 Anthony Edwards 2.00 5.00
8 Cade Cunningham 1.25 3.00
9 Devin Booker 1.00 2.50
10 RJ Barrett .60 1.50
11 Zach LaVine .75 2.00
12 Julius Randle .50 1.25
13 Keldon Johnson .50 1.25
14 Kyrie Irving .75 2.00
15 Luka Doncic 2.50 6.00
16 Trae Young 1.00 2.50
17 Pascal Siakam .60 1.50
18 Evan Mobley 1.00 2.50
19 Jordan Poole .60 1.50
20 Bradley Beal .50 1.25
21 Jrue Holiday .50 1.25
22 Jimmy Butler .60 1.50
23 Alperen Sengun .50 1.25
24 Klay Thompson 1.00 2.50
25 Russell Westbrook .60 1.50
26 Damian Lillard 1.00 2.50
27 Mikal Bridges .50 1.25
28 Kawhi Leonard 1.00 2.50
29 Donovan Mitchell .75 2.00
30 Jayson Tatum 1.50 4.00
31 LeBron James 3.00 8.00
32 Anfernee Simons .50 1.25
33 Anthony Davis 1.00 2.50
34 Jalen Green 1.25 3.00
35 Ja Morant 1.25 3.00
36 Dejounte Murray .50 1.25
37 Kevin Durant 1.25 3.00
38 D'Angelo Russell .30 .75
39 CJ McCollum .40 1.00
40 James Harden .75 2.00
41 Chris Paul .75 2.00
42 Josh Giddey .60 1.50
43 Spencer Dinwiddie .30 .75
44 Darius Garland .60 1.50
45 Joel Embiid .60 1.50
46 LaMelo Ball 1.00 2.50
47 Shai Gilgeous-Alexander 2.00 5.00
48 Brandon Ingram .50 1.25
49 Giannis Antetokounmpo 2.00 5.00
50 Tyrese Haliburton .75 2.00
51 De'Aaron Fox .75 2.00
52 Tyler Herro .60 1.50
53 Jaylen Brown .75 2.00
54 Scottie Barnes .60 1.50
55 Lauri Markkanen .60 1.50
56 Tyrese Maxey .75 2.00
57 Nikola Jokic 2.00 5.00
58 Jalen Brunson .75 2.00
59 Franz Wagner 1.00 2.50
60 Karl-Anthony Towns .60 1.50
61 Marcus Smart .50 1.25
62 Immanuel Quickley .40 1.00
63 Khris Middleton .50 1.25
64 Jamal Murray .60 1.50
65 Michael Porter Jr. .50 1.25
66 Paolo Banchero RC 6.00 15.00
67 Max Christie RC 1.50 4.00
68 Jabari Smith Jr. RC 2.00 5.00
69 Keegan Murray RC 1.50 4.00
70 Jaden Ivey RC 2.00 5.00
71 Patrick Baldwin Jr. RC .60 1.50
72 Bennedict Mathurin RC 2.00 5.00
73 David Roddy RC .75 2.00
74 Dyson Daniels RC 1.50 4.00
75 Jeremy Sochan RC 1.50 4.00
76 MarJon Beauchamp RC .60 1.50
77 Kennedy Chandler RC .60 1.50
78 Jalen Williams RC 3.00 8.00
79 AJ Griffin RC .50 1.25
80 Mark Williams RC 1.25 3.00
81 Ochai Agbaji RC .75 2.00
82 Dalen Terry RC .60 1.50
83 Jalen Duren RC 2.00 5.00
84 Tari Eason RC 1.50 4.00
85 Walker Kessler RC 1.25 3.00
86 Ousmane Dieng RC .75 2.00
87 Jaden Hardy RC .75 2.00
88 Christian Braun RC 1.50 4.00
89 Shaedon Sharpe RC 2.50 6.00
90 TyTy Washington Jr. RC .60 1.50
91 Nikola Jovic RC 1.25 3.00
92 Malaki Branham RC .60 1.50
93 Andrew Nembhard RC 1.25 3.00
94 Chet Holmgren RC 3.00 8.00
95 Jaylin Williams RC .75 2.00

2022-23 Panini Black Rookie Jumbo Memorabilia Autographs

COMPLETE SET (20)
STATED PRINT RUN 20-25 SER.#'d SETS
1 Paolo Banchero/20 300.00 600.00
2 Chet Holmgren/20 200.00 500.00
3 Jabari Smith Jr./20 50.00 125.00
4 Keegan Murray/20 40.00 100.00
5 Jaden Ivey/20 50.00 125.00
6 Bennedict Mathurin/25 50.00 120.00
7 Shaedon Sharpe/20 60.00 150.00
8 Dyson Daniels/25 40.00 100.00
9 Jeremy Sochan/25 50.00 125.00
10 Jalen Williams/25 80.00 200.00
11 Jalen Duren/20 50.00 125.00
12 Ochai Agbaji/25 20.00 50.00
13 AJ Griffin/25 12.00 30.00
14 Tari Eason/25 40.00 100.00
15 Malaki Branham/25 15.00 40.00
16 Walker Kessler/25 30.00 80.00
17 MarJon Beauchamp/25 15.00 40.00
18 Patrick Baldwin Jr./25 15.00 40.00
19 Andrew Nembhard/25 30.00 80.00
20 Jaden Hardy/20 25.00 60.00

2022-23 Panini Black Rookie Memorabilia Autographs

COMPLETE SET (30)
STATED PRINT RUN 25-49 SER.#'d SETS
*SILVER/25: .5X TO 1.25X BASIC
1 Paolo Banchero/25 200.00 500.00
2 Chet Holmgren/25 150.00 400.00
3 Jabari Smith Jr./35 40.00 100.00
4 Keegan Murray/35 30.00 80.00
5 Jaden Ivey/25 40.00 100.00
6 Bennedict Mathurin/35 40.00 100.00
7 Shaedon Sharpe/35 50.00 125.00
8 Dyson Daniels/49 30.00 80.00
9 Jeremy Sochan/49 40.00 100.00
10 Johnny Davis/25 12.00 30.00
11 Ousmane Dieng/49 15.00 40.00
12 Jalen Williams/49 60.00 150.00
13 Jalen Duren/35 40.00 100.00
14 Ochai Agbaji/49 12.00 30.00
15 Mark Williams/49 25.00 60.00
16 AJ Griffin/35 10.00 25.00
17 Tari Eason/49 30.00 80.00
18 Dalen Terry/49 12.00 30.00
19 Jake LaRavia/49 12.00 30.00
20 Malaki Branham/49 12.00 30.00
21 Christian Braun/49 30.00 80.00
22 Walker Kessler/49 25.00 60.00
23 MarJon Beauchamp/49 12.00 30.00
24 Blake Wesley/49 12.00 30.00
25 Nikola Jovic/49 25.00 60.00
26 Andrew Nembhard/49 25.00 60.00
27 Christian Koloko/49 12.00 30.00
28 Patrick Baldwin Jr./49 12.00 30.00
29 Max Christie/49 50.00 120.00
30 Jaden Hardy/25 20.00 50.00

2022-23 Panini Black Smoke Show Signatures

COMPLETE SET (50)
STATED PRINT RUN 15-35 SER.#'d SETS
*SILVER/20-25: .5X TO 1.2X BASIC
1 Paolo Banchero/25 125.00 300.00
2 Chet Holmgren/25 100.00 250.00
3 Jabari Smith Jr./25 30.00 80.00
4 Keegan Murray/35 25.00 60.00
5 Jaden Ivey/30 30.00 80.00
6 Bennedict Mathurin/30 30.00 80.00
7 Shaedon Sharpe/30 40.00 100.00
8 Dyson Daniels/35 25.00 60.00
9 Jeremy Sochan/35 30.00 80.00
10 Ousmane Dieng/35 12.00 30.00
11 Jalen Williams/35 50.00 125.00
12 Jalen Duren/25 30.00 80.00
13 Ochai Agbaji/35 12.00 30.00
14 Mark Williams/35 20.00 50.00
15 AJ Griffin/35 8.00 20.00
16 Tari Eason/35 25.00 60.00
17 Dalen Terry/35 10.00 25.00
18 Jake LaRavia/35 10.00 25.00
19 Malaki Branham/35 10.00 25.00
20 Christian Braun/35 25.00 60.00
21 Walker Kessler/35 20.00 50.00
22 David Roddy/35 12.00 30.00
23 MarJon Beauchamp/35 12.00 30.00
24 Blake Wesley/35 10.00 25.00
25 Nikola Jovic/35 20.00 50.00
26 Patrick Baldwin Jr./35 10.00 25.00
27 Andrew Nembhard/35 20.00 50.00
28 Christian Koloko/35 10.00 25.00
29 Max Christie/35 40.00 100.00
30 Jaden Hardy/20 15.00 40.00
31 Luka Doncic/15 300.00 600.00
32 Austin Reaves/35 60.00 150.00
33 Josh Giddey/35 15.00 40.00
34 Lauri Markkanen/25 15.00 40.00
35 Nikola Vucevic/30 10.00 25.00
36 Anthony Edwards/15 150.00 400.00
37 Tyrese Haliburton/25 40.00 100.00
38 Jordan Poole/25 15.00 40.00
39 Bojan Bogdanovic/35 10.00 25.00
40 Patty Mills/35 15.00 40.00
41 Jose Alvarado/35 10.00 25.00
42 Kelly Oubre Jr./35 10.00 25.00
43 Malcolm Brogdon/35 8.00 20.00
44 Jordan Clarkson/35 20.00 50.00
45 Saddiq Bey/35 8.00 20.00
46 Gary Payton/25 25.00 60.00
47 Shawn Kemp/35 25.00 60.00
48 Anfernee Hardaway/25 50.00 120.00
49 Clyde Drexler/25 25.00 60.00
50 Paul Pierce/30 25.00 60.00

2022-23 Panini Black White Night

COMPLETE SET (5)
1 Luka Doncic 500.00 1,000.00
2 Stephen Curry 600.00 1,200.00
3 Giannis Antetokounmpo 400.00 800.00
4 LeBron James 600.00 1,200.00
5 Paolo Banchero 600.00 1,200.00

2023-24 Panini Black

*SHINE: 1.25X TO 3X BASIC
*SILVER/75: 2X TO 5X BASIC
*COPPER/35: 3X TO 8X BASIC
*GOLD/25: 4X TO 10X BASIC
1 Mikal Bridges .50 1.25
2 Jalen Williams .75 2.00
3 RJ Barrett .60 1.50
4 Lauri Markkanen .60 1.50
5 Jordan Poole .60 1.50
6 Ja Morant 1.25 3.00
7 Anthony Edwards 2.00 5.00
8 Anthony Davis 1.00 2.50
9 Trae Young .75 2.00
10 Donovan Mitchell .75 2.00
11 Shai Gilgeous-Alexander 2.00 5.00
12 Joel Embiid 1.00 2.50
13 Darius Garland .60 1.50
14 Devin Booker 1.00 2.50
15 Zion Williamson 1.00 2.50
16 Tyrese Maxey .75 2.00
17 Kyrie Irving .75 2.00
18 Keldon Johnson .50 1.25
19 Jayson Tatum 1.50 4.00
20 Paolo Banchero 1.00 2.50
21 DeMar DeRozan .60 1.50
22 Anfernee Simons .50 1.25
23 Kevin Durant 1.25 3.00
24 Bam Adebayo .60 1.50
25 LeBron James 3.00 8.00
26 Jamal Murray .75 2.00
27 Luka Doncic 2.50 6.00
28 Klay Thompson 1.00 2.50
29 Alperen Sengun .60 1.50
30 Jalen Brunson .75 2.00
31 Chet Holmgren 1.00 2.50
32 Jimmy Butler .60 1.50
33 Bradley Beal .50 1.25
34 Kawhi Leonard 1.00 2.50
35 Jalen Green .60 1.50
36 Giannis Antetokounmpo 2.00 5.00
37 Cameron Thomas .50 1.25
38 Pascal Siakam .60 1.50
39 James Harden .75 2.00
40 Cade Cunningham 1.00 2.50
41 Franz Wagner .60 1.50
42 Tyler Herro .60 1.50
43 Jaylen Brown .75 2.00
44 Nikola Jokic 2.00 5.00
45 Zach LaVine .60 1.50
46 Cameron Johnson .40 1.00
47 Jaren Jackson Jr. .60 1.50
48 Chris Paul .75 2.00
49 De'Aaron Fox .75 2.00
50 Tyrese Haliburton .75 2.00
51 LaMelo Ball 1.00 2.50
52 Domantas Sabonis .60 1.50
53 Dejounte Murray .60 1.50
54 Scottie Barnes .60 1.50
55 Stephen Curry 3.00 8.00
56 Damian Lillard 1.00 2.50
57 Julius Randle .50 1.25
58 Karl-Anthony Towns .60 1.50
59 Paul George .60 1.50
60 Brandon Ingram .50 1.25
61 Anthony Black RC 1.50 4.00
62 Dereck Lively II RC 1.50 4.00
63 Jalen Hood-Schifino RC .75 2.00
64 Jaime Jaquez Jr. RC 1.25 3.00
65 Kris Murray RC .75 2.00
66 Gradey Dick RC 1.50 4.00
67 Cason Wallace RC 1.50 4.00
68 Julian Strawther RC 1.00 2.50
69 Cam Whitmore RC 2.00 5.00
70 Brandin Podziemski RC 2.50 6.00
71 Jett Howard RC 1.00 2.50
72 Toumani Camara RC 1.50 4.00
73 Brandon Miller RC 3.00 8.00
74 Taylor Hendricks RC .75 2.00
75 GG Jackson II RC 1.50 4.00
76 Marcus Sasser RC 1.25 3.00
77 Keyonte George RC 2.50 6.00
78 Amen Thompson RC 4.00 10.00
79 Kobe Bufkin RC 1.00 2.50
80 Trayce Jackson-Davis RC 1.00 2.50
81 Andre Jackson Jr. RC 1.25 3.00
82 Jarace Walker RC 1.50 4.00
83 Dariq Whitehead RC 1.00 2.50
84 Ausar Thompson RC 2.00 5.00
85 Jordan Hawkins RC 1.25 3.00
86 Ben Sheppard RC .75 2.00
87 Victor Wembanyama RC 20.00 50.00
88 Bilal Coulibaly RC 2.00 5.00
89 Nick Smith Jr. RC 1.00 2.50
90 Scoot Henderson RC 2.50 6.00

2023-24 Panini Black Dead of Night Autographs

1 De'Aaron Fox/25 40.00 100.00
2 Alperen Sengun/25 30.00 80.00
3 Ja Morant/25 125.00 300.00
4 Brandon Ingram/25 20.00 50.00
5 Shai Gilgeous-Alexander/15 400.00 800.00
8 Jalen Brunson/25 60.00 150.00
9 Tyrese Maxey/25 60.00 150.00
10 Anthony Edwards/15 300.00 600.00

2023-24 Panini Black Dead of Night Autographs Ruby FOTL

1 De'Aaron Fox/15 40.00 100.00
2 Alperen Sengun/15 30.00 80.00
3 Ja Morant/15 125.00 300.00
4 Brandon Ingram/15 20.00 50.00
8 Jalen Brunson/15 60.00 150.00
9 Tyrese Maxey/15 60.00 150.00
10 Anthony Edwards/15 300.00 600.00

2023-24 Panini Black Dead of Night Autographs Silver

1 De'Aaron Fox 40.00 100.00
2 Alperen Sengun 30.00 80.00
3 Ja Morant 125.00 300.00
4 Brandon Ingram 20.00 50.00
8 Jalen Brunson 60.00 150.00
9 Tyrese Maxey 60.00 150.00

2023-24 Panini Black Rookie Jumbo Memorabilia Autographs

STATED PRINT RUN 25 SER.#'d SETS
1 Dariq Whitehead 20.00 50.00
2 GG Jackson II 30.00 80.00
3 Kobe Bufkin 20.00 50.00
4 Sasha Vezenkov 12.00 30.00
5 Keyonte George 50.00 125.00
6 Cason Wallace 30.00 80.00
7 Trayce Jackson-Davis 20.00 50.00
8 Ben Sheppard 15.00 40.00
9 Ausar Thompson 40.00 100.00
10 Kris Murray 15.00 40.00
11 Bilal Coulibaly 40.00 100.00
12 Julian Strawther 20.00 50.00
13 Brandin Podziemski 50.00 125.00
14 Amen Thompson 80.00 200.00
15 Jordan Walsh 15.00 40.00
16 Toumani Camara 30.00 80.00
17 Dereck Lively II 30.00 80.00
18 Vasilije Micic 15.00 40.00
19 Andre Jackson Jr. 25.00 60.00
20 Marcus Sasser 25.00 60.00

2023-24 Panini Black Rookie Memorabilia Autographs

STATED PRINT RUN 49 SER.#'d SETS
*SILVER/25: .5X TO 1.25X BASIC
*CITRINE FOTL/21: .5X TO 1.25X BASIC
1 Brandin Podziemski 40.00 100.00
2 Marcus Sasser 20.00 50.00
3 Ben Sheppard 12.00 30.00
4 Brice Sensabaugh 20.00 50.00
5 Keyonte George 40.00 100.00
6 Hunter Tyson 12.00 30.00
8 Jordan Walsh 12.00 30.00
9 Andre Jackson Jr. 20.00 50.00
10 Bilal Coulibaly 30.00 80.00
11 Dereck Lively II 25.00 60.00
12 Ausar Thompson 30.00 80.00
13 Sasha Vezenkov 10.00 25.00
14 Kobe Brown 12.00 30.00
15 Noah Clowney 15.00 40.00
16 Julian Strawther 15.00 40.00
18 Toumani Camara 25.00 60.00
19 Kobe Bufkin 15.00 40.00
20 Amen Thompson 60.00 150.00
21 Dariq Whitehead 15.00 40.00
22 Kris Murray 12.00 30.00
23 Vasilije Micic 12.00 30.00
25 GG Jackson II 25.00 60.00
27 Maxwell Lewis 10.00 25.00
28 Trayce Jackson-Davis 15.00 40.00
29 Olivier-Maxence Prosper 12.00 30.00
30 Cason Wallace 25.00 60.00

2023-24 Panini Black Smoke Show Signatures

STATED PRINT RUN 25-35 SER.#'d SETS
*SILVER/25: .4X TO 1X BASIC
1 Jalen Johnson/35 12.00 30.00
2 John Wall/35 12.00 30.00
3 Julius Randle/35 12.00 30.00
5 Scottie Barnes/35 12.00 30.00
6 Quentin Grimes/35 10.00 25.00
7 Kevin Huerter/35 8.00 20.00
8 Ayo Dosunmu/35 10.00 25.00
9 Marcus Sasser/35 15.00 40.00
10 Trayce Jackson-Davis/35 12.00 30.00
11 Cason Wallace/35 20.00 50.00
12 Dyson Daniels/35 12.00 30.00
13 Chris Livingston/35 12.00 30.00
14 Grant Hill/25 15.00 40.00
15 Norman Powell/35 10.00 25.00
16 Maxwell Lewis/35 8.00 20.00
17 Grant Williams/35 8.00 20.00
19 Al Horford/35 10.00 25.00
20 Kristaps Porzingis/25 12.00 30.00
21 Fred VanVleet/35 15.00 40.00
22 JJ Redick/35 10.00 25.00
23 GG Jackson II/35 20.00 50.00
24 Donte DiVincenzo/35 10.00 25.00
25 Mahmoud Abdul-Rauf/35 8.00 20.00
26 Lauri Markkanen/35 15.00 40.00
27 Anfernee Simons/35 12.00 30.00
29 Desmond Bane/35 12.00 30.00
30 Markelle Fultz/35 8.00 20.00
31 De'Anthony Melton/35 10.00 25.00
32 Cameron Thomas/35 12.00 30.00
33 Alex Caruso/35 10.00 25.00
34 RJ Barrett/25 15.00 40.00
35 Keegan Murray/35 12.00 30.00
36 Tim Hardaway/35 12.00 30.00
37 Lester Quinones/35 8.00 20.00
38 Duop Reath/35 10.00 25.00
39 Craig Porter Jr. /35 12.00 30.00
40 Keldon Johnson/35 12.00 30.00

2023-24 Panini Black Vanta

1 LeBron James 350.00 700.00
2 Victor Wembanyama 500.00 1,000.00
3 Luka Doncic 350.00 700.00
4 Stephen Curry 350.00 700.00
5 Scoot Henderson 125.00 300.00

2023-24 Panini Black White Night

1 Stephen Curry 300.00 600.00
2 Brandon Miller 300.00 600.00
3 Luka Doncic 300.00 600.00
4 Victor Wembanyama 800.00 1,500.00
5 LeBron James 300.00 600.00

2011 Panini Black Friday Autographs

BJ Brandon Jennings Adrenalyn 10.00 25.00
KB Kobe Bryant Patch/30* 125.00 300.00
OC Omri Casspi Adrenalyn 3.00 8.00

2012 Panini Black Friday Rookie Materials Shoes

1 Harrison Barnes 15.00 40.00
2 Jared Sullinger 8.00 20.00

2012 Panini Black Friday Rookie of the Year Materials

ROYKI Kyrie Irving 12.00 30.00

2012 Panini Black Friday Spokesman Jumbo Jerseys

KB Kobe Bryant 15.00 40.00

2012 Panini Black Friday Tools of the Trade Towels

1 Anthony Davis 12.00 30.00
2 Michael Kidd-Gilchrist 8.00 20.00
3 Thomas Robinson 10.00 25.00
4 Harrison Barnes 10.00 25.00
5 Terrence Ross 6.00 15.00
6 Austin Rivers 8.00 20.00

2013 Panini Black Friday Inked Autographs

AB Anthony Bennett 12.00 30.00
AL Alex Len 4.00 10.00
BM Ben McLemore 5.00 12.00
CZ Cody Zeller 4.00 10.00
MCW Michael Carter-Williams 20.00 50.00
NN Nerlens Noel 30.00 80.00
OP Otto Porter 5.00 12.00
TB Trey Burke 25.00 60.00
TH Tim Hardaway Jr. 6.00 15.00
VO Victor Oladipo 25.00 60.00

2013 Panini Black Friday Hot Rookies

ISSUED VIA BLACK FRIDAY PROMOTION
1 Anthony Bennett .60 1.50
2 Trey Burke .50 1.25
3 Nerlens Noel .75 2.00
4 Michael Carter-Williams .50 1.25
5 Shabazz Muhammad .50 1.25
6 Cody Zeller .50 1.25
7 Victor Oladipo .75 2.00
8 Kentavious Caldwell-Pope .50 1.25
9 Alex Len .50 1.25
10 Otto Porter .60 1.50

2013 Panini Black Friday Hot Rookies Cracked Ice

*CRACKED ICE: 1.5X TO 4X BASIC
ISSUED VIA BLACK FRIDAY PROMOTION
ANNOUNCED PRINT RUN 35 OR LESS

2013 Panini Black Friday Hot Rookies Lava Flow

*LAVA FLOW: .75X TO 2X BASIC
ISSUED VIA BLACK FRIDAY PROMOTION
ANNOUNCED PRINT RUN 150 OR LESS

2013 Panini Black Friday NBA Championship Materials

ISSUED VIA BLACK FRIDAY PROMOTION
1 LeBron James 25.00 60.00
2 Dwyane Wade 6.00 15.00
3 Chris Bosh 3.00 8.00
4 Shane Battier 2.50 6.00
5 Mario Chalmers 2.50 6.00
6 Ray Allen 4.00 10.00

2013 Panini Black Friday Rookie Materials

BK1 Anthony Bennett BK 5.00 12.00
BK2 Michael Carter-Williams BK 10.00 25.00
BK3 Otto Porter BK 3.00 8.00
BK4 Trey Burke BK 5.00 12.00
BK5 Tim Hardaway Jr. BK 4.00 10.00
BK6 Nerlens Noel BK 5.00 12.00
BK7 Kentavious Caldwell-Pope BK 2.50 6.00

2013 Panini Black Friday Rookie Materials Headbands

ISSUED VIA BLACK FRIDAY PROMOTION
1 Anthony Bennett 2.50 6.00
2 Victor Oladipo 3.00 8.00
3 Nerlens Noel 3.00 8.00
4 Trey Burke 2.00 5.00
5 Ben McLemore 2.50 6.00
6 Otto Porter 2.50 6.00

2013 Panini Black Friday Tools of the Trade Materials

ISSUED VIA BLACK FRIDAY PROMOTION
1 Anthony Bennett 2.00 5.00
2 Victor Oladipo 2.50 6.00
3 Alex Len 1.50 4.00
4 C.J. McCollum 2.50 6.00
5 Tim Hardaway Jr. 2.50 6.00
6 Trey Burke 1.50 4.00
KB Kobe Bryant 10.00 25.00

2014 Panini Black Friday Manufactured Patch Autographs

SN Shabazz Napier 10.00 25.00

2014 Panini Black Friday Manufactured Patch Autographs Team Logo

JR Julius Randle 15.00 40.00
MS Marcus Smart 15.00 40.00
SN Shabazz Napier 10.00 25.00

2014 Panini Black Friday Manufactured Patches NBA

AW Andrew Wiggins 4.00 10.00
KB Kobe Bryant 6.00 15.00
KD Kevin Durant 4.00 10.00

2014 Panini Black Friday Rookie Materials Jerseys

*CRACKED ICE/25: 1.2X TO 3X BASIC
1 Dante Exum 1.50 4.00
2 Joel Embiid 8.00 20.00
3 Aaron Gordon 4.00 10.00
4 Shabazz Napier 1.50 4.00
5 Doug McDermott 2.50 6.00
6 Nik Stauskas 2.00 5.00
7 Noah Vonleh 2.00 5.00
8 Elfrid Payton 2.50 6.00
9 Adreian Payne 1.25 3.00
10 Andrew Wiggins 6.00 15.00

2014 Panini Black Friday Rookie Materials Wristbands

*CRACKED ICE/25: 1.2X TO 3X BASIC
1 Jabari Parker 3.00 8.00
2 Julius Randle 3.00 8.00
3 Marcus Smart 2.50 6.00
4 Doug McDermott 2.50 6.00
5 Zach Lavine 3.00 8.00
6 Rodney Hood 2.50 6.00

2014 Panini Black Friday Tools of the Trade Towels

*CRACKED ICE/25: .6X TO 1.5X BASIC
1 Joel Embiid 10.00 25.00
2 Nik Stauskas 2.50 6.00
3 Jabari Parker 6.00 15.00
4 Joe Harris 2.50 6.00
5 Glenn Robinson III 2.00 5.00
6 Zach Lavine 4.00 10.00
7 Shabazz Napier 2.00 5.00
8 Doug McDermott 3.00 8.00
9 Aaron Gordon 5.00 12.00
10 Elfrid Payton 3.00 8.00
11 James Young 2.00 5.00
12 Marcus Smart 3.00 8.00
2 Julius Randle 4.00 10.00

2016 Panini Black Friday Happy Holidays Materials

*CRACKED/25: .8X TO 2X BASE MEM
1 D'Angelo Russell 2.50 6.00
2 Georgios Papagiannis 2.50 6.00
3 Emmanuel Mudiay 2.50 6.00
4 Devin Booker 2.50 6.00
5 Kris Dunn 2.50 6.00
6 Jaylen Brown 2.50 6.00
7 Brandon Ingram 2.50 6.00
8 Tyler Ulis 2.50 6.00
9 Denzel Valentine 2.50 6.00
10 Isaiah Whitehead 2.50 6.00
11 Thon Maker 2.50 6.00
12 Buddy Hield 2.50 6.00
13 Jamal Murray 2.50 6.00
14 Stephen Zimmerman 2.50 6.00
15 Jakob Poeltl 2.50 6.00

2016 Panini Black Friday Jerseys

*CRACKED/25: .8X TO 2X BASE JSY
BK1 Kris Dunn 2.50 6.00
BK2 Thon Maker 2.50 6.00
BK3 Jamal Murray 2.50 6.00
BK4 Buddy Hield 2.50 6.00
BK5 Dragan Bender 2.50 6.00
BK6 Marquese Chriss 2.50 6.00
BK7 Brandon Ingram 2.50 6.00
BK8 Jaylen Brown 2.50 6.00
BK9 Henry Ellenson 2.50 6.00
BK10 Caris LeVert 2.50 6.00
BK11 Malik Beasley 2.50 6.00
BK12 Dejounte Murray 2.50 6.00
BK13 Damian Jones 2.50 6.00
BK14 Wade Baldwin IV 2.50 6.00
BK15 Juan Hernangomez 2.50 6.00

2016 Panini Black Friday Tools of the Trade Combine Towels

*CRACKED/25: .8X TO 2X BASE TOWEL
C1 Patrick McCaw 2.50 6.00
C2 DeAndre' Bembry 2.50 6.00
C3 Taurean Prince 2.50 6.00
C4 Chinanu Onuaku 2.50 6.00
C5 Cheick Diallo 2.50 6.00
C6 Damian Jones 2.50 6.00
C7 Malcolm Brogdon 2.50 6.00
C8 Pascal Siakam 2.50 6.00
C9 Marquese Chriss 2.50 6.00
C10 Kay Felder 2.50 6.00

2016 Panini Black Friday Tools of the Trade Towels

*CRACKED/25: .8X TO 2X BASIC TOWEL
1 Jaylen Brown 2.50 6.00
2 A.J. Hammons 2.50 6.00
3 Denzel Valentine 2.50 6.00
4 Taurean Prince 2.50 6.00
5 Jamal Murray 2.50 6.00

2015-16 Panini Black Gold
1 Larry Bird 5.00 12.00
2 Reggie Jackson 1.00 2.50
3 DeAndre Jordan 1.00 2.50
4 Jonas Valanciunas 1.00 2.50
5 Dwyane Wade 2.50 6.00
6 Brook Lopez 1.25 3.00
7 Nicolas Batum .75 2.00
8 Rudy Gobert 1.50 4.00
9 Zaza Pachulia .75 2.00
10 LeBron James 10.00 25.00
11 Magic Johnson 5.00 12.00
12 Kentavious Caldwell-Pope 1.00 2.50
13 Rudy Gay 1.25 3.00
14 DeMar DeRozan 1.50 4.00
15 Chris Bosh 1.50 4.00
16 Thaddeus Young .75 2.00
17 Al Jefferson .75 2.00
18 Kenneth Faried 1.00 2.50
19 Mike Conley 1.25 3.00
20 Kyrie Irving 2.50 6.00
21 Julius Erving 3.00 8.00
22 Giannis Antetokounmpo 6.00 15.00
23 DeMarcus Cousins 1.25 3.00
24 Kyle Lowry 1.25 3.00
25 Hassan Whiteside 1.00 2.50
26 Nerlens Noel .75 2.00
27 John Wall 1.50 4.00
28 Danilo Gallinari 1.00 2.50
29 Marc Gasol 1.25 3.00
30 Kevin Love 1.25 3.00
31 Wilt Chamberlain 5.00 12.00
32 Jabari Parker .75 2.00
33 Rajon Rondo 1.50 4.00
34 Avery Bradley .75 2.00
35 Al Horford 1.25 3.00
36 Robert Covington 1.00 2.50
37 Bradley Beal 1.50 4.00
38 Will Barton .75 2.00
39 Zach Randolph 1.25 3.00
40 Jimmy Butler 2.50 6.00
41 Pete Maravich 3.00 8.00
42 Michael Carter-Williams .75 2.00
43 Eric Bledsoe 1.00 2.50
44 Isaiah Thomas 1.00 2.50
45 Paul Millsap 1.00 2.50
46 Isaiah Canaan .75 2.00
47 Marcin Gortat .75 2.00
48 Andrew Wiggins 1.50 4.00
49 James Harden 2.50 6.00
50 Derrick Rose 2.00 5.00
51 Scottie Pippen 3.00 8.00
52 Stephen Curry 8.00 20.00
53 Brandon Knight .75 2.00
54 Jared Sullinger .75 2.00
55 Jeff Teague .75 2.00
56 Russell Westbrook 2.00 5.00
57 Tony Parker 2.00 5.00
58 Ricky Rubio 1.00 2.50
59 Trevor Ariza .75 2.00
60 Pau Gasol 2.00 5.00
61 Kareem Abdul-Jabbar 4.00 10.00
62 Klay Thompson 3.00 8.00
63 T.J. Warren 1.25 3.00
64 Carmelo Anthony 2.00 5.00
65 Tobias Harris 1.00 2.50
66 Kevin Durant 5.00 12.00
67 Tim Duncan 3.00 8.00
68 Kevin Garnett 3.00 8.00
69 Dwight Howard 1.50 4.00
70 Paul George 2.00 5.00
71 Allen Iverson 3.00 8.00
72 Draymond Green 1.50 4.00
73 Kobe Bryant 10.00 25.00
74 Arron Afflalo .75 2.00
75 Nikola Vucevic 1.00 2.50
76 Serge Ibaka 1.00 2.50
77 Kawhi Leonard 4.00 10.00
78 Damian Lillard 3.00 8.00
79 Anthony Davis 3.00 8.00
80 George Hill 1.00 2.50
81 John Stockton 2.50 6.00
82 Blake Griffin 1.25 3.00
83 Roy Hibbert 1.00 2.50
84 Robin Lopez .75 2.00
85 Victor Oladipo 1.00 2.50
86 Gordon Hayward 1.25 3.00
87 Dirk Nowitzki 3.00 8.00
88 C.J. McCollum 1.25 3.00
89 Tyreke Evans 1.00 2.50
90 Monta Ellis 1.00 2.50
91 Chris Webber 1.50 4.00
92 Chris Paul 2.50 6.00
93 Jordan Clarkson 1.25 3.00
94 Joe Johnson 1.00 2.50
95 Kemba Walker 1.25 3.00
96 Derrick Favors 1.00 2.50
97 Deron Williams 1.00 2.50
98 Mason Plumlee .75 2.00
99 Eric Gordon 1.00 2.50
100 Andre Drummond 1.25 3.00

2015-16 Panini Black Gold Rare
*RARE: .6X TO 1.5X BASIC

2015-16 Panini Black Gold Uncommon
*UNCOMMON: .6X TO 1.5X BASIC

2015-16 Panini Black Gold Bronze
*BRONZE: .4X TO 1X BASIC

2015-16 Panini Black Gold Gold Discs
1 LeBron James 100.00 250.00
2 Stephen Curry 100.00 250.00
3 Kobe Bryant 75.00 200.00
4 Kyrie Irving 30.00 80.00
5 Dwyane Wade 50.00 120.00
6 James Harden 30.00 80.00
7 Tim Duncan 40.00 100.00
8 Russell Westbrook 50.00 120.00
9 Kevin Durant 60.00 150.00
10 Anthony Davis 40.00 100.00

2015-16 Panini Black Gold Golden Jams Materials
STATED PRINT RUN 99 SER.#'d SETS
*PRIME/25: 1X TO 2.5X BASIC
1 Aaron Gordon 4.00 10.00
2 Andre Drummond 4.00 10.00
3 Blake Griffin 4.00 10.00
4 Bradley Beal 5.00 12.00
5 Chandler Parsons 2.50 6.00
6 DeAndre Jordan 3.00 8.00
7 DeMar DeRozan 5.00 12.00
8 Gary Harris 3.00 8.00
9 Grant Hill 6.00 15.00
10 Harrison Barnes 3.00 8.00
11 J.R. Smith 4.00 10.00
12 Jimmy Butler 8.00 20.00
13 Jonathon Simmons 3.00 8.00
14 Julius Erving 10.00 25.00
15 Karl-Anthony Towns 10.00 25.00
16 Kemba Walker 4.00 10.00
17 Kenneth Faried 3.00 8.00
18 Kevin Durant 8.00 20.00
19 Kobe Bryant 30.00 80.00
20 Larry Johnson 5.00 12.00
21 LeBron James 20.00 50.00
22 Marcus Smart 5.00 12.00
23 Mario Hezonja 3.00 8.00
24 Nerlens Noel 2.50 6.00
25 Norman Powell 2.50 6.00
26 Rudy Gobert 5.00 12.00
27 Russell Westbrook 8.00 20.00
28 Scottie Pippen 10.00 25.00
29 Victor Oladipo 3.00 8.00
30 Zach LaVine 10.00 25.00

2015-16 Panini Black Gold Golden Opportunity Memorabilia
STATED PRINT RUN 199 SER.#'d SETS
*PRIME/25: 1X TO 2.5X BASIC
1 Aaron Gordon 4.00 10.00
2 Alec Burks 2.50 6.00
3 Anthony Davis 6.00 15.00
4 Bobby Portis 6.00 15.00
5 Bradley Beal 5.00 12.00
6 Cameron Payne 4.00 10.00
7 D'Angelo Russell 8.00 20.00
8 Devin Booker 8.00 20.00
9 Emmanuel Mudiay 3.00 8.00
10 Frank Kaminsky 3.00 8.00
11 Gary Harris 3.00 8.00
12 Jahlil Okafor 5.00 12.00
13 James Harden 8.00 20.00
14 Jarell Martin 2.50 6.00
15 Enes Kanter 2.50 6.00
16 Jerian Grant 2.50 6.00
17 Joe Young 2.50 6.00
18 Jonathon Simmons 3.00 8.00
19 Jordan Adams 2.50 6.00
20 Jordan Clarkson 4.00 10.00
21 Josh Richardson 4.00 10.00
22 Jrue Holiday 5.00 12.00
23 Julius Randle 5.00 12.00
24 Justin Anderson 2.50 6.00
25 Justise Winslow 4.00 10.00
26 Karl-Anthony Towns 10.00 25.00
27 Kelly Oubre Jr. 8.00 20.00
28 Kenneth Faried 3.00 8.00
29 Kevon Looney 8.00 20.00
30 Doug McDermott 3.00 8.00
31 Langston Galloway 2.50 6.00
33 Mario Hezonja 2.50 6.00
34 Mitch McGary 2.50 6.00
35 Myles Turner 10.00 25.00
36 Nick Young 2.50 6.00
38 Otto Porter 3.00 8.00
39 Rajon Rondo 5.00 12.00
41 Richaun Holmes 4.00 10.00
42 Rodney Hood 3.00 8.00
43 Rondae Hollis-Jefferson 3.00 8.00
44 Shane Larkin 2.50 6.00
45 Stanley Johnson 3.00 8.00
46 Trey Lyles 3.00 8.00
47 Tyreke Evans 3.00 8.00
48 Victor Oladipo 3.00 8.00
49 Willie Cauley-Stein 4.00 10.00
50 Zach Randolph 4.00 10.00

2015-16 Panini Black Gold Grand Debut Signatures
PRINT RUNS B/WN 13-199 COPIES PER
NO PRICING ON QTY 13
EXCHANGE DEADLINE 1/6/2018
1 Tyus Jones/199 5.00 12.00
4 Jahlil Okafor/140 5.00 12.00
5 Emmanuel Mudiay/199 5.00 12.00
6 Boban Marjanovic/199 12.00 30.00
7 Bobby Portis/199 10.00 25.00
8 Jonathon Simmons/199 5.00 12.00
9 Raul Neto/199 4.00 10.00
10 R.J. Hunter/199 4.00 10.00
11 Devin Booker/199 200.00 500.00
12 D'Angelo Russell/124 25.00 60.00
13 Jerian Grant/199 4.00 10.00
14 Stanley Johnson/199 5.00 12.00
15 Larry Nance Jr./199 8.00 20.00
16 Justin Anderson/140 4.00 10.00
17 Myles Turner/199 15.00 40.00
18 Montrezl Harrell/199 12.00 30.00
19 Jordan Mickey/199 4.00 10.00
20 Terry Rozier/100 15.00 40.00
21 Rashad Vaughn/199 4.00 10.00
22 Kelly Oubre Jr./199 12.00 30.00
23 Rondae Hollis-Jefferson/199 5.00 12.00
24 Sam Dekker/199 4.00 10.00
25 Norman Powell/199 8.00 20.00

2015-16 Panini Black Gold Massive Materials
PRINT RUNS B/WN 49-199 COPIES PER
1 Al Horford/199 4.00 10.00
2 Al Jefferson/199 2.50 6.00
3 Allen Iverson/99 8.00 20.00
4 Andre Drummond/199 4.00 10.00
5 Avery Bradley/199 2.50 6.00
6 Blake Griffin/199 4.00 10.00
7 Bradley Beal/199 5.00 12.00
8 Brandon Jennings/199 2.50 6.00
9 Chris Bosh/199 5.00 12.00
10 Damian Lillard/99 6.00 15.00
11 Dante Exum/49 3.00 8.00
12 DeAndre Jordan/199 3.00 8.00
13 Devin Booker/199 6.00 15.00
14 Dirk Nowitzki/199 10.00 25.00
15 Dwyane Wade/99 8.00 20.00
16 Gordon Hayward/49 4.00 10.00
17 Grant Hill/149 6.00 15.00
18 James Harden/49 8.00 20.00
19 Joe Johnson/199 3.00 8.00
20 John Stockton/49 8.00 20.00
21 Julius Erving/49 10.00 25.00
22 Karl Malone/49 6.00 15.00
23 Kemba Walker/199 4.00 10.00
24 Kevin Garnett/49 10.00 25.00
25 Kevin Love/199 4.00 10.00
26 Kevin McHale/49 6.00 15.00
27 Kobe Bryant/199 30.00 80.00
28 LaMarcus Aldridge/199 4.00 10.00
29 Marcin Gortat/49 2.50 6.00
30 Marcus Smart/49 5.00 12.00
31 Nerlens Noel/49 2.50 6.00
32 Patrick Ewing/49 6.00 15.00
33 Rajon Rondo/49 5.00 12.00
34 Ricky Rubio/49 3.00 8.00
35 Rudy Gobert/199 5.00 12.00
36 Tony Parker/49 6.00 15.00
37 Victor Oladipo/49 3.00 8.00
38 Alonzo Mourning/49 6.00 15.00
39 Brook Lopez/99 4.00 10.00
40 Chandler Parsons/99 2.50 6.00
41 Deron Williams/49 3.00 8.00
42 Robert Covington/199 3.00 8.00
43 J.J. Redick/199 4.00 10.00
44 Jrue Holiday/199 5.00 12.00
45 Kelly Oubre Jr./199 8.00 20.00
46 Khris Middleton/199 5.00 12.00
47 Kyrie Irving/99 6.00 15.00
48 Lance Stephenson/199 3.00 8.00
49 Thaddeus Young/99 2.50 6.00
50 Trey Lyles/199 3.00 8.00

2015-16 Panini Black Gold Memorabilia
STATED PRINT RUN 99 SER.#'d SETS
*PRIME/25: 1X TO 2.5X BASIC
1 Aaron Gordon 4.00 10.00
2 Al Horford 4.00 10.00
3 Al Jefferson 2.50 6.00
4 Allen Iverson 8.00 20.00
5 Andre Drummond 4.00 10.00
6 Avery Bradley 2.50 6.00
7 Blake Griffin 4.00 10.00
8 Bradley Beal 5.00 12.00
9 Brandon Jennings 2.50 6.00
10 Chris Bosh 5.00 12.00
11 Damian Lillard 6.00 15.00
12 Dante Exum 3.00 8.00
13 DeAndre Jordan 3.00 8.00
14 Devin Booker 8.00 20.00
15 Dirk Nowitzki 10.00 25.00
16 Dwyane Wade 8.00 20.00
17 Emmanuel Mudiay 3.00 8.00
18 Gary Harris 3.00 8.00
19 Goran Dragic 4.00 10.00
20 Gordon Hayward 4.00 10.00
21 Grant Hill 6.00 15.00
22 James Harden 8.00 20.00
23 Jerian Grant 2.50 6.00
24 Joe Johnson 3.00 8.00
25 John Stockton 8.00 20.00
26 Jose Calderon 2.50 6.00
27 Julius Erving 10.00 25.00
28 Jusuf Nurkic 3.00 8.00
29 Karl Malone 6.00 15.00
30 Kemba Walker 4.00 10.00
31 Kenneth Faried 3.00 8.00
32 Kevin Garnett 10.00 25.00
33 Kevin Love 4.00 10.00
34 Kevin McHale 6.00 15.00
35 Kobe Bryant 30.00 80.00
36 LaMarcus Aldridge 4.00 10.00
37 Langston Galloway 2.50 6.00
38 Marcin Gortat 2.50 6.00
39 Marcus Smart 5.00 12.00
40 Nerlens Noel 2.50 6.00
41 Patrick Ewing 6.00 15.00
42 Rajon Rondo 5.00 12.00
43 Ricky Rubio 3.00 8.00
44 Rudy Gobert 5.00 12.00
45 Russell Westbrook 8.00 20.00
46 Stephen Curry 20.00 50.00
47 Tim Hardaway Jr. 3.00 8.00
48 Tony Parker 6.00 15.00
49 Tyreke Evans 3.00 8.00
50 Victor Oladipo 3.00 8.00

2015-16 Panini Black Gold Pick and Roll Materials
STATED PRINT RUN 99 SER.#'d SETS
*PRIME/25: 1X TO 2.5X BASIC
1 A.Horford/J.Teague 4.00 10.00
2 M.Smart/J.Sullinger 5.00 12.00
3 Rose/Gasol 10.00 25.00
4 Mudiay/Faried 3.00 8.00
5 A.Drummond/R.Jackson 4.00 10.00
6 Green/Curry 20.00 50.00
7 Howard/Harden 8.00 20.00
8 Russell/Randle 6.00 15.00
9 Z.Randolph/M.Conley 4.00 10.00
10 Bosh/Wade 8.00 20.00
11 G.Dieng/R.Rubio 3.00 8.00
12 Davis/Holiday 8.00 20.00
13 Jackson/Ewing 6.00 15.00
14 Westbrook/Ibaka 6.00 15.00
15 N.Vucevic/E.Payton 3.00 8.00
16 A.Len/B.Knight 2.50 6.00
17 A.Stoudemire/S.Nash 6.00 15.00
18 D.Cousins/R.Rondo 5.00 12.00
19 Duncan/Parker 10.00 25.00
20 Stockton/Malone 8.00 20.00

2015-16 Panini Black Gold Rookie Jersey Autographs
PRINT RUNS B/WN 65-199 COPIES PER
EXCHANGE DEADLINE 1/6/2018
*PRIME/21-25: 1.2X TO 3X BASIC
1 Karl-Anthony Towns/199 60.00 150.00
2 D'Angelo Russell/199 15.00 40.00
3 Jahlil Okafor/199 5.00 12.00
4 Emmanuel Mudiay/199 5.00 12.00
5 Kristaps Porzingis/199 30.00 80.00
6 Mario Hezonja/199 5.00 12.00
7 Justise Winslow/65 20.00 50.00
8 Willie Cauley-Stein/199 12.00 30.00
9 Tyus Jones/199 5.00 12.00
10 Stanley Johnson/199 5.00 12.00
11 Frank Kaminsky/78 8.00 20.00
12 Devin Booker/199 300.00 600.00
13 Myles Turner/199 12.00 30.00
14 Trey Lyles/199 5.00 12.00
15 Jerian Grant/199 4.00 10.00
16 Kevon Looney/199 12.00 30.00
17 Cameron Payne/118 6.00 15.00
18 Kelly Oubre Jr./199 12.00 30.00
19 Terry Rozier/199 15.00 40.00
20 Rondae Hollis-Jefferson/199 5.00 12.00
21 Bobby Portis/199 4.00 10.00
22 Nikola Jokic/157 800.00 1,500.00
23 Justin Anderson/199 4.00 10.00
24 R.J. Hunter/199 4.00 10.00
25 Raul Neto/199 4.00 10.00
26 Marcelo Huertas/165 4.00 10.00
27 Anthony Brown/199 4.00 10.00
28 Norman Powell/199 8.00 20.00
29 Sasha Kaun/199 4.00 10.00
30 Pat Connaughton/199 6.00 15.00

2015-16 Panini Black Gold Signatures
PRINT RUNS B/WN 60-99 COPIES PER
EXCHANGE DEADLINE 1/6/2018
BGN Nene/99 5.00 12.00
BGAD Andre Drummond/99 12.00 30.00
BGAD Anthony Davis/60 40.00 100.00
BGAH Anfernee Hardaway/75 25.00 60.00
BGAM Alonzo Mourning/60 20.00 50.00
BGBB Bradley Beal/75 EXCH 12.00 30.00
BGBK Brandon Knight/99 4.00 10.00
BGDE Dante Exum/75 10.00 25.00
BGDG Danny Green/99 5.00 12.00
BGDM Dikembe Mutombo/99 10.00 25.00
BGDR Dennis Rodman/75 25.00 60.00
BGDS Dennis Schroder/99 6.00 15.00
BGEJ Eddie Jones/99 6.00 15.00
BGEP Elfrid Payton/99 12.00 30.00
BGGD Goran Dragic/99 6.00 15.00
BGGH Gordon Hayward/99 12.00 30.00
BGGH Grant Hill/75 20.00 50.00
BGGN Gary Neal/99 4.00 10.00
BGJC Jordan Clarkson/99 EXCH 10.00 25.00
BGJE Julius Erving/60 40.00 100.00
BGJP Jabari Parker/60 12.00 30.00
BGJR Julius Randle/75 10.00 25.00
BGJS J.R. Smith/99 EXCH 6.00 15.00
BGJS John Stockton/60 20.00 50.00
BGJS Jared Sullinger/75 4.00 10.00
BGJW John Wall/60 15.00 40.00
BGKB Kent Bazemore/99 EXCH 4.00 10.00
BGKB Kobe Bryant/60 500.00 1,000.00
BGKD Kevin Durant/60 60.00 150.00
BGKI Kyrie Irving/60 50.00 120.00
BGKL Kevin Love/75 20.00 50.00
BGKM Karl Malone/60 20.00 50.00
BGKT Klay Thompson/75 30.00 80.00
BGMD M. Dellavedova/99 EXCH 10.00 25.00
BGMJ Mark Jackson/99 5.00 12.00
BGMS Marcus Smart/75 8.00 20.00
BGNM Nikola Mirotic/99 4.00 10.00
BGNS Nik Stauskas/99 4.00 10.00
BGNY Nick Young/99 4.00 10.00
BGRA Ray Allen/75 20.00 50.00
BGRM Ray McCallum/99 4.00 10.00
BGRS Rod Strickland/99 4.00 10.00
BGTM Tracy McGrady/75 20.00 50.00
BGTP Tony Parker/75 25.00 60.00
BGTW T.J. Warren/99 6.00 15.00
BGTY Thaddeus Young/99 4.00 10.00
BGWM Wesley Matthews/99 4.00 10.00
BGABK Alec Burks/99 4.00 10.00
BGAHF Al Horford/99 6.00 15.00
BGBGF Blake Griffin/60 25.00 60.00
BGCBS Chris Bosh/75 8.00 20.00
BGCJW C.J. Watson/99 4.00 10.00
BGDCL DeMarre Carroll/99 4.00 10.00
BGDMJ Donatas Motiejunas/99 4.00 10.00
BGDPW Dwight Powell/99 4.00 10.00
BGDRS David Robinson/60 25.00 60.00
BGEBS Eric Bledsoe/99 5.00 12.00
BGFEZ Festus Ezeli/99 4.00 10.00
BGGGE George Gervin/75 8.00 20.00
BGGHS Gary Harris/99 5.00 12.00
BGGPT Gary Payton/75 EXCH 10.00 25.00
BGITH Isaiah Thomas/99 12.00 30.00
BGJET Jason Terry/99 5.00 12.00
BGJHD Jrue Holiday/75 8.00 20.00
BGJKD Jason Kidd/75 10.00 25.00
BGMGT Marcin Gortat/99 4.00 10.00
BGMHL Maurice Harkless/99 4.00 10.00
BGMJS Magic Johnson/60 30.00 80.00
BGNCL Norris Cole/99 4.00 10.00
BGSON Shaquille O'Neal/60 40.00 100.00
BGTKU Toni Kukoc/99 6.00 15.00
BGVOD Victor Oladipo/75 5.00 12.00
BGZLV Zach LaVine/99 20.00 50.00

2015-16 Panini Black Gold Sizeable Signatures Jerseys
STATED PRINT RUN 99 SER.#'d SETS
EXCHANGE DEADLINE 1/6/2018
RSSAB Anthony Brown 5.00 12.00
RSSBP Bobby Portis 12.00 30.00
RSSCP Cameron Payne 8.00 20.00
RSSDB Devin Booker 300.00 600.00
RSSDR D'Angelo Russell EXCH 25.00 60.00
RSSEM Emmanuel Mudiay 6.00 15.00
RSSJG Jerian Grant 5.00 12.00
RSSJO Jahlil Okafor 12.00 30.00
RSSJS Jonathon Simmons 6.00 15.00
RSSJW Justise Winslow 8.00 20.00
RSSKP Kristaps Porzingis 40.00 100.00
RSSKT Karl-Anthony Towns 60.00 150.00
RSSMH Montrezl Harrell 15.00 40.00
RSSMH Mario Hezonja 6.00 15.00
RSSMH Marcelo Huertas 5.00 12.00
RSSMT Myles Turner 20.00 50.00
RSSNB Nemanja Bjelica 8.00 20.00
RSSNJ Nikola Jokic 1,500.00 3,000.00
RSSNP Norman Powell 10.00 25.00
RSSRH R.J. Hunter 5.00 12.00
RSSRH Richaun Holmes 8.00 20.00
RSSRN Raul Neto 5.00 12.00
RSSSJ Stanley Johnson 6.00 15.00
RSSTR Terry Rozier 20.00 50.00
RSSWC Willie Cauley-Stein 6.00 15.00

2015-16 Panini Black Gold Sizeable Signatures Jerseys Prime
*PRIME: 1.5X TO 4X BASIC
STATED PRINT RUN 25 SER.#'d SETS
EXCHANGE DEADLINE 1/6/2018
RSSDB Devin Booker 1,000.00 2,000.00

2015-16 Panini Black Gold Team Emblems
1 Kobe Bryant 75.00 200.00
2 Kristaps Porzingis 30.00 80.00
3 Kevin Durant 30.00 80.00
4 D'Angelo Russell 30.00 80.00
5 Kyrie Irving 40.00 100.00
6 Jahlil Okafor 6.00 15.00
7 Anthony Davis 20.00 50.00
8 Nemanja Bjelica 8.00 20.00
9 LeBron James 75.00 200.00
10 Justise Winslow 12.00 30.00
11 Stephen Curry 100.00 250.00
12 Russell Westbrook 25.00 60.00
13 James Harden 30.00 80.00
14 DeMarcus Cousins 8.00 20.00
15 Chris Paul 20.00 50.00
16 John Wall 10.00 25.00
17 Carmelo Anthony 20.00 50.00
18 Jimmy Butler 20.00 50.00
19 Dwight Howard 10.00 25.00
20 Paul George 20.00 50.00
21 Julius Erving 20.00 50.00
22 Artis Gilmore 10.00 25.00
23 George Gervin 10.00 25.00
24 Connie Hawkins 8.00 20.00
25 David Thompson 10.00 25.00
26 Mack Calvin 5.00 12.00
27 Dan Issel 10.00 25.00
28 George McGinnis 8.00 20.00
29 Louie Dampier 8.00 20.00
30 Larry Brown 8.00 20.00

2015-16 Panini Black Gold Vintage Gold Autographs
PRINT RUNS B/WN 28-149 COPIES PER
EXCHANGE DEADLINE 1/6/2018
1 Elvin Hayes/149 10.00 25.00
2 Walt Frazier/55 8.00 20.00
3 Jalen Rose/149 5.00 12.00
4 Jamaal Wilkes/149 6.00 15.00
5 Dan Issel/149 8.00 20.00
6 Tim Hardaway/149 8.00 20.00
7 Glen Rice/115 5.00 12.00
8 George Gervin/149 10.00 25.00
9 Hal Greer/50 8.00 20.00
10 Jason Kidd/65 20.00 50.00
11 Bob McAdoo/70 8.00 20.00
12 David Thompson/149 8.00 20.00
13 Ray Allen/125 12.00 30.00
14 Jerry West/28 25.00 60.00
15 Dennis Rodman/75 25.00 60.00
16 John Stockton/99 20.00 50.00
17 James Worthy/75 12.00 30.00
18 David Robinson/75 20.00 50.00
19 Nate Archibald/99 6.00 15.00
20 Clyde Drexler/65 15.00 40.00
21 Dikembe Mutombo/149 15.00 40.00
22 Grant Hill/105 12.00 30.00
23 John Salley/149 4.00 10.00
24 Steve Smith/149 5.00 12.00
25 Eddie Jones/149 6.00 15.00
26 Charles Oakley/149 5.00 12.00
27 Toni Kukoc/149 6.00 15.00
28 Jo Jo White/125 6.00 15.00
29 Wayne Embry/125 4.00 10.00
30 Ron Harper/125 6.00 15.00
31 Maurice Cheeks/125 5.00 12.00
32 Norm Nixon/99 4.00 10.00
33 Darrell Griffith/99 5.00 12.00
34 Jim Jackson/149 4.00 10.00
35 Bill Laimbeer/149 6.00 15.00
36 Isiah Thomas/125 10.00 25.00
37 Tracy McGrady/75 12.00 30.00
38 Anfernee Hardaway/50 25.00 60.00
39 Tom Heinsohn/149 25.00 60.00
40 Muggsy Bogues/125 5.00 12.00
41 John Starks/149 6.00 15.00
42 Thurl Bailey/149 4.00 10.00
43 Theo Ratliff/49 4.00 10.00
44 Kelly Tripucka/149 4.00 10.00
45 Rolando Blackman/149 5.00 12.00

2012-13 Panini Brilliance
COMPLETE SET (300) 60.00 150.00
1 Al Horford .40 1.00
2 Kevin Durant 1.50 4.00
3 DeShawn Stevenson .25 .60
4 Devin Harris .25 .60
5 Jeff Teague .25 .60
6 Josh Smith .25 .60
7 Kyle Korver .30 .75
8 Kevin Martin .30 .75
9 Avery Bradley .25 .60
10 Brandon Bass .25 .60
11 Courtney Lee .25 .60
12 Jason Terry .30 .75
13 Jeff Green .25 .60
14 Kevin Garnett 1.00 2.50
15 Leandro Barbosa .30 .75
16 Paul Pierce .60 1.50
17 Rajon Rondo .50 1.25
18 Andray Blatche .25 .60
19 Brook Lopez .30 .75
20 C.J. Watson .25 .60
21 Serge Ibaka .30 .75
22 Deron Williams .30 .75
23 Gerald Wallace .30 .75
24 Jerry Stackhouse .30 .75
25 Joe Johnson .30 .75
26 Reggie Evans .25 .60
27 Kris Humphries .25 .60
28 Ben Gordon .25 .60
29 Byron Mullens .25 .60
30 Gerald Henderson .25 .60
31 Tyson Chandler .30 .75
32 Ramon Sessions .25 .60
33 Russell Westbrook .60 1.50
34 Carlos Boozer .30 .75
35 Daequan Cook .25 .60
36 Derrick Rose .60 1.50
37 Joakim Noah .30 .75
38 Kirk Hinrich .30 .75
39 Luol Deng .25 .60
40 Marco Belinelli .25 .60
41 Richard Hamilton .40 1.00
42 Taj Gibson .25 .60
43 Alonzo Gee .25 .60
44 Anderson Varejao .25 .60
45 Daniel Gibson .25 .60
46 Thabo Sefolosha .25 .60
47 Chris Kaman .30 .75
48 Dahntay Jones .25 .60
49 Darren Collison .25 .60
50 Dirk Nowitzki 1.00 2.50
51 Elton Brand .30 .75
52 O.J. Mayo .30 .75
53 Shawn Marion .40 1.00
54 Vince Carter .75 2.00
55 Andre Iguodala .40 1.00
56 Andre Miller .30 .75
57 Corey Brewer .25 .60
58 Danilo Gallinari .30 .75
59 JaVale McGee .30 .75
60 Ty Lawson .25 .60
61 Kendrick Perkins .25 .60
62 Greg Monroe .25 .60
63 Jason Maxiell .25 .60
64 Rodney Stuckey .25 .60
65 Tayshaun Prince .40 1.00
66 Will Bynum .25 .60
67 Andrew Bogut .30 .75
68 Andris Biedrins .25 .60
69 Brandon Rush .25 .60
70 Carl Landry .25 .60
71 David Lee .25 .60
72 Stephen Curry 3.00 8.00
73 James Harden .75 2.00
74 Jeremy Lin .60 1.50
75 Omer Asik .25 .60
76 Patrick Patterson .25 .60
77 Toney Douglas .25 .60
78 Danny Granger .25 .60
79 George Hill .30 .75
80 Gerald Green .25 .60
81 Lance Stephenson .30 .75
82 Roy Hibbert .30 .75
83 Tyler Hansbrough .25 .60
84 Blake Griffin .40 1.00
85 Caron Butler .30 .75
86 Chauncey Billups .50 1.25
87 Chris Paul .75 2.00
88 DeAndre Jordan .30 .75
89 Eric Bledsoe .30 .75
90 Grant Hill .60 1.50
91 Jamal Crawford .40 1.00
92 Matt Barnes .25 .60
93 Antawn Jamison .30 .75
94 Devin Ebanks .25 .60
95 Earl Clark .25 .60
96 Jodie Meeks .25 .60
97 Dwight Howard .50 1.25
98 Kobe Bryant 3.00 8.00
99 Metta World Peace .30 .75
100 Pau Gasol .60 1.50
101 Steve Blake .25 .60
102 Steve Nash .75 2.00
103 Darrell Arthur .25 .60
104 Jerryd Bayless .25 .60
105 Marc Gasol .40 1.00
106 Marreese Speights .25 .60
107 Mike Conley .30 .75
108 Rudy Gay .40 1.00
109 Tony Allen .30 .75
110 Wayne Ellington .25 .60
111 Zach Randolph .40 1.00
112 Chris Bosh .50 1.25
113 Dwyane Wade .75 2.00
114 James Jones .25 .60
115 Joel Anthony .25 .60
116 LeBron James 3.00 8.00
117 Mario Chalmers .30 .75
118 Mike Miller .30 .75
119 Rashard Lewis .40 1.00
120 Udonis Haslem .30 .75
121 Beno Udrih .25 .60
122 Brandon Jennings .30 .75
123 Drew Gooden .25 .60
124 Ekpe Udoh .25 .60
125 Ersan Ilyasova .25 .60
126 Larry Sanders .25 .60
127 Luc Mbah a Moute .25 .60
128 Andrei Kirilenko .30 .75
129 Brandon Roy .30 .75
130 J.J. Barea .30 .75
131 Kevin Love .40 1.00
132 Luke Ridnour .30 .75
133 Nikola Pekovic .25 .60
134 Ricky Rubio .30 .75
135 Al-Farouq Aminu .25 .60
136 Eric Gordon .30 .75
137 Greivis Vasquez .25 .60
138 Robin Lopez .25 .60
139 Xavier Henry .25 .60
140 Amar'e Stoudemire .40 1.00
141 Carmelo Anthony .60 1.50
142 J.R. Smith .40 1.00
143 Jason Kidd .60 1.50
144 Marcus Camby .40 1.00
145 Raymond Felton .25 .60
146 Steve Novak .25 .60
147 Glen Davis .25 .60
148 Hedo Turkoglu .30 .75
149 J.J. Redick .40 1.00
150 Jameer Nelson .25 .60
151 Arron Afflalo .25 .60
152 Andrew Bynum .25 .60
153 Evan Turner .25 .60
154 Jason Richardson .40 1.00
155 Jrue Holiday .50 1.25
156 Nick Young .25 .60
157 Spencer Hawes .25 .60
158 Thaddeus Young .25 .60
159 Goran Dragic .40 1.00
160 Jared Dudley .25 .60
161 Jermaine O'Neal .30 .75
162 Luis Scola .30 .75
163 Marcin Gortat .25 .60
164 P.J. Tucker .25 .60
165 Shannon Brown .25 .60
166 J.J. Hickson .25 .60
167 Joel Freeland .25 .60
168 LaMarcus Aldridge .40 1.00
169 Nicolas Batum .30 .75
170 Wesley Matthews .25 .60
171 DeMarcus Cousins .40 1.00
172 Francisco Garcia .30 .75
173 James Johnson .25 .60
174 Jason Thompson .25 .60
175 John Salmons .30 .75
176 Marcus Thornton .25 .60
177 Tyreke Evans .30 .75
178 Boris Diaw .30 .75
179 Danny Green .30 .75
180 DeJuan Blair .25 .60
181 Manu Ginobili .75 2.00
182 Stephen Jackson .30 .75
183 Tiago Splitter .25 .60
184 Tim Duncan 1.00 2.50
185 Tony Parker .60 1.50
186 Alan Anderson .25 .60
187 Amir Johnson .25 .60
188 Andrea Bargnani .25 .60
189 DeMar DeRozan .50 1.25
190 Ed Davis .25 .60
191 Kyle Lowry .40 1.00
192 Randy Foye .25 .60
193 Al Jefferson .25 .60
194 Derrick Favors .30 .75
195 Gordon Hayward .40 1.00
196 Marvin Williams .25 .60
197 Emeka Okafor .30 .75
198 John Wall .50 1.25
199 Jordan Crawford .25 .60
200 Nene .30 .75
201 Adrian Dantley .30 .75
202 Allan Houston .30 .75
203 Allen Iverson .60 1.50
204 B.J. Armstrong .40 1.00
205 Bernard King .50 1.25
206 Bob McAdoo .30 .75
207 Clyde Drexler .60 1.50
208 Dan Majerle .30 .75
209 Earl Monroe .50 1.25
210 Gary Payton .50 1.25
211 George Gervin .60 1.50
212 Hakeem Olajuwon .75 2.00
213 Horace Grant .40 1.00
214 Isiah Thomas .75 2.00
215 James Worthy .60 1.50
216 Jeff Hornacek .30 .75
217 John Starks .30 .75
218 John Stockton .75 2.00
219 Larry Bird 1.25 3.00
220 Mark Aguirre .30 .75
221 Mitch Richmond .40 1.00
222 Moses Malone .60 1.50
223 Nate McMillan .25 .60
224 Ralph Sampson .30 .75
225 Reggie Theus .25 .60
226 Rick Mahorn .25 .60
227 Sam Cassell .30 .75
228 Sam Perkins .30 .75
229 Shaquille O'Neal 1.25 3.00
230 Tim Hardaway .50 1.25
231 Norris Cole RC .50 1.25
232 Alexey Shved RC .50 1.25
233 Greg Stiemsma RC .50 1.25
234 Anthony Davis RC 6.00 15.00
235 Austin Rivers RC .75 2.00
236 Brian Roberts RC .50 1.25
237 Lance Thomas RC .50 1.25
238 Chris Copeland RC .50 1.25
239 Iman Shumpert RC .60 1.50
240 Jeremy Lamb RC .75 2.00
241 Perry Jones RC .50 1.25
242 Reggie Jackson RC .75 2.00
243 Andrew Nicholson RC .50 1.25
244 DeQuan Jones RC .50 1.25
245 E'Twaun Moore RC .60 1.50
246 Gustavo Ayon RC .50 1.25
247 Maurice Harkless RC .60 1.50
248 Nikola Vucevic RC 2.00 5.00
249 John Jenkins RC .50 1.25
250 Jared Sullinger RC .50 1.25
251 MarShon Brooks RC .50 1.25
252 Mirza Teletovic RC .60 1.50
253 Tornike Shengelia RC .50 1.25
254 Tyshawn Taylor RC .50 1.25
255 Kemba Walker RC 2.00 5.00
256 Michael Kidd-Gilchrist RC .60 1.50
257 Jimmy Butler RC 5.00 12.00
258 Marquis Teague RC .50 1.25
259 Dion Waiters RC .60 1.50
260 Kyrie Irving RC 8.00 20.00
261 Tristan Thompson RC .75 2.00
262 Tyler Zeller RC .50 1.25
263 Bernard James RC .50 1.25
264 Jae Crowder RC 1.00 2.50
265 Kenneth Faried RC .60 1.50
266 Jordan Hamilton RC .50 1.25
267 Andre Drummond RC 1.25 3.00
268 Brandon Knight RC .60 1.50
269 Kyle Singler RC .50 1.25
270 Kent Bazemore RC .75 2.00
271 Klay Thompson RC 8.00 20.00
272 Chandler Parsons RC .60 1.50
273 Donatas Motiejunas RC .60 1.50
274 Terrence Jones RC .50 1.25
275 Miles Plumlee RC .50 1.25
276 Orlando Johnson RC .50 1.25
277 Darius Morris RC .60 1.50
278 Robert Sacre RC .50 1.25
279 Ivan Johnson RC .50 1.25
280 Tony Wroten RC .50 1.25
281 Lavoy Allen RC .50 1.25

282 Markieff Morris RC .75 2.00
283 Damian Lillard RC 5.00 12.00
284 Meyers Leonard RC .60 1.50
285 Nolan Smith RC .50 1.25
286 Will Barton RC 1.00 2.50
287 Thomas Robinson RC .50 1.25
288 Kawhi Leonard RC 6.00 15.00
289 Nando De Colo RC .50 1.25
290 Jonas Valanciunas RC 1.00 2.50
291 Quincy Acy RC .50 1.25
292 Terrence Ross RC 1.25 3.00
293 Alec Burks RC .75 2.00
294 Bradley Beal RC 4.00 10.00
295 Chris Singleton RC .50 1.25
296 Pablo Prigioni RC .50 1.25
297 John Henson RC .60 1.50
298 Tobias Harris RC 1.50 4.00
299 Marcus Morris RC .75 2.00
300 Viacheslav Kravtsov RC .50 1.25

2012-13 Panini Brilliance Starburst

*STARBURST VET: 1.5X TO 4X BASIC
*STARBURST RC: 1.5X TO 4X BASIC RC
283 Damian Lillard 50.00 120.00

2012-13 Panini Brilliance Accolades

COMPLETE SET (20) 10.00 25.00
1 Jason Kidd 1.25 3.00
2 Paul Pierce 1.25 3.00
3 Dirk Nowitzki 2.00 5.00
4 Kevin Garnett 2.00 5.00
5 Ray Allen 1.25 3.00
6 Marcus Camby .75 2.00
7 Kobe Bryant 6.00 15.00
8 Grant Hill 1.25 3.00
9 Steve Nash 1.50 4.00
10 Andre Miller .60 1.50
11 Vince Carter 1.50 4.00
12 Tim Duncan 2.00 5.00
13 Shawn Marion .75 2.00
14 Andrei Kirilenko .60 1.50
15 Antawn Jamison .60 1.50
16 Rasheed Wallace 1.00 2.50
17 Jason Terry .60 1.50
18 Chauncey Billups 1.00 2.50
19 Jerry Stackhouse .60 1.50
20 LeBron James 6.00 15.00

2012-13 Panini Brilliance Brilliant Beginnings Autographs

EXCHANGE DEADLINE 11/22/2014
1 Alec Burks 5.00 12.00
2 Alexey Shved 3.00 8.00
3 Andre Drummond 8.00 20.00
4 Andrew Nicholson 3.00 8.00
5 Anthony Davis 125.00 300.00
6 Austin Rivers 5.00 12.00
7 Bernard James 3.00 8.00
8 Bismack Biyombo 4.00 10.00
9 Bradley Beal 25.00 60.00
10 Brandon Knight 4.00 10.00
11 Chandler Parsons 4.00 10.00
12 Charles Jenkins 3.00 8.00
13 Chris Singleton 3.00 8.00
14 Darius Morris 4.00 10.00
15 Brian Roberts 3.00 8.00
16 Derrick Williams 3.00 8.00
17 Dion Waiters 4.00 10.00
18 Doron Lamb 3.00 8.00
19 Draymond Green 20.00 50.00
20 Enes Kanter 5.00 12.00
21 E'Twaun Moore 4.00 10.00
22 Evan Fournier 5.00 12.00
23 Gustavo Ayon 3.00 8.00
24 Harrison Barnes 6.00 15.00
25 Iman Shumpert 4.00 10.00
26 Isaiah Thomas 6.00 15.00
27 Jae Crowder 6.00 15.00
28 Jan Vesely 3.00 8.00
29 Tyler Zeller 3.00 8.00
30 Jared Sullinger 3.00 8.00
31 Jeff Taylor 3.00 8.00
32 Tristan Thompson 5.00 12.00
33 Jimmer Fredette 5.00 12.00
34 John Henson 4.00 10.00
35 Jonas Valanciunas 6.00 15.00
36 Jordan Hamilton 3.00 8.00
37 Kawhi Leonard 125.00 300.00
38 Kemba Walker 12.00 30.00
39 Kendall Marshall 3.00 8.00
40 Kenneth Faried 4.00 10.00
41 Kent Bazemore 5.00 12.00
42 Klay Thompson 100.00 250.00
43 Kyrie Irving 60.00 150.00
44 Lance Thomas 3.00 8.00
45 Marquis Teague 3.00 8.00
46 MarShon Brooks 3.00 8.00
47 Maurice Harkless 4.00 10.00
48 Meyers Leonard 4.00 10.00
49 Michael Kidd-Gilchrist 4.00 10.00
50 Tobias Harris 10.00 25.00
51 Nando De Colo 3.00 8.00
52 Nikola Vucevic 12.00 30.00
53 Nolan Smith 3.00 8.00
54 Norris Cole EXCH 3.00 8.00
55 Orlando Johnson 3.00 8.00
56 Quincy Acy 3.00 8.00
57 Robert Sacre 3.00 8.00
58 Will Barton 6.00 15.00
59 Terrence Ross 8.00 20.00
60 Thomas Robinson 3.00 8.00

2012-13 Panini Brilliance City to City Jerseys

PRIME PRINT RUNS 10-25 COPIES PER
1 Vince Carter 8.00 20.00
2 Dwight Howard 5.00 12.00
3 LeBron James 40.00 100.00
4 Chris Paul 8.00 20.00
5 Carmelo Anthony 8.00 20.00
6 Steve Nash 8.00 20.00
7 Andre Iguodala 4.00 10.00
8 Shaquille O'Neal 20.00 50.00
9 Andrei Kirilenko 3.00 8.00
10 Joe Johnson 3.00 8.00
11 Metta World Peace 3.00 8.00
12 Kyle Lowry 4.00 10.00
13 Ben Gordon 3.00 8.00
14 Andrew Bogut 3.00 8.00
15 Brandon Roy 3.00 8.00
16 Amar'e Stoudemire 4.00 10.00
17 Ray Allen 6.00 15.00
18 Grant Hill 6.00 15.00
19 Stephen Jackson 3.00 8.00
20 Goran Dragic 4.00 10.00

2012-13 Panini Brilliance City to City Jerseys Prime

*PRIME: 1.25X TO 3X BASIC
PRINT RUNS B/WN 10-25 COPIES PER

2012-13 Panini Brilliance Game Time Jerseys

PRIME PRINT RUNS 1-25 COPIES PER
1 Greg Monroe 2.50 6.00
2 Jose Calderon 2.50 6.00
3 Stephen Curry 30.00 80.00
4 Metta World Peace 3.00 8.00
5 J.J. Barea 3.00 8.00
6 Gordon Hayward 4.00 10.00
7 Andrea Bargnani 2.50 6.00
8 Jason Kidd 6.00 15.00
9 Al-Farouq Aminu 2.50 6.00
10 JaVale McGee 3.00 8.00
11 Kevin Love 4.00 10.00
12 Rajon Rondo 5.00 12.00
13 David Lee 2.50 6.00
14 Zach Randolph 4.00 10.00
15 Ryan Anderson 2.50 6.00
16 John Wall 5.00 12.00
17 Kevin Garnett 10.00 25.00
18 Kevin Durant 15.00 40.00
19 Josh Smith 2.50 6.00
20 Ty Lawson 2.50 6.00
21 Steve Novak 2.50 6.00
22 Paul Pierce 6.00 15.00
23 Blake Griffin 4.00 10.00
24 Marc Gasol 4.00 10.00
25 Robin Lopez 2.50 6.00
26 Goran Dragic 4.00 10.00
27 Paul George 6.00 15.00
28 Russell Westbrook 6.00 15.00
29 Al Horford 4.00 10.00
30 Derrick Favors 3.00 8.00
31 Rasheed Wallace 5.00 12.00
32 Derrick Rose 6.00 15.00
33 Grant Hill 6.00 15.00
34 Chris Bosh 5.00 12.00
35 Tyson Chandler 3.00 8.00
36 Luis Scola 3.00 8.00
37 Anderson Varejao 2.50 6.00
38 Glen Davis 2.50 6.00
39 Nene 3.00 8.00
40 Rudy Gay 4.00 10.00
41 David West 3.00 8.00
42 Darren Collison 2.50 6.00
43 Eric Bledsoe 3.00 8.00
44 DeMarcus Cousins 4.00 10.00
45 Kyle Lowry 4.00 10.00
46 LaMarcus Aldridge 4.00 10.00
47 Elton Brand 3.00 8.00
48 Hedo Turkoglu 3.00 8.00
49 Andre Iguodala 4.00 10.00
50 Brandon Roy 3.00 8.00
51 Tim Duncan 10.00 25.00
52 Rodney Stuckey 2.50 6.00
53 Kobe Bryant 50.00 120.00
54 LeBron James 50.00 120.00
55 Al Jefferson 2.50 6.00
56 Tyreke Evans 3.00 8.00
57 Chris Kaman 3.00 8.00
58 J.J. Redick 4.00 10.00
59 Andre Miller 3.00 8.00
60 Pau Gasol 6.00 15.00
61 Dirk Nowitzki 10.00 25.00
62 Damian Lillard 25.00 60.00
63 Steve Nash 10.00 25.00
64 O.J. Mayo 2.50 6.00
65 J.J. Hickson 2.50 6.00
66 Louis Williams 3.00 8.00
67 Chris Paul 8.00 20.00
68 Bradley Beal 20.00 50.00
69 Marcin Gortat 2.50 6.00
70 Thabo Sefolosha 2.50 6.00
71 Vince Carter 8.00 20.00
72 Anthony Davis 30.00 80.00
73 Emeka Okafor 3.00 8.00
74 Michael Kidd-Gilchrist 3.00 8.00
75 Kenneth Faried 3.00 8.00
76 DeMar DeRozan 8.00 20.00
77 Paul Millsap 3.00 8.00
78 Serge Ibaka 3.00 8.00
79 Eric Gordon 4.00 10.00
80 Jeff Teague 2.50 6.00

2012-13 Panini Brilliance Magic Numbers

COMPLETE SET (15) 12.00 30.00
1 Kobe Bryant 8.00 20.00
2 Blake Griffin 1.00 2.50
3 Anthony Davis 8.00 20.00
4 James Harden 2.00 5.00
5 Ty Lawson .60 1.50
6 Kyrie Irving 6.00 15.00
7 Kevin Garnett 2.50 6.00
8 John Wall 1.25 3.00
9 Tim Duncan 2.50 6.00
10 Damian Lillard 6.00 15.00
11 Kevin Love 1.00 2.50
12 LeBron James 8.00 20.00
13 Jeremy Lin 1.50 4.00
14 Stephen Curry 8.00 20.00
15 Brandon Knight .75 2.00

2012-13 Panini Brilliance Marks of Brilliance

PRINT RUNS B/WN 25-199 COPIES PER
EXCHANGE DEADLINE 11/22/2014
1 Kareem Abdul-Jabbar/199 60.00 150.00
2 Keith Erickson/199 5.00 12.00
3 Kelly Tripucka/25 4.00 10.00
4 Kemba Walker/25 40.00 100.00
5 Kenny Anderson/199 4.00 10.00
6 Kevin Durant/199 125.00 300.00
7 Kevin Love/25 10.00 25.00
8 Kevin Martin/25 4.00 10.00
9 Kevin McHale/25 12.00 30.00
11 Klay Thompson/25 150.00 400.00
12 Kobe Bryant/199 1,500.00 3,000.00
14 Kwame Brown/199 10.00 25.00
15 Kyle Lowry/199 10.00 25.00
16 LaMarcus Aldridge/25 10.00 25.00
17 Lance Stephenson/199 5.00 12.00
18 Landry Fields/199 3.00 8.00
19 Larry Bird/199 60.00 150.00
20 Larry Johnson/199 12.00 30.00
21 Larry Sanders/199 3.00 8.00
22 Len Elmore/199 3.00 8.00
23 Truck Robinson/199 3.00 8.00
24 Luc Longley/199 4.00 10.00
25 Marcin Gortat/199 3.00 8.00
26 Marco Belinelli/199 EXCH 3.00 8.00
27 Marcus Camby/199 5.00 12.00
28 Mario Chalmers/25 4.00 10.00
29 Leandro Barbosa/199 4.00 10.00
30 Mark Jackson/25 4.00 10.00
31 Mark Price/199 5.00 12.00
32 Marreese Speights/199 3.00 8.00
33 Maurice Cheeks/199 4.00 10.00
35 Michael Cooper/199 5.00 12.00
38 Muggsy Bogues/199 4.00 10.00
39 Nate Thurmond/25 10.00 25.00
40 Nick Anderson/199 4.00 10.00
41 Nick Collison/199 3.00 8.00
42 Nick Van Exel/25 15.00 40.00
43 Nick Young/25 3.00 8.00
44 Norris Cole/199 3.00 8.00
45 Peja Stojakovic/25 4.00 10.00
46 Rashard Lewis/199 EXCH 5.00 12.00
47 Raymond Felton/25 3.00 8.00
48 Reggie Evans/25 3.00 8.00
49 Reggie Theus/199 4.00 10.00
50 Rex Chapman/199 4.00 10.00
51 Richard Hamilton/25 5.00 12.00
52 Rick Mahorn/199 3.00 8.00
53 Robert Horry/25 12.00 30.00
54 Robert Parish/25 12.00 30.00
55 Rod Strickland/199 10.00 25.00
56 Ronnie Brewer/199 3.00 8.00
58 Scottie Pippen/25 60.00 150.00
59 Sean Elliott/199 4.00 10.00
60 Shane Battier/25 4.00 10.00
61 Spencer Haywood/199 5.00 12.00
62 Stephen Curry/25 500.00 1,000.00
63 Steve Francis/199 4.00 10.00
64 Steve Smith/199 4.00 10.00
65 Taj Gibson/25 3.00 8.00
66 Thabo Sefolosha/25 3.00 8.00
67 Tiago Splitter/199 3.00 8.00
68 Timofey Mozgov/199 3.00 8.00
69 Tom Chambers/25 5.00 12.00
71 Tristan Thompson/25 5.00 12.00
72 Tyronn Lue/199 4.00 10.00
73 Udonis Haslem/199 4.00 10.00
74 Vernon Maxwell/199 3.00 8.00
75 Victor Claver/199 3.00 8.00
76 Vin Baker/199 3.00 8.00
77 Vince Carter/25 50.00 120.00
80 Wesley Johnson/25 3.00 8.00
81 Will Bynum/199 3.00 8.00
82 Will Perdue/199 3.00 8.00
83 Zach Randolph/25 5.00 12.00
84 Zaza Pachulia/199 3.00 8.00
85 Zydrunas Ilgauskas/199 4.00 10.00
86 A.C. Green/25 5.00 12.00
87 Adrian Dantley/25 4.00 10.00
88 Alan Anderson/199 3.00 8.00
89 Alex English/25 6.00 15.00
90 Al-Farouq Aminu/199 3.00 8.00
91 Allan Houston/25 4.00 10.00
92 Alonzo Gee/199 3.00 8.00
93 Alonzo Mourning/25 20.00 50.00
94 Andray Blatche/199 3.00 8.00
95 Andre Drummond/25 20.00 50.00
97 Andre Miller/25 4.00 10.00
98 Andrea Bargnani/25 3.00 8.00
99 Andrew Bogut/25 4.00 10.00
100 Anfernee Hardaway/25 50.00 120.00
101 Anthony Davis/199 150.00 400.00
102 Anthony Mason/199 4.00 10.00
103 Anthony Morrow/199 3.00 8.00
104 Antoine Walker/199 4.00 10.00
105 Antonio Davis/199 6.00 15.00
106 Arron Afflalo/25 3.00 8.00
107 Artis Gilmore/25 6.00 15.00
108 Austin Daye/199 3.00 8.00
109 B.J. Armstrong/25 8.00 20.00
110 Bailey Howell/25 8.00 20.00
111 Ben Gordon/25 4.00 10.00
112 Beno Udrih/199 3.00 8.00
113 Bernard King/25 6.00 15.00
114 Bill Cartwright/25 4.00 10.00
115 Bill Walton/25 20.00 50.00
116 Blake Griffin/199 12.00 30.00
117 Bob Love/199 EXCH 5.00 12.00
119 Bobby Jackson/199 3.00 8.00
120 Bobby Jones/199 12.00 30.00
121 Brad Daugherty/199 4.00 10.00
122 Bradley Beal/25 50.00 120.00
123 Brandon Bass/25 3.00 8.00
124 Brandon Knight/25 4.00 10.00
125 Brandon Rush/199 3.00 8.00
126 Brent Barry/25 3.00 8.00
127 Brook Lopez/25 4.00 10.00
128 Bruce Bowen/199 4.00 10.00
129 Buck Williams/199 3.00 8.00
130 Byron Mullens/199 3.00 8.00
131 Byron Scott/25 15.00 40.00
132 C.J. Watson/199 3.00 8.00
134 Carl Landry/25 3.00 8.00
135 Carlos Boozer/25 4.00 10.00
136 Caron Butler/25 4.00 10.00
137 Cazzie Russell/199 4.00 10.00
138 Cedric Ceballos/199 4.00 10.00
139 Cedric Maxwell/199 3.00 8.00
140 Charles Oakley/199 8.00 20.00
141 Charlie Villanueva/25 3.00 8.00
142 Charlie Ward/199 5.00 12.00
143 Chase Budinger/25 3.00 8.00
145 Chris Wilcox/199 3.00 8.00
146 Clyde Drexler/25 25.00 60.00
148 Corey Brewer/199 3.00 8.00
149 Courtney Lee/199 3.00 8.00
150 Dahntay Jones/199 3.00 8.00
151 Dan Issel/199 5.00 12.00
152 Dana Barros/199 3.00 8.00
153 Danilo Gallinari/25 3.00 8.00
154 Danny Granger/25 3.00 8.00
155 Danny Green/199 4.00 10.00
156 Danny Manning/25 4.00 10.00
157 Darrell Armstrong/199 3.00 8.00
158 Darryl Dawkins/199 3.00 8.00
159 Dave Cowens/25 12.00 30.00
160 David Robinson/49 40.00 100.00
162 David West/25 4.00 10.00
163 DeMarre Carroll/199 3.00 8.00
164 Dennis Rodman/25 50.00 120.00
165 Dennis Scott/199 3.00 8.00
166 Deron Williams/25 4.00 10.00
167 Derrick Favors/25 4.00 10.00
168 Derrick Williams/25 3.00 8.00
169 Detlef Schrempf/199 5.00 12.00
170 Devin Harris/25 3.00 8.00
171 Dikembe Mutombo/25 12.00 30.00
172 Dominique Wilkins/25 15.00 40.00
173 Dwyane Wade/49 75.00 200.00
174 Yao Ming/25 150.00 400.00
175 Earl Lloyd/25 12.00 30.00
176 Earl Monroe/25 6.00 15.00
177 Ed Davis/199 3.00 8.00
178 Ekpe Udoh/199 3.00 8.00
179 Elgin Baylor/25 25.00 60.00
180 Enes Kanter/25 5.00 12.00
181 Eric Gordon/25 4.00 10.00
182 Ersan Ilyasova/199 3.00 8.00
183 Fat Lever/199 4.00 10.00
184 J.J. Hickson/199 3.00 8.00
185 J.J. Redick/25 15.00 40.00
186 Jamaal Tinsley/199 3.00 8.00
187 Jamaal Wilkes/25 8.00 20.00
188 Jameer Nelson/25 3.00 8.00
189 James Johnson/199 3.00 8.00
190 James Worthy/25 15.00 40.00
191 Jared Dudley/25 3.00 8.00
192 Jared Sullinger/25 3.00 8.00
193 Jason Kidd/25 25.00 60.00
195 Jason Smith/199 3.00 8.00
196 Jason Terry/25 12.00 30.00
197 Jason Thompson/199 3.00 8.00
198 JaVale McGee/25 4.00 10.00
199 Jayson Williams/199 3.00 8.00
200 Jeff Teague/199 3.00 8.00
201 Jeremy Evans/199 3.00 8.00
202 Jerome Williams/199 3.00 8.00
203 Jerry West/149 40.00 100.00
204 Jim Jackson/199 4.00 10.00
205 Joakim Noah/25 4.00 10.00
206 Joe Johnson/25 4.00 10.00
207 Johan Petro/199 3.00 8.00
208 John Havlicek/25 60.00 150.00
209 John Henson/25 4.00 10.00
210 John Salmons/199 4.00 10.00
211 John Stockton/25 40.00 100.00
212 Magic Johnson/199 60.00 150.00
213 Johnny Newman/199 6.00 15.00
214 Jonas Jerebko/199 3.00 8.00
215 Jonas Valanciunas/199 6.00 15.00
216 Jonathan Bender/199 3.00 8.00
217 Jordan Crawford/199 3.00 8.00
218 Josh Smith/25 3.00 8.00
219 Julius Erving/49 40.00 100.00
220 Gail Goodrich/25 12.00 30.00
221 Gary Payton/25 20.00 50.00
222 George Gervin/25 12.00 30.00
223 George Hill/25 4.00 10.00
224 Gerald Henderson/25 3.00 8.00
225 George McGinnis/25 5.00 12.00
227 Gordon Hayward/199 5.00 12.00
228 Grant Hill/49 20.00 50.00
229 Greg Monroe/25 3.00 8.00
230 Greg Ostertag/199 4.00 10.00
231 Greivis Vasquez/199 3.00 8.00
232 Hakeem Olajuwon/25 40.00 100.00
234 Harrison Barnes/25 12.00 30.00
236 Henry Bibby/199 3.00 8.00
237 Herb Williams/199 3.00 8.00
238 Iman Shumpert/199 4.00 10.00
239 Isaiah Rider/199 4.00 10.00
240 Isiah Thomas/25 30.00 80.00

2012-13 Panini Brilliance Scorers Inc.

COMPLETE SET (20) 30.00 80.00
1 Dwyane Wade 1.50 4.00
2 Brandon Jennings .50 1.25
3 Paul Pierce 1.25 3.00
4 LeBron James 10.00 25.00
5 Stephen Curry 8.00 20.00
6 Kobe Bryant 10.00 25.00
7 Kevin Durant 3.00 8.00
8 James Harden 1.50 4.00
9 Russell Westbrook 1.25 3.00
10 O.J. Mayo .50 1.25
11 Carmelo Anthony 1.25 3.00
12 Kemba Walker 2.00 5.00
13 Jamal Crawford .75 2.00
14 Eric Gordon .60 1.50
15 Monta Ellis .60 1.50
16 Chris Paul 1.50 4.00
17 Klay Thompson 12.00 30.00
18 J.R. Smith .75 2.00
19 Jrue Holiday 1.00 2.50
20 Damian Lillard 10.00 25.00

2012-13 Panini Brilliance Spellbound

ALL LETTERS EQUALLY PRICED
1 Russell Westbrook 1.25 3.00
2 Russell Westbrook 1.25 3.00
3 Russell Westbrook 1.25 3.00
4 Russell Westbrook 1.25 3.00
5 Russell Westbrook 1.25 3.00
6 Russell Westbrook 1.25 3.00
7 Russell Westbrook 1.25 3.00
8 Russell Westbrook 1.25 3.00
9 Russell Westbrook 1.25 3.00
10 Kobe Bryant 15.00 40.00
11 Kobe Bryant 15.00 40.00
12 Kobe Bryant 15.00 40.00
13 Kobe Bryant 15.00 40.00
14 Kobe Bryant 15.00 40.00
15 Kobe Bryant 15.00 40.00
16 Kevin Durant 3.00 8.00
17 Kevin Durant 3.00 8.00
18 Kevin Durant 3.00 8.00
19 Kevin Durant 3.00 8.00
20 Kevin Durant 3.00 8.00
21 Kevin Durant 3.00 8.00
22 Kevin Love .75 2.00
23 Kevin Love .75 2.00
24 Kevin Love .75 2.00
25 Kevin Love .75 2.00
26 Anthony Davis 10.00 25.00
27 Anthony Davis 10.00 25.00
28 Anthony Davis 10.00 25.00
29 Anthony Davis 10.00 25.00
30 Anthony Davis 10.00 25.00
31 Blake Griffin .75 2.00
32 Blake Griffin .75 2.00
33 Blake Griffin .75 2.00
34 Blake Griffin .75 2.00
35 Blake Griffin .75 2.00
36 Blake Griffin .75 2.00
37 Blake Griffin .75 2.00
38 LeBron James 15.00 40.00
39 LeBron James 15.00 40.00
40 LeBron James 15.00 40.00
41 LeBron James 15.00 40.00
42 LeBron James 15.00 40.00
43 Dwyane Wade 1.50 4.00
44 Dwyane Wade 1.50 4.00
45 Dwyane Wade 1.50 4.00
46 Dwyane Wade 1.50 4.00
47 Dwight Howard 1.00 2.50
48 Dwight Howard 1.00 2.50
49 Dwight Howard 1.00 2.50
50 Dwight Howard 1.00 2.50
51 Dwight Howard 1.00 2.50
52 Dwight Howard 1.00 2.50
53 Paul Pierce 1.25 3.00
54 Paul Pierce 1.25 3.00
55 Paul Pierce 1.25 3.00
56 Paul Pierce 1.25 3.00
57 Paul Pierce 1.25 3.00
58 Paul Pierce 1.25 3.00
59 Bradley Beal 4.00 10.00
60 Bradley Beal 4.00 10.00
61 Bradley Beal 4.00 10.00
62 Bradley Beal 4.00 10.00
63 Jeremy Lin 1.25 3.00
64 Jeremy Lin 1.25 3.00
65 Jeremy Lin 1.25 3.00
66 Kyrie Irving 5.00 12.00
67 Kyrie Irving 5.00 12.00
68 Kyrie Irving 5.00 12.00
69 Kyrie Irving 5.00 12.00
70 Kyrie Irving 5.00 12.00
71 Kyrie Irving 5.00 12.00
72 Carmelo Anthony 1.25 3.00
73 Carmelo Anthony 1.25 3.00
74 Carmelo Anthony 1.25 3.00
75 Carmelo Anthony 1.25 3.00
76 Carmelo Anthony 1.25 3.00
77 Carmelo Anthony 1.25 3.00
78 Carmelo Anthony 1.25 3.00
79 Kemba Walker 2.00 5.00
80 Kemba Walker 2.00 5.00
81 Kemba Walker 2.00 5.00
82 Kemba Walker 2.00 5.00
83 Kemba Walker 2.00 5.00
84 Kemba Walker 2.00 5.00
85 Serge Ibaka .60 1.50
86 Serge Ibaka .60 1.50
87 Serge Ibaka .60 1.50
88 Serge Ibaka .60 1.50
89 Serge Ibaka .60 1.50
90 Dion Waiters .60 1.50
91 Dion Waiters .60 1.50
92 Dion Waiters .60 1.50
93 Dion Waiters .60 1.50
94 Dion Waiters .60 1.50
95 Dion Waiters .60 1.50
96 Dion Waiters .60 1.50
97 Derrick Rose 1.25 3.00
98 Derrick Rose 1.25 3.00
99 Derrick Rose 1.25 3.00
100 Derrick Rose 1.25 3.00

2012-13 Panini Brilliance Springfield

COMPLETE SET (25) 20.00 50.00
1 Bill Russell 2.50 6.00
2 Kevin McHale 1.00 2.50
3 Larry Bird 2.50 6.00
4 Clyde Drexler 1.25 3.00
5 Alex English 1.00 2.50
6 Kareem Abdul-Jabbar 2.50 6.00
7 Hakeem Olajuwon 1.50 4.00
8 Magic Johnson 2.50 6.00
9 Pete Maravich 1.50 4.00
10 Patrick Ewing 1.25 3.00
11 Earl Monroe 1.00 2.50
12 Dominique Wilkins 1.00 2.50
13 Chris Mullin 1.00 2.50
14 John Stockton 1.50 4.00
15 David Thompson .75 2.00
16 Isiah Thomas 1.50 4.00
17 Wes Unseld 1.00 2.50
18 Bill Walton 1.25 3.00
19 James Worthy 1.25 3.00
20 Calvin Murphy .60 1.50
21 Julius Erving 2.00 5.00
22 Joe Dumars 1.00 2.50
23 David Robinson 1.25 3.00
24 Oscar Robertson 1.50 4.00
25 Drazen Petrovic .75 2.00

2012-13 Panini Brilliance Team Tomorrow

COMPLETE SET (20) 40.00 100.00
1 Kemba Walker 2.00 5.00
2 MarShon Brooks .50 1.25
3 Dion Waiters .60 1.50
4 Kyrie Irving 5.00 12.00
5 Kenneth Faried .60 1.50
6 Bradley Beal 4.00 10.00
7 Andre Drummond 1.25 3.00
8 Tobias Harris 1.50 4.00
9 Damian Lillard 12.00 30.00
10 Kawhi Leonard 15.00 40.00
11 Michael Kidd-Gilchrist .60 1.50
12 Tristan Thompson .75 2.00
13 Jared Sullinger .50 1.25
14 Alexey Shved .50 1.25
15 Andrew Nicholson .50 1.25
16 Meyers Leonard .60 1.50
17 Isaiah Thomas 1.00 2.50
18 Thomas Robinson .50 1.25
19 Anthony Davis 15.00 40.00
20 Nikola Vucevic 2.00 5.00

2017-18 Panini Brilliance

STATED PRINT RUN 249 SER.#'d SETS
351 T.J. Leaf .75 2.00
352 Jonathan Isaac 2.00 5.00
353 Dwayne Bacon .75 2.00
354 Lonzo Ball 3.00 8.00
355 Luke Kennard 1.50 4.00
356 Ante Zizic 1.00 2.50
357 Frank Jackson .75 2.00
358 De'Aaron Fox 6.00 15.00
359 Justin Jackson .60 1.50
360 Frank Ntilikina 1.00 2.50
361 Tyler Lydon .75 2.00
362 Josh Jackson 1.00 2.50
363 Ivan Rabb .75 2.00
364 Malik Monk 3.00 8.00
365 Sindarius Thornwell .75 2.00
366 D.J. Wilson .75 2.00
367 Jarrett Allen 2.00 5.00
368 Dennis Smith Jr. 1.00 2.50
369 Milos Teodosic 1.00 2.50
370 Jayson Tatum 10.00 25.00
371 Caleb Swanigan .75 2.00
372 Lauri Markkanen 5.00 12.00
373 Josh Hart 2.00 5.00
374 Markelle Fultz 2.00 5.00
375 Tyler Dorsey .75 2.00

2017-18 Panini Brilliance Blue Starbursts

*BLUE: .5X TO 1.2X BASIC
STATED PRINT RUN 149 SER.#'d SETS

2024 Panini Caitlin Clark Collection Donruss

*METALIZED: .6X TO 1.5X BASIC
*DOT: .75X TO 2X BASIC
*TARGET: .75X TO 2X BASIC
*VORTEX/399: 3X TO 8X BASIC
*POINTED STARS/299: 4X TO 10X BASIC
*FLOATING HEARTS/199: 5X TO 12X BASIC
*GOLD/99: 6X TO 15X BASIC
*PINK/50: 8X TO 20X BASIC
*BLUE/22: 12X TO 30X BASIC
1 Caitlin Clark 2.50 6.00
2 Caitlin Clark 2.50 6.00
3 Caitlin Clark 2.50 6.00
4 Caitlin Clark 2.50 6.00
5 Caitlin Clark 2.50 6.00
6 Caitlin Clark 2.50 6.00
7 Caitlin Clark 2.50 6.00
8 Caitlin Clark 2.50 6.00
9 Caitlin Clark 2.50 6.00
10 Caitlin Clark 2.50 6.00
11 Caitlin Clark 2.50 6.00
12 Caitlin Clark 2.50 6.00
13 Caitlin Clark 2.50 6.00
14 Caitlin Clark 2.50 6.00
15 Caitlin Clark 2.50 6.00
16 Caitlin Clark 2.50 6.00
17 Caitlin Clark 2.50 6.00
18 Caitlin Clark 2.50 6.00
19 Caitlin Clark 2.50 6.00
20 Caitlin Clark 2.50 6.00

2024 Panini Caitlin Clark Collection College Contenders

*METALIZED: .6X TO 1.5X BASIC
*DOT: .75X TO 2X BASIC
*TARGET: .75X TO 2X BASIC
*VORTEX/399: 3X TO 8X BASIC
*POINTED STARS/299: 4X TO 10X BASIC
*FLOATING HEARTS/199: 5X TO 12X BASIC
*PINK/50: 8X TO 20X BASIC
*BLUE/22: 12X TO 30X BASIC
CC1 Caitlin Clark 2.50 6.00
CC2 Caitlin Clark 2.50 6.00
CC3 Caitlin Clark 2.50 6.00
CC4 Caitlin Clark 2.50 6.00

2024 Panini Caitlin Clark Collection Contenders Campus Legends

*METALIZED: .6X TO 1.5X BASIC
*DOT: .75X TO 2X BASIC
*TARGET: .75X TO 2X BASIC
*VORTEX/399: 3X TO 8X BASIC
*POINTED STARS/299: 4X TO 10X BASIC
*FLOATING HEARTS/199: 5X TO 12X BASIC
*GOLD/99: 8X TO 20X BASIC
*PINK/50: 8X TO 20X BASIC
*BLUE/22: 12X TO 30X BASIC
CL1 Caitlin Clark 2.50 6.00
CL2 Caitlin Clark 2.50 6.00
CL3 Caitlin Clark 2.50 6.00

2024 Panini Caitlin Clark Collection Contenders School Colors

*METALIZED: .6X TO 1.5X BASIC
*DOT: .75X TO 2X BASIC
*TARGET: .75X TO 2X BASIC
*VORTEX/399: 3X TO 8X BASIC
*POINTED STARS/299: 4X TO 10X BASIC
*FLOATING HEARTS/199: 5X TO 12X BASIC
*GOLD/99: 8X TO 20X BASIC
*PINK/50: 8X TO 20X BASIC
*BLUE/22: 12X TO 30X BASIC
SC1 Caitlin Clark 2.50 6.00
SC2 Caitlin Clark 2.50 6.00
SC3 Caitlin Clark 2.50 6.00
SC4 Caitlin Clark 2.50 6.00

2024 Panini Caitlin Clark Collection Donruss Crunch Time

*METALIZED: .6X TO 1.5X BASIC
*DOT: .75X TO 2X BASIC
*TARGET: .75X TO 2X BASIC
*VORTEX/399: 3X TO 8X BASIC
*POINTED STARS/299: 4X TO 10X BASIC
*FLOATING HEARTS/199: 5X TO 12X BASIC
*GOLD/99: 8X TO 20X BASIC
*PINK/50: 8X TO 20X BASIC
*BLUE/22: 12X TO 30X BASIC
CT1 Caitlin Clark 4.00 10.00
CT2 Caitlin Clark 4.00 10.00

2024 Panini Caitlin Clark Collection Donruss Highlights

*METALIZED: .6X TO 1.5X BASIC
*DOT: .75X TO 2X BASIC
*TARGET: .75X TO 2X BASIC
*VORTEX/399: 3X TO 8X BASIC
*POINTED STARS/299: 4X TO 10X BASIC
*FLOATING HEARTS/199: 5X TO 12X BASIC
*GOLD/99: 8X TO 20X BASIC
*PINK/50: 8X TO 20X BASIC
*BLUE/22: 12X TO 30X BASIC
H1 Caitlin Clark 2.50 6.00
H2 Caitlin Clark 2.50 6.00
H3 Caitlin Clark 2.50 6.00
H4 Caitlin Clark 2.50 6.00
H5 Caitlin Clark 2.50 6.00
H6 Caitlin Clark 2.50 6.00
H7 Caitlin Clark 2.50 6.00
H8 Caitlin Clark 2.50 6.00
H9 Caitlin Clark 2.50 6.00
H10 Caitlin Clark 2.50 6.00
H11 Caitlin Clark 2.50 6.00
H12 Caitlin Clark 2.50 6.00
H13 Caitlin Clark 2.50 6.00
H14 Caitlin Clark 2.50 6.00
H15 Caitlin Clark 2.50 6.00
H16 Caitlin Clark 2.50 6.00
H17 Caitlin Clark 2.50 6.00
H18 Caitlin Clark 2.50 6.00
H19 Caitlin Clark 2.50 6.00
H20 Caitlin Clark 2.50 6.00

2024 Panini Caitlin Clark Collection Donruss Raining 3's

*METALIZED: .6X TO 1.5X BASIC
*DOT: .75X TO 2X BASIC
*TARGET: .75X TO 2X BASIC
*VORTEX/399: 3X TO 8X BASIC
*POINTED STARS/299: 4X TO 10X BASIC
*FLOATING HEARTS/199: 5X TO 12X BASIC
*GOLD/99: 8X TO 20X BASIC
*PINK/50: 8X TO 20X BASIC
*BLUE/22: 12X TO 30X BASIC
R1 Caitlin Clark 2.50 6.00
R2 Caitlin Clark 2.50 6.00

2024 Panini Caitlin Clark Collection Mosaic Razzle Dazzle

RD1 Caitlin Clark 15.00 40.00
RD2 Caitlin Clark 15.00 40.00

2024 Panini Caitlin Clark Collection On-Campus Exclusive

OCCC Caitlin Clark
Pink Uniform 150.00 400.00

2024 Panini Caitlin Clark Collection On-Campus Hy-Vee Exclusive

CCH Caitlin Clark
Black Uniform 150.00 400.00

2024 Panini Caitlin Clark Collection On-Campus Panini Exclusive

CCP Caitlin Clark
Yellow Uniform 150.00 400.00

2024 Panini Caitlin Clark Collection On-Campus Target Exclusive

CCT1 Caitlin Clark
White Uniform 150.00 400.00
CCT2 Caitlin Clark
White Uniform 150.00 400.00

2024 Panini Caitlin Clark Collection Prizm Autograph

RBCC Caitlin Clark 600.00 1,200.00

2024 Panini Caitlin Clark Collection Prizm Fearless

F1 Caitlin Clark 10.00 25.00
F2 Caitlin Clark 10.00 25.00

2024 Panini Caitlin Clark Collection Record Breaker

RBCC Caitlin Clark 4.00 10.00

2024 Panini Caitlin Clark Collection Select Artistic Selections

AS1 Caitlin Clark 10.00 25.00
AS2 Caitlin Clark 10.00 25.00

2010 Panini Century Sports Stamp Autographs

STATED PRINT RUN 5-100
NO PRICING ON QTY 25 OR LESS
12A Bill Walton/36 10.00 25.00
13A Bobby Wanzer/75 6.00 15.00
14A George Gervin/67 6.00 15.00
14B George Gervin/33 8.00 20.00
15A Kevin McHale/33 10.00 25.00
23A Al Cervi/65 6.00 15.00
23B Al Cervi/35 8.00 20.00
28A Elvin Hayes/30 10.00 25.00
29A Bailey Howell/50 10.00 25.00
30A Dan Issel/50 15.00 40.00
31A Clyde Lovellette/75 15.00 40.00
34A Arnie Risen/80 10.00 25.00
35A Dolph Schayes/75 8.00 20.00
36A David Thompson/75 10.00 25.00

2010 Panini Century Sports Stamp Materials Autographs

STATED PRINT RUN 2-50
NO PRICING ON QTY 25 OR LESS
27B Cliff Hagan/40 15.00 40.00

2015-16 Panini Clear Vision

COMP.SET w/o SPs (81) 60.00 150.00
1 Victor Oladipo .50 1.25
2 Kevin Love .60 1.50
3 Wesley Matthews .40 1.00
4 Jabari Parker .40 1.00
5 Chris Paul 1.25 3.00
6 Kyle Lowry .60 1.50
7 Kobe Bryant 5.00 12.00
8 Nerlens Noel .40 1.00
9 Dwyane Wade 1.25 3.00
10 Andrew Wiggins .75 2.00
11 Marcin Gortat .40 1.00
12 Jimmy Butler 1.25 3.00
13 Marc Gasol .60 1.50
14 Giannis Antetokounmpo 3.00 8.00
15 DeAndre Jordan .50 1.25
16 DeMar DeRozan .75 2.00
17 Jordan Clarkson .60 1.50
18 Robert Covington .50 1.25
19 Paul Millsap .50 1.25
20 Ricky Rubio .50 1.25
21 Kawhi Leonard 2.00 5.00
22 Derrick Rose 1.00 2.50
23 Mike Conley .60 1.50
24 Greg Monroe .50 1.25
25 Paul Pierce 1.00 2.50
26 Isaiah Thomas .50 1.25
27 Julius Randle .75 2.00
28 Kevin Durant 2.50 6.00
29 Al Horford .60 1.50
30 Damian Lillard 1.50 4.00
31 Tony Parker 1.00 2.50
32 Pau Gasol 1.00 2.50
33 Zach Randolph .60 1.50
34 Stephen Curry 5.00 12.00
35 Brandon Knight .40 1.00
36 Marcus Smart .75 2.00
37 Nicolas Batum .40 1.00
38 Russell Westbrook 1.00 2.50
39 Jeff Teague .40 1.00
40 C.J. McCollum .60 1.50
41 LaMarcus Aldridge .60 1.50
42 Paul George 1.00 2.50
43 James Harden 1.25 3.00
44 Klay Thompson 1.50 4.00
45 Eric Bledsoe .50 1.25
46 Carmelo Anthony 1.00 2.50
47 Kemba Walker .60 1.50
48 Serge Ibaka .50 1.25
49 Tobias Harris .50 1.25
50 Kenneth Faried .50 1.25
51 Tim Duncan 1.50 4.00
52 Monta Ellis .50 1.25
53 Dwight Howard .75 2.00
54 Draymond Green .75 2.00
55 Rajon Rondo .75 2.00
56 Arron Afflalo .40 1.00
57 Jeremy Lin 1.25 3.00
58 Gordon Hayward .60 1.50
59 Nikola Vucevic .50 1.25
60 Danilo Gallinari .50 1.25
61 Deron Williams .50 1.25
62 Andre Drummond .60 1.50
63 Anthony Davis 1.50 4.00
64 Andre Iguodala .60 1.50
65 DeMarcus Cousins .60 1.50
66 Brook Lopez .60 1.50
67 Chris Bosh .75 2.00
68 Derrick Favors .50 1.25
69 John Wall .75 2.00
70 LeBron James 5.00 12.00
71 Dirk Nowitzki 1.50 4.00
72 Reggie Jackson .50 1.25
73 Eric Gordon .50 1.25
74 Blake Griffin .60 1.50
75 Rudy Gay .60 1.50
76 Thaddeus Young .40 1.00
77 Goran Dragic .60 1.50
78 Kevin Garnett 1.50 4.00
79 Bradley Beal .75 2.00
80 Kyrie Irving 1.25 3.00
81 Jrue Holiday .75 2.00
82A Karl-Anthony Towns RC 6.00 15.00
82B K.Towns White Jsy 8.00 20.00
83 Jonathon Simmons RC 1.25 3.00
84 Kelly Oubre Jr. RC 3.00 8.00
85 Jerian Grant RC 1.00 2.50
86 Myles Turner RC 4.00 10.00
87 Tyus Jones RC 1.25 3.00
88 Mario Hezonja RC 1.25 3.00
89A Raul Neto RC 1.00 2.50
89B Raul Neto
Purple jersey 1.25 3.00
90A Stanley Johnson RC 1.25 3.00
90B Johnson Wht jrsy 1.50 4.00
91 Montrezl Harrell RC 3.00 8.00
92 Trey Lyles RC 1.25 3.00
93 Joe Young RC 1.00 2.50
94 Terry Rozier RC 4.00 10.00
95 Justin Anderson RC 1.00 2.50
96A D'Angelo Russell RC 4.00 10.00
96B D.Russell Prpl Jsy 5.00 12.00
97A T.J. McConnell RC 4.00 10.00
97B T.J. McConnell
Blue jersey 5.00 12.00
98A Willie Cauley-Stein RC 1.25 3.00
98B W.Cauley-Stein Prpl Jsy 1.50 4.00
99 Nikola Jokic RC 100.00 250.00
100 Frank Kaminsky RC 1.25 3.00
101 Marcelo Huertas RC 1.00 2.50
102 Devin Booker RC 12.00 30.00
103 Boban Marjanovic RC 3.00 8.00
104 Rashad Vaughn RC 1.00 2.50
105 Bobby Portis RC 2.50 6.00
106A Jahlil Okafor RC 1.25 3.00
106B J.Okafor White Jsy 1.50 4.00
107A Nemanja Bjelica RC 1.50 4.00
107B Nemanja Bjelica
White jersey 2.00 5.00
108A Emmanuel Mudiay RC 1.25 3.00
108B E.Mudiay Blue Jsy 1.50 4.00
109 Larry Nance Jr. RC 2.00 5.00
110A Justise Winslow RC 1.50 4.00
110B Justise Winslow
Black jersey 2.00 5.00
111 R.J. Hunter RC 1.00 2.50
112 Cameron Payne RC 1.50 4.00
113 Richaun Holmes RC 1.50 4.00
114 Sam Dekker RC 1.00 2.50
115 Rondae Hollis-Jefferson RC 1.25 3.00
116A Kristaps Porzingis RC 6.00 15.00
116B K.Porzingis White Jsy 8.00 20.00
117A Kobe Bryant RR 10.00 25.00
117B K.Bryant Yllw jersey 12.00 30.00
118A Steve Nash RR 2.00 5.00
118B Steve Nash
Purple jersey 2.50 6.00
119A Anthony Davis RR 3.00 8.00
119B A.Davis Yllw jersey 4.00 10.00
120A Dwight Howard RR 1.50 4.00
120B Dwight Howard
Blue jersey 2.00 5.00
121A Dirk Nowitzki RR 3.00 8.00
121B D.Nowitzki Blue Jsy 4.00 10.00
122A Grant Hill RR 2.00 5.00
122B G.Hill Blue Jsy 2.50 6.00
123A Shaquille O'Neal RR 4.00 10.00
123B S.O'Neal Blk Jsy 5.00 12.00
124A Carmelo Anthony RR 2.00 5.00
124B C.Anthony Whte Jsy 2.50 6.00
125A Gary Payton RR 2.00 5.00
125B Gary Payton
Ball in left hand 2.50 6.00
126A Jason Kidd RR 2.00 5.00
126B Jason Kidd
White jersey 2.50 6.00
127A Kevin Durant RR 5.00 12.00
127B K.Durant White Jsy 6.00 15.00
128A Vince Carter RR 2.50 6.00
128B V.Carter White Jsy 3.00 8.00
129A Stephen Curry RR 10.00 25.00
129B S.Curry Whte Jsy 12.00 30.00
130A Tony Parker RR 2.00 5.00
130B Tony Parker
White jersey 2.50 6.00
131A Kevin Garnett RR 3.00 8.00
131B K.Garnett Blue Jsy 4.00 10.00
132A Allen Iverson RR 3.00 8.00
132B A.Iverson Red jersey 4.00 10.00
133A Paul Pierce RR 2.00 5.00
133B Paul Pierce
Green jersey 2.50 6.00
134A Chris Webber RR 1.50 4.00
134B Chris Webber
White jersey 2.00 5.00
135A Ray Allen RR 1.50 4.00
135B Ray Allen
Purple jersey 2.00 5.00
136A Chris Paul RR 2.50 6.00
136B C.Paul Blue Jsy 3.00 8.00
137A Kyrie Irving RR 2.50 6.00
137B K.Irving White Jsy 3.00 8.00
138A Dwyane Wade RR 2.50 6.00
138B D.Wade Blk Jsy 3.00 8.00
139A Tim Duncan RR 3.00 8.00
139B T.Duncan White Jsy 4.00 10.00
140A Chris Bosh RR 1.50 4.00
140B Chris Bosh
Red jersey 2.00 5.00
141A LeBron James RR 10.00 25.00
141B L.James Red jersey 12.00 30.00

2015-16 Panini Clear Vision Blue

*BLUE 1-81: 1.2X TO 3X BASIC
*BLUE 82-116: .5X TO 1.2X BASIC
*BLUE 82-116 VAR: .4X TO 1X BASIC
*BLUE RR: .6X TO 1.5X BASIC
*BLUE RR VAR: .5X TO 1.2X BASIC
STATED PRINT RUN 149 SER.#'d SETS

2015-16 Panini Clear Vision Bronze

*BRNZ 1-81: 3X TO 8X BASIC
*BRNZ 82-116: 1.2X TO 3X BASIC
*BRNZ 82-116 VAR: 1X TO 2.5X BASIC

2015-16 Panini Clear Vision Purple

*PRPL 1-81: 3X TO 8X BASIC
*PRPL 82-116: 1.2X TO 3X BASIC
*PRPL 82-116 VAR: 1X TO 2.5X BASIC
*PRPL RR: 1.5X TO 4X BASIC
*PRPL RR VAR: 1.2X TO 3X BASIC
STATED PRINT RUN 25 SER.#'d SETS
14 Giannis Antetokounmpo 40.00 100.00
21 Kawhi Leonard 20.00 50.00
70 LeBron James 75.00 200.00
91 Montrezl Harrell 10.00 25.00
141A LeBron James RR 25.00 60.00
141B LeBron James
Red jersey 25.00 60.00

2015-16 Panini Clear Vision Red

*RED 1-81: 1.5X TO 4X BASIC
*RED 82-116: .6X TO 1.5X BASIC
*RED 82-116 VAR: .5X TO 1.2X BASIC
*RED RR: .75X TO 2X BASIC
*RED RR VAR: .6X TO 1.5X BASIC
STATED PRINT RUN 99 SER.#'d SETS

2015-16 Panini Clear Vision Clear Vision Signatures

PRINT RUNS B/WN 94-119 COPIES PER
*GOLD/25: .5X TO 1.2X BASIC
1 Kobe Bryant/119 400.00 800.00
2 Carmelo Anthony/119 15.00 40.00
3 Chris Paul/119 40.00 100.00
4 Dwyane Wade/119 30.00 80.00
5 Kevin Durant/119 50.00 120.00
7 Anthony Davis/119 30.00 80.00
8 Kyrie Irving/118 30.00 80.00
9 Blake Griffin/119 20.00 50.00
10 Dirk Nowitzki/119 60.00 150.00
11 John Wall/119 15.00 40.00
12 Jabari Parker/119 10.00 25.00
13 Andrew Wiggins/119 25.00 60.00
14 Chris Bosh/118 8.00 20.00
15 Kevin Love/119 8.00 20.00
16 Tony Parker/119 10.00 25.00
17 Vince Carter/99 12.00 30.00
18 Marcus Smart/117 8.00 20.00
19 Julius Randle/102 10.00 25.00
21 Karl-Anthony Towns/115 75.00 200.00
22 D'Angelo Russell/94 20.00 50.00
23 Jahlil Okafor/119 12.00 30.00
24 Emmanuel Mudiay/116 5.00 12.00
25 Kristaps Porzingis/119 50.00 120.00
26 Mario Hezonja/119 5.00 12.00
27 Justise Winslow/119 12.00 30.00
28 Willie Cauley-Stein/119 8.00 20.00

2015-16 Panini Clear Vision Standouts

*BLUE/149: .5X TO 1.2X BASIC
*RED/99: .6X TO 1.5X BASIC
*PURPLE/25: 2X TO 5X BASIC
1 LeBron James 6.00 15.00
2 Kevin Durant 3.00 8.00
3 Chris Paul 1.50 4.00
4 Kyrie Irving 1.50 4.00
5 Carmelo Anthony 1.25 3.00
6 Anthony Davis 2.00 5.00
7 Stephen Curry 6.00 15.00
8 Kobe Bryant 6.00 15.00
9 Tim Duncan 2.00 5.00
10 Kevin Garnett 2.00 5.00

2015-16 Panini Clear Vision Visionaries

*BLUE/149: .5X TO 1.2X BASIC
*RED/99: .6X TO 1.5X BASIC
*PURPLE/25: 1.2X TO 3X BASIC
1 David Robinson 3.00 8.00
2 Steve Nash 2.50 6.00
3 John Stockton 3.00 8.00
4 Grant Hill 2.50 6.00
5 Allen Iverson 4.00 10.00
6 Clyde Drexler 2.50 6.00
7 Gary Payton 2.50 6.00
8 Hakeem Olajuwon 3.00 8.00
9 Karl Malone 2.50 6.00
10 Tracy McGrady 2.50 6.00
11 Dennis Rodman 4.00 10.00
12 Julius Erving 4.00 10.00
13 Scottie Pippen 4.00 10.00
14 Dominique Wilkins 2.50 6.00
15 Isiah Thomas 1.50 4.00
16 Larry Bird 6.00 15.00
17 Kareem Abdul-Jabbar 5.00 12.00
18 Moses Malone 2.50 6.00
19 Shawn Kemp 2.50 6.00
20 Patrick Ewing 2.50 6.00
21 Jason Kidd 2.50 6.00

2015-16 Panini Clear Vision Visionary Signatures

PRINT RUNS B/WN 99-122 COPIES PER
1 Allen Iverson/122 60.00 150.00
2 Alonzo Mourning/99 20.00 50.00
3 Anfernee Hardaway/112 20.00 50.00
4 Clyde Drexler/108 20.00 50.00
5 David Robinson/101 20.00 50.00
6 Dennis Rodman/103 30.00 80.00
7 Dominique Wilkins/110 12.00 30.00
8 Gary Payton/99 30.00 80.00
9 Hakeem Olajuwon/99 20.00 50.00
10 Jason Kidd/99 25.00 60.00
11 Jerry West/112 25.00 60.00
12 Julius Erving/99 30.00 80.00
13 John Stockton/122 20.00 50.00
14 Karl Malone/99 20.00 50.00
16 Larry Bird/99 60.00 120.00
17 Magic Johnson/109 40.00 100.00
18 Oscar Robertson/112 25.00 60.00
19 Shaquille O'Neal/112 50.00 120.00
20 Tracy McGrady/99 40.00 100.00

2015-16 Panini Complete

1 Al Horford .40 1.00
2 Jared Sullinger .25 .60
3 Al Jefferson .25 .60
4 Jimmy Butler .75 2.00
5 Kevin Love .40 1.00
6 Raymond Felton .25 .60
7 Wilson Chandler .30 .75
8 Andre Iguodala .40 1.00
9 Clint Capela .30 .75
10 George Hill .30 .75
11 Josh Smith .25 .60
12 Tarik Black .25 .60
13 Chris Andersen .30 .75
14 Jabari Parker .30 .75
15 Nikola Pekovic .25 .60
16 Tyreke Evans .30 .75
17 Enes Kanter .25 .60
18 Nikola Vucevic .30 .75
19 Robert Covington .30 .75
20 Al-Farouq Aminu .25 .60
21 Caron Butler .25 .60
22 David West .30 .75
23 DeMarre Carroll .25 .60
24 Rudy Gobert .50 1.25
25 Nene .30 .75
26 Kelly Olynyk .30 .75
27 Cody Zeller .25 .60
28 Joakim Noah .30 .75
29 Kyrie Irving .75 2.00
30 Wesley Matthews .25 .60
31 Andre Drummond .40 1.00
32 Andrew Bogut .30 .75
33 Corey Brewer .25 .60
34 Monta Ellis .30 .75
35 Lance Stephenson .30 .75
36 Beno Udrih .25 .60
37 Chris Bosh .50 1.25
38 Jerryd Bayless .25 .60
39 Ricky Rubio .30 .75
40 Arron Afflalo .25 .60
41 Kevin Durant 1.50 4.00
42 Shabazz Napier .25 .60
43 Tony Wroten .25 .60
44 Allen Crabbe .25 .60
45 Darren Collison .25 .60
46 Kawhi Leonard 1.25 3.00
47 Jonas Valanciunas .30 .75
48 Trevor Booker .25 .60
49 Otto Porter .30 .75
50 Marcus Smart .50 1.25
51 Jeremy Lamb .25 .60
52 Kirk Hinrich .25 .60
53 LeBron James 3.00 8.00
54 Zaza Pachulia .25 .60
55 Brandon Jennings .25 .60
56 Draymond Green .50 1.25
57 Donatas Motiejunas .25 .60
58 Paul George .60 1.50
59 Paul Pierce .60 1.50
60 Courtney Lee .25 .60
61 Dwyane Wade .75 2.00
62 John Henson .25 .60
63 Shabazz Muhammad .25 .60
64 Carmelo Anthony .60 1.50
65 Mitch McGary .25 .60
66 Tobias Harris .30 .75
67 Alex Len .25 .60
68 C.J. McCollum .40 1.00
69 DeMarcus Cousins .40 1.00
70 Kyle Anderson .25 .60
71 Kyle Lowry .40 1.00
72 Trey Burke .25 .60
73 Kyle Korver .30 .75
74 Andrea Bargnani .25 .60
75 Jeremy Lin .75 2.00
76 Mike Dunleavy .25 .60
77 Matthew Dellavedova .30 .75
78 Danilo Gallinari .30 .75
79 Aron Baynes RC .25 .60
80 Festus Ezeli .25 .60
81 Dwight Howard .50 1.25
82 Rodney Stuckey .25 .60
83 Wesley Johnson .25 .60
84 Jeff Green .25 .60
85 Gerald Green .30 .75
86 Johnny O'Bryant .25 .60
87 Zach LaVine 1.00 2.50
88 Cleanthony Early .25 .60
89 Nick Collison .25 .60
90 Victor Oladipo .30 .75
91 Archie Goodwin .25 .60
92 Damian Lillard 1.00 2.50
93 Kosta Koufos .25 .60
94 LaMarcus Aldridge .40 1.00
95 Patrick Patterson .25 .60
96 Alan Anderson .25 .60
97 Tim Hardaway Jr. .30 .75
98 Bojan Bogdanovic .30 .75
99 Kemba Walker .40 1.00
100 Nikola Mirotic .30 .75
101 Mo Williams .30 .75
102 Gary Harris .30 .75
103 Ersan Ilyasova .25 .60
104 C.J. Watson .25 .60
105 Ish Smith .25 .60
106 Shayne Whittington RC .25 .60
107 Jordan Clarkson .40 1.00
108 Jordan Adams .25 .60
109 Goran Dragic .40 1.00
110 Khris Middleton .50 1.25
111 Alexis Ajinca .25 .60
112 Derrick Williams .25 .60
113 Russell Westbrook .60 1.50
114 Furkan Aldemir RC .25 .60
115 Brandon Knight .25 .60
116 Ed Davis .25 .60
117 Marco Belinelli .25 .60
118 Manu Ginobili .75 2.00
119 Terrence Ross .30 .75
120 Bradley Beal .50 1.25
121 Paul Millsap .30 .75
122 Brook Lopez .40 1.00
123 Michael Kidd-Gilchrist .25 .60
124 Pau Gasol .60 1.50
125 Timofey Mozgov .25 .60
126 J.J. Hickson .25 .60
127 Jodie Meeks .25 .60
128 Harrison Barnes .30 .75
129 James Harden .75 2.00
130 Austin Rivers .30 .75
131 Julius Randle .50 1.25
132 Marc Gasol .40 1.00
133 Hassan Whiteside .30 .75
134 Michael Carter-Williams .25 .60
135 Anthony Davis 1.00 2.50
136 Jose Calderon .25 .60
137 Serge Ibaka .30 .75
138 Hollis Thompson .30 .75
139 Eric Bledsoe .30 .75
140 Gerald Henderson .25 .60
141 Omri Casspi .25 .60
142 Matt Bonner .25 .60
143 Alec Burks .25 .60
144 DeJuan Blair .25 .60
145 Thabo Sefolosha .25 .60
146 Jarrett Jack .30 .75
147 Nicolas Batum .30 .75
148 Taj Gibson .30 .75
149 Tristan Thompson .30 .75
150 Jameer Nelson .25 .60
151 Kentavious Caldwell-Pope .25 .60
152 Klay Thompson 1.00 2.50
153 Patrick Beverley .25 .60
154 Blake Griffin .40 1.00
155 Kobe Bryant 3.00 8.00
156 Matt Barnes .25 .60
157 Luol Deng .30 .75
158 O.J. Mayo .25 .60
159 Eric Gordon .30 .75
160 Langston Galloway .25 .60
161 Steven Adams .30 .75
162 Isaiah Canaan .25 .60
163 Markieff Morris .25 .60
164 Mason Plumlee .25 .60
165 Quincy Acy .25 .60
166 Patty Mills .40 1.00
167 Dante Exum .30 .75
168 Drew Gooden III .30 .75
169 Avery Bradley .25 .60
170 Joe Johnson .30 .75
171 Spencer Hawes .25 .60
172 Tony Snell .25 .60
173 Chandler Parsons .25 .60
174 Jusuf Nurkic .30 .75
175 Marcus Morris .25 .60
176 Leandro Barbosa .25 .60
177 Terrence Jones .25 .60
178 Chris Paul .75 2.00
179 Lou Williams .30 .75
180 Mike Conley .40 1.00
181 Mario Chalmers .30 .75
182 Adreian Payne .25 .60
183 Jrue Holiday .50 1.25
184 Lou Amundson .25 .60
185 Aaron Gordon .40 1.00
186 JaKarr Sampson .25 .60
187 Mirza Teletovic .25 .60
188 Maurice Harkless .25 .60
189 Rajon Rondo .50 1.25
190 Tim Duncan 1.00 2.50
191 Derrick Favors .30 .75
192 Gary Neal .25 .60
193 David Lee .25 .60
194 Markel Brown .25 .60
195 Tyler Hansbrough .25 .60
196 Anderson Varejao .25 .60
197 Deron Williams .30 .75
198 Kenneth Faried .30 .75
199 Reggie Jackson .30 .75
200 Marreese Speights .25 .60
201 Trevor Ariza .25 .60
202 Cole Aldrich .25 .60
203 Nick Young .30 .75
204 Tony Allen .25 .60
205 Tyler Johnson RC .30 .75
206 Andrew Wiggins .50 1.25
207 Omer Asik .25 .60
208 Robin Lopez .25 .60
209 Andrew Nicholson .25 .60
210 Jerami Grant .40 1.00
211 P.J. Tucker .25 .60
212 Meyers Leonard .25 .60
213 Rudy Gay .40 1.00
214 Tony Parker .60 1.50
215 Gordon Hayward .40 1.00
216 Jared Dudley .25 .60
217 Evan Turner .25 .60
218 Shane Larkin .25 .60
219 Derrick Rose .60 1.50
220 Iman Shumpert .25 .60
221 Devin Harris .25 .60
222 Nick Johnson .25 .60
223 Spencer Dinwiddie .30 .75
224 Shaun Livingston .30 .75
225 Ty Lawson .25 .60
226 DeAndre Jordan .30 .75
227 Robert Sacre .25 .60
228 Vince Carter .75 2.00
229 Chris Copeland .25 .60
230 Gorgui Dieng .25 .60
231 Quincy Pondexter .25 .60
232 Anthony Morrow .25 .60
233 Elfrid Payton .30 .75
234 Nerlens Noel .25 .60
235 T.J. Warren .40 1.00
236 Noah Vonleh .25 .60
237 Boris Diaw .30 .75
238 Bruno Caboclo .25 .60
239 Joe Ingles .25 .60
240 John Wall .50 1.25
241 Isaiah Thomas .30 .75
242 Thaddeus Young .25 .60
243 Doug McDermott .30 .75
244 J.R. Smith .40 1.00
245 Dirk Nowitzki 1.00 2.50
246 Randy Foye .25 .60
247 Steve Blake .25 .60
248 Stephen Curry 3.00 8.00
249 C.J. Miles .25 .60
250 J.J. Redick .40 1.00
251 Roy Hibbert .25 .60
252 Zach Randolph .40 1.00
253 Giannis Antetokounmpo 2.00 5.00
254 Kevin Garnett 1.00 2.50
255 Ryan Anderson .25 .60
256 D.J. Augustin .25 .60
257 Evan Fournier .30 .75
258 Nik Stauskas .30 .75
259 Tyson Chandler .30 .75
260 Ben McLemore .25 .60
261 Danny Green .30 .75
262 DeMar DeRozan .50 1.25
263 Rodney Hood .30 .75
264 Marcin Gortat .25 .60
265 Jae Crowder .25 .60
266 Thomas Robinson .25 .60
267 E'Twaun Moore .25 .60
268 James Jones .25 .60
269 J.J. Barea .30 .75
270 Will Barton .25 .60
271 Jeff Teague .25 .60
272 Dennis Schroder .40 1.00
273 Chase Budinger .25 .60
274 Jamal Crawford .40 1.00
275 Ryan Kelly .25 .60
276 Amar'e Stoudemire .40 1.00
277 Greg Monroe .30 .75
278 Kevin Martin .30 .75
279 Dante Cunningham .25 .60
280 Dion Waiters .25 .60
281 Lamar Patterson RC .40 1.00
282 Justin Anderson RC .40 1.00
283 Larry Nance Jr. RC .75 2.00
284 Jahlil Okafor RC .50 1.25
285 Terran Petteway RC .40 1.00
286 Dwight Powell .25 .60
287 Jarell Martin RC .40 1.00
288 Pierre Jackson RC .40 1.00
289 Walter Tavares RC .40 1.00
290 Emmanuel Mudiay RC .50 1.25
291 Josh Richardson RC .60 1.50
292 Richaun Holmes RC .60 1.50
293 Jordan Mickey RC .40 1.00
294 Darrun Hilliard RC .40 1.00
295 Justise Winslow RC .60 1.50
296 Devin Booker RC 20.00 50.00
297 R.J. Hunter RC .40 1.00
298 Stanley Johnson RC .50 1.25
299 Rashad Vaughn RC .40 1.00
300 Cliff Alexander RC .40 1.00
301 Terry Rozier RC 1.50 4.00
302 Kevon Looney RC 1.25 3.00
303 Karl-Anthony Towns RC 2.50 6.00
304 Pat Connaughton RC .60 1.50
305 Chris McCullough RC .40 1.00
306 Sam Dekker RC .40 1.00
307 Nemanja Bjelica RC .60 1.50
308 Willie Cauley-Stein RC .50 1.25
309 Rondae Hollis-Jefferson RC .50 1.25
310 Joe Young RC .40 1.00
311 Tyus Jones RC .50 1.25
312 Jonathon Simmons RC .50 1.25
313 Ryan Boatright RC .40 1.00
314 Myles Turner RC 1.50 4.00
315 Jerian Grant RC .50 1.25
316 Delon Wright RC .50 1.25
317 Aaron Harrison RC .50 1.25
318 Rakeem Christmas RC .40 1.00
319 Kristaps Porzingis RC 2.50 6.00
320 Norman Powell RC .75 2.00
321 Frank Kaminsky RC .50 1.25
322 Branden Dawson RC .40 1.00
323 Cameron Payne RC .60 1.50
324 Trey Lyles RC .50 1.25
325 Bobby Portis RC 1.00 2.50
326 Anthony Brown RC .40 1.00
327 Mario Hezonja RC .50 1.25
328 Kelly Oubre Jr. RC 1.25 3.00
329 Brandon Ashley RC .40 1.00
330 D'Angelo Russell RC 1.50 4.00

2015-16 Panini Complete Gold

*GOLD: 2.5X TO 6X BASIC
*GOLD RC: 1.5X TO 4X BASIC RC
STATED ODDS 1:37 RETAIL
296 Devin Booker 125.00 300.00

2015-16 Panini Complete Silver

*SILVER: 1.25X TO 3X BASIC
*SILVER RC: .75X TO 2X BASIC RC

2015-16 Panini Complete Autographs

STATED ODDS 1:220 RETAIL
1 Kobe Bryant 400.00 800.00
2 Dwyane Wade 15.00 40.00
3 Carmelo Anthony 12.00 30.00
4 Chris Paul 40.00 100.00
5 Kevin Durant 40.00 100.00
6 Anthony Davis 30.00 80.00
8 Kyrie Irving 25.00 60.00
10 John Wall 15.00 40.00
12 James Harden 25.00 60.00
13 Andrew Wiggins 12.00 30.00
14 Karl-Anthony Towns 30.00 80.00
15 D'Angelo Russell 12.00 30.00
16 Jahlil Okafor 3.00 8.00
17 Emmanuel Mudiay 3.00 8.00
18 Kristaps Porzingis 60.00 150.00
19 Mario Hezonja 3.00 8.00
20 Justise Winslow 4.00 10.00
21 Willie Cauley-Stein 8.00 20.00
22 Stanley Johnson 6.00 15.00
23 Frank Kaminsky 8.00 20.00
24 Devin Booker 200.00 500.00
25 Myles Turner 10.00 25.00
26 Jerian Grant 2.50 6.00
27 Trey Lyles 3.00 8.00
28 Delon Wright 3.00 8.00
29 Rashad Vaughn 2.50 6.00
30 Cameron Payne 4.00 10.00

2015-16 Panini Complete Away

STATED ODDS 1:112 RETAIL
1 Carmelo Anthony 1.50 4.00
2 Greg Monroe .75 2.00
3 Gordon Hayward 1.00 2.50
4 Eric Bledsoe .75 2.00
5 Vince Carter 2.00 5.00
6 Al Horford 1.00 2.50
7 Jimmy Butler 2.00 5.00
8 Kemba Walker 1.00 2.50
9 Kyle Lowry 1.00 2.50
10 Dirk Nowitzki 2.50 6.00
11 Damian Lillard 2.50 6.00
12 Stephen Curry 8.00 20.00
13 Ty Lawson .60 1.50
14 Rajon Rondo 1.25 3.00
15 Kevin Love 1.00 2.50
16 John Wall 1.25 3.00
17 Pau Gasol 1.50 4.00
18 Elfrid Payton .75 2.00
19 DeMar DeRozan 1.25 3.00
20 Tim Duncan 2.50 6.00
21 LaMarcus Aldridge 1.00 2.50
22 Klay Thompson 2.50 6.00
23 Kenneth Faried .75 2.00
24 DeMarcus Cousins 1.00 2.50
25 Kyrie Irving 2.00 5.00
26 Bradley Beal 1.25 3.00
27 Giannis Antetokounmpo 5.00 12.00
28 Victor Oladipo .75 2.00
29 Marcus Smart 1.25 3.00
30 Tony Parker 1.50 4.00
31 Russell Westbrook 1.50 4.00
32 Blake Griffin 1.00 2.50
33 Andrew Wiggins 1.25 3.00
34 Kobe Bryant 8.00 20.00
35 LeBron James 10.00 25.00
36 Dwyane Wade 2.00 5.00
37 Paul George 1.50 4.00
38 James Harden 2.00 5.00
39 Manu Ginobili 2.00 5.00
40 Anthony Davis 2.50 6.00
41 Kevin Durant 4.00 10.00
42 Chris Paul 2.00 5.00
43 Zach LaVine 2.50 6.00
44 Jeff Teague .60 1.50
45 Derrick Rose 1.50 4.00
46 Chris Bosh 1.25 3.00
47 Andre Drummond 1.00 2.50
48 Dwight Howard 1.25 3.00
49 Nerlens Noel .60 1.50
50 Marc Gasol 1.00 2.50

2015-16 Panini Complete Court Vision

STATED ODDS 1:40 RETAIL
1 Marcus Smart .75 2.00
2 Emmanuel Mudiay .50 1.25
3 Dante Exum .50 1.25
4 John Wall .75 2.00
5 Kyrie Irving 1.25 3.00
6 Mike Conley .60 1.50
7 Brandon Jennings .40 1.00
8 Chris Paul 1.25 3.00
9 Kyle Lowry .60 1.50
10 Rajon Rondo .75 2.00
11 Damian Lillard 1.50 4.00
12 Jerian Grant .40 1.00
13 Zach LaVine 1.50 4.00
14 Kemba Walker .60 1.50
15 Derrick Rose 1.00 2.50
16 Tony Parker 1.00 2.50
17 Stephen Curry 5.00 12.00
18 Eric Bledsoe .50 1.25
19 Goran Dragic .60 1.50
20 D'Angelo Russell 1.50 4.00
21 Russell Westbrook 1.00 2.50
22 Jeff Teague .40 1.00
23 Ty Lawson .40 1.00
24 Elfrid Payton .50 1.25
25 Michael Carter-Williams .40 1.00

2015-16 Panini Complete Craftsmen

STATED ODDS 1:562 RETAIL
1 Tony Allen 2.00 5.00
2 Stephen Curry 25.00 60.00
3 LeBron James 25.00 60.00
4 Chris Paul 6.00 15.00
5 Zach LaVine 8.00 20.00
6 DeAndre Jordan 2.50 6.00
7 Kyrie Irving 6.00 15.00
8 DeMarcus Cousins 3.00 8.00
9 Anthony Davis 8.00 20.00
10 Marc Gasol 3.00 8.00

2015-16 Panini Complete Home

STATED ODDS 1:21 RETAIL
1 Carmelo Anthony 1.50 4.00
2 Greg Monroe .75 2.00
3 Gordon Hayward 1.00 2.50
4 Eric Bledsoe .75 2.00
5 Kevin Garnett 2.50 6.00
6 Al Horford 1.00 2.50
7 Jimmy Butler 2.00 5.00
8 Kemba Walker 1.00 2.50
9 Kyle Lowry 1.00 2.50
10 Dirk Nowitzki 2.50 6.00
11 Damian Lillard 2.50 6.00
12 Stephen Curry 8.00 20.00
13 Ty Lawson .60 1.50
14 Rajon Rondo 1.25 3.00
15 Kevin Love 1.00 2.50
16 John Wall 1.25 3.00
17 Pau Gasol 1.50 4.00
18 Elfrid Payton .75 2.00
19 DeMar DeRozan 1.25 3.00
20 Tim Duncan 2.50 6.00
21 LaMarcus Aldridge 1.00 2.50
22 Klay Thompson 2.50 6.00
23 Kenneth Faried .75 2.00
24 DeMarcus Cousins 1.00 2.50
25 Kyrie Irving 2.00 5.00
26 Bradley Beal 1.25 3.00
27 Giannis Antetokounmpo 5.00 12.00
28 Victor Oladipo .75 2.00
29 Marcus Smart 1.25 3.00
30 Tony Parker 1.50 4.00
31 Russell Westbrook 1.50 4.00
32 Blake Griffin 1.00 2.50
33 Andrew Wiggins 1.25 3.00
34 Kobe Bryant 8.00 20.00
35 LeBron James 10.00 25.00
36 Dwyane Wade 2.00 5.00
37 Paul George 1.50 4.00
38 James Harden 2.00 5.00
39 Deron Williams .75 2.00
40 Anthony Davis 2.50 6.00
41 Kevin Durant 4.00 10.00
42 Chris Paul 2.00 5.00
43 Zach LaVine 2.50 6.00
44 Jeff Teague .60 1.50
45 Derrick Rose 1.50 4.00
46 Chris Bosh 1.25 3.00
47 Andre Drummond 1.00 2.50
48 Dwight Howard 1.25 3.00
49 Nerlens Noel .60 1.50
50 Marc Gasol 1.00 2.50

2015-16 Panini Complete NBA Cares

STATED ODDS 1:40 RETAIL
1 Bob Lanier .75 2.00
2 Dikembe Mutombo 1.00 2.50
3 Felipe Lopez .40 1.00
5 Tim Duncan 1.50 4.00
6 Kevin Durant 2.50 6.00
7 Russell Westbrook 1.00 2.50
8 Chris Paul 1.25 3.00
9 Marc Gasol .60 1.50
10 Draymond Green .75 2.00
11 Stephen Curry 5.00 12.00
12 Ryan Anderson .40 1.00
13 LeBron James 5.00 12.00
14 Dwyane Wade 1.25 3.00
15 Pau Gasol 1.00 2.50
16 Dwight Howard .75 2.00
17 Anthony Davis 1.50 4.00
18 Zach Randolph .60 1.50
19 Damian Lillard 1.50 4.00
20 Kenneth Faried .50 1.25
21 Kyle Korver .50 1.25
22 James Harden 1.25 3.00
23 Michael Carter-Williams .40 1.00
24 Jeremy Lin 1.25 3.00
25 Klay Thompson 1.50 4.00

2015-16 Panini Complete Prime Numbers

STATED ODDS 1:563 RETAIL
1 Andre Drummond 3.00 8.00
2 Russell Westbrook 5.00 12.00
3 Kawhi Leonard 10.00 25.00
4 James Harden 6.00 15.00
5 Stephen Curry 25.00 60.00
6 Chris Paul 6.00 15.00
7 Anthony Davis 8.00 20.00
8 John Wall 4.00 10.00
9 Rudy Gobert 4.00 10.00
10 DeAndre Jordan 2.50 6.00

2016-17 Panini Complete

1 Joel Embiid 1.00 2.50
2 Jerryd Bayless .25 .60
3 Robert Covington .30 .75
4 Ben Simmons RC 1.00 2.50
5 Dario Saric RC .50 1.25
6 Jahlil Okafor .25 .60
7 Jerami Grant .40 1.00
8 Nerlens Noel .25 .60
9 Richaun Holmes .30 .75
10 Timothe Luwawu-Cabarrot RC .50 1.25
11 Gerald Henderson .25 .60
12 T.J. McConnell .30 .75
13 Anthony Barber .25 .60
14 Giannis Antetokounmpo 2.00 5.00
15 Malcolm Brogdon RC 1.00 2.50
16 Michael Carter-Williams .25 .60
17 Matthew Dellavedova .30 .75
18 Tyler Ennis .25 .60
19 John Henson .25 .60
20 Thon Maker RC .40 1.00
21 Khris Middleton .40 1.00
22 Greg Monroe .25 .60
23 Jabari Parker .25 .60
24 Miles Plumlee .25 .60
25 Rashad Vaughn .25 .60
26 Mirza Teletovic .25 .60
27 Jimmy Butler .75 2.00
28 Isaiah Canaan .25 .60
29 Cristiano Felicio .25 .60
30 Taj Gibson .25 .60
31 Jerian Grant .25 .60
32 Robin Lopez .25 .60
33 Doug McDermott .30 .75
34 Nikola Mirotic .25 .60
35 Bobby Portis .40 1.00
36 Rajon Rondo .50 1.25
37 Denzel Valentine RC .30 .75
38 Dwyane Wade .75 2.00
39 Tony Snell .25 .60
40 Spencer Dinwiddie .30 .75
41 Chris Andersen .30 .75
42 Mike Dunleavy .25 .60
43 Kay Felder RC .30 .75
44 Channing Frye .30 .75
45 Kyrie Irving .75 2.00
46 LeBron James 3.00 8.00
47 Richard Jefferson .30 .75
48 Kevin Love .40 1.00
49 Iman Shumpert .25 .60
50 Tristan Thompson .30 .75
51 J.R. Smith .40 1.00
52 James Jones .25 .60
53 Jordan McRae .25 .60
54 Ben Bentil RC .30 .75
55 Avery Bradley .25 .60
56 Jaylen Brown RC 4.00 10.00
57 Jae Crowder .25 .60
58 Gerald Green .30 .75
59 Al Horford .40 1.00
60 Demetrius Jackson RC .30 .75
61 R.J. Hunter .25 .60
62 Jordan Mickey .25 .60
63 Kelly Olynyk RC .30 .75
64 Terry Rozier .40 1.00
65 Marcus Smart .50 1.25
66 Isaiah Thomas .30 .75
67 Brandon Bass .25 .60
68 Jamal Crawford .40 1.00
69 Raymond Felton .25 .60
70 Blake Griffin .40 1.00
71 Brice Johnson RC .30 .75
72 Wesley Johnson .25 .60
73 DeAndre Jordan .30 .75
74 Chris Paul .60 1.50
75 J.J. Redick .40 1.00
76 Paul Pierce .60 1.50
77 Austin Rivers .30 .75
78 Marreese Speights .25 .60
79 Diamond Stone RC .30 .75
80 Jordan Adams .25 .60
81 Tony Allen .25 .60
82 Wade Baldwin IV RC .30 .75
83 Vince Carter .75 2.00
84 Mike Conley .30 .75
85 Deyonta Davis RC .30 .75
86 James Ennis .25 .60
87 Marc Gasol .40 1.00
88 Jarell Martin .25 .60
89 Chandler Parsons .25 .60
90 Zach Randolph .40 1.00
91 Tony Wroten .25 .60
92 Brandan Wright .25 .60
93 Kent Bazemore .25 .60
94 DeAndre' Bembry RC .50 1.25
95 Tim Hardaway Jr. .30 .75
96 Dwight Howard .50 1.25
97 Kris Humphries .25 .60
98 Jarrett Jack .30 .75
99 Kyle Korver .30 .75
100 Paul Millsap .30 .75
101 Taurean Prince RC .40 1.00
102 Dennis Schroder .40 1.00
103 Thabo Sefolosha .25 .60
104 Walter Tavares .25 .60
105 Mike Scott .25 .60
106 Luke Babbitt .25 .60
107 Chris Bosh .50 1.25
108 Goran Dragic .40 1.00
109 Wayne Ellington .25 .60
110 Udonis Haslem .30 .75
111 James Johnson .25 .60
112 Tyler Johnson .25 .60
113 Josh Richardson .30 .75
114 Dion Waiters .25 .60
115 Hassan Whiteside .30 .75
116 Derrick Williams .25 .60
117 Justise Winslow .30 .75
118 Josh McRoberts .25 .60
119 Nicolas Batum .30 .75
120 Marco Belinelli .25 .60
121 Aaron Harrison .25 .60
122 Spencer Hawes .25 .60
123 Roy Hibbert .30 .75
124 Frank Kaminsky .25 .60
125 Michael Kidd-Gilchrist .25 .60
126 Jeremy Lamb .25 .60
127 Kemba Walker .30 .75
128 Marvin Williams .25 .60
129 Cody Zeller .25 .60
130 Brian Roberts .25 .60
131 Ramon Sessions .25 .60
132 Joel Bolomboy RC .30 .75
133 Alec Burks .30 .75
134 Boris Diaw .30 .75
135 Dante Exum .30 .75
136 Derrick Favors .25 .60
137 Rudy Gobert .50 1.25
138 Gordon Hayward .40 1.00
139 George Hill .30 .75
140 Rodney Hood .30 .75
141 Trey Lyles .30 .75
142 Joe Johnson .40 1.00
143 Marcus Paige RC .30 .75
144 Jeff Withey .25 .60
145 Raul Neto .25 .60
146 Arron Afflalo .25 .60
147 Matt Barnes .25 .60
148 Omri Casspi .25 .60
149 Willie Cauley-Stein .30 .75
150 Darren Collison .25 .60
151 DeMarcus Cousins .30 .75
152 Rudy Gay .40 1.00
153 Skal Labissiere RC .30 .75
154 Ben McLemore .25 .60
155 Georgios Papagiannis RC .30 .75
156 Malachi Richardson RC .30 .75
157 Isaiah Cousins RC .30 .75
158 Carmelo Anthony .60 1.50
159 Ron Baker RC .30 .75
160 Brandon Jennings .25 .60
161 Marshall Plumlee RC .30 .75
162 Courtney Lee .25 .60
163 Joakim Noah .25 .60
164 Kyle O'Quinn .25 .60
165 Kristaps Porzingis .60 1.50
166 Derrick Rose .60 1.50
167 Lance Thomas .25 .60
168 Sasha Vujacic .25 .60
169 Justin Holiday RC .40 1.00
170 Anthony Brown .25 .60
171 Jose Calderon .25 .60
172 Jordan Clarkson .40 1.00
173 Luol Deng .30 .75
174 Marcelo Huertas .25 .60
175 Brandon Ingram RC 1.25 3.00
176 Timofey Mozgov .25 .60
177 Larry Nance Jr. .25 .60
178 Julius Randle .50 1.25
179 D'Angelo Russell .50 1.25
180 Lou Williams .40 1.00
181 Ivica Zubac RC .75 2.00
182 D.J. Augustin .25 .60
183 Bismack Biyombo .25 .60
184 Evan Fournier .25 .60
185 Aaron Gordon .40 1.00
186 Jeff Green .25 .60
187 Mario Hezonja .25 .60
188 Serge Ibaka .30 .75
189 C.J. Wilcox .25 .60
190 Jodie Meeks .25 .60
191 Elfrid Payton .30 .75
192 Nikola Vucevic .40 1.00
193 C.J. Watson .25 .60
194 Stephen Zimmerman RC .30 .75
195 Dirk Nowitzki 1.00 2.50
196 Harrison Barnes .30 .75
197 Andrew Bogut .40 1.00
198 Deron Williams .30 .75
199 Wesley Matthews .30 .75
200 J.J. Barea .25 .60
201 Justin Anderson .25 .60
202 Seth Curry .30 .75
203 Salah Mejri .30 .75
204 Dwight Powell .25 .60
205 A.J. Hammons RC .30 .75
206 Devin Harris .25 .60
207 Quincy Acy .25 .60
208 Anthony Bennett .25 .60
209 Bojan Bogdanovic .30 .75
210 Trevor Booker .25 .60
211 Randy Foye .30 .75
212 Rondae Hollis-Jefferson .25 .60
213 Sean Kilpatrick RC .30 .75
214 Caris LeVert RC .75 2.00
215 Jeremy Lin .75 2.00
216 Brook Lopez .30 .75
217 Chris McCullough .25 .60
218 Isaiah Whitehead RC .30 .75
219 Luis Scola .30 .75
220 Greivis Vasquez .25 .60
221 Darrell Arthur .25 .60
222 Will Barton .25 .60
223 Malik Beasley RC .60 1.50
224 Wilson Chandler .30 .75
225 Kenneth Faried .30 .75
226 Danilo Gallinari .30 .75
227 Gary Harris .30 .75
228 Juan Hernangomez RC .60 1.50
229 Nikola Jokic 2.00 5.00
230 Emmanuel Mudiay .25 .60
231 Jamal Murray RC 2.50 6.00
232 JaKarr Sampson .25 .60
233 Jusuf Nurkic .50 1.25
234 Jameer Nelson .25 .60
235 Lavoy Allen .25 .60
236 Aaron Brooks .30 .75
237 Monta Ellis .30 .75
238 Paul George .60 1.50
239 Al Jefferson .25 .60
240 C.J. Miles .25 .60
241 Georges Niang RC .50 1.25
242 Glenn Robinson III .25 .60
243 Rodney Stuckey .30 .75
244 Jeff Teague .25 .60
245 Myles Turner .40 1.00
246 Joe Young .25 .60
247 Thaddeus Young .25 .60
248 Ty Lawson .25 .60
249 Alexis Ajinca .25 .60
250 Omer Asik .25 .60
251 Dante Cunningham .25 .60
252 Anthony Davis 1.25 3.00
253 Cheick Diallo RC .30 .75
254 Tyreke Evans .30 .75
255 Langston Galloway .25 .60
256 Alonzo Gee .25 .60
257 Lance Stephenson .30 .75
258 Buddy Hield RC 1.00 2.50
259 Solomon Hill .25 .60
260 Jrue Holiday .50 1.25
261 Terrence Jones .25 .60
262 E'Twaun Moore .25 .60
263 Ray McCallum .25 .60
264 Aron Baynes .25 .60
265 Lorenzo Brown .25 .60
266 Reggie Bullock .25 .60
267 Kentavious Caldwell-Pope .30 .75
268 Andre Drummond .40 1.00
269 Henry Ellenson RC .30 .75
270 Michael Gbinije RC .30 .75
271 Tobias Harris .40 1.00
272 Reggie Jackson .30 .75
273 Stanley Johnson .25 .60
274 Boban Marjanovic .30 .75
275 Marcus Morris .25 .60
276 Ish Smith .25 .60
277 Bruno Caboclo .25 .60
278 DeMarre Carroll .25 .60
279 DeMar DeRozan .50 1.25
280 Cory Joseph .25 .60
281 Kyle Lowry .40 1.00
282 Patrick Patterson .25 .60
283 Jakob Poeltl RC .60 1.50
284 Norman Powell .40 1.00
285 Terrence Ross .30 .75
286 Pascal Siakam RC 2.00 5.00
287 Jared Sullinger .25 .60
288 Jonas Valanciunas .30 .75
289 Delon Wright .30 .75
290 Ryan Anderson .30 .75
291 Trevor Ariza .25 .60
292 Michael Beasley .25 .60
293 Patrick Beverley .25 .60
294 Corey Brewer .25 .60
295 Clint Capela .30 .75
296 Sam Dekker .25 .60
297 Eric Gordon .30 .75
298 James Harden .75 2.00
299 Chinanu Onuaku .25 .60
300 Nene .30 .75
301 Montrezl Harrell .40 1.00
302 Pablo Prigioni .25 .60
303 LaMarcus Aldridge .40 1.00
304 Kyle Anderson .25 .60
305 Pau Gasol .60 1.50
306 Manu Ginobili .75 2.00
307 Danny Green .30 .75
308 Livio Jean-Charles .25 .60
309 David Lee .25 .60
310 Kawhi Leonard 1.00 2.50
311 Kevin Martin .30 .75
312 Patty Mills .40 1.00
313 Dejounte Murray RC 1.50 4.00
314 Tony Parker .60 1.50
315 Jonathon Simmons .25 .60
316 Dewayne Dedmon RC .30 .75
317 Leandro Barbosa .25 .60
318 Dragan Bender RC .30 .75
319 Eric Bledsoe .30 .75
320 Devin Booker 1.50 4.00
321 Tyson Chandler .30 .75
322 Marquese Chriss RC .40 1.00
323 Jared Dudley .25 .60
324 Archie Goodwin .25 .60
325 Brandon Knight .30 .75
326 Alex Len .25 .60
327 P.J. Tucker .25 .60
328 Tyler Ulis RC .40 1.00
329 T.J. Warren .30 .75
330 Steven Adams .30 .75
331 Nick Collison .25 .60
332 Daniel Hamilton RC .30 .75
333 Josh Huestis .25 .60
334 Ersan Ilyasova .25 .60
335 Enes Kanter .25 .60
336 Anthony Morrow .25 .60
337 Mitch McGary .25 .60
338 Victor Oladipo .30 .75
339 Cameron Payne .40 1.00
340 Andre Roberson .25 .60
341 Domantas Sabonis RC 2.00 5.00
342 Russell Westbrook .60 1.50
343 Kyle Singler .25 .60
344 Cole Aldrich .25 .60
345 Nemanja Bjelica .25 .60
346 Gorgui Dieng .25 .60
347 Kris Dunn RC .50 1.25
348 Damjan Rudez .25 .60
349 Jordan Hill .25 .60
350 Tyus Jones .25 .60
351 Zach LaVine .75 2.00
352 Andrew Wiggins .50 1.25
353 Karl-Anthony Towns .75 2.00
354 Ricky Rubio .30 .75
355 Brandon Rush .25 .60
356 Shabazz Muhammad .25 .60
357 Adreian Payne .25 .60
358 Nikola Pekovic .25 .60
359 Al-Farouq Aminu .25 .60
360 Pat Connaughton .25 .60
361 Allen Crabbe .25 .60
362 Ed Davis .25 .60
363 Festus Ezeli .25 .60
364 Maurice Harkless .25 .60
365 Jake Layman RC .40 1.00
366 Meyers Leonard .25 .60
367 Damian Lillard 1.00 2.50
368 C.J. McCollum .40 1.00
369 Evan Turner .25 .60
370 Noah Vonleh .25 .60
371 Mason Plumlee .25 .60
372 Shabazz Napier .25 .60
373 Ian Clark .25 .60
374 Stephen Curry 3.00 8.00
375 Kevin Durant 1.50 4.00
376 Draymond Green .50 1.25
377 Andre Iguodala .40 1.00
378 Damian Jones RC .30 .75
379 Shaun Livingston .25 .60
380 Kevon Looney .40 1.00
381 Patrick McCaw RC .30 .75
382 James Michael McAdoo .25 .60
383 Zaza Pachulia .25 .60
384 Klay Thompson 1.00 2.50
385 Anderson Varejao .25 .60
386 David West .30 .75
387 Bradley Beal .50 1.25
388 Trey Burke .25 .60
389 Marcin Gortat .25 .60
390 Danuel House .40 1.00
391 Ian Mahinmi .25 .60
392 Sheldon McClellan RC .30 .75
393 Markieff Morris .25 .60
394 Andrew Nicholson .25 .60
395 Kelly Oubre Jr. .50 1.25
396 Otto Porter .30 .75
397 Jason Smith .25 .60
398 John Wall .50 1.25
399 Marcus Thornton .25 .60
400 Tomas Satoransky RC .50 1.25

2016-17 Panini Complete Gold

*GOLD: 2.5X TO 6X BASIC
*GOLD RC: 2X TO 5X BASIC RC

2016-17 Panini Complete No Back

*NO BACK: 4X TO 10X BASIC
*NO BACK RC: 2X TO 5X BASIC RC

2016-17 Panini Complete Silver

*SILVER: 1X TO 2.5X BASIC
*SILVER RC: .75X TO 2X BASIC RC

2016-17 Panini Complete Autographs

1 Brandon Ingram 12.00 30.00
2 Jaylen Brown 75.00 200.00
3 Kris Dunn 5.00 12.00
4 Buddy Hield 10.00 25.00
5 Jamal Murray 50.00 120.00
6 Thon Maker 4.00 10.00
7 Marquese Chriss 4.00 10.00
8 Taurean Prince 4.00 10.00
9 Denzel Valentine 3.00 8.00
10 Malachi Richardson 3.00 8.00
11 Dejounte Murray 75.00 200.00
12 Jakob Poeltl 6.00 15.00
13 Dragan Bender 3.00 8.00
14 Caris LeVert 8.00 20.00
15 Henry Ellenson 3.00 8.00
16 Dwyane Wade 40.00 100.00
17 Kevin Durant 100.00 250.00
18 Chris Paul 40.00 100.00
19 Kyrie Irving 30.00 80.00
20 Anthony Davis 40.00 100.00
21 DeMar DeRozan 6.00 15.00
22 Kevin Love 5.00 12.00
23 Isaiah Thomas 4.00 10.00
24 Blake Griffin 5.00 12.00
25 Dennis Schroder 5.00 12.00
26 Karl-Anthony Towns 10.00 25.00
27 Andrew Wiggins 10.00 25.00
28 Kristaps Porzingis 15.00 40.00
29 Devin Booker 75.00 200.00
30 Dirk Nowitzki 100.00 250.00

2016-17 Panini Complete Complete Players

1 Anthony Davis 2.00 5.00
2 LeBron James 5.00 12.00
3 Stephen Curry 5.00 12.00
4 James Harden 1.25 3.00
5 Kevin Durant 2.50 6.00
6 Chris Paul 1.00 2.50
7 Dwyane Wade 1.25 3.00
8 Carmelo Anthony 1.00 2.50
9 Kyrie Irving 1.25 3.00
10 Damian Lillard 1.50 4.00
11 Russell Westbrook 1.50 4.00
12 Andre Drummond .60 1.50
13 Dirk Nowitzki 1.50 4.00
14 DeMar DeRozan .75 2.00
15 Kawhi Leonard 1.50 4.00

2016-17 Panini Complete First Steps

1 Juan Hernangomez .75 2.00
2 Denzel Valentine .40 1.00
3 Georgios Papagiannis .40 1.00
4 Taurean Prince .50 1.25
5 Domantas Sabonis 2.50 6.00
6 Thon Maker .50 1.25
7 Jakob Poeltl .75 2.00
8 Marquese Chriss .50 1.25
9 Jamal Murray 3.00 8.00
10 Buddy Hield 1.25 3.00
11 Kris Dunn .60 1.50
12 Dragan Bender .40 1.00
13 Jaylen Brown 3.00 8.00
14 Brandon Ingram 1.50 4.00
15 Ben Simmons 1.25 3.00

2016-17 Panini Complete Home

*AWAY: .75X TO 2X BASIC
1 John Wall 1.25 3.00
2 DeAndre Jordan .75 2.00
3 Jimmy Butler 2.00 5.00
4 Dwight Howard 1.25 3.00
5 Klay Thompson 2.50 6.00
6 LaMarcus Aldridge 1.00 2.50
7 Dirk Nowitzki 2.50 6.00
8 Chris Bosh 1.25 3.00
9 Andrew Wiggins 1.25 3.00
10 Stephen Curry 8.00 20.00
11 Mike Conley .75 2.00
12 DeMarcus Cousins .75 2.00
13 LeBron James 8.00 20.00
14 Russell Westbrook 1.50 4.00
15 Chris Paul 1.50 4.00
16 Kyle Lowry 1.00 2.50
17 Karl-Anthony Towns 2.00 5.00
18 Kristaps Porzingis 1.50 4.00
19 C.J. McCollum 1.00 2.50
20 Kevin Love 1.00 2.50

2012-13 Panini Contenders

COMP.SET w/o RCs (200) 15.00 40.00
1 Al Horford .40 1.00
2 Al Jefferson .25 .60
3 Al-Farouq Aminu .25 .60
4 Alonzo Gee .25 .60
5 Amare Stoudemire .40 1.00
6 Anderson Varejao .25 .60
7 Andre Iguodala .40 1.00
8 Andre Miller .30 .75
9 Andrea Bargnani .30 .75
10 Andrei Kirilenko .30 .75
11 John Salmons .30 .75
12 Joe Johnson .30 .75
13 Joakim Noah .30 .75
14 J.J. Hickson .25 .60
15 J.J. Barea .25 .60
16 Jermaine O'Neal .30 .75
17 Jeff Teague .25 .60
18 JaVale McGee .30 .75
19 Jason Thompson .25 .60
20 Jason Terry .30 .75
21 Jason Richardson .40 1.00
22 Steve Blake .25 .60
23 Stephen Jackson .30 .75
24 Stephen Curry 3.00 8.00
25 Spencer Hawes .25 .60
26 Shawn Marion .40 1.00
27 Shane Battier .30 .75
28 Serge Ibaka .30 .75
29 Samuel Dalembert .25 .60
30 Ryan Anderson .25 .60
31 Russell Westbrook .60 1.50
32 Rudy Gay .40 1.00
33 Ricky Rubio .30 .75
34 Roy Hibbert .30 .75
35 Rodney Stuckey .25 .60
36 Raymond Felton .25 .60
37 Ray Allen .60 1.50
38 Rashard Lewis .40 1.00
39 Randy Foye .25 .60
40 Ramon Sessions .25 .60
41 Rajon Rondo .50 1.25
42 Al Harrington .30 .75
43 Paul Pierce .60 1.50
44 Paul Millsap .30 .75
45 Paul George .60 1.50
46 Pau Gasol .60 1.50
47 Patrick Patterson .25 .60
48 Omri Casspi .25 .60
49 Omer Asik .25 .60
50 O.J. Mayo .30 .75
51 Nikola Pekovic .30 .75
52 Nicolas Batum .30 .75
53 Nick Young .25 .60
54 Nick Collison .25 .60
55 Nene .30 .75
56 Nate Robinson .25 .60
57 Monta Ellis .30 .75
58 Mo Williams .30 .75
59 Mike Miller .30 .75
60 Mike Dunleavy .25 .60
61 Mike Conley .30 .75
62 Michael Beasley .25 .60
63 Metta World Peace .30 .75
64 Marvin Williams .25 .60
65 Marreese Speights .25 .60
66 Mario Chalmers .30 .75
67 Marcus Thornton .25 .60
68 Marcus Camby .40 1.00
69 Marco Belinelli .25 .60
70 Marcin Gortat .25 .60
71 Marc Gasol .40 1.00
72 Manu Ginobili .75 2.00
73 Luol Deng .25 .60
74 Luke Ridnour .25 .60
75 Luke Harangody .25 .60
76 Luke Babbitt .25 .60
77 Luis Scola .30 .75
78 Louis Williams .30 .75
79 Linas Kleiza .25 .60
80 LeBron James 3.00 8.00
81 Landry Fields .25 .60
82 LaMarcus Aldridge .40 1.00
83 Lamar Odom .30 .75
84 Kyle Lowry .40 1.00
85 Kyle Korver .30 .75
86 Kris Humphries .25 .60
87 Kobe Bryant 3.00 8.00
88 Kirk Hinrich .30 .75
89 Kevin Martin .30 .75
90 Kevin Love .40 1.00
91 Kevin Garnett 1.00 2.50
92 Kevin Durant 1.50 4.00
93 Kendrick Perkins .25 .60
94 Jrue Holiday .50 1.25
95 Josh Smith .25 .60
96 Jose Calderon .25 .60
97 Jordan Crawford .25 .60
98 Leandro Barbosa .25 .60
99 John Wall .50 1.25
100 Trevor Ariza .25 .60
101 Tony Parker .60 1.50
102 Tony Allen .25 .60
103 Timofey Mozgov .25 .60
104 Tim Duncan 1.00 2.50
105 Thaddeus Young .25 .60
106 Thabo Sefolosha .25 .60
107 Jerry Stackhouse .30 .75
108 Tayshaun Prince .40 1.00
109 Taj Gibson .25 .60
110 Steve Nash .75 2.00
111 Jason Kidd .60 1.50
112 Jarrett Jack .30 .75
113 Jeremy Lin .60 1.50
114 James Johnson .25 .60
115 James Harden .75 2.00
116 Jameer Nelson .25 .60
117 J.R. Smith .40 1.00
118 J.J. Redick .40 1.00
119 Hedo Turkoglu .30 .75
120 Hakim Warrick .25 .60
121 Greivis Vasquez .25 .60
122 Greg Monroe .25 .60
123 Grant Hill .60 1.50
124 Gordon Hayward .40 1.00
125 Goran Dragic .40 1.00
126 Glen Davis .25 .60
127 Gerald Wallace .30 .75
128 Gerald Henderson .25 .60
129 Gerald Green .30 .75
130 George Hill .30 .75
131 Gary Neal .25 .60
132 Toney Douglas .25 .60
133 Evan Turner .25 .60
134 Ersan Ilyasova .25 .60
135 Eric Gordon .30 .75
136 Emeka Okafor .25 .60
137 Elton Brand .30 .75
138 Ed Davis .25 .60
139 Dwyane Wade .75 2.00
140 Dwight Howard .50 1.25
141 Drew Gooden .30 .75
142 Dorell Wright .25 .60
143 Dirk Nowitzki 1.00 2.50
144 Devin Harris .25 .60
145 Derrick Rose .60 1.50
146 Derrick Favors .30 .75
147 Deron Williams .30 .75
148 DeMarcus Cousins .40 1.00
149 DeMar DeRozan .50 1.25
150 DeJuan Blair .25 .60
151 DeAndre Jordan .30 .75
152 David West .30 .75
153 David Lee .25 .60
154 Darren Collison .25 .60
155 Darrell Arthur .25 .60
156 Danny Green .30 .75
157 Danny Granger .25 .60
158 Daniel Gibson .25 .60
159 Daequan Cook .25 .60
160 D.J. Augustin .25 .60
161 Courtney Lee .25 .60
162 Corey Maggette .30 .75
163 Corey Brewer .25 .60
164 Chris Paul .75 2.00
165 Chris Kaman .30 .75
166 Chris Bosh .50 1.25
167 Chauncey Billups .50 1.25
168 Chase Budinger .25 .60
169 Charlie Villanueva .25 .60
170 Channing Frye .25 .60
171 Caron Butler .30 .75
172 Carmelo Anthony .60 1.50
173 Carlos Delfino .25 .60
174 Carlos Boozer .30 .75
175 Carl Landry .25 .60
176 C.J. Watson .25 .60
177 Brook Lopez .30 .75
178 Brendan Haywood .25 .60
179 Brandon Rush .25 .60
180 Brandon Roy .30 .75
181 Brandon Jennings .25 .60
182 Brandon Bass .25 .60
183 Blake Griffin .40 1.00
184 Ben Gordon .30 .75
185 Avery Bradley .30 .75
186 Arron Afflalo .25 .60
187 Anthony Morrow .25 .60
188 Antawn Jamison .30 .75
189 Andrew Bynum .30 .75
190 Andrew Bogut .30 .75
191 Trevor Booker .25 .60
192 Ty Lawson .25 .60
193 Tyreke Evans .30 .75
194 Tyrus Thomas .25 .60
195 Tyson Chandler .30 .75
196 Vince Carter .75 2.00
197 Wesley Matthews .25 .60
198 Will Bynum .25 .60
199 Xavier Henry .25 .60
200 Zach Randolph .40 1.00
201 Anthony Davis AU RC 125.00 300.00
202 M.Kidd-Gilchrist AU RC 3.00 8.00
203 Bradley Beal AU RC 15.00 40.00
204 Dion Waiters AU RC EXCH 3.00 8.00
205 Thomas Robinson AU RC 2.50 6.00
206 Harrison Barnes AU RC 10.00 25.00
207 Terrence Ross AU RC 6.00 15.00
208 Andre Drummond AU RC 6.00 15.00
209 Austin Rivers AU RC 4.00 10.00
210 M.Leonard AU RC EXCH 3.00 8.00
211 Jeremy Lamb AU RC 4.00 10.00
212 Kendall Marshall AU RC 2.50 6.00
213 John Henson AU RC 3.00 8.00
214 Moe Harkless AU RC 3.00 8.00
215 Royce White AU RC 2.50 6.00
216 Tyler Zeller AU RC 2.50 6.00
217 Terrence Jones AU RC 2.50 6.00
218 Andrew Nicholson AU RC 2.50 6.00
219 Evan Fournier AU RC 4.00 10.00
220 Jared Sullinger AU RC 2.50 6.00
221 Fab Melo AU RC 2.50 6.00
222 John Jenkins AU RC 2.50 6.00
223 Jared Cunningham AU RC 2.50 6.00
224 Tony Wroten AU RC 2.50 6.00
225 Miles Plumlee AU RC 2.50 6.00
226 Arnett Moultrie AU RC 2.50 6.00
227 Perry Jones AU RC 2.50 6.00
228 Marquis Teague AU RC 2.50 6.00
229 Festus Ezeli AU RC 2.50 6.00
230 Jeff Taylor AU RC 2.50 6.00
231 Bernard James AU RC 2.50 6.00
232 Jae Crowder AU RC 5.00 12.00
233 Draymond Green AU RC 50.00 120.00
234 Orlando Johnson AU RC 2.50 6.00
235 Quincy Acy AU RC 2.50 6.00
236 Quincy Miller AU RC 2.50 6.00
237 Khris Middleton AU RC 12.00 30.00
238 Will Barton AU RC 5.00 12.00
239 Tyshawn Taylor AU RC 2.50 6.00
240 Doron Lamb AU RC 2.50 6.00
241 Mike Scott AU RC 3.00 8.00
242 Kim English AU RC 2.50 6.00
243 Maalik Wayns AU RC 3.00 8.00
244 Darius Miller AU RC 3.00 8.00
245 Kevin Murphy AU RC 2.50 6.00
246 Kyle O'Quinn AU RC 2.50 6.00
247 Kris Joseph AU RC 2.50 6.00
248 Lance Thomas AU RC 2.50 6.00
249 D.Johnson-Odom AU RC 2.50 6.00
250 Kyrie Irving AU RC 100.00 250.00
251 Bismack Biyombo AU RC 3.00 8.00
252 MarShon Brooks AU RC 2.50 6.00
253 Alec Burks AU RC 4.00 10.00
254 Jimmy Butler AU RC 60.00 150.00
255 Norris Cole AU RC 2.50 6.00
256 Kenneth Faried AU RC 3.00 8.00
257 Jimmer Fredette AU RC 4.00 10.00
258 Jordan Hamilton AU RC 2.50 6.00
259 Tobias Harris AU RC 8.00 20.00
260 Reggie Jackson AU RC 4.00 10.00
261 Enes Kanter AU RC 4.00 10.00
262 Brandon Knight AU RC 3.00 8.00
263 Kawhi Leonard AU RC 100.00 250.00
264 Marcus Morris AU RC 4.00 10.00
265 Markieff Morris AU RC EXCH 4.00 10.00
266 Chandler Parsons AU RC 3.00 8.00
267 Iman Shumpert AU RC 3.00 8.00
268 Chris Singleton AU RC 2.50 6.00
269 Nolan Smith AU RC 2.50 6.00
270 Isaiah Thomas AU RC 5.00 12.00
271 Klay Thompson AU RC 100.00 250.00
272 Tristan Thompson AU RC 4.00 10.00
273 Jan Vesely AU RC 2.50 6.00
274 Kemba Walker AU RC 10.00 25.00
275 Derrick Williams AU RC 2.50 6.00
276 Cory Joseph AU RC 3.00 8.00
277 Chris Copeland AU RC 2.50 6.00
278 Gustavo Ayon AU RC 2.50 6.00
279 Charles Jenkins AU RC 2.50 6.00
280 Jeremy Tyler AU RC 2.50 6.00
281 Lavoy Allen AU RC 2.50 6.00
282 Josh Selby AU RC 2.50 6.00
283 Ivan Johnson AU RC 2.50 6.00
284 J.Valanciunas AU RC 5.00 12.00
285 Greg Stiemsma AU RC 2.50 6.00
286 DeAndre Liggins AU RC 2.50 6.00
287 Malcolm Lee AU RC 2.50 6.00
288 Darius Morris AU RC 3.00 8.00
289 Jon Leuer AU RC 2.50 6.00
290 Trey Thompkins AU RC 2.50 6.00
291 D.Motiejunas AU RC 3.00 8.00
292 Tyler Honeycutt AU RC 2.50 6.00
293 Robert Sacre AU RC 2.50 6.00
294 Victor Claver AU RC 2.50 6.00
295 Julyan Stone AU RC 2.50 6.00

2012-13 Panini Contenders Silver

*SILVER: 5X TO 12X BASE HI
STATED PRINT RUN 25 SER.#'d SETS
123 Grant Hill 10.00 25.00

2012-13 Panini Contenders Contemporary Contenders Autographs

STATED PRINT RUN 10 TO 99 SER.#'d SETS
2 Kevin Love/25 15.00 40.00
3 Brook Lopez/49 5.00 12.00
4 Steve Nash/25 40.00 100.00
5 Kobe Bryant/99 500.00 1,000.00
6 Tony Parker/25 EXCH 12.00 30.00
7 Marcin Gortat/99 15.00 40.00
9 James Harden/49 40.00 100.00
10 Josh Smith/49 5.00 12.00
11 LaMarcus Aldridge/25 15.00 40.00
13 Drew Gooden/99 EXCH 4.00 10.00
14 Antawn Jamison/49 8.00 20.00
15 Jason Kidd/25 8.00 20.00
17 Stephen Curry/49 400.00 800.00
18 Tyreke Evans/25 4.00 10.00
19 Ty Lawson/99 5.00 12.00
21 Tyson Chandler/49 8.00 20.00
22 Brandon Rush/99 6.00 15.00
23 Brandon Jennings/49 EXCH 12.00 30.00
24 Mario Chalmers/99 4.00 10.00
25 Grant Hill/25 20.00 50.00
27 Chris Bosh/25 15.00 40.00
28 Andre Iguodala/49 8.00 20.00
29 Kyrie Irving/25 150.00 275.00
30 Stephen Jackson/99 EXCH 4.00 10.00
32 Andrea Bargnani/49 4.00 10.00
34 Zach Randolph/49 8.00 20.00
37 Wesley Matthews/99 4.00 10.00
38 David West/49 EXCH 8.00 20.00
39 Roy Hibbert/99 8.00 20.00
40 J.R. Smith/99 12.00 30.00
41 Gordon Hayward/99 8.00 20.00
42 Al-Farouq Aminu/99 4.00 10.00
43 D.J. Augustin/49 4.00 10.00
44 Jameer Nelson/99 4.00 10.00
45 Nick Young/99 EXCH 4.00 10.00
46 Brandon Bass/99 4.00 10.00
48 Goran Dragic/99 12.00 30.00
49 Greivis Vasquez/99 12.00 30.00
50 DeAndre Jordan/99 4.00 10.00

2012-13 Panini Contenders Historic Contenders Autographs

STATED PRINT RUN 10 TO 149 SER.#'d SETS
1 Bill Russell/25 500.00 1,000.00
2 Magic Johnson/25 40.00 100.00
3 Scottie Pippen/25 125.00 250.00
4 Anfernee Hardaway/49 15.00 40.00
6 Alvan Adams/149 4.00 10.00
7 Oscar Robertson/25 30.00 80.00
8 George McGinnis/99 6.00 15.00
9 Rick Mahorn/149 4.00 10.00
10 Elgin Baylor/25 8.00 20.00
11 Bob McAdoo/99 10.00 25.00
12 Spencer Haywood/149 4.00 10.00
13 Sleepy Floyd/149 4.00 10.00
14 Jeff Hornacek/149 4.00 10.00
15 Rolando Blackman/99 6.00 15.00
16 Bailey Howell/99 8.00 20.00
17 Otis Birdsong/149 4.00 10.00
18 Sidney Moncrief/99 4.00 10.00
19 Charles Oakley/99 4.00 10.00
20 Cedric Maxwell/99 4.00 10.00
21 Ralph Sampson/149 4.00 10.00
22 Vernon Maxwell/149 6.00 15.00
23 Nick Van Exel/49 20.00 50.00
24 Muggsy Bogues/99 4.00 10.00
25 Kevin Willis/149 4.00 10.00
27 Bob Love/149 4.00 10.00
28 Kurt Rambis/149 4.00 10.00
29 Spud Webb/149 4.00 10.00
30 Sam Perkins/99 EXCH 6.00 15.00
31 Bill Laimbeer/149 4.00 10.00
32 David Robinson/25 15.00 40.00
33 Larry Bird/25 40.00 100.00
34 Hersey Hawkins/99 EXCH 4.00 10.00
35 Frank Ramsey/99 12.00 30.00

36 Jalen Rose/99 EXCH 8.00 20.00
38 Tom Heinsohn/99 25.00 60.00
39 Kelly Tripucka/99 4.00 10.00
40 Darryl Dawkins/149 4.00 10.00
41 Dan Issel/99 4.00 10.00
42 Alonzo Mourning/25 25.00 60.00
43 Tim Hardaway/99 4.00 10.00
44 Kiki Vandeweghe/149 EXCH 4.00 10.00
45 Bernard King/99 4.00 10.00
46 World B. Free/49 4.00 10.00
47 Robert Horry/49 8.00 20.00
48 Bill Sharman/49 12.00 30.00
49 Paul Silas/99 8.00 20.00
50 Bobby Wanzer/99 4.00 10.00

2012-13 Panini Contenders HOF Contenders

1 Carmelo Anthony 8.00 20.00
2 Dwight Howard 6.00 15.00
3 Steve Nash 10.00 25.00
4 Ben Wallace 4.00 10.00
5 Ray Allen 8.00 20.00
6 Jason Kidd 8.00 20.00
7 Dwyane Wade 10.00 25.00
8 LeBron James 40.00 100.00
9 Paul Pierce 8.00 20.00
10 Dirk Nowitzki 12.00 30.00
11 Kevin Garnett 12.00 30.00
12 Kobe Bryant 40.00 100.00
13 Tim Duncan 12.00 30.00
14 Allen Iverson 8.00 20.00
15 Vince Carter 10.00 25.00
16 Kevin Durant 20.00 50.00
17 Derrick Rose 8.00 20.00
18 Chris Paul 10.00 25.00
19 Dikembe Mutombo 8.00 20.00
20 Tony Parker 8.00 20.00
21 Pau Gasol 8.00 20.00
22 Grant Hill 8.00 20.00
23 Manu Ginobili 10.00 25.00
24 Shaquille O'Neal 15.00 40.00
25 Yao Ming 10.00 25.00

2012-13 Panini Contenders Legendary Contenders

COMPLETE SET (50) 30.00 80.00
1 Patrick Ewing 1.50 4.00
2 Moses Malone 1.50 4.00
3 Wilt Chamberlain 3.00 8.00
4 Bernard King 1.25 3.00
5 Shaquille O'Neal 3.00 8.00
6 Karl Malone 1.50 4.00
7 Dikembe Mutombo 1.50 4.00
8 George Mikan 3.00 8.00
9 Bill Laimbeer 1.25 3.00
10 Clyde Drexler 1.50 4.00
11 Rik Smits .75 2.00
12 Shawn Kemp 1.50 4.00
13 Anfernee Hardaway 2.50 6.00
14 George Gervin 1.50 4.00
15 David Thompson 1.00 2.50
16 Bill Russell 3.00 8.00
17 Gary Payton 1.25 3.00
18 Jeff Malone .60 1.50
19 Julius Erving 2.50 6.00
20 Rolando Blackman .75 2.00
21 Jo Jo White .75 2.00
22 Jerry West 2.00 5.00
23 Bob Pettit 1.00 2.50
24 Rick Barry .75 2.00
25 Elvin Hayes 1.25 3.00
26 Bob Cousy 1.50 4.00
27 Kevin McHale 1.25 3.00
28 Nate Thurmond 1.00 2.50
29 Dolph Schayes 1.25 3.00
30 Walt Frazier 1.50 4.00
31 Jerry Lucas 1.00 2.50
32 Billy Cunningham 1.00 2.50
33 Dominique Wilkins 1.25 3.00
34 Nate Archibald 1.25 3.00
35 Connie Hawkins 1.00 2.50
36 James Worthy 1.50 4.00
37 Hal Greer 1.25 3.00
38 Pete Maravich 2.00 5.00
39 Alonzo Mourning 1.50 4.00
40 Bill Walton 1.50 4.00
41 Joe Dumars 1.25 3.00
42 Chris Webber 1.00 2.50
43 Tim Hardaway 1.25 3.00
44 Chris Mullin 1.25 3.00
45 Mitch Richmond 1.00 2.50
46 Yao Ming 2.00 5.00
47 Toni Kukoc 1.00 2.50
48 Cedric Maxwell .60 1.50
49 Buck Williams .60 1.50
50 Doug Collins 1.00 2.50

2012-13 Panini Contenders Materials

STATED PRINT RUN 10 TO 149 SER.#'d SETS
1 Kobe Bryant/99 25.00 60.00
2 Dwyane Wade/99 6.00 15.00
3 LeBron James/99 25.00 60.00
4 Tim Duncan/149 8.00 20.00
5 Kevin Love/49 3.00 8.00
6 Zach Randolph/149 3.00 8.00
7 Raymond Felton/79 2.00 5.00
8 Deron Williams/49 2.50 6.00
9 Stephen Curry/79 25.00 60.00
10 Blake Griffin/79 3.00 8.00
11 Tyreke Evans/79 2.50 6.00
12 Gordon Hayward/79 3.00 8.00
13 Evan Turner/79 2.00 5.00
14 George Hill/79 2.50 6.00
15 Andre Iguodala/79 3.00 8.00
16 Paul Pierce/49 5.00 12.00
17 Kevin Garnett/99 8.00 20.00
18 Brook Lopez/29 2.50 6.00
19 Derrick Rose/49 5.00 12.00
21 Jameer Nelson/149 2.00 5.00
22 Tony Parker/149 5.00 12.00
23 Kevin Martin/149 2.50 6.00
24 Amare Stoudemire/49 3.00 8.00
26 Rudy Gay/49 3.00 8.00
27 Al Jefferson/149 2.00 5.00
28 Josh Smith/149 2.00 5.00
29 Kirk Hinrich/99 2.50 6.00
30 Manu Ginobili/149 6.00 15.00
31 Luol Deng/149 2.50 6.00
32 Rajon Rondo/49 4.00 10.00
33 Marc Gasol/79 3.00 8.00
34 Metta World Peace/99 4.00 10.00
35 Pau Gasol/99 5.00 12.00
36 Chris Paul/49 6.00 15.00
37 Greg Monroe/49 2.50 6.00
38 Shane Battier/99 2.50 6.00
39 J.J. Redick/149 3.00 8.00
40 Serge Ibaka/19 6.00 15.00
41 Tayshaun Prince/149 3.00 8.00
42 Karl Malone/49 5.00 12.00
43 David Lee/149 2.00 5.00
44 Thaddeus Young/79 2.00 5.00
45 Josh Howard/149 2.50 6.00
46 John Wall/49 4.00 10.00
47 Devin Harris/79 2.00 5.00
48 Kyrie Irving/49 12.00 30.00
49 Brandon Knight/49 2.50 6.00
50 MarShon Brooks/149 2.50 6.00
51 David West/49 2.50 6.00
52 Taj Gibson/49 2.50 6.00
53 Patrick Ewing/49 15.00 40.00
54 Caron Butler/79 2.50 6.00
55 Carlos Boozer/149 2.50 6.00
56 Derrick Favors/49 2.50 6.00
57 Hedo Turkoglu/149 2.50 6.00
58 Ben Wallace/149 2.50 6.00
59 Russell Westbrook/49 5.00 12.00
60 Carlos Delfino/149 2.00 5.00
61 Eric Gordon/149 2.50 6.00
62 Hakeem Olajuwon/49 6.00 15.00
63 Ty Lawson/49 2.00 5.00
64 Spencer Hawes/149 2.00 5.00
65 Al Horford/99 3.00 8.00
66 Channing Frye/99 2.00 5.00
67 Danny Granger/99 2.00 5.00
68 Jeff Teague/99 2.00 5.00
69 Brandon Jennings/49 2.00 5.00
71 DeJuan Blair/49 2.00 5.00
72 Wesley Matthews/49 2.00 5.00
74 Daniel Gibson/99 2.00 5.00
75 John Stockton/49 6.00 15.00
76 Ed Davis/149 2.00 5.00
77 James Harden/49 6.00 15.00
79 Gary Neal/99 2.00 5.00
80 Jose Calderon/149 2.00 5.00
81 Jrue Holiday/49 4.00 10.00
82 DeMarcus Cousins/49 3.00 8.00
83 J.J. Barea/49 2.00 5.00
84 Tyson Chandler/49 2.50 6.00
85 Mike Conley/49 2.50 6.00
86 Anderson Varejao/29 2.00 5.00
87 Luke Ridnour/49 2.50 6.00
88 Rodrigue Beaubois/99 2.00 5.00
89 Andrea Bargnani/99 2.00 5.00
90 DeAndre Jordan/79 2.50 6.00
91 Rick Mahorn/49 2.00 5.00
92 Manute Bol/49 3.00 8.00
93 Kenny Anderson/99 2.50 6.00
94 Chris Mullin/49 4.00 10.00
95 Reggie Lewis/99 3.00 8.00
96 Sean Elliott/29 2.50 6.00
97 Alex English/49 4.00 10.00
98 Ron Harper/99 3.00 8.00
99 Kevin McHale/49 3.00 8.00

2012-13 Panini Contenders Playoff Contenders

COMPLETE SET (25) 15.00 40.00
1 Tim Duncan 2.00 5.00
2 Kobe Bryant 6.00 15.00
3 Kevin Durant 3.00 8.00
4 LeBron James 6.00 15.00
5 Tony Parker 1.25 3.00
6 Karl Malone 1.25 3.00
7 Scottie Pippen 2.00 5.00
8 Magic Johnson 2.50 6.00
9 Dennis Rodman 2.00 5.00
10 Paul Pierce 1.25 3.00
11 Shaquille O'Neal 2.50 6.00
12 Hakeem Olajuwon 1.50 4.00
13 John Stockton 1.50 4.00
14 Robert Horry .75 2.00
15 Jason Kidd 1.50 4.00
16 Sam Jones 1.00 2.50
17 Tom Heinsohn .75 2.00
18 Derek Fisher .60 1.50
19 Kareem Abdul-Jabbar 2.50 6.00
20 Danny Ainge .75 2.00
21 Robert Parish 1.25 3.00
22 Chauncey Billups 1.00 2.50
23 Bill Russell 2.50 6.00
24 Jerry West 1.50 4.00
25 John Havlicek 1.50 4.00

2012-13 Panini Contenders Rookie Remembrance

COMPLETE SET (35) 20.00 50.00
1 Blake Griffin .75 2.00
2 Tyreke Evans .60 1.50
3 Derrick Rose 1.25 3.00
4 Kevin Durant 3.00 8.00
5 Brandon Roy .60 1.50
6 Chris Paul 1.50 4.00
7 Emeka Okafor .60 1.50
8 LeBron James 6.00 15.00
9 Amare Stoudemire .75 2.00
10 Pau Gasol 1.25 3.00
11 Elton Brand .60 1.50
12 Vince Carter 1.50 4.00
13 Tim Duncan 2.00 5.00
14 Damon Stoudamire .75 2.00
15 Jason Kidd 1.25 3.00
16 Grant Hill 1.25 3.00
17 Chris Webber .75 2.00
18 Shaquille O'Neal 2.50 6.00
19 Larry Johnson 1.00 2.50
20 Derrick Coleman .75 2.00
21 David Robinson 1.25 3.00
22 Mitch Richmond .75 2.00
23 Mark Jackson .60 1.50
24 Patrick Ewing 1.25 3.00
25 Ralph Sampson .60 1.50
26 Larry Bird 2.50 6.00
27 Bob McAdoo .60 1.50
28 Kareem Abdul-Jabbar 2.50 6.00
29 Wes Unseld 1.00 2.50
30 Earl Monroe 1.00 2.50
31 Allen Iverson 1.25 3.00
32 Oscar Robertson 1.50 4.00
33 Wilt Chamberlain 2.50 6.00
34 Elgin Baylor 2.00 5.00
35 Bob Pettit .75 2.00

2012-13 Panini Contenders ROY Contenders

COMPLETE SET (15) 15.00 40.00
1 Andre Drummond 1.25 3.00
2 Anthony Davis 6.00 15.00
3 Austin Rivers .75 2.00
4 Bradley Beal 4.00 10.00
5 Damian Lillard 5.00 12.00
6 Dion Waiters .60 1.50
7 Harrison Barnes 1.00 2.50
8 Jeremy Lamb .75 2.00
9 John Henson .60 1.50
10 Kendall Marshall .50 1.25
11 Meyers Leonard .60 1.50
12 Michael Kidd-Gilchrist .60 1.50
13 Moe Harkless .60 1.50
14 Terrence Ross 1.25 3.00
15 Thomas Robinson .50 1.25

2012-13 Panini Contenders Statistical Contenders

1 LeBron James 5.00 12.00
2 Russell Westbrook 1.00 2.50
3 Kevin Durant 2.50 6.00
4 Kobe Bryant 5.00 12.00
5 Kevin Love .60 1.50
6 Rajon Rondo .75 2.00
7 Steve Nash 1.25 3.00
8 Chris Paul 1.25 3.00
9 Ricky Rubio .50 1.25
10 Deron Williams .50 1.25
11 Dwight Howard .75 2.00
12 Andrew Bynum .40 1.00
13 DeMarcus Cousins .60 1.50
14 Kris Humphries .40 1.00
15 Blake Griffin .60 1.50
16 Mike Conley .50 1.25
17 Paul Millsap .50 1.25
18 Derrick Rose 1.00 2.50
19 Andre Iguodala .60 1.50
20 Iman Shumpert .50 1.25
21 Serge Ibaka .50 1.25
22 Carmelo Anthony 1.00 2.50
23 DeAndre Jordan .50 1.25
24 Roy Hibbert .50 1.25
25 Marc Gasol .60 1.50

2012-13 Panini Contenders Substantial Signatures Materials

STATED PRINT RUN 10 TO 149 SER.#'d SETS
1 Pau Gasol/25 15.00 40.00
3 Kevin Love/25 10.00 25.00
4 Chris Bosh/25 10.00 25.00
5 Chris Paul/25 EXCH 75.00 200.00
6 Al Horford/99 6.00 15.00
8 Jared Dudley/49 4.00 10.00
9 John Wall/25 25.00 60.00
10 Tyler Hansbrough/99 6.00 15.00
11 Vince Carter/49 25.00 60.00
12 Blake Griffin/25 30.00 80.00
13 DeMarcus Cousins/49 12.00 30.00
15 Tayshaun Prince/49 6.00 15.00
16 Brandon Knight/99 5.00 12.00
17 DeJuan Blair/149 EXCH 4.00 10.00
18 Derrick Williams/25 4.00 10.00
19 Kemba Walker/99 30.00 80.00
20 Kevin Martin/99 6.00 15.00
21 Zach Randolph/49 10.00 25.00
22 Tristan Thompson/99 6.00 15.00
23 Derrick Favors/99 5.00 12.00
24 Taj Gibson/149 4.00 10.00
25 Gary Neal/149 EXCH 4.00 10.00
26 Tyreke Evans/99 5.00 12.00
28 Udonis Haslem/149 5.00 12.00
29 MarShon Brooks/149 4.00 10.00
30 Kyrie Irving/49 75.00 200.00
31 Ed Davis/149 4.00 10.00
32 Jose Calderon/99 EXCH 4.00 10.00
33 Ty Lawson/49 4.00 10.00
34 Josh Smith/99 4.00 10.00
35 Norris Cole/149 4.00 10.00
36 Josh Howard/99 EXCH 5.00 12.00
37 Brandon Jennings/49 4.00 10.00
38 Eric Gordon/49 6.00 15.00
39 Austin Rivers/49 6.00 15.00
40 Andrea Bargnani/49 6.00 15.00
41 Markieff Morris/149 EXCH 6.00 15.00
42 Anthony Davis/25 500.00 1,000.00
43 Kawhi Leonard/149 200.00 500.00
44 Bradley Beal/99 15.00 40.00
45 Tony Parker/25 15.00 40.00
46 Tobias Harris/149 12.00 30.00
47 Hedo Turkoglu/99 6.00 15.00
50 Bismack Biyombo/149 5.00 12.00
51 Al Jefferson/25 EXCH 4.00 10.00
52 Jimmer Fredette/149 6.00 15.00
53 Channing Frye/149 4.00 10.00
54 Caron Butler/49 5.00 12.00
55 Jameer Nelson/99 4.00 10.00
56 Wesley Matthews/149 4.00 10.00
57 J.J. Redick/99 12.00 30.00
58 Danny Granger/49 EXCH 4.00 10.00
59 Jrue Holiday/149 8.00 20.00
60 LaMarcus Aldridge/49 8.00 20.00
61 George Hill/149 5.00 12.00
62 Ivan Johnson/149 4.00 10.00
63 Luke Ridnour/99 EXCH 5.00 12.00
65 Shane Battier/25 5.00 12.00
66 Rodrigue Beaubois/149 EXCH 4.00 10.00
67 Brook Lopez/49 5.00 12.00
68 Devin Harris/49 4.00 10.00
69 Jeff Teague/149 4.00 10.00
70 Mark Jackson/49 6.00 15.00
71 Nate Thurmond/25 12.00 30.00
72 Artis Gilmore/49 6.00 15.00
73 Fat Lever/49 5.00 12.00
76 Robert Parish/99 15.00 40.00
78 Larry Johnson/99 12.00 30.00
79 Dikembe Mutombo/49 20.00 50.00
80 Toni Kukoc/49 12.00 30.00
81 Chris Mullin/49 20.00 50.00
83 Larry Bird/25 50.00 125.00
84 Danny Manning/49 6.00 15.00
85 Dominique Wilkins/25 12.00 30.00
86 Sean Elliott/149 6.00 15.00
87 Zydrunas Ilgauskas/49 5.00 12.00
88 Alex English/49 6.00 15.00
89 David Robinson/25 50.00 125.00
90 Jeff Hornacek/49 8.00 20.00
91 John Starks/49 10.00 25.00
92 Kareem Abdul-Jabbar/25 40.00 100.00
94 Isaiah Thomas/99 8.00 20.00
95 Kendall Marshall/99 4.00 10.00
96 Michael Kidd-Gilchrist/25 5.00 12.00
97 Allan Houston/49 8.00 20.00
99 Mark Price/49 15.00 40.00
100 Thomas Robinson/25 4.00 10.00

2012-13 Panini Contenders Throwback Rookies

2 LeBron James 100.00 250.00
3 Kevin Garnett 30.00 80.00
4 Dwight Howard 15.00 40.00
5 Dwyane Wade 25.00 60.00
6 Steve Nash 20.00 50.00
7 Deron Williams 10.00 25.00
8 Paul Pierce 20.00 50.00
9 Dirk Nowitzki 30.00 80.00
12 LaMarcus Aldridge 12.00 30.00
13 Kareem Abdul-Jabbar 40.00 100.00
14 Larry Bird 15.00 40.00
15 Vince Carter 25.00 60.00
16 Kevin Durant 15.00 40.00
19 Amare Stoudemire 12.00 30.00
20 Carmelo Anthony 20.00 50.00
21 Tim Duncan 30.00 80.00
22 Jason Kidd 20.00 50.00

2017-18 Panini Contenders

AU PRINT RUNS B/WN 75-125 COPIES PER
EXCHANGE DEADLINE 8/21/2019
1 Justise Winslow .20 .50
2 Victor Oladipo .25 .60
3 Giannis Antetokounmpo 1.50 4.00
4 Chandler Parsons .20 .50
5 TJ Warren .25 .60
6 Gordon Hayward .25 .60
7 Elfrid Payton .20 .50
8 Jabari Parker .20 .50
9 George Hill .25 .60
10 Myles Turner .30 .75
11 Stephen Curry 2.50 6.00
12 Paul Millsap .25 .60
13 Pau Gasol .50 1.25
14 Kristaps Porzingis .40 1.00
15 LaMarcus Aldridge .30 .75
16 Rodney Hood .20 .50
17 Jeremy Lin .50 1.25
18 Kevin Durant 1.25 3.00
19 Bojan Bogdanovic .25 .60
20 LeBron James 2.50 6.00
21 Tyson Chandler .25 .60
22 Isaiah Thomas .25 .60
23 Eric Bledsoe .25 .60
24 Anthony Davis .75 2.00
25 Ben Simmons .30 .75
26 Jimmy Butler .50 1.25
27 Kyrie Irving .60 1.50
28 Kevin Love .30 .75
29 D'Angelo Russell .25 .60
30 Zach Randolph .30 .75
31 JJ Redick .30 .75
32 Nikola Vucevic .25 .60
33 Reggie Jackson .25 .60
34 Goran Dragic .25 .60
35 Aaron Gordon .30 .75
36 Damian Lillard .75 2.00
37 Klay Thompson .75 2.00
38 Chris Paul .50 1.25
39 Blake Griffin .30 .75
40 Serge Ibaka .25 .60
41 Jeff Teague .20 .50
42 Julius Randle .30 .75
43 Marc Gasol .30 .75
44 Joel Embiid .60 1.50
45 Andre Drummond .25 .60
46 Harrison Barnes .25 .60
47 Avery Bradley .20 .50
48 Paul George .50 1.25
49 Ersan Ilyasova .20 .50
50 Marcus Morris .20 .50
51 Russell Westbrook .50 1.25
52 Rudy Gobert .40 1.00
53 Dwight Howard .40 1.00
54 John Wall .40 1.00
55 Dennis Schroder .25 .60
56 Tobias Harris .25 .60
57 Steven Adams .25 .60
58 Jordan Clarkson .30 .75
59 Malcolm Brogdon .25 .60
60 Carmelo Anthony .50 1.25
61 Jusuf Nurkic .25 .60
62 Dirk Nowitzki .75 2.00
63 Hassan Whiteside .25 .60
64 Ricky Rubio .25 .60
65 Danilo Gallinari .25 .60
66 Al Horford .30 .75
67 DeMar DeRozan .40 1.00
68 Kyle Lowry .30 .75
69 Dario Saric .25 .60
70 DeMarcus Cousins .25 .60
71 Joakim Noah .20 .50
72 Mike Conley .20 .50
73 Clint Capela .25 .60
74 Dwyane Wade .60 1.50
75 Wesley Matthews .20 .50
76 Kawhi Leonard .75 2.00
77 James Harden .60 1.50
78 Kemba Walker .25 .60
79 Kent Bazemore .20 .50
80 Brook Lopez .25 .60
81 Trevor Booker .20 .50
82 Rajon Rondo .40 1.00
83 Brandon Ingram .40 1.00
84 Vince Carter .60 1.50
85 Zach LaVine .50 1.25
86 Robin Lopez .20 .50
87 Draymond Green .40 1.00
88 Nikola Jokic 2.00 5.00
89 Karl-Anthony Towns .50 1.25
90 Bradley Beal .40 1.00
91 CJ McCollum .30 .75
92 Derrick Rose .50 1.25
93 Emmanuel Mudiay .20 .50
94 Marcin Gortat .20 .50
95 Andrew Wiggins .40 1.00
96 Devin Booker .75 2.00
97 Nicolas Batum .20 .50
98 Kris Dunn .20 .50
99 Willie Cauley-Stein .20 .50
100 DeAndre Jordan .25 .60
101A Fultz AU/125 RC 6.00 15.00
101B Fultz AU VAR/75 6.00 15.00
102A Ball AU/125 RC 50.00 120.00
102B Ball AU VAR/75 50.00 120.00
103A Tatum AU/125 RC 600.00 1,200.00
103B Tatum AU VAR/75 800.00 1,500.00
104A Jackson AU/125 RC EX 3.00 8.00
104B Jackson AU VAR/75 EX 3.00 8.00
105A Fox AU/125 RC 50.00 120.00
105B Fox AU VAR/75 50.00 120.00
106A Isaac AU/125 RC 10.00 25.00
106B Isaac AU VAR/75 10.00 25.00
107A Markkanen AU/125 RC 50.00 120.00
107B Markkanen AU VAR/75 50.00 120.00
108A Ntilikina AU/125 RC 3.00 8.00
108B Ntilikina AU VAR/75 3.00 8.00
109A Smith Jr. AU/125 RC 3.00 8.00
109B Smith Jr. AU VAR/75 3.00 8.00
110A Collins AU/125 RC 4.00 10.00
110B Collins AU VAR/75 4.00 10.00
111A Monk AU/125 RC 12.00 30.00
111B Monk AU VAR/75 12.00 30.00
112A Kennard AU/125 RC 5.00 12.00
112B Kennard AU VAR/75 5.00 12.00
113A Mitchell AU/125 RC 300.00 600.00
113B Mitchell AU VAR/75 350.00 700.00
114A Adebayo AU/125 RC 30.00 80.00
114B Adebayo AU VAR/75 30.00 80.00
115A Jackson AU/125 RC 2.50 6.00
115B Jackson AU VAR/75 2.50 6.00
116A Patton AU/125 RC 2.50 6.00
116B Patton AU VAR/75 2.50 6.00
117A Wilson AU/125 RC 2.50 6.00
117B Wilson AU VAR/75 2.50 6.00
118A Leaf AU/125 RC 2.50 6.00
118B Leaf AU VAR/75 2.50 6.00
119A Collins AU/125 RC 6.00 15.00
119B Collins AU VAR/75 6.00 15.00
120A Giles AU/125 RC 2.50 6.00
120B Giles AU VAR/75 2.50 6.00
121A Ferguson AU/125 RC 2.50 6.00
121B Ferguson AU VAR/75 2.50 6.00
122A Allen AU/125 RC 6.00 15.00
122B Allen AU VAR/75 6.00 15.00
123A Anunoby AU/125 RC 8.00 20.00
123B Anunoby AU VAR/75 8.00 20.00
124A Lydon AU/125 RC 2.50 6.00
124B Lydon AU VAR/75 2.50 6.00
125A Swanigan AU/125 RC 2.50 6.00
125B Swanigan AU VAR/75 2.50 6.00
126A Kuzma AU/125 RC 10.00 25.00
126B Kuzma AU VAR/75 10.00 25.00
127A Bradley AU/125 RC EX 2.50 6.00
127B Bradley AU VAR/75 EX 2.50 6.00
128A White AU/125 RC 15.00 40.00
128B White AU VAR/75 15.00 40.00
129A Hart AU/125 RC 20.00 50.00
129B Hart AU VAR/75 20.00 50.00
130A Jackson AU/125 RC 2.50 6.00
130B Jackson AU VAR/75 2.50 6.00
131A Reed AU/125 RC 2.50 6.00
131B Reed AU VAR/75 2.50 6.00
132A Iwundu AU/125 RC 2.50 6.00
132B Iwundu AU VAR/75 2.50 6.00
133A Mason III AU/125 RC 2.50 6.00
133B Mason III AU VAR/75 2.50 6.00
134A Rabb AU/125 RC 2.50 6.00
134B Rabb AU VAR/75 2.50 6.00
135A Ojeleye AU/125 RC 3.00 8.00
135B Ojeleye AU VAR/75 3.00 8.00
136A Bell AU/125 RC 2.50 6.00
136B Bell AU VAR/75 2.50 6.00
137A Evans AU/125 RC 2.50 6.00
137B Evans AU VAR/75 2.50 6.00
138A Bacon AU/125 RC 2.50 6.00
138B Bacon AU VAR/75 2.50 6.00
139A Dorsey AU/125 RC 2.50 6.00
139B Dorsey AU VAR/75 2.50 6.00
140A Bryant AU/125 RC 4.00 10.00
140B Bryant AU VAR/75 4.00 10.00
141A Brooks AU/125 RC EX 6.00 15.00
141B Brooks AU VAR/75 EX 6.00 15.00
142A Brown AU/125 RC 2.50 6.00
142B Brown AU VAR/75 2.50 6.00
143A Thornwell AU/125 RC EX 2.50 6.00
143B Thornwell AU VAR/75 EX 2.50 6.00
144A Teodosic AU/125 RC 3.00 8.00
144B Teodosic AU VAR/75 3.00 8.00
145A Bogdanovic AU/125 RC 10.00 25.00
145B Bogdanovic AU VAR/75 10.00 25.00

2017-18 Panini Contenders Prizms

*PRIZMS 1-100: 1X TO 2.5X BASIC
*PRIZMS 101-145: .75X TO 2X BASIC
122A Jarrett Allen AU 25.00 60.00
122B Jarrett Allen AU VAR 25.00 60.00

2017-18 Panini Contenders Cracked Ice Ticket

*CRACKED ICE 1-100: 5X TO 12X BASIC
*CRACKED ICE 101-145: 2X TO 5X BASIC
1-100 PRINT RUN 25 SER.#'d SETS
11 Stephen Curry/25 40.00 100.00
20 LeBron James/25 60.00 150.00
25 Ben Simmons/25 4.00 10.00
103A Jayson Tatum AU/25 2,500.00 5,000.00
103B J.Tatum AU VAR/20 2,500.00 5,000.00
113A D.Mitchell AU/25 2,000.00 4,000.00
113B D.Mitchell AU VAR/20 2,000.00 4,000.00
122A Jarrett Allen AU/25 60.00 150.00
122B Jarrett Allen AU VAR/20 60.00 150.00

2017-18 Panini Contenders Front Row Seat

*RETAIL: .3X TO .8X BASIC
1 Kristaps Porzingis .75 2.00
2 Mike Conley .50 1.25
3 DeMar DeRozan .75 2.00
4 James Harden 1.25 3.00
5 John Wall .75 2.00
6 Kawhi Leonard 1.50 4.00
7 Myles Turner .60 1.50
8 Russell Westbrook 1.00 2.50
9 DeMarcus Cousins .50 1.25
10 Giannis Antetokounmpo 3.00 8.00
11 Andrew Wiggins .75 2.00
12 DeAndre Jordan .50 1.25
13 Anthony Davis 1.50 4.00
14 Karl-Anthony Towns 1.00 2.50
15 Blake Griffin .60 1.50
16 Damian Lillard 1.50 4.00
17 Klay Thompson 1.50 4.00
18 Dwyane Wade 1.25 3.00
19 Carmelo Anthony 1.00 2.50
20 Kyle Lowry .60 1.50
21 Hassan Whiteside .50 1.25
22 Bradley Beal .75 2.00
23 Kemba Walker .50 1.25
24 LeBron James 5.00 12.00
25 Goran Dragic .50 1.25
26 Stephen Curry 5.00 12.00
27 Kevin Love .60 1.50
28 Kevin Durant 2.50 6.00
29 Draymond Green .75 2.00
30 Nikola Jokic 4.00 10.00

2017-18 Panini Contenders Front Row Seat Cracked Ice

*CRACKED ICE: 1.5X TO 4X BASIC
STATED PRINT RUN 25 SER.#'d SETS
24 LeBron James 20.00 50.00
26 Stephen Curry 20.00 50.00

2017-18 Panini Contenders Game Ticket

*GAME TICKET: .75X TO 2X BASIC

2017-18 Panini Contenders Hall of Fame Contenders

1 Dwight Howard .75 2.00
2 Tim Duncan 1.50 4.00
3 Steve Nash 1.00 2.50
4 Kobe Bryant 5.00 12.00
5 Carmelo Anthony 1.00 2.50
6 LeBron James 5.00 12.00
7 Stephen Curry 5.00 12.00
8 Dwyane Wade 1.25 3.00
9 Russell Westbrook 1.00 2.50
10 Dirk Nowitzki 1.50 4.00
11 Vince Carter 1.25 3.00
12 Kevin Garnett 1.50 4.00
13 Tony Parker 1.00 2.50
14 Chris Paul 1.00 2.50
15 Pau Gasol 1.00 2.50
16 Jason Kidd 1.00 2.50
17 James Harden 1.25 3.00
18 Kevin Durant 2.50 6.00
19 Grant Hill 1.00 2.50
20 Ray Allen 1.00 2.50

2017-18 Panini Contenders Hall of Fame Contenders Cracked Ice

*CRACKED ICE: 1.5X TO 4X BASIC
STATED PRINT RUN 25 SER.#'d SETS
4 Kobe Bryant 20.00 50.00
6 LeBron James 20.00 50.00
7 Stephen Curry 20.00 50.00

2017-18 Panini Contenders Historic Rookie Season Ticket

PRINT RUNS B/WN 49-99 COPIES PER
EXCHANGE DEADLINE 8/21/2019
*PRIZMS: .5X TO 1.2X BASIC
*FINALS/20-25: .6X TO 1.5X BASIC
1 Kevin Durant/49 400.00 800.00
2 Kobe Bryant/49 4,000.00 8,000.00
3 Giannis Antetokounmpo/99 400.00 800.00
4 Carmelo Anthony/49 125.00 300.00
6 Anthony Davis/99 75.00 200.00
7 Kyrie Irving/49 100.00 250.00
9 Dwyane Wade/49 125.00 300.00
10 Chris Paul/49 125.00 300.00

2017-18 Panini Contenders Legendary Contenders Autographs

PRINT RUNS B/WN 10-99 COPIES PER
NO PRICING ON QTY 10
EXCHANGE DEADLINE 8/21/2019
*BRNZE/25: .5X TO 1.2X BASE p/r 49-99
*BRNZE/25: .4X TO 1X BASE p/r 25
1 Willis Reed/49 40.00 100.00
2 Rolando Blackman/99 4.00 10.00
3 Robert Horry/49 6.00 15.00
4 Ben Wallace/49 8.00 20.00
6 Lenny Wilkens/49 6.00 15.00
7 Magic Johnson/25 25.00 60.00
8 Allan Houston/99 5.00 12.00
9 Dominique Wilkins/49 8.00 20.00
10 John Starks/99 4.00 10.00
11 Steve Kerr/49 6.00 15.00
12 Jamal Mashburn/99 4.00 10.00
13 Latrell Sprewell/49 6.00 15.00
14 Joe Dumars/49 6.00 15.00
16 Michael Cooper/99 4.00 10.00
17 Larry Bird/25 40.00 100.00
18 Alex English/99 6.00 15.00
19 Anfernee Hardaway/49 15.00 40.00
20 Tim Hardaway/99 6.00 15.00

2017-18 Panini Contenders Lottery Ticket

*RETAIL: .2X TO .5X BASIC
1 Markelle Fultz 3.00 8.00
2 Lonzo Ball 5.00 12.00
3 Jayson Tatum 25.00 60.00
4 Josh Jackson 1.50 4.00
5 De'Aaron Fox 10.00 25.00
6 Jonathan Isaac 3.00 8.00
7 Lauri Markkanen 8.00 20.00
8 Frank Ntilikina 1.50 4.00
9 Dennis Smith Jr. 1.50 4.00
10 Zach Collins 2.00 5.00
11 Malik Monk 5.00 12.00
12 Luke Kennard 2.50 6.00
13 Donovan Mitchell 20.00 50.00
14 Bam Adebayo 8.00 20.00

2017-18 Panini Contenders Lottery Ticket Cracked Ice

*CRACKED ICE: 2.5X TO 6X BASIC
STATED PRINT RUN 25 SER.#'D SETS
2 Lonzo Ball 75.00 200.00
3 Jayson Tatum 125.00 300.00
5 De'Aaron Fox 30.00 80.00
6 Jonathan Isaac 30.00 80.00
7 Lauri Markkanen 75.00 200.00
8 Frank Ntilikina 30.00 80.00
10 Zach Collins 20.00 50.00
13 Donovan Mitchell 150.00 400.00

2017-18 Panini Contenders Most Valuable Contenders

1 James Harden 1.25 3.00
2 Giannis Antetokounmpo 3.00 8.00
3 Russell Westbrook 1.00 2.50
4 Anthony Davis 1.50 4.00
5 Kevin Durant 2.50 6.00
6 Stephen Curry 5.00 12.00
7 LeBron James 5.00 12.00
8 Kyrie Irving 1.25 3.00
9 Damian Lillard 1.50 4.00
10 Karl-Anthony Towns 1.00 2.50

2017-18 Panini Contenders Most Valuable Contenders Cracked Ice

*CRACKED ICE: 2X TO 5X BASIC
STATED PRINT RUN 25 SER.#'d SETS
6 Stephen Curry 20.00 50.00
7 LeBron James 25.00 60.00

2017-18 Panini Contenders MVP Contenders Autographs

PRINT RUNS B/WN 10-49 COPIES PER
NO PRICING ON QTY 10
EXCHANGE DEADLINE 8/21/2019
*BRNZE/25: .5X TO 1.2X BASE p/r 49
1 Anthony Davis/25 30.00 80.00
3 Damian Lillard/25 30.00 80.00
5 Giannis Antetokounmpo/25 50.00 120.00
7 Kyrie Irving/25 30.00 80.00
8 Chris Paul/25 25.00 60.00
9 Karl-Anthony Towns/25 30.00 80.00
10 Nikola Jokic/49 125.00 300.00

2017-18 Panini Contenders NBA Ink

PRINT RUNS B/WN 10-199 COPIES PER
NO PRICING ON QTY 10
EXCHANGE DEADLINE 8/21/2019
*BRNZE/25: .5X TO 1.2X BASE p/r 49-199
*BRNZE/25: .4X TO 1X BASE p/r 25
1 Dirk Nowitzki/25 40.00 100.00
3 Elfrid Payton/199 3.00 8.00
4 Manu Ginobili/49 20.00 50.00
5 Udonis Haslem/199 3.00 8.00
6 Cody Zeller/199 3.00 8.00
7 Rondae Hollis-Jefferson/199 3.00 8.00
8 Andre Drummond/99 4.00 10.00
9 Dwyane Wade/25 20.00 50.00
10 Victor Oladipo/99 10.00 25.00
11 Anthony Davis/25 25.00 60.00
12 Damian Jones/199 3.00 8.00
13 Seth Curry/199 5.00 12.00
14 LaMarcus Aldridge/49 8.00 20.00
17 Taurean Prince/199 3.00 8.00
18 Gordon Hayward/99 8.00 20.00
19 Chris Paul/25 40.00 100.00
20 Jason Terry/99 4.00 10.00
21 Giannis Antetokounmpo/25 50.00 120.00
22 Mario Hezonja/199 3.00 8.00
23 Zaza Pachulia/199 3.00 8.00
24 Marcus Smart/49 5.00 12.00
25 Corey Brewer/199 3.00 8.00
26 Zach Randolph/49 5.00 12.00
28 Nikola Jokic/99 125.00 300.00
29 Damian Lillard/25 30.00 80.00
30 Reggie Jackson/99 4.00 10.00
31 Andrew Wiggins/25 12.00 30.00
32 Frank Kaminsky/199 3.00 8.00
33 Justin Anderson/199 3.00 8.00
34 Buddy Hield/49 5.00 12.00
35 Denzel Valentine/199 3.00 8.00
36 Kemba Walker/49 4.00 10.00
37 Carmelo Anthony/25 15.00 40.00
38 Nikola Vucevic/199 4.00 10.00
39 Kyrie Irving/25 30.00 80.00

2017-18 Panini Contenders NBA Ink Bronze

*BRONZE: .5X TO 1.2X BASE p/r 49-199
*BRONZE: .4X TO 1X BASE p/r 25
STATED PRINT RUN 25 SER.#'d SETS
EXCHANGE DEADLINE 8/21/2019
40 Kyle Korver 5.00 12.00

2017-18 Panini Contenders Playing the Numbers Game

*CRACKED ICE: 3X TO 8X BASIC
1 Rajon Rondo .75 2.00
2 Stephen Curry 5.00 12.00
3 Rudy Gobert .75 2.00
4 Tyson Chandler .50 1.25
5 Anthony Davis 1.50 4.00
6 Devin Booker 1.50 4.00
7 Chris Paul 1.00 2.50
8 Russell Westbrook 1.00 2.50
9 James Harden 1.25 3.00
10 Jimmy Butler 1.00 2.50
11 Draymond Green .75 2.00
12 Rudy Gobert .75 2.00
13 Brook Lopez .50 1.25
14 Andre Drummond .50 1.25
15 Nikola Jokic 4.00 10.00
16 Klay Thompson 1.50 4.00
17 John Wall .75 2.00
18 DeMarcus Cousins .50 1.25
19 LeBron James 5.00 12.00
20 Isaiah Thomas .50 1.25
21 Marcus Smart .60 1.50
22 DeAndre Jordan .50 1.25
23 Giannis Antetokounmpo 3.00 8.00

24 Dwight Howard .75 2.00
25 Jusuf Nurkic .50 1.25
26 Damian Lillard 1.50 4.00
27 Ricky Rubio .50 1.25
28 James Harden 1.25 3.00
29 Jeff Teague .40 1.00
30 Andrew Wiggins .75 2.00
31 Stephen Curry 5.00 12.00
32 Hassan Whiteside .50 1.25
33 Stephen Curry 5.00 12.00
34 Jonas Valanciunas .50 1.25
35 Russell Westbrook 1.00 2.50

2017-18 Panini Contenders Rookie Game Ticket Retail Autographs

STATED PRINT RUN 25 SER.#'d SETS
EXCHANGE DEADLINE 8/21/2019
1 Semi Ojeleye 8.00 20.00
2 Donovan Mitchell 150.00 400.00
3 Treveon Graham 8.00 20.00
4 Ike Anigbogu 6.00 15.00
5 Jonathan Isaac 15.00 40.00
6 Abdel Nader 8.00 20.00
7 Kyle Kuzma 25.00 60.00
8 Brandon Paul 6.00 15.00
9 Matt Costello 8.00 20.00
10 Davon Reed 6.00 15.00
11 Sindarius Thornwell 6.00 15.00
12 Dwayne Bacon 6.00 15.00
13 Tyler Cavanaugh 6.00 15.00
14 Ivan Rabb 6.00 15.00
15 Jordan Bell 6.00 15.00
16 Alex Caruso 75.00 200.00
17 Lauri Markkanen 50.00 120.00
18 Caleb Swanigan 6.00 15.00
19 Maxi Kleber 10.00 25.00
20 De'Aaron Fox 50.00 120.00
21 Sterling Brown 6.00 15.00
22 Frank Jackson 6.00 15.00
23 Tyler Dorsey 6.00 15.00
24 Jarrett Allen 15.00 40.00
25 Josh Hart 25.00 60.00
26 Alfonzo McKinnie 10.00 25.00
27 Lonzo Ball 25.00 60.00
28 Cedi Osman 12.00 30.00
30 Dennis Smith Jr. 8.00 20.00
31 TJ Leaf 6.00 15.00
32 Frank Mason III 6.00 15.00
33 Tyler Lydon 6.00 15.00
34 Jawun Evans 6.00 15.00
35 Justin Jackson 6.00 15.00
36 Ante Zizic 8.00 20.00
37 Luke Kennard 12.00 30.00
38 D.J. Wilson 6.00 15.00
39 Milos Teodosic 8.00 20.00
40 Damyean Dotson 8.00 20.00
41 Thomas Bryant 10.00 25.00
42 Frank Ntilikina 8.00 20.00
43 Wes Iwundu 6.00 15.00
45 Justin Patton 6.00 15.00
46 Bam Adebayo 40.00 100.00
47 Malik Monk 25.00 60.00
48 Daniel Theis 12.00 30.00
49 Royce O'Neale 8.00 20.00
50 Derrick White 25.00 60.00
51 Tony Bradley 6.00 15.00
52 Guerschon Yabusele 6.00 15.00
53 Zach Collins 10.00 25.00
54 John Collins 15.00 40.00
55 Kadeem Allen 6.00 15.00
56 Bogdan Bogdanovic 15.00 40.00
57 Markelle Fultz 15.00 40.00
58 David Nwaba 6.00 15.00
59 Ryan Arcidiacono 10.00 25.00
60 Dillon Brooks 20.00 50.00

2017-18 Panini Contenders Rookie of the Year Contenders

*RETAIL: .2X TO .5X BASIC
1 Lauri Markkanen 8.00 20.00
2 De'Aaron Fox 10.00 25.00
3 Kyle Kuzma 5.00 12.00
4 Josh Jackson 1.50 4.00
5 Dillon Brooks 4.00 10.00
6 Lonzo Ball 5.00 12.00
7 Justin Jackson 1.25 3.00
8 Markelle Fultz 3.00 8.00
9 Luke Kennard 2.50 6.00
10 Jonathan Isaac 3.00 8.00
11 Frank Ntilikina 1.50 4.00
12 Donovan Mitchell 12.00 30.00
13 Mike James 1.25 3.00
14 Malik Monk 5.00 12.00
15 John Collins 3.00 8.00
16 Dennis Smith Jr. 1.50 4.00
17 Ben Simmons 2.00 5.00
18 Jayson Tatum 15.00 40.00

2017-18 Panini Contenders Rookie of the Year Contenders Cracked Ice

*CRACKED ICE: 1.2X TO 3X BASIC
STATED PRINT RUN 25 SER.#'D SETS
1 Lauri Markkanen 40.00 100.00
12 Donovan Mitchell 75.00 200.00
16 Dennis Smith Jr. 5.00 12.00
17 Ben Simmons 6.00 15.00
18 Jayson Tatum 75.00 200.00

2017-18 Panini Contenders Rookie Season Ticket Retail Autographs

EXCHANGE DEADLINE 8/21/2019
1 Semi Ojeleye 4.00 10.00
2 Donovan Mitchell 75.00 200.00
3 Treveon Graham 4.00 10.00
4 Ike Anigbogu 3.00 8.00
5 Jonathan Isaac 8.00 20.00
6 Abdel Nader 4.00 10.00
7 Kyle Kuzma 12.00 30.00
8 Brandon Paul 3.00 8.00
9 Matt Costello 4.00 10.00
10 Davon Reed 3.00 8.00
11 Sindarius Thornwell 3.00 8.00
12 Dwayne Bacon 3.00 8.00
13 Tyler Cavanaugh 3.00 8.00
14 Ivan Rabb 3.00 8.00
15 Jordan Bell 3.00 8.00
16 Alex Caruso 40.00 100.00
17 Lauri Markkanen 25.00 60.00
18 Caleb Swanigan 3.00 8.00
19 Maxi Kleber 5.00 12.00
20 De'Aaron Fox 25.00 60.00
21 Sterling Brown 3.00 8.00
22 Frank Jackson 3.00 8.00
23 Tyler Dorsey 3.00 8.00
24 Jarrett Allen 8.00 20.00
25 Josh Hart 12.00 30.00
26 Alfonzo McKinnie 5.00 12.00
27 Lonzo Ball 12.00 30.00
28 Cedi Osman 6.00 15.00
30 Dennis Smith Jr. 4.00 10.00
31 TJ Leaf 3.00 8.00
32 Frank Mason III 3.00 8.00
33 Tyler Lydon 3.00 8.00
34 Jawun Evans 3.00 8.00
35 Justin Jackson 3.00 8.00
36 Ante Zizic 4.00 10.00
37 Luke Kennard 6.00 15.00
38 D.J. Wilson 3.00 8.00
39 Milos Teodosic 4.00 10.00
40 Damyean Dotson 4.00 10.00
41 Thomas Bryant 5.00 12.00
42 Frank Ntilikina 4.00 10.00
43 Wes Iwundu 3.00 8.00
45 Justin Patton 3.00 8.00
46 Bam Adebayo 20.00 50.00
47 Malik Monk 12.00 30.00
48 Daniel Theis 6.00 15.00
49 Royce O'Neale 4.00 10.00
50 Derrick White 12.00 30.00
51 Tony Bradley 3.00 8.00
53 Zach Collins 5.00 12.00
54 John Collins 8.00 20.00
55 Kadeem Allen 3.00 8.00
56 Bogdan Bogdanovic 8.00 20.00
57 Markelle Fultz 8.00 20.00
58 David Nwaba 3.00 8.00
59 Ryan Arcidiacono 5.00 12.00

2017-18 Panini Contenders Rookie Ticket Dual Swatches

*PRIME/25: 1X TO 2.5X BASIC
1 Jackson/Tatum 20.00 50.00
2 Jackson/Reed 2.00 5.00
3 Smith Jr./Ntilikina 2.00 5.00
4 Fox/Giles 12.00 30.00
5 Fox/Mason III 12.00 30.00
6 John Collins
Tyler Dorsey 4.00 10.00
7 Tatum/Kennard 20.00 50.00
8 Bacon/Monk 6.00 15.00
9 Ball/Tatum 20.00 50.00
10 D.J. Wilson
Sterling Brown 1.50 4.00
11 Jonathan Isaac
Dwayne Bacon 4.00 10.00
12 Zach Collins
Caleb Swanigan 2.50 6.00
13 Fultz/Mitchell 15.00 40.00
14 Frank Mason III
Harry Giles 1.50 4.00
15 Mitchell/Bradley 15.00 40.00
16 Tatum/Ojeleye 20.00 50.00
17 Adebayo/Monk 10.00 25.00
18 Sindarius Thornwell
Jawun Evans 1.50 4.00
19 Fultz/Ball 6.00 15.00
20 Jonathan Isaac
Wes Iwundu 4.00 10.00

2017-18 Panini Contenders Rookie Ticket Swatches

*PRIME/25: 1X TO 2.5X BASIC
1 Markelle Fultz 4.00 10.00
2 Lonzo Ball 6.00 15.00
3 Jayson Tatum 20.00 50.00
4 Josh Jackson 2.00 5.00
5 De'Aaron Fox 12.00 30.00
6 Jonathan Isaac 4.00 10.00
7 Frank Ntilikina 2.00 5.00
8 Dennis Smith Jr. 2.00 5.00
9 Zach Collins 2.50 6.00
10 Malik Monk 6.00 15.00
11 Luke Kennard 3.00 8.00
12 Donovan Mitchell 15.00 40.00
13 Bam Adebayo 10.00 25.00
14 Justin Patton 1.50 4.00
15 D.J. Wilson 1.50 4.00
16 TJ Leaf 1.50 4.00
17 John Collins 4.00 10.00
18 Harry Giles 1.50 4.00
19 Terrance Ferguson 1.50 4.00
20 Caleb Swanigan 1.50 4.00

2017-18 Panini Contenders Superstar Die Cuts

*RETAIL: .4X TO 1X BASIC
*CRACKED ICE/25: 2.5X TO 6X BASIC
1 Kobe Bryant 15.00 40.00
2 Giannis Antetokounmpo 10.00 25.00
3 Stephen Curry 15.00 40.00
4 James Harden 4.00 10.00
5 Kevin Durant 8.00 20.00
6 LeBron James 15.00 40.00
7 Klay Thompson 5.00 12.00
8 Damian Lillard 5.00 12.00
9 Russell Westbrook 3.00 8.00
10 John Wall 2.50 6.00

2017-18 Panini Contenders The Finals Ticket

*FINALS 1-100: 1.5X TO 4X BASIC
1-100 PRINT RUN 99 SER.#'d SETS
20 LeBron James/99 15.00 40.00
25 Ben Simmons/99 1.25 3.00
103B Jayson Tatum AU VAR/25 2,000.00 4,000.00
113B Donovan Mitchell
AU VAR/25 600.00 1,200.00

2017-18 Panini Contenders Up and Coming Contenders Autographs

PRINT RUNS B/WN 10-49 COPIES PER
NO PRICING ON QTY 10
EXCHANGE DEADLINE 8/21/2019
1 De'Aaron Fox/99 15.00 40.00
2 Donovan Mitchell/199 40.00 100.00
3 Dennis Smith Jr./99 4.00 10.00
4 John Collins/199 8.00 20.00
5 Bam Adebayo/199 15.00 40.00
7 Justin Jackson/199 3.00 8.00
8 Jarrett Allen/199 8.00 20.00
9 Jayson Tatum/99 50.00 120.00
10 Caleb Swanigan/199 3.00 8.00
13 Kyle Kuzma/199 12.00 30.00
14 D.J. Wilson/199 3.00 8.00
15 Frank Ntilikina/99 4.00 10.00
16 Luke Kennard/199 6.00 15.00
17 Zach Collins/99 5.00 12.00
19 Harry Giles/199 3.00 8.00
20 Tony Bradley/199 3.00 8.00
21 Derrick White/199 12.00 30.00
23 Frank Jackson/199 3.00 8.00
24 TJ Leaf/199 3.00 8.00
25 Tyler Lydon/199 3.00 8.00
26 Jonathan Isaac/99 8.00 20.00
27 Markelle Fultz/99 12.00 30.00
28 Lonzo Ball/149 15.00 40.00
30 Lauri Markkanen/99 15.00 40.00

2017-18 Panini Contenders Up and Coming Contenders Autographs Bronze

*BRONZE: .6X TO 1.5X BASE
STATED PRINT RUN 25 SER.#'d SETS
EXCHANGE DEADLINE 8/21/2019
11 OG Anunoby 10.00 25.00
12 Justin Patton 5.00 12.00
18 Malik Monk 20.00 50.00
22 Josh Hart 12.00 30.00

2017-18 Panini Contenders Winning Tickets

*CRACKED ICE: 3X TO 8X BASIC
1 Dennis Rodman 1.50 4.00
2 Isiah Thomas 1.00 2.50
3 Stephen Curry 5.00 12.00
4 Kareem Abdul-Jabbar 2.00 5.00
5 Tim Duncan 1.50 4.00
6 Wilt Chamberlain 2.00 5.00
7 Kobe Bryant 5.00 12.00
8 Andre Iguodala .60 1.50
9 Chauncey Billups .75 2.00
10 Ray Allen 1.00 2.50
11 Scottie Pippen 1.50 4.00
12 Joe Dumars .75 2.00
13 Kevin Durant 2.50 6.00
14 Larry Bird 2.50 6.00
15 Tony Parker 1.00 2.50
16 Willis Reed 1.00 2.50
17 Kevin Garnett 1.50 4.00
18 Jason Kidd 1.00 2.50
19 David Robinson 1.25 3.00
20 Klay Thompson 1.50 4.00
21 Clyde Drexler 1.00 2.50
22 James Worthy .75 2.00
23 LeBron James 5.00 12.00
24 Cedric Maxwell .50 1.25
25 Dwyane Wade 1.25 3.00
26 Kawhi Leonard 1.50 4.00
27 Shaquille O'Neal 2.00 5.00
28 Ben Wallace .50 1.25
29 Manu Ginobili 1.25 3.00
30 Draymond Green .75 2.00
31 Hakeem Olajuwon 1.25 3.00
32 Magic Johnson 2.50 6.00
33 Kyrie Irving 1.25 3.00
34 Wes Unseld .60 1.50
35 Dirk Nowitzki 1.50 4.00

2017-18 Panini Contenders Winning Tickets Cracked Ice

*CRACKED ICE: 3X TO 8X BASIC
STATED PRINT RUN 25 SER.#'D SETS
23 LeBron James 50.00 120.00

2018-19 Panini Contenders

EXCHANGE DEADLINE 6/26/2020
*PREMIUM: 1.2X TO 3X BASIC
*PREMIUM RC AU: .5X TO 1.2X BASIC
*PLAYOFF TCK/199: 1.25X TO 3X BASIC
*PLAYOFF AU/65: .6X TO 1.5X BASIC
*FINALS TCK/99: 1.5X TO 4X BASIC
*FINALS RC AU/49: .6X TO 1.5X BASIC
CRACKED ICE TCK/25: 6X TO 15X BASIC
*CRACKED ICE RC AU/25: 1.5X TO 4X BASIC
1 Hassan Whiteside .25 .60
2 Jeremy Lin .50 1.25
3 Elfrid Payton .25 .60
4 Kemba Walker .25 .60
5 Nikola Vucevic .25 .60
6 Dirk Nowitzki .75 2.00
7 Jusuf Nurkic .25 .60
8 Kevin Durant 1.25 3.00
9 Danny Green .25 .60
10 Tobias Harris .25 .60
11 Giannis Antetokounmpo 1.50 4.00
12 John Collins .40 1.00
13 Kristaps Porzingis .30 .75
14 Tony Parker .50 1.25
15 Ben Simmons .75 2.00
16 DeAndre Jordan .25 .60
17 De'Aaron Fox .60 1.50
18 Draymond Green .40 1.00
19 Serge Ibaka .25 .60
20 Lonzo Ball .30 .75
21 Eric Bledsoe .25 .60
22 Vince Carter .60 1.50
23 Enes Kanter .25 .60
24 Nicolas Batum .25 .60
25 Joel Embiid .75 2.00
26 Nikola Jokic 1.50 4.00
27 Bogdan Bogdanovic .30 .75
28 Chris Paul .60 1.50
29 Ricky Rubio .30 .75
30 LeBron James 2.50 6.00
31 Khris Middleton .30 .75
32 Kyrie Irving .75 2.00
33 Tim Hardaway Jr. .20 .50
34 Kris Dunn .20 .50
35 JJ Redick .30 .75
36 Isaiah Thomas .25 .60
37 Zach Randolph .25 .60
38 James Harden .60 1.50
39 Donovan Mitchell 1.00 2.50
40 Brandon Ingram .30 .75
41 Jimmy Butler .50 1.25
42 Jaylen Brown .50 1.25
43 Russell Westbrook .50 1.25
44 Zach LaVine .50 1.25
45 Markelle Fultz .25 .60
46 Paul Millsap .25 .60
47 DeMar DeRozan .40 1.00
48 Carmelo Anthony .50 1.25
49 Joe Ingles .25 .60
50 Kyle Kuzma .30 .75
51 Andrew Wiggins .40 1.00
52 Jayson Tatum 1.25 3.00
53 Dennis Schroder .25 .60
54 Lauri Markkanen .50 1.25
55 Devin Booker .75 2.00
56 Reggie Jackson .25 .60
57 LaMarcus Aldridge .30 .75
58 Victor Oladipo .25 .60
59 Rudy Gobert .40 1.00
60 Mike Conley .25 .60
61 Karl-Anthony Towns .50 1.25
62 Al Horford .30 .75
63 Paul George .50 1.25
64 Kevin Love .25 .60
65 TJ Warren .20 .50
66 Blake Griffin .30 .75
67 Pau Gasol .50 1.25
68 Myles Turner .30 .75
69 John Wall .40 1.00
70 Dillon Brooks .30 .75
71 Derrick Rose .60 1.50
72 D'Angelo Russell .30 .75
73 Steven Adams .25 .60
74 JR Smith .30 .75
75 Trevor Ariza .20 .50
76 Andre Drummond .25 .60
77 Rudy Gay .30 .75
78 Tyreke Evans .20 .50
79 Bradley Beal .40 1.00
80 Marc Gasol .30 .75
81 Anthony Davis .75 2.00
82 Jarrett Allen .30 .75
83 Evan Fournier .25 .60
84 Kyle Korver .25 .60
85 Damian Lillard .75 2.00
86 Stephen Curry 2.50 6.00
87 Kyle Lowry .30 .75
88 Lou Williams .25 .60
89 Dwight Howard .40 1.00
90 Goran Dragic .25 .60
91 Jrue Holiday .40 1.00
92 DeMarre Carroll .20 .50
93 Aaron Gordon .30 .75
94 Dennis Smith Jr. .20 .50
95 CJ McCollum .30 .75
96 Klay Thompson .75 2.00
97 Kawhi Leonard .75 2.00
98 Marcin Gortat .20 .50
99 DeMarcus Cousins .25 .60
100 Dion Waiters .20 .50
101 Aaron Holiday AU RC 6.00 15.00
102 Deandre Ayton AU RC 12.00 30.00
103 Jacob Evans III AU RC 4.00 10.00
104 Mo Bamba AU RC 6.00 15.00
105 Jalen Brunson AU RC 150.00 400.00
106 Gilgeous-Alexander AU RC 600.00 1,200.00
107 Hamidou Diallo AU RC 6.00 15.00
108 Troy Brown Jr. AU RC 5.00 12.00
109 Khyri Thomas AU RC 4.00 10.00
110 Kevin Huerter AU RC 8.00 20.00
111 Anfernee Simons AU RC 20.00 50.00
112 M.Bagley III AU RC 6.00 15.00
113 Dzanan Musa AU RC 4.00 10.00
114 W.Carter Jr. AU RC 10.00 25.00
115 Devonte' Graham AU RC 6.00 15.00
116 Kevin Hervey AU RC 4.00 10.00
117 De'Anthony Melton AU RC 8.00 20.00
118 Zhaire Smith AU RC 4.00 10.00
119 K.Antetokounmpo AU RC 5.00 12.00
120 Josh Okogie AU RC 6.00 15.00
121 Moritz Wagner AU RC 8.00 20.00
122 Luka Doncic AU RC 1,000.00 2,000.00
123 Omari Spellman AU RC 4.00 10.00
124 Collin Sexton AU RC 12.00 30.00
125 Gary Trent Jr. AU RC 8.00 20.00
126 Jerome Robinson AU RC 4.00 10.00
127 Keita Bates-Diop AU RC 5.00 12.00
128 Donte DiVincenzo AU RC 10.00 25.00
129 M.Robinson AU RC EXCH 10.00 25.00
130 Grayson Allen AU RC 8.00 20.00
131 Landry Shamet AU RC 6.00 15.00
132 J.Jackson Jr. AU RC 125.00 300.00
133 Elie Okobo AU RC 4.00 10.00
134 Kevin Knox AU RC 5.00 12.00
135 Melvin Frazier Jr. AU RC 4.00 10.00
136 Vincent Edwards AU RC 4.00 10.00
137 M.Porter Jr. AU RC 15.00 40.00
138 Walker IV AU RC 8.00 20.00
139 Svi Mykhailiuk AU RC 5.00 12.00
140 Chandler Hutchison AU RC EXCH 5.00 12.00
141 Williams III AU RC EXCH 8.00 20.00
142 Trae Young AU RC 400.00 800.00
143 Jevon Carter AU RC 6.00 15.00
144 Mikal Bridges AU RC 20.00 50.00
145 Bruce Brown AU RC 8.00 20.00

2018-19 Panini Contenders Conference Finals Ticket

*CONF FINALS: 1.2X TO 3X BASIC
STATED PRINT RUN 135 SER.#'d SETS
30 LeBron James 20.00 50.00

2018-19 Panini Contenders Game Ticket Blue

*BLUE: 1.5X TO 4X BASIC
STATED PRINT RUN 49 SER.#'d SETS
30 LeBron James 8.00 20.00

2018-19 Panini Contenders Game Ticket Green

*GREEN: .6X TO 1.5X BASIC

2018-19 Panini Contenders Game Ticket Purple

*PURPLE: 2.5X TO 6X BASIC
STATED PRINT RUN 25 SER.#'d SETS
30 LeBron James 12.00 30.00

2018-19 Panini Contenders Game Ticket Red

*RED: .6X TO 1.5X BASIC

2018-19 Panini Contenders Variations

*VAR: .4X TO 1X BASIC
EXCHANGE DEADLINE 6/26/2020

2018-19 Panini Contenders Variations Cracked Ice Ticket

*VAR CRACKED: 1.5X TO 4X BASIC
STATED PRINT RUN 20 SER.#'d SETS
EXCHANGE DEADLINE 6/26/2020
101 Aaron Holiday AU 30.00 80.00
102 Deandre Ayton AU 400.00 800.00
104 Mo Bamba AU 100.00 250.00
105 Jalen Brunson AU 30.00 80.00
107 Hamidou Diallo AU 60.00 150.00
108 Troy Brown Jr. AU 20.00 50.00
110 Kevin Huerter AU 60.00 150.00
111 Anfernee Simons AU 30.00 80.00
112 Marvin Bagley III AU 15.00 40.00
113 Dzanan Musa AU 30.00 80.00
114 Wendell Carter Jr. AU 100.00 250.00
117 De'Anthony Melton AU 25.00 60.00
118 Zhaire Smith AU 40.00 100.00
119 Kostas Antetokounmpo AU 60.00 150.00
120 Josh Okogie AU 40.00 100.00
121 Moritz Wagner AU 50.00 120.00
122 Luka Doncic AU 5,000.00 10,000.00
124 Collin Sexton AU 100.00 250.00
127 Keita Bates-Diop AU 25.00 60.00
128 Donte DiVincenzo AU 40.00 100.00
129 Mitchell Robinson AU 60.00 150.00
130 Grayson Allen AU 30.00 80.00
131 Landry Shamet AU 60.00 150.00
132 Jaren Jackson Jr. AU 400.00 800.00
137 Michael Porter Jr. AU 250.00 500.00
138 Lonnie Walker IV AU 200.00 400.00
139 Svi Mykhailiuk AU 40.00 100.00
141 Robert Williams III AU EXCH 50.00 120.00
142 Trae Young AU 800.00 1,500.00
143 Jevon Carter AU 40.00 100.00
144 Mikal Bridges AU 40.00 100.00

2018-19 Panini Contenders Variations Playoff Ticket

*VAR PLAYOFF: .6X TO 1.5X BASIC
STATED PRINT RUN 35 SER.#'d SETS
EXCHANGE DEADLINE 6/26/2020
113 Dzanan Musa AU 10.00 25.00
114 Wendell Carter Jr. AU 20.00 50.00
122 Luka Doncic AU 3,000.00 6,000.00

2018-19 Panini Contenders Variations Premium

*VAR PREM: .5X TO 1.2X BASIC
EXCHANGE DEADLINE 6/26/2020

2018-19 Panini Contenders Variations The Finals Ticket

*VAR FINALS: .75X TO 2X BASIC
STATED PRINT RUN 25 SER.#'d SETS
EXCHANGE DEADLINE 6/26/2020
113 Dzanan Musa AU 15.00 40.00
114 Wendell Carter Jr. AU 25.00 60.00
122 Luka Doncic AU 4,000.00 8,000.00

2018-19 Panini Contenders Front Row Seat

*RETAIL: .4X TO 1X BASIC
1 Joel Embiid 1.50 4.00
2 Stephen Curry 5.00 12.00
3 De'Aaron Fox 1.25 3.00
4 Chris Paul 1.25 3.00
5 Giannis Antetokounmpo 3.00 8.00
6 Kyrie Irving 1.50 4.00
7 LeBron James 5.00 12.00
8 Zach LaVine 1.00 2.50
9 Russell Westbrook 1.00 2.50
10 Dennis Smith Jr. .40 1.00
11 Devin Booker 1.50 4.00
12 Kevin Durant 2.50 6.00
13 Donovan Mitchell 2.00 5.00
14 James Harden 1.25 3.00
15 Jimmy Butler 1.00 2.50
16 Jayson Tatum 2.50 6.00
17 Anthony Davis 1.50 4.00
18 Lauri Markkanen 1.00 2.50
19 Paul George 1.00 2.50
20 Dirk Nowitzki 1.50 4.00
21 Damian Lillard 1.50 4.00
22 Klay Thompson 1.50 4.00
23 John Wall .75 2.00
24 Lonzo Ball .60 1.50
25 Karl-Anthony Towns 1.00 2.50
26 Kemba Walker .50 1.25
27 Kristaps Porzingis .75 2.00
28 Kevin Love .50 1.25
29 Ben Simmons .60 1.50
30 Blake Griffin .60 1.50

2018-19 Panini Contenders Front Row Seat Cracked Ice

*CRACKED ICE: 1.5X TO 4X BASIC
STATED PRINT RUN 25 SER.#'d SETS
7 LeBron James 40.00 100.00

2018-19 Panini Contenders Hall of Fame Contenders

1 Dirk Nowitzki 1.50 4.00
2 Tony Parker 1.00 2.50
3 Kevin Durant 2.50 6.00
4 Kyrie Irving 1.50 4.00
5 Russell Westbrook 1.00 2.50
6 Draymond Green .75 2.00
7 James Harden 1.25 3.00
8 Kobe Bryant 5.00 12.00
9 LeBron James 5.00 12.00
10 Kevin Garnett 1.50 4.00
11 Chris Paul 1.25 3.00
12 Anthony Davis 1.50 4.00
13 Stephen Curry 5.00 12.00
14 John Wall .75 2.00
15 Carmelo Anthony 1.00 2.50
16 Klay Thompson 1.50 4.00
17 Vince Carter 1.25 3.00
18 Tim Duncan 1.50 4.00
19 Dwyane Wade 1.25 3.00
20 Paul Pierce 1.00 2.50

2018-19 Panini Contenders Hall of Fame Contenders Cracked Ice

*CRACKED ICE: 2X TO 5X BASIC
STATED PRINT RUN 25 SER.#'d SETS
8 Kobe Bryant 20.00 50.00
9 LeBron James 40.00 100.00
13 Stephen Curry 20.00 50.00

2018-19 Panini Contenders Historic Rookie Season Ticket

EXCHANGE DEADLINE 6/26/2020
*PREMIUM: .5X TO 1.2X BASIC
*PLAYOFF/49: .5X TO 1.2X BASIC
*FINALS/25: .6X TO 1.5X BASIC
1 Shaquille O'Neal EXCH 100.00 250.00
2 Grant Hill 40.00 100.00
3 Allen Iverson 100.00 250.00
5 Dirk Nowitzki 100.00 250.00
6 Karl-Anthony Towns 20.00 50.00
8 David Robinson 60.00 150.00
9 Charles Barkley 100.00 250.00
10 Kobe Bryant 500.00 1,000.00

2018-19 Panini Contenders Legendary Contenders Autographs

PRINT RUN B/WN 99-199 COPIES PER
EXCHANGE DEADLINE 6/26/2020
*BRONZE/25: .6X TO 1.5X BASIC
1 B.J. Armstrong/199 4.00 10.00
2 Larry Bird/99 25.00 60.00
3 Kevin Willis/199 3.00 8.00
4 Ray Allen/99 8.00 20.00
5 Stephen Jackson/199 3.00 8.00
6 Walt Frazier/99 5.00 12.00
7 Tom Heinsohn/199 10.00 25.00
8 Jalen Rose/99 3.00 8.00
9 Marques Johnson/199 3.00 8.00
10 Robert Parish/99 6.00 15.00
11 Allan Houston/199 4.00 10.00
12 Magic Johnson/99 20.00 50.00
13 Bill Cartwright/199 3.00 8.00
14 Paul Pierce/99 15.00 40.00
15 George McGinnis/199 5.00 12.00
16 Richard Hamilton/99 3.00 8.00
17 David Thompson/199 5.00 12.00
18 Avery Johnson/99 3.00 8.00
19 Rolando Blackman/199 3.00 8.00
20 Ralph Sampson/99 3.00 8.00
21 Mark Aguirre/199 3.00 8.00
22 Alonzo Mourning/99 8.00 20.00
23 Mitch Richmond/199 5.00 12.00
24 Christian Laettner/99 4.00 10.00
25 Toni Kukoc/199 5.00 12.00
26 George Gervin/99 6.00 15.00
27 A.C. Green/199 4.00 10.00
28 Rick Fox/99 3.00 8.00
29 Tom Gugliotta/199 2.50 6.00
30 Gail Goodrich/99 4.00 10.00
31 Kenny "Sky" Walker/199 2.50 6.00
32 David Robinson/99 12.00 30.00
33 Sam Cassell/199 3.00 8.00
34 Jerry Lucas/99 5.00 12.00
35 Alex English/199 4.00 10.00
36 Nick Van Exel/99 4.00 10.00
37 Alvan Adams/199 3.00 8.00
38 Chauncey Billups/99 5.00 12.00
39 Damon Stoudamire/199 4.00 10.00
40 Horace Grant/199 4.00 10.00

2018-19 Panini Contenders Lottery Ticket

*RETAIL: .4X TO 1X BASIC
1 Deandre Ayton 1.25 3.00
2 Marvin Bagley III .60 1.50
3 Luka Doncic 30.00 80.00
4 Jaren Jackson Jr. 3.00 8.00
5 Trae Young 8.00 20.00
6 Mo Bamba .60 1.50
7 Wendell Carter Jr. 1.00 2.50
8 Collin Sexton 1.25 3.00
9 Kevin Knox .50 1.25
10 Mikal Bridges 2.00 5.00
11 Shai Gilgeous-Alexander 4.00 10.00
12 Miles Bridges 1.00 2.50
13 Jerome Robinson .40 1.00
14 Michael Porter Jr. 1.50 4.00

2018-19 Panini Contenders Lottery Ticket Cracked Ice

*CRACKED ICE: 3X TO 8X BASIC
STATED PRINT RUN 25 SER.#'D SETS
3 Luka Doncic 400.00 800.00
5 Trae Young 75.00 200.00

2018-19 Panini Contenders Most Valuable Contenders

1 Kevin Durant 2.50 6.00
2 Stephen Curry 5.00 12.00
3 Anthony Davis 1.50 4.00
4 Giannis Antetokounmpo 3.00 8.00
5 Kawhi Leonard 1.50 4.00
6 Kyrie Irving 1.50 4.00
7 Joel Embiid 1.50 4.00
8 LeBron James 5.00 12.00
9 Russell Westbrook 1.00 2.50
10 James Harden 1.25 3.00

2018-19 Panini Contenders Most Valuable Contenders Cracked Ice

*CRACKED ICE: 1.5X TO 4X BASIC
STATED PRINT RUN 25 SER.#'d SETS
2 Stephen Curry 20.00 50.00
8 LeBron James 40.00 100.00

2018-19 Panini Contenders MVP Contenders Autographs

PRINT RUNS B/WN 183-199 COPIES PER
EXCHANGE DEADLINE 6/26/2020
1 Kevin Durant/199 EXCH 40.00 100.00
2 Stephen Curry/199 EXCH 500.00 1,000.00
3 Nikola Jokic/199 125.00 300.00
4 Giannis Antetokounmpo/188 60.00 150.00
5 Kawhi Leonard/183 60.00 150.00
6 Kyrie Irving/199 15.00 40.00
7 Joel Embiid/199 20.00 50.00
8 Damian Lillard/199 10.00 25.00
9 Karl-Anthony Towns/199 12.00 30.00

2018-19 Panini Contenders MVP Contenders Autographs Bronze

*BRONZE: .6X TO 1.5X BASIC
STATED PRINT RUN 25 SER.#'d SETS
EXCHANGE DEADLINE 6/26/2020
10 Donovan Mitchell 30.00 80.00

2018-19 Panini Contenders Playing the Numbers Game

1 Russell Westbrook 1.00 2.50
2 James Harden 1.25 3.00
3 Nikola Jokic 3.00 8.00
4 DeMar DeRozan .75 2.00
5 Andre Drummond .50 1.25
6 CJ McCollum .60 1.50
7 Lou Williams .50 1.25
8 Kyrie Irving 1.50 4.00
9 Anthony Davis 1.50 4.00
10 Devin Booker 1.50 4.00
11 LeBron James 5.00 12.00
12 Nicolas Batum .40 1.00
13 Dwight Howard .75 2.00
14 Bradley Beal .75 2.00
15 Clint Capela .50 1.25
16 Lou Williams .50 1.25
17 Willie Cauley-Stein .40 1.00
18 Victor Oladipo .50 1.25
19 Kevin Durant 2.50 6.00
20 Joel Embiid 1.50 4.00
21 James Harden 1.25 3.00
22 Karl-Anthony Towns 1.00 2.50
23 John Wall .75 2.00
24 Kevin Durant 2.50 6.00
25 DeAndre Jordan .50 1.25
26 Stephen Curry 5.00 12.00
27 Chris Paul 1.25 3.00
28 Kemba Walker .50 1.25
29 Joel Embiid 1.50 4.00
30 Rajon Rondo .75 2.00
31 Jrue Holiday .75 2.00
32 Anthony Davis 1.50 4.00
33 LeBron James 5.00 12.00
34 Damian Lillard 1.50 4.00
35 DeMarcus Cousins .50 1.25

2018-19 Panini Contenders Playing the Numbers Game Cracked Ice

*CRACKED ICE: 1.5X TO 4X BASIC
STATED PRINT RUN 25 SER.#'D SETS
11 LeBron James 40.00 100.00
26 Stephen Curry 20.00 50.00
33 LeBron James 40.00 100.00

2018-19 Panini Contenders Rookie of the Year Contenders

*RETAIL: .4X TO 1X BASIC
1 Mikal Bridges 2.00 5.00
2 Miles Bridges 1.00 2.50
3 Deandre Ayton 1.25 3.00
4 Luka Doncic 20.00 50.00
5 Michael Porter Jr. 1.50 4.00
6 Trae Young 3.00 8.00
7 Zhaire Smith .40 1.00
8 Wendell Carter Jr. 1.00 2.50
9 Lonnie Walker IV .75 2.00
10 Kevin Knox .50 1.25
11 Shai Gilgeous-Alexander 4.00 10.00
12 Marvin Bagley III .60 1.50
13 Jerome Robinson .40 1.00
14 Jaren Jackson Jr. 3.00 8.00
15 Troy Brown Jr. .50 1.25
16 Mo Bamba .60 1.50
17 Donte DiVincenzo 1.00 2.50
18 Collin Sexton 1.25 3.00

2018-19 Panini Contenders Rookie of the Year Contenders Cracked Ice

*CRACKED ICE: 3X TO 8X BASIC
STATED PRINT RUN 25 SER.#'D SETS
4 Luka Doncic 300.00 600.00

2018-19 Panini Contenders Rookie Ticket Dual Swatches

1 Donte DiVincenzo
Mikal Bridges 6.00 15.00
2 Ayton/Bagley III 4.00 10.00
3 Gilgeous-Alexander/Robinson 12.00 30.00
4 Doncic/Young 200.00 500.00
5 Ayton/Bridges 4.00 10.00
6 Bagley III/Carter Jr. 3.00 8.00
7 Huerter/Young 12.00 30.00
8 Knox/Gilgeous-Alexander 3.00 8.00
9 Doncic/Brunson 20.00 50.00
10 Svi Mykhailiuk
Devonte' Graham 2.00 5.00

2018-19 Panini Contenders Rookie Ticket Swatches

1 Bruce Brown 2.50 6.00
2 Jevon Carter 2.00 5.00
3 Landry Shamet 2.00 5.00
4 Donte DiVincenzo 3.00 8.00
5 Chandler Hutchison 1.50 4.00
6 Michael Porter Jr. 5.00 12.00
7 Gary Trent Jr. 2.50 6.00
8 Omari Spellman 1.25 3.00
9 Kevin Knox 1.50 4.00
10 Jaren Jackson Jr. 3.00 10.00
11 Luka Doncic 25.00 60.00
12 Josh Okogie 2.00 5.00
13 Troy Brown Jr. 1.50 4.00
14 Shai Gilgeous-Alexander 2.50 6.00
15 Svi Mykhailiuk 1.50 4.00
16 Wendell Carter Jr. 3.00 8.00
17 Jacob Evans III 1.25 3.00
18 Aaron Holiday 2.00 5.00
19 Marvin Bagley III 3.00 10.00
20 Kevin Huerter 2.50 6.00
21 Jerome Robinson 1.25 3.00
22 Collin Sexton 3.00 8.00
23 Jarred Vanderbilt 2.50 6.00
24 Elie Okobo 1.25 3.00
25 Mikal Bridges 6.00 15.00
26 Trae Young 20.00 50.00
27 Grayson Allen 2.50 6.00
28 Keita Bates-Diop 1.50 4.00
29 Robert Williams III 2.50 6.00
30 Lonnie Walker IV 2.50 6.00

31 Mo Bamba 2.00 5.00
32 Deandre Ayton 4.00 10.00
33 Dzanan Musa 1.25 3.00
34 Anfernee Simons 6.00 15.00
35 Moritz Wagner 2.50 6.00
36 Zhaire Smith 1.25 3.00
37 Hamidou Diallo 2.00 5.00
38 Jalen Brunson 10.00 25.00
39 De'Anthony Melton 2.50 6.00
40 Devonte' Graham 2.00 5.00

2018-19 Panini Contenders Sophomore Contenders Autographs

PRINT RUNW B/WN 49-199 COPIES PER
EXCHANGE DEADLINE 6/26/2020
2 Lonzo Ball/49 15.00 40.00
3 Jayson Tatum/99 25.00 60.00
4 De'Aaron Fox/99 15.00 40.00
7 Frank Ntilikina/199 2.50 6.00
8 Jonathan Isaac/199 4.00 10.00
9 Dillon Brooks/199 4.00 10.00
10 Zhou Qi/199 2.50 6.00

2018-19 Panini Contenders Sophomore Contenders Autographs Bronze

*BRONZE: .6X TO 1.5X BASIC
STATED PRINT RUN 25 SER.#'d SETS
EXCHANGE DEADLINE 6/26/2020
6 Donovan Mitchell 30.00 80.00

2018-19 Panini Contenders Superstar Die Cuts

*RETAIL: .4X TO 1X BASIC
1 Stephen Curry 8.00 20.00
2 LeBron James 8.00 20.00
3 Kyrie Irving 2.50 6.00
4 Kevin Durant 4.00 10.00
5 Ben Simmons 1.00 2.50
6 James Harden 2.00 5.00
7 Joel Embiid 2.50 6.00
8 Russell Westbrook 1.50 4.00
9 Anthony Davis 2.50 6.00
10 Donovan Mitchell 3.00 8.00

2018-19 Panini Contenders Superstar Die Cuts Cracked Ice

*CRACKED ICE: 4X TO 10X TO BASIC
STATED PRINT RUN 25 SER.#'d SETS
1 Stephen Curry 50.00 120.00
2 LeBron James 100.00 250.00
5 Ben Simmons 50.00 120.00

2018-19 Panini Contenders Up and Coming Contenders Autographs

STATED PRINT RUN 199 SER.#'d SETS
EXCHANGE DEADLINE 6/26/2020
*BRONZE/25: .75X TO 2X BASIC
1 Michael Porter Jr. 12.00 30.00
2 Wendell Carter Jr. 8.00 20.00
3 Trae Young 200.00 500.00
4 Zhaire Smith 3.00 8.00
5 Omari Spellman 3.00 8.00
6 Aaron Holiday 5.00 12.00
7 Keita Bates-Diop 4.00 10.00
8 Jalen Brunson 25.00 60.00
9 Jaren Jackson Jr. 125.00 300.00
10 Kevin Huerter 6.00 15.00
11 Lonnie Walker IV 6.00 15.00
12 Devonte' Graham 5.00 12.00
13 Jevon Carter 5.00 12.00
14 Josh Okogie 5.00 12.00
15 Collin Sexton 10.00 25.00
16 Deandre Ayton 10.00 25.00
17 Donte DiVincenzo 8.00 20.00
18 Shai Gilgeous-Alexander 400.00 800.00
19 Elie Okobo 3.00 8.00
20 Anfernee Simons 15.00 40.00
21 Chandler Hutchison 4.00 10.00
22 Svi Mykhailiuk 4.00 10.00
23 Mikal Bridges 15.00 40.00
24 Moritz Wagner 6.00 15.00
25 Gary Trent Jr. 6.00 15.00
26 Jacob Evans III 3.00 8.00
27 Grayson Allen 6.00 15.00
28 Hamidou Diallo 5.00 12.00
29 Kevin Knox 4.00 10.00
30 Marvin Bagley III 5.00 12.00
31 Robert Williams III 6.00 15.00
32 De'Anthony Melton 6.00 15.00
33 Bruce Brown 6.00 15.00
34 Luka Doncic 1,000.00 2,000.00
36 Mo Bamba 5.00 12.00
38 Troy Brown Jr. 4.00 10.00
39 Jarred Vanderbilt 6.00 15.00
40 Dzanan Musa 3.00 8.00

2018-19 Panini Contenders Winning Tickets

1 Alonzo Mourning 1.00 2.50
2 Kevin Love .50 1.25
3 Ben Wallace .50 1.25
4 Jerry West 1.25 3.00
5 Hakeem Olajuwon .75 2.00
6 Dirk Nowitzki 1.50 4.00
7 Pau Gasol 1.00 2.50
8 Kevin Durant 2.50 6.00
9 Rajon Rondo .75 2.00
10 Draymond Green .75 2.00
11 Tony Parker 1.00 2.50
12 Gary Payton .75 2.00
13 David Robinson 1.25 3.00
14 Clyde Drexler 1.00 2.50
15 Kawhi Leonard 1.50 4.00
16 Jason Kidd 1.00 2.50
17 Paul Pierce 1.00 2.50
18 Stephen Curry 5.00 12.00
19 Robert Horry .60 1.50
20 LeBron James 5.00 12.00
21 Richard Hamilton .50 1.25
22 Tim Duncan 1.50 4.00
23 Scottie Pippen 1.50 4.00
24 Andre Iguodala .50 1.25
25 Larry Bird 2.50 6.00
26 Kobe Bryant 5.00 12.00
27 Kevin Garnett 1.50 4.00
28 Klay Thompson 1.50 4.00
29 Shaquille O'Neal 2.00 5.00
30 Kyrie Irving 1.50 4.00
31 Chauncey Billups .75 2.00
32 Dwyane Wade 1.25 3.00
33 Dennis Rodman 6.00 15.00
34 Ray Allen .75 2.00
35 Magic Johnson 2.50 6.00

2018-19 Panini Contenders Winning Tickets Cracked Ice

*CRACKED ICE: 2X TO 5X BASIC
STATED PRINT RUN 25 SER.#'d SETS
18 Stephen Curry 20.00 50.00
20 LeBron James 40.00 100.00
26 Kobe Bryant 20.00 50.00

2019-20 Panini Contenders

EXCHANGE DEADLINE 6/27/2021
*GAME TICKET GREEN: .6X TO 1.5X BASIC
*GAME TICKET RED: .6X TO 1.5X BASIC
*PLAYOFF TCKT 1-100/199: 1X TO 2.5X BASIC
*PLAYOFF TCKT AU/99: .4X TO 1X BASIC
*SEMIFINAL TCKT/149: 1.2X TO 3X BASIC
*CONF FINALS TCKT/125: 1.2X TO 3X BASIC
*GAME TICKET BLUE/99: 1.2X TO 3X BASIC
*FINALS TCKT/65: 1.5X TO 4X BASIC
*FINALS TCKT AU/49: .5X TO 1.2X BASIC
*GAME TCKT PURPLE/49: 2X TO 5X BASIC
CRACKED ICE 1-100/25: 7.5X TO 20X BASIC
*CRACKED ICE AU/25: 1.5X TO 4X BASIC
1 Trae Young .75 2.00
2 Aaron Gordon .30 .75
3 Al Horford .30 .75
4 Allonzo Trier .20 .50
5 Andre Drummond .25 .60
6 Andrew Wiggins .40 1.00
7 Anthony Davis .75 2.00
8 Bam Adebayo .50 1.25
9 Ben Simmons .30 .75
10 Blake Griffin .30 .75
11 Bradley Beal .40 1.00
12 Brandon Ingram .30 .75
13 Brook Lopez .25 .60
14 Buddy Hield .25 .60
15 Caris LeVert .25 .60
16 Chris Paul .60 1.50
17 CJ McCollum .30 .75
18 Clint Capela .25 .60
19 Collin Sexton .40 1.00
20 Damian Lillard .75 2.00
21 D'Angelo Russell .25 .60
22 De'Aaron Fox .50 1.25
23 Deandre Ayton .30 .75
24 DeAndre Jordan .25 .60
25 DeMar DeRozan .40 1.00
26 DeMarcus Cousins .25 .60
27 Dennis Smith Jr. .20 .50
28 Derrick Rose .60 1.50
29 Devin Booker .07 .20
30 Domantas Sabonis .40 1.00
31 Donovan Mitchell .60 1.50
32 Draymond Green .40 1.00
33 Giannis Antetokounmpo 1.50 4.00
34 Goran Dragic .25 .60
35 Gordon Hayward .25 .60
36 Hassan Whiteside .20 .50
37 Jae Crowder .20 .50
38 Jahlil Okafor .20 .50
39 Jamal Murray .50 1.25
40 James Harden .60 1.50
41 Jaren Jackson Jr. .50 1.25
42 Jaylen Brown .50 1.25
43 Jayson Tatum 1.25 3.00
44 Jimmy Butler .60 1.50
45 Joel Embiid .60 1.50
46 John Collins .30 .75
47 John Wall .40 1.00
48 Jonas Valanciunas .25 .60
49 Jonathan Isaac .30 .75
50 Jordan Clarkson .30 .75
51 Josh Hart .25 .60
52 Josh Okogie .25 .60
53 Julius Randle .40 1.00
54 Karl-Anthony Towns .50 1.25
55 Kawhi Leonard .75 2.00
56 Kemba Walker .25 .60
57 Kevin Durant 1.00 2.50
58 Kevin Huerter .30 .75
59 Kevin Knox II .20 .50
60 Kevin Love .30 .75
61 Khris Middleton .30 .75
62 Klay Thompson .75 2.00
63 Kris Dunn .20 .50
64 Kristaps Porzingis .40 1.00
65 Kyle Kuzma .40 1.00
66 Kyle Lowry .30 .75
67 Kyrie Irving .60 1.50
68 LaMarcus Aldridge .30 .75
69 Lauri Markkanen .40 1.00
70 LeBron James 2.50 6.00
71 Lonnie Walker IV .25 .60
72 Lonzo Ball .30 .75
73 Luka Doncic 2.00 5.00
74 Malcolm Brogdon .25 .60
75 Malik Monk .30 .75
76 Marc Gasol .30 .75
77 Marvin Bagley III .25 .60
78 Michael Porter Jr. .50 1.25
79 Mike Conley .25 .60
80 Miles Bridges .30 .75
81 Mitchell Robinson .30 .75
82 Mo Bamba .25 .60
83 Montrezl Harrell .25 .60
84 Myles Turner .30 .75
85 Nikola Jokic 1.50 4.00
86 Nikola Vucevic .25 .60
87 Pascal Siakam .50 1.25
88 Paul George .50 1.25
89 Rudy Gobert .40 1.00
90 Russell Westbrook .50 1.25
91 Shai Gilgeous-Alexander 1.50 4.00
92 Stephen Curry 2.50 6.00
93 Steven Adams .25 .60
94 Terry Rozier .25 .60
95 Thomas Bryant .25 .60
96 Tim Hardaway Jr. .20 .50
97 Tobias Harris .25 .60
98 Tyler Johnson .20 .50
99 Victor Oladipo .25 .60
100 Zach LaVine .50 1.25
101 Jordan Poole AU RC 15.00 40.00
102 Jaxson Hayes AU RC 6.00 15.00
103 Alen Smailagic AU RC 4.00 10.00
104 Matisse Thybulle AU RC 8.00 20.00
105 Talen Horton-Tucker AU RC 6.00 15.00
106 Nickeil Alexander-Walker AU RC 6.00 15.00
107 Keldon Johnson AU RC 12.00 30.00
108 Zion Williamson AU RC 300.00 600.00
109 Grant Williams AU RC 6.00 15.00
110 De'Andre Hunter AU RC 15.00 40.00
111 Kevin Porter Jr. AU RC 8.00 20.00
112 Bol Bol AU RC 10.00 25.00
113 Cody Martin AU RC 6.00 15.00
114 Nassir Little AU RC 6.00 15.00
115 Jaylen Nowell AU RC 5.00 12.00
116 Sekou Doumbouya AU RC 4.00 10.00
117 Luka Samanic AU RC 5.00 12.00
118 Ja Morant AU RC 400.00 800.00
119 Ty Jerome AU RC 8.00 20.00
120 Cam Reddish AU RC 6.00 15.00
121 KZ Okpala AU RC 5.00 12.00
122 Cameron Johnson AU RC 10.00 25.00
123 Ignas Brazdeikis AU RC 5.00 12.00
124 Romeo Langford AU RC 4.00 10.00
125 Quinndary Weatherspoon AU RC 4.00 10.00
126 Carsen Edwards AU RC 5.00 12.00
127 Admiral Schofield AU RC 5.00 12.00
128 RJ Barrett AU RC 15.00 40.00
129 Dylan Windler AU RC 5.00 12.00
130 Jarrett Culver AU RC 4.00 10.00
131 Mfiondu Kabengele AU RC 5.00 12.00
132 PJ Washington Jr. AU RC 12.00 30.00
133 Isaiah Roby AU RC 4.00 10.00
134 Brandon Clarke AU RC 8.00 20.00
135 Terance Mann AU RC 8.00 20.00
136 Goga Bitadze AU RC 6.00 15.00
137 Bruno Fernando AU RC 4.00 10.00
138 Rui Hachimura AU RC 15.00 40.00
139 Eric Paschall AU RC 5.00 12.00
140 Coby White AU RC 40.00 100.00
141 Darius Bazley AU RC 4.00 10.00
142 Tyler Herro AU RC 40.00 100.00
143 Kyle Guy AU RC 4.00 10.00
144 Chuma Okeke AU RC 6.00 15.00
145 Tremont Waters AU RC 5.00 12.00
146 Amir Coffey AU RC 6.00 15.00
147 Marial Shayok AU RC 4.00 10.00
148 Nicolas Claxton AU RC 8.00 20.00
149 Jalen Lecque AU RC 4.00 10.00
150 Brian Bowen II AU RC 4.00 10.00
151 Justin Robinson AU RC 4.00 10.00
152 Jaylen Hoard AU RC 4.00 10.00
153 Jordan Bone AU RC 4.00 10.00
154 Josh Reaves AU RC 4.00 10.00
155 Zach Norvell Jr. AU RC 5.00 12.00
156 Ky Bowman AU RC 5.00 12.00
157 Luguentz Dort AU RC 15.00 40.00
158 Jalen McDaniels AU RC 10.00 25.00
159 Naz Reid AU RC 30.00 80.00
160 Justin James AU RC 4.00 10.00
161 Robert Franks AU RC 4.00 10.00
162 Miye Oni AU RC 4.00 10.00
163 Tacko Fall AU RC 5.00 12.00
164 Louis King AU RC 5.00 12.00
165 Daniel Gafford AU RC 8.00 20.00

2019-20 Panini Contenders Photo Variations

*VAR: .4X TO 1X BASIC
EXCHANGE DEADLINE 6/27/2021

2019-20 Panini Contenders Premium

*PREMIUM AU: .5X TO 1.2X BASIC
EXCHANGE DEADLINE 6/27/2021
108 Zion Williamson AU 2,000.00 4,000.00

2019-20 Panini Contenders Premium Blue Shimmer

*PREMIUM BLUE SHIMMER AU: 1.2X TO 3X BASIC
STATED PRINT RUN 20 SER.#'d SETS
EXCHANGE DEADLINE 6/27/2021
104 Matisse Thybulle AU 100.00 250.00
108 Zion Williamson AU 6,000.00 10,000.00
110 De'Andre Hunter AU 100.00 250.00
111 Kevin Porter Jr. AU 15.00 40.00
116 Sekou Doumbouya AU 8.00 20.00
118 Ja Morant AU 2,000.00 5,000.00
132 PJ Washington Jr. AU 100.00 250.00
134 Brandon Clarke AU 100.00 250.00
136 Goga Bitadze AU 20.00 50.00

2019-20 Panini Contenders Premium Green Shimmer

*PREMIUM AU: .75X TO 2X BASIC
EXCHANGE DEADLINE 6/27/2021
101 Jordan Poole AU 25.00 60.00
104 Matisse Thybulle AU 60.00 150.00
108 Zion Williamson AU 3,000.00 6,000.00
110 De'Andre Hunter AU 60.00 150.00
111 Kevin Porter Jr. AU 10.00 25.00
116 Sekou Doumbouya AU 5.00 12.00
118 Ja Morant AU 1,000.00 3,000.00
132 PJ Washington Jr. AU 60.00 150.00
134 Brandon Clarke AU 60.00 150.00
136 Goga Bitadze AU 12.00 30.00

2019-20 Panini Contenders Semifinal Ticket

*SEMIFINAL TCKT: 1.2X TO 3X BASIC
STATED PRINT RUN 149 SER.#'d SETS

2019-20 Panini Contenders '19 Draft Class Contenders

*CRACKED ICE/25: 4X TO 10X BASIC
1 Zion Williamson 2.50 6.00
2 Ja Morant 3.00 8.00
3 RJ Barrett 1.25 3.00
4 De'Andre Hunter 1.25 3.00
5 Darius Garland 1.25 3.00
6 Jarrett Culver .30 .75
7 Coby White 1.00 2.50
8 Jaxson Hayes .50 1.25
9 Rui Hachimura 1.25 3.00
10 Cam Reddish .50 1.25
11 Cameron Johnson .75 2.00
12 PJ Washington Jr. 1.00 2.50
13 Tyler Herro 1.50 4.00
14 Romeo Langford .30 .75
15 Sekou Doumbouya .30 .75
16 Carsen Edwards .40 1.00
17 Nickeil Alexander-Walker .50 1.25
18 Goga Bitadze .50 1.25
19 Luka Samanic .40 1.00
20 Matisse Thybulle .60 1.50
21 Brandon Clarke .60 1.50
22 Grant Williams .50 1.25
23 Ty Jerome .60 1.50
24 Nassir Little .50 1.25
25 Dylan Windler .40 1.00
26 Jordan Poole 1.25 3.00
27 Keldon Johnson 1.00 2.50
28 Kevin Porter Jr. .60 1.50
29 Darius Bazley .30 .75
30 Bol Bol .75 2.00

2019-20 Panini Contenders Contenders Autographs

STATED PRINT RUN 49-199 SER.#'d SETS
EXCHANGE DEADLINE 6/27/2021
1 Luka Doncic/99 300.00 600.00
2 Nemanja Bjelica/199 3.00 8.00
3 Eric Bledsoe/99 4.00 10.00
4 Quinn Cook/199 4.00 10.00
5 Malcolm Brogdon/99 4.00 10.00
6 Reggie Jackson/99 4.00 10.00
7 Andrew Wiggins/49 8.00 20.00
8 Jonas Valanciunas/199 4.00 10.00
9 LaMarcus Aldridge/49 6.00 15.00
10 Michael Porter Jr./199 8.00 20.00
11 Danilo Gallinari/99 4.00 10.00
12 Rudy Gobert/199 6.00 15.00
13 Julius Randle/99 6.00 15.00
14 Joe Harris/199 4.00 10.00
15 Pascal Siakam/99 10.00 25.00
16 Kevin Knox II/99 3.00 8.00
17 DeMarcus Cousins/49 5.00 12.00
18 Montrezl Harrell/199 4.00 10.00
19 Lauri Markkanen/49 8.00 20.00
20 Evan Turner/199 3.00 8.00
21 Nikola Vucevic/99 4.00 10.00
22 Gerald Green/199 4.00 10.00
23 Avery Bradley/99 3.00 8.00
24 Jarrett Allen/199 5.00 12.00
25 Willie Cauley-Stein/99 3.00 8.00
26 Danny Green/199 4.00 10.00
27 Markelle Fultz/49 5.00 12.00
28 Thaddeus Young/199 3.00 8.00
29 Khris Middleton/99 5.00 12.00
30 Dario Saric/199 4.00 10.00
31 Kentavious Caldwell-Pope/99 4.00 10.00
32 Domantas Sabonis/199 6.00 15.00
33 Otto Porter Jr./99 3.00 8.00
34 Kelly Olynyk/199 3.00 8.00
35 Nerlens Noel/99 3.00 8.00
36 Allonzo Trier/199 3.00 8.00
37 Trae Young/49 100.00 250.00
38 Terrence Ross/199 5.00 12.00
39 Alex Len/99 3.00 8.00
40 Ersan Ilyasova/199 3.00 8.00

2019-20 Panini Contenders Contenders Autographs Bronze

STATED PRINT RUN 25 SER.#'d SETS
EXCHANGE DEADLINE 6/27/2021
1 Luka Doncic 600.00 1,200.00
10 Michael Porter Jr. 12.00 30.00
37 Trae Young 150.00 400.00

2019-20 Panini Contenders Front Row Seat

1 Jayson Tatum 2.50 6.00
2 Giannis Antetokounmpo 3.00 8.00
3 LeBron James 5.00 12.00
4 Anthony Davis 1.50 4.00
5 James Harden 1.25 3.00
6 Russell Westbrook 1.00 2.50
7 Paul George 1.00 2.50
8 Kawhi Leonard 1.50 4.00
9 Nikola Jokic 3.00 8.00
10 Trae Young 1.50 4.00
11 Luka Doncic 4.00 10.00
12 Ben Simmons .60 1.50
13 Joel Embiid 1.25 3.00
14 Kyrie Irving 1.25 3.00
15 Donovan Mitchell 1.25 3.00
16 De'Aaron Fox 1.00 2.50
17 Bradley Beal .75 2.00
18 Devin Booker .15 .40
19 Jimmy Butler 1.25 3.00
20 Stephen Curry 5.00 12.00

2019-20 Panini Contenders Front Row Seat Cracked Ice

*CRACKED ICE: 1.5X TO 4X BASIC
STATED PRINT RUN 25 SER.#'d SETS
2 Giannis Antetokounmpo 12.00 30.00
3 LeBron James 75.00 200.00
10 Trae Young 20.00 50.00
11 Luka Doncic 40.00 100.00

2019-20 Panini Contenders Kobe Bryant Autographs

COMMON CARD 800.00 1,500.00

2019-20 Panini Contenders Legendary Contenders

COMMON CARD .60 1.50
SEMISTARS .75 2.00
UNLISTED STARS 1.00 2.50
1 Kobe Bryant 12.00 30.00
2 Bill Russell 3.00 8.00
3 Kareem Abdul-Jabbar 3.00 8.00
4 Shaquille O'Neal 4.00 10.00
5 Larry Bird 4.00 10.00
6 Walt Frazier 1.50 4.00
7 Magic Johnson 3.00 8.00
8 Dominique Wilkins 1.50 4.00
9 Wilt Chamberlain 4.00 10.00
10 Hakeem Olajuwon 2.00 5.00
11 Allen Iverson 2.50 6.00
12 David Robinson 2.00 5.00
13 Dwyane Wade 2.00 5.00
14 Dirk Nowitzki 2.50 6.00
15 Scottie Pippen 2.50 6.00
16 Shawn Kemp 1.50 4.00
17 Pete Maravich 2.50 6.00
18 Kevin Garnett 2.50 6.00
19 Grant Hill 1.50 4.00
20 Ray Allen 1.50 4.00
21 Chris Webber 1.25 3.00
22 Tim Duncan 2.50 6.00
23 Dennis Rodman 2.50 6.00
24 Charles Barkley 2.00 5.00
25 Robert Parish 1.25 3.00

2019-20 Panini Contenders Legendary Contenders Autographs

COMMON p/r 99-199 3.00 8.00
SEMIS p/r 99-199 4.00 10.00
UNLISTED p/r 99-199 5.00 12.00
COMMON p/r 49 4.00 10.00
SEMIS p/r 49 5.00 12.00
UNLISTED p/r 49 6.00 15.00
STATED PRINT RUN 49-199 SER.#'d SETS
EXCHANGE DEADLINE 6/27/2021
*BRONZE: .75X TO 2X p/r 99-199
*BRONZE: .6X TO 1.5X p/r 49
1 Jerome Williams/199 3.00 8.00
2 Lenny Wilkens/99 6.00 15.00
3 Mychal Thompson/199 3.00 8.00
4 Chuck Person/199 4.00 10.00
5 Tom Chambers/199 5.00 12.00
6 Magic Johnson/49 60.00 150.00
7 Toni Kukoc/199 6.00 15.00
8 Chris Bosh/49 8.00 20.00
9 Tree Rollins/199 3.00 8.00
10 Jalen Rose/99 4.00 10.00
11 Charlie Ward/199 4.00 10.00
12 George Gervin/99 8.00 20.00
13 Antonio McDyess/199 4.00 10.00
14 Elvin Hayes/199 6.00 15.00
15 Alvan Adams/199 3.00 8.00
16 Jerry West/49 25.00 60.00
17 Cedric Maxwell/199 4.00 10.00
18 Artis Gilmore/99 6.00 15.00
19 Rashard Lewis/199 4.00 10.00
20 Latrell Sprewell/99 6.00 15.00
21 Charlie Scott/199 4.00 10.00
22 Carlos Boozer/199 4.00 10.00
23 Rudy Tomjanovich/199 4.00 10.00
24 Nate McMillan/199 4.00 10.00
25 Bill Cartwright/199 4.00 10.00
26 Hakeem Olajuwon/49 25.00 60.00
27 Glen Rice/199 4.00 10.00
28 Kenny Smith/99 4.00 10.00
29 Sidney Moncrief/199 5.00 12.00
30 Robert Parish/99 6.00 15.00
31 Sarunas Marciulionis/199 3.00 8.00
32 Shane Battier/199 4.00 10.00
33 Scott Skiles/199 4.00 10.00
34 Sam Cassell/199 4.00 10.00
35 Alex English/199 6.00 15.00
36 David Robinson/49 25.00 60.00
37 M.L. Carr/199 5.00 12.00
38 Jason Terry/99 4.00 10.00
39 Paul Silas/199 4.00 10.00
40 Louie Dampier/99 6.00 15.00

2019-20 Panini Contenders License to Dominate

1 Jayson Tatum 30.00 80.00
2 LeBron James 400.00 800.00
3 Kevin Durant 40.00 100.00
4 Anthony Davis 30.00 80.00
5 James Harden 25.00 60.00
6 Stephen Curry 60.00 150.00
7 Giannis Antetokounmpo 60.00 150.00
8 Joel Embiid 25.00 60.00
9 Russell Westbrook 20.00 50.00
10 Paul George 20.00 50.00
11 Kawhi Leonard 30.00 80.00
12 Damian Lillard 30.00 80.00
13 Chris Paul 25.00 60.00
14 Jimmy Butler 25.00 60.00
15 Rudy Gobert 15.00 40.00
16 Ben Simmons 12.00 30.00
17 Klay Thompson 30.00 80.00
18 Victor Oladipo 10.00 25.00
19 Karl-Anthony Towns 20.00 50.00
20 Nikola Jokic 60.00 150.00
21 Kyrie Irving 25.00 60.00
22 John Wall 15.00 40.00
23 Kemba Walker 25.00 60.00
24 Bradley Beal 15.00 40.00
25 Kevin Love 12.00 30.00
26 Blake Griffin 12.00 30.00
27 Devin Booker 3.00 8.00
28 Trae Young 125.00 300.00
29 Luka Doncic 200.00 500.00
30 Donovan Mitchell 25.00 60.00

2019-20 Panini Contenders Lottery Ticket

*RETAIL: .4X TO 1X BASIC
1 Zion Williamson 20.00 50.00
2 Ja Morant 8.00 20.00
3 RJ Barrett 1.50 4.00
4 De'Andre Hunter 1.50 4.00
5 Darius Garland 1.50 4.00
6 Jarrett Culver .40 1.00
7 Coby White 1.25 3.00
8 Jaxson Hayes .60 1.50
9 Rui Hachimura 1.50 4.00
10 Cam Reddish .60 1.50
11 Cameron Johnson 1.00 2.50
12 PJ Washington Jr. 1.25 3.00
13 Tyler Herro 2.00 5.00
14 Romeo Langford .40 1.00

2019-20 Panini Contenders Lottery Ticket Cracked Ice

*CRACKED ICE: 3X TO 8X BASIC
STATED PRINT RUN 25 SER.#'D SETS
1 Zion Williamson 400.00 800.00
2 Ja Morant 200.00 500.00
3 RJ Barrett 60.00 150.00
4 De'Andre Hunter 12.00 30.00
5 Darius Garland 12.00 30.00
6 Jarrett Culver 3.00 8.00
7 Coby White 60.00 150.00
8 Jaxson Hayes 10.00 25.00
9 Rui Hachimura 20.00 50.00
10 Cam Reddish 5.00 12.00
11 Cameron Johnson 10.00 25.00
12 PJ Washington Jr. 12.00 30.00
13 Tyler Herro 60.00 150.00

2019-20 Panini Contenders MVP Contenders

COMMON CARD .60 1.50
SEMISTARS .75 2.00
UNLISTED STARS 1.00 2.50
1 Giannis Antetokounmpo 5.00 12.00
2 Stephen Curry 8.00 20.00
3 LeBron James 12.00 30.00
4 Nikola Jokic 5.00 12.00
5 Kawhi Leonard 2.50 6.00
6 Anthony Davis 2.50 6.00
7 James Harden 2.00 5.00
8 Joel Embiid 2.00 5.00
9 Paul George 1.50 4.00
10 Damian Lillard 2.50 6.00
11 Kyrie Irving 2.00 5.00
12 Donovan Mitchell 2.00 5.00
13 Luka Doncic 20.00 50.00
14 Ben Simmons 1.00 2.50
15 Blake Griffin 1.00 2.50
16 Russell Westbrook 1.50 4.00
17 Pascal Siakam 1.50 4.00
18 Kemba Walker .75 2.00
19 Bradley Beal 1.25 3.00
20 Trae Young 8.00 20.00
21 Karl-Anthony Towns 1.50 4.00
22 Victor Oladipo .75 2.00
23 Devin Booker .25 .60
24 Jimmy Butler 2.00 5.00
25 Julius Randle 1.25 3.00

2019-20 Panini Contenders MVP Contenders Autographs

COMMON p/r 99 3.00 8.00
SEMIS p/r 99 4.00 10.00
UNLISTED p/r 99 5.00 12.00
COMMON p/r 46-49 4.00 10.00
SEMIS p/r 46-49 5.00 12.00
UNLISTED p/r 46-49 6.00 15.00
STATED PRINT RUN 46-99 SER.#'d SETS
EXCHANGE DEADLINE 6/27/2021
1 Damian Lillard/49 20.00 50.00
2 Kyrie Irving/49 15.00 40.00
3 Giannis Antetokounmpo/49 75.00 200.00
4 Anthony Davis/49 30.00 80.00
5 Kawhi Leonard/49 30.00 80.00
6 Karl-Anthony Towns/49 10.00 25.00
7 Donovan Mitchell/49 20.00 50.00
8 Bradley Beal/46 8.00 20.00
9 Nikola Jokic/99 125.00 300.00
10 Luka Doncic/99 500.00 1,000.00

2019-20 Panini Contenders MVP Contenders Autographs Bronze

*BRONZE: .6X TO 1.5X p/r 99
*BRONZE: .5X TO 1.2X p/r 46-49
STATED PRINT RUN 25 SER.#'d SETS
EXCHANGE DEADLINE 6/27/2021
5 Kawhi Leonard 50.00 120.00
10 Luka Doncic 1,000.00 2,000.00

2019-20 Panini Contenders Permit to Dominate

1 Brandon Clarke 40.00 100.00
2 Luka Samanic 10.00 25.00
3 Nassir Little 20.00 50.00
4 Nickeil Alexander-Walker 12.00 30.00
5 Carsen Edwards 10.00 25.00
6 Sekou Doumbouya 60.00 150.00
7 Romeo Langford 8.00 20.00
8 Tyler Herro 50.00 120.00
9 PJ Washington Jr. 25.00 60.00
10 Cameron Johnson 20.00 50.00
11 Cam Reddish 12.00 30.00
12 Rui Hachimura 25.00 60.00
13 Jaxson Hayes 12.00 30.00
14 Coby White 50.00 120.00
15 Jarrett Culver 8.00 20.00
16 Darius Garland 25.00 60.00
17 De'Andre Hunter 40.00 100.00
18 RJ Barrett 60.00 150.00
19 Ja Morant 150.00 400.00
20 Zion Williamson 400.00 800.00

2019-20 Panini Contenders Photo Variation Autographs Premium Green Shimmer

*PREMIUM GREEN SHIMMER AU: .75X TO 2X BASIC
EXCHANGE DEADLINE 6/27/2021
101 Jordan Poole AU 25.00 60.00
104 Matisse Thybulle AU 60.00 150.00
108 Zion Williamson AU 3,000.00 6,000.00
110 De'Andre Hunter AU 60.00 150.00
111 Kevin Porter Jr. AU 10.00 25.00
116 Sekou Doumbouya AU 5.00 12.00
118 Ja Morant AU 1,000.00 3,000.00
132 PJ Washington Jr. AU 60.00 150.00
134 Brandon Clarke AU 60.00 150.00
136 Goga Bitadze AU 12.00 30.00

2019-20 Panini Contenders Photo Variation Autographs The Finals Ticket

101 Jordan Poole AU 20.00 50.00
108 Zion Williamson AU 3,000.00 6,000.00
110 De'Andre Hunter AU 30.00 80.00
111 Kevin Porter Jr. AU 8.00 20.00
116 Sekou Doumbouya AU 4.00 10.00
118 Ja Morant AU 800.00 1,500.00
132 PJ Washington Jr. AU 30.00 80.00
134 Brandon Clarke AU 50.00 120.00

2019-20 Panini Contenders Photo Variations Autographs

*VAR: .4X TO 1X BASIC
EXCHANGE DEADLINE 6/27/2021

2019-20 Panini Contenders Photo Variations Autographs Cracked Ice Ticket

*CRACKED ICE AU: 1.5X TO 4X BASIC
STATED PRINT RUN 25 SER.#'d SETS
EXCHANGE DEADLINE 6/27/2021
101 Jordan Poole AU 60.00 150.00
102 Jaxson Hayes AU 125.00 300.00
103 Alen Smailagic AU 75.00 200.00
104 Matisse Thybulle AU 125.00 300.00
106 Nickeil Alexander-Walker AU 60.00 150.00
107 Keldon Johnson AU 60.00 150.00
108 Zion Williamson AU 6,000.00 10,000.00
109 Grant Williams AU 50.00 120.00
110 De'Andre Hunter AU 150.00 400.00
111 Kevin Porter Jr. AU 20.00 50.00
112 Bol Bol AU 100.00 250.00
113 Cody Martin AU 30.00 80.00
114 Nassir Little AU 75.00 200.00
115 Jaylen Nowell AU 30.00 80.00
116 Sekou Doumbouya AU 10.00 25.00
118 Ja Morant AU 2,000.00 5,000.00
119 Ty Jerome AU 30.00 80.00
121 KZ Okpala AU 12.00 30.00
122 Cameron Johnson AU 50.00 120.00
123 Ignas Brazdeikis AU 30.00 80.00
125 Quinndary Weatherspoon AU 25.00 60.00
127 Admiral Schofield AU 30.00 80.00
128 RJ Barrett AU 800.00 1,500.00
129 Dylan Windler AU 12.00 30.00
131 Mfiondu Kabengele AU 12.00 30.00
132 PJ Washington Jr. AU 125.00 300.00
133 Isaiah Roby AU 12.00 30.00
134 Brandon Clarke AU 150.00 400.00
135 Terance Mann AU 20.00 50.00
136 Goga Bitadze AU 40.00 100.00
137 Bruno Fernando AU 30.00 80.00
138 Rui Hachimura AU 200.00 500.00
140 Coby White AU 200.00 500.00
141 Darius Bazley AU 10.00 25.00
142 Tyler Herro AU 400.00 800.00
143 Kyle Guy AU 40.00 100.00
144 Chuma Okeke AU 100.00 250.00
145 Tremont Waters AU 40.00 100.00

2019-20 Panini Contenders Photo Variations Autographs Playoff Ticket

101 Jordan Poole AU 12.00 30.00
102 Jaxson Hayes AU 20.00 50.00
103 Alen Smailagic AU 12.00 30.00
104 Matisse Thybulle AU 25.00 60.00
106 Nickeil Alexander-Walker AU 6.00 15.00
107 Keldon Johnson AU 12.00 30.00
108 Zion Williamson AU 1,500.00 4,500.00
109 Grant Williams AU 6.00 15.00
110 De'Andre Hunter AU 25.00 60.00
111 Kevin Porter Jr. AU 8.00 20.00
112 Bol Bol AU 20.00 50.00
113 Cody Martin AU 6.00 15.00
114 Nassir Little AU 12.00 30.00
115 Jaylen Nowell AU 5.00 12.00
116 Sekou Doumbouya AU 4.00 10.00
118 Ja Morant AU 600.00 1,200.00
119 Ty Jerome AU 8.00 20.00
121 KZ Okpala AU 5.00 12.00
122 Cameron Johnson AU 12.00 30.00
123 Ignas Brazdeikis AU 5.00 12.00
124 Romeo Langford AU 4.00 10.00
125 Quinndary Weatherspoon AU 4.00 10.00
127 Admiral Schofield AU 5.00 12.00
128 RJ Barrett AU 150.00 400.00
129 Dylan Windler AU 5.00 12.00
131 Mfiondu Kabengele AU 5.00 12.00
132 PJ Washington Jr. AU 20.00 50.00
133 Isaiah Roby AU 5.00 12.00
134 Brandon Clarke AU 8.00 20.00
135 Terance Mann AU 8.00 20.00
136 Goga Bitadze AU 6.00 15.00
137 Bruno Fernando AU 5.00 12.00
138 Rui Hachimura AU 125.00 300.00
140 Coby White AU 125.00 300.00
141 Darius Bazley AU 4.00 10.00
142 Tyler Herro AU 125.00 300.00
143 Kyle Guy AU 5.00 12.00
144 Chuma Okeke AU 6.00 15.00
145 Tremont Waters AU 5.00 12.00

2019-20 Panini Contenders Photo Variations Autographs Premium

*PREMIUM AU: .5X TO 1.2X BASIC
EXCHANGE DEADLINE 6/27/2021
101 Jordan Poole AU 10.00 25.00
102 Jaxson Hayes AU 15.00 40.00
103 Alen Smailagic AU 10.00 25.00
104 Matisse Thybulle AU 20.00 50.00
106 Nickeil Alexander-Walker AU 5.00 12.00
107 Keldon Johnson AU 10.00 25.00
108 Zion Williamson AU 2,000.00 4,000.00
109 Grant Williams AU 5.00 12.00
110 De'Andre Hunter AU 20.00 50.00
111 Kevin Porter Jr. AU 6.00 15.00
112 Bol Bol AU 15.00 40.00
113 Cody Martin AU 5.00 12.00
114 Nassir Little AU 10.00 25.00
115 Jaylen Nowell AU 4.00 10.00
116 Sekou Doumbouya AU 3.00 8.00
118 Ja Morant AU 500.00 1,000.00
119 Ty Jerome AU 6.00 15.00
121 KZ Okpala AU 4.00 10.00
122 Cameron Johnson AU 10.00 25.00
123 Ignas Brazdeikis AU 4.00 10.00
124 Romeo Langford AU 3.00 8.00
125 Quinndary Weatherspoon AU 3.00 8.00
126 Carsen Edwards AU 4.00 10.00
127 Admiral Schofield AU 4.00 10.00
128 RJ Barrett AU 125.00 300.00
129 Dylan Windler AU 4.00 10.00
131 Mfiondu Kabengele AU 4.00 10.00
132 PJ Washington Jr. AU 15.00 40.00
133 Isaiah Roby AU 4.00 10.00
134 Brandon Clarke AU 25.00 60.00
135 Terance Mann AU 6.00 15.00
136 Goga Bitadze AU 5.00 12.00
137 Bruno Fernando AU 4.00 10.00
138 Rui Hachimura AU 100.00 250.00
140 Coby White AU 100.00 250.00
141 Darius Bazley AU 3.00 8.00
142 Tyler Herro AU 100.00 250.00

2019-20 Panini Contenders Photo Variations Autographs Premium Blue Shimmer

*PREMIUM BLUE SHIMMER AU: 1.2X TO 3X BASIC
STATED PRINT RUN 20 SER.#'d SETS
EXCHANGE DEADLINE 6/27/2021
104 Matisse Thybulle AU 100.00 250.00
108 Zion Williamson AU 6,000.00 10,000.00

132 PJ Washington Jr. AU 100.00 250.00
134 Brandon Clarke AU 100.00 250.00

2019-20 Panini Contenders Rookie of the Year Contenders
1 Zion Williamson 25.00 60.00
2 Ja Morant 10.00 25.00
3 RJ Barrett 1.50 4.00
4 De'Andre Hunter 1.50 4.00
5 Darius Garland 1.50 4.00
6 Jarrett Culver .40 1.00
7 Coby White 1.25 3.00
8 Jaxson Hayes .60 1.50
9 Rui Hachimura 1.50 4.00
10 Cam Reddish .60 1.50
11 Cameron Johnson 1.00 2.50
12 PJ Washington Jr. 1.25 3.00
13 Tyler Herro 2.00 5.00
14 Romeo Langford .40 1.00
15 Sekou Doumbouya .40 1.00
16 Michael Porter Jr. 1.00 2.50
17 Nickeil Alexander-Walker .60 1.50
18 Brandon Clarke .75 2.00

2019-20 Panini Contenders Rookie of the Year Contenders Cracked Ice
1 Zion Williamson 300.00 600.00
2 Ja Morant 125.00 300.00
3 RJ Barrett 30.00 80.00
6 Jarrett Culver 3.00 8.00
7 Coby White 25.00 60.00
9 Rui Hachimura 25.00 60.00
10 Cam Reddish 5.00 12.00
12 PJ Washington Jr. 10.00 25.00
13 Tyler Herro 25.00 60.00
15 Sekou Doumbouya 3.00 8.00
16 Michael Porter Jr. 10.00 25.00
18 Brandon Clarke 12.00 30.00

2019-20 Panini Contenders Rookie Ticket Dual Swatches
1 D.Hunter/C.Reddish 5.00 12.00
2 R.Barrett/Z.Williamson 20.00 50.00
3 J.Hayes/Z.Williamson 10.00 25.00
4 B.Clarke/R.Hachimura 5.00 12.00
5 C.White/N.Little 4.00 10.00
6 B.Clarke/J.Morant 12.00 30.00
7 J.Culver/D.Hunter 5.00 12.00
8 C.Johnson/C.White 4.00 10.00
9 T.Herro/P.Washington Jr. 6.00 15.00
10 T.Jerome/K.Guy 2.50 6.00

2019-20 Panini Contenders Rookie Ticket Swatches
1 Carsen Edwards 1.50 4.00
2 Cam Reddish 2.00 5.00
3 Admiral Schofield 1.50 4.00
4 Romeo Langford 1.25 3.00
5 Ignas Brazdeikis 1.50 4.00
6 Goga Bitadze 2.00 5.00
7 Ty Jerome 2.50 6.00
8 Zion Williamson 50.00 120.00
9 Jordan Poole 5.00 12.00
10 Jarrett Culver 1.25 3.00
11 Bruno Fernando 1.50 4.00
12 Cameron Johnson 3.00 8.00
13 Jaylen Nowell 1.50 4.00
14 Sekou Doumbouya 1.25 3.00
15 Quinndary Weatherspoon 1.25 3.00
16 Luka Samanic 1.50 4.00
17 Nassir Little 2.00 5.00
18 Ja Morant 15.00 40.00
19 Keldon Johnson 4.00 10.00
20 Coby White 4.00 10.00
21 Cody Martin 2.00 5.00
22 PJ Washington Jr. 4.00 10.00
23 Bol Bol 3.00 8.00
24 Chuma Okeke 2.00 5.00
25 Tremont Waters 1.50 4.00
26 Brandon Clarke 2.50 6.00
27 Dylan Windler 1.50 4.00
28 RJ Barrett 5.00 12.00
29 Kevin Porter Jr. 2.50 6.00
30 Jaxson Hayes 2.00 5.00
31 Eric Paschall 1.50 4.00
32 Tyler Herro 6.00 15.00
33 Isaiah Roby 1.50 4.00
34 Nickeil Alexander-Walker 2.00 5.00
35 Matisse Thybulle 2.50 6.00
36 Grant Williams 2.00 5.00
37 Mfiondu Kabengele 1.50 4.00
38 De'Andre Hunter 5.00 12.00
39 KZ Okpala 1.50 4.00
40 Rui Hachimura 5.00 12.00

2019-20 Panini Contenders Sophomore Contenders Autographs
STATED PRINT RUN 99 SER.#'d SETS
EXCHANGE DEADLINE 6/27/2021
1 Deandre Ayton 30.00 80.00
2 Marvin Bagley III 4.00 10.00
3 Luka Doncic 400.00 800.00
4 Jaren Jackson Jr. 12.00 30.00
5 Trae Young 125.00 300.00
6 Wendell Carter Jr. 5.00 12.00
7 Collin Sexton 6.00 15.00
8 Kevin Knox II 3.00 8.00
9 Michael Porter Jr. 8.00 20.00
10 Jalen Brunson 12.00 30.00

2019-20 Panini Contenders Superstar Die Cuts
1 LeBron James 15.00 40.00
2 Giannis Antetokounmpo 5.00 12.00
3 Stephen Curry 8.00 20.00
4 James Harden 2.00 5.00
5 Russell Westbrook 1.50 4.00
6 Anthony Davis 2.50 6.00
7 Kawhi Leonard 2.50 6.00
8 Zion Williamson 30.00 80.00
9 Ja Morant 15.00 40.00
10 RJ Barrett 2.50 6.00

2019-20 Panini Contenders Superstar Die Cuts Cracked Ice
*CRACKED ICE: 4X TO 10X TO BASIC
STATED PRINT RUN 25 SER.#'d SETS
1 LeBron James 200.00 500.00

2019-20 Panini Contenders Team Quads
1 Reddish/Hunter/Young/Collins 3.00 8.00
2 Walker/Hayward/Brown/Tatum 3.00 8.00
3 Allen/LeVert/Jordan/Irving 1.50 4.00
4 Rozier/Monk/Bridges/Washington Jr. 1.50 4.00
5 LaVine/Markkanen/Carter Jr./White 1.50 4.00
6 Garland/Sexton/Love/Thompson 2.00 5.00
7 Hardaway Jr./Curry/Doncic/Porzingis 5.00 12.00
8 Murray/Beasley/Jokic/Porter Jr. 4.00 10.00
9 Griffin/Kennard Drummond/Doumbouya .75 2.00
10 Curry/Thompson/Russell/Green 6.00 15.00
11 Capela/Gordon/Harden/Westbrook 1.50 4.00
12 Sabonis/Brogdon/Turner/Oladipo 1.00 2.50
13 Leonard/Harrell/Beverley/George 2.00 5.00
14 Davis/Kuzma/Green/James 6.00 15.00
15 Valanciunas/Clarke Morant/Jackson Jr. 5.00 12.00
16 Herro/Butler/Adebayo/Dragic 2.50 6.00
17 Bledsoe/Middleton Antetokounmpo/Lopez 4.00 10.00
18 Wiggins/Culver/Teague/Towns 1.25 3.00
19 Ingram/Hayes/Williamson/Ball 12.00 30.00
20 Smith Jr./Barrett/Robinson/Randle 2.00 5.00
21 Paul/Bazley/Gilgeous-Alexander/Adams 4.00 10.00
22 Fournier/Isaac/Bamba/Gordon .75 2.00
23 Horford/Simmons/Embiid/Harris 1.50 4.00
24 Rubio/Ayton/Booker/Johnson 1.25 3.00
25 Little/McCollum/Whiteside/Lillard 2.00 5.00
26 Hield/Fox/Barnes/Bagley III 1.25 3.00
27 Aldridge/Walker IV/White/DeRozan 1.00 2.50
28 Lowry/Gasol/VanVleet/Siakam 1.25 3.00
29 Ingles/Mitchell/Gobert/Conley 1.50 4.00
30 Beal/Bryant/Wall/Hachimura 2.00 5.00

2019-20 Panini Contenders Team Quads Cracked Ice
*CRACKED ICE: 2X TO 5X BASIC
STATED PRINT RUN 25 SER.#'d SETS
14 Davis/Kuzma/Green/James 60.00 150.00
17 Bledsoe/Middleton Antetokounmpo/Lopez 20.00 50.00
19 Ingram/Hayes/Williamson/Ball 75.00 200.00

2019-20 Panini Contenders Veteran Autographs
COMMON CARD 3.00 8.00
SEMISTARS 4.00 10.00
UNLISTED STARS 5.00 12.00
EXCHANGE DEADLINE 6/27/2021
1 Kobe Bryant 800.00 1,500.00
2 Charles Barkley 75.00 200.00
3 Kevin Durant 60.00 150.00
4 Dwyane Wade 50.00 120.00
5 Kyrie Irving 60.00 150.00
6 Damian Lillard 40.00 100.00
7 Anthony Davis 60.00 150.00
8 Kevin Garnett 75.00 200.00
9 Karl-Anthony Towns 15.00 40.00
10 Shaquille O'Neal 75.00 200.00

2019-20 Panini Contenders Veteran Autographs Playoff Ticket
*PLAYOFF TICKET: .6X TO 1.5X BASIC
STATED PRINT RUN 35 SER.#'d SETS
EXCHANGE DEADLINE 6/27/2021
1 Kobe Bryant 2,500.00 5,000.00

2019-20 Panini Contenders Veteran Autographs Premium
*PREMIUM AU: .5X TO 1.2X BASIC
EXCHANGE DEADLINE 6/27/2021
1 Kobe Bryant 1,000.00 2,000.00

2019-20 Panini Contenders Veteran Autographs Premium Green Shimmer
1 Kobe Bryant 1,000.00 2,000.00

2019-20 Panini Contenders Veteran Autographs The Finals Ticket
*FINALS TICKET: .6X TO 1.5X BASIC
STATED PRINT RUN 25 SER.#'d SETS
EXCHANGE DEADLINE 6/27/2021
1 Kobe Bryant 3,000.00 6,000.00

2019-20 Panini Contenders Winning Ticket
1 Kawhi Leonard 1.50 4.00
2 LeBron James 5.00 12.00
3 Robert Horry .50 1.25
4 Kobe Bryant 5.00 12.00
5 Scottie Pippen 1.50 4.00
6 Shaquille O'Neal 2.50 6.00
7 Stephen Curry 5.00 12.00
8 Chris Bosh .75 2.00
9 Kevin Durant 2.00 5.00
10 Kyrie Irving 1.25 3.00
11 Kareem Abdul-Jabbar 2.00 5.00
12 Bill Russell 2.00 5.00
13 Willis Reed 1.00 2.50
14 Rick Barry .75 2.00
15 Jo Jo White .50 1.25
16 Bill Walton 1.00 2.50
17 Kyle Lowry .60 1.50
18 Dennis Johnson .75 2.00
19 Magic Johnson 2.00 5.00
20 Cedric Maxwell .50 1.25
21 Moses Malone 1.00 2.50
22 Hakeem Olajuwon 1.25 3.00
23 Tim Duncan 1.50 4.00
24 Dwyane Wade 1.25 3.00
25 John Salley .40 1.00
26 Derek Fisher .60 1.50
27 Steve Kerr .75 2.00
28 Bruce Bowen .60 1.50
29 Ron Harper .60 1.50
30 Robert Parish .75 2.00

2019-20 Panini Contenders Winning Ticket Cracked Ice
*CRACKED ICE: 2X TO 5X BASIC
STATED PRINT RUN 25 SER.#'D SETS
1 Kawhi Leonard 20.00 50.00
2 LeBron James 150.00 400.00
4 Kobe Bryant 40.00 100.00
7 Stephen Curry 20.00 50.00
11 Kareem Abdul-Jabbar 8.00 20.00
12 Bill Russell 15.00 40.00
22 Hakeem Olajuwon 8.00 20.00
24 Dwyane Wade 8.00 20.00

2020-21 Panini Contenders
EXCHANGE DEADLINE 11/19/2022
GM TCKT BRNZ: .6X TO 1.5X BASIC
GM TCKT RED: .6X TO 1.5X BASIC
*FIRST ROUND TCKT/149: 1.2X TO 3X BASIC
*SEMIFINAL TICKET/99: 1.5X TO 4X BASIC
1 Kevin Love .40 1.00
2 Bojan Bogdanovic .30 .75
3 Jusuf Nurkic .40 1.00
4 Tyler Herro .75 2.00
5 Trae Young 1.00 2.50
6 Kelly Oubre Jr. .40 1.00
7 Lauri Markkanen .50 1.25
8 Malcolm Brogdon .40 1.00
9 Andrew Wiggins .50 1.25
10 Collin Sexton .40 1.00
11 Joel Embiid 1.00 2.50
12 Eric Gordon .30 .75
13 Khris Middleton .50 1.25
14 Gordon Hayward .40 1.00
15 Zach LaVine .60 1.50
16 Deandre Ayton .40 1.00
17 Damian Lillard 1.00 2.50
18 Bradley Beal .50 1.25
19 Marvin Bagley III .30 .75
20 Stephen Curry 3.00 8.00
21 Brandon Ingram .50 1.25
22 Donovan Mitchell .75 2.00
23 Mitchell Robinson .40 1.00
24 De'Andre Hunter .40 1.00
25 Rui Hachimura .50 1.25
26 Chris Paul .75 2.00
27 Derrick Rose .60 1.50
28 Buddy Hield .40 1.00
29 Caris LeVert .40 1.00
30 Sekou Doumbouya .25 .60
31 Nikola Vucevic .40 1.00
32 Lonzo Ball .50 1.25
33 Jarrett Culver .25 .60
34 Goran Dragic .40 1.00
35 Terry Rozier .40 1.00
36 Jimmy Butler .75 2.00
37 Devin Booker 1.00 2.50
38 D'Angelo Russell .40 1.00
39 Al Horford .40 1.00
40 Steven Adams .40 1.00
41 Draymond Green .50 1.25
42 Kristaps Porzingis .50 1.25
43 Patty Mills .40 1.00
44 Coby White .50 1.25
45 Devonte' Graham .30 .75
46 Markelle Fultz .30 .75
47 Jaren Jackson Jr. .60 1.50
48 Christian Wood .30 .75
49 Kevin Durant 1.50 4.00
50 Paul George .60 1.50
51 Julius Randle .40 1.00
52 Bam Adebayo .60 1.50
53 John Wall .50 1.25
54 Miles Bridges .40 1.00
55 Kyle Lowry .50 1.25
56 Ben Simmons .50 1.25
57 Myles Turner .40 1.00
58 Zion Williamson 1.25 3.00
59 CJ McCollum .40 1.00
60 Russell Westbrook .75 2.00
61 Rudy Gobert .50 1.25
62 Davis Bertans .30 .75
63 John Collins .40 1.00
64 Seth Curry .40 1.00
65 Jamal Murray .60 1.50
66 DeMar DeRozan .50 1.25
67 Karl-Anthony Towns .60 1.50
68 Domantas Sabonis .50 1.25
69 PJ Washington Jr. .40 1.00
70 Tobias Harris .40 1.00
71 Kawhi Leonard 1.00 2.50
72 Klay Thompson 1.00 2.50
73 Kyrie Irving .75 2.00
74 Shai Gilgeous-Alexander 2.00 5.00
75 Ja Morant 1.25 3.00
76 Kemba Walker .40 1.00
77 Jrue Holiday .40 1.00
78 Blake Griffin .40 1.00
79 Andre Drummond .40 1.00
80 RJ Barrett .60 1.50
81 LeBron James 3.00 8.00
82 Victor Oladipo .30 .75
83 Aaron Gordon .40 1.00
84 Jaylen Brown .60 1.50
85 Luka Doncic 2.50 6.00
86 Pascal Siakam .60 1.50
87 Jayson Tatum 1.50 4.00
88 De'Aaron Fox .60 1.50
89 Anthony Davis 1.00 2.50
90 Fred VanVleet .60 1.50
91 Montrezl Harrell .40 1.00
92 Carmelo Anthony .60 1.50
93 Eric Bledsoe .30 .75
94 James Harden .75 2.00
95 LaMarcus Aldridge .40 1.00
96 Nikola Jokic 2.00 5.00
97 Michael Porter Jr. .50 1.25
98 Jonas Valanciunas .30 .75
99 Giannis Antetokounmpo 2.00 5.00
100 Kyle Kuzma .50 1.25
101 Aaron Nesmith AU RC 10.00 25.00
103 Saddiq Bey AU RC 10.00 25.00
104 RJ Hampton AU RC 5.00 12.00
105 Anthony Edwards AU RC 600.00 1,200.00
106 Killian Hayes AU RC 5.00 12.00
107 Onyeka Okongwu AU RC 10.00 25.00
108 Daniel Oturu AU RC 5.00 12.00
109 Jalen Smith AU RC 10.00 25.00
110 Robert Woodard II AU RC 5.00 12.00
111 Cole Anthony AU RC 12.00 30.00
112 Jahmi'us Ramsey AU RC 5.00 12.00
113 Precious Achiuwa AU RC 10.00 25.00
114 Immanuel Quickley AU RC 12.00 30.00
115 James Wiseman AU RC 6.00 15.00
116 Desmond Bane AU RC 15.00 40.00
117 Killian Hayes AU RC 5.00 12.00
118 Theo Maledon AU RC 5.00 12.00
119 Devin Vassell AU RC 15.00 40.00
120 Tre Jones AU RC 8.00 20.00
121 Isaiah Stewart AU RC 10.00 25.00
122 Kenyon Martin Jr. AU RC 8.00 20.00
123 Tyrese Maxey AU RC 150.00 400.00
124 Payton Pritchard AU RC 15.00 40.00
125 LaMelo Ball AU RC 150.00 400.00
126 Tyrell Terry AU RC 4.00 10.00
127 Obi Toppin AU RC 10.00 25.00
128 Xavier Tillman AU RC 6.00 15.00
129 Tyrese Haliburton AU RC 150.00 400.00
130 Jordan Nwora AU RC 6.00 15.00
131 Aleksej Pokusevski AU RC 6.00 15.00
132 Cassius Stanley AU RC 5.00 12.00
133 Zeke Nnaji AU RC 6.00 15.00
134 Udoka Azubuike AU RC 6.00 15.00
135 Patrick Williams AU RC 12.00 30.00
136 Vernon Carey Jr. AU RC 5.00 12.00
137 Deni Avdija AU RC 12.00 30.00
138 Tyler Bey AU RC 5.00 12.00
139 Kira Lewis Jr. AU RC 5.00 12.00
140 Nico Mannion AU RC 5.00 12.00
141 Josh Green AU RC 10.00 25.00
142 Cassius Winston AU RC 5.00 12.00
143 Devon Dotson AU RC 5.00 12.00
144 Jaden McDaniels AU RC 15.00 40.00
145 Isaac Okoro AU RC 8.00 20.00
146 CJ Elleby AU RC 5.00 12.00
147 Saben Lee AU RC 5.00 12.00
148 Nick Richards AU RC 6.00 15.00
149 Skylar Mays AU RC 5.00 12.00
150 Grant Riller AU RC 5.00 12.00
151 Dakota Mathias AU RC 4.00 10.00
152 Paul Reed AU RC 6.00 15.00
153 Sam Merrill AU RC 8.00 20.00
154 Caleb Martin AU RC 10.00 25.00
155 Reggie Perry AU RC 5.00 12.00
156 Karim Mane AU RC 4.00 10.00
157 Mason Jones AU RC 4.00 10.00
158 Isaiah Joe AU RC 6.00 15.00
159 Ashton Hagans AU RC 6.00 15.00
160 Nathan Knight AU RC 5.00 12.00
161 Jae'Sean Tate AU RC 6.00 15.00
162 Killian Tillie AU RC 6.00 15.00
163 Markus Howard AU RC 6.00 15.00
164 Naji Marshall AU RC 5.00 12.00
165 Lamar Stevens AU RC 6.00 15.00

2020-21 Panini Contenders Conference Finals Ticket
*CONFERENCE FINALS: 1.5X TO 4X BASIC
STATED PRINT RUN 75 SER.#'d SETS
5 Trae Young 10.00 25.00
20 Stephen Curry 15.00 40.00
26 Chris Paul 8.00 20.00
37 Devin Booker 12.00 30.00
58 Zion Williamson 20.00 50.00
75 Ja Morant 15.00 40.00
81 LeBron James 20.00 50.00
85 Luka Doncic 20.00 50.00
99 Giannis Antetokounmpo 12.00 30.00

2020-21 Panini Contenders Cracked Ice Ticket
STATED PRINT RUN 25 SER.#'d SETS
EXCHANGE DEADLINE 11/19/2022
5 Trae Young 30.00 80.00
20 Stephen Curry 75.00 200.00
26 Chris Paul 20.00 50.00
37 Devin Booker 40.00 100.00
58 Zion Williamson 75.00 200.00
75 Ja Morant 60.00 150.00
81 LeBron James 150.00 400.00
85 Luka Doncic 150.00 400.00
87 Jayson Tatum 30.00 80.00
99 Giannis Antetokounmpo 40.00 100.00
101 Aaron Nesmith AU 100.00 250.00
103 Saddiq Bey AU 200.00 500.00
109 Jalen Smith AU 60.00 150.00
111 Cole Anthony AU 200.00 500.00
113 Precious Achiuwa AU 60.00 150.00
119 Devin Vassell AU 150.00 400.00
124 Payton Pritchard AU 150.00 400.00
125 LaMelo Ball AU 3,000.00 6,000.00
135 Patrick Williams AU 300.00 600.00
139 Kira Lewis Jr. AU 100.00 250.00
140 Nico Mannion AU 75.00 200.00
143 Devon Dotson AU 40.00 100.00
144 Jaden McDaniels AU 125.00 300.00
145 Isaac Okoro AU 150.00 400.00
161 Jae'Sean Tate AU 100.00 250.00
163 Markus Howard AU 60.00 150.00

2020-21 Panini Contenders Game Ticket Blue
*GM TCK BLUE: 1.5X TO 4X BASIC
STATED PRINT RUN 49 SER.#'d SETS
20 Stephen Curry 12.00 30.00
26 Chris Paul 8.00 20.00
37 Devin Booker 8.00 20.00
58 Zion Williamson 12.00 30.00
75 Ja Morant 12.00 30.00
81 LeBron James 15.00 40.00
85 Luka Doncic 15.00 40.00

2020-21 Panini Contenders Game Ticket Purple
*GM TCK PRPL: 2.5X TO 6X BASIC
STATED PRINT RUN 25 SER.#'d SETS
20 Stephen Curry 25.00 60.00
26 Chris Paul 15.00 40.00
37 Devin Booker 15.00 40.00
58 Zion Williamson 25.00 60.00
75 Ja Morant 25.00 60.00
81 LeBron James 40.00 100.00
85 Luka Doncic 40.00 100.00

2020-21 Panini Contenders Opening Night Ticket
OPEN NGT TCK: 4X TO 10X BASIC
STATED PRINT RUN 25 SER.#'d SETS
5 Trae Young 30.00 80.00
20 Stephen Curry 75.00 200.00
26 Chris Paul 20.00 50.00
37 Devin Booker 40.00 100.00
58 Zion Williamson 75.00 200.00
75 Ja Morant 60.00 150.00
81 LeBron James 150.00 400.00
85 Luka Doncic 150.00 400.00
87 Jayson Tatum 30.00 80.00
99 Giannis Antetokounmpo 40.00 100.00

2020-21 Panini Contenders Panini Contenders Photo Variations
20 Stephen Curry 15.00 40.00
26 Chris Paul 10.00 25.00
37 Devin Booker 10.00 25.00
58 Zion Williamson 25.00 60.00
75 Ja Morant 10.00 25.00
81 LeBron James 40.00 100.00
85 Luka Doncic 40.00 100.00
103 Saddiq Bey 15.00 40.00
104 RJ Hampton 1.50 4.00
105 Anthony Edwards 125.00 300.00
106 Malachi Flynn 1.50 4.00
107 Onyeka Okongwu 3.00 8.00
108 Daniel Oturu 1.50 4.00
109 Jalen Smith 3.00 8.00
111 Cole Anthony 20.00 50.00
113 Precious Achiuwa 3.00 8.00
114 Immanuel Quickley 20.00 50.00
115 James Wiseman 2.00 5.00
116 Desmond Bane 12.00 30.00
117 Killian Hayes 1.50 4.00
118 Theo Maledon 12.00 30.00
119 Devin Vassell 12.00 30.00
120 Tre Jones 2.50 6.00
121 Isaiah Stewart 12.00 30.00
123 Tyrese Maxey 25.00 60.00
124 Payton Pritchard 15.00 40.00
125 LaMelo Ball 200.00 500.00
127 Obi Toppin 15.00 40.00
128 Xavier Tillman 2.00 5.00
129 Tyrese Haliburton 40.00 100.00
133 Zeke Nnaji 2.00 5.00
135 Patrick Williams 40.00 100.00
137 Deni Avdija 15.00 40.00
139 Kira Lewis Jr. 1.50 4.00
141 Josh Green 3.00 8.00
144 Jaden McDaniels 12.00 30.00
145 Isaac Okoro 15.00 40.00

2020-21 Panini Contenders Playoff Ticket
1-100 PRINT RUN 249 SER.#'d SETS
101-165 PRINT RUN 99 SER.#'d SETS
EXCHANGE DEADLINE 11/19/2022
20 Stephen Curry 12.00 30.00
26 Chris Paul 10.00 25.00
37 Devin Booker 10.00 25.00
58 Zion Williamson 12.00 30.00
75 Ja Morant 10.00 25.00
81 LeBron James 15.00 40.00
85 Luka Doncic 15.00 40.00

2020-21 Panini Contenders The Finals Ticket
*FINALS 1-100: 2X TO 5X BASIC
*FINALS AU: .75X TO 2X BASIC
1-100 PRINT RUN 49 SER.#'d SETS
101-165 PRINT RUN 49 SER.#'d SETS
EXCHANGE DEADLINE 11/19/2022
5 Trae Young 15.00 40.00
20 Stephen Curry 40.00 100.00
26 Chris Paul 10.00 25.00
37 Devin Booker 15.00 40.00
58 Zion Williamson 25.00 60.00
75 Ja Morant 20.00 50.00
81 LeBron James 40.00 100.00
85 Luka Doncic 40.00 100.00
99 Giannis Antetokounmpo 15.00 40.00
101 Aaron Nesmith AU 40.00 100.00
103 Saddiq Bey AU 75.00 200.00

2020-21 Panini Contenders '20 Draft Class Contenders
*RED: .4X TO 1X BASIC
*CRACKED ICE/25: 3X TO 8X BASIC
1 Jalen Smith .75 2.00
2 Udoka Azubuike .50 1.25
3 Kira Lewis Jr. .50 1.25
4 Isaiah Stewart .75 2.00
5 Anthony Edwards 4.00 10.00
6 Saddiq Bey .75 2.00
7 Patrick Williams 1.00 2.50
8 Zeke Nnaji .50 1.25
9 Killian Hayes .40 1.00
10 Immanuel Quickley 1.00 2.50
11 Devin Vassell 1.25 3.00
12 Jaden McDaniels 1.25 3.00
13 Aaron Nesmith .75 2.00
14 Aleksej Pokusevski .50 1.25
15 James Wiseman .50 1.25
16 Precious Achiuwa .75 2.00
17 Isaac Okoro .60 1.50
18 Jordan Nwora .50 1.25
19 Obi Toppin .60 1.50
20 Desmond Bane 1.25 3.00
21 Tyrese Haliburton 3.00 8.00
22 Malachi Flynn .40 1.00
23 Cole Anthony 1.00 2.50
24 Josh Green .75 2.00
25 LaMelo Ball 3.00 8.00
26 Tyrese Maxey 3.00 8.00
27 Onyeka Okongwu .75 2.00
28 RJ Hampton .40 1.00
29 Deni Avdija 1.00 2.50
30 Payton Pritchard 1.25 3.00

2020-21 Panini Contenders Autographs
STATED PRINT RUN 49-199 SER.#'d SETS
EXCHANGE DEADLINE 11/19/2022
*BRONZE: .75X TO 2X BASIC
1 Bradley Beal/99 12.00 30.00
2 Anfernee Simons/199 12.00 30.00
3 Markelle Fultz/99 10.00 25.00
4 Doug McDermott/199 4.00 10.00
5 Torrey Craig/199 4.00 10.00
6 Kevin Huerter/199 4.00 10.00
7 Devonte' Graham/99 4.00 10.00
8 Meyers Leonard/149 3.00 8.00
9 Jarrett Allen/199 5.00 12.00
10 John Collins/99 8.00 20.00
11 Boban Marjanovic/99 10.00 25.00
12 Tobias Harris/99 5.00 12.00
13 Kelly Oubre Jr./99 5.00 12.00
14 Mo Bamba/99 5.00 12.00
15 Eric Bledsoe/99 4.00 10.00
16 Lauri Markkanen/99 6.00 15.00
17 JR Smith/99 20.00 50.00
18 Karl-Anthony Towns/99 12.00 30.00
19 Jayson Tatum/49 100.00 250.00
20 Julius Randle/99 5.00 12.00
21 Michael Porter Jr./99 6.00 15.00
22 Joe Harris/99 4.00 10.00
23 Michael Kidd-Gilchrist/99 3.00 8.00
24 Gordon Hayward/99 5.00 12.00
25 Dewayne Dedmon/149 3.00 8.00
26 Maxi Kleber/99 4.00 10.00
27 T.J. McConnell/149 4.00 10.00
28 Keita Bates-Diop/149 3.00 8.00
30 Trae Young/49 75.00 200.00
31 Lonzo Ball/99 12.00 30.00
32 RJ Barrett/99 30.00 80.00
33 Alex Caruso/149 20.00 50.00
34 LaMarcus Aldridge/99 5.00 12.00
35 Justin Holiday/149 3.00 8.00
36 Ricky Rubio/99 8.00 20.00
37 Zach Collins/99 4.00 10.00
38 Patrick Beverley/99 3.00 8.00
39 Thomas Bryant/149 4.00 10.00
40 Donte DiVincenzo/99 5.00 12.00

2020-21 Panini Contenders Game Night Ticket
*RED: .5X TO 1.25X BASIC
1 James Harden 1.25 3.00
2 Damian Lillard 1.50 4.00
3 Anthony Davis 1.50 4.00
4 Kyrie Irving 1.25 3.00
5 LeBron James 5.00 12.00
6 Joel Embiid 1.50 4.00
7 Khris Middleton .75 2.00
8 T.J. Warren .50 1.25
9 Luka Doncic 4.00 10.00
10 D'Angelo Russell .60 1.50
11 Nikola Jokic 3.00 8.00
12 Giannis Antetokounmpo 3.00 8.00
13 Devin Booker 1.50 4.00
14 Jamal Murray 1.00 2.50
15 Trae Young 1.50 4.00
16 Donovan Mitchell 1.25 3.00
17 Jayson Tatum 2.50 6.00
18 Jimmy Butler 1.25 3.00
19 Zion Williamson 2.00 5.00
20 Ja Morant 2.00 5.00

2020-21 Panini Contenders Game Night Ticket Cracked Ice
STATED PRINT RUN 25 SER.#'d SETS

2020-21 Panini Contenders International Ticket
*RED: .5X TO 1.25X BASIC
1 Aron Baynes .40 1.00
2 Drazen Petrovic .60 1.50
3 Kyrie Irving 1.25 3.00
4 Patty Mills .60 1.50
5 Ben Simmons .60 1.50
6 Buddy Hield .60 1.50
7 Jusuf Nurkic .60 1.50
8 Joel Embiid 1.50 4.00
9 Pascal Siakam 1.00 2.50
10 RJ Barrett 1.00 2.50
11 Goran Dragic .60 1.50
12 Jamal Murray 1.00 2.50
13 Shai Gilgeous-Alexander 3.00 8.00
14 Andrew Wiggins .75 2.00
15 Deni Avdija 1.25 3.00
16 Bojan Bogdanovic .50 1.25
17 Lauri Markkanen .75 2.00
18 Rudy Gobert .75 2.00
19 Dennis Schroder .60 1.50
20 Giannis Antetokounmpo 3.00 8.00
21 Rui Hachimura .75 2.00
22 Dirk Nowitzki 1.50 4.00
23 Kristaps Porzingis .75 2.00
24 Steven Adams .60 1.50
25 Nikola Vucevic .60 1.50
26 Bogdan Bogdanovic .60 1.50
27 Nikola Jokic 3.00 8.00
28 Luka Doncic 4.00 10.00
29 Ricky Rubio .60 1.50
30 OG Anunoby .60 1.50

2020-21 Panini Contenders International Ticket Cracked Ice
STATED PRINT RUN 25 SER.#'d SETS
3 Kyrie Irving 15.00 40.00
10 RJ Barrett 25.00 60.00
15 Deni Avdija 60.00 150.00
20 Giannis Antetokounmpo 50.00 120.00
22 Dirk Nowitzki 40.00 100.00
27 Nikola Jokic 15.00 40.00
28 Luka Doncic 200.00 500.00

2020-21 Panini Contenders Legendary Contenders
1 Shaquille O'Neal 8.00 20.00
2 Wilt Chamberlain 6.00 15.00
3 Dominique Wilkins 3.00 8.00
4 Larry Bird 8.00 20.00
5 Hakeem Olajuwon 4.00 10.00
6 Oscar Robertson 5.00 12.00
7 John Stockton 4.00 10.00
8 Walt Frazier 3.00 8.00
9 Clyde Drexler 3.00 8.00
10 Charles Barkley 5.00 12.00
11 Pete Maravich 5.00 12.00
12 Dwyane Wade 4.00 10.00
13 Tim Duncan 5.00 12.00
14 Bill Russell 6.00 15.00
15 Dennis Rodman 5.00 12.00
16 Anfernee Hardaway 5.00 12.00
17 Isiah Thomas 3.00 8.00
18 Julius Erving 5.00 12.00
19 Magic Johnson 8.00 20.00
20 Tracy McGrady 3.00 8.00
21 Kevin Garnett 5.00 12.00
22 Steve Nash 4.00 10.00
23 Dirk Nowitzki 5.00 12.00
24 Kareem Abdul-Jabbar 6.00 15.00
25 Allen Iverson 5.00 12.00

2020-21 Panini Contenders Legendary Contenders Autographs
STATED PRINT RUN 49-199 SER.#'d SETS
EXCHANGE DEADLINE 11/19/2022
1 Magic Johnson 50.00 120.00
2 Shawn Kemp 30.00 80.00
3 Rod Strickland 4.00 10.00
4 Anderson Varejao 3.00 8.00
5 Mike Miller 4.00 10.00
6 Jeff Mullins 4.00 10.00
7 Mehmet Okur 3.00 8.00
8 Kevin Garnett 75.00 200.00
9 Kenny Smith 4.00 10.00
10 Robert Horry 10.00 25.00
11 Isaiah Rider 4.00 10.00
12 Nate Archibald 6.00 15.00
13 Darius Miles 3.00 8.00
14 Dick Barnett 4.00 10.00
15 Steve Francis 10.00 5.00
16 Spud Webb 10.00 25.00
17 Dwyane Wade 60.00 150.00
18 Danny Granger 3.00 8.00
19 Charles Oakley 5.00 12.00
20 Elgin Baylor 12.00 30.00
21 Tim Hardaway 12.00 30.00
22 Larry Bird 60.00 150.00
24 Kirk Hinrich 4.00 10.00
25 Ray Allen 25.00 60.00
26 Pat Riley 12.00 30.00
27 Stephon Marbury 12.00 30.00
28 Dave Bing 8.00 20.00
29 Avery Johnson 4.00 10.00
30 Jason Williams 40.00 100.00
31 Jeff Malone 3.00 8.00
32 Xavier McDaniel 4.00 10.00
33 Jerry West 12.00 30.00
34 Terry Porter 4.00 10.00
35 Jason Richardson 5.00 12.00
36 Matt Bonner 3.00 8.00
37 Baron Davis 10.00 25.00
38 Jason Terry 4.00 10.00
39 Brian Winters 3.00 8.00
40 Caron Butler 4.00 10.00

2020-21 Panini Contenders Lottery Ticket
1 Jalen Smith 1.50 4.00
2 Isaac Okoro 1.25 3.00
3 Patrick Williams 2.00 5.00
4 LaMelo Ball 6.00 15.00
5 Deni Avdija 2.00 5.00
6 Devin Vassell 2.50 6.00
7 Aaron Nesmith 1.50 4.00
8 Killian Hayes .75 2.00
9 Obi Toppin 1.50 4.00
10 James Wiseman 1.00 2.50
11 Anthony Edwards 8.00 20.00
12 Tyrese Haliburton 6.00 15.00
13 Kira Lewis Jr. .75 2.00
14 Onyeka Okongwu 1.50 4.00

2020-21 Panini Contenders Lottery Ticket Cracked Ice
STATED PRINT RUN 25 SER.#'d SETS
4 LaMelo Ball 125.00 300.00
11 Anthony Edwards 125.00 300.00
12 Tyrese Haliburton 75.00 200.00

2020-21 Panini Contenders MVP Contenders
COMMON CARD .60 1.50
SEMISTARS .75 2.00
UNLISTED STARS 1.00 2.50
1 Luka Doncic 20.00 50.00
2 LeBron James 20.00 50.00
3 Giannis Antetokounmpo 5.00 12.00
4 Kawhi Leonard 2.50 6.00
5 Nikola Jokic 5.00 12.00
6 James Harden 2.00 5.00
7 Damian Lillard 2.50 6.00
8 Anthony Davis 2.50 6.00
9 Stephen Curry 10.00 25.00
10 Devin Booker 10.00 25.00
11 Chris Paul 10.00 25.00
12 Bradley Beal 1.25 3.00
13 Jayson Tatum 4.00 10.00
14 Donovan Mitchell 2.00 5.00
15 Zion Williamson 12.00 30.00
16 Bam Adebayo 1.50 4.00
17 Pascal Siakam 1.50 4.00
18 Russell Westbrook 2.00 5.00
19 Ja Morant 12.00 30.00
20 Kevin Durant 8.00 20.00
21 Ben Simmons 1.00 2.50
22 Jamal Murray 1.50 4.00
23 Jimmy Butler 2.00 5.00
24 Joel Embiid 2.50 6.00
25 Kyrie Irving 2.00 5.00

2020-21 Panini Contenders MVP Contenders Autographs
COMMON CARD 6.00 15.00
SEMISTARS 8.00 20.00
UNLISTED STARS 10.00 25.00
STATED PRINT RUN 49 SER.#'d SETS
EXCHANGE DEADLINE 11/19/2022
*BRONZE: .5X TO 1.2X BASIC
1 Stephen Curry 400.00 800.00
2 Trae Young 100.00 250.00
3 Karl-Anthony Towns 25.00 60.00
4 Ja Morant 200.00 500.00
6 De'Aaron Fox 25.00 60.00
7 RJ Barrett 40.00 100.00
8 Bradley Beal 30.00 80.00
9 Jayson Tatum 125.00 300.00
10 Anthony Davis 125.00 300.00

2020-21 Panini Contenders Permit to Dominate
1 Killian Hayes 10.00 25.00
2 RJ Hampton 10.00 25.00
3 Aaron Nesmith 30.00 80.00
4 Isaac Okoro 40.00 100.00
5 Jalen Smith 20.00 50.00
6 Tyrese Haliburton 125.00 300.00
7 Isaiah Stewart 20.00 50.00
8 Josh Green 20.00 50.00
9 Saddiq Bey 60.00 150.00

10 Tyrese Maxey 80.00 200.00
11 Devin Vassell 50.00 120.00
12 Deni Avdija 75.00 200.00
13 James Wiseman 12.00 30.00
14 Obi Toppin 20.00 50.00
15 Kira Lewis Jr. 10.00 25.00
16 Cole Anthony 50.00 120.00
17 Anthony Edwards 400.00 800.00
18 LaMelo Ball 800.00 1,500.00
19 Patrick Williams 60.00 150.00
20 Onyeka Okongwu 20.00 50.00

2020-21 Panini Contenders Photo Variation Autographs

*VAR: .4X TO 1X BASIC
EXCHANGE DEADLINE 11/19/2022

2020-21 Panini Contenders Photo Variation Autographs Clear Ticket

*VAR CLEAR: .75X TO 2X BASIC
EXCHANGE DEADLINE 11/19/2022

2020-21 Panini Contenders Photo Variation Autographs Cracked Ice Ticket

STATED PRINT RUN 25 SER.#'d SETS
EXCHANGE DEADLINE 11/19/2022
101 Aaron Nesmith AU 100.00 250.00
103 Saddiq Bey AU 200.00 500.00
109 Jalen Smith AU 60.00 150.00
111 Cole Anthony AU 200.00 500.00
113 Precious Achiuwa AU 60.00 150.00
119 Devin Vassell AU 150.00 400.00
124 Payton Pritchard AU 150.00 400.00
125 LaMelo Ball AU 3,000.00 6,000.00
135 Patrick Williams AU 300.00 600.00
139 Kira Lewis Jr. AU 100.00 250.00
143 Devon Dotson AU 40.00 100.00
144 Jaden McDaniels AU 125.00 300.00
145 Isaac Okoro AU 150.00 400.00

2020-21 Panini Contenders Photo Variation Autographs Playoff Ticket

*PLAYOFF AU VAR: .75X TO 2X BASIC
PRINT RUN 99 SER.#'d SETS
EXCHANGE DEADLINE 11/19/2022

2020-21 Panini Contenders Photo Variation Autographs The Finals Ticket

*FINALS AU VAR: .75X TO 2X BASIC
STATED PRINT RUN 49 SER.#'d SETS
EXCHANGE DEADLINE 11/19/2022
101 Aaron Nesmith AU 40.00 100.00
103 Saddiq Bey AU 75.00 200.00

2020-21 Panini Contenders Rookie Clear Ticket

EXCHANGE DEADLINE 11/19/2022

2020-21 Panini Contenders Rookie of the Year Contenders

1 Devin Vassell 1.50 4.00
2 Killian Hayes .50 1.25
3 James Wiseman .60 1.50
4 Isaac Okoro .75 2.00
5 Cole Anthony 1.25 3.00
6 Tyrese Haliburton 4.00 10.00
7 LaMelo Ball 20.00 50.00
8 Josh Green 1.00 2.50
9 Onyeka Okongwu 1.00 2.50
10 Tyrese Maxey 4.00 10.00
11 Deni Avdija 1.25 3.00
12 Aaron Nesmith 1.00 2.50
13 Obi Toppin 1.00 2.50
14 Jalen Smith 1.00 2.50
15 Anthony Edwards 15.00 40.00
16 Isaiah Stewart 1.00 2.50
17 Patrick Williams 1.25 3.00
18 Saddiq Bey 1.00 2.50

2020-21 Panini Contenders Rookie Ticket Dual Swatches

1 Anthony Edwards
LaMelo Ball 75.00 200.00
2 James Wiseman
LaMelo Ball 12.00 30.00
3 LaMelo Ball
RJ Hampton 12.00 30.00
4 Isaiah Stewart
Saddiq Bey 10.00 25.00
5 Immanuel Quickley
Obi Toppin 8.00 20.00
6 Anthony EdwardsJ
ames Wiseman 15.00 40.00
7 RJ Hampton
Zeke Nnaji 2.00 5.00
8 Isaiah Stewart
Killian Hayes 8.00 20.00
9 Killian Hayes
Saddiq Bey 10.00 25.00
10 Devin Vassell
Tre Jones 5.00 12.00

2020-21 Panini Contenders Rookie Ticket Swatches

1 Deni Avdija 4.00 10.00
2 James Wiseman 2.00 5.00
3 Josh Green 3.00 8.00
4 Devin Vassell 5.00 12.00
5 Payton Pritchard 5.00 12.00
6 Aaron Nesmith 3.00 8.00
7 Xavier Tillman 2.00 5.00
8 Malachi Flynn 1.50 4.00
9 Zeke Nnaji 2.00 5.00
10 Robert Woodard II 1.50 4.00
11 CJ Elleby 1.50 4.00
12 Desmond Bane 5.00 12.00
13 Jahmi'us Ramsey 1.50 4.00
14 Tre Jones 2.50 6.00
15 LaMelo Ball 40.00 100.00
16 Saddiq Bey 3.00 8.00
17 Tyrese Haliburton 12.00 30.00
18 Onyeka Okongwu 3.00 8.00
19 Udoka Azubuike 2.00 5.00
20 Cole Anthony 4.00 10.00
21 Kira Lewis Jr. 1.50 4.00
22 Killian Hayes 1.50 4.00
23 Jaden McDaniels 5.00 12.00
24 Isaiah Stewart 3.00 8.00
25 Tyrell Terry 1.25 3.00
26 RJ Hampton 1.50 4.00
27 Jordan Nwora 2.00 5.00
28 Daniel Oturu 1.50 4.00
29 Patrick Williams 4.00 10.00
30 Precious Achiuwa 3.00 8.00
31 Nico Mannion 1.50 4.00
32 Theo Maledon 1.50 4.00
33 Isaac Okoro 2.50 6.00
34 Tyrese Maxey 12.00 30.00
35 Obi Toppin 3.00 8.00
36 Anthony Edwards 15.00 40.00
37 Aleksej Pokusevski 2.00 5.00
38 Jalen Smith 3.00 8.00
39 Vernon Carey Jr. 1.50 4.00
40 Immanuel Quickley 4.00 10.00

2020-21 Panini Contenders Sophomore Contenders Autographs

STATED PRINT RUN 25-199 SER.#'d SETS
EXCHANGE DEADLINE 11/19/2022
1 Chuma Okeke/199 5.00 12.00
2 Ja Morant/49 125.00 300.00
3 Coby White/99 6.00 15.00
4 RJ Barrett/49 10.00 25.00
5 Kendrick Nunn/99 4.00 10.00
6 Jaxson Hayes/99 4.00 10.00
7 Sekou Doumbouya/99 3.00 8.00
8 Zion Williamson/25 125.00 300.00
9 Nickeil Alexander-Walker/199 5.00 12.00
10 Jordan Poole/199 8.00 20.00

2020-21 Panini Contenders Suite Shots

1 Anthony Davis 1.50 4.00
2 Kawhi Leonard 1.50 4.00
3 Bradley Beal .75 2.00
4 Paul George 1.00 2.50
5 Klay Thompson 1.50 4.00
6 Kyle Lowry .75 2.00
7 Kyrie Irving 1.25 3.00
8 Ben Simmons .60 1.50
9 Devin Booker 1.50 4.00
10 Ja Morant 2.00 5.00
11 Jayson Tatum 2.50 6.00
12 Trae Young 1.50 4.00
13 James Harden 1.25 3.00
14 Jamal Murray 1.00 2.50
15 LeBron James 5.00 12.00
16 Joel Embiid 1.50 4.00
17 Donovan Mitchell 1.25 3.00
18 Damian Lillard 1.50 4.00
19 Zion Williamson 2.00 5.00
20 Russell Westbrook 1.25 3.00
21 Luka Doncic 4.00 10.00
22 Chris Paul 1.25 3.00
23 Pascal Siakam 1.00 2.50
24 Bam Adebayo 1.00 2.50
25 Giannis Antetokounmpo 3.00 8.00
26 Stephen Curry 5.00 12.00
27 Jimmy Butler 1.25 3.00
28 Kemba Walker .60 1.50
29 Kevin Durant 2.50 6.00
30 Nikola Jokic 3.00 8.00

2020-21 Panini Contenders Suite Shots Cracked Ice

STATED PRINT RUN 25 SER.#'d SETS
12 Trae Young 25.00 60.00
15 LeBron James 50.00 120.00
18 Damian Lillard 15.00 40.00
21 Luka Doncic 50.00 120.00
26 Stephen Curry 25.00 60.00

2020-21 Panini Contenders Superstar Die-Cuts

1 Luka Doncic 15.00 40.00
2 Jayson Tatum 10.00 25.00
3 LeBron James 15.00 40.00
4 Stephen Curry 15.00 40.00
5 Damian Lillard 10.00 25.00
6 Kevin Durant 10.00 25.00
7 Kawhi Leonard 8.00 20.00
8 Anthony Davis 8.00 20.00
9 Zion Williamson 15.00 40.00
10 Giannis Antetokounmpo 10.00 25.00

2020-21 Panini Contenders Superstar Die-Cuts Cracked Ice

*CRACKED ICE: 3X TO 8X TO BASIC
STATED PRINT RUN 25 SER.#'d SETS
1 Luka Doncic 200.00 500.00
3 LeBron James 200.00 500.00
9 Zion Williamson 200.00 500.00

2020-21 Panini Contenders Veteran Autographs

EXCHANGE DEADLINE 11/19/2022
1 Stephen Curry 400.00 800.00
2 Ja Morant 125.00 300.00
3 Luka Doncic 500.00 1,000.00
4 Kevin Garnett 125.00 300.00
5 Anthony Davis 75.00 200.00
6 Trae Young 75.00 200.00
7 Charles Barkley 75.00 200.00
8 Allen Iverson 75.00 200.00
9 Shaquille O'Neal 125.00 300.00
10 Dirk Nowitzki 125.00 300.00

2020-21 Panini Contenders Veteran Autographs Clear Ticket

EXCHANGE DEADLINE 11/19/2022
3 Luka Doncic 1,000.00 2,000.00

2020-21 Panini Contenders Veteran Autographs Playoff Ticket

STATED PRINT RUN 49 SER.#'d SETS
EXCHANGE DEADLINE 11/19/2022
3 Luka Doncic 1,250.00 2,500.00

2020-21 Panini Contenders Veteran Autographs Premium Green Shimmer

EXCHANGE DEADLINE 11/19/2022
3 Luka Doncic 1,000.00 2,000.00

2020-21 Panini Contenders Veteran Autographs The Finals Ticket

STATED PRINT RUN 25 SER.#'d SETS
EXCHANGE DEADLINE 11/19/2022
1 Stephen Curry 1,000.00 2,000.00
3 Luka Doncic 1,500.00 3,000.00

2020-21 Panini Contenders Veteran Autographs Ticket Stub

STATED PRINT RUN 3-41 SER.#'d SETS
NO PRICING ON QTY BELOW 20
EXCHANGE DEADLINE 11/19/2022
1 Stephen Curry/30 1,000.00 2,000.00

2021-22 Panini Contenders

COMMON CARD (1-100) .30 .75
SEMISTARS .40 1.00
UNLISTED STARS .50 1.25
COMMON RC AU (101-165) 4.00 10.00
AU SEMIS 5.00 12.00
AU UNLISTED 6.00 15.00
*CLEAR TICKET AU RC: .6X TO 1.5X BASIC
GM TCKT BRNZ: .6X TO 1.5X BASIC
GM TCKT GREEN: .6X TO 1.5X BASIC
GM TCKT RED: .6X TO 1.5X BASIC
*75TH ANN TCKT (1-100): .75X TO 2X BASIC
*75TH ANN TCKT RC AU (101-145): .6X TO 1.5X BASIC
*PLAYOFF TCKT/249 (1-100): .75X TO 2X BASIC
*PLAYOFF TCKT RC AU/99 (101-165): .6X TO 1.5X BASIC
GM TCKT GREEN ICE: 1X TO 2.5X BASIC
*FIRST ROUND TCKT/149: 1.2X TO 3X BASIC
*SEMIFINAL TCKT/99: 1.5X TO 4X BASIC
*CONFERENCE FNLS TCKT/75: 2X TO 5X BASIC
*FINALS TCKT/49 (1-100): 2.5X TO 6X BASIC
*GAMETCKT BLUE/49: 2.5X TO 6X BASIC
*PLAYOFF TCKT RC AU/49 (101-165): 1.25X TO 3X BASIC
1 Keldon Johnson .60 1.50
2 Domantas Sabonis .60 1.50
3 Ja Morant 1.50 4.00
4 Trae Young 1.25 3.00
5 Anthony Edwards 2.50 6.00
6 LaMelo Ball 1.25 3.00
7 Darius Bazley .30 .75
8 Kevin Love .50 1.25
9 Devin Booker 1.25 3.00
10 Stephen Curry 3.00 8.00
11 Fred VanVleet .60 1.50
12 Myles Turner .50 1.25
13 Jaren Jackson Jr. .75 2.00
14 John Collins .50 1.25
15 Karl-Anthony Towns .75 2.00
16 Gordon Hayward .40 1.00
17 Markelle Fultz .30 .75
18 Luka Doncic 3.00 8.00
19 Deandre Ayton .50 1.25
20 Klay Thompson 1.25 3.00
21 Gary Trent Jr. .40 1.00
22 Kawhi Leonard 1.25 3.00
23 Kyle Lowry .50 1.25
24 Clint Capela .50 1.25
25 Devonte' Graham .40 1.00
26 Terry Rozier .40 1.00
27 Wendell Carter Jr. .50 1.25
28 Tim Hardaway Jr. .30 .75
29 Damian Lillard 1.25 3.00
30 James Wiseman .40 1.00
31 Pascal Siakam .75 2.00
32 Paul George .75 2.00
33 Duncan Robinson .40 1.00
34 Jaylen Brown .75 2.00
35 Zion Williamson 1.25 3.00
36 Lonzo Ball .50 1.25
37 Chuma Okeke .50 1.25
38 Kristaps Porzingis .60 1.50
39 CJ McCollum .40 1.00
40 Draymond Green .60 1.50
41 Donovan Mitchell 1.00 2.50
42 Eric Bledsoe .40 1.00
43 Bam Adebayo .75 2.00
44 Jayson Tatum 2.00 5.00
45 Brandon Ingram .60 1.50
46 Zach LaVine .75 2.00
47 Terrence Ross .40 1.00
48 Michael Porter Jr. .60 1.50
49 Norman Powell .40 1.00
50 Andrew Wiggins .60 1.50
51 Mike Conley .40 1.00
52 Russell Westbrook .75 2.00
53 Jimmy Butler .75 2.00
54 Dennis Schroder .50 1.25
55 Kemba Walker .50 1.25
56 DeMar DeRozan .60 1.50
57 Seth Curry .40 1.00
58 Aaron Gordon .50 1.25
59 De'Aaron Fox .75 2.00
60 John Wall .60 1.50
61 Rudy Gobert .60 1.50
62 LeBron James 4.00 10.00
63 Jrue Holiday .60 1.50
64 James Harden 1.00 2.50
65 RJ Barrett .75 2.00
66 Nikola Vucevic .50 1.25
67 Joel Embiid 1.25 3.00
68 Nikola Jokic 2.50 6.00
69 Buddy Hield .40 1.00
70 Kevin Porter Jr. .40 1.00
71 Bradley Beal .60 1.50
72 Anthony Davis 1.25 3.00
73 Giannis Antetokounmpo 2.50 6.00
74 Kyrie Irving 1.00 2.50
75 Julius Randle .60 1.50
76 Darius Garland .75 2.00
77 Ben Simmons .50 1.25
78 Killian Hayes .50 1.25
79 Harrison Barnes .40 1.00
80 Christian Wood .40 1.00
81 Kyle Kuzma .60 1.50
82 Carmelo Anthony .75 2.00
83 Khris Middleton .50 1.25
84 Kevin Durant 1.50 4.00
85 Shai Gilgeous-Alexander 2.50 6.00
86 Collin Sexton .50 1.25
87 Tobias Harris .40 1.00
88 Jerami Grant .50 1.25
89 Dejounte Murray .50 1.25
90 Malcolm Brogdon .40 1.00
91 Rui Hachimura .50 1.25
92 Steven Adams .40 1.00
93 D'Angelo Russell .50 1.25
94 Blake Griffin .50 1.25
95 Aleksej Pokusevski .40 1.00
96 Isaac Okoro .40 1.00
97 Chris Paul 1.00 2.50
98 Saddiq Bey .40 1.00
99 Derrick White .50 1.25
100 T.J. Warren .30 .75
101 Cade Cunningham AU RC 200.00 500.00
102 Jalen Green AU RC 150.00 400.00
103 Evan Mobley AU RC 100.00 250.00
104 Scottie Barnes AU RC 100.00 250.00
105 Jalen Suggs AU RC 40.00 100.00
106 Josh Giddey AU RC 100.00 250.00
107 Jonathan Kuminga AU RC 75.00 200.00
108 Franz Wagner AU RC 75.00 200.00
109 Davion Mitchell AU RC 6.00 15.00
110 Ziaire Williams AU RC 8.00 20.00
111 James Bouknight AU RC 5.00 12.00
112 Joshua Primo AU RC 5.00 12.00
113 Chris Duarte AU RC 5.00 12.00
114 Moses Moody AU RC 12.00 30.00
115 Corey Kispert AU RC 8.00 20.00
116 Alperen Sengun AU RC 60.00 150.00
117 Trey Murphy III AU RC 20.00 50.00
118 Tre Mann AU RC 10.00 25.00
119 Kai Jones AU RC 5.00 12.00
120 Jalen Johnson AU RC 20.00 50.00
121 Keon Johnson AU RC 6.00 15.00
122 Isaiah Jackson AU RC 6.00 15.00
123 Usman Garuba AU RC 5.00 12.00
124 Josh Christopher AU RC 5.00 12.00
125 Quentin Grimes AU RC 12.00 30.00
126 Bones Hyland AU RC 8.00 20.00
127 Cameron Thomas AU RC 40.00 100.00
128 Jaden Springer AU RC 6.00 15.00
129 Day'Ron Sharpe AU RC 6.00 15.00
130 Santi Aldama AU RC 8.00 20.00
131 Jeremiah Robinson-Earl AU RC 6.00 15.00
132 Miles McBride AU RC 10.00 25.00
133 Ayo Dosunmu AU RC 12.00 30.00
134 Jared Butler AU RC 6.00 15.00
135 Isaiah Livers AU RC 6.00 15.00
136 Greg Brown III AU RC 5.00 12.00
137 Brandon Boston Jr. AU RC 6.00 15.00
138 Luka Garza AU RC 6.00 15.00
139 Charles Bassey AU RC 6.00 15.00
140 Scottie Lewis AU RC 5.00 12.00
141 JT Thor AU RC 6.00 15.00
142 Jason Preston AU RC 5.00 12.00
143 Herbert Jones AU RC 8.00 20.00
144 Neemias Queta AU RC 6.00 15.00
145 Joe Wieskamp AU RC 5.00 12.00
146 Kessler Edwards AU RC 6.00 15.00
147 David Johnson AU RC 5.00 12.00
148 David Duke Jr. AU RC 6.00 15.00
149 Sandro Mamukelashvili AU RC 8.00 20.00
150 Aaron Wiggins AU RC 8.00 20.00
151 Jericho Sims AU RC 8.00 20.00
152 Juan Toscano-Anderson AU RC 6.00 15.00
153 Dalano Banton AU RC 8.00 20.00
154 Arnoldas Kulboka AU RC 6.00 15.00
155 Duane Washington Jr. AU RC 6.00 15.00
156 Dejon Jarreau AU RC 4.00 10.00
157 Marko Simonovic AU RC 5.00 12.00
158 Jose Alvarado AU RC 15.00 40.00
159 Trendon Watford AU RC 8.00 20.00
160 Isaiah Todd AU RC 8.00 20.00
161 Eugene Omoruyi AU RC 5.00 12.00
162 Austin Reaves AU RC 75.00 200.00
163 Sam Hauser AU RC 15.00 40.00
164 Joel Ayayi AU RC 5.00 12.00
165 Aaron Henry AU RC 4.00 10.00

2021-22 Panini Contenders Cracked Ice Ticket

*CRCKD ICE TCKT/25 (1-100): 5X TO 12X BASIC
*CRCKD ICE TCKT RC AU/25 (101-165): 2.5X TO 6X BASIC
3 Ja Morant 50.00 120.00
10 Stephen Curry 60.00 150.00
18 Luka Doncic 60.00 150.00
62 LeBron James 75.00 200.00

2021-22 Panini Contenders Game Ticket Purple

*GAME TCKT PRPL/25: 5X TO 12X BASIC
3 Ja Morant 50.00 120.00
10 Stephen Curry 60.00 150.00
18 Luka Doncic 60.00 150.00
62 LeBron James 75.00 200.00

2021-22 Panini Contenders Opening Night Ticket

*OPENING NIGHT TCKT/25: 5X TO 12X BASIC
3 Ja Morant 50.00 120.00
10 Stephen Curry 60.00 150.00
18 Luka Doncic 60.00 150.00
62 LeBron James 75.00 200.00

2021-22 Panini Contenders '21 Draft Class Contenders

COMMON CARD .50 1.25
SEMISTARS .60 1.50
UNLISTED STARS .75 2.00
1 Cade Cunningham 5.00 12.00
2 Jalen Green 4.00 10.00
3 Evan Mobley 3.00 8.00
4 Scottie Barnes 2.50 6.00
5 Jalen Suggs 2.00 5.00
6 Josh Giddey 2.50 6.00
7 Jonathan Kuminga 2.50 6.00
8 Franz Wagner 2.50 6.00
9 Davion Mitchell .75 2.00
10 Ziaire Williams 1.00 2.50
11 James Bouknight .60 1.50
12 Joshua Primo .60 1.50
13 Chris Duarte .60 1.50
14 Moses Moody 1.50 4.00
15 Corey Kispert 1.00 2.50
16 Alperen Sengun 2.50 6.00
17 Trey Murphy III 2.50 6.00
18 Tre Mann 1.25 3.00
19 Kai Jones .60 1.50
20 Jalen Johnson 2.50 6.00
21 Keon Johnson .75 2.00
22 Isaiah Jackson .75 2.00
23 Usman Garuba .60 1.50
24 Josh Christopher .60 1.50
25 Quentin Grimes 1.50 4.00
26 Bones Hyland 1.00 2.50
27 Cameron Thomas 1.50 4.00
28 Jaden Springer .75 2.00
29 Day'Ron Sharpe .75 2.00
30 Santi Aldama 1.00 2.50

2021-22 Panini Contenders '21 Draft Class Contenders Cracked Ice

*CRACKED ICE: 4X TO 10X BASIC
STATED PRINT RUN 25 SER.#'d SETS

2021-22 Panini Contenders '21 Draft Class Contenders Green Ice

*GREEN ICE: .75X TO 2X BASIC

2021-22 Panini Contenders Autographs

COMMON CARD 4.00 10.00
SEMISTARS 5.00 12.00
UNLISTED STARS 6.00 15.00
STATED PRINT RUN 49-199 SER.#'d SETS
EXCHANGE DEADLINE 09/30/2023
*BRONZE/25: .75X TO 2X BASIC
1 Kristaps Porzingis/92 8.00 20.00
2 Rodney Hood/199 4.00 10.00
3 Luguentz Dort/199 6.00 15.00
4 Dennis Smith Jr./199 4.00 10.00
5 Nassir Little/199 6.00 15.00
6 Eric Bledsoe/143 5.00 12.00
7 T.J. McConnell/199 5.00 12.00
8 Harrison Barnes/146 5.00 12.00
9 Udonis Haslem/199 4.00 10.00
10 Jonas Valanciunas/199 5.00 12.00
11 Kyle Kuzma/132 8.00 20.00
12 Caris LeVert/199 5.00 12.00
13 Luke Kennard/199 5.00 12.00
14 Derrick White/143 6.00 15.00
15 Nikola Vucevic/199 6.00 15.00
16 Frank Jackson/199 4.00 10.00
17 Taj Gibson/199 4.00 10.00
18 Jalen Brunson/199 12.00 30.00
19 Wendell Carter Jr./199 6.00 15.00
20 Josh Jackson/199 4.00 10.00
21 Larry Nance Jr./199 5.00 12.00
22 Chris Boucher/199 6.00 15.00
23 Michael Carter-Williams/199 4.00 10.00
24 Devonte' Graham/199 5.00 12.00
25 Patty Mills/199 12.00 30.00
26 Gary Harris/188 5.00 12.00
27 Tim Hardaway Jr./109 4.00 10.00
28 Jamal Murray/49 20.00 50.00
29 Will Barton/199 4.00 10.00
30 Jrue Holiday/49 8.00 20.00
31 Lou Williams/199 6.00 15.00
32 Collin Sexton/199 12.00 30.00
33 Mike Conley/49 5.00 12.00
34 Doug McDermott/199 5.00 12.00
35 Rudy Gay/164 6.00 15.00
36 Gordon Hayward/49 5.00 12.00
37 Tomas Satoransky/199 4.00 10.00
38 Jaren Jackson Jr./102 30.00 80.00
39 Zach LaVine/102 40.00 100.00
40 Khris Middleton/49 6.00 15.00

2021-22 Panini Contenders Game Night Ticket

COMMON CARD .40 1.00
SEMISTARS .50 1.25
UNLISTED STARS .60 1.50
*GREEN ICE: .75X TO 2X BASIC
*CRACKED ICE TCKT/25: 5X TO 12X BASIC
1 De'Aaron Fox 1.00 2.50
2 Joel Embiid 1.50 4.00
3 Trae Young 1.50 4.00
4 Jamal Murray 1.00 2.50
5 Donovan Mitchell 1.25 3.00
6 Bojan Bogdanovic .50 1.25
7 Luka Doncic 4.00 10.00
8 Stephen Curry 4.00 10.00
9 Zach LaVine 1.00 2.50
10 Fred VanVleet .75 2.00
11 James Harden 1.25 3.00
12 Damian Lillard 1.50 4.00
13 Kevin Durant 2.00 5.00
14 Kevin Porter Jr. .50 1.25
15 Giannis Antetokounmpo 3.00 8.00
16 Nikola Jokic 3.00 8.00
17 LeBron James 5.00 12.00
18 Jayson Tatum 2.50 6.00
19 Devin Booker 1.50 4.00
20 Bradley Beal .75 2.00

2021-22 Panini Contenders International Ticket

COMMON CARD .40 1.00
SEMISTARS .50 1.25
UNLISTED STARS .60 1.50
*GREEN ICE: .75X TO 2X BASIC
*CRACKED ICE TCKT/25: 5X TO 12X BASIC
1 Kristaps Porzingis .75 2.00
2 Tony Parker 1.00 2.50
3 Boban Marjanovic .60 1.50
4 Giannis Antetokounmpo 3.00 8.00
5 Ben Simmons .60 1.50
6 Marc Gasol .60 1.50
7 RJ Barrett 1.00 2.50
8 Andrei Kirilenko .50 1.25
9 Luka Doncic 4.00 10.00
10 Steve Nash 1.25 3.00
11 Clint Capela .60 1.50
12 Drazen Petrovic .75 2.00
13 Aleksej Pokusevski .50 1.25
14 Vlade Divac .50 1.25
15 Jamal Murray 1.00 2.50
16 Rudy Gobert .75 2.00
17 Dominique Wilkins 1.00 2.50
18 Toni Kukoc .75 2.00
19 Deni Avdija .60 1.50
20 Dirk Nowitzki 1.50 4.00
21 Wang Zhi-zhi .60 1.50
22 Nikola Jokic 3.00 8.00
23 Kyrie Irving 1.25 3.00
24 Joel Embiid 1.50 4.00
25 Shai Gilgeous-Alexander 3.00 8.00
26 Manu Ginobili 1.25 3.00
27 Andrew Wiggins .75 2.00
28 Dikembe Mutombo .75 2.00
29 Killian Hayes .60 1.50
30 Hakeem Olajuwon 1.25 3.00

2021-22 Panini Contenders Legendary Contenders

1 Dennis Rodman 5.00 12.00
2 Charles Barkley 5.00 12.00
3 Bill Bradley 2.00 5.00
4 Karl Malone 4.00 10.00
5 Patrick Ewing 3.00 8.00
6 John Stockton 4.00 10.00
7 Moses Malone 3.00 8.00
8 Magic Johnson 6.00 15.00
9 Tracy McGrady 3.00 8.00
10 David Robinson 4.00 10.00
11 Jerry West 4.00 10.00
12 Shaquille O'Neal 6.00 15.00
13 Wilt Chamberlain 6.00 15.00
14 Allen Iverson 5.00 12.00
15 Kevin Garnett 5.00 12.00
16 Oscar Robertson 4.00 10.00
17 Stephon Marbury 2.50 6.00
18 Jason Kidd 3.00 8.00
19 Pete Maravich 5.00 12.00
20 Ray Allen 3.00 8.00
21 Anfernee Hardaway 5.00 12.00
22 Bill Russell 6.00 15.00
23 Tim Duncan 5.00 12.00
24 Larry Bird 6.00 15.00
25 Dennis Johnson 2.00 5.00

2021-22 Panini Contenders Legendary Contenders Autographs

COMMON CARD 4.00 10.00
SEMISTARS 5.00 12.00
UNLISTED STARS 6.00 15.00
STATED PRINT RUN 49-199 SER. #'d SETS
EXCHANGE DEADLINE 9/30/2023
*BRONZE/25: .6X TO 1.5X BASIC
1 Dee Brown/199 5.00 12.00
2 Sam Perkins/199 5.00 12.00
3 Dominique Wilkins/99 15.00 40.00
4 Tim Hardaway/199 8.00 20.00
5 Horace Grant/199 6.00 15.00
6 Juwan Howard/199 5.00 12.00
7 Al Attles/199 5.00 12.00
8 Mark Eaton/199 6.00 15.00
9 Bob Dandridge/199 6.00 15.00
10 Rasheed Wallace/49 25.00 60.00
11 Dennis Rodman/49 40.00 100.00
12 Shawn Kemp/199 25.00 60.00
13 Drew Gooden/199 5.00 12.00
14 Tom Gugliotta/199 5.00 12.00
15 Jack Sikma/199 6.00 15.00
16 Kevin Willis/199 5.00 12.00
17 Alvan Adams/199 5.00 12.00
18 Mark Price/199 6.00 15.00
19 Caron Butler/199 5.00 12.00
20 Rex Chapman/199 5.00 12.00
21 Derek Fisher/99 6.00 15.00
22 Spencer Haywood/199 6.00 15.00
23 Glen Rice/199 6.00 15.00
24 Tree Rollins/199 5.00 12.00
25 Joakim Noah/199 5.00 12.00
26 Mario Chalmers/199 5.00 12.00
27 Arvydas Sabonis/199 8.00 20.00
28 Mitch Kupchak/199 5.00 12.00
29 Charles Oakley/199 5.00 12.00
30 Rod Strickland/199 5.00 12.00
31 Detlef Schrempf/199 6.00 15.00
32 Maurice Cheeks/199 5.00 12.00
33 Hedo Turkoglu/199 5.00 12.00
34 Wang Zhi-zhi/199 15.00 40.00
35 John Salley/199 5.00 12.00
36 Mark Aguirre/199 5.00 12.00
37 Bill Laimbeer/199 6.00 15.00
38 Ralph Sampson/99 6.00 15.00
39 Dan Issel/199 6.00 15.00
40 Ron Harper/199 6.00 15.00

2021-22 Panini Contenders License to Dominate

COMMON CARD 6.00 15.00
SEMISTARS 8.00 20.00
UNLISTED STARS 10.00 25.00
1 Kevin Durant 30.00 80.00
2 Julius Randle 12.00 30.00
3 Bradley Beal 12.00 30.00
4 Anthony Davis 25.00 60.00
5 Brandon Ingram 12.00 30.00
6 Kawhi Leonard 25.00 60.00
7 Nikola Jokic 50.00 120.00
8 Donovan Mitchell 20.00 50.00
9 De'Aaron Fox 15.00 40.00
10 Giannis Antetokounmpo 50.00 120.00
11 Kyrie Irving 20.00 50.00
12 Trae Young 25.00 60.00
13 Nikola Vucevic 10.00 25.00
14 Jayson Tatum 40.00 100.00
15 Jaylen Brown 15.00 40.00
16 Stephen Curry 60.00 150.00
17 Russell Westbrook 15.00 40.00
18 Luka Doncic 60.00 150.00
19 Devin Booker 25.00 60.00
20 Ja Morant 30.00 80.00
21 Damian Lillard 25.00 60.00
22 Karl-Anthony Towns 15.00 40.00
23 Collin Sexton 10.00 25.00
24 Joel Embiid 25.00 60.00
25 Anthony Edwards 50.00 120.00
26 Zach LaVine 15.00 40.00
27 James Harden 20.00 50.00
28 Zion Williamson 25.00 60.00
29 Paul George 15.00 40.00
30 LeBron James 80.00 200.00

2021-22 Panini Contenders Lottery Ticket

COMMON CARD .60 1.50
SEMISTARS .75 2.00
UNLISTED STARS 1.00 2.50
1 Cade Cunningham 6.00 15.00
2 Jalen Green 5.00 12.00
3 Evan Mobley 4.00 10.00
4 Scottie Barnes 3.00 8.00
5 Jalen Suggs 2.50 6.00
6 Josh Giddey 3.00 8.00
7 Jonathan Kuminga 3.00 8.00
8 Franz Wagner 3.00 8.00
9 Davion Mitchell 1.00 2.50
10 Ziaire Williams 1.25 3.00
11 James Bouknight .75 2.00
12 Joshua Primo .75 2.00
13 Chris Duarte .75 2.00
14 Moses Moody 2.00 5.00

2021-22 Panini Contenders Lottery Ticket Cracked Ice

*CRACKED ICE: 3X TO 8X BASIC
STATED PRINT RUN 25 SER.#'d SETS
1 Cade Cunningham 125.00 300.00
2 Jalen Green 125.00 300.00
6 Josh Giddey 100.00 250.00

2021-22 Panini Contenders MVP Contenders

COMMON CARD 1.25 3.00
SEMISTARS 1.50 4.00
UNLISTED STARS 2.00 5.00
1 Donovan Mitchell 4.00 10.00
2 Luka Doncic 12.00 30.00
3 Zion Williamson 5.00 12.00
4 Giannis Antetokounmpo 10.00 25.00
5 Ja Morant 6.00 15.00
6 LeBron James 15.00 40.00
7 Julius Randle 2.50 6.00
8 Trae Young 5.00 12.00
9 Karl-Anthony Towns 3.00 8.00
10 Anthony Davis 5.00 12.00
11 Jayson Tatum 8.00 20.00
12 Joel Embiid 5.00 12.00
13 Jimmy Butler 3.00 8.00
14 Stephen Curry 12.00 30.00
15 Zach LaVine 3.00 8.00
16 Nikola Jokic 10.00 25.00
17 Russell Westbrook 3.00 8.00
18 James Harden 4.00 10.00
19 De'Aaron Fox 3.00 8.00
20 Devin Booker 5.00 12.00
21 Paul George 3.00 8.00
22 Kevin Durant 6.00 15.00
23 Chris Paul 4.00 10.00
24 Damian Lillard 5.00 12.00
25 Bradley Beal 2.50 6.00

2021-22 Panini Contenders MVP Contenders Autographs

STATED PRINT RUN 15-25 SER. #'d SETS
EXCHANGE DEADLINE 09/30/2023
1 Luka Doncic/15 600.00 1,200.00
2 Stephen Curry/15 600.00 1,200.00
3 Nikola Jokic/25 150.00 400.00
4 Zion Williamson/15 300.00 600.00
5 Trae Young/25 150.00 400.00
6 Kevin Durant/15 150.00 400.00
7 Anthony Davis/15 60.00 150.00
8 Jayson Tatum/15 150.00 400.00
9 Julius Randle/25 15.00 40.00
10 De'Aaron Fox/25 25.00 60.00

2021-22 Panini Contenders Permit to Dominate

COMMON CARD 6.00 15.00
SEMISTARS 8.00 20.00
UNLISTED STARS 10.00 25.00
1 Cade Cunningham 40.00 100.00
2 Jalen Green 30.00 80.00
3 Evan Mobley 25.00 60.00
4 Scottie Barnes 20.00 50.00
5 Jalen Suggs 15.00 40.00
6 Josh Giddey 20.00 50.00
7 Jonathan Kuminga 20.00 50.00
8 Franz Wagner 20.00 50.00
9 Davion Mitchell 6.00 15.00
10 Ziaire Williams 8.00 20.00
11 James Bouknight 5.00 12.00
12 Joshua Primo 5.00 12.00
13 Chris Duarte 5.00 12.00
14 Moses Moody 12.00 30.00
15 Corey Kispert 8.00 20.00
16 Bones Hyland 8.00 20.00
17 Trey Murphy III 20.00 50.00
18 Tre Mann 10.00 25.00
19 Kai Jones 5.00 12.00
20 Jalen Johnson 20.00 50.00

2021-22 Panini Contenders Photo Variation Autographs

*PHOTO VAR AUTO (101-:145) .4X TO 1X BASIC

2021-22 Panini Contenders Photo Variations

*PHOTO VARIATIONS 4-97: .75X TO 2X BASIC
PHOTO VARIATION RC (101-145) 2.00 5.00
RC SEMIS 2.50 6.00
RC UNLISTED 3.00 8.00
101 Cade Cunningham 60.00 150.00
102 Jalen Green 50.00 120.00
103 Evan Mobley 40.00 100.00
104 Scottie Barnes 50.00 120.00
105 Jalen Suggs 8.00 20.00
106 Josh Giddey 40.00 100.00
107 Jonathan Kuminga 30.00 80.00
108 Franz Wagner 10.00 25.00
109 Davion Mitchell 3.00 8.00
110 Ziaire Williams 4.00 10.00
111 James Bouknight 2.50 6.00
112 Joshua Primo 2.50 6.00
113 Chris Duarte 2.50 6.00
114 Moses Moody 6.00 15.00
115 Corey Kispert 4.00 10.00
116 Alperen Sengun 10.00 25.00
117 Trey Murphy III 10.00 25.00
118 Tre Mann 5.00 12.00
119 Kai Jones 2.50 6.00
120 Jalen Johnson 10.00 25.00
121 Keon Johnson 3.00 8.00
122 Isaiah Jackson 3.00 8.00
123 Usman Garuba 2.50 6.00
124 Josh Christopher 2.50 6.00
125 Quentin Grimes 6.00 15.00
126 Bones Hyland 4.00 10.00
127 Cameron Thomas 6.00 15.00
128 Jaden Springer 3.00 8.00
129 Day'Ron Sharpe 3.00 8.00
130 Santi Aldama 4.00 10.00
131 Jeremiah Robinson-Earl 3.00 8.00

132 Miles McBride 5.00 12.00
133 Ayo Dosunmu 6.00 15.00
134 Jared Butler 3.00 8.00
135 Isaiah Livers 3.00 8.00
136 Greg Brown III 2.50 6.00
137 Brandon Boston Jr. 3.00 8.00
138 Luka Garza 3.00 8.00
139 Charles Bassey 3.00 8.00
140 Scottie Lewis 2.50 6.00

2021-22 Panini Contenders Rookie of the Year Contenders

COMMON CARD .60 1.50
SEMISTARS .75 2.00
UNLISTED STARS 1.00 2.50
*CRACKED ICE/25: 4X TO 10X BASIC
1 Cade Cunningham 6.00 15.00
2 Jalen Green 5.00 12.00
3 Evan Mobley 4.00 10.00
4 Scottie Barnes 3.00 8.00
5 Jalen Suggs 2.50 6.00
6 Josh Giddey 3.00 8.00
7 Jonathan Kuminga 3.00 8.00
8 Franz Wagner 3.00 8.00
9 Davion Mitchell 1.00 2.50
10 Ziaire Williams 1.25 3.00
11 James Bouknight .75 2.00
12 Joshua Primo .75 2.00
13 Chris Duarte .75 2.00
14 Moses Moody 2.00 5.00
15 Corey Kispert 1.25 3.00
16 Bones Hyland 1.25 3.00
17 Trey Murphy III 3.00 8.00
18 Tre Mann 1.50 4.00

2021-22 Panini Contenders Rookie Ticket Dual Swatches

COMMON CARD 1.25 3.00
SEMISTARS 1.50 4.00
UNLISTED STARS 2.00 5.00
2 Jalen Green
Jonathan Kuminga 10.00 25.00
3 Evan Mobley
Scottie Barnes 8.00 20.00
4 Josh Giddey
Tre Mann 6.00 15.00
5 Jonathan Kuminga
Moses Moody 6.00 15.00
6 Chris Duarte
Isaiah Jackson 2.00 5.00
8 Corey Kispert
Jalen Suggs 5.00 12.00
9 Cameron Thomas
Joshua Primo 4.00 10.00

2021-22 Panini Contenders Rookie Ticket Swatches

1 Cade Cunningham 12.00 30.00
2 Jalen Green 10.00 25.00
3 Evan Mobley 8.00 20.00
4 Scottie Barnes 6.00 15.00
5 Jalen Suggs 5.00 12.00
6 Josh Giddey 6.00 15.00
7 Jonathan Kuminga 6.00 15.00
8 Franz Wagner 6.00 15.00
9 Davion Mitchell 2.00 5.00
10 Ziaire Williams 2.50 6.00
11 James Bouknight 1.50 4.00
12 Joshua Primo 1.50 4.00
13 Chris Duarte 1.50 4.00
14 Moses Moody 4.00 10.00
15 Corey Kispert 2.50 6.00
16 Alperen Sengun 6.00 15.00
17 Trey Murphy III 6.00 15.00
18 Tre Mann 3.00 8.00
19 Kai Jones 1.50 4.00
20 Jalen Johnson 6.00 15.00
21 Keon Johnson 2.00 5.00
22 Isaiah Jackson 2.00 5.00
23 Usman Garuba 1.50 4.00
24 Josh Christopher 1.50 4.00
25 Quentin Grimes 4.00 10.00
26 Bones Hyland 2.50 6.00
27 Cameron Thomas 4.00 10.00
28 Jaden Springer 2.00 5.00
29 Day'Ron Sharpe 2.00 5.00
30 Santi Aldama 2.50 6.00
31 Jeremiah Robinson-Earl 2.00 5.00
32 Miles McBride 3.00 8.00
33 Ayo Dosunmu 4.00 10.00
34 Jared Butler 2.00 5.00
35 Isaiah Livers 2.00 5.00
36 Greg Brown III 1.50 4.00
37 Brandon Boston Jr. 2.00 5.00
38 Luka Garza 2.00 5.00
39 Charles Bassey 2.00 5.00
40 Scottie Lewis 1.50 4.00

2021-22 Panini Contenders Sophomore Contenders Autographs

COMMON CARD 4.00 10.00
SEMISTARS 5.00 12.00
UNLISTED STARS 6.00 15.00
STATED PRINT RUN 25-199 SER. #'d SETS
EXCHANGE DEADLINE 9/30/2023
*BRONZE/25: .75X TO 2X BASIC
1 Anthony Edwards/25 125.00 300.00
2 Jae'Sean Tate/199 6.00 15.00
3 James Wiseman/25 5.00 12.00
4 Onyeka Okongwu/49 6.00 15.00
5 Isaac Okoro/49 5.00 12.00
6 Facundo Campazzo/199 6.00 15.00
7 Deni Avdija/49 6.00 15.00
9 Zeke Nnaji/199 5.00 12.00
10 Saben Lee/199 5.00 12.00

2021-22 Panini Contenders Suite Shots

COMMON CARD .40 1.00
SEMISTARS .50 1.25
UNLISTED STARS .60 1.50
*CRACKED ICE/25: 4X TO 10X BASIC
1 Jaylen Brown 1.00 2.50
2 Mike Conley .50 1.25
3 Nikola Jokic 3.00 8.00
4 Carmelo Anthony 1.00 2.50
5 Kyrie Irving 1.25 3.00
6 Ray Allen 1.00 2.50
7 Damian Lillard 1.50 4.00
8 Steve Nash 1.25 3.00
9 Jayson Tatum 2.50 6.00
10 Stephen Curry 4.00 10.00
11 Bradley Beal .75 2.00
12 Julius Randle .75 2.00
13 Devin Booker 1.50 4.00
14 Tyrese Haliburton 1.25 3.00
15 RJ Barrett 1.00 2.50
16 Larry Bird 2.00 5.00
17 Terry Rozier .50 1.25
18 Anfernee Hardaway 1.50 4.00
19 Donovan Mitchell 1.25 3.00
20 Zach LaVine 1.00 2.50
21 Luka Doncic 4.00 10.00
22 Paul George 1.00 2.50
23 Trae Young 1.50 4.00
24 Duncan Robinson .50 1.25
25 Buddy Hield .50 1.25
26 Allen Iverson 1.50 4.00
27 Giannis Antetokounmpo 3.00 8.00
28 Michael Porter Jr. .75 2.00
29 Lonzo Ball .60 1.50
30 Khris Middleton .60 1.50

2021-22 Panini Contenders Superstar Die-Cuts

COMMON CARD 1.00 2.50
SEMISTARS 1.25 3.00
UNLISTED STARS 1.50 4.00
*CRACKED ICE/25: 3X TO 8X BASIC
1 LaMelo Ball 4.00 10.00
2 Luka Doncic 10.00 25.00
3 Kawhi Leonard 4.00 10.00
4 Jayson Tatum 6.00 15.00
5 Stephen Curry 10.00 25.00
6 LeBron James 12.00 30.00
7 Trae Young 4.00 10.00
8 Giannis Antetokounmpo 8.00 20.00
9 Zion Williamson 4.00 10.00
10 Kevin Durant 5.00 12.00

2021-22 Panini Contenders Veteran Autographs

COMMON CARD 4.00 10.00
SEMISTARS 5.00 12.00
UNLISTED STARS 6.00 15.00
EXCHANGE DEADLINE 09/30/2023
*PREMIUM AU: .5X TO 1.2X BASIC
*FINALS TICKET AU/35: .5X TO 1.2X BASIC
1 Luka Doncic 500.00 1,000.00
3 Anthony Davis 50.00 120.00
4 Larry Bird 125.00 300.00
5 Ja Morant 300.00 600.00
6 Zion Williamson 200.00 500.00
7 Anthony Edwards 200.00 500.00
8 Trae Young 125.00 300.00
9 Shaquille O'Neal 125.00 300.00
10 Oscar Robertson 50.00 120.00

2022-23 Panini Contenders

COMMON CARD (1-100) .30 .75
SEMISTARS .40 1.00
UNLISTED STARS .50 1.25
COMMON RC AU (101-145) 5.00 12.00
AU SEMIS 6.00 15.00
AU UNLISTED 8.00 20.00
*GM TCKT BRNZ: .6X TO 1.5X BASIC
*GM TCKT GREEN: .6X TO 1.5X BASIC
*GM TCKT RED: .6X TO 1.5X BASIC
*PLAY-IN TCKT: .75X TO 2X BASIC
*PREMIUM (1-100): .75X TO 2X BASIC
*PREMIUM RC AU (101-145): .5X TO 1.2X BASIC
*PLAYOFF TCKT/249 (1-100): .75X TO 2X BASIC
*PLAYOFF TCKT RC AU/99 (101-145): .6X TO 1.5X BASIC
*FIRST ROUND TCKT/199: .75X TO 2X BASIC
*GM TCKT GREEN ICE: 1X TO 2.5X BASIC
*SEMIFINAL TCKT/99: 1.25X TO 3X BASIC
*CONFERENCE FNLS TCKT/75: 1.5X TO 4X BASIC
*GM TCKT BLUE/49: 2X TO 5X BASIC
*FINALS TCKT/49 (1-100): 2X TO 5X BASIC
*FINALS TCKT RC AU/49 (101-145): .75X TO 2X BASIC
*GM TCKT PRPL/25: 4X TO 10X BASIC
*OPN NGHT TCKT FOTLL/25: 4X TO 10X BASIC
1 Rudy Gobert .60 1.50
2 Anthony Edwards 2.50 6.00
3 Marcus Smart .60 1.50
4 Kevin Durant 1.50 4.00
5 Kyrie Irving 1.00 2.50
6 Damian Lillard 1.25 3.00
7 Luguentz Dort .50 1.25
8 James Harden 1.00 2.50
9 Joel Embiid .75 2.00
10 Jayson Tatum 2.00 5.00
11 Michael Porter Jr. .60 1.50
12 Scottie Barnes .75 2.00
13 Ben Simmons .50 1.25
14 Julius Randle .60 1.50
15 Fred VanVleet .60 1.50
16 Josh Giddey .75 2.00
17 Nikola Jokic 2.50 6.00
18 Shai Gilgeous-Alexander 2.50 6.00
19 RJ Barrett .75 2.00
20 Karl-Anthony Towns .75 2.00
21 Jaylen Brown 1.00 2.50
22 Pascal Siakam .75 2.00
23 Jamal Murray .75 2.00
24 Jalen Brunson 1.00 2.50
25 Anfernee Simons .60 1.50
26 Darius Garland .75 2.00
27 Kawhi Leonard 1.25 3.00
28 Anthony Davis 1.25 3.00
29 Bojan Bogdanovic .50 1.25
30 Paul George .75 2.00
31 Stephen Curry 4.00 10.00
32 Tyrese Haliburton 1.00 2.50
33 Collin Sexton .60 1.50
34 Lonzo Ball .50 1.25
35 Giannis Antetokounmpo 2.50 6.00
36 LeBron James 4.00 10.00
37 Khris Middleton .60 1.50
38 Jonathan Kuminga 1.25 3.00
39 Donovan Mitchell 1.00 2.50
40 Saddiq Bey .40 1.00
41 James Wiseman .40 1.00
42 Zach LaVine 1.00 2.50
43 DeMar DeRozan .60 1.50
44 Cade Cunningham 1.50 4.00
45 Myles Turner .50 1.25
46 Mike Conley .40 1.00
47 Evan Mobley 1.25 3.00
48 Chris Duarte .40 1.00
49 Jrue Holiday .60 1.50
50 Russell Westbrook .75 2.00
51 Christian Wood .30 .75
52 Cole Anthony .50 1.25
53 Dejounte Murray .60 1.50
54 Kevin Porter Jr. .40 1.00
55 Franz Wagner 1.25 3.00
56 De'Aaron Fox 1.00 2.50
57 Luka Doncic 3.00 8.00
58 Jalen Suggs .60 1.50
59 Davion Mitchell .40 1.00
60 Kristaps Porzingis .60 1.50
61 Spencer Dinwiddie .40 1.00
62 Chris Paul 1.00 2.50
63 Bam Adebayo .75 2.00
64 Bradley Beal .60 1.50
65 Tyler Herro .75 2.00
66 Trae Young 1.25 3.00
67 Devin Booker 1.25 3.00
68 Kyle Kuzma .60 1.50
69 Deandre Ayton .50 1.25
70 Jalen Green 1.50 4.00
71 John Wall .60 1.50
72 LaMelo Ball 1.25 3.00
73 Domantas Sabonis .60 1.50
74 Gordon Hayward .40 1.00
75 Jimmy Butler 1.00 2.50
76 Jaren Jackson Jr. .75 2.00
77 Ja Morant 1.50 4.00
78 Devin Vassell .60 1.50
79 Klay Thompson 1.25 3.00
80 Cameron Thomas .75 2.00
81 Tre Mann .40 1.00
82 Buddy Hield .50 1.25
83 Terry Rozier III .60 1.50
84 Ayo Dosunmu .60 1.50
85 Zion Williamson 1.25 3.00
86 Markelle Fultz .40 1.00
87 Lauri Markkanen .75 2.00
88 Jusuf Nurkic .50 1.25
89 Desmond Bane .60 1.50
90 Kyle Lowry .60 1.50
91 Alperen Sengun .60 1.50
92 D'Angelo Russell .40 1.00
93 Jerami Grant .60 1.50
94 CJ McCollum .50 1.25
95 Brandon Ingram .60 1.50
96 Marvin Bagley III .40 1.00
97 Keldon Johnson .60 1.50
98 Tim Hardaway Jr. .40 1.00
99 Tobias Harris .40 1.00
100 Malcolm Brogdon .40 1.00
101 Jaden Ivey RC 25.00 60.00
102 Jalen Duren RC 25.00 60.00
103 Wendell Moore Jr. RC 8.00 20.00
104 Ochai Agbaji RC 10.00 25.00
105 David Roddy RC 10.00 25.00
106 Christian Braun RC 20.00 50.00
107 Peyton Watson RC 12.00 30.00
108 Tyrese Martin RC 6.00 15.00
109 Caleb Houstan RC 6.00 15.00
110 Shaedon Sharpe RC 30.00 80.00
111 Moussa Diabate RC 8.00 20.00
112 Paolo Banchero RC 150.00 400.00
113 Trevor Keels RC 6.00 15.00
114 Jabari Walker RC 6.00 15.00
115 Jalen Williams RC 40.00 100.00
116 Tari Eason RC 20.00 50.00
117 Jabari Smith Jr. RC 25.00 60.00
118 Bennedict Mathurin RC 25.00 60.00
119 Andrew Nembhard RC 15.00 40.00
120 Jake LaRavia RC 8.00 20.00
121 Ryan Rollins RC 8.00 20.00
122 Ousmane Dieng RC 10.00 25.00
123 Jeremy Sochan RC 25.00 60.00
124 E.J. Liddell RC 8.00 20.00
125 Malaki Branham RC 8.00 20.00
126 Isaiah Mobley RC 8.00 20.00
127 Kennedy Chandler RC 8.00 20.00
128 TyTy Washington Jr. RC 8.00 20.00
129 AJ Griffin RC 6.00 15.00
130 Johnny Davis RC 8.00 20.00
131 Josh Minott RC 8.00 20.00
132 Patrick Baldwin Jr. RC 8.00 20.00
133 Blake Wesley RC 8.00 20.00
134 Walker Kessler RC 15.00 40.00
135 Nikola Jovic RC 15.00 40.00
136 Mark Williams RC 15.00 40.00
137 Chet Holmgren RC 125.00 300.00
138 Jaylin Williams RC 10.00 25.00
139 Christian Koloko RC 8.00 20.00
140 Keegan Murray RC 20.00 50.00
141 Dalen Terry RC 8.00 20.00
142 Dyson Daniels RC 20.00 50.00
143 MarJon Beauchamp RC 8.00 20.00
144 Max Christie RC 20.00 50.00
145 Jaden Hardy RC 12.00 30.00
146 Collin Gillespie 6.00 15.00
147 Bryce McGowens 6.00 15.00
148 Jordan Hall 5.00 12.00
149 Julian Champagnie 8.00 20.00
150 Justin Lewis 6.00 15.00
151 Vince Williams Jr. 8.00 20.00
152 Kendall Brown 5.00 12.00
153 Kenneth Lofton Jr. 8.00 20.00
154 Michael Foster Jr. 5.00 12.00
155 Simone Fontecchio 6.00 15.00
156 Vlatko Cancar 8.00 20.00
157 Johnny Juzang 8.00 20.00
158 Scotty Pippen Jr. 8.00 20.00
159 Alondes Williams 6.00 15.00
160 Devin Cannady 6.00 15.00
161 Keon Ellis 6.00 15.00
162 Dereon Seabron 5.00 12.00
163 Cole Swider 8.00 20.00
164 Ron Harper Jr. 8.00 20.00
165 Buddy Boeheim 6.00 15.00

2022-23 Panini Contenders Cracked Ice Ticket

COMPLETE SET (164)
*CRCKD ICE TCKT/25 (1-100): 5X TO 12X BASIC
*CRCKD ICE TCKT RC AU/25 (101-145): 3X TO 8X BASIC
*CRCKD ICE TCKT RC AU/25 (146-165): 2X TO 5X BASIC
31 Stephen Curry 75.00 200.00
36 LeBron James 75.00 200.00
112 Paolo Banchero 2,000.00 4,000.00

2022-23 Panini Contenders Retail

COMMON CARD (1-100) .30 .75
SEMISTARS .40 1.00
UNLISTED STARS .50 1.25
COMMON RC AU (101-120) 4.00 10.00
AU SEMIS 5.00 12.00
AU UNLISTED 6.00 15.00
*GREEN ICE RC AU: .5X TO 1.2X BASIC
*PLAYOFF TCKT RC AU/99: .6X TO 1.5X BASIC
*FINALS TCKT RC AU/49): .6X TO 1.5X BASIC
*CRCKD ICE TCKT RC AU/25: 2X TO 5X BASIC

2022-23 Panini Contenders Contenders Autographs

COMMON CARD 4.00 10.00
SEMISTARS 5.00 12.00
UNLISTED STARS 6.00 15.00
1 Jonathan Kuminga/49 20.00 50.00
2 Tim Hardaway Jr./199 5.00 12.00
3 Tyrese Haliburton/49 50.00 120.00
4 Ayo Dosunmu/99 8.00 20.00
5 Franz Wagner/99 15.00 40.00
6 Chris Duarte/199 5.00 12.00
7 Steven Adams/99 6.00 15.00
8 Ivica Zubac/99 6.00 15.00
9 Chris Paul/49 40.00 100.00
10 RJ Hampton/99 5.00 12.00
11 Lauri Markkanen/49 40.00 100.00
12 Grayson Allen/199 6.00 15.00
13 Duncan Robinson/99 6.00 15.00
14 Cameron Thomas/199 10.00 25.00
15 Marcus Smart/99 20.00 50.00
16 Tre Mann/199 5.00 12.00
17 Moses Moody/99 8.00 20.00
18 Jalen Brunson/99 40.00 100.00
19 RJ Barrett/49 12.00 30.00
20 Danny Green/199 5.00 12.00
21 Rajon Rondo/49 12.00 30.00
22 Ziaire Williams/199 5.00 12.00
23 Michael Porter Jr./99 8.00 20.00
24 Chris Boucher/199 6.00 15.00
25 Keldon Johnson/99 8.00 20.00
26 Herbert Jones/199 6.00 15.00
27 Avery Bradley/99 4.00 10.00
28 Nickeil Alexander-Walker/99 5.00 12.00
29 Brandon Ingram/49 40.00 100.00
30 Lonnie Walker IV/199 5.00 12.00
31 Andre Drummond/49 6.00 15.00
32 Alperen Sengun/199 20.00 50.00
33 Jordan Clarkson/99 12.00 30.00
34 Evan Fournier/199 5.00 12.00
35 Obi Toppin/99 6.00 15.00
36 Bones Hyland/199 5.00 12.00
37 Bogdan Bogdanovic/99 6.00 15.00
38 Pat Connaughton/99 5.00 12.00
39 Dejounte Murray/49 20.00 50.00
40 Aleksej Pokusevski/199 6.00 15.00

2022-23 Panini Contenders Contenders Autographs Bronze

*BRONZE/25: .75X TO 2X BASIC
1 Jonathan Kuminga 25.00 60.00
3 Tyrese Haliburton 100.00 250.00
9 Chris Paul 50.00 120.00
11 Lauri Markkanen 50.00 120.00
19 RJ Barrett 15.00 40.00
21 Rajon Rondo 15.00 40.00
29 Brandon Ingram 50.00 120.00
39 Dejounte Murray 25.00 60.00

2022-23 Panini Contenders Draft Class Contenders

COMMON CARD .50 1.25
SEMISTARS .60 1.50
UNLISTED STARS .75 2.00
*CRKD ICE/25: 4X TO 10X BASIC
1 Bennedict Mathurin 2.50 6.00
2 Jeremy Sochan 2.50 6.00
3 Jake LaRavia .75 2.00
4 Jabari Smith Jr. 2.50 6.00
5 Shaedon Sharpe 3.00 8.00
6 Malaki Branham .75 2.00
7 Ochai Agbaji 1.00 2.50
8 Dyson Daniels 2.00 5.00
9 Jaden Ivey 2.50 6.00
10 Keegan Murray 2.00 5.00
11 Tari Eason 2.00 5.00
12 MarJon Beauchamp .75 2.00
13 David Roddy 1.00 2.50
14 Paolo Banchero 5.00 12.00
15 Mark Williams 1.50 4.00
16 Johnny Davis .75 2.00
17 AJ Griffin .60 1.50
18 Jalen Duren 2.50 6.00
19 Jalen Williams 4.00 10.00
20 Dalen Terry .75 2.00
21 Christian Braun 2.00 5.00
22 Ousmane Dieng 1.00 2.50
23 Chet Holmgren 4.00 10.00
24 Blake Wesley .75 2.00
25 Walker Kessler 1.50 4.00

2022-23 Panini Contenders Game Night Ticket

COMMON CARD .30 .75
SEMISTARS .40 1.00
UNLISTED STARS .50 1.25
*CRKD ICE/25: 4X TO 10X BASIC
1 De'Aaron Fox 1.00 2.50
2 Jayson Tatum 2.00 5.00
3 James Harden 1.00 2.50
4 DeMar DeRozan .60 1.50
5 Stephen Curry 4.00 10.00
6 Anthony Edwards 2.50 6.00
7 LaMelo Ball 1.25 3.00
8 Cade Cunningham 1.50 4.00
9 Trae Young 1.25 3.00
10 Kevin Durant 1.50 4.00
11 Damian Lillard 1.25 3.00
12 Ja Morant 1.50 4.00
13 Devin Booker 1.25 3.00
14 Scottie Barnes .75 2.00
15 Joel Embiid .75 2.00
16 Nikola Jokic 2.50 6.00
17 Jalen Green 1.50 4.00
18 Tyrese Haliburton 1.00 2.50
19 Donovan Mitchell 1.00 2.50
20 Bradley Beal .60 1.50
21 LeBron James 4.00 10.00
22 Anthony Davis 1.25 3.00
23 Giannis Antetokounmpo 2.50 6.00
24 Luka Doncic 3.00 8.00
25 Shai Gilgeous-Alexander 2.50 6.00

2022-23 Panini Contenders Historic Draft Class Contenders

COMMON CARD .30 .75
SEMISTARS .40 1.00
UNLISTED STARS .50 1.25
*CRKD ICE/25: 4X TO 10X BASIC
1 Shaquille O'Neal 2.00 5.00
2 Allen Iverson 1.25 3.00
3 Tim Duncan 1.25 3.00
4 Gary Payton .75 2.00
5 Anfernee Hardaway 1.25 3.00
6 Jason Kidd .75 2.00
7 Grant Hill .75 2.00
8 Kevin Garnett 1.25 3.00
9 Ray Allen .75 2.00
10 Steve Nash 1.00 2.50
11 Vince Carter 1.00 2.50
12 Dirk Nowitzki 1.25 3.00
13 Paul Pierce .75 2.00
14 Pau Gasol .75 2.00
15 Dwyane Wade 1.00 2.50
16 David Robinson 1.00 2.50
17 Karl Malone 1.00 2.50
18 Stephen Curry 4.00 10.00
19 Chris Webber .60 1.50
20 LeBron James 4.00 10.00
21 Kevin Durant 1.50 4.00
22 Tracy McGrady .75 2.00
23 Hakeem Olajuwon 1.00 2.50
24 Charles Barkley 1.25 3.00
25 John Stockton 1.00 2.50

2022-23 Panini Contenders Legendary Contenders Autographs

COMMON CARD 4.00 10.00
SEMISTARS 5.00 12.00
UNLISTED STARS 6.00 15.00
1 Brad Miller/199 5.00 12.00
2 Grant Hill/49 20.00 50.00
3 Michael Olowokandi /199 5.00 12.00
4 Steve Francis/99 6.00 15.00
5 John Lucas/99 6.00 15.00
6 Morris Peterson/199 5.00 12.00
7 Harold Miner/99 6.00 15.00
8 Jamaal Wilkes/99 6.00 15.00
9 Willie Green/199 6.00 15.00
10 Antawn Jamison/99 6.00 15.00
11 Jamal Crawford/49 6.00 15.00
12 Oscar Robertson/49 30.00 80.00
13 Jim Paxson/199 6.00 15.00
14 Kareem Abdul-Jabbar/49 75.00 200.00
15 Carl Landry/99 6.00 15.00
16 Charlie Ward/99 6.00 15.00
17 Manu Ginobili/49 40.00 100.00
18 Mark Price/199 6.00 15.00
19 David Wesley/199 5.00 12.00
20 Jason Kidd/49 15.00 40.00
21 Pervis Ellison/199 5.00 12.00
22 Tim Hardaway/99 8.00 20.00
23 Luis Scola/199 5.00 12.00
24 Muggsy Bogues/199 15.00 40.00
25 Adam Morrison/199 5.00 12.00
26 Greg Anthony/199 5.00 12.00
27 Billy Knight/199 6.00 15.00
28 Shawn Kemp/99 20.00 50.00
29 Juwan Howard/99 6.00 15.00
30 Lenny Wilkens/99 8.00 20.00
31 Frank Selvy/199 6.00 15.00
32 Hakeem Olajuwon/49 40.00 100.00
33 Carlos Boozer/99 5.00 12.00
34 Glen Rice/99 6.00 15.00
35 Eddy Curry/199 5.00 12.00
36 Jack Sikma/99 8.00 20.00
37 Quentin Richardson/99 5.00 12.00
38 Adrian Dantley/99 6.00 15.00
39 Willie Anderson/199 5.00 12.00
40 Walt Frazier/49 12.00 30.00

2022-23 Panini Contenders Legendary Contenders Autographs Bronze

*BRONZE/25: .75X TO 2X BASIC
2 Grant Hill 25.00 60.00
12 Oscar Robertson 40.00 100.00
14 Kareem Abdul-Jabbar 100.00 250.00
17 Manu Ginobili 50.00 120.00
20 Jason Kidd 20.00 50.00
32 Hakeem Olajuwon 50.00 120.00
40 Walt Frazier 15.00 40.00

2022-23 Panini Contenders License to Dominate

1 Trae Young 15.00 40.00
2 Jalen Green 40.00 100.00
3 DeMar DeRozan 8.00 20.00
4 Zach LaVine 12.00 30.00
5 Devin Booker 15.00 40.00
6 James Harden 12.00 30.00
7 Donovan Mitchell 12.00 30.00
8 Ja Morant 20.00 50.00
9 LaMelo Ball 15.00 40.00
10 LeBron James 125.00 300.00
11 Bradley Beal 8.00 20.00
12 Scottie Barnes 10.00 25.00
13 Damian Lillard 15.00 40.00
14 Zion Williamson 15.00 40.00
15 Shai Gilgeous-Alexander 30.00 80.00
16 Stephen Curry 75.00 200.00
17 Nikola Jokic 30.00 80.00
18 Anthony Edwards 30.00 80.00
19 Giannis Antetokounmpo 60.00 150.00
20 Luka Doncic 40.00 100.00
21 Kawhi Leonard 15.00 40.00
22 Cade Cunningham 20.00 50.00
23 Kevin Durant 20.00 50.00
24 Anthony Davis 15.00 40.00
25 Jayson Tatum 25.00 60.00

2022-23 Panini Contenders Lottery Ticket

COMMON CARD .60 1.50
SEMISTARS .75 2.00
UNLISTED STARS 1.00 2.50
1 Paolo Banchero 6.00 15.00
2 Chet Holmgren 5.00 12.00
3 Jabari Smith Jr. 3.00 8.00
4 Keegan Murray 2.50 6.00
5 Jaden Ivey 3.00 8.00
6 Bennedict Mathurin 3.00 8.00
7 Shaedon Sharpe 4.00 10.00
8 Dyson Daniels 2.50 6.00
9 Jeremy Sochan 3.00 8.00
10 Johnny Davis 1.00 2.50
11 Ousmane Dieng 1.25 3.00
12 Jalen Williams 5.00 12.00
13 Jalen Duren 3.00 8.00
14 Ochai Agbaji 1.25 3.00

2022-23 Panini Contenders Lottery Ticket Cracked Ice

*CRKD ICE/25: 4X TO 10X BASIC
1 Paolo Banchero 200.00 500.00
2 Chet Holmgren 125.00 300.00
7 Shaedon Sharpe 75.00 200.00
12 Jalen Williams 75.00 200.00

2022-23 Panini Contenders Permit to Dominate

1 AJ Griffin 6.00 15.00
2 Patrick Baldwin Jr. 8.00 20.00
3 Dyson Daniels 20.00 50.00
4 Dalen Terry 8.00 20.00
5 Blake Wesley 8.00 20.00
6 Jalen Williams 50.00 120.00
7 Paolo Banchero 100.00 250.00
8 Bennedict Mathurin 50.00 120.00
9 Jabari Smith Jr. 40.00 100.00
10 Nikola Jovic 15.00 40.00
11 Jalen Duren 30.00 80.00
12 Tari Eason 20.00 50.00
13 Jaden Ivey 60.00 150.00
14 Christian Braun 20.00 50.00
15 Jake LaRavia 8.00 20.00
16 Ousmane Dieng 10.00 25.00
17 Malaki Branham 8.00 20.00
18 Wendell Moore Jr. 8.00 20.00
19 Keegan Murray 50.00 120.00
20 Jeremy Sochan 50.00 120.00
21 Chet Holmgren 60.00 150.00
22 Johnny Davis 8.00 20.00
23 Shaedon Sharpe 60.00 150.00
24 Ochai Agbaji 50.00 120.00
25 Jaden Hardy 30.00 80.00

2022-23 Panini Contenders Premium Blue Shimmer FOTL

*BLUE SHIMMER FOTL/21 (101-145): 1.5X TO 4X BASIC
107 Peyton Watson 125.00 300.00
112 Paolo Banchero 3,000.00 6,000.00
116 Tari Eason 150.00 400.00
123 Jeremy Sochan 500.00 1,000.00
134 Walker Kessler 600.00 1,200.00
138 Jaylin Williams 125.00 300.00

2022-23 Panini Contenders Rookie of the Year Contenders

COMMON CARD .60 1.50
SEMISTARS .75 2.00
UNLISTED STARS 1.00 2.50
1 Paolo Banchero 6.00 15.00
2 Jabari Smith Jr. 3.00 8.00
3 Walker Kessler 3.00 8.00
4 Jeremy Sochan 3.00 8.00
5 Ousmane Dieng 1.25 3.00
6 Keegan Murray 2.50 6.00
7 Christian Koloko 1.00 2.50
8 Tari Eason 2.50 6.00
9 Ochai Agbaji 1.25 3.00
10 AJ Griffin .75 2.00
11 Bennedict Mathurin 3.00 8.00
12 Malaki Branham 1.00 2.50
13 Shaedon Sharpe 4.00 10.00
14 Dyson Daniels 2.50 6.00
15 Jaden Ivey 3.00 8.00
16 Jalen Williams 5.00 12.00
17 Andrew Nembhard 2.00 5.00
18 Jalen Duren 3.00 8.00

2022-23 Panini Contenders Rookie of the Year Contenders Cracked Ice

*CRKD ICE/25: 4X TO 10X BASIC
1 Paolo Banchero 200.00 500.00
13 Shaedon Sharpe 60.00 150.00
16 Jalen Williams 75.00 200.00

2022-23 Panini Contenders Rookie Stallions

COMMON CARD .60 1.50
SEMISTARS .75 2.00
UNLISTED STARS 1.00 2.50
1 Bennedict Mathurin 3.00 8.00
2 Peyton Watson 1.50 4.00
3 Malaki Branham 1.00 2.50
4 Johnny Davis 1.00 2.50
5 Keegan Murray 2.50 6.00
6 Dyson Daniels 2.50 6.00
7 Wendell Moore Jr. 1.00 2.50
8 Jalen Williams 5.00 12.00
9 Mark Williams 2.00 5.00
10 Jeremy Sochan 3.00 8.00
11 Jalen Duren 3.00 8.00
12 Dalen Terry 1.00 2.50
13 Ochai Agbaji 1.25 3.00
14 Patrick Baldwin Jr. 1.00 2.50
15 Nikola Jovic 2.00 5.00
16 Jaden Hardy 1.50 4.00
17 Tari Eason 2.50 6.00
18 AJ Griffin .75 2.00
19 Paolo Banchero 6.00 15.00
20 Chet Holmgren 5.00 12.00
21 Ousmane Dieng 1.25 3.00
22 Jabari Smith Jr. 3.00 8.00
23 Shaedon Sharpe 4.00 10.00
24 Jake LaRavia 1.00 2.50
25 Jaden Ivey 3.00 8.00

2022-23 Panini Contenders Rookie Stallions Cracked Ice

*CRKD ICE/25: 4X TO 10X BASIC
8 Jalen Williams 75.00 200.00
19 Paolo Banchero 200.00 500.00
20 Chet Holmgren 125.00 300.00
23 Shaedon Sharpe 60.00 150.00

2022-23 Panini Contenders Rookie Ticket Dual Swatches

1 Jaden Ivey
Paolo Banchero 20.00 50.00
2 Ousmane Dieng
Chet Holmgren 15.00 40.00
3 Jabari Smith Jr.
Keegan Murray 10.00 25.00
4 AJ Griffin
Ochai Agbaji 4.00 10.00
5 Chet Holmgren
Paolo Banchero 20.00 50.00
6 Bennedict Mathurin
Dalen Terry 10.00 25.00
7 Shaedon Sharpe
Jalen Williams 15.00 40.00
8 Dyson Daniels
Johnny Davis 8.00 20.00
9 Malaki Branham
Jeremy Sochan 10.00 25.00
10 Jaden Ivey
Jalen Duren 10.00 25.00

2022-23 Panini Contenders Rookie Ticket Swatches

COMMON CARD 2.00 5.00
SEMISTARS 2.50 6.00
UNLISTED STARS 3.00 8.00
1 Tari Eason 8.00 20.00
2 Malaki Branham 3.00 8.00
3 Jaden Ivey 10.00 25.00
4 Jabari Smith Jr. 10.00 25.00
5 Paolo Banchero 20.00 50.00
6 Shaedon Sharpe 12.00 30.00
7 Jeremy Sochan 10.00 25.00
8 Bennedict Mathurin 10.00 25.00
9 Jake LaRavia 3.00 8.00
10 Dyson Daniels 8.00 20.00
11 Johnny Davis 3.00 8.00
12 AJ Griffin 2.50 6.00
13 Keegan Murray 8.00 20.00
14 Jalen Duren 10.00 25.00
15 Jalen Williams 15.00 40.00
16 Dalen Terry 3.00 8.00
17 Mark Williams 6.00 15.00
18 Ochai Agbaji 4.00 10.00
19 Chet Holmgren 15.00 40.00
20 Ousmane Dieng 4.00 10.00
21 Wendell Moore Jr. 3.00 8.00
22 Caleb Houstan 3.00 8.00
23 E.J. Liddell 3.00 8.00
24 Walker Kessler 6.00 15.00
25 Trevor Keels 2.50 6.00
26 Blake Wesley 3.00 8.00
27 Max Christie 8.00 20.00
28 Andrew Nembhard 6.00 15.00
29 Jaden Hardy 5.00 12.00
30 Peyton Watson 5.00 12.00
31 Kennedy Chandler 3.00 8.00
32 Nikola Jovic 6.00 15.00
33 Isaiah Mobley 3.00 8.00
34 TyTy Washington Jr. 3.00 8.00
35 Christian Braun 8.00 20.00
36 Patrick Baldwin Jr. 3.00 8.00
37 Moussa Diabate 3.00 8.00
38 David Roddy 4.00 10.00
39 MarJon Beauchamp 3.00 8.00
40 Christian Koloko 3.00 8.00

2022-23 Panini Contenders Sophomore Contenders Autographs

COMMON CARD 4.00 10.00
SEMISTARS 5.00 12.00
UNLISTED STARS 6.00 15.00
*BRONZE/25: .5X TO 1.2X BASIC
1 Scottie Barnes/99 20.00 50.00
2 Franz Wagner/99 20.00 50.00
3 Herbert Jones/99 6.00 15.00
4 Jalen Green/49 40.00 100.00
5 Ayo Dosunmu/99 8.00 20.00
6 Davion Mitchell/99 5.00 12.00
7 Corey Kispert/99 6.00 15.00
8 Josh Giddey/99 30.00 80.00
9 Alperen Sengun/99 20.00 50.00
10 Ziaire Williams/99 5.00 12.00

2022-23 Panini Contenders Suite Shots

COMMON CARD .30 .75
SEMISTARS .40 1.00
UNLISTED STARS .50 1.25
*CRKD ICE/25: 4X TO 10X BASIC
1 Cade Cunningham 1.50 4.00
2 Luka Doncic 3.00 8.00
3 Allen Iverson 1.25 3.00
4 Stephen Curry 4.00 10.00
5 Paul George .75 2.00
6 Buddy Hield .50 1.25
7 Anthony Edwards 2.50 6.00
8 Jayson Tatum 2.00 5.00
9 Jamal Murray .75 2.00
10 James Harden 1.00 2.50
11 Shaquille O'Neal 2.00 5.00
12 Duncan Robinson .50 1.25
13 Donovan Mitchell 1.00 2.50
14 Bradley Beal .60 1.50
15 Jaylen Brown 1.00 2.50
16 CJ McCollum .50 1.25
17 LaMelo Ball 1.25 3.00
18 LeBron James 4.00 10.00
19 Kyrie Irving 1.00 2.50
20 Dwyane Wade 1.00 2.50
21 Nikola Jokic 2.50 6.00
22 Ja Morant 1.50 4.00
23 Devin Booker 1.25 3.00

24 Jordan Poole .75 2.00
25 Dirk Nowitzki 1.25 3.00
26 Trae Young 1.25 3.00
27 DeMar DeRozan .60 1.50
28 Khris Middleton .60 1.50
29 Tyrese Haliburton 1.00 2.50
30 Damian Lillard 1.25 3.00

2022-23 Panini Contenders Superstar Die-Cuts

*CRKD ICE/25: 4X TO 10X BASIC
1 Jayson Tatum 3.00 8.00
2 Luka Doncic 5.00 12.00
3 Kevin Durant 2.50 6.00
4 Stephen Curry 6.00 15.00
5 LeBron James 6.00 15.00
6 Zion Williamson 2.00 5.00
7 Anthony Edwards 4.00 10.00
8 Giannis Antetokounmpo 4.00 10.00
9 Trae Young 2.00 5.00
10 Ja Morant 2.50 6.00

2022-23 Panini Contenders Ticket to the Hall

COMMON CARD .30 .75
SEMISTARS .40 1.00
UNLISTED STARS .50 1.25
*CRKD ICE/25: 4X TO 10X BASIC
1 Dwyane Wade 1.00 2.50
2 Dirk Nowitzki 1.25 3.00
3 Giannis Antetokounmpo 2.50 6.00
4 Damian Lillard 1.25 3.00
5 Stephen Curry 4.00 10.00
6 Shawn Marion .50 1.25
7 Pau Gasol .75 2.00
8 Carmelo Anthony .75 2.00
9 Kawhi Leonard 1.25 3.00
10 Draymond Green .60 1.50
11 Anthony Davis 1.25 3.00
12 Nikola Jokic 2.50 6.00
13 Tony Parker .75 2.00
14 James Harden 1.00 2.50
15 Chauncey Billups .60 1.50
16 Dwight Howard .60 1.50
17 Rajon Rondo .60 1.50
18 Kevin Durant 1.50 4.00
19 Luka Doncic 3.00 8.00
20 Russell Westbrook .75 2.00
21 Kyrie Irving 1.00 2.50
22 Amar'e Stoudemire .50 1.25
23 Klay Thompson 1.25 3.00
24 LeBron James 4.00 10.00
25 Kevin Love .50 1.25
26 Rudy Gobert .60 1.50
27 Vince Carter 1.00 2.50
28 Chris Paul 1.00 2.50

2022-23 Panini Contenders Veteran Autographs Season Ticket

*PREMIUM: .5X TO 1.2X BASIC
*GREEN SHMR: .5X TO 1.2X BASIC
*THE FINALS TCKT/49: .6X TO 1.5X BASIC
*PREMIUM BLUE SHMR FOTL/21: .75X TO 2X BASIC
VTAE Anthony Edwards 125.00 300.00
VTAI Allen Iverson 75.00 200.00
VTDW Dwyane Wade 75.00 200.00
VTJM Ja Morant 125.00 300.00
VTJT Jayson Tatum 125.00 300.00
VTLD Luka Doncic 400.00 800.00
VTPP Paul Pierce 40.00 100.00
VTZW Zion Williamson 125.00 300.00
VTHHR Hakeem Olajuwon 40.00 100.00

2023-24 Panini Contenders

*PREMIUM ED GRN SHMR RC AU (101-144): .6X TO 1.5X BASIC
*PLAY-IN TCK: 1.25X TO 3X BASIC
*PREMIUM ED(1-100): 1.25X TO 3X BASIC
*PREMIUM ED RC AU (101-145): .6X TO 1.5X BASIC
1 Dariq Whitehead AU RC 10.00 25.00
1 Nikola Jokic 1.50 4.00
2 Julian Strawther AU RC 10.00 25.00
2 RJ Barrett .50 1.25
3 Lauri Markkanen .50 1.25
3 Rayan Rupert AU RC 8.00 20.00
4 Jrue Holiday .40 1.00
5 Klay Thompson .75 2.00
6 Jerami Grant .40 1.00
7 Tyrese Maxey .60 1.50
8 Josh Giddey .40 1.00
9 Damian Lillard .75 2.00
10 Bennedict Mathurin .50 1.25
11 Victor Wembanyama 4.00 10.00
12 Anthony Davis .75 2.00
13 Fred VanVleet .50 1.25
14 Bradley Beal .40 1.00
15 Austin Reaves .75 2.00
16 Jalen Green .50 1.25
17 Marcus Smart .40 1.00
18 Julius Randle .40 1.00
19 Cameron Johnson .30 .75
20 Cade Cunningham .75 2.00
21 Jordan Poole .50 1.25
22 Paul George .50 1.25
23 Paolo Banchero .75 2.00
24 Brandon Miller 2.00 5.00
25 Kyrie Irving .60 1.50
26 LaMelo Ball .75 2.00
27 Scoot Henderson 1.50 4.00
28 Michael Porter Jr. .40 1.00
29 Darius Garland .50 1.25
30 Pascal Siakam .50 1.25
31 CJ McCollum .30 .75
32 Kyle Kuzma .40 1.00
33 Chet Holmgren .75 2.00
34 Jordan Clarkson .30 .75
35 Anthony Black 1.00 2.50
36 Alperen Sengun .50 1.25
37 Scottie Barnes .40 1.00
38 Brandon Ingram .40 1.00
39 Jarace Walker .60 1.50
40 De'Aaron Fox .60 1.50
41 Zach LaVine .50 1.25
42 Karl-Anthony Towns .50 1.25
43 Taylor Hendricks .50 1.25
44 Jaden Ivey .40 1.00
45 Kristaps Porzingis .40 1.00
46 LeBron James 2.50 6.00
47 Aaron Gordon .30 .75
48 DeMar DeRozan .50 1.25
49 Khris Middleton .30 .75
50 Mikal Bridges .40 1.00
51 Jaden Hardy .40 1.00
52 Shai Gilgeous-Alexander 1.50 4.00
53 Jett Howard .60 1.50
54 Anfernee Simons .40 1.00
55 Stephen Curry 2.50 6.00
56 Joel Embiid .75 2.00
57 Dejounte Murray .40 1.00
58 Jarrett Allen .30 .75
59 Jalen Brunson .60 1.50
60 Tyler Herro .50 1.25
61 Luka Doncic 2.00 5.00
62 Anthony Edwards 1.50 4.00
63 D'Angelo Russell .30 .75
64 Rudy Gobert .40 1.00
65 Andrew Wiggins .40 1.00
66 Giannis Antetokounmpo 1.50 4.00
67 Jalen Williams .60 1.50
68 Keldon Johnson .40 1.00
69 Jimmy Butler .50 1.25
70 Jeremy Sochan .40 1.00
71 Gradey Dick 1.00 2.50
72 Jaylen Brown .60 1.50
73 Immanuel Quickley .30 .75
74 Ja Morant 1.00 2.50
75 Donovan Mitchell .60 1.50
76 Jordan Hawkins .75 2.00
77 Jayson Tatum 1.25 3.00
78 Bam Adebayo .50 1.25
79 Zion Williamson .75 2.00
80 Kawhi Leonard .75 2.00
81 Markelle Fultz .25 .60
82 James Harden .50 1.25
83 Jalen Hood-Schifino .50 1.25
84 Jaime Jaquez Jr. .75 2.00
85 Devin Booker .75 2.00
86 Russell Westbrook .50 1.25
87 Kevin Durant 1.00 2.50
88 Jabari Smith Jr. .50 1.25
89 Deandre Ayton .30 .75
90 Tyrese Haliburton .60 1.50
91 Domantas Sabonis .50 1.25
92 Trae Young .60 1.50
93 Jaren Jackson Jr. .50 1.25
94 Caleb Martin .25 .60
95 Cam Whitmore 1.25 3.00
96 Desmond Bane .40 1.00
97 Franz Wagner .50 1.25
98 Jamal Murray .60 1.50
99 Walker Kessler .30 .75
100 Nick Smith Jr. .60 1.50
101 Julian Phillips RC 8.00 20.00
102 Ben Sheppard RC 8.00 20.00
103 Jordan Miller RC 10.00 25.00
106 Oscar Tshiebwe RC 10.00 25.00
107 Trayce Jackson-Davis RC 10.00 25.00
108 Andre Jackson Jr. RC 12.00 30.00
110 Hunter Tyson RC 8.00 20.00
111 Amen Thompson RC 100.00 250.00
112 Jalen Wilson RC 8.00 20.00
113 Bilal Coulibaly RC 20.00 50.00
114 Mike Miles Jr. RC 6.00 15.00
116 Tristan Vukcevic RC 8.00 20.00
117 Noah Clowney RC 10.00 25.00
118 Marcus Sasser RC 12.00 30.00
119 Colby Jones RC 8.00 20.00
120 Jalen Slawson RC 8.00 20.00
121 Maxwell Lewis RC 6.00 15.00
122 Brandin Podziemski RC 25.00 60.00
123 Cason Wallace RC 15.00 40.00
124 Leonard Miller RC 8.00 20.00
125 Kris Murray RC 8.00 20.00
126 James Nnaji RC 6.00 15.00
127 GG Jackson II RC 15.00 40.00
129 Toumani Camara RC 15.00 40.00
130 Kobe Brown RC 8.00 20.00
131 Olivier-Maxence Prosper RC 8.00 20.00
132 Brice Sensabaugh RC 12.00 30.00
133 Ausar Thompson RC 20.00 50.00
134 Jalen Pickett RC 6.00 15.00
135 Mouhamed Gueye RC 8.00 20.00
136 Markquis Nowell RC 8.00 20.00
137 Sidy Cissoko RC 8.00 20.00
138 Keyontae Johnson RC 8.00 20.00
139 Jaylen Clark RC 8.00 20.00
140 Kobe Bufkin RC 10.00 25.00
141 Jordan Walsh RC 8.00 20.00
142 Chris Livingston RC 8.00 20.00
143 Dereck Lively II RC 15.00 40.00
144 Keyonte George RC 25.00 60.00
145 Terquavion Smith RC 8.00 20.00

2023-24 Panini Contenders Conference Finals Ticket

*CONFERENCE FINALS TCK: 2.5X TO 6X BASIC
STATED PRINT RUN 75 SER. #'D SETS
11 Victor Wembanyama 125.00 300.00

2023-24 Panini Contenders Cracked Ice Ticket

*CRCKD ICE TCKT/25 (1-100): 5X TO 12X BASIC
*CRCKD ICE TCKT RC AU/25 (101-165): 2X TO 5X BASIC
11 Victor Wembanyama 1,000.00 2,000.00

2023-24 Panini Contenders First Round Ticket

*FIRST ROUND TCK: 1.5X TO 4X BASIC
STATED PRINT RUN 149 SER. #'D SETS
11 Victor Wembanyama 60.00 150.00

2023-24 Panini Contenders Game Ticket Blue

*GAME TCK BLUE: 3X TO 8X BASIC
STATED PRINT RUN 49 SER. #'D SETS
11 Victor Wembanyama 400.00 800.00
24 Brandon Miller 60.00 150.00

2023-24 Panini Contenders Game Ticket Bronze

11 Victor Wembanyama 12.00 30.00

2023-24 Panini Contenders Game Ticket Green

GM TCKT GREEN: .75X TO 2X BASIC
11 Victor Wembanyama 20.00 50.00

2023-24 Panini Contenders Game Ticket Pink

*GAME TICKET PINK: 1.5X TO 4X BASIC
STATED PRINT RUN 199 SER. #'D SETS
11 Victor Wembanyama 100.00 250.00

2023-24 Panini Contenders Game Ticket Purple

*GAME TCK PURPLE: 5X TO 12X BASIC
STATED PRINT RUN 25 SER. #'D SETS
11 Victor Wembanyama 600.00 1,200.00
24 Brandon Miller 100.00 250.00

2023-24 Panini Contenders Game Ticket Red

GM TCKT RED: .75X TO 2X BASIC
11 Victor Wembanyama 12.00 30.00

2023-24 Panini Contenders Opening Night Ticket FOTL

*OPENING NIGHT TCK: 5X TO 12X BASIC
STATED PRINT RUN 25 SER. #'D SETS
11 Victor Wembanyama 1000.00 2000.00

2023-24 Panini Contenders Playoff Ticket

*PLAYOFF TCK (1-100): 1.25X TO 3X BASIC
STATED PRINT RUN 249 SER. #'D SETS
*PLAYOFF TCK RC AU (101-145): .6X TO 1.5X BASIC
STATED PRINT RUN 99 SER. #'D SETS
*PLAYOFF TCK RC AU (146-165): .5X TO 1.2X BASIC
STATED PRINT RUN 99 SER. #'D SETS
11 Victor Wembanyama 50.00 120.00

2023-24 Panini Contenders Retail

*RETAIL: .4X TO 1X BASIC
COMMON RETAIL RC AU (146-165) 4.00 10.00
AU SEMIS 5.00 12.00
AU UNLISTED 6.00 15.00
157 Vasilije Micic 6.00 15.00

2023-24 Panini Contenders Semifinal Ticket

*SEMIFINAL TCK: 2X TO 5X BASIC
STATED PRINT RUN 99 SER. #'D SETS
11 Victor Wembanyama 75.00 200.00

2023-24 Panini Contenders The Finals Ticket

*PLAYOFF TCK (1-100): 3X TO 8X BASIC
STATED PRINT RUN 49 SER. #'D SETS
*PLAYOFF TCK RC AU (101-145): .75X TO 2X BASIC
STATED PRINT RUN 49 SER. #'D SETS
*PLAYOFF TCK RC AU (146-165): .6X TO 1.5X BASIC
STATED PRINT RUN 49 SER. #'D SETS
11 Victor Wembanyama 200.00 500.00

2023-24 Panini Contenders Contenders Autographs

STATED PRINT RUN 75-99 SER. #'d SETS
*RED/49: .5X TO 1.2X BASIC
*BRONZE/25: .6X TO 1.5X BASIC
1 RJ Barrett/75 10.00 25.00
2 D'Angelo Russell/75 6.00 15.00
3 Jonathan Kuminga/75 15.00 40.00
4 Jrue Holiday/75 25.00 60.00
5 James Wiseman/75 5.00 12.00
6 Keegan Murray/75 8.00 20.00
7 Rudy Gobert/75 8.00 20.00
8 Desmond Bane/75 8.00 20.00
9 AJ Griffin/75 5.00 12.00
10 Max Christie/99 6.00 15.00
12 Markelle Fultz/75 5.00 12.00
13 Immanuel Quickley/75 6.00 15.00
14 Jordan Clarkson/75 6.00 15.00
15 Obi Toppin/75 6.00 15.00
16 Tari Eason/99 8.00 20.00
17 Nikola Vucevic/75 6.00 15.00
18 Onyeka Okongwu/75 5.00 12.00
19 Malaki Branham/99 8.00 20.00
20 Robin Lopez/99 5.00 12.00
21 Ayo Dosunmu/75 6.00 15.00
22 Dyson Daniels/75 8.00 20.00
23 Blake Wesley/75 4.00 10.00
24 Bobby Portis/75 8.00 20.00
26 Gary Harris/99 5.00 12.00
27 Isaac Okoro/75 5.00 12.00
29 Precious Achiuwa/99 5.00 12.00
30 Walker Kessler/99 6.00 15.00
31 Daniel Gafford/99 6.00 15.00
32 Dorian Finney-Smith/75 5.00 12.00
33 Evan Fournier/99 5.00 12.00
34 Herbert Jones/99 6.00 15.00
35 Landry Shamet/99 4.00 10.00
36 Michael Porter Jr./75 8.00 20.00
37 Dalen Terry/99 6.00 15.00
38 Jake LaRavia/99 5.00 12.00
39 Bradley Beal/75 8.00 20.00
40 Kevon Looney/99 6.00 15.00

2023-24 Panini Contenders Crown Jewels

1 Luka Doncic 80.00 200.00
2 Ja Morant 40.00 100.00
3 LeBron James 100.00 250.00
4 Stephen Curry 100.00 250.00
5 Nikola Jokic 60.00 150.00
6 Jayson Tatum 50.00 120.00
7 Trae Young 25.00 60.00
8 Giannis Antetokounmpo 60.00 150.00
9 Kevin Durant 40.00 100.00
10 Damian Lillard 30.00 80.00
11 Scoot Henderson 75.00 200.00
12 Ausar Thompson 30.00 80.00
13 Bilal Coulibaly 30.00 80.00
14 Cam Whitmore 30.00 80.00
15 Anthony Black 25.00 60.00
16 Amen Thompson 60.00 150.00
17 Jarace Walker 25.00 60.00
18 Taylor Hendricks 12.00 30.00
19 Jett Howard 15.00 40.00
20 Gradey Dick 25.00 60.00
21 Jordan Hawkins 20.00 50.00
22 Brandon Miller 125.00 300.00
23 Jalen Hood-Schifino 12.00 30.00
24 Jaime Jaquez Jr. 75.00 200.00
25 Victor Wembanyama 800.00 1500.00

2023-24 Panini Contenders Draft Class Contenders

1 Olivier-Maxence Prosper .75 2.00
2 Kobe Bufkin 1.00 2.50
3 Noah Clowney 1.00 2.50
4 Jaime Jaquez Jr. 1.25 3.00
5 Amen Thompson 4.00 10.00
6 Dariq Whitehead 1.00 2.50
7 Gradey Dick 1.50 4.00
8 Bilal Coulibaly 2.00 5.00
9 Victor Wembanyama 6.00 15.00
10 Anthony Black 1.50 4.00
11 Cason Wallace 1.50 4.00
12 Jarace Walker 1.50 4.00
13 Jalen Hood-Schifino .75 2.00
14 Jordan Hawkins 1.25 3.00
15 Keyonte George 2.50 6.00
16 Scoot Henderson 2.50 6.00
17 Taylor Hendricks .75 2.00
18 Marcus Sasser 1.25 3.00
19 Brandin Podziemski 2.50 6.00
20 Brandon Miller 3.00 8.00
21 Jett Howard 1.00 2.50
22 Dereck Lively II 1.50 4.00
23 Cam Whitmore 2.00 5.00
24 Kris Murray .75 2.00
25 Ausar Thompson 2.00 5.00

2023-24 Panini Contenders Draft Class Contenders Cracked Ice

*CRACKED ICE: 4X TO 10X BASIC
STATED PRINT RUN 25 SER. #'D SETS
9 Victor Wembanyama 400.00 800.00
20 Brandon Miller 75.00 200.00

2023-24 Panini Contenders Game Night Ticket

*CRKD ICE/25: 8X TO 20X BASIC
1 James Harden .60 1.50
2 De'Aaron Fox .60 1.50
3 Ja Morant 1.00 2.50
4 Jaylen Brown .60 1.50
5 LaMelo Ball .75 2.00
6 Nikola Jokic 1.50 4.00
7 Anthony Edwards 1.50 4.00
8 Stephen Curry 2.50 6.00
9 Scottie Barnes .40 1.00
10 Damian Lillard .75 2.00
11 Shai Gilgeous-Alexander 1.50 4.00
12 Kawhi Leonard .75 2.00
13 LeBron James 2.50 6.00
14 Trae Young .60 1.50
15 Zach LaVine .50 1.25
16 Jayson Tatum 1.25 3.00
17 Paolo Banchero .75 2.00
18 Kevin Durant 1.00 2.50
19 Donovan Mitchell .60 1.50
20 Julius Randle .40 1.00
21 Luka Doncic 2.00 5.00
22 Tyrese Haliburton .60 1.50
23 Giannis Antetokounmpo 1.50 4.00
24 Joel Embiid .75 2.00
25 Kyrie Irving .60 1.50

2023-24 Panini Contenders Historic Draft Class Contenders

*CRKD ICE/25: 5X TO 12X BASIC
1 Kyrie Irving 1.00 2.50
2 Kevin Garnett 1.25 3.00
3 Dwyane Wade 1.00 2.50
4 LeBron James 4.00 10.00
5 Stephen Curry 4.00 10.00
6 Chris Bosh .60 1.50
7 Allen Iverson 1.25 3.00
8 Derrick Rose .75 2.00
9 Carmelo Anthony .75 2.00
10 Dirk Nowitzki 1.25 3.00
11 Charles Barkley 1.25 3.00
12 Tracy McGrady .75 2.00
13 Yao Ming 1.25 3.00
14 Pau Gasol .75 2.00
15 Magic Johnson 2.00 5.00
16 Kevin Durant 1.50 4.00
17 Julius Erving 1.25 3.00
18 Tony Parker .75 2.00
19 Vince Carter 1.00 2.50
20 Patrick Ewing .75 2.00
21 Larry Bird 2.00 5.00
22 Tim Duncan 1.25 3.00
23 Brandon Roy .60 1.50
24 Paul Pierce .75 2.00
25 Shaquille O'Neal 1.50 4.00

2023-24 Panini Contenders Legendary Contenders Autographs

STATED PRINT RUN 49-99 SER. #'d SETS
*RED/49: .5X TO 1.2X BASIC
*BRONZE/25: .6X TO 1.5X BASIC
1 Chris Mullin/75 8.00 20.00
2 Derek Fisher/49 6.00 15.00
4 Dick Van Arsdale/75 6.00 15.00
5 Ben Wallace/75 15.00 40.00
6 John Lucas/99 5.00 12.00
7 Rick Fox/75 6.00 15.00
8 Wally Szczerbiak/99 5.00 12.00
9 Steve Francis/75 6.00 15.00
10 Rolando Blackman/75 5.00 12.00
11 Carlos Boozer/75 5.00 12.00
12 David Thompson/75 8.00 20.00
13 Harold Miner/99 6.00 15.00
14 Caron Butler/99 5.00 12.00
15 Antawn Jamison/75 6.00 15.00
16 Jason Williams/75 15.00 40.00
17 B.J. Armstrong/75 6.00 15.00
18 Amar'e Stoudemire/75 8.00 20.00
19 Steve Kerr/75 8.00 20.00
20 Clyde Drexler/75 20.00 50.00

2023-24 Panini Contenders License to Dominate

1 Paolo Banchero 25.00 60.00
2 Bennedict Mathurin 15.00 40.00
3 Jabari Smith Jr. 15.00 40.00
4 Keegan Murray 12.00 30.00
5 Shaedon Sharpe 20.00 50.00
6 LeBron James 80.00 200.00
7 Luka Doncic 60.00 150.00
8 Jayson Tatum 40.00 100.00
9 Giannis Antetokounmpo 50.00 125.00
10 Ja Morant 30.00 80.00
11 Nikola Jokic 50.00 125.00
12 Stephen Curry 80.00 200.00
13 Zion Williamson 25.00 60.00
14 Donovan Mitchell 20.00 50.00
15 Shai Gilgeous-Alexander 50.00 120.00
16 Kevin Durant 30.00 80.00
17 Kyrie Irving 20.00 50.00
18 LaMelo Ball 25.00 60.00
19 Anthony Edwards 50.00 125.00
20 Trae Young 20.00 50.00
21 Damian Lillard 25.00 60.00
22 Jamal Murray 20.00 50.00
23 Joel Embiid 25.00 60.00
24 Jimmy Butler 15.00 40.00
25 De'Aaron Fox 20.00 50.00

2023-24 Panini Contenders Lottery Ticket

1 Victor Wembanyama 15.00 40.00
2 Brandon Miller 2.50 6.00
3 Scoot Henderson 2.00 5.00
4 Amen Thompson 3.00 8.00
5 Ausar Thompson 1.50 4.00
6 Anthony Black 1.25 3.00
7 Bilal Coulibaly 1.50 4.00
8 Jarace Walker 1.25 3.00
9 Taylor Hendricks .60 1.50
10 Cason Wallace 1.25 3.00
11 Jett Howard .75 2.00
12 Dereck Lively II 1.25 3.00
13 Gradey Dick 1.25 3.00
14 Jordan Hawkins 1.00 2.50

2023-24 Panini Contenders Lottery Ticket Cracked Ice

*CRACKED ICE: 5X TO 12X BASIC
STATED PRINT RUN 25 SER. #'D SETS
1 Victor Wembanyama 200.00 500.00

2023-24 Panini Contenders Lottery Ticket Playoff Edition

*PLAYOFF EDITION: 1.5X TO 4X BASIC
STATED PRINT RUN 99 SER. #'D SETS
1 Victor Wembanyama 100.00 250.00

2023-24 Panini Contenders MVP Contenders Autographs

STATED PRINT RUN 25-49 SER. #'d SETS
*RED/25: .5X TO 1.2X BASIC
*BRONZE/15: .5X TO 1.2X BASIC
1 Luka Doncic/49 400.00 800.00
2 Zion Williamson/49 75.00 200.00
3 Nikola Jokic/49 125.00 300.00
4 Russell Westbrook/49 60.00 150.00
5 Stephen Curry/25 500.00 1000.00
6 Anthony Edwards/49 125.00 300.00
7 Paul George/49 75.00 200.00
8 James Harden/49 60.00 150.00
9 Brandon Ingram/49 10.00 25.00
10 Tyrese Maxey/49 40.00 100.00

2023-24 Panini Contenders NBA Ink Autographs

STATED PRINT RUN 49-99 SER. #'d SETS
*RED/25-49: .5X TO 1.2X BASIC
*BRONZE/25: .6X TO 1.5X BASIC
1 Jabari Smith Jr./75 10.00 25.00
2 Jaden Ivey/75 10.00 25.00
3 Jordan Poole/75 10.00 25.00
4 Deandre Ayton/75 6.00 15.00
5 Jaren Jackson Jr./75 10.00 25.00
6 Keegan Murray/75 8.00 20.00
7 Shaedon Sharpe/75 12.00 30.00
8 Marcus Smart/75 8.00 20.00
10 Josh Giddey/75 8.00 20.00
11 Alperen Sengun/75 10.00 25.00
14 Bojan Bogdanovic/75 6.00 15.00
15 Jeremy Sochan/75 8.00 20.00
16 Kentavious Caldwell-Pope/99 5.00 12.00
17 Mo Bamba/75 5.00 12.00
18 Bruce Brown/99 6.00 15.00
19 Jalen Williams/99 12.00 30.00
20 Austin Reaves/99 15.00 40.00
21 Dorian Finney-Smith/75 5.00 12.00
22 Tim Hardaway Jr./75 5.00 12.00
23 Malik Monk/99 8.00 20.00
24 Dan Issel/99 8.00 20.00
25 Antawn Jamison/75 6.00 15.00
26 Nick Van Exel/75 6.00 15.00
27 Peja Stojakovic/75 6.00 15.00
28 Bill Walton/75 20.00 50.00
29 Derek Fisher/75 6.00 15.00
30 Steve Kerr/49 8.00 20.00

2023-24 Panini Contenders Permit to Dominate

1 Victor Wembanyama 600.00 1200.00
2 Keyonte George 60.00 150.00
3 Amen Thompson 60.00 150.00
4 Scoot Henderson 60.00 150.00
5 Gradey Dick 25.00 60.00
6 Jordan Hawkins 20.00 50.00
7 Ausar Thompson 30.00 80.00
8 Brandon Miller 125.00 300.00
9 Anthony Black 25.00 60.00
10 Bilal Coulibaly 30.00 80.00
11 Kobe Bufkin 15.00 40.00
12 Cam Whitmore 30.00 80.00
13 Jalen Hood-Schifino 12.00 30.00
14 Jaime Jaquez Jr. 60.00 150.00
15 Jett Howard 15.00 40.00
16 Cason Wallace 25.00 60.00
17 Brandin Podziemski 40.00 100.00
18 Dereck Lively II 60.00 150.00
19 Taylor Hendricks 12.00 30.00
20 Jarace Walker 25.00 60.00
21 Noah Clowney 15.00 40.00
22 Dariq Whitehead 15.00 40.00
23 Nick Smith Jr. 15.00 40.00
24 Olivier-Maxence Prosper 12.00 30.00
25 Kris Murray 12.00 30.00

2023-24 Panini Contenders Retail Veteran Autographs

*PLAYOFF TCKT/99: .5X TO 1.2X BASIC
*THE FINALS TICKET/49: .6X TO 1.5X BASIC
*CRACKED ICE TICKET/25: .75X TO 2X BASIC
1 Torrey Craig 3.00 8.00
2 Max Strus 4.00 10.00
3 Daniel Gafford 4.00 10.00
4 Jock Landale 3.00 8.00
5 Jevon Carter 3.00 8.00
6 Will Barton 3.00 8.00
7 Jose Alvarado 4.00 10.00
8 Landry Shamet 2.50 6.00
9 Thomas Bryant 3.00 8.00
10 Isaiah Roby 2.50 6.00
11 Precious Achiuwa 3.00 8.00
12 Dalen Terry 4.00 10.00
13 Larry Nance Jr. 2.50 6.00
14 Herbert Jones 4.00 10.00
15 Bruno Fernando 2.50 6.00
16 Chuma Okeke 3.00 8.00
17 Jalen McDaniels 3.00 8.00
18 Drew Eubanks 2.50 6.00
19 Edmond Sumner 2.50 6.00
20 Georges Niang 2.50 6.00

2023-24 Panini Contenders Rookie of the Year Contenders

1 Cam Whitmore 2.00 5.00
2 Nick Smith Jr. 1.00 2.50
3 Victor Wembanyama 12.00 30.00
4 Scoot Henderson 2.50 6.00
5 Amen Thompson 4.00 10.00
7 Brandon Miller 3.00 8.00
8 Bilal Coulibaly 2.00 5.00
9 Anthony Black 1.50 4.00
10 Jarace Walker 1.50 4.00
11 Cason Wallace 1.50 4.00
12 Jett Howard 1.00 2.50
13 Keyonte George 2.50 6.00
14 Jordan Hawkins 1.25 3.00
15 Jalen Hood-Schifino 0.75 2.00
16 Kobe Bufkin 1.00 2.50
17 Dereck Lively II 1.50 4.00
18 Gradey Dick 1.50 4.00

2023-24 Panini Contenders Rookie of the Year Contenders Cracked Ice

*CRACKED ICE: 4X TO 10X BASIC
STATED PRINT RUN 25 SER. #'D SETS
3 Victor Wembanyama 500.00 1,000.00
7 Brandon Miller 75.00 200.00

2023-24 Panini Contenders Rookie of the Year Contenders Playoff Edition

*PLAYOFF EDITION: 1.5X TO 4X BASIC
STATED PRINT RUN 99 SER. #'D SETS
1 Cam Whitmore 150.00 400.00

2023-24 Panini Contenders Rookie Stallions

1 Kobe Bufkin 1.00 2.50
2 Jaime Jaquez Jr. 1.25 3.00
3 Dariq Whitehead 1.00 2.50
4 Bilal Coulibaly 2.00 5.00
5 Anthony Black 1.50 4.00
6 Jarace Walker 1.50 4.00
7 Jordan Hawkins 1.25 3.00
8 Scoot Henderson 2.50 6.00
9 Marcus Sasser 1.25 3.00
10 Brandon Miller 3.00 8.00
11 Dereck Lively II 1.50 4.00
12 Kris Murray .75 2.00
13 Ausar Thompson 2.00 5.00
14 Cam Whitmore 2.00 5.00
15 Jett Howard 1.00 2.50
16 Taylor Hendricks .75 2.00
17 Brandin Podziemski 2.50 6.00
18 Keyonte George 2.50 6.00
19 Jalen Hood-Schifino .75 2.00
20 Cason Wallace 1.50 4.00
21 Victor Wembanyama 6.00 15.00
22 Gradey Dick 1.50 4.00
23 Amen Thompson 4.00 10.00
24 Noah Clowney 1.00 2.50
25 Olivier-Maxence Prosper .75 2.00

2023-24 Panini Contenders Rookie Stallions Cracked Ice

*CRACKED ICE: 4X TO 10X BASIC
STATED PRINT RUN 25 SER. #'D SETS
10 Brandon Miller 75.00 200.00
21 Victor Wembanyama 400.00 800.00

2023-24 Panini Contenders Rookie Ticket Dual Swatches

1 Kobe Bufkin
Brandon Miller 8.00 20.00
2 Scoot Henderson
Cason Wallace 6.00 15.00
3 Amen Thompson
Ausar Thompson 10.00 25.00
4 Dereck Lively II
Olivier-Maxence Prosper 4.00 10.00
5 Brandin Podziemski
Jarace Walker 6.00 15.00
6 Noah Clowney
Dariq Whitehead 2.50 6.00
7 Victor Wembanyama
Bilal Coulibaly 15.00 40.00
8 Jett Howard
Anthony Black 4.00 10.00
9 Keyonte George
Taylor Hendricks 6.00 15.00
10 Gradey Dick
Jordan Hawkins 4.00 10.00

2023-24 Panini Contenders Rookie Ticket Swatches

1 Julian Strawther 2.00 5.00
2 Gradey Dick 3.00 8.00
3 Julian Phillips 1.50 4.00
4 Brandon Miller 6.00 15.00
5 Kobe Brown 1.50 4.00
6 Victor Wembanyama 15.00 40.00
7 Keyonte George 5.00 12.00
8 Leonard Miller 1.50 4.00
9 Jordan Hawkins 2.50 6.00
10 Jalen Hood-Schifino 1.50 4.00
11 Nick Smith Jr. 2.00 5.00
12 Jordan Walsh 1.50 4.00
13 Olivier-Maxence Prosper 1.50 4.00
14 Taylor Hendricks 1.50 4.00
15 Noah Clowney 2.00 5.00
16 Dereck Lively II 3.00 8.00
17 Scoot Henderson 5.00 12.00
18 Maxwell Lewis 1.25 3.00
19 Cam Whitmore 4.00 10.00
20 James Nnaji 1.25 3.00
21 Cason Wallace 3.00 8.00
22 Anthony Black 3.00 8.00
23 Brandin Podziemski 5.00 12.00
24 Brice Sensabaugh 2.50 6.00
25 Dariq Whitehead 2.00 5.00
26 Jaime Jaquez Jr. 2.50 6.00
27 Ben Sheppard 1.50 4.00
28 Marcus Sasser 2.50 6.00
29 Jarace Walker 3.00 8.00
30 Kobe Bufkin 2.00 5.00
31 Bilal Coulibaly 4.00 10.00
32 Jett Howard 2.00 5.00
33 Andre Jackson Jr. 2.50 6.00
34 Colby Jones 1.50 4.00
35 Hunter Tyson 1.50 4.00
36 Amen Thompson 8.00 20.00
37 Kris Murray 1.50 4.00
38 Ausar Thompson 4.00 10.00
39 Jalen Pickett 1.25 3.00
40 GG Jackson II 3.00 8.00

2023-24 Panini Contenders Suite Shots

*PLAYOFF EDTN/99: 1.5X TO 4X BASIC
*CRKD ICE/25: 4X TO 10X BASIC
1 Allen Iverson 1.25 3.00
2 Shaquille O'Neal 1.50 4.00
3 Yao Ming 1.25 3.00
4 Carmelo Anthony .75 2.00
5 Dwyane Wade 1.00 2.50
6 Tony Parker .75 2.00
7 Dirk Nowitzki 1.25 3.00
8 Pau Gasol .75 2.00
9 Larry Bird 2.00 5.00
10 Kevin Garnett 1.25 3.00
11 Cade Cunningham 1.25 3.00
12 Jamal Murray 1.00 2.50
13 Tyrese Haliburton 1.00 2.50
14 Devin Booker 1.25 3.00
15 Jimmy Butler .75 2.00
16 Anthony Edwards 2.50 6.00
17 De'Aaron Fox 1.00 2.50
18 Kevin Durant 1.50 4.00
19 Zion Williamson 1.25 3.00
20 LeBron James 4.00 10.00
21 Joel Embiid 1.25 3.00
22 Stephen Curry 4.00 10.00
23 Ja Morant 1.50 4.00
24 Luka Doncic 3.00 8.00
25 Jayson Tatum 2.00 5.00
26 Shai Gilgeous-Alexander 2.50 6.00
27 Kyrie Irving 1.00 2.50
28 Damian Lillard 1.25 3.00
29 Giannis Antetokounmpo 2.50 6.00
30 Trae Young 1.00 2.50

2023-24 Panini Contenders Supernatural

1 Victor Wembanyama 20.00 50.00
2 Bilal Coulibaly 2.00 5.00
3 Scoot Henderson 2.50 6.00
4 Anthony Black 1.50 4.00
5 Keyonte George 2.50 6.00
6 Kobe Bufkin 1.00 2.50
7 Amen Thompson 4.00 10.00
8 Ausar Thompson 2.00 5.00
9 Jett Howard 1.00 2.50
10 Dereck Lively II 1.50 4.00
11 Jordan Hawkins 1.25 3.00
12 Cason Wallace 1.50 4.00
13 Jaime Jaquez Jr. 1.25 3.00
14 Jalen Hood-Schifino .75 2.00
15 Cam Whitmore 2.00 5.00
16 Nikola Jokic 4.00 10.00
17 LeBron James 6.00 15.00
18 Luka Doncic 5.00 12.00
19 Ja Morant 2.50 6.00
20 Stephen Curry 6.00 15.00
21 Trae Young 1.50 4.00
22 Donovan Mitchell 1.50 4.00
23 Jayson Tatum 3.00 8.00
24 Kevin Durant 2.50 6.00
25 Giannis Antetokounmpo 4.00 10.00
26 Kyrie Irving 1.50 4.00
27 Zion Williamson 2.00 5.00
28 Shai Gilgeous-Alexander 4.00 10.00

2023-24 Panini Contenders Supernatural Playoff Edition

*PLAYOFF EDITION: 1.5X TO 4X BASIC
STATED PRINT RUN 99 SER. #'D SETS
1 Victor Wembanyama 150.00 400.00

2023-24 Panini Contenders Supernaturall Cracked Ice

*CRACKED ICE: 3X TO 8X BASIC
STATED PRINT RUN 25 SER. #'D SETS
1 Victor Wembanyama 400.00 800.00

2023-24 Panini Contenders Superstar Die-Cuts

*PLAYOFF EDTN/99: 1.5X TO 4X BASIC
*CRKD ICE/25: 4X TO 10X BASIC
1 Luka Doncic 5.00 12.00
2 Donovan Mitchell 1.50 4.00
3 Stephen Curry 6.00 15.00
4 LeBron James 6.00 15.00
5 Giannis Antetokounmpo 4.00 10.00
6 Jayson Tatum 3.00 8.00
7 Nikola Jokic 4.00 10.00
8 Kevin Durant 2.50 6.00
9 Damian Lillard 2.00 5.00
10 Ja Morant 2.50 6.00

2023-24 Panini Contenders Variations

*VARIATIONS 1-100: .75X TO 2X BASIC
*VARIATIONS AU RC 101-145: .4X TO 1X BASIC
*VAR PREM ED RC AU (101-145): .6X TO 1.5X BASIC
*VAR PREM ED GRN SHMR RC AU (101-145): .6X TO 1.5X BASIC

*VAR PLAYOFF TCK RC AU/99 (101-145): .6X TO 1.5X BASIC
*VAR THE FINALS TCK RC AU/49 (101-145): .75X TO 2X BASIC

2023-24 Panini Contenders Variations Cracked Ice Ticket

*VAR CRCKD ICE TCKT RC AU/25 (101-145): 2X TO 5X BASIC

2023-24 Panini Contenders Variations Premium Edition Blue FOTL

*VAR PRM ED BLUE FOTL RC AU/21 (101-145): 2X TO 5X BASIC

2023-24 Panini Contenders Veteran Autographs

*PREMIUM EDITION: .5X TO 1.2X BASIC
*PREMIUM ED GRN SHMR: .5X TO 1.2X BASIC
*PLAYOFF TCK/75: .5X TO 1.2X BASIC
*CRACKED ICE TCK/25: .75X TO 2X BASIC
*PREMIUM ED BLUE FOTL/21: .75X TO 2X BASIC
1 Luka Doncic 300.00 600.00
3 Nikola Jokic 125.00 300.00
4 Paul George 75.00 200.00
5 Pau Gasol 50.00 120.00
6 Carmelo Anthony 100.00 250.00
7 Tony Parker 50.00 120.00
8 Dennis Rodman 75.00 200.00
9 Dwyane Wade 75.00 200.00
10 Kevin Garnett 75.00 200.00

2015-16 Panini Contenders Draft Picks

OVERALL FIVE AUTOS PER HOBBY BOX
1 Aaron Brooks .20 .50
2 Aaron Gordon .30 .75
3 Al Horford .30 .75
4 Al-Farouq Aminu .20 .50
5 Andre Drummond .30 .75
6 Andre Iguodala .30 .75
7 Andrew Bogut .25 .60
8 Andrew Wiggins .40 1.00
9 Anthony Davis .75 2.00
10 Ben Gordon .25 .60
11 Blake Griffin .30 .75
12 Bradley Beal .40 1.00
13 Brook Lopez .30 .75
14 Carlos Boozer .25 .60
15 Carmelo Anthony .50 1.25
16 Chandler Parsons .20 .50
17 Channing Frye .20 .50
18 Chris Bosh .40 1.00
19 Chris Paul .60 1.50
20 Damian Lillard .75 2.00
21 Darren Collison .20 .50
22 David Lee .20 .50
23 DeAndre Jordan .25 .60
24 DeMar DeRozan .40 1.00
25 DeMarcus Cousins .30 .75
26 Deron Williams .25 .60
27 Derrick Favors .25 .60
28 Derrick Rose .50 1.25
29 Doug McDermott .25 .60
30 Draymond Green .40 1.00
31 Dwyane Wade .60 1.50
32 Elfrid Payton .25 .60
33 Eric Bledsoe .25 .60
34 Gary Harris .25 .60
35 Greg Monroe .25 .60
36 Gordon Hayward .30 .75
37 Harrison Barnes .25 .60
38 Hassan Whiteside .25 .60
39 J.J. Redick .30 .75
40 Jabari Brown .20 .50
41 Jabari Parker .20 .50
42 Jamal Crawford .30 .75
43 James Harden .60 1.50
44 Jimmer Fredette .20 .50
45 Jimmy Butler .60 1.50
46 Joakim Noah .20 .50
47 Joe Johnson .25 .60
48 Joel Embiid .75 2.00
49 John Wall .40 1.00
50 Jordan Clarkson .30 .75
51 Jrue Holiday .40 1.00
52 Julius Randle .40 1.00
53 Kawhi Leonard 1.00 2.50
54 Kemba Walker .30 .75
55 Kenneth Faried .25 .60
56 Kentavious Caldwell-Pope .25 .60
57 Kevin Durant 1.25 3.00
58 Kevin Love .30 .75
59 Arron Afflalo .20 .50
60 Kirk Hinrich .25 .60
61 Klay Thompson .75 2.00
62 Kyle Korver .30 .75
63 Kyrie Irving .60 1.50
64 LaMarcus Aldridge .30 .75
65 Marcus Morris .20 .50
66 Marcus Smart .40 1.00
67 Markieff Morris .20 .50
68 Mason Plumlee .20 .50
69 Matt Barnes .20 .50
70 Michael Carter-Williams .20 .50
71 Michael Kidd-Gilchrist .20 .50
72 Mike Conley .30 .75
73 Mike Dunleavy .20 .50
74 Mo Williams .25 .60
75 Nerlens Noel .20 .50
76 Nikola Vucevic .25 .60
77 Noah Vonleh .20 .50
78 Paul George .50 1.25
79 Paul Millsap .20 .50
80 Paul Pierce .50 1.25
81 Rajon Rondo .40 1.00
82 Richard Jefferson .25 .60
83 Rodney Hood .25 .60
84 Roy Hibbert .25 .60
85 Russell Westbrook .50 1.25
86 Shabazz Napier .20 .50
87 Stephen Curry 2.50 6.00
88 Tayshaun Prince .25 .60
89 Tim Duncan .75 2.00
90 Tim Hardaway Jr. .25 .60
91 Trevor Ariza .20 .50
92 Trey Burke .20 .50
93 Ty Lawson .20 .50
94 Tyler Hansbrough .20 .50
95 Tyreke Evans .25 .60
96 Victor Oladipo .25 .60
97 Vince Carter .60 1.50
98 Wesley Matthews .25 .60
99 Zach LaVine .75 2.00
100 Zach Randolph .30 .75
102A Alan Williams AU Ball at head 3.00 8.00
102B Alan Williams AU Ball at waist 3.00 8.00
104A Anthony Brown AU Red jersey 3.00 8.00
104B Anthony Brown AU Black jersey 3.00 8.00
105A Portis AU White jsy 8.00 20.00
105B Portis AU Red jsy 8.00 20.00
106A Brandon Ashley AU Dribbling 3.00 8.00
106B Brandon Ashley AU Hands on ball 3.00 8.00
107A Cameron Payne AU White jersey 5.00 12.00
107B Cameron Payne AU Yellow jersey 5.00 12.00
108A Chris McCullough AU Facing right 3.00 8.00
108B Chris McCullough AU Facing left 3.00 8.00
109A Aaron White AU Black jersey 4.00 10.00
109B Aaron White AU White jersey 4.00 10.00
110A Christian Wood AU Left hand dribbling 5.00 12.00
110B Christian Wood AU Two hands on balll 5.00 12.00
111A Cliff Alexander AU Facing right 3.00 8.00
111B Cliff Alexander AU Facing left 3.00 8.00
112A Russell AU White jsy 20.00 50.00
112B Russell AU Red jsy 20.00 50.00
113A Dakari Johnson AU Number hidden 3.00 8.00
113B Dakari Johnson AU Number partially visable 3.00 8.00
114A Delon Wright AU Dribbling right hand 4.00 10.00
114B Delon Wright AU Dribbling left hand 4.00 10.00
115A Booker AU Face left 150.00 400.00
115B Booker AU Face right 150.00 400.00
116A Kmnsky AU Face left 4.00 10.00
116B Kmnsky AU Face right 4.00 10.00
117A J.P. Tokoto AU Blue jersey 3.00 8.00
117B J.P. Tokoto AU White jersey 3.00 8.00
118A Okafor AU Face left 4.00 10.00
118B Okafor AU Face right 4.00 10.00
119A Jarell Martin AU Yellow jersey 3.00 8.00
119B Jarell Martin AU White jersey 3.00 8.00
120A Jordan Mickey AU Black jersey 3.00 8.00
120B Jordan Mickey AU White jersey 3.00 8.00
121A Joe Young AU Yellow jersey 3.00 8.00
121B Joe Young AU 3.00 8.00
122A Andrsn AU White jsy 3.00 8.00
122B Andrsn AU Dark jsy 3.00 8.00
123A Winslow AU Blue jsy 5.00 12.00
123B Winslow AU White jsy 5.00 12.00
124A Towns AU Face right 40.00 100.00
124B Towns AU Face left 40.00 100.00
125A Oubre AU Blue jsy 10.00 25.00
125B Oubre AU White jsy 10.00 25.00
126A Branden Dawson AU White jersey 3.00 8.00
126B Branden Dawson AU Green jersey 3.00 8.00
127A Kevon Looney AU White jersey 10.00 25.00
127B Kevon Looney AU Blue jersey 10.00 25.00
128A Michael Frazier II AU White jersey 4.00 10.00
128B Michael Frazier II AU Blue jersey 4.00 10.00
129A Michael Qualls AU Dribbling 4.00 10.00
129B Michael Qualls AU Dunking 4.00 10.00
130A Montrezl Harrell AU White jersey 10.00 25.00
130B Montrezl Harrell AU Black jersey 10.00 25.00
131A Turner AU Ornge jsy 12.00 30.00
131B Turner AU White jsy 12.00 30.00
133A Olivier Hanlan AU Left arm out 3.00 8.00
133B Olivier Hanlan AU Left arm crooked 3.00 8.00
134A Cook AU Arm down 6.00 15.00
134B Cook AU Arm up 6.00 15.00
135A R.J. Hunter AU Blue jersey 3.00 8.00
135B R.J. Hunter AU White jersey 3.00 8.00
136A Rakeem Christmas AU White jersey 3.00 8.00
136B Rakeem Christmas AU Orange jersey 3.00 8.00
137A Rashad Vaughn AU Black jersey 3.00 8.00
137B Rashad Vaughn AU Red jersey 3.00 8.00
138A Richaun Holmes AU Pointing 5.00 12.00
138B Richaun Holmes AU Two hands on ball 5.00 12.00
140A Rondae Hollis-Jefferson AU Blue jersey 4.00 10.00
140B Rondae Hollis-Jefferson AU Red jersey 4.00 10.00
141A Dkkr AU Hands on ball 3.00 8.00
141B Dkkr AU Hand on ball 3.00 8.00
142A Jhnsn AU Face forward 4.00 10.00
142B Jhnsn AU Face left 4.00 10.00
144A Rozier AU White jsy 12.00 30.00
144B Rozier AU Black jsy 12.00 30.00
145A Nance Jr. AU Reb 6.00 15.00
145B Nance Jr. AU Drive 6.00 15.00
146A Lyles AU Hands on ball 4.00 10.00
146B Lyles AU Dribble 4.00 10.00
147A Tyler Harvey AU Red jersey 3.00 8.00
147B Tyler Harvey AU Dark jersey 3.00 8.00
148A Jones AU Blue jsy 4.00 10.00
148B Jones AU White jsy 4.00 10.00
149A Jonathan Holmes AU White jersey 3.00 8.00
149B Jonathan Holmes AU Orange jersey 3.00 8.00
150A Cly-Stn AU Hands on ball 4.00 10.00
150B Cly-Stn AU Dribble 4.00 10.00
151 Darrun Hilliard AU 3.00 8.00
152 Josh Richardson AU 5.00 12.00
153 Kevin Pangos AU 3.00 8.00
156 Dez Wells AU 3.00 8.00
157 Marcus Thornton AU 3.00 8.00
158 Chasson Randle AU 3.00 8.00
159 Sir'Dominic Pointer AU 3.00 8.00
160 TaShawn Thomas AU 3.00 8.00
161 Christian Wood AU 5.00 12.00
162 Michael Frazier II AU 4.00 10.00
165 Emmanuel Mudiay AU 4.00 10.00
166 Cliff Alexander AU 3.00 8.00
167 Kristaps Porzingis AU 25.00 60.00
168 Mario Hezonja AU 4.00 10.00
169 Aleighsa Welch AU 3.00 8.00
170 Josh Richardson AU 5.00 12.00
171 Ally Malott AU 3.00 8.00
172 Amanda Zahui B. AU 4.00 10.00
173 Amber Orrange AU 3.00 8.00
174 Andrea Hoover AU 3.00 8.00
175 Darrun Hilliard AU 3.00 8.00
176 Betnijah Laney AU 3.00 8.00
177 Brianna Kiesel AU 3.00 8.00
178 Brittany Boyd AU 3.00 8.00
179 Brittany Hrynko AU 3.00 8.00
180 Chelsea Gardner AU 3.00 8.00
181 Cheyenne Parker AU 3.00 8.00
182 Cierra Burdick AU 4.00 10.00
183 Crystal Bradford AU 3.00 8.00
184 Dearica Hamby AU 4.00 10.00
185 Elizabeth Williams AU 3.00 8.00
186 Isabelle Harrison AU 3.00 8.00
187 Kaleena Mosqueda-Lewis AU 3.00 8.00
188 Kiah Stokes AU 4.00 10.00
189 Shannon Scott AU 3.00 8.00
190 Laurin Mincy AU 3.00 8.00
191 Dez Wells AU 3.00 8.00
192 Mimi Mungedi AU 3.00 8.00
193 Natasha Cloud AU 3.00 8.00
194 Nikki Moody AU 3.00 8.00
195 Nneka Enemkpali AU 3.00 8.00
196 Promise Amukamara AU 3.00 8.00
197 Reshanda Gray AU 3.00 8.00
198 Samantha Logic AU 3.00 8.00
199 Shae Kelley AU 3.00 8.00
200 Duje Dukan AU 3.00 8.00

2015-16 Panini Contenders Draft Picks Cracked Ice Ticket

*CRCKD ICE 1-100: 5X TO 12X BASIC
*CRCKD ICE 101-150: .75X TO 2X BASIC
*CRCKD ICE 151-200: .75X TO 2X BASIC
OVERALL FIVE AUTOS PER HOBBY BOX
STATED PRINT RUN 23 SER.#'d SETS
101A Hrrsn AU White jsy 8.00 20.00
101B Hrrsn AU Blue jsy 8.00 20.00
103A Hrrsn AU No number 8.00 20.00
103B Hrrsn AU Number 8.00 20.00
112A D'Angelo Russell AU White jersey 75.00 200.00
112B D'Angelo Russell AU Red jersey 75.00 200.00
115A Devin Booker AU Facing left 400.00 800.00
115B Devin Booker AU Facing right 400.00 800.00
124A Towns AU Face right 100.00 250.00
124B Towns AU Face left 100.00 250.00
163 Aaron Harrison AU 8.00 20.00

2015-16 Panini Contenders Draft Picks Draft Ticket

*DRFT 1-100: 2X TO 5X BASIC
*DRFT 101-150: .5X TO 1.2X BASIC
*DRFT 151-200: .5X TO 1.2X BASIC
OVERALL FIVE AUTOS PER HOBBY BOX
STATED PRINT RUN 99 SER.#'d SETS
101A Hrrsn AU White jsy 5.00 12.00
101B Hrrsn AU Blue jsy 5.00 12.00
103A Hrrsn AU No number 5.00 12.00
103B Hrrsn AU Number 5.00 12.00
163 Aaron Harrison AU 5.00 12.00

2015-16 Panini Contenders Draft Picks Alumni Ink

OVERALL FIVE AUTOS PER HOBBY BOX
2 Al-Farouq Aminu 3.00 8.00
3 Andre Drummond 25.00 60.00
5 Jabari Brown 3.00 8.00
7 Joel Embiid 12.00 30.00
8 Jordan Clarkson 5.00 12.00
11 Kentavious Caldwell-Pope 4.00 10.00
12 Victor Oladipo 8.00 20.00
14 Marcus Smart 6.00 15.00
15 Mason Plumlee 3.00 8.00
16 Michael Carter-Williams 10.00 25.00
17 Michael Kidd-Gilchrist 20.00 50.00
18 Mo Williams 4.00 10.00
19 Nerlens Noel 3.00 8.00
20 Noah Vonleh 3.00 8.00
24 Trey Burke 3.00 8.00

2015-16 Panini Contenders Draft Picks Class Reunion

APPX.ODDS 1:8 HOBBY
1 Andrew Wiggins .60 1.50
2 Anthony Davis 1.25 3.00
3 Blake Griffin .50 1.25
4 Carmelo Anthony .75 2.00
5 Chris Paul 1.00 2.50
6 Damian Lillard 1.25 3.00
7 DeMar DeRozan .60 1.50
8 Derrick Rose .75 2.00
9 Dwyane Wade 1.00 2.50
10 Hassan Whiteside .40 1.00
11 James Harden 1.00 2.50
12 Jimmy Butler 1.00 2.50
13 John Wall .60 1.50
14 Kawhi Leonard 1.50 4.00
15 Kevin Durant 2.00 5.00
16 Kevin Love .50 1.25
17 Klay Thompson 1.25 3.00
18 Kyrie Irving 1.00 2.50
19 Nerlens Noel .30 .75
20 Paul George .75 2.00
21 Russell Westbrook .75 2.00
22 Stephen Curry 4.00 10.00
23 Tim Duncan 1.25 3.00
24 Victor Oladipo .40 1.00
25 Zach LaVine 1.25 3.00

2015-16 Panini Contenders Draft Picks Collegiate Connections

APPX.ODDS 1:8 HOBBY
1 Hlls-Jffrsn/Jhnsn .40 1.00
2 Portis/Qualls .75 2.00
3 McDermott/Korver .40 1.00
4 Parker/Irving 1.00 2.50
5 Okafor/Winslow .50 1.25
6 Beal/Frazier II .60 1.50
7 Wiggins/Embiid 1.25 3.00
8 Davis/Wall 1.25 3.00
9 Harrison/Harrison .40 1.00
10 Towns/Cauley-Stein 2.00 5.00
11 Booker/Lyles 4.00 10.00
12 Harrell/Rozier 1.25 3.00
13 Martin/Mickey .30 .75
14 Wade/Butler 1.00 2.50
15 Rose/Evans .75 2.00
16 Crawford/Booker .50 1.25
17 Barnes/Carter 1.00 2.50
18 Russell/Turner 1.25 3.00
19 Brooks/Young .30 .75
20 Anthony/Carter-Williams .75 2.00
21 Durant/Turner 2.00 5.00
22 Love/Westbrook .75 2.00
23 Looney/LaVine 1.25 3.00
24 Paul/Duncan 1.25 3.00
25 Kaminsky/Dekker .40 1.00

2015-16 Panini Contenders Draft Picks Collegiate Connections Signatures

OVERALL FIVE AUTOS PER HOBBY BOX
1 Hollis-Jefferson/Johnson 30.00 80.00
5 Beal/Frazier II 25.00 60.00
9 Booker/Lyles 75.00 200.00
10 Harrell/Rozier 30.00 80.00
14 Kaminsky/Dekker 50.00 120.00
15 Cook/Jones 40.00 100.00
16 Alexander/Oubre 12.00 30.00
17 Kidd-Gilchrist/Noel 25.00 60.00
20 Holmes/Turner 30.00 80.00
21 Looney/Wood 12.00 30.00
25 Barnes/Tokoto 12.00 30.00

2015-16 Panini Contenders Draft Picks Game Day

APPX.ODDS 1:4 HOBBY
1 Aaron Harrison .50 1.25
2 Alan Williams .40 1.00
3 Andrew Harrison .50 1.25
4 Anthony Brown .40 1.00
5 Bobby Portis 1.00 2.50
6 Cameron Payne .60 1.50
7 Chris McCullough .40 1.00
8 Aaron White .50 1.25
9 Christian Wood .60 1.50
10 Cliff Alexander .40 1.00
11 D'Angelo Russell 1.50 4.00
12 Dakari Johnson .40 1.00
13 Delon Wright .50 1.25
14 Devin Booker 5.00 12.00
15 Frank Kaminsky .50 1.25
16 Jahlil Okafor .50 1.25
17 Jarell Martin .40 1.00
18 Jordan Mickey .40 1.00
19 Joe Young .40 1.00
20 Justin Anderson .40 1.00
21 Justise Winslow .60 1.50
22 Karl-Anthony Towns 2.50 6.00
23 Kelly Oubre Jr. 1.25 3.00
24 Branden Dawson .40 1.00
25 Kevon Looney 1.25 3.00
26 Michael Frazier II .50 1.25
27 Michael Qualls .50 1.25
28 Montrezl Harrell 1.25 3.00
29 Myles Turner 1.50 4.00
30 Norman Powell .75 2.00
31 Olivier Hanlan .40 1.00
32 Quinn Cook .75 2.00
33 R.J. Hunter .40 1.00
34 Rakeem Christmas .40 1.00
35 Rashad Vaughn .40 1.00
36 Richaun Holmes .60 1.50
37 Robert Upshaw .40 1.00
38 Rondae Hollis-Jefferson .50 1.25
39 Sam Dekker .40 1.00
40 Stanley Johnson .50 1.25
41 Terry Rozier 1.50 4.00
42 Trey Lyles .50 1.25
43 Tyler Harvey .40 1.00
44 Tyus Jones .50 1.25
45 Larry Nance Jr. .75 2.00
46 Willie Cauley-Stein .50 1.25
47 Darrun Hilliard .40 1.00

2015-16 Panini Contenders Draft Picks Old School Colors

COMPLETE SET (50) 12.00 30.00
1 Andrew Wiggins .50 1.25
2 Anthony Davis 1.00 2.50
3 Blake Griffin .40 1.00
4 Carmelo Anthony .60 1.50
5 Chris Paul .75 2.00
6 Damian Lillard 1.00 2.50
7 DeMar DeRozan .50 1.25
8 DeMarcus Cousins .40 1.00
9 Derrick Rose .60 1.50
10 Dwyane Wade .75 2.00
11 Hassan Whiteside .30 .75
12 Jabari Parker .25 .60
13 James Harden .75 2.00
14 Jimmy Butler .75 2.00
15 John Wall .50 1.25
16 Julius Randle .50 1.25
17 Kawhi Leonard 1.25 3.00
18 Kevin Durant 1.50 4.00
19 Kevin Love .40 1.00
20 Klay Thompson 1.00 2.50
21 Kyrie Irving .75 2.00
22 Marcus Smart .50 1.25
23 Michael Carter-Williams .25 .60
24 Michael Kidd-Gilchrist .25 .60
25 Nerlens Noel .25 .60
26 Paul George .60 1.50
27 Paul Pierce .60 1.50
28 Russell Westbrook .60 1.50
29 Stephen Curry 3.00 8.00
30 Tim Duncan 1.00 2.50
31 Victor Oladipo .30 .75
32 Zach LaVine 1.00 2.50
33 Aaron Gordon .40 1.00
34 Bradley Beal .50 1.25
35 Chris Bosh .50 1.25
36 DeAndre Jordan .30 .75
37 Joe Johnson .30 .75
38 Nikola Vucevic .30 .75
39 Noah Vonleh .25 .60
40 Shabazz Napier .25 .60
41 Trey Burke .25 .60
42 Vince Carter .75 2.00
43 Andre Iguodala .40 1.00
44 Deron Williams .30 .75
45 Derrick Favors .30 .75
46 Doug McDermott .30 .75
47 Gordon Hayward .40 1.00
48 Harrison Barnes .30 .75
49 Jimmer Fredette .25 .60
50 Joel Embiid 1.00 2.50

2015-16 Panini Contenders Draft Picks Old School Colors Signatures

OVERALL FIVE AUTOS PER HOBBY BOX
1 Aaron Gordon 10.00 25.00
2 Al-Farouq Aminu 3.00 8.00
4 Ben Gordon 4.00 10.00
5 Harrison Barnes 10.00 25.00
6 Jabari Brown 3.00 8.00
7 Joel Embiid 25.00 60.00
11 Kentavious Caldwell-Pope 4.00 10.00
12 Victor Oladipo 10.00 25.00
13 Kyle Korver 6.00 15.00
14 Marcus Smart 6.00 15.00
16 Michael Carter-Williams 3.00 8.00
18 Mo Williams 4.00 10.00
19 Nerlens Noel 8.00 20.00
20 Noah Vonleh 3.00 8.00
24 Trey Burke 3.00 8.00

2015-16 Panini Contenders Draft Picks Passports

1 Emmanuel Mudiay .50 1.25
2 Kristaps Porzingis 2.50 6.00
3 Mario Hezonja .50 1.25

2015-16 Panini Contenders Draft Picks School Colors

COMPLETE SET (50) 12.00 30.00
1 Aaron Harrison .30 .75
2 Alan Williams .25 .60
3 Andrew Harrison .30 .75
4 Anthony Brown .25 .60
5 Bobby Portis .60 1.50
6 Brandon Ashley .25 .60
7 Cameron Payne .40 1.00
8 Chris McCullough .25 .60
9 Aaron White .30 .75
10 Christian Wood .40 1.00
11 Cliff Alexander .25 .60
12 D'Angelo Russell 1.00 2.50
13 Dakari Johnson .25 .60
14 Delon Wright .30 .75
15 Devin Booker 3.00 8.00
16 Frank Kaminsky .30 .75
17 J.P. Tokoto .25 .60
18 Jahlil Okafor .30 .75
19 Jarell Martin .25 .60
20 Jordan Mickey .25 .60
21 Joe Young .25 .60
22 Justin Anderson .25 .60
23 Justise Winslow .40 1.00
24 Karl-Anthony Towns 1.50 4.00
25 Kelly Oubre Jr. .75 2.00
26 Branden Dawson .25 .60
27 Kevon Looney .75 2.00
28 Michael Frazier II .30 .75
29 Michael Qualls .30 .75
30 Montrezl Harrell .75 2.00
31 Myles Turner 1.00 2.50
32 Norman Powell .50 1.25
33 Olivier Hanlan .25 .60
34 Quinn Cook .50 1.25
35 R.J. Hunter .25 .60
36 Rakeem Christmas .25 .60
37 Rashad Vaughn .25 .60
38 Richaun Holmes .40 1.00
39 Robert Upshaw .25 .60
40 Rondae Hollis-Jefferson .30 .75
41 Sam Dekker .30 .75
42 Stanley Johnson .30 .75
43 Terran Petteway .25 .60
44 Terry Rozier 1.00 2.50
45 Josh Richardson .40 1.00
46 Trey Lyles .30 .75
47 Tyler Harvey .25 .60
48 Tyus Jones .30 .75
49 Larry Nance Jr. .50 1.25
50 Willie Cauley-Stein .30 .75

2015-16 Panini Contenders Draft Picks School Colors Signatures

OVERALL FIVE AUTOS PER HOBBY BOX
1 Karl-Anthony Towns 75.00 200.00
3 D'Angelo Russell 12.00 30.00
4 Willie Cauley-Stein 10.00 25.00
5 Justise Winslow 25.00 60.00
7 Stanley Johnson 15.00 40.00
8 Myles Turner 12.00 30.00
9 Trey Lyles 4.00 10.00
11 Cameron Payne 5.00 12.00
15 Tyus Jones 6.00 15.00
17 R.J. Hunter 3.00 8.00
18 Delon Wright 4.00 10.00
19 Montrezl Harrell 10.00 25.00
20 Rondae Hollis-Jefferson 4.00 10.00
21 Christian Wood 5.00 12.00
22 Justin Anderson 3.00 8.00
23 Rashad Vaughn 3.00 8.00
24 Chris McCullough 3.00 8.00
25 Terry Rozier 12.00 30.00

2016-17 Panini Contenders Draft Picks

OVERALL FIVE AUTOS PER HOBBY BOX
1 Aaron Gordon .30 .75
2 Al-Farouq Aminu .20 .50
3 Andre Drummond .30 .75
4 Andre Iguodala .30 .75
5 Andrew Wiggins .40 1.00
6 Anthony Davis 1.00 2.50
7 Arron Afflalo .20 .50
8 Ben Gordon .25 .60
9 Blake Griffin .30 .75
10 Bobby Portis .30 .75
11 Bradley Beal .40 1.00
12 Brook Lopez .25 .60
13 Cameron Payne .25 .60
14 Zach LaVine .60 1.50
15 Carmelo Anthony .50 1.25
16 Chris Bosh .40 1.00
17 Chris McCullough .20 .50
18 Chris Paul .50 1.25
19 D'Angelo Russell .40 1.00
20 Damian Lillard .75 2.00
21 Dante Exum .20 .50
22 DeAndre Jordan .25 .60
23 Delon Wright .25 .60
24 DeMar DeRozan .40 1.00
25 DeMarcus Cousins .25 .60
26 Deron Williams .25 .60
27 Derrick Favors .20 .50
28 Derrick Rose .50 1.25
29 Devin Booker 1.25 3.00
30 Doug McDermott .25 .60
31 Draymond Green .40 1.00
32 Dwyane Wade .60 1.50
33 Frank Kaminsky .20 .50
34 Gordon Hayward .30 .75
35 Harrison Barnes .25 .60
36 Hassan Whiteside .25 .60
37 Willie Cauley-Stein .25 .60
38 Jabari Parker .20 .50
39 Jahlil Okafor .20 .50
40 James Harden .60 1.50
41 Vince Carter .60 1.50
42 Jimmy Butler .60 1.50
43 Joakim Noah .20 .50
44 Joe Johnson .25 .60
45 Joel Embiid .75 2.00
46 John Wall .40 1.00
47 Jordan Clarkson .30 .75
48 Josh Richardson .25 .60
49 Jrue Holiday .40 1.00
50 Julius Randle .40 1.00
51 Justin Anderson .20 .50
52 Justise Winslow .20 .50
53 Karl-Anthony Towns .60 1.50
54 Kawhi Leonard .75 2.00
55 Kelly Oubre Jr. .40 1.00
56 Kentavious Caldwell-Pope .25 .60
57 Kevin Durant 1.25 3.00
58 Kevin Love .30 .75
59 Kevon Looney .30 .75
60 Klay Thompson .75 2.00
61 Kyle Korver .25 .60
62 Kyrie Irving .60 1.50
63 LaMarcus Aldridge .30 .75
64 Larry Nance Jr. .20 .50
65 Marcus Smart .40 1.00
66 Mason Plumlee .20 .50
67 Michael Carter-Williams .20 .50
68 Victor Oladipo .25 .60
69 Michael Kidd-Gilchrist .20 .50
70 Mike Conley .25 .60
71 Mo Williams .20 .50
72 Myles Turner .30 .75
73 Nerlens Noel .20 .50
74 Nikola Vucevic .25 .60
75 Noah Vonleh .20 .50
76 Paul George .50 1.25
77 Paul Pierce .50 1.25
78 R.J. Hunter .20 .50
79 Rajon Rondo .40 1.00
80 Rashad Vaughn .20 .50
81 Richard Jefferson .25 .60
82 Rondae Hollis-Jefferson .20 .50
83 Roy Hibbert .25 .60
84 Russell Westbrook .50 1.25
85 Sam Dekker .20 .50
86 Shabazz Napier .20 .50
87 Stanley Johnson .20 .50
88 Stephen Curry 2.50 6.00
89 Terry Rozier .30 .75
90 Tim Duncan .60 1.50
91 Tim Hardaway Jr. .25 .60
92 Trevor Ariza .20 .50
93 Trey Burke .25 .60
94 Trey Lyles .25 .60
95 Tyreke Evans .25 .60
96 Tyus Jones .20 .50
102A Ingram AU Wht jsy 25.00 60.00
102B Ingram AU Blk jsy 25.00 60.00
103A Murray AU Wht jsy 60.00 150.00
103B Murray AU Blue jsy 60.00 150.00
104A Hield AU Red jsy 10.00 25.00
104B Hield AU Wht jsy 10.00 25.00
105A Henry Ellenson AU Blue jersey 3.00 8.00
105B Henry Ellenson AU Yellow jersey 3.00 8.00
106A Dunn AU Gray jsy 5.00 12.00
106B Dunn AU Wht jsy 5.00 12.00
107A Chriss AU Wht jsy 4.00 10.00
107B Chriss AU Prpl jsy 4.00 10.00
108A Brown AU Wht jsy 50.00 120.00
108B Brown AU Ylw jsy 50.00 120.00
109A Jakob Poeltl AU Black jersey 6.00 15.00
109B Jakob Poeltl AU White jersey 6.00 15.00
110A Labissiere AU Wht jsy 3.00 8.00
110B Labissiere AU Blue jsy 3.00 8.00
111A Deyonta Davis AU Dribbling 3.00 8.00
111B Deyonta Davis AU No ball 3.00 8.00
112A Valentine AU Wht jsy 3.00 8.00
112B Valentine AU Grn jsy 3.00 8.00
113A Ulis AU Blue jsy 4.00 10.00
113B Ulis AU Wht jsy 4.00 10.00
114A Diamond Stone AU Yellow jersey 3.00 8.00
114B Diamond Stone AU White jersey 3.00 8.00
115A Murray AU Gld jsy 60.00 150.00
115B Murray AU Blk jsy 60.00 150.00
116A Sabonis AU Ball on side 20.00 50.00
116B Sabonis AU Ball at mid 20.00 50.00
117A Wade Baldwin IV AU White jersey 3.00 8.00
117B Wade Baldwin IV AU Gold jersey 3.00 8.00
118A DeAndre Bembry AU Red jersey 5.00 12.00
118B DeAndre Bembry AU White jersey 5.00 12.00
119A Stephen Zimmerman AU Two hands on ball 3.00 8.00
119B Stephen Zimmerman AU Dunking 3.00 8.00
120A Demetrius Jackson AU 3.00 8.00
120B Demetrius Jackson AU 3.00 8.00
121A Ben Bentil AU Dribbling 3.00 8.00
121B Ben Bentil AU Ball over head 3.00 8.00
122A Johnson AU Lt blue jsy 3.00 8.00
122B Johnson AU Blk jsy 3.00 8.00
123A Cheick Diallo AU Ball over head 3.00 8.00
123B Cheick Diallo AU Ball at hip 3.00 8.00
124A Malik Beasley AU Red jersey 6.00 15.00
124B Malik Beasley AU Black jersey 6.00 15.00
125A LeVert AU Dark jsy 8.00 20.00
125B LeVert AU Wht jsy 8.00 20.00
127A Taurean Prince AU Green jersey 4.00 10.00
127B Taurean Prince AU Black jersey 4.00 10.00
128A Richardson AU Orng jsy 3.00 8.00
128B Richardson AU Wht jsy 3.00 8.00
129A McCaw AU Wht jsy 3.00 8.00
129B McCaw AU Blk jsy 3.00 8.00
130A Jarrod Uthoff AU Black jersey 3.00 8.00
130B Jarrod Uthoff AU White jersey 3.00 8.00
131A Damian Jones AU Ball at midsection 3.00 8.00
131B Damian Jones AU Facing right 3.00 8.00
132A Anthony Barber AU Facing forward 3.00 8.00
132B Anthony Barber AU Facing left 3.00 8.00
133A Brogdon AU Dark jsy 10.00 25.00
133B Brogdon AU Wht jsy 10.00 25.00
134A Elgin Cook AU Ball in right hand 3.00 8.00
134B Elgin Cook AU Ball in left hand 3.00 8.00
135A Gary Payton II AU Orange jersey 8.00 20.00
135B Gary Payton II AU White jersey 8.00 20.00
136A Kay Felder AU Driving 3.00 8.00
136B Kay Felder AU Making fist 3.00 8.00
137A Robert Carter AU Ball at midsection 3.00 8.00
137B Robert Carter AU Ball at head 3.00 8.00
138A James Webb III AU Ball in right hand 3.00 8.00
138B James Webb III AU Two hands on ball 3.00 8.00
139A Baker AU Wht jsy 3.00 8.00
139B Baker AU Ylw jsy 3.00 8.00
140A Jake Layman AU Yellow jersey 4.00 10.00
140B Jake Layman AU White jersey 4.00 10.00
141A Paige AU Ball at head 3.00 8.00
141B Paige AU Dribbling 3.00 8.00
142A Jalen Reynolds AU White jersey 3.00 8.00
142B Jalen Reynolds AU Black jersey 3.00 8.00
143A Pascal Siakam AU Red jersey 20.00 50.00
143B Pascal Siakam AU White jersey 20.00 50.00
144A VanVleet AU Wht jsy 50.00 120.00
144B VanVleet AU Blk jsy 50.00 120.00
146A Tim Quarterman AU

White jersey 3.00 8.00
146B Tim Quarterman AU
Yellow jersey 3.00 8.00
148A Wayne Selden Jr. AU
White jersey 4.00 10.00
148B Wayne Selden Jr. AU
Blue jersey 4.00 10.00
149A Perry Ellis AU
White jersey 3.00 8.00
149B Perry Ellis AU
Blue jersey 3.00 8.00
150A Chinanu Onuaku AU
Red jersey 3.00 8.00
150B Chinanu Onuaku AU
White jersey 3.00 8.00
151 Daniel Hamilton AU 3.00 8.00
152 Rasheed Sulaimon AU 4.00 10.00
153 Rosco Allen AU 3.00 8.00
154 A.J. Hammons AU 3.00 8.00
156 Alex Poythress AU 4.00 10.00
157 Georges Niang AU 5.00 12.00
158 A.J. Hammons AU 3.00 8.00
159 Dorian Finney-Smith AU 4.00 10.00
160 Troy Williams AU 3.00 8.00
161 Danuel House AU 5.00 12.00
162 Devin Williams AU 3.00 8.00
163 David Walker AU 3.00 8.00
164 Rico Gathers AU 3.00 8.00
165 Kyle Wiltjer AU 3.00 8.00
166 Shawn Long AU 3.00 8.00
167 Isaiah Taylor AU 3.00 8.00
168 Yogi Ferrell AU 4.00 10.00
169 Prince Ibeh AU 3.00 8.00
171 Damion Lee AU 4.00 10.00
172 Sheldon McClellan AU 3.00 8.00
173 Joel Bolomboy AU 3.00 8.00
176 Stefan Jankovic AU 3.00 8.00
178 Abdel Nader AU 3.00 8.00
179 Marshall Plumlee AU 3.00 8.00
180 Tre Demps AU 3.00 8.00
181 Nikola Jovanovic AU 3.00 8.00
182 Derrick Jones AU 4.00 10.00
183 Cameron Ridley AU 3.00 8.00
184 Daniel Ochefu AU 3.00 8.00
190 Dragan Bender AU 3.00 8.00
192 Georgios Papagiannis AU 3.00 8.00
193 Timothe Luwawu-Cabarrot AU 5.00 12.00
195 Mindaugas Kuzminskas AU 3.00 8.00
197 Ivica Zubac AU 8.00 20.00
198 Isaia Cordinier AU 3.00 8.00
199 Thon Maker AU 4.00 10.00

2016-17 Panini Contenders Draft Picks Cracked Ice Ticket

*CRCKD ICE 1-96: 5X TO 12X BASIC
*CRCKD ICE 102-199: .75X TO 2X BASIC
OVERALL FIVE AUTOS PER HOBBY BOX
STATED PRINT RUN 23 SER.#'d SETS

2016-17 Panini Contenders Draft Picks Draft Ticket

*DRFT 1-96: 2X TO 5X BASIC
*DRFT 102-199: .5X TO 1.2X BASIC
OVERALL FIVE AUTOS PER HOBBY BOX
STATED PRINT RUN 99 SER.#'d SETS

2016-17 Panini Contenders Draft Picks Alumni Ink

OVERALL FIVE AUTOS PER HOBBY BOX
14 Danny Manning 4.00 10.00

2016-17 Panini Contenders Draft Picks Class Reunion

1 Ben Simmons .75 2.00
2 Brandon Ingram 1.00 2.50
3 Jamal Murray 2.00 5.00
4 Buddy Hield .75 2.00
5 Henry Ellenson .25 .60
6 Kris Dunn .40 1.00
7 Marquese Chriss .30 .75
8 Jaylen Brown 2.00 5.00
9 Jakob Poeltl .50 1.25
10 Skal Labissiere .25 .60
11 Deyonta Davis .25 .60
12 Denzel Valentine .25 .60
13 Tyler Ulis .30 .75
14 Diamond Stone .25 .60
15 Dejounte Murray 1.25 3.00
16 Domantas Sabonis 1.50 4.00
17 Wade Baldwin IV .25 .60
18 DeAndre Bembry .50 1.25
19 Stephen Zimmerman .25 .60
20 Malachi Richardson .25 .60

2016-17 Panini Contenders Draft Picks Collegiate Connections

1 Murray/Labissiere 2.00 5.00
2 Murray/Chriss 1.25 3.00
3 Valentine/Davis .25 .60
4 Bentil/Dunn .40 1.00
5 Simmons/Quarterman .75 2.00
6 McCaw/Zimmerman .25 .60
7 Damian Jones
Wade Baldwin IV .25 .60
8 Diamond Stone
Robert Carter .25 .60
9 Brown/Wallace 2.00 5.00
10 Hield/Cousins .75 2.00
11 Murray/Ulis 2.00 5.00
12 Cheick Diallo
Wayne Selden Jr. .30 .75
13 Brice Johnson
Marcus Paige .25 .60
14 Daniel Ochefu
Ryan Arcidiacono .40 1.00
15 Ingram/Plumlee 1.00 2.50
16 Sabonis/Wiltjer 1.50 4.00
17 Jake Layman
Robert Carter .30 .75
18 Fred VanVleet
Ron Baker 1.25 3.00
19 Rico Gathers
Taurean Prince .30 .75
20 Malachi Richardson
Michael Gbinije .25 .60

2016-17 Panini Contenders Draft Picks Collegiate Connections Signatures

OVERALL FIVE AUTOS PER HOBBY BOX
1 Murray/Labissiere 60.00 150.00
7 Jones/Baldwin IV 12.00 30.00
8 Stone/Carter 20.00 50.00

2016-17 Panini Contenders Draft Picks Game Day

1 Ben Simmons .75 2.00
2 Brandon Ingram 1.00 2.50
3 Jamal Murray 2.00 5.00
4 Buddy Hield .75 2.00
5 Henry Ellenson .25 .60
6 Kris Dunn .40 1.00
7 Marquese Chriss .30 .75
8 Jaylen Brown 2.00 5.00
9 Jakob Poeltl .50 1.25
10 Skal Labissiere .25 .60
11 Deyonta Davis .25 .60
12 Denzel Valentine .25 .60
13 Tyler Ulis .30 .75
14 Diamond Stone .25 .60
15 Dejounte Murray 1.25 3.00
16 Domantas Sabonis 1.50 4.00
17 Wade Baldwin IV .25 .60
18 DeAndre Bembry .40 1.00
19 Stephen Zimmerman .25 .60
20 Malachi Richardson .25 .60

2016-17 Panini Contenders Draft Picks Old School Colors

1 Andrew Wiggins .50 1.25
2 Anthony Davis 1.25 3.00
3 Blake Griffin .40 1.00
4 Carmelo Anthony .60 1.50
5 Chris Paul .60 1.50
6 DeMar DeRozan .50 1.25
7 DeMarcus Cousins .30 .75
8 James Harden .75 2.00
9 Jimmy Butler .75 2.00
10 John Wall .50 1.25
11 Karl-Anthony Towns .75 2.00
12 Kawhi Leonard 1.00 2.50
13 Kevin Durant 1.50 4.00
14 Klay Thompson 1.00 2.50
15 Kyrie Irving .75 2.00
16 Myles Turner .40 1.00
17 Paul George .60 1.50
18 Russell Westbrook .60 1.50
19 Stephen Curry 3.00 8.00

2016-17 Panini Contenders Draft Picks Old School Colors Signatures

OVERALL FIVE AUTOS PER HOBBY BOX
6 James Worthy 6.00 15.00

2016-17 Panini Contenders Draft Picks School Colors

1 Ben Simmons .75 2.00
2 Brandon Ingram 1.00 2.50
3 Jamal Murray 2.00 5.00
4 Buddy Hield .75 2.00
5 Henry Ellenson .25 .60
6 Kris Dunn .40 1.00
7 Marquese Chriss .30 .75
8 Jaylen Brown 2.00 5.00
9 Jakob Poeltl .50 1.25
10 Skal Labissiere .25 .60
11 Deyonta Davis .25 .60
12 Denzel Valentine .25 .60
13 Tyler Ulis .30 .75
14 Diamond Stone .25 .60
15 Dejounte Murray 1.25 3.00
16 Domantas Sabonis 1.50 4.00
17 Wade Baldwin IV .25 .60
18 DeAndre Bembry .40 1.00
19 Stephen Zimmerman .25 .60
20 Malachi Richardson .25 .60

2016-17 Panini Contenders Draft Picks School Colors Signatures

OVERALL FIVE AUTOS PER HOBBY BOX
4 Buddy Hield 10.00 25.00
5 Henry Ellenson 3.00 8.00
6 Kris Dunn 5.00 12.00
7 Marquese Chriss 4.00 10.00
9 Jakob Poeltl 6.00 15.00

2017-18 Panini Contenders Draft Picks

COMPLETE SET (230) 10.00 25.00
OVERALL SIX AUTOS PER HOBBY BOX
1A Andrew Wiggins .40 1.00
1B Andrew Wiggins .40 1.00
2A Anthony Davis .75 2.00
2B Anthony Davis .75 2.00
3A Ben Simmons .30 .75
3B Ben Simmons .30 .75
4A Blake Griffin .30 .75
4B Blake Griffin .30 .75
5A Brandon Ingram .40 1.00
5B Brandon Ingram .40 1.00
6A Buddy Hield .30 .75
6B Buddy Hield .30 .75
7A Carmelo Anthony .50 1.25
7B Carmelo Anthony .50 1.25
8A Chris Paul .50 1.25
8B Chris Paul .50 1.25
9A Damian Lillard .75 2.00
9B Damian Lillard .75 2.00
10A D'Angelo Russell .25 .60
10B D'Angelo Russell .25 .60
11A Dario Saric .25 .60
11B Dario Saric .25 .60
12A DeMar DeRozan .40 1.00
12B DeMar DeRozan .40 1.00
13A Derrick Rose .50 1.25
13B Derrick Rose .50 1.25
14A Devin Booker .75 2.00
14B Devin Booker .75 2.00
15A Dirk Nowitzki .75 2.00
15B Dirk Nowitzki .75 2.00
16A Draymond Green .40 1.00
16B Draymond Green .40 1.00
17A Dwyane Wade .60 1.50
17B Dwyane Wade .60 1.50
18A Giannis Antetokounmpo 1.50 4.00
18B Giannis Antetokounmpo 1.50 4.00
19A Isaiah Thomas .25 .60
19B Isaiah Thomas .25 .60
20A Jabari Parker .20 .50
20B Jabari Parker .20 .50
21A Jamal Murray .50 1.25
21B Jamal Murray .50 1.25
22A James Harden .60 1.50
22B James Harden .60 1.50
23A Jaylen Brown .75 2.00
23B Jaylen Brown .75 2.00
24A Jimmy Butler .50 1.25
24B Jimmy Butler .50 1.25
25A Joel Embiid .60 1.50
25B Joel Embiid .60 1.50
26A John Wall .40 1.00
26B John Wall .40 1.00
27A Karl-Anthony Towns .50 1.25
27B Karl-Anthony Towns .50 1.25
28A Kawhi Leonard .75 2.00
28B Kawhi Leonard .75 2.00
29A Kevin Durant 1.25 3.00
29B Kevin Durant 1.25 3.00
30A Klay Thompson .75 2.00
30B Klay Thompson .75 2.00
31A Kobe Bryant 2.50 6.00
31B Kobe Bryant 2.50 6.00
32A Kris Dunn .20 .50
32B Kris Dunn .20 .50
33A Kristaps Porzingis .40 1.00
33B Kristaps Porzingis .40 1.00
34A Kyrie Irving .60 1.50
34B Kyrie Irving .60 1.50
35A Larry Bird 1.25 3.00
35B Larry Bird 1.25 3.00
36A LeBron James 2.50 6.00
36B LeBron James 2.50 6.00
37A Magic Johnson 1.25 3.00
37B Magic Johnson 1.25 3.00
38A Malcolm Brogdon .25 .60
38B Malcolm Brogdon .25 .60
39A Marquese Chriss .20 .50
39B Marquese Chriss .20 .50
40A Paul George .50 1.25
40B Paul George .50 1.25
41A Reggie Miller .60 1.50
41B Reggie Miller .60 1.50
42A Rodney McGruder .20 .50
42B Rodney McGruder .20 .50
43A Russell Westbrook .50 1.25
43B Russell Westbrook .50 1.25
44A Scottie Pippen .75 2.00
44B Scottie Pippen .75 2.00
45A Shaquille O'Neal 1.00 2.50
45B Shaquille O'Neal 1.00 2.50
46A Stephen Curry 2.50 6.00
46B Stephen Curry 2.50 6.00
47A Thon Maker .20 .50
47B Thon Maker .20 .50
48A Vince Carter .60 1.50
48B Vince Carter .60 1.50
49A Willy Hernangomez .20 .50
49B Willy Hernangomez .20 .50
50A Yogi Ferrell .20 .50
50B Yogi Ferrell .20 .50
51 Lonzo Ball AU 12.00 30.00
51A Lonzo Ball AU 12.00 30.00
51B Lonzo Ball AU 12.00 30.00
51C Lonzo Ball AU 12.00 30.00
52 Markelle Fultz AU 8.00 20.00
52A Markelle Fultz AU 8.00 20.00
52B Markelle Fultz AU 8.00 20.00
52C Markelle Fultz AU 8.00 20.00
53 Josh Jackson AU 4.00 10.00
53A Josh Jackson AU 4.00 10.00
53B Josh Jackson AU 4.00 10.00
53C Josh Jackson AU 4.00 10.00
54 Jayson Tatum AU 75.00 200.00
54A Jayson Tatum AU 75.00 200.00
54B Jayson Tatum AU 75.00 200.00
54C Jayson Tatum AU 75.00 200.00
55 De'Aaron Fox AU 40.00 100.00
55A De'Aaron Fox AU 40.00 100.00
55B De'Aaron Fox AU 40.00 100.00
55C De'Aaron Fox AU 40.00 100.00
56 Malik Monk AU 12.00 30.00
56A Malik Monk AU 12.00 30.00
56B Malik Monk AU 12.00 30.00
56C Malik Monk AU 12.00 30.00
57 Lauri Markkanen AU 20.00 50.00
57A Lauri Markkanen AU 20.00 50.00
57B Lauri Markkanen AU 20.00 50.00
57C Lauri Markkanen AU 20.00 50.00
58 Zach Collins AU 5.00 12.00
58A Zach Collins AU 5.00 12.00
58B Zach Collins AU 5.00 12.00
58C Zach Collins AU 5.00 12.00
59 Jonathan Isaac AU 8.00 20.00
59A Jonathan Isaac AU 8.00 20.00
59B Jonathan Isaac AU 8.00 20.00
59C Jonathan Isaac AU 8.00 20.00
60 Dennis Smith Jr. AU 4.00 10.00
60A Dennis Smith Jr. AU 4.00 10.00
60B Dennis Smith Jr. AU 4.00 10.00
60C Dennis Smith Jr. AU 4.00 10.00
61 Harry Giles AU 3.00 8.00
61A Harry Giles AU 3.00 8.00
61B Harry Giles AU 3.00 8.00
61C Harry Giles AU 3.00 8.00
62 Justin Patton AU 3.00 8.00
62A Justin Patton AU 3.00 8.00
62B Justin Patton AU 3.00 8.00
62C Justin Patton AU 3.00 8.00
63 T.J. Leaf AU 3.00 8.00
63A T.J. Leaf AU 3.00 8.00
63B T.J. Leaf AU 3.00 8.00
63C T.J. Leaf AU 3.00 8.00
64 Bam Adebayo AU 20.00 50.00
64A Bam Adebayo AU 20.00 50.00
64B Bam Adebayo AU 20.00 50.00
64C Bam Adebayo AU 20.00 50.00
65 Jarrett Allen AU 8.00 20.00
65A Jarrett Allen AU 8.00 20.00
65B Jarrett Allen AU 8.00 20.00
65C Jarrett Allen AU 8.00 20.00
66A OG Anunoby AU 15.00 40.00
66B OG Anunoby AU 15.00 40.00
67A Ivan Rabb AU 3.00 8.00
67B Ivan Rabb AU 3.00 8.00
68A Justin Jackson AU 3.00 8.00
68B Justin Jackson AU 3.00 8.00
69 Tyler Lydon AU 3.00 8.00
70 Marcus Keene AU 3.00 8.00
71 Monte Morris AU 8.00 20.00
72 Josh Hart AU 8.00 20.00
73 Alec Peters AU 3.00 8.00
74 Cameron Oliver AU 3.00 8.00
75 Dillon Brooks AU 10.00 25.00
76A John Collins AU 8.00 20.00
76B John Collins AU 8.00 20.00
77A Caleb Swanigan AU 3.00 8.00
77B Caleb Swanigan AU 3.00 8.00
78A Luke Kennard AU 6.00 15.00
78B Luke Kennard AU 6.00 15.00
79A Donovan Mitchell AU 50.00 120.00
79B Donovan Mitchell AU 50.00 120.00
80 Johnathan Motley AU 3.00 8.00
81A Jawun Evans AU 3.00 8.00
81B Jawun Evans AU 3.00 8.00
82 Tyler Dorsey AU 3.00 8.00
83 Thomas Bryant AU 5.00 12.00
84 Dwayne Bacon AU 3.00 8.00
86A Frank Jackson AU 3.00 8.00
86B Frank Jackson AU 3.00 8.00
87 Jaron Blossomgame AU 3.00 8.00
89 Devin Robinson AU 3.00 8.00
90A Jordan Bell AU 3.00 8.00
90B Jordan Bell AU 3.00 8.00
91 Wesley Iwundu AU 3.00 8.00
92 Sindarius Thornwell AU 3.00 8.00
93 Edmond Sumner AU 5.00 12.00
94 Derrick White AU 12.00 30.00
96 Frank Mason III AU 3.00 8.00
97A Tony Bradley AU 3.00 8.00
97B Tony Bradley AU 3.00 8.00
98 Moses Kingsley AU 3.00 8.00
99 Sterling Brown AU 3.00 8.00
101 L.J. Peak AU 3.00 8.00
102A D.J. Wilson AU 3.00 8.00
102B D.J. Wilson AU 3.00 8.00
103A Ike Anigbogu AU 3.00 8.00
103B Ike Anigbogu AU 3.00 8.00
104 Semi Ojeleye AU 4.00 10.00
105 Nigel Hayes AU 3.00 8.00
106 Eric Mika AU 3.00 8.00
107 Luke Kornet AU 4.00 10.00
108 Kyle Kuzma AU 12.00 30.00
109 Nigel Williams-Goss AU 3.00 8.00
110 Isaiah Hicks AU 5.00 12.00
111 Frank Ntilikina AU 4.00 10.00
113 Terrance Ferguson AU 3.00 8.00
114 Isaiah Hartenstein AU 10.00 25.00
116 Andrew White III AU 3.00 8.00
117 Isaiah Briscoe AU 4.00 10.00
118 Damyean Dotson AU 4.00 10.00
119 Zak Irvin AU 3.00 8.00
121 Deonte Burton AU 3.00 8.00
122 Malcolm Hill AU 3.00 8.00
124 Bronson Koenig AU 5.00 12.00
125 Derrick Walton Jr. AU 3.00 8.00
126 Kennedy Meeks AU 5.00 12.00
128 Amile Jefferson AU 4.00 10.00
129 London Perrantes AU 3.00 8.00
134 Davon Reed AU 3.00 8.00

2017-18 Panini Contenders Draft Picks Cracked Ice Ticket

*CRCKD ICE 1-50: 4X TO 10X BASIC
*CRCKD ICE 51-134: 2X TO 5X BASIC
OVERALL SIX AUTOS PER HOBBY BOX
STATED PRINT RUN 23 SER.#'d SETS
71 Monte Morris AU 40.00 100.00

2017-18 Panini Contenders Draft Picks Draft Ticket

*DRFT 1-50: 1.5X TO 4X BASIC
*DRFT 51-134/98-99: .5X TO 1.2X BASIC
*DRFT 51-134/25: .75X TO 2X BASIC
OVERALL SIX AUTOS PER HOBBY BOX
STATED PRINT RUN 99 SER.#'d SETS

2017-18 Panini Contenders Draft Picks Game Day Tickets

COMMON CARD .25 .60
SEMISTARS .30 .75
UNLISTED STARS .40 1.00
1 Markelle Fultz .60 1.50
2 Lonzo Ball 1.00 2.50
3 Josh Jackson .30 .75
4 Malik Monk 1.00 2.50
5 Jayson Tatum 3.00 8.00
6 Lauri Markkanen 1.50 4.00
7 De'Aaron Fox 2.00 5.00
8 Dennis Smith Jr. .30 .75
9 Jonathan Isaac .60 1.50
10 Harry Giles .25 .60
11 Zach Collins .40 1.00
12 OG Anunoby 1.25 3.00
13 T.J. Leaf .25 .60
14 Justin Patton .25 .60
15 Jarrett Allen .60 1.50
16 Bam Adebayo 1.50 4.00
17 Luke Kennard .50 1.25
18 Ike Anigbogu .25 .60
19 Justin Jackson .25 .60
20 Dwayne Bacon .25 .60
21 John Collins .60 1.50
22 Frank Jackson .25 .60
23 Jawun Evans .25 .60
24 Tyler Dorsey .25 .60
25 Tony Bradley .25 .60
26 D.J. Wilson .25 .60
27 Caleb Swanigan .25 .60
28 Tyler Lydon .25 .60
29 Donovan Mitchell 2.50 6.00
30 Monte Morris .60 1.50
31 Dillon Brooks .75 2.00
32 Jordan Bell .25 .60
33 Sindarius Thornwell .25 .60
34 Josh Hart .60 1.50
35 Frank Mason III .25 .60

2017-18 Panini Contenders Draft Picks Collegiate Connections Signatures

1 Ball/Leaf 40.00 100.00
2 Giles/Tatum 100.00 250.00
3 Fox/Monk 75.00 200.00
4 Isaac/Bacon 25.00 60.00
5 Mason III/Jackson 12.00 30.00
6 Collins/Williams-Goss 15.00 40.00
7 Jackson/Bradley 10.00 25.00
8 Jackson/Kennard 20.00 50.00
9 Bell/Brooks 30.00 80.00
10 Sterling Brown/Semi Ojeleye 12.00 30.00

2017-18 Panini Contenders Draft Picks Legacy

COMPLETE SET (30) 8.00 20.00
1 Andrew Wiggins .50 1.25
2 Anthony Davis 1.00 2.50
3 Blake Griffin .40 1.00
4 Carmelo Anthony .60 1.50
5 Chris Paul .60 1.50
6 Damian Lillard 1.00 2.50
7 DeMar DeRozan .50 1.25
8 Derrick Rose .60 1.50
9 Devin Booker 1.00 2.50
10 Bill Walton .60 1.50
11 Draymond Green .50 1.25
12 Dwyane Wade .75 2.00
13 Paul George .60 1.50
14 Isaiah Thomas .30 .75
15 Jabari Parker .25 .60
16 James Harden .75 2.00
17 Jimmy Butler .60 1.50
18 John Wall .50 1.25
19 Karl-Anthony Towns .60 1.50
20 Kawhi Leonard 1.00 2.50
21 Kevin Durant 1.50 4.00
22 Klay Thompson 1.00 2.50
23 Ben Simmons .40 1.00
24 Kyrie Irving .75 2.00
25 Larry Bird 1.50 4.00
26 Reggie Miller .75 2.00
27 Magic Johnson 1.50 4.00
28 Russell Westbrook .60 1.50
29 Shaquille O'Neal 1.25 3.00
30 Stephen Curry 3.00 8.00

2017-18 Panini Contenders Draft Picks Legacy Signatures

OVERALL SIX AUTOS PER HOBBY BOX
1 Isaiah Thomas 20.00 50.00
2 Magic Johnson 50.00 120.00
3 Shaquille O'Neal 75.00 200.00
4 Stephen Curry 400.00 800.00
5 James Harden 75.00 200.00
6 Reggie Miller 75.00 200.00
7 Kareem Abdul-Jabbar 50.00 120.00
8 Larry Bird 50.00 120.00
9 Bill Walton 15.00 40.00

2017-18 Panini Contenders Draft Picks School Colors

1 Markelle Fultz .60 1.50
2 Lonzo Ball 1.00 2.50
3 Josh Jackson .30 .75
4 Malik Monk 1.00 2.50
5 Jayson Tatum 3.00 8.00
6 Lauri Markkanen 1.50 4.00
7 De'Aaron Fox 2.00 5.00
8 Dennis Smith Jr. .30 .75
9 Jonathan Isaac .60 1.50
10 Harry Giles .25 .60
11 Zach Collins .40 1.00
12 OG Anunoby 1.25 3.00
13 T.J. Leaf .25 .60
14 Justin Patton .25 .60
15 Jarrett Allen .60 1.50
16 Bam Adebayo 1.50 4.00
17 Luke Kennard .50 1.25
18 Ike Anigbogu .25 .60
19 Justin Jackson .25 .60
20 Dwayne Bacon .25 .60
21 John Collins .60 1.50
22 Frank Jackson .25 .60
23 Jawun Evans .25 .60
24 Tyler Dorsey .25 .60
25 Tony Bradley .25 .60
26 D.J. Wilson .25 .60
27 Caleb Swanigan .25 .60
28 Tyler Lydon .25 .60
29 Donovan Mitchell 2.50 6.00
30 Monte Morris .60 1.50
31 Dillon Brooks .75 2.00
32 Jordan Bell .25 .60
33 Sindarius Thornwell .25 .60
34 Josh Hart .60 1.50
35 Frank Mason III .25 .60

2017-18 Panini Contenders Draft Picks School Colors Signatures

1 Markelle Fultz 50.00 120.00
2 Lonzo Ball 75.00 200.00
3 Josh Jackson 10.00 25.00
4 Malik Monk 30.00 80.00
5 Jayson Tatum 150.00 400.00
6 Lauri Markkanen 50.00 120.00
7 De'Aaron Fox 100.00 250.00
8 Dennis Smith Jr. 10.00 25.00
9 Jonathan Isaac 20.00 50.00
10 Harry Giles 8.00 20.00
11 Zach Collins 12.00 30.00
12 OG Anunoby 40.00 100.00
13 T.J. Leaf 8.00 20.00
14 Justin Patton 8.00 20.00
15 Jarrett Allen 20.00 50.00
16 Bam Adebayo 50.00 120.00
17 Luke Kennard 15.00 40.00
18 Ike Anigbogu 8.00 20.00
19 Justin Jackson 8.00 20.00
20 Ivan Rabb 8.00 20.00

2017-18 Panini Contenders Draft Picks Season Ticket Signatures

OVERALL SIX AUTOS PER HOBBY BOX
1 Brandon Ingram 15.00 40.00
2 Buddy Hield 5.00 12.00
3 Damian Lillard 40.00 100.00
4 D'Angelo Russell 20.00 50.00
5 Giannis Antetokounmpo 125.00 300.00
6 Isaiah Thomas 4.00 10.00
7 James Harden 30.00 80.00
8 Jaylen Brown 25.00 60.00
9 Joel Embiid 40.00 100.00
10 John Wall 10.00 25.00
12 Kobe Bryant 500.00 1,000.00
13 Kyrie Irving 30.00 80.00
15 Malcolm Brogdon 4.00 10.00
16 Rodney McGruder 3.00 8.00
17 Shaquille O'Neal 75.00 200.00
18 Stephen Curry 400.00 800.00
19 Willy Hernangomez 3.00 8.00
20 Yogi Ferrell 3.00 8.00

2017-18 Panini Contenders Draft Picks Season Ticket Signatures Cracked Ice

*CRACKED ICE: .75X TO 2X BASIC
STATED PRINT RUN 23 SER.#'d SETS
1 Brandon Ingram 30.00 80.00
2 Buddy Hield 10.00 25.00
11 Karl-Anthony Towns 150.00 400.00
14 Magic Johnson 60.00 150.00
15 Malcolm Brogdon 20.00 50.00
17 Shaquille O'Neal 125.00 300.00
18 Stephen Curry 600.00 1,200.00

2017-18 Panini Contenders Draft Picks Turning Pro Signatures

OVERALL SIX AUTOS PER HOBBY BOX
1 Karl-Anthony Towns 20.00 50.00
2 Malcolm Brogdon 4.00 10.00
3 Yogi Ferrell 3.00 8.00
4 Jaylen Brown 40.00 100.00
5 Brandon Ingram 40.00 100.00
6 Buddy Hield 5.00 12.00
7 Damian Lillard 60.00 150.00
8 Kyrie Irving 60.00 150.00
9 Stephen Curry 400.00 800.00
10 John Wall 12.00 30.00

2018-19 Panini Contenders Draft Picks

1 Andrew Wiggins .40 1.00
2 Anthony Davis .75 2.00
3 Bam Adebayo .50 1.25
4 Ben Simmons .30 .75
5 Brandon Ingram .30 .75
6 Caleb Swanigan .20 .50
7 Carmelo Anthony .50 1.25
8 Charles Barkley .60 1.50
9 Chris Paul .60 1.50
10 Damian Lillard .75 2.00
11 De'Aaron Fox .60 1.50
12 Dennis Smith Jr. .20 .50
13 Devin Booker .75 2.00
14 Dirk Nowitzki .75 2.00
15 Donovan Mitchell 1.00 2.50
16 Draymond Green .40 1.00
17 Dwyane Wade .60 1.50
18 Giannis Antetokounmpo 1.50 4.00
19 Jabari Parker .20 .50
20 Jamal Murray .60 1.50
21 James Harden .60 1.50
22 Jaylen Brown .50 1.25
23 Jayson Tatum 1.25 3.00
24 Joel Embiid .75 2.00
25 John Collins .30 .75
26 John Wall .40 1.00
27 Jonathan Isaac .30 .75
28 Jordan Bell .20 .50
29 Josh Jackson .20 .50
30 Karl-Anthony Towns .50 1.25
31 Kawhi Leonard .75 2.00
32 Kevin Durant 1.25 3.00
33 Klay Thompson .75 2.00
34 Kobe Bryant 2.50 6.00
35 Kris Dunn .20 .50
36 Kristaps Porzingis .40 1.00
37 Kyle Kuzma .30 .75
38 Kyrie Irving .75 2.00
39 Larry Bird 1.25 3.00
40 Lauri Markkanen .50 1.25
41 LeBron James 2.50 6.00
42 Lonzo Ball .30 .75
43 Magic Johnson 1.25 3.00
44 Malik Monk .30 .75
45 Markelle Fultz .25 .60
46 Paul George .50 1.25
47 Russell Westbrook .50 1.25
48 Shaquille O'Neal 1.00 2.50
49 Stephen Curry 2.50 6.00
50 Vince Carter .60 1.50
51 Deandre Ayton AU RC 10.00 25.00
52 Mo Bamba AU RC 5.00 12.00
53 Marvin Bagley III AU RC 5.00 12.00
54 Jaren Jackson Jr. AU RC 40.00 100.00
55 Michael Porter Jr. AU RC 12.00 30.00
56 Trae Young AU RC 60.00 150.00
57 Wendell Carter Jr. AU RC 8.00 20.00
59 Collin Sexton AU RC 10.00 25.00
60 Mikal Bridges AU RC 15.00 40.00
61 Kevin Knox AU RC 4.00 10.00
62 Robert Williams III AU RC 6.00 15.00
63 Lonnie Walker IV AU RC 6.00 15.00
64 Shai Gilgeous-Alexander AU RC 150.00 400.00
65 Zhaire Smith AU RC 3.00 8.00
66 Khyri Thomas AU RC 3.00 8.00
67 Gary Trent Jr. AU RC 6.00 15.00
68 Malik Newman AU RC 3.00 8.00
69 Troy Brown Jr. AU RC 4.00 10.00
70 Chandler Hutchison AU RC 4.00 10.00
71 Bruce Brown AU RC 6.00 15.00
74 De'Anthony Melton AU RC 6.00 15.00
75 Keita Bates-Diop AU RC 4.00 10.00
76 Hamidou Diallo AU RC 5.00 12.00
77 Landry Shamet AU RC 5.00 12.00
78 Brandon McCoy AU RC 3.00 8.00
79 Grayson Allen AU RC 6.00 15.00
80 Chimezie Metu AU RC 4.00 10.00
81 Devonte' Graham AU RC 5.00 12.00
82 Jacob Evans III AU RC 3.00 8.00
83 Aaron Holiday AU RC 5.00 12.00
84 Jalen Brunson AU RC 40.00 100.00
85 Omari Spellman AU RC 3.00 8.00
86 Dakota Mathias AU RC 3.00 8.00
87 Moritz Wagner AU RC 6.00 15.00
88 Melvin Frazier AU RC 3.00 8.00
89 Braian Angola AU RC 3.00 8.00
90 Jevon Carter AU RC 5.00 12.00
91 Donte DiVincenzo AU RC 8.00 20.00
92 Tony Carr AU RC 3.00 8.00
93 Svi Mykhailiuk AU RC 4.00 10.00
94 Donte Ingram AU RC 3.00 8.00
95 Alize Johnson AU RC 5.00 12.00
96 Bonzie Colson AU RC 3.00 8.00
97 Bryant McIntosh AU RC 3.00 8.00
98 Keenan Evans AU RC 3.00 8.00
99 Jared Terrell AU RC 3.00 8.00
100 Kelan Martin AU RC 4.00 10.00
101 Kenrich Williams AU RC 4.00 10.00
102 Yante Maten AU RC 3.00 8.00
103 Jonathan Stark AU RC 3.00 8.00
104 Joel Berry II AU RC 3.00 8.00
106 Kevin Hervey AU RC 3.00 8.00
108 Deng Adel AU RC 3.00 8.00
109 Justin Tillman AU RC 3.00 8.00
110 Malik Pope AU RC 3.00 8.00
111 Gary Clark AU RC 3.00 8.00
112 Jerome Robinson AU RC 3.00 8.00
113 Ray Spalding AU RC 3.00 8.00
114 Vincent Edwards AU RC 3.00 8.00
115 DJ Hogg AU RC 3.00 8.00
116 Devon Hall AU RC 3.00 8.00
117 Marcus Derrickson AU RC 3.00 8.00
118 Nuni Omot AU RC 3.00 8.00
119 Theo Pinson AU RC 3.00 8.00
120 Kevin Huerter AU RC 6.00 15.00
121 Angel Delgado AU RC 3.00 8.00
122 Kostas Antetokounmpo AU RC 4.00 10.00
123 Josh Okogie AU RC 5.00 12.00
124 Zach Lofton AU RC 3.00 8.00
125 Anfernee Simons AU RC 15.00 40.00
126 Luka Doncic AU RC 400.00 800.00
127 Dzanan Musa AU RC 3.00 8.00
128 Rodions Kurucs AU RC 4.00 10.00
129 Elie Okobo AU RC 3.00 8.00
130 Isaac Bonga AU RC 4.00 10.00

2018-19 Panini Contenders Draft Picks College Cracked Ice Ticket Signature Variations A

*CRK ICE VAR A: .75X TO 2X BASIC
STATED PRINT RUN 23 SER.#'d SETS

2018-19 Panini Contenders Draft Picks College Draft Ticket Signature Variations A

*DFT VAR A: .75X TO 2X BASIC
STATED PRINT RUN 25 SER.#'d SETS

2018-19 Panini Contenders Draft Picks College Draft Ticket Signature Variations B

*DFT VAR B: .75X TO 2X BASIC
STATED PRINT RUN 25 SER.#'d SETS

2018-19 Panini Contenders Draft Picks College Draft Ticket Signature Variations C

*DFT VAR C: .75X TO 2X BASIC
STATED PRINT RUN 25 SER.#'d SETS

2018-19 Panini Contenders Draft Picks College Ticket Signature Variations A

*VAR A: .4X TO 1X BASIC

2018-19 Panini Contenders Draft Picks College Ticket Signature Variations B

*VAR B: .4X TO 1X BASIC

2018-19 Panini Contenders Draft Picks College Ticket Signature Variations C

*VAR C: .4X TO 1X BASIC

2018-19 Panini Contenders Draft Picks Cracked Ice Ticket

*CRCKD ICE: 4X TO 10X BASIC
*CRCKD ICE AU: .75X TO 2X BASIC
STATED PRINT RUN 23 SER.#'d SETS
126 Luka Doncic AU 2,000.00 4,000.00

2018-19 Panini Contenders Draft Picks Draft Ticket

*DRAFT: 1.5X TO 4X BASIC
*DRAFT AU: .5X TO 1.2X BASIC
STATED PRINT RUN 99 SER.#'d SETS
126 Luka Doncic AU 600.00 1,200.00

2018-19 Panini Contenders Draft Picks Collegiate Connections Signatures

*CRACKED ICE/23: .6X TO 1.5X BASIC
1 Ayton/Markkanen 10.00 25.00
2 Bamba/Allen 5.00 12.00
3 Bagley/Carter 8.00 20.00
4 Young/Hield 25.00 60.00
6 Bell/Brown 4.00 10.00
7 Patton/Thomas 3.00 8.00
8 Holiday/Ball 5.00 12.00
9 Gilgs-Alxndr/Knox 125.00 300.00

2018-19 Panini Contenders Draft Picks Game Day Ticket Signatures

*DRFT TCKT/99: .5X TO 1.2X
*CRCKD ICE/23: .6X TO 1.5X
1 Deandre Ayton 10.00 25.00
2 Mo Bamba 5.00 12.00
3 Marvin Bagley III 5.00 12.00
4 Jaren Jackson Jr. 30.00 80.00
5 Kevin Knox 4.00 10.00
6 Trae Young 60.00 150.00
7 Wendell Carter Jr. 8.00 20.00
8 Shai Gilgeous-Alexander 150.00 400.00
9 Collin Sexton 10.00 25.00
10 Mikal Bridges 15.00 40.00

2018-19 Panini Contenders Draft Picks Game Day Tickets

*CRCKD ICE/23: 6X TO 15X BASIC
1 Deandre Ayton .75 2.00
2 Mo Bamba .40 1.00
3 Marvin Bagley III .40 1.00
4 Jaren Jackson Jr. 2.00 5.00
5 Michael Porter Jr. 1.00 2.50
6 Trae Young 2.00 5.00
7 Donte DiVincenzo .60 1.50
8 Mitchell Robinson .60 1.50
9 Collin Sexton .75 2.00
10 Mikal Bridges 1.25 3.00
11 Kevin Knox .30 .75
12 Robert Williams III .50 1.25
13 Lonnie Walker IV .50 1.25

14 Shai Gilgeous-Alexander 2.50 6.00
15 Zhaire Smith .25 .60
16 Khyri Thomas .25 .60
17 Gary Trent Jr. .50 1.25
18 Kevin Huerter .50 1.25
19 Troy Brown Jr. .30 .75
20 Chandler Hutchison .30 .75
21 Bruce Brown .50 1.25
22 Trevon Duval .40 1.00
23 Shake Milton .40 1.00
24 Anfernee Simons 1.25 3.00
25 Kelta Bates-Diop .30 .75
26 Hamidou Diallo .40 1.00
27 Landry Shamet .40 1.00
28 Brandon McCoy .25 .60
29 Grayson Allen .50 1.25
30 Chimezie Metu .30 .75
31 Devonte' Graham .40 1.00
32 Jacob Evans III .25 .60
33 Aaron Holiday .40 1.00
34 Jalen Brunson 2.00 5.00
35 Melvin Frazier .25 .60

2018-19 Panini Contenders Draft Picks Season Ticket Signatures
*CRACKED ICE/23: 1.25X TO 3X BASIC
1 Charles Barkley 125.00 300.00
2 Dan Issel 6.00 15.00
3 Dwyane Wade 25.00 60.00
4 Gail Goodrich 5.00 12.00
5 Jamaal Wilkes 5.00 12.00
6 Joel Embiid 40.00 100.00
7 Magic Johnson 30.00 80.00
8 Marques Johnson 4.00 10.00
9 Rick Barry 6.00 15.00
10 Victor Oladipo 4.00 10.00

2018-19 Panini Contenders Draft Picks Variations
*VAR: .4X TO 1X BASIC
*VAR AU: .4X TO 1X BASIC AU

2018-19 Panini Contenders Draft Picks Variations Cracked Ice Ticket
*CRACKED ICE VAR: 4X TO 10X BASIC
*CRACKED ICE VAR AU: .75X TO 2X BASIC
STATED PRINT RUN 23 SER.#'d SETS

2018-19 Panini Contenders Draft Picks Variations Draft Ticket
*DRAFT VAR: 1.5X TO 4X BASIC
*DRAFT VAR AU: .5X TO 1.2X BASIC
STATED PRINT RUN 99 SER.#'d SETS

2018-19 Panini Contenders Draft Picks Legacy
1 Andrew Wiggins .50 1.25
2 Anthony Davis 1.00 2.50
3 Ben Simmons .40 1.00
4 Charles Barkley .75 2.00
5 Chris Paul .75 2.00
6 Damian Lillard 1.00 2.50
7 De'Aaron Fox .75 2.00
8 Dennis Smith Jr. .25 .60
9 Devin Booker 1.00 2.50
10 Donovan Mitchell 1.25 3.00
11 Draymond Green .50 1.25
12 Jabari Parker .25 .60
13 James Harden .75 2.00
14 Jayson Tatum 1.50 4.00
15 John Wall .50 1.25
16 Josh Jackson .25 .60
17 Karl-Anthony Towns .60 1.50
18 Kawhi Leonard 1.00 2.50
19 Kevin Durant 1.50 4.00
20 Klay Thompson 1.00 2.50
21 Kyle Kuzma .40 1.00
22 Kyrie Irving 1.00 2.50
23 Larry Bird 1.50 4.00
24 Lauri Markkanen .60 1.50
25 Lonzo Ball .40 1.00
26 Magic Johnson 1.50 4.00
27 Markelle Fultz .30 .75
28 Russell Westbrook .60 1.50
29 Shaquille O'Neal 1.25 3.00
30 Stephen Curry 3.00 8.00

2018-19 Panini Contenders Draft Picks Legacy Cracked Ice Signatures
*CRACKED ICE: .6X TO 1.5X BASIC
STATED PRINT RUN 23 SER.#'d SETS
3 Damian Lillard 40.00 100.00
4 Devin Booker 60.00 150.00

2018-19 Panini Contenders Draft Picks Legacy Signatures
1 Anthony Davis 25.00 60.00
2 Charles Barkley 60.00 150.00
3 Damian Lillard 25.00 60.00
4 Devin Booker 40.00 100.00
6 Kyrie Irving 20.00 50.00
7 Lauri Markkanen 20.00 50.00
8 Lonzo Ball 5.00 12.00
9 Magic Johnson 30.00 80.00
10 Victor Oladipo 4.00 10.00

2018-19 Panini Contenders Draft Picks School Colors
*CRCKD ICE/23: 6X TO 15X BASIC
1 Deandre Ayton .75 2.00
2 Mo Bamba .40 1.00
3 Marvin Bagley III .40 1.00
4 Jaren Jackson Jr. 2.00 5.00
5 Michael Porter Jr. 1.00 2.50
6 Trae Young 2.00 5.00
7 Wendell Carter Jr. .60 1.50
8 Donte DiVincenzo .60 1.50
9 Collin Sexton .75 2.00
10 Mikal Bridges 1.25 3.00
11 Kevin Knox .30 .75
12 Robert Williams III .50 1.25
13 Lonnie Walker IV .50 1.25
14 Shai Gilgeous-Alexander 2.50 6.00
15 Zhaire Smith .25 .60
16 Khyri Thomas .25 .60
17 Gary Trent Jr. .50 1.25
18 Kevin Huerter .50 1.25
19 Troy Brown Jr. .30 .75
20 Chandler Hutchison .30 .75
21 Bruce Brown .50 1.25
22 Trevon Duval .40 1.00
23 Shake Milton .40 1.00
24 De'Anthony Melton .50 1.25
25 Keita Bates-Diop .30 .75
26 Hamidou Diallo .40 1.00
27 Landry Shamet .40 1.00
28 Brandon McCoy .25 .60
29 Grayson Allen .50 1.25
30 Chimezie Metu .30 .75
31 Devonte' Graham .40 1.00
32 Jacob Evans III .25 .60
33 Aaron Holiday .40 1.00
34 Jalen Brunson 2.00 5.00
35 Melvin Frazier .25 .60

2018-19 Panini Contenders Draft Picks School Colors Signatures
*CRCKD ICE/23: 1.5X TO 4X
1 Deandre Ayton 10.00 25.00
2 Mo Bamba 5.00 12.00
3 Marvin Bagley III 5.00 12.00
4 Jaren Jackson Jr. 40.00 100.00
5 Michael Porter Jr. 12.00 30.00
6 Trae Young 75.00 200.00
7 Wendell Carter Jr. 8.00 20.00
9 Collin Sexton 10.00 25.00
10 Mikal Bridges 15.00 40.00
11 Kevin Knox 4.00 10.00
12 Robert Williams III 6.00 15.00
13 Lonnie Walker IV 6.00 15.00
14 Shai Gilgeous-Alexander 150.00 400.00
15 Zhaire Smith 3.00 8.00
16 Khyri Thomas 3.00 8.00
17 Gary Trent Jr. 6.00 15.00
18 Kevin Huerter 6.00 15.00
19 Troy Brown Jr. 4.00 10.00
20 Chandler Hutchison 4.00 10.00

2018-19 Panini Contenders Draft Picks Turning Pro Signatures
*CRCKD ICE/23: .5X TO 1.2X BASIC
1 De'Aaron Fox 40.00 100.00
3 Donovan Mitchell 100.00 250.00
4 Jayson Tatum 40.00 100.00
6 Kyle Kuzma 40.00 100.00
7 Lauri Markkanen 20.00 50.00
8 Lonzo Ball 30.00 80.00
9 Markelle Fultz 40.00 100.00
10 Jordan Bell 20.00 50.00

2019-20 Panini Contenders Draft Picks
EXCHANGE DEADLINE 3/4/2021
1 Allonzo Trier .20 .50
2 Anthony Davis .75 2.00
3 Ben Simmons .30 .75
4 Blake Griffin .30 .75
5 Bradley Beal .40 1.00
6 Buddy Hield .25 .60
7 Charles Barkley .60 1.50
8 Chris Paul .60 1.50
9 Collin Sexton .40 1.00
10 D'Angelo Russell .25 .60
11 Damian Lillard .75 2.00
12 De'Aaron Fox .50 1.25
13 Deandre Ayton .30 .75
14 DeMar DeRozan .40 1.00
15 Devin Booker .07 .20
16 Donovan Mitchell .60 1.50
17 Giannis Antetokounmpo 1.50 4.00
18 James Harden .60 1.50
19 Jaren Jackson Jr. .50 1.25
20 Jayson Tatum 1.25 3.00
21 Joel Embiid .60 1.50
22 John Wall .40 1.00
23 Jrue Holiday .40 1.00
24 Julius Randle .40 1.00
25 Karl-Anthony Towns .50 1.25
26 Kawhi Leonard .75 2.00
27 Kemba Walker .25 .60
28 Kevin Durant 1.00 2.50
29 Kevin Huerter .30 .75
30 Kevin Knox II .20 .50
31 Klay Thompson .75 2.00
32 Kobe Bryant 2.50 6.00
33 Kyle Kuzma .40 1.00
34 Kyrie Irving .60 1.50
35 LaMarcus Aldridge .30 .75
36 Landry Shamet .25 .60
37 Larry Bird 1.25 3.00
38 LeBron James 2.50 6.00
39 Luka Doncic 2.00 5.00
40 Magic Johnson 1.00 2.50
41 Marvin Bagley III .25 .60
42 Mikal Bridges .50 1.25
43 Miles Bridges .30 .75
44 Paul George .50 1.25
45 Russell Westbrook .50 1.25
46 Shai Gilgeous-Alexander 1.50 4.00
47 Shaquille O'Neal 1.25 3.00
48 Stephen Curry 2.50 6.00
49 Trae Young .75 2.00
50 Zach LaVine .50 1.25
51 Zion Williamson AU RC 75.00 200.00
52 Ja Morant AU RC 100.00 250.00
53 RJ Barrett AU RC 12.00 30.00
54 Cam Reddish AU RC 5.00 12.00
56 Jarrett Culver AU RC 3.00 8.00
57 De'Andre Hunter AU RC 12.00 30.00
58 Coby White AU RC 10.00 25.00
59 Romeo Langford AU RC 3.00 8.00
60 Jaxson Hayes AU RC 5.00 12.00
61 Rui Hachimura AU RC EXCH 12.00 30.00
62 Nassir Little AU RC 5.00 12.00
63 Keldon Johnson AU RC 10.00 25.00
64 Bol Bol AU RC 8.00 20.00
65 PJ Washington Jr. AU RC 10.00 25.00
66 Kevin Porter Jr. AU RC 6.00 15.00
67 Cameron Johnson AU RC 8.00 20.00
69 Tyler Herro AU RC 15.00 40.00
70 Nickeil Alexander-Walker AU RC 5.00 12.00
71 Brandon Clarke AU RC 6.00 15.00
72 KZ Okpala AU RC 4.00 10.00
73 Jontay Porter AU RC 3.00 8.00
74 Matisse Thybulle AU RC 6.00 15.00
75 Grant Williams AU RC 5.00 12.00
76 Ty Jerome AU RC 6.00 15.00
77 Luguentz Dort AU RC 12.00 30.00
78 Bruno Fernando AU RC 4.00 10.00
79 Kyle Guy AU RC 4.00 10.00
80 Chuma Okeke AU RC 5.00 12.00
81 Eric Paschall AU RC 4.00 10.00
82 Admiral Schofield AU RC 4.00 10.00
83 Dylan Windler AU RC 4.00 10.00
84 Jalen McDaniels AU RC 8.00 20.00
85 Daniel Gafford AU RC 6.00 15.00
86 Isaiah Roby AU RC 4.00 10.00
87 Jordan Bone AU RC 3.00 8.00
88 Zach Norvell Jr. AU RC 4.00 10.00
89 Dedric Lawson AU RC 3.00 8.00
90 Shamorie Ponds AU RC 3.00 8.00
92 Carsen Edwards AU RC 4.00 10.00
93 Jaylen Hoard AU RC 3.00 8.00
94 Quinndary Weatherspoon AU RC 3.00 8.00
95 James Palmer AU RC 3.00 8.00
96 Simi Shittu AU RC 3.00 8.00
97 Kris Wilkes AU RC 3.00 8.00
99 Robert Franks AU RC 3.00 8.00
100 Sagaba Konate AU RC 3.00 8.00
101 Max Strus AU RC 6.00 15.00
102 Ky Bowman AU RC 4.00 10.00
103 Tyler Cook AU RC 3.00 8.00
104 Kaleb Johnson AU RC 3.00 8.00
105 Bennie Boatwright AU RC 3.00 8.00
106 Aric Holman AU RC 3.00 8.00
107 Luke Maye AU RC 4.00 10.00
108 Justin Robinson AU RC 3.00 8.00
109 DaQuan Jeffries AU RC 3.00 8.00
110 Terance Mann AU RC 6.00 15.00
111 Ignas Brazdeikis AU RC 4.00 10.00
112 Jaylen Hands AU RC 3.00 8.00
113 Moses Brown AU RC 5.00 12.00
114 Oshae Brissett AU RC 4.00 10.00
115 Tyus Battle AU RC 3.00 8.00
116 Amir Coffey AU RC 5.00 12.00
117 Ethan Happ AU RC 3.00 8.00
118 Tacko Fall AU RC 4.00 10.00
119 Jalen Lecque AU RC 3.00 8.00
120 Miye Oni AU RC 3.00 8.00
121 Terence Davis AU RC 5.00 12.00
122 Louis King AU RC 4.00 10.00
123 Charles Matthews AU RC 5.00 12.00
124 Mfiondu Kabengele AU RC 4.00 10.00
125 Nic Claxton AU RC 6.00 15.00
126 Tremont Waters AU RC 4.00 10.00
127 Zylan Cheatham AU RC 3.00 8.00
128 Kerwin Roach AU RC 3.00 8.00
129 Justin Wright-Foreman AU RC 3.00 8.00
130 Fletcher Magee AU RC 3.00 8.00
131 Jordan Poole AU RC 12.00 30.00
132 Phil Booth AU RC 3.00 8.00
133 Justin James AU RC 3.00 8.00
134 Cody Martin AU RC 5.00 12.00
135 Marial Shayok AU RC 3.00 8.00
136 Dewan Hernandez AU RC 3.00 8.00

2019-20 Panini Contenders Draft Picks Cracked Ice Ticket
*CRCKD ICE: 2X TO 5X BASIC
*CRCKD ICE AU: .75X TO 2X BASIC
STATED PRINT RUN 23 SER.#'d SETS
EXCHANGE DEADLINE 3/4/2021

2019-20 Panini Contenders Draft Picks Draft Hyper Ticket
*DRAFT HYPER: 1X TO 2.5X BASIC
STATED PRINT RUN 75 SER.#'d SETS

2019-20 Panini Contenders Draft Picks Draft Ticket
*DRAFT: 1X TO 2.5X BASIC
*DRAFT AU/99: .5X TO 1.2X BASIC
*DRAFT AU/25: .75X TO 2X BASIC
PRINT RUNS B/WN 5-99 COPIES PER
NO PRICING ON QTY 5
EXCHANGE DEADLINE 3/4/2021

2019-20 Panini Contenders Draft Picks Draft Ticket Blue Foil
*BLUE FOIL: .4X TO 1X BASIC
*BLUE FOIL AU: .4X TO 1X BASIC
EXCHANGE DEADLINE 3/4/2021

2019-20 Panini Contenders Draft Picks Draft Ticket Red Foil
*RED FOIL: .4X TO 1X BASIC
*RED FOIL AU: .4X TO 1X BASIC
EXCHANGE DEADLINE 3/4/2021

2019-20 Panini Contenders Draft Picks College Ticket Autograph Variations
EXCHANGE DEADLINE 3/4/2021
*BLUE FOIL: .4X TO 1X BASIC
*RED FOIL: .4X TO 1X BASIC
*DRAFT/99: .5X TO 1.2X BASIC
*CRCKD ICE/23: .75X TO 2X BASIC
68 Cameron Johnson 8.00 20.00
70 Nickeil Alexander-Walker 5.00 12.00
71 Brandon Clarke 6.00 15.00
74 Matisse Thybulle 6.00 15.00
75 Grant Williams 5.00 12.00
76 Ty Jerome 6.00 15.00
124 Mfiondu Kabengele 4.00 10.00

2019-20 Panini Contenders Draft Picks RPS College Ticket Autograph Variations A
EXCHANGE DEADLINE 3/4/2021
*BLUE FOIL: .4X TO 1X BASIC
*RED FOIL: .4X TO 1X BASIC
*DRAFT/25: .75X TO 2X BASIC
*CRCKD ICE/23: .75X TO 2X BASIC
51 Zion Williamson 100.00 250.00
52 Ja Morant 100.00 250.00
53 RJ Barrett 12.00 30.00
54 Cam Reddish 5.00 12.00
56 Jarrett Culver 3.00 8.00
57 De'Andre Hunter 12.00 30.00
58 Coby White 10.00 25.00
59 Romeo Langford 3.00 8.00
60 Jaxson Hayes 5.00 12.00
61 Rui Hachimura EXCH 12.00 30.00
62 Nassir Little 5.00 12.00
63 Keldon Johnson 10.00 25.00
64 Bol Bol 8.00 20.00
65 PJ Washington Jr. 10.00 25.00
66 Kevin Porter Jr. 6.00 15.00
69 Tyler Herro 25.00 60.00

2019-20 Panini Contenders Draft Picks RPS College Ticket Autograph Variations B
EXCHANGE DEADLINE 3/4/2021
*BLUE FOIL: .4X TO 1X BASIC
*RED FOIL: .4X TO 1X BASIC
*DRAFT/25: .75X TO 2X BASIC
*CRCKD ICE/23: .75X TO 2X BASIC
51 Zion Williamson 75.00 200.00
52 Ja Morant 100.00 250.00
53 RJ Barrett 12.00 30.00
54 Cam Reddish 5.00 12.00
56 Jarrett Culver 3.00 8.00
57 De'Andre Hunter 12.00 30.00
58 Coby White 10.00 25.00
59 Romeo Langford 3.00 8.00
60 Jaxson Hayes 5.00 12.00
61 Rui Hachimura EXCH 12.00 30.00
62 Nassir Little 5.00 12.00
63 Keldon Johnson 10.00 25.00
64 Bol Bol 8.00 20.00
65 PJ Washington Jr. 10.00 25.00
66 Kevin Porter Jr. 6.00 15.00
69 Tyler Herro 25.00 60.00

2019-20 Panini Contenders Draft Picks RPS College Ticket Autograph Variations C
EXCHANGE DEADLINE 3/4/2021
*BLUE FOIL: .4X TO 1X BASIC
*RED FOIL: .4X TO 1X BASIC
*DRAFT/25: .75X TO 2X BASIC
*CRCKD ICE/23: .75X TO 2X BASIC
51 Zion Williamson 75.00 200.00
52 Ja Morant 100.00 250.00
54 Cam Reddish 5.00 12.00
56 Jarrett Culver 3.00 8.00
57 De'Andre Hunter 12.00 30.00
58 Coby White 10.00 25.00
59 Romeo Langford 3.00 8.00
60 Jaxson Hayes 5.00 12.00
61 Rui Hachimura EXCH 12.00 30.00
62 Nassir Little 5.00 12.00
63 Keldon Johnson 10.00 25.00
64 Bol Bol 8.00 20.00
65 PJ Washington Jr. 10.00 25.00
66 Kevin Porter Jr. 6.00 15.00
69 Tyler Herro 15.00 40.00

2019-20 Panini Contenders Draft Picks Variations
*VAR: .4X TO 1X BASIC

2019-20 Panini Contenders Draft Picks Variations Cracked Ice Ticket
*CRCKD ICE VAR: 2X TO 5X BASIC
STATED PRINT RUN 23 SER.#'d SETS

2019-20 Panini Contenders Draft Picks Variations Draft Hyper Ticket
*DRAFT HYPER VAR: 1X TO 2.5X
STATED PRINT RUN 75 SER.#'d SETS
38 LeBron James 15.00 40.00

2019-20 Panini Contenders Draft Picks Variations Draft Ticket
*DRAFT VAR: 1X TO 2.5X BASIC
STATED PRINT RUN 99 SER.#'d SETS

2019-20 Panini Contenders Draft Picks Variations Draft Ticket Blue Foil
*BLUE FOIL VAR: .4X TO 1X BASIC

2019-20 Panini Contenders Draft Picks Variations Draft Ticket Red Foil
*RED FOIL VAR: .4X TO 1X BASIC

2019-20 Panini Contenders Draft Picks Collegiate Connections Signatures
EXCHANGE DEADLINE 3/4/2021
*CRCKD ICE/23: .75X TO 2X BASIC
1 Clarke/Hachimura 15.00 40.00
2 Hunter/Jerome 15.00 40.00
3 Barrett/Williamson 125.00 300.00
4 White/Little 12.00 30.00
5 Culver/Smith 4.00 10.00
6 Schofield/Williams 6.00 15.00
7 Hield/Young EXCH 40.00 100.00
8 Porter/Porter Jr. 10.00 25.00
9 Fernando/Huerter 6.00 15.00
10 Johnson/Herro 20.00 50.00

2019-20 Panini Contenders Draft Picks Game Day Ticket Signatures
EXCHANGE DEADLINE 3/4/2021
*BLUE FOIL: .4X TO 1X
*RED FOIL: .4X TO 1X
*DRAFT/99: .5X TO 1.2X
*CRCKD ICE/23: .75X TO 2X
1 Zion Williamson 100.00 250.00
2 Ja Morant 100.00 250.00
3 RJ Barrett 12.00 30.00
4 Cam Reddish 5.00 12.00
5 Jaxson Hayes 5.00 12.00
6 Jarrett Culver 3.00 8.00
7 De'Andre Hunter 12.00 30.00
8 Coby White 10.00 25.00
9 Rui Hachimura 12.00 30.00

2019-20 Panini Contenders Draft Picks Game Day Tickets
*CRACKED ICE/23: 6X TO 15X BASIC
1 Zion Williamson 2.00 5.00
2 Ja Morant 2.50 6.00
3 RJ Barrett 1.00 2.50
4 Cam Reddish .40 1.00
5 Mfiondu Kabengele .30 .75
6 Jarrett Culver .25 .60
7 De'Andre Hunter 1.00 2.50
8 Coby White .75 2.00
9 Romeo Langford .25 .60
10 Jaxson Hayes .40 1.00
11 Rui Hachimura 1.00 2.50
12 Nassir Little .40 1.00
13 Keldon Johnson .75 2.00
14 Bol Bol .60 1.50
15 PJ Washington Jr. .75 2.00
16 Kevin Porter Jr. .50 1.25
17 Jordan Poole 1.00 2.50
18 Cameron Johnson .60 1.50
19 Tyler Herro 1.25 3.00
20 Nickeil Alexander-Walker .40 1.00
21 Brandon Clarke .50 1.25
22 KZ Okpala .30 .75
23 Jontay Porter .25 .60
24 Naz Reid 1.00 2.50
25 Grant Williams .40 1.00
26 Ty Jerome .50 1.25
27 Luguentz Dort 1.00 2.50
28 Bruno Fernando .30 .75
29 Carsen Edwards .30 .75
30 Chuma Okeke .40 1.00
31 Eric Paschall .30 .75
32 Admiral Schofield .30 .75
33 Dylan Windler .30 .75
34 Jalen McDaniels .60 1.50
35 Daniel Gafford .50 1.25

2019-20 Panini Contenders Draft Picks International Ticket Autographs
EXCHANGE DEADLINE 3/4/2021
*BLUE FOIL: .4X TO 1X
*RED FOIL: .4X TO 1X
*DRAFT/99: .5X TO 1.2X
*CRCKD ICE/23: .75X TO 2X
1 Sekou Doumbouya 3.00 8.00
2 Goga Bitadze 5.00 12.00
3 Luka Samanic 4.00 10.00
4 Alen Smailagic 3.00 8.00
5 Deividas Sirvydis 3.00 8.00

2019-20 Panini Contenders Draft Picks Legacy
*CRCKD ICE/23: 1.5X TO 4X
1 David Robinson .75 2.00
2 Hakeem Olajuwon .75 2.00
3 Jerry West .60 1.50
4 Kyrie Irving .75 2.00
5 Magic Johnson 1.25 3.00
6 Oscar Robertson 1.00 2.50
7 Bill Russell 1.25 3.00
8 Allen Iverson 1.00 2.50
9 James Worthy .60 1.50
10 Karl-Anthony Towns .60 1.50
11 Ben Simmons .40 1.00
12 Stephen Curry 3.00 8.00
13 Charles Barkley .75 2.00
14 James Harden .75 2.00
15 Kawhi Leonard 1.00 2.50
16 Kevin Durant 1.25 3.00
17 Larry Bird 1.50 4.00
18 Russell Westbrook .60 1.50
19 Shaquille O'Neal 1.50 4.00
20 Trae Young 1.00 2.50
21 De'Aaron Fox .60 1.50
22 Deandre Ayton .40 1.00
23 Devin Booker .10 .25
24 Donovan Mitchell .75 2.00
25 Jayson Tatum 1.50 4.00
26 Joel Embiid .75 2.00
27 Kyle Kuzma .50 1.25
29 Kevin Knox II .25 .60
30 Marvin Bagley III .30 .75

2019-20 Panini Contenders Draft Picks Legacy Signatures
EXCHANGE DEADLINE 3/4/2021
*CRCKD ICE/23: .75X TO 2X
1 David Robinson 20.00 50.00
2 Hakeem Olajuwon 20.00 50.00
3 Jerry West 20.00 50.00
4 Kyrie Irving 25.00 60.00
5 Magic Johnson 25.00 60.00
6 Oscar Robertson 25.00 60.00
7 Bill Russell 125.00 300.00
8 Allen Iverson 30.00 80.00
9 James Worthy 8.00 20.00
10 Karl-Anthony Towns 8.00 20.00

2019-20 Panini Contenders Draft Picks School Colors
1 Zion Williamson 2.00 5.00
2 Ja Morant 2.50 6.00
3 RJ Barrett 1.00 2.50
4 Cam Reddish .40 1.00
5 Mfiondu Kabengele .30 .75
6 Jarrett Culver .25 .60
7 De'Andre Hunter 1.00 2.50
8 Coby White .75 2.00
9 Romeo Langford .25 .60
10 Jaxson Hayes .40 1.00
11 Rui Hachimura 1.00 2.50
12 Nassir Little .40 1.00
13 Keldon Johnson .75 2.00
14 Bol Bol .60 1.50
15 PJ Washington Jr. .75 2.00
16 Kevin Porter Jr. .50 1.25
17 Jordan Poole 1.00 2.50
18 Cameron Johnson .60 1.50
19 Tyler Herro 1.25 3.00
20 Nickeil Alexander-Walker .40 1.00
21 Brandon Clarke .50 1.25
22 KZ Okpala .30 .75
23 Jontay Porter .25 .60
24 Naz Reid 1.00 2.50
25 Grant Williams .40 1.00
26 Ty Jerome .50 1.25
27 Luguentz Dort 1.00 2.50
28 Bruno Fernando .30 .75
29 Carsen Edwards .30 .75
30 Chuma Okeke .40 1.00
31 Eric Paschall .30 .75
32 Admiral Schofield .30 .75
33 Dylan Windler .30 .75
34 Jalen McDaniels .60 1.50
35 Daniel Gafford .50 1.25

2019-20 Panini Contenders Draft Picks School Colors Cracked Ice
*CRACKED ICE: 6X TO 15X BASIC
STATED PRINT RUN 23 SER.#'d SETS

2019-20 Panini Contenders Draft Picks School Colors Signatures
EXCHANGE DEADLINE 3/4/2021
*CRCKD ICE/23: .75X TO 2X
1 Zion Williamson 75.00 200.00
2 Ja Morant 100.00 250.00
3 RJ Barrett 12.00 30.00
4 Cam Reddish 5.00 12.00
6 Jarrett Culver 3.00 8.00
7 De'Andre Hunter 12.00 30.00
8 Coby White 10.00 25.00
9 Romeo Langford 3.00 8.00
10 Jaxson Hayes 5.00 12.00
11 Rui Hachimura 12.00 30.00
12 Nassir Little 5.00 12.00
13 Keldon Johnson 10.00 25.00
14 Bol Bol 8.00 20.00
15 PJ Washington Jr. 10.00 25.00
16 Kevin Porter Jr. 6.00 15.00
18 Cameron Johnson 8.00 20.00
19 Tyler Herro 25.00 60.00
20 Brandon Clarke 6.00 15.00

2019-20 Panini Contenders Draft Picks Season Ticket Autographs Draft Ticket Blue Foil
EXCHANGE DEADLINE 3/4/2021
*RED FOIL: .4X TO 1X BASIC
*DRAFT/25: .75X TO 2X BASIC
CRCKD ICE/23: .75X TO 2X BASIC
1 Calvin Murphy 5.00 12.00
2 Christian Laettner 8.00 20.00
3 David Robinson 20.00 50.00
4 Elvin Hayes 6.00 15.00
5 Eric Bledsoe 4.00 10.00
6 Hakeem Olajuwon 20.00 50.00
7 Jerry West 20.00 50.00
8 Magic Johnson 25.00 60.00
9 Monte Morris 5.00 12.00
10 Sam Perkins 4.00 10.00

2019-20 Panini Contenders Draft Picks Turning Pro Signatures
EXCHANGE DEADLINE 3/4/2021
*CRCKD ICE/23: .75X TO 2X
1 Deandre Ayton 5.00 12.00
2 Trae Young 50.00 120.00
3 Marvin Bagley III 4.00 10.00
4 Kevin Knox II 3.00 8.00
5 Collin Sexton 6.00 15.00
6 Shai Gilgeous-Alexander 100.00 250.00
7 Jaren Jackson Jr. 25.00 60.00
8 Kevin Huerter 5.00 12.00
10 Allonzo Trier 3.00 8.00

2020-21 Panini Contenders Draft Picks
COMMON CARD (1-50) .20 .50
SEMISTARS .25 .60
UNLISTED STARS .30 .80
COMMON AUTO (51-139) 3.00 8.00
SEMISTARS 4.00 10.00
UNLISTED STARS 5.00 12.00
EXCHANGE DEADLINE 4/2/2022
*CAMPUS TICKET: .6X TO 1.5X BASIC
1 Stephen Curry 2.50 6.00
2 James Harden .60 1.50
3 Russell Westbrook .60 1.50
4 Derrick Rose .50 1.25
5 Kevin Durant 1.25 3.00
6 Klay Thompson .75 2.00
7 Anthony Davis .75 2.00
8 Jayson Tatum 1.25 3.00
9 Kemba Walker .30 .75
10 Jaylen Brown .50 1.25
11 Kyrie Irving .60 1.50
12 RJ Barrett .50 1.25
13 Zion Williamson 1.00 2.50
14 Ben Simmons .30 .75
15 Joel Embiid .75 2.00
16 Al Horford .30 .75
17 Pascal Siakam .30 .75
18 Kawhi Leonard .75 2.00
19 Paul George .50 1.25
20 Devin Booker .75 2.00
21 Deandre Ayton .30 .75
22 De'Aaron Fox .50 1.25
23 Trae Young .75 2.00
24 Buddy Hield .30 .75
25 Zach LaVine .50 1.25
26 Lauri Markkanen .40 1.00
27 Kevin Love .30 .75
28 Blake Griffin .30 .75
29 Victor Oladipo .25 .60
30 Khris Middleton .40 1.00
31 Devonte' Graham .25 .60
32 Jimmy Butler .60 1.50
33 Rui Hachimura .40 1.00
34 John Wall .40 1.00
35 Bradley Beal .40 1.00
36 Karl-Anthony Towns .50 1.25
37 D'Angelo Russell .30 .75
38 Chris Paul .60 1.50
39 Shai Gilgeous-Alexander 1.50 4.00
40 Damian Lillard .75 2.00
41 CJ McCollum .30 .75
42 Carmelo Anthony .50 1.25
43 Donovan Mitchell .60 1.50
44 Ja Morant 1.00 2.50
45 Jaren Jackson Jr. .50 1.25
46 Lonzo Ball .50 1.25
47 Jrue Holiday .30 .75
48 LaMarcus Aldridge .30 .75
49 DeMar DeRozan .40 1.00
50 JJ Redick .30 .75
51 Anthony Edwards AU 100.00 250.00
52 Obi Toppin AU 8.00 20.00
53 James Wiseman AU 5.00 12.00
54 LaMelo Ball AU 75.00 200.00
55 Onyeka Okongwu AU 8.00 20.00
56 Cole Anthony AU 10.00 25.00
57 Deni Avdija AU 10.00 25.00
58 Theo Maledon AU 4.00 10.00
59 Nico Mannion AU 4.00 10.00
60 Isaac Okoro AU 6.00 15.00
61 Tyrese Haliburton AU 75.00 200.00
62 Vernon Carey Jr. AU 4.00 10.00
63 Killian Hayes AU 4.00 10.00
64 Jaden McDaniels AU 12.00 30.00
65 Josh Green AU 8.00 20.00
66 RJ Hampton AU 4.00 10.00
67 Precious Achiuwa AU 8.00 20.00
68 Tyrese Maxey AU 40.00 100.00
69 Isaiah Stewart AU 8.00 20.00
70 Cassius Winston AU 4.00 10.00
71 Tyler Bey AU 4.00 10.00
72 Jahmi'us Ramsey AU 4.00 10.00
73 Markus Howard AU 5.00 12.00
74 Aaron Nesmith AU 8.00 20.00
75 Devin Vassell AU 12.00 30.00
76 Patrick Williams AU 10.00 25.00
77 Payton Pritchard AU 12.00 30.00
78 Saddiq Bey AU 8.00 20.00
79 Robert Woodard II AU 4.00 10.00
80 Kira Lewis Jr. AU 4.00 10.00
81 Daniel Oturu AU 4.00 10.00
82 Reggie Perry AU 4.00 10.00
83 Jordan Nwora AU 5.00 12.00
84 Zeke Nnaji AU 5.00 12.00
85 Immanuel Quickley AU 10.00 25.00
86 Isaiah Moss AU 3.00 8.00
87 Udoka Azubuike AU 5.00 12.00
88 Jay Scrubb AU 5.00 12.00
89 Elijah Hughes AU 4.00 10.00
90 Nick Richards AU 5.00 12.00
91 Devon Dotson AU 4.00 10.00
92 Tre Jones AU 6.00 15.00
93 Paul Reed AU 5.00 12.00
94 Killian Tillie AU 5.00 12.00
95 Mamadi Diakite AU 4.00 10.00
96 Jalen Smith AU 8.00 20.00
97 Malachi Flynn AU 4.00 10.00
98 Ashton Hagans AU 5.00 12.00
99 Cassius Stanley AU 4.00 10.00
100 Omer Yurtseven AU 12.00 30.00
101 Freddie Gillespie AU 4.00 10.00
102 Austin Wiley AU 3.00 8.00
103 Steven Enoch AU 3.00 8.00
104 Romaro Gill AU 3.00 8.00
105 Dwayne Sutton AU 3.00 8.00
106 Malik Fitts AU 3.00 8.00
107 Josh Hall AU 3.00 8.00
108 Lamar Stevens AU 5.00 12.00
109 Ty-Shon Alexander AU 4.00 10.00
110 Rayshaun Hammonds AU 3.00 8.00
111 Mustapha Heron AU 3.00 8.00
112 Myles Powell AU 6.00 15.00
113 Yoeli Childs AU 4.00 10.00
114 JJ Culver AU 4.00 10.00
115 John Mooney AU 3.00 8.00
116 Josh Nebo AU 3.00 8.00
117 Kristian Doolittle AU 3.00 8.00
118 Tyrique Jones AU 3.00 8.00
119 Sean McDermott AU 3.00 8.00
120 Naji Marshall AU 4.00 10.00
121 Kenyon Martin Jr. AU 6.00 15.00
122 EJ Montgomery AU 3.00 8.00
123 Grant Riller AU 4.00 10.00
124 Skylar Mays AU 4.00 10.00
125 Jordan Bowden AU 3.00 8.00
126 Ryan Woolridge AU 3.00 8.00
127 Desmond Bane AU 12.00 30.00
128 Jake Toolson AU 3.00 8.00
129 Trent Forrest AU 5.00 12.00
130 Haanif Cheatham AU 4.00 10.00
131 Sam Merrill AU 6.00 15.00
132 Braxton Key AU 3.00 8.00
133 Mason Jones AU 3.00 8.00
134 Saben Lee AU 4.00 10.00
135 Kerry Blackshear Jr. AU 3.00 8.00
136 Brandon Robinson AU 3.00 8.00
137 Kaleb Wesson AU 4.00 10.00
138 Javin DeLaurier AU 3.00 8.00
139 Xavier Sneed AU 4.00 10.00

2020-21 Panini Contenders Draft Picks Conference Finals Ticket
*CONF.FINALS: 1X TO 2.5X BASIC
*CONF.FINALS AU: .5X TO 1.2X BASIC
PRINT RUNS B/WN 5-75 COPIES PER
NO PRICING QTY 20 OR LESS
EXCHANGE DEADLINE 4/2/2022
85 Immanuel Quickley AU/75 12.00 30.00
92 Tre Jones AU/75 8.00 20.00
97 Malachi Flynn AU/75 5.00 12.00
99 Cassius Stanley AU/75 10.00 25.00
121 Kenyon Martin Jr. AU/75 8.00 20.00
127 Desmond Bane AU/75 15.00 40.00

2020-21 Panini Contenders Draft Picks Conference Ticket
*CONF.: 1X TO 2.5X BASIC
*CONF.AU/99: .5X TO 1.2X BASIC
*CONF.AU/30: .6X TO 1.5X BASIC
PRINT RUNS B/WN 10-99 COPIES PER
NO PRICING QTY 15 OR LESS
EXCHANGE DEADLINE 4/2/2022

2020-21 Panini Contenders Draft Picks Cracked Ice Ticket
*CRKD ICE.: 2X TO 5X BASIC
*CRKD ICE AU: .8X TO 2X BASIC
STATED PRINT RUN 23 SER.#'d SETS
EXCHANGE DEADLINE 4/2/2022

2020-21 Panini Contenders Draft Picks Game Ticket Blue
*BLUE: 1X TO 2.5X BASIC
*BLUE AU: .5X TO 1.2X BASIC
STATED PRINT RUN 99 SER.#'d SETS
EXCHANGE DEADLINE 4/2/2022

2020-21 Panini Contenders Draft Picks Game Ticket Purple
*PURPLE: .6X TO 1.5X BASIC
*PURPLE AU: .5X TO 1.2X BASIC
AU PRINT RUN 99 SER.#'d SETS
EXCHANGE DEADLINE 4/2/2022

2020-21 Panini Contenders Draft Picks Gold Cracked Ice Ticket
*GOLD ICE: 2X TO 5X BASIC
*GOLD ICE AU: .8X TO 2X BASIC
STATED PRINT RUN 23 SER.#'d SETS
EXCHANGE DEADLINE 4/2/2022

2020-21 Panini Contenders Draft Picks Prospect Ticket Autographs Variations Ticket Stubs
*VAR.STUBS/33-50: .5X TO 1.2X BASIC
*VAR.STUBS/22-25: .8X TO 2X BASIC
STATED PRINT RUN 1-50 SER.#'d SETS
NO PRICING QTY 20 OR LESS
EXCHANGE DEADLINE 4/2/2022
84 Zeke Nnaji/22 20.00 50.00
96 Jalen Smith/25 30.00 80.00
97 Malachi Flynn/22 8.00 20.00

2020-21 Panini Contenders Draft Picks RPS Prospect Ticket Autographs Premium Edition
*PREMIUM: .5X TO 1.2X BASIC
EXCHANGE DEADLINE 4/2/2022

2020-21 Panini Contenders Draft Picks RPS Prospect Ticket Autographs Variation A Cracked Ice Ticket
*VAR.A CRKD ICE: .8X TO 2X BASIC
STATED PRINT RUN 23 SER.#'d SETS
EXCHANGE DEADLINE 4/2/2022

2020-21 Panini Contenders Draft Picks RPS Prospect Ticket Autographs Variation A Premium Edition
*VAR.A PREM.: .5X TO 1.2X BASIC
EXCHANGE DEADLINE 4/2/2022

2020-21 Panini Contenders Draft Picks RPS Prospect Ticket Autographs Variation A Ticket Stubs
*VAR.A STUBS/32-55: .5X TO 1.2X BASIC
*VAR.A STUBS/21-24: .8X TO 2X BASIC
STATED PRINT RUN 1-55 SER.#'d SETS
NO PRICING QTY 15 OR LESS
EXCHANGE DEADLINE 4/2/2022
55 Onyeka Okongwu/21 75.00 200.00

2020-21 Panini Contenders Draft Picks RPS Prospect Ticket Autographs Variation B Cracked Ice Ticket
*VAR.B CRKD ICE: .8X TO 2X BASIC
STATED PRINT RUN 23 SER.#'d SETS
EXCHANGE DEADLINE 4/2/2022

2020-21 Panini Contenders Draft Picks RPS Prospect Ticket Autographs Variation B Premium Edition
*VAR.B PREM.: .5X TO 1.2X BASIC
EXCHANGE DEADLINE 4/2/2022

2020-21 Panini Contenders Draft Picks RPS Prospect Ticket Autographs Variation B Ticket Stubs
*VAR.B STUBS/32-55: .5X TO 1.2X BASIC
*VAR.B STUBS/21-24: .8X TO 2X BASIC
STATED PRINT RUN 1-55 SER.#'d SETS
NO PRICING QTY 15 OR LESS
EXCHANGE DEADLINE 4/2/2022
55 Onyeka Okongwu/21 75.00 200.00

2020-21 Panini Contenders Draft Picks Campus ID
1 Tyrese Haliburton 60.00 150.00
2 Anthony Edwards 125.00 300.00
3 Obi Toppin 75.00 200.00
4 James Wiseman 3.00 8.00
5 Onyeka Okongwu 30.00 80.00
6 Cole Anthony 60.00 150.00
7 Nico Mannion 10.00 25.00
8 Aaron Nesmith 15.00 40.00
9 Isaac Okoro 20.00 50.00
10 Vernon Carey Jr. 12.00 30.00
11 Tyrese Maxey 60.00 150.00
12 Precious Achiuwa 12.00 30.00
13 Nick Richards 20.00 50.00
14 Saddiq Bey 25.00 60.00
15 LaMelo Ball 75.00 200.00
16 Deni Avdija 125.00 300.00
17 Killian Hayes 40.00 100.00
18 RJ Hampton 2.50 6.00
19 Theo Maledon 12.00 30.00
20 Josh Green 20.00 50.00
21 Jaden McDaniels 10.00 25.00
22 Devin Vassell 15.00 40.00
23 Patrick Williams 30.00 80.00
24 Devon Dotson 15.00 40.00
25 Cassius Winston 30.00 80.00

2020-21 Panini Contenders Draft Picks Campus Legends
1 Zion Williamson 1.25 3.00
2 RJ Barrett .60 1.50
3 Rui Hachimura .50 1.25
4 Ja Morant 1.25 3.00
5 Charles Barkley 1.00 2.50
6 Stephen Curry 3.00 8.00
7 Shaquille O'Neal 1.50 4.00
8 Bill Russell 1.25 3.00
9 Allen Iverson 1.00 2.50
10 Karl Malone .75 2.00
11 Dwyane Wade .75 2.00
12 Larry Bird 1.50 4.00
13 John Stockton .75 2.00
14 Jayson Tatum 1.50 4.00
15 Magic Johnson 1.50 4.00
16 Oscar Robertson 1.00 2.50
17 Jerry West .75 2.00
18 David Robinson .75 2.00
19 Hakeem Olajuwon .75 2.00
20 Clyde Drexler .60 1.50
21 Jason Kidd .60 1.50
22 Paul Pierce .60 1.50
23 Ray Allen .60 1.50
24 Kevin Durant 1.50 4.00
25 Anthony Davis 1.00 2.50
26 John Wall .50 1.25
27 Derrick Rose .60 1.50
28 Trae Young 1.00 2.50
29 Donovan Mitchell .75 2.00
30 Vince Carter .75 2.00
31 Chris Paul .75 2.00
32 Carmelo Anthony .60 1.50
33 James Harden .75 2.00
34 Russell Westbrook .75 2.00
35 Kawhi Leonard 1.00 2.50

2020-21 Panini Contenders Draft Picks Campus Legends Cracked Ice
*CRACKED ICE: 2X TO 5X BASIC
STATED PRINT RUN 23 SER.#'d SETS
1 Zion Williamson 20.00 50.00
2 RJ Barrett 10.00 25.00
3 Rui Hachimura 12.00 30.00
4 Ja Morant 30.00 80.00
5 Charles Barkley 12.00 30.00
6 Stephen Curry 15.00 40.00
8 Bill Russell 15.00 40.00
9 Allen Iverson 15.00 40.00
10 Karl Malone 8.00 20.00
11 Dwyane Wade 6.00 15.00
12 Larry Bird 12.00 30.00
14 Jayson Tatum 15.00 40.00
15 Magic Johnson 15.00 40.00
17 Jerry West 12.00 30.00
18 David Robinson 10.00 25.00
19 Hakeem Olajuwon 10.00 25.00
20 Clyde Drexler 25.00 60.00
25 Anthony Davis 10.00 25.00
26 John Wall 5.00 12.00
29 Donovan Mitchell 6.00 15.00
30 Vince Carter 10.00 25.00
35 Kawhi Leonard 15.00 40.00

2020-21 Panini Contenders Draft Picks Draft Class
*GREEN: .6X TO 1.5X BASIC
*RED: .6X TO 1.5X BASIC
*BLUE/99: 1.25X TO 3X BASIC
*PURPLE/99: 1.25X TO 3X BASIC
*CRACKED ICE/23: 2.5X TO 6X BASIC
*GOLD CRKD ICE/23: 2.5X TO 6X BASIC
1 Tyrese Haliburton 2.50 6.00
2 Anthony Edwards 3.00 8.00
3 James Wiseman .40 1.00
4 LaMelo Ball 2.50 6.00
5 Onyeka Okongwu .60 1.50
6 Isaac Okoro .50 1.25
7 Deni Avdija .75 2.00
8 Obi Toppin .60 1.50
9 Precious Achiuwa .60 1.50
10 Tyrese Maxey 2.50 6.00

2020-21 Panini Contenders Draft Picks Front-Row Seats
*GREEN: .6X TO 1.5X BASIC
*RED: .6X TO 1.5X BASIC
*BLUE/99: 1.25X TO 3X BASIC
*PURPLE/99: 1.25X TO 3X BASIC
*CRACKED ICE/23: 2.5X TO 6X BASIC
*GOLD CRKD ICE/23: 2.5X TO 6X BASIC
1 Josh Green .60 1.50
2 Anthony Edwards 3.00 8.00
3 James Wiseman .40 1.00
4 LaMelo Ball 2.50 6.00
5 Obi Toppin .60 1.50
6 Deni Avdija .75 2.00
7 Killian Hayes .30 .75
8 Tyrese Haliburton 2.50 6.00
9 Tyrese Maxey 2.50 6.00
10 Cole Anthony .75 2.00
11 Isaac Okoro .50 1.25
12 Onyeka Okongwu .60 1.50
13 RJ Hampton .30 .75
14 Aaron Nesmith .60 1.50
15 Devin Vassell 1.00 2.50
16 Jaden McDaniels 1.00 2.50
17 Theo Maledon .30 .75
18 Nico Mannion .30 .75
19 Saddiq Bey .60 1.50
20 Patrick Williams .75 2.00
21 Precious Achiuwa .60 1.50
22 Killian Tillie .40 1.00
23 Kira Lewis Jr. .30 .75
24 Nick Richards .40 1.00
25 Isaiah Stewart .60 1.50
26 Vernon Carey Jr. .30 .75
27 Cassius Winston .30 .75
28 Jalen Smith .60 1.50
29 Udoka Azubuike .40 1.00
30 Devon Dotson .30 .75

2020-21 Panini Contenders Draft Picks Game Day Prospect Ticket Autographs
EXCHANGE DEADLINE 4/2/2022
*GREEN: .4X TO 1X BASIC
*RED: .4X TO 1X BASIC
*STUBS/32: .5X TO 1.2X BASIC
*STUBS/21-23: .8X TO 2X BASIC
*CRKD ICE/23: .8X TO 2X BASIC
*GOLD CRKD ICE/23: .8X TO 2X BASIC
*RED CRKD ICE/23: .8X TO 2X BASIC
1 Anthony Edwards 100.00 250.00
2 Obi Toppin 8.00 20.00
3 James Wiseman 5.00 12.00
4 LaMelo Ball EXCH 75.00 200.00
5 Onyeka Okongwu 8.00 20.00
6 Cole Anthony 10.00 25.00
7 Deni Avdija 10.00 25.00
8 Theo Maledon 4.00 10.00
9 Nico Mannion 4.00 10.00
10 Isaac Okoro 6.00 15.00

2020-21 Panini Contenders Draft Picks International Prospect Ticket Autographs
EXCHANGE DEADLINE 4/2/2022
*GREEN: .4X TO 1X BASIC
*RED: .4X TO 1X BASIC
4 Aleksej Pokusevski 5.00 12.00

2020-21 Panini Contenders Draft Picks International Prospect Ticket Autographs Blue
*BLUE: .5X TO 1.2X BASIC
STATED PRINT RUN 99 SER.#'d SETS
EXCHANGE DEADLINE 4/2/2022

2020-21 Panini Contenders Draft Picks International Prospect Ticket Autographs Conference Finals Ticket
*CNFRNCE FNLS: .5X TO 1.2X BASIC
STATED PRINT RUN 75 SER.#'d SETS
EXCHANGE DEADLINE 4/2/2022

2020-21 Panini Contenders Draft Picks International Prospect Ticket Autographs Conference Ticket
*CNFRNCE: .5X TO 1.2X BASIC
STATED PRINT RUN 99 SER.#'d SETS
EXCHANGE DEADLINE 4/2/2022

2020-21 Panini Contenders Draft Picks International Prospect Ticket Autographs Purple
*PURPLE: .5X TO 1.2X BASIC
STATED PRINT RUN 99 SER.#'d SETS
EXCHANGE DEADLINE 4/2/2022

2020-21 Panini Contenders Draft Picks International Prospect Ticket Autographs Tournament Ticket
*TOURN.: .5X TO 1.2X BASIC
STATED PRINT RUN 49 SER.#'d SETS
EXCHANGE DEADLINE 4/2/2022

2020-21 Panini Contenders Draft Picks Legacy Ticket Autographs
EXCHANGE DEADLINE 4/2/2022
1 Magic Johnson 40.00 100.00
2 Ray Allen 30.00 80.00
4 Jerry West 20.00 50.00
5 Anthony Davis 20.00 50.00
7 RJ Barrett 8.00 20.00

2020-21 Panini Contenders Draft Picks Legacy Ticket Autographs Premium Edition
*PREMIUM: .5X TO 1.2X BASIC
EXCHANGE DEADLINE 4/2/2022

2020-21 Panini Contenders Draft Picks Legacy Ticket Autographs Ticket Stubs
*TICKET STUBS/30-44: .6X TO 1.5X BASIC
*TICKET STUBS/23: .8X TO 2X BASIC
STATED PRINT RUN 1-44 SER.#'d SETS
NO PRICING QTY 15 OR LESS
EXCHANGE DEADLINE 4/2/2022

2020-21 Panini Contenders Draft Picks Mascots
*GREEN: .5X TO 1.2X BASIC
*RED: .5X TO 1.2X BASIC
*BLUE/99: 1X TO 2.5X BASIC
*PURPLE/99: 1X TO 2.5X BASIC
*CRACKED ICE/23: 2.5X TO 6X BASIC
*GOLD CRACKED ICE/23: 2.5X TO 6X BASIC
1 Uga 1.25 3.00
2 The Duck 1.25 3.00
3 Mike The Tiger 1.25 3.00
4 Sparty 1.25 3.00
5 Brutus Buckeye 1.25 3.00
6 Albert 1.25 3.00
7 Sebastian The Ibis 1.25 3.00
8 Aubie The Tiger 1.25 3.00
9 Duke Blue Devil 1.25 3.00
10 Sparky The Sun Devil 1.25 3.00
11 Big Jay 1.25 3.00
12 Otto the Orange 1.25 3.00
13 Joe Bruin 1.25 3.00
14 Duke Blue Devil 1.25 3.00
15 Rameses 1.25 3.00
16 Hink 1.25 3.00
17 Smokey 1.25 3.00
18 Big Red 1.25 3.00
19 The Wildcat 1.25 3.00
20 Rudy Flyer 1.25 3.00

2020-21 Panini Contenders Draft Picks Playing the Numbers Game
*CRACKED ICE/23: 2.5X TO 6X BASIC
1 Devon Dotson .30 .75
2 Anthony Edwards 3.00 8.00
3 James Wiseman .40 1.00
4 LaMelo Ball 2.50 6.00
5 Obi Toppin .60 1.50
6 Deni Avdija .75 2.00
7 Killian Hayes .30 .75
8 Tyrese Haliburton 2.50 6.00
9 Tyrese Maxey 2.50 6.00
10 Cole Anthony .75 2.00
11 Isaac Okoro .50 1.25
12 Onyeka Okongwu .60 1.50
13 RJ Hampton .30 .75
14 Aaron Nesmith .60 1.50
15 Devin Vassell 1.00 2.50
16 Jaden McDaniels 1.00 2.50
17 Theo Maledon .30 .75
18 Nico Mannion .30 .75
19 Saddiq Bey .60 1.50
20 Patrick Williams .75 2.00
21 Precious Achiuwa .60 1.50
22 Killian Tillie .40 1.00
23 Kira Lewis Jr. .30 .75
24 Nick Richards .40 1.00
25 Isaiah Stewart .60 1.50
26 Vernon Carey Jr. .30 .75
27 Cassius Winston .30 .75
28 Markus Howard .40 1.00
29 Udoka Azubuike .40 1.00
30 Josh Green .60 1.50

2020-21 Panini Contenders Draft Picks School Colors
*CRACKED ICE/23: 2.5X TO 6X BASIC
1 Josh Green .60 1.50
2 Anthony Edwards 3.00 8.00
3 Ashton Hagans .40 1.00
4 Tyler Bey .30 .75
5 Obi Toppin .60 1.50
6 Udoka Azubuike .40 1.00
7 Devon Dotson .30 .75
8 Tyrese Haliburton 2.50 6.00
9 Tyrese Maxey 2.50 6.00
10 Cole Anthony .75 2.00
11 Isaac Okoro .50 1.25
12 Onyeka Okongwu .60 1.50
13 Jalen Smith .60 1.50
14 Aaron Nesmith .60 1.50
15 Devin Vassell 1.00 2.50
16 Jaden McDaniels 1.00 2.50
17 Cassius Winston .30 .75
18 Nico Mannion .30 .75
19 Saddiq Bey .60 1.50
20 Patrick Williams .75 2.00
21 Precious Achiuwa .60 1.50
22 Killian Tillie .40 1.00
23 Kira Lewis Jr. .30 .75
24 Nick Richards .40 1.00
25 Isaiah Stewart .60 1.50
26 Vernon Carey Jr. .30 .75
27 Daniel Oturu .30 .75
28 Zeke Nnaji .40 1.00
29 Payton Pritchard 1.00 2.50
30 Tre Jones .50 1.25
31 Jordan Nwora .40 1.00
32 Cassius Stanley .30 .75
33 Markus Howard .40 1.00
34 Paul Reed .40 1.00
35 Reggie Perry .30 .75

2020-21 Panini Contenders Draft Picks Ticket Stubs
*TICKET STUBS/32-50: .5X TO 1.5X BASIC
*TICKET STUBS/21-24: .8X TO 2X BASIC
STATED PRINT RUN 1-55 SER.#'d SETS
NO PRICING QTY 15 OR LESS
EXCHANGE DEADLINE 4/2/2022

2020-21 Panini Contenders Draft Picks Tournament Ticket
*TOUR.: 1.2X TO 3X BASIC
*TOUR. AU: .5X TO 1.2X BASIC
PRINT RUNS B/WN 5-49 COPIES PER
NO PRICING ON QTY 15 OR LESS
EXCHANGE DEADLINE 4/2/2022
85 Immanuel Quickley AU/49 12.00 30.00
92 Tre Jones AU/49 8.00 20.00
96 Jalen Smith AU/49 20.00 50.00
97 Malachi Flynn AU/49 5.00 12.00
99 Cassius Stanley AU/49 12.00 30.00
121 Kenyon Martin Jr. AU/49 8.00 20.00
127 Desmond Bane AU/49 15.00 40.00

2020-21 Panini Contenders Draft Picks Variations Conference Finals Ticket
*VAR.CONF.FINALS.: 1X TO 2.5X BASIC
*VAR.CONF.FINALS.AU: .5X TO 1.2X BASIC
STATED PRINT RUN 75 SER.#'d SETS
EXCHANGE DEADLINE 4/2/2022

2020-21 Panini Contenders Draft Picks Variations Conference Ticket
*VAR.CONF.: 1X TO 2.5X BASIC
*VAR.CONF.AU: .5X TO 1.2X BASIC
STATED PRINT RUN 99 SER.#'d SETS
EXCHANGE DEADLINE 4/2/2022

2020-21 Panini Contenders Draft Picks Variations Cracked Ice Ticket
*VAR.CRKD ICE: 2X TO 5X BASIC
*VAR.CRKD ICE AU: .8X TO 2X BASIC
STATED PRINT RUN 23 SER.#'d SETS
EXCHANGE DEADLINE 4/2/2022

2020-21 Panini Contenders Draft Picks Variations Game Ticket Blue
*VAR.BLUE: 1X TO 2.5X BASIC
*VAR.BLUE AU: .5X TO 1.2X BASIC
STATED PRINT RUN 99 SER.#'d SETS
EXCHANGE DEADLINE 4/2/2022

2020-21 Panini Contenders Draft Picks Variations Game Ticket Purple
*VAR.PURPLE: .6X TO 1.5X BASIC
*VAR.PURPLE AU: .5X TO 1.2X BASIC
AU PRINT RUN 99 SER.#'d SETS
EXCHANGE DEADLINE 4/2/2022

2020-21 Panini Contenders Draft Picks Variations Gold Cracked Ice Ticket
*VAR.GOLD ICE: 2X TO 5X BASIC
*VAR.GOLD ICE AU: .8X TO 2X BASIC
STATED PRINT RUN 23 SER.#'d SETS
EXCHANGE DEADLINE 4/2/2022

2020-21 Panini Contenders Draft Picks Variations Red Cracked Ice Ticket
*VAR.RED ICE: 2X TO 5X BASIC
*VAR.RED ICE AU: .8X TO 2X BASIC
STATED PRINT RUN 23 SER.#'d SETS
EXCHANGE DEADLINE 4/2/2022

2020-21 Panini Contenders Draft Picks Variations Tournament Ticket
*VAR.TOUR.: 1.2X TO 3X BASIC
*VAR.TOUR.AU: .5X TO 1.2X BASIC
STATED PRINT RUN 49 SER.#'d SETS
EXCHANGE DEADLINE 4/2/2022

2020-21 Panini Contenders Draft Picks Winning Tickets
*GREEN: .6X TO 1.5X BASIC
*RED: .6X TO 1.5X BASIC
*BLUE/99: 1.2X TO 3X BASIC
*PURPLE/99: 1.2X TO 3X BASIC
*CRACKED ICE/23: 2.5X TO 6X BASIC
*GOLD CRACKED ICE/23: 2.5X TO 6X BASIC
1 Zion Williamson 1.25 3.00
2 De'Andre Hunter .40 1.00
3 Ty Jerome .25 .60
4 Jalen Brunson .60 1.50
5 Donte DiVincenzo .40 1.00
6 Justin Jackson .25 .60
7 Josh Hart .30 .75
8 Justise Winslow .30 .75
9 Shabazz Napier .25 .60
10 Montrezl Harrell .40 1.00
11 Anthony Davis 1.00 2.50
12 Michael Kidd-Gilchrist .25 .60
13 Jeremy Lamb .25 .60
14 Kemba Walker .40 1.00
15 Seth Curry .40 1.00
16 Danny Green .30 .75
17 Ed Davis .25 .60
18 Al Horford .40 1.00
19 Corey Brewer .25 .60
20 Marvin Williams .25 .60
21 Carmelo Anthony .60 1.50
22 Richard Hamilton .40 1.00
23 Mike Bibby .40 1.00
24 Tony Delk .30 .75
25 Christian Laettner .40 1.00
26 James Worthy .60 1.50
27 Magic Johnson 1.50 4.00
28 Bill Walton .60 1.50
29 Kareem Abdul-Jabbar 1.25 3.00
30 Gail Goodrich .40 1.00
31 Jerry Lucas .50 1.25
32 Bill Russell 1.25 3.00
33 JJ Redick .40 1.00
34 Tyrese Haliburton 2.50 6.00
35 Devonte' Graham .30 .75
36 Allen Iverson 1.00 2.50
37 Jerry West .75 2.00
38 David Robinson .75 2.00
39 Hakeem Olajuwon .75 2.00
40 Ray Allen .60 1.50

2018-19 Panini Contenders Optic
EXCHANGE DEADLINE 1/31/2021
1 Brandon Ingram .40 1.00
2 Lonzo Ball .40 1.00
3 DeMar DeRozan .50 1.25
4 Paul George .60 1.50
5 Elfrid Payton .30 .75
6 Steven Adams .30 .75
7 James Harden .75 2.00
8 Josh Richardson .30 .75
9 Aaron Gordon .40 1.00
10 Kevin Love .30 .75
11 Buddy Hield .40 1.00
12 Lou Williams .30 .75
13 DeMarcus Cousins .30 .75
14 Paul Millsap .30 .75
15 Emmanuel Mudiay .25 .60
16 T.J. Warren .30 .75
17 Jayson Tatum 1.50 4.00
18 Jrue Holiday .50 1.25
19 Al Horford .40 1.00
20 Khris Middleton .40 1.00
21 Chris Paul .75 2.00
22 Malcolm Brogdon .40 1.00
23 Dennis Smith Jr. .25 .60
24 Reggie Jackson .30 .75
25 Eric Bledsoe .30 .75
26 Taurean Prince .25 .60
27 Jeremy Lamb .25 .60
28 Julius Randle .40 1.00
29 Andre Drummond .30 .75
30 Klay Thompson 1.00 2.50
31 CJ McCollum .40 1.00
32 Mike Conley .30 .75
33 Derrick Rose .75 2.00
34 Ricky Rubio .30 .75
35 Eric Gordon .30 .75
36 Tim Hardaway Jr. .25 .60
37 Jimmy Butler .60 1.50
38 Jusuf Nurkic .30 .75
39 Andrew Wiggins .50 1.25
40 Kristaps Porzingis .50 1.25
41 Clint Capela .30 .75
42 Montrezl Harrell .40 1.00
43 Devin Booker 1.00 2.50
44 Rudy Gay .40 1.00
45 Evan Fournier .30 .75
46 Tobias Harris .30 .75
47 Joe Harris .30 .75
48 Karl-Anthony Towns .60 1.50
49 Anthony Davis 1.00 2.50
50 Kyle Kuzma .40 1.00
51 Damian Lillard 1.00 2.50
52 Nikola Jokic 2.00 5.00
53 Dirk Nowitzki 1.00 2.50
54 Rudy Gobert .50 1.25
55 Giannis Antetokounmpo 2.00 5.00
56 Tony Parker .60 1.50
57 Joel Embiid 1.00 2.50
58 Kawhi Leonard 1.00 2.50
59 Avery Bradley .25 .60
60 Kyle Lowry .40 1.00
61 D'Angelo Russell .40 1.00
62 Nikola Vucevic .30 .75
63 Domantas Sabonis .50 1.25
64 Russell Westbrook .60 1.50
65 Goran Dragic .30 .75
66 Tristan Thompson .25 .60
67 John Collins .40 1.00
68 Kelly Oubre Jr. .40 1.00
69 Ben Simmons .40 1.00
70 Kyrie Irving 1.00 2.50
71 Danilo Gallinari .30 .75
72 Otto Porter Jr. .30 .75
73 Donovan Mitchell 1.25 3.00
74 Serge Ibaka .30 .75
75 Harrison Barnes .30 .75
76 Victor Oladipo .30 .75
77 John Wall .50 1.25
78 Kemba Walker .30 .75
79 Blake Griffin .40 1.00
80 LaMarcus Aldridge .40 1.00
81 De'Aaron Fox .75 2.00
82 Pascal Siakam .60 1.50
83 Draymond Green .50 1.25
84 Spencer Dinwiddie .30 .75
85 Jabari Parker .25 .60
86 Vince Carter .75 2.00
87 Jonas Valanciunas .40 1.00
88 Kent Bazemore .25 .60
89 Bojan Bogdanovic .30 .75
90 Lauri Markkanen .60 1.50
91 DeAndre Jordan .30 .75
92 Pau Gasol .60 1.50
93 Dwyane Wade .75 2.00
94 Stephen Curry 3.00 8.00
95 Jamal Murray .75 2.00
96 Zach LaVine .60 1.50
97 Jordan Clarkson .40 1.00
98 Kevin Durant 1.50 4.00
99 Bradley Beal .50 1.25
100 LeBron James 15.00 40.00
101 Collin Sexton AU RC 20.00 50.00
102 Bruce Brown AU RC 5.00 12.00
103 Dzanan Musa AU RC 2.50 6.00
104 Rodions Kurucs AU RC EXCH 3.00 8.00
105 Jalen Brunson AU RC 20.00 50.00
106 Troy Brown Jr. AU RC 5.00 12.00
107 Josh Okogie AU RC 4.00 10.00
108 Landry Shamet AU RC 10.00 25.00
109 Aaron Holiday AU RC 4.00 10.00
110 Marvin Bagley III AU RC 4.00 10.00
111 Deandre Ayton AU RC 25.00 60.00
112 Mo Bamba AU RC 4.00 10.00
113 Grayson Allen AU RC 5.00 12.00
114 Shai Gilgeous-Alexander AU RC 800.00 1,500.00
115 Jaren Jackson Jr. AU RC 150.00 400.00
116 Wendell Carter Jr. AU RC 15.00 40.00
117 Kevin Huerter AU RC 5.00 12.00
118 Lonnie Walker IV AU RC 25.00 60.00
119 Allonzo Trier AU RC 2.50 6.00
120 Michael Porter Jr. AU RC 200.00 500.00
121 Donte DiVincenzo AU RC 5.00 12.00
122 Omari Spellman AU RC 2.50 6.00
123 Hamidou Diallo AU RC 6.00 15.00
124 Trae Young AU RC 125.00 300.00
125 Jerome Robinson AU RC 2.50 6.00
126 Zhaire Smith AU RC 2.50 6.00
127 Kevin Knox II AU RC 12.00 30.00
128 Luka Doncic AU RC 2,000.00 4,000.00
129 Chandler Hutchison AU RC 3.00 8.00
130 Mikal Bridges AU RC 12.00 30.00

2018-19 Panini Contenders Optic Blue
*BLUE: 1.2X TO 3X BASIC
*BLUE AU: .5X TO 1.2X BASIC
STATED PRINT RUN 99 SER.#'d SETS
EXCHANGE DEADLINE 1/31/2021
100 LeBron James 60.00 150.00
108 Landry Shamet AU 20.00 50.00
120 Michael Porter Jr. AU 400.00 800.00
124 Trae Young AU 200.00 500.00
128 Luka Doncic AU 3,000.00 6,000.00

2018-19 Panini Contenders Optic Orange
*ORANGE: 1.5X TO 4X BASIC
*ORANGE AU: 1X TO 2.5X BASIC
1-100 STATED PRINT RUN 49 SER.#'d SETS
101-130 STATED PRINT RUN 25 SER.#'d SETS
EXCHANGE DEADLINE 1/31/2021
94 Stephen Curry/49 15.00 40.00
100 LeBron James/49 125.00 300.00
106 Troy Brown Jr. AU/25 15.00 40.00
108 Landry Shamet AU/25 40.00 100.00
111 Deandre Ayton AU/25 100.00 250.00
113 Grayson Allen AU/25 15.00 40.00
117 Kevin Huerter AU/25 25.00 60.00
120 Michael Porter Jr. AU/25 1,000.00 2,000.00
123 Hamidou Diallo AU/25 20.00 50.00
124 Trae Young AU/25 400.00 800.00
127 Kevin Knox II AU/25 40.00 100.00
128 Luka Doncic AU/25 8,000.00 12,000.00

2018-19 Panini Contenders Optic Red
*RED: .6X TO 1.5X BASIC
*RED AU: .5X TO 1.2X BASIC
101-130 STATED PRINT RUN 149 SER.#'d SETS
EXCHANGE DEADLINE 1/31/2021
100 LeBron James 25.00 60.00
124 Trae Young AU/149 200.00 500.00

2018-19 Panini Contenders Optic Silver
*SILVER: 1X TO 2.5X BASIC
100 LeBron James 40.00 100.00

2018-19 Panini Contenders Optic Variations
*VAR: .4X TO 1X BASIC
EXCHANGE DEADLINE 1/31/2021
101 Collin Sexton 20.00 50.00
106 Troy Brown Jr. 5.00 12.00
110 Marvin Bagley III 4.00 10.00
114 Shai Gilgeous-Alexander 800.00 1,500.00
115 Jaren Jackson Jr. 150.00 400.00
116 Wendell Carter Jr. 15.00 40.00

2018-19 Panini Contenders Optic Variations Blue
*VAR.BLUE: .6X TO 1.5X BASIC
STATED PRINT RUN 49 SER.#'d SETS
EXCHANGE DEADLINE 1/31/2021
108 Landry Shamet 25.00 60.00
111 Deandre Ayton 60.00 150.00
117 Kevin Huerter 15.00 40.00
120 Michael Porter Jr. 500.00 1,000.00
123 Hamidou Diallo 12.00 30.00
124 Trae Young 250.00 600.00
128 Luka Doncic EXCH 3,000.00 6,000.00

2018-19 Panini Contenders Optic Variations Orange
*VAR.ORANGE: 1X TO 2.5X BASIC
STATED PRINT RUN 25 SER.#'d SETS
EXCHANGE DEADLINE 1/31/2021
106 Troy Brown Jr. 15.00 40.00
108 Landry Shamet 40.00 100.00
111 Deandre Ayton 100.00 250.00
113 Grayson Allen 15.00 40.00
117 Kevin Huerter 25.00 60.00
120 Michael Porter Jr. 1,000.00 2,000.00
123 Hamidou Diallo 20.00 50.00
124 Trae Young 400.00 800.00
127 Kevin Knox II 40.00 100.00
128 Luka Doncic EXCH 8,000.00 12,000.00

2018-19 Panini Contenders Optic Variations Red
*VAR.RED: .5X TO 1.2X BASIC
STATED PRINT RUN 99 SER.#'d SETS
EXCHANGE DEADLINE 1/31/2021
108 Landry Shamet 20.00 50.00
111 Deandre Ayton 50.00 120.00
120 Michael Porter Jr. 400.00 800.00
124 Trae Young 200.00 500.00
128 Luka Doncic EXCH 2,500.00 5,000.00

2018-19 Panini Contenders Optic Class Acts
*BLUE CRKD ICE: .6X TO 1.5X BASIC
1 Jayson Tatum 2.50 6.00
2 Steve Nash 1.25 3.00
3 Deandre Ayton 1.25 3.00
4 LeBron James 25.00 60.00
5 Kevin Durant 2.50 6.00
6 Gary Payton .75 2.00
7 Blake Griffin .60 1.50
8 Anfernee Hardaway 1.50 4.00
9 Anthony Davis 1.50 4.00
10 Grant Hill 1.00 2.50
11 Donovan Mitchell 2.00 5.00
12 Tracy McGrady 1.00 2.50
13 Luka Doncic 40.00 100.00
14 Dwyane Wade 1.25 3.00
15 James Harden 1.25 3.00
16 Shaquille O'Neal 2.00 5.00
17 DeMar DeRozan .75 2.00
18 Jason Kidd 1.00 2.50
19 Giannis Antetokounmpo 3.00 8.00
20 Allen Iverson 1.50 4.00
21 Lonzo Ball .60 1.50
22 Tim Duncan 1.50 4.00
23 Trae Young 12.00 30.00
24 Chris Paul 1.25 3.00
25 Stephen Curry 10.00 25.00
26 Larry Johnson .75 2.00
27 Kyrie Irving 1.50 4.00
28 Jalen Rose .50 1.25

2018-19 Panini Contenders Optic Front Row Seat
*BLUE CRKD ICE: .6X TO 1.5X BASIC
1 Joel Embiid 1.50 4.00
2 Stephen Curry 5.00 12.00
3 De'Aaron Fox 1.25 3.00
4 Chris Paul 1.25 3.00
5 Giannis Antetokounmpo 3.00 8.00
6 Kyrie Irving 1.50 4.00
7 LeBron James 15.00 40.00
8 Zach LaVine 1.00 2.50
9 Russell Westbrook 1.00 2.50
10 Dennis Smith Jr. .40 1.00
11 Devin Booker 1.50 4.00
12 Kevin Durant 2.50 6.00
13 Donovan Mitchell 2.00 5.00
14 James Harden 1.25 3.00
15 Jimmy Butler 1.00 2.50
16 Jayson Tatum 2.50 6.00
17 Anthony Davis 1.50 4.00
18 Lauri Markkanen 1.00 2.50
19 Paul George 1.00 2.50
20 Dirk Nowitzki 1.50 4.00
21 Damian Lillard 1.50 4.00
22 Klay Thompson 1.50 4.00
23 John Wall .75 2.00
24 Lonzo Ball .60 1.50
25 Karl-Anthony Towns 1.00 2.50
26 Kemba Walker .50 1.25
27 Luka Doncic 25.00 60.00
28 Kevin Love .50 1.25
29 Ben Simmons .60 1.50
30 Blake Griffin .60 1.50

2018-19 Panini Contenders Optic Hall of Fame Contenders
*BLUE CRKD ICE: .6X TO 1.5X BASIC
*RED CRKD ICE: .6X TO 1.5X BASIC
1 Dirk Nowitzki 1.50 4.00
2 Tony Parker 1.00 2.50
3 Kevin Durant 2.50 6.00
4 Kyrie Irving 1.50 4.00
5 Russell Westbrook 1.00 2.50
6 Draymond Green .75 2.00
7 James Harden 1.25 3.00
8 Kobe Bryant 4.00 10.00
9 LeBron James 8.00 20.00
10 Pau Gasol 1.00 2.50
11 Chris Paul 1.25 3.00
12 Anthony Davis 1.50 4.00
13 Stephen Curry 5.00 12.00
14 John Wall .75 2.00
15 Chris Bosh .60 1.50
16 Klay Thompson 1.50 4.00
17 Vince Carter 1.25 3.00
18 Tim Duncan 1.50 4.00
19 Dwyane Wade 1.25 3.00
20 Paul Pierce 1.00 2.50

2018-19 Panini Contenders Optic Historic MVPs
*BLUE CRKD ICE: .6X TO 1.5X BASIC
*RED CRKD ICE: .6X TO 1.5X BASIC
1 James Harden 1.25 3.00
2 Russell Westbrook 1.00 2.50
3 Stephen Curry 25.00 60.00
4 Kevin Durant 2.50 6.00
5 LeBron James 40.00 100.00
6 Kobe Bryant 15.00 40.00
7 Kevin Garnett 1.50 4.00
8 Allen Iverson 1.50 4.00
9 Shaquille O'Neal 2.00 5.00
10 Charles Barkley 1.25 3.00

2018-19 Panini Contenders Optic Historic MVPs Blue Cracked Ice
*BLUE CRKD ICE: .6X TO 1.5X BASIC
6 Kobe Bryant 40.00 100.00

2018-19 Panini Contenders Optic Historic MVPs Red Cracked Ice
*RED CRKD ICE: .6X TO 1.5X BASIC
6 Kobe Bryant 40.00 100.00

2018-19 Panini Contenders Optic Historic Rookies of the Year
*BLUE CRKD ICE: .6X TO 1.5X BASIC
*RED CRKD ICE: .6X TO 1.5X BASIC
1 Ben Simmons .60 1.50
2 Karl-Anthony Towns 1.00 2.50
3 Damian Lillard 1.50 4.00
4 Kyrie Irving 1.50 4.00
5 Kevin Durant 2.50 6.00
6 LeBron James 15.00 40.00
7 Vince Carter 1.25 3.00
8 Tim Duncan 1.50 4.00
9 Allen Iverson 1.50 4.00
10 Chris Webber .75 2.00

11 Shaquille O'Neal 2.00 5.00
12 David Robinson 1.25 3.00
13 Patrick Ewing 1.00 2.50
14 Larry Bird 2.50 6.00
15 Kareem Abdul-Jabbar 2.00 5.00
16 Oscar Robertson 1.25 3.00
17 Jason Kidd 1.00 2.50
18 Grant Hill 1.00 2.50

2018-19 Panini Contenders Optic Legendary Autographs

PRINT RUNS B/WN 49-99 COPIES PER
EXCHANGE DEADLINE 1/31/2021
1 Hakeem Olajuwon/99 12.00 30.00
2 John Starks/99 4.00 10.00
3 Jason Williams/99 10.00 25.00
4 Tim Hardaway/99 6.00 15.00
5 Doc Rivers/99 5.00 12.00
6 Sarunas Marciulionis/99 5.00 12.00
7 Jermaine O'Neal/99 4.00 10.00
8 Glen Rice/99 5.00 12.00
9 Jerry West/49 15.00 40.00
10 Juwan Howard/99 4.00 10.00
11 Dominique Wilkins/99 8.00 20.00
12 Jamaal Wilkes/99 5.00 12.00
13 Kenny Smith/99 4.00 10.00
14 Damon Stoudamire/99 5.00 12.00
15 Lenny Wilkens/99 6.00 15.00
16 Gerald Henderson Sr./99 3.00 8.00
17 George Karl/99 5.00 12.00
18 A.C. Green/99 5.00 12.00
19 Magic Johnson/49 20.00 50.00
20 Allan Houston/99 5.00 12.00
21 Rick Barry/99 6.00 15.00
22 Tom Chambers/99 4.00 10.00
23 George Gervin/99 8.00 20.00
24 Charlie Scott/99 5.00 12.00
25 Rick Fox/99 4.00 10.00
26 Mychal Thompson/99 3.00 8.00
27 Cliff Hagan/99 5.00 12.00
28 Dikembe Mutombo/99 8.00 20.00
29 Grant Hill/49 10.00 25.00
30 B.J. Armstrong/99 5.00 12.00
31 Bob Lanier/99 6.00 15.00
32 Jerry Stackhouse/99 6.00 15.00
33 Robert Parish/99 8.00 20.00
34 Arvydas Sabonis/99 5.00 12.00
35 Avery Johnson/99 4.00 10.00
36 Spud Webb/99 5.00 12.00
37 George McGinnis/99 6.00 15.00
38 Michael Cooper/99 5.00 12.00
39 Dennis Rodman/99 15.00 40.00
40 Kurt Rambis/99 4.00 10.00

2018-19 Panini Contenders Optic Lottery Ticket

*BLUE CRKD ICE: .6X TO 1.5X BASIC
*RED CRKD ICE: .6X TO 1.5X BASIC
1 Deandre Ayton 2.00 5.00
2 Marvin Bagley III 1.00 2.50
3 Luka Doncic 100.00 250.00
4 Jaren Jackson Jr. 12.00 30.00
5 Trae Young 50.00 120.00
6 Mo Bamba 1.00 2.50
7 Wendell Carter Jr. 1.50 4.00
8 Collin Sexton 2.00 5.00
9 Kevin Knox II .75 2.00
10 Mikal Bridges 3.00 8.00
11 Shai Gilgeous-Alexander 12.00 30.00
12 Miles Bridges 1.50 4.00
13 Jerome Robinson .60 1.50
14 Michael Porter Jr. 12.00 30.00

2018-19 Panini Contenders Optic NBA Ink

PRINT RUNS B/WN 25-99 COPIES PER
EXCHANGE DEADLINE 1/31/2021
1 Andrew Wiggins/49 8.00 20.00
2 DeMarcus Cousins/49 5.00 12.00
3 Kevin Love/99 4.00 10.00
4 Josh Jackson/99 3.00 8.00
5 Nikola Jokic/99 150.00 400.00
6 Khris Middleton/99 5.00 12.00
7 Dwyane Wade/25 40.00 100.00
8 Jamal Murray/99 10.00 25.00
9 JJ Redick/99 5.00 12.00
10 Eric Bledsoe/99 4.00 10.00
11 Lonzo Ball/99 5.00 12.00
12 Damian Lillard/25 40.00 100.00
13 Reggie Jackson/99 4.00 10.00
14 Otto Porter Jr./99 4.00 10.00
15 Gary Harris/99 4.00 10.00
16 Serge Ibaka/99 4.00 10.00
17 Joel Embiid/49 15.00 40.00
18 Andre Drummond/99 4.00 10.00
19 Jonas Valanciunas/99 5.00 12.00
20 Lauri Markkanen/99 8.00 20.00
22 Willie Cauley-Stein/99 3.00 8.00
23 DeMarre Carroll/99 3.00 8.00
24 Kevin Durant/25 EXCH 75.00 200.00
25 Kristaps Porzingis/99 6.00 15.00
26 Stephen Curry/25 500.00 1,000.00
27 Jayson Tatum/49 75.00 200.00
28 Kawhi Leonard/25 50.00 120.00
29 Spencer Dinwiddie/99 4.00 10.00
30 Donovan Mitchell/49 25.00 60.00

2018-19 Panini Contenders Optic Playing the Numbers Game

*BLUE CRKD ICE: .6X TO 1.5X BASIC
*RED CRKD ICE: .6X TO 1.5X BASIC
1 James Harden 1.25 3.00
2 Kemba Walker .50 1.25
3 LaMarcus Aldridge .60 1.50
4 Klay Thompson 1.50 4.00
5 Stephen Curry 5.00 12.00
6 LeBron James 5.00 12.00
7 Blake Griffin .60 1.50
8 Derrick Rose 1.25 3.00
9 Kevin Durant 2.50 6.00
10 Anthony Davis 1.50 4.00
11 Jamal Murray 1.25 3.00
12 Paul George 1.00 2.50
13 Kawhi Leonard 1.50 4.00
14 Giannis Antetokounmpo 3.00 8.00
15 Karl-Anthony Towns 1.00 2.50
16 Anthony Davis 1.50 4.00
17 Enes Kanter .50 1.25
18 Rudy Gobert .75 2.00
19 Jarrett Allen .60 1.50
20 Steven Adams .50 1.25
21 Clint Capela .50 1.25
22 DeAndre Jordan .50 1.25
23 Andre Drummond .50 1.25
24 Russell Westbrook 1.00 2.50
25 Kyrie Irving 1.50 4.00
26 Jeff Teague .40 1.00
27 Darren Collison .40 1.00
28 Kyle Lowry .60 1.50
29 Trae Young 8.00 20.00
30 James Harden 1.25 3.00
31 Kyrie Irving 1.50 4.00
32 Klay Thompson 1.50 4.00
33 Stephen Curry 5.00 12.00
34 James Harden 1.25 3.00
35 Damian Lillard 1.50 4.00

2018-19 Panini Contenders Optic Playing the Numbers Game Blue Cracked Ice

*BLUE CRKD ICE: .6X TO 1.5X BASIC
6 LeBron James 20.00 50.00

2018-19 Panini Contenders Optic Playing the Numbers Game Red Cracked Ice

*RED CRKD ICE: .6X TO 1.5X BASIC
6 LeBron James 20.00 50.00

2018-19 Panini Contenders Optic Sophomore Autographs

STATED PRINT RUN 99 SER.#'d SETS
EXCHANGE DEADLINE 1/31/2021
1 Lonzo Ball 5.00 12.00
3 Lauri Markkanen 8.00 20.00
4 Jayson Tatum 15.00 40.00
5 Donovan Mitchell 20.00 50.00

2018-19 Panini Contenders Optic Up and Coming Autographs

STATED PRINT RUN 99 SER.#'d SETS
EXCHANGE DEADLINE 1/31/2021
1 Jarred Vanderbilt 6.00 15.00
2 De'Anthony Melton 6.00 15.00
3 Troy Brown Jr. 4.00 10.00
4 Hamidou Diallo 5.00 12.00
5 Trae Young 200.00 500.00
6 Allonzo Trier 3.00 8.00
7 Mo Bamba 5.00 12.00
8 Gary Clark 3.00 8.00
9 Jalen Brunson 25.00 60.00
10 Monte Morris 8.00 20.00
11 Mitchell Robinson 8.00 20.00
12 Michael Porter Jr. 12.00 30.00
13 Devonte' Graham 5.00 12.00
14 Kevin Knox II 4.00 10.00
15 Svi Mykhailiuk 4.00 10.00
16 Luka Doncic 1,000.00 2,000.00
17 Zhaire Smith 3.00 8.00
18 Jevon Carter 5.00 12.00
19 Gary Trent Jr. 6.00 15.00
20 Lonnie Walker IV 6.00 15.00
21 Robert Williams III 6.00 15.00
22 Moritz Wagner 6.00 15.00
23 Omari Spellman 3.00 8.00
24 Anfernee Simons 15.00 40.00
25 Aaron Holiday 5.00 12.00

2018-19 Panini Contenders Optic Veteran Ticket Autographs

EXCHANGE DEADLINE 1/31/2021
*RED/49: .6X TO 1.5X
*BLUE/35: .6X TO 1.5X
*ORANGE/25: .75X TO 2X
1 Serge Ibaka 3.00 8.00
2 Anthony Davis 20.00 50.00
3 Nemanja Bjelica 2.50 6.00
4 Andrew Wiggins 5.00 12.00
5 Lonzo Ball 4.00 10.00
6 Kobe Bryant EXCH 300.00 600.00
7 Jamal Murray 8.00 20.00
8 Magic Johnson 12.00 30.00
9 JJ Redick 4.00 10.00
10 Dwyane Wade 15.00 40.00
11 Lauri Markkanen 6.00 15.00
12 Karl-Anthony Towns 6.00 15.00
13 Willie Cauley-Stein 2.50 6.00
14 Joel Embiid 10.00 25.00
15 Kristaps Porzingis 5.00 12.00
16 Kevin Durant EXCH 25.00 60.00
17 Andre Drummond 3.00 8.00
18 Charles Barkley 75.00 200.00
19 Nikola Jokic 125.00 300.00
20 Damian Lillard 6.00 15.00
21 DeMarre Carroll 2.50 6.00
23 Devin Booker 75.00 200.00
24 Kevin Love 3.00 8.00
25 Khris Middleton 4.00 10.00
26 Kyrie Irving 10.00 25.00
27 Paul Millsap 3.00 8.00
28 James Harden 50.00 120.00
29 Gary Harris 3.00 8.00
30 Chris Paul 30.00 80.00

2018-19 Panini Contenders Optic Winning Tickets

*BLUE CRKD ICE: .6X TO 1.5X BASIC
*RED CRKD ICE: .6X TO 1.5X BASIC
1 Alonzo Mourning 1.00 2.50
2 Kevin Love .50 1.25
3 Ben Wallace .50 1.25
4 Jerry West 1.25 3.00
5 Hakeem Olajuwon .75 2.00
6 Dirk Nowitzki 1.50 4.00
7 Pau Gasol 1.00 2.50
8 Kevin Durant 2.50 6.00
9 Rajon Rondo .75 2.00
10 Draymond Green .75 2.00
11 Tony Parker 1.00 2.50
12 Gary Payton .75 2.00
13 David Robinson 1.25 3.00
14 Clyde Drexler 1.00 2.50
15 Kawhi Leonard 1.50 4.00
16 Jason Kidd 1.00 2.50
17 Paul Pierce 1.00 2.50
18 Stephen Curry 5.00 12.00
19 Robert Horry .60 1.50
20 LeBron James 20.00 50.00
21 Richard Hamilton .50 1.25
22 Tim Duncan 1.50 4.00
23 Scottie Pippen 1.50 4.00
24 Andre Iguodala .50 1.25
25 Larry Bird 2.50 6.00
26 Kobe Bryant 5.00 12.00
27 Kevin Garnett 1.50 4.00
28 Klay Thompson 1.50 4.00
29 Shaquille O'Neal 2.00 5.00
30 Kyrie Irving 1.50 4.00
31 Chauncey Billups .75 2.00
32 Dwyane Wade 1.25 3.00
33 Wilt Chamberlain 2.00 5.00
34 Ray Allen .75 2.00
35 Magic Johnson 2.50 6.00

2019-20 Panini Contenders Optic

EXCHANGE DEADLINE 6/01/2023
1 Kemba Walker .40 1.00
2 Bam Adebayo .75 2.00
3 Bradley Beal .60 1.50
4 Christian Wood .40 1.00
5 Mitchell Robinson .50 1.25
6 Gordon Hayward .40 1.00
7 Terry Rozier .40 1.00
8 John Collins .50 1.25
9 Deandre Ayton .50 1.25
10 Damian Lillard 1.25 3.00
11 Tobias Harris .40 1.00
12 Bojan Bogdanovic .40 1.00
13 Kyle Lowry .50 1.25
14 Karl-Anthony Towns .75 2.00
15 Davis Bertans .30 .75
16 Buddy Hield .40 1.00
17 Chris Paul 1.00 2.50
18 Al Horford .50 1.25
19 De'Aaron Fox .75 2.00
20 Khris Middleton .50 1.25
21 Jayson Tatum 2.00 5.00
22 Kyrie Irving 1.00 2.50
23 Devin Booker .12 .30
24 Jaylen Brown .75 2.00
25 Jrue Holiday .60 1.50
26 Julius Randle .60 1.50
27 Andre Drummond .40 1.00
28 Kristaps Porzingis .60 1.50
29 Aaron Gordon .50 1.25
30 DeMar DeRozan .60 1.50
31 Myles Turner .50 1.25
32 Stephen Curry 4.00 10.00
33 Eric Bledsoe .40 1.00
34 Luka Doncic 20.00 50.00
35 Jaren Jackson Jr. .75 2.00
36 Andrew Wiggins .60 1.50
37 Malik Beasley .40 1.00
38 Malcolm Brogdon .40 1.00
39 Draymond Green .60 1.50
40 CJ McCollum .50 1.25
41 Bogdan Bogdanovic .50 1.25
42 Trae Young 1.25 3.00
43 Derrick Rose 1.00 2.50
44 Nikola Vucevic .40 1.00
45 Marc Gasol .50 1.25
46 Donovan Mitchell 1.00 2.50
47 John Wall .60 1.50
48 Kevin Love .50 1.25
49 Nikola Jokic 2.50 6.00
50 Collin Sexton .60 1.50
51 Joel Embiid 1.00 2.50
52 Hassan Whiteside .30 .75
53 LaMarcus Aldridge .50 1.25
54 Shai Gilgeous-Alexander 2.50 6.00
55 Victor Oladipo .40 1.00
56 Goran Dragic .40 1.00
57 Domantas Sabonis .60 1.50
58 Jamal Murray .75 2.00
59 Devonte' Graham .40 1.00
60 Rudy Gobert .60 1.50
61 Michael Porter Jr. .75 2.00
62 Ben Simmons .75 2.00
63 Anthony Davis 1.25 3.00
64 Zach LaVine .75 2.00
65 Vince Carter 1.00 2.50
66 Lauri Markkanen .60 1.50
67 Caris LeVert .40 1.00
68 Russell Westbrook .75 2.00
69 Lonzo Ball .50 1.25
70 Miles Bridges .50 1.25
71 Mike Conley .40 1.00
72 Kevin Durant 1.50 4.00
73 Brandon Ingram .50 1.25
74 Carmelo Anthony .75 2.00
75 Dejounte Murray .50 1.25
76 Paul George .75 2.00
77 Rudy Gay .40 1.00
78 Robert Covington .30 .75
79 Markelle Fultz .40 1.00
80 Klay Thompson 1.25 3.00
81 Darius Garland 1.25 3.00
82 Wendell Carter Jr. .50 1.25
83 Kelly Oubre Jr. .40 1.00
84 Giannis Antetokounmpo 2.50 6.00
85 D'Angelo Russell .50 1.25
86 Alex Caruso .50 1.25
87 Kawhi Leonard 1.25 3.00
88 LeBron James 15.00 40.00
89 Blake Griffin .50 1.25
90 Jimmy Butler 1.00 2.50
91 Montrezl Harrell .40 1.00
92 Dillon Brooks .40 1.00
93 Danilo Gallinari .40 1.00
94 Fred VanVleet .60 1.50
95 Steven Adams .40 1.00
96 Jonas Valanciunas .40 1.00
97 Pascal Siakam .75 2.00
98 Elfrid Payton .30 .75
99 Tim Hardaway Jr. .30 .75
100 James Harden 1.00 2.50
101 Nassir Little AU RC 5.00 12.00
102 Coby White AU RC 40.00 100.00
103 PJ Washington Jr. AU RC 25.00 60.00
104 Eric Paschall AU RC 4.00 10.00
105 Talen Horton-Tucker AU RC 5.00 12.00
106 Ja Morant AU RC 1,250.00 2,500.00
107 Keldon Johnson AU RC 40.00 100.00
108 Admiral Schofield AU RC 4.00 10.00
109 KZ Okpala AU RC EXCH 4.00 10.00
111 Nickeil Alexander-Walker AU RC 5.00 12.00
112 Cody Martin AU RC 5.00 12.00
113 RJ Barrett AU RC 75.00 200.00
114 Goga Bitadze AU RC 5.00 12.00
115 Ty Jerome AU RC 6.00 15.00
116 Jarrett Culver AU RC 3.00 8.00
117 Kendrick Nunn AU RC 5.00 12.00
118 Bol Bol AU RC 20.00 50.00
119 Luka Samanic AU RC 4.00 10.00
120 Cameron Johnson AU RC 30.00 80.00
121 Nicolas Claxton AU RC 15.00 40.00
122 De'Andre Hunter AU RC 25.00 60.00
123 Rui Hachimura AU RC 40.00 100.00
124 Grant Williams AU RC 12.00 30.00
125 Tyler Herro AU RC EXCH 150.00 400.00
126 Jaxson Hayes AU RC 12.00 30.00
127 Kevin Porter Jr. AU RC 6.00 15.00
128 Brandon Clarke AU RC 15.00 40.00
129 Matisse Thybulle AU RC EXCH 40.00 100.00
130 Carsen Edwards AU RC 4.00 10.00
131 Nicolo Melli AU RC 4.00 10.00
132 Dylan Windler AU RC 4.00 10.00
133 Sekou Doumbouya AU RC 3.00 8.00
134 Isaiah Roby AU RC 4.00 10.00
135 Zion Williamson AU RC 800.00 1,500.00
136 Jaylen Nowell AU RC 4.00 10.00
137 Kyle Guy AU RC 8.00 20.00
138 Bruno Fernando AU RC 4.00 10.00
139 Mfiondu Kabengele AU RC 4.00 10.00
140 Chuma Okeke AU RC 12.00 30.00

2019-20 Panini Contenders Optic Blue

*BLUE/99: 1.2X TO 3X BASIC
*BLUE AU/99: .5X TO 1.2X BASIC
*BLUE AU/35-75: .6X TO 1.5X BASIC
1-100 STATED PRINT RUN 99 SER.#'d SETS
AU PRINT RUN BTW 35-99 COPIES PER
EXCHANGE DEADLINE 3/23/2022
32 Stephen Curry/99 50.00 120.00
34 Luka Doncic/99 150.00 400.00
88 LeBron James/99 125.00 300.00
102 Coby White AU/35 300.00 600.00
103 PJ Washington Jr. AU/49 60.00 150.00
106 Ja Morant AU/99 2,000.00 4,000.00
107 Keldon Johnson AU/99 125.00 300.00
109 KZ Okpala AU/35 EXCH 40.00 100.00
118 Bol Bol AU/99 100.00 250.00
122 De'Andre Hunter AU/35 60.00 150.00
127 Kevin Porter Jr. AU/99 8.00 20.00
135 Zion Williamson AU/35 1,500.00 3,000.00

2019-20 Panini Contenders Optic Orange

*ORANGE/49: 1.5X TO 4X BASIC
*ORANGE AU/25: .75X TO 2X BASIC
1-100 PRINT RUN 49 SER.#'d SETS
AU PRINT RUN 25 SER.#'d SETS
EXCHANGE DEADLINE 3/23/2022
32 Stephen Curry/49 60.00 150.00
34 Luka Doncic/49 200.00 500.00
88 LeBron James/49 300.00 800.00
102 Coby White AU/25 500.00 1,000.00
103 PJ Washington Jr. AU/25 75.00 200.00
106 Ja Morant AU/25 5,000.00 10,000.00
107 Keldon Johnson AU/25 200.00 500.00
109 KZ Okpala AU/25 EXCH 125.00 300.00
111 Nickeil Alexander-Walker AU/25 75.00 200.00
118 Bol Bol AU/25 150.00 400.00
122 De'Andre Hunter AU/25 75.00 200.00
124 Grant Williams AU/25 40.00 100.00
126 Jaxson Hayes AU/25 100.00 250.00
127 Kevin Porter Jr. AU/25 12.00 30.00
133 Sekou Doumbouya AU/25 6.00 15.00
135 Zion Williamson AU/25 4,000.00 8,000.00
137 Kyle Guy AU/25 25.00 60.00
139 Mfiondu Kabengele AU/25 30.00 80.00
140 Chuma Okeke AU/25 150.00 400.00

2019-20 Panini Contenders Optic Red

*RED: .6X TO 1.5X BASIC
*RED AU/99-149: .5X TO 1.2X BASIC
*RED AU/49-75: .6X TO 1.5X BASIC
AU PRINT RUN BTW 49-149 COPIES PER
EXCHANGE DEADLINE 3/23/2022
32 Stephen Curry 8.00 20.00
34 Luka Doncic 60.00 150.00
102 Coby White AU/49 300.00 600.00
103 PJ Washington Jr. AU/75 50.00 120.00
109 KZ Okpala AU/49 EXCH 30.00 80.00
122 De'Andre Hunter AU/49 60.00 150.00
127 Kevin Porter Jr. AU/149 8.00 20.00
135 Zion Williamson AU/49 1,250.00 2,500.00

2019-20 Panini Contenders Optic Silver

*SILVER: 1X TO 2.5X BASIC
32 Stephen Curry 15.00 40.00
34 Luka Doncic 20.00 50.00

2019-20 Panini Contenders Optic '82 Tribute Autographs

EXCHANGE DEADLINE 3/23/2022
*RED: .6X TO 1.5X BASIC
1 Damian Lillard 75.00 200.00
2 Allen Iverson 100.00 250.00
3 Anthony Davis 100.00 250.00
4 Charles Barkley 125.00 300.00
5 Kevin Garnett 125.00 300.00
6 Kevin Durant 125.00 300.00
7 Bill Russell 400.00 800.00
8 Stephen Curry 500.00 1,000.00
9 Dwyane Wade 100.00 250.00
10 Giannis Antetokounmpo 200.00 500.00

2019-20 Panini Contenders Optic All-Star Aspirations

*BLUE CRKD ICE: .6X TO 1.5X BASIC
*RED CRKD ICE: .6X TO 1.5X BASIC
1 Tim Duncan 5.00 12.00
2 Chris Webber 2.50 6.00
3 Allen Iverson 5.00 12.00
4 Charles Barkley 4.00 10.00
5 Scottie Pippen 5.00 12.00
6 Dwyane Wade 4.00 10.00
7 Kevin Garnett 5.00 12.00
8 Magic Johnson 6.00 15.00
9 Wilt Chamberlain 8.00 20.00
10 Anfernee Hardaway 5.00 12.00
11 Kevin Durant 6.00 15.00
12 Anthony Davis 5.00 12.00
13 Joel Embiid 4.00 10.00
14 Paul George 3.00 8.00
15 Kawhi Leonard 5.00 12.00
16 James Harden 4.00 10.00
17 Russell Westbrook 3.00 8.00
18 Giannis Antetokounmpo 10.00 25.00
19 Stephen Curry 15.00 40.00
20 LeBron James 15.00 40.00
21 Trae Young 5.00 12.00
22 Luka Doncic 12.00 30.00
23 Pascal Siakam 3.00 8.00
24 Donovan Mitchell 4.00 10.00
25 Jayson Tatum 8.00 20.00

2019-20 Panini Contenders Optic Front Row Seat

*BLUE CRKD ICE: .6X TO 1.5X BASIC
*RED CRKD ICE: .6X TO 1.5X BASIC
1 Jayson Tatum 8.00 20.00
2 Giannis Antetokounmpo 10.00 25.00
3 LeBron James 40.00 100.00
4 Anthony Davis 5.00 12.00
5 James Harden 4.00 10.00
6 Russell Westbrook 3.00 8.00
7 Paul George 3.00 8.00
8 Nikola Jokic 10.00 25.00
9 Trae Young 5.00 12.00
10 Luka Doncic 25.00 60.00
11 Kawhi Leonard 5.00 12.00
12 Ben Simmons 2.00 5.00
13 Joel Embiid 4.00 10.00
14 Kyrie Irving 4.00 10.00
15 Donovan Mitchell 4.00 10.00
16 Pascal Siakam 3.00 8.00
17 Bradley Beal 2.50 6.00
18 Jimmy Butler 4.00 10.00
19 Stephen Curry 15.00 40.00
20 Devin Booker .50 1.25

2019-20 Panini Contenders Optic Historic Picks

*BLUE CRKD ICE: .6X TO 1.5X BASIC
*RED CRKD ICE: .6X TO 1.5X BASIC
1 Zion WilliamsonLeBron James 500.00 1,000.00
2 Kevin DurantJa Morant 125.00 300.00
3 James HardenRJ Barrett 15.00 40.00
4 Russell Westbrook
Stephon Marbury 10.00 25.00
5 Charles Barkley
Kevin Garnett 15.00 40.00
6 Damian Lillard
Larry Bird 25.00 60.00
7 Jason Williams
Stephen Curry 30.00 80.00
8 Luka Doncic
Jayson Tatum 125.00 300.00
9 Rui Hachimura
Dirk Nowitzki 30.00 80.00
10 Paul George
Paul Pierce 10.00 25.00
11 Dwyane Wade
Scottie Pippen 20.00 50.00
12 Dennis Rodman
Pascal Siakam 15.00 40.00
13 Donovan Mitchell
Devin Booker 12.00 30.00
14 Kyrie Irving
Allen Iverson 20.00 50.00
15 Giannis Antetokounmpo
Kawhi Leonard 30.00 80.00
16 Anthony Davis
Chris Webber 15.00 40.00

2019-20 Panini Contenders Optic Historic Slams

*BLUE CRKD ICE: .6X TO 1.5X BASIC
*RED CRKD ICE: .6X TO 1.5X BASIC
1 Zach LaVine 10.00 25.00
2 Vince Carter 40.00 100.00
3 Aaron Gordon 8.00 20.00
4 Jason Richardson 6.00 15.00
5 Spud Webb 3.00 8.00
6 Dwight Howard 8.00 20.00
7 Dee Brown 2.00 5.00
8 Dominique Wilkins 5.00 12.00
9 Shawn Kemp 8.00 20.00
10 Isaiah Rider 2.50 6.00
11 Tracy McGrady 8.00 20.00
12 Andre Iguodala 2.50 6.00
13 DeMar DeRozan 4.00 10.00
14 Blake Griffin 6.00 15.00
15 Terrence Ross 3.00 8.00
16 Zach LaVine 10.00 25.00
17 Paul George 8.00 20.00
18 John Wall 4.00 10.00
19 Aaron Gordon 8.00 20.00
20 Donovan Mitchell 8.00 20.00

2019-20 Panini Contenders Optic Legendary Contenders Autographs

PRINT RUNS B/WN 49-125 COPIES PER
EXCHANGE DEADLINE 3/23/2022
1 Jason Kidd/49 15.00 40.00
2 Larry Johnson/125 12.00 30.00
3 Stephon Marbury/99 12.00 30.00
4 Avery Johnson/125 3.00 8.00
5 Calvin Murphy/125 5.00 12.00
6 Deron Williams/125 4.00 10.00
7 George McGinnis/125 8.00 20.00
8 Ralph Sampson/125 8.00 20.00
9 Oscar Robertson/49 40.00 100.00
10 Danny Manning/125 4.00 10.00
11 Jerry West/49 40.00 100.00
12 Louie Dampier/125 5.00 12.00
13 Gary Payton/99 10.00 25.00
14 Jason Richardson/125 8.00 20.00
15 Elvin Hayes/125 8.00 20.00
16 Doc Rivers/125 8.00 20.00
17 Danny Granger/125 3.00 8.00
18 Jason Terry/125 4.00 10.00
19 Magic Johnson/49 50.00 120.00
20 Joe Dumars/125 8.00 20.00
21 Dennis Rodman/99 50.00 120.00
22 Robert Parish/125 8.00 20.00
23 Derek Fisher/125 8.00 20.00
24 Shawn Kemp/125 25.00 60.00
25 Steve Francis/125 5.00 12.00
26 Rick Fox/125 4.00 10.00
27 Charles Oakley/125 4.00 10.00
28 Chauncey Billups/125 10.00 25.00
29 David Robinson/49 40.00 100.00
30 Gail Goodrich/125 10.00 25.00

2019-20 Panini Contenders Optic Lottery Ticket

*BLUE CRKD ICE: .6X TO 1.5X BASIC
*RED CRKD ICE: .6X TO 1.5X BASIC
1 Zion Williamson 30.00 80.00
2 Ja Morant 40.00 100.00
3 RJ Barrett 2.50 6.00
4 De'Andre Hunter 2.50 6.00
5 Darius Garland 8.00 20.00
6 Jarrett Culver .60 1.50
7 Coby White 2.00 5.00
8 Jaxson Hayes 1.00 2.50
9 Rui Hachimura 2.50 6.00
10 Cam Reddish 1.00 2.50
11 Cameron Johnson 1.50 4.00
12 PJ Washington Jr. 2.00 5.00
13 Tyler Herro 8.00 20.00
14 Romeo Langford .60 1.50

2019-20 Panini Contenders Optic NBA Ink

STATED PRINT RUN 125 SER.#'d SETS
EXCHANGE DEADLINE 3/23/2022
1 Andrew Wiggins 8.00 20.00
2 Markelle Fultz 8.00 20.00
3 D'Angelo Russell 12.00 30.00
4 Dwight Howard 25.00 60.00
5 Jrue Holiday 6.00 15.00
6 Al Horford 5.00 12.00
7 Buddy Hield 4.00 10.00
8 Danilo Gallinari 4.00 10.00
9 Eric Gordon 4.00 10.00
10 Brook Lopez 4.00 10.00
11 Julius Randle 6.00 15.00
12 Eric Bledsoe 4.00 10.00
13 JJ Redick 8.00 20.00
14 Reggie Jackson 4.00 10.00
15 Pascal Siakam 20.00 50.00
16 Elfrid Payton 3.00 8.00
17 Allonzo Trier 3.00 8.00
18 Otto Porter Jr. 3.00 8.00
19 Mo Bamba 4.00 10.00
20 Trevor Ariza 3.00 8.00
21 Ryan Anderson 3.00 8.00
22 Cody Zeller 3.00 8.00
23 Joe Harris 4.00 10.00
24 Terrence Ross 5.00 12.00
25 Bam Adebayo 20.00 50.00
26 Avery Bradley 3.00 8.00
27 Wesley Matthews 3.00 8.00
28 Montrezl Harrell 4.00 10.00
29 Patrick Beverley 4.00 10.00
30 Bogdan Bogdanovic 5.00 12.00

2019-20 Panini Contenders Optic Playing the Numbers Game

*BLUE CRKD ICE: .6X TO 1.5X BASIC
*RED CRKD ICE: .6X TO 1.5X BASIC
1 Damian Lillard 5.00 12.00
2 James Harden 4.00 10.00
3 Kyrie Irving 4.00 10.00
4 D'Angelo Russell 1.50 4.00
5 Giannis Antetokounmpo 10.00 25.00
6 Anthony Davis 5.00 12.00
7 Brandon Ingram 2.00 5.00
8 Zach LaVine 3.00 8.00
9 Trae Young 5.00 12.00
10 Bradley Beal 2.50 6.00
11 Paul George 3.00 8.00
12 Donovan Mitchell 4.00 10.00
13 Russell Westbrook 3.00 8.00
14 Pascal Siakam 3.00 8.00
15 Luka Doncic 12.00 30.00
16 LeBron James 12.00 30.00
17 Kawhi Leonard 5.00 12.00
18 Nikola Jokic 10.00 25.00
19 Anthony Davis 5.00 12.00
20 Giannis Antetokounmpo 10.00 25.00
21 Shai Gilgeous-Alexander 10.00 25.00
22 LeBron James 12.00 30.00
23 Trae Young 5.00 12.00
24 Luka Doncic 12.00 30.00
25 Ben Simmons 2.00 5.00
26 Giannis Antetokounmpo 10.00 25.00
27 Ja Morant 20.00 50.00
28 Zion Williamson 15.00 40.00
29 RJ Barrett 5.00 12.00
30 Anthony Davis 5.00 12.00

2019-20 Panini Contenders Optic Rookie Ticket Variation Autographs

EXCHANGE DEADLINE 3/23/2022
101 Nassir Little 5.00 12.00
102 Coby White 40.00 100.00
103 PJ Washington Jr. 25.00 60.00
104 Eric Paschall 4.00 10.00
105 Talen Horton-Tucker 5.00 12.00
106 Ja Morant 1,250.00 2,500.00
107 Keldon Johnson 40.00 100.00
108 Admiral Schofield 4.00 10.00
109 KZ Okpala EXCH 4.00 10.00
110 Cam Reddish 5.00 12.00
111 Nickeil Alexander-Walker 5.00 12.00
112 Cody Martin 5.00 12.00
113 RJ Barrett 75.00 200.00
114 Goga Bitadze 5.00 12.00
115 Ty Jerome 6.00 15.00
116 Jarrett Culver 3.00 8.00
117 Kendrick Nunn 5.00 12.00
118 Bol Bol 20.00 50.00
120 Cameron Johnson 30.00 80.00
121 Nicolas Claxton 15.00 40.00
122 De'Andre Hunter 25.00 60.00
123 Rui Hachimura 40.00 100.00
124 Grant Williams 12.00 30.00
125 Tyler Herro EXCH 150.00 400.00
126 Jaxson Hayes 12.00 30.00
127 Kevin Porter Jr. 6.00 15.00
128 Brandon Clarke 15.00 40.00
129 Matisse Thybulle EXCH 40.00 100.00
130 Carsen Edwards 4.00 10.00
131 Nicolo Melli 4.00 10.00
132 Dylan Windler 4.00 10.00
133 Sekou Doumbouya 3.00 8.00
134 Isaiah Roby 4.00 10.00
135 Zion Williamson 800.00 1,500.00
136 Jaylen Nowell 4.00 10.00
137 Kyle Guy 8.00 20.00
138 Bruno Fernando 4.00 10.00
139 Mfiondu Kabengele 4.00 10.00
140 Chuma Okeke 12.00 30.00

2019-20 Panini Contenders Optic Rookie Ticket Variation Autographs Blue

*BLUE/99: .5X TO 1.2X BASIC
*BLUE/35-75: .6X TO 1.5X BASIC
PRINT RUN BTW 35-99 COPIES PER
EXCHANGE DEADLINE 3/23/2022
102 Coby White 300.00 600.00
103 PJ Washington Jr. 60.00 150.00
106 Ja Morant 1,500.00 3,000.00
107 Keldon Johnson 125.00 300.00
109 KZ Okpala AU/35 EXCH 40.00 100.00
118 Bol Bol 100.00 250.00
122 De'Andre Hunter 60.00 150.00
127 Kevin Porter Jr. 8.00 20.00
135 Zion Williamson 2,500.00 5,000.00

2019-20 Panini Contenders Optic Rookie Ticket Variation Autographs Orange

*ORANGE: .75X TO 2X BASIC
STATED PRINT RUN 25 SER.#'d SETS
EXCHANGE DEADLINE 3/23/2022
102 Coby White 500.00 1,000.00
103 PJ Washington Jr. 75.00 200.00
106 Ja Morant 4,000.00 8,000.00
107 Keldon Johnson 200.00 500.00
109 KZ Okpala AU/25 EXCH 125.00 300.00
111 Nickeil Alexander-Walker 75.00 200.00
118 Bol Bol 150.00 400.00
122 De'Andre Hunter 75.00 200.00
124 Grant Williams 40.00 100.00
126 Jaxson Hayes 100.00 250.00
127 Kevin Porter Jr. 12.00 30.00
135 Zion Williamson 4,000.00 8,000.00
137 Kyle Guy 25.00 60.00
139 Mfiondu Kabengele 30.00 80.00
140 Chuma Okeke 150.00 400.00

2019-20 Panini Contenders Optic Rookie Ticket Variation Autographs Red

*RED/99-149: .5X TO 1.2X BASIC
*RED/49-75: .6X TO 1.5X BASIC
PRINT RUN BTW 49-149 COPIES PER
EXCHANGE DEADLINE 3/23/2022
102 Coby White 60.00 150.00
103 PJ Washington Jr. 40.00 100.00

2019-20 Panini Contenders Optic Sophomore Contenders Autographs

STATED PRINT RUN 125 SER.#'d SETS
EXCHANGE DEADLINE 3/23/2022
1 Landry Shamet 5.00 12.00
2 Collin Sexton 8.00 20.00
3 Shai Gilgeous-Alexander 125.00 300.00
4 Jalen Brunson 15.00 40.00
5 Troy Brown Jr. 4.00 10.00
6 Josh Okogie 5.00 12.00
7 Kevin Huerter 6.00 15.00
8 Anfernee Simons 10.00 25.00
9 Kevin Knox II 4.00 10.00
10 Bruce Brown 6.00 15.00
11 Mo Bamba 5.00 12.00
12 Devonte' Graham 5.00 12.00
13 Trae Young 125.00 300.00
14 Jaren Jackson Jr. 25.00 60.00
15 Wendell Carter Jr. 6.00 15.00

2019-20 Panini Contenders Optic Superstars

*BLUE CRKD ICE: .6X TO 1.5X BASIC
*RED CRKD ICE: .6X TO 1.5X BASIC
1 LeBron James 15.00 40.00
2 Anthony Davis 5.00 12.00
3 James Harden 6.00 15.00
4 Giannis Antetokounmpo 10.00 25.00
5 Luka Doncic 12.00 30.00
6 Trae Young 5.00 12.00
7 Kawhi Leonard 5.00 12.00
8 Jayson Tatum 8.00 20.00
9 Stephen Curry 15.00 40.00
10 Joel Embiid 10.00 25.00
11 Zion Williamson 40.00 100.00
12 Ja Morant 50.00 120.00
13 RJ Barrett 12.00 30.00
14 Rui Hachimura 5.00 12.00
15 Kendrick Nunn 2.00 5.00

2019-20 Panini Contenders Optic Uniformity

*BLUE CRKD ICE: .6X TO 1.5X BASIC
*RED CRKD ICE: .6X TO 1.5X BASIC
1 Kendrick Nunn 2.00 5.00
2 Rui Hachimura 12.00 30.00
3 RJ Barrett 20.00 50.00
4 Ja Morant 100.00 250.00
5 Zion Williamson 125.00 300.00
6 Draymond Green 2.50 6.00
7 Rudy Gobert 2.50 6.00
8 Andre Drummond 1.50 4.00
9 Shai Gilgeous-Alexander 10.00 25.00
10 Zach LaVine 3.00 8.00
11 Brandon Ingram 2.00 5.00
12 Trae Young 15.00 40.00
13 Jayson Tatum 25.00 60.00
14 Devin Booker 12.00 30.00
15 Chris Paul 4.00 10.00
16 Pascal Siakam 3.00 8.00
17 Donovan Mitchell 10.00 25.00
18 Luka Doncic 100.00 250.00
19 Ben Simmons 2.00 5.00
20 Russell Westbrook 3.00 8.00
21 Kemba Walker 1.50 4.00
22 Kyrie Irving 4.00 10.00
23 Jimmy Butler 8.00 20.00
24 Bradley Beal 2.50 6.00

25 Karl-Anthony Towns 3.00 8.00
26 Nikola Jokic 10.00 25.00
27 Damian Lillard 5.00 12.00
28 Paul George 3.00 8.00
29 Joel Embiid 4.00 10.00
30 James Harden 4.00 10.00
31 Anthony Davis 15.00 40.00
32 Giannis Antetokounmpo 20.00 50.00
33 Stephen Curry 20.00 50.00
34 Kawhi Leonard 12.00 30.00
35 LeBron James 100.00 250.00

2019-20 Panini Contenders Optic Up and Coming Autographs

STATED PRINT RUN 35-125 SER.#'d SETS
EXCHANGE DEADLINE 3/23/2022
1 Nassir Little/125 6.00 15.00
2 Daniel Gafford/125 8.00 20.00
3 PJ Washington Jr./125 15.00 40.00
4 Grant Williams/125 6.00 15.00
5 Talen Horton-Tucker/125 6.00 15.00
6 Jarrett Culver/125 4.00 10.00
7 Kendrick Nunn/125 6.00 15.00
8 Alen Smailagic/125 4.00 10.00
9 Kyle Guy/125 15.00 40.00
10 Cameron Johnson/125 20.00 50.00
11 Nickeil Alexander-Walker/125 6.00 15.00
12 Nicolo Melli/125 5.00 12.00
13 RJ Barrett/125 100.00 250.00
14 Isaiah Roby/125 5.00 12.00
15 Terance Mann/125 8.00 20.00
16 Keldon Johnson/125 20.00 50.00
17 Kevin Porter Jr./125 8.00 20.00
18 Bruno Fernando/125 5.00 12.00
19 Matisse Thybulle/125 25.00 60.00
20 Coby White/125 100.00 250.00
21 Nicolas Claxton/125 8.00 20.00
22 Goga Bitadze/125 6.00 15.00
23 Sekou Doumbouya/125 4.00 10.00
24 Ja Morant/125 300.00 600.00

2019-20 Panini Contenders Optic Winning Tickets

*BLUE CRKD ICE: .6X TO 1.5X BASIC
*RED CRKD ICE: .6X TO 1.5X BASIC
1 Kawhi Leonard 5.00 12.00
2 LeBron James 30.00 80.00
3 Robert Horry 1.50 4.00
4 Scottie Pippen 5.00 12.00
5 Shaquille O'Neal 8.00 20.00
6 Stephen Curry 12.00 30.00
7 Chris Bosh 2.50 6.00
8 Kevin Durant 6.00 15.00
9 Kyrie Irving 4.00 10.00
10 Kareem Abdul-Jabbar 6.00 15.00
11 Bill Russell 6.00 15.00
12 Dennis Rodman 5.00 12.00
13 Klay Thompson 5.00 12.00
14 Dirk Nowitzki 5.00 12.00
15 Kyle Lowry 2.00 5.00
16 Ray Allen 3.00 8.00
17 Magic Johnson 6.00 15.00
18 Hakeem Olajuwon 4.00 10.00
19 Tim Duncan 5.00 12.00
20 Dwyane Wade 4.00 10.00
21 Alonzo Mourning 3.00 8.00
22 Ron Harper 2.00 5.00
23 Robert Parish 2.50 6.00
24 Pascal Siakam 3.00 8.00
25 Kevin Garnett 5.00 12.00

2019-20 Panini Contenders Optic College Ticket Autographs

EXCHANGE DEADLINE 3/4/2021
*HYPER/20: .75X TO 2X BASIC
51 Zion Williamson 600.00 1,200.00
52 Ja Morant 150.00 400.00
53 RJ Barrett 125.00 300.00
54 Cam Reddish 5.00 12.00
56 Jarrett Culver 3.00 8.00
57 De'Andre Hunter 20.00 50.00
58 Coby White 20.00 50.00
59 Romeo Langford 3.00 8.00
60 Jaxson Hayes 12.00 30.00
61 Rui Hachimura 125.00 300.00
62 Nassir Little 12.00 30.00
63 Keldon Johnson 8.00 20.00
64 Bol Bol 15.00 40.00
65 PJ Washington Jr. 12.00 30.00
66 Kevin Porter Jr. 6.00 15.00
67 Talen Horton-Tucker 5.00 12.00
68 Cameron Johnson 10.00 25.00
69 Tyler Herro 25.00 60.00
70 Nickeil Alexander-Walker 12.00 30.00
71 Brandon Clarke 10.00 25.00
72 KZ Okpala 4.00 10.00
74 Eric Paschall 4.00 10.00
75 Grant Williams 10.00 25.00
76 Bruno Fernando 4.00 10.00
78 Admiral Schofield 10.00 25.00
79 Ty Jerome 6.00 15.00
80 Carsen Edwards 4.00 10.00

2020-21 Panini Contenders Optic

COMMON CARD (1-100) .30 .75
SEMISTARS .40 1.00
UNLISTED STARS .50 1.25
COMMON AU RC(101-140) 4.00 10.00
AU RC SEMIS 5.00 12.00
AU RC UNLISTED 6.00 15.00
EXCHANGE DEADLINE 6/01/2023
*RED: .75X TO 2X BASIC
*RED/149: .5X TO 1.2X BASIC
*RED WAVE (1-100): .75X TO 2X BASIC
*RED WAVE (101-139): .5X TO 1.2X BASIC
1 Darius Garland .75 2.00
2 Mike Conley .40 1.00
3 Norman Powell .40 1.00
4 Tyler Herro 1.00 2.50
5 Trae Young 1.25 3.00
6 Josh Jackson .30 .75
7 Jordan Clarkson .50 1.25
8 Malcolm Brogdon .50 1.25
9 Andrew Wiggins .60 1.50
10 Collin Sexton .50 1.25
11 Joel Embiid 1.25 3.00
12 Kevin Porter Jr. .40 1.00
13 Khris Middleton .60 1.50
14 Gordon Hayward .50 1.25
15 Zach LaVine .75 2.00
16 Deandre Ayton .50 1.25
17 Damian Lillard 1.25 3.00
18 Bradley Beal .60 1.50
19 Richaun Holmes .40 1.00
20 Stephen Curry 4.00 10.00
21 Brandon Ingram .60 1.50
22 Donovan Mitchell 1.00 2.50
23 Gary Trent Jr. .50 1.25
24 De'Andre Hunter .50 1.25
25 Rui Hachimura .60 1.50
26 Chris Paul 1.00 2.50
27 Derrick Rose .75 2.00
28 Buddy Hield .50 1.25
29 Caris LeVert .50 1.25
30 Jerami Grant .50 1.25
31 Nikola Vucevic .50 1.25
32 Lonzo Ball .60 1.50
33 Malik Beasley .40 1.00
34 Patrick Beverley .30 .75
35 Terry Rozier .50 1.25
36 Jimmy Butler 1.00 2.50
37 Devin Booker 1.25 3.00
38 D'Angelo Russell .50 1.25
39 Luguentz Dort .75 2.00
40 Chuma Okeke .50 1.25
41 Draymond Green .60 1.50
42 Kristaps Porzingis .60 1.50
43 Keldon Johnson .75 2.00
44 Coby White .60 1.50
45 Devonte' Graham .40 1.00
46 Markelle Fultz .40 1.00
47 Jaren Jackson Jr. .75 2.00
48 Christian Wood .40 1.00
49 Kevin Durant 2.00 5.00
50 Paul George .75 2.00
51 Julius Randle .50 1.25
52 Bam Adebayo .75 2.00
53 John Wall .60 1.50
54 Tim Hardaway Jr. .30 .75
55 Kyle Lowry .60 1.50
56 Ben Simmons .60 1.50
57 Rajon Rondo .50 1.25
58 Zion Williamson 1.50 4.00
59 CJ McCollum .50 1.25
60 Russell Westbrook 1.00 2.50
61 Rudy Gobert .60 1.50
62 Jarrett Allen .50 1.25
63 John Collins .50 1.25
64 Seth Curry .50 1.25
65 Jamal Murray .75 2.00
66 DeMar DeRozan .60 1.50
67 Karl-Anthony Towns .75 2.00
68 Domantas Sabonis .60 1.50
69 Hamidou Diallo .40 1.00
70 Tobias Harris .50 1.25
71 Kawhi Leonard 1.25 3.00
72 Evan Fournier .40 1.00
73 Kyrie Irving 1.00 2.50
74 Shai Gilgeous-Alexander 2.50 6.00
75 Ja Morant 1.50 4.00
76 Kemba Walker .50 1.25
77 Jrue Holiday .50 1.25
78 Blake Griffin .50 1.25
79 Andre Drummond .50 1.25
80 RJ Barrett .75 2.00
81 LeBron James 4.00 10.00
82 Victor Oladipo .40 1.00
83 Aaron Gordon .50 1.25
84 Jaylen Brown .75 2.00
85 Luka Doncic 3.00 8.00
86 Pascal Siakam .75 2.00
87 Jayson Tatum 2.00 5.00
88 De'Aaron Fox .75 2.00
89 Anthony Davis 1.25 3.00
90 Fred VanVleet .75 2.00
91 Darius Bazley .30 .75
92 Carmelo Anthony .75 2.00
93 Terrence Ross .40 1.00
94 James Harden 1.00 2.50
95 Dejounte Murray .50 1.25
96 Nikola Jokic 2.50 6.00
97 Michael Porter Jr. .60 1.50
98 Jonas Valanciunas .40 1.00
99 Giannis Antetokounmpo 2.50 6.00
100 Kyle Kuzma .60 1.50
101 Jaden McDaniels AU RC 15.00 40.00
102 Isaac Okoro AU RC 8.00 20.00
103 Xavier Tillman AU RC 6.00 15.00
104 Jordan Nwora AU RC 6.00 15.00
105 LaMelo Ball AU RC 600.00 1,200.00
106 Robert Woodard II AU RC 5.00 12.00
107 Nico Mannion AU RC 5.00 12.00
108 CJ Elleby AU RC 5.00 12.00
109 James Wiseman AU RC 6.00 15.00
110 Deni Avdija AU RC 12.00 30.00
111 Paul Reed AU RC 6.00 15.00
112 Precious Achiuwa AU RC 10.00 25.00
113 Saddiq Bey AU RC 40.00 100.00
114 Onyeka Okongwu AU RC 10.00 25.00
115 Cole Anthony AU RC 60.00 150.00
116 Theo Maledon AU RC 5.00 12.00
117 Killian Hayes AU RC 5.00 12.00
118 Obi Toppin AU RC 30.00 80.00
119 Aaron Nesmith AU RC 10.00 25.00
120 Tyrese Maxey AU RC 300.00 600.00
121 Kira Lewis Jr. AU RC 5.00 12.00
122 Devon Dotson AU RC 5.00 12.00
123 Jae'Sean Tate AU RC 6.00 15.00
124 Josh Green AU RC 10.00 25.00
125 Tyrese Haliburton AU RC 125.00 300.00
126 Desmond Bane AU RC 100.00 250.00
127 Zeke Nnaji AU RC 6.00 15.00
128 Immanuel Quickley AU RC 40.00 100.00
130 Devin Vassell AU RC 40.00 100.00
131 Cassius Stanley AU RC 5.00 12.00
132 Facundo Campazzo AU RC 6.00 15.00
133 Jay Scrubb AU RC 6.00 15.00
134 Isaiah Stewart AU RC 10.00 25.00
135 Malachi Flynn AU RC 5.00 12.00
136 RJ Hampton AU RC 5.00 12.00
137 Anthony Edwards AU RC 500.00 1,000.00
138 Ty-Shon Alexander AU RC 5.00 12.00
139 Tyrell Terry AU RC 4.00 10.00
140 Payton Pritchard AU RC 15.00 40.00

2020-21 Panini Contenders Optic Blue

*BLUE/99: 2X TO 5X BASIC
*BLUE AU/99: .75X TO 2X BASIC
1-100 STATED PRINT RUN 99 SER.#'d SETS
AU PRINT RUN BTW 49-99 COPIES PER
EXCHANGE DEADLINE 6/01/2023
20 Stephen Curry 40.00 100.00
75 Ja Morant 40.00 100.00
81 LeBron James 40.00 100.00
85 Luka Doncic 40.00 100.00

2020-21 Panini Contenders Optic Green Pulsar

*GREEN PULSAR: 4X TO 10X BASIC
STATED PRINT RUN 25 SER.#'d SETS
15 Zach LaVine 20.00 50.00
20 Stephen Curry 100.00 250.00
37 Devin Booker 20.00 50.00
49 Kevin Durant 40.00 100.00
75 Ja Morant 125.00 300.00
81 LeBron James 150.00 400.00
85 Luka Doncic 100.00 250.00
99 Giannis Antetokounmpo 60.00 150.00

2020-21 Panini Contenders Optic Orange

*ORANGE/49: 2.5X TO 6X BASIC
*ORANGE AU/25: 1.5X TO 4X BASIC
1-100 STATED PRINT RUN 49 SER.#'d SETS
AU PRINT RUN 25 COPIES PER
EXCHANGE DEADLINE 6/01/2023
20 Stephen Curry 50.00 120.00
75 Ja Morant 50.00 120.00
81 LeBron James 60.00 150.00
85 Luka Doncic 50.00 120.00
105 LaMelo Ball AU 2,500.00 5,000.00

2020-21 Panini Contenders Optic Silver

*SILVER: 1.25X TO 3X BASIC
20 Stephen Curry 15.00 40.00
75 Ja Morant 15.00 40.00
81 LeBron James 25.00 60.00
85 Luka Doncic 20.00 50.00

2020-21 Panini Contenders Optic '83 Tribute Autographs

*RED/25: .6X TO 1.5X BASIC
*BLUE/20: .6X TO 1.5X BASIC
1 Luka Doncic 500.00 1,000.00
2 Bill Russell 500.00 1,000.00
3 Kareem Abdul-Jabbar 200.00 500.00
4 Kevin Garnett 125.00 300.00
5 Shaquille O'Neal 200.00 500.00
6 John Stockton 50.00 120.00
7 Ja Morant 300.00 600.00
8 Dwyane Wade 100.00 250.00
9 Allen Iverson 100.00 250.00
10 Oscar Robertson 75.00 200.00

2020-21 Panini Contenders Optic All-Star Aspirations

COMMON CARD 1.00 2.50
SEMISTARS 1.25 3.00
UNLISTED STARS 1.50 4.00
*BLUE CRKD ICE: .6X TO 1.5X BASIC
*RED CRKD ICE: .6X TO 1.5X BASIC
1 LeBron James 12.00 30.00
2 Kevin Durant 6.00 15.00
3 Giannis Antetokounmpo 8.00 20.00
4 Luka Doncic 10.00 25.00
5 Stephen Curry 12.00 30.00
6 Chris Paul 3.00 8.00
7 Damian Lillard 4.00 10.00
8 Anthony Davis 4.00 10.00
9 Ben Simmons 1.50 4.00
10 Jayson Tatum 6.00 15.00
11 Donovan Mitchell 3.00 8.00
12 Bradley Beal 2.00 5.00
13 James Harden 3.00 8.00
14 Zion Williamson 5.00 12.00
15 Julius Randle 1.50 4.00
16 Allen Iverson 4.00 10.00
17 Dirk Nowitzki 4.00 10.00
18 Vince Carter 3.00 8.00
19 Karl Malone 3.00 8.00
20 Larry Bird 6.00 15.00
21 Shaquille O'Neal 6.00 15.00
22 Dwyane Wade 3.00 8.00
23 Paul Pierce 2.50 6.00
24 Kevin Garnett 4.00 10.00
25 Tracy McGrady 2.50 6.00

2020-21 Panini Contenders Optic Hoop Dreams

COMMON CARD 1.00 2.50
SEMISTARS 1.25 3.00
UNLISTED STARS 1.50 4.00
*BLUE CRKD ICE: .6X TO 1.5X BASIC
*RED CRKD ICE: .6X TO 1.5X BASIC
1 RJ Hampton 1.25 3.00
2 Jae'Sean Tate 1.50 4.00
3 Immanuel Quickley 3.00 8.00
4 Aleksej Pokusevski 1.50 4.00
5 Isaiah Stewart 2.50 6.00
6 Tyrese Haliburton 10.00 25.00
7 Desmond Bane 10.00 25.00
8 Patrick Williams 3.00 8.00
9 Precious Achiuwa 2.50 6.00
10 James Wiseman 1.50 4.00
11 Saddiq Bey 2.50 6.00
12 Devin Vassell 4.00 10.00
13 Kenyon Martin Jr. 2.00 5.00
14 Payton Pritchard 4.00 10.00
15 Facundo Campazzo 5.00 12.00
16 Deni Avdija 3.00 8.00
17 Theo Maledon 1.25 3.00
18 Anthony Edwards 30.00 80.00
19 Tyrese Maxey 10.00 25.00
20 Cole Anthony 10.00 25.00
21 LaMelo Ball 50.00 120.00
22 Obi Toppin 2.50 6.00
23 Isaac Okoro 2.00 5.00
24 Onyeka Okongwu 2.50 6.00
25 Malachi Flynn 1.25 3.00

2020-21 Panini Contenders Optic Legendary Contenders Autographs

COMPLETE SET (35)
PRINT RUNS B/WN 49-149 COPIES PER
EXCHANGE DEADLINE 3/23/2022
*ORANGE/25: .6X TO 1.5X BASIC
1 Rick Fox/149 5.00 12.00
2 Rick Mahorn/149 5.00 12.00
3 Juwan Howard/149 5.00 12.00
4 Quentin Richardson/149 4.00 10.00
5 Jerry West/99 30.00 80.00
6 Kenny Sky Walker/149 5.00 12.00
7 Charles Oakley/149 6.00 15.00
8 Maurice Cheeks/149 6.00 15.00
9 Dee Brown/149 5.00 12.00
10 Mark Price/99 6.00 15.00
11 Josh Howard/149 5.00 12.00
12 Harold Miner/149 5.00 12.00
13 Dennis Rodman/99 40.00 100.00
14 Lamar Odom/149 6.00 15.00
15 Rasheed Wallace/99 40.00 100.00
16 Sam Perkins/149 5.00 12.00
17 Dikembe Mutombo/99 15.00 40.00
18 Calvin Murphy/149 6.00 15.00
19 James Worthy/99 15.00 40.00
20 Elvin Hayes/99 8.00 20.00
21 Anfernee Hardaway/99 60.00 150.00
22 Carlos Boozer/149 5.00 12.00
23 Wang Zhi-zhi/99 15.00 40.00
24 Slick Watts/149 5.00 12.00
25 Kurt Rambis/149 5.00 12.00
26 Jason Williams/99 30.00 80.00
27 David Robinson/49 30.00 80.00
28 Stephen Jackson/99 5.00 12.00
29 Jason Richardson/149 6.00 15.00
30 Chris Mullin/99 8.00 20.00
31 Kenny Smith/149 5.00 12.00
32 Toni Kukoc/99 12.00 30.00
33 Ben Wallace/99 30.00 80.00
34 Danny Manning/149 5.00 12.00
35 Gheorghe Muresan/149 5.00 12.00

2020-21 Panini Contenders Optic Lottery Ticket

COMMON CARD .60 1.50
SEMISTARS .75 2.00
UNLISTED STARS 1.00 2.50
*BLUE CRKD ICE: .6X TO 1.5X BASIC
*RED CRKD ICE: .6X TO 1.5X BASIC
1 Anthony Edwards 30.00 80.00
2 James Wiseman 1.00 2.50
3 LaMelo Ball 50.00 120.00
4 Patrick Williams 2.00 5.00
5 Isaac Okoro 1.25 3.00
6 Onyeka Okongwu 1.50 4.00
7 Killian Hayes .75 2.00
8 Obi Toppin 1.50 4.00
9 Deni Avdija 2.00 5.00
10 Jalen Smith 1.50 4.00
11 Devin Vassell 2.50 6.00
12 Tyrese Haliburton 8.00 20.00
13 Kira Lewis Jr. .75 2.00
14 Aaron Nesmith 1.50 4.00

2020-21 Panini Contenders Optic Perennial Contenders Autographs

COMMON CARD 4.00 10.00
SEMISTARS 5.00 12.00
UNLISTED STARS 6.00 15.00
PRINT RUNS B/WN 49-99 COPIES PER
EXCHANGE DEADLINE 3/23/2022
*ORANGE/25: .6X TO 1.5X BASIC
1 Latrell Sprewell/99 8.00 20.00
2 Gordon Hayward/99 6.00 15.00
3 Michael Cooper/99 5.00 12.00
4 Jalen Brunson/99 10.00 25.00
5 Arvydas Sabonis/99 12.00 30.00
6 Jason Williams/99 30.00 80.00
7 Collin Sexton/99 12.00 30.00
8 Andrea Bargnani/99 4.00 10.00
9 Juwan Howard/99 5.00 12.00
10 Ben McLemore/99 4.00 10.00
11 Clint Capela/99 5.00 12.00
12 Glen Rice/99 5.00 12.00
13 Ja Morant/49 300.00 600.00
14 Lonnie Walker IV/99 8.00 20.00
15 Bernard King/99 8.00 20.00
16 Peja Stojakovic/99 6.00 15.00
17 Luka Doncic/49 500.00 1,000.00
18 Buddy Hield/99 6.00 15.00
19 T.J. Warren/99 5.00 12.00
20 Jerry West/49 30.00 80.00
21 J.J. Barea/99 8.00 20.00
22 Nick Van Exel/99 12.00 30.00
23 Larry Bird/49 100.00 250.00
24 Anthony Davis/49 75.00 200.00
25 Joe Harris/99 5.00 12.00
26 Julius Randle/99 10.00 25.00
27 Jamaal Wilkes/99 6.00 15.00
28 Kevin McHale/99 12.00 30.00
29 Derrick White/99 6.00 15.00
30 Pat Riley/49 12.00 30.00

2020-21 Panini Contenders Optic Pick n Roll

COMMON CARD .75 2.00
SEMISTARS 1.00 2.50
UNLISTED STARS 1.25 3.00
*BLUE CRKD ICE: .6X TO 1.5X BASIC
*RED CRKD ICE: .6X TO 1.5X BASIC
1 K.Abdul-Jabbar/M.Johnson 5.00 12.00
2 J.Stockton/K.Malone 2.50 6.00
3 T.Parker/T.Duncan 3.00 8.00
4 S.Nash/A.Stoudemire 2.50 6.00
5 D.Nowitzki/J.Terry 3.00 8.00
6 J.Murray/N.Jokic 6.00 15.00
7 D.Wade/L.James 10.00 25.00
8 D.Mitchell/R.Gobert 2.50 6.00
9 Z.Williamson/L.Ball 4.00 10.00
10 K.Durant/K.Irving 5.00 12.00
11 B.Griffin/C.Paul 2.50 6.00
12 L.Doncic/K.Porzingis 8.00 20.00
13 C.Capela/T.Young 3.00 8.00
14 C.Anthony/D.Lillard 3.00 8.00
15 R.Rondo/K.Garnett 3.00 8.00
16 J.Jackson Jr./J.Morant 4.00 10.00
17 S.Curry/K.Durant 10.00 25.00
18 A.Davis/L.James 10.00 25.00
19 J.Embiid/B.Simmons 3.00 8.00
20 N.Vucevic/Z.LaVine 2.00 5.00

2020-21 Panini Contenders Optic Playing the Numbers Game

COMMON CARD 1.25 3.00
SEMISTARS 1.50 4.00
UNLISTED STARS 2.00 5.00
*BLUE CRKD ICE: .6X TO 1.5X BASIC
*RED CRKD ICE: .6X TO 1.5X BASIC
1 Jayson Tatum 8.00 20.00
2 Stephen Curry 15.00 40.00
3 LeBron James 15.00 40.00
4 Kevin Durant 8.00 20.00
5 Zach LaVine 3.00 8.00
6 Joel Embiid 5.00 12.00
7 Nikola Jokic 10.00 25.00
8 Bradley Beal 2.50 6.00
9 Fred VanVleet 3.00 8.00
10 Damian Lillard 5.00 12.00
11 Jamal Murray 3.00 8.00
12 Giannis Antetokounmpo 10.00 25.00
13 Kevin Porter Jr. 1.50 4.00
14 Luka Doncic 12.00 30.00
15 Zion Williamson 6.00 15.00
16 Ja Morant 6.00 15.00
17 Russell Westbrook 4.00 10.00
18 LaMelo Ball 20.00 50.00
19 Anthony Edwards 12.00 30.00
20 Isaiah Stewart 3.00 8.00
21 Tyrese Maxey 12.00 30.00
22 Rudy Gobert 2.50 6.00
23 Chris Paul 4.00 10.00
24 Devin Booker 5.00 12.00
25 James Harden 4.00 10.00
26 Julius Randle 2.00 5.00
27 Anthony Davis 5.00 12.00
28 Luka Doncic 12.00 30.00
29 Tyrese Haliburton 12.00 30.00
30 James Wiseman 2.00 5.00

2020-21 Panini Contenders Optic Sophomore Contenders Autographs

COMMON CARD 4.00 10.00
SEMISTARS 5.00 12.00
UNLISTED STARS 6.00 15.00
PRINT RUNS B/WN 99-149 COPIES PER
EXCHANGE DEADLINE 3/23/2022
*ORANGE/25: .6X TO 1.5X BASIC
1 Jarrett Culver/149 4.00 10.00
2 PJ Washington Jr./149 6.00 15.00
3 Ty Jerome/99 4.00 10.00
4 Chuma Okeke/99 6.00 15.00
5 Ja Morant/99 300.00 600.00
6 Daniel Gafford/99 5.00 12.00
7 Carsen Edwards/149 5.00 12.00
8 Brandon Clarke/149 6.00 15.00
9 Cam Reddish/99 8.00 20.00
10 Grant Williams/99 5.00 12.00
11 De'Andre Hunter/99 6.00 15.00
12 Nassir Little/149 5.00 12.00
13 Terence Davis II/149 6.00 15.00
14 Kendrick Nunn/99 5.00 12.00
15 RJ Barrett/99 25.00 60.00

2020-21 Panini Contenders Optic Suite Shots

COMMON CARD 1.25 3.00
SEMISTARS 1.50 4.00
UNLISTED STARS 2.00 5.00
*BLUE CRKD ICE: .6X TO 1.5X BASIC
*RED CRKD ICE: .6X TO 1.5X BASIC
1 Anthony Davis 5.00 12.00
2 Kawhi Leonard 5.00 12.00
3 Bradley Beal 2.50 6.00
4 Paul George 3.00 8.00
5 Stephen Curry 15.00 40.00
6 Giannis Antetokounmpo 10.00 25.00
7 Kevin Durant 8.00 20.00
8 Ben Simmons 2.00 5.00
9 Devin Booker 5.00 12.00
10 Ja Morant 6.00 15.00
11 Jayson Tatum 8.00 20.00
12 Trae Young 5.00 12.00
13 James Harden 4.00 10.00
14 Nikola Jokic 10.00 25.00
15 LeBron James 15.00 40.00
16 Joel Embiid 5.00 12.00
17 Donovan Mitchell 4.00 10.00
18 Damian Lillard 5.00 12.00
19 Zion Williamson 6.00 15.00
20 Russell Westbrook 4.00 10.00
21 Luka Doncic 12.00 30.00

2020-21 Panini Contenders Optic Superstars

COMMON CARD 1.25 3.00
SEMISTARS 1.50 4.00
UNLISTED STARS 2.00 5.00
*BLUE CRKD ICE: .6X TO 1.5X BASIC
*RED CRKD ICE: .6X TO 1.5X BASIC
1 Luka Doncic 12.00 30.00
2 LaMelo Ball 40.00 100.00
3 LeBron James 15.00 40.00
4 Stephen Curry 15.00 40.00
5 Damian Lillard 5.00 12.00
6 Kevin Durant 8.00 20.00
7 Anthony Edwards 25.00 60.00
8 Nikola Jokic 10.00 25.00
9 Zion Williamson 6.00 15.00
10 Giannis Antetokounmpo 10.00 25.00

2020-21 Panini Contenders Optic Team Tandems

COMMON CARD 1.25 3.00
SEMISTARS 1.50 4.00
UNLISTED STARS 2.00 5.00
*BLUE CRKD ICE: .6X TO 1.5X BASIC
*RED CRKD ICE: .6X TO 1.5X BASIC
1 A.Davis/L.James 15.00 40.00
2 K.Porzingis/L.Doncic 12.00 30.00
3 J.Harden/K.Durant 8.00 20.00
4 C.Paul/D.Booker 5.00 12.00
5 J.Brown/J.Tatum 8.00 20.00
6 B.Adebayo/J.Butler 4.00 10.00
7 N.Vucevic/Z.LaVine 3.00 8.00
8 C.McCollum/D.Lillard 5.00 12.00
9 R.Barrett/J.Randle 3.00 8.00
10 B.Beal/R.Westbrook 4.00 10.00
11 P.George/K.Leonard 5.00 12.00
12 D.Mitchell/R.Gobert 4.00 10.00
13 Z.Williamson/B.Ingram 6.00 15.00
14 B.Simmons/J.Embiid 5.00 12.00
15 J.Murray/N.Jokic 10.00 25.00
16 K.Middleton/G.Antetokounmpo 10.00 25.00
17 S.Curry/J.Wiseman 15.00 40.00
18 A.Edwards/K.Towns 15.00 40.00
19 D.Fox/T.Haliburton 12.00 30.00
20 L.Ball/T.Rozier 12.00 30.00

2020-21 Panini Contenders Optic Uniformity

COMMON CARD 1.25 3.00
SEMISTARS 1.50 4.00
UNLISTED STARS 2.00 5.00
*BLUE CRKD ICE: .6X TO 1.5X BASIC
*RED CRKD ICE: .6X TO 1.5X BASIC
1 Zion Williamson 6.00 15.00
2 Stephen Curry 15.00 40.00
3 Ja Morant 20.00 50.00
4 Luka Doncic 15.00 40.00
5 Giannis Antetokounmpo 10.00 25.00
6 Damian Lillard 5.00 12.00
7 Jayson Tatum 8.00 20.00
8 Julius Randle 2.00 5.00
9 Russell Westbrook 4.00 10.00
10 LeBron James 20.00 50.00
11 Kawhi Leonard 5.00 12.00
12 Nikola Jokic 10.00 25.00
13 Donovan Mitchell 4.00 10.00
14 Zach LaVine 3.00 8.00
15 Jimmy Butler 4.00 10.00
16 Trae Young 5.00 12.00
17 Chris Paul 4.00 10.00
18 Pascal Siakam 3.00 8.00
19 Bradley Beal 2.50 6.00
20 DeMar DeRozan 2.50 6.00
21 Ben Simmons 2.00 5.00
22 James Harden 4.00 10.00
23 Anthony Davis 5.00 12.00
24 Joel Embiid 5.00 12.00
25 Kevin Durant 8.00 20.00
26 Aleksej Pokusevski 2.00 5.00
27 Immanuel Quickley 4.00 10.00
28 Isaac Okoro 2.50 6.00
29 Jae'Sean Tate 2.00 5.00
30 James Wiseman 2.00 5.00
31 LaMelo Ball 50.00 120.00
32 Anthony Edwards 25.00 60.00
33 Tyrese Haliburton 12.00 30.00
34 Cole Anthony 4.00 10.00
35 Saddiq Bey 3.00 8.00

2020-21 Panini Contenders Optic Up and Coming Autographs

COMMON CARD 4.00 10.00
SEMISTARS 5.00 12.00
UNLISTED STARS 6.00 15.00
PRINT RUN 99 COPIES PER
EXCHANGE DEADLINE 3/23/2022
*ORANGE/25: .6X TO 1.5X BASIC
1 Jae'Sean Tate 25.00 60.00
2 Facundo Campazzo 6.00 15.00
3 Nathan Knight 5.00 12.00
4 Patrick Williams 12.00 30.00
5 LaMelo Ball 500.00 1,000.00
6 Mychal Mulder 5.00 12.00
7 Isaiah Joe 6.00 15.00
8 Onyeka Okongwu 10.00 25.00
9 James Wiseman 6.00 15.00
10 Moses Brown 4.00 10.00
11 Mason Jones 4.00 10.00
12 Saben Lee 5.00 12.00
13 Markus Howard 6.00 15.00
14 Deni Avdija 12.00 30.00
15 Freddie Gillespie 5.00 12.00
16 Trent Forrest 6.00 15.00
17 Mamadi Diakite 5.00 12.00
18 Anthony Edwards 300.00 600.00
19 Gabe Vincent 10.00 25.00
20 Lamar Stevens 6.00 15.00

2020-21 Panini Contenders Optic Variations

COMMON CARD 4.00 10.00
SEMISTARS 5.00 12.00
UNLISTED STARS 6.00 15.00
EXCHANGE DEADLINE 6/01/2023
101 Jaden McDaniels AU 30.00 80.00
102 Isaac Okoro AU 30.00 80.00
103 Xavier Tillman AU 6.00 15.00
104 Jordan Nwora AU 20.00 50.00
105 LaMelo Ball AU 600.00 1,200.00
106 Robert Woodard II AU 5.00 12.00
107 Nico Mannion AU 5.00 12.00
108 CJ Elleby AU 5.00 12.00
109 James Wiseman AU 6.00 15.00
110 Deni Avdija AU 25.00 60.00
111 Paul Reed AU 6.00 15.00
112 Precious Achiuwa AU 10.00 25.00
113 Saddiq Bey AU 40.00 100.00
114 Onyeka Okongwu AU 10.00 25.00
115 Cole Anthony AU 60.00 150.00
116 Theo Maledon AU 12.00 30.00
117 Killian Hayes AU 5.00 12.00
118 Obi Toppin AU 30.00 80.00
119 Aaron Nesmith AU 10.00 25.00
120 Tyrese Maxey AU 125.00 300.00
121 Kira Lewis Jr. AU 5.00 12.00
122 Devon Dotson AU 5.00 12.00
123 Jae'Sean Tate AU 25.00 60.00
124 Josh Green AU 10.00 25.00
125 Tyrese Haliburton AU 125.00 300.00
126 Desmond Bane AU 60.00 150.00
127 Zeke Nnaji AU 6.00 15.00
129 Immanuel Quickley AU 40.00 100.00
130 Devin Vassell AU 40.00 100.00
131 Cassius Stanley AU 5.00 12.00
132 Facundo Campazzo AU 6.00 15.00
133 Jay Scrubb AU 6.00 15.00
134 Isaiah Stewart AU 10.00 25.00
135 Malachi Flynn AU 5.00 12.00
136 RJ Hampton AU 5.00 12.00
137 Anthony Edwards AU 800.00 1,500.00
138 Ty-Shon Alexander AU 5.00 12.00
139 Tyrell Terry AU 4.00 10.00
140 Payton Pritchard AU 30.00 80.00

2020-21 Panini Contenders Optic Variations Blue

*BLUE VAR: 1.25X TO 3X BASIC
PRINT RUN BTW 35-49 COPIES PER
EXCHANGE DEADLINE 6/01/2023
105 LaMelo Ball AU/35 2,000.00 4,000.00

2020-21 Panini Contenders Optic Variations Orange

*ORANGE VAR: 1.5X TO 4X BASIC
PRINT RUN 25 COPIES PER
EXCHANGE DEADLINE 6/01/2023
105 LaMelo Ball AU 2,500.00 5,000.00

2020-21 Panini Contenders Optic Variations Red

*RED VAR: .75X TO 2X BASIC
PRINT RUN BTW 49-99 COPIES PER
EXCHANGE DEADLINE 6/01/2023
105 LaMelo Ball AU/49 1,250.00 2,500.00

2020-21 Panini Contenders Optic Variations Red Wave

*RED WAVE VAR: .6X TO 1.5X BASIC
105 LaMelo Ball AU 800.00 1,500.00

2020-21 Panini Contenders Optic Veteran Ticket Autographs

EXCHANGE DEADLINE 6/01/2023
*RED/25: .6X TO 1.5X BASIC
1 Ja Morant 300.00 600.00
2 Karl-Anthony Towns 50.00 120.00
3 Nikola Jokic 200.00 500.00
4 Allen Iverson 100.00 250.00
5 Anthony Davis 100.00 250.00
6 Anfernee Hardaway 125.00 300.00
7 Karl Malone 50.00 120.00
8 Jayson Tatum 125.00 300.00
9 Dwyane Wade 100.00 250.00
10 Luka Doncic 500.00 1,000.00

2020-21 Panini Contenders Optic Veteran Ticket Autographs Blue

*BLUE: .6X TO 1.5X BASIC
PRINT RUN 20 SER.#'d SETS
EXCHANGE DEADLINE 6/01/2023
1 Ja Morant 500.00 1,000.00

2021-22 Panini Contenders Optic Gold Rush

COMPLETE SET (5)
1 Stephen Curry 75.00 200.00
2 Luka Doncic 50.00 120.00
3 Jayson Tatum 40.00 100.00
4 Ja Morant 30.00 80.00
5 LeBron James 75.00 200.00

2021-22 Panini Contenders Optic '84 Tribute Autographs

COMPLETE SET (10)
*RED WAVE: .4X TO 1X BASIC
*RED/35: .5X TO 1.2X BASIC
*BLUE/25: .6X TO 1.5X BASIC
1 Kevin Garnett 100.00 250.00
2 Dwyane Wade 75.00 200.00
3 Allen Iverson 100.00 250.00
4 Zion Williamson 200.00 500.00
5 Charles Barkley 100.00 250.00
6 Stephen Curry 500.00 1,000.00
7 Luka Doncic 500.00 1,000.00
8 Larry Bird 100.00 250.00
9 Dirk Nowitzki 100.00 250.00
10 Karl Malone 60.00 150.00

2021-22 Panini Contenders Optic All Star Aspirations

COMPLETE SET (25)
*RED CRACKED ICE: .6X TO 1.5X BASIC
*BLUE CRACKED ICE/75: 2.5X TO 6X BASIC
1 LeBron James 6.00 15.00
2 Chris Paul 1.50 4.00
3 Giannis Antetokounmpo 4.00 10.00
4 Joel Embiid 2.00 5.00
5 Ja Morant 2.50 6.00
6 Stephen Curry 5.00 12.00
7 DeMar DeRozan 1.00 2.50
8 Jayson Tatum 3.00 8.00
9 Luka Doncic 5.00 12.00
10 Nikola Jokic 4.00 10.00
11 Trae Young 2.00 5.00
12 LaMelo Ball 2.00 5.00
13 Devin Booker 2.00 5.00
14 Zach LaVine 1.25 3.00
15 Karl-Anthony Towns 1.25 3.00
16 Kevin Durant 2.50 6.00
17 Kyrie Irving 1.50 4.00
18 James Harden 1.50 4.00
19 Donovan Mitchell 1.50 4.00
20 Russell Westbrook 1.25 3.00
21 Klay Thompson 2.00 5.00
22 Damian Lillard 2.00 5.00
23 Paul George 1.25 3.00
24 Kawhi Leonard 2.00 5.00
25 Derrick Rose 1.25 3.00

2021-22 Panini Contenders Optic Legendary Contenders Autographs

COMPLETE SET (33)
PRINT RUNS B/WN 49-149 COPIES PER
*BLUE/49-75: .5X TO 1.25X BASIC
*ORANGE/25: .6X TO 1.5X BASIC
1 Bob McAdoo/149 8.00 20.00
2 Isiah Thomas/99 15.00 40.00
3 Rick Barry/149 8.00 20.00
4 Jerry West/99 25.00 60.00
5 Amar'e Stoudemire/149 6.00 15.00
6 Jason Williams/149 25.00 60.00
7 Arvydas Sabonis/149 8.00 20.00
8 Elvin Hayes/149 8.00 20.00
9 Tony Parker/149 15.00 40.00
10 Rick Fox/149 6.00 15.00
11 Karl Malone/75 40.00 100.00
12 John Stockton/99 40.00 100.00
13 Latrell Sprewell/149 6.00 15.00
14 Dennis Rodman/99 40.00 100.00
15 Hakeem Olajuwon/75 40.00 100.00
16 Bill Walton/149 15.00 40.00
17 Robert Horry/149 6.00 15.00

18 Nate Archibald/149 6.00 15.00
19 David Robinson/99 20.00 50.00
20 Robert Parish/149 8.00 20.00
22 Kevin Garnett/75 40.00 100.00
23 Clyde Drexler/75 20.00 50.00
24 Gary Payton/49 12.00 30.00
25 David Thompson/149 8.00 20.00
26 Jerry Lucas/149 8.00 20.00
27 Dell Curry/149 6.00 15.00
28 Stephen Jackson/149 5.00 12.00
29 Bill Laimbeer/149 6.00 15.00
30 Dino Radja/149 5.00 12.00
31 Tim Hardaway/149 8.00 20.00
32 Steve Kerr/149 8.00 20.00
33 Larry Bird/99 75.00 200.00
34 Derek Fisher/149 6.00 15.00

2021-22 Panini Contenders Optic Legendary Tandems

COMPLETE SET (20)
*RED CRACKED ICE: .6X TO 1.5X BASIC
*BLUE CRACKED ICE/75: 2X TO 5X BASIC
1 J.Stockton/K.Malone 1.50 4.00
2 L.James/D.Wade 6.00 15.00
3 K.McHale/L.Bird 2.50 6.00
4 M.Johnson/K.Abdul-Jabbar 2.50 6.00
5 W.Chamberlain/J.West 2.50 6.00
6 S.Curry/K.Thompson 5.00 12.00
7 T.Duncan/T.Parker 2.00 5.00
8 J.Williams/C.Webber 1.00 2.50
9 G.Payton/S.Kemp 1.25 3.00
10 C.Drexler/H.Olajuwon 1.50 4.00
11 A.Stoudemire/S.Nash 1.50 4.00
12 A.Hardaway/S.O'Neal 2.50 6.00
13 P.Pierce/K.Garnett 2.00 5.00
14 C.Barkley/K.Johnson 2.00 5.00
15 W.Reed/W.Frazier 1.00 2.50
16 J.Dumars/I.Thomas 1.25 3.00
17 A.Iverson/C.Anthony 2.00 5.00
18 R.Westbrook/K.Durant 2.50 6.00
19 J.Kidd/D.Nowitzki 2.00 5.00
20 T.McGrady/V.Carter 1.50 4.00

2021-22 Panini Contenders Optic Lottery Ticket

COMPLETE SET (14)
*RED CRACKED ICE: .5X TO 1.25X BASIC
*BLUE CRACKED ICE/75: 2X TO 5X BASIC
1 Cade Cunningham 6.00 15.00
2 Jalen Green 5.00 12.00
3 Evan Mobley 4.00 10.00
4 Scottie Barnes 3.00 8.00
5 Jalen Suggs 2.50 6.00
6 Josh Giddey 3.00 8.00
7 Jonathan Kuminga 3.00 8.00
8 Franz Wagner 3.00 8.00
9 Davion Mitchell 1.00 2.50
10 Ziaire Williams 1.25 3.00
11 James Bouknight .75 2.00
12 Joshua Primo .75 2.00
13 Chris Duarte .75 2.00
14 Moses Moody 2.00 5.00

2021-22 Panini Contenders Optic Perennial Contenders Autographs

COMPLETE SET (28)
*BLUE/49-75: .5X TO 1.25X BASIC
*ORANGE/25: .6X TO 1.5X BASIC
1 Marcus Smart/99 6.00 15.00
2 De'Aaron Fox/75 12.00 30.00
3 Rajon Rondo/99 8.00 20.00
4 Bradley Beal/75 8.00 20.00
5 Myles Turner/99 6.00 15.00
6 Robert Williams III/99 6.00 15.00
7 Dillon Brooks/99 6.00 15.00
8 Rudy Gobert/99 8.00 20.00
9 RJ Barrett/99 10.00 25.00
10 Wendell Carter Jr./99 6.00 15.00
11 Keldon Johnson/99 8.00 20.00
12 Michael Porter Jr./99 8.00 20.00
13 Spencer Dinwiddie/99 5.00 12.00
14 John Collins/99 6.00 15.00
15 CJ McCollum/75 5.00 12.00
18 Desmond Bane/99 12.00 30.00
19 Jalen Brunson/99 12.00 30.00
20 Jonas Valanciunas/99 5.00 12.00
21 Tyrese Haliburton/75 25.00 60.00
22 Karl-Anthony Towns/99 10.00 25.00
23 Anfernee Simons/99 10.00 25.00
24 Anthony Edwards/99 100.00 250.00
25 Duncan Robinson/99 5.00 12.00
26 Anthony Davis/75 40.00 100.00
27 Jrue Holiday/99 12.00 30.00
28 Clint Capela/99 6.00 15.00
29 Kevin Porter Jr./75 5.00 12.00
30 Jaren Jackson Jr./99 25.00 60.00

2021-22 Panini Contenders Optic Pick n Roll

COMPLETE SET (20)
*RED CRACKED ICE: .5X TO 1.25X BASIC
*BLUE CRACKED ICE/75: 2X TO 5X BASIC
1 J.Tatum/R.Williams III 4.00 10.00
2 G.Antetokounmpo/K.Middleton 5.00 12.00
3 T.Maxey/J.Embiid 2.50 6.00
4 A.Davis/L.James 8.00 20.00
5 S.Curry/J.Kuminga 6.00 15.00
6 D.Booker/D.Ayton 2.50 6.00
7 S.Dinwiddie/L.Doncic 6.00 15.00
8 K.Durant/K.Irving 3.00 8.00
9 B.Hyland/N.Jokic 5.00 12.00
10 K.Towns/A.Edwards 5.00 12.00
11 R.Gobert/D.Mitchell 2.00 5.00
12 J.Randle/R.Barrett 1.50 4.00
13 S.Gilgeous-Alexander/J.Giddey 5.00 12.00
14 B.Adebayo/T.Herro 1.50 4.00
15 J.Johnson/T.Young 3.00 8.00
16 Z.LaVine/D.DeRozan 1.50 4.00
17 J.Morant/J.Jackson Jr. 3.00 8.00
18 D.Sabonis/D.Mitchell 1.25 3.00
19 D.Garland/E.Mobley 4.00 10.00
20 P.Siakam/S.Barnes 3.00 8.00

2021-22 Panini Contenders Optic Playing the Numbers Game

COMPLETE SET (30)
*RED CRACKED ICE: .5X TO 1.25X BASIC
*BLUE CRACKED ICE/75: 2X TO 5X BASIC
1 Kyrie Irving 2.00 5.00
2 Karl-Anthony Towns 1.50 4.00
3 LeBron James 8.00 20.00
4 Trae Young 2.50 6.00
5 Jayson Tatum 4.00 10.00
6 Kevin Durant 3.00 8.00
7 Ja Morant 3.00 8.00
8 Luka Doncic 6.00 15.00
9 Giannis Antetokounmpo 5.00 12.00
10 Jaylen Brown 1.50 4.00
11 Stephen Curry 6.00 15.00
12 Joel Embiid 2.50 6.00
13 Devin Booker 2.50 6.00
14 Nikola Jokic 5.00 12.00
15 Anthony Edwards 5.00 12.00
16 RJ Barrett 1.50 4.00
17 Franz Wagner 3.00 8.00
18 Cade Cunningham 6.00 15.00
19 Jalen Green 5.00 12.00
20 Scottie Barnes 3.00 8.00
21 Josh Giddey 3.00 8.00
22 Chris Paul 2.00 5.00
23 Darius Garland 1.50 4.00
24 Tyrese Haliburton 2.00 5.00
25 Fred VanVleet 1.25 3.00
26 James Harden 2.00 5.00
27 Robert Williams III 1.00 2.50
28 Rudy Gobert 1.25 3.00
29 Evan Mobley 4.00 10.00
30 Paul George 1.50 4.00

2021-22 Panini Contenders Optic Sophomore Contenders Autographs

COMPLETE SET (13)
PRINT RUN B/WN 99-149 COPIES PER
*BLUE/49-75: .5X TO 1.25X BASIC
*ORANGE/25: .6X TO 1.5X BASIC
1 Desmond Bane/149 12.00 30.00
2 Anthony Edwards/99 100.00 250.00
3 Onyeka Okongwu/149 6.00 15.00
4 Jae'Sean Tate/149 6.00 15.00
5 RJ Hampton/149 4.00 10.00
7 Aleksej Pokusevski/149 5.00 12.00
9 Payton Pritchard/149 6.00 15.00
10 Kenyon Martin Jr./149 6.00 15.00
11 Jordan Nwora/149 6.00 15.00
12 Zeke Nnaji/149 5.00 12.00
13 Tyrese Haliburton/99 40.00 100.00
14 Kira Lewis Jr./149 4.00 10.00
15 Deni Avdija/149 6.00 15.00

2021-22 Panini Contenders Optic Suite Shots

COMPLETE SET (21)
*RED CRACKED ICE: .5X TO 1.25X BASIC
*BLUE CRACKED ICE/75: 2X TO 5X BASIC
1 Luka Doncic 6.00 15.00
2 Trae Young 2.50 6.00
3 Ja Morant 3.00 8.00
4 James Harden 2.00 5.00
5 Damian Lillard 2.50 6.00
6 Donovan Mitchell 2.00 5.00
7 LeBron James 8.00 20.00
8 Kevin Durant 3.00 8.00
9 Kyrie Irving 2.00 5.00
10 Jayson Tatum 4.00 10.00
11 Devin Booker 2.50 6.00
12 Bradley Beal 1.25 3.00
13 Paul George 1.50 4.00
14 Stephen Curry 6.00 15.00
15 Giannis Antetokounmpo 5.00 12.00
16 Nikola Jokic 5.00 12.00
17 Joel Embiid 2.50 6.00
18 Zach LaVine 1.50 4.00
19 RJ Barrett 1.50 4.00
20 Anthony Edwards 5.00 12.00
21 LaMelo Ball 2.50 6.00

2021-22 Panini Contenders Optic Superstars

COMPLETE SET (10)
*RED CRACKED ICE: .5X TO 1.25X BASIC
*BLUE CRACKED ICE/75: 2X TO 5X BASIC
1 Kevin Durant 3.00 8.00
2 LaMelo Ball 2.50 6.00
3 Anthony Edwards 5.00 12.00
4 Luka Doncic 6.00 15.00
5 LeBron James 8.00 20.00
6 Giannis Antetokounmpo 5.00 12.00
7 Nikola Jokic 5.00 12.00
8 Stephen Curry 6.00 15.00
9 Ja Morant 3.00 8.00
10 Jayson Tatum 4.00 10.00

2021-22 Panini Contenders Optic Uniformity

COMPLETE SET (30)
*RED CRACKED ICE: .5X TO 1.25X BASIC
*BLUE CRACKED ICE/75: 2X TO 5X BASIC
1 Trae Young 2.50 6.00
2 Giannis Antetokounmpo 5.00 12.00
3 Damian Lillard 2.50 6.00
4 Jayson Tatum 4.00 10.00
5 Luka Doncic 6.00 15.00
6 Ja Morant 3.00 8.00
7 Stephen Curry 6.00 15.00
8 LeBron James 8.00 20.00
9 RJ Barrett 1.50 4.00
10 Nikola Jokic 5.00 12.00
11 Donovan Mitchell 2.00 5.00
12 Zach LaVine 1.50 4.00
13 Jimmy Butler 1.50 4.00
14 Devin Booker 2.50 6.00
15 Bradley Beal 1.25 3.00
16 Kevin Durant 3.00 8.00
17 Kyrie Irving 2.00 5.00
18 Anthony Edwards 5.00 12.00
19 LaMelo Ball 2.50 6.00
20 Tyrese Haliburton 2.00 5.00
21 Shai Gilgeous-Alexander 5.00 12.00
22 Joel Embiid 2.50 6.00
23 Dejounte Murray 1.00 2.50
24 Chris Paul 2.00 5.00
25 Jonathan Kuminga 3.00 8.00
26 Jalen Green 5.00 12.00
27 Cade Cunningham 6.00 15.00
28 Evan Mobley 4.00 10.00
29 Scottie Barnes 3.00 8.00
30 Josh Giddey 3.00 8.00

2021-22 Panini Contenders Optic Veteran Ticket Autographs

COMPLETE SET (10)
*RED WAVE: .4X TO 1X BASIC
*RED/60: .5X TO 1.2X BASIC
*BLUE/25: .6X TO 1.5X BASIC
1 Karl-Anthony Towns 25.00 60.00
2 Anthony Davis 60.00 150.00
3 Zion Williamson 200.00 500.00
4 RJ Barrett 25.00 60.00
5 Ja Morant 300.00 600.00
6 Chris Paul 75.00 200.00
7 Luka Doncic 600.00 1,200.00
8 Jayson Tatum 200.00 500.00
9 Anthony Edwards 125.00 300.00
10 Stephen Curry 600.00 1,200.00

2017-18 Panini Cornerstones

1-100 STATED PRINT RUN 165 SER.#'d SETS
JSY AU RC STATED PRINT RUN B/WN 80-199 COPIES PER
EXCHANGE DEADLINE 01/25/2020
1 Kemba Walker/165 .75 2.00
2 D.J. Augustin/165 .60 1.50
3 J.J. Barea/165 .75 2.00
4 Damian Lillard/165 2.50 6.00
5 Andre Iguodala/165 .60 1.50
6 Kyle Lowry/165 1.00 2.50
7 Danilo Gallinari/165 .75 2.00
8 Goran Dragic/165 .75 2.00
9 Dennis Schroder/165 .75 2.00
10 Rajon Rondo/165 1.25 3.00
11 Nicolas Batum/165 .60 1.50
12 Evan Fournier/165 .75 2.00
13 Wesley Matthews/165 .60 1.50
14 CJ McCollum/165 1.00 2.50
15 Draymond Green/165 1.25 3.00
16 DeMar DeRozan/165 1.25 3.00
17 Avery Bradley/165 .60 1.50
18 Tyler Johnson/165 .60 1.50
19 Kent Bazemore/165 .60 1.50
20 Jrue Holiday/165 1.25 3.00
21 Michael Kidd-Gilchrist/165 .60 1.50
22 Mario Hezonja/165 .60 1.50
23 Dirk Nowitzki/165 2.50 6.00
24 Maurice Harkless/165 .60 1.50
25 Klay Thompson/165 2.50 6.00
26 Serge Ibaka/165 .75 2.00
27 Tobias Harris/165 .75 2.00
28 Josh Richardson/165 .75 2.00
29 Taurean Prince/165 .60 1.50
30 Nikola Mirotic/165 .60 1.50
31 Marvin Williams/165 .60 1.50
32 Aaron Gordon/165 1.00 2.50
33 Harrison Barnes/165 .75 2.00
34 Jusuf Nurkic/165 .75 2.00
35 Kevin Durant/165 4.00 10.00
36 Pascal Siakam/165 .75 2.00
37 Lou Williams/165 .75 2.00
38 Justise Winslow/165 .60 1.50
39 Ersan Ilyasova/165 .60 1.50
40 Anthony Davis/165 2.50 6.00
41 Dwight Howard/165 1.25 3.00
42 Nikola Vucevic/165 .75 2.00
43 Doug McDermott/165 .60 1.50
44 Al-Farouq Aminu/165 .60 1.50
45 Stephen Curry/165 8.00 20.00
46 Jonas Valanciunas/165 .75 2.00
47 DeAndre Jordan/165 .75 2.00
48 Hassan Whiteside/165 .75 2.00
49 Dewayne Dedmon/165 .60 1.50
50 DeMarcus Cousins/165 .75 2.00
51 Kris Dunn/165 .60 1.50
52 Ben Simmons/165 1.00 2.50
53 Jamal Murray/165 1.50 4.00
54 Buddy Hield/165 1.00 2.50
55 Chris Paul/165 1.50 4.00
56 Ricky Rubio/165 .75 2.00
57 Brandon Ingram/165 1.25 3.00
58 Eric Bledsoe/165 .75 2.00
59 Kyrie Irving/165 2.00 5.00
60 Courtney Lee/165 .60 1.50
61 Zach LaVine/165 1.50 4.00
62 JJ Redick/165 1.00 2.50
63 Gary Harris/165 .75 2.00
64 Vince Carter/165 2.00 5.00
65 James Harden/165 2.00 5.00
66 Jae Crowder/165 .75 2.00
67 Isaiah Thomas/165 .75 2.00
68 Malcolm Brogdon/165 .75 2.00
69 Jaylen Brown/165 2.50 6.00
70 Tim Hardaway Jr./165 .75 2.00
71 Robin Lopez/165 .60 1.50
72 Dario Saric/165 .75 2.00
73 Will Barton/165 .60 1.50
74 Zach Randolph/165 1.00 2.50
75 Trevor Ariza/165 .60 1.50
76 Joe Ingles/165 .75 2.00
77 Kentavious Caldwell-Pope/165 .75 2.00
78 Khris Middleton/165 1.25 3.00
79 Al Horford/165 1.00 2.50
80 Kristaps Porzingis/165 1.25 3.00
81 Denzel Valentine/165 .60 1.50
82 Robert Covington/165 .60 1.50
83 Wilson Chandler/165 .75 2.00
84 Willie Cauley-Stein/165 .60 1.50
85 Ryan Anderson/165 .60 1.50
86 Derrick Favors/165 .60 1.50
87 Julius Randle/165 1.00 2.50
88 Giannis Antetokounmpo/165 5.00 12.00
89 Gordon Hayward/165 .75 2.00
90 Michael Beasley/165 .60 1.50
91 Bobby Portis/165 .60 1.50
92 Joel Embiid/165 2.00 5.00
93 Nikola Jokic/165 6.00 15.00
94 Iman Shumpert/165 .60 1.50
95 Clint Capela/165 .75 2.00
96 Rudy Gobert/165 1.25 3.00
97 Brook Lopez/165 .75 2.00
98 Thon Maker/165 .60 1.50
99 Marcus Smart/165 1.00 2.50
100 Enes Kanter/165 .75 2.00
101 George Hill/165 .75 2.00
102 Devin Booker/165 2.50 6.00
103 Reggie Jackson/165 .75 2.00
104 Tony Parker/165 1.50 4.00
105 Domantas Sabonis/165 2.00 5.00
106 John Wall/165 1.25 3.00
107 Mike Conley/165 .75 2.00
108 Jeff Teague/165 .60 1.50
109 Spencer Dinwiddie/165 .75 2.00
110 Russell Westbrook/165 1.50 4.00
111 JR Smith/165 .75 2.00
112 Elfrid Payton/165 .60 1.50
113 Stanley Johnson/165 .60 1.50
114 Danny Green/165 .75 2.00
115 Victor Oladipo/165 .75 2.00
116 Bradley Beal/165 1.25 3.00
117 Tyreke Evans/165 .60 1.50
118 Jimmy Butler/165 1.50 4.00
119 D'Angelo Russell/165 .75 2.00
120 Paul George/165 1.50 4.00
121 Jordan Clarkson/165 1.00 2.50
122 TJ Warren/165 .75 2.00
123 Blake Griffin/165 1.00 2.50
124 Kawhi Leonard/165 2.50 6.00
125 Bojan Bogdanovic/165 .75 2.00
126 Otto Porter Jr./165 .75 2.00
127 Ben McLemore/165 .60 1.50
128 Andrew Wiggins/165 1.25 3.00
129 Allen Crabbe/165 .60 1.50
130 Carmelo Anthony/165 1.50 4.00
131 LeBron James/165 8.00 20.00
132 Dragan Bender/165 .60 1.50
133 Andre Drummond/165 .75 2.00
134 LaMarcus Aldridge/165 1.00 2.50
135 Thaddeus Young/165 .60 1.50
136 Markieff Morris/165 .60 1.50
137 JaMychal Green/165 .60 1.50
138 Taj Gibson/165 .60 1.50
139 DeMarre Carroll/165 .60 1.50
140 Jerami Grant/165 .75 2.00
141 Kevin Love/165 1.00 2.50
142 Tyson Chandler/165 .75 2.00
143 Ish Smith/165 .60 1.50
144 Pau Gasol/165 1.50 4.00
145 Myles Turner/165 .75 2.00
146 Marcin Gortat/165 .60 1.50
147 Marc Gasol/165 1.00 2.50
148 Karl-Anthony Towns/165 1.50 4.00
149 Rondae Hollis-Jefferson/165 .60 1.50
150 Steven Adams/165 .75 2.00
151 Markelle Fultz JSY AU/199 RC 12.00 30.00
152 Lonzo Ball JSY AU/199 RC 20.00 50.00
153 Jayson Tatum JSY AU/199 RC 400.00 800.00
154 Josh Jackson JSY AU/199 RC 6.00 15.00
155 De'Aaron Fox JSY AU/199 RC 30.00 80.00
156 Jonathan Isaac JSY AU/199 RC 12.00 30.00
157 Lauri Markkanen JSY AU/199 RC 40.00 100.00
158 Frank Ntilikina JSY AU/199 RC 6.00 15.00
159 Dennis Smith Jr. JSY AU/199 RC 6.00 15.00
160 Zach Collins JSY AU/199 RC 8.00 20.00
161 Malik Monk JSY AU/199 RC 20.00 50.00
162 Luke Kennard JSY AU/199 RC 10.00 25.00
163 Donovan Mitchell
JSY AU/199 RC 60.00 150.00
164 Bam Adebayo JSY AU/199 RC 20.00 50.00
165 Justin Jackson JSY AU/199 RC 5.00 12.00
166 Justin Patton JSY AU/199 RC 5.00 12.00
167 John Collins JSY AU/199 RC 12.00 30.00
168 Harry Giles JSY AU/199 RC 5.00 12.00
169 Kyle Kuzma JSY AU/199 RC 20.00 50.00
170 Jordan Bell JSY AU/199 RC 5.00 12.00
172 Milos Teodosic JSY AU/199 RC 6.00 15.00
173 Semi Ojeleye JSY AU/199 RC 6.00 15.00
174 TJ Leaf JSY AU/199 RC 5.00 12.00
175 OG Anunoby JSY AU/199 RC 25.00 60.00
176 Frank Mason III JSY AU/199 RC 5.00 12.00
177 Josh Hart JSY AU/80 RC 30.00 80.00
178 Jarrett Allen JSY AU/199 RC 12.00 30.00
179 D.J. Wilson JSY AU/199 RC 5.00 12.00
180 Wes Iwundu JSY AU/199 RC 5.00 12.00
181 Davon Reed JSY AU/199 RC 5.00 12.00
182 Tyler Lydon JSY AU/199 RC 5.00 12.00
183 Ike Anigbogu JSY AU/99 RC 5.00 12.00
184 Frank Jackson JSY AU/199 RC 5.00 12.00
185 Bogdan Bogdanovic
JSY AU/199 RC 12.00 30.00
186 Sterling Brown JSY AU/199 RC 5.00 12.00
187 Tyler Dorsey JSY AU/199 RC 5.00 12.00
188 Dwayne Bacon JSY AU/199 RC 5.00 12.00
189 Dillon Brooks JSY AU/199 RC 15.00 40.00

2017-18 Panini Cornerstones Crystal

*CRYSTAL 1-150: .5X TO 1.2X BASIC
*CRYSTAL 151-189: .5X TO 1.2X BASIC
1-150 STATED PRINT RUN 89 SER.#'d SETS
JSY AU STATED PRINT RUN B/WN 59-75 COPIES PER
EXCHANGE DEADLINE 01/25/2020

2017-18 Panini Cornerstones Quartz

*QUARTZ 1-150: .6X TO 1.5X BASIC
*QUARTZ 151-189: .6X TO 1.5X BASIC
1-150 STATED PRINT RUN 49 SER.#'d SETS
JSU AU STATED PRINT RUN B/WN 42-49 COPIES PER
EXCHANGE DEADLINE 01/25/2020

2017-18 Panini Cornerstones Building Blocks Memorabilia

1 Tony Bradley 1.50 4.00
2 Frank Mason III 1.50 4.00
3 Josh Hart 4.00 10.00
4 Jayson Tatum 20.00 50.00
5 Ante Zizic 2.00 5.00
6 Markelle Fultz 4.00 10.00
7 Dwayne Bacon 1.50 4.00
8 Jonathan Isaac 4.00 10.00
9 Justin Patton 1.50 4.00
10 Malik Monk 6.00 15.00
11 Tyler Dorsey 1.50 4.00
12 Harry Giles 1.50 4.00
13 Luke Kennard 3.00 8.00
14 Kyle Kuzma 6.00 15.00
15 Caleb Swanigan 1.50 4.00
16 De'Aaron Fox 12.00 30.00
17 Frank Jackson 1.50 4.00
18 Jordan Bell 1.50 4.00
19 Semi Ojeleye 2.00 5.00
20 OG Anunoby 8.00 20.00
21 Tyler Lydon 1.50 4.00
22 Jawun Evans 1.50 4.00
23 TJ Leaf 1.50 4.00
24 Lonzo Ball 6.00 15.00
25 D.J. Wilson 1.50 4.00
26 Dennis Smith Jr. 2.00 5.00
27 Ivan Rabb 1.50 4.00
28 Josh Jackson 2.00 5.00
29 Sindarius Thornwell 1.50 4.00
30 Terrance Ferguson 1.50 4.00
31 Wes Iwundu 1.50 4.00
32 John Collins 4.00 10.00
33 Zach Collins 2.50 6.00
34 Donovan Mitchell 15.00 40.00
35 Davon Reed 1.50 4.00
36 Frank Ntilikina 2.00 5.00
37 Jarrett Allen 4.00 10.00
38 Bam Adebayo 10.00 25.00
39 Sterling Brown 1.50 4.00
40 Derrick White 3.00 8.00

2017-18 Panini Cornerstones Downtown

DT1 Lonzo Ball 150.00 400.00
DT2 LeBron James 1,000.00 2,000.00
DT3 De'Aaron Fox 150.00 400.00
DT4 Reggie Miller 150.00 400.00
DT5 Kyrie Irving 100.00 250.00
DT6 Giannis Antetokounmpo 500.00 1,000.00
7 Anthony Davis 125.00 300.00
DT8 Shaquille O'Neal 400.00 800.00
DT9 Kevin Durant 400.00 800.00
DT10 Donovan Mitchell 400.00 800.00
DT11 Jayson Tatum 1,000.00 2,000.00
DT12 John Wall 60.00 150.00
DT13 Kawhi Leonard 200.00 500.00
DT14 Kristaps Porzingis 50.00 120.00
DT15 Josh Jackson 25.00 60.00
DT16 Markelle Fultz 50.00 125.00
DT17 Russell Westbrook 75.00 200.00
DT18 James Harden 75.00 200.00
DT19 Dennis Smith Jr. 25.00 60.00
DT20 Stephen Curry 800.00 1,500.00

2017-18 Panini Cornerstones Elusive Ink

PRINT RUNS 159 SER. #'d SETS
EXCHANGE DEADLINE 01/25/2020
*BRONZE/75: .5X TO 1.2X BASIC
*SILVER/49: .6X TO 1.5X BASIC
1 Tom Meschery 2.50 6.00
2 Jason Williams 12.00 30.00
3 Eric Snow 2.50 6.00
4 Gerald Henderson Sr. 2.50 6.00
5 Elden Campbell 2.50 6.00
6 Purvis Short 2.50 6.00
7 Ron Mercer 2.50 6.00
8 Felipe Lopez 2.50 6.00
9 Al Attles 4.00 10.00
10 Michael Adams 2.50 6.00

2017-18 Panini Cornerstones Fractured Memorabilia

1 Blake Griffin 2.50 6.00
2 Kemba Walker 2.00 5.00
3 Caris LeVert 2.50 6.00
4 Klay Thompson 6.00 15.00
5 DeAndre Jordan 2.00 5.00
6 Malcolm Brogdon 2.00 5.00
7 Doug McDermott 1.50 4.00
8 Eric Bledsoe 2.00 5.00
9 Al Jefferson 2.00 5.00
10 Jarell Martin 1.50 4.00
11 Brandon Ingram 3.00 8.00
12 Kevin Durant 10.00 25.00
13 Courtney Lee 1.50 4.00
14 Kyle Lowry 2.50 6.00
15 DeMar DeRozan 3.00 8.00
16 Marc Gasol 2.50 6.00
17 Draymond Green 3.00 8.00
18 Giannis Antetokounmpo 12.00 30.00
19 Andre Drummond 2.00 5.00
20 Jrue Holiday 3.00 8.00
21 Brook Lopez 2.00 5.00
22 Khris Middleton 3.00 8.00
23 Danilo Gallinari 2.00 5.00
24 LeBron James 20.00 50.00
25 Dirk Nowitzki 6.00 15.00
26 Michael Beasley 1.50 4.00
27 Dwight Howard 3.00 8.00
28 Harrison Barnes 2.00 5.00
29 Anthony Davis 6.00 15.00
30 Julius Randle 2.50 6.00

2017-18 Panini Cornerstones Franchise Foundations Signatures

COMPLETE SET (35)
STATED PRINT RUN B/WN 25-159 COPIES PER
EXCHANGE DEADLINE 01/25/2020
*BRONZE/75: .5X TO 1.2X BASIC
*SILVER/49: .6X TO 1.5X BASIC
1 Shareef Abdur-Rahim/159 3.00 8.00
2 Magic Johnson/25 12.00 30.00
3 Elvin Hayes/99 5.00 12.00
4 Fat Lever/159 3.00 8.00
5 Sam Jones/99 5.00 12.00
6 Jermaine O'Neal/99 4.00 10.00
7 Antoine Walker/159 3.00 8.00
8 Dennis Rodman/99 12.00 30.00
9 Artis Gilmore/99 5.00 12.00
10 Jerry West/25 20.00 50.00
11 Marques Johnson/159 3.00 8.00
12 Alonzo Mourning/25 15.00 40.00
13 Rolando Blackman/159 3.00 8.00
14 Stacey Augmon/159 3.00 8.00
15 Spud Webb/159 3.00 8.00
16 Jo Jo White/159 4.00 10.00
17 Jeff Hornacek/159 3.00 8.00
18 Cuttino Mobley/159 2.50 6.00
19 Gail Goodrich/99 4.00 10.00
20 Charlie Ward/159 2.50 6.00
21 Vinny Del Negro/99 2.50 6.00
22 Vlade Divac/159 4.00 10.00
23 Glen Rice/159 3.00 8.00
24 Kenny "Sky" Walker/159 2.50 6.00
25 Damon Stoudamire/159 4.00 10.00
26 Tom Gugliotta/159 2.50 6.00
27 Cedric Ceballos/159 2.50 6.00
28 Jamaal Wilkes/159 4.00 10.00
29 Antawn Jamison/159 3.00 8.00
30 Corey Maggette/159 3.00 8.00
31 Junior Bridgeman/159 3.00 8.00
32 Nate Thurmond/99 4.00 10.00
33 Kurt Thomas/159 2.50 6.00
34 Horace Grant/159 4.00 10.00
35 Walter McCarty/159 2.50 6.00

2017-18 Panini Cornerstones Keystone Signatures

STATED PRINT RUN B/WN 25-159 COPIES PER
EXCHANGE DEADLINE 01/25/2020
*BRONZE/75: .5X TO 1.2X p/r 99-159
*SILVER/49: .6X TO 1.5X pr 99-159
1 Milos Teodosic/99 3.00 8.00
2 Kelly Oubre Jr./159 4.00 10.00
3 Andrew Wiggins/25 10.00 25.00
4 Caris LeVert/159 4.00 10.00
5 Malcolm Brogdon/159 3.00 8.00
6 Sterling Brown/159 2.50 6.00
7 Brandon Ingram/25 12.00 30.00
8 Bogdan Bogdanovic/159 6.00 15.00
9 Ivica Zubac/159 3.00 8.00
10 Davon Reed/159 2.50 6.00
11 Karl-Anthony Towns/25 12.00 30.00
12 Alex Caruso/159 40.00 100.00
13 Norman Powell/159 4.00 10.00
14 Zhou Qi/159 5.00 12.00
15 Domantas Sabonis/159 8.00 20.00
17 Fred VanVleet/159 75.00 200.00
18 Evan Fournier/159 3.00 8.00
19 Sindarius Thornwell/159 2.50 6.00
20 Derrick White/159 10.00 25.00
21 Cedi Osman/159 5.00 12.00
22 Guerschon Yabusele/159 2.50 6.00
23 Abdel Nader/159 3.00 8.00
24 Ante Zizic/159 3.00 8.00
25 Kadeem Allen/159 2.50 6.00
26 Donovan Mitchell/99 EXCH 50.00 120.00
27 Lonzo Ball/99 15.00 40.00
28 Markelle Fultz/99 6.00 15.00
29 Jayson Tatum/99 50.00 120.00

2017-18 Panini Cornerstones Legendary Quad Relic Autographs

STATED PRINT RUN B/WN 25-129 COPIES PER
EXCHANGE DEADLINE 01/25/2020
*CRYSTAL/75: .5X TO 1.2X p/r 129
*CRYSTAL/20: .4X TO 1X p/r 25
*QUARTZ/45-49: .6X TO 1.5X p/r 129
*QUARTZ/45-49: .4X TO 1X p/r 49
*QUARTZ/25-35: .8X TO 2X p/r 129
*QUARTZ/25-35: .5X TO 1.2X p/r 49
*GRANITE/25: .8X TO 2X p/r 129
*GRANITE/25: .5X TO 1.2X p/r 49
1 Kobe Bryant/25 3,000.00 6,000.00
2 Allen Iverson/49 100.00 250.00
3 James Worthy/49 20.00 50.00
4 Mike Bibby/129 10.00 25.00
5 Bernard King/129 12.00 30.00
6 Hakeem Olajuwon/49 30.00 80.00
7 Antoine Walker/129 8.00 20.00
8 Grant Hill/129 15.00 40.00
9 Antawn Jamison/129 8.00 20.00
10 Gary Payton/129 15.00 40.00
11 Sam Perkins/129 8.00 20.00
12 Stephen Jackson/129 8.00 20.00
13 Christian Laettner/129 10.00 25.00
14 Jermaine O'Neal/129 10.00 25.00
15 Jason Williams/129 15.00 40.00

2017-18 Panini Cornerstones Memorabilia

1 Artis Gilmore 3.00 8.00
2 Patrick Beverley 1.50 4.00
3 Isiah Thomas 4.00 10.00
4 Serge Ibaka 2.00 5.00
5 Karl Malone 5.00 12.00
6 Tyreke Evans 1.50 4.00
7 Andrew Wiggins 3.00 8.00
8 Michael Kidd-Gilchrist 1.50 4.00
9 Nikola Jokic 15.00 40.00
10 Nerlens Noel 1.50 4.00
11 Clyde Drexler 4.00 10.00
12 Rajon Rondo 3.00 8.00
13 Alonzo Mourning 4.00 10.00
14 Thaddeus Young 1.50 4.00
15 Mark Price 2.50 6.00
16 Victor Oladipo 2.00 5.00
17 Gordon Hayward 2.00 5.00
18 Mike Conley 2.00 5.00
19 Rudy Gobert 3.00 8.00
20 Nicolas Batum 1.50 4.00
21 Larry Bird 10.00 25.00
22 Reggie Jackson 2.00 5.00
23 Robert Parish 3.00 8.00
24 Tobias Harris 2.00 5.00
25 Allen Iverson 6.00 15.00
26 Aaron Gordon 2.00 5.00
27 Jimmy Butler 4.00 10.00
28 Myles Turner 2.50 6.00
29 Julius Erving 6.00 15.00
30 Pascal Siakam 5.00 12.00

2017-18 Panini Cornerstones Pillars of Power Autographs

STATED PRINT RUN B/WN 25-159 COPIES PER
EXCHANGE DEADLINE 01/25/2020
*BRONZE/75: .5X TO 1.2X p/r 99-159
*SILVER/49: .6X TO 1.5X p/r 99-159
*SILVER/25: .4X TO 1X p/r 25-49
1 Kyle Kuzma/49 15.00 40.00
2 Shaquille O'Neal/25 40.00 100.00
3 Aaron Gordon/49 6.00 15.00
4 Dillon Brooks/159 8.00 20.00
5 Semi Ojeleye/159 3.00 8.00
6 Guerschon Yabusele/159 3.00 8.00
8 Isaiah Thomas/49 5.00 12.00
9 Tyson Chandler/159 3.00 8.00
10 Myles Turner/99 4.00 10.00
11 Lauri Markkanen/159 20.00 50.00
12 Avery Bradley/99 2.50 6.00
13 Willie Cauley-Stein/159 2.50 6.00
14 Michael Kidd-Gilchrist/99 2.50 6.00
15 Ike Anigbogu/159 2.50 6.00
16 Nene/159 3.00 8.00
17 Dwight Powell/159 2.50 6.00
18 Zaza Pachulia/159 2.50 6.00
20 Larry Nance Jr./159 3.00 8.00
22 Darrell Arthur/159 2.50 6.00
23 Enes Kanter/159 3.00 8.00
24 DeMarre Carroll/159 2.50 6.00
25 Marvin Williams/159 2.50 6.00

2017-18 Panini Cornerstones Quad Relic Autographs

STATED PRINT RUN B/WN 49-129 COPIES PER
EXCHANGE DEADLINE 01/25/2020
*CRYSTAL/65-75: .5X TO 1.2X p/r 129
*CRYSTAL/40: .4X TO 1X p/r 49
*QUARTZ/49: .6X TO 1.5X p/r 129
*QUARTZ/49: .5X TO 1.2X p/r 75
*QUARTZ/25: .8X TO 2X p/r 129
*QUARTZ/25: .5X TO 1.2X p/r 49
*GRANITE/19-25: .8X TO 2X p/r 129
*GRANITE/19-25: .6X TO 1.5X p/r 75
*GRANITE/19-25: .5X TO 1.2X p/r 49
1 Kyrie Irving/49 30.00 80.00
2 Damian Lillard/49 40.00 100.00
3 Isaiah Thomas/129 8.00 20.00
4 Myles Turner/129 10.00 25.00
5 Kristaps Porzingis/49 20.00 50.00
6 Rudy Gobert/129 12.00 30.00
7 Seth Curry/129 10.00 25.00
8 Avery Bradley/129 6.00 15.00
9 Giannis Antetokounmpo/49 60.00 150.00
10 Patrick Beverley/129 6.00 15.00
11 Karl-Anthony Towns/129 20.00 50.00
12 Trevor Ariza/129 6.00 15.00
13 Mike Conley/129 8.00 20.00
14 Aaron Gordon/129 10.00 25.00
15 Kevin Love/129 10.00 25.00
16 Rudy Gay/129 8.00 20.00
18 Reggie Jackson/129 8.00 20.00
19 Nikola Jokic/129 200.00 500.00
20 Gary Harris/129 8.00 20.00
22 Kemba Walker/129 8.00 20.00
23 Evan Turner/129 6.00 15.00
24 Chris Paul/49 40.00 100.00
25 Eric Gordon/129 8.00 20.00
26 Vince Carter/129 20.00 50.00
27 D'Angelo Russell/129 8.00 20.00
28 LaMarcus Aldridge/129 10.00 25.00
29 Anthony Davis/49 40.00 100.00
30 Joel Embiid/129 30.00 80.00
31 Ryan Anderson/129 6.00 15.00
32 Malcolm Brogdon/129 8.00 20.00
33 Michael Kidd-Gilchrist/129 6.00 15.00
34 Jeremy Lin/129 15.00 40.00
35 Marcus Smart/129 10.00 25.00
36 Zach LaVine/129 15.00 40.00
37 Harrison Barnes/129 8.00 20.00
38 Kevin Durant/49 60.00 150.00
39 Brandon Ingram/75 25.00 60.00
41 Tim Hardaway Jr./129 8.00 20.00
43 Elfrid Payton/129 6.00 15.00
44 Devin Booker/129 200.00 500.00
45 Kawhi Leonard/49 40.00 100.00
46 Ricky Rubio/129 15.00 40.00

2017-18 Panini Cornerstones Startups

1 Denzel Valentine .60 1.50
2 Bogdan Bogdanovic 1.50 4.00
3 Caris LeVert 1.00 2.50
4 Milos Teodosic .75 2.00
5 Terrance Ferguson .60 1.50
6 Jayson Tatum 8.00 20.00
7 TJ Leaf .60 1.50
8 Lauri Markkanen 4.00 10.00
9 Jamal Murray 1.50 4.00
10 Dennis Smith Jr. .75 2.00
11 Domantas Sabonis 2.00 5.00
12 Jonathan Isaac 1.50 4.00
13 Buddy Hield 1.00 2.50
14 Bam Adebayo 4.00 10.00
15 John Collins 1.50 4.00
16 Kyle Kuzma 2.50 6.00
17 Ben Simmons 1.00 2.50
18 Markelle Fultz 1.50 4.00
19 Jaylen Brown 2.50 6.00
20 Maxi Kleber 1.00 2.50
21 Malcolm Brogdon .75 2.00
22 Jordan Bell .60 1.50
23 Kris Dunn .60 1.50
24 Malik Monk 2.50 6.00
25 Josh Hart 1.50 4.00
26 Lonzo Ball 2.50 6.00
27 Brandon Ingram 1.25 3.00
28 Zhou Qi 1.25 3.00
29 Yogi Ferrell .60 1.50
30 Cedi Osman 1.25 3.00
31 Dragan Bender .60 1.50
32 Josh Jackson .60 1.50
33 Dejounte Murray 1.00 2.50
34 OG Anunoby 3.00 8.00
35 Luke Kennard 1.25 3.00
36 Donovan Mitchell 6.00 15.00
37 Taurean Prince .60 1.50
38 De'Aaron Fox 5.00 12.00
39 Dario Saric .75 2.00
40 Frank Ntilikina .75 2.00

2017-18 Panini Cornerstones Unbreakables

1 Ben Wallace .75 2.00
2 LeBron James 8.00 20.00
3 Brook Lopez .75 2.00
4 Hassan Whiteside .75 2.00
5 Kevin Garnett 2.50 6.00
6 Andre Drummond .75 2.00
7 Kevin McHale 1.25 3.00
8 Anthony Davis 2.50 6.00
9 Alonzo Mourning 1.50 4.00
10 Marc Gasol 1.00 2.50
11 Dikembe Mutombo 1.25 3.00
12 Dirk Nowitzki 2.50 6.00
13 Artis Gilmore 1.25 3.00
14 Shaquille O'Neal 3.00 8.00
15 Patrick Ewing 1.50 4.00
16 DeAndre Jordan .75 2.00
17 Chris Webber 1.50 4.00
18 Nikola Jokic 6.00 15.00
19 Vlade Divac 1.00 2.50

20 Marcin Gortat .60 1.50
21 Zach Randolph 1.00 2.50
22 Blake Griffin 1.00 2.50
23 DeMarcus Cousins .75 2.00
24 Hakeem Olajuwon 2.00 5.00
25 David Robinson 2.00 5.00
26 Karl-Anthony Towns 1.50 4.00
27 Kareem Abdul-Jabbar 3.00 8.00
28 Joel Embiid 2.00 5.00
29 Wilt Chamberlain 3.00 8.00
30 LaMarcus Aldridge 1.00 2.50
31 Al Jefferson .75 2.00
32 Draymond Green 1.25 3.00
33 Kristaps Porzingis 1.25 3.00
34 Tim Duncan 2.50 6.00
35 Robert Parish 1.25 3.00
36 Dwight Howard 1.25 3.00
37 Shawn Kemp 1.50 4.00
38 Pau Gasol 1.50 4.00
39 Dennis Rodman 2.50 6.00
40 Al Horford 1.00 2.50

2018-19 Panini Cornerstones

1-100 STATED PRINT RUN 139 SER.#'d SETS
JSY AU RC STATED PRINT RUN 199 SER.#'d SETS
EXCHANGE DEADLINE 09/20/2020
1 Aaron Gordon 1.00 2.50
2 Al Horford 1.00 2.50
3 Allen Crabbe .60 1.50
4 Andre Drummond .75 2.00
5 Andrew Wiggins 1.25 3.00
6 Anthony Davis 2.50 6.00
7 Avery Bradley .60 1.50
8 Ben Simmons 1.00 2.50
9 Blake Griffin 1.00 2.50
10 Bobby Portis 1.00 2.50
11 Bojan Bogdanovic .75 2.00
12 Bradley Beal 1.25 3.00
13 Brandon Ingram 1.00 2.50
14 Brook Lopez .75 2.00
15 Bryn Forbes .75 2.00
16 Buddy Hield 1.00 2.50
17 CJ McCollum 1.00 2.50
18 Harrison Barnes .75 2.00
19 Tyson Chandler .75 2.00
20 Charles Barkley 2.00 5.00
21 Chris Paul 2.00 5.00
22 Clint Capela .75 2.00
23 D.J. Augustin .60 1.50
24 Damian Lillard 2.50 6.00
25 Damyean Dotson .60 1.50
26 D'Angelo Russell 1.00 2.50
27 Danilo Gallinari .75 2.00
28 Danny Green .75 2.00
29 Darren Collison .60 1.50
30 Dennis Rodman 2.00 5.00
31 De'Aaron Fox 2.00 5.00
32 DeAndre Jordan .75 2.00
33 DeMar DeRozan 1.25 3.00
34 DeMarre Carroll .60 1.50
35 Dennis Rodman 2.50 6.00
36 Dennis Schroder .75 2.00
37 Dennis Smith Jr. .60 1.50
38 Derrick Rose 2.00 5.00
39 Devin Booker 2.50 6.00
40 Dillon Brooks 1.00 2.50
41 Dirk Nowitzki 2.50 6.00
42 Domantas Sabonis 1.25 3.00
43 Dominique Wilkins 1.50 4.00
44 Donovan Mitchell 3.00 8.00
45 Draymond Green 1.25 3.00
46 Dwyane Wade 2.00 5.00
47 Ed Davis .60 1.50
48 Enes Kanter .75 2.00
49 Eric Bledsoe .75 2.00
50 Eric Gordon .75 2.00
51 E'Twaun Moore .60 1.50
52 Evan Fournier .75 2.00
53 Frank Ntilikina .60 1.50
54 Garrett Temple .60 1.50
55 Gary Harris .75 2.00
56 Giannis Antetokounmpo 5.00 12.00
57 Goran Dragic .75 2.00
58 Gordon Hayward 1.00 2.50
59 Hassan Whiteside .75 2.00
60 Henry Ellenson .60 1.50
61 Iman Shumpert .60 1.50
62 J.J. Barea 1.00 2.50
63 JJ Redick 1.00 2.50
64 JR Smith 1.00 2.50
65 Jabari Parker .60 1.50
66 Jae Crowder .60 1.50
67 Jamal Murray 2.00 5.00
68 James Harden 2.00 5.00
69 Jarrett Allen 1.00 2.50
70 Jaylen Brown 1.50 4.00
71 Jayson Tatum 4.00 10.00
72 Jeff Teague .60 1.50
73 Jeremy Lamb .60 1.50
74 Jeremy Lin 1.50 4.00
75 Jimmy Butler 1.50 4.00
76 Joe Ingles .75 2.00
77 Joel Embiid 2.50 6.00
78 John Collins 1.00 2.50
79 John Wall 1.25 3.00
80 Jonas Valanciunas 1.00 2.50
81 Jordan Clarkson 1.00 2.50
82 Josh Jackson .60 1.50
83 Josh Richardson .75 2.00
84 Jrue Holiday 1.25 3.00
85 Julius Randle 1.00 2.50
86 Jusuf Nurkic .75 2.00
87 Karl-Anthony Towns 1.50 4.00
88 Kawhi Leonard 2.50 6.00
89 Kelly Oubre Jr. 1.00 2.50
90 Kemba Walker .75 2.00
91 Kevin Durant 4.00 10.00
92 Kevin Love .75 2.00
93 Khris Middleton 1.00 2.50
94 Klay Thompson 2.50 6.00
95 Kobe Bryant 8.00 20.00
96 Kyle Korver .75 2.00
97 Kyle Kuzma 1.00 2.50
98 Kyle Lowry 1.00 2.50
99 Kyrie Irving 2.50 6.00
100 LaMarcus Aldridge 1.00 2.50
101 Lauri Markkanen 1.50 4.00
102 LeBron James 8.00 20.00
103 Lonzo Ball 1.00 2.50
104 Lou Williams .75 2.00
105 Luke Kennard .75 2.00
106 Malcolm Brogdon 1.00 2.50
107 Marc Gasol 1.00 2.50
108 Markelle Fultz .75 2.00
109 Markieff Morris .60 1.50
110 Michael Kidd-Gilchrist .60 1.50
111 Mike Conley .75 2.00
112 Montrezl Harrell 1.00 2.50
113 Myles Turner 1.00 2.50
114 Nemanja Bjelica .60 1.50
115 Nicolas Batum .60 1.50
116 Nik Stauskas .60 1.50
117 Nikola Jokic 5.00 12.00
118 Nikola Mirotic .60 1.50
119 Nikola Vucevic .75 2.00
120 Otto Porter Jr. .75 2.00
121 Paul George 1.50 4.00
122 Paul Millsap .75 2.00
123 Raymond Felton .60 1.50
124 Reggie Jackson .75 2.00
125 Ricky Rubio .75 2.00
126 Robert Covington .75 2.00
127 Rodney McGruder .60 1.50
128 Rudy Gay 1.00 2.50
129 Rudy Gobert 1.25 3.00
130 Russell Westbrook 1.50 4.00
131 Serge Ibaka .75 2.00
132 Shaun Livingston .75 2.00
133 Stephen Curry 8.00 20.00
134 Steven Adams .75 2.00
135 T.J. Warren .75 2.00
136 Taurean Prince .60 1.50
137 Terrence Ross .75 2.00
138 Tim Hardaway Jr. .60 1.50
139 Tobias Harris .75 2.00
140 Tony Parker 1.50 4.00
141 Trevor Ariza .60 1.50
142 Trey Burke .60 1.50
143 Trey Lyles .60 1.50
144 Tristan Thompson .60 1.50
145 Victor Oladipo .75 2.00
146 Vince Carter 2.00 5.00
147 Wesley Matthews .60 1.50
148 Willie Cauley-Stein .60 1.50
149 Zach Collins .60 1.50
150 Zach LaVine 1.50 4.00
151 Deandre Ayton JSY AU RC 12.00 30.00
152 Marvin Bagley III JSY AU RC EXCH 6.00 15.00
153 Luka Doncic JSY AU RC 800.00 1,500.00
154 Jaren Jackson Jr. JSY AU RC 200.00 500.00
155 Trae Young JSY AU RC 50.00 120.00
156 Mo Bamba JSY AU RC 6.00 15.00
157 Wendell Carter Jr. JSY AU RC 10.00 25.00
158 Collin Sexton JSY AU RC 12.00 30.00
159 Kevin Knox JSY AU RC 5.00 12.00
160 Mikal Bridges JSY AU RC 20.00 50.00
161 Shai Gilgeous-Alexander JSY AU RC 600.00 1,200.00
162 Jerome Robinson JSY AU RC 4.00 10.00
163 Michael Porter Jr. JSY AU RC 15.00 40.00
164 Troy Brown Jr. JSY AU RC 5.00 12.00
165 Donte DiVincenzo JSY AU RC 10.00 25.00
166 Lonnie Walker IV JSY AU RC 12.00 30.00
167 Kevin Huerter JSY AU RC 8.00 20.00
168 Josh Okogie JSY AU RC 12.00 30.00
169 Grayson Allen JSY AU RC 8.00 20.00
170 Chandler Hutchison JSY AU RC 5.00 12.00
171 Aaron Holiday JSY AU RC 6.00 15.00
172 Anfernee Simons JSY AU RC 12.00 30.00
173 Landry Shamet JSY AU RC 6.00 15.00
174 Robert Williams III JSY AU RC 8.00 20.00
175 Jacob Evans III JSY AU RC 4.00 10.00
176 Dzanan Musa JSY AU RC 4.00 10.00
177 Omari Spellman JSY AU RC 4.00 10.00
178 Elie Okobo JSY AU RC 4.00 10.00
179 Jalen Brunson JSY AU RC 30.00 80.00
180 Devonte' Graham JSY AU RC 6.00 15.00
181 Gary Trent Jr. JSY AU RC 8.00 20.00
182 Bruce Brown JSY AU RC 8.00 20.00
183 Hamidou Diallo JSY AU RC 6.00 15.00
184 Svi Mykhailiuk JSY AU RC 5.00 12.00
185 Keita Bates-Diop JSY AU RC 5.00 12.00

2018-19 Panini Cornerstones Crystal

*CRYSTAL 1-150: .5X TO 1.2X BASIC
*CRYSTAL 151-185: .6X TO 1.5X BASIC
1-150 STATED PRINT RUN 79 SER.#'d SETS
JSY AU STATED PRINT RUN 75 SER.#'d SETS
EXCHANGE DEADLINE 09/20/2020
152 Marvin Bagley III JSY AU EXCH 10.00 25.00
153 Luka Doncic JSY AU 1,500.00 3,000.00
155 Trae Young JSY AU 75.00 200.00
158 Collin Sexton JSY AU 40.00 100.00

2018-19 Panini Cornerstones Downtown

1 Stephen Curry 300.00 600.00
2 LeBron James 800.00 1,500.00
3 Kyrie Irving 100.00 250.00
4 Kevin Durant 150.00 400.00
5 Giannis Antetokounmpo 200.00 500.00
6 Chris Paul 100.00 250.00
7 Ben Simmons 75.00 200.00
8 Russell Westbrook 60.00 150.00
9 Kawhi Leonard 150.00 400.00
10 Deandre Ayton 150.00 400.00
11 Luka Doncic 1,250.00 2,500.00
12 Trae Young 500.00 1,000.00
13 Kevin Knox 15.00 40.00
14 Wendell Carter Jr. 30.00 80.00
15 Jaren Jackson Jr. 125.00 300.00
16 Collin Sexton 40.00 100.00
17 Kevin Garnett 125.00 300.00
18 Tim Duncan 125.00 300.00
19 Charles Barkley 125.00 300.00
20 Kobe Bryant 800.00 1,500.00

2018-19 Panini Cornerstones Quartz

*QUARTZ 1-150: .6X TO 1.5X BASIC
*QUARTZ 151-185: .8X TO 2X BASIC
STATED PRINT RUN 49 SER.#'d SETS
EXCHANGE DEADLINE 09/20/2020
152 Marvin Bagley III JSY AU EXCH 12.00 30.00
153 Luka Doncic JSY AU 2,000.00 4,000.00
155 Trae Young JSY AU 125.00 300.00
156 Mo Bamba JSY AU 25.00 60.00
157 Wendell Carter Jr. JSY AU 20.00 50.00
158 Collin Sexton JSY AU 50.00 120.00
161 Shai Gilgeous-Alexander JSY AU 1,500.00 3,000.00

2018-19 Panini Cornerstones Startups

1 Deandre Ayton 2.00 5.00
2 Marvin Bagley III 1.00 2.50
3 Luka Doncic 100.00 250.00
4 Jaren Jackson Jr. 5.00 12.00
5 Trae Young 15.00 40.00
6 Mo Bamba 1.00 2.50
7 Wendell Carter Jr. 1.50 4.00
8 Collin Sexton 2.00 5.00
9 Kevin Knox .75 2.00
10 Mikal Bridges 3.00 8.00
11 Shai Gilgeous-Alexander 6.00 15.00
12 Jerome Robinson .60 1.50
13 Michael Porter Jr. 2.50 6.00
14 Troy Brown Jr. .75 2.00
15 Zhaire Smith .60 1.50
16 Donte DiVincenzo 1.50 4.00
17 Lonnie Walker IV 1.25 3.00
18 Kevin Huerter 1.25 3.00
19 Josh Okogie 1.00 2.50
20 Grayson Allen 1.25 3.00
21 Chandler Hutchison .75 2.00
22 Aaron Holiday 1.00 2.50
23 Anfernee Simons 3.00 8.00
24 Moritz Wagner 1.25 3.00
25 Landry Shamet 1.00 2.50
26 Robert Williams III 1.25 3.00
27 Jacob Evans III .60 1.50
28 Dzanan Musa .60 1.50
29 Elie Okobo .60 1.50
30 Jevon Carter 1.00 2.50
31 Omari Spellman .60 1.50
32 Jalen Brunson 5.00 12.00
33 Devonte' Graham 1.00 2.50
34 Mitchell Robinson 1.50 4.00
35 Gary Trent Jr. 1.25 3.00
36 Rodions Kurucs .75 2.00
37 Bruce Brown 1.25 3.00
38 Hamidou Diallo 1.00 2.50
39 Allonzo Trier .60 1.50
40 Svi Mykhailiuk .75 2.00

2018-19 Panini Cornerstones Building Blocks Memorabilia

1 Mikal Bridges 8.00 20.00
2 Gary Trent Jr. 3.00 8.00
3 Trae Young 12.00 30.00
4 Moritz Wagner 3.00 8.00
5 Omari Spellman 1.50 4.00
6 Josh Okogie 2.50 6.00
7 Svi Mykhailiuk 2.00 5.00
8 Troy Brown Jr. 2.00 5.00
9 Keita Bates-Diop 2.00 5.00
10 Kevin Knox 2.00 5.00
11 Devonte' Graham 2.50 6.00
12 Anfernee Simons 8.00 20.00
13 Jaren Jackson Jr. 12.00 30.00
14 Mo Bamba 2.50 6.00
15 Dzanan Musa 1.50 4.00
16 Kevin Huerter 3.00 8.00
17 Luka Doncic 25.00 60.00
18 Marvin Bagley III 2.50 6.00
19 Deandre Ayton 5.00 12.00
20 Jacob Evans III 1.50 4.00
21 Michael Porter Jr. 6.00 15.00
22 De'Anthony Melton 3.00 8.00
23 Collin Sexton 5.00 12.00
24 Jalen Brunson 12.00 30.00
25 Aaron Holiday 2.50 6.00
26 Lonnie Walker IV 3.00 8.00
27 Hamidou Diallo 2.50 6.00
28 Wendell Carter Jr. 4.00 10.00
29 Jevon Carter 2.50 6.00
30 Robert Williams III 3.00 8.00
31 Chandler Hutchison 2.00 5.00
32 Donte DiVincenzo 4.00 10.00
33 Shai Gilgeous-Alexander 15.00 40.00
34 Bruce Brown 3.00 8.00
35 Elie Okobo 1.50 4.00
36 Landry Shamet 2.50 6.00
37 Grayson Allen 3.00 8.00
38 Zhaire Smith 1.50 4.00
39 Jerome Robinson 1.50 4.00
40 Jarred Vanderbilt 3.00 8.00

2018-19 Panini Cornerstones Elemental Signatures

STATED PRINT RUN B/WN 25-129 COPIES PER
EXCHANGE DEADLINE 09/20/2020
*CRYSTAL/49: .6X TO 1.5X p/r 129
*CRYSTAL/35: .6X TO 1.5X p/r 129
*CRYSTAL/35: .4X TO 1X p/r 49
*QUARTZ/25: .8X TO 2X p/r 129
*QUARTZ/25: .5X TO 1.2X p/r 49
1 Thaddeus Young/129 2.50 6.00
2 Kentavious Caldwell-Pope/129 2.50 6.00
3 Caris LeVert/129 4.00 10.00
4 Gary Harris/129 3.00 8.00
5 Myles Turner/129 4.00 10.00
6 Dwyane Wade/25 25.00 60.00
7 Enes Kanter/129 3.00 8.00
8 Andrew Wiggins/129 5.00 12.00
9 Rudy Gobert/129 5.00 12.00
10 Dion Waiters/129 2.50 6.00
11 Willie Cauley-Stein/129 2.50 6.00
12 Al Horford/129 4.00 10.00
13 Lou Williams/129 3.00 8.00
14 Serge Ibaka/129 3.00 8.00
15 Mario Hezonja/129 2.50 6.00
16 Damian Lillard/25 20.00 50.00
17 Frank Ntilikina/129 2.50 6.00
18 Josh Jackson/129 2.50 6.00
19 T.J. Warren/129 3.00 8.00
20 JJ Redick/129 4.00 10.00
21 Al-Farouq Aminu/129 2.50 6.00
22 Eric Gordon/129 3.00 8.00
23 Tim Hardaway Jr./129 2.50 6.00
24 Terry Rozier/129 2.50 6.00
25 Kyle Korver/129 3.00 8.00
26 Blake Griffin/49 8.00 20.00
27 Reggie Jackson/129 3.00 8.00
28 Jeremy Lin/49 10.00 25.00
29 Gerald Green/129 3.00 8.00
30 Eric Bledsoe/129 3.00 8.00
31 Udonis Haslem/129 2.50 6.00
32 Derrick Favors/129 2.50 6.00
33 Wayne Ellington/129 2.50 6.00
35 Lauri Markkanen/129 6.00 15.00

2018-19 Panini Cornerstones Elemental Signatures Crystal

*CRYSTAL/49: .6X TO 1.5X p/r 129
*CRYSTAL/35: .6X TO 1.5X p/r 129
*CRYSTAL/35: .4X TO 1X p/r 49
STATED PRINT RUN B/WN 15-49 COPIES PER
NO PRICING QTY 15 OR LESS
EXCHANGE DEADLINE 09/20/2020
26 Blake Griffin/35 10.00 25.00

2018-19 Panini Cornerstones Elemental Signatures Quartz

*QUARTZ/25: .8X TO 2X p/r 129
*QUARTZ/25: .5X TO 1.2X p/r 49
STATED PRINT RUN B/WN 10-25 COPIES PER
NO PRICING QTY 15 OR LESS
EXCHANGE DEADLINE 09/20/2020
26 Blake Griffin/25 12.00 30.00

2018-19 Panini Cornerstones Elusive Ink

STATED PRINT RUN 129 SER.#'d SETS
EXCHANGE DEADLINE 09/20/2020
*CRYSTAL/49: .6X TO 1.5X BASIC
*QUARTZ/25: .8X TO 2X BASIC
1 Derek Fisher 3.00 8.00
2 Tyronn Lue 3.00 8.00
3 Nate McMillan 3.00 8.00
4 Lionel Hollins 3.00 8.00
5 Quinn Buckner 2.50 6.00
7 Devean George 3.00 8.00
8 Kenyon Martin 3.00 8.00
9 Don Chaney 8.00 20.00

2018-19 Panini Cornerstones Foundations Memorabilia

1 Danny Granger 1.50 4.00
2 Tim Duncan 6.00 15.00
3 Kevin Garnett 6.00 15.00
4 Dominique Wilkins 4.00 10.00
5 Paul Pierce 4.00 10.00
6 Joe Smith 2.00 5.00
7 Larry Bird 8.00 20.00
8 John Stockton 5.00 12.00
9 Grant Hill 4.00 10.00
10 Chris Webber 3.00 8.00
11 Shaquille O'Neal 8.00 20.00
12 Peja Stojakovic 2.00 5.00
13 Stephon Marbury 3.00 8.00
14 Shawn Marion 2.00 5.00
15 Anfernee Hardaway 6.00 15.00
16 Kareem Abdul-Jabbar 8.00 20.00
17 Mark Price 2.50 6.00
18 Ernie DiGregorio 2.00 5.00
19 World B. Free 2.00 5.00
20 Mark Aguirre 2.00 5.00
21 Vinnie Johnson 2.50 6.00
22 Steve Kerr 3.00 8.00
23 Isiah Thomas 4.00 10.00
24 Toni Kukoc 3.00 8.00
25 Mark Jackson 2.00 5.00
26 Glen Rice 2.50 6.00
27 Tracy McGrady 4.00 10.00
28 Dee Brown 2.00 5.00
29 Horace Grant 2.50 6.00
30 Steve Nash 5.00 12.00

2018-19 Panini Cornerstones Franchise Pillars Autographs

STATED PRINT RUN B/WN 25-129 COPIES PER
EXCHANGE DEADLINE 09/20/2020
*CRYSTAL/49: .6X TO 1.5X p/r 129
*CRYSTAL/35: .6X TO 1.5X p/r 129
*CRYSTAL/35: .4X TO 1X p/r 49
*QUARTZ/25: .8X TO 2X p/r 129
*QUARTZ/25: .5X TO 1.2X p/r 49
3 Kyrie Irving/25 20.00 50.00
4 Ray Allen/49 12.00 30.00
5 Dennis Rodman/49 20.00 50.00
6 Rick Barry/129 5.00 12.00
7 Willis Reed/49 20.00 50.00
8 Rick Fox/129 3.00 8.00
9 Sam Jones/129 10.00 25.00
10 Robert Horry/129 4.00 10.00
11 Bob Lanier/129 5.00 12.00
12 Walt Frazier/129 6.00 15.00
13 Richard Hamilton/129 3.00 8.00
14 Chris Mullin/129 5.00 12.00
15 George Gervin/129 6.00 15.00
16 Nick Van Exel/129 4.00 10.00
17 Calvin Murphy/129 3.00 8.00
18 Peja Stojakovic/129 3.00 8.00
19 Elvin Hayes/129 5.00 12.00
20 Louie Dampier/129 4.00 10.00
21 Horace Grant/129 6.00 15.00
22 Allan Houston/129 4.00 10.00
23 Chauncey Billups/129 5.00 12.00
24 Latrell Sprewell/129 5.00 12.00
25 Joe Dumars/129 5.00 12.00

2018-19 Panini Cornerstones Keystone Signatures

STATED PRINT RUN 129 SER.#'d SETS
EXCHANGE DEADLINE 09/20/2020
*CRYSTAL/49: .6X TO 1.5X BASIC
*QUARTZ/25: .8X TO 2X BASIC
1 Walter Davis 4.00 10.00
2 Rick Mahorn 2.50 6.00
3 Marcus Camby 5.00 12.00
4 Bryon Russell 2.50 6.00
5 Scott Skiles 3.00 8.00
6 Sean Elliott 3.00 8.00
7 Doug Christie 3.00 8.00
8 Darrell Griffith 3.00 8.00
9 Vin Baker 2.50 6.00
10 Herb Williams 2.50 6.00
11 Charlie Ward 3.00 8.00
12 Clifford Robinson 4.00 10.00
13 Brad Davis 3.00 8.00
14 Muggsy Bogues 5.00 12.00
15 Larry Nance 3.00 8.00
16 Nick Anderson 3.00 8.00
17 Wally Szczerbiak 3.00 8.00
18 Jim Jackson 3.00 8.00
19 John Salley 3.00 8.00
20 Jerome Williams 2.50 6.00
21 Kenny Anderson 3.00 8.00
22 Rudy Tomjanovich 3.00 8.00
23 Sarunas Marciulionis 4.00 10.00
24 Theo Ratliff 2.50 6.00
25 Tree Rollins 2.50 6.00
26 Mark Eaton 4.00 10.00
27 Antonio McDyess 3.00 8.00
28 Brent Barry 2.50 6.00
29 Dee Brown 3.00 8.00
30 Cuttino Mobley 2.50 6.00

2018-19 Panini Cornerstones Legendary Quad Relic Autographs

STATED PRINT RUN B/WN 25-129 COPIES PER
EXCHANGE DEADLINE 09/20/2020
*CRYSTAL/35-49: .6X TO 1.5X p/r 129
*CRYSTAL/35-49: .4X TO 1X p/r 49
*QUARTZ/25: .8X TO 2X p/r 129
*QUARTZ/25: .5X TO 1.2X p/r 49
1 Dominique Wilkins/49 25.00 60.00
2 Reggie Miller/25 50.00 120.00
3 John Stockton/25 40.00 100.00
4 Kareem Abdul-Jabbar/25 40.00 100.00
5 Robert Parish/129 15.00 40.00
6 Shaquille O'Neal /25 60.00 150.00
7 Kevin McHale/49 EXCH 25.00 60.00
8 James Worthy/49 25.00 60.00
9 Artis Gilmore/129 12.00 30.00
10 Louie Dampier/129 10.00 25.00
11 Allen Iverson/25 30.00 80.00
12 Charles Barkley/25 EXCH 75.00 200.00
13 Dan Issel/129 12.00 30.00
15 Peja Stojakovic/129 8.00 20.00
16 Walter Davis/129 10.00 25.00
17 Jason Kidd/25 30.00 80.00
18 Danny Manning/129 8.00 20.00
19 Stephen Jackson/129 8.00 20.00
20 Kelly Tripucka/129 6.00 15.00
21 Erick Dampier/129 6.00 15.00
22 Mike Bibby/129 10.00 25.00
23 Herb Williams/129 6.00 15.00
24 Bill Cartwright/129 8.00 20.00
25 Tom Gugliotta/129 6.00 15.00
26 Mark Price/129 10.00 25.00
27 Jack Sikma/129 8.00 20.00
28 World B. Free/129 8.00 20.00
30 Kevin Johnson/129 10.00 25.00

2018-19 Panini Cornerstones Memorabilia

1 Vince Carter 5.00 12.00
2 Jaylen Brown 4.00 10.00
3 Rondae Hollis-Jefferson 1.50 4.00
4 Michael Kidd-Gilchrist 1.50 4.00
5 Jabari Parker 1.50 4.00
6 Kyle Korver 2.00 5.00
7 DeAndre Jordan 2.00 5.00
8 Gary Harris 2.00 5.00
9 Andre Drummond 2.00 5.00
10 Draymond Green 3.00 8.00
11 James Harden 5.00 12.00
12 Victor Oladipo 2.00 5.00
13 Brandon Ingram 2.50 6.00
14 Dillon Brooks 2.50 6.00
15 Hassan Whiteside 2.00 5.00
16 Eric Bledsoe 2.00 5.00
17 Jimmy Butler 4.00 10.00
18 Elfrid Payton 2.00 5.00
19 Tim Hardaway Jr. 1.50 4.00
20 Russell Westbrook 4.00 10.00
21 Nikola Vucevic 2.00 5.00
22 Dario Saric 2.00 5.00
23 Devin Booker 6.00 15.00
24 CJ McCollum 2.50 6.00
25 Buddy Hield 2.50 6.00
26 DeMar DeRozan 3.00 8.00
27 Danny Green 2.00 5.00
28 Rudy Gobert 3.00 8.00
29 John Wall 3.00 8.00
30 Lou Williams 2.00 5.00

2018-19 Panini Cornerstones Quad Relic Autographs

STATED PRINT RUN B/WN 25-129 COPIES PER
EXCHANGE DEADLINE 09/20/2020
*CRYSTAL/35-49: .6X TO 1.5X p/r 129
*CRYSTAL/35-49: .4X TO 1X p/r 49
*QUARTZ/22-25: .8X TO 2X p/r 129
*QUARTZ/22-25: .5X TO 1.2X p/r 49
1 Enes Kanter/129 8.00 20.00
2 Tyus Jones/129 6.00 15.00
3 Dirk Nowitzki/25 60.00 150.00
4 Gordon Hayward/129 10.00 25.00
5 Karl-Anthony Towns/25 30.00 80.00
6 Andrew Wiggins/25 25.00 60.00
7 Joe Ingles/129 8.00 20.00
8 J.J. Barea/129 8.00 20.00
9 Dion Waiters/129 6.00 15.00
10 Caris LeVert/129 6.00 15.00
11 Harrison Barnes/129 8.00 20.00
12 Allen Crabbe/129 6.00 15.00
13 Cody Zeller/129 6.00 15.00
14 Joel Embiid/25 50.00 120.00
15 JJ Redick/129 10.00 25.00
17 Justin Jackson/129 6.00 15.00
18 Tim Hardaway Jr./129 6.00 15.00
19 Kristaps Porzingis/49 20.00 50.00
20 John Collins/129 10.00 25.00
23 TJ Leaf/129 6.00 15.00
24 Kelly Oubre Jr./129 10.00 25.00
26 Shaun Livingston/129 8.00 20.00
27 Buddy Hield/129 10.00 25.00
28 Terry Rozier/129 8.00 20.00
29 Marc Gasol/25 EXCH 20.00 50.00
30 Damian Lillard/25 50.00 120.00
31 Zach LaVine/129 15.00 40.00
32 Lonzo Ball/49 15.00 40.00
33 Kyle Kuzma/129 10.00 25.00
34 De'Aaron Fox/129 20.00 50.00
35 Donovan Mitchell/25 60.00 150.00

2018-19 Panini Cornerstones Unbreakables

1 Joel Embiid 2.50 6.00
2 Ben Simmons 1.00 2.50
3 Giannis Antetokounmpo 5.00 12.00
4 Zach LaVine 1.50 4.00
5 Jayson Tatum 4.00 10.00
6 Kyrie Irving 2.50 6.00
7 Tobias Harris .75 2.00
8 Mike Conley .75 2.00
9 Dwyane Wade 2.00 5.00
10 Kemba Walker .75 2.00
11 Donovan Mitchell 3.00 8.00
12 Rudy Gobert 1.25 3.00
13 De'Aaron Fox 2.00 5.00
14 Buddy Hield 1.00 2.50
15 Enes Kanter .75 2.00
16 LeBron James 6.00 15.00
17 Brandon Ingram 1.00 2.50
18 Dirk Nowitzki 2.50 6.00
19 Dennis Smith Jr. .60 1.50
20 Stephen Curry 8.00 20.00
21 Nikola Jokic 5.00 12.00
22 Jamal Murray 2.00 5.00
23 Victor Oladipo .75 2.00
24 Anthony Davis 2.50 6.00
25 Blake Griffin 1.00 2.50
26 Kawhi Leonard 2.50 6.00
27 James Harden 2.00 5.00
28 Russell Westbrook 1.50 4.00
29 Karl-Anthony Towns 1.50 4.00
30 Kevin Durant 4.00 10.00
31 John Wall 1.25 3.00
32 Vince Carter 2.00 5.00
33 Jrue Holiday 1.25 3.00
34 Andre Drummond .75 2.00
35 Kyle Lowry 1.00 2.50
36 Chris Paul 2.00 5.00
37 DeMar DeRozan 1.25 3.00
38 Devin Booker 2.50 6.00
39 Paul George 1.50 4.00
40 Lauri Markkanen 1.50 4.00

2012-13 Panini Crusade

COMPLETE SET (100) 20.00 50.00
1 Blake Griffin .50 1.25
2 Chris Paul 1.00 2.50
3 Grant Hill .75 2.00
4 Dwight Howard .60 1.50
5 Kobe Bryant 60.00 150.00
6 Pau Gasol .75 2.00
7 Steve Nash 1.00 2.50
8 Marc Gasol .50 1.25
9 Rudy Gay .50 1.25
10 Zach Randolph .50 1.25
11 Chris Bosh .60 1.50
12 Dwyane Wade 1.00 2.50
13 LeBron James 4.00 10.00
14 Brandon Jennings .30 .75
15 Mike Dunleavy .30 .75
16 Monta Ellis .40 1.00
17 Andrei Kirilenko .40 1.00
18 Kevin Love .50 1.25
19 Ricky Rubio .40 1.00
20 Al-Farouq Aminu .30 .75
21 Eric Gordon .40 1.00
22 Greivis Vasquez .30 .75
23 Amar'e Stoudemire .50 1.25
24 Carmelo Anthony .75 2.00
25 Jason Kidd .75 2.00
26 Rasheed Wallace .60 1.50
27 Raymond Felton .30 .75
28 Kendrick Perkins .30 .75
29 Kevin Durant 2.00 5.00
30 Russell Westbrook .75 2.00
31 Serge Ibaka .40 1.00
32 Thabo Sefolosha .30 .75
33 Evan Turner .30 .75
34 Jrue Holiday .60 1.50
35 Nick Young .30 .75
36 Goran Dragic .50 1.25
37 Jared Dudley .30 .75
38 Marcin Gortat .30 .75
39 LaMarcus Aldridge .50 1.25
40 Nicolas Batum .40 1.00
41 Wesley Matthews .30 .75
42 DeMarcus Cousins .50 1.25
43 Tyreke Evans .40 1.00
44 Manu Ginobili 1.00 2.50
45 Tim Duncan 1.25 3.00
46 Tony Parker .75 2.00
47 DeMar DeRozan .60 1.50
48 Kyle Lowry .50 1.25
49 Jose Calderon .30 .75
50 Al Jefferson .30 .75
51 Gordon Hayward .50 1.25
52 John Wall .60 1.50
53 Jordan Crawford .30 .75
54 Al Horford .50 1.25
55 Josh Smith .30 .75
56 Kevin Garnett 1.25 3.00
57 Paul Pierce .75 2.00
58 Rajon Rondo .60 1.50
59 Brook Lopez .40 1.00
60 Deron Williams .40 1.00
61 Gerald Wallace .40 1.00
62 Kris Humphries .30 .75
63 Ben Gordon .40 1.00
64 Gerald Henderson .30 .75
65 Derrick Rose .75 2.00
66 Joakim Noah .40 1.00
67 Luol Deng .40 1.00
68 Taj Gibson .30 .75
69 Alonzo Gee .30 .75
70 Anderson Varejao .30 .75
71 Dirk Nowitzki 1.25 3.00
72 Vince Carter 1.00 2.50
73 Andre Iguodala .50 1.25
74 Ty Lawson .30 .75
75 Greg Monroe .30 .75
76 Rodney Stuckey .30 .75
77 Tayshaun Prince .50 1.25
78 David Lee .30 .75
79 Stephen Curry 4.00 10.00
80 James Johnson 1.00 2.50
81 Jeremy Lin .75 2.00
82 Omer Asik .30 .75
83 David West .40 1.00
84 George Hill .40 1.00
85 Paul George .75 2.00
86 Alexey Shved RC .40 1.00
87 Andre Drummond RC 1.00 2.50
88 Anthony Davis RC 5.00 12.00
89 Bradley Beal RC 3.00 8.00
90 Brandon Knight RC .50 1.25
91 Chandler Parsons RC .50 1.25
92 Damian Lillard RC 20.00 50.00
93 Harrison Barnes RC .75 2.00
94 Jared Sullinger RC .40 1.00
95 Kemba Walker RC 1.50 4.00
96 Kenneth Faried RC .50 1.25
97 Klay Thompson RC 4.00 10.00
98 Kyrie Irving RC 4.00 10.00
99 Michael Kidd-Gilchrist RC .50 1.25
100 Tristan Thompson RC .60 1.50

2012-13 Panini Crusade Insert Blue

1 Jared Sullinger 1.25 3.00
2 Anthony Davis 20.00 50.00
3 Will Barton 2.50 6.00
4 Nolan Smith 1.25 3.00
5 Enes Kanter 2.00 5.00
6 Jeff Taylor 1.25 3.00
7 Kevin Murphy 1.25 3.00
8 Klay Thompson 40.00 100.00
9 Draymond Green 8.00 20.00
10 Andrew Nicholson 1.25 3.00
11 Tyler Zeller 1.25 3.00
12 Austin Rivers 2.00 5.00
13 E'Twaun Moore 1.50 4.00
14 Nikola Vucevic 5.00 12.00
15 Kyle Singler 1.25 3.00
16 Nando De Colo 1.25 3.00
17 Kenneth Faried 1.50 4.00
18 Jared Cunningham 1.25 3.00
19 Dion Waiters 1.50 4.00
20 Andre Drummond 3.00 8.00
21 Tristan Thompson 1.25 3.00
22 Bradley Beal 10.00 25.00
23 Evan Fournier 2.00 5.00
24 Tornike Shengelia 1.25 3.00
25 Kyrie Irving 12.00 30.00
26 Jimmer Fredette 2.00 5.00
27 Kendall Marshall 1.25 3.00
28 Jan Vesely 1.25 3.00
29 Derrick Williams 1.25 3.00
30 Fab Melo 1.25 3.00
31 Tobias Harris 4.00 10.00
32 Brandon Knight 1.50 4.00
33 Alexey Shved 1.25 3.00
34 Mirza Teletovic 1.50 4.00
35 Lance Thomas 1.25 3.00
36 Jeremy Lamb 2.00 5.00
37 Kemba Walker 5.00 12.00
38 Jae Crowder 2.50 6.00
39 DeAndre Liggins 1.25 3.00
40 Alec Burks 2.00 5.00
41 Thomas Robinson 1.25 3.00
42 Brian Roberts 1.25 3.00
43 Festus Ezeli 1.25 3.00
44 Miles Plumlee 1.25 3.00
45 Lavoy Allen 1.25 3.00
46 Jimmy Butler 12.00 30.00
47 Kawhi Leonard 20.00 50.00
48 Isaiah Thomas 2.50 6.00
49 Darius Morris 1.50 4.00
50 Orlando Johnson 1.25 3.00
51 Terrence Ross 3.00 8.00
52 Chandler Parsons 1.50 4.00
53 Greg Stiemsma 1.25 3.00
54 Meyers Leonard 1.50 4.00
55 Marcus Morris 2.00 5.00
56 MarShon Brooks 1.25 3.00
57 Jordan Hamilton 1.25 3.00
58 Iman Shumpert 1.50 4.00
59 Darius Miller 1.50 4.00
60 Pablo Prigioni 1.25 3.00
61 Terrence Jones 1.25 3.00
62 Chris Copeland 1.25 3.00
63 Gustavo Ayon 1.25 3.00
64 John Henson 1.50 4.00
65 Markieff Morris 2.00 5.00
66 Norris Cole 1.25 3.00
67 John Jenkins 1.25 3.00
68 Harrison Barnes 2.50 6.00
69 Damian Lillard 40.00 100.00
70 Reggie Jackson 2.00 5.00
71 Dominique Wilkins 2.50 6.00
72 Karl Malone 3.00 8.00
73 Hakeem Olajuwon 4.00 10.00
74 James Worthy 3.00 8.00
75 Larry Bird 6.00 15.00
76 Toni Kukoc 2.00 5.00
77 Rick Mahorn 1.25 3.00
78 Len Elmore 1.25 3.00
79 Julius Erving 5.00 12.00
80 Vlade Divac 2.00 5.00
81 Doc Rivers 2.00 5.00
82 Manute Bol 2.00 5.00
83 Robert Horry 2.00 5.00
84 Jerry West 4.00 10.00
85 Kevin McHale 2.50 6.00
86 Zydrunas Ilgauskas 1.50 4.00
87 Joe Dumars 2.50 6.00
88 Moses Malone 3.00 8.00
89 Allen Iverson 3.00 8.00
90 Wilt Chamberlain 6.00 15.00
91 Gary Payton 2.50 6.00
92 Rod Strickland 1.25 3.00
93 Sam Cassell 1.50 4.00
94 Kareem Abdul-Jabbar 6.00 15.00
95 Bob Cousy 3.00 8.00
96 Mark Price 2.00 5.00
97 Isiah Thomas 4.00 10.00
98 Sidney Moncrief 1.25 3.00
99 Willis Reed 3.00 8.00
100 Horace Grant 2.00 5.00
101 Shawn Kemp 3.00 8.00
102 Wes Unseld 2.50 6.00
103 Steve Francis 1.50 4.00
104 Magic Johnson 6.00 15.00
105 Bill Russell 6.00 15.00

106 Larry Nance 1.50 4.00
107 Dennis Rodman 5.00 12.00
108 Clyde Lovellette 2.50 6.00
109 Patrick Ewing 3.00 8.00
110 Shareef Abdur-Rahim 1.50 4.00
111 Detlef Schrempf 2.00 5.00
112 Chris Webber 2.00 5.00
113 Chris Mullin 2.50 6.00
114 Michael Cooper 2.00 5.00
115 Larry Johnson 2.50 6.00
116 Dell Curry 1.25 3.00
117 Bob Lanier 1.50 4.00
118 Anfernee Hardaway 5.00 12.00
119 John Starks 1.50 4.00
120 Bobby Jackson 1.25 3.00
121 Dolph Schayes 2.50 6.00
122 Tim Hardaway 2.50 6.00
123 A.C. Green 2.00 5.00
124 Nick Van Exel 2.00 5.00
125 Glen Rice 1.50 4.00
126 Michael Finley 2.00 5.00
127 Bill Laimbeer 2.50 6.00
128 Bill Walton 3.00 8.00
129 Jason Kidd 3.00 8.00
130 Cedric Maxwell 1.25 3.00
131 Jeff Hornacek 1.50 4.00
132 Calvin Murphy 1.50 4.00
133 Bob McAdoo 1.50 4.00
134 Shaquille O'Neal 6.00 15.00
135 Anthony Mason 1.50 4.00
136 Jim Jackson 1.50 4.00
137 George Gervin 3.00 8.00
138 Tom Chambers 1.25 3.00
139 Allan Houston 1.50 4.00
140 Bernard King 2.50 6.00
141 John Stockton 4.00 10.00
142 Yao Ming 4.00 10.00
143 Cedric Ceballos 1.50 4.00
144 Pete Maravich 4.00 10.00
145 Alonzo Mourning 3.00 8.00
146 Alex English 2.50 6.00
147 David Robinson 3.00 8.00
148 Kevin Johnson 2.00 5.00
149 Mark Jackson 1.50 4.00
150 Rick Barry 1.50 4.00
151 Kirk Hinrich 1.50 4.00
152 Shawn Marion 2.00 5.00
153 Nene 1.50 4.00
154 Richard Jefferson 1.50 4.00
155 Tiago Splitter 1.25 3.00
156 Kyle Lowry 2.00 5.00
157 Chris Paul 4.00 10.00
158 Kevin Love 2.00 5.00
159 O.J. Mayo 1.25 3.00
160 Brandon Jennings 1.25 3.00
161 LeBron James 30.00 80.00
162 Rasheed Wallace 2.50 6.00
163 Jamal Crawford 2.00 5.00
164 J.R. Smith 2.00 5.00
165 Danny Granger 1.25 3.00
166 Mike Dunleavy 1.25 3.00
167 Dwight Howard 2.50 6.00
168 Kevin Durant 8.00 20.00
169 Tim Duncan 5.00 12.00
170 Grant Hill 3.00 8.00
171 Mike Conley 1.50 4.00
172 Thabo Sefolosha 1.25 3.00
173 Josh Smith 1.25 3.00
174 Arron Afflalo 1.25 3.00
175 Dwyane Wade 4.00 10.00
176 Amar'e Stoudemire 2.00 5.00
177 Stephen Curry 30.00 80.00
178 Kevin Garnett 5.00 12.00
179 Anderson Varejao 1.25 3.00
180 Jarrett Jack 1.50 4.00
181 Tyler Hansbrough 1.25 3.00
182 Marcus Camby 2.00 5.00
183 DeAndre Jordan 1.50 4.00
184 Corey Brewer 1.25 3.00
185 Eric Bledsoe 1.50 4.00
186 Kendrick Perkins 1.25 3.00
187 Deron Williams 1.50 4.00
188 Paul Pierce 3.00 8.00
189 J.J. Hickson 1.25 3.00
190 Patrick Patterson 1.25 3.00
191 Raymond Felton 1.25 3.00
192 Russell Westbrook 3.00 8.00
193 Louis Williams 1.50 4.00
194 Kobe Bryant 30.00 80.00
195 Beno Udrih 1.25 3.00
196 Glen Davis 1.25 3.00
197 Nick Collison 1.25 3.00
198 Carl Landry 1.25 3.00
199 Hedo Turkoglu 1.50 4.00
200 Kevin Martin 1.50 4.00
201 Zaza Pachulia 1.25 3.00
202 Joe Johnson 1.50 4.00
203 Jeff Teague 1.25 3.00
204 Trevor Ariza 1.25 3.00
205 J.J. Redick 2.00 5.00
206 Greivis Vasquez 1.25 3.00
207 Earl Clark 1.25 3.00
208 Jose Calderon 1.25 3.00
209 Larry Sanders 1.25 3.00
210 Andrew Bynum 1.25 3.00
211 Jameer Nelson 1.25 3.00
212 Udonis Haslem 1.50 4.00
213 JaVale McGee 1.50 4.00
214 Thaddeus Young 1.25 3.00
215 Goran Dragic 2.00 5.00
216 Eric Gordon 1.50 4.00
217 Brandon Roy 1.50 4.00
218 Jamaal Tinsley 1.25 3.00
219 Jordan Crawford 1.25 3.00
220 Ty Lawson 1.25 3.00
221 Evan Turner 1.25 3.00
222 LaMarcus Aldridge 2.00 5.00
223 DeMarcus Cousins 2.00 5.00
224 Darrell Arthur 1.25 3.00
225 Derrick Favors 1.50 4.00
226 Nick Young 1.25 3.00
227 P.J. Tucker 1.25 3.00
228 Paul George 3.00 8.00
229 Danny Green 1.50 4.00
230 Jrue Holiday 2.50 6.00
231 Tyreke Evans 1.50 4.00
232 Andrei Kirilenko 1.50 4.00
233 Marc Gasol 2.00 5.00
234 Jason Richardson 2.00 5.00
235 Nicolas Batum 1.50 4.00
236 Shannon Brown 1.25 3.00
237 Brandon Bass 1.25 3.00
238 Blake Griffin 2.00 5.00
239 Tyrus Thomas 1.25 3.00
240 Rudy Gay 2.00 5.00
241 Al Horford 2.00 5.00
242 Marcus Thornton 1.25 3.00
243 Metta World Peace 1.50 4.00
244 Ed Davis 1.25 3.00
245 DeJuan Blair 1.25 3.00
246 John Wall 2.50 6.00
247 Manu Ginobili 4.00 10.00
248 Greg Monroe 1.25 3.00
249 George Hill 1.50 4.00
250 Andrea Bargnani 1.25 3.00
251 Roy Hibbert 1.50 4.00
252 Ersan Ilyasova 1.25 3.00
253 Andre Iguodala 2.00 5.00
254 Zach Randolph 2.00 5.00
255 Chase Budinger 1.25 3.00
256 Tony Parker 3.00 8.00
257 Rodney Stuckey 1.25 3.00
258 Shane Battier 1.50 4.00
259 Andre Miller 1.50 4.00
260 Richard Hamilton 2.00 5.00
261 Rashard Lewis 2.00 5.00
262 Tayshaun Prince 2.00 5.00
263 Amir Johnson 1.25 3.00
264 Al-Farouq Aminu 1.25 3.00
265 Brook Lopez 1.50 4.00
266 Jason Terry 1.50 4.00
267 Gerald Henderson 1.25 3.00
268 Marcin Gortat 1.25 3.00
269 Ray Allen 3.00 8.00
270 Jeremy Lin 3.00 8.00
271 Drew Gooden 1.50 4.00
272 Wilson Chandler 1.50 4.00
273 Ricky Rubio 1.50 4.00
274 Darren Collison 1.25 3.00
275 Spencer Hawes 1.25 3.00
276 Al Jefferson 1.25 3.00
277 Dirk Nowitzki 5.00 12.00
278 Alan Anderson 1.25 3.00
279 Jared Dudley 1.25 3.00
280 Derrick Rose 3.00 8.00
281 Luis Scola 1.50 4.00
282 Marvin Williams 1.25 3.00
283 Vince Carter 4.00 10.00
284 James Harden 4.00 10.00
285 Steve Nash 4.00 10.00
286 Chris Bosh 2.50 6.00
287 Luol Deng 1.50 4.00
288 Linas Kleiza 1.25 3.00
289 Joakim Noah 1.50 4.00
290 David Lee 1.25 3.00
291 Rajon Rondo 2.50 6.00
292 Serge Ibaka 1.50 4.00
293 Taj Gibson 1.25 3.00
294 Gordon Hayward 2.00 5.00
295 Tyson Chandler 1.50 4.00
296 David West 1.50 4.00
297 Caron Butler 1.50 4.00
298 Andrew Bogut 1.50 4.00
299 Carmelo Anthony 3.00 8.00
300 Chauncey Billups 2.50 6.00

2012-13 Panini Crusade Insert Green

*GREEN: 1.5X TO 4X BLUE
STATED PRINT RUN 25 SER.#'d SETS
69 Damian Lillard 200.00 500.00
89 Allen Iverson 25.00 60.00
110 Shareef Abdur-Rahim 12.00 30.00
161 LeBron James 125.00 300.00
177 Stephen Curry 125.00 300.00
194 Kobe Bryant 125.00 300.00

2012-13 Panini Crusade Insert Purple

*PURPLE: 1X TO 2.5X BLUE
STATED PRINT RUN 49 SER.#'d SETS
69 Damian Lillard 125.00 300.00
161 LeBron James 75.00 200.00
177 Stephen Curry 75.00 200.00
194 Kobe Bryant 75.00 200.00

2012-13 Panini Crusade Insert Red

*RED: .6X TO 1.5X BLUE
STATED PRINT RUN 99 SER.#'d SETS
69 Damian Lillard 75.00 200.00
161 LeBron James 50.00 120.00
177 Stephen Curry 50.00 120.00
194 Kobe Bryant 50.00 120.00

2012-13 Panini Crusade Knight Court

1 Kobe Bryant 12.00 30.00
2 Jason Kidd 2.50 6.00
3 LeBron James 12.00 30.00
4 Tim Duncan 4.00 10.00
5 Dwyane Wade 3.00 8.00
6 Kevin Love 1.50 4.00
7 James Harden 3.00 8.00
8 Carmelo Anthony 2.50 6.00
9 Derrick Rose 2.50 6.00
10 Russell Westbrook 2.50 6.00
11 Blake Griffin 1.50 4.00
12 Ricky Rubio 1.25 3.00
13 DeMarcus Cousins 1.25 3.00
14 Chris Paul 3.00 8.00
15 Steve Nash 3.00 8.00
16 Stephen Curry 12.00 30.00
17 Joakim Noah 1.25 3.00
18 Amar'e Stoudemire 1.50 4.00
19 Deron Williams 1.25 3.00
20 Kevin Garnett 4.00 10.00
21 Ray Allen 2.50 6.00
22 Greg Monroe 1.00 2.50
23 Zach Randolph 1.50 4.00
24 Dwight Howard 2.00 5.00
25 John Wall 2.00 5.00
26 LaMarcus Aldridge 1.50 4.00
27 Josh Smith 1.00 2.50
28 Tony Parker 2.50 6.00
29 Kevin Durant 6.00 15.00
30 Al Horford 1.50 4.00
31 Vince Carter 3.00 8.00
32 Rajon Rondo 2.00 5.00
33 Al Jefferson 1.00 2.50
34 Chris Bosh 2.00 5.00
35 Pau Gasol 2.50 6.00
36 Manu Ginobili 3.00 8.00
37 Jrue Holiday 2.00 5.00
38 Dirk Nowitzki 4.00 10.00
39 David Lee 1.00 2.50
40 Joe Johnson 1.25 3.00
41 Danny Granger 1.00 2.50
42 Paul Pierce 2.50 6.00
43 Antawn Jamison 1.25 3.00
44 Grant Hill 2.50 6.00
45 Jason Terry 1.25 3.00
46 Chauncey Billups 2.00 5.00
47 Shawn Marion 1.50 4.00
48 Roy Hibbert 1.25 3.00
49 Marc Gasol 1.50 4.00
50 Andrew Bynum 1.00 2.50

2012-13 Panini Crusade Majestic Materials

1 Blake Griffin 3.00 8.00
2 Andre Miller 2.50 6.00
3 Dennis Rodman 8.00 20.00
4 Trevor Ariza 2.00 5.00
5 Tim Duncan 8.00 20.00
6 Jalen Rose 2.50 6.00
7 Doc Rivers 3.00 8.00
8 Earl Monroe 4.00 10.00
9 Ricky Rubio 2.50 6.00
10 Alvan Adams 2.00 5.00
11 Patrick Ewing 5.00 12.00
12 Metta World Peace 2.50 6.00
13 Gary Payton 4.00 10.00
14 Dan Issel 3.00 8.00
15 Glen Rice 2.50 6.00
16 Julius Erving 8.00 20.00
17 Al Jefferson 2.00 5.00
18 Clyde Drexler 5.00 12.00
19 Rasheed Wallace 4.00 10.00
20 Kobe Bryant 40.00 100.00
21 Caron Butler 2.50 6.00
22 Jim Jackson 2.50 6.00
23 Alex English 4.00 10.00
24 Hakeem Olajuwon 6.00 15.00
25 Larry Johnson 4.00 10.00
26 Zydrunas Ilgauskas 2.50 6.00
27 Jason Kidd 5.00 12.00
28 Dwyane Wade 6.00 15.00
29 Paul Millsap 2.50 6.00
30 Chris Kaman 2.50 6.00
31 Amar'e Stoudemire 3.00 8.00
32 David Robinson 5.00 12.00
33 Alonzo Mourning 5.00 12.00
34 Roy Hibbert 2.50 6.00
35 Chris Paul 6.00 15.00
36 Rudy Gay 3.00 8.00
37 James Harden 6.00 15.00
38 Sean Elliott 2.50 6.00
39 Andrei Kirilenko 2.50 6.00
40 Dominique Wilkins 4.00 10.00
41 Jeff Hornacek 2.50 6.00
42 David Lee 2.00 5.00
43 Tyreke Evans 2.50 6.00
44 Zach Randolph 3.00 8.00
45 Marc Gasol 3.00 8.00
46 Lucius Allen 3.00 8.00
47 Dwight Howard 4.00 10.00
48 Detlef Schrempf 3.00 8.00
49 Danny Manning 3.00 8.00
50 Andrew Bogut 2.50 6.00
51 Paul Pierce 5.00 12.00
52 LeBron James 40.00 100.00
53 Nene 2.50 6.00
54 Deron Williams 2.50 6.00
55 Gerald Wallace 2.50 6.00
56 Elton Brand 2.50 6.00
57 Steve Nash 6.00 15.00
58 Stephen Curry 40.00 100.00
59 Dirk Nowitzki 8.00 20.00
60 Jason Terry 2.50 6.00
61 Ty Lawson 2.00 5.00
62 Kevin Durant 12.00 30.00
63 Tim Hardaway 4.00 10.00
64 Derrick Rose 5.00 12.00
65 Rick Mahorn 2.00 5.00
66 Allen Iverson 5.00 12.00
67 Kevin Garnett 8.00 20.00
68 Chris Bosh 4.00 10.00
69 J.J. Redick 3.00 8.00
70 Russell Westbrook 5.00 12.00
71 Drew Gooden 2.50 6.00
72 Rajon Rondo 4.00 10.00
73 Karl Malone 5.00 12.00
74 LaMarcus Aldridge 3.00 8.00
75 Tayshaun Prince 3.00 8.00
76 Vince Carter 6.00 15.00
77 James Worthy 5.00 12.00
78 Kelly Tripucka 2.50 6.00
79 Carmelo Anthony 5.00 12.00
80 Al Horford 3.00 8.00
81 Grant Hill 5.00 12.00
82 Mark Aguirre 2.50 6.00
83 Marcus Camby 3.00 8.00
84 Shawn Marion 3.00 8.00
85 Emeka Okafor 2.50 6.00
86 John Wall 4.00 10.00
87 Manu Ginobili 6.00 15.00
88 Bernard King 4.00 10.00
89 Bill Laimbeer 4.00 10.00
90 Shaquille O'Neal 10.00 25.00
92 Andre Iguodala 3.00 8.00
93 Kevin Love 3.00 8.00
94 Robert Parish 5.00 12.00
95 Anthony Mason 2.50 6.00
96 Chris Mullin 4.00 10.00
97 Mark Eaton 2.50 6.00
98 Peja Stojakovic 2.50 6.00
99 Shawn Kemp 12.00 30.00
100 Michael Cage 2.00 5.00

2012-13 Panini Crusade Majestic Materials Prime

*PRIME: 1.2X TO 3X BASIC
PRINT RUNS B/WN 1-25 COPIES PER
NO PRICING ON QTY 15 OR LESS

2012-13 Panini Crusade Majestic Signatures

EXCHANGE DEADLINE 12/12/2014
1 Kevin Durant 125.00 300.00
2 Kobe Bryant 1,000.00 2,000.00
3 Jared Dudley 3.00 8.00
4 Blake Griffin 12.00 30.00
5 Deron Williams 4.00 10.00
6 Marcus Camby 5.00 12.00
7 Vince Carter 25.00 60.00
8 Andre Iguodala 5.00 12.00
9 Grant Hill 30.00 80.00
10 Gerald Wallace 4.00 10.00
11 Jason Kidd 15.00 40.00
13 Marcin Gortat 3.00 8.00
14 Tyson Chandler 4.00 10.00
15 Danny Granger 3.00 8.00
16 Jason Terry 4.00 10.00
17 Anderson Varejao 3.00 8.00
18 Andrei Kirilenko 4.00 10.00
19 Andrew Bogut 4.00 10.00
20 Kevin Love 5.00 12.00
21 Brook Lopez 4.00 10.00
22 Jeff Green 4.00 10.00
23 Ed Davis 3.00 8.00
24 Tyreke Evans 4.00 10.00
25 David West 4.00 10.00
26 J.J. Redick 5.00 12.00
27 Joakim Noah 4.00 10.00
28 Greg Monroe 3.00 8.00
29 Ty Lawson 3.00 8.00
30 Stephen Curry EXCH 1,000.00 2,000.00
31 Taj Gibson 3.00 8.00
32 Kendrick Perkins 3.00 8.00
33 Kyle Lowry 5.00 12.00
34 Danilo Gallinari 3.00 8.00
35 Nick Collison 3.00 8.00
36 Corey Brewer 3.00 8.00
37 Gordon Hayward 5.00 12.00
38 Rodney Stuckey 3.00 8.00
39 Jeff Teague 3.00 8.00
40 Raymond Felton 3.00 8.00
41 Ryan Anderson 3.00 8.00
42 DeMarcus Cousins 5.00 12.00
43 Udonis Haslem 4.00 10.00
44 Gerald Henderson 3.00 8.00
45 Caron Butler 4.00 10.00
46 Jamaal Tinsley 3.00 8.00
47 Jason Thompson 3.00 8.00
48 Kevin Martin 4.00 10.00
49 Jason Maxiell 3.00 8.00
50 Thabo Sefolosha 3.00 8.00
51 Alex English 6.00 15.00
52 Allan Houston 8.00 20.00
53 Alonzo Mourning 20.00 50.00
54 Anfernee Hardaway 40.00 100.00
55 Anthony Mason 4.00 10.00
56 Bernard King 6.00 15.00
57 Bill Walton 15.00 40.00
58 Bob McAdoo 8.00 20.00
59 Bobby Jackson 3.00 8.00
60 Buck Williams 3.00 8.00
61 Cedric Ceballos 4.00 10.00
62 Cedric Maxwell 3.00 8.00
63 Chris Mullin 6.00 15.00
64 Clyde Drexler 20.00 50.00
65 Darryl Dawkins 8.00 20.00
66 David Robinson 30.00 80.00
67 David Thompson 5.00 12.00
68 Dennis Scott 3.00 8.00
69 Detlef Schrempf 5.00 12.00
70 Dikembe Mutombo 12.00 30.00
71 Dominique Wilkins 15.00 40.00
72 Fat Lever 4.00 10.00
73 Gary Payton 20.00 50.00
74 George Gervin 10.00 25.00
75 Gus Williams 3.00 8.00
76 Hakeem Olajuwon 40.00 100.00
77 Horace Grant 5.00 12.00
78 Julius Erving 40.00 100.00
79 Kurt Rambis 5.00 12.00
80 Larry Bird 100.00 250.00
81 Larry Johnson 15.00 40.00
82 Len Elmore 3.00 8.00
83 Luc Longley 4.00 10.00
84 Mark Price 5.00 12.00
85 Michael Cooper 5.00 12.00
86 Michael Finley 5.00 12.00
87 Nick Anderson 4.00 10.00
89 Rick Mahorn 3.00 8.00
90 Sam Cassell 4.00 10.00
91 Sean Elliott 3.00 8.00
92 Sidney Moncrief 3.00 8.00
93 Sleepy Floyd 3.00 8.00
94 Spencer Haywood 5.00 12.00
95 Steve Smith 4.00 10.00
96 Tim Hardaway 12.00 30.00
97 Vernon Maxwell 3.00 8.00
98 Vin Baker 3.00 8.00
99 Walt Frazier 12.00 30.00
100 Will Perdue 3.00 8.00

2012-13 Panini Crusade Majestic Signatures Gold

*GOLD: .6X TO 1.5X BASIC
PRINT RUNS B/WN 10-25 COPIES PER
EXCHANGE DEADLINE 12/12/2014
30 Stephen Curry/25 1,500.00 3,000.00

2012-13 Panini Crusade Nobility

1 Paul Pierce 2.50 6.00
2 John Wall 2.00 5.00
3 James Harden 3.00 8.00
4 Kobe Bryant 12.00 30.00
5 Dwight Howard 2.00 5.00
6 Chris Paul 3.00 8.00
7 Carmelo Anthony 2.50 6.00
8 Jason Kidd 2.50 6.00
9 Zach Randolph 1.50 4.00
10 Steve Nash 3.00 8.00
11 Derrick Rose 2.50 6.00
12 LeBron James 12.00 30.00
13 Greg Monroe 1.00 2.50
14 Stephen Curry 12.00 30.00
15 Russell Westbrook 2.50 6.00
16 Tim Duncan 4.00 10.00
17 Rajon Rondo 2.00 5.00
18 Ray Allen 2.50 6.00
19 Blake Griffin 1.50 4.00
20 Dwyane Wade 3.00 8.00
21 Dirk Nowitzki 4.00 10.00
22 Kevin Durant 6.00 15.00
23 Kevin Garnett 4.00 10.00
24 Kevin Love 1.50 4.00
25 Deron Williams 1.25 3.00

2012-13 Panini Crusade Quest Autographs

EXCHANGE DEADLINE 12/12/2014
1 Nikola Vucevic 12.00 30.00
2 Jae Crowder 6.00 15.00
3 Anthony Davis 75.00 200.00
4 Kyrie Irving 40.00 100.00
5 Klay Thompson 100.00 250.00
6 Marquis Teague 3.00 8.00
7 Tristan Thompson 5.00 12.00
8 Alexey Shved 3.00 8.00
9 Bernard James 3.00 8.00
10 Nando De Colo 3.00 8.00
11 Victor Claver 3.00 8.00
12 Brian Roberts 3.00 8.00
13 Jimmy Butler 30.00 80.00
14 Brandon Knight 4.00 10.00
15 Chandler Parsons 4.00 10.00
16 Harrison Barnes 6.00 15.00
17 Jared Sullinger 3.00 8.00
18 Jimmer Fredette 5.00 12.00
19 Andrew Nicholson 3.00 8.00
20 Andre Drummond 8.00 20.00
21 Isaiah Thomas 6.00 15.00
22 Mirza Teletovic 4.00 10.00
23 Lance Thomas 3.00 8.00
24 Bradley Beal 25.00 60.00
25 Michael Kidd-Gilchrist 4.00 10.00
26 Tyler Zeller 3.00 8.00
27 Iman Shumpert 4.00 10.00
28 Jonas Valanciunas 6.00 15.00
29 Kenneth Faried 4.00 10.00
30 Terrence Ross 8.00 20.00
31 Tobias Harris 10.00 25.00
32 Kyle Singler 3.00 8.00
33 Tornike Shengelia 3.00 8.00
34 Robert Sacre 3.00 8.00
35 Kent Bazemore 5.00 12.00
36 Austin Rivers 5.00 12.00
37 Thomas Robinson 3.00 8.00
38 Kemba Walker 15.00 40.00
39 Alec Burks 5.00 12.00
40 Kawhi Leonard 75.00 200.00
41 Doron Lamb 3.00 8.00
42 Darius Morris 4.00 10.00
43 Kendall Marshall 3.00 8.00
44 Will Barton 6.00 15.00
45 MarShon Brooks 3.00 8.00
46 Draymond Green 30.00 80.00
47 Orlando Johnson 3.00 8.00
48 Jeff Taylor 3.00 8.00
49 DeQuan Jones 3.00 8.00
50 Chris Copeland 3.00 8.00
51 John Henson 4.00 10.00
52 Dion Waiters 4.00 10.00
53 Derrick Williams 3.00 8.00
54 Enes Kanter 5.00 12.00
55 Ben Hansbrough 3.00 8.00
56 Greg Stiemsma 3.00 8.00
57 Kevin Jones 3.00 8.00
58 E'Twaun Moore 4.00 10.00
59 Festus Ezeli 3.00 8.00
60 Chris Singleton 3.00 8.00
61 DeAndre Liggins 3.00 8.00
62 Jan Vesely 3.00 8.00
63 Maurice Harkless 4.00 10.00
64 Miles Plumlee 3.00 8.00
65 Nolan Smith 3.00 8.00
66 Norris Cole 3.00 8.00
67 Quincy Acy 3.00 8.00
68 Meyers Leonard 4.00 10.00
69 Jordan Hamilton 3.00 8.00
70 Jon Leuer 3.00 8.00
71 Reggie Jackson 5.00 12.00
72 Lavoy Allen 3.00 8.00
73 Bismack Biyombo 4.00 10.00
74 Evan Fournier 5.00 12.00
75 Earl Clark 3.00 8.00
76 Lance Stephenson 4.00 10.00
77 Joel Anthony 3.00 8.00
78 Marvin Williams 3.00 8.00
79 Jason Smith 3.00 8.00
80 Ronnie Brewer 3.00 8.00
81 Austin Daye 3.00 8.00
82 Chase Budinger 3.00 8.00
83 Courtney Lee 3.00 8.00
84 J.J. Hickson 3.00 8.00
85 George Hill 4.00 10.00
86 Leandro Barbosa 4.00 10.00
87 Mario Chalmers 4.00 10.00
88 Wesley Matthews 3.00 8.00
89 Will Bynum 3.00 8.00
90 Brandon Rush 3.00 8.00
91 Landry Fields 3.00 8.00
92 Alan Anderson 3.00 8.00
93 Anthony Morrow 3.00 8.00
94 Andray Blatche 3.00 8.00
95 Tiago Splitter 3.00 8.00
96 Larry Sanders 3.00 8.00
97 Randy Foye 3.00 8.00
98 Greivis Vasquez 3.00 8.00
99 Byron Mullens 3.00 8.00
100 Ersan Ilyasova 3.00 8.00

2012-13 Panini Crusade Quest Autographs Gold

*GOLD: .6X TO 1.5X BASIC
PRINT RUNS B/WN 10-25 COPIES PER
EXCHANGE DEADLINE 12/12/2014

2012-13 Panini Crusade Quest Memorabilia

*PRIME/25: 1.2X TO 3X BASIC
1 Eric Bledsoe 2.50 6.00
2 Taj Gibson 2.00 5.00
3 Eric Gordon 2.50 6.00
4 Tony Allen 2.00 5.00
5 Robin Lopez 2.00 5.00
6 Tyson Chandler 2.50 6.00
7 Courtney Lee 2.00 5.00
8 Derrick Favors 2.50 6.00
9 DeAndre Jordan 2.50 6.00
10 Luis Scola 2.50 6.00
11 J.J. Barea 2.50 6.00
12 DeMarcus Cousins 3.00 8.00
13 Luke Ridnour 2.50 6.00
14 Jamal Crawford 3.00 8.00
15 Gordon Hayward 3.00 8.00
16 Goran Dragic 3.00 8.00
17 Brook Lopez 2.50 6.00
18 Wesley Matthews 2.00 5.00
19 Hedo Turkoglu 2.00 5.00
20 Brandon Roy 2.50 6.00
21 Tyrus Thomas 2.00 5.00
22 Gerald Henderson 2.00 5.00
23 Marcin Gortat 2.00 5.00
24 Thabo Sefolosha 2.00 5.00
25 Enes Kanter 3.00 8.00
26 Andrea Bargnani 2.00 5.00
27 Jason Maxiell 2.00 5.00
28 Brandon Jennings 2.00 5.00
29 Ryan Anderson 2.00 5.00
30 Michael Beasley 2.00 5.00
31 Anderson Varejao 2.00 5.00
32 Mike Conley 2.50 6.00
33 Serge Ibaka 2.50 6.00
34 Jonas Jerebko 2.00 5.00
35 Anthony Davis 25.00 60.00
36 Xavier Henry 2.00 5.00
37 Evan Fournier 3.00 8.00
38 Kyrie Irving 20.00 50.00
39 DeMar DeRozan 4.00 10.00
40 Jose Calderon 2.00 5.00
41 Linas Kleiza 2.00 5.00
42 Brandon Bass 2.00 5.00
43 Chase Budinger 2.00 5.00
44 Arron Afflalo 2.00 5.00
45 Tristan Thompson 3.00 8.00
46 George Hill 2.50 6.00
47 Kevin Martin 2.50 6.00
48 Landry Fields 2.00 5.00
49 Nicolas Batum 2.50 6.00
50 Nikola Pekovic 2.00 5.00
51 Greg Monroe 2.00 5.00
52 David West 2.50 6.00
53 Glen Davis 2.00 5.00
54 Jameer Nelson 2.00 5.00
55 Markieff Morris 3.00 8.00
56 Thomas Robinson 2.00 5.00
57 Jeremy Lin 5.00 12.00
58 Thaddeus Young 2.00 5.00
59 Ed Davis 2.00 5.00
60 Darrell Arthur 2.00 5.00
61 Michael Kidd-Gilchrist 2.50 6.00
62 Louis Williams 2.50 6.00
63 Draymond Green 12.00 30.00
64 Austin Rivers 3.00 8.00
65 JaVale McGee 2.50 6.00
66 Paul George 5.00 12.00
67 Bismack Biyombo 2.50 6.00
68 Jonas Valanciunas 4.00 10.00
69 Udonis Haslem 2.50 6.00
70 Mo Williams 2.50 6.00
71 Rodney Stuckey 2.00 5.00
72 Jared Sullinger 2.00 5.00
73 Jeff Teague 2.00 5.00
74 Kemba Walker 8.00 20.00
75 Kyle Lowry 3.00 8.00
76 Harrison Barnes 4.00 10.00
77 Josh Smith 2.00 5.00
78 Darren Collison 2.00 5.00
79 Jeff Green 2.00 5.00
80 Kawhi Leonard 25.00 60.00
81 Bradley Beal 15.00 40.00
82 Shane Battier 2.50 6.00
83 Antawn Jamison 2.50 6.00
84 J.J. Hickson 2.00 5.00
85 Ben Gordon 2.50 6.00
86 Devin Harris 2.00 5.00
87 Pau Gasol 5.00 12.00
88 Gary Neal 2.00 5.00
89 Chris Copeland 2.00 5.00
90 Raymond Felton 2.00 5.00
91 Omer Asik 2.00 5.00
92 Carl Landry 2.00 5.00
93 DeShawn Stevenson 2.00 5.00
94 Kris Humphries 2.00 5.00
95 Charlie Villanueva 2.00 5.00
96 Pablo Prigioni 2.00 5.00
97 O.J. Mayo 2.00 5.00
98 Damian Lillard 20.00 50.00
99 Kenneth Faried 2.50 6.00
100 Daniel Gibson 2.00 5.00

2012-13 Panini Crusade Royalty

1 Bill Russell 6.00 15.00
2 Magic Johnson 6.00 15.00
3 Larry Bird 6.00 15.00
4 Dennis Rodman 5.00 12.00
5 Clyde Drexler 3.00 8.00
6 Earl Monroe 2.50 6.00
7 Kareem Abdul-Jabbar 6.00 15.00
8 Patrick Ewing 3.00 8.00
9 John Stockton 4.00 10.00
10 Julius Erving 5.00 12.00
11 Shaquille O'Neal 6.00 15.00
12 Nate Thurmond 2.00 5.00
13 Hal Greer 2.50 6.00
14 Isiah Thomas 4.00 10.00
15 Wes Unseld 2.00 5.00
16 Wilt Chamberlain 6.00 15.00
17 Nate Archibald 2.50 6.00
18 Walt Frazier 3.00 8.00
19 Hakeem Olajuwon 4.00 10.00
20 Jerry West 4.00 10.00
21 Willis Reed 3.00 8.00
22 Oscar Robertson 4.00 10.00
23 Paul Arizin 2.00 5.00
24 Kevin McHale 2.50 6.00
25 Pete Maravich 4.00 10.00

2013-14 Panini Crusade

1 Chris Paul 1.00 2.50
2 Al Horford .50 1.25
3 Pau Gasol .75 2.00
4 Nikola Vucevic .60 1.50
5 Monta Ellis .40 1.00
6 Tyreke Evans .40 1.00
7 Rajon Rondo .60 1.50
8 Carmelo Anthony .75 2.00
9 Kevin Love .50 1.25
10 Andre Drummond .50 1.25
11 J.J. Redick .50 1.25
12 Jeff Teague .30 .75
13 Steve Nash 1.00 2.50
14 Jameer Nelson .30 .75
15 Dirk Nowitzki 1.25 3.00
16 Amir Johnson .30 .75
17 Jeff Green .30 .75
18 Tyson Chandler .40 1.00
19 Kevin Martin .40 1.00
20 Luol Deng .40 1.00
21 Goran Dragic .40 1.00
22 Nick Young .30 .75
23 Paul Millsap .40 1.00
24 Tony Parker .75 2.00
25 Shawn Marion .40 1.00
26 Spencer Hawes .30 .75
27 Jordan Crawford .30 .75
28 Andrea Bargnani .30 .75
29 Derrick Favors .30 .75
30 Derrick Rose .75 2.00
31 Eric Bledsoe .40 1.00
32 DeMarcus Cousins .50 1.25
33 Kemba Walker .50 1.25
34 Tim Duncan 1.25 3.00
35 Vince Carter 1.00 2.50
36 Wesley Matthews .30 .75
37 DeMar DeRozan .60 1.50
38 Damian Lillard 1.50 4.00
39 Enes Kanter .40 1.00
40 Carlos Boozer .40 1.00
41 Gerald Green .40 1.00
42 Isaiah Thomas .40 1.00
43 Gerald Henderson .30 .75
44 Manu Ginobili 1.00 2.50
45 Mike Conley .50 1.25
46 Nicolas Batum .40 1.00
47 Kyle Lowry .50 1.25
48 LaMarcus Aldridge .50 1.25
49 Gordon Hayward .40 1.00
50 Kyrie Irving 1.50 4.00
51 Stephen Curry 4.00 10.00
52 Rudy Gay .40 1.00
53 Al Jefferson .30 .75
54 Kawhi Leonard 1.50 4.00
55 Zach Randolph .40 1.00
56 J.J. Hickson .30 .75
57 Evan Turner .30 .75
58 Kevin Durant 1.50 4.00
59 Paul George .75 2.00
60 Dion Waiters .30 .75
61 Klay Thompson 1.50 4.00
62 LeBron James 4.00 10.00
63 John Wall .60 1.50
64 James Harden 1.00 2.50
65 Marc Gasol .50 1.25
66 Ricky Rubio .40 1.00
67 Thaddeus Young .30 .75
68 Russell Westbrook .75 2.00
69 David West .40 1.00
70 Tristan Thompson .30 .75
71 David Lee .30 .75
72 Chris Bosh .60 1.50
73 Marcin Gortat .30 .75
74 Dwight Howard .60 1.50
75 Eric Gordon .40 1.00
76 Caron Butler .40 1.00
77 Kevin Garnett 1.25 3.00
78 Serge Ibaka .40 1.00
79 Roy Hibbert .30 .75
80 O.J. Mayo .30 .75
81 Harrison Barnes .50 1.25
82 Dwyane Wade 1.00 2.50
83 Bradley Beal .75 2.00
84 Chandler Parsons .30 .75
85 Anthony Davis 1.50 4.00
86 DeAndre Jordan .40 1.00
87 Paul Pierce .75 2.00
88 Ty Lawson .30 .75
89 Brandon Jennings .30 .75
90 Larry Sanders .30 .75
91 Kobe Bryant 4.00 10.00
92 Ray Allen .75 2.00
93 Arron Afflalo .30 .75
94 Jeremy Lin .75 2.00
95 Jrue Holiday .60 1.50
96 Robin Lopez .30 .75
97 Deron Williams .40 1.00
98 Kenneth Faried .40 1.00
99 Greg Monroe .30 .75
100 Blake Griffin .50 1.25
101 Nemanja Nedovic RC .40 1.00
102 Ryan Kelly RC .40 1.00
103 Jeff Withey RC .40 1.00
104 Ben McLemore RC .50 1.25
105 Brandon Davies RC .40 1.00
106 Rudy Gobert RC 1.50 4.00
107 Pero Antic RC .40 1.00
108 Cody Zeller RC .50 1.25
109 Sergey Karasev RC .40 1.00
110 Kentavious Caldwell-Pope RC .60 1.50
111 Isaiah Canaan RC .40 1.00
112 Jamaal Franklin RC .40 1.00
113 Tim Hardaway Jr. RC .75 2.00
114 Victor Oladipo RC 1.00 2.50
115 Archie Goodwin RC .40 1.00
116 Otto Porter RC .60 1.50
117 Dennis Schroder RC 1.25 3.00
118 Erik Murphy RC .40 1.00
119 Carrick Felix RC .40 1.00
120 Luigi Datome RC .40 1.00
121 Robert Covington RC .60 1.50
122 G.Antetokounmpo RC 60.00 150.00
123 Steven Adams RC 1.00 2.50
124 Dwight Buycks RC .40 1.00
125 Alex Len RC .50 1.25

126 Glen Rice Jr. RC .40 1.00
127 Vitor Faverani RC .40 1.00
128 Tony Snell RC .50 1.25
129 Ricky Ledo RC .40 1.00
130 Tony Mitchell RC .40 1.00
131 Solomon Hill RC .50 1.25
132 Miroslav Raduljica RC .40 1.00
133 Andre Roberson RC .50 1.25
134 Gorgui Dieng RC .50 1.25
135 Ian Clark RC .50 1.25
136 C.J. McCollum RC 1.50 4.00
137 Kelly Olynyk RC .50 1.25
138 Anthony Bennett RC .40 1.00
139 Shane Larkin RC .40 1.00
140 Peyton Siva RC .40 1.00
141 Reggie Bullock RC .50 1.25
142 Nate Wolters RC .40 1.00
143 Ray McCallum RC .40 1.00
144 M.Carter-Williams RC .50 1.25
145 Trey Burke RC .50 1.25
146 Lorenzo Brown RC .40 1.00
147 Phil Pressey RC .40 1.00
148 Matthew Dellavedova RC .60 1.50
149 Gal Mekel RC .40 1.00
150 Ognjen Kuzmic RC .40 1.00
151 Hakeem Olajuwon 1.00 2.50
152 Bill Russell 1.50 4.00
153 Shaquille O'Neal 2.00 5.00
154 Yao Ming 1.00 2.50
155 Joe Dumars .60 1.50
156 Lenny Wilkens .50 1.25
157 Robert Horry .50 1.25
158 Clyde Drexler .75 2.00
159 George Gervin .75 2.00
160 Grant Hill .75 2.00
161 Jason Kidd .75 2.00
162 Arvydas Sabonis .60 1.50
163 Larry Johnson .60 1.50
164 Rick Fox .40 1.00
165 Detlef Schrempf .50 1.25
166 Scottie Pippen 1.25 3.00
167 Moses Malone .75 2.00
168 Shawn Kemp .75 2.00
169 Karl Malone 1.00 2.50
170 Spud Webb .50 1.25
171 Chris Mullin .60 1.50
172 Drazen Petrovic .60 1.50
173 Dave Bing .50 1.25
174 Oscar Robertson .75 2.00
175 Jack Sikma .50 1.25
176 Dennis Johnson .40 1.00
177 Jerry Lucas .50 1.25
178 Isiah Thomas .75 2.00
179 Dominique Wilkins .75 2.00
180 Bernard King .60 1.50
181 Wilt Chamberlain 1.50 4.00
182 John Stockton 1.00 2.50
183 Dan Majerle .40 1.00
184 Allen Iverson 1.00 2.50
185 Dennis Rodman 1.25 3.00
186 Nick Van Exel .50 1.25
187 Kareem Abdul-Jabbar 1.50 4.00
188 Adrian Dantley .50 1.25
189 Alonzo Mourning .75 2.00
190 James Worthy .60 1.50
191 Pete Maravich .75 2.00
192 Vlade Divac .50 1.25
193 Gary Payton .75 2.00
194 John Havlicek 1.25 3.00
195 David Robinson 1.00 2.50
196 Larry Bird 2.00 5.00
197 Jerry West 1.25 3.00
198 Anfernee Hardaway 1.25 3.00
199 Magic Johnson 2.00 5.00
200 Julius Erving 1.25 3.00

2013-14 Panini Crusade Silver

*SILVER VET: 2X TO 5X BASIC
*SILVER RC: 1.5X TO 4X BASIC RC
STATED PRINT RUN 25 SER.#'d SETS
21 Goran Dragic 8.00 20.00
122 Giannis Antetokounmpo 1,000.00 2,000.00

2013-14 Panini Crusade Apprentice Signatures

EXCHANGE DEADLINE 11/21/2015
1 Shabazz Muhammad 3.00 8.00
2 Kentavious Caldwell-Pope 5.00 12.00
3 Enes Kanter 4.00 10.00
4 Kawhi Leonard 75.00 200.00
5 Steven Adams 8.00 20.00
6 Nerlens Noel 4.00 10.00
7 C.J. McCollum 12.00 30.00
8 Derrick Williams 3.00 8.00
9 Tony Snell 4.00 10.00
10 Ben McLemore 4.00 10.00
11 Harrison Barnes 5.00 12.00
12 Gorgui Dieng 4.00 10.00
13 Stephen Curry 500.00 1,000.00
14 Trey Burke 4.00 10.00
15 Andre Drummond 5.00 12.00
16 Jason Smith 3.00 8.00
17 Anthony Bennett 3.00 8.00
18 Bradley Beal 12.00 30.00
19 Anthony Davis 60.00 150.00
20 Kelly Olynyk 4.00 10.00
21 Victor Oladipo 8.00 20.00
22 Andrew Nicholson 3.00 8.00
23 Matthew Dellavedova 5.00 12.00
24 Giannis Antetokounmpo 800.00 1,500.00
25 Michael Carter-Williams 4.00 10.00
26 Khris Middleton 10.00 25.00
27 Phil Pressey 3.00 8.00
28 Patrick Beverley 3.00 8.00
29 Cody Zeller 4.00 10.00
30 Hollis Thompson 3.00 8.00
31 Gal Mekel 3.00 8.00
32 Otto Porter 5.00 12.00
33 Shane Larkin 3.00 8.00
34 Robbie Hummel 3.00 8.00
35 Dwight Buycks 3.00 8.00
36 Mason Plumlee 4.00 10.00
37 Alex Len 4.00 10.00
38 Reggie Jackson 4.00 10.00
39 Danny Green 4.00 10.00
40 Jrue Holiday 6.00 15.00

2013-14 Panini Crusade Apprentice Signatures Silver

*SILVER: .5X TO 1.2X BASIC
PRINT RUNS B/WN 25-49 COPIES PER
EXCHANGE DEADLINE 11/21/2015
13 Stephen Curry/25 1,000.00 2,000.00
24 Giannis Antetokounmpo/49 1,500.00 3,000.00

2013-14 Panini Crusade Hardwood Homage Autographs

PRINT RUNS B/WN 10-199 COPIES PER
NO PRICING ON QTY 10
EXCHANGE DEADLINE 11/21/2015
1 Bob Dandridge/199 5.00 12.00
2 Kobe Bryant/25 1,000.00 2,000.00
8 Dikembe Mutombo/99 25.00 60.00
9 Kenny Anderson/199 5.00 12.00
10 Campy Russell/199 5.00 12.00
11 Larry Johnson/199 12.00 30.00
13 Antawn Jamison/199 5.00 12.00
14 Jason Kidd/25 30.00 80.00
18 Jalen Rose/199 5.00 12.00
19 Larry Nance/199 5.00 12.00
20 Fat Lever/199 5.00 12.00
21 Mark Aguirre/199 5.00 12.00
23 Kevin Willis/199 5.00 12.00

2013-14 Panini Crusade Hardwood Homage Autographs Silver

*SILVER: .5X TO 1.2X BASIC
PRINT RUNS B/WN 5-25 COPIES PER
NO PRICING ON QTY 10 OR LESS
EXCHANGE DEADLINE 11/21/2015

2013-14 Panini Crusade High Praise Ink

PRINT RUNS B/WN 10-25 COPIES PER
NO PRICING ON QTY 10
EXCHANGE DEADLINE 11/21/2015
2 Karl Malone/25 50.00 120.00
3 Jason Kidd/25 30.00 80.00
4 Anfernee Hardaway/25 60.00 150.00
6 Scottie Pippen/25 75.00 200.00
10 Kevin Durant/25 100.00 250.00
11 Grant Hill/25 30.00 80.00
12 Arvydas Sabonis 6.00 15.00
13 Magic Johnson/25 100.00 250.00
15 Kobe Bryant/25 1,000.00 2,000.00
16 Bob Dandridge 4.00 10.00
17 Larry Bird/25 100.00 250.00
18 Kyrie Irving/25 60.00 150.00

2013-14 Panini Crusade High Praise Ink Silver

*SILVER: .5X TO 1.2X BASIC
PRINT RUNS B/WN 5-49 COPIES PER
NO PRICING ON QTY 10 OR LESS
EXCHANGE DEADLINE 11/21/2015
12 Arvydas Sabonis/49 12.00 30.00

2013-14 Panini Crusade Insert Blue

1 C.J. McCollum 3.00 8.00
2 Toni Kukoc 1.50 4.00
3 Chris Mullin 1.50 4.00
4 Alex English 1.50 4.00
5 Thaddeus Young .75 2.00
6 JaVale McGee 1.00 2.50
7 Joakim Noah 1.25 3.00
8 P.J. Tucker 1.25 3.00
9 Norris Cole .75 2.00
10 Tiago Splitter .75 2.00
11 Vitor Faverani .75 2.00
12 Rick Mahorn .75 2.00
13 Michael Cooper 1.25 3.00
14 David Robinson 2.50 6.00
15 Spencer Hawes .75 2.00
16 Kevin Love 1.25 3.00
17 Derrick Rose 2.00 5.00
18 Miles Plumlee .75 2.00
19 Al Horford 1.25 3.00
20 Boris Diaw 1.00 2.50
21 Gal Mekel .75 2.00
22 Julius Erving 3.00 8.00
23 Larry Johnson 1.50 4.00
24 Tom Gugliotta 1.00 2.50
25 Tony Wroten .75 2.00
26 Kevin Martin 1.00 2.50
27 Kirk Hinrich 1.00 2.50
28 Klay Thompson 4.00 10.00
29 Jeff Teague .75 2.00
30 James Harden 2.50 6.00
31 Otto Porter 1.25 3.00
32 Arvydas Sabonis 1.50 4.00
33 Dell Curry .75 2.00
34 Mark Jackson 1.00 2.50
35 Lavoy Allen .75 2.00
36 Nikola Pekovic .75 2.00
37 Jimmy Butler 2.50 6.00
38 Stephen Curry 12.00 30.00
39 Paul Millsap 1.00 2.50
40 Dwight Howard 1.50 4.00
41 Nerlens Noel 1.00 2.50
42 Doc Rivers 1.00 2.50
43 Bob Lanier 1.50 4.00
44 Rick Barry 1.50 4.00
45 Jason Richardson 1.25 3.00
46 Corey Brewer .75 2.00
47 Kyrie Irving 4.00 10.00
48 David Lee .75 2.00
49 Kyle Korver 1.00 2.50
50 Jeremy Lin 2.00 5.00
51 Rudy Gobert 3.00 8.00
52 Robert Horry 1.25 3.00
53 Anfernee Hardaway 3.00 8.00
54 Drazen Petrovic 1.50 4.00
55 Carmelo Anthony 2.00 5.00
56 Ricky Rubio 1.00 2.50
57 Dion Waiters .75 2.00
58 Harrison Barnes 1.25 3.00
59 DeMarre Carroll .75 2.00
60 Chandler Parsons .75 2.00
61 Giannis Antetokounmpo 200.00 500.00
62 Jerry West 3.00 8.00
63 John Starks 1.25 3.00
64 Grant Hill 2.00 5.00
65 Andrea Bargnani .75 2.00
66 J.J. Barea 1.00 2.50
67 Tristan Thompson .75 2.00
68 Andre Iguodala 1.25 3.00
69 Louis Williams 1.00 2.50
70 Patrick Beverley .75 2.00
71 Steven Adams 2.00 5.00
72 Kevin McHale 2.00 5.00
73 Peja Stojakovic 1.00 2.50
74 Dennis Johnson 1.00 2.50
75 J.R. Smith 1.25 3.00
76 Gordon Hayward 1.00 2.50
77 Jarrett Jack 1.00 2.50
78 Andrew Bogut 1.00 2.50
79 Kemba Walker 1.25 3.00
80 Omer Asik .75 2.00
81 Kentavious Caldwell-Pope 1.25 3.00
82 Mitch Richmond 1.50 4.00
83 Joe Dumars 1.50 4.00
84 Kelly Tripucka 1.00 2.50
85 Raymond Felton .75 2.00
86 Alec Burks 1.00 2.50
87 Anderson Varejao .75 2.00
88 Jermaine O'Neal 1.00 2.50
89 Gerald Henderson .75 2.00
90 Terrence Jones .75 2.00
91 Tim Hardaway Jr. 1.50 4.00
92 Moses Malone 2.00 5.00
93 A.C. Green 1.25 3.00
94 Robert Parish 1.50 4.00
95 Iman Shumpert .75 2.00
96 Enes Kanter 1.00 2.50
97 Andrew Bynum .75 2.00
98 Draymond Green 2.00 5.00
99 Ramon Sessions .75 2.00
100 Monta Ellis 1.00 2.50
101 Anthony Bennett .75 2.00
102 Allen Iverson 2.50 6.00
103 Nick Van Exel 1.25 3.00
104 Jeff Green .75 2.00
105 Amare Stoudemire 1.25 3.00
106 Derrick Favors .75 2.00
107 O.J. Mayo .75 2.00
108 Kobe Bryant 20.00 50.00
109 Al Jefferson .75 2.00
110 Dirk Nowitzki 3.00 8.00
111 Cody Zeller 1.00 2.50
112 Wilt Chamberlain 4.00 10.00
113 Glen Rice 1.00 2.50
114 Jordan Crawford .75 2.00
115 Tyson Chandler 1.00 2.50
116 Richard Jefferson 1.00 2.50
117 John Henson .75 2.00
118 Pau Gasol 2.00 5.00
119 Michael Kidd-Gilchrist .75 2.00
120 Shawn Marion 1.00 2.50
121 Glen Rice Jr. .75 2.00
122 Gary Payton 2.00 5.00
123 Michael Finley 1.25 3.00
124 Avery Bradley .75 2.00
125 LaMarcus Aldridge 1.25 3.00
126 John Lucas III .75 2.00
127 Khris Middleton 2.50 6.00
128 Steve Nash 2.50 6.00
129 Bismack Biyombo .75 2.00
130 Vince Carter 2.50 6.00
131 Alex Len 1.00 2.50
132 Keith Van Horn 1.00 2.50
133 Vernon Maxwell 1.00 2.50
134 Jared Sullinger .75 2.00
135 Damian Lillard 4.00 10.00
136 Paul George 2.00 5.00
137 Caron Butler 1.00 2.50
138 Nick Young .75 2.00
139 John Wall 1.50 4.00
140 Jose Calderon .75 2.00
141 Mason Plumlee 1.00 2.50
142 Kareem Abdul-Jabbar 4.00 10.00
143 Bill Walton 2.00 5.00
144 Wesley Matthews .75 2.00
145 Brandon Bass .75 2.00
146 David West 1.00 2.50
147 Brandon Knight 1.00 2.50
148 Steve Blake .75 2.00
149 Marcin Gortat .75 2.00
150 Samuel Dalembert .75 2.00
151 Ben McLemore 1.00 2.50
152 Mark Price 1.25 3.00
153 Jason Kidd 2.00 5.00
154 Rajon Rondo 1.50 4.00
155 Nicolas Batum 1.00 2.50
156 Roy Hibbert .75 2.00
157 Ersan Ilyasova .75 2.00
158 Jordan Hill .75 2.00
159 Bradley Beal 2.00 5.00
160 DeJuan Blair .75 2.00
161 Reggie Bullock 1.00 2.50
162 Isiah Thomas 2.00 5.00
163 Cedric Maxwell 1.00 2.50
164 DeMar DeRozan 1.50 4.00
165 Robin Lopez .75 2.00
166 Lance Stephenson 1.00 2.50
167 Larry Sanders .75 2.00
168 Xavier Henry .75 2.00
169 Trevor Ariza .75 2.00
170 Zach Randolph 1.00 2.50
171 Tony Snell 1.00 2.50
172 Sidney Moncrief 1.25 3.00
173 Jeff Hornacek 1.00 2.50
174 Kyle Lowry 1.25 3.00
175 Mo Williams 1.00 2.50
176 George Hill 1.00 2.50
177 Blake Griffin 1.25 3.00
178 DeMarcus Cousins 1.25 3.00
179 Nene 1.00 2.50
180 Marc Gasol 1.25 3.00
181 Shabazz Muhammad .75 2.00
182 Willis Reed 2.00 5.00
183 Calvin Murphy 1.00 2.50
184 Amir Johnson .75 2.00
185 Kevin Durant 4.00 10.00
186 Luis Scola 1.00 2.50
187 Chris Paul 2.50 6.00
188 Isaiah Thomas 1.00 2.50
189 Martell Webster .75 2.00
190 Mike Conley 1.25 3.00
191 Michael Carter-Williams 1.00 2.50
192 Horace Grant 1.25 3.00
193 Shaquille O'Neal 5.00 12.00
194 Jonas Valanciunas 1.00 2.50
195 Russell Westbrook 2.00 5.00
196 Ian Mahinmi .75 2.00
197 Jamal Crawford 1.25 3.00
198 Jimmer Fredette 1.25 3.00
199 Arron Afflalo .75 2.00
200 Kosta Koufos .75 2.00
201 Victor Oladipo 2.00 5.00
202 Shawn Kemp 2.00 5.00
203 Jamal Mashburn 1.00 2.50
204 Terrence Ross 1.00 2.50
205 Serge Ibaka 1.00 2.50
206 Brandon Jennings .75 2.00
207 J.J. Redick 1.25 3.00
208 Rudy Gay 1.00 2.50
209 Nikola Vucevic 1.50 4.00
210 Tony Allen .75 2.00
211 Trey Burke 1.00 2.50
212 Steve Francis 1.00 2.50
213 George Gervin 2.00 5.00
214 Tyler Hansbrough .75 2.00
215 Reggie Jackson 1.00 2.50
216 Josh Smith .75 2.00
217 DeAndre Jordan 1.00 2.50
218 Jason Thompson .75 2.00
219 Jameer Nelson .75 2.00
220 Jon Leuer .75 2.00
221 Kelly Olynyk 1.00 2.50
222 Magic Johnson 5.00 12.00
223 Tom Chambers 1.25 3.00
224 Joe Johnson 1.00 2.50
225 Kendrick Perkins .75 2.00
226 Greg Monroe .75 2.00
227 Jared Dudley .75 2.00
228 Derrick Williams .75 2.00
229 Tobias Harris 1.25 3.00
230 Tayshaun Prince 1.25 3.00
231 Nate Wolters .75 2.00
232 Bill Russell 4.00 10.00
233 Allan Houston 1.25 3.00
234 Brook Lopez 1.25 3.00
235 Derek Fisher 1.00 2.50
236 Rodney Stuckey .75 2.00
237 Antawn Jamison 1.00 2.50
238 LeBron James 20.00 50.00
239 Glen Davis .75 2.00
240 Eric Gordon 1.00 2.50
241 Archie Goodwin .75 2.00
242 Larry Nance 1.00 2.50
243 Bernard King 1.50 4.00
244 Paul Pierce 2.00 5.00
245 Thabo Sefolosha 1.00 2.50
246 Andre Drummond 1.25 3.00
247 Goran Dragic 1.00 2.50
248 Dwyane Wade 2.50 6.00
249 Maurice Harkless .75 2.00
250 Anthony Davis 4.00 10.00
251 Dominique Wilkins 2.00 5.00
252 Dennis Rodman 3.00 8.00
253 John Stockton 2.50 6.00
254 Kevin Garnett 3.00 8.00
255 Ty Lawson .75 2.00
256 Kyle Singler .75 2.00
257 Eric Bledsoe 1.00 2.50
258 Chris Bosh 1.50 4.00
259 Tony Parker 2.00 5.00
260 Jrue Holiday 1.50 4.00
261 Karl Malone 2.50 6.00
262 Patrick Ewing 2.00 5.00
263 Yao Ming 2.50 6.00
264 Jason Terry 1.00 2.50
265 Nate Robinson .75 2.00
266 Chauncey Billups 1.50 4.00
267 Gerald Green 1.00 2.50
268 Ray Allen 2.00 5.00
269 Tim Duncan 3.00 8.00
270 Tyreke Evans 1.00 2.50
271 Hakeem Olajuwon 2.50 6.00
272 Mahmoud Abdul-Rauf .75 2.00
273 Byron Scott 1.25 3.00
274 Andray Blatche .75 2.00
275 J.J. Hickson .75 2.00
276 Luol Deng 1.00 2.50
277 Marcus Morris 1.00 2.50
278 Mario Chalmers 1.00 2.50
279 Manu Ginobili 2.50 6.00
280 Ryan Anderson .75 2.00
281 James Worthy 1.50 4.00
282 Detlef Schrempf 1.25 3.00
283 Pete Maravich 2.00 5.00
284 Andrei Kirilenko 1.25 3.00
285 Kenneth Faried 1.00 2.50
286 Carlos Boozer 1.00 2.50
287 Markieff Morris .75 2.00
288 Michael Beasley .75 2.00
289 Kawhi Leonard 4.00 10.00
290 Jason Smith .75 2.00
291 Larry Bird 5.00 12.00
292 Tim Hardaway 1.50 4.00
293 Alonzo Mourning 2.00 5.00
294 Evan Turner .75 2.00
295 Danilo Gallinari 1.00 2.50
296 Taj Gibson .75 2.00
297 Channing Frye .75 2.00
298 Chris Andersen 1.00 2.50
299 Danny Green 1.00 2.50
300 Al-Farouq Aminu .75 2.00

2013-14 Panini Crusade Insert Orange Die Cut

*ORANGE: 1X TO 2.5X BASIC
STATED PRINT RUN 99 SER.#'d SETS
108 Kobe Bryant 50.00 120.00
238 LeBron James 50.00 120.00

2013-14 Panini Crusade Insert Purple

*PURPLE: 1.2X TO 3X BASIC
STATED PRINT RUN 49 SER.#'d SETS
185 Kevin Durant 25.00 60.00

2013-14 Panini Crusade Insert Red

*RED: .5X TO 1.2X BASIC
STATED PRINT RUN 349 SER.#'d SETS

2013-14 Panini Crusade Insert Teal

*TEAL: .6X TO 1.5X BASIC
STATED PRINT RUN 249 SER.#'d SETS
185 Kevin Durant 12.00 30.00

2013-14 Panini Crusade Knight Court

*SILVER: 1.5X TO 4X BASIC
1 DeAndre Jordan .60 1.50
2 Monta Ellis .60 1.50
3 Kevin Durant 2.50 6.00
4 Kyrie Irving 2.50 6.00
5 Derrick Rose 1.25 3.00
6 Kevin Love .75 2.00
7 Al Horford .75 2.00
8 Serge Ibaka .60 1.50
9 Kenneth Faried .60 1.50
10 Greg Monroe .50 1.25
11 Kawhi Leonard 2.50 6.00
12 Jrue Holiday 1.00 2.50
13 Chris Paul 1.50 4.00
14 James Harden 1.50 4.00
15 Blake Griffin .75 2.00
16 Stephen Curry 6.00 15.00
17 Mike Conley .75 2.00
18 Paul George 1.25 3.00
19 Ty Lawson .50 1.25
20 Andre Drummond .75 2.00
21 George Hill .60 1.50
22 Nikola Vucevic 1.00 2.50
23 Dwight Howard 1.00 2.50
24 Anthony Davis 2.50 6.00
25 Russell Westbrook 1.25 3.00
26 LaMarcus Aldridge .75 2.00
27 Luol Deng .60 1.50
28 Brook Lopez .75 2.00
29 Jimmy Butler 1.50 4.00
30 Rajon Rondo 1.00 2.50

2013-14 Panini Crusade Majestic Marks

PRINT RUNS B/WN 10-199 COPIES PER
NO PRICING ON QTY 10
EXCHANGE DEADLINE 11/21/2015
*SILVER: .5X TO 1.2X BASIC
1 Kyle Korver/199 10.00 25.00
2 John Havlicek/25 75.00 200.00
5 George McGinnis/199 5.00 12.00
6 Antoine Walker/199 4.00 10.00
7 Kobe Bryant/25 1,000.00 2,000.00
9 Andre Iguodala/49 10.00 25.00
11 John Lucas/199 4.00 10.00
14 David Robinson/25 40.00 100.00
15 Dan Majerle/199 4.00 10.00
16 Larry Bird/25 100.00 250.00
17 Jason Kidd/25 40.00 100.00
19 Bradley Beal/49 12.00 30.00
21 Nikola Vucevic/199 6.00 15.00
24 Anfernee Hardaway/49 60.00 150.00
25 Darryl Dawkins/199 4.00 10.00
26 Magic Johnson/25 100.00 250.00
27 Anthony Davis/25 60.00 150.00
30 Roy Hibbert/199 3.00 8.00
31 Kenyon Martin/199 5.00 12.00
33 B.J. Armstrong/199 8.00 20.00
34 Kyrie Irving/25 75.00 200.00
35 Cazzie Russell/199 4.00 10.00
36 Julius Erving/25 40.00 100.00
37 Tom Chambers/199 5.00 12.00
38 Stephen Curry/49 500.00 1,000.00
40 Amir Johnson/199 3.00 8.00
41 Nick Young/199 3.00 8.00
43 Harrison Barnes/49 5.00 12.00
44 Kevin Durant/25 125.00 300.00
45 Muggsy Bogues/199 12.00 30.00
46 Joe Dumars/49 6.00 15.00
47 Kenny Sky Walker/199 3.00 8.00
48 James Harden/49 20.00 50.00
49 Jared Sullinger/49 3.00 8.00
50 Kawhi Leonard/199 60.00 150.00

2013-14 Panini Crusade Majestic Memorabilia

PRINT RUNS B/WN 49-299 COPIES PER
*PRIME: .75X TO 2X BASIC
1 Derrick Favors/99 2.50 6.00
2 Tiago Splitter/299 2.50 6.00
3 Sidney Moncrief/99 4.00 10.00
4 David Robinson/99 8.00 20.00
5 Ricky Rubio/199 3.00 8.00
6 DeMarcus Cousins/199 4.00 10.00
7 Kenny Sky Walker/99 2.50 6.00
8 Kareem Abdul-Jabbar/49 12.00 30.00
9 Gary Payton/99 6.00 15.00
10 Chris Kaman/299 3.00 8.00
11 Kirk Hinrich /299 3.00 8.00
12 Alex English/99 5.00 12.00
13 Larry Nance/99 3.00 8.00
14 Robert Horry/99 4.00 10.00
15 Damian Lillard/99 12.00 30.00
16 Kawhi Leonard/149 12.00 30.00
17 John Starks/99 4.00 10.00
18 Larry Bird/49 15.00 40.00
19 Patrick Ewing/49 6.00 15.00
20 John Stockton/99 8.00 20.00
21 Gerald Wallace/299 3.00 8.00
22 Danny Green/199 3.00 8.00
23 Larry Johnson/99 5.00 12.00
24 Kelly Tripucka/99 3.00 8.00
25 Enes Kanter/199 3.00 8.00
26 Brandon Jennings/199 2.50 6.00
27 Charles Oakley/99 4.00 10.00
28 Shaquille O'Neal/99 15.00 40.00
29 Hakeem Olajuwon/99 8.00 20.00
30 Mo Williams/199 3.00 8.00
31 Michael Beasley/199 2.50 6.00
32 Fat Lever/99 3.00 8.00
33 Shane Battier/299 3.00 8.00
34 Bill Laimbeer/99 4.00 10.00
35 Jeff Teague/49 2.50 6.00
36 Josh Smith/199 2.50 6.00
37 Larry Johnson/99 5.00 12.00
38 Magic Johnson/49 15.00 40.00
39 John Wall/199 5.00 12.00
40 Anderson Varejao/199 2.50 6.00
41 Terrence Ross/99 3.00 8.00
42 Bismack Biyombo/199 2.50 6.00
43 Rick Mahorn/99 2.50 6.00
44 Shawn Kemp/99 6.00 15.00
45 Andre Iguodala/99 4.00 10.00
46 Jeremy Lin/99 12.00 30.00
47 Iman Shumpert/199 2.50 6.00
48 Kobe Bryant/99 40.00 100.00
49 Shaquille O'Neal /99 15.00 40.00
50 Vince Carter/99 8.00 20.00
51 Dominique Wilkins/99 6.00 15.00
52 Randy Foye/199 2.50 6.00
53 Pablo Prigioni/299 2.50 6.00
54 Will Perdue/99 2.50 6.00
55 David Lee/99 2.50 6.00
56 George Hill/199 3.00 8.00
57 Tim Duncan/99 10.00 25.00
58 Kevin Durant/299 12.00 30.00
59 Tracy McGrady/99 6.00 15.00
60 Chris Mullin/99 5.00 12.00
61 Danilo Gallinari/299 3.00 8.00
62 Luis Scola/299 3.00 8.00
63 Evan Fournier/299 3.00 8.00
64 Shawn Bradley/99 2.50 6.00
65 Mike Conley/99 4.00 10.00
66 Pau Gasol/299 6.00 15.00
67 LeBron James/199 40.00 100.00
68 Scottie Pippen/99 10.00 25.00
69 Dwyane Wade/199 8.00 20.00
70 Amare Stoudemire/299 4.00 10.00
71 Andre Miller/199 3.00 8.00
72 Beno Udrih/299 2.50 6.00
73 Darren Collison/199 2.50 6.00
74 Reggie Lewis/99 12.00 30.00
75 Marc Gasol/199 4.00 10.00
76 Nick Young/99 2.50 6.00
77 Joe Dumars/99 5.00 12.00
78 Kyrie Irving/199 12.00 30.00
79 Clyde Drexler/99 6.00 15.00
80 Tristan Thompson/199 2.50 6.00
81 Thaddeus Young/99 2.50 6.00
82 Martell Webster/299 2.50 6.00
83 Kevin Love/299 4.00 10.00
84 Kenneth Faried/99 3.00 8.00
85 Zach Randolph/99 3.00 8.00
86 Tony Parker/99 6.00 15.00
87 Karl Malone/99 8.00 20.00
88 Blake Griffin/199 4.00 10.00
89 Grant Hill/99 6.00 15.00
90 Tayshaun Prince/199 4.00 10.00
91 Gordon Hayward/99 3.00 8.00
92 James Jones/299 2.50 6.00
93 Kurt Rambis/99 4.00 10.00
94 Dwight Howard/99 5.00 12.00
95 LaMarcus Aldridge/199 4.00 10.00
96 DeMar DeRozan/199 5.00 12.00
97 Kevin McHale/99 6.00 15.00
98 Anthony Davis/99 12.00 30.00
99 Walter Davis/99 3.00 8.00
100 Robert Parish/99 5.00 12.00

2013-14 Panini Crusade Nobility

*SILVER: 1.2X TO 3X BASIC
1 Tony Parker 1.25 3.00
2 Robert Horry .75 2.00
3 Dennis Rodman 2.00 5.00
4 Isiah Thomas 1.25 3.00
5 Bob McAdoo 1.00 2.50
6 Tyson Chandler .60 1.50
7 Anthony Davis 2.50 6.00
8 Russell Westbrook 1.25 3.00
9 LeBron James 6.00 15.00
10 Pau Gasol 1.25 3.00
11 Tayshaun Prince .75 2.00
12 Glen Rice .60 1.50
13 Hakeem Olajuwon 1.50 4.00
14 Kareem Abdul-Jabbar 2.50 6.00
15 Kevin McHale 1.25 3.00
16 Kevin Durant 2.50 6.00
17 Damian Lillard 2.50 6.00
18 Dikembe Mutombo 1.25 3.00
19 Dwyane Wade 1.50 4.00
20 Paul Pierce 1.25 3.00
21 Manu Ginobili 1.50 4.00
22 Clyde Drexler 1.25 3.00
23 David Robinson 1.50 4.00
24 Magic Johnson 3.00 8.00
25 Maurice Cheeks .60 1.50
26 Kyrie Irving 2.50 6.00
27 Chris Bosh 1.00 2.50
28 Kevin Garnett 2.00 5.00
29 Dirk Nowitzki 2.00 5.00
30 Tim Duncan 2.00 5.00
31 Shaquille O'Neal 3.00 8.00
32 Scottie Pippen 2.00 5.00
33 Joe Dumars 1.00 2.50
34 Larry Bird 3.00 8.00
35 Blake Griffin .75 2.00
36 Rajon Rondo 1.00 2.50
37 Serge Ibaka .60 1.50
38 Bill Walton 1.25 3.00
39 Kobe Bryant 6.00 15.00
40 Alonzo Mourning 1.25 3.00

2013-14 Panini Crusade Nobility Silver

*SILVER: 1.2X TO 3X BASIC
STATED PRINT RUN 25 SER.#'d SETS

2013-14 Panini Crusade Quest Autographs

PRINT RUNS B/WN 10-199 COPIES PER
NO PRICING ON QTY 10
EXCHANGE DEADLINE 11/21/2015
*SILVER: .5X TO 1.2X BASIC
1 Jerry West/25 30.00 80.00
2 David Robinson/25 30.00 80.00
4 Steve Blake 4.00 10.00
5 Anthony Davis/25 60.00 150.00
6 Kareem Abdul-Jabbar/25 100.00 250.00
8 Kenny Anderson 5.00 12.00
9 Kobe Bryant/25 1,000.00 2,000.00
10 Danny Manning/25 5.00 12.00
11 Elgin Baylor/49 15.00 40.00
12 Jack Sikma 6.00 15.00
13 Kevin Durant/25 100.00 250.00
16 Larry Nance 5.00 12.00
17 Dennis Rodman/49 40.00 100.00
18 Kyrie Irving/25 60.00 150.00
20 Magic Johnson/25 100.00 250.00
21 Rael LaFrentz 4.00 10.00
22 Vince Carter/49 20.00 50.00
23 Kyle Korver 5.00 12.00
24 Mark Aguirre 5.00 12.00
25 Larry Bird/25 100.00 250.00
27 Nick Young 6.00 15.00
28 Spud Webb 6.00 15.00
29 Julius Erving/25 30.00 80.00
31 Kevin Willis 5.00 12.00
32 Clifford Robinson 6.00 15.00
33 Karl Malone/25 30.00 80.00
35 Tobias Harris 6.00 15.00
36 Jared Dudley 4.00 10.00
37 Scottie Pippen/25 75.00 200.00
39 Darryl Dawkins 10.00 25.00

2013-14 Panini Crusade Quest Autographs Silver

*SILVER: .5X TO 1.2X BASIC
PRINT RUNS B/WN 5-25 COPIES PER
NO PRICING ON QTY 5-25 OR LESS
EXCHANGE DEADLINE 11/21/2015

2013-14 Panini Crusade Quest Memorabilia

PRINT RUNS B/WN 15-299 COPIES PER
NO PRICING ON QTY 15
1 Andre Drummond/299 4.00 10.00
2 Kareem Abdul-Jabbar/49 12.00 30.00
3 Blake Griffin/199 4.00 10.00
4 MarShon Brooks/199 2.50 6.00
5 Samuel Dalembert/299 2.50 6.00
6 Norris Cole/299 2.50 6.00
7 Jared Sullinger/299 2.50 6.00
8 O.J. Mayo/299 2.50 6.00
9 Ricky Pierce/99 3.00 8.00
10 Dirk Nowitzki/299 10.00 25.00
11 Harrison Barnes/99 4.00 10.00
12 Patrick Ewing/49 6.00 15.00
13 Anthony Davis/99 12.00 30.00
14 John Salmons/199 3.00 8.00
15 Kevin Garnett/199 10.00 25.00
16 Antawn Jamison/299 3.00 8.00
17 Paul Pierce/199 6.00 15.00
18 Dikembe Mutombo/25 6.00 15.00
19 Deron Williams/99 3.00 8.00
20 James Harden/99 8.00 20.00
21 Steve Nash/49 8.00 20.00
22 Tracy McGrady/99 6.00 15.00
23 Gary Payton/49 6.00 15.00
24 Rashard Lewis/199 3.00 8.00
25 Carmelo Anthony/99 6.00 15.00
26 Luc Mbah a Moute/199 2.50 6.00
27 Evan Turner/99 2.50 6.00
28 Steve Novak/299 2.50 6.00
29 Brad Daugherty/49 4.00 10.00
30 Paul George/99 6.00 15.00
31 Iman Shumpert/249 2.50 6.00
32 David Robinson/49 8.00 20.00
33 Larry Bird/49 15.00 40.00
34 Boris Diaw/299 3.00 8.00
35 Vinnie Johnson/99 4.00 10.00
36 Caron Butler/299 3.00 8.00
37 Nene/99 3.00 8.00
38 Jordan Farmar/149 2.50 6.00
39 Bill Cartwright/99 3.00 8.00
40 Kevin Love/299 4.00 10.00
41 Tim Duncan/299 10.00 25.00
42 Clyde Drexler/99 6.00 15.00
43 DeJuan Blair/299 2.50 6.00
44 Scottie Pippen/149 10.00 25.00
45 Anthony Randolph/299 2.50 6.00
46 Brandon Bass/299 2.50 6.00
47 Maurice Harkless/15 2.50 6.00
48 Julius Erving/49 10.00 25.00
49 Mark Jackson/75 3.00 8.00
50 Russell Westbrook/199 6.00 15.00
51 LeBron James/99 40.00 100.00
52 Magic Johnson/49 15.00 40.00
53 Hakeem Olajuwon/99 8.00 20.00
54 Dwyane Wade/99 8.00 20.00
55 Carlos Delfino/299 2.50 6.00
56 Tobias Harris/199 4.00 10.00
57 Udonis Haslem/299 3.00 8.00
58 Andrei Kirilenko/99 4.00 10.00
59 Anthony Mason/99 3.00 8.00
60 Al Horford/99 4.00 10.00
61 Shaquille O'Neal /99 15.00 40.00
62 Kobe Bryant/199 40.00 100.00
63 Grant Hill/99 6.00 15.00
64 Michael Kidd-Gilchrist/199 2.50 6.00
65 Moses Malone/99 6.00 15.00
66 Ben Gordon/90 3.00 8.00
67 Jerryd Bayless/199 2.50 6.00
68 Terry Cummings/99 3.00 8.00
69 Rory Sparrow/99 2.50 6.00
70 Monta Ellis/99 3.00 8.00
71 Joe Dumars/99 5.00 12.00
72 Kevin Durant/199 12.00 30.00
73 John Wall/199 5.00 12.00
74 Isiah Thomas/49 6.00 15.00
75 Matt Barnes/299 2.50 6.00
76 Luol Deng /99 3.00 8.00
77 Chris Paul/99 8.00 20.00
78 Norm Nixon/99 3.00 8.00
79 Kiki VanDeWeghe/99 3.00 8.00
80 Bradley Beal/99 6.00 15.00
81 Karl Malone/99 8.00 20.00
82 Vince Carter/99 8.00 20.00
83 Devin Harris/99 2.50 6.00
84 Ray Allen/199 6.00 15.00
85 Channing Frye/199 2.50 6.00
86 Nate Robinson/299 2.50 6.00
87 Patty Mills/99 2.50 6.00
88 Dan Majerle/99 3.00 8.00
89 Buck Williams/99 3.00 8.00
90 Al Jefferson/60 2.50 6.00
91 Kevin McHale/99 6.00 15.00
92 Kyrie Irving/199 12.00 30.00
93 Jason Richardson/99 4.00 10.00
94 Kevin Martin/99 3.00 8.00
95 JaVale McGee/299 3.00 8.00
96 David West/199 3.00 8.00
97 Earl Clark/299 2.50 6.00
98 Jeff Malone/99 3.00 8.00
99 Rajon Rondo/99 5.00 12.00
100 Kemba Walker/99 4.00 10.00

2013-14 Panini Crusade Quest Memorabilia Prime
*PRIME: .75X TO 2X BASIC
PRINT RUNS B/WN 2-25 COPIES PER
NO PRICING ON QTY 15 OR LESS

2013-14 Panini Crusade Royalty
*SILVER: 1.2X TO 3X BASIC
1 Carmelo Anthony 1.25 3.00
2 Paul George 1.25 3.00
3 Jerry West 2.00 5.00
4 Wilt Chamberlain 2.50 6.00
5 Bill Walton 1.25 3.00
6 James Worthy 1.00 2.50
7 Cedric Maxwell .60 1.50
8 Kobe Bryant 6.00 15.00
9 Blake Griffin .75 2.00
10 James Harden 1.50 4.00
11 Derrick Rose 1.25 3.00
12 Dirk Nowitzki 2.00 5.00
13 Willis Reed 1.25 3.00
14 John Havlicek 2.00 5.00
15 Moses Malone 1.25 3.00
16 Dennis Johnson .60 1.50
17 Grant Hill 1.25 3.00
18 Kevin Durant 2.50 6.00
19 Damian Lillard 2.50 6.00
20 Kevin Love .75 2.00
21 Rudy Gay .60 1.50
22 Steve Nash 1.50 4.00
23 Kareem Abdul-Jabbar 2.50 6.00
24 Rick Barry 1.00 2.50
25 Magic Johnson 3.00 8.00
26 Larry Bird 3.00 8.00
27 Anfernee Hardaway 2.00 5.00
28 Kyrie Irving 2.50 6.00
29 Dwight Howard 1.25 3.00
30 Stephen Curry 6.00 15.00

2013-14 Panini Crusade Sultans of Springfield Signatures
PRINT RUNS B/WN 10-199 COPIES PER
NO PRICING ON QTY 10
EXCHANGE DEADLINE 11/21/2015
*SILVER: .5X TO 1.2X BASIC
3 Bob McAdoo/199 8.00 20.00
4 Kareem Abdul-Jabbar/25 30.00 80.00
5 Karl Malone/25 25.00 60.00
7 Dan Issel/199 6.00 15.00
10 Joe Dumars/75 6.00 15.00
12 Julius Erving/25 40.00 100.00
13 Scottie Pippen/25 60.00 150.00
14 Bernard King/49 6.00 15.00
15 James Worthy/49 15.00 40.00
17 Robert Parish/75 6.00 15.00
22 Magic Johnson/25 40.00 100.00
24 Dennis Rodman/49 25.00 60.00

2017-18 Panini Dominion
1-100 PRINT RUN 75 SER.#'d SETS
101-140 PRINT RUN 199 SER.#'d SETS
141-180 PRINT RUN 199 SER.#'d SETS
EXCHANGE DEADLINE 11/23/2019
1 Damian Lillard 4.00 10.00
2 Stephen Curry 12.00 30.00
3 LaMarcus Aldridge 1.50 4.00
4 Blake Griffin 1.50 4.00
5 Hassan Whiteside 1.25 3.00
6 Taurean Prince 1.00 2.50
7 Anthony Davis 4.00 10.00
8 Kemba Walker 1.25 3.00
9 Steven Adams 1.25 3.00
10 Harrison Barnes 1.25 3.00
11 CJ McCollum 1.50 4.00
12 Kevin Durant 6.00 15.00
13 DeMar DeRozan 2.00 5.00
14 DeAndre Jordan 1.25 3.00
15 Dion Waiters 1.00 2.50
16 Dennis Schroder 1.25 3.00
17 DeMarcus Cousins 1.25 3.00
18 Nicolas Batum 1.00 2.50
19 Aaron Gordon 1.50 4.00
20 Nerlens Noel 1.00 2.50
21 Jusuf Nurkic 1.25 3.00
22 Klay Thompson 4.00 10.00
23 Serge Ibaka 1.25 3.00
24 Danilo Gallinari 1.25 3.00
25 Giannis Antetokounmpo 8.00 20.00
26 Kent Bazemore 1.00 2.50
27 Jrue Holiday 2.00 5.00
28 Kris Dunn 1.00 2.50
29 Elfrid Payton 1.00 2.50
30 Nikola Jokic 10.00 25.00
31 Evan Turner 1.00 2.50
32 Draymond Green 2.00 5.00
33 Kyle Lowry 1.50 4.00
34 Brandon Ingram 2.00 5.00
35 Khris Middleton 2.00 5.00
36 Kyrie Irving 3.00 8.00
37 Rajon Rondo 2.00 5.00
38 Zach LaVine 2.50 6.00
39 Nikola Vucevic 1.25 3.00
40 Gary Harris 1.25 3.00
41 Buddy Hield 1.50 4.00
42 Chris Paul 2.50 6.00
43 Rudy Gobert 2.00 5.00
44 Brook Lopez 1.25 3.00
45 Malcolm Brogdon 1.25 3.00
46 Al Horford 1.50 4.00
47 Kristaps Porzingis 2.00 5.00
48 Nikola Mirotic 1.00 2.50
49 Ben Simmons 1.50 4.00
50 Paul Millsap 1.25 3.00
51 Vince Carter 3.00 8.00
52 James Harden 3.00 8.00
53 Rodney Hood 1.00 2.50
54 Jordan Clarkson 1.50 4.00
55 Thon Maker 1.00 2.50
56 Jaylen Brown 4.00 10.00
57 Enes Kanter 1.25 3.00
58 LeBron James 12.00 30.00
59 Joel Embiid 3.00 8.00
60 Jamal Murray 2.50 6.00
61 Willie Cauley-Stein 1.00 2.50
62 Eric Gordon 1.25 3.00
63 Ricky Rubio 1.25 3.00
64 Mike Conley 1.25 3.00
65 Karl-Anthony Towns 2.50 6.00
66 D'Angelo Russell 1.25 3.00
67 Tim Hardaway Jr. 1.25 3.00
68 Dwyane Wade 3.00 8.00
69 Dario Saric 1.25 3.00
70 Avery Bradley 1.00 2.50
71 Kawhi Leonard 4.00 10.00
72 Myles Turner 1.50 4.00
73 John Wall 2.00 5.00
74 Marc Gasol 1.50 4.00
75 Andrew Wiggins 2.00 5.00
76 Jeremy Lin 2.50 6.00
77 Carmelo Anthony 2.50 6.00
78 Kevin Love 1.50 4.00
79 Devin Booker 4.00 10.00
80 Andre Drummond 1.25 3.00
81 Pau Gasol 2.50 6.00
82 Victor Oladipo 1.25 3.00
83 Bradley Beal 2.00 5.00
84 Tyreke Evans 1.00 2.50
85 Jimmy Butler 2.50 6.00
86 DeMarre Carroll 1.00 2.50
87 Russell Westbrook 2.50 6.00
88 Julius Randle 1.50 4.00
89 Marquese Chriss 1.00 2.50
90 Tobias Harris 1.25 3.00
91 Rudy Gay 1.25 3.00
92 Thaddeus Young 1.00 2.50
93 Otto Porter Jr. 1.25 3.00
94 Goran Dragic 1.25 3.00
95 Jeff Teague 1.00 2.50
96 Dwight Howard 2.00 5.00
97 Paul George 2.50 6.00
98 Dirk Nowitzki 4.00 10.00
99 Tyson Chandler 1.25 3.00
100 Reggie Jackson 1.25 3.00
101 Tyler Dorsey MET RC 1.50 4.00
102 Frank Ntilikina MET RC 2.00 5.00
103 Semi Ojeleye MET RC 2.00 5.00
104 Luke Kennard MET RC 3.00 8.00
105 Harry Giles MET RC 1.50 4.00
106 Lauri Markkanen MET RC 10.00 25.00
107 OG Anunoby MET RC 8.00 20.00
108 Milos Teodosic MET RC 2.00 5.00
109 Derrick White MET RC 6.00 15.00
110 Lonzo Ball MET RC 6.00 15.00
111 Frank Mason III MET RC 1.50 4.00
112 Dennis Smith Jr. MET RC 2.00 5.00
113 Wes Iwundu MET RC 1.50 4.00
114 Donovan Mitchell MET RC 75.00 200.00
115 John Collins MET RC 4.00 10.00
116 Justin Jackson MET RC 1.50 4.00
117 Terrance Ferguson MET RC 1.50 4.00
118 Maxi Kleber MET RC 2.50 6.00
119 Josh Hart MET RC 4.00 10.00
120 Jayson Tatum MET RC 25.00 60.00
121 Bam Adebayo MET RC 10.00 25.00
122 Zach Collins MET RC 2.50 6.00
123 Sindarius Thornwell MET RC 1.50 4.00
124 Ante Zizic MET RC 2.00 5.00
125 TJ Leaf MET RC 1.50 4.00
126 Justin Patton MET RC 1.50 4.00
127 Zhou Qi MET RC 3.00 8.00
128 Markelle Fultz MET RC 4.00 10.00
129 Kyle Kuzma MET RC 6.00 15.00
130 De'Aaron Fox MET RC 12.00 30.00
131 Jordan Bell MET RC 1.50 4.00
132 Malik Monk MET RC 6.00 15.00
133 Sterling Brown MET RC 1.50 4.00
134 D.J. Wilson MET RC 1.50 4.00
135 Jarrett Allen MET RC 4.00 10.00
136 Bogdan Bogdanovic MET RC 4.00 10.00
137 Caleb Swanigan MET RC 1.50 4.00
138 Josh Jackson MET RC 2.00 5.00
139 Dillon Brooks MET RC 5.00 12.00
140 Jonathan Isaac MET RC 4.00 10.00
141 Dwayne Bacon JSY AU RC 3.00 8.00
142 Sterling Brown JSY AU 3.00 8.00
143 Harry Giles JSY AU 3.00 8.00
144 Tyler Dorsey JSY AU 3.00 8.00
145 Jayson Tatum JSY AU EXCH 75.00 200.00
146 Josh Hart JSY AU 20.00 50.00
147 Bam Adebayo JSY AU 20.00 50.00
148 Kyle Kuzma JSY AU EXCH 12.00 30.00
149 De'Aaron Fox JSY AU 40.00 100.00
150 Malik Monk JSY AU 12.00 30.00
151 Frank Jackson JSY AU RC 3.00 8.00
152 TJ Leaf JSY AU 3.00 8.00
153 Ivan Rabb JSY AU RC 3.00 8.00
154 Tyler Lydon JSY AU RC 3.00 8.00
155 John Collins JSY AU 10.00 25.00
156 Josh Jackson JSY AU 4.00 10.00
157 Ante Zizic JSY AU 3.00 8.00
158 Lauri Markkanen JSY AU 40.00 100.00
159 Dennis Smith Jr. JSY AU 4.00 10.00
160 Markelle Fultz JSY AU 15.00 40.00
161 Frank Mason III JSY AU 3.00 8.00
162 Terrance Ferguson JSY AU 3.00 8.00
163 Jarrett Allen JSY AU 8.00 20.00
164 Wes Iwundu JSY AU 3.00 8.00
165 Jonathan Isaac JSY AU 8.00 20.00
167 D.J. Wilson JSY AU 3.00 8.00
168 Lonzo Ball JSY AU 25.00 60.00
169 Derrick White JSY AU 10.00 25.00
170 OG Anunoby JSY AU EXCH 15.00 40.00
171 Frank Ntilikina JSY AU 4.00 10.00
172 Tony Bradley JSY AU RC 3.00 8.00
173 Jawun Evans JSY AU RC 3.00 8.00
174 Zach Collins JSY AU 5.00 12.00
175 Jordan Bell JSY AU 3.00 8.00
176 Justin Patton JSY AU 3.00 8.00
177 Davon Reed JSY AU RC 3.00 8.00
178 Luke Kennard JSY AU 6.00 15.00
179 Donovan Mitchell JSY AU 75.00 200.00
180 Semi Ojeleye JSY AU 4.00 10.00

2017-18 Panini Dominion Bronze
*BRNZ 101-140: .75X TO 2X BASIC
*BRNZ 141-180: .6X TO 1.5X BASIC
STATED PRINT RUN 49 SER.#'d SETS
EXCHANGE DEADLINE 11/23/2019

2017-18 Panini Dominion Gold
*GOLD 1-100: 1.2X TO 3X BASIC
1-100 PRINT RUN 25 SER.#'d SETS
101-180 PRINT RUN 10 SER.#'d SETS
EXCHANGE DEADLINE 11/23/2019

2017-18 Panini Dominion Franchise Favorites Dual Signatures
PRINT RUNS B/WN 10-25 COPIES PER
NO PRICING ON QTY 15 OR LESS
EXCHANGE DEADLINE 11/23/2019
2 Michael Kidd-Gilchrist
Cody Zeller/25 5.00 12.00
3 Kerr/Kukoc/25 20.00 50.00
4 Love/Thompson/25 12.00 30.00
5 Derek Harper
Rolando Blackman/25 6.00 15.00
6 Fat Lever
Michael Adams/25 10.00 25.00
7 Laimbeer/Dumars/25 12.00 30.00
11 Gasol/Conley/25 12.00 30.00
12 Houston/Sprewell/25 30.00 80.00
13 Aaron Gordon
Nikola Vucevic/25 8.00 20.00
14 Aaron McKie
Eric Snow/25 10.00 25.00
15 Adams/Davis/25 12.00 30.00
16 Divac/Williams/25 40.00 100.00
18 Payton/Kemp25 50.00 120.00
20 Reeves/Abdur-Rahim/25 15.00 40.00

2017-18 Panini Dominion Main Exhibit Autographs
PRINT RUNS B/WN 25-49 COPIES PER
EXCHANGE DEADLINE 11/23/20109
1 Danny Green/49 4.00 10.00
2 Ricky Rubio/25 10.00 25.00
3 Tim Hardaway Jr./49 EXCH 4.00 10.00
4 Rodney Hood/49 3.00 8.00
5 Nikola Jokic/49 125.00 300.00
8 Damian Lillard/25 25.00 60.00
10 Giannis Antetokounmpo/25 50.00 120.00
11 Willie Cauley-Stein/49 3.00 8.00
12 Kristaps Porzingis/49 15.00 40.00
13 Larry Nance Jr./49 6.00 15.00
14 Gordon Hayward/49 12.00 30.00
15 Khris Middleton/49 6.00 15.00
16 Kevin Durant/25 60.00 150.00
17 Justise Winslow/49 3.00 8.00
20 Karl-Anthony Towns/25 25.00 60.00
21 Rudy Gobert/49 8.00 20.00
23 Norman Powell/49 5.00 12.00
24 Aaron Gordon/49 5.00 12.00
25 Avery Bradley/49 3.00 8.00
26 Kyrie Irving/25 30.00 80.00
28 Dirk Nowitzki/25 60.00 150.00
29 Iman Shumpert/49 3.00 8.00
30 Marc Gasol/25 12.00 30.00

2017-18 Panini Dominion Main Exhibit Autographs Bronze
*BRONZE/25: .5X TO 1.2X p/r 49
PRINT RUNS B/WN 15-25 COPIES PER
NO PRICING ON QTY 15 OR LESS
EXCHANGE DEADLINE 11/23/2019
7 Victor Oladipo/25 20.00 50.00

2017-18 Panini Dominion Main Exhibit Legends Autographs
PRINT RUNS B/WN 25-49 COPIES PER
EXCHANGE DEADLINE 11/23/2019
*BRONZE/25: .5X TO 1.2X BASE p/r 49
1 Shaquille O'Neal/25 60.00 150.00
2 Allen Iverson/25 60.00 150.00
3 Kareem Abdul-Jabbar/25 50.00 120.00
4 Tracy McGrady/49 20.00 50.00
5 Rick Barry/49 6.00 15.00
6 Walt Frazier/49 12.00 30.00
7 Robert Parish/49 6.00 15.00
8 Frank Ramsey/49 12.00 30.00
9 Bill Walton/49 6.00 15.00
10 Ralph Sampson/49 5.00 12.00
11 Cliff Hagan/49 6.00 15.00
12 Adrian Dantley/49 5.00 12.00
13 Arvydas Sabonis/49 8.00 20.00
14 Jason Kidd/49 12.00 30.00
16 Robert Horry/49 5.00 12.00
17 Chauncey Billups/49 6.00 15.00
18 Glen Rice/49 4.00 10.00
19 Juwan Howard/49 4.00 10.00
20 Tom Chambers/49 5.00 12.00
21 Jerry Stackhouse/49 8.00 20.00
22 John Starks/49 8.00 20.00
23 Kobe Bryant/49 500.00 1,000.00
24 Larry Hughes/49 6.00 15.00
25 Eddie Jones/49 6.00 15.00
26 Jason Williams/49 40.00 100.00
27 Andrei Kirilenko/49 4.00 10.00
28 Stacey Augmon/49 5.00 12.00
29 Detlef Schrempf/49 6.00 15.00
30 Isaiah Rider/49 6.00 15.00

2017-18 Panini Dominion Main Exhibit Rookie Autographs
STATED PRINT RUN 49 SER.#'d SETS
EXCHANGE DEADLINE 11/23/20109
*BRONZE/25: .5X TO 1.2X BASIC
1 Ante Zizic 4.00 10.00
2 Bam Adebayo 20.00 50.00
3 Bogdan Bogdanovic 10.00 25.00
4 Dillon Brooks 10.00 25.00
5 D.J. Wilson 3.00 8.00
6 De'Aaron Fox 15.00 40.00
7 Dennis Smith Jr. 4.00 10.00
8 Derrick White 6.00 15.00
9 Frank Mason III 6.00 15.00
10 Frank Ntilikina 10.00 25.00
11 Guerschon Yabusele 3.00 8.00
12 Harry Giles 3.00 8.00
13 Ike Anigbogu 3.00 8.00
14 Ivan Rabb 3.00 8.00
15 Jarrett Allen 6.00 15.00
16 John Collins 10.00 25.00
17 Jonathan Isaac 6.00 15.00
18 Jordan Bell EXCH 3.00 8.00
19 Jayson Tatum EXCH 125.00 300.00
20 Josh Hart 15.00 40.00
21 Josh Jackson 4.00 10.00
23 Justin Patton EXCH 3.00 8.00
24 Kyle Kuzma 12.00 30.00
25 Lauri Markkanen 40.00 100.00
26 Lonzo Ball 50.00 120.00
27 Luke Kennard 6.00 15.00
28 Malik Monk 20.00 50.00
29 Markelle Fultz 30.00 80.00
30 OG Anunoby EXCH 10.00 25.00
31 Daniel Theis 10.00 25.00
32 TJ Leaf 3.00 8.00
33 Terrance Ferguson 3.00 8.00
34 Tony Bradley 3.00 8.00
35 Tyler Dorsey 3.00 8.00
37 Wayne Selden 3.00 8.00
39 Zach Collins 5.00 12.00
40 Zhou Qi 15.00 40.00

2017-18 Panini Dominion Mammoth Materials
STATED PRINT RUN 49 SER.#'d SETS
1 Chris Paul 5.00 12.00
2 Stephen Curry 20.00 50.00
3 Kevin Durant 12.00 30.00
4 Giannis Antetokounmpo 15.00 40.00
5 Russell Westbrook 5.00 12.00
6 Kyrie Irving 6.00 15.00
7 Dwight Howard 4.00 10.00
8 Dirk Nowitzki 8.00 20.00
9 James Harden 5.00 12.00
10 LeBron James 25.00 60.00
11 Blake Griffin 3.00 8.00
12 Brandon Ingram 4.00 10.00
13 Karl-Anthony Towns 5.00 12.00
14 Andrew Wiggins 4.00 10.00
15 Kristaps Porzingis 4.00 10.00
16 Anthony Davis 5.00 12.00
17 Paul George 5.00 12.00
19 Damian Lillard 8.00 20.00
20 John Wall 4.00 10.00

2017-18 Panini Dominion NBA Champions Dual Signatures
PRINT RUNS B/WN 4-25 COPIES PER
NO PRICING ON QTY 15 OR LESS
EXCHANGE DEADLINE 11/23/2019
1 Fox/Horry/25 15.00 40.00
2 Armstrong/Grant/25 20.00 50.00
3 Billups/Hamilton/25 15.00 40.00
6 Johnson/Elliott/25 15.00 40.00
8 Hayes/Unseld/24 15.00 40.00
9 Cedric Maxwell
Nate Archibald/25 12.00 30.00
10 McAdoo/Wilkes/25 25.00 60.00
11 Rodman/Harper/25 25.00 60.00
12 Williams/Haslem/25 40.00 100.00
15 Shane Battier
Mario Chalmers/25 8.00 20.00
18 Rick Barry
Jamaal Wilkes/25 12.00 30.00

2017-18 Panini Dominion Peerless Jersey Autographs
PRINT RUNS B/WN 25-49 COPIES PER
EXCHANGE DEADLINE 11/23/2019
*BRONZE/25: .5X TO 1.2X p/r 49
1 Ryan Anderson/49 5.00 12.00
2 Joel Embiid/49 30.00 80.00
3 CJ McCollum/49 8.00 20.00
4 Nikola Mirotic/49 3.00 8.00
5 Jrue Holiday/49 6.00 15.00
6 Rudy Gay/49 4.00 10.00
7 Dirk Nowitzki/25 40.00 100.00
8 Tim Hardaway Jr./49 5.00 12.00
9 DeMarre Carroll/49 3.00 8.00
10 Zach LaVine/49 6.00 15.00
12 D'Angelo Russell/49 6.00 15.00
13 Dwyane Wade/25 20.00 50.00
14 Rudy Gobert/49 6.00 15.00
15 Eric Gordon/49 4.00 10.00
16 Gordon Hayward/49 12.00 30.00
17 Harrison Barnes/49 4.00 10.00
19 Aaron Gordon/49 6.00 15.00
20 Khris Middleton/49 6.00 15.00
23 Reggie Miller/25 60.00 150.00
24 JJ Redick/49 6.00 15.00
26 Victor Oladipo/49 12.00 30.00
27 Devin Booker/49 125.00 300.00
28 Reggie Jackson/49 4.00 10.00
29 Kristaps Porzingis/49 15.00 40.00
30 Jamal Murray/49 12.00 30.00
31 Kevin Love/25 12.00 30.00
32 Evan Turner/49 3.00 8.00
33 Chris Paul/25 25.00 60.00
34 Hakeem Olajuwon/25 15.00 40.00
35 Avery Bradley/49 3.00 8.00
36 Vince Carter/25 20.00 50.00
37 Willie Cauley-Stein/49 3.00 8.00
38 Rodney Hood/49 3.00 8.00
39 Thaddeus Young/49 3.00 8.00
40 Ricky Rubio/25 10.00 25.00
42 Mike Conley/49 4.00 10.00
43 Seth Curry/49 5.00 12.00
44 Nikola Jokic/49 200.00 500.00
45 Giannis Antetokounmpo/25 50.00 120.00
46 Marc Gasol/25 8.00 20.00
48 Karl-Anthony Towns/25 20.00 50.00
49 Damian Lillard/25 25.00 60.00
50 Kyrie Irving/25 30.00 80.00
51 Kobe Bryant/25 1,000.00 2,000.00
52 Dion Waiters/49 3.00 8.00
53 Doug Collins/49 6.00 15.00
54 Tom Chambers/49 5.00 12.00
55 Detlef Schrempf/49 5.00 12.00
56 Sam Perkins/49 4.00 10.00
57 Jack Sikma/49 5.00 12.00
58 Shawn Bradley/49 4.00 10.00
59 Mitch Richmond/49 6.00 15.00
60 B.J. Armstrong/49 6.00 15.00

2017-18 Panini Dominion Power Players Autograph Memorabilia
PRINT RUNS B/WN 15-49 COPIES PER
NO PRICING ON QTY 15
EXCHANGE DEADLINE 11/23/2019
9 Kristaps Porzingis/25 20.00 50.00
10 LaMarcus Aldridge/25 10.00 25.00
11 Dennis Rodman/25 20.00 50.00
12 Christian Laettner/25 12.00 30.00
13 Artis Gilmore/49 6.00 15.00
14 Aaron Gordon/49 5.00 12.00
15 Tyson Chandler/49 4.00 10.00
16 Jermaine O'Neal/49 5.00 12.00
17 Bill Walton/49 6.00 15.00
18 Robert Parish/49 6.00 15.00
19 Ralph Sampson/49 5.00 12.00
20 Myles Turner/49 5.00 12.00
22 Nerlens Noel/49 3.00 8.00
23 Jonas Valanciunas/49 4.00 10.00
24 Antawn Jamison/49 4.00 10.00
25 Shawn Kemp/25 20.00 50.00
26 Ronny Turiaf/49 10.00 25.00
27 Willie Cauley-Stein/49 3.00 8.00
28 Rudy Gobert/49 6.00 15.00
29 Brad Daugherty/49 4.00 10.00
30 Rick Mahorn/49 3.00 8.00

2017-18 Panini Dominion Quad Materials
STATED PRINT RUN 75 SER.#'d SETS
*BRONZE/25: .75X TO 2X BASIC
1 Bembry/Bzmre/Prince/Schroder 3.00 8.00
2 Hrfrd/Brown/Irvng/Smart 10.00 25.00
3 Russell/Carroll/Crabbe/Lin 6.00 15.00
4 Howard/Kdd-Glchrst/Wlkr/Batum 5.00 12.00
5 Vlntne/LaVine/Portis/Dunn 6.00 15.00
6 Smith/Love/James/Thmpsn 20.00 50.00
7 Nowitzki/Barnes/Noel/Curry 10.00 25.00
8 Harris/Murray/Jokic/Millsap 25.00 60.00
9 Drmmnd/Griffin/Jcksn/Jhnsn 4.00 10.00
10 Green/Curry/Drnt/Thmpsn 50.00 120.00
11 Hrdn/Paul/Gordon/Ariza 6.00 15.00
12 Jefferson/Oladipo/Turner/Young 4.00 10.00
13 Beverley/Harris/Gllnri/Jordan 3.00 8.00
14 Ingrm/Lpz/Cldwll-Ppe/Rndle 6.00 15.00
15 Martin/Gasol/Conley/Evans 4.00 10.00
16 Dragic/Haslem/Waiters/Whtsde 4.00 10.00
17 Giannis/Mkr/Mddltn/Brgdn 6.00 15.00
18 Butler/Wggns/Tge/Towns 6.00 15.00
19 Davis/Rondo/Csns/Holiday 6.00 15.00
20 Lee/Hrdwy/Kanter/Przngs 5.00 12.00
21 Anthny/Grge/Wstbrk/Adams 6.00 15.00
22 Gordon/Fournier/Vucevic/Ross 4.00 10.00
23 Saric/Rdck/Embd/McCnnll 8.00 20.00
25 McCllm/Llrd/Nrkc/Trnr 10.00 25.00
26 Hield/Carter/Caly-Stn/Lbssre 8.00 20.00
27 Lnrd/Aldrge/Gsl/Gay 10.00 25.00
28 Lowry/DeRozan/Siakam/Ibaka 8.00 20.00
29 Burks/Fvrs/Rbo/Gbrt 6.00 15.00
30 Wall/Morris/Porter/Jr./Beal 5.00 12.00
31 Jms/Wstbrk/Giannis/Crry 20.00 50.00
32 Lllrd/Giannis/James/Hrdn 12.00 30.00
33 Curry/Csns/Booker/Irving 30.00 80.00
34 Davis/Beal/Oladipo/Alddge 5.00 12.00
35 Capela/Jordan/Drmmnd/Csns 3.00 8.00
36 Towns/Love/Jokic/Howard 4.00 10.00
37 Vcvc/Davis/Giannis/Embd 8.00 20.00
38 Green/Hrdn/James/Wstbrk 30.00 80.00
39 Teague/Wall/Lowry/Rondo 5.00 12.00
40 Lllrd/Holiday/Jcksn/Curry 8.00 20.00

2017-18 Panini Dominion Quad Rookies Materials
STATED PRINT RUN 99 SER.#'d SETS
*BRONZE/25: .75X TO 2X BASIC
1 Ttm/Ball/Jcksn/Fultz 20.00 50.00
2 Ntlkna/Isaac/Mrkknn/Fox 4.00 10.00
3 Cllns/Smith/Knnrd/Monk 6.00 15.00
4 Adb/Wilson/Patton/Mtchll 5.00 12.00
5 Wilson/Giles/Cllns/Leaf 4.00 10.00
6 Allen/Annby/Lydon/Frgsn 8.00 20.00
7 White/Kzma/Swngn/Brdly 6.00 15.00
8 White/Jackson/Iwundu/Reed 6.00 15.00
9 Jcksn/Giles/Knnrd/Ttm 20.00 50.00
10 Bacon/Giles/Isaac/Brdly 4.00 10.00
11 Reed/Smith/Mtchll/Cllns 15.00 40.00
13 Mason/Jcksn/Sldn/Iwnd 2.00 5.00
14 Allen/Evans/Jcksn/Iwnd 3.00 8.00
15 White/Rabb/Bell/Dorsey 6.00 15.00
16 Kzma/Ball/Angbgu/Leaf 6.00 15.00
17 Adb/Thrnwll/Fox/Monk 3.00 8.00
18 Wlsn/Angbgu/Mrkknn/Brwn 4.00 10.00
19 Knnrd/Leaf/Mrkknn/Brown 4.00 10.00
20 Dorsey/Adb/Isaac/Iwnd 10.00 25.00
21 Bacon/Monk/Dorsey/Cllns 6.00 15.00
22 Ntlkna/Allen/Ttm/Fultz 6.00 15.00
23 Ojeleye/Dotson/Ttm/Fultz 6.00 15.00
24 Frgsn/Swngn/Mtchll/Brdly 15.00 40.00
25 Patton/Lydon/Swngn/Cllns 2.50 6.00
26 Bell/Jcksn/Evans/Ball 6.00 15.00
27 Reed/Evans/Giles/Jcksn 2.00 5.00
28 Fox/Mason//Kzma/Thrnwll 12.00 30.00
29 Fox/Mason//Jcksn/Ball 12.00 30.00
30 White/Rabb/Smith/Jr/Sldn 6.00 15.00
32 Mtchll/Ttm/Kzma/Mrkknn 20.00 50.00
33 Fox/Smith/Cllns/Jcksn 12.00 30.00
34 Ball/Annby/Mtchll/Monk 8.00 20.00
35 Ball/Fox/Smith/Mtchll 15.00 40.00
36 Msn/Ntlkna/Fultz/Monk 4.00 10.00
37 Cllns/Mrkknn/Ball/Kzma 10.00 25.00
38 Smith/Jcksn/Fox/Ttm 20.00 50.00
39 Smith/Ttm/Mrkknn/Ball 20.00 50.00
40 Fox/Mtchll/Mason//Kzma 15.00 40.00

2017-18 Panini Dominion Rookie Dual Signatures
STATED PRINT RUN 25 SER.#'d SETS
EXCHANGE DEADLINE 11/23/2019
1 Dillon Brooks
Tyler Dorsey 10.00 25.00
2 Bogdanovic/Fox 50.00 120.00
3 Kadeem Allen
Daniel Theis 12.00 30.00
4 Fultz/Ball 50.00 120.00
5 Bryant/Anunoby 12.00 30.00
6 Tyler Dorsey
John Collins 15.00 40.00
7 Monk/Adebayo 15.00 40.00
8 Kuzma/Ball 25.00 60.00
9 Frank Jackson
Tony Bradley EXCH 6.00 15.00
10 D.J. Wilson
Sterling Brown 6.00 15.00
12 Frank Mason III
Justin Jackson 6.00 15.00
13 Johnathan Motley
Royce O'Neale 8.00 20.00
14 Tatum/Ball EXCH 150.00 400.00
15 Jackson/Selden EXCH 8.00 20.00
17 Fox/Monk 50.00 120.00
18 Hart/Ball 25.00 60.00
20 Jonathan Isaac
Wes Iwundu 15.00 40.00
21 Ball/Leaf 30.00 80.00
22 Brandon Paul
Derrick White 25.00 60.00
23 Tatum/Kennard EXCH 60.00 150.00
24 Mitchell/Ball 150.00 400.00
25 Jackson/Mason III 8.00 20.00
26 Dwayne Bacon
Malik Monk 25.00 60.00
27 Adebayo/Fox 50.00 120.00
28 Hart/Kuzma 25.00 60.00
29 Bell/Dorsey EXCH 6.00 15.00
30 Smith Jr./Kleber EXCH 10.00 25.00
31 Josh Hart
Ryan Arcidiacono 15.00 40.00
32 Allonzo McKinnie
OG Anunoby 12.00 30.00
33 Dwayne Bacon
Jonathan Isaac 15.00 40.00
34 Smith Jr./Ball EXCH 25.00 60.00
35 Frank Mason III
Wayne Selden EXCH 6.00 15.00
36 Zizic/Osman 12.00 30.00
37 Justin Jackson
Frank Jackson 6.00 15.00
38 Dillon Brooks
Wayne Selden EXCH 20.00 50.00
39 Brooks/Bell EXCH 20.00 50.00
40 Caleb Swanigan
Zach Collins 10.00 25.00

2017-18 Panini Dominion Rookie Showcase Jersey Autographs
PRINT RUNS B/WN 25-49 COPIES PER
EXCHANGE DEADLINE 11/23/2019
1 Markelle Fultz/25 30.00 80.00
2 Josh Jackson/25 5.00 12.00
3 Lonzo Ball/25 40.00 100.00
4 Jayson Tatum/25 150.00 400.00
5 De'Aaron Fox/49 20.00 50.00
6 Jonathan Isaac/49 8.00 20.00
7 Lauri Markkanen/25 60.00 150.00
8 Frank Ntilikina/49 6.00 15.00
9 Dennis Smith Jr./49 EXCH 4.00 10.00
10 Zach Collins/49 5.00 12.00
11 Caleb Swanigan/49 3.00 8.00
12 Malik Monk/49 12.00 30.00
13 Luke Kennard/49 6.00 15.00
14 Bam Adebayo/49 20.00 50.00
15 Ante Zizic/49 4.00 10.00
16 D.J. Wilson/49 3.00 8.00
17 Sindarius Thornwell/49 3.00 8.00
18 Justin Patton/49 3.00 8.00
19 Harry Giles/49 3.00 8.00
20 John Collins/49 10.00 25.00
21 TJ Leaf/49 3.00 8.00
22 Sterling Brown/49 3.00 8.00
23 Jarrett Allen/49 8.00 20.00
24 OG Anunoby/49 15.00 40.00
25 Terrance Ferguson/49 3.00 8.00
26 Tyler Lydon/49 3.00 8.00
28 Jordan Bell/49 EXCH 3.00 8.00
29 Derrick White/49 12.00 30.00
31 Kyle Kuzma/49 12.00 30.00
33 Tyler Dorsey/49 3.00 8.00
34 Davon Reed/49 3.00 8.00
35 Dwayne Bacon/49 3.00 8.00
36 Frank Jackson/49 3.00 8.00
37 Frank Mason III/49 3.00 8.00
38 Donovan Mitchell/49 100.00 250.00
39 Ivan Rabb/49 3.00 8.00
40 Jawun Evans/49 3.00 8.00

2017-18 Panini Dominion Triple Threat Trio Signatures
PRINT RUNS B/WN 10-25 COPIES PER
NO PRICING ON QTY 15 OR LESS
EXCHANGE DEADLINE 11/23/2019
2 Russell/Carroll/Lin/25 25.00 60.00
3 Kidd-Gilchrist/Zeller/Walker/25 10.00 25.00
6 Harris/Plumlee/Jokic/25 125.00 300.00
7 Smith/Jackson/Drummond/25 10.00 25.00
8 Kanter/Ntilikina/Porzingis/25 40.00 100.00
10 Young/Turner/Oladipo/25 20.00 50.00
15 Redick/Embiid/Fultz/25 60.00 150.00

2017-18 Panini Dominion With Authority Jersey Autographs
PRINT RUNS B/WN 15-49 COPIES PER
NO PRICING ON QTY 15
EXCHANGE DEADLINE 11/23/2019
10 Brent Barry/49 5.00 12.00
11 Dominique Wilkins/25 12.00 30.00
12 Donovan Mitchell/49 100.00 250.00
13 Harrison Barnes/49 4.00 10.00
14 Andre Drummond/49 4.00 10.00
15 Nick Anderson/49 4.00 10.00
16 Aaron Gordon/49 5.00 12.00
17 Michael Finley/24 6.00 15.00
18 Eric Bledsoe/49 4.00 10.00
19 Zach LaVine/49 6.00 15.00
20 Victor Oladipo/49 12.00 30.00
21 Dennis Smith Jr./49 4.00 10.00
22 Rudy Gay/49 4.00 10.00
23 JR Smith/49 4.00 10.00
24 Shawn Kemp/25 20.00 50.00
25 Kenny "Sky" Walker/49 3.00 8.00
26 Tom Chambers/49 5.00 12.00
27 Jayson Tatum/49 125.00 300.00
28 David Thompson/49 6.00 15.00
29 Larry Nance/49 4.00 10.00
30 Mason Plumlee/49 3.00 8.00

2018-19 Panini Dominion
1-100 PRINT RUN 75 SER.#'d SETS
101-140 PRINT RUN 199 SER.#'d SETS
141-180 PRINT RUN 199 SER.#'d SETS
EXCHANGE DEADLINE 07/04/2020
1 Elfrid Payton 1.25 3.00
2 John Collins 1.50 4.00
3 Evan Fournier 1.25 3.00
4 Harrison Barnes 1.25 3.00
5 Damian Lillard 4.00 10.00
6 Klay Thompson 4.00 10.00
7 Danny Green 1.25 3.00
8 Lou Williams 1.25 3.00
9 Goran Dragic 1.25 3.00
10 Kemba Walker 1.25 3.00
11 Jrue Holiday 2.00 5.00
12 Jeremy Lin 2.50 6.00
13 Aaron Gordon 1.50 4.00
14 Dirk Nowitzki 4.00 10.00
15 CJ McCollum 1.50 4.00
16 Kevin Durant 6.00 15.00
17 Serge Ibaka 1.25 3.00
18 Tobias Harris 1.25 3.00
19 Dion Waiters 1.00 2.50
20 Tony Parker 2.50 6.00
21 Anthony Davis 4.00 10.00
22 Taurean Prince 1.00 2.50
23 Nikola Vucevic 1.25 3.00
24 DeAndre Jordan 1.25 3.00
25 Jusuf Nurkic 1.25 3.00
26 Draymond Green 2.00 5.00
27 Ricky Rubio 1.25 3.00
28 Marcin Gortat 1.00 2.50
29 Hassan Whiteside 1.25 3.00
30 Nicolas Batum 1.00 2.50
31 Tim Hardaway Jr. 1.00 2.50
32 Kyrie Irving 4.00 10.00
33 Ben Simmons 10.00 25.00
34 Jamal Murray 3.00 8.00
35 De'Aaron Fox 3.00 8.00
36 Chris Paul 3.00 8.00
37 Donovan Mitchell 5.00 12.00
38 Lonzo Ball 1.50 4.00
39 Eric Bledsoe 1.25 3.00
40 Kris Dunn 1.00 2.50
41 Kristaps Porzingis 2.00 5.00
42 Jaylen Brown 2.50 6.00
43 Joel Embiid 4.00 10.00
44 Nikola Jokic 8.00 20.00
45 Buddy Hield 1.50 4.00
46 James Harden 3.00 8.00
47 Joe Ingles 1.25 3.00
48 LeBron James 10.00 25.00
49 Giannis Antetokounmpo 8.00 20.00
50 Zach LaVine 2.50 6.00
51 Enes Kanter 1.25 3.00
52 Jayson Tatum 6.00 15.00
53 Markelle Fultz 1.25 3.00
54 Isaiah Thomas 1.25 3.00
55 Zach Randolph 1.25 3.00
56 Carmelo Anthony 2.50 6.00
57 Rudy Gobert 2.00 5.00
58 Kyle Kuzma 1.50 4.00
59 Khris Middleton 1.50 4.00
60 Lauri Markkanen 2.50 6.00
61 Russell Westbrook 2.50 6.00
62 Al Horford 1.50 4.00
63 JJ Redick 1.50 4.00
64 Reggie Jackson 1.25 3.00
65 DeMar DeRozan 2.00 5.00
66 Clint Capela 1.25 3.00
67 John Wall 2.00 5.00
68 Josh Hart 1.25 3.00
69 Jimmy Butler 2.50 6.00
70 Kevin Love 1.25 3.00
71 Dennis Schroder 1.25 3.00
72 D'Angelo Russell 1.50 4.00
73 Devin Booker 4.00 10.00
74 Blake Griffin 1.50 4.00
75 LaMarcus Aldridge 1.50 4.00
76 Tyreke Evans 1.00 2.50
77 Bradley Beal 2.00 5.00
78 Mike Conley 1.25 3.00
79 Derrick Rose 3.00 8.00
80 JR Smith 1.50 4.00
81 Paul George 2.50 6.00
82 Jarrett Allen 1.50 4.00
83 TJ Warren 1.00 2.50
84 Andre Drummond 1.25 3.00
85 Pau Gasol 2.50 6.00
86 Victor Oladipo 1.25 3.00
87 Otto Porter Jr. 1.25 3.00
88 Dillon Brooks 1.50 4.00
89 Karl-Anthony Towns 2.50 6.00
90 Kyle Korver 1.25 3.00
91 Steven Adams 1.25 3.00
92 DeMarre Carroll 1.00 2.50
93 Josh Jackson 1.00 2.50
94 Stephen Curry 12.00 30.00
95 Kyle Lowry 1.50 4.00
96 Myles Turner 1.50 4.00
97 Dwight Howard 2.00 5.00
98 Marc Gasol 1.50 4.00
99 Andrew Wiggins 2.00 5.00
100 Dennis Smith Jr. 1.00 2.50
101 Jalen Brunson MET RC 12.00 30.00
102 Jerome Robinson MET RC 1.50 4.00
103 Bruce Brown MET RC 3.00 8.00
104 Donte DiVincenzo MET RC 4.00 10.00
105 Grayson Allen MET RC 2.00 5.00
106 Deandre Ayton MET RC 5.00 12.00
107 Moritz Wagner MET RC 3.00 8.00
108 Trae Young MET RC 12.00 30.00
109 Dzanan Musa MET RC 1.50 4.00
110 Kevin Knox MET RC 2.00 5.00
111 Devonte' Graham MET RC 2.50 6.00
112 Michael Porter Jr. MET RC 6.00 15.00
113 Hamidou Diallo MET RC 2.50 6.00
114 Lonnie Walker IV MET RC 3.00 8.00
115 Chandler Hutchison MET RC 2.00 5.00
116 Marvin Bagley III MET RC 2.50 6.00
117 Landry Shamet MET RC 2.50 6.00
118 Mo Bamba MET RC 2.50 6.00
119 Omari Spellman MET RC 1.50 4.00
120 Mikal Bridges MET RC 8.00 20.00
121 Gary Trent Jr. MET RC 3.00 8.00
122 Troy Brown Jr. MET RC 2.00 5.00
123 De'Anthony Melton MET RC 3.00 8.00
124 Kevin Huerter MET RC 3.00 8.00
125 Aaron Holiday MET RC 2.50 6.00
126 Luka Doncic MET RC 30.00 80.00
127 Robert Williams III MET RC 3.00 8.00
128 Wendell Carter Jr. MET RC 4.00 10.00
129 Elie Okobo MET RC 1.50 4.00
130 Shai Gilgeous-Alexander MET RC 15.00 40.00
131 Kostas Antetokounmpo MET RC 2.00 5.00
132 Zhaire Smith MET RC 1.50 4.00
133 Keita Bates-Diop MET RC 2.00 5.00
134 Josh Okogie MET RC 2.50 6.00
135 Anfernee Simons MET RC 8.00 20.00
136 Jaren Jackson Jr. MET RC 12.00 30.00
137 Jacob Evans III MET RC 1.50 4.00
138 Collin Sexton MET RC 5.00 12.00
139 Jevon Carter MET RC 2.50 6.00

140 Miles Bridges MET RC 4.00 10.00
141 Elie Okobo JSY AU 3.00 8.00
142 Dzanan Musa JSY AU 3.00 8.00
143 Keita Bates-Diop JSY AU 4.00 10.00
144 Hamidou Diallo JSY AU 5.00 12.00
145 Jacob Evans III JSY AU 3.00 8.00
146 Landry Shamet JSY AU 5.00 12.00
147 Gary Trent Jr. JSY AU 6.00 15.00
148 Jalen Brunson JSY AU 25.00 60.00
149 Aaron Holiday JSY AU 5.00 12.00
150 Grayson Allen JSY AU 6.00 15.00
151 Shai Gilgeous-
Alexander JSY AU 500.00 1,000.00
152 Kevin Knox JSY AU 4.00 10.00
153 Josh Okogie JSY AU 5.00 12.00
154 Lonnie Walker IV JSY AU 6.00 15.00
155 Collin Sexton JSY AU 10.00 25.00
156 Mo Bamba JSY AU 5.00 12.00
157 Troy Brown Jr. JSY AU 4.00 10.00
158 Jerome Robinson JSY AU 3.00 8.00
159 Luka Doncic JSY AU 500.00 1,000.00
160 Deandre Ayton JSY AU 10.00 25.00
161 Jarred Vanderbilt JSY AU RC 6.00 15.00
162 Devonte' Graham JSY AU 5.00 12.00
163 Anfernee Simons JSY AU 15.00 40.00
164 Chandler Hutchison JSY AU 4.00 10.00
165 Jevon Carter JSY AU 5.00 12.00
166 Omari Spellman JSY AU 3.00 8.00
167 De'Anthony Melton JSY AU 6.00 15.00
168 Bruce Brown JSY AU 6.00 15.00
169 Robert Williams III JSY AU 6.00 15.00
170 Moritz Wagner JSY AU 6.00 15.00
171 Zhaire Smith JSY AU 3.00 8.00
172 Michael Porter Jr. JSY AU 10.00 25.00
173 Jaren Jackson Jr. JSY AU 125.00 300.00
174 Marvin Bagley III JSY AU 5.00 12.00
175 Svi Mykhailiuk JSY AU RC 4.00 10.00
176 Mikal Bridges JSY AU 15.00 40.00
177 Kevin Huerter JSY AU 6.00 15.00
178 Donte DiVincenzo JSY AU 8.00 20.00
179 Wendell Carter Jr. JSY AU 8.00 20.00
180 Trae Young JSY AU 40.00 100.00

2018-19 Panini Dominion Gold

*GOLD 1-100: 1X TO 2.5X BASIC
1-100 PRINT RUN 25 SER.#'d SETS
101-180 PRINT RUN 10 SER.#'d SETS
EXCHANGE DEADLINE 07/04/2020
5 Damian Lillard 10.00 25.00
33 Ben Simmons 20.00 50.00
46 James Harden 12.00 30.00
48 LeBron James 40.00 100.00

2018-19 Panini Dominion Red

*RED 101-140: .75X TO 2X BASIC
*RED 141-180: .6X TO 1.5X BASIC
STATED PRINT RUN 49 SER.#'d SETS
EXCHANGE DEADLINE 07/04/2020
126 Luka Doncic MET 75.00 200.00

2018-19 Panini Dominion Court Supremacy Material Signatures

PRINT RUNS B/WN 25-49 COPIES PER
EXCHANGE DEADLINE 07/04/2020
1 Larry Bird/49 40.00 100.00
2 John Stockton/49 15.00 40.00
4 Steve Kerr/49 8.00 20.00
5 Louie Dampier/49 6.00 15.00
7 J.J. Barea/49 6.00 15.00
8 Reggie Miller/25 50.00 120.00
9 Damian Lillard/49 25.00 60.00
10 Brandon Ingram/49 8.00 20.00
11 Lonzo Ball/49 15.00 40.00
12 Harrison Barnes/49 5.00 12.00
13 Kyle Kuzma/49 15.00 40.00
14 Bernard King/49 6.00 15.00
15 Al Horford/49 6.00 15.00
16 Calvin Murphy/49 5.00 12.00
17 Chauncey Billups/49 8.00 20.00
18 Jalen Rose/49 5.00 12.00
19 Michael Kidd-Gilchrist/49 4.00 10.00
20 Myles Turner/49 6.00 15.00
21 Robert Parish/49 10.00 25.00
22 Lauri Markkanen/49 10.00 25.00
23 John Collins/49 6.00 15.00
24 Alvan Adams/49 5.00 12.00
25 Thaddeus Young/49 4.00 10.00
26 Toni Kukoc/49 8.00 20.00
27 Allen Crabbe/49 4.00 10.00
28 John Henson/49 4.00 10.00
29 Tim Hardaway Jr./49 4.00 10.00
30 Dan Issel/49 8.00 20.00

2018-19 Panini Dominion Franchise Favorites Dual Signatures

STATED PRINT RUN 25 SER.#'d SETS
EXCHANGE DEADLINE 07/04/2020
1 Walker/Pierce 20.00 50.00
2 McAdoo/DiGregorio 25.00 60.00
3 Wade/Shaq 125.00 300.00
4 Davis/Blackman 8.00 20.00
5 Kareem/Magic 75.00 200.00
6 Hakeem/Drexler 25.00 60.00
7 Wallace/Hamilton 15.00 40.00
8 McHale/Parish 15.00 40.00
9 Monroe/Reed 50.00 120.00
10 Chris Mullin
Mitch Richmond 15.00 40.00

2018-19 Panini Dominion Main Exhibit Autographs

PRINT RUNS B/WN 15-49 COPIES PER
NO PRICING QTY 15 OR LESS
EXCHANGE DEADLINE 07/04/2020
1 Thaddeus Young/49 3.00 8.00
2 Giannis Antetokounmpo/25 60.00 150.00
3 Seth Curry/49 4.00 10.00
4 Kristaps Porzingis/25 8.00 20.00
5 J.J. Barea/49 6.00 15.00
6 Jason Terry/49 4.00 10.00
7 Trevor Ariza/49 3.00 8.00
9 Danny Green/49 4.00 10.00
11 Willie Cauley-Stein/49 3.00 8.00
12 Karl-Anthony Towns/25 12.00 30.00
13 Courtney Lee/49 3.00 8.00
14 Gordon Hayward/25 8.00 20.00
15 Caris LeVert/49 5.00 12.00
16 Myles Turner/49 5.00 12.00
17 JR Smith/49 5.00 12.00
METMK Thon Maker/49 3.00 8.00
21 Patrick Beverley/49 3.00 8.00
22 Joel Embiid/25 25.00 60.00
23 Matthew Dellavedova/49 4.00 10.00
24 Avery Bradley/49 3.00 8.00
25 Lou Williams/49 4.00 10.00
26 Clint Capela/49 4.00 10.00
27 Enes Kanter/49 4.00 10.00
29 Gerald Green/49 4.00 10.00

2018-19 Panini Dominion Main Exhibit Legends Autographs

PRINT RUNS B/WN 15-49 COPIES PER
NO PRICING QTY 15 OR LESS
EXCHANGE DEADLINE 07/04/2020
2 Rolando Blackman/49 4.00 10.00
4 Brad Daugherty/49 4.00 10.00
5 Bob Lanier/49 6.00 15.00
6 Arvydas Sabonis/49 5.00 12.00
7 George Gervin/49 8.00 20.00
8 Sidney Moncrief/49 3.00 8.00
9 Dave Cowens/49 6.00 15.00
10 Dikembe Mutombo/49 10.00 25.00
12 Charlie Scott/49 5.00 12.00
14 Mark Price/49 5.00 12.00
15 Steve Kerr/49 8.00 20.00
16 Zydrunas Ilgauskas/49 4.00 10.00
17 Robert Parish/49 6.00 15.00
18 Kevin Johnson/49 5.00 12.00
19 Rick Fox/49 4.00 10.00
20 Allan Houston/49 5.00 12.00
22 Terrell Brandon/49 4.00 10.00
24 Vlade Divac/49 6.00 15.00
25 Bernard King/49 5.00 12.00
26 Rafer Alston/49 4.00 10.00
27 Bill Walton/49 15.00 40.00
28 Spencer Haywood/49 5.00 12.00
29 Chauncey Billups/49 6.00 15.00
30 Rik Smits/49 4.00 10.00

2018-19 Panini Dominion Main Exhibit Rookie Autographs

STATED PRINT RUN 49 SER.#'d SETS
EXCHANGE DEADLINE 07/04/2020
1 Jalen Brunson 25.00 60.00
2 Aaron Holiday 5.00 12.00
3 Grayson Allen 6.00 15.00
4 Elie Okobo 3.00 8.00
5 Dzanan Musa 3.00 8.00
6 Keita Bates-Diop 4.00 10.00
7 Hamidou Diallo 5.00 12.00
8 Jacob Evans III 3.00 8.00
9 Landry Shamet 5.00 12.00
10 Gary Trent Jr. 6.00 15.00
11 Jerome Robinson 3.00 8.00
12 Luka Doncic 400.00 800.00
13 Deandre Ayton 10.00 25.00
14 Shai Gilgeous-Alexander 400.00 800.00
15 Kevin Knox 4.00 10.00
16 Josh Okogie 5.00 12.00
17 Lonnie Walker IV 6.00 15.00
18 Collin Sexton 10.00 25.00
19 Mo Bamba 5.00 12.00
20 Troy Brown Jr. 4.00 10.00
21 Bruce Brown 6.00 15.00
22 Robert Williams III 6.00 15.00
23 Moritz Wagner 6.00 15.00
24 Isaac Bonga 4.00 10.00
25 Devonte' Graham 5.00 12.00
26 Anfernee Simons 15.00 40.00
27 Chandler Hutchison 4.00 10.00
28 Jevon Carter 5.00 12.00
29 Omari Spellman 3.00 8.00
30 De'Anthony Melton 6.00 15.00
31 Donte DiVincenzo 8.00 20.00
32 Wendell Carter Jr. 15.00 30.00
33 Trae Young 200.00 500.00
34 Zhaire Smith 3.00 8.00
35 Michael Porter Jr. 15.00 40.00
36 Jaren Jackson Jr. 75.00 200.00
37 Marvin Bagley III 6.00 15.00
38 Svi Mykhailiuk 4.00 10.00
39 Mikal Bridges 15.00 40.00
40 Kevin Huerter 8.00 20.00

2018-19 Panini Dominion Mammoth Materials

STATED PRINT RUN 75 SER.#'d SETS
1 Jimmy Butler 5.00 12.00
2 Karl-Anthony Towns 5.00 12.00
3 Andrew Wiggins 4.00 10.00
4 Dirk Nowitzki 8.00 20.00
5 LeBron James 15.00 40.00
6 Bradley Beal 4.00 10.00
7 Paul George 5.00 12.00
8 Rudy Gobert 4.00 10.00
9 Harrison Barnes 2.50 6.00
10 Markelle Fultz 2.50 6.00
11 Deandre Ayton 6.00 15.00
12 Marvin Bagley III 3.00 8.00
13 Luka Doncic 30.00 80.00
14 Jaren Jackson Jr. 15.00 40.00
15 Trae Young 25.00 60.00
16 Mo Bamba 3.00 8.00
17 Wendell Carter Jr. 5.00 12.00
18 Collin Sexton 6.00 15.00
19 Kevin Knox 2.50 6.00
20 Mikal Bridges 10.00 25.00

2018-19 Panini Dominion NBA Champions Dual Signatures

STATED PRINT RUN 25 SER.#'d SETS
EXCHANGE DEADLINE 07/04/2020
1 Green/Cooper 10.00 25.00
2 Frazier/Barnett 15.00 40.00
3 Curry/Durant 800.00 1,500.00
4 Cowens/Scott 12.00 30.00
5 Cartwright/King 12.00 30.00
6 Wilkes/Nixon 10.00 25.00
7 Horry/Cassell 12.00 30.00
8 Robinson/Elliott 20.00 50.00
9 Heinsohn/Sanders 30.00 80.00
10 Rodman/Kukoc 40.00 100.00

2018-19 Panini Dominion Peerless Jersey Autographs

PRINT RUNS B/WN 25-49 COPIES PER
EXCHANGE DEADLINE 07/04/2020
*RED/25: .5X TO 1.2X p/r 49
1 Myles Turner/49 6.00 15.00
2 Charles Barkley/25 EXCH 125.00 300.00
3 Danny Green/49 5.00 12.00
4 Larry Bird/49 40.00 100.00
5 Seth Curry/49 5.00 12.00
6 Jayson Tatum/49 30.00 80.00
7 Caris LeVert/49 6.00 15.00
8 Buddy Hield/49 6.00 15.00
9 Jamal Mashburn/49 5.00 12.00
10 Goran Dragic/49 5.00 12.00
11 Robert Parish/49 10.00 25.00
12 Kobe Bryant/25 500.00 1,000.00
13 Thon Maker/49 4.00 10.00
14 Dirk Nowitzki/49 EXCH 40.00 100.00
15 Thaddeus Young/49 4.00 10.00
16 Kevin McHale/49 10.00 25.00
17 Charlie Scott/49 6.00 15.00
18 Harrison Barnes/49 5.00 12.00
19 Kevin Johnson/49 6.00 15.00
20 Nick Van Exel/49 12.00 30.00
21 Trevor Ariza/49 4.00 10.00
22 Kevin Durant/25 50.00 120.00
23 Alvan Adams/49 5.00 12.00
24 Julius Erving/49 25.00 60.00
25 Tom Chambers/49 5.00 12.00
26 Tony Parker/49 10.00 25.00
27 J.J. Barea/49 6.00 15.00
28 Zach LaVine/49 10.00 25.00
29 Mike Bibby/49 6.00 15.00
30 Derrick Favors/49 4.00 10.00
31 JR Smith/49 6.00 15.00
32 Allen Iverson/49 30.00 80.00
33 Courtney Lee/49 4.00 10.00
34 Kareem Abdul-Jabbar/49 40.00 100.00
35 Willie Cauley-Stein/49 4.00 10.00
36 Jeremy Lin/49 75.00 200.00
37 Tim Hardaway Jr./49 4.00 10.00
38 Brook Lopez/49 5.00 12.00
39 Sam Perkins/49 5.00 12.00
40 Clint Capela/49 5.00 12.00
41 Cody Zeller/49 4.00 10.00
42 Dwyane Wade/49 30.00 80.00
43 Kenny "Sky" Walker/49 4.00 10.00
44 Giannis Antetokounmpo/49 75.00 200.00
45 Matthew Dellavedova/49 5.00 12.00
46 Dominique Wilkins/49 10.00 25.00
47 Arvydas Sabonis/49 6.00 15.00
48 Kyle Kuzma/49 15.00 40.00
49 Spencer Dinwiddie/49 5.00 12.00
50 Elfrid Payton/49 5.00 12.00
51 Enes Kanter/49 5.00 12.00
52 Damian Lillard/49 30.00 80.00
53 Marvin Williams/49 4.00 10.00
54 Donovan Mitchell/49 20.00 50.00
55 Allen Crabbe/49 4.00 10.00
56 Kristaps Porzingis/49 8.00 20.00
57 Detlef Schrempf/49 8.00 20.00
58 Al Horford/49 6.00 15.00
59 Yogi Ferrell/49 4.00 10.00
60 Michael Kidd-Gilchrist/49 4.00 10.00

2018-19 Panini Dominion Peerless Jersey Autographs Red

*RED/25: .5X TO 1.2X p/r 49
PRINT RUN B/WN 15-25 COPIES PER
NO PRICING QTY 15 OR LESS
EXCHANGE DEADLINE 07/04/2020
26 Tony Parker/25 20.00 50.00

2018-19 Panini Dominion Quad Rookies Relics

STATED PRINT RUN 99 SER.#'d SETS
1 Simons/Musa/Doncic/Okobo 40.00 100.00
2 Deandre Ayton
Luka Doncic
Jaren Jackson Jr.
Marvin Bagley III 40.00 100.00
3 Collin Sexton
Kevin Knox
Michael Porter Jr.
Shai Gilgeous-Alexander 20.00 50.00
4 Jerome Robinson
Kevin Knox
Mikal Bridges
Shai Gilgeous-Alexander 20.00 50.00
5 Donte DiVincenzo
Michael Porter Jr.
Troy Brown Jr.
Zhaire Smith 8.00 20.00
6 Hamidou Diallo
Jarred Vanderbilt
Kevin Knox
Shai Gilgeous-Alexander 20.00 50.00
7 Holiday/Simons/Hutch/Allen 10.00 25.00
8 Lonnie Walker IV
Marvin Bagley III
Jerome Robinson
Wendell Carter Jr. 5.00 12.00
9 Dzanan Musa
Elie Okobo
Jevon Carter
Omari Spellman 3.00 8.00
10 Zhaire Smith
Jevon Carter
Mo Bamba
Trae Young 15.00 40.00
11 De'Anthony Melton
Deandre Ayton
Troy Brown Jr.
Aaron Holiday 6.00 15.00
12 Collin Sexton
Mo Bamba
Wendell Carter Jr.
Trae Young 25.00 60.00
13 Michael Porter Jr.
Hamidou Diallo
Jarred Vanderbilt
Robert Williams III 8.00 20.00
14 Marvin Bagley III
Gary Trent Jr.
Grayson Allen
Wendell Carter Jr. 5.00 12.00
15 Donte DiVincenzo
Josh Okogie
Kevin Huerter
Lonnie Walker IV 5.00 12.00
16 Donte DiVincenzo
Omari Spellman
Jalen Brunson
Mikal Bridges 15.00 40.00
17 Landry Shamet
Jacob Evans III
Moritz Wagner
Robert Williams III 4.00 10.00
18 Bruce Brown
Gary Trent Jr.
Grayson Allen
Josh Okogie 4.00 10.00
19 Shai Gilgeous-Alexander
Trae Young
Collin Sexton
Luka Doncic 75.00 200.00
20 Keita Bates-Diop
Jaren Jackson Jr.
Kevin Huerter
Moritz Wagner 15.00 40.00

2018-19 Panini Dominion Regal Rookie Signatures

STATED PRINT RUN 49 SER.#'d SETS
EXCHANGE DEADLINE 07/04/2020
1 Trae Young 150.00 400.00
2 Deandre Ayton 10.00 25.00
3 Marvin Bagley III 5.00 12.00
4 Lonnie Walker IV 6.00 15.00
5 Bruce Brown 6.00 15.00
6 Jalen Brunson 25.00 60.00
7 Devonte' Graham 5.00 12.00
8 Dzanan Musa 3.00 8.00
9 Omari Spellman 3.00 8.00
11 Zhaire Smith 3.00 8.00
12 Shai Gilgeous-Alexander 400.00 800.00
13 Svi Mykhailiuk 4.00 10.00
14 Collin Sexton 10.00 25.00
15 Robert Williams III 6.00 15.00
16 Aaron Holiday 5.00 12.00
17 Anfernee Simons 15.00 40.00
18 Keita Bates-Diop 4.00 10.00
19 De'Anthony Melton 6.00 15.00
20 Gary Trent Jr. 6.00 15.00
21 Michael Porter Jr. 125.00 300.00
22 Kevin Knox 4.00 10.00
23 Mikal Bridges 15.00 40.00
24 Mo Bamba 5.00 12.00
25 Moritz Wagner 6.00 15.00
26 Grayson Allen 6.00 15.00
27 Chandler Hutchison 4.00 10.00
28 Hamidou Diallo 5.00 12.00
29 Donte DiVincenzo 8.00 20.00
31 Jaren Jackson Jr. 150.00 400.00
32 Josh Okogie 5.00 12.00
33 Kevin Huerter 6.00 15.00
34 Troy Brown Jr. 4.00 10.00
35 Jarred Vanderbilt 6.00 15.00
36 Elie Okobo 3.00 8.00
37 Jevon Carter 5.00 12.00
38 Jacob Evans III 3.00 8.00
39 Wendell Carter Jr. 8.00 20.00
40 Luka Doncic 400.00 800.00

2018-19 Panini Dominion Reigning Threes Relics

STATED PRINT RUN 75 SER.#'d SETS
1 Larry Bird 12.00 30.00
2 Reggie Miller 8.00 20.00
3 Kyle Korver 2.50 6.00
4 Klay Thompson 8.00 20.00
5 Stephen Curry 15.00 40.00
6 Vince Carter 6.00 15.00
7 Jason Kidd 5.00 12.00
8 Dirk Nowitzki 8.00 20.00
9 Peja Stojakovic 2.50 6.00
10 James Harden 6.00 15.00
11 LeBron James 15.00 40.00
12 Mike Bibby 3.00 8.00
13 JJ Redick 3.00 8.00
14 Rashard Lewis 2.50 6.00
15 Glen Rice 3.00 8.00
17 Nick Van Exel 3.00 8.00
18 Wesley Matthews 2.00 5.00
19 Kyle Lowry 3.00 8.00
20 Ryan Anderson 2.00 5.00

2018-19 Panini Dominion Rookie Dual Signatures

STATED PRINT RUN 25 SER.#'d SETS
EXCHANGE DEADLINE 07/04/2020
1 Jackson/Huerter 15.00 40.00
2 Wagner/Mykhailiuk 15.00 40.00
3 Bridges/DiVincenzo 40.00 100.00
4 Smith/Shamet 12.00 30.00
5 Carter Jr./Bagley 20.00 50.00
6 Huerter/Young 125.00 300.00
7 Robinson/Simons 20.00 50.00
8 Robinson/Knox 20.00 50.00
9 Knox/Gilgeous 200.00 500.00
10 Jarred Vanderbilt
Michael Porter Jr. 30.00 80.00
11 Brown/Walker 15.00 40.00
12 Jackson Jr./Carter 60.00 150.00
13 DiVincenzo/Spellman 20.00 50.00
14 Deandre Ayton
Mikal Bridges 25.00 60.00
15 Carter Jr./Allen 20.00 50.00
16 Huerter/Spellman 15.00 40.00
17 Musa/Doncic 400.00 800.00
18 Hutchison/Carter Jr. 20.00 50.00
19 Vanderbilt/Gilgeous 200.00 500.00
20 Brown/Thomas 15.00 40.00
21 Jackson Jr./Wagner 25.00 60.00
22 Okogie/Bates 12.00 30.00
23 Spellman/Brunson 60.00 150.00
24 Simons/Trent Jr. 40.00 100.00
25 Trent Jr./Allen 15.00 40.00
26 Young/Doncic 2,000.00 4,000.00
27 Graham/Mykhailiuk 12.00 30.00
28 Brunson/Doncic 400.00 800.00
29 Diallo/Vanderbilt 15.00 40.00
30 Gilgeous/Robinson 150.00 400.00

2018-19 Panini Dominion Rookie Materials

STATED PRINT RUN 99 SER.#'d SETS
1 Bruce Brown 4.00 10.00
2 Donte DiVincenzo 5.00 12.00
3 Omari Spellman 2.00 5.00
4 Kevin Huerter 4.00 10.00
5 Svi Mykhailiuk 2.50 6.00
6 Jevon Carter 3.00 8.00
7 Anfernee Simons 10.00 25.00
8 Michael Porter Jr. 8.00 20.00
9 Trae Young 40.00 100.00
10 Moritz Wagner 4.00 10.00
11 Jalen Brunson 15.00 40.00
12 Jerome Robinson 2.00 5.00
13 Landry Shamet 3.00 8.00
14 Troy Brown Jr. 2.50 6.00
15 Collin Sexton 6.00 15.00
16 Jacob Evans III 2.00 5.00
17 Keita Bates-Diop 2.50 6.00
18 Kevin Knox 2.50 6.00
19 Deandre Ayton 6.00 15.00
20 Grayson Allen 4.00 10.00
21 Devonte' Graham 3.00 8.00
22 Jaren Jackson Jr. 15.00 40.00
23 Zhaire Smith 2.00 5.00
24 Jarred Vanderbilt 4.00 10.00
25 Robert Williams III 4.00 10.00
26 Wendell Carter Jr. 5.00 12.00
27 De'Anthony Melton 4.00 10.00
28 Mikal Bridges 10.00 25.00
29 Marvin Bagley III 3.00 8.00
30 Chandler Hutchison 2.50 6.00
31 Dzanan Musa 2.00 5.00
32 Josh Okogie 3.00 8.00
33 Shai Gilgeous-Alexander 20.00 50.00
34 Elie Okobo 2.00 5.00
35 Aaron Holiday 3.00 8.00
36 Luka Doncic 75.00 200.00
37 Gary Trent Jr. 4.00 10.00
38 Mo Bamba 3.00 8.00
39 Lonnie Walker IV 4.00 10.00
40 Hamidou Diallo 3.00 8.00

2018-19 Panini Dominion Rookie Quad Signatures

STATED PRINT RUN 25 SER.#'d SETS
EXCHANGE DEADLINE 07/04/2020
1 Carter Jr/Trent Jr/Allen/Bagley 20.00 50.00
2 Doncic/Bagley/Ayton/Jackson Jr 500.00 1,000.00
3 Diallo/Vanderbilt/Knox/Gilgeous 125.00 300.00
4 Sexton/Bamba/Young/Carter Jr 150.00 400.00
5 DiVincenzo/Brunson
Spellman/Bridges 20.00 50.00

2018-19 Panini Dominion Rookie Showcase Jersey Autographs

STATED PRINT RUN 49 SER.#'d SETS
EXCHANGE DEADLINE 07/04/2020
1 Michael Porter Jr. 200.00 500.00
2 Trae Young 200.00 500.00
3 Moritz Wagner 8.00 20.00
5 Donte DiVincenzo 10.00 25.00
6 Omari Spellman 4.00 10.00
7 Kevin Huerter 8.00 20.00
8 Svi Mykhailiuk 5.00 12.00
9 Jevon Carter 6.00 15.00
10 Anfernee Simons 20.00 50.00
11 Kevin Knox 5.00 12.00
12 Deandre Ayton 12.00 30.00
13 Grayson Allen 8.00 20.00
14 Jalen Brunson 30.00 80.00
17 Troy Brown Jr. 5.00 12.00
18 Collin Sexton 12.00 30.00
19 Jacob Evans III 4.00 10.00
20 Keita Bates-Diop 5.00 12.00
21 Mikal Bridges 20.00 50.00
22 Marvin Bagley III 6.00 15.00
24 Devonte' Graham 6.00 15.00
25 Jaren Jackson Jr. 150.00 400.00
26 Zhaire Smith 4.00 10.00
27 Jarred Vanderbilt 8.00 20.00
28 Robert Williams III 8.00 20.00
29 Wendell Carter Jr. 10.00 25.00
30 De'Anthony Melton 8.00 20.00
31 Mo Bamba 6.00 15.00
32 Lonnie Walker IV 8.00 20.00
33 Hamidou Diallo 6.00 15.00
34 Dzanan Musa 4.00 10.00
35 Josh Okogie 6.00 15.00
36 Shai Gilgeous-Alexander 500.00 1,000.00
37 Elie Okobo 4.00 10.00
38 Aaron Holiday 6.00 15.00
39 Luka Doncic 1,500.00 3,000.00
40 Gary Trent Jr. 8.00 20.00

2018-19 Panini Dominion Rookie Triple Signatures

STATED PRINT RUN 25 SER.#'d SETS
EXCHANGE DEADLINE 07/04/2020
1 Ayton/Bagley/Doncic 300.00 600.00
2 Knox/Gilgeous/Vanderbilt 125.00 300.00
3 Huerter/Spellman/Young 125.00 300.00
4 DiVincenzo/Bridges/Spellman 40.00 100.00
5 Allen/Carter Jr/Bagley 20.00 50.00

2018-19 Panini Dominion With Authority Material Signatures

PRINT RUNS B/WN 32-49 COPIES PER
EXCHANGE DEADLINE 07/04/2020
1 Allen Iverson/49 30.00 80.00
2 Dwyane Wade/49 25.00 60.00
3 Magic Johnson/49 25.00 60.00
4 Alonzo Mourning/32 25.00 60.00
5 Andrew Wiggins/49 8.00 20.00
6 Hakeem Olajuwon/49 12.00 30.00
7 Paul Pierce/49 20.00 50.00
8 De'Aaron Fox/49 20.00 50.00
9 Artis Gilmore/49 8.00 20.00
10 Chris Mullin/49 8.00 20.00
11 Nick Van Exel/49 6.00 15.00
12 Bill Walton/49 20.00 50.00
13 Clint Capela/49 5.00 12.00
14 Ralph Sampson/49 5.00 12.00
15 Dikembe Mutombo/49 10.00 25.00
16 Antawn Jamison/49 5.00 12.00
17 Alex English/49 6.00 15.00
18 David Thompson/49 8.00 20.00
19 Stephen Jackson/49 5.00 12.00
20 Tom Chambers/49 5.00 12.00
21 Willie Cauley-Stein/49 4.00 10.00
22 Luke Kennard/49 5.00 12.00
23 Tom Gugliotta/49 4.00 10.00
24 Blake Griffin/49 15.00 40.00
25 Julius Erving/49 25.00 60.00
26 Giannis Antetokounmpo/49 75.00 200.00
27 Kareem Abdul-Jabbar/48 25.00 60.00
28 David Robinson/49 15.00 40.00
29 Tracy McGrady/49 15.00 40.00
30 Kenny "Sky" Walker/49 4.00 10.00

2014-15 Panini Eminence All Star Signatures Silver

PRINT RUNS B/WN 9-10 COPIES PER
3 Chris Webber/10 250.00 400.00
4 Chris Webber/10 250.00 400.00
8 Chris Bosh/10 90.00 150.00
9 Chris Bosh/10 90.00 150.00
10 Kareem Abdul-Jabbar/10 150.00 300.00
11 Kareem Abdul-Jabbar/10 150.00 300.00
14 Karl Malone/10 125.00 250.00
17 Magic Johnson/10 175.00 350.00
21 Jason Kidd/10 150.00 300.00
22 Jason Kidd/10 150.00 300.00
23 Jason Kidd/10 150.00 300.00
24 Pau Gasol/10 100.00 200.00
25 Pau Gasol/10 100.00 200.00
26 Pau Gasol/10 100.00 200.00
28 Stephen Curry/10 1,000.00 2,000.00
30 David Robinson/10 150.00 300.00
31 Kobe Bryant/10 500.00 1,000.00
33 Steve Nash/10 100.00 250.00
34 Steve Nash/10 100.00 250.00
35 Julius Erving/10 200.00 400.00
36 Julius Erving/10 200.00 400.00
37 Julius Erving/10 200.00 400.00
40 Jerry West/10 200.00 400.00
42 Alonzo Mourning/10 125.00 250.00
43 Alonzo Mourning/10 125.00 250.00
44 Chris Paul/10 150.00 400.00
45 Chris Paul/10 150.00 400.00
46 Bill Russell/10 800.00 1,500.00
48 Ray Allen/10 150.00 300.00
49 Ray Allen/10 150.00 300.00
50 Ray Allen/10 150.00 300.00
54 Shaquille O'Neal/10 200.00 400.00
55 Shaquille O'Neal/10 200.00 400.00
56 Shaquille O'Neal/10 200.00 400.00
57 Shaquille O'Neal/10 200.00 400.00
58 Grant Hill/10 150.00 300.00
59 Grant Hill/10 150.00 300.00
60 Larry Bird/10 175.00 350.00
62 Allen Iverson/10 250.00 500.00
63 Allen Iverson/10 250.00 500.00
64 Allen Iverson/10 250.00 500.00
66 Dwight Howard/10 100.00 200.00
67 Dwight Howard/10 100.00 200.00
68 Dwight Howard/10 100.00 200.00
69 Dwyane Wade/10 175.00 350.00
72 Oscar Robertson/10 100.00 200.00
73 Oscar Robertson/10 100.00 200.00
74 Scottie Pippen/10 200.00 400.00
76 Bill Walton/10 100.00 200.00
77 Wes Unseld/10 100.00 200.00
78 Wes Unseld/10 100.00 200.00
79 Dave Cowens/10 90.00 150.00

2014-15 Panini Eminence Finals MVP Signatures Silver

STATED PRINT RUN 10 SER.#'d SETS
1 Magic Johnson 175.00 350.00
2 Magic Johnson 175.00 350.00
3 Magic Johnson 175.00 350.00
4 Shaquille O'Neal 200.00 400.00
5 Shaquille O'Neal 200.00 400.00
6 Shaquille O'Neal 200.00 400.00
7 Kareem Abdul-Jabbar 150.00 300.00
8 Kareem Abdul-Jabbar 150.00 300.00
9 Larry Bird 175.00 350.00
10 Larry Bird 175.00 350.00
11 Kobe Bryant 500.00 1,000.00
12 Kobe Bryant 500.00 1,000.00
13 Jerry West 200.00 400.00
15 Hakeem Olajuwon 150.00 300.00
16 Hakeem Olajuwon 150.00 300.00
19 Bill Walton 100.00 200.00
20 Wes Unseld 100.00 200.00

2014-15 Panini Eminence Larry O'Brien Trophy Signatures Silver

STATED PRINT RUN 10 SER.#'d SETS
1 Scottie Pippen 200.00 400.00
2 Scottie Pippen 200.00 400.00
3 Scottie Pippen 200.00 400.00
4 Scottie Pippen 200.00 400.00
5 Scottie Pippen 200.00 400.00
6 Scottie Pippen 200.00 400.00
7 Dwyane Wade 175.00 350.00
8 Dwyane Wade 175.00 350.00
9 Dwyane Wade 175.00 350.00
10 Kareem Abdul-Jabbar 150.00 300.00
11 Kareem Abdul-Jabbar 150.00 300.00
12 Kareem Abdul-Jabbar 150.00 300.00
13 Kareem Abdul-Jabbar 150.00 300.00
14 Kareem Abdul-Jabbar 150.00 300.00
15 Kareem Abdul-Jabbar 150.00 300.00
16 Kobe Bryant 500.00 1,000.00
17 Kobe Bryant 500.00 1,000.00
18 Kobe Bryant 500.00 1,000.00
19 Kobe Bryant 500.00 1,000.00
20 Kobe Bryant 500.00 1,000.00
21 Larry Bird 175.00 350.00
22 Larry Bird 175.00 350.00
23 Larry Bird 175.00 350.00
24 Magic Johnson 175.00 350.00
25 Magic Johnson 175.00 350.00
26 Magic Johnson 175.00 350.00
27 Magic Johnson 175.00 350.00
28 Magic Johnson 175.00 350.00
29 Shaquille O'Neal 200.00 400.00
30 Shaquille O'Neal 200.00 400.00
31 Shaquille O'Neal 200.00 400.00
32 Shaquille O'Neal 200.00 400.00

2014-15 Panini Eminence MVP Signatures Silver

STATED PRINT RUN 10 SER.#'d SETS
1 Bill Russell 800.00 1,500.00
2 Bill Russell 800.00 1,500.00
3 Bill Russell 800.00 1,500.00
4 Bill Russell 800.00 1,500.00
5 Bill Russell 800.00 1,500.00
6 Kareem Abdul-Jabbar 150.00 300.00
7 Kareem Abdul-Jabbar 150.00 300.00
8 Kareem Abdul-Jabbar 150.00 300.00
9 Kareem Abdul-Jabbar 150.00 300.00
10 Kareem Abdul-Jabbar 150.00 300.00
11 Kareem Abdul-Jabbar 150.00 300.00
12 Larry Bird 175.00 350.00
13 Larry Bird 175.00 350.00
14 Larry Bird 175.00 350.00
15 Magic Johnson 175.00 350.00
16 Magic Johnson 175.00 350.00
17 Magic Johnson 175.00 350.00
18 Julius Erving 200.00 400.00
19 Karl Malone 125.00 250.00
20 Karl Malone 125.00 250.00
21 Steve Nash 100.00 250.00
22 Steve Nash 100.00 250.00
23 Shaquille O'Neal 200.00 400.00
25 David Robinson 150.00 300.00
26 Kobe Bryant 500.00 1,000.00
27 Hakeem Olajuwon 150.00 300.00
28 Allen Iverson 250.00 500.00
30 Stephen Curry 1,000.00 2,000.00
32 Oscar Robertson 100.00 200.00
33 Bill Walton 100.00 200.00
34 Wes Unseld 100.00 200.00
35 Dave Cowens 90.00 150.00

2017-18 Panini Encased

STATED PRINT RUN 99 SER.#'d SETS
*RED/25: .6X TO 1.5X BASIC
1 Stephen Curry 10.00 25.00
2 Tyson Chandler 1.00 2.50
3 Dirk Nowitzki 3.00 8.00
4 Carmelo Anthony 2.00 5.00
5 Dwight Howard 1.50 4.00
6 Karl-Anthony Towns 2.00 5.00
7 Dennis Schroder 1.00 2.50
8 Goran Dragic 1.00 2.50
9 Blake Griffin 1.25 3.00
10 Manu Ginobili 2.50 6.00
11 Klay Thompson 3.00 8.00
12 Damian Lillard 3.00 8.00
13 Harrison Barnes 1.00 2.50
14 Steven Adams 1.00 2.50
15 Marvin Williams .75 2.00
16 Jrue Holiday 1.50 4.00
17 Kent Bazemore .75 2.00
18 Dion Waiters .75 2.00
19 DeAndre Jordan 1.00 2.50
20 Kyle Lowry 1.25 3.00
21 Kevin Durant 5.00 12.00
22 CJ McCollum 1.25 3.00
23 Wesley Matthews .75 2.00
24 Elfrid Payton .75 2.00
25 Zach LaVine 2.00 5.00
26 Rajon Rondo 1.50 4.00
27 Taurean Prince .75 2.00
28 Justise Winslow .75 2.00
29 Patrick Beverley .75 2.00
30 DeMar DeRozan 1.50 4.00
31 Draymond Green 1.50 4.00
32 Jusuf Nurkic 1.00 2.50
33 Jamal Murray 2.00 5.00
34 Aaron Gordon 1.25 3.00
35 Robin Lopez .75 2.00
36 Anthony Davis 3.00 8.00
37 Kyrie Irving 2.50 6.00
38 Eric Bledsoe 1.00 2.50
39 Brook Lopez 1.00 2.50
40 Serge Ibaka 1.00 2.50
41 Chris Paul 2.00 5.00
42 Zach Randolph 1.25 3.00
43 Will Barton .75 2.00
44 Nikola Vucevic 1.00 2.50
45 Kris Dunn .75 2.00
46 DeMarcus Cousins 1.00 2.50
47 Jaylen Brown 3.00 8.00
48 Khris Middleton 1.50 4.00
49 Brandon Ingram 1.50 4.00
50 Ricky Rubio 1.00 2.50
51 James Harden 2.50 6.00
52 Vince Carter 2.50 6.00
53 Gary Harris 1.00 2.50
54 Ben Simmons 1.25 3.00
55 Gordon Hayward 1.00 2.50
56 Kristaps Porzingis 1.50 4.00
57 Al Horford 1.25 3.00
58 Giannis Antetokounmpo 6.00 15.00
59 Kentavious Caldwell-Pope 1.00 2.50
60 Rudy Gobert 1.50 4.00
61 Clint Capela 1.00 2.50
62 Buddy Hield 1.25 3.00
63 Tobias Harris 1.00 2.50
64 Dario Saric 1.00 2.50
65 LeBron James 10.00 25.00
66 Enes Kanter 1.00 2.50
67 Jeremy Lin 2.00 5.00
68 Malcolm Brogdon 1.00 2.50
69 Jordan Clarkson 1.25 3.00
70 Derrick Favors .75 2.00
71 Victor Oladipo 1.00 2.50
72 Tony Parker 2.00 5.00
73 Reggie Jackson 1.00 2.50
74 Joel Embiid 2.50 6.00
75 Kevin Love 1.25 3.00
76 Tim Hardaway Jr. 1.00 2.50
77 DeMarre Carroll .75 2.00
78 Jeff Teague .75 2.00
79 Mike Conley 1.00 2.50
80 John Wall 1.50 4.00
81 Myles Turner 1.25 3.00
82 LaMarcus Aldridge 1.25 3.00
83 Andre Drummond 1.00 2.50
84 Devin Booker 3.00 8.00
85 Isaiah Thomas 1.00 2.50
86 Russell Westbrook 2.00 5.00
87 D'Angelo Russell 1.00 2.50
88 Jimmy Butler 2.00 5.00
89 Marc Gasol 1.25 3.00
90 Bradley Beal 1.50 4.00
91 Thaddeus Young .75 2.00
92 Pau Gasol 2.00 5.00
93 Avery Bradley .75 2.00
94 TJ Warren 1.00 2.50
95 Dwyane Wade 2.50 6.00
96 Paul George 2.00 5.00
97 Kemba Walker 1.00 2.50

2018-19 Panini Dominion Gold

98 Andrew Wiggins 1.50 4.00
99 Tyreke Evans .75 2.00
100 Marcin Gortat .75 2.00
101 J.Bell AU RC EXCH 5.00 12.00
102 D.Mitchell AU RC EXCH 75.00 200.00
103 G.Yabusele AU RC 5.00 12.00
104 D.J. Wilson AU RC 5.00 12.00
105 T.Ferguson AU RC 5.00 12.00
106 Markelle Fultz AU RC 12.00 30.00
107 Dillon Brooks AU RC 15.00 40.00
108 De'Aaron Fox AU RC 50.00 120.00
109 Josh Hart AU RC 12.00 30.00
110 D.Smith Jr. AU RC 6.00 15.00
111 Sterling Brown AU RC 5.00 12.00
112 Bam Adebayo AU RC 30.00 80.00
113 B.Bogdanovic AU RC 12.00 30.00
114 TJ Leaf AU RC 5.00 12.00
115 Jarrett Allen AU RC 12.00 30.00
116 Lonzo Ball AU RC 20.00 50.00
117 Kyle Kuzma AU RC 20.00 50.00
118 Jonathan Isaac AU RC 12.00 30.00
119 Frank Jackson AU RC 5.00 12.00
120 Zach Collins AU RC 8.00 20.00
121 Sindarius Thornwell AU RC 5.00 12.00
122 Justin Jackson AU RC 5.00 12.00
123 Wayne Selden AU RC 5.00 12.00
124 John Collins AU RC 12.00 30.00
125 OG Anunoby AU RC 25.00 60.00
126 Jayson Tatum AU RC 400.00 800.00
127 Tony Bradley AU RC 5.00 12.00
128 L.Markkanen AU RC 30.00 80.00
129 Frank Mason AU RC 5.00 12.00
130 Malik Monk AU RC 20.00 50.00
131 Milos Teodosic AU RC 6.00 15.00
132 Justin Patton AU RC 5.00 12.00
133 Cedi Osman AU RC 10.00 25.00
134 Harry Giles AU RC 5.00 12.00
135 Tyler Lydon AU RC 5.00 12.00
136 Josh Jackson AU RC 6.00 15.00
137 Derrick White AU RC 25.00 60.00
138 Frank Ntilikina AU RC 6.00 15.00
139 Ivan Rabb AU RC 5.00 12.00
140 Luke Kennard AU RC 10.00 25.00
141 Derrick White AU RC 25.00 60.00
142 Markelle Fultz AU RC 12.00 30.00
143 Justin Jackson AU RC 5.00 12.00
144 Josh Jackson AU RC 6.00 15.00
145 D.J. Wilson AU RC 5.00 12.00
146 L.Markkanen AU RC 30.00 80.00
147 Harry Giles AU RC 5.00 12.00
148 Zach Collins AU RC 8.00 20.00
149 Ante Zizic AU RC 6.00 15.00
150 D.Mitchell AU RC EXCH 75.00 200.00
151 Kyle Kuzma AU RC 20.00 50.00
152 Lonzo Ball AU RC 20.00 50.00
153 Frank Mason AU RC 5.00 12.00
154 De'Aaron Fox AU RC 50.00 120.00
155 TJ Leaf AU RC 5.00 12.00
156 Frank Ntilikina AU RC 6.00 15.00
157 Wes Iwundu AU RC 5.00 12.00
158 Malik Monk AU RC 20.00 50.00
159 Dwayne Bacon AU RC 5.00 12.00
160 Bam Adebayo AU RC 30.00 80.00
161 Josh Hart AU RC 12.00 30.00
162 Jayson Tatum AU RC 400.00 800.00
163 Justin Patton AU RC 5.00 12.00
164 Jonathan Isaac AU RC 12.00 30.00
165 John Collins AU RC 12.00 30.00
166 D.Smith Jr. AU RC 6.00 15.00
167 Semi Ojeleye AU RC 6.00 15.00
168 Luke Kennard AU RC 10.00 25.00
169 Davon Reed AU RC 5.00 12.00
170 Milos Teodosic AU RC 6.00 15.00
171 Jayson Tatum AU RC 400.00 800.00
172 D.J. Wilson AU RC 5.00 12.00
173 De'Aaron Fox AU RC 50.00 120.00
174 Kyle Kuzma AU RC 20.00 50.00
175 TJ Leaf AU RC 5.00 12.00
176 John Collins AU RC 12.00 30.00
177 D.Smith Jr. AU RC 6.00 15.00
178 Malik Monk AU RC 20.00 50.00
179 Markelle Fultz AU RC 12.00 30.00
180 D.Mitchell AU RC EXCH 75.00 200.00
181 Josh Jackson AU RC 6.00 15.00
182 Derrick White AU RC 25.00 60.00
183 Jonathan Isaac AU RC 12.00 30.00
184 Josh Hart AU RC 12.00 30.00
185 Frank Ntilikina AU RC 6.00 15.00
186 Frank Mason AU RC 5.00 12.00
187 Zach Collins AU RC 8.00 20.00
188 Luke Kennard AU RC 10.00 25.00
189 Lonzo Ball AU RC 20.00 50.00
190 Bam Adebayo AU RC 30.00 80.00

2017-18 Panini Encased Dual Jerseys

STATED PRINT RUN 99 SER.#'d SETS
1 Pau Gasol 5.00 12.00
2 Tyreke Evans 2.00 5.00
3 Rudy Gobert 4.00 10.00
4 Enes Kanter 2.50 6.00
5 Jimmy Butler 5.00 12.00
6 Aaron Gordon 3.00 8.00
7 Kevin Durant 12.00 30.00
8 Blake Griffin 3.00 8.00
9 Marc Gasol 3.00 8.00
10 Damian Lillard 8.00 20.00
11 Paul George 6.00 15.00
12 Devin Booker 8.00 20.00
13 Russell Westbrook 5.00 12.00
14 Eric Bledsoe 2.50 6.00
15 Joel Embiid 6.00 15.00
16 Andre Drummond 2.50 6.00
17 Kris Dunn 2.00 5.00
18 Bradley Beal 4.00 10.00
19 Mike Conley 2.50 6.00
20 D'Angelo Russell 2.50 6.00
21 Paul Millsap 2.50 6.00
22 Dion Waiters 2.00 5.00
23 Serge Ibaka 2.50 6.00
24 Giannis Antetokounmpo 15.00 40.00
25 John Wall 4.00 10.00
26 Andrew Wiggins 4.00 10.00
27 Kristaps Porzingis 4.00 10.00
28 Brandon Ingram 4.00 10.00
29 Myles Turner 3.00 8.00
30 DeAndre Jordan 2.50 6.00
31 Ricky Rubio 2.50 6.00
32 Dirk Nowitzki 8.00 20.00
33 Stephen Curry 25.00 60.00
34 Goran Dragic 2.50 6.00
35 Jrue Holiday 4.00 10.00
36 Anthony Davis 8.00 20.00
37 Kyle Lowry 3.00 8.00
38 Buddy Hield 3.00 8.00
39 Nikola Jokic 20.00 50.00
40 DeMar DeRozan 4.00 10.00
41 Rodney Hood 2.00 5.00
42 Dwight Howard 4.00 10.00
43 Taurean Prince 2.00 5.00
44 Hassan Whiteside 2.50 6.00
45 Karl-Anthony Towns 5.00 12.00
46 Avery Bradley 2.00 5.00
47 Kyrie Irving 6.00 15.00
48 CJ McCollum 3.00 8.00
49 Nikola Vucevic 2.50 6.00
50 DeMarcus Cousins 2.50 6.00
51 Rudy Gay 2.50 6.00
52 Elfrid Payton 2.00 5.00
53 Victor Oladipo 2.50 6.00
54 James Harden 6.00 15.00
55 Kemba Walker 2.50 6.00
57 LeBron James 50.00 120.00
58 Chris Paul 5.00 12.00
59 Otto Porter Jr. 2.50 6.00
60 Dennis Schroder 2.50 6.00

2017-18 Panini Encased Dual Rookie Jerseys

1 Sterling Brown/149 1.50 4.00
2 Frank Ntilikina/99 2.00 5.00
3 Tyler Dorsey/149 1.50 4.00
4 Jawun Evans/149 1.50 4.00
5 Jordan Bell/99 2.00 5.00
6 Ante Zizic/149 2.00 5.00
7 Kyle Kuzma/99 6.00 15.00
8 Davon Reed/149 1.50 4.00
9 Markelle Fultz/99 4.00 10.00
10 Donovan Mitchell/99 15.00 40.00
11 TJ Leaf/99 1.50 4.00
12 Harry Giles/99 1.50 4.00
13 Tyler Lydon/99 1.50 4.00
14 Jayson Tatum/99 40.00 100.00
15 Josh Hart/99 4.00 10.00
16 Bam Adebayo/149 10.00 25.00
17 Lonzo Ball/99 6.00 15.00
18 De'Aaron Fox/99 12.00 30.00
19 OG Anunoby/149 8.00 20.00
20 Dwayne Bacon/149 1.50 4.00
21 Terrance Ferguson/99 1.50 4.00
22 Ivan Rabb/149 1.50 4.00
23 Wes Iwundu/99 1.50 4.00
24 John Collins/99 4.00 10.00
25 Josh Jackson/99 2.00 5.00
26 Caleb Swanigan/99 1.50 4.00
27 Luke Kennard/99 3.00 8.00
28 Dennis Smith Jr./99 2.00 5.00
29 Semi Ojeleye/99 2.00 5.00
30 Frank Jackson/99 1.50 4.00
31 Tony Bradley/149 1.50 4.00
32 Jarrett Allen/99 4.00 10.00
33 Zach Collins/99 2.50 6.00
34 Jonathan Isaac/99 4.00 10.00
35 Justin Patton/99 1.50 4.00
36 D.J. Wilson/99 1.50 4.00
37 Malik Monk/99 6.00 15.00
38 Derrick White/99 6.00 15.00
39 Sindarius Thornwell/99 1.50 4.00
40 Frank Mason III/99 1.50 4.00

2017-18 Panini Encased Endorsements

PRINT RUNS B/WN 25-99 COPIES PER
EXCHANGE DEADLINE 12/27/2019
*RED/25: .5X TO 1.2X p/r 49-99
*RED/15-25: .4X TO 1X p/r 25
1 Jose Calderon/99 6.00 15.00
2 Giannis Antetokounmpo/49 150.00 400.00
3 Bob Dandridge/99 10.00 25.00
4 Elvin Hayes/99 12.00 30.00
5 Tyson Chandler/49 8.00 20.00
7 Gary Harris/99 8.00 20.00
8 Reggie Miller/25 EXCH 150.00 400.00
9 B.J. Armstrong/99 10.00 25.00
10 Karl Malone/25 40.00 100.00
11 Cedric Maxwell/99 8.00 20.00
12 Hakeem Olajuwon/49 40.00 100.00
13 Eddie Jones/99 10.00 25.00
14 Mike Conley/49 8.00 20.00
15 JJ Redick/99 15.00 40.00
17 Kyle Korver/99 EXCH 8.00 20.00
18 Blake Griffin/25 EXCH 12.00 30.00
19 Michael Cooper/99 8.00 20.00
20 Kyrie Irving/25 EXCH 75.00 200.00
21 Corey Maggette/99 8.00 20.00
22 Tracy McGrady/49 75.00 200.00
23 Shareef Abdur-Rahim/99 8.00 20.00
24 Gordon Hayward/49 8.00 20.00
25 Jason Terry/99 8.00 20.00
26 Bill Russell/25 500.00 1,000.00
27 Rudy Gay/99 8.00 20.00
28 Dwyane Wade/25 75.00 200.00
29 Thaddeus Young/99 6.00 15.00
30 John Stockton/25 40.00 100.00
31 Tim Hardaway Jr./99 8.00 20.00
32 D'Angelo Russell/49 8.00 20.00
33 Stacey Augmon/99 8.00 20.00
34 Bernard King/49 12.00 30.00
35 Dave Cowens/99 15.00 40.00
37 Iman Shumpert/99 6.00 15.00
39 David Thompson/99 12.00 30.00
40 Larry Bird/25 125.00 300.00
41 Arvydas Sabonis/99 12.00 30.00
42 Joel Embiid/49 40.00 100.00
43 Vlade Divac/99 10.00 25.00
44 Chris Middleton/49 12.00 30.00
45 Danny Manning/99 8.00 20.00
46 Allen Iverson/25 100.00 250.00
47 Zaza Pachulia/99 6.00 15.00
48 Damian Lillard/25 75.00 200.00
49 Mark Aguirre/99 6.00 15.00
50 Magic Johnson/25 125.00 300.00

2017-18 Panini Encased Legendary Swatch Signatures

STATED PRINT RUN 49 SER.#'d SETS
EXCHANGE DEADLINE 12/27/2019
1 Doug Collins 12.00 30.00
2 Detlef Schrempf 12.00 30.00
3 Sam Perkins 10.00 25.00
4 Jack Sikma 12.00 30.00
5 Larry Bird 150.00 400.00
6 Mitch Richmond 15.00 40.00
7 Shawn Bradley 8.00 20.00
8 B.J. Armstrong 12.00 30.00
9 Tom Gugliotta 8.00 20.00
10 Christian Laettner 12.00 30.00
11 Grant Hill 20.00 50.00
12 Dominique Wilkins 20.00 50.00
13 Kobe Bryant 1,500.00 3,000.00
14 Glen Rice 10.00 25.00
15 Kenny Smith 10.00 25.00
16 Jeff Hornacek 10.00 25.00
17 Danny Manning 10.00 25.00
18 Joe Dumars 15.00 40.00
19 Jason Kidd 40.00 100.00
20 Reggie Miller EXCH 150.00 400.00

2017-18 Panini Encased Perfect 10 Autographs

STATED PRINT RUN 49 SER.#'d SETS
EXCHANGE DEADLINE 12/27/2019
*RED/25: .5X TO 1.2X BASIC
P10AD Anthony Davis 40.00 100.00
P10GA Giannis Antetokounmpo 125.00 300.00
P10JT Jayson Tatum 500.00 1,[illegible]
P10KB Kobe Bryant 1,000.00 2,[illegible]
P10KD Kevin Durant 125.00 300.00
P10KI Kyrie Irving 75.00 200.00
P10KL Kawhi Leonard 75.00 200.00
P10LB Lonzo Ball 25.00 60.00
P10MF Markelle Fultz 15.00 40.00
P10SC Stephen Curry 1,000.00 2,[illegible]

2017-18 Panini Encased Rookie Triple Jerseys

PRINT RUNS B/WN 25-99 COPIES PER
1 Jordan Bell/99 2.50 6.00
2 Ante Zizic/99 3.00 8.00
3 Kyle Kuzma/59 10.00 25.00
4 Davon Reed/99 2.50 6.00
5 Markelle Fultz/99 6.00 15.00
6 Donovan Mitchell/99 25.00 60.00
7 Sterling Brown/99 2.50 6.00
8 Frank Ntilikina/99 3.00 8.00
9 Tyler Dorsey/99 2.50 6.00
10 Jawun Evans/99 2.50 6.00
11 Josh Hart/25 6.00 15.00
12 Bam Adebayo/99 15.00 40.00
13 Lonzo Ball/99 10.00 25.00
14 De'Aaron Fox/99 20.00 50.00
15 OG Anunoby/99 12.00 30.00
16 Dwayne Bacon/99 2.50 6.00
17 TJ Leaf/99 2.50 6.00
18 Harry Giles/99 2.50 6.00
19 Tyler Lydon/99 2.50 6.00
20 Jayson Tatum/99 60.00 150.00
21 Josh Jackson/99 3.00 8.00
22 Caleb Swanigan/99 2.50 6.00
23 Luke Kennard/99 5.00 12.00
24 Dennis Smith Jr./99 3.00 8.00
25 Semi Ojeleye/99 3.00 8.00
26 Frank Jackson/99 2.50 6.00
27 Terrance Ferguson/99 2.50 6.00
28 Ivan Rabb/99 2.50 6.00
29 Wes Iwundu/99 2.50 6.00
30 John Collins/99 6.00 15.00
31 Justin Patton/99 2.50 6.00
32 D.J. Wilson/99 2.50 6.00
33 Malik Monk/99 10.00 25.00
34 Derrick White/99 10.00 25.00
35 Sindarius Thornwell/99 2.50 6.00
36 Frank Mason III/99 2.50 6.00
37 Tony Bradley/99 2.50 6.00
38 Jarrett Allen/99 6.00 15.00
39 Zach Collins/99 4.00 10.00
40 Jonathan Isaac/99 6.00 15.00

2017-18 Panini Encased Sculpted Signatures

PRINT RUNS B/WN 25-99 COPIES PER
EXCHANGE DEADLINE 12/27/2019
*RED/25: .5X TO 1.2X p/r 49-99
*RED/15-25: .4X TO 1X p/r 25
1 Steve Kerr/49 12.00 30.00
2 Kobe Bryant/25 1,500.00 [illegible],000.00
3 Jermaine O'Neal/99 10.00 25.00
4 Reggie Miller/25 EXCH 150.00 400.00
5 Allan Houston/99 10.00 25.00
6 Kyrie Irving/25 EXCH 75.00 200.00
7 Matthew Dellavedova/99 8.00 20.00
8 Karl-Anthony Towns/49 25.00 60.00
9 Bill Laimbeer/99 10.00 25.00
10 Kristaps Porzingis/49 12.00 30.00
11 Zach LaVine/49 50.00 120.00
13 Jeff Teague/99 8.00 20.00
14 Giannis Antetokounmpo/25 200.00 500.00
15 Juwan Howard/99 8.00 20.00
16 John Stockton/25 40.00 100.00
17 Omri Casspi/99 6.00 15.00
18 Ricky Rubio/49 8.00 20.00
19 Dennis Scott/99 6.00 15.00
20 Andre Drummond/49 8.00 20.00
21 Clint Capela/99 8.00 20.00
22 Bill Russell/25 500.00 1,000.00
23 Richard Jefferson/99 EXCH 8.00 20.00
24 Dwyane Wade/25 75.00 200.00
25 D.J. Augustin/99 6.00 15.00
26 Larry Bird/25 125.00 300.00
27 Dwight Powell/99 6.00 15.00
28 Isaiah Thomas/49 8.00 20.00
29 Junior Bridgeman/99 8.00 20.00
31 Reggie Jackson/99 8.00 20.00
33 Ryan Anderson/99 6.00 15.00
35 Adrian Dantley/99 10.00 25.00
36 Magic Johnson/25 125.00 300.00
37 Jason Williams/99 25.00 60.00
38 Dominique Wilkins/49 20.00 50.00
39 Vin Baker/99 8.00 20.00
40 Devin Booker/99 125.00 300.00
41 Robert Parish/99 12.00 30.00
42 Allen Iverson/25 100.00 250.00
43 Evan Turner/99 6.00 15.00
44 Karl Malone/25 40.00 100.00
45 Tom Heinsohn/99 20.00 50.00
46 Anthony Davis/25 60.00 150.00
47 Will Barton/99 EXCH 6.00 15.00
48 Willis Reed/49 40.00 100.00
49 Damian Lillard/25 75.00 200.00
50 Nikola Jokic/49 150.00 400.00

2017-18 Panini Encased Substantial Swatches

STATED PRINT RUN 99 SER.#'d SETS
1 Danny Granger 1.50 4.00
2 Dirk Nowitzki 6.00 15.00
3 Vince Carter 5.00 12.00
4 Kevin Garnett 6.00 15.00
5 Tim Duncan 6.00 15.00
6 Lance Stephenson 2.00 5.00
7 Rudy Gobert 3.00 8.00
8 Carmelo Anthony 4.00 10.00
9 Gordon Hayward 2.00 5.00
10 LeBron James 50.00 120.00

2017-18 Panini Encased Substantial Swatches Rookies

STATED PRINT RUN 99 SER.#'d SETS
1 Tyler Lydon 1.50 4.00
2 Bam Adebayo 10.00 25.00
3 Frank Ntilikina 2.00 5.00
4 Lonzo Ball 6.00 15.00
5 Zach Collins 2.50 6.00
6 Jordan Bell 1.50 4.00
7 Jayson Tatum 40.00 100.00
8 Terrance Ferguson 1.50 4.00
9 Malik Monk 6.00 15.00
10 De'Aaron Fox 12.00 30.00
11 Josh Jackson 2.00 5.00
12 TJ Leaf 1.50 4.00
13 Ivan Rabb 1.50 4.00
14 Jonathan Isaac 4.00 10.00
15 John Collins 4.00 10.00
16 Donovan Mitchell 15.00 40.00
17 Tony Bradley 1.50 4.00
18 Markelle Fultz 4.00 10.00
19 Justin Patton 1.50 4.00
20 Dennis Smith Jr. 2.00 5.00
21 Derrick White 6.00 15.00
22 Jarrett Allen 4.00 10.00
23 Luke Kennard 3.00 8.00
24 Frank Jackson 1.50 4.00
25 OG Anunoby 8.00 20.00
26 D.J. Wilson 1.50 4.00
27 Frank Mason III 1.50 4.00
28 Caleb Swanigan 1.50 4.00
29 Harry Giles 1.50 4.00
30 Sterling Brown 1.50 4.00

2017-18 Panini Encased Triple Jerseys

STATED PRINT RUN 99 SER.#'d SETS
1 Aaron Gordon 4.00 10.00
2 Kevin Durant 15.00 40.00
3 Blake Griffin 4.00 10.00
4 Marc Gasol 4.00 10.00
5 Damian Lillard 10.00 25.00
6 Pau Gasol 6.00 15.00
7 Tyreke Evans 2.50 6.00
8 Rudy Gobert 5.00 12.00
9 Enes Kanter 3.00 8.00
10 Jimmy Butler 6.00 15.00
11 Andre Drummond 3.00 8.00
12 Kris Dunn 2.50 6.00
13 Bradley Beal 5.00 12.00
14 Mike Conley 3.00 8.00
15 D'Angelo Russell 2.50 6.00
16 Paul George 6.00 15.00
17 Devin Booker 10.00 25.00
18 Russell Westbrook 6.00 15.00
19 Eric Bledsoe 3.00 8.00
20 Joel Embiid 8.00 20.00
21 Andrew Wiggins 5.00 12.00
22 Kristaps Porzingis 5.00 12.00
23 Brandon Ingram 5.00 12.00
24 Myles Turner 4.00 10.00
25 DeAndre Jordan 3.00 8.00
26 Paul Millsap 3.00 8.00
27 Dion Waiters 2.50 6.00
28 Serge Ibaka 3.00 8.00
29 Giannis Antetokounmpo 20.00 50.00
30 John Wall 5.00 12.00
31 Anthony Davis 10.00 25.00
32 Kyle Lowry 4.00 10.00
33 Buddy Hield 4.00 10.00
34 Nikola Jokic 25.00 60.00
35 DeMar DeRozan 5.00 12.00
36 Ricky Rubio 3.00 8.00
37 Dirk Nowitzki 10.00 25.00
38 Stephen Curry 30.00 80.00
39 Goran Dragic 3.00 8.00
40 Jrue Holiday 5.00 12.00
41 Avery Bradley 2.50 6.00
42 Kyrie Irving 8.00 20.00
43 CJ McCollum 4.00 10.00
44 Nikola Vucevic 3.00 8.00
45 DeMarcus Cousins 3.00 8.00
46 Rodney Hood 2.50 6.00
47 Dwight Howard 3.00 8.00
48 Taurean Prince 2.50 6.00
49 Hassan Whiteside 3.00 8.00
50 Karl-Anthony Towns 6.00 15.00
52 LeBron James 50.00 120.00
53 Chris Paul 6.00 15.00
54 Otto Porter Jr. 3.00 8.00
55 Dennis Schroder 3.00 8.00
56 Rudy Gay 3.00 8.00
57 Elfrid Payton 2.50 6.00
58 Victor Oladipo 3.00 8.00
59 James Harden 8.00 20.00
60 Kemba Walker 3.00 8.00

2017-18 Panini Encased Vaulted Veteran Materials Signatures

STATED PRINT RUN 49 SER.#'d SETS
EXCHANGE DEADLINE 12/27/2019
1 Malcolm Brogdon 10.00 25.00
3 Patrick Beverley 8.00 20.00
4 Khris Middleton 15.00 40.00
5 JJ Redick 12.00 30.00
6 Kyrie Irving EXCH 100.00 250.00
7 Myles Turner 12.00 30.00
8 Karl-Anthony Towns 25.00 60.00
9 Gary Harris 10.00 25.00
10 Mike Conley 10.00 25.00
11 Rudy Gobert 15.00 40.00
12 Zach LaVine 20.00 50.00
13 Seth Curry 12.00 30.00
14 Elfrid Payton 8.00 20.00
15 Victor Oladipo 10.00 25.00
16 Kevin Durant 125.00 300.00
17 Ryan Anderson 8.00 20.00
18 Kevin Love 12.00 30.00
19 Jeff Teague 8.00 20.00
20 Kemba Walker 10.00 25.00
21 Willie Cauley-Stein 8.00 20.00
22 Eric Gordon 10.00 25.00
23 Tim Hardaway Jr. 10.00 25.00
24 Nikola Jokic 300.00 600.00
25 Reggie Jackson 10.00 25.00
26 Anthony Davis 75.00 200.00
27 Jrue Holiday 15.00 40.00
28 Joel Embiid EXCH 40.00 100.00
29 DeMarre Carroll 8.00 20.00
30 Harrison Barnes 10.00 25.00
31 Thaddeus Young 8.00 20.00
32 Aaron Gordon 12.00 30.00
33 James Johnson 8.00 20.00
34 Avery Bradley 8.00 20.00
35 Michael Kidd-Gilchrist 8.00 20.00
36 Giannis Antetokounmpo 200.00 500.00
37 Rudy Gay 10.00 25.00
38 Kristaps Porzingis 25.00 60.00
39 Evan Turner 8.00 20.00
40 Andre Drummond 10.00 25.00

2018-19 Panini Encased

1-100 STATED PRINT RUN 99 SER.#'d SETS
101-190 STATED PRINT RUN 75 SER.#'d SETS
191-223 STATED PRINT RUN 99 SER.#'d SETS
EXCHANGE DEADLINE 1/26/2021
*RED/25-35: .6X TO 1.5X BASIC
1 Al Horford 1.25 3.00
2 Aaron Gordon 1.25 3.00
3 Damian Lillard 3.00 8.00
4 Kent Bazemore .75 2.00
5 Derrick Rose 2.50 6.00
6 Jrue Holiday 1.50 4.00
7 Andre Drummond 1.00 2.50
8 Klay Thompson 3.00 8.00
9 Kawhi Leonard 3.00 8.00
10 Kyle Kuzma 1.25 3.00
11 D'Angelo Russell 1.25 3.00
12 Evan Fournier 1.00 2.50
13 CJ McCollum 1.25 3.00
14 James Harden 2.50 6.00
15 Andrew Wiggins 1.50 4.00
16 Elfrid Payton 1.00 2.50
17 Reggie Jackson 1.00 2.50
18 DeMarcus Cousins 1.00 2.50
19 Pascal Siakam 2.00 5.00
20 Brandon Ingram 1.25 3.00
21 Spencer Dinwiddie 1.00 2.50
22 Kemba Walker 1.00 2.50
23 Jusuf Nurkic 1.00 2.50
24 Chris Paul 2.50 6.00
25 Giannis Antetokounmpo 6.00 15.00
26 Dirk Nowitzki 3.00 8.00
27 Zach LaVine 2.00 5.00
28 Draymond Green 1.50 4.00
29 Serge Ibaka 1.00 2.50
30 Lonzo Ball 1.25 3.00
31 Joe Harris 1.00 2.50
32 Jeremy Lamb .75 2.00
33 Paul George 2.00 5.00
34 Eric Gordon 1.00 2.50
35 Khris Middleton 1.25 3.00
36 Tim Hardaway Jr. .75 2.00
37 Lauri Markkanen 2.00 5.00
38 Lou Williams 1.00 2.50
39 Kyle Lowry 1.25 3.00
40 Devin Booker 3.00 8.00
41 Dennis Smith Jr. .75 2.00
42 Tony Parker 2.00 5.00
43 Russell Westbrook 2.00 5.00
44 Clint Capela 1.00 2.50
45 Eric Bledsoe 1.00 2.50
46 Kristaps Porzingis 1.50 4.00
47 Otto Porter Jr. 1.00 2.50
48 Danilo Gallinari 1.00 2.50
49 Joel Embiid 3.00 8.00
50 T.J. Warren 1.00 2.50
51 DeAndre Jordan 1.00 2.50
52 John Wall 1.50 4.00
53 Steven Adams 1.00 2.50
54 DeMar DeRozan 1.50 4.00
55 Malcolm Brogdon 1.25 3.00
56 Mike Conley 1.00 2.50
57 Kevin Love 1.00 2.50
58 Montrezl Harrell 1.25 3.00
59 Tobias Harris 1.00 2.50
60 Kelly Oubre Jr. 1.25 3.00
61 Emmanuel Mudiay .75 2.00
62 Bradley Beal 1.50 4.00
63 Donovan Mitchell 4.00 10.00
64 LaMarcus Aldridge 1.25 3.00
65 Victor Oladipo 1.00 2.50
66 Jonas Valanciunas 1.25 3.00
67 Jordan Clarkson 1.25 3.00
68 Buddy Hield 1.25 3.00
69 Jimmy Butler 2.00 5.00
70 Josh Richardson 1.00 2.50
71 Nikola Jokic 6.00 15.00
72 Jabari Parker .75 2.00
73 Rudy Gobert 1.50 4.00
74 Rudy Gay 1.25 3.00
75 Bojan Bogdanovic 1.00 2.50
76 Avery Bradley .75 2.00
77 Tristan Thompson .75 2.00
78 De'Aaron Fox 2.50 6.00
79 Ben Simmons 1.25 3.00
80 Goran Dragic 1.00 2.50
81 Jamal Murray 2.50 6.00
82 John Collins 1.25 3.00
83 Ricky Rubio 1.00 2.50
84 Anthony Davis 3.00 8.00
85 Domantas Sabonis 1.50 4.00
86 Pau Gasol 2.00 5.00
87 Stephen Curry 10.00 25.00
88 Harrison Barnes 1.00 2.50
89 Kyrie Irving 3.00 8.00
90 Dwyane Wade 2.50 6.00
91 Paul Millsap 1.00 2.50
92 Taurean Prince .75 2.00
93 Karl-Anthony Towns 2.00 5.00
94 Julius Randle 1.25 3.00
95 Blake Griffin 1.25 3.00
96 Vince Carter 2.50 6.00
97 Kevin Durant 5.00 12.00
98 LeBron James 10.00 25.00
99 Jayson Tatum 5.00 12.00
100 Nikola Vucevic 1.00 2.50
101 Donte DiVincenzo RE AU RC 12.00 30.00
102 Robert Williams III RE AU RC 10.00 25.00
103 Jalen Brunson RE AU RC 40.00 100.00
104 Troy Brown Jr. RE AU RC 6.00 15.00
105 Josh Okogie RE AU RC 8.00 20.00
106 Kevin Knox RE AU RC 6.00 15.00
107 Aaron Holiday RE AU RC 8.00 20.00
108 Luka Doncic RE AU RC 600.00 1,200.00
109 Collin Sexton RE AU RC 15.00 40.00
110 Mikal Bridges RE AU RC 25.00 60.00
111 Grayson Allen RE AU RC 10.00 25.00
112 Shai Gilgeous-Alexander RE AU RC 600.00 1,200.00
113 Jaren Jackson Jr. RE AU RC 75.00 200.00
114 Wendell Carter Jr. RE AU RC 12.00 30.00
115 Keita Bates-Diop RE AU RC 6.00 15.00
116 Landry Shamet RE AU RC 8.00 20.00
117 Anfernee Simons RE AU RC 25.00 60.00
118 Marvin Bagley III RE AU RC 8.00 20.00
119 Deandre Ayton RE AU RC 15.00 40.00
120 Mo Bamba RE AU RC 8.00 20.00
122 Trae Young RE AU RC 125.00 300.00
123 Jerome Robinson RE AU RC 5.00 12.00
124 Zhaire Smith RE AU RC 5.00 12.00
125 Kevin Huerter RE AU RC 10.00 25.00
126 Lonnie Walker IV RE AU RC 10.00 25.00
127 Chandler Hutchison RE AU RC 6.00 15.00
128 Michael Porter Jr. RE AU RC 20.00 50.00
129 Devonte' Graham RE AU RC 8.00 20.00
130 Moritz Wagner RE AU RC 10.00 25.00
131 Kevin Knox SS AU 6.00 15.00
132 Aaron Holiday SS AU 8.00 20.00
133 Luka Doncic SS AU 600.00 1,200.00
134 Collin Sexton SS AU 15.00 40.00
135 Mikal Bridges SS AU 25.00 60.00
136 Donte DiVincenzo SS AU 12.00 30.00
137 Robert Williams III SS AU 10.00 25.00
138 Jalen Brunson SS AU 100.00 250.00
139 Troy Brown Jr. SS AU 6.00 15.00
140 Josh Okogie SS AU 8.00 20.00
141 Svi Mykhailiuk SS AU RC 6.00 15.00
142 Anfernee Simons SS AU 25.00 60.00
143 Marvin Bagley III SS AU 8.00 20.00
144 Deandre Ayton SS AU 15.00 40.00
145 Mo Bamba SS AU 8.00 20.00
146 Grayson Allen SS AU 10.00 25.00
147 Shai Gilgeous-Alexander SS AU 600.00 1,200.00
148 Jaren Jackson Jr. SS AU 75.00 200.00
149 Allonzo Trier SS AU RC 5.00 12.00
150 Jarred Vanderbilt SS AU RC 10.00 25.00
151 Lonnie Walker IV SS AU 10.00 25.00
152 Dzanan Musa SS AU RC 5.00 12.00
153 Michael Porter Jr. SS AU 20.00 50.00
154 Omari Spellman SS AU RC 5.00 12.00
155 Moritz Wagner SS AU 10.00 25.00
157 Trae Young SS AU 125.00 300.00
158 Elie Okobo SS AU RC 5.00 12.00
159 Zhaire Smith SS AU 5.00 12.00
160 Hamidou Diallo SS AU RC 8.00 20.00
161 Mitchell Robinson NS AU RC EXCH 12.00 30.00
162 Mikal Bridges NS AU 25.00 60.00
163 Donte DiVincenzo NS AU 12.00 30.00
164 Robert Williams III NS AU 10.00 25.00
165 Jalen Brunson NS AU 100.00 250.00
166 Troy Brown Jr. NS AU 6.00 15.00
167 Josh Okogie NS AU 8.00 20.00
168 Kevin Knox NS AU 6.00 15.00
169 Aaron Holiday NS AU 8.00 20.00
170 Luka Doncic NS AU 600.00 1,200.00
171 Deandre Ayton NS AU 15.00 40.00
172 Mo Bamba NS AU 8.00 20.00
173 Grayson Allen NS AU 10.00 25.00
174 Shai Gilgeous-Alexander NS AU 600.00 1,200.00
175 Kostas Antetokounmpo NS AU RC 6.00 15.00
176 De'Anthony Melton NS AU RC 10.00 25.00
177 Kevin Huerter NS AU 10.00 25.00
178 Keita Bates-Diop NS AU 6.00 15.00
179 Anfernee Simons NS AU 25.00 60.00
180 Marvin Bagley III NS AU 8.00 20.00
181 Gary Trent Jr. NS AU RC 10.00 25.00
182 Moritz Wagner NS AU 10.00 25.00
184 Trae Young NS AU 125.00 300.00
185 Landry Shamet NS AU 8.00 20.00
186 Zhaire Smith NS AU 5.00 12.00
187 Devonte' Graham NS AU 8.00 20.00
188 Lonnie Walker IV NS AU 10.00 25.00
189 Bruce Brown NS AU RC 10.00 25.00
190 Michael Porter Jr. NS AU 20.00 50.00
191 Shai Gilgeous-Alexander JSY AU 1,000.00 2,000.00
192 Jalen Brunson JSY AU 200.00 500.00
193 Zhaire Smith JSY AU 8.00 20.00
194 Keita Bates-Diop JSY AU 10.00 25.00
195 Landry Shamet JSY AU 12.00 30.00
196 Aaron Holiday JSY AU 12.00 30.00
197 Marvin Bagley III JSY AU 12.00 30.00
198 Collin Sexton JSY AU 25.00 60.00
199 Mo Bamba JSY AU 12.00 30.00
200 Donte DiVincenzo JSY AU 20.00 50.00
201 Trae Young JSY AU 200.00 500.00
202 Jaren Jackson Jr. JSY AU 125.00 300.00
203 Hamidou Diallo JSY AU 12.00 30.00
204 Kevin Huerter JSY AU 15.00 40.00
205 Lonnie Walker IV JSY AU 15.00 40.00
206 Anfernee Simons JSY AU 40.00 100.00
207 Michael Porter Jr. JSY AU 30.00 80.00
208 Deandre Ayton JSY AU 25.00 60.00
209 Moritz Wagner JSY AU 15.00 40.00
210 Grayson Allen JSY AU 15.00 40.00
211 Troy Brown Jr. JSY AU 10.00 25.00
212 Jerome Robinson JSY AU 8.00 20.00
213 Svi Mykhailiuk JSY AU 10.00 25.00
214 Kevin Knox JSY AU 10.00 25.00
215 Luka Doncic JSY AU 1,250.00 2,500.00
216 Chandler Hutchison JSY AU 10.00 25.00
217 Mikal Bridges JSY AU 40.00 100.00
218 Devonte' Graham JSY AU 12.00 30.00
219 Robert Williams III JSY AU 15.00 40.00
221 Wendell Carter Jr. JSY AU 20.00 50.00
222 Josh Okogie JSY AU 12.00 30.00
223 Omari Spellman JSY AU 8.00 20.00

2018-19 Panini Encased Endorsements

PRINT RUNS B/WN 25-99 COPIES PER
EXCHANGE DEADLINE 1/26/2021
*RED/15-25: .6X TO 1.5X p/r 99
*RED/15-25: .5X TO 1.2X p/r 35-49
*RED/15-25: .4X TO 1X p/r 25
1 Khris Middleton/49 10.00 25.00
2 Bruce Bowen/99 6.00 15.00
3 Gary Harris/49 8.00 20.00
4 Jerry Stackhouse/49 12.00 30.00
5 Kobe Bryant/25 EXCH 1,000.00 2,000.00
6 Rik Smits/49 8.00 20.00
7 Magic Johnson/35 100.00 250.00
8 Larry Nance/99 6.00 15.00
9 Brandon Ingram/35 10.00 25.00
10 Antonio McDyess/99 6.00 15.00
11 Walt Frazier/49 15.00 40.00
13 Joe Dumars/49 12.00 30.00
14 Kurt Rambis/49 8.00 20.00
15 Charles Barkley/25 EXCH 100.00 250.00
16 Isaiah Rider/99 6.00 15.00
18 Jerome Williams/99 5.00 12.00
19 Ray Allen/35 40.00 100.00
20 Cuttino Mobley/99 5.00 12.00
21 Chris Mullin/49 12.00 30.00
22 Doug Collins/99 8.00 20.00
23 Ralph Sampson/49 8.00 20.00
24 Mark Aguirre/49 8.00 20.00
25 Karl Malone/35 40.00 100.00
26 Sean Elliott/99 6.00 15.00
27 Jerry West/35 30.00 80.00
28 Sarunas Marciulionis/99 8.00 20.00
29 Kevin Love/35 8.00 20.00
30 Rafer Alston/99 6.00 15.00
31 JJ Redick/49 10.00 25.00
32 Dennis Scott/99 EXCH 6.00 15.00
33 George McGinnis/49 12.00 30.00
34 Kevin Willis/49 8.00 20.00
35 Larry Bird/35 100.00 250.00
36 Herb Williams/99 5.00 12.00
38 Tree Rollins/99 5.00 12.00
39 Isaiah Thomas/35 8.00 20.00
40 Zydrunas Ilgauskas/99 6.00 15.00
41 Nate Archibald/49 12.00 30.00
42 Larry Hughes/99 6.00 15.00
43 Allan Houston/49 10.00 25.00
44 Stephen Jackson/49 8.00 20.00
45 Kyrie Irving/35 75.00 200.00
46 Muggsy Bogues/99 15.00 40.00

2018-19 Panini Encased Jerseys

STATED PRINT RUN 99 SER.#'d SETS
*PRIME: .75X TO 2X BASIC
1 A.C. Green 4.00 10.00
2 Aaron Gordon 4.00 10.00
3 Al Horford 4.00 10.00
4 Al-Farouq Aminu 2.50 6.00
5 Allen Crabbe 2.50 6.00
8 Andre Drummond 3.00 8.00
9 Andre Iguodala 3.00 8.00
11 Andrew Wiggins 5.00 12.00
12 Anfernee Hardaway 10.00 25.00
13 Anthony Davis 10.00 25.00
15 Bam Adebayo 6.00 15.00
16 Ben Simmons 4.00 10.00
17 Bismack Biyombo 2.50 6.00
18 Blake Griffin 4.00 10.00
19 Bobby Portis 4.00 10.00
22 Brandon Ingram 4.00 10.00
23 Bradley Beal 5.00 12.00
24 Brook Lopez 3.00 8.00
25 Buddy Hield 4.00 10.00
26 Caris LeVert 4.00 10.00
27 Karl-Anthony Towns 6.00 15.00
28 Chris Bosh 4.00 10.00
29 Chris Paul 8.00 20.00
30 CJ McCollum 4.00 10.00
32 Clyde Drexler 6.00 15.00
33 Damian Lillard 10.00 25.00
34 D'Angelo Russell 4.00 10.00
36 David Robinson 8.00 20.00
37 De'Aaron Fox 8.00 20.00
38 DeAndre Jordan 3.00 8.00
39 DeMar DeRozan 5.00 12.00
40 DeMarcus Cousins 3.00 8.00
42 Dennis Schroder 3.00 8.00
43 Dennis Smith Jr. 2.50 6.00
45 Derrick Rose 8.00 20.00
46 Devin Booker 10.00 25.00
47 Dirk Nowitzki 10.00 25.00
48 Domantas Sabonis 5.00 12.00
49 Donovan Mitchell 12.00 30.00
50 Dragan Bender 2.50 6.00
51 Draymond Green 5.00 12.00
52 Dwight Howard 5.00 12.00
53 Dwyane Wade 8.00 20.00
54 Elfrid Payton 3.00 8.00
55 Enes Kanter 3.00 8.00
56 Eric Bledsoe 3.00 8.00
57 Eric Gordon 3.00 8.00
58 Evan Fournier 3.00 8.00
59 Evan Turner 2.50 6.00
60 Frank Ntilikina 2.50 6.00

2018-19 Panini Encased Legendary Swatch Signatures

PRINT RUNS B/WN 35-99 COPIES PER
EXCHANGE DEADLINE 1/26/2021
*RED/25: .6X TO 1.5X p/r 99
*RED/25: .5X TO 1.2X p/r 35-49
1 Toni Kukoc/99 20.00 50.00
2 Chris Mullin/49 20.00 50.00
3 Dee Brown/99 8.00 20.00

2018-19 Panini Encased Legendary Swatch Signatures

4 Calvin Murphy/49 10.00 25.00
5 World B. Free/49 10.00 25.00
7 Robert Parish/49 20.00 50.00
8 Kevin McHale/35 EXCH 20.00 50.00
9 Horace Grant/99 10.00 25.00
10 Dominique Wilkins/35 20.00 50.00
11 A.C. Green/99 10.00 25.00
12 Nick Van Exel/49 12.00 30.00
13 Mark Price/99 10.00 25.00
15 Mark Jackson/49 10.00 25.00
16 Jason Kidd/35 40.00 100.00
17 Glen Rice/99 10.00 25.00
18 James Worthy/35 20.00 50.00
19 Mark Aguirre/99 8.00 20.00
20 Steve Kerr/49 15.00 40.00

2018-19 Panini Encased Legendary Swatch Signatures Prime

*RED/25: .6X TO 1.5X p/r 99
*RED/25: .5X TO 1.2X p/r 35-49
STATED PRINT RUN 25 SER.#'d SETS
EXCHANGE DEADLINE 1/26/2021
1 Toni Kukoc 20.00 50.00
2 Chris Mullin 20.00 50.00
8 Kevin McHale EXCH 25.00 60.00
9 Horace Grant 15.00 40.00
10 Dominique Wilkins 25.00 60.00
12 Nick Van Exel 15.00 40.00
13 Mark Price 15.00 40.00
16 Jason Kidd 25.00 60.00
17 Glen Rice 15.00 40.00

2018-19 Panini Encased Materials

STATED PRINT RUN 99 SER.#'d SETS
*PRIME/25: .75X TO 2X BASIC
1 Fred VanVleet 5.00 12.00
2 Gary Harris 3.00 8.00
3 Gerald Green 3.00 8.00
4 Giannis Antetokounmpo 20.00 50.00
5 Goran Dragic 3.00 8.00
6 Harrison Barnes 3.00 8.00
7 Harry Giles 2.50 6.00
8 Hassan Whiteside 3.00 8.00
9 Ivica Zubac 3.00 8.00
10 J.J. Barea 4.00 10.00
11 Jabari Parker 2.50 6.00
12 Jamal Murray 8.00 20.00
13 James Harden 8.00 20.00
14 Jarrett Allen 4.00 10.00
15 Jaylen Brown 6.00 15.00
16 Jayson Tatum 15.00 40.00
17 Jeff Teague 2.50 6.00
18 Jerami Grant 4.00 10.00
19 Jeremy Lin 6.00 15.00
20 Jimmy Butler 6.00 15.00
21 JJ Redick 4.00 10.00
22 Joe Harris 3.00 8.00
23 Joel Embiid 10.00 25.00
24 John Collins 4.00 10.00
25 John Wall 5.00 12.00
26 Jonathan Isaac 4.00 10.00
27 Jordan Bell 2.50 6.00
28 Josh Jackson 2.50 6.00
29 Jrue Holiday 5.00 12.00
30 Julius Randle 4.00 10.00
31 Jusuf Nurkic 3.00 8.00
32 Karl-Anthony Towns 6.00 15.00
33 Kawhi Leonard 10.00 25.00
34 Kelly Oubre Jr. 4.00 10.00
35 Kevin Durant 15.00 40.00
36 Kevin Love 3.00 8.00
37 Khris Middleton 4.00 10.00
38 Klay Thompson 10.00 25.00
39 Kobe Bryant 50.00 120.00
40 Kristaps Porzingis 5.00 12.00
41 Kyle Kuzma 4.00 10.00
42 Kyle Lowry 4.00 10.00
43 LaMarcus Aldridge 4.00 10.00
44 LeBron James 50.00 120.00
45 Lonzo Ball 4.00 10.00
46 Lou Williams 3.00 8.00
47 Magic Johnson 15.00 40.00
48 Marc Gasol 4.00 10.00
49 Marcus Morris 2.50 6.00
50 Marcus Smart 4.00 10.00
51 Mike Conley 3.00 8.00
52 Myles Turner 4.00 10.00
53 Nerlens Noel 2.50 6.00
54 Nikola Jokic 20.00 50.00
55 Nikola Mirotic 2.50 6.00
56 Otto Porter Jr. 3.00 8.00
57 Pascal Siakam 6.00 15.00
58 Paul George 6.00 15.00
59 Russell Westbrook 6.00 15.00
60 Stephen Curry 50.00 120.00

2018-19 Panini Encased Rookie Jerseys

STATED PRINT RUN 99 SER.#'d SETS
*PRIME: .75X TO 2X BASIC
1 Luka Doncic 100.00 250.00
2 Trae Young 20.00 50.00
3 Deandre Ayton 8.00 20.00
4 Wendell Carter Jr. 6.00 15.00
5 Marvin Bagley III 4.00 10.00
6 Jaren Jackson Jr. 20.00 50.00
7 Lonnie Walker IV 5.00 12.00
8 Kevin Huerter 5.00 12.00
9 Omari Spellman 2.50 6.00
10 Shai Gilgeous-Alexander 75.00 200.00
11 Jerome Robinson 2.50 6.00
12 Kevin Knox II 3.00 8.00
13 Allonzo Trier 2.50 6.00
14 Mitchell Robinson 6.00 15.00
15 Josh Okogie 4.00 10.00
16 Keita Bates-Diop 3.00 8.00
17 Mo Bamba 4.00 10.00
18 Mikal Bridges 12.00 30.00
19 Michael Porter Jr. 10.00 25.00
20 Grayson Allen 5.00 12.00
21 Zhaire Smith 2.50 6.00
22 Donte DiVincenzo 6.00 15.00
23 Aaron Holiday 4.00 10.00
24 Anfernee Simons 12.00 30.00
25 Moritz Wagner 5.00 12.00
26 Landry Shamet 4.00 10.00
27 Robert Williams III 5.00 12.00
28 Jacob Evans III 2.50 6.00
29 Dzanan Musa 2.50 6.00
30 Devonte' Graham 4.00 10.00
31 Jalen Brunson 20.00 50.00
32 Svi Mykhailiuk 3.00 8.00
33 Hamidou Diallo 4.00 10.00
34 Rodions Kurucs 3.00 8.00
35 De'Anthony Melton 5.00 12.00
36 Chimezie Metu 3.00 8.00
37 Troy Brown Jr. 3.00 8.00
38 Elie Okobo 2.50 6.00
39 Jevon Carter 4.00 10.00
40 Jarred Vanderbilt 5.00 12.00

2018-19 Panini Encased Rookie Materials

STATED PRINT RUN 99 SER.#'d SETS
*PRIME/25: .75X TO 2X BASIC
1 Luka Doncic 100.00 250.00
2 Trae Young 20.00 50.00
3 Deandre Ayton 8.00 20.00
4 Wendell Carter Jr. 6.00 15.00
5 Marvin Bagley III 4.00 10.00
6 Jaren Jackson Jr. 20.00 50.00
7 Lonnie Walker IV 5.00 12.00
8 Kevin Huerter 5.00 12.00
9 Omari Spellman 2.50 6.00
10 Shai Gilgeous-Alexander 75.00 200.00
11 Jerome Robinson 2.50 6.00
12 Kevin Knox II 3.00 8.00
13 Allonzo Trier 2.50 6.00
14 Mitchell Robinson 6.00 15.00
15 Josh Okogie 4.00 10.00
16 Keita Bates-Diop 3.00 8.00
17 Mo Bamba 4.00 10.00
18 Mikal Bridges 12.00 30.00
19 Michael Porter Jr. 10.00 25.00
20 Grayson Allen 5.00 12.00
21 Zhaire Smith 2.50 6.00
22 Donte DiVincenzo 6.00 15.00
23 Aaron Holiday 4.00 10.00
24 Anfernee Simons 12.00 30.00
25 Moritz Wagner 5.00 12.00
26 Landry Shamet 4.00 10.00
27 Robert Williams III 5.00 12.00
28 Jacob Evans III 2.50 6.00
29 Dzanan Musa 2.50 6.00
30 Devonte' Graham 4.00 10.00
31 Jalen Brunson 20.00 50.00
32 Svi Mykhailiuk 4.00 10.00
33 Hamidou Diallo 4.00 10.00
34 Rodions Kurucs 3.00 8.00
35 De'Anthony Melton 4.00 10.00
36 Chimezie Metu 3.00 8.00
37 Troy Brown Jr. 3.00 8.00
38 Elie Okobo 2.50 6.00
39 Jevon Carter 4.00 10.00
40 Jarred Vanderbilt 5.00 12.00

2018-19 Panini Encased Scripted Signatures

PRINT RUNS B/WN 25-99 COPIES PER
EXCHANGE DEADLINE 1/26/2021
*RED/15-25: .6X TO 1.5X p/r 99
*RED/15-25: .5X TO 1.2X p/r 35-49
*RED/15-25: .4X TO 1X p/r 25
1 Kareem Abdul-Jabbar/35 100.00 250.00
2 Nick Anderson/99 6.00 15.00
SC-DML Donovan Mitchell/35 40.00 100.00
4 Dee Brown/99 6.00 15.00
5 Jerry Lucas/49 12.00 30.00
9 Kyrie Irving/35 75.00 200.00
10 Charlie Scott/49 10.00 25.00
11 Karl-Anthony Towns/35 25.00 60.00
12 Rudy Tomjanovich/99 6.00 15.00
13 Jason Kidd/35 15.00 40.00
14 Dino Radja/99 5.00 12.00
15 Kyle Kuzma/49 10.00 25.00
16 Reggie Jackson/49 8.00 20.00
17 Gail Goodrich/49 10.00 25.00
18 David Thompson/49 12.00 30.00
19 Kevin Durant/25 125.00 300.00
20 Scott Skiles/99 6.00 15.00
21 Alonzo Mourning/35 15.00 40.00
22 Theo Ratliff/99 5.00 12.00
23 Dennis Rodman/35 60.00 150.00
24 Jason Williams/99 20.00 50.00
25 Bernard King/49 10.00 25.00
26 Keith Van Horn/99 6.00 15.00
27 Doc Rivers/49 10.00 25.00
28 Tom Satch Sanders/49 10.00 25.00
29 Dwyane Wade/25 75.00 200.00
30 Mychal Thompson/99 5.00 12.00
32 Wally Szczerbiak/99 6.00 15.00
33 Lonzo Ball/35 10.00 25.00
34 Rony Seikaly/99 5.00 12.00
35 Elvin Hayes/49 12.00 30.00
36 Rashard Lewis/99 EXCH 6.00 15.00
37 Glen Rice/49 10.00 25.00
38 Bill Cartwright/49 8.00 20.00
39 Damian Lillard/25 75.00 200.00
40 Charlie Ward/99 4.00 10.00
41 Grant Hill/35 15.00 40.00
42 Clifford Robinson/99 5.00 12.00
43 Nikola Jokic/49 150.00 400.00
44 Vlade Divac/99 5.00 12.00
46 Brad Daugherty/99 4.00 10.00
47 Horace Grant/49 10.00 25.00
48 Tim Hardaway/49 12.00 30.00
49 Julius Erving/35 60.00 150.00
50 Xavier McDaniel/99 6.00 15.00

2018-19 Panini Encased Slabbed Signatures

STATED PRINT RUN 49 SER.#'d SETS
EXCHANGE DEADLINE 1/26/2021
*RED: .5X TO 1.2X BASIC
1 Charles Barkley 75.00 200.00
2 Kobe Bryant EXCH 1,000.00 2,000.00
3 Kevin Durant 100.00 250.00
4 Kyrie Irving 75.00 200.00
6 Shaquille O'Neal 100.00 250.00
7 Deandre Ayton 20.00 50.00
8 Marvin Bagley III 10.00 25.00
9 Luka Doncic 1,000.00 2,000.00
10 Trae Young 400.00 800.00

2018-19 Panini Encased Substantial Swatches

STATED PRINT RUN 99 SER.#'d SETS
*PRIME: .75X TO 2X BASIC
1 Kevin Durant 15.00 40.00
2 Stephen Curry 50.00 120.00
3 Giannis Antetokounmpo 20.00 50.00
4 Kyrie Irving 10.00 25.00
5 Donovan Mitchell 12.00 30.00
6 Zach LaVine 6.00 15.00
7 Karl-Anthony Towns 6.00 15.00
8 Andrew Wiggins 5.00 12.00
9 Kyle Lowry 4.00 10.00
10 Jayson Tatum 15.00 40.00
11 Jimmy Butler 6.00 15.00
12 Nikola Jokic 20.00 50.00
13 Mike Conley 3.00 8.00
14 Damian Lillard 10.00 25.00
15 LaMarcus Aldridge 4.00 10.00
16 CJ McCollum 4.00 10.00
17 Anthony Davis 10.00 25.00
18 DeMar DeRozan 5.00 12.00
19 Kemba Walker 3.00 8.00
20 Jrue Holiday 5.00 12.00

2018-19 Panini Encased Substantial Swatches Rookies

STATED PRINT RUN 99 SER.#'d SETS
*PRIME: .75X TO 2X BASIC
1 Bruce Brown 5.00 12.00
2 Mikal Bridges 12.00 30.00
3 Anfernee Simons 12.00 30.00
4 Michael Porter Jr. 10.00 25.00
5 Lonnie Walker IV 5.00 12.00
6 Deandre Ayton 8.00 20.00
7 Chandler Hutchison 3.00 8.00
8 Jaren Jackson Jr. 20.00 50.00
9 Omari Spellman 2.50 6.00
10 Wendell Carter Jr. 6.00 15.00
11 Hamidou Diallo 4.00 10.00
12 Shai Gilgeous-Alexander 75.00 200.00
13 Jacob Evans III 2.50 6.00
14 Troy Brown Jr. 3.00 8.00
15 Kevin Huerter 5.00 12.00
16 Marvin Bagley III 4.00 10.00
17 Aaron Holiday 4.00 10.00
18 Trae Young 20.00 50.00
19 Elie Okobo 2.50 6.00
20 Collin Sexton 8.00 20.00
21 Jevon Carter 4.00 10.00
22 Jerome Robinson 2.50 6.00
23 Zhaire Smith 2.50 6.00
24 Donte DiVincenzo 6.00 15.00
25 Josh Okogie 4.00 10.00
26 Luka Doncic 100.00 250.00
27 Landry Shamet 4.00 10.00
28 Mo Bamba 4.00 10.00
29 Jalen Brunson 20.00 50.00
30 Kevin Knox II 3.00 8.00

2018-19 Panini Encased Vaulted Veteran Material Signatures

PRINT RUNS B/WN 35-99 COPIES PER
*RED/25: .6X TO 1.5X p/r 99
*RED/25: .5X TO 1.2X p/r 35-49
1 Khris Middleton/49 12.00 30.00
2 Anthony Davis/35 60.00 150.00
4 Damian Lillard/35 75.00 200.00
5 Gary Harris/49 10.00 25.00
7 Cody Zeller/99 6.00 15.00
8 Kevin Love/35 10.00 25.00
9 Nene/99 8.00 20.00
10 Lonzo Ball/35 12.00 30.00
11 Zach LaVine/49 20.00 50.00
12 Kevin Durant/35 EXCH 125.00 300.00
13 JJ Redick/49 12.00 30.00
14 Kyrie Irving/35 100.00 250.00
17 Bam Adebayo/99 EXCH 15.00 40.00
18 Jayson Tatum/35 125.00 300.00
19 Caris LeVert/99 10.00 25.00
20 LaMarcus Aldridge/35 12.00 30.00
21 Kyle Kuzma/49 12.00 30.00
22 Dwyane Wade/35 100.00 250.00
23 Nikola Mirotic/49 8.00 20.00
24 Karl-Anthony Towns/35 20.00 50.00
25 Reggie Jackson/49 10.00 25.00
26 Donovan Mitchell/35 40.00 100.00
27 John Collins/99 10.00 25.00
28 Isaiah Thomas/35 10.00 25.00
30 Nikola Jokic/49 125.00 300.00

2019-20 Panini Encased

COMMON VET (1-100) .75 2.00
SEMISTARS 1.00 2.50
UNLISTED STARS 1.25 3.00
1-100 STATED PRINT RUN 99 SER.#'d SETS
COMMON AU (101-190) 5.00 12.00
AU RC SEMIS 6.00 15.00
AU RC UNLISTED 8.00 20.00
101-190 STATED PRINT RUN 25-99 SER.#'d SETS
COMMON JSY AU (191-274) 5.00 12.00
AU RC SEMIS 6.00 15.00
AU RC UNLISTED 8.00 20.00
191-274 STATED PRINT RUN 25-99 SER.#'d SETS
EXCHANGE DEADLINE 4/21/2022
1 Aaron Gordon 1.25 3.00
2 Darius Garland 3.00 8.00
3 Dejounte Murray 1.25 3.00
4 Vince Carter 2.50 6.00
5 Jonas Valanciunas 1.00 2.50
6 Caris LeVert 1.00 2.50
7 Devin Booker .30 .75
8 Rudy Gay 1.00 2.50
9 Kyrie Irving 2.50 6.00
10 Paul George 2.00 5.00
11 Deandre Ayton 1.25 3.00
12 Bojan Bogdanovic 1.00 2.50
13 Andrew Wiggins 1.50 4.00
14 Tim Hardaway Jr. .75 2.00
15 Eric Bledsoe 1.00 2.50
16 Bam Adebayo 2.00 5.00
17 Christian Wood 1.00 2.50
18 Victor Oladipo 1.00 2.50
19 James Harden 2.50 6.00
20 Jaylen Brown 2.00 5.00
21 Michael Porter Jr. 2.00 5.00
22 Devonte' Graham 1.00 2.50
23 Mitchell Robinson 1.25 3.00
24 Danilo Gallinari 1.00 2.50
25 Robert Covington .75 2.00
26 Tobias Harris 1.00 2.50
27 DeMar DeRozan 1.50 4.00
28 Jrue Holiday 1.50 4.00
29 Elfrid Payton .75 2.00
30 Alex Caruso 1.25 3.00
31 Nikola Jokic 6.00 15.00
32 Kevin Love 1.25 3.00
33 Khris Middleton 1.25 3.00
34 Shai Gilgeous-Alexander 6.00 15.00
35 Hassan Whiteside .75 2.00
36 Collin Sexton 1.50 4.00
37 Zach LaVine 2.00 5.00
38 D'Angelo Russell 1.00 2.50
39 Trae Young 3.00 8.00
40 Kyle Lowry 1.25 3.00
41 Damian Lillard 3.00 8.00
42 De'Aaron Fox 2.00 5.00
43 Kawhi Leonard 3.00 8.00
44 Domantas Sabonis 1.50 4.00
45 Kevin Durant 10.00 25.00
46 Terry Rozier 1.00 2.50
47 Stephen Curry 10.00 25.00
48 Pascal Siakam 2.00 5.00
49 Goran Dragic 1.00 2.50
50 John Wall 1.50 4.00
51 Kemba Walker 1.00 2.50
52 Karl-Anthony Towns 2.00 5.00
53 Bradley Beal 1.50 4.00
54 Wendell Carter Jr. 1.25 3.00
55 Andre Drummond 1.00 2.50
56 Joel Embiid 2.50 6.00
57 Marc Gasol 1.25 3.00
58 Brandon Ingram 1.25 3.00
59 Al Horford 1.25 3.00
60 Lonzo Ball 1.25 3.00
61 LaMarcus Aldridge 1.25 3.00
62 Carmelo Anthony 2.00 5.00
63 Lonnie Walker IV 1.00 2.50
64 Kelly Oubre Jr. 1.00 2.50
65 Jamal Murray 2.00 5.00
66 Bogdan Bogdanovic 1.25 3.00
67 Ben Simmons 1.25 3.00
68 Jayson Tatum 5.00 12.00
69 Fred VanVleet 1.50 4.00
70 CJ McCollum 1.25 3.00
71 Russell Westbrook 2.00 5.00
72 Miles Bridges 1.25 3.00
73 Lauri Markkanen 1.50 4.00
74 Steven Adams 1.00 2.50
75 Mike Conley 1.00 2.50
76 Markelle Fultz 1.00 2.50
77 Malik Beasley 1.00 2.50
78 Kristaps Porzingis 1.50 4.00
79 John Collins 1.25 3.00
80 Montrezl Harrell 1.00 2.50
81 Julius Randle 1.50 4.00
82 Dillon Brooks 1.00 2.50
83 Nikola Vucevic 1.00 2.50
84 Donovan Mitchell 2.50 6.00
85 Jaren Jackson Jr. 2.00 5.00
86 Klay Thompson 3.00 8.00
87 LeBron James 60.00 150.00
88 Gordon Hayward 1.00 2.50
89 Blake Griffin 1.25 3.00
90 Luka Doncic 75.00 200.00
91 Malcolm Brogdon 1.00 2.50
92 Chris Paul 2.50 6.00
93 Myles Turner 1.25 3.00
94 Giannis Antetokounmpo 10.00 25.00
95 Jimmy Butler 2.50 6.00
96 Anthony Davis 3.00 8.00
97 Draymond Green 1.50 4.00
98 Davis Bertans .75 2.00
99 Derrick Rose 2.50 6.00
100 Buddy Hield 1.00 2.50
101 Goga Bitadze RE AU/99 RC 10.00 25.00
102 Kendrick Nunn RE AU/99 RC 8.00 20.00
103 Brandon Clarke RE AU/99 RC 10.00 25.00
104 RJ Barrett RE AU/49 RC 125.00 300.00
105 Ty Jerome RE AU/99 RC 10.00 25.00
106 Jaxson Hayes RE AU/99 RC 15.00 40.00
107 Mfiondu Kabengele RE AU/99 RC 6.00 15.00
108 Cameron Johnson RE AU/99 RC 50.00 120.00
109 Carsen Edwards RE AU/99 RC 6.00 15.00
110 Sekou Doumbouya RE AU/99 RC 5.00 12.00
111 Luka Samanic RE AU/99 RC 6.00 15.00
112 Zion Williamson
RE AU/25 RC 1,000.00 2,000.00
113 Grant Williams RE AU/99 RC 8.00 20.00
114 Jarrett Culver RE AU/49 RC 5.00 12.00
115 Nassir Little RE AU/99 RC 8.00 20.00
116 Rui Hachimura RE AU/49 RC 20.00 50.00
117 Keldon Johnson RE AU/99 RC 50.00 120.00
118 PJ Washington Jr. RE AU/99 RC 15.00 40.00
119 KZ Okpala RE AU/99 RC 6.00 15.00
120 Chuma Okeke RE AU/99 RC 8.00 20.00
121 Matisse Thybulle RE AU/99 RC 30.00 80.00
122 Ja Morant RE AU/49 RC 1,500.00 3,000.00
123 Darius Bazley RE AU/99 RC 5.00 12.00
124 Coby White RE AU/49 RC 15.00 40.00
125 Dylan Windler RE AU/99 RC 6.00 15.00
126 Cam Reddish RE AU/99 RC 8.00 20.00
127 Kevin Porter Jr. RE AU/99 RC 10.00 25.00
128 Tyler Herro RE AU/99 RC 125.00 300.00
129 Bol Bol RE AU/99 RC 12.00 30.00
130 Nickeil Alexander-Walker
RE AU/99 RC 8.00 20.00
131 Coby White SS AU/49 15.00 40.00
132 Isaiah Roby SS AU/99 RC 6.00 15.00
133 Cameron Johnson SS AU/99 50.00 120.00
134 Quinndary Weatherspoon
SS AU/99 RC 5.00 12.00
135 Brandon Clarke SS AU/99 10.00 25.00
136 Oshae Brissett SS AU/99 RC 8.00 20.00
137 Kevin Porter Jr. SS AU/99 10.00 25.00
138 Bruno Fernando SS AU/99 RC 6.00 15.00
139 Kendrick Nunn SS AU/99 8.00 20.00
140 Justin James SS AU/99 RC 5.00 12.00
141 Jaxson Hayes SS AU/99 15.00 40.00
142 Talen Horton-Tucker SS AU/99 RC 8.00 20.00
143 Goga Bitadze SS AU/99 10.00 25.00
144 Kyle Guy SS AU/99 RC 6.00 15.00
145 Dylan Windler SS AU/99 8.00 20.00
146 Naz Reid SS AU/99 RC 40.00 100.00
147 Nicolas Claxton SS AU/99 RC 10.00 25.00
148 Daniel Gafford SS AU/99 RC 10.00 25.00
149 Ja Morant SS AU/49 1,500.00 3,000.00
150 Admiral Schofield SS AU/99 RC 6.00 15.00
151 Cam Reddish SS AU/99 8.00 20.00
152 Terance Mann SS AU/99 RC 10.00 25.00
153 Matisse Thybulle SS AU/99 10.00 25.00
154 Jalen Lecque SS AU/99 RC 5.00 12.00
155 Mfiondu Kabengele SS AU/99 6.00 15.00
156 Terence Davis SS AU/99 RC 8.00 20.00
157 Carsen Edwards SS AU/99 6.00 15.00
158 Alen Smailagic SS AU/99 RC 5.00 12.00
159 RJ Barrett SS AU/49 125.00 300.00
160 Jaylen Nowell SS AU/99 RC 6.00 15.00
161 Jaylen Nowell NS AU/99 6.00 15.00
162 Cam Reddish NS AU/99 8.00 20.00
163 Kyle Guy NS AU/99 6.00 15.00
164 Ty Jerome NS AU/99 10.00 25.00
165 Naz Reid NS AU/99 40.00 100.00
166 Nicolas Claxton NS AU/99 10.00 25.00
167 Cody Martin NS AU/99 RC 8.00 20.00
168 Kendrick Nunn NS AU/99 8.00 20.00
169 Justin James NS AU/99 5.00 12.00
170 Jarrett Culver NS AU/49 5.00 12.00
171 Talen Horton-Tucker NS AU/99 8.00 20.00
172 PJ Washington Jr. NS AU/99 15.00 40.00
173 Jalen Lecque NS AU/99 5.00 12.00
174 Dylan Windler NS AU/99 6.00 15.00
175 Terence Davis NS AU/99 8.00 20.00
176 Bol Bol NS AU/99 12.00 30.00
177 Daniel Gafford NS AU/99 10.00 25.00
178 Ja Morant NS AU/49 1,500.00 3,000.00
179 Eric Paschall NS AU/99 RC 6.00 15.00
180 Jaxson Hayes NS AU/99 15.00 40.00
181 Terance Mann NS AU/99 10.00 25.00
182 Luka Samanic NS AU/99 6.00 15.00
183 Oshae Brissett NS AU/99 8.00 20.00
184 Keldon Johnson NS AU/99 50.00 120.00
185 Tacko Fall NS AU/99 RC 6.00 15.00
186 Bruno Fernando NS AU/99 6.00 15.00
187 Alen Smailagic NS AU/99 5.00 12.00
188 RJ Barrett NS AU/49 125.00 300.00
189 Admiral Schofield NS AU/99 6.00 15.00
190 Rui Hachimura NS AU/49 20.00 50.00
191 Zion Williamson JSY AU/25 1,000.00 2,000.00
192 Dylan Windler JSY AU/99 6.00 15.00
193 Jarrett Culver JSY AU/99 5.00 12.00
194 KZ Okpala JSY AU/99 6.00 15.00
195 Cam Reddish JSY AU/99 8.00 20.00
196 Eric Paschall JSY AU/99 6.00 15.00
197 Romeo Langford JSY AU/99 RC 5.00 12.00
198 Isaiah Roby JSY AU/99 6.00 15.00
199 Goga Bitadze JSY AU/99 10.00 25.00
200 Grant Williams JSY AU/99 8.00 20.00
201 Ja Morant JSY AU/49 1,500.00 3,000.00
202 Mfiondu Kabengele JSY AU/99 6.00 15.00
203 Coby White JSY AU/99 15.00 40.00
204 Carsen Edwards JSY AU/99 6.00 15.00
205 Cameron Johnson JSY AU/99 50.00 120.00
206 Admiral Schofield JSY AU/99 6.00 15.00
207 Sekou Doumbouya JSY AU/99 5.00 12.00
208 Tacko Fall JSY AU/99 6.00 15.00
209 Luka Samanic JSY AU/99 6.00 15.00
210 Darius Bazley JSY AU/99 5.00 12.00
211 RJ Barrett JSY AU/49 125.00 300.00
212 Jordan Poole JSY AU/99 RC 100.00 250.00
213 Jaxson Hayes JSY AU/99 15.00 40.00
214 Bruno Fernando JSY AU/99 6.00 15.00
215 PJ Washington Jr. JSY AU/99 15.00 40.00
216 Jaylen Nowell JSY AU/99 6.00 15.00
217 Chuma Okeke JSY AU/99 8.00 20.00
218 Quinndary
Weatherspoon JSY AU/99 5.00 12.00
219 Matisse Thybulle JSY AU/99 30.00 80.00
220 Ty Jerome JSY AU/99 10.00 25.00
221 De'Andre Hunter JSY AU/49 RC 25.00 60.00
222 Keldon Johnson JSY AU/99 50.00 120.00
223 Rui Hachimura JSY AU/99 20.00 50.00
224 Cody Martin JSY AU/99 8.00 20.00
225 Tyler Herro JSY AU/99 125.00 300.00
226 Bol Bol JSY AU/99 12.00 30.00
227 Nickeil Alexander-
Walker JSY AU/99 8.00 20.00
228 Tremont Waters JSY AU/99 RC 6.00 15.00
229 Brandon Clarke JSY AU/99 10.00 25.00
230 Nassir Little JSY AU/99 RC 8.00 20.00
231 Kevin Porter Jr. JSY AU/99 10.00 25.00
232 Kyle Guy JSY AU/99 6.00 15.00
233 Matisse Thybulle JSY AU/99 30.00 80.00
234 Goga Bitadze JSY AU/99 10.00 25.00
235 Rui Hachimura JSY AU/99 20.00 50.00
236 Coby White JSY AU/99 15.00 40.00
237 Nickeil Alexander-
Walker JSY AU/99 8.00 20.00
238 Sekou Doumbouya JSY AU/99 5.00 12.00
239 Kevin Porter Jr. JSY AU/99 10.00 25.00
240 Dylan Windler JSY AU/99 6.00 15.00
241 RJ Barrett JSY AU/49 125.00 300.00
242 Jaylen Nowell JSY AU/99 6.00 15.00
243 Eric Paschall JSY AU/99 6.00 15.00
244 Ty Jerome JSY AU/99 10.00 25.00
245 Grant Williams JSY AU/99 8.00 20.00
246 Cody Martin JSY AU/99 8.00 20.00
247 Carsen Edwards JSY AU/99 6.00 15.00
248 Tremont Waters JSY AU/99 6.00 15.00
249 Tacko Fall JSY AU/99 6.00 15.00
250 Kyle Guy JSY AU/99 6.00 15.00
251 Jordan Poole JSY AU/99 100.00 250.00
252 Jarrett Culver JSY AU/99 5.00 12.00
253 Chuma Okeke JSY AU/99 8.00 20.00
254 Romeo Langford JSY AU/99 5.00 12.00
255 De'Andre Hunter JSY AU/49 25.00 60.00
256 Ja Morant JSY AU/49 1,500.00 3,000.00
257 Tyler Herro JSY AU/99 125.00 300.00
258 Cameron Johnson JSY AU/99 50.00 120.00
259 Brandon Clarke JSY AU/99 10.00 25.00
260 Luka Samanic JSY AU/99 6.00 15.00
261 KZ Okpala JSY AU/99 6.00 15.00
262 Jaxson Hayes JSY AU/99 15.00 40.00
263 Quinndary
Weatherspoon JSY AU/99 5.00 12.00
264 Isaiah Roby JSY AU/99 6.00 15.00
265 Keldon Johnson JSY AU/99 50.00 120.00
266 Mfiondu Kabengele JSY AU/99 6.00 15.00
267 Bol Bol JSY AU/99 12.00 30.00
268 Admiral Schofield JSY AU/99 6.00 15.00
269 Nassir Little JSY AU/99 8.00 20.00
270 Darius Bazley JSY AU/99 5.00 12.00
271 Bruno Fernando JSY AU/99 6.00 15.00
272 Zion Williamson JSY AU/25 1,000.00 2,000.00
273 PJ Washington Jr. JSY AU/99 15.00 40.00
274 Cam Reddish JSY AU/99 8.00 20.00

2019-20 Panini Encased Bronze

*BRONZE/35: .6X TO 1.5X p/r 99
*BRONZE/35: .5X TO 1.2X p/r 49
*BRONZE/35: .4X TO 1X p/r 25
STATED PRINT RUN 35 COPIES PER
EXCHANGE DEADLINE 4/21/2022
231 Kevin Porter Jr. JSY AU 15.00 40.00
239 Kevin Porter Jr. JSY AU 15.00 40.00

2019-20 Panini Encased Purple

*PURPLE: .6X TO 1.5X BASIC
STATED PRINT RUN 35 COPIES PER
87 LeBron James 125.00 300.00
94 Giannis Antetokounmpo 20.00 50.00

2019-20 Panini Encased Red

*RED/25: .75X TO 2X p/r 99
*RED/25: .6X TO 1.5X p/r 49
STATED PRINT RUN 15-25 COPIES PER
NO PRICING ON QTY 15 OR LESS
EXCHANGE DEADLINE 4/21/2022
87 LeBron James 150.00 400.00
94 Giannis Antetokounmpo 25.00 60.00

2019-20 Panini Encased Endorsements

COMMON p/r 99 3.00 8.00
SEMIS p/r 99 4.00 10.00
UNLISTED p/r 99 5.00 12.00
COMMON p/r 49 4.00 10.00
SEMIS p/r 49 5.00 12.00
UNLISTED p/r 49 6.00 15.00
COMMON p/r 25 5.00 12.00
SEMIS p/r 25 6.00 15.00
UNLISTED p/r 25 8.00 20.00
PRINT RUNS B/WN 25-99 COPIES PER
EXCHANGE DEADLINE 4/21/2022
*RED/25: .6X TO 1.5X p/r 99
*RED/25: .5X TO 1.2X p/r 35-49
1 Arvydas Sabonis/99 10.00 25.00
2 Eric Gordon/49 5.00 12.00
3 Gary Harris/49 5.00 12.00
4 Charles Barkley/25 100.00 250.00
5 Caris LeVert/99 20.00 50.00
6 Larry Bird/25 125.00 300.00
7 Luke Walton/99 4.00 10.00
8 Paul Pierce/25 40.00 100.00
9 Nemanja Bjelica/99 3.00 8.00
10 Rick Barry/49 12.00 30.00
11 Eddie Jones/99 12.00 30.00
12 Julius Randle/49 12.00 30.00
13 Kevin Johnson/49 12.00 30.00
14 Stephen Curry/49 800.00 1,500.00
15 Allan Houston/99 6.00 15.00
16 John Stockton/25 50.00 120.00
17 Thon Maker/99 3.00 8.00
18 Elgin Baylor/25 40.00 100.00
19 Toni Kukoc/99 12.00 30.00
20 Christian Laettner/49 8.00 20.00
21 Jason Williams/99 50.00 120.00
22 Calvin Murphy/49 6.00 15.00
23 Louie Dampier/49 6.00 15.00
24 Kevin Durant/49 125.00 300.00
25 Carlos Boozer/99 4.00 10.00
26 Kevin Garnett/25 125.00 300.00
27 Alex English/99 12.00 30.00
28 Vince Carter/25 60.00 150.00
29 Cedi Osman/99 4.00 10.00
30 Jaren Jackson Jr./49 30.00 80.00
31 Lionel Hollins/99 3.00 8.00
32 Bill Walton/49 20.00 50.00
33 Ralph Sampson/49 5.00 12.00
34 Allen Iverson/25 125.00 300.00
35 J.J. Barea/99 12.00 30.00
36 Oscar Robertson/25 75.00 200.00
37 Bogdan Bogdanovic/99 5.00 12.00
38 Gary Payton/25 30.00 80.00
39 Jalen Brunson/99 8.00 20.00
40 Artis Gilmore/49 12.00 30.00
41 Mike Bibby/99 12.00 30.00
42 Danny Manning/49 5.00 12.00
43 Steve Francis/49 12.00 30.00
44 Dwyane Wade/25 50.00 120.00
45 Joe Harris/99 4.00 10.00
46 Clyde Drexler/25 25.00 60.00
47 Ersan Ilyasova/99 3.00 8.00
48 DeAndre Jordan/49 5.00 12.00
49 Rondae Hollis-Jefferson/99 3.00 8.00
50 Richard Hamilton/49 12.00 30.00

2019-20 Panini Encased Label Materials

COMMON CARD 2.50 6.00
SEMISTARS 3.00 8.00
UNLISTED STARS 4.00 10.00
STATED PRINT RUN 99-199 SER.#'d SETS
1 Karl-Anthony Towns/199 8.00 20.00
2 Andrew Wiggins/199 5.00 12.00
3 LaMarcus Aldridge/199 4.00 10.00
4 Kevin Love/199 4.00 10.00
5 Zach LaVine/199 8.00 20.00
6 Derrick Rose/99 8.00 20.00
7 Carmelo Anthony/99 6.00 15.00
8 Jarrett Allen/199 4.00 10.00
9 DeAndre Jordan/199 3.00 8.00
10 Rudy Gobert/199 5.00 12.00
11 Josh Okogie/99 3.00 8.00
12 Kyrie Irving/199 8.00 20.00
13 Nikola Vucevic/199 3.00 8.00
14 Serge Ibaka/199 3.00 8.00
15 Bojan Bogdanovic/199 3.00 8.00
16 Bradley Beal/99 5.00 12.00
17 Kristaps Porzingis/199 5.00 12.00
18 Kyle Lowry/99 4.00 10.00
19 Anthony Davis/199 15.00 40.00
20 John Wall/99 5.00 12.00
21 Enes Kanter/199 2.50 6.00
22 Domantas Sabonis/199 5.00 12.00
23 Kawhi Leonard/199 10.00 25.00
24 Marc Gasol/199 4.00 10.00
25 Nikola Jokic/199 15.00 40.00
26 LeBron James/199 50.00 120.00
27 Myles Turner/199 4.00 10.00
28 Aaron Gordon/199 4.00 10.00
29 Draymond Green/199 5.00 12.00
30 CJ McCollum/99 4.00 10.00
31 Terrence Ross/99 4.00 10.00
32 Kris Dunn/199 2.50 6.00
33 Jamal Murray/199 6.00 15.00
34 Steven Adams/199 3.00 8.00
35 Harrison Barnes/199 3.00 8.00
36 Jimmy Butler/99 8.00 20.00
37 Mitchell Robinson/199 4.00 10.00
38 Victor Oladipo/99 3.00 8.00
39 Jonas Valanciunas/199 3.00 8.00
40 Luka Doncic/199 60.00 150.00
41 Rudy Gay/199 3.00 8.00
42 Mo Bamba/199 3.00 8.00
43 Blake Griffin/99 4.00 10.00
44 D'Angelo Russell/199 3.00 8.00
45 Eric Bledsoe/99 3.00 8.00
46 Lou Williams/99 4.00 10.00
47 DeMar DeRozan/199 5.00 12.00
48 Paul George/199 6.00 15.00
49 Eric Gordon/199 3.00 8.00
50 Khris Middleton/199 4.00 10.00
51 Miles Bridges/199 4.00 10.00
52 Kyle Kuzma/199 5.00 12.00
53 Lauri Markkanen/99 5.00 12.00
54 Donovan Mitchell/99 8.00 20.00
55 Giannis Antetokounmpo/99 30.00 80.00
56 Devin Booker/99 1.00 2.50
57 Seth Curry/199 3.00 8.00
58 Damian Lillard/99 10.00 25.00

2019-20 Panini Encased Legendary Swatches

COMMON CARD 2.50 6.00
SEMISTARS 3.00 8.00
UNLISTED STARS 4.00 10.00
STATED PRINT RUN 149 SER.#'d SETS
1 Shaquille O'Neal 25.00 60.00
2 Richard Jefferson 2.50 6.00
3 Kevin Garnett 10.00 25.00
4 Deron Williams 3.00 8.00
5 Hakeem Olajuwon 8.00 20.00
6 Grant Hill 6.00 15.00
7 Larry Bird 25.00 60.00
8 David Robinson 8.00 20.00
9 Scottie Pippen 15.00 40.00
10 Karl Malone 8.00 20.00
11 Magic Johnson 25.00 60.00
12 Michael Redd 3.00 8.00
13 Larry Johnson 5.00 12.00
14 Paul Pierce 6.00 15.00
15 Chris Bosh 5.00 12.00
16 Patrick Ewing 6.00 15.00
17 Clyde Drexler 6.00 15.00
18 Shawn Marion 3.00 8.00
19 Jason Kidd 6.00 15.00
20 Dwyane Wade 8.00 20.00

2019-20 Panini Encased Rookie Label Materials

COMMON CARD 2.00 5.00
SEMISTARS 2.50 6.00
UNLISTED STARS 3.00 8.00
STATED PRINT RUN 199 SER.#'d SETS
*PRIME: .75X TO 2X BASIC
1 Ignas Brazdeikis 2.50 6.00
2 De'Andre Hunter 8.00 20.00
3 RJ Barrett 15.00 40.00
4 Cody Martin 3.00 8.00
5 Nickeil Alexander-Walker 3.00 8.00
6 Romeo Langford 2.00 5.00
7 Zion Williamson 40.00 100.00
8 Ty Jerome 4.00 10.00
9 Jaxson Hayes 3.00 8.00
10 Eric Paschall 2.50 6.00
11 Bol Bol 5.00 12.00
12 Jarrett Culver 2.00 5.00
13 Cameron Johnson 5.00 12.00
14 Sekou Doumbouya 2.00 5.00
15 Coby White 25.00 60.00
16 Goga Bitadze 3.00 8.00
17 KZ Okpala 2.50 6.00
18 Carsen Edwards 2.50 6.00
19 Cam Reddish 3.00 8.00
20 Ja Morant 75.00 200.00
21 Bruno Fernando 2.50 6.00
22 Brandon Clarke 4.00 10.00
23 Isaiah Roby 2.50 6.00
24 Luka Samanic 2.50 6.00
25 Mfiondu Kabengele 2.50 6.00
26 Rui Hachimura 8.00 20.00
27 Jaylen Nowell 2.50 6.00
28 Kyle Guy 2.50 6.00
29 Chuma Okeke 3.00 8.00
30 Grant Williams 3.00 8.00
31 Darius Bazley 2.00 5.00
32 Keldon Johnson 6.00 15.00
33 Nassir Little 3.00 8.00
34 Tyler Herro 25.00 60.00
35 Admiral Schofield 2.50 6.00
36 Quinndary Weatherspoon 2.00 5.00
37 Jordan Poole 8.00 20.00
38 PJ Washington Jr. 6.00 15.00
39 Matisse Thybulle 4.00 10.00
40 Kevin Porter Jr. 4.00 10.00
41 Tremont Waters 2.50 6.00
42 Dylan Windler 2.50 6.00

2019-20 Panini Encased Rookie Label Materials Prime

*PRIME: .75X TO 2X BASIC
PRINT RUN 25 COPIES PER
40 Kevin Porter Jr. 8.00 20.00

2019-20 Panini Encased Scripted Signatures

COMMON p/r 99 3.00 8.00
SEMIS p/r 99 4.00 10.00
UNLISTED p/r 99 5.00 12.00
COMMON p/r 49 4.00 10.00
SEMIS p/r 49 5.00 12.00
UNLISTED p/r 49 6.00 15.00
COMMON p/r 25 5.00 12.00
SEMIS p/r 25 6.00 15.00
UNLISTED p/r 25 8.00 20.00
PRINT RUNS B/WN 25-99 COPIES PER
EXCHANGE DEADLINE 4/21/2022

*RED/25: .6X TO 1.5X p/r 99
*RED/25: .5X TO 1.2X p/r 49
1 Dave Cowens/49 8.00 20.00
2 Vlade Divac/99 5.00 12.00
3 Willie Cauley-Stein/49 4.00 10.00
4 Kyrie Irving/25 75.00 200.00
5 Josh Hart/99 4.00 10.00
6 Jason Kidd/25 15.00 40.00
7 Kenny "Sky" Walker/99 4.00 10.00
8 Nikola Jokic/49 150.00 400.00
9 Al Harrington/99 5.00 12.00
10 Bernard King/49 8.00 20.00
11 Jalen Rose/49 8.00 20.00
13 Mo Bamba/99 4.00 10.00
14 Anthony Davis/25 100.00 250.00
15 Montrezl Harrell/99 4.00 10.00
16 Kevin McHale/25 15.00 40.00
17 Stephen Jackson/99 3.00 8.00
18 Zach LaVine/49 25.00 60.00
19 Bob Dandridge/99 3.00 8.00
20 George Gervin/49 12.00 30.00
21 Latrell Sprewell/49 12.00 30.00
22 Shaquille O'Neal/25 150.00 400.00
23 Avery Bradley/99 3.00 8.00
24 Julius Erving/25 100.00 250.00
25 A.C. Green/99 5.00 12.00
26 Lonzo Ball/25 25.00 60.00
27 Matthew Dellavedova/99 4.00 10.00
28 Dwight Howard/49 10.00 25.00
29 Ernie DiGregorio/99 4.00 10.00
30 Nick Van Exel/49 15.00 40.00
31 Mark Jackson/49 5.00 12.00
32 Giannis Antetokounmpo/49 300.00 600.00
33 Evan Turner/99 3.00 8.00
34 Kareem Abdul-Jabbar/25 125.00 300.00
35 Alvan Adams/99 3.00 8.00
36 Kristaps Porzingis/25 15.00 40.00
37 Cedric Maxwell/99 4.00 10.00
38 Jrue Holiday/49 8.00 20.00
39 Mark Price/99 10.00 25.00
40 Elvin Hayes/49 10.00 25.00
41 Rick Fox/49 5.00 12.00
42 Karl Malone/25 100.00 250.00
43 Jarrett Allen/99 5.00 12.00
44 Karl-Anthony Towns/25 25.00 60.00
45 Charles Oakley/99 4.00 10.00
46 Lauri Markkanen/25 10.00 25.00
47 Rik Smits/99 4.00 10.00
48 Walt Frazier/49 12.00 30.00
49 Wally Szczerbiak/99 4.00 10.00
50 Chauncey Billups/49 12.00 30.00

2019-20 Panini Encased Scripted Signatures Red

*RED/25: .6X TO 1.5X p/r 99
*RED/25: .5X TO 1.2X p/r 49
PRINT RUNS B/WN 15-25 COPIES PER
NO PRICING ON QTY 15 OR LESS
EXCHANGE DEADLINE 4/21/2022
8 Nikola Jokic/25 200.00 500.00

2019-20 Panini Encased Slabbed Signatures

COMMON CARD 5.00 12.00
SEMISTARS 6.00 15.00
UNLISTED STARS 8.00 20.00
STATED PRINT RUN 25-99 SER.#'d SETS
EXCHANGE DEADLINE 4/21/2022
*RED/25: .6X TO 1.5X p/r 99
*RED/25: .5X TO 1.2X p/r 49
2 Kevin Durant/49 125.00 300.00
3 Kyrie Irving/25 75.00 200.00
4 Stephen Curry/25 500.00 1,000.00
5 Kevin Garnett/25 150.00 400.00
6 Zion Williamson/25 1,000.00 2,000.00
7 RJ Barrett/49 100.00 250.00
8 Ja Morant/49 1,000.00 2,000.00
9 Coby White/99 40.00 100.00
10 Charles Barkley/25 100.00 250.00

2019-20 Panini Encased Slabbed Signatures Red

*RED/25: .6X TO 1.5X p/r 99
*RED/25: .5X TO 1.2X p/r 49
PRINT RUNS B/WN 15-25 COPIES PER
NO PRICING ON QTY 15 OR LESS
EXCHANGE DEADLINE 4/21/2022
2 Kevin Durant/25 200.00 500.00

2019-20 Panini Encased Substantial Swatches

COMMON CARD 2.50 6.00
SEMISTARS 3.00 8.00
UNLISTED STARS 4.00 10.00
STATED PRINT RUN 99 SER.#'d SETS
1 Karl-Anthony Towns 6.00 15.00
2 Andrew Wiggins 5.00 12.00
3 Kevin Love 4.00 10.00
4 Zach LaVine 6.00 15.00
5 Derrick Rose 8.00 20.00
6 Carmelo Anthony 6.00 15.00
7 Jamal Murray 6.00 15.00
8 Rudy Gobert 5.00 12.00
9 Kyrie Irving 8.00 20.00
10 Bradley Beal 5.00 12.00
11 Kristaps Porzingis 5.00 12.00
12 Kyle Lowry 4.00 10.00
13 Anthony Davis 10.00 25.00
14 John Wall 5.00 12.00
15 Domantas Sabonis 5.00 12.00
16 Kawhi Leonard 10.00 25.00
17 Nikola Jokic 20.00 50.00
18 Myles Turner 4.00 10.00
19 Draymond Green 5.00 12.00
20 CJ McCollum 4.00 10.00

2019-20 Panini Encased Substantial Swatches Rookies

COMMON CARD 2.00 5.00
SEMISTARS 2.50 6.00
UNLISTED STARS 3.00 8.00
STATED PRINT RUN 199 SER.#'d SETS
*PRIME: .75X TO 2X BASIC
1 Nickeil Alexander-Walker 3.00 8.00
2 Brandon Clarke 4.00 10.00
3 Goga Bitadze 3.00 8.00
4 Rui Hachimura 8.00 20.00
5 Ja Morant 75.00 200.00
6 Cody Martin 3.00 8.00
7 Kevin Porter Jr. 4.00 10.00
8 Tyler Herro 25.00 60.00
9 Cameron Johnson 5.00 12.00
10 Coby White 6.00 15.00
11 Chuma Okeke 3.00 8.00
12 PJ Washington Jr. 6.00 15.00
13 RJ Barrett 20.00 50.00
14 Zion Williamson 40.00 100.00
15 Keldon Johnson 6.00 15.00
16 Sekou Doumbouya 2.00 5.00
17 Nassir Little 3.00 8.00
18 Grant Williams 3.00 8.00
19 Jaxson Hayes 3.00 8.00
20 De'Andre Hunter 8.00 20.00
21 Jordan Poole 8.00 20.00
22 Cam Reddish 3.00 8.00
23 Matisse Thybulle 4.00 10.00
24 Jarrett Culver 2.00 5.00
25 Eric Paschall 2.50 6.00
26 Romeo Langford 2.00 5.00
27 Bol Bol 5.00 12.00
28 Luka Samanic 2.50 6.00
29 Ty Jerome 4.00 10.00
30 Carsen Edwards 2.50 6.00

2019-20 Panini Encased Vaulted Veteran Material

COMMON CARD 2.00 5.00
SEMISTARS 2.50 6.00
UNLISTED STARS 3.00 8.00
STATED PRINT RUN 149 SER.#'d SETS
1 Harry Giles III 2.00 5.00
2 Ben Simmons 3.00 8.00
3 Frank Ntilikina 2.00 5.00
4 Jaylen Brown 5.00 12.00
5 Trae Young 15.00 40.00
6 Maxi Kleber 2.00 5.00
7 Luka Doncic 60.00 150.00
8 Terry Rozier 2.50 6.00
9 LeBron James 50.00 120.00
10 OG Anunoby 2.50 6.00
11 Jonathan Isaac 3.00 8.00
12 Malcolm Brogdon 2.50 6.00
13 Klay Thompson 15.00 40.00
14 Kevin Knox II 2.00 5.00
15 Jusuf Nurkic 2.50 6.00
16 Kemba Walker 2.50 6.00
17 Reggie Jackson 2.50 6.00
18 Pascal Siakam 5.00 12.00
19 John Collins 3.00 8.00
20 Giannis Antetokounmpo 25.00 60.00
21 Andre Drummond 2.50 6.00
22 Donovan Mitchell 15.00 40.00
23 Joel Embiid 6.00 15.00
24 Markelle Fultz 2.50 6.00
25 Gordon Hayward 2.50 6.00
26 Patrick Beverley 2.50 6.00
27 Dennis Schroder 2.50 6.00
28 Jaren Jackson Jr. 5.00 12.00
29 Jayson Tatum 20.00 50.00
30 Chris Paul 6.00 15.00

2017-18 Panini Essentials

201-240 PRINT RUN 99 SER.#'d SETS
EXCHANGE DEADLINE 11/30/2019
1 Thomas Bryant .40 1.00
2 Patrick Beverley .25 .60
3 Quinn Cook .30 .75
4 Eric Bledsoe .30 .75
5 Russell Westbrook .60 1.50
6 Dennis Schroder .30 .75
7 Damian Lillard 1.00 2.50
8 Kris Dunn .25 .60
9 Ricky Rubio .30 .75
10 Reggie Jackson .25 .60
11 Bogdan Bogdanovic .60 1.50
12 Austin Rivers .30 .75
13 Jordan Bell RC .40 1.00
14 Malcolm Brogdon .30 .75
15 Carmelo Anthony .60 1.50
16 Kent Bazemore .25 .60
17 CJ McCollum .40 1.00
18 Zach LaVine .60 1.50
19 Alec Burks .25 .60
20 Avery Bradley .25 .60
21 John Collins RC 1.00 2.50
22 Blake Griffin .40 1.00
23 Zach Collins RC .60 1.50
24 Khris Middleton .50 1.25
25 Paul George .60 1.50
26 Taurean Prince .25 .60
27 Noah Vonleh .25 .60
28 Justin Holiday .25 .60
29 Derrick Favors .25 .60
30 Stanley Johnson .25 .60
31 OG Anunoby RC 2.00 5.00
32 DeAndre Jordan .30 .75
33 Justin Patton RC .40 1.00
34 Giannis Antetokounmpo 2.00 5.00
35 Steven Adams .30 .75
36 Ersan Ilyasova .25 .60
37 Jusuf Nurkic .30 .75
38 Denzel Valentine .25 .60
39 Rudy Gobert .50 1.25
40 Tobias Harris .30 .75
41 Frank Ntilikina RC .50 1.25
42 Danilo Gallinari .30 .75
43 D.J. Wilson RC .40 1.00
44 Thon Maker .25 .60
45 Raymond Felton .25 .60
46 Dewayne Dedmon .25 .60
47 Evan Turner .25 .60
48 Robin Lopez .25 .60
49 Joe Ingles .30 .75
50 Andre Drummond .30 .75
51 Dwayne Bacon RC .40 1.00
52 Jordan Clarkson .40 1.00
53 Harry Giles RC .40 1.00
54 Jeff Teague .25 .60
55 Elfrid Payton .25 .60
56 Kyrie Irving .75 2.00
57 George Hill .30 .75
58 Kyle Collinsworth RC .40 1.00
59 John Wall .50 1.25
60 Stephen Curry 3.00 8.00
61 Markelle Fultz RC 1.00 2.50
62 Kentavious Caldwell-Pope .30 .75
63 Terrance Ferguson RC .40 1.00
64 Jimmy Butler .60 1.50
65 Evan Fournier .30 .75
66 Gordon Hayward .30 .75
67 Buddy Hield .40 1.00
68 Isaiah Thomas .30 .75
69 Bradley Beal .50 1.25
70 Klay Thompson 1.00 2.50
71 Sindarius Thornwell RC .40 1.00
72 Brandon Ingram .50 1.25
73 Tyler Lydon RC .40 1.00
74 Andrew Wiggins .50 1.25
75 Aaron Gordon .40 1.00
76 Jaylen Brown 1.00 2.50
77 Vince Carter .75 2.00
78 LeBron James 3.00 8.00
79 Otto Porter Jr. .30 .75
80 Kevin Durant 1.50 4.00
81 Semi Ojeleye .30 .75
82 Brook Lopez .30 .75
83 Caleb Swanigan RC .40 1.00
84 Karl-Anthony Towns .60 1.50
85 Nikola Vucevic .30 .75
86 Al Horford .40 1.00
87 Zach Randolph .40 1.00
88 Dwyane Wade .75 2.00
89 Marcin Gortat .25 .60
90 Draymond Green .50 1.25
91 Malik Monk RC 1.50 4.00
92 Julius Randle .40 1.00
93 Tony Bradley .25 .60
94 Taj Gibson .25 .60
95 Jonathon Simmons RC .40 1.00
96 Marcus Morris .25 .60
97 Willie Cauley-Stein .25 .60
98 Kevin Love .40 1.00
99 Markieff Morris .25 .60
100 Andre Iguodala .40 1.00
101 Frank Mason III RC .40 1.00
102 Tyreke Evans .25 .60
103 Derrick White RC 1.50 4.00
104 Rajon Rondo .50 1.25
105 Ben Simmons .40 1.00
106 D'Angelo Russell .30 .75
107 Tony Parker .60 1.50
108 Yogi Ferrell .25 .60
109 Maxi Kleber .40 1.00
110 Chris Paul .60 1.50
111 Luke Kennard RC .75 2.00
112 Mike Conley .30 .75
113 Jawun Evans RC .40 1.00
114 Jrue Holiday .50 1.25
115 JJ Redick .40 1.00
116 Jeremy Lin .60 1.50
117 Kawhi Leonard 1.00 2.50
118 Wesley Matthews .25 .60
119 Josh Jackson RC .50 1.25
120 James Harden .75 2.00
121 Justin Jackson RC .40 1.00
122 Marc Gasol .40 1.00
123 Royce O'Neale .30 .75
124 Anthony Davis 1.00 2.50
125 Dario Saric .30 .75
126 Rondae Hollis-Jefferson .25 .60
127 Manu Ginobili .75 2.00
128 Harrison Barnes .30 .75
129 Jayson Tatum RC 5.00 12.00
130 Eric Gordon .30 .75
131 Brandon Paul .25 .60
132 Chandler Parsons .25 .60
133 Zhou Qi RC .75 2.00
134 DeMarcus Cousins .30 .75
135 Robert Covington .25 .60
136 DeMarre Carroll .25 .60
137 LaMarcus Aldridge .40 1.00
138 Seth Curry .40 1.00
139 Lonzo Ball RC 1.50 4.00
140 Clint Capela .30 .75
141 Daniel Theis .50 1.25
142 Ben McLemore .25 .60
143 Antonio Blakeney .40 1.00
144 E'Twaun Moore .25 .60
145 Joel Embiid .75 2.00
146 Spencer Dinwiddie .30 .75
147 Pau Gasol .60 1.50
148 Dirk Nowitzki 1.00 2.50
149 Donovan Mitchell RC 4.00 10.00
150 Ryan Anderson .25 .60
151 Josh Hart RC 1.00 2.50
152 Goran Dragic .30 .75
153 Damyean Dotson .30 .75
154 Kristaps Porzingis .50 1.25
155 Tyler Ulis .25 .60
156 Kemba Walker .30 .75
157 Kyle Lowry .40 1.00
158 Jamal Murray .60 1.50
159 Lauri Markkanen RC 2.50 6.00
160 Victor Oladipo .30 .75
161 Jarrett Allen RC 1.00 2.50
162 Dion Waiters .25 .60
163 Cedi Osman .50 1.25
164 Enes Kanter .30 .75
165 Devin Booker 1.00 2.50
166 Nicolas Batum .25 .60
167 DeMar DeRozan .50 1.25
168 Will Barton .25 .60
169 Dillon Brooks .75 2.00
170 Domantas Sabonis .75 2.00
171 Bam Adebayo RC 2.50 6.00
172 Josh Richardson .30 .75
173 Abdel Nader .30 .75
174 Tim Hardaway Jr. .30 .75
175 TJ Warren .30 .75
176 Michael Kidd-Gilchrist .25 .60
177 Serge Ibaka .30 .75
178 Wilson Chandler .30 .75
179 Kyle Kuzma RC 1.50 4.00
180 Darren Collison .25 .60
181 Jonathan Isaac RC 1.00 2.50
182 Justise Winslow .25 .60
183 Wes Iwundu RC .40 1.00
184 Jarrett Jack .30 .75
185 Marquese Chriss .25 .60
186 Marvin Williams .25 .60
187 Jonas Valanciunas .30 .75
188 Nikola Jokic 2.50 6.00
189 De'Aaron Fox RC 3.00 8.00
190 Thaddeus Young .25 .60
191 TJ Leaf RC .40 1.00
192 Hassan Whiteside .30 .75
193 Milos Teodosic .30 .75
194 Courtney Lee .25 .60
195 Tyson Chandler .30 .75
196 Dwight Howard .50 1.25
197 Norman Powell .40 1.00
198 Paul Millsap .30 .75
199 Dennis Smith Jr. RC .50 1.25
200 Myles Turner .40 1.00
201 Jonathan Isaac AU/99 6.00 15.00
202 Ante Zizic AU RC/99 3.00 8.00
203 Dennis Smith Jr. AU/99 EXCH 3.00 8.00
204 Bam Adebayo AU/99 10.00 25.00
205 Markelle Fultz AU/99 EXCH 8.00 20.00
206 Tyler Dorsey AU RC/99 2.50 6.00
207 Sterling Brown AU RC/99 2.50 6.00
208 Lonzo Ball AU/99 20.00 50.00
209 Davon Reed AU RC/99 2.50 6.00
210 Derrick White AU/99 10.00 25.00
211 Jawun Evans AU/99 2.50 6.00
212 Lauri Markkanen AU/99 20.00 50.00
213 OG Anunoby AU/99 12.00 30.00
214 Justin Patton AU/99 2.50 6.00
215 Zach Collins AU/99 4.00 10.00
216 Josh Jackson AU/99 3.00 8.00
217 Donovan Mitchell AU/99 60.00 150.00
218 De'Aaron Fox AU/99 20.00 50.00
219 John Collins AU/99 6.00 15.00
220 Josh Hart AU/99 6.00 15.00
221 Jarrett Allen AU/99 6.00 15.00
223 Jayson Tatum AU/99 125.00 300.00
224 Tyler Lydon AU/99 2.50 6.00
225 Sindarius Thornwell AU/99 2.50 6.00
226 Kyle Kuzma AU/99 10.00 25.00
228 Wes Iwundu AU/99 2.50 6.00
229 Luke Kennard AU/99 5.00 12.00
230 Frank Ntilikina AU/99 3.00 8.00
231 Dwayne Bacon AU/99 2.50 6.00
232 Malik Monk AU/99 10.00 25.00
233 Frank Jackson AU RC/99 2.50 6.00
234 TJ Leaf AU/99 2.50 6.00
235 Terrance Ferguson AU/99 2.50 6.00
236 Frank Mason III AU/99 2.50 6.00
237 D.J. Wilson AU/99 2.50 6.00
238 Harry Giles AU/99 2.50 6.00
240 Ivan Rabb AU RC/99 2.50 6.00

2017-18 Panini Essentials Green

*GREEN: 1X TO 2.5X BASIC
*GREEN RC: .6X TO 1.5X BASIC RC
129 Jayson Tatum 8.00 20.00
149 Donovan Mitchell 10.00 25.00

2017-18 Panini Essentials Orange

*ORANGE: .75X TO 2X BASIC
*ORANGE RC: .5X TO 1.2X BASIC RC
129 Jayson Tatum 6.00 15.00
149 Donovan Mitchell 10.00 25.00

2017-18 Panini Essentials Red

*RED: .75X TO 2X BASIC
*RED RC: .5X TO 1.2X BASIC RC
129 Jayson Tatum 6.00 15.00
149 Donovan Mitchell 10.00 25.00

2017-18 Panini Essentials Retail

*RETAIL 1-200: .4X TO 1X BASIC
*RETAIL RC 1-200: .4X TO 1X BASIC RC
*RETAIL AU 201-240: .4X TO 1X BASIC RC
EXCHANGE DEADLINE 11/30/2019

2017-18 Panini Essentials Silver

*SILVER: 1.5X TO 4X BASIC
*SILVER RC: 1X TO 2.5X BASIC RC
STATED PRINT RUN 99 SER.#'d SETS
129 Jayson Tatum 12.00 30.00
149 Donovan Mitchell 20.00 50.00

2017-18 Panini Essentials Spiral

*SPIRAL: 1X TO 2.5X BASIC
*SPIRAL RC: .6X TO 1.5X BASIC RC
129 Jayson Tatum 8.00 20.00
149 Donovan Mitchell 8.00 20.00

2017-18 Panini Essentials Called to Excellence Autographs

STATED PRINT RUN 49 SER.#'d SETS
EXCHANGE DEADLINE 11/30/2019
*GOLD/35: .5X TO 1.2X BASIC
*GOLD/22: .6X TO 1.5X BASIC
*SILVER/25: .6X TO 1.5X BASIC
1 Kobe Bryant EXCH 400.00 800.00
2 Zaza Pachulia 2.50 6.00
3 Ray Allen 10.00 25.00
4 Sam Cassell 3.00 8.00
5 Dennis Rodman 10.00 25.00
6 Bill Laimbeer 5.00 12.00
7 Bill Walton 6.00 15.00
8 Will Perdue 2.50 6.00
9 Channing Frye 2.50 6.00
10 B.J. Armstrong 4.00 10.00
11 Magic Johnson 20.00 50.00
12 Danny Green 3.00 8.00
13 Gary Payton 6.00 15.00
14 Jamaal Wilkes 4.00 10.00
15 Rick Fox 3.00 8.00
16 Bob Dandridge 4.00 10.00
17 Dave Cowens 6.00 15.00
18 Antoine Walker 3.00 8.00
19 Iman Shumpert 2.50 6.00
20 Michael Cooper 3.00 8.00
21 Alonzo Mourning 10.00 25.00
22 Toni Kukoc 5.00 12.00
23 Steve Kerr 8.00 20.00
24 J.J. Barea 5.00 12.00
25 Robert Horry 4.00 10.00
26 Brian Scalabrine 4.00 10.00
27 Tristan Thompson 2.50 6.00
28 Jason Williams 15.00 40.00
29 Juwan Howard 3.00 8.00
30 Jo Jo White 4.00 10.00

2017-18 Panini Essentials Claim to Fame Signatures

EXCHANGE DEADLINE 11/30/2019
1 Kobe Bryant/49 EXCH 400.00 800.00
2 Kevin Durant/49 40.00 100.00
3 Shaquille O'Neal/99 30.00 80.00
4 Damian Lillard/99 15.00 40.00
5 Jerry West/99 20.00 50.00
6 Alonzo Mourning/99 10.00 25.00
7 Karl-Anthony Towns/99 12.00 30.00
8 Ray Allen/99 10.00 25.00
9 Sam Jones/99 15.00 40.00
10 Richard Hamilton/99 5.00 12.00
11 Artis Gilmore/99 5.00 12.00
12 Nate Archibald/99 4.00 10.00
13 Cliff Hagan/99 5.00 12.00
14 Elvin Hayes/99 5.00 12.00
15 Ralph Sampson/99 4.00 10.00
16 Bill Walton/99 6.00 15.00
17 Dave Cowens/99 6.00 15.00
18 Robert Horry/99 4.00 10.00
19 Bill Russell/99 300.00 600.00
20 Reggie Miller/99 25.00 60.00

2017-18 Panini Essentials Destined for Greatness Signatures

EXCHANGE DEADLINE 11/30/2019
1 Brandon Ingram/99 EXCH 12.00 30.00
2 Frank Jackson/99 2.50 6.00
3 Dragan Bender/57 2.50 6.00
4 D.J. Wilson/99 2.50 6.00
5 Ryan Arcidiacono/99 4.00 10.00
6 Jarrett Allen/99 6.00 15.00
7 Alfonzo McKinnie/99 4.00 10.00
8 Sindarius Thornwell/99 2.50 6.00
9 Maxi Kleber/99 4.00 10.00
10 Luke Kennard/99 5.00 12.00
11 D'Angelo Russell/99 3.00 8.00
12 TJ Leaf/99 2.50 6.00
13 Aaron Gordon/99 4.00 10.00
14 Harry Giles/99 2.50 6.00
15 Alex Caruso/99 40.00 100.00
17 Royce O'Neale/99 3.00 8.00
18 Kyle Kuzma/99 10.00 25.00
19 Damian Lillard/99 15.00 40.00
20 Frank Ntilikina/99 3.00 8.00
21 Buddy Hield/99 4.00 10.00
22 Terrance Ferguson/99 2.50 6.00
23 Nikola Jokic/99 125.00 300.00
25 Matt Costello/99 3.00 8.00
26 Jayson Tatum/99 EXCH 125.00 300.00
27 Tyrone Wallace/99 2.50 6.00
29 Karl-Anthony Towns/99 12.00 30.00
30 Dwayne Bacon/99 2.50 6.00
31 Ivica Zubac/99 3.00 8.00
32 Frank Mason III/99 2.50 6.00
33 Kristaps Porzingis/99 12.00 30.00
34 Ivan Rabb/99 2.50 6.00
35 Alec Peters/99 2.50 6.00
36 Tyler Lydon/99 2.50 6.00
37 Dillon Brooks/99 5.00 12.00
38 Wes Iwundu/99 2.50 6.00
39 Andrew Wiggins/99 8.00 20.00
40 Malik Monk/99 10.00 25.00

2017-18 Panini Essentials Dynamic Duos

1 Bird/McHale 2.00 5.00
2 Brad Daugherty
Mark Price .50 1.25
3 Kemba Walker
Dwight Howard .60 1.50
4 Paul/Harden 1.00 2.50
5 Rodman/Pippen 1.25 3.00
6 Giannis/Bledsoe 2.50 6.00
7 Starks/Ewing .75 2.00
8 Carmelo/Westbrook .75 2.00
9 Cowens/Havlicek 1.00 2.50
10 McCollum/Lillard 1.25 3.00
11 Magic/Worthy 2.00 5.00
12 Clifford Robinson
Rod Strickland .30 .75
13 James/Love 4.00 10.00
14 Andre Drummond
Blake Griffin .50 1.25
16 Wiggins/Towns .75 2.00
17 Hardaway/O'Neal 1.50 4.00
18 Jonathan Isaac
Aaron Gordon .75 2.00
19 Walt Frazier
Willis Reed .75 2.00
20 Pau Gasol
LaMarcus Aldridge .75 2.00
21 Bryant/O'Neal 4.00 10.00
22 Reggie Miller
Rik Smits 1.00 2.50
23 Nowitzki/Smith Jr. 1.25 3.00
24 Kuzma/Ball 1.25 3.00
25 Payton/Kemp .75 2.00
26 Davis/Cousins 1.25 3.00
27 Isiah Thomas
Joe Dumars .75 2.00
28 Fultz/Simmons .75 2.00
29 West/Chamberlain 1.50 4.00
30 DeMar DeRozan
Kyle Lowry .60 1.50
31 Irving/Tatum 4.00 10.00
32 Ben Wallace
Chauncey Billups .60 1.50
33 Curry/Durant 4.00 10.00
34 Marc Gasol
Mike Conley .50 1.25
35 Drexler/Olajuwon 1.00 2.50
36 Ntilikina/Porzingis .60 1.50
37 Robinson/Duncan 1.25 3.00
38 Booker/Warren 1.25 3.00
39 Malone/Stockton 1.00 2.50
40 Wall/Beal .60 1.50

2017-18 Panini Essentials Essential Legends

1 Wilt Chamberlain 1.50 4.00
EL2 Dennis Rodman 1.25 3.00
EL3 Tim Duncan 1.25 3.00
4 Alonzo Mourning .75 2.00
EL5 David Robinson 1.00 2.50
EL6 Jerry West 1.00 2.50
EL7 Larry Bird 2.00 5.00
EL8 Allen Iverson 1.25 3.00
EL9 Kobe Bryant 4.00 10.00
EL10 Oscar Robertson 1.00 2.50
EL11 Karl Malone 1.00 2.50
EL12 Dominique Wilkins .75 2.00
EL13 Kevin Garnett 1.25 3.00
EL14 Chris Webber .75 2.00
EL15 Reggie Miller 1.00 2.50
EL16 Jason Kidd .75 2.00
EL17 Hakeem Olajuwon 1.00 2.50
EL18 Scottie Pippen 1.25 3.00
EL19 Shaquille O'Neal 1.50 4.00
EL20 Paul Pierce .75 2.00
EL21 John Stockton 1.00 2.50
EL22 Grant Hill .75 2.00
EL23 Julius Erving 1.25 3.00
EL24 James Worthy .60 1.50
EL25 Magic Johnson 2.00 5.00
EL26 Anfernee Hardaway 1.25 3.00
EL27 Clyde Drexler .75 2.00
EL28 Patrick Ewing .75 2.00
EL29 Kareem Abdul-Jabbar 1.50 4.00
EL30 Tracy McGrady .75 2.00

2017-18 Panini Essentials Essential Rookies

1 Markelle Fultz .75 2.00
ER2 Jarrett Allen .75 2.00
ER3 De'Aaron Fox 2.50 6.00
ER4 Daniel Theis .60 1.50
5 Jordan Bell .30 .75
ER6 Wes Iwundu .30 .75
ER7 Terrance Ferguson .30 .75
ER8 Luke Kennard .60 1.50
ER9 Jayson Tatum 4.00 10.00
ER10 Josh Hart .75 2.00
ER11 Zhou Qi .60 1.50
ER12 Maxi Kleber .50 1.25
ER13 Frank Ntilikina .40 1.00
ER14 Royce O'Neale .40 1.00
ER15 Milos Teodosic .40 1.00
ER16 Tyler Dorsey .30 .75
ER17 Malik Monk 1.25 3.00
ER18 Harry Giles .30 .75
ER19 Lonzo Ball 1.25 3.00
ER20 Zach Collins .50 1.25
ER21 Lauri Markkanen 2.00 5.00
ER22 Sindarius Thornwell .30 .75
ER23 Jonathan Isaac .75 2.00
ER24 Semi Ojeleye .40 1.00
ER25 Bogdan Bogdanovic .75 2.00
ER26 Caleb Swanigan .30 .75
ER27 Bam Adebayo 2.00 5.00
ER28 John Collins .75 2.00
ER29 Kyle Kuzma 1.25 3.00
ER30 TJ Leaf .30 .75
ER31 Dennis Smith Jr. .40 1.00
ER32 Cedi Osman .60 1.50
ER33 Josh Jackson .40 1.00
ER34 Jawun Evans .30 .75
ER35 OG Anunoby 1.50 4.00
ER36 Dwayne Bacon .30 .75
ER37 Justin Jackson .30 .75
ER38 Frank Mason III .30 .75
ER39 Donovan Mitchell 3.00 8.00
ER40 Dillon Brooks 1.00 2.50

2017-18 Panini Essentials Essential Stars

1 LeBron James 4.00 10.00
2 Kristaps Porzingis .60 1.50
3 Nikola Jokic 3.00 8.00
4 Paul George .75 2.00
5 Stephen Curry 4.00 10.00
6 Damian Lillard 1.25 3.00
7 Chris Paul .75 2.00
8 Giannis Antetokounmpo 2.50 6.00
9 Kyrie Irving 1.00 2.50
10 Karl-Anthony Towns .75 2.00
11 Kevin Love .50 1.25
12 Russell Westbrook .75 2.00
13 Andre Drummond .40 1.00
14 Ben Simmons .50 1.25
15 Klay Thompson 1.25 3.00
16 DeMar DeRozan .60 1.50
17 James Harden 1.00 2.50
18 Victor Oladipo .40 1.00
19 Dwight Howard .60 1.50
20 Andrew Wiggins .60 1.50
21 Dirk Nowitzki 1.25 3.00
22 Carmelo Anthony .60 1.50
23 Kevin Durant 2.00 5.00
24 Joel Embiid 1.00 2.50
25 Draymond Green .60 1.50
26 John Wall .60 1.50
27 Blake Griffin .50 1.25
28 Jimmy Butler .75 2.00
29 Kemba Walker .40 1.00
30 Anthony Davis 1.25 3.00

2017-18 Panini Essentials Franchise Foundations

1 Kemba Walker .40 1.00
2 John Stockton 1.00 2.50
3 Tim Duncan 1.25 3.00
4 Isiah Thomas .75 2.00
5 Scottie Pippen 1.25 3.00
6 Dirk Nowitzki 1.25 3.00
7 Kobe Bryant 4.00 10.00
8 Allen Iverson 1.25 3.00
9 John Wall .60 1.50
10 Kevin Garnett 1.25 3.00
11 Dominique Wilkins .75 2.00
12 Russell Westbrook .75 2.00
13 Anthony Davis 1.25 3.00
14 Kareem Abdul-Jabbar 1.50 4.00
15 Stephen Curry 4.00 10.00
16 Bill Russell 1.50 4.00
17 Steve Nash .75 2.00
18 Patrick Ewing .75 2.00
19 Alonzo Mourning .75 2.00
20 Alex English .60 1.50
21 Hakeem Olajuwon 1.00 2.50
22 LeBron James 4.00 10.00
23 Mike Conley .40 1.00
24 Reggie Miller 1.00 2.50
25 DeAndre Jordan .40 1.00
26 DeMar DeRozan .60 1.50
27 Chris Webber .75 2.00
28 Jason Kidd .75 2.00
29 Shaquille O'Neal 1.50 4.00
30 Clyde Drexler .75 2.00

2017-18 Panini Essentials Future Legends

1 Jayson Tatum 4.00 10.00
FL2 Ben Simmons .50 1.25
FL3 Jaylen Brown 1.25 3.00
FL4 Donovan Mitchell 3.00 8.00
FL5 Malcolm Brogdon .40 1.00
FL6 Kyle Kuzma 1.25 3.00
FL7 Devin Booker 1.25 3.00
FL8 Kristaps Porzingis .60 1.50
FL9 Josh Jackson .40 1.00
FL10 Markelle Fultz .75 2.00
FL11 Lonzo Ball 1.25 3.00
FL12 Joel Embiid 1.00 2.50
FL13 Jamal Murray .75 2.00
FL14 Lauri Markkanen 2.00 5.00
15 Taurean Prince .30 .75
FL16 Dennis Smith Jr. .40 1.00
FL17 Karl-Anthony Towns .75 2.00
FL18 De'Aaron Fox 2.50 6.00
FL19 Brandon Ingram .60 1.50
FL20 Malik Monk 1.25 3.00

2017-18 Panini Essentials Glorified Signatures

STATED PRINT RUN 49 SER.#'d SETS
EXCHANGE DEADLINE 11/30/2019
*GOLD/33-35: .5X TO 1.2X BASIC
*SILVER/25: .6X TO 1.5X BASIC
1 Reggie Miller 25.00 60.00
2 Allen Iverson 30.00 80.00
3 Karl Malone 20.00 50.00
4 Magic Johnson 20.00 50.00
5 Larry Bird 30.00 80.00
6 Jerry West 20.00 50.00
7 Alonzo Mourning 10.00 25.00
8 Hakeem Olajuwon 10.00 25.00
9 Clyde Drexler 10.00 25.00
10 Gary Payton 6.00 15.00
11 James Worthy 8.00 20.00
12 Bernard King 5.00 12.00
13 Artis Gilmore 5.00 12.00
14 Elvin Hayes 5.00 12.00
15 Nate Archibald 4.00 10.00
16 Shaquille O'Neal 30.00 80.00
17 Dave Cowens 6.00 15.00
18 Nate Thurmond 4.00 10.00
19 Lenny Wilkens 5.00 12.00
20 Robert Parish 5.00 12.00
21 Frank Ramsey 10.00 25.00
22 John Stockton 12.00 30.00
23 Jamaal Wilkes 4.00 10.00
24 Adrian Dantley 4.00 10.00
25 David Robinson 10.00 25.00
26 Bob McAdoo 5.00 12.00
27 Damon Stoudamire 4.00 10.00
28 Arvydas Sabonis 5.00 12.00
29 Isaiah Rider 3.00 8.00
30 Cedric Ceballos 2.50 6.00

2017-18 Panini Essentials Indispensable Rookies

1 Maxi Kleber .50 1.25
2 Dillon Brooks 1.00 2.50
3 Luke Kennard .60 1.50
4 Dennis Smith Jr. .40 1.00
5 Frank Mason III .30 .75
6 Markelle Fultz .75 2.00
7 Bogdan Bogdanovic .75 2.00
8 Jayson Tatum 4.00 10.00
9 OG Anunoby 1.50 4.00
10 Donovan Mitchell 3.00 8.00
11 Malik Monk 1.25 3.00
12 Kyle Kuzma 1.25 3.00
13 Jonathan Isaac .75 2.00
14 De'Aaron Fox 2.50 6.00
15 Justin Jackson .30 .75
16 Josh Jackson .40 1.00
17 John Collins .75 2.00
18 Lonzo Ball 1.25 3.00
19 Frank Ntilikina .40 1.00
20 Lauri Markkanen 2.00 5.00

2017-18 Panini Essentials Indispensable Stars

1 Draymond Green .60 1.50
2 Dirk Nowitzki 1.25 3.00
3 John Wall .60 1.50
4 Damian Lillard 1.25 3.00
5 LeBron James 4.00 10.00
6 Klay Thompson 1.25 3.00
7 Kawhi Leonard 1.25 3.00
8 DeMarcus Cousins .40 1.00
9 Chris Paul .75 2.00
10 Carmelo Anthony .75 2.00
11 Jimmy Butler .75 2.00
12 Andrew Wiggins .60 1.50
13 Karl-Anthony Towns .75 2.00
14 Mike Conley .40 1.00
15 Kevin Durant 2.00 5.00
16 Kyrie Irving 1.00 2.50
17 James Harden 1.00 2.50
18 Kemba Walker .40 1.00
19 Anthony Davis 1.25 3.00
20 Joel Embiid 1.00 2.50
21 Paul George .75 2.00
22 Myles Turner .50 1.25
23 Rudy Gobert .60 1.50
24 Kyle Lowry .50 1.25
25 Stephen Curry 4.00 10.00
26 Blake Griffin .50 1.25
27 Russell Westbrook .75 2.00
28 Kristaps Porzingis .60 1.50
29 Giannis Antetokounmpo 2.50 6.00
30 Ben Simmons .50 1.25

2017-18 Panini Essentials Kings of the Court

KC1 Larry Bird 2.00 5.00
KC2 Kyrie Irving 1.00 2.50
KC3 Hakeem Olajuwon 1.00 2.50
KC4 Paul George .75 2.00
KC5 Blake Griffin .50 1.25
KC6 Dirk Nowitzki 1.25 3.00
KC7 Giannis Antetokounmpo 2.50 6.00
KC8 LeBron James 4.00 10.00
KC9 Kobe Bryant 4.00 10.00
KC10 Chris Paul .75 2.00

KC11 Kareem Abdul-Jabbar 1.50 4.00
KC12 James Harden 1.00 2.50
KC13 Pete Maravich 1.25 3.00
KC14 Rudy Gobert .60 1.50
KC15 Russell Westbrook .75 2.00
KC16 John Wall .60 1.50
KC17 Ben Simmons .50 1.25
KC18 Klay Thompson 1.25 3.00
KC19 Magic Johnson 2.00 5.00
KC20 Karl-Anthony Towns .75 2.00
KC21 Wilt Chamberlain 1.50 4.00
KC22 Anthony Davis 1.25 3.00
KC23 Kevin Garnett 1.25 3.00
KC24 Stephen Curry 4.00 10.00
KC25 Kristaps Porzingis .60 1.50
KC26 Damian Lillard 1.25 3.00
KC27 Tim Duncan 1.25 3.00
KC28 Kawhi Leonard 1.25 3.00
KC29 Shaquille O'Neal 1.50 4.00
KC30 Kevin Durant 2.00 5.00

2017-18 Panini Essentials Kobe's All Rookie Team

1 Markelle Fultz 15.00 40.00
2 Lonzo Ball 25.00 60.00
3 Josh Jackson 8.00 20.00
4 De'Aaron Fox 50.00 120.00
5 Dennis Smith Jr. 8.00 20.00
6 Donovan Mitchell 125.00 300.00
7 Jayson Tatum 75.00 200.00
8 Lauri Markkanen 40.00 100.00
9 Kyle Kuzma 25.00 60.00
10 Bogdan Bogdanovic 15.00 40.00
11 Dillon Brooks 20.00 50.00
12 John Collins 12.00 30.00

2017-18 Panini Essentials License to Dominate

1 LaMarcus Aldridge 5.00 12.00
2 Chris Paul 8.00 20.00
3 Jonathan Isaac 10.00 25.00
4 Brandon Ingram 8.00 20.00
5 Karl-Anthony Towns 15.00 40.00
6 Dennis Schroder 4.00 10.00
7 Carmelo Anthony 8.00 20.00
8 Malik Monk 12.00 30.00
9 Joel Embiid 15.00 40.00
10 Nikola Jokic 12.00 30.00
11 Tony Parker 8.00 20.00
12 James Harden 15.00 40.00
13 Frank Ntilikina 4.00 10.00
14 Marc Gasol 5.00 12.00
15 Jimmy Butler 8.00 20.00
16 Kyrie Irving 10.00 25.00
17 Paul George 8.00 20.00
18 Lauri Markkanen 15.00 40.00
19 Devin Booker 15.00 40.00
20 Andre Drummond 4.00 10.00
21 Kyle Lowry 5.00 12.00
22 Victor Oladipo 4.00 10.00
23 Luke Kennard 6.00 15.00
24 Goran Dragic 4.00 10.00
25 Anthony Davis 15.00 40.00
26 D'Angelo Russell 4.00 10.00
27 Aaron Gordon 5.00 12.00
28 LeBron James 150.00 400.00
29 Josh Jackson 4.00 10.00
30 Stephen Curry 40.00 100.00
31 Donovan Mitchell 40.00 100.00
32 Blake Griffin 5.00 12.00
33 Kyle Kuzma 12.00 30.00
34 Giannis Antetokounmpo 30.00 80.00
35 Kristaps Porzingis 15.00 40.00
36 Kemba Walker 6.00 15.00
37 Ben Simmons 5.00 12.00
38 Dennis Smith Jr. 4.00 10.00
39 Damian Lillard 12.00 30.00
40 Klay Thompson 10.00 25.00
41 John Wall 6.00 15.00
42 Lonzo Ball 20.00 50.00
43 DeMar DeRozan 6.00 15.00
44 Andrew Wiggins 6.00 15.00
45 Russell Westbrook 8.00 20.00
46 Jayson Tatum 40.00 100.00
47 Markelle Fultz 8.00 20.00
48 Dirk Nowitzki 20.00 50.00
49 De'Aaron Fox 25.00 60.00
50 Kevin Durant 30.00 80.00

2017-18 Panini Essentials Rock the Rim

1 Shaquille O'Neal 10.00 25.00
2 Andre Drummond 2.50 6.00
3 Amar'e Stoudemire 3.00 8.00
4 Blake Griffin 3.00 8.00
5 Malik Monk 8.00 20.00
6 LeBron James 125.00 300.00
7 Julius Erving 8.00 20.00
8 Devin Booker 6.00 15.00
9 Kobe Bryant 30.00 80.00
10 Dwight Howard 4.00 10.00
11 Scottie Pippen 8.00 20.00
12 Myles Turner 3.00 8.00
13 Spud Webb 2.50 6.00
14 Draymond Green 4.00 10.00
15 Josh Jackson 2.50 6.00
16 James Harden 10.00 25.00
17 Dominique Wilkins 5.00 12.00
18 Kevin Durant 15.00 40.00
19 Tracy McGrady 6.00 15.00
20 Anthony Davis 8.00 20.00
21 John Wall 4.00 10.00
22 Kristaps Porzingis 4.00 10.00
23 Paul George 5.00 12.00
24 Donovan Mitchell 15.00 40.00
25 De'Aaron Fox 20.00 50.00
26 Giannis Antetokounmpo 30.00 80.00
27 Clyde Drexler 5.00 12.00
28 DeAndre Jordan 2.50 6.00
29 Russell Westbrook 5.00 12.00
30 Karl-Anthony Towns 5.00 12.00
31 Ben Simmons 3.00 8.00
32 Andrew Wiggins 4.00 10.00
33 DeMar DeRozan 4.00 10.00
34 Dennis Smith Jr. 2.50 6.00
35 Jayson Tatum 25.00 60.00
36 DeMarcus Cousins 2.50 6.00
37 Shawn Kemp 8.00 20.00
38 Rudy Gobert 4.00 10.00

2017-18 Panini Essentials Swish Kings

SK1 Peja Stojakovic .40 1.00
SK2 Dirk Nowitzki 1.25 3.00
SK3 Stephen Curry 4.00 10.00
SK4 Kevin Durant 2.00 5.00
SK5 LeBron James 6.00 15.00
SK6 Ray Allen .75 2.00
SK7 Larry Bird 2.00 5.00
SK8 Reggie Miller 1.00 2.50
SK9 Kyle Korver .40 1.00
SK10 Kobe Bryant 4.00 10.00
SK11 Devin Booker 1.25 3.00
SK12 Pete Maravich 1.25 3.00
SK13 George Gervin .75 2.00
SK14 Rick Barry .60 1.50
SK15 James Harden 1.00 2.50
SK16 Oscar Robertson 1.00 2.50
SK17 Dominique Wilkins .75 2.00
SK18 Jerry West 1.00 2.50
SK19 Klay Thompson 1.25 3.00
SK20 Carmelo Anthony .75 2.00

2017-18 Panini Essentials True Potential Signatures

STATED PRINT RUN 49 SER.#'d SETS
EXCHANGE DEADLINE 11/30/2019
*GOLD/35: .5X TO 1.2X BASIC
*SILVER/25: .6X TO 1.5X BASIC
1 Zhou Qi 8.00 20.00
2 Davon Reed 2.50 6.00
3 Ike Anigbogu 2.50 6.00
4 OG Anunoby 12.00 30.00
5 Damyean Dotson 3.00 8.00
6 Donovan Mitchell 50.00 120.00
7 Milos Teodosic 3.00 8.00
8 Jonathan Isaac 6.00 15.00
9 Tyler Cavanaugh 2.50 6.00
10 Markelle Fultz 12.00 30.00
11 Tyrone Wallace 2.50 6.00
12 Derrick White 10.00 25.00
13 Edmond Sumner 4.00 10.00
14 Justin Patton 2.50 6.00
15 Luke Kornet 3.00 8.00
16 De'Aaron Fox 25.00 60.00
17 Guerschon Yabusele 2.50 6.00
18 Ante Zizic 3.00 8.00
19 Cedi Osman 5.00 12.00
20 Tyler Dorsey 2.50 6.00
21 Justin Jackson 2.50 6.00
22 Jawun Evans 2.50 6.00
23 Thomas Bryant 4.00 10.00
24 Zach Collins 4.00 10.00
25 Brandon Paul 2.50 6.00
26 John Collins 6.00 15.00
27 Johnathan Motley 2.50 6.00
28 Dennis Smith Jr. EXCH 3.00 8.00
29 Kadeem Allen 2.50 6.00
30 Sterling Brown 2.50 6.00
31 Maxi Kleber 4.00 10.00
32 Lauri Markkanen 15.00 40.00
33 Daniel Theis 10.00 25.00
34 Josh Jackson 3.00 8.00
35 David Nwaba 2.50 6.00
36 Josh Hart 6.00 15.00
37 Abdel Nader 3.00 8.00
38 Bam Adebayo 15.00 40.00
39 Bogdan Bogdanovic 6.00 15.00
40 Lonzo Ball 25.00 60.00

2017-18 Panini Essentials Worldwide Wonders

1 Dikembe Mutombo 2.50 6.00
2 Kristaps Porzingis 2.50 6.00
3 Dirk Nowitzki 5.00 12.00
4 Nikola Jokic 12.00 30.00
5 Kyrie Irving 4.00 10.00
6 Giannis Antetokounmpo 10.00 25.00
7 Joel Embiid 4.00 10.00
8 Hakeem Olajuwon 4.00 10.00
9 Yao Ming 4.00 10.00
10 Steve Nash 3.00 8.00

2014-15 Panini Excalibur

1 John Wall .50 1.25
2 Brandon Knight .25 .60
3 Nikola Vucevic .30 .75
4 Kyle Lowry .50 1.25
5 Monta Ellis .30 .75
6 Michael Carter-Williams .25 .60
7 Stephen Curry 3.00 8.00
8 Serge Ibaka .30 .75
9 Ben McLemore .25 .60
10 Thaddeus Young .25 .60
11 Bradley Beal .60 1.50
12 Giannis Antetokounmpo 2.50 6.00
13 Victor Oladipo .30 .75
14 Jonas Valanciunas .30 .75
15 Chandler Parsons .30 .75
16 Nerlens Noel .25 .60
17 Harrison Barnes .30 .75
18 Steven Adams .50 1.25
19 Rudy Gay .40 1.00
20 Gorgui Dieng .25 .60
21 Paul Pierce .60 1.50
22 Khris Middleton .50 1.25
23 Tobias Harris .30 .75
24 Amir Johnson .25 .60
25 Tyson Chandler .40 1.00
26 Luc Mbah a Moute .25 .60
27 Draymond Green .50 1.25
28 Kevin Durant 1.25 3.00
29 DeMarcus Cousins .30 .75
30 Nikola Pekovic .30 .75
31 Marcin Gortat .25 .60
32 O.J. Mayo .25 .60
33 Evan Fournier .25 .60
34 Terrence Ross .30 .75
35 Dirk Nowitzki 1.00 2.50
36 Robert Covington .30 .75
37 Klay Thompson 1.00 2.50
38 Russell Westbrook .60 1.50
39 Darren Collison .25 .60
40 Ricky Rubio .30 .75
41 Nene .25 .60
42 Ersan Ilyasova .25 .60
43 Channing Frye .25 .60
44 DeMar DeRozan .50 1.25
45 Rajon Rondo .50 1.25
46 Tony Wroten .25 .60
47 Andrew Bogut .30 .75
48 Reggie Jackson .30 .75
49 Jason Thompson .25 .60
50 Anthony Bennett .25 .60
51 Kemba Walker .40 1.00
52 Kentavious Caldwell-Pope .30 .75
53 Marc Gasol .40 1.00
54 Kevin Garnett 1.00 2.50
55 Tim Duncan 1.00 2.50
56 Carmelo Anthony .60 1.50
57 Chris Paul .60 1.50
58 Arron Afflalo .25 .60
59 Kobe Bryant 3.00 8.00
60 Pau Gasol .60 1.50
61 Gerald Henderson .25 .60
62 Andre Drummond .30 .75
63 Courtney Lee .25 .60
64 Deron Williams .30 .75
65 Tony Parker .60 1.50
66 Jose Calderon .25 .60
67 Blake Griffin .40 1.00
68 Kenneth Faried .25 .60
69 Carlos Boozer .30 .75
70 Derrick Rose .75 2.00
71 Al Jefferson .25 .60
72 Brandon Jennings .25 .60
73 Mike Conley .30 .75
74 Joe Johnson .30 .75
75 Manu Ginobili .75 2.00
76 Jason Smith .25 .60
77 DeAndre Jordan .30 .75
78 Wilson Chandler .25 .60
79 Jeremy Lin .75 2.00
80 Jimmy Butler .60 1.50
81 Michael Kidd-Gilchrist .25 .60
82 Greg Monroe .25 .60
83 Zach Randolph .40 1.00
84 Brook Lopez .40 1.00
85 Kawhi Leonard 1.00 2.50
86 Tim Hardaway Jr. .30 .75
87 J.J. Redick .40 1.00
88 Ty Lawson .25 .60
89 Jordan Hill .25 .60
90 Taj Gibson .25 .60
91 Lance Stephenson .30 .75
92 Kyle Singler .25 .60
93 Vince Carter .75 2.00
94 Jarrett Jack .30 .75
95 Danny Green .30 .75
96 Andrea Bargnani .25 .60
97 Jamal Crawford .40 1.00
98 J.J. Hickson .25 .60
99 Steve Nash .75 2.00
100 Joakim Noah .40 1.00
101 Chris Bosh .50 1.25
102 David West .30 .75
103 Dwight Howard .50 1.25
104 Jared Sullinger .25 .60
105 Ryan Anderson .25 .60
106 Damian Lillard 1.00 2.50
107 Markieff Morris .30 .75
108 Gordon Hayward .30 .75
109 Paul Millsap .30 .75
110 Kevin Love .40 1.00
111 Luol Deng .30 .75
112 Roy Hibbert .30 .75
113 James Harden .75 2.00
114 Avery Bradley .30 .75
115 Anthony Davis 1.00 2.50
116 Wesley Matthews .25 .60
117 Marcus Morris .25 .60
118 Derrick Favors .25 .60
119 Kyle Korver .30 .75
120 Kyrie Irving .75 2.00
121 Dwyane Wade .75 2.00
122 Solomon Hill .25 .60
123 Trevor Ariza .25 .60
124 Tyler Zeller .25 .60
125 Jrue Holiday .50 1.25
126 LaMarcus Aldridge .40 1.00
127 Eric Bledsoe .40 1.00
128 Enes Kanter .30 .75
129 Al Horford .40 1.00
130 LeBron James 3.00 8.00
131 Mario Chalmers .25 .60
132 George Hill .30 .75
133 Jason Terry .30 .75
134 Evan Turner .25 .60
135 Tyreke Evans .30 .75
136 Nicolas Batum .30 .75
137 Goran Dragic .40 1.00
138 Trey Burke .25 .60
139 Jeff Teague .25 .60
140 Tristan Thompson .25 .60
141 Hassan Whiteside .25 .60
142 Paul George .60 1.50
143 Josh Smith .25 .60
144 Brandon Bass .25 .60
145 Omer Asik .25 .60
146 Robin Lopez .25 .60
147 Isaiah Thomas .60 1.50
148 Alec Burks .25 .60
149 DeMarre Carroll .25 .60
150 Timofey Mozgov .25 .60
151 Jordan Clarkson RC 2.00 5.00
152 Dante Exum RC .75 2.00
153 Aaron Gordon RC 2.50 6.00
154 Zach LaVine RC 3.00 8.00
155 Jarnell Stokes RC .50 1.25
156 Sim Bhullar RC .50 1.25
157 Jabari Parker RC .60 1.50
158 James Young RC .50 1.25
159 C.J. Wilcox RC .50 1.25
160 Cleanthony Early RC .50 1.25
161 Noah Vonleh RC .50 1.25
162 Rodney Hood RC .60 1.50
163 Elfrid Payton RC .75 2.00
164 Adreian Payne RC .50 1.25
165 Russ Smith RC .50 1.25
166 Bruno Caboclo RC .60 1.50
167 Damien Inglis RC .50 1.25
168 Marcus Smart RC 2.00 5.00
169 Zoran Dragic RC .60 1.50
170 Langston Galloway RC .75 2.00
171 P.J. Hairston RC .50 1.25
172 Joe Ingles RC .75 2.00
173 Clint Capela RC 2.00 5.00
174 Glenn Robinson III RC .60 1.50
175 Dwight Powell RC .60 1.50
176 Bojan Bogdanovic RC .75 2.00
177 Johnny O'Bryant RC .50 1.25
178 Joel Embiid RC 5.00 12.00
179 Nik Stauskas RC .50 1.25
180 Mitch McGary RC .50 1.25
181 James Ennis RC .50 1.25
182 Elijah Millsap RC .50 1.25
183 Kostas Papanikolaou RC .50 1.25
184 Doug McDermott RC .75 2.00
185 Kyle Anderson RC .75 2.00
186 Cory Jefferson RC .50 1.25
187 Spencer Dinwiddie RC .75 2.00
188 K.J. McDaniels RC .50 1.25
189 Julius Randle RC 2.50 6.00
190 Gary Harris RC .75 2.00
191 Shabazz Napier RC .60 1.50
192 Andrew Wiggins RC 2.50 6.00
193 Jordan Adams RC .50 1.25
194 Nikola Mirotic RC .75 2.00
195 JaKarr Sampson RC .50 1.25
196 Markel Brown RC .50 1.25
197 Damjan Rudez RC .50 1.25
198 Jerami Grant RC 2.50 6.00
199 Tarik Black RC .50 1.25
200 Jusuf Nurkic RC 1.50 4.00

2014-15 Panini Excalibur Blue

*BLUE 1-150: .75X TO 2X BASIC
*BLUE RC 151-200: .75X TO 2X BASIC RC

2014-15 Panini Excalibur Knights Templar

*TEMPLAR 1-150: .6X TO 1.5X BASIC
*TEMPLAR RC 151-200: .6X TO 1.5X BASIC RC

2014-15 Panini Excalibur Orange

*ORANGE 1-150: .6X TO 1.5X BASIC
*ORANGE RC 151-200: .6X TO 1.5X BASIC RC

2014-15 Panini Excalibur Red

*RED 1-150: .5X TO 1.2X BASIC
*RED RC 151-200: .5X TO 1.2X BASIC RC

2014-15 Panini Excalibur Silver

*SILVER 1-150: 1.2X TO 3X BASIC
*SILVER RC 151-200: 1.2X TO 3X BASIC RC
STATED PRINT RUN 49 SER.#'d SETS
178 Joel Embiid 75.00 200.00

2014-15 Panini Excalibur Crusade Camouflage

1 Serge Ibaka 1.25 3.00
2 Marcin Gortat 1.00 2.50
3 Gorgui Dieng 1.00 2.50
4 Tobias Harris 1.25 3.00
5 Giannis Antetokounmpo 10.00 25.00
6 Dirk Nowitzki 4.00 10.00
7 Kyle Lowry 2.00 5.00
8 Draymond Green 2.00 5.00
9 Michael Carter-Williams 1.00 2.50
10 DeMarcus Cousins 1.25 3.00
11 Reggie Jackson 1.25 3.00
12 Bradley Beal 2.50 6.00
13 Mo Williams 1.25 3.00
14 Victor Oladipo 1.25 3.00
15 O.J. Mayo 1.00 2.50
16 Tyson Chandler 1.50 4.00
17 DeMar DeRozan 2.00 5.00
18 Klay Thompson 4.00 10.00
19 Tony Wroten 1.00 2.50
20 Darren Collison 1.00 2.50
21 Ty Lawson 1.00 2.50
22 Paul Pierce 2.50 6.00
23 Jimmy Butler 2.50 6.00
24 Marc Gasol 1.50 4.00
25 Khris Middleton 2.00 5.00
26 Rajon Rondo 2.00 5.00
27 Jonas Valanciunas 1.25 3.00
28 Harrison Barnes 1.25 3.00
29 Carmelo Anthony 2.50 6.00
30 Ben McLemore 1.00 2.50
31 Arron Afflalo 1.00 2.50
32 Kemba Walker 1.50 4.00
33 Pau Gasol 2.50 6.00
34 Vince Carter 3.00 8.00
35 Greg Monroe 1.00 2.50
36 Kawhi Leonard 4.00 10.00
37 Terrence Ross 1.25 3.00
38 Chris Paul 2.50 6.00
39 Tim Hardaway Jr. 1.25 3.00
40 Kobe Bryant 20.00 50.00
41 Wilson Chandler 1.00 2.50
42 Al Jefferson 1.00 2.50
43 Derrick Rose 3.00 8.00
44 Zach Randolph 1.50 4.00
45 Andre Drummond 1.50 4.00
46 Tim Duncan 4.00 10.00
47 Joe Johnson 1.25 3.00
48 Blake Griffin 1.50 4.00
49 Amare Stoudemire 1.50 4.00
50 Steve Nash 3.00 8.00
51 Kenneth Faried 1.00 2.50
52 Gerald Henderson 1.00 2.50
53 Taj Gibson 1.00 2.50
54 Mike Conley 1.25 3.00
55 Brandon Jennings 1.00 2.50
56 Tony Parker 2.50 6.00
57 Kevin Garnett 4.00 10.00
58 DeAndre Jordan 1.25 3.00
59 Jose Calderon 1.00 2.50
60 Carlos Boozer 1.25 3.00
61 Gordon Hayward 1.25 3.00
62 Lance Stephenson 1.25 3.00
63 Joakim Noah 1.50 4.00
64 Dwight Howard 2.00 5.00
65 Kentavious Caldwell-Pope 1.25 3.00
66 Manu Ginobili 3.00 8.00
67 Deron Williams 1.25 3.00
68 J.J. Redick 1.50 4.00
69 Damian Lillard 4.00 10.00
70 Jordan Hill 1.00 2.50
71 Trey Burke 1.00 2.50
72 Chris Bosh 2.00 5.00
73 Kyrie Irving 3.00 8.00
74 Trevor Ariza 1.00 2.50
75 Paul George 2.50 6.00
76 Danny Green 1.25 3.00
77 Mason Plumlee 1.00 2.50
78 Eric Bledsoe 1.25 3.00
79 LaMarcus Aldridge 1.50 4.00
80 Paul Millsap 1.25 3.00
81 Derrick Favors 1.00 2.50
82 Dwyane Wade 3.00 8.00
83 Kevin Love 1.50 4.00
84 James Harden 3.00 8.00
85 Roy Hibbert 1.25 3.00
86 Anthony Davis 4.00 10.00
87 Jared Sullinger 1.00 2.50
88 Goran Dragic 1.50 4.00
89 Wesley Matthews 1.00 2.50
90 Kyle Korver 1.25 3.00
91 Rudy Gobert 2.50 6.00
92 Luol Deng 1.25 3.00
93 LeBron James 12.00 30.00
94 Donatas Motiejunas 1.00 2.50
95 Solomon Hill 1.00 2.50
96 Ryan Anderson 1.00 2.50
97 Avery Bradley 1.00 2.50
98 Markieff Morris 1.00 2.50
99 Nicolas Batum 1.25 3.00
100 Al Horford 1.50 4.00
101 Thaddeus Young 1.00 2.50
102 Hassan Whiteside 1.25 3.00
103 Shawn Marion 1.25 3.00
104 Monta Ellis 1.25 3.00
105 David West 1.25 3.00
106 Jrue Holiday 2.00 5.00
107 Evan Turner 1.00 2.50
108 Isaiah Thomas 1.25 3.00
109 Kevin Durant 5.00 12.00
110 Jeff Teague 1.00 2.50
111 Ricky Rubio 1.25 3.00
112 Nikola Vucevic 1.25 3.00
113 Brandon Knight 1.00 2.50
114 Chandler Parsons 1.00 2.50
115 Stephen Curry 12.00 30.00
116 Tyreke Evans 1.25 3.00
117 Nerlens Noel 1.00 2.50
118 Rudy Gay 1.50 4.00
119 Russell Westbrook 2.50 6.00
120 John Wall 2.00 5.00
121 George Gervin 2.50 6.00
122 Scottie Pippen 4.00 10.00
123 James Worthy 2.50 6.00
124 Toni Kukoc 2.00 5.00
125 Allen Iverson 4.00 10.00
126 John Stockton 3.00 8.00
127 Baron Davis 1.50 4.00
128 Larry Bird 6.00 15.00
129 Dikembe Mutombo 2.50 6.00
130 Patrick Ewing 2.50 6.00
131 Grant Hill 2.50 6.00
132 Shaquille O'Neal 6.00 15.00
133 Jason Kidd 2.50 6.00
134 Tracy McGrady 2.50 6.00
135 Alonzo Mourning 2.50 6.00
136 Julius Erving 4.00 10.00
137 Clifford Robinson 1.50 4.00
138 Latrell Sprewell 2.00 5.00
139 Dominique Wilkins 2.50 6.00
140 Pete Maravich 5.00 12.00
141 Hakeem Olajuwon 3.00 8.00
142 Shawn Kemp 2.50 6.00
143 Jerry West 4.00 10.00
144 Yao Ming 4.00 10.00
145 Anfernee Hardaway 4.00 10.00
146 Kareem Abdul-Jabbar 5.00 12.00
147 Clyde Drexler 2.50 6.00
148 Magic Johnson 6.00 15.00
149 Drazen Petrovic 2.00 5.00
150 Rony Seikaly 1.25 3.00
151 Isiah Thomas 2.50 6.00
152 Tim Hardaway 2.00 5.00
153 John Havlicek 3.00 8.00
154 Oscar Robertson 3.00 8.00
155 Arvydas Sabonis 2.00 5.00
156 Karl Malone 3.00 8.00
157 David Robinson 3.00 8.00
158 Moses Malone 2.50 6.00
159 Gary Payton 2.50 6.00
160 Dennis Rodman 4.00 10.00
161 Andrew Wiggins 5.00 12.00
162 K.J. McDaniels 1.00 2.50
163 Elfrid Payton 1.50 4.00
164 Bojan Bogdanovic 1.50 4.00
165 Nikola Mirotic 1.50 4.00
166 Zach LaVine 6.00 15.00
167 Jabari Parker 1.25 3.00
168 Jusuf Nurkic 3.00 8.00
169 Dante Exum 1.50 4.00
170 Marcus Smart 4.00 10.00
171 Jordan Clarkson 4.00 10.00
172 Julius Randle 5.00 12.00
173 Joel Embiid 25.00 60.00
174 Jerami Grant 5.00 12.00
175 Shabazz Napier 1.25 3.00
176 Aaron Gordon 5.00 12.00
177 Nik Stauskas 1.00 2.50
178 Noah Vonleh 1.00 2.50
179 Doug McDermott 1.50 4.00
180 James Young 1.00 2.50
181 T.J. Warren 1.50 4.00
182 Gary Harris 1.50 4.00
183 Tyler Ennis 1.00 2.50
184 Bruno Caboclo 1.25 3.00
185 Mitch McGary 1.00 2.50
186 Rodney Hood 1.25 3.00
187 P.J. Hairston 1.00 2.50
188 Kyle Anderson 1.50 4.00
189 Glenn Robinson III 1.25 3.00
190 Cameron Bairstow 1.00 2.50
191 Langston Galloway 1.50 4.00
192 JaKarr Sampson 1.00 2.50
193 Kostas Papanikolaou 1.00 2.50
194 Tarik Black 1.00 2.50
195 Joe Ingles 1.50 4.00
196 Cleanthony Early 1.00 2.50
197 James Ennis 1.00 2.50
198 Zoran Dragic 1.25 3.00
199 Cory Jefferson 1.00 2.50
200 Travis Wear 1.00 2.50

2014-15 Panini Excalibur Crusade Blue

*BLUE: .75.X TO 2X BASIC
STATED PRINT RUN 149 SER.#'d SETS
40 Kobe Bryant 60.00 150.00

2014-15 Panini Excalibur Crusade Orange Die-Cuts

*ORANGE: 1.25X TO 3X BASIC
STATED PRINT RUN 60 SER.#'d SETS
40 Kobe Bryant 100.00 250.00

2014-15 Panini Excalibur Crusade Purple

*PURPLE: 1.25X TO 3X BASIC
STATED PRINT RUN 75 SER.#'d SETS
40 Kobe Bryant 100.00 250.00

2014-15 Panini Excalibur Crusade Red

*RED: 1X TO 2.5X BASIC
STATED PRINT RUN 99 SER.#'d SETS
40 Kobe Bryant 75.00 200.00

2014-15 Panini Excalibur Crusade Teal

*TEAL: 1.5X TO 4X BASIC
STATED PRINT RUN 35 SER.#'d SETS
40 Kobe Bryant 125.00 300.00

2014-15 Panini Excalibur Dunk Company Jerseys

*PRIME/25: 1.25X TO 3X BASIC
1 Jimmy Butler 5.00 12.00
2 Kevin Garnett 8.00 20.00
3 Chandler Parsons 2.00 5.00
4 LeBron James 40.00 100.00
5 Kobe Bryant 40.00 100.00
6 Giannis Antetokounmpo 20.00 50.00
7 Victor Oladipo 2.50 6.00
8 Zach LaVine 12.00 30.00
9 Mason Plumlee 2.00 5.00
10 Andrew Wiggins 10.00 25.00
11 Aaron Gordon 10.00 25.00
12 Adreian Payne 2.00 5.00
13 Bruno Caboclo 2.50 6.00
14 Jabari Parker 2.50 6.00
15 Russell Westbrook 5.00 12.00
16 Terrence Ross 2.50 6.00
17 Blake Griffin 3.00 8.00
18 Dwight Howard 4.00 10.00
19 Derrick Rose 6.00 15.00
20 Kevin Durant 10.00 25.00

2014-15 Panini Excalibur Fresh Faces Die-Cut Jerseys

*PRIME/25: 1.25X TO 3X BASIC
1 Jordan Adams 1.50 4.00
2 Kyle Anderson 2.50 6.00
3 Bruno Caboclo 2.00 5.00
4 Cleanthony Early 1.50 4.00
5 Joel Embiid 20.00 50.00
6 Tyler Ennis 1.50 4.00
7 Dante Exum 2.50 6.00
8 Aaron Gordon 8.00 20.00
9 P.J. Hairston 1.50 4.00
10 Gary Harris 2.50 6.00
11 Joe Harris 2.50 6.00
12 Rodney Hood 2.00 5.00
13 Damien Inglis 1.50 4.00
14 Zach LaVine 10.00 25.00
15 K.J. McDaniels 1.50 4.00
16 Doug McDermott 2.50 6.00
17 Mitch McGary 1.50 4.00
18 Shabazz Napier 2.00 5.00
19 Spencer Dinwiddie 2.50 6.00
20 Jabari Parker 2.00 5.00
21 Adreian Payne 1.50 4.00
22 Elfrid Payton 2.50 6.00
23 Julius Randle 8.00 20.00
24 Marcus Smart 6.00 15.00
25 Nik Stauskas 1.50 4.00
26 Noah Vonleh 1.50 4.00
27 T.J. Warren 2.50 6.00
28 Andrew Wiggins 8.00 20.00
29 C.J. Wilcox 1.50 4.00
30 James Young 1.50 4.00

2014-15 Panini Excalibur High Praise Signatures

1 George Gervin 10.00 25.00
2 Kevin McHale 8.00 20.00
3 John Stockton 20.00 50.00
4 Terry Cummings 4.00 10.00
5 David Robinson 20.00 50.00
6 Artis Gilmore 6.00 15.00
7 Spud Webb 5.00 12.00
8 Tom Satch Sanders 5.00 12.00
9 Robert Horry 5.00 12.00
10 Grant Hill 12.00 30.00
11 Latrell Sprewell 15.00 40.00
12 Wayne Embry 4.00 10.00
13 Oscar Robertson 40.00 100.00
14 Anthony Mason 4.00 10.00
15 Chris Webber 75.00 200.00
16 Gary Payton 8.00 20.00
17 Tim Hardaway 8.00 20.00
18 Robert Parish 6.00 15.00
19 Joe Dumars 6.00 15.00
20 Dolph Schayes 5.00 12.00
21 Allen Iverson 75.00 200.00
22 Dan Issel 8.00 20.00
23 Karl Malone 20.00 50.00
24 Eddie Jones 5.00 12.00
25 Hakeem Olajuwon 20.00 50.00
26 Bernard King 6.00 15.00
27 John Starks 5.00 12.00
28 Walt Frazier 10.00 25.00
29 Rick Fox 4.00 10.00
30 Clyde Drexler 15.00 40.00

2014-15 Panini Excalibur Juggernauts

*BLUE/99: 1.2X TO 3X BASIC
*ORANGE/99: 1.2X TO 3X BASIC
*SILVER/49: 1.5X TO 4X BASIC
1 Stephen Curry 5.00 12.00
2 Kareem Abdul-Jabbar 2.00 5.00
3 Damian Lillard 1.50 4.00
4 Julius Erving 1.50 4.00
5 LeBron James 5.00 12.00
6 Tim Duncan 1.50 4.00
7 Carmelo Anthony 1.00 2.50
8 Kevin Love .60 1.50
9 Blake Griffin .60 1.50
10 Derrick Rose 1.25 3.00
11 Jerry West 1.50 4.00
12 Larry Bird 2.50 6.00
13 Chris Bosh .75 2.00
14 Patrick Ewing 1.00 2.50
15 Kobe Bryant 5.00 12.00
16 Anthony Davis 1.50 4.00
17 Dwyane Wade 1.25 3.00
18 Chris Paul 1.00 2.50
19 Paul Pierce 1.00 2.50
20 Allen Iverson 1.50 4.00
21 Russell Westbrook 1.00 2.50
22 Pete Maravich 2.00 5.00
23 Vince Carter 1.25 3.00
24 Chris Webber .75 2.00
25 Kevin Durant 2.00 5.00
26 James Harden 1.25 3.00
27 Dirk Nowitzki 1.50 4.00
28 Wilt Chamberlain 2.00 5.00
29 Kyrie Irving 1.25 3.00
30 Karl Malone 1.25 3.00

2014-15 Panini Excalibur Kaboom

1 LeBron James 2,000.00 4,000.00
2 Kevin Durant 500.00 1,000.00
3 Kevin Garnett 500.00 1,000.00
4 Chris Paul 200.00 500.00
5 Tim Duncan 400.00 800.00
6 Dirk Nowitzki 400.00 800.00
7 Vince Carter 400.00 800.00
8 Stephen Curry 1,500.00 3,000.00
9 Jimmy Butler 125.00 300.00
10 Blake Griffin 75.00 200.00
11 James Harden 200.00 500.00
12 Dwight Howard 125.00 300.00
13 Kevin Love 75.00 200.00
14 Steve Nash 200.00 500.00
15 Derrick Rose 150.00 400.00
16 Dwyane Wade 300.00 600.00
17 Russell Westbrook 125.00 300.00
18 Carmelo Anthony 400.00 800.00
19 Chris Bosh 125.00 300.00
20 Kobe Bryant 2,000.00 4,000.00
21 Anthony Davis 300.00 600.00
22 Tony Parker 200.00 500.00
23 John Wall 100.00 250.00
24 Kyrie Irving 200.00 500.00
25 Damian Lillard 300.00 600.00
26 Pau Gasol 75.00 200.00
27 DeMar DeRozan 150.00 400.00
28 Klay Thompson 500.00 1,000.00
29 Manu Ginobili 200.00 500.00
30 Rajon Rondo 150.00 400.00
31 Paul George 300.00 600.00
32 Andrew Wiggins 150.00 400.00
33 Jabari Parker 75.00 200.00
34 Allen Iverson 500.00 1,000.00
35 Shaquille O'Neal 500.00 1,000.00
36 Karl Malone 300.00 600.00
37 Magic Johnson 500.00 1,000.00
38 Larry Bird 500.00 1,000.00
39 Julius Erving 300.00 600.00
40 Kareem Abdul-Jabbar 400.00 800.00
41 Jason Kidd 200.00 500.00
42 Anfernee Hardaway 800.00 1,500.00
43 Chris Webber 300.00 600.00
44 Patrick Ewing 300.00 600.00
45 Gary Payton 200.00 500.00
46 John Stockton 300.00 600.00
47 Scottie Pippen 400.00 800.00
48 Dominique Wilkins 200.00 500.00
49 Dennis Rodman 400.00 800.00
50 Grant Hill 300.00 600.00

2014-15 Panini Excalibur Knight Court

*BLUE/99: 1.2X TO 3X BASIC
*ORANGE/99: 1.2X TO 3X BASIC
*SILVER/49: 1.5X TO 4X BASIC
1 Pau Gasol .75 2.00
2 Kyrie Irving 1.00 2.50
3 Tim Duncan 1.25 3.00
4 Klay Thompson 1.25 3.00
5 Dirk Nowitzki 1.25 3.00
6 John Wall .60 1.50
7 Derrick Rose 1.00 2.50
8 James Harden 1.00 2.50
9 Eric Bledsoe .40 1.00
10 Stephen Curry 4.00 10.00
11 Kevin Love .50 1.25
12 Monta Ellis .40 1.00
13 Kobe Bryant 4.00 10.00
14 Jimmy Butler .75 2.00
15 Kevin Garnett 1.25 3.00
16 Chris Paul .75 2.00
17 Dwight Howard .60 1.50
18 Blake Griffin .50 1.25
19 Russell Westbrook .75 2.00
20 Anthony Davis 1.25 3.00
21 DeMarcus Cousins .40 1.00
22 LaMarcus Aldridge .50 1.25
23 Kevin Durant 1.50 4.00
24 Carmelo Anthony .75 2.00
25 Dwyane Wade 1.00 2.50
26 Jeff Teague .30 .75
27 Tony Parker .75 2.00
28 Damian Lillard 1.25 3.00
29 Kemba Walker .50 1.25
30 LeBron James 4.00 10.00

2014-15 Panini Excalibur Knights of the Round Die-Cuts

1 John Wall 20.00 50.00
2 Kyle Lowry 15.00 40.00
3 Monta Ellis 8.00 20.00
4 Michael Carter-Williams 6.00 15.00
5 Stephen Curry 600.00 1,200.00
6 Bradley Beal 40.00 100.00
7 Nerlens Noel 6.00 15.00
8 Paul Pierce 20.00 50.00
9 Kevin Durant 100.00 250.00
10 Dirk Nowitzki 100.00 250.00

11 Klay Thompson 100.00 250.00
12 Russell Westbrook 40.00 100.00
13 Ricky Rubio 4.00 10.00
14 Rajon Rondo 20.00 50.00
15 Kevin Garnett 100.00 250.00
16 Tim Duncan 100.00 250.00
17 Carmelo Anthony 40.00 100.00
18 Chris Paul 40.00 100.00
19 Kobe Bryant 600.00 1,200.00
20 Pau Gasol 15.00 40.00
21 Tony Parker 20.00 50.00
22 Blake Griffin 10.00 25.00
23 Derrick Rose 40.00 100.00
24 Manu Ginobili 40.00 100.00
25 Jeremy Lin 20.00 50.00
26 Jimmy Butler 30.00 80.00
27 Kawhi Leonard 150.00 400.00
28 Vince Carter 75.00 200.00
29 Steve Nash 75.00 200.00
30 Chris Bosh 20.00 50.00
31 Dwight Howard 20.00 50.00
32 Damian Lillard 75.00 200.00
33 Kevin Love 10.00 25.00
34 James Harden 75.00 200.00
35 Anthony Davis 75.00 200.00
36 Kyrie Irving 75.00 200.00
37 Dwyane Wade 60.00 150.00
38 LaMarcus Aldridge 10.00 25.00
39 LeBron James 600.00 1,200.00
40 Goran Dragic 15.00 40.00
41 Paul George 20.00 50.00
42 Dante Exum 10.00 25.00
43 Zach LaVine 150.00 400.00
44 Jabari Parker 8.00 20.00
45 Elfrid Payton 10.00 25.00
46 Marcus Smart 25.00 60.00
47 Doug McDermott 10.00 25.00
48 Julius Randle 30.00 80.00
49 Andrew Wiggins 50.00 120.00
50 Nikola Mirotic 10.00 25.00

2014-15 Panini Excalibur Majectic Marks Signatures

2 Brad Daugherty 3.00 8.00
3 Gary Payton 6.00 15.00
4 Spud Webb 4.00 10.00
6 Luc Longley 3.00 8.00
7 Roy Hibbert 3.00 8.00
8 Kendall Gill 4.00 10.00
10 Lance Stephenson 3.00 8.00
11 Paul George 30.00 80.00
12 Anthony Mason 3.00 8.00
13 Grant Hill 15.00 40.00
14 Mahmoud Abdul-Rauf 3.00 8.00
15 Trey Burke 2.50 6.00
16 Mychal Thompson 3.00 8.00
17 Kurt Rambis 3.00 8.00
18 Donatas Motiejunas 2.50 6.00
20 David Thompson 4.00 10.00
21 Kareem Abdul-Jabbar 25.00 60.00
22 Eddie Jones 4.00 10.00
23 Victor Oladipo 3.00 8.00
24 Bill Laimbeer 4.00 10.00
25 Rick Fox 3.00 8.00
26 Sarunas Marciulionis 4.00 10.00
27 Alex English 5.00 12.00
28 Khris Middleton 5.00 12.00
30 Cedric Ceballos 3.00 8.00
31 Anthony Davis 50.00 120.00
32 Mark Price 4.00 10.00
34 Zydrunas Ilgauskas 3.00 8.00
35 Latrell Sprewell 15.00 40.00
36 Michael Cooper 4.00 10.00
38 Rudy Gobert 6.00 15.00
39 Julius Erving 25.00 60.00
40 Ricky Pierce 2.50 6.00
41 Kyrie Irving 25.00 60.00
42 Sean Elliott 4.00 10.00
43 Nerlens Noel 2.50 6.00
44 Jack Sikma 4.00 10.00
45 Allan Houston 4.00 10.00
46 Clifford Robinson 4.00 10.00
47 Robert Horry 4.00 10.00
48 Robert Covington 3.00 8.00
49 Karl Malone 20.00 50.00
50 Tim Hardaway Jr. 3.00 8.00

2014-15 Panini Excalibur Nobility

*BLUE/99: 1.2X TO 3X BASIC
*ORANGE/99: 1.2X TO 3X BASIC
*SILVER/49: 1.5X TO 4X BASIC
1 Shaquille O'Neal 2.00 5.00
2 Rick Barry .60 1.50
3 Larry Bird 2.00 5.00
4 Willis Reed .75 2.00
5 Manu Ginobili 1.00 2.50
6 Bill Walton .75 2.00
7 Kawhi Leonard 1.25 3.00
8 Rajon Rondo .60 1.50
9 Paul Pierce .75 2.00
10 Clyde Drexler .75 2.00
11 Kareem Abdul-Jabbar 1.50 4.00
12 Tim Duncan 1.25 3.00
13 Hakeem Olajuwon 1.00 2.50
14 Robert Horry .50 1.25
15 Chris Bosh .60 1.50
16 Kobe Bryant 4.00 10.00
17 LeBron James 4.00 10.00
18 Alonzo Mourning .75 2.00
19 Tony Parker .75 2.00
20 Dennis Rodman 1.25 3.00
21 Isiah Thomas .75 2.00
22 Kevin Garnett 1.25 3.00
23 Joe Dumars .60 1.50
24 Moses Malone .75 2.00
25 Jason Kidd .75 2.00
26 Magic Johnson 2.00 5.00
27 Dirk Nowitzki 1.25 3.00
28 Gary Payton .75 2.00
29 Scottie Pippen 1.25 3.00
30 Dwyane Wade 1.00 2.50

2014-15 Panini Excalibur Quest Signatures

1 Michael Carter-Williams 2.50 6.00
2 Marcus Smart 10.00 25.00
3 Tim Hardaway Jr. 3.00 8.00
4 Trey Burke 2.50 6.00
5 Robert Covington 3.00 8.00
6 Donatas Motiejunas 2.50 6.00
7 K.J. McDaniels 2.50 6.00
8 Reggie Jackson 4.00 10.00
9 Mason Plumlee 2.50 6.00
10 Nikola Mirotic 4.00 10.00
12 Joel Embiid 75.00 200.00
13 Lance Stephenson 3.00 8.00
14 Nerlens Noel 2.50 6.00
15 Jordan Clarkson 10.00 25.00
16 Rudy Gobert 6.00 15.00
17 James Ennis 2.50 6.00
18 Taj Gibson 2.50 6.00
19 Victor Oladipo 3.00 8.00
20 Julius Randle 6.00 15.00

2014-15 Panini Excalibur Red White and Blue Jerseys

*PRIME/24-25: 1X TO 2.5X BASIC
1 DeMarcus Cousins 5.00 12.00
2 Stephen Curry 50.00 125.00
3 Anthony Davis 15.00 40.00
4 DeMar DeRozan 8.00 20.00
5 Andre Drummond 5.00 12.00
6 Kenneth Faried 4.00 10.00
7 Rudy Gay 6.00 15.00
8 James Harden 12.00 30.00
9 Kyrie Irving 12.00 30.00
10 Mason Plumlee 4.00 10.00
11 Derrick Rose 12.00 30.00
12 Klay Thompson 15.00 40.00
13 Larry Bird 25.00 60.00
14 Karl Malone 12.00 30.00
15 Magic Johnson 25.00 60.00
16 Scottie Pippen 15.00 40.00
17 Clyde Drexler 10.00 25.00
18 David Robinson 12.00 30.00
19 Chris Mullin 8.00 20.00
20 Shaquille O'Neal 25.00 60.00

2014-15 Panini Excalibur Ringing Endorsements Jerseys

*PRIME/25: 1.25X TO 3X BASIC
1 Kobe Bryant 25.00 60.00
2 Kevin Durant 10.00 25.00
3 Anthony Davis 8.00 20.00
4 Stephen Curry 25.00 60.00
5 James Harden 6.00 15.00
6 LeBron James 25.00 60.00
7 Carmelo Anthony 5.00 12.00
8 Chris Paul 5.00 12.00
9 John Wall 4.00 10.00
10 Derrick Rose 6.00 15.00
11 Jeff Teague 2.00 5.00
12 Klay Thompson 8.00 20.00
13 Blake Griffin 3.00 8.00
14 LaMarcus Aldridge 3.00 8.00
15 Dwyane Wade 6.00 15.00
16 Russell Westbrook 5.00 12.00
17 Kyrie Irving 6.00 15.00
18 Damian Lillard 8.00 20.00
19 Dirk Nowitzki 8.00 20.00
20 Al Horford 3.00 8.00

2014-15 Panini Excalibur Rookie Rampage Autograph Dual Jerseys

STATED PRINT RUN 349 SER.#'d SETS
1 Jordan Adams 4.00 10.00
3 Markel Brown 4.00 10.00
5 Spencer Dinwiddie 6.00 15.00
6 Cleanthony Early 4.00 10.00
7 Joel Embiid 75.00 200.00
8 Tyler Ennis 4.00 10.00
9 Russ Smith 4.00 10.00
10 Aaron Gordon 20.00 50.00
11 Jerami Grant 20.00 50.00
13 Gary Harris 6.00 15.00
16 Damien Inglis 4.00 10.00
18 K.J. McDaniels 4.00 10.00
19 Doug McDermott 6.00 15.00
22 Johnny O'Bryant 4.00 10.00
23 Jabari Parker 5.00 12.00
24 Adreian Payne 4.00 10.00
25 Elfrid Payton 6.00 15.00
26 Julius Randle 8.00 20.00
27 Marcus Smart 15.00 40.00
28 Nik Stauskas 4.00 10.00
29 Jarnell Stokes 4.00 10.00
30 T.J. Warren 6.00 15.00
31 Andrew Wiggins 25.00 60.00
32 C.J. Wilcox 4.00 10.00
33 James Young 4.00 10.00

2014-15 Panini Excalibur Rookie Rampage Autograph Dual Jerseys Prime

*PRIME: .6X TO 1.5X BASIC
STATED PRINT RUN 25 SER.#'d SETS
4 Bruno Caboclo 8.00 20.00
7 Joel Embiid 150.00 400.00

2014-15 Panini Excalibur Rookie Rampage Autograph Jerseys

1 Aaron Gordon 15.00 40.00
2 Adreian Payne 3.00 8.00
3 Andrew Wiggins 40.00 100.00
4 Bruno Caboclo 4.00 10.00
5 C.J. Wilcox 3.00 8.00
6 Cleanthony Early 3.00 8.00
7 Damien Inglis 3.00 8.00
8 Dante Exum 5.00 12.00
9 Doug McDermott 5.00 12.00
10 Elfrid Payton 5.00 12.00
11 Gary Harris 5.00 12.00
12 Jabari Parker 4.00 10.00
13 James Young 3.00 8.00
14 Jarnell Stokes 3.00 8.00
15 Jerami Grant 15.00 40.00
17 Joel Embiid 75.00 200.00
18 Johnny O'Bryant 3.00 8.00
19 Jordan Adams 3.00 8.00
20 Julius Randle 15.00 40.00
21 K.J. McDaniels 3.00 8.00
22 Kyle Anderson 5.00 12.00
23 Marcus Smart 12.00 30.00
24 Markel Brown 3.00 8.00
26 Nik Stauskas 3.00 8.00
30 Spencer Dinwiddie 5.00 12.00
31 T.J. Warren 5.00 12.00
32 Tyler Ennis 3.00 8.00

2014-15 Panini Excalibur Rookie Rampage Autograph Jerseys Prime

*PRIME: .6X TO 1.5X BASIC
STATED PRINT RUN 25 SER.#'d SETS
3 Andrew Wiggins 75.00 200.00
27 P.J. Hairston 5.00 12.00
29 Shabazz Napier 6.00 15.00

2014-15 Panini Excalibur Rookie Rampage Autograph Jumbo Jerseys

1 Adreian Payne 5.00 12.00
2 Marcus Smart 20.00 50.00
3 James Young 5.00 12.00
4 Markel Brown 5.00 12.00
5 P.J. Hairston 5.00 12.00
6 Doug McDermott 8.00 20.00
8 Gary Harris 8.00 20.00
9 Spencer Dinwiddie 8.00 20.00
10 C.J. Wilcox 5.00 12.00
11 Julius Randle 25.00 60.00
12 Jordan Adams 5.00 12.00
13 Jarnell Stokes 5.00 12.00
15 Damien Inglis 5.00 12.00
16 Johnny O'Bryant 5.00 12.00
17 Jabari Parker 6.00 15.00
18 Zach LaVine 100.00 250.00
19 Andrew Wiggins 40.00 100.00
20 Cleanthony Early 5.00 12.00
22 Aaron Gordon 25.00 60.00
23 Elfrid Payton 8.00 20.00
24 Joel Embiid 100.00 250.00
25 Jerami Grant 25.00 60.00
26 K.J. McDaniels 5.00 12.00
27 Tyler Ennis 5.00 12.00
28 T.J. Warren 8.00 20.00
29 Nik Stauskas 5.00 12.00
30 Kyle Anderson 8.00 20.00
31 Bruno Caboclo 6.00 15.00
32 Dante Exum 8.00 20.00
33 Rodney Hood 6.00 15.00

2014-15 Panini Excalibur Rookie Rampage Autograph Jumbo Jerseys Prime

*PRIME: .75X TO 2X BASIC
STATED PRINT RUN 25 SER.#'d SETS
18 Zach LaVine 300.00 600.00
24 Joel Embiid 300.00 600.00

2014-15 Panini Excalibur Royalty Jerseys

*PRIME/25: 1.25X TO 3X BASIC
1 Avery Johnson 2.50 6.00
2 Tyson Chandler 3.00 8.00
3 Kevin McHale 5.00 12.00
4 Hakeem Olajuwon 6.00 15.00
5 Chris Andersen 2.50 6.00
6 Mark Aguirre 2.50 6.00
7 Boris Diaw 2.50 6.00
8 Byron Scott 3.00 8.00
9 Tayshaun Prince 3.00 8.00
10 Tim Duncan 8.00 20.00
11 Luc Longley 2.50 6.00
12 Danny Green 2.50 6.00
13 Kawhi Leonard 8.00 20.00
14 Robert Horry 3.00 8.00
15 Chris Bosh 4.00 10.00
16 Adrian Dantley 3.00 8.00
17 Kobe Bryant 40.00 100.00
18 James Worthy 5.00 12.00
19 David Robinson 6.00 15.00
20 Robert Parish 4.00 10.00
21 Scottie Pippen 8.00 20.00
22 Patty Mills 3.00 8.00
23 Tony Parker 5.00 12.00
24 Isiah Thomas 5.00 12.00
25 Dwyane Wade 6.00 15.00
26 Kareem Abdul-Jabbar 10.00 25.00
27 Robert Horry 3.00 8.00
28 Danny Ainge 3.00 8.00
29 Robert Horry 3.00 8.00
30 Julius Erving 8.00 20.00
31 Robert Parish 4.00 10.00
32 Marco Belinelli 2.00 5.00
33 Manu Ginobili 6.00 15.00
34 Bill Laimbeer 3.00 8.00
35 Shane Battier 2.50 6.00
36 Magic Johnson 12.00 30.00
37 Shaquille O'Neal 12.00 30.00
38 Larry Bird 12.00 30.00
39 Shaquille O'Neal 12.00 30.00
40 Moses Malone 5.00 12.00
41 Clyde Drexler 5.00 12.00
42 Mario Chalmers 2.50 6.00
43 Tiago Splitter 2.00 5.00
44 Joe Dumars 4.00 10.00
45 Dirk Nowitzki 8.00 20.00
46 Kurt Rambis 2.50 6.00
47 Udonis Haslem 2.50 6.00
48 Dennis Johnson 3.00 8.00
49 Ray Allen 5.00 12.00
50 Fred Brown 2.00 5.00

2014-15 Panini Excalibur Slam Inc.

*BLUE/99: 1.2X TO 3X BASIC
*ORANGE/99: 1.2X TO 3X BASIC
*SILVER/49: 1.5X TO 4X BASIC
1 Dwight Howard .60 1.50
2 Kobe Bryant 4.00 10.00
3 LeBron James 4.00 10.00
4 DeAndre Jordan .40 1.00
5 DeMar DeRozan .60 1.50
6 Dominique Wilkins .75 2.00
7 Vince Carter 1.00 2.50
8 Julius Erving 1.25 3.00
9 Anthony Davis 1.25 3.00
10 Blake Griffin .50 1.25

2014-15 Panini Excalibur Sultans of Springfield Jerseys

PRINT RUNS B/WN 25-49 COPIES PER
1 Pete Maravich/25 20.00 50.00
2 Julius Erving/25 15.00 40.00
3 Karl Malone/49 12.00 30.00
4 Larry Bird/25 25.00 60.00
5 Jerry Lucas/25 8.00 20.00
6 David Robinson/49 12.00 30.00
7 Hakeem Olajuwon/49 12.00 30.00
8 Kareem Abdul-Jabbar/25 20.00 50.00
9 Moses Malone/49 10.00 25.00
10 Clyde Drexler/49 10.00 25.00

2014-15 Panini Excalibur Top Flight Jerseys

*PRIME/25: 1X TO 2.5X BASIC
1 Damian Lillard 8.00 20.00
2 Larry Nance 2.50 6.00
3 Dwight Howard 4.00 10.00
4 Michael Finley 3.00 8.00
5 Harrison Barnes 2.50 6.00
6 Shawn Kemp 5.00 12.00
7 Aaron Gordon 10.00 25.00
8 Joe Johnson 2.50 6.00
9 Andre Drummond 2.50 6.00
10 Kenny Sky Walker 2.00 5.00
11 DeAndre Jordan 2.50 6.00
12 Larry Johnson 4.00 10.00
13 Dwyane Wade 6.00 15.00
14 Monta Ellis 2.50 6.00
15 J.R. Smith 3.00 8.00
16 Terrence Ross 2.50 6.00
17 Julius Randle 10.00 25.00
18 John Wall 4.00 10.00
19 Anthony Davis 8.00 20.00
20 Kevin Durant 10.00 25.00
21 DeMar DeRozan 4.00 10.00
22 LeBron James 40.00 100.00
23 Julius Erving 8.00 20.00
24 Jimmy Butler 5.00 12.00
25 James Harden 6.00 15.00
26 Victor Oladipo 2.50 6.00
27 Al Horford 3.00 8.00
28 John Starks 3.00 8.00
29 Blake Griffin 3.00 8.00
30 Kobe Bryant 40.00 100.00
31 DeMarcus Cousins 2.50 6.00
32 Marcus Smart 8.00 20.00
33 Giannis Antetokounmpo 20.00 50.00
34 Nick Young 2.00 5.00
35 James Young 2.00 5.00
36 Vince Carter 6.00 15.00
37 Al Jefferson 2.00 5.00
38 Josh Smith 2.00 5.00
39 Chandler Parsons 2.00 5.00
40 Kyrie Irving 6.00 15.00
41 Derrick Rose 6.00 15.00
42 Michael Carter-Williams 2.00 5.00
43 Mason Plumlee 2.00 5.00
44 Russell Westbrook 5.00 12.00
45 Jeff Teague 2.00 5.00
46 Zach LaVine 12.00 30.00
47 Amare Stoudemire 3.00 8.00
48 Kenneth Faried 2.00 5.00
49 Chris Andersen 2.50 6.00
50 LaMarcus Aldridge 3.00 8.00

2015-16 Panini Excalibur

COMPLETE SET (200) 15.00 40.00
1 DeMar DeRozan .40 1.00
2 Kyle Lowry .30 .75
3 Luis Scola .25 .60
4 DeMarre Carroll .20 .50
5 Jonas Valanciunas .25 .60
6 Isaiah Thomas .25 .60
7 Jae Crowder .20 .50
8 Jared Sullinger .20 .50
9 Amir Johnson .20 .50
10 Avery Bradley .20 .50
11 Jose Calderon .20 .50
12 Robin Lopez .20 .50
13 Carmelo Anthony .50 1.25
14 Arron Afflalo .20 .50
15 Lance Thomas .20 .50
16 Joe Johnson .25 .60
17 Brook Lopez .30 .75
18 Thaddeus Young .20 .50
19 Jarrett Jack .25 .60
20 Bojan Bogdanovic .25 .60
21 Hollis Thompson .20 .50
22 Nerlens Noel .20 .50
23 Jerami Grant .30 .75
24 Isaiah Canaan .20 .50
25 Robert Covington .25 .60
26 Russell Westbrook .50 1.25
27 Serge Ibaka .25 .60
28 Kevin Durant 1.25 3.00
29 Dion Waiters .20 .50
30 Steven Adams .20 .50
31 Gordon Hayward .30 .75
32 Rodney Hood .25 .60
33 Derrick Favors .25 .60
34 Trey Burke .20 .50
35 Alec Burks .20 .50
36 C.J. McCollum .20 .50
37 Al-Farouq Aminu .20 .50
38 Damian Lillard .75 2.00
39 Mason Plumlee .20 .50
40 Allen Crabbe .20 .50
41 Kevin Garnett .75 2.00
42 Andrew Wiggins .40 1.00
43 Ricky Rubio .25 .60
44 Gorgui Dieng .20 .50
45 Zach LaVine .75 2.00
46 Will Barton .20 .50
47 Danilo Gallinari .25 .60
48 Gary Harris .25 .60
49 Kenneth Faried .25 .60
50 Jameer Nelson .20 .50
51 LeBron James 2.50 6.00
52 Kevin Love .30 .75
53 Kyrie Irving .60 1.50
54 Tristan Thompson .20 .50
55 Matthew Dellavedova .25 .60
56 Jimmy Butler .50 1.25
57 Pau Gasol .50 1.25
58 Derrick Rose .50 1.25
59 Joakim Noah .25 .60
60 Nikola Mirotic .20 .50
61 Paul George .50 1.25
62 Monta Ellis .25 .60
63 George Hill .25 .60
64 C.J. Miles .20 .50
65 Ian Mahinmi .20 .50
66 Kentavious Caldwell-Pope .25 .60
67 Marcus Morris .20 .50
68 Andre Drummond .30 .75
69 Reggie Jackson .25 .60
70 Ersan Ilyasova .20 .50
71 Khris Middleton .40 1.00
72 Giannis Antetokounmpo 1.50 4.00
73 Greg Monroe .25 .60
74 Michael Carter-Williams .20 .50
75 Jabari Parker .20 .50
76 Stephen Curry 2.50 6.00
77 Klay Thompson .75 2.00
78 Draymond Green .40 1.00
79 Andre Iguodala .30 .75
80 Harrison Barnes .25 .60
81 DeAndre Jordan .25 .60
82 Blake Griffin .30 .75
83 Chris Paul .60 1.50
84 J.J. Redick .30 .75
85 Paul Pierce .50 1.25
86 Rajon Rondo .40 1.00
87 Rudy Gay .30 .75
88 Omri Casspi .20 .50
89 DeMarcus Cousins .30 .75
90 Ben McLemore .20 .50
91 Brandon Knight .20 .50
92 Eric Bledsoe .25 .60
93 P.J. Tucker .20 .50
94 T.J. Warren .30 .75
95 Tyson Chandler .25 .60
96 Jordan Clarkson .25 .60
97 Lou Williams .25 .60
98 Roy Hibbert .25 .60
99 Julius Randle .40 1.00
100 Kobe Bryant 2.50 6.00
101 Chris Bosh .40 1.00
102 Goran Dragic .30 .75
103 Hassan Whiteside .30 .75
104 Dwyane Wade .60 1.50
105 Luol Deng .25 .60
106 Paul Millsap .25 .60
107 Al Horford .30 .75
108 Kyle Korver .25 .60
109 Jeff Teague .20 .50
110 Kent Bazemore .20 .50
111 Tobias Harris .25 .60
112 Evan Fournier .25 .60
113 Elfrid Payton .25 .60
114 Nikola Vucevic .25 .60
115 Victor Oladipo .25 .60
116 Kemba Walker .30 .75
117 Nicolas Batum .20 .50
118 Marvin Williams .20 .50
119 Jeremy Lin .60 1.50
120 Al Jefferson .20 .50
121 John Wall .40 1.00
122 Otto Porter .25 .60
123 Marcin Gortat .25 .60
124 Bradley Beal .40 1.00
125 Jared Dudley .20 .50
126 Kawhi Leonard 1.00 2.50
127 LaMarcus Aldridge .30 .75
128 Tony Parker .50 1.25
129 Tim Duncan .75 2.00
130 Manu Ginobili .60 1.50
131 Wesley Matthews .25 .60
132 Dirk Nowitzki .75 2.00
133 Zaza Pachulia .20 .50
134 Deron Williams .25 .60
135 Chandler Parsons .25 .60
136 Marc Gasol .30 .75
137 Mike Conley .30 .75
138 Vince Carter .60 1.50
139 Jeff Green .25 .60
140 Zach Randolph .30 .75
141 James Harden .60 1.50
142 Dwight Howard .40 1.00
143 Trevor Ariza .20 .50
144 Ty Lawson .20 .50
145 Clint Capela .25 .60
146 Eric Gordon .25 .60
147 Anthony Davis .75 2.00
148 Ryan Anderson .20 .50
149 Jrue Holiday .40 1.00
150 Tyreke Evans .20 .50
151 Larry Nance Jr. RC .75 2.00
152 Delon Wright RC .50 1.25
153 Trey Lyles RC .50 1.25
154 Salah Mejri RC .40 1.00
155 Kelly Oubre Jr. RC 1.25 3.00
156 Bobby Portis RC 1.00 2.50
157 Jahlil Okafor RC .50 1.25
158 Anthony Brown RC .40 1.00
159 Justise Winslow RC .60 1.50
160 Norman Powell RC .75 2.00
161 Raul Neto RC .40 1.00
162 Jarell Martin RC .40 1.00
163 Rondae Hollis-Jefferson RC .50 1.25
164 Luis Montero RC .40 1.00
165 Jonathon Simmons RC .50 1.25
166 Myles Turner RC 1.50 4.00
167 Karl-Anthony Towns RC 2.50 6.00
168 Stanley Johnson RC .50 1.25
169 Josh Richardson RC .60 1.50
170 Darrun Hilliard RC .40 1.00
171 Nemanja Bjelica RC .60 1.50
172 Sam Dekker RC .40 1.00
173 Mario Hezonja RC .50 1.25
174 Branden Dawson RC .40 1.00
175 Rashad Vaughn RC .40 1.00
176 Montrezl Harrell RC 1.25 3.00
177 D'Angelo Russell RC 1.50 4.00
178 Justin Anderson RC .40 1.00
179 Emmanuel Mudiay RC .50 1.25
180 Joe Young RC .40 1.00
181 Devin Booker RC 12.00 30.00
182 Jordan Mickey RC .40 1.00
183 Willie Cauley-Stein RC .50 1.25
184 Cliff Alexander RC .40 1.00
185 R.J. Hunter RC .40 1.00
186 Boban Marjanovic RC 1.25 3.00
187 Kristaps Porzingis RC 2.50 6.00
188 Tyus Jones RC .50 1.25
189 Frank Kaminsky RC .50 1.25
190 Pat Connaughton RC .60 1.50
191 Jerian Grant RC .40 1.00
192 Sasha Kaun RC .40 1.00
193 Richaun Holmes RC .60 1.50
194 Jarell Eddie RC .60 1.50
195 Marcelo Huertas RC .40 1.00
196 Cameron Payne RC .60 1.50
197 T.J. McConnell RC 1.50 4.00
198 Terry Rozier RC 1.50 4.00
199 Nikola Jokic RC 60.00 150.00
200 Aaron Harrison RC .50 1.25

2015-16 Panini Excalibur Gold

*GOLD 1-150: 2.5X TO 6X BASIC
*GOLD RC 151-200: 2.5X TO 6X BASIC RC
STATED PRINT 25 SER.#'d SETS
181 Devin Booker 100.00 250.00
199 Nikola Jokic 500.00 1,000.00

2015-16 Panini Excalibur Light Blue

*LT BLUE 1-150: .5X TO 1.2X BASIC
*LT BLUE RC 151-200: .5X TO 1.2X BASIC RC

2015-16 Panini Excalibur Silver

*SILVER 1-150: 1X TO 2.5X BASIC
*SILVER RC 151-200: 1X TO 2.5X BASIC RC
STATED PRINT 70 SER.#'d SETS
181 Devin Booker 40.00 100.00
199 Nikola Jokic 150.00 400.00

2015-16 Panini Excalibur Class Masters

1 LeBron James 10.00 25.00
2 Allen Iverson 3.00 8.00
3 Shaquille O'Neal 4.00 10.00
4 Kyrie Irving 2.50 6.00
5 Derrick Rose 2.00 5.00

2015-16 Panini Excalibur Crusade Camo

*BLUE/199: .5X TO 1.2X BASIC
*RED/149: .6X TO 1.5X BASIC
*PURPLE/60: 1X TO 2.5X BASIC
1 Nemanja Bjelica 1.50 4.00
2 Giannis Antetokounmpo 5.00 12.00
3 Patrick Ewing 1.50 4.00
4 DeMarcus Cousins 1.00 2.50
5 Al Horford 1.00 2.50
6 DeMar DeRozan 1.25 3.00
7 Tim Duncan 2.50 6.00
8 Russell Westbrook 1.50 4.00
9 Jahlil Okafor .75 2.00
10 LeBron James 8.00 20.00
11 Devin Booker 30.00 80.00
12 Michael Carter-Williams .60 1.50
13 Dominique Wilkins 1.50 4.00
14 Brandon Knight .60 1.50
15 Elfrid Payton .75 2.00
16 Kyle Lowry 1.00 2.50
17 Dirk Nowitzki 2.50 6.00
18 Kevin Durant 4.00 10.00
19 Karl-Anthony Towns 8.00 20.00
20 Kevin Love 1.00 2.50
21 Jerian Grant .60 1.50
22 Jabari Parker .60 1.50
23 Jason Kidd 1.50 4.00
24 Eric Bledsoe .75 2.00
25 Nikola Vucevic .75 2.00
26 Isaiah Thomas .75 2.00
27 Deron Williams .75 2.00
28 Gordon Hayward 1.00 2.50
29 D'Angelo Russell 2.50 6.00
30 Kyrie Irving 2.00 5.00
31 Mario Hezonja .75 2.00
32 Stephen Curry 8.00 20.00
33 Grant Hill 1.50 4.00
34 Jordan Clarkson 1.00 2.50
35 Victor Oladipo .75 2.00
36 Avery Bradley .60 1.50
37 Marc Gasol 1.00 2.50
38 Rodney Hood .75 2.00
39 Kristaps Porzingis 4.00 10.00
40 Jimmy Butler 2.00 5.00
41 Willie Cauley-Stein .75 2.00
42 Klay Thompson 2.50 6.00
43 Magic Johnson 4.00 10.00
44 Julius Randle 1.25 3.00
45 Kemba Walker 1.00 2.50
46 Carmelo Anthony 1.50 4.00
47 Mike Conley 1.00 2.50
48 C.J. McCollum 1.50 4.00
49 T.J. McConnell 2.50 6.00
50 Pau Gasol 1.50 4.00
51 Larry Bird 4.00 10.00
52 Draymond Green 1.25 3.00
53 Anfernee Hardaway 2.50 6.00
54 Kobe Bryant 8.00 20.00
55 Nicolas Batum .60 1.50
56 Arron Afflalo .60 1.50
57 James Harden 2.00 5.00
58 Damian Lillard 2.00 5.00
59 Justise Winslow 1.00 2.50
60 Derrick Rose 1.50 4.00
61 John Stockton 2.00 5.00
62 DeAndre Jordan .75 2.00
63 Steve Nash 1.50 4.00
64 Chris Bosh 1.25 3.00
65 John Wall 1.25 3.00
66 Joe Johnson .75 2.00
67 Dwight Howard 1.25 3.00
68 Kevin Garnett 2.50 6.00
69 Stanley Johnson .75 2.00
70 Paul George 1.50 4.00
71 Karl Malone 1.50 4.00
72 Blake Griffin 1.00 2.50
73 Shawn Kemp 1.50 4.00
74 Hassan Whiteside .75 2.00
75 Bradley Beal 1.25 3.00
76 Brook Lopez 1.00 2.50
77 Anthony Davis 2.50 6.00
78 Andrew Wiggins 1.25 3.00
79 Emmanuel Mudiay .75 2.00
80 Monta Ellis .75 2.00
81 Julius Erving 2.50 6.00
82 Chris Paul 2.00 5.00
83 Ben Wallace .75 2.00
84 Dwyane Wade 2.00 5.00
85 Kawhi Leonard 2.00 5.00
86 Nerlens Noel .60 1.50
87 Jrue Holiday 1.25 3.00
88 Danilo Gallinari .75 2.00
89 Frank Kaminsky .75 2.00
90 Andre Drummond 1.00 2.50
91 Scottie Pippen 2.50 6.00
92 Rajon Rondo 1.25 3.00
93 Dennis Rodman 2.50 6.00
94 Paul Millsap .75 2.00
95 Tony Parker 1.50 4.00
96 Robert Covington .75 2.00
97 Tyreke Evans .75 2.00
98 Kenneth Faried .75 2.00
99 Raul Neto .60 1.50
100 Reggie Jackson .75 2.00

2015-16 Panini Excalibur Gamers Jerseys

PRINT RUNS B/WN 49-99 COPIES PER
1 Tony Parker/99 5.00 12.00
2 Damian Lillard/99 5.00 12.00
3 Brandon Jennings/99 2.00 5.00
4 DeMarcus Cousins/99 3.00 8.00
5 Kemba Walker/49 3.00 8.00
6 Kyrie Irving/99 5.00 12.00
7 Klay Thompson/49 8.00 20.00
8 James Harden/75 6.00 15.00
9 Marc Gasol/49 3.00 8.00
10 Andrew Wiggins/75 4.00 10.00
11 Rudy Gobert/99 4.00 10.00
12 Blake Griffin/99 3.00 8.00
13 Victor Oladipo/99 2.50 6.00
14 Tim Duncan/75 8.00 20.00
15 Chandler Parsons/49 2.00 5.00
16 Dirk Nowitzki/75 8.00 20.00
17 Monta Ellis/49 2.50 6.00
18 Chris Paul/99 6.00 15.00
19 Elfrid Payton/49 2.50 6.00
20 Kevin Durant/99 5.00 12.00
21 Bojan Bogdanovic/49 2.50 6.00
23 Kawhi Leonard/99 10.00 25.00
24 Marcus Smart/99 4.00 10.00
25 Andre Drummond/74 3.00 8.00

2015-16 Panini Excalibur Head to Toe Signatures

STATED PRINT RUN 75 SER.#'d SETS
1 Anthony Brown 4.00 10.00
2 D'Angelo Russell 15.00 40.00
3 Delon Wright 5.00 12.00
4 Jahlil Okafor 5.00 12.00
5 Frank Kaminsky 5.00 12.00
6 Jarell Martin 4.00 10.00
7 Joe Young 4.00 10.00
8 Jordan Mickey 4.00 10.00
9 Josh Richardson 6.00 15.00
10 Justin Anderson 4.00 10.00
11 Karl-Anthony Towns 50.00 120.00
12 Justise Winslow 6.00 15.00
13 Kelly Oubre Jr. 12.00 30.00
14 Kevon Looney 12.00 30.00
15 Kristaps Porzingis 25.00 60.00
16 Pat Connaughton 6.00 15.00
17 Richaun Holmes 6.00 15.00
18 Rondae Hollis-Jefferson 5.00 12.00
19 Sam Dekker 4.00 10.00
20 Stanley Johnson 5.00 12.00
21 Terry Rozier 12.00 30.00
22 Trey Lyles 5.00 12.00
23 Tyus Jones 5.00 12.00
24 Walter Tavares 4.00 10.00
25 Willie Cauley-Stein 5.00 12.00

2015-16 Panini Excalibur Head to Toe Swatches

PRINT RUNS B/WN 10-75 COPIES PER
NO PRICING ON QTY 10
1 Karl Malone/25 10.00 25.00
3 Rick Fox/75 5.00 12.00
4 Joe Johnson/75 5.00 12.00
5 Anfernee Hardaway/75 15.00 40.00
6 Grant Hill/75 12.00 30.00
7 Derrick Rose/75 8.00 20.00
8 Joakim Noah/75 4.00 10.00
9 Larry Johnson/25 12.00 30.00
10 Scottie Pippen/25 20.00 50.00
12 Kevin Garnett/25 15.00 40.00
13 Dwight Howard/25 8.00 20.00
14 Deron Williams/75 5.00 12.00
15 John Stockton/25 15.00 40.00
16 Gerald Henderson/49 4.00 10.00
17 Tyler Ennis/75 4.00 10.00
20 Blake Griffin/49 6.00 15.00
24 Michael Kidd-Gilchrist/75 4.00 10.00
25 Shawn Kemp/25 50.00 120.00

2015-16 Panini Excalibur Jamfest

*SILVER/70: 1X TO 2.5X BASIC
1 Kobe Bryant 4.00 10.00
2 Dwight Howard .60 1.50
3 Andre Drummond .50 1.25
4 Kevin Durant 2.00 5.00
5 Blake Griffin .50 1.25
6 Russell Westbrook .75 2.00
7 Anthony Davis 1.25 3.00
8 Kristaps Porzingis 2.50 6.00
9 Andrew Wiggins .60 1.50
10 LeBron James 4.00 10.00
11 Kawhi Leonard 1.50 4.00
12 Jimmy Butler 1.00 2.50
13 Stanley Johnson .40 1.00
14 Mario Hezonja .40 1.00
15 DeAndre Jordan .50 1.25
16 Marc Gasol .50 1.25
17 DeMarcus Cousins .50 1.25
18 Karl-Anthony Towns 2.00 5.00
19 Darryl Dawkins .30 .75
20 Dwyane Wade 1.00 2.50
21 Julius Erving 1.25 3.00
22 Dominique Wilkins .75 2.00
23 Shawn Kemp .75 2.00
24 Spud Webb .40 1.00
25 Isaiah Rider .40 1.00
26 Tracy McGrady .75 2.00
27 Dee Brown .30 .75
28 Shaquille O'Neal 1.50 4.00
29 Allen Iverson 1.25 3.00
30 Clyde Drexler .50 1.25

2015-16 Panini Excalibur Jamfest Gold
*GOLD: 1.5X TO 4X BASIC
STATED PRINT RUN 25 SER.#'d SETS
8 Kristaps Porzingis 15.00 40.00
18 Karl-Anthony Towns 25.00 60.00

2015-16 Panini Excalibur Kaboom
1 Kobe Bryant 1,500.00 3,000.00
2 Kevin Durant 400.00 800.00
3 Kyrie Irving 125.00 300.00
4 John Wall 75.00 200.00
5 Anthony Davis 125.00 300.00
6 Stephen Curry 500.00 1,000.00
7 Andrew Wiggins 75.00 200.00
8 Chris Paul 125.00 300.00
9 LeBron James 1,500.00 3,000.00
10 Tim Duncan 200.00 500.00
11 Derrick Rose 125.00 300.00
12 Russell Westbrook 125.00 300.00
13 James Harden 150.00 400.00
14 Dwyane Wade 150.00 400.00
15 Carmelo Anthony 125.00 300.00
16 Karl-Anthony Towns 400.00 800.00
17 D'Angelo Russell 150.00 400.00
18 Kristaps Porzingis 150.00 400.00
19 Jahlil Okafor 40.00 100.00
20 Patrick Ewing 100.00 250.00
21 Allen Iverson 150.00 400.00
22 Wilt Chamberlain 400.00 800.00
23 Pete Maravich 200.00 500.00
24 Shaquille O'Neal 200.00 500.00
25 Scottie Pippen 125.00 300.00

2015-16 Panini Excalibur Knight School Jerseys
PRINT RUNS B/WN 49-99 COPIES PER
*PRIME/25: .75X TO 2X BASIC
1 Rondae Hollis-Jefferson 2.50 6.00
2 Josh Huestis 2.00 5.00
3 Emmanuel Mudiay 2.50 6.00
4 Cameron Payne 3.00 8.00
6 D'Angelo Russell 8.00 20.00
7 Devin Booker 30.00 80.00
8 Justise Winslow 3.00 8.00
9 Karl-Anthony Towns 12.00 30.00
10 Trey Lyles 2.50 6.00
11 Richaun Holmes 3.00 8.00
12 Bobby Portis 5.00 12.00
13 Willie Cauley-Stein 2.50 6.00
14 Jordan Mickey 2.00 5.00
15 Kristaps Porzingis 12.00 30.00
16 Terry Rozier 8.00 20.00
17 Frank Kaminsky 2.50 6.00
18 Myles Turner 8.00 20.00
19 Stanley Johnson 2.50 6.00
20 Mario Hezonja 2.50 6.00
21 Kelly Oubre Jr. 6.00 15.00
22 Josh Richardson 3.00 8.00
23 Jerian Grant 2.00 5.00
24 R.J. Hunter 2.00 5.00
25 Justin Anderson 2.00 5.00

2015-16 Panini Excalibur Knight's Templar
*TEMPLAR 1-150: .5X TO 1.2X BASIC
*TEMPLAR RC 151-200: .5X TO 1.2X BASIC RC

2015-16 Panini Excalibur Knights of the Round Die Cuts
1 D'Angelo Russell 25.00 60.00
2 Anthony Davis 75.00 200.00
3 Patrick Ewing 30.00 80.00
4 Chris Paul 40.00 100.00
5 Pete Maravich 60.00 150.00
6 Derrick Rose 40.00 100.00
7 James Harden 60.00 150.00
8 Kobe Bryant 400.00 800.00
9 Carmelo Anthony 40.00 100.00
10 Kyrie Irving 50.00 120.00
11 Kristaps Porzingis 25.00 60.00
12 Stephen Curry 400.00 800.00
13 Allen Iverson 100.00 250.00
14 LeBron James 500.00 1,000.00
15 Shaquille O'Neal 100.00 250.00
16 Russell Westbrook 40.00 100.00
17 Dwyane Wade 60.00 150.00
18 Kevin Durant 100.00 250.00
19 Karl-Anthony Towns 75.00 200.00
20 John Wall 20.00 50.00
21 Jahlil Okafor 8.00 20.00
22 Andrew Wiggins 20.00 50.00
23 Wilt Chamberlain 100.00 250.00
24 Tim Duncan 100.00 250.00
25 Scottie Pippen 50.00 120.00

2015-16 Panini Excalibur Memorable Memorabilia
1 Nerlens Noel 1.50 4.00
2 Russell Westbrook 4.00 10.00
3 Joe Johnson 2.00 5.00
4 Carmelo Anthony 4.00 10.00
5 Isaiah Thomas 2.00 5.00
6 Derrick Rose 4.00 10.00
7 Reggie Jackson 2.00 5.00
8 Stephen Curry 20.00 50.00
9 Mike Conley 2.50 6.00
10 Kobe Bryant 20.00 50.00
11 Kyle Lowry 2.50 6.00
12 John Wall 3.00 8.00
13 Aaron Gordon 2.50 6.00
14 Rajon Rondo 3.00 8.00
15 Jimmy Butler 5.00 12.00
16 LeBron James 20.00 50.00
17 Dwight Howard 3.00 8.00
18 Paul George 4.00 10.00
19 Zach Randolph 2.50 6.00
20 Anthony Davis 6.00 15.00
21 Gordon Hayward 2.50 6.00
22 Dwyane Wade 5.00 12.00
23 LaMarcus Aldridge 2.50 6.00
24 Bradley Beal 3.00 8.00
25 Kenneth Faried 2.00 5.00

2015-16 Panini Excalibur Monumental Marks
PRINT RUNS B/WN 35-299 COPIES PER
1 Chris Paul/35 75.00 200.00
2 Jeff Green/165 2.50 6.00
3 Dirk Nowitzki/35 50.00 120.00
4 Emmanuel Mudiay/149 3.00 8.00
5 Paul George/35 15.00 40.00
6 Frank Kaminsky/99 4.00 10.00
7 Cody Zeller/299 2.50 6.00
8 Tyson Chandler/199 3.00 8.00
9 Kobe Bryant/35 1,000.00 2,000.00
10 Tyler Ennis/299 2.50 6.00
11 Dwyane Wade/35 40.00 100.00
12 Ryan Anderson/225 2.50 6.00
13 Blake Griffin/35 15.00 40.00
14 Justise Winslow/49 5.00 12.00
15 Michael Kidd-Gilchrist/299 2.50 6.00
16 Myles Turner/149 10.00 25.00
17 Dante Exum/199 3.00 8.00
18 Kentavious Caldwell-Pope/149 3.00 8.00
MM-KDR Kevin Durant/35 100.00 250.00
20 Gordon Hayward/149 4.00 10.00
21 Anthony Davis/35 40.00 100.00
22 D'Angelo Russell/149 20.00 50.00
23 Kyrie Irving/35 25.00 60.00
24 Tyus Jones/199 3.00 8.00
25 Marcus Smart/115 5.00 12.00
26 Trey Lyles/149 3.00 8.00
27 Al Horford/199 4.00 10.00
28 Trey Burke/199 2.50 6.00
29 Carmelo Anthony/35 15.00 40.00
30 Jose Calderon/146 2.50 6.00

2015-16 Panini Excalibur Old School Swatches
PRINT RUNS B/WN 32-99 COPIES PER
1 Rick Fox/99 2.50 6.00
2 Kenny Walker/99 2.00 5.00
3 Shawn Marion/99 2.50 6.00
4 Walter Davis/99 2.00 5.00
5 Ben Wallace/99 2.50 6.00
6 Dominique Wilkins/99 5.00 12.00
7 Calvin Murphy/32 2.50 6.00
8 James Worthy/99 5.00 12.00
9 Mike Bibby/99 2.50 6.00
10 Kenny Anderson/99 2.50 6.00
11 Dennis Rodman/35 5.00 12.00
12 Mark Jackson/99 2.50 6.00
13 Michael Finley/99 3.00 8.00
14 Clyde Drexler/99 5.00 12.00
15 Grant Hill/99 5.00 12.00
16 Karl Malone/99 5.00 12.00
17 Danny Manning/99 2.50 6.00
18 Ray Allen/99 4.00 10.00
19 Danny Ainge/99 3.00 8.00
20 Bernard King/99 4.00 10.00
21 Brad Daugherty/99 2.50 6.00
22 Doug Collins/99 3.00 8.00
23 Dan Issel/99 4.00 10.00
24 Scottie Pippen/99 5.00 12.00
25 Chris Mullin/99 4.00 10.00

2015-16 Panini Excalibur Regal Endorsements
PRINT RUNS B/WN 1-300 COPIES PER
NO PRICING ON QTY 15 OR LESS
1 Oscar Robertson/35 30.00 80.00
2 Gail Goodrich/149 5.00 12.00
3 Grant Hill/135 10.00 25.00
4 Shane Battier/200 3.00 8.00
6 Walt Frazier/165 6.00 15.00
7 Scottie Pippen/35 40.00 100.00
8 Cliff Hagan/300 4.00 10.00
10 Don Nelson/234 10.00 25.00
11 Ray Allen/99 12.00 30.00
12 Bobby Wanzer/273 2.50 6.00
13 Anfernee Hardaway/49 20.00 50.00
14 Wes Unseld/200 5.00 12.00
15 Kareem Abdul-Jabbar/35 25.00 60.00
16 Peja Stojakovic/147 3.00 8.00
17 John Stockton/35 30.00 80.00
18 Dolph Schayes/277 4.00 10.00
19 Larry Bird/35 30.00 80.00
20 George Gervin/300 6.00 15.00
21 Tracy McGrady/99 12.00 30.00
22 Slick Watts/260 2.50 6.00
23 Christian Laettner/123 3.00 8.00
24 Isiah Thomas/299 8.00 20.00
25 Allen Iverson/35 30.00 80.00
26 Elvin Hayes/254 6.00 15.00
27 Julius Erving/32 25.00 60.00
28 Calvin Murphy/149 3.00 8.00
29 Karl Malone/35 15.00 40.00
30 Dave Cowens/165 5.00 12.00

2015-16 Panini Excalibur Rookie Rampage Jersey Autographs
*PRIME/25: .75X TO 2X BASIC
1 Karl-Anthony Towns 60.00 150.00
2 D'Angelo Russell 20.00 50.00
3 Jahlil Okafor 4.00 10.00
4 Emmanuel Mudiay 4.00 10.00
5 Kristaps Porzingis 40.00 100.00
6 Mario Hezonja 4.00 10.00
8 Willie Cauley-Stein 4.00 10.00
9 Stanley Johnson 4.00 10.00
10 Frank Kaminsky 4.00 10.00
11 Devin Booker 200.00 500.00
12 Myles Turner 8.00 20.00
13 Trey Lyles 4.00 10.00
14 Jerian Grant 3.00 8.00
15 Cameron Payne 5.00 12.00
16 Delon Wright 4.00 10.00
17 Terry Rozier 10.00 25.00
18 Kelly Oubre Jr. 10.00 25.00
19 Rondae Hollis-Jefferson 4.00 10.00
20 Bobby Portis 8.00 20.00
21 Justin Anderson 3.00 8.00
22 R.J. Hunter 3.00 8.00
23 Jarell Martin 3.00 8.00
24 Anthony Brown 3.00 8.00
25 Jordan Mickey 3.00 8.00
26 Josh Huestis 3.00 8.00
27 Pat Connaughton 5.00 12.00
28 Josh Richardson 5.00 12.00
29 Rakeem Christmas 3.00 8.00
30 Richaun Holmes 5.00 12.00

2015-16 Panini Excalibur Rookie Rampage Jumbo Jersey Autographs
*PRIME/21-25: 1.2X TO 3X BASIC
1 Josh Huestis 3.00 8.00
2 Bobby Portis 8.00 20.00
3 Pat Connaughton 5.00 12.00
4 Josh Richardson 5.00 12.00
5 Cameron Payne 5.00 12.00
6 Joe Young 3.00 8.00
7 Jordan Mickey 3.00 8.00
8 R.J. Hunter 3.00 8.00
9 D'Angelo Russell 15.00 40.00
10 Terry Rozier 12.00 30.00
11 Rakeem Christmas 3.00 8.00
12 Anthony Brown 3.00 8.00
13 Justise Winslow 5.00 12.00
14 Myles Turner 10.00 25.00
15 Trey Lyles 4.00 10.00
16 Chris McCullough 3.00 8.00
17 Mario Hezonja 4.00 10.00
18 Rondae Hollis-Jefferson 4.00 10.00
19 Jarell Martin 3.00 8.00
20 Richaun Holmes 5.00 12.00
21 Kelly Oubre Jr. 10.00 25.00
22 Emmanuel Mudiay 4.00 10.00
23 Willie Cauley-Stein 4.00 10.00
24 Jerian Grant 3.00 8.00
25 Jahlil Okafor 4.00 10.00
26 Delon Wright 4.00 10.00
27 Kristaps Porzingis 30.00 80.00
28 Justin Anderson 3.00 8.00
29 Devin Booker 300.00 600.00
30 Frank Kaminsky 4.00 10.00
31 Karl-Anthony Towns 40.00 100.00
32 Stanley Johnson 4.00 10.00
33 Nemanja Bjelica 5.00 12.00
35 Nikola Jokic 500.00 1,000.00

2015-16 Panini Excalibur Rookie Rampage Jumbo Jerseys
STATED PRINT RUN 49 SER.#'d SETS
*PRIME/25: .75X TO 2X BASIC
1 Trey Lyles 2.50 6.00
2 Jarell Martin 2.00 5.00
3 Josh Huestis 2.00 5.00
4 Willie Cauley-Stein 2.50 6.00
5 Cameron Payne 3.00 8.00
7 D'Angelo Russell 8.00 20.00
8 Frank Kaminsky 2.50 6.00
9 Anthony Brown 2.00 5.00
10 Nemanja Bjelica 3.00 8.00
11 Chris McCullough 2.00 5.00
12 Richaun Holmes 3.00 8.00
13 Bobby Portis 5.00 12.00
14 Jerian Grant 2.00 5.00
15 Joe Young 2.00 5.00
16 Justin Anderson 2.00 5.00
17 Terry Rozier 8.00 20.00
18 Karl-Anthony Towns 12.00 30.00
19 Justise Winslow 3.00 8.00
21 Mario Hezonja 2.50 6.00
22 Kelly Oubre Jr. 6.00 15.00
23 Pat Connaughton 3.00 8.00
24 Jahlil Okafor 4.00 10.00
25 Jordan Mickey 2.00 5.00
26 Devin Booker 25.00 60.00
27 Rakeem Christmas 2.00 5.00
28 Stanley Johnson 2.50 6.00
29 Myles Turner 8.00 20.00
31 Rondae Hollis-Jefferson 2.50 6.00
32 Emmanuel Mudiay 2.50 6.00
33 Josh Richardson 3.00 8.00
34 Delon Wright 2.50 6.00
35 R.J. Hunter 2.00 5.00

2015-16 Panini Excalibur Team 2020
*SILVER/70: 1X TO 2.5X BASIC
1 Anthony Davis 1.25 3.00
2 Kyrie Irving 1.00 2.50
3 Andre Drummond .50 1.25
4 Damian Lillard 1.25 3.00
5 Kawhi Leonard 1.50 4.00
6 Rudy Gobert .60 1.50
7 John Wall .60 1.50
8 DeMarcus Cousins .50 1.25
9 Stephen Curry 4.00 10.00
10 Blake Griffin .50 1.25
11 Giannis Antetokounmpo 2.50 6.00
12 Nikola Mirotic .30 .75
13 Ricky Rubio .40 1.00
14 Reggie Jackson .40 1.00
15 Nerlens Noel .30 .75
16 Bradley Beal .60 1.50
17 Jordan Clarkson .50 1.25
18 Tobias Harris .40 1.00
19 Klay Thompson 1.25 3.00
20 Andrew Wiggins .60 1.50
21 Jabari Parker .30 .75
22 Elfrid Payton .40 1.00
23 Marcus Smart .60 1.50
24 Aaron Gordon .50 1.25
25 Jusuf Nurkic .40 1.00
26 Karl-Anthony Towns 2.00 5.00
27 D'Angelo Russell 1.25 3.00
28 Jahlil Okafor .40 1.00
29 Kristaps Porzingis 2.00 5.00
30 Mario Hezonja .40 1.00
31 Willie Cauley-Stein .40 1.00
32 Emmanuel Mudiay .40 1.00
33 Stanley Johnson .40 1.00
34 Frank Kaminsky .40 1.00
35 Justise Winslow .50 1.25
36 T.J. McConnell 1.25 3.00
37 Nikola Jokic 25.00 60.00
38 Raul Neto .30 .75
39 Devin Booker 4.00 10.00
40 Jerian Grant .30 .75

2015-16 Panini Excalibur Team 2020 Gold
*GOLD: 1.5X TO 4X BASIC
STATED PRINT RUN 25 SER.#'d SETS
26 Karl-Anthony Towns 25.00 60.00
37 Nikola Jokic 125.00 300.00

2015-16 Panini Excalibur Team Titans
*SILVER/70: 1X TO 2.5X BASIC
*GOLD/25: 1.5X TO 4X BASIC
1 Karl Malone .75 2.00
2 Magic Johnson 2.00 5.00
3 Dominique Wilkins .75 2.00
4 Kevin McHale .75 2.00
5 Tony Parker .75 2.00
6 John Stockton 1.00 2.50
7 Kyrie Irving 1.00 2.50
8 Tim Duncan 1.25 3.00
9 Stephen Curry 4.00 10.00
10 Kobe Bryant 4.00 10.00
11 Hakeem Olajuwon 1.00 2.50
12 Larry Bird 2.00 5.00
13 Russell Westbrook .75 2.00
14 Dwyane Wade 1.00 2.50
15 Manu Ginobili 1.00 2.50
16 Dirk Nowitzki 1.25 3.00
17 Anthony Davis 1.25 3.00
18 David Robinson 1.00 2.50
19 John Wall .60 1.50
20 Jerry West .75 2.00
21 Patrick Ewing .75 2.00
22 John Havlicek .60 1.50
23 Blake Griffin .50 1.25
24 Bill Russell 1.50 4.00
25 Kevin Durant 2.00 5.00

2015-16 Panini Excalibur Treasured Ink
PRINT RUNS B/WN 15-299 COPIES PER
NO PRICING ON QTY 15
1 Otto Porter/299 3.00 8.00
2 Duje Dukan/299 2.50 6.00
3 C.J. McCollum/199 4.00 10.00
4 Danny Green/175 3.00 8.00
5 Kobe Bryant/35 500.00 1,000.00
7 Dwyane Wade/35 25.00 60.00
8 Luis Montero/299 2.50 6.00
9 Kyrie Irving/35 25.00 60.00
10 Norman Powell/299 5.00 12.00
11 Alex Len/299 2.50 6.00
12 Branden Dawson/299 2.50 6.00
13 Goran Dragic/249 4.00 10.00
14 Karl-Anthony Towns/99 60.00 150.00
15 Kevin Durant/35 50.00 120.00
16 Stanley Johnson/199 3.00 8.00
17 Anthony Davis/35 30.00 80.00
18 Salah Mejri/299 2.50 6.00
19 Paul George/35 15.00 40.00
20 Sasha Kaun/299 2.50 6.00
21 Bradley Beal/99 6.00 15.00
22 T.J. McConnell/299 12.00 30.00
23 Kevin Martin/299 3.00 8.00
24 Jahlil Okafor/75 4.00 10.00
25 Carmelo Anthony/35 15.00 40.00
26 Devin Booker/199 200.00 500.00
27 Dirk Nowitzki/35 50.00 120.00
28 Larry Nance Jr./299 5.00 12.00
29 Jabari Parker/60 3.00 8.00
30 Boban Marjanovic/199 8.00 20.00
31 Ben McLemore/275 2.50 6.00
32 Robert Covington/299 3.00 8.00
33 Gary Harris/299 3.00 8.00
34 Kristaps Porzingis/99 40.00 100.00
35 Chris Paul/35 40.00 100.00
36 Jerian Grant/199 2.50 6.00
37 Blake Griffin/35 5.00 12.00
38 Gorgui Dieng/299 2.50 6.00
39 Victor Oladipo/199 12.00 30.00
40 Jonathon Simmons/299 3.00 8.00

2016-17 Panini Excalibur
COMPLETE SET (200) 15.00 40.00
1 Dwight Howard .40 1.00
2 Paul Millsap .25 .60
3 Tim Hardaway Jr. .25 .60
4 DeAndre' Bembry RC .60 1.50
5 Kent Bazemore .20 .50
6 Taurean Prince RC .50 1.25
7 Isaiah Thomas .25 .60
8 Al Horford .30 .75
9 Jaylen Brown RC 3.00 8.00
10 Gerald Green .25 .60
11 Marcus Smart .40 1.00
12 Kelly Olynyk .20 .50
13 Brook Lopez .25 .60
14 Jeremy Lin .60 1.50
15 Caris LeVert RC 1.00 2.50
16 Bojan Bogdanovic .25 .60
17 Isaiah Whitehead RC .40 1.00
18 Trevor Booker .20 .50
19 Kemba Walker .25 .60
20 Nicolas Batum .25 .60
21 Michael Kidd-Gilchrist .20 .50
22 Marco Belinelli .20 .50
23 Miles Plumlee .20 .50
24 Cody Zeller .20 .50
25 Jimmy Butler .60 1.50
26 Dwyane Wade .60 1.50
27 Paul Zipser RC .40 1.00
28 Taj Gibson .20 .50
29 Denzel Valentine RC .40 1.00
30 Robin Lopez .20 .50
31 LeBron James 2.50 6.00
32 Kyrie Irving .60 1.50
33 Kay Felder RC .40 1.00
34 Kevin Love .30 .75
35 Tristan Thompson .25 .60
36 Kyle Korver .25 .60
37 Dirk Nowitzki .75 2.00
38 Harrison Barnes .25 .60
39 Yogi Ferrell RC .50 1.25
40 Wesley Matthews .20 .50
41 Devin Harris .20 .50
42 Deron Williams .25 .60
43 Nikola Jokic 1.50 4.00
44 Emmanuel Mudiay .20 .50
45 Jamal Murray RC 6.00 15.00
46 Kenneth Faried .25 .60
47 Juan Hernangomez RC .75 2.00
48 Danilo Gallinari .25 .60
49 Andre Drummond .30 .75
50 Tobias Harris .30 .75
51 Henry Ellenson RC .40 1.00
52 Stanley Johnson .20 .50
53 Michael Gbinije RC .40 1.00
54 Reggie Jackson .25 .60
55 Stephen Curry 2.50 6.00
56 Kevin Durant 1.25 3.00
57 Klay Thompson .75 2.00
58 Patrick McCaw RC .40 1.00
59 Draymond Green .40 1.00
60 Andre Iguodala .30 .75
61 James Harden .60 1.50
62 Eric Gordon .25 .60
63 Chinanu Onuaku RC .40 1.00
64 Ryan Anderson .20 .50
65 Patrick Beverley .20 .50
66 Clint Capela .25 .60
67 Paul George .50 1.25
68 Monta Ellis .25 .60
69 Georges Niang RC .60 1.50
70 Myles Turner .30 .75
71 Jeff Teague .20 .50
72 Al Jefferson .20 .50
73 Chris Paul .50 1.25
74 Blake Griffin .30 .75
75 DeAndre Jordan .25 .60
76 J.J. Redick .30 .75
77 Diamond Stone RC .40 1.00
78 Jamal Crawford .30 .75
79 Jordan Clarkson .30 .75
80 Brandon Ingram RC 1.50 4.00
81 Julius Randle .40 1.00
82 D'Angelo Russell .40 1.00
83 Lou Williams .30 .75
84 Larry Nance Jr. .20 .50
85 Mike Conley .25 .60
86 Deyonta Davis RC .40 1.00
87 Marc Gasol .30 .75
88 Zach Randolph .30 .75
89 Chandler Parsons .20 .50
90 Wade Baldwin IV RC .40 1.00
91 Goran Dragic .30 .75
92 Hassan Whiteside .25 .60
93 Josh Richardson .25 .60
94 Tyler Johnson .20 .50
95 Justise Winslow .25 .60
96 James Johnson .20 .50
97 Giannis Antetokounmpo 1.50 4.00
98 Malcolm Brogdon RC 1.25 3.00
99 Thon Maker RC .50 1.25
100 Jabari Parker .20 .50
101 Greg Monroe .20 .50
102 Michael Beasley .20 .50
103 Karl-Anthony Towns .60 1.50
104 Andrew Wiggins .40 1.00
105 Kris Dunn RC .60 1.50
106 Zach LaVine .60 1.50
107 Ricky Rubio .25 .60
108 Shabazz Muhammad .20 .50
109 Anthony Davis 1.00 2.50
110 Buddy Hield RC 1.25 3.00
111 Jrue Holiday .40 1.00
112 Cheick Diallo RC .40 1.00
113 Tyreke Evans .25 .60
114 Solomon Hill .20 .50
115 Carmelo Anthony .50 1.25
116 Derrick Rose .50 1.25
117 Willy Hernangomez RC .50 1.25
118 Kristaps Porzingis .50 1.25
119 Ron Baker RC .40 1.00
120 Courtney Lee .20 .50
121 Russell Westbrook .50 1.25
122 Victor Oladipo .25 .60
123 Steven Adams .25 .60
124 Enes Kanter .20 .50
125 Alex Abrines RC .50 1.25
126 Domantas Sabonis RC 2.50 6.00
127 Aaron Gordon .30 .75
128 Nikola Vucevic .30 .75
129 Serge Ibaka .25 .60
130 Elfrid Payton .25 .60
131 Evan Fournier .25 .60
132 Jeff Green .20 .50
133 Joel Embiid .75 2.00
134 Ben Simmons RC 1.25 3.00
135 Dario Saric RC .60 1.50
136 Nerlens Noel .20 .50
137 Ersan Ilyasova .20 .50
138 T. Luwawu-Cabarrot RC .60 1.50
139 Devin Booker 1.25 3.00
140 Marquese Chriss RC .50 1.25
141 Eric Bledsoe .25 .60
142 Dragan Bender RC .40 1.00
143 Tyson Chandler .25 .60
144 Brandon Knight .25 .60
145 Damian Lillard .75 2.00
146 C.J. McCollum .30 .75
147 Jake Layman RC .50 1.25
148 Allen Crabbe .20 .50
149 Al-Farouq Aminu .20 .50
150 Noah Vonleh .20 .50
151 DeMarcus Cousins .25 .60
152 Darren Collison .20 .50
153 Malachi Richardson RC .40 1.00
154 Willie Cauley-Stein .25 .60
155 Rudy Gay .30 .75
156 Georgios Papagiannis RC .40 1.00
157 Kawhi Leonard .75 2.00
158 LaMarcus Aldridge .30 .75
159 Dejounte Murray RC 2.00 5.00
160 Pau Gasol .50 1.25
161 Tony Parker .50 1.25
162 Manu Ginobili .60 1.50
163 DeMar DeRozan .40 1.00
164 Kyle Lowry .30 .75
165 Pascal Siakam RC 2.50 6.00
166 Jakob Poeltl RC .75 2.00
167 DeMarre Carroll .20 .50
168 Jonas Valanciunas .20 .50
169 Gordon Hayward .30 .75
170 Rudy Gobert .40 1.00
171 Derrick Favors .20 .50
172 Joel Bolomboy RC .40 1.00
173 Rodney Hood .25 .60
174 Alec Burks .25 .60
175 John Wall .40 1.00
176 Bradley Beal .40 1.00
177 Marcin Gortat .20 .50
178 Tomas Satoransky RC .60 1.50
179 Markieff Morris .20 .50
180 Otto Porter .25 .60
181 Alex English .25 .60
182 Allen Iverson .50 1.25
183 Artis Gilmore .40 1.00
184 Shaquille O'Neal 1.00 2.50
185 Grant Hill .40 1.00
186 Scottie Pippen .60 1.50
187 David Robinson .60 1.50
188 Dave Cowens .25 .60
189 George Gervin .50 1.25
190 Hakeem Olajuwon .60 1.50
191 John Havlicek .75 2.00
192 Jerry Lucas .30 .75
193 Lenny Wilkens .30 .75
194 John Stockton .50 1.25
195 Wilt Chamberlain 1.00 2.50
196 Patrick Ewing .40 1.00
197 Dominique Wilkins .40 1.00
198 Karl Malone .50 1.25
199 Gary Payton .50 1.25
200 Charles Oakley .25 .60

2016-17 Panini Excalibur Count
*COUNT: 1.2X TO 3X BASIC
*COUNT RC: .6X TO 1.5X BASIC

2016-17 Panini Excalibur Duke
*DUKE: 2X TO 5X BASIC
*DUKE RC: 1X TO 2.5X BASIC
STATED PRINT RUN 49 SER.#'d SETS
45 Jamal Murray 25.00 60.00

2016-17 Panini Excalibur Lord
*LORD: 1.2X TO 3X BASIC
*LORD RC: .6X TO 1.5X BASIC

2016-17 Panini Excalibur Marquis
*MARQUIS: 1.5X TO 4X BASIC
*MARQUIS RC: .75X TO 2X BASIC
STATED PRINT RUN 199 SER.#'d SETS
45 Jamal Murray 15.00 40.00

2016-17 Panini Excalibur Prince
*PRINCE: 1.5X TO 4X BASIC
*PRINCE RC: .75X TO 2X BASIC
STATED PRINT RUN 149 SER.#'d SETS
45 Jamal Murray 15.00 40.00

2016-17 Panini Excalibur Squire
1 Karl-Anthony Towns 1.25 3.00
2 Anthony Davis 2.00 5.00
3 Ben Simmons 1.25 3.00
4 Brandon Ingram 1.50 4.00
5 Devin Booker 2.50 6.00
6 Kristaps Porzingis 1.00 2.50
7 Patrick McCaw .40 1.00
8 Julius Randle .75 2.00
9 Yogi Ferrell .50 1.25
10 Kris Dunn .60 1.50
11 Jaylen Brown 3.00 8.00
12 Buddy Hield 1.25 3.00
13 Myles Turner .60 1.50
14 Andrew Wiggins .75 2.00
15 Dario Saric .60 1.50

2016-17 Panini Excalibur Squire Red
*RED: .6X TO 1.5X BASIC
STATED PRINT RUN 99 SER.#'d SETS

2016-17 Panini Excalibur Viscount
*VISCOUNT: 1.5X TO 4X BASIC
*VISCOUNT RC: .75X TO 2X BASIC

2016-17 Panini Excalibur Apprentice Shield Jerseys
STATED PRINT RUN 149 SER.#'d SETS
1 Brandon Ingram 8.00 20.00
2 Jaylen Brown 15.00 40.00
3 Dragan Bender 2.00 5.00
4 Kris Dunn 3.00 8.00
5 Buddy Hield 6.00 15.00
6 Jamal Murray 15.00 40.00
7 Marquese Chriss 2.50 6.00
8 Jakob Poeltl 4.00 10.00
9 Thon Maker 2.50 6.00
10 Domantas Sabonis 12.00 30.00
11 Paul Zipser 2.00 5.00
12 Georgios Papagiannis 2.00 5.00
13 Denzel Valentine 2.00 5.00
14 Juan Hernangomez 4.00 10.00
15 Wade Baldwin IV 2.00 5.00
16 Henry Ellenson 2.00 5.00
17 Malik Beasley 4.00 10.00
18 Caris LeVert 5.00 12.00
19 Malachi Richardson 2.00 5.00
20 Timothe Luwawu-Cabarrot 3.00 8.00
21 Brice Johnson 2.00 5.00
22 Pascal Siakam 12.00 30.00
23 Skal Labissiere 2.00 5.00
24 Dejounte Murray 10.00 25.00
25 Damian Jones 2.00 5.00
26 Malcolm Brogdon 6.00 15.00
27 Michael Gbinije 2.00 5.00
28 Georges Niang 3.00 8.00
29 Jake Layman 2.50 6.00
30 Patrick McCaw 2.00 5.00
31 Kay Felder 2.00 5.00
32 Tyler Ulis 2.50 6.00
33 Marshall Plumlee 2.00 5.00
34 Joel Bolomboy 2.00 5.00
35 Ivica Zubac 5.00 12.00

2016-17 Panini Excalibur Apprentice Signature Shield Jerseys
1 Brandon Ingram 25.00 60.00
2 Jaylen Brown 75.00 200.00
3 Dragan Bender 2.50 6.00
5 Buddy Hield 8.00 20.00
8 Jakob Poeltl 5.00 12.00
9 Thon Maker 3.00 8.00
10 Domantas Sabonis 15.00 40.00
11 Paul Zipser 2.50 6.00
12 Georgios Papagiannis 2.50 6.00
13 Denzel Valentine 2.50 6.00
14 Juan Hernangomez 12.00 30.00
15 Wade Baldwin IV 2.50 6.00
16 Henry Ellenson 2.50 6.00
17 Malik Beasley 5.00 12.00
18 Caris LeVert 6.00 15.00
20 Timothe Luwawu-Cabarrot 4.00 10.00
21 Brice Johnson 2.50 6.00
22 Pascal Siakam 15.00 40.00
23 Skal Labissiere 2.50 6.00
25 Damian Jones 2.50 6.00
26 Malcolm Brogdon 8.00 20.00
27 Michael Gbinije 2.50 6.00
28 Georges Niang 4.00 10.00
29 Jake Layman 3.00 8.00
30 Patrick McCaw 2.50 6.00
31 Kay Felder 2.50 6.00
33 Marshall Plumlee 2.50 6.00
34 Joel Bolomboy 2.50 6.00
35 Ivica Zubac 6.00 15.00

2016-17 Panini Excalibur Apprentice Signatures
STATED PRINT RUN 199 SER.#'d SETS
1 Brandon Ingram 25.00 60.00
2 Jaylen Brown 100.00 250.00
4 Buddy Hield 10.00 25.00
7 Jakob Poeltl 6.00 15.00
8 Thon Maker 4.00 10.00
9 Domantas Sabonis 20.00 50.00
10 Taurean Prince 4.00 10.00
11 Denzel Valentine 3.00 8.00
12 Juan Hernangomez 6.00 15.00
13 Wade Baldwin IV 3.00 8.00
14 Henry Ellenson 3.00 8.00
15 Malik Beasley 6.00 15.00
16 Caris LeVert 8.00 20.00
17 DeAndre' Bembry 5.00 12.00
19 Timothe Luwawu-Cabarrot 5.00 12.00
20 Brice Johnson 3.00 8.00
21 Pascal Siakam 20.00 50.00
22 Skal Labissiere 3.00 8.00
24 Malcolm Brogdon 10.00 25.00
25 Ivica Zubac 8.00 20.00
26 Jake Layman 4.00 10.00
27 Paul Zipser 3.00 8.00
28 Patrick McCaw 3.00 8.00
29 Chinanu Onuaku 3.00 8.00
30 Deyonta Davis 3.00 8.00

2016-17 Panini Excalibur Armory Jerseys
STATED PRINT RUN 99 SER.#'d SETS
1 Paul Millsap 2.50 6.00
2 Marcus Smart 4.00 10.00
3 Brook Lopez 2.50 6.00
4 Nicolas Batum 2.50 6.00
5 Dwyane Wade 6.00 15.00
6 Kevin Love 3.00 8.00
7 Harrison Barnes 2.50 6.00
8 Nikola Jokic 15.00 40.00
9 Reggie Jackson 2.50 6.00
10 Draymond Green 4.00 10.00
11 Patrick Beverley 2.00 5.00
12 Myles Turner 3.00 8.00
13 J.J. Redick 3.00 8.00
14 Julius Randle 4.00 10.00
15 Mike Conley 2.50 6.00
16 Goran Dragic 3.00 8.00
17 Jabari Parker 2.00 5.00
18 Ricky Rubio 2.50 6.00
19 Jrue Holiday 4.00 10.00
20 Derrick Rose 5.00 12.00
21 Victor Oladipo 2.50 6.00
22 Aaron Gordon 3.00 8.00
23 Jahlil Okafor 2.00 5.00
24 Eric Bledsoe 2.50 6.00
25 C.J. McCollum 3.00 8.00
26 Rudy Gay 3.00 8.00
27 LaMarcus Aldridge 3.00 8.00
28 Kyle Lowry 3.00 8.00
29 Rudy Gobert 4.00 10.00
30 Markieff Morris 2.00 5.00
31 Jamal Crawford 3.00 8.00
32 Jordan Clarkson 3.00 8.00
33 Marc Gasol 3.00 8.00
34 Hassan Whiteside 2.50 6.00
35 Kristaps Porzingis 5.00 12.00
36 Serge Ibaka 2.50 6.00
37 Pau Gasol 5.00 12.00
38 Bradley Beal 4.00 10.00

2016-17 Panini Excalibur Battlements
*RED/99: .6X TO 1.5X BASIC
1 Hassan Whiteside .50 1.25
2 Andre Drummond .60 1.50
3 DeAndre Jordan .50 1.25
4 Dwight Howard .75 2.00
5 Rudy Gobert .75 2.00
6 Anthony Davis 2.00 5.00
7 Karl-Anthony Towns 1.25 3.00
8 Tyson Chandler .50 1.25
9 Marcin Gortat .40 1.00
10 Kevin Love .60 1.50
11 DeMarcus Cousins .50 1.25
12 Russell Westbrook 1.00 2.50
13 Jonas Valanciunas .50 1.25
14 Nikola Vucevic .60 1.50
15 Tristan Thompson .50 1.25
16 Giannis Antetokounmpo 3.00 8.00
17 Joakim Noah .40 1.00
18 Trevor Booker .40 1.00
19 Draymond Green .75 2.00
20 Kevin Durant 2.50 6.00
21 Nikola Jokic 3.00 8.00
22 Zach Randolph .60 1.50
23 James Harden 1.25 3.00
24 Kenneth Faried .50 1.25
25 Julius Randle .75 2.00
26 Paul Millsap .50 1.25
27 Pau Gasol 1.00 2.50
28 Steven Adams .50 1.25
29 Michael Kidd-Gilchrist .40 1.00
30 Kawhi Leonard 1.50 4.00

2016-17 Panini Excalibur Calligraphy Autographs
STATED PRINT RUN 149 SER.#'d SETS
CALAI Allen Iverson 75.00 200.00
CALBB Bojan Bogdanovic 4.00 10.00
CALBW Bill Willoughby 4.00 10.00
CALDC Dell Curry 5.00 12.00
CALDL Damian Lillard 40.00 100.00
CALDS Dennis Scott 3.00 8.00
CALDS Damon Stoudamire 5.00 12.00
CALGH Gary Harris 4.00 10.00
CALGR Glen Rice 5.00 12.00
CALJR Julius Randle 6.00 15.00
CALMG Marc Gasol 5.00 12.00
CALMJ Magic Johnson 75.00 200.00

CALMT Myles Turner 5.00 12.00
CALRA Ryan Anderson 3.00 8.00
CALRF Rick Fox 4.00 10.00
CALRS Ralph Sampson 4.00 10.00
CALSE Sean Elliott 4.00 10.00
CALSK Shawn Kemp 30.00 80.00
CALSW Spud Webb 5.00 12.00
CALTD Tony Delk 3.00 8.00
CALTG Tom Gugliotta 3.00 8.00
CALVB Vin Baker 4.00 10.00
CALZL Zach LaVine 40.00 100.00

2016-17 Panini Excalibur Coat of Arms

*BLUE/199: .6X TO 1.5X BASIC
*PURPLE/49: .75X TO 2X BASIC
1 Stephen Curry 5.00 12.00
2 Andrew Wiggins 1.25 3.00
3 Chris Paul 1.50 4.00
4 Kristaps Porzingis 1.50 4.00
5 Kemba Walker .75 2.00
6 Karl-Anthony Towns 2.00 5.00
7 Aaron Gordon 1.00 2.50
8 Nikola Jokic 5.00 12.00
9 Joel Embiid 2.50 6.00
10 Kyrie Irving 2.00 5.00
11 Devin Booker 4.00 10.00
12 D'Angelo Russell 1.25 3.00
13 Damian Lillard 2.50 6.00
14 Dwight Howard 1.25 3.00
15 DeMarcus Cousins .75 2.00
16 Paul George 1.50 4.00
17 Kawhi Leonard 2.50 6.00
18 Giannis Antetokounmpo 5.00 12.00
19 Dirk Nowitzki 2.50 6.00
20 DeMar DeRozan 1.25 3.00
21 Marc Gasol 1.00 2.50
22 James Harden 2.00 5.00
23 Pau Gasol 1.50 4.00
24 Isaiah Thomas .75 2.00
25 Gordon Hayward 1.00 2.50
26 Kevin Durant 4.00 10.00
27 Kyle Lowry 1.00 2.50
28 LeBron James 5.00 12.00
29 Jabari Parker .60 1.50
30 C.J. McCollum 1.00 2.50
31 Klay Thompson 2.50 6.00
32 Russell Westbrook 1.50 4.00
33 Dwyane Wade 2.00 5.00
34 Carmelo Anthony 1.50 4.00
35 Goran Dragic 1.00 2.50
36 Anthony Davis 3.00 8.00
37 Andre Drummond 1.00 2.50
38 Mike Conley .75 2.00
39 Myles Turner 1.00 2.50
40 Jeremy Lin 2.00 5.00
41 Ben Simmons 2.00 5.00
42 Brandon Ingram 5.00 12.00
43 Thon Maker .75 2.00
44 Jaylen Brown 5.00 12.00
45 Buddy Hield 2.00 5.00
46 Yogi Ferrell .75 2.00
47 Malcolm Brogdon 2.00 5.00
48 Marquese Chriss .75 2.00
49 Jamal Murray 8.00 20.00
50 Kris Dunn 1.00 2.50

2016-17 Panini Excalibur Coat of Arms Blue

*BLUE: .6X TO 1.5X BASIC

2016-17 Panini Excalibur Coat of Arms Purple

*PURPLE: .75X TO 2X BASIC
49 Jamal Murray 20.00 50.00

2016-17 Panini Excalibur Crusade Blue

*BLUE: .6X TO 1.5X BASIC
STATED PRINT RUN 149 SER.#'d SETS
1 LeBron James 10.00 25.00
2 Stephen Curry 10.00 25.00
92 Brandon Ingram 8.00 20.00
96 Jaylen Brown 4.00 10.00
97 Jamal Murray 25.00 60.00

2016-17 Panini Excalibur Crusade Orange

*ORANGE: 1.2X TO 3X BASIC
STATED PRINT RUN 25 SER.#'d SETS
1 LeBron James 20.00 50.00
2 Stephen Curry 20.00 50.00
92 Brandon Ingram 15.00 40.00
96 Jaylen Brown 15.00 40.00
97 Jamal Murray 125.00 300.00

2016-17 Panini Excalibur Crusade Purple

*PURPLE: 1X TO 2.5X BASIC
STATED PRINT RUN 49 SER.#'d SETS
1 LeBron James 15.00 40.00
2 Stephen Curry 15.00 40.00
92 Brandon Ingram 12.00 30.00
96 Jaylen Brown 6.00 15.00
97 Jamal Murray 60.00 150.00

2016-17 Panini Excalibur Crusade Red

*RED: .75X TO 2X BASIC
STATED PRINT RUN 99 SER.#'d SETS
1 LeBron James 12.00 30.00
2 Stephen Curry 12.00 30.00
92 Brandon Ingram 10.00 25.00
96 Jaylen Brown 5.00 12.00
97 Jamal Murray 40.00 100.00

2016-17 Panini Excalibur Crusade Silver

*CAMO: .4X TO 1X BASIC
1 LeBron James 8.00 20.00
2 Stephen Curry 8.00 20.00
3 Kevin Durant 4.00 10.00
4 James Harden 2.00 5.00
5 Russell Westbrook 1.50 4.00
6 Anthony Davis 3.00 8.00
7 Isaiah Thomas .75 2.00
8 DeMarcus Cousins .75 2.00
9 DeMar DeRozan 1.25 3.00
10 Damian Lillard 2.50 6.00
11 Kawhi Leonard 2.50 6.00
12 C.J. McCollum 1.00 2.50
13 Kyrie Irving 2.00 5.00
14 Giannis Antetokounmpo 5.00 12.00
15 Karl-Anthony Towns 2.00 5.00
16 Jimmy Butler 2.00 5.00
17 Kyle Lowry 1.00 2.50
18 John Wall 1.25 3.00
19 Carmelo Anthony 1.50 4.00
20 Kemba Walker .75 2.00
21 Paul George 1.50 4.00
22 Andrew Wiggins 1.25 3.00
23 Gordon Hayward 1.00 2.50
24 Bradley Beal 1.25 3.00
25 Eric Bledsoe .75 2.00
26 Klay Thompson 2.50 6.00
27 Devin Booker 4.00 10.00
28 Marc Gasol 1.00 2.50
29 Brook Lopez .75 2.00
30 Harrison Barnes .75 2.00
31 Jabari Parker .60 1.50
32 Kevin Love 1.00 2.50
33 Dirk Nowitzki 2.50 6.00
34 Goran Dragic 1.00 2.50
35 Mike Conley .75 2.00
36 Dwyane Wade 2.00 5.00
37 Chris Paul 1.50 4.00
38 Paul Millsap .75 2.00
39 Zach LaVine 2.00 5.00
40 Blake Griffin 1.00 2.50
41 Kristaps Porzingis 1.50 4.00
42 Lou Williams 1.00 2.50
43 Derrick Rose 1.50 4.00
44 Avery Bradley .60 1.50
45 LaMarcus Aldridge 1.00 2.50
46 Eric Gordon .75 2.00
47 Danilo Gallinari .75 2.00
48 Dennis Schroder 1.00 2.50
49 Evan Fournier .75 2.00
50 Hassan Whiteside .75 2.00
51 Joel Embiid 2.50 6.00
52 Myles Turner 1.00 2.50
53 Al Horford 1.00 2.50
54 Nicolas Batum .75 2.00
55 Andre Drummond 1.00 2.50
56 Zach Randolph 1.00 2.50
57 Kentavious Caldwell-Pope .75 2.00
58 Dwight Howard 1.25 3.00
59 DeAndre Jordan .75 2.00
60 Pau Gasol 1.50 4.00
61 Michael Kidd-Gilchrist .60 1.50
62 Tony Allen .60 1.50
63 Jeff Teague .60 1.50
64 Bojan Bogdanovic .75 2.00
65 Enes Kanter .60 1.50
66 Serge Ibaka .75 2.00
67 J.J. Redick 1.00 2.50
68 Rudy Gobert 1.25 3.00
69 Rodney Hood .75 2.00
70 Draymond Green 1.25 3.00
71 Deron Williams .75 2.00
72 Julius Randle 1.25 3.00
73 Jordan Clarkson 1.00 2.50
74 Tim Hardaway Jr. .75 2.00
75 Steven Adams .75 2.00
76 Jamal Crawford 1.00 2.50
77 Jonas Valanciunas .75 2.00
78 Marcin Gortat .60 1.50
79 Victor Oladipo .75 2.00
80 Pete Maravich 1.50 4.00
81 Wilt Chamberlain 3.00 8.00
82 Bill Russell 3.00 8.00
83 George Mikan 2.00 5.00
84 Jerry West 2.50 6.00
85 Scottie Pippen 2.00 5.00
86 Tim Duncan 2.00 5.00
87 Shaquille O'Neal 3.00 8.00
88 Kobe Bryant 30.00 80.00
89 David Robinson 2.00 5.00
90 Allen Iverson 1.50 4.00
92 Brandon Ingram 2.50 6.00
93 Malcolm Brogdon 2.00 5.00
94 Buddy Hield 2.00 5.00
95 Kris Dunn 1.00 2.50
96 Jaylen Brown 5.00 12.00
97 Jamal Murray 15.00 40.00
98 Dario Saric 1.00 2.50
99 Marquese Chriss .75 2.00
100 Yogi Ferrell .75 2.00

2016-17 Panini Excalibur Emblem Jerseys

STATED PRINT RUN 99 SER.#'d SETS
1 Giannis Antetokounmpo 15.00 40.00
2 Carmelo Anthony 5.00 12.00
3 Jimmy Butler 6.00 15.00
4 DeMarcus Cousins 2.50 6.00
5 Stephen Curry 25.00 60.00
6 Anthony Davis 4.00 10.00
7 DeMar DeRozan 4.00 10.00
8 Andre Drummond 3.00 8.00
9 Kevin Durant 6.00 15.00
10 Paul George 5.00 12.00
11 James Harden 6.00 15.00
12 Kyrie Irving 6.00 15.00
13 LeBron James 25.00 60.00
14 Kawhi Leonard 8.00 20.00
15 Damian Lillard 4.00 10.00
16 Nikola Jokic 15.00 40.00
17 Dirk Nowitzki 8.00 20.00
18 Chris Paul 5.00 12.00
19 Kristaps Porzingis 4.00 10.00
20 Isaiah Thomas 2.50 6.00
21 Klay Thompson 8.00 20.00
22 Karl-Anthony Towns 4.00 10.00
23 Dwyane Wade 4.00 10.00
24 Russell Westbrook 5.00 12.00
25 Hassan Whiteside 2.50 6.00

2016-17 Panini Excalibur Jousting

1 LeBron James 5.00 12.00
2 Kawhi Leonard 1.50 4.00
3 Kevin Durant 2.50 6.00
4 Russell Westbrook 1.50 4.00
5 Dirk Nowitzki 1.50 4.00
6 Dwyane Wade 1.25 3.00
7 DeMarcus Cousins .50 1.25
8 Joel Embiid 1.50 4.00
9 Klay Thompson 1.50 4.00
10 James Harden 1.25 3.00
11 Damian Lillard 1.50 4.00
12 Stephen Curry 5.00 12.00
13 John Wall .75 2.00
14 Kyrie Irving 1.25 3.00
15 Kevin Love .60 1.50
16 Andre Drummond .60 1.50
17 Karl-Anthony Towns 1.25 3.00
18 Ben Simmons 1.25 3.00
19 Giannis Antetokounmpo 3.00 8.00
20 Anthony Davis 2.00 5.00
21 Wilt Chamberlain 2.00 5.00
22 Bill Russell 2.00 5.00
23 Oscar Robertson 1.50 4.00
24 Jerry West 1.50 4.00
25 Larry Bird 2.50 6.00
26 Magic Johnson 2.50 6.00
27 Kobe Bryant
Jousting Left 5.00 12.00
28 Allen Iverson 1.00 2.50
29 Shaquille O'Neal 2.00 5.00
30 Hakeem Olajuwon 1.25 3.00

2016-17 Panini Excalibur Jousting Red

*RED: .6X TO 1.5X BASIC
STATED PRINT RUN 99 SER.#'d SETS

2016-17 Panini Excalibur Kaboom

1 LeBron James 1,500.00 3,000.00
2 Stephen Curry 800.00 1,500.00
3 James Harden 125.00 300.00
4 Russell Westbrook 75.00 200.00
5 Kevin Durant 400.00 [illegible]00.00
6 Anthony Davis 125.00 [illegible]00.00
7 DeMarcus Cousins 40.00 [illegible]00.00
8 Joel Embiid 400.00 [illegible]00.00
9 Damian Lillard 125.00 [illegible]00.00
10 Kawhi Leonard 300.00 [illegible]00.00
11 Jimmy Butler 75.00 200.00
12 Giannis Antetokounmpo 1,000.00 2,[illegible]00.00
13 Karl-Anthony Towns 300.00 [illegible]00.00
14 John Wall 75.00 200.00
15 Carmelo Anthony 150.00 400.00
16 Kyrie Irving 150.00 400.00
17 Paul George 125.00 300.00
18 Klay Thompson 400.00 300.00
19 Ben Simmons 150.00 400.00
20 Brandon Ingram 300.00 500.00
21 Buddy Hield 60.00 150.00
22 Tim Duncan 150.00 400.00
23 Kobe Bryant 1,500.00 3,000.00
24 Kareem Abdul-Jabbar 200.00 500.00
25 Dominique Wilkins 125.00 300.00

2016-17 Panini Excalibur Knight in Shining Armor

*BLUE/199: .6X TO 1.5X BASIC
*PURPLE/49: .75X TO 2X BASIC
1 James Harden 3.00 8.00
2 Russell Westbrook 2.50 6.00
3 Kevin Durant 6.00 15.00
4 Stephen Curry 12.00 30.00
5 LeBron James 12.00 30.00
6 Anthony Davis 5.00 12.00
7 Damian Lillard 4.00 10.00
8 Isaiah Thomas 1.25 3.00
9 DeMarcus Cousins 1.25 3.00
10 Dirk Nowitzki 4.00 10.00
11 Dwyane Wade 3.00 8.00
12 Chris Paul 2.50 6.00
13 Klay Thompson 4.00 10.00
14 Karl-Anthony Towns 3.00 8.00
15 DeMar DeRozan 2.00 5.00
16 Jimmy Butler 3.00 8.00
17 Paul George 2.50 6.00
18 Giannis Antetokounmpo 8.00 20.00
19 Kawhi Leonard 3.00 8.00
20 Kyrie Irving 3.00 8.00
21 C.J. McCollum 1.50 4.00
22 Kyle Lowry 1.50 4.00
23 John Wall 1.50 4.00
24 Carmelo Anthony 2.50 6.00
25 Kemba Walker 1.25 3.00

2016-17 Panini Excalibur Knights Cloak Jerseys

*PRIME/25: .75X TO 2X BASIC
1 Kevin Durant 10.00 25.00
2 LeBron James 20.00 50.00
3 Russell Westbrook 4.00 10.00
4 James Harden 5.00 12.00
5 Stephen Curry 20.00 50.00
6 Damian Lillard 6.00 15.00
7 Isaiah Thomas 2.00 5.00
8 DeMarcus Cousins 2.00 5.00
9 Dirk Nowitzki 6.00 15.00
10 Anthony Davis 6.00 15.00
11 Klay Thompson 6.00 15.00
12 Dwyane Wade 5.00 12.00
13 Chris Paul 4.00 10.00
14 DeMar DeRozan 3.00 8.00
15 Karl-Anthony Towns 3.00 8.00
16 Jimmy Butler 5.00 12.00
17 Paul George 4.00 10.00
18 Giannis Antetokounmpo 12.00 30.00
19 Kawhi Leonard 6.00 15.00
20 C.J. McCollum 2.50 6.00
21 Kyrie Irving 5.00 12.00
22 Carmelo Anthony 4.00 10.00
23 John Wall 3.00 8.00
24 Andrew Wiggins 3.00 8.00
25 Kristaps Porzingis 4.00 10.00

2016-17 Panini Excalibur Manuscripts Autographs

STATED PRINT RUN 149 SER.#'d SETS
1 C.J. McCollum 8.00 20.00
2 Joel Embiid 75.00 200.00
3 Vince Carter 40.00 100.00
5 Tony Allen 3.00 8.00
6 Ricky Rubio 8.00 20.00
9 Zaza Pachulia 3.00 8.00
11 Zach Randolph 5.00 12.00
12 Marcin Gortat 3.00 8.00
13 Nikola Vucevic 5.00 12.00
14 Danilo Gallinari 4.00 10.00
15 Tristan Thompson 4.00 10.00
16 Tobias Harris 5.00 12.00
17 Dwyane Wade 40.00 100.00
18 Karl-Anthony Towns 20.00 50.00
20 D'Angelo Russell 10.00 25.00
21 Yogi Ferrell 4.00 10.00
22 Buddy Hield 10.00 25.00
23 Malcolm Brogdon 10.00 25.00
24 Brandon Ingram 20.00 50.00
25 Anfernee Hardaway 60.00 150.00
26 Marcus Camby 4.00 10.00
27 Dominique Wilkins 15.00 40.00
28 Kenny Smith 4.00 10.00
29 Kareem Abdul-Jabbar 75.00 200.00
30 Alex English 4.00 10.00
31 Sidney Moncrief 4.00 10.00
32 Jeff Hornacek 4.00 10.00
33 Horace Grant 5.00 12.00
34 Rashard Lewis 4.00 10.00
35 Hakeem Olajuwon 40.00 100.00
36 Alonzo Mourning 40.00 100.00
37 Jo Jo White 4.00 10.00
38 Antoine Carr 3.00 8.00
39 Kobe Bryant 800.00 1,500.00
40 Jaylen Brown 100.00 250.00

2016-17 Panini Excalibur Run the Gauntlet

*RED/99: .6X TO 1.5X BASIC
1 James Harden 1.25 3.00
2 John Wall .75 2.00
3 Russell Westbrook 1.00 2.50
4 LeBron James 5.00 12.00
5 Ricky Rubio .50 1.25
6 Jeff Teague .40 1.00
7 Jrue Holiday .75 2.00
8 Draymond Green .75 2.00
9 Deron Williams .50 1.25
10 Kyle Lowry .60 1.50
11 Rajon Rondo .75 2.00
12 Goran Dragic .60 1.50
13 Isaiah Thomas .50 1.25
14 Stephen Curry 5.00 12.00
15 Dennis Schroder .60 1.50
16 Mike Conley .50 1.25
17 Eric Bledsoe .50 1.25
18 Nicolas Batum .50 1.25
19 Tim Frazier .40 1.00
20 T.J. McConnell .50 1.25
21 Kyrie Irving 1.25 3.00
22 Elfrid Payton .50 1.25
23 Damian Lillard 1.50 4.00
24 Giannis Antetokounmpo 3.00 8.00
25 Kemba Walker .50 1.25

2016-17 Panini Excalibur Signature Knights Autographs

1 E'Twaun Moore 2.50 6.00
2 Trey Lyles 3.00 8.00
3 Sean Kilpatrick 2.50 6.00
4 Jason Terry 3.00 8.00
5 Victor Oladipo 3.00 8.00
6 Gordon Hayward 6.00 15.00
7 James Johnson 2.50 6.00
8 Doug McDermott 8.00 20.00
9 Michael Kidd-Gilchrist 2.50 6.00
10 Eric Gordon 3.00 8.00
11 Yogi Ferrell 8.00 20.00
12 J.J. Barea 10.00 25.00
13 D'Angelo Russell 8.00 20.00
14 Justise Winslow 3.00 8.00
15 Karl-Anthony Towns 30.00 80.00
16 Larry Nance Jr. 2.50 6.00
17 Chinanu Onuaku 2.50 6.00
18 Buddy Hield 8.00 20.00
19 Taurean Prince 3.00 8.00
20 Tim Hardaway Jr. 3.00 8.00
21 Michael Gbinije 2.50 6.00
22 Willy Hernangomez 3.00 8.00
23 Diamond Stone 2.50 6.00
24 Rodney McGruder 3.00 8.00
25 Joel Bolomboy 2.50 6.00

2016-17 Panini Excalibur Storm the Castle

*BLUE/199: .5X TO 1.2X BASIC
*PURPLE/49: .6X TO 1.5X BASIC
1 Isaiah Thomas 1.25 3.00
2 Jimmy Butler 1.50 4.00
3 Dwyane Wade 3.00 8.00
4 Kyrie Irving 3.00 8.00
5 LeBron James 12.00 30.00
6 Dirk Nowitzki 4.00 10.00
7 Nikola Jokic 8.00 20.00
8 Andre Drummond 1.50 4.00
9 Stephen Curry 12.00 30.00
10 Kevin Durant 6.00 15.00
11 Klay Thompson 4.00 10.00
12 James Harden 5.00 12.00
13 Paul George 2.50 6.00
14 Chris Paul 2.50 6.00
15 Hassan Whiteside 1.25 3.00
16 Giannis Antetokounmpo 8.00 20.00
17 Karl-Anthony Towns 3.00 8.00
18 Anthony Davis 5.00 12.00
19 Carmelo Anthony 2.50 6.00
20 Kristaps Porzingis 2.50 6.00
21 Russell Westbrook 2.50 6.00
22 Damian Lillard 4.00 10.00
23 DeMarcus Cousins 1.25 3.00
24 Kawhi Leonard 4.00 10.00
25 DeMar DeRozan 2.00 5.00

2016-17 Panini Excalibur Storm the Castle Blue

*BLUE: .6X TO 1.5X BASIC
5 LeBron James 12.00 30.00

2016-17 Panini Excalibur Storm the Castle Purple

*PURPLE: .75X TO 2X BASIC
5 LeBron James 15.00 40.00

2016-17 Panini Excalibur Team USA Jerseys

STATED PRINT RUN 99 SER.#'d SETS
1 Carmelo Anthony 10.00 25.00
2 Harrison Barnes 4.00 10.00
5 DeMar DeRozan 6.00 15.00
6 Kevin Durant 8.00 20.00
9 Kyrie Irving 8.00 20.00

2012 Panini Father's Day Draft Day Hats

1 DeMarcus Cousins 8.00 20.00
2 Cole Aldrich 4.00 10.00
3 Derrick Favors 6.00 15.00
4 Ekpe Udoh 4.00 10.00
5 Evan Turner 6.00 15.00
6 Gordon Hayward 6.00 15.00
7 Greg Monroe 6.00 15.00
8 Paul George 6.00 15.00
9 Wesley Johnson 5.00 12.00
10 Xavier Henry 5.00 12.00
BG Blake Griffin 12.00 30.00

2012 Panini Father's Day Kobe Bryant Shoes

KB1 Kobe Bryant 40.00 70.00
KB2 Kobe Bryant 40.00 70.00

2012 Panini Father's Day NBA Finals Memorabilia

1 Dirk Nowitzki 20.00 50.00
2 Jason Kidd 20.00 50.00
3 Jason Terry 20.00 50.00
4 LeBron James 50.00 120.00
5 Dwyane Wade 40.00 100.00
MVP Dirk Nowitzki 40.00 100.00
NNO Net Card 50.00 120.00

2013-14 Panini Father's Day March Memories Autographs

STATED PRINT RUN 50 SER.#'d SETS
CD Clyde Drexler 15.00 40.00
CL Christian Laettner 4.00 10.00
NR Nolan Richardson 15.00 40.00
RS Ralph Sampson 4.00 10.00

2013-14 Panini Father's Day NBA Draft Combine Jerseys

*CRACKED ICE/25: .6X TO 1.5X BASIC
1 Michael Carter-Williams 1.50 4.00
2 Victor Oladipo 3.00 8.00
3 Trey Burke 1.50 4.00
4 Ben McLemore 1.50 4.00
5 Tim Hardaway Jr. 2.50 6.00
6 Tony Snell 1.50 4.00
7 Kelly Olynyk 1.50 4.00
8 Nate Wolters 1.25 3.00
9 Steven Adams 3.00 8.00
10 Kentavious Caldwell-Pope 2.00 5.00
11 Mason Plumlee 1.50 4.00
12 Shane Larkin 1.25 3.00
13 Otto Porter 2.00 5.00
14 Cody Zeller 1.50 4.00
15 Peyton Siva 1.25 3.00

2013-14 Panini Father's Day NBA Patch Autographs

AB Anthony Bennett 60.00 150.00
CM C.J. McCollum 4.00 10.00
SM Shabazz Muhammad 3.00 8.00
TB Trey Burke 20.00 50.00
TM Tracy McGrady 15.00 40.00

2014 Panini Father's Day Tools of the Trade

*CRACKED ICE/25: 1X TO 2.5X BASIC
DN Dirk Nowitzki 5.00 12.00
MCW Michael Carter-Williams 3.00 8.00

2012-13 Panini Finals Private Signings

PRINT RUNS B/WN 1-25 COPIES PER
NO PRICING ON QTY 10 OR LESS
AM Alonzo Mourning/25 20.00 50.00
BW Bill Walton/25 20.00 50.00
CD Clyde Drexler/15 30.00 80.00
DN Don Nelson/25 20.00 50.00
HO Hakeem Olajuwon/15 40.00 100.00
IT Isiah Thomas/20 20.00 50.00
JS John Salley/25 6.00 15.00
JW James Worthy/25 12.00 30.00
TS Satch Sanders/25 20.00 50.00

2013-14 Panini Finals Private Signings

PRINT RUNS B/WN 2-25 COPIES PER
NO PRICING ON QTY 10 OR LESS
AH Anfernee Hardaway/25 20.00 50.00
BL Bill Laimbeer/25 10.00 25.00
BW Bill Walton/25 10.00 25.00
DD Darryl Dawkins/25 4.00 10.00
DR David Robinson/25 15.00 40.00
GD Gorgui Dieng/25 8.00 20.00
GH Grant Hill/25 12.00 30.00
HO Hakeem Olajuwon/25 15.00 40.00
JK Jason Kidd/20 20.00 50.00
JW James Worthy/15 10.00 25.00
MP Mason Plumlee/25 10.00 25.00
MR Mitch Richmond/15 20.00 50.00
PA Pero Antic/25 8.00 20.00
SC Stephen Curry/25 500.00 1,000.00
SN Steve Nash/20 20.00 50.00
SP Scottie Pippen/20 60.00 120.00
TB Trey Burke/15 30.00 60.00
TH Tim Hardaway Jr./15 30.00 60.00
VO Victor Oladipo/15 50.00 100.00

2013-14 Panini Finals Rookie Memorabilia Autographs

STATED PRINT RUN 25 SER.#'d SETS
AB Anthony Bennett 10.00 25.00
AL Alex Len 10.00 25.00
BM Ben McLemore 10.00 25.00
CJM C.J. McCollum 40.00 100.00
CZ Cody Zeller 10.00 25.00
GA Giannis Antetokounmpo 400.00 800.00
KO Kelly Olynyk 15.00 40.00
MCW Michael Carter-Williams 10.00 25.00
OP Otto Porter 20.00 50.00
SA Steven Adams 40.00 100.00
SM Shabazz Muhammad 10.00 25.00
TB Trey Burke 20.00 50.00
TH Tim Hardaway Jr. 20.00 50.00
VO Victor Oladipo 75.00 200.00

2014-15 Panini Finals Private Signings

STATED PRINT RUN B/WN 2-25 COPIES PER
NO PRICING ON QTY 15 OR LESS
AP Adreian Payne/25 12.00 30.00
GP Gary Patyon/25 20.00 50.00
JC Jordan Clarkson/25 50.00 120.00
JN Jusuf Nurkic/25 15.00 40.00
MM Mitch McGary/25 12.00 30.00
NM Nikola Mirotic/25 20.00 50.00
SC Stephen Curry/25 500.00 1,000.00
BB2 Bojan Bogdanovic/25 20.00 50.00
JE2 James Ennis/25 12.00 30.00
JH1 Joe Harris/25 20.00 50.00
KA2 Kyle Anderson/25 12.00 30.00
KM1 K.J. McDaniels/25 12.00 30.00
SN2 Steve Nash/25 40.00 100.00

2012-13 Panini Flawless

STATED PRINT RUN 20 SER.#'d SETS
1 Carlos Boozer 40.00 100.00
2 Chris Bosh 50.00 120.00
3 Eric Gordon 40.00 100.00
4 Gordon Hayward 60.00 150.00
5 Kevin Garnett 125.00 250.00
6 Zach Randolph 50.00 120.00
7 Kevin Love 100.00 200.00
8 Rajon Rondo 100.00 200.00
9 Ricky Rubio 50.00 120.00
10 Andre Iguodala 50.00 120.00
11 Carmelo Anthony 150.00 300.00
12 Chris Paul 175.00 350.00
13 Dwyane Wade 250.00 400.00
14 Greg Monroe 40.00 100.00
15 Kevin Durant 400.00 800.00
16 Vince Carter 125.00 250.00
17 Kobe Bryant 600.00 1,200.00
18 Paul Pierce 60.00 150.00
19 Roy Hibbert 50.00 120.00
20 Anderson Varejao 50.00 120.00
21 Brook Lopez 50.00 120.00
22 Danny Granger 40.00 100.00
23 Dwight Howard 100.00 200.00
24 Jameer Nelson 40.00 100.00
25 John Wall 100.00 200.00
26 Tyson Chandler 50.00 120.00
27 LaMarcus Aldridge 60.00 150.00
28 Paul George 300.00 500.00
29 Rudy Gay 40.00 100.00
30 Amar'e Stoudemire 50.00 120.00
31 Brandon Jennings 50.00 120.00
32 David Lee 50.00 120.00
33 Dirk Nowitzki 150.00 300.00
34 James Harden 150.00 300.00
35 Joe Johnson 40.00 100.00
36 Tyreke Evans 60.00 150.00
37 LeBron James 1,500.00 2,000.00
38 Pau Gasol 100.00 200.00
39 Russell Westbrook 125.00 250.00
40 Al Jefferson 40.00 100.00
41 Blake Griffin 100.00 200.00
42 DeMar DeRozan 100.00 250.00
43 Derrick Rose 250.00 500.00
44 Jason Kidd 50.00 120.00
45 Joakim Noah 60.00 120.00
46 Tony Parker 40.00 100.00
47 Manu Ginobili 60.00 150.00
48 Nick Young 40.00 100.00
49 Shawn Marion 50.00 150.00
50 Al Horford 60.00 150.00
51 Ben Gordon 40.00 100.00
52 DeMarcus Cousins 60.00 150.00
53 Deron Williams 60.00 150.00
54 JaVale McGee 40.00 100.00
55 Jeremy Lin 125.00 250.00
56 Tim Duncan 150.00 300.00
57 Marcin Gortat 40.00 100.00
58 Monta Ellis 50.00 120.00
59 Stephen Curry 400.00 800.00
60 Steve Nash 60.00 150.00
61 Allen Iverson 200.00 400.00
62 Elgin Baylor 60.00 150.00
63 James Worthy 50.00 120.00
64 Pete Maravich 125.00 300.00
65 Yao Ming 300.00 600.00
66 Anfernee Hardaway 125.00 250.00
67 Gary Payton 100.00 200.00
68 Jerry West 60.00 150.00
69 Patrick Ewing 150.00 300.00
70 Wilt Chamberlain 200.00 400.00
71 Bill Russell 100.00 200.00
72 George Gervin 60.00 150.00
73 John Havlicek 60.00 150.00
74 Oscar Robertson 40.00 100.00
75 Willis Reed 60.00 150.00
76 Bob Pettit 50.00 120.00
77 George Mikan 125.00 250.00
78 John Stockton 100.00 200.00
79 Magic Johnson 200.00 400.00
80 Walt Frazier 40.00 100.00
81 David Robinson 60.00 150.00
82 Isiah Thomas 200.00 400.00
83 Julius Erving 125.00 250.00
84 Larry Bird 100.00 200.00
85 Shaquille O'Neal 100.00 200.00
86 Dennis Rodman 50.00 120.00
87 Hakeem Olajuwon 125.00 250.00
88 Kareem Abdul-Jabbar 125.00 250.00
89 Karl Malone 100.00 200.00
90 Scottie Pippen 200.00 400.00
91 Bradley Beal RC 300.00 600.00
92 Brandon Knight RC 60.00 150.00
93 Chandler Parsons RC 50.00 120.00
94 Andre Drummond RC 200.00 500.00
95 Anthony Davis RC 1,000.00 3,000.00
96 Kyrie Irving RC 800.00 1,500.00
97 Kenneth Faried RC 60.00 150.00
98 Damian Lillard RC 1,000.00 3,000.00
99 Harrison Barnes RC 100.00 250.00
100 Michael Kidd-Gilchrist RC 40.00 100.00

2012-13 Panini Flawless All-Star Ink

PRINT RUNS B/WN 15-25 COPIES PER
NO PRICING ON QTY 15
1 Magic Johnson/20 300.00 600.00
3 Blake Griffin/20 50.00 120.00
4 Kyrie Irving/20 600.00 1,200.00
7 Kobe Bryant/20 2,000.00 4,000.00
8 Grant Hill/20 50.00 120.00
11 Kevin Durant/20 500.00 1,000.00
14 Julius Erving/20 125.00 300.00
15 Jerry West/20 125.00 300.00
17 Isiah Thomas/15 75.00 200.00
18 Alonzo Mourning/15 75.00 200.00
19 David Robinson/15 125.00 300.00
20 Hakeem Olajuwon/15 125.00 300.00

2012-13 Panini Flawless Greats Autographs

STATED PRINT RUN 20 SER.#'d SETS
1 Yao Ming 500.00 1,000.00
2 Sam Jones 20.00 50.00
3 Rick Barry 20.00 50.00
4 Larry Johnson 20.00 50.00
5 Kevin McHale 30.00 80.00
6 Gary Payton 50.00 120.00
7 Gail Goodrich 15.00 40.00
8 Clyde Lovellette 15.00 40.00
10 Adrian Dantley 20.00 50.00
11 Walt Frazier 15.00 40.00
12 Sidney Moncrief 15.00 40.00
13 Robert Parish 15.00 40.00
14 Magic Johnson 125.00 300.00
15 John Thompson 25.00 60.00
16 George Gervin 25.00 60.00
17 Dominique Wilkins 50.00 120.00
18 Dan Issel 15.00 40.00
19 Chris Mullin 25.00 60.00
20 Alex English 15.00 40.00
21 Wes Unseld 15.00 40.00
22 Spencer Haywood 15.00 40.00
23 Nate Thurmond 15.00 40.00
24 Mark Eaton 25.00 60.00
25 Larry Bird 125.00 300.00
26 Hal Greer 15.00 40.00
27 Elgin Baylor 50.00 120.00
28 Darryl Dawkins 15.00 40.00
29 Bill Walton 20.00 50.00
30 Anfernee Hardaway 75.00 200.00
31 Willis Reed 100.00 250.00
32 Spud Webb 20.00 50.00
33 Nate Archibald 15.00 40.00
34 Mark Jackson 15.00 40.00
35 John Stockton 75.00 200.00
36 Jeff Hornacek 15.00 40.00
37 Elvin Hayes 25.00 60.00
38 David Thompson 10.00 25.00
39 Bill Russell 1,500.00 3,000.00
40 Artis Gilmore 20.00 50.00
41 Tim Hardaway 20.00 50.00
42 Sean Elliott 20.00 50.00
43 Mitch Richmond 15.00 40.00
44 Michael Finley 20.00 50.00
45 John Starks 20.00 50.00
46 John Havlicek 100.00 250.00
47 Dolph Schayes 15.00 40.00
48 Doc Rivers 10.00 25.00
49 Bill Laimbeer 15.00 40.00

2012-13 Panini Flawless Greats Dual Patches Autographs

PRINT RUNS B/WN 15-25 COPIES PER
NO PRICING ON QTY 15
1 Kobe Bryant/25 5,000.00 10,000.00
2 Kareem Abdul-Jabbar/25 1,000.00 2,000.00
3 Julius Erving/25 500.00 1,000.00
4 Grant Hill/20 150.00 400.00
5 David Robinson/25 200.00 500.00
6 Shaquille O'Neal/20 1,000.00 2,000.00
8 Danny Manning/25 30.00 80.00
9 Scottie Pippen/20 1,000.00 2,000.00
10 Grant Hill/20 150.00 400.00
11 John Stockton/25 200.00 500.00
13 Artis Gilmore/20 40.00 100.00
14 Clyde Drexler/20 150.00 400.00
15 Larry Bird/20 1,000.00 2,000.00
16 Mitch Richmond/20 125.00 300.00
17 Anfernee Hardaway/25 400.00 800.00
18 Ralph Sampson/20 25.00 60.00
19 Robert Parish/20 40.00 100.00
20 Larry Johnson/25 125.00 300.00
21 World B. Free/20 25.00 60.00
22 Calvin Murphy/20 30.00 80.00
23 Bill Laimbeer/20 75.00 200.00
24 Paul Westphal/25 40.00 100.00

2012-13 Panini Flawless Greats Patches Autographs

STATED PRINT RUN 25 SER.#'d SETS
1 Karl Malone 150.00 400.00
2 Larry Johnson 75.00 200.00
3 Earl Monroe 40.00 100.00
4 Mark Jackson 20.00 50.00
5 Robert Parish 40.00 100.00
6 Larry Bird 400.00 800.00
7 Gail Goodrich 25.00 60.00
8 Doc Rivers 25.00 60.00
9 Sean Elliott 30.00 80.00
10 Kevin McHale 75.00 200.00
11 Kiki VanDeWeghe 20.00 50.00
12 Danny Manning 20.00 50.00
14 Julius Erving 200.00 500.00
16 Dan Issel 20.00 50.00
17 Bill Laimbeer 40.00 100.00
18 John Stockton 125.00 300.00
19 Jamaal Wilkes 40.00 100.00
20 Clyde Drexler 100.00 250.00
21 Bob Lanier 30.00 80.00
22 Jerry West 150.00 400.00
23 James Worthy 75.00 200.00
24 Chris Mullin 50.00 120.00
25 Calvin Murphy 25.00 60.00

2012-13 Panini Flawless Hall of Fame Autographs

STATED PRINT RUN 20 SER.#'d SETS
1 Jamaal Wilkes 20.00 50.00
2 Ralph Sampson 15.00 40.00
3 Don Nelson 25.00 60.00
4 Artis Gilmore 20.00 50.00
5 David Robinson 100.00 250.00
6 John Stockton 75.00 200.00
7 Hakeem Olajuwon 100.00 250.00
8 Dominique Wilkins 40.00 100.00
9 Clyde Drexler 60.00 150.00
10 Joe Dumars 25.00 60.00
11 Robert Parish 40.00 100.00
12 Isiah Thomas 60.00 150.00
13 Bob McAdoo 40.00 100.00
14 Gail Goodrich 15.00 40.00
15 Kareem Abdul-Jabbar 400.00 800.00

16 Bill Walton 40.00 100.00
17 Dan Issel 15.00 40.00
18 Earl Monroe 40.00 100.00
19 Wes Unseld 40.00 100.00
20 Willis Reed 100.00 250.00

2012-13 Panini Flawless Inscriptions

PRINT RUNS B/WN 20-25 COPIES PER
1 Zach Randolph/20 15.00 40.00
2 Vince Carter/20 150.00 400.00
3 Kobe Bryant/25 2,000.00 4,000.00
4 Kevin Love/20 30.00 80.00
5 Deron Williams/20 20.00 50.00
6 Tobias Harris/20 40.00 100.00
7 Tyson Chandler/20 15.00 40.00
8 Kyrie Irving/25 400.00 800.00
9 Kevin Durant/25 400.00 800.00
10 Chris Bosh/20 40.00 100.00
11 Grant Hill/25 60.00 150.00
12 Tyreke Evans/20 15.00 40.00
13 LaMarcus Aldridge/20 25.00 60.00
14 Andre Drummond/20 100.00 250.00
15 Blake Griffin/20 40.00 100.00
16 Greg Monroe/20 15.00 40.00
17 Tony Parker/20 40.00 100.00
18 Rick Fox/20 20.00 50.00
19 Joakim Noah/20 15.00 40.00
20 Anthony Davis/20 400.00 800.00
21 James Harden/20 150.00 400.00
22 Steve Nash/20 100.00 250.00
23 Stephen Curry/20 1,500.00 3,000.00
24 Jason Kidd/20 60.00 150.00
25 Andre Iguodala/20 15.00 40.00

2012-13 Panini Flawless Memorable Marks

PRINT RUNS B/WN 20-25 COPIES PER
1 Hakeem Olajuwon 100.00 250.00
2 Larry Bird 150.00 400.00
3 Magic Johnson 150.00 400.00
4 Jerry West 75.00 200.00
5 Gail Goodrich 15.00 40.00
6 Jamaal Wilkes 20.00 50.00
7 Mark Price 30.00 80.00
8 Kareem Abdul-Jabbar 150.00 400.00
9 Isiah Thomas 40.00 100.00
10 Nate Thurmond 15.00 40.00
11 Glen Rice 20.00 50.00
12 Walt Frazier 25.00 60.00
13 Julius Erving 125.00 300.00
14 Sidney Moncrief 15.00 40.00
15 Calvin Murphy 15.00 40.00
16 Dikembe Mutombo 25.00 60.00
17 Scottie Pippen 150.00 400.00
18 Anfernee Hardaway 75.00 200.00
19 Rick Barry 20.00 50.00
20 Mitch Richmond 25.00 60.00
21 Rolando Blackman 12.00 30.00
22 George Gervin 20.00 50.00
23 Elgin Baylor 40.00 100.00
24 Elvin Hayes 20.00 50.00
25 Alonzo Mourning 60.00 150.00
26 Joe Dumars 20.00 50.00
27 Chris Mullin 20.00 50.00
28 Bill Walton 25.00 60.00
29 Spencer Haywood 15.00 40.00
30 Dolph Schayes 12.00 30.00
31 Connie Hawkins 20.00 50.00
32 Gary Payton 40.00 100.00
33 Larry Johnson 25.00 60.00
34 Sam Jones 20.00 50.00
36 Tim Hardaway 20.00 50.00
37 John Havlicek 75.00 200.00
38 Artis Gilmore 20.00 50.00
39 Nate Archibald 15.00 40.00
40 John Starks 12.00 30.00
41 Spud Webb 20.00 50.00
42 David Robinson 100.00 250.00
43 Bill Russell 1,500.00 3,000.00
44 James Worthy 40.00 100.00
45 Robert Parish 40.00 100.00
46 Kobe Bryant 1,500.00 3,000.00
47 Kevin Durant 200.00 500.00
48 Kyrie Irving 200.00 500.00
49 Grant Hill 50.00 120.00
50 Blake Griffin 40.00 100.00

2012-13 Panini Flawless Signatures

PRINT RUNS B/WN 20-25 COPIES PER
1 Tyreke Evans/20 15.00 40.00
2 Roy Hibbert/20 15.00 40.00
3 Raymond Felton/20 15.00 40.00
4 Joakim Noah/20 15.00 40.00
5 Jason Kidd/20 60.00 150.00
6 Scottie Pippen/25 150.00 400.00
7 Deron Williams/20 20.00 50.00
8 Anderson Varejao/20 15.00 40.00
9 Stephen Curry/20 1,500.00 3,000.00
10 Steve Francis/20 15.00 40.00
11 John Starks/20 20.00 50.00
12 Kenneth Faried/20 15.00 40.00
13 Harrison Barnes/20 20.00 50.00
14 DeMarcus Cousins/20 25.00 60.00
15 Antawn Jamison/20 15.00 40.00
16 Steve Nash/20 125.00 300.00
17 LaMarcus Aldridge/20 25.00 60.00
18 Jose Calderon/20 15.00 40.00
19 James Harden/20 300.00 600.00
20 Goran Dragic/20 15.00 40.00
21 Zach Randolph/20 15.00 40.00
22 Anthony Davis/20 600.00 1,200.00
23 Tony Parker/20 40.00 100.00
24 Kobe Bryant/25 1,500.00 3,000.00
25 Bradley Beal/20 150.00 400.00
26 J.R. Smith/20 15.00 40.00
27 Tyson Chandler/20 15.00 40.00
28 Danny Granger/20 15.00 40.00
29 Blake Griffin/20 25.00 60.00
30 Ty Lawson/20 15.00 40.00
31 Kyrie Irving/25 600.00 1,200.00
32 Kevin Durant/25 500.00 1,000.00
33 Greg Monroe/20 15.00 40.00
34 Grant Hill/25 40.00 100.00
35 Karl Malone/25 100.00 250.00
37 Bill Russell/25 1,500.00 3,000.00
38 David Robinson/20 125.00 300.00
39 Wes Unseld/20 15.00 40.00
40 Anfernee Hardaway/25 75.00 200.00
41 Clyde Drexler/20 40.00 100.00
42 Kevin McHale/20 30.00 80.00
43 Dominique Wilkins/20 50.00 120.00
44 Julius Erving/20 100.00 250.00
45 Tom Chambers/20 15.00 40.00
46 Larry Bird/20 125.00 300.00
47 Hakeem Olajuwon/20 125.00 300.00
48 Walt Frazier/20 20.00 50.00
49 Jerry West/20 125.00 300.00
50 Elgin Baylor/25 50.00 120.00

2012-13 Panini Flawless Patches

PRINT RUNS B/WN 9-25 COPIES PER
NO PRICING ON QTY 19 OR LESS
1 Russell Westbrook/25 60.00 150.00
2 Amar'e Stoudemire/25 25.00 60.00
3 Andrei Kirilenko/25 20.00 50.00
4 David Lee/25 20.00 50.00
5 David West/25 25.00 60.00
7 Grant Hill/25 50.00 120.00
8 Alex English/25 20.00 50.00
9 LaMarcus Aldridge/25 40.00 100.00
10 Roy Hibbert/25 15.00 40.00
11 Ricky Rubio/25 60.00 150.00
12 Jason Terry/25 20.00 50.00
14 Reggie Lewis/25 75.00 200.00
15 DeMarcus Cousins/25 20.00 50.00
16 Glen Davis/25 15.00 40.00
17 Greg Monroe/25 20.00 50.00
18 Kevin Love/25 25.00 60.00
19 Magic Johnson/25 75.00 200.00
20 Tim Duncan/25 50.00 120.00
21 Ray Allen/25 40.00 100.00
22 Andre Iguodala/25 20.00 50.00
23 Blake Griffin/25 40.00 100.00
24 John Wall/25 50.00 120.00
25 Derrick Favors/25 15.00 40.00
26 Eric Gordon/21 40.00 100.00
27 James Harden/21 75.00 200.00
28 Kevin Garnett/25 125.00 300.00
30 Tony Parker/25 40.00 100.00
31 Rajon Rondo/25 50.00 120.00
32 Al Jefferson/25 15.00 40.00
33 Brandon Jennings/25 20.00 50.00
36 Dwyane Wade/25 200.00 500.00
37 Jeremy Lin/25 75.00 200.00
38 Kevin Durant/25 125.00 300.00
40 Tyreke Evans/25 20.00 50.00
41 Paul Pierce/25 60.00 150.00
42 Manu Ginobili/25 60.00 150.00
43 Carlos Boozer/25 20.00 50.00
44 Carmelo Anthony/25 60.00 150.00
45 Dirk Nowitzki/25 100.00 250.00
46 Dwight Howard/25 50.00 120.00
47 Joakim Noah/25 15.00 40.00
49 O.J. Mayo/25 20.00 50.00
50 LeBron James/25 500.00 1,000.00
52 Karl Malone/25 60.00 150.00
54 Shaquille O'Neal/22 200.00 500.00
55 David Robinson/24 60.00 150.00
56 Kevin McHale/25 30.00 80.00
58 Manute Bol/25 60.00 150.00
59 Fat Lever/24 30.00 80.00
60 Larry Bird/25 100.00 250.00
61 Gus Williams/25 20.00 50.00
62 John Stockton/25 50.00 120.00
64 Lou Hudson/23 25.00 60.00
67 Hakeem Olajuwon/25 60.00 150.00
70 Jamaal Wilkes/20 40.00 100.00
73 Patrick Ewing/25 100.00 250.00
75 Isiah Thomas/25 40.00 100.00

2012-13 Panini Flawless Patches Autographs

PRINT RUNS B/WN 15-25 COPIES PER
NO PRICING ON QTY 15
2 Kevin Durant/25 300.00 600.00
3 Grant Hill/25 100.00 250.00
4 Alex English/25 30.00 80.00
5 Hakeem Olajuwon/25 60.00 150.00
6 Hal Greer/20 40.00 100.00
7 Jason Kidd/25 60.00 150.00
9 Jeff Hornacek/25 40.00 100.00
10 Joe Dumars/25 30.00 80.00
11 Joe Johnson/25 20.00 50.00
12 LaMarcus Aldridge/25 25.00 60.00
14 Monta Ellis/25 20.00 50.00
15 Paul George/25 125.00 300.00
16 Raymond Felton/25 15.00 40.00
17 Robert Parish/25 40.00 100.00
18 Jalen Rose/25 25.00 60.00
19 Tom Chambers/25 30.00 80.00
20 Tyson Chandler/25 25.00 60.00
22 Dennis Rodman/25 150.00 400.00
23 Robert Parish/25 40.00 100.00
24 Luol Deng /25 25.00 60.00
25 Tony Parker/25 60.00 150.00
26 Deron Williams/25 25.00 60.00
27 Ron Harper/25 30.00 80.00
28 Derrick Favors/25 20.00 50.00
29 Joakim Noah/25 20.00 50.00
30 Jameer Nelson/25 20.00 50.00
31 Kenneth Faried/25 20.00 50.00
32 Chandler Parsons/25 25.00 60.00
33 Rolando Blackman/25 25.00 60.00
34 Bill Cartwright/25 25.00 60.00
35 Ty Lawson/25 15.00 40.00
39 Doc Rivers/25 20.00 50.00
40 Jeff Teague/25 25.00 60.00
41 Cazzie Russell/25 30.00 80.00
42 Rick Mahorn/25 20.00 50.00
43 Derrick Coleman/25 40.00 100.00
44 Sleepy Floyd/25 30.00 80.00
45 Buck Williams/25 30.00 80.00
48 Chris Bosh/25 40.00 100.00
49 Karl Malone/25 75.00 200.00
50 Damian Lillard/25 1,500.00 3,000.00

2012-13 Panini Flawless Rookie Autographs

STATED PRINT RUN 25 SER.#'d SETS
1 Kenneth Faried 40.00 100.00
2 Kyrie Irving 400.00 800.00
3 Anthony Davis 500.00 1,000.00
4 Iman Shumpert 30.00 80.00
5 Isaiah Thomas 50.00 120.00
6 Kemba Walker 125.00 300.00
7 Harrison Barnes 60.00 150.00
8 Austin Rivers 40.00 100.00
9 Michael Kidd-Gilchrist 30.00 80.00
10 Jared Sullinger 25.00 60.00
11 Kawhi Leonard 500.00 1,000.00
12 Nikola Vucevic 50.00 120.00
13 Bradley Beal 150.00 400.00
14 Dion Waiters 40.00 100.00
15 Andre Drummond 100.00 250.00
16 Jonas Valanciunas 40.00 100.00
17 Klay Thompson 200.00 500.00
18 Brandon Knight 30.00 80.00
19 Jimmer Fredette 25.00 60.00
20 Jimmy Butler 125.00 300.00
21 Tobias Harris 50.00 120.00
22 Tristan Thompson 40.00 100.00
23 Chandler Parsons 30.00 80.00
24 Alexey Shved 25.00 60.00
25 Damian Lillard 500.00 1,000.00

2012-13 Panini Flawless Rookie Patches

STATED PRINT RUN 25 SER.#'d SETS
1 Harrison Barnes 40.00 100.00
2 Kenneth Faried 30.00 80.00
3 Chandler Parsons 20.00 50.00
4 Damian Lillard 500.00 1,000.00
5 Klay Thompson 300.00 600.00
6 Andre Drummond 40.00 100.00
7 Jared Sullinger 20.00 50.00
8 Anthony Davis 600.00 1,200.00
9 Jonas Valanciunas 30.00 80.00
10 Michael Kidd-Gilchrist 20.00 50.00
11 Isaiah Thomas 40.00 100.00
12 Austin Rivers 30.00 80.00
13 Kawhi Leonard 600.00 1,200.00
14 John Henson 25.00 60.00
15 Iman Shumpert 30.00 80.00
16 Bradley Beal 150.00 400.00
17 Kemba Walker 150.00 400.00
18 Kyrie Irving 300.00 600.00
19 Dion Waiters 30.00 80.00
20 Brandon Knight 20.00 50.00
21 Thomas Robinson 20.00 50.00
22 Tristan Thompson 20.00 50.00
23 Jimmer Fredette 30.00 60.00
24 Kyrie Irving 300.00 600.00
25 Damian Lillard 500.00 1,000.00

2012-13 Panini Flawless Spokesmen Patches Autographs

PRINT RUNS B/WN 20-25 COPIES PER
1 Kevin Durant/25 1,000.00 2,000.00
2 Kobe Bryant/25 4,000.00 8,000.00
3 Blake Griffin/20 75.00 200.00
4 Kyrie Irving/25 1,500.00 3,000.00
5 Anthony Davis/20 1,000.00 2,000.00
6 Kevin Durant/25 1,000.00 2,000.00
7 Kobe Bryant/25 4,000.00 8,000.00
8 Blake Griffin/20 75.00 200.00
9 Kyrie Irving/25 1,000.00 2,000.00
10 Anthony Davis/20 1,500.00 3,000.00

2012-13 Panini Flawless Team Panini Autographs

STATED PRINT RUN 10 SER.#'d SETS
ALL VERSIONS EQUALLY PRICED
1 Kobe Bryant 2,000.00 4,000.00
2 Kobe Bryant 2,000.00 4,000.00
3 Kobe Bryant 2,000.00 4,000.00
4 Kobe Bryant 2,000.00 4,000.00
5 Kobe Bryant 2,000.00 4,000.00
6 Kobe Bryant 2,000.00 4,000.00
7 Kobe Bryant 2,000.00 4,000.00
8 Kobe Bryant 2,000.00 4,000.00
9 Kobe Bryant 2,000.00 4,000.00
10 Kobe Bryant 2,000.00 4,000.00
11 Kevin Durant 500.00 1,000.00
12 Kevin Durant 500.00 1,000.00
13 Kevin Durant 500.00 1,000.00
14 Kevin Durant 500.00 1,000.00
15 Kevin Durant 500.00 1,000.00
16 Kevin Durant 500.00 1,000.00
17 Kevin Durant 500.00 1,000.00
18 Kevin Durant 500.00 1,000.00
19 Kevin Durant 500.00 1,000.00
20 Kevin Durant 500.00 1,000.00
21 Blake Griffin 60.00 150.00
22 Blake Griffin 60.00 150.00
23 Blake Griffin 60.00 150.00
24 Blake Griffin 60.00 150.00
25 Blake Griffin 60.00 150.00
26 Blake Griffin 60.00 150.00
27 Blake Griffin 60.00 150.00
28 Blake Griffin 60.00 150.00
29 Blake Griffin 60.00 150.00
30 Blake Griffin 60.00 150.00
31 Kyrie Irving 400.00 800.00
32 Kyrie Irving 400.00 800.00
33 Kyrie Irving 400.00 800.00
34 Kyrie Irving 400.00 800.00
35 Kyrie Irving 400.00 800.00
36 Kyrie Irving 400.00 800.00
37 Kyrie Irving 400.00 800.00
38 Kyrie Irving 400.00 800.00
39 Kyrie Irving 400.00 800.00
40 Kyrie Irving 400.00 800.00
41 Anthony Davis 400.00 800.00
42 Anthony Davis 400.00 800.00
43 Anthony Davis 400.00 800.00
44 Anthony Davis 400.00 800.00
45 Anthony Davis 400.00 800.00
46 Anthony Davis 400.00 800.00
47 Anthony Davis 400.00 800.00
48 Anthony Davis 400.00 800.00
49 Anthony Davis 400.00 800.00
50 Anthony Davis 400.00 800.00

2012-13 Panini Flawless Team Panini Autographs Emerald

*EMERALD: .6X TO 1.5X BASIC
STATED PRINT RUN 5 SER.#'d SETS
ALL VERSIONS EQUALLY PRICED

2013-14 Panini Flawless

STATED PRINT RUN 20 SER.#'d SETS
1 Kobe Bryant 600.00 1,200.00
2A Kevin Durant 500.00 1,000.00
2B Kevin Durant MVP 500.00 1,000.00
3 Kyrie Irving 125.00 300.00
4 Blake Griffin 40.00 100.00
5 Anthony Davis 150.00 400.00
6 Carmelo Anthony 100.00 250.00
7 Dwyane Wade 150.00 400.00
8 Chris Paul 80.00 200.00
9 Russell Westbrook 60.00 150.00
10 Tim Duncan 100.00 250.00
11 Tony Parker 25.00 60.00
12 Kevin Love 40.00 100.00
13 Kevin Garnett 100.00 250.00
14 Deron Williams 30.00 80.00
15 Rajon Rondo 50.00 120.00
16 Ricky Rubio 40.00 100.00
17 Andre Drummond 40.00 100.00
18 Brandon Jennings 25.00 60.00
19 Damian Lillard 120.00 300.00
20 LaMarcus Aldridge 40.00 100.00
21 DeMarcus Cousins 40.00 100.00
22 Stephen Curry 500.00 1,000.00
23 Klay Thompson 120.00 300.00
24 Andre Iguodala 40.00 100.00
25 Pau Gasol 40.00 100.00
26 Goran Dragic 30.00 80.00
27 Eric Bledsoe 30.00 80.00
28 Dirk Nowitzki 50.00 120.00
29 Monta Ellis 30.00 80.00
30 Vince Carter 40.00 100.00
31 LeBron James 600.00 1,200.00
32 Chris Bosh 50.00 120.00
33 Arron Afflalo 25.00 60.00
34 John Wall 50.00 125.00
35 Bradley Beal 60.00 150.00
36 Marcin Gortat 25.00 60.00
37 Derrick Rose 60.00 150.00
38 Jimmy Butler 50.00 120.00
39 Joakim Noah 25.00 60.00
40 DeMar DeRozan 50.00 125.00
41 Kyle Lowry 40.00 100.00
42 Paul George 60.00 150.00
43 Roy Hibbert 25.00 60.00
44 Lance Stephenson 30.00 80.00
45 Jeremy Lin 60.00 150.00
47 James Harden 75.00 150.00
48 Marc Gasol 40.00 100.00
49 Zach Randolph 25.00 60.00
50 Tyson Chandler 40.00 100.00
51 Ty Lawson 30.00 80.00
52 Kenneth Faried 30.00 80.00
53 Gordon Hayward 40.00 100.00
54 Ray Allen 60.00 150.00
55 O.J. Mayo 40.00 100.00
56 Brandon Knight 30.00 80.00
57 Kemba Walker 40.00 100.00
58 Al Jefferson 25.00 60.00
59 Thaddeus Young 25.00 60.00
60 Al Horford 40.00 100.00
61 Paul Millsap 30.00 80.00
62 Chandler Parsons 25.00 60.00
63 Isaiah Thomas 50.00 120.00
64 Paul Pierce 60.00 150.00
65 Manu Ginobili 80.00 200.00
66 Hakeem Olajuwon 100.00 200.00
67 Arvydas Sabonis 50.00 120.00
68 Bill Walton 60.00 150.00
69 Anfernee Hardaway 100.00 250.00
70 Dominique Wilkins 40.00 100.00
71 Bill Russell 120.00 300.00
72 Tim Hardaway 50.00 120.00
73 Alonzo Mourning 50.00 125.00
74 Shaquille O'Neal 150.00 400.00
75 Karl Malone 80.00 200.00
76 Moses Malone 40.00 100.00
77 Scottie Pippen 100.00 250.00
78 Grant Hill 60.00 150.00
79 Kareem Abdul-Jabbar 100.00 250.00
80 John Stockton 50.00 120.00
81 Julius Erving 100.00 250.00
82 Dikembe Mutombo 60.00 150.00
83 Clyde Drexler 60.00 150.00
84 Wilt Chamberlain 125.00 300.00
85 Pete Maravich 60.00 150.00
86 Larry Bird 150.00 400.00
87 Magic Johnson 150.00 400.00
88 Jason Kidd 60.00 150.00
89 Oscar Robertson 60.00 150.00
90 Allen Iverson 150.00 400.00
91 Anthony Bennett RC 25.00 60.00
92 Ben McLemore RC 30.00 80.00
93 Tim Hardaway Jr. RC 50.00 125.00
94 Nerlens Noel RC 30.00 80.00
95 Dennis Schroder RC 100.00 250.00
96 C.J. McCollum RC 200.00 500.00
97A M.Carter-Williams RC 30.00 80.00
97B M.Carter-Williams ROY 30.00 80.00
98 Victor Oladipo RC 50.00 120.00
99 Giannis Antetokounmpo RC 3,000.00 6,000.00
100 Trey Burke RC 30.00 80.00

2013-14 Panini Flawless All-Star Achievements Autographs

STATED PRINT RUN 20 SER.#'D SETS
1 Kyrie Irving 150.00 400.00
2 Blake Griffin 25.00 60.00
3 Magic Johnson 125.00 300.00
4 Kobe Bryant 1,500.00 3,000.00
5 Isiah Thomas 40.00 100.00
6 Allen Iverson 150.00 400.00
8 Steve Nash 75.00 200.00
9 Kareem Abdul-Jabbar 150.00 400.00
10 Jerry West 75.00 200.00
11 Clyde Drexler 40.00 100.00
12 Julius Erving 100.00 250.00
13 Jason Kidd 40.00 100.00
14 Chris Bosh 40.00 100.00
15 Larry Bird 125.00 300.00

2013-14 Panini Flawless Autographs

PRINT RUNS B/WN 20-25 COPIES PER
1 Artis Gilmore/20 25.00 60.00
2 Kobe Bryant/25 1,500.00 3,000.00
3 Blake Griffin/25 40.00 100.00
4 Jason Kidd/20 40.00 100.00
5 Grant Hill/20 50.00 120.00
6 Anfernee Hardaway/20 60.00 150.00
7 Chris Mullin/20 25.00 60.00
8 Rick Barry/20 25.00 60.00
10 Gary Payton/20 30.00 80.00
11 Allen Iverson/20 125.00 300.00
12 John Havlicek/20 75.00 200.00
13 David Robinson/20 75.00 200.00
14 Bill Russell/25 1,500.00 3,000.00
15 Kareem Abdul-Jabbar/25 125.00 300.00
16 Julius Erving/25 75.00 200.00
18 Dennis Rodman/20 75.00 200.00
19 John Wall/25 60.00 150.00
20 Chris Bosh/20 40.00 100.00
21 Tony Parker/20 40.00 100.00
22 Vince Carter/20 75.00 200.00
24 Deron Williams/20 15.00 40.00
25 Joakim Noah/20 20.00 50.00
26 Chris Andersen/20 40.00 100.00
28 Josh Smith/20 12.00 30.00
29 Manu Ginobili/25 40.00 100.00
30 Mark Aguirre/20 15.00 40.00
31 Jose Calderon/20 12.00 30.00
32 Oscar Robertson/20 75.00 200.00
33 Eric Gordon/20 12.00 30.00
34 Goran Dragic/20 15.00 40.00
35 Marcin Gortat/20 12.00 30.00
36 Harrison Barnes/20 20.00 50.00
37 Dwyane Wade/25 125.00 300.00
38 Baron Davis/20 12.00 30.00
39 George Gervin/20 20.00 50.00
40 Christian Laettner/20 20.00 50.00
41 Kevin Love/25 20.00 50.00
42 Horace Grant/20 20.00 50.00
43 Byron Scott/20 20.00 50.00
44 Robert Horry/20 20.00 50.00
45 Carmelo Anthony/25 40.00 100.00
46 Jerry West/25 40.00 100.00
47 Nick Anderson/20 15.00 40.00
48 Wes Unseld/20 40.00 100.00
51 Chris Webber/25 125.00 300.00

2013-14 Panini Flawless Franchise Greats Autographs

STATED PRINT RUN 20 SER.#'D SETS
1 Larry Bird 125.00 300.00
2 Dominique Wilkins 30.00 80.00
3 Alex English 20.00 50.00
4 Isiah Thomas 40.00 100.00
5 Hakeem Olajuwon 75.00 200.00
6 Kobe Bryant 1,000.00 2,000.00
7 Gary Payton 30.00 80.00
8 Walt Frazier 25.00 60.00
9 Karl Malone 40.00 100.00
10 Manu Ginobili 40.00 100.00
11 Bob McAdoo 25.00 60.00
12 Terry Porter 15.00 40.00
13 Allen Iverson 125.00 300.00
14 Dick Van Arsdale 15.00 40.00
15 George Gervin 25.00 60.00
16 Blake Griffin 40.00 100.00
17 Baron Davis 12.00 30.00
18 Dwyane Wade 75.00 200.00
19 John Wall 40.00 100.00
20 Stephen Curry 600.00 1,200.00
21 Oscar Robertson 60.00 150.00

2013-14 Panini Flawless Greats Dual Memorabilia Autographs

STATED PRINT RUN 25 SER.#'d SETS
1 David Robinson 75.00 200.00
2 Glen Rice 40.00 100.00
3 Isiah Thomas 125.00 300.00
4 Bill Laimbeer 75.00 200.00
5 Kevin Love 30.00 80.00
6 Larry Johnson 40.00 100.00
7 Steve Nash 125.00 300.00
8 Dwyane Wade 600.00 1,200.00
9 Deron Williams 25.00 60.00
11 Kobe Bryant 5,000.00 10,000.00
12 Kevin Durant 1,000.00 2,000.00
13 Anthony Davis 600.00 1,200.00
14 Carmelo Anthony 400.00 800.00
15 Kyrie Irving 500.00 1,000.00
16 John Wall 75.00 200.00
17 Grant Hill 100.00 250.00
18 John Stockton 125.00 300.00
19 Shaquille O'Neal 1,000.00 2,000.00
20 Tracy McGrady 300.00 600.00
21 Manu Ginobili 300.00 600.00
22 Blake Griffin 75.00 200.00
23 Tony Parker 100.00 250.00
GRPG Paul George 300.00 600.00

2013-14 Panini Flawless Hall of Fame Autographs Memorabilia

STATED PRINT RUN 25 SER.#'d SETS
1 Larry Bird 150.00 400.00
2 Dominique Wilkins 50.00 120.00
3 David Robinson 125.00 300.00
5 Karl Malone 100.00 250.00
6 Gary Payton 50.00 120.00
7 Hakeem Olajuwon 125.00 300.00
8 Alex English 30.00 80.00
9 Clyde Drexler 75.00 200.00
10 Chris Mullin 40.00 100.00
11 Dennis Rodman 125.00 300.00
12 Magic Johnson 150.00 400.00
13 Gail Goodrich 25.00 60.00
14 Kareem Abdul-Jabbar 200.00 500.00
15 Bob Lanier 30.00 80.00
16 Joe Dumars 30.00 80.00
17 John Stockton 75.00 200.00
18 Kevin McHale 40.00 100.00
19 Isiah Thomas 75.00 200.00
20 Artis Gilmore 30.00 80.00

2013-14 Panini Flawless NBA Signatures

PRINT RUNS B/WN 20-25 COPIES PER
1 Dwyane Wade 150.00 400.00
3 Blake Griffin 40.00 100.00
4 Gordon Hayward 12.00 30.00
6 Carmelo Anthony 60.00 150.00
7 John Havlicek 75.00 200.00
8 Manu Ginobili 75.00 200.00
9 Kevin McHale 25.00 60.00
10 LaMarcus Aldridge 20.00 50.00
11 Connie Hawkins 15.00 40.00
12 Andre Drummond 30.00 80.00
13 Stephen Curry 600.00 1,200.00
14 Mark Aguirre 15.00 40.00
15 Alex English 20.00 50.00
16 Chris Bosh 40.00 100.00
17 Tony Parker 40.00 100.00
18 Anthony Davis 125.00 300.00
19 Artis Gilmore 25.00 60.00
21 Allen Iverson 125.00 300.00
22 Bradley Beal 40.00 100.00
23 Tim Hardaway 25.00 60.00
25 Marcin Gortat 12.00 30.00
26 John Wall 40.00 100.00
27 Andrea Bargnani 12.00 30.00
29 Baron Davis 15.00 40.00
30 Chris Mullin 25.00 60.00
32 Oscar Robertson 75.00 200.00
33 Jon McGlocklin 12.00 30.00
35 Jose Calderon 12.00 30.00
36 Glen Rice 15.00 40.00
37 Byron Scott 12.00 30.00
38 Elgin Baylor 40.00 100.00
39 J.R. Smith 20.00 50.00
40 Mark Jackson 30.00 80.00
41 Sean Elliott 20.00 50.00
42 David Robinson 75.00 200.00
43 Shaquille O'Neal 200.00 500.00
44 James Worthy 40.00 100.00
45 Anfernee Hardaway 75.00 200.00
46 Gary Payton 40.00 100.00
47 Christian Laettner 12.00 30.00
48 Grant Hill 60.00 150.00
49 Vince Carter 40.00 100.00
50 Kevin Love 20.00 50.00
51 Chris Webber 100.00 250.00

2013-14 Panini Flawless Patch Autographs

PRINT RUNS B/WN 20-25 COPIES PER
2 Fred Brown/25 20.00 50.00
3 Rick Barry/25 30.00 80.00
5 Mark Price/25 25.00 60.00
7 Bradley Beal/25 75.00 200.00
8 Josh Smith/25 15.00 40.00
9 LaMarcus Aldridge/25 60.00 150.00
10 Zach Randolph/25 20.00 50.00
11 Tyson Chandler/25 20.00 50.00
12 Kawhi Leonard/25 500.00 1,000.00
13 Jose Calderon/25 15.00 40.00
14 Vince Carter/25 60.00 150.00
15 Ty Lawson/25 15.00 40.00
16 Goran Dragic/25 20.00 50.00
17 Dwyane Wade/25 400.00 800.00
18 Robert Horry/25 25.00 60.00
19 Nick Anderson/25 20.00 50.00
20 Kyle Lowry/25 25.00 60.00
23 John Wall/25 60.00 150.00
24 Allen Iverson/25 300.00 600.00
25 Joakim Noah/25 25.00 60.00
26 Gordon Hayward/25 40.00 100.00
28 Al Horford/25 25.00 60.00
29 Harrison Barnes/25 30.00 80.00
30 Andre Drummond/25 25.00 60.00
31 Carmelo Anthony/25 75.00 200.00
33 Dikembe Mutombo/25 40.00 100.00
34 Grant Hill/25 60.00 150.00
35 Jason Kidd/25 60.00 150.00
36 Manu Ginobili/25 150.00 400.00
37 Kemba Walker/25 25.00 60.00
38 Mark Jackson/25 20.00 50.00
39 Nikola Vucevic/25 30.00 80.00
40 J.R. Smith/25 25.00 60.00
41 Anfernee Hardaway/25 100.00 250.00
42 Eric Gordon/25 20.00 50.00
43 Tyreke Evans/25 20.00 50.00
45 Andrei Kirilenko/25 25.00 60.00
46 Anthony Davis/20 500.00 1,000.00
47 Kobe Bryant/25 1,500.00 3,000.00
48 Kevin Durant/25 800.00 1,500.00
49 Kyrie Irving/20 400.00 800.00
50 Kevin Martin/25 15.00 40.00
51 Kevin Love/25 50.00 120.00
52 Jrue Holiday/25 25.00 60.00
53 Stephen Curry/25 1,500.00 3,000.00
54 Dominique Wilkins/25 50.00 120.00
55 Kenneth Faried/25 20.00 50.00
56 Chris Webber/25 200.00 500.00
PAPG Paul George/25 200.00 500.00

2013-14 Panini Flawless Patches

PRINT RUNS B/WN 9-25 COPIES PER
NO PRICING ON QTY 15 OR LESS
1 Louie Dampier/25 12.00 30.00
2 LeBron James/25 400.00 800.00
3 Kawhi Leonard/25 125.00 300.00
4 James Harden/25 100.00 250.00
5 Kevin Durant/20 200.00 500.00
7 Vince Carter/20 100.00 250.00
8 Tyson Chandler/25 15.00 40.00
9 Jimmy Butler/25 60.00 150.00
10 Russell Westbrook/25 75.00 200.00
11 Ricky Rubio/20 15.00 40.00
13 Rajon Rondo/25 40.00 100.00
14 Paul George/25 75.00 200.00
15 Patrick Ewing/25 75.00 200.00
16 Monta Ellis/25 15.00 40.00
17 Harrison Barnes/25 20.00 50.00
18 LaMarcus Aldridge/25 30.00 80.00
20 Kyrie Irving/20 125.00 300.00
21 Paul Millsap/20 15.00 40.00
22 Kevin Garnett/20 60.00 150.00
23 Kenneth Faried/25 15.00 40.00
24 Kevin Love/25 20.00 50.00
25 Jrue Holiday/20 25.00 60.00
26 Josh Smith/20 12.00 30.00
27 Jonas Valanciunas/25 15.00 40.00
28 John Wall/20 40.00 100.00
29 Joe Johnson/25 15.00 40.00
30 Eric Bledsoe/25 15.00 40.00
31 Damian Lillard/25 100.00 250.00
32 Nicolas Batum/25 15.00 40.00
33 Brandon Knight/25 15.00 40.00
34 Goran Dragic/20 15.00 40.00
35 Dwight Howard/25 50.00 120.00
36 Chris Paul/25 60.00 150.00
37 Pau Gasol/25 40.00 100.00
38 Dennis Johnson/20 40.00 100.00
39 Kevin McHale/20 40.00 100.00
40 Michael Finley/25 20.00 50.00
41 Chandler Parsons/25 12.00 30.00
42 Stephen Curry/25 400.00 800.00
43 Kobe Bryant/20 400.00 800.00
44 Karl Malone/25 60.00 150.00
45 Kareem Abdul-Jabbar/25 125.00 300.00
46 Larry Bird/25 100.00 250.00
47 DeMar DeRozan/25 30.00 80.00
48 Dwyane Wade/25 100.00 250.00
49 Zach Randolph/25 15.00 40.00
51 Andre Iguodala/25 25.00 60.00
52 Ty Lawson/25 12.00 30.00
53 Bradley Beal/25 30.00 80.00
54 Klay Thompson/20 100.00 250.00
55 Joakim Noah/25 20.00 50.00
56 Blake Griffin/25 40.00 100.00
57 Paul Pierce/25 60.00 150.00
58 Dirk Nowitzki/25 60.00 150.00
59 Andre Drummond/25 20.00 50.00
60 Jeremy Lin/25 60.00 150.00
61 Hakeem Olajuwon/25 60.00 150.00
62 Ray Allen/25 60.00 150.00
63 Tim Duncan/25 60.00 150.00
64 Anthony Davis/25 75.00 150.00
65 Gordon Hayward/25 15.00 40.00
66 Serge Ibaka/25 15.00 40.00
67 O.J. Mayo/25 12.00 30.00
68 DeMarcus Cousins/20 20.00 50.00
69 Kemba Walker/20 20.00 50.00
70 David Robinson/25 60.00 150.00
71 Scottie Pippen/25 150.00 400.00
72 John Stockton/25 60.00 150.00
73 Jason Kidd/25 40.00 100.00
74 James Worthy/25 40.00 100.00
75 Allen Iverson/25 125.00 300.00
76 Larry Johnson/25 40.00 100.00
77 Arron Afflalo/25 12.00 30.00
78 Shawn Kemp/25 60.00 150.00
79 John Starks/20 40.00 100.00
80 Charles Oakley/20 25.00 60.00
81 Joe Dumars/20 25.00 60.00
82 Shawn Bradley/25 12.00 30.00
83 Shawn Marion/20 15.00 40.00
84 Pat Riley/20 40.00 100.00
85 Alex English/20 25.00 60.00
86 LeBron James/25 400.00 800.00

2013-14 Panini Flawless Retired Numbers Autographs

STATED PRINT RUN 20 SER.#'d SETS
1 Dominique Wilkins 25.00 60.00
4 John Havlicek 75.00 200.00
5 Don Nelson 40.00 100.00
6 Karl Malone 60.00 150.00
7 Jason Kidd 40.00 100.00
8 Julius Erving 75.00 200.00
9 Zydrunas Ilgauskas 12.00 30.00
10 Alex English 12.00 30.00
11 David Thompson 15.00 40.00
12 Bob Lanier 20.00 50.00
13 Bill Laimbeer 25.00 60.00
14 Rick Barry 25.00 60.00
16 Clyde Drexler 60.00 150.00
17 Hakeem Olajuwon 75.00 200.00
18 Gail Goodrich 12.00 30.00
19 Jamaal Wilkes 12.00 30.00
20 Jerry West 40.00 100.00
21 Kareem Abdul-Jabbar 125.00 300.00
23 Oscar Robertson 75.00 200.00
24 Walt Frazier 25.00 60.00
26 Bobby Jones 12.00 30.00
27 Dan Majerle 12.00 30.00
28 Connie Hawkins 20.00 50.00
29 Dick Van Arsdale 12.00 30.00
30 Bill Walton 25.00 60.00
31 Terry Porter 15.00 40.00
32 John Stockton 60.00 150.00
34 Avery Johnson 12.00 30.00
35 Sean Elliott 20.00 50.00
37 Spencer Haywood 15.00 40.00
38 Fred Brown 12.00 30.00
39 George Gervin 20.00 50.00
40 Jeff Hornacek 12.00 30.00

2013-14 Panini Flawless Rookie Autographs

STATED PRINT RUN 20 SER.#'d SETS
1 Anthony Bennett 12.00 30.00
2 Victor Oladipo 100.00 250.00
3 Trey Burke 15.00 40.00
4 Tim Hardaway Jr. 25.00 60.00
5 Giannis Antetokounmpo 3,000.00 6,000.00
6 Nerlens Noel 15.00 40.00
7 Ben McLemore 15.00 40.00
8 C.J. McCollum 150.00 400.00
9 Michael Carter-Williams 15.00 40.00
10 Steven Adams 50.00 120.00

2013-14 Panini Flawless Rookie Patches

STATED PRINT RUN 25 SER.#'d SETS
1 Victor Oladipo 30.00 80.00
2 Kelly Olynyk 15.00 40.00
3 Anthony Bennett 12.00 30.00
4 Tim Hardaway Jr. 25.00 60.00
5 C.J. McCollum 50.00 120.00
6 Ben McLemore 15.00 40.00
7 Trey Burke 15.00 40.00
8 Steven Adams 30.00 80.00
9 Tony Snell 15.00 40.00
10 Michael Carter-Williams 15.00 40.00
11 Reggie Bullock 15.00 40.00
12 Gorgui Dieng 15.00 40.00
13 Dennis Schroder 40.00 100.00
14 Cody Zeller 15.00 40.00
15 Otto Porter 20.00 50.00

2013-14 Panini Flawless Super Signatures

PRINT RUNS B/WN 20-25 COPIES PER
2 Kobe Bryant/25 4,000.00 8,000.00
3 Kevin Durant/25 600.00 1,200.00
4 Kyrie Irving/25 150.00 400.00
6 John Wall/25 60.00 150.00
7 Blake Griffin/25 40.00 100.00
8 Anthony Davis/25 150.00 400.00
9 Karl Malone/20 100.00 250.00
10 Kareem Abdul-Jabbar/20 200.00 500.00
12 Bill Russell/25 1,500.00 3,000.00
13 Magic Johnson/25 200.00 500.00

14 Larry Bird/25 200.00 500.00
15 Julius Erving/25 150.00 400.00
16 Oscar Robertson/25 125.00 300.00
17 Chris Webber/25 150.00 400.00

2013-14 Panini Flawless Team Panini Autographs

STATED PRINT RUN 10 SER.#'D SETS
ALL VERSIONS EQUALLY PRICED
*EMERALD/5: .5X TO 1.2X BASIC
1 Kyrie Irving 150.00 400.00
6 Kobe Bryant 1,500.00 3,000.00
11 Kevin Durant 400.00 800.00
16 Anthony Davis 150.00 400.00
21 Trey Burke 25.00 60.00
26 Victor Oladipo 75.00 200.00
31 Michael Carter-Williams 25.00 60.00

2013-14 Panini Flawless Transitions Autographs

STATED PRINT RUN 10 SER.#'D SETS
ALL VERSIONS EQUALLY PRICED
*EMERALD/5: .5X TO 1.2X BASIC
TM1 Tracy McGrady 100.00 250.00
SO1 Shaquille O'Neal 150.00 400.00
JE1 Julius Erving 75.00 200.00
TH1 Tim Hardaway 25.00 60.00
DM1 Dikembe Mutombo 50.00 120.00
CW1 Chris Webber 150.00 400.00

2015-16 Panini Flawless

1-150 PRINT RUN 20 SER.#'d SETS
151-170 PRINT RUN 10 SER.#'d SETS
NO PRICING AVAILABLE ON 151-170
1 Kobe Bryant 400.00 800.00
2 Kevin Durant 60.00 150.00
3 Kyrie Irving 30.00 80.00
4 Jimmy Butler 30.00 80.00
5 Damian Lillard 40.00 100.00
6 Dirk Nowitzki 40.00 100.00
7 Eric Bledsoe 12.00 30.00
8 Brandon Knight 10.00 25.00
9 Dwyane Wade 30.00 80.00
10 Chris Bosh 20.00 50.00
11 Paul George 25.00 60.00
12 Monta Ellis 12.00 30.00
13 Russell Westbrook 25.00 60.00
14 Anthony Davis 40.00 100.00
15 Gordon Hayward 15.00 40.00
16 Kemba Walker 15.00 40.00
17 Nicolas Batum 10.00 25.00
18 Lance Stephenson 12.00 30.00
19 LeBron James 400.00 800.00
20 Kevin Love 15.00 40.00
21 Stephen Curry 300.00 600.00
22 Klay Thompson 40.00 100.00
23 Draymond Green 20.00 50.00
24 Kenneth Faried 12.00 30.00
25 James Harden 30.00 80.00
26 Dwight Howard 20.00 50.00
27 Giannis Antetokounmpo 125.00 300.00
28 Jabari Parker 10.00 25.00
29 Chris Paul 30.00 80.00
30 Blake Griffin 15.00 40.00
31 Paul Pierce 25.00 60.00
32 DeMar DeRozan 20.00 50.00
33 Kyle Lowry 15.00 40.00
34 Tim Duncan 40.00 100.00
35 Manu Ginobili 30.00 80.00
36 Tony Parker 25.00 60.00
37 LaMarcus Aldridge 15.00 40.00
38 Jrue Holiday 20.00 50.00
39 Marc Gasol 15.00 40.00
40 Mike Conley 15.00 40.00
41 C.J. McCollum 15.00 40.00
42 Andrew Wiggins 20.00 50.00
43 Zach LaVine 40.00 100.00
44 Greg Monroe 12.00 30.00
45 Carmelo Anthony 75.00 200.00
46 Goran Dragic 15.00 40.00
47 John Wall 20.00 50.00
48 Bradley Beal 20.00 50.00
49 Marcin Gortat 10.00 25.00
50 Brook Lopez 15.00 40.00
51 Thaddeus Young 10.00 25.00
52 Rudy Gobert 20.00 50.00
53 Allen Crabbe 10.00 25.00
54 Al Horford 15.00 40.00
55 Dennis Schroder 15.00 40.00
56 Jeff Teague 10.00 25.00
57 Jeremy Lin 30.00 80.00
58 Derrick Rose 75.00 200.00
59 Pau Gasol 25.00 60.00
60 Hassan Whiteside 10.00 25.00
61 Deron Williams 12.00 30.00
62 Wesley Matthews 10.00 25.00
63 J.R. Smith 15.00 40.00
64 Will Barton 10.00 25.00
65 Danilo Gallinari 12.00 30.00
66 Reggie Jackson 12.00 30.00
67 Andre Drummond 15.00 40.00
68 Kentavious Caldwell-Pope 12.00 30.00
69 Harrison Barnes 12.00 30.00
70 J.J. Redick 15.00 40.00
71 DeAndre Jordan 12.00 30.00
72 Jordan Clarkson 15.00 40.00
73 Lou Williams 12.00 30.00
74 Khris Middleton 20.00 50.00
75 Kevin Garnett 40.00 100.00
76 Ryan Anderson 10.00 25.00
77 Enes Kanter 10.00 25.00
78 Isaiah Thomas 12.00 30.00
79 Avery Bradley 10.00 25.00
80 Jae Crowder 10.00 25.00
81 Arron Afflalo 10.00 25.00
82 Robin Lopez 10.00 25.00
83 Nikola Vucevic 12.00 30.00
84 Victor Oladipo 12.00 30.00
85 Elfrid Payton 12.00 30.00
86 Aaron Gordon 15.00 40.00
87 Ish Smith 10.00 25.00
88 Nerlens Noel 10.00 25.00
89 Rajon Rondo 20.00 50.00
90 DeMarcus Cousins 15.00 40.00
91 Rudy Gay 15.00 40.00
92 DeMarre Carroll 10.00 25.00
93 Rodney Hood 12.00 30.00
94 Alec Burks 10.00 25.00
95 Paul Millsap 12.00 30.00
96 Evan Turner 10.00 25.00
97 Al Jefferson 10.00 25.00
98 Nikola Mirotic 10.00 25.00
99 Doug McDermott 12.00 30.00
100 Tobias Harris 12.00 30.00
101 Trevor Ariza 10.00 25.00
102 Alex Len 10.00 25.00
103 Chandler Parsons 10.00 25.00
104 Zaza Pachulia 10.00 25.00
105 George Hill 12.00 30.00
106 Omri Casspi 10.00 25.00
107 Tristan Thompson 10.00 25.00
108 Zach Randolph 15.00 40.00
109 Norris Cole 10.00 25.00
110 Bojan Bogdanovic 12.00 30.00
111 Dion Waiters 10.00 25.00
112 Serge Ibaka 12.00 30.00
113 Matthew Dellavedova 12.00 30.00
114 Andre Iguodala 15.00 40.00
115 Andrew Bogut 12.00 30.00
116 Kawhi Leonard 50.00 125.00
117 Ricky Rubio 12.00 30.00
118 Patrick Beverley 10.00 25.00
119 Gerald Henderson 10.00 25.00
120 Otto Porter 12.00 30.00
121 Jonas Valanciunas 12.00 30.00
122 Marcus Morris 10.00 25.00
123 Austin Rivers 12.00 30.00
124 Danny Green 12.00 30.00
125 Vince Carter 30.00 80.00
126 Scottie Pippen 40.00 100.00
127 Larry Bird 60.00 150.00
128 Magic Johnson 60.00 150.00
129 Wilt Chamberlain 60.00 150.00
130 Patrick Ewing 25.00 60.00
131 Oscar Robertson 40.00 100.00
132 Shaquille O'Neal 50.00 125.00
133 John Stockton 30.00 80.00
134 Julius Erving 40.00 100.00
135 Pete Maravich 40.00 100.00
136 Karl-Anthony Towns RC 50.00 125.00
137 D'Angelo Russell RC 30.00 80.00
138 Jahlil Okafor RC 10.00 25.00
139 Kristaps Porzingis RC 50.00 125.00
140 Justise Winslow RC 12.00 30.00
141 Devin Booker RC 400.00 800.00
142 Emmanuel Mudiay RC 10.00 25.00
143 Myles Turner RC 30.00 80.00
144 Bobby Portis RC 20.00 50.00
145 Nikola Jokic RC 1,500.00 3,000.00
146 Willie Cauley-Stein RC 10.00 25.00
147 Mario Hezonja RC 10.00 25.00
148 Cameron Payne RC 12.00 30.00
149 Stanley Johnson RC 10.00 25.00
150 Stephen Curry MVP 300.00 600.00

2015-16 Panini Flawless Ruby

*RUBY 1-135/150: .4X TO 1X BASIC
*RUBY 136-149: .4X TO 1X BASIC
STATED PRINT RUN 15 SER.#'d SETS

2015-16 Panini Flawless Dual Diamond Memorabilia

PRINT RUNS B/WN 16-25 COPIES PER
NO PRICING ON QTY 12 OR LESS
2 Towns/Porzingis/25 75.00 200.00
5 Durant/Westbrook/25 125.00 300.00
7 Leonard/Duncan/25 200.00 500.00
8 McCollum/Lillard/25 60.00 150.00
9 Ellis/George/25 25.00 60.00
10 Cousins/Rondo/25 20.00 50.00
13 Beal/Wall/16 30.00 80.00
15 Love/Westbrook/25 40.00 100.00
16 Russell/Clarkson/25 25.00 60.00
17 Paul/Duncan/25 100.00 250.00
18 Wiggins/Towns/25 60.00 150.00
19 Bird/Johnson/25 400.00 800.00

2015-16 Panini Flawless Dual Diamond Memorabilia Ruby

*RUBY: .4X TO 1X BASIC
PRINT RUNS B/WN 12-15 COPIES PER
NO PRICING ON QTY 14 OR LESS
1 Thompson/Curry/15 400.00 800.00
12 Williams/Nowitzki/15 40.00 100.00

2015-16 Panini Flawless Dual Patch Autographs

STATED PRINT RUN 16-25 SER.#'d SETS
DPAAD Anthony Davis 150.00 400.00
DPAAW Andrew Wiggins 75.00 200.00
DPABG Blake Griffin 75.00 200.00
DPACM C.J. McCollum 50.00 120.00
DPACW Chris Webber 125.00 300.00
DPADC DeMarre Carroll 15.00 40.00
DPADH Dwight Howard 100.00 250.00
DPADR David Robinson 150.00 400.00
DPAGH Grant Hill 100.00 250.00
DPAGP Gary Payton 125.00 300.00
DPAHW Hassan Whiteside 20.00 50.00
DPAJB Jimmy Butler 100.00 250.00
DPAJG Jerian Grant 15.00 40.00
DPAJM Jamal Mashburn 20.00 50.00
DPAJP Jabari Parker 15.00 40.00
DPAJR Julius Randle 60.00 150.00
DPAJS John Stockton 125.00 300.00
DPAJV Jonas Valanciunas 20.00 50.00
DPAJV Gary Harris 20.00 50.00
DPAJW John Wall 30.00 80.00
DPAKB Kobe Bryant 2,500.00 5,000.00
DPAKD Kevin Durant 500.00 1,000.00
DPAKI Kyrie Irving 400.00 800.00
DPAKL Kevin Love 40.00 100.00
DPAKM Khris Middleton 60.00 150.00
DPAKP Kristaps Porzingis 125.00 300.00
DPAKT Klay Thompson 150.00 400.00
DPALB Larry Bird 400.00 800.00
DPAMC Michael Carter-Williams 15.00 40.00
DPAMC Mike Conley 25.00 60.00
DPAMP Mark Price 25.00 60.00
DPAMS Marcus Smart 30.00 80.00
DPAPG Pau Gasol 100.00 250.00
DPAPM Paul Millsap 20.00 50.00
DPAWC Willie Cauley-Stein 20.00 50.00
DPAZL Zach LaVine 100.00 250.00

2015-16 Panini Flawless Flawless Autographs

STATED PRINT RUN 25 SER.#'D SETS
*RUBY/15: .4X TO 1X BASIC
FAAA Alvan Adams 8.00 20.00
FAAB Alec Burks 8.00 20.00
FAAB Andrew Bogut 10.00 25.00
FAAH Anfernee Hardaway 100.00 250.00
FAAW Andrew Wiggins 15.00 40.00
FABG Blake Griffin 20.00 50.00
FABK Brandon Knight 8.00 20.00
FABW Bill Walton 60.00 150.00
FACA Carmelo Anthony 100.00 250.00
FACD Clyde Drexler 40.00 100.00
FACM Cedric Maxwell 10.00 25.00
FACP Chris Paul 125.00 300.00
FADC Dell Curry 10.00 25.00
FADD DeMar DeRozan 40.00 100.00
FADH Dwight Howard 40.00 100.00
FADR David Robinson 75.00 200.00
FADR Dennis Rodman 100.00 250.00
FADS Dennis Scott 8.00 20.00
FADT David Thompson 15.00 40.00
FADW Dwyane Wade 100.00 250.00
FAEB Eric Bledsoe 10.00 25.00
FAET Evan Turner 8.00 20.00
FAGG George Gervin 40.00 100.00
FAGH Grant Hill 40.00 100.00
FAGH Gordon Hayward 12.00 30.00
FAGP Gary Payton 30.00 80.00
FAHO Hakeem Olajuwon 75.00 200.00
FAHW Hassan Whiteside 10.00 25.00
FAIT Isiah Thomas 40.00 100.00
FAJB Jimmy Butler 50.00 120.00
FAJB Junior Bridgeman 8.00 20.00
FAJD Joe Dumars 25.00 60.00
FAJK Jason Kidd 40.00 100.00
FAJM Jamal Mashburn 10.00 25.00
FAJR Jalen Rose 10.00 25.00
FAJS John Stockton 75.00 200.00
FAJS Jerry Stackhouse 12.00 30.00
FAJW James Worthy 30.00 80.00
FAJW Jerry West 100.00 250.00
FAJW John Wall 15.00 40.00
FAKB Kobe Bryant 2,000.00 4,000.00
FAKD Kevin Durant 150.00 400.00
FAKI Kyrie Irving 100.00 250.00
FAKL Kevin Love 12.00 30.00
FAKM Karl Malone 75.00 200.00
FAKM Khris Middleton 15.00 40.00
FALA LaMarcus Aldridge 12.00 30.00
FALB Larry Bird 200.00 500.00
FAMD Matthew Dellavedova 10.00 25.00
FAMJ Magic Johnson 150.00 400.00
FAMJ Marques Johnson 10.00 25.00
FAMR Mitch Richmond 25.00 60.00
FAPE Patrick Ewing 150.00 400.00
FAPG Pau Gasol 40.00 100.00
FARA Ray Allen 100.00 250.00
FARH Robert Horry 25.00 60.00
FASP Scottie Pippen 125.00 300.00
FATH Tim Hardaway 25.00 60.00
FATK Toni Kukoc 40.00 100.00
FATW T.J. Warren 12.00 30.00
FAVO Victor Oladipo 10.00 25.00

2015-16 Panini Flawless Greats Dual Memorabilia Autographs

STATED PRINT RUN 18-25 SER.#'d SETS
GRCD Clyde Drexler/18 200.00 500.00
GRDR David Robinson/25 200.00 500.00
GRGH Grant Hill/25 125.00 300.00
GRHO Hakeem Olajuwon/25 200.00 500.00
GRJK Jason Kidd/18 150.00 400.00
GRJS John Stockton/25 150.00 400.00
GRKB Kobe Bryant/25 4,000.00 8,000.00
GRKD Kevin Durant/25 2,000.00 4,000.00
GRKM Karl Malone/25 200.00 500.00
GRMJ Magic Johnson/18 400.00 800.00
GRPG Pau Gasol/25 125.00 300.00
GRSC Stephen Curry/25 3,000.00 6,000.00

2015-16 Panini Flawless Now and Then Signatures

STATED PRINT RUN 25 SER.#'D SETS
*RUBY/15: .4X TO 1X BASIC
NTAB Avery Bradley 10.00 25.00
NTAB Andrew Bogut 12.00 30.00
NTAW Andrew Wiggins 60.00 150.00
NTBK Brandon Knight 10.00 25.00
NTDD DeMar DeRozan 100.00 250.00
NTDH Dwight Howard 125.00 300.00
NTDW Dwyane Wade 200.00 500.00
NTEB Eric Bledsoe 12.00 30.00
NTEP Elfrid Payton 12.00 30.00
NTET Evan Turner 10.00 25.00
NTHW Hassan Whiteside 12.00 30.00
NTJB Jimmy Butler 125.00 300.00
NTJP Jabari Parker 10.00 25.00
NTJR Julius Randle 60.00 150.00
NTJS Josh Smith 10.00 25.00
NTJS J.R. Smith 15.00 40.00
NTKB Kobe Bryant 2,000.00 4,000.00
NTKI Kyrie Irving 300.00 600.00
NTKL Kevin Love 15.00 40.00
NTLA LaMarcus Aldridge 15.00 40.00
NTMC Michael Carter-Williams 10.00 25.00
NTVO Victor Oladipo 12.00 30.00
NTZL Zach LaVine 150.00 400.00
NTZR Zach Randolph 15.00 40.00

2015-16 Panini Flawless Now and Then Signatures Ruby

*RUBY: .4X TO 1X BASIC
STATED PRINT RUN 15 SER.#'d SETS
NTAW Andrew Wiggins 60.00 150.00
NTDW Dwyane Wade 200.00 500.00
NTJB Jimmy Butler 125.00 300.00
NTJR Julius Randle 60.00 150.00
NTKB Kobe Bryant 2,000.00 4,000.00
NTKI Kyrie Irving 300.00 600.00
NTZL Zach LaVine 150.00 400.00

2015-16 Panini Flawless Patches

PRINT RUNS B/WN 10-25 COPIES PER
NO PRICING ON QTY 12 OR LESS
3 Kevin Durant/25 300.00 600.00
4 Grant Hill/17 60.00 150.00
5 DeAndre Jordan/25 10.00 25.00
6 Marcus Smart/23 15.00 40.00
9 Andre Drummond/12 12.00 30.00
10 Goran Dragic/21 12.00 30.00
11 Jeremy Lin/25 125.00 300.00
12 Kyle Lowry/23 40.00 100.00
13 Dwyane Wade/25 125.00 300.00
15 Damian Lillard/25 125.00 300.00
16 LeBron James/25 500.00 1,000.00
17 Isaiah Thomas/25 10.00 25.00
18 DeMarcus Cousins/25 12.00 30.00
19 Vince Carter/25 125.00 300.00
22 Harrison Barnes/23 10.00 25.00
23 Blake Griffin/19 50.00 120.00
24 O.J. Mayo/25 8.00 20.00
27 T.J. Warren/25 12.00 30.00
28 Al Jefferson/25 8.00 20.00
29 Anthony Davis/25 125.00 300.00
30 Kyrie Irving/25 125.00 300.00
31 Pau Gasol/24 50.00 120.00
32 Derrick Rose/25 125.00 300.00
33 Jimmy Butler/25 75.00 200.00
34 Rudy Gobert/25 40.00 100.00
35 Stephen Curry/23 500.00 1,000.00
36 Russell Westbrook/25 125.00 300.00
39 Aaron Gordon/25 40.00 100.00
41 Jabari Parker/25 8.00 20.00

2015-16 Panini Flawless Patches Ruby

*RUBY: .4X TO 1X BASIC
PRINT RUNS B/WN 8-15 COPIES PER
NO PRICING ON QTY 14 OR LESS
7 Marcus Morris/15 8.00 20.00
8 Reggie Jackson/15 10.00 25.00
14 Kevin Love/15 12.00 30.00
20 James Harden/15 125.00 300.00
21 Mike Conley/15 12.00 30.00
37 Rodney Hood/15 10.00 25.00
42 Tyson Chandler/15 10.00 25.00

2015-16 Panini Flawless Premium Ink

STATED PRINT RUN 25 SER.#'D SETS
*RUBY/15: .4X TO 1X BASIC
PIAA Alvan Adams 8.00 20.00
PIAB Avery Bradley 8.00 20.00
PIAB Alec Burks 8.00 20.00
PIAD Anthony Davis 100.00 250.00
PIAH Al Horford 20.00 50.00
PIAI Allen Iverson 150.00 400.00
PIAM Antonio McDyess 10.00 25.00
PIAW Andrew Wiggins 15.00 40.00
PIBG Blake Griffin 12.00 30.00
PIBK Brandon Knight 8.00 20.00
PIBK Bernard King 15.00 40.00
PIBM Boban Marjanovic 50.00 120.00
PIBP Bobby Portis 20.00 50.00
PIBW Bill Walton 60.00 150.00
PICA Carmelo Anthony 100.00 250.00
PICB Chauncey Billups 25.00 60.00
PICB Chris Bosh 20.00 50.00
PICD Clyde Drexler 40.00 100.00
PICM Cedric Maxwell 10.00 25.00
PICP Cameron Payne 12.00 30.00
PICP Chris Paul 125.00 300.00
PIDB Devin Booker 600.00 1,200.00
PIDC Dell Curry 10.00 25.00
PIDC DeMarre Carroll 8.00 20.00
PIDG Danilo Gallinari 10.00 25.00
PIDG Draymond Green 40.00 100.00
PIDH Dwight Howard 30.00 80.00
PIDM Dan Majerle 12.00 30.00
PIDM Dikembe Mutombo 60.00 150.00
PIDR D'Angelo Russell 75.00 200.00
PIDR David Robinson 75.00 200.00
PIDR Dennis Rodman 100.00 250.00
PIDT David Thompson 15.00 40.00
PIDW Dwyane Wade 100.00 250.00
PIEB Eric Bledsoe 10.00 25.00
PIEH Elvin Hayes 20.00 50.00
PIEM Emmanuel Mudiay 10.00 25.00
PIGG George Gervin 40.00 100.00
PIGH Gordon Hayward 12.00 30.00
PIGH Grant Hill 40.00 100.00
PIGP Gary Payton 25.00 60.00
PIHG Horace Grant 40.00 100.00
PIHO Hakeem Olajuwon 75.00 200.00
PIHW Hassan Whiteside 10.00 25.00
PIIT Isiah Thomas 40.00 100.00
PIJB Jimmy Butler 30.00 80.00
PIJD Joe Dumars 15.00 40.00
PIJE Julius Erving 100.00 250.00
PIJK Jason Kidd 40.00 100.00
PIJM Jamal Mashburn 10.00 25.00
PIJO Jahlil Okafor 10.00 25.00
PIJR Jalen Rose 10.00 25.00
PIJR Julius Randle 15.00 40.00
PIJS J.R. Smith 40.00 100.00
PIJS John Stockton 75.00 200.00
PIJS John Starks 20.00 50.00
PIJS Jerry Stackhouse 12.00 30.00
PIJW Jerry West 100.00 250.00
PIJW Justise Winslow 12.00 30.00
PIJW James Worthy 20.00 50.00
PIKB Kobe Bryant 2,000.00 4,000.00
PIKD Kevin Durant 150.00 400.00
PIKF Kenneth Faried 10.00 25.00
PIKI Kyrie Irving 100.00 250.00
PIKL Kevin Love 12.00 30.00
PIKM Karl Malone 75.00 200.00
PIKP Kristaps Porzingis 125.00 300.00
PIKT Klay Thompson 125.00 300.00
PIKT Karl-Anthony Towns 125.00 300.00
PILA LaMarcus Aldridge 12.00 30.00
PILB Larry Bird 200.00 500.00
PIMD Matthew Dellavedova 10.00 25.00
PIMH Mario Hezonja 10.00 25.00
PIMJ Magic Johnson 150.00 400.00
PIMJ Marques Johnson 10.00 25.00
PIMR Mitch Richmond 15.00 40.00
PIMS Marcus Smart 15.00 40.00
PIMT Myles Turner 30.00 80.00
PINJ Nikola Jokic 4,000.00 8,000.00
PIPE Patrick Ewing 150.00 400.00
PIPG Pau Gasol 50.00 120.00
PIRA Ray Allen 100.00 250.00
PIRH Robert Horry 25.00 60.00
PISC Stephen Curry 1,000.00 2,000.00
PISP Scottie Pippen 100.00 250.00
PITH Tim Hardaway 25.00 60.00
PITK Toni Kukoc 40.00 100.00
PITL Trey Lyles 10.00 25.00
PITM Tracy McGrady 100.00 250.00
PIVO Victor Oladipo 10.00 25.00
PIWC Willie Cauley-Stein 10.00 25.00
PIZL Zach LaVine 60.00 150.00

2015-16 Panini Flawless Rookie Autographs

STATED PRINT RUN 25 SER.#'D SETS
*RUBY/15: .4X TO 1X BASIC
RABM Boban Marjanovic 25.00 60.00
RABP Bobby Portis 20.00 50.00
RACP Cameron Payne 12.00 30.00
RADB Devin Booker 800.00 1,500.00
RADR D'Angelo Russell 100.00 250.00
RAEM Emmanuel Mudiay 10.00 25.00
RAJO Jahlil Okafor 10.00 25.00
RAJW Justise Winslow 12.00 30.00
RAKP Kristaps Porzingis 150.00 400.00
RAKT Karl-Anthony Towns 150.00 400.00
RAMH Mario Hezonja 10.00 25.00
RAMT Myles Turner 30.00 80.00
RANJ Nikola Jokic 4,000.00 8,000.00
RATL Trey Lyles 10.00 25.00
RAWC Willie Cauley-Stein 6.00 15.00

2015-16 Panini Flawless Rookie Patches

PRINT RUNS B/WN 22-25 COPIES PER
1 Delon Wright/22 8.00 20.00
2 Jahlil Okafor/25 8.00 20.00
3 T.J. McConnell/25 25.00 60.00
4 Richaun Holmes/25 10.00 25.00
5 D'Angelo Russell/25 25.00 60.00
6 Karl-Anthony Towns/25 100.00 250.00
7 Mario Hezonja/25 8.00 20.00
9 Emmanuel Mudiay/25 8.00 20.00
10 Kelly Oubre Jr./25 20.00 50.00
11 Frank Kaminsky/25 8.00 20.00
13 Willie Cauley-Stein/25 8.00 20.00
14 Myles Turner/25 25.00 60.00
16 Stanley Johnson/25 8.00 20.00

2015-16 Panini Flawless Rookie Patches Ruby

*RUBY: .4X TO 1X BASIC
STATED PRINT RUN 15 SER.#'d SETS
8 Justise Winslow 10.00 25.00
15 Montrezl Harrell 20.00 50.00

2015-16 Panini Flawless Super Signatures

STATED PRINT RUN 25 SER.#'D SETS
*RUBY/15: .4X TO 1X BASIC
SSAB Andrew Bogut 12.00 30.00
SSAB Alec Burks 10.00 25.00
SSAD Anthony Davis 100.00 250.00
SSAH Al Horford 15.00 40.00
SSAH Anfernee Hardaway 75.00 200.00
SSAI Allen Iverson 125.00 300.00
SSBG Blake Griffin 20.00 50.00
SSBK Bernard King 20.00 50.00
SSBM Boban Marjanovic 20.00 50.00
SSBP Bobby Portis 20.00 50.00
SSCA Carmelo Anthony 100.00 250.00
SSCB Chris Bosh 20.00 50.00
SSCD Clyde Drexler 40.00 100.00
SSCP Chris Paul 125.00 300.00
SSCW Chris Webber 75.00 200.00
SSDB Devin Booker 1,000.00 2,000.00
SSDC DeMarre Carroll 10.00 25.00
SSDD DeMar DeRozan 40.00 100.00
SSDM Doug McDermott 12.00 30.00
SSDM Dan Majerle 15.00 40.00
SSDM Dikembe Mutombo 40.00 100.00
SSDR David Robinson 60.00 150.00
SSDR D'Angelo Russell 40.00 100.00
SSDS Dennis Scott 10.00 25.00
SSDW Dwyane Wade 100.00 250.00
SSEH Elvin Hayes 25.00 60.00
SSEP Elfrid Payton 12.00 30.00
SSGA Giannis Antetokounmpo 200.00 500.00
SSGH Grant Hill 40.00 100.00
SSGH Gary Harris 12.00 30.00
SSGH Gordon Hayward 15.00 40.00
SSGP Gary Payton 40.00 100.00
SSHO Hakeem Olajuwon 60.00 150.00
SSHW Hassan Whiteside 12.00 30.00
SSIT Isiah Thomas 40.00 100.00
SSJB Jimmy Butler 50.00 120.00
SSJD Joe Dumars 15.00 40.00
SSJE Julius Erving 60.00 150.00
SSJK Jason Kidd 40.00 100.00
SSJO Jahlil Okafor 12.00 30.00
SSJR Jalen Rose 12.00 30.00
SSJR Julius Randle 20.00 50.00
SSJS John Stockton 60.00 150.00
SSJS John Starks 15.00 40.00
SSJV Jonas Valanciunas 12.00 30.00
SSJW James Worthy 40.00 100.00
SSJW Jerry West 100.00 250.00
SSKB Kobe Bryant 1,500.00 3,000.00
SSKD Kevin Durant 125.00 300.00
SSKI Kyrie Irving 100.00 250.00
SSKL Kevin Love 15.00 40.00
SSKM Karl Malone 60.00 150.00
SSKM Khris Middleton 20.00 50.00
SSKP Kristaps Porzingis 100.00 250.00
SSKT Karl-Anthony Towns 75.00 200.00
SSKT Klay Thompson 100.00 250.00
SSKV Keith Van Horn 12.00 30.00
SSLA LaMarcus Aldridge 15.00 40.00
SSLB Larry Bird 125.00 300.00
SSMC Michael Carter-Williams 10.00 25.00
SSMC Mike Conley 15.00 40.00
SSMD Matthew Dellavedova 12.00 30.00
SSMG Marc Gasol 20.00 50.00
SSMJ Magic Johnson 125.00 300.00
SSMJ Marques Johnson 12.00 30.00
SSMR Mitch Richmond 20.00 50.00
SSPG Pau Gasol 40.00 100.00
SSPM Paul Millsap 12.00 30.00
SSRA Ray Allen 100.00 250.00
SSRH Robert Horry 20.00 50.00
SSSC Stephen Curry 1,000.00 2,000.00
SSSP Scottie Pippen 125.00 300.00
SSTH Tim Hardaway 20.00 50.00
SSTM Tracy McGrady 100.00 250.00
SSVO Victor Oladipo 12.00 30.00

2015-16 Panini Flawless Transitions Autographs

STATED PRINT RUN 25 SER.#'D SETS
ALL VERSIONS EQUALLY PRICED
TRAB Andrew Bogut 20.00 50.00
TRAB Andrew Bogut 20.00 50.00
TRAB Andrew Bogut 20.00 50.00
TRAM Antonio McDyess 12.00 30.00
TRAM Antonio McDyess 12.00 30.00
TRAM Antonio McDyess 12.00 30.00
TRAM Antonio McDyess 12.00 30.00
TRAM Antonio McDyess 12.00 30.00
TRAM Antonio McDyess 12.00 30.00
TRBK Brandon Knight 10.00 25.00
TRBK Brandon Knight 10.00 25.00
TRBK Brandon Knight 10.00 25.00
TRBK Brandon Knight 10.00 25.00
TRCB Chauncey Billups 40.00 100.00
TRCB Chauncey Billups 40.00 100.00
TRCB Chauncey Billups 40.00 100.00
TRCB Chauncey Billups 40.00 100.00
TRCB Chauncey Billups 40.00 100.00
TRCB Chauncey Billups 40.00 100.00
TRCB Chauncey Billups 40.00 100.00
TRCB Chauncey Billups 40.00 100.00
TRCB Chauncey Billups 40.00 100.00
TRDH Dwight Howard 40.00 100.00
TRDH Dwight Howard 40.00 100.00
TRDH Dwight Howard 40.00 100.00
TREB Eric Bledsoe 12.00 30.00
TREB Eric Bledsoe 12.00 30.00
TREB Eric Bledsoe 12.00 30.00
TREH Elvin Hayes 25.00 60.00
TREH Elvin Hayes 25.00 60.00
TREH Elvin Hayes 25.00 60.00
TRET Evan Turner 10.00 25.00
TRET Evan Turner 10.00 25.00
TRET Evan Turner 10.00 25.00
TRET Evan Turner 10.00 25.00
TRHG Horace Grant 40.00 100.00
TRHG Horace Grant 40.00 100.00
TRHG Horace Grant 40.00 100.00
TRHG Horace Grant 40.00 100.00
TRHW Hassan Whiteside 12.00 30.00
TRHW Hassan Whiteside 12.00 30.00
TRHW Hassan Whiteside 12.00 30.00
TRJM Jamal Mashburn 12.00 30.00
TRJM Jamal Mashburn 12.00 30.00
TRJM Jamal Mashburn 12.00 30.00
TRJM Jamal Mashburn 12.00 30.00
TRJM Jamal Mashburn 12.00 30.00
TRKB Kobe Bryant 2,000.00 4,000.00
TRKB Kobe Bryant 2,000.00 4,000.00
TRKB Kobe Bryant 2,000.00 4,000.00
TRKB Kobe Bryant 2,000.00 4,000.00
TRKI Kyrie Irving 300.00 600.00
TRKI Kyrie Irving 300.00 600.00
TRKI Kyrie Irving 300.00 600.00
TRKM Khris Middleton 20.00 50.00
TRKM Khris Middleton 20.00 50.00
TRKM Khris Middleton 20.00 50.00
TRKV Keith Van Horn 12.00 30.00
TRKV Keith Van Horn 12.00 30.00
TRKV Keith Van Horn 12.00 30.00
TRKV Keith Van Horn 12.00 30.00
TRKV Keith Van Horn 12.00 30.00
TRLA LaMarcus Aldridge 20.00 50.00
TRLA LaMarcus Aldridge 20.00 50.00
TRLA LaMarcus Aldridge 20.00 50.00
TRPE2 Patrick Ewing 125.00 300.00
TRPE Patrick Ewing 125.00 300.00
TRPE4 Patrick Ewing 125.00 300.00
TRPE3 Patrick Ewing 125.00 300.00
TRSC Stephen Curry 1,000.00 2,000.00
TRSC Stephen Curry 1,000.00 2,000.00
TRSC Stephen Curry 1,000.00 2,000.00
TRSP Scottie Pippen 125.00 300.00
TRSP Scottie Pippen 125.00 300.00
TRSP Scottie Pippen 125.00 300.00
TRSP Scottie Pippen 125.00 300.00
TRSP Scottie Pippen 125.00 300.00
TRTK Toni Kukoc 40.00 100.00
TRTK Toni Kukoc 40.00 100.00
TRTK Toni Kukoc 40.00 100.00
TRTK Toni Kukoc 40.00 100.00

2016-17 Panini Flawless Momentous Patch Autographs

COMMON CARD 10.00 25.00
SEMISTARS 12.00 30.00
UNLISTED STARS 15.00 40.00
STATED PRINT RUN 10-25 SER.#'D SETS
1 Harrison Barnes/25 12.00 30.00
2 Joel Embiid/25 400.00 800.00
3 Buddy Hield/25 30.00 80.00
5 John Wall/25 60.00 150.00
6 Damian Lillard/25 100.00 250.00
7 Dwyane Wade/25 100.00 250.00
10 Julius Randle/16 40.00 100.00
11 Chris Paul/25 100.00 250.00
13 Dario Saric/25 15.00 40.00
15 Brandon Ingram/25 800.00 1,500.00
16 Nikola Jokic/23 500.00 1,000.00
17 Dirk Nowitzki/25 400.00 800.00
18 Marc Gasol/25 15.00 40.00
19 Carmelo Anthony/25 100.00 250.00
20 Kyrie Irving/25 100.00 250.00
21 D'Angelo Russell/25 40.00 100.00
26 Jamal Murray/25 800.00 1,500.00
28 Rudy Gay/25 15.00 40.00
29 Pau Gasol/16 30.00 80.00
30 Ricky Rubio/20 25.00 60.00
31 Tony Parker/25 75.00 200.00
32 Vince Carter/25 150.00 400.00
33 Tim Hardaway Jr./24 12.00 30.00
34 C.J. McCollum/25 75.00 200.00
35 Eric Gordon/20 12.00 30.00
36 Khris Middleton/22 15.00 40.00
37 Justise Winslow/25 12.00 30.00
41 Myles Turner/25 100.00 250.00
45 Allen Iverson/18 500.00 1,000.00
46 Jordan Clarkson/25 40.00 100.00
50 David Robinson/25 125.00 300.00
55 Grant Hill/25 75.00 200.00
57 Bojan Bogdanovic/25 12.00 30.00
58 Thon Maker/25 12.00 30.00
59 Domantas Sabonis/25 60.00 150.00
60 Willy Hernangomez/25 12.00 30.00

2017-18 Panini Flawless Momentous Autographs

COMMON CARD 8.00 20.00
SEMISTARS 10.00 25.00
UNLISTED STARS 12.00 30.00
STATED PRINT RUN 25 SER.#'D SETS
*RUBY/15: .4X TO 1X BASIC
1 Bill Russell 400.00 800.00
2 Allen Iverson 150.00 400.00
3 Magic Johnson 200.00 500.00
4 John Stockton 100.00 250.00
5 Kareem Abdul-Jabbar 200.00 500.00
6 Oscar Robertson 100.00 250.00
7 Alonzo Mourning 75.00 200.00
8 Hakeem Olajuwon 100.00 250.00
9 Tracy McGrady 150.00 400.00
10 Kevin McHale 40.00 100.00
11 Jason Kidd 75.00 200.00
12 Dennis Rodman 125.00 300.00
13 Anfernee Hardaway 125.00 300.00
14 Gary Payton 75.00 200.00
15 Grant Hill 75.00 200.00
16 James Worthy 40.00 100.00
17 Rick Barry 40.00 100.00
18 Bob Lanier 40.00 100.00
19 Sam Jones 40.00 100.00
20 Kyrie Irving 125.00 300.00
21 Damian Lillard 100.00 250.00
22 Isaiah Thomas 20.00 50.00
23 Gordon Hayward 10.00 25.00
24 Paul Pierce 75.00 200.00
25 Kristaps Porzingis 40.00 100.00
26 Myles Turner 12.00 30.00
27 Dwyane Wade 100.00 250.00
28 Joel Embiid 150.00 400.00
29 Giannis Antetokounmpo 400.00 800.00
30 Jrue Holiday 30.00 80.00
31 Domantas Sabonis 40.00 100.00
32 Al Horford 25.00 60.00
33 Dirk Nowitzki 300.00 600.00
34 Harrison Barnes 10.00 25.00
35 Brandon Ingram 100.00 250.00
36 Jeremy Lin 150.00 400.00
37 Steve Kerr 40.00 100.00
38 Richard Hamilton 40.00 100.00
39 Bernard King 15.00 40.00
40 Artis Gilmore 15.00 40.00
41 George Gervin 40.00 100.00
42 Walt Frazier 40.00 100.00
43 Calvin Murphy 12.00 30.00
44 Elvin Hayes 15.00 40.00
45 Nate Archibald 15.00 40.00
46 Gail Goodrich 12.00 30.00
47 Lenny Wilkens 15.00 40.00
48 Glen Rice 10.00 25.00
49 Antawn Jamison 10.00 25.00
50 Clint Capela 10.00 25.00
51 Trevor Ariza 8.00 20.00
52 JR Smith 25.00 60.00
53 Rudy Gay 10.00 25.00
54 Kobe Bryant 2,000.00 4,000.00
55 Charles Barkley 150.00 400.00
56 Kurt Thomas 8.00 20.00
57 Mike Bibby 20.00 50.00
58 Jason Williams 100.00 250.00
59 Eric Snow 8.00 20.00
60 Jamal Mashburn 20.00 50.00

2020-21 Panini Flux Deja Vu

*SILVER: 1.25X TO 3X BASIC
*BLUE/99: 2.5X TO 6X BASIC
1 Charles Barkley
Zion Williamson 1.50 4.00
2 Carmelo Anthony
LaMelo Ball 3.00 8.00
3 Deni Avdija
Hedo Turkoglu 1.00 2.50
4 Anthony Davis
Tim Duncan 1.25 3.00
5 Magic Johnson
Russell Westbrook 2.00 5.00
6 Isiah Thomas
Ja Morant 1.50 4.00
7 Shai Gilgeous-Alexander
Tyrese Haliburton 3.00 8.00
8 Anthony Edwards
Dwyane Wade 4.00 10.00
9 Bam Adebayo
Onyeka Okongwu .75 2.00
10 Christian Wood
Obi Toppin .75 2.00
11 Brandon Ingram
Devin Vassell 1.25 3.00
12 Khris Middleton
Saddiq Bey .75 2.00
13 Aaron Nesmith
Klay Thompson 1.25 3.00
14 Cole Anthony
Steve Francis 1.00 2.50
15 Damian Lillard
Darius Garland 1.25 3.00
16 Stephen Curry
Trae Young 4.00 10.00
17 LeBron James
Luka Doncic 15.00 40.00
18 Deandre Ayton
James Wiseman .50 1.25
19 D'Angelo Russell
Killian Hayes .50 1.25
20 Ben Wallace
Isaiah Stewart .75 2.00
21 Anfernee Hardaway
RJ Barrett 1.25 3.00
22 Devin Booker
Tyler Herro 1.25 3.00
23 Jimmy Butler
Keldon Johnson 1.00 2.50
24 De'Andre Hunter

Pascal Siakam .75 2.00
25 Goran Dragic
Nico Mannion .50 1.25
26 Collin Sexton
Tyrese Maxey 3.00 8.00
27 Immanuel Quickley
Tony Parker 1.00 2.50
28 Michael Porter Jr
Paul George .75 2.00
29 Kawhi Leonard
Kevin Durant 2.00 5.00
30 Allen Iverson
Kyrie Irving 1.25 3.00
31 De'Aaron Fox
John Wall .75 2.00
32 James Harden
Paul Pierce 1.00 2.50
33 Giannis Antetokounmpo
Kevin Garnett 2.50 6.00
34 Karl-Anthony Towns
LaMarcus Aldridge .75 2.00
35 Josh Green
Patty Mills .75 2.00
36 OG Anunoby
Patrick Williams 1.00 2.50
37 Aleksej Pokusevski
Detlef Schrempf .50 1.25
38 Jalen Smith
James Worthy .75 2.00
39 Desmond Bane
Malcolm Brogdon 1.25 3.00
40 Fred VanVleet
Malachi Flynn .75 2.00

2020-21 Panini Flux Exosphere

COMPLETE SET (5)
96 LeBron James 40.00 100.00
97 Luka Doncic 30.00 80.00
98 Stephen Curry 40.00 100.00
99 Giannis Antetokounmpo 30.00 80.00
100 LaMelo Ball 40.00 100.00

2022-23 Panini Flux

COMPLETE SET (250)
*RED: .75X TO 2X BASIC
*RED CRACKED ICE: .75X TO 2X BASIC
*SILVER: .75X TO 2X BASIC
*SILVER MOJO: 1X TO 2.5X BASIC
*MOONLIGHT: 1.25X TO 3X BASIC
*SUNRISE: 1.25X TO 3X BASIC
*BLUE/99: 2X TO 5X BASIC
*RED MOJO/99: 2X TO 5X BASIC
*SUPERNOVA/75: 2.5X TO 6X BASIC
1 Khris Middleton .50 1.25
2 Bobby Portis .40 1.00
3 Cameron Johnson .30 .75
4 Aaron Gordon .40 1.00
5 Scottie Barnes .60 1.50
6 Dorian Finney-Smith .30 .75
7 Deni Avdija .40 1.00
8 Nikola Vucevic .40 1.00
9 Jarred Vanderbilt .30 .75
10 Immanuel Quickley .40 1.00
11 Cole Anthony .40 1.00
12 Franz Wagner 1.00 2.50
13 Darius Garland .60 1.50
14 James Harden .75 2.00
15 Bam Adebayo .60 1.50
16 Dejounte Murray .50 1.25
17 Joel Embiid .60 1.50
18 Jimmy Butler .75 2.00
19 RJ Barrett .60 1.50
20 Tyrese Haliburton .75 2.00
21 Markelle Fultz .30 .75
22 Zach LaVine .75 2.00
23 Cameron Thomas .60 1.50
24 Bradley Beal .50 1.25
25 Kevin Love .40 1.00
26 Max Strus .40 1.00
27 Jalen Suggs .50 1.25
28 Kelly Oubre Jr. .40 1.00
29 Jalen McDaniels .40 1.00
30 Marvin Bagley III .30 .75
31 Tobias Harris .30 .75
32 Buddy Hield .40 1.00
33 Isaac Okoro .30 .75
34 De'Andre Hunter .40 1.00
35 Bol Bol .40 1.00
36 Ben Simmons .40 1.00
37 Tyler Herro .60 1.50
38 Monte Morris .25 .60
39 Lonnie Walker IV .30 .75
40 Robert Williams III .30 .75
41 LaMelo Ball 1.00 2.50
42 Dwight Powell .25 .60
43 James Wiseman .30 .75
44 Gary Trent Jr. .40 1.00
45 Bruce Brown .40 1.00
46 Karl-Anthony Towns .60 1.50
47 Pascal Siakam .60 1.50
48 Naji Marshall .40 1.00
49 Quentin Grimes .30 .75
50 Kyle Lowry .50 1.25
51 Myles Turner .40 1.00
52 Ayo Dosunmu .50 1.25
53 Patrick Williams .40 1.00
54 John Collins .40 1.00
55 Nikola Jokic 2.00 5.00
56 Jarrett Allen .40 1.00
57 Kyle Kuzma .50 1.25
58 Donovan Mitchell .75 2.00
59 Terry Rozier III .50 1.25
60 Kristaps Porzingis .50 1.25
61 Jakob Poeltl .30 .75
62 Jaylen Brown .75 2.00
63 Grayson Allen .40 1.00
64 Jrue Holiday .50 1.25
65 Jamal Murray .60 1.50
66 Gordon Hayward .30 .75
67 Coby White .30 .75
68 DeMar DeRozan .50 1.25
69 Mike Conley .30 .75
70 Tyrese Maxey .75 2.00
71 Al Horford .40 1.00
72 Mikal Bridges .50 1.25
73 Bogdan Bogdanovic .40 1.00
74 Malcolm Brogdon .30 .75
75 De'Anthony Melton .30 .75
76 Aaron Nesmith .40 1.00
77 Julius Randle .50 1.25
78 Brook Lopez .40 1.00
79 Jayson Tatum 1.50 4.00
80 Trae Young 1.00 2.50
81 Fred VanVleet .50 1.25
82 Caris LeVert .30 .75
83 Rudy Gobert .50 1.25
84 OG Anunoby .50 1.25
85 Marcus Smart .50 1.25
86 Wendell Carter Jr. .40 1.00
87 Evan Mobley 1.00 2.50
88 Michael Porter Jr. .50 1.25
89 Saddiq Bey .30 .75
90 Spencer Dinwiddie .30 .75
91 Kentavious Caldwell-Pope .30 .75
92 Corey Kispert .40 1.00
93 Cade Cunningham 1.25 3.00
94 Anthony Edwards 2.00 5.00
95 Bojan Bogdanovic .40 1.00
96 Jalen Brunson .75 2.00
97 Jalen Smith .40 1.00
98 Giannis Antetokounmpo 2.00 5.00
99 PJ Washington Jr. .40 1.00
100 Josh Hart .40 1.00
101 LeBron James 3.00 8.00
102 Tre Jones .40 1.00
103 Jonas Valanciunas .30 .75
104 Josh Giddey .60 1.50
105 Luka Doncic 2.50 6.00
106 Maxi Kleber .30 .75
107 Tyus Jones .30 .75
108 Domantas Sabonis .50 1.25
109 Brandon Ingram .50 1.25
110 Keldon Johnson .50 1.25
111 Harrison Barnes .30 .75
112 Russell Westbrook .60 1.50
113 Devonte' Graham .30 .75
114 Malik Monk .40 1.00
115 Zion Williamson 1.00 2.50
116 Dillon Brooks .40 1.00
117 Josh Green .40 1.00
118 Jerami Grant .50 1.25
119 Kelly Olynyk .30 .75
120 Trey Murphy III .50 1.25
121 Tre Mann .30 .75
122 Jaylen Nowell .40 1.00
123 Reggie Bullock .30 .75
124 Terance Mann .30 .75
125 Kevin Porter Jr. .30 .75
126 Devin Vassell .50 1.25
127 Norman Powell .40 1.00
128 Marcus Morris Sr. .25 .60
129 Jae'Sean Tate .25 .60
130 Luke Kennard .30 .75
131 D'Angelo Russell .30 .75
132 Talen Horton-Tucker .30 .75
133 Obi Toppin .40 1.00
134 Damian Lillard 1.00 2.50
135 Alex Caruso .40 1.00
136 Steven Adams .40 1.00
137 Alperen Sengun .50 1.25
138 T.J. Warren .30 .75
139 Anthony Davis 1.00 2.50
140 Kevin Durant 1.25 3.00
141 CJ McCollum .40 1.00
142 Kyrie Irving .75 2.00
143 Devin Booker 1.00 2.50
144 Moses Moody .50 1.25
145 Deandre Ayton .40 1.00
146 Donte DiVincenzo .40 1.00
147 Stephen Curry 3.00 8.00
148 Nicolas Claxton .40 1.00
149 Andrew Wiggins .50 1.25
150 Anfernee Simons .50 1.25
151 Tim Hardaway Jr. .30 .75
152 Jalen Green 1.25 3.00
153 Mitchell Robinson .40 1.00
154 Shai Gilgeous-Alexander 2.00 5.00
155 Christian Wood .25 .60
156 Kevin Huerter .40 1.00
157 Jaren Jackson Jr. .60 1.50
158 Chris Paul .75 2.00
159 Ja Morant 1.25 3.00
160 Desmond Bane .50 1.25
161 Josh Richardson .30 .75
162 Dennis Smith Jr. .30 .75
163 Klay Thompson 1.00 2.50
164 Naz Reid .30 .75
165 Davion Mitchell .40 1.00
166 Derrick White .40 1.00
167 Malik Beasley .30 .75
168 Draymond Green .50 1.25
169 De'Aaron Fox .75 2.00
170 Seth Curry .30 .75
171 Jordan Poole .60 1.50
172 Lauri Markkanen .60 1.50
173 Pat Connaughton .30 .75
174 Kawhi Leonard 1.00 2.50
175 Luguentz Dort .40 1.00
176 Jonathan Kuminga 1.00 2.50
177 Matisse Thybulle .30 .75
178 Doug McDermott .25 .60
179 Killian Hayes .25 .60
180 Rui Hachimura .40 1.00
181 Kenyon Martin Jr. .40 1.00
182 Cam Reddish .30 .75
183 Torrey Craig .25 .60
184 Bones Hyland .40 1.00
185 Joe Harris .30 .75
186 Jose Alvarado .40 1.00
187 Mo Bamba .30 .75
188 Josh Christopher .25 .60
189 Jaden McDaniels .40 1.00
190 Santi Aldama .40 1.00
191 Cameron Payne .30 .75
192 Dennis Schroder .40 1.00
193 Collin Sexton .50 1.25
194 Jordan Clarkson .40 1.00
195 Paul George .60 1.50
196 Eric Gordon .30 .75
197 Herbert Jones .40 1.00
198 Onyeka Okongwu .40 1.00
199 Jusuf Nurkic .40 1.00
200 Austin Reaves 1.00 2.50
201 Jabari Smith Jr. RC 2.00 5.00
202 Johnny Davis RC .60 1.50
203 Kennedy Chandler RC .60 1.50
204 Tyrese Martin RC .50 1.25
205 Jeremy Sochan RC 2.00 5.00
206 Christian Braun RC 1.50 4.00
207 Shaedon Sharpe RC 2.50 6.00
208 Jabari Walker RC .50 1.25
209 Dyson Daniels RC 1.50 4.00
210 Bryce McGowens RC .60 1.50
211 Max Christie RC 1.50 4.00
212 Bennedict Mathurin RC 2.00 5.00
213 Simone Fontecchio RC .60 1.50
214 Jaden Ivey RC 2.00 5.00
215 Jaylin Williams RC .75 2.00
216 Nikola Jovic RC 1.25 3.00
217 Julian Champagnie RC .75 2.00
218 Peyton Watson RC 1.00 2.50
219 Malaki Branham RC .60 1.50
220 Wendell Moore Jr. RC .60 1.50
221 Blake Wesley RC .60 1.50
222 Caleb Houstan RC .60 1.50
223 Moussa Diabate RC .60 1.50
224 Jalen Williams RC 3.00 8.00
225 Kevon Harris RC .50 1.25
226 Jalen Duren RC 2.00 5.00
227 Jaden Hardy RC 1.00 2.50
228 Keegan Murray RC 1.50 4.00
229 A.J. Green RC .75 2.00
230 Orlando Robinson RC .50 1.25
231 AJ Griffin RC .50 1.25
232 MarJon Beauchamp RC .60 1.50
233 Ousmane Dieng RC .75 2.00
234 Kenneth Lofton Jr. RC .75 2.00
235 Dalen Terry RC .60 1.50
236 Mark Williams RC 1.25 3.00
237 Paolo Banchero RC 4.00 10.00
238 David Roddy RC .75 2.00
239 Ryan Rollins RC .60 1.50
240 Johnny Juzang RC .75 2.00
241 Christian Koloko RC .60 1.50
242 Jake LaRavia RC .60 1.50
243 Chet Holmgren RC 3.00 8.00
244 Andrew Nembhard RC 1.25 3.00
245 Ochai Agbaji RC .75 2.00
246 Patrick Baldwin Jr. RC .60 1.50
247 TyTy Washington Jr. RC .60 1.50
248 Josh Minott RC .60 1.50
249 Tari Eason RC 1.50 4.00
250 Walker Kessler RC 1.25 3.00

2022-23 Panini Flux Blue Cracked Ice

COMPLETE SET (250)
*BLUE CRACKED ICE: 5X TO 12X BASIC
STATED PRINT RUN 25 SER.#'d SETS
237 Paolo Banchero 75.00 200.00
243 Chet Holmgren 100.00 250.00

2022-23 Panini Flux Blue Mojo

COMPLETE SET (250)
*BLUE MOJO: 5X TO 12X BASIC
STATED PRINT RUN 25 SER.#'d SETS
237 Paolo Banchero 75.00 200.00
243 Chet Holmgren 100.00 250.00

2022-23 Panini Flux Lunar Eclipse

COMPLETE SET (250)
*LUNAR ECLIPSE: 5X TO 12X BASIC
STATED PRINT RUN 25 SER.#'d SETS
237 Paolo Banchero 75.00 200.00
243 Chet Holmgren 100.00 250.00

2022-23 Panini Flux Solar Eclipse

COMPLETE SET (250)
*SOLAR ECLIPSE: 3X TO 8X BASIC
STATED PRINT RUN 49 SER.#'d SETS
237 Paolo Banchero 40.00 100.00
243 Chet Holmgren 50.00 120.00

2022-23 Panini Flux Autograph Influx

COMPLETE SET (27)
*RED/49: .6X TO 1.5X BASIC
1 Norman Powell 5.00 12.00
2 Lauri Markkanen 8.00 20.00
3 Gabe Vincent 5.00 12.00
5 James Worthy 8.00 20.00
6 Franz Wagner 12.00 30.00
7 Charles Barkley 50.00 120.00
8 Antawn Jamison 5.00 12.00
9 Bones Hyland 4.00 10.00
10 Jalen Green 40.00 100.00
11 Bobby Portis 5.00 12.00
12 Paolo Banchero 75.00 200.00
13 Keegan Murray 12.00 30.00
14 Bennedict Mathurin 15.00 40.00
15 Jalen Williams 25.00 60.00
16 Cade Cunningham 40.00 100.00
17 Manu Ginobili 30.00 80.00
18 Christian Laettner 5.00 12.00
19 Walker Kessler 10.00 25.00
21 Ralph Sampson 4.00 10.00
22 George McGinnis 5.00 12.00
23 Austin Reaves 40.00 100.00
25 Boban Marjanovic 10.00 25.00
26 Clyde Drexler 25.00 60.00
27 Buddy Hield 5.00 12.00
28 Davion Mitchell 4.00 10.00
29 Deni Avdija 5.00 12.00
30 Bogdan Bogdanovic 5.00 12.00

2022-23 Panini Flux Best of the Best Signatures

*RED/49: .6X TO 1.5X BASIC
1 Luka Doncic 200.00 500.00
2 Tyrese Haliburton 50.00 120.00
3 Kevin Garnett 40.00 100.00
4 Nikola Jokic 50.00 120.00
5 Allen Iverson 40.00 100.00
6 Anthony Edwards 50.00 120.00
7 Carmelo Anthony 40.00 100.00
8 Kareem Abdul-Jabbar 40.00 100.00
9 Karl Malone 25.00 60.00
10 James Harden 40.00 100.00

2022-23 Panini Flux D Lux

COMPLETE SET (20)
*SILVER: .75X TO 2X BASIC
*SILVER MOJO: .75X TO 2X BASIC
1 Giannis Antetokounmpo 2.50 6.00
2 Jaren Jackson Jr. .75 2.00
3 Jarrett Allen .50 1.25
4 Nicolas Claxton .50 1.25
5 Marcus Smart .60 1.50
6 Joel Embiid .75 2.00
7 Bam Adebayo .75 2.00
8 Jayson Tatum 2.00 5.00
9 Jimmy Butler 1.00 2.50
10 Rudy Gobert .60 1.50
11 Mikal Bridges .60 1.50
12 Paul George .75 2.00
13 Evan Mobley 1.25 3.00
14 Jrue Holiday .60 1.50
15 Donovan Mitchell 1.00 2.50
16 Deandre Ayton .50 1.25
17 Derrick White .50 1.25
18 Anthony Davis 1.25 3.00
19 Nikola Jokic 2.50 6.00
20 Brook Lopez .50 1.25

2022-23 Panini Flux Equinox Autographs

COMPLETE SET (96)
*RED/35: .6X TO 1.5X BASIC
1 RJ Barrett 10.00 25.00
2 Deandre Ayton 6.00 15.00
3 Patty Mills 6.00 15.00
4 Josh Giddey 10.00 25.00
5 Udonis Haslem 5.00 12.00
6 Jason Williams 12.00 30.00
7 Wally Szczerbiak 5.00 12.00
8 Cole Anthony 6.00 15.00
9 Monte Morris 4.00 10.00
10 Bruce Brown 6.00 15.00
11 John Starks 6.00 15.00
12 Bill Walton 10.00 25.00
13 Mario Chalmers 5.00 12.00
14 Jrue Holiday 8.00 20.00
15 Gary Trent Jr. 6.00 15.00
16 T.J. Warren 5.00 12.00
17 Joakim Noah 5.00 12.00
18 Evan Mobley 15.00 40.00
19 Bradley Beal 8.00 20.00
20 Hakeem Olajuwon 20.00 50.00
21 Richard Hamilton 8.00 20.00
22 Devonte' Graham 5.00 12.00
23 Robert Parish 8.00 20.00
24 Kevin Huerter 6.00 15.00
25 Dillon Brooks 6.00 15.00
26 Michael Cooper 6.00 15.00
27 Max Strus 6.00 15.00
28 Ayo Dosunmu 8.00 20.00
30 Alperen Sengun 8.00 20.00
31 Dell Curry 6.00 15.00
32 James Wiseman 5.00 12.00
33 Oscar Robertson 20.00 50.00
34 Jalen Suggs 8.00 20.00
35 Steve Kerr 8.00 20.00
36 Saddiq Bey 5.00 12.00
37 Seth Curry 5.00 12.00
38 Jordan Clarkson 6.00 15.00
39 Onyeka Okongwu 6.00 15.00
40 Joe Harris 5.00 12.00
41 Devin Vassell 8.00 20.00
42 Nick Van Exel 10.00 25.00
43 Bojan Bogdanovic 6.00 15.00
44 Calvin Murphy 6.00 15.00
45 Nate Archibald 8.00 20.00
46 David Thompson 8.00 20.00
47 Pat Connaughton 5.00 12.00
48 Robert Horry 6.00 15.00
49 Doug McDermott 4.00 10.00
50 Isaiah Stewart 5.00 12.00
51 Precious Achiuwa 6.00 15.00
52 Derrick Coleman 6.00 15.00
53 Toni Kukoc 8.00 20.00
54 Herbert Jones 6.00 15.00
55 Jonathan Kuminga 15.00 40.00
56 Gary Payton 10.00 25.00
57 Rudy Gobert 8.00 20.00
58 Scottie Barnes 10.00 25.00
59 Chris Mullin 8.00 20.00
60 Peja Stojakovic 6.00 15.00
61 Paolo Banchero 75.00 200.00
62 Jalen Williams 30.00 80.00
63 Jalen Duren 20.00 50.00
64 Johnny Davis 6.00 15.00
65 Walker Kessler 12.00 30.00
66 Nikola Jovic 12.00 30.00
67 Ousmane Dieng 8.00 20.00
68 Malaki Branham 6.00 15.00
69 Kennedy Chandler 6.00 15.00
70 Bennedict Mathurin 20.00 50.00
71 Chet Holmgren 75.00 200.00
72 Dyson Daniels 15.00 40.00
73 Shaedon Sharpe 40.00 100.00
74 AJ Griffin 5.00 12.00
75 Jake LaRavia 6.00 15.00
76 MarJon Beauchamp 6.00 15.00
78 Jaden Ivey 20.00 50.00
79 Jeremy Sochan 20.00 50.00
80 Max Christie 15.00 40.00
81 Patrick Baldwin Jr. 6.00 15.00
82 Keegan Murray 15.00 40.00
83 Jaylin Williams 8.00 20.00
84 Blake Wesley 6.00 15.00
85 Andrew Nembhard 12.00 30.00
86 Ochai Agbaji 8.00 20.00
88 Jaden Hardy 10.00 25.00
89 Caleb Houstan 6.00 15.00
90 Christian Koloko 6.00 15.00
91 Christian Braun 15.00 40.00
92 Johnny Juzang 8.00 20.00
93 Tari Eason 15.00 40.00
94 Simone Fontecchio 6.00 15.00
95 Moussa Diabate 6.00 15.00
96 Jabari Smith Jr. 20.00 50.00
97 Julian Champagnie 8.00 20.00
99 Bryce McGowens 6.00 15.00
100 Mark Williams 12.00 30.00

2022-23 Panini Flux Fade to Black

1 LeBron James 80.00 200.00
2 Kyrie Irving 20.00 50.00
3 Luka Doncic 60.00 150.00
4 Devin Booker 25.00 60.00
5 Giannis Antetokounmpo 50.00 120.00
6 Damian Lillard 25.00 60.00
7 Trae Young 25.00 60.00
8 Kevin Durant 30.00 80.00
9 Shai Gilgeous-Alexander 50.00 120.00
10 Anthony Edwards 50.00 120.00
11 Ja Morant 30.00 80.00
12 Jayson Tatum 40.00 100.00
13 Stephen Curry 80.00 200.00
14 Donovan Mitchell 20.00 50.00
15 Jaylen Brown 20.00 50.00

2022-23 Panini Flux Flow Motion

COMPLETE SET (20)
*SILVER: .75X TO 2X BASIC
1 Jalen Williams 2.50 6.00
2 Ja Morant 1.50 4.00
3 De'Aaron Fox 1.00 2.50
4 Darius Garland .75 2.00
5 Bennedict Mathurin 1.50 4.00
6 Shai Gilgeous-Alexander 2.50 6.00
7 Chris Paul 1.00 2.50
8 James Harden 1.00 2.50
9 Trae Young 1.25 3.00
10 Jaden Ivey 1.50 4.00
11 Bradley Beal .60 1.50
12 Damian Lillard 1.25 3.00
13 Kyrie Irving 1.00 2.50
14 Paolo Banchero 3.00 8.00
15 Jalen Brunson 1.00 2.50
16 Tyrese Haliburton 1.00 2.50
17 Stephen Curry 4.00 10.00
18 LaMelo Ball 1.25 3.00
19 Luka Doncic 3.00 8.00
20 Shaedon Sharpe 2.00 5.00

2022-23 Panini Flux Fluid

COMPLETE SET (20)
*SILVER: .75X TO 2X BASIC
1 Giannis Antetokounmpo 2.50 6.00
2 Jabari Smith Jr. 1.50 4.00
3 Nikola Jokic 2.50 6.00
4 Jayson Tatum 2.00 5.00
5 Anthony Edwards 2.50 6.00
6 Kevin Durant 1.50 4.00
7 Jaden Ivey 1.50 4.00
8 Stephen Curry 4.00 10.00
9 Bennedict Mathurin 1.50 4.00
10 LeBron James 4.00 10.00
11 Trae Young 1.25 3.00
12 Jeremy Sochan 1.50 4.00
13 Ja Morant 1.50 4.00
14 Luka Doncic 3.00 8.00
15 Allen Iverson 1.25 3.00
16 Keegan Murray 1.25 3.00
17 Dirk Nowitzki 1.25 3.00
18 Donovan Mitchell 1.00 2.50
19 Zach LaVine 1.00 2.50
20 Paolo Banchero 3.00 8.00

2022-23 Panini Flux Flux Appeal

COMPLETE SET (20)
*SILVER: .75X TO 2X BASIC
*SILVER MOJO: .75X TO 2X BASIC
1 Keegan Murray 1.25 3.00
2 Jayson Tatum 2.00 5.00
3 Kyrie Irving 1.00 2.50
4 Damian Lillard 1.25 3.00
5 LeBron James 4.00 10.00
6 James Harden 1.00 2.50
7 Donovan Mitchell 1.00 2.50
8 Shaedon Sharpe 2.00 5.00
9 Zach LaVine 1.00 2.50
10 Ja Morant 1.50 4.00
11 Bennedict Mathurin 1.50 4.00
12 Stephen Curry 4.00 10.00
13 Shai Gilgeous-Alexander 2.50 6.00
14 Jaden Ivey 1.50 4.00
15 Trae Young 1.25 3.00
16 Luka Doncic 3.00 8.00
17 Kevin Durant 1.50 4.00
18 Giannis Antetokounmpo 2.50 6.00
19 Anthony Edwards 2.50 6.00
20 Paolo Banchero 3.00 8.00

2022-23 Panini Flux Flux Freshman Signatures

1 Chet Holmgren 125.00 300.00
2 Paolo Banchero 75.00 200.00
3 Keegan Murray 15.00 40.00
6 Jaden Ivey 20.00 50.00
7 Jabari Smith Jr. 20.00 50.00
8 Shaedon Sharpe 25.00 60.00
10 Jeremy Sochan 20.00 50.00

2022-23 Panini Flux Flux Rookie Signatures

1 Paolo Banchero 75.00 200.00
3 Jalen Duren 15.00 40.00
4 Jeremy Sochan 15.00 40.00
5 Shaedon Sharpe 20.00 50.00
6 Ochai Agbaji 6.00 15.00
7 Jaden Hardy 8.00 20.00
8 Blake Wesley 5.00 12.00
9 Jalen Williams 25.00 60.00
10 Jaden Ivey 15.00 40.00
11 Tari Eason 12.00 30.00
14 Scotty Pippen Jr. 6.00 15.00
15 Trevor Keels 4.00 10.00
16 Jaylin Williams 6.00 15.00
18 Buddy Boeheim 5.00 12.00
19 Max Christie 12.00 30.00
20 Keegan Murray 12.00 30.00
23 Jamal Cain 5.00 12.00
24 Julian Champagnie 6.00 15.00
25 Tyrese Martin 4.00 10.00
26 Ron Harper Jr. 6.00 15.00
27 Wendell Moore Jr. 5.00 12.00
29 Dyson Daniels 12.00 30.00
30 Bennedict Mathurin 15.00 40.00
32 Ousmane Dieng 6.00 15.00
34 Bryce McGowens 5.00 12.00
35 Josh Minott 5.00 12.00
36 Ryan Rollins 5.00 12.00
37 Darius Days 4.00 10.00
38 Trevelin Queen 3.00 8.00
39 Lindy Waters III 4.00 10.00
40 Chet Holmgren 125.00 300.00
41 Vince Williams Jr. 6.00 15.00
43 Johnny Juzang 6.00 15.00
44 MarJon Beauchamp 5.00 12.00
45 Kennedy Chandler 5.00 12.00
46 Jabari Walker 4.00 10.00
47 Jordan Hall 4.00 10.00
48 A.J. Green 6.00 15.00
49 Dominick Barlow 4.00 10.00
50 Jabari Smith Jr. 15.00 40.00

2022-23 Panini Flux Flux Signatures

1 Jose Alvarado 5.00 12.00
2 Ish Wainright 4.00 10.00
3 Kevon Looney 5.00 12.00
4 Moses Brown 3.00 8.00
5 Frank Ntilikina 3.00 8.00
6 Max Strus 5.00 12.00
7 Day'Ron Sharpe 4.00 10.00
8 Xavier Tillman 5.00 12.00
9 Jeremiah Robinson-Earl 4.00 10.00
10 Keon Johnson 3.00 8.00
11 Jalen Green 20.00 50.00
12 Chris Duarte 4.00 10.00
13 Furkan Korkmaz 4.00 10.00
14 Naji Marshall 5.00 12.00
15 Tony Allen 3.00 8.00
16 Jae'Sean Tate 3.00 8.00
17 Sam Hauser 5.00 12.00
18 Corey Kispert 5.00 12.00
19 Jericho Sims 4.00 10.00
20 Lauri Markkanen 12.00 30.00
21 Brandon Ingram 12.00 30.00
22 Davion Mitchell 4.00 10.00
23 Moses Moody 6.00 15.00
24 Tobias Harris 4.00 10.00
25 Jarrett Allen 5.00 12.00
26 M.L. Carr 4.00 10.00
27 Jeff Malone 4.00 10.00
28 Vin Baker 4.00 10.00
29 Cedric Ceballos 4.00 10.00
30 Doc Rivers 6.00 15.00
31 Deron Williams 4.00 10.00
32 Bradley Beal 6.00 15.00
34 Buddy Hield 5.00 12.00
35 Gordon Hayward 4.00 10.00
36 Andre Drummond 5.00 12.00
37 Jason Terry 4.00 10.00
38 Kurt Rambis 5.00 12.00
39 Drew Gooden 4.00 10.00
40 Greg Anthony 4.00 10.00

2022-23 Panini Flux Fluxuations

COMPLETE SET (20)
*SILVER: .75X TO 2X BASIC
*SILVER MOJO: .75X TO 2X BASIC
1 James Harden 1.00 2.50
2 LeBron James 4.00 10.00
3 Donovan Mitchell 1.00 2.50
4 Kevin Durant 1.50 4.00
5 Kyrie Irving 1.00 2.50
6 Tyrese Haliburton 1.00 2.50
7 Zach LaVine 1.00 2.50
8 Rudy Gobert .60 1.50
9 Kawhi Leonard 1.25 3.00
10 Jalen Brunson 1.00 2.50
11 Domantas Sabonis .60 1.50
12 Russell Westbrook .75 2.00
13 Anthony Davis 1.25 3.00
14 CJ McCollum .50 1.25
15 Shai Gilgeous-Alexander 2.50 6.00
16 Paul George .75 2.00
17 Brandon Ingram .60 1.50
18 DeMar DeRozan .60 1.50
19 Julius Randle .60 1.50
20 Lauri Markkanen .75 2.00

2022-23 Panini Flux Freshman Year

COMPLETE SET (30)
*SILVER: .75X TO 2X BASIC
*SILVER MOJO: 1X TO 2.5X BASIC
1 Jabari Smith Jr. 1.50 4.00
2 MarJon Beauchamp .50 1.25
3 Jake LaRavia .50 1.25
4 Bennedict Mathurin 1.50 4.00
5 Shaedon Sharpe 2.00 5.00
6 David Roddy .60 1.50
7 Keegan Murray 1.25 3.00
8 Jeremy Sochan 1.50 4.00
9 Chet Holmgren 2.50 6.00
10 Jaden Ivey 1.50 4.00
11 Tari Eason 1.25 3.00
12 Walker Kessler 1.00 2.50
13 Jalen Williams 2.50 6.00
14 Andrew Nembhard 1.00 2.50
15 Christian Braun 1.25 3.00
16 Christian Koloko .50 1.25
17 Paolo Banchero 3.00 8.00
18 Nikola Jovic 1.00 2.50
19 AJ Griffin .40 1.00
20 Dyson Daniels 1.25 3.00
21 Ochai Agbaji .60 1.50
22 Jaylin Williams .60 1.50
23 Max Christie 1.25 3.00
24 Peyton Watson .75 2.00
25 Caleb Houstan .50 1.25
26 Mark Williams 1.00 2.50
27 Jalen Duren 1.50 4.00
28 Malaki Branham .50 1.25
29 Ousmane Dieng .60 1.50
30 Jaden Hardy .75 2.00

2022-23 Panini Flux Full Capacity

1 Anfernee Hardaway 40.00 100.00
2 Joel Embiid 25.00 60.00
3 Charles Barkley 40.00 100.00
4 Giannis Antetokounmpo 80.00 200.00
5 Damian Lillard 40.00 100.00
6 Trae Young 40.00 100.00
7 Ja Morant 50.00 120.00
8 Anthony Edwards 80.00 200.00
9 Jayson Tatum 60.00 150.00
10 Nikola Jokic 80.00 200.00
11 Devin Booker 40.00 100.00
12 Vince Carter 30.00 80.00
13 Magic Johnson 60.00 150.00
14 Kevin Durant 50.00 120.00
15 Kyrie Irving 30.00 80.00
16 Luka Doncic 100.00 250.00
17 Donovan Mitchell 30.00 80.00
18 LeBron James 125.00 300.00
19 Dwyane Wade 30.00 80.00
20 Stephen Curry 125.00 300.00

2022-23 Panini Flux Hall Influx

COMPLETE SET (10)
*SILVER: .75X TO 2X BASIC
*SILVER MOJO: .75X TO 2X BASIC
1 Dirk Nowitzki 1.50 4.00
2 Pau Gasol 1.00 2.50
3 Tim Duncan 1.50 4.00
4 Allen Iverson 1.50 4.00
5 Larry Bird 2.50 6.00
6 Dwyane Wade 1.25 3.00
7 Tracy McGrady 1.00 2.50
8 Shaquille O'Neal 2.50 6.00
9 Tony Parker 1.00 2.50
10 Yao Ming 1.50 4.00

2022-23 Panini Flux Hot Stock Signatures

*RED/49: .6X TO 1.5X BASIC
1 Chet Holmgren 125.00 300.00
2 Keegan Murray 12.00 30.00
3 Jalen Duren 15.00 40.00
4 Johnny Davis 5.00 12.00
5 Jeremy Sochan 15.00 40.00
6 Nikola Jovic 10.00 25.00
7 Paolo Banchero 75.00 200.00
8 AJ Griffin 4.00 10.00
9 Dyson Daniels 12.00 30.00
10 Malaki Branham 5.00 12.00
11 David Roddy 6.00 15.00
12 Jaden Ivey 15.00 40.00
13 Ochai Agbaji 6.00 15.00
14 Walker Kessler 10.00 25.00
15 Jalen Williams 25.00 60.00
16 Mark Williams 10.00 25.00
17 Jaden Hardy 8.00 20.00
18 Ousmane Dieng 6.00 15.00
19 Tari Eason 12.00 30.00
20 Andrew Nembhard 10.00 25.00
21 Christian Braun 12.00 30.00
22 Jabari Smith Jr. 15.00 40.00
23 Max Christie 12.00 30.00
25 MarJon Beauchamp 5.00 12.00
26 Shaedon Sharpe 20.00 50.00
27 Patrick Baldwin Jr. 5.00 12.00
28 Jaylin Williams 6.00 15.00
30 Bennedict Mathurin 15.00 40.00

2022-23 Panini Flux Incoming

*SILVER: .75X TO 2X BASIC
1 Jalen Williams 2.50 6.00
2 Keegan Murray 1.25 3.00
3 Bennedict Mathurin 1.50 4.00
4 Jalen Duren 1.50 4.00
5 Jabari Smith Jr. 1.50 4.00
6 Jeremy Sochan 1.50 4.00
7 Shaedon Sharpe 2.00 5.00
8 Paolo Banchero 3.00 8.00
9 Walker Kessler 1.00 2.50
10 Jaden Ivey 1.50 4.00

2022-23 Panini Flux Rookie Influx

*SILVER: .75X TO 2X BASIC
1 Jeremy Sochan 1.50 4.00
2 Andrew Nembhard 1.00 2.50
3 Jaden Ivey 1.50 4.00
4 Mark Williams 1.00 2.50
5 Jalen Williams 2.50 6.00
6 Christian Braun 1.25 3.00
7 Nikola Jovic 1.00 2.50
8 Bennedict Mathurin 1.50 4.00
9 Dyson Daniels 1.25 3.00
10 Shaedon Sharpe 2.00 5.00
11 Johnny Davis .50 1.25
12 Tari Eason 1.25 3.00
13 Ochai Agbaji .60 1.50
14 Jabari Smith Jr. 1.50 4.00
15 Keegan Murray 1.25 3.00
16 Malaki Branham .50 1.25
17 Bryce McGowens .50 1.25
18 Ousmane Dieng .60 1.50
19 Patrick Baldwin Jr. .50 1.25
20 Paolo Banchero 3.00 8.00
21 Jaden Hardy .75 2.00
22 MarJon Beauchamp .50 1.25
23 Chet Holmgren 2.50 6.00
24 Jaylin Williams .60 1.50
25 Jalen Duren 1.50 4.00
26 Max Christie 1.25 3.00
27 AJ Griffin .40 1.00
28 Christian Koloko .50 1.25
29 Jake LaRavia .50 1.25
30 Walker Kessler 1.00 2.50

2022-23 Panini Flux Titan

*SILVER: .75X TO 2X BASIC
1 Kevin Durant 2.00 5.00
2 Anthony Edwards 3.00 8.00
3 Orlando Robinson .50 1.25
4 Karl-Anthony Towns 1.00 2.50
5 De'Aaron Fox 1.25 3.00
6 Jaylen Brown 1.25 3.00
7 Kenneth Lofton Jr. .75 2.00
8 Johnny Davis .60 1.50
9 Kevon Harris .50 1.25
10 Stephen Curry 5.00 12.00
11 LaMelo Ball 1.50 4.00
12 Ochai Agbaji .75 2.00
13 Shaedon Sharpe 2.50 6.00
14 Tyrese Martin .50 1.25
15 Peyton Watson 1.00 2.50
16 Anthony Davis 1.50 4.00
17 Tari Eason 1.50 4.00
18 Caleb Houstan .60 1.50
19 Jalen Williams 3.00 8.00
20 Max Christie 1.50 4.00
21 Shaquille O'Neal 2.50 6.00
22 Jaden Hardy 1.00 2.50
23 Patrick Baldwin Jr. .60 1.50
24 Paul George 1.00 2.50
25 Yao Ming 1.50 4.00
26 Jeremy Sochan 2.00 5.00
27 Allen Iverson 1.50 4.00
28 Christian Braun 1.50 4.00
29 Kareem Abdul-Jabbar 2.00 5.00

30 A.J. Green .75 2.00
31 Jalen Duren 2.00 5.00
32 Vince Carter 1.25 3.00
33 Shai Gilgeous-Alexander 3.00 8.00
34 Nikola Jokic 3.00 8.00
35 Simone Fontecchio .60 1.50
36 Julius Randle .75 2.00
37 Jalen Brunson 1.25 3.00
38 Jaylin Williams .75 2.00
39 Ryan Rollins .60 1.50
40 Paolo Banchero 4.00 10.00
41 Moussa Diabate .60 1.50
42 AJ Griffin .50 1.25
43 Zion Williamson 1.50 4.00
44 Christian Koloko .60 1.50
45 TyTy Washington Jr. .60 1.50
46 Ousmane Dieng .75 2.00
47 Tony Parker 1.00 2.50
48 Bradley Beal .75 2.00
49 Larry Bird 2.50 6.00
50 Jabari Walker .50 1.25
51 Donovan Mitchell 1.25 3.00
52 Tyrese Haliburton 1.25 3.00
53 Johnny Juzang .75 2.00
54 Zach LaVine 1.25 3.00
55 Ja Morant 2.00 5.00
56 Pau Gasol 1.00 2.50
57 Dwyane Wade 1.25 3.00
58 Keldon Johnson .75 2.00
59 LeBron James 5.00 12.00
60 Trae Young 1.50 4.00
61 Luka Doncic 4.00 10.00
62 Scottie Barnes 1.00 2.50
63 Jaden Ivey 2.00 5.00
64 Kennedy Chandler .60 1.50
65 Kyrie Irving 1.25 3.00
66 Andrew Nembhard 1.25 3.00
67 Spencer Dinwiddie .50 1.25
68 Klay Thompson 1.50 4.00
69 Franz Wagner 1.50 4.00
70 Devin Booker 1.50 4.00
71 Dyson Daniels 1.50 4.00
72 Blake Wesley .60 1.50
73 Josh Minott .60 1.50
74 Dalen Terry .60 1.50
75 Bennedict Mathurin 2.00 5.00
76 Dirk Nowitzki 1.50 4.00
77 Keegan Murray 1.50 4.00
78 MarJon Beauchamp .60 1.50
79 Walker Kessler 1.25 3.00
80 Nikola Jovic 1.25 3.00
81 Vince Williams Jr. .75 2.00
82 Jalen Green 2.00 5.00
83 Wendell Moore Jr. .60 1.50
84 Chet Holmgren 3.00 8.00
85 Mark Williams 1.25 3.00
86 Jimmy Butler 1.25 3.00
87 Lauri Markkanen 1.00 2.50
88 Cade Cunningham 2.00 5.00
89 James Harden 1.25 3.00
90 Jake LaRavia .60 1.50
91 Damian Lillard 1.50 4.00
92 Kawhi Leonard 1.50 4.00
93 Joel Embiid 1.00 2.50
94 Bryce McGowens .60 1.50
95 Jayson Tatum 2.50 6.00
96 Jabari Smith Jr. 2.00 5.00
97 David Roddy .75 2.00
98 Giannis Antetokounmpo 3.00 8.00
99 Brandon Ingram .75 2.00
100 Malaki Branham .60 1.50

2022-23 Panini Flux Triumph

*SILVER: .75X TO 2X BASIC
1 Luka Doncic 2.50 6.00
2 Kawhi Leonard 1.00 2.50
3 Damian Lillard 1.00 2.50
4 Trae Young 1.00 2.50
5 Joel Embiid .60 1.50
6 Stephen Curry 3.00 8.00
7 LeBron James 3.00 8.00
8 Jaylen Brown .75 2.00
9 Julius Randle .50 1.25
10 Kyrie Irving .75 2.00
11 Kevin Durant 1.25 3.00
12 Anthony Edwards 2.00 5.00
13 Giannis Antetokounmpo 2.00 5.00
14 Jayson Tatum 1.50 4.00
15 Anthony Davis 1.00 2.50
16 Klay Thompson 1.00 2.50
17 Ja Morant 1.25 3.00
18 Nikola Jokic 2.00 5.00
19 Donovan Mitchell .75 2.00
20 Devin Booker 1.00 2.50

2022-23 Panini Flux Ultraviolet Signatures

*RED/49: .6X TO 1.5X BASIC
1 Christian Wood 3.00 8.00
2 Brandon Ingram 12.00 30.00
3 Austin Reaves 20.00 50.00
4 Ivica Zubac 5.00 12.00
5 Marcus Smart 6.00 15.00
6 Domantas Sabonis 6.00 15.00
7 Metta World Peace 5.00 12.00
8 Dennis Rodman 25.00 60.00
9 Chet Holmgren 125.00 300.00
10 Jaden Ivey 15.00 40.00
11 Shaedon Sharpe 20.00 50.00
12 Magic Johnson 40.00 100.00
13 Rasheed Wallace 12.00 30.00
14 Zach Randolph 5.00 12.00
15 Steve Francis 5.00 12.00
16 Larry Johnson 10.00 25.00
17 Louie Dampier 5.00 12.00
18 Jaden Hardy 8.00 20.00
19 Jabari Smith Jr. 15.00 40.00
20 Jason Williams 8.00 20.00
21 Goran Dragic 4.00 10.00
22 Malik Monk 5.00 12.00
23 Jose Alvarado 5.00 12.00
24 Kendrick Perkins 3.00 8.00
25 Josh Giddey 8.00 20.00
26 Kevin Garnett 40.00 100.00
27 Kenyon Martin 5.00 12.00
28 Artis Gilmore 6.00 15.00
29 De'Aaron Fox 25.00 60.00
30 Moses Moody 6.00 15.00

2014-15 Panini Gala

1-83 PRINT RUN 79 SER.#'d SETS
83-100 PRINT RUN 8 SER.#'d SETS
1 Kobe Bryant 15.00 40.00
2 John Wall 2.50 6.00
3 Goran Dragic 2.00 5.00
4 Victor Oladipo 1.50 4.00
5 Nerlens Noel 1.25 3.00
6 Monta Ellis 1.50 4.00
7 James Harden 4.00 10.00
8 DeMar DeRozan 2.50 6.00
9 Mike Conley 1.50 4.00
10 Dennis Schroeder 2.50 6.00
11 Kevin Durant 6.00 15.00
12 Anthony Davis 5.00 12.00
13 O.J. Mayo 1.25 3.00
14 David West 1.50 4.00
15 Tim Duncan 5.00 12.00
16 Jimmy Butler 3.00 8.00
17 Gordon Hayward 1.50 4.00
18 Zach Randolph 2.00 5.00
19 Markieff Morris 1.25 3.00
20 Avery Bradley 1.25 3.00
21 Draymond Green 2.50 6.00
22 Bradley Beal 3.00 8.00
23 LaMarcus Aldridge 2.00 5.00
24 J.R. Smith 2.00 5.00
25 DeAndre Jordan 1.50 4.00
26 Greg Monroe 1.25 3.00
27 Jeremy Lin 4.00 10.00
28 Kyrie Irving 4.00 10.00
29 Ty Lawson 2.00 5.00
30 Derrick Rose 4.00 10.00
31 Damian Lillard 5.00 12.00
32 Rudy Gay 2.00 5.00
33 Trey Burke 1.25 3.00
34 Luol Deng 1.25 3.00
35 Tyreke Evans 1.50 4.00
36 Joe Johnson 1.50 4.00
37 Klay Thompson 5.00 12.00
38 Nikola Vucevic 1.50 4.00
39 Tim Hardaway Jr. 1.50 4.00
40 Arron Afflalo 1.25 3.00
41 Paul Millsap 1.50 4.00
42 Dwight Howard 2.50 6.00
43 Chandler Parsons 1.25 3.00
44 Blake Griffin 2.00 5.00
45 Tony Parker 3.00 8.00
46 Kemba Walker 2.00 5.00
47 Michael Carter-Williams 1.25 3.00
48 Ricky Rubio 1.50 4.00
49 Jared Sullinger 1.25 3.00
50 Chris Paul 3.00 8.00
51 Kenneth Faried 1.25 3.00
52 Kevin Love 2.00 5.00
53 C.J. Miles 1.25 3.00
54 Andrea Bargnani 1.25 3.00
55 DeMarcus Cousins 1.50 4.00
56 Al Horford 2.00 5.00
57 Brandon Jennings 1.25 3.00
58 Serge Ibaka 1.50 4.00
59 Joakim Noah 2.00 5.00
60 Tyson Chandler 2.00 5.00
61 Dwyane Wade 4.00 10.00
62 Eric Bledsoe 1.50 4.00
63 Deron Williams 1.50 4.00
64 Manu Ginobili 4.00 10.00
65 Jrue Holiday 2.50 6.00
66 Jeff Teague 1.25 3.00
67 Marc Gasol 2.00 5.00
68 Kevin Garnett 5.00 12.00
69 Kyle Lowry 2.50 6.00
70 Stephen Curry 15.00 40.00
71 Paul Pierce 3.00 8.00
72 Russell Westbrook 5.00 12.00
73 Pau Gasol 3.00 8.00
74 Kawhi Leonard 5.00 12.00
75 Carmelo Anthony 3.00 8.00
76 Dirk Nowitzki 5.00 12.00
77 George Hill 1.50 4.00
78 LeBron James 20.00 50.00
79 Al Jefferson 1.25 3.00
80 Lou Williams 1.50 4.00
81 Chris Bosh 2.50 6.00
82 Andre Drummond 1.50 4.00
83 Giannis Antetokounmpo 8.00 20.00

2014-15 Panini Gala Award Winning Autographs

PRINT RUNS B/WN 40-60 COPIES PER
INSCRIPTIONS NOT SER.#'d
EXCHANGE DEADLINE 2/19/2017
1 Kevin Durant/40 75.00 150.00
2 Kobe Bryant/40 100.00 200.00
3 Shaquille O'Neal/40 100.00 200.00
5 Magic Johnson/40 40.00 100.00
7 David Robinson/40 15.00 40.00
9 Larry Nance/50 5.00 12.00
12 Tyson Chandler/40 6.00 15.00
13 Dikembe Mutombo/50 12.00 30.00
15 Sidney Moncrief/60 6.00 15.00
16 J.R. Smith/60 10.00 25.00
17 Jason Terry/50 5.00 12.00
18 Clifford Robinson/60 6.00 15.00
19 Bill Walton/50 10.00 25.00
20A Bobby Jones/60 5.00 12.00
20B B.Jones Inscription 30.00 80.00
21 George Karl/50 15.00 40.00
22 Byron Scott/40 8.00 20.00
23 Avery Johnson/40 8.00 20.00
24 Don Nelson/50 20.00 50.00
25 Larry Bird/40 50.00 120.00

2014-15 Panini Gala Cinematic Rookie Signatures

STATED PRINT RUN 60 SER.#'d SETS
EXCHANGE DEADLINE 2/19/2017
*JADE/25: .5X TO 1.2X BASIC
1 Andrew Wiggins 20.00 50.00
2 Jabari Parker 5.00 12.00
3 Joel Embiid 150.00 400.00
4 K.J. McDaniels 4.00 10.00
5 Aaron Gordon 20.00 50.00
6 Marcus Smart 15.00 40.00
7 Nikola Mirotic 6.00 15.00
8 Bojan Bogdanovic 6.00 15.00
9 Jarnell Stokes 4.00 10.00
10 Jordan Adams 4.00 10.00
11 Tyler Ennis 4.00 10.00
12 Travis Wear 4.00 10.00
13 Jordan Clarkson 15.00 40.00
15 Bruno Caboclo 5.00 12.00
16 Doug McDermott 6.00 15.00
17 Joe Harris 6.00 15.00
18 James Ennis 4.00 10.00
19 Dante Exum 6.00 15.00
20 Cory Jefferson 4.00 10.00
21 Noah Vonleh 4.00 10.00
22 Julius Randle 20.00 50.00
23 Zach LaVine 150.00 400.00
24 Tarik Black 4.00 10.00
26 Shabazz Napier 5.00 12.00
27 Kyle Anderson 6.00 15.00
28 Elfrid Payton 6.00 15.00
29 Glenn Robinson III 5.00 12.00
30 Nik Stauskas 4.00 10.00

2014-15 Panini Gala Cinematic Signatures

PRINT RUNS B/WN 35-60 COPIES PER
INSCRIPTIONS NOT SER.#'d
EXCHANGE DEADLINE 2/19/2017
*JADE/25: .5X TO 1.2X BASIC
1 Kobe Bryant/49 2,000.00 4,000.00
2 Kevin Durant/49 150.00 400.00
3 Kyrie Irving/35 60.00 150.00
4 Stephen Curry/35 600.00 1,200.00
5 John Wall/35 40.00 100.00
6 Anthony Davis/35 100.00 250.00
7 Jeff Green/35 6.00 15.00
9 Vince Carter/49 100.00 250.00
10 Zach Randolph/49 8.00 20.00
12 P.J. Tucker/60 6.00 15.00
13 Jason Terry/60 6.00 15.00
16 Reggie Jackson/60 6.00 15.00
18 Maurice Harkless/60 5.00 12.00
19 Kyle Korver/60 6.00 15.00
20 Alec Burks/60 6.00 15.00
21 Blake Griffin/35 8.00 20.00
22 Mike Conley/35 6.00 15.00
23 Tyson Chandler/49 8.00 20.00
24 Jeff Teague/60 5.00 12.00
26 Mike Muscala/60 5.00 12.00
27 Lance Stephenson/35 6.00 15.00
29 Phil Pressey/60 5.00 12.00
30 DeMarre Carroll/60 5.00 12.00
33 Victor Oladipo/60 6.00 15.00
34 Thaddeus Young/60 5.00 12.00
35 Mason Plumlee/60 5.00 12.00
37 Andrew Nicholson/60 5.00 12.00
38 Tobias Harris/60 6.00 15.00
39 Michael Kidd-Gilchrist/35 6.00 15.00
40 Kevin Love/35 8.00 20.00
41 Harrison Barnes/49 6.00 15.00
44 Spencer Hawes/60 5.00 12.00
45 Taj Gibson/60 5.00 12.00
46 Derrick Favors/60 5.00 12.00
47 Chris Andersen/49 6.00 15.00
48 Randy Foye/60 5.00 12.00
50 Gordon Hayward/60 12.00 30.00
51 Marcin Gortat/60 5.00 12.00
53A Tim Hardaway/60 20.00 50.00
53B T.Hardaway Inscription 25.00 60.00
54 Bill Walton/60 12.00 30.00
55 Grant Hill/35 30.00 80.00
56 Jason Kidd/49 25.00 60.00
57 Dan Issel/60 10.00 25.00
58 Kendall Gill/60 10.00 25.00
59 Glen Rice/60 8.00 20.00
60 Gary Payton/35 20.00 50.00
61 Isiah Thomas/60 20.00 50.00
63 Antoine Walker/60 6.00 15.00
64 Sean Elliott/60 8.00 20.00
65 Robert Horry/60 10.00 25.00
66 Muggsy Bogues/60 20.00 50.00
67 Jim Jackson/60 6.00 15.00
68 Mychal Thompson/60 6.00 15.00
69 Tracy McGrady/39 60.00 150.00
70 Sam Perkins/35 6.00 15.00

2014-15 Panini Gala Coming Attractions Memorabilia

STATED PRINT RUN 35 SER.#'d SETS
*JADE/25: 1.2X TO 3X BASIC
1 Doug McDermott 3.00 8.00
2 Joel Embiid 5.00 12.00
3 Glenn Robinson III 2.50 6.00
4 Marcus Smart 8.00 20.00
5 James Young 2.00 5.00
6 Nik Stauskas 2.00 5.00
7 Aaron Gordon 10.00 25.00
8 Rodney Hood 2.50 6.00
9 Bruno Caboclo 2.50 6.00
10 T.J. Warren 3.00 8.00
11 Elfrid Payton 3.00 8.00
12 Julius Randle 10.00 25.00
13 Jabari Parker 2.50 6.00
14 Markel Brown 2.00 5.00
15 Jerami Grant 10.00 25.00
16 Noah Vonleh 2.00 5.00
17 Adreian Payne 2.00 5.00
18 Shabazz Napier 2.50 6.00
19 Cleanthony Early 2.00 5.00
20 Tyler Ennis 2.00 5.00
21 Gary Harris 3.00 8.00
22 Kyle Anderson 3.00 8.00
23 James Ennis 2.00 5.00
24 Mitch McGary 2.00 5.00
25 Joe Harris 3.00 8.00
26 P.J. Hairston 2.00 5.00
27 Andrew Wiggins 6.00 15.00
28 Spencer Dinwiddie 3.00 8.00
29 Dante Exum 5.00 12.00
30 Zach LaVine 12.00 30.00

2014-15 Panini Gala Double Feature Memorabilia

PRINT RUNS B/WN 35-45 COPIES PER
*JADE/25: .75X TO 2X BASIC
1 T.Duncan/T.Parker/49 8.00 20.00
2 D.Howard/J.Harden/35 8.00 20.00
3 J.Stockton/K.Malone/35 10.00 25.00
4 B.Griffin/C.Paul/35 6.00 15.00
5 T.Lawson/K.Faried/35 2.50 6.00
6 A.Horford/J.Teague/49 4.00 10.00
7 K.Bryant/S.Nash/49 30.00 80.00
8 D.Rose/J.Butler/49 8.00 20.00
9 A.Davis/T.Evans/35 6.00 15.00
10 D.Nowitzki/M.Ellis/49 10.00 25.00
11 D.DeRozan/K.Lowry/35 5.00 12.00
12 C.Drexler/H.Olajuwon/35 8.00 20.00
13 P.Ewing/L.Johnson/35 6.00 15.00
14 M.Gasol/Z.Randolph/49 4.00 10.00
15 M.Morris/M.Morris/35 2.50 6.00
16 G.Rice/V.Divac/49 4.00 10.00
17 D.Lillard/L.Aldridge/35 10.00 25.00
18 K.Irving/L.James/49 30.00 80.00
19 K.Durant/R.Westbrook/49 12.00 30.00
20 A.Drummond/B.Jennings/35 3.00 8.00

2014-15 Panini Gala Main Attraction Memorabilia

PRINT RUNS B/WN 35-49 COPIES PER
*JADE/15-25: 1.2X TO 3X BASIC
1 DeMarcus Cousins/35 3.00 8.00
2 Kevin Durant/49 6.00 15.00
3 Monta Ellis/35 3.00 8.00
4 Tim Duncan/35 10.00 25.00
5 Jeremy Lin/35 8.00 20.00
6 Roy Hibbert/35 3.00 8.00
7 Joakim Noah/35 4.00 10.00
8 Kobe Bryant/35 12.00 30.00
9 Kyle Lowry/35 5.00 12.00
10 Rajon Rondo/49 5.00 12.00
11 John Wall/35 5.00 12.00
12 Anthony Davis/35 8.00 20.00
13 LaMarcus Aldridge/35 4.00 10.00
14 Chandler Parsons/35 2.50 6.00
15 Jeff Teague/35 2.50 6.00
16 Tobias Harris/49 3.00 8.00
17 Gordon Hayward/35 3.00 8.00
18 Dwyane Wade/35 6.00 15.00
19 Blake Griffin/35 4.00 10.00
20 Grant Hill/49 6.00 15.00
21 James Harden/35 8.00 20.00
22 Dwight Howard/35 5.00 12.00
23 Al Horford/49 4.00 10.00
24 Bradley Beal/35 6.00 15.00
25 Michael Carter-Williams/35 2.50 6.00
26 Dirk Nowitzki/49 10.00 25.00
27 Allen Iverson/49 10.00 25.00
28 Patrick Ewing/49 6.00 15.00
29 Marc Gasol/49 4.00 10.00
30 Russell Westbrook/35 6.00 15.00
31 Ricky Rubio/35 3.00 8.00
32 Kenneth Faried/35 2.50 6.00
33 Manu Ginobili/35 8.00 20.00
34 Jimmy Butler/49 6.00 15.00
35 Chris Andersen/35 3.00 8.00
36 Carmelo Anthony/35 6.00 15.00
37 Ralph Sampson/35 4.00 10.00
38 Chris Paul/35 6.00 15.00
39 Kemba Walker/35 4.00 10.00
40 Derrick Rose/35 6.00 15.00
41 Hakeem Olajuwon/35 8.00 20.00
42 Pau Gasol/35 6.00 15.00
43 Nerlens Noel/35 2.50 6.00
44 Joe Johnson/35 3.00 8.00
45 Taj Gibson/35 2.50 6.00
46 DeMar DeRozan/35 5.00 12.00
47 Damian Lillard/35 6.00 15.00
48 Shaquille O'Neal/35 15.00 40.00
49 Victor Oladipo/35 3.00 8.00
50 Trey Burke/35 2.50 6.00

2014-15 Panini Gala Silver Screen Rookie Signatures

STATED PRINT RUN 50 SER.#'d SETS
EXCHANGE DEADLINE 2/19/2017
1 Spencer Dinwiddie 6.00 15.00
2 Jordan Adams 4.00 10.00
3 Andrew Wiggins 20.00 50.00
4 Jabari Parker 20.00 50.00
5 Dante Exum 6.00 15.00
6 Nik Stauskas 4.00 10.00
7 Zach LaVine 20.00 50.00
8 Julius Randle 10.00 25.00
9 Langston Galloway 6.00 15.00
10 Devyn Marble 4.00 10.00
11 Elfrid Payton 6.00 15.00
12 Aaron Gordon 20.00 50.00
13 Shabazz Napier 5.00 12.00
14 Cory Jefferson 4.00 10.00
15 Jordan Clarkson 15.00 40.00
16 Nikola Mirotic 6.00 15.00
17 Johnny O'Bryant 4.00 10.00
18 K.J. McDaniels 4.00 10.00
19 Joe Harris 6.00 15.00
21 Markel Brown 4.00 10.00
22 Travis Wear 4.00 10.00
23 C.J. Wilcox 4.00 10.00
24 Doug McDermott 6.00 15.00
25 Bojan Bogdanovic 6.00 15.00

2014-15 Panini Gala Silver Screen Signatures

PRINT RUNS B/WN 35-60 COPIES PER
INSCRIPTIONS NOT SER.#'d
EXCHANGE DEADLINE 2/19/2017
1 Shaquille O'Neal/35 75.00 150.00
3 Maurice Harkless/60 4.00 10.00
6 Dikembe Mutombo/49 8.00 20.00
7 Bill Laimbeer/60 8.00 20.00
8 Vin Baker/60 5.00 12.00
10 Jalen Rose/60 8.00 20.00
11 Kenny Smith/60 5.00 12.00
12A Cedric Maxwell/60 5.00 12.00
13 Rick Mahorn/60 5.00 12.00
15 C.J. McCollum/49 10.00 25.00
16 Kelly Olynyk/60 5.00 12.00
17 Mason Plumlee/60 4.00 10.00
18 J.R. Smith/60 6.00 15.00
20 Enes Kanter/60 5.00 12.00
21 Tristan Thompson/60 4.00 10.00
22 John Wall/35 20.00 50.00
24 Deron Williams/35 5.00 12.00
25 Klay Thompson/49 30.00 80.00
26 Troy Daniels/60 4.00 10.00
28 Josh Smith/49 4.00 10.00
30 DeMarre Carroll/60 4.00 10.00
32 Nick Collison/60 5.00 12.00
33 James Jones/60 4.00 10.00
34A Gail Goodrich/49 6.00 15.00
35 Bernard King/49 8.00 20.00
36A Bill Cartwright/60 5.00 12.00
37 Michael Finley/35 8.00 20.00
38 Keith Van Horn/60 5.00 12.00
39 Magic Johnson/35 40.00 100.00
40 Larry Bird/35 50.00 120.00
41 Byron Scott/35 6.00 15.00
42 A.C. Green/60 10.00 25.00
43A Kenny Anderson/60 5.00 12.00
44 Ron Harper/60 6.00 15.00
45 Grant Hill/35 25.00 60.00
46 Jason Kidd/35 20.00 50.00
47 Larry Nance/60 5.00 12.00
48 Harvey Grant/60 4.00 10.00
49 Vinny Del Negro/49 5.00 12.00
50 Rick Fox/49 5.00 12.00
51A Bob Dandridge/60 6.00 15.00
52 Kiki Vandeweghe/60 5.00 12.00
53 Tom Gugliotta/60 4.00 10.00
54 Toni Kukoc/60 8.00 20.00
55 Mychal Thompson/60 5.00 12.00
56 Doug Collins/49 6.00 15.00
57 Calvin Murphy/35 5.00 12.00
58 Dick Van Arsdale/60 6.00 15.00
59 Campy Russell/60 5.00 12.00
61 Phil Chenier/60 5.00 12.00
63A Anfernee Hardaway/35 25.00 60.00
64 Allan Houston/49 6.00 15.00
65 Giannis Antetokounmpo/60 100.00 250.00
66 Alec Burks/60 5.00 12.00
67 E'Twaun Moore/60 10.00 25.00
70 Kobe Bryant/49 150.00 400.00
71 Kevin Durant/49 60.00 150.00
72 Kyrie Irving/49 30.00 80.00
73 Stephen Curry/35 400.00 800.00
74 Anthony Davis/35 60.00 150.00
75 Alex Len/49 4.00 10.00

2014-15 Panini Gala Starring Role Signatures

PRINT RUNS B/WN 32-60 COPIES PER
INSCRIPTIONS NOT SER.#'d
EXCHANGE DEADLINE 2/19/2017
1 Ty Lawson/47 4.00 10.00
2 Isaiah Thomas/60 10.00 25.00
8 Stephen Curry/40 500.00 1,000.00
9 Deron Williams/40 5.00 12.00
10 Andre Drummond/40 5.00 12.00
12 Chris Andersen/40 5.00 12.00
15 Jason Terry/50 5.00 12.00
16 Gordon Hayward/60 12.00 30.00
17 Ben McLemore/50 4.00 10.00
18 Blake Griffin/40 25.00 60.00
19 Kyrie Irving/40 30.00 80.00
20 D.J. Augustin/60 5.00 12.00
22 Tony Snell/60 4.00 10.00
25A A.C. Green/60 10.00 25.00
25B A.Green Inscription 50.00 120.00
26 Bernard King/40 8.00 20.00
27 John Starks/60 6.00 15.00
28A Jamaal Wilkes/60 6.00 15.00
29 Bob McAdoo/60 6.00 15.00
30 Rick Barry/40 8.00 20.00
31 Jerry Lucas/40 8.00 20.00
32 Toni Kukoc/60 8.00 20.00
33 Danny Manning/32 5.00 12.00
34 Michael Finley/40 8.00 20.00
35 Dave Cowens/50 8.00 20.00
36A Dolph Schayes/50 6.00 15.00
37 Walter Davis/60 5.00 12.00
38 Grant Hill/40 25.00 60.00
39 Dominique Wilkins/40 10.00 25.00
40 Jason Kidd/40 20.00 50.00
41 Rony Seikaly/60 5.00 12.00
42 Chris Mullin/50 8.00 20.00
44 Gary Payton/40 15.00 40.00
45 Mark Aguirre/60 5.00 12.00
46A Alex English/60 6.00 15.00
49 Clifford Robinson/60 6.00 15.00
50 Steve Smith/60 5.00 12.00

2014-15 Panini Gala World Premiere Autographs

STATED PRINT RUN 50 SER.#'d SETS
EXCHANGE DEADLINE 2/19/2017
1 Nik Stauskas 4.00 10.00
2 Andrew Wiggins 75.00 200.00
3 Jabari Parker 15.00 40.00
4 Dante Exum 6.00 15.00
5 Marcus Smart 8.00 20.00
6 Tarik Black 4.00 10.00
7 James Ennis 4.00 10.00
8 Zach LaVine 30.00 80.00
9 Doug McDermott 6.00 15.00
11 Jarnell Stokes 4.00 10.00
12 T.J. Warren 6.00 15.00
13 K.J. McDaniels 4.00 10.00
16 Johnny O'Bryant 4.00 10.00
17 Travis Wear 4.00 10.00
18 Shabazz Napier 5.00 12.00
19 Spencer Dinwiddie 6.00 15.00
20 Langston Galloway 6.00 15.00
21 Nikola Mirotic 15.00 40.00
22 Elfrid Payton 12.00 30.00
23 Aaron Gordon 15.00 40.00
24 Jordan Clarkson 25.00 60.00
25 Kyle Anderson 6.00 15.00

2015-16 Panini Gala

1-120 PRINT RUN 99 SER.#'d SETS
121-150 PRINT RUN 8 SER.#'d SETS
1 Anthony Davis 6.00 15.00
2 Deron Williams 2.00 5.00
3 Elfrid Payton 2.00 5.00
4 James Harden 5.00 12.00
5 Damian Lillard 6.00 15.00
6 Jordan Clarkson 2.50 6.00
7 Rudy Gay 2.50 6.00
8 Marcus Smart 3.00 8.00
9 Ricky Rubio 3.00 8.00
10 Kemba Walker 2.50 6.00
11 Jrue Holiday 3.00 8.00
12 Danilo Gallinari 2.00 5.00
13 Victor Oladipo 2.00 5.00
14 Dwight Howard 3.00 8.00
15 Mason Plumlee 1.50 4.00
16 Julius Randle 3.00 8.00
17 DeMar DeRozan 3.00 8.00
18 Joe Johnson 2.00 5.00
19 Jabari Parker 1.50 4.00
20 Michael Kidd-Gilchrist 1.50 4.00
21 Carmelo Anthony 4.00 10.00
22 Kenneth Faried 2.00 5.00
23 Tobias Harris 2.00 5.00
24 Ty Lawson 1.50 4.00
25 Gerald Henderson 1.50 4.00
26 Mike Conley 2.50 6.00
27 Kyle Lowry 2.50 6.00
28 Brook Lopez 2.50 6.00
29 Giannis Antetokounmpo 12.00 30.00
30 Derrick Rose 4.00 10.00
31 Arron Afflalo 1.50 4.00
32 Gary Harris 2.00 5.00
33 Nikola Vucevic 2.00 5.00
34 Monta Ellis 2.00 5.00
35 Tony Parker 4.00 10.00
36 Zach Randolph 2.50 6.00
37 Jonas Valanciunas 2.00 5.00
38 Avery Bradley 1.50 4.00
39 Michael Carter-Williams 1.50 4.00
40 Pau Gasol 4.00 10.00
41 Robin Lopez 1.50 4.00
42 Andre Drummond 2.50 6.00
43 Isaiah Canaan 1.50 4.00
44 Paul George 4.00 10.00
45 Manu Ginobili 5.00 12.00
46 Marc Gasol 2.50 6.00
47 Trey Burke 1.50 4.00
48 Amir Johnson 1.50 4.00
49 Greg Monroe 2.00 5.00
50 Jimmy Butler 5.00 12.00
51 Langston Galloway 1.50 4.00
52 Reggie Jackson 2.00 5.00
53 Robert Covington 2.00 5.00
54 George Hill 2.00 5.00
55 Kawhi Leonard 8.00 20.00
56 Dwyane Wade 5.00 12.00
57 Gordon Hayward 2.50 6.00
58 Bojan Bogdanovic 2.00 5.00
59 Zach LaVine 6.00 15.00
60 Kyrie Irving 5.00 12.00
61 Russell Westbrook 4.00 10.00
62 Kentavious Caldwell-Pope 2.00 5.00
63 Nerlens Noel 1.50 4.00
64 Chris Paul 5.00 12.00
65 LaMarcus Aldridge 2.50 6.00
66 Chris Bosh 3.00 8.00
67 Rudy Gobert 3.00 8.00
68 Jeff Teague 1.50 4.00
69 DeAndre Jordan 2.00 5.00
70 LeBron James 15.00 40.00
71 Kevin Durant 10.00 25.00
72 Stephen Curry 15.00 40.00
73 Brandon Knight 1.50 4.00
74 Blake Griffin 2.50 6.00
75 Tim Duncan 6.00 15.00
76 Goran Dragic 2.50 6.00
77 John Wall 3.00 8.00
78 Al Horford 2.50 6.00
79 Andre Iguodala 2.50 6.00
80 Kevin Love 2.50 6.00
81 Enes Kanter 1.50 4.00
82 Klay Thompson 6.00 15.00
83 Eric Bledsoe 2.00 5.00
84 Paul Pierce 4.00 10.00
85 Rajon Rondo 3.00 8.00
86 Andrew Wiggins 3.00 8.00
87 Bradley Beal 3.00 8.00
88 Kyle Korver 2.00 5.00
89 Joakim Noah 1.50 4.00
90 Dirk Nowitzki 6.00 15.00
91 Serge Ibaka 2.00 5.00
92 Harrison Barnes 2.00 5.00
93 Tyson Chandler 2.00 5.00
94 Kobe Bryant 15.00 40.00
95 DeMarcus Cousins 2.50 6.00
96 Kevin Garnett 6.00 15.00
97 Marcin Gortat 1.50 4.00
98 Al Jefferson 1.50 4.00
99 Tyreke Evans 2.00 5.00
100 Chandler Parsons 1.50 4.00
101 John Stockton 5.00 12.00
102 Dominique Wilkins 4.00 10.00
103 Kareem Abdul-Jabbar 8.00 20.00
104 Pete Maravich 6.00 15.00
105 Alonzo Mourning 4.00 10.00
106 James Worthy 4.00 10.00
107 Dennis Rodman 6.00 15.00
108 Drazen Petrovic 2.50 6.00
109 Scottie Pippen 6.00 15.00
110 Larry Bird 10.00 25.00
111 Patrick Ewing 4.00 10.00
112 Julius Erving 6.00 15.00
113 Clyde Drexler 4.00 10.00
114 Chris Mullin 3.00 8.00
115 Gary Payton 4.00 10.00
116 Magic Johnson 10.00 25.00
117 Karl Malone 4.00 10.00
118 Isiah Thomas 2.50 6.00
119 David Robinson 5.00 12.00
120 George Gervin 4.00 10.00

2015-16 Panini Gala Action Autographs

STATED PRINT RUN 40 SER.#'d SETS
EXCHANGE DEADLINE 12/22/2017
1 Kobe Bryant 500.00 1,000.00
2 Kevin Durant 50.00 120.00
3 Anthony Davis 25.00 60.00
4 Blake Griffin 15.00 40.00
5 John Wall 15.00 40.00
6 Andrew Wiggins 10.00 25.00
7 Dennis Rodman 15.00 40.00
8 Anfernee Hardaway 30.00 80.00
9 Julius Randle 8.00 20.00
10 Ben McLemore 4.00 10.00
11 Aaron Gordon 6.00 15.00
12 Byron Scott 5.00 12.00
13 Langston Galloway 4.00 10.00
14 Jonas Valanciunas 5.00 12.00
15 Robert Parish 8.00 20.00
16 Mark Jackson 5.00 12.00
17 Peja Stojakovic 5.00 12.00
18 J.R. Smith 6.00 15.00
20 Nene 5.00 12.00
21 Allan Houston 5.00 12.00
22 Klay Thompson 25.00 60.00
23 Doug McDermott 5.00 12.00
24 Gary Harris 5.00 12.00
25 Mike Conley 6.00 15.00
26 Wilson Chandler 5.00 12.00
27 Mitch Richmond 12.00 30.00
28 Jerry Stackhouse 12.00 30.00
29 Danny Green 5.00 12.00
30 Kemba Walker 4.00 10.00
31 Robert Horry 5.00 12.00
32 Alex English 8.00 20.00
33 Dennis Schroder 6.00 15.00
34 Antonio McDyess 5.00 12.00
35 Nick Young 4.00 10.00
36 Bill Laimbeer 6.00 15.00
37 Eddie Jones 6.00 15.00
38 Gary Neal 4.00 10.00
39 Mason Plumlee 4.00 10.00
40 Bojan Bogdanovic 5.00 12.00

2015-16 Panini Gala Award Winning Autographs

PRINT RUNS B/WN 30-60 COPIES PER
EXCHANGE DEADLINE 12/22/2017
1 Dwight Howard/30 20.00 50.00
3 Zach LaVine/50 40.00 100.00
4 Steve Nash/30 EXCH 30.00 80.00
5 Andrew Wiggins/30 8.00 20.00
6 Dennis Rodman/30 30.00 80.00
7 Vince Carter/30 75.00 200.00
8 Gary Payton/30 25.00 60.00
9 Allen Iverson/30 250.00 400.00
12 Kobe Bryant/30 600.00 1,200.00
13 Joe Dumars/30 10.00 25.00
14 Glen Rice/60 8.00 20.00
15 Mitch Richmond/60 12.00 30.00
16 Dikembe Mutombo/60 15.00 40.00
17 Michael Cooper/60 4.00 10.00
19 Blake Griffin/30 30.00 80.00
20 Bob McAdoo/60 12.00 30.00

2015-16 Panini Gala Cinematic Rookie Signatures

STATED PRINT RUN 60 SER.#'d SETS
EXCHANGE DEADLINE 12/22/2017
*JADE/25: .6X TO 1.5X BASIC
1 Karl-Anthony Towns 40.00 100.00
2 D'Angelo Russell 20.00 50.00
3 Jahlil Okafor 4.00 10.00
4 Emmanuel Mudiay 4.00 10.00
5 Kristaps Porzingis 30.00 80.00
6 Mario Hezonja 4.00 10.00
7 Justise Winslow 5.00 12.00
8 Willie Cauley-Stein 4.00 10.00
9 Stanley Johnson 4.00 10.00
10 Bobby Portis 8.00 20.00
11 Frank Kaminsky 4.00 10.00
12 Devin Booker 200.00 500.00
13 Myles Turner 12.00 30.00
14 Joe Young 3.00 8.00
15 Jerian Grant 3.00 8.00
16 Trey Lyles 4.00 10.00
17 Delon Wright 4.00 10.00
18 Cameron Payne 5.00 12.00
19 Norman Powell 6.00 15.00
20 Sam Dekker 3.00 8.00
21 Terry Rozier 12.00 30.00
22 Kelly Oubre Jr. 10.00 25.00
23 Rondae Hollis-Jefferson 4.00 10.00
24 Kevon Looney 10.00 25.00
25 Justin Anderson 3.00 8.00

2015-16 Panini Gala Cinematic Signatures

PRINT RUNS B/WN 35-60 COPIES PER
EXCHANGE DEADLINE 12/22/2017
*JADE/25: .6X TO 1.5X p/r 50-60
*JADE/25: .5X TO 1.2X p/r 35-40
1 Chris Paul/40 100.00 250.00
2 Clyde Drexler/40 30.00 80.00
3 Blake Griffin/40 20.00 50.00
4 John Wall/40 15.00 40.00
5 Alonzo Mourning/40 12.00 30.00
6 Andrew Wiggins/40 30.00 80.00
7 Tracy McGrady/40 30.00 80.00
8 Rick Barry/35 8.00 20.00
9 Jason Kidd/40 15.00 40.00
10 Marcus Smart/40 8.00 20.00
11 David Robinson/40 20.00 50.00
13 Victor Oladipo/40 5.00 12.00
14 Julius Randle/40 8.00 20.00
15 Dwyane Wade/40 30.00 80.00
16 Marques Johnson/60 4.00 10.00
17 Joe Dumars/50 5.00 12.00
18 Michael Finley/50 5.00 12.00
19 Dennis Schroder/60 5.00 12.00
20 Anfernee Hardaway/40 30.00 80.00
21 Gary Neal/60 3.00 8.00
22 Courtney Lee/60 3.00 8.00
23 Kenny Smith/50 4.00 10.00
24 Rick Fox/50 6.00 15.00
25 Patrick Patterson/60 3.00 8.00
26 Steve Kerr/50 8.00 20.00
27 Gordon Hayward/60 6.00 15.00
28 Glen Rice/60 4.00 10.00
29 Nene/60 4.00 10.00
30 Kevin Love/40 15.00 40.00
31 Nikola Mirotic/60 3.00 8.00
32 Allan Houston/60 4.00 10.00
33 Joe Ingles/60 4.00 10.00
34 Wilson Chandler/60 4.00 10.00
35 Zach LaVine/60 12.00 30.00
36 A.C. Green/60 4.00 10.00
37 Jerry Stackhouse/60 10.00 25.00
38 Aaron Gordon/60 10.00 25.00
39 Mitch Richmond/60 10.00 25.00
40 Dikembe Mutombo/60 10.00 25.00
41 Doug McDermott/60 4.00 10.00
42 Gary Harris/60 4.00 10.00
43 Giannis Antetokounmpo/60 60.00 150.00
44 Tony Allen/60 3.00 8.00
45 Rolando Blackman/60 5.00 12.00
46 Kyrie Irving/40 30.00 80.00
47 Mo Williams/60 4.00 10.00
48 Elfrid Payton/50 4.00 10.00

49 Thaddeus Young/60 3.00 8.00
50 Timofey Mozgov/60 3.00 8.00
51 Mike Conley/60 5.00 12.00
53 Kenneth Faried/60 4.00 10.00
54 Tom Chambers/60 4.00 10.00
55 Antonio McDyess/60 4.00 10.00
56 Alec Burks/60 3.00 8.00
57 Cuttino Mobley/60 3.00 8.00
58 Damon Stoudamire/60 5.00 12.00
59 Spud Webb/60 4.00 10.00
61 Rafer Alston/60 3.00 8.00
62 Jordan Adams/60 3.00 8.00
63 Gary Payton/40 25.00 60.00
65 Sam Bowie/60 3.00 8.00
66 Michael Cooper/60 4.00 10.00
67 Anthony Davis/40 40.00 100.00
68 Mason Plumlee/60 3.00 8.00
69 Bojan Bogdanovic/60 4.00 10.00
70 Langston Galloway/60 3.00 8.00
71 Grant Hill/40 20.00 50.00
72 Bradley Beal/40 12.00 30.00
73 Tarik Black/60 3.00 8.00
74 Andre Drummond/60 5.00 12.00

2015-16 Panini Gala Coming Attractions Memorabilia

PRINT RUNS B/WN 45-60 COPIES PER
*PURPLE/40: .5X TO 1.2X BASIC
*JADE/21-25: .75X TO 2X BASIC
1 Kristaps Porzingis/60 12.00 30.00
2 Justin Anderson/60 2.00 5.00
3 Stanley Johnson/60 2.50 6.00
4 Jarell Martin/60 2.00 5.00
5 Trey Lyles/60 2.50 6.00
6 Montrezl Harrell/60 6.00 15.00
7 Kelly Oubre Jr./60 6.00 15.00
8 Jordan Mickey/60 2.00 5.00
9 Karl-Anthony Towns/60 12.00 30.00
10 Sam Dekker/60 2.00 5.00
11 Mario Hezonja/60 2.50 6.00
12 Bobby Portis/60 5.00 12.00
13 Frank Kaminsky/60 2.50 6.00
14 R.J. Hunter/60 2.00 5.00
15 Devin Booker/60 6.00 15.00
16 Anthony Brown/60 2.00 5.00
17 Terry Rozier/60 8.00 20.00
18 Rakeem Christmas/60 2.00 5.00
19 D'Angelo Russell/45 6.00 15.00
20 Jerian Grant/60 2.00 5.00
21 Willie Cauley-Stein/60 2.50 6.00
22 Rondae Hollis-Jefferson/60 2.50 6.00
23 Justise Winslow/60 3.00 8.00
24 Chris McCullough/60 2.50 6.00
25 Cameron Payne/60 3.00 8.00
26 Joe Young/60 2.00 5.00
27 Nikola Jokic/60 75.00 200.00
28 Pat Connaughton/60 3.00 8.00
29 Jahlil Okafor/60 5.00 12.00
30 Delon Wright/60 2.50 6.00
31 Emmanuel Mudiay/60 2.50 6.00
32 Tyus Jones/60 2.50 6.00
33 Myles Turner/60 8.00 20.00

2015-16 Panini Gala Double Feature Memorabilia

PRINT RUNS B/WN 35-60 COPIES PER
*PURPLE/40: .5X TO 1.2X BASIC
*JADE/23-25: .75X TO 2X BASIC
1 K.Duckworth/C.Robinson/60 3.00 8.00
2 Nowitzki/Nash/60 8.00 20.00
3 Schrempf/Payton/60 8.00 20.00
4 Davis/Griffin/60 3.00 8.00
5 D.Favors/T.Burke/60 2.50 6.00
6 Wiggins/Garnett/60 8.00 20.00
7 D.Manning/M.Jackson/60 2.50 6.00
8 Bird/Ainge/60 10.00 25.00
9 Oakley/Ewing/35 8.00 20.00
10 Johnson/Mourning/60 5.00 12.00
11 Duncan/Parker/60 6.00 15.00
12 D.Gallinari/K.Faried/60 2.50 6.00
13 T.Ross/D.DeRozan/60 4.00 10.00
14 K.Bryant/J.Clarkson/60 25.00 60.00
16 Davis/Gordon/60 4.00 10.00
17 A.Gordon/E.Payton/60 3.00 8.00
18 J.Young/M.Smart/60 4.00 10.00
19 Wstbrk/Drnt/60 10.00 25.00
20 Rodman/Pippen/60 10.00 25.00
21 Leonard/Ginobili/60 8.00 20.00
22 A.Dantley/I.Thomas/35 3.00 8.00
23 Stockton/Malone/60 12.00 30.00
24 Wade/O'Neal/60 10.00 25.00
25 Hill/George/60 5.00 12.00
26 Starks/Ewing/60 5.00 12.00
27 A.Adams/W.Davis/60 2.00 5.00
28 K.McHale/R.Lewis/60 5.00 12.00
29 E.Bledsoe/T.Warren/60 3.00 8.00
30 Rose/Butler/60 6.00 15.00
32 H.Olajuwon/C.Drexler/60 10.00 25.00

2015-16 Panini Gala Genregraphs Classics

STATED PRINT RUN 25 SER.#'d SETS
EXCHANGE DEADLINE 12/22/2017
1 Larry Bird 50.00 120.00
2 Julius Erving 40.00 100.00
3 Magic Johnson 30.00 80.00
4 Michael Cooper 6.00 15.00
5 Dominique Wilkins 15.00 40.00
6 Hersey Hawkins 5.00 12.00
7 Wes Unseld 10.00 25.00
8 Sam Bowie 5.00 12.00
9 Bob McAdoo 20.00 50.00
10 David Robinson 25.00 60.00
11 Mark Aguirre 6.00 15.00
12 John Stockton 30.00 80.00
14 Steve Kerr 12.00 30.00
15 Dennis Rodman 30.00 80.00
16 Hakeem Olajuwon 15.00 40.00
17 Clyde Drexler 40.00 100.00
19 Jerry West 25.00 60.00
20 Artis Gilmore 8.00 20.00
21 Nate Archibald 10.00 25.00
23 Robert Parish 10.00 25.00
24 Walt Frazier 10.00 25.00
26 Byron Scott 6.00 15.00
27 Bill Laimbeer 8.00 20.00
28 Dan Issel 10.00 25.00
29 Anfernee Hardaway 40.00 100.00
30 Gary Payton 30.00 80.00
31 Rick Fox 6.00 15.00
33 Ralph Sampson 6.00 15.00
34 Jerry Stackhouse 20.00 50.00
35 Marques Johnson 8.00 20.00
36 Dikembe Mutombo 15.00 40.00
37 Bill Walton 40.00 100.00
38 Dave Cowens 10.00 25.00
40 Joe Dumars 8.00 20.00

2015-16 Panini Gala Genregraphs Comedy

STATED PRINT RUN 25 SER.#'d SETS
EXCHANGE DEADLINE 12/22/2017
1 Andrew Wiggins 30.00 80.00
2 John Wall 30.00 80.00
3 Kevin Durant 60.00 150.00
4 Tony Allen 5.00 12.00
5 Vlade Divac 8.00 20.00
6 Kevin Love 12.00 30.00
7 J.R. Smith 8.00 20.00
8 Steve Nash 60.00 150.00
9 Zach Randolph 8.00 20.00
10 Kenneth Faried 6.00 15.00
11 Zach LaVine 30.00 80.00
12 Elfrid Payton 6.00 15.00
13 Kobe Bryant 800.00 1,500.00
14 Magic Johnson 30.00 80.00
15 Grant Hill 25.00 60.00
16 Shaquille O'Neal 40.00 100.00
17 Dikembe Mutombo 15.00 40.00
18 Jason Kidd 20.00 50.00
19 Allen Iverson 150.00 400.00
20 Kyrie Irving 50.00 120.00
21 Blake Griffin 25.00 60.00
22 Anthony Davis 60.00 150.00
23 Damon Stoudamire 10.00 25.00
24 Rick Fox 6.00 15.00
25 Chris Bosh 12.00 30.00

2015-16 Panini Gala Genregraphs Drama

STATED PRINT RUN 25 SER.#'d SETS
EXCHANGE DEADLINE 12/22/2017
1 Kobe Bryant 600.00 1,200.00
2 Kevin Durant 60.00 150.00
3 Andrew Wiggins 30.00 80.00
4 Anthony Davis 60.00 150.00
5 Vince Carter 40.00 100.00
6 Tracy McGrady 40.00 100.00
7 John Wall 20.00 50.00
8 Julius Randle 10.00 25.00
10 Jrue Holiday 10.00 25.00
11 Zach Randolph 8.00 20.00
12 Klay Thompson 30.00 80.00
13 Bradley Beal 15.00 40.00
14 Tony Parker 25.00 60.00
15 Jabari Parker 25.00 60.00
16 Victor Oladipo 20.00 50.00
17 Zach LaVine 30.00 80.00

2015-16 Panini Gala Genregraphs Thriller

STATED PRINT RUN 25 SER.#'d SETS
EXCHANGE DEADLINE 12/22/2017
1 Kevin Durant 60.00 150.00
2 Kobe Bryant 500.00 1,000.00
3 Kyrie Irving 50.00 120.00
4 John Wall 20.00 50.00
5 Anthony Davis 60.00 150.00
6 Bradley Beal 15.00 40.00
7 Gordon Hayward 10.00 25.00
8 Blake Griffin 25.00 60.00
9 Chris Paul 75.00 200.00
10 Courtney Lee 5.00 12.00
11 Tracy McGrady 40.00 100.00
12 Chris Bosh 12.00 30.00
13 Ray Allen 30.00 80.00
14 Steve Nash 40.00 100.00
15 Robert Horry 6.00 15.00
16 Magic Johnson 30.00 80.00
17 Danny Green 6.00 15.00
18 Alonzo Mourning 15.00 40.00

2015-16 Panini Gala Main Attraction Memorabilia

PRINT RUNS B/WN 34-60 COPIES PER
*PURPLE/40: .5X TO 1.2X BASIC
*JADE/20-25: .75X TO 2X BASIC
1 Kevin Durant/60 5.00 12.00
2 Damian Lillard/60 5.00 12.00
3 Markieff Morris/60 2.00 5.00
4 Detlef Schrempf/60 3.00 8.00
5 Rafer Alston/60 2.00 5.00
6 Isaiah Thomas/60 2.50 6.00
7 Terrence Ross/60 2.50 6.00
8 Alex Len/60 2.00 5.00
9 John Starks/60 3.00 8.00
10 Blake Griffin/60 3.00 8.00
11 Kawhi Leonard/60 10.00 25.00
12 Kobe Bryant/60 25.00 60.00
13 LeBron James/60 20.00 50.00
14 Doug McDermott/60 2.50 6.00
15 Richard Hamilton/60 3.00 8.00
16 James Harden/60 6.00 15.00
17 Toni Kukoc/60 3.00 8.00
18 Andrew Bogut/60 2.50 6.00
19 Jordan Clarkson/60 3.00 8.00
20 Brook Lopez/60 3.00 8.00
21 Manute Bol/60 3.00 8.00
22 David Thompson/44 4.00 10.00
23 Mo Williams/60 2.50 6.00
24 Eric Gordon/60 2.50 6.00
25 Ron Harper/34 3.00 8.00
26 Jeff Teague/60 2.00 5.00
27 Wilson Chandler/60 2.50 6.00
28 Avery Bradley/60 2.00 5.00
29 Kenneth Faried/60 2.50 6.00
30 Clifford Robinson/60 3.00 8.00
31 Larry Johnson/60 4.00 10.00
33 Patrick Ewing/60 5.00 12.00
34 Gordon Hayward/60 3.00 8.00
35 Shaquille O'Neal/60 8.00 20.00

2015-16 Panini Gala Primetime Memorabilia

STATED PRINT RUN 60 SER.#'d SETS
*PURPLE/40: .5X TO 1.2X BASIC
1 Allen Iverson 8.00 20.00
2 Jimmy Butler 6.00 15.00
3 Carmelo Anthony 5.00 12.00
4 Karl Malone 5.00 12.00
5 David Robinson 6.00 15.00
6 Manu Ginobili 6.00 15.00
7 Dirk Nowitzki 8.00 20.00
8 Scottie Pippen 8.00 20.00
9 Kyrie Irving 6.00 15.00
10 Grant Hill 5.00 12.00
11 Anthony Davis 4.00 10.00
12 John Stockton 6.00 15.00
13 Chris Paul 6.00 15.00
14 Kobe Bryant 25.00 60.00
15 DeMar DeRozan 4.00 10.00
16 Marcus Smart 4.00 10.00
17 Dominique Wilkins 5.00 12.00
18 Steve Nash 5.00 12.00
20 Hakeem Olajuwon 6.00 15.00
21 Chris Bosh 4.00 10.00
22 John Wall 4.00 10.00
23 Clyde Drexler 5.00 12.00
24 LaMarcus Aldridge 3.00 8.00
25 Dennis Rodman 8.00 20.00
27 Dwyane Wade 6.00 15.00
28 Tim Duncan 8.00 20.00
29 Aaron Gordon 3.00 8.00
31 Ben Wallace 2.50 6.00
32 Kareem Abdul-Jabbar 10.00 25.00
33 Danny Manning 2.50 6.00
34 Larry Bird 12.00 30.00
35 Derrick Rose 5.00 12.00
36 Russell Westbrook 5.00 12.00
37 Gary Payton 5.00 12.00
38 Tony Parker 5.00 12.00
40 Jason Kidd 5.00 12.00

2015-16 Panini Gala Primetime Rookie Memorabilia

STATED PRINT RUN 60 SER.#'d SETS
*PURPLE/40: .5X TO 1.2X BASIC
*PRIME/24-25: .75X TO 2X BASIC
1 Justise Winslow 3.00 8.00
2 Jarell Martin 2.00 5.00
3 Devin Booker 6.00 15.00
4 Montrezl Harrell 6.00 15.00
6 Terry Rozier 8.00 20.00
8 Jerian Grant 2.00 5.00
9 Emmanuel Mudiay 2.50 6.00
10 Bobby Portis 5.00 12.00
11 Myles Turner 8.00 20.00
12 R.J. Hunter 2.00 5.00
13 Cameron Payne 3.00 8.00
14 Anthony Brown 2.00 5.00
15 D'Angelo Russell 8.00 20.00
16 Nemanja Bjelica 3.00 8.00
17 Mario Hezonja 2.50 6.00
18 Delon Wright 2.50 6.00
19 Stanley Johnson 2.50 6.00
20 Rondae Hollis-Jefferson 2.50 6.00
21 Trey Lyles 2.50 6.00
22 Chris McCullough 2.00 5.00
23 Kelly Oubre Jr. 6.00 15.00
24 Joe Young 2.00 5.00
25 Jahlil Okafor 2.50 6.00
26 Sam Dekker 2.00 5.00
27 Willie Cauley-Stein 2.50 6.00
28 Justin Anderson 2.00 5.00
29 Frank Kaminsky 2.50 6.00
30 Tyus Jones 2.50 6.00

2015-16 Panini Gala Red Carpet Signatures

STATED PRINT RUN 30 SER.#'d SETS
EXCHANGE DEADLINE 12/22/2017
1 Kobe Bryant 500.00 1,000.00
2 Chris Paul 100.00 250.00
3 Blake Griffin 20.00 50.00
4 John Wall 20.00 50.00
5 Jabari Parker 20.00 50.00
6 Kevin Love 12.00 30.00
7 Kevin Durant 50.00 120.00
8 Dominique Wilkins 12.00 30.00
9 Nick Young 10.00 25.00
10 Andre Drummond 8.00 20.00
11 Chris Bosh 10.00 25.00
12 Steve Nash 60.00 150.00
13 Victor Oladipo 15.00 40.00
14 Ralph Sampson 5.00 12.00
15 Julius Erving 30.00 80.00
16 Zach LaVine 20.00 50.00
17 Frank Kaminsky 12.00 30.00
18 Shaquille O'Neal 40.00 100.00
19 Walt Frazier 5.00 12.00
20 Justise Winslow 15.00 40.00

2015-16 Panini Gala Signatures

STATED PRINT RUN 40 SER.#'d SETS
EXCHANGE DEADLINE 12/22/2017
1 Chris Paul 20.00 50.00
2 Joe Ingles 10.00 25.00
3 Elfrid Payton 5.00 12.00
4 Andrew Wiggins 15.00 40.00
5 Antoine Walker 5.00 12.00
6 Antonio McDyess 5.00 12.00
7 Bill Laimbeer 6.00 15.00
8 Ray Allen 25.00 60.00
9 Mike Conley 6.00 15.00
10 DeMarre Carroll 4.00 10.00
11 Gary Harris 5.00 12.00
12 Tracy McGrady 30.00 80.00
13 Dan Issel 8.00 20.00
14 Jerry West 20.00 50.00
15 Tony Allen 4.00 10.00
16 Doug McDermott 4.00 10.00
17 Dwight Powell 4.00 10.00
19 Julius Randle 8.00 20.00
20 Giannis Antetokounmpo 75.00 200.00
21 Dennis Schroder 6.00 15.00
22 Nick Van Exel 20.00 50.00
23 Jabari Parker 12.00 30.00
24 Jerami Grant 6.00 15.00
25 Jrue Holiday 8.00 20.00
26 Marques Johnson 5.00 12.00
28 John Wall 15.00 40.00
29 Jordan Adams 4.00 10.00
30 K.J. McDaniels 4.00 10.00
31 Timofey Mozgov 4.00 10.00
32 Nick Young 4.00 10.00
33 Kenny Smith 5.00 12.00
34 Kevin Love 6.00 15.00
35 Kobe Bryant 500.00 1,000.00
36 Michael Cooper 5.00 12.00
37 Gary Neal 4.00 10.00
38 Michael Finley 6.00 15.00
39 Kenneth Faried 5.00 12.00
40 Mo Williams 5.00 12.00
41 Antoine Carr 4.00 10.00
42 Jonas Valanciunas 5.00 12.00
43 Mark Aguirre 5.00 12.00
44 Nene 5.00 12.00
45 Rafer Alston 4.00 10.00
46 Hersey Hawkins 4.00 10.00
47 Robert Horry 5.00 12.00
48 Rolando Blackman 6.00 15.00
49 Ron Harper 6.00 15.00
50 Spud Webb 5.00 12.00
52 Sam Bowie 4.00 10.00
53 Patrick Patterson 4.00 10.00
54 J.R. Smith 6.00 15.00
55 Tarik Black 4.00 10.00
56 Thaddeus Young 4.00 10.00
57 Tom Chambers 5.00 12.00
58 Tony Delk 4.00 10.00
59 Marcus Smart 8.00 20.00
60 Wilson Chandler 5.00 12.00

2015-16 Panini Gala Silver Screen Autographs

PRINT RUNS B/WN 30-60 COPIES PER
EXCHANGE DEADLINE 12/22/2017
1 Kobe Bryant/35 500.00 1,000.00
2 Kevin Durant/35 60.00 150.00
3 Dwyane Wade/35 30.00 80.00
4 John Stockton/30 25.00 60.00
5 Tracy McGrady/30 30.00 80.00
6 Anthony Davis/35 40.00 100.00
8 Kyrie Irving/35 30.00 80.00
9 Dennis Rodman/35 25.00 60.00
10 Jabari Parker/35 10.00 25.00
11 Andrew Wiggins/35 15.00 40.00
12 Kevin Love/35 15.00 40.00
13 Jrue Holiday/35 8.00 20.00
14 Andre Drummond/35 8.00 20.00
15 Aaron Gordon/35 12.00 30.00
16 Mark Aguirre/60 4.00 10.00
17 Wesley Matthews/60 3.00 8.00
18 Jason Kidd/35 15.00 40.00
19 Mike Conley/60 5.00 12.00
20 Danny Green/60 4.00 10.00
21 Taj Gibson/60 3.00 8.00
23 Jerry Stackhouse/60 5.00 12.00
24 Kenny Walker/60 3.00 8.00
25 Robert Horry/60 4.00 10.00
26 Bill Walton/35 30.00 80.00
27 Dennis Schroder/60 5.00 12.00
28 Tom Chambers/60 4.00 10.00
29 Alec Burks/60 3.00 8.00
30 Kenneth Faried/60 4.00 10.00
31 Jusuf Nurkic/60 4.00 10.00
32 Patrick Patterson/60 3.00 8.00
33 Elfrid Payton/35 5.00 12.00
34 Klay Thompson/60 20.00 50.00
35 Dan Issel/60 6.00 15.00
36 Doug McDermott/60 4.00 10.00
37 Antonio McDyess/60 4.00 10.00
38 Ron Harper/60 5.00 12.00
39 Bill Laimbeer/60 5.00 12.00
41 Rafer Alston/60 3.00 8.00
42 Dino Radja/60 8.00 20.00
43 Cuttino Mobley/60 3.00 8.00
44 Antoine Carr/60 3.00 8.00
45 Keith Van Horn/60 4.00 10.00
46 Damon Stoudamire/60 10.00 25.00
47 Rony Seikaly/60 4.00 10.00
48 Sam Bowie/60 3.00 8.00
49 Tony Delk/60 3.00 8.00
50 Timofey Mozgov/60 3.00 8.00
51 Tony Allen/60 4.00 10.00
52 Sean Elliott/60 4.00 10.00
53 Thaddeus Young/60 4.00 10.00
54 Kendall Gill/60 10.00 25.00
55 Nick Young/60 3.00 8.00
56 Zach LaVine/60 12.00 30.00
57 Michael Finley/35 6.00 15.00
58 Jordan Adams/60 3.00 8.00
59 Rick Barry/35 8.00 20.00
60 Wilson Chandler/60 3.00 8.00
61 Mark Jackson/60 4.00 10.00
62 Dan Majerle/60 4.00 10.00
63 Victor Oladipo/35 5.00 12.00
65 Jerami Grant/60 5.00 12.00
66 J.R. Smith/60 5.00 12.00
67 Dikembe Mutombo/60 10.00 25.00
68 Zach Randolph/35 6.00 15.00
69 Dwight Powell/60 3.00 8.00
70 Michael Cooper/60 4.00 10.00
71 Marques Johnson/35 5.00 12.00
72 Enes Kanter/60 3.00 8.00
74 Nick Van Exel/35 25.00 60.00

2015-16 Panini Gala Silver Screen Rookie Autographs

STATED PRINT RUN 60 SER.#'d SETS
EXCHANGE DEADLINE 12/22/2017
1 Karl-Anthony Towns 60.00 150.00
2 D'Angelo Russell 15.00 40.00
3 Jahlil Okafor 4.00 10.00
4 Emmanuel Mudiay 4.00 10.00
5 Kristaps Porzingis 50.00 120.00
6 Mario Hezonja 4.00 10.00
7 Justise Winslow 10.00 25.00
8 Willie Cauley-Stein 8.00 20.00
9 Stanley Johnson 4.00 10.00
10 Bobby Portis 8.00 20.00
11 Frank Kaminsky 4.00 10.00
12 Devin Booker 200.00 500.00
13 Myles Turner 10.00 25.00
14 Justin Anderson 3.00 8.00
15 Jerian Grant 3.00 8.00
16 Trey Lyles 3.00 8.00
17 Delon Wright 4.00 10.00
18 R.J. Hunter 3.00 8.00
19 Jarell Martin 3.00 8.00
20 Anthony Brown 3.00 8.00
21 Norman Powell 6.00 15.00
22 Larry Nance Jr. 6.00 15.00
23 Walter Tavares 3.00 8.00
24 Montrezl Harrell 10.00 25.00
25 Joe Young 3.00 8.00

2015-16 Panini Gala Starring Role Signatures

PRINT RUNS B/WN 35-50 COPIES PER
EXCHANGE DEADLINE 12/22/2017
1 Kobe Bryant/35 500.00 1,000.00
2 Kevin Durant/35 50.00 120.00
3 Anthony Davis/35 40.00 100.00
4 Kyrie Irving/35 30.00 80.00
5 John Wall/35 15.00 40.00
6 Nikola Mirotic/35 8.00 20.00
7 Victor Oladipo/35 5.00 12.00
8 Zach Randolph/35 6.00 15.00
9 Elfrid Payton/35 5.00 12.00
10 Jordan Clarkson/35 12.00 30.00
11 Danny Green/35 5.00 12.00
12 Matthew Dellavedova/35 15.00 40.00
13 Giannis Antetokounmpo/35 60.00 150.00
15 Dennis Schroder/35 12.00 30.00
16 Marcus Smart/35 8.00 20.00
17 Julius Randle/35 8.00 20.00
18 Gordon Hayward/35 8.00 20.00
19 Kevin Love/35 15.00 40.00
20 Blake Griffin/35 20.00 50.00
21 Mike Conley/50 5.00 12.00
22 Kenneth Faried/50 4.00 10.00
23 Norris Cole/50 3.00 8.00
24 Tony Parker/50 15.00 40.00
25 Andre Drummond/50 10.00 25.00
26 Ray Allen/50 20.00 50.00
27 Dominique Wilkins/50 10.00 25.00
28 Nate Archibald/50 6.00 15.00
29 Anfernee Hardaway/50 25.00 60.00
30 Grant Hill/50 20.00 50.00
31 David Robinson/50 20.00 50.00
32 Bill Walton/50 25.00 60.00
33 Wes Unseld/50 6.00 15.00
34 Dave Cowens/50 6.00 15.00
35 Joe Dumars/50 5.00 12.00

2015-16 Panini Gala Studio Swatches

STATED PRINT RUN 60 SER.#'d SETS
*PURPLE/40: .5X TO 1.2X BASIC
*PRIME/25: .75X TO 2X BASIC
1 Anderson Varejao 2.00 5.00
2 Danny Green 2.50 6.00
3 LeBron James 20.00 50.00
4 Steven Adams 2.50 6.00
5 Derrick Favors 2.50 6.00
6 James Young 2.00 5.00
7 Kevin Garnett 8.00 20.00
8 Alex Len 2.00 5.00
9 Shane Battier 2.50 6.00
10 Eric Gordon 2.50 6.00
11 Boris Diaw 2.50 6.00
12 DeMar DeRozan 4.00 10.00
13 Darren Collison 2.00 5.00
14 Al Jefferson 2.00 5.00
15 Joe Smith 2.50 6.00
16 John Henson 2.00 5.00
17 Nicolas Batum 2.00 5.00
18 Avery Bradley 2.00 5.00
19 Tim Hardaway Jr. 2.50 6.00
21 Cody Zeller 2.00 5.00
22 Marcus Smart 4.00 10.00
23 David West 2.50 6.00
24 Brandon Jennings 2.00 5.00
25 Jusuf Nurkic 2.50 6.00
26 Aaron Gordon 3.00 8.00
27 Paul George 5.00 12.00
28 Doug McDermott 2.50 6.00
29 Trey Burke 2.00 5.00
30 Stephen Curry 10.00 25.00

2010-11 Panini Gold Standard

STATED PRINT RUN 299 SER.#'d SETS
EWING, MARAVICH, RODMAN HAVE VAR
ALL VAR STILL TOTAL JUST 299 CARDS
EXCH.EXPIRATION 1/14/2013
1 Kevin Durant 6.00 15.00
2 Kobe Bryant 50.00 120.00
3 Derrick Rose 3.00 8.00
4 Paul Pierce 2.50 6.00
5 Ty Lawson 1.00 2.50
6 Amare Stoudemire 1.50 4.00
7 Deron Williams 1.25 3.00
8 Blake Griffin 1.50 4.00
9 Kevin Love 1.50 4.00
10 Russell Westbrook 2.50 6.00
11 Monta Ellis 1.25 3.00
12 Tim Duncan 4.00 10.00
13 Steve Nash 3.00 8.00
14 Jrue Holiday 2.00 5.00
15 Kevin Martin 1.25 3.00
16 Dirk Nowitzki 4.00 10.00
17 Stephen Jackson 1.25 3.00
18 LeBron James 50.00 120.00
19 Eric Gordon 1.25 3.00
20 Tayshaun Prince 1.50 4.00
21 Derek Fisher 1.50 4.00
22 Vince Carter 3.00 8.00
23 Antawn Jamison 1.25 3.00
24 Tyreke Evans 1.25 3.00
25 Al Horford 1.50 4.00
26 Danny Granger 1.00 2.50
27 Marcus Camby 1.00 2.50
28 Rajon Rondo 2.00 5.00
29 Carmelo Anthony 2.50 6.00
30 Michael Beasley 1.00 2.50
31 Dwight Howard 2.00 5.00
32 Tony Parker 2.50 6.00
33 Chris Bosh 2.00 5.00
34 LaMarcus Aldridge 1.50 4.00
35 Stephen Curry 50.00 120.00
36 Brook Lopez 1.25 3.00
37 Tyson Chandler 1.25 3.00
38 Jason Richardson 1.50 4.00
39 Anderson Varejao 1.00 2.50
40 Andre Iguodala 1.50 4.00
41 Marc Gasol 1.50 4.00
42 Danilo Gallinari 1.25 3.00
43 Joe Johnson 1.25 3.00
44 DeMar DeRozan 2.50 6.00
45 Devin Harris 1.00 2.50
46 Andrei Kirilenko 1.25 3.00
47 Brandon Roy 2.00 5.00
48 Raymond Felton 1.00 2.50
49 Pau Gasol 2.50 6.00
50 Dwyane Wade 3.00 8.00
51 Aaron Brooks 1.00 2.50
52 Zach Randolph 1.50 4.00
53 Jason Terry 1.25 3.00
54 Charlie Villanueva 1.00 2.50
55 Jeff Green 1.25 3.00
56 Channing Frye 1.00 2.50
57 Al Thornton 1.00 2.50
58 Manu Ginobili 3.00 8.00
59 David West 1.25 3.00
60 Andrew Bogut 1.25 3.00
61 Jonny Flynn 1.00 2.50
62 David Lee 1.00 2.50
63 Tracy McGrady 2.50 6.00
64 Luol Deng 1.25 3.00
65 Elton Brand 1.25 3.00
66 Emeka Okafor 1.25 3.00
67 Kevin Garnett 4.00 10.00
68 Carl Landry 1.00 2.50
69 Jameer Nelson 1.00 2.50
70 Joakim Noah 1.50 4.00
71 Chris Kaman 1.00 2.50
72 Rudy Gay 1.50 4.00
73 Richard Jefferson 1.00 2.50
74 Andrea Bargnani 1.00 2.50
75 Jamal Crawford 1.50 4.00
76 Grant Hill 2.50 6.00
77 Lamar Odom 1.25 3.00
78 Paul Millsap 1.25 3.00
79 Luis Scola 1.25 3.00
80 J.R. Smith 1.50 4.00
81 Ray Allen 2.50 6.00
82 Tyler Hansbrough 1.00 2.50
83 Ben Wallace 2.00 5.00
84 J.J. Hickson 1.00 2.50
85 Al Jefferson 1.00 2.50
86 Jason Kidd 2.50 6.00
87 Luke Ridnour 1.00 2.50
88 Nene 1.25 3.00
89 Sasha Vujacic 1.00 2.50
90 Rashard Lewis 1.25 3.00
91 D.J. Augustin 1.00 2.50
92 Ron Artest 1.50 4.00
93 Yao Ming 3.00 8.00
94 Juwan Howard 1.25 3.00
95 Roy Hibbert 1.25 3.00
96 Carlos Boozer 1.25 3.00
97 Wilson Chandler 1.25 3.00
98 DeJuan Blair 1.00 2.50
99 Shaquille O'Neal 6.00 15.00
100 Chris Paul 3.00 8.00
101 Baron Davis 1.50 4.00
102 Leandro Barbosa 1.25 3.00
103 Josh Smith 1.25 3.00
104 John Salmons 1.00 2.50
105 Hedo Turkoglu 1.25 3.00
106 Ben Gordon 1.25 3.00
107 Gerald Henderson 1.00 2.50
108 Serge Ibaka 1.25 3.00
109 Shane Battier 1.25 3.00
110 Andrew Bynum 1.25 3.00
111 Chauncey Billups 2.00 5.00
112 Nick Young 1.00 2.50
113 Dorell Wright 1.00 2.50
114 Gilbert Arenas 1.50 4.00
115 Darko Milicic 1.00 2.50
116 Caron Butler 1.25 3.00
117 Zydrunas Ilgauskas 1.25 3.00
118 Trevor Ariza 1.00 2.50
119 Troy Murphy 1.00 2.50
120 J.J. Redick 1.50 4.00
121 Gerald Wallace 1.25 3.00
122 Samuel Dalembert 1.00 2.50
123 Shawn Marion 1.50 4.00
124 Rudy Fernandez 1.25 3.00
125 Brandon Jennings 1.25 3.00
126 JaVale McGee 1.25 3.00
127 O.J. Mayo 1.00 2.50
128 James Harden 4.00 10.00
129 Chris Andersen 1.50 4.00
130 Toney Douglas 1.00 2.50
131 Glen Davis 1.00 2.50
132 Richard Hamilton 2.00 5.00
133 George Hill 1.25 3.00
134 Louis Williams 1.25 3.00
135 Al Harrington 1.00 2.50
136 Anthony Morrow 1.00 2.50
137 Daniel Gibson 1.00 2.50
138 Wesley Matthews 1.00 2.50
139 Kris Humphries 1.00 2.50
140 Rodrigue Beaubois 1.00 2.50
141 A.J. Price 1.00 2.50
142 Chase Budinger 1.00 2.50
143 Donte Greene 1.00 2.50
144 Andre Miller 1.25 3.00
145 Ryan Gomes 1.00 2.50
146 Jodie Meeks 1.00 2.50
147 Kendrick Perkins 1.00 2.50
148 Taj Gibson 1.00 2.50
149 Boris Diaw 1.00 2.50
150 Derrick Brown 1.00 2.50
151 Jeff Teague 1.00 2.50
152 Wayne Ellington 1.00 2.50
153 Terrence Williams 1.00 2.50
154 Robin Lopez 1.00 2.50
155 Jermaine O'Neal 1.50 4.00
156 Austin Daye 1.00 2.50
157 J.J. Barea 1.25 3.00
158 Darren Collison 1.00 2.50
159 Goran Dragic 2.00 5.00
160 Beno Udrih 1.00 2.50
161 Earl Clark 1.00 2.50
162 Hakim Warrick 1.00 2.50
163 Sam Young 1.00 2.50
164 Ronnie Brewer 1.00 2.50
165 Omri Casspi 1.00 2.50
166 T.J. Ford 1.00 2.50
167 Chris Douglas-Roberts 1.00 2.50
168 Eric Maynor 1.00 2.50
169 James Johnson 1.00 2.50
170 Patrick Mills 1.50 4.00
171 Mark Jackson 1.25 3.00
172 Chris Webber 2.00 5.00
173 Derek Harper 1.25 3.00
174A Patrick Ewing Knicks 2.50 6.00
175 Brad Daugherty 1.25 3.00
176 Kenny Anderson 1.25 3.00
177 Scott Skiles 1.25 3.00
178 Charles Oakley 1.50 4.00
179 Dan Majerle 1.25 3.00
180A Pete Maravich Hawks 4.00 10.00
180C P.Maravich Jazz SP 6.00 15.00
181 Wilt Chamberlain 5.00 12.00
182 Horace Grant 1.50 4.00
183 Glen Rice 1.50 4.00
184 Shawn Kemp 2.50 6.00
185 Jo Jo White 1.25 3.00
186 Jalen Rose 1.25 3.00
187A Dennis Rodman Pistons 6.00 15.00
187B D.Rodman Bulls SP 6.00 15.00
187C D.Rodman Lakers SP 6.00 15.00
187E D.Rodman Spurs SP 6.00 15.00
188 Dave DeBusschere 1.50 4.00
189 Oscar Robertson 4.00 10.00
190 Bill Walton 2.50 6.00
191 Kareem Abdul-Jabbar 5.00 12.00
192 Larry Bird 6.00 15.00
193 Dan Issel 2.00 5.00
194 Doc Rivers 1.50 4.00
195 George McGinnis 1.50 4.00
196 Bill Russell 5.00 12.00
197 Christian Laettner 1.50 4.00
198 Dolph Schayes 2.00 5.00
199 M.L. Carr 1.50 4.00
200 Darryl Dawkins 1.50 4.00
201 David Thompson 1.50 4.00
202 Bob Lanier 2.50 6.00
203 Michael Cooper 1.50 4.00
204 Bernard King 2.00 5.00
205 Bailey Howell 1.50 4.00
206 Al Attles 1.50 4.00
207 Dikembe Mutombo 2.50 6.00
208 Bob McAdoo 2.00 5.00
209 Artis Gilmore 2.00 5.00
210 A.C. Green 1.50 4.00
211 Dominique Wilkins 2.50 6.00
212 Alonzo Mourning 2.50 6.00
213 John Wall AU RC 20.00 50.00
214 Evan Turner AU RC 5.00 12.00
215 Derrick Favors AU RC 6.00 15.00
216 Wesley Johnson AU RC 4.00 10.00
217 DeMarcus Cousins AU RC 12.00 30.00
218 Ekpe Udoh AU RC 4.00 10.00
219 Greg Monroe AU RC 5.00 12.00
220 Al-Farouq Aminu AU RC 4.00 10.00
221 Gordon Hayward AU RC 15.00 40.00
222 Paul George AU RC 50.00 120.00
223 Cole Aldrich AU RC 4.00 10.00
224 Xavier Henry AU RC 4.00 10.00
225 Ed Davis AU RC 5.00 12.00
226 Patrick Patterson AU RC 5.00 12.00
227 Larry Sanders AU RC 4.00 10.00
228 Luke Babbitt AU RC 4.00 10.00
229 Kevin Seraphin AU RC 4.00 10.00
230 Eric Bledsoe AU RC 8.00 20.00
231 Avery Bradley AU RC 6.00 15.00
232 James Anderson AU RC 4.00 10.00
233 Elliot Williams AU RC 4.00 10.00
234 Landry Fields AU RC 4.00 10.00
235 Greivis Vasquez AU RC 4.00 10.00
236 Dominique Jones AU RC 4.00 10.00
237 Gary Neal AU RC 5.00 12.00
238 Daniel Orton AU RC 4.00 10.00
239 Lazar Hayward AU RC 4.00 10.00
240 Devin Ebanks AU RC 4.00 10.00
241 Timofey Mozgov AU RC 5.00 12.00
242 Luke Harangody AU RC 4.00 10.00
243 Omer Asik AU RC 6.00 15.00
244 Eugene Jeter AU RC 6.00 15.00
245 Gary Forbes AU RC 4.00 10.00
246 Nikola Pekovic AU RC 6.00 15.00
247 Jordan Crawford AU RC 4.00 10.00

2010-11 Panini Gold Standard Platinum Gold

*STARS: 2X TO 5X BASE HI
*RETIRED: 1.25X TO 3X BASE HI
*ROOKIES: .75X TO 2X BASE HI
STATED PRINT RUN 25 SER.#'d SETS
184 Shawn Kemp 30.00 80.00
212 Alonzo Mourning 12.00 30.00
213 John Wall AU 150.00 300.00

2010-11 Panini Gold Standard 24-Karat Kobe

COMMON CARD (1-15) 60.00 150.00
STATED PRINT RUN 299 SER.#'d SETS

2010-11 Panini Gold Standard 24-Karat Kobe Materials Signatures

COMMON CARD 200.00 500.00
STATED PRINT RUN 49 SER.#'d SETS

2010-11 Panini Gold Standard 24-Karat Kobe Materials Signatures Prime

COMMON CARD 300.00 600.00
STATED PRINT RUN 24 SER.#'d SETS

2010-11 Panini Gold Standard 24-Karat Kobe Signatures

COMMON CARD 200.00 500.00
STATED PRINT RUN 49 SER.#'d SETS

2010-11 Panini Gold Standard Gold Bars

STATED PRINT RUN 299 SER.#'d SETS
1 Kevin Durant 12.00 30.00
2 Dwight Howard 4.00 10.00
3 Dwyane Wade 6.00 15.00
4 Kobe Bryant 60.00 150.00
5 LaMarcus Aldridge 3.00 8.00
6 Brandon Jennings 2.00 5.00
7 Kevin Garnett 8.00 20.00
8 Eric Gordon 2.50 6.00
9 Deron Williams 2.50 6.00
10 Kevin Love 3.00 8.00
11 Monta Ellis 2.50 6.00
12 Carmelo Anthony 5.00 12.00
13 Chris Paul 6.00 15.00
14 Kevin Martin 2.50 6.00
15 Derrick Rose 6.00 15.00

2010-11 Panini Gold Standard Gold Bars Materials
STATED PRINT RUN 199 SER.#'d SETS
1 Kevin Durant 12.00 30.00
2 Dwight Howard 4.00 10.00
3 Dwyane Wade 6.00 15.00
4 Kobe Bryant 100.00 250.00
5 LaMarcus Aldridge 3.00 8.00
6 Brandon Jennings 2.00 5.00
7 Kevin Garnett 8.00 20.00
8 Eric Gordon 2.50 6.00
10 Kevin Love 3.00 8.00
11 Monta Ellis 2.50 6.00
13 Chris Paul 6.00 15.00
15 Derrick Rose 6.00 15.00

2010-11 Panini Gold Standard Gold Bars Materials Prime
*PRIME: .75X TO 2X BASE HI
STATED PRINT RUN ONE TO 25 SER.#'d SETS
1 Kevin Durant/25 25.00 60.00

2010-11 Panini Gold Standard Gold Bars Materials Signatures
STATED PRINT RUN 5 TO 49 SER.#'d SETS
4 Kobe Bryant/24 1,500.00 3,000.00
5 LaMarcus Aldridge/49 12.00 30.00
8 Eric Gordon/49 8.00 20.00
10 Kevin Love/25 20.00 50.00

2010-11 Panini Gold Standard Gold Bars Materials Signatures Prime
STATED PRINT RUN ONE TO 25 SER.#'d SETS
5 LaMarcus Aldridge/25 20.00 50.00
10 Kevin Love/15 25.00 60.00

2010-11 Panini Gold Standard Gold Bars Signatures
STATED PRINT RUN 5 TO 49 SER.#'d SETS
4 Kobe Bryant/24 1,500.00 3,000.00
5 LaMarcus Aldridge/49 10.00 25.00
8 Eric Gordon/40 10.00 25.00
10 Kevin Love/25 15.00 40.00
14 Kevin Martin/49 6.00 15.00

2010-11 Panini Gold Standard Gold Crowns
STATED PRINT RUN 299 SER.#'d SETS
1 Kevin Durant 6.00 15.00
2 Dwight Howard 2.00 5.00
3 Stephen Curry 40.00 100.00
4 Amare Stoudemire 1.50 4.00
5 Rajon Rondo 2.00 5.00
6 Kevin Love 1.50 4.00
7 Andrew Bogut 1.25 3.00
8 Chris Paul 3.00 8.00
9 Steve Nash 3.00 8.00
10 Kobe Bryant 60.00 150.00
11 Serge Ibaka 1.25 3.00
12 Deron Williams 1.25 3.00
13 Luke Ridnour 1.00 2.50
14 Monta Ellis 1.25 3.00
15 LeBron James 40.00 100.00
16 JaVale McGee 1.25 3.00
17 Emeka Okafor 1.25 3.00
18 Chauncey Billups 2.00 5.00
19 Raymond Felton 1.00 2.50
20 Tyson Chandler 1.25 3.00
21 Russell Westbrook 2.50 6.00
22 Dwyane Wade 3.00 8.00
23 Tim Duncan 4.00 10.00
24 Jose Calderon 1.00 2.50
25 Pau Gasol 2.50 6.00

2010-11 Panini Gold Standard Gold Crowns Materials
STATED PRINT RUN 99 TO 249 SER.#'d SETS
1 Kevin Durant/249 15.00 40.00
2 Dwight Howard/249 5.00 12.00
3 Stephen Curry/49 75.00 200.00
4 Amare Stoudemire/249 4.00 10.00
5 Rajon Rondo/249 5.00 12.00
6 Kevin Love/249 4.00 10.00
7 Andrew Bogut/249 3.00 8.00
8 Chris Paul/249 8.00 20.00
9 Steve Nash/249 8.00 20.00
10 Kobe Bryant/249 75.00 200.00
11 Serge Ibaka/249 3.00 8.00
13 Luke Ridnour/249 2.50 6.00
14 Monta Ellis/249 3.00 8.00
15 LeBron James/249 40.00 100.00
16 JaVale McGee/249 3.00 8.00
17 Emeka Okafor/249 3.00 8.00
20 Tyson Chandler/249 3.00 8.00
21 Russell Westbrook/249 6.00 15.00
22 Dwyane Wade/249 8.00 20.00
23 Tim Duncan/249 10.00 25.00
24 Jose Calderon/249 2.50 6.00
25 Pau Gasol/249 6.00 15.00

2010-11 Panini Gold Standard Gold Crowns Materials Prime
*PRIME: .1.25X TO 3X BASE HI
STATED PRINT RUN ONE TO 25 SER.#'d SETS
1 Kevin Durant/25 50.00 125.00

2010-11 Panini Gold Standard Gold Crowns Materials Signatures
STATED PRINT RUN 5 TO 199 SER.#'d SETS
3 Stephen Curry/199 1,500.00 3,000.00
5 Rajon Rondo/25 25.00 60.00
6 Kevin Love/49 20.00 50.00
7 Andrew Bogut/199 6.00 15.00
10 Kobe Bryant/24 1,500.00 3,000.00
11 Serge Ibaka/199 4.00 10.00
13 Luke Ridnour/199 4.00 10.00
16 JaVale McGee/199 5.00 12.00
17 Emeka Okafor/25 5.00 12.00
20 Tyson Chandler/199 5.00 12.00

2010-11 Panini Gold Standard Gold Crowns Materials Signatures Prime
STATED PRINT RUN 3 TO 25 SER.#'d SETS
3 Stephen Curry/25 1,500.00 3,000.00
5 Rajon Rondo/25 25.00 60.00
6 Kevin Love/25 20.00 50.00
7 Andrew Bogut/25 12.00 30.00
10 Kobe Bryant/24 2,000.00 4,000.00
11 Serge Ibaka/25 20.00 50.00
13 Luke Ridnour/25 8.00 20.00
16 JaVale McGee/25 8.00 20.00
17 Emeka Okafor/25 8.00 20.00
20 Tyson Chandler/25 10.00 25.00
21 Russell Westbrook/25 125.00 300.00

2010-11 Panini Gold Standard Gold Crowns Signatures
STATED PRINT RUN 5 TO 69 SER.#'d SETS
3 Stephen Curry/69 1,000.00 2,000.00
5 Rajon Rondo/25 15.00 40.00
6 Kevin Love/49 12.00 30.00
10 Kobe Bryant/49 1,500.00 3,000.00
11 Serge Ibaka/69 8.00 20.00
13 Luke Ridnour/69 4.00 10.00
16 JaVale McGee/69 4.00 10.00
17 Emeka Okafor/49 4.00 10.00
18 Chauncey Billups/25 6.00 15.00
19 Raymond Felton/69 4.00 10.00
20 Tyson Chandler/49 5.00 12.00

2010-11 Panini Gold Standard Gold Medalists
STATED PRINT RUN 299 SER.#'d SETS
1 Dwight Howard 2.00 5.00
2 Tayshaun Prince 1.50 4.00
3 Michael Redd 1.25 3.00
4 LeBron James 40.00 100.00
5 Dwyane Wade 3.00 8.00
6 Jason Kidd 2.50 6.00
7 Carlos Boozer 1.25 3.00
8 Chris Bosh 2.00 5.00
9 Chris Paul 3.00 8.00
10 Kevin Garnett 4.00 10.00
11 Larry Johnson 2.00 5.00
12 Mark Price 1.50 4.00
13 Shaquille O'Neal 6.00 15.00
14 Steve Smith 1.25 3.00
15 Dan Majerle 1.25 3.00
16 Dominique Wilkins 2.50 6.00
17 Joe Dumars 1.50 4.00
18 Kevin Johnson 1.50 4.00
19 Alonzo Mourning 2.50 6.00
20 David Robinson 3.00 8.00

2010-11 Panini Gold Standard Gold Medalists Materials
STATED PRINT RUN 299 SER.#'d SETS
*PRIME/25: 1X TO 2.5X BASE HI
1 Dwight Howard 5.00 12.00
2 Tayshaun Prince 4.00 10.00
3 Michael Redd 3.00 8.00
4 LeBron James 60.00 150.00
5 Dwyane Wade 8.00 20.00
6 Jason Kidd 6.00 15.00
7 Carlos Boozer 3.00 8.00
8 Chris Bosh 5.00 12.00
9 Chris Paul 8.00 20.00
10 Kevin Garnett 10.00 25.00
11 Larry Johnson 5.00 12.00
12 Mark Price 4.00 10.00
13 Shaquille O'Neal 15.00 40.00
14 Steve Smith 3.00 8.00
15 Dan Majerle 3.00 8.00
16 Dominique Wilkins 6.00 15.00
17 Joe Dumars 4.00 10.00
18 Kevin Johnson 4.00 10.00
19 Alonzo Mourning 6.00 15.00

2010-11 Panini Gold Standard Gold Medalists Materials Signatures
STATED PRINT RUN 10 TO 99 SER.#'d SETS
*PRIME/25: .6X TO 1.5X BASE HI
7 Carlos Boozer/49 25.00 60.00
11 Larry Johnson/99 60.00 150.00
12 Mark Price/49 30.00 80.00
14 Steve Smith/99 25.00 60.00
15 Dan Majerle/49 25.00 60.00
17 Joe Dumars/25 30.00 80.00
18 Kevin Johnson/49 30.00 80.00

2010-11 Panini Gold Standard Gold Medalists Signatures
STATED PRINT RUN 10 TO 199 SER.#'d SETS
7 Carlos Boozer/49 6.00 15.00
12 Mark Price/180 8.00 20.00
15 Dan Majerle/199 6.00 15.00
17 Joe Dumars/25 8.00 20.00
18 Kevin Johnson/49 8.00 20.00

2010-11 Panini Gold Standard Gold Medalists Signatures Dual
STATED PRINT RUN 5 TO 50 SER.#'d SETS
3 B.Davis/R.Westbrook/50 100.00 250.00
4 M.Bogues/J.Flynn/50 20.00 50.00
5 W.Bellamy/T.Chandler/50 20.00 50.00
6 M.Bibby/S.Curry/50 1,000.00 2,000.00
8 J.West/K.Bryant/25 2,000.00 4,000.00
9 K.Love/V.Carter/35 60.00 150.00
11 D.Williams/E.Gordon/35 12.00 30.00
12 C.Mullin/C.Laettner/50 30.00 80.00
13 D.Wilkins/D.Majerle/35 30.00 80.00
16 C.Drexler/D.Wilkins/25 100.00 250.00
19 E.Gordon/A.Iguodala/50 20.00 50.00
20 I.Thomas/S.Elliott/50 40.00 100.00

2010-11 Panini Gold Standard Gold Mining
STATED PRINT RUN 299 SER.#'d SETS
1 Chris Paul 2.50 6.00
2 Bernard King 1.50 4.00
3 Derrick Rose 2.50 6.00
4 Blake Griffin 1.25 3.00
5 Magic Johnson 5.00 12.00
6 Tim Duncan 3.00 8.00
7 Kobe Bryant 40.00 100.00
8 Kareem Abdul-Jabbar 4.00 10.00
9 Stephen Curry 25.00 60.00
10 Dwyane Wade 2.50 6.00
11 Amare Stoudemire 1.25 3.00
12 Oscar Robertson 3.00 8.00
13 Chris Bosh 1.50 4.00
14 Dirk Nowitzki 3.00 8.00
15 Derek Fisher 1.25 3.00
16 Larry Bird 5.00 12.00
17 Kevin Love 1.25 3.00
18 Wilt Chamberlain 4.00 10.00
19 Kevin Durant 5.00 12.00
20 LeBron James 10.00 25.00

2010-11 Panini Gold Standard Gold Mining Materials
STATED PRINT RUN 49 TO 299 SER.#'d SETS
*PRIME: .75X TO 2X BASE HI
1 Chris Paul/299 6.00 15.00
2 Bernard King/299 4.00 10.00
4 Blake Griffin/299 3.00 8.00
5 Magic Johnson/99 20.00 50.00
6 Tim Duncan/299 8.00 20.00
7 Kobe Bryant/299 75.00 200.00
9 Stephen Curry/99 50.00 120.00
10 Dwyane Wade/299 6.00 15.00
11 Amare Stoudemire/299 3.00 8.00
13 Chris Bosh/299 4.00 10.00
14 Dirk Nowitzki/299 8.00 20.00
15 Derek Fisher/299 3.00 8.00
16 Larry Bird/49 20.00 50.00
17 Kevin Love/299 3.00 8.00
19 Kevin Durant/299 12.00 30.00
20 LeBron James/299 40.00 100.00

2010-11 Panini Gold Standard Gold Mining Materials Signatures
STATED PRINT RUN 3 TO 49 SER.#'d SETS
2 Bernard King/49 10.00 25.00
7 Kobe Bryant/24 1,500.00 3,000.00
9 Stephen Curry/49 1,000.00 2,000.00
15 Derek Fisher/49 12.00 30.00

2010-11 Panini Gold Standard Gold Mining Materials Signatures Prime
STATED PRINT RUN 3 TO 25 SER.#'d SETS
2 Bernard King/25 15.00 40.00
7 Kobe Bryant/24 2,000.00 4,000.00
9 Stephen Curry/25 1,500.00 3,000.00
15 Derek Fisher/25 20.00 50.00

2010-11 Panini Gold Standard Gold Mining Signatures
STATED PRINT RUN 3 TO 99 SER.#'d SETS
2 Bernard King/99 12.00 30.00
7 Kobe Bryant/24 1,500.00 3,000.00
9 Stephen Curry/99 1,000.00 2,000.00
15 Derek Fisher/99 10.00 25.00
17 Kevin Love/25 15.00 40.00

2010-11 Panini Gold Standard Gold Mining Signatures Dual
STATED PRINT RUN 10 TO 50 SER.#'d SETS
1 D.Fisher/P.Gasol/20 30.00 80.00
3 C.Bosh/L.Odom/25 25.00 60.00
6 I.Thomas/J.Dumars/50 20.00 50.00
7 K.Love/D.Granger/50 12.00 30.00
8 J.Noah/T.Chandler/50 15.00 40.00
9 B.King/D.Thompson/50 15.00 40.00
10 J.Rose/J.Howard/50 12.00 30.00

2010-11 Panini Gold Standard Gold NBA Logos
STATED PRINT RUN 5 TO 199 SER.#'d SETS
1 Al Attles/199 12.00 30.00
2 Alex English/199 12.00 30.00
5 Artis Gilmore/199 12.00 30.00
7 Bill Walton/99 40.00 100.00
10 Connie Hawkins/199 30.00 80.00
11 Dave Cowens/99 25.00 60.00
14 Dolph Schayes/99 10.00 25.00
16 Elvin Hayes/99 15.00 40.00
17 Gail Goodrich/99 10.00 25.00
19 George Gervin/99 30.00 80.00
20 Isiah Thomas/99 30.00 80.00
21 Jack Twyman/199 6.00 15.00
22 Jalen Rose/199 12.00 30.00
24 Jeff Hornacek/199 10.00 25.00
30 Kelly Tripucka/199 6.00 15.00
32 Kobe Bryant/99 2,000.00 [illegible],000.00
33 Lenny Wilkens/99 12.00 30.00
36 Michael Beasley/25 8.00 20.00
38 Nate Archibald/99 12.00 30.00
41 Rick Barry/199 12.00 30.00
42 Robert Horry/99 40.00 100.00
43 Robert Parish/199 20.00 50.00
44 Rolando Blackman/199 8.00 20.00
45 Sam Perkins/199 12.00 30.00
47 Stephen Curry/199 1,250.00 2,500.00
49 Tyreke Evans/25 6.00 15.00
50 Walt Frazier/25 25.00 60.00

2010-11 Panini Gold Standard Gold Nuggets
STATED PRINT RUN 299 SER.#'d SETS
1 LeBron James 10.00 25.00
2 Kobe Bryant 10.00 25.00
3 Blake Griffin 1.25 3.00
4 Kevin Durant 5.00 12.00
5 Paul Pierce 2.00 5.00
6 Dirk Nowitzki 3.00 8.00
7 Derrick Rose 2.50 6.00
8 Kevin Love 1.25 3.00
9 Tyreke Evans 1.00 2.50
10 Carmelo Anthony 2.00 5.00
11 Amare Stoudemire 1.25 3.00
12 Dwyane Wade 2.50 6.00
13 Deron Williams 1.00 2.50
14 LaMarcus Aldridge 1.25 3.00
15 Rajon Rondo 1.50 4.00
16 Russell Westbrook 2.00 5.00
17 Brandon Jennings .75 2.00
18 Eric Gordon 1.00 2.50
19 Pau Gasol 2.00 5.00
20 Steve Nash 2.50 6.00
21 Al Jefferson .75 2.00
22 D.J. Augustin .75 2.00
23 Raymond Felton .75 2.00
24 Kevin Garnett 3.00 8.00
25 Aaron Brooks .75 2.00
26 Chris Paul 2.50 6.00
27 Tim Duncan 3.00 8.00
28 Monta Ellis 1.00 2.50
29 Tracy McGrady 2.00 5.00
30 Dwight Howard 1.50 4.00
31 Andrea Bargnani .75 2.00
32 Antawn Jamison 1.00 2.50
33 Joe Johnson 1.25 3.00
34 Lamar Odom 1.00 2.50
35 Tyson Chandler 1.00 2.50
36 Andre Miller 1.00 2.50
37 Devin Harris .75 2.00
38 Roy Hibbert 1.00 2.50
39 Rudy Gay 1.25 3.00
40 David West 1.00 2.50
41 Kevin Martin 1.00 2.50
42 Jameer Nelson .75 2.00
43 Nene 1.00 2.50
44 Al Horford 1.25 3.00
45 Manu Ginobili 2.50 6.00
46 Shaquille O'Neal 5.00 12.00
47 Stephen Curry 10.00 15.00
48 Jeff Green 1.00 2.50
49 Joakim Noah 1.25 3.00
50 Jason Richardson 1.25 3.00

2010-11 Panini Gold Standard Gold Nuggets Materials
STATED PRINT RUN 49 TO 199 SER.#'d SETS
1 LeBron James/199 40.00 100.00
2 Kobe Bryant/199 40.00 100.00
3 Blake Griffin/199 2.50 6.00
4 Kevin Durant/199 10.00 25.00
5 Paul Pierce/199 4.00 10.00
6 Dirk Nowitzki/199 6.00 15.00
7 Derrick Rose/199 5.00 12.00
8 Kevin Love/199 2.50 6.00
9 Tyreke Evans/199 2.00 5.00
11 Amare Stoudemire/199 2.50 6.00
12 Dwyane Wade/199 5.00 12.00
14 LaMarcus Aldridge/199 2.50 6.00
15 Rajon Rondo/199 3.00 8.00
16 Russell Westbrook/199 4.00 10.00
17 Brandon Jennings/199 1.50 4.00
18 Eric Gordon/199 2.00 5.00
19 Pau Gasol/199 4.00 10.00
20 Steve Nash/199 5.00 12.00
21 Al Jefferson/199 1.50 4.00
22 D.J. Augustin/199 1.50 4.00
24 Kevin Garnett/199 6.00 15.00
26 Chris Paul/199 5.00 12.00
27 Tim Duncan/199 6.00 15.00
28 Monta Ellis/199 2.00 5.00
30 Dwight Howard/199 3.00 8.00
31 Andrea Bargnani/199 1.50 4.00
32 Antawn Jamison/199 2.00 5.00
33 Joe Johnson/199 2.50 6.00
34 Lamar Odom/199 2.00 5.00
35 Tyson Chandler/199 2.00 5.00
36 Andre Miller/199 2.00 5.00
39 Rudy Gay/49 2.50 6.00
40 David West/199 2.00 5.00
42 Jameer Nelson/199 1.50 4.00
43 Nene/199 2.00 5.00
44 Al Horford/199 2.50 6.00
45 Manu Ginobili/199 5.00 12.00
46 Shaquille O'Neal/199 10.00 25.00
47 Stephen Curry/99 40.00 100.00
49 Joakim Noah/75 2.50 6.00

2010-11 Panini Gold Standard Gold Nuggets Materials Prime
*PRIME: .75X TO 2X BASE HI
STATED PRINT RUN 10 TO 25 SER.#'d SETS

2010-11 Panini Gold Standard Gold Nuggets Materials Signatures
STATED PRINT RUN 3 TO 99 SER.#'d SETS
2 Kobe Bryant/24 1,500.00 3,000.00
8 Kevin Love/25 15.00 40.00
9 Tyreke Evans/25 5.00 12.00
14 LaMarcus Aldridge/25 10.00 25.00
15 Rajon Rondo/25 15.00 40.00
16 Russell Westbrook/25 40.00 100.00
17 Brandon Jennings/25 5.00 12.00
21 Al Jefferson/25 5.00 12.00
22 D.J. Augustin/49 5.00 12.00
31 Andrea Bargnani/25 5.00 21.00
32 Antawn Jamison/25 6.00 15.00
33 Joe Johnson/25 6.00 15.00
36 Andre Miller/49 5.00 12.00
39 Rudy Gay/25 6.00 15.00
42 Jameer Nelson/49 5.00 12.00
44 Al Horford/25 12.00 30.00
47 Stephen Curry/49 600.00 1,200.00
49 Joakim Noah/25 5.00 12.00

2010-11 Panini Gold Standard Gold Nuggets Materials Signatures Prime
STATED PRINT RUN ONE TO 25 SER.#'d SETS
2 Kobe Bryant/24 2,000.00 4,000.00
8 Kevin Love/15 25.00 60.00
14 LaMarcus Aldridge/15 12.00 30.00
15 Rajon Rondo/15 20.00 50.00
16 Russell Westbrook/25 50.00 120.00
21 Al Jefferson/25 8.00 20.00
22 D.J. Augustin/15 8.00 20.00
31 Andrea Bargnani/15 8.00 20.00
32 Antawn Jamison/15 10.00 25.00
33 Joe Johnson/15 10.00 25.00
35 Tyson Chandler/15 8.00 20.00
36 Andre Miller/15 8.00 20.00
42 Jameer Nelson/15 8.00 20.00
44 Al Horford/25 8.00 20.00
47 Stephen Curry/25 1,500.00 3,000.00

2010-11 Panini Gold Standard Gold Nuggets Signatures
STATED PRINT RUN ONE TO 99 SER.#'d SETS
2 Kobe Bryant/24 1,500.00 3,000.00
8 Kevin Love/25 12.00 30.00
9 Tyreke Evans/25 4.00 10.00
17 Brandon Jennings/49 6.00 15.00
18 Eric Gordon/99 4.00 10.00
21 Al Jefferson/25 6.00 15.00
22 D.J. Augustin/99 4.00 10.00
23 Raymond Felton/49 4.00 10.00
25 Aaron Brooks/99 4.00 10.00
31 Andrea Bargnani/49 4.00 10.00
32 Antawn Jamison/49 4.00 10.00
33 Joe Johnson/25 6.00 15.00
35 Tyson Chandler/49 5.00 12.00
36 Andre Miller/99 5.00 12.00
37 Devin Harris/99 4.00 10.00
38 Roy Hibbert/99 4.00 10.00
39 Rudy Gay/49 8.00 20.00
42 Jameer Nelson/49 4.00 10.00
44 Al Horford/99 8.00 20.00
47 Stephen Curry/99 400.00 800.00
48 Jeff Green/99 5.00 12.00
49 Joakim Noah/25 6.00 15.00

2010-11 Panini Gold Standard Gold Records
STATED PRINT RUN 299 SER.#'d SETS
1 Ray Allen 2.50 6.00
2 John Stockton 2.50 6.00
3 Wilt Chamberlain 5.00 12.00
4 Hakeem Olajuwon 3.00 8.00
5 Steve Nash 3.00 8.00
6 Mark Eaton 1.50 4.00
7 John Stockton 2.50 6.00
8 Kareem Abdul-Jabbar 5.00 12.00
9 Wilt Chamberlain 5.00 12.00
10 Karl Malone 3.00 8.00
11 Robert Parish 2.50 6.00
12 John Stockton 2.50 6.00
13 Jerry West 3.00 8.00
14 Moses Malone 2.50 6.00
15 Kareem Abdul-Jabbar 5.00 12.00

2010-11 Panini Gold Standard Gold Records Materials
STATED PRINT RUN 49 TO 299 SER.#'d SETS
1 Ray Allen/299 5.00 12.00
2 John Stockton/49 8.00 20.00
5 Steve Nash/299 6.00 15.00
6 Mark Eaton/299 3.00 8.00
7 John Stockton/49 8.00 20.00
8 Kareem Abdul-Jabbar/99 10.00 25.00
10 Karl Malone/299 6.00 15.00
11 Robert Parish/299 5.00 12.00
12 John Stockton/49 8.00 20.00
14 Moses Malone/299 5.00 12.00

2010-11 Panini Gold Standard Gold Records Materials Prime
*PRIME: 1.25X TO 3X BASE HI
STATED PRINT RUN 10 TO 25 SER.#'d SETS
4 Hakeem Olajuwon/25 12.00 30.00
5 Steve Nash/25 15.00 40.00
10 Karl Malone/25 12.00 30.00

2010-11 Panini Gold Standard Gold Records Materials Signatures
STATED PRINT RUN 2 TO 25 SER.#'d SETS
6 Mark Eaton/25 12.00 30.00
11 Robert Parish/25 12.00 30.00

2010-11 Panini Gold Standard Gold Records Materials Signatures Prime
STATED PRINT RUN ONE TO 25 SER.#'d SETS
6 Mark Eaton/25 20.00 50.00
11 Robert Parish/25 20.00 50.00

2010-11 Panini Gold Standard Gold Records Signatures
STATED PRINT RUN 5 TO 99 SER.#'d SETS
6 Mark Eaton/99 12.00 30.00
11 Robert Parish/25 12.00 30.00

2010-11 Panini Gold Standard Gold Rings
STATED PRINT RUN 299 SER.#'d SETS
1 Magic Johnson 6.00 15.00
2 Tim Duncan 4.00 10.00
3 Rajon Rondo 2.00 5.00
4 Dwyane Wade 3.00 8.00
5 Kobe Bryant 12.00 30.00
6 Scottie Pippen 4.00 10.00
7 Alonzo Mourning 2.50 6.00
8 Isiah Thomas 2.50 6.00
9 Dennis Rodman 3.00 8.00
10 Pau Gasol 2.50 6.00
11 Ray Allen 2.50 6.00
12 Hakeem Olajuwon 3.00 8.00
13 Tony Parker 2.50 6.00
14 Bill Walton 2.50 6.00
15 Kareem Abdul-Jabbar 5.00 12.00
16 Richard Hamilton 2.00 5.00
17 Julius Erving 3.00 8.00
18 Elvin Hayes 2.00 5.00
19 Paul Pierce 2.50 6.00
20 Robert Horry 1.50 4.00

2010-11 Panini Gold Standard Gold Rings Materials
STATED PRINT RUN 49 TO 299 SER.#'d SETS
1 Magic Johnson/99 10.00 25.00
2 Tim Duncan/299 10.00 25.00
3 Rajon Rondo/299 5.00 12.00
4 Dwyane Wade/299 8.00 20.00
5 Kobe Bryant/299 12.00 30.00
6 Scottie Pippen/299 10.00 25.00
7 Alonzo Mourning/299 6.00 15.00
8 Isiah Thomas/199 6.00 15.00
9 Dennis Rodman/49 8.00 20.00
10 Pau Gasol/299 6.00 15.00
11 Ray Allen/299 6.00 15.00
12 Hakeem Olajuwon/299 8.00 20.00
13 Tony Parker/299 6.00 15.00
15 Kareem Abdul-Jabbar/99 12.00 30.00
16 Richard Hamilton/299 5.00 12.00
17 Julius Erving/149 8.00 20.00
19 Paul Pierce/299 6.00 15.00
20 Robert Horry/299 4.00 10.00

2010-11 Panini Gold Standard Gold Rings Materials Prime
*PRIME: .75X TO 2X BASE HI
STATED PRINT RUN 5 TO 25 SER.#'d SETS
6 Scottie Pippen/25 40.00 100.00
7 Alonzo Mourning/25 30.00 80.00
12 Hakeem Olajuwon/25 12.00 30.00

2010-11 Panini Gold Standard Gold Rings Materials Signatures
STATED PRINT RUN 5 TO 49 SER.#'d SETS
3 Rajon Rondo/49 15.00 40.00
5 Kobe Bryant/24 1,500.00 3,000.00
8 Isiah Thomas/49 10.00 25.00
9 Dennis Rodman/25 30.00 80.00
11 Ray Allen/25 30.00 60.00
12 Hakeem Olajuwon/25 25.00 60.00
13 Tony Parker/25 12.00 30.00
16 Richard Hamilton/49 6.00 15.00
20 Robert Horry/49 15.00 40.00

2010-11 Panini Gold Standard Gold Rings Materials Signatures Prime
STATED PRINT RUN 3 TO 25 SER.#'d SETS
3 Rajon Rondo/25 25.00 60.00
5 Kobe Bryant/24 2,000.00 4,000.00
8 Isiah Thomas/25 12.00 30.00
13 Tony Parker/25 20.00 50.00
16 Richard Hamilton/25 10.00 25.00
20 Robert Horry/25 30.00 80.00

2010-11 Panini Gold Standard Gold Rings Signatures
STATED PRINT RUN 5 TO 69 SER.#'d SETS
3 Rajon Rondo/49 15.00 40.00
5 Kobe Bryant/49 1,500.00 3,000.00
7 Alonzo Mourning/25 30.00 80.00
8 Isiah Thomas/49 EXCH 12.00 30.00
9 Dennis Rodman/25 30.00 80.00
12 Hakeem Olajuwon/25 20.00 50.00
13 Tony Parker/49 10.00 25.00
14 Bill Walton/49 20.00 50.00
16 Richard Hamilton/49 6.00 15.00
18 Elvin Hayes/49 6.00 15.00
20 Robert Horry/69 8.00 20.00

2010-11 Panini Gold Standard Gold Rings Signatures Dual
STATED PRINT RUN 10 TO 50 SER.#'d SETS
1 P.Pierce/R.Rondo/20 30.00 80.00
2 I.Thomas/B.Laimbeer/50 EXCH 12.00 30.00
3 R.Rondo/R.Allen/20 25.00 60.00
5 K.Bryant/P.Gasol/50 800.00 1,500.00
6 K.Bryant/D.Fisher/25 800.00 1,500.00
7 T.Parker/R.Horry/50 25.00 60.00
8 H.Olajuwon/C.Drexler/20 50.00 120.00
9 C.Billups/R.Hamilton/50 12.00 30.00
10 G.Payton/A.Mourning/20 50.00 120.00

2010-11 Panini Gold Standard Gold Stars
STATED PRINT RUN 299 SER.#'d SETS
1 Blake Griffin 1.25 3.00
2 Dwight Howard 1.50 4.00
3 Russell Westbrook 2.00 5.00
4 Lamar Odom 1.00 2.50
5 Jonny Flynn .75 2.00
6 Carlos Boozer 1.00 2.50
7 Raymond Felton .75 2.00
8 Ray Allen 2.00 5.00
9 Ben Gordon 1.00 2.50
10 Jameer Nelson .75 2.00
11 Dirk Nowitzki 3.00 8.00
12 Marc Gasol 1.25 3.00
13 Monta Ellis 1.00 2.50
14 Shane Battier 1.00 2.50
15 Andre Iguodala 1.25 3.00
16 Andrei Kirilenko 1.00 2.50
17 Nene 1.00 2.50
18 Steve Nash 2.50 6.00
19 Jordan Farmar .75 2.00
20 Andrea Bargnani .75 2.00
21 Kevin Durant 5.00 12.00
22 Tyson Chandler 1.00 2.50
23 Derrick Rose 2.50 6.00
24 Kobe Bryant 10.00 25.00
25 Amare Stoudemire 1.25 3.00

2010-11 Panini Gold Standard Gold Stars Materials
STATED PRINT RUN 99 SER.#'d SETS
1 Blake Griffin 2.50 6.00
2 Dwight Howard 3.00 8.00
3 Russell Westbrook 4.00 10.00
4 Lamar Odom 2.00 5.00
5 Jonny Flynn 1.50 4.00
8 Ray Allen 4.00 10.00
9 Ben Gordon 2.00 5.00
10 Jameer Nelson 1.50 4.00
11 Dirk Nowitzki 6.00 15.00
12 Marc Gasol 2.50 6.00
13 Monta Ellis 2.00 5.00
15 Andre Iguodala 2.50 6.00
16 Andrei Kirilenko 2.00 5.00
17 Nene 2.00 5.00
18 Steve Nash 5.00 12.00
20 Andrea Bargnani 1.50 4.00
21 Kevin Durant 10.00 25.00
22 Tyson Chandler 2.00 5.00
23 Derrick Rose 5.00 12.00
24 Kobe Bryant 20.00 50.00
25 Amare Stoudemire 2.50 6.00

2010-11 Panini Gold Standard Gold Stars Materials Prime
*PRIME: .75X TO 2X BASE HI
STATED PRINT RUN 2 TO 25 SER.#'d SETS
11 Dirk Nowitzki/25 10.00 25.00

2010-11 Panini Gold Standard Gold Stars Materials Signatures
STATED PRINT RUN 5 TO 49 SER.#'d SETS
3 Russell Westbrook/25 40.00 100.00
4 Lamar Odom/30 10.00 25.00
5 Jonny Flynn/35 5.00 12.00
9 Ben Gordon/49 5.00 12.00
10 Jameer Nelson/49 5.00 12.00
15 Andre Iguodala/49 6.00 15.00
16 Andrei Kirilenko/25 6.00 15.00
22 Tyson Chandler/20 8.00 20.00
24 Kobe Bryant/15 1,500.00 3,000.00

2010-11 Panini Gold Standard Gold Stars Materials Signatures Prime
STATED PRINT RUN 2 TO 25 SER.#'d SETS
5 Jonny Flynn/20 8.00 20.00
9 Ben Gordon/25 8.00 20.00
10 Jameer Nelson/20 8.00 20.00
15 Andre Iguodala/20 8.00 20.00
22 Tyson Chandler/20 12.00 30.00

2010-11 Panini Gold Standard Gold Stars Signatures
STATED PRINT RUN 5 TO 99 SER.#'d SETS
4 Lamar Odom/25 10.00 25.00
5 Jonny Flynn/50 4.00 10.00
6 Carlos Boozer/49 6.00 15.00
7 Raymond Felton/99 4.00 10.00
8 Ray Allen/25 30.00 60.00
10 Jameer Nelson/99 4.00 10.00
14 Shane Battier/99 5.00 12.00
15 Andre Iguodala/99 4.00 10.00
16 Andrei Kirilenko/49 4.00 10.00
20 Andrea Bargnani/25 5.00 12.00
22 Tyson Chandler/49 5.00 12.00
24 Kobe Bryant/24 1,500.00 3,000.00

2010-11 Panini Gold Standard Gold Team Logos
STATED PRINT RUN 5 TO 199 SER.#'d SETS
1 Aaron Brooks/199 6.00 15.00
2 Alvan Adams/199 6.00 15.00
4 Andre Iguodala/99 6.00 15.00
5 Andrew Bogut/199 6.00 15.00
6 Andrew Bynum/49 12.00 30.00
7 Baron Davis/49 8.00 20.00
8 Bernard King/199 4.00 10.00
9 Bill Laimbeer/199 8.00 20.00
10 Bill Walton/99 15.00 40.00
11 Billy Cunningham/99 15.00 40.00
13 Boris Diaw/199 6.00 15.00
14 Brandon Jennings/49 12.00 30.00
15 Brook Lopez/99 6.00 15.00
16 Carl Landry/199 6.00 15.00
17 Carlos Boozer/199 10.00 25.00
18 Channing Frye/199 6.00 15.00
20 Danilo Gallinari/199 6.00 15.00
21 David Lee/99 6.00 15.00
22 DeMar DeRozan/199 15.00 40.00
23 Derek Fisher/199 6.00 15.00
26 Elvin Hayes/199 6.00 15.00
27 Emeka Okafor/49 8.00 20.00
28 Eric Gordon/199 8.00 20.00
29 J.J. Barea/199 EXCH 12.00 30.00
30 Jalen Rose/199 6.00 15.00
31 Jeff Green/199 6.00 15.00
32 Joakim Noah/99 12.00 30.00
33 Juwan Howard/199 8.00 20.00
34 Kendrick Perkins/199 4.00 10.00
36 LaMarcus Aldridge/199 20.00 50.00
37 Michael Cooper/199 8.00 20.00
41 Raymond Felton/199 6.00 15.00
42 Russell Westbrook/199 75.00 200.00
43 Stephen Curry/199 500.00 1,000.00
44 Tony Parker/25 10.00 25.00
45 Tracy McGrady/25 40.00 100.00
47 Walter Berry/199 6.00 15.00
48 Zach Randolph/99 10.00 25.00
49 Tyson Chandler/199 6.00 15.00
50 Robin Lopez/199 6.00 15.00

2010-11 Panini Gold Standard Golden Age
STATED PRINT RUN 299 SER.#'d SETS
1 Magic Johnson 5.00 12.00
2 Tim Hardaway 1.50 4.00
3 David Robinson 2.50 6.00
4 Dikembe Mutombo 2.00 5.00
5 Jerry West 2.50 6.00
6 Tom Heinsohn 1.25 3.00
7 Dennis Rodman 2.50 6.00
8 Rick Barry 1.50 4.00
9 Bob Lanier 2.00 5.00
10 Oscar Robertson 3.00 8.00
11 Larry Bird 5.00 12.00
12 John Stockton 2.00 5.00
13 Julius Erving 2.50 6.00
14 Hakeem Olajuwon 2.50 6.00
15 David Thompson 1.25 3.00
16 Elvin Hayes 1.50 4.00
17 Walt Bellamy 1.50 4.00
18 Elgin Baylor 2.50 6.00
19 Darryl Dawkins 1.25 3.00
20 Bill Russell 4.00 10.00

2010-11 Panini Gold Standard Golden Age Materials
STATED PRINT RUN 49 TO 299 SER.#'d SETS
1 Magic Johnson/99 12.00 30.00
2 Tim Hardaway/299 4.00 10.00
4 Dikembe Mutombo/299 5.00 12.00
7 Dennis Rodman/99 6.00 15.00
9 Bob Lanier/99 5.00 12.00
11 Larry Bird/49 12.00 30.00
12 John Stockton/299 5.00 12.00
13 Julius Erving/149 6.00 15.00
14 Hakeem Olajuwon/299 6.00 15.00

2010-11 Panini Gold Standard Golden Age Materials Prime
*PRIME: .75X TO 2X BASE HI
STATED PRINT RUN 5 TO 25 SER.#'d SETS
4 Dikembe Mutombo/25 10.00 25.00
14 Hakeem Olajuwon/25 10.00 25.00

2010-11 Panini Gold Standard Golden Age Materials Signatures
STATED PRINT RUN 3 TO 49 SER.#'d SETS
4 Dikembe Mutombo/49 15.00 40.00
9 Bob Lanier/25 10.00 25.00

2010-11 Panini Gold Standard Golden Age Materials Signatures Prime
STATED PRINT RUN ONE TO 25 SER.#'d SETS
4 Dikembe Mutombo/25 30.00 80.00
6 Tom Heinsohn/25 50.00 120.00
8 Rick Barry/25 20.00 50.00
9 Bob Lanier/25 20.00 50.00

2010-11 Panini Gold Standard Golden Age Signatures
STATED PRINT RUN 2 TO 99 SER.#'d SETS
2 Tim Hardaway/99 12.00 30.00
4 Dikembe Mutombo/99 30.00 80.00
6 Tom Heinsohn/99 20.00 50.00
8 Rick Barry/99 10.00 25.00
9 Bob Lanier/50 30.00 80.00
15 David Thompson/99 10.00 25.00
16 Elvin Hayes/75 12.00 30.00
17 Walt Bellamy/75 12.00 30.00
19 Darryl Dawkins/99 15.00 40.00

2010-11 Panini Gold Standard Golden Age Signatures Dual
STATED PRINT RUN 5 TO 50 SER.#'d SETS
5 D.Dawkins/M.Cheeks/50 10.00 25.00
6 D.Griffith/M.Eaton/50 10.00 25.00
8 A.Dantley/R.Blackman/50 10.00 25.00
10 I.Thomas/J.Dumars/50 20.00 50.00

2010-11 Panini Gold Standard Golden Anniversary
STATED PRINT RUN 299 SER.#'d SETS
1 Kareem Abdul-Jabbar 4.00 10.00
2 Elgin Baylor 2.50 6.00

3 Rick Barry 1.50 4.00
4 Larry Bird 5.00 12.00
5 Sam Jones 1.50 4.00
6 Oscar Robertson 3.00 8.00
7 Bill Russell 4.00 10.00
8 Jerry West 2.50 6.00
9 Bill Walton 2.00 5.00
10 Lenny Wilkens 1.25 3.00
11 Scottie Pippen 3.00 8.00
12 David Robinson 2.50 6.00
13 Hakeem Olajuwon 2.50 6.00
14 Dolph Schayes 1.50 4.00
15 Julius Erving 2.50 6.00
16 Clyde Drexler 2.00 5.00
17 George Gervin 2.00 5.00
18 Dave Cowens 2.00 5.00
19 John Havlicek 2.50 6.00
20 Magic Johnson 5.00 12.00

2010-11 Panini Gold Standard Golden Anniversary Materials

STATED PRINT RUN 49 TO 299 SER.#'d SETS
1 Kareem Abdul-Jabbar/99 10.00 25.00
4 Larry Bird/49 12.00 30.00
11 Scottie Pippen/299 8.00 20.00
12 David Robinson/299 6.00 15.00
13 Hakeem Olajuwon/149 6.00 15.00
15 Julius Erving/149 6.00 15.00
16 Clyde Drexler/299 5.00 12.00
17 George Gervin/299 5.00 12.00
18 Dave Cowens/125 5.00 12.00
20 Magic Johnson/99 12.00 30.00

2010-11 Panini Gold Standard Golden Anniversary Materials Prime

*PRIME: .75X TO 2X BASE HI
STATED PRINT RUN ONE TO 25 SER.#'d SETS
11 Scottie Pippen/25 50.00 125.00
13 Hakeem Olajuwon/25 10.00 25.00

2010-11 Panini Gold Standard Golden Anniversary Materials Signatures

STATED PRINT RUN 10 TO 49 SER.#'d SETS
12 David Robinson/49 12.00 30.00
13 Hakeem Olajuwon/25 25.00 60.00
17 George Gervin/49 12.00 30.00

2010-11 Panini Gold Standard Golden Anniversary Materials Signatures Prime

STATED PRINT RUN 5 TO 25 SER.#'d SETS
12 David Robinson/25 40.00 100.00
13 Hakeem Olajuwon/25 30.00 80.00
17 George Gervin/25 15.00 40.00

2010-11 Panini Gold Standard Golden Anniversary Signatures

STATED PRINT RUN 5 TO 49 SER.#'d SETS
2 Elgin Baylor/25 20.00 50.00
3 Rick Barry/49 10.00 25.00
5 Sam Jones/49 15.00 40.00
6 Oscar Robertson/25 50.00 120.00
9 Bill Walton/49 20.00 50.00
10 Lenny Wilkens/49 8.00 20.00
12 David Robinson/25 40.00 100.00
14 Dolph Schayes/49 8.00 20.00
16 Clyde Drexler/25 25.00 60.00
17 George Gervin/30 10.00 25.00
18 Dave Cowens/49 10.00 25.00

2010-11 Panini Gold Standard Golden Anniversary Signatures Dual

STATED PRINT RUN 5 TO 50 SER.#'d SETS
3 D.Robinson/G.Gervin/20 75.00 200.00
4 W.Frazier/E.Monroe/25 40.00 100.00
6 H.Greer/D.Schayes/50 20.00 50.00
7 D.Cowens/R.Parish/50 15.00 40.00
8 E.Hayes/H.Olajuwon/25 40.00 100.00
9 J.Worthy/E.Baylor/25 50.00 120.00
10 S.Moncrief/O.Robertson/25 50.00 120.00
13 W.Frazier/W.Reed/50 50.00 120.00
15 R.Barry/N.Thurmond/50 20.00 50.00

2010-11 Panini Gold Standard Golden Threads

STATED PRINT RUN 299 SER.#'d SETS
1 S.Jones/R.Rondo 1.50 4.00
2 M.Johnson/K.Bryant 12.00 30.00
3 J.Erving/A.Iguodala 2.50 6.00
4 D.Rodman/D.Blair 2.50 6.00
5 R.Blackman/J.Kidd 2.00 5.00
6 W.Frazier/C.Billups 2.00 5.00
7 S.Pippen/D.Rose 5.00 12.00
8 R.Parish/P.Pierce 2.00 5.00
9 A.Mourning/C.Bosh 2.50 6.00
10 W.Reed/A.Stoudemire 2.00 5.00

2010-11 Panini Gold Standard Golden Threads Materials

STATED PRINT RUN 25 TO 299 SER.#'d SETS
2 M.Johnson/K.Bryant/299 12.00 30.00
3 J.Erving/A.Iguodala/99 6.00 15.00
5 R.Blackman/J.Kidd/25 5.00 12.00
8 R.Parish/P.Pierce/299 4.00 10.00
9 A.Mourning/C.Bosh/299 5.00 12.00

2010-11 Panini Gold Standard Golden Threads Materials Prime

*PRIME: 1X TO 2.5X BASE HI
STATED PRINT RUN 3 TO 25 SER.#'d SETS
9 A.Mourning/C.Bosh/25 20.00 50.00

2010-11 Panini Gold Standard Golden Threads Signatures

STATED PRINT RUN 10 TO 25 SER.#'d SETS
1 S.Jones/R.Rondo/25 30.00 80.00
4 D.Rodman/D.Blair/25 40.00 100.00
5 R.Blackman/J.Kidd/25 25.00 60.00
6 W.Frazier/C.Billups/25 40.00 100.00
9 A.Mourning/C.Bosh/25 40.00 100.00

2010-11 Panini Gold Standard Signatures

STATED PRINT RUN 5 TO 299 SER.#'d SETS
2 Kobe Bryant/75 1,000.00 2,000.00
5 Ty Lawson/299 4.00 10.00
9 Kevin Love/25 15.00 40.00
15 Kevin Martin/299 5.00 12.00
17 Stephen Jackson/299 5.00 12.00
19 Eric Gordon/299 5.00 12.00
23 Antawn Jamison/199 5.00 12.00
24 Tyreke Evans/25 5.00 12.00
25 Al Horford/99 15.00 40.00
26 Danny Granger/50 4.00 10.00
28 Rajon Rondo/49 20.00 50.00
30 Michael Beasley/25 4.00 10.00
32 Tony Parker/25 25.00 60.00
34 LaMarcus Aldridge/299 6.00 15.00
35 Stephen Curry/299 600.00 1,200.00
36 Brook Lopez/99 5.00 12.00
37 Tyson Chandler/199 5.00 12.00
40 Andre Iguodala/299 6.00 15.00
42 Danilo Gallinari/299 5.00 12.00
43 Joe Johnson/49 6.00 15.00
44 DeMar DeRozan/299 50.00 120.00
45 Devin Harris/299 4.00 10.00
46 Andrei Kirilenko/199 5.00 12.00
47 Brandon Roy/25 25.00 60.00
48 Raymond Felton/199 4.00 10.00
51 Aaron Brooks/299 4.00 10.00
52 Zach Randolph/49 6.00 15.00
54 Charlie Villanueva/49 4.00 10.00
55 Jeff Green/299 5.00 12.00
56 Channing Frye/220 4.00 10.00
57 Al Thornton/299 4.00 10.00
62 David Lee/199 4.00 10.00
66 Emeka Okafor/25 5.00 12.00
68 Carl Landry/299 4.00 10.00
69 Jameer Nelson/199 4.00 10.00
70 Joakim Noah/99 6.00 15.00
71 Chris Kaman/99 4.00 10.00
74 Andrea Bargnani/49 4.00 10.00
76 Grant Hill/25 100.00 250.00
77 Lamar Odom/25 15.00 40.00
80 J.R. Smith/299 6.00 15.00
82 Tyler Hansbrough/199 4.00 10.00
85 Al Jefferson/49 4.00 10.00
87 Luke Ridnour/199 4.00 10.00
91 D.J. Augustin/299 4.00 10.00
94 Juwan Howard/299 5.00 12.00
95 Roy Hibbert/299 5.00 12.00
98 DeJuan Blair/299 4.00 10.00
101 Baron Davis/49 6.00 15.00
103 Josh Smith/199 4.00 10.00
105 Hedo Turkoglu/299 5.00 12.00
106 Ben Gordon/49 4.00 10.00
107 Gerald Henderson/299 4.00 10.00
108 Serge Ibaka/299 5.00 12.00
109 Shane Battier/149 5.00 12.00
111 Chauncey Billups/23 20.00 50.00
115 Darko Milicic/299 4.00 10.00
116 Caron Butler/49 5.00 12.00
118 Trevor Ariza/49 4.00 10.00
120 J.J. Redick/299 6.00 15.00
121 Gerald Wallace/99 5.00 12.00
122 Samuel Dalembert/299 4.00 10.00
125 Brandon Jennings/149 4.00 10.00
126 JaVale McGee/299 5.00 12.00
128 James Harden/149 100.00 250.00
129 Chris Andersen/25 8.00 20.00
130 Toney Douglas/299 4.00 10.00
132 Richard Hamilton/49 8.00 20.00
133 George Hill/299 5.00 12.00
137 Daniel Gibson/299 4.00 10.00
138 Wesley Matthews/299 4.00 10.00
139 Kris Humphries/49 4.00 10.00
140 Rodrigue Beaubois/299 4.00 10.00
141 A.J. Price/299 4.00 10.00
142 Chase Budinger/299 4.00 10.00
143 Donte Greene/99 4.00 10.00
144 Andre Miller/199 5.00 12.00
145 Ryan Gomes/299 4.00 10.00
146 Jodie Meeks/299 4.00 10.00
147 Kendrick Perkins/99 4.00 10.00
148 Taj Gibson/199 4.00 10.00
149 Boris Diaw/199 5.00 12.00
150 Derrick Brown/299 4.00 10.00
151 Jeff Teague/299 4.00 10.00
152 Wayne Ellington/199 4.00 10.00
153 Terrence Williams/199 4.00 10.00
154 Robin Lopez/149 4.00 10.00
155 Jermaine O'Neal/25 10.00 25.00
156 Austin Daye/299 4.00 10.00
157 J.J. Barea/199 10.00 25.00
158 Darren Collison/299 4.00 10.00
159 Goran Dragic/149 8.00 20.00
160 Beno Udrih/149 4.00 10.00
161 Earl Clark/99 4.00 10.00
162 Hakim Warrick/149 4.00 10.00
163 Sam Young/99 4.00 10.00
164 Ronnie Brewer/199 4.00 10.00
165 Omri Casspi/299 4.00 10.00
166 T.J. Ford/199 4.00 10.00
167 Chris Douglas-Roberts/99 4.00 10.00
168 Eric Maynor/79 4.00 10.00
169 James Johnson/99 4.00 10.00
170 Patrick Mills/99 25.00 60.00
179 Dan Majerle/199 5.00 12.00
183 Glen Rice/299 6.00 15.00
186 Jalen Rose/299 5.00 12.00
190 Bill Walton/49 25.00 60.00
193 Dan Issel/49 8.00 20.00
194 Doc Rivers/49 10.00 25.00
195 George McGinnis/42 6.00 15.00
197 Christian Laettner/25 15.00 40.00
198 Dolph Schayes/49 8.00 20.00
199 M.L. Carr/99 6.00 15.00
200 Darryl Dawkins/99 12.00 30.00
201 David Thompson/99 6.00 15.00
202 Bob Lanier/49 20.00 50.00
204 Bernard King/99 8.00 20.00
206 Al Attles/99 6.00 15.00
207 Dikembe Mutombo/49 20.00 50.00
208 Bob McAdoo/99 12.00 30.00
209 Artis Gilmore/99 10.00 25.00
210 A.C. Green/99 8.00 20.00
211 Dominique Wilkins/99 15.00 40.00
212 Alonzo Mourning/99 20.00 50.00

2011-12 Panini Gold Standard

COMMON CARD (1-225) 1.25 3.00
STATED PRINT RUN 299 SER.#'d SETS
170/179/183/210/213/214 HAVE VAR
ALL VAR STILL TOTAL JUST 299 CARDS
1 Paul Pierce 3.00 8.00
2 LaMarcus Aldridge 2.00 5.00
3 Al Jefferson 1.25 3.00
4 Pau Gasol 3.00 8.00
5 DeMarcus Cousins 2.00 5.00
6 Danilo Gallinari 1.50 4.00
7 Dwight Howard 2.50 6.00
8 Ty Lawson 1.25 3.00
9 Luke Ridnour 1.50 4.00
10 Emeka Okafor 1.50 4.00
11 Ray Allen 3.00 8.00
12 LeBron James 15.00 40.00
13 Eric Gordon 1.50 4.00
14 Nate Robinson 2.00 5.00
15 Kobe Bryant 15.00 40.00
16 Damion James 1.25 3.00
17 Kevin Garnett 5.00 12.00
18 DeJuan Blair 1.25 3.00
19 Jeremy Lin 12.00 30.00
20 Kris Humphries 1.25 3.00
21 Andre Iguodala 2.00 5.00
22 Andrea Bargnani 1.25 3.00
23 Evan Turner 1.25 3.00
24 Carmelo Anthony 3.00 8.00
25 DeAndre Jordan 1.50 4.00
26 Rajon Rondo 2.50 6.00
27 Kevin Durant 8.00 20.00
28 John Wall 2.50 6.00
29 Mo Williams 1.50 4.00
30 Marcin Gortat 1.25 3.00
31 Chauncey Billups 2.50 6.00
32 Tyson Chandler 1.50 4.00
33 Steve Nash 4.00 10.00
34 Caron Butler 1.25 3.00
35 Derek Fisher 2.00 5.00
36 Marcus Thornton 1.25 3.00
37 Jose Calderon 1.25 3.00
38 Zach Randolph 1.50 4.00
39 Grant Hill 3.00 8.00
40 Avery Bradley 2.00 5.00
41 Channing Frye 1.25 3.00
42 Matt Barnes 1.25 3.00
43 Jason Thompson 1.25 3.00
44 Chris Paul 4.00 10.00
45 Tyreke Evans 1.50 4.00
46 Carlos Boozer 1.50 4.00
47 Brandon Rush 1.25 3.00
48 Joakim Noah 2.00 5.00
49 Rudy Gay 2.00 5.00
50 Luol Deng 1.50 4.00
51 Amare Stoudemire 2.00 5.00
52 Taj Gibson 1.50 4.00
53 Anderson Varejao 1.25 3.00
54 Deron Williams 1.50 4.00
55 Antawn Jamison 1.50 4.00
56 Ramon Sessions 1.25 3.00
57 Rodney Stuckey 1.25 3.00
58 Chris Bosh 2.50 6.00
59 Trevor Booker 1.25 3.00
60 Ben Gordon 1.50 4.00
61 Tony Parker 2.50 6.00
62 Danny Granger 1.50 4.00
63 Jodie Meeks 1.50 4.00
64 George Hill 1.50 4.00
65 Ed Davis 1.25 3.00
66 Paul George 3.00 8.00
67 Landry Fields 1.25 3.00
68 Roy Hibbert 1.50 4.00
69 Russell Westbrook 3.00 8.00
70 Thabo Sefolosha 1.25 3.00
71 Darren Collison 1.25 3.00
72 Delonte West 1.25 3.00
73 Jerryd Bayless 1.25 3.00
74 Stephen Jackson 1.50 4.00
75 Dirk Nowitzki 5.00 12.00
76 Tim Duncan 5.00 12.00
77 Drew Gooden 1.50 4.00
78 Shawn Marion 2.00 5.00
79 Brook Lopez 2.00 5.00
80 Kevin Martin 1.50 4.00
81 Manu Ginobili 4.00 10.00
82 Marc Gasol 2.00 5.00
83 Al-Farouq Aminu 1.25 3.00
84 Gary Neal 1.25 3.00
85 Patrick Patterson 1.25 3.00
86 Mike Conley 1.50 4.00
87 Stephen Curry 15.00 40.00
88 Michael Beasley 1.25 3.00
89 Al Harrington 1.50 4.00
90 Larry Sanders 1.25 3.00
91 Ryan Anderson 1.25 3.00
92 Nicolas Batum 1.25 3.00
93 Dwyane Wade 4.00 10.00
94 Gerald Wallace 1.50 4.00
95 Monta Ellis 1.50 4.00
96 Jared Dudley 1.50 4.00
97 Jrue Holiday 2.50 6.00
98 Nick Young 1.25 3.00
99 Nene 1.50 4.00
100 Vince Carter 4.00 10.00
101 Elton Brand 2.00 5.00
102 Andrew Bynum 1.25 3.00
103 Greg Monroe 1.25 3.00
104 Tyler Hansbrough 1.25 3.00
105 Andrew Bogut 1.50 4.00
106 Jeff Teague 1.25 3.00
107 D.J. Augustin 1.25 3.00
108 Jason Terry 1.50 4.00
109 Austin Daye 1.25 3.00
110 Brandon Jennings 1.25 3.00
111 Gordon Hayward 2.00 5.00
112 Kyle Lowry 2.00 5.00
113 Jamal Crawford 2.00 5.00
114 Jason Richardson 2.00 5.00
115 James Harden 4.00 10.00
116 Boris Diaw 1.50 4.00
117 Chris Andersen 1.50 4.00
118 Kevin Love 2.00 5.00
119 Kirk Hinrich 1.50 4.00
120 Shane Battier 1.50 4.00
121 Ersan Ilyasova 1.25 3.00
122 Jason Kidd 3.00 8.00
123 Wesley Matthews 1.25 3.00
124 Serge Ibaka 1.50 4.00
125 Hedo Turkoglu 1.25 3.00
126 Paul Millsap 1.50 4.00
127 JaVale McGee 1.50 4.00
128 Timofey Mozgov 1.25 3.00
129 Nikola Pekovic 1.25 3.00
130 Luis Scola 1.50 4.00
131 Mario Chalmers 1.50 4.00
132 Jameer Nelson 1.25 3.00
133 Tayshaun Prince 2.00 5.00
134 Blake Griffin 2.00 5.00
135 Wesley Johnson 1.25 3.00
136 Derrick Favors 1.50 4.00
137 Kendrick Perkins 1.25 3.00
138 Chase Budinger 1.25 3.00
139 Devin Harris 1.25 3.00
140 Tiago Splitter 1.25 3.00
141 DeMar DeRozan 2.50 6.00
142 Derrick Rose 3.00 8.00
143 Josh Smith 1.25 3.00
144 Ricky Rubio 2.00 5.00
145 Jordan Crawford 1.25 3.00
146 J.J. Redick 2.00 5.00
147 Greivis Vasquez 1.25 3.00
148 Al Horford 2.00 5.00
149 Brandon Bass 1.25 3.00
150 Anthony Morrow 1.25 3.00
151 Baron Davis 1.50 4.00
152 Thaddeus Young 1.25 3.00
153 James Johnson 1.25 3.00
154 Ekpe Udoh 1.25 3.00
155 Metta World Peace 1.50 4.00
156 Michael Redd 1.50 4.00
157 John Salmons 1.50 4.00
158 Omri Casspi 1.25 3.00
159 Richard Hamilton 2.50 6.00
160 Alonzo Gee RC 1.25 3.00
161 J.J. Hickson 1.25 3.00
162 Rodrigue Beaubois 1.25 3.00
163 Marreese Speights 1.25 3.00
164 Xavier Henry 1.25 3.00
165 Reggie Williams 1.50 4.00
166 Raja Bell 1.50 4.00
167 Raymond Felton 1.25 3.00
168 Daequan Cook 1.25 3.00
169 David Lee 1.25 3.00
170A T.McGrady Hawks/149* 5.00 12.00
170C T.McGrady Magic/45* 12.00 30.00
170E T.McGrady Raptors/30* 25.00 60.00
170F T.McGrady Rockets/55* 5.00 12.00
171 Joel Anthony 1.25 3.00
172 Tyrus Thomas 1.25 3.00
173 Joe Johnson 1.50 4.00
174 Randy Foye 1.25 3.00
175 Gerald Henderson 1.25 3.00
176 Jack Sikma 2.00 5.00
177 Paul Silas 2.00 5.00
178 Harry Gallatin 2.00 5.00
179A G.Payton Sonics/199* 4.00 10.00
179B G.Payton Bucks/30* 25.00 60.00
179C G.Payton Celtics/25* 25.00 60.00
179D G.Payton Heat/25* 30.00 80.00
179E G.Payton Lakers/20* 25.00 60.00
180 Detlef Schrempf 2.00 5.00
181 John Salley 1.50 4.00
182 Earl Monroe 3.00 8.00
183A B.Walton Blazers/209* 4.00 10.00
183B B.Walton Celtics/40* 20.00 50.00
183C B.Walton LA Clips/30* 12.00 30.00
183D B.Walton SD Clips/20* 15.00 40.00
184 Shawn Kemp 5.00 12.00
185 Wilt Chamberlain 6.00 15.00
186 Dan Issel 2.50 6.00
187 Jerry West 4.00 10.00
188 Bill Russell 6.00 15.00
189 Robert Parish 2.50 6.00
190 Maurice Cheeks 1.50 4.00
191 Allen Iverson 3.00 8.00
192 Anfernee Hardaway 5.00 12.00
193 Horace Grant 2.00 5.00
194 Walt Frazier 3.00 8.00
195 Yao Ming 4.00 10.00
196 Sean Elliott 1.50 4.00
197 Rod Strickland 1.50 4.00
198 Magic Johnson 8.00 20.00
199 Sam Jones 2.50 6.00
200 Tom Sanders 2.00 5.00
201 George Mikan 6.00 15.00
202 Steve Kerr 2.50 6.00
203 Walt Bellamy 2.00 5.00
204 Bruce Bowen 1.25 3.00
205 Larry Johnson 4.00 10.00
206 Cedric Ceballos 1.50 4.00
207 Vlade Divac 2.00 5.00
208 Rex Chapman 1.50 4.00
209 Karl Malone 4.00 10.00
210A S.O'Neal Magic/79* 12.00 30.00
210B S.O'Neal Cavs/50* 10.00 25.00
210C S.O'Neal Celtics/20* 50.00 125.00
210E S.O'Neal Lakers/70* 12.00 30.00
210F S.O'Neal Suns/40* 40.00 70.00
211 John Starks 2.00 5.00
212 Zydrunas Ilgauskas 1.25 3.00
213A R.Horry Rockets/129* 4.00 10.00
213B R.Horry Lakers/60* 10.00 25.00
213C R.Horry Spurs/40* 12.00 30.00
213D R.Horry Suns/70* 4.00 10.00
214A Mutombo Nuggets/99* 5.00 12.00
214B Mutombo 76ers/30* 12.00 30.00
214C Mutombo Hawks/80* 8.00 20.00
214D Mutombo Knicks/20* 20.00 50.00
214F Mutombo Rockets/60* 12.00 30.00
215 Brad Davis 1.25 3.00
216 Jonny Flynn 1.25 3.00
217 Jamal Mashburn 1.50 4.00
218 Marvin Williams 1.25 3.00
219 John Lucas III 1.25 3.00
220 Nick Collison 1.25 3.00
221 J.J. Barea 2.00 5.00
222 Jonas Jerebko 1.25 3.00
223 Danny Green 1.50 4.00
224 Omer Asik 1.25 3.00
225 Dorell Wright 1.25 3.00

2011-12 Panini Gold Standard 14K Autographs

STATED PRINT RUN 25 TO 149 SER.#'d SETS
1 Allan Houston/149 6.00 15.00
2 Robert Parish/49 8.00 20.00
3 Adrian Dantley/149 5.00 12.00
4 Elgin Baylor/74 40.00 100.00
5 Ray Allen/49 EXCH 30.00 80.00
6 Clyde Drexler/49 15.00 40.00
7 Paul Pierce/49 15.00 40.00
8 Gary Payton/49 15.00 40.00
9 Larry Bird/49 75.00 200.00
10 Hal Greer/49 12.00 30.00
11 Walt Bellamy/49 6.00 15.00
12 Bob Pettit/49 15.00 40.00
13 Vince Carter/49 40.00 100.00
14 David Robinson/49 30.00 80.00
15 Mitch Richmond/149 8.00 20.00
16 Tom Chambers/149 6.00 15.00
17 John Stockton/25 40.00 100.00
18 Bernard King/149 8.00 20.00
19 Bob Lanier/49 15.00 40.00
20 Gail Goodrich/49 6.00 15.00
21 Dale Ellis/149 5.00 12.00
22 Scottie Pippen/49 40.00 100.00
23 Isiah Thomas/49 25.00 60.00
24 Bob McAdoo/149 8.00 20.00
25 Antawn Jamison/149 5.00 12.00
26 Mark Aguirre/149 6.00 15.00
27 Dolph Schayes/49 6.00 15.00
28 Glen Rice/149 6.00 15.00
29 Tracy McGrady/25 40.00 100.00
30 World B. Free/49 5.00 12.00
31 Calvin Murphy/49 5.00 12.00
32 Chris Mullin/149 8.00 20.00
33 Lenny Wilkens/49 8.00 20.00
34 Bailey Howell/49 8.00 20.00
35 Magic Johnson/49 75.00 200.00
36 Rolando Blackman/149 5.00 12.00
37 Earl Monroe/49 10.00 25.00
38 Kevin McHale/49 10.00 25.00
39 Michael Finley/149 6.00 15.00
41 Kevin Willis/149 5.00 12.00
42 Spencer Haywood/149 6.00 15.00
43 George McGinnis/149 6.00 15.00
44 Hersey Hawkins/149 5.00 12.00
45 Jason Kidd/25 20.00 50.00
46 Grant Hill/49 20.00 50.00
47 Nate Archibald/49 8.00 20.00
48 Joe Dumars/49 6.00 15.00
49 James Worthy/49 10.00 25.00
50 Billy Cunningham/49 6.00 15.00
51 Steve Nash/25 30.00 80.00
52 Juwan Howard/149 5.00 12.00
53 Rod Strickland/149 5.00 12.00
54 Kiki Vandeweghe/49 5.00 12.00
55 Jack Twyman/99 6.00 15.00
56 Detlef Schrempf/149 6.00 15.00
57 Jeff Hornacek/49 5.00 12.00
58 Terry Porter/149 5.00 12.00
59 Walt Frazier/49 10.00 25.00
60 Tim Hardaway/149 8.00 20.00

2011-12 Panini Gold Standard 14K Memorabilia

STATED PRINT RUN 2 TO 149 SER.#'d SETS
1 LeBron James/99 50.00 125.00
2 Chris Webber/99 8.00 20.00
3 Scottie Pippen/75 15.00 40.00
4 Chauncey Billups/49 8.00 20.00
5 Dennis Johnson/25 8.00 20.00
7 Shawn Marion/99 6.00 15.00
8 Elton Brand/99 6.00 15.00
9 Shawn Kemp/49 10.00 25.00
10 LeBron James/25 60.00 150.00
11 Vince Carter/99 12.00 30.00
12 Carmelo Anthony/149 10.00 25.00
13 Richard Hamilton/25 8.00 20.00
14 Rashard Lewis/99 5.00 12.00
15 Chauncey Billups/99 8.00 20.00
16 Mike Bibby/99 6.00 15.00
17 Jamaal Wilkes/25 6.00 15.00
18 Allan Houston/49 6.00 15.00
19 Dwyane Wade/149 12.00 30.00
21 Andre Miller/99 5.00 12.00
22 Alonzo Mourning/99 10.00 25.00
23 Pau Gasol/99 10.00 25.00
24 Joe Johnson/149 5.00 12.00
25 Eddie Jones/49 6.00 15.00
26 Paul Pierce/149 10.00 25.00
27 David Robinson/49 12.00 30.00
28 Ray Allen/99 10.00 25.00
29 Scottie Pippen/49 15.00 40.00
30 Tracy McGrady/35 12.00 30.00
31 Vince Carter/99 12.00 30.00
32 Tracy McGrady/99 12.00 30.00
33 Jason Terry/99 5.00 12.00
34 Steve Nash/49 12.00 30.00
35 Jason Kidd/49 10.00 25.00
36 Jason Richardson/99 6.00 15.00
37 Robert Parish/49 8.00 20.00
38 Clyde Drexler/49 10.00 25.00
40 Tom Chambers/49 6.00 15.00
41 Grant Hill/99 10.00 25.00
42 Kiki Vandeweghe/99 5.00 12.00
43 Chris Mullin/25 8.00 20.00
44 Mark Aguirre/49 6.00 15.00
45 Joe Dumars/25 6.00 15.00
46 Kevin Willis/49 5.00 12.00
47 Kevin McHale/49 10.00 25.00
48 Earl Monroe/25 10.00 25.00
49 Antawn Jamison/99 5.00 12.00
50 Isiah Thomas/25 10.00 25.00
51 John Stockton/49 12.00 30.00
52 Mitch Richmond/20 8.00 20.00
53 Larry Bird/25 25.00 60.00
55 James Worthy/25 10.00 25.00
57 Glen Rice/49 6.00 15.00

2011-12 Panini Gold Standard 14K Memorabilia Prime

STATED PRINT RUN ONE TO 25 SER.#'d SETS
12 Carmelo Anthony/25 20.00 50.00
19 Dwyane Wade/25 50.00 120.00
26 Paul Pierce/25 20.00 50.00

2011-12 Panini Gold Standard Golden Futures Autographs

AB Alec Burks 5.00 12.00
BB Bismack Biyombo 4.00 10.00
BK Brandon Knight 4.00 10.00
CHJ Charles Jenkins 3.00 8.00
CJ Cory Joseph 4.00 10.00
CP Chandler Parsons 4.00 10.00
CS Chris Singleton 3.00 8.00
DW Derrick Williams 3.00 8.00
EK Enes Kanter 5.00 12.00
GA Gustavo Ayon 3.00 8.00
IS Iman Shumpert 5.00 12.00
IT Isaiah Thomas 6.00 15.00
JB Jimmy Butler 60.00 150.00
JF Jimmer Fredette 5.00 12.00
JH Justin Harper 3.00 8.00
JJ JaJuan Johnson 3.00 8.00
JOH Jordan Hamilton 3.00 8.00
JT Jeremy Tyler 3.00 8.00
JV Jan Vesely 3.00 8.00
KF Kenneth Faried 5.00 12.00
KI Kyrie Irving 100.00 250.00
KL Kawhi Leonard 100.00 250.00
KS Kyle Singler 4.00 10.00
KT Klay Thompson 100.00 250.00
KW Kemba Walker 8.00 20.00
LA Lavoy Allen 4.00 10.00
MB MarShon Brooks 4.00 10.00
MCM Marcus Morris 5.00 12.00
MM Markieff Morris 5.00 12.00
NC Norris Cole 4.00 10.00
NS Nolan Smith 3.00 8.00
RJ Reggie Jackson 4.00 10.00
SM Shelvin Mack 3.00 8.00
TH Tobias Harris 8.00 20.00
TT Tristan Thompson 5.00 12.00
XRCF Josh Harrellson 3.00 8.00

2011-12 Panini Gold Standard 2012 Draft Pick Redemptions

XRC1 Anthony Davis 30.00 80.00
XRC2 Michael Kidd-Gilchrist 4.00 10.00
XRC3 Bradley Beal 8.00 20.00
XRC4 Dion Waiters 4.00 10.00
XRC5 Thomas Robinson 2.50 6.00
XRC6 Damian Lillard 25.00 60.00
XRC7 Harrison Barnes 10.00 25.00
XRC8 Terrence Ross 4.00 10.00
XRC9 Andre Drummond 12.00 30.00
XRC10 Austin Rivers 5.00 12.00
XRC11 Meyers Leonard 3.00 8.00
XRC12 Jeremy Lamb 4.00 10.00
XRC13 Kendall Marshall 2.50 6.00
XRC14 John Henson 4.00 10.00
XRC15 Maurice Harkless 4.00 10.00
XRC16 Royce White 2.50 6.00
XRC17 Tyler Zeller 3.00 8.00
XRC18 Terrence Jones 3.00 8.00
XRC19 Andrew Nicholson 2.50 6.00
XRC20 Evan Fournier 4.00 10.00
XRC21 Jared Sullinger 3.00 8.00
XRC22 Fab Melo 2.50 6.00
XRC23 John Jenkins 2.50 6.00
XRC24 Jared Cunningham 2.50 6.00
XRC25 Tony Wroten 2.50 6.00
XRC26 Miles Plumlee 3.00 8.00
XRC27 Arnett Moultrie 3.00 8.00
XRC28 Perry Jones 2.50 6.00
XRC29 Marquis Teague 2.50 6.00
XRC30 Festus Ezeli 3.00 8.00

2011-12 Panini Gold Standard 24K Autographs

STATED PRINT RUN 10 TO 149 SER.#'d SETS
1 Kareem Abdul-Jabbar/25 75.00 200.00
2 Julius Erving/25 75.00 200.00
3 Hakeem Olajuwon/25 40.00 100.00
4 Kobe Bryant/49 1,000.00 2,000.00
5 Dan Issel/149 10.00 25.00
6 Elvin Hayes/49 8.00 20.00
7 Dirk Nowitzki/25 100.00 250.00
8 Oscar Robertson/25 40.00 100.00
9 Dominique Wilkins/25 25.00 60.00
10 George Gervin/149 12.00 30.00
11 John Havlicek/25 50.00 120.00
12 Alex English/25 8.00 20.00
13 Rick Barry/149 12.00 30.00
14 Jerry West/25 40.00 100.00
15 Shaquille O'Neal/20 100.00 250.00

2011-12 Panini Gold Standard 24K Memorabilia

STATED PRINT RUN 10 TO 149 SER.#'d SETS
1 Kareem Abdul-Jabbar/49 20.00 50.00
2 Karl Malone/49 12.00 30.00
4 Kobe Bryant/49 75.00 200.00
5 Shaquille O'Neal/149 25.00 60.00
6 Moses Malone/49 10.00 25.00
7 Kevin Garnett/149 15.00 40.00
8 Hakeem Olajuwon/49 12.00 30.00
9 Dirk Nowitzki/149 15.00 40.00
10 Dominique Wilkins/149 10.00 25.00
11 George Gervin/149 10.00 25.00
12 Alex English/149 8.00 20.00
13 Jerry West/25 12.00 30.00
14 Patrick Ewing/149 10.00 25.00
15 Shaquille O'Neal/121 25.00 60.00
16 Allen Iverson/30 12.00 30.00

2011-12 Panini Gold Standard 24K Memorabilia Prime

*PRIME: 1X TO 2.5X BASE HI
STATED PRINT RUN 5 TO 25 SER.#'d SETS
5 Shaquille O'Neal/25 75.00 200.00
7 Kevin Garnett/25 75.00 200.00
9 Dirk Nowitzki/25 75.00 200.00

2011-12 Panini Gold Standard Black Gold Threads

STATED PRINT RUN 10 TO 149 SER.#'d SETS
100 Tony Parker/49 8.00 20.00
BG1 Dirk Nowitzki/149 15.00 40.00
BG2 Brandon Jennings/49 4.00 10.00
BG3 Ricky Rubio/49 6.00 15.00
BG4 Russell Westbrook/149 10.00 25.00
BG5 Shawn Marion/49 6.00 15.00
BG6 Shawn Kemp/49 10.00 25.00
BG7 Stephen Curry/149 50.00 125.00
BG8 Tim Duncan/49 15.00 40.00
BG9 Toni Kukoc/49 8.00 20.00
BG10 Tracy McGrady/49 12.00 30.00
BG11 Tyler Hansbrough/30 4.00 10.00
BG12 LeBron James/149 50.00 125.00
BG13 Dwight Howard/149 8.00 20.00
BG14 Drew Gooden/49 5.00 12.00
BG15 Dwyane Wade/149 12.00 30.00
BG16 Gary Payton/25 8.00 20.00
BG17 Jason Terry/25 5.00 12.00
BG18 Joakim Noah/25 6.00 15.00
BG19 Al Jefferson/149 4.00 10.00
BG20 Alonzo Mourning/49 10.00 25.00
BG21 Amare Stoudemire/49 6.00 15.00
BG22 Andre Iguodala/49 6.00 15.00
BG23 Andrew Bynum/149 4.00 10.00
BG24 Derrick Rose/149 10.00 25.00
BG25 Kobe Bryant/149 50.00 125.00
BG26 Kevin Garnett/49 15.00 40.00
BG27 Kevin Love/49 6.00 15.00
BG28 LaMarcus Aldridge/49 6.00 15.00
BG29 Manu Ginobili/49 12.00 30.00
BG30 Marc Gasol/49 6.00 15.00
BG31 Pau Gasol/49 10.00 25.00
BG32 Paul Pierce/149 10.00 25.00
BG33 Ben Gordon/49 5.00 12.00
BG34 Serge Ibaka/149 5.00 12.00
BG35 David Lee/49 4.00 10.00
BG36 DeMarcus Cousins/149 6.00 15.00
BG37 Andrew Bogut/49 5.00 12.00
BG38 Bill Cartwright/49 5.00 12.00
BG39 Blake Griffin/149 6.00 15.00
BG40 Brendan Haywood/149 4.00 10.00
BG41 Brook Lopez/149 6.00 15.00
BG42 Carlos Boozer/149 5.00 12.00
BG43 Carmelo Anthony/149 10.00 25.00
BG44 Chris Bosh/149 8.00 20.00
BG45 Chris Webber/49 8.00 20.00
BG46 Chuck Hayes/99 4.00 10.00
BG47 Courtney Lee/99 4.00 10.00
BG48 Darren Collison/49 4.00 10.00
BG49 Roy Hibbert/82 5.00 12.00
BG50 Derrick Favors/99 5.00 12.00
BG51 Danny Granger/99 5.00 12.00
BG52 Eddie Jones/49 6.00 15.00
BG53 Evan Turner/149 4.00 10.00
BG54 Glen Davis/99 5.00 12.00
BG55 Grant Hill/99 10.00 25.00
BG56 Greg Monroe/149 4.00 10.00
BG57 James Harden/149 12.00 30.00
BG58 Jason Kidd/99 10.00 25.00
BG59 JaVale McGee/149 5.00 12.00
BG60 Joe Dumars/25 6.00 15.00
BG61 John Wall/149 8.00 20.00
BG62 Jrue Holiday/149 8.00 20.00
BG63 Julius Erving/25 15.00 40.00
BG64 Karl Malone/49 12.00 30.00
BG65 Kevin Durant/149 25.00 60.00
BG66 Kevin Willis/49 5.00 12.00
BG67 Nicolas Batum/149 4.00 10.00
BG68 Luis Scola/99 5.00 12.00
BG69 Luol Deng/99 5.00 12.00
BG70 Tyreke Evans/49 5.00 12.00
BG71 Vince Carter/99 12.00 30.00
BG72 Patrick Ewing/99 10.00 25.00
BG74 Omri Casspi/49 4.00 10.00
BG75 Nick Van Exel/49 6.00 15.00
BG76 Moses Malone/25 10.00 25.00
BG77 Michael Beasley/49 4.00 10.00
BG78 Mario Chalmers/49 5.00 12.00
BG79 Rajon Rondo/49 8.00 20.00
BG80 Josh Smith/99 4.00 10.00
BG81 Rudy Gay/99 6.00 15.00
BG82 Landry Fields/149 4.00 10.00
BG83 Kiki Vandeweghe/99 5.00 12.00
BG84 Kevin Johnson/149 6.00 15.00
BG86 Chris Paul/149 12.00 30.00
BG87 Andrea Bargnani/99 4.00 10.00
BG88 Patrick Patterson/149 4.00 10.00
BG89 Chris Kaman/99 5.00 12.00
BG90 Nene/49 5.00 12.00
BG91 Spencer Hawes/149 4.00 10.00
BG92 Sleepy Floyd/149 6.00 15.00
BG93 Shawn Bradley/99 4.00 10.00
BG94 Alex English/25 8.00 20.00
BG95 Bill Laimbeer/49 6.00 15.00
BG96 Chris Andersen/49 5.00 12.00
BG97 Danilo Gallinari/49 5.00 12.00
BG98 DeMar DeRozan/149 8.00 20.00
BG99 Yao Ming/49 12.00 30.00

2011-12 Panini Gold Standard Gold Rush

STATED PRINT RUN 49 SER.#'d SETS
1 Kobe Bryant 80.00 200.00
2 Paul Pierce 15.00 40.00
3 LaMarcus Aldridge 10.00 25.00
4 Tony Parker 12.00 30.00
5 Tyreke Evans 8.00 20.00
6 Nick Young 6.00 15.00
7 Marc Gasol 10.00 25.00
8 Josh Smith 6.00 15.00
9 Kevin Durant 40.00 100.00
10 Chris Bosh 12.00 30.00
11 Amare Stoudemire 10.00 25.00
12 Kevin Martin 8.00 20.00
13 LeBron James 80.00 200.00
14 James Harden 20.00 50.00
15 Andrew Bogut 8.00 20.00
16 Al Jefferson 8.00 20.00
17 Jason Terry 8.00 20.00
18 Jason Kidd 15.00 40.00
19 Danny Granger 8.00 20.00
20 Dwyane Wade 20.00 50.00
21 Ty Lawson 6.00 15.00
22 Vlade Divac 10.00 25.00
23 John Starks 10.00 25.00
24 Gary Payton 12.00 30.00
25 Blake Griffin 10.00 25.00
26 Stephen Curry 80.00 200.00
27 Jordan Crawford 6.00 15.00
28 Gordon Hayward 10.00 25.00
29 Chris Paul 20.00 50.00
30 Pau Gasol 15.00 40.00
31 Brandon Jennings 6.00 15.00
32 Toni Kukoc 12.00 30.00
33 Landry Fields 6.00 15.00
34 Derrick Rose 15.00 40.00
35 Scottie Pippen 25.00 60.00
36 David Lee 6.00 15.00
37 Vince Carter 20.00 50.00
38 Shawn Marion 10.00 25.00
39 Andre Iguodala 10.00 25.00
40 Andre Miller 8.00 20.00
41 Jrue Holiday 12.00 30.00
42 Earl Monroe 15.00 40.00
43 David Robinson 20.00 50.00
44 Jerry West 20.00 50.00

45 Julius Erving 25.00 60.00
46 Wilt Chamberlain 30.00 80.00
47 Dwight Howard 12.00 30.00
48 George Mikan 30.00 80.00
49 Chris Mullin 12.00 30.00
50 Shaquille O'Neal 40.00 100.00

2011-12 Panini Gold Standard Gold Stars Materials

STATED PRINT RUN 9 TO 149 SER.#'d SETS
1 Kevin Durant/149 12.00 30.00
2 Ricky Rubio/149 3.00 8.00
3 Rajon Rondo/149 4.00 10.00
4 Derrick Rose/149 5.00 12.00
5 LeBron James/149 25.00 60.00
6 Tony Parker/149 4.00 10.00
7 Steve Nash/149 6.00 15.00
8 Dirk Nowitzki/149 8.00 20.00
9 Amare Stoudemire/149 3.00 8.00
10 Chris Paul/149 6.00 15.00
11 Dwight Howard/149 4.00 10.00
12 Dwyane Wade/149 6.00 15.00
13 Deron Williams/149 2.50 6.00
14 Andrea Bargnani/149 2.00 5.00
15 Tim Duncan/149 8.00 20.00
16 Carlos Boozer/149 2.50 6.00
17 Kevin Garnett/149 8.00 20.00
18 Kevin Love/149 3.00 8.00
19 LaMarcus Aldridge/149 3.00 8.00
20 Greg Monroe/149 2.00 5.00
21 Roy Hibbert/149 2.50 6.00
22 Russell Westbrook/149 5.00 12.00
23 Brandon Jennings/149 2.00 5.00
24 Kobe Bryant/149 25.00 60.00
25 Josh Smith/149 2.00 5.00
26 Monta Ellis/149 2.50 6.00
27 Chris Bosh/149 4.00 10.00
28 D.J. Augustin/40 2.00 5.00
29 Al Jefferson/149 2.00 5.00
30 Andrew Bynum/149 2.00 5.00
31 Ryan Anderson/149 2.00 5.00
32 Brook Lopez/149 3.00 8.00
33 Marcin Gortat/149 2.00 5.00
34 John Wall/149 4.00 10.00
35 Tyreke Evans/149 2.50 6.00
36 Kevin Martin/149 2.50 6.00
37 Carmelo Anthony/149 5.00 12.00
38 Paul Pierce/149 5.00 12.00
40 Marcus Thornton/149 2.00 5.00

2011-12 Panini Gold Standard Gold Stars Materials Prime

*PRIME: 1.25X TO 3X BASE HI
STATED PRINT RUN 3 TO 25 SER.#'d SETS
5 LeBron James/19 125.00 300.00
24 Kobe Bryant/15 125.00 300.00

2011-12 Panini Gold Standard Golden 50 Materials

STATED PRINT RUN 5 TO 149 SER.#'d SETS
1 James Worthy/25 8.00 20.00
2 Robert Parish/99 6.00 15.00
3 Kevin McHale/99 8.00 20.00
4 Kareem Abdul-Jabbar/25 15.00 40.00
5 Karl Malone/99 10.00 25.00
6 Sam Jones/25 6.00 15.00
7 George Gervin/149 8.00 20.00
8 Patrick Ewing/149 8.00 20.00
9 Shaquille O'Neal/149 20.00 50.00
10 Earl Monroe/99 8.00 20.00
11 Scottie Pippen/149 25.00 60.00
12 Clyde Drexler/149 8.00 20.00
13 David Robinson/99 10.00 25.00
14 Julius Erving/25 12.00 30.00
15 John Stockton/99 10.00 25.00
16 Isiah Thomas/99 8.00 20.00
18 George Mikan/25 60.00 150.00
19 Hakeem Olajuwon/149 10.00 25.00
20 Julius Erving/25 12.00 30.00
21 Shaquille O'Neal/149 20.00 50.00
22 Shaquille O'Neal/57 20.00 50.00
23 Shaquille O'Neal/149 20.00 50.00
24 Scottie Pippen/149 12.00 30.00
25 Clyde Drexler/149 8.00 20.00

2011-12 Panini Gold Standard Golden 50 Materials Prime

*PRIME: 1.25X TO 3X BASE HI
STATED PRINT RUN ONE TO 25 SER.#'d SETS

2011-12 Panini Gold Standard Greatest Graphs

STATED PRINT RUN 10 TO 149 SER.#'d SETS
1 John Havlicek/25 75.00 200.00
2 Kareem Abdul-Jabbar/25 75.00 200.00
3 Julius Erving/25 75.00 200.00
4 Lenny Wilkens/149 6.00 15.00
5 Nate Archibald/149 6.00 15.00
6 Rick Barry/25 12.00 30.00
7 Elgin Baylor/49 15.00 40.00
8 Larry Bird/25 100.00 250.00
9 Dave Cowens/149 8.00 20.00
10 Billy Cunningham/149 15.00 40.00
11 Clyde Drexler/25 30.00 80.00
12 Walt Frazier/149 12.00 30.00
13 Hal Greer/149 10.00 25.00
14 Elvin Hayes/149 15.00 40.00
15 Magic Johnson/25 100.00 250.00
16 Sam Jones/25 20.00 50.00
17 Bob Pettit/25 50.00 120.00
18 Kevin McHale/25 30.00 80.00
19 Earl Monroe/25 20.00 50.00
20 Hakeem Olajuwon/25 30.00 80.00
21 Robert Parish/149 8.00 20.00
22 Scottie Pippen/25 125.00 300.00
23 Willis Reed/25 40.00 100.00
24 Oscar Robertson/25 75.00 200.00
25 David Robinson/25 75.00 200.00
27 Dolph Schayes/149 6.00 15.00
29 John Stockton/25 60.00 150.00
30 Isiah Thomas/149 10.00 25.00
31 Nate Thurmond/149 6.00 15.00
32 Wes Unseld/149 10.00 25.00
33 Bill Walton/99 12.00 30.00
35 James Worthy/25 30.00 80.00

2011-12 Panini Gold Standard Hall of Gold Materials

STATED PRINT RUN 5 TO 149 SER.#'d SETS
1 Dominique Wilkins/149 8.00 20.00
2 Dennis Rodman/149 12.00 30.00
3 Clyde Drexler/149 8.00 20.00
4 Joe Dumars/149 5.00 12.00
5 George Gervin/149 8.00 20.00
6 Alex English/149 6.00 15.00
8 Patrick Ewing/149 8.00 20.00
10 Artis Gilmore/25 6.00 15.00
11 David Robinson/149 10.00 25.00
13 James Worthy/25 8.00 20.00
15 Dan Issel/25 6.00 15.00
17 Karl Malone/149 10.00 25.00
18 Kevin McHale/99 8.00 20.00
21 Scottie Pippen/149 12.00 30.00
22 John Stockton/149 10.00 25.00
23 Isiah Thomas/149 8.00 20.00
24 Dennis Johnson/149 6.00 15.00
25 Chris Mullin/49 6.00 15.00

2011-12 Panini Gold Standard Hall of Gold Materials Prime

*PRIME: 1X TO 2.5X BASE HI
STATED PRINT RUN ONE TO 25 SER.#'d SETS

2011-12 Panini Gold Standard Marks of the Hall Autographs

STATED PRINT RUN 10 TO 149 SER.#'d SETS
1 Pat Riley/25 50.00 120.00
2 Kareem Abdul-Jabbar/25 75.00 200.00
3 Nate Archibald/99 6.00 15.00
4 Bobby Wanzer/149 6.00 15.00
5 Elgin Baylor/24 40.00 100.00
7 Dolph Schayes/149 8.00 20.00
8 Bob Pettit/25 40.00 100.00
9 Arnie Risen/149 30.00 80.00
10 Robert Parish/149 12.00 30.00
11 Oscar Robertson/25 75.00 200.00
13 Hal Greer/149 12.00 30.00
14 Frank Ramsey/149 25.00 60.00
15 Willis Reed/25 75.00 200.00
16 John Havlicek/25 75.00 200.00
17 Chris Mullin/149 12.00 30.00
18 Bob McAdoo/149 15.00 40.00
20 Clyde Lovellette/149 12.00 30.00
21 Harry Gallatin/149 8.00 20.00
23 Dan Issel/149 12.00 30.00
26 James Worthy/25 40.00 100.00
27 Dominique Wilkins/25 40.00 100.00
28 Lenny Wilkens/25 8.00 20.00
29 Bill Walton/99 12.00 30.00
30 Wes Unseld/99 12.00 30.00
31 David Thompson/99 10.00 25.00
32 Isiah Thomas/149 EXCH 25.00 60.00
33 John Stockton/25 75.00 200.00
34 Scottie Pippen/25 125.00 300.00
35 Calvin Murphy/149 6.00 15.00
36 Earl Monroe/149 12.00 30.00
37 Bob Lanier/25 40.00 100.00
38 Sam Jones/25 60.00 150.00
39 K.C. Jones/25 50.00 120.00
40 George Gervin/149 12.00 30.00
41 Elvin Hayes/149 12.00 30.00
42 Gail Goodrich/149 8.00 20.00
43 Walt Frazier/99 12.00 30.00
45 Joe Dumars/149 12.00 30.00
46 Dave Cowens/99 12.00 30.00
47 Clyde Drexler/25 60.00 150.00
48 Alex English/99 10.00 25.00
49 Adrian Dantley/149 6.00 15.00
50 Artis Gilmore/25 12.00 30.00

2011-12 Panini Gold Standard Private Signings

1 Oscar Robertson 75.00 200.00
2 John Wall 40.00 100.00
3 Elgin Baylor 75.00 200.00
4 Kareem Abdul-Jabbar 100.00 250.00
5 John Stockton 75.00 200.00
6 Magic Johnson 100.00 250.00
7 Kevin Durant 125.00 300.00
8 Julius Erving 100.00 250.00
9 Derrick Rose 40.00 100.00
10 David Robinson 50.00 125.00
11 Bill Russell 600.00 1,200.00
12 Jerry West 75.00 200.00
13 John Havlicek 75.00 200.00
14 Pat Riley 75.00 200.00
15 Grant Hill 75.00 200.00
16 Toni Kukoc 40.00 100.00

2011-12 Panini Gold Standard Signs of Gold

STATED PRINT RUN 10 TO 149 SER.#'d SETS
1 Chris Paul/25 EXCH 75.00 200.00
4 Andrew Bynum/25 10.00 25.00
5 Russell Westbrook/49 EXCH 50.00 120.00
6 Ray Allen/25 EXCH 40.00 100.00
7 DeMarcus Cousins/49 12.00 30.00
8 Kobe Bryant/49 600.00 1,200.00
11 Artis Gilmore/25 8.00 20.00
12 Ronnie Brewer/149 4.00 10.00
14 Mike Bibby/49 10.00 25.00
15 Danny Granger/49 4.00 10.00
16 Al Jefferson/49 4.00 10.00
17 David Lee/149 6.00 15.00
18 LaMarcus Aldridge/49 6.00 15.00
19 Jamal Crawford/149 4.00 10.00
20 Joe Johnson/25 6.00 15.00
21 Deron Williams/25 8.00 20.00
22 Jason Kidd/25 25.00 60.00
23 Luol Deng/49 4.00 10.00
24 Andrea Bargnani/49 4.00 10.00
25 Kevin Love/25 15.00 40.00
26 Glen Rice/149 6.00 15.00
27 David Thompson/49 6.00 15.00
28 David Robinson/25 30.00 80.00
29 Paul George/149 60.00 150.00
30 Greg Monroe/149 4.00 10.00
31 Walt Frazier/49 12.00 30.00
32 Larry Bird/10 75.00 200.00
33 Detlef Schrempf/149 8.00 20.00
34 Stephen Curry/149 600.00 1,200.00
35 Tyreke Evans/49 10.00 25.00
36 Marcin Gortat/149 5.00 12.00
37 Kevin Martin/149 4.00 10.00
38 Michael Beasley/49 EXCH 5.00 12.00
39 Blake Griffin/25 20.00 50.00
40 Brandon Jennings/49 EXCH 4.00 10.00
41 Mike Conley/149 4.00 10.00
42 Chauncey Billups/25 12.00 30.00
43 Ty Lawson/149 EXCH 4.00 10.00
44 Tony Parker/25 20.00 50.00
45 O.J. Mayo/149 4.00 10.00
46 Vince Carter/25 40.00 100.00
47 Clyde Drexler/25 15.00 40.00
48 Mo Williams/25 6.00 15.00
49 Jeff Teague/149 4.00 10.00
50 Dikembe Mutombo/49 15.00 40.00
51 James Harden/49 40.00 100.00
52 Serge Ibaka/149 6.00 15.00
53 Juwan Howard/149 5.00 12.00
54 Bernard King/149 12.00 30.00
55 Robert Parish/49 12.00 30.00
56 Mark Price/149 6.00 15.00
57 Danilo Gallinari/49 4.00 10.00
58 Jason Richardson/49 5.00 12.00
59 Andre Iguodala/49 12.00 30.00
60 Grant Hill/25 40.00 100.00
61 George Gervin/49 12.00 30.00
62 World B. Free/49 6.00 15.00
63 Metta World Peace/25 12.00 30.00
64 Spencer Haywood/149 10.00 25.00
65 Gerald Wallace/49 4.00 10.00
66 Dave Cowens/49 12.00 30.00
67 Hal Greer/49 12.00 30.00
68 Delonte West/149 4.00 10.00
69 Shane Battier/49 6.00 15.00
70 Ben Gordon/25 4.00 10.00
71 Kyle Lowry/149 12.00 30.00
72 Ersan Ilyasova/149 4.00 10.00
73 Kris Humphries/149 4.00 10.00
74 Chris Kaman/49 4.00 10.00
75 Trevor Ariza/49 4.00 10.00
76 J.R. Smith/149 8.00 20.00
77 DeJuan Blair/149 EXCH 4.00 10.00
78 DeMar DeRozan/49 20.00 50.00
79 Gordon Hayward/149 8.00 20.00
80 Nick Young/149 4.00 10.00
81 D.J. Augustin/49 4.00 10.00
82 Richard Hamilton/25 12.00 30.00
83 Joakim Noah/49 4.00 10.00
84 Paul Westphal/49 5.00 12.00
85 Jose Calderon/149 4.00 10.00
86 Isiah Thomas/149 25.00 60.00
87 Mitch Richmond/149 10.00 25.00
88 Alonzo Mourning/25 30.00 80.00
89 Xavier Henry/149 4.00 10.00
90 Marc Gasol/25 EXCH 15.00 40.00
91 Tayshaun Prince/49 8.00 20.00
93 Bill Walton/49 20.00 50.00
94 K.C. Jones/25 20.00 50.00
95 Elvin Hayes/25 12.00 30.00
96 Jalen Rose/149 5.00 12.00
97 Jamal Mashburn/149 6.00 15.00
98 James Worthy/49 20.00 50.00
99 Mark Aguirre/149 6.00 15.00
100 Muggsy Bogues/149 12.00 30.00

2011-12 Panini Gold Standard Superscribe Autographs

STATED PRINT RUN 25 TO 149 SER.#'d SETS
1 Stephen Curry/149 600.00 1,200.00
2 Brandon Jennings/49 EXCH 4.00 10.00
3 DeMar DeRozan/49 40.00 100.00
4 Antawn Jamison/149 4.00 10.00
5 Stephen Jackson/149 8.00 20.00
6 Luis Scola/149 EXCH 6.00 15.00
7 Kevin Love/25 12.00 30.00
8 Kyle Lowry/149 12.00 30.00
9 Ryan Anderson/149 4.00 10.00
10 Roy Hibbert/149 4.00 10.00
11 Tyson Chandler/99 6.00 15.00
12 Paul George/149 40.00 100.00
13 Gary Neal/149 EXCH 4.00 10.00
14 Evan Turner/25 4.00 10.00
15 David Thompson/149 8.00 20.00
16 Jameer Nelson/149 8.00 20.00
17 Channing Frye/149 4.00 10.00
18 Luke Ridnour/149 4.00 10.00
19 Chris Kaman/149 4.00 10.00
20 Jeff Teague/149 4.00 10.00
21 Rajon Rondo/49 EXCH 15.00 40.00
22 Gerald Wallace/49 4.00 10.00
23 Josh Smith/49 4.00 10.00
24 Kobe Bryant/149 800.00 1,500.00
24A K.Bryant USA Inscription 3,000.00 5,000.00
25 Jrue Holiday/149 12.00 30.00
26 Wesley Matthews/149 4.00 10.00
27 Devin Harris/149 4.00 10.00
28 Shane Battier/149 6.00 15.00
29 Russell Westbrook/49 60.00 150.00
30 Chase Budinger/149 4.00 10.00
31 DeJuan Blair/149 EXCH 4.00 10.00
32 Blake Griffin/49 20.00 50.00
33 Jodie Meeks/149 EXCH 4.00 10.00
34 Caron Butler/49 4.00 10.00
35 Kevin Durant/49 125.00 300.00
36 Landry Fields/149 4.00 10.00
37 Derek Fisher/149 12.00 30.00
38 Rudy Gay/149 EXCH 6.00 15.00
39 Nene/149 EXCH 4.00 10.00
40 Tyler Hansbrough/149 4.00 10.00
41 Ty Lawson/149 4.00 10.00
42 Kris Humphries/149 4.00 10.00
43 Marcin Gortat/149 6.00 15.00
44 DeMarcus Cousins/149 8.00 20.00
45 Eric Gordon/149 8.00 20.00
46 Serge Ibaka/149 EXCH 10.00 25.00
47 Chris Andersen/49 40.00 100.00
48 DeAndre Jordan/149 8.00 20.00
49 Zach Randolph/49 10.00 25.00
50 J.R. Smith/149 8.00 20.00

2012-13 Panini Gold Standard

1-225 PRINT RUN 349 SER.#'d SETS
EXCHANGE DEADLINE 12/26/2014
1 Kevin Love 1.50 4.00
3 LeBron James 12.00 30.00
4 Carmelo Anthony 2.50 6.00
5 Paul Pierce 2.50 6.00
6 Dirk Nowitzki 4.00 10.00
7 Kevin Durant 6.00 15.00
8 Kobe Bryant 12.00 30.00
9 Dwyane Wade 3.00 8.00
10 Blake Griffin 1.50 4.00
11 James Harden 3.00 8.00
12 Deron Williams 1.25 3.00
13 Ricky Rubio 1.25 3.00
14 Dwight Howard 2.00 5.00
15 Russell Westbrook 2.50 6.00
16 Rajon Rondo 2.00 5.00
17 Ray Allen 2.50 6.00
18A Grant Hill Clippers 30.00 80.00
18B Grant Hill Magic 12.00 30.00
18C Grant Hill Suns 10.00 25.00
19 LaMarcus Aldridge 1.50 4.00
20 Chris Bosh 2.00 5.00
21 Tim Duncan 4.00 10.00
22 Tyson Chandler 1.25 3.00
23 Joe Johnson 1.25 3.00
25 Brandon Jennings 1.00 2.50
26 DeMarcus Cousins 1.50 4.00
27 Stephen Curry 12.00 30.00
28 Kevin Garnett 4.00 10.00
29 Chris Paul 3.00 8.00
30 Tyreke Evans 1.25 3.00
31 Andrew Bynum 1.00 2.50
32 Marcin Gortat 1.00 2.50
33 Jeremy Lin 2.50 6.00
34 Derrick Rose 2.50 6.00
35 Ty Lawson 1.00 2.50
36 Al Jefferson 1.00 2.50
37 Tony Parker 2.50 6.00
38 John Wall 2.00 5.00
39 Kevin Martin 1.25 3.00
40 Marc Gasol 1.50 4.00
41 Amar'e Stoudemire 1.50 4.00
42 Josh Smith 1.00 2.50
43 Andrea Bargnani 1.00 2.50
44 Nicolas Batum 1.25 3.00
45 Zach Randolph 1.50 4.00
46A Jason Kidd Knicks 12.00 30.00
46B Jason Kidd Mavericks 12.00 30.00
46C Jason Kidd Nets 12.00 30.00
46D Jason Kidd Suns 12.00 30.00
46E Jason Kidd Mavericks 12.00 30.00
47 Luol Deng 1.25 3.00
48 Jrue Holiday 2.00 5.00
49 Danny Granger 1.00 2.50
50 Pau Gasol 2.50 6.00
51 O.J. Mayo 1.00 2.50
52 Corey Brewer 1.00 2.50
53 Anderson Varejao 1.00 2.50
54 Serge Ibaka 1.25 3.00
55 Metta World Peace 1.25 3.00
56 Jordan Crawford 1.00 2.50
57 Jamal Crawford 1.50 4.00
58 Jason Terry 1.25 3.00
59 David West 1.25 3.00
60 Manu Ginobili 3.00 8.00
61 Andre Iguodala 1.50 4.00
62 Evan Turner 1.00 2.50
63 Greg Monroe 1.00 2.50
64 Roy Hibbert 1.50 4.00
65 Rudy Gay 1.50 4.00
66 Chris Kaman 1.25 3.00
67 Joakim Noah 1.25 3.00
68 Gordon Hayward 1.50 4.00
69 JaVale McGee 1.25 3.00
70 Darren Collison 1.00 2.50
71 Mike Conley 1.25 3.00
72 Louis Williams 1.25 3.00
73 Paul George 2.50 6.00
74 Monta Ellis 1.25 3.00
75 Brook Lopez 1.25 3.00
76 Kyle Lowry 1.50 4.00
77 Ryan Anderson 1.00 2.50
78 DeMar DeRozan 2.00 5.00
79 Al Horford 1.50 4.00
80 Arron Afflalo 1.00 2.50
81 Wesley Matthews 1.00 2.50
82 Raymond Felton 1.00 2.50
83 DeAndre Jordan 1.00 2.50
84 Glen Davis 1.00 2.50
85 Brandon Bass 1.00 2.50
86 Jose Calderon 1.00 2.50
87 Goran Dragic 1.50 4.00
88 Ramon Sessions 1.00 2.50
89 Thaddeus Young 1.00 2.50
90 Marcus Thornton 1.00 2.50
91 Paul Millsap 1.25 3.00
92 Nikola Pekovic 1.00 2.50
93 Jameer Nelson 1.00 2.50
94 Richard Hamilton 1.50 4.00
95 J.R. Smith 1.50 4.00
96 Carlos Boozer 1.25 3.00
97 Jeff Teague 1.00 2.50
98 J.J. Redick 1.50 4.00
99 Andrei Kirilenko 1.25 3.00
100 Tayshaun Prince 1.00 2.50
101 Jason Richardson 1.50 4.00
102 J.J. Hickson 1.00 2.50
103 Kirk Hinrich 1.25 3.00
104 Omer Asik 1.00 2.50
105 Nene 1.00 2.50
106 Antawn Jamison 1.25 3.00
107 Chauncey Billups 2.00 5.00
108 Devin Harris 1.00 2.50
109 Mario Chalmers 1.25 3.00
110 Nick Collison 1.00 2.50
111 Darrell Arthur 1.00 2.50
112 Earl Clark 1.00 2.50
113 Taj Gibson 1.00 2.50
114 Shane Battier 1.25 3.00
115 Gerald Wallace 1.25 3.00
116 Gary Neal 1.00 2.50
117 Andre Miller 1.00 2.50
118 Nick Young 1.00 2.50
119 Mo Williams 1.25 3.00
120 Ersan Ilyasova 1.00 2.50
121 Dorell Wright 1.00 2.50
122 J.J. Barea 1.25 3.00
123 Michael Beasley 1.00 2.50
124 Eric Bledsoe 1.25 3.00
125 Ekpe Udoh 1.00 2.50
126 Jared Dudley 1.00 2.50
127 DeJuan Blair 1.00 2.50
128 Thabo Sefolosha 1.00 2.50
129 Mike Miller 1.25 3.00
130 Marcus Camby 1.50 4.00
131 Rodney Stuckey 1.00 2.50
132 Kris Humphries 1.00 2.50
133 Randy Foye 1.00 2.50
134 Tiago Splitter 1.00 2.50
135 Patrick Patterson 1.00 2.50
136 Emeka Okafor 1.25 3.00
137 Steve Novak 1.00 2.50
138 George Hill 1.25 3.00
139 Derrick Favors 1.25 3.00
140 Lamar Odom 1.25 3.00
141 Shannon Brown 1.00 2.50
142 Ben Gordon 1.25 3.00
143 Carl Landry 1.00 2.50
144 Greivis Vasquez 1.00 2.50
145 Stephen Jackson 1.25 3.00
147 Byron Mullens 1.00 2.50
148 Caron Butler 1.25 3.00
149 Robin Lopez 1.00 2.50
150 Gerald Henderson 1.00 2.50
151 Danny Green 1.25 3.00
152 Samuel Dalembert 1.00 2.50
153 Luis Scola 1.25 3.00
154 Shawn Marion 1.50 4.00
155 Elton Brand 1.25 3.00
156 Jerry Stackhouse 1.25 3.00
157 David Lee 1.00 2.50
158 Larry Sanders 1.00 2.50
159 D.J. Augustin 1.00 2.50
160 Al-Farouq Aminu 1.00 2.50
161 Jarrett Jack 1.25 3.00
162 Kyle Korver 1.25 3.00
163 Nate Robinson 1.00 2.50
164 Marco Belinelli 1.00 2.50
165 Mike Dunleavy 1.00 2.50
166 Kevin Seraphin 1.00 2.50
167 Luke Ridnour 1.25 3.00
168 Jeff Green 1.00 2.50
169 Kendrick Perkins 1.00 2.50
170 Matt Barnes 1.00 2.50
171 Chase Budinger 1.00 2.50
172 Linas Kleiza 1.00 2.50
173 Gerald Green 1.25 3.00
174 Brandon Rush 1.00 2.50
175 Ronnie Brewer 1.00 2.50
176 Kosta Koufos 1.00 2.50
177 Marreese Speights 1.00 2.50
178 Ed Davis 1.00 2.50
179 Landry Fields 1.00 2.50
180 Andray Blatche 1.00 2.50
181 C.J. Watson 1.00 2.50
182 Tony Allen 1.00 2.50
183 Damian Lillard RC 15.00 40.00
184 DeShawn Stevenson 1.00 2.50
185 Courtney Lee 1.00 2.50
186 Tyler Hansbrough 1.00 2.50
187 Lance Stephenson 1.25 3.00
188 Jason Smith 1.00 2.50
189 Brandan Wright 1.00 2.50
190 Marvin Williams 1.00 2.50
191 Kareem Abdul-Jabbar 5.00 12.00
192 Larry Bird 5.00 12.00
193 Wilt Chamberlain 5.00 12.00
194 Yao Ming 3.00 8.00
195 Elgin Baylor 4.00 10.00
196 Isiah Thomas 3.00 8.00
197 Magic Johnson 5.00 12.00
198 Oscar Robertson 3.00 8.00
199 Jerry West 3.00 8.00
200 John Havlicek 3.00 8.00
201 Julius Erving 4.00 10.00
202 Bill Russell 5.00 12.00
203 Scottie Pippen 4.00 10.00
204C Anfernee Hardaway Knicks 15.00 40.00
204D Anfernee Hardaway Suns 4.00 10.00
205 Shaquille O'Neal 5.00 12.00
206 Dennis Rodman 4.00 10.00
207 Pete Maravich 3.00 8.00
208 Karl Malone 2.50 6.00
210 Hakeem Olajuwon 3.00 8.00
211 Dikembe Mutombo 2.50 6.00
212 John Stockton 3.00 8.00
213 Gary Payton 2.00 5.00
214 Bob Pettit 1.50 4.00
215 Moses Malone 2.50 6.00
216 Rick Barry 1.25 3.00
217 David Robinson 2.50 6.00
218 Elvin Hayes 2.50 6.00
219 Bob Cousy 2.50 6.00
220 George Mikan 5.00 12.00
221 Patrick Ewing 2.50 6.00
222 Allen Iverson 5.00 12.00
223 Earl Monroe 2.00 5.00
224 Bob Love 1.50 4.00
225 Bill Walton 2.50 6.00
226 A. Drummond JSY AU RC 10.00 25.00
227 Kyrie Irving JSY AU RC 150.00 400.00
228 Anthony Davis JSY AU RC 300.00 600.00
229 Arnett Moultrie JSY AU RC 4.00 10.00
230 M.Kidd-Gilchrist JSY AU RC 5.00 12.00
231 Bernard James JSY AU RC 4.00 10.00
232 Bismack Biyombo JSY AU RC 5.00 12.00
233 Bradley Beal JSY AU RC 25.00 60.00
234 Will Barton JSY AU RC 8.00 20.00
235 Parsons JSY AU RC EXCH 5.00 12.00
236 Chris Copeland JSY AU RC 4.00 10.00
237 Darius Johnson-Odom JSY AU RC 4.00 10.00
238 Darius Miller JSY AU RC 5.00 12.00
239 Darius Morris JSY AU RC 5.00 12.00
240 Austin Rivers JSY AU RC 6.00 15.00
241 D.Williams JSY AU RC EXCH 4.00 10.00
242 Dion Waiters JSY AU RC EXCH 5.00 12.00
243 Kenneth Faried JSY AU RC 5.00 12.00
244 Dray Green JSY AU RC 20.00 50.00
245 Jae Crowder JSY AU RC 8.00 20.00
246 E'Twaun Moore JSY AU RC 5.00 12.00
247 Evan Fournier JSY AU RC 6.00 15.00
248 Fab Melo JSY AU RC 4.00 10.00
249 Festus Ezeli JSY AU RC 4.00 10.00
250 J.Hamilton JSY AU RC EXCH 4.00 10.00
251 H.Barnes JSY AU RC 8.00 20.00
252 I.Shumpert JSY AU RC EXCH 5.00 12.00
253 Isaiah Thomas JSY AU RC 8.00 20.00
254 Ivan Johnson JSY AU RC EXCH 4.00 10.00
255 Marcus Morris JSY AU RC EXCH 6.00 15.00
256 Jan Vesely JSY AU RC 4.00 10.00
257 Jared Cunningham JSY AU RC 4.00 10.00
258 Jared Sullinger JSY AU RC 4.00 10.00
259 Kawhi Leonard JSY AU RC 300.00 600.00
260 Jeremy Pargo JSY AU RC 4.00 10.00
261 Jeremy Tyler JSY AU RC EXCH 4.00 10.00
262 Jimmer Fredette JSY AU RC 6.00 15.00
263 J.Butler JSY AU RC EXCH 125.00 300.00
264 Kevin Murphy JSY AU RC 4.00 10.00
265 John Jenkins JSY AU RC EXCH 4.00 10.00
266 Jonas Valanciunas JSY AU RC 8.00 20.00
267 Jeremy Lamb JSY AU RC 6.00 15.00
268 K.Walker JSY AU RC EXCH 30.00 80.00
269 Kendall Marshall JSY AU RC 4.00 10.00
270 Doron Lamb JSY AU RC 4.00 10.00
271 Thomas Robinson JSY AU RC 4.00 10.00
272 Khris Middleton JSY AU RC 20.00 50.00
273 Kim English JSY AU RC 4.00 10.00
274 Klay Thompson JSY AU RC 200.00 500.00
275 Kris Joseph JSY AU RC 4.00 10.00
276 Andrew Nicholson JSY AU RC 4.00 10.00
277 Lance Thomas JSY AU RC EXCH 4.00 10.00
278 Lavoy Allen JSY AU RC 4.00 10.00
279 Malcolm Lee JSY AU RC 4.00 10.00
280 Nolan Smith JSY AU RC 4.00 10.00
281 Markieff Morris JSY AU RC EXCH 6.00 15.00
282 Marquis Teague JSY AU RC 4.00 10.00
283 MarShon Brooks JSY AU RC 4.00 10.00
284 Meyers Leonard JSY AU RC 5.00 12.00
285 Kyle Singler JSY AU RC 4.00 10.00
286 Mike Scott JSY AU RC EXCH 5.00 12.00
287 Miles Plumlee JSY AU RC EXCH 4.00 10.00
288 Maurice Harkless JSY AU RC 5.00 12.00
289 Nikola Vucevic JSY AU RC 75.00 200.00
290 Enes Kanter JSY AU RC 6.00 15.00
291 Norris Cole JSY AU RC 4.00 10.00
292 Orlando Johnson JSY AU RC 4.00 10.00
293 Perry Jones JSY AU RC 4.00 10.00
294 Quincy Acy JSY AU RC 4.00 10.00
295 Tyler Honeycutt JSY AU RC 4.00 10.00
296 Reggie Jackson JSY AU RC 6.00 15.00
297 Robert Sacre JSY AU RC 4.00 10.00
298 Terrence Jones JSY AU RC 4.00 10.00
299 Terrence Ross JSY AU RC 10.00 25.00
300 Tobias Harris JSY AU RC 20.00 50.00
301 Trey Thompkins JSY AU RC 4.00 10.00
302 Tristan Thompson JSY AU RC 6.00 15.00
303 Tyler Zeller JSY AU RC 4.00 10.00
304 Brandon Knight JSY AU RC 5.00 12.00
305 John Henson JSY AU RC EXCH 5.00 12.00
306 Damian Lillard JSY AU 200.00 500.00

2012-13 Panini Gold Standard Black Gold Threads

PRINT RUNS B/WN 8-199 COPIES PER
NO PRICING ON QTY 10 OR LESS
1 Ricky Rubio/49 4.00 10.00
2 LeBron James/49 40.00 100.00
3 Tim Duncan/149 6.00 15.00
4 Raymond Felton/149 3.00 8.00
5 Paul Pierce/99 8.00 20.00
6 Kareem Abdul-Jabbar/25 12.00 30.00
7 J.R. Smith/99 5.00 12.00
8 Evan Turner/149 3.00 8.00
9 Kevin Love/99 5.00 12.00
10 Kevin Durant/49 15.00 40.00
11 Carmelo Anthony/49 12.00 30.00
12 Jameer Nelson/199 3.00 8.00
13 Kevin McHale/99 8.00 20.00
14 Marc Gasol/149 5.00 12.00
15 Stephen Curry/149 8.00 20.00
16 Greg Monroe/149 3.00 8.00
17 Arron Afflalo/199 3.00 8.00
18 Andrei Kirilenko/149 4.00 10.00
19 Rudy Gay/199 5.00 12.00
20 Rodney Stuckey/199 3.00 8.00
21 Julius Erving/49 10.00 25.00
22 Kobe Bryant/49 20.00 50.00
23 Robert Parish/49 8.00 20.00
24 Marcus Camby/149 5.00 12.00
25 Dwyane Wade/49 10.00 25.00
26 John Wall/149 6.00 15.00
27 Jalen Rose/49 4.00 10.00
28 Kevin Martin/149 4.00 10.00
29 Pau Gasol/149 8.00 20.00
30 Metta World Peace/149 4.00 10.00
31 Dirk Nowitzki/49 12.00 30.00
32 Tayshaun Prince/199 5.00 12.00
33 Derrick Rose/49 20.00 50.00
34 Josh Smith/149 3.00 8.00
35 Kevin Garnett/99 6.00 15.00
36 Alex English/49 6.00 15.00
37 DeMar DeRozan/199 6.00 15.00
38 Ty Lawson/149 3.00 8.00
40 Thaddeus Young/199 3.00 8.00
41 Scottie Pippen/49 30.00 60.00
42 Zydrunas Ilgauskas/49 4.00 10.00
43 Blake Griffin/49 5.00 12.00
45 Jason Terry/149 4.00 10.00
46 Robin Lopez/199 3.00 8.00
47 Clyde Drexler/49 8.00 20.00
48 Brandon Roy/99 4.00 10.00
49 Allen Iverson/49 20.00 50.00
50 Tony Parker/49 8.00 20.00
51 J.J. Redick/199 5.00 12.00
52 Joe Dumars/49 6.00 15.00
53 Isiah Thomas/49 10.00 25.00
54 Ron Harper/49 5.00 12.00
56 Amar'e Stoudemire/149 5.00 12.00
57 Alonzo Mourning/49 12.00 30.00
58 Kenneth Faried/99 6.00 15.00
59 Patrick Ewing/49 8.00 20.00
60 Elton Brand/199 4.00 10.00
61 David Lee/149 3.00 8.00
62 Hedo Turkoglu/199 4.00 10.00
63 JaVale McGee/199 4.00 10.00
64 Nene/199 4.00 10.00
66 Jamaal Wilkes/25 20.00 50.00
67 DeMarcus Cousins/149 5.00 12.00
69 Vinnie Johnson/49 5.00 12.00
71 Pablo Prigioni/99 5.00 12.00
72 Steve Novak/199 3.00 8.00
73 DeAndre Jordan/149 4.00 10.00
74 Tyrus Thomas/199 3.00 8.00
75 Alvan Adams/49 3.00 8.00
76 Larry Johnson/49 8.00 20.00
77 Danny Manning/49 4.00 10.00
78 Larry Bird/25 12.00 30.00
79 Michael Kidd-Gilchrist/99 6.00 15.00
80 Andre Iguodala/149 5.00 12.00
81 Kyle Lowry/199 5.00 12.00
82 Al Jefferson/199 3.00 8.00
83 Kemba Walker/99 6.00 15.00
84 Andre Miller/149 4.00 10.00
85 Jose Calderon/199 3.00 8.00
86 Brandon Knight/99 4.00 10.00
87 Gordon Hayward/149 5.00 12.00
88 Ben Gordon/199 4.00 10.00
89 Derrick Favors/199 4.00 10.00
90 Andrea Bargnani/149 3.00 8.00
91 Bismack Biyombo/199 4.00 10.00
92 Ramon Sessions/199 3.00 8.00
93 Reggie Lewis/49 12.00 30.00
94 Gary Payton/49 15.00 40.00
95 Dennis Rodman/25 12.00 30.00
96 Bill Laimbeer/49 6.00 15.00
97 Kenny Anderson/49 4.00 10.00
98 Manu Ginobili/149 10.00 25.00
99 Shawn Bradley/49 6.00 15.00
100 Rajon Rondo/49 6.00 15.00

2012-13 Panini Gold Standard Gold Rush

STATED PRINT RUN 25 SER.#'d SETS
1 Dwyane Wade 12.00 30.00
2 Steve Nash 12.00 30.00
3 Deron Williams 5.00 12.00
4 Chris Paul 12.00 30.00
5 Rajon Rondo 8.00 20.00
6 Russell Westbrook 10.00 25.00
7 Ricky Rubio 15.00 40.00
8 Kyrie Irving 100.00 250.00
9 Stephen Curry 60.00 150.00
10 James Harden 12.00 30.00
11 Tim Duncan 15.00 40.00
12 Dwight Howard 8.00 20.00
13 Brook Lopez 5.00 12.00
14 Chris Bosh 8.00 20.00
15 Al Jefferson 4.00 10.00
16 Joakim Noah 5.00 12.00
17 Marc Gasol 6.00 15.00
18 Pau Gasol 10.00 25.00
19 Zach Randolph 6.00 15.00
20 Serge Ibaka 5.00 12.00
21 Derrick Rose 10.00 25.00
22 Kevin Durant 30.00 80.00
23 LeBron James 60.00 150.00
24 Kobe Bryant 100.00 200.00
25 Joe Johnson 5.00 12.00
26 Luol Deng 5.00 12.00
27 Mario Chalmers 5.00 12.00
28 Carmelo Anthony 20.00 50.00
29 Andre Iguodala 6.00 15.00
30 Paul Pierce 10.00 25.00
31 Amar'e Stoudemire 6.00 15.00
32 Tony Parker 15.00 40.00
33 Kevin Love 6.00 15.00
34 Steve Smith 5.00 12.00
35 O.J. Mayo 4.00 10.00
36 Danny Granger 4.00 10.00
37 Greg Monroe 4.00 10.00
38 Vince Carter 12.00 30.00
39 Ray Allen 10.00 25.00
40 Rudy Gay 6.00 15.00
41 Jrue Holiday 8.00 20.00
42 Monta Ellis 5.00 12.00
43 David Lee 4.00 10.00
44 Raymond Felton 4.00 10.00
45 DeMar DeRozan 8.00 20.00
46 Kemba Walker 15.00 40.00
47 J.R. Smith 6.00 15.00
48 Jamal Crawford 12.00 30.00
49 Paul George 25.00 60.00
50 Klay Thompson 40.00 100.00
51 Al Horford 6.00 15.00
52 Shaquille O'Neal 20.00 50.00
53 Metta World Peace 5.00 12.00
54 DeMarcus Cousins 15.00 40.00
55 Ty Lawson 4.00 10.00
56 Goran Dragic 6.00 15.00
57 Anderson Varejao 4.00 10.00
58 Kenneth Faried 5.00 12.00
59 Roy Hibbert 5.00 12.00
60 Marcin Gortat 20.00 50.00
61 Mike Conley 8.00 20.00
62 Steve Francis 5.00 12.00
63 Shawn Kemp 10.00 25.00
64 Alonzo Mourning 20.00 50.00
65 Allen Iverson 25.00 60.00
66 Isiah Thomas 12.00 30.00
67 Larry Bird 15.00 40.00
68 Horace Grant 6.00 15.00
69 Yao Ming 12.00 30.00
70 Bill Russell 20.00 50.00
71 Wilt Chamberlain 20.00 50.00
72 Pete Maravich 20.00 50.00
73 Patrick Ewing 10.00 25.00
74 David Robinson 10.00 25.00
75 Julius Erving 15.00 40.00
76 Anthony Davis 50.00 120.00
77 Chris Webber 8.00 20.00
78 Vlade Divac 6.00 15.00
79 Hakeem Olajuwon 12.00 30.00
80 Magic Johnson 20.00 50.00
81 Gary Payton 8.00 20.00
82 Karl Malone 10.00 25.00
83 Damian Lillard 400.00 800.00
84 Glen Rice 20.00 50.00
85 Dennis Rodman 15.00 40.00
86 Oscar Robertson 12.00 30.00
87 Moses Malone 10.00 25.00
88 John Stockton 12.00 30.00
89 Michael Kidd-Gilchrist 5.00 12.00
90 Gerald Wallace 5.00 12.00
91 Evan Turner 4.00 10.00
92 Tim Hardaway 8.00 20.00
93 Kevin McHale 8.00 20.00
94 Jerry West 12.00 30.00
95 Kareem Abdul-Jabbar 20.00 50.00

96 Bill Walton 10.00 25.00
97 Bob Cousy 10.00 25.00
98 Clyde Drexler 10.00 25.00
99 LaMarcus Aldridge 6.00 15.00
100 Anfernee Hardaway 15.00 40.00

2012-13 Panini Gold Standard Gold Standard Insert

STATED PRINT RUN 199 SER.#'d SETS
1 Chris Paul 5.00 12.00
2 Dwyane Wade 5.00 12.00
3 Rajon Rondo 3.00 8.00
4 Deron Williams 2.00 5.00
5 Steve Nash 5.00 12.00
6 Derrick Rose 4.00 10.00
7 Russell Westbrook 4.00 10.00
8 Mario Chalmers 2.00 5.00
9 Raymond Felton 1.50 4.00
10 Marc Gasol 2.50 6.00
11 Kobe Bryant 12.00 30.00
12 Kevin Durant 10.00 25.00
13 LeBron James 12.00 30.00
14 James Harden 8.00 20.00
15 Carmelo Anthony 4.00 10.00
16 Damian Lillard 125.00 300.00
17 Tyreke Evans 2.00 5.00
18 Stephen Curry 20.00 50.00
19 LaMarcus Aldridge 2.50 6.00
20 Blake Griffin 2.50 6.00
21 Paul George 8.00 20.00
22 Rudy Gay 2.50 6.00
23 Brandon Jennings 1.50 4.00
24 Tim Duncan 6.00 15.00
25 David Lee 1.50 4.00
26 Kyrie Irving 15.00 40.00
27 Paul Pierce 4.00 10.00
28 Tony Parker 6.00 15.00
29 Monta Ellis 2.00 5.00
30 Jrue Holiday 3.00 8.00
31 Brook Lopez 2.00 5.00
32 Kevin Love 2.50 6.00
33 Chris Bosh 3.00 8.00
34 Dwight Howard 3.00 8.00
35 Klay Thompson 25.00 60.00
36 Joe Johnson 2.00 5.00
37 J.R. Smith 2.50 6.00
38 Dirk Nowitzki 6.00 15.00
39 Serge Ibaka 2.00 5.00
40 Chandler Parsons 2.00 5.00
41 Tyson Chandler 2.00 5.00
42 Anthony Davis 30.00 80.00
43 Danny Granger 1.50 4.00
44 Eric Gordon 2.00 5.00
45 Al Jefferson 1.50 4.00
46 Marcin Gortat 1.50 4.00
47 Amar'e Stoudemire 2.50 6.00
48 David West 2.00 5.00

2012-13 Panini Gold Standard Gold Strike Signatures

PRINT RUNS B/WN 49-249 COPIES PER
EXCHANGE DEADLINE 12/26/2014
1 Derrick Favors/75 4.00 10.00
2 DeMarcus Cousins/75 EXCH 8.00 20.00
3 Al-Farouq Aminu/199 3.00 8.00
4 E'Twaun Moore/249 4.00 10.00
5 Paul George/149 20.00 50.00
6 Ed Davis/249 3.00 8.00
7 Eric Bledsoe/199 EXCH 6.00 15.00
8 Jordan Crawford/249 EXCH 3.00 8.00
9 Greivis Vasquez/249 3.00 8.00
10 Landry Fields/199 3.00 8.00
11 James Harden/75 50.00 120.00
12 Tyreke Evans/75 4.00 10.00
13 Stephen Curry/75 EXCH 400.00 800.00
14 Gerald Henderson/149 3.00 8.00
15 Brandon Rush/249 3.00 8.00
16 Taj Gibson/149 3.00 8.00
17 DeJuan Blair/149 3.00 8.00
18 Nando De Colo/249 3.00 8.00
19 Eric Gordon/75 4.00 10.00
20 JaVale McGee/149 EXCH 4.00 10.00
21 Ryan Anderson/249 3.00 8.00
22 DeAndre Jordan/99 4.00 10.00
23 Omer Asik/249 3.00 8.00
24 Goran Dragic/99 12.00 30.00
25 Kyrie Irving/49 125.00 300.00
26 Jeff Teague/199 3.00 8.00
27 Ty Lawson/249 3.00 8.00
28 Alexey Shved/249 3.00 8.00
29 Marcus Thornton/149 3.00 8.00
30 Chase Budinger/149 3.00 8.00
31 Avery Bradley/199 EXCH 3.00 8.00
32 Enes Kanter/249 5.00 12.00
33 Jonas Valanciunas/199 6.00 15.00
34 Jimmer Fredette/199 6.00 15.00
35 Klay Thompson/199 150.00 400.00
36 Kawhi Leonard/249 150.00 400.00
37 Iman Shumpert/249 EXCH 4.00 10.00
38 Tobias Harris/249 5.00 12.00
39 Chandler Parsons/249 EXCH 4.00 10.00
40 Isaiah Thomas/249 6.00 15.00
41 Gordon Hayward/149 12.00 30.00
42 Brandon Knight/75 4.00 10.00
43 Nikola Vucevic/249 12.00 30.00
44 Anthony Davis/49 300.00 600.00
45 Andre Drummond/75 8.00 20.00
46 Harrison Barnes/75 6.00 15.00
47 Kenneth Faried/249 3.00 8.00
48 Nolan Smith/249 3.00 8.00
49 Jordan Hamilton/249 3.00 8.00
50 Norris Cole/249 3.00 8.00
51 MarShon Brooks/249 3.00 8.00
52 Derrick Williams/75 EXCH 3.00 8.00
53 Tristan Thompson/99 5.00 12.00
54 Tiago Splitter/199 3.00 8.00
55 Andray Blatche/199 3.00 8.00
56 Victor Claver/249 3.00 8.00
57 Eric Maynor/249 3.00 8.00
58 Michael Kidd-Gilchrist/49 4.00 10.00
59 Jared Sullinger/75 3.00 8.00
60 Kemba Walker/75 EXCH 25.00 60.00

2012-13 Panini Gold Standard Hall of Gold

STATED PRINT RUN 199 SER.#'d SETS
1 Julius Erving 6.00 15.00
2 Scottie Pippen 6.00 15.00
3 David Robinson 4.00 10.00
4 Larry Bird 8.00 20.00
5 Hakeem Olajuwon 5.00 12.00
6 Isiah Thomas 5.00 12.00
7 Kareem Abdul-Jabbar 8.00 20.00
8 Bob Cousy 4.00 10.00
9 Magic Johnson 8.00 20.00
10 Patrick Ewing 4.00 10.00
11 Bill Russell 8.00 20.00
12 Karl Malone 4.00 10.00
13 Wilt Chamberlain 8.00 20.00
14 Elgin Baylor 6.00 15.00
15 Dave Cowens 4.00 10.00
16 Ralph Sampson 2.00 5.00
17 Bob McAdoo 2.00 5.00
18 Drazen Petrovic 2.50 6.00
19 Frank Ramsey 2.50 6.00
20 John Stockton 5.00 12.00
21 Dennis Rodman 6.00 15.00
22 Joe Dumars 3.00 8.00
23 David Thompson 2.50 6.00
24 Nate Thurmond 2.50 6.00
25 Chet Walker 2.50 6.00
26 James Worthy 4.00 10.00
27 Jerry West 5.00 12.00
28 Arvydas Sabonis 2.50 6.00
29 Chris Mullin 3.00 8.00
30 Oscar Robertson 5.00 12.00
31 Bob Pettit 2.50 6.00
32 Earl Monroe 3.00 8.00
33 Dave Bing 2.50 6.00
34 Bill Bradley 3.00 8.00
35 Clyde Drexler 4.00 10.00
36 George Gervin 4.00 10.00
37 Artis Gilmore 3.00 8.00
38 Harry Gallatin 2.50 6.00
39 Tom Heinsohn 2.50 6.00
40 Dominique Wilkins 3.00 8.00
41 Jamaal Wilkes 2.50 6.00
42 Moses Malone 4.00 10.00
43 Alex English 3.00 8.00
44 Pete Maravich 5.00 12.00
45 Jerry Lucas 2.50 6.00
46 George Mikan 8.00 20.00
47 Robert Parish 4.00 10.00
48 Don Nelson 2.50 6.00

2012-13 Panini Gold Standard Marks of Gold Autographs

PRINT RUNS B/WN 25-149 COPIES PER
EXCHANGE DEADLINE 12/26/2014
1 Joe Johnson/25 8.00 20.00
2 Kobe Bryant/75 500.00 1,000.00
3 Steve Kerr/49 8.00 20.00
4 Bob Lanier/25 6.00 15.00
5 Mitch Richmond/99 8.00 20.00
6 Fat Lever/149 4.00 10.00
7 Rashard Lewis/99 EXCH 5.00 12.00
8 Darryl Dawkins/149 3.00 8.00
9 Joe Dumars/49 6.00 15.00
10 Kevin Durant/49 60.00 150.00
11 Andre Iguodala/25 5.00 12.00
12 Caron Butler/25 4.00 10.00
14 Kemba Walker/49 25.00 60.00
15 David West/99 6.00 15.00
16 Tayshaun Prince/25 5.00 12.00
17 Rod Strickland/149 6.00 15.00
18 Ersan Ilyasova/99 3.00 8.00
19 Kyle Lowry/99 5.00 12.00
20 Monta Ellis/49 4.00 10.00
21 Tom Gugliotta/149 3.00 8.00
22 Jamaal Wilkes/99 5.00 12.00
23 Al-Farouq Aminu/99 3.00 8.00
24 Tom Chambers/99 5.00 12.00
25 John Paxson/149 6.00 15.00
26 Cedric Ceballos/149 8.00 20.00
27 David Robinson/25 20.00 50.00
28 Arron Afflalo/49 3.00 8.00
29 Metta World Peace/49 10.00 25.00
30 Robert Horry/99 10.00 25.00
31 Kyrie Irving/25 150.00 400.00
32 Detlef Schrempf/99 10.00 25.00
33 Willis Reed/25 50.00 120.00
34 Bradley Beal/49 25.00 60.00
35 Blake Griffin/75 30.00 60.00
36 Corey Brewer/99 3.00 8.00
37 Dennis Rodman/49 20.00 50.00
38 Ed Davis/99 3.00 8.00
39 Kevin Love/25 12.00 30.00
40 Nick Anderson/99 4.00 10.00
41 James Johnson/99 3.00 8.00
42 Byron Mullens/99 3.00 8.00
43 Wes Unseld/25 6.00 15.00
44 Ben Gordon/25 6.00 15.00
45 Bernard King/99 6.00 15.00
46 Connie Hawkins/99 6.00 15.00
47 Alonzo Gee/99 3.00 8.00
48 Alan Anderson/99 3.00 8.00
49 Luke Ridnour/99 4.00 10.00
50 Adrian Dantley/99 4.00 10.00
51 Antawn Jamison/99 4.00 10.00
52 Udonis Haslem/99 4.00 10.00
53 Nick Collison/99 3.00 8.00
54 Dolph Schayes/49 6.00 15.00
55 Sam Perkins/99 4.00 10.00
56 Dominique Wilkins/25 12.00 30.00
57 Grant Hill/49 30.00 60.00
58 Spud Webb/99 6.00 15.00
59 Dikembe Mutombo/49 12.00 30.00
60 Courtney Lee/99 3.00 8.00
61 Brandon Rush/99 3.00 8.00
62 Tiago Splitter/99 3.00 8.00
63 Lance Stephenson/149 10.00 25.00
64 Jason Thompson/99 EXCH 3.00 8.00
65 Jared Dudley/99 3.00 8.00
66 J.J. Hickson/99 3.00 8.00
67 Jeff Teague/99 3.00 8.00
68 Eric Bledsoe/99 6.00 15.00
69 Greivis Vasquez/99 3.00 8.00
70 Bobby Jackson/99 3.00 8.00
71 Dave Stallworth/99 3.00 8.00
72 Zydrunas Ilgauskas/99 4.00 10.00
73 Harrison Barnes/25 20.00 50.00
74 Charlie Ward/99 6.00 15.00
75 Marcus Camby/99 5.00 12.00
76 Len Elmore/99 8.00 20.00
77 Kevin Martin/49 6.00 15.00
78 Nikola Pekovic/149 3.00 8.00
79 Jordan Crawford/149 EXCH 3.00 8.00
80 Deron Williams/25 10.00 25.00
81 Taj Gibson/99 3.00 8.00
82 Johan Petro/99 5.00 12.00
83 Gerald Wallace/25 4.00 10.00
85 Gerald Henderson/99 3.00 8.00
86 Mario Chalmers/99 4.00 10.00
87 Danny Granger/25 6.00 15.00
88 Joel Anthony/99 3.00 8.00
89 John Salmons/99 4.00 10.00
90 Bill Walton/49 25.00 60.00
91 Danny Green/149 6.00 15.00
92 Raymond Felton/49 3.00 8.00
93 World B. Free/49 4.00 10.00
94 Carl Landry/49 3.00 8.00
95 J.J. Redick/49 10.00 25.00
96 Anthony Morrow/99 EXCH 3.00 8.00
97 Dwyane Wade/25 25.00 60.00
98 Kiki Vandeweghe/99 4.00 10.00
99 Brandon Knight/49 4.00 10.00
100 Hakeem Olajuwon/25 20.00 50.00

2012-13 Panini Gold Standard Mother Lode Autographs

PRINT RUNS B/WN 19-99 COPIES PER
NO PRICING ON QTY 20 OR LESS
EXCHANGE DEADLINE 12/26/2014
1 Steve Francis/99 6.00 15.00
2 John Havlicek/25 20.00 50.00
4 Larry Bird/75 40.00 100.00
5 Kareem Abdul-Jabbar/75 40.00 100.00
6 Larry Johnson/99 8.00 20.00
7 Magic Johnson/75 30.00 80.00
8 Brent Barry/75 8.00 20.00
9 Jerry West/75 15.00 40.00
10 Zach Randolph/75 5.00 12.00
11 Alex English/99 5.00 12.00
12 Alonzo Mourning/75 10.00 25.00
13 Micheal Ray Richardson/99 5.00 12.00
14 Kobe Bryant/99 400.00 800.00
15 Brook Lopez/99 5.00 12.00
16 Eric Gordon/99 5.00 12.00
17 Allan Houston/99 5.00 12.00
18 Scottie Pippen/25 75.00 200.00
19 Charles Oakley/99 5.00 12.00
20 Clyde Drexler/75 15.00 40.00
21 Thabo Sefolosha/99 4.00 10.00
22 Blake Griffin/75 12.00 30.00
23 Derrick Favors/99 5.00 12.00
24 Danny Manning/99 5.00 12.00
25 Hakeem Olajuwon/75 20.00 50.00
26 Vince Carter/75 10.00 25.00
27 Dwyane Wade/49 30.00 80.00
28 Michael Finley/99 6.00 15.00
29 Gary Payton/99 12.00 30.00
30 Yao Ming/25 40.00 100.00
31 Artis Gilmore/99 5.00 12.00
32 Kevin Durant/75 60.00 150.00
33 Steve Nash/25 20.00 50.00
34 Isiah Thomas/99 8.00 20.00
35 David Robinson/49 15.00 40.00
36 David Thompson/99 5.00 12.00
37 Jason Kidd/49 15.00 40.00
38 Peja Stojakovic/99 6.00 15.00
39 Allen Iverson/25 200.00 300.00
40 Chris Bosh/99 5.00 12.00
41 Stephen Curry/99 EXCH 400.00 800.00
42 Joakim Noah/99 5.00 12.00
43 Kurt Rambis/99 5.00 12.00
44 Dominique Wilkins/99 10.00 25.00
45 Elgin Baylor/75 12.00 30.00
46 Andre Iguodala/99 5.00 12.00
47 DeMarcus Cousins/99 12.00 30.00
48 LaMarcus Aldridge/99 12.00 30.00
49 Oscar Robertson/25 60.00 150.00
50 Josh Smith/99 5.00 12.00

2012-13 Panini Gold Standard Superscribe Autographs

PRINT RUNS B/WN 10-99 COPIES PER
NO PRICING ON QTY 20 OR LESS
EXCHANGE DEADLINE 12/26/2014
1 James Harden/49 30.00 80.00
2 Grant Hill/49 60.00 120.00
3 Kyrie Irving/25 150.00 400.00
5 Kevin Martin/49 4.00 10.00
7 Muggsy Bogues/99 6.00 15.00
8 Brandon Jennings/25 EXCH 3.00 8.00
9 Luol Deng/25 EXCH 4.00 10.00
10 LaMarcus Aldridge/49 10.00 25.00
11 DeMarcus Cousins/49 EXCH 10.00 25.00
13 Andrei Kirilenko/25 4.00 10.00
14 Goran Dragic/99 8.00 20.00
15 Horace Grant/99 12.00 30.00
16 Anfernee Hardaway/25 125.00 300.00
17 Al-Farouq Aminu/99 5.00 12.00
18 Bob McAdoo/99 8.00 20.00
19 Courtney Lee/99 5.00 12.00
20 Dan Majerle/99 6.00 15.00
21 Dave Cowens/49 6.00 15.00
23 Ersan Ilyasova/99 5.00 12.00
24 Kobe Bryant/75 1,000.00 2,000.00
25 Glen Rice/99 10.00 25.00
27 Mario Chalmers/99 5.00 12.00
29 Toni Kukoc/99 8.00 20.00
30 Lenny Wilkens/49 10.00 20.00
31 Monta Ellis/49 EXCH 4.00 10.00
32 Blake Griffin/75 12.00 30.00
33 Rick Fox/49 4.00 10.00
34 Steve Kerr/49 10.00 25.00
38 Mark Price/99 5.00 12.00
39 Luis Scola/25 12.00 30.00
40 Larry Johnson/99 12.00 30.00

2012-13 Panini Gold Standard White Gold Threads

PRINT RUNS B/WN 25-99 COPIES PER
1 Yao Ming/99 10.00 25.00
2 Paul Pierce/99 8.00 20.00
3 Steve Novak/99 3.00 8.00
4 James Harden/99 6.00 15.00
5 Nate Thurmond/25 30.00 60.00
6 Evan Turner/99 3.00 8.00
7 Brandon Jennings/99 3.00 8.00
8 Danny Manning/99 4.00 10.00
9 Channing Frye/99 3.00 8.00
10 George Hill/99 4.00 10.00
11 Tim Duncan/99 6.00 15.00
12 Patrick Ewing/99 8.00 20.00
13 Ricky Rubio/99 8.00 20.00
14 Andray Blatche/99 3.00 8.00
15 Brook Lopez/99 4.00 10.00
16 Jrue Holiday/99 6.00 15.00
17 Al-Farouq Aminu/99 3.00 8.00
18 Jimmer Fredette/99 5.00 12.00
19 Brandon Knight/99 4.00 10.00
20 Greg Monroe/99 3.00 8.00
21 Josh Smith/99 3.00 8.00
22 Kevin Love/99 5.00 12.00
23 Andrea Bargnani/99 3.00 8.00
24 Mike Dunleavy/99 3.00 8.00
25 Jordan Crawford/99 3.00 8.00
26 Carlos Boozer/99 4.00 10.00
27 Isiah Thomas/49 10.00 25.00
28 Toni Kukoc/99 6.00 15.00
29 DeMarcus Cousins/99 5.00 12.00
30 Thomas Robinson/99 3.00 8.00
31 Dennis Scott/99 3.00 8.00
32 Marc Gasol/99 5.00 12.00
33 Zach Randolph/99 5.00 12.00
34 Ty Lawson/99 3.00 8.00
35 Steve Smith/99 4.00 10.00
36 Ben Gordon/99 4.00 10.00
37 David Lee/99 3.00 8.00
38 Darren Collison/99 3.00 8.00
39 Trevor Booker/99 3.00 8.00
40 LeBron James/99 12.00 30.00
41 Dirk Nowitzki/99 12.00 30.00
42 Jalen Rose/99 4.00 10.00
43 Dwyane Wade/99 10.00 25.00
44 Robert Parish/49 8.00 20.00
45 Pau Gasol/99 8.00 20.00
46 Ed Davis/99 3.00 8.00
47 Chris Paul/99 6.00 15.00
48 John Wall/99 6.00 15.00
49 Wesley Johnson/99 3.00 8.00
50 Tayshaun Prince/99 5.00 12.00

2012-13 Panini Gold Standard Metal

1 Kobe Bryant 20.00 50.00
2 Kevin Durant 10.00 25.00
3 Kyrie Irving 30.00 80.00
4 Blake Griffin 2.50 6.00
5 LeBron James 20.00 50.00
6 Rajon Rondo 3.00 8.00
7 Russell Westbrook 4.00 10.00
8 Kevin Love 2.50 6.00
9 James Harden 5.00 12.00
10 Chris Paul 5.00 12.00
11 Derrick Rose 4.00 10.00
12 Carmelo Anthony 4.00 10.00
13 Dwight Howard 3.00 8.00
14 Zach Randolph 2.50 6.00
15 Tyson Chandler 2.00 5.00
16 Jeremy Lin 4.00 10.00
17 DeMarcus Cousins 2.50 6.00
18 Steve Nash 5.00 12.00
19 Paul Pierce 4.00 10.00
20 John Wall 3.00 8.00
21 Ty Lawson 2.00 5.00
22 Roy Hibbert 2.00 5.00
23 Dirk Nowitzki 6.00 15.00
24 Brandon Jennings 1.50 4.00
25 Luol Deng 2.00 5.00
26 Joe Johnson 2.00 5.00
27 Grant Hill 4.00 10.00
28 Jason Kidd 4.00 10.00
29 Paul George 4.00 10.00
30 Eric Gordon 2.00 5.00
31 J.R. Smith 2.50 6.00
32 Andre Iguodala 2.50 6.00
33 Tim Duncan 6.00 15.00
34 Ricky Rubio 2.00 5.00
35 Klay Thompson 60.00 150.00
36 Kemba Walker 6.00 15.00
37 Raymond Felton 1.50 4.00
38 Josh Smith 1.50 4.00
39 Greg Monroe 1.50 4.00
40 Tyreke Evans 2.00 5.00
41 Brandon Knight 2.00 5.00
42 Tony Parker 4.00 10.00
43 Pau Gasol 3.00 8.00
44 Chandler Parsons 2.00 5.00
45 Kenneth Faried 2.00 5.00
46 Brook Lopez 2.00 5.00
47 Damian Lillard 125.00 300.00
48 Bradley Beal 12.00 30.00
49 Greivis Vasquez 1.50 4.00
50 Dwyane Wade 5.00 12.00
51 Goran Dragic 2.50 6.00
52 Shawn Marion 2.50 6.00
53 Anthony Davis 20.00 50.00
54 Kevin Garnett 6.00 15.00
55 Deron Williams 2.00 5.00
56 Nikola Vucevic 6.00 15.00
57 Metta World Peace 2.00 5.00
58 Marc Gasol 2.50 6.00
59 Vince Carter 5.00 12.00
60 Ray Allen 4.00 10.00
61 Tyler Zeller 1.50 4.00
62 Mario Chalmers 2.00 5.00
63 Thomas Robinson 1.50 4.00
64 Michael Kidd-Gilchrist 2.00 5.00
65 Alexey Shved 1.50 4.00
66 Jared Sullinger 1.50 4.00
67 Harrison Barnes 3.00 8.00
68 Jonas Valanciunas 3.00 8.00
69 Andre Drummond 4.00 10.00
70 Wilt Chamberlain 8.00 20.00
71 Bill Russell 8.00 20.00
72 Pete Maravich 5.00 12.00
73 Anfernee Hardaway 6.00 15.00
74 Allen Iverson 4.00 10.00
75 Yao Ming 5.00 12.00
76 Karl Malone 4.00 10.00
77 John Stockton 5.00 12.00
78 Magic Johnson 8.00 20.00
79 Larry Bird 8.00 20.00
80 Dennis Rodman 6.00 15.00
81 Shaquille O'Neal 8.00 20.00
82 Oscar Robertson 5.00 12.00
83 Elgin Baylor 6.00 15.00
84 Jerry West 5.00 12.00
85 Hakeem Olajuwon 5.00 12.00
86 Julius Erving 6.00 15.00
87 David Robinson 4.00 10.00
88 Bill Walton 4.00 10.00
89 Bob Cousy 4.00 10.00
90 Scottie Pippen 6.00 15.00

2013-14 Panini Gold Standard

226-260 ARE NOT SERIAL NUMBERED
EXCHANGE DEADLINE 8/19/2015
286-310 PRINT RUN 199 SER.#'d SETS
VARIATION PRINT RUN 225 SER.#'d SETS
1 Gordon Hayward 1.25 3.00
2 John Wall 2.00 5.00
3 Louis Williams 1.25 3.00
4 JaVale McGee 1.25 3.00
5 Nikola Vucevic 2.00 5.00
6 Jamal Crawford 1.50 4.00
7 Terrence Ross 1.25 3.00
8 Channing Frye 1.00 2.50
9 Jimmer Fredette 1.50 4.00
10 Danilo Gallinari 1.25 3.00
11 Joakim Noah 1.50 4.00
12 Jason Maxiell 1.00 2.50
13 Austin Rivers 1.25 3.00
14 Tony Wroten 1.00 2.50
15 Larry Sanders 1.00 2.50
16 Kent Bazemore 1.00 2.50
17 Kirk Hinrich 1.25 3.00
18 Arnett Moultrie 1.00 2.50
19 Amir Johnson 1.00 2.50
20 LaMarcus Aldridge 1.50 4.00
21 Andrea Bargnani 1.00 2.50
22 Andrew Bynum 1.00 2.50
23 Marcin Gortat 1.00 2.50
24 Kyrie Irving 5.00 12.00
25 Robert Sacre 1.00 2.50
26 Luke Ridnour 1.25 3.00
27 Greg Oden 1.00 2.50
28 P.J. Tucker 1.50 4.00
29 Kyle Korver 1.25 3.00
30 David West 1.25 3.00
31 Kemba Walker 1.50 4.00
32 George Hill 1.25 3.00
33 Andrew Bogut 1.25 3.00
34 Eric Bledsoe 1.25 3.00
35 Ben Gordon 1.25 3.00
36 Boris Diaw 1.00 2.50
37 Rodney Stuckey 1.00 2.50
38 Kevin Seraphin 1.00 2.50
39 Jrue Holiday 2.00 5.00
40 Dirk Nowitzki 4.00 10.00
41 Bradley Beal 2.50 6.00
42A R.Allen MIA 2.50 6.00
42B R.Allen MIL 6.00 15.00
42C R.Allen SEA 15.00 40.00
42D R.Allen BOS 15.00 40.00
43 Ersan Ilyasova 1.00 2.50
44 Festus Ezeli 1.00 2.50
45 Josh McRoberts 1.00 2.50
46 Ricky Rubio 1.25 3.00
47 Nando De Colo 1.00 2.50
48 Draymond Green 2.50 6.00
49 Bismack Biyombo 1.00 2.50
50 LeBron James 12.00 30.00
51 Will Barton 1.00 2.50
52 Reggie Jackson 1.25 3.00
53 Arron Afflalo 1.00 2.50
54 Kosta Koufos 1.00 2.50
55 Derrick Favors 1.00 2.50
56 Shawn Marion 1.25 3.00
57 J.J. Redick 1.50 4.00
58 Andrei Kirilenko 1.50 4.00
59 Klay Thompson 5.00 12.00
60 Jose Calderon 1.00 2.50
61 Shane Battier 1.25 3.00
62 Kevin Durant 5.00 12.00
63 Blake Griffin 1.50 4.00
64 Marquis Teague 1.00 2.50
65 Tony Parker 2.50 6.00
66 John Jenkins 1.00 2.50
67 Perry Jones 1.00 2.50
68 Harrison Barnes 1.50 4.00
69 Nick Collison 1.00 2.50
70 Udonis Haslem 1.00 2.50
71 Lance Stephenson 1.25 3.00
72 Enes Kanter 1.25 3.00
73 Jae Crowder 1.00 2.50
74 Thabo Sefolosha 1.25 3.00
75 Jared Sullinger 1.25 3.00
76 Goran Dragic 1.25 3.00
77 Marco Belinelli 1.25 3.00
78A D.Howard HOU 2.00 5.00
78C D.Howard ORL 4.00 10.00
78D D.Howard LAL 8.00 20.00
79 Reggie Evans 1.00 2.50
80 Paul Millsap 1.25 3.00
81 Stephen Curry 12.00 30.00
82 Andray Blatche 1.00 2.50
83 Richard Jefferson 1.25 3.00
84 Brandon Bass 1.00 2.50
85 Thomas Robinson 1.00 2.50
86 DeMar DeRozan 2.00 5.00
87 Wilson Chandler 1.25 3.00
88 Matt Barnes 1.00 2.50
89 Vince Carter 3.00 8.00
90 Earl Clark 1.00 2.50
91 Avery Bradley 1.00 2.50
92 Deron Williams 1.25 3.00
93 Josh Smith 1.25 3.00
94 Jerryd Bayless 1.00 2.50
95 Emeka Okafor 1.25 3.00
96 C.J. Watson 1.00 2.50
97 Jeff Taylor 1.00 2.50
98 Brandon Jennings 1.00 2.50
99 Anderson Varejao 1.00 2.50
100 Matt Bonner 1.00 2.50
101 J.J. Hickson 1.00 2.50
102 Raymond Felton 1.00 2.50
103 Evan Turner 1.00 2.50
104 Amar'e Stoudemire 1.50 4.00
105 Brandon Knight 1.00 2.50
106 Ryan Anderson 1.25 3.00
107 O.J. Mayo 1.00 2.50
108 Markieff Morris 1.00 2.50
109 Derek Fisher 1.25 3.00
110 Paul George 2.50 6.00
111 Jodie Meeks 1.00 2.50
112 Danny Green 1.25 3.00
113 Dion Waiters 1.00 2.50
114 David Lee 1.00 2.50
115 Gerald Green 1.25 3.00
116 Steve Novak 1.00 2.50
117 Jimmy Butler 3.00 8.00
118 Al Horford 1.50 4.00
119 Chris Paul 3.00 8.00
120 Jeff Teague 1.00 2.50
121 Martell Webster 1.00 2.50
122 Luis Scola 1.25 3.00
123 Kris Humphries 1.00 2.50
124 Monta Ellis 1.25 3.00
125 Carlos Boozer 1.25 3.00
126 Miles Plumlee 1.00 2.50
127 Glen Davis 1.00 2.50
128 Trevor Ariza 1.00 2.50
129 E'Twaun Moore 1.00 2.50
130 Zach Randolph 1.25 3.00
131 Elton Brand 1.25 3.00
132 Derrick Rose 2.50 6.00
133 John Henson 1.00 2.50
134 Chris Andersen 1.25 3.00
135 Nicolas Batum 1.25 3.00
136 Jonas Jerebko 1.00 2.50
137 Jason Thompson 1.00 2.50
138 Tiago Splitter 1.00 2.50
139 Danny Granger 1.25 3.00
140 Al-Farouq Aminu 1.00 2.50
141A C.Billups DET 2.00 5.00
141B C.Billups DEN 6.00 15.00
141C C.Billups BOS 6.00 15.00
141F C.Billups MIN 6.00 15.00
142 Wayne Ellington 1.00 2.50
143 Marcus Morris 1.25 3.00
144 Chris Kaman 1.25 3.00
145 DeMarcus Cousins 1.50 4.00
146 Kevin Martin 1.25 3.00
147 Tim Duncan 4.00 10.00
148 Tristan Thompson 1.00 2.50
149 Carlos Delfino 1.00 2.50
150 Kawhi Leonard 5.00 12.00
151 Jordan Hill 1.00 2.50
152 Luc Mbah a Moute 1.00 2.50
153 Pau Gasol 2.50 6.00
154 Greivis Vasquez 1.00 2.50
155 Kendrick Perkins 1.00 2.50
156 Brandan Wright 1.00 2.50
157 Robin Lopez 1.00 2.50
158 Mike Miller 1.25 3.00
159 Nate Robinson 1.00 2.50
160 Jonas Valanciunas 1.25 3.00
161 Kobe Bryant 12.00 30.00
162 Meyers Leonard 1.00 2.50
163 Thaddeus Young 1.00 2.50
164 Russell Westbrook 2.50 6.00
165 Tyreke Evans 1.25 3.00
166 Chandler Parsons 1.25 3.00
167 Taj Gibson 1.00 2.50
168 Terrence Jones 1.00 2.50
169 Corey Brewer 1.00 2.50
170 Iman Shumpert 1.00 2.50
171 Willie Green 1.00 2.50
172 Anthony Davis 5.00 12.00
173 Nene 1.25 3.00
174 Chris Bosh 2.00 5.00
175 Kyle Singler 1.00 2.50
176 John Salmons 1.00 2.50
177 Andrew Nicholson 1.00 2.50
178 Evan Fournier 1.25 3.00
179 Isaiah Thomas 1.25 3.00
180 J.J. Barea 1.25 3.00
181 Donatas Motiejunas 1.00 2.50
182 Wesley Matthews 1.00 2.50
183 Derrick Williams 1.00 2.50
184 C.J. Miles 1.00 2.50
185 Steve Nash 3.00 8.00
186 Aaron Brooks 1.00 2.50
187 Dwyane Wade 3.00 8.00
188 Nick Calathes 1.00 2.50
189 Lavoy Allen 1.00 2.50
190 Metta World Peace 1.00 2.50
191 Jan Vesely 1.00 2.50
192 Kevin Love 1.50 4.00
193 Jason Richardson 1.50 4.00
194 Roy Hibbert 1.00 2.50
195 Marcus Thornton 1.00 2.50
196 Carmelo Anthony 2.50 6.00
197 Brook Lopez 1.50 4.00
198 Damian Lillard 5.00 12.00
199 Jeff Green 1.00 2.50
200 Marc Gasol 1.50 4.00
201 Rajon Rondo 2.00 5.00
202 Spencer Hawes 1.00 2.50
203 Jameer Nelson 1.00 2.50
204A A.Miller DEN 1.25 3.00
204B A.Miller CLE 6.00 15.00
204F A.Miller POR 6.00 15.00
205 Kevin Garnett 4.00 10.00
206 Nikola Pekovic 1.00 2.50
207 Gerald Henderson 1.00 2.50
208 Rudy Gay 1.25 3.00
209 Greg Monroe 1.00 2.50
210 Ty Lawson 1.00 2.50
211 Alonzo Gee 1.00 2.50
212 Kenneth Faried 1.25 3.00
213 DeMarre Carroll 1.00 2.50
214 Serge Ibaka 1.25 3.00
215 Maurice Harkless 1.00 2.50
216 Andre Iguodala 1.50 4.00
217 Kyle Lowry 1.50 4.00
218 James Harden 3.00 8.00
219 Luol Deng 1.25 3.00
220 Dante Cunningham 1.00 2.50
221 Gerald Wallace 1.25 3.00
222 Brian Roberts 1.00 2.50
223 Paul Pierce 2.50 6.00
224 Jeremy Lin 2.50 6.00
225 DeAndre Jordan 1.25 3.00
226 V.Oladipo JSY AU RC 8.00 20.00
227 Archie Goodwin JSY AU RC 3.00 8.00
228 Caldwell-Pope JSY AU RC 5.00 12.00
229 Nate Wolters JSY AU RC 3.00 8.00
230 Isaiah Canaan JSY AU RC 3.00 8.00
231 G.Antkmp JSY AU RC EXCH 1,000.00 2,000.00
232 Carter-Williams JSY AU RC 4.00 10.00
233 Cody Zeller JSY AU RC 4.00 10.00
234 Glen Rice Jr. JSY AU RC 3.00 8.00
235 S.Muhammad JSY AU RC 3.00 8.00
236 Jeff Withey JSY AU RC 3.00 8.00
237 Alex Len JSY AU RC 4.00 10.00
238 Allen Crabbe JSY AU RC 3.00 8.00
239 Reggie Bullock JSY AU RC 4.00 10.00
240 N.Noel JSY AU RC EXCH 4.00 10.00
241 Tony Snell JSY AU RC 4.00 10.00
242 Kelly Olynyk JSY AU RC 4.00 10.00
243 Solomon Hill JSY AU RC 4.00 10.00
244 Andre Roberson JSY AU RC EXCH 4.00 10.00
245 C.J. McCollum JSY AU RC 15.00 40.00
246 Tony Mitchell JSY AU RC 3.00 8.00
247 Mason Plumlee JSY AU RC 4.00 10.00
248 A.Bennett JSY AU RC 3.00 8.00
249 Ricky Ledo JSY AU RC 3.00 8.00
250 Erik Murphy JSY AU RC 3.00 8.00
251 Peyton Siva JSY AU RC 3.00 8.00
252 Hardaway Jr. JSY AU RC 6.00 15.00
253 Dennis Schroder JSY AU RC 10.00 25.00
254 Ryan Kelly JSY AU RC 3.00 8.00
255 B.McLemore JSY AU RC 4.00 10.00
256 Jamaal Franklin JSY AU RC 3.00 8.00
257 Shane Larkin JSY AU RC EXCH 3.00 8.00
258 Steven Adams JSY AU RC 12.00 30.00
259 Trey Burke JSY AU RC 4.00 10.00
260 Otto Porter JSY AU RC 5.00 12.00
261 Omer Asik 1.00 2.50
262 Carl Landry 1.00 2.50
263 Orlando Johnson 1.00 2.50
264 Andre Drummond 1.50 4.00
265 Norris Cole 1.00 2.50
266 Al Jefferson 1.00 2.50
267 Byron Mullens 1.00 2.50
268 Jason Terry 1.25 3.00
269 Michael Kidd-Gilchrist 1.00 2.50
270 Tayshaun Prince 1.50 4.00
271 Joe Johnson 1.25 3.00
272 Mike Conley 1.50 4.00
273 Nick Young 1.00 2.50
274 Marvin Williams 1.00 2.50
275 Ekpe Udoh 1.00 2.50
276 Tyson Chandler 1.25 3.00
277 Eric Gordon 1.25 3.00
278 Devin Harris 1.00 2.50
279 Alec Burks 1.25 3.00
280 Mario Chalmers 1.25 3.00
281 Andris Biedrins 1.00 2.50
282 Tyler Hansbrough 1.00 2.50
283 J.R. Smith 1.50 4.00
284 Manu Ginobili 3.00 8.00
285 Tony Allen 1.00 2.50
286 Shaquille O'Neal 8.00 20.00
287 David Robinson 4.00 10.00
288 Wilt Chamberlain 6.00 15.00
289 Larry Bird 8.00 20.00
290 Magic Johnson 8.00 20.00
291 Hakeem Olajuwon 4.00 10.00
292 Drazen Petrovic 2.50 6.00
293 Walt Frazier 3.00 8.00
294A M.Cheeks PHI 1.50 4.00
294D M.Cheeks ATL 6.00 15.00
295 Yao Ming 4.00 10.00
296 George Gervin 3.00 8.00
297 Dominique Wilkins 3.00 8.00
298 Anfernee Hardaway 5.00 12.00
299 Oscar Robertson 3.00 8.00
300 Kevin McHale 3.00 8.00
301 Julius Erving 5.00 12.00
302 Bill Russell 6.00 15.00
303 Alonzo Mourning 3.00 8.00
304 Clyde Drexler 3.00 8.00
305 Jerry West 5.00 12.00
306 Moses Malone 3.00 8.00
307 Karl Malone 4.00 10.00
308 Elgin Baylor 2.00 5.00
309 John Stockton 4.00 10.00
310A M.Finley DAL 2.00 5.00
310B M.Finley PHO 25.00 60.00
310C M.Finley SA 6.00 15.00

2013-14 Panini Gold Standard Black Gold Threads

PRINT RUNS B/WN 1-75 COPIES PER
NO PRICING ON QTY 10 OR LESS
1 Dwight Howard/49 8.00 20.00
2 Bill Laimbeer/49 6.00 15.00
3 Dion Waiters/49 4.00 10.00
4 LeBron James/49 75.00 200.00
5 Tristan Thompson/49 4.00 10.00
6 Pau Gasol/49 10.00 25.00
7 Thaddeus Young/20 4.00 10.00
8 Kevin McHale/49 10.00 25.00
9 Brook Lopez/49 6.00 15.00
11 Jeff Green/25 4.00 10.00
12 Andre Miller/20 5.00 12.00
13 Nikola Vucevic/25 8.00 20.00
14 Kevin Garnett/25 15.00 40.00
15 Alex English/25 8.00 20.00
16 Luol Deng/25 5.00 12.00
17 World B. Free/49 5.00 12.00
18 Chris Paul/25 12.00 30.00
19 Al Horford/25 6.00 15.00
20 Zach Randolph/49 5.00 12.00
21 Ray Allen/25 10.00 25.00
23 Earl Monroe/25 10.00 25.00
24 Paul Pierce/25 10.00 25.00
25 Damian Lillard/49 20.00 50.00
26 Ryan Anderson/25 4.00 10.00
27 Kawhi Leonard/25 20.00 50.00
28 Kareem Abdul-Jabbar/25 20.00 50.00
29 Hakeem Olajuwon/25 12.00 30.00
30 Sidney Moncrief/25 6.00 15.00
31 Rajon Rondo/25 8.00 20.00
32 Roy Hibbert/75 4.00 10.00
33 Jamal Mashburn/25 5.00 12.00
34 Carlos Boozer/25 5.00 12.00
35 Carmelo Anthony/25 10.00 25.00
36 Reggie Lewis/49 6.00 15.00
37 Ralph Sampson/25 5.00 12.00
38 Fat Lever/25 5.00 12.00
40 Russell Westbrook/25 10.00 25.00
42 Moses Malone/49 10.00 25.00
43 Vince Carter/20 12.00 30.00
44 Tyson Chandler/25 5.00 12.00

45 Paul Millsap/20 5.00 12.00
46 Blake Griffin/49 6.00 15.00
48 Joakim Noah/25 6.00 15.00
49 Tim Duncan/25 15.00 40.00
50 Monta Ellis/49 5.00 12.00
51 Klay Thompson/49 20.00 50.00
52 J.R. Smith/25 6.00 15.00
53 Mike Conley/25 6.00 15.00
54 Rasheed Wallace/20 6.00 15.00
55 Andrei Kirilenko/25 6.00 15.00
56 Isiah Thomas/25 10.00 25.00
57 David Robinson/49 12.00 30.00
58 Steve Nash/25 12.00 30.00
59 Metta World Peace/25 5.00 12.00
60 Bradley Beal/49 10.00 25.00
61 Andre Drummond/25 6.00 15.00
62 Anfernee Hardaway/49 15.00 40.00
63 Robert Horry/49 6.00 15.00
64 John Wall/25 8.00 20.00
66 James Harden/25 12.00 30.00
67 John Stockton/25 12.00 30.00
68 Raymond Felton/25 4.00 10.00
69 Jalen Rose/25 5.00 12.00
70 Marc Gasol/49 6.00 15.00
71 Clyde Drexler/49 10.00 25.00
72 Joe Dumars/25 8.00 20.00
73 DeMar DeRozan/25 8.00 20.00
74 Artis Gilmore/25 8.00 20.00
75 Kobe Bryant/25 75.00 200.00
76 Kemba Walker/25 6.00 15.00
77 Serge Ibaka/25 5.00 12.00
78 Shaquille O'Neal /49 25.00 60.00
79 Gerald Wallace/25 5.00 12.00
80 Kevin Durant/25 20.00 50.00
81 George Mikan/25 20.00 50.00
82 Chris Bosh/25 8.00 20.00
83 Josh Smith/25 4.00 10.00
84 Deron Williams/25 5.00 12.00
85 Jose Calderon/25 4.00 10.00
86 Dwyane Wade/25 12.00 30.00
87 Dirk Nowitzki/25 15.00 40.00
88 Harrison Barnes/49 6.00 15.00
89 LaMarcus Aldridge/49 6.00 15.00
90 Magic Johnson/49 25.00 60.00
91 Kyrie Irving/49 20.00 50.00
92 Manu Ginobili/25 12.00 30.00
93 Ricky Rubio/49 5.00 12.00
94 Larry Bird/49 25.00 60.00
95 Andre Iguodala/49 6.00 15.00
96 Jameer Nelson/49 4.00 10.00
97 Anthony Davis/49 20.00 50.00
98 Patrick Ewing/49 10.00 25.00
99 Dominique Wilkins/49 10.00 25.00
100 Karl Malone/49 12.00 30.00

2013-14 Panini Gold Standard Claim to Fame Duals

STATED PRINT RUN 49 SER.#'d SETS
1 C.Anthony/K.Durant 12.00 30.00
2 D.Howard/N.Vucevic 5.00 12.00
3 R.Rondo/C.Paul 8.00 20.00
4 C.Paul/R.Rubio 8.00 20.00
5 S.Ibaka/L.Sanders 3.00 8.00
6 K.Thompson/S.Curry 40.00 100.00
7 D.Lillard/A.Davis 12.00 30.00
8 K.Faried/K.Leonard 12.00 30.00
9 J.Wall/D.Cousins 5.00 12.00
10 J.Harden/S.Curry 30.00 80.00
11 B.Pettit/D.Wilkins 6.00 15.00
12 B.Russell/L.Bird 15.00 40.00
13 S.O'Neal /W.Chamberlain 15.00 40.00
14 W.Reed/P.Ewing 6.00 15.00
15 K.Malone/J.Stockton 8.00 20.00
16 K.Bryant/K.Garnett 30.00 80.00
17 K.Garnett/T.Duncan 10.00 25.00
18 S.Nash/A.Miller 8.00 20.00
19 C.Paul/M.Peace 8.00 20.00
20 T.Duncan/K.Garnett 10.00 25.00
21 M.Johnson/L.Bird 15.00 40.00
22 J.Erving/M.Malone 10.00 25.00
23 D.Nowitzki/R.Blackman 10.00 25.00
24 B.Russell/D.Cowens 12.00 30.00
25 L.James/O.Robertson 30.00 80.00
26 S.Curry/K.Durant 30.00 80.00
27 R.Rondo/B.Jennings 5.00 12.00
28 N.Vucevic/T.Chandler 5.00 12.00
29 R.Rubio/K.Walker 4.00 10.00
30 J.Noah/R.Hibbert 4.00 10.00
31 A.English/D.Issel 5.00 12.00
32 I.Thomas/J.Dumars 6.00 15.00
33 W.Chamberlain/R.Barry 12.00 30.00
34 H.Olajuwon/C.Murphy 8.00 20.00
35 C.Drexler/T.Porter 6.00 15.00
36 J.Wilkes/R.Sampson 3.00 8.00
37 D.Rodman/C.Mullin 10.00 25.00
38 K.Malone/S.Pippen 10.00 25.00
39 H.Olajuwon/P.Ewing 8.00 20.00
40 D.Wilkins/J.Dumars 6.00 15.00

2013-14 Panini Gold Standard Finals MVP

STATED PRINT RUN 20 SER.#'d SETS
1 LeBron James 100.00 250.00
2 Dirk Nowitzki 30.00 80.00
3 Kobe Bryant 100.00 250.00
4 Paul Pierce 20.00 50.00
5 Tony Parker 20.00 50.00
6 Dwyane Wade 25.00 60.00
7 Tim Duncan 30.00 80.00
8 Chauncey Billups 15.00 40.00
9 Shaquille O'Neal 50.00 125.00
10 Hakeem Olajuwon 25.00 60.00
11 Isiah Thomas 20.00 50.00
12 Joe Dumars 15.00 40.00
13 James Worthy 15.00 40.00
14 Magic Johnson 50.00 125.00
15 Larry Bird 50.00 125.00
16 Kareem Abdul-Jabbar 40.00 100.00
17 Moses Malone 20.00 50.00
18 Bill Walton 20.00 50.00
19 Willis Reed 20.00 50.00
20 Wilt Chamberlain 40.00 100.00

2013-14 Panini Gold Standard Gold Prospects

STATED PRINT RUN 49 SER.#'d SETS
1 Blake Griffin 4.00 10.00
2 Jimmy Butler 8.00 20.00
3 Greg Monroe 2.50 6.00
4 Anthony Davis 12.00 30.00
5 Paul George 6.00 15.00
6 Damian Lillard 12.00 30.00
7 Nikola Vucevic 5.00 12.00
8 Kawhi Leonard 12.00 30.00
9 Kyrie Irving 12.00 30.00
10 Thomas Robinson 2.50 6.00
11 Tristan Thompson 2.50 6.00
12 Kemba Walker 4.00 10.00
13 Kenneth Faried 3.00 8.00
14 Dion Waiters 2.50 6.00
15 Andre Drummond 4.00 10.00
16 Nikola Pekovic 2.50 6.00
17 Isaiah Thomas 3.00 8.00
18 Klay Thompson 12.00 30.00
19 Iman Shumpert 2.50 6.00
20 Michael Kidd-Gilchrist 2.50 6.00
21 Kelly Olynyk 3.00 8.00
22 John Wall 5.00 12.00
23 Victor Oladipo 6.00 15.00
24 Chandler Parsons 2.50 6.00
25 Jonas Valanciunas 3.00 8.00
26 Jonas Jerebko 2.50 6.00
27 Otto Porter 4.00 10.00
28 Derrick Favors 2.50 6.00
29 Ricky Rubio 3.00 8.00
30 Alex Len 3.00 8.00
31 Avery Bradley 2.50 6.00
32 Bradley Beal 6.00 15.00
33 Derrick Williams 2.50 6.00
34 Anthony Bennett 2.50 6.00
35 Harrison Barnes 4.00 10.00
36 Meyers Leonard 2.50 6.00
37 Nerlens Noel 3.00 8.00
38 Cody Zeller 3.00 8.00
39 Greivis Vasquez 2.50 6.00
40 Jared Sullinger 2.50 6.00

2013-14 Panini Gold Standard Gold Records

STATED PRINT RUN 20 SER.#'d SETS
1 Kobe Bryant 100.00 250.00
2 Chris Bosh 15.00 40.00
3 Carmelo Anthony 20.00 50.00
4 Kyrie Irving 40.00 100.00
5 Kevin Garnett 30.00 80.00
6 Tim Duncan 30.00 80.00
7 Ricky Rubio 10.00 25.00
8 Blake Griffin 12.00 30.00
9 Dwight Howard 15.00 40.00
10 Paul Pierce 20.00 50.00
11 Kevin Durant 40.00 100.00
12 Derrick Rose 20.00 50.00
13 Anthony Davis 40.00 100.00
14 Tony Parker 20.00 50.00
15 Kenneth Faried 10.00 25.00
16 LeBron James 100.00 250.00
17 Damian Lillard 40.00 100.00
18 Russell Westbrook 20.00 50.00
19 Steve Nash 25.00 60.00
20 Chris Paul 25.00 60.00

2013-14 Panini Gold Standard Gold Rush

STATED PRINT RUN 20 SER.#'d SETS
1 Kevin Garnett 30.00 80.00
2 J.R. Smith 12.00 30.00
3 Zach Randolph 10.00 25.00
4 Ray Allen 20.00 50.00
5 David Lee 8.00 20.00
6 Luol Deng 10.00 25.00
7 David West 10.00 25.00
8 Pau Gasol 20.00 50.00
9 LaMarcus Aldridge 12.00 30.00
10 Andre Iguodala 12.00 30.00
11 Amar'e Stoudemire 12.00 30.00
12 Chauncey Billups 15.00 40.00
13 Paul Millsap 10.00 25.00
14 Tim Duncan 30.00 80.00
15 Carlos Boozer 10.00 25.00
16 Al Jefferson 8.00 20.00
17 Nicolas Batum 10.00 25.00
18 Josh Smith 8.00 20.00
19 Paul Pierce 20.00 50.00
20 Gerald Wallace 10.00 25.00
21 Joakim Noah 12.00 30.00
22 Jeff Green 8.00 20.00
23 Andre Miller 10.00 25.00
24 Jose Calderon 8.00 20.00
25 Dwyane Wade 25.00 60.00
26 Danny Granger 8.00 20.00
27 Mike Conley 12.00 30.00
28 Emeka Okafor 10.00 25.00
29 Dirk Nowitzki 30.00 80.00
30 Thaddeus Young 8.00 20.00
31 Rajon Rondo 15.00 40.00
32 Jameer Nelson 8.00 20.00
33 Steve Nash 25.00 60.00
34 Andrei Kirilenko 12.00 30.00
35 Tyson Chandler 10.00 25.00
36 Ryan Anderson 8.00 20.00
37 Al Horford 12.00 30.00
38 Serge Ibaka 10.00 25.00
39 Dwight Howard 15.00 40.00
40 Anderson Varejao 8.00 20.00
41 Carmelo Anthony 20.00 50.00
42 Marcin Gortat 8.00 20.00
43 Kyrie Irving 40.00 100.00
44 Monta Ellis 10.00 25.00
45 Kobe Bryant 100.00 250.00
46 Damian Lillard 40.00 100.00
47 Marc Gasol 12.00 30.00
48 DeMar DeRozan 15.00 40.00
49 Kemba Walker 12.00 30.00
50 Shawn Marion 10.00 25.00
51 Blake Griffin 12.00 30.00
52 Derrick Rose 20.00 50.00
53 Brook Lopez 12.00 30.00
54 Tony Parker 20.00 50.00
55 Brandon Jennings 8.00 20.00
56 Kevin Durant 40.00 100.00
57 Paul George 20.00 50.00
58 Russell Westbrook 20.00 50.00
59 Klay Thompson 40.00 100.00
60 LeBron James 100.00 250.00
61 Kawhi Leonard 40.00 100.00
62 Ty Lawson 8.00 20.00
63 Joe Johnson 10.00 25.00
64 Chris Paul 25.00 50.00
65 Nikola Vucevic 15.00 40.00
66 Tyreke Evans 10.00 25.00
67 Vince Carter 25.00 60.00
68 Ricky Rubio 10.00 25.00
69 Raymond Felton 8.00 20.00
70 Deron Williams 10.00 25.00
71 Anthony Davis 40.00 100.00
72 Manu Ginobili 25.00 60.00
73 Dion Waiters 8.00 20.00
74 James Harden 25.00 60.00
75 Robin Lopez 8.00 20.00
76 Metta World Peace 10.00 25.00
77 Tristan Thompson 8.00 20.00
78 Kevin Love 12.00 30.00
79 Roy Hibbert 8.00 20.00
80 Chris Bosh 15.00 40.00

2013-14 Panini Gold Standard Gold Scripts

PRINT RUNS B/WN 3-149 COPIES PER
NO PRICING ON QTY 10 OR LESS
EXCHANGE DEADLINE 8/19/2015
1 D.Cousins/25 EXCH 6.00 15.00
2 Kemba Walker/25 EXCH 6.00 15.00
3 Kevin Willis/49 5.00 12.00
4 Charlie Scott/49 6.00 15.00
6 Kobe Bryant/25 EXCH 1,000.00 2,000.00
7 Marvin Williams/49 4.00 10.00
9 Jrue Holiday/25 8.00 20.00
10 Stephen Curry/35 800.00 1,500.00
11 Brandon Knight/50 5.00 12.00
14 Kevin Durant/35 EXCH 125.00 300.00
15 Festus Ezeli/149 4.00 10.00
16 Patrick Beverley/149 4.00 10.00
17 Andre Miller/100 5.00 12.00
18 Jordan Hamilton/149 4.00 10.00
19 Serge Ibaka/25 10.00 25.00
21 Kyrie Irving/35 EXCH 100.00 250.00
22 Hakeem Olajuwon/25 50.00 120.00
23 Al-Farouq Aminu/25 4.00 10.00
25 J.R. Smith/100 6.00 15.00
26 Joakim Noah/25 6.00 15.00
27 Greivis Vasquez/25 4.00 10.00
28 Greg Monroe/149 4.00 10.00
29 Khris Middleton/149 12.00 30.00
30 Iman Shumpert/25 4.00 10.00
31 Chris Bosh/25 8.00 20.00
32 Donatas Motiejunas/149 5.00 12.00
33 Kent Bazemore/149 4.00 10.00
34 Kawhi Leonard/125 75.00 200.00
35 Andre Drummond/50 6.00 15.00
37 Tom Chambers/49 6.00 15.00
38 Draymond Green/49 40.00 100.00
39 Deron Williams/25 5.00 12.00
41 Michael Finley/25 6.00 15.00
42 Anthony Davis/35 40.00 100.00
43 Luis Scola/35 5.00 12.00
44 Andrei Kirilenko/25 6.00 15.00
45 Courtney Lee/149 4.00 10.00
46 Blake Griffin/25 15.00 40.00
47 Perry Jones/49 4.00 10.00
48 Lavoy Allen/49 4.00 10.00
49 Alec Burks/49 5.00 12.00
50 P.J. Tucker/49 6.00 15.00

2013-14 Panini Gold Standard Gold Season Autographs

PRINT RUNS B/WN 25-299 COPIES PER
EXCHANGE DEADLINE 8/19/2015
1 Larry Bird/35 125.00 300.00
2 Alonzo Mourning/35 40.00 100.00
3 Magic Johnson/35 125.00 300.00
4 Dikembe Mutombo/100 20.00 50.00
5 Stephen Curry/25 800.00 1,500.00
6 Elvin Hayes/25 8.00 20.00
7 Allan Houston/100 6.00 15.00
8 Bill Sharman/25 30.00 80.00
9 Antoine Walker/299 5.00 12.00
10 Adrian Dantley/299 6.00 15.00
11 Buck Williams/299 5.00 12.00
12 Kevin Durant/50 125.00 300.00
13 Alex English/299 8.00 20.00
14 Greivis Vasquez/299 4.00 10.00
15 Kyrie Irving/50 100.00 250.00
16 Kareem Abdul-Jabbar/25 100.00 250.00
17 D.Cousins/25 EXCH 12.00 30.00
18 Dennis Rodman/25 75.00 200.00
19 Dan Majerle/249 5.00 12.00
20 Kevin Love/25 12.00 30.00
21 Gary Payton/26 40.00 100.00
22 Micheal Ray Richardson/299 5.00 12.00
23 Blake Griffin/25 30.00 80.00
24 Marcus Camby/299 5.00 12.00
25 Kobe Bryant/50 EXCH 1,000.00 2,000.00

2013-14 Panini Gold Standard Gold Strike Signatures

PRINT RUNS B/WN 15-299 COPIES PER
EXCHANGE DEADLINE 8/19/2015
1 Kawhi Leonard/100 100.00 250.00
2 Iman Shumpert/250 4.00 10.00
3 J.J. Hickson/299 4.00 10.00
4 Stephen Curry/75 600.00 1,200.00
5 Jan Vesely/299 4.00 10.00
6 C.Parsons/299 EXCH 4.00 10.00
7 Kevin Love/25 15.00 40.00
8 Dennis Schroder/250 12.00 30.00
9 Ray McCallum/299 4.00 10.00
10 Gal Mekel/299 4.00 10.00
11 MarShon Brooks/298 4.00 10.00
12 Alexey Shved/299 4.00 10.00
13 Robert Sacre/299 4.00 10.00
14 Dwight Howard/25 30.00 80.00
15 Gorgui Dieng/299 5.00 12.00
16 Jared Sullinger/25 4.00 10.00
17 Al-Farouq Aminu/250 4.00 10.00
18 Tobias Harris/250 6.00 15.00
19 Elias Harris/299 4.00 10.00
20 Meyers Leonard/299 4.00 10.00
21 Dwight Buycks/299 4.00 10.00
22 Rudy Gobert/299 15.00 40.00
23 James Harden/25 EXCH 100.00 250.00
24 Phil Pressey/299 4.00 10.00
25 Reggie Jackson/299 5.00 12.00
26 K.Thompson/100 EXCH 100.00 250.00
27 Kyrie Irving/75 75.00 200.00
28 Norris Cole/299 4.00 10.00
29 Tornike Shengelia/299 4.00 10.00
30 Lavoy Allen/299 4.00 10.00
31 Nando De Colo/299 4.00 10.00
32 Kent Bazemore/299 4.00 10.00
33 Jordan Crawford/299 4.00 10.00
34 Brandon Knight/25 5.00 12.00
35 Kenneth Faried/100 5.00 12.00
36 Harrison Barnes/75 6.00 15.00
37 Jimmer Fredette/299 6.00 15.00
38 John Henson/25 4.00 10.00
39 Alonzo Gee/299 4.00 10.00
40 Quincy Acy/299 4.00 10.00
41 Greivis Vasquez/299 4.00 10.00
42 Nikola Pekovic/299 4.00 10.00
43 DeMarcus Cousins/15 12.00 30.00
44 Nemanja Nedovic/299 4.00 10.00
45 Isaiah Thomas/299 5.00 12.00
46 Andrew Nicholson/299 4.00 10.00
47 Andre Drummond/75 6.00 15.00
48 Michael Kidd-Gilchrist/25 4.00 10.00
49 Nikola Vucevic/299 8.00 20.00
50 James Anderson/299 4.00 10.00
51 Carrick Felix/299 4.00 10.00
52 Tyreke Evans/15 5.00 12.00
53 Sergey Karasev/299 4.00 10.00
54 Jrue Holiday/25 20.00 50.00
55 Jordan Hamilton/299 4.00 10.00
56 Terrence Ross/150 5.00 12.00
57 Evan Fournier/299 5.00 12.00
58 Enes Kanter/299 5.00 12.00
59 Jonas Valanciunas/299 5.00 12.00
60 Draymond Green/299 40.00 100.00

2013-14 Panini Gold Standard Marks of Gold

PRINT RUNS B/WN 4-99 COPIES PER
NO PRICING ON QTY 10 OR LESS
EXCHANGE DEADLINE 8/19/2015
1 Henry Bibby/49 4.00 10.00
2 James Harden/49 75.00 200.00
5 Maurice Harkless/49 4.00 10.00
6 Orlando Johnson/99 4.00 10.00
7 Kyrie Irving/49 60.00 150.00
8 Eric Gordon/25 5.00 12.00
11 Satch Sanders/25 12.00 30.00
12 Goran Dragic/25 15.00 40.00
13 Tyreke Evans/25 5.00 12.00
14 Andrea Bargnani/25 4.00 10.00
16 Draymond Green/49 40.00 100.00
17 Anthony Davis/35 50.00 120.00
18 Eddie Johnson/49 4.00 10.00
19 Jan Vesely/49 4.00 10.00
20 Michael Kidd-Gilchrist/25 4.00 10.00
21 Juwan Howard/49 5.00 12.00
23 Nick Collison/49 4.00 10.00
24 Vernon Maxwell/49 5.00 12.00
25 Marquis Teague/49 4.00 10.00
26 Kobe Bryant/25 EXCH 1,000.00 2,000.00
27 E'Twaun Moore/49 4.00 10.00
28 Kenny Walker/49 4.00 10.00
29 Gail Goodrich/49 6.00 15.00
30 Tony Parker/25 30.00 80.00
31 Chris Andersen/49 12.00 30.00
32 Peja Stojakovic/25 5.00 12.00
33 John Starks/49 12.00 30.00
34 Miles Plumlee/99 4.00 10.00
35 Vince Carter/49 75.00 200.00
38 Derrick Favors/25 4.00 10.00
39 Blake Griffin/25 15.00 40.00
40 Andrew Nicholson/25 4.00 10.00
41 Raymond Felton/15 4.00 10.00
42 Josh Smith/15 4.00 10.00
43 Kevin Durant/25 125.00 300.00
45 Harrison Barnes/49 6.00 15.00
46 Kenneth Faried/25 5.00 12.00
47 Kurt Rambis/49 6.00 15.00
48 C.J. Watson/49 4.00 10.00

2013-14 Panini Gold Standard Metal

1 Rajon Rondo 4.00 10.00
2 Magic Johnson 12.00 30.00
3 Derrick Rose 5.00 12.00
4 John Havlicek 8.00 20.00
5 Nerlens Noel 2.50 6.00
6 Al Horford 3.00 8.00
7 Larry Bird 12.00 30.00
8 Paul Pierce 5.00 12.00
9 Elvin Hayes 4.00 10.00
10 Kyrie Irving 10.00 25.00
11 Isiah Thomas 5.00 12.00
12 LeBron James 60.00 150.00
13 Bob Cousy 8.00 20.00
14 Anthony Bennett 2.00 5.00
15 Kemba Walker 3.00 8.00
16 Wilt Chamberlain 10.00 25.00
17 Carmelo Anthony 5.00 12.00
18 Jason Kidd 5.00 12.00
19 Josh Smith 2.00 5.00
20 Scottie Pippen 8.00 20.00
21 Alex Len 2.50 6.00
22 Roy Hibbert 2.00 5.00
23 Julius Erving 8.00 20.00
24 Nikola Vucevic 4.00 10.00
25 Willis Reed 5.00 12.00
26 Kevin Garnett 8.00 20.00
27 Anfernee Hardaway 8.00 20.00
28 Michael Carter-Williams 2.50 6.00
29 Larry Sanders 2.00 5.00
30 Walt Frazier 5.00 12.00
31 John Wall 4.00 10.00
32 George Gervin 5.00 12.00
33 Dwyane Wade 6.00 15.00
34 Patrick Ewing 5.00 12.00
35 Ty Lawson 2.00 5.00
36 Shaquille O'Neal 12.00 30.00
37 Stephen Curry 60.00 150.00
38 Gary Payton 5.00 12.00
39 Dirk Nowitzki 8.00 20.00
40 Clyde Drexler 5.00 12.00
41 Deron Williams 2.50 6.00
42 Alonzo Mourning 5.00 12.00
43 Victor Oladipo 5.00 12.00
44 Kevin Love 3.00 8.00
45 Earl Monroe 5.00 12.00
46 Blake Griffin 3.00 8.00
47 Drazen Petrovic 4.00 10.00
48 Brandon Jennings 2.00 5.00
49 Dennis Rodman 8.00 20.00
50 Ben McLemore 2.50 6.00
51 Dwight Howard 4.00 10.00
52 David Robinson 6.00 15.00
53 Kevin Durant 10.00 25.00
54 Maurice Cheeks 2.50 6.00
55 Marc Gasol 3.00 8.00
56 James Worthy 4.00 10.00
57 Chris Bosh 4.00 10.00
58 Bill Russell 10.00 25.00
59 Kobe Bryant 60.00 150.00
60 Bernard King 4.00 10.00
61 Tyreke Evans 2.50 6.00
62 John Stockton 6.00 15.00
63 Chris Paul 6.00 15.00
64 Bill Walton 5.00 12.00
65 Shabazz Muhammad 2.00 5.00
66 Damian Lillard 10.00 25.00
67 Jerry West 8.00 20.00
68 Russell Westbrook 5.00 12.00
69 Adrian Dantley 3.00 8.00
70 Otto Porter 3.00 8.00
71 James Harden 6.00 15.00
72 Alex English 4.00 10.00
73 DeMarcus Cousins 3.00 8.00
74 Dominique Wilkins 5.00 12.00
75 Tony Parker 5.00 12.00
76 Artis Gilmore 4.00 10.00
77 Monta Ellis 2.50 6.00
78 Tim Hardaway 4.00 10.00
79 Steve Nash 6.00 15.00
80 Yao Ming 15.00 40.00
81 Kelly Olynyk 2.50 6.00
82 Anthony Davis 10.00 25.00
83 Chris Mullin 4.00 10.00
84 Tim Duncan 8.00 20.00
85 Karl Malone 6.00 15.00
86 Jeremy Lin 10.00 25.00
87 Dikembe Mutombo 5.00 12.00
88 Cody Zeller 2.50 6.00
89 Manu Ginobili 6.00 15.00
90 Hakeem Olajuwon 6.00 15.00

2013-14 Panini Gold Standard Metal Black

*BLACK: 1.5X TO 4X BASIC

2013-14 Panini Gold Standard Mother Lode Autographs

PRINT RUNS B/WN 25-299 COPIES PER
EXCHANGE DEADLINE 8/19/2015
1 Kevin Durant/50 125.00 300.00
2 J.R. Smith/50 6.00 15.00
3 Kenny Walker/249 4.00 10.00
4 Jayson Williams/249 4.00 10.00
5 Satch Sanders/249 8.00 20.00
6 Nick Van Exel/25 15.00 40.00
7 John Havlicek/25 40.00 100.00
8 Gail Goodrich/49 6.00 15.00
9 Terry Porter/249 6.00 15.00
10 Andre Drummond/49 6.00 15.00
11 LaMarcus Aldridge/25 20.00 50.00
12 James Harden/25 EXCH 75.00 200.00
13 Kobe Bryant/25 EXCH 1,000.00 2,000.00
14 J.J. Redick/75 6.00 15.00
15 Maalik Wayns/250 4.00 10.00
16 Charlie Ward/299 5.00 12.00
17 Alan Anderson/299 4.00 10.00
18 Tom Gugliotta/225 5.00 12.00
19 Elgin Baylor/25 40.00 100.00
20 Charlie Scott/249 6.00 15.00
21 K.Thompson/149 EXCH 60.00 150.00
22 C.Parsons/249 EXCH 4.00 10.00
23 Stephen Curry/49 800.00 1,500.00
24 Kyrie Irving/50 EXCH 100.00 250.00
25 Tony Parker/25 30.00 80.00
26 Harrison Barnes/75 6.00 15.00
27 Karl Malone/25 50.00 120.00
28 Sleepy Floyd/249 5.00 12.00
29 Jared Cunningham/299 4.00 10.00
31 Vlade Divac/249 6.00 15.00
32 Jarrett Jack/249 5.00 12.00
33 Kenyon Martin/249 6.00 15.00
34 Blake Griffin/25 EXCH 20.00 50.00
35 Tyson Chandler/25 10.00 25.00
36 Anthony Davis/49 40.00 100.00
37 Micheal Ray Richardson/249 5.00 12.00
39 Anfernee Hardaway/25 75.00 200.00
40 Al Horford/25 6.00 15.00
41 Wes Unseld/25 12.00 30.00
42 Herb Williams/249 4.00 10.00
43 Danilo Gallinari/25 6.00 15.00
44 George Hill/249 5.00 12.00
45 Nikola Vucevic/249 8.00 20.00
46 James Worthy/25 30.00 80.00
47 Rick Barry/25 15.00 40.00
48 Jon Leuer/299 4.00 10.00
49 Muggsy Bogues/249 12.00 30.00
50 David Thompson/299 6.00 15.00

2013-14 Panini Gold Standard Ring Bearers Autographs

PRINT RUNS B/WN 10-299 COPIES PER
NO PRICING ON QTY 10
EXCHANGE DEADLINE 8/19/2015
2 Dwyane Wade/15 75.00 200.00
4 Jon McGlocklin/299 5.00 12.00
5 Mark Landsberger/299 15.00 40.00
6 Kenny Smith/25 8.00 20.00
7 Kareem Abdul-Jabbar/25 75.00 200.00
8 Toni Kukoc/249 8.00 20.00
9 Kobe Bryant/25 800.00 1,500.00
10 Dennis Rodman/25 75.00 200.00
11 Jason Terry/25 20.00 50.00
13 Joe Dumars/25 20.00 50.00
14 Alonzo Mourning/25 40.00 100.00
15 Sean Elliott/299 6.00 15.00
16 Magic Johnson/25 125.00 300.00
17 Steve Kerr/25 40.00 100.00
18 Hakeem Olajuwon/25 60.00 150.00
19 Tony Parker/25 40.00 100.00
20 Ron Harper/299 6.00 15.00
21 Kurt Rambis/249 6.00 15.00
22 Robert Horry/249 EXCH 6.00 15.00
23 Antoine Walker/299 5.00 12.00
24 Fred Brown/299 5.00 12.00
25 Michael Cooper/299 6.00 15.00

2013-14 Panini Gold Standard Superscribe Autographs

PRINT RUNS B/WN 25-299 COPIES PER
EXCHANGE DEADLINE 8/19/2015
1 Magic Johnson/49 100.00 250.00
2 Jerry Lucas/50 12.00 30.00
3 Eddie Jones/249 5.00 12.00
4 Scottie Pippen/49 100.00 250.00
6 John Starks/299 12.00 30.00
7 Adrian Dantley/225 6.00 15.00
8 Chris Andersen/35 EXCH 40.00 100.00
9 Spencer Haywood/299 6.00 15.00
10 Kawhi Leonard/75 75.00 200.00
11 J.J. Redick/99 10.00 25.00
12 Mario Chalmers/75 5.00 12.00
13 Dikembe Mutombo/99 20.00 50.00
14 Tony Parker/25 40.00 100.00
15 Dwight Howard/49 25.00 60.00
16 Kobe Bryant/75 1,000.00 2,000.00
17 Blake Griffin/25 20.00 50.00
18 John Lucas/225 5.00 12.00
19 Bob Lanier/15 60.00 150.00
20 David Robinson/25 60.00 150.00
21 Jason Terry/25 20.00 50.00
22 Ryan Anderson/199 4.00 10.00
23 World B. Free/25 15.00 40.00
24 Larry Bird/49 100.00 250.00
25 Jamaal Wilkes/25 10.00 25.00
26 Jon McGlocklin/299 5.00 12.00
27 Brook Lopez/15 15.00 40.00
28 James Worthy/15 EXCH 30.00 80.00
29 Kyrie Irving/49 75.00 200.00
30 Kevin Durant/49 100.00 250.00
31 Harrison Barnes/75 6.00 15.00
32 Anfernee Hardaway/50 75.00 200.00
34 Kenneth Faried/99 5.00 12.00
35 Spud Webb/299 6.00 15.00
36 James Harden/50 EXCH 75.00 200.00
37 Keith Van Horn/299 5.00 12.00
38 J.R. Smith/99 6.00 15.00
39 Dominique Wilkins/15 20.00 50.00
40 Jeff Hornacek/299 5.00 12.00

2013-14 Panini Gold Standard White Gold Threads

PRINT RUNS B/WN 25-199 COPIES PER
1 Deron Williams/99 3.00 8.00
2 World B. Free/49 3.00 8.00
3 Vince Carter/99 8.00 20.00
4 Zach Randolph/99 3.00 8.00
5 Andre Iguodala/99 4.00 10.00
6 Kyrie Irving/149 12.00 30.00
7 Mike Conley/149 4.00 10.00
8 Blake Griffin/125 4.00 10.00
9 Josh Smith/75 2.50 6.00
10 Gerald Wallace/75 3.00 8.00
11 Marc Gasol/99 4.00 10.00
12 DeMar DeRozan/149 5.00 12.00
13 Carlos Boozer/149 3.00 8.00
14 Raymond Felton/99 2.50 6.00
15 Hakeem Olajuwon/49 8.00 20.00
16 Kemba Walker/75 4.00 10.00
17 Rajon Rondo/99 5.00 12.00
18 Shaquille O'Neal /99 15.00 40.00
19 Damian Lillard/99 12.00 30.00
20 Artis Gilmore/25 5.00 12.00
21 Steve Nash/125 8.00 20.00
22 Kawhi Leonard/199 12.00 30.00
23 Joakim Noah/149 4.00 10.00
24 Ryan Anderson/75 2.50 6.00
25 Luol Deng/75 3.00 8.00
26 Kevin Garnett/199 10.00 25.00
27 Jameer Nelson/99 2.50 6.00
28 Dirk Nowitzki/199 10.00 25.00
29 Al Horford/199 4.00 10.00
30 Amar'e Stoudemire/199 4.00 10.00
31 Ty Lawson/75 2.50 6.00
32 LeBron James/125 40.00 100.00
33 Pau Gasol/199 6.00 15.00
34 Larry Bird/49 15.00 40.00
35 Anfernee Hardaway/49 10.00 25.00
36 Ray Allen/199 6.00 15.00
37 Andre Miller/199 3.00 8.00
38 Clyde Drexler/99 6.00 15.00
39 Manu Ginobili/125 8.00 20.00
40 Joe Dumars/49 5.00 12.00
41 Brook Lopez/149 4.00 10.00
42 Russell Westbrook/99 6.00 15.00
43 Monta Ellis/75 3.00 8.00
44 Ricky Rubio/125 3.00 8.00
45 Carmelo Anthony/199 6.00 15.00
46 Jose Calderon/199 2.50 6.00
47 Andrei Kirilenko/199 4.00 10.00
48 Dwyane Wade/199 8.00 20.00
49 Danny Granger/49 2.50 6.00
50 Serge Ibaka/199 3.00 8.00
51 Magic Johnson/49 15.00 40.00
52 LaMarcus Aldridge/199 4.00 10.00
53 Anthony Davis/199 12.00 30.00
54 Jeff Green/199 2.50 6.00
55 Tim Duncan/199 10.00 25.00
56 Dwight Howard/199 5.00 12.00
57 Tony Parker/99 6.00 15.00
58 Paul Millsap/149 3.00 8.00
59 Kevin Durant/199 12.00 30.00
60 Paul Pierce/199 6.00 15.00
61 J.R. Smith/199 4.00 10.00
62 Klay Thompson/199 12.00 30.00
63 Earl Monroe/49 6.00 15.00
64 Thaddeus Young/50 2.50 6.00
65 Tyson Chandler/199 3.00 8.00

2014-15 Panini Gold Standard

COMPLETE SET (347)
201-266 PRINT RUN B/WN 149-199 COPIES PER
267-299 PRINT RUN 99 SER.#'d SETS
VARIATION PRINT RUN 285 SER.#'d SETS
EXCHANGE DEADLINE 8/19/2015
1 Kawhi Leonard 4.00 10.00
2 Dirk Nowitzki 4.00 10.00
3 DeMarcus Cousins 1.25 3.00
4A Kobe Bryant 12.00 30.00
4B Kobe Bryant VAR 20.00 50.00
5A Damian Lillard 4.00 10.00
5B Damian Lillard VAR 6.00 15.00
6 Kentavious Caldwell-Pope 1.25 3.00
7 Jose Calderon 1.00 2.50
8 Derrick Favors 1.00 2.50
9 David Lee 1.00 2.50
10 Kevin Love 1.50 4.00
11 Amir Johnson 1.00 2.50
12 Zach Randolph 1.50 4.00
13 Ryan Anderson 1.00 2.50
14 Avery Bradley 1.00 2.50
15 Randy Foye 1.00 2.50
16 Andre Iguodala 1.50 4.00
17 Al Jefferson 1.00 2.50
18 Stephen Curry 12.00 30.00
19 Roy Hibbert 1.25 3.00
20A Anthony Davis 4.00 10.00
20B Anthony Davis VAR 6.00 15.00
21 Isaiah Thomas 1.25 3.00
22 Gerald Henderson 1.00 2.50
23A L.James CLE 12.00 30.00
23B L.James CLE 20.00 50.00
23C L.James MIA 20.00 50.00
24 Monta Ellis 1.25 3.00
25 Enes Kanter 1.25 3.00
26 Marc Gasol 1.50 4.00
27A Kyrie Irving 3.00 8.00
27B Kyrie Irving VAR 5.00 12.00
28 Gordon Hayward 1.25 3.00
29 Ersan Ilyasova 1.00 2.50
30 Matt Barnes 1.25 3.00
31 Brandon Knight 1.00 2.50
32 Victor Oladipo 1.25 3.00
33 Tony Parker 2.50 6.00
34 Cody Zeller 1.00 2.50
35 Terrence Ross 1.25 3.00
36 Carlos Boozer 1.25 3.00
37 Bradley Beal 2.50 6.00
38 Ty Lawson 1.00 2.50
39 Tim Duncan 4.00 10.00
40 Channing Frye 1.00 2.50
41 Nicolas Batum 1.25 3.00
42 Joe Johnson 1.25 3.00
43 Jeff Green 1.25 3.00
44 Paul Pierce 2.50 6.00
45 Jamal Crawford 1.50 4.00
46 Norris Cole 1.00 2.50
47 Nerlens Noel 1.00 2.50
48 Jimmy Butler 2.50 6.00
49 Jared Sullinger 1.00 2.50
50 Deron Williams 1.25 3.00
51A P.Gasol CHI 2.50 6.00
51B P.Gasol MEM 4.00 10.00
51C P.Gasol LAL 4.00 10.00
52 DeMar DeRozan 2.00 5.00
53 Klay Thompson 4.00 10.00
54 Kenneth Faried 1.25 3.00
55A Dwyane Wade 3.00 8.00
55B Dwyane Wade VAR 5.00 12.00
56 Kevin Garnett 4.00 10.00
57 Jrue Holiday 2.00 5.00
58 Dion Waiters 1.00 2.50
59 Russell Westbrook 2.50 6.00
60 Arron Afflalo 1.00 2.50
61 Andre Drummond 1.25 3.00
62 Tayshaun Prince 1.50 4.00
63 Al Horford 1.50 4.00
64 Ricky Rubio 6.00 15.00
65A S.Marion CLE 1.25 3.00
65B S.Marion MIA 2.00 5.00
65C S.Marion DAL 2.00 5.00
65D S.Marion TOR 2.00 5.00
65E S.Marion PHO 2.00 5.00
66 Anthony Bennett 1.00 2.50
67 Amar'e Stoudemire 1.50 4.00
68 Steven Adams 2.00 5.00
69 Gerald Green 1.25 3.00
70 Mike Conley 1.25 3.00
71 Manu Ginobili 3.00 8.00
72 J.R. Smith 1.50 4.00
73 Kyle Lowry 2.00 5.00
74 Goran Dragic 1.50 4.00
75 Eric Gordon 1.25 3.00
76 Marco Belinelli 1.00 2.50
77 Lance Stephenson 1.25 3.00
78 Harrison Barnes 1.25 3.00
79 Tobias Harris 1.25 3.00
80A Chris Paul 2.50 6.00
80B Chris Paul VAR 4.00 10.00
81 C.J. McCollum 1.50 4.00
82A Blake Griffin 1.50 4.00
82B Blake Griffin VAR 2.50 6.00
83 Wesley Matthews 1.00 2.50
84 Tristan Thompson 1.00 2.50
85 Tiago Splitter 1.00 2.50
86 Chandler Parsons 1.00 2.50
87 Brandon Jennings 1.00 2.50
88 David West 1.25 3.00
89 Jordan Hill 1.00 2.50
90 Tyson Chandler 1.50 4.00
91 JaVale McGee 1.25 3.00
92 Paul Millsap 1.25 3.00
93 Nikola Pekovic 1.00 2.50
94 Jonas Valanciunas 1.25 3.00
95 Nene 1.25 3.00
96A J.Lin NYK 10.00 25.00
96B J.Lin LAL 5.00 12.00
96C J.Lin HOU 5.00 12.00
96D J.Lin GSW 5.00 12.00
97A James Harden 6.00 15.00
97B James Harden VAR 5.00 12.00
98 Otto Porter 1.25 3.00
99 Nick Young 1.00 2.50
100 Jodie Meeks 1.00 2.50
101 Kemba Walker 1.50 4.00
102 Dwight Howard 2.00 5.00
103 Dennis Schroder 1.50 4.00
104 Danilo Gallinari 1.00 2.50
105 Kyle Korver 1.25 3.00
106A Kevin Durant 5.00 12.00
106B Kevin Durant VAR 8.00 20.00
107 Josh Smith 1.00 2.50
108 Derrick Rose 3.00 8.00
109 DeAndre Jordan 1.25 3.00
110 Kevin Martin 1.25 3.00
111 Anderson Varejao 1.00 2.50
112 Taj Gibson 1.00 2.50
113 Serge Ibaka 1.25 3.00

114 Ben McLemore 1.00 2.50
115 Patrick Beverley 1.00 2.50
116 Andrew Bogut 1.25 3.00
117 Alex Len 1.00 2.50
118 Steve Nash 3.00 8.00
119 Rudy Gay 1.50 4.00
120 Archie Goodwin 1.00 2.50
121 Brook Lopez 1.50 4.00
122 J.J. Redick 1.50 4.00
123 Giannis Antetokounmpo 12.00 30.00
124 Michael Kidd-Gilchrist 1.00 2.50
125 Eric Bledsoe 1.25 3.00
126 Marcin Gortat 1.00 2.50
127 LaMarcus Aldridge 1.50 4.00
128 Greg Monroe 1.00 2.50
129 Michael Carter-Williams 1.00 2.50
130 Luol Deng 1.25 3.00
131 Vince Carter 3.00 8.00
132 Trey Burke 1.00 2.50
133 Corey Brewer 1.00 2.50
134A Carmelo Anthony 2.50 6.00
134B Carmelo Anthony VAR 4.00 10.00
135 Thaddeus Young 1.00 2.50
136 Brandon Bass 1.00 2.50
137 Tyreke Evans 1.25 3.00
138 Tim Hardaway Jr. 1.25 3.00
139 Chris Bosh 2.00 5.00
140 Nikola Vucevic 1.25 3.00
141 John Wall 2.00 5.00
142 Jeff Teague 1.00 2.50
143 Rajon Rondo 2.00 5.00
144 Trevor Ariza 1.00 2.50
145 O.J. Mayo 1.00 2.50
146 Nick Collison 1.25 3.00
147 Joakim Noah 1.50 4.00
148 Paul George 2.50 6.00
149 Tony Wroten 1.00 2.50
150 George Hill 1.25 3.00
151 Robert Horry 1.50 4.00
152 Hakeem Olajuwon 3.00 8.00
153 Tim Hardaway 2.00 5.00
154A A.Iverson PHI 40.00 100.00
154B A.Iverson PHI 6.00 15.00
154C A.Iverson MEM 6.00 15.00
154D A.Iverson DEN 6.00 15.00
154E A.Iverson DET 6.00 15.00
155 John Havlicek 3.00 8.00
156A B.Davis CLE 1.50 4.00
156B B.Davis LAC 2.50 6.00
156C B.Davis CHA 2.50 6.00
156D B.Davis NOH 2.50 6.00
156E B.Davis NYK 2.50 6.00
156F B.Davis GSW 2.50 6.00
157 Kevin McHale 2.50 6.00
158 Clyde Drexler 2.50 6.00
159 Oscar Robertson 3.00 8.00
160 Drazen Petrovic 2.00 5.00
161 Robert Parish 2.00 5.00
162 Isiah Thomas 2.50 6.00
163A Tracy McGrady 2.50 6.00
163B Tracy McGrady VAR 4.00 10.00
164A A.Mourning MIA 2.50 6.00
164B A.Mourning MIA 4.00 10.00
164C A.Mourning CHA 4.00 10.00
164D A.Mourning NJN 4.00 10.00
165 John Stockton 3.00 8.00
166 Bernard King 2.00 5.00
167A Larry Bird 6.00 15.00
167B Larry Bird VAR 10.00 25.00
168 David Robinson 3.00 8.00
169 Patrick Ewing 2.50 6.00
170 Elgin Baylor 3.00 8.00
171A S.Pippen CHI 4.00 10.00
171B S.Pippen CHI 6.00 15.00
171C S.Pippen HOU 6.00 15.00
171D S.Pippen POR 6.00 15.00
172 James Worthy 2.50 6.00
173A Anfernee Hardaway 4.00 10.00
173B Anfernee Hardaway VAR 4.00 10.00
174 Wilt Chamberlain 5.00 12.00
175 Julius Erving 4.00 10.00
176 Bill Russell 5.00 12.00
177A L.Sprewell NYK 2.00 5.00
177B L.Sprewell MIN 3.00 8.00
177C L.Sprewell GSW 3.00 8.00
178 Dennis Rodman 4.00 10.00
179 Pete Maravich 5.00 12.00
180 Gary Payton 2.50 6.00
181A Shaquille O'Neal 6.00 15.00
181B Shaquille O'Neal VAR 10.00 25.00
182 Jason Kidd 2.50 6.00
183 Yao Ming 4.00 10.00
184A C.Webber PHI 3.00 8.00
184B C.Webber WSH 3.00 8.00
184C C.Webber SAC 3.00 8.00
184D C.Webber DET 3.00 8.00
184E C.Webber GSW 3.00 8.00
184F C.Webber WSH 3.00 8.00
185 Kareem Abdul-Jabbar 5.00 12.00
186 Bill Walton 2.50 6.00
187A Magic Johnson 6.00 15.00
187B Magic Johnson VAR 6.00 15.00
188 Dikembe Mutombo 2.50 6.00
189 Phil Jackson 2.50 6.00
190 George Gervin 2.50 6.00
191 Shawn Kemp 2.50 6.00
192 Jerry West 4.00 10.00
193 Arvydas Sabonis 2.00 5.00
194 Karl Malone 3.00 8.00
195 Chris Mullin 2.00 5.00
196 Michael Finley 1.50 4.00
197 Rick Barry 2.00 5.00
198 Grant Hill 2.50 6.00
199 Joe Dumars 2.00 5.00
200 Dominique Wilkins 2.50 6.00
201 A.Wiggins JSY AU/199 RC 30.00 80.00
202 J.Parker JSY AU/199 RC 5.00 12.00
203 J.Randle JSY AU/199 RC 20.00 50.00
204 J.Embiid JSY AU/199 RC 200.00 500.00
205 D.Exum JSY AU/199 RC 6.00 15.00
206 S.Napier JSY AU/199 RC 5.00 12.00
207 M.Smart JSY AU/199 RC 15.00 40.00
208 C.Early JSY AU/199 RC 4.00 10.00
209 J.Young JSY AU/199 RC 4.00 10.00
210 A.Gordon JSY AU/199 RC 20.00 50.00
211 E.Payton JSY AU/199 RC 6.00 15.00
212 B.Caboclo JSY AU/199 RC 5.00 12.00
213 J.Ennis JSY AU/199 RC 4.00 10.00
214 G.Harris JSY AU/199 RC 6.00 15.00
215 G.Robinson III JSY AU/199 RC 5.00 12.00
216 C.Jefferson JSY AU/199 RC 4.00 10.00
217 K.Anderson JSY AU/199 RC 6.00 15.00
218 R.Smith JSY AU/199 RC 4.00 10.00
219 Z.LaVine JSY AU/199 RC 25.00 60.00
220 S.Dinwiddie JSY AU/199 RC 6.00 15.00
221 R.Hood JSY AU/199 RC 5.00 12.00
222 T.Warren JSY AU/199 RC 6.00 15.00
223 T.Ennis JSY AU/199 RC 4.00 10.00
224 J.Adams JSY AU/199 RC 4.00 10.00
225 D.McDermott JSY AU/199 RC 6.00 15.00
226 A.Payne JSY AU/199 RC 4.00 10.00
227 K.McDaniels JSY AU/199 RC 4.00 10.00
228 N.Stauskas JSY AU/199 RC 4.00 10.00
229 N.Vonleh JSY AU/199 RC 4.00 10.00
230 M.McGary JSY AU/199 RC 4.00 10.00
231 J.O'Bryant JSY AU/199 RC 4.00 10.00
232 J.Stokes JSY AU/199 RC 4.00 10.00
233 D.Inglis JSY AU/199 RC 4.00 10.00
234 A.Wiggins JSY AU/149 30.00 80.00
235 J.Parker JSY AU/149 5.00 12.00
236 J.Randle JSY AU/149 20.00 50.00
237 J.Embiid JSY AU/149 200.00 500.00
238 D.Exum JSY AU/149 6.00 15.00
239 S.Napier JSY AU/149 5.00 12.00
240 M.Smart JSY AU/149 15.00 40.00
241 C.Early JSY AU/149 4.00 10.00
242 J.Young JSY AU/149 4.00 10.00
243 A.Gordon JSY AU/149 20.00 50.00
244 E.Payton JSY AU/149 6.00 15.00
245 B.Caboclo JSY AU/149 5.00 12.00
246 J.Ennis JSY AU/149 4.00 10.00
247 G.Harris JSY AU/149 6.00 15.00
248 G.Robinson III JSY AU/149 5.00 12.00
249 C.Jefferson JSY AU/149 4.00 10.00
250 K.Anderson JSY AU/149 6.00 15.00
251 R.Smith JSY AU/149 4.00 10.00
252 Z.LaVine JSY AU/149 25.00 60.00
253 S.Dinwiddie JSY AU/149 6.00 15.00
254 R.Hood JSY AU/149 5.00 12.00
255 T.Warren JSY AU/149 6.00 15.00
256 T.Ennis JSY AU/149 4.00 10.00
257 J.Adams JSY AU/149 4.00 10.00
258 D.McDermott JSY AU/149 6.00 15.00
259 A.Payne JSY AU/149 4.00 10.00
260 K.McDaniels JSY AU/149 4.00 10.00
261 N.Stauskas JSY AU/149 4.00 10.00
262 N.Vonleh JSY AU/149 4.00 10.00
263 M.McGary JSY AU/149 4.00 10.00
264 J.O'Bryant JSY AU/149 4.00 10.00
265 J.Stokes JSY AU/149 4.00 10.00
266 D.Inglis JSY AU/149 4.00 10.00
267 A.Wiggins JSY AU/99 40.00 100.00
268 J.Parker JSY AU/99 6.00 15.00
269 J.Randle JSY AU/99 25.00 60.00
270 J.Embiid JSY AU/99 300.00 600.00
271 D.Exum JSY AU/99 8.00 20.00
272 S.Napier JSY AU/99 6.00 15.00
273 M.Smart JSY AU/99 20.00 50.00
274 C.Early JSY AU/99 5.00 12.00
275 J.Young JSY AU/99 5.00 12.00
276 A.Gordon JSY AU/99 25.00 60.00
277 E.Payton JSY AU/99 8.00 20.00
278 B.Caboclo JSY AU/99 6.00 15.00
279 J.Ennis JSY AU/99 5.00 12.00
280 G.Harris JSY AU/99 8.00 20.00
281 G.Robinson III JSY AU/99 6.00 15.00
282 C.Jefferson JSY AU/99 5.00 12.00
283 K.Anderson JSY AU/99 8.00 20.00
284 R.Smith JSY AU/99 5.00 12.00
285 Z.LaVine JSY AU/99 30.00 80.00
286 S.Dinwiddie JSY AU/99 8.00 20.00
287 R.Hood JSY AU/99 6.00 15.00
288 T.Warren JSY AU/99 8.00 20.00
289 T.Ennis JSY AU/99 5.00 12.00
290 J.Adams JSY AU/99 5.00 12.00
291 D.McDermott JSY AU/99 8.00 20.00
292 A.Payne JSY AU/99 5.00 12.00
293 K.McDaniels JSY AU/99 5.00 12.00
294 N.Stauskas JSY AU/99 5.00 12.00
295 N.Vonleh JSY AU/99 5.00 12.00
296 M.McGary JSY AU/99 5.00 12.00
297 J.O'Bryant JSY AU/99 5.00 12.00
298 J.Stokes JSY AU/99 5.00 12.00
299 D.Inglis JSY AU/99 5.00 12.00

2014-15 Panini Gold Standard Black

*BLACK: 1.5X TO 4X BASE HI
4 Kobe Bryant 75.00 200.00
123 Giannis Antetokounmpo 75.00 200.00

2014-15 Panini Gold Standard Gold

*GOLD: .8X TO 2X BASE HI
STATED PRINT RUN 79 SER.#'d SETS
27 Kyrie Irving 6.00 15.00
96 Jeremy Lin 6.00 15.00
154 Allen Iverson 8.00 20.00

2014-15 Panini Gold Standard 14K Autographs

STATED PRINT RUN B/WN 25-199 COPIES PER
3 Kyrie Irving/25 100.00 250.00
4 Kobe Bryant/25 1,000.00 2,000.00
5 Mike Conley/75 6.00 15.00
6 Kendall Gill/199 6.00 15.00
7 Tyler Zeller/199 5.00 12.00
8 Kevin Durant/25 125.00 300.00
9 Larry Bird/25 125.00 300.00
10 Isiah Thomas/50 12.00 30.00
11 George Gervin/35 20.00 50.00
12 Peja Stojakovic/35 6.00 15.00
13 Dan Issel/199 10.00 25.00
14 Marques Johnson/199 6.00 15.00
15 Sam Perkins/99 6.00 15.00
16 Shaquille O'Neal/25 125.00 300.00
17 Spud Webb/199 8.00 20.00
18 Steve Smith/199 6.00 15.00
19 Bill Walton/35 12.00 30.00
20 Satch Sanders/99 8.00 20.00
21 Ralph Sampson/35 12.00 30.00
22 David Thompson/99 8.00 20.00
23 Bradley Beal/35 20.00 50.00
24 Jason Terry/35 6.00 15.00
25 Alex English/99 10.00 25.00
26 Mark Aguirre/99 6.00 15.00
27 Thaddeus Young/199 5.00 12.00

2014-15 Panini Gold Standard AU Autographs

STATED PRINT RUN 79 SER.#'d SETS
1 Kobe Bryant 800.00 1,500.00
2 Kevin Durant 100.00 250.00
3 Kareem Abdul-Jabbar 75.00 200.00
4 Kyrie Irving 75.00 200.00
5 John Wall 20.00 50.00
6 Kelly Olynyk 5.00 12.00
7 Tim Hardaway Jr. 6.00 15.00
8 Isaiah Thomas 6.00 15.00
9 Andre Drummond 6.00 15.00
10 Bradley Beal 12.00 30.00
11 Nick Van Exel 15.00 40.00
12 Danny Green 6.00 15.00
14 Mychal Thompson 6.00 15.00
16 Iman Shumpert 5.00 12.00
17 Jonas Valanciunas 5.00 12.00
20 Marcin Gortat 5.00 12.00
21 Marvin Williams 5.00 12.00
22 Nick Young 5.00 12.00
24 P.J. Tucker 6.00 15.00
26 Reggie Jackson 6.00 15.00
27 Richard Jefferson 6.00 15.00
29 Stephen Curry 600.00 1,200.00
30 Steve Blake 5.00 12.00
31 Taj Gibson 5.00 12.00
33 Spencer Hawes 5.00 12.00
35 Tony Parker 20.00 50.00
36 Ty Lawson 5.00 12.00
37 Tom Gugliotta 5.00 12.00
38 Vince Carter 75.00 200.00
39 Archie Goodwin 5.00 12.00
40 Vin Baker 6.00 15.00
41 Wayne Embry 6.00 15.00
43 Adrian Dantley 8.00 20.00
44 Antoine Walker 6.00 15.00
45 Alex English 10.00 25.00
46 Bailey Howell 10.00 25.00
47 Bill Laimbeer 8.00 20.00
48 Joe Dumars 10.00 25.00
51 Bruce Bowen 8.00 20.00
52 Eddie Johnson 5.00 12.00
53 Cedric Maxwell 6.00 15.00
54 Charlie Scott 8.00 20.00
55 Dolph Schayes 8.00 20.00
56 Darryl Dawkins 8.00 20.00
57 Dave Cowens 10.00 25.00
58 Dick Van Arsdale 8.00 20.00
59 Doug Collins 8.00 20.00
61 Fred Brown 5.00 12.00
62 Grant Hill 15.00 40.00
63 Jamal Mashburn 6.00 15.00
65 Jim Jackson 6.00 15.00
66 John Salley 6.00 15.00
67 John Starks 12.00 30.00
68 Keith Van Horn 6.00 15.00
69 Kendall Gill 8.00 20.00
70 David Thompson 8.00 20.00
71 Muggsy Bogues 12.00 30.00
72 Phil Chenier 6.00 15.00
73 Rick Mahorn 6.00 15.00
74 Sam Perkins 6.00 15.00
75 Scott Skiles 6.00 15.00
76 Spud Webb 8.00 20.00
77 Tom Van Arsdale 6.00 15.00
78 Vernon Maxwell 6.00 15.00
79 Vlade Divac 8.00 20.00

2014-15 Panini Gold Standard Black Gold Threads

STATED PRINT RUN B/WN 19-25 COPIES PER
1 Tim Duncan/25 15.00 40.00
2 Alonzo Mourning/25 10.00 25.00
3 Kevin Love/25 6.00 15.00
4 Bradley Beal/25 10.00 25.00
5 John Wall/25 8.00 20.00
6 Dwyane Wade/25 12.00 30.00
7 LeBron James/25 100.00 250.00
8 Kobe Bryant/25 100.00 250.00
9 Kevin Durant/25 20.00 50.00
10 Russell Westbrook/25 10.00 25.00
13 Dirk Nowitzki/25 15.00 40.00
14 Blake Griffin/25 6.00 15.00
15 Chris Paul/25 10.00 25.00
17 Joakim Noah/25 6.00 15.00
18 Brandon Jennings/25 6.00 15.00
19 Victor Oladipo/25 5.00 12.00
20 M.Carter-Williams/25 4.00 10.00
23 Stephen Curry/25 100.00 250.00
24 Deron Williams/25 5.00 12.00
25 Eric Gordon/25 5.00 12.00
26 Paul George/25 10.00 25.00
28 James Harden/25 12.00 30.00
30 DeMar DeRozan/25 8.00 20.00
31 LaMarcus Aldridge/25 6.00 15.00
32 John Stockton/25 12.00 30.00
33 Dominique Wilkins/25 10.00 25.00
34 Kevin McHale/25 10.00 25.00
35 Magic Johnson/25 25.00 60.00
36 Karl Malone/25 12.00 30.00
37 David Robinson/25 12.00 30.00
38 Isiah Thomas/25 12.00 30.00
39 Allen Iverson/25 15.00 40.00
40 Kevin Duckworth/25 10.00 25.00
41 Larry Johnson/25 8.00 20.00
42 Grant Hill/25 10.00 25.00
43 Shaquille O'Neal/25 25.00 60.00
44 Dikembe Mutombo/25 10.00 25.00
45 Antoine Walker/25 5.00 12.00
46 Dan Majerle/25 5.00 12.00
48 Kenneth Faried/25 4.00 10.00
49 Doc Rivers/25 6.00 15.00
50 Mark Jackson/25 5.00 12.00

2014-15 Panini Gold Standard Etched in Gold Autographs

STATED PRINT RUN B/WN 35-99 COPIES PER
2 Dan Issel/99 10.00 25.00
3 Vlade Divac/99 8.00 20.00
5 Jamaal Wilkes/99 8.00 20.00
6 Shaquille O'Neal/35 100.00 250.00
7 Latrell Sprewell/99 10.00 25.00
8 Adrian Dantley/99 8.00 20.00
9 Bobby Jones/99 6.00 15.00
10 Byron Scott/99 8.00 20.00
11 Cedric Maxwell/99 6.00 15.00
12 George Karl/60 8.00 20.00
13 Grant Hill/35 20.00 50.00
14 Jack Sikma/99 8.00 20.00
18 Mark Aguirre/99 6.00 15.00
19 Marques Johnson/99 6.00 15.00
20 Peja Stojakovic/35 6.00 15.00
21 Anfernee Hardaway/35 60.00 150.00

2014-15 Panini Gold Standard Freshly Minted

STATED PRINT RUN 25 SER.#'d SETS
1 Marcus Smart 25.00 60.00
2 Nikola Mirotic 10.00 25.00
3 Julius Randle 30.00 80.00
4 Elfrid Payton 10.00 25.00
5 K.J. McDaniels 6.00 15.00
6 Andrew Wiggins 30.00 80.00
7 Rodney Hood 8.00 20.00
8 T.J. Warren 10.00 25.00
9 Nik Stauskas 6.00 15.00
10 Noah Vonleh 6.00 15.00
11 Jabari Parker 8.00 20.00
12 Doug McDermott 10.00 25.00
13 Nick Johnson 6.00 15.00
14 Dante Exum 10.00 25.00
15 Zach LaVine 40.00 100.00
16 Jordan Adams 6.00 15.00
17 Shabazz Napier 8.00 20.00
18 Aaron Gordon 30.00 80.00
20 Mitch McGary 6.00 15.00
21 Gary Harris 10.00 25.00
22 P.J. Hairston 6.00 15.00
23 Adreian Payne 6.00 15.00
24 Joel Embiid 125.00 300.00
25 Bruno Caboclo 8.00 20.00
26 Cleanthony Early 6.00 15.00
27 C.J. Wilcox 6.00 15.00
28 Johnny O'Bryant 6.00 15.00
29 Glenn Robinson III 8.00 20.00

2014-15 Panini Gold Standard Gold Records

STATED PRINT RUN 25 SER.#'d SETS
1 Robert Parish 20.00 50.00
2 Kareem Abdul-Jabbar 50.00 125.00
3 John Stockton 30.00 80.00
4 Wilt Chamberlain 50.00 125.00
5 Hakeem Olajuwon 30.00 80.00
6 Oscar Robertson 30.00 80.00
7 Ray Allen 25.00 60.00
8 LeBron James 125.00 300.00
9 Kevin Durant 50.00 120.00
10 Artis Gilmore 20.00 50.00
11 Kobe Bryant 125.00 300.00
12 Elgin Baylor 30.00 80.00
13 Carmelo Anthony 25.00 60.00
14 Dave Cowens 20.00 50.00
15 Karl Malone 30.00 80.00
16 Dennis Rodman 40.00 100.00
17 Steve Nash 30.00 80.00
18 George Gervin 25.00 60.00
19 Stephen Curry 125.00 300.00
20 Moses Malone 25.00 60.00
21 Chris Paul 25.00 60.00
22 Dwight Howard 20.00 50.00
23 Scott Skiles 12.00 30.00
24 Michael Carter-Williams 10.00 25.00
25 Nate Archibald 20.00 50.00

2014-15 Panini Gold Standard Gold Rush Autographs

STATED PRINT RUN B/WN 50-199 COPIES PER
1 Isaiah Thomas/199 5.00 12.00
2 Maurice Harkless/199 4.00 10.00
3 Troy Daniels/199 4.00 10.00
4 Gorgui Dieng/199 4.00 10.00
5 M.Carter-Williams/75 4.00 10.00
6 Matthew Dellavedova/199 5.00 12.00
7 Pero Antic/199 4.00 10.00
8 Ryan Kelly/199 4.00 10.00
9 Mike Muscala/199 4.00 10.00
10 Gerald Henderson/199 4.00 10.00
11 Kendall Marshall/199 4.00 10.00
12 P.J. Tucker/199 5.00 12.00
14 Kevin Durant/50 125.00 300.00
15 Steve Blake/199 4.00 10.00
17 Robin Lopez/199 4.00 10.00
18 Taj Gibson/199 4.00 10.00
21 Draymond Green/199 20.00 50.00
22 Kenneth Faried/199 4.00 10.00
24 Jared Sullinger/75 4.00 10.00
25 Bradley Beal/75 15.00 40.00
26 Nate Wolters/199 4.00 10.00
27 Steven Adams/199 8.00 20.00
29 Goran Dragic/99 6.00 15.00
30 G.Antetokounmpo/199 300.00 600.00

2014-15 Panini Gold Standard Gold Scripts

STATED PRINT RUN B/WN 15-199 COPIES PER
NO PRICING ON QTY 15 OR LESS
1 K.J. McDaniels/199 4.00 10.00
2 Rodney Hood/199 5.00 12.00
3 T.J. Warren/199 6.00 15.00
4 Jordan Adams/199 4.00 10.00
5 Glenn Robinson III/199 5.00 12.00
6 Joe Harris/199 6.00 15.00
7 Russ Smith/199 4.00 10.00
8 Gary Harris/199 6.00 15.00
9 C.J. Wilcox/199 4.00 10.00
10 Zach LaVine/199 25.00 60.00
11 Mitch McGary/199 4.00 10.00
12 Dennis Schroder/199 6.00 15.00
13 Gorgui Dieng/199 4.00 10.00
14 Spencer Hawes/199 4.00 10.00
15 Reggie Bullock/199 4.00 10.00
16 P.J. Hairston/199 4.00 10.00
17 Tyler Ennis/99 4.00 10.00
18 Patric Young/199 4.00 10.00
19 Doug McDermott/199 6.00 15.00
20 Johnny O'Bryant/199 4.00 10.00
21 Nerlens Noel/199 6.00 15.00
22 Will Cherry/199 4.00 10.00
23 Erick Green/199 4.00 10.00
24 Jordan Clarkson/199 15.00 40.00
25 Jusuf Nurkic/199 12.00 30.00
26 Cameron Bairstow/199 4.00 10.00
27 Aaron Gordon/125 20.00 50.00
28 James Young/199 4.00 10.00
29 Shabazz Napier/199 5.00 12.00
30 Danny Green/199 5.00 12.00
31 Al-Farouq Aminu/199 4.00 10.00
32 Jason Terry/199 5.00 12.00
33 JaVale McGee/149 5.00 12.00
34 Jeff Green/149 5.00 12.00
35 Evan Fournier/149 4.00 10.00
36 Mason Plumlee/199 6.00 15.00
38 Tristan Thompson/199 4.00 10.00
39 Victor Oladipo/99 5.00 12.00
40 Udonis Haslem/199 5.00 12.00

2014-15 Panini Gold Standard Gold Strike Jersey Autographs

STATED PRINT RUN B/WN 49-199 COPIES PER
1 Nick Anderson/199 5.00 12.00
2 Glen Rice/199 6.00 15.00
3 Bill Laimbeer/199 12.00 30.00
7 Danny Green/149 5.00 12.00
8 Gerald Henderson/99 4.00 10.00
9 James Harden/49 60.00 150.00
10 Jimmy Butler/49 40.00 100.00
11 Jose Calderon/99 4.00 10.00
12 Dennis Schroder/199 6.00 15.00
13 Gorgui Dieng/199 4.00 10.00
14 Cleanthony Early/199 4.00 10.00
15 Russ Smith/199 4.00 10.00
16 Cory Jefferson/199 4.00 10.00
17 Johnny O'Bryant/199 4.00 10.00
18 Doug McDermott/199 6.00 15.00
19 Zach LaVine/199 25.00 60.00
20 T.J. Warren/199 6.00 15.00
21 Rodney Hood/199 5.00 12.00
22 P.J. Hairston/199 4.00 10.00
23 Jordan Adams/199 4.00 10.00
24 Bruno Caboclo/199 5.00 12.00
25 Adreian Payne/199 4.00 10.00
26 Marcus Smart/149 15.00 40.00
27 C.J. Wilcox/199 4.00 10.00
28 James Young/199 4.00 10.00
29 Elfrid Payton/199 6.00 15.00
30 Glenn Robinson III/199 5.00 12.00
31 Gary Harris/199 6.00 15.00
32 Joe Harris/199 6.00 15.00
33 Julius Randle/149 20.00 50.00
34 Markel Brown/199 4.00 10.00
35 James Ennis/199 4.00 10.00
36 Shabazz Napier/199 5.00 12.00
37 Spencer Dinwiddie/199 6.00 15.00
38 Jarell Stokes/199 4.00 10.00
39 Nik Stauskas/199 4.00 10.00
40 Mitch McGary/199 4.00 10.00

2014-15 Panini Gold Standard Gold Strike Jersey Autographs Prime

*PRIME: .8X TO 2X BASE HI
STATED PRINT RUN 25 SER.#'d SETS
9 James Harden 50.00 120.00
10 Jimmy Butler 30.00 80.00

2014-15 Panini Gold Standard Golden Debuts

STATED PRINT RUN 50 SER.#'d SETS
1 Jusuf Nurkic 12.00 30.00
2 C.J. Wilcox 4.00 10.00
3 Nik Stauskas 4.00 10.00
4 Bruno Caboclo 5.00 12.00
5 Jarnell Stokes 4.00 10.00
6 Andrew Wiggins 20.00 50.00
7 Zach LaVine 25.00 60.00
8 Shabazz Napier 5.00 12.00
9 Dante Exum 6.00 15.00
10 Nick Johnson 4.00 10.00
11 James Young 4.00 10.00
12 Kyle Anderson 6.00 15.00
13 Noah Vonleh 4.00 10.00
14 Mitch McGary 4.00 10.00
15 Spencer Dinwiddie 6.00 15.00
16 Jabari Parker 5.00 12.00
17 T.J. Warren 6.00 15.00
18 Clint Capela 15.00 40.00
19 Marcus Smart 15.00 40.00
20 Markel Brown 4.00 10.00
21 Tyler Ennis 4.00 10.00
22 Cleanthony Early 4.00 10.00
23 Elfrid Payton 6.00 15.00
24 Jordan Adams 4.00 10.00
25 Glenn Robinson III 5.00 12.00
26 Aaron Gordon 20.00 50.00
27 Adreian Payne 4.00 10.00
28 P.J. Hairston 4.00 10.00
29 Julius Randle 20.00 50.00
30 Cory Jefferson 4.00 10.00
31 Gary Harris 6.00 15.00
32 Doug McDermott 6.00 15.00
33 Rodney Hood 5.00 12.00
34 Jordan Clarkson 15.00 40.00
35 Damien Inglis 4.00 10.00

2014-15 Panini Gold Standard Golden Pairs

STATED PRINT RUN 25 SER.#'d SETS
1 T.Duncan/T.Parker 20.00 50.00
2 A.Jefferson/K.Walker 8.00 20.00
3 C.Anthony/I.Shumpert 12.00 30.00
5 K.Durant/R.Westbrook 25.00 60.00
6 D.West/P.George 12.00 30.00
7 K.Thompson/S.Curry 100.00 250.00
8 D.Howard/J.Harden 15.00 40.00
9 D.Nowitzki/M.Ellis 20.00 50.00
10 M.Harkless/V.Oladipo 6.00 15.00
11 B.Griffin/C.Paul 12.00 30.00
12 E.Bledsoe/G.Dragic 8.00 20.00
14 B.Griffin/D.Jordan 8.00 20.00
15 M.Gasol/Z.Randolph 8.00 20.00
16 B.McLemore/D.Cousins 6.00 15.00
17 A.Horford/J.Teague 8.00 20.00
18 B.Beal/J.Wall 12.00 30.00
19 D.Williams/K.Garnett 20.00 50.00
20 C.Bosh/D.Wade 15.00 40.00
21 A.Davis/J.Holiday 20.00 50.00
22 D.DeRozan/K.Lowry 10.00 25.00
23 G.Hayward/T.Burke 6.00 15.00
24 D.Rose/J.Noah 15.00 40.00
25 B.Jennings/J.Smith 5.00 12.00
26 B.Knight/L.Sanders 5.00 12.00
27 K.Faried/T.Lawson 5.00 12.00
28 D.Lillard/L.Aldridge 20.00 50.00
29 J.Richardson/M.Carter-Williams 8.00 20.00
30 A.Bradley/J.Sullinger 5.00 12.00
31 D.Rodman/S.Pippen 20.00 50.00
32 J.Stockton/K.Malone 15.00 40.00
33 I.Thomas/J.Dumars 12.00 30.00
34 T.McGrady/Y.Ming 20.00 50.00
35 A.Hardaway/S.O'Neal 30.00 80.00
36 J.Starks/P.Ewing 12.00 30.00
37 K.McHale/L.Bird 30.00 80.00
38 C.Robinson/K.Duckworth 8.00 20.00
39 K.Bryant/S.O'Neal 100.00 250.00
40 G.Robinson/R.Allen 12.00 30.00
41 D.Robinson/S.Elliott 15.00 40.00
42 C.Mullin/T.Hardaway 10.00 25.00
43 A.Iverson/D.Mutombo 20.00 50.00
44 K.Abdul-Jabbar/M.Johnson 30.00 80.00
45 B.Laimbeer/R.Mahorn 8.00 20.00

2014-15 Panini Gold Standard Golden Quads

STATED PRINT RUN B/WN 9-25 COPIES PER
NO PRICING ON QTY 10 OR LESS
3 Jffrsn/Csns/Hwrd/Nh/25 20.00 50.00
4 Dvs/Grffn/Nwtzki/Aldrdge/25 40.00 100.00
5 Pl/Rse/Wstbrk/Crry/25 120.00 300.00
6 Rse/Nh/Hnrch/Gbsn/25 30.00 80.00
7 Bgl/Le/Thmpsn/Crry/25 125.00 300.00
8 Lnrd/Gnbli/Dncn/Prkr/25 40.00 100.00
9 Grffn/Pl/Jrdn/Rdck/25 25.00 60.00
10 Llrd/Aldrdge/Btm/Mtthws/25 40.00 100.00
11 Bl/Rce/Wll/Nne/25 25.00 60.00
13 Andrsn/Bsh/Wde/Chlmrs/25 30.00 80.00
14 Drnt/Cllsn/Wstbrk/Ibka/20 50.00 120.00
16 Gsl/Cnly/Alln/Rndlph/25 15.00 40.00
18 Grdn/Prkr/Smrt/Vnlh/25 50.00 120.00
19 Wggns/McDrmtt/Rndle/Stsks/25 50.00 120.00
20 Wggns/Pytn/Prkr/LVne/25 60.00 150.00

2014-15 Panini Gold Standard Golden Trios

STATED PRINT RUN B/WN 3-25 COPIES PER
NO PRICING ON QTY 3 OR LESS
2 Gordon/Exum/Smart 30.00 80.00
3 Wiggins/Parker/Randle 30.00 80.00
4 Wiggins/Embiid/Smart 60.00 150.00
5 McDermott/Payton/Stauskas 10.00 25.00
7 Durant/Westbrook/Ibaka 30.00 80.00
8 Rose/Butler/Noah 20.00 50.00
9 Ginobili/Duncan/Parker 25.00 60.00
10 Hill/Bryant/Sacre 80.00 200.00
11 Griffin/Paul/Jordan 15.00 40.00
12 Andersen/Bosh/Wade 20.00 50.00
13 Lee/Thompson/Curry 80.00 200.00
16 Howard/Harden/Jones 20.00 50.00
17 Sullinger/Green/Rondo 12.00 30.00
18 Gasol/Conley/Randolph 10.00 25.00
19 Lillard/Aldridge/Matthews 25.00 60.00
21 Jefferson/Walker/Kidd-Gilchrist 10.00 25.00
22 Wright/Nowitzki/Ellis 25.00 60.00
23 DeRozan/Lowry/Ross 12.00 30.00
24 Lopez/Williams/Johnson 10.00 25.00
25 West/George/Hibbert 15.00 40.00
26 Paul/Wall/Rondo 15.00 40.00
27 Durant/Bryant/James 125.00 300.00
28 Cousins/Howard/Noah 12.00 30.00
29 Davis/Griffin/Duncan 25.00 60.00
30 Wade/Harden/Thompson 25.00 60.00
31 Lillard/Westbrook/Curry 80.00 200.00
32 Anthony/Wade/James 80.00 200.00
33 Erving/Bird/Johnson 40.00 100.00
34 Olajuwon/Malone/Ewing 20.00 50.00

2014-15 Panini Gold Standard Good as Gold Jersey Autographs

STATED PRINT RUN B/WN 35-199 COPIES PER
1 Archie Goodwin/199 5.00 12.00
2 Bradley Beal/49 12.00 30.00
3 Enes Kanter/149 6.00 15.00
4 Chris Copeland/199 5.00 12.00
5 Dennis Rodman/35 40.00 100.00
6 Dennis Schroder/199 6.00 15.00
7 Zydrunas Ilgauskas/199 6.00 15.00
9 Greg Monroe/99 6.00 15.00
10 Isiah Thomas/50 12.00 30.00
12 James Worthy/35 12.00 30.00
13 John Henson/35 5.00 12.00
14 John Wall/35 10.00 25.00
15 Kelly Olynyk/199 5.00 12.00
16 Nate Wolters/199 4.00 10.00
17 Mike Conley/49 6.00 15.00
18 Larry Johnson/199 10.00 25.00
19 Xavier McDaniel/199 6.00 15.00
20 Jordan Hill/49 5.00 12.00
21 Jonas Valanciunas/60 6.00 15.00
22 Jeff Hornacek/149 6.00 15.00
23 Hakeem Olajuwon/35 40.00 100.00
25 Rolando Blackman/149 6.00 15.00

2014-15 Panini Gold Standard Good as Gold Jersey Autographs Prime

*PRIME: .8X TO 2X BASE HI
STATED PRINT RUN 25 SER.#'d SETS
5 Dennis Rodman 75.00 200.00
6 Dennis Schroder 15.00 40.00
14 John Wall 20.00 50.00
22 Jeff Hornacek 12.00 30.00
23 Hakeem Olajuwon 75.00 200.00

2014-15 Panini Gold Standard Marks of Gold Jersey Autographs

STATED PRINT RUN B/WN 49-199 COPIES PER
1 A.C. Green/99 6.00 15.00
2 Anfernee Hardaway/49 40.00 100.00
3 Antoine Walker/199 5.00 12.00
4 Bill Laimbeer/199 6.00 15.00
5 Byron Scott/99 6.00 15.00
6 Carmelo Anthony/49 40.00 100.00
7 Chris Mullin/199 8.00 20.00
8 Dan Majerle/199 5.00 12.00
9 David West/49 5.00 12.00
10 Dikembe Mutombo/99 20.00 50.00
11 Fred Brown/199 4.00 10.00
12 Grant Hill/75 20.00 50.00
13 Harrison Barnes/49 5.00 12.00
14 Jodie Meeks/199 4.00 10.00
15 JaVale McGee/75 5.00 12.00
16 Jeff Green/99 5.00 12.00
18 Alan Anderson/199 4.00 10.00
19 Clifford Robinson/199 6.00 15.00
21 LaMarcus Aldridge/49 6.00 15.00
22 Klay Thompson/75 40.00 100.00
25 M.Carter-Williams/125 4.00 10.00
27 Reggie Jackson/199 5.00 12.00
29 Stephen Curry/49 500.00 1,000.00
30 Brandan Wright/199 4.00 10.00
31 Thaddeus Young/199 4.00 10.00
32 Tim Hardaway/199 5.00 12.00
33 Tony Snell/199 4.00 10.00
34 Trey Burke/125 4.00 10.00
35 Marques Johnson/199 5.00 12.00

2014-15 Panini Gold Standard Marks of Gold Jersey Autographs Prime

*PRIME: .6X TO 1.5X BASE HI
STATED PRINT RUN B/WN 12-25 SER.#'d SETS
NO PRICING ON QTY 12 OR LESS
28 Sidney Moncrief/25 12.00 30.00

2014-15 Panini Gold Standard Mother Lode Autographs

STATED PRINT RUN B/WN 35-199 COPIES PER
1 Dan Issel 8.00 20.00
2 Adrian Dantley 6.00 15.00
3 Alex English 8.00 20.00
4 David Thompson 6.00 15.00
5 Arvydas Sabonis 8.00 20.00
6 John Salley 5.00 12.00
7 Jamaal Wilkes 6.00 15.00
8 B.J. Armstrong 6.00 15.00
9 Bruce Bowen 6.00 15.00
10 Charlie Scott 6.00 15.00
11 Chet Walker 5.00 12.00
12 Eddie Jones 6.00 15.00
13 Horace Grant 6.00 15.00
14 Jon McGlocklin 5.00 12.00
15 Mark Price 6.00 15.00
16 Marques Johnson 5.00 12.00
17 Michael Cooper 6.00 15.00
18 Sam Perkins 5.00 12.00
19 Spud Webb 6.00 15.00
20 Tim Hardaway 8.00 20.00
21 Tracy McGrady 10.00 25.00
22 Vlade Divac 6.00 15.00
23 Zydrunas Ilgauskas 5.00 12.00
24 Toni Kukoc 8.00 20.00
25 Robert Horry 6.00 15.00
26 Larry Johnson 8.00 20.00
27 Nick Van Exel 6.00 15.00
28 Bill Walton 10.00 25.00
29 Anfernee Hardaway 40.00 100.00
30 John Stockton 40.00 100.00

2014-15 Panini Gold Standard Newly Minted Memorabilia

STATED PRINT RUN 25 SER.#'d SETS
NMMS Marcus Smart 12.00 30.00
NMRH Rodney Hood 4.00 10.00
NMDM Doug McDermott 5.00 12.00
NMCW C.J. Wilcox 3.00 8.00
NMAP Adreian Payne 3.00 8.00
NMAG Aaron Gordon 15.00 40.00
NMTE Tyler Ennis 3.00 8.00
NMJE Joel Embiid 30.00 80.00
NMJP Jabari Parker 4.00 10.00
NMMM Mitch McGary 3.00 8.00
NMNV Noah Vonleh 3.00 8.00
NMSN Shabazz Napier 4.00 10.00
NMZL Zach LaVine 20.00 50.00
NMCE Cleanthony Early 3.00 8.00
NMJY James Young 3.00 8.00
NMAW Andrew Wiggins 15.00 40.00
NMGH Gary Harris 5.00 12.00
NMDE Dante Exum 5.00 12.00
NMJA Jordan Adams 3.00 8.00
NMEP Elfrid Payton 5.00 12.00
NMPH P.J. Hairston 3.00 8.00

2014-15 Panini Gold Standard Newly Minted Memorabilia Duals

STATED PRINT RUN 25 SER.#'d SETS
1 J.Parker/J.Randle 20.00 50.00
2 J.Young/M.Smart 15.00 40.00
3 C.Jefferson/M.Brown 4.00 10.00
4 N.Vonleh/P.Hairston 4.00 10.00
5 J.Stokes/J.Adams 4.00 10.00
6 J.Ennis/S.Napier 5.00 12.00
7 A.Gordon/E.Payton 20.00 50.00
8 T.Warren/T.Ennis 6.00 15.00
10 A.Wiggins/J.Embiid 40.00 100.00
12 M.Smart/M.Brown 15.00 40.00
13 J.Grant/T.Ennis 20.00 50.00
14 P.Hairston/R.Hood 5.00 12.00
15 C.Jefferson/D.McDermott 6.00 15.00
16 G.Harris/N.Stauskas 6.00 15.00
17 A.Payne/M.McGary 4.00 10.00
18 A.Wiggins/J.Randle 20.00 50.00
20 A.Gordon/Z.LaVine 25.00 60.00
21 A.Wiggins/J.Parker 20.00 50.00
22 A.Gordon/J.Embiid 40.00 100.00
23 D.Exum/M.Smart 15.00 40.00
24 J.Randle/N.Stauskas 8.00 20.00

2014-15 Panini Gold Standard Newly Minted Memorabilia Quads

STATED PRINT RUN 25 SER.#'d SETS
1 Jffrsn/Yng/Smrt/Brwn 30.00 80.00
2 Cbclo/Ealy/Embd/McDnls 80.00 200.00
3 McDrmtt/Prkr/Hrrs/Dnwdde 12.00 30.00
4 Grdn/Pytn/Enns/Npr 40.00 100.00
7 Enns/Vnlh/Hrstn/Npr 10.00 25.00
8 Wggns/Exm/Hod/LVne 50.00 120.00
9 Wlcx/Rndle/Wrrn/Enns 40.00 100.00
11 Prkr/Hrstn/Hod/Wrrn 12.00 30.00
12 Wggns/Yng/Embd/Rndle 80.00 200.00
13 Pyne/Hrrs/McGry/Stsks 12.00 30.00
14 Rbnsn/Yng/Rndle/Stsks 40.00 100.00
15 Prkr/Hrrs/McDnls/Wrrn 12.00 30.00
16 Grdn/Wggns/Prkr/Embd 80.00 200.00
17 Exm/Rndle/Smrt/Stsks 40.00 100.00
18 McDrmtt/Pytn/Vnlh/LVne 50.00 120.00
19 Pyne/Yng/Wrrn/Enns 12.00 30.00
21 Wlcx/Rndle/Hrrs/McDnls 10.00 25.00
22 Ealy/Ingls/Hrrs/McDnls 12.00 30.00

2014-15 Panini Gold Standard Newly Minted Memorabilia Triples

STATED PRINT RUN 25 SER.#'d SETS
2 Wiggins/Robinson III/LaVine 25.00 60.00
3 Grant/Embiid/McDaniels 40.00 100.00
4 Caboclo/Inglis/Exum 6.00 15.00
5 Robinson/McGary/Stauskas 5.00 12.00
6 Adams/Anderson/LaVine 25.00 60.00
7 Parker/Hairston/Hood 5.00 12.00
8 Grant/Napier/Ennis 20.00 50.00
10 Harris/McDaniels/Warren 6.00 15.00
11 Randle/Smith/Napier 20.00 50.00
12 Jefferson/Smart/Brown 15.00 40.00
14 Gordon/Wilcox/Dinwiddie 20.00 50.00
15 Early/McDermott/Ennis 6.00 15.00
16 Wiggins/Parker/Embiid 40.00 100.00
17 Gordon/Exum/Smart 20.00 50.00
18 Randle/Stauskas/Vonleh 20.00 50.00
19 McDermott/Payton/LaVine 25.00 60.00
20 Payne/Young/Warren 6.00 15.00
21 Caboclo/Harris/Ennis 6.00 15.00
22 Adams/McGary/Hood 5.00 12.00
23 Wilcox/Hairston/Napier 5.00 12.00
24 Wiggins/Parker/Randle 20.00 50.00
25 Wiggins/Exum/Parker 20.00 50.00

2014-15 Panini Gold Standard Ring Bearers Autographs

STATED PRINT RUN B/WN 25-199 COPIES PER
1 Phil Jackson 350.00 700.00
3 Rick Carlisle 20.00 50.00
4 Doc Rivers 10.00 25.00
5 Lenny Wilkens 10.00 25.00
6 Patrick Mills 20.00 50.00
7 Magic Johnson 75.00 200.00
8 Kobe Bryant 800.00 1,500.00
9 Bill Wennington 8.00 20.00
10 Tony Parker 30.00 80.00
11 Bruce Bowen 10.00 25.00
12 Shaquille O'Neal 125.00 300.00
13 Udonis Haslem 8.00 20.00
14 Antoine Walker 8.00 20.00
15 Derek Anderson 6.00 15.00
16 Gary Payton 25.00 60.00
17 Tiago Splitter 6.00 15.00
18 Robert Horry 10.00 25.00
19 Jason Kidd 30.00 80.00
20 Hakeem Olajuwon 40.00 100.00
21 Kawhi Leonard 125.00 300.00
22 Toni Kukoc 12.00 30.00
23 David Robinson 40.00 100.00
24 Kareem Abdul-Jabbar 75.00 200.00
25 James Worthy 20.00 50.00
26 Ray Allen 40.00 100.00
27 Mark Aguirre 8.00 20.00
28 John Salley 8.00 20.00
29 James Jones 6.00 15.00
30 Sean Elliott 10.00 25.00

2014-15 Panini Gold Standard Rookie Jersey Autographs Prime

*PRIME/25: .75X TO 2X JSY AU/149-199
*PRIME/25: .75X TO 2X JSY AU/99
STATED PRINT RUN 25 SER.#'d SETS
201 Andrew Wiggins 100.00 250.00
210 Aaron Gordon 40.00 100.00
234 Andrew Wiggins 100.00 250.00
243 Aaron Gordon 40.00 100.00
267 Andrew Wiggins 75.00 200.00
273 Marcus Smart 60.00 150.00
276 Aaron Gordon 60.00 150.00
280 Gary Harris 12.00 30.00
285 Zach LaVine 75.00 200.00

2014-15 Panini Gold Standard Superscribe Autographs

STATED PRINT RUN B/WN 50-199 COPIES PER
1 Victor Oladipo 6.00 15.00
2 Kenneth Faried 5.00 12.00
3 Xavier Henry 5.00 12.00
4 John Wall 10.00 25.00
5 Luigi Datome 5.00 12.00
6 Tony Parker 25.00 60.00
7 Stephen Curry 600.00 1,200.00
8 Phil Chenier 6.00 15.00
10 Sidney Moncrief 8.00 20.00
11 Toni Kukoc 10.00 25.00
12 Travis Best 6.00 15.00
13 Will Perdue 5.00 12.00
14 World B. Free 6.00 15.00
15 Thabo Sefolosha 5.00 12.00
16 Mychal Thompson 6.00 15.00
17 Archie Goodwin 5.00 12.00
18 Kelly Olynyk 6.00 15.00
19 Ryan Kelly 5.00 12.00
20 Steven Adams 10.00 25.00
21 Tim Hardaway 10.00 25.00
22 Danilo Gallinari 5.00 12.00
23 Mike Conley 6.00 15.00
24 Gorgui Dieng 5.00 12.00
25 Cory Jefferson 5.00 12.00
26 Latrell Sprewell 20.00 50.00
28 Devyn Marble 5.00 12.00
29 Lance Stephenson 6.00 15.00
30 Brook Lopez 8.00 20.00
31 Bradley Beal 12.00 30.00
32 Mike Muscala 5.00 12.00
33 Troy Daniels 5.00 12.00
36 Andre Miller 6.00 15.00
37 Danny Green 6.00 15.00
38 Richard Jefferson 6.00 15.00
39 Robin Lopez 5.00 12.00
40 Michael Kidd-Gilchrist 5.00 12.00

2014-15 Panini Gold Standard Vintage Gold

STATED PRINT RUN 20 SER.#'d SETS
1 Kareem Abdul-Jabbar 30.00 80.00
2 Larry Bird 40.00 100.00
3 Shaquille O'Neal 40.00 100.00
4 David Robinson 20.00 50.00
5 John Stockton 20.00 50.00
6 Julius Erving 25.00 60.00
7 Magic Johnson 40.00 100.00
8 Hakeem Olajuwon 20.00 50.00
9 Patrick Ewing 15.00 40.00
10 Rick Barry 12.00 30.00
11 Clyde Drexler 15.00 40.00
12 John Havlicek 20.00 50.00
13 Karl Malone 20.00 50.00
14 Scottie Pippen 25.00 60.00
15 Isiah Thomas 15.00 40.00
16 Dominique Wilkins 15.00 40.00
17 Bill Walton 15.00 40.00
18 Nate Thurmond 10.00 25.00
19 Bill Russell 30.00 80.00
20 Tracy McGrady 15.00 40.00
21 Dikembe Mutombo 15.00 40.00
22 Allen Iverson 25.00 60.00
23 Shawn Kemp 15.00 40.00
24 Grant Hill 15.00 40.00
25 Chris Webber 12.00 30.00

2014-15 Panini Gold Standard White Gold Threads

STATED PRINT RUN 49 SER.#'d SETS
1 Tim Duncan 15.00 40.00
4 Eric Bledsoe 5.00 12.00
5 Nikola Vucevic 5.00 12.00
6 LeBron James 50.00 125.00
7 Kevin Love 6.00 15.00
8 Dwight Howard 8.00 20.00
9 Nicolas Batum 5.00 12.00
10 Kemba Walker 4.00 10.00
11 Victor Oladipo 5.00 12.00
13 Josh Smith 4.00 10.00
14 J.R. Smith 6.00 15.00
15 Kelly Olynyk 4.00 10.00
17 Carmelo Anthony 10.00 25.00
19 Tony Parker 10.00 25.00
20 Mike Conley 5.00 12.00
23 Dirk Nowitzki 15.00 40.00
24 Kevin Durant 20.00 50.00
25 Tiago Splitter 4.00 10.00
27 Otto Porter 5.00 12.00
28 Markieff Morris 4.00 10.00
32 Michael Carter-Williams 4.00 10.00
33 Marc Gasol 6.00 15.00
34 Russell Westbrook 10.00 25.00
36 Gary Payton 10.00 25.00
39 Clyde Drexler 10.00 25.00
40 Chris Mullin 8.00 20.00
43 Dikembe Mutombo 10.00 25.00
44 Clifford Robinson 6.00 15.00
47 Yao Ming 15.00 40.00
49 Bobby Jackson 4.00 10.00
50 Michael Finley 6.00 15.00

2014-15 Panini Gold Standard White Gold Threads Prime

*PRIME: .6X TO 1.5X BASE HI
STATED PRINT RUN B/WN 6-25 COPIES PER
NO PRICING ON QTY 6 OR LESS
12 Manu Ginobili/25 25.00 60.00
19 Tony Parker/25 20.00 50.00
27 Otto Porter/25 10.00 25.00
30 Kentavious Caldwell-Pope/25 10.00 25.00
32 M.Carter-Williams/25 8.00 20.00
36 Gary Payton/25 20.00 50.00
37 Bill Cartwright/25 10.00 25.00
38 Alvan Adams/25 8.00 20.00
42 Jason Kidd/25 20.00 50.00
50 Michael Finley/25 12.00 30.00

2015-16 Panini Gold Standard

1-200 PRINT RUN 299 SER.#'d SETS
PHT VAR COMBINED P/R OF 299
TEAM VAR COMBINED P/R OF 299
TEAM VAR SP COMBINED P/R OF 299
JSY AU PRINT RUNS B/WN 49-199
EXCHANGE DEADLINE 8/17/2017
1A Curry Black jsy 12.00 30.00
1B Curry White jsy 12.00 30.00
1C Curry Blue jsy 12.00 30.00
2 Tony Parker 2.50 6.00
3 Randy Foye 1.00 2.50
4 Brandon Knight 1.00 2.50
5 Jrue Holiday 2.00 5.00
6A Irving Yellow jsy 3.00 8.00
6B Irving Red jsy 3.00 8.00
6C Irving White jsy 3.00 8.00
7 Jeff Teague 1.00 2.50
8 Ricky Rubio 1.25 3.00
9 Kyle Lowry 1.50 4.00
10 Mike Conley 1.50 4.00
11 Klay Thompson 4.00 10.00
12 Manu Ginobili 3.00 8.00
13 Wilson Chandler 1.00 2.50
14 Eric Bledsoe 1.25 3.00
15 Eric Gordon 1.25 3.00
16A LeBron Yellow jsy 12.00 30.00
16B LeBron White jsy 12.00 30.00
16C LeBron Red jsy 12.00 30.00
17 Kyle Korver 1.25 3.00
18 Zach LaVine 4.00 10.00
19 DeMar DeRozan 2.00 5.00
20 Vince Carter 3.00 8.00
21 Andre Iguodala 1.50 4.00
22 Kawhi Leonard 5.00 12.00
23 Danilo Gallinari 1.25 3.00
24 P.J. Tucker 1.00 2.50
25 Tyreke Evans 1.25 3.00
26 Kevin Love 1.50 4.00
27 Thabo Sefolosha 1.00 2.50
28 Kevin Martin 1.25 3.00
29 Terrence Ross 1.25 3.00
30 Tony Allen 1.00 2.50
31 Draymond Green 2.00 5.00
32 LaMarcus Aldridge 1.50 4.00
33 Kenneth Faried 1.25 3.00
34 Markieff Morris 1.00 2.50
35A A.Davis Red jsy 4.00 10.00
35B A.Davis Blue jsy 4.00 10.00
35C A.Davis White jsy 4.00 10.00
36 Tristan Thompson 1.00 2.50
37 Paul Millsap 1.25 3.00
38A Wiggins Black jsy 2.00 5.00
38B Wiggins Blue jsy 2.00 5.00
38C Wiggins White jsy 2.00 5.00
39 DeMarre Carroll 1.00 2.50
40 Zach Randolph 1.50 4.00
41 Andrew Bogut 1.25 3.00
42 Tim Duncan 4.00 10.00
43 Jusuf Nurkic 1.25 3.00
44 Tyson Chandler 1.25 3.00
45 Omer Asik 1.00 2.50
46 Matthew Dellavedova 1.25 3.00
47 Al Horford 1.50 4.00
48A Garnett T'wolves 4.00 10.00
48B Garnett Celtics 6.00 15.00
48C Garnett Nets SP 50.00 120.00
48D Garnett USA 8.00 20.00
48E Garnett Wolves Blk 8.00 20.00
49 Jonas Valanciunas 1.25 3.00
50 Marc Gasol 1.50 4.00
51 J.J. Redick 1.50 4.00
52 Alec Burks 1.00 2.50
53 Ty Lawson 1.00 2.50
54A Rajon Rondo Kings 2.00 5.00
54B Rajon Rondo Mavericks 4.00 10.00
54C Rajon Rondo Celtics 4.00 10.00
54D Rondo Wildcats SP 25.00 60.00
55 Elfrid Payton 1.25 3.00
56 Reggie Jackson 1.25 3.00
57 Kemba Walker 1.50 4.00
58 Jose Calderon 1.00 2.50
59 Jarrett Jack 1.25 3.00
60 Michael Carter-Williams 1.00 2.50
61A Pierce Clippers 2.50 6.00
61D Pierce Wizards 5.00 12.00
61E Pierce Celtics 5.00 12.00
62 Trey Burke 1.00 2.50
63A Harden Rockets 3.00 8.00
63B Harden Sun Devils SP 40.00 100.00
63C Harden Thunder 6.00 15.00
63D Harden USA SP 40.00 100.00
64 Ben McLemore 1.00 2.50
65 Victor Oladipo 1.25 3.00
66 Brandon Jennings 1.00 2.50
67 Nicolas Batum 1.00 2.50
68 Arron Afflalo 1.00 2.50
69 Joe Johnson 1.25 3.00
70 Giannis Antetokounmpo 8.00 20.00
71A C.Paul Dribbling 3.00 8.00
71B C.Paul Holding ball 3.00 8.00
71C C.Paul Red jsy 3.00 8.00
72 Gordon Hayward 1.50 4.00
73 Trevor Ariza 1.00 2.50
74 Rudy Gay 1.50 4.00
75 Tobias Harris 1.25 3.00
76 Kentavious Caldwell-Pope 1.25 3.00
77 Michael Kidd-Gilchrist 1.00 2.50
78A Carmelo Ornge sleeve 2.50 6.00
78B Carmelo Black sleeve 2.50 6.00
78C Carmelo White jsy 2.50 6.00
79 Bojan Bogdanovic 1.25 3.00
80 Khris Middleton 2.00 5.00
81 Blake Griffin 1.50 4.00
82 Derrick Favors 1.25 3.00
83 Terrence Jones 1.00 2.50
84 DeMarcus Cousins 1.50 4.00
85 Aaron Gordon 1.50 4.00
86 Andre Drummond 1.50 4.00
87 Jeremy Lin 3.00 8.00
88 Langston Galloway 1.00 2.50
89 Thaddeus Young 1.00 2.50
90 Jabari Parker 1.00 2.50
91 DeAndre Jordan 1.25 3.00
92 Rudy Gobert 2.00 5.00
93 Dwight Howard 2.00 5.00
94 Darren Collison 1.00 2.50
95 Nikola Vucevic 1.25 3.00
96 Ersan Ilyasova 1.00 2.50
97 Al Jefferson 1.00 2.50
98 Robin Lopez 1.00 2.50
99 Brook Lopez 1.50 4.00
100 Greg Monroe 1.25 3.00
101A Goran Dragic Heat 1.50 4.00
101B Goran Dragic Suns 3.00 8.00
101C Goran Dragic Rockets 3.00 8.00
102 Marcus Smart 2.00 5.00
103 Jordan Clarkson 1.50 4.00
104A Wall Blue shorts 2.00 5.00
104B Wall White shorts 2.00 5.00
104C Wall Red shorts 2.00 5.00
105A Lillard Red jsy 4.00 10.00
105B Lillard Black jsy 4.00 10.00
106 George Hill 1.25 3.00
107 Deron Williams 1.25 3.00
108 Tony Wroten 1.00 2.50
109A D.Rose Black jsy 2.50 6.00
109B D.Rose Red jsy 2.50 6.00
109C D.Rose White jsy 2.50 6.00
110A Westbrook Orange jsy 2.50 6.00
110B Westbrook Blue jsy 2.50 6.00
110C Westbrook White jsy 2.50 6.00
111A D.Wade Red jsy 3.00 8.00
111B D.Wade Black jsy 3.00 8.00
111C D.Wade White jsy 3.00 8.00
112 Avery Bradley 1.00 2.50
113A Kobe Black jsy 12.00 30.00
113B Kobe Purple jsy 12.00 30.00
113C Kobe Yellow jsy 12.00 30.00
114 Bradley Beal 2.00 5.00
115 Gerald Henderson 1.00 2.50
116 Monta Ellis 1.25 3.00
117 Wesley Matthews 1.00 2.50
118 Robert Covington 1.25 3.00
119 Jimmy Butler 3.00 8.00
120 Dion Waiters 1.00 2.50
121 Luol Deng 1.25 3.00
122 Evan Turner 1.00 2.50
123 Nick Young 1.00 2.50
124 Otto Porter Jr. 1.25 3.00
125 Al-Farouq Aminu 1.00 2.50
126 Paul George 2.50 6.00
127 Chandler Parsons 1.00 2.50
128 Nerlens Noel 1.00 2.50
129 Pau Gasol 2.50 6.00
130A Durant Two hand on ball 6.00 15.00
130B Durant Dribbling 6.00 15.00
130C Durant White jsy 6.00 15.00
131 Chris Bosh 2.00 5.00
132 David Lee 1.00 2.50
133 Julius Randle 2.00 5.00
134 Nene 1.25 3.00
135 Mason Plumlee 1.00 2.50
136 Chase Budinger 1.00 2.50
137A Dirk Dark blue jsy 4.00 10.00
137B Dirk White jsy 4.00 10.00
137C Dirk Blue jsy 4.00 10.00
138 Nik Stauskas 1.00 2.50
139 Nikola Mirotic 1.00 2.50
140 Serge Ibaka 1.25 3.00
141 Hassan Whiteside 1.25 3.00
142 Jared Sullinger 1.00 2.50
143 Roy Hibbert 1.25 3.00
144 Marcin Gortat 1.00 2.50
145 Noah Vonleh 1.00 2.50
146 Jordan Hill 1.00 2.50
147 Devin Harris 1.00 2.50
148 JaKarr Sampson 1.00 2.50
149 Joakim Noah 1.00 2.50
150 Enes Kanter 1.00 2.50
151A Damon Stoudamire Raptors 1.50 4.00
151B Damon Stoudamire Trail Blazers 3.00 8.00
151C Stdmre Spurs SP 40.00 100.00
151D Stdmre Wildcats SP 40.00 100.00
151E Damon Stoudamire Grizzlies 3.00 8.00
152 Jerry West 2.50 6.00
153 Dino Radja 1.00 2.50
154 Kevin McHale 2.50 6.00
155 Grant Hill 2.50 6.00
156 Mike Bibby 1.25 3.00
157 Allen Iverson 4.00 10.00
158 Robert Horry 1.25 3.00
159 Baron Davis 1.25 3.00
160 Steve Kerr 1.50 4.00
161 David Robinson 3.00 8.00
162 John Starks 1.50 4.00
163 Dominique Wilkins 2.50 6.00
164 Larry Bird 6.00 15.00
165 Hakeem Olajuwon 3.00 8.00
166 Patrick Ewing 2.50 6.00
167 Alonzo Mourning 2.50 6.00
168 Rony Seikaly 1.25 3.00
169 Bill Russell 5.00 12.00
170 Tracy McGrady 2.50 6.00
171 Dennis Johnson 1.25 3.00
172 John Stockton 3.00 8.00
173 Drazen Petrovic 1.50 4.00
174 Latrell Sprewell 1.25 3.00
175 Jason Kidd 2.50 6.00
176A Maravich Hawks 4.00 10.00
176C Maravich Celtics SP 50.00 120.00
176D Maravich Jazz 6.00 15.00
177 Anfernee Hardaway 4.00 10.00
178 Scottie Pippen 4.00 10.00
179 Chris Mullin 2.00 5.00
180 Vlade Divac 1.50 4.00
181 Dennis Rodman 4.00 10.00
182 Julius Erving 4.00 10.00
183 Gary Payton 2.50 6.00
184 Magic Johnson 6.00 15.00
185 Elgin Baylor 3.00 8.00
186 Ralph Sampson 1.25 3.00
187 Antonio McDyess 1.25 3.00
188 Shaquille O'Neal 5.00 12.00
189 Christian Laettner 1.25 3.00
190A Wilt Lakers 6.00 15.00
190B Wilt Jayhawks SP 60.00 150.00
190C Wilt 76ers 20.00 50.00
190D Wilt Phil.Warriors 20.00 50.00
190E Wilt SF Warriors 10.00 25.00
191 Dikembe Mutombo 2.50 6.00
192 Kareem Abdul-Jabbar 5.00 12.00
193 George Gervin 2.50 6.00
194 Michael Redd 1.25 3.00
195A Jerry Stackhouse 76ers 1.50 4.00
195B Jerry Stackhouse Mavericks 3.00 8.00
195C Jerry Stackhouse Pistons 3.00 8.00
195D Jerry Stackhouse Heat 3.00 8.00
195E Jerry Stackhouse Wizards 3.00 8.00
195F Stackhouse Hawks SP 60.00 150.00
196 Richard Hamilton 1.50 4.00
197 Arvydas Sabonis 1.50 4.00
198 Shawn Kemp 2.50 6.00
199 Clyde Drexler 2.50 6.00
200 Yao Ming 4.00 10.00
201 Russell JSY AU/199 RC 15.00 40.00
202 Rashad Vaughn JSY AU/199 RC 4.00 10.00
203 Porzingis JSY AU/199 RC 50.00 120.00
204 Delon Wright JSY AU/199 RC 5.00 12.00
205 Kaminsky JSY AU/199 RC 8.00 20.00
206 Chris McCullough JSY AU/199 RC 4.00 10.00
207 Booker JSY AU/199 RC 400.00 800.00
209 Okafor JSY AU/199 RC 5.00 12.00
210 Montrezl Harrell JSY AU/199 RC 12.00 30.00
211 Winslow JSY AU/199 RC 12.00 30.00
212 Jarell Martin JSY AU/199 RC 4.00 10.00
213 Johnson JSY AU/199 RC 5.00 12.00
214 Justin Anderson JSY AU/199 RC 4.00 10.00
215 Dekker JSY AU/199 RC 4.00 10.00
216 Pat Connaughton JSY AU/199 RC 6.00 15.00
217 Lyles JSY AU/199 RC 5.00 12.00
218 Rakeem Christmas JSY AU/199 RC 4.00 10.00
219 Towns JSY AU/199 RC 75.00 200.00
220 Looney JSY AU/199 RC 12.00 30.00
221 Hezonja JSY AU/199 RC 5.00 12.00
222 Payne JSY AU/199 RC 6.00 15.00
223 Kelly Oubre Jr. JSY AU/199 RC 6.00 15.00
224 Anthony Brown JSY AU/199 RC 4.00 10.00
225 Portis JSY AU/199 RC 10.00 25.00
226 Terry Rozier JSY AU/199 RC 6.00 15.00
227 Jerian Grant JSY AU/199 RC 4.00 10.00
228 Rondae Hollis-Jefferson JSY AU/199 RC 5.00 12.00
229 Mudiay JSY AU/199 RC 5.00 12.00
230 R.J. Hunter JSY AU/199 RC 4.00 10.00
231 Cauley-Stein JSY AU/199 RC 12.00 30.00
232 Joe Young JSY AU/199 RC 4.00 10.00
233 Turner JSY AU/199 RC 10.00 25.00
234 Jordan Mickey JSY AU/199 RC 4.00 10.00
235 Richardson JSY AU/199 RC 6.00 15.00
237 Jones JSY AU/199 RC 5.00 12.00
238 Walter Tavares JSY AU/199 RC 4.00 10.00
239 Russell JSY AU/149 15.00 40.00
240 Rashad Vaughn JSY AU/149 4.00 10.00
241 Porzingis JSY AU/149 60.00 150.00
242 Delon Wright JSY AU/149 5.00 12.00
243 Jordan Mickey JSY AU/149 4.00 10.00
244 Chris McCullough JSY AU/149 4.00 10.00
245 D.Booker JSY AU/149 400.00 800.00
246 F.Kaminsky JSY AU/149 5.00 12.00
247 Okafor JSY AU/149 5.00 12.00
248 Montrezl Harrell JSY AU/149 12.00 30.00
249 J.Winslow JSY AU/149 10.00 25.00
250 Jarell Martin JSY AU/149 4.00 10.00
251 S.Johnson JSY AU/149 5.00 12.00
252 Justin Anderson JSY AU/149 4.00 10.00
253 S.Dekker JSY AU/149 4.00 10.00
254 Pat Connaughton JSY AU/149 6.00 15.00
255 T.Lyles JSY AU/149 8.00 20.00
256 Rakeem Christmas JSY AU/149 4.00 10.00
257 Towns JSY AU/149 100.00 250.00
258 Rondae Hollis-Jefferson JSY AU/149 5.00 12.00
259 C.Payne JSY AU/149 8.00 20.00
260 Kelly Oubre Jr. JSY AU/149 6.00 15.00
261 Anthony Brown JSY AU/149 4.00 10.00
262 B.Portis JSY AU/149 10.00 25.00
263 Terry Rozier JSY AU/149 15.00 40.00
264 Jerian Grant JSY AU/149 4.00 10.00
265 Richardson JSY AU/149 6.00 15.00
266 Mudiay JSY AU/149 5.00 12.00
267 R.J. Hunter JSY AU/149 4.00 10.00
268 Cauley-Stein JSY AU/149 12.00 30.00
269 Joe Young JSY AU/149 4.00 10.00
270 M.Turner JSY AU/149 10.00 25.00
271 Russell JSY AU/99 20.00 50.00
272 Rashad Vaughn JSY AU/99 4.00 10.00
273 Porzingis JSY AU/99 75.00 150.00
274 Delon Wright JSY AU/99 5.00 12.00
275 Chris McCullough JSY AU/99 4.00 10.00
276 D.Booker JSY AU/99 400.00 800.00
277 F.Kaminsky JSY AU/99 8.00 20.00
278 Okafor JSY AU/99 5.00 12.00
279 Montrezl Harrell JSY AU/99 12.00 30.00
280 J.Winslow JSY AU/99 12.00 30.00
281 Jordan Mickey JSY AU/99 4.00 10.00
282 S.Johnson JSY AU/99 5.00 12.00
283 Justin Anderson JSY AU/99 4.00 10.00
284 S.Dekker JSY AU/99 4.00 10.00
285 Pat Connaughton JSY AU/99 6.00 15.00
286 T.Lyles JSY AU/99 5.00 12.00
287 Rakeem Christmas JSY AU/99 4.00 10.00
288 Towns JSY AU/99 125.00 250.00
289 Rondae Hollis-Jefferson JSY AU/99 5.00 12.00
290 C.Payne JSY AU/99 8.00 20.00
291 Kelly Oubre Jr. JSY AU/99 6.00 15.00
292 Anthony Brown JSY AU/99 4.00 10.00
293 B.Portis JSY AU/99 12.00 30.00
294 Terry Rozier JSY AU/99 6.00 15.00
295 Jerian Grant JSY AU/99 4.00 10.00
296 Mudiay JSY AU/99 5.00 12.00
297 Josh Richardson JSY AU/99 6.00 15.00
298 Cauley-Stein JSY AU/99 12.00 30.00
299 Joe Young JSY AU/99 4.00 10.00
300 M.Turner JSY AU/99 12.00 30.00
301 Russell JSY AU/49 25.00 60.00
302 Rashad Vaughn JSY AU/49 4.00 10.00
303 Porzingis JSY AU/49 75.00 150.00
304 Delon Wright JSY AU/49 5.00 12.00
305 F.Kaminsky JSY AU/49 5.00 12.00
306 Chris McCullough JSY AU/49 4.00 10.00
307 D.Booker JSY AU/49 400.00 800.00
309 Okafor JSY AU/49 5.00 12.00
310 Montrezl Harrell JSY AU/49 12.00 30.00
311 J.Winslow JSY AU/49 6.00 15.00
312 Jarell Martin JSY AU/49 4.00 10.00
313 S.Johnson JSY AU/49 5.00 12.00
314 Justin Anderson JSY AU/49 4.00 10.00
315 S.Dekker JSY AU/49 4.00 10.00
316 Pat Connaughton JSY AU/49 6.00 15.00
317 T.Lyles JSY AU/49 8.00 20.00
318 Rakeem Christmas JSY AU/49 4.00 10.00
319 Towns JSY AU/49 150.00 300.00
320 K.Looney JSY AU/49 12.00 30.00
321 M.Hezonja JSY AU/49 8.00 20.00
322 C.Payne JSY AU/49 8.00 20.00
323 Kelly Oubre Jr. JSY AU/49 6.00 15.00
324 Anthony Brown JSY AU/49 4.00 10.00
325 B.Portis JSY AU/49 12.00 30.00
326 Terry Rozier JSY AU/49 6.00 15.00
327 Jerian Grant JSY AU/49 4.00 10.00
328 Rondae Hollis-Jefferson JSY AU/49 5.00 12.00
329 Mudiay JSY AU/49 5.00 12.00
330 R.J. Hunter JSY AU/49 4.00 10.00
331 Cauley-Stein JSY AU/49 12.00 30.00
332 Joe Young JSY AU/49 4.00 10.00
333 M.Turner JSY AU/49 12.00 30.00
334 Jordan Mickey JSY AU/49 4.00 10.00
335 Josh Richardson JSY AU/49 6.00 15.00
337 T.Jones JSY AU/49 8.00 20.00
338 Walter Tavares JSY AU/49 4.00 10.00

2015-16 Panini Gold Standard Gold

*GOLD: .6X TO 1.5X BASE HI
STATED PRINT RUN 79 SER.#'d SETS

2015-16 Panini Gold Standard 14K Autographs

PRINT RUNS B/WN 40-99 COPIES PER
EXCHANGE DEADLINE 8/17/2017
14KAD Anthony Davis/40 50.00 120.00
14KAL Alex Len/40 5.00 12.00
14KAW Andrew Wiggins/40 25.00 60.00
14KBB Bradley Beal/40 12.00 30.00
14KBG Blake Griffin/40 20.00 50.00
14KBW Bill Walton/40 25.00 60.00
14KDI Dan Issel/99 8.00 20.00
14KDW Dwyane Wade/40 40.00 100.00
14KEP Elfrid Payton/40 12.00 30.00
14KGG Gail Goodrich/40 8.00 20.00
14KGH Grant Hill/40 15.00 40.00
14KGH Gordon Hayward/99 10.00 25.00
14KGH Gary Harris/99 5.00 12.00
14KJE James Ennis/99 4.00 10.00
14KJK Jason Kidd/40 20.00 50.00
14KJP Jabari Parker/40 20.00 50.00
14KJR Julius Randle/40 12.00 30.00
14KJW John Wall/40 20.00 50.00
14KKB Kobe Bryant/40 500.00 1,000.00
14KKD Kevin Durant/40 60.00 150.00
14KMA Mark Aguirre/99 5.00 12.00
14KMF Michael Finley/40 5.00 12.00
14KNC Norris Cole/99 4.00 10.00
14KNV Nick Van Exel/40 10.00 25.00
14KRH Rodney Hood/99 5.00 12.00
14KSN Shabazz Napier/99 4.00 10.00
14KTB Tarik Black/99 4.00 10.00
14KTH Tobias Harris/99 5.00 12.00
14KWF Walt Frazier/40 12.00 30.00

2015-16 Panini Gold Standard AU Autographs

STATED PRINT RUN 79 SER.#'d SETS
EXCHANGE DEADLINE 8/17/2017
AUAB Alec Burks 4.00 10.00
AUAD Anthony Davis 40.00 100.00
AUAL Alex Len 4.00 10.00
AUAM Antonio McDyess 5.00 12.00
AUAN Andrew Nicholson 4.00 10.00
AUAW Andrew Wiggins 20.00 50.00
AUBBD Bojan Bogdanovic 5.00 12.00
AUBB Bradley Beal 8.00 20.00
AUBC Bill Cartwright 5.00 12.00
AUBD Brad Daugherty 5.00 12.00
AUBG Blake Griffin 15.00 40.00
AUBL Bill Laimbeer 6.00 15.00
AUBS Byron Scott 5.00 12.00
AUCB Chris Bosh 10.00 25.00
AUCC Cedric Ceballos 4.00 10.00
AUCR Cazzie Russell 5.00 12.00
AUCW C.J. Watson 4.00 10.00
AUDC Dave Cowens 8.00 20.00
AUDCR DeMarre Carroll 4.00 10.00
AUDH Darrun Hilliard 4.00 10.00
AUDI Dan Issel 8.00 20.00
AUDR Dino Radja 12.00 30.00
AUDS Damon Stoudamire 6.00 15.00
AUDSH Dennis Schroder 6.00 15.00
AUED Ed Davis 4.00 10.00
AUEP Elfrid Payton 5.00 12.00
AUGA Giannis Antetokounmpo 75.00 200.00
AUGHR Gary Harris 5.00 12.00
AUGH Gordon Hayward 6.00 15.00
AUGR Glen Rice 5.00 12.00
AUHG Horace Grant 6.00 15.00
AUJC Jordan Clarkson 6.00 15.00
AUJE James Ennis 4.00 10.00
AUJG Jeff Green 4.00 10.00
AUJH Jeff Hornacek 5.00 12.00
AUJHR Joe Harris 5.00 12.00
AUJI Joe Ingles 5.00 12.00
AUJP Jabari Parker 10.00 25.00
AUJV Jonas Valanciunas 5.00 12.00
AUJW John Wall 15.00 40.00
AUJY James Young 4.00 10.00
AUKB Kobe Bryant 500.00 1,000.00
AUKD Kevin Durant 40.00 100.00
AUKF Kenneth Faried 5.00 12.00
AULG Langston Galloway 4.00 10.00
AULN Larry Nance 5.00 12.00
AUMA Mark Aguirre 5.00 12.00
AUMC Maurice Cheeks 5.00 12.00
AUMCL Mike Conley 6.00 15.00
AUMF Michael Finley 6.00 15.00
AUMH Maurice Harkless 4.00 10.00
AUMJ Marques Johnson 5.00 12.00
AUMP Mason Plumlee 4.00 10.00
AUNA Nate Archibald 8.00 20.00
AUNJ Nikola Jokic 1,500.00 3,000.00
AUNM Nikola Mirotic 4.00 10.00
AUNV Nick Van Exel 6.00 15.00
AUPP Patrick Patterson 4.00 10.00
AURA Rafer Alston 4.00 10.00
AURF Rick Fox 5.00 12.00
AURH Robert Horry 5.00 12.00
AURN Raul Neto 4.00 10.00
AURP Robert Parish 8.00 20.00
AURS Ralph Sampson 5.00 12.00
AUSE Sean Elliott 5.00 12.00
AUSS Satch Sanders 6.00 15.00
AUSW Scott Wedman 5.00 12.00
AUTA Tony Allen 4.00 10.00
AUTB Tarik Black 4.00 10.00
AUTD Troy Daniels 4.00 10.00
AUTG Tom Gugliotta 4.00 10.00
AUTM Timofey Mozgov 4.00 10.00
AUWC Wilson Chandler 5.00 12.00
AUWE Wayne Embry 4.00 10.00
AUWF Walt Frazier 10.00 25.00
AUWT Walter Tavares 4.00 10.00

2015-16 Panini Gold Standard Gold Scripts

PRINT RUNS B/WN 35-99 COPIES PER
EXCHANGE DEADLINE 8/17/2017
SCAL Alex Len/49 4.00 10.00
SCAM Andre Miller/99 5.00 12.00
SCBB Bojan Bogdanovic/99 5.00 12.00
SCBR Brian Roberts/99 4.00 10.00
SCBW Bill Walton/99 25.00 60.00
SCCL Courtney Lee/99 4.00 10.00
SCCM Calvin Murphy/99 5.00 12.00
SCDC Dave Cowens/99 8.00 20.00
SCDC DeMarre Carroll/99 4.00 10.00
SCDE Dante Exum/49 5.00 12.00
SCDR David Robinson/35 15.00 40.00
SCDS Dennis Schroder/99 6.00 15.00
SCEK Enes Kanter/99 4.00 10.00
SCFE Festus Ezeli/99 4.00 10.00
SCGG Gail Goodrich/99 6.00 15.00
SCGH Gerald Henderson/99 4.00 10.00
SCJC Jordan Clarkson/99 8.00 20.00
SCJE James Ennis/99 4.00 10.00
SCJW Jerry West/35 20.00 50.00
SCJW Jamaal Wilkes/99 6.00 15.00
SCKM Kevin McHale/35 12.00 30.00
SCLG Langston Galloway/99 4.00 10.00
SCMD Matthew Dellavedova/99 5.00 12.00
SCMH Maurice Harkless/99 4.00 10.00
SCMK Michael Kidd-Gilchrist/49 4.00 10.00
SCMP Mason Plumlee/99 4.00 10.00
SCMW Mo Williams/99 5.00 12.00
SCNA Nate Archibald/99 8.00 20.00
SCNS Nik Stauskas/99 4.00 10.00
SCPG Pau Gasol/35 10.00 25.00
SCRG Rudy Gobert/99 8.00 20.00
SCRH Roy Hibbert/99 5.00 12.00
SCRP Robert Parish/99 8.00 20.00
SCRR Ricky Rubio/35 12.00 30.00
SCSC Seth Curry/99 8.00 20.00
SCSM Shabazz Muhammad/49 4.00 10.00
SCTA Tony Allen/99 4.00 10.00
SCTM Timofey Mozgov/99 4.00 10.00
SCVO Victor Oladipo/49 5.00 12.00
SCWF Walt Frazier/99 10.00 25.00

2015-16 Panini Gold Standard Gold Strike Jersey Autographs

PRINT RUNS B/WN 30-99 COPIES PER
EXCHANGE DEADLINE 8/17/2017
*PRIME/25: .75X TO 2X BASIC
1 Rashad Vaughn/99 4.00 10.00
2 Mario Hezonja/99 5.00 12.00
3 Mitch McGary/45 4.00 10.00
4 Jusuf Nurkic/99 5.00 12.00
5 Rakeem Christmas/99 4.00 10.00
6 D'Angelo Russell/49 30.00 80.00
7 Andrew Nicholson/99 4.00 10.00
8 Anthony Bennett/49 4.00 10.00
9 Glenn Robinson III/99 4.00 10.00
10 Bernard King/99 8.00 20.00
11 Kelly Oubre Jr./99 6.00 15.00
12 Luol Deng/30 5.00 12.00
13 Robert Sacre/99 4.00 10.00
14 Jared Dudley/99 4.00 10.00
15 Joe Young/99 4.00 10.00
16 Chris Webber/49 50.00 120.00
17 Tony Allen/99 4.00 10.00
18 Victor Oladipo/49 8.00 20.00
19 Kiki Vandeweghe/92 5.00 12.00
20 Kristaps Porzingis/99 60.00 150.00
21 Sam Dekker/99 4.00 10.00
22 Michael Cooper/99 5.00 12.00
23 Montrezl Harrell/99 12.00 30.00
24 Kenny Walker/99 4.00 10.00
25 Terry Rozier/99 15.00 40.00
26 Karl-Anthony Towns/49 125.00 250.00
27 Mo Williams/99 5.00 12.00
28 Harrison Barnes/49 10.00 25.00
29 Norm Nixon/99 4.00 10.00
30 C.J. McCollum/99 10.00 25.00
31 Chris Copeland/99 4.00 10.00
32 Stanley Johnson/99 12.00 30.00
33 Pat Connaughton/99 6.00 15.00
34 Myles Turner/99 12.00 30.00
35 R.J. Hunter/99 4.00 10.00
36 Chris Bosh/49 10.00 25.00
37 Darrell Griffith/99 5.00 12.00
38 Tyreke Evans/49 5.00 12.00
39 Will Perdue/99 4.00 10.00
40 Tyler Ennis/99 4.00 10.00

2015-16 Panini Gold Standard Golden Debuts

STATED PRINT RUN 50 SER.#'d SETS
1 Emmanuel Mudiay 3.00 8.00
2 Jerian Grant 2.50 6.00
3 Myles Turner 10.00 25.00
4 Rondae Hollis-Jefferson 3.00 8.00
5 Kelly Oubre Jr. 8.00 20.00
6 R.J. Hunter 2.50 6.00
7 Karl-Anthony Towns 25.00 60.00
8 Jordan Mickey 2.50 6.00
9 Kristaps Porzingis 15.00 40.00
10 Walter Tavares 2.50 6.00
11 Stanley Johnson 3.00 8.00
12 Delon Wright 3.00 8.00
13 Trey Lyles 3.00 8.00
14 Tyus Jones 3.00 8.00
15 Terry Rozier 10.00 25.00
16 Chris McCullough 2.50 6.00
17 D'Angelo Russell 10.00 25.00
18 Mario Hezonja 3.00 8.00
19 Anthony Brown 2.50 6.00
20 Kevon Looney 8.00 20.00
21 Frank Kaminsky 3.00 8.00
22 Justin Anderson 2.50 6.00
23 Devin Booker 15.00 40.00
24 Jarell Martin 2.50 6.00
25 Rashad Vaughn 2.50 6.00
26 Montrezl Harrell 8.00 20.00
27 Jahlil Okafor 3.00 8.00
28 Rakeem Christmas 2.50 6.00
29 Willie Cauley-Stein 3.00 8.00
30 Nemanja Bjelica 4.00 10.00
31 Justise Winslow 4.00 10.00
32 Bobby Portis 6.00 15.00
33 Cameron Payne 4.00 10.00
34 Larry Nance Jr. 5.00 12.00
35 Sam Dekker 2.50 6.00

2015-16 Panini Gold Standard Golden Graphs

PRINT RUNS B/WN 35-75 COPIES PER
EXCHANGE DEADLINE 8/17/2017
GGAG A.C. Green/75 6.00 15.00
GGAH Anfernee Hardaway/35 25.00 60.00
GGBW Bill Walton/35 25.00 60.00
GGCH Cliff Hagan/35 8.00 20.00
GGCM Cedric Maxwell/75 5.00 12.00
GGCR Cazzie Russell/75 5.00 12.00
GGDG Danny Green/75 5.00 12.00
GGDR David Robinson/35 20.00 50.00
GGDS Dennis Schroder/75 6.00 15.00
GGJW Jo Jo White/75 6.00 15.00
GGJY James Young/75 4.00 10.00
GGKG Kendall Gill/75 4.00 10.00
GGMC Michael Cage/75 4.00 10.00
GGMJ Magic Johnson/35 25.00 60.00
GGMJ Mark Jackson/35 6.00 15.00
GGNA Nate Archibald/35 10.00 25.00
GGPP Patrick Patterson/75 4.00 10.00
GGRB Rick Barry/35 10.00 25.00
GGRH Ron Harper/75 10.00 25.00
GGRS Rik Smits/75 5.00 12.00
GGSB Sam Bowie/75 4.00 10.00
GGSM Sidney Moncrief/75 4.00 10.00
GGSS Steve Smith/75 5.00 12.00
GGTB Tarik Black/75 4.00 10.00
GGTP Tony Parker/35 20.00 50.00
GGTT Tristan Thompson/35 5.00 12.00
GGVM Vernon Maxwell/75 4.00 10.00

2015-16 Panini Gold Standard Golden Pairs
PRINT RUNS B/WN 5-14 COPIES PER
NO PRICING ON QTY 14 OR LESS
1 Iverson/Erving/25 15.00 40.00
2 Griffin/Davis/25 12.00 25.00
3 Johnson/Lopez/25 8.00 20.00
5 Holiday/Davis/25 12.00 30.00
6 Bird/Parish/25 25.00 60.00
7 Vucevic/Harris/25 8.00 20.00
8 Aguirre/Blackman/25 12.00 30.00
9 Payton/Allen/25 15.00 40.00
10 Thompson/Curry/25 75.00 150.00
11 King/Anthony/25 15.00 40.00
12 Bryant/O'Neal/25 125.00 250.00
13 D.Gallinari/K.Faried/25 5.00 12.00
14 Westbrook/Durant/25 25.00 60.00
16 Pippen/Rodman/25 40.00 100.00
17 Hill/Nash/25 25.00 60.00
18 Hill/Dumars/25 15.00 40.00
19 Malone/Stockton/25 30.00 80.00
20 Drexler/Olajuwon/25 25.00 60.00
21 J.Teague/A.Horford/25 6.00 15.00
22 Wade/O'Neal/25 30.00 80.00
25 Oakley/Ewing/25 20.00 50.00

2015-16 Panini Gold Standard Golden Quads
PRINT RUNS B/WN 5-25 COPIES PER
NO PRICING ON QTY 5
1 Tge/Mllsp/Hrfrd/Knvr/25 20.00 50.00
2 Bgdnvc/Jack/Jhnsn/Lpz/25 10.00 25.00
3 Jffrsn/Hrstn/Zllr/Wlkr/25 10.00 25.00
4 Btlr/Rose/McDrmtt/Noah/25 20.00 50.00
8 Grffn/Jrdn/Crwfrd/Paul/25 30.00 80.00
9 Gsl/Cnly/Rndlph/Alln/25 12.00 30.00
10 Andrsn/Wade/Bosh/Chlmrs/25 25.00 60.00
12 Wggns/Grntt/Pkvc/Rbo/25 30.00 80.00
13 Drnl/Adms/Wstbrk/Ibka/25 15.00 40.00
14 Vcvc/Hrrs/Oldpo/Pytn/25 20.00 50.00
15 Len/Morris/Warren/Bledsoe/25 6.00 15.00
16 McLmre/Cllsn/Csns/Csspi/25 10.00 25.00
17 Lnrd/Gnbli/Dncn/Prkr/25 25.00 60.00
18 Vlncns/DRzn/Lowry/Ross/25 15.00 40.00
19 Exum/Fvrs/Hywrd/Brke/25 10.00 25.00
20 Mhnm/Grge/Hill/Hill/25 10.00 25.00
22 Clrksn/Brynt/Yng/Scre/25 60.00 150.00
23 Grdn/Hldy/Evns/Dvs/25 15.00 40.00
24 Bird/Lws/Rdja/McHle/25 40.00 100.00

2015-16 Panini Gold Standard Golden Trios
STATED PRINT RUN 25 SER.#'d SETS
1 Walker/Jefferson/Hairston 6.00 15.00
2 McLmre/Csns/Cllsn 8.00 20.00
3 Igdla/Green/Barnes 12.00 30.00
4 Burke/Favors/Hayward 8.00 20.00
5 Gasol/Conley/Randolph 12.00 30.00
6 Rdmn/Thms/Dmrs 15.00 40.00
7 Starks/Jackson/Ewing 25.00 60.00
8 Robinson/Kerr/Duncan 25.00 60.00
9 Hrfrd/Sflsha/Mllsp 6.00 15.00
10 Mourning/Rice/Johnson 15.00 40.00
11 Nash/Nwtzki/Finley 40.00 100.00
12 Prkr/Ginobili/Duncan 40.00 100.00
13 Paul/Griffin/Jordan 20.00 50.00
14 Beal/Wall/Porter Jr. 12.00 30.00
15 Andersen/Bosh/Wade 15.00 40.00
16 Smith/Drexler/Olajuwon 30.00 80.00
17 Payton/Gordon/Oladipo 30.00 80.00
18 Jnnngs/Cldwll-Pope/Drmmnd 12.00 30.00
19 Bradley/Sullinger/Smart 8.00 20.00
20 Mlne/Hrnck/Socktn 25.00 60.00
21 Gallinari/Nurkic/Faried 5.00 12.00
22 DRzn/Ross/Vlnciuns 15.00 40.00
23 Young/Clarkson/Bryant 60.00 150.00
24 Rbnsn/Dckwrth/Pppn 20.00 50.00
25 Davis/Evans/Holiday 10.00 25.00

2015-16 Panini Gold Standard Good as Gold Jersey Autographs
PRINT RUNS B/WN 30-99 COPIES PER
EXCHANGE DEADLINE 8/17/2017
*PRIME/25: .75X TO 2X BASIC
1 Josh Richardson/99 6.00 15.00
2 Manu Ginobili/38 30.00 80.00
3 George Hill/99 5.00 12.00
4 Jrue Holiday/49 8.00 20.00
5 Mitch Richmond/99 8.00 20.00
6 Tayshaun Prince/99 5.00 12.00
7 James Jones/99 4.00 10.00
8 Danilo Gallinari/99 5.00 12.00
9 Jerian Grant/99 4.00 10.00
10 Shabazz Muhammad/99 4.00 10.00
11 Justin Anderson/99 4.00 10.00
12 Marcus Smart/49 8.00 20.00
13 Thabo Sefolosha/99 4.00 10.00
14 Al Horford/99 6.00 15.00
15 Wilson Chandler/99 5.00 12.00
16 Jordan Hill/99 4.00 10.00
17 Devin Booker/99 400.00 800.00
18 Kenny Smith/99 5.00 12.00
19 Jordan Mickey/99 4.00 10.00
20 Kyle Korver/99 5.00 12.00
21 Pat Connaughton/99 6.00 15.00
22 Alex Len/49 5.00 12.00
23 Chase Budinger/99 4.00 10.00
24 Andre Iguodala/98 6.00 15.00
25 Patty Mills/67 10.00 25.00

2015-16 Panini Gold Standard Marks of Gold Jersey Autographs
PRINT RUNS B/WN 49-99 COPIES PER
EXCHANGE DEADLINE 8/17/2017
*PRIME/25: .75X TO 2X BASIC
1 Dante Exum/49 5.00 12.00
2 Jack Sikma/99 5.00 12.00
3 Eric Gordon/99 5.00 12.00
4 Donatas Motiejunas/99 4.00 10.00
5 J.R. Smith/75 8.00 20.00
6 Fat Lever/99 5.00 12.00
7 Kurt Rambis/99 5.00 12.00
8 Brad Daugherty/99 5.00 12.00
9 Dennis Rodman/49 25.00 60.00
10 Alan Anderson/99 4.00 10.00
11 Ben McLemore/99 4.00 10.00
12 Rafer Alston/99 4.00 10.00
13 Byron Scott/99 5.00 12.00
14 Jodie Meeks/99 4.00 10.00
15 Nikola Mirotic/99 4.00 10.00
16 Keith Van Horn/99 5.00 12.00
17 Taj Gibson/65 4.00 10.00
18 World B. Free/99 5.00 12.00
19 Grant Hill/49 15.00 40.00
20 Bill Laimbeer/99 6.00 15.00
21 Chris Mullin/99 10.00 25.00
22 Scott Wedman/99 5.00 12.00
23 Joe Dumars/99 8.00 20.00
24 Kent Bazemore/99 10.00 25.00
25 Bill Cartwright/99 5.00 12.00
26 Rik Smits/99 5.00 12.00
27 Cedric Maxwell/99 5.00 12.00
28 Jalen Rose/99 5.00 12.00
29 Richard Hamilton/49 6.00 15.00
30 Dino Radja/84 12.00 30.00
31 Nick Van Exel/99 10.00 25.00
32 Terry Cummings/99 5.00 12.00
33 Rick Fox/99 5.00 12.00
34 K.J. McDaniels/99 4.00 10.00
35 Jason Thompson/99 4.00 10.00

2015-16 Panini Gold Standard Mother Lode Autographs
PRINT RUNS B/WN 35-99 COPIES PER
EXCHANGE DEADLINE 8/17/2017
MLAH Allan Houston/99 4.00 10.00
MLAH Anfernee Hardaway/35 20.00 50.00
MLAI Allen Iverson/35 60.00 150.00
MLAM Antonio McDyess/99 4.00 10.00
MLAN Andrew Nicholson/99 3.00 8.00
MLBB Brandon Bass/99 3.00 8.00
MLBC Bruno Caboclo/99 3.00 8.00
MLBS Byron Scott/99 4.00 10.00
MLCR Cazzie Russell/99 4.00 10.00
MLDH Dwight Howard/35 10.00 25.00
MLDM Dikembe Mutombo/99 8.00 20.00
MLDM Donatas Motiejunas/99 3.00 8.00
MLDN Don Nelson/99 10.00 25.00
MLFL Fat Lever/99 4.00 10.00
MLGD Gorgui Dieng/99 3.00 8.00
MLGH George Hill/99 4.00 10.00
MLGH Grant Hill/35 15.00 40.00
MLGK George Karl/99 5.00 12.00
MLGR Glen Rice/49 4.00 10.00
MLHB Henry Bibby/99 3.00 8.00
MLJC Jordan Clarkson/99 5.00 12.00
MLJJ Jim Jackson/99 3.00 8.00
MLJK Jason Kidd/35 12.00 30.00
MLJS Jerry Stackhouse/99 5.00 12.00
MLJS J.R. Smith/99 5.00 12.00
MLJW Jay Williams/99 3.00 8.00
MLKG Kendall Gill/99 3.00 8.00
MLKK Kyle Korver/99 4.00 10.00
MLKM Kevin McHale/35 6.00 15.00
MLLB Larry Brown/99 5.00 12.00
MLLD Luol Deng/99 4.00 10.00
MLLS Lance Stephenson/99 4.00 10.00
MLMC Maurice Cheeks/99 4.00 10.00
MLMD Matthew Dellavedova/99 4.00 10.00
MLMG Manu Ginobili/35 20.00 50.00
MLMM Mike Muscala/99 3.00 8.00
MLNN Norm Nixon/99 3.00 8.00
MLPM Patty Mills/99 10.00 25.00
MLPS Peja Stojakovic/99 4.00 10.00
MLPS Paul Silas/99 5.00 12.00
MLPT P.J. Tucker/99 3.00 8.00
MLRC Robert Covington/99 4.00 10.00
MLRC Rick Carlisle/50 12.00 30.00
MLRG Rudy Gobert/90 6.00 15.00
MLRH Roy Hibbert/99 4.00 10.00
MLRM Ray McCallum/99 3.00 8.00
MLRS Rik Smits/99 4.00 10.00
MLRS Rod Strickland/99 3.00 8.00
MLRT Rudy Tomjanovich/99 4.00 10.00
MLSD Spencer Dinwiddie/99 4.00 10.00
MLSE Sean Elliott/99 4.00 10.00
MLSF Steve Francis/99 5.00 12.00
MLSL Shane Larkin/99 3.00 8.00
MLSW Sonny Weems/99 3.00 8.00
MLTB Trey Burke/50 3.00 8.00
MLTM Tracy McGrady/35 15.00 40.00
MLTM Timofey Mozgov/99 3.00 8.00
MLTS Thabo Sefolosha/99 3.00 8.00
MLVD Vinny Del Negro/99 4.00 10.00
MLVD Vlade Divac/99 5.00 12.00

2015-16 Panini Gold Standard Newly Minted Memorabilia
STATED PRINT RUN 25 SER.#'d SETS
1 Kelly Oubre Jr. 12.00 30.00
2 Justise Winslow 6.00 15.00
3 Sam Dekker 4.00 10.00
4 Karl-Anthony Towns 25.00 60.00
5 Justin Anderson 4.00 10.00
6 Kristaps Porzingis 25.00 60.00
7 Tyus Jones 5.00 12.00
8 Willie Cauley-Stein 10.00 25.00
9 Devin Booker 50.00 125.00
10 Stanley Johnson 5.00 12.00
11 Terry Rozier 15.00 40.00
12 Myles Turner 15.00 40.00
13 Jerian Grant 4.00 10.00
14 D'Angelo Russell 15.00 40.00
15 Bobby Portis 10.00 25.00
16 Mario Hezonja 5.00 12.00
17 R.J. Hunter 4.00 10.00
18 Emmanuel Mudiay 5.00 12.00
19 Cameron Payne 6.00 15.00
20 Frank Kaminsky 5.00 12.00
22 Trey Lyles 5.00 12.00
23 Delon Wright 5.00 12.00
24 Jahlil Okafor 12.00 30.00
25 Rondae Hollis-Jefferson 5.00 12.00

2015-16 Panini Gold Standard Newly Minted Memorabilia Duals
STATED PRINT RUN 25 SER.#'d SETS
3 J.Grant/P.Connaughton 10.00 25.00
4 C.Payne/J.Huestis 10.00 25.00
5 K.Towns/D.Russell 20.00 50.00
6 T.Rozier/R.Hunter 15.00 40.00
7 Hlls-Jffrsn/Jhnsn 5.00 12.00
8 S.Dekker/M.Harrell 12.00 30.00
9 K.Towns/W.Cauley-Stein 25.00 60.00
10 A.Brown/D.Russell 12.00 30.00
13 A.Brown/J.Huestis 4.00 10.00
14 K.Porzingis/M.Hezonja 25.00 60.00
15 J.Okafor/K.Porzingis 20.00 50.00
16 R.Hollis-Jefferson/C.McCullough 5.00 12.00
17 J.Okafor/J.Winslow 12.00 30.00
20 B.Portis/J.Martin 10.00 25.00
21 J.Martin/J.Mickey 4.00 10.00
22 J.Grant/K.Porzingis 15.00 40.00
23 F.Kaminsky/S.Dekker 15.00 40.00
24 J.Okafor/R.Holmes 12.00 30.00
25 M.Hezonja/W.Cauley-Stein 5.00 12.00

2015-16 Panini Gold Standard Newly Minted Memorabilia Quads
STATED PRINT RUN 25 SER.#'d SETS
2 Yng/Jhnsn/Wrght/Lny 12.00 30.00
3 Portis/Anderson/Hollis-Jefferson/Jones 10.00 25.00
5 Twns/Cly-Stn/Kmnsky/Dkkr 20.00 50.00
6 Kmnsky/Hznja/Rchrdsn/Wnsow 6.00 15.00
7 Grnt/Hrrll/Wnslw/Jns 12.00 30.00
8 Connaughton/Mudiay/Lyles/Jones 6.00 15.00
9 Rssll/Okfr/Przngs/Twns 60.00 150.00
10 Anderson/Dekker/Martin/Harrell 12.00 30.00
11 Pyne/Bkr/Obre/Rzr 50.00 120.00
12 Prts/Twns/Mrtn/Cly-Stn 20.00 50.00
13 Harrell/McCullough/Looney/Hunter 12.00 30.00
15 Przngs/Mdy/Hznja/Tvrs 15.00 40.00
16 Pyne/Hsis/Twns/Jns 25.00 60.00
17 Brwn/Hsts/Hlls-Jffrsn/Jhnsn 15.00 40.00
18 Brwn/Rssll/Lny/Cly-Stn 12.00 30.00
19 Mdy/Hznja/Jhnsn/Cly-Stn 10.00 25.00
20 Mdy/Wnslw/Twns/Okfr 50.00 120.00
22 Mrtn/Mcky/Towns/Cly-Stn 15.00 40.00
23 Bkr/Twns/Lyles/Cly-Stn 60.00 150.00
24 Prts/Trnr/Chstms/Jhnsn 15.00 40.00
25 McCllgh/Okfr/Andrsn/Rzr 8.00 20.00

2015-16 Panini Gold Standard Newly Minted Memorabilia Triples
STATED PRINT RUN 25 SER.#'d SETS
1 Booker/Lyles/Cly-Stein 20.00 50.00
2 Russell/Okafor/Towns 60.00 150.00
3 Russell/Kmnsky/Dekker 25.00 60.00
4 Winslow/Turner/Lyles 15.00 40.00
5 Portis/Martin/Booker 12.00 30.00
6 Wright/Grant/Anderson 5.00 12.00
7 Towns/Cly-Stein/Okafor 25.00 60.00
8 Mickey/Rozier/Hunter 15.00 40.00
10 Okafor/Winslow/Jones 15.00 40.00
11 Rozier/Okafor/Grant 8.00 20.00
12 Przngs/Cly-Stein/Hznja 25.00 60.00
13 Wright/Looney/Johnson 6.00 15.00
14 Payne/Booker/Oubre 12.00 30.00
15 Richardson/Lyles/Mickey 6.00 15.00
16 Portis/Hollis-Jefferson/Jones 10.00 25.00
17 Mudiay/Russell/Hezonja 15.00 40.00
18 Mudiay/Huestis/Payne 8.00 20.00
19 Booker/Lyles/Towns 50.00 120.00
20 Towns/Lyles/Cly-Stein 20.00 50.00
21 Jones/McCullough/Anderson 5.00 12.00
22 Kmnsky/Johnson/Mudiay 15.00 40.00
23 Young/Brown/Hollis-Jefferson 5.00 12.00
25 Mudiay/Hznja/Porzingis 25.00 60.00

2015-16 Panini Gold Standard Ring Bearers Autographs
PRINT RUNS B/WN 25-49 COPIES PER
EXCHANGE DEADLINE 8/17/2017
RBAW Antoine Walker/49 8.00 20.00
RBBL Bill Laimbeer/49 6.00 15.00
RBDG Danny Green/49 8.00 20.00
RBDR David Robinson/25 25.00 60.00
RBDW Dwyane Wade/25 150.00 300.00
RBGP Gary Payton/25 12.00 30.00
RBGR Glen Rice/49 5.00 12.00
RBJD Joe Dumars/49 6.00 15.00
RBJM J. Michael McAdoo/25 5.00 12.00
RBJT Jason Terry/25 15.00 40.00
RBKB Kobe Bryant/25 500.00 1,000.00
RBKT Klay Thompson/49 60.00 150.00
RBMA Mark Aguirre/49 5.00 12.00
RBMJ Magic Johnson/25 40.00 100.00
RBRF Rick Fox/49 8.00 20.00
RBRH Robert Horry/49 10.00 25.00
RBSE Sean Elliott/49 5.00 12.00
RBTP Tony Parker/25 40.00 100.00

2015-16 Panini Gold Standard Rookie Jersey Autographs Prime
*PRIME: 1X TO 2.5X BASIC
STATED PRINT RUN 25 SER.#'d SETS
EXCHANGE DEADLINE 8/17/2017
201 D'Angelo Russell 150.00 400.00
203 Kristaps Porzingis 300.00 600.00
219 Karl-Anthony Towns 400.00 800.00
233 Myles Turner 60.00 150.00
239 D'Angelo Russell 125.00 300.00
241 Kristaps Porzingis 350.00 700.00
257 Karl-Anthony Towns 400.00 800.00
270 Myles Turner 125.00 300.00
271 D'Angelo Russell 150.00 400.00
273 Kristaps Porzingis 350.00 700.00
288 Karl-Anthony Towns 400.00 800.00
300 Myles Turner 125.00 300.00
301 D'Angelo Russell 150.00 400.00
303 Kristaps Porzingis 350.00 700.00
319 Karl-Anthony Towns 400.00 800.00
333 Myles Turner 125.00 300.00

2015-16 Panini Gold Standard White Gold Threads
STATED PRINT RUN 25 SER.#'d SETS
1 Grant Hill 12.00 30.00
2 Damian Lillard 15.00 40.00
3 Marc Gasol 6.00 15.00
4 DeMarcus Cousins 20.00 50.00
5 Michael Redd 5.00 12.00
6 Tim Duncan 25.00 60.00
7 Russell Westbrook 20.00 50.00
8 Manu Ginobili 15.00 40.00
9 Rajon Rondo 8.00 20.00
11 Hakeem Olajuwon 15.00 40.00
12 DeMar DeRozan 10.00 25.00
14 John Stockton 15.00 40.00
15 Patrick Ewing 25.00 60.00

2016-17 Panini Gold Standard
1-200 PRINT RUN 269 SER.#'d SETS
201-238 PRINT RUN 199 SER.#'d SETS
239-269 PRINT RUN 149 SER.#'d SETS
270-300 PRINT RUN 99 SER.#'d SETS
301-338 PRINT RUN 49 SER.#'d SETS
339-373 PRINT RUN 25 SER.#'d SETS
EXCHANGE DEADLINE 6/28/2018
1B Durant Thunder 6.00 15.00
2 Emmanuel Mudiay 1.00 2.50
3 Jordan Clarkson 1.50 4.00
4 Brook Lopez 1.25 3.00
5A Kawhi Leonard 4.00 10.00
5B Kawhi Leonard VAR 4.00 10.00
6 John Wall 2.00 5.00
7 Anthony Bennett 1.00 2.50
8 Julius Randle 2.00 5.00
9 Andrew Bogut 1.50 4.00
10 Gary Harris 1.25 3.00
11 Luol Deng 1.25 3.00
12 Bojan Bogdanovic 1.25 3.00
13 Kyle Anderson 1.00 2.50
14 LaMarcus Aldridge 1.50 4.00
15 Lance Thomas 1.00 2.50
16 D'Angelo Russell 2.00 5.00
17 Wesley Matthews 1.00 2.50
18 Dennis Schroder 1.50 4.00
19 Kenneth Faried 1.25 3.00
20 Lou Williams 1.50 4.00
21 Jeremy Lin 3.00 8.00
22 Willie Cauley-Stein 1.25 3.00
23 Manu Ginobili 2.00 5.00
24 Kelly Oubre Jr. 2.00 5.00
25A Kristaps Porzingis 2.50 6.00
25B Kristaps Porzingis VAR 2.50 6.00
26 Paul Pierce 2.50 6.00
27 Harrison Barnes 1.25 3.00
28 Kent Bazemore 1.00 2.50
29 Nikola Jokic 8.00 20.00
30 Chandler Parsons 1.00 2.50
31 Rondae Hollis-Jefferson 1.00 2.50
32 Rudy Gay 1.50 4.00
33 Tony Parker 2.50 6.00
34 Marcin Gortat 1.00 2.50
35 Joakim Noah 1.00 2.50
36 Mike Conley 1.50 4.00
37A Dirk Nowitzki 4.00 10.00
37B Dirk Nowitzki VAR 4.00 10.00
38 Paul Millsap 1.25 3.00
39 Wilson Chandler 1.25 3.00
40 Marc Gasol 1.50 4.00
41 Thomas Robinson 1.00 2.50
42A DeMarcus Cousins 1.25 3.00
42B DeMarcus Cousins VAR 1.25 3.00
43A DeMar DeRozan 2.00 5.00
43B DeMar DeRozan VAR 2.00 5.00
44 Markieff Morris 1.00 2.50
45 Derrick Rose 2.50 6.00
46 J.J. Redick 1.50 4.00
47 Deron Williams 1.25 3.00
48 Al Horford 1.50 4.00
49 Aron Baynes 1.00 2.50
50 DeMarre Carroll 1.00 2.50
51 Cameron Payne 1.50 4.00
52 Darren Collison 1.00 2.50
53A Jamal Crawford Clippers 1.50 4.00
53C Jamal Crawford Bulls 1.50 4.00
53G Jamal Crawford Knicks 1.50 4.00
54 Thabo Sefolosha 1.00 2.50
55A Carmelo Anthony 2.50 6.00
55B Carmelo Anthony VAR 2.50 6.00
55C Anthony Nuggets 2.50 6.00
56 DeAndre Jordan 1.25 3.00
57 Tristan Thompson 1.25 3.00
58A Isaiah Thomas 1.25 3.00
58B Isaiah Thomas VAR 1.25 3.00
59 Boban Marjanovic 1.25 3.00
60 Vince Carter 3.00 8.00
61 Ersan Ilyasova 1.00 2.50
62 Mason Plumlee 1.00 2.50
63 Jonas Valanciunas 1.25 3.00
64 J.J. Barea 1.25 3.00
65 Solomon Hill 1.00 2.50
66A Chris Paul 2.50 6.00
66B Chris Paul VAR 2.50 6.00
67 Richard Jefferson 1.25 3.00
68 Jae Crowder 1.00 2.50
69 Marcus Morris 1.00 2.50
70 Zach Randolph 1.50 4.00
71A Russell Westbrook 2.50 6.00
71B Russell Westbrook VAR 2.50 6.00
72 Evan Turner 1.00 2.50
73A Kyle Lowry 1.50 4.00
73B Kyle Lowry VAR 1.50 4.00
74 Clint Capela 1.25 3.00
75 Langston Galloway 1.00 2.50
76A Blake Griffin 1.50 4.00
76B Blake Griffin VAR 1.50 4.00
77 Chris Andersen 1.25 3.00
78 Kemba Walker 1.25 3.00
79 Reggie Jackson 1.25 3.00
80 Tyler Johnson 1.00 2.50
81 Steven Adams 1.25 3.00
82A Damian Lillard 4.00 10.00
82B Damian Lillard VAR 4.00 10.00
83 Terrence Ross 1.25 3.00
84 John Henson 1.00 2.50
85 Jrue Holiday 2.00 5.00
86 Thaddeus Young 1.00 2.50
87A LeBron James 30.00 80.00
87B LeBron James VAR 150.00 400.00
88 Michael Kidd-Gilchrist 1.00 2.50
89 Stanley Johnson 1.00 2.50
90 Goran Dragic 1.50 4.00
91 Victor Oladipo 1.25 3.00
92 Allen Crabbe 1.00 2.50
93 Dante Exum 1.25 3.00
94 Gorgui Dieng 1.00 2.50
95A Anthony Davis 5.00 12.00
95B Anthony Davis VAR 5.00 12.00
96A Paul George 2.50 6.00
96B Paul George VAR 2.50 6.00
97A Kyrie Irving 3.00 8.00
97B Kyrie Irving VAR 3.00 8.00
98 Nicolas Batum 1.25 3.00
99 Tobias Harris 1.50 4.00
100 Hassan Whiteside 1.25 3.00
101 Aaron Gordon 1.50 4.00
102 Alex Len 1.00 2.50
103 George Hill 1.25 3.00
104 Joel Embiid 4.00 10.00
105 Alexis Ajinca 1.00 2.50
106 Myles Turner 1.50 4.00
107 Kevin Love 1.50 4.00
108C Wade Heat 3.00 8.00
109 Andre Iguodala 1.50 4.00
110 Josh Richardson 1.25 3.00
111 Elfrid Payton 1.25 3.00
112 Eric Bledsoe 1.25 3.00
113 Gordon Hayward 1.50 4.00
114 Alan Williams RC 1.00 2.50
115A Zach LaVine 3.00 8.00
115B Zach LaVine VAR 3.00 8.00
116 Monta Ellis 1.25 3.00
117 Robin Lopez 1.00 2.50
118A Jimmy Butler 3.00 8.00
118B Jimmy Butler VAR 3.00 8.00
119A Draymond Green 2.00 5.00
119B Draymond Green VAR 2.00 5.00
120A Justise Winslow 1.25 3.00
120B Justise Winslow VAR 1.25 3.00
121 Evan Fournier 1.25 3.00
122A Devin Booker 6.00 15.00
122B Devin Booker VAR 6.00 15.00
123 Joe Johnson 1.50 4.00
124 Maurice Harkless 1.00 2.50
125 Ricky Rubio 1.25 3.00
126 Jeff Teague 1.00 2.50
127 Taj Gibson 1.00 2.50
128 Rajon Rondo 2.00 5.00
129A Klay Thompson 4.00 10.00
129B Klay Thompson VAR 4.00 10.00
130A Giannis Antetokounmpo 10.00 25.00
130B G. Antetokounmpo VAR 100.00 250.00
131 Mario Hezonja 1.00 2.50
132 Brandon Knight 1.25 3.00
133A Rodney Hood 1.25 3.00
133B Rodney Hood VAR 1.25 3.00
134 C.J. McCollum 1.50 4.00
135 Shaun Livingston 1.00 2.50
136 Trevor Ariza 1.00 2.50
137 Frank Kaminsky 1.00 2.50
138 Bobby Portis 1.50 4.00
139A Stephen Curry 12.00 30.00
139B Stephen Curry VAR 12.00 30.00
140 Jabari Parker 1.00 2.50
141 Nikola Vucevic 1.50 4.00
142 Robert Covington 1.25 3.00
143 Rudy Gobert 2.00 5.00
144 Ben McLemore 1.00 2.50
145A Karl-Anthony Towns 3.00 8.00
145B Karl-Anthony Towns VAR 3.00 8.00
146 Ryan Anderson 1.00 2.50
147 Cody Zeller 1.00 2.50
148 Marcus Smart 2.00 5.00
149 Zaza Pachulia 1.00 2.50
150 Khris Middleton 1.50 4.00
151 Serge Ibaka 1.25 3.00
152 Nik Stauskas 1.00 2.50
153 Bradley Beal 2.00 5.00
154 Patty Mills 1.50 4.00
155A Andrew Wiggins 2.00 5.00
155B Andrew Wiggins VAR 2.00 5.00
156 Patrick Beverley 1.00 2.50
157 Amir Johnson 1.00 2.50
158 Kyle Korver 1.25 3.00
159 Eric Gordon 1.25 3.00
160 Michael Carter-Williams 1.00 2.50
161 Jahlil Okafor 1.00 2.50
162 Nerlens Noel 1.00 2.50
163 Ian Mahinmi 1.00 2.50
164 Patrick Patterson 1.00 2.50
165 Miles Plumlee 1.00 2.50
166 Jonas Jerebko 1.00 2.50
167A James Harden 3.00 8.00
167B James Harden VAR 3.00 8.00
168 Rodney Stuckey 1.00 2.50
169 Mike Muscala 1.00 2.50
170 Will Barton 1.00 2.50
171A Kobe Bryant 12.00 30.00
171B Kobe Bryant VAR 12.00 30.00
172 David Robinson 3.00 8.00
173 Tracy McGrady 2.50 6.00
174 Larry Johnson 2.00 5.00
175A Scottie Pippen 3.00 8.00
175B Scottie Pippen VAR 3.00 8.00
176 Wilt Chamberlain 5.00 12.00
177E Rick Barry GS Warriors 2.00 5.00
178 Shareef Abdur-Rahim 1.25 3.00
179A Olajuwon Rockets 3.00 8.00
180 Pete Maravich 2.50 6.00
181 Shaquille O'Neal 5.00 12.00
182 Dave DeBusschere 1.50 4.00
183A Erving 76ers 4.00 10.00
184 Gary Payton 2.50 6.00
185 Chris Webber 1.50 4.00
186 Larry Bird 6.00 15.00
187 Magic Johnson 6.00 15.00
188A Dikembe Mutombo Nuggets 2.50 6.00
188B Dikembe Mutombo Hawks 2.50 6.00
188E Dikembe Mutombo Rockets 2.50 6.00
189 Clyde Drexler 2.50 6.00
190 Anfernee Hardaway 4.00 10.00
191 Connie Hawkins 1.50 4.00
192 Isiah Thomas 2.50 6.00
193 Chris Mullin 2.50 6.00
194A Ben Wallace 2.00 5.00
194C Ben Wallace Pistons 2.00 5.00
195 Jason Kidd 2.50 6.00
196 John Stockton 2.50 6.00
197 Bill Bradley 2.00 5.00
198A Robert Parish Celtics 2.00 5.00
199 Bob Cousy 2.50 6.00
200 Oscar Robertson 4.00 10.00
201 Ingram JSY AU/199 RC 40.00 100.00
202 Brown JSY AU/199 RC 125.00 300.00
203 Bender JSY AU/199 RC 3.00 8.00
204 Dunn JSY AU/199 RC 5.00 12.00
205 Hield JSY AU/199 RC 10.00 25.00
206 Murray JSY AU/199 RC 30.00 80.00
207 Chriss JSY AU/199 RC 4.00 10.00
208 Jakob Poeltl JSY AU/199 RC 6.00 15.00
209 Maker JSY AU/199 RC 4.00 10.00
210 A.J. Hammons JSY AU/199 RC 3.00 8.00
211 Taurean Prince JSY AU/199 RC 4.00 10.00
212 Georgios Papagiannis JSY AU/199 RC 3.00 8.00
213 Valentine JSY AU/199 RC 3.00 8.00
214 Hernangomez JSY AU/199 RC 15.00 40.00
215 Cheick Diallo JSY AU/199 RC 3.00 8.00
216 Wade Baldwin IV JSY AU/199 RC 3.00 8.00
217 Henry Ellenson JSY AU/199 RC 3.00 8.00
218 Malik Beasley JSY AU/199 RC 6.00 15.00
219 LeVert JSY AU/199 RC 8.00 20.00
220 DeAndre' Bembry JSY AU/199 RC 5.00 12.00
221 Malachi Richardson JSY AU/199 RC 3.00 8.00
222 Stephen Zimmerman JSY AU/199 RC 3.00 8.00
224 Brice Johnson JSY AU/199 RC 3.00 8.00
225 Murray JSY AU/199 RC 300.00 600.00
226 Pascal Siakam JSY AU/199 RC 25.00 60.00
227 Labissiere JSY AU/199 RC 3.00 8.00
228 Zubac JSY AU/199 RC 8.00 20.00
229 Jones JSY AU/199 RC 3.00 8.00
230 Deyonta Davis JSY AU/199 RC 3.00 8.00
231 Diamond Stone JSY AU/199 RC 3.00 8.00
232 Ulis JSY AU/199 RC 4.00 10.00
233 Whitehead JSY AU/199 RC 3.00 8.00
234 Demetrius Jackson JSY AU/199 RC 3.00 8.00
235 Brogdon JSY AU/199 RC 12.00 30.00
236 Felder JSY AU/199 RC 3.00 8.00
237 Gary Payton II JSY AU/199 RC 30.00 80.00
238 Saric JSY AU/199 RC 5.00 12.00
239 Ingram JSY AU/149 40.00 100.00
240 Brown JSY AU/149 125.00 300.00
241 Bender JSY AU/149 3.00 8.00
242 Dunn JSY AU/149 5.00 12.00
243 Hield JSY AU/149 10.00 25.00
244 Murray JSY AU/149 50.00 120.00
245 Chriss JSY AU/149 4.00 10.00
246 Jakob Poeltl JSY AU/149 6.00 15.00
247 Maker JSY AU/149 4.00 10.00
248 A.J. Hammons JSY AU/149 3.00 8.00
249 Taurean Prince JSY AU/149 4.00 10.00
250 Valentine JSY AU/149 3.00 8.00
251 Hernangomez JSY AU/149 15.00 40.00
252 Wade Baldwin IV JSY AU/149 3.00 8.00
253 Henry Ellenson JSY AU/149 3.00 8.00
254 Malik Beasley JSY AU/149 6.00 15.00
255 LeVert JSY AU/149 8.00 20.00
256 DeAndre' Bembry JSY AU/149 5.00 12.00
257 Malachi Richardson JSY AU/149 3.00 8.00
258 Lwwu-Cbrrt JSY AU/149 5.00 12.00
259 Brice Johnson JSY AU/149 3.00 8.00
260 Labissiere JSY AU/149 3.00 8.00
261 Jones JSY AU/149 3.00 8.00
262 Deyonta Davis JSY AU/149 3.00 8.00
263 Diamond Stone JSY AU/149 3.00 8.00
264 Ulis JSY AU/149 4.00 10.00
265 Whitehead JSY AU/149 3.00 8.00
266 Demetrius Jackson JSY AU/149 3.00 8.00
267 Brogdon JSY AU/149 12.00 30.00
268 Gary Payton II JSY AU/149 40.00 100.00
269 Saric JSY AU/149 5.00 12.00
270 Ingram JSY AU/99 50.00 120.00
271 Brown JSY AU/99 150.00 400.00
272 Bender JSY AU/99 4.00 10.00
273 Dunn JSY AU/99 6.00 15.00
274 Hield JSY AU/99 12.00 30.00
275 Murray JSY AU/99 60.00 150.00
276 Chriss JSY AU/99 5.00 12.00
277 Jakob Poeltl JSY AU/99 8.00 20.00
278 Maker JSY AU/99 5.00 12.00
279 A.J. Hammons JSY AU/99 4.00 10.00
280 Taurean Prince JSY AU/99 5.00 12.00
281 Valentine JSY AU/99 4.00 10.00
282 Hernangomez JSY AU/99 20.00 50.00
283 Wade Baldwin IV JSY AU/99 4.00 10.00
284 Henry Ellenson JSY AU/99 4.00 10.00
285 Malik Beasley JSY AU/99 8.00 20.00
286 LeVert JSY AU/99 10.00 25.00
287 DeAndre' Bembry JSY AU/99 6.00 15.00
288 Malachi Richardson JSY AU/99 4.00 10.00
289 Lwwu-Cbrrt JSY AU/99 6.00 15.00
290 Brice Johnson JSY AU/99 4.00 10.00
291 Labissiere JSY AU/99 4.00 10.00
292 Jones JSY AU/99 4.00 10.00
293 Deyonta Davis JSY AU/99 4.00 10.00
294 Diamond Stone JSY AU/99 4.00 10.00
295 Ulis JSY AU/99 5.00 12.00
296 Whitehead JSY AU/99 4.00 10.00
297 Demetrius Jackson JSY AU/99 4.00 10.00
298 Brogdon JSY AU/99 15.00 40.00
299 Gary Payton II JSY AU/99 50.00 120.00
300 Saric JSY AU/99 6.00 15.00
301 B. Ingram JSY AU/49 50.00 120.00
302 Brown JSY AU/49 150.00 400.00
303 Bender JSY AU/49 5.00 12.00
304 Dunn JSY AU/49 6.00 15.00
305 Hield JSY AU/49 12.00 30.00
306 Murray JSY AU/49 60.00 150.00
307 Chriss JSY AU/49 5.00 12.00
308 Jakob Poeltl JSY AU/49 8.00 20.00
309 Maker JSY AU/49 5.00 12.00
310 A.J. Hammons JSY AU/49 4.00 10.00
311 Taurean Prince JSY AU/49 5.00 12.00
312 Georgios Papagiannis JSY AU/49 4.00 10.00
313 Valentine JSY AU/49 4.00 10.00
314 Hernangomez JSY AU/49 20.00 50.00
315 Cheick Diallo JSY AU/49 4.00 10.00
316 Wade Baldwin IV JSY AU/49 4.00 10.00
317 Henry Ellenson JSY AU/49 4.00 10.00
318 Malik Beasley JSY AU/49 8.00 20.00
319 LeVert JSY AU/49 10.00 25.00
320 DeAndre' Bembry JSY AU/49 6.00 15.00
321 Malachi Richardson JSY AU/49 4.00 10.00
322 Stephen Zimmerman JSY AU/49 4.00 10.00
323 Lwwu-Cbrrt JSY AU/49 6.00 15.00
324 Brice Johnson JSY AU/49 4.00 10.00
325 Murray JSY AU/49 350.00 700.00
326 Pascal Siakam JSY AU/49 40.00 100.00
327 Labissiere JSY AU/49 4.00 10.00
328 Zubac JSY AU/49 10.00 25.00
329 Jones JSY AU/49 4.00 10.00
330 Deyonta Davis JSY AU/49 4.00 10.00
331 Diamond Stone JSY AU/49 4.00 10.00
332 Ulis JSY AU/49 5.00 12.00
333 Whitehead JSY AU/49 4.00 10.00
334 Demetrius Jackson JSY AU/49 4.00 10.00
335 Brogdon JSY AU/49 15.00 40.00
336 Felder JSY AU/49 4.00 10.00
337 Gary Payton II JSY AU/49 60.00 150.00
338 Saric JSY AU/49 6.00 15.00
339 Brandon Ingram GD 40.00 100.00
340 Ben Simmons GD 15.00 40.00
341 Jaylen Brown GD 60.00 150.00
342 Kris Dunn GD 8.00 20.00
343 Dragan Bender GD 5.00 12.00
344 Marquese Chriss GD 6.00 15.00
345 Buddy Hield GD 15.00 40.00
346 Jamal Murray GD 75.00 200.00
347 Jakob Poeltl GD 10.00 25.00
348 Thon Maker GD 6.00 15.00
349 Taurean Prince GD 6.00 15.00
350 Domantas Sabonis GD 30.00 80.00
351 Denzel Valentine GD 5.00 12.00
352 Wade Baldwin IV GD 5.00 12.00
353 Henry Ellenson GD 5.00 12.00
354 Caris LeVert GD 12.00 30.00
355 Isaiah Whitehead GD 5.00 12.00
356 Dejounte Murray GD 50.00 120.00
357 Skal Labissiere GD 5.00 12.00
358 Brice Johnson GD 5.00 12.00
359 Malachi Richardson GD 5.00 12.00
360 Malik Beasley GD 10.00 25.00
361 T. Luwawu-Cabarrot GD 8.00 20.00
362 DeAndre' Bembry GD 8.00 20.00
363 Cheick Diallo GD 5.00 12.00
364 Georgios Papagiannis GD 5.00 12.00
365 Juan Hernangomez GD 10.00 25.00
366 Pascal Siakam GD 30.00 80.00
367 Ivica Zubac GD 12.00 30.00
368 Damian Jones GD 5.00 12.00
369 Deyonta Davis GD 5.00 12.00
370 Malcolm Brogdon GD 15.00 40.00
371 Tyler Ulis GD 6.00 15.00
372 Patrick McCaw GD 5.00 12.00
373 Diamond Stone GD 5.00 12.00

2016-17 Panini Gold Standard Gold
*GOLD: .5X TO 1.2X BASE HI
STATED PRINT RUN 79 SER.#'d SETS

2016-17 Panini Gold Standard 14K Autographs
PRINT RUNS B/WN 25-49 COPIES PER
EXCHANGE DEADLINE 6/28/2018
14KNVE Nick Van Exel/49 10.00 25.00
1 Jimmy Butler/25 40.00 100.00
2 Avery Bradley/49 3.00 8.00
3 Jae Crowder/49 3.00 8.00
4 Dwight Powell/49 3.00 8.00
5 Kyrie Irving/25 60.00 150.00
6 Devin Booker/49 200.00 500.00
7 Kobe Bryant/25 1,500.00 3,000.00
8 Kevin Durant/25 125.00 300.00
10 Tom Gugliotta/49 3.00 8.00
11 Tim Hardaway/49 10.00 25.00
12 Cedric Maxwell/49 4.00 10.00
13 John Starks/49 5.00 12.00
14 Robert Horry/49 10.00 25.00
15 Vin Baker/49 4.00 10.00
16 Reggie Jackson/49 3.00 8.00
17 Andrei Kirilenko/49 4.00 10.00
18 Zach LaVine/49 40.00 100.00
19 Clint Capela/49 6.00 15.00
20 Evan Fournier/49 4.00 10.00
21 Evan Turner/49 3.00 8.00
23 Boban Marjanovic/49 12.00 30.00
25 David Robinson/25 40.00 100.00
26 Gary Payton/25 25.00 60.00
27 Sean Elliott/49 4.00 10.00
29 Spud Webb/49 10.00 25.00
30 Jamal Mashburn/49 4.00 10.00

2016-17 Panini Gold Standard AU Autographs
STATED PRINT RUN 79 SER.#'d SETS
EXCHANGE DEADLINE 6/28/2018
1 Kevin Durant 100.00 250.00
2 Kyrie Irving 40.00 100.00
3 Carmelo Anthony 60.00 150.00
4 Dwyane Wade 75.00 200.00
5 Chris Paul 75.00 200.00
6 Mike Conley 8.00 20.00
7 Anthony Davis 40.00 100.00
8 Andrew Wiggins 15.00 40.00
9 Blake Griffin 15.00 40.00
10 John Wall 15.00 40.00
12 Karl-Anthony Towns 40.00 100.00
13 Isaiah Thomas 20.00 50.00
14 Jimmy Butler 40.00 100.00
16 Tony Parker 20.00 50.00
19 Klay Thompson 125.00 300.00
20 Tobias Harris 5.00 12.00
21 Draymond Green 20.00 50.00
23 Kristaps Porzingis 15.00 40.00
24 Paul Millsap 4.00 10.00
25 Brandon Knight 4.00 10.00
27 Khris Middleton 10.00 25.00
28 Evan Turner 3.00 8.00
29 Jae Crowder 3.00 8.00
30 Matthew Dellavedova 8.00 20.00
31 Michael Carter-Williams 3.00 8.00
33 DeMarre Carroll 3.00 8.00
34 Nikola Vucevic 10.00 25.00
35 Devin Booker 100.00 250.00
36 Myles Turner 5.00 12.00
38 Marcus Smart 6.00 15.00
39 Zach LaVine 30.00 80.00
41 Bobby Portis 5.00 12.00
42 Cameron Payne 8.00 20.00
44 Nemanja Bjelica 3.00 8.00
45 Evan Fournier 10.00 25.00
46 Trey Lyles 4.00 10.00
47 D'Angelo Russell 12.00 30.00
49 Clint Capela 8.00 20.00
50 Thaddeus Young 3.00 8.00
51 Glen Rice 5.00 12.00

52 Dikembe Mutombo 10.00 25.00
53 Horace Grant 8.00 20.00
54 Jo Jo White 4.00 10.00
55 Allan Houston 12.00 30.00
56 Alvan Adams 4.00 10.00
57 Mark Aguirre 4.00 10.00
58 A.C. Green 6.00 15.00
59 Bill Cartwright 8.00 20.00
60 Tom Gugliotta 3.00 8.00
61 Tim Hardaway 10.00 25.00
62 Cedric Maxwell 4.00 10.00
63 Mark Price 8.00 20.00
64 Jim Chones 3.00 8.00
65 Jamal Mashburn 4.00 10.00
66 David Robinson 30.00 80.00
67 Ray Allen 25.00 60.00
68 Alex English 4.00 10.00
69 Dell Curry 8.00 20.00
70 Andrei Kirilenko 4.00 10.00
71 Robert Horry 10.00 25.00
72 Junior Bridgeman 4.00 10.00
73 Gary Payton 15.00 40.00
74 Toni Kukoc 12.00 30.00
75 Patrick Ewing 60.00 150.00
76 John Starks 5.00 12.00
77 Chauncey Billups 10.00 25.00
78 Larry Bird 100.00 250.00
79 Magic Johnson 100.00 250.00

2016-17 Panini Gold Standard Gold Scripts

PRINT RUNS B/WN 25-99 COPIES PER
EXCHANGE DEADLINE 6/28/2018
1 Latrell Sprewell/25 12.00 30.00
2 Rashad Vaughn/99 3.00 8.00
3 Kobe Bryant/25 1,000.00 2,000.00
4 Tom Heinsohn/99 40.00 100.00
5 Scottie Pippen/25 75.00 200.00
6 Adrian Smith/99 3.00 8.00
7 Tom Van Arsdale/99 4.00 10.00
8 Sean Elliott/99 4.00 10.00
9 Seth Curry/99 4.00 10.00
10 Bob Lanier/25 8.00 20.00
11 Jason Terry/25 5.00 12.00
12 Calvin Murphy/25 6.00 15.00
13 George Gervin/25 12.00 30.00
14 Yao Ming/25 200.00 500.00
15 Jusuf Nurkic/47 4.00 10.00
16 Jordan Clarkson/25 6.00 15.00
17 Gail Goodrich/25 6.00 15.00
18 Vince Carter/25 75.00 200.00
19 Mario Chalmers/25 5.00 12.00
20 Brian Grant/99 4.00 10.00
21 Rony Seikaly/99 3.00 8.00
22 Michael Carter-Williams/25 4.00 10.00
23 Junior Bridgeman/99 4.00 10.00
25 Robert Covington/99 4.00 10.00
26 Andrew Nicholson/99 3.00 8.00
27 Joel Embiid/25 125.00 300.00
28 T.J. McConnell/99 4.00 10.00
29 Jahlil Okafor/25 4.00 10.00
30 JaKarr Sampson/99 3.00 8.00
31 Dan Issel/99 6.00 15.00
32 David Thompson/99 6.00 15.00
33 Jalen Rose/25 5.00 12.00
34 Spencer Haywood/99 3.00 8.00
35 Kevin McHale/25 10.00 25.00
36 Paul Millsap/25 5.00 12.00
37 Shawn Kemp/25 40.00 100.00
38 Chuck Person/25 5.00 12.00
39 Steve Blake/99 3.00 8.00
40 Jim Chones/99 3.00 8.00

2016-17 Panini Gold Standard Gold Standard Autographs

PRINT RUNS B/WN 25-75 COPIES PER
EXCHANGE DEADLINE 6/28/2018
1 Jimmy Butler/25 40.00 100.00
2 Kobe Bryant/25 1,500.00 3,000.00
3 Kevin Durant/25 125.00 300.00
4 Kyrie Irving/25 60.00 150.00
5 Andrew Wiggins/25 25.00 60.00
6 Nikola Vucevic/75 12.00 30.00
7 Andrei Kirilenko/75 4.00 10.00
8 Draymond Green/25 40.00 100.00
10 Tobias Harris/75 8.00 20.00
11 Adrian Dantley/75 5.00 12.00
12 Chauncey Billups/75 12.00 30.00
13 Bill Walton/75 25.00 60.00
15 Antonio McDyess/75 4.00 10.00
16 Bill Laimbeer/75 8.00 20.00
17 Jeff Hornacek/75 8.00 20.00
18 Kiki Vandeweghe/75 4.00 10.00
19 Spud Webb/75 12.00 30.00
20 Robert Horry/75 5.00 12.00
21 Jo Jo White/75 8.00 20.00
GSVC Vince Carter/25 75.00 200.00

2016-17 Panini Gold Standard Gold Strike Jersey Autographs

PRINT RUNS B/WN 25-149 COPIES PER
EXCHANGE DEADLINE 6/28/2018
1 Carmelo Anthony/25 20.00 50.00
3 Patrick Ewing/25 60.00 150.00
4 Dirk Nowitzki/25 75.00 200.00
5 Kyrie Irving/25 40.00 100.00
6 David Robinson/25 40.00 100.00
7 Karl-Anthony Towns/25 40.00 100.00
8 D'Angelo Russell/25 20.00 50.00
9 Deron Williams/25 5.00 12.00
10 Vince Carter/25 12.00 30.00
11 Alex Len/25 6.00 15.00
12 Tyson Chandler/25 5.00 12.00
13 Michael Carter-Williams/25 4.00 10.00
16 Dikembe Mutombo/35 10.00 25.00
18 Reggie Bullock/149 3.00 8.00
19 Dan Majerle/85 4.00 10.00
20 Jerry Stackhouse/25 5.00 12.00
21 Gary Harris/35 4.00 10.00
22 Langston Galloway/149 3.00 8.00
24 Walter Davis/149 5.00 12.00
25 Bill Laimbeer/149 5.00 12.00
26 Kelly Olynyk/149 3.00 8.00
27 Dwight Powell/149 3.00 8.00
28 Archie Goodwin/149 3.00 8.00
29 T.J. McConnell/149 6.00 15.00
30 Robert Covington/149 4.00 10.00

2016-17 Panini Gold Standard Golden Graphs

PRINT RUNS B/WN 25-99 COPIES PER
EXCHANGE DEADLINE 6/28/2018
1 Jimmy Butler/25 25.00 60.00
2 Tobias Harris/49 5.00 12.00
4 Jonas Valanciunas/99 4.00 10.00
5 Chauncey Billups/75 6.00 15.00
6 Reggie Jackson/99 4.00 10.00
7 Mike Conley/99 4.00 10.00
8 Tyus Jones/99 3.00 8.00
9 Avery Bradley/99 3.00 8.00
10 Gary Harris/75 4.00 10.00
11 Evan Turner/99 3.00 8.00
13 DeMarre Carroll/99 3.00 8.00
14 Kevin Durant/25 100.00 250.00
15 Kyrie Irving/25 40.00 100.00
16 Andrew Wiggins/25 25.00 60.00
19 Rondae Hollis-Jefferson/99 3.00 8.00
21 Nate Archibald/49 5.00 12.00
22 Devin Booker/75 150.00 400.00
23 Jamal Mashburn/49 4.00 10.00
24 David Thompson/99 6.00 15.00
25 Alex English/99 4.00 10.00
26 Bob McAdoo/99 6.00 15.00
28 Dan Issel/99 6.00 15.00
29 Sarunas Marciulionis/99 5.00 12.00
30 Glen Rice/99 5.00 12.00
31 Michael Cooper/99 5.00 12.00
32 Allan Houston/99 4.00 10.00

2016-17 Panini Gold Standard Golden Jumbo Threads

STATED PRINT RUN 49 SER.#'d SETS
1 Tim Duncan/49 5.00 12.00
2 Grant Hill/49 5.00 12.00
3 Michael Redd/49 3.00 8.00
4 Shaquille O'Neal/49 12.00 30.00
5 Patrick Ewing/49 5.00 12.00
6 Andrei Kirilenko/49 3.00 8.00
7 Hakeem Olajuwon/49 8.00 20.00
8 Scottie Pippen/49 8.00 20.00
9 Richard Hamilton/49 3.00 8.00
10 Larry Bird/49 15.00 40.00

2016-17 Panini Gold Standard Golden Pairs

STATED PRINT RUN 49 SER.#'d SETS
1 A.Gordon/Z.LaVine 6.00 15.00
2 M.Gasol/Z.Randolph 4.00 10.00
3 L.Aldridge/T.Parker 6.00 15.00
4 C.Anthony/L.James 12.00 30.00
5 D.Favors/G.Hayward 4.00 10.00
6 H.Olajuwon/G.Hill 8.00 20.00
7 M.Smart/I.Thomas 5.00 12.00
8 G.Dragic/H.Whiteside 4.00 10.00
9 J.Holiday/K.Love 5.00 12.00
10 P.Millsap/K.Korver 3.00 8.00
11 M.Ellis/P.George 6.00 15.00
12 D.Cousins/R.Gay 4.00 10.00
13 D.Robinson/T.Duncan 10.00 25.00
14 J.Butler/R.Westbrook 8.00 20.00
15 L.James/K.Irving 20.00 50.00
16 J.Okafor/N.Noel 2.50 6.00
17 V.Carter/K.Garnett 10.00 25.00
18 D.Lillard/K.Leonard 10.00 25.00
19 K.Faried/D.Gallinari 3.00 8.00
20 A.Wiggins/K.Towns 10.00 25.00
21 S.Pippen/S.O'Neal 12.00 30.00
22 M.Conley/R.Rubio 3.00 8.00
23 E.Kanter/S.Adams 3.00 8.00
24 A.Mourning/D.Wilkins 6.00 15.00

2016-17 Panini Gold Standard Golden Quads

STATED PRINT RUN 49 SER.#'d SETS
1 Ro/Gi/Du/Pa 10.00 25.00
2 Le/An/Bu/Ge 10.00 25.00
3 To/Jo/La/Wi 12.00 30.00
4 Burks/Favors/Hood/Gobert 5.00 12.00
5 Lo/Ja/Sh/Ir 30.00 80.00
6 Ga/Ca/Co/Ra 8.00 20.00
7 Ga/Al/El/Gay 10.00 25.00
8 Ro/Ka/We/Al 6.00 15.00
9 Ol/Ew/Hi/O'N 12.00 30.00
10 Ha/He/Ba/Co 10.00 25.00
11 Mickey/Rozier/Young/Hunter 4.00 10.00
12 Thomas/Fournier/Smart/Hezonja 5.00 12.00
13 Ha/Ze/Ol/Go 10.00 25.00
15 Gordon/Drummond/Beal/Ross 5.00 12.00
16 Exum/Lamb/Holiday/Dragic 5.00 12.00
17 Bogdanovic/Casspi/Porter/Stuckey 3.00 8.00
18 Okafor/Winslow
Turner/Hollis-Jefferson 4.00 10.00
20 Bi/Pi/Al/Ha 15.00 40.00
21 Mirotic/Vucevic/Noel/Millsap 4.00 10.00
22 Korver/Morris/Gallinari/Neto 3.00 8.00
23 Li/Wh/Po/Ru 10.00 25.00
24 Plumlee/Ariza/Plumlee/Sefolosha 2.50 6.00

2016-17 Panini Gold Standard Golden Trios

STATED PRINT RUN 49 SER.#'d SETS
1 Hill/Allen/Duncan 8.00 20.00
2 Anthony/DeRozan/Butler 8.00 20.00
3 Love/Shumpert/James 30.00 80.00
4 Favors/Hood/Gobert 5.00 12.00
5 Carter/Gasol/Randolph 8.00 20.00
6 Leonard/Ginobili/Parker 10.00 25.00
7 Jordan/Walker/Carroll 3.00 8.00
8 Wiggins/Towns/Garnett 25.00 60.00
9 Kanter/Westbrook/Adams 6.00 15.00
10 Randle/Gay/LaVine 8.00 20.00
11 Stuckey/Ellis/George 6.00 15.00
12 Burks/Exum/Hayward 4.00 10.00
13 Beal/Gortat/Porter 5.00 12.00
14 Thomas/Hunter/Smart 5.00 12.00
15 Olajuwon/O'Neal/Ewing 12.00 30.00
16 Hezonja/Gordon/Fournier 4.00 10.00
17 Parker/Aldridge/Irving 6.00 15.00
18 Lillard/Dragic/Conley 5.00 12.00
19 Thompson/Lowry/Griffin 10.00 25.00
20 Drummond/Whiteside/Noel 4.00 10.00
21 Bird/Stockton/Pippen 15.00 40.00
22 Nurkic/Gallinari/Faried 3.00 8.00
23 Bazemore/Millsap/Sefolosha 8.00 20.00
24 Russell/Winslow/Turner 5.00 12.00
25 Oubre Jr./Portis/Hollis-Jefferson 5.00 12.00

2016-17 Panini Gold Standard Good as Gold Jersey Autographs

PRINT RUNS B/WN 49-149 COPIES PER
EXCHANGE DEADLINE 6/28/2018
*PRIME/25: 1X TO 2.5X BASIC
1 Brandon Ingram/49 30.00 80.00
2 Juan Hernangomez/149 6.00 15.00
3 Jaylen Brown/49 100.00 250.00
4 Dragan Bender/49 3.00 8.00
5 Cheick Diallo/149 3.00 8.00
6 Kris Dunn/49 5.00 12.00
7 Henry Ellenson/149 3.00 8.00
8 Buddy Hield/49 15.00 40.00
9 Jamal Murray/49 50.00 120.00
10 Malik Beasley/149 6.00 15.00
11 Marquese Chriss/49 4.00 10.00
12 DeAndre' Bembry/149 5.00 12.00
13 Jakob Poeltl/49 6.00 15.00
14 Thon Maker/49 4.00 10.00
15 T. Luwawu-Cabarrot/149 5.00 12.00
16 Pascal Siakam/149 20.00 50.00
17 Ivica Zubac/149 8.00 20.00
18 Demetrius Jackson/149 3.00 8.00
19 Malcolm Brogdon/149 10.00 25.00
20 Kay Felder/149 3.00 8.00

2016-17 Panini Gold Standard Mother Lode Autographs

PRINT RUNS B/WN 25-99 COPIES PER
EXCHANGE DEADLINE 6/28/2018
1 Kobe Bryant/25 500.00 1,000.00
2 T.J. McConnell/99 4.00 10.00
3 Scott Skiles/99 4.00 10.00
4 Hollis Thompson/99 3.00 8.00
5 Bobby Jones/99 4.00 10.00
6 Hersey Hawkins/99 3.00 8.00
7 Satch Sanders/99 5.00 12.00
8 Anthony Bennett/25 4.00 10.00
9 Scottie Pippen/25 60.00 150.00
10 Toni Kukoc/99 5.00 12.00
11 Reggie Jackson/75 4.00 10.00
12 Terrence Jones/99 3.00 8.00
13 Yao Ming/25 40.00 100.00
14 Vernon Maxwell/99 3.00 8.00
15 Cuttino Mobley/99 3.00 8.00
16 Jordan Clarkson/49 5.00 12.00
17 Jamaal Wilkes/99 5.00 12.00
18 Eddie Jones/99 4.00 10.00
19 Bob Dandridge/99 5.00 12.00
20 Karl-Anthony Towns/25 30.00 80.00
21 Archie Goodwin/99 3.00 8.00
22 C.J. McCollum/49 5.00 12.00
23 Allen Crabbe/99 3.00 8.00
24 Rod Strickland/99 3.00 8.00
25 Vlade Divac/99 5.00 12.00
26 Michael Kidd-Gilchrist/25 4.00 10.00
27 Steve Francis/27 5.00 12.00
28 C.J. Miles/99 3.00 8.00
29 Cedric Maxwell/88 4.00 10.00
30 Glenn Robinson III/99 3.00 8.00
31 Kendall Gill/99 5.00 12.00
32 Tristan Thompson/25 5.00 12.00
33 Mike Bibby/65 4.00 10.00
34 Latrell Sprewell/49 10.00 25.00
35 Mario Elie/99 3.00 8.00
36 Herb Williams/99 3.00 8.00
37 James Ennis/99 3.00 8.00
38 Chauncey Billups/49 6.00 15.00
39 Dennis Scott/99 3.00 8.00
40 Nick Anderson/99 4.00 10.00
41 Shawn Kemp/75 25.00 60.00
42 Norman Powell/99 5.00 12.00
43 Dante Exum/25 5.00 12.00
44 Thabo Sefolosha/75 3.00 8.00
45 Steve Smith/99 4.00 10.00
46 Spud Webb/99 5.00 12.00
47 Kent Bazemore/86 5.00 12.00
48 Glen Rice/75 6.00 15.00
49 Junior Bridgeman/99 4.00 10.00
50 Johnny Newman/99 3.00 8.00
51 Dick Barnett/99 4.00 10.00
52 Brian Grant/99 4.00 10.00
53 Gail Goodrich/39 5.00 12.00
54 Sidney Moncrief/99 4.00 10.00
55 Spencer Haywood/99 3.00 8.00
56 Michael Carter-Williams/25 4.00 10.00
57 Cazzie Russell/99 4.00 10.00
58 Kiki Vandeweghe/99 4.00 10.00
59 Tony Snell/99 3.00 8.00
60 Frank Ramsey/25 12.00 30.00

2016-17 Panini Gold Standard Newly Minted Memorabilia

STATED PRINT RUN 25 SER.#'d SETS
1 Brandon Ingram 10.00 25.00
2 Jaylen Brown 20.00 50.00
3 Kris Dunn 4.00 10.00
4 Dragan Bender 2.50 6.00
5 Buddy Hield 8.00 20.00
6 Jamal Murray 20.00 50.00
7 Marquese Chriss 3.00 8.00
8 Jakob Poeltl 5.00 12.00
9 Thon Maker 3.00 8.00
10 Domantas Sabonis 15.00 40.00
11 Dario Saric 4.00 10.00
12 Georgios Papagiannis 2.50 6.00
13 Denzel Valentine 2.50 6.00
14 Juan Hernangomez 5.00 12.00
15 Wade Baldwin IV 2.50 6.00
16 Henry Ellenson 2.50 6.00
17 Malik Beasley 5.00 12.00
18 Caris LeVert 6.00 15.00
19 Malachi Richardson 2.50 6.00
20 Timothe Luwawu-Cabarrot 4.00 10.00
21 Brice Johnson 5.00 12.00
22 Skal Labissiere 2.50 6.00
23 Dejounte Murray 12.00 30.00
24 Cheick Diallo 2.50 6.00
25 Kay Felder 2.50 6.00

2016-17 Panini Gold Standard Newly Minted Memorabilia Duals

STATED PRINT RUN 25 SER.#'d SETS
1 B.Ingram/J.Brown 20.00 50.00
2 D.Bender/G.Papagiannis 4.00 10.00
3 B.Hield/T.Prince 8.00 20.00
4 M.Chriss/D.Murray 10.00 25.00
5 S.Labissiere/J.Murray 15.00 40.00
6 H.Ellenson/K.Dunn 6.00 15.00
7 C.LeVert/D.Valentine 10.00 25.00
8 B.Johnson/D.Stone 4.00 10.00
9 J.Hernangomez/M.Beasley 8.00 20.00
10 P.McCaw/S.Zimmerman 4.00 10.00
11 D.Jones/W.Baldwin IV 4.00 10.00
12 D.Valentine/D.Davis 8.00 20.00
13 J.Murray/T.Ulis 15.00 40.00
14 Luwawu-Cabarrot/Saric 6.00 15.00
15 I.Zubac/B.Ingram 15.00 40.00
16 M.Brogdon/T.Maker 25.00 60.00
17 D.Jackson/J.Brown 12.00 30.00
18 I.Whitehead/C.LeVert 10.00 25.00
19 D.Jones/P.McCaw 4.00 10.00
20 C.Onuaku/G.Payton II 10.00 25.00
21 D.Davis/W.Baldwin IV 4.00 10.00
22 C.Diallo/B.Hield 8.00 20.00
23 P.Siakam/J.Poeltl 25.00 60.00
24 D.Bender/T.Ulis 5.00 12.00
25 D.Saric/D.Sabonis 25.00 60.00

2016-17 Panini Gold Standard Newly Minted Memorabilia Quads

STATED PRINT RUN 25 SER.#'d SETS
1 Be/Br/In/Du 15.00 40.00
2 Ma/Sa/Be/Pa 8.00 20.00
3 Hi/Du/Ch/Mu 15.00 40.00
4 Mu/Va/Ba/Br 12.00 30.00
5 In/Ja/Ch/Be 12.00 30.00
6 Br/Mc/Jo/Ja 12.00 30.00
7 Hield/Poeltl/Diallo/Siakam 25.00 60.00
8 In/Zu/He/Lu 15.00 40.00
9 Pa/Br/Ma/On 8.00 20.00
10 Johnson/Davis/Stone/Baldwin IV 4.00 10.00
11 Ch/Mu/Va/Da 20.00 50.00
12 In/Ch/Be/Zu 15.00 40.00
13 Hi/Va/Du/Mu 30.00 80.00
14 Hammons/Ellenson
Zimmerman/Prince 5.00 12.00
15 Jo/Ri/In/Fe 15.00 40.00
16 Bender/Labissiere/Poeltl/Felder 8.00 20.00
17 Mu/Be/Ul/Du 12.00 30.00
18 Br/Va/Pa/Wh 12.00 30.00
19 LeVert/Bembry/Jhsn/Hield 12.00 30.00
20 Be/Di/Mu/Ri 15.00 40.00
21 Ch/Mc/He/La 8.00 20.00
22 Hammons/Stone/Ellenson/Poeltl 8.00 20.00
23 Si/Fe/Zi/Ma 8.00 20.00
24 Ja/Lu-Ca/On/Pr 6.00 15.00
25 Ul/Sa/Pa/Br 8.00 20.00

2016-17 Panini Gold Standard Newly Minted Memorabilia Triples

STATED PRINT RUN 25 SER.#'d SETS
1 Murray/Hernangomez/Beasley 12.00 30.00
2 Bender/Chriss/Ulis 8.00 20.00
3 Richardson/Papagiannis/Labissiere 4.00 10.00
4 Bender/Hernangomez/Papagiannis 8.00 20.00
5 Zubac/Maker/Luwawu-Cabarrot 8.00 20.00
6 Labissiere/Ulis/Murray 15.00 40.00
7 Prince/Hield/Diallo 12.00 30.00
8 Brogdon/Johnson/Jackson 8.00 20.00
9 Ingram/Bender/Brown 12.00 30.00
10 Hield/Murray/Dunn 15.00 40.00
11 Poeltl/Maker/Bender 8.00 20.00
12 Pa/He/Lu-Ca 8.00 20.00
13 Ingram/Hield/Dunn 15.00 40.00
14 Poeltl/Saric/Papagiannis 8.00 20.00
15 LeVert/Valentine/Murray 30.00 80.00
16 Chriss/Prince/Maker 5.00 12.00
17 Murray/Dunn/Baldwin IV 8.00 20.00
19 Johnson/Ellenson/Maker 5.00 12.00
20 Valentine/Ingram/Hield 20.00 50.00
21 Be/He/Lu-Ca 8.00 20.00
22 Ingram/Murray/Murray 25.00 60.00
23 Dunn/Johnson/Valentine 6.00 15.00
24 Stone/Maker/Bender 5.00 12.00
25 Murray/Murray/Brown 15.00 40.00

2016-17 Panini Gold Standard Rookie Jersey Autographs Prime

*PRIME: 1X TO 2.5X BASIC
STATED PRINT RUN 25 SER.#'d SETS
EXCHANGE DEADLINE 6/28/2018

2016-17 Panini Gold Standard White Gold Threads

STATED PRINT RUN 49 SER.#'d SETS
1 Tim Duncan 6.00 15.00
2 Carmelo Anthony 5.00 12.00
3 LeBron James 30.00 80.00
4 Vince Carter 6.00 15.00
5 Kevin Garnett 8.00 20.00
6 Russell Westbrook 5.00 12.00
7 Grant Hill 4.00 10.00
8 Kawhi Leonard 8.00 20.00
9 Dwyane Wade 5.00 12.00
10 Derrick Rose 5.00 12.00
11 Patrick Ewing 4.00 10.00
12 Shaquille O'Neal 10.00 25.00
13 Thaddeus Young 2.00 5.00
14 Zach LaVine 6.00 15.00
15 Bradley Beal 4.00 10.00

2017-18 Panini Gold Standard

STATED PRINT RUN 99 SER.#'d SETS
151 Lonzo Ball 25.00 60.00
152 T.J. Leaf 2.50 6.00
153 Abdel Nader 3.00 8.00
154 Derrick White 10.00 25.00
155 De'Aaron Fox 20.00 50.00
156 Ivan Rabb 2.50 6.00
157 Jayson Tatum 50.00 125.00
158 Josh Hart 6.00 15.00
159 Josh Jackson 3.00 8.00
160 Milos Teodosic 3.00 8.00
161 Malik Monk 10.00 25.00
162 Tyler Dorsey 2.50 6.00
163 Bogdan Bogdanovic 8.00 20.00
164 Cedi Osman 8.00 20.00
165 Dennis Smith Jr. 3.00 8.00
166 John Collins 6.00 15.00
167 Jonathan Isaac 6.00 15.00
168 Khem Birch 6.00 15.00
169 Lauri Markkanen 40.00 100.00
170 Semi Ojeleye 3.00 8.00
171 Markelle Fultz 6.00 15.00
172 Wesley Iwundu 2.50 6.00
173 D.J. Wilson 2.50 6.00
174 Guerschon Yabusele 2.50 6.00
175 Frank Ntilikina 3.00 8.00

2017-18 Panini Gold Standard AU

*AU: .5X TO 1.2X BASIC
STATED PRINT RUN 49 SER.#'d SETS

2016-17 Panini Grand Reserve

COMP.SET w/o AU's (100) 40.00 100.00
101-140 PRINT 99 SER.#'d SETS
EXCHANGE DEADLIN 1/19/2019
1 Ben Simmons RC 4.00 10.00
2 Joel Embiid 1.50 4.00
3 Giannis Antetokounmpo 3.00 8.00
4 Jabari Parker .40 1.00
5 Khris Middleton .60 1.50
6 Jimmy Butler 1.25 3.00
7 Dwyane Wade 1.25 3.00
8 Cameron Payne .60 1.50
9 LeBron James 5.00 12.00
10 Kyrie Irving 1.25 3.00
11 Kevin Love .60 1.50
12 Isaiah Thomas .50 1.25
13 Al Horford .60 1.50
14 Marcus Smart .75 2.00
15 Chris Paul 1.00 2.50
16 Blake Griffin .60 1.50
17 DeAndre Jordan .50 1.25
18 Marc Gasol .60 1.50
19 Mike Conley .50 1.25
20 Zach Randolph .60 1.50
21 Malcolm Delaney .40 1.00
22 Dennis Schroder .60 1.50
23 Paul Millsap .50 1.25
24 Goran Dragic .60 1.50
25 Hassan Whiteside .50 1.25
26 James Johnson .40 1.00
27 Kemba Walker .50 1.25
28 Michael Kidd-Gilchrist .40 1.00
29 Nicolas Batum .50 1.25
30 Gordon Hayward .60 1.50
31 Rudy Gobert .75 2.00
32 George Hill .50 1.25
33 Darren Collison .40 1.00
34 Willie Cauley-Stein .50 1.25
35 Ben McLemore .40 1.00
36 Carmelo Anthony 1.00 2.50
37 Kristaps Porzingis 1.00 2.50
38 Derrick Rose 1.00 2.50
39 D'Angelo Russell .75 2.00
40 Julius Randle .75 2.00
41 Jordan Clarkson .60 1.50
42 Elfrid Payton .50 1.25
43 Aaron Gordon .60 1.50
44 Nikola Vucevic .60 1.50
45 Yogi Ferrell RC 1.50 4.00
46 Dirk Nowitzki 1.50 4.00
47 Harrison Barnes .50 1.25
48 Jeremy Lin 1.25 3.00
49 Brook Lopez .50 1.25
50 Sean Kilpatrick .40 1.00
51 Kenneth Faried .50 1.25
52 Emmanuel Mudiay .40 1.00
53 Danilo Gallinari .40 1.00
54 Paul George 1.00 2.50
55 Jeff Teague .60 1.50
56 Myles Turner .60 1.50
57 Anthony Davis 2.00 5.00
58 DeMarcus Cousins .75 2.00
59 Jrue Holiday .50 1.25
60 Reggie Jackson .50 1.25
61 Kentavious Caldwell-Pope .50 1.25
62 Andre Drummond .60 1.50
63 Kyle Lowry .60 1.50
64 DeMar DeRozan .75 2.00
65 Serge Ibaka .60 1.50
66 James Harden 1.25 3.00
67 Eric Gordon .40 1.00
68 Ryan Anderson .40 1.00
69 Tony Parker 1.00 2.50
70 LaMarcus Aldridge .60 1.50
71 Kawhi Leonard 1.50 4.00
72 Devin Booker 2.50 6.00
73 Tyson Chandler .50 1.25
74 Eric Bledsoe .50 1.25
75 Russell Westbrook 1.00 2.50
76 Doug McDermott .50 1.25
77 Victor Oladipo .75 2.00
78 Andrew Wiggins .50 1.25
79 Karl-Anthony Towns 1.25 3.00
80 Ricky Rubio .50 1.25
81 Damian Lillard 1.50 4.00
82 C.J. McCollum .60 1.50
83 Jusuf Nurkic .50 1.25
84 Stephen Curry 5.00 12.00
85 Kevin Durant 2.50 6.00
86 Draymond Green .75 2.00
87 Klay Thompson 1.50 4.00
88 John Wall .75 2.00
89 Markieff Morris .40 1.00
90 Otto Porter .50 1.25
91 Bradley Beal .75 2.00
92 Robert Covington .50 1.25
93 Kyle Korver .50 1.25
94 Steven Adams .40 1.00
95 Wesley Matthews .40 1.00
96 Gary Harris .50 1.25
97 Jamal Crawford .60 1.50
98 Jae Crowder .40 1.00
99 DeMarre Carroll .40 1.00
100 Andre Iguodala .60 1.50
101 Ingram JSY AU/99 RC 30.00 80.00
102 Dunn JSY AU/99 RC 6.00 15.00
103 Hield JSY AU/99 RC 12.00 30.00
104 Murray JSY AU/99 RC 150.00 400.00
105 Brown JSY AU/99 RC 125.00 300.00
107 Kay Felder JSY AU/99 RC 4.00 10.00
108 Stephen Zimmerman JSY AU/99 RC 4.00 10.00
109 Labissiere JSY AU/99 RC 4.00 10.00
110 Richardson JSY AU/99 RC 4.00 10.00
111 Chriss JSY AU/99 RC 5.00 12.00
112 J.Hrnngmz JSY AU/99 RC 6.00 15.00
113 Sabonis JSY AU/99 RC 25.00 60.00
114 Brogdon JSY AU/99 RC 15.00 40.00
115 Zipser JSY AU/99 RC 4.00 10.00
116 Pascal Siakam JSY AU/99 RC 12.00 30.00
117 W.Hrnngmz JSY AU/99 RC 5.00 12.00
118 Caris LeVert JSY AU/99 RC 10.00 25.00
119 Brice Johnson JSY AU/99 RC 4.00 10.00
120 Maker JSY AU/99 RC 5.00 12.00
121 Plumlee JSY AU/99 RC 4.00 10.00
122 Jakob Poeltl JSY AU/99 RC 8.00 20.00
123 Jake Layman JSY AU/99 RC 5.00 12.00
124 McCaw JSY AU/99 RC 4.00 10.00
125 Demetrius Jackson JSY AU/99 RC 4.00 10.00
126 Wade Baldwin IV JSY AU/99 RC 4.00 10.00
127 Niang JSY AU/99 RC 6.00 15.00
128 Kuzminskas JSY AU/99 RC 4.00 10.00
129 Isaiah Whitehead JSY AU/99 RC 4.00 10.00
130 Damian Jones JSY AU/99 RC 4.00 10.00
131 Valentine JSY AU/99 RC 4.00 10.00
132 A.J. Hammons JSY AU/99 RC 4.00 10.00
133 Lwwu-Cbrrt JSY AU/99 RC 6.00 15.00
134 Saric JSY AU/99 RC 6.00 15.00
135 Deyonta Davis JSY AU/99 RC 4.00 10.00
136 Zubac JSY AU/99 RC 10.00 25.00
137 Malik Beasley JSY AU/99 RC 8.00 20.00
138 Ulis JSY AU/99 RC 5.00 12.00
139 Cheick Diallo JSY AU/99 RC 4.00 10.00
140 Henry Ellenson JSY AU/99 RC 4.00 10.00

2016-17 Panini Grand Reserve Vintage

*VNTGE: 2.5X TO 6X BASIC
*VNTGE RC: 2X TO 5X BASIC RC
1 Ben Simmons 20.00 50.00
9 LeBron James 20.00 50.00
84 Stephen Curry 20.00 50.00

2016-17 Panini Grand Reserve All Systems Go

1 Tony Parker 8.00 20.00
2 Mike Conley 4.00 10.00
3 Kyrie Irving 10.00 25.00
4 Isaiah Thomas 4.00 10.00
5 John Wall 6.00 15.00
6 Stephen Curry 25.00 60.00
7 Darren Collison 3.00 8.00
8 D'Angelo Russell 6.00 15.00
9 George Hill 4.00 10.00
10 Emmanuel Mudiay 3.00 8.00
11 Goran Dragic 5.00 12.00
12 Devin Booker 12.00 30.00
13 T.J. McConnell 4.00 10.00
14 Dennis Schroder 5.00 12.00
15 Jimmy Butler 10.00 25.00

2016-17 Panini Grand Reserve Closing Statements

1 Kobe Bryant 120.00 300.00
2 Wilt Chamberlain 50.00 120.00
3 Bill Russell 50.00 120.00
4 Larry Bird 60.00 150.00
5 David Robinson 30.00 80.00

2016-17 Panini Grand Reserve Cornerstones Quad Jersey Autographs

PRINT RUNS B/WN 35-99 COPIES PER
EXCHANGE DEADLINE 1/19/2019
*QRTZ/30-49: .5X TO 1.2X p/r 75-99
*QRTZ/30-49: .4X TO 1X p/r 35-49
*QRTZ/25: .75X TO 2X p/r 75-99
*QRTZ/25: .6X TO 1.5X p/r 35-49
*GRNTE/20-25: .75X TO 2X p/r 75-99
*GRNTE/20-25: .6X TO 1.5X p/r 35-49
2 Myles Turner/99 6.00 15.00
3 Kristaps Porzingis/35 30.00 80.00
4 Karl-Anthony Towns/35 40.00 100.00
5 Clint Capela/99 10.00 25.00
6 Matthew Dellavedova/99 5.00 12.00
7 Devin Booker/75 200.00 500.00
8 Udonis Haslem/99 5.00 12.00
9 J.J. Barea/99 15.00 40.00
10 Elfrid Payton/75 5.00 12.00
11 Bobby Portis/99 6.00 15.00
12 Jimmy Butler/35 20.00 50.00
14 George Hill/99 5.00 12.00
15 Evan Turner/99 5.00 12.00
16 Kevin Durant/35 100.00 250.00
17 Kyrie Irving/35 40.00 100.00
18 John Wall/35 10.00 25.00
19 Tony Parker/35 15.00 40.00
20 Kenneth Faried/75 5.00 12.00
21 Evan Fournier/99 5.00 12.00
22 Goran Dragic/75 6.00 15.00
23 Eric Gordon/75 5.00 12.00
24 Michael Kidd-Gilchrist/99 4.00 10.00
25 Ryan Anderson/99 4.00 10.00
26 Carmelo Anthony/35 20.00 50.00
27 Dwyane Wade/35 25.00 60.00
28 Chris Paul/35 50.00 120.00
29 D'Angelo Russell/40 10.00 25.00
30 Anthony Davis/35 30.00 80.00
31 C.J. McCollum/35 20.00 50.00
32 Gordon Hayward/40 12.00 30.00
33 Zach LaVine/99 10.00 25.00
34 Jordan Clarkson/75 6.00 15.00
35 Luol Deng/99 5.00 12.00
36 Justin Anderson/99 4.00 10.00
37 Nikola Mirotic/75 4.00 10.00
38 Jeremy Lin/35 30.00 80.00
39 Isaiah Thomas/49 6.00 15.00
40 Jrue Holiday/35 10.00 25.00

2016-17 Panini Grand Reserve Difference Makers Autographs

PRINT RUNS B/WN 10-99 COPIES PER
NO PRICING ON QTY 10
EXCHANGE DEADLINE 1/19/2019
2 Joe Dumars/75 5.00 12.00
3 Kareem Abdul-Jabbar/25 40.00 100.00
4 James Worthy/35 10.00 25.00
5 Troy Daniels/99 3.00 8.00
7 Isaiah Thomas/75 8.00 20.00
8 Tony Parker/35 25.00 60.00
10 Anthony Davis/25 25.00 60.00
11 Chris Paul/25 50.00 120.00
12 Carmelo Anthony/25 12.00 30.00
13 Dwyane Wade/25 30.00 80.00
15 Kevin Durant/35 75.00 200.00
16 Andrew Wiggins/35 20.00 50.00
17 Karl-Anthony Towns/35 40.00 100.00
18 Alex English/99 4.00 10.00
19 Hakeem Olajuwon/35 15.00 40.00
20 Walt Frazier/75 8.00 20.00
21 Bob Lanier/75 6.00 15.00
22 Oscar Robertson/35 30.00 80.00
23 George Gervin/75 6.00 15.00
24 David Robinson/35 20.00 50.00
25 Cedric Maxwell/99 4.00 10.00
26 Tim Hardaway/99 6.00 15.00
27 Glen Rice/99 5.00 12.00
29 Latrell Sprewell/75 12.00 30.00
30 Yao Ming/35 60.00 150.00
31 Arvydas Sabonis/99 10.00 25.00
33 Justise Winslow/75 5.00 12.00
36 John Wall/35 20.00 50.00
38 Devin Booker/75 100.00 250.00
39 Clint Capela/99 4.00 10.00
40 Elfrid Payton/75 4.00 10.00
41 Tristan Thompson/75 4.00 10.00
44 Matthew Dellavedova/99 4.00 10.00
45 Nikola Mirotic/75 3.00 8.00
46 Vince Carter/35 20.00 50.00
47 Evan Fournier/99 4.00 10.00
50 Frank Ramsey/75 10.00 25.00

2016-17 Panini Grand Reserve Dominating Performances

1 John Wall 1.50 4.00
2 Jimmy Butler 2.50 6.00
3 Kevin Durant 5.00 12.00
4 Kevin Love 1.25 3.00
5 Klay Thompson 3.00 8.00
6 James Harden 2.50 6.00
7 Anthony Davis 4.00 10.00
8 Russell Westbrook 2.00 5.00
9 Isaiah Thomas 1.00 2.50
10 Andrew Wiggins 1.50 4.00
11 Stephen Curry 10.00 25.00
12 Rudy Gobert 1.50 4.00
13 DeAndre Jordan 1.00 2.50
14 Russell Westbrook 2.00 5.00
15 LeBron James 10.00 25.00
16 Giannis Antetokounmpo 6.00 15.00
17 Damian Lillard 3.00 8.00
18 Kyrie Irving 2.50 6.00
19 Anthony Davis 4.00 10.00
20 Andre Drummond 1.25 3.00
21 Kevin Love 1.25 3.00
22 John Stockton 2.00 5.00
23 Draymond Green 1.50 4.00
24 Eric Bledsoe 1.00 2.50
25 Malcolm Brogdon 2.50 6.00
26 Stephen Curry 10.00 25.00
27 Dion Waiters .75 2.00
28 Carmelo Anthony 2.00 5.00
29 DeMar DeRozan 1.50 4.00
30 Kyrie Irving 2.50 6.00
31 David Thompson 1.50 4.00
32 Pete Maravich 5.00 12.00
33 Glen Rice 1.25 3.00
34 Gary Payton 2.00 5.00
35 Tim Duncan 2.50 6.00
36 Magic Johnson 5.00 12.00
37 Dennis Rodman 2.50 6.00
38 Shaquille O'Neal 4.00 10.00
39 John Havlicek 3.00 8.00
40 Damon Stoudamire 1.25 3.00
41 Wilt Chamberlain 4.00 10.00
42 Steve Nash 2.00 5.00
43 Shawn Marion 1.00 2.50
44 Vince Carter 2.50 6.00
45 Allen Iverson 2.50 6.00
46 David Robinson 2.50 6.00
47 Larry Bird 5.00 12.00
48 Dominique Wilkins 1.50 4.00
49 Karl Malone 2.00 5.00
50 Hakeem Olajuwon 2.50 6.00

2016-17 Panini Grand Reserve Grand Autographs

PRINT RUNS B/WN 35-99 COPIES PER
EXCHANGE DEADLINE 1/19/2019
*GRNTE/25: .6X TO 1.5X p/r 99
*GRNTE/25: .5X TO 1.2X p/r 35-49
1 Buddy Hield/35 12.00 30.00
2 Denzel Valentine/49 4.00 10.00
3 Eric Gordon/49 5.00 12.00
4 Juan Hernangomez/49 15.00 40.00
6 Tim Hardaway Jr./99 4.00 10.00
7 Zydrunas Ilgauskas/99 4.00 10.00
8 Frank Ramsey/49 12.00 30.00
9 Kyle Wiltjer/99 3.00 8.00
10 C.J. McCollum/35 12.00 30.00
11 Glen Rice/49 6.00 15.00
12 Allan Houston/99 4.00 10.00
13 DeMarre Carroll/99 3.00 8.00
14 Doug McDermott/99 3.00 8.00
15 Larry Nance/99 4.00 10.00
16 Jason Terry/49 5.00 12.00
17 Trey Lyles/99 4.00 10.00
18 Walter Berry/99 3.00 8.00
19 Gordon Hayward/49 8.00 20.00
20 Alec Burks/99 4.00 10.00
21 Ron Harper/99 5.00 12.00
22 Victor Oladipo/35 5.00 12.00
23 Kenny "Sky" Walker/99 5.00 12.00
24 Dennis Schroder/99 5.00 12.00
25 Dennis Scott/99 3.00 8.00
26 John Starks/99 5.00 12.00
27 Dan Issel/99 6.00 15.00
28 Will Barton/99 3.00 8.00
29 Georgios Papagiannis/49 4.00 10.00
30 Cedric Ceballos/99 3.00 8.00
31 Semaj Christon/99 3.00 8.00
32 Brandon Ingram/35 60.00 150.00
33 Taurean Prince/99 4.00 10.00
34 Cody Zeller/35 4.00 10.00
35 DeAndre' Bembry/99 5.00 12.00
36 Rondae Hollis-Jefferson/99 3.00 8.00
37 Rodney McGruder/99 4.00 10.00
38 Malcolm Delaney/99 3.00 8.00
39 Larry Nance Jr./99 3.00 8.00
40 Dan Majerle/99 5.00 12.00

2016-17 Panini Grand Reserve Hickory Memorabilia

STATED PRINT RUN 39 SER.#'d SETS
1 Monta Ellis 12.00 30.00
2 Myles Turner 15.00 40.00
3 Paul George 25.00 60.00
4 Glenn Robinson III 10.00 25.00
5 C.J. Miles 10.00 25.00

2016-17 Panini Grand Reserve Highly Revered Autographs

PRINT RUNS B/WN 25-99 COPIES PER
EXCHANGE DEADLINE 1/19/2019
1 Karl-Anthony Towns/35 40.00 100.00
2 Myles Turner/99 5.00 12.00
3 John Wall/35 20.00 50.00
5 Devin Booker/60 200.00 500.00
6 Michael Kidd-Gilchrist/99 3.00 8.00
7 Tristan Thompson/99 4.00 10.00
8 Kevin Durant/25 75.00 200.00
10 Nikola Mirotic/99 3.00 8.00
11 Oscar Robertson/35 30.00 80.00
12 Bill Walton/99 25.00 60.00
13 Kareem Abdul-Jabbar/35 30.00 80.00
14 Gail Goodrich/99 5.00 12.00
15 Hakeem Olajuwon/35 15.00 40.00
16 Magic Johnson/25 30.00 80.00
17 Larry Bird/25 50.00 120.00
18 Adrian Dantley/99 5.00 12.00
19 James Worthy/49 10.00 25.00
20 Nate Archibald/99 5.00 12.00
21 Arvydas Sabonis/99 10.00 25.00
22 Walt Frazier/60 8.00 20.00
23 Rick Barry/35 8.00 20.00
24 Dave Cowens/99 8.00 20.00

2016-17 Panini Grand Reserve Legendary Cornerstones Quad Jersey Autographs

PRINT RUNS B/WN 34-99 COPIES PER
EXCHANGE DEADLINE 1/19/2019
*GRANITE/23-25: .75X TO 2X BASIC
1 Kareem Abdul-Jabbar/35 50.00 120.00
2 David Robinson/35 20.00 50.00
4 Dan Issel/99 8.00 20.00
5 Grant Hill/35 20.00 50.00
6 Bernard King/60 8.00 20.00
7 Louie Dampier/49 5.00 12.00
8 Gary Payton/35 12.00 30.00
9 Arvydas Sabonis/99 10.00 25.00
10 Robert Horry/34 10.00 25.00
11 Vlade Divac/99 6.00 15.00
12 Mark Aguirre/99 5.00 12.00
14 Tim Hardaway/99 10.00 25.00
15 Glen Rice/99 8.00 20.00
17 Jason Kidd/35 20.00 50.00
19 Hakeem Olajuwon/35 20.00 50.00
20 Alex English/99 6.00 15.00

2016-17 Panini Grand Reserve Local Legends Autographs

STATED PRINT RUN 25 SER.#'d SETS
EXCHANGE DEADLINE 1/19/2019
1 Larry Bird 50.00 120.00
2 Oscar Robertson 40.00 100.00
3 Allen Iverson 50.00 120.00
4 Magic Johnson 30.00 80.00
5 Kobe Bryant 500.00 1,000.00
6 Kevin Durant 75.00 200.00
7 Stephen Curry 400.00 800.00
8 Anthony Davis 25.00 60.00
9 John Wall 25.00 60.00
10 Paul George 15.00 40.00

2016-17 Panini Grand Reserve Reserve Materials

STATED PRINT RUN 35 SER.#'d SETS
*GRANITE/25: .75X TO 2X BASIC
1 Thabo Sefolosha 2.00 5.00
2 Dwight Howard 4.00 10.00
3 Amir Johnson 2.00 5.00
4 James Young 2.00 5.00
5 Kelly Olynyk 2.00 5.00
6 Rondae Hollis-Jefferson 2.00 5.00
7 LeBron James 20.00 50.00
8 Stephen Curry 20.00 50.00
9 Kevin Durant 12.00 30.00
10 Russell Westbrook 6.00 15.00
11 James Harden 6.00 15.00
12 Jeremy Lamb 2.00 5.00
13 Giannis Antetokounmpo 15.00 40.00
14 Nicolas Batum 2.50 6.00
15 Kemba Walker 2.50 6.00
16 Nikola Mirotic 2.00 5.00
17 Dirk Nowitzki 8.00 20.00
18 Devin Harris 2.00 5.00
19 Wesley Matthews 2.00 5.00
20 Danilo Gallinari 2.50 6.00
21 Jameer Nelson 2.00 5.00
22 Jusuf Nurkic 2.50 6.00
23 Nikola Jokic 15.00 40.00
24 Rudy Gay 3.00 8.00
25 Cory Joseph 2.00 5.00
26 Kyle Lowry 3.00 8.00
27 Bradley Beal 4.00 10.00
28 John Wall 4.00 10.00
29 Trey Burke 2.00 5.00
30 DeMarcus Cousins 2.50 6.00
31 Joakim Noah 2.00 5.00
32 Derrick Rose 5.00 12.00
33 Kristaps Porzingis 5.00 12.00
34 Carmelo Anthony 5.00 12.00
35 Al Horford 3.00 8.00
36 Jeff Teague 2.00 5.00
37 Omri Casspi 2.00 5.00
38 Manu Ginobili 6.00 15.00
39 Marcus Smart 4.00 10.00
40 Harrison Barnes 2.50 6.00
41 Jahlil Okafor 2.00 5.00
42 Kentavious Caldwell-Pope 2.50 6.00
43 Brook Lopez 2.50 6.00
44 Shaun Livingston 2.00 5.00
45 Tyreke Evans 2.50 6.00
46 Jabari Parker 2.00 5.00
47 Willie Cauley-Stein 2.50 6.00
48 Danny Ainge 3.00 8.00
49 Grant Hill 4.00 10.00
50 Patrick Ewing 4.00 10.00
51 Tim Duncan 6.00 15.00
52 David Robinson 6.00 15.00
53 Draymond Green 4.00 10.00
54 Shaquille O'Neal 10.00 25.00
55 Klay Thompson 8.00 20.00
56 DeMar DeRozan 4.00 10.00
57 Cody Zeller 2.00 5.00
58 Greg Monroe 2.00 5.00
59 Derrick Favors 2.00 5.00
60 Vince Carter 6.00 15.00
61 Domantas Sabonis 12.00 30.00
62 Patrick McCaw 2.00 5.00
63 Dejounte Murray 10.00 25.00
64 Jaylen Brown 5.00 12.00
65 Brandon Ingram 6.00 15.00
66 Willy Hernangomez 2.50 6.00
67 Tyler Ulis 2.50 6.00
68 Denzel Valentine 2.00 5.00
69 Wade Baldwin IV 2.00 5.00
70 Juan Hernangomez 4.00 10.00
71 Malcolm Brogdon 4.00 10.00
72 Mindaugas Kuzminskas 2.00 5.00
73 Kay Felder 2.00 5.00
74 Malik Beasley 4.00 10.00
75 Skal Labissiere 2.00 5.00

2016-17 Panini Grand Reserve Reserve Signatures

PRINT RUNS B/WN 25-75 COPIES PER
EXCHANGE DEADLINE 1/19/2019
*GRNTE/25: .6X TO 1.5X p/r 75-99
*GRNTE/25: .5X TO 1.2X p/r 35-49
*GRNTE/25: .4X TO 1X p/r 20-25
1 Kevin Durant/25 75.00 200.00
2 Anthony Davis/25 25.00 60.00
3 Karl-Anthony Towns/25 50.00 120.00
4 John Wall/25 25.00 60.00
6 Tony Parker/25 30.00 80.00
7 Paul George/20 15.00 40.00
8 Buddy Hield/49 10.00 25.00
9 Joel Embiid/49 60.00 150.00
10 Cody Zeller/99 3.00 8.00
11 C.J. McCollum/49 12.00 30.00
12 Zach LaVine/49 10.00 25.00
13 Noah Vonleh/99 3.00 8.00
14 Goran Dragic/35 6.00 15.00
15 George Hill/20 6.00 15.00
16 Michael Kidd-Gilchrist/20 5.00 12.00
17 Gary Harris/75 4.00 10.00
18 Jonas Valanciunas/99 4.00 10.00
19 Jrue Holiday/99 6.00 15.00
20 Tyus Jones/99 3.00 8.00
21 Myles Turner/99 5.00 12.00
22 Danny Green/99 4.00 10.00
23 Jared Dudley/99 3.00 8.00
24 Taurean Prince/99 4.00 10.00
25 Denzel Valentine/99 3.00 8.00
26 Trey Lyles/99 4.00 10.00
27 Nemanja Bjelica/99 3.00 8.00
28 Timofey Mozgov/99 3.00 8.00
29 Tim Hardaway Jr./99 4.00 10.00
30 Matthew Dellavedova/99 5.00 12.00
31 James Johnson/99 3.00 8.00
32 Donatas Motiejunas/99 3.00 8.00
33 Cameron Payne/99 5.00 12.00
34 E'Twaun Moore/99 3.00 8.00
35 Dwight Powell/99 3.00 8.00
36 Justin Holiday/99 4.00 10.00
37 Isaiah Canaan/99 3.00 8.00
38 Deyonta Davis/99 3.00 8.00
39 Brice Johnson/99 3.00 8.00
40 Tarik Black/99 3.00 8.00
41 Lucas Nogueira/99 3.00 8.00
43 Rodney McGruder/99 4.00 10.00
44 Malcolm Delaney/99 3.00 8.00
45 Joe Young/99 3.00 8.00
46 Jake Layman/99 4.00 10.00
47 Boban Marjanovic/99 4.00 10.00
48 Mike Muscala/99 5.00 12.00
49 Sean Kilpatrick/99 3.00 8.00
50 Chasson Randle/99 3.00 8.00

2016-17 Panini Grand Reserve Rookie Cornerstones Quad Jersey Autographs Granite

*GRANITE: .75X TO 2X BASIC
STATED PRINT RUN 25 SER.#'d SETS
EXCHANGE DEADLIN 1/19/2019
101 Brandon Ingram 125.00 300.00
116 Pascal Siakam 40.00 100.00

2016-17 Panini Grand Reserve Rookie Cornerstones Quad Jersey Autographs Quartz

*QUARTZ: .5X TO 1.2X BASIC
STATED PRINT RUN 49 SER.#'d SETS
EXCHANGE DEADLIN 1/19/2019

2016-17 Panini Grand Reserve Startups

1 Dennis Schroder 1.50 4.00
2 Isaiah Thomas 1.25 3.00
3 Malcolm Brogdon 3.00 8.00
4 Yogi Ferrell 1.25 3.00
5 Isaiah Whitehead 1.00 2.50
6 Victor Oladipo 1.25 3.00
7 Kay Felder 1.00 2.50
8 Jaylen Brown 8.00 20.00
9 C.J. McCollum 1.50 4.00
10 Ben McLemore 1.00 2.50
11 Andrew Wiggins 2.00 5.00
12 Jordan Clarkson 1.50 4.00
13 Dejounte Murray 5.00 12.00
14 Wade Baldwin IV 1.00 2.50
15 Tyler Johnson 1.00 2.50
16 Elfrid Payton 1.25 3.00
17 Doug McDermott 1.25 3.00
18 Giannis Antetokounmpo 8.00 20.00
19 Kemba Walker 1.25 3.00
20 Bradley Beal 2.00 5.00

2016-17 Panini Grand Reserve The Ascent Autographs

PRINT RUNS B/WN 25-75 COPIES PER
EXCHANGE DEADLINE 1/19/2019
1 Andrew Wiggins/75 15.00 40.00
4 Evan Fournier/75 4.00 10.00
5 Anthony Davis/25 25.00 60.00
6 Eric Bledsoe/75 4.00 10.00
8 Karl-Anthony Towns/35 40.00 100.00
9 Justise Winslow/75 5.00 12.00
11 Kristaps Porzingis/35 30.00 80.00
13 Myles Turner/75 5.00 12.00
14 Tyler Johnson/75 3.00 8.00
15 Allen Crabbe/75 3.00 8.00
18 Clint Capela/75 4.00 10.00
19 Tristan Thompson/75 4.00 10.00
21 Justin Anderson/75 3.00 8.00
22 Robert Covington/75 4.00 10.00
23 Nikola Mirotic/75 3.00 8.00
25 Matthew Dellavedova/75 5.00 12.00
26 John Wall/35 20.00 50.00
27 Kevin Durant/25 75.00 200.00
28 Kyrie Irving/25 30.00 80.00
29 Elfrid Payton/75 4.00 10.00
30 George Hill/75 4.00 10.00
31 Brandon Ingram/35 40.00 100.00
32 Kris Dunn/35 6.00 15.00
33 Jaylen Brown/35 125.00 300.00
34 Buddy Hield/35 12.00 30.00
35 Malcolm Delaney/75 3.00 8.00
36 Rodney McGruder/75 4.00 10.00
37 Kay Felder/75 3.00 8.00
38 Patrick McCaw/75 3.00 8.00
39 Tomas Satoransky/75 5.00 12.00
40 Paul Zipser/75 3.00 8.00
41 Domantas Sabonis/75 5.00 12.00
43 Ron Baker/75 3.00 8.00
44 Pascal Siakam/75 20.00 50.00
45 Willy Hernangomez/75 4.00 10.00
46 Dorian Finney-Smith/75 4.00 10.00
47 Thon Maker/75 4.00 10.00
49 Denzel Valentine/75 3.00 8.00
50 Malcolm Brogdon/75 10.00 25.00

2016-17 Panini Grand Reserve Unbreakable

1 James Harden 4.00 10.00
2 Russell Westbrook 3.00 8.00
3 DeMarcus Cousins 1.50 4.00
4 LeBron James 15.00 40.00
5 Giannis Antetokounmpo 10.00 25.00
6 Kevin Durant 8.00 20.00
7 Isaiah Thomas 1.50 4.00
8 Karl-Anthony Towns 4.00 10.00
9 John Wall 2.50 6.00
10 Dennis Schroder 2.00 5.00

2016-17 Panini Grand Reserve Upper Tier Signatures

PRINT RUNS B/WN 10-99 COPIES PER
NO PRICING ON QTY 10
EXCHANGE DEADLINE 1/19/2019
3 Magic Johnson/25 30.00 80.00
4 Larry Bird/25 50.00 120.00
5 Hakeem Olajuwon/25 20.00 50.00
6 Kareem Abdul-Jabbar/25 40.00 100.00
7 Alex English/99 4.00 10.00
8 George Gervin/99 6.00 15.00
9 Adrian Dantley/99 5.00 12.00
10 David Thompson/99 6.00 15.00
11 James Worthy/30 10.00 25.00
12 Nate Archibald/99 5.00 12.00
13 Bob Lanier/60 6.00 15.00
14 Damon Stoudamire/99 10.00 25.00
15 Mark Aguirre/99 4.00 10.00
16 Cedric Maxwell/99 4.00 10.00
17 Sidney Moncrief/99 4.00 10.00
18 Horace Grant/99 6.00 15.00
19 Bill Laimbeer/99 6.00 15.00
20 Glen Rice/99 5.00 12.00
21 Latrell Sprewell/99 12.00 30.00
22 Yao Ming/25 75.00 200.00
23 Grant Hill/30 20.00 50.00
24 Frank Ramsey/99 10.00 25.00
25 Spud Webb/99 5.00 12.00
26 Tim Hardaway/99 6.00 15.00
27 Louie Dampier/99 12.00 30.00
28 Arvydas Sabonis/99 10.00 25.00
29 Myles Turner/99 5.00 12.00
30 C.J. McCollum/60 10.00 25.00
31 John Wall/25 25.00 60.00
34 Devin Booker/99 100.00 250.00
35 Elfrid Payton/99 4.00 10.00
36 Zach Randolph/60 5.00 12.00
39 Kyrie Irving/25 30.00 80.00
40 Kevin Durant/25 100.00 250.00
41 Karl-Anthony Towns/25 50.00 120.00
42 Kristaps Porzingis/60 30.00 80.00
43 Carmelo Anthony/25 12.00 30.00
44 Chris Paul/25 40.00 100.00
45 Dwyane Wade/25 30.00 80.00

2015-16 Panini HV KB20 Unleash the Hero

COMPLETE SET (21) 12.00 30.00
COMMON CARD 2.50 6.00
ONE COMPLETE SET PER BOX

2015-16 Panini HV KB20 Unleash the Hero Black Mamba

*BLACK MAMBA: 20X TO 50X BASIC

2015-16 Panini HV KB20 Unleash the Hero Blue Larry O'Brien Trophy

*BLUE: 1X TO 2.5X BASIC

2015-16 Panini HV KB20 Unleash the Hero Gold 24

*GOLD: 1.2X TO 3X BASIC

2015-16 Panini HV KB20 Unleash the Hero Purple 8

*PURPLE: 1.2X TO 3X BASIC

2015-16 Panini HV KB20 Unleash the Hero Red MVP

*RED: 1X TO 2.5X BASIC

2015-16 Panini HV KB20 Channel the Villain

COMPLETE SET (21) 12.00 30.00
*VILLAIN: .4X TO 1X HERO
ONE COMPLETE SET PER BOX

2015-16 Panini HV KB20 Channel the Villain Black Mamba

*BLACK MAMBA: 20X TO 50X BASIC

2015-16 Panini HV KB20 Channel the Villain Blue Larry O'Brien Trophy

*BLUE: 1X TO 2.5X BASIC

2015-16 Panini HV KB20 Channel the Villain Gold 24

*GOLD: 1.2X TO 3X BASIC

2015-16 Panini HV KB20 Channel the Villain Purple 8

*PURPLE: 1.2X TO 3X BASIC

2015-16 Panini HV KB20 Channel the Villain Red MVP

*RED: 1X TO 2.5X BASIC

2019-20 Panini Illusions

COMPLETE SET (200)
*EMERALD: .6X TO 1.5X BASIC
*ORANGE: .6X TO 1.5X BASIC
*SAPPHIRE: .6X TO 1.5X BASIC
1 Hassan Whiteside .20 .50
2 Donovan Mitchell .60 1.50
3 Chris Paul .60 1.50
4 Devonte' Graham .25 .60
5 Kyle Kuzma .40 1.00
6 Donte DiVincenzo .25 .60
7 De'Aaron Fox .50 1.25
8 John Collins .30 .75
9 Derrick Rose .60 1.50
10 Terrence Ross .30 .75
11 Lonzo Ball .30 .75
12 D'Angelo Russell .25 .60
13 Mitchell Robinson .30 .75
14 Kevin Huerter .30 .75
15 Kevin Love .30 .75
16 Devin Booker .07 .20
17 Malcolm Brogdon .25 .60
18 Kelly Oubre Jr. .25 .60
19 Eric Bledsoe .25 .60
20 LeBron James 2.50 6.00
21 Brook Lopez .25 .60
22 Andrew Wiggins .40 1.00
23 Dennis Schroder .25 .60
24 Montrezl Harrell .25 .60
25 Julius Randle .40 1.00
26 Giannis Antetokounmpo 1.50 4.00
27 Myles Turner .30 .75
28 Thaddeus Young .20 .50
29 Domantas Sabonis .40 1.00
30 Danilo Gallinari .25 .60
31 Khris Middleton .30 .75
32 Cody Zeller .20 .50
33 Al Horford .30 .75
34 Josh Okogie .20 .50
35 James Harden .60 1.50
36 Jrue Holiday .40 1.00
37 P.J. Tucker .25 .60
38 Klay Thompson .75 2.00
39 Derrick Jones Jr. .20 .50
40 Nikola Vucevic .25 .60
41 Miles Bridges .30 .75
42 Josh Jackson .25 .60
43 Will Barton .20 .50
44 Draymond Green .40 1.00
45 Wendell Carter Jr. .30 .75
46 Frank Ntilikina .20 .50
47 Robert Covington .20 .50
48 Deandre Ayton .30 .75
49 Jonathan Isaac .30 .75
50 Spencer Dinwiddie .25 .60
51 Tobias Harris .25 .60
52 Paul George .50 1.25
53 CJ McCollum .30 .75
54 Anthony Davis .75 2.00
55 OG Anunoby .25 .60
56 Dejounte Murray .30 .75
57 T.J. Warren .25 .60
58 Kristaps Porzingis .40 1.00
59 Steven Adams .25 .60
60 Nikola Jokic 1.50 4.00
61 Lauri Markkanen .40 1.00
62 LaMarcus Aldridge .30 .75
63 Joel Embiid .60 1.50
64 Christian Wood .25 .60
65 Collin Sexton .40 1.00
66 Duncan Robinson .50 1.25
67 Marcus Morris Sr. .20 .50
68 Bruce Brown .30 .75
69 Anfernee Simons .50 1.25
70 Goran Dragic .25 .60
71 Ben Simmons .30 .75
72 Tristan Thompson .20 .50
73 Jonas Valanciunas .20 .50
74 Kevin Knox II .25 .60
75 Gary Harris .20 .50
76 Bogdan Bogdanovic .30 .75
77 Victor Oladipo .25 .60
78 Derrick Favors .20 .50
79 Andre Drummond .25 .60
80 Blake Griffin .30 .75
81 Dillon Brooks .25 .60
82 Danuel House Jr. .20 .50
83 Ricky Rubio .25 .60
84 Jake Layman .20 .50
85 John Wall .40 1.00
86 Gordon Hayward .25 .60
87 Marc Gasol .30 .75
88 Damian Lillard .75 2.00
89 Troy Brown Jr. .20 .50
90 Josh Richardson .20 .50
91 Pascal Siakam .50 1.25
92 Seth Curry .25 .60
93 Mike Conley .25 .60
94 Thomas Bryant .25 .60
95 Elfrid Payton .20 .50
96 Shai Gilgeous-Alexander 1.50 4.00
97 Buddy Hield .25 .60
98 Jayson Tatum 1.25 3.00
99 Terry Rozier .25 .60
100 Jaren Jackson Jr. .50 1.25
101 Brandon Ingram .30 .75
102 Kevin Durant 1.00 2.50
103 Danny Green .25 .60
104 Joe Ingles .25 .60
105 Otto Porter Jr. .20 .50
106 Fred VanVleet .40 1.00
107 Aaron Gordon .30 .75
108 Carmelo Anthony .50 1.25
109 Marvin Bagley III .25 .60
110 Russell Westbrook .50 1.25
111 Kemba Walker .25 .60
112 Bam Adebayo .50 1.25
113 Davis Bertans .20 .50
114 Malik Beasley .25 .60
115 Dorian Finney-Smith .25 .60
116 Jeff Teague .20 .50
117 Harry Giles III .20 .50
118 Vince Carter .60 1.50
119 DeMar DeRozan .40 1.00
120 Tim Hardaway Jr. .20 .50
121 Matthew Dellavedova .25 .60
122 Lonnie Walker IV .25 .60
123 Jamal Murray .50 1.25
124 Kevon Looney .20 .50
125 Kawhi Leonard .75 2.00
126 Bojan Bogdanovic .25 .60
127 Jae Crowder .20 .50
128 Marcus Smart .25 .60
129 Taurean Prince .20 .50
130 Aron Baynes .20 .50
131 Karl-Anthony Towns .50 1.25
132 Lou Williams .30 .75
133 JJ Redick .30 .75
134 Luka Doncic 2.00 5.00
135 Kyle Lowry .30 .75
136 Trae Young .75 2.00
137 Luke Kennard .25 .60
138 Rudy Gobert .40 1.00
139 Jimmy Butler .60 1.50
140 Bismack Biyombo .20 .50
141 Jaylen Brown .50 1.25
142 Michael Porter Jr. .50 1.25
143 Caris LeVert .25 .60
144 Patty Mills .30 .75
145 Kyrie Irving .60 1.50
146 Stephen Curry 2.50 6.00
147 Alex Caruso .30 .75
148 Markelle Fultz .25 .60
149 Zach LaVine .50 1.25
150 Bradley Beal .40 1.00
151 Zion Williamson RC 8.00 20.00
152 Carsen Edwards RC .50 1.25
153 Jarrett Culver RC .40 1.00
154 Jaylen Nowell RC .50 1.25
155 Cameron Johnson RC 1.00 2.50
156 Tremont Waters RC .50 1.25
157 Nickeil Alexander-Walker RC .60 1.50
158 Terence Davis RC .60 1.50
159 Grant Williams RC .60 1.50
160 Mfiondu Kabengele RC .50 1.25
161 Ja Morant RC 8.00 20.00
162 Bruno Fernando RC .50 1.25
163 Coby White RC 1.25 3.00
164 Bol Bol RC 1.00 2.50
165 PJ Washington Jr. RC 1.25 3.00
166 Kyle Guy RC .50 1.25
167 Goga Bitadze RC .60 1.50
168 Terance Mann RC .75 2.00
169 Darius Bazley RC .40 1.00
170 Jordan Poole RC 1.50 4.00
171 RJ Barrett RC 1.50 4.00
172 Cody Martin RC .60 1.50
173 Jaxson Hayes RC .60 1.50
174 Isaiah Roby RC .50 1.25
175 Tyler Herro RC 2.00 5.00
176 Kendrick Nunn RC .60 1.50
177 Luka Samanic RC .50 1.25
178 Daniel Gafford RC .75 2.00
179 Ty Jerome RC .75 2.00
180 Keldon Johnson RC 1.25 3.00
181 De'Andre Hunter RC 1.50 4.00
182 Eric Paschall RC .50 1.25
183 Rui Hachimura RC 1.50 4.00
184 Ignas Brazdeikis RC .50 1.25
185 Romeo Langford RC .75 2.00
186 Nicolo Melli RC .50 1.25
187 Matisse Thybulle RC .75 2.00
188 Ky Bowman RC .50 1.25
189 Nassir Little RC .60 1.50
190 Kevin Porter Jr. RC .75 2.00
191 Darius Garland RC 1.50 4.00
192 Admiral Schofield RC .50 1.25
193 Cam Reddish RC .60 1.50
194 Quinndary Weatherspoon RC .40 1.00
195 Sekou Doumbouya RC .40 1.00
196 Tacko Fall RC .50 1.25
197 Brandon Clarke RC .75 2.00
198 Naz Reid RC 1.50 4.00
199 Dylan Windler RC .50 1.25
200 KZ Okpala RC .50 1.25

2019-20 Panini Illusions Trophy Collection Black

PRINT RUN 49 SER.#'d SETS
20 LeBron James 40.00 100.00
26 Giannis Antetokounmpo 20.00 50.00
102 Kevin Durant 12.00 30.00
134 Luka Doncic 40.00 100.00
146 Stephen Curry 25.00 60.00
151 Zion Williamson 60.00 150.00
161 Ja Morant 75.00 200.00
175 Tyler Herro 20.00 50.00

2019-20 Panini Illusions Trophy Collection Blue

PRINT RUN 25 SER.#'d SETS
20 LeBron James 75.00 200.00
26 Giannis Antetokounmpo 30.00 80.00
102 Kevin Durant 20.00 50.00
134 Luka Doncic 75.00 200.00
146 Stephen Curry 40.00 100.00
151 Zion Williamson 100.00 250.00
161 Ja Morant 125.00 300.00
175 Tyler Herro 30.00 80.00

2019-20 Panini Illusions Trophy Collection Bronze

*BRONZE: .75X TO 2X BASIC
20 LeBron James 12.00 30.00
26 Giannis Antetokounmpo 6.00 15.00
102 Kevin Durant 6.00 15.00
134 Luka Doncic 12.00 30.00
136 Trae Young 6.00 15.00
151 Zion Williamson 30.00 80.00
161 Ja Morant 25.00 60.00

2019-20 Panini Illusions Trophy Collection Pink

*PINK: 1.25X TO 3X BASIC
20 LeBron James 30.00 80.00
26 Giannis Antetokounmpo 10.00 25.00
102 Kevin Durant 8.00 20.00
125 Kawhi Leonard 8.00 20.00
134 Luka Doncic 30.00 80.00
146 Stephen Curry 8.00 20.00
151 Zion Williamson 100.00 250.00
161 Ja Morant 75.00 200.00
175 Tyler Herro 50.00 120.00

2019-20 Panini Illusions Trophy Collection Red

*RED: 1.5X TO 4X BASIC
PRINT RUN 99 SER.#'d SETS
20 LeBron James 25.00 60.00
26 Giannis Antetokounmpo 15.00 40.00
102 Kevin Durant 10.00 25.00
134 Luka Doncic 25.00 60.00
146 Stephen Curry 20.00 50.00
151 Zion Williamson 40.00 100.00
161 Ja Morant 50.00 120.00
175 Tyler Herro 15.00 40.00

2019-20 Panini Illusions Trophy Collection Ruby

*RUBY: 1X TO 2.5X BASIC
PRINT RUN 199 SER.#'d SETS
20 LeBron James 15.00 40.00
26 Giannis Antetokounmpo 10.00 25.00
102 Kevin Durant 6.00 15.00
134 Luka Doncic 15.00 40.00
146 Stephen Curry 12.00 30.00
151 Zion Williamson 25.00 60.00
161 Ja Morant 25.00 60.00
175 Tyler Herro 8.00 20.00

2019-20 Panini Illusions Trophy Collection Starlight

*STARLIGHT: 1.5X TO 4X BASIC
20 LeBron James 30.00 80.00
26 Giannis Antetokounmpo 20.00 50.00
134 Luka Doncic 30.00 80.00
146 Stephen Curry 30.00 80.00
151 Zion Williamson 50.00 120.00
161 Ja Morant 60.00 150.00
175 Tyler Herro 12.00 30.00

2019-20 Panini Illusions Trophy Collection Teal

*TEAL: 1.25X TO 3X BASIC
PRINT RUN 125 SER.#'d SETS
20 LeBron James 20.00 50.00
26 Giannis Antetokounmpo 12.00 30.00
102 Kevin Durant 8.00 20.00
134 Luka Doncic 20.00 50.00
146 Stephen Curry 15.00 40.00
151 Zion Williamson 30.00 80.00
161 Ja Morant 40.00 100.00
175 Tyler Herro 12.00 30.00

2019-20 Panini Illusions Trophy Collection Yellow

*YELLOW: 1.25X TO 3X BASIC
PRINT RUN 149 SER.#'d SETS
20 LeBron James 20.00 50.00
26 Giannis Antetokounmpo 12.00 30.00
102 Kevin Durant 8.00 20.00
134 Luka Doncic 20.00 50.00
146 Stephen Curry 15.00 40.00
151 Zion Williamson 30.00 80.00
161 Ja Morant 30.00 80.00
175 Tyler Herro 10.00 25.00

2019-20 Panini Illusions Astounding

*EMERALD: .75X TO 2X BASIC
*ORANGE: .75X TO 2X BASIC
*SAPPHIRE: 1X TO 2.5X BASIC
1 Stephen Curry 4.00 10.00
2 Bradley Beal .60 1.50
3 James Harden 1.00 2.50
4 Zach LaVine .75 2.00
5 Kawhi Leonard 1.25 3.00
6 Donovan Mitchell 1.00 2.50
7 Joel Embiid 1.00 2.50
8 Ben Simmons .50 1.25
9 LeBron James 4.00 10.00
10 Kemba Walker .40 1.00
11 Jayson Tatum 2.00 5.00
12 Damian Lillard 1.25 3.00
13 Luka Doncic 3.00 8.00
14 Devin Booker .12 .30
15 Anthony Davis 1.25 3.00
16 CJ McCollum .50 1.25
17 Kyrie Irving 1.00 2.50
18 Russell Westbrook .75 2.00
19 Giannis Antetokounmpo 2.50 6.00
20 Trae Young 1.25 3.00

2019-20 Panini Illusions Astounding Pink

*PINK: 1.25X TO 3X BASIC
9 LeBron James 25.00 60.00
11 Jayson Tatum 10.00 25.00
13 Luka Doncic 25.00 60.00
15 Anthony Davis 8.00 20.00
19 Giannis Antetokounmpo 12.00 30.00
20 Trae Young 10.00 25.00

2019-20 Panini Illusions Career Lineage

*EMERALD: .75X TO 2X BASIC
1 James Harden 1.00 2.50
2 Kevin Garnett 1.25 3.00
3 Damian Lillard 1.25 3.00
4 David Robinson 1.00 2.50
5 Russell Westbrook .75 2.00
6 Tracy McGrady .75 2.00
7 Kemba Walker .40 1.00
8 Gary Payton .75 2.00
9 Tim Duncan 1.25 3.00
10 Dwyane Wade 1.00 2.50
11 Giannis Antetokounmpo 2.50 6.00
12 Charles Barkley 1.00 2.50
13 Stephen Curry 4.00 10.00
14 Paul Pierce .75 2.00
15 Chris Paul .75 2.00
16 Jason Kidd .75 2.00
17 Kawhi Leonard 1.25 3.00
18 Ray Allen .75 2.00
19 Shaquille O'Neal 2.00 5.00
20 Karl Malone 1.00 2.50
21 Anthony Davis 1.25 3.00
22 Steve Nash 1.00 2.50
23 LeBron James 4.00 10.00
24 Grant Hill .75 2.00
25 Dwight Howard .60 1.50

2019-20 Panini Illusions Career Lineage Orange

*ORANGE: 1.5X TO 4X BASIC
PRINT RUN 125 SER.#'d SETS
2 Kevin Garnett 8.00 20.00
9 Tim Duncan 8.00 20.00
12 Charles Barkley 8.00 20.00
19 Shaquille O'Neal 10.00 25.00
21 Anthony Davis 10.00 25.00
23 LeBron James 30.00 80.00

2019-20 Panini Illusions Career Lineage Pink

*PINK: 4X TO 10X BASIC
PRINT RUN 25 SER.#'d SETS
2 Kevin Garnett 20.00 50.00
9 Tim Duncan 20.00 50.00
12 Charles Barkley 20.00 50.00
19 Shaquille O'Neal 40.00 100.00
21 Anthony Davis 40.00 100.00
23 LeBron James 75.00 200.00

2019-20 Panini Illusions Career Lineage Sapphire

*SAPPHIRE: 1.25X TO 3X BASIC
PRINT RUN 199 SER.#'d SETS
12 Charles Barkley 6.00 15.00
23 LeBron James 25.00 60.00

2019-20 Panini Illusions Clear Shots

*EMERALD: .75X TO 2X BASIC
*ORANGE: .75X TO 2X BASIC
*SAPPHIRE: 1X TO 2.5X BASIC
1 LeBron James 4.00 10.00
2 CJ McCollum .50 1.25
3 Ray Allen .75 2.00
4 Kawhi Leonard 1.25 3.00
5 Trae Young 1.25 3.00
6 Bojan Bogdanovic .40 1.00
7 Bradley Beal .60 1.50
8 Devin Booker .12 .30
9 Stephen Curry 4.00 10.00
10 Luka Doncic 3.00 8.00
11 James Harden 1.00 2.50
12 Jayson Tatum 2.00 5.00
13 Steve Nash 1.00 2.50
14 Khris Middleton .50 1.25
15 Giannis Antetokounmpo 2.50 6.00
16 Brandon Ingram .50 1.25
17 Zach LaVine .75 2.00
18 Donovan Mitchell 1.00 2.50
19 Damian Lillard 1.25 3.00
20 Russell Westbrook .75 2.00

2019-20 Panini Illusions Clear Shots Pink

*PINK: 1.25X TO 3X BASIC
1 LeBron James 25.00 60.00
5 Trae Young 10.00 25.00
10 Luka Doncic 25.00 60.00
12 Jayson Tatum 10.00 25.00
15 Giannis Antetokounmpo 12.00 30.00

2019-20 Panini Illusions Double Vision

1 Kyle Lowry
Pascal Siakam 2.50 6.00
2 Jayson Tatum
Kemba Walker 6.00 15.00
3 Ben Simmons
Joel Embiid 3.00 8.00
4 Kyrie Irving
Kevin Durant 10.00 25.00
5 Julius Randle
RJ Barrett 4.00 10.00
6 Nikola Jokic
Jamal Murray 6.00 15.00
7 Donovan Mitchell
Rudy Gobert 3.00 8.00
8 Chris Paul
Shai Gilgeous-Alexander 8.00 20.00
9 CJ McCollum
Damian Lillard 4.00 10.00
10 Karl-Anthony Towns
D'Angelo Russell 2.50 6.00
11 Giannis Antetokounmpo
Khris Middleton 10.00 25.00
12 Domantas Sabonis
Malcolm Brogdon 2.00 5.00
13 Coby White
Zach LaVine 3.00 8.00
14 Derrick Rose
Blake Griffin 3.00 8.00
15 Collin Sexton
Darius Garland 4.00 10.00
16 Anthony Davis
LeBron James 75.00 200.00
17 Paul George
Kawhi Leonard 4.00 10.00
18 De'Aaron Fox
Buddy Hield 2.50 6.00
19 Devin Booker
Deandre Ayton 1.50 4.00
20 Klay Thompson
Stephen Curry 12.00 30.00
21 Jimmy Butler
Bam Adebayo 5.00 12.00
22 Nikola Vucevic
Aaron Gordon 1.50 4.00
23 Rui Hachimura
Bradley Beal 4.00 10.00
24 Devonte' Graham
Terry Rozier 1.25 3.00
25 Trae Young
John Collins 4.00 10.00
26 Russell Westbrook
James Harden 3.00 8.00
27 Luka Doncic
Kristaps Porzingis 15.00 40.00
28 Jaren Jackson Jr.
Ja Morant 25.00 60.00
29 Zion Williamson
Brandon Ingram 40.00 100.00
30 DeMar DeRozan
LaMarcus Aldridge 2.00 5.00

2019-20 Panini Illusions Draft Night Signatures

STATED PRINT RUN 32 SER.#'d SETS
EXCHANGE DEADLINE 2/05/2022
3 Bol Bol 100.00 250.00
4 Quinndary Weatherspoon 8.00 20.00
5 Cam Reddish 12.00 30.00
6 Rui Hachimura 100.00 250.00
8 Terance Mann 40.00 100.00
10 Tyler Herro 150.00 400.00
11 Mfiondu Kabengele 10.00 25.00
12 Nicolas Claxton 15.00 40.00
13 Brandon Clarke 50.00 120.00
14 RJ Barrett 150.00 400.00
15 De'Andre Hunter 50.00 120.00
16 Coby White 150.00 400.00
20 Zion Williamson 3,000.00 6,000.00
21 Nassir Little 12.00 30.00
22 PJ Washington Jr. 75.00 200.00
23 Bruno Fernando 12.00 30.00
24 Romeo Langford 8.00 20.00
25 Goga Bitadze 25.00 60.00
27 Jordan Poole 25.00 60.00

2019-20 Panini Illusions Fantasy Matchups

1 Charles Barkley
Zion Williamson 25.00 60.00
2 Pete Maravich
Trae Young 12.00 30.00
3 Dwight Howard
Shawn Kemp 2.50 6.00
4 Magic Johnson
LeBron James 15.00 40.00
5 Donovan Mitchell
John Stockton 3.00 8.00
6 Kevin Garnett
Karl-Anthony Towns 6.00 15.00
7 Jayson Tatum
Paul Pierce 6.00 15.00
8 Kareem Abdul-Jabbar
Anthony Davis 8.00 20.00
9 Walt Frazier
RJ Barrett 4.00 10.00
10 Wilt Chamberlain
Joel Embiid 6.00 15.00

2019-20 Panini Illusions First Impressions Jersey Autographs

1 Zion Williamson 400.00 800.00
2 Rui Hachimura 40.00 100.00
3 Ja Morant 400.00 800.00
4 RJ Barrett 75.00 200.00
5 De'Andre Hunter 20.00 50.00
6 Jarrett Culver 5.00 12.00
7 Cam Reddish 8.00 20.00
8 Coby White 75.00 200.00
10 Cameron Johnson 12.00 30.00
11 PJ Washington Jr. 15.00 40.00
12 Tyler Herro 150.00 400.00
13 Romeo Langford 5.00 12.00
14 Matisse Thybulle 10.00 25.00
15 Nassir Little 8.00 20.00
16 Brandon Clarke 10.00 25.00
17 Sekou Doumbouya 5.00 12.00
18 Darius Bazley 5.00 12.00
19 Chuma Okeke 8.00 20.00
20 Nickeil Alexander-Walker 8.00 20.00
21 Keldon Johnson 15.00 40.00
22 Carsen Edwards 6.00 15.00
23 Grant Williams 8.00 20.00
24 Bruno Fernando 6.00 15.00
25 Nicolo Melli 6.00 15.00
26 Kevin Porter Jr. 10.00 25.00
27 KZ Okpala 6.00 15.00
28 Mfiondu Kabengele 6.00 15.00
29 Eric Paschall 6.00 15.00
30 Kyle Guy 6.00 15.00
31 Isaiah Roby 6.00 15.00
32 Cody Martin 8.00 20.00
33 Quinndary Weatherspoon 5.00 12.00

2019-20 Panini Illusions Illumination

1 Joel Embiid 3.00 8.00
2 Nikola Jokic 8.00 20.00
3 Kemba Walker 1.25 3.00
4 Carmelo Anthony 2.50 6.00
5 Luka Doncic 25.00 60.00
6 CJ McCollum 1.50 4.00
7 Stephen Curry 10.00 25.00
8 Giannis Antetokounmpo 10.00 25.00
9 Zach LaVine 2.50 6.00
10 Nikola Vucevic 1.25 3.00
11 Ben Simmons 1.50 4.00
12 Jamal Murray 2.50 6.00
13 Jayson Tatum 10.00 25.00
14 Brandon Ingram 1.50 4.00
15 Devin Booker .40 1.00
16 Kyrie Irving 3.00 8.00
17 Bradley Beal 2.00 5.00
18 Trae Young 10.00 25.00
19 Kawhi Leonard 10.00 25.00
20 D'Angelo Russell 1.25 3.00
21 LeBron James 25.00 60.00
22 De'Aaron Fox 2.50 6.00
23 Damian Lillard 8.00 20.00
24 DeMar DeRozan 2.00 5.00
25 Anthony Davis 10.00 25.00
26 Russell Westbrook 2.50 6.00
27 James Harden 8.00 20.00
28 Chris Paul 3.00 8.00
29 Donovan Mitchell 3.00 8.00
30 Karl-Anthony Towns 2.50 6.00

2019-20 Panini Illusions Instant Impact

1 Zion Williamson 5.00 12.00
2 Sekou Doumbouya .60 1.50
3 Nassir Little 1.00 2.50
4 De'Andre Hunter 2.50 6.00
5 Cam Reddish 1.00 2.50
6 Darius Bazley .60 1.50
7 Ja Morant 6.00 15.00
8 Kendrick Nunn 1.00 2.50
9 Tyler Herro 3.00 8.00
10 Cameron Johnson 1.50 4.00
11 Matisse Thybulle 1.25 3.00
12 RJ Barrett 2.50 6.00
13 Darius Garland 2.50 6.00
14 Kevin Porter Jr. 1.25 3.00
15 Romeo Langford .60 1.50
16 PJ Washington Jr. 2.00 5.00
17 Brandon Clarke 1.25 3.00
18 Jarrett Culver .60 1.50
19 Nickeil Alexander-Walker 1.00 2.50
20 Tacko Fall .75 2.00
21 Eric Paschall .75 2.00
22 Grant Williams 1.00 2.50
23 Carsen Edwards .75 2.00
24 Rui Hachimura 2.50 6.00
25 Goga Bitadze 1.00 2.50

2019-20 Panini Illusions Instant Impact Sapphire

STATED PRINT RUN 199 COPIES PER

2019-20 Panini Illusions Living Legends

*EMERALD: .4X TO 1X BASIC
*ORANGE: .6X TO 1.5X BASIC
*PINK: 1.25X TO 3X BASIC
*SAPPHIRE: .6X TO 1.5X BASIC
1 Scottie Pippen 1.50 4.00
2 Larry Bird 2.50 6.00
3 Chris Webber .75 2.00
4 Julius Erving 1.50 4.00
5 Kevin Garnett 1.50 4.00
6 Charles Barkley 1.25 3.00
7 Oscar Robertson 1.50 4.00
8 Bill Russell 2.00 5.00
9 Tim Duncan 1.50 4.00
10 Karl Malone 1.25 3.00
11 Steve Nash 1.25 3.00
12 Magic Johnson 2.00 5.00
13 Yao Ming 1.50 4.00
14 John Stockton 1.25 3.00
15 Kareem Abdul-Jabbar 2.00 5.00
16 Shaquille O'Neal 2.50 6.00
17 Patrick Ewing 1.00 2.50
18 Allen Iverson 1.50 4.00
19 Tracy McGrady 1.00 2.50
20 Dwyane Wade 1.25 3.00

2019-20 Panini Illusions Mystique

*EMERALD: .5X TO 1.25X BASIC
*ORANGE: .5X TO 1.25X BASIC
*PINK: 1.25X TO 3X BASIC
*SAPPHIRE: .5X TO 1.25X BASIC
1 James Harden 3.00 8.00
2 Anthony Davis 4.00 10.00
3 Kawhi Leonard 4.00 10.00
4 Kyrie Irving 3.00 8.00
5 Joel Embiid 3.00 8.00
6 Giannis Antetokounmpo 8.00 20.00
7 LeBron James 12.00 30.00
8 Jayson Tatum 6.00 15.00
9 Stephen Curry 12.00 30.00
10 Luka Doncic 10.00 25.00
11 Zach LaVine 2.50 6.00
12 CJ McCollum 1.50 4.00
13 Donovan Mitchell 3.00 8.00
14 Russell Westbrook 2.50 6.00
15 Ben Simmons 1.50 4.00
16 Trae Young 4.00 10.00
17 Kemba Walker 1.25 3.00
18 Damian Lillard 4.00 10.00
19 Bradley Beal 2.00 5.00
20 Devin Booker .40 1.00

2019-20 Panini Illusions Rookie Reflections

*EMERALD: .5X TO 1.25X BASIC
1 Latrell Sprewell
RJ Barrett 2.50 6.00
2 Brandon Clarke
Shane Battier 1.25 3.00
3 Jarrett Culver
Paul George 1.50 4.00
4 Danilo Gallinari
Darius Bazley .75 2.00
5 Antawn Jamison
Rui Hachimura 2.50 6.00
6 Dwyane Wade
Kendrick Nunn 2.00 5.00
7 Blake Griffin
Sekou Doumbouya 1.00 2.50
8 Jrue Holiday
Nickeil Alexander-Walker 1.25 3.00
9 Zion Williamson
Charles Barkley 5.00 12.00
10 Luka Samanic
LaMarcus Aldridge 1.00 2.50
11 Dominique Wilkins
De'Andre Hunter 2.50 6.00
12 Grant Williams
Tobias Harris 1.00 2.50
13 Derrick Rose
Coby White 2.00 5.00
14 Clyde Drexler
Nassir Little 1.50 4.00
15 Cam Reddish
Vince Carter 2.00 5.00
16 Kevin Porter Jr.
DeMar DeRozan 1.25 3.00
17 Tyler Herro
Dwyane Wade 3.00 8.00
18 Goga Bitadze
Jermaine O'Neal 1.00 2.50
19 De'Aaron Fox
Ja Morant 6.00 15.00
20 Bruce Bowen
Matisse Thybulle 1.25 3.00
21 Darius Garland
Mark Price 2.50 6.00
22 Draymond Green
Eric Paschall 1.25 3.00
23 Anthony Davis
Jaxson Hayes 2.50 6.00
24 Manute Bol
Bol Bol 1.50 4.00
25 Larry Johnson
PJ Washington Jr. 2.00 5.00

2019-20 Panini Illusions Rookie Reflections Orange

*ORANGE: 1X TO 2.5X BASIC
PRINT RUN 125 SER.#'d SETS
9 Zion Williamson
Charles Barkley 30.00 80.00
19 De'Aaron Fox
Ja Morant 25.00 60.00

2019-20 Panini Illusions Rookie Reflections Pink

*PINK: 2X TO 5X BASIC
PRINT RUN 25 SER.#'d SETS
9 Zion Williamson
Charles Barkley 300.00 600.00
13 Derrick Rose
Coby White 30.00 80.00
17 Tyler Herro
Dwyane Wade 75.00 200.00
19 De'Aaron Fox
Ja Morant 150.00 400.00
24 Manute Bol
Bol Bol 20.00 50.00

2019-20 Panini Illusions Rookie Reflections Sapphire

*SAPPHIRE: .75X TO 2X BASIC
PRINT RUN 199 SER.#'d SETS
9 Zion Williamson
Charles Barkley 25.00 60.00
19 De'Aaron Fox
Ja Morant 20.00 50.00

2019-20 Panini Illusions Rookie Signs

EXCHANGE DEADLINE 2/05/2022
*EMERALD/25: .75X TO 2X BASIC
2 Zion Williamson 200.00 500.00
3 Dylan Windler 5.00 12.00
4 De'Andre Hunter 15.00 40.00
5 Kyle Guy 12.00 30.00
7 Miye Oni 4.00 10.00
9 Terance Mann 8.00 20.00
10 Nicolo Melli 5.00 12.00
12 Rui Hachimura 15.00 40.00
13 Alen Smailagic 4.00 10.00
14 Jarrett Culver 4.00 10.00
16 Cameron Johnson 10.00 25.00
17 Naz Reid 15.00 40.00
18 Brandon Clarke 8.00 20.00
20 Kendrick Nunn 6.00 15.00
22 Ja Morant 200.00 500.00
23 Daniel Gafford 8.00 20.00
24 Cam Reddish 6.00 15.00
26 PJ Washington Jr. 12.00 30.00
27 Amir Coffey 6.00 15.00
28 Sekou Doumbouya 4.00 10.00
29 Marial Shayok 4.00 10.00
31 Mfiondu Kabengele 5.00 12.00
32 RJ Barrett 15.00 40.00
33 Nicolas Claxton 8.00 20.00
34 Coby White 12.00 30.00
35 Jordan Bone 4.00 10.00
37 Brian Bowen II 4.00 10.00
38 Carsen Edwards 5.00 12.00
39 Terence Davis 6.00 15.00
40 Talen Horton-Tucker 6.00 15.00

2019-20 Panini Illusions Rookie Vision

1 Jordan Poole 5.00 12.00
2 Tyler Herro 25.00 60.00
3 Nickeil Alexander-Walker 2.00 5.00
4 Zion Williamson 75.00 200.00
5 Matisse Thybulle 2.50 6.00
6 Eric Paschall 1.50 4.00
7 Nassir Little 2.00 5.00
8 Darius Garland 5.00 12.00
9 Carsen Edwards 1.50 4.00
10 Cam Reddish 2.00 5.00
11 Admiral Schofield 1.50 4.00
12 Romeo Langford 1.25 3.00
13 Goga Bitadze 2.00 5.00
14 Ja Morant 60.00 150.00
15 Brandon Clarke 2.50 6.00
16 Kendrick Nunn 2.00 5.00
17 Keldon Johnson 4.00 10.00
18 Jarrett Culver 1.25 3.00
19 Bol Bol 8.00 20.00
20 Cameron Johnson 3.00 8.00
21 Tacko Fall 1.50 4.00
22 Sekou Doumbouya 1.25 3.00
23 Luka Samanic 1.50 4.00
24 RJ Barrett 15.00 40.00
25 Grant Williams 2.00 5.00
26 De'Andre Hunter 5.00 12.00
27 Kevin Porter Jr. 2.50 6.00
28 Rui Hachimura 5.00 12.00
29 Darius Bazley 1.25 3.00
30 PJ Washington Jr. 4.00 10.00

2019-20 Panini Illusions Season Highlights

*EMERALD: .6X TO 1.5X BASIC
1 Giannis Antetokounmpo 2.50 6.00
2 Anthony Davis 1.25 3.00
3 Caris LeVert .40 1.00
4 Buddy Hield .40 1.00
5 Zion Williamson 10.00 25.00
6 Bojan Bogdanovic .40 1.00
7 Anthony Davis 1.25 3.00
8 Kawhi Leonard 1.25 3.00
9 Damian Lillard 1.25 3.00
10 Jaylen Brown .75 2.00
11 Trae Young 1.25 3.00
12 Derrick Jones Jr. .30 .75
13 Khris Middleton .50 1.25
14 Miles Bridges .50 1.25
15 Jae Crowder .30 .75
16 Nemanja Bjelica .30 .75
17 Eric Gordon .40 1.00
18 Joel Embiid 1.00 2.50
19 James Harden 1.00 2.50
20 Giannis Antetokounmpo 2.50 6.00
21 Kyrie Irving 1.00 2.50
22 Bam Adebayo .75 2.00
23 Anthony Davis 1.25 3.00
24 Kawhi Leonard 1.25 3.00
25 Bojan Bogdanovic .40 1.00

2019-20 Panini Illusions Season Highlights Orange

*ORANGE: 1X TO 2.5X BASIC
PRINT RUN 125 SER.#'d SETS
5 Zion Williamson 50.00 120.00

2019-20 Panini Illusions Season Highlights Pink

*PINK: 2X TO 5X BASIC
PRINT RUN 25 SER.#'d SETS
5 Zion Williamson 75.00 200.00

2019-20 Panini Illusions Season Highlights Sapphire

*SAPPHIRE: .75X TO 2X BASIC
PRINT RUN 199 SER.#'d SETS
5 Zion Williamson 40.00 100.00

2019-20 Panini Illusions Shining Stars

*EMERALD: .6X TO 1.5X BASIC
*ORANGE: .6X TO 1.5X BASIC
*PINK: 1.25X TO 3X BASIC
*SAPPHIRE: .6X TO 1.5X BASIC
1 Kawhi Leonard 1.50 4.00
2 Ben Simmons .60 1.50
3 Joel Embiid 1.25 3.00
4 Kemba Walker .50 1.25
5 LeBron James 10.00 25.00
6 Bradley Beal .75 2.00
7 Stephen Curry 5.00 12.00
8 Zach LaVine 1.00 2.50
9 James Harden 1.25 3.00
10 Donovan Mitchell 1.25 3.00
11 Kyrie Irving 1.25 3.00
12 Trae Young 1.50 4.00
13 Giannis Antetokounmpo 3.00 8.00
14 Damian Lillard 1.50 4.00
15 Jayson Tatum 2.50 6.00
16 Devin Booker .15 .40
17 Luka Doncic 10.00 25.00
18 CJ McCollum .60 1.50
19 Anthony Davis 1.50 4.00
20 Russell Westbrook 1.00 2.50

2019-20 Panini Illusions Superlatives Signatures

EXCHANGE DEADLINE 2/05/2022
1 Damian Lillard 40.00 100.00
2 Devonte' Graham 10.00 25.00
3 Anthony Davis 40.00 100.00
4 Dave Bing 25.00 60.00
5 Oscar Robertson 30.00 80.00
6 Stephon Marbury 8.00 20.00
7 Charles Barkley 75.00 200.00
8 Nerlens Noel 4.00 10.00
9 Allen Iverson 50.00 120.00
10 Austin Rivers 4.00 10.00
11 Larry Bird 50.00 120.00
12 M.L. Carr 6.00 15.00
13 John Stockton 40.00 100.00
14 Brook Lopez 5.00 12.00
15 Hakeem Olajuwon 20.00 50.00
16 Eric Bledsoe 5.00 12.00
17 Stephen Curry 300.00 600.00
18 Shawn Kemp 15.00 40.00
19 Karl Malone 20.00 50.00
20 Luke Kennard 5.00 12.00
21 Magic Johnson 50.00 120.00
22 Anfernee Simons 10.00 25.00
23 Kevin Garnett 100.00 250.00
24 Derek Fisher 8.00 20.00
25 Trae Young 60.00 150.00
26 Bojan Marjanovic 6.00 15.00
27 Kevin Durant 75.00 200.00
28 Danuel House Jr. 4.00 10.00
29 Dwyane Wade 40.00 100.00
30 Robin Lopez 4.00 10.00
31 Julius Erving 40.00 100.00
32 Gheorghe Muresan 4.00 10.00
33 Kareem Abdul-Jabbar 40.00 100.00
34 Deron Williams 5.00 12.00
35 David Robinson 20.00 50.00
36 Larry Johnson 12.00 30.00
38 Gerald Henderson Sr. 4.00 10.00
40 Craig Ehlo 4.00 10.00

2019-20 Panini Illusions Trophy Collection Signatures

EXCHANGE DEADLINE 2/05/2022
*EMERALD: .75X TO 2X BASIC
1 Ron Harper 6.00 15.00
3 Kevin Willis 4.00 10.00
4 Dennis Rodman 25.00 60.00
5 Boris Diaw 5.00 12.00
6 Derek Fisher 6.00 15.00
7 Royce O'Neale 4.00 10.00
8 Ivica Zubac 5.00 12.00
9 E'Twaun Moore 4.00 10.00
10 Danny Granger 4.00 10.00
11 Austin Rivers 4.00 10.00
12 Stephen Curry 200.00 500.00
13 Matthew Dellavedova 5.00 12.00
14 Stephon Marbury 8.00 20.00
15 Drew Gooden 4.00 10.00
16 Larry Johnson 12.00 30.00
17 Mario Hezonja 4.00 10.00
18 Trevor Ariza 4.00 10.00
19 Ish Smith 4.00 10.00
20 Kevin Martin 4.00 10.00
21 Nate McMillan 5.00 12.00
23 Kelly Olynyk 4.00 10.00
24 Jerry Lucas 8.00 20.00
25 Kris Humphries 4.00 10.00
26 Allonzo Trier 4.00 10.00
27 Grayson Allen 6.00 15.00
28 Shawn Kemp 15.00 40.00
29 Vin Baker 5.00 12.00
30 Michael Kidd-Gilchrist 4.00 10.00
31 Derrick White 6.00 15.00
32 Magic Johnson 50.00 120.00
33 Delon Wright 4.00 10.00
34 Dave Bing 25.00 60.00
35 Rolando Blackman 5.00 12.00
36 David Lee 5.00 12.00
37 Dewayne Dedmon 4.00 10.00
38 Joe Harris 5.00 12.00
39 Kevin Huerter 6.00 15.00
40 Zach Collins 4.00 10.00
41 Derrick Coleman 5.00 12.00
42 Hakeem Olajuwon 20.00 50.00
43 Luke Kennard 5.00 12.00
44 Eric Bledsoe 5.00 12.00
45 Mason Plumlee 4.00 10.00
46 Deron Williams 5.00 12.00
47 Dwayne Bacon 4.00 10.00
48 Andrea Bargnani 4.00 10.00
49 Dale Ellis 5.00 12.00
50 Gerald Henderson Sr. 4.00 10.00
51 Mark Aguirre 5.00 12.00
52 Jerry West 25.00 60.00
53 Robin Lopez 4.00 10.00
54 Brook Lopez 5.00 12.00
55 Jakob Poeltl 4.00 10.00
56 Dana Barros 4.00 10.00
57 Moritz Wagner 4.00 10.00
58 Chris Kaman 4.00 10.00
59 Shake Milton 4.00 10.00
60 P.J. Tucker 5.00 12.00

2020-21 Panini Illusions

COMPLETE SET (200)
COMMON CARD (1-150) .20 .50
SEMISTARS .25 .60
UNLISTED STARS .30 .75
COMMON RC (151-200) .40 1.00
RC SEMIS .50 1.25
RC UNLISTED .60 1.50
*EMERALD: .5X TO 1.2X BASIC
*ORANGE: .6X TO 1.5X BASIC
*SAPPHIRE: .6X TO 1.5X BASIC
*BRONZE: .6X TO 1.5X BASIC
*PINK: .6X TO 1.5X BASIC
1 Ja Morant 1.00 2.50
2 Goran Dragic .30 .75
3 Serge Ibaka .25 .60
4 Bobby Portis .30 .75
5 Kemba Walker .30 .75
6 Keldon Johnson .50 1.25
7 Rui Hachimura .40 1.00
8 Josh Richardson .25 .60
9 Eric Gordon .25 .60
10 Trae Young .75 2.00
11 Julius Randle .30 .75
12 Rudy Gobert .40 1.00
13 Nikola Vucevic .30 .75
14 Kawhi Leonard .75 2.00
15 Norman Powell .25 .60
16 Jordan Clarkson .30 .75
17 Jamal Murray .50 1.25
18 Ricky Rubio .30 .75
19 Terrence Ross .25 .60
20 Devin Booker .75 2.00
21 Kelly Oubre Jr. .30 .75
22 Myles Turner .30 .75
23 Montrezl Harrell .30 .75
24 Aaron Gordon .30 .75
25 Lonzo Ball .40 1.00
26 Paul George .50 1.25
27 De'Andre Hunter .30 .75
28 Devonte' Graham .25 .60
29 Draymond Green .40 1.00
30 Eric Bledsoe .25 .60
31 Fred VanVleet .50 1.25
32 John Collins .30 .75
33 Tobias Harris .30 .75
34 Eric Paschall .25 .60
35 Shai Gilgeous-Alexander 1.50 4.00
36 Danny Green .25 .60
37 Dillon Brooks .30 .75
38 Zach LaVine .50 1.25
39 Clint Capela .25 .60
40 Kevin Durant 1.25 3.00
41 Rajon Rondo .30 .75
42 Michael Porter Jr. .40 1.00
43 Luka Doncic 2.00 5.00
44 Kendrick Nunn .25 .60
45 Tyler Herro .60 1.50
46 Lou Williams .30 .75
47 Darius Bazley .20 .50
48 Lauri Markkanen .40 1.00
49 Bam Adebayo .50 1.25
50 DeMar DeRozan .40 1.00
51 Khris Middleton .40 1.00
52 Kyrie Irving .60 1.50
53 Joel Embiid .75 2.00
54 Al Horford .30 .75
55 Carmelo Anthony .50 1.25
56 Mikal Bridges .40 1.00
57 Dennis Schroder .30 .75
58 JJ Redick .30 .75
59 Seth Curry .30 .75
60 Jae Crowder .20 .50
61 Mason Plumlee .20 .50
62 Andre Drummond .30 .75
63 Harrison Barnes .30 .75
64 Gordon Hayward .30 .75
65 James Harden .60 1.50
66 Lonnie Walker IV .30 .75
67 Marvin Bagley III .25 .60
68 Bradley Beal .40 1.00
69 Bojan Bogdanovic .25 .60
70 Anthony Davis .75 2.00
71 Danilo Gallinari .25 .60
72 Malik Monk .30 .75
73 Stephen Curry 2.50 6.00
74 OG Anunoby .30 .75
75 Brandon Clarke .30 .75
76 Josh Jackson .20 .50
77 Jaylen Brown .50 1.25
78 Jarrett Allen .30 .75
79 Chuma Okeke .30 .75
80 Blake Griffin .30 .75
81 Jordan Poole .50 1.25
82 Jerami Grant .50 1.25
83 John Wall .40 1.00
84 Marcus Smart .30 .75
85 Hamidou Diallo .30 .75
86 Coby White .40 1.00
87 Donte DiVincenzo .30 .75
88 Terry Rozier .30 .75
89 Kristaps Porzingis .40 1.00
90 Kevin Porter Jr. .30 .75
91 Tristan Thompson .20 .50
92 Rudy Gay .30 .75
93 D'Angelo Russell .30 .75
94 Ben Simmons .30 .75
95 Elfrid Payton .25 .60
96 Luguentz Dort .50 1.25
97 Brandon Ingram .40 1.00
98 Paul Millsap .25 .60
99 Jarrett Culver .20 .50
100 Domantas Sabonis .40 1.00
101 LeBron James 2.50 6.00
102 Jrue Holiday .30 .75
103 Deandre Ayton .30 .75
104 Buddy Hield .30 .75
105 Thaddeus Young .20 .50
106 Gary Trent Jr. .30 .75
107 Tim Hardaway Jr. .20 .50
108 Giannis Antetokounmpo 1.50 4.00
109 Jonas Valanciunas .25 .60
110 Kyle Lowry .40 1.00
111 Chris Paul .60 1.50
112 Darius Garland .50 1.25
113 Russell Westbrook .60 1.50
114 Andrew Wiggins .40 1.00
115 Robert Covington .25 .60
116 Zion Williamson 1.00 2.50
117 Kyle Kuzma .40 1.00
118 Collin Sexton .30 .75
119 Mike Conley .25 .60
120 Victor Oladipo .25 .60
121 CJ McCollum .30 .75
122 Christian Wood .30 .75
123 RJ Barrett .50 1.25
124 Damian Lillard .75 2.00
125 Jalen Brunson .50 1.25
126 Jimmy Butler .60 1.50
127 Isaiah Roby .20 .50
128 Dejounte Murray .30 .75
129 Joe Ingles .25 .60
130 Wendell Carter Jr. .25 .60
131 Kevin Love .30 .75
132 Donovan Mitchell .60 1.50
133 Thomas Bryant .25 .60
134 Duncan Robinson .30 .75
135 De'Aaron Fox .50 1.25
136 Malcolm Brogdon .30 .75
137 Jayson Tatum 1.25 3.00
138 Derrick Rose .50 1.25
139 Patrick Beverley .20 .50
140 Shake Milton .25 .60
141 PJ Washington Jr. .30 .75
142 Markelle Fultz .25 .60
143 Nikola Jokic 1.50 4.00
144 Caris LeVert .30 .75
145 Enes Kanter .25 .60
146 Joe Harris .25 .60
147 Chris Boucher RC .60 1.50
148 Pascal Siakam .50 1.25
149 Evan Fournier .25 .60
150 Karl-Anthony Towns .50 1.25
151 LaMelo Ball RC 4.00 10.00
152 Anthony Edwards RC 5.00 12.00
153 Tyrese Haliburton RC 4.00 10.00
154 Immanuel Quickley RC 1.25 3.00
155 James Wiseman RC .60 1.50
156 Cole Anthony RC 1.25 3.00
157 Patrick Williams RC 1.25 3.00
158 Desmond Bane RC 1.50 4.00
159 Saddiq Bey RC 1.00 2.50
160 Jae'Sean Tate RC .60 1.50
161 Isaac Okoro RC .75 2.00
162 Tyrese Maxey RC 4.00 10.00
163 Theo Maledon RC .50 1.25
164 Robert Woodard II RC .50 1.25
165 Saben Lee RC .50 1.25
166 Precious Achiuwa RC 1.00 2.50
167 Deni Avdija RC 1.25 3.00
168 Paul Reed RC .60 1.50
169 Mason Jones RC .40 1.00
170 Facundo Campazzo RC .60 1.50
171 Devin Vassell RC 1.50 4.00
172 Isaiah Stewart RC 1.00 2.50
173 Jaden McDaniels RC 1.50 4.00
174 Jordan Nwora RC .60 1.50
175 Kira Lewis Jr. RC .50 1.25
176 Obi Toppin RC 1.00 2.50
177 Killian Hayes RC .50 1.25
178 Isaiah Joe RC .60 1.50
179 Aaron Nesmith RC 1.00 2.50
180 Lamar Stevens RC .50 1.25
181 Devon Dotson RC .50 1.25
182 Skylar Mays RC .50 1.25
183 Zeke Nnaji RC .60 1.50
184 Reggie Perry RC .50 1.25
185 Moses Brown RC .40 1.00
186 Onyeka Okongwu RC 1.00 2.50
187 Kenyon Martin Jr. RC .75 2.00
188 Aleksej Pokusevski RC .60 1.50
189 Josh Green RC 1.00 2.50
190 RJ Hampton RC .50 1.25
191 Jalen Smith RC 1.00 2.50
192 Payton Pritchard RC 1.50 4.00
193 Udoka Azubuike RC .60 1.50
194 Xavier Tillman RC .60 1.50
195 Malachi Flynn RC .50 1.25
196 CJ Elleby RC .50 1.25
197 Naji Marshall RC .50 1.25
198 Tre Jones RC .75 2.00
199 Sam Merrill RC .75 2.00
200 Nathan Knight RC .50 1.25

2020-21 Panini Illusions Black

PRINT RUN 49 SER.#'d SETS
1 Ja Morant 12.00 30.00
43 Luka Doncic 40.00 100.00
73 Stephen Curry 25.00 60.00
101 LeBron James 40.00 100.00
108 Giannis Antetokounmpo 15.00 40.00
151 LaMelo Ball 125.00 300.00
152 Anthony Edwards 75.00 200.00

2020-21 Panini Illusions Blue

*BLUE: 3X TO 8X BASIC
PRINT RUN 25 SER.#'d SETS
1 Ja Morant 20.00 50.00
43 Luka Doncic 60.00 150.00
73 Stephen Curry 40.00 100.00
101 LeBron James 60.00 150.00
108 Giannis Antetokounmpo 25.00 60.00
151 LaMelo Ball 200.00 500.00
152 Anthony Edwards 125.00 300.00

2020-21 Panini Illusions Red

PRINT RUN 99 SER.#'d SETS
101 LeBron James 12.00 30.00

2020-21 Panini Illusions Ruby

PRINT RUN 125 SER.#'d SETS
151 LaMelo Ball 40.00 100.00
152 Anthony Edwards 40.00 100.00

2020-21 Panini Illusions Starlight

1 Ja Morant 12.00 30.00
43 Luka Doncic 40.00 100.00
73 Stephen Curry 20.00 50.00
101 LeBron James 50.00 120.00
108 Giannis Antetokounmpo 12.00 30.00
151 LaMelo Ball 100.00 250.00
152 Anthony Edwards 60.00 150.00
153 Tyrese Haliburton 40.00 100.00
156 Cole Anthony 25.00 60.00
162 Tyrese Maxey 25.00 60.00

2020-21 Panini Illusions Teal

PRINT RUN 75 SER.#'d SETS
151 LaMelo Ball 60.00 150.00
152 Anthony Edwards 60.00 150.00

2020-21 Panini Illusions Yellow

PRINT RUN 149 SER.#'d SETS
151 LaMelo Ball 40.00 100.00
152 Anthony Edwards 40.00 100.00

2020-21 Panini Illusions Amazing

*EMERALD: .5X TO 1.2X BASIC
*ORANGE: .5X TO 1.2X BASIC
*PINK: .5X TO 1.2X BASIC
*SAPPHIRE: .5X TO 1.2X BASIC
*ASIS RED & YELLOW: .6X TO 1.5X BASIC
1 Donovan Mitchell 1.25 3.00
2 Ja Morant 2.00 5.00
3 Luka Doncic 4.00 10.00
4 Chris Paul 1.25 3.00
5 Kevin Durant 2.50 6.00
6 Nikola Jokic 3.00 8.00
7 De'Aaron Fox 1.00 2.50
8 Ben Simmons .60 1.50
9 James Harden 1.25 3.00
10 Russell Westbrook 1.25 3.00
11 Damian Lillard 1.50 4.00
12 LeBron James 5.00 12.00
13 Stephen Curry 5.00 12.00
14 Anthony Davis 1.50 4.00
15 Jayson Tatum 2.50 6.00
16 Zion Williamson 2.00 5.00
17 Trae Young 1.50 4.00
18 Kawhi Leonard 1.50 4.00
19 Giannis Antetokounmpo 3.00 8.00
20 Jimmy Butler 1.25 3.00

2020-21 Panini Illusions Career Lineage

*EMERALD: .5X TO 1.2X BASIC
*SAPPHIRE/149: 1.25X TO 3X BASIC
*ORANGE/75: 1.5X TO 4X BASIC
*PINK/25: 3X TO 8X BASIC
*RED & YELLOW/25: 3X TO 8X BASIC
1 James Harden 1.25 3.00
2 LeBron James 5.00 12.00
3 Kevin Durant 2.50 6.00
4 Chris Paul 1.25 3.00
5 Kristaps Porzingis .75 2.00
6 Kyrie Irving 1.25 3.00
7 Paul George 1.00 2.50
8 Giannis Antetokounmpo 3.00 8.00
9 Vince Carter 1.25 3.00
10 Russell Westbrook 1.25 3.00
11 Rasheed Wallace .60 1.50
12 Dirk Nowitzki 1.50 4.00
13 Kareem Abdul-Jabbar 2.00 5.00
14 Charles Barkley 1.50 4.00
15 Ray Allen 1.00 2.50
16 DeMar DeRozan 1.00 2.50
17 Jimmy Butler 1.25 3.00
18 Kawhi Leonard 1.50 4.00
19 Carmelo Anthony 1.00 2.50
20 Kevin Garnett 1.50 4.00
21 Mike Conley .50 1.25
22 Tracy McGrady 1.00 2.50
23 Shaquille O'Neal 2.50 6.00
24 Julius Randle .60 1.50
25 Zach LaVine 1.00 2.50

2020-21 Panini Illusions Clear Shots

*EMERALD: .5X TO 1.2X BASIC
*ORANGE: .5X TO 1.2X BASIC
*PINK: .5X TO 1.2X BASIC
*SAPPHIRE: .5X TO 1.2X BASIC
1 Stephen Curry 8.00 20.00
2 Damian Lillard 2.50 6.00
3 Kyrie Irving 2.00 5.00
4 Devin Booker 2.50 6.00
5 Ray Allen 1.50 4.00
6 Zach LaVine 1.50 4.00
7 Larry Bird 4.00 10.00
8 Donovan Mitchell 2.00 5.00
9 Jayson Tatum 4.00 10.00
10 Trae Young 2.50 6.00
11 James Harden 2.00 5.00
12 Klay Thompson 2.50 6.00
13 Paul George 1.50 4.00
14 Bradley Beal 1.25 3.00
15 Allen Iverson 2.50 6.00
16 Fred VanVleet 1.50 4.00
17 Luka Doncic 6.00 15.00
18 Khris Middleton 1.25 3.00
19 Jamal Murray 1.50 4.00
20 Kevin Durant 4.00 10.00

2020-21 Panini Illusions Double Vision

1 Luka Doncic
Kristaps Porzingis 5.00 12.00
2 Kevin Durant
James Harden 3.00 8.00
3 Jaylen Brown
Jayson Tatum 3.00 8.00
4 Chris Paul
Devin Booker 2.00 5.00
5 Zach LaVine
Nikola Vucevic 1.25 3.00
6 Bradley Beal
Russell Westbrook 1.50 4.00
7 Brandon Ingram
Zion Williamson 2.50 6.00

8 Damian Lillard
CJ McCollum 2.00 5.00
9 Giannis Antetokounmpo
Khris Middleton 4.00 10.00
10 Joel Embiid
Ben Simmons 2.00 5.00
11 Nikola Jokic
Jamal Murray 4.00 10.00
12 Paul George
Kawhi Leonard 2.00 5.00
13 Donovan Mitchell
Rudy Gobert 1.50 4.00
14 Collin Sexton
Darius Garland 1.25 3.00
15 Bam Adebayo
Jimmy Butler 1.50 4.00
16 Kyle Lowry
Pascal Siakam 1.25 3.00
17 Julius Randle
RJ Barrett 1.25 3.00
18 Draymond Green
Stephen Curry 6.00 15.00
19 Trae Young
John Collins 2.00 5.00
20 Domantas Sabonis
Malcolm Brogdon 1.00 2.50

2020-21 Panini Illusions Fantasy Matchups

1 Larry Bird
Luka Doncic 20.00 50.00
2 Stephen Curry
Ray Allen 20.00 50.00
3 Joel Embiid
Hakeem Olajuwon 5.00 12.00
4 Karl Malone
Zion Williamson 4.00 10.00
5 Allen Iverson
Ja Morant 4.00 10.00
6 Steve Nash
Chris Paul 8.00 20.00
7 Zach LaVine
Dominique Wilkins 4.00 10.00
8 Kareem Abdul-Jabbar
Giannis Antetokounmpo 8.00 20.00
9 Clyde Drexler
Damian Lillard 3.00 8.00
10 Allen Iverson
Ben Simmons 3.00 8.00
11 Anthony Davis
Tim Duncan 3.00 8.00
12 James Harden
Jerry West 2.50 6.00
13 Draymond Green
Rasheed Wallace 1.50 4.00
14 Dwyane Wade
Anthony Edwards 15.00 40.00
15 Shaquille O'Neal
Wilt Chamberlain 8.00 20.00
16 Tracy McGrady
Bradley Beal 2.00 5.00
17 John Stockton
Trae Young 3.00 8.00
18 Kevin Garnett
Nikola Jokic 6.00 15.00
19 Bill Russell
LeBron James 15.00 40.00
20 LaMelo Ball
Magic Johnson 30.00 80.00

2020-21 Panini Illusions First Impressions Jersey Autographs

EXCHANGE DEADLINE 5/17/2023
1 Onyeka Okongwu 12.00 30.00
2 Anthony Edwards 200.00 500.00
3 Isaiah Stewart 12.00 30.00
4 Immanuel Quickley 15.00 40.00
5 Xavier Tillman 8.00 20.00
6 Tyrese Haliburton 75.00 200.00
7 Zeke Nnaji 8.00 20.00
8 Aaron Nesmith 12.00 30.00
9 Mason Jones 5.00 12.00
10 Karim Mane 5.00 12.00
11 Patrick Williams 15.00 40.00
12 Isaiah Joe 8.00 20.00
13 Robert Woodard II 6.00 15.00
14 Payton Pritchard 20.00 50.00
15 Cole Anthony 75.00 200.00
16 Kenyon Martin Jr. 10.00 25.00
17 Devin Vassell 20.00 50.00
18 Malachi Flynn 6.00 15.00
19 Killian Hayes 6.00 15.00
21 Kira Lewis Jr. 6.00 15.00
22 Aleksej Pokusevski 8.00 20.00
23 James Wiseman 8.00 20.00
25 Daniel Oturu 6.00 15.00
26 Nico Mannion 6.00 15.00
27 LaMelo Ball 400.00 800.00
28 Jahmi'us Ramsey 6.00 15.00
29 Deni Avdija 15.00 40.00
30 Obi Toppin 12.00 30.00
31 RJ Hampton 6.00 15.00
32 Precious Achiuwa 12.00 30.00
33 Tyrese Maxey 75.00 200.00
34 Skylar Mays 6.00 15.00
35 Jordan Nwora 8.00 20.00
36 Tre Jones 10.00 25.00
37 Vernon Carey Jr. 6.00 15.00
38 Theo Maledon 6.00 15.00
39 Isaac Okoro 10.00 25.00
40 Facundo Campazzo 8.00 20.00

2020-21 Panini Illusions Illuminated

1 Donovan Mitchell 1.25 3.00
2 Ja Morant 2.00 5.00
3 Julius Randle .60 1.50
4 Jaylen Brown 1.00 2.50
5 Collin Sexton .60 1.50
6 Shai Gilgeous-Alexander 3.00 8.00
7 Luka Doncic 4.00 10.00
8 Chris Paul 1.25 3.00
9 Kevin Durant 2.50 6.00
10 Nikola Jokic 3.00 8.00
11 De'Aaron Fox 1.00 2.50
12 Paul George 1.00 2.50
13 Bradley Beal .75 2.00
14 Kyrie Irving 1.25 3.00
15 Ben Simmons .60 1.50
16 James Harden 1.25 3.00
17 Russell Westbrook 1.25 3.00
18 Damian Lillard 1.50 4.00
19 LeBron James 5.00 12.00
20 Stephen Curry 5.00 12.00
21 Anthony Davis 1.50 4.00
22 Jayson Tatum 2.50 6.00
23 Zion Williamson 2.00 5.00
24 Trae Young 1.50 4.00
25 Kawhi Leonard 1.50 4.00
26 Giannis Antetokounmpo 3.00 8.00
27 Jimmy Butler 1.25 3.00
28 Joel Embiid 1.50 4.00
29 Zach LaVine 1.00 2.50
30 Devin Booker 1.50 4.00

2020-21 Panini Illusions Instant Impact

*EMERALD: .5X TO 1.2X BASIC
*SAPPHIRE/149: 1.5X TO 4X BASIC
*ORANGE/75: 2X TO 5X BASIC
*PINK/25: 3X TO 8X BASIC
*RED & YELLOW/25: 3X TO 8X BASIC
1 Jaden McDaniels 1.50 4.00
2 Obi Toppin 1.00 2.50
3 Nico Mannion .50 1.25
4 Facundo Campazzo .60 1.50
5 Killian Hayes .50 1.25
6 RJ Hampton .50 1.25
7 Anthony Edwards 5.00 12.00
8 LaMelo Ball 4.00 10.00
9 Tyrese Haliburton 4.00 10.00
10 Kira Lewis Jr. .50 1.25
11 Saddiq Bey 1.00 2.50
12 Desmond Bane 1.50 4.00
13 Malachi Flynn .50 1.25
14 Isaac Okoro .75 2.00
15 Theo Maledon .50 1.25
16 Patrick Williams 1.25 3.00
17 Immanuel Quickley 1.25 3.00
18 Deni Avdija 1.25 3.00
19 James Wiseman .60 1.50
20 Tyrese Maxey 4.00 10.00
21 Jae'Sean Tate .60 1.50
22 Aleksej Pokusevski .60 1.50
23 Payton Pritchard 1.50 4.00
24 Cole Anthony 1.25 3.00
25 Jordan Nwora .60 1.50

2020-21 Panini Illusions Living Legends

*EMERALD: .5X TO 1.2X BASIC
*ORANGE: .5X TO 1.2X BASIC
*PINK: .5X TO 1.2X BASIC
*SAPPHIRE: .5X TO 1.2X BASIC
1 Dirk Nowitzki 2.50 6.00
2 Tim Duncan 2.50 6.00
3 Kevin Garnett 2.50 6.00
4 Charles Barkley 2.50 6.00
5 Shaquille O'Neal 4.00 10.00
6 Tracy McGrady 1.50 4.00
7 Gary Payton 1.50 4.00
8 Jason Kidd 1.50 4.00
9 Hakeem Olajuwon 2.00 5.00
10 Dennis Rodman 2.50 6.00
11 Dominique Wilkins 1.50 4.00
12 Steve Nash 2.00 5.00
13 Allen Iverson 2.50 6.00
14 Tony Parker 1.50 4.00
15 Isiah Thomas 1.50 4.00
16 Clyde Drexler 1.50 4.00
17 Vince Carter 2.00 5.00
18 Paul Pierce 1.50 4.00
19 Ben Wallace 1.25 3.00
20 Jerry West 2.00 5.00

2020-21 Panini Illusions Mystique

*EMERLAD: .5X TO 1.2X BASIC
*ORANGE: .5X TO 1.2X BASIC
*PINK: .5X TO 1.2X BASIC
*SAPPHIRE: .5X TO 1.2X BASIC
1 Collin Sexton 1.00 2.50
2 Devin Booker 2.50 6.00
3 Bradley Beal 1.25 3.00
4 Joel Embiid 2.50 6.00
5 Damian Lillard 2.50 6.00
6 Donovan Mitchell 2.00 5.00
7 Zach LaVine 1.50 4.00
8 Julius Randle 1.00 2.50
9 James Harden 2.00 5.00
10 LeBron James 8.00 20.00
11 Giannis Antetokounmpo 5.00 12.00
12 Karl-Anthony Towns 1.50 4.00
13 Stephen Curry 8.00 20.00
14 Zion Williamson 3.00 8.00
15 Anthony Davis 2.50 6.00
16 Paul George 1.50 4.00
17 Jaylen Brown 1.50 4.00
18 Kyrie Irving 2.00 5.00
19 Kawhi Leonard 2.50 6.00
20 Luka Doncic 6.00 15.00

2020-21 Panini Illusions Rookie Reflections

*EMERLAD: .5X TO 1.2X BASIC
*SAPPHIRE/149: 1.25X TO 3X BASIC
*ORANGE/75: 1.5X TO 4X BASIC
*PINK/25: 2.5X TO 6X BASIC
*RED & YELLOW/25: 2.5X TO 6X BASIC
1 Kawhi Leonard
Patrick Williams 2.50 6.00
2 LaMelo Ball
Lonzo Ball 8.00 20.00
3 Collin Sexton
Kira Lewis Jr. 1.00 2.50
4 Kristaps Porzingis
Aleksej Pokusevski 1.25 3.00
5 Tony Parker
Theo Maledon 1.50 4.00
6 Saddiq Bey
Khris Middleton 1.50 4.00
7 Shai Gilgeous-Alexander
Tyrese Maxey 6.00 15.00
8 Facundo Campazzo
J.J. Barea 1.00 2.50
9 Fred VanVleet
Malachi Flynn 1.50 4.00
10 Immanuel Quickley
John Wall 2.00 5.00
11 Carmelo Anthony
Obi Toppin 1.50 4.00
12 Tyrese Haliburton
De'Aaron Fox 6.00 15.00
13 Vince Carter
Anthony Edwards 8.00 20.00
14 Onyeka Okongwu
Bam Adebayo 1.50 4.00
15 Cole Anthony
Jamal Murray 2.00 5.00
16 Ja Morant
Desmond Bane 3.00 8.00
17 James Wiseman
Anthony Davis 2.50 6.00
18 Isaac Okoro
Jaylen Brown 1.50 4.00
19 Zach LaVine
RJ Hampton 1.50 4.00
20 Draymond Green
Jae'Sean Tate 1.25 3.00
21 Kenyon Martin
Kenyon Martin Jr. 1.25 3.00
22 Karl-Anthony Towns
Jaden McDaniels 2.50 6.00
23 Amar'e Stoudemire
Jalen Smith 1.50 4.00
24 Deni Avdija
Gordon Hayward 2.00 5.00
25 Isiah Thomas
Killian Hayes 1.50 4.00

2020-21 Panini Illusions Rookie Retro Signatures

EXCHANGE DEADLINE 5/17/2023
1 Paul Pierce 20.00 50.00
2 David Robinson 60.00 150.00
3 Kevin Durant 150.00 400.00
4 Karl-Anthony Towns 20.00 50.00
5 Allen Iverson 100.00 250.00
6 John Stockton 40.00 100.00
7 Luka Doncic 400.00 800.00
8 Jason Kidd 20.00 50.00
9 Hakeem Olajuwon 60.00 150.00
10 Vince Carter 100.00 250.00
11 Anfernee Hardaway 75.00 200.00
12 Ja Morant 200.00 500.00
13 Grant Hill 30.00 80.00
14 Tony Parker 30.00 80.00
15 CJ McCollum 15.00 40.00
16 Jayson Tatum 125.00 300.00
17 Shaquille O'Neal 125.00 300.00
18 De'Aaron Fox 20.00 50.00
19 Trae Young 100.00 250.00
20 Rasheed Wallace 60.00 150.00

2020-21 Panini Illusions Rookie Signs

EXCHANGE DEADLINE 5/17/2023
1 Caleb Martin 10.00 25.00
2 Paul Reed 6.00 15.00
3 Reggie Perry 5.00 12.00
4 Naji Marshall 5.00 12.00
5 James Wiseman 6.00 15.00
6 Nico Mannion 5.00 12.00
8 Mamadi Diakite 5.00 12.00
9 Karim Mane 4.00 10.00
11 Ashton Hagans 6.00 15.00
13 Trent Forrest 6.00 15.00
14 Devon Dotson 5.00 12.00
15 Isaac Okoro 8.00 20.00
16 Myles Powell 8.00 20.00
17 Kaleb Wesson 5.00 12.00
18 Lamar Stevens 6.00 15.00
19 Mychal Mulder 5.00 12.00
20 Gabe Vincent 12.00 30.00
21 Jae'Sean Tate 6.00 15.00
22 Sean McDermott 4.00 10.00
24 Obi Toppin 25.00 60.00
25 Zeke Nnaji 6.00 15.00
26 Jahmi'us Ramsey 5.00 12.00
27 Devin Vassell 15.00 40.00
28 Tyrese Maxey 40.00 100.00
30 Moses Brown 4.00 10.00
31 Cole Anthony 40.00 100.00
32 Anthony Lamb 5.00 12.00
33 Freddie Gillespie 5.00 12.00
35 Ty-Shon Alexander 5.00 12.00
36 Tyrese Haliburton 40.00 100.00
37 Robert Woodard II 5.00 12.00
38 Killian Tillie 6.00 15.00
39 Markus Howard 6.00 15.00
40 Sam Merrill 8.00 20.00

2020-21 Panini Illusions Rookie Signs Emerald

*EMERALD: .75X TO 2X BASIC
PRINT RUN 25 SER.#'d SETS
EXCHANGE DEADLINE 5/17/2023
27 Tyrese Maxey 100.00 250.00
31 Cole Anthony 100.00 250.00

2020-21 Panini Illusions Rookie Vision

1 LaMelo Ball 12.00 30.00
2 James Wiseman 1.00 2.50
3 Anthony Edwards 10.00 25.00
4 Tyrese Haliburton 6.00 15.00
5 Obi Toppin 1.50 4.00
6 Deni Avdija 1.50 4.00
7 Immanuel Quickley 2.50 6.00
8 Tyrese Maxey 6.00 15.00
9 Patrick Williams 2.00 5.00
10 Payton Pritchard 2.50 6.00
11 Cole Anthony 2.00 5.00
12 Isaac Okoro 1.25 3.00
13 Aaron Nesmith 1.50 4.00
14 Onyeka Okongwu 1.50 4.00
15 Saddiq Bey 1.50 4.00
16 Jae'Sean Tate 1.00 2.50
17 Facundo Campazzo 1.00 2.50
18 Killian Hayes .75 2.00
19 RJ Hampton .75 2.00
20 Precious Achiuwa 1.50 4.00
21 Devin Vassell 2.50 6.00
22 Kira Lewis Jr. .75 2.00
23 Desmond Bane 2.50 6.00
24 Jaden McDaniels 2.50 6.00
25 Nico Mannion .75 2.00
26 Isaiah Stewart 1.50 4.00
27 Aleksej Pokusevski 1.00 2.50
28 Malachi Flynn .75 2.00
29 Theo Maledon .75 2.00
30 Kenyon Martin Jr. 1.25 3.00

2020-21 Panini Illusions Season Highlights

*EMERLAD: .5X TO 1.2X BASIC
*SAPPHIRE/149: 1.25X TO 3X BASIC
*ORANGE/75: 1.5X TO 4X BASIC
*PINK/25: 2.5X TO 6X BASIC
*RED & YELLOW/25: 2.5X TO 6X BASIC
1 Luka Doncic 2.50 6.00
2 Cole Anthony .75 2.00
3 Stephen Curry 3.00 8.00
4 Russell Westbrook .75 2.00
5 Devin Booker 1.00 2.50
6 Collin Sexton .40 1.00
7 Damian Lillard 1.00 2.50
8 LeBron James 3.00 8.00
9 LaMelo Ball 2.50 6.00
10 Giannis Antetokounmpo 2.00 5.00
11 Bradley Beal .50 1.25
12 Fred VanVleet .60 1.50
13 Jayson Tatum 1.50 4.00
14 Anthony Edwards 3.00 8.00
15 Damian Lillard 1.00 2.50
16 Domantas Sabonis .50 1.25
17 Chris Paul .75 2.00
18 Anfernee Simons .50 1.25
19 Terry Rozier .40 1.00
20 Luguentz Dort .60 1.50
21 Nikola Jokic 2.00 5.00
22 Zach LaVine .60 1.50
23 James Harden .75 2.00
24 Bam Adebayo .60 1.50
25 Stephen Curry 3.00 8.00

2020-21 Panini Illusions Shining Stars

*EMERLAD: .5X TO 1.2X BASIC
*ORANGE: .5X TO 1.2X BASIC
*PINK: .5X TO 1.2X BASIC
*SAPPHIRE: .5X TO 1.2X BASIC
1 LeBron James 8.00 20.00
2 Luka Doncic 6.00 15.00
3 Damian Lillard 2.50 6.00
4 Anthony Davis 2.50 6.00
5 Kawhi Leonard 2.50 6.00
6 James Harden 2.00 5.00
7 Jayson Tatum 4.00 10.00
8 Donovan Mitchell 2.00 5.00
9 Bradley Beal 1.25 3.00
10 Kevin Durant 4.00 10.00
11 Giannis Antetokounmpo 5.00 12.00
12 Stephen Curry 8.00 20.00
13 Zion Williamson 3.00 8.00
14 Devin Booker 2.50 6.00
15 Kyrie Irving 2.00 5.00
16 Nikola Jokic 5.00 12.00
17 Ben Simmons 1.00 2.50
18 Joel Embiid 2.50 6.00
19 Paul George 1.50 4.00
20 Zach LaVine 1.50 4.00

2020-21 Panini Illusions Superlatives Signatures

EXCHANGE DEADLINE 5/17/2023
1 Luguentz Dort 15.00 40.00
2 Clint Capela 5.00 12.00
3 Khris Middleton 8.00 20.00
4 Bill Walton 12.00 30.00
5 Kendrick Nunn 5.00 12.00
6 Jarrett Culver 4.00 10.00
7 Sarunas Marciulionis 6.00 15.00
8 Kawhi Leonard 40.00 100.00
9 Furkan Korkmaz 5.00 12.00
10 Devonte' Graham 5.00 12.00
11 Ricky Davis 5.00 12.00
12 Rasheed Wallace 40.00 100.00
13 Wang Zhi-zhi 100.00 250.00
14 Rex Chapman 5.00 12.00
15 Elvin Hayes 12.00 30.00
16 Jerry West 20.00 50.00
17 Tony Parker 15.00 40.00
18 CJ McCollum 6.00 15.00
19 Rick Mahorn 5.00 12.00
21 Glen Rice 5.00 12.00
22 Jason Richardson 6.00 15.00
23 Gary Harris 5.00 12.00
24 Pat Riley 12.00 30.00
25 Mike Bibby 6.00 15.00
26 Dino Radja 5.00 12.00
27 Thaddeus Young 4.00 10.00
28 Tony Snell 4.00 10.00
29 Maurice Harkless 5.00 12.00
30 Collin Sexton 12.00 30.00
31 Christian Laettner 10.00 25.00
32 PJ Washington Jr. 6.00 15.00
33 Boban Marjanovic 10.00 25.00
34 Cam Reddish 8.00 20.00
35 Myles Turner 6.00 15.00
36 Ja Morant 75.00 200.00
37 Jamal Murray 15.00 40.00
38 Brian Scalabrine 4.00 10.00
39 Stephen Jackson 5.00 12.00
40 Ben Wallace 40.00 100.00

2020-21 Panini Illusions Trophy Collection Signatures

EXCHANGE DEADLINE 5/17/2023
*EMERALD/25: .75X TO 2X BASIC
1 Thanasis Antetokounmpo 20.00 50.00
2 Alvin Robertson 5.00 12.00
3 Ersan Ilyasova 4.00 10.00
4 Jalen Brunson 10.00 25.00
5 James Silas 5.00 12.00
6 Gheorghe Muresan 5.00 12.00
7 Grant Williams 5.00 12.00
8 James Ennis III 4.00 10.00
9 Calvin Natt 5.00 12.00
10 Daniel Gafford 5.00 12.00
11 B.J. Armstrong 5.00 12.00
12 Tony Delk 5.00 12.00
13 Lonnie Walker IV 6.00 15.00
14 Tim Legler 4.00 10.00
15 Carsen Edwards 5.00 12.00
16 Larry Nance Jr. 5.00 12.00
17 Reggie Bullock 5.00 12.00
19 Rasheed Wallace 40.00 100.00
20 Isaiah Hartenstein 4.00 10.00
21 Elton Brand 6.00 15.00
23 John Shumate 5.00 12.00
24 Elmore Smith 20.00 50.00
25 Bobby Portis 6.00 15.00
26 Cody Martin 4.00 10.00
27 Dorian Finney-Smith 5.00 12.00
28 Jason Williams 30.00 80.00
29 Louis King 5.00 12.00
30 Terence Davis II 6.00 15.00
31 Jarrett Culver 4.00 10.00
32 Alex Caruso 20.00 50.00
33 LaPhonso Ellis 4.00 10.00
34 Luguentz Dort 15.00 40.00
35 Harold Miner 5.00 12.00
37 Dwight Powell 4.00 10.00
38 Juwan Howard 5.00 12.00
39 Khem Birch 5.00 12.00
40 Justin Holiday 4.00 10.00
41 Magic Johnson 60.00 150.00
42 Robin Lopez 4.00 10.00
43 Chimezie Metu 5.00 12.00
44 Otis Birdsong 5.00 12.00
45 Dale Davis 5.00 12.00
46 Isaiah Roby 4.00 10.00
47 Jakob Poeltl 5.00 12.00
48 Spencer Haywood 6.00 15.00
49 Slick Watts 5.00 12.00
50 Zach Collins 5.00 12.00
51 Troy Brown Jr. 5.00 12.00
53 Ron Harper 6.00 15.00
54 Artis Gilmore 10.00 25.00
55 Kyle Guy 4.00 10.00
56 Drew Eubanks 6.00 15.00
57 Greg Ostertag 4.00 10.00
59 Tomas Satoransky 4.00 10.00
60 Oshae Brissett 6.00 15.00

2016-17 Panini Impeccable

1-100 PRINT RUN 99 SER.#'d SETS
101-135 PRINT RUNS B/WN 75-99 PER
101-135 PRINT RUN 99 SER.#'d SET
EXCHANGE DEADLINE 3/20/2019
1 Stephen Curry/99 12.00 30.00
2 George Hill/99 2.00 5.00
3 Patrick Ewing/99 3.00 8.00
4 Kemba Walker/99 2.00 5.00
5 Danilo Gallinari/99 2.00 5.00
6 Kyrie Irving/99 5.00 12.00
7 George Gervin/99 4.00 10.00
8 Chris Paul/99 4.00 10.00
9 Lenny Wilkens/99 2.50 6.00
10 Elvin Hayes/99 3.00 8.00
11 Hassan Whiteside/99 2.00 5.00
12 Kevin McHale/99 4.00 10.00
13 Kobe Bryant/99 75.00 200.00
14 Paul George/99 4.00 10.00
15 Gordon Hayward/99 2.50 6.00
16 John Havlicek/99 6.00 15.00
17 Lou Williams/99 2.50 6.00
18 Victor Oladipo/99 2.50 6.00
19 Giannis Antetokounmpo/99 6.00 15.00
20 Larry Bird/99 10.00 25.00
21 Walt Frazier/99 2.50 6.00
22 Myles Turner/99 2.50 6.00
23 Hakeem Olajuwon/99 5.00 12.00
24 Russell Westbrook/99 4.00 10.00
25 Marc Gasol/99 2.50 6.00
26 Pete Maravich/99 4.00 10.00
27 Jimmy Butler/99 5.00 12.00
28 Seth Curry/99 2.00 5.00
29 David Robinson/99 5.00 12.00
30 Nikola Jokic/99 12.00 30.00
31 Mike Conley/99 2.00 5.00
32 Willis Reed/99 2.00 5.00
33 Tracy McGrady/99 4.00 10.00
34 James Worthy/99 3.00 8.00
35 Reggie Miller/99 4.00 10.00
36 Jordan Clarkson/99 2.50 6.00
37 John Stockton/99 4.00 10.00
38 Bradley Beal/99 3.00 8.00
39 Jrue Holiday/99 3.00 8.00
40 Kristaps Porzingis/99 4.00 10.00
41 Anthony Davis/99 8.00 20.00
42 Pau Gasol/99 4.00 10.00
43 Jeremy Lin/99 5.00 12.00
44 Bob Pettit/99 2.50 6.00
45 LaMarcus Aldridge/99 2.50 6.00
46 DeMarcus Cousins/99 2.00 5.00
47 Kareem Abdul-Jabbar/99 8.00 20.00
48 Magic Johnson/99 10.00 25.00
49 Dirk Nowitzki/99 6.00 15.00
50 Julius Erving/99 6.00 15.00
51 George Mikan/99 5.00 12.00
52 Blake Griffin/99 2.50 6.00
53 Wes Unseld/99 2.50 6.00
54 Draymond Green/99 3.00 8.00
55 Wilt Chamberlain/99 8.00 20.00
56 Isaiah Thomas/99 2.00 5.00
57 Eric Gordon/99 2.00 5.00
58 Bill Walton/99 4.00 10.00
59 Earl Monroe/99 4.00 10.00
60 Joel Embiid/99 6.00 15.00
61 Karl Malone/99 4.00 10.00
62 Robert Parish/99 3.00 8.00
63 Jerry West/99 6.00 15.00
64 John Wall/99 3.00 8.00
65 Elgin Baylor/99 5.00 12.00
66 Kawhi Leonard/99 6.00 15.00
67 Ben Simmons/99 RC 5.00 12.00
68 Karl-Anthony Towns/99 5.00 12.00
69 Goran Dragic/99 2.50 6.00
70 Harrison Barnes/99 2.00 5.00
71 Klay Thompson/99 6.00 15.00
72 Bill Russell/99 8.00 20.00
73 James Harden/99 5.00 12.00
74 Oscar Robertson/99 6.00 15.00
75 Devin Booker/99 10.00 25.00
76 Dwyane Wade/99 5.00 12.00
77 Derrick Rose/99 4.00 10.00
78 Jeff Teague/99 1.50 4.00
79 D'Angelo Russell/99 3.00 8.00
80 C.J. McCollum/99 2.50 6.00
81 Eric Bledsoe/99 2.00 5.00
82 Damian Lillard/99 6.00 15.00
83 Rick Barry/99 3.00 8.00
84 Shaquille O'Neal/99 8.00 20.00
85 Clyde Drexler/99 4.00 10.00
86 Kevin Love/99 2.50 6.00
87 Brook Lopez/99 2.00 5.00
88 Julius Randle/99 3.00 8.00
89 Anfernee Hardaway/99 6.00 15.00
90 Kevin Durant/99 10.00 25.00
91 DeMar DeRozan/99 3.00 8.00
92 Scottie Pippen/99 5.00 12.00
93 Paul Millsap/99 2.00 5.00
94 LeBron James/99 15.00 40.00
95 Andrew Wiggins/99 3.00 8.00
96 Robert Covington/99 2.00 5.00
97 Vince Carter/99 5.00 12.00
98 Jabari Parker/99 1.50 4.00
99 Carmelo Anthony/99 4.00 10.00
100 Kyle Lowry/99 2.50 6.00
101 Yogi Ferrell AU/99 RC 5.00 12.00
102 Brandon Ingram AU/75 40.00 100.00
104 Thon Maker AU/99 5.00 12.00
105 Malcolm Brogdon AU/99 20.00 50.00
106 Kris Dunn AU/75 6.00 15.00
107 Buddy Hield AU/75 20.00 50.00
108 Ivica Zubac AU/99 10.00 25.00
109 Patrick McCaw AU/99 RC 4.00 10.00
110 Jamal Murray AU/75 125.00 300.00
111 Georgios Papagiannis AU/99 RC 4.00 10.00
112 Marquese Chriss AU/99 5.00 12.00
113 Dario Saric AU/99 RC 6.00 15.00
114 Taurean Prince AU/99 RC 5.00 12.00
115 Paul Zipser AU/99 RC 4.00 10.00
116 Michael Gbinije AU/99 RC 4.00 10.00
117 Tomas Satoransky AU/99 RC 6.00 15.00
118 Dragan Bender AU/99 RC 6.00 15.00
119 Luwawu-Cabarrot AU/99 RC 6.00 15.00
120 J.Hernangomez AU/99 8.00 20.00
121 DeAndre' Bembry AU/99 RC 6.00 15.00
122 Cheick Diallo AU/99 RC 4.00 10.00
123 Henry Ellenson AU/99 4.00 10.00
124 Marshall Plumlee AU/99 RC 4.00 10.00
125 W.Hernangomez AU/99 RC 5.00 12.00
126 Dorian Finney-Smith AU/99 RC 5.00 12.00
127 Brice Johnson AU/99 4.00 10.00
128 Diamond Stone AU/99 RC 4.00 10.00
129 Deyonta Davis AU/99 RC 4.00 10.00
130 Pascal Siakam AU/99 40.00 100.00
131 Ron Baker AU/99 RC 4.00 10.00
132 Jake Layman AU/99 RC 5.00 12.00
133 Jakob Poeltl AU/99 8.00 20.00
134 Mindaugas Kuzminskas AU/99 RC 4.00 10.00
135 Georges Niang AU/99 RC 6.00 15.00
136 B.Ingram JSY AU/99 15.00 40.00
138 Kris Dunn JSY AU/99 6.00 15.00
139 Buddy Hield JSY AU/99 12.00 30.00
140 Jamal Murray JSY AU/99 60.00 150.00
141 Chriss JSY AU/99 5.00 12.00
142 Jakob Poeltl JSY AU/99 8.00 20.00
143 Thon Maker JSY AU/99 5.00 12.00
144 Sabonis JSY AU/99 RC 40.00 100.00
145 Kay Felder JSY AU/99 RC 4.00 10.00
146 Valentine JSY AU/99 RC 4.00 10.00
147 J.Hrnngmz JSY AU/99 8.00 20.00
148 Wade Baldwin IV JSY AU/99 RC 4.00 10.00
149 Henry Ellenson JSY AU/99 4.00 10.00
150 Malik Beasley JSY AU/99 RC 8.00 20.00
151 Caris LeVert JSY AU/99 RC 10.00 25.00
152 Tyler Ulis JSY AU/99 RC 5.00 12.00
153 Malachi Richardson JSY AU/99 RC 4.00 10.00
154 Damian Jones JSY AU/99 RC 4.00 10.00
155 Brice Johnson JSY AU/99 4.00 10.00
156 Pascal Siakam JSY AU/99 40.00 100.00
157 Lbssre JSY AU/99 RC 4.00 10.00
158 Murray JSY AU/99 RC 40.00 100.00
159 Brogdon JSY AU/99 12.00 30.00
160 Ivica Zubac JSY AU/99 10.00 25.00

2016-17 Panini Impeccable Holo Silver

*HOLO.SLVR 1-100: .6X TO 1.5X BASIC
*HOLO.SLVR 101-135: .5X TO 1.2X BASIC
*HOLO.SLVR 136-160: .5X TO 1.2X BASIC
STATED PRINT RUN 25 SER.#'d SETS
94 LeBron James 40.00 100.00

2016-17 Panini Impeccable Silver

*SLVR 101-135: .4X TO 1X BASIC
*SLVR 136-160: .4X TO 1X BASIC
STATED PRINT RUN 49 SER.#'d SETS
EXCHANGE DEADLINE 3/20/2019
110 Jamal Murray AU 150.00 400.00
130 Pascal Siakam AU 60.00 150.00
140 Jamal Murray JSY AU 150.00 400.00
156 Pascal Siakam JSY AU 75.00 200.00

2016-17 Panini Impeccable Elegance Retired Jersey Autographs

STATED PRINT RUN 99 SER.#'d SETS
EXCHANGE DEADLINE 3/20/2019
1 George Gervin 15.00 40.00
2 Ray Allen 40.00 100.00
4 Kurt Thomas 4.00 10.00
5 Kenny Smith 5.00 12.00
6 Rashard Lewis 5.00 12.00
8 Chauncey Billups 15.00 40.00

2016-17 Panini Impeccable Elegance Retired Jersey Autographs Holo Silver

*HOLO.SLVR: .5X TO 1.2X BASIC
STATED PRINT RUN 25 SER.#'d SETS
EXCHANGE DEADLINE 3/20/2019
9 David Robinson 125.00 300.00
10 Allen Iverson 400.00 800.00

2016-17 Panini Impeccable Elegance Retired Jersey Autographs Silver

*SILVER: .4X TO 1X BASIC
STATED PRINT RUN 49 SER.#'d SETS
EXCHANGE DEADLINE 3/20/2019
3 Anfernee Hardaway 25.00 60.00
7 Alonzo Mourning 20.00 50.00
9 David Robinson 20.00 50.00
10 Allen Iverson 75.00 200.00

2016-17 Panini Impeccable Elegance Veteran Jersey Autographs

PRINT RUNS B/WN 75-99 COPIES PER
EXCHANGE DEADLINE 3/20/2019
*SILVER/49: .4X TO 1X BASIC
*HOLO.SLVR/25: .75X TO 2X BASIC
1 Karl-Anthony Towns/75 40.00 100.00
2 DeMarre Carroll/99 4.00 10.00
3 Justise Winslow/99 6.00 15.00
4 D'Angelo Russell/99 10.00 25.00
5 Ryan Anderson/99 4.00 10.00
6 Bojan Bogdanovic/99 5.00 12.00
7 Marc Gasol/75 8.00 20.00
8 Gordon Hayward/99 10.00 25.00
9 Joel Embiid/75 125.00 300.00
10 Kristaps Porzingis/99 20.00 50.00
11 Zach LaVine/99 15.00 40.00
12 Jordan Clarkson/99 6.00 15.00
13 John Wall/75 20.00 50.00
14 Harrison Barnes/99 6.00 15.00
15 Devin Harris/99 4.00 10.00
16 Julius Randle/75 8.00 20.00
17 Michael Kidd-Gilchrist/99 4.00 10.00
18 Tobias Harris/99 6.00 15.00
19 Andre Drummond/99 6.00 15.00
20 Vince Carter/75 20.00 50.00
21 Elfrid Payton/99 5.00 12.00
22 Jason Terry/99 6.00 15.00
23 Nikola Mirotic/99 4.00 10.00
25 Goran Dragic/99 6.00 15.00
26 Myles Turner/99 10.00 25.00
27 Kyrie Irving/75 40.00 100.00
28 Marcin Gortat/99 4.00 10.00
29 Nicolas Batum/99 6.00 15.00
30 Isaiah Thomas/99 12.00 30.00

2016-17 Panini Impeccable Impeccable Jersey Numbers Autographs

PRINT RUNS B/WN 1-91 COPIES PER
NO PRICING ON QTY 14 OR LESS
EXCHANGE DEADLINE 3/20/2019
1 Dennis Rodman/91 125.00 300.00
2 Kobe Bryant/24 6,000.00 12,000.00
3 Shaquille O'Neal/32 300.00 600.00
4 Kevin Durant/35 400.00 800.00
5 Myles Turner/33 30.00 80.00
6 Karl-Anthony Towns/32 125.00 300.00
7 Julius Randle/30 75.00 200.00
8 Stephen Curry/30 EXCH 1,000.00 2,000.00
9 Jamal Murray/27 300.00 600.00
10 Buddy Hield/24 60.00 150.00
11 Anthony Davis/23 125.00 300.00
12 Andrew Wiggins/22 75.00 200.00
13 Joel Embiid/21 150.00 400.00
14 Gordon Hayward/20 75.00 200.00

2016-17 Panini Impeccable Impeccable Season Autographs

PRINT RUNS B/WN 19-21 COPIES PER
EXCHANGE DEADLINE 3/20/2019
1 Kobe Bryant/20 5,000.00 10,000.00
2 Robert Parish/21 60.00 150.00
3 Kareem Abdul-Jabbar/20 400.00 800.00
4 John Stockton/19 300.00 600.00
5 Charles Oakley/19 20.00 50.00
6 Juwan Howard/19 75.00 200.00
7 Jason Kidd/19 200.00 500.00
8 Shaquille O'Neal/19 400.00 800.00
9 Vince Carter/19 150.00 400.00
10 Dirk Nowitzki/19 400.00 800.00

2016-17 Panini Impeccable Impeccable Stats Autographs

PRINT RUNS B/WN 7-81 COPIES PER
NO PRICING ON QTY 13 OR LESS
EXCHANGE DEADLINE 3/20/2019
1 Kobe Bryant/81 6,000.00 12,000.00
2 Rick Barry/64 60.00 150.00
3 David Thompson/73 40.00 100.00
4 Jerry West/63 75.00 200.00
5 George Gervin/63 50.00 120.00
6 Tracy McGrady/62 150.00 400.00
7 Shaquille O'Neal/61 300.00 600.00
8 Bernard King/60 40.00 100.00
9 Larry Bird/60 125.00 300.00
10 Allen Iverson/60 300.00 600.00
14 Jason Kidd/25 150.00 400.00
15 Magic Johnson/24 300.00 600.00
16 Nick Van Exel/23 125.00 300.00

2016-17 Panini Impeccable Indelible Ink

PRINT RUNS B/WN 75-99 COPIES PER
EXCHANGE DEADLINE 3/20/2019
*SILVER/49: .4X TO 1X BASIC
*HOLO.SLVR/25: .5X TO 1.2X BASIC
1 Gail Goodrich/75 8.00 20.00
2 DeMarre Carroll/75 5.00 12.00
3 Marcus Camby/99 8.00 20.00
4 Glen Rice/99 6.00 15.00
5 Damon Stoudamire/99 8.00 20.00
6 Dan Majerle/99 6.00 15.00
7 Dominique Wilkins/75 15.00 40.00
8 Gary Harris/75 6.00 15.00
9 Eric Gordon/75 6.00 15.00
10 Kiki Vandeweghe/99 6.00 15.00
11 Rick Fox/99 8.00 20.00
12 Sidney Moncrief/99 6.00 15.00
13 Bob Dandridge/99 5.00 12.00
14 Jeff Hornacek/99 6.00 15.00
15 Zydrunas Ilgauskas/99 6.00 15.00
16 Cedric Ceballos/99 6.00 15.00
17 Hersey Hawkins/99 5.00 12.00
18 Kyle Korver/75 10.00 25.00
19 Mark Aguirre/99 6.00 15.00
20 Horace Grant/99 8.00 20.00
21 Richard Jefferson/99 12.00 30.00
22 Junior Bridgeman/99 6.00 15.00
23 Jo Jo White/99 6.00 15.00
24 James Worthy/75 10.00 25.00
25 Dennis Scott/99 5.00 12.00
26 Hakeem Olajuwon/75 25.00 60.00
27 Alex English/99 6.00 15.00
28 Ryan Anderson/99 5.00 12.00
29 Robert Covington/99 6.00 15.00
30 Nick Van Exel/99 12.00 30.00

31 Cedric Maxwell/99 6.00 15.00
32 Latrell Sprewell/99 15.00 40.00
33 Allan Houston/99 6.00 15.00
34 Sean Elliott/99 6.00 15.00
35 Tony Delk/99 5.00 12.00
36 D'Angelo Russell/75 15.00 40.00
37 Jalen Rose/99 6.00 15.00
38 Chauncey Billups/75 10.00 25.00
39 Devin Booker/75 125.00 300.00
40 Dennis Rodman/75 25.00 60.00
41 Bojan Bogdanovic/99 6.00 15.00
42 Dwyane Wade/75 100.00 250.00
43 Darren Collison/99 5.00 12.00
44 J.J. Barea/99 6.00 15.00
45 Jrue Holiday/99 10.00 25.00
46 James Johnson/99 5.00 12.00
47 Paul Millsap/99 6.00 15.00
48 Danilo Gallinari/99 6.00 15.00
49 Stephen Curry/75 500.00 1,000.00
50 Anthony Davis/75 100.00 250.00

2017-18 Panini Impeccable

STATED PRINT RUN 99 SER.#'d SETS
EXCHANGE DEADLINE 04/03/2020
1 Aaron Gordon 2.00 5.00
2 Al Horford 2.00 5.00
3 Andre Drummond 1.50 4.00
4 Andrew Wiggins 2.50 6.00
5 Anthony Davis 5.00 12.00
6 Avery Bradley 1.25 3.00
7 Ben Simmons 2.00 5.00
8 Blake Griffin 2.00 5.00
9 Bradley Beal 2.50 6.00
10 Brandon Ingram 2.50 6.00
11 Buddy Hield 2.00 5.00
12 CJ McCollum 2.00 5.00
13 Carmelo Anthony 3.00 8.00
14 Chris Paul 3.00 8.00
15 Clint Capela 1.50 4.00
16 Damian Lillard 5.00 12.00
17 D'Angelo Russell 1.50 4.00
18 Dario Saric 1.50 4.00
19 De'Aaron Fox RC 12.00 30.00
20 DeAndre Jordan 1.50 4.00
21 DeMar DeRozan 2.50 6.00
22 DeMarcus Cousins 1.50 4.00
23 Dennis Schroder 1.50 4.00
24 Dennis Smith Jr. RC 2.00 5.00
25 Derrick Favors 1.25 3.00
26 Derrick Rose 3.00 8.00
27 Devin Booker 5.00 12.00
28 Dirk Nowitzki 5.00 12.00
29 Donovan Mitchell RC 40.00 100.00
30 Draymond Green 2.50 6.00
31 Dwight Howard 2.50 6.00
32 Dwyane Wade 4.00 10.00
33 Enes Kanter 1.50 4.00
34 Eric Bledsoe 1.50 4.00
35 Eric Gordon 1.50 4.00
36 Evan Fournier 1.50 4.00
37 George Hill 1.50 4.00
38 Giannis Antetokounmpo 10.00 25.00
39 Goran Dragic 1.50 4.00
40 Gordon Hayward 1.50 4.00
41 Harrison Barnes 1.50 4.00
42 Hassan Whiteside 1.50 4.00
43 Jamal Murray 3.00 8.00
44 James Harden 4.00 10.00
45 Jayson Tatum RC 40.00 100.00
46 Jimmy Butler 3.00 8.00
47 Joel Embiid 4.00 10.00
48 John Wall 2.50 6.00
49 Jonas Valanciunas 1.50 4.00
50 Jrue Holiday 2.50 6.00
51 Julius Randle 2.00 5.00
52 Jusuf Nurkic 1.50 4.00
53 Karl-Anthony Towns 3.00 8.00
54 Kawhi Leonard 5.00 12.00
55 Kemba Walker 1.50 4.00
56 Kent Bazemore 1.25 3.00
57 Kevin Durant 8.00 20.00
58 Kevin Love 2.00 5.00
59 Khris Middleton 2.50 6.00
60 Klay Thompson 5.00 12.00
61 Kris Dunn 1.25 3.00
62 Kristaps Porzingis 2.50 6.00
63 Kyle Kuzma RC 6.00 15.00
64 Kyle Lowry 2.00 5.00
65 Kyrie Irving 4.00 10.00
66 LaMarcus Aldridge 2.00 5.00
67 Larry Nance Jr. 1.50 4.00
68 Lauri Markkanen RC 10.00 25.00
69 LeBron James 15.00 40.00
70 Lonzo Ball RC 6.00 15.00
71 Lou Williams 1.50 4.00
72 Marc Gasol 2.00 5.00
73 Markelle Fultz RC 4.00 10.00
74 MarShon Brooks 1.25 3.00
75 Michael Beasley 1.25 3.00
76 Mike Conley 1.50 4.00
77 Myles Turner 2.00 5.00
78 Nicolas Batum 1.25 3.00
79 Nikola Jokic 12.00 30.00
80 Nikola Vucevic 1.50 4.00
81 Otto Porter Jr. 1.50 4.00
82 Pau Gasol 3.00 8.00
83 Paul George 3.00 8.00
84 Paul Millsap 1.50 4.00
85 Reggie Jackson 1.50 4.00
86 Ricky Rubio 1.50 4.00
87 Rondae Hollis-Jefferson 1.25 3.00
88 Rudy Gay 1.50 4.00
89 Rudy Gobert 2.50 6.00
90 Russell Westbrook 3.00 8.00
91 Spencer Dinwiddie 1.50 4.00
92 Stephen Curry 15.00 40.00
93 TJ Warren 1.50 4.00
94 Taurean Prince 1.25 3.00
95 Thaddeus Young 1.25 3.00
96 Tyson Chandler 1.50 4.00
97 Victor Oladipo 1.50 4.00
98 Wesley Matthews 1.25 3.00
99 Willie Cauley-Stein 1.25 3.00
100 Zach LaVine 3.00 8.00
101 Donovan Mitchell AU 75.00 200.00
102 Jayson Tatum AU 75.00 200.00
103 Lonzo Ball AU 30.00 80.00
104 Kyle Kuzma AU 15.00 40.00
105 Dennis Smith Jr. AU 5.00 12.00
106 Markelle Fultz AU 25.00 60.00
107 De'Aaron Fox AU 40.00 100.00
108 Josh Jackson AU RC 5.00 12.00
109 Bam Adebayo AU RC 8.00 20.00
110 Harry Giles AU RC 4.00 10.00
111 Jordan Bell AU RC 4.00 10.00
112 Frank Ntilikina AU RC 5.00 12.00
113 Jarrett Allen AU RC 10.00 25.00
114 John Collins AU RC 30.00 80.00
115 Malik Monk AU RC 15.00 40.00
116 Zhou Qi AU RC 20.00 50.00
117 Maxi Kleber AU RC 6.00 15.00
118 Bogdan Bogdanovic AU RC 10.00 25.00
119 Dillon Brooks AU RC 12.00 30.00
120 Milos Teodosic AU RC 5.00 12.00
121 Semi Ojeleye JSY AU RC 5.00 12.00
122 Dwayne Bacon JSY AU RC 4.00 10.00
123 TJ Leaf JSY AU RC 4.00 10.00
124 Harry Giles JSY AU RC 4.00 10.00
125 Tyler Lydon JSY AU RC 4.00 10.00
126 John Collins JSY AU 30.00 80.00
127 Josh Jackson JSY AU 5.00 12.00
128 Bam Adebayo JSY AU 10.00 25.00
129 Luke Kennard JSY AU RC 8.00 20.00
130 Dennis Smith Jr. JSY AU 5.00 12.00
131 Sindarius Thornwell JSY AU RC 4.00 10.00
132 Frank Jackson JSY AU RC 4.00 10.00
133 Terrance Ferguson JSY AU RC 4.00 10.00
135 Wes Iwundu JSY AU RC 4.00 10.00
136 Jonathan Isaac JSY AU RC 12.00 30.00
137 Justin Patton JSY AU RC 4.00 10.00
138 Caleb Swanigan JSY AU RC 4.00 10.00
139 Malik Monk JSY AU 15.00 40.00
140 Derrick White JSY AU RC 30.00 80.00
141 Sterling Brown JSY AU RC 4.00 10.00
142 Frank Mason III JSY AU RC 4.00 10.00
143 Tony Bradley JSY AU RC 4.00 10.00
144 Jarrett Allen JSY AU 10.00 25.00
145 Zach Collins JSY AU RC 8.00 20.00
146 Jordan Bell JSY AU 4.00 10.00
147 Kyle Kuzma JSY AU 15.00 40.00
148 D.J. Wilson JSY AU RC 4.00 10.00
149 Markelle Fultz JSY AU 25.00 60.00
150 Donovan Mitchell JSY AU 400.00 800.00
151 Jawun Evans JSY AU RC 4.00 10.00
152 Frank Ntilikina JSY AU 5.00 12.00
153 Tyler Dorsey JSY AU RC 4.00 10.00
154 Jayson Tatum JSY AU 125.00 300.00
155 Lauri Markkanen JSY AU 40.00 100.00
156 Josh Hart JSY AU RC 30.00 80.00
157 Lonzo Ball JSY AU 30.00 80.00
158 Davon Reed JSY AU RC 4.00 10.00
159 OG Anunoby JSY AU RC 8.00 20.00
160 De'Aaron Fox JSY AU 60.00 150.00

2017-18 Panini Impeccable Holo Silver

*SILVER: .5X TO 1.2X BASE
*SILVER RC: .5X TO 1.2X BASE RC
*SILVER AU: .6X TO 1.5X BASE AU
*SILVER JSY AU: .6X TO 1.5X JSY AU
1-100 PRINT RUN 49 SER.#'d SETS
101-160 PRINT RUN 25 SER.#'d SETS
EXCHANGE DEADLINE 04/03/2020
147 Kyle Kuzma JSY AU 25.00 60.00
155 Lauri Markkanen JSY AU 100.00 250.00
157 Lonzo Ball JSY AU 75.00 200.00
160 De'Aaron Fox JSY AU 150.00 400.00

2017-18 Panini Impeccable Elegance Retired Jersey Autographs

PRINT RUNS B/WN 25-99 COPIES PER
EXCHANGE DEADLINE 04/03/2020
*SILVER/20-25: .6X TO 1.5X p/r 99
1 Mark Price/99 6.00 15.00
2 Alonzo Mourning/25 15.00 40.00
4 Clyde Drexler/25 20.00 50.00
5 Dominique Wilkins/25 12.00 30.00
6 Kobe Bryant/25 6,000.00 12,000.00
7 Artis Gilmore/99 6.00 15.00
8 Allen Iverson/25 50.00 120.00
9 B.J. Armstrong/99 6.00 15.00
10 Julius Erving/25 40.00 100.00
11 Shawn Bradley/99 3.00 8.00
12 David Robinson/25 20.00 50.00
13 Detlef Schrempf/99 5.00 12.00
14 Grant Hill/25 25.00 60.00
15 Christian Laettner/99 5.00 12.00
16 Shaquille O'Neal/25 75.00 200.00
17 Robert Parish/99 6.00 15.00
18 Karl Malone/25 20.00 50.00
19 Tom Gugliotta/99 3.00 8.00
20 Larry Bird/25 50.00 120.00

2017-18 Panini Impeccable Elegance Veteran Jersey Autographs

PRINT RUNS B/WN 25-99 COPIES PER
EXCHANGE DEADLINE 04/03/2020
*SILVER/25: .6X TO 1.5X p/r 99
1 Kevin Durant/25 200.00 500.00
2 Aaron Gordon/99 5.00 12.00
3 Kyrie Irving/25 60.00 150.00
4 Myles Turner/99 5.00 12.00
5 Blake Griffin/25 15.00 40.00
6 Thaddeus Young/99 3.00 8.00
7 Brandon Ingram/25 50.00 120.00
8 Allen Crabbe/99 3.00 8.00
9 Kristaps Porzingis/25 10.00 25.00
10 Khris Middleton/99 6.00 15.00
11 Damian Lillard/25 75.00 200.00
12 Zach LaVine/99 40.00 100.00
13 Dirk Nowitzki/25 100.00 250.00
14 Courtney Lee/99 3.00 8.00
15 Giannis Antetokounmpo/25 200.00 500.00
16 Seth Curry/99 5.00 12.00
17 Kevin Love/25 12.00 30.00
18 Rondae Hollis-Jefferson/99 3.00 8.00
19 Harrison Barnes/99 4.00 10.00
20 Mike Conley/99 4.00 10.00

2017-18 Panini Impeccable Draft Picks Autographs

PRINT RUNS B/WN 1-27 COPIES PER
NO PRICING ON QTY 13 OR LESS
EXCHANGE DEADLINE 04/03/2020
11 Kyle Kuzma/27 12.00 30.00

2017-18 Panini Impeccable Impeccable Numbers Autographs

PRINT RUNS B/WN 1-34 COPIES PER
NO PRICING ON QTY 13 OR LESS
EXCHANGE DEADLINE 04/03/2020
8 Bernard King/30 12.00 30.00
10 Blake Griffin/23 25.00 60.00
16 Karl-Anthony Towns/32 100.00 250.00
18 Steve Kerr/25 40.00 100.00
20 Clyde Drexler/22 50.00 120.00
26 Richard Hamilton/32 25.00 60.00
28 Sam Jones/24 30.00 80.00
30 Gordon Hayward/20 40.00 100.00
31 Charles Barkley/34 300.00 500.00

2017-18 Panini Impeccable Impeccable Stats Autographs

PRINT RUNS B/WN 3-60 COPIES PER
NO PRICING ON QTY 13 OR LESS
EXCHANGE DEADLINE 04/03/2020
1 Ernie DiGregorio/25 30.00 80.00
2 Kevin Johnson/25 40.00 100.00
3 John Stockton/28 60.00 150.00
4 Dennis Rodman/34 60.00 150.00
6 Lou Williams/50 12.00 30.00
7 Andre Drummond/27 20.00 50.00
8 Bernard King/55 5.00 12.00
9 Nate Archibald/55 10.00 25.00
10 Glen Rice/56 10.00 25.00
11 Adrian Dantley/57 6.00 15.00
12 Jerry Stackhouse/57 15.00 40.00
13 Purvis Short/59 5.00 12.00
14 Tom Chambers/60 8.00 20.00
23 Aaron Gordon/41 20.00 50.00
24 Kemba Walker/41 30.00 80.00
25 Khris Middleton/40 12.00 30.00
26 Kristaps Porzingis/40 30.00 80.00
27 Calvin Murphy/57 12.00 30.00
31 Charles Barkley/33 300.00 600.00

2017-18 Panini Impeccable Impeccable Victory Signatures

PRINT RUNS B/WN 15-99 COPIES PER
NO PRICING ON QTY 15
EXCHANGE DEADLINE 04/03/2020
*SILVER/49: .5X TO 1.2X p/r 99
2 Antawn Jamison/99 3.00 8.00
3 Dirk Nowitzki/25 200.00 400.00
4 Mark Aguirre/99 3.00 8.00
5 Jason Kidd/99 20.00 50.00
6 Jamal Mashburn/99 3.00 8.00
7 Rick Barry/99 6.00 15.00
8 Rick Fox/99 3.00 8.00
10 Dave Cowens/99 6.00 15.00
11 Kyrie Irving/25 60.00 150.00
12 Allan Houston/99 4.00 10.00
14 Alex English/99 5.00 12.00
15 Tony Parker/99 10.00 25.00
16 Shareef Abdur-Rahim/99 3.00 8.00
17 Richard Hamilton/99 5.00 12.00
18 Jermaine O'Neal/99 4.00 10.00
20 B.J. Armstrong/99 4.00 10.00
21 Larry Bird/25 60.00 150.00
22 A.C. Green/99 4.00 10.00
23 Hakeem Olajuwon/25 30.00 80.00
24 Cedric Maxwell/99 3.00 8.00
25 Dennis Rodman/99 30.00 80.00
26 Spencer Haywood/99 4.00 10.00
27 Walt Frazier/99 8.00 20.00
28 Gail Goodrich/99 4.00 10.00
30 Danny Green/99 3.00 8.00
31 Magic Johnson/25 50.00 120.00
32 Bob McAdoo/99 5.00 12.00
33 Clyde Drexler/25 50.00 120.00
34 Paul Silas/99 4.00 10.00
35 James Worthy/99 8.00 20.00
37 Avery Johnson/99 3.00 8.00
38 Joe Dumars/99 5.00 12.00
40 Michael Cooper/99 3.00 8.00

2017-18 Panini Impeccable Indelible Ink

PRINT RUNS B/WN 15-99 COPIES PER
NO PRICING ON QTY 15
EXCHANGE DEADLINE 04/03/2020
*SILVER/49: .5X TO 1.2X p/r 99
1 Serge Ibaka/99 8.00 20.00
3 Stephen Jackson/99 3.00 8.00
4 Jerry West/25 20.00 50.00
5 Lou Williams/99 3.00 8.00
6 Anfernee Hardaway/99 20.00 50.00
7 Vlade Divac/99 4.00 10.00
8 Jayson Tatum/99 75.00 200.00
9 Isaiah Rider/99 5.00 12.00
10 Josh Jackson/99 3.00 8.00
11 Channing Frye/99 2.50 6.00
13 Patrick Beverley/99 2.50 6.00
14 Giannis Antetokounmpo/25 60.00 150.00
15 Gerald Henderson Sr./99 2.50 6.00
16 Isaiah Thomas/99 5.00 12.00
17 Antoine Walker/99 3.00 8.00
18 Lonzo Ball/99 30.00 80.00
19 Jamal Mashburn/99 3.00 8.00
20 Bam Adebayo/99 15.00 40.00
21 Danny Green/99 5.00 12.00
23 Sam Cassell/99 3.00 8.00
24 Karl-Anthony Towns/25 25.00 60.00
25 Mike Bibby/99 4.00 10.00
26 Grant Hill/99 15.00 40.00
27 Bill Laimbeer/99 5.00 12.00
28 Kyle Kuzma/99 10.00 25.00
29 Kevin Johnson/99 12.00 30.00
30 Harry Giles/99 2.50 6.00
31 Juwan Howard/99 3.00 8.00
33 Rik Smits/99 3.00 8.00
34 David Robinson/25 15.00 40.00
35 Sam Perkins/99 3.00 8.00
36 James Worthy/99 8.00 20.00
37 Detlef Schrempf/99 4.00 10.00
38 Dennis Smith Jr./99 3.00 8.00
39 Shawn Bradley/99 2.50 6.00
40 Jordan Bell/99 2.50 6.00
41 Michael Cooper/99 3.00 8.00
42 Dwyane Wade/25 30.00 80.00
43 Rolando Blackman/99 3.00 8.00
44 Brandon Ingram/25 30.00 80.00
45 Shareef Abdur-Rahim/99 5.00 12.00
46 Kristaps Porzingis/99 12.00 30.00
47 Doug Collins/99 4.00 10.00
48 Markelle Fultz/99 20.00 50.00
49 Spud Webb/99 4.00 10.00
50 Frank Ntilikina/99 3.00 8.00
51 Nene/99 3.00 8.00
52 Magic Johnson/25 50.00 120.00
53 Tom Gugliotta/99 2.50 6.00
54 Clyde Drexler/25 50.00 120.00
55 Spencer Haywood/99 4.00 10.00
56 Donovan Mitchell/99 75.00 200.00
57 Felipe Lopez/99 2.50 6.00
58 De'Aaron Fox/99 75.00 200.00
59 Terrell Brandon/99 2.50 6.00
60 Robert Horry/99 4.00 10.00

2017-18 Panini Impeccable Stainless Stars

STATED PRINT RUN 99 SER.#'d SETS
1 Donovan Mitchell 30.00 80.00
2 Magic Johnson 6.00 15.00
3 Lonzo Ball 8.00 20.00
4 Giannis Antetokounmpo 15.00 40.00
5 Kevin Durant 12.00 30.00
6 Russell Westbrook 5.00 12.00
7 LeBron James 50.00 120.00
8 Dennis Smith Jr. 2.50 6.00
9 Chris Paul 5.00 12.00
10 Tim Duncan 10.00 25.00
11 James Harden 6.00 15.00
12 Kawhi Leonard 8.00 20.00
13 Markelle Fultz 5.00 12.00
14 Charles Barkley 12.00 30.00
15 Jayson Tatum 75.00 200.00
16 De'Aaron Fox 25.00 60.00
17 Kobe Bryant 75.00 200.00
18 Kyrie Irving 6.00 15.00
19 Reggie Miller 6.00 15.00
20 Larry Bird 12.00 30.00
21 Anthony Davis 8.00 20.00
22 Josh Jackson 2.50 6.00
23 Kristaps Porzingis 4.00 10.00
24 Ben Simmons 3.00 8.00
25 Frank Ntilikina 2.50 6.00
26 Shaquille O'Neal 10.00 25.00
27 Kyle Kuzma 8.00 20.00
28 Jordan Bell 2.00 5.00
29 Damian Lillard 3.00 8.00
30 Stephen Curry 25.00 60.00

2018-19 Panini Impeccable

STATED PRINT RUN 99 SER.#'d SETS
EXCHANGE DEADLINE 08/20/2020
1 Kyle Lowry 2.00 5.00
2 Myles Turner 2.00 5.00
3 Elfrid Payton 1.50 4.00
4 Chris Paul 4.00 10.00
5 Devin Booker 5.00 12.00
6 Karl-Anthony Towns 3.00 8.00
7 T.J. Warren 1.50 4.00
8 Joel Embiid 5.00 12.00
9 Nicolas Batum 1.25 3.00
10 Dejounte Murray 2.50 6.00
11 Evan Fournier 1.50 4.00
12 James Harden 4.00 10.00
13 Jeremy Lin 3.00 8.00
14 Andrew Wiggins 2.50 6.00
15 De'Aaron Fox 4.00 10.00
16 Lou Williams 1.50 4.00
17 JR Smith 2.00 5.00
18 Clint Capela 1.50 4.00
19 Lauri Markkanen 3.00 8.00
20 Nikola Jokic 10.00 25.00
21 Jimmy Butler 3.00 8.00
22 John Collins 2.00 5.00
23 Draymond Green 2.50 6.00
24 Dario Saric 1.50 4.00
25 Stephen Curry 15.00 40.00
26 Ricky Rubio 1.50 4.00
27 Evan Turner 1.25 3.00
28 Kevin Durant 8.00 20.00
29 Kyle Kuzma 2.00 5.00
30 Tyreke Evans 1.25 3.00
31 Klay Thompson 5.00 12.00
32 DeAndre Jordan 1.50 4.00
33 Eric Bledsoe 1.50 4.00
34 LaMarcus Aldridge 2.00 5.00
35 Dirk Nowitzki 5.00 12.00
36 Zach LaVine 3.00 8.00
37 Marcin Gortat 1.25 3.00
38 Trevor Ariza 1.25 3.00
39 Zach Randolph 1.50 4.00
40 Pau Gasol 3.00 8.00
41 LeBron James 25.00 60.00
42 Tony Parker 3.00 8.00
43 Rudy Gobert 2.50 6.00
44 Eric Gordon 1.50 4.00
45 Buddy Hield 2.00 5.00
46 Tim Hardaway Jr. 1.25 3.00
47 DeMarcus Cousins 1.50 4.00
48 Kris Dunn 1.25 3.00
49 Jarrett Allen 2.00 5.00
50 Aaron Gordon 2.00 5.00
51 Kemba Walker 1.50 4.00
52 DeMar DeRozan 2.50 6.00
53 Kyle Korver 1.50 4.00
54 CJ McCollum 2.00 5.00
55 Isaiah Thomas 1.50 4.00
56 Giannis Antetokounmpo 10.00 25.00
57 Hassan Whiteside 1.50 4.00
58 Fred VanVleet 2.50 6.00
59 Jonathan Isaac 1.50 4.00
60 Bogdan Bogdanovic 2.00 5.00
61 Blake Griffin 2.00 5.00
62 Jamal Murray 4.00 10.00
63 Khris Middleton 2.00 5.00
64 Marc Gasol 1.50 4.00
65 Dennis Smith Jr. 1.25 3.00
66 Nikola Vucevic 1.50 4.00
67 Dennis Schroder 1.50 4.00
68 Anthony Davis 5.00 12.00
69 Ben Simmons 2.00 5.00
70 Kawhi Leonard 5.00 12.00
71 Kristaps Porzingis 2.50 6.00
72 D'Angelo Russell 2.00 5.00
73 Lonzo Ball 2.00 5.00
74 Donovan Mitchell 6.00 15.00
75 Russell Westbrook 3.00 8.00
76 Caris LeVert 2.00 5.00
77 Vince Carter 4.00 10.00
78 Dwight Howard 2.50 6.00
79 Andre Drummond 1.50 4.00
80 Kevin Love 1.50 4.00
81 Dillon Brooks 2.00 5.00
82 Tobias Harris 1.50 4.00
83 Dion Waiters 1.25 3.00
84 Nikola Mirotic 1.25 3.00
85 Derrick Rose 4.00 10.00
86 Damian Lillard 5.00 12.00
87 Markelle Fultz 1.50 4.00
88 Steven Adams 1.50 4.00
89 Kyrie Irving 5.00 12.00
90 Paul George 3.00 8.00
91 Gordon Hayward 2.00 5.00
92 Victor Oladipo 1.50 4.00
93 Jayson Tatum 8.00 20.00
94 Reggie Jackson 1.50 4.00
95 Mike Conley 1.50 4.00
96 John Wall 2.50 6.00
97 Jaylen Brown 3.00 8.00
98 Bradley Beal 2.50 6.00
99 Enes Kanter 1.50 4.00
100 Brandon Ingram 2.00 5.00
101 Kostas Antetokounmpo AU RC EXCH 15.00 40.00
102 Khyri Thomas AU RC 4.00 10.00
103 Isaac Bonga AU RC 5.00 12.00
104 Melvin Frazier Jr. AU RC 4.00 10.00
105 Billy Preston AU RC 4.00 10.00
106 Chimezie Metu AU RC 5.00 12.00
107 Kevin Hervey AU RC 4.00 10.00
108 Vincent Edwards AU RC 4.00 10.00
109 Rodions Kurucs AU RC 10.00 25.00
110 Allonzo Trier AU RC 4.00 10.00
111 Deandre Ayton JSY AU RC 100.00 250.00
112 Marvin Bagley III JSY AU RC 8.00 20.00
113 Luka Doncic JSY AU RC 8,000.00 12,000.00
114 Jaren Jackson Jr. JSY AU RC 600.00 1,200.00
115 Trae Young JSY AU RC 1,500.00 3,000.00
116 Mo Bamba JSY AU RC 20.00 50.00
117 Wendell Carter Jr. JSY AU RC 30.00 80.00
118 Collin Sexton JSY AU RC 100.00 250.00
119 Kevin Knox JSY AU RC 15.00 40.00
120 Mikal Bridges JSY AU RC 25.00 60.00
121 Shai Gilgeous-Alexander JSY AU RC 2,000.00 4,000.00
122 Svi Mykhailiuk JSY AU RC 6.00 15.00
123 Jerome Robinson JSY AU RC 5.00 12.00
124 Michael Porter Jr. JSY AU RC 500.00 1,000.00
125 Troy Brown Jr. JSY AU RC 6.00 15.00
126 Zhaire Smith JSY AU RC 20.00 50.00
127 Donte DiVincenzo JSY AU RC 12.00 30.00
128 Lonnie Walker IV JSY AU RC EXCH 30.00 80.00
129 Kevin Huerter JSY AU RC EXCH 25.00 60.00
130 Josh Okogie JSY AU RC 25.00 60.00
131 Grayson Allen JSY AU RC 25.00 60.00
132 Chandler Hutchison JSY AU RC 15.00 40.00
133 Aaron Holiday JSY AU RC 8.00 20.00
134 Anfernee Simons JSY AU RC 12.00 30.00
135 Moritz Wagner JSY AU RC 25.00 60.00
136 Landry Shamet JSY AU RC 20.00 50.00
137 Robert Williams III JSY AU RC 15.00 40.00
138 Jacob Evans III JSY AU RC 5.00 12.00
139 Dzanan Musa JSY AU RC 8.00 20.00
140 Omari Spellman JSY AU RC 10.00 25.00
142 Jevon Carter JSY AU RC 15.00 40.00
143 Jalen Brunson JSY AU RC 15.00 40.00
144 Devonte' Graham JSY AU RC 8.00 20.00
145 Gary Trent Jr. JSY AU RC 8.00 20.00
146 Jarred Vanderbilt JSY AU RC 8.00 20.00
147 Keita Bates-Diop JSY AU RC 10.00 25.00
148 Bruce Brown JSY AU RC 10.00 25.00
149 De'Anthony Melton JSY AU RC 10.00 25.00
150 Hamidou Diallo JSY AU RC 20.00 50.00

2018-19 Panini Impeccable Gold

*GOLD: .6X TO 1.5X BASE
PRINT RUN 35 SER.#'d SETS
25 Stephen Curry 40.00 100.00
41 LeBron James 40.00 100.00
69 Ben Simmons 3.00 8.00
70 Kawhi Leonard 8.00 20.00

2018-19 Panini Impeccable Silver

*SILVER: .5X TO 1.2X BASE
PRINT RUN 49 SER.#'d SETS
25 Stephen Curry 20.00 50.00
41 LeBron James 30.00 80.00
56 Giannis Antetokounmpo 12.00 30.00
69 Ben Simmons 12.00 30.00

2018-19 Panini Impeccable Immortal Ink

STATED PRINT RUN B/WN 10-99 SER.#'d SETS
EXCHANGE DEADLINE 08/20/2020
1 John Salley/99 6.00 15.00
2 B.J. Armstrong/49 6.00 15.00
3 Sam Bowie/99 3.00 8.00
4 Mitch Richmond/49 EXCH 8.00 20.00
5 Brad Davis/99 4.00 10.00
7 Craig Hodges/99 4.00 10.00
8 Alonzo Mourning/25 30.00 80.00
9 Jack Sikma/99 4.00 10.00
10 Avery Johnson/49 8.00 20.00
11 Mark Eaton/99 5.00 12.00
12 Alex English/49 6.00 15.00
13 Spencer Haywood/99 4.00 10.00
14 Toni Kukoc/49 8.00 20.00
15 Bryant Reeves/99 5.00 12.00
17 Doug Collins/99 5.00 12.00
18 Jerry Lucas/49 8.00 20.00
19 Jeff Hornacek/99 4.00 10.00
20 Jalen Rose/99 5.00 12.00
21 Rod Strickland/99 4.00 10.00
23 Vin Baker/99 3.00 8.00
24 Rolando Blackman/49 5.00 12.00
25 Charlie Ward/99 4.00 10.00
27 Ernie DiGregorio/99 2.00 5.00
28 Bernard King/49 6.00 15.00
29 Keyon Dooling/99 3.00 8.00
30 Rick Fox/49 5.00 12.00

2018-19 Panini Impeccable 76ers Autographs

STATED PRINT RUN B/WN 10-99 SER.#'d SETS
EXCHANGE DEADLINE 08/20/2020
5 JJ Redick/49 12.00 30.00
8 Doug Collins/99 5.00 12.00
9 Zhaire Smith/99 3.00 8.00
10 Landry Shamet/99 5.00 12.00

2018-19 Panini Impeccable Celtics Autographs

STATED PRINT RUN B/WN 10-99 SER.#'d SETS
EXCHANGE DEADLINE 08/20/2020
4 Paul Pierce/25 60.00 150.00
7 Jayson Tatum/49 30.00 80.00
9 Al Horford/49 5.00 12.00
12 Robert Parish/49 8.00 20.00
14 Bill Walton/49 40.00 100.00
15 Tom Satch Sanders/99 10.00 25.00
17 Antoine Walker/99 5.00 12.00
18 Gerald Henderson Sr./99 3.00 8.00

2018-19 Panini Impeccable Jersey Number Autographs

STATED PRINT RUN B/WN 1-45 SER.#'d SETS
EXCHANGE DEADLINE 08/20/2020
11 Andrew Wiggins/22 30.00 80.00
13 Paul Pierce/34 100.00 250.00
15 Jason Kidd/32 100.00 250.00
18 Dominique Wilkins/21 EXCH 75.00 200.00
19 Donovan Mitchell/45 50.00 120.00

2018-19 Panini Impeccable Knicks Autographs

STATED PRINT RUN B/WN 25-99 SER.#'d SETS
EXCHANGE DEADLINE 08/20/2020
1 Kristaps Porzingis/25 40.00 100.00
3 Jerry Lucas/49 8.00 20.00
4 Walt Frazier/49 10.00 25.00
5 Bernard King/49 8.00 20.00
6 Latrell Sprewell/49 12.00 30.00
7 Mark Jackson/49 8.00 20.00
8 Enes Kanter/99 4.00 10.00
9 Allan Houston/99 5.00 12.00
10 Frank Ntilikina/99 3.00 8.00
11 Kevin Knox/99 4.00 10.00
12 Kenny Sky Walker/99 3.00 8.00
14 Bill Cartwright/99 4.00 10.00
15 Bob McAdoo/99 8.00 20.00
16 Courtney Lee/99 3.00 8.00
17 John Starks/99 8.00 20.00
19 Mel Davis/99 3.00 8.00
20 Charlie Ward/99 4.00 10.00

2018-19 Panini Impeccable Lakers Autographs

STATED PRINT RUN B/WN 10-99 SER.#'d SETS
EXCHANGE DEADLINE 08/20/2020
9 Kyle Kuzma/49 20.00 50.00
10 Nick Van Exel/49 12.00 30.00
11 Kurt Rambis/49 5.00 12.00
12 Gail Goodrich/49 6.00 15.00
13 Rick Fox/49 8.00 20.00
14 Luke Walton/99 8.00 20.00
15 A.C. Green/99 5.00 12.00
16 Jamaal Wilkes/99 5.00 12.00
17 Cedric Ceballos/99 5.00 12.00
18 Eddie Jones/99 8.00 20.00
19 Moritz Wagner/99 6.00 15.00
20 Svi Mykhailiuk/99 4.00 10.00

2018-19 Panini Impeccable Pistons Autographs

STATED PRINT RUN B/WN 25-99 SER.#'d SETS
EXCHANGE DEADLINE 08/20/2020
1 Dennis Rodman/25 60.00 150.00
2 Grant Hill/25 25.00 60.00
4 Bob Lanier/49 8.00 20.00
5 Richard Hamilton/49 8.00 20.00
7 Chauncey Billups/49 8.00 20.00
8 Reggie Jackson/49 5.00 12.00
9 Joe Dumars/49 8.00 20.00
10 Kelly Tripucka/99 3.00 8.00

2018-19 Panini Impeccable Points Autographs

2 Ray Allen/26 100.00 250.00
3 Donovan Mitchell/20 150.00 400.00
4 Giannis Antetokounmpo/26 300.00 800.00
6 Kristaps Porzingis/22 60.00 150.00
7 Kyrie Irving/24 150.00 400.00
8 Stephen Curry/26 1,000.00 2,000.00
11 Bernard King/32 12.00 30.00
12 Dominique Wilkins/30 EXCH 25.00 60.00
13 George Gervin/33 25.00 60.00
14 Kareem Abdul-Jabbar/34 100.00 250.00
15 Karl Malone/31 50.00 120.00
16 Oscar Robertson/29 40.00 100.00
17 Tracy McGrady/32 250.00 500.00
19 Chris Mullin/26 EXCH 25.00 60.00
20 Paul Pierce/26 EXCH 75.00 200.00

2018-19 Panini Impeccable Rookie Signatures

STATED PRINT RUN 99 SER.#'d SETS
EXCHANGE DEADLINE 08/20/2020
1 Deandre Ayton 40.00 100.00
2 Marvin Bagley III 8.00 20.00
3 Luka Doncic 1,500.00 3,000.00
4 Jaren Jackson Jr. 150.00 400.00
5 Trae Young 400.00 800.00
6 Mo Bamba 15.00 40.00
7 Wendell Carter Jr. 20.00 50.00
8 Collin Sexton 30.00 80.00
9 Kevin Knox 6.00 15.00
10 Mikal Bridges 25.00 60.00
11 Shai Gilgeous-Alexander 500.00 1,000.00
12 Svi Mykhailiuk 5.00 12.00
13 Jerome Robinson 5.00 12.00
14 Michael Porter Jr. 200.00 500.00
15 Troy Brown Jr. 6.00 15.00
16 Zhaire Smith 5.00 12.00
17 Donte DiVincenzo 12.00 30.00
18 Lonnie Walker IV EXCH 15.00 40.00
19 Kevin Huerter EXCH 10.00 25.00
20 Josh Okogie 12.00 30.00
21 Grayson Allen 10.00 25.00
22 Chandler Hutchison 6.00 15.00
23 Aaron Holiday 10.00 25.00
24 Anfernee Simons 25.00 60.00
25 Moritz Wagner 10.00 25.00
26 Landry Shamet 10.00 25.00
27 Robert Williams III 10.00 25.00
28 Jacob Evans III 5.00 12.00
29 Dzanan Musa 5.00 12.00
30 Omari Spellman 5.00 12.00
31 Elie Okobo 5.00 12.00
32 Jevon Carter 8.00 20.00
33 Jalen Brunson 40.00 100.00
34 Devonte' Graham 8.00 20.00
35 Gary Trent Jr. 10.00 25.00
36 Jarred Vanderbilt 10.00 25.00
37 Keita Bates-Diop 6.00 15.00
38 Bruce Brown 10.00 25.00
39 De'Anthony Melton 10.00 25.00
40 Hamidou Diallo 8.00 20.00

2018-19 Panini Impeccable Rookie Signatures Holo Silver

STATED PRINT RUN 25 SER.#'d SETS
EXCHANGE DEADLINE 08/20/2020
20 Josh Okogie 12.00 30.00

2018-19 Panini Impeccable Stars Signatures

STATED PRINT RUN B/WN 10-49 SER.#'d SETS
EXCHANGE DEADLINE 08/20/2020
2 Brook Lopez/49 8.00 20.00
4 Goran Dragic/49 5.00 12.00
6 Myles Turner/49 6.00 15.00
8 Lauri Markkanen/49 20.00 50.00
9 Isaiah Thomas/25 12.00 30.00
12 Kyle Kuzma/49 25.00 60.00
14 JJ Redick/49 6.00 15.00
18 Willie Cauley-Stein/49 10.00 25.00
19 Lonzo Ball/25 25.00 60.00
20 Harrison Barnes/49 5.00 12.00
22 Nikola Jokic/49 150.00 400.00
24 Clint Capela/49 5.00 12.00
26 Enes Kanter/49 5.00 12.00
27 Tony Parker/25 EXCH 20.00 50.00
28 J.J. Barea/49 12.00 30.00
29 Jeremy Lin/25 25.00 60.00
30 Mike Conley/49 5.00 12.00

2018-19 Panini Impeccable Victory Signatures

STATED PRINT RUN B/WN 10-99 SER.#'d SETS
EXCHANGE DEADLINE 08/20/2020
2 Robert Parish/49 10.00 25.00
4 A.C. Green/49 6.00 15.00
8 Tom Satch Sanders/49 10.00 25.00
10 Chauncey Billups/49 8.00 20.00
12 B.J. Armstrong/49 10.00 25.00
14 Bill Cartwright/49 5.00 12.00
16 Toni Kukoc/49 25.00 60.00
17 Alonzo Mourning/25 40.00 100.00
18 Gerald Henderson Sr./99 3.00 8.00
19 Steve Kerr/49 8.00 20.00
20 Jason Terry/49 15.00 40.00
22 Horace Grant/49 10.00 25.00
24 Mark Aguirre/49 5.00 12.00
26 Bruce Bowen/99 4.00 10.00
27 Paul Pierce/25 EXCH 50.00 120.00
28 John Salley/99 4.00 10.00
29 Avery Johnson/49 6.00 15.00
30 Rick Fox/49 8.00 20.00

2018-19 Panini Impeccable Victory Signatures Holo Silver

8 Tom Satch Sanders/25 12.00 30.00
16 Toni Kukoc/25 30.00 80.00
20 Jason Terry/25 20.00 50.00
22 Horace Grant/25 12.00 30.00
30 Rick Fox/25 10.00 25.00

2018-19 Panini Impeccable Warriors Autographs

STATED PRINT RUN B/WN 10-99 SER.#'d SETS
EXCHANGE DEADLINE 08/20/2020
3 Mitch Richmond/99 EXCH 8.00 20.00
5 Jerry Lucas/49 15.00 40.00
7 Antawn Jamison/49 6.00 15.00
8 Jamaal Wilkes/99 6.00 15.00
9 Tim Hardaway/99 12.00 30.00
10 Sarunas Marciulionis/99 5.00 12.00

2018-19 Panini Impeccable Indelible Ink

STATED PRINT RUN B/WN 15-99 SER.#'d SETS
EXCHANGE DEADLINE 08/20/2020
1 Bruce Bowen/99 4.00 10.00
3 Detlef Schrempf/99 8.00 20.00
4 Tracy McGrady/25 50.00 125.00
5 James Silas/99 5.00 12.00
6 Dave Cowens/49 6.00 15.00
7 Larry Nance/99 3.00 8.00
8 A.C. Green/49 5.00 12.00
9 Rudy Tomjanovich/99 4.00 10.00
11 Cedric Ceballos/99 4.00 10.00
13 Erick Dampier/99 3.00 8.00
14 Artis Gilmore/49 8.00 20.00
15 Joe Smith/99 8.00 20.00
16 Ralph Sampson/49 5.00 12.00
17 Muggsy Bogues/99 6.00 15.00
18 David Thompson/49 8.00 20.00
19 Sidney Moncrief/99 3.00 8.00
20 Rik Smits/49 5.00 12.00
21 Corey Maggette/99 4.00 10.00
23 Gerald Henderson Sr./99 3.00 8.00
24 Nick Van Exel/49 10.00 25.00
25 Kerry Kittles/99 3.00 8.00
26 Antawn Jamison/49 5.00 12.00
27 Rick Mahorn/99 3.00 8.00
28 Mark Aguirre/49 5.00 12.00
29 Terrell Brandon/99 3.00 8.00
30 Brad Daugherty/99 4.00 10.00

2018-19 Panini Impeccable Indelible Ink Holo Silver

STATED PRINT RUN B/TW 5-25 SER.#'d SETS
EXCHANGE DEADLINE 08/20/2020
3 Detlef Schrempf/25 12.00 30.00
15 Joe Smith/25 12.00 30.00
17 Muggsy Bogues/25 10.00 25.00
24 Nick Van Exel/25 12.00 30.00

2018-19 Panini Impeccable Stainless Stars
STATED PRINT RUN 99 SER.#'d SETS
1 Kyrie Irving 8.00 20.00
3 James Harden 6.00 15.00
4 Jaren Jackson Jr. 15.00 40.00
5 Russell Westbrook 5.00 12.00
6 Wendell Carter Jr. 5.00 12.00
7 Draymond Green 8.00 20.00
8 Anthony Davis 8.00 20.00
9 Stephen Curry 15.00 40.00
10 Deandre Ayton 6.00 15.00
11 Kevin Durant 12.00 30.00
12 Trae Young 40.00 100.00
13 Jayson Tatum 12.00 30.00
14 Collin Sexton 6.00 15.00
15 Klay Thompson 8.00 20.00
18 Donovan Mitchell 12.00 30.00
19 LeBron James 40.00 100.00
20 Marvin Bagley III 12.00 30.00
21 Ben Simmons 20.00 50.00
22 Mo Bamba 8.00 20.00
23 Joel Embiid 8.00 20.00
24 Kevin Knox 2.50 6.00
25 Chris Paul 6.00 15.00

2018-19 Panini Impeccable Stainless Stars Autographs
STATED PRINT RUN B/WN 15-99 SER.#'d SETS
EXCHANGE DEADLINE 08/20/2020
2 Mikal Bridges/99 8.00 20.00
4 Troy Brown Jr./99 4.00 10.00
5 Deandre Ayton/99 60.00 150.00
6 Grayson Allen/99 10.00 25.00
7 Jaren Jackson Jr./99 150.00 400.00
8 Lonnie Walker IV/99 EXCH 12.00 30.00
9 Wendell Carter Jr./99 20.00 50.00
10 Michael Porter Jr./99 30.00 80.00
12 Shai Gilgeous-Alexander/99 500.00 1,000.00
13 Reggie Miller/25 75.00 200.00
14 Zhaire Smith/99 5.00 12.00
15 Marvin Bagley III/99 8.00 20.00
16 Josh Okogie/99 8.00 20.00
17 Mo Bamba/99 8.00 20.00
19 Collin Sexton/99 25.00 60.00
20 Kevin Knox/99 4.00 10.00
22 Jerome Robinson/99 3.00 8.00
23 Trae Young/99 200.00 500.00
24 Donte DiVincenzo/99 8.00 20.00
25 Luka Doncic/99 800.00 1,500.00

2019-20 Panini Impeccable
1-100 PRINT RUN 99 SER.#'d SETS
AU PRINT RUN B/WN 49-99 COPIES PER
JSY AU PRINT RUN B/WN 75-99 COPIES PER
EXCHANGE DEADLINE 9/11/2021
1 Luka Samanic/99 RC 2.00 5.00
2 Romeo Langford/99 RC 1.50 4.00
3 Matisse Thybulle/99 RC 3.00 8.00
4 Sekou Doumbouya/99 RC 1.50 4.00
5 Carsen Edwards/99 RC 2.00 5.00
6 Cameron Johnson/99 RC 4.00 10.00
7 Nickeil Alexander-Walker/99 RC 2.50 6.00
8 PJ Washington Jr./99 RC 5.00 12.00
9 Goga Bitadze/99 RC 2.50 6.00
10 Tyler Herro/99 RC 8.00 20.00
11 Deandre Ayton/99 2.00 5.00
12 Nikola Vucevic/99 1.50 4.00
13 Damian Lillard/99 5.00 12.00
14 Ben Simmons/99 2.00 5.00
15 Joel Embiid/99 4.00 10.00
16 Chris Paul/99 4.00 10.00
17 Josh Richardson/99 1.25 3.00
18 Steven Adams/99 1.50 4.00
19 Devin Booker/99 .50 1.25
20 Aaron Gordon/99 2.00 5.00
21 Jayson Tatum/99 8.00 20.00
22 Keldon Johnson/99 RC 5.00 12.00
23 Kyrie Irving/99 4.00 10.00
24 Kevin Porter Jr./99 RC 3.00 8.00
25 Trae Young/99 5.00 12.00
26 Darius Bazley/99 RC 1.50 4.00
27 John Collins/99 2.00 5.00
28 Ty Jerome/99 RC 3.00 8.00
29 Kemba Walker/99 1.50 4.00
30 Nassir Little/99 RC 2.50 6.00
31 Marc Gasol/99 2.00 5.00
32 Buddy Hield/99 1.50 4.00
33 Kyle Lowry/99 2.00 5.00
34 Marvin Bagley III/99 1.50 4.00
35 DeMar DeRozan/99 2.50 6.00
36 CJ McCollum/99 2.00 5.00
37 LaMarcus Aldridge/99 2.00 5.00
38 Kendrick Nunn/99 RC 2.50 6.00
39 Pascal Siakam/99 3.00 8.00
40 De'Aaron Fox/99 3.00 8.00
41 Kevin Love/99 2.00 5.00
42 Miles Bridges/99 2.00 5.00
43 Luka Doncic/99 75.00 200.00
44 Zach LaVine/99 3.00 8.00
45 Lauri Markkanen/99 2.50 6.00
46 Kevin Durant/99 6.00 15.00
47 Wendell Carter Jr./99 2.00 5.00
48 DeAndre Jordan/99 1.50 4.00
49 Collin Sexton/99 2.50 6.00
50 Terry Rozier/99 1.50 4.00
51 Dennis Smith Jr./99 1.25 3.00
52 John Wall/99 2.50 6.00
53 Jrue Holiday/99 2.50 6.00
54 Bradley Beal/99 2.50 6.00
55 Isaiah Thomas/99 1.50 4.00
56 Mike Conley/99 1.50 4.00
57 Ricky Rubio/99 1.50 4.00
58 Donovan Mitchell/99 4.00 10.00
59 Tobias Harris/99 1.50 4.00
60 Rudy Gobert/99 2.50 6.00
61 D'Angelo Russell/99 1.50 4.00
62 Nikola Jokic/99 5.00 12.00
63 Draymond Green/99 2.50 6.00
64 Blake Griffin/99 2.00 5.00
65 Andre Drummond/99 1.50 4.00
66 Kristaps Porzingis/99 2.50 6.00
67 Stephen Curry/99 20.00 50.00
68 Jamal Murray/99 3.00 8.00
69 Klay Thompson/99 5.00 12.00
70 Paul Millsap/99 1.50 4.00
71 Jaren Jackson Jr./99 3.00 8.00
72 Malcolm Brogdon/99 1.50 4.00
73 Jonas Valanciunas/99 1.50 4.00
74 Paul George/99 3.00 8.00
75 Kawhi Leonard/99 5.00 12.00
76 Russell Westbrook/99 3.00 8.00
77 LeBron James/99 75.00 200.00
78 James Harden/99 8.00 20.00
79 Anthony Davis/99 12.00 30.00
80 Victor Oladipo/99 1.50 4.00
81 Rui Hachimura/99 RC 12.00 30.00
82 RJ Barrett/99 RC 12.00 30.00
83 Cam Reddish/99 RC 2.50 6.00
84 De'Andre Hunter/99 RC 12.00 30.00
85 Jarrett Culver/99 RC 1.50 4.00
86 Darius Garland/99 RC 12.00 30.00
87 Coby White/99 RC 15.00 40.00
88 Zion Williamson/99 RC 200.00 500.00
89 Jaxson Hayes/99 RC 2.50 6.00
90 Ja Morant/99 RC 100.00 250.00
91 Kevin Knox II/99 1.25 3.00
92 Khris Middleton/99 2.00 5.00
93 Julius Randle/99 2.50 6.00
94 Andrew Wiggins/99 2.50 6.00
95 Karl-Anthony Towns/99 5.00 12.00
96 Goran Dragic/99 1.50 4.00
97 Brandon Ingram/99 2.00 5.00
98 Jimmy Butler/99 6.00 15.00
99 Lonzo Ball/99 2.00 5.00
100 Giannis Antetokounmpo/99 15.00 40.00
101 Kevin Porter Jr. AU/99 8.00 20.00
102 Cam Reddish AU/99 6.00 15.00
103 Cody Martin AU/99 RC 6.00 15.00
104 Romeo Langford AU/99 4.00 10.00
105 Bol Bol AU/99 RC 40.00 100.00
106 Goga Bitadze AU/99 6.00 15.00
107 Grant Williams AU/99 RC 10.00 25.00
108 Zion Williamson AU/49 800.00 1,500.00
109 Dylan Windler AU/99 RC 15.00 40.00
110 Jarrett Culver AU/99 4.00 10.00
111 KZ Okpala AU/99 RC 20.00 50.00
112 Cameron Johnson AU/99 20.00 50.00
113 Eric Paschall AU/99 RC 5.00 12.00
114 Sekou Doumbouya AU/99 4.00 10.00
115 Isaiah Roby AU/99 RC 6.00 15.00
116 Luka Samanic AU/99 5.00 12.00
117 Darius Bazley AU/99 4.00 10.00
118 Ja Morant AU/99 400.00 1,000.00
119 Mfiondu Kabengele AU/99 RC 10.00 25.00
120 Coby White AU/99 100.00 250.00
121 Carsen Edwards AU/99 5.00 12.00
122 PJ Washington Jr. AU/99 20.00 50.00
123 Admiral Schofield AU/99 RC 12.00 30.00
124 Chuma Okeke AU/99 RC 30.00 80.00
125 Ignas Brazdeikis AU/99 RC 5.00 12.00
126 Matisse Thybulle AU/99 40.00 100.00
127 Ty Jerome AU/99 10.00 25.00
128 RJ Barrett AU/99 100.00 250.00
129 Jordan Poole AU/99 RC 15.00 40.00
130 Jaxson Hayes AU/99 20.00 50.00
131 Bruno Fernando AU/99 RC 8.00 20.00
132 Tyler Herro AU/99 200.00 500.00
133 Jaylen Nowell AU/99 RC 5.00 12.00
134 Nickeil Alexander-Walker AU/99 15.00 40.00
135 Quinndary Weatherspoon AU/99 RC 4.00 10.00
136 Brandon Clarke AU/99 RC 75.00 200.00
137 Nassir Little AU/99 15.00 40.00
138 De'Andre Hunter AU/99 25.00 60.00
139 Keldon Johnson AU/99 40.00 100.00
140 Rui Hachimura AU/99 75.00 200.00
141 Goga Bitadze JSY AU/99 8.00 20.00
142 Grant Williams JSY AU/99 15.00 40.00
143 Zion Williamson JSY AU/75 1,000.00 2,000.00
144 Mfiondu Kabengele JSY AU/99 12.00 30.00
145 Jarrett Culver JSY AU/99 6.00 15.00
146 Carsen Edwards JSY AU/99 6.00 15.00
147 Cam Reddish JSY AU/99 8.00 20.00
148 Admiral Schofield JSY AU/99 12.00 30.00
149 Romeo Langford JSY AU/99 5.00 12.00
150 Ignas Brazdeikis JSY AU/99 6.00 15.00
151 Luka Samanic JSY AU/99 6.00 15.00
152 Ty Jerome JSY AU/99 10.00 25.00
153 Ja Morant JSY AU/99 500.00 1,200.00
154 Keldon Johnson JSY AU/99 100.00 250.00
155 Coby White JSY AU/99 125.00 300.00
156 Bruno Fernando JSY AU/99 12.00 30.00
157 Cameron Johnson JSY AU/99 25.00 60.00
158 Jaylen Nowell JSY AU/99 6.00 15.00
159 Sekou Doumbouya JSY AU/99 5.00 12.00
160 Quinndary Weatherspoon JSY AU/99 5.00 12.00
161 Matisse Thybulle JSY AU/99 40.00 100.00
162 Nassir Little JSY AU/99 15.00 40.00
163 RJ Barrett JSY AU/99 100.00 250.00
164 Kevin Porter Jr. JSY AU/99 10.00 25.00
165 Jaxson Hayes JSY AU/99 30.00 80.00
166 Cody Martin JSY AU/99 8.00 20.00
167 PJ Washington Jr. JSY AU/99 15.00 40.00
168 Bol Bol JSY AU/99 50.00 120.00
169 Chuma Okeke JSY AU/99 60.00 150.00
170 Tremont Waters JSY AU/99 RC 15.00 40.00
171 Brandon Clarke JSY AU/99 40.00 100.00
172 Dylan Windler JSY AU/99 15.00 40.00
173 De'Andre Hunter JSY AU/99 30.00 80.00
174 KZ Okpala JSY AU/99 15.00 40.00
175 Rui Hachimura JSY AU/99 125.00 300.00
176 Eric Paschall JSY AU/99 6.00 15.00
177 Tyler Herro JSY AU/99 250.00 600.00
178 Isaiah Roby JSY AU/99 6.00 15.00
179 Nickeil Alexander-Walker JSY AU/99 25.00 60.00
180 Kyle Guy JSY AU/99 RC 20.00 50.00

2019-20 Panini Impeccable Gold
*GOLD: .6X TO 1.5X BASIC
*GOLD RC: .5X TO 1.2X BASIC
STATED PRINT RUN 49 SER.#'d SETS

2019-20 Panini Impeccable Holo Silver
*HOLO SLVR: .8X TO 2X BASIC
*HOLO SLVR RC: .6X TO 1.5X BASIC
*HOLO SLVR AU: .6X TO 1.5X BASIC
*HOLO SLVR JSY AU: .6X TO 1.5X BASIC
STATED PRINT RUN 25 SER.#'d SETS
EXCHANGE DEADLINE 04/03/2020
83 Cam Reddish 4.00 10.00
88 Zion Williamson 600.00 1,200.00
108 Zion Williamson AU 1,000.00 2,000.00
112 Cameron Johnson AU 20.00 120.00
130 Jaxson Hayes AU 60.00 150.00
132 Tyler Herro AU 400.00 1,000.00
142 Grant Williams JSY AU 30.00 80.00
159 Sekou Doumbouya JSY AU 8.00 20.00
165 Jaxson Hayes JSY AU 60.00 150.00
168 Bol Bol JSY AU 100.00 250.00
170 Tremont Waters JSY AU 30.00 80.00
177 Tyler Herro JSY AU 500.00 1,200.00

2019-20 Panini Impeccable Canvas Creations Autographs
NO PRICING QTY 15 OR LESS
EXCHANGE DEADLINE 9/11/2021
EXCHANGE DEADLINE 9/11/2021
*HOLO SLVR: .6X TO 1.5X p/r 49-99
*HOLO SLVR: .4X TO 1X p/r 25
1 Grant Hill/25 20.00 50.00
2 Dino Radja/99 3.00 8.00
3 Sam Jones/25 25.00 60.00
4 Rik Smits/99 4.00 10.00
5 Danny Manning/49 4.00 10.00
6 Jamaal Wilkes/99 6.00 15.00
8 Dan Issel/99 6.00 15.00
10 Quinn Buckner/99 3.00 8.00
11 Elgin Baylor/25 30.00 80.00
13 Kenny Smith/49 6.00 15.00
14 Wally Szczerbiak/99 4.00 10.00
15 Bob McAdoo/99 10.00 25.00
16 Bill Cartwright/99 4.00 10.00
18 Bob Dandridge/99 3.00 8.00
20 Eddie Jones/99 6.00 15.00
21 Latrell Sprewell/25 15.00 40.00
22 Rony Seikaly/99 3.00 8.00
23 Derek Fisher/49 10.00 25.00
24 Jamal Mashburn/99 8.00 20.00
26 Fred VanVleet/99 15.00 40.00
28 Raja Bell/99 4.00 10.00
29 Kevin Garnett/25 200.00 500.00
30 Tyronn Lue/99 3.00 8.00

2019-20 Panini Impeccable Elegance Retired Jersey Autographs
PRINT RUNS B/WN 10-99 COPIES PER
NO PRICING QTY 15 OR LESS
EXCHANGE DEADLINE 9/11/2021
*HOLO SLVR: .6X TO 1.5X p/r 49-99
*HOLO SLVR: .4X TO 1X p/r 25
5 Mike Bibby/99 8.00 20.00
6 Richard Hamilton/49 15.00 40.00
7 Tony Parker/25 20.00 50.00
8 Kareem Abdul-Jabbar/25 100.00 250.00
9 Magic Johnson/25 50.00 120.00

2019-20 Panini Impeccable Elegance Veteran Jersey Autographs
PRINT RUNS B/WN 10-49 COPIES PER
NO PRICING QTY 15 OR LESS
EXCHANGE DEADLINE 9/11/2021
*HOLO SLVR: .6X TO 1.5X p/r 49
*HOLO SLVR: .4X TO 1X p/r 25
2 Nikola Vucevic/49 10.00 25.00
3 Nikola Jokic/25 300.00 600.00
4 Lauri Markkanen/25 15.00 40.00
6 Collin Sexton/49 15.00 40.00
7 Wendell Carter Jr./49 8.00 20.00
8 Myles Turner/49 8.00 20.00

2019-20 Panini Impeccable Extravagance Autographs
PRINT RUNS B/WN 10-99 COPIES PER
NO PRICING QTY 15 OR LESS
EXCHANGE DEADLINE 9/11/2021
*HOLO SLVR: .6X TO 1.5X p/r 49-99
*HOLO SLVR: .4X TO 1X p/r 25
7 Kevin Garnett/25 200.00 500.00
8 Pat Riley/25 20.00 50.00
9 Chris Bosh/25 30.00 80.00
11 Gordon Hayward/25 15.00 40.00
12 Danilo Gallinari/49 4.00 10.00
13 Nikola Vucevic/49 4.00 10.00
14 Jalen Rose/49 10.00 25.00
15 Gail Goodrich/49 5.00 12.00
16 Horace Grant/99 12.00 30.00
17 Lonzo Ball/25 20.00 50.00
18 Alex English/99 6.00 15.00
19 Cedric Maxwell/99 4.00 10.00
20 Maurice Cheeks/99 4.00 10.00
21 Caron Butler/99 4.00 10.00
22 Don Chaney/99 5.00 12.00
23 Lionel Hollins/99 3.00 8.00
24 Devean George/99 4.00 10.00
25 Cuttino Mobley/99 3.00 8.00
26 Brad Daugherty/99 4.00 10.00
27 Dell Curry/99 3.00 8.00
28 Mark Price/99 10.00 25.00
29 Arvydas Sabonis/99 5.00 12.00
30 A.C. Green/99 5.00 12.00

2019-20 Panini Impeccable Illustrious Ink
PRINT RUNS B/WN 10-99 COPIES PER
NO PRICING QTY 15 OR LESS
EXCHANGE DEADLINE 9/11/2021
1 Wally Szczerbiak/99 4.00 10.00
3 Raja Bell/99 4.00 10.00
4 Bob Lanier/25 10.00 25.00
5 Tyronn Lue/99 3.00 8.00
6 Gail Goodrich/49 5.00 12.00
7 Chris Mullin/99 15.00 40.00
9 Bill Cartwright/99 4.00 10.00
10 Walt Frazier/25 10.00 25.00
11 Bob Dandridge/99 3.00 8.00
12 Dennis Rodman/25 60.00 150.00
13 Caron Butler/99 4.00 10.00
14 Derek Fisher/49 10.00 25.00
15 Kelly Tripucka/99 4.00 10.00
16 Dave Cowens/49 8.00 20.00
17 Shane Battier/99 4.00 10.00
19 Alvan Adams/99 3.00 8.00
20 Hakeem Olajuwon/25 250.00 600.00
21 Horace Grant/99 12.00 30.00
22 Rick Barry/25 15.00 40.00
23 Quinn Buckner/99 3.00 8.00
24 Bob McAdoo/49 10.00 25.00
25 Dino Radja/99 3.00 8.00
26 Robert Parish/49 6.00 15.00
27 Kurt Rambis/99 12.00 30.00
29 Cedric Maxwell/99 4.00 10.00
30 David Robinson/25 100.00 250.00
31 Stromile Swift/99 3.00 8.00
32 Christian Laettner/25 30.00 80.00
33 Eddie Jones/99 6.00 15.00
34 Lenny Wilkens/49 6.00 15.00
35 Jamal Mashburn/99 8.00 20.00
36 Mark Jackson/49 4.00 10.00
37 Tom Heinsohn/99 40.00 100.00
38 Kevin Garnett/25 200.00 500.00
39 Dan Issel/99 6.00 15.00
40 Grant Hill/25 20.00 50.00

2019-20 Panini Impeccable Illustrious Ink Holo Silver
*HOLO SLVR: .6X TO 1.5X p/r 49-99
*HOLO SLVR: .4X TO 1X p/r 25
PRINT RUNS B/WN 5-25 COPIES PER
NO PRICING QTY 15 OR LESS
EXCHANGE DEADLINE 9/11/2021
37 Tom Heinsohn/25 100.00 250.00

2019-20 Panini Impeccable Immortal Ink
PRINT RUNS B/WN 10-99 COPIES PER
NO PRICING QTY 15 OR LESS
EXCHANGE DEADLINE 9/11/2021
*HOLO SLVR: .6X TO 1.5X p/r 49-99
*HOLO SLVR: .4X TO 1X p/r 25
2 Ralph Sampson/49 4.00 10.00
4 Jalen Rose/49 10.00 25.00
5 David Robinson/25 100.00 250.00
6 World B. Free/49 4.00 10.00
7 Elgin Baylor/25 30.00 80.00
9 Sam Jones/25 25.00 60.00
10 Kenny Smith/49 6.00 15.00
12 Lenny Wilkens/49 6.00 15.00
13 Walt Frazier/25 10.00 25.00
14 Dave Cowens/49 8.00 20.00
15 Pat Riley/25 20.00 50.00
16 Mark Jackson/49 4.00 10.00
17 Dennis Rodman/25 60.00 150.00
18 Shane Battier/99 4.00 10.00
19 Christian Laettner/25 30.00 80.00
20 Derek Fisher/49 10.00 25.00
22 Danny Manning/49 4.00 10.00
23 Jerry West/25 60.00 150.00
24 Louie Dampier/49 5.00 12.00
25 Grant Hill/25 20.00 50.00
26 Avery Johnson/49 3.00 8.00
27 Dominique Wilkins/25 20.00 50.00
28 Ernie DiGregorio/99 4.00 10.00
29 Steve Kerr/25 20.00 50.00
30 Nick Van Exel/49 12.00 30.00
32 Horace Grant/99 12.00 30.00
33 Hakeem Olajuwon/25 250.00 600.00
34 Robert Parish/49 6.00 15.00
36 Allan Houston/99 10.00 25.00
37 Rick Barry/25 15.00 40.00
38 Jamaal Wilkes/99 6.00 15.00
39 Bob Lanier/49 6.00 15.00
40 Kevin Johnson/49 5.00 12.00

2019-20 Panini Impeccable Impeccable Career Points Autographs
PRINT RUNS B/WN 15-27 COPIES PER
NO PRICING QTY 15 OR LESS
EXCHANGE DEADLINE 9/11/2021
1 Elgin Baylor/27 125.00 300.00
2 Jerry West/27 60.00 150.00
3 Kevin Durant/27 200.00 500.00
4 Allen Iverson/26 500.00 1,000.00
6 George Gervin/25 75.00 200.00
7 Karl Malone/25 100.00 250.00
9 Dominique Wilkins/24 75.00 200.00
10 Rick Barry/24 15.00 40.00
11 Kareem Abdul-Jabbar/24 100.00 250.00
12 Larry Bird/24 300.00 600.00
13 Adrian Dantley/24 40.00 100.00
14 Julius Erving/24 200.00 500.00
15 Anthony Davis/23 500.00 1,000.00
16 Shaquille O'Neal/23 300.00 600.00
17 Damian Lillard/23 500.00 1,000.00
18 David Thompson/22 50.00 120.00
19 Dan Issel/22 100.00 250.00
20 Charles Barkley/22 300.00 600.00

2019-20 Panini Impeccable Impeccable Jersey Number Autographs
PRINT RUNS B/WN 1-44 COPIES PER
NO PRICING QTY 15 OR LESS
EXCHANGE DEADLINE 9/11/2021
2 Elgin Baylor/22 125.00 300.00
8 Jerry West/44 100.00 250.00
9 Hakeem Olajuwon/34 150.00 400.00
12 Grant Hill/33 200.00 500.00
14 Charles Barkley/34 200.00 500.00
16 Dominique Wilkins/21 75.00 200.00

2019-20 Panini Impeccable Impeccable Rookie Signatures
STATED PRINT RUN B/WN 49-99 COPIES PER
EXCHANGE DEADLINE 9/11/2021
1 Kevin Porter Jr./99 8.00 20.00
2 Cam Reddish/99 6.00 15.00
3 Cody Martin/99 6.00 15.00
4 Romeo Langford/99 EXCH 4.00 10.00
5 Bol Bol/99 40.00 100.00
6 Goga Bitadze/99 6.00 15.00
7 Grant Williams/99 10.00 25.00
8 Zion Williamson/49 800.00 1,500.00
9 Dylan Windler/99 15.00 40.00
10 Jarrett Culver/99 4.00 10.00
11 KZ Okpala/99 20.00 50.00
12 Cameron Johnson/99 20.00 50.00
13 Eric Paschall/99 5.00 12.00
14 Sekou Doumbouya/99 4.00 10.00
15 Isaiah Roby/99 6.00 15.00
16 Luka Samanic/99 5.00 12.00
17 Darius Bazley/99 4.00 10.00
18 Ja Morant/99 400.00 1,000.00
19 Mfiondu Kabengele/99 10.00 25.00
20 Coby White/99 100.00 250.00
21 Carsen Edwards/99 5.00 12.00
22 PJ Washington Jr./99 30.00 80.00
23 Admiral Schofield/99 12.00 30.00
24 Chuma Okeke/99 30.00 80.00
25 Ignas Brazdeikis/99 5.00 12.00
26 Matisse Thybulle/99 40.00 100.00
27 Ty Jerome/99 10.00 25.00
28 RJ Barrett/99 100.00 250.00
29 Jordan Poole/99 15.00 40.00
30 Jaxson Hayes/99 EXCH 20.00 50.00
31 Bruno Fernando/99 8.00 20.00
32 Tyler Herro/99 EXCH 200.00 500.00
33 Jaylen Nowell/99 5.00 12.00
34 Nickeil Alexander-Walker/99 15.00 40.00
35 Quinndary Weatherspoon/99 4.00 10.00
36 Brandon Clarke/99 75.00 200.00
37 Nassir Little/99 15.00 40.00
38 De'Andre Hunter/99 25.00 60.00
39 Keldon Johnson/99 40.00 100.00
40 Rui Hachimura/99 75.00 200.00

2019-20 Panini Impeccable Impeccable Rookie Signatures Holo Silver
*HOLO SLVR: .6X TO 1.5X BASIC
STATED PRINT RUN 25 SER.#'d SETS
EXCHANGE DEADLINE 9/11/2021
8 Zion Williamson 1,000.00 2,000.00
12 Cameron Johnson 50.00 120.00
30 Jaxson Hayes EXCH 60.00 150.00
32 Tyler Herro EXCH 400.00 1,000.00

2019-20 Panini Impeccable Impeccable Shots Signatures
PRINT RUNS B/WN 10-99 COPIES PER
NO PRICING QTY 15 OR LESS
EXCHANGE DEADLINE 9/11/2021
*HOLO SLVR: .6X TO 1.5X p/r 49-99
*HOLO SLVR: .4X TO 1X p/r 25
1 Peja Stojakovic/49 15.00 40.00
3 Gary Harris/99 4.00 10.00
5 Allan Houston/99 10.00 25.00
6 Ray Allen/25 100.00 250.00
8 Kristaps Porzingis/25 40.00 100.00
9 Dell Curry/99 3.00 8.00
10 Chris Mullin/49 15.00 40.00
11 Chauncey Billups/49 20.00 50.00
13 Lauri Markkanen/25 15.00 40.00
15 Dan Majerle/99 4.00 10.00
16 Kevin Love/25 25.00 60.00
17 Wally Szczerbiak/99 4.00 10.00
18 Steve Kerr/25 20.00 50.00
19 Mark Price/99 10.00 25.00
21 Jason Terry/49 20.00 50.00
23 B.J. Armstrong/99 10.00 25.00
24 Paul Pierce/25 100.00 250.00
25 Nick Van Exel/99 12.00 30.00
26 Isaiah Thomas/25 6.00 15.00
27 Dennis Scott/99 3.00 8.00
28 Kenny Smith/49 6.00 15.00
29 Rashard Lewis/99 4.00 10.00
30 Nikola Jokic/49 150.00 400.00

2019-20 Panini Impeccable Impeccable Stars Signatures
PRINT RUNS B/WN 10-99 COPIES PER
NO PRICING QTY 15 OR LESS
EXCHANGE DEADLINE 9/11/2021
*HOLO SLVR: .6X TO 1.5X p/r 49-99
*HOLO SLVR: .4X TO 1X p/r 25
2 Cedric Maxwell/99 4.00 10.00
3 Kevin Garnett/25 200.00 500.00
4 Eddie Jones/99 6.00 15.00
6 Brad Daugherty/99 4.00 10.00
7 Kenny Smith/49 6.00 15.00
8 Robert Horry/49 8.00 20.00
12 Bob Dandridge/99 3.00 8.00
13 Grant Hill/25 20.00 50.00
14 Dino Radja/99 3.00 8.00
15 Julius Randle/25 10.00 25.00
16 Rony Seikaly/99 3.00 8.00
17 Nikola Vucevic/49 4.00 10.00
18 Gail Goodrich/49 5.00 12.00
20 Antoine Walker/99 4.00 10.00
22 Maurice Cheeks/99 4.00 10.00
23 Elgin Baylor/25 30.00 80.00
24 Vince Carter/25 125.00 300.00
25 Sam Jones/25 25.00 60.00
26 Dell Curry/99 3.00 8.00
27 Lenny Wilkens/49 6.00 15.00
28 Zach LaVine/99 25.00 60.00
30 Alex English/99 6.00 15.00

2019-20 Panini Impeccable Impeccable Stats Autographs
PRINT RUNS B/WN 2-50 COPIES PER
NO PRICING QTY 15 OR LESS
EXCHANGE DEADLINE 9/11/2021
7 Anthony Davis/48 300.00 600.00
11 Karl-Anthony Towns/27 100.00 250.00
15 Donovan Mitchell/46 200.00 500.00
16 Paul Pierce/50 150.00 400.00
18 Pascal Siakam/44 50.00 120.00
19 Zach LaVine/47 150.00 400.00

2019-20 Panini Impeccable Impeccable Victory Signatures
PRINT RUNS B/WN 10-99 COPIES PER
NO PRICING QTY 15 OR LESS
EXCHANGE DEADLINE 9/11/2021
*HOLO SLVR: .6X TO 1.5X p/r 49-99
*HOLO SLVR: .4X TO 1X p/r 25
1 Pascal Siakam/49 50.00 120.00
2 Kareem Abdul-Jabbar/25 100.00 250.00
3 Robert Horry/49 8.00 20.00
4 Magic Johnson/25 125.00 300.00
5 Wesley Matthews/99 6.00 15.00
6 Lauri Markkanen/25 15.00 40.00
7 Gordon Hayward/25 15.00 40.00
9 Julius Randle/49 6.00 15.00
11 Chauncey Billups/49 20.00 50.00
12 Karl-Anthony Towns/25 30.00 80.00
14 Paul Pierce/25 100.00 250.00
15 Toni Kukoc/99 6.00 15.00
16 Nikola Jokic/25 200.00 500.00
17 Zach LaVine/25 40.00 100.00
19 Derek Fisher/49 10.00 25.00
21 Ralph Sampson/49 4.00 10.00
23 Danny Green/99 12.00 30.00
24 Vince Carter/25 125.00 300.00
25 Rondae Hollis-Jefferson/99 3.00 8.00
26 Khris Middleton/25 10.00 25.00
27 Steve Kerr/49 12.00 30.00

2019-20 Panini Impeccable Indelible Ink
PRINT RUNS B/WN 10-99 COPIES PER
NO PRICING QTY 15 OR LESS
EXCHANGE DEADLINE 9/11/2021
*HOLO SLVR: .6X TO 1.5X p/r 49-99
*HOLO SLVR: .4X TO 1X p/r 25
1 Raja Bell/99 4.00 10.00
2 Sam Jones/25 25.00 60.00
3 Don Chaney/99 5.00 12.00
4 Lenny Wilkens/49 6.00 15.00
5 Tyronn Lue/99 3.00 8.00
6 Rik Smits/99 4.00 10.00
7 B.J. Armstrong/99 10.00 25.00
9 Bob Dandridge/99 3.00 8.00
10 Pat Riley/25 20.00 50.00
11 Caron Butler/99 4.00 10.00
12 Kenny Smith/49 6.00 15.00
13 Eddie Jones/99 6.00 15.00
14 Robert Horry/49 8.00 20.00
15 Devean George/99 4.00 10.00
17 Bill Cartwright/99 4.00 10.00
19 Maurice Cheeks/99 4.00 10.00
20 Grant Hill/25 20.00 50.00
21 Quinn Buckner/99 3.00 8.00
22 Derek Fisher/49 10.00 25.00
23 Lionel Hollins/99 3.00 8.00
24 Gail Goodrich/49 5.00 12.00
25 Dino Radja/99 3.00 8.00
26 Antoine Walker/99 4.00 10.00
27 Cedric Maxwell/99 4.00 10.00
28 Kevin Garnett/25 200.00 500.00
29 Stromile Swift/99 3.00 8.00
30 Elgin Baylor/25 30.00 80.00

2019-20 Panini Impeccable Silver Draft Logo
STATED PRINT RUN 25 SER.#'d SETS
1 PJ Washington Jr. 75.00 200.00
2 Zion Williamson 1,000.00 2,500.00
3 Romeo Langford 15.00 40.00
4 RJ Barrett 125.00 300.00
5 Nickeil Alexander-Walker 50.00 120.00
6 Jarrett Culver 15.00 40.00
8 Jaxson Hayes 25.00 60.00
9 Darius Garland 60.00 150.00
10 Cam Reddish 25.00 60.00
11 Tyler Herro 80.00 200.00
12 Ja Morant 300.00 600.00
13 Sekou Doumbouya 15.00 40.00
14 De'Andre Hunter 60.00 150.00
15 Goga Bitadze 40.00 100.00
16 Coby White 50.00 125.00
17 Matisse Thybulle 75.00 200.00
18 Rui Hachimura 150.00 400.00
19 Brandon Clarke 125.00 300.00
20 Cameron Johnson 75.00 200.00

2019-20 Panini Impeccable Silver HOF Logo
STATED PRINT RUN 25 SER.#'d SETS
1 Pete Maravich 100.00 250.00
2 Patrick Ewing 60.00 150.00
3 Gary Payton 40.00 100.00
4 Yao Ming 100.00 250.00
5 Hakeem Olajuwon 60.00 150.00
6 Charles Barkley 75.00 200.00
7 Jerry West 75.00 200.00
8 Allen Iverson 150.00 400.00
9 Wilt Chamberlain 100.00 250.00
10 Larry Bird 75.00 200.00
11 George Mikan 50.00 125.00
12 Kareem Abdul-Jabbar 75.00 200.00
13 Isiah Thomas 50.00 120.00
14 Alonzo Mourning 50.00 120.00
15 David Robinson 50.00 125.00
16 Shaquille O'Neal 100.00 250.00
17 Clyde Drexler 75.00 200.00
18 Karl Malone 50.00 125.00
19 Dennis Johnson 50.00 120.00
20 John Stockton 75.00 200.00
21 Tracy McGrady 75.00 200.00
22 Oscar Robertson 50.00 120.00
23 Jason Kidd 50.00 120.00
24 Magic Johnson 75.00 200.00
25 Dennis Rodman 125.00 300.00
26 Bill Russell 60.00 150.00
27 Bill Bradley 30.00 80.00
28 Scottie Pippen 75.00 200.00
29 Moses Malone 40.00 100.00
30 Julius Erving 75.00 200.00

2019-20 Panini Impeccable Silver NBA Logo
STATED PRINT RUN 25 SER.#'d SETS
1 Russell Westbrook 40.00 100.00
2 Tyler Herro 80.00 200.00
3 Trae Young 60.00 150.00
4 Coby White 50.00 125.00
5 Karl-Anthony Towns 60.00 150.00
7 Stephon Marbury 40.00 100.00
8 PJ Washington Jr. 75.00 200.00
9 Stephen Curry 200.00 500.00
10 Jarrett Culver 15.00 40.00
11 Jimmy Butler 60.00 150.00
12 Ja Morant 300.00 600.00
13 Paul George 75.00 200.00
14 Matisse Thybulle 75.00 200.00
15 Donovan Mitchell 50.00 125.00
16 Kevin Garnett 75.00 200.00
17 Drazen Petrovic 150.00 400.00
18 Zion Williamson 1,000.00 2,500.00
19 Kyrie Irving 75.00 200.00
21 Kevin Durant 80.00 200.00
22 Sekou Doumbouya 15.00 40.00
23 Kawhi Leonard 60.00 150.00
24 Rui Hachimura 150.00 400.00
25 Anthony Davis 150.00 400.00
26 Steve Nash 50.00 120.00
27 Paul Pierce 40.00 100.00
28 Romeo Langford 15.00 40.00
29 Giannis Antetokounmpo 100.00 250.00
30 Jaxson Hayes 25.00 60.00
31 Ben Simmons 25.00 60.00
32 De'Andre Hunter 60.00 150.00
33 Bradley Beal 30.00 80.00
34 Brandon Clarke 125.00 300.00
35 Devin Booker 75.00 200.00
36 Chris Webber 30.00 80.00
37 Amar'e Stoudemire 40.00 100.00
38 RJ Barrett 125.00 300.00
39 Joel Embiid 50.00 125.00
40 Darius Garland 60.00 150.00
41 Luka Doncic 800.00 1,500.00
42 Goga Bitadze 40.00 100.00
43 Damian Lillard 125.00 300.00
44 Cameron Johnson 75.00 200.00
45 Kemba Walker 50.00 120.00
46 Tim Duncan 100.00 250.00
47 LeBron James 500.00 1,000.00
48 Nickeil Alexander-Walker 50.00 120.00
49 James Harden 50.00 125.00
50 Cam Reddish 25.00 60.00

2019-20 Panini Impeccable Stainless Stars
STATED PRINT RUN 99 SER.#'d SETS
1 Zion Williamson 100.00 250.00
2 James Harden 6.00 15.00
3 De'Andre Hunter 10.00 25.00
4 Kevin Durant 10.00 25.00
5 Coby White 6.00 15.00
6 Kawhi Leonard 8.00 20.00
7 Cam Reddish 3.00 8.00
9 Stephen Curry 25.00 60.00
10 Giannis Antetokounmpo 15.00 40.00
11 Ja Morant 50.00 120.00
12 Russell Westbrook 5.00 12.00
13 Jarrett Culver 2.00 5.00
14 Ben Simmons 6.00 15.00
15 Jaxson Hayes 3.00 8.00
16 Charles Barkley 5.00 12.00
17 LeBron James 75.00 200.00
18 Shaquille O'Neal 12.00 30.00
19 Kyrie Irving 8.00 20.00
20 Joel Embiid 6.00 15.00
21 RJ Barrett 15.00 40.00
22 Jimmy Butler 8.00 20.00
23 Darius Garland 8.00 20.00
24 Paul George 5.00 12.00
25 Rui Hachimura 12.00 30.00

2019-20 Panini Impeccable Stainless Stars Purple
*PURPLE: .6X TO 1.5X BASIC
STATED PRINT RUN 49 SER.#'d SETS
11 Ja Morant 100.00 250.00
17 LeBron James 125.00 300.00
18 Shaquille O'Neal 20.00 50.00
23 Darius Garland 15.00 40.00

2019-20 Panini Impeccable Stainless Stars Red
*RED: .6X TO 1.5X BASIC
STATED PRINT RUN 60 SER.#'d SETS
11 Ja Morant 100.00 250.00
23 Darius Garland 15.00 40.00

2019-20 Panini Impeccable Stainless Stars Autographs
STATED PRINT RUN 49-99 SER.#'d SETS
EXCHANGE DEADLINE 9/11/2021
1 RJ Barrett/99 60.00 150.00
2 Luka Samanic/99 8.00 20.00
3 Coby White/99 75.00 200.00
4 Grant Williams/99 10.00 25.00
5 Cam Reddish/99 10.00 25.00
6 Nassir Little/99 10.00 25.00
7 Tyler Herro/99 125.00 300.00
8 Sekou Doumbouya/99 6.00 15.00
9 Zion Williamson/49 800.00 1,500.00
10 Nickeil Alexander-Walker/99 20.00 50.00
11 De'Andre Hunter/99 15.00 40.00
12 Matisse Thybulle/99 30.00 80.00
13 Jaxson Hayes/99 15.00 40.00
14 Darius Bazley/99 6.00 15.00
15 Cameron Johnson/99 15.00 40.00
16 Bol Bol/99 40.00 100.00
17 Romeo Langford/99 6.00 15.00
18 Chuma Okeke/99 20.00 50.00
19 Ja Morant/99 300.00 800.00
20 Goga Bitadze/99 12.00 30.00
21 Jarrett Culver/99 6.00 15.00
22 Brandon Clarke/99 50.00 120.00
23 Rui Hachimura/99 50.00 120.00
24 Ty Jerome/99 12.00 30.00
25 PJ Washington Jr./99 25.00 60.00

2019-20 Panini Impeccable Stainless Stars Autographs Purple
*PURPLE: .4X TO 1X BASIC
STATED PRINT RUN 49 SER.#'d SETS
EXCHANGE DEADLINE 9/11/2021
6 Nassir Little/49 15.00 40.00
11 De'Andre Hunter/49 40.00 100.00
18 Chuma Okeke/49 30.00 80.00
23 Rui Hachimura/49 75.00 200.00
25 PJ Washington Jr./49 50.00 120.00

2019-20 Panini Impeccable Stainless Stars Autographs Red
*RED: .4X TO 1X BASIC
STATED PRINT RUN 60 SER.#'d SETS
EXCHANGE DEADLINE 9/11/2021
11 De'Andre Hunter 40.00 100.00
23 Rui Hachimura 75.00 200.00

2020-21 Panini Impeccable
1-100 PRINT RUN 99 SER.#'d SETS
JSY AU PRINT RUN 99 COPIES PER
EXCHANGE DEADLINE 12/16/2022
*GOLD/60: .6X TO 1.5X BASIC
*SILVER/75: .5X TO 1.2X BASIC
*HOLO SILVER/25-35: .75X TO 2X BASIC
1 Devin Booker 10.00 25.00
2 Zion Williamson 25.00 60.00
3 Mitchell Robinson 4.00 10.00
4 Fred VanVleet 6.00 15.00
5 Davis Bertans 3.00 8.00
6 Paul George 6.00 15.00
7 Jaylen Brown 6.00 15.00
8 Aaron Gordon 4.00 10.00
9 Kyle Lowry 5.00 12.00
10 Giannis Antetokounmpo 20.00 50.00
11 Andrew Wiggins 5.00 12.00
12 Coby White 5.00 12.00
13 Jimmy Butler 8.00 20.00

14 Domantas Sabonis 5.00 12.00
15 Derrick Rose 6.00 15.00
16 Chris Paul 8.00 20.00
17 Kemba Walker 4.00 10.00
18 Anthony Davis 10.00 25.00
19 Brandon Ingram 5.00 12.00
20 Damian Lillard 10.00 25.00
21 Tyler Herro 8.00 20.00
22 Collin Sexton 4.00 10.00
23 Caris LeVert 4.00 10.00
24 Zach LaVine 6.00 15.00
25 Russell Westbrook 8.00 20.00
26 Myles Turner 4.00 10.00
27 Michael Porter Jr. 5.00 12.00
28 Luka Doncic 50.00 120.00
29 Ben Simmons 4.00 10.00
30 Nikola Jokic 20.00 50.00
31 Kawhi Leonard 10.00 25.00
32 D'Angelo Russell 4.00 10.00
33 Klay Thompson 10.00 25.00
34 Victor Oladipo 3.00 8.00
35 Christian Wood 3.00 8.00
36 Lonnie Walker IV 4.00 10.00
37 Brandon Clarke 4.00 10.00
38 RJ Barrett 6.00 15.00
39 Kyrie Irving 8.00 20.00
40 Joel Embiid 10.00 25.00
41 CJ McCollum 4.00 10.00
42 John Collins 4.00 10.00
43 Pascal Siakam 6.00 15.00
44 Kristaps Porzingis 5.00 12.00
45 Stephen Curry 50.00 120.00
46 Jayson Tatum 15.00 40.00
47 Deandre Ayton 4.00 10.00
48 Carmelo Anthony 6.00 15.00
49 Khris Middleton 5.00 12.00
50 Jamal Murray 6.00 15.00
51 Kevin Love 4.00 10.00
52 LaMarcus Aldridge 4.00 10.00
53 Danilo Gallinari 3.00 8.00
54 LeBron James 50.00 120.00
55 Andre Drummond 4.00 10.00
56 Lauri Markkanen 5.00 12.00
57 Blake Griffin 4.00 10.00
58 Trae Young 10.00 25.00
59 Shai Gilgeous-Alexander 20.00 50.00
60 Rudy Gobert 5.00 12.00
61 DeMar DeRozan 5.00 12.00
62 James Harden 8.00 20.00
63 Kevin Durant 15.00 40.00
64 Kyle Kuzma 5.00 12.00
65 John Wall 5.00 12.00
66 Bam Adebayo 6.00 15.00
67 Lou Williams 4.00 10.00
68 Jrue Holiday 4.00 10.00
69 Buddy Hield 4.00 10.00
70 Julius Randle 4.00 10.00
71 Bradley Beal 5.00 12.00
72 Miles Bridges 4.00 10.00
73 Donovan Mitchell 8.00 20.00
74 Karl-Anthony Towns 6.00 15.00
75 Nikola Vucevic 4.00 10.00
76 Jaren Jackson Jr. 6.00 15.00
77 Cam Reddish 5.00 12.00
78 De'Aaron Fox 6.00 15.00
79 Devonte' Graham 3.00 8.00
80 Ja Morant 50.00 120.00
81 Tyrese Maxey 25.00 60.00
82 Precious Achiuwa 6.00 15.00
83 RJ Hampton 3.00 8.00
84 Aleksej Pokusevski 4.00 10.00
85 Isaiah Stewart 6.00 15.00
86 Cole Anthony 8.00 20.00
87 Aaron Nesmith 6.00 15.00
88 Kira Lewis Jr. 3.00 8.00
89 Tyrese Haliburton 30.00 80.00
90 Devin Vassell 12.00 30.00
91 Jalen Smith 6.00 15.00
92 Deni Avdija 8.00 20.00
93 Obi Toppin 6.00 15.00
94 Killian Hayes 3.00 8.00
95 Onyeka Okongwu 6.00 15.00
96 Isaac Okoro 5.00 12.00
97 Patrick Williams 8.00 20.00
98 LaMelo Ball 100.00 250.00
99 James Wiseman 3.00 8.00
100 Anthony Edwards 75.00 200.00
101 Nico Mannion JSY AU RC 10.00 25.00
102 Jordan Nwora JSY AU RC 12.00 30.00
103 Tre Jones JSY AU RC 15.00 40.00
104 Robert Woodard II JSY AU RC 10.00 25.00
105 Caleb Martin JSY AU RC 20.00 50.00
106 Xavier Tillman JSY AU RC 12.00 30.00
107 Theo Maledon JSY AU RC 10.00 25.00
108 Daniel Oturu JSY AU RC 10.00 25.00
109 Vernon Carey Jr. JSY AU RC 10.00 25.00
110 Tyrell Terry JSY AU RC 8.00 20.00
111 Desmond Bane JSY AU RC 125.00 300.00
112 Malachi Flynn JSY AU RC 10.00 25.00
113 Jaden McDaniels JSY AU RC 60.00 150.00
114 Udoka Azubuike JSY AU RC 12.00 30.00
115 Payton Pritchard JSY AU RC 30.00 80.00
116 Immanuel Quickley JSY AU RC 60.00 150.00
117 RJ Hampton JSY AU RC 10.00 25.00
118 CJ Elleby JSY AU RC 10.00 25.00
119 Zeke Nnaji JSY AU RC 12.00 30.00
120 Tyrese Maxey JSY AU RC 200.00 500.00
121 Precious Achiuwa JSY AU RC 20.00 50.00
122 Saddiq Bey JSY AU RC 100.00 250.00
123 Josh Green JSY AU RC 20.00 50.00
124 Aleksej Pokusevski JSY AU RC 12.00 30.00
125 Isaiah Stewart JSY AU RC 60.00 150.00
126 Cole Anthony JSY AU RC 100.00 250.00
127 Aaron Nesmith JSY AU RC 20.00 50.00
128 Kira Lewis Jr. JSY AU RC 10.00 25.00
129 Tyrese Haliburton JSY AU RC 150.00 400.00
130 Devin Vassell JSY AU RC 60.00 150.00
131 Jalen Smith JSY AU RC 20.00 50.00
132 Deni Avdija JSY AU RC 60.00 150.00
133 Obi Toppin JSY AU RC 60.00 150.00
134 Killian Hayes JSY AU RC 10.00 25.00
135 Onyeka Okongwu JSY AU RC 20.00 50.00
136 Isaac Okoro JSY AU RC 15.00 40.00
137 Patrick Williams JSY AU RC 100.00 250.00
138 LaMelo Ball JSY AU RC 1,000.00 2,000.00
139 James Wiseman JSY AU RC 12.00 30.00
140 Anthony Edwards JSY AU RC 800.00 1,500.00

2020-21 Panini Impeccable Award-Winning Autographs

EXCHANGE DEADLINE 12/16/2022
14 Karl-Anthony Towns 40.00 100.00
24 George Gervin 30.00 80.00
33 Jason Williams 150.00 400.00
37 John Stockton 75.00 200.00
38 Kareem Abdul-Jabbar 150.00 400.00
40 Paul Pierce 75.00 200.00
46 Dwyane Wade 150.00 400.00

2020-21 Panini Impeccable Canvas Creations Autographs

STATED PRINT RUN 10-99 SER.#'d SETS
EXCHANGE DEADLINE 12/16/2022
2 Dwyane Wade/25 150.00 400.00
4 Robert Covington/99 8.00 20.00
6 Thaddeus Young/99 4.00 10.00
7 Spud Webb/49 20.00 50.00
8 De'Aaron Fox/49 60.00 150.00
9 Clyde Drexler/49 40.00 100.00
10 Walt Frazier/99 12.00 30.00
12 Wendell Carter Jr./49 5.00 12.00
13 Collin Sexton/25 40.00 100.00
15 RJ Barrett/25 40.00 100.00
16 Kendrick Nunn/49 5.00 12.00
18 Maxi Kleber/99 5.00 12.00
19 Larry Bird/25 150.00 400.00
21 John Collins/49 25.00 60.00
22 Robert Parish/49 15.00 40.00
23 Kareem Abdul-Jabbar/25 150.00 400.00
24 Jaren Jackson Jr./49 30.00 80.00
25 Troy Daniels/99 4.00 10.00
26 Roy Hibbert/99 4.00 10.00
27 Chris Mullin/49 8.00 20.00
28 Kevin Garnett/25 150.00 400.00
29 Trae Young/49 200.00 500.00
30 Ja Morant/49 800.00 1,500.00

2020-21 Panini Impeccable Elegance Retired Jersey Autographs

STATED PRINT RUN 25-49 SER.#'d SETS
EXCHANGE DEADLINE 12/16/2022
1 Mike Miller/49 8.00 20.00
2 Bernard King/49 12.00 30.00
3 Mike Bibby/49 10.00 25.00
4 Shaquille O'Neal /25 200.00 500.00
5 Deron Williams/49 12.00 30.00
6 Hedo Turkoglu/49 8.00 20.00
7 Dirk Nowitzki/25 200.00 500.00
8 Xavier McDaniel/49 8.00 20.00
9 Toni Kukoc/49 50.00 120.00
10 Elton Brand/49 12.00 30.00

2020-21 Panini Impeccable Elegance Veteran Jersey Autographs

STATED PRINT RUN 49-99 SER.#'d SETS
EXCHANGE DEADLINE 12/16/2022
*HOLO SILVER: .75X TO 2X BASIC
1 Anthony Davis/49 150.00 400.00
2 PJ Washington Jr./99 20.00 50.00
3 LaMarcus Aldridge/99 15.00 40.00
4 Jordan Poole/99 20.00 50.00
5 Trae Young/49 300.00 600.00
6 Matthew Dellavedova/99 6.00 15.00
7 Shai Gilgeous-Alexander/49 500.00 1,000.00
8 Maxi Kleber/99 6.00 15.00
9 Brook Lopez/99 12.00 30.00
10 Karl-Anthony Towns/49 60.00 150.00

2020-21 Panini Impeccable Extravagance Autographs

STATED PRINT RUN 10-49 SER.#'d SETS
NO PRICING ON QTY 10
EXCHANGE DEADLINE 12/16/2022
1 Kendrick Nunn/25 8.00 20.00
4 Karl-Anthony Towns/25 25.00 60.00
5 Stephen Curry/25 2,000.00 4,000.00
6 Coby White/25 30.00 80.00
7 Nikola Vucevic/49 15.00 40.00
8 Roy Hibbert/49 6.00 15.00
10 RJ Barrett/49 60.00 150.00
11 Trae Young/25 75.00 200.00
12 Lauri Markkanen/49 15.00 40.00
13 Kevin Knox II/49 6.00 15.00
14 Kurt Rambis/49 8.00 20.00
15 LaMarcus Aldridge/25 10.00 25.00
16 Ricky Rubio/49 20.00 50.00
17 Gordon Hayward/25 20.00 50.00
18 Kristaps Porzingis/25 20.00 50.00
19 Wendell Carter Jr./49 8.00 20.00
20 Shai Gilgeous-Alexander/25 500.00 1,000.00
21 De'Aaron Fox/49 40.00 100.00
22 Thaddeus Young/49 6.00 15.00
23 James Worthy/49 15.00 40.00
26 Robert Covington/49 8.00 20.00
27 Ja Morant/49 300.00 600.00
29 Dwyane Wade/49 125.00 300.00
30 Jaylen Nowell/49 8.00 20.00

2020-21 Panini Impeccable Illustrious Ink

STATED PRINT RUN 10-49 SER.#'d SETS
EXCHANGE DEADLINE 12/16/2022
1 James Worthy/25 30.00 80.00
2 Adrian Dantley/49 10.00 25.00
3 Dominique Wilkins/25 25.00 60.00
4 Bill Russell/25 800.00 1,500.00
5 Lenny Wilkens/49 10.00 25.00
6 Joe Dumars/25 12.00 30.00
7 John Stockton/25 75.00 200.00
8 Boris Diaw/49 8.00 20.00
9 Kenny ""Sky"" Walker/49 8.00 20.00
10 Tim Hardaway/49 25.00 60.00
11 Bill Walton/25 15.00 40.00
12 Magic Johnson/25 40.00 100.00
14 Jerry West/49 40.00 100.00
16 Robert Parish/49 15.00 40.00
17 Andre Miller/49 8.00 20.00
20 Clyde Drexler/25 40.00 100.00
21 Kevin McHale/25 20.00 50.00
22 Mike Miller/49 8.00 20.00
23 Chauncey Billups/25 40.00 100.00
24 Charles Barkley/25 150.00 400.00
25 Avery Johnson/25 8.00 20.00
26 Al Harrington/49 6.00 15.00
27 Walt Frazier/25 15.00 40.00
29 Rolando Blackman/49 8.00 20.00
30 Mark Price/49 15.00 40.00
31 Jarrett Jack/49 6.00 15.00
32 Jason Kidd/25 40.00 100.00
33 Calvin Murphy/49 10.00 25.00
34 Allen Iverson/25 125.00 300.00
35 Ralph Sampson/25 8.00 20.00
36 Jason Williams/25 75.00 200.00
37 Isiah Thomas/49 40.00 100.00
38 Karl Malone/49 40.00 100.00
39 Jerry Lucas/25 12.00 30.00
40 Dino Radja/49 8.00 20.00

2020-21 Panini Impeccable Immortal Ink

STATED PRINT RUN 10-49 SER.#'d SETS
EXCHANGE DEADLINE 12/16/2022
1 Adrian Dantley/49 10.00 25.00
2 Chris Mullin/49 15.00 40.00
3 Dwyane Wade/49 150.00 400.00
4 Marcus Camby/49 8.00 20.00
5 Dave Cowens/49 12.00 30.00
6 John Stockton/25 75.00 200.00
7 Walt Frazier/25 15.00 40.00
8 Kareem Abdul-Jabbar/25 150.00 400.00
10 Robert Parish/25 20.00 50.00
11 Calvin Murphy/49 10.00 25.00
12 Tim Hardaway/49 25.00 60.00
13 Richard Jefferson/49 12.00 30.00
14 Ray Allen/49 60.00 150.00
15 David Thompson/49 12.00 30.00
17 David Robinson/25 75.00 200.00
18 Stephen Jackson/49 8.00 20.00
19 Jason Kidd/49 40.00 100.00
20 Kevin Martin/49 8.00 20.00
21 Boris Diaw/49 15.00 40.00
22 Drew Gooden/49 6.00 15.00
25 Ralph Sampson/49 8.00 20.00
26 Elton Brand/49 10.00 25.00
27 Kenny ""Sky"" Walker/49 8.00 20.00
28 Jerry Lucas/49 12.00 30.00
29 Lenny Wilkens/49 10.00 25.00
30 Derek Fisher/49 20.00 50.00
31 Clyde Drexler/25 60.00 150.00
32 Paul Pierce/49 60.00 150.00
33 Isiah Thomas/49 40.00 100.00
35 Rolando Blackman/49 8.00 20.00
37 Jarrett Jack/49 6.00 15.00
38 Rick Fox/49 15.00 40.00
39 Larry Bird/25 150.00 400.00
40 Kevin Garnett/25 150.00 400.00

2020-21 Panini Impeccable Impeccable Hall of Fame Autographs

STATED PRINT RUN 1-96 SER.#'d SETS
EXCHANGE DEADLINE 12/16/2022
3 David Thompson/96 25.00 60.00
7 George Gervin/96 40.00 100.00
9 Jerry West/80 150.00 400.00
10 Dave Cowens/91 25.00 60.00
15 Bill Walton/93 60.00 150.00
16 Lenny Wilkens/89 25.00 60.00
18 Larry Bird/98 200.00 500.00
25 Gail Goodrich/96 40.00 100.00

2020-21 Panini Impeccable Impeccable Jersey Number Autographs

STATED PRINT RUN 1-44 SER.#'d SETS
EXCHANGE DEADLINE 12/16/2022
1 Charles Barkley/34 400.00 800.00
7 Jerry West/44 300.00 600.00
8 Grant Hill/33 300.00 600.00
11 Gary Payton/20 200.00 500.00
17 Dirk Nowitzki/41 1,000.00 2,000.00

2020-21 Panini Impeccable Impeccable Rookie Signatures

STATED PRINT RUN 99 SER.#'d SETS
EXCHANGE DEADLINE 12/16/2022
*HOLO SILVER/25: .75X TO 2X BASIC
1 Anthony Edwards 300.00 600.00
2 LaMelo Ball 400.00 800.00
3 Isaac Okoro 12.00 30.00
4 Killian Hayes 8.00 20.00
5 Deni Avdija 20.00 50.00
6 Devin Vassell 25.00 60.00
7 Kira Lewis Jr. 8.00 20.00
8 Cole Anthony 50.00 120.00
9 Aleksej Pokusevski 10.00 25.00
10 Saddiq Bey 15.00 40.00
11 Tyrese Maxey 125.00 300.00
12 CJ Elleby 8.00 20.00
13 Immanuel Quickley 20.00 50.00
14 Udoka Azubuike 10.00 25.00
15 Daniel Oturu 8.00 20.00
16 Malachi Flynn 8.00 20.00
17 Tyrell Terry 6.00 15.00
18 Xavier Tillman 10.00 25.00
19 Robert Woodard II 8.00 20.00
20 Jordan Nwora 8.00 20.00
21 Nico Mannion 8.00 20.00
22 Tre Jones 12.00 30.00
23 Tyler Bey 8.00 20.00
24 Theo Maledon 8.00 20.00
25 Vernon Carey Jr. 8.00 20.00
26 Desmond Bane 25.00 60.00
27 Jaden McDaniels 25.00 60.00
28 Payton Pritchard 25.00 60.00
29 RJ Hampton 8.00 20.00
30 Zeke Nnaji 10.00 25.00
31 Precious Achiuwa 15.00 40.00
32 Josh Green 15.00 40.00
33 Isaiah Stewart 15.00 40.00
34 Aaron Nesmith 15.00 40.00
35 Tyrese Haliburton 100.00 250.00
36 Jalen Smith 15.00 40.00
37 Obi Toppin 15.00 40.00
38 Onyeka Okongwu 15.00 40.00
39 Patrick Williams 60.00 150.00
40 James Wiseman 10.00 25.00

2020-21 Panini Impeccable Impeccable Shots Signatures

PRINT RUNS B/WN 25-99 COPIES PER
EXCHANGE DEADLINE 12/16/2022
1 Ja Morant/49 300.00 600.00
2 Christian Laettner/99 10.00 25.00
3 Coby White/49 25.00 60.00
4 Paul Pierce/49 60.00 150.00
5 De'Aaron Fox/99 40.00 100.00
6 Rick Barry/99 30.00 80.00
7 Collin Sexton/49 40.00 100.00
8 Mike Bibby/99 12.00 30.00
9 Kristaps Porzingis/49 20.00 50.00
10 Ray Allen/49 60.00 150.00
11 Donte DiVincenzo/99 12.00 30.00
12 Mike Miller/99 6.00 15.00
13 Jason Terry/99 15.00 40.00
14 Steve Kerr/49 25.00 60.00
17 Jordan Poole/99 25.00 60.00
18 Lou Williams/99 15.00 40.00
19 Robert Horry/99 15.00 40.00
20 Larry Bird/25 200.00 500.00
21 Quinn Cook/99 5.00 12.00
22 Jayson Tatum/49 200.00 500.00
23 Andrew Wiggins/49 20.00 50.00
24 Malcolm Brogdon/99 12.00 30.00
25 Allan Houston/99 12.00 30.00
27 Lauri Markkanen/99 12.00 30.00
28 RJ Barrett/49 50.00 120.00
29 Kendrick Nunn/99 6.00 15.00
30 Stephen Curry/25 2,000.00 4,000.00

2020-21 Panini Impeccable Impeccable Stars Signatures

STATED PRINT RUN 10-49 SER.#'d SETS
EXCHANGE DEADLINE 12/16/2022
1 Gordon Hayward/49 10.00 25.00
2 JJ Redick/49 10.00 25.00
3 Ivica Zubac/49 10.00 25.00
4 Domantas Sabonis/49 20.00 50.00
6 Lonzo Ball/49 40.00 100.00
7 Justin Holiday/49 6.00 15.00
8 Trevor Ariza/49 6.00 15.00
10 Kevin Knox II/49 6.00 15.00
11 Donte DiVincenzo/49 12.00 30.00
12 Nickeil Alexander-Walker/49 15.00 40.00
13 Kristaps Porzingis/49 20.00 50.00
14 Andrew Wiggins/49 20.00 50.00
15 Wendell Carter Jr./49 8.00 20.00
16 Malcolm Brogdon/49 12.00 30.00
17 Collin Sexton/49 40.00 100.00
18 Jaren Jackson Jr./49 20.00 50.00
19 LaMarcus Aldridge/49 10.00 25.00
20 Jayson Tatum/25 200.00 500.00
21 John Collins/49 20.00 50.00
22 Ricky Rubio/49 20.00 50.00
24 Eric Gordon/49 8.00 20.00
25 JR Smith/49 40.00 100.00
26 Quinn Cook/49 6.00 15.00
27 Lou Williams/49 15.00 40.00
29 Trae Young/25 200.00 500.00
30 Matthew Dellavedova/49 8.00 20.00

2020-21 Panini Impeccable Impeccable Stats Autographs

STATED PRINT RUN 18-64 SER.#'d SETS
EXCHANGE DEADLINE 12/16/2022
1 Trae Young/50 600.00 1,200.00
2 Kevin Garnett/25 400.00 800.00
3 Kristaps Porzingis/18 75.00 200.00
4 Khris Middleton/51 75.00 200.00
5 Rick Barry/64 75.00 200.00
6 Nikola Vucevic/29 60.00 150.00
7 Jason Williams/38 400.00 800.00
8 RJ Barrett/27 300.00 600.00
9 Damian Lillard/61 400.00 800.00
10 Stephen Curry/54 2,000.00 4,000.00
11 Magic Johnson/46 400.00 800.00
12 Clyde Drexler/50 100.00 250.00
13 Dwyane Wade/55 500.00 1,000.00
14 Zion Williamson/35 2,000.00 4,000.00
16 George Gervin/63 75.00 200.00
17 Andrew Wiggins/47 60.00 150.00
18 Dennis Rodman/34 400.00 800.00
19 Allen Iverson/60 400.00 800.00
20 Anthony Davis/59 400.00 800.00

2020-21 Panini Impeccable Impeccable Victory Signatures

PRINT RUNS B/WN 10-99 COPIES PER
NO PRICING ON QTY 10
EXCHANGE DEADLINE 12/16/2022
1 Bogdan Bogdanovic/99 12.00 30.00
2 David Robinson/49 60.00 150.00
3 Chauncey Billups/99 20.00 50.00
4 Gary Payton/99 30.00 80.00
5 T.J. Ford/99 4.00 10.00
6 JJ Redick/49 10.00 25.00
7 Andre Miller/99 5.00 12.00
8 Domantas Sabonis/99 12.00 30.00
9 Lonzo Ball/49 30.00 80.00
10 Allen Iverson/25 125.00 300.00
12 David Lee/99 4.00 10.00
13 Jason Terry/99 12.00 30.00
15 Kurt Rambis/99 5.00 12.00
16 Latrell Sprewell/99 15.00 40.00
17 Shai Gilgeous-Alexander/49 400.00 800.00
19 Karl-Anthony Towns/25 40.00 100.00
20 Jayson Tatum/25 200.00 500.00
21 Karl Malone/25 60.00 150.00
22 Brook Lopez/99 10.00 25.00
23 Derek Fisher/99 15.00 40.00
24 Arron Afflalo/99 4.00 10.00
26 Jrue Holiday/99 12.00 30.00
27 Hedo Turkoglu/99 12.00 30.00
29 Trae Young/25 200.00 500.00
30 Steven Adams/99 6.00 15.00

2020-21 Panini Impeccable Indelible Ink

PRINT RUNS B/WN 25-99 COPIES PER
EXCHANGE DEADLINE 12/16/2022
1 Grant Hill/99 30.00 80.00
2 Charles Barkley/25 125.00 300.00
3 Christian Laettner/99 6.00 15.00
4 Marcus Camby/99 5.00 12.00
5 Mike Bibby/99 10.00 25.00
6 Avery Johnson/99 5.00 12.00
7 Richard Jefferson/99 4.00 10.00
8 John Salmons/99 4.00 10.00
9 Kris Humphries/99 4.00 10.00
10 Isaiah Rider/99 5.00 12.00
11 Kirk Hinrich /99 5.00 12.00
12 Kevin Johnson/99 15.00 40.00
13 Matt Bonner/99 4.00 10.00
14 Magic Johnson/49 100.00 250.00
15 Mark Price/49 12.00 30.00
16 Al Harrington/99 4.00 10.00
17 Steve Kerr/99 20.00 50.00
18 Bill Walton/49 40.00 100.00
19 Pat Riley/99 20.00 50.00
20 Stephen Jackson/99 5.00 12.00
21 Rick Fox/99 5.00 12.00
22 Shaquille O'Neal /25 200.00 500.00
23 Drew Gooden/99 4.00 10.00
24 Allan Houston/99 6.00 15.00
25 Bernard King/99 12.00 30.00
26 Kevin Garnett/25 200.00 500.00
27 Spud Webb/99 10.00 25.00
28 Sam Cassell/99 5.00 12.00
29 Dwyane Wade/49 150.00 400.00
30 Gail Goodrich/99 6.00 15.00

2020-21 Panini Impeccable Rookie Autographs

STATED PRINT RUN 99 SER.#'d SETS
EXCHANGE DEADLINE 12/16/2022
1 Nico Mannion 8.00 20.00
2 Jordan Nwora 10.00 25.00
3 Tre Jones 12.00 30.00
4 Robert Woodard II 8.00 20.00
5 Tyler Bey 8.00 20.00
6 Xavier Tillman 10.00 25.00
7 Theo Maledon 8.00 20.00
8 Daniel Oturu 8.00 20.00
9 Vernon Carey Jr. 8.00 20.00
10 Tyrell Terry 6.00 15.00
11 Desmond Bane 25.00 60.00
12 Malachi Flynn 8.00 20.00
13 Jaden McDaniels 25.00 60.00
14 Udoka Azubuike 10.00 25.00
15 Payton Pritchard 25.00 60.00
16 Immanuel Quickley 20.00 50.00
17 RJ Hampton 8.00 20.00
18 Jahmi'us Ramsey 8.00 20.00
19 Zeke Nnaji 10.00 25.00
20 Tyrese Maxey 60.00 150.00
21 Precious Achiuwa 15.00 40.00
22 Saddiq Bey 15.00 40.00
23 Josh Green 15.00 40.00
24 Aleksej Pokusevski 10.00 25.00
25 Isaiah Stewart 15.00 40.00
26 Cole Anthony 20.00 50.00
27 Aaron Nesmith 15.00 40.00
28 Kira Lewis Jr. 8.00 20.00
29 Tyrese Haliburton 125.00 300.00
30 Devin Vassell 25.00 60.00
31 Jalen Smith 15.00 40.00
32 Deni Avdija 20.00 50.00
33 Obi Toppin 15.00 40.00
34 Killian Hayes 8.00 20.00
35 Onyeka Okongwu 15.00 40.00
36 Isaac Okoro 12.00 30.00
37 Patrick Williams 75.00 200.00
38 LaMelo Ball 400.00 800.00
39 James Wiseman 10.00 25.00
40 Anthony Edwards 300.00 600.00

2020-21 Panini Impeccable Spectra Hall of Fame Signatures

EXCHANGE DEADLINE 12/16/2022
22 George Gervin 30.00 80.00
30 John Stockton 75.00 200.00
32 Kareem Abdul-Jabbar 150.00 400.00
39 Magic Johnson 125.00 300.00

2020-21 Panini Impeccable Stainless Stars

STATED PRINT RUN 99 SER.#'d SETS
1 Jamal Murray 8.00 20.00
2 Pascal Siakam 8.00 20.00
3 Nikola Jokic 25.00 60.00
4 LeBron James 60.00 150.00
5 Zion Williamson 15.00 40.00
6 Ja Morant 50.00 120.00
7 Stephen Curry 60.00 150.00
8 James Harden 10.00 25.00
9 Paul George 8.00 20.00
10 Giannis Antetokounmpo 25.00 60.00
11 Devin Booker 25.00 60.00
12 Ben Simmons 5.00 12.00
13 Anthony Davis 12.00 30.00
14 Donovan Mitchell 10.00 25.00
15 Trae Young 12.00 30.00
16 Jayson Tatum 25.00 60.00
17 Kevin Durant 20.00 50.00
18 Jimmy Butler 10.00 25.00
19 Kawhi Leonard 12.00 30.00
20 Luka Doncic 60.00 150.00
21 Anthony Edwards 60.00 150.00
22 LaMelo Ball 100.00 250.00
23 Deni Avdija 10.00 25.00
24 Obi Toppin 8.00 20.00
25 James Wiseman 5.00 12.00

2020-21 Panini Impeccable Stainless Stars Orange

STATED PRINT RUN 25 SER.#'d SETS
4 LeBron James 150.00 400.00
20 Luka Doncic 150.00 400.00
21 Anthony Edwards 150.00 400.00
22 LaMelo Ball 300.00 600.00

2020-21 Panini Impeccable Stainless Stars Autographs

STATED PRINT RUN 99 SER.#'d SETS
EXCHANGE DEADLINE 12/16/2022
1 Malachi Flynn 8.00 20.00
2 Payton Pritchard 25.00 60.00
3 Immanuel Quickley 20.00 50.00
4 RJ Hampton 8.00 20.00
5 Zeke Nnaji 10.00 25.00
6 Tyrese Maxey 60.00 150.00
7 Precious Achiuwa 15.00 40.00
8 Josh Green 15.00 40.00
9 Aleksej Pokusevski 10.00 25.00
10 Isaiah Stewart 15.00 40.00
11 Cole Anthony 20.00 50.00
12 Aaron Nesmith 15.00 40.00
13 Kira Lewis Jr. 8.00 20.00
14 Tyrese Haliburton 100.00 250.00
15 Devin Vassell 25.00 60.00
16 Jalen Smith 15.00 40.00
17 Deni Avdija 20.00 50.00
18 Obi Toppin 15.00 40.00
19 Killian Hayes 8.00 20.00
20 Onyeka Okongwu 15.00 40.00
21 Isaac Okoro 12.00 30.00
22 Patrick Williams 75.00 200.00
23 LaMelo Ball 400.00 800.00
24 James Wiseman 10.00 25.00
25 Anthony Edwards 300.00 600.00

2020-21 Panini Impeccable Stainless Stars Autographs Orange

STATED PRINT RUN 25 SER.#'d SETS
EXCHANGE DEADLINE 12/16/2022
23 LaMelo Ball 1,000.00 2,000.00

2021-22 Panini Impeccable

COMMON CARD (1-80) 2.50 6.00
SEMISTARS 3.00 8.00
UNLISTED STARS 4.00 10.00
COMMON RC (80-100) 2.50 6.00
RC SEMIS 3.00 8.00
RC UNLISTED 4.00 10.00
COMMON JSY AU (101-140) 10.00 25.00
JSY AU SEMIS 12.00 30.00
JSY AU UNL 15.00 40.00
1-100 PRINT RUN 99 SER.#'d SETS
JSY AU PRINT RUN 99 COPIES PER
EXCHANGE DEADLINE 11/25/2023
*ASIA: .4X TO 1X BASIC
*SILVER/75: .5X TO 1.2X BASIC
*GOLD/49: .6X TO 1.5X BASIC
*GREEN/35: .6X TO 1.5X BASIC
*HOLO SILVER/25: .75X TO 2X BASIC
1 Rui Hachimura 4.00 10.00
2 Pascal Siakam 6.00 15.00
3 Michael Porter Jr. 5.00 12.00
4 John Collins 4.00 10.00
5 Tim Hardaway Jr. 2.50 6.00
6 Tyrese Haliburton 8.00 20.00
7 Joel Embiid 10.00 25.00
8 Jaren Jackson Jr. 6.00 15.00
9 Nikola Vucevic 4.00 10.00
10 Zion Williamson 10.00 25.00
11 Jimmy Butler 6.00 15.00
12 DeMar DeRozan 5.00 12.00
13 Devin Booker 10.00 25.00
14 James Harden 8.00 20.00
15 Kawhi Leonard 10.00 25.00
16 Mike Conley 3.00 8.00
17 Khris Middleton 4.00 10.00
18 Aleksej Pokusevski 3.00 8.00
19 Keldon Johnson 5.00 12.00
20 Terry Rozier III 3.00 8.00
21 Kyrie Irving 8.00 20.00
22 Victor Oladipo 3.00 8.00
23 Devin Vassell 6.00 15.00
24 Jayson Tatum 15.00 40.00
25 Aaron Gordon 4.00 10.00
26 Deandre Ayton 4.00 10.00
27 Blake Griffin 4.00 10.00
28 Bradley Beal 5.00 12.00
29 LeBron James 30.00 80.00
30 Shai Gilgeous-Alexander 20.00 50.00
31 RJ Barrett 6.00 15.00
32 Jaylen Brown 6.00 15.00
33 Kristaps Porzingis 5.00 12.00
34 Fred VanVleet 5.00 12.00
35 Nikola Jokic 20.00 50.00
36 Lonzo Ball 4.00 10.00
37 LaMelo Ball 10.00 25.00
38 CJ McCollum 3.00 8.00
39 Carmelo Anthony 6.00 15.00
40 Malcolm Brogdon 3.00 8.00
41 Rudy Gobert 5.00 12.00
42 Zach LaVine 6.00 15.00
43 Ja Morant 12.00 30.00
44 De'Aaron Fox 6.00 15.00
45 Damian Lillard 10.00 25.00
46 John Wall 5.00 12.00
47 Jamal Murray 6.00 15.00
48 Karl-Anthony Towns 6.00 15.00
49 Julius Randle 5.00 12.00
50 Jerami Grant 4.00 10.00
51 Kyle Lowry 4.00 10.00
52 Trae Young 10.00 25.00
53 RJ Hampton 2.50 6.00
54 Donovan Mitchell 8.00 20.00
55 Tobias Harris 3.00 8.00
56 Bam Adebayo 6.00 15.00
57 D'Angelo Russell 4.00 10.00
58 Domantas Sabonis 5.00 12.00
59 Ben Simmons 4.00 10.00
60 Stephen Curry 25.00 60.00
61 Jrue Holiday 5.00 12.00
62 Dennis Schroder 4.00 10.00
63 Russell Westbrook 6.00 15.00
64 Saddiq Bey 3.00 8.00
65 Derrick Rose 6.00 15.00
66 Paul George 6.00 15.00
67 Chris Paul 8.00 20.00
68 Luka Doncic 25.00 60.00
69 Darius Garland 6.00 15.00
70 Brandon Ingram 5.00 12.00
71 Anthony Davis 10.00 25.00
72 Collin Sexton 4.00 10.00
73 Giannis Antetokounmpo 20.00 50.00
74 Kemba Walker 4.00 10.00
75 Cole Anthony 5.00 12.00
76 Kevin Durant 12.00 30.00
77 Anthony Edwards 20.00 50.00
78 Tyrese Maxey 10.00 25.00
79 Klay Thompson 10.00 25.00
80 Kevin Porter Jr. 3.00 8.00
81 Cade Cunningham 25.00 60.00
82 Jalen Green 20.00 50.00
83 Scottie Barnes 12.00 30.00
84 Evan Mobley 15.00 40.00
85 Josh Giddey 12.00 30.00
86 Jonathan Kuminga 12.00 30.00
87 Davion Mitchell 4.00 10.00
88 Franz Wagner 12.00 30.00
89 James Bouknight 3.00 8.00
90 Ziaire Williams 5.00 12.00
91 Joshua Primo 3.00 8.00
92 Chris Duarte 3.00 8.00
93 Corey Kispert 5.00 12.00
94 Moses Moody 8.00 20.00
95 Alperen Sengun 12.00 30.00
96 Trey Murphy III 12.00 30.00
97 Tre Mann 6.00 15.00
98 Bones Hyland 5.00 12.00
99 Jalen Johnson 12.00 30.00
100 Jalen Suggs 10.00 25.00
101 Cade Cunningham JSY AU RC 300.00 600.00
102 Jalen Green JSY AU RC 200.00 500.00
103 Evan Mobley JSY AU RC 150.00 400.00
104 Scottie Barnes JSY AU RC 150.00 400.00
105 Jalen Suggs JSY AU RC 125.00 300.00
106 Josh Giddey JSY AU RC 125.00 300.00
107 Jonathan Kuminga JSY AU RC 150.00 400.00
108 Franz Wagner JSY AU RC 150.00 400.00
109 Davion Mitchell JSY AU RC 15.00 40.00
110 Ziaire Williams JSY AU RC 20.00 50.00
111 James Bouknight JSY AU RC 12.00 30.00
112 Joshua Primo JSY AU RC 12.00 30.00
113 Chris Duarte JSY AU RC 12.00 30.00
114 Moses Moody JSY AU RC 125.00 300.00
115 Corey Kispert JSY AU RC 20.00 50.00
116 Alperen Sengun JSY AU RC 200.00 500.00
117 Trey Murphy III JSY AU RC 50.00 125.00
118 Tre Mann JSY AU RC 25.00 60.00
119 Kai Jones JSY AU RC 12.00 30.00
120 Jalen Johnson JSY AU RC 100.00 250.00
121 Keon Johnson JSY AU RC 15.00 40.00
122 Isaiah Jackson JSY AU RC 15.00 40.00
123 Usman Garuba JSY AU RC 12.00 30.00
124 Josh Christopher JSY AU RC 12.00 30.00
125 Quentin Grimes JSY AU RC 30.00 80.00
126 Bones Hyland JSY AU RC 20.00 50.00
127 Cameron Thomas JSY AU RC 100.00 250.00
128 Jaden Springer JSY AU RC 15.00 40.00
129 Day'Ron Sharpe JSY AU RC 15.00 40.00
130 Santi Aldama JSY AU RC 20.00 50.00
131 Jeremiah Robinson-Earl JSY AU RC 15.00 40.00
132 Miles McBride JSY AU RC 25.00 60.00
133 Ayo Dosunmu JSY AU RC 30.00 80.00
134 Jared Butler JSY AU RC 15.00 40.00
135 Isaiah Livers JSY AU RC 15.00 40.00
136 Greg Brown III JSY AU RC 12.00 30.00
137 Brandon Boston Jr. JSY AU RC 15.00 40.00
138 Luka Garza JSY AU RC 15.00 40.00
139 Charles Bassey JSY AU RC 15.00 40.00
140 Scottie Lewis JSY AU RC 12.00 30.00

2021-22 Panini Impeccable Canvas Creations Autographs

COMMON CARD 6.00 15.00
SEMISTARS 8.00 20.00
UNLISTED STARS 10.00 25.00
STATED PRINT RUN 35-99 SER.#'d SETS
EXCHANGE DEADLINE 11/25/2023
*HOLO SILVER: .5X TO 1.2X BASIC
1 Eric Gordon/49 8.00 20.00
2 Steve Kerr/35 12.00 30.00
3 Ja Morant/35 600.00 1,200.00
4 Joe Harris/99 8.00 20.00
6 Kristaps Porzingis/35 12.00 30.00
8 Mike Bibby/99 20.00 50.00
10 Richard Hamilton/49 12.00 30.00
11 Frank Kaminsky/99 6.00 15.00
13 Jamal Murray/35 15.00 40.00
14 Jrue Holiday/49 20.00 50.00
16 Luka Doncic/25 800.00 1,500.00
17 Charlie Ward/99 8.00 20.00
19 Derek Fisher/49 20.00 50.00
20 Roy Hibbert/99 8.00 20.00
21 Hedo Turkoglu/99 8.00 20.00
22 Trae Young/35 300.00 600.00
24 Kenny ""Sky"" Walker/99 6.00 15.00
25 Bill Laimbeer/99 15.00 40.00
26 Mark Price/99 10.00 25.00
28 Onyeka Okongwu/49 10.00 25.00
29 Drew Gooden/99 8.00 20.00

2021-22 Panini Impeccable Elegance Retired Jersey Autographs

COMMON CARD 8.00 20.00
SEMISTARS 10.00 25.00
UNLISTED STARS 12.00 30.00
STATED PRINT RUN 25-99 SER.#'d SETS
EXCHANGE DEADLINE 11/25/2023
*HOLO SILVER: .5X TO 1.2X BASIC
1 James Worthy/49 30.00 80.00
2 Christian Laettner/99 12.00 30.00
3 Charles Barkley/25 150.00 400.00
4 Ralph Sampson/99 12.00 30.00
5 David Robinson/49 50.00 120.00
6 Carlos Boozer/99 10.00 25.00
7 Clyde Drexler/49 50.00 120.00
8 Elton Brand/99 12.00 30.00
9 Vince Carter/49 125.00 300.00
10 Xavier McDaniel/99 10.00 25.00

2021-22 Panini Impeccable Elegance Veteran Jersey Autographs

COMMON CARD 8.00 20.00
SEMISTARS 10.00 25.00
UNLISTED STARS 12.00 30.00
STATED PRINT RUN 25-99 SER.#'d SETS
EXCHANGE DEADLINE 11/25/2023
*HOLO SILVER: .5X TO 1.2X BASIC
1 Kristaps Porzingis/49 15.00 40.00
3 Luka Doncic/25 1,000.00 2,000.00
5 Anthony Davis/25 125.00 300.00
6 Domantas Sabonis/99 25.00 60.00
7 Trae Young/49 400.00 800.00
8 Rudy Gay/99 12.00 30.00
9 Nikola Jokic/49 200.00 500.00
10 Lonnie Walker IV/99 10.00 25.00

2021-22 Panini Impeccable Extravagance Autographs

COMMON CARD 6.00 15.00
SEMISTARS 8.00 20.00
UNLISTED STARS 10.00 25.00
STATED PRINT RUN 25-99 SER.#'d SETS
EXCHANGE DEADLINE 11/25/2023
*HOLO SILVER/25: .5X TO 1.2X BASIC
2 Anthony Davis/25 125.00 300.00
3 Lauri Markkanen/35 12.00 30.00
4 Cam Reddish/49 10.00 25.00

7 Rick Fox/49 10.00 25.00
8 Glen Rice/99 10.00 25.00
9 T.J. Warren/49 6.00 15.00
10 James Wiseman/35 8.00 20.00
11 Justin Holiday/99 6.00 15.00
12 Avery Johnson/99 8.00 20.00
13 Marcus Camby/99 8.00 20.00
14 Chauncey Billups/99 12.00 30.00
15 Nikola Jokic/35 150.00 400.00
16 Detlef Schrempf/99 10.00 25.00
17 Rudy Gay/99 10.00 25.00
19 Thaddeus Young/99 6.00 15.00
20 Jason Richardson/99 10.00 25.00
22 Boban Marjanovic/99 10.00 25.00
23 Maxi Kleber/99 8.00 20.00
24 CJ McCollum/35 20.00 50.00
26 Duncan Robinson/49 8.00 20.00
27 Spud Webb/99 10.00 25.00
28 Jae'Sean Tate/99 10.00 25.00
30 John Collins/49 10.00 25.00

2021-22 Panini Impeccable Illustrious Ink

COMMON CARD 6.00 15.00
SEMISTARS 8.00 20.00
UNLISTED STARS 10.00 25.00
STATED PRINT RUN 35-99 SER.#'d SETS
EXCHANGE DEADLINE 11/25/2023
*HOLO SILVER: .5X TO 1.2X BASIC
1 Al Horford/49 30.00 80.00
3 Bill Walton/99 25.00 60.00
4 Michael Porter Jr./49 12.00 30.00
5 Chauncey Billups/99 20.00 50.00
6 Oscar Robertson/35 60.00 150.00
7 Deni Avdija/99 10.00 25.00
8 Rui Hachimura/35 30.00 80.00
10 Jerry Lucas/49 12.00 30.00
11 Andrea Bargnani/99 6.00 15.00
12 Khris Middleton/35 10.00 25.00
13 Brandon Clarke/49 10.00 25.00
15 CJ McCollum/35 20.00 50.00
16 Paul Pierce/35 60.00 150.00
17 Duncan Robinson/49 8.00 20.00
18 Tony Parker/35 40.00 100.00
19 Hakeem Olajuwon/35 75.00 200.00
20 JJ Redick/49 10.00 25.00
21 Avery Johnson/99 8.00 20.00
22 Larry Bird/35 125.00 300.00
24 Myles Turner/49 10.00 25.00
25 Clint Capela/99 10.00 25.00
26 Ricky Rubio/49 20.00 50.00
27 Gail Goodrich/99 10.00 25.00
28 Trae Young/35 300.00 600.00
30 Jonas Valanciunas/99 8.00 20.00
31 Bill Russell/25 500.00 1,000.00
32 Lauri Markkanen/35 12.00 30.00
33 Cam Reddish/49 10.00 25.00
34 Onyeka Okongwu/49 10.00 25.00
35 Clyde Drexler/35 60.00 150.00
36 Robert Parish/99 20.00 50.00
37 Gary Payton/35 40.00 100.00
38 Vince Carter/35 125.00 300.00
39 Jason Williams/49 60.00 150.00
40 Jrue Holiday/49 20.00 50.00

2021-22 Panini Impeccable Immortal Ink

COMMON CARD 6.00 15.00
SEMISTARS 8.00 20.00
UNLISTED STARS 10.00 25.00
STATED PRINT RUN 25-99 SER.#'d SETS
EXCHANGE DEADLINE 11/25/2023
*HOLO SILVER: .5X TO 1.2X BASIC
1 Oscar Robertson/35 60.00 150.00
2 Clyde Drexler/35 60.00 150.00
3 Ray Allen/35 75.00 200.00
4 Dino Radja/99 8.00 20.00
5 Shaquille O'Neal /25 300.00 600.00
6 Hakeem Olajuwon/35 75.00 200.00
7 Jerry Lucas/49 12.00 30.00
9 Louie Dampier/99 10.00 25.00
10 Bill Walton/99 25.00 60.00
11 Pat Riley/35 40.00 100.00
13 Raymond Felton/99 6.00 15.00
14 Gail Goodrich/99 10.00 25.00
15 Toni Kukoc/99 20.00 50.00
16 James Worthy/35 40.00 100.00
18 Arvydas Sabonis/99 20.00 50.00
20 Bob Dandridge/99 10.00 25.00
21 Paul Pierce/35 60.00 150.00
22 David Lee/99 8.00 20.00
23 Robert Parish/99 12.00 30.00
24 Gary Payton/35 40.00 100.00
25 Tony Parker/35 40.00 100.00
26 Jason Kidd/35 50.00 120.00
27 Kirk Hinrich /99 10.00 25.00
28 Ben Wallace/49 50.00 120.00
29 Maurice Cheeks/99 8.00 20.00
30 Carlos Boozer/99 8.00 20.00
31 Ralph Sampson/49 10.00 25.00
32 David Thompson/99 12.00 30.00
33 Brad Miller/99 6.00 15.00
34 George McGinnis/99 10.00 25.00
35 Vince Carter/35 125.00 300.00
36 Jason Williams/49 60.00 150.00
37 Larry Bird/35 125.00 300.00
38 Bill Russell/25 500.00 1,000.00
39 Nate Archibald/49 10.00 25.00
40 Charles Barkley/25 150.00 400.00

2021-22 Panini Impeccable Impeccable Impressions Signatures

COMMON CARD
SEMISTARS
UNLISTED STARS
STATED PRINT RUN 99 SER.#'d SETS
EXCHANGE DEADLINE 11/25/2023
*HOLO SILVER/25: .75X TO 2X BASIC
1 Cade Cunningham 400.00 800.00
2 Evan Mobley 200.00 500.00
3 Jalen Suggs 75.00 200.00
4 Jonathan Kuminga 200.00 500.00
5 Davion Mitchell 50.00 120.00
6 James Bouknight 8.00 20.00
7 Chris Duarte 8.00 20.00
8 Corey Kispert 12.00 30.00
9 Trey Murphy III 30.00 80.00
10 Kai Jones 8.00 20.00
11 Keon Johnson 10.00 25.00
12 Usman Garuba 8.00 20.00
13 Isaiah Todd 8.00 20.00
14 Cameron Thomas 60.00 150.00
15 Day'Ron Sharpe 10.00 25.00
16 Jeremiah Robinson-Earl 10.00 25.00
17 Ayo Dosunmu 20.00 50.00
18 Kessler Edwards 10.00 25.00
19 Brandon Boston Jr. 10.00 25.00
20 Charles Bassey 10.00 25.00
22 Luka Garza 10.00 25.00
23 Greg Brown III 8.00 20.00
24 Jared Butler 10.00 25.00
25 Miles McBride 15.00 40.00
26 Neemias Queta 10.00 25.00
27 Jaden Springer 10.00 25.00
28 Dalano Banton 12.00 30.00
29 Josh Christopher 8.00 20.00
30 Isaiah Jackson 10.00 25.00
31 Jalen Johnson 30.00 80.00
32 Tre Mann 15.00 40.00
33 Alperen Sengun 100.00 250.00
34 Moses Moody 75.00 200.00
35 Sandro Mamukelashvili 12.00 30.00
36 Ziaire Williams 12.00 30.00
37 Franz Wagner 100.00 250.00
38 Josh Giddey 200.00 500.00
39 Scottie Barnes 300.00 600.00
40 Jalen Green 300.00 600.00

2021-22 Panini Impeccable Impeccable NBA 75th Anniversary Autographs

COMMON CARD 20.00 50.00
SEMISTARS 25.00 60.00
UNLISTED STARS 30.00 80.00
STATED PRINT RUN 25-75 SER.#'d SETS
EXCHANGE DEADLINE 11/25/2023
2 Kareem Abdul-Jabbar/25 1,500.00 3,000.00
3 David Robinson/49 400.00 800.00
4 Isiah Thomas/49 400.00 800.00
5 Clyde Drexler/49 400.00 800.00
6 Bill Russell/25 1,500.00 3,000.00
7 Jason Kidd/25 600.00 1,200.00
8 Kevin Garnett/25 1,500.00 3,000.00
9 Rick Barry/75 300.00 600.00
10 Dirk Nowitzki/25 1,500.00 3,000.00
11 Robert Parish/75 300.00 600.00
12 Magic Johnson/25 1,500.00 3,000.00
13 Hakeem Olajuwon/49 400.00 800.00
14 Charles Barkley/25 1,500.00 3,000.00
16 Allen Iverson/25 1,500.00 3,000.00
17 Gary Payton/75 400.00 800.00
18 Dwyane Wade/25 600.00 1,200.00
19 Dominique Wilkins/75 300.00 600.00
20 John Stockton/25 600.00 1,200.00
21 Bill Walton/49 300.00 600.00
22 Ray Allen/49 500.00 1,000.00
23 Bob McAdoo/49 200.00 500.00
24 Shaquille O'Neal /25 1,500.00 3,000.00
25 Jerry West/49 500.00 1,000.00
26 Karl Malone/25 600.00 1,200.00
27 James Worthy/75 300.00 600.00
28 Larry Bird/25 1,500.00 3,000.00
29 Walt Frazier/75 300.00 600.00
30 Oscar Robertson/25 500.00 1,000.00

2021-22 Panini Impeccable Impeccable Selections Signatures

COMMON CARD 8.00 20.00
SEMISTARS 10.00 25.00
UNLISTED STARS 12.00 30.00
STATED PRINT RUN 15-99 SER.#'d SETS
NO PRICING ON QTY 15
EXCHANGE DEADLINE 11/25/2023
*HOLO SILVER/25: .75X TO 2X BASIC
1 David Robinson/49 75.00 200.00
2 Cazzie Russell/99 12.00 30.00
3 Magic Johnson/25 150.00 400.00
5 LaRue Martin/99 10.00 25.00
6 Kwame Brown/99 10.00 25.00
7 Anthony Edwards/49 200.00 500.00
8 Derrick Coleman/99 15.00 40.00
10 Brad Daugherty/99 12.00 30.00
11 Hakeem Olajuwon/49 75.00 200.00
12 Joe Smith/99 10.00 25.00
14 Pervis Ellison/99 25.00 60.00
15 Michael Olowokandi /99 10.00 25.00
16 Andrew Bogut/99 12.00 30.00
18 Larry Johnson/99 75.00 200.00
20 Doug Collins/99 10.00 25.00
21 Ralph Sampson/99 12.00 30.00
22 Austin Carr/99 12.00 30.00
25 Frank Selvy/99 12.00 30.00
27 Karl-Anthony Towns/25 60.00 150.00
28 Kenyon Martin/99 25.00 60.00
30 Mychal Thompson/99 10.00 25.00

2021-22 Panini Impeccable Impeccable Stars Signatures

COMMON CARD 8.00 20.00
SEMISTARS 10.00 25.00
UNLISTED STARS 12.00 30.00
STATED PRINT RUN 25-49 SER.#'d SETS
EXCHANGE DEADLINE 11/25/2023
*HOLO SILVER: .5X TO 1.2X BASIC
1 Coby White/49 12.00 30.00
3 Duncan Robinson/49 10.00 25.00
4 T.J. Warren/49 8.00 20.00
5 Jamal Murray/35 50.00 120.00
7 Al Horford/49 20.00 50.00
9 Cam Reddish/49 12.00 30.00
12 Ricky Rubio/49 20.00 50.00
14 Trae Young/35 200.00 500.00
15 Jayson Tatum/35 200.00 500.00
16 Khris Middleton/35 12.00 30.00
17 Anthony Davis/25 125.00 300.00
18 Luka Doncic/25 1,000.00 2,000.00
20 Myles Turner/49 12.00 30.00
21 Domantas Sabonis/49 20.00 50.00
22 Stephen Curry/25 1,000.00 2,000.00
23 Ja Morant/35 500.00 1,000.00
25 Jrue Holiday/49 20.00 50.00
26 Kristaps Porzingis/35 15.00 40.00
28 Michael Porter Jr./49 15.00 40.00
29 CJ McCollum/35 20.00 50.00
30 Nikola Jokic/35 150.00 400.00

2021-22 Panini Impeccable Impeccable Victory Signatures

COMMON CARD 6.00 15.00
SEMISTARS 8.00 20.00
UNLISTED STARS 10.00 25.00
STATED PRINT RUN 25-99 SER.#'d SETS
EXCHANGE DEADLINE 11/25/2023
*HOLO SILVER/25: .5X TO 1.2X BASIC
2 Grant Hill/35 100.00 250.00
4 Adrian Dantley/99 10.00 25.00
7 Mark Aguirre/99 8.00 20.00
8 Devin Harris/99 6.00 15.00
12 Jamal Crawford/49 10.00 25.00
13 John Stockton/35 100.00 250.00
14 Alex English/99 12.00 30.00
15 Latrell Sprewell/99 30.00 80.00
17 Nikola Jokic/35 150.00 400.00
19 Robert Horry/99 25.00 60.00
21 Vince Carter/35 150.00 400.00
22 Jason Richardson/99 10.00 25.00
25 Luka Doncic/25 1,000.00 2,000.00
26 Charles Barkley/25 200.00 500.00
27 Paul Pierce/35 100.00 250.00
28 Dwyane Wade/35 200.00 500.00
30 Glen Rice/99 10.00 25.00

2021-22 Panini Impeccable Indelible Ink

COMMON CARD
SEMISTARS
UNLISTED STARS
STATED PRINT RUN 35-99 SER.#'d SETS
EXCHANGE DEADLINE 11/25/2023
*HOLO SILVER/25: .5X TO 1.2X BASIC
1 Brandon Clarke/49 10.00 25.00
2 Michael Porter Jr./49 12.00 30.00
3 Clint Capela/99 10.00 25.00
5 Elton Brand/99 10.00 25.00
6 Stephen Jackson/99 8.00 20.00
7 Ivica Zubac/99 10.00 25.00
8 JJ Redick/49 10.00 25.00
9 Al Horford/49 10.00 25.00
10 Khris Middleton/35 10.00 25.00
12 Myles Turner/49 10.00 25.00
13 Deni Avdija/99 10.00 25.00
14 Ricky Rubio/49 20.00 50.00
15 Fat Lever/99 8.00 20.00
16 Taj Gibson/99 6.00 15.00
17 Jalen Rose/99 8.00 20.00
18 Jonas Valanciunas/99 8.00 20.00
19 Anthony Edwards/35 300.00 600.00
20 Lonnie Walker IV/99 8.00 20.00
21 Christian Laettner/49 10.00 25.00
23 Domantas Sabonis/49 20.00 50.00
24 Rui Hachimura/35 25.00 60.00
27 Jaren Jackson Jr./49 40.00 100.00
28 Kendrick Nunn/99 8.00 20.00
29 B.J. Armstrong/99 10.00 25.00
30 Mark Aguirre/99 8.00 20.00

2021-22 Panini Impeccable Rookie Autographs

COMMON CARD 6.00 15.00
SEMISTARS 8.00 20.00
UNLISTED STARS 10.00 25.00
STATED PRINT RUN 99 SER.#'d SETS
EXCHANGE DEADLINE 11/25/2023
*HOLO SILVER/25: .75X TO 2X BASIC
*ASIA/88: .4X TO 1X BASIC
1 Cade Cunningham 400.00 800.00
2 Evan Mobley 200.00 500.00
3 Jalen Suggs 75.00 200.00
4 Jonathan Kuminga 200.00 500.00
5 Davion Mitchell 50.00 120.00
6 James Bouknight 8.00 20.00
7 Chris Duarte 8.00 20.00
8 Corey Kispert 12.00 30.00
9 Trey Murphy III 30.00 80.00
10 Kai Jones 8.00 20.00
11 Keon Johnson 10.00 25.00
12 Usman Garuba 8.00 20.00
13 Quentin Grimes 20.00 50.00
14 Cameron Thomas 60.00 150.00
15 Day'Ron Sharpe 10.00 25.00
16 Jeremiah Robinson-Earl 10.00 25.00
17 Ayo Dosunmu 20.00 50.00
18 Isaiah Livers 10.00 25.00
19 Brandon Boston Jr. 10.00 25.00
20 Charles Bassey 10.00 25.00
22 Luka Garza 10.00 25.00
23 Greg Brown III 8.00 20.00
24 Jared Butler 10.00 25.00
25 Miles McBride 15.00 40.00
26 Santi Aldama 12.00 30.00
27 Jaden Springer 10.00 25.00
28 Bones Hyland 12.00 30.00
29 Josh Christopher 8.00 20.00
30 Isaiah Jackson 10.00 25.00
31 Jalen Johnson 30.00 80.00
32 Tre Mann 15.00 40.00
33 Alperen Sengun 100.00 250.00
34 Moses Moody 75.00 200.00
35 Joshua Primo 8.00 20.00
36 Ziaire Williams 12.00 30.00
37 Franz Wagner 100.00 250.00
38 Josh Giddey 200.00 500.00
39 Scottie Barnes 300.00 600.00
40 Jalen Green 300.00 600.00

2021-22 Panini Impeccable Stainless Stars

COMMON CARD 4.00 10.00
SEMISTARS 5.00 12.00
UNLISTED STARS 6.00 15.00
STATED PRINT RUN 99 SER.#'d SETS
*ASIA: .4X TO 1X BASIC
*BLUE/75: .5X TO 1.2X BASIC
*PURPLE/49: .6X TO 1.5X BASIC
ORANGE/30: .6X TO 1.5X BASIC
1 LeBron James 40.00 100.00
2 Luka Doncic 30.00 80.00
3 Giannis Antetokounmpo 25.00 60.00
4 Trae Young 12.00 30.00
5 Zion Williamson 12.00 30.00
6 Ja Morant 15.00 40.00
7 Anthony Davis 12.00 30.00
8 Kevin Durant 15.00 40.00
9 Devin Booker 12.00 30.00
10 Nikola Jokic 25.00 60.00
11 Joel Embiid 12.00 30.00
12 Kawhi Leonard 12.00 30.00
13 Damian Lillard 12.00 30.00
14 Larry Bird 15.00 40.00
15 Magic Johnson 15.00 40.00
16 Charles Barkley 12.00 30.00
17 Shaquille O'Neal 15.00 40.00
18 David Robinson 10.00 25.00
19 Kevin Garnett 12.00 30.00
20 Cade Cunningham 30.00 80.00
21 Jalen Green 25.00 60.00
22 Evan Mobley 20.00 50.00
23 Jonathan Kuminga 15.00 40.00
24 Jalen Suggs 12.00 30.00
25 Davion Mitchell 5.00 12.00

2022-23 Panini Impeccable

COMMON CARD (1-100) 2.50 6.00
SEMISTARS 3.00 8.00
UNLISTED STARS 4.00 10.00
COMMON RC (1-100) 2.50 6.00
RC SEMIS 3.00 8.00
RC UNLISTED 4.00 10.00
COMMON JSY AU (101-140) 10.00 25.00
JSY AU SEMIS 12.00 30.00
JSY AU UNL 15.00 40.00
1-100 PRINT RUN 99 SER.#'d SETS
JSY AU PRINT RUN 99 COPIES PER
*ASIA: .4X TO 1X BASIC
*SILVER/75: .5X TO 1.2X BASIC
*GOLD/49: .6X TO 1.5X BASIC
*GREEN/35: .75X TO 2X BASIC
*HOLO SILVER/25 (1-100): 1X TO 2.5X BASIC
*HOLO SILVER/25 (101-140): .6X TO 1.5X BASIC
1 Anthony Davis 10.00 25.00
2 Paolo Banchero 25.00 60.00
3 Jaylen Brown 8.00 20.00
4 Donovan Mitchell 8.00 20.00
5 Anthony Edwards 20.00 50.00
6 Kevin Porter Jr. 3.00 8.00
7 Jalen Suggs 5.00 12.00
8 Dejounte Murray 5.00 12.00
9 Zach LaVine 8.00 20.00
10 Kevin Durant 12.00 30.00
11 Chris Paul 8.00 20.00
12 Julius Randle 5.00 12.00
13 Josh Giddey 6.00 15.00
14 Nikola Jokic 20.00 50.00
15 Shaedon Sharpe 15.00 40.00
16 Luka Doncic 25.00 60.00
17 Bam Adebayo 6.00 15.00
18 Khris Middleton 5.00 12.00
19 Jalen Williams 20.00 50.00
20 Ja Morant 12.00 30.00
21 David Roddy 5.00 12.00
22 Shai Gilgeous-Alexander 20.00 50.00
23 Giannis Antetokounmpo 20.00 50.00
24 Deandre Ayton 4.00 10.00
25 AJ Griffin 3.00 8.00
26 Bradley Beal 5.00 12.00
27 Christian Braun 10.00 25.00
28 Joel Embiid 6.00 15.00
29 Malaki Branham 4.00 10.00
30 Jeremy Sochan 12.00 30.00
31 Tyrese Haliburton 8.00 20.00
32 Jimmy Butler 8.00 20.00
33 Walker Kessler 8.00 20.00
34 Damian Lillard 10.00 25.00
35 Karl-Anthony Towns 6.00 15.00
36 Scottie Barnes 6.00 15.00
37 Franz Wagner 10.00 25.00
38 Christian Wood 2.50 6.00
39 James Harden 8.00 20.00
40 Kristaps Porzingis 5.00 12.00
41 Devin Vassell 5.00 12.00
42 Brandon Ingram 5.00 12.00
43 Marcus Smart 5.00 12.00
44 Keldon Johnson 5.00 12.00
45 DeMar DeRozan 5.00 12.00
46 Keegan Murray 10.00 25.00
47 Andrew Wiggins 5.00 12.00
48 Bojan Bogdanovic 4.00 10.00
49 Malcolm Brogdon 3.00 8.00
50 Jabari Smith Jr. 12.00 30.00
51 Jamal Murray 6.00 15.00
52 Jrue Holiday 5.00 12.00
53 Kawhi Leonard 10.00 25.00
54 Desmond Bane 5.00 12.00
55 Dyson Daniels 10.00 25.00
56 Anfernee Simons 5.00 12.00
57 Michael Porter Jr. 5.00 12.00
58 Stephen Curry 30.00 80.00
59 Kyrie Irving 8.00 20.00
60 Klay Thompson 10.00 25.00
61 LaMelo Ball 10.00 25.00
62 Tyrese Maxey 8.00 20.00
63 Ayo Dosunmu 5.00 12.00
64 Jalen Green 12.00 30.00
65 Terry Rozier III 5.00 12.00
66 TyTy Washington Jr. 4.00 10.00
67 Ochai Agbaji 5.00 12.00
68 Bennedict Mathurin 12.00 30.00
69 Andrew Nembhard 8.00 20.00
70 Trae Young 10.00 25.00
71 Jalen Brunson 8.00 20.00
72 Fred VanVleet 5.00 12.00
73 Quentin Grimes 3.00 8.00
74 Jordan Poole 6.00 15.00
75 Zion Williamson 10.00 25.00
76 Lauri Markkanen 6.00 15.00
77 MarJon Beauchamp 4.00 10.00
78 Jaden Hardy 6.00 15.00
79 Evan Mobley 10.00 25.00
80 Jayson Tatum 15.00 40.00
81 Pascal Siakam 6.00 15.00
82 Tyler Herro 6.00 15.00
83 Cameron Thomas 6.00 15.00
84 Christian Koloko 4.00 10.00
85 Chet Holmgren 20.00 50.00
86 Tari Eason 10.00 25.00
87 RJ Barrett 6.00 15.00
88 Paul George 6.00 15.00
89 Darius Garland 6.00 15.00
90 LeBron James 30.00 80.00
91 De'Aaron Fox 8.00 20.00
92 Ben Simmons 4.00 10.00
93 Trey Murphy III 5.00 12.00
94 Cade Cunningham 12.00 30.00
95 Devin Booker 10.00 25.00
96 Jaren Jackson Jr. 6.00 15.00
97 Johnny Davis 4.00 10.00
98 Jaden Ivey 12.00 30.00
99 Russell Westbrook 6.00 15.00
100 Jalen Duren 12.00 30.00
101 Paolo Banchero JSY AU RC 400.00 800.00
102 Chet Holmgren JSY AU RC 300.00 600.00
103 Jabari Smith Jr. JSY AU RC 50.00 125.00
104 Keegan Murray JSY AU RC 40.00 100.00
105 Jaden Ivey JSY AU RC 50.00 125.00
106 Bennedict Mathurin JSY AU RC 50.00 120.00
107 Shaedon Sharpe JSY AU RC 200.00 500.00
108 Dyson Daniels JSY AU RC 40.00 100.00
109 Jeremy Sochan JSY AU RC 50.00 125.00
110 Johnny Davis JSY AU RC 15.00 40.00
111 Ousmane Dieng JSY AU RC 20.00 50.00
112 Jalen Williams JSY AU RC 200.00 500.00
113 Jalen Duren JSY AU RC 50.00 125.00
114 Ochai Agbaji JSY AU RC 20.00 50.00
115 Mark Williams JSY AU RC 30.00 80.00
116 AJ Griffin JSY AU RC 12.00 30.00
117 Tari Eason JSY AU RC 40.00 100.00
118 Dalen Terry JSY AU RC 15.00 40.00
119 Jake LaRavia JSY AU RC 15.00 40.00
120 Malaki Branham JSY AU RC 15.00 40.00
121 Christian Braun JSY AU RC 40.00 100.00
122 Walker Kessler JSY AU RC 30.00 80.00
123 David Roddy JSY AU RC 20.00 50.00
124 MarJon Beauchamp JSY AU RC 15.00 40.00
125 Blake Wesley JSY AU RC 15.00 40.00
126 Wendell Moore Jr. JSY AU RC 15.00 40.00
127 Nikola Jovic JSY AU RC 30.00 80.00
128 Patrick Baldwin Jr. JSY AU RC 15.00 40.00
129 TyTy Washington Jr. JSY AU RC 15.00 40.00
130 Peyton Watson JSY AU RC 25.00 60.00
131 Andrew Nembhard JSY AU RC 30.00 80.00
132 Caleb Houstan JSY AU RC 15.00 40.00
133 Christian Koloko JSY AU RC 15.00 40.00
134 Max Christie JSY AU RC 75.00 200.00
135 Jaden Hardy JSY AU RC 25.00 60.00
136 Kennedy Chandler JSY AU RC 15.00 40.00
137 Moussa Diabate JSY AU RC 15.00 40.00
138 E.J. Liddell JSY AU RC 15.00 40.00
139 Trevor Keels JSY AU RC 12.00 30.00
140 Isaiah Mobley JSY AU RC 15.00 40.00

2022-23 Panini Impeccable Canvas Creations Signatures

COMMON CARD 6.00 15.00
SEMISTARS 8.00 20.00
UNLISTED STARS 10.00 25.00
STATED PRINT RUN 25-99 SER.#'d SETS
*HOLO SILVER/10-25: .5X TO 1.2X BASIC
1 Jalen Brunson/99 60.00 150.00
2 Evan Mobley/99 50.00 120.00
3 Anfernee Hardaway/35 125.00 300.00
4 Lenny Wilkens/75 12.00 30.00
6 RJ Barrett/35 25.00 60.00
7 Elton Brand/99 10.00 25.00
8 Ja Morant/25 200.00 500.00
9 Dirk Nowitzki/25 200.00 500.00
10 Calvin Murphy/99 10.00 25.00
14 Anthony Edwards/25 200.00 500.00
15 Isiah Thomas/99 40.00 100.00
16 B.J. Armstrong/99 10.00 25.00
17 Matt Barnes/99 8.00 20.00
18 Jamal Murray/99 60.00 150.00
20 Bill Walton/99 30.00 80.00
21 Bill Laimbeer/99 10.00 25.00
23 Glen Rice/99 10.00 25.00
24 Mark Aguirre/99 10.00 25.00
25 Ralph Sampson/99 8.00 20.00
26 Dejounte Murray/35 40.00 100.00
27 James Worthy/35 20.00 50.00
28 Detlef Schrempf/99 10.00 25.00
30 Wally Szczerbiak/99 8.00 20.00

2022-23 Panini Impeccable Elegance Retired Jersey Autographs

COMMON CARD 6.00 15.00
SEMISTARS 8.00 20.00
UNLISTED STARS 10.00 25.00
STATED PRINT RUN 25-99 SER.#'d SETS
*HOLO SILVER/15-25: .5X TO 1.2X BASIC
1 Adrian Dantley/99 10.00 25.00
2 Pau Gasol/35 75.00 200.00
3 Shawn Kemp/99 75.00 200.00
4 Vince Carter/25 150.00 400.00
5 Charles Barkley/25 150.00 400.00
6 Sam Cassell/99 10.00 25.00
7 Clyde Drexler/25 75.00 200.00
9 Joe Dumars/99 12.00 30.00
10 Jamal Crawford/99 10.00 25.00

2022-23 Panini Impeccable Elegance Veteran Jersey Autographs

COMMON CARD 6.00 15.00
SEMISTARS 8.00 20.00
UNLISTED STARS 10.00 25.00
STATED PRINT RUN 25-99 SER.#'d SETS
*HOLO SILVER/10-25: .5X TO 1.2X BASIC
1 Karl-Anthony Towns/49 40.00 100.00
2 James Harden/25 125.00 300.00
3 Jalen Brunson/99 60.00 150.00
4 Stephen Curry/25 1,000.00 2,000.00
5 Lonnie Walker IV/99 8.00 20.00
8 Khris Middleton/35 20.00 50.00
9 RJ Barrett/49 25.00 60.00
10 Myles Turner/99 10.00 25.00

2022-23 Panini Impeccable Extravagance Autographs

COMMON CARD 6.00 15.00
SEMISTARS 8.00 20.00
UNLISTED STARS 10.00 25.00
STATED PRINT RUN 25-99 SER.#'d SETS
*HOLO SILVER/10-25: .5X TO 1.2X BASIC
1 Marcus Smart/99 40.00 100.00
2 CJ McCollum/35 10.00 25.00
7 Al Horford/75 10.00 25.00
8 Jonas Valanciunas/99 8.00 20.00
9 Elvin Hayes/99 12.00 30.00
10 Dino Radja/99 8.00 20.00
11 Avery Johnson/99 8.00 20.00
12 Hakeem Olajuwon/35 75.00 200.00
13 Gail Goodrich/75 10.00 25.00
14 Jason Richardson/99 10.00 25.00
15 Bogdan Bogdanovic/99 10.00 25.00
16 Michael Porter Jr./75 12.00 30.00
17 Chris Paul/25 75.00 200.00
20 Jalen Green/35 75.00 200.00
21 Dennis Rodman/25 100.00 250.00
22 Ray Allen/25 100.00 250.00
23 Dwyane Wade/25 125.00 300.00
24 Sam Cassell/99 10.00 25.00
25 Cameron Payne/99 8.00 20.00
26 Hedo Turkoglu/99 10.00 25.00
27 Luguentz Dort/99 10.00 25.00
28 Jordan Poole/75 15.00 40.00
29 Myles Turner/99 10.00 25.00

2022-23 Panini Impeccable Illustrious Ink

COMMON CARD 6.00 15.00
SEMISTARS 8.00 20.00
UNLISTED STARS 10.00 25.00
STATED PRINT RUN 25-99 SER.#'d SETS
*HOLO SILVER/10-25: .5X TO 1.2X BASIC
1 Robert Parish/75 12.00 30.00
2 Bernard King/75 12.00 30.00
3 Jamal Murray/35 60.00 150.00
4 Jerry Stackhouse/99 12.00 30.00
5 John Stockton/25 60.00 150.00
6 Kevin Porter Jr./99 8.00 20.00
7 Derrick White/49 10.00 25.00
8 Dejounte Murray/35 40.00 100.00
9 Jamal Crawford/75 10.00 25.00
10 Deni Avdija/99 10.00 25.00
11 Nikola Jokic/25 200.00 500.00
12 James Harden/25 150.00 400.00
13 Nate Archibald/75 12.00 30.00
14 Anfernee Hardaway/25 125.00 300.00
15 Richard Hamilton/75 20.00 50.00
16 Jalen Green/35 125.00 300.00
17 Kristaps Porzingis/99 12.00 30.00
18 Jason Williams/75 75.00 200.00
19 Jordan Clarkson/99 25.00 60.00
20 Louie Dampier/99 10.00 25.00
21 Caron Butler/99 8.00 20.00
22 Karl-Anthony Towns/35 30.00 80.00
23 David Robinson/35 60.00 150.00
24 Khris Middleton/35 20.00 50.00
25 Jerry West/25 60.00 150.00
26 Paul Pierce/35 50.00 120.00
27 Cazzie Russell/99 12.00 30.00
29 Karl Malone/25 75.00 200.00
30 Herbert Jones/99 10.00 25.00
33 Josh Giddey/75 75.00 200.00
34 T.J. Warren/99 8.00 20.00
35 Anfernee Simons/99 30.00 80.00
36 Desmond Bane/75 40.00 100.00
40 Peja Stojakovic/99 10.00 25.00

2022-23 Panini Impeccable Immortal Ink

COMMON CARD 6.00 15.00
SEMISTARS 8.00 20.00
UNLISTED STARS 10.00 25.00
STATED PRINT RUN 25-99 SER.#'d SETS
*HOLO SILVER/10-25: .5X TO 1.2X BASIC
1 Dirk Nowitzki/25 200.00 500.00
2 Ray Allen/25 100.00 250.00
3 Paul Pierce/25 60.00 150.00
4 Clyde Drexler/35 40.00 100.00
5 Jason Kidd/35 40.00 100.00
6 John Stockton/25 75.00 200.00
7 Nate Archibald/75 12.00 30.00
8 Bob McAdoo/99 10.00 25.00
9 Gail Goodrich/75 10.00 25.00
10 Rick Barry/49 12.00 30.00
11 Joe Dumars/99 12.00 30.00
12 Walt Frazier/75 15.00 40.00
13 Dominique Wilkins/35 25.00 60.00
14 Robert Parish/99 12.00 30.00
15 Adrian Dantley/99 10.00 25.00
16 Tony Parker/35 40.00 100.00
17 Glen Rice/99 10.00 25.00
18 Tony Allen/99 6.00 15.00
19 Derek Fisher/75 20.00 50.00
20 Lenny Wilkens/99 12.00 30.00
21 Pau Gasol/35 100.00 250.00
23 Shawn Kemp/49 60.00 150.00
24 Elvin Hayes/99 12.00 30.00
25 Sam Cassell/99 12.00 30.00
26 Jason Richardson/99 10.00 25.00
27 Bernard King/99 12.00 30.00
28 Jerry West/25 60.00 150.00
29 Dennis Rodman/25 125.00 300.00
30 James Worthy/35 25.00 60.00

2022-23 Panini Impeccable Impeccable Honors Signatures

COMMON CARD 6.00 15.00
SEMISTARS 8.00 20.00
UNLISTED STARS 10.00 25.00
STATED PRINT RUN 25-75 SER.#'d SETS
*HOLO SILVER/10-25: .5X TO 1.2X BASIC
1 Nikola Jokic/25 200.00 500.00
2 Stephen Curry/25 1,000.00 2,000.00
3 Grant Hill/35 60.00 150.00
4 Karl-Anthony Towns/35 40.00 100.00
6 Larry Bird/35 125.00 300.00
7 Magic Johnson/25 125.00 300.00
8 David Robinson/35 75.00 200.00
9 Allen Iverson/25 200.00 500.00
10 Paul Pierce/35 125.00 300.00
11 Joe Dumars/75 25.00 60.00
12 Ja Morant/35 300.00 600.00
13 Bill Walton/49 25.00 60.00
14 Jayson Tatum/25 300.00 600.00
15 Kevin Garnett/25 150.00 400.00
16 Jason Kidd/35 75.00 200.00
17 Karl Malone/25 125.00 300.00
18 Rudy Gobert/49 25.00 60.00
19 Manu Ginobili/35 200.00 500.00
20 Jason Terry/75 40.00 100.00

2022-23 Panini Impeccable Impeccable Rookie Signatures

COMMON CARD 6.00 15.00
SEMISTARS 8.00 20.00
UNLISTED STARS 10.00 25.00
STATED PRINT RUN 25-99 SER.#'d SETS
*HOLO SILVER/25: .5X TO 1.2X BASIC
1 Jabari Smith Jr. 100.00 250.00
2 Jake LaRavia 10.00 25.00
3 E.J. Liddell 10.00 25.00
4 Malaki Branham 10.00 25.00
5 MarJon Beauchamp 10.00 25.00
6 Christian Braun 25.00 60.00
7 Jaden Ivey 75.00 200.00
8 Jeremy Sochan 60.00 150.00
9 Ousmane Dieng 12.00 30.00
10 Ochai Agbaji 12.00 30.00
11 Jaden Hardy 75.00 200.00
12 Moussa Diabate 10.00 25.00
13 Paolo Banchero 200.00 500.00
14 Isaiah Mobley 10.00 25.00
15 Bennedict Mathurin 100.00 250.00
16 Andrew Nembhard 20.00 50.00
17 Dyson Daniels 25.00 60.00
18 Christian Koloko 10.00 25.00
19 Caleb Houstan 10.00 25.00
20 Trevor Keels 8.00 20.00
21 Patrick Baldwin Jr. 10.00 25.00
22 AJ Griffin 8.00 20.00
23 Dalen Terry 10.00 25.00
24 Wendell Moore Jr. 10.00 25.00
25 Max Christie 40.00 100.00
26 TyTy Washington Jr. 10.00 25.00
27 Peyton Watson 15.00 40.00
28 Jalen Duren 30.00 80.00
29 Keegan Murray 100.00 250.00
30 Bryce McGowens 10.00 25.00
31 Shaedon Sharpe 100.00 250.00
32 Jaylin Williams 12.00 30.00
33 Johnny Davis 10.00 25.00
34 Blake Wesley 10.00 25.00
35 Mark Williams 20.00 50.00
36 Tari Eason 25.00 60.00
37 Jalen Williams 100.00 250.00
38 Walker Kessler 75.00 200.00
39 Nikola Jovic 40.00 100.00
40 Kennedy Chandler 10.00 25.00

2022-23 Panini Impeccable Indelible Ink

COMMON CARD 6.00 15.00
SEMISTARS 8.00 20.00
UNLISTED STARS 10.00 25.00
STATED PRINT RUN 25-99 SER.#'d SETS
*HOLO SILVER/10-25: .5X TO 1.2X BASIC
2 Anthony Edwards/25 200.00 500.00
4 Jordan Clarkson/99 20.00 50.00
5 T.J. Warren/99 8.00 20.00
6 Jonas Valanciunas/99 8.00 20.00
7 Latrell Sprewell/99 25.00 60.00
8 Lonnie Walker IV/99 8.00 20.00
9 Jayson Tatum/25 200.00 500.00
11 Jaren Jackson Jr./49 60.00 150.00
12 Shai Gilgeous-Alexander/35 400.00 800.00
13 Jonathan Kuminga/49 50.00 120.00
15 Al Horford/49 10.00 25.00
16 Michael Porter Jr./49 12.00 30.00
17 Ralph Sampson/75 8.00 20.00
18 Caris LeVert/99 8.00 20.00
19 Jamaal Wilkes/99 10.00 25.00
20 Kevin Porter Jr./99 8.00 20.00
21 Kenny "Sky" Walker/99 8.00 20.00
22 Luka Doncic/25 800.00 1,500.00
23 Anfernee Simons/49 20.00 50.00
24 Vince Carter/35 100.00 250.00
25 Nikola Jokic/25 200.00 500.00
26 Ray Allen/35 100.00 250.00
27 Hedo Turkoglu/99 10.00 25.00
28 Jason Williams/75 60.00 150.00
29 Bill Walton/99 25.00 60.00
30 Collin Sexton/75 12.00 30.00
31 Antawn Jamison/99 10.00 25.00
34 Caron Butler/99 8.00 20.00
35 Manu Ginobili/25 100.00 250.00
37 Shawn Kemp/99 60.00 150.00
38 Franz Wagner/75 50.00 120.00

2022-23 Panini Impeccable Rookie Autographs

COMMON CARD 6.00 15.00
SEMISTARS 8.00 20.00
UNLISTED STARS 10.00 25.00
STATED PRINT RUN 99 SER.#'d SETS
*HOLO SILVER/25: .5X TO 1.2X BASIC
1 Chet Holmgren 150.00 400.00
2 Shaedon Sharpe 100.00 250.00
3 AJ Griffin 8.00 20.00
4 Dalen Terry 10.00 25.00
5 Wendell Moore Jr. 10.00 25.00
6 Max Christie 40.00 100.00
7 Dyson Daniels 25.00 60.00
8 Christian Koloko 10.00 25.00
9 Caleb Houstan 10.00 25.00
10 Jabari Smith Jr. 100.00 250.00
11 Jake LaRavia 10.00 25.00
12 E.J. Liddell 10.00 25.00
13 Malaki Branham 10.00 25.00
14 MarJon Beauchamp 10.00 25.00
15 Christian Braun 25.00 60.00
16 Jaden Ivey 75.00 200.00
17 Jeremy Sochan 60.00 150.00
18 Ousmane Dieng 12.00 30.00
19 Ochai Agbaji 12.00 30.00
20 Isaiah Mobley 10.00 25.00
21 Moussa Diabate 10.00 25.00
22 Paolo Banchero 200.00 500.00
23 TyTy Washington Jr. 10.00 25.00
24 Bennedict Mathurin 100.00 250.00
25 Andrew Nembhard 20.00 50.00
26 Trevor Keels 8.00 20.00
27 Keegan Murray 100.00 250.00
28 Patrick Baldwin Jr. 10.00 25.00
29 Jaylin Williams 12.00 30.00
30 Johnny Davis 10.00 25.00
31 Blake Wesley 10.00 25.00
32 Mark Williams 20.00 50.00
33 Tari Eason 25.00 60.00
34 Jalen Williams 100.00 250.00
35 Walker Kessler 75.00 200.00
36 Nikola Jovic 40.00 100.00

37 Kennedy Chandler 10.00 25.00
38 David Roddy 12.00 30.00
39 Peyton Watson 15.00 40.00
40 Jalen Duren 30.00 80.00

2022-23 Panini Impeccable Stainless Stars

COMMON CARD 2.50 6.00
SEMISTARS 3.00 8.00
UNLISTED STARS 4.00 10.00
STATED PRINT RUN 99 SER.#'d SETS
*ASIA RED: .4X TO 1X BASIC
*BLUE/75: .5X TO 1.2X BASIC
*PURPLE/49: .6X TO 1.5X BASIC
ORANGE/30: .75X TO 2X BASIC
1 Luka Doncic 25.00 60.00
2 LeBron James 30.00 80.00
3 Ja Morant 12.00 30.00
4 Trae Young 10.00 25.00
5 Kevin Durant 12.00 30.00
6 Stephen Curry 30.00 80.00
7 Jayson Tatum 15.00 40.00
8 Giannis Antetokounmpo 20.00 50.00
9 Nikola Jokic 20.00 50.00
10 Joel Embiid 6.00 15.00
11 Anthony Edwards 20.00 50.00
12 Zion Williamson 10.00 25.00
13 Devin Booker 10.00 25.00
14 Donovan Mitchell 8.00 20.00
15 LaMelo Ball 10.00 25.00
16 Johnny Davis 4.00 10.00
17 Dyson Daniels 10.00 25.00
18 Paolo Banchero 40.00 100.00
19 Chet Holmgren 20.00 50.00
20 Jabari Smith Jr. 12.00 30.00
21 Keegan Murray 10.00 25.00
22 Jaden Ivey 12.00 30.00
23 Bennedict Mathurin 12.00 30.00
24 Shaedon Sharpe 15.00 40.00
25 Jeremy Sochan 12.00 30.00

2022-23 Panini Impeccable Stainless Stars Autographs

COMMON CARD 6.00 15.00
SEMISTARS 8.00 20.00
UNLISTED STARS 10.00 25.00
STATED PRINT RUN 75-99 SER.#'d SETS
*BLUE/49-75: .4X TO 1X BASIC
*PURPLE/35-49: .5X TO 1.2X BASIC
ORANGE/25: .5X TO 1.2X BASIC
1 Keegan Murray/75 100.00 250.00
2 Jalen Williams/99 100.00 250.00
3 Jaden Ivey/75 75.00 200.00
4 Jeremy Sochan/99 60.00 150.00
5 Chet Holmgren/75 150.00 400.00
6 Ochai Agbaji/99 12.00 30.00
7 Ousmane Dieng/99 12.00 30.00
8 Mark Williams/99 20.00 50.00
9 Jalen Duren/75 30.00 80.00
10 AJ Griffin/99 8.00 20.00
11 Tari Eason/99 25.00 60.00
12 Paolo Banchero /75 200.00 500.00
13 Dalen Terry/99 10.00 25.00
14 Dyson Daniels/99 25.00 60.00
15 Jake LaRavia/99 10.00 25.00
16 Johnny Davis/75 10.00 25.00
17 MarJon Beauchamp/99 10.00 25.00
18 Malaki Branham/99 10.00 25.00
19 Jabari Smith Jr./75 100.00 250.00
20 Christian Braun/99 25.00 60.00
21 Walker Kessler/99 75.00 200.00
22 Shaedon Sharpe/99 100.00 250.00
23 David Roddy/99 12.00 30.00
24 Nikola Jovic/99 40.00 100.00
25 Bennedict Mathurin/99 100.00 250.00

2022-23 Panini Impeccable Watercolor Signatures

COMMON CARD 6.00 15.00
SEMISTARS 8.00 20.00
UNLISTED STARS 10.00 25.00
STATED PRINT RUN 25-99 SER.#'d SETS
*HOLO SILVER/10-25: .5X TO 1.2X BASIC
1 Jonathan Kuminga/49 50.00 120.00
2 Nikola Jokic/25 200.00 500.00
3 Caris LeVert/99 8.00 20.00
4 Dominique Wilkins/35 25.00 60.00
5 Richard Hamilton/49 20.00 50.00
6 Robert Horry/75 15.00 40.00
7 Tyrese Haliburton/49 75.00 200.00
8 Antawn Jamison/99 10.00 25.00
9 Kevin Garnett/25 125.00 300.00
10 Jason Kidd/35 40.00 100.00
11 George McGinnis/99 10.00 25.00
12 Bob McAdoo/99 12.00 30.00
13 Jamaal Wilkes/99 10.00 25.00
14 Bobby Portis/99 10.00 25.00
15 Jason Terry/99 8.00 20.00
16 Allen Iverson/25 150.00 400.00
17 Tony Parker/35 40.00 100.00
20 Khris Middleton/35 20.00 50.00
21 Mark Price/99 10.00 25.00
22 Collin Sexton/49 12.00 30.00
24 Grant Williams/99 8.00 20.00
25 Walt Frazier/75 15.00 40.00
26 Rudy Gobert/49 12.00 30.00
27 Dell Curry/99 10.00 25.00
29 Grayson Allen/99 10.00 25.00
30 Charles Barkley/25 150.00 400.00
32 Chris Paul/25 75.00 200.00
34 Dino Radja/99 8.00 20.00
35 Latrell Sprewell/99 40.00 100.00
36 Rolando Blackman/99 8.00 20.00
37 Dirk Nowitzki/25 200.00 500.00
38 Shawn Kemp/99 75.00 200.00
40 Franz Wagner/75 50.00 120.00

2023-24 Panini Impeccable

1-100 PRINT RUN 99 SER.#'d SETS
JSY AU PRINT RUN 99 COPIES PER
*INTERNATIONAL: .4X TO 1X BASIC
*SILVER/75: .5X TO 1.2X BASIC
*GOLD/49: .6X TO 1.5X BASIC
*GREEN/35: .75X TO 2X BASIC
*HOLO SILVER/25: 1X TO 2.5X BASIC
*HOLO SILVER RC JSY AU/25: .75X TO 2X BASIC
1 Karl-Anthony Towns 4.00 10.00
2 Jordan Walsh RC 4.00 10.00
3 Giannis Antetokounmpo 12.00 30.00
4 Cade Cunningham 6.00 15.00
5 Chet Holmgren 6.00 15.00
6 Noah Smith Jr. RC 5.00 12.00
7 Tyler Herro 4.00 10.00
8 Scoot Henderson RC 12.00 30.00
9 Kevin Durant 8.00 20.00
10 Kris Murray RC 4.00 10.00
11 DeMar DeRozan 4.00 10.00
12 LaMelo Ball 6.00 15.00
13 Andre Jackson Jr. RC 6.00 15.00
14 Tyrese Haliburton 5.00 12.00
15 Jimmy Butler 4.00 10.00
16 Jalen Williams 5.00 12.00
17 Julius Randle 3.00 8.00
18 Anthony Black RC 8.00 20.00
19 Dejounte Murray 3.00 8.00
20 Shaedon Sharpe 5.00 12.00
21 De'Aaron Fox 5.00 12.00
22 RJ Barrett 4.00 10.00
23 Kyrie Irving 5.00 12.00
24 Jarace Walker RC 8.00 20.00
25 Kristaps Porzingis 3.00 8.00
26 Scottie Barnes 3.00 8.00
27 Julian Phillips RC 4.00 10.00
28 LeBron James 20.00 50.00
29 Jaden Ivey 3.00 8.00
30 Jordan Hawkins RC 5.00 12.00
31 Jalen Hood-Schifino RC 4.00 10.00
32 Ausar Thompson RC 10.00 25.00
33 Amen Thompson RC 20.00 50.00
34 Zion Williamson 6.00 15.00
35 Jalen Brunson 6.00 15.00
36 Devin Booker 5.00 12.00
37 Donovan Mitchell 5.00 12.00
38 Tyrese Maxey 5.00 12.00
39 Luka Doncic 15.00 40.00
40 Gradey Dick RC 8.00 20.00
41 Joel Embiid 6.00 15.00
42 Jayson Tatum 10.00 25.00
43 Kobe Brown RC 4.00 10.00
44 Mikal Bridges 3.00 8.00
45 Jaren Jackson Jr. 4.00 10.00
46 Nikola Jokic 12.00 30.00
47 Taylor Hendricks RC 4.00 10.00
48 Hunter Tyson RC 4.00 10.00
49 Marcus Sasser RC 6.00 15.00
50 Olivier-Maxence Prosper RC 4.00 10.00
51 Bilal Coulibaly RC 10.00 25.00
52 Gary Trent Jr. 2.50 6.00
53 Shai Gilgeous-Alexander 12.00 30.00
54 Leonard Miller RC 4.00 10.00
55 Jett Howard RC 5.00 12.00
56 Colby Jones RC 4.00 10.00
57 Bradley Beal 3.00 8.00
58 Brice Sensabaugh RC 6.00 15.00
59 James Harden 5.00 12.00
60 Jamal Murray 5.00 12.00
61 Darius Garland 4.00 10.00
62 Kyle Kuzma 3.00 8.00
63 Amari Bailey RC 4.00 10.00
64 Noah Clowney RC 5.00 12.00
65 Maxwell Lewis RC 3.00 8.00
66 Cam Whitmore RC 10.00 25.00
67 Dereck Lively II RC 8.00 20.00
68 Chris Paul 5.00 12.00
69 Ben Simmons 2.50 6.00
70 Brandin Podziemski RC 12.00 30.00
71 Brandon Ingram 3.00 8.00
72 Jrue Holiday 3.00 8.00
73 Fred VanVleet 4.00 10.00
74 Jordan Poole 4.00 10.00
75 Stephen Curry 20.00 50.00
76 Lauri Markkanen 4.00 10.00
77 Zach LaVine 4.00 10.00
78 Paul George 4.00 10.00
79 Keyonte George RC 12.00 30.00
80 Julian Strawther RC 4.00 10.00
81 Ben Sheppard RC 5.00 12.00
82 Russell Westbrook 4.00 10.00
83 Victor Wembanyama RC 75.00 200.00
84 Kawhi Leonard 6.00 15.00
85 Kobe Bufkin RC 5.00 12.00
86 Austin Reaves 6.00 15.00
87 Anthony Davis 6.00 15.00
88 GG Jackson II RC 6.00 15.00
89 Paolo Banchero 6.00 15.00
90 Cason Wallace RC 8.00 20.00
91 Jaime Jaquez Jr. RC 6.00 15.00
92 Ja Morant 8.00 20.00
93 Damian Lillard 6.00 15.00
94 Jaylen Brown 5.00 12.00
95 Anthony Edwards 12.00 30.00
96 Jabari Smith Jr. 4.00 10.00
97 Desmond Bane 3.00 8.00
98 Dariq Whitehead RC 5.00 12.00
99 Trae Young 5.00 12.00
100 Keegan Murray 3.00 8.00
101 Amen Thompson JSY AU 100.00 250.00
102 Ausar Thompson JSY AU 50.00 125.00
103 Bilal Coulibaly JSY AU 50.00 125.00
104 Cason Wallace JSY AU 40.00 100.00
105 Dereck Lively II JSY AU 40.00 100.00
106 Kobe Bufkin JSY AU 25.00 60.00
107 Keyonte George JSY AU 60.00 150.00
108 Brandin Podziemski JSY AU 60.00 150.00
109 Noah Clowney JSY AU 25.00 60.00
110 Dariq Whitehead JSY AU 25.00 60.00
111 Kris Murray JSY AU 20.00 50.00
112 Olivier-Maxence Prosper JSY AU 20.00 50.00
113 Marcus Sasser JSY AU 30.00 80.00
114 Ben Sheppard JSY AU 20.00 50.00
115 Brice Sensabaugh JSY AU 30.00 80.00
116 Julian Strawther JSY AU 25.00 60.00
117 Kobe Brown JSY AU 20.00 50.00
118 James Nnaji JSY AU RC 15.00 40.00
119 Jalen Pickett JSY AU RC 15.00 40.00
120 Sasha Vezenkov JSY AU RC 15.00 40.00
121 Colby Jones JSY AU 20.00 50.00
122 Julian Phillips JSY AU 20.00 50.00
123 Andre Jackson Jr. JSY AU 30.00 80.00
124 Hunter Tyson JSY AU 20.00 50.00
125 Jordan Walsh JSY AU 20.00 50.00
126 Mouhamed Gueye JSY AU RC 20.00 50.00
127 Maxwell Lewis JSY AU 15.00 40.00
128 Tristan Vukcevic JSY AU RC 20.00 50.00
130 Sidy Cissoko JSY AU RC 20.00 50.00
131 GG Jackson II JSY AU 40.00 100.00
132 Vasilije Micic JSY AU RC 20.00 50.00
133 Jordan Miller JSY AU RC 25.00 60.00
134 Keyontae Johnson JSY AU RC 20.00 50.00
135 Jalen Wilson JSY AU 20.00 50.00
136 Toumani Camara JSY AU RC 40.00 100.00
137 Jaylen Clark JSY AU RC 20.00 50.00
138 Jalen Slawson JSY AU RC 20.00 50.00
139 Isaiah Wong JSY AU RC 20.00 50.00
140 Trayce Jackson-Davis JSY AU RC 25.00 60.00

2023-24 Panini Impeccable Canvas Creations Signatures

STATED PRINT RUN 25-99 SER.#'d SETS
*HOLO SILVER/15-25: .5X TO 1.2X BASIC
1 Markelle Fultz/99 10.00 25.00
4 Ayo Dosunmu/99 12.00 30.00
6 Josh Giddey/49 15.00 40.00
7 RJ Barrett/49 20.00 50.00
8 Gary Harris/99 10.00 25.00
9 De'Aaron Fox/25 75.00 200.00
10 Bones Hyland/75 10.00 25.00
11 Bennedict Mathurin/75 20.00 50.00
12 Jeremy Sochan/75 15.00 40.00
13 Dalen Terry/75 12.00 30.00
14 Malaki Branham/75 10.00 25.00
15 Cole Anthony/75 12.00 30.00
16 Jalen Duren/25 15.00 40.00
17 Jaden Hardy/25 15.00 40.00
18 Russell Westbrook/49 75.00 200.00
20 Johnny Davis/75 10.00 25.00
21 Larry Johnson/75 15.00 40.00
22 B.J. Armstrong/99 12.00 30.00
23 Brandon Roy/25 15.00 40.00
24 Isaac Okoro/99 10.00 25.00
25 Kevin Garnett/25 125.00 300.00
26 Joakim Noah/49 12.00 30.00
27 Mark Aguirre/99 10.00 25.00
28 Jason Williams/75 75.00 200.00
29 Antoine Walker/99 12.00 30.00
30 Toni Kukoc/25 15.00 40.00

2023-24 Panini Impeccable Elegance Retired Jersey Autographs

*HOLO SILVER/10-25: .5X TO 1.2X BASIC
NO PRICING ON QTY 10
1 Jason Kidd/49 40.00 100.00
2 Amar'e Stoudemire/99 15.00 40.00
3 Joakim Noah/99 30.00 80.00
4 Larry Bird/15 200.00 500.00
5 Dirk Nowitzki/15 200.00 500.00
6 Steve Kerr/49 40.00 100.00
7 Carmelo Anthony/15 100.00 250.00
8 Isiah Thomas/25 40.00 100.00
9 Manu Ginobili/25 100.00 250.00
10 Jason Terry/49 20.00 50.00

2023-24 Panini Impeccable Elegance Veteran Jersey Autographs

*HOLO SILVER/10-25: .5X TO 1.2X BASIC
NO PRICING ON QTY 10
EVJJAM Ja Morant/15 500.00 1,000.00
2 Stephen Curry/15 1,250.00 2,500.00
3 Brandon Ingram/35 20.00 50.00
5 Jrue Holiday/75 40.00 100.00
6 Jalen Brunson/75 75.00 200.00
7 Immanuel Quickley/99 15.00 40.00
8 Deandre Ayton/99 15.00 40.00
9 Devin Vassell/99 25.00 60.00
10 Damian Lillard/35 100.00 250.00

2023-24 Panini Impeccable Extravagance Autographs

STATED PRINT RUN 25-99 SER.#'d SETS
*HOLO SILVER/15-25: .5X TO 1.2X BASIC
1 Zion Williamson/25 200.00 500.00
2 Jordan Poole/49 20.00 50.00
3 Bones Hyland/99 10.00 25.00
5 Jonas Valanciunas/75 10.00 25.00
6 Jaden Ivey/25 60.00 150.00
7 Alperen Sengun/75 40.00 100.00
9 Kelly Oubre Jr./75 12.00 30.00
10 Tyrese Maxey/25 75.00 200.00
11 Desmond Bane/25 15.00 40.00
13 Jalen Williams/75 75.00 200.00
15 Jabari Smith Jr./25 20.00 50.00
16 Luka Doncic/49 600.00 1,200.00
17 Ja Morant/49 500.00 1,000.00
18 Donovan Mitchell/25 60.00 150.00
19 Ray Allen/25 75.00 200.00
20 Bill Laimbeer/99 12.00 30.00
21 Robert Parish/99 15.00 40.00
22 Mike Bibby/99 12.00 30.00
23 Julius Erving/25 75.00 200.00
24 Magic Johnson/25 75.00 200.00
25 Kevin McHale/25 25.00 60.00
26 Doc Rivers/49 12.00 30.00
27 Steve Kerr/25 25.00 60.00
28 Nick Van Exel/25 20.00 50.00
29 Dale Ellis/99 12.00 30.00
30 Jeff Hornacek/99 10.00 25.00

2023-24 Panini Impeccable Illustrious Ink

STATED PRINT RUN 10-99 SER.#'d SETS
NO PRICING ON QTY 10
*HOLO SILVER/15-25: .5X TO 1.2X BASIC
2 Onyeka Okongwu/75 10.00 25.00
3 Jose Alvarado/99 12.00 30.00
4 Jabari Smith Jr./25 20.00 50.00
5 Jordan Clarkson/25 12.00 30.00
7 Jalen Duren/49 15.00 40.00
10 Wendell Moore Jr./99 10.00 25.00
12 Caleb Martin/99 10.00 25.00
13 Shaedon Sharpe/75 40.00 100.00
15 Walker Kessler/99 12.00 30.00
16 Jordan Poole/25 20.00 50.00
17 Paul George/25 60.00 150.00
19 Deandre Ayton/25 12.00 30.00
20 Michael Porter Jr./75 15.00 40.00
23 Bobby Portis/25 15.00 40.00
24 Precious Achiuwa/99 10.00 25.00
26 Nicolas Batum/99 8.00 20.00
27 Bob Dandridge/99 12.00 30.00
30 Stephen Jackson/99 10.00 25.00
31 Yao Ming/25 200.00 500.00
32 Ben Wallace/25 40.00 100.00
33 Dwyane Wade/25 100.00 250.00
34 Antoine Carr/99 10.00 25.00
35 Wally Szczerbiak/99 10.00 25.00
36 Tracy McGrady/25 125.00 300.00
37 Calvin Murphy/99 12.00 30.00
38 Fat Lever/99 12.00 30.00
39 Dell Curry/99 12.00 30.00
40 Rolando Blackman/99 10.00 25.00

2023-24 Panini Impeccable Immortal Ink

STATED PRINT RUN 25-99 SER.#'d SETS
*HOLO SILVER/15-25: .5X TO 1.2X BASIC
1 Magic Johnson/25 75.00 200.00
2 Nick Van Exel/49 20.00 50.00
3 Hakeem Olajuwon/25 60.00 150.00
4 Tom Chambers/99 12.00 30.00
5 Antawn Jamison/99 12.00 30.00
6 Wally Szczerbiak/99 10.00 25.00
7 Fat Lever/49 12.00 30.00
8 Dan Issel/99 15.00 40.00
9 Nate Archibald/99 15.00 40.00
10 Dave Bing/99 15.00 40.00
11 Rolando Blackman/99 10.00 25.00
13 Ray Allen/49 75.00 200.00
15 Maurice Cheeks/99 12.00 30.00
16 Calvin Murphy/99 12.00 30.00
17 Brandon Roy/25 15.00 40.00
18 Metta World Peace/49 12.00 30.00
19 Antoine Carr/99 10.00 25.00
20 Rod Strickland/99 12.00 30.00
21 Artis Gilmore/99 15.00 40.00
22 Michael Cooper/49 12.00 30.00
23 Anfernee Hardaway/49 75.00 200.00
24 Jeff Hornacek/99 10.00 25.00
25 Dell Curry/99 12.00 30.00
27 Doc Rivers/99 12.00 30.00
29 Dennis Rodman/49 150.00 400.00
30 Allen Iverson/25 150.00 400.00

2023-24 Panini Impeccable Impeccable All Time Signatures

1 Stephen Curry 1,500.00 3,000.00

2023-24 Panini Impeccable Impeccable Championship

7 Magic Johnson/87 50.00 120.00
8 Larry Bird/86 50.00 120.00
9 Kareem Abdul-Jabbar/85 50.00 120.00
10 Julius Erving/83 50.00 120.00

2023-24 Panini Impeccable Impeccable Honors Signatures

*HOLO SILVER/10-25: .5X TO 1.2X BASIC
NO PRICING ON QTY 10
1 De'Aaron Fox/35 100.00 250.00
2 Russell Westbrook/35 125.00 300.00
3 Julius Erving/25 100.00 250.00
4 Chauncey Billups/35 75.00 200.00
5 Pau Gasol/35 75.00 200.00
6 Tony Parker/35 75.00 200.00
7 Ben Wallace/35 75.00 200.00
8 Marcus Smart/35 25.00 60.00
10 Hakeem Olajuwon/35 100.00 250.00
11 Stephen Curry/35 1,500.00 3,000.00
13 Dwyane Wade/35 125.00 300.00
14 Kareem Abdul-Jabbar/25 100.00 250.00
15 Jaren Jackson Jr./35 60.00 150.00
16 Amar'e Stoudemire/35 60.00 150.00
17 Ben Simmons/35 75.00 200.00
18 Gary Payton/25 60.00 150.00
19 Jason Kidd/25 75.00 200.00
20 Toni Kukoc/35 40.00 100.00

2023-24 Panini Impeccable Impeccable Rookie Signatures

STATED PRINT RUN 75-99 SER.#'d SETS
*HOLO SILVER/25: .75X TO 2X BASIC
1 Sidy Cissoko/99 8.00 20.00
2 Keyonte George/75 25.00 60.00
3 Brice Sensabaugh/99 12.00 30.00
4 Jordan Walsh/99 8.00 20.00
5 Andre Jackson Jr./99 12.00 30.00
6 James Nnaji/99 6.00 15.00
7 Seth Lundy/99 6.00 15.00
8 Noah Clowney/99 10.00 25.00
9 Keyontae Johnson/99 8.00 20.00
10 Jalen Slawson/99 8.00 20.00
11 Julian Strawther/99 10.00 25.00
12 Dariq Whitehead/75 10.00 25.00
13 Oscar Tshiebwe/99 10.00 25.00
14 Dereck Lively II/99 15.00 40.00
15 Hunter Tyson/99 8.00 20.00
16 Trayce Jackson-Davis/99 10.00 25.00
17 Jordan Miller/99 10.00 25.00
18 Julian Phillips/99 8.00 20.00
19 Bilal Coulibaly/99 20.00 50.00
20 Jaylen Clark/99 8.00 20.00
21 Jalen Pickett/99 6.00 15.00
22 Tristan Vukcevic/99 8.00 20.00
23 Brandin Podziemski/99 25.00 60.00
24 Kobe Bufkin/99 10.00 25.00
25 Marcus Sasser/99 12.00 30.00
26 Cason Wallace/99 15.00 40.00
27 Ben Sheppard/99 8.00 20.00
28 Colby Jones/99 8.00 20.00
29 Jalen Wilson/99 8.00 20.00
30 Ausar Thompson/75 20.00 50.00
31 Kris Murray/99 8.00 20.00
32 Mouhamed Gueye/99 8.00 20.00
33 Olivier-Maxence Prosper/99 8.00 20.00
35 Isaiah Wong/99 8.00 20.00
36 Kobe Brown/99 8.00 20.00
37 Toumani Camara/99 15.00 40.00
38 Amen Thompson/75 60.00 150.00
39 Leonard Miller/99 8.00 20.00
40 Maxwell Lewis/99 6.00 15.00

2023-24 Panini Impeccable Impeccable Stars Signatures

STATED PRINT RUN 25-99 SER.#'d SETS
*HOLO SILVER/15-25: .5X TO 1.2X BASIC
1 Stephen Curry/25 1,000.00 2,000.00
2 Luka Doncic/25 600.00 1,200.00
3 Isaac Okoro/99 10.00 25.00
4 Carmelo Anthony/25 125.00 300.00
5 Desmond Bane/49 15.00 40.00
6 Julius Erving/25 75.00 200.00
7 Donovan Mitchell/25 60.00 150.00
8 Yuta Watanabe/99 40.00 100.00
9 Shawn Kemp/75 40.00 100.00
10 Toni Kukoc/99 15.00 40.00
11 Kareem Abdul-Jabbar/25 100.00 250.00
12 Anthony Edwards/49 500.00 1,000.00
13 Dale Ellis/99 12.00 30.00
14 Jaren Jackson Jr./49 75.00 200.00
15 Chris Mullin/49 20.00 50.00
16 Josh Giddey/49 25.00 60.00
17 Alperen Sengun/49 60.00 150.00
18 Peja Stojakovic/75 12.00 30.00
20 Jason Williams/99 75.00 200.00
22 Chauncey Billups/99 25.00 60.00
24 Jrue Holiday/25 40.00 100.00
25 Chris Paul/25 150.00 400.00
26 Tracy McGrady/25 150.00 400.00
29 Bradley Beal/49 25.00 60.00

2023-24 Panini Impeccable Impeccable Stats

1 LeBron James/61 200.00 500.00
2 LeBron James/27 300.00 600.00
3 LeBron James/57 200.00 500.00
4 Joel Embiid/59 20.00 50.00
5 Damian Lillard/71 75.00 200.00
6 Giannis Antetokounmpo/50 125.00 300.00
7 Anthony Davis/50 75.00 200.00
8 Jayson Tatum/51 100.00 250.00
9 Kyrie Irving/60 100.00 250.00
10 Klay Thompson/37 100.00 250.00
11 Devin Booker/70 100.00 250.00
12 Shai Gilgeous-Alexander/44 200.00 500.00
13 Tim Duncan/53 125.00 300.00
14 Pete Maravich/68 75.00 200.00
15 Wilt Chamberlain/100 150.00 400.00
16 Dirk Nowitzki/53 125.00 300.00
17 Allen Iverson/48 125.00 300.00
18 John Stockton/28 100.00 250.00
19 David Robinson/71 100.00 250.00
20 Carmelo Anthony/62 150.00 400.00
21 Vince Carter/51 100.00 250.00
22 Kevin Durant/55 125.00 300.00
23 Victor Wembanyama/38 800.00 1,500.00
24 Brandon Miller/29 200.00 500.00
25 Scoot Henderson/25 100.00 250.00

2023-24 Panini Impeccable Indelible Ink

STATED PRINT RUN 25-99 SER.#'d SETS
*HOLO SILVER/15-25: .5X TO 1.2X BASIC
1 Tyrese Haliburton/25 100.00 250.00
2 Dejounte Murray/75 15.00 40.00
3 Oscar Tshiebwe/99 15.00 40.00
5 Ivica Zubac/25 12.00 30.00
6 Wendell Moore Jr./99 10.00 25.00
7 Keegan Murray/75 15.00 40.00
8 Jaden Hardy/25 15.00 40.00
9 Bennedict Mathurin/75 20.00 50.00
10 Tari Eason/75 15.00 40.00
11 Dalen Terry/75 12.00 30.00
12 Precious Achiuwa/99 10.00 25.00
13 Ousmane Dieng/75 12.00 30.00
14 Chris Livingston/99 12.00 30.00
15 Tyrese Maxey/25 100.00 250.00
16 Jaden Ivey/25 75.00 200.00
21 Cole Anthony/99 12.00 30.00
22 Peyton Watson/99 12.00 30.00
23 Andrew Nembhard/99 12.00 30.00
24 Jaylin Williams/99 12.00 30.00
26 Jake LaRavia/99 10.00 25.00
27 Nikola Jovic/99 12.00 30.00
28 Jose Alvarado/99 12.00 30.00
30 Markelle Fultz/49 10.00 25.00
35 Kentavious Caldwell-Pope/75 10.00 25.00
36 T.J. McConnell/99 12.00 30.00
37 Caleb Martin/99 10.00 25.00
38 Paul George/25 100.00 250.00
39 Bobby Portis/75 15.00 40.00
40 Ayo Dosunmu/99 12.00 30.00

2023-24 Panini Impeccable Rookie Autographs

STATED PRINT RUN 99 SER.#'d SETS
*INTERNATIONAL/88: .5X TO 1.2X BASIC
*HOLO SILVER/25: .75X TO 2X BASIC
1 Andre Jackson Jr. 12.00 30.00
2 Marcus Sasser 12.00 30.00
3 Mouhamed Gueye 8.00 20.00
4 Seth Lundy 6.00 15.00
5 Jalen Wilson 8.00 20.00
6 Ausar Thompson 20.00 50.00
7 Jalen Slawson 8.00 20.00
8 Tristan Vukcevic 8.00 20.00
9 Jordan Walsh 8.00 20.00
10 Brandin Podziemski 25.00 60.00
11 Olivier-Maxence Prosper 8.00 20.00
12 Keyontae Johnson 8.00 20.00
13 Kobe Bufkin 10.00 25.00
14 Kobe Brown 8.00 20.00
15 Dariq Whitehead 10.00 25.00
16 James Nnaji 6.00 15.00
17 Noah Clowney 10.00 25.00
18 Toumani Camara 15.00 40.00
19 Maxwell Lewis 6.00 15.00
20 Leonard Miller 8.00 20.00
21 Dereck Lively II 15.00 40.00
22 Julian Strawther 10.00 25.00
23 Brice Sensabaugh 12.00 30.00
24 Colby Jones 8.00 20.00
25 Cason Wallace 15.00 40.00
26 Trayce Jackson-Davis 10.00 25.00
27 GG Jackson II 15.00 40.00
28 Sidy Cissoko 8.00 20.00
29 Jaylen Clark 8.00 20.00
31 Hunter Tyson 8.00 20.00
32 Amen Thompson 60.00 150.00
33 Julian Phillips 8.00 20.00
34 Bilal Coulibaly 20.00 50.00
35 Kris Murray 8.00 20.00
36 Jalen Pickett 6.00 15.00
37 Keyonte George 25.00 60.00
38 Isaiah Wong 8.00 20.00
39 Jordan Miller 10.00 25.00
40 Ben Sheppard 8.00 20.00

2023-24 Panini Impeccable Stainless Stars

STATED PRINT RUN 75 SER.#'d SETS
*INTERNATIONAL RED: .4X TO 1X BASIC
*BLUE/49: .5X TO 1.2X BASIC
*ORANGE/25: .6X TO 1.5X BASIC
1 Victor Wembanyama 100.00 250.00
2 Giannis Antetokounmpo 15.00 40.00
3 Jordan Hawkins 5.00 12.00
4 Brandon Miller 12.00 30.00
5 Cam Whitmore 8.00 20.00
6 Stephen Curry 25.00 60.00
7 Anthony Edwards 15.00 40.00
8 Gradey Dick 6.00 15.00
9 Jayson Tatum 12.00 30.00
10 Luka Doncic 20.00 50.00
11 Kevin Durant 10.00 25.00
12 Trae Young 6.00 15.00
13 Anthony Black 6.00 15.00
14 Shai Gilgeous-Alexander 15.00 40.00
15 LeBron James 25.00 60.00
16 Damian Lillard 8.00 20.00
17 Cason Wallace 6.00 15.00
18 Ja Morant 10.00 25.00
19 Ausar Thompson 8.00 20.00
20 Jaime Jaquez Jr. 5.00 12.00
21 Bilal Coulibaly 8.00 20.00
22 Scoot Henderson 10.00 25.00
23 Nikola Jokic 15.00 40.00
24 Amen Thompson 15.00 40.00
25 Keyonte George 10.00 25.00

2023-24 Panini Impeccable Stainless Stars Autographs

STATED PRINT RUN 75-99 SER.#'d SETS
*BLUE/49-75: .5X TO 1.2X BASIC
*PURPLE/35-49: .6X TO 1.5X BASIC
*ORANGE/25: .75X TO 2X BASIC
1 Dereck Lively II/99 15.00 40.00
2 Hunter Tyson/99 8.00 20.00
3 Andre Jackson Jr./99 12.00 30.00
4 Maxwell Lewis/99 6.00 15.00
5 Bilal Coulibaly/99 20.00 50.00
6 Olivier-Maxence Prosper/99 8.00 20.00
7 Keyonte George/75 25.00 60.00
8 Julian Phillips/99 8.00 20.00
9 Kobe Bufkin/99 10.00 25.00
10 Marcus Sasser/99 12.00 30.00
11 Rayan Rupert/99 8.00 20.00
12 Noah Clowney/99 10.00 25.00
13 Ben Sheppard/99 8.00 20.00
14 Brice Sensabaugh/99 12.00 30.00
15 Toumani Camara/99 15.00 40.00
16 Ausar Thompson/75 20.00 50.00
17 Brandin Podziemski/99 25.00 60.00
18 Jordan Walsh/99 8.00 20.00
19 Amen Thompson/75 60.00 150.00
20 Julian Strawther/99 10.00 25.00
21 Kris Murray/99 8.00 20.00
22 Cason Wallace/99 15.00 40.00
23 Kobe Brown/99 8.00 20.00
24 GG Jackson II/99 15.00 40.00
25 Tristan Vukcevic/99 8.00 20.00

2023-24 Panini Impeccable Watercolor Signatures

STATED PRINT RUN 25-99 SER.#'d SETS
*HOLO SILVER/15-25: .5X TO 1.2X BASIC
4 Ivica Zubac/75 12.00 30.00
5 Devin Vassell/49 25.00 60.00
8 Jarred Vanderbilt/99 10.00 25.00
9 Dell Curry/99 12.00 30.00
10 Marcus Smart/49 15.00 40.00
12 Dejounte Murray/75 15.00 40.00
13 Ochai Agbaji/75 12.00 30.00
14 Tari Eason/75 15.00 40.00
15 MarJon Beauchamp/75 10.00 25.00
16 Mark Williams/75 12.00 30.00
17 Nikola Jovic/75 12.00 30.00
19 Ayo Dosunmu/99 12.00 30.00
21 Onyeka Okongwu/25 10.00 25.00
22 Jose Alvarado/99 12.00 30.00
23 Jordan Clarkson/49 12.00 30.00
24 Bradley Beal/25 15.00 40.00
25 James Harden/49 150.00 400.00
27 James Wiseman/75 10.00 25.00
28 Larry Bird/25 125.00 300.00
29 Clyde Drexler/75 40.00 100.00
30 Dan Issel/99 15.00 40.00
31 B.J. Armstrong/99 12.00 30.00
32 Xavier McDaniel/99 12.00 30.00
33 Bob Dandridge/49 12.00 30.00
34 Mike Miller/99 10.00 25.00
35 Tom Chambers/99 12.00 30.00
36 Manu Ginobili/25 50.00 120.00
37 Antawn Jamison/99 12.00 30.00
38 Maurice Cheeks/99 12.00 30.00
39 Chauncey Billups/75 15.00 40.00
40 Luke Kennard/99 10.00 25.00

2012-13 Panini Intrigue

JSY AU RC B/WN 15-199 COPIES PER
NO PRICING ON QTY 15 OR LESS
EXCHANGE DEADLINE 3/18/2015
1 Ty Lawson .25 .60
2 Derrick Rose .60 1.50
3 Alonzo Gee .25 .60
4 Brook Lopez .30 .75
5 Dwyane Wade .75 2.00
6 Anderson Varejao .25 .60
7 Joakim Noah .30 .75
8 Shane Battier .30 .75
9 Deron Williams .30 .75
10 Jason Kidd .60 1.50
11 Dirk Nowitzki 1.00 2.50
12 Jarrett Jack .30 .75
13 Jeremy Lin .60 1.50
14 Blake Griffin .40 1.00
15 Ekpe Udoh .25 .60
16 Russell Westbrook .60 1.50
17 Jrue Holiday .50 1.25
18 Tony Parker .60 1.50
19 Jamaal Tinsley .25 .60
20 Jeff Teague .25 .60
21 Shawn Marion .40 1.00
22 Ray Allen .60 1.50
23 Roy Hibbert .30 .75
24 Steve Nash .75 2.00
25 Brandon Jennings .25 .60
26 Kevin Martin .30 .75
27 Marcin Gortat .25 .60
28 Tim Duncan 1.00 2.50
29 Gordon Hayward .40 1.00
30 Josh Smith .25 .60
31 Luol Deng .30 .75
32 Greg Monroe .25 .60
33 James Harden .75 2.00
34 Pau Gasol .60 1.50
35 Ricky Rubio .30 .75
36 Kevin Durant 1.50 4.00
37 Luis Scola .30 .75
38 Tiago Splitter .25 .60
39 DeMarre Carroll .25 .60
40 Avery Bradley .25 .60
41 Taj Gibson .25 .60
42 Jose Calderon .25 .60
43 Paul George .60 1.50
44 Kobe Bryant 3.00 8.00
45 Nikola Pekovic .25 .60
46 Kendrick Perkins .25 .60
47 Goran Dragic .40 1.00
48 Manu Ginobili .75 2.00
49 Trevor Booker .25 .60
50 Kevin Garnett 1.00 2.50
51 Ben Gordon .30 .75
52 Stephen Curry 3.00 8.00
53 David West .30 .75
54 Dwight Howard .50 1.25
55 Chase Budinger .25 .60
56 Jameer Nelson .25 .60
57 LaMarcus Aldridge .40 1.00
58 Rudy Gay .40 1.00
59 Trevor Ariza .25 .60
60 Paul Pierce .60 1.50
61 Byron Mullens .25 .60
62 Andre Iguodala .40 1.00
63 Danny Granger .25 .60
64 Zach Randolph .40 1.00
65 Ryan Anderson .25 .60
66 Glen Davis .25 .60
67 J.J. Hickson .25 .60
68 Landry Fields .25 .60
69 John Wall .50 1.25
70 Rajon Rondo .50 1.25
71 Gerald Wallace .30 .75
72 Andre Miller .30 .75
73 Eric Bledsoe .30 .75
74 Mike Conley .30 .75
75 Robin Lopez .25 .60
76 Arron Afflalo .25 .60
77 Tyreke Evans .30 .75
78 Kyle Lowry .40 1.00
79 Tyson Chandler .30 .75
80 Amar'e Stoudemire .40 1.00
81 Joe Johnson .30 .75
82 LeBron James 3.00 8.00
83 DeAndre Jordan .30 .75
84 Monta Ellis .30 .75
85 Greivis Vasquez .25 .60
86 Spencer Hawes .25 .60
87 Marcus Thornton .25 .60
88 DeMar DeRozan .50 1.25
89 Steve Novak .25 .60
90 Carmelo Anthony .60 1.50
91 Chris Bosh .50 1.25
92 David Lee .25 .60
93 Chris Paul .75 2.00
94 J.J. Redick .40 1.00
95 Serge Ibaka .30 .75
96 Nick Young .25 .60
97 DeMarcus Cousins .40 1.00
98 Marvin Williams .25 .60
99 Raymond Felton .25 .60
100 Damian Lillard RC 25.00 60.00
101 Jared Sullinger JSY AU/99 RC 4.00 10.00
104 Kevin Murphy JSY AU RC 4.00 10.00
106 Marquis Teague JSY AU/25 RC 4.00 10.00
107 Nolan Smith JSY AU/99 RC 4.00 10.00
108 Evan Fournier JSY AU/99 RC 6.00 15.00
109 Mirza Teletovic JSY AU/25 RC 5.00 12.00
110 Iman Shumpert JSY AU/149 RC 5.00 12.00
111 H.Barnes JSY AU/149 RC 8.00 20.00
112 Lavoy Allen JSY AU/199 RC 4.00 10.00
113 Irving JSY AU/199 RC 60.00 150.00
114 K.Leonard JSY AU/149 RC 150.00 400.00
115 K.Faried JSY AU/125 RC 5.00 12.00
116 Kim English JSY AU RC 4.00 10.00
117 Bradley Beal JSY AU/99 RC 12.00 30.00
118 A.Davis JSY AU/25 RC 200.00 500.00
119 Damian Lillard JSY AU/49 150.00 400.00
120 Meyers Leonard JSY AU/99 RC 5.00 12.00
121 Orlando Johnson JSY AU/99 RC 4.00 10.00
122 T.Robinson JSY AU/49 RC 4.00 10.00
123 Chris Copeland JSY AU/99 RC 4.00 10.00
124 Austin Rivers JSY AU/49 RC 6.00 15.00
127 Valanciunas JSY AU/199 RC 8.00 20.00
128 Viacheslav Kravtsov JSY AU RC 4.00 10.00
129 Lance Thomas JSY AU RC 4.00 10.00
130 Tornike Shengelia JSY AU/75 RC 4.00 10.00
131 Kent Bazemore JSY AU/199 RC 6.00 15.00
132 Gustavo Ayon JSY AU RC 4.00 10.00
133 Tobias Harris JSY AU/199 RC 12.00 30.00
134 Robert Sacre JSY AU RC 4.00 10.00
135 Victor Claver JSY AU/199 RC 4.00 10.00
136 A.Drummond JSY AU/149 RC 10.00 25.00
137 Brian Roberts JSY AU/199 RC 4.00 10.00
138 M.Brooks JSY AU/199 RC 4.00 10.00
140 Quincy Acy JSY AU/199 RC 4.00 10.00
142 Will Barton JSY AU RC 8.00 20.00
143 DeQuan Jones JSY AU/199 RC 4.00 10.00
144 Malcolm Lee JSY AU RC 4.00 10.00
146 N.Vucevic JSY AU/149 RC 15.00 40.00
147 Norris Cole JSY AU/199 RC 4.00 10.00
148 Tyler Zeller JSY AU/49 RC 4.00 10.00
150 Brandon Knight JSY AU/99 RC 5.00 12.00
151 A.Nicholson JSY AU/99 RC 4.00 10.00
154 Darius Morris JSY AU RC 5.00 12.00
155 T.Thompson JSY AU/99 RC 6.00 15.00
157 Khris Middleton JSY AU RC 50.00 120.00
159 R.Jackson JSY AU/49 RC 6.00 15.00
160 John Henson JSY AU/99 RC 5.00 12.00

2012-13 Panini Intrigue Autograph Jerseys

PRINT RUNS B/WN 15-199 COPIES PER
NO PRICING ON QTY 20 OR LESS
EXCHANGE DEADLINE 3/18/2015
4 Alvan Adams/49 4.00 10.00
5 Chase Budinger/49 4.00 10.00
6 James Worthy/25 10.00 25.00

7 Clyde Drexler/25 15.00 40.00
8 Taj Gibson/49 4.00 10.00
9 Anderson Varejao/25 4.00 10.00
10 Greg Monroe/49 4.00 10.00
11 Kiki Vandeweghe/199 5.00 12.00
12 Ron Harper/199 6.00 15.00
13 Courtney Lee/25 4.00 10.00
14 Detlef Schrempf/199 8.00 20.00
15 Gail Goodrich/25 5.00 12.00
16 Shawn Bradley/75 4.00 10.00
17 Kevin Love/25 15.00 40.00
18 Mike Conley/25 10.00 25.00
19 James Harden/25 EXCH 75.00 200.00
20 Devin Harris/25 4.00 10.00
21 Chris Kaman/25 5.00 12.00
22 Jason Maxiell/25 4.00 10.00
23 Ty Lawson/25 4.00 10.00
24 Kobe Bryant/49 500.00 1,000.00
25 Jason Terry/25 5.00 12.00
26 Alan Anderson/25 4.00 10.00
27 Larry Nance/199 5.00 12.00
28 Nick Anderson/99 5.00 12.00
29 Al-Farouq Aminu/25 4.00 10.00
31 David West/99 5.00 12.00
33 Vince Carter/25 25.00 60.00
34 Rick Mahorn/199 4.00 10.00
38 Andrea Bargnani/25 4.00 10.00
39 Tom Chambers/49 6.00 15.00
40 Arron Afflalo/25 4.00 10.00
41 Ryan Anderson/49 4.00 10.00
43 George Hill/49 5.00 12.00
44 Brandon Bass/25 4.00 10.00
46 Rodney Stuckey/125 4.00 10.00
47 Carl Landry/25 4.00 10.00
48 Dwyane Wade/49 30.00 80.00
50 Kyle Lowry/99 6.00 15.00
51 Xavier McDaniel/199 4.00 10.00
52 Serge Ibaka/25 8.00 20.00
53 Bernard King/49 10.00 25.00
54 Udonis Haslem/25 6.00 15.00
55 Roy Hibbert/25 5.00 12.00
56 Jeff Green/25 4.00 10.00
57 Andre Miller/25 5.00 12.00
58 Will Bynum/99 4.00 10.00
59 Calvin Murphy/25 5.00 12.00
60 Andrei Kirilenko/25 5.00 12.00
61 Gerald Henderson/49 4.00 10.00
62 Landry Fields/99 4.00 10.00
63 Wesley Matthews/49 4.00 10.00
64 Kevin Martin/25 5.00 12.00
65 Marcus Camby/25 6.00 15.00
66 Ekpe Udoh/25 4.00 10.00
67 Danny Manning/25 5.00 12.00
68 Robert Parish/25 8.00 20.00
69 Dan Issel/199 6.00 15.00
70 Andrew Bogut/25 8.00 20.00
71 Hakeem Olajuwon/25 25.00 60.00
72 Greivis Vasquez/25 4.00 10.00
73 Mark Price/99 8.00 20.00
74 Derrick Favors/25 5.00 12.00
75 Bobby Jackson/99 4.00 10.00
76 Kevin Durant/49 60.00 150.00
77 Mark Jackson/25 5.00 12.00
78 Jack Sikma/99 5.00 12.00
79 Grant Hill/49 25.00 60.00
81 Fat Lever/99 5.00 12.00
82 Chris Mullin/25 10.00 25.00
84 Xavier Henry/25 4.00 10.00
85 Jim Jackson/75 5.00 12.00
86 Josh Smith/25 4.00 10.00
87 John Salmons/99 5.00 12.00
88 Tyson Chandler/25 5.00 12.00
89 Spencer Haywood/99 6.00 15.00
91 Ronny Turiaf/49 4.00 10.00
92 Kelly Tripucka/25 5.00 12.00
94 Carlos Delfino/49 4.00 10.00
95 Caron Butler/25 5.00 12.00
96 Blake Griffin/49 EXCH 20.00 50.00
97 Alex English/49 8.00 20.00
98 Maurice Cheeks/99 5.00 12.00
100 Steve Novak/25 4.00 10.00

2012-13 Panini Intrigue Dunk Company Autographs

PRINT RUNS B/WN 15-199 COPIES PER
NO PRICING ON QTY 20 OR LESS
EXCHANGE DEADLINE 3/18/2015

1 Harrison Barnes/49 8.00 20.00
3 Kobe Bryant/49 500.00 1,000.00
4 Kevin Durant/49 60.00 150.00
8 Vince Carter/25 30.00 60.00
9 Dominique Wilkins/49 8.00 20.00
10 Kenneth Faried/49 5.00 12.00
11 Cedric Ceballos/25 12.00 30.00
13 David Robinson/49 15.00 40.00
15 Darryl Dawkins/199 4.00 10.00
16 Tom Chambers/199 6.00 15.00
17 Larry Nance/199 5.00 12.00
18 Spud Webb/199 5.00 12.00
19 Kenny Walker/99 4.00 10.00
20 Larry Johnson/75 12.00 30.00
21 Clyde Drexler/25 20.00 50.00
22 Darrell Griffith/199 4.00 10.00
24 Anthony Davis/25 300.00 600.00

2012-13 Panini Intrigue Fearless Foursomes

PRINT RUNS B/WN 25-49 COPIES PER

1 Ant/Dur/Kobe/James/49 40.00 80.00
2 How/Bran/James/Dunc/49 12.00 30.00
3 Davis/Griffin/Wall/Irving/49 10.00 25.00
5 Paul/Will/Vasq/Rubio/49 12.00 30.00
6 Noah/Hibb/Ibaka/Dunc/49 15.00 40.00
7 Hard/Walk/Ellis/Westb/49 15.00 40.00
8 Hard/Batum/Ander/Cur/25 50.00 120.00
9 Rob/Rod/Olaj/Ewing/49 10.00 25.00

2012-13 Panini Intrigue First Flight Unis

PRINT RUNS B/WN 5-99 COPIES PER
NO PRICING ON QTY 10 OR LESS

2 Clyde Drexler/99 8.00 20.00
3 Tyrus Thomas/99 3.00 8.00
5 Carmelo Anthony/49 8.00 20.00
6 Shaquille O'Neal/49 12.00 30.00
7 David Lee/49 3.00 8.00
8 Andrei Kirilenko/25 4.00 10.00
10 Deron Williams/99 4.00 10.00
12 Michael Beasley/99 3.00 8.00
13 Dikembe Mutombo/25 20.00 50.00
17 Al-Farouq Aminu/99 3.00 8.00
18 Landry Fields/75 3.00 8.00
20 Kevin Martin/25 4.00 10.00
21 Kevin Durant/25 20.00 50.00
22 Grant Hill/99 8.00 20.00
23 Derrick Favors/99 4.00 10.00
24 Jeff Green/99 3.00 8.00
25 JaVale McGee/99 4.00 10.00

2012-13 Panini Intrigue Immortalized Autographs

PRINT RUNS B/WN 15-299 COPIES PER
NO PRICING ON QTY 15 OR LESS
EXCHANGE DEADLINE 3/18/2015

2 Cedric Maxwell/299 4.00 10.00
3 Connie Hawkins/25 12.00 30.00
5 Terry Porter/299 5.00 12.00
9 George McGinnis/25 8.00 20.00
10 Tom Heinsohn/25 25.00 60.00
12 Nick Anderson/199 5.00 12.00
13 Mitch Richmond/25 15.00 40.00
14 Spud Webb/299 5.00 12.00
15 Adrian Dantley/25 8.00 20.00
16 Rory Sparrow/299 4.00 10.00
17 Larry Nance/199 5.00 12.00
18 Tim Hardaway/299 8.00 20.00
19 Mark Price/249 6.00 15.00
20 Mel Davis/299 4.00 10.00
21 Jack Sikma/299 5.00 12.00
22 Darryl Dawkins/199 4.00 10.00
23 Scott Skiles/299 5.00 12.00
24 Rolando Blackman/199 5.00 12.00
25 Sam Perkins/25 5.00 12.00
26 Bob McAdoo/25 15.00 40.00
27 Satch Sanders/25 10.00 25.00
28 Alex English/25 20.00 50.00
29 Tom Chambers/25 12.00 30.00
30 Kurt Rambis/25 6.00 15.00
31 Buck Williams/299 4.00 10.00
41 Gary Payton/15 20.00 50.00
43 Larry Bird/25 50.00 120.00
45 Vlade Divac/299 6.00 15.00
46 Herb Williams/299 4.00 10.00
47 Muggsy Bogues/299 5.00 12.00
48 Sean Elliott/299 5.00 12.00
49 Cedric Ceballos/299 5.00 12.00
51 Bob Dandridge/299 4.00 10.00
52 Anthony Mason/299 5.00 12.00
53 Charles Oakley/299 6.00 15.00
54 Bill Cartwright/25 12.00 30.00
56 Jamaal Wilkes/25 12.50 30.00
58 Michael Cage/299 4.00 10.00
60 Mark Aguirre/199 5.00 12.00

2012-13 Panini Intrigue Impact Rookie Autographs

PRINT RUNS B/WN 15-299 COPIES PER
NO PRICING ON QTY 15 OR LESS
EXCHANGE DEADLINE 3/18/2015

1 Harrison Barnes/99 6.00 15.00
3 Iman Shumpert/149 4.00 10.00
4 Alexey Shved/49 3.00 8.00
5 Jordan Hamilton/299 3.00 8.00
6 E'Twaun Moore/249 4.00 10.00
7 Reggie Jackson/49 5.00 12.00
9 Festus Ezeli/149 3.00 8.00
10 MarShon Brooks/199 3.00 8.00
11 Kent Bazemore/299 5.00 12.00
12 Chris Copeland/199 3.00 8.00
15 Kendall Marshall/299 3.00 8.00
17 Jared Cunningham/199 EXCH 3.00 8.00
19 Draymond Green/249 20.00 50.00
20 Brian Roberts/299 3.00 8.00
25 DeAndre Liggins/299 3.00 8.00
26 Ben Hansbrough/299 3.00 8.00
27 Khris Middleton/299 15.00 40.00
28 Brandon Knight/49 4.00 10.00
29 DeQuan Jones/199 EXCH 3.00 8.00
30 Andre Drummond/99 8.00 20.00
31 Lance Thomas/299 3.00 8.00
32 Orlando Johnson/49 3.00 8.00
34 Jared Sullinger/99 3.00 8.00
35 Nando De Colo/249 3.00 8.00
36 Damian Lillard/25 200.00 500.00
39 Will Barton/199 6.00 15.00
40 Victor Claver/199 3.00 8.00
42 Meyers Leonard/149 4.00 10.00
43 Kyrie Irving/99 60.00 150.00
44 Kevin Murphy/299 3.00 8.00
45 Bismack Biyombo/299 4.00 10.00
46 Alec Burks/99 5.00 12.00
48 Tyler Zeller/25 3.00 8.00
50 Robert Sacre/299 3.00 8.00
51 Jonas Valanciunas/99 6.00 15.00
52 Isaiah Thomas/299 6.00 15.00
53 Kawhi Leonard/99 60.00 150.00
55 Mike Scott/299 4.00 10.00
56 John Henson/25 4.00 10.00
57 Darius Morris/299 4.00 10.00
58 Norris Cole/125 3.00 8.00
59 Quincy Acy/279 3.00 8.00
60 Tobias Harris/99 10.00 25.00
61 Jae Crowder/99 EXCH 6.00 15.00
63 Kenneth Faried/99 4.00 10.00
64 Marquis Teague/25 EXCH 3.00 8.00
66 Enes Kanter/25 10.00 25.00
68 Nikola Vucevic/125 12.00 30.00
69 Chandler Parsons/15 12.00 30.00
70 Gustavo Ayon/299 3.00 8.00
72 Bradley Beal/49 25.00 60.00
73 Kim English/299 3.00 8.00
75 Jan Vesely/299 3.00 8.00

2012-13 Panini Intrigue Intriguing Pairs Jerseys

PRINT RUNS B/WN 25-99 COPIES PER

1 Bryant/Irving/99 12.00 30.00
2 Dragic.Scola/25 5.00 12.00
3 Wade/James/99 25.00 60.00
4 M.Gasol/Z.Randolph/25 5.00 12.00
5 Howard/Nash/49 10.00 25.00
6 Griffin/Paul/49 10.00 25.00
7 J.Harden/J.Lin/49 10.00 25.00
8 A.Drummond/G.Monroe/99 5.00 12.00
10 D.Williams/G.Wallace/99 4.00 10.00
11 Garnett/Pierce/25 12.00 30.00
12 A.Horford/J.Noah/25 5.00 12.00
13 B.Beal/J.Wall/25 6.00 15.00
14 Favors/Hayw/25 6.00 15.00
15 D.DeRozan/T.Ross/25 8.00 20.00
16 J.Fredette/T.Evans/25 5.00 12.00
17 Lillard/Aldridge/49 20.00 50.00
18 Durant/Westb/99 10.00 25.00
19 Anthony/Durant/99 10.00 25.00
20 Davis/Rivers/25 8.00 20.00
21 C.Anthony/T.Chandler/99 5.00 12.00
22 Love/Rubio/25 5.00 12.00
23 Howard/Love/25 6.00 15.00
24 Rubio/Nash/99 10.00 25.00
25 Hill/George/25 8.00 20.00
26 Thompson/Curry/25 40.00 100.00
27 B.Knight/K.Irving/99 6.00 15.00
28 D.Lillard/K.Irving/49 30.00 80.00
29 Howard/Shaq/99 6.00 15.00
31 Griffin/Howard/25 6.00 15.00
32 James/Pierce/25 40.00 100.00
33 Bryant/James/99 40.00 100.00
34 Stoud/Melo/99 8.00 20.00
35 Durant/James/99 40.00 100.00
36 Harden/Curry/99 15.00 40.00
37 Griffin/Duncan/25 8.00 20.00
38 D.Howard/R.Hibbert/99 6.00 15.00
39 B.Jennings/T.Lawson/99 3.00 8.00
40 Lawson/Evans/25 4.00 10.00
41 E.Gordon/R.Westbrook/25 5.00 12.00
42 C.Paul/D.Williams/25 5.00 12.00
43 Bryant/Rondo/99 8.00 20.00
44 J.Kidd/S.Nash/99 10.00 25.00
45 A.Stoudemire/S.Marion/25 5.00 12.00
46 Nicholson/Thomp/25 5.00 12.00
47 B.Griffin/D.Lee/25 5.00 12.00
48 Thomas/Crawford/25 10.00 25.00
49 Bogut/Redick/25 5.00 12.00
50 Barnes/Carter/49 6.00 15.00
51 C.Kaman/D.Nowitzki/99 5.00 12.00
52 Leonard/Elliott/25 40.00 100.00
53 Durant/Aldridge/99 6.00 15.00
54 Love/Westb/25 8.00 20.00
55 Davis/Irving/99 40.00 100.00
56 B.Gordon/R.Allen/25 8.00 20.00
57 Hill/Irving/99 30.00 80.00
58 D.Collison/K.Love/99 5.00 12.00
59 D.Cousins/J.Wall/25 6.00 15.00
60 DeRozan/Mayo/25 6.00 15.00

2012-13 Panini Intrigue Intriguing Players

ALL VERSIONS EQUALLY PRICED

1 Kyrie Irving 3.00 8.00
11 Anthony Davis 12.00 30.00
21 Kobe Bryant 6.00 15.00
31 Kevin Durant 2.00 5.00
41 Blake Griffin .50 1.25
51 LeBron James 6.00 15.00
61 Tim Duncan 1.25 3.00
71 Dirk Nowitzki 1.25 3.00
81 Dwyane Wade 1.00 2.50
91 Dwight Howard .60 1.50
101 Rajon Rondo .60 1.50
111 Russell Westbrook .75 2.00
121 Derrick Rose .75 2.00
131 Damian Lillard 25.00 60.00
141 Carmelo Anthony .75 2.00
151 Stephen Curry 4.00 10.00
161 Kevin Garnett 1.25 3.00
171 Chris Paul 1.00 2.50
181 Paul Pierce .75 2.00
191 John Wall .60 1.50

2012-13 Panini Intrigue Intriguing Players Gold

*GOLD: 8X TO 20X BASIC
STATED PRINT RUN 10 SER.#'d SETS
ALL VERSION EQUALLY PRICED

2012-13 Panini Intrigue Red White and Blue Autographs

PRINT RUNS B/WN 15-299 COPIES PER
NO PRICING ON QTY 15 OR LESS
EXCHANGE DEADLINE 3/18/2015

1 Kevin Durant/125 60.00 150.00
2 Kobe Bryant/99 1,000.00 2,000.00
3 Tyson Chandler/25 15.00 40.00
4 Andre Iguodala/25 15.00 40.00
8 Antawn Jamison/99 5.00 12.00
9 Vin Baker/299 4.00 10.00
10 Allan Houston/99 5.00 12.00
11 Alonzo Mourning/25 60.00 150.00
12 Derrick Coleman/199 12.00 30.00
13 Gary Payton/25 40.00 80.00
14 Steve Smith/299 5.00 12.00
15 Tim Hardaway/299 8.00 20.00
16 Anfernee Hardaway/49 50.00 120.00
17 Grant Hill/49 20.00 50.00
22 Chris Mullin/199 8.00 20.00
23 Magic Johnson/25 60.00 150.00
25 Danny Manning/25 5.00 12.00
26 Mitch Richmond/199 6.00 15.00
27 Sam Perkins/199 5.00 12.00
28 Larry Bird/25 60.00 120.00
30 Carlos Boozer/25 5.00 12.00
32 Adrian Dantley/199 5.00 12.00
33 Bobby Jones/299 5.00 12.00
34 Spencer Haywood/299 6.00 15.00
35 Jo Jo White/299 6.00 15.00

2012-13 Panini Intrigue Rookie Memorabilia

STATED PRINT RUN 99 SER.#'d SETS

1 Anthony Davis 8.00 20.00
2 Kenneth Faried 3.00 8.00
3 Jonas Valanciunas 5.00 12.00
4 Kawhi Leonard 6.00 15.00
5 Jae Crowder 6.00 15.00
6 Austin Rivers 4.00 10.00
7 Andre Drummond 6.00 15.00
8 Quincy Acy 2.50 6.00
9 Will Barton 5.00 12.00
10 Tyler Zeller 2.50 6.00
11 Iman Shumpert 4.00 10.00
12 Brandon Knight 6.00 15.00
13 Terrence Ross 6.00 15.00
14 Meyers Leonard 3.00 8.00
15 Tristan Thompson 4.00 10.00
16 John Henson 3.00 8.00
17 Kim English 2.50 6.00
18 Kevin Murphy 2.50 6.00
19 Damian Lillard 30.00 80.00
20 Kyrie Irving 6.00 15.00
21 Norris Cole 2.50 6.00
22 Kyle Singler 2.50 6.00
23 Bradley Beal 6.00 15.00
24 Markieff Morris 4.00 10.00
25 Marquis Teague 2.50 6.00
26 Tony Wroten 2.50 6.00
27 Harrison Barnes 5.00 12.00
28 Chris Singleton 2.50 6.00
29 Perry Jones 2.50 6.00
30 Jimmy Butler 5.00 12.00
31 Dion Waiters 3.00 8.00
32 Klay Thompson 12.00 30.00
33 Andrew Nicholson 2.50 6.00
34 Reggie Jackson 4.00 10.00
35 Michael Kidd-Gilchrist 3.00 8.00
36 John Jenkins 2.50 6.00
37 Orlando Johnson 2.50 6.00
38 Chandler Parsons 3.00 8.00
39 Robert Sacre 2.50 6.00
40 Kemba Walker 5.00 12.00

2012-13 Panini Intrigue Slam Ink

PRINT RUNS B/WN 15-299 COPIES PER
NO PRICING ON QTY 15 OR LESS
EXCHANGE DEADLINE 3/18/2015

3 Kobe Bryant/99 500.00 1,000.00
4 Kevin Durant/49 60.00 150.00
5 Anthony Davis/25 300.00 600.00
6 Terrence Ross/49 10.00 25.00
9 Tyson Chandler/25 8.00 20.00
11 Chris Copeland/299 4.00 10.00
12 Harrison Barnes/25 30.00 80.00
13 Taj Gibson/49 EXCH 4.00 10.00
15 Andre Iguodala/25 6.00 15.00
16 Jonas Valanciunas/99 8.00 20.00
17 Michael Kidd-Gilchrist/25 10.00 25.00
19 JaVale McGee/99 5.00 12.00
21 Jerryd Bayless/199 4.00 10.00
22 Maurice Harkless/199 5.00 12.00
23 Tobias Harris/199 12.00 30.00
24 Anthony Randolph/25 EXCH 5.00 12.00
25 Al-Farouq Aminu/199 4.00 10.00
27 J.R. Smith/25 12.00 30.00
28 Jeff Green/25 12.00 30.00
29 Darryl Dawkins/199 4.00 10.00
31 Jason Maxiell/299 4.00 10.00
32 Steve Francis/25 20.00 50.00
33 Alonzo Gee/199 4.00 10.00
34 George Gervin/25 25.00 60.00
35 Dion Waiters/25 20.00 50.00
36 Kenny Walker/199 4.00 10.00
37 Darrell Griffith/199 4.00 10.00
38 Dee Brown/199 8.00 20.00
40 Larry Nance/199 5.00 12.00
42 Nick Young/49 4.00 10.00
43 Tristan Thompson/25 EXCH 8.00 20.00
44 Will Barton/299 8.00 20.00
45 John Henson/25 EXCH 10.00 25.00
46 Andre Drummond/49 25.00 60.00
47 Jimmy Butler/199 20.00 50.00
48 Draymond Green/199 20.00 50.00
50 David Thompson/199 6.00 15.00

2012-13 Panini Intrigue Terrific Trios Jerseys

PRINT RUNS B/WN 25-49 COPIES PER

1 Bosh/Wade/James/49 30.00 80.00
2 Griffin/Paul/Hill/49 10.00 25.00
3 Garn/Pierce/Rondo/49 12.00 30.00
4 Melo/Kidd/Chand/49 8.00 20.00
5 Howard/Bryant/Nash/49 12.00 30.00
6 Durant/Martin/Westb/49 10.00 25.00
7 Kirilen/Love/Rubio/49 5.00 12.00
8 DeRozan/Valanciunas/Lowry/49 6.00 15.00
9 Beal/Wall/Nene/49 6.00 15.00
10 Parsons/Harden/Lin/49 10.00 25.00
11 Lopez/Williams/Johnson/49 4.00 10.00
12 Lee/Barnes/Curry/49 15.00 40.00
13 Gasol/Gasol/Rubio/49 15.00 40.00
14 Scola/Ginobili/Prigioni/49 10.00 25.00
15 Fourn/Batum/Parker/49 8.00 20.00
16 Davis/Kidd-Gilk/Jones/49 10.00 25.00
17 Horford/Beal/Noah/49 5.00 12.00
18 Howard/Smith/Garn/49 12.00 30.00
19 Durant/Aldrid/Thomp/49 20.00 50.00
20 Mourning/Rice/Smith/49 15.00 40.00
21 Griffin/Howard/James/25 15.00 40.00
22 Barnes/Felton/Carter/49 5.00 12.00
23 Rivers/Hill/Irving/49 50.00 120.00
24 Melo/Durant/Bryant/49 15.00 40.00
25 Knight/Wall/Rondo/49 6.00 15.00
26 Monroe/Ewing/Hib/49 15.00 40.00
27 Melo/Durant/James/49 40.00 100.00
28 Paul/Will/Rondo/49 10.00 25.00
29 Drum/Okafor/Walk/49 12.00 30.00
30 Iguo/Williams/Terry/49 5.00 12.00

2012-13 Panini Intrigue Top Flight Unis

PRINT RUNS B/WN 25-99 COPIES PER

1 Dwight Howard/99 5.00 12.00
2 Hakeem Olajuwon/49 8.00 20.00
3 Jimmy Butler/99 8.00 20.00
4 Kevin Garnett/99 6.00 15.00
5 Tyrus Thomas/25 2.50 6.00
6 Kevin Durant/99 5.00 12.00
7 Blake Griffin/99 6.00 15.00
8 Anderson Varejao/99 2.50 6.00
9 Paul Pierce/99 6.00 15.00
10 Clyde Drexler/49 6.00 15.00
12 Harrison Barnes/49 8.00 20.00
13 Jeff Green/25 5.00 12.00
14 Kobe Bryant/99 30.00 80.00
15 Tristan Thompson/25 10.00 25.00
16 Kenneth Faried/25 3.00 8.00
17 Anthony Davis/25 12.00 30.00
18 Amir Johnson/25 2.50 6.00
19 Paul Millsap/25 3.00 8.00
21 Dikembe Mutombo/25 12.00 30.00
22 Grant Hill/99 6.00 15.00
23 JaVale McGee/99 3.00 8.00
24 Landry Fields/49 2.50 6.00
25 Thaddeus Young/49 2.50 6.00
28 Amar'e Stoudemire/99 4.00 10.00
29 Paul George/49 6.00 15.00
30 Caron Butler/25 3.00 8.00
31 Devin Harris/25 2.50 6.00
32 Gerald Henderson/99 2.50 6.00
33 Jared Sullinger/99 5.00 12.00
35 Thabo Sefolosha/99 2.50 6.00
38 Alex English/99 5.00 12.00
39 Patrick Ewing/49 6.00 15.00
40 Carmelo Anthony/99 6.00 15.00
42 Gerald Wallace/25 3.00 8.00
43 Jan Vesely/99 2.50 6.00
44 LeBron James/49 10.00 25.00
46 Karl Malone/99 6.00 15.00
48 Kevin Martin/49 3.00 8.00
50 Brandon Jennings/25 2.50 6.00
51 Deron Williams/25 3.00 8.00
53 James White/99 2.50 6.00
54 Markieff Morris/99 4.00 10.00
55 Shaquille O'Neal/49 6.00 15.00
56 Jordan Hamilton/99 2.50 6.00
58 Al-Farouq Aminu/99 2.50 6.00
59 Michael Kidd-Gilchrist/25 6.00 15.00
60 Brandon Bass/49 2.50 6.00
66 John Wall/25 5.00 12.00
67 Andre Drummond/99 5.00 12.00
68 Joakim Noah/49 3.00 8.00
69 Michael Beasley/99 2.50 6.00
70 Bradley Beal/99 5.00 12.00
72 Dwyane Wade/25 8.00 20.00
73 Iman Shumpert/49 3.00 8.00
74 Matt Barnes/99 2.50 6.00
75 Roy Hibbert/25 3.00 8.00

2012-13 Panini Intrigue Winning Ink

PRINT RUNS B/WN 15-299 COPIES PER
NO PRICING ON QTY 15 OR LESS
EXCHANGE DEADLINE 3/18/2015

1 Julius Erving/25 60.00 150.00
2 Robert Parish/25 10.00 25.00
3 Rick Mahorn/299 4.00 10.00
4 David Robinson/25 50.00 120.00
5 Udonis Haslem/49 5.00 12.00
7 Toni Kukoc/25 12.00 30.00
8 Bill Laimbeer/299 8.00 20.00
9 Beno Udrih/299 4.00 10.00
12 Dennis Rodman/25 40.00 100.00
13 Mark Aguirre/299 5.00 12.00
14 Antoine Walker/299 5.00 12.00
15 Kobe Bryant/49 1,000.00 2,000.00
16 Larry Bird/25 125.00 300.00
18 Joe Dumars/25 10.00 25.00
19 Gary Payton/25 20.00 50.00
22 Will Perdue/299 4.00 10.00
23 Bill Cartwright/25 15.00 40.00
24 Alonzo Mourning/25 25.00 60.00
25 Mario Chalmers/25 5.00 12.00
26 A.C. Green/25 12.00 30.00
27 Sean Elliott/199 8.00 20.00
28 B.J. Armstrong/25 10.00 25.00
31 Spencer Haywood/299 6.00 15.00
32 Glen Rice/25 20.00 50.00
33 John Paxson/299 8.00 20.00
34 Bruce Bowen/299 5.00 12.00
36 Magic Johnson/25 EXCH 125.00 300.00
37 Horace Grant/25 20.00 50.00
38 Clyde Drexler/25 30.00 80.00
39 Michael Finley/25 6.00 15.00
40 Jason Kidd/25 50.00 120.00
42 Rick Fox/25 10.00 25.00
43 Vernon Maxwell/299 4.00 10.00
44 Hakeem Olajuwon/25 60.00 150.00
46 Michael Cooper/299 6.00 15.00
47 Stephen Jackson/25 EXCH 5.00 12.00
48 Luc Longley/299 5.00 12.00
49 Robert Horry/25 12.00 30.00

2013-14 Panini Intrigue

1 Jameer Nelson .25 .60
2 Vince Carter .75 2.00
3 George Hill .30 .75
4 Gerald Green .30 .75
5 Gerald Henderson .25 .60
6 Manu Ginobili .75 2.00
7 Kenneth Faried .30 .75
8 LaMarcus Aldridge .40 1.00
9 Monta Ellis .30 .75
10 Carmelo Anthony .60 1.50
11 Dwight Howard .50 1.25
12 DeAndre Jordan .30 .75
13 Russell Westbrook .60 1.50
14 Tyreke Evans .30 .75
15 O.J. Mayo .25 .60
16 Andre Drummond .40 1.00
17 Greivis Vasquez .25 .60
18 Al Horford .40 1.00
19 Serge Ibaka .30 .75
20 Rodney Stuckey .25 .60
21 Isaiah Thomas .30 .75
22 Glen Davis .25 .60
23 Paul Pierce .60 1.50
24 Chris Bosh .50 1.25
25 Harrison Barnes .40 1.00
26 Rudy Gay .30 .75
27 Rajon Rondo .50 1.25
28 Andre Miller .30 .75
29 Marc Gasol .40 1.00
30 Kawhi Leonard 1.25 3.00
31 LeBron James 3.00 8.00
32 Derrick Favors .25 .60
33 John Wall .50 1.25
34 James Harden .75 2.00
35 Randy Foye .25 .60
36 Andre Iguodala .40 1.00
37 Luol Deng .30 .75
38 DeMar DeRozan .50 1.25
39 Kevin Garnett 1.00 2.50
40 Gordon Hayward .30 .75
41 Al Jefferson .25 .60
42 Steve Nash .75 2.00
43 Tony Parker .60 1.50
44 Nikola Pekovic .25 .60
45 Shawn Marion .30 .75
46 Evan Turner .25 .60
47 Derrick Rose .60 1.50
48 Bradley Beal .60 1.50
49 Kemba Walker .40 1.00
50 Goran Dragic .30 .75
51 Brandon Jennings .25 .60
52 Deron Williams .30 .75
53 Jason Richardson .40 1.00
54 J.R. Smith .40 1.00
55 Anderson Varejao .25 .60
56 Tyson Chandler .30 .75
57 Gerald Wallace .30 .75
58 Nikola Vucevic .50 1.25
59 Lance Stephenson .30 .75
60 Dwyane Wade .75 2.00
61 Kobe Bryant 3.00 8.00
62 Marcin Gortat .25 .60
63 Pau Gasol .60 1.50
64 Carlos Boozer .30 .75
65 Paul George .60 1.50
66 Anthony Davis 1.25 3.00
67 Klay Thompson 1.25 3.00
68 Nicolas Batum .30 .75
69 Kevin Martin .30 .75
70 Dion Waiters .25 .60
71 Jeremy Lin .60 1.50
72 Paul Millsap .30 .75
73 Kevin Love .40 1.00
74 DeMarcus Cousins .40 1.00
75 Joakim Noah .40 1.00
76 Ricky Rubio .30 .75
77 Brandon Knight .30 .75
78 Kevin Durant 1.25 3.00
79 Brook Lopez .40 1.00
80 Roy Hibbert .25 .60
81 Thaddeus Young .25 .60
82 Blake Griffin .40 1.00
83 Jeff Teague .25 .60
84 Mike Conley .40 1.00
85 Eric Bledsoe .30 .75
86 Larry Sanders .25 .60
87 Kyrie Irving 1.25 3.00
88 Austin Rivers .30 .75
89 Amar'e Stoudemire .40 1.00
90 Chris Paul .75 2.00
91 Dirk Nowitzki 1.00 2.50
92 Ty Lawson .25 .60
93 Damian Lillard 1.25 3.00
94 Avery Bradley .25 .60
95 Tim Duncan 1.00 2.50
96 Zach Randolph .30 .75
97 Jrue Holiday .50 1.25
98 Stephen Curry 3.00 8.00
99 Ersan Ilyasova .25 .60
100 Kyle Lowry .40 1.00

2013-14 Panini Intrigue '14 Draft X-Change

EXCHANGE DEADLINE 12/12/2015

1 Andrew Wiggins
Pick 1 6.00 15.00
2 Jabari Parker
Pick 2 10.00 25.00
3 Joel Embiid
Pick 3 12.00 30.00
4 Aaron Gordon
Pick 4 10.00 25.00
5 Dante Exum
Pick 5 8.00 20.00
6 Marcus Smart
Pick 6 8.00 20.00
7 Julius Randle
Pick 7 25.00 60.00
8 Nik Stauskas
Pick 8 5.00 12.00
9 Noah Vonleh
Pick 9 6.00 15.00
10 Elfrid Payton
Pick 10 6.00 15.00
11 Doug McDermott
Pick 11 5.00 12.00
12 Dario Saric
Pick 12 8.00 20.00
13 Zach LaVine
Pick 13 8.00 20.00
14 T. J. Warren
Pick 14 8.00 20.00
15 Adreian Payne
Pick 15 5.00 12.00
16 Jusuf Nurkic
Pick 16 8.00 20.00
17 James Young
Pick 17 5.00 12.00
18 Tyler Ennis
Pick 18 5.00 12.00
19 Gary Harris
Pick 19 10.00 25.00
20 Bruno Caboclo
Pick 20 6.00 15.00
21 Mitch McGary
Pick 21 5.00 12.00
22 Jordan Adams
Pick 22 5.00 12.00
23 Rodney Hood
Pick 23 10.00 25.00
24 Shabazz Napier
Pick 24 5.00 12.00
25 Clint Capela
Pick 25 10.00 25.00

2013-14 Panini Intrigue Autograph Jerseys

PRINT RUNS B/WN 12-149 COPIES PER
NO PRICING ON QTY 15 OR LESS
EXCHANGE DEADLINE 10/23/2015

1 DeMarre Carroll/149 4.00 10.00
2 Derrick Williams/25 4.00 10.00
3 Kenyon Martin/149 6.00 15.00
4 Anthony Davis/25 60.00 120.00
6 Darrell Griffith/149 5.00 12.00
8 Kevin Durant/25 50.00 120.00
9 Spencer Haywood/99 6.00 15.00
10 Jason Kidd/25 20.00 50.00
11 John Wall/99 10.00 25.00
14 Bernard King/49 8.00 20.00
15 Anthony Mason/149 8.00 20.00
16 Fat Lever/149 5.00 12.00
17 James Jones/149 4.00 10.00
18 Ramon Sessions/149 4.00 10.00
19 Eddie Jones/149 10.00 25.00
20 Nick Young/149 8.00 20.00
21 John Stockton/25 40.00 80.00
22 Udonis Haslem/149 5.00 12.00
23 Kevin Love/25 15.00 40.00
24 Tracy McGrady/25 30.00 60.00
26 Brad Daugherty/149 6.00 15.00
27 Ron Harper/149 6.00 15.00
28 Al Horford/25 6.00 15.00
29 John Havlicek/25 40.00 80.00
34 Alex English/75 8.00 20.00
37 Dennis Rodman/25 20.00 50.00
38 Jordan Crawford/149 10.00 25.00
39 Steve Smith/149 5.00 12.00
40 Kenny Anderson/149 5.00 12.00
42 Dwight Howard/25 10.00 25.00
43 Juwan Howard/75 5.00 12.00
44 Mitch Richmond/75 12.00 30.00
46 Tyson Chandler/25 5.00 12.00
49 Tony Parker/25 20.00 50.00
50 Boris Diaw/75 5.00 12.00

2013-14 Panini Intrigue Dual Jersey Autographs

PRINT RUNS B/WN 12-149 COPIES PER
NO PRICING ON QTY 15 OR LESS
EXCHANGE DEADLINE 10/23/2015

1 Dee Brown/99 5.00 12.00
2 Chris Kaman/25 5.00 12.00
3 Al Horford/25 6.00 15.00
4 Reggie Jackson/25 5.00 12.00
5 World B. Free/25 5.00 12.00
6 Ralph Sampson/25 5.00 12.00
7 Andrea Bargnani/49 4.00 10.00
8 Larry Johnson/25 8.00 20.00
9 J.J. Redick/25 12.00 30.00
10 Kyrie Irving/49 50.00 120.00
11 Tracy McGrady/49 75.00 200.00
12 Nick Young/99 4.00 10.00
13 Clyde Drexler/25 40.00 100.00
14 Chuck Person/25 5.00 12.00
15 Artis Gilmore/25 10.00 25.00
16 Jason Terry/25 5.00 12.00
17 Spencer Haywood/99 6.00 15.00
18 Gerald Henderson/25 4.00 10.00
19 Shane Battier/25 5.00 12.00
20 Jae Crowder/99 4.00 10.00
21 Jrue Holiday/25 8.00 20.00
22 Kawhi Leonard/25 125.00 300.00
23 Danny Manning/25 5.00 12.00
24 Alonzo Mourning/25 25.00 60.00
25 Kareem Abdul-Jabbar/25 100.00 250.00
26 Deron Williams/25 5.00 12.00
27 Evan Fournier/99 5.00 12.00
28 John Lucas/25 5.00 12.00
29 Grant Hill/25 25.00 60.00
30 Andre Iguodala/25 12.00 30.00
31 Ron Harper/75 6.00 15.00
32 Udonis Haslem/99 5.00 12.00
33 Steve Smith/99 5.00 12.00
34 Jayson Williams/99 4.00 10.00
35 Joe Dumars/25 8.00 20.00
36 Kevin Durant/49 125.00 300.00
37 Kobe Bryant/49 800.00 1,500.00

2013-14 Panini Intrigue Dunk Company Autographs

PRINT RUNS B/WN 12-149 COPIES PER
NO PRICING ON QTY 15 OR LESS
EXCHANGE DEADLINE 10/23/2015

1 Luc Longley/99 4.00 10.00
2 Vlade Divac/99 5.00 12.00
3 Kobe Bryant/25 1,000.00 2,000.00
5 Daniel Orton/99 3.00 8.00
6 Nick Collison/99 3.00 8.00
7 Kawhi Leonard/75 75.00 200.00
9 Vince Carter/49 40.00 100.00
10 Iman Shumpert/99 3.00 8.00
14 Darryl Dawkins/99 10.00 25.00
16 Nick Anderson/99 6.00 15.00
17 Mark Aguirre/99 4.00 10.00
18 Tom Chambers/99 5.00 12.00
21 Derrick Coleman/99 5.00 12.00
22 Michael Cooper/99 5.00 12.00
24 Udonis Haslem/99 4.00 10.00
25 Larry Nance/99 4.00 10.00
26 Ron Harper/99 5.00 12.00
28 Toni Kukoc/99 12.00 30.00
29 Kevin Willis/99 4.00 10.00
32 Mahmoud Abdul-Rauf/99 10.00 25.00
33 Greg Monroe/99 3.00 8.00
37 Isaiah Rider/25 15.00 40.00
39 Kenny Walker/99 3.00 8.00
40 Scottie Pippen/25 75.00 200.00
41 Dee Brown/99 6.00 15.00
42 Chris Andersen/49 15.00 40.00
44 Spud Webb/99 12.00 30.00
45 Tyson Chandler/25 5.00 12.00
46 Anfernee Hardaway/49 60.00 150.00
49 Larry Johnson/75 12.00 30.00
50 David Thompson/99 10.00 25.00
51 Tracy McGrady/49 40.00 100.00
52 Kenyon Martin/99 5.00 12.00
53 Jan Vesely/99 3.00 8.00
54 Kevin Love/49 6.00 15.00
55 Connie Hawkins/99 12.00 30.00
57 Vernon Maxwell/99 4.00 10.00
58 Al-Farouq Aminu/99 3.00 8.00
59 Fred Jones/99 3.00 8.00
60 Nick Young/99 3.00 8.00

2013-14 Panini Intrigue Fearless Foursomes

PRINT RUNS B/WN 25-199 COPIES PER

1 Std/Brg/Anth/Fltn/199 10.00 25.00
2 Dvs/Csns/Wll/Glc/199 20.00 50.00
3 Bsh/Wde/Jms/Alln/99 75.00 200.00
4 Le/Brns/Thmp/Crry/149 50.00 120.00
5 Dml/Wstb/Ibka/Sfl/199 20.00 50.00
6 Vrjo/Wtrs/Jck/Irvng/50 10.00 25.00
7 Bnntt/Zllr/Prtr/Oldpo/199 10.00 25.00
8 Nwtzki/Wde/Brynt/Jms/50 125.00 300.00
9 Grffn/Llrd/Irvng/Evns/25 20.00 50.00
10 Grffn/Drnt/Brynt/Irvng/25 40.00 100.00

2013-14 Panini Intrigue Fearless Foursomes Prime

*PRIME: .6X TO 1.5X BASIC
PRINT RUNS B/WN 2-25 COPIES PER
NO PRICING ON QTY 8 OR LESS

8 Nwtzki/Wde/Brynt/Jms/25 200.00 500.00

2013-14 Panini Intrigue First Flight Unis
PRINT RUNS B/WN 99-199 COPIES PER
NO PRICING ON QTY 15 OR LESS
*PRIME: .75X TO 2X BASIC
1 Eric Gordon/199 3.00 8.00
2 David Lee/199 2.50 6.00
3 Vince Carter/199 8.00 20.00
4 Amar'e Stoudemire/199 4.00 10.00
5 JaVale McGee/199 3.00 8.00
6 Andre Iguodala/199 4.00 10.00
7 Derrick Favors/199 2.50 6.00
8 Andrei Kirilenko/199 4.00 10.00
9 Chris Kaman/199 3.00 8.00
10 David West/199 3.00 8.00
11 Dwight Howard/199 5.00 12.00
12 Carl Landry/199 2.50 6.00
13 Jose Calderon/199 2.50 6.00
14 Andray Blatche/199 2.50 6.00
15 Kevin Martin/199 3.00 8.00
16 James Harden/199 8.00 20.00
17 LeBron James/99 30.00 80.00
18 O.J. Mayo/199 2.50 6.00
19 Deron Williams/199 3.00 8.00
20 Danilo Gallinari/199 3.00 8.00
21 Andrew Bynum/199 2.50 6.00
22 Nene/199 3.00 8.00
23 Luis Scola/199 3.00 8.00
24 Samuel Dalembert/199 2.50 6.00
25 Kevin Garnett/149 5.00 12.00

2013-14 Panini Intrigue Hall Dwellers Jersey Autographs
PRINT RUNS B/WN 15-49 COPIES PER
NO PRICING ON QTY 15 OR LESS
EXCHANGE DEADLINE 10/23/2015
3 Julius Erving/25 40.00 100.00
5 Karl Malone/25 40.00 80.00
10 Kareem Abdul-Jabbar/25 50.00 100.00
14 Jerry West/25 60.00 120.00
15 Dan Issel/49 8.00 20.00
19 Scottie Pippen/25 50.00 120.00
22 Alex English/49 10.00 25.00
28 Larry Bird/25 50.00 120.00

2013-14 Panini Intrigue Immortalized Autographs
PRINT RUNS B/WN 15-99 COPIES PER
NO PRICING ON QTY 15 OR LESS
EXCHANGE DEADLINE 10/23/2015
1 Wes Unseld/35 8.00 20.00
2 Muggsy Bogues/99 12.00 30.00
3 Micheal Ray Richardson/99 5.00 12.00
4 Jason Kidd/25 30.00 80.00
5 Clyde Drexler/25 25.00 60.00
6 Spencer Haywood/99 6.00 15.00
7 Nate Thurmond/25 6.00 15.00
8 Tom Chambers/25 6.00 15.00
9 George McGinnis/25 6.00 15.00
10 Fat Lever/99 5.00 12.00
11 Eddie Jones/99 8.00 20.00
13 Toni Kukoc/25 20.00 50.00
14 Bob McAdoo/25 15.00 40.00
15 Kevin McHale/25 15.00 40.00
16 James Worthy/25 15.00 40.00
17 Dan Issel/99 8.00 20.00
20 Tom Gugliotta/99 5.00 12.00
21 Darryl Dawkins/99 8.00 20.00
22 Hakeem Olajuwon/25 50.00 120.00
24 Earl Monroe/25 25.00 60.00
26 Sam Cassell/25 10.00 25.00
28 Elgin Baylor/25 30.00 80.00
29 Dikembe Mutombo/25 20.00 50.00
30 Bernard King/35 12.00 30.00
31 David Robinson/25 30.00 80.00
32 Rex Chapman/99 6.00 15.00
33 Gary Payton/25 12.00 30.00
34 Tracy McGrady/25 50.00 120.00
35 Michael Cooper/49 6.00 15.00
36 Mitch Richmond/25 25.00 60.00
37 Dennis Rodman/25 50.00 120.00
38 Eddie Johnson/99 4.00 10.00
39 Derrick Coleman/25 6.00 15.00
41 Detlef Schrempf/99 6.00 15.00
42 Dan Majerle/25 12.00 30.00
43 Sleepy Floyd/99 5.00 12.00
44 Grant Hill/25 30.00 80.00
45 Allan Houston/25 6.00 15.00
46 Scottie Pippen/35 75.00 200.00
47 Dana Barros/99 4.00 10.00
48 Michael Finley/35 6.00 15.00
50 Reggie Theus/99 5.00 12.00
51 Jalen Rose/25 12.00 30.00
52 Dominique Wilkins/25 25.00 60.00
53 Karl Malone/35 50.00 120.00
54 Magic Johnson/25 100.00 250.00
56 Isiah Thomas/35 30.00 80.00
57 Cedric Maxwell/99 5.00 12.00
58 Julius Erving/25 50.00 120.00
59 Sean Elliott/99 6.00 15.00
60 Ron Harper/99 6.00 15.00

2013-14 Panini Intrigue Impact Rookie Autographs
PRINT RUNS B/WN 49-149 COPIES PER
EXCHANGE DEADLINE 10/23/2015
1 Cody Zeller/75 4.00 10.00
2 Peyton Siva/149 3.00 8.00
3 Shabazz Muhammad/75 3.00 8.00
4 M.Carter-Williams/149 4.00 10.00
5 Ben McLemore/49 4.00 10.00
6 Andre Roberson/149 4.00 10.00
7 Matthew Dellavedova/149 5.00 12.00
8 Carrick Felix/149 3.00 8.00
9 Nemanja Nedovic/149 3.00 8.00
10 Jamaal Franklin/149 3.00 8.00
11 Tim Hardaway Jr./149 6.00 15.00
12 Glen Rice Jr./149 3.00 8.00
13 C.J. McCollum/75 12.00 30.00
14 Ricky Ledo/149 3.00 8.00
15 Kelly Olynyk/149 4.00 10.00
16 Anthony Bennett/75 3.00 8.00
17 Kentavious Caldwell-Pope/75 5.00 12.00
18 Rudy Gobert/149 8.00 20.00
19 Tony Snell/149 4.00 10.00
20 Isaiah Canaan/149 3.00 8.00
21 G.Antetokounmpo/149 400.00 800.00
22 Gorgui Dieng/149 8.00 20.00
23 Victor Oladipo/75 8.00 20.00
24 Alex Len/75 4.00 10.00
25 Dennis Schroder/149 10.00 25.00
26 Erik Murphy/149 3.00 8.00
27 Gal Mekel/149 3.00 8.00
28 Solomon Hill/149 4.00 10.00
29 Nate Wolters/149 3.00 8.00
30 Steven Adams/149 12.00 30.00
31 Archie Goodwin/149 3.00 8.00
32 Trey Burke/75 4.00 10.00
33 Mason Plumlee/149 4.00 10.00
34 Shane Larkin/149 3.00 8.00
35 Tony Mitchell/149 3.00 8.00
36 Ryan Kelly/149 3.00 8.00
37 Jeff Withey/149 3.00 8.00
38 Nerlens Noel/49 4.00 10.00
39 Allen Crabbe/149 3.00 8.00
40 Otto Porter/49 5.00 12.00

2013-14 Panini Intrigue Intriguing Pairs Jerseys
PRINT RUNS B/WN 25-199 COPIES PER
*PRIME: .75X TO 2X BASIC
1 K.Hinrich/N.Collison/199 3.00 8.00
2 K.Walker/M.Gilchrist/199 4.00 10.00
3 B.Beal/J.Wall/99 6.00 15.00
4 T.Splitter/T.Duncan/99 10.00 25.00
5 K.Durant/S.Ibaka/199 12.00 30.00
6 K.Bryant/K.Irving/25 30.00 80.00
7 B.McLemore/J.Withey/199 5.00 12.00
8 C.Zeller/D.Porter/199 3.00 8.00
9 T.Hardaway Jr./T.Burke/199 6.00 15.00
10 B.Griffin/J.Redick/169 4.00 10.00
11 D.Lillard/K.Irving/25 12.00 30.00
12 T.Prince/Z.Randolph/49 4.00 10.00
13 E.Ilyasova/J.Henson/199 2.50 6.00
14 L.Allen/T.Young/199 2.50 6.00
15 J.Green/R.Rondo/99 5.00 12.00
16 G.Hill/K.Irving/25 10.00 25.00
17 M.Beasley/U.Haslem/199 3.00 8.00
18 A.Davis/A.Rivers/99 6.00 15.00
19 D.Williams/J.Terry/199 3.00 8.00
20 C.Paul/J.Crawford/25 8.00 20.00
21 A.Bennett/K.Olynyk/199 3.00 8.00
22 R.Ledo/S.Larkin/199 2.50 6.00
23 C.McCollum/M.Williams/199 6.00 15.00
24 M.Gasol/P.Gasol/99 6.00 15.00
25 R.Jackson/R.Westbrook/199 6.00 15.00
26 B.Griffin/K.Durant/199 8.00 20.00
27 D.Wade/M.Chalmers/199 5.00 12.00
28 J.Noah/T.Gibson/199 4.00 10.00
29 B.Bass/J.Sullinger/199 2.50 6.00
30 K.Durant/K.Bryant/199 12.00 30.00
32 J.McGee/K.Faried/199 3.00 8.00
33 K.Bryant/S.Nash/25 15.00 40.00
34 C.Zeller/V.Oladipo/199 6.00 15.00
35 A.Goodwin/B.McLemore/199 4.00 10.00
36 H.Barnes/K.Thompson/49 12.00 30.00
37 A.Shved/R.Rubio/99 3.00 8.00
38 J.Harden/J.Lin/99 8.00 20.00
39 C.Bosh/L.James/49 8.00 20.00
40 A.Drummond/C.Villanueva/199 4.00 10.00
41 D.Williams/J.Johnson/199 3.00 8.00
42 D.West/G.Hill/49 3.00 8.00
43 D.Blair/D.Nowitzki/199 10.00 25.00
44 F.Lever/T.Lawson/99 3.00 8.00
45 D.Lee/D.Green/199 6.00 15.00
46 D.Cousins/I.Thomas/99 4.00 10.00
47 A.Bennett/L.Johnson/49 5.00 12.00
48 J.Dumars/K.Pope/99 5.00 12.00
49 A.Iverson/M.Williams/99 8.00 20.00
50 N.De Colo/T.Parker/49 10.00 25.00
51 N.Cole/R.Allen/199 6.00 15.00
52 A.Johnson/D.DeRozan/199 5.00 12.00
53 I.Shumpert/R.Felton/199 2.50 6.00
54 A.Len/N.Noel/199 3.00 8.00
55 M.Gortat/Nene/35 12.00 30.00
56 A.Bennett/V.Oladipo/199 5.00 12.00
57 Marc.Morris/Mark.Morris/199 3.00 8.00
58 A.Goodwin/N.Noel/199 4.00 10.00
59 C.Anthony/J.Smith/99 6.00 15.00
60 E.Murphy/T.Snell/199 3.00 8.00

2013-14 Panini Intrigue Intriguing Players
ALL VERSIONS EQUALLY PRICED
1 LeBron James 5.00 12.00
11 Kevin Durant 2.00 5.00
21 Stephen Curry 5.00 12.00
31 Russell Westbrook 1.00 2.50
41 James Harden 1.25 3.00
51 Carmelo Anthony 1.00 2.50
61 Kyrie Irving 2.00 5.00
71 Chris Paul 1.25 3.00
81 Derrick Rose 1.00 2.50
91 Dwyane Wade 1.25 3.00
101 Dirk Nowitzki 1.50 4.00
111 Tim Duncan 1.50 4.00
121 Anthony Davis 2.00 5.00
131 Dwight Howard .75 2.00
141 Paul George 1.00 2.50
151 Kobe Bryant 5.00 12.00
161 Damian Lillard 2.00 5.00
171 Paul Pierce 1.00 2.50
181 John Wall .75 2.00
191 Tony Parker 1.00 2.50

2013-14 Panini Intrigue Intriguing Players Die Cuts
*DIE CUT: .75X TO 2X BASIC

2013-14 Panini Intrigue Intriguing Players Die Cuts Gold
*DIE CUT GOLD: 6X TO 15X
STATED PRINT RUN 10 SER.#'d SETS

2013-14 Panini Intrigue Intriguing Players Gold
*DIE CUT: 6X TO 15X
STATED PRINT RUN 10 SER.#'d SETS

2013-14 Panini Intrigue Red White and Blue Autographs
PRINT RUNS B/WN 15-99 COPIES PER
NO PRICING ON QTY 15 OR LESS
EXCHANGE DEADLINE 10/23/2015
1 Tim Hardaway/99 6.00 15.00
2 Kenny Anderson/99 4.00 10.00
3 Rick Mahorn/99 3.00 8.00
5 Jason Kidd/25 30.00 80.00
8 Larry Bird/25 75.00 200.00
9 Terry Porter/99 5.00 12.00
12 Kendall Gill/99 10.00 25.00
15 Spencer Haywood/99 5.00 12.00
16 Bobby Jones/99 6.00 15.00
17 Kobe Bryant/25 1,000.00 2,000.00
18 Bill Russell/25 500.00 1,000.00
19 Karl Malone/25 30.00 80.00
20 Buck Williams/99 4.00 10.00
21 David Robinson/25 40.00 100.00
24 Scottie Pippen/25 75.00 200.00
25 Jeff Hornacek/99 4.00 10.00
26 Steve Blake/99 3.00 8.00
29 Mark Price/99 20.00 50.00
32 John Starks/99 5.00 12.00
34 Anfernee Hardaway/25 60.00 150.00
35 Charlie Scott/99 5.00 12.00
36 Mark Aguirre/99 4.00 10.00
38 Grant Hill/25 EXCH 40.00 100.00

2013-14 Panini Intrigue Rookie Autographed Memorabilia
PRINT RUNS B/WN 49-149 COPIES PER
EXCHANGE DEADLINE 10/23/2015
1 Tony Mitchell/99 4.00 10.00
2 M.Carter-Williams/99 5.00 12.00
3 Otto Porter/25 10.00 25.00
4 G.Antetokounmpo/99 300.00 600.00
5 Tony Snell/99 5.00 12.00
6 Peyton Siva/99 4.00 10.00
7 Jeff Withey/99 4.00 10.00
8 C.J. McCollum/25 10.00 25.00
9 Kelly Olynyk/99 5.00 12.00
10 Ricky Ledo/99 4.00 10.00
11 Jamaal Franklin/99 4.00 10.00
12 Victor Oladipo/25 20.00 50.00
13 Trey Burke/25 5.00 12.00
14 Isaiah Canaan/99 4.00 10.00
15 Mason Plumlee/99 5.00 12.00
16 Reggie Bullock/99 5.00 12.00
17 Alex Len/25 5.00 12.00
18 Erik Murphy/99 4.00 10.00
19 Andre Roberson/99 5.00 12.00
20 Archie Goodwin/99 4.00 10.00
21 Ben McLemore/25 5.00 12.00
22 Dennis Schroder/99 12.00 30.00
23 Anthony Bennett/25 4.00 10.00
24 Kentavious Caldwell-Pope/25 6.00 15.00
25 Ryan Kelly/99 4.00 10.00
26 Shabazz Muhammad/25 4.00 10.00
27 Steven Adams/99 10.00 25.00
28 Allen Crabbe/99 4.00 10.00
29 Cody Zeller/25 5.00 12.00
30 Shane Larkin/99 4.00 10.00
31 Solomon Hill/99 4.00 10.00
32 Nate Wolters/99 4.00 10.00
33 Tim Hardaway Jr./99 8.00 20.00
34 Nerlens Noel/25 8.00 20.00
35 Glen Rice Jr./99 4.00 10.00

2013-14 Panini Intrigue Slam Ink
PRINT RUNS B/WN 15-49 COPIES PER
NO PRICING ON QTY 15 OR LESS
EXCHANGE DEADLINE 10/23/2015
1 Lavoy Allen/49 5.00 12.00
2 Jeff Green/20 5.00 12.00
3 Derrick Favors/20 5.00 12.00
4 Raef LaFrentz/49 5.00 12.00
5 Nick Collison/49 5.00 12.00
6 Jason Richardson/25 EXCH 8.00 20.00
7 Michael Finley/20 EXCH 8.00 20.00
8 Harrison Barnes/49 8.00 20.00
9 George Gervin/20 20.00 50.00
10 Kenny Smith/20 6.00 15.00
11 David Thompson/25 15.00 40.00
12 Michael Cooper/49 12.00 30.00
14 Jerome Williams/49 5.00 12.00
15 Clyde Drexler/20 25.00 60.00
17 John Starks/49 8.00 20.00
18 J.J. Hickson/49 5.00 12.00
19 Terrence Ross/25 6.00 15.00
20 Darryl Dawkins/49 8.00 20.00
21 Cedric Ceballos/49 5.00 12.00
22 Andre Iguodala/20 20.00 50.00
23 Tom Chambers/25 8.00 20.00
24 Allan Houston/20 8.00 20.00
25 Kobe Bryant/25 1,500.00 3,000.00
26 Rex Chapman/49 8.00 20.00
27 Artis Gilmore/20 10.00 25.00
28 Xavier Henry/49 5.00 12.00
29 Spud Webb/49 8.00 20.00
30 Kenny Walker/25 5.00 12.00
31 JaVale McGee/20 6.00 15.00
32 Steve Francis/20 6.00 15.00
33 Larry Nance/49 6.00 15.00
34 Reggie Jackson/25 6.00 15.00
35 Ralph Sampson/20 15.00 40.00
36 Jonas Jerebko/49 5.00 12.00
37 Doug Christie/49 5.00 12.00
38 Ron Harper/49 8.00 20.00
39 Dominique Wilkins/20 30.00 60.00
40 Vince Carter/20 100.00 250.00
41 Chase Budinger/25 5.00 12.00
42 Bismack Biyombo/49 5.00 12.00
43 Kawhi Leonard/20 EXCH 125.00 300.00
44 Julius Erving/20 100.00 250.00
45 Tracy McGrady/20 100.00 250.00
46 Andrew Nicholson/49 5.00 12.00
47 J.R. Smith/25 5.00 12.00
48 Larry Johnson/20 20.00 50.00
49 Dee Brown/49 6.00 15.00
50 Gerald Henderson/25 5.00 12.00

2013-14 Panini Intrigue Terrific Trios
PRINT RUNS B/WN 25-199 COPIES PER
1 Bss/Grn/Rndo/199 5.00 12.00
2 Bltchw/Wllms/Jhn/199 3.00 8.00
3 Anth/Smth/Chnd/149 6.00 15.00
4 Rse/Btlr/Hnrch/25 8.00 20.00
5 Bsh/Wde/Jms/199 30.00 80.00
6 Bl/Wll/Arza/199 6.00 15.00
7 Prsns/Hrdn/Ln/199 8.00 20.00
8 Lnrd/Dncn/Prkr/25 12.00 30.00
9 Gllnri/Frd/Lwsn/199 3.00 8.00
10 Shvd/Lve/Rbo/199 4.00 10.00
11 Drnt/Wst/Ibka/199 12.00 30.00
12 Brns/Thmpsn/Crry/149 30.00 80.00
13 Grffn/Pl/Jrdn/49 8.00 20.00
14 Brynt/Gsl/Nsh/199 30.00 80.00
15 Jhn/Chnd/Rndl/199 3.00 8.00
16 Anthny/Bsh/Jms/49 60.00 150.00
17 Pl/Wllms/Fltn/199 8.00 20.00
18 Hrfrd/Nh/Drnt/199 12.00 30.00
19 Gllnri/Lve/Wstbrk/199 6.00 15.00
20 Grffn/Hrdn/Rbo/199 8.00 20.00
21 Shmprt/Lnrd/Wlkr/199 12.00 30.00
22 Dvs/Lllrd/Brns/199 12.00 30.00
23 Bnntt/Prtr/Oldpo/199 6.00 15.00
24 Ln/Zllr/Nl/199 3.00 8.00
25 McLmre/Ppe/Brke/199 4.00 10.00
26 Schrdr/Gian/Adms/199 75.00 200.00
27 Nwtzki/Wde/Dncn/199 30.00 80.00
28 Wll/Irvng/Evns/199 12.00 30.00
29 Dvs/Grffn/Lve/199 12.00 30.00
30 Grffn/Drnt/Brynt/199 30.00 80.00

2013-14 Panini Intrigue Terrific Trios Prime
*PRIME: .75X TO 2X BASIC
PRINT RUNS B/WN 1-25 COPIES PER
NO PRICING ON QTY 15 OR LESS
13 Grffn/Pl/Jrdn/25 15.00 40.00
27 Nwtzki/Wde/Dncn/25 60.00 150.00

2013-14 Panini Intrigue Top Flight Unis
PRINT RUNS B/WN 49-199 COPIES PER
*PRIME: .75X TO 2X BASIC
1 Michael Kidd-Gilchrist/49 2.50 6.00
2 Tristan Thompson/49 2.50 6.00
3 DeAndre Jordan/99 3.00 8.00
4 LeBron James/99 40.00 100.00
5 Andrea Bargnani/49 2.50 6.00
6 Nick Young/49 2.50 6.00
7 Kevin Garnett/99 10.00 25.00
8 Jrue Holiday/49 5.00 12.00
9 Tiago Splitter/49 2.50 6.00
10 Serge Ibaka/99 3.00 8.00
11 Evan Turner/49 2.50 6.00
12 JaVale McGee/199 3.00 8.00
13 Dirk Nowitzki/199 10.00 25.00
14 Kobe Bryant/199 40.00 100.00
15 Udonis Haslem/199 3.00 8.00
16 Tayshaun Prince/49 4.00 10.00
17 Blake Griffin/199 4.00 10.00
18 Kyrie Irving/49 12.00 30.00
19 Damian Lillard/49 12.00 30.00
20 Joakim Noah/49 4.00 10.00
21 Courtney Lee/99 2.50 6.00
22 Jamal Crawford/49 4.00 10.00
23 Gordon Hayward/49 3.00 8.00
24 Chris Kaman/49 3.00 8.00
25 Samuel Dalembert/49 2.50 6.00
26 Nate Robinson/49 2.50 6.00
27 Rudy Gay/49 3.00 8.00
28 Eric Bledsoe/99 3.00 8.00
29 Andre Iguodala/49 4.00 10.00
30 Thaddeus Young/99 2.50 6.00
31 Gerald Henderson/49 2.50 6.00
32 Norris Cole/199 2.50 6.00
33 Iman Shumpert/49 2.50 6.00
34 Tobias Harris/49 4.00 10.00
35 Harrison Barnes/49 4.00 10.00
36 Kirk Hinrich/99 3.00 8.00
37 Brandon Bass/99 2.50 6.00
38 Amar'e Stoudemire/49 4.00 10.00
39 Jameer Nelson/49 2.50 6.00
40 Joe Johnson/199 3.00 8.00
41 Andre Miller/49 2.50 6.00
42 Jared Sullinger/49 2.50 6.00
43 Austin Rivers/49 3.00 8.00
44 Channing Frye/49 2.50 6.00
45 Reggie Jackson/99 3.00 8.00
46 Kevin Love/199 4.00 10.00
47 John Wall/99 3.00 8.00
48 Bismack Biyombo/49 2.50 6.00
49 O.J. Mayo/49 2.50 6.00
50 Andrew Bynum/199 2.50 6.00
51 Chris Paul/99 8.00 20.00
52 Mike Miller/99 3.00 8.00
53 Michael Beasley/49 2.50 6.00
54 Carmelo Anthony/99 6.00 15.00
55 Glen Davis/49 2.50 6.00
56 Deron Williams/49 3.00 8.00
57 Kenneth Faried/49 3.00 8.00
58 Rodney Stuckey/49 2.50 6.00
59 Kawhi Leonard/49 12.00 30.00
60 Kevin Durant/99 12.00 30.00
61 Draymond Green/49 6.00 15.00
62 Eric Gordon/49 3.00 8.00
63 Luol Deng/49 3.00 8.00
64 Gerald Wallace/99 3.00 8.00
65 J.J. Redick/49 4.00 10.00
66 Dwyane Wade/199 8.00 20.00
67 Raymond Felton/49 2.50 6.00
68 Shane Battier/99 3.00 8.00
69 DeJuan Blair/49 2.50 6.00
70 Paul Pierce/49 6.00 15.00
71 Alec Burks/49 3.00 8.00
72 Jason Richardson/49 4.00 10.00
73 Tim Duncan/49 10.00 25.00
74 Thabo Sefolosha/99 3.00 8.00
75 Klay Thompson/49 12.00 30.00

2013-14 Panini Intrigue Winning Ink
PRINT RUNS B/WN 15-49 COPIES PER
NO PRICING ON QTY 15 OR LESS
EXCHANGE DEADLINE 10/23/2015
1 Scottie Pippen/20 125.00 300.00
2 Udonis Haslem/49 12.00 30.00
3 Rick Fox/20 12.00 30.00
5 James Jones/49 EXCH 6.00 15.00
6 Joe Dumars/20 25.00 60.00
7 Willis Reed/20 75.00 200.00
8 Robert Parish/20 30.00 60.00
9 Horace Grant/25 30.00 80.00
10 Jerry Lucas/20 25.00 60.00
11 Michael Cooper/49 12.00 30.00
12 George McGinnis/25 20.00 50.00
13 Sean Elliott/49 15.00 40.00
14 Robert Horry/25 EXCH 30.00 80.00
15 Kobe Bryant/20 1,500.00 3,000.00
17 Luc Longley/49 15.00 40.00
18 Bill Walton/20 50.00 120.00
19 Kendrick Perkins/25 5.00 12.00
20 Chris Bosh/15 20.00 50.00
21 Kareem Abdul-Jabbar/20 125.00 300.00
22 Vernon Maxwell/49 10.00 25.00
23 David Robinson/20 40.00 100.00
24 Peja Stojakovic/20 20.00 50.00
25 Glen Rice/25 8.00 20.00
26 Bailey Howell/25 8.00 20.00
27 Jon McGlocklin/49 8.00 20.00
28 Byron Scott/20 12.00 30.00
29 Mark Aguirre/49 8.00 20.00
30 Avery Johnson/20 12.00 30.00
31 Bobby Jones/49 20.00 50.00
33 Magic Johnson/20 125.00 300.00
34 Bruce Bowen/49 12.00 30.00
35 Toni Kukoc/25 40.00 100.00
36 Naz Mohammed/49 EXCH 5.00 12.00
37 Sam Cassell/25 EXCH 15.00 40.00
38 Isiah Thomas/20 40.00 100.00
39 Jason Terry/20 12.00 30.00
40 Gail Goodrich/20 10.00 25.00
41 Walt Frazier/20 25.00 60.00
42 Dan Issel/49 10.00 25.00
44 Steve Kerr/20 25.00 60.00
46 Tayshaun Prince/20 20.00 50.00
47 Spencer Haywood/49 25.00 60.00
48 Nate Archibald/20 15.00 40.00
49 Kevin Willis/25 6.00 15.00
50 Larry Bird/20 EXCH 125.00 300.00

2012-13 Panini Kobe Anthology
COMMON CARD (1-201) 1.50 4.00

2012-13 Panini Kobe Anthology Gold
COMMON CARD (1-200) 12.00 30.00
STATED PRINT RUN 24 SER.#'d SETS

2012-13 Panini Kobe Anthology Platinum
COMMON CARD (1-200) 15.00 40.00
STATED PRINT RUN 8 SER.#'d SETS

2012-13 Panini Kobe Anthology Autographs
COMMON CARD (1-25) 1,000.00 2,000.00
STATED PRINT RUN 24 SER.#'d SETS

2012-13 Panini Kobe Anthology Memorabilia
COMMON CARD (1-50) 25.00 60.00
STATED PRINT RUN 24 SER.#'d SETS
*PRIME: .6X TO 1.5X BASIC
PRIME PRINT RUN 8 SETS

2012-13 Panini Kobe Anthology Memorabilia Autographs
COMMON CARD (1-25) 500.00 1,000.00
STATED PRINT RUN 24 SER.#'d SETS

2017 Panini Kobe Eminence 33643 Autographs Diamond
COMMON CARD 600.00 1,200.00
STATED PRINT RUN 10 SER.#'d SETS
ALL VERSIONS EQUALLY PRICED

2017 Panini Kobe Eminence 33643 Autographs Double Diamond
DBLE DMND: .5X TO 1.2X BASIC
STATED PRINT RUN 3 SER.#'d SETS
ALL VERSIONS EQUALLY PRICED

2017 Panini Kobe Eminence All-Time Buckets Autographs Diamond
COMMON CARD 600.00 1,200.00
STATED PRINT RUN 10 SER.#'d SETS
ALL VERSIONS EQUALLY PRICED
DBLE DMND/5: .5X TO 1.2X BASIC

2017 Panini Kobe Eminence Black Mamba Moments Autographs Diamond
COMMON CARD 800.00 1,500.00
STATED PRINT RUN 10 SER.#'d SETS
ALL VERSIONS EQUALLY PRICED

2017 Panini Kobe Eminence Crown Jewels Autographs Diamond
COMMON CARD 800.00 1,500.00
STATED PRINT RUN 8 SER.#'d SETS
ALL VERSIONS EQUALLY PRICED

2017 Panini Kobe Eminence Five Fold Autographs
COMMON CARD 1,500.00 3,000.00
STATED PRINT RUN 2 SER.#'d SETS
ALL VERSIONS EQUALLY PRICED

2017 Panini Kobe Eminence Game Winners Autographs
COMMON CARD 1,500.00 3,000.00
STATED PRINT RUN 3 SER.#'d SETS
ALL VERSIONS EQUALLY PRICED

2017 Panini Kobe Eminence Signature Sketches Autographs Diamond
COMMON CARD 800.00 1,500.00
STATED PRINT RUN 10 SER.#'d SETS
ALL VERSIONS EQUALLY PRICED

2017 Panini Kobe Eminence Triple Double Autographs Diamond
COMMON CARD 800.00 1,500.00
STATED PRINT RUN 8 SER.#'d SETS
ALL VERSIONS EQUALLY PRICED

2014-15 Panini Luxe Autographs
OVERALL THREE AUTOS PER BOX
PRINT RUNS B/WN 40-65 COPIES PER
EXCHANGE DEADLINE 3/2/2017
1 Aaron Gordon/40 30.00 80.00
2 Andrew Wiggins/40 50.00 120.00
3 Elfrid Payton/40 5.00 12.00
4 James Ennis/60 3.00 8.00
5 Bojan Bogdanovic/60 5.00 12.00
6 Damjan Rudez/60 3.00 8.00
8 Zoran Dragic/60 4.00 10.00
9 Jordan Clarkson/60 12.00 30.00
10 T.J. Warren/40 40.00 100.00
11 Kyle Anderson/60 5.00 12.00
12 Nikola Mirotic/40 5.00 12.00
13 Doug McDermott/49 5.00 12.00
14 Spencer Dinwiddie/60 5.00 12.00
15 Joel Embiid/40 150.00 400.00
16 K.J. McDaniels/49 3.00 8.00
17 Jerami Grant/60 15.00 40.00
18 Langston Galloway/60 5.00 12.00
19 Shabazz Napier/60 4.00 10.00
20 Jabari Parker/40 4.00 10.00
21 Johnny O'Bryant/60 3.00 8.00
22 Cory Jefferson/60 3.00 8.00
23 Devyn Marble/60 3.00 8.00
24 Russ Smith/65 3.00 8.00
25 Jarnell Stokes/60 3.00 8.00
26 Lucas Nogueira/60 3.00 8.00
27 Gary Harris/49 5.00 12.00
28 Jusuf Nurkic/49 12.00 30.00
29 Erick Green/60 3.00 8.00
30 Zach LaVine/49 25.00 60.00
31 Rodney Hood/60 4.00 10.00
32 Bruno Caboclo/60 4.00 10.00
33 Marcus Smart/40 12.00 30.00
34 James Young/49 3.00 8.00
35 Dante Exum/40 5.00 12.00
36 Cleanthony Early/40 3.00 8.00
37 Kobe Bryant/40 500.00 1,000.00
38 Kyrie Irving/40 30.00 80.00
39 Carmelo Anthony/40 25.00 60.00
40 Michael Carter-Williams/40 3.00 8.00
41 Julius Randle/40 12.00 30.00
42 Trey Burke/40 3.00 8.00
43 Michael Kidd-Gilchrist/40 3.00 8.00
44 Tyson Chandler/40 5.00 12.00
46 John Wall/40 12.00 30.00
47 Kelly Olynyk/60 3.00 8.00
48 Tyler Zeller/40 3.00 8.00
49 Kyle Korver/49 6.00 15.00
50 Stephen Curry/40 500.00 1,000.00
51 Carl Landry/40 3.00 8.00
52 Ben McLemore/40 3.00 8.00
53 Blake Griffin/40 20.00 50.00
54 Goran Dragic/40 5.00 12.00
55 Ty Lawson/40 3.00 8.00
56 LaMarcus Aldridge/40 6.00 15.00
58 Latrell Sprewell/40 15.00 40.00
61 Steven Adams/40 6.00 15.00
62 Giannis Antetokounmpo/49 300.00 600.00
63 Tim Hardaway Jr./49 4.00 10.00
64 Shabazz Muhammad/40 3.00 8.00
65 Tracy McGrady/40 25.00 60.00
66 Mason Plumlee/60 3.00 8.00
67 Rudy Gobert/60 10.00 25.00
68 Brook Lopez/40 5.00 12.00
69 Kevin Durant/40 60.00 150.00
70 Kareem Abdul-Jabbar/40 25.00 60.00
71 Tom Van Arsdale/49 4.00 10.00
72 Rudy Tomjanovich/49 6.00 15.00
73 Scott Brooks/40 3.00 8.00
74 Mark Price/49 10.00 25.00
75 Zydrunas Ilgauskas/49 5.00 12.00
76 Clifford Robinson/49 5.00 12.00
77 Steve Smith/49 4.00 10.00
78 Dikembe Mutombo/40 10.00 25.00
79 Rod Strickland/49 4.00 10.00
80 Cedric Maxwell/49 3.00 8.00
81 Mark Aguirre/49 4.00 10.00
82 Adrian Dantley/40 5.00 12.00
83 Alex English/40 6.00 15.00
84 Horace Grant/40 10.00 25.00
85 Dan Issel/49 6.00 15.00
86 Mychal Thompson/49 4.00 10.00
87 Ron Harper/49 6.00 15.00
88 Michael Finley/40 8.00 20.00
89 Mahmoud Abdul-Rauf/49 10.00 25.00
90 Larry Bird/40 40.00 100.00
91 Hakeem Olajuwon/40 15.00 40.00
92 Magic Johnson/40 30.00 80.00
93 Kevin Love/40 5.00 12.00
94 Steve Nash/40 40.00 100.00
95 George Gervin/40 12.00 30.00
96 Bill Walton/40 8.00 20.00
97 Gary Payton/40 8.00 20.00
98 Clyde Drexler/40 8.00 20.00
99 Bernard King/40 6.00 15.00
100 Scott Skiles/49 4.00 10.00

2014-15 Panini Luxe Autographs Silver
*SILVER: .6X TO 1.5X BASIC
OVERALL THREE AUTOS PER BOX
STATED PRINT RUN 25 SER.#'d SETS
EXCHANGE DEADLINE 3/2/2017

2014-15 Panini Luxe Die Cut Autographs
OVERALL THREE AUTOS PER BOX
PRINT RUNS B/WN 25-60 COPIES PER
EXCHANGE DEADLINE 3/2/2017
1 Kyrie Irving/40 30.00 80.00
2 Kobe Bryant/25 500.00 1,000.00
3 Kevin Durant/35 100.00 250.00
4 Kevin Love/40 12.00 30.00
5 Carmelo Anthony/35 12.00 30.00
7 Anthony Davis/25 50.00 120.00
8 Trey Burke/40 3.00 8.00
9 Ty Lawson/50 3.00 8.00
11 Andre Drummond/40 6.00 15.00
12 Gordon Hayward/40 6.00 15.00
13 Derrick Favors/40 3.00 8.00
15 Tony Parker/40 20.00 50.00
16 DeMarre Carroll/60 6.00 15.00
18 Isaiah Thomas/60 8.00 20.00
19 Gary Harris/60 5.00 12.00
20 Chris Bosh/40 6.00 15.00
21 Reggie Jackson/60 8.00 20.00
22 Blake Griffin/35 25.00 60.00
23 John Wall/40 15.00 40.00
24 Gary Payton/40 10.00 25.00
25 Clyde Drexler/40 15.00 40.00
26 Jason Kidd/40 15.00 40.00
27 Grant Hill/40 15.00 40.00
28 Jonas Valanciunas/60 4.00 10.00
30 Kenneth Faried/50 3.00 8.00
31 Josh Smith/50 3.00 8.00
35 Mason Plumlee/50 3.00 8.00
36 Enes Kanter/60 4.00 10.00
37 Taj Gibson/60 3.00 8.00
39 Jeff Green/50 4.00 10.00
40 Alec Burks/60 4.00 10.00
41 Erick Green/60 3.00 8.00
42 Zoran Dragic/60 4.00 10.00
43 Jusuf Nurkic/60 10.00 25.00
44 Cory Jefferson/60 3.00 8.00
46 Jarnell Stokes/60 3.00 8.00
47 Bruno Caboclo/60 3.00 8.00
48 Andrew Wiggins/60 50.00 120.00
49 Jabari Parker/40 4.00 10.00
50 Julius Randle/40 20.00 50.00
51 Joel Embiid/40 75.00 200.00
52 Marcus Smart/40 12.00 30.00
53 Zach LaVine/60 25.00 60.00
54 Elfrid Payton/60 5.00 12.00
55 Aaron Gordon/40 12.00 30.00
58 Glenn Robinson III/60 4.00 10.00
59 Jordan Clarkson/60 6.00 15.00
61 James Ennis/60 3.00 8.00
62 Shabazz Napier/60 4.00 10.00
63 Tyler Ennis/40 3.00 8.00
64 T.J. Warren/60 12.00 30.00
65 James Young/60 3.00 8.00
66 Devyn Marble/60 3.00 8.00
68 Dante Exum/40 5.00 12.00
70 P.J. Hairston/60 3.00 8.00
71 Lucas Nogueira/60 3.00 8.00
72 Adreian Payne/60 3.00 8.00
73 Johnny O'Bryant/60 3.00 8.00
74 Nikola Mirotic/50 5.00 12.00
75 Bojan Bogdanovic/60 5.00 12.00
76 World B. Free/50 4.00 10.00
77 Terry Porter/50 3.00 8.00
78 Wayne Embry/60 4.00 10.00
79 Charles Oakley/60 5.00 12.00
80 Horace Grant/50 6.00 15.00
81 Dikembe Mutombo/50 10.00 25.00
82 Bernard King/40 6.00 15.00
83 Julius Erving/35 30.00 80.00
84 Dolph Schayes/50 5.00 12.00
85 Adrian Dantley/50 5.00 12.00
86 Walt Frazier/40 10.00 25.00
87 Dave Cowens/50 6.00 15.00
88 Hal Greer/50 6.00 15.00
89 Mark Aguirre/60 4.00 10.00
90 Latrell Sprewell/50 12.00 30.00
91 Tim Hardaway/60 6.00 15.00
92 Rick Fox/50 4.00 10.00
93 George Karl/50 5.00 12.00
94 Bob Dandridge/60 5.00 12.00
95 Jo Jo White/60 5.00 12.00
96 Tracy McGrady/40 25.00 60.00
97 Shaquille O'Neal/25 60.00 150.00
98 Larry Bird/35 40.00 100.00
99 Keith Van Horn/60 4.00 10.00
100 Eddie Jones/60 6.00 15.00

2014-15 Panini Luxe Memorabilia Autographs
OVERALL THREE AUTOS PER BOX
PRINT RUNS B/WN 30-60 COPIES PER
EXCHANGE DEADLINE 3/2/2017
1 Jabari Parker/49 6.00 15.00
2 Jarnell Stokes/60 5.00 12.00
3 Julius Randle/49 15.00 40.00
4 Andrew Wiggins/49 25.00 60.00
5 Aaron Gordon/49 25.00 60.00
6 Marcus Smart/49 20.00 50.00
7 James Young/49 5.00 12.00
8 Elfrid Payton/49 8.00 20.00
9 Cleanthony Early/60 5.00 12.00
10 Bruno Caboclo/60 6.00 15.00
11 Jordan Adams/60 5.00 12.00
12 James Ennis/60 5.00 12.00
13 Adreian Payne/60 5.00 12.00
14 Gary Harris/60 8.00 20.00
16 Noah Vonleh/49 8.00 20.00
17 Spencer Dinwiddie/60 8.00 20.00
18 Doug McDermott/60 8.00 20.00
19 Cory Jefferson/60 5.00 12.00
20 Zach LaVine/60 30.00 80.00
22 Johnny O'Bryant/60 5.00 12.00
23 Jerami Grant/60 25.00 60.00
24 Dante Exum/49 8.00 20.00
25 Joel Embiid/49 75.00 200.00
26 Joe Harris/60 8.00 20.00
28 P.J. Hairston/60 5.00 12.00
30 Tyler Ennis/49 5.00 12.00
32 Glenn Robinson III/60 6.00 15.00
33 Russ Smith/60 5.00 12.00
34 T.J. Warren/49 40.00 100.00
35 Shabazz Napier/60 6.00 15.00
36 Larry Bird/35 40.00 100.00
37 Kevin McHale/35 12.00 30.00
38 Clyde Drexler/35 15.00 40.00
39 Alonzo Mourning/35 20.00 50.00
40 Jeff Green/49 6.00 15.00
42 Tim Hardaway Jr./60 6.00 15.00
43 Kyle Korver/35 6.00 15.00
44 Gordon Hayward/49 6.00 15.00
45 Kevin Martin/35 6.00 15.00
46 Andre Drummond/35 6.00 15.00
49 Danilo Gallinari/35 6.00 15.00
50 Charles Oakley/60 8.00 20.00
51 Michael Kidd-Gilchrist/35 5.00 12.00
52 Hakeem Olajuwon/35 15.00 40.00
53 Kevin Love/35 15.00 40.00
54 Clifford Robinson/49 8.00 20.00
55 Michael Finley/35 8.00 20.00
56 Thaddeus Young/60 5.00 12.00
57 Tyson Chandler/35 8.00 20.00
59 Kyrie Irving/35 40.00 100.00
60 Carmelo Anthony/35 20.00 50.00
61 Blake Griffin/35 25.00 60.00
62 Kevin Durant/35 125.00 300.00
63 Kobe Bryant/35 500.00 1,000.00
64 Karl Malone/35 25.00 60.00
65 John Stockton/35 25.00 60.00
66 James Worthy/35 15.00 40.00
67 Adrian Dantley/49 8.00 20.00
68 Bernard King/35 10.00 25.00
69 Gerald Henderson/49 5.00 12.00
71 Marcin Gortat/49 12.00 30.00
72 John Wall/35 20.00 50.00
74 Ben McLemore/35 5.00 12.00
75 Chris Andersen/35 6.00 15.00
76 Stephen Curry/35 500.00 1,000.00
78 Reggie Jackson/49 6.00 15.00

79 Spencer Hawes/60 5.00 12.00
80 Mike Conley/35 6.00 15.00
81 Ryan Anderson/49 5.00 12.00
82 Tony Parker/35 20.00 50.00
83 Thabo Sefolosha/30 5.00 12.00
84 Alec Burks/60 6.00 15.00
85 Tiago Splitter/49 5.00 12.00
86 Steve Nash/35 75.00 200.00
87 Harrison Barnes/35 6.00 15.00
89 Andrew Nicholson/60 5.00 12.00
90 Jonas Valanciunas/49 6.00 15.00
91 Joe Dumars/35 10.00 25.00
92 Magic Johnson/35 30.00 80.00
93 Alex English/49 10.00 25.00
94 Brad Daugherty/60 6.00 15.00
95 Tom Chambers/49 8.00 20.00
96 Dan Majerle/49 6.00 15.00
97 Jason Kidd/35 15.00 40.00
98 Xavier McDaniel/60 6.00 15.00
99 Robert Horry/49 8.00 20.00
100 Shaquille O'Neal/35 75.00 200.00

2014-15 Panini Luxe Memorabilia Prime

OVERALL ONE MEM PER BOX
PRINT RUNS B/WN 10-25 COPIES PER
NO PRICING ON QTY 10
EXCHANGE DEADLINE 3/2/2017
1 Manu Ginobili/25 12.00 30.00
2 Jarrell Stokes/25 4.00 10.00
3 Rajon Rondo/25 8.00 20.00
4 Mitch McGary/25 4.00 10.00
5 Detlef Schrempf/25 20.00 50.00
6 Tiago Splitter/25 4.00 10.00
7 Danny Manning/20 5.00 12.00
9 Joe Johnson/25 5.00 12.00
10 Cory Jefferson/25 4.00 10.00
11 Manute Bol/25 20.00 50.00
12 Jerami Grant/25 20.00 50.00
13 Rick Mahorn/25 4.00 10.00
14 Nik Stauskas/25 4.00 10.00
15 Dikembe Mutombo/25 10.00 25.00
16 Tom Chambers/25 6.00 15.00
17 Derrick Rose/25 12.00 30.00
18 Chris Andersen/25 5.00 12.00
19 Kareem Abdul-Jabbar/25 20.00 50.00
20 Damien Inglis/25 10.00 25.00
21 Markieff Morris/25 4.00 10.00
22 Joe Harris/25 6.00 15.00
23 Robert Horry/25 6.00 15.00
24 Noah Vonleh/25 10.00 25.00
25 Allen Iverson/25 20.00 50.00
27 Earl Monroe/25 10.00 25.00
28 Jeff Teague/25 4.00 10.00
29 Kevin Duckworth/25 4.00 10.00
30 Dante Exum/25 6.00 15.00
31 Matt Barnes/25 5.00 12.00
32 Joel Embiid/25 40.00 100.00
34 P.J. Hairston/25 4.00 10.00
35 Andre Iguodala/25 6.00 15.00
36 Tristan Thompson/25 4.00 10.00
37 Eric Bledsoe/25 5.00 12.00
38 Paul Millsap/25 5.00 12.00
40 Doug McDermott/25 6.00 15.00
41 Monta Ellis/25 5.00 12.00
42 Johnny O'Bryant/25 4.00 10.00
43 Roy Hibbert/25 5.00 12.00
44 Rodney Hood/25 5.00 12.00
45 Anthony Davis/25 15.00 40.00
46 Tyreke Evans/25 5.00 12.00
47 Fat Lever/25 6.00 15.00
48 Kenneth Faried/25 4.00 10.00
49 Kiki Vandeweghe/25 5.00 12.00
50 Elfrid Payton/25 6.00 15.00
51 Moses Malone/25 10.00 25.00
52 Jordan Adams/25 4.00 10.00
53 Russell Westbrook/25 15.00 40.00
54 Shabazz Napier/25 5.00 12.00
55 Bernard King/25 8.00 20.00
57 Grant Hill/25 10.00 25.00
58 Aaron Gordon/25 8.00 20.00
59 Kevin Durant/25 25.00 60.00
60 Gary Harris/25 6.00 15.00
61 Nick Young/25 4.00 10.00
62 Julius Randle/25 20.00 50.00
64 Spencer Dinwiddie/25 6.00 15.00
65 Bradley Beal/25 10.00 25.00
66 Walter Davis/25 8.00 20.00
68 Andrew Wiggins/25 20.00 50.00
70 Glenn Robinson III/25 5.00 12.00
71 Nicolas Batum/25 8.00 20.00
72 K.J. McDaniels/25 4.00 10.00
73 Steve Nash/25 12.00 30.00
74 T.J. Warren/25 6.00 15.00
75 Chandler Parsons/25 6.00 15.00
76 Jimmy Butler/25 8.00 20.00
77 Hakeem Olajuwon/25 12.00 30.00
78 Bruno Caboclo/25 5.00 12.00
79 Larry Johnson/25 12.00 30.00
80 Jabari Parker/25 5.00 12.00
81 Norm Nixon/25 5.00 12.00
83 Terry Cummings/25 5.00 12.00
84 Tyler Ennis/25 4.00 10.00
85 Damian Lillard/25 15.00 40.00
86 Xavier McDaniel/25 6.00 15.00
87 Jeff Hornacek/25 5.00 12.00
88 C.J. Wilcox/25 4.00 10.00
89 LeBron James/25 50.00 120.00
90 James Ennis/25 4.00 10.00
91 Patrick Ewing/25 20.00 50.00
92 Marcus Smart/25 15.00 40.00
93 Thaddeus Young/25 4.00 10.00
94 Zach LaVine/25 25.00 60.00
95 Danny Ainge/25 6.00 15.00
96 Kirk Hinrich/25 5.00 12.00
97 Joakim Noah/25 6.00 15.00
98 Cleanthony Early/25 4.00 10.00
99 Anderson Varejao/25 4.00 10.00
100 James Young/25 4.00 10.00

2015-16 Panini Luxe Autographs

PRINT RUNS B/WN 34-75 COPIES PER
EXCHANGE DEADLINE 10/20/2017
1 Karl-Anthony Towns/75 75.00 200.00
2 D'Angelo Russell/75 20.00 50.00
3 Jahlil Okafor/75 6.00 15.00
4 Emmanuel Mudiay/49 6.00 15.00
5 Kristaps Porzingis/49 60.00 150.00
6 Mario Hezonja/49 6.00 15.00
7 Justise Winslow/49 8.00 20.00
8 Willie Cauley-Stein/49 6.00 15.00
9 Stanley Johnson/49 6.00 15.00
10 Frank Kaminsky/49 6.00 15.00
11 Devin Booker/49 200.00 500.00
12 Myles Turner/49 20.00 50.00
13 Jerian Grant/49 5.00 12.00
14 Trey Lyles/49 6.00 15.00
15 Nemanja Bjelica/49 8.00 20.00
16 Cameron Payne/75 8.00 20.00
17 Delon Wright/75 6.00 15.00
18 Rashad Vaughn/75 5.00 12.00
19 Sam Dekker/75 5.00 12.00
20 Kelly Oubre Jr./75 15.00 40.00
21 Terry Rozier/75 20.00 50.00
22 Rondae Hollis-Jefferson/75 6.00 15.00
23 Nikola Jokic/75 1,000.00 2,000.00
24 Bobby Portis/75 12.00 30.00
25 Kevon Looney/75 15.00 40.00
26 Justin Anderson/75 5.00 12.00
27 Jarell Martin/75 5.00 12.00
28 R.J. Hunter/75 5.00 12.00
29 Anthony Brown/75 5.00 12.00
30 Raul Neto/75 5.00 12.00
31 Jordan Mickey/75 5.00 12.00
32 Montrezl Harrell/75 15.00 40.00
33 Larry Nance Jr./75 10.00 25.00
34 Walter Tavares/75 5.00 12.00
35 Josh Richardson/75 8.00 20.00
36 Norman Powell/75 10.00 25.00
37 Jonathon Simmons/75 6.00 15.00
38 Joe Young/75 5.00 12.00
39 Duje Dukan/75 5.00 12.00
41 Kobe Bryant/35 800.00 1,500.00
42 Chris Paul/35 40.00 100.00
43 Carmelo Anthony/35 40.00 100.00
44 Larry Bird/35 100.00 250.00
45 Julius Erving/35 50.00 120.00
46 Anthony Davis/35 50.00 120.00
47 Kyrie Irving/35 40.00 100.00
48 Alonzo Mourning/35 40.00 100.00
49 John Wall/35 15.00 40.00
50 Jabari Parker/35 5.00 12.00
51 Clyde Drexler/34 30.00 80.00
52 Chris Bosh/49 30.00 80.00
53 Tony Parker/49 30.00 80.00
54 Tracy McGrady/49 125.00 300.00
55 Dominique Wilkins/49 30.00 80.00
56 Victor Oladipo/49 6.00 15.00
57 Anfernee Hardaway/49 60.00 150.00
58 Harrison Barnes/49 6.00 15.00
59 Larry Brown/49 20.00 50.00
60 Andre Drummond/49 8.00 20.00
61 Steve Kerr/49 8.00 20.00
62 Walt Frazier/49 20.00 50.00
63 Byron Scott/49 10.00 25.00
64 Jared Sullinger/49 5.00 12.00
65 Gail Goodrich/49 8.00 20.00
66 Dave Cowens/49 10.00 25.00
67 Robert Parish/49 10.00 25.00
68 Frank Ramsey/49 10.00 25.00
69 Calvin Murphy/49 6.00 15.00
70 Joe Dumars/49 10.00 25.00
71 Bill Walton/49 25.00 60.00
72 Mark Jackson/49 6.00 15.00
73 Mike Conley/49 6.00 15.00
74 Gordon Hayward/49 8.00 20.00
75 Nikola Mirotic/49 5.00 12.00
76 Danny Green/49 6.00 15.00
77 Chuck Person/49 6.00 15.00
78 Michael Cooper/49 6.00 15.00
79 Wesley Matthews/49 5.00 12.00
80 Al-Farouq Aminu/49 5.00 12.00
81 Zach LaVine/49 75.00 200.00
82 Bob McAdoo/45 10.00 25.00
83 Kenny Walker/49 5.00 12.00
84 George McGinnis/49 8.00 20.00
85 Marques Johnson/49 8.00 20.00
86 A.C. Green/49 8.00 20.00
87 Mitch Richmond/49 10.00 25.00
88 Doug McDermott/49 6.00 15.00
89 Gary Harris/49 6.00 15.00
90 Giannis Antetokounmpo/49 800.00 1,500.00
91 DeMarre Carroll/75 5.00 12.00
92 Sonny Weems/75 5.00 12.00
93 Dennis Schroder/75 8.00 20.00
94 Rony Seikaly/75 6.00 15.00
95 Antonio McDyess/75 6.00 15.00
96 Bobby Jones/75 6.00 15.00
97 Ron Harper/75 8.00 20.00
98 Raef LaFrentz/75 5.00 12.00
99 Tony Delk/75 5.00 12.00
100 Paul Westphal/75 8.00 20.00

2015-16 Panini Luxe Autographs Ruby

*RUBY: .5X TO 1.2X BASIC
PRINT RUNS B/WN 25-49 COPIES PER
EXCHANGE DEADLINE 10/20/2017
EXCHANGE DEADLINE 10/20/2017

2015-16 Panini Luxe Autographs Sapphire

*SAPPHIRE: .6X TO 1.5X BASIC
PRINT RUNS B/WN 15-25 COPIES PER
NO PRICING ON QTY 15
EXCHANGE DEADLINE 10/20/2017

2015-16 Panini Luxe Crown Jewels Autographs

PRINT RUNS B/WN 35-49 COPIES PER
EXCHANGE DEADLINE 10/20/2017
2 Magic Johnson/35 30.00 80.00
3 Blake Griffin/35 20.00 50.00
5 Andrew Wiggins/35 40.00 100.00
7 Klay Thompson/49 150.00 400.00
8 Gary Payton/49 25.00 60.00
10 Wes Unseld/49 15.00 40.00
11 Nick Van Exel/49 15.00 40.00
12 Kenneth Faried/49 12.00 30.00
13 Ralph Sampson/49 6.00 15.00
14 Elfrid Payton/49 6.00 15.00
17 Dikembe Mutombo/49 20.00 50.00
19 Allan Houston/49 6.00 15.00
20 Wilson Chandler/49 6.00 15.00
21 Satch Sanders/49 8.00 20.00
24 James Young/49 5.00 12.00
25 Tony Allen/49 5.00 12.00
26 Thaddeus Young/49 5.00 12.00
27 Dino Radja/49 5.00 12.00
28 Scott Wedman/49 5.00 12.00
29 Brad Daugherty/49 6.00 15.00
31 Norm Nixon/49 6.00 15.00
35 Kenny Anderson/49 6.00 15.00
37 Cuttino Mobley/49 5.00 12.00
38 Bojan Bogdanovic/49 6.00 15.00
39 Hersey Hawkins/49 5.00 12.00
42 Tarik Black/49 5.00 12.00
43 James Ennis/49 5.00 12.00
44 Oscar Robertson/35 40.00 100.00
47 Nick Young/49 5.00 12.00
50 Enes Kanter/49 5.00 12.00

2015-16 Panini Luxe DeLuxe Autographs

STATED PRINT RUN 25 SER.#'d SETS
EXCHANGE DEADLINE 10/20/2017
1 Karl-Anthony Towns 200.00 500.00
2 D'Angelo Russell 60.00 150.00
3 Jahlil Okafor 6.00 15.00
4 Emmanuel Mudiay 6.00 15.00
5 Kristaps Porzingis 60.00 150.00
6 Mario Hezonja 6.00 15.00
7 Justise Winslow 8.00 20.00
8 Willie Cauley-Stein 6.00 15.00
9 Stanley Johnson 6.00 15.00
11 Devin Booker 400.00 800.00
12 Myles Turner 60.00 150.00
13 Jerian Grant 5.00 12.00
14 Trey Lyles 6.00 15.00
15 Nemanja Bjelica 10.00 25.00
16 Cameron Payne 20.00 50.00
18 Rashad Vaughn 5.00 12.00
19 Sam Dekker 5.00 12.00
22 Rondae Hollis-Jefferson 6.00 15.00
24 Bobby Portis 15.00 40.00
25 Kevon Looney 15.00 40.00
26 Justin Anderson 20.00 50.00
27 Jarell Martin 5.00 12.00
33 Larry Nance Jr. 15.00 40.00
35 Josh Richardson 8.00 20.00
38 Joe Young 5.00 12.00
41 Kobe Bryant 1,500.00 3,000.00
42 Chris Paul 75.00 200.00
43 Carmelo Anthony 75.00 200.00
48 Alonzo Mourning 60.00 150.00
49 John Wall 30.00 80.00
51 Clyde Drexler 40.00 100.00
55 Dominique Wilkins EXCH 20.00 50.00
56 Victor Oladipo 6.00 15.00
58 Harrison Barnes 6.00 15.00
59 Larry Brown 15.00 40.00
61 Steve Kerr 20.00 50.00
63 Byron Scott 6.00 15.00
64 Jared Sullinger 5.00 12.00
65 Gail Goodrich 15.00 40.00
68 Frank Ramsey 20.00 50.00
70 Joe Dumars 10.00 25.00
74 Gordon Hayward 10.00 25.00
75 Nikola Mirotic 10.00 25.00
76 Danny Green 20.00 50.00
82 Bob McAdoo 20.00 50.00
83 Kenny Walker 5.00 12.00
84 George McGinnis 8.00 20.00
85 Marques Johnson 6.00 15.00
88 Doug McDermott 6.00 15.00
89 Gary Harris 6.00 15.00
90 Giannis Antetokounmpo 1,500.00 3,000.00
91 DeMarre Carroll 5.00 12.00
92 Sonny Weems 5.00 12.00
93 Dennis Schroder 8.00 20.00
94 Rony Seikaly 6.00 15.00
96 Bobby Jones 6.00 15.00
98 Raef LaFrentz 5.00 12.00
99 Tony Delk 5.00 12.00

2015-16 Panini Luxe Die Cut Autographs

PRINT RUNS B/WN 35-49 COPIES PER
EXCHANGE DEADLINE 10/20/2017
1 Marcus Smart/49 10.00 25.00
2 Julius Randle/49 10.00 25.00
3 Michael Finley/49 8.00 20.00
4 Michael Carter-Williams/49 5.00 12.00
5 Cliff Hagan/49 8.00 20.00
7 Lenny Wilkens/49 8.00 20.00
8 Rick Fox/49 6.00 15.00
9 Antoine Carr/49 5.00 12.00
10 Bojan Bogdanovic/49 6.00 15.00
11 Hersey Hawkins/49 5.00 12.00
12 Joe Ingles/49 6.00 15.00
13 James Ennis/49 5.00 12.00
14 Gerald Henderson/49 5.00 12.00
15 Aaron Gordon/49 8.00 20.00
16 Dennis Rodman/49 40.00 100.00
17 Maurice Harkless/49 5.00 12.00
19 Shaquille O'Neal/35 75.00 200.00
20 Kevin Durant/35 75.00 200.00
21 Karl Malone/35 30.00 80.00
22 Jerry West/35 30.00 80.00
23 Hakeem Olajuwon/35 40.00 100.00
24 Kevin McHale/49 12.00 30.00
25 Kevin Love/49 8.00 20.00
26 Grant Hill/49 25.00 60.00
27 Terry Cummings/49 6.00 15.00
28 Keith Van Horn/49 6.00 15.00
29 Langston Galloway/49 5.00 12.00
30 Gary Neal/49 5.00 12.00
31 Kenny Anderson/49 6.00 15.00
32 Cuttino Mobley/49 5.00 12.00
33 Shabazz Napier/49 5.00 12.00
34 Tarik Black/49 5.00 12.00
35 Oscar Robertson/35 30.00 80.00
36 Isaiah Thomas/49 10.00 25.00
37 Marcin Gortat/49 5.00 12.00
38 Nik Stauskas/49 5.00 12.00
39 Scott Brooks/49 5.00 12.00
40 T.J. Warren/49 8.00 20.00
41 Norris Cole/49 5.00 12.00
42 Wayne Embry/49 5.00 12.00
43 Bill Cartwright/49 6.00 15.00
44 Dan Majerle/49 8.00 20.00
45 Timofey Mozgov/49 5.00 12.00
46 Tim Hardaway Jr./49 6.00 15.00
47 Cazzie Russell/49 6.00 15.00
48 Rafer Alston/49 5.00 12.00
49 Fred Brown/49 5.00 12.00
50 Will Perdue/49 5.00 12.00

2015-16 Panini Luxe Memorabilia

STATED PRINT RUN 99 SER.#'d SETS
1 Zach LaVine/99 10.00 25.00
2 Ricky Rubio/99 3.00 8.00
3 Avery Bradley/99 2.50 6.00
4 Marcus Smart/99 5.00 12.00
5 Evan Turner/99 2.50 6.00
6 Dirk Nowitzki/99 10.00 25.00
7 Matthew Dellavedova/99 3.00 8.00
8 Iman Shumpert/99 2.50 6.00
9 Tristan Thompson/99 2.50 6.00
10 Tiago Splitter/99 2.50 6.00
11 Deron Williams/99 3.00 8.00
12 Andre Iguodala/99 4.00 10.00
13 Gary Neal/99 2.50 6.00
14 Andre Miller/99 3.00 8.00
15 Moses Malone/99 6.00 15.00
16 Kent Bazemore/99 2.50 6.00
17 Thaddeus Young/99 2.50 6.00
18 Nene/99 2.50 6.00
19 T.J. Warren/99 4.00 10.00
20 Lou Williams/99 3.00 8.00
21 Mirza Teletovic/99 2.50 6.00
22 Kevin Love/99 4.00 10.00
23 Luol Deng/99 3.00 8.00
24 Kelly Olynyk/99 2.50 6.00
25 DeMar DeRozan/99 5.00 12.00
26 Damian Lillard/99 10.00 25.00
27 Rajon Rondo/99 5.00 12.00
28 Tobias Harris/99 3.00 8.00
29 Mike Conley/99 4.00 10.00
30 Dwyane Wade/99 6.00 15.00
31 LeBron James/99 30.00 80.00
32 Gary Payton/99 6.00 15.00
33 Serge Ibaka/99 4.00 10.00
34 Andre Drummond/99 4.00 10.00
35 Tyson Chandler/99 3.00 8.00
36 Trey Burke/99 2.50 6.00
37 Dante Exum/99 3.00 8.00
38 Klay Thompson/99 12.00 30.00
39 Russell Westbrook/99 6.00 15.00
40 Dennis Rodman/99 10.00 25.00
41 Kevin Durant/99 15.00 40.00
42 Larry Bird/99 12.00 30.00
43 Mark Jackson/99 3.00 8.00
44 Dan Issel/99 5.00 12.00
45 Chris Andersen/99 3.00 8.00
46 Glenn Robinson/99 2.50 6.00
47 Adreian Payne/99 2.50 6.00
48 Alex Len/99 2.50 6.00
49 Allen Iverson/99 12.00 30.00
50 Jordan Clarkson/99 4.00 10.00
51 Magic Johnson/99 15.00 40.00
52 Alonzo Mourning/99 6.00 15.00
53 Glen Rice/99 3.00 8.00
54 Karl Malone/99 6.00 15.00
55 Shaquille O'Neal/99 12.00 30.00
56 Blake Griffin/99 4.00 10.00
57 John Wall/99 5.00 12.00
58 Kentavious Caldwell-Pope/99 3.00 8.00
59 Ty Lawson/99 2.50 6.00
60 Tony Allen/99 2.50 6.00

2015-16 Panini Luxe Memorabilia Die Cuts Red

PRINT RUNS B/WN 85-99 COPIES PER
*BLUE/25: .75X TO 2X BASIC
1 Tim Duncan/99 12.00 30.00
2 Kevin Garnett/99 12.00 30.00
3 Jimmy Butler/99 10.00 25.00
4 Bojan Bogdanovic/99 4.00 10.00
5 Russell Westbrook/99 8.00 20.00
6 Khris Middleton/99 6.00 15.00
7 Kemba Walker/99 5.00 12.00
8 Enes Kanter/99 3.00 8.00
9 Kawhi Leonard/99 15.00 40.00
10 Thaddeus Young/99 3.00 8.00
11 Vince Carter/99 12.00 30.00
12 Festus Ezeli/99 3.00 8.00
13 Kobe Bryant/99 40.00 100.00
14 Harrison Barnes/99 4.00 10.00
15 Kyrie Irving/99 10.00 25.00
16 Joe Johnson/99 4.00 10.00
17 John Wall/99 6.00 15.00
18 Nicolas Batum/99 3.00 8.00
19 Michael Carter-Williams/99 3.00 8.00
20 Paul George/99 8.00 20.00
21 LeBron James/99 40.00 100.00
22 Shane Larkin/99 3.00 8.00
23 Zach Randolph/99 5.00 12.00
24 Andre Drummond/99 5.00 12.00
25 Iman Shumpert/99 3.00 8.00
26 Victor Oladipo/99 4.00 10.00
27 Derrick Favors/99 4.00 10.00
28 Serge Ibaka/99 4.00 10.00
29 Bradley Beal/99 6.00 15.00
30 Andrew Wiggins/99 6.00 15.00
31 Thomas Robinson/99 3.00 8.00
32 Timofey Mozgov/99 3.00 8.00
33 George Hill/99 4.00 10.00
34 Evan Fournier/99 4.00 10.00
35 Marcus Smart/99 6.00 15.00
36 Terrence Jones/99 3.00 8.00
37 Rudy Gay/99 5.00 12.00
38 Marc Gasol/99 5.00 12.00
39 Jordan Clarkson/99 5.00 12.00
40 DeMarcus Cousins/99 5.00 12.00
41 Paul Millsap/99 4.00 10.00
42 Boris Diaw/99 4.00 10.00
43 Damian Lillard/99 12.00 30.00
44 Markieff Morris/99 3.00 8.00
45 Kenneth Faried/99 4.00 10.00
46 Carmelo Anthony/99 8.00 20.00
47 Gordon Hayward/85 5.00 12.00
48 David Lee/99 3.00 8.00
49 Klay Thompson/99 12.00 30.00
50 Jose Calderon/99 3.00 8.00
51 Paul Pierce/99 8.00 20.00
52 Tony Parker/99 8.00 20.00
53 Reggie Jackson/99 4.00 10.00
54 Terrence Ross/99 4.00 10.00
55 Corey Brewer/99 3.00 8.00
56 Anthony Davis/99 12.00 30.00
57 Manu Ginobili/99 10.00 25.00
58 Draymond Green/99 6.00 15.00
59 James Harden/99 10.00 25.00
60 Shabazz Napier/99 3.00 8.00
61 C.J. McCollum/99 5.00 12.00
62 Chris Paul/99 10.00 25.00
63 Eric Gordon/99 4.00 10.00
64 Goran Dragic/99 5.00 12.00
65 Otto Porter/99 4.00 10.00
66 Dwight Howard/99 6.00 15.00
67 Stephen Curry/99 40.00 100.00
68 Greg Monroe/99 4.00 10.00
69 Chris Bosh/99 6.00 15.00
70 Gary Harris/99 4.00 10.00
71 Karl-Anthony Towns/99 20.00 50.00
72 Jahlil Okafor/99 4.00 10.00
73 D'Angelo Russell/99 12.00 30.00
74 Kristaps Porzingis/99 20.00 50.00
75 Mario Hezonja/99 4.00 10.00
76 Frank Kaminsky/99 4.00 10.00
77 Justise Winslow/99 5.00 12.00
78 Jerian Grant/99 3.00 8.00
79 Stanley Johnson/99 4.00 10.00
80 Emmanuel Mudiay/99 4.00 10.00
81 Devin Booker/99 40.00 100.00
82 Willie Cauley-Stein/99 4.00 10.00
83 Jonathon Simmons/99 4.00 10.00
84 Myles Turner/99 12.00 30.00
85 Tyus Jones/99 4.00 10.00
86 Larry Bird/99 20.00 50.00
87 Jason Kidd/99 8.00 20.00
88 Larry Johnson/99 6.00 15.00
89 Joe Smith/99 4.00 10.00
90 Danny Manning/99 4.00 10.00
91 Gary Payton/99 8.00 20.00
92 John Stockton/99 10.00 25.00
93 Scottie Pippen/99 12.00 30.00
94 David Robinson/99 10.00 25.00
95 Shaquille O'Neal/99 15.00 40.00
96 Patrick Ewing/99 8.00 20.00
97 Alonzo Mourning/99 8.00 20.00
98 Grant Hill/99 8.00 20.00
99 Hakeem Olajuwon/99 10.00 25.00
100 Karl Malone/99 8.00 20.00

2015-16 Panini Luxe Memorabilia Prime

*PRIME/17-25: .75X TO 2X BASIC
PRINT RUNS B/WN 5-25 COPIES PER
NO PRICING ON QTY 15 OR LESS

2015-16 Panini Luxe Rookie Jerseys

PRINT RUNS B/WN 30-99 COPIES PER
*PRIME/25: 1X TO 2.5X BASIC
1 Jahlil Okafor/99 2.50 6.00
2 Tyus Jones/99 2.50 6.00
3 Terry Rozier/99 8.00 20.00
4 Pat Connaughton/99 3.00 8.00
5 Norman Powell/99 4.00 10.00
6 Anthony Brown/99 2.00 5.00
7 Frank Kaminsky/99 2.50 6.00
8 Kevon Looney/99 6.00 15.00
9 Justise Winslow/99 3.00 8.00
10 Justin Anderson/99 2.00 5.00
11 Jerian Grant/99 2.00 5.00
12 Trey Lyles/99 2.50 6.00
13 Stanley Johnson/99 2.50 6.00
14 R.J. Hunter/99 2.00 5.00
15 Nikola Jokic/99 125.00 300.00
16 Bobby Portis/99 5.00 12.00
17 Emmanuel Mudiay/99 2.50 6.00
18 Marcelo Huertas/99 2.00 5.00
19 Kelly Oubre Jr./99 6.00 15.00
20 Josh Richardson/99 3.00 8.00
21 Joe Young/99 2.00 5.00
22 Walter Tavares/99 2.00 5.00
23 Sam Dekker/99 2.00 5.00
24 Raul Neto/99 2.00 5.00
25 Nemanja Bjelica/99 3.00 8.00
26 Cameron Payne/99 3.00 8.00
27 Devin Booker/99 100.00 250.00
28 Mario Hezonja/99 2.50 6.00
29 Karl-Anthony Towns/99 20.00 50.00
30 Josh Huestis/99 2.00 5.00
31 Jonathon Simmons/99 2.50 6.00
32 Willie Cauley-Stein/99 2.50 6.00
33 Rondae Hollis-Jefferson/99 2.50 6.00
34 Richaun Holmes/99 3.00 8.00
35 Myles Turner/99 8.00 20.00
36 D'Angelo Russell/99 8.00 20.00
37 Delon Wright/99 2.50 6.00
38 Montrezl Harrell/99 6.00 15.00
39 Kristaps Porzingis/30 12.00 30.00
40 Jordan Mickey/99 2.00 5.00

2015-16 Panini Luxe Rookie Jumbo Jersey Autographs

STATED PRINT RUN 35 SER.#'d SETS
EXCHANGE DEADLINE 10/20/2017
*PRIME: .6X TO 1.5X BASIC
1 Karl-Anthony Towns 100.00 250.00
2 D'Angelo Russell 15.00 40.00
3 Jahlil Okafor 5.00 12.00
4 Emmanuel Mudiay 5.00 12.00
5 Kristaps Porzingis 50.00 120.00
6 Mario Hezonja 5.00 12.00
7 Justise Winslow 6.00 15.00
8 Willie Cauley-Stein 5.00 12.00
9 Stanley Johnson 5.00 12.00
10 Tyus Jones 5.00 12.00
11 Frank Kaminsky 5.00 12.00
12 Devin Booker 400.00 800.00
13 Myles Turner 15.00 40.00
14 Jerian Grant 4.00 10.00
15 Trey Lyles 5.00 12.00
16 Cameron Payne 6.00 15.00
17 Delon Wright 5.00 12.00
18 Rashad Vaughn 4.00 10.00
19 Kelly Oubre Jr. 12.00 30.00
20 Sam Dekker 4.00 10.00
21 Terry Rozier 15.00 40.00
22 Rondae Hollis-Jefferson 5.00 12.00
23 Bobby Portis 10.00 25.00
24 Justin Anderson 4.00 10.00
25 Kevon Looney 12.00 30.00
26 Jarell Martin 4.00 10.00
27 R.J. Hunter 4.00 10.00
28 Jordan Mickey 4.00 10.00
29 Walter Tavares 4.00 10.00
30 Josh Richardson 6.00 15.00
31 Joe Young 4.00 10.00
32 Pat Connaughton 6.00 15.00
33 Rakeem Christmas 4.00 10.00

2015-16 Panini Luxe Rookie Memorabilia Autographs

STATED PRINT RUN 49 SER.#'d SETS
EXCHANGE DEADLINE 10/20/2017
*PRIME: .6X TO 1.5X BASIC
1 Karl-Anthony Towns 75.00 200.00
2 D'Angelo Russell 15.00 40.00
3 Jahlil Okafor 5.00 12.00
4 Emmanuel Mudiay 5.00 12.00
5 Kristaps Porzingis 50.00 120.00
6 Mario Hezonja 5.00 12.00
7 Justise Winslow 6.00 15.00
8 Willie Cauley-Stein 5.00 12.00
9 Stanley Johnson 5.00 12.00
10 Tyus Jones 5.00 12.00
11 Frank Kaminsky 5.00 12.00
12 Devin Booker 400.00 800.00
13 Myles Turner 15.00 40.00
14 Jerian Grant 4.00 10.00
15 Trey Lyles 5.00 12.00
16 Cameron Payne 6.00 15.00
17 Delon Wright 5.00 12.00
18 Rashad Vaughn 4.00 10.00
19 Kelly Oubre Jr. 12.00 30.00
20 Sam Dekker 4.00 10.00
21 Terry Rozier 15.00 40.00
22 Rondae Hollis-Jefferson 5.00 12.00
23 Bobby Portis 10.00 25.00
24 Justin Anderson 4.00 10.00
25 Kevon Looney 12.00 30.00
26 Jarell Martin 4.00 10.00
27 R.J. Hunter 4.00 10.00
28 Jordan Mickey 4.00 10.00
29 Walter Tavares 4.00 10.00
30 Josh Richardson 6.00 15.00
31 Joe Young 4.00 10.00
32 Pat Connaughton 6.00 15.00
33 Rakeem Christmas 4.00 10.00

2017-18 Panini Majestic

301 Lonzo Ball 2.00 5.00
302 T.J. Leaf .50 1.25
303 Ante Zizic .60 1.50
304 Donovan Mitchell 5.00 12.00
305 De'Aaron Fox 4.00 10.00
306 Jarrett Allen 1.25 3.00
307 Jayson Tatum 6.00 15.00
308 Justin Jackson .50 1.25
309 Josh Jackson .60 1.50
310 Milos Teodosic .60 1.50
311 Malik Monk 2.00 5.00
312 Tony Bradley .50 1.25
313 Bogdan Bogdanovic 1.25 3.00
314 Frank Jackson .50 1.25
315 Dennis Smith Jr. .60 1.50
316 Jordan Bell .50 1.25
317 Jonathan Isaac 1.25 3.00
318 Kyle Kuzma 2.00 5.00
319 Lauri Markkanen 3.00 8.00
320 Semi Ojeleye .60 1.50
321 Markelle Fultz 1.25 3.00
322 Tyler Lydon .50 1.25
323 D.J. Wilson .50 1.25
324 Harry Giles .50 1.25
325 Frank Ntilikina .60 1.50

2017-18 Panini Majestic Blue

*BLUE: .5X TO 1.2X BASIC
STATED PRINT RUN 199 SER.#'d SETS

2017-18 Panini Majestic Red

*RED: .5X TO 1.2X BASIC
STATED PRINT RUN 249 SER.#'d SETS

2017-18 Panini Majestic Silver

*SILVER: .6X TO 1.5X BASIC
STATED PRINT RUN 99 SER.#'d SETS

2012-13 Panini Marquee

1 Kobe Bryant 8.00 20.00
2 Kevin Durant 2.00 5.00
3 LeBron James 4.00 10.00
4 Goran Dragic .50 1.25
5 Chris Paul 1.00 2.50
6 Derrick Rose .75 2.00
7 Dirk Nowitzki 1.25 3.00
8 Kevin Love .50 1.25
9 Amare Stoudemire .50 1.25
10 Dwight Howard .60 1.50
11 Greg Monroe .30 .75
12 Andrew Bogut .40 1.00
13 Daniel Gibson .30 .75
14 James Harden 1.00 2.50
15 John Wall .60 1.50
16 Deron Williams .40 1.00
17 Blake Griffin .50 1.25
18 Ben Gordon .40 1.00
19 David West .40 1.00
20 Eric Gordon .40 1.00
21 Andrew Bynum .30 .75
22 Serge Ibaka .40 1.00
23 Dwyane Wade 1.00 2.50
24 Paul Pierce .75 2.00
25 Paul Millsap .40 1.00
26 Brandon Jennings .30 .75
27 DeAndre Jordan .40 1.00
28 Andrea Bargnani .30 .75
29 Stephen Jackson .30 .75
30 DeMarcus Cousins .50 1.25
31 J.J. Hickson .30 .75
32 Luol Deng .40 1.00
33 Stephen Curry 4.00 10.00
34 Joe Johnson .40 1.00
35 Andre Iguodala .50 1.25
36 Roy Hibbert .40 1.00
37 Manu Ginobili 1.00 2.50
38 Carmelo Anthony 1.00 2.50
39 J.J. Redick .50 1.25
40 Tyrus Thomas .30 .75
41 Kevin Garnett 1.25 3.00
42 Rudy Gay .50 1.25
43 Rodney Stuckey .30 .75
44 Ryan Anderson .30 .75
45 Al Horford .50 1.25
46 Joakim Noah .40 1.00
47 O.J. Mayo .30 .75
48 Ray Allen .75 2.00
49 Evan Turner .30 .75
50 Jeremy Lin .75 2.00
51 Danny Granger .30 .75
52 Ricky Rubio .40 1.00
53 Anderson Varejao .30 .75
54 Ersan Ilyasova .30 .75
55 Nene Hilario .40 1.00
56 Tyson Chandler .40 1.00
57 Tony Parker .75 2.00
58 Kevin Martin .40 1.00
59 DeMar DeRozan .60 1.50
60 Wesley Matthews .30 .75
61 JaVale McGee .40 1.00
62 Marc Gasol .50 1.25
63 Jason Terry .40 1.00
64 Al Jefferson .30 .75
65 Grant Hill .75 2.00
66 Luc Mbah a Moute .30 .75
67 Carl Landry .30 .75
68 Charlie Villanueva .30 .75
69 Steve Nash 1.00 2.50
70 Daequan Cook .30 .75
71 Hedo Turkoglu .40 1.00
72 Brook Lopez .40 1.00
73 Andrei Kirilenko .40 1.00
74 Al-Farouq Aminu .30 .75
75 Josh Smith .30 .75
76 Tim Duncan 1.25 3.00
77 Gordon Hayward .50 1.25
78 Carlos Boozer .40 1.00
79 David Lee .30 .75
80 Tyreke Evans .40 1.00
81 Darren Collison .30 .75
82 Rajon Rondo .60 1.50
83 Emeka Okafor .40 1.00
84 Chris Bosh .60 1.50
85 Marcin Gortat .30 .75
86 Ty Lawson .30 .75
87 LaMarcus Aldridge .50 1.25
88 Jason Kidd .75 2.00
89 Danny Green .40 1.00
90 Luis Scola .40 1.00
91 Pau Gasol .75 2.00
92 Ed Davis .30 .75
93 Zach Randolph .60 1.50
94 Paul George .75 2.00
95 Vince Carter 1.00 2.50
96 Gerald Wallace .40 1.00
97 Arron Afflalo .30 .75
98 Louis Williams .40 1.00
99 Travis Outlaw .40 1.00
100 Thaddeus Young .30 .75
101 Pete Maravich 2.00 5.00
102 Wilt Chamberlain 3.00 8.00
103 Bill Russell 3.00 8.00
104 Patrick Ewing 1.50 4.00
105 Jerry West 2.00 5.00
106 Larry Bird 3.00 8.00
107 Magic Johnson 3.00 8.00
108 Bob Cousy 1.50 4.00
109 George Mikan 3.00 8.00
110 Julius Erving 2.50 6.00
111 Ralph Sampson .75 2.00
112 David Thompson 1.00 2.50
113 Hakeem Olajuwon 2.00 5.00
114 Kareem Abdul-Jabbar 3.00 8.00
115 Bill Walton 1.50 4.00
116 Isiah Thomas 2.00 5.00
117 Mookie Blaylock .60 1.50
118 Clyde Lovellette 1.25 3.00
119 Scottie Pippen 2.50 6.00
120 Shaquille O'Neal 3.00 8.00
121 Chris Webber 1.00 2.50
122 Jalen Rose .75 2.00
123 Elvin Hayes 1.25 3.00
124 Karl Malone 1.50 4.00
125 Drazen Petrovic 1.00 2.50
126 Calvin Murphy .75 2.00
127 John Stockton 2.00 5.00
128 Doug Collins 1.00 2.50
129 Sean Elliott .75 2.00
130 David Robinson 1.50 4.00
131 Dolph Schayes 1.25 3.00
132 Dominique Wilkins 1.25 3.00
133 Jamal Mashburn .75 2.00
134 Danny Manning .75 2.00
135 Elgin Baylor 2.50 6.00
136 Greg Anthony .60 1.50
137 Cedric Maxwell .60 1.50
138 Mitch Richmond 1.00 2.50
139 Dennis Rodman 2.50 6.00
140 Rolando Blackman .75 2.00
141 Glen Rice .75 2.00
142 Clyde Drexler 1.50 4.00
143 Jerry Lucas 1.00 2.50
144 Oscar Robertson 2.00 5.00
145 Gary Payton 1.25 3.00
146 Kevin McHale 1.25 3.00
147 Rex Chapman .75 2.00
148 Christian Laettner 1.00 2.50
149 Antoine Walker .75 2.00
150 Allen Iverson 1.50 4.00
151 Damian Lillard RC 30.00 80.00
152 Anthony Davis RC 40.00 100.00
153 Dion Waiters RC .60 1.50
154 Bradley Beal RC 4.00 10.00
155 Michael Kidd-Gilchrist RC .60 1.50
156 Alexey Shved RC .50 1.25
157 Harrison Barnes RC 1.00 2.50
158 Jonas Valanciunas RC 2.00 5.00
159 Kyle Singler RC .50 1.25
160 Tyler Zeller RC .50 1.25
161 Kyrie Irving RC 25.00 60.00
162 Kemba Walker RC 2.00 5.00
163 Klay Thompson RC 20.00 50.00
164 Brandon Knight RC .60 1.50
165 Kenneth Faried RC .60 1.50
166 Kawhi Leonard RC 30.00 80.00
167 Nikola Vucevic RC 2.00 5.00
168 Markieff Morris RC .75 2.00

169 Derrick Williams RC .50 1.25
170 Jimmer Fredette RC .75 2.00
171 Austin Rivers RC .75 2.00
172 Jae Crowder RC 1.00 2.50
173 Jeff Taylor RC .50 1.25
174 Andrew Nicholson RC .50 1.25
175 Brian Roberts RC .50 1.25
176 Andre Drummond RC 1.25 3.00
177 Jared Sullinger RC .50 1.25
178 Terrence Ross RC 1.25 3.00
179 John Henson RC .60 1.50
180 Thomas Robinson RC .50 1.25
181 Marcus Morris RC .75 2.00
182 Tristan Thompson RC .75 2.00
183 Isaiah Thomas RC 1.00 2.50
184 Tobias Harris RC 1.50 4.00
185 MarShon Brooks RC .50 1.25
186 Enes Kanter RC .75 2.00
187 Lavoy Allen RC .50 1.25
188 Jimmy Butler RC 5.00 12.00
189 Norris Cole RC .50 1.25
190 Bismack Biyombo RC .60 1.50
191 Doron Lamb RC .50 1.25
192 Meyers Leonard RC .60 1.50
193 Bernard James RC .50 1.25
194 Chris Copeland RC .50 1.25
195 Evan Fournier RC .75 2.00
196 Maurice Harkless RC .60 1.50
197 Draymond Green RC 3.00 8.00
198 Kyle O'Quinn RC .60 1.50
199 Mirza Teletovic RC .60 1.50
200 Festus Ezeli RC .50 1.25
201 Jan Vesely RC .50 1.25
202 Lance Thomas RC .50 1.25
203 Alec Burks RC .75 2.00
204 Ivan Johnson RC .50 1.25
205 Jordan Hamilton RC .50 1.25
206 Kent Bazemore RC .75 2.00
207 Greg Stiemsma RC .50 1.25
208 Reggie Jackson RC .75 2.00
209 Gustavo Ayon RC .50 1.25
210 Charles Jenkins RC .50 1.25
211 Nando De Colo RC .50 1.25
212 Pablo Prigioni RC .50 1.25
213 Kim English RC .50 1.25
214 DeQuan Jones RC .50 1.25
215 Darius Miller RC .60 1.50
216 Luke Zeller RC .50 1.25
217 Perry Jones RC .50 1.25
218 Kendall Marshall RC .60 1.50
219 Tyshawn Taylor RC .50 1.25
220 Terrence Jones RC .50 1.25
221 Chandler Parsons RC .60 1.50
222 Will Barton RC 1.00 2.50
223 Josh Selby RC .50 1.25
224 DeAndre Liggins RC .50 1.25
225 Iman Shumpert RC .60 1.50
226 Nolan Smith RC .50 1.25
227 Malcolm Lee RC .50 1.25
228 Marquis Teague RC .50 1.25
229 Miles Plumlee RC .50 1.25
230 Orlando Johnson RC .50 1.25
231 Damian Lillard RC 12.00 30.00
232 Anthony Davis RC 12.00 30.00
233 Dion Waiters RC .60 1.50
234 Bradley Beal RC 4.00 10.00
235 Michael Kidd-Gilchrist RC .60 1.50
236 Alexey Shved RC .50 1.25
237 Harrison Barnes RC 1.00 2.50
238 Jonas Valanciunas RC 1.00 2.50
239 Kyle Singler RC .50 1.25
240 Tyler Zeller RC .50 1.25
241 Kyrie Irving RC 5.00 12.00
242 Kemba Walker RC 2.00 5.00
243 Klay Thompson RC 20.00 50.00
244 Brandon Knight RC .60 1.50
245 Kenneth Faried RC .60 1.50
246 Kawhi Leonard RC 8.00 20.00
247 Nikola Vucevic RC 2.00 5.00
248 Markieff Morris RC .75 2.00
249 Derrick Williams RC .50 1.25
250 Jimmer Fredette RC .75 2.00
251 Austin Rivers RC .75 2.00
252 Jae Crowder RC 1.00 2.50
253 Jeff Taylor RC .50 1.25
254 Andrew Nicholson RC .50 1.25
255 Brian Roberts RC .50 1.25
256 Andre Drummond RC 1.25 3.00
257 Jared Sullinger RC .50 1.25
258 Terrence Ross RC 1.25 3.00
259 John Henson RC .60 1.50
260 Thomas Robinson RC .50 1.25
261 Marcus Morris RC .75 2.00
262 Tristan Thompson RC .75 2.00
263 Isaiah Thomas RC 1.00 2.50
264 Tobias Harris RC 1.50 4.00
265 MarShon Brooks RC .50 1.25
266 Enes Kanter RC .75 2.00
267 Lavoy Allen RC .50 1.25
268 Jimmy Butler RC 5.00 12.00
269 Norris Cole RC .50 1.25
270 Bismack Biyombo RC .60 1.50
271 Doron Lamb RC .50 1.25
272 Meyers Leonard RC .60 1.50
273 Bernard James RC .50 1.25
274 Chris Copeland RC .50 1.25
275 Evan Fournier RC .75 2.00
276 Maurice Harkless RC .60 1.50
277 Draymond Green RC 3.00 8.00
278 Kyle O'Quinn RC .60 1.50
279 Mirza Teletovic RC .60 1.50
280 Festus Ezeli RC .50 1.25
281 Jan Vesely RC .50 1.25
282 Lance Thomas RC .50 1.25
283 Alec Burks RC .75 2.00
284 Ivan Johnson RC .50 1.25
285 Jordan Hamilton RC .50 1.25
286 Kent Bazemore RC .75 2.00
287 Greg Stiemsma RC .50 1.25
288 Reggie Jackson RC .75 2.00
289 Gustavo Ayon RC .50 1.25
290 Charles Jenkins RC .50 1.25
291 Nando De Colo RC .50 1.25
292 Pablo Prigioni RC .50 1.25
293 Kim English RC .50 1.25
294 DeQuan Jones RC .50 1.25
295 Darius Miller RC .60 1.50
296 Luke Zeller RC .50 1.25
297 Perry Jones RC .50 1.25
298 Kendall Marshall RC .50 1.25
299 Tyshawn Taylor RC .50 1.25
300 Terrence Jones RC .50 1.25
301 Chandler Parsons RC .60 1.50
302 Will Barton RC 1.00 2.50
303 Josh Selby RC .50 1.25
304 DeAndre Liggins RC .50 1.25
305 Iman Shumpert RC .60 1.50
306 Nolan Smith RC .50 1.25
307 Malcolm Lee RC .50 1.25
308 Marquis Teague RC .50 1.25
309 Miles Plumlee RC .50 1.25
310 Orlando Johnson RC .50 1.25
311 Damian Lillard RC 10.00 25.00
312 Anthony Davis RC 12.00 30.00
313 Dion Waiters RC .60 1.50
314 Bradley Beal RC 4.00 10.00
315 Michael Kidd-Gilchrist RC .60 1.50
316 Alexey Shved RC .50 1.25
317 Harrison Barnes RC 1.00 2.50
318 Jonas Valanciunas RC 1.00 2.50
319 Kyle Singler RC .50 1.25
320 Tyler Zeller RC .50 1.25
321 Kyrie Irving RC 5.00 12.00
322 Kemba Walker RC 2.00 5.00
323 Klay Thompson RC 15.00 40.00
324 Brandon Knight RC .60 1.50
325 Kenneth Faried RC .60 1.50
326 Kawhi Leonard RC 12.00 30.00
327 Nikola Vucevic RC 2.00 5.00
328 Markieff Morris RC .75 2.00
329 Derrick Williams RC .50 1.25
330 Jimmer Fredette RC .75 2.00
331 Austin Rivers RC .75 2.00
332 Jae Crowder RC 1.00 2.50
333 Jeff Taylor RC .50 1.25
334 Andrew Nicholson RC .50 1.25
335 Brian Roberts RC .50 1.25
336 Andre Drummond RC 1.25 3.00
337 Jared Sullinger RC .50 1.25
338 Terrence Ross RC 1.25 3.00
339 John Henson RC .60 1.50
340 Thomas Robinson RC .50 1.25
341 Marcus Morris RC .75 2.00
342 Tristan Thompson RC .75 2.00
343 Isaiah Thomas RC 1.00 2.50
344 Tobias Harris RC 1.50 4.00
345 MarShon Brooks RC .50 1.25
346 Enes Kanter RC .75 2.00
347 Lavoy Allen RC .50 1.25
348 Jimmy Butler RC 5.00 12.00
349 Norris Cole RC .50 1.25
350 Bismack Biyombo RC .60 1.50
351 Doron Lamb RC .50 1.25
352 Meyers Leonard RC .60 1.50
353 Bernard James RC .50 1.25
354 Chris Copeland RC .50 1.25
355 Evan Fournier RC .75 2.00
356 Maurice Harkless RC .60 1.50
357 Draymond Green RC 3.00 8.00
358 Kyle O'Quinn RC .60 1.50
359 Mirza Teletovic RC .60 1.50
360 Festus Ezeli RC .50 1.25
361 Jan Vesely RC .50 1.25
362 Lance Thomas RC .50 1.25
363 Alec Burks RC .75 2.00
364 Ivan Johnson RC .50 1.25
365 Jordan Hamilton RC .50 1.25
366 Kent Bazemore RC .75 2.00
367 Greg Stiemsma RC .50 1.25
368 Reggie Jackson RC .75 2.00
369 Gustavo Ayon RC .50 1.25
370 Charles Jenkins RC .50 1.25
371 Nando De Colo RC .50 1.25
372 Pablo Prigioni RC .50 1.25
373 Kim English RC .50 1.25
374 DeQuan Jones RC .50 1.25
375 Darius Miller RC .60 1.50
376 Luke Zeller RC .50 1.25
377 Perry Jones RC .50 1.25
378 Kendall Marshall RC .60 1.50
379 Tyshawn Taylor RC .50 1.25
380 Terrence Jones RC .50 1.25
381 Chandler Parsons RC .60 1.50
382 Will Barton RC 1.00 2.50
383 Josh Selby RC .50 1.25
384 DeAndre Liggins RC .50 1.25
385 Iman Shumpert RC .60 1.50
386 Nolan Smith RC .50 1.25
387 Malcolm Lee RC .50 1.25
388 Marquis Teague RC .50 1.25
389 Miles Plumlee RC .50 1.25
390 Orlando Johnson RC .50 1.25
391 Damian Lillard RC 30.00 80.00
392 Anthony Davis RC 30.00 80.00
393 Dion Waiters RC 2.00 5.00
394 Bradley Beal RC 12.00 30.00
395 Michael Kidd-Gilchrist RC 2.00 5.00
396 Alexey Shved RC 1.50 4.00
397 Harrison Barnes RC 3.00 8.00
398 Jonas Valanciunas RC 3.00 8.00
399 Kyle Singler RC 1.50 4.00
400 Tyler Zeller RC 1.50 4.00
401 Kyrie Irving RC 15.00 40.00
402 Kemba Walker RC 6.00 15.00
403 Klay Thompson RC 20.00 50.00
404 Brandon Knight RC 2.00 5.00
405 Kenneth Faried RC 2.00 5.00
406 Kawhi Leonard RC 30.00 80.00
407 Nikola Vucevic RC 6.00 15.00
408 Markieff Morris RC 2.50 6.00
409 Derrick Williams RC 1.50 4.00
410 Jimmer Fredette RC 2.50 6.00
411 Austin Rivers RC 2.50 6.00
412 Jae Crowder RC 3.00 8.00
413 Jeff Taylor RC 1.50 4.00
414 Andrew Nicholson RC 1.50 4.00
415 Brian Roberts RC 1.50 4.00
416 Andre Drummond RC 4.00 10.00
417 Jared Sullinger RC 1.50 4.00
418 Terrence Ross RC 4.00 10.00
419 John Henson RC 2.00 5.00
420 Thomas Robinson RC 1.50 4.00
421 Marcus Morris RC 2.50 6.00
422 Tristan Thompson RC 2.50 6.00
423 Isaiah Thomas RC 3.00 8.00
424 Tobias Harris RC 5.00 12.00
425 MarShon Brooks RC 1.50 4.00
426 Enes Kanter RC 2.50 6.00
427 Lavoy Allen RC 1.50 4.00
428 Jimmy Butler RC 15.00 40.00
429 Norris Cole RC 1.50 4.00
430 Bismack Biyombo RC 2.00 5.00
431 Doron Lamb RC 1.50 4.00
432 Meyers Leonard RC 2.00 5.00
433 Bernard James RC 1.50 4.00
434 Chris Copeland RC 1.50 4.00
435 Evan Fournier RC 2.50 6.00
436 Maurice Harkless RC 2.00 5.00
437 Draymond Green RC 10.00 25.00
438 Kyle O'Quinn RC 2.00 5.00
439 Mirza Teletovic RC 2.00 5.00
440 Festus Ezeli RC 1.50 4.00
441 Jan Vesely RC 1.50 4.00
442 Lance Thomas RC 1.50 4.00
443 Alec Burks RC 2.50 6.00
444 Ivan Johnson RC 1.50 4.00
445 Jordan Hamilton RC 1.50 4.00
446 Kent Bazemore RC 2.50 6.00
447 Greg Stiemsma RC 1.50 4.00
448 Reggie Jackson RC 2.50 6.00
449 Gustavo Ayon RC 1.50 4.00
450 Charles Jenkins RC 1.50 4.00
451 Nando De Colo RC 1.50 4.00
452 Pablo Prigioni RC 1.50 4.00
453 Kim English RC 1.50 4.00
454 DeQuan Jones RC 1.50 4.00
455 Darius Miller RC 2.00 5.00
456 Luke Zeller RC 1.50 4.00
457 Perry Jones RC 1.50 4.00
458 Kendall Marshall RC 1.50 4.00
459 Tyshawn Taylor RC 1.50 4.00
460 Terrence Jones RC 1.50 4.00
461 Damian Lillard RC 12.00 30.00
462 Anthony Davis RC 12.00 30.00
463 Dion Waiters RC .75 2.00
464 Bradley Beal RC 5.00 12.00
465 Michael Kidd-Gilchrist RC .75 2.00
466 Alexey Shved RC .60 1.50
467 Harrison Barnes RC 1.25 3.00
468 Jonas Valanciunas RC 1.25 3.00
469 Kyle Singler RC .60 1.50
470 Tyler Zeller RC .60 1.50
471 Kyrie Irving RC 6.00 15.00
472 Kemba Walker RC 2.50 6.00
473 Klay Thompson RC 15.00 40.00
474 Brandon Knight RC .75 2.00
475 Kenneth Faried RC .75 2.00
476 Kawhi Leonard RC 12.00 30.00
477 Nikola Vucevic RC 2.50 6.00
478 Markieff Morris RC 1.00 2.50
479 Derrick Williams RC .60 1.50
480 Jimmer Fredette RC 1.00 2.50
481 Austin Rivers RC 1.00 2.50
482 Jae Crowder RC 1.25 3.00
483 Jeff Taylor RC .60 1.50
484 Andrew Nicholson RC .60 1.50
485 Brian Roberts RC .60 1.50
486 Andre Drummond RC 1.50 4.00
487 Jared Sullinger RC .60 1.50
488 Terrence Ross RC 1.50 4.00
489 John Henson RC .75 2.00
490 Thomas Robinson RC .60 1.50
491 Marcus Morris RC 1.00 2.50
492 Tristan Thompson RC 1.00 2.50
493 Isaiah Thomas RC 1.25 3.00
494 Tobias Harris RC 2.00 5.00
495 MarShon Brooks RC .60 1.50
496 Enes Kanter RC 1.00 2.50
497 Lavoy Allen RC .60 1.50
498 Jimmy Butler RC 6.00 15.00
499 Norris Cole RC .60 1.50
500 Bismack Biyombo RC .75 2.00
501 Doron Lamb RC .60 1.50
502 Meyers Leonard RC .75 2.00
503 Bernard James RC .60 1.50
504 Chris Copeland RC .60 1.50
505 Evan Fournier RC 1.00 2.50
506 Maurice Harkless RC .75 2.00
507 Draymond Green RC 4.00 10.00
508 Kyle O'Quinn RC .75 2.00
509 Mirza Teletovic RC .75 2.00
510 Festus Ezeli RC .60 1.50
511 Jan Vesely RC .60 1.50
512 Lance Thomas RC .60 1.50
513 Alec Burks RC 1.00 2.50
514 Ivan Johnson RC .60 1.50
515 Jordan Hamilton RC .60 1.50
516 Kent Bazemore RC 1.00 2.50
517 Greg Stiemsma RC .60 1.50
518 Reggie Jackson RC 1.00 2.50
519 Gustavo Ayon RC .60 1.50
520 Charles Jenkins RC .60 1.50
521 Nando De Colo RC .60 1.50
522 Pablo Prigioni RC .60 1.50
523 Kim English RC .60 1.50
524 DeQuan Jones RC .60 1.50
525 Darius Miller RC .75 2.00
526 Luke Zeller RC .60 1.50
527 Perry Jones RC .60 1.50
528 Kendall Marshall RC .60 1.50
529 Tyshawn Taylor RC .60 1.50
530 Terrence Jones RC .60 1.50
531 Chandler Parsons RC .75 2.00
532 Will Barton RC 1.25 3.00
533 Josh Selby RC .60 1.50
534 DeAndre Liggins RC .60 1.50
535 Iman Shumpert RC .75 2.00
536 Nolan Smith RC .60 1.50
537 Malcolm Lee RC .60 1.50
538 Marquis Teague RC .60 1.50
539 Miles Plumlee RC .60 1.50
540 Orlando Johnson RC .60 1.50

2012-13 Panini Marquee All-Rookie Team Laser Cut

COMPLETE SET (20) 30.00 60.00
1 Kareem Abdul-Jabbar 3.00 8.00
2 Larry Bird 3.00 8.00
3 Wilt Chamberlain 3.00 8.00
4 Kyrie Irving 6.00 15.00
5 Blake Griffin 1.00 2.50
6 Patrick Ewing 1.50 4.00
7 Shaquille O'Neal 3.00 8.00
8 Grant Hill 1.50 4.00
9 Jason Kidd 1.50 4.00
10 Allen Iverson 1.50 4.00
11 LeBron James 8.00 20.00
12 Kevin Durant 4.00 10.00
13 Chris Paul 2.00 5.00
14 Vince Carter 2.00 5.00
15 Tim Duncan 2.50 6.00
16 David Robinson 1.50 4.00
17 Elgin Baylor 2.50 6.00
18 Derrick Rose 1.50 4.00
19 Amare Stoudemire 1.00 2.50
20 Chris Webber 1.00 2.50

2012-13 Panini Marquee Champions

COMPLETE SET (20) 25.00 60.00
COMMON CARD .75 2.00
SEMISTARS 1.00 2.50
UNLISTED STARS 1.25 3.00
1 Kobe Bryant 10.00 25.00
2 Bill Russell 4.00 10.00
3 Tim Duncan 3.00 8.00
4 Larry Bird 4.00 10.00
5 Scottie Pippen 3.00 8.00
6 Dirk Nowitzki 3.00 8.00
7 LeBron James 10.00 25.00
8 Hakeem Olajuwon 2.50 6.00
9 Kareem Abdul-Jabbar 4.00 10.00
10 Dwyane Wade 2.50 6.00
11 Isiah Thomas 2.50 6.00
12 David Robinson 2.50 6.00
13 Kevin Garnett 3.00 8.00
14 James Worthy 2.00 5.00
15 Moses Malone 2.00 5.00
16 Dennis Rodman 3.00 8.00
17 John Havlicek 2.50 6.00
18 Horace Grant 1.25 3.00
19 Magic Johnson 4.00 10.00
20 Bill Walton 2.00 5.00

2012-13 Panini Marquee Coach's Autographs

PRINT RUNS B/WN 10-299 COPIES PER
NO JACKSON PRICING AVAILABLE
EXCHANGE DEADLINE 10/10/2014
1 Larry Bird/49 75.00 200.00
2 Bill Russell/46 600.00 1,200.00
3 Bill Sharman/25 40.00 100.00
4 Kiki VanDeWeghe/299 EXCH 4.00 10.00
5 Dave Cowens/25 10.00 25.00
6 Doc Rivers/25 15.00 40.00
7 Don Nelson/25 15.00 40.00
8 Vinny Del Negro/25 15.00 40.00
9 Maurice Cheeks/299 4.00 10.00
10 George Karl/25 40.00 100.00
11 Harry Gallatin/199 5.00 12.00
12 Isiah Thomas/25 40.00 100.00
13 Pat Riley/49 30.00 80.00
15 Jerry West/49 40.00 100.00
18 Kevin McHale/25 12.00 30.00
19 Lenny Wilkens/25 12.00 30.00
20 Magic Johnson/49 EXCH 75.00 200.00
21 Paul Westphal/299 EXCH 12.00 30.00
23 Byron Scott/25 25.00 60.00
24 Al Attles/299 4.00 10.00
25 Mark Jackson/25 12.00 30.00

2012-13 Panini Marquee Election Night Autographs

PRINT RUNS B/WN 10-299 COPIES PER
EXCHANGE DEADLINE 10/10/2014
1 Kareem Abdul-Jabbar/49 75.00 200.00
3 Magic Johnson/49 75.00 200.00
4 David Robinson/49 30.00 80.00
5 Hakeem Olajuwon/49 40.00 100.00
6 George Gervin/25 15.00 40.00
7 Scottie Pippen/49 60.00 150.00
8 James Worthy/49 15.00 40.00
9 Clyde Drexler/49 20.00 50.00
10 Larry Bird/49 75.00 200.00
11 Bob Lanier/25 20.00 50.00
12 Tom Heinsohn/199 20.00 50.00
13 Bill Russell/49 400.00 800.00
14 Jamaal Wilkes/199 8.00 20.00
15 Joe Dumars/25 10.00 25.00
16 Julius Erving/49 40.00 100.00
17 Robert Parish/25 20.00 50.00
18 Adrian Dantley/199 4.00 10.00
19 Bob McAdoo/199 10.00 25.00
20 Alex English/199 6.00 15.00
21 Jerry West/49 40.00 100.00
22 Artis Gilmore/25 20.00 50.00
24 Bailey Howell/199 6.00 15.00
25 Nate Archibald/25 10.00 25.00

2012-13 Panini Marquee Legends Signatures

EXCHANGE DEADLINE 10/10/2014
1 Elgin Baylor SP 12.00 30.00
2 George McGinnis 5.00 12.00
3 Nick Anderson 4.00 10.00
4 Walt Frazier SP 30.00 80.00
5 Muggsy Bogues 8.00 20.00
6 Bill Walton SP 10.00 25.00
8 Alonzo Mourning 20.00 50.00
9 Buck Williams 3.00 8.00
11 Robert Horry 5.00 12.00
12 Alex English 6.00 15.00
13 Hakeem Olajuwon SP 25.00 60.00
14 Michael Cooper 6.00 15.00
16 Cedric Maxwell 3.00 8.00
17 Rick Fox SP 40.00 100.00
18 Bruce Bowen 4.00 10.00
19 Luc Longley 4.00 10.00
20 Glen Rice SP 4.00 10.00
21 Tom Sanders 5.00 12.00
22 Steve Smith 4.00 10.00
23 Bailey Howell 6.00 15.00
24 Tom Chambers 5.00 12.00
25 Gary Payton 20.00 50.00
26 Darryl Dawkins 3.00 8.00
27 Walt Bellamy SP 6.00 15.00
28 Magic Johnson 60.00 150.00
29 Julius Erving 25.00 60.00
30 Sam Jones SP 15.00 40.00
31 Sam Perkins 4.00 10.00
32 Nick Van Exel SP 15.00 40.00
33 Leonard Robinson 3.00 8.00
35 Fat Lever 4.00 10.00
36 Bob Love 5.00 12.00
38 James Worthy 12.00 30.00
39 John Starks 4.00 10.00
40 John Havlicek SP 30.00 80.00
41 Bernard King 6.00 15.00
42 Toni Kukoc 15.00 40.00
43 Anfernee Hardaway 20.00 50.00
44 Dave Cowens SP 10.00 25.00
45 Dale Ellis 5.00 12.00
46 Sidney Moncrief 3.00 8.00
47 Zydrunas Ilgauskas 4.00 10.00
48 Bill Cartwright 4.00 10.00
49 Tom Heinsohn 15.00 40.00
50 George Gervin SP 12.00 30.00

2012-13 Panini Marquee Rookie Rivals Leather

1 G.Hill/J.Kidd 3.00 8.00
2 L.James/C.Anthony 15.00 40.00
3 S.O'Neal /A.Mourning 6.00 15.00
4 L.Bird/M.Johnson 6.00 15.00
5 K.Bryant/R.Allen 15.00 40.00
6 V.Carter/P.Pierce 4.00 10.00
7 Wes Unseld
Elvin Hayes 2.50 6.00
8 C.Paul/D.Williams 4.00 10.00
9 D.Rose/R.Westbrook 3.00 8.00
10 A.Davis/D.Lillard 30.00 80.00
11 J.Kidd/G.Hill 3.00 8.00
12 C.Anthony/L.James 15.00 40.00
13 A.Mourning/S.O'Neal 6.00 15.00
14 M.Johnson/L.Bird 6.00 15.00
15 R.Allen/K.Bryant 15.00 40.00
16 P.Pierce/V.Carter 4.00 10.00
17 Elvin Hayes
Wes Unseld 2.50 6.00
18 D.Williams/C.Paul 4.00 10.00
19 R.Westbrook/D.Rose 3.00 8.00
20 D.Lillard/A.Davis 30.00 80.00

2012-13 Panini Marquee Rookie Signatures

EXCHANGE DEADLINE 10/10/2014
1 Kyrie Irving 30.00 80.00
2 Anthony Davis 150.00 400.00
3 Dion Waiters SP EXCH 4.00 10.00
4 Thomas Robinson 3.00 8.00
5 Chandler Parsons 4.00 10.00
6 Michael Kidd-Gilchrist 4.00 10.00
7 Bradley Beal 25.00 60.00
8 Kemba Walker 12.00 30.00
9 Brandon Knight SP 4.00 10.00
10 Harrison Barnes 6.00 15.00
11 Andre Drummond 8.00 20.00
12 Austin Rivers 5.00 12.00
13 Derrick Williams SP 3.00 8.00
14 Markieff Morris SP 5.00 12.00
15 Donatas Motiejunas 4.00 10.00
16 Victor Claver 3.00 8.00
17 Kyle Singler 3.00 8.00
18 John Henson SP 4.00 10.00
19 Jeremy Lamb SP EXCH 5.00 12.00
20 Kawhi Leonard 150.00 400.00
21 Chris Copeland 3.00 8.00
22 Kenneth Faried 4.00 10.00
23 Klay Thompson 100.00 250.00
24 Jonas Valanciunas 6.00 15.00
25 Nikola Vucevic 12.00 30.00
26 Isaiah Thomas 6.00 15.00
27 Marcus Morris SP EXCH 5.00 12.00
29 Jimmer Fredette 5.00 12.00
30 Enes Kanter 5.00 12.00
31 Lavoy Allen 3.00 8.00
32 Tobias Harris 10.00 25.00
33 MarShon Brooks SP 3.00 8.00
34 Jimmy Butler SP 60.00 150.00
35 Bismack Biyombo 4.00 10.00
36 Tyler Zeller 3.00 8.00
37 Andrew Nicholson 3.00 8.00
38 Terrence Ross 8.00 20.00
39 Brian Roberts 3.00 8.00
40 Doron Lamb 3.00 8.00
41 Maurice Harkless 4.00 10.00
42 Jeff Taylor 3.00 8.00
43 Jae Crowder 6.00 15.00
44 Jared Sullinger 4.00 10.00
45 Meyers Leonard 4.00 10.00
46 Alexey Shved 3.00 8.00
47 John Jenkins 3.00 8.00
48 Nando De Colo 3.00 8.00
49 Evan Fournier 10.00 25.00
50 Bernard James 3.00 8.00
51 Terrence Jones 3.00 8.00
52 Draymond Green 15.00 40.00
53 Will Barton 6.00 15.00
54 Festus Ezeli 3.00 8.00
55 Marquis Teague 3.00 8.00
56 Kyle O'Quinn 4.00 10.00
57 DeQuan Jones 3.00 8.00
58 Kent Bazemore 5.00 12.00
59 Shelvin Mack 4.00 10.00
60 Gustavo Ayon 3.00 8.00
61 Khris Middleton 15.00 40.00
62 Fab Melo SP 3.00 8.00
63 Tornike Shengelia 3.00 8.00
64 Arnett Moultrie 3.00 8.00
65 Julyan Stone 3.00 8.00
66 Cory Joseph SP EXCH 4.00 10.00
67 Kendall Marshall 3.00 8.00
68 Iman Shumpert 4.00 10.00
69 DeAndre Liggins 3.00 8.00
70 Orlando Johnson 3.00 8.00
71 Perry Jones 3.00 8.00
72 Robert Sacre 3.00 8.00
73 Mike Scott 4.00 10.00
74 Nolan Smith 3.00 8.00
75 Charles Jenkins SP 3.00 8.00
76 Ben Hansbrough 3.00 8.00
77 Jon Leuer 3.00 8.00
78 Norris Cole 3.00 8.00
79 Miles Plumlee 3.00 8.00
80 Alec Burks 5.00 12.00
81 Darius Miller 4.00 10.00
82 Greg Stiemsma 3.00 8.00
83 Jan Vesely 3.00 8.00
84 Jared Cunningham 3.00 8.00
85 Kim English 3.00 8.00
86 Lance Thomas 3.00 8.00
87 Chris Singleton 3.00 8.00
88 Quincy Acy SP 3.00 8.00
89 Tyshawn Taylor SP EXCH 3.00 8.00
90 Reggie Jackson 5.00 12.00

2012-13 Panini Marquee Signatures

EXCHANGE DEADLINE 10/10/2014
1 Grant Hill EXCH 60.00 120.00
2 Andrea Bargnani SP 3.00 8.00
3 Joe Johnson SP 10.00 25.00
4 Kobe Bryant 1,500.00 3,000.00
6 Ersan Ilyasova 3.00 8.00
7 Greivis Vasquez 3.00 8.00
8 Kevin Durant 150.00 400.00
9 Mario Chalmers SP 4.00 10.00
10 Joakim Noah SP 4.00 10.00
11 Jeff Teague 3.00 8.00
14 Stephen Curry SP 500.00 1,000.00
15 Blake Griffin 10.00 25.00
16 Nick Collison 3.00 8.00
17 Metta World Peace SP 6.00 15.00
18 Kevin Martin SP 4.00 10.00
22 Elliot Williams 3.00 8.00
23 Kevin Love 10.00 25.00
26 Greg Monroe SP 3.00 8.00
28 Gordon Hayward 5.00 12.00
29 Danny Green 8.00 20.00
30 Jordan Crawford 3.00 8.00
31 Marcus Thornton 3.00 8.00
32 Andre Iguodala SP 5.00 12.00
33 Courtney Lee 3.00 8.00
34 Tiago Splitter 3.00 8.00
35 Jason Kidd 30.00 60.00
36 Vince Carter 40.00 100.00
37 Raymond Felton SP 3.00 8.00
38 Jason Richardson SP 5.00 12.00
39 Tyreke Evans SP 4.00 10.00
40 Gerald Henderson 3.00 8.00
41 Andre Miller SP 4.00 10.00
42 Tyson Chandler SP 5.00 12.00
43 Anderson Varejao SP 3.00 8.00
44 Monta Ellis SP 4.00 10.00
45 Landry Fields 3.00 8.00
46 Ekpe Udoh EXCH 3.00 8.00
47 Corey Brewer 3.00 8.00
48 Thabo Sefolosha SP 3.00 8.00
49 Hedo Turkoglu SP 4.00 10.00
50 Eric Gordon SP 4.00 10.00

2012-13 Panini Marquee Slam Dunk Legends

COMPLETE SET (20) 40.00 100.00
1 LeBron James 20.00 50.00
2 Vince Carter 2.50 6.00
3 Kobe Bryant 20.00 50.00
4 Dominique Wilkins 1.50 4.00
5 Clyde Drexler 2.00 5.00
6 Shawn Kemp 2.00 5.00
7 Julius Erving 3.00 8.00
8 Blake Griffin 1.25 3.00
9 Steve Francis 1.00 2.50
10 Shaquille O'Neal 4.00 10.00
11 Kevin Durant 5.00 12.00
12 David Thompson 1.25 3.00
13 Dwyane Wade 2.50 6.00
14 Dwight Howard 1.50 4.00
15 Spud Webb 1.00 2.50
16 Tom Chambers 1.25 3.00
17 Brent Barry .75 2.00
18 Larry Nance 1.00 2.50
19 Darryl Dawkins .75 2.00
20 Amare Stoudemire 1.25 3.00

2012-13 Panini Marquee Stars of the Night

COMPLETE SET (20) 20.00 50.00
1 Blake Griffin 1.00 2.50
2 Kobe Bryant 12.00 30.00
3 Kevin Durant 4.00 10.00
4 Kyrie Irving 6.00 15.00
5 Paul Pierce 1.50 4.00
6 Grant Hill 1.50 4.00
7 Carmelo Anthony 1.50 4.00
8 James Harden 2.00 5.00
9 Rajon Rondo 1.25 3.00
10 Russell Westbrook 1.50 4.00
11 Derrick Rose 1.50 4.00
12 Kenneth Faried .75 2.00
13 Jeremy Lin 1.50 4.00
14 Kevin Love 1.00 2.50
15 Chris Paul 2.00 5.00
16 Dwight Howard 1.25 3.00
17 Deron Williams .75 2.00
18 DeMarcus Cousins 1.00 2.50
19 Stephen Curry 8.00 20.00
20 Dirk Nowitzki 2.50 6.00

2017-18 Panini Marquee

STATED PRINT RUN 99 SER.#'d SETS
226 T.J. Leaf 1.25 3.00
227 Lauri Markkanen 8.00 20.00
228 Guerschon Yabusele 1.25 3.00
229 Markelle Fultz 3.00 8.00
230 Derrick White 5.00 12.00
231 De'Aaron Fox 10.00 25.00
232 John Collins 3.00 8.00
233 Frank Ntilikina 1.50 4.00
234 Luke Kennard 2.50 6.00
235 Jonathan Isaac 3.00 8.00
236 Tyler Dorsey 1.25 3.00
237 Lonzo Ball 10.00 25.00
238 Wayne Selden Jr. 1.25 3.00
239 Ante Zizic 1.50 4.00
240 Frank Jackson 1.25 3.00
241 Dennis Smith Jr. 1.50 4.00
242 Justin Jackson 1.25 3.00
243 Jayson Tatum 10.00 25.00
244 Semi Ojeleye 1.50 4.00
245 Josh Jackson 1.50 4.00
246 Zach Collins 2.00 5.00
247 Malik Monk 5.00 12.00
248 Johnathan Motley 1.25 3.00
249 Caleb Swanigan 1.25 3.00
250 Ivan Rabb 1.25 3.00

2017-18 Panini Marquee Tier 2

*TIER 2: .5X TO 1.2X BASIC
STATED PRINT RUN 49 SER.#'d SETS

2019-20 Panini Mosaic

COMPLETE SET (300)
*BLUE REACTIVE: 1X TO 2.5X BASIC
*GREEN: 1X TO 2.5X BASIC
*ORANGE REACTIVE: 1X TO 2.5X BASIC
*PINK CAMO: 1X TO 2.5X BASIC
*RED: 1X TO 2.5X BASIC
*MOSAIC: 1.2X TO 3X BASIC
*MOSAIC RED WAVE: 1.2X TO 3X BASIC
*FB SILVER: 1.2X TO 3X BASIC
*SILVER: 1.25X TO 3X BASIC
*BLUE/99: 4X TO 10X BASIC
*RED FUSION/88: 5X TO 12X BASIC
*FB BLUE/85: 5X TO 12X BASIC
1 Kevin Durant 1.25 3.00
2 Evan Fournier .30 .75
3 Mason Plumlee .25 .60
4 Jabari Parker .25 .60
5 Damian Lillard 1.00 2.50
6 Bryn Forbes .30 .75
7 Aaron Holiday .30 .75
8 LeBron James 3.00 8.00
9 Fred VanVleet .50 1.25
10 De'Aaron Fox .60 1.50
11 Kyrie Irving .75 2.00
12 Aaron Gordon .40 1.00
13 Donovan Mitchell .75 2.00
14 DeAndre' Bembry .25 .60
15 CJ McCollum .40 1.00
16 Derrick White .40 1.00
17 Andre Drummond .30 .75
18 Anthony Davis 1.00 2.50
19 Pascal Siakam .60 1.50
20 Marvin Bagley III .30 .75
21 Jarrett Allen .40 1.00
22 Nikola Vucevic .30 .75
23 Rudy Gobert .50 1.25
24 Kevin Huerter .40 1.00
25 Carmelo Anthony .60 1.50
26 Rudy Gay .30 .75
27 Luke Kennard .30 .75
28 Kyle Kuzma .50 1.25
29 Kyle Lowry .40 1.00
30 Richaun Holmes .25 .60
31 Joe Harris .30 .75
32 D.J. Augustin .25 .60
33 Bojan Bogdanovic .30 .75
34 Damian Jones .25 .60
35 Rodney Hood .30 .75
36 Patty Mills .40 1.00
37 Blake Griffin .40 1.00
38 Danny Green .30 .75
39 OG Anunoby .30 .75
40 Bogdan Bogdanovic .40 1.00
41 Spencer Dinwiddie .30 .75
42 Markelle Fultz .30 .75
43 Mike Conley .30 .75
44 Luka Doncic 2.50 6.00
45 Zach Collins .25 .60
46 Dejounte Murray .40 1.00
47 Langston Galloway .25 .60
48 Kentavious Caldwell-Pope .30 .75
49 Marc Gasol .40 1.00
50 Nemanja Bjelica .25 .60
51 Caris LeVert .30 .75
52 Terrence Ross .40 1.00
53 Royce O'Neale .25 .60
54 Kristaps Porzingis .50 1.25
55 Hassan Whiteside .25 .60
56 Jae Crowder .25 .60
57 Bruce Brown .40 1.00
58 Dwight Howard .50 1.25
59 Norman Powell .30 .75
60 Glenn Robinson III .25 .60
61 Taurean Prince .25 .60
62 Devonte' Graham .30 .75
63 Joe Ingles .30 .75
64 Dorian Finney-Smith .30 .75
65 Anfernee Simons .60 1.50
66 Dillon Brooks .25 .60
67 Derrick Rose .75 2.00
68 Lou Williams .40 1.00
69 Serge Ibaka .30 .75
70 Stephen Curry 3.00 8.00
71 Marcus Morris Sr. .25 .60
72 Terry Rozier .30 .75
73 Andrew Wiggins .50 1.25
74 Dwight Powell .25 .60
75 Giannis Antetokounmpo 2.00 5.00
76 Jaren Jackson Jr. .60 1.50
77 Markieff Morris .25 .60
78 Kawhi Leonard 1.00 2.50
79 Jayson Tatum 1.50 4.00
80 Klay Thompson 1.00 2.50
81 Julius Randle .50 1.25
82 Miles Bridges .40 1.00
83 Karl-Anthony Towns .60 1.50
84 Tim Hardaway Jr. .25 .60
85 Khris Middleton .40 1.00
86 Jonas Valanciunas .30 .75
87 Zach LaVine .60 1.50
88 Patrick Beverley .30 .75
89 Jaylen Brown .60 1.50
90 D'Angelo Russell .30 .75
91 Frank Ntilikina .25 .60
92 Cody Zeller .25 .60
93 Jeff Teague .25 .60
94 Delon Wright .25 .60
95 Eric Bledsoe .30 .75
96 Kyle Anderson .25 .60
97 Lauri Markkanen .50 1.25
98 Montrezl Harrell .30 .75
99 Kemba Walker .30 .75
100 Draymond Green .50 1.25
101 Elfrid Payton .25 .60
102 Nicolas Batum .25 .60
103 Robert Covington .25 .60
104 Seth Curry .30 .75
105 Brook Lopez .30 .75
106 Tyus Jones .25 .60

2019-20 Panini Mosaic

107 Wendell Carter Jr. .40 1.00
108 Paul George .60 1.50
109 Marcus Smart .30 .75
110 Willie Cauley-Stein .25 .60
111 Bobby Portis .25 .60
112 Malik Monk .40 1.00
113 Josh Okogie .30 .75
114 James Harden .75 2.00
115 Wesley Matthews .25 .60
116 Grayson Allen .40 1.00
117 Tomas Satoransky .25 .60
118 Landry Shamet .30 .75
119 Gordon Hayward .30 .75
120 Alec Burks .25 .60
121 Taj Gibson .25 .60
122 John Wall .50 1.25
123 Jake Layman .25 .60
124 P.J. Tucker .30 .75
125 George Hill .30 .75
126 Jrue Holiday .50 1.25
127 Otto Porter Jr. .25 .60
128 Devin Booker .10 .25
129 Daniel Theis .40 1.00
130 Jimmy Butler .75 2.00
131 Kevin Knox II .25 .60
132 Bradley Beal .50 1.25
133 Shai Gilgeous-Alexander 2.00 5.00
134 Russell Westbrook .60 1.50
135 Donte DiVincenzo .30 .75
136 Brandon Ingram .40 1.00
137 Thaddeus Young .25 .60
138 Deandre Ayton .40 1.00
139 Enes Kanter .25 .60
140 Justise Winslow .25 .60
141 Jamal Murray .60 1.50
142 Thomas Bryant .30 .75
143 Chris Paul .75 2.00
144 Clint Capela .30 .75
145 Victor Oladipo .30 .75
146 JJ Redick .40 1.00
147 Tristan Thompson .25 .60
148 Kelly Oubre Jr. .30 .75
149 Ben Simmons .40 1.00
150 Bam Adebayo .60 1.50
151 Will Barton .25 .60
152 Isaiah Thomas .30 .75
153 Danilo Gallinari .30 .75
154 Danuel House Jr. .25 .60
155 Domantas Sabonis .50 1.25
156 Josh Hart .30 .75
157 Kevin Love .40 1.00
158 Ricky Rubio .30 .75
159 Tobias Harris .30 .75
160 Goran Dragic .30 .75
161 Gary Harris .30 .75
162 Troy Brown Jr. .25 .60
163 Dennis Schroder .30 .75
164 Eric Gordon .30 .75
165 T.J. Warren .30 .75
166 Lonzo Ball .40 1.00
167 Collin Sexton .50 1.25
168 Dario Saric .30 .75
169 Josh Richardson .25 .60
170 Duncan Robinson .60 1.50
171 Nikola Jokic 2.00 5.00
172 Davis Bertans .25 .60
173 Steven Adams .30 .75
174 Austin Rivers .25 .60
175 Jeremy Lamb .25 .60
176 Kenrich Williams .30 .75
177 Cedi Osman .30 .75
178 Aron Baynes .25 .60
179 Al Horford .40 1.00
180 Kelly Olynyk .25 .60
181 Paul Millsap .30 .75
182 Trae Young 1.00 2.50
183 Terrance Ferguson .25 .60
184 DeMar DeRozan .50 1.25
185 Malcolm Brogdon .30 .75
186 Derrick Favors .25 .60
187 Larry Nance Jr. .30 .75
188 Harrison Barnes .30 .75
189 Joel Embiid .75 2.00
190 Meyers Leonard .25 .60
191 Jerami Grant .40 1.00
192 John Collins .40 1.00
193 Hamidou Diallo .30 .75
194 LaMarcus Aldridge .40 1.00
195 Myles Turner .40 1.00
196 Rajon Rondo .50 1.25
197 Jordan Clarkson .40 1.00
198 Buddy Hield .30 .75
199 Furkan Korkmaz .30 .75
200 Jonathan Isaac .40 1.00
201 Jarrett Culver RC .50 1.25
202 Admiral Schofield RC .60 1.50
203 Cameron Johnson RC 1.25 3.00
204 Quinndary Weatherspoon RC .50 1.25
205 Nickeil Alexander-Walker RC .75 2.00
206 Ky Bowman RC .60 1.50
207 Brandon Clarke RC 1.00 2.50
208 Dylan Windler RC .60 1.50
209 Zion Williamson RC 4.00 10.00
210 KZ Okpala RC .60 1.50
211 Coby White RC 1.50 4.00
212 Jaylen Nowell RC .60 1.50
213 PJ Washington Jr. RC 1.50 4.00
214 Tremont Waters RC .60 1.50
215 Talen Horton-Tucker RC .75 2.00
216 Nicolo Melli RC .60 1.50
217 Grant Williams RC .75 2.00
218 Mfiondu Kabengele RC .60 1.50
219 Ja Morant RC 5.00 12.00
220 Carsen Edwards RC .60 1.50
221 Jaxson Hayes RC .75 2.00
222 Bol Bol RC 1.25 3.00
223 Tyler Herro RC 2.50 6.00
224 Kyle Guy RC .60 1.50
225 Goga Bitadze RC .75 2.00
226 Terence Davis RC .75 2.00
227 Darius Bazley RC .60 1.50
228 Jordan Poole RC 2.00 5.00
229 RJ Barrett RC 2.00 5.00
230 Bruno Fernando RC .60 1.50
231 Rui Hachimura RC 2.00 5.00
232 Isaiah Roby RC .60 1.50
233 Romeo Langford RC .50 1.25
234 Kendrick Nunn RC .75 2.00
235 Luka Samanic RC .60 1.50
236 Nicolas Claxton RC 1.00 2.50
237 Ty Jerome RC 1.00 2.50
238 Keldon Johnson RC 1.50 4.00
239 De'Andre Hunter RC 2.00 5.00
240 Cody Martin RC .75 2.00
241 Cam Reddish RC .75 2.00
242 Ignas Brazdeikis RC .60 1.50
243 Sekou Doumbouya RC .50 1.25
244 Tacko Fall RC .60 1.50
245 Matisse Thybulle RC 1.00 2.50
246 Terance Mann RC 1.00 2.50
247 Nassir Little RC .75 2.00
248 Kevin Porter Jr. RC 1.00 2.50
249 Darius Garland RC 2.00 5.00
250 Eric Paschall RC .60 1.50
251 Kevin Durant 1.25 3.00
252 Charles Barkley .75 2.00
253 Patrick Ewing .60 1.50
254 Larry Bird 1.50 4.00
255 Magic Johnson 1.25 3.00
256 Scottie Pippen 1.00 2.50
257 Karl Malone .75 2.00
258 Vince Carter .75 2.00
259 Dwyane Wade .75 2.00
260 Stephen Curry 3.00 8.00
261 Jordan Poole 2.00 5.00
262 Darius Garland 2.00 5.00
263 Jarrett Culver .50 1.25
264 Coby White 1.50 4.00
265 Cameron Johnson 1.25 3.00
266 De'Andre Hunter 2.00 5.00
267 Jaxson Hayes .75 2.00
268 Kendrick Nunn .75 2.00
269 Zion Williamson 4.00 10.00
270 RJ Barrett 2.00 5.00
272 Eric Paschall .60 1.50
273 Ty Jerome 1.00 2.50
274 Ja Morant 5.00 12.00
275 Rui Hachimura 2.00 5.00
276 Tacko Fall .60 1.50
277 Brandon Clarke 1.00 2.50
278 PJ Washington Jr. 1.50 4.00
279 Nicolo Melli .60 1.50
280 Tyler Herro 2.50 6.00
281 Shaquille O'Neal HOF 1.50 4.00
282 Charles Barkley HOF .75 2.00
283 Kareem Abdul-Jabbar HOF 1.25 3.00
284 Karl Malone HOF .75 2.00
285 Wilt Chamberlain HOF 1.50 4.00
286 Oscar Robertson HOF 1.00 2.50
287 Allen Iverson HOF 1.00 2.50
288 Julius Erving HOF 1.00 2.50
289 Patrick Ewing HOF .60 1.50
290 Larry Bird HOF 1.50 4.00
291 Magic Johnson HOF 1.25 3.00
292 Scottie Pippen HOF 1.00 2.50
293 John Stockton HOF .75 2.00
294 Dominique Wilkins HOF .60 1.50
295 Pete Maravich HOF 1.00 2.50
296 James Harden MVP .75 2.00
297 Giannis Antetokounmpo MVP 2.00 5.00
298 LeBron James MVP 3.00 8.00
299 Stephen Curry MVP 3.00 8.00
300 Wilt Chamberlain MVP 1.50 4.00

2019-20 Panini Mosaic Mosaic Choice Red and Green

*CH RED & GREEN: 1.2X TO 3X BASIC
209 Zion Williamson 50.00 120.00
219 Ja Morant 60.00 150.00

2019-20 Panini Mosaic Mosaic Fast Break Purple

COMPLETE SET (300)
*FB PURPLE: 5X TO 12X BASIC
STATED PRINT RUN 50 SER.#'d SETS
209 Zion Williamson 125.00 300.00
219 Ja Morant 125.00 300.00

2019-20 Panini Mosaic Mosaic Genesis

*GENESIS: 6X TO 15X BASIC
*GENESIS RC: 12X TO 30X BASIC RC
STATED PRINT RUN 25 SER.#'d SETS
1 Kevin Durant 150.00 400.00
5 Damian Lillard 20.00 50.00
8 LeBron James 2,000.00 4,000.00
13 Donovan Mitchell 25.00 60.00
18 Anthony Davis 125.00 300.00
19 Pascal Siakam 30.00 80.00
44 Luka Doncic 800.00 1,500.00
54 Kristaps Porzingis 25.00 60.00
67 Derrick Rose 20.00 50.00
70 Stephen Curry 400.00 800.00
75 Giannis Antetokounmpo 500.00 1,000.00
78 Kawhi Leonard 400.00 800.00
79 Jayson Tatum 150.00 400.00
80 Klay Thompson 40.00 100.00
87 Zach LaVine 25.00 60.00
89 Jaylen Brown 20.00 50.00
99 Kemba Walker 15.00 40.00
108 Paul George 30.00 80.00
114 James Harden 50.00 120.00
133 Shai Gilgeous-Alexander 60.00 150.00
134 Russell Westbrook 30.00 80.00
136 Brandon Ingram 30.00 80.00
138 Deandre Ayton 15.00 40.00
141 Jamal Murray 15.00 40.00
143 Chris Paul 20.00 50.00
148 Kelly Oubre Jr. 12.00 30.00
149 Ben Simmons 50.00 120.00
150 Bam Adebayo 25.00 60.00
166 Lonzo Ball 20.00 50.00
170 Duncan Robinson 125.00 300.00
198 Buddy Hield 10.00 25.00
201 Jarrett Culver 75.00 200.00
207 Brandon Clarke 150.00 400.00
209 Zion Williamson 5,000.00 8,000.00
211 Coby White 400.00 800.00
213 PJ Washington Jr. 75.00 200.00
219 Ja Morant 2,000.00 4,000.00
221 Jaxson Hayes 60.00 150.00
222 Bol Bol 75.00 200.00
223 Tyler Herro 200.00 500.00
228 Jordan Poole 40.00 100.00
229 RJ Barrett 300.00 600.00
231 Rui Hachimura 150.00 400.00
238 Keldon Johnson 50.00 120.00
239 De'Andre Hunter 100.00 250.00
245 Matisse Thybulle 125.00 300.00
248 Kevin Porter Jr. 30.00 80.00
249 Darius Garland 125.00 300.00
250 Eric Paschall 75.00 200.00
251 Kevin Durant 150.00 400.00
252 Charles Barkley 40.00 100.00
253 Patrick Ewing 20.00 50.00
254 Larry Bird 40.00 100.00
255 Magic Johnson 40.00 100.00
256 Scottie Pippen 50.00 120.00
257 Karl Malone 25.00 60.00
258 Vince Carter 30.00 80.00
259 Dwyane Wade 60.00 150.00
260 Stephen Curry 200.00 500.00
269 Zion Williamson 1,500.00 3,000.00
274 Ja Morant 400.00 800.00
281 Shaquille O'Neal HOF 50.00 120.00
282 Charles Barkley HOF 50.00 120.00
284 Karl Malone HOF 15.00 40.00
287 Allen Iverson HOF 60.00 150.00
288 Julius Erving HOF 50.00 120.00
290 Larry Bird HOF 50.00 120.00
291 Magic Johnson HOF 50.00 120.00
292 Scottie Pippen HOF 50.00 120.00
296 James Harden MVP 125.00 300.00
297 Giannis Antetokounmpo MVP 400.00 800.00
298 LeBron James MVP 1,500.00 3,000.00
299 Stephen Curry MVP 400.00 800.00

2019-20 Panini Mosaic Mosaic Orange Fluorescent

*ORANGE FLUORESCENT: 12X TO 30X BASIC
*ORANGE FLUORESCENT RC: 12X TO 30X BASIC RC
STATED PRINT RUN 25 SER.#'d SETS
8 LeBron James 400.00 800.00
44 Luka Doncic 300.00 600.00
70 Stephen Curry 400.00 800.00
209 Zion Williamson 600.00 1,200.00
219 Ja Morant 600.00 1,200.00
298 LeBron James MVP 200.00 500.00
299 Stephen Curry MVP 200.00 500.00

2019-20 Panini Mosaic Mosaic Purple

*PURPLE: 6X TO 15X BASIC
*PURPLE RC: 6X TO 15X BASIC RC
STATED PRINT RUN 49 SER.#'d SETS
209 Zion Williamson 125.00 300.00
219 Ja Morant 125.00 300.00

2019-20 Panini Mosaic Mosaic White

*MOSAIC WHITE: 12X TO 30X BASIC
*MOSAIC WHITE RC: 12X TO 30X BASIC RC
STATED PRINT RUN 25 SER.#'d SETS
8 LeBron James 400.00 800.00
44 Luka Doncic 300.00 600.00
70 Stephen Curry 400.00 800.00
209 Zion Williamson 600.00 1,200.00
219 Ja Morant 600.00 1,200.00
298 LeBron James MVP 200.00 500.00
299 Stephen Curry MVP 200.00 500.00

2019-20 Panini Mosaic Autographs Fast Break

COMMON CARD 3.00 8.00
SEMISTARS 4.00 10.00
UNLISTED STARS 5.00 12.00
EXCHANGE DEADLINE 10/22/2021
1 Mfiondu Kabengele 4.00 10.00
2 De'Aaron Fox 30.00 80.00
3 Jaren Jackson Jr. 20.00 50.00
4 Charles Barkley 125.00 300.00
5 Larry Johnson 15.00 40.00
6 Damian Lillard 75.00 200.00
7 PJ Washington Jr. 10.00 25.00
8 Karl-Anthony Towns 15.00 40.00
9 Darius Bazley 3.00 8.00
10 Chris Bosh 12.00 30.00
11 Jordan Poole 20.00 50.00
12 Gary Payton 25.00 60.00
13 Kevin Knox II 3.00 8.00
14 Hakeem Olajuwon 40.00 100.00
15 Dave Cowens 6.00 15.00
16 Larry Bird 125.00 300.00
17 Bol Bol 8.00 20.00
18 Ja Morant 400.00 800.00
19 Goga Bitadze 5.00 12.00
20 Clyde Drexler 30.00 80.00
21 Kevin Porter Jr. 6.00 15.00
22 Deandre Ayton 30.00 80.00
23 Jarrett Culver 3.00 8.00
25 Bill Walton 25.00 60.00
26 Anthony Davis 125.00 300.00
27 Tyler Herro 50.00 120.00
28 Andrew Wiggins 12.00 30.00
29 Luka Samanic 4.00 10.00
30 Grant Hill 20.00 50.00
31 KZ Okpala 4.00 10.00
32 James Worthy 12.00 30.00
33 Cam Reddish 5.00 12.00
34 Zion Williamson 500.00 1,000.00
35 Gail Goodrich 5.00 12.00
36 John Stockton 40.00 100.00
37 Romeo Langford 3.00 8.00
38 Magic Johnson 75.00 200.00
39 Keldon Johnson 50.00 120.00
40 Kevin McHale 15.00 40.00
41 Eric Paschall 4.00 10.00
42 Lauri Markkanen 6.00 15.00
43 Coby White 30.00 80.00
44 Shaquille O'Neal 150.00 400.00
45 Malcolm Brogdon 4.00 10.00
46 Julius Erving 60.00 150.00
47 Matisse Thybulle 20.00 50.00
48 RJ Barrett 50.00 120.00
49 Carsen Edwards 4.00 10.00
50 Rui Hachimura 50.00 120.00
51 Talen Horton-Tucker 5.00 12.00
52 Nikola Jokic 125.00 300.00
53 Eric Bledsoe 4.00 10.00
54 Kevin Durant 125.00 300.00
55 Collin Sexton 20.00 50.00
56 Kevin Garnett 100.00 250.00
57 Nassir Little 5.00 12.00
58 David Robinson 40.00 100.00
59 Grant Williams 5.00 12.00
60 Dennis Rodman 40.00 100.00
61 Kendrick Nunn 5.00 12.00
63 Derek Fisher 12.00 30.00
64 Giannis Antetokounmpo 150.00 400.00
65 Myles Turner 5.00 12.00
66 Kareem Abdul-Jabbar 125.00 300.00
67 Sekou Doumbouya 3.00 8.00
68 Trae Young 100.00 250.00
69 Ty Jerome 6.00 15.00
70 Tony Parker 12.00 30.00
71 Cody Martin 5.00 12.00
72 De'Andre Hunter 20.00 50.00
73 George Gervin 12.00 30.00
74 Allen Iverson 100.00 250.00
76 John Wall 25.00 60.00
78 Jerry West 40.00 100.00
79 Bruno Fernando 4.00 10.00
80 Elgin Baylor 20.00 50.00
81 Isaiah Roby 12.00 30.00
82 Steve Kerr 15.00 40.00
83 Kevin Johnson 12.00 30.00
84 Karl Malone 40.00 100.00
86 Oscar Robertson 75.00 200.00
87 Nickeil Alexander-Walker 15.00 40.00
88 Jason Kidd 15.00 40.00
89 Admiral Schofield 4.00 10.00
90 CJ McCollum 12.00 30.00
92 Dwight Howard 12.00 30.00
93 Latrell Sprewell 10.00 25.00
94 Dwyane Wade 75.00 200.00
95 Cameron Johnson 20.00 50.00
96 Kawhi Leonard 75.00 299.00
97 Brandon Clarke 12.00 30.00
98 DeMarcus Cousins 4.00 10.00
99 Dylan Windler 4.00 10.00
100 Stephon Marbury 12.00 30.00

2019-20 Panini Mosaic Autographs Mosaic

COMMON CARD 2.50 6.00
SEMISTARS 3.00 8.00
UNLISTED STARS 4.00 10.00
EXCHANGE DEADLINE 10/22/2021
1 Bill Walton 20.00 50.00
2 Dennis Rodman 60.00 150.00
3 De'Aaron Fox 30.00 80.00
4 Charles Barkley 75.00 200.00
5 Steve Kerr 15.00 40.00
6 Karl Malone 25.00 60.00
7 Jaren Jackson Jr. 15.00 40.00
8 Anthony Davis 50.00 120.00
9 Chris Mullin 5.00 12.00
10 David Robinson 50.00 120.00
11 Lou Williams 4.00 10.00
12 Tony Parker 15.00 40.00
13 Gary Payton 20.00 50.00
14 Magic Johnson 40.00 100.00
15 Zach LaVine 15.00 40.00
16 Dwyane Wade 40.00 100.00
17 Kevin Knox II 2.50 6.00
18 Julius Erving 50.00 120.00
19 Bernard King 5.00 12.00
20 Trae Young 100.00 250.00
21 Collin Sexton 25.00 60.00
22 Elgin Baylor 25.00 60.00
23 James Worthy 15.00 40.00
24 Stephen Curry 300.00 600.00
25 Al Horford 4.00 10.00
26 Larry Bird 40.00 100.00
27 Jrue Holiday 5.00 12.00
28 Kevin Garnett 100.00 250.00
29 George Gervin 6.00 15.00
30 Jason Kidd 12.00 30.00
31 Myles Turner 4.00 10.00
32 Vince Carter 50.00 120.00
33 Lauri Markkanen 5.00 12.00
34 Kevin Durant 60.00 150.00
35 Dwight Howard 50.00 120.00
36 Damian Lillard 75.00 200.00
37 Walt Frazier 12.00 30.00
38 Kareem Abdul-Jabbar 75.00 200.00
39 Kevin Johnson 12.00 30.00
40 Chris Bosh 12.00 30.00
42 Lonzo Ball 20.00 50.00
44 Giannis Antetokounmpo 150.00 400.00
45 Christian Laettner 8.00 20.00
46 Kyrie Irving 40.00 100.00
47 Richard Hamilton 8.00 20.00
48 Oscar Robertson 50.00 120.00
49 Dave Cowens 5.00 12.00
50 Clyde Drexler 20.00 50.00
51 Steve Francis 8.00 20.00
52 Kristaps Porzingis 15.00 40.00
54 Allen Iverson 75.00 200.00
55 Harrison Barnes 3.00 8.00
56 John Stockton 60.00 150.00
57 Goran Dragic 3.00 8.00
58 Karl-Anthony Towns 12.00 30.00
59 Latrell Sprewell 8.00 20.00
60 Kevin McHale 10.00 25.00

2019-20 Panini Mosaic Autographs Mosaic Choice Red Fusion

*CHOICE RED FUSION: .5X TO 1.2X BASIC
EXCHANGE DEADLINE 10/22/2021

2019-20 Panini Mosaic Blue Chips

COMMON CARD .50 1.25
SEMISTARS .60 1.50
UNLISTED STARS .75 2.00
*FB SILVER: .75X TO 2X BASIC
*MOSAIC: 1.2X TO 3X BASIC
*MOSAIC WHITE/25: 5X TO 12X BASIC
1 Cam Reddish .75 2.00
2 RJ Barrett 2.00 5.00
3 Tyler Herro 2.50 6.00
4 Jarrett Culver .50 1.25
5 Kendrick Nunn .75 2.00
6 Coby White 1.50 4.00
7 Jaxson Hayes .75 2.00
8 Zion Williamson 4.00 10.00
9 Rui Hachimura 2.00 5.00
10 Ja Morant 5.00 12.00
11 PJ Washington Jr. 1.50 4.00
12 De'Andre Hunter 2.00 5.00
13 Eric Paschall .60 1.50
14 Darius Garland 2.00 5.00
15 Cameron Johnson 1.25 3.00

2019-20 Panini Mosaic Center Stage Prizms

COMMON CARD 1.00 2.50
SEMISTARS 1.25 3.00
UNLISTED STARS 1.50 4.00
1 James Harden 12.00 30.00
2 LeBron James 125.00 300.00
3 Kyrie Irving 12.00 30.00
4 Derrick Rose 3.00 8.00
5 Joel Embiid 8.00 20.00
6 Damian Lillard 8.00 20.00
7 Chris Paul 3.00 8.00
8 Russell Westbrook 5.00 12.00
9 Paul George 2.50 6.00
10 Anthony Davis 12.00 30.00
11 Karl-Anthony Towns 2.50 6.00
12 D'Angelo Russell 1.25 3.00
13 CJ McCollum 1.50 4.00
14 Stephen Curry 25.00 60.00
15 Ben Simmons 8.00 20.00
16 Nikola Vucevic 1.25 3.00
17 Luka Doncic 75.00 200.00
18 Draymond Green 2.00 5.00
19 Donovan Mitchell 8.00 20.00
20 Kawhi Leonard 10.00 25.00
21 Blake Griffin 1.50 4.00
22 Pascal Siakam 2.50 6.00
23 Nikola Jokic 6.00 15.00
24 Giannis Antetokounmpo 30.00 80.00
25 Kemba Walker 1.25 3.00
26 DeMar DeRozan 2.00 5.00
27 De'Aaron Fox 2.50 6.00
28 Jayson Tatum 20.00 50.00
29 Trae Young 25.00 60.00
30 Bradley Beal 2.00 5.00

2019-20 Panini Mosaic Give and Go

COMMON CARD .50 1.25
SEMISTARS .60 1.50
UNLISTED STARS .75 2.00
*MOSAIC GREEN: .75X TO 2X BASIC
*MOSAIC: 1.2X TO 3X BASIC
*MOSAIC BLUE REACTIVE/99: 2X TO 5X BASIC
*MOSAIC ORANGE FLUORESCENT/25: 5X TO 12X BASIC
1 Kyrie Irving 1.50 4.00
2 Ben Simmons .75 2.00
3 De'Aaron Fox 1.25 3.00
4 Trae Young 2.00 5.00
5 Jrue Holiday 1.00 2.50
6 James Harden 1.50 4.00
7 Damian Lillard 1.25 3.00
8 LeBron James 6.00 15.00
9 Bradley Beal 1.00 2.50
10 Luka Doncic 5.00 12.00
11 Russell Westbrook 1.25 3.00
12 Ricky Rubio .60 1.50
13 Kyle Lowry .75 2.00
14 Malcolm Brogdon .60 1.50
15 Jimmy Butler 1.50 4.00

2019-20 Panini Mosaic Got Game?

COMMON CARD .50 1.25
SEMISTARS .60 1.50
UNLISTED STARS .75 2.00
*MOSAIC GREEN: .75X TO 2X BASIC
*MOSAIC: 1.2X TO 3X BASIC
*MOSAIC BLUE REACTIVE/99: 1.5X TO 4X BASIC
*MOSAIC ORANGE FLUORESCENT/25: 5X TO 12X BASIC
1 Ben Simmons .75 2.00
2 Derrick Rose 1.50 4.00
3 Paul George 1.25 3.00
4 Kemba Walker .60 1.50
5 Pascal Siakam 1.25 3.00
6 Anthony Davis 2.00 5.00
7 LeBron James 6.00 15.00
8 Russell Westbrook 1.25 3.00
9 Stephen Curry 6.00 15.00
10 Bradley Beal 1.00 2.50
11 Luka Doncic 5.00 12.00
12 CJ McCollum .75 2.00
13 Kawhi Leonard 2.00 5.00
14 Damian Lillard 2.00 5.00
15 Kyrie Irving 1.50 4.00
16 Trae Young 2.00 5.00
17 Blake Griffin .75 2.00
18 Donovan Mitchell 1.50 4.00
19 Nikola Jokic 4.00 10.00
20 Karl-Anthony Towns 1.25 3.00
21 Nikola Vucevic .60 1.50
22 Joel Embiid 1.50 4.00
23 James Harden 1.50 4.00
24 De'Aaron Fox 1.25 3.00
25 Giannis Antetokounmpo 4.00 10.00

2019-20 Panini Mosaic In It to Win It

COMMON CARD .75 2.00
SEMISTARS 1.00 2.50
UNLISTED STARS 1.25 3.00
1 Karl-Anthony Towns 2.00 5.00
2 Giannis Antetokounmpo 6.00 15.00
3 Kawhi Leonard 3.00 8.00
4 Stephen Curry 10.00 25.00
5 Anthony Davis 3.00 8.00
6 Donovan Mitchell 2.50 6.00
7 Pascal Siakam 2.00 5.00
8 Paul George 2.00 5.00
9 Russell Westbrook 2.00 5.00
10 James Harden 2.50 6.00
11 CJ McCollum 1.25 3.00
12 Trae Young 3.00 8.00
13 Kyrie Irving 2.50 6.00
14 Luka Doncic 8.00 20.00
15 Blake Griffin 1.25 3.00
16 Ben Simmons 3.00 8.00
17 LeBron James 10.00 25.00
18 Joel Embiid 2.50 6.00
19 Nikola Jokic 6.00 15.00
20 Damian Lillard 3.00 8.00

2019-20 Panini Mosaic International Men of Mastery

COMMON CARD .50 1.20
SEMISTARS .60 1.50
UNLISTED STARS .75 2.00
*FAST BREAK SILVER: 1.2X TO 3X BASIC
*MOSAIC: 1.2X TO 3X BASIC
*MOSAIC WHITE/25: 5X TO 12X BASIC
1 Joel Embiid 1.50 4.00
2 Peja Stojakovic .60 1.50
3 Ben Simmons .75 2.00
4 Tony Parker 1.00 2.50
5 Toni Kukoc 1.00 2.50
6 Steve Nash 1.50 4.00
7 Hakeem Olajuwon 1.50 4.00
8 Arvydas Sabonis .75 2.00
9 Nikola Jokic 4.00 10.00
10 Hedo Turkoglu .60 1.50
11 Luka Doncic 5.00 12.00
12 Dikembe Mutombo .75 2.00
13 Kyrie Irving 1.50 4.00
14 Kristaps Porzingis 1.00 2.50
15 Dirk Nowitzki 2.00 5.00
16 Drazen Petrovic 1.00 2.50
17 Giannis Antetokounmpo 4.00 10.00
18 Vlade Divac .75 2.00
19 Ricky Rubio .60 1.50
20 Marc Gasol .75 2.00

2019-20 Panini Mosaic Introductions

COMMON CARD .50 1.25
SEMISTARS .60 1.50
UNLISTED STARS .75 2.00
*FB SILVER: .75X TO 2X BASIC
*MOSAIC: 1X TO 2.5X BASIC
1 RJ Barrett 2.00 5.00
2 Tyler Herro 2.50 6.00
3 Jarrett Culver .50 1.25
4 Coby White 1.50 4.00
5 Zion Williamson 4.00 10.00
6 Rui Hachimura 2.00 5.00
7 Ja Morant 5.00 12.00
8 PJ Washington Jr. 1.50 4.00
9 De'Andre Hunter 2.00 5.00
10 Eric Paschall .60 1.50

2019-20 Panini Mosaic Introductions Mosaic White

*MOSAIC WHITE: 5X TO 12X BASIC
STATED PRINT RUN 25 SER.#'d SETS
7 Ja Morant 125.00 300.00

2019-20 Panini Mosaic Jam Masters

COMMON CARD .50 1.25
SEMISTARS .60 1.50
UNLISTED STARS .75 2.00
1 Spud Webb .75 2.00
2 Julius Erving 2.00 5.00
3 DeAndre Jordan .60 1.50
4 Clyde Drexler 1.25 3.00
5 Russell Westbrook 1.25 3.00
6 Aaron Gordon .75 2.00
7 Donovan Mitchell 1.50 4.00
8 Blake Griffin .75 2.00
9 DeMar DeRozan 1.00 2.50
10 Jason Richardson .75 2.00
11 Tracy McGrady 1.25 3.00
12 Dominique Wilkins 1.25 3.00
13 Terrence Ross .75 2.00
14 Shawn Kemp 1.25 3.00
15 Paul George 1.25 3.00
16 LeBron James 8.00 20.00
17 Anthony Davis 2.00 5.00
18 Zach LaVine 1.25 3.00
19 Giannis Antetokounmpo 4.00 10.00
20 Dwight Howard 1.00 2.50

2019-20 Panini Mosaic Jam Masters Mosaic

*MOSAIC: 1.2X TO 3X BASIC
16 LeBron James 75.00 200.00
17 Anthony Davis 8.00 20.00
19 Giannis Antetokounmpo 40.00 100.00

2019-20 Panini Mosaic Jam Masters Mosaic Blue Reactive

*MOSAIC BLUE REACTIVE: 1.5X TO 4X BASIC
2 Julius Erving 12.00 30.00
11 Tracy McGrady 12.00 30.00
15 Paul George 15.00 40.00
16 LeBron James 400.00 800.00
17 Anthony Davis 30.00 80.00
18 Zach LaVine 20.00 50.00
19 Giannis Antetokounmpo 150.00 400.00
20 Dwight Howard 12.00 30.00

2019-20 Panini Mosaic Jam Masters Mosaic Green

*MOSAIC GREEN: .75X TO 2X BASIC
16 LeBron James 60.00 150.00
19 Giannis Antetokounmpo 20.00 50.00

2019-20 Panini Mosaic Jam Masters Mosaic Orange Fluorescent

*MOSAIC ORANGE FLUORESCENT: 5X TO 12X BASIC
STATED PRINT RUN 25 SER.#'d SETS
1 Spud Webb 20.00 50.00
2 Julius Erving 40.00 100.00
3 DeAndre Jordan 20.00 50.00
4 Clyde Drexler 40.00 100.00
5 Russell Westbrook 40.00 100.00
6 Aaron Gordon 20.00 50.00
7 Donovan Mitchell 50.00 120.00
9 DeMar DeRozan 30.00 80.00
10 Jason Richardson 10.00 25.00
11 Tracy McGrady 40.00 100.00
12 Dominique Wilkins 40.00 100.00
14 Shawn Kemp 25.00 60.00
15 Paul George 40.00 100.00
16 LeBron James 800.00 1,500.00
17 Anthony Davis 75.00 200.00
18 Zach LaVine 60.00 150.00
19 Giannis Antetokounmpo 200.00 500.00
20 Dwight Howard 40.00 100.00

2019-20 Panini Mosaic Montage

COMMON CARD .50 1.25
SEMISTARS .60 1.50
UNLISTED STARS .75 2.00
*FB SILVER: .75X TO 2X BASIC
1 Damian Lillard 2.00 5.00
2 Nikola Vucevic .60 1.50
3 DeMar DeRozan 1.00 2.50
4 Russell Westbrook 1.25 3.00
5 Draymond Green 1.00 2.50
6 Jayson Tatum 3.00 8.00
7 Anthony Davis 2.00 5.00
8 Kawhi Leonard 2.00 5.00
9 Bradley Beal 1.00 2.50
10 LeBron James 6.00 15.00
11 D'Angelo Russell .60 1.50
12 Pascal Siakam 1.25 3.00
13 Derrick Rose 1.50 4.00
14 Stephen Curry 6.00 15.00
15 Giannis Antetokounmpo 4.00 10.00
16 Joel Embiid 1.50 4.00
17 Ben Simmons .75 2.00
18 Kemba Walker .60 1.50
19 Chris Paul 1.50 4.00
20 Luka Doncic 5.00 12.00
21 De'Aaron Fox 1.25 3.00
22 Paul George 1.25 3.00
23 Donovan Mitchell 1.50 4.00
24 Trae Young 2.00 5.00
25 James Harden 1.50 4.00
26 Karl-Anthony Towns 1.25 3.00
27 Blake Griffin .75 2.00
28 Kyrie Irving 1.50 4.00
29 CJ McCollum .75 2.00
30 Nikola Jokic 4.00 10.00

2019-20 Panini Mosaic Montage Mosaic

*MOSAIC: 1.2X TO 3X BASIC
10 LeBron James 30.00 80.00
20 Luka Doncic 30.00 80.00

2019-20 Panini Mosaic Montage Mosaic White

*MOSAIC WHITE: 5X TO 12X BASIC
STATED PRINT RUN 25 SER.#'d SETS
6 Jayson Tatum 60.00 150.00
7 Anthony Davis 60.00 150.00
8 Kawhi Leonard 75.00 200.00
10 LeBron James 400.00 800.00
14 Stephen Curry 125.00 300.00
15 Giannis Antetokounmpo 150.00 400.00
17 Ben Simmons 30.00 80.00
20 Luka Doncic 300.00 600.00
24 Trae Young 100.00 250.00

2019-20 Panini Mosaic Old School

COMMON CARD .50 1.25
SEMISTARS .60 1.50
UNLISTED STARS .75 2.00
1 Steve Nash 1.50 4.00
2 Patrick Ewing 1.25 3.00
3 Dennis Rodman 2.00 5.00
4 Anfernee Hardaway 2.00 5.00
5 John Stockton 1.50 4.00
6 Dennis Johnson 1.00 2.50
7 Moses Malone 1.25 3.00
8 Larry Bird 3.00 8.00
9 Stephon Marbury 1.00 2.50
10 Darryl Dawkins .75 2.00
11 Scottie Pippen 2.00 5.00
12 Kevin Garnett 2.00 5.00
13 Chris Webber 1.00 2.50
14 Allen Iverson 2.00 5.00
15 Amar'e Stoudemire .60 1.50
16 Magic Johnson 2.50 6.00
17 Pete Maravich 2.00 5.00
18 Wilt Chamberlain 3.00 8.00
19 Tracy McGrady 1.25 3.00
20 Tim Duncan 2.00 5.00

2019-20 Panini Mosaic Old School Mosaic Blue Reactive

*MOSAIC BLUE REACTIVE: 1.5X TO 4X BASIC

2019-20 Panini Mosaic Old School Mosaic Green

*MOSAIC GREEN: .75X TO 2X BASIC

2019-20 Panini Mosaic Old School Mosaic Orange Fluorescent

*MOSAIC ORANGE FLUORESCENT: 5X TO 12X BASIC
STATED PRINT RUN 25 SER.#'d SETS

2019-20 Panini Mosaic Overdrive

COMMON CARD .75 2.00
SEMISTARS 1.00 2.50
UNLISTED STARS 1.25 3.00
1 Pascal Siakam 2.00 5.00
2 De'Aaron Fox 2.00 5.00
3 LeBron James 300.00 600.00
4 Russell Westbrook 2.00 5.00
5 Nikola Jokic 6.00 15.00
6 Karl-Anthony Towns 2.00 5.00
7 Nikola Vucevic 1.00 2.50
8 CJ McCollum 1.25 3.00
9 Kawhi Leonard 15.00 40.00
10 Kemba Walker 1.00 2.50
11 Kyrie Irving 2.50 6.00
12 Anthony Davis 12.00 30.00
13 Blake Griffin 1.25 3.00
14 Donovan Mitchell 8.00 20.00
15 Ben Simmons 6.00 15.00
16 Derrick Rose 2.50 6.00
17 Paul George 2.00 5.00
18 Joel Embiid 2.50 6.00
19 James Harden 8.00 20.00
20 Damian Lillard 8.00 20.00
21 Giannis Antetokounmpo 75.00 200.00
22 Trae Young 20.00 50.00
23 Stephen Curry 20.00 50.00
24 Bradley Beal 1.50 4.00
25 Luka Doncic 75.00 200.00

2019-20 Panini Mosaic Rookie Autographs Mosaic

COMMON CARD 3.00 8.00
SEMISTARS 4.00 10.00

UNLISTED STARS 5.00 12.00
EXCHANGE DEADLINE 10/22/2021
1 Zion Williamson 150.00 400.00
2 Carsen Edwards 4.00 10.00
3 De'Andre Hunter 12.00 30.00
4 Admiral Schofield 4.00 10.00
5 Jaxson Hayes 5.00 12.00
6 Kevin Porter Jr. 6.00 15.00
7 Tyler Herro 15.00 40.00
8 Kendrick Nunn 5.00 12.00
9 Sekou Doumbouya 3.00 8.00
10 Darius Bazley 3.00 8.00
11 Ja Morant 500.00 1,000.00
12 Grant Williams 5.00 12.00
13 Jarrett Culver 3.00 8.00
14 Dylan Windler 4.00 10.00
15 Cameron Johnson 8.00 20.00
16 KZ Okpala 4.00 10.00
18 Cody Martin 5.00 12.00
19 Chuma Okeke 5.00 12.00
20 Goga Bitadze 5.00 12.00
21 RJ Barrett 12.00 30.00
22 Ty Jerome 6.00 15.00
23 Cam Reddish 5.00 12.00
24 Mfiondu Kabengele 4.00 10.00
25 PJ Washington Jr. 10.00 25.00
26 Eric Paschall 4.00 10.00
27 Matisse Thybulle 6.00 15.00
28 Isaiah Roby 4.00 10.00
29 Nickeil Alexander-Walker 5.00 12.00
30 Luka Samanic 4.00 10.00
31 Rui Hachimura 12.00 30.00
32 Bruno Fernando 4.00 10.00
33 Coby White 10.00 25.00
34 Jordan Poole 12.00 30.00
35 Bol Bol 8.00 20.00
36 Talen Horton-Tucker 5.00 12.00
37 Nassir Little 5.00 12.00
38 Jaylen Nowell 4.00 10.00
39 Brandon Clarke 6.00 15.00
40 Keldon Johnson 10.00 25.00

2019-20 Panini Mosaic Rookie Scripts

COMMON CARD 3.00 8.00
SEMISTARS 4.00 10.00
UNLISTED STARS 5.00 12.00
EXCHANGE DEADLINE 10/22/2021
1 De'Andre Hunter 12.00 30.00
2 Dean Wade 4.00 10.00
3 Louis King 4.00 10.00
4 Jarrett Culver 3.00 8.00
5 Tacko Fall 4.00 10.00
6 Chris Clemons 3.00 8.00
7 Jaylen Hoard 3.00 8.00
8 Zion Williamson 150.00 400.00
9 Amir Coffey 5.00 12.00
10 Brian Bowen II 3.00 8.00
11 PJ Washington Jr. 10.00 25.00
12 Luka Samanic 4.00 10.00
13 Ja Morant 500.00 1,000.00
14 Sekou Doumbouya 3.00 8.00
15 Romeo Langford 3.00 8.00
16 Darius Bazley 3.00 8.00
17 Miye Oni 3.00 8.00
18 Garrison Mathews 5.00 12.00
20 Bruno Fernando 4.00 10.00
21 Nicolas Claxton 6.00 15.00
22 Isaiah Roby 4.00 10.00
RS-KDN Kendrick Nunn 5.00 12.00
25 Terence Davis 5.00 12.00
26 Rui Hachimura 12.00 30.00
27 Jordan Bone 3.00 8.00
28 RJ Barrett 12.00 30.00
29 Cameron Johnson 8.00 20.00
30 Nicolo Melli 4.00 10.00
31 Nickeil Alexander-Walker 5.00 12.00
32 Brandon Clarke 6.00 15.00
33 Matisse Thybulle 6.00 15.00
34 Alen Smailagic 3.00 8.00
35 Daniel Gafford 6.00 15.00
36 Goga Bitadze 5.00 12.00
37 Keldon Johnson 10.00 25.00
38 Coby White 10.00 25.00
39 Justin Wright-Foreman 3.00 8.00
40 Terance Mann 6.00 15.00

2019-20 Panini Mosaic Rookie Scripts Gold

*GOLD: 1.25X TO 3X BASIC
EXCHANGE DEADLINE 10/22/2021
25 Terence Davis 30.00 80.00
37 Keldon Johnson 100.00 250.00

2019-20 Panini Mosaic Rookie Scripts Orange

*ORANGE: .5X TO 1.2X BASIC
EXCHANGE DEADLINE 10/22/2021

2019-20 Panini Mosaic Rookie Variations

COMMON CARD 1.00 2.50
SEMISTARS 1.25 3.00
UNLISTED STARS 1.50 4.00
*FB: .75X TO 2X BASIC
201 Jarrett Culver 1.00 2.50
209 Zion Williamson 8.00 20.00
211 Coby White 3.00 8.00
213 PJ Washington Jr. 3.00 8.00
219 Ja Morant 10.00 25.00
221 Jaxson Hayes 1.50 4.00
223 Tyler Herro 5.00 12.00
229 RJ Barrett 4.00 10.00
231 Rui Hachimura 4.00 10.00
234 Kendrick Nunn 1.50 4.00
239 De'Andre Hunter 4.00 10.00
241 Cam Reddish 1.50 4.00
249 Darius Garland 4.00 10.00
250 Eric Paschall 1.25 3.00

2019-20 Panini Mosaic Scripts

COMMON CARD 3.00 8.00
SEMISTARS 4.00 10.00
UNLISTED STARS 5.00 12.00
EXCHANGE DEADLINE 10/22/2021
*RED WAVE: .5X TO 1.5X BASIC
1 Erick Strickland 3.00 8.00
2 John Stockton 30.00 80.00
3 Devonte' Graham 4.00 10.00
5 Delon Wright 3.00 8.00
6 Josh Okogie 4.00 10.00
7 Ish Smith 3.00 8.00
9 M.L. Carr 5.00 12.00
10 Allen Iverson 75.00 200.00
11 Mario Hezonja 3.00 8.00
12 Julius Erving 50.00 120.00
13 Meyers Leonard 3.00 8.00
14 Magic Johnson 75.00 200.00
15 Tyus Jones 3.00 8.00
16 Dorian Finney-Smith 4.00 10.00
17 Daniel Theis 5.00 12.00
18 David Robinson 25.00 60.00
19 Bruce Brown 5.00 12.00
20 Karl Malone 30.00 80.00
21 DeAndre' Bembry 3.00 8.00
23 Alex Caruso 25.00 60.00
24 Stephon Marbury 15.00 40.00
25 Jakob Poeltl 3.00 8.00
26 Rodney Hood 4.00 10.00
27 Tony Snell 3.00 8.00
29 Gheorghe Muresan 3.00 8.00
30 Dwyane Wade 60.00 150.00
31 Mason Plumlee 3.00 8.00
32 Kareem Abdul-Jabbar 75.00 200.00
33 Bonzi Wells 4.00 10.00
34 Larry Johnson 12.00 30.00
35 Royce O'Neale 3.00 8.00
36 Kevin Huerter 5.00 12.00
37 Sterling Brown 3.00 8.00
39 Mike Scott 3.00 8.00
41 James Johnson 3.00 8.00
42 Oscar Robertson 30.00 80.00
43 Grayson Allen 12.00 30.00
44 Zach Collins 3.00 8.00
45 Vin Baker 4.00 10.00
46 Damian Jones 3.00 8.00
47 Anfernee Simons 15.00 40.00
49 Torrey Craig 3.00 8.00
50 Larry Bird 75.00 200.00
51 Larry Nance Jr. 4.00 10.00
52 Kawhi Leonard 75.00 200.00
53 Troy Brown Jr. 3.00 8.00
54 Gerald Henderson Sr. 3.00 8.00
55 E'Twaun Moore 3.00 8.00
56 Wes Iwundu 3.00 8.00
57 Alec Burks 3.00 8.00
59 Sam Mack 3.00 8.00

2019-20 Panini Mosaic Scripts Gold

*GOLD: .75X TO 2X BASIC
STATED PRINT RUN 25 SER.#'d SETS
EXCHANGE DEADLINE 10/22/2021
24 Stephon Marbury 40.00 100.00

2019-20 Panini Mosaic Scripts Orange

*ORANGE: .5X TO 1.2X BASIC
EXCHANGE DEADLINE 10/22/2021
4 Karl-Anthony Towns 30.00 80.00
22 Kevin Garnett 100.00 250.00
58 Giannis Antetokounmpo 150.00 400.00

2019-20 Panini Mosaic Stained Glass

COMMON CARD 8.00 20.00
SEMISTARS 10.00 25.00
UNLISTED STARS 12.00 30.00
1 Stephen Curry 300.00 600.00
2 Russell Westbrook 20.00 50.00
3 LeBron James 300.00 600.00
4 Trae Young 75.00 200.00
5 James Harden 60.00 150.00
6 Kyrie Irving 40.00 100.00
7 Giannis Antetokounmpo 75.00 200.00
8 Kawhi Leonard 50.00 120.00
9 Luka Doncic 200.00 500.00
10 Anthony Davis 40.00 100.00

2019-20 Panini Mosaic Stare Masters

COMMON CARD .50 1.25
SEMISTARS .60 1.50
UNLISTED STARS .75 2.00
1 Russell Westbrook 1.25 3.00
2 Donovan Mitchell 1.50 4.00
3 Bradley Beal 1.00 2.50
4 Karl-Anthony Towns 1.25 3.00
5 Derrick Rose 1.50 4.00
6 CJ McCollum .75 2.00
7 Joel Embiid 1.50 4.00
8 Kemba Walker .60 1.50
9 Damian Lillard 2.00 5.00
10 De'Aaron Fox 1.25 3.00
11 Anthony Davis 2.00 5.00
12 Trae Young 2.00 5.00
13 LeBron James 6.00 15.00
14 Blake Griffin .75 2.00
15 Stephen Curry 6.00 15.00
16 Nikola Jokic 4.00 10.00
17 Ben Simmons .75 2.00
18 Luka Doncic 5.00 12.00
19 Nikola Vucevic .60 1.50
20 Paul George 1.25 3.00
21 Kawhi Leonard 2.00 5.00
22 James Harden 1.50 4.00
23 Pascal Siakam 1.25 3.00
24 Kyrie Irving 1.50 4.00
25 Giannis Antetokounmpo 4.00 10.00

2019-20 Panini Mosaic Stare Masters Mosaic

*MOSAIC: 1.2X TO 3X BASIC
11 Anthony Davis 10.00 25.00
12 Trae Young 8.00 20.00
13 LeBron James 60.00 150.00
18 Luka Doncic 30.00 80.00
25 Giannis Antetokounmpo 20.00 50.00

2019-20 Panini Mosaic Stare Masters Mosaic White

*MOSAIC WHITE: 5X TO 12X BASIC
STATED PRINT RUN 25 SER.#'d SETS
11 Anthony Davis 100.00 250.00
13 LeBron James 500.00 1,000.00
15 Stephen Curry 125.00 300.00
17 Ben Simmons 40.00 100.00
18 Luka Doncic 200.00 500.00
21 Kawhi Leonard 100.00 250.00
25 Giannis Antetokounmpo 150.00 400.00

2019-20 Panini Mosaic Swagger

COMMON CARD .75 2.00
SEMISTARS 1.00 2.50
UNLISTED STARS 1.25 3.00
1 Kawhi Leonard 8.00 20.00
2 Ben Simmons 1.25 3.00
3 Anthony Davis 8.00 20.00
4 Joel Embiid 2.50 6.00
5 Russell Westbrook 2.00 5.00
6 Damian Lillard 3.00 8.00
7 Trae Young 10.00 25.00
8 Kyrie Irving 2.50 6.00
9 Giannis Antetokounmpo 40.00 100.00
10 Luka Doncic 75.00 200.00
11 Karl-Anthony Towns 2.00 5.00
12 LeBron James 125.00 300.00
13 Paul George 2.00 5.00
14 Nikola Jokic 6.00 15.00
15 James Harden 6.00 15.00

2019-20 Panini Mosaic Will to Win

COMMON CARD .50 1.25
SEMISTARS .60 1.50
UNLISTED STARS .75 2.00
1 CJ McCollum .75 2.00
2 Karl-Anthony Towns 1.25 3.00
3 Kyrie Irving 1.50 4.00
4 Kawhi Leonard 2.00 5.00
5 Blake Griffin .75 2.00
6 Anthony Davis 2.00 5.00
7 LeBron James 6.00 15.00
8 Pascal Siakam 1.25 3.00
9 Nikola Jokic 4.00 10.00
10 Russell Westbrook 1.25 3.00
11 Trae Young 2.00 5.00
12 Giannis Antetokounmpo 4.00 10.00
13 Luka Doncic 5.00 12.00
14 Stephen Curry 6.00 15.00
15 Ben Simmons .75 2.00
16 Donovan Mitchell 1.50 4.00
17 Joel Embiid 1.50 4.00
18 Paul George 1.25 3.00
19 Damian Lillard 2.00 5.00
20 James Harden 1.50 4.00

2019-20 Panini Mosaic Will to Win Mosaic

*MOSAIC: 1.2X TO 3X BASIC
7 LeBron James 25.00 60.00

2019-20 Panini Mosaic Will to Win Mosaic Blue Reactive

*MOSAIC BLUE REACTIVE: 1.5X TO 4X BASIC
4 Kawhi Leonard 12.00 30.00
7 LeBron James 125.00 300.00
11 Trae Young 12.00 30.00
12 Giannis Antetokounmpo 25.00 60.00
13 Luka Doncic 50.00 120.00

2019-20 Panini Mosaic Will to Win Mosaic Green

*MOSAIC GREEN: .75X TO 2X BASIC
7 LeBron James 12.00 30.00

2019-20 Panini Mosaic Will to Win Mosaic Orange Fluorescent

*MOSAIC ORANGE FLUORESCENT: 5X TO 12X BASIC
STATED PRINT RUN 25 SER.#'d SETS
7 LeBron James 500.00 1,000.00
11 Trae Young 40.00 100.00
12 Giannis Antetokounmpo 100.00 250.00
13 Luka Doncic 125.00 300.00

2020-21 Panini Mosaic

COMPLETE SET (300)
*CAMO PINK: .75X TO 2X BASIC
*FB SILVER: 1.25X TO 3X BASIC
*SILVER: 1.25X TO 3X BASIC
*GREEN ICE: 1.5X TO 4X BASIC
*BLUE/99: 4X TO 10X BASIC
*RED & YLW FUSION/88: 5X TO 12X BASIC RC
*FB BLUE/85: 5X TO 12X BASIC RC
1 Kyle Kuzma .50 1.25
2 Jordan Clarkson .40 1.00
3 Nemanja Bjelica .25 .60
4 Lauri Markkanen .50 1.25
5 Tyler Herro .75 2.00
6 Spencer Dinwiddie .30 .75
7 Kevin Durant 1.50 4.00
8 Joe Ingles .30 .75
9 Brook Lopez .30 .75
10 Davis Bertans .30 .75
11 Troy Brown Jr. .30 .75
12 Josh Okogie .30 .75
13 Donte DiVincenzo .30 .75
14 Cody Zeller .25 .60
15 Domantas Sabonis .50 1.25
16 Michael Porter Jr. .50 1.25
17 Grayson Allen .40 1.00
18 Trae Young 1.00 2.50
19 P.J. Tucker .30 .75
21 Nikola Jokic 2.00 5.00
22 Aaron Gordon .40 1.00
23 T.J. Warren .30 .75
24 Isaiah Roby .25 .60
25 Myles Turner .40 1.00
26 Malcolm Brogdon .40 1.00
27 PJ Washington Jr. .40 1.00
28 Duncan Robinson .40 1.00
29 Jaren Jackson Jr. .60 1.50
30 CJ McCollum .40 1.00
31 Derrick Jones Jr. .30 .75
32 Wendell Carter Jr. .30 .75
33 Devin Booker 1.00 2.50
34 Coby White .50 1.25
35 Thaddeus Young .25 .60
36 Goran Dragic .40 1.00
37 Lonzo Ball .50 1.25
38 Mo Bamba .40 1.00
39 Russell Westbrook .75 2.00
40 Ja Morant 1.25 3.00
41 Ben McLemore .25 .60
42 Paul Millsap .30 .75
43 Andrew Wiggins .50 1.25
44 Kent Bazemore .25 .60
45 John Wall .50 1.25
46 Dejounte Murray .40 1.00
47 Luka Doncic 2.50 6.00
48 Robin Lopez .25 .60
49 Zion Williamson 1.25 3.00
50 De'Andre Hunter .40 1.00
51 Jeff Teague .25 .60
52 JJ Redick .40 1.00
53 Landry Shamet .30 .75
54 Markelle Fultz .30 .75
55 Draymond Green .50 1.25
56 Shake Milton .30 .75
57 Fred VanVleet .60 1.50
58 Rudy Gobert .50 1.25
59 Nikola Vucevic .40 1.00
60 Ivica Zubac .40 1.00
61 Rajon Rondo .40 1.00
62 Matisse Thybulle .30 .75
63 Derrick White .40 1.00
64 Donovan Mitchell .75 2.00
65 Kentavious Caldwell-Pope .30 .75
66 Zach LaVine .60 1.50
67 Buddy Hield .40 1.00
68 RJ Barrett .60 1.50
69 Bradley Beal .50 1.25
70 Pascal Siakam .60 1.50
71 Ricky Rubio .40 1.00
72 Tyus Jones .30 .75
73 Otto Porter Jr. .25 .60
74 Kristaps Porzingis .50 1.25
75 Paul George .60 1.50
76 Terry Rozier .40 1.00
77 Blake Griffin .40 1.00
78 Royce O'Neale .25 .60
79 Lonnie Walker IV .40 1.00
80 Giannis Antetokounmpo 2.00 5.00
81 LeBron James 3.00 8.00
82 Nicolas Batum .25 .60
83 Danny Green .30 .75
84 Elfrid Payton .30 .75
85 Collin Sexton .40 1.00
86 Jamal Murray .60 1.50
87 Monte Morris .25 .60
88 Josh Hart .30 .75
89 Sekou Doumbouya .25 .60
90 Miles Bridges .40 1.00
91 Larry Nance Jr. .30 .75
92 Chris Paul .75 2.00
93 Damian Lillard 1.00 2.50
94 Jonas Valanciunas .30 .75
95 Caris LeVert .40 1.00
96 Jusuf Nurkic .40 1.00
97 Seth Curry .40 1.00
98 Kemba Walker .40 1.00
99 Marcus Smart .40 1.00
100 Darius Garland .60 1.50
101 Kevin Love .40 1.00
102 Clint Capela .30 .75
103 Shai Gilgeous-Alexander 2.00 5.00
104 Ben Simmons .40 1.00
105 Khris Middleton .50 1.25
106 Marvin Bagley III .30 .75
107 Jayson Tatum 1.50 4.00
108 Brandon Clarke .40 1.00
109 Lou Williams .40 1.00
110 Trey Burke .30 .75
111 Robert Covington .30 .75
112 Luguentz Dort .60 1.50
113 Aron Baynes .25 .60
114 Reggie Bullock .30 .75
115 Serge Ibaka .30 .75
116 Jerami Grant .40 1.00
117 Kyle Anderson .25 .60
118 Mason Plumlee .25 .60
119 Danilo Gallinari .30 .75
120 Enes Kanter .30 .75
121 Tristan Thompson .25 .60
122 JaMychal Green .25 .60
123 Derrick Rose .60 1.50
124 Karl-Anthony Towns .60 1.50
125 Mike Conley .30 .75
126 Gordon Hayward .40 1.00
127 Boban Marjanovic .30 .75
128 Kelly Oubre Jr. .40 1.00
129 Alex Caruso .40 1.00
130 Tim Hardaway Jr. .25 .60
131 Dennis Schroder .40 1.00
132 Evan Fournier .30 .75
133 DeMar DeRozan .50 1.25
134 Terrence Ross .30 .75
135 Gary Trent Jr. .40 1.00
136 Keldon Johnson .60 1.50
137 Cam Reddish .50 1.25
138 Eric Bledsoe .30 .75
139 Daniel Theis .30 .75
140 Cameron Payne .25 .60
141 Anthony Davis 1.00 2.50
142 Richaun Holmes .30 .75
143 Josh Jackson .25 .60
144 Kawhi Leonard 1.00 2.50
145 Hamidou Diallo .30 .75
146 Luke Kennard .30 .75
147 D'Angelo Russell .40 1.00
148 Josh Richardson .30 .75
149 Eric Paschall .30 .75
150 Doug McDermott .30 .75
151 Talen Horton-Tucker .40 1.00
152 Julius Randle .40 1.00
153 DeAndre Jordan .30 .75
154 Zach Collins .30 .75
155 Jaylen Brown .60 1.50
156 Jrue Holiday .40 1.00
157 Kyle Lowry .50 1.25
158 Will Barton .25 .60
159 Tobias Harris .40 1.00
160 Rudy Gay .40 1.00
161 Rui Hachimura .50 1.25
162 Malik Beasley .30 .75
163 Eric Gordon .30 .75
164 Joel Embiid 1.00 2.50
165 Christian Wood .30 .75
166 Jabari Parker .25 .60
167 Thanasis Antetokounmpo .30 .75
168 De'Aaron Fox .60 1.50
169 Bol Bol .40 1.00
170 Andre Drummond .40 1.00
171 Bam Adebayo .60 1.50
172 Cameron Johnson .50 1.25
173 James Harden .75 2.00
174 Mikal Bridges .50 1.25
175 Stephen Curry 3.00 8.00
176 Jarrett Culver .25 .60
177 Jimmy Butler .75 2.00
178 Mitchell Robinson .40 1.00
179 Steven Adams .40 1.00
180 Harrison Barnes .30 .75
181 Kevin Knox II .25 .60
182 LaMarcus Aldridge .40 1.00
183 Joe Harris .30 .75
184 Brandon Ingram .50 1.25
185 Jae Crowder .25 .60
186 Victor Oladipo .30 .75
187 Bojan Bogdanovic .30 .75
188 Darius Bazley .25 .60
189 Jakob Poeltl .30 .75
190 OG Anunoby .40 1.00
191 Al Horford .40 1.00
192 Maxi Kleber .30 .75
193 Kelly Olynyk .25 .60
194 Thomas Bryant .30 .75
195 Norman Powell .30 .75
196 Devonte' Graham .30 .75
197 Jarrett Allen .40 1.00
198 Kyrie Irving .75 2.00
199 Deandre Ayton .40 1.00
200 Bogdan Bogdanovic .40 1.00
201 Anthony Edwards RC 6.00 15.00
202 LaMelo Ball RC 5.00 12.00
203 Tyrese Maxey RC 5.00 12.00
204 Tyrese Haliburton RC 5.00 12.00
205 James Wiseman RC .75 2.00
206 Patrick Williams RC 1.50 4.00
207 Cole Anthony RC 1.50 4.00
208 Immanuel Quickley RC 1.50 4.00
209 Saddiq Bey RC 1.25 3.00
210 Payton Pritchard RC 2.00 5.00
211 Desmond Bane RC 2.00 5.00
212 Isaac Okoro RC 1.00 2.50
213 Xavier Tillman RC .75 2.00
214 Jae'Sean Tate RC .75 2.00
215 Precious Achiuwa RC 1.25 3.00
216 Isaiah Joe RC .75 2.00
217 Deni Avdija RC 1.50 4.00
218 Theo Maledon RC .60 1.50
219 Jordan Nwora RC .75 2.00
220 Obi Toppin RC 1.25 3.00
221 Devin Vassell RC 2.00 5.00
222 Killian Hayes RC .60 1.50
223 Isaiah Stewart RC 1.25 3.00
224 Kira Lewis Jr. RC .60 1.50
225 Onyeka Okongwu RC 1.25 3.00
226 Aleksej Pokusevski RC .75 2.00
227 Aaron Nesmith RC 1.25 3.00
228 Jalen Smith RC 1.25 3.00
229 Nico Mannion RC .60 1.50
230 Josh Green RC 1.25 3.00
231 Zeke Nnaji RC .75 2.00
232 CJ Elleby RC .60 1.50
233 RJ Hampton RC .60 1.50
234 Udoka Azubuike RC .75 2.00
235 Jaden McDaniels RC 2.00 5.00
236 Malachi Flynn RC .60 1.50
237 Facundo Campazzo RC .75 2.00
238 Lamar Stevens RC .75 2.00
239 Jahmi'us Ramsey RC .60 1.50
240 Sam Merrill RC 1.00 2.50
241 Mason Jones RC .50 1.25
242 Vernon Carey Jr. RC .60 1.50
243 Tre Jones RC 1.00 2.50
244 Reggie Perry RC .60 1.50
245 Paul Reed RC .75 2.00
246 Damian Lillard 1.00 2.50
247 LeBron James 3.00 8.00
248 Kevin Durant 1.50 4.00
249 Stephen Curry 3.00 8.00
250 Anthony Davis 1.00 2.50
251 Chris Paul .75 2.00
252 Anthony Edwards 6.00 15.00
253 Russell Westbrook .75 2.00
254 Jayson Tatum 1.50 4.00
255 Paul George .60 1.50
256 James Harden .75 2.00
257 LaMelo Ball 5.00 12.00
258 Tyrese Haliburton 5.00 12.00
259 Tyrese Maxey 5.00 12.00
260 James Wiseman .75 2.00
261 Anthony Edwards 6.00 15.00
262 LaMelo Ball 5.00 12.00
263 Tyrese Maxey 5.00 12.00
264 Tyrese Haliburton 5.00 12.00
265 Jae'Sean Tate .75 2.00
266 James Wiseman .75 2.00
267 Patrick Williams 1.50 4.00
268 Cole Anthony 1.50 4.00
269 Payton Pritchard 2.00 5.00
270 Killian Hayes .60 1.50
271 Isaac Okoro 1.00 2.50
272 Deni Avdija 1.50 4.00
273 Obi Toppin 1.25 3.00
274 Onyeka Okongwu 1.25 3.00
275 Jalen Smith 1.25 3.00
276 Saddiq Bey 1.25 3.00
277 Immanuel Quickley 1.50 4.00
278 Devin Vassell 2.00 5.00
279 Aaron Nesmith 1.25 3.00
280 Kira Lewis Jr. .60 1.50
281 Charles Barkley 1.00 2.50
282 Tony Parker .60 1.50
283 Kevin Garnett 1.00 2.50
284 Hakeem Olajuwon .75 2.00
285 Paul Pierce .60 1.50
286 Steve Nash .75 2.00
287 Tracy McGrady .60 1.50
288 Magic Johnson 1.50 4.00
289 Tim Duncan 1.00 2.50
290 Vince Carter .75 2.00
291 Gary Payton .60 1.50
292 Allen Iverson 1.00 2.50
293 Jerry West .75 2.00
294 Jason Kidd .60 1.50
295 Larry Bird 1.50 4.00
296 Kevin Durant 1.50 4.00
297 LeBron James 3.00 8.00
298 Dirk Nowitzki 1.00 2.50
299 Kawhi Leonard 1.00 2.50
300 Shaquille O'Neal 1.50 4.00

2020-21 Panini Mosaic Mosaic

*MOSAIC: .75X TO 2X BASIC
201 Anthony Edwards 15.00 40.00
202 LaMelo Ball 40.00 100.00
252 Anthony Edwards 6.00 15.00
257 LaMelo Ball 20.00 50.00
261 Anthony Edwards 15.00 40.00
262 LaMelo Ball 25.00 60.00

2020-21 Panini Mosaic Mosaic Choice Red and Green

*CHC RED & GREEN: 1.5X TO 4X BASIC
201 Anthony Edwards 30.00 80.00
202 LaMelo Ball 150.00 400.00
203 Tyrese Maxey 30.00 80.00
204 Tyrese Haliburton 30.00 80.00
206 Patrick Williams 25.00 60.00
207 Cole Anthony 25.00 60.00
209 Saddiq Bey 25.00 60.00
211 Desmond Bane 25.00 60.00

2020-21 Panini Mosaic Mosaic Fast Break Purple

COMPLETE SET (300)
*FB PURPLE RC: 6X TO 15X BASIC RC
STATED PRINT RUN 50 SER.#'d SETS
201 Anthony Edwards 200.00 500.00
252 Anthony Edwards 200.00 500.00
261 Anthony Edwards 200.00 500.00

2020-21 Panini Mosaic Mosaic Green

*GREEN: .75X TO 2X BASIC
201 Anthony Edwards 15.00 40.00
202 LaMelo Ball 10.00 25.00
252 Anthony Edwards 12.00 30.00
257 LaMelo Ball 10.00 25.00

2020-21 Panini Mosaic Mosaic Orange Fluorescent

*ORANGE FLUORESCENT: 10X TO 25X BASIC
STATED PRINT RUN 25 SER.#'d SETS
40 Ja Morant 200.00 500.00
47 Luka Doncic 300.00 600.00
49 Zion Williamson 100.00 250.00
80 Giannis Antetokounmpo 75.00 200.00
81 LeBron James 400.00 800.00
175 Stephen Curry 300.00 600.00
201 Anthony Edwards 400.00 800.00
202 LaMelo Ball 1,500.00 3,000.00
203 Tyrese Maxey 350.00 700.00
204 Tyrese Haliburton 350.00 700.00
207 Cole Anthony 300.00 600.00
211 Desmond Bane 200.00 500.00
247 LeBron James 400.00 800.00
249 Stephen Curry 300.00 600.00
252 Anthony Edwards 400.00 800.00
257 LaMelo Ball 1,000.00 2,000.00
261 Anthony Edwards 400.00 800.00
262 LaMelo Ball 1,000.00 2,000.00
292 Allen Iverson 50.00 120.00
296 Kevin Durant 60.00 150.00
297 LeBron James 500.00 1,000.00
298 Dirk Nowitzki 100.00 250.00
299 Kawhi Leonard 60.00 150.00
300 Shaquille O'Neal 60.00 150.00

2020-21 Panini Mosaic Mosaic Purple

*PURPLE RC: 5X TO 12X BASIC RC
STATED PRINT RUN 49 SER.#'d SETS
40 Ja Morant 100.00 250.00
47 Luka Doncic 125.00 300.00
49 Zion Williamson 50.00 120.00
80 Giannis Antetokounmpo 40.00 100.00
81 LeBron James 125.00 300.00
175 Stephen Curry 125.00 300.00
201 Anthony Edwards 150.00 400.00
202 LaMelo Ball 150.00 400.00
247 LeBron James 100.00 250.00
249 Stephen Curry 100.00 250.00
252 Anthony Edwards 150.00 400.00
257 LaMelo Ball 150.00 400.00
261 Anthony Edwards 150.00 400.00
262 LaMelo Ball 150.00 400.00
297 LeBron James 100.00 250.00
298 Dirk Nowitzki 60.00 150.00
300 Shaquille O'Neal 30.00 80.00

2020-21 Panini Mosaic Mosaic Reactive Blue

*REACTIVE BLUE: 1.25X TO 3X BASIC
201 Anthony Edwards 25.00 60.00
202 LaMelo Ball 75.00 200.00
203 Tyrese Maxey 20.00 50.00
204 Tyrese Haliburton 20.00 50.00
207 Cole Anthony 20.00 50.00
211 Desmond Bane 20.00 50.00
252 Anthony Edwards 25.00 60.00
257 LaMelo Ball 50.00 120.00
261 Anthony Edwards 25.00 60.00
262 LaMelo Ball 50.00 120.00

2020-21 Panini Mosaic Mosaic Reactive Green

*REACTIVE GREEN: .75X TO 2X BASIC
201 Anthony Edwards 15.00 40.00
202 LaMelo Ball 40.00 100.00
252 Anthony Edwards 6.00 15.00
257 LaMelo Ball 20.00 50.00
261 Anthony Edwards 15.00 40.00
262 LaMelo Ball 25.00 60.00

2020-21 Panini Mosaic Mosaic Reactive Orange

*REACTIVE ORANGE: .75X TO 2X BASIC
201 Anthony Edwards 15.00 40.00
202 LaMelo Ball 40.00 100.00
252 Anthony Edwards 12.00 30.00
257 LaMelo Ball 20.00 50.00
261 Anthony Edwards 15.00 40.00
262 LaMelo Ball 25.00 60.00

2020-21 Panini Mosaic Mosaic Reactive Red

*REACTIVE RED: 1.25X TO 3X BASIC
201 Anthony Edwards 25.00 60.00
202 LaMelo Ball 75.00 200.00
203 Tyrese Maxey 20.00 50.00
204 Tyrese Haliburton 20.00 50.00
207 Cole Anthony 20.00 50.00
211 Desmond Bane 20.00 50.00
252 Anthony Edwards 25.00 60.00
257 LaMelo Ball 50.00 120.00
261 Anthony Edwards 25.00 60.00
262 LaMelo Ball 50.00 120.00

2020-21 Panini Mosaic Mosaic Reactive Yellow

*REACTIVE YELLOW: 1.25X TO 3X BASIC
201 Anthony Edwards 25.00 60.00
202 LaMelo Ball 75.00 200.00
203 Tyrese Maxey 20.00 50.00
204 Tyrese Haliburton 20.00 50.00
207 Cole Anthony 20.00 50.00
211 Desmond Bane 20.00 50.00
252 Anthony Edwards 25.00 60.00
257 LaMelo Ball 50.00 120.00
261 Anthony Edwards 25.00 60.00
262 LaMelo Ball 50.00 120.00

2020-21 Panini Mosaic Mosaic Red

*RED: 1X TO 2.5X BASIC
201 Anthony Edwards 20.00 50.00

2020-21 Panini Mosaic Mosaic Red Wave

*MOSAIC RED WAVE: 1.2X TO 3X BASIC

2020-21 Panini Mosaic Mosaic White

COMPLETE SET (300)
*WHITE: 12X TO 30X BASIC
STATED PRINT RUN 25 SER.#'d SETS
201 Anthony Edwards 500.00 1,000.00
252 Anthony Edwards 500.00 1,000.00
261 Anthony Edwards 500.00 1,000.00

2020-21 Panini Mosaic Autographs Fast Break

COMMON CARD 3.00 8.00
SEMISTARS 4.00 10.00
UNLISTED STARS 5.00 12.00
EXCHANGE DEADLINE 06/03/2023
1 Greg Ostertag 3.00 8.00
2 Donte DiVincenzo 5.00 12.00
3 Horace Grant 12.00 30.00
4 Mitch Richmond 10.00 25.00
5 Isiah Thomas 30.00 80.00
6 Mark Jackson 4.00 10.00
7 De'Andre Hunter 5.00 12.00
8 Josh Jackson 3.00 8.00
9 Jordan Poole 40.00 100.00
10 Gary Payton 15.00 40.00
11 Cam Reddish 6.00 15.00
12 Maxi Kleber 4.00 10.00
13 Kevin Garnett 100.00 250.00
14 Lauri Markkanen 6.00 15.00
15 Duncan Robinson 5.00 12.00
16 Isaiah Rider 4.00 10.00
17 Elton Brand 5.00 12.00
18 Nate Archibald 6.00 15.00
19 Avery Johnson 4.00 10.00
20 Al Harrington 3.00 8.00
21 Elfrid Payton 4.00 10.00
22 Al-Farouq Aminu 3.00 8.00
23 Buddy Hield 8.00 20.00
24 Tim Legler 3.00 8.00
25 Shawn Kemp 30.00 80.00
26 Darius Miles 3.00 8.00
27 Luguentz Dort 12.00 30.00
28 Michael Porter Jr. 6.00 15.00
29 Danilo Gallinari 4.00 10.00
30 Dominique Wilkins 15.00 40.00
31 Chris Mullin 10.00 25.00
32 Bradley Beal 15.00 40.00
33 Dennis Rodman 40.00 100.00
34 Tim Hardaway 10.00 25.00
35 Artis Gilmore 8.00 20.00
36 Domantas Sabonis 15.00 40.00
37 Aron Baynes 3.00 8.00
38 Larry Nance Jr. 4.00 10.00
39 Nassir Little 4.00 10.00
40 Tony Parker 12.00 30.00
41 Ja Morant 150.00 400.00
42 Luka Doncic 500.00 1,000.00
43 Shake Milton 4.00 10.00
44 Boban Marjanovic 10.00 25.00
45 Kendrick Nunn 4.00 10.00
46 Alex Caruso 20.00 50.00
47 Aaron Holiday 4.00 10.00
48 Spencer Dinwiddie 4.00 10.00
49 Rasheed Wallace 40.00 100.00
50 Kristaps Porzingis 12.00 30.00
51 Allen Iverson 75.00 200.00
52 Magic Johnson 75.00 200.00
53 Nico Mannion 4.00 10.00
54 Robert Woodard II 4.00 10.00
55 Jaden McDaniels 12.00 30.00
56 Kira Lewis Jr. 4.00 10.00
57 Kenyon Martin Jr. 6.00 15.00
58 Malachi Flynn 4.00 10.00
59 Tyrell Terry 3.00 8.00
60 Jalen Harris 3.00 8.00
61 Aleksej Pokusevski 5.00 12.00
62 Elijah Hughes 4.00 10.00
63 Caleb Martin 8.00 20.00
64 Cassius Stanley 4.00 10.00
65 Jahmi'us Ramsey 4.00 10.00
66 CJ Elleby 4.00 10.00
67 Vernon Carey Jr. 4.00 10.00
68 Josh Green 8.00 20.00
69 LaMelo Ball 400.00 800.00
70 Cole Anthony 75.00 200.00
71 RJ Hampton 4.00 10.00
72 Obi Toppin 8.00 20.00
73 Payton Pritchard 12.00 30.00
74 Killian Hayes 4.00 10.00
75 Tyrese Haliburton 75.00 200.00
76 Tre Jones 6.00 15.00
77 Jordan Nwora 5.00 12.00
78 Isaiah Joe 5.00 12.00
79 Immanuel Quickley 10.00 25.00
80 Sam Merrill 6.00 15.00
81 Cassius Winston 4.00 10.00
82 Nick Richards 5.00 12.00
83 Desmond Bane 50.00 120.00
84 Onyeka Okongwu 8.00 20.00
85 Daniel Oturu 4.00 10.00
86 Patrick Williams 10.00 25.00

87 Saddiq Bey 8.00 20.00
88 Mason Jones 3.00 8.00
89 Isaiah Stewart 8.00 20.00
90 Devin Vassell 12.00 30.00
91 Theo Maledon 4.00 10.00
92 Aaron Nesmith 8.00 20.00
93 Tyler Bey 4.00 10.00
94 Tyrese Maxey 75.00 200.00
95 Deni Avdija 10.00 25.00
96 Isaac Okoro 6.00 15.00
97 James Wiseman 5.00 12.00
98 Anthony Edwards 300.00 600.00
99 Markus Howard 5.00 12.00
100 Jae'Sean Tate 5.00 12.00

2020-21 Panini Mosaic Autographs Mosaic

COMMON CARD 3.00 8.00
SEMISTARS 4.00 10.00
UNLISTED STARS 5.00 12.00
*CHC FSN RED & YELLOW: .6X TO 1.5X BASIC
1 Jarrett Culver 3.00 8.00
2 Robin Lopez 3.00 8.00
3 Robert Covington 4.00 10.00
4 Horace Grant 8.00 20.00
5 De'Andre Hunter 5.00 12.00
6 Josh Jackson 3.00 8.00
7 Jack Sikma 5.00 12.00
8 Jarrett Jack 3.00 8.00
9 Jordan Poole 40.00 100.00
10 Cam Reddish 6.00 15.00
11 Shake Milton 4.00 10.00
12 Kiki Vandeweghe 4.00 10.00
13 M.L. Carr 4.00 10.00
14 Jason Terry 4.00 10.00
15 Nickeil Alexander-Walker 5.00 12.00
16 Kevin Garnett 100.00 250.00
17 Lenny Wilkens 5.00 12.00
18 Duncan Robinson 10.00 25.00
19 Calvin Murphy 5.00 12.00
20 Quentin Richardson 3.00 8.00
21 Calvin Natt 4.00 10.00
22 Brent Barry 4.00 10.00
23 Ish Smith 3.00 8.00
25 Brian Winters 3.00 8.00
26 Otto Porter Jr. 3.00 8.00
27 Dominique Wilkins 12.00 30.00
28 Mason Plumlee 3.00 8.00
29 Baron Davis 8.00 20.00
30 Andrea Bargnani 3.00 8.00
31 Caron Butler 4.00 10.00
32 Roy Hibbert 3.00 8.00
33 Sarunas Marciulionis 5.00 12.00
34 Delon Wright 3.00 8.00
35 Justin Holiday 3.00 8.00
36 Jarrett Allen 8.00 20.00
37 Carsen Edwards 4.00 10.00
38 Ben McLemore 3.00 8.00
39 Danny Manning 4.00 10.00
40 Hakeem Olajuwon 40.00 100.00
41 Dorian Finney-Smith 4.00 10.00
42 Luka Doncic 500.00 1,000.00
43 Richard Hamilton 5.00 12.00
44 Jrue Holiday 8.00 20.00
45 Kelly Oubre Jr. 8.00 20.00
46 Elvin Hayes 10.00 25.00
47 Gordon Hayward 8.00 20.00
48 Domantas Sabonis 15.00 40.00
49 Kawhi Leonard 75.00 200.00
50 Myles Turner 5.00 12.00
51 Ryan Arcidiacono 3.00 8.00
52 Malik Beasley 4.00 10.00
53 Mike Conley 4.00 10.00
54 Gary Payton 15.00 40.00
55 Kyle Kuzma 10.00 25.00
56 Jerry West 30.00 80.00
57 Tim Hardaway 10.00 25.00
58 Magic Johnson 75.00 200.00
59 Allen Iverson 75.00 200.00
60 Sterling Brown 3.00 8.00

2020-21 Panini Mosaic Award-Winning Autographs

7 Zion Williamson 400.00 800.00
12 Ja Morant 400.00 800.00
22 Jayson Tatum 200.00 500.00
28 Joe Dumars 12.00 30.00

2020-21 Panini Mosaic Bang!

COMPLETE SET (15)
*MOSAIC: .75X TO 2X BASIC
*GREEN: .75X TO 2X BASIC
1 Luka Doncic 2.50 6.00
2 Stephen Curry 3.00 8.00
3 Damian Lillard 1.00 2.50
4 Ray Allen .60 1.50
5 Derrick Rose .60 1.50
6 Jason Terry .30 .75
7 Carmelo Anthony .60 1.50
8 Kawhi Leonard 1.00 2.50
9 Kyrie Irving 1.25 3.00
10 Paul Pierce .60 1.50
11 LeBron James 3.00 8.00
12 Dwyane Wade .75 2.00
13 Trae Young 1.00 2.50
14 Kevin Durant 1.50 4.00
15 Derek Fisher .40 1.00

2020-21 Panini Mosaic Bang! Mosaic Orange Fluorescent

*ORANGE: 8X TO 20X BASIC
PRINT RUN 25 SER.#'d SETS
2 Stephen Curry 125.00 300.00
9 Kyrie Irving 75.00 200.00
11 LeBron James 125.00 300.00

2020-21 Panini Mosaic Bang! Mosaic Reactive Blue

*REACTIVE BLUE: 2X TO 5X BASIC
PRINT RUN 99 SER.#'d SETS
2 Stephen Curry 60.00 150.00
9 Kyrie Irving 40.00 100.00
11 LeBron James 60.00 150.00

2020-21 Panini Mosaic Bang! Mosaic Reactive Yellow

*YELLOW: 4X TO 10X BASIC
PRINT RUN 99 SER.#'d SETS
2 Stephen Curry 60.00 150.00
9 Kyrie Irving 40.00 100.00
11 LeBron James 60.00 150.00

2020-21 Panini Mosaic Blue Chips

COMPLETE SET (15)
1 Onyeka Okongwu 1.25 3.00
2 Killian Hayes .60 1.50
3 Deni Avdija 1.50 4.00
4 Saddiq Bey 1.25 3.00
5 Tyrese Haliburton 5.00 12.00
6 Patrick Williams 1.50 4.00
7 Isaac Okoro 1.00 2.50
8 Tyrese Maxey 5.00 12.00
9 LaMelo Ball 5.00 12.00
10 Obi Toppin 1.25 3.00
11 Cole Anthony 1.50 4.00
12 James Wiseman .75 2.00
13 Payton Pritchard 2.00 5.00
14 Anthony Edwards 6.00 15.00
15 Desmond Bane 2.00 5.00

2020-21 Panini Mosaic Blue Chips Mosaic White

*WHITE: 4X TO 10X BASIC
STATED PRINT RUN 25 SER.#'d SETS
5 Tyrese Haliburton 100.00 250.00
9 LaMelo Ball 100.00 250.00
14 Anthony Edwards 125.00 300.00

2020-21 Panini Mosaic Center Stage

COMMON CARD 1.00 2.50
SEMISTARS 1.25 3.00
UNLISTED STARS 1.50 4.00
1 Damian Lillard 4.00 10.00
2 Russell Westbrook 3.00 8.00
3 Kyrie Irving 3.00 8.00
4 Kristaps Porzingis 2.00 5.00
5 Donovan Mitchell 3.00 8.00
6 Kawhi Leonard 4.00 10.00
7 Zion Williamson 5.00 12.00
8 Devin Booker 4.00 10.00
9 Kevin Durant 6.00 15.00
10 Giannis Antetokounmpo 8.00 20.00
11 Joel Embiid 4.00 10.00
12 Jamal Murray 2.50 6.00
13 Paul George 2.50 6.00
14 Kemba Walker 1.50 4.00
15 DeMar DeRozan 2.00 5.00
16 LeBron James 12.00 30.00
17 Stephen Curry 12.00 30.00
18 Ja Morant 5.00 12.00
19 Luka Doncic 10.00 25.00
20 Trae Young 4.00 10.00
21 Bradley Beal 2.00 5.00
22 Khris Middleton 2.00 5.00
23 Anthony Davis 4.00 10.00
24 Jimmy Butler 3.00 8.00
25 James Harden 3.00 8.00
26 Kyle Lowry 2.00 5.00
27 Karl-Anthony Towns 2.50 6.00
28 De'Aaron Fox 2.50 6.00
29 Jayson Tatum 6.00 15.00
30 Ben Simmons 1.50 4.00

2020-21 Panini Mosaic Elevate

COMPLETE SET (25)
*MOSAIC: .75X TO 2X BASIC
*GREEN: .75X TO 2X BASIC
*REACTIVE BLUE/99: 3X TO 8X BASIC
*REACTIVE YELLOW/99: 3X TO 8X BASIC
*ORANGE FL/25: 8X TO 20X BASIC
1 Zach LaVine .60 1.50
2 Giannis Antetokounmpo 2.00 5.00
3 Zion Williamson 1.25 3.00
4 Derrick Jones Jr. .30 .75
5 James Wiseman .40 1.00
6 Domantas Sabonis .50 1.25
7 Kristaps Porzingis .50 1.25
8 Jaylen Brown .60 1.50
9 Kevin Durant 1.50 4.00
10 Christian Wood .30 .75
11 De'Aaron Fox .60 1.50
12 Anthony Edwards 3.00 8.00
13 Ja Morant 1.25 3.00
14 Russell Westbrook .75 2.00
15 Karl-Anthony Towns .60 1.50
16 Aaron Gordon .40 1.00
17 Bam Adebayo .60 1.50
18 Anthony Davis 1.00 2.50
19 Deandre Ayton .40 1.00
20 Joel Embiid 1.00 2.50
21 Miles Bridges .40 1.00
22 Ben Simmons .40 1.00
23 LeBron James 3.00 8.00
24 Donovan Mitchell .75 2.00
25 Jayson Tatum 1.50 4.00

2020-21 Panini Mosaic HoloFame

COMPLETE SET (20)
*MOSAIC: .75X TO 2X BASIC
*GREEN: .75X TO 2X BASIC
*REACTIVE BLUE/99: 3X TO 8X BASIC
*REACTIVE YELLOW/99: 3X TO 8X BASIC
*ORANGE FL/25: 8X TO 20X BASIC
1 Allen Iverson 1.00 2.50
2 Charles Barkley 1.00 2.50
3 Shaquille O'Neal 1.50 4.00
4 Larry Bird 1.50 4.00
5 Tim Duncan 1.00 2.50
6 Kevin Garnett 1.00 2.50
7 Tracy McGrady .60 1.50
8 Dennis Rodman 1.00 2.50
9 Jason Kidd .60 1.50
10 Steve Nash .75 2.00
11 Magic Johnson 1.50 4.00
12 Ray Allen .60 1.50
13 John Stockton .75 2.00
14 David Robinson .75 2.00
15 Karl Malone .75 2.00
16 Grant Hill .60 1.50
17 Kareem Abdul-Jabbar 1.25 3.00
18 Hakeem Olajuwon .75 2.00
19 Dominique Wilkins .60 1.50
20 Clyde Drexler .60 1.50

2020-21 Panini Mosaic Introductions

COMPLETE SET (10)
*FB: .75X TO 2X BASIC
*MOSAIC: .75X TO 2X BASIC
*RED: .75X TO 2X BASIC
1 Tyrese Haliburton 5.00 12.00
2 Patrick Williams 1.50 4.00
3 Isaac Okoro 1.00 2.50
4 Tyrese Maxey 5.00 12.00
5 LaMelo Ball 5.00 12.00
6 Obi Toppin 1.25 3.00
7 Cole Anthony 1.50 4.00
8 James Wiseman .75 2.00
9 Payton Pritchard 2.00 5.00
10 Anthony Edwards 6.00 15.00

2020-21 Panini Mosaic Introductions Mosaic White

COMPLETE SET (10)
*WHITE: 4X TO 10X BASIC
STATED PRINT RUN 25 SER.#'d SETS
1 Tyrese Haliburton 100.00 250.00
5 LaMelo Ball 100.00 250.00
10 Anthony Edwards 125.00 300.00

2020-21 Panini Mosaic Jam Masters

COMPLETE SET (20)
*MOSAIC: .75X TO 2X BASIC
*GREEN: .75X TO 2X BASIC
*REACTIVE BLUE/99: 4X TO 10X BASIC
*REACTIVE YELLOW/99: 4X TO 10X BASIC
*ORNG FL/25: 8X TO 20X BASIC
1 Zion Williamson 1.25 3.00
2 Blake Griffin .40 1.00
3 John Wall .50 1.25
4 Russell Westbrook .75 2.00
5 Aaron Gordon .40 1.00
6 Zach LaVine .60 1.50
7 Donovan Mitchell .75 2.00
8 Paul George .60 1.50
9 Giannis Antetokounmpo 2.00 5.00
10 LeBron James 3.00 8.00
11 Vince Carter .75 2.00
12 Luka Doncic 2.50 6.00
13 Dominique Wilkins .60 1.50
14 Shaquille O'Neal 1.50 4.00
15 Shawn Kemp .60 1.50
16 Spud Webb .40 1.00
17 Clyde Drexler .60 1.50
18 Tracy McGrady .60 1.50
19 Anthony Davis 1.00 2.50
20 Jason Richardson .40 1.00

2020-21 Panini Mosaic Men of Mastery

COMPLETE SET (20)
*FB: .75X TO 2X BASIC
*MOSAIC: .75X TO 2X BASIC
*RED: .75X TO 2X BASIC
1 Kevin Durant 1.50 4.00
2 Kawhi Leonard 1.00 2.50
3 Shai Gilgeous-Alexander 2.00 5.00
4 Ben Simmons .40 1.00
5 Kyrie Irving .75 2.00
6 Trae Young 1.00 2.50
7 Bradley Beal .50 1.25
8 Donovan Mitchell .75 2.00
9 Chris Paul .75 2.00
10 Pascal Siakam .60 1.50
11 Anthony Davis 1.00 2.50
12 Nikola Jokic 2.00 5.00
13 Jayson Tatum 1.50 4.00
14 Zion Williamson 1.25 3.00
15 Damian Lillard 1.00 2.50
16 Stephen Curry 3.00 8.00
17 Ja Morant 1.25 3.00
18 Luka Doncic 2.50 6.00
19 Giannis Antetokounmpo 2.00 5.00
20 LeBron James 3.00 8.00

2020-21 Panini Mosaic Men of Mastery Mosaic White

*WHITE: 4X TO 10X BASIC
STATED PRINT RUN 25 SER.#'d SETS
1 Kevin Durant 60.00 150.00
9 Chris Paul 20.00 50.00
16 Stephen Curry 100.00 250.00
17 Ja Morant 125.00 300.00
18 Luka Doncic 125.00 300.00
19 Giannis Antetokounmpo 60.00 150.00
20 LeBron James 125.00 300.00

2020-21 Panini Mosaic Montage

COMMON CARD .40 1.00
SEMISTARS .50 1.25
UNLISTED STARS .60 1.50
*FB: .6X TO 1.5X BASIC
*MOSAIC: .6X TO 1.5X BASIC
1 De'Aaron Fox 1.00 2.50
2 Collin Sexton .60 1.50
3 Jaylen Brown 1.00 2.50
4 Paul George 1.00 2.50
5 Jamal Murray 1.00 2.50
6 CJ McCollum .60 1.50
7 Bradley Beal .75 2.00
8 Pascal Siakam 1.00 2.50
9 Joel Embiid 1.50 4.00
10 Kristaps Porzingis .75 2.00
11 D'Angelo Russell .60 1.50
12 Chris Paul 1.25 3.00
13 Kyrie Irving 1.25 3.00
14 RJ Barrett 1.00 2.50
15 Shai Gilgeous-Alexander 3.00 8.00
16 Brandon Ingram .75 2.00
17 LeBron James 5.00 12.00
18 Giannis Antetokounmpo 3.00 8.00
19 Luka Doncic 4.00 10.00
20 Bam Adebayo 1.00 2.50
21 John Wall .75 2.00
22 Zion Williamson 2.00 5.00
23 Zach LaVine 1.00 2.50
24 Ja Morant 2.00 5.00
25 Malcolm Brogdon .60 1.50
26 Gordon Hayward .60 1.50
27 Keldon Johnson 1.00 2.50
28 Stephen Curry 5.00 12.00
29 Trae Young 1.50 4.00
30 Derrick Rose 1.00 2.50

2020-21 Panini Mosaic Montage Mosaic White

*WHITE: 4X TO 10X BASIC
STATED PRINT RUN 25 SER.#'d SETS
17 LeBron James 125.00 300.00
18 Giannis Antetokounmpo 50.00 120.00
19 Luka Doncic 100.00 250.00
24 Ja Morant 100.00 250.00
28 Stephen Curry 100.00 250.00

2020-21 Panini Mosaic Overdrive

COMMON CARD 1.00 2.50
SEMISTARS 1.25 3.00
UNLISTED STARS 1.50 4.00
1 Nikola Jokic 8.00 20.00
2 Joel Embiid 4.00 10.00
3 Kawhi Leonard 4.00 10.00
4 Kevin Durant 6.00 15.00
5 LeBron James 12.00 30.00
6 Anthony Davis 4.00 10.00
7 Giannis Antetokounmpo 8.00 20.00
8 Paul George 2.50 6.00
9 Luka Doncic 10.00 25.00
10 Trae Young 4.00 10.00
11 Donovan Mitchell 3.00 8.00
12 Jayson Tatum 6.00 15.00
13 Zion Williamson 5.00 12.00
14 Ja Morant 5.00 12.00
15 Russell Westbrook 3.00 8.00
16 Bradley Beal 2.00 5.00
17 James Harden 3.00 8.00
18 Kyrie Irving 3.00 8.00
19 Bam Adebayo 2.50 6.00
20 Devin Booker 4.00 10.00
21 Karl-Anthony Towns 2.50 6.00
22 Domantas Sabonis 2.00 5.00
23 Damian Lillard 4.00 10.00
24 De'Aaron Fox 2.50 6.00
25 Ben Simmons 1.50 4.00

2020-21 Panini Mosaic Rookie Autographs Mosaic

COMMON CARD 4.00 10.00
SEMISTARS 5.00 12.00
UNLISTED STARS 6.00 15.00
EXCHANGE DEADLINE 06/03/2023
*CHC FSN RED & YELLOW: .6X TO 1.5X BASIC
1 Anthony Edwards 300.00 600.00
2 Jae'Sean Tate 6.00 15.00
3 Markus Howard 6.00 15.00
4 James Wiseman 6.00 15.00
5 Isaac Okoro 8.00 20.00
6 Deni Avdija 12.00 30.00
7 Tyrese Maxey 75.00 200.00
8 Tyler Bey 6.00 15.00
9 Aaron Nesmith 10.00 25.00
10 Killian Tillie 6.00 15.00
11 Theo Maledon 6.00 15.00
12 Devin Vassell 15.00 40.00
13 Isaiah Stewart 10.00 25.00
14 Mason Jones 4.00 10.00
15 Saddiq Bey 10.00 25.00
16 Patrick Williams 12.00 30.00
17 Lamar Stevens 6.00 15.00
18 Onyeka Okongwu 10.00 25.00
19 Desmond Bane 50.00 120.00
20 Killian Hayes 5.00 12.00
21 Payton Pritchard 15.00 40.00
22 Obi Toppin 10.00 25.00
23 RJ Hampton 5.00 12.00
24 Cole Anthony 40.00 100.00
25 LaMelo Ball 400.00 800.00
26 Josh Green 10.00 25.00
27 Precious Achiuwa 10.00 25.00
28 Xavier Tillman 6.00 15.00
29 Vernon Carey Jr. 5.00 12.00
30 Aleksej Pokusevski 6.00 15.00
31 Jalen Harris 4.00 10.00
33 Udoka Azubuike 6.00 15.00
34 Tyrese Haliburton 60.00 150.00
35 Tre Jones 8.00 20.00
36 Isaiah Joe 6.00 15.00
37 Immanuel Quickley 12.00 30.00
38 Devon Dotson 5.00 12.00
39 Cassius Winston 5.00 12.00
40 Nick Richards 6.00 15.00

2020-21 Panini Mosaic Rookie Scripts

COMMON CARD 4.00 10.00
SEMISTARS 5.00 12.00
UNLISTED STARS 6.00 15.00
EXCHANGE DEADLINE 06/03/2023
1 Markus Howard 6.00 15.00
2 Anthony Edwards 400.00 800.00
3 Freddie Gillespie 5.00 12.00
4 Tyler Bey 5.00 12.00
5 Theo Maledon 5.00 12.00
6 Ty-Shon Alexander 5.00 12.00
7 Mason Jones 4.00 10.00
8 Trent Forrest 6.00 15.00
9 Patrick Williams 12.00 30.00
10 Daniel Oturu 5.00 12.00
11 Lamar Stevens 6.00 15.00
12 Onyeka Okongwu 10.00 25.00
13 Nathan Knight 5.00 12.00
14 Sam Merrill 8.00 20.00
15 Deni Avdija 12.00 30.00
16 Anthony Lamb 5.00 12.00
17 Tyrese Maxey 75.00 200.00
18 Sean McDermott 4.00 10.00
19 Jordan Nwora 6.00 15.00
20 Tyrese Haliburton 75.00 200.00
21 Reggie Perry 5.00 12.00
22 Killian Hayes 5.00 12.00
23 Ashton Hagans 6.00 15.00
24 Payton Pritchard 15.00 40.00
25 Obi Toppin 10.00 25.00
26 LaMelo Ball 400.00 800.00
27 CJ Elleby 5.00 12.00
28 Jahmi'us Ramsey 5.00 12.00
30 Jalen Harris 4.00 10.00
31 Kira Lewis Jr. 5.00 12.00
33 Paul Reed 6.00 15.00
34 Grant Riller 5.00 12.00
35 Nico Mannion 5.00 12.00
36 Udoka Azubuike 6.00 15.00
37 Tyrell Terry 4.00 10.00
38 Killian Tillie 6.00 15.00
39 Skylar Mays 5.00 12.00
40 James Wiseman 6.00 15.00

2020-21 Panini Mosaic Rookie Scripts Green Ice

*GREEN ICE: .5X TO 1.2X BASIC

2020-21 Panini Mosaic Rookie Scripts Orange

*ORANGE: .5X TO 1.2X BASIC

2020-21 Panini Mosaic Rookie Scripts Red Wave

*RED WAVE: .5X TO 1.2X BASIC

2020-21 Panini Mosaic Rookie Variations

COMPLETE SET (14)
*FB: .75X TO 2X BASIC
201 Anthony Edwards 12.00 30.00
202 LaMelo Ball 10.00 25.00
203 Tyrese Maxey 10.00 25.00
204 Tyrese Haliburton 10.00 25.00
205 James Wiseman 1.50 4.00
206 Patrick Williams 3.00 8.00
207 Cole Anthony 3.00 8.00
208 Immanuel Quickley 3.00 8.00
210 Payton Pritchard 4.00 10.00
211 Desmond Bane 4.00 10.00
212 Isaac Okoro 2.00 5.00
217 Deni Avdija 3.00 8.00
220 Obi Toppin 2.50 6.00
221 Onyeka Okongwu 2.50 6.00

2020-21 Panini Mosaic Scripts

COMMON CARD 3.00 8.00
SEMISTARS 4.00 10.00
UNLISTED STARS 5.00 12.00
*GREEN ICE: .5X TO 1.2X BASIC
*ORANGE: .5X TO 1.2X BASIC
1 E'Twaun Moore 3.00 8.00
2 John Salmons 3.00 8.00
3 Marcus Camby 4.00 10.00
4 Kevin Willis 4.00 10.00
5 Nerlens Noel 3.00 8.00
6 Wally Szczerbiak 4.00 10.00
7 James Johnson 3.00 8.00
8 Jarred Vanderbilt 4.00 10.00
9 David Nwaba 3.00 8.00
10 Mike Miller 4.00 10.00
11 Bruce Brown 4.00 10.00
12 Alex English 5.00 12.00
13 Calvin Natt 4.00 10.00
14 James Ennis III 3.00 8.00
15 Fat Lever 5.00 12.00
16 Quinndary Weatherspoon 3.00 8.00
17 Wes Iwundu 3.00 8.00
18 Jack Sikma 5.00 12.00
19 Kenny "Sky" Walker 4.00 10.00
20 Sekou Doumbouya 3.00 8.00
21 Christian Laettner 5.00 12.00
22 Kevin Garnett 100.00 250.00
23 Arron Afflalo 3.00 8.00
24 Yuta Watanabe 20.00 50.00
25 DeShawn Stevenson 3.00 8.00
26 Keita Bates-Diop 3.00 8.00
27 Dwayne Bacon 3.00 8.00
28 Mike Scott 3.00 8.00
29 Alec Burks 3.00 8.00
30 Micheal Ray Richardson 3.00 8.00
31 Danilo Gallinari 4.00 10.00
32 Quentin Richardson 3.00 8.00
33 Brent Barry 4.00 10.00
34 Ish Smith 3.00 8.00
35 Tim Legler 3.00 8.00
36 Ricky Pierce 3.00 8.00
37 Terry Cummings 5.00 12.00
38 Darius Miles 3.00 8.00
39 Kevin Porter 3.00 8.00
40 Mitch Kupchak 3.00 8.00
41 Dominique Wilkins 12.00 30.00
43 Buddy Hield 8.00 20.00
44 Brian Scalabrine 3.00 8.00
45 Bradley Beal 12.00 30.00
46 Jarrett Culver 3.00 8.00
47 Thanasis Antetokounmpo 12.00 30.00
48 Solomon Hill 3.00 8.00
49 Jerry West 25.00 60.00
50 Tony Bradley 3.00 8.00
51 Cody Martin 3.00 8.00
52 Daniel Theis 4.00 10.00
53 Dennis Rodman 40.00 100.00
54 Dee Brown 4.00 10.00
55 Khem Birch 4.00 10.00
56 Ja Morant 200.00 500.00
57 PJ Washington Jr. 5.00 12.00
58 Langston Galloway 3.00 8.00
60 Sterling Brown 3.00 8.00

2020-21 Panini Mosaic Stained Glass

COMPLETE SET (10)
1 LeBron James 100.00 250.00
2 Anthony Davis 30.00 80.00
3 Kevin Durant 50.00 125.00
4 Stephen Curry 100.00 250.00
5 Giannis Antetokounmpo 60.00 150.00
6 Ja Morant 40.00 100.00
7 Kawhi Leonard 30.00 80.00
8 James Harden 25.00 60.00
9 Luka Doncic 80.00 200.00
10 Zion Williamson 40.00 100.00

2020-21 Panini Mosaic Stare Masters

COMPLETE SET (25)
*MOSAIC: .75X TO 2X BASIC
*FAST BREAK: .75X TO 2X BASIC
*RED: .75X TO 2X BASIC
*WHITE/25: 8X TO 20X BASIC
1 Tyler Herro .75 2.00
2 Russell Westbrook .75 2.00
3 LeBron James 3.00 8.00
4 Giannis Antetokounmpo 2.00 5.00
5 Luka Doncic 2.50 6.00
6 Ja Morant 1.25 3.00
7 Stephen Curry 3.00 8.00
8 Damian Lillard 1.00 2.50
9 Joel Embiid 1.00 2.50
10 Zion Williamson 1.25 3.00
11 Jayson Tatum 1.50 4.00
12 Jimmy Butler .75 2.00
13 Anthony Davis 1.00 2.50
14 James Harden .75 2.00
15 Devin Booker 1.00 2.50
16 Donovan Mitchell .75 2.00
17 Jamal Murray .60 1.50
18 Trae Young 1.00 2.50
19 De'Aaron Fox .60 1.50
20 Karl-Anthony Towns .60 1.50
21 Zach LaVine .60 1.50
22 Brandon Ingram .50 1.25
23 Kevin Durant 1.50 4.00
24 RJ Barrett .60 1.50
25 Paul George .60 1.50

2020-21 Panini Mosaic Straight Fire

COMPLETE SET (20)
1 Devin Booker 4.00 10.00
2 LeBron James 12.00 30.00
3 Giannis Antetokounmpo 8.00 20.00
4 Tyler Herro 3.00 8.00
5 Stephen Curry 12.00 30.00
6 Kevin Durant 6.00 15.00
7 Damian Lillard 4.00 10.00
8 Luka Doncic 10.00 25.00
9 Nikola Jokic 8.00 20.00
10 Zion Williamson 5.00 12.00
11 Ja Morant 5.00 12.00
12 Ben Simmons 1.50 4.00
13 Anthony Davis 4.00 10.00
14 Jayson Tatum 6.00 15.00
15 Kawhi Leonard 4.00 10.00
16 Donovan Mitchell 3.00 8.00
17 Trae Young 4.00 10.00
18 James Harden 3.00 8.00
19 Russell Westbrook 3.00 8.00
20 Jimmy Butler 3.00 8.00

2020-21 Panini Mosaic Swagger

COMPLETE SET (15)
1 James Harden 2.00 5.00
2 Giannis Antetokounmpo 5.00 12.00
3 LeBron James 8.00 20.00
4 Kevin Durant 4.00 10.00
5 Jayson Tatum 4.00 10.00
6 Russell Westbrook 2.00 5.00
7 Trae Young 2.50 6.00
8 Nikola Jokic 5.00 12.00
9 Stephen Curry 8.00 20.00
10 Kawhi Leonard 2.50 6.00
11 Luka Doncic 6.00 15.00
12 Zion Williamson 3.00 8.00
13 Damian Lillard 2.50 6.00
14 Ja Morant 3.00 8.00
15 Anthony Davis 2.50 6.00

2020-21 Panini Mosaic Will to Win

COMPLETE SET (20)
*MOSAIC: .75X TO 2X BASIC
*GREEN: .75X TO 2X BASIC
*REACTIVE BLUE/99: 3X TO 8X BASIC
*REACTIVE YELLOW/99: 3X TO 8X BASIC
*ORANGE FL/25: 8X TO 20X BASIC
1 Kevin Durant 1.50 4.00
2 Damian Lillard 1.00 2.50
3 Kawhi Leonard 1.00 2.50
4 Jimmy Butler .75 2.00
5 Bradley Beal .50 1.25
6 Stephen Curry 3.00 8.00
7 Jamal Murray .60 1.50
8 James Harden .75 2.00
9 Zach LaVine .60 1.50
10 LeBron James 3.00 8.00
11 D'Angelo Russell .40 1.00
12 Luka Doncic 2.50 6.00
13 Zion Williamson 1.25 3.00
14 Kyrie Irving .75 2.00
15 Giannis Antetokounmpo 2.00 5.00
16 Deandre Ayton .40 1.00
17 Nikola Vucevic .40 1.00
18 Ja Morant 1.25 3.00
19 Domantas Sabonis .50 1.25
20 Anthony Davis 1.00 2.50

2020-21 Panini Mosaic Will to Win Mosaic Reactive Yellow

*REACTIVE YELLOW: 2X TO 5X BASIC
PRINT RUN 99 SER.#'d SETS

2021-22 Panini Mosaic

COM CARD .25 .60
SEMISTARS .30 .75
UNLISTED STARS .40 1.00
COMMON RC .50 1.25
RC SEMIS .60 1.50
RC UNLISTED .75 2.00
*GREEN: .6X TO 1.5X BASIC
*MOSAIC: .75X TO 2X BASIC
*FB SILVER: 1.25X TO 3X BASIC
*RED: 1.25X TO 3X BASIC
*RED WAVE: 1.25X TO 3X BASIC
*SILVER: 1.25X TO 3X BASIC
*GREEN ICE: 1.5X TO 4X BASIC
1 Lonnie Walker IV .30 .75
2 Carmelo Anthony .60 1.50
3 Cameron Johnson .40 1.00
4 Jordan Clarkson .40 1.00
5 CJ McCollum .30 .75
6 Luka Doncic 2.50 6.00
7 Coby White .40 1.00
8 Tobias Harris .30 .75
9 Ben Simmons .40 1.00
10 Terrence Ross .30 .75
11 LaMarcus Aldridge .40 1.00
12 Ja Morant 1.25 3.00
13 Al Horford .40 1.00
14 Kyle Lowry .40 1.00
15 Christian Wood .30 .75
16 Kevin Durant 1.25 3.00
17 Jaden McDaniels .40 1.00
18 Julius Randle .50 1.25
19 RJ Hampton .25 .60
20 Patty Mills .40 1.00
21 Ivica Zubac .40 1.00
22 Rudy Gay .40 1.00
23 Terry Rozier III .30 .75
24 Michael Porter Jr. .50 1.25
25 LaMelo Ball 1.00 2.50
26 Seth Curry .30 .75
27 James Harden .75 2.00
28 Jrue Holiday .50 1.25
29 Jordan Poole .60 1.50
30 Patrick Beverley .25 .60
31 Luguentz Dort .40 1.00
32 Malcolm Brogdon .30 .75
33 Lonzo Ball .40 1.00
34 Steven Adams .30 .75
35 Jaylen Brown .60 1.50
36 Devin Vassell .60 1.50
37 Cameron Payne .40 1.00
38 Deni Avdija .40 1.00
39 Gary Trent Jr. .30 .75
40 Kevin Porter Jr. .30 .75
41 Shai Gilgeous-Alexander 2.00 5.00
42 Domantas Sabonis .50 1.25
43 Jonas Valanciunas .30 .75
44 P.J. Tucker .30 .75
45 Kenyon Martin Jr. .40 1.00
46 Jakob Poeltl .30 .75
47 Jordan Nwora .40 1.00
48 Richaun Holmes .25 .60
49 Tyrese Maxey 1.00 2.50
50 Damian Lillard 1.00 2.50
51 Russell Westbrook .60 1.50
52 John Collins .40 1.00
53 Tyler Herro .60 1.50
54 Hamidou Diallo .30 .75
55 Jarrett Allen .40 1.00
56 Aaron Gordon .40 1.00
57 Robert Williams III .40 1.00
58 Jimmy Butler .60 1.50
59 D'Angelo Russell .40 1.00
60 OG Anunoby .40 1.00
61 De'Anthony Melton .30 .75
62 Jamal Murray .60 1.50
63 Pascal Siakam .60 1.50
64 Killian Hayes .40 1.00
65 DeMarcus Cousins .30 .75
66 Clint Capela .40 1.00
67 Fred VanVleet .50 1.25
68 Kyle Kuzma .50 1.25
69 Cole Anthony .50 1.25
70 Dwight Howard .50 1.25
71 Isaiah Stewart .40 1.00
72 Buddy Hield .30 .75
73 Marcus Smart .40 1.00
74 Rajon Rondo .50 1.25
75 Alex Caruso .40 1.00
76 Jae Crowder .25 .60
77 Monte Morris .30 .75
78 Nikola Vucevic .40 1.00
79 Anthony Edwards 2.00 5.00
80 Draymond Green .50 1.25
81 Kyrie Irving .75 2.00
82 Joel Embiid 1.00 2.50
83 Kemba Walker .40 1.00
84 Derrick Rose .60 1.50
85 Terance Mann .40 1.00
86 Gary Harris .30 .75
87 Dillon Brooks .40 1.00
88 Bogdan Bogdanovic .40 1.00
89 Jerami Grant .40 1.00
90 Immanuel Quickley .40 1.00
91 Harrison Barnes .30 .75
92 Bojan Bogdanovic .30 .75
93 Mo Bamba .30 .75
94 Robert Covington .25 .60
95 Darius Garland .60 1.50
96 Kevin Huerter .30 .75
97 Miles Bridges .30 .75
98 Giannis Antetokounmpo 2.00 5.00
99 De'Aaron Fox .60 1.50
100 Yuta Watanabe .40 1.00
101 Stephen Curry 2.50 6.00
102 Anfernee Simons .60 1.50
103 Matisse Thybulle .30 .75
104 Caris LeVert .30 .75
105 Grayson Allen .40 1.00
106 Obi Toppin .40 1.00
107 Eric Gordon .30 .75
108 Will Barton .25 .60
109 Nickeil Alexander-Walker .30 .75
110 Facundo Campazzo .40 1.00
111 Nikola Jokic 2.00 5.00
112 Jayson Tatum 1.50 4.00
113 Chris Boucher .40 1.00
114 Patrick Williams .40 1.00
115 John Wall .50 1.25
116 Josh Hart .30 .75
117 Jalen Brunson .75 2.00
118 Chris Paul .75 2.00
119 Klay Thompson 1.00 2.50
120 Zach LaVine .60 1.50
121 Luke Kennard .30 .75
122 Maxi Kleber .30 .75
123 Precious Achiuwa .40 1.00
124 Zion Williamson 1.00 2.50
125 Blake Griffin .40 1.00
126 Kevin Love .40 1.00
127 Desmond Bane .75 2.00
128 Ricky Rubio .40 1.00
129 Trae Young 1.00 2.50
130 Cam Reddish .40 1.00
131 Payton Pritchard .40 1.00
132 Gordon Hayward .30 .75
133 Paul George .60 1.50
134 Deandre Ayton .40 1.00
135 James Wiseman .30 .75
136 Joe Ingles .30 .75
137 Dennis Schroder .40 1.00
138 Alec Burks .25 .60
139 Mike Conley .30 .75
140 RJ Barrett .60 1.50
141 Kawhi Leonard 1.00 2.50
142 Lauri Markkanen .50 1.25
143 Malik Beasley .30 .75
144 Rudy Gobert .50 1.25
145 Danny Green .30 .75
146 LeBron James 3.00 8.00
147 Karl-Anthony Towns .60 1.50
148 Jaren Jackson Jr. .60 1.50
149 Dorian Finney-Smith .25 .60
150 Saddiq Bey .30 .75
151 Marcus Morris Sr. .25 .60
152 Rui Hachimura .40 1.00

153 Kristaps Porzingis .50 1.25
154 Dejounte Murray .40 1.00
155 Khris Middleton .40 1.00
156 Tim Hardaway Jr. .50 1.25
157 PJ Washington Jr. .40 1.00
158 Tyrese Haliburton .75 2.00
159 Andrew Wiggins .50 1.25
160 Keldon Johnson .50 1.25
161 Donovan Mitchell .75 2.00
162 Anthony Davis 1.00 2.50
163 Evan Fournier .30 .75
164 DeMar DeRozan .50 1.25
165 Kira Lewis Jr. .25 .60
166 Nicolas Claxton .40 1.00
167 Jusuf Nurkic .30 .75
168 Duncan Robinson .30 .75
169 Frank Jackson .25 .60
170 Mikal Bridges .50 1.25
171 Montrezl Harrell .30 .75
172 T.J. McConnell .30 .75
173 Derrick White .40 1.00
174 Kentavious Caldwell-Pope .25 .60
175 Spencer Dinwiddie .30 .75
176 Nassir Little .40 1.00
177 Kelly Olynyk .25 .60
178 Isaac Okoro .30 .75
179 Devonte' Graham .30 .75
180 Joe Harris .30 .75
181 Andre Iguodala .40 1.00
182 Bobby Portis .30 .75
183 Reggie Jackson .30 .75
184 Marvin Bagley III .30 .75
185 Collin Sexton .40 1.00
186 Justin Holiday .25 .60
187 Talen Horton-Tucker .40 1.00
188 Kelly Oubre Jr. .40 1.00
189 Wendell Carter Jr. .40 1.00
190 Aleksej Pokusevski .30 .75
191 Bradley Beal .50 1.25
192 De'Andre Hunter .40 1.00
193 Devin Booker 1.00 2.50
194 Norman Powell .30 .75
195 Bam Adebayo .60 1.50
196 Myles Turner .40 1.00
197 Jae'Sean Tate .40 1.00
198 Dorius Bazley .25 .60
199 Boban Marjanovic .40 1.00
200 Brandon Ingram .50 1.25
201 Evan Mobley RC 3.00 8.00
202 James Bouknight RC .60 1.50
203 Cade Cunningham RC 5.00 12.00
204 Joshua Primo RC .60 1.50
205 Jonathan Kuminga RC 2.50 6.00
206 Jalen Green RC 4.00 10.00
207 Scottie Barnes RC 2.50 6.00
208 Davion Mitchell RC .75 2.00
209 Jalen Suggs RC 2.00 5.00
210 Josh Giddey RC 2.50 6.00
211 Moses Moody RC 1.50 4.00
212 Tre Mann RC 1.25 3.00
213 Corey Kispert RC 1.00 2.50
214 Bones Hyland RC 1.00 2.50
215 Cameron Thomas RC 1.50 4.00
216 Ziaire Williams RC 1.00 2.50
217 Chris Duarte RC .60 1.50
218 Alperen Sengun RC 2.50 6.00
219 Trey Murphy III RC 2.50 6.00
220 Franz Wagner RC 2.50 6.00
221 Kai Jones RC .60 1.50
222 Usman Garuba RC .60 1.50
223 Quentin Grimes RC 1.50 4.00
224 Josh Christopher RC .60 1.50
225 Keon Johnson RC .75 2.00
226 Jaden Springer RC .75 2.00
227 Day'Ron Sharpe RC .75 2.00
228 Jalen Johnson RC 2.50 6.00
229 Santi Aldama RC 1.00 2.50
230 Isaiah Jackson RC .75 2.00
231 Herbert Jones RC 1.00 2.50
232 Jeremiah Robinson-Earl RC .75 2.00
233 Ayo Dosunmu RC 1.50 4.00
234 Dalano Banton RC 1.00 2.50
235 Brandon Boston Jr. RC .75 2.00
236 Sandro Mamukelashvili RC 1.00 2.50
237 Aaron Wiggins RC 1.00 2.50
238 Luka Garza RC .75 2.00
239 Jared Butler RC .75 2.00
240 Isaiah Todd RC .60 1.50
241 Austin Reaves RC 4.00 10.00
242 Charles Bassey RC .75 2.00
243 Miles McBride RC 1.25 3.00
244 JT Thor RC .75 2.00
245 Greg Brown III RC .60 1.50
246 LeBron James NP 3.00 8.00
247 Stephen Curry NP 2.50 6.00
248 Kevin Durant NP 1.25 3.00
249 Ja Morant NP 1.25 3.00
250 Trae Young NP 1.00 2.50
251 LaMelo Ball NP 1.00 2.50
252 Zach LaVine NP .60 1.50
253 Donovan Mitchell NP .75 2.00
254 Davion Mitchell NP .75 2.00
255 Cameron Thomas NP 1.50 4.00
256 Jalen Suggs NP 2.00 5.00
257 Scottie Barnes NP 2.50 6.00
258 Evan Mobley NP 3.00 8.00
259 Jalen Green NP 4.00 10.00
260 Cade Cunningham NP 5.00 12.00
261 Cade Cunningham DEB 5.00 12.00
262 Jalen Green DEB 4.00 10.00
263 Evan Mobley DEB 3.00 8.00
264 Scottie Barnes DEB 2.50 6.00
265 Josh Giddey DEB 2.50 6.00
266 Jalen Suggs DEB 2.00 5.00
267 Franz Wagner DEB 2.50 6.00
268 Jonathan Kuminga DEB 2.50 6.00
269 Davion Mitchell DEB .75 2.00
270 Chris Duarte DEB .60 1.50
271 Bones Hyland DEB 1.00 2.50
272 Alperen Sengun DEB 2.50 6.00
273 Ziaire Williams DEB 1.00 2.50
274 James Bouknight DEB .60 1.50
275 Joshua Primo DEB .60 1.50
276 Corey Kispert DEB 1.00 2.50
277 Moses Moody DEB 1.50 4.00
278 Trey Murphy III DEB 2.50 6.00
279 Ayo Dosunmu DEB 1.50 4.00
280 Herbert Jones DEB 1.00 2.50
281 Giannis Antetokounmpo ALL 2.00 5.00
282 Luka Doncic ALL 2.50 6.00
283 Nikola Jokic ALL 1.50 4.00
284 Stephen Curry ALL 2.50 6.00
285 Kawhi Leonard ALL 1.00 2.50
286 LeBron James ALL 3.00 8.00
287 Damian Lillard ALL 1.00 2.50
288 Chris Paul ALL .75 2.00
289 Julius Randle ALL .50 1.25
290 Joel Embiid ALL 1.00 2.50
291 Jimmy Butler ALL .60 1.50
292 Paul George ALL .60 1.50
293 Rudy Gobert ALL .50 1.25
294 Bradley Beal ALL .50 1.25
295 Kyrie Irving ALL .75 2.00
296 Giannis Antetokounmpo MVP 2.00 5.00
297 Shaquille O'Neal MVP 1.25 3.00
298 LeBron James MVP 3.00 8.00
299 Dwyane Wade MVP .75 2.00
300 Kawhi Leonard MVP 1.00 2.50

2021-22 Panini Mosaic Mosaic Blue

*BLUE: 2.5X TO 6X BASIC
STATED PRINT RUN 99 SER.#'d SETS
203 Cade Cunningham 50.00 120.00
298 LeBron James MVP 50.00 120.00

2021-22 Panini Mosaic Mosaic Choice Fusion Red and Yellow

*CHOICE FUSION R & Y: 3X TO 8X BASIC
STATED PRINT RUN 88 SER.#'d SETS
6 Luka Doncic 50.00 120.00
101 Stephen Curry 50.00 120.00
146 LeBron James 50.00 120.00
203 Cade Cunningham 100.00 250.00
206 Jalen Green 100.00 250.00
246 LeBron James NP 50.00 120.00
247 Stephen Curry NP 50.00 120.00
259 Jalen Green NP 100.00 250.00
260 Cade Cunningham NP 100.00 250.00
261 Cade Cunningham DEB 100.00 250.00
262 Jalen Green DEB 100.00 250.00
282 Luka Doncic ALL 50.00 120.00
284 Stephen Curry ALL 50.00 120.00
286 LeBron James ALL 50.00 120.00
298 LeBron James MVP 60.00 150.00

2021-22 Panini Mosaic Mosaic Fast Break Blue

*FB BLUE: 4X TO 10X BASIC
STATED PRINT RUN 85 SER.#'d SETS
6 Luka Doncic 60.00 150.00
101 Stephen Curry 60.00 150.00
146 LeBron James 60.00 150.00
203 Cade Cunningham 125.00 300.00
206 Jalen Green 125.00 300.00
246 LeBron James NP 60.00 150.00
247 Stephen Curry NP 60.00 150.00
259 Jalen Green NP 125.00 300.00
260 Cade Cunningham NP 125.00 300.00
261 Cade Cunningham DEB 125.00 300.00
262 Jalen Green DEB 125.00 300.00
282 Luka Doncic ALL 60.00 150.00
284 Stephen Curry ALL 60.00 150.00
286 LeBron James ALL 60.00 150.00
298 LeBron James MVP 75.00 200.00

2021-22 Panini Mosaic Mosaic Fast Break Purple

*FB PURPLE: 5X TO 12X BASIC
STATED PRINT RUN 50 SER.#'d SETS
6 Luka Doncic 75.00 200.00
101 Stephen Curry 75.00 200.00
146 LeBron James 75.00 200.00
203 Cade Cunningham 150.00 400.00
206 Jalen Green 150.00 400.00
246 LeBron James NP 75.00 200.00
247 Stephen Curry NP 75.00 200.00
259 Jalen Green NP 150.00 400.00
260 Cade Cunningham NP 150.00 400.00
261 Cade Cunningham DEB 150.00 400.00
262 Jalen Green DEB 150.00 400.00
282 Luka Doncic ALL 75.00 200.00
284 Stephen Curry ALL 75.00 200.00
286 LeBron James ALL 75.00 200.00
298 LeBron James MVP 100.00 250.00

2021-22 Panini Mosaic Mosaic Gold Wave

*GOLD WAVE: 2.5X TO 6X BASIC RC
6 Luka Doncic 40.00 100.00
101 Stephen Curry 40.00 100.00
146 LeBron James 40.00 100.00
203 Cade Cunningham 75.00 200.00
206 Jalen Green 75.00 200.00
246 LeBron James NP 40.00 100.00
247 Stephen Curry NP 40.00 100.00
259 Jalen Green NP 75.00 200.00
260 Cade Cunningham NP 75.00 200.00
261 Cade Cunningham DEB 75.00 200.00
262 Jalen Green DEB 75.00 200.00
282 Luka Doncic ALL 40.00 100.00
284 Stephen Curry ALL 40.00 100.00
286 LeBron James ALL 40.00 100.00
298 LeBron James MVP 50.00 120.00

2021-22 Panini Mosaic Mosaic Orange Fluorescent

*ORNG FLO: 10X TO 25X BASIC
STATED PRINT RUN 25 SER.#'d SETS
6 Luka Doncic 150.00 400.00
101 Stephen Curry 150.00 400.00
146 LeBron James 150.00 400.00
203 Cade Cunningham 500.00 1,000.00
206 Jalen Green 500.00 1,000.00
246 LeBron James NP 150.00 400.00
247 Stephen Curry NP 150.00 400.00
259 Jalen Green NP 400.00 800.00
260 Cade Cunningham NP 400.00 800.00
261 Cade Cunningham DEB 400.00 800.00
262 Jalen Green DEB 400.00 800.00
282 Luka Doncic ALL 150.00 400.00
284 Stephen Curry ALL 150.00 400.00
286 LeBron James ALL 150.00 400.00
298 LeBron James MVP 200.00 500.00

2021-22 Panini Mosaic Mosaic Purple

*PURPLE: 5X TO 12X BASIC
STATED PRINT RUN 49 SER.#'d SETS
6 Luka Doncic 75.00 200.00
101 Stephen Curry 75.00 200.00
146 LeBron James 75.00 200.00
203 Cade Cunningham 150.00 400.00
206 Jalen Green 150.00 400.00
246 LeBron James NP 75.00 200.00
247 Stephen Curry NP 75.00 200.00
259 Jalen Green NP 150.00 400.00
260 Cade Cunningham NP 150.00 400.00
261 Cade Cunningham DEB 150.00 400.00
262 Jalen Green DEB 150.00 400.00
282 Luka Doncic ALL 75.00 200.00
284 Stephen Curry ALL 75.00 200.00
286 LeBron James ALL 75.00 200.00
298 LeBron James MVP 100.00 250.00

2021-22 Panini Mosaic Mosaic White

*WHITE: 10X TO 25X BASIC
STATED PRINT RUN 25 SER.#'d SETS
6 Luka Doncic 150.00 400.00
101 Stephen Curry 150.00 400.00
146 LeBron James 150.00 400.00
203 Cade Cunningham 500.00 1,000.00
206 Jalen Green 500.00 1,000.00
246 LeBron James NP 150.00 400.00
247 Stephen Curry NP 150.00 400.00
259 Jalen Green NP 400.00 800.00
260 Cade Cunningham NP 400.00 800.00
261 Cade Cunningham DEB 400.00 800.00
262 Jalen Green DEB 400.00 800.00
282 Luka Doncic ALL 150.00 400.00
284 Stephen Curry ALL 150.00 400.00
286 LeBron James ALL 150.00 400.00
298 LeBron James MVP 200.00 500.00

2021-22 Panini Mosaic Autographs Fast Break

COMMON CARD 4.00 10.00
SEMISTARS 5.00 12.00
UNLISTED STARS 6.00 15.00
1 Stephen Curry 500.00 1,000.00
2 Malik Monk 6.00 15.00
3 Anthony Edwards 100.00 250.00
4 Dwyane Wade 60.00 150.00
5 Jaren Jackson Jr. 30.00 80.00
6 Robert Williams III 6.00 15.00
7 Luka Doncic 400.00 800.00
8 Myles Turner 6.00 15.00
9 Aleksej Pokusevski 5.00 12.00
10 Joe Ingles 5.00 12.00
11 Tyrese Haliburton 50.00 120.00
12 Zeke Nnaji 5.00 12.00
13 Bobby Portis 5.00 12.00
14 Allen Iverson 75.00 200.00
15 Joe Harris 5.00 12.00
16 RJ Barrett 15.00 40.00
17 Jae'Sean Tate 6.00 15.00
18 Robert Horry 6.00 15.00
19 Caris LeVert 5.00 12.00
20 Wang Zhi-zhi 60.00 150.00
21 Kevin Porter Jr. 5.00 12.00
22 Amar'e Stoudemire 6.00 15.00
23 Kristaps Porzingis 6.00 15.00
24 Talen Horton-Tucker 6.00 15.00
25 Kevin Garnett 75.00 200.00
26 Jerry Lucas 8.00 20.00
27 Keldon Johnson 8.00 20.00
28 Montrezl Harrell 5.00 12.00
29 Devin Vassell 10.00 25.00
30 Marcus Smart 6.00 15.00
31 Ricky Rubio 6.00 15.00
32 Robert Parish 8.00 20.00
33 Bogdan Bogdanovic 6.00 15.00
34 Bradley Beal 8.00 20.00
35 Larry Johnson 15.00 40.00
36 Steve Francis 6.00 15.00
37 Jalen Rose 5.00 12.00
38 Christian Laettner 6.00 15.00
39 Arvydas Sabonis 8.00 20.00
40 Dillon Brooks 6.00 15.00
41 Luis Scola 5.00 12.00
42 Deni Avdija 6.00 15.00
43 Isiah Thomas 12.00 30.00
44 Sarunas Marciulionis 6.00 15.00
45 Elton Brand 6.00 15.00
46 Anthony Davis 40.00 100.00
47 Grant Williams 6.00 15.00
48 Al Horford 6.00 15.00
49 Clyde Drexler 15.00 40.00
50 Karl Malone 40.00 100.00
51 Moses Brown 4.00 10.00
52 Brad Miller 4.00 10.00
53 Jamal Crawford 6.00 15.00
54 Rex Chapman 5.00 12.00
55 Paul Pierce 20.00 50.00
56 Marcus Camby 5.00 12.00
57 Juan Toscano-Anderson 6.00 15.00
58 Jayson Tatum 150.00 400.00
59 Bill Laimbeer 6.00 15.00
60 Dennis Rodman 40.00 100.00
61 Alperen Sengun 40.00 100.00
62 Quentin Grimes 12.00 30.00
63 Jalen Green 150.00 400.00
64 Trey Murphy III 20.00 50.00
65 Jason Preston 5.00 12.00
66 James Bouknight 5.00 12.00
67 Cameron Thomas 75.00 200.00
68 Scottie Barnes 40.00 100.00
69 Jonathan Kuminga 40.00 100.00
70 Duane Washington Jr. 6.00 15.00
71 Dalano Banton 8.00 20.00
72 Josh Giddey 75.00 200.00
73 Isaiah Livers 6.00 15.00
74 Brandon Boston Jr. 6.00 15.00
75 Evan Mobley 75.00 200.00
76 Tre Mann 10.00 25.00
77 Joshua Primo 5.00 12.00
78 Jalen Johnson 20.00 50.00
79 Ayo Dosunmu 12.00 30.00
80 Day'Ron Sharpe 6.00 15.00
81 Corey Kispert 8.00 20.00
82 Miles McBride 10.00 25.00
83 Jalen Suggs 30.00 80.00
84 Luka Garza 6.00 15.00
85 Ziaire Williams 8.00 20.00
86 Herbert Jones 8.00 20.00
87 Davion Mitchell 6.00 15.00
88 Joe Wieskamp 5.00 12.00
89 Joel Ayayi 5.00 12.00
90 Kessler Edwards 6.00 15.00
91 David Duke Jr. 6.00 15.00
92 Omer Yurtseven 6.00 15.00
93 Moses Moody 12.00 30.00
94 Armoni Brooks 6.00 15.00
95 Franz Wagner 40.00 100.00
96 Santi Aldama 8.00 20.00
97 Chris Duarte 5.00 12.00
98 Josh Christopher 5.00 12.00
99 Cade Cunningham 150.00 400.00
100 Austin Reaves 30.00 80.00

2021-22 Panini Mosaic Autographs Mosaic

COMMON CARD 4.00 10.00
SEMISTARS 5.00 12.00
UNLISTED STARS 6.00 15.00
1 Wendell Carter Jr. 6.00 15.00
2 Landry Shamet 5.00 12.00
3 Allen Iverson 75.00 200.00
4 Thanasis Antetokounmpo 12.00 30.00
5 Dave Bing 8.00 20.00
6 Steve Francis 6.00 15.00
7 Luc Longley 5.00 12.00
8 Kevin Garnett 75.00 200.00
9 Robert Parish 8.00 20.00
10 Keldon Johnson 8.00 20.00
11 Facundo Campazzo 6.00 15.00
12 Kevin Porter Jr. 5.00 12.00
13 Jayson Tatum 150.00 400.00
14 Montrezl Harrell 5.00 12.00
15 Kelly Oubre Jr. 6.00 15.00
16 Bradley Beal 8.00 20.00
17 Dominique Wilkins 10.00 25.00
18 Nassir Little 6.00 15.00
19 Mark Price 6.00 15.00
20 Anthony Edwards 100.00 250.00
21 Metta World Peace 6.00 15.00
22 Caris LeVert 5.00 12.00
23 Dennis Rodman 30.00 80.00
24 Dillon Brooks 6.00 15.00
25 Rudy Gobert 8.00 20.00
26 Quentin Richardson 5.00 12.00
27 Luka Doncic 400.00 800.00
28 Gary Payton 15.00 40.00
29 Aleksej Pokusevski 5.00 12.00
30 Stephen Curry 500.00 1,000.00
31 Sam Jones 12.00 30.00
32 Malik Monk 6.00 15.00
33 Kenny Walker 4.00 10.00
34 Nicolas Claxton 6.00 15.00
35 Jerry West 30.00 80.00
36 Latrell Sprewell 6.00 15.00
37 Elvin Hayes 8.00 20.00
38 Manu Ginobili 30.00 80.00
39 Avery Bradley 4.00 10.00
40 Zion Williamson 150.00 400.00
41 Jae'Sean Tate 6.00 15.00
42 Bobby Portis 5.00 12.00
43 Amar'e Stoudemire 6.00 15.00
44 Larry Johnson 15.00 40.00
45 Dell Curry 6.00 15.00
46 Joakim Noah 5.00 12.00
47 Charles Barkley 100.00 250.00
48 Ron Harper 6.00 15.00
49 RJ Hampton 4.00 10.00
50 David Robinson 25.00 60.00
51 Dirk Nowitzki 100.00 250.00
52 Magic Johnson 60.00 150.00
53 Theo Maledon 5.00 12.00
54 Nate Archibald 6.00 15.00
55 Joe Ingles 5.00 12.00
56 Anthony Davis 40.00 100.00
57 Jalen Brunson 12.00 30.00
58 Horace Grant 6.00 15.00
59 Karl Malone 30.00 80.00
60 Alex English 8.00 20.00

2021-22 Panini Mosaic Bang

COMMON CARD .40 1.00
SEMISTARS .50 1.25
UNLISTED STARS .60 1.50
*MOSAIC: .6X TO 1.5X BASIC
*GREEN: .6X TO 1.5X BASIC
*ORNG FL/25: 6X TO 15X BASIC
1 Robert Horry .60 1.50
2 Nikola Jokic 3.00 8.00
3 Cole Anthony .75 2.00
4 Tracy McGrady 1.00 2.50
5 Gary Payton 1.00 2.50
6 Klay Thompson 1.50 4.00
7 Paul George 1.00 2.50
8 John Stockton 1.25 3.00
9 Jayson Tatum 2.50 6.00
10 DeMar DeRozan .75 2.00
11 Allen Iverson 1.50 4.00
12 LeBron James 5.00 12.00
13 Stephen Curry 4.00 10.00
14 Kawhi Leonard 1.50 4.00
15 Damian Lillard 1.50 4.00

2021-22 Panini Mosaic Elevate

COMMON CARD .40 1.00
SEMISTARS .50 1.25
UNLISTED STARS .60 1.50
*MOSAIC: .6X TO 1.5X BASIC
*GREEN: .6X TO 1.5X BASIC
*ORNG FL/25: 6X TO 15X BASIC
1 Ja Morant 2.00 5.00
2 Anthony Edwards 3.00 8.00
3 Kevin Durant 2.00 5.00
4 Donovan Mitchell 1.25 3.00
5 Jayson Tatum 2.50 6.00
6 LeBron James 5.00 12.00
7 Bam Adebayo 1.00 2.50
8 Julius Randle .75 2.00
9 Zach LaVine 1.00 2.50
10 Anthony Davis 1.50 4.00
11 Kawhi Leonard 1.50 4.00
12 Ben Simmons .60 1.50
13 Giannis Antetokounmpo 3.00 8.00
14 Paul George 1.00 2.50
15 Blake Griffin .60 1.50
16 DeMar DeRozan .75 2.00
17 Jaylen Brown 1.00 2.50
18 Karl-Anthony Towns 1.00 2.50
19 Jarrett Allen .60 1.50
20 Zion Williamson 1.50 4.00
21 Joel Embiid 1.50 4.00
22 Russell Westbrook 1.00 2.50
23 Jamal Murray 1.00 2.50
24 Damian Lillard 1.50 4.00
25 Deandre Ayton .60 1.50

2021-22 Panini Mosaic Epic Performers

COMMON CARD .40 1.00
SEMISTARS .50 1.25
UNLISTED STARS .60 1.50
*MOSAIC: .6X TO 1.5X BASIC
*GREEN: .6X TO 1.5X BASIC
*ORNG FL/25: 6X TO 15X BASIC
1 Luka Doncic 4.00 10.00
2 Ja Morant 2.00 5.00
3 Nikola Jokic 3.00 8.00
4 James Harden 1.25 3.00
5 Trae Young 1.50 4.00
6 LeBron James 5.00 12.00
7 Stephen Curry 4.00 10.00
8 Dirk Nowitzki 1.50 4.00
9 Kevin Durant 2.00 5.00
10 Tim Duncan 1.50 4.00
11 Shaquille O'Neal 2.00 5.00
12 Larry Bird 2.00 5.00
13 Charles Barkley 1.50 4.00
14 Allen Iverson 1.50 4.00
15 Paul George 1.00 2.50
16 Magic Johnson 2.00 5.00
17 Chris Paul 1.25 3.00
18 Damian Lillard 1.50 4.00
19 Giannis Antetokounmpo 3.00 8.00
20 Dwyane Wade 1.25 3.00

2021-22 Panini Mosaic Introductions

COMMON CARD .30 .75
SEMISTARS .40 1.00
UNLISTED STARS .50 1.25
*MOSAIC: .75X TO 2X BASIC
*FB SILVER: .75X TO 2X BASIC
*WHITE/25: 8X TO 20X BASIC
1 Jalen Green 2.50 6.00
2 Evan Mobley 2.00 5.00
3 Cade Cunningham 3.00 8.00
4 Scottie Barnes 1.50 4.00
5 Franz Wagner 1.50 4.00
6 Jalen Suggs 1.25 3.00
7 Josh Giddey 1.50 4.00
8 Jonathan Kuminga 1.50 4.00
9 Davion Mitchell .50 1.25
10 Chris Duarte .40 1.00

2021-22 Panini Mosaic Jam Masters

COMMON CARD .40 1.00
SEMISTARS .50 1.25
UNLISTED STARS .60 1.50
*MOSAIC: .6X TO 1.5X BASIC
*GREEN: .6X TO 1.5X BASIC
*ORNG FL/25: 6X TO 15X BASIC
1 LeBron James 5.00 12.00
2 Ja Morant 2.00 5.00
3 Zach LaVine 1.00 2.50
4 Anthony Edwards 3.00 8.00
5 Zion Williamson 1.50 4.00
6 Giannis Antetokounmpo 3.00 8.00
7 Donovan Mitchell 1.25 3.00
8 Russell Westbrook 1.00 2.50
9 Obi Toppin .60 1.50
10 Miles Bridges .50 1.25
11 Jalen Green 3.00 8.00
12 John Collins .60 1.50
13 Shaquille O'Neal 2.00 5.00
14 Paul George 1.00 2.50
15 Vince Carter 1.25 3.00
16 Cade Cunningham 4.00 10.00
17 Shawn Kemp 1.00 2.50
18 Jonathan Kuminga 2.00 5.00
19 Tracy McGrady 1.00 2.50
20 Aaron Gordon .60 1.50

2021-22 Panini Mosaic Moments in Time

COMMON CARD .40 1.00
SEMISTARS .50 1.25
UNLISTED STARS .60 1.50
*MOSAIC: .75X TO 2X BASIC
*FB SILVER: .75X TO 2X BASIC
*WHITE/25: 6X TO 15X BASIC
1 Ja Morant 2.00 5.00
2 Aaron Gordon .60 1.50
3 Blake Griffin .60 1.50
4 LeBron James 5.00 12.00
5 Jalen Green 3.00 8.00
6 Derrick Rose 1.00 2.50
7 Dwight Howard .75 2.00
8 Russell Westbrook 1.00 2.50
9 Tim Duncan 1.50 4.00
10 Josh Giddey 2.00 5.00
11 Klay Thompson 1.50 4.00
12 Devin Booker 1.50 4.00
13 Carmelo Anthony 1.00 2.50
14 Chris Paul 1.25 3.00
15 Jamal Murray 1.00 2.50
16 Deandre Ayton .60 1.50
17 Kawhi Leonard 1.50 4.00
18 Damian Lillard 1.50 4.00
19 Larry Bird 2.00 5.00
20 Magic Johnson 2.00 5.00

2021-22 Panini Mosaic Montage

COMMON CARD .40 1.00
SEMISTARS .50 1.25
UNLISTED STARS .60 1.50
*MOSAIC: .75X TO 2X BASIC
*FB SILVER: .75X TO 2X BASIC
*WHITE/25: 6X TO 15X BASIC
1 Jayson Tatum 2.50 6.00
2 Kevin Durant 2.00 5.00
3 Julius Randle .75 2.00
4 Joel Embiid 1.50 4.00
5 Fred VanVleet .75 2.00
6 Zach LaVine 1.00 2.50
7 Darius Garland 1.00 2.50
8 DeMar DeRozan .75 2.00
9 Domantas Sabonis .75 2.00
10 Giannis Antetokounmpo 3.00 8.00
11 Trae Young 1.50 4.00
12 LaMelo Ball 1.50 4.00
13 Jimmy Butler 1.00 2.50
14 Cole Anthony .75 2.00
15 Bradley Beal .75 2.00
16 Nikola Jokic 3.00 8.00
17 Anthony Edwards 3.00 8.00
18 Shai Gilgeous-Alexander 3.00 8.00
19 Damian Lillard 1.50 4.00
20 Donovan Mitchell 1.25 3.00
21 Stephen Curry 4.00 10.00
22 Paul George 1.00 2.50
23 LeBron James 5.00 12.00
24 Devin Booker 1.50 4.00
25 De'Aaron Fox 1.00 2.50
26 Luka Doncic 4.00 10.00
27 Anthony Davis 1.50 4.00
28 Ja Morant 2.00 5.00
29 Zion Williamson 1.50 4.00
30 Kyrie Irving 1.25 3.00

2021-22 Panini Mosaic Overdrive

1 Ja Morant 4.00 10.00
2 Josh Giddey 4.00 10.00
3 Luka Doncic 8.00 20.00
4 LeBron James 10.00 25.00
5 LaMelo Ball 3.00 8.00
6 Zion Williamson 3.00 8.00
7 Anthony Edwards 6.00 15.00
8 Jalen Green 6.00 15.00
9 Kevin Durant 4.00 10.00
10 Giannis Antetokounmpo 6.00 15.00
11 Stephen Curry 8.00 20.00
12 Zach LaVine 2.00 5.00
13 James Harden 2.50 6.00
14 Evan Mobley 5.00 12.00
15 Trae Young 3.00 8.00
16 Bones Hyland 1.50 4.00
17 Franz Wagner 4.00 10.00
18 Cade Cunningham 8.00 20.00
19 Jalen Suggs 3.00 8.00
20 Alperen Sengun 4.00 10.00
21 Devin Booker 3.00 8.00
22 Chris Duarte 1.00 2.50
23 Damian Lillard 3.00 8.00
24 Davion Mitchell 1.25 3.00
25 Jonathan Kuminga 4.00 10.00

2021-22 Panini Mosaic Rising Stars

COMMON CARD .50 1.25
SEMISTARS .60 1.50
UNLISTED STARS .75 2.00
*MOSAIC: .75X TO 2X BASIC
*FB SILVER: .75X TO 2X BASIC
*WHITE/25: 8X TO 20X BASIC
1 LaMelo Ball 2.00 5.00
2 Cade Cunningham 4.00 10.00
3 Anthony Edwards 4.00 10.00
4 Jalen Green 4.00 10.00
5 Tyrese Maxey 2.00 5.00
6 Evan Mobley 3.00 8.00
7 Josh Giddey 2.50 6.00
8 Jalen Suggs 2.00 5.00
9 Scottie Barnes 2.50 6.00
10 Saddiq Bey .60 1.50
11 Tyrese Haliburton 1.50 4.00
12 Ja Morant 2.50 6.00
13 Zion Williamson 2.00 5.00
14 Tyler Herro 1.25 3.00
15 Franz Wagner 2.00 5.00

2021-22 Panini Mosaic Rookie Autographs Mosaic

COMMON CARD 4.00 10.00
SEMISTARS 5.00 12.00
UNLISTED STARS 6.00 15.00
*FUSION R&Y: .5X TO 1.25X BASIC
1 Jason Preston 5.00 12.00
2 Cade Cunningham 150.00 400.00
3 Keon Johnson 6.00 15.00
4 Evan Mobley 75.00 200.00
5 Josh Christopher 5.00 12.00
6 Quentin Grimes 12.00 30.00
7 Chris Duarte 5.00 12.00
8 Herbert Jones 8.00 20.00
9 Corey Kispert 8.00 20.00
10 Jalen Suggs 15.00 40.00
11 Jonathan Kuminga 40.00 100.00
12 Brandon Boston Jr. 6.00 15.00
13 Omer Yurtseven 6.00 15.00
14 Davion Mitchell 6.00 15.00
15 Franz Wagner 40.00 100.00
16 Miles McBride 10.00 25.00
17 James Bouknight 5.00 12.00
18 Cameron Thomas 75.00 200.00
19 Ayo Dosunmu 12.00 30.00
20 Ziaire Williams 8.00 20.00
21 Armoni Brooks 6.00 15.00
22 Bones Hyland 8.00 20.00
23 Josh Giddey 75.00 200.00
24 Usman Garuba 5.00 12.00
25 Scottie Barnes 75.00 200.00
26 Isaiah Todd 5.00 12.00
27 Alperen Sengun 40.00 100.00
28 Jared Butler 6.00 15.00
29 Trey Murphy III 20.00 50.00
30 Greg Brown III 5.00 12.00
31 Jalen Johnson 20.00 50.00
32 Luka Garza 6.00 15.00
33 Moses Moody 12.00 30.00
34 Charles Bassey 6.00 15.00
35 Jalen Green 150.00 400.00
36 Jaden Springer 6.00 15.00
37 Austin Reaves 30.00 80.00
38 Joshua Primo 5.00 12.00
39 Isaiah Jackson 6.00 15.00
40 Kai Jones 5.00 12.00

2021-22 Panini Mosaic Rookie Scripts

COMMON CARD 4.00 10.00
SEMISTARS 5.00 12.00
UNLISTED STARS 6.00 15.00
*GREEN ICE: .5X TO 1.25X BASIC
*GOLD: .5X TO 1.25X BASIC
*RED WAVE: .5X TO 1.25X BASIC
1 Neemias Queta 6.00 15.00
2 Joe Wieskamp 5.00 12.00
3 Corey Kispert 8.00 20.00
4 Jaden Springer 6.00 15.00
5 Scottie Barnes 20.00 50.00
6 Isaiah Todd 5.00 12.00
7 Justin Champagnie 5.00 12.00
8 Trendon Watford 8.00 20.00
9 Jonathan Kuminga 20.00 50.00
10 JT Thor 6.00 15.00
11 David Duke Jr. 6.00 15.00
12 Ayo Dosunmu 12.00 30.00
13 Davion Mitchell 6.00 15.00
15 Chris Duarte 5.00 12.00
16 Trey Murphy III 20.00 50.00
17 Josh Christopher 5.00 12.00
18 Franz Wagner 20.00 50.00
19 Charles Bassey 6.00 15.00
20 Jalen Green 30.00 80.00
21 Austin Reaves 30.00 80.00
22 Ziaire Williams 8.00 20.00
23 Josh Giddey 20.00 50.00
24 Joel Ayayi 5.00 12.00
25 Evan Mobley 25.00 60.00
26 Herbert Jones 8.00 20.00
27 Jared Butler 6.00 15.00
28 Jock Landale 10.00 25.00
29 Moses Moody 12.00 30.00
30 Scottie Lewis 5.00 12.00
31 Alperen Sengun 20.00 50.00
32 Aaron Wiggins 8.00 20.00
33 Jamorko Pickett 5.00 12.00
34 Cade Cunningham 40.00 100.00
35 Greg Brown III 5.00 12.00
36 Cameron Thomas 12.00 30.00
37 Jalen Suggs 15.00 40.00
38 Bones Hyland 8.00 20.00
39 Duane Washington Jr. 6.00 15.00
40 Marcus Garrett 5.00 12.00

2021-22 Panini Mosaic Scripts

*GREEN ICE: .5X TO 1.25X BASIC
*GOLD: .5X TO 1.25X BASIC
*RED WAVE: .5X TO 1.25X BASIC
1 David Wesley 6.00 15.00
2 Kwame Brown 5.00 12.00
3 Luka Doncic 400.00 800.00
4 Willie Anderson 5.00 12.00
5 Kirk Hinrich 6.00 15.00
7 Markus Howard 6.00 15.00
8 Georges Niang 4.00 10.00
9 Jim Paxson 5.00 12.00
10 Ricky Davis 5.00 12.00
11 Anthony Davis 40.00 100.00
12 Xavier Tillman 5.00 12.00
13 Daniel Gafford 5.00 12.00
14 Jarred Vanderbilt 6.00 15.00
17 Micheal Ray Richardson 5.00 12.00
18 Jahmi'us Ramsey 5.00 12.00
20 T.J. McConnell 5.00 12.00
21 Moses Brown 4.00 10.00
22 Zion Williamson 100.00 250.00
26 Robert Woodard II 5.00 12.00
27 Michael Olowokandi 5.00 12.00
28 Brad Miller 4.00 10.00
30 Gerald Henderson Sr. 4.00 10.00
31 Billy Knight 5.00 12.00
32 Matt Barnes 5.00 12.00
33 Dylan Windler 4.00 10.00
34 Landry Shamet 5.00 12.00
35 Skylar Mays 4.00 10.00
36 Fat Lever 5.00 12.00
37 Mychal Thompson 5.00 12.00
39 Pervis Ellison 5.00 12.00
40 Walter McCarty 6.00 15.00
41 Luis Scola 5.00 12.00
43 Brian Scalabrine 5.00 12.00
44 Nicolas Claxton 6.00 15.00
46 Tom Gugliotta 5.00 12.00
47 Derrick Coleman 6.00 15.00
48 Joe Smith 5.00 12.00
49 Karl Malone 25.00 60.00
50 Enes Freedom 5.00 12.00
51 Dennis Rodman 40.00 100.00
52 Killian Tillie 5.00 12.00
53 Tony Delk 5.00 12.00
54 Bogdan Bogdanovic 6.00 15.00
59 John Lucas 5.00 12.00
60 Bingo Smith 5.00 12.00

2021-22 Panini Mosaic Stained Glass

1 LeBron James 125.00 300.00
2 Luka Doncic 100.00 250.00
3 Stephen Curry 100.00 250.00
4 Giannis Antetokounmpo 80.00 200.00
5 Ja Morant 50.00 120.00
6 LaMelo Ball 40.00 100.00
7 Kevin Durant 50.00 120.00
8 Cade Cunningham 100.00 250.00
9 Jalen Green 80.00 200.00
10 Evan Mobley 60.00 150.00

2021-22 Panini Mosaic Stare Masters

COMMON CARD .40 1.00
SEMISTARS .50 125.00
UNLISTED STARS .60 1.50
*MOSAIC: .75X TO 2X BASIC
*FB SILVER: .75X TO 2X BASIC
*WHITE/25: 6X TO 15X BASIC
1 Giannis Antetokounmpo 3.00 8.00
2 Russell Westbrook 1.00 2.50
3 Zion Williamson 1.50 4.00
4 Chris Paul 1.25 3.00
5 LaMelo Ball 1.50 4.00
6 LeBron James 5.00 12.00
7 Klay Thompson 1.50 4.00
8 Zach LaVine 1.00 2.50
9 Donovan Mitchell 1.25 3.00
10 Anthony Edwards 3.00 8.00
11 Luka Doncic 4.00 10.00
12 Nikola Jokic 3.00 8.00

13 Jayson Tatum 2.50 6.00
14 Kevin Durant 2.00 5.00
15 Trae Young 1.50 4.00
16 Ja Morant 2.00 5.00
17 Khris Middleton .60 1.50
18 Stephen Curry 4.00 10.00
19 Dejounte Murray .60 1.50
20 Rudy Gobert .75 2.00
21 Jamal Murray 1.00 2.50
22 Kristaps Porzingis .75 2.00
23 Fred VanVleet .75 2.00
24 James Harden 1.25 3.00
25 Kawhi Leonard 1.50 4.00

2021-22 Panini Mosaic Straight Fire

1 Trae Young 4.00 10.00
2 Stephen Curry 10.00 25.00
3 Ja Morant 5.00 12.00
4 Jayson Tatum 6.00 15.00
5 Zach LaVine 2.50 6.00
6 LeBron James 12.00 30.00
7 Kevin Durant 5.00 12.00
8 Jalen Suggs 4.00 10.00
9 Giannis Antetokounmpo 8.00 20.00
10 Josh Giddey 5.00 12.00
11 Anthony Edwards 8.00 20.00
12 LaMelo Ball 4.00 10.00
13 Luka Doncic 10.00 25.00
14 Kawhi Leonard 4.00 10.00
15 Zion Williamson 4.00 10.00
16 Anthony Davis 4.00 10.00
17 Jalen Green 8.00 20.00
18 Cade Cunningham 10.00 25.00
19 Evan Mobley 6.00 15.00
20 Scottie Barnes 5.00 12.00

2021-22 Panini Mosaic Swagger

1 Stephen Curry 10.00 25.00
2 LeBron James 12.00 30.00
3 Trae Young 4.00 10.00
4 LaMelo Ball 4.00 10.00
5 Giannis Antetokounmpo 8.00 20.00
6 Anthony Edwards 8.00 20.00
7 Ja Morant 5.00 12.00
8 Kevin Durant 5.00 12.00
9 Cade Cunningham 10.00 25.00
10 Kawhi Leonard 4.00 10.00
11 Jalen Green 8.00 20.00
12 Josh Giddey 5.00 12.00
13 Klay Thompson 4.00 10.00
14 Evan Mobley 6.00 15.00
15 Scottie Barnes 5.00 12.00

2021-22 Panini Mosaic Thunder Lane

COMMON CARD .40 1.00
SEMISTARS .50 1.25
UNLISTED STARS .60 1.50
*MOSAIC: .6X TO 1.5X BASIC
*GREEN: .6X TO 1.5X BASIC
*ORNG FL/25: 6X TO 15X BASIC
1 Giannis Antetokounmpo 3.00 8.00
2 Jayson Tatum 2.50 6.00
3 Anthony Davis 1.50 4.00
4 Donovan Mitchell 1.25 3.00
5 James Harden 1.25 3.00
6 LeBron James 5.00 12.00
7 Kevin Durant 2.00 5.00
8 LaMelo Ball 1.50 4.00
9 Damian Lillard 1.50 4.00
10 Zach LaVine 1.00 2.50
11 Luka Doncic 4.00 10.00
12 Ja Morant 2.00 5.00
13 Shai Gilgeous-Alexander 3.00 8.00
14 Zion Williamson 1.50 4.00
15 Trae Young 1.50 4.00
16 De'Aaron Fox 1.00 2.50
17 Stephen Curry 4.00 10.00
18 Devin Booker 1.50 4.00
19 Kawhi Leonard 1.50 4.00
20 Anthony Edwards 3.00 8.00

2021-22 Panini Mosaic Translucence

1 LeBron James 200.00 500.00
2 Luka Doncic 200.00 500.00
3 Stephen Curry 200.00 500.00
4 Giannis Antetokounmpo 75.00 200.00
5 Kevin Durant 40.00 100.00
6 LaMelo Ball 60.00 150.00
7 Ja Morant 150.00 400.00
8 Trae Young 40.00 100.00
9 Damian Lillard 40.00 100.00
10 Devin Booker 40.00 100.00
11 Julius Randle 40.00 100.00
12 Nikola Jokic 60.00 150.00
13 Anthony Edwards 60.00 150.00
14 Jimmy Butler 40.00 100.00
15 Joel Embiid 40.00 100.00
16 Paul George 40.00 100.00
17 Chris Paul 40.00 100.00
18 Kawhi Leonard 40.00 100.00
19 Jamal Murray 40.00 100.00
20 Karl-Anthony Towns 40.00 100.00
21 Shai Gilgeous-Alexander 60.00 150.00
22 Kyrie Irving 40.00 100.00
23 Zion Williamson 40.00 100.00
24 Pascal Siakam 40.00 100.00
25 Donovan Mitchell 40.00 100.00

2022-23 Panini Mosaic

COMPLETE SET (250)
*GREEN: .6X TO 1.5X BASIC
*MOSAIC: .6X TO 1.5X BASIC
*BLUE WAVE: 1.25X TO 3X BASIC
*REACTIVE BLUE: 1.25X TO 3X BASIC
*REACTIVE YELLOW: 1.25X TO 3X BASIC
*RED: 1.25X TO 3X BASIC
*RED WAVE: 1.25X TO 3X BASIC
*FB SILVER: 1.25X TO 3X BASIC
*SILVER: 1.25X TO 3X BASIC
*BLUE/199: 2.5X TO 6X BASIC
*PINK/149: 3X TO 8X BASIC
*PURPLE/99: 4X TO 10X BASIC
*RED & YLW CHC/88: 5X TO 12X BASIC
*FB BLUE/85: 5X TO 12X BASIC
*FB PURPLE/50: 6X TO 15X BASIC
1 Luka Doncic 2.50 6.00
2 Mikal Bridges .50 1.25
3 RJ Barrett .60 1.50
4 Shai Gilgeous-Alexander 2.00 5.00
5 Donovan Mitchell .75 2.00
6 Cade Cunningham 1.25 3.00
7 Jordan Poole .60 1.50
8 Trae Young 1.00 2.50
9 Jaylen Brown .75 2.00
10 Cole Anthony .40 1.00
11 Anfernee Simons .50 1.25
12 Patrick Beverley .25 .60
13 Kyrie Irving .75 2.00
14 Cameron Johnson .30 .75
15 Giannis Antetokounmpo 2.00 5.00
16 Spencer Dinwiddie .30 .75
17 Gary Trent Jr. .40 1.00
18 Paul George .60 1.50
19 Jimmy Butler .75 2.00
20 Zach LaVine .75 2.00
21 Jarred Vanderbilt .30 .75
22 CJ McCollum .40 1.00
23 Dennis Schroder .40 1.00
24 Jordan Nwora .40 1.00
25 Saddiq Bey .30 .75
26 Anthony Edwards 2.00 5.00
27 Norman Powell .40 1.00
28 Tobias Harris .30 .75
29 Kenyon Martin Jr. .40 1.00
30 Devin Booker 1.00 2.50
31 Jayson Tatum 1.50 4.00
32 Bradley Beal .50 1.25
33 Terry Rozier III .50 1.25
34 Klay Thompson 1.00 2.50
35 Julius Randle .50 1.25
36 Myles Turner .40 1.00
37 Tim Hardaway Jr. .30 .75
38 Damian Lillard 1.00 2.50
39 Franz Wagner 1.00 2.50
40 Andrew Wiggins .50 1.25
41 Alperen Sengun .50 1.25
42 Kevin Love .40 1.00
43 Jusuf Nurkic .40 1.00
44 Michael Porter Jr. .50 1.25
45 Isaac Okoro .30 .75
46 Buddy Hield .40 1.00
47 Nicolas Claxton .40 1.00
48 Austin Reaves 1.00 2.50
49 Jalen Suggs .50 1.25
50 Devonte' Graham .30 .75
51 Bones Hyland .30 .75
52 Reggie Jackson .30 .75
53 Malik Beasley .30 .75
54 Kevin Huerter .40 1.00
55 James Harden .75 2.00
56 Marvin Bagley III .30 .75
57 Aaron Nesmith .40 1.00
58 Jaden McDaniels .40 1.00
59 Jaren Jackson Jr. .60 1.50
60 Jalen Smith .40 1.00
61 Brandon Ingram .50 1.25
62 Kelly Olynyk .30 .75
63 Immanuel Quickley .40 1.00
64 Coby White .30 .75
65 Domantas Sabonis .50 1.25
66 Khris Middleton .50 1.25
67 Caris LeVert .30 .75
68 Pascal Siakam .60 1.50
69 Collin Sexton .50 1.25
70 Devin Vassell .50 1.25
71 Monte Morris .25 .60
72 Kelly Oubre Jr. .40 1.00
73 Luke Kennard .30 .75
74 Talen Horton-Tucker .30 .75
75 Corey Kispert .40 1.00
76 Pat Connaughton .30 .75
77 Chris Paul .75 2.00
78 Bam Adebayo .60 1.50
79 James Wiseman .30 .75
80 Danny Green .30 .75
81 Mo Bamba .30 .75
82 Ja Morant 1.25 3.00
83 Joe Harris .30 .75
84 Onyeka Okongwu .40 1.00
85 Evan Mobley 1.00 2.50
86 Kentavious Caldwell-Pope .30 .75
87 Bojan Bogdanovic .40 1.00
88 Boban Marjanovic .40 1.00
89 Tyrese Maxey .75 2.00
90 Bogdan Bogdanovic .40 1.00
91 Kyle Kuzma .50 1.25
92 Stephen Curry 3.00 8.00
93 Bol Bol .40 1.00
94 Bobby Portis .40 1.00
95 Jalen Brunson .75 2.00
96 Markelle Fultz .30 .75
97 Dejounte Murray .50 1.25
98 LeBron James 3.00 8.00
99 Max Strus .40 1.00
100 Killian Hayes .25 .60
101 Mike Conley .30 .75
102 Josh Green .40 1.00
103 Luguentz Dort .40 1.00
104 Tyler Herro .60 1.50
105 Jerami Grant .50 1.25
106 Ivica Zubac .40 1.00
107 Jamal Murray .60 1.50
108 Naz Reid .40 1.00
109 Santi Aldama .40 1.00
110 Anthony Davis 1.00 2.50
111 Donte DiVincenzo .40 1.00
112 Cam Reddish .30 .75
113 Scottie Barnes .60 1.50
114 Jakob Poeltl .30 .75
115 Karl-Anthony Towns .60 1.50
116 Reggie Bullock .30 .75
117 De'Anthony Melton .30 .75
118 Kawhi Leonard 1.00 2.50
119 Malik Monk .40 1.00
120 Zion Williamson 1.00 2.50
121 PJ Washington Jr. .40 1.00
122 Derrick White .40 1.00
123 Jordan Clarkson .40 1.00
124 Darius Garland .60 1.50
125 Christian Wood .25 .60
126 Kevin Durant 1.25 3.00
127 Gordon Hayward .30 .75
128 Grant Williams .30 .75
129 Josh Giddey .60 1.50
130 Victor Oladipo .30 .75
131 Patrick Williams .40 1.00
132 Dorian Finney-Smith .30 .75
133 Kevin Porter Jr. .30 .75
134 Mason Plumlee .30 .75
135 Al Horford .40 1.00
136 OG Anunoby .50 1.25
137 Lonnie Walker IV .30 .75
138 Rudy Gobert .50 1.25
139 Rui Hachimura .40 1.00
140 Steven Adams .40 1.00
141 Joel Embiid .60 1.50
142 Robert Williams III .30 .75
143 Draymond Green .50 1.25
144 Grayson Allen .40 1.00
145 John Collins .40 1.00
146 Josh Christopher .25 .60
147 Lauri Markkanen .60 1.50
148 P.J. Tucker .30 .75
149 Isaiah Stewart .30 .75
150 Seth Curry .30 .75
151 LaMelo Ball 1.00 2.50
152 Deandre Ayton .40 1.00
153 Obi Toppin .40 1.00
154 Josh Hart .40 1.00
155 Kristaps Porzingis .50 1.25
156 Desmond Bane .50 1.25
157 Quentin Grimes .30 .75
158 Jrue Holiday .50 1.25
159 Cameron Thomas .60 1.50
160 Aaron Gordon .40 1.00
161 Moses Moody .50 1.25
162 Tyrese Haliburton .75 2.00
163 Zaire Williams .30 .75
164 Russell Westbrook .60 1.50
165 Brandon Clarke .30 .75
166 Kyle Lowry .50 1.25
167 Herbert Jones .40 1.00
168 Nikola Jokic 2.00 5.00
169 Cameron Payne .30 .75
170 DeMar DeRozan .50 1.25
171 Joe Ingles .30 .75
172 Eric Gordon .30 .75
173 Tre Jones .40 1.00
174 Wendell Carter Jr. .40 1.00
175 Jalen McDaniels .40 1.00
176 Jarrett Allen .40 1.00
177 Jeff Green .25 .60
178 Trey Murphy III .50 1.25
179 Keldon Johnson .50 1.25
180 Josh Okogie .40 1.00
181 De'Aaron Fox .75 2.00
182 Jonas Valanciunas .30 .75
183 Ben Simmons .40 1.00
184 Jonathan Kuminga 1.00 2.50
185 Jose Alvarado .40 1.00
186 Tre Mann .30 .75
187 Nikola Vucevic .40 1.00
188 Marcus Smart .50 1.25
189 Dillon Brooks .40 1.00
190 D'Angelo Russell .30 .75
191 Harrison Barnes .30 .75
192 De'Andre Hunter .40 1.00
193 Jalen Green 1.25 3.00
194 Tyus Jones .30 .75
195 Deni Avdija .40 1.00
196 Malcolm Brogdon .30 .75
197 Ayo Dosunmu .50 1.25
198 Davion Mitchell .30 .75
199 Fred VanVleet .50 1.25
200 Robin Lopez .30 .75
201 AJ Griffin RC .50 1.25
202 Malaki Branham RC .60 1.50
203 Dyson Daniels RC 1.50 4.00
204 Jake LaRavia RC .60 1.50
205 TyTy Washington Jr. RC .60 1.50
206 Ousmane Dieng RC .75 2.00
207 Jordan Goodwin RC .60 1.50
208 Ochai Agbaji RC .75 2.00
209 Dalen Terry RC .60 1.50
210 Bennedict Mathurin RC 2.00 5.00
211 Kennedy Chandler RC .60 1.50
212 Walker Kessler RC 1.25 3.00
213 Shaedon Sharpe RC 2.50 6.00
214 Tyrese Martin RC .50 1.25
215 Jabari Walker RC .50 1.25
216 Jaden Ivey RC 2.00 5.00
217 Jalen Williams RC 3.00 8.00
218 MarJon Beauchamp RC .60 1.50
219 Patrick Baldwin Jr. RC .60 1.50
220 Vince Williams Jr. RC .75 2.00
221 Peyton Watson RC 1.00 2.50
222 Wendell Moore Jr. RC .60 1.50
223 David Roddy RC .75 2.00
224 Moussa Diabate RC .60 1.50
225 Jalen Duren RC 2.00 5.00
226 Jeremy Sochan RC 2.00 5.00
227 Keegan Murray RC 1.50 4.00
228 Andrew Nembhard RC 1.25 3.00
229 Max Christie RC 1.50 4.00
230 Mark Williams RC 1.25 3.00
231 Paolo Banchero RC 4.00 10.00
232 Simone Fontecchio RC .60 1.50
233 Christian Koloko RC .60 1.50
234 Jaden Hardy RC 1.00 2.50
235 Alondes Williams RC .60 1.50
236 Chet Holmgren RC 3.00 8.00
237 Josh Minott RC .60 1.50
238 Mac McClung RC 1.50 4.00
239 Jabari Smith Jr. RC 2.00 5.00
240 Christian Braun RC 1.50 4.00
241 Jaylin Williams RC .75 2.00
242 Bryce McGowens RC .60 1.50
243 Johnny Davis RC .60 1.50
244 Nikola Jovic RC 1.25 3.00
245 Ryan Rollins RC .60 1.50
246 Caleb Houstan RC .60 1.50
247 Isaiah Mobley RC .60 1.50
248 Tari Eason RC 1.50 4.00
249 Blake Wesley RC .60 1.50
250 Kenneth Lofton Jr. RC .75 2.00

2022-23 Panini Mosaic Mosaic White

COMPLETE SET (250)
*WHITE: 12X TO 30X BASIC
STATED PRINT RUN 25 SER.#'d SETS
92 Stephen Curry 125.00 300.00
98 LeBron James 125.00 300.00
210 Bennedict Mathurin 200.00 500.00
213 Shaedon Sharpe 200.00 500.00
216 Jaden Ivey 200.00 500.00
217 Jalen Williams 200.00 500.00
227 Keegan Murray 150.00 400.00
231 Paolo Banchero 400.00 800.00
236 Chet Holmgren 400.00 800.00
239 Jabari Smith Jr. 150.00 400.00

2022-23 Panini Mosaic Autographs Fast Break

COMPLETE SET (96)
*RED/49: .5X TO 1.25X BASIC
*BLUE/25: .75X TO 2X BASIC
1 Luka Doncic 300.00 600.00
2 Anthony Edwards 75.00 200.00
3 Jordan Poole 10.00 25.00
4 Louie Dampier 6.00 15.00
5 Hakeem Olajuwon 30.00 80.00
6 Jalen Rose 6.00 15.00
7 Kevin Garnett 60.00 150.00
8 Brandon Ingram 15.00 40.00
9 Tyrese Haliburton 50.00 120.00
11 Jerry Lucas 8.00 20.00
12 Rasheed Wallace 20.00 50.00
13 Buddy Hield 6.00 15.00
14 Richard Hamilton 8.00 20.00
15 Peja Stojakovic 8.00 20.00
16 Domantas Sabonis 12.00 30.00
17 Pat Connaughton 5.00 12.00
18 Jose Alvarado 6.00 15.00
19 Alperen Sengun 12.00 30.00
20 Kenyon Martin 6.00 15.00
21 Toni Kukoc 12.00 30.00
22 Patty Mills 15.00 40.00
23 Jason Richardson 6.00 15.00
24 Josh Giddey 10.00 25.00
25 Marcus Smart 8.00 20.00
26 Max Strus 6.00 15.00
27 Bones Hyland 5.00 12.00
28 Quentin Grimes 5.00 12.00
29 James Silas 5.00 12.00
30 Brad Miller 5.00 12.00
31 Joe Ingles 5.00 12.00
32 Ayo Dosunmu 8.00 20.00
34 Austin Reaves 50.00 120.00
35 Dillon Brooks 6.00 15.00
36 Danny Green 5.00 12.00
37 Alex English 8.00 20.00
38 Moses Moody 8.00 20.00
39 Nick Van Exel 6.00 15.00
40 Zach Randolph 6.00 15.00
41 Onyeka Okongwu 6.00 15.00
42 Jaren Jackson Jr. 20.00 50.00
43 Gary Payton 15.00 40.00
44 Deandre Ayton 6.00 15.00
45 Jrue Holiday 8.00 20.00
46 Dennis Rodman 40.00 100.00
47 Evan Mobley 15.00 40.00
48 Derrick Coleman 6.00 15.00
49 Dale Ellis 6.00 15.00
50 Thanasis Antetokounmpo 6.00 15.00
51 Devonte' Graham 5.00 12.00
53 Juwan Howard 6.00 15.00
54 Kevin Huerter 6.00 15.00
55 Boban Marjanovic 6.00 15.00
56 Mac McClung 15.00 40.00
57 Jason Williams 15.00 40.00
58 Bradley Beal 8.00 20.00
60 E.J. Liddell 6.00 15.00
61 Scotty Pippen Jr. 8.00 20.00
62 Moussa Diabate 6.00 15.00
63 Kennedy Chandler 6.00 15.00
64 Jake LaRavia 6.00 15.00
65 Nikola Jovic 12.00 30.00
66 Patrick Baldwin Jr. 6.00 15.00
67 Dalen Terry 6.00 15.00
68 MarJon Beauchamp 6.00 15.00
69 Caleb Houstan 6.00 15.00
70 Blake Wesley 6.00 15.00
71 Simone Fontecchio 6.00 15.00
72 Christian Koloko 6.00 15.00
73 Jabari Walker 5.00 12.00
74 Bryce McGowens 6.00 15.00
75 Max Christie 20.00 50.00
76 Mark Williams 12.00 30.00
77 Ochai Agbaji 8.00 20.00
78 Jalen Duren 20.00 50.00
79 Andrew Nembhard 12.00 30.00
80 Malaki Branham 6.00 15.00
81 Dyson Daniels 15.00 40.00
82 TyTy Washington Jr. 6.00 15.00
83 Tari Eason 15.00 40.00
84 Ousmane Dieng 8.00 20.00
85 AJ Griffin 8.00 20.00
86 Christian Braun 15.00 40.00
87 Jabari Smith Jr. 50.00 120.00
88 Jeremy Sochan 40.00 100.00
89 David Roddy 8.00 20.00
90 Walker Kessler 12.00 30.00
91 Johnny Davis 6.00 15.00
92 Jaylin Williams 8.00 20.00
93 Paolo Banchero 150.00 400.00
94 Keegan Murray 40.00 100.00
95 Jalen Williams 40.00 100.00
96 Bennedict Mathurin 50.00 120.00
97 Shaedon Sharpe 60.00 150.00
98 Chet Holmgren 125.00 300.00
99 Jaden Ivey 50.00 120.00
100 Jaden Hardy 10.00 25.00

2022-23 Panini Mosaic Autographs Mosaic

COMPLETE SET (55)
*CHOICE: .5X TO 1.2X BASIC
*RED WAVE: .5X TO 1.2X BASIC
*BLUE/25-49: .75X TO 2X BASIC
1 Austin Reaves 50.00 120.00
2 James Wiseman 4.00 10.00
4 Dorian Finney-Smith 4.00 10.00
5 Josh Giddey 20.00 50.00
6 Chris Mullin 6.00 15.00
7 Jose Alvarado 5.00 12.00
8 Steve Francis 5.00 12.00
9 Jaren Jackson Jr. 20.00 50.00
11 Malik Monk 5.00 12.00
12 Franz Wagner 15.00 40.00
13 Evan Mobley 15.00 40.00
14 Cameron Payne 4.00 10.00
15 Marcus Smart 6.00 15.00
16 Richard Hamilton 6.00 15.00
17 Buddy Hield 5.00 12.00
19 Seth Curry 4.00 10.00
20 Jordan Clarkson 12.00 30.00
21 Peja Stojakovic 5.00 12.00
22 Jonathan Kuminga 12.00 30.00
23 Cole Anthony 5.00 12.00
24 Davion Mitchell 4.00 10.00
25 Gary Trent Jr. 5.00 12.00
27 Domantas Sabonis 12.00 30.00
28 Calvin Murphy 5.00 12.00
29 Goran Dragic 4.00 10.00
30 George McGinnis 5.00 12.00
31 Robert Parish 8.00 20.00
32 Joakim Noah 4.00 10.00
33 Shawn Kemp 15.00 40.00
34 Dillon Brooks 5.00 12.00
35 Ayo Dosunmu 6.00 15.00
36 Alperen Sengun 12.00 30.00
37 Ralph Sampson 4.00 10.00
38 Bojan Bogdanovic 5.00 12.00
39 Bradley Beal 6.00 15.00
40 Clyde Drexler 15.00 40.00
41 Antawn Jamison 5.00 12.00
42 Nate Archibald 6.00 15.00
43 David Thompson 6.00 15.00
44 Cade Cunningham 40.00 100.00
45 Kevin Garnett 60.00 150.00
46 Corey Kispert 5.00 12.00
47 Jalen Green 40.00 100.00
48 Oscar Robertson 30.00 80.00
50 Derrick White 8.00 20.00
51 Zach Randolph 5.00 12.00
52 Alex English 6.00 15.00
53 Carlos Boozer 4.00 10.00
54 Danny Green 4.00 10.00
55 Boban Marjanovic 5.00 12.00
56 Aaron Nesmith 5.00 12.00
57 Herbert Jones 5.00 12.00
58 Tony Allen 3.00 8.00
59 T.J. McConnell 4.00 10.00
60 Karl Malone 40.00 100.00

2022-23 Panini Mosaic Breakaway

COMPLETE SET (20)
*FAST BREAK: .75X TO 2X BASIC
*MOSAIC: .75X TO 2X BASIC
*PURPLE/99: 3X TO 8X BASIC
*WHITE/25: 8X TO 20X BASIC
1 LaMelo Ball 1.00 2.50
2 LeBron James 3.00 8.00
3 Stephen Curry 3.00 8.00
4 Trae Young 1.00 2.50
5 Kyrie Irving .75 2.00
6 Ja Morant 1.25 3.00
7 Cade Cunningham 1.25 3.00
8 Jalen Williams 2.00 5.00
9 Bradley Beal .50 1.25
10 Tyrese Haliburton .75 2.00
11 Jalen Green 1.25 3.00
12 De'Aaron Fox .75 2.00
13 Bennedict Mathurin 1.25 3.00
14 Jalen Brunson .75 2.00
15 Jaden Ivey 1.25 3.00
16 Zach LaVine .75 2.00
17 Keegan Murray 1.00 2.50
18 Damian Lillard 1.00 2.50
19 Paolo Banchero 2.50 6.00
20 Chris Paul .75 2.00

2022-23 Panini Mosaic Collage Autographs Mosaic

COMPLETE SET (47)
*CHOICE: .5X TO 1.2X BASIC
*RED WAVE: .5X TO 1.2X BASIC
*BLUE/25-49: .75X TO 2X BASIC
1 Tyrese Haliburton 40.00 100.00
2 Kareem Abdul-Jabbar 100.00 250.00
3 Luka Doncic 300.00 600.00
4 Wendell Carter Jr. 5.00 12.00
5 De'Aaron Fox 30.00 80.00
6 Gary Payton 15.00 40.00
7 Rudy Gobert 6.00 15.00
8 Bill Walton 8.00 20.00
9 Brandon Clarke 4.00 10.00
10 Michael Cooper 5.00 12.00
11 Jarred Vanderbilt 4.00 10.00
12 Fat Lever 4.00 10.00
14 James Harden 75.00 200.00
15 Rasheed Wallace 20.00 50.00
16 Avery Johnson 4.00 10.00
17 RJ Hampton 4.00 10.00
19 Toni Kukoc 12.00 30.00
20 Luke Kennard 4.00 10.00
22 Nicolas Batum 4.00 10.00
23 Arvydas Sabonis 6.00 15.00
24 Pat Connaughton 5.00 12.00
25 Glen Rice 5.00 12.00
26 Charles Barkley 50.00 120.00
27 Paolo Banchero 150.00 400.00
28 Bennedict Mathurin 50.00 120.00
29 Jeremy Sochan 30.00 80.00
30 Shaedon Sharpe 60.00 150.00
31 Andrew Nembhard 10.00 25.00
32 Jrue Holiday 12.00 30.00
33 Artis Gilmore 6.00 15.00
34 Jabari Smith Jr. 50.00 120.00
35 James Worthy 12.00 30.00
36 Devin Vassell 12.00 30.00
37 Jaden Hardy 8.00 20.00
38 Chet Holmgren 125.00 300.00
39 Christian Laettner 5.00 12.00
40 Bernard King 6.00 15.00
41 Deni Avdija 5.00 12.00
42 Elvin Hayes 6.00 15.00
43 Bob Dandridge 5.00 12.00
44 Hedo Turkoglu 5.00 12.00
45 Quentin Grimes 4.00 10.00
46 Dino Radja 4.00 10.00
47 Derek Harper 4.00 10.00
48 Sidney Moncrief 4.00 10.00
49 Tari Eason 12.00 30.00
50 Jaden Ivey 50.00 120.00

2022-23 Panini Mosaic Elevate

COMPLETE SET (25)
*GREEN: .75X TO 2X BASIC
*MOSAIC: .75X TO 2X BASIC
*REACTIVE BLUE/99: 3X TO 8X BASIC
*REACTIVE YELLOW/99: 3X TO 8X BASIC
*ORNG FL/25: 8X TO 20X BASIC
1 Jayson Tatum 1.50 4.00
2 Ja Morant 1.25 3.00
3 Kevin Durant 1.25 3.00
4 LeBron James 3.00 8.00
5 Anthony Edwards 2.00 5.00
6 Jalen Brunson .75 2.00
7 Brandon Ingram .50 1.25
8 Julius Randle .50 1.25
9 Paul George .60 1.50
10 Anthony Davis 1.00 2.50
11 Zach LaVine .75 2.00
12 Joel Embiid .60 1.50
13 Shai Gilgeous-Alexander 2.00 5.00
14 Jonathan Kuminga 1.00 2.50
15 Scottie Barnes .60 1.50
16 Russell Westbrook .60 1.50
17 Damian Lillard 1.00 2.50
18 DeMar DeRozan .50 1.25
19 Luka Doncic 2.50 6.00
20 Domantas Sabonis .50 1.25
21 Jimmy Butler .75 2.00
22 Kevin Porter Jr. .30 .75
23 Bradley Beal .50 1.25
24 Donovan Mitchell .75 2.00
25 Jaylen Brown .75 2.00

2022-23 Panini Mosaic Epic Performers

COMPLETE SET (20)
*GREEN: .75X TO 2X BASIC
*MOSAIC: .75X TO 2X BASIC
*REACTIVE BLUE/99: 3X TO 8X BASIC
*REACTIVE YELLOW/99: 3X TO 8X BASIC
*ORNG FL/25: 8X TO 20X BASIC
1 Stephen Curry 3.00 8.00
2 Giannis Antetokounmpo 2.00 5.00
3 Nikola Jokic 2.00 5.00
4 Jayson Tatum 1.50 4.00
5 Kevin Durant 1.25 3.00
6 LeBron James 3.00 8.00
7 Luka Doncic 2.50 6.00
8 Ja Morant 1.25 3.00
9 Joel Embiid .60 1.50
10 Devin Booker 1.00 2.50
11 Damian Lillard 1.00 2.50
12 Dirk Nowitzki 1.00 2.50
13 Kevin Garnett 1.00 2.50
14 Magic Johnson 1.50 4.00
15 Trae Young 1.00 2.50
16 Anthony Edwards 2.00 5.00
17 Larry Bird 1.50 4.00
18 Kawhi Leonard 1.00 2.50
19 DeMar DeRozan .50 1.25
20 Allen Iverson 1.00 2.50

2022-23 Panini Mosaic Give and Go

COMPLETE SET (15)
*GREEN: .75X TO 2X BASIC
*MOSAIC: .75X TO 2X BASIC
*REACTIVE BLUE/99: 3X TO 8X BASIC
*REACTIVE YELLOW/99: 3X TO 8X BASIC
*ORNG FL/25: 8X TO 20X BASIC
1 LaMelo Ball 1.00 2.50
2 Darius Garland .60 1.50
3 LeBron James 3.00 8.00
4 Trae Young 1.00 2.50
5 Luka Doncic 2.50 6.00
6 Damian Lillard 1.00 2.50
7 Josh Giddey .60 1.50
8 De'Aaron Fox .75 2.00
9 Ja Morant 1.25 3.00
10 Shai Gilgeous-Alexander 2.00 5.00
11 Stephen Curry 3.00 8.00
12 Kyrie Irving .75 2.00
13 Tyrese Haliburton .75 2.00
14 James Harden .75 2.00
15 Nikola Jokic 2.00 5.00

2022-23 Panini Mosaic Introductions

COMPLETE SET (15)
*FB: .75X TO 2X BASIC
*MOSAIC: .75X TO 2X BASIC
*PURPLE/99: 3X TO 8X BASIC
*WHITE/25: 8X TO 20X BASIC
1 Jeremy Sochan 1.50 4.00
2 Paolo Banchero 3.00 8.00
3 Jalen Duren 1.50 4.00
4 Jalen Williams 2.50 6.00
5 Jaden Hardy .75 2.00
6 AJ Griffin .40 1.00
7 Keegan Murray 1.25 3.00
8 Tari Eason 1.25 3.00
9 Bennedict Mathurin 1.50 4.00
10 Jabari Smith Jr. 1.50 4.00
11 Shaedon Sharpe 2.00 5.00
12 Chet Holmgren 2.50 6.00
13 Walker Kessler 1.00 2.50
14 Ochai Agbaji .60 1.50
15 Jaden Ivey 1.50 4.00

2022-23 Panini Mosaic Jam Masters

COMPLETE SET (20)
*GREEN: .75X TO 2X BASIC
*MOSAIC: .75X TO 2X BASIC
*REACTIVE BLUE/99: 3X TO 8X BASIC
*REACTIVE YELLOW/99: 3X TO 8X BASIC
*ORNG FL/25: 8X TO 20X BASIC
1 LeBron James 3.00 8.00
2 Giannis Antetokounmpo 2.00 5.00
3 Jayson Tatum 1.50 4.00
4 Anthony Edwards 2.00 5.00
5 De'Aaron Fox .75 2.00
6 Ja Morant 1.25 3.00
7 Jaden Ivey 1.25 3.00
8 Donovan Mitchell .75 2.00
9 Paul George .60 1.50
10 Shaquille O'Neal 1.50 4.00
11 Bennedict Mathurin 1.25 3.00
12 Zach LaVine .75 2.00
13 Aaron Gordon .40 1.00
14 Jalen Green 1.25 3.00
15 Paolo Banchero 2.50 6.00
16 Tracy McGrady .60 1.50
17 Jalen Williams 2.00 5.00
18 Zion Williamson 1.00 2.50
19 Shaedon Sharpe 1.50 4.00
20 Vince Carter .75 2.00

2022-23 Panini Mosaic Montage

COMPLETE SET (30)
*FB: .75X TO 2X BASIC
*MOSAIC: .75X TO 2X BASIC
*PURPLE/99: 3X TO 8X BASIC
*WHITE/25: 8X TO 20X BASIC
1 Kyrie Irving .75 2.00
2 Kevin Durant 1.25 3.00
3 LeBron James 3.00 8.00
4 Joel Embiid .60 1.50
5 Zion Williamson 1.00 2.50
6 Shai Gilgeous-Alexander 2.00 5.00
7 Donovan Mitchell .75 2.00
8 Ja Morant 1.25 3.00
9 Jabari Smith Jr. 1.25 3.00
10 Zach LaVine .75 2.00
11 Stephen Curry 3.00 8.00
12 Damian Lillard 1.00 2.50
13 Paul George .60 1.50
14 Julius Randle .50 1.25
15 Devin Booker 1.00 2.50
16 De'Aaron Fox .75 2.00
17 Luka Doncic 2.50 6.00
18 Jayson Tatum 1.50 4.00
19 Paolo Banchero 2.50 6.00
20 Jalen Green 1.25 3.00
21 Giannis Antetokounmpo 2.00 5.00
22 Josh Giddey .60 1.50
23 Jaden Ivey 1.25 3.00
24 Nikola Jokic 2.00 5.00
25 Bennedict Mathurin 1.25 3.00
26 Trae Young 1.00 2.50
27 Keegan Murray 1.00 2.50
28 Anthony Edwards 2.00 5.00
29 Jalen Williams 2.00 5.00
30 Tyrese Haliburton .75 2.00

2022-23 Panini Mosaic Notoriety

COMPLETE SET (10)
*FB: .75X TO 2X BASIC
*MOSAIC: .75X TO 2X BASIC
*PURPLE/99: 3X TO 8X BASIC
*WHITE/25: 8X TO 20X BASIC
1 Stephen Curry 3.00 8.00
2 LeBron James 3.00 8.00
3 Giannis Antetokounmpo 2.00 5.00
4 Luka Doncic 2.50 6.00
5 Ja Morant 1.25 3.00
6 Paolo Banchero 2.50 6.00
7 Jaden Ivey 1.25 3.00
8 Bennedict Mathurin 1.25 3.00
9 Keegan Murray 1.00 2.50
10 Jalen Williams 2.00 5.00

2022-23 Panini Mosaic Overdrive

COMPLETE SET (25)
1 Jalen Duren 4.00 10.00
2 Stephen Curry 10.00 25.00
3 Paolo Banchero 8.00 20.00
4 LeBron James 10.00 25.00
5 De'Aaron Fox 2.50 6.00
6 Jaden Ivey 4.00 10.00
7 Trae Young 3.00 8.00
8 Jabari Smith Jr. 4.00 10.00
9 Luka Doncic 8.00 20.00
10 Ja Morant 4.00 10.00
11 Bennedict Mathurin 4.00 10.00
12 Giannis Antetokounmpo 6.00 15.00
13 Devin Booker 3.00 8.00
14 Shai Gilgeous-Alexander 6.00 15.00
15 Keegan Murray 3.00 8.00
16 Donovan Mitchell 2.50 6.00
17 Walker Kessler 2.50 6.00
18 Anthony Edwards 6.00 15.00
19 Jalen Williams 6.00 15.00
20 Damian Lillard 3.00 8.00
21 Kevin Durant 4.00 10.00
22 Zach LaVine 2.50 6.00
23 Shaedon Sharpe 5.00 12.00
24 Kyrie Irving 2.50 6.00
25 Jeremy Sochan 4.00 10.00

2022-23 Panini Mosaic Pictographs Mosaic

COMPLETE SET (47)
*CHOICE: .5X TO 1.2X BASIC
*RED WAVE: .5X TO 1.2X BASIC
*BLUE/25-49: .75X TO 2X BASIC
1 Deandre Ayton 5.00 12.00
2 Brandon Ingram 15.00 40.00
3 Carmelo Anthony 60.00 150.00
4 Magic Johnson 40.00 100.00
5 Anthony Edwards 60.00 150.00
6 Onyeka Okongwu 5.00 12.00
7 Nikola Jokic 100.00 250.00
8 Jordan Poole 20.00 50.00
9 Steve Kerr 12.00 30.00
10 Andre Drummond 5.00 12.00
11 Metta World Peace 5.00 12.00
12 Cam Reddish 4.00 10.00
13 Moses Moody 6.00 15.00
14 Robert Horry 5.00 12.00
15 Precious Achiuwa 5.00 12.00
16 Brian Scalabrine 3.00 8.00
17 Allen Iverson 40.00 100.00
18 Gary Harris 4.00 10.00
20 Kyle Anderson 4.00 10.00
22 Muggsy Bogues 10.00 25.00
23 Nicolas Claxton 5.00 12.00
24 Bones Hyland 4.00 10.00
25 Brook Lopez 5.00 12.00
26 Manu Ginobili 20.00 50.00

27 Lauri Markkanen 10.00 25.00
28 Jalen Williams 40.00 100.00
29 Jaden Ivey 40.00 100.00
30 Jabari Smith Jr. 40.00 100.00
31 Keegan Murray 40.00 100.00
32 AJ Griffin 4.00 10.00
33 Walker Kessler 10.00 25.00
34 RJ Barrett 8.00 20.00
35 T.J. Warren 4.00 10.00
36 Bobby Portis 5.00 12.00
37 Jason Williams 15.00 40.00
38 Malaki Branham 5.00 12.00
39 TyTy Washington Jr. 5.00 12.00
40 Alex Caruso 12.00 30.00
41 Marcus Camby 4.00 10.00
43 Rod Strickland 4.00 10.00
44 Rashard Lewis 4.00 10.00
45 Bogdan Bogdanovic 5.00 12.00
46 Dennis Smith Jr. 4.00 10.00
47 Norman Powell 5.00 12.00
48 Christian Wood 3.00 8.00
49 Caleb Martin 5.00 12.00
50 Paolo Banchero 100.00 250.00

2022-23 Panini Mosaic Razzle Dazzle

COMPLETE SET (15)
1 Ja Morant 25.00 60.00
2 Stephen Curry 60.00 150.00
3 Luka Doncic 50.00 125.00
4 Jaden Ivey 25.00 60.00
5 LeBron James 60.00 150.00
6 Jalen Green 25.00 60.00
7 Bennedict Mathurin 25.00 60.00
8 Kyrie Irving 15.00 40.00
9 Jalen Williams 40.00 100.00
10 Trae Young 20.00 50.00
11 Keegan Murray 20.00 50.00
12 Giannis Antetokounmpo 40.00 100.00
13 Paolo Banchero 50.00 120.00
14 Jayson Tatum 30.00 80.00
15 LaMelo Ball 20.00 50.00

2022-23 Panini Mosaic Rookie Autographs Mosaic

COMPLETE SET (40)
*CHOICE: .5X TO 1.2X BASIC
*RED WAVE: .5X TO 1.2X BASIC
*BLUE/49: .75X TO 2X BASIC
1 Johnny Davis 5.00 12.00
2 Ousmane Dieng 6.00 15.00
3 Jabari Smith Jr. 40.00 100.00
4 Blake Wesley 5.00 12.00
5 Shaedon Sharpe 40.00 100.00
6 Walker Kessler 10.00 25.00
7 AJ Griffin 4.00 10.00
8 Mark Williams 10.00 25.00
9 Dalen Terry 5.00 12.00
10 Paolo Banchero 125.00 300.00
11 Ochai Agbaji 6.00 15.00
12 TyTy Washington Jr. 5.00 12.00
13 Simone Fontecchio 5.00 12.00
14 Nikola Jovic 10.00 25.00
15 Chet Holmgren 100.00 250.00
16 Moussa Diabate 5.00 12.00
17 Dyson Daniels 12.00 30.00
18 Jalen Williams 40.00 100.00
19 Tari Eason 12.00 30.00
20 Keegan Murray 40.00 100.00
21 Malaki Branham 5.00 12.00
22 Kennedy Chandler 5.00 12.00
23 Bennedict Mathurin 40.00 100.00
24 Patrick Baldwin Jr. 5.00 12.00
25 Andrew Nembhard 10.00 25.00
26 Max Christie 20.00 50.00
27 Jeremy Sochan 40.00 100.00
28 Caleb Houstan 5.00 12.00
29 Jaden Ivey 40.00 100.00
30 Jake LaRavia 5.00 12.00
31 MarJon Beauchamp 5.00 12.00
32 Bryce McGowens 5.00 12.00
33 David Roddy 6.00 15.00
34 Christian Braun 12.00 30.00
35 Jabari Walker 4.00 10.00
36 Jalen Duren 15.00 40.00
37 Mac McClung 15.00 40.00
38 Jaylin Williams 6.00 15.00
39 Wendell Moore Jr. 5.00 12.00
40 Jaden Hardy 8.00 20.00

2022-23 Panini Mosaic Rookie Scripts

COMPLETE SET (36)
*GRREN ICE: .5X TO 1.2X BASIC
1 Julian Champagnie 15.00 40.00
2 Paolo Banchero 125.00 300.00
4 Jalen Duren 15.00 40.00
5 Ryan Rollins 5.00 12.00
6 Buddy Boeheim 5.00 12.00
7 Bennedict Mathurin 40.00 100.00
8 Jaden Ivey 40.00 100.00
10 Jordan Goodwin 4.00 10.00
11 Johnny Juzang 6.00 15.00
12 Jalen Williams 40.00 100.00
13 Kendall Brown 4.00 10.00
14 Dominick Barlow 15.00 40.00
15 Ochai Agbaji 6.00 15.00
16 Keegan Murray 40.00 100.00
17 MarJon Beauchamp 5.00 12.00
18 A.J. Green 30.00 80.00
19 Darius Days 4.00 10.00
21 Malaki Branham 5.00 12.00
22 Walker Kessler 10.00 25.00
23 Jaylin Williams 6.00 15.00
24 Jamal Cain 5.00 12.00
25 Nikola Jovic 10.00 25.00
26 Jabari Smith Jr. 40.00 100.00
28 Scotty Pippen Jr. 6.00 15.00
29 Dyson Daniels 12.00 30.00
30 Matt Ryan 5.00 12.00
31 Cole Swider 6.00 15.00
32 Jordan Hall 4.00 10.00
33 Jeremy Sochan 40.00 100.00
34 Simone Fontecchio 5.00 12.00
35 Dereon Seabron 4.00 10.00
36 Kevon Harris 4.00 10.00
37 Josh Minott 5.00 12.00
38 Tyrese Martin 4.00 10.00
39 Trevor Keels 4.00 10.00
40 Shaedon Sharpe 40.00 100.00

2022-23 Panini Mosaic Rookie Variations Fast Break

COMPLETE SET (14)

2022-23 Panini Mosaic Scripts

COMPLETE SET (56)
*GREN ICE: .5X TO 1.2X BASIC
1 Kendrick Perkins 3.00 8.00
3 Wally Szczerbiak 4.00 10.00
4 Maurice Cheeks 5.00 12.00
5 Ivica Zubac 5.00 12.00
6 Monte Morris 3.00 8.00
8 Patty Mills 15.00 40.00
9 Gary Trent Jr. 5.00 12.00
10 Chuma Okeke 5.00 12.00
11 Edmond Sumner 3.00 8.00
12 Jalen McDaniels 5.00 12.00
13 Devin Vassell 6.00 15.00
14 Evan Fournier 4.00 10.00
15 Goran Dragic 4.00 10.00
16 Thomas Bryant 4.00 10.00
17 Udonis Haslem 4.00 10.00
18 Juan Toscano-Anderson 3.00 8.00
19 Tim Hardaway Jr. 4.00 10.00
20 Landry Shamet 3.00 8.00
21 Bobby Portis 5.00 12.00
22 Isaiah Roby 3.00 8.00
23 Kevon Looney 5.00 12.00
24 Torrey Craig 3.00 8.00
25 Max Strus 5.00 12.00
26 Mo Bamba 4.00 10.00
27 Doug McDermott 3.00 8.00
28 Isaiah Stewart 4.00 10.00
29 Darius Miles 4.00 10.00
30 Sandro Mamukelashvili 5.00 12.00
31 Duane Washington Jr. 3.00 8.00
32 Dan Majerle 5.00 12.00
33 Santi Aldama 5.00 12.00
34 Devonte' Graham 4.00 10.00
35 Adam Morrison 4.00 10.00
36 Nicolas Batum 4.00 10.00
37 Miles McBride 5.00 12.00
38 Grayson Allen 5.00 12.00
39 Dell Curry 5.00 12.00
40 Mario Chalmers 4.00 10.00
41 Will Barton 3.00 8.00
42 John Starks 10.00 25.00
43 Nick Van Exel 5.00 12.00
45 Larry Johnson 12.00 30.00
46 Dan Issel 6.00 15.00
47 Tom Chambers 5.00 12.00
48 Stephen Jackson 5.00 12.00
49 David Thompson 6.00 15.00
50 Bill Laimbeer 5.00 12.00
51 Caron Butler 4.00 10.00
52 Mason Plumlee 4.00 10.00
53 Kevin Huerter 5.00 12.00
54 Gabe Vincent 5.00 12.00
55 Furkan Korkmaz 4.00 10.00
56 Lauri Markkanen 15.00 40.00
57 Jalen Suggs 6.00 15.00
59 James Worthy 12.00 30.00
60 Jrue Holiday 12.00 30.00

2022-23 Panini Mosaic Stained Glass

COMPLETE SET (10)
1 Bennedict Mathurin 60.00 150.00
2 LeBron James 150.00 400.00
3 Stephen Curry 150.00 400.00
4 Jalen Williams 100.00 250.00
5 Ja Morant 60.00 150.00
6 Luka Doncic 125.00 300.00
7 Jaden Ivey 60.00 150.00
8 Giannis Antetokounmpo 100.00 250.00
9 Kevin Durant 60.00 150.00
10 Paolo Banchero 125.00 300.00

2022-23 Panini Mosaic Stare Masters

COMPLETE SET (25)
*FB: .75X TO 2X BASIC
*MOSAIC: .75X TO 2X BASIC
*PURPLE/99: 3X TO 8X BASIC
*WHITE/25: 8X TO 20X BASIC
1 Zion Williamson 1.00 2.50
2 Kevin Durant 1.25 3.00
3 Stephen Curry 3.00 8.00
4 James Harden .75 2.00
5 Kawhi Leonard 1.00 2.50
6 Giannis Antetokounmpo 2.00 5.00
7 LeBron James 3.00 8.00
8 Darius Garland .60 1.50
9 DeMar DeRozan .50 1.25
10 Jamal Murray .60 1.50
11 Jayson Tatum 1.50 4.00
12 Luka Doncic 2.50 6.00
13 Ja Morant 1.25 3.00
14 Anthony Edwards 2.00 5.00
15 Josh Giddey .60 1.50
16 Trae Young 1.00 2.50
17 Damian Lillard 1.00 2.50
18 Jalen Brunson .75 2.00
19 Jimmy Butler .75 2.00
20 Kyrie Irving .75 2.00
21 Nikola Jokic 2.00 5.00
22 Lauri Markkanen .60 1.50
23 Tyrese Maxey .75 2.00
24 Klay Thompson 1.00 2.50
25 Anthony Davis 1.00 2.50

2022-23 Panini Mosaic Storm Chasers

COMPLETE SET (15)
1 Keegan Murray 10.00 25.00
2 LeBron James 30.00 80.00
3 Stephen Curry 30.00 80.00
4 Ja Morant 12.00 30.00
5 Paolo Banchero 25.00 60.00
6 Kevin Durant 12.00 30.00
7 Luka Doncic 25.00 60.00
8 Jalen Williams 20.00 50.00
9 Devin Booker 10.00 25.00
10 Jaden Ivey 12.00 30.00
11 Jayson Tatum 15.00 40.00
12 Giannis Antetokounmpo 20.00 50.00
13 Kyrie Irving 8.00 20.00
14 Donovan Mitchell 8.00 20.00
15 Bennedict Mathurin 12.00 30.00

2022-23 Panini Mosaic Straight Fire

COMPLETE SET (20)
1 Ja Morant 5.00 12.00
2 Kevin Durant 5.00 12.00
3 Paolo Banchero 10.00 25.00
4 Giannis Antetokounmpo 8.00 20.00
5 Jayson Tatum 6.00 15.00
6 Keegan Murray 4.00 10.00
7 LeBron James 12.00 30.00
8 Bennedict Mathurin 5.00 12.00
9 Stephen Curry 12.00 30.00
10 Donovan Mitchell 3.00 8.00
11 Klay Thompson 4.00 10.00
12 Shai Gilgeous-Alexander 8.00 20.00
13 Jaden Ivey 5.00 12.00
14 Nikola Jokic 8.00 20.00
15 Trae Young 4.00 10.00
16 Damian Lillard 4.00 10.00
17 Jalen Williams 8.00 20.00
18 Julius Randle 2.00 5.00
19 Kyrie Irving 3.00 8.00
20 Jabari Smith Jr. 5.00 12.00

2022-23 Panini Mosaic Swagger

COMPLETE SET (15)
1 Paolo Banchero 6.00 15.00
2 Giannis Antetokounmpo 5.00 12.00
3 Trae Young 2.50 6.00
4 Damian Lillard 2.50 6.00
5 Jaden Ivey 3.00 8.00
6 Luka Doncic 6.00 15.00
7 LeBron James 8.00 20.00
8 Kevin Durant 3.00 8.00
9 Stephen Curry 8.00 20.00
10 Jabari Smith Jr. 3.00 8.00
11 De'Aaron Fox 2.00 5.00
12 Ja Morant 3.00 8.00
13 Bennedict Mathurin 3.00 8.00
14 Joel Embiid 1.50 4.00
15 Keegan Murray 2.50 6.00

2022-23 Panini Mosaic Thunder Road

COMPLETE SET (20)
*GREEN: .75X TO 2X BASIC
*MOSAIC: .75X TO 2X BASIC
*REACTIVE BLUE/99: 3X TO 8X BASIC
*REACTIVE YELLOW/99: 3X TO 8X BASIC
*ORNG FL/25: 8X TO 20X BASIC
1 LeBron James 3.00 8.00
2 Devin Booker 1.00 2.50
3 Tyrese Haliburton .75 2.00
4 Trae Young 1.00 2.50
5 Kevin Durant 1.25 3.00
6 Giannis Antetokounmpo 2.00 5.00
7 Lauri Markkanen .60 1.50
8 Kawhi Leonard 1.00 2.50
9 Luka Doncic 2.50 6.00
10 Jayson Tatum 1.50 4.00
11 Ja Morant 1.25 3.00
12 Stephen Curry 3.00 8.00
13 Zion Williamson 1.00 2.50
14 Shai Gilgeous-Alexander 2.00 5.00
15 Anthony Edwards 2.00 5.00
16 LaMelo Ball 1.00 2.50
17 Nikola Jokic 2.00 5.00
18 Damian Lillard 1.00 2.50
19 Kyrie Irving .75 2.00
20 Donovan Mitchell .75 2.00

2023-24 Panini Mosaic

*GREEN: .6X TO 1.5X BASIC
*MOSAIC: .6X TO 1.5X BASIC
*REACTIVE BLUE: .75X TO 2X BASIC
*REACTIVE YELLOW: .75X TO 2X BASIC
*RED: .75X TO 2X BASIC
*FB SILVER: 1.25X TO 3X BASIC
*GREEN ICE: 1.25X TO 3X BASIC
*SILVER: 1.25X TO 3X BASIC
1 Matisse Thybulle .30 .75
2 Tyrese Haliburton .75 2.00
3 Stephen Curry 3.00 8.00
4 Derrick Jones Jr. .30 .75
5 D'Angelo Russell .40 1.00
6 Pascal Siakam .60 1.50
7 Jabari Smith Jr. .60 1.50
8 Naz Reid .40 1.00
9 Jalen Johnson .50 1.25
10 Kevin Huerter .30 .75
11 Tyler Herro .60 1.50
12 Trey Murphy III .50 1.25
13 Gordon Hayward .40 1.00
14 Terance Mann .30 .75
15 Paolo Banchero 1.00 2.50
16 De'Andre Hunter .40 1.00
17 Max Strus .40 1.00
18 Mark Williams .40 1.00
19 Russell Westbrook .60 1.50
20 Kentavious Caldwell-Pope .30 .75
21 Jarrett Allen .40 1.00
22 Jonathan Kuminga 1.00 2.50
23 Dillon Brooks .40 1.00
24 Bogdan Bogdanovic .40 1.00
25 John Collins .40 1.00
26 Bam Adebayo .60 1.50
27 Jordan Poole .60 1.50
28 Austin Reaves 1.00 2.50
29 Ben Simmons .40 1.00
30 Chet Holmgren 1.00 2.50
31 Luka Doncic 2.50 6.00
32 Zion Williamson 1.00 2.50
33 Anthony Edwards 2.00 5.00
34 Precious Achiuwa .30 .75
35 Jeremy Sochan .50 1.25
36 Mike Conley .30 .75
37 Quentin Grimes .40 1.00
38 Lauri Markkanen .60 1.50
39 Malik Monk .60 1.50
40 Malik Beasley .40 1.00
41 Jalen Williams .75 2.00
42 Jordan Clarkson .40 1.00
43 Jamal Murray .75 2.00
44 Bradley Beal .50 1.25
45 Klay Thompson 1.00 2.50
46 Caris LeVert .40 1.00
47 Nikola Jokic 2.00 5.00
48 Derrick Rose .60 1.50
49 Corey Kispert .30 .75
50 Paul George .60 1.50
51 Jalen Green .60 1.50
52 Rudy Gobert .50 1.25
53 RJ Barrett .60 1.50
54 Marvin Bagley III .30 .75
55 Duncan Robinson .40 1.00
56 Scottie Barnes .50 1.25
57 Desmond Bane .50 1.25
58 Kelly Oubre Jr. .40 1.00
59 Khris Middleton .40 1.00
60 Deni Avdija .40 1.00
61 Julius Randle .50 1.25
62 Collin Sexton .50 1.25
63 Tari Eason .50 1.25
64 Evan Mobley .60 1.50
65 Anfernee Simons .50 1.25
66 Clint Capela .30 .75
67 Jalen Brunson .75 2.00
68 Ayo Dosunmu .40 1.00
69 Grayson Allen .40 1.00
70 Saddiq Bey .40 1.00
71 Bennedict Mathurin .60 1.50
72 Jusuf Nurkic .40 1.00
73 Anthony Davis 1.00 2.50
74 Herbert Jones .40 1.00
75 Harrison Barnes .30 .75
76 Domantas Sabonis .60 1.50
77 Giannis Antetokounmpo 2.00 5.00
78 Karl-Anthony Towns .60 1.50
79 Tyrese Maxey .75 2.00
80 P.J. Washington Jr. .40 1.00
81 Cade Cunningham 1.00 2.50
82 DeMar DeRozan .60 1.50
83 Onyeka Okongwu .30 .75
84 Buddy Hield .40 1.00
85 Shai Gilgeous-Alexander 2.00 5.00
86 Isaiah Joe .40 1.00
87 Jaden McDaniels .40 1.00
88 Kyle Anderson .30 .75
89 Tobias Harris .40 1.00
90 Marcus Smart .50 1.25
91 Josh Hart .40 1.00
92 LeBron James 3.00 8.00
93 Jaren Jackson Jr. .60 1.50
94 Isaac Okoro .30 .75
95 Caleb Martin .30 .75
96 Spencer Dinwiddie .30 .75
97 Zach Collins .30 .75
98 Rui Hachimura .40 1.00
99 Dorian Finney-Smith .30 .75
100 Zach LaVine .60 1.50
101 Andrew Wiggins .50 1.25
102 Malaki Branham .30 .75
103 Daniel Gafford .40 1.00
104 Eric Gordon .30 .75
105 Darius Garland .60 1.50
106 Coby White .40 1.00
107 Trae Young .75 2.00
108 Miles Bridges .40 1.00
109 Damian Lillard 1.00 2.50
110 Michael Porter Jr. .50 1.25
111 Alex Caruso .40 1.00
112 Brook Lopez .30 .75
113 Cam Reddish .30 .75
114 Immanuel Quickley .40 1.00
115 Kyrie Irving .75 2.00
116 Jakob Poeltl .30 .75
117 Cameron Thomas .50 1.25
118 Patrick Beverley .30 .75
119 Keldon Johnson .50 1.25
120 Al Horford .40 1.00
121 Jimmy Butler .60 1.50
122 LaMelo Ball 1.00 2.50
123 Nikola Vucevic .40 1.00
124 Gary Harris .30 .75
125 Devin Booker 1.00 2.50
126 Keegan Murray .50 1.25
127 Ja Morant 1.25 3.00
128 Aaron Gordon .40 1.00
129 De'Anthony Melton .40 1.00
130 Draymond Green .50 1.25
131 Jalen Suggs .50 1.25
132 Jaden Hardy .50 1.25
133 Simone Fontecchio .40 1.00
134 Dejounte Murray .50 1.25
135 OG Anunoby .50 1.25
136 Chris Paul .50 1.25
137 Jaden Ivey .50 1.25
138 Norman Powell .40 1.00
139 Terry Rozier III .50 1.25
140 Fred VanVleet .60 1.50
141 Deandre Ayton .40 1.00
142 Jalen Duren .50 1.25
143 Donovan Mitchell .75 2.00
144 Obi Toppin .40 1.00
145 Talen Horton-Tucker .40 1.00
146 Dante Exum .30 .75
147 Jayson Tatum 1.50 4.00
148 Dennis Schroder .40 1.00
149 Kawhi Leonard 1.00 2.50
150 Josh Giddey .50 1.25
151 Donte DiVincenzo .40 1.00
152 James Harden .75 2.00
153 CJ McCollum .40 1.00
154 Devin Vassell .50 1.25
155 Jerami Grant .50 1.25
156 Mikal Bridges .50 1.25
157 David Roddy .30 .75
158 Gary Trent Jr. .40 1.00
159 Jrue Holiday .50 1.25
160 Dyson Daniels .50 1.25
161 Kyle Lowry .50 1.25
162 Tim Hardaway Jr. .30 .75
163 De'Aaron Fox .75 2.00
164 Reggie Jackson .25 .60
165 Cole Anthony .40 1.00
166 Derrick White .50 1.25
167 Bojan Bogdanovic .40 1.00
168 Christian Braun .40 1.00
169 Kristaps Porzingis .50 1.25
170 Joel Embiid 1.00 2.50
171 Alperen Sengun .60 1.50
172 Tre Jones .40 1.00
173 Ziaire Williams .40 1.00
174 Brandon Ingram .50 1.25
175 Kyle Kuzma .50 1.25
176 Tyus Jones .30 .75
177 Shaedon Sharpe .75 2.00
178 Lonnie Walker IV .40 1.00
179 Nicolas Claxton .40 1.00
180 Kevin Durant 1.25 3.00
181 Bobby Portis .50 1.25
182 Jaylen Brown .75 2.00
183 Patrick Williams .30 .75
184 Franz Wagner .60 1.50
185 Bruce Brown .40 1.00
186 Jose Alvarado .40 1.00
187 Gabe Vincent .40 1.00
188 Cameron Johnson .40 1.00
189 Josh Richardson .25 .60
190 Malcolm Brogdon .40 1.00
191 Luguentz Dort .40 1.00
192 Markelle Fultz .30 .75
193 Jonas Valanciunas .30 .75
194 Grant Williams .30 .75
195 Kevon Looney .40 1.00
196 Taurean Prince .25 .60
197 Nicolas Batum .25 .60
198 Myles Turner .40 1.00
199 Isaiah Stewart .40 1.00
200 Ivica Zubac .40 1.00
201 Kobe Bufkin RC .75 2.00
202 Brandon Miller RC 2.50 6.00
203 Jalen Wilson RC .60 1.50
204 Craig Porter Jr. RC .75 2.00
205 Trayce Jackson-Davis RC .75 2.00
206 Jalen Slawson RC .60 1.50
207 Kris Murray RC .60 1.50
208 Jaylen Clark RC .60 1.50
209 Kobe Brown RC .60 1.50
210 Jarace Walker RC 1.25 3.00
211 Colby Jones RC .60 1.50
212 Olivier-Maxence Prosper RC .60 1.50
213 Leonard Miller RC .60 1.50
214 Julian Strawther RC .75 2.00
215 Vasilije Micic RC .60 1.50
216 Scoot Henderson RC 2.00 5.00
217 Cam Whitmore RC 1.50 4.00
218 Cason Wallace RC 1.25 3.00
219 Emoni Bates RC .75 2.00
220 Chris Livingston RC .60 1.50
221 Taylor Hendricks RC .60 1.50
222 Keyonte George RC 2.00 5.00
223 Jalen Hood-Schifino RC .60 1.50
224 Julian Phillips RC .60 1.50
225 Anthony Black RC 1.25 3.00
226 Ausar Thompson RC 1.50 4.00
227 Maxwell Lewis RC .50 1.25
228 GG Jackson II RC 1.25 3.00
229 Marcus Sasser RC 1.00 2.50
230 Amen Thompson RC 3.00 8.00
231 Amari Bailey RC .60 1.50
232 Rayan Rupert RC .60 1.50
233 Sidy Cissoko RC .60 1.50
234 Andre Jackson Jr. RC 1.00 2.50
235 Bilal Coulibaly RC 1.50 4.00
236 Sasha Vezenkov RC .50 1.25
237 Jalen Pickett RC .50 1.25
238 Victor Wembanyama RC 5.00 12.00
239 Gradey Dick RC 1.25 3.00
240 Jett Howard RC .75 2.00
241 Hunter Tyson RC .60 1.50
242 Nick Smith Jr. RC .75 2.00
243 Jordan Hawkins RC 1.00 2.50
244 Ben Sheppard RC .60 1.50
245 Brandin Podziemski RC 2.00 5.00
246 Jaime Jaquez Jr. RC 1.00 2.50
247 Dariq Whitehead RC .75 2.00
248 Dereck Lively II RC 1.25 3.00
249 Toumani Camara RC 1.25 3.00
250 Noah Clowney RC .75 2.00
251 Keyonte George NBA Debut 2.00 5.00
252 Brandon Miller NBA Debut 2.50 6.00
253 Jordan Hawkins NBA Debut 1.00 2.50
254 Trayce Jackson-Davis NBA Debut .75 2.00
255 Scoot Henderson NBA Debut 2.00 5.00
256 Julian Strawther NBA Debut .75 2.00
257 Victor Wembanyama NBA Debut 5.00 12.00
258 Cason Wallace NBA Debut 1.25 3.00
259 Andre Jackson Jr. NBA Debut 1.00 2.50
260 Gradey Dick NBA Debut 1.25 3.00
261 Taylor Hendricks NBA Debut .60 1.50
262 Ausar Thompson NBA Debut 1.50 4.00
263 Anthony Black NBA Debut 1.25 3.00
264 Marcus Sasser NBA Debut 1.00 2.50
265 Dereck Lively II NBA Debut 1.25 3.00
266 Brandin Podziemski NBA Debut 2.00 5.00
267 Jaime Jaquez Jr. NBA Debut 1.00 2.50
268 Bilal Coulibaly NBA Debut 1.50 4.00
269 Amen Thompson NBA Debut 3.00 8.00
270 Toumani Camara NBA Debut 1.25 3.00
271 Zion Williamson City Edition 1.00 2.50
272 Shai Gilgeous-Alexander City Edition 2.00 5.00
273 Anthony Edwards City Edition 2.00 5.00
274 Trae Young City Edition .75 2.00
275 Scoot Henderson City Edition 2.00 5.00
276 Stephen Curry City Edition 3.00 8.00
277 Brandon Miller City Edition 2.50 6.00
278 LeBron James City Edition 3.00 8.00
279 Giannis Antetokounmpo City Edition 2.00 5.00
280 Jaime Jaquez Jr. City Edition 1.00 2.50
281 Amen Thompson City Edition 3.00 8.00
282 Victor Wembanyama City Edition 5.00 12.00
283 Joel Embiid City Edition 1.00 2.50
284 Jayson Tatum City Edition 1.50 4.00
285 Luka Doncic City Edition 2.50 6.00
286 Kevin Durant City Edition 1.25 3.00
287 Nikola Jokic City Edition 2.00 5.00
288 Ja Morant City Edition 1.25 3.00
289 Tyrese Haliburton City Edition .75 2.00
290 Ausar Thompson City Edition 1.50 4.00
291 Tim Duncan NBA Greats 1.00 2.50
292 Julius Erving NBA Greats 1.00 2.50
293 Charles Barkley NBA Greats 1.00 2.50
294 Yao Ming NBA Greats 1.00 2.50
295 Magic Johnson NBA Greats 1.50 4.00
296 Shaquille O'Neal NBA Greats 1.25 3.00
297 Karl Malone NBA Greats .75 2.00
298 Dirk Nowitzki NBA Greats 1.00 2.50
299 Kareem Abdul-Jabbar NBA Greats 1.25 3.00
300 Allen Iverson NBA Greats 1.00 2.50

2023-24 Panini Mosaic Mosaic Blue

*BLUE: 1.5X TO 4X BASIC
STATED PRINT RUN 199 SER.#'d SETS
202 Brandon Miller 30.00 80.00
238 Victor Wembanyama 150.00 400.00
252 Brandon Miller NBA Debut 15.00 40.00
257 Victor Wembanyama NBA Debut 75.00 200.00
277 Brandon Miller City Edition 15.00 40.00
282 Victor Wembanyama City Edition 75.00 200.00

2023-24 Panini Mosaic Mosaic Blue International

*BLUE INT: 6X TO 15X BASIC
STATED PRINT RUN 25 SER.#'d SETS
202 Brandon Miller 125.00 300.00
238 Victor Wembanyama 1,000.00 2,000.00
252 Brandon Miller NBA Debut 60.00 150.00
257 Victor Wembanyama NBA Debut 500.00 1,000.00
277 Brandon Miller City Edition 60.00 150.00
282 Victor Wembanyama City Edition 500.00 1,000.00

2023-24 Panini Mosaic Mosaic Choice Fusion Red and Yellow

*CHOICE FUSION RD & YLW: 2.5X TO 6X BASIC
STATED PRINT RUN 75 SER.#'d SETS
202 Brandon Miller 50.00 120.00
238 Victor Wembanyama 300.00 600.00
252 Brandon Miller NBA Debut 25.00 60.00
257 Victor Wembanyama NBA Debut 125.00 300.00
277 Brandon Miller City Edition 25.00 60.00
282 Victor Wembanyama City Edition 125.00 300.00

2023-24 Panini Mosaic Mosaic Fast Break Blue

*FB BLUE: 2.5X TO 6X BASIC
STATED PRINT RUN 85 SER.#'d SETS
202 Brandon Miller 50.00 120.00
238 Victor Wembanyama 300.00 600.00
252 Brandon Miller NBA Debut 25.00 60.00
257 Victor Wembanyama NBA Debut 125.00 300.00
277 Brandon Miller City Edition 25.00 60.00
282 Victor Wembanyama City Edition 125.00 300.00

2023-24 Panini Mosaic Mosaic Fast Break Pink

*FB PINK: 8X TO 20X BASIC
STATED PRINT RUN 20 SER.#'d SETS
202 Brandon Miller 200.00 500.00
238 Victor Wembanyama 1,250.00 2,500.00
252 Brandon Miller NBA Debut 100.00 250.00
257 Victor Wembanyama NBA Debut 600.00 1,200.00
277 Brandon Miller City Edition 100.00 250.00
282 Victor Wembanyama City Edition 600.00 1,200.00

2023-24 Panini Mosaic Mosaic Fast Break Purple

*FB PURPLE: 4X TO 10X BASIC
STATED PRINT RUN 50 SER.#'d SETS
202 Brandon Miller 75.00 200.00
238 Victor Wembanyama 500.00 1,000.00
252 Brandon Miller NBA Debut 40.00 100.00
257 Victor Wembanyama NBA Debut 200.00 500.00
277 Brandon Miller City Edition 40.00 100.00
282 Victor Wembanyama City Edition 200.00 500.00

2023-24 Panini Mosaic Mosaic Fast Break Silver

*FB SILVER: 1.25X TO 3X BASIC

2023-24 Panini Mosaic Mosaic Glitter

*GLITTER: 6X TO 15X BASIC
202 Brandon Miller 150.00 400.00
238 Victor Wembanyama 1,000.00 2,000.00
252 Brandon Miller NBA Debut 75.00 200.00
257 Victor Wembanyama NBA Debut 500.00 1,000.00
277 Brandon Miller City Edition 75.00 200.00
282 Victor Wembanyama City Edition 500.00 1,000.00

2023-24 Panini Mosaic Mosaic Ice

*ICE: 2X TO 5X BASIC
STATED PRINT RUN 125 SER.#'d SETS
202 Brandon Miller 40.00 100.00
238 Victor Wembanyama 200.00 500.00
252 Brandon Miller NBA Debut 20.00 50.00
257 Victor Wembanyama NBA Debut 100.00 250.00
277 Brandon Miller City Edition 20.00 50.00
282 Victor Wembanyama City Edition 100.00 250.00

2023-24 Panini Mosaic Mosaic Orange Fluorescent

*ORANGE FLRSC: 6X TO 15X BASIC
STATED PRINT RUN 25 SER.#'d SETS
202 Brandon Miller 125.00 300.00
238 Victor Wembanyama 1,000.00 2,000.00
252 Brandon Miller NBA Debut 60.00 150.00
257 Victor Wembanyama NBA Debut 500.00 1,000.00
277 Brandon Miller City Edition 60.00 150.00
282 Victor Wembanyama City Edition 500.00 1,000.00

2023-24 Panini Mosaic Mosaic Pink

*PINK: 2X TO 5X BASIC
STATED PRINT RUN 149 SER.#'d SETS
202 Brandon Miller 40.00 100.00
238 Victor Wembanyama 200.00 500.00
252 Brandon Miller NBA Debut 20.00 50.00
257 Victor Wembanyama NBA Debut 100.00 250.00
277 Brandon Miller City Edition 20.00 50.00
282 Victor Wembanyama City Edition 100.00 250.00

2023-24 Panini Mosaic Mosaic Purple

*PURPLE: 2.5X TO 6X BASIC
STATED PRINT RUN 99 SER.#'d SETS
202 Brandon Miller 50.00 120.00
238 Victor Wembanyama 300.00 600.00
252 Brandon Miller NBA Debut 25.00 60.00
257 Victor Wembanyama NBA Debut 125.00 300.00
277 Brandon Miller City Edition 25.00 60.00
282 Victor Wembanyama City Edition 125.00 300.00

2023-24 Panini Mosaic Mosaic Red International

*RED INTL: 2.5X TO 6X BASIC
STATED PRINT RUN 75 SER.#'d SETS
202 Brandon Miller 50.00 120.00
238 Victor Wembanyama 300.00 600.00
252 Brandon Miller NBA Debut 25.00 60.00
257 Victor Wembanyama NBA Debut 125.00 300.00
277 Brandon Miller City Edition 25.00 60.00
282 Victor Wembanyama City Edition 125.00 300.00

2023-24 Panini Mosaic Mosaic Teal

*TEAL: 2.5X TO 6X BASIC
STATED PRINT RUN 75 SER.#'d SETS
202 Brandon Miller 50.00 120.00
238 Victor Wembanyama 300.00 600.00
252 Brandon Miller NBA Debut 25.00 60.00
257 Victor Wembanyama NBA Debut 125.00 300.00
277 Brandon Miller City Edition 25.00 60.00
282 Victor Wembanyama City Edition 125.00 300.00

2023-24 Panini Mosaic Mosaic White

*WHITE: 6X TO 15X BASIC
STATED PRINT RUN 25 SER.#'d SETS
202 Brandon Miller 150.00 400.00
238 Victor Wembanyama 1,000.00 2,000.00
252 Brandon Miller NBA Debut 75.00 200.00
257 Victor Wembanyama

NBA Debut 500.00 1,000.00
277 Brandon Miller
City Edition 75.00 200.00
282 Victor Wembanyama
City Edition 500.00 1,000.00

2023-24 Panini Mosaic Red Seismic

*RED SEISMIC: 1.5X TO 4X BASIC
STATED PRINT RUN 299 SER.#'d SETS
202 Brandon Miller 30.00 80.00
238 Victor Wembanyama 150.00 400.00
252 Brandon Miller
NBA Debut 15.00 40.00
257 Victor Wembanyama
NBA Debut 75.00 200.00
277 Brandon Miller
City Edition 15.00 40.00
282 Victor Wembanyama
City Edition 75.00 200.00

2023-24 Panini Mosaic Autographs Fast Break

*FB BLUE/25: .6X TO 1.5X BASIC
1 Trae Young 40.00 100.00
2 Luka Doncic 200.00 500.00
3 Kristaps Porzingis 12.00 30.00
4 Rudy Gobert 8.00 20.00
5 Moritz Wagner 6.00 15.00
7 T.J. McConnell 6.00 15.00
8 Steven Adams 6.00 15.00
9 Clint Capela 5.00 12.00
10 Andrew Wiggins 8.00 20.00
11 Luke Kennard 5.00 12.00
12 Donte DiVincenzo 12.00 30.00
13 Malik Beasley 6.00 15.00
14 Coby White 6.00 15.00
15 Josh Giddey 8.00 20.00
16 Malik Monk 8.00 20.00
17 Jaren Jackson Jr. 10.00 25.00
18 Ja Morant 75.00 200.00
19 Cameron Thomas 8.00 20.00
20 Anthony Davis 40.00 100.00
21 Paolo Banchero 40.00 100.00
22 Shaedon Sharpe 12.00 30.00
23 Chet Holmgren 75.00 200.00
24 Deandre Ayton 6.00 15.00
25 Obi Toppin 6.00 15.00
27 Marcus Smart 8.00 20.00
28 Jalen Duren 8.00 20.00
29 Jeremy Sochan 8.00 20.00
30 Bojan Bogdanovic 6.00 15.00
32 Myles Turner 6.00 15.00
33 Jrue Holiday 12.00 30.00
34 Jordan Clarkson 6.00 15.00
36 Markelle Fultz 5.00 12.00
37 Dorian Finney-Smith 5.00 12.00
38 Ayo Dosunmu 6.00 15.00
39 Ben Simmons 6.00 15.00
41 Yuta Tabuse 12.00 30.00
42 Buddy Hield 6.00 15.00
44 Doc Rivers 6.00 15.00
45 DeMarcus Cousins 6.00 15.00
46 Larry Johnson 8.00 20.00
47 Jerry Stackhouse 6.00 15.00
48 Dee Brown 5.00 12.00
49 Elvin Hayes 8.00 20.00
50 Kerry Kittles 5.00 12.00
51 Adrian Dantley 6.00 15.00
52 Bill Laimbeer 6.00 15.00
53 Steve Francis 6.00 15.00
54 Taj Gibson 4.00 10.00
55 Arvydas Sabonis 8.00 20.00
56 Dell Curry 6.00 15.00
57 Keon Ellis 5.00 12.00
58 Kevin McHale 10.00 25.00
59 Steve Kerr 8.00 20.00
60 Jalen Wilson 6.00 15.00
61 Colby Jones 6.00 15.00
62 Leonard Miller 6.00 15.00
63 Jordan Miller 8.00 20.00
64 Kobe Brown 6.00 15.00
65 Keyonte George 30.00 80.00
66 Amen Thompson 30.00 80.00
67 Kobe Bufkin 8.00 20.00
68 Dereck Lively II 12.00 30.00
69 Ausar Thompson 15.00 40.00
70 Brandin Podziemski 40.00 100.00
71 Kris Murray 6.00 15.00
72 Bilal Coulibaly 15.00 40.00
73 GG Jackson II 12.00 30.00
74 Hunter Tyson 6.00 15.00
75 Maxwell Lewis 5.00 12.00
76 Jalen Pickett 5.00 12.00
77 Dariq Whitehead 8.00 20.00
78 Jordan Walsh 6.00 15.00
80 Craig Porter Jr. 8.00 20.00
81 Trayce Jackson-Davis 8.00 20.00
82 Brice Sensabaugh 10.00 25.00
83 Andre Jackson Jr. 10.00 25.00
84 Chris Livingston 6.00 15.00
85 Rayan Rupert 6.00 15.00
86 Keyontae Johnson 6.00 15.00
87 Cason Wallace 12.00 30.00
88 Noah Clowney 8.00 20.00
89 Ben Sheppard 6.00 15.00
90 Ricky Council IV 8.00 20.00
91 Sidy Cissoko 6.00 15.00
92 Mouhamed Gueye 6.00 15.00
93 Isaiah Wong 6.00 15.00
94 Jaylen Clark 6.00 15.00
95 Sasha Vezenkov 5.00 12.00
96 Duop Reath 6.00 15.00
97 Vasilije Micic 6.00 15.00
98 Lester Quinones 5.00 12.00
99 Toumani Camara 12.00 30.00
100 Amari Bailey 6.00 15.00

2023-24 Panini Mosaic Autographs Fast Break Red

*FB RED: .5X TO 1.2X BASIC
STATED PRINT RUN 25-499 SER.#'d SETS
1 Trae Young/25 60.00 150.00
41 Yuta Tabuse/25 20.00 50.00

2023-24 Panini Mosaic Autographs Mosaic

*CHOICE: .5X TO 1.25X BASIC
*INTERNATIONAL: .5X TO 1.2X BASIC
*BLUE/49: .6X TO 1.5X BASIC
*WHITE/25: .75X TO 2X BASIC
1 Latrell Sprewell 6.00 15.00
2 Nicolas Batum 3.00 8.00
3 Evan Fournier 4.00 10.00
4 Ben Simmons 5.00 12.00
5 Jaden Hardy 6.00 15.00
6 Evan Mobley 8.00 20.00
7 Andrew Wiggins 6.00 15.00
8 Gabe Vincent 5.00 12.00
9 Scottie Barnes 15.00 40.00
12 Bogdan Bogdanovic 5.00 12.00
13 Quentin Grimes 5.00 12.00
15 Dante Exum 4.00 10.00
16 Brook Lopez 4.00 10.00
17 Isaac Okoro 4.00 10.00
19 Al Horford 5.00 12.00
20 Davion Mitchell 4.00 10.00
21 Yuta Watanabe 8.00 20.00
22 Moses Moody 6.00 15.00
23 Christian Wood 4.00 10.00
25 Josh Green 4.00 10.00
26 Lonnie Walker IV 5.00 12.00
27 Corey Kispert 4.00 10.00
28 Doug McDermott 4.00 10.00
30 Bruce Brown 5.00 12.00
31 Cameron Thomas 6.00 15.00
32 Damian Lillard 40.00 100.00
33 Jose Alvarado 5.00 12.00
34 Isaiah Hartenstein 5.00 12.00
35 John Wall 6.00 15.00
36 Fred VanVleet 8.00 20.00
38 Mark Williams 5.00 12.00
39 Jabari Smith Jr. 8.00 20.00
40 Kelly Olynyk 3.00 8.00
41 Ziaire Williams 5.00 12.00
42 Norman Powell 5.00 12.00
43 Jonathan Kuminga 12.00 30.00
44 James Wiseman 4.00 10.00
46 Patty Mills 5.00 12.00
47 Monte Morris 5.00 12.00
48 Jason Terry 5.00 12.00
49 MarJon Beauchamp 4.00 10.00
50 Christian Braun 5.00 12.00
51 Tyus Jones 4.00 10.00
52 Drew Eubanks 3.00 8.00
53 Daniel Gafford 5.00 12.00
54 Jalen Suggs 6.00 15.00
55 Jeff Hornacek 4.00 10.00
56 Charles Oakley 5.00 12.00
57 Carlos Boozer 4.00 10.00
58 Joe Dumars 6.00 15.00
59 Bruce Bowen 4.00 10.00
60 Glen Rice 5.00 12.00

2023-24 Panini Mosaic Bank Shot

1 Kawhi Leonard 1.50 4.00
2 Jalen Brunson 1.25 3.00
3 Giannis Antetokounmpo 3.00 8.00
4 Stephen Curry 5.00 12.00
5 Nikola Jokic 3.00 8.00
6 Amen Thompson 3.00 8.00
7 Ausar Thompson 1.50 4.00
8 Zach LaVine 1.00 2.50
9 Zion Williamson 1.50 4.00
10 Kevin Durant 2.00 5.00
11 Jaime Jaquez Jr. 1.00 2.50
12 Ja Morant 2.00 5.00
13 LeBron James 5.00 12.00
14 Brandon Miller 2.50 6.00
15 Chet Holmgren 1.50 4.00
16 Luka Doncic 4.00 10.00
17 Victor Wembanyama 8.00 20.00
18 Scoot Henderson 2.00 5.00
19 Tyrese Haliburton 1.25 3.00
20 Jayson Tatum 2.50 6.00

2023-24 Panini Mosaic Bank Shot Fast Break

*FAST BREAK: .5X TO 1.2X BASIC
17 Victor Wembanyama 25.00 60.00

2023-24 Panini Mosaic Bank Shot Fast Break Blue

*FB BLUE: 1.5X TO 4X BASIC
STATED PRINT RUN 85 SER.#'d SETS
14 Brandon Miller 25.00 60.00
17 Victor Wembanyama 150.00 400.00

2023-24 Panini Mosaic Bank Shot Mosaic

*MOSAIC: .5X TO 1.2X BASIC
17 Victor Wembanyama 20.00 50.00

2023-24 Panini Mosaic Bank Shot Mosaic Orange

*ORANGE: 2.5X TO 6X BASIC
STATED PRINT RUN 49 SER.#'d SETS
14 Brandon Miller 40.00 100.00
17 Victor Wembanyama 400.00 800.00

2023-24 Panini Mosaic Bank Shot Mosaic Purple

*PURPLE: 1.5X TO 4X BASIC
STATED PRINT RUN 99 SER.#'d SETS
14 Brandon Miller 20.00 50.00
17 Victor Wembanyama 125.00 300.00

2023-24 Panini Mosaic Bank Shot Mosaic Teal

*TEAL: 2X TO 5X BASIC
STATED PRINT RUN 75 SER.#'d SETS
14 Brandon Miller 30.00 80.00
17 Victor Wembanyama 300.00 600.00

2023-24 Panini Mosaic Bank Shot Mosaic White

*WHITE: 4X TO 10X BASIC
STATED PRINT RUN 25 SER.#'d SETS
14 Brandon Miller 60.00 150.00
17 Victor Wembanyama 600.00 1,200.00

2023-24 Panini Mosaic Collage Autographs Mosaic

*CHOICE: .5X TO 1.25X BASIC
*INTERNATIONAL: .5X TO 1.25X BASIC
*BLUE/25-49: .6X TO 1.5X BASIC
*WHITE/15-25: .75X TO 2X BASIC
1 Stephen Curry 300.00 600.00
2 Dejounte Murray 6.00 15.00
3 Jonas Valanciunas 4.00 10.00
5 Donovan Mitchell 25.00 60.00
6 Jaden Ivey 6.00 15.00
7 Walker Kessler 5.00 12.00
8 CJ McCollum 5.00 12.00
9 Tyler Herro 8.00 20.00
10 Cade Cunningham 25.00 60.00
11 Lauri Markkanen 8.00 20.00
12 Michael Porter Jr. 6.00 15.00
13 Anfernee Simons 6.00 15.00
14 Dyson Daniels 6.00 15.00
15 Payton Pritchard 5.00 12.00
16 Terance Mann 4.00 10.00
17 Caris LeVert 5.00 12.00
18 Tre Jones 5.00 12.00
19 Isiah Thomas 12.00 30.00
20 Calvin Murphy 5.00 12.00
21 Shawn Kemp 12.00 30.00
22 Spud Webb 5.00 12.00
23 Mike Bibby 5.00 12.00
24 Toni Kukoc 10.00 25.00
25 Amen Thompson 25.00 60.00
26 Brandin Podziemski 25.00 60.00
27 Marcus Sasser 8.00 20.00
28 Bilal Coulibaly 12.00 30.00
29 Ausar Thompson 12.00 30.00
30 Toumani Camara 10.00 25.00
31 Kobe Bufkin 6.00 15.00
32 Dereck Lively II 10.00 25.00
33 Kris Murray 5.00 12.00
34 Cason Wallace 10.00 25.00
35 Keyonte George 30.00 80.00

2023-24 Panini Mosaic Elevate

1 Tyrese Haliburton 1.25 3.00
2 Luka Doncic 4.00 10.00
3 Jayson Tatum 2.50 6.00
4 Joel Embiid 1.50 4.00
5 Nikola Jokic 3.00 8.00
6 Stephen Curry 5.00 12.00
7 Shai Gilgeous-Alexander 3.00 8.00
8 Zion Williamson 1.50 4.00
9 Scoot Henderson 2.00 5.00
10 Ausar Thompson 1.50 4.00
11 Trae Young 1.25 3.00
12 Giannis Antetokounmpo 3.00 8.00
13 Amen Thompson 3.00 8.00
14 Damian Lillard 1.50 4.00
15 Paolo Banchero 1.50 4.00
16 Kevin Durant 2.00 5.00
17 Brandon Miller 2.50 6.00
18 Victor Wembanyama 8.00 20.00
19 Anthony Edwards 3.00 8.00
20 Donovan Mitchell 1.25 3.00
21 Jaime Jaquez Jr. 1.00 2.50
22 Keyonte George 2.00 5.00
23 LeBron James 5.00 12.00
24 Anthony Davis 1.50 4.00
25 Ja Morant 2.00 5.00

2023-24 Panini Mosaic Elevate Mosaic

*MOSAIC: .5X TO 1.2X BASIC
18 Victor Wembanyama 20.00 50.00

2023-24 Panini Mosaic Elevate Mosaic Green

*GREEN: .5X TO 1.2X BASIC
18 Victor Wembanyama 25.00 60.00

2023-24 Panini Mosaic Elevate Mosaic Orange Fluorescent

*ORANGE FL: 4X TO 10X BASIC
STATED PRINT RUN 25 SER.#'d SETS
17 Brandon Miller 60.00 150.00
18 Victor Wembanyama 600.00 1,200.00

2023-24 Panini Mosaic Elevate Mosaic Reactive Blue

*REACTIVE BLUE: 1.5X TO 4X BASIC
STATED PRINT RUN 99 SER.#'d SETS
17 Brandon Miller 20.00 50.00
18 Victor Wembanyama 125.00 300.00

2023-24 Panini Mosaic Elevate Mosaic Reactive Yellow

*REACTIVE YELLOW: 1.5X TO 4X BASIC
STATED PRINT RUN 99 SER.#'d SETS
17 Brandon Miller 20.00 50.00
18 Victor Wembanyama 125.00 300.00

2023-24 Panini Mosaic Epic Performers

1 Shai Gilgeous-Alexander 3.00 8.00
2 LeBron James 5.00 12.00
3 Jayson Tatum 2.50 6.00
4 Tyrese Haliburton 1.25 3.00
5 Ja Morant 2.00 5.00
6 Trae Young 1.25 3.00
7 Tracy McGrady 1.00 2.50
8 Giannis Antetokounmpo 3.00 8.00
9 Luka Doncic 4.00 10.00
10 Zion Williamson 1.50 4.00
11 Charles Barkley 1.50 4.00
12 Victor Wembanyama 8.00 20.00
13 Kevin Durant 2.00 5.00
14 Stephen Curry 5.00 12.00
15 Nikola Jokic 3.00 8.00
16 Magic Johnson 2.50 6.00
17 Dwyane Wade 1.25 3.00
18 Joel Embiid 1.50 4.00
19 Tim Duncan 1.50 4.00
20 Anthony Edwards 3.00 8.00

2023-24 Panini Mosaic Epic Performers Mosaic

*MOSAIC: .5X TO 1.2X BASIC
12 Victor Wembanyama 20.00 50.00

2023-24 Panini Mosaic Epic Performers Mosaic Green

*GREEN: .5X TO 1.2X BASIC
12 Victor Wembanyama 25.00 60.00

2023-24 Panini Mosaic Epic Performers Mosaic Orange Fluorescent

*ORANGE FL: 4X TO 10X BASIC
STATED PRINT RUN 25 SER.#'d SETS
12 Victor Wembanyama 600.00 1,200.00

2023-24 Panini Mosaic Epic Performers Mosaic Reactive Blue

*REACTIVE BLUE: 1.5X TO 4X BASIC
STATED PRINT RUN 99 SER.#'d SETS
12 Victor Wembanyama 125.00 300.00

2023-24 Panini Mosaic Epic Performers Mosaic Reactive Yellow

*REACTIVE YELLOW: 1.5X TO 4X BASIC
STATED PRINT RUN 99 SER.#'d SETS
12 Victor Wembanyama 125.00 300.00

2023-24 Panini Mosaic Give and Go

1 Stephen Curry 5.00 12.00
2 Damian Lillard 1.50 4.00
3 LeBron James 5.00 12.00
4 De'Aaron Fox 1.25 3.00
5 Shai Gilgeous-Alexander 3.00 8.00
6 Nikola Jokic 3.00 8.00
7 Tyrese Haliburton 1.25 3.00
8 Kyrie Irving 1.25 3.00
9 Ja Morant 2.00 5.00
10 Trae Young 1.25 3.00
11 Luka Doncic 4.00 10.00
12 Victor Wembanyama 8.00 20.00
13 LaMelo Ball 1.50 4.00
14 Tyrese Maxey 1.25 3.00
15 James Harden 1.25 3.00

2023-24 Panini Mosaic Give and Go Mosaic

*MOSAIC: .5X TO 1.2X BASIC
12 Victor Wembanyama 20.00 50.00

2023-24 Panini Mosaic Give and Go Mosaic Green

*GREEN: .5X TO 1.2X BASIC
12 Victor Wembanyama 25.00 60.00

2023-24 Panini Mosaic Give and Go Mosaic Orange Fluorescent

*ORANGE FL: 4X TO 10X BASIC
STATED PRINT RUN 25 SER.#'d SETS
12 Victor Wembanyama 600.00 1,200.00

2023-24 Panini Mosaic Give and Go Mosaic Reactive Blue

*REACTIVE BLUE: 1.5X TO 4X BASIC
STATED PRINT RUN 99 SER.#'d SETS
12 Victor Wembanyama 125.00 300.00

2023-24 Panini Mosaic Give and Go Mosaic Reactive Yellow

*REACTIVE YELLOW: 1.5X TO 4X BASIC
STATED PRINT RUN 99 SER.#'d SETS
12 Victor Wembanyama 125.00 300.00

2023-24 Panini Mosaic Heat Check

1 Brandon Miller 4.00 10.00
2 LeBron James 8.00 20.00
3 Victor Wembanyama 30.00 80.00
4 Scoot Henderson 3.00 8.00
5 Donovan Mitchell 2.00 5.00
6 Damian Lillard 2.50 6.00
7 Paolo Banchero 2.50 6.00
8 Ausar Thompson 2.50 6.00
9 Ja Morant 3.00 8.00
10 Stephen Curry 8.00 20.00
11 Trae Young 2.00 5.00
12 Amen Thompson 5.00 12.00
13 Luka Doncic 6.00 15.00
14 Tyrese Haliburton 2.00 5.00
15 Jayson Tatum 4.00 10.00

2023-24 Panini Mosaic Introductions

1 Dereck Lively II 1.25 3.00
2 Anthony Black 1.25 3.00
3 Amen Thompson 3.00 8.00
4 Marcus Sasser 1.00 2.50
5 Trayce Jackson-Davis .75 2.00
6 Gradey Dick 1.25 3.00
7 Andre Jackson Jr. 1.00 2.50
8 Victor Wembanyama 8.00 20.00
9 Cason Wallace 1.25 3.00
10 Julian Strawther .75 2.00
11 Taylor Hendricks .60 1.50
12 Ausar Thompson 1.50 4.00
13 Brandon Miller 2.50 6.00
14 Jordan Hawkins 1.00 2.50
15 Toumani Camara 1.25 3.00
16 Brandin Podziemski 2.00 5.00
17 Jaime Jaquez Jr. 1.00 2.50
18 Scoot Henderson 2.00 5.00
19 Bilal Coulibaly 1.50 4.00
20 Keyonte George 2.00 5.00

2023-24 Panini Mosaic Introductions Fast Break

*FB: .5X TO 1.2X BASIC
8 Victor Wembanyama 25.00 60.00

2023-24 Panini Mosaic Introductions Fast Break Blue

*FB BLUE: 1.5X TO 4X BASIC
STATED PRINT RUN 85 SER.#'d SETS
8 Victor Wembanyama 150.00 400.00
13 Brandon Miller 25.00 60.00

2023-24 Panini Mosaic Introductions Mosaic

*MOSAIC: .5X TO 1.2X BASIC
8 Victor Wembanyama 20.00 50.00

2023-24 Panini Mosaic Introductions Mosaic Orange

*ORANGE: 2.5X TO 6X BASIC
STATED PRINT RUN 49 SER.#'d SETS
8 Victor Wembanyama 400.00 800.00
13 Brandon Miller 40.00 100.00

2023-24 Panini Mosaic Introductions Mosaic Purple

*PURPLE: 1.5X TO 4X BASIC
STATED PRINT RUN 99 SER.#'d SETS
8 Victor Wembanyama 125.00 300.00
13 Brandon Miller 20.00 50.00

2023-24 Panini Mosaic Introductions Mosaic Teal

*TEAL: 2X TO 5X BASIC
STATED PRINT RUN 75 SER.#'d SETS
8 Victor Wembanyama 300.00 600.00
13 Brandon Miller 30.00 80.00

2023-24 Panini Mosaic Introductions Mosaic White

*WHITE: 4X TO 10X BASIC
STATED PRINT RUN 25 SER.#'d SETS
8 Victor Wembanyama 600.00 1,200.00
13 Brandon Miller 60.00 150.00

2023-24 Panini Mosaic Jam Masters Mosaic

*MOSAIC: .5X TO 1.2X BASIC
3 Victor Wembanyama 20.00 50.00

2023-24 Panini Mosaic Jam Masters Mosaic Green

*GREEN: .5X TO 1.2X BASIC
3 Victor Wembanyama 25.00 60.00

2023-24 Panini Mosaic Jam Masters Mosaic Orange Fluorescent

*ORANGE FL: 4X TO 10X BASIC
STATED PRINT RUN 25 SER.#'d SETS
1 Brandon Miller 60.00 150.00
3 Victor Wembanyama 600.00 1,200.00

2023-24 Panini Mosaic Jam Masters Mosaic Reactive Blue

*REACTIVE BLUE: 1.5X TO 4X BASIC
STATED PRINT RUN 99 SER.#'d SETS
1 Brandon Miller 20.00 50.00
3 Victor Wembanyama 125.00 300.00

2023-24 Panini Mosaic Micro Mosaic

1 De'Aaron Fox 100.00 250.00
2 Ausar Thompson 200.00 500.00
3 Scoot Henderson 350.00 700.00
4 Luka Doncic 600.00 1,200.00
5 Brandon Miller 800.00 1,500.00
6 Giannis Antetokounmpo 300.00 600.00
7 Keyonte George 300.00 600.00
8 Dereck Lively II 200.00 500.00
9 Chet Holmgren 150.00 400.00
10 Anthony Edwards 600.00 1,200.00
11 Tyrese Haliburton 200.00 500.00
12 Brandin Podziemski 300.00 600.00
13 Shai Gilgeous-Alexander 400.00 800.00
14 Ja Morant 350.00 700.00
15 LeBron James 1,000.00 2,000.00
16 Jayson Tatum 400.00 800.00
17 Jordan Hawkins 150.00 400.00
18 Cason Wallace 200.00 500.00
19 Jaime Jaquez Jr. 300.00 600.00
20 Nikola Jokic 500.00 1,000.00
21 Amen Thompson 300.00 600.00
22 Victor Wembanyama 4,000.00 8,000.00
23 Donovan Mitchell 100.00 250.00
24 Tyrese Maxey 300.00 600.00
25 Stephen Curry 600.00 1,200.00

2023-24 Panini Mosaic Montage

1 De'Aaron Fox 1.25 3.00
2 Joel Embiid 1.50 4.00
3 Keyonte George 2.00 5.00
4 Zion Williamson 1.50 4.00
5 Luka Doncic 4.00 10.00
6 Kevin Durant 2.00 5.00
7 Victor Wembanyama 8.00 20.00
8 Ausar Thompson 1.50 4.00
9 Trae Young 1.25 3.00
10 Damian Lillard 1.50 4.00
11 Shai Gilgeous-Alexander 3.00 8.00
12 Brandon Miller 2.50 6.00
13 Nikola Jokic 3.00 8.00
14 James Harden 1.25 3.00
15 Giannis Antetokounmpo 3.00 8.00
16 Jaylen Brown 1.25 3.00
17 Anthony Davis 1.50 4.00
18 Jayson Tatum 2.50 6.00
19 Anthony Edwards 3.00 8.00
20 Tyrese Haliburton 1.25 3.00
21 Bilal Coulibaly 1.50 4.00
22 Scoot Henderson 2.00 5.00
23 Jordan Hawkins 1.00 2.50
24 LeBron James 5.00 12.00
25 Stephen Curry 5.00 12.00
26 Amen Thompson 3.00 8.00
27 Brandin Podziemski 2.00 5.00
28 Jaime Jaquez Jr. 1.00 2.50
29 Tyrese Maxey 1.25 3.00
30 Ja Morant 2.00 5.00

2023-24 Panini Mosaic Montage Fast Break

*FB: .5X TO 1.2X BASIC
7 Victor Wembanyama 25.00 60.00

2023-24 Panini Mosaic Montage Fast Break Blue

*FB BLUE: 1.5X TO 4X BASIC
STATED PRINT RUN 85 SER.#'d SETS
7 Victor Wembanyama 150.00 400.00
12 Brandon Miller 25.00 60.00

2023-24 Panini Mosaic Montage Mosaic

*MOSAIC: .5X TO 1.2X BASIC
7 Victor Wembanyama 20.00 50.00

2023-24 Panini Mosaic Montage Mosaic Orange

*ORANGE: 2.5X TO 6X BASIC
STATED PRINT RUN 49 SER.#'d SETS
7 Victor Wembanyama 400.00 800.00
12 Brandon Miller 40.00 100.00

2023-24 Panini Mosaic Montage Mosaic Purple

*PURPLE: 1.5X TO 4X BASIC
STATED PRINT RUN 99 SER.#'d SETS
7 Victor Wembanyama 125.00 300.00
12 Brandon Miller 20.00 50.00

2023-24 Panini Mosaic Montage Mosaic Teal

*TEAL: 2X TO 5X BASIC
STATED PRINT RUN 75 SER.#'d SETS
7 Victor Wembanyama 300.00 600.00
12 Brandon Miller 30.00 80.00

2023-24 Panini Mosaic Montage Mosaic White

*WHITE: 4X TO 10X BASIC
STATED PRINT RUN 25 SER.#'d SETS
7 Victor Wembanyama 600.00 1,200.00
12 Brandon Miller 60.00 150.00

2023-24 Panini Mosaic Notoriety

1 Ausar Thompson 1.50 4.00
2 Stephen Curry 5.00 12.00
3 LeBron James 5.00 12.00
4 Scoot Henderson 2.00 5.00
5 Victor Wembanyama 8.00 20.00
6 Jayson Tatum 2.50 6.00
7 Amen Thompson 3.00 8.00
8 Luka Doncic 4.00 10.00
9 Ja Morant 2.00 5.00
10 Brandon Miller 2.50 6.00

2023-24 Panini Mosaic Notoriety Mosaic

*MOSAIC: .5X TO 1.2X BASIC
5 Victor Wembanyama 20.00 50.00

2023-24 Panini Mosaic Notoriety Mosaic Fast Break

*FB: .5X TO 1.2X BASIC
5 Victor Wembanyama 25.00 60.00

2023-24 Panini Mosaic Notoriety Mosaic Fast Break Blue

*FB BLUE: 1.5X TO 4X BASIC
STATED PRINT RUN 85 SER.#'d SETS
5 Victor Wembanyama 150.00 400.00
10 Brandon Miller 25.00 60.00

2023-24 Panini Mosaic Notoriety Mosaic Orange

*ORANGE: 2.5X TO 6X BASIC
STATED PRINT RUN 49 SER.#'d SETS
5 Victor Wembanyama 400.00 800.00
10 Brandon Miller 40.00 100.00

2023-24 Panini Mosaic Notoriety Mosaic Purple

*PURPLE: 1.5X TO 4X BASIC
STATED PRINT RUN 99 SER.#'d SETS
5 Victor Wembanyama 125.00 300.00
10 Brandon Miller 20.00 50.00

2023-24 Panini Mosaic Notoriety Mosaic Teal

*TEAL: 2X TO 5X BASIC
STATED PRINT RUN 75 SER.#'d SETS
5 Victor Wembanyama 300.00 600.00
10 Brandon Miller 30.00 80.00

2023-24 Panini Mosaic Notoriety Mosaic White

*WHITE: 4X TO 10X BASIC
STATED PRINT RUN 25 SER.#'d SETS
5 Victor Wembanyama 600.00 1,200.00
10 Brandon Miller 60.00 150.00

2023-24 Panini Mosaic Overdrive

1 Paolo Banchero 2.00 5.00
2 Tyrese Haliburton 1.50 4.00
3 Shai Gilgeous-Alexander 4.00 10.00
4 Luka Doncic 5.00 12.00
5 Stephen Curry 6.00 15.00
6 Cade Cunningham 2.00 5.00
7 Keyonte George 2.50 6.00
8 Ausar Thompson 2.00 5.00
9 Dereck Lively II 1.50 4.00
10 Zion Williamson 2.00 5.00
11 Brandin Podziemski 2.50 6.00
12 Nikola Jokic 4.00 10.00
13 LeBron James 6.00 15.00
14 Anthony Edwards 4.00 10.00
15 Giannis Antetokounmpo 4.00 10.00
16 Victor Wembanyama 25.00 60.00
17 Jayson Tatum 3.00 8.00
18 Amen Thompson 4.00 10.00
19 Jordan Hawkins 1.25 3.00
20 Ja Morant 2.50 6.00
21 Jaime Jaquez Jr. 1.25 3.00
22 Scoot Henderson 2.50 6.00
23 Brandon Miller 3.00 8.00
24 Kevin Durant 2.50 6.00
25 Trae Young 1.50 4.00

2023-24 Panini Mosaic Pictographs Mosaic

*CHOICE: .5X TO 1.25X BASIC
*INTERNATIONAL: .5X TO 1.2X BASIC
*BLUE/49: .6X TO 1.5X BASIC
*WHITE/25: .75X TO 2X BASIC
1 Tyrese Maxey 20.00 50.00
3 Franz Wagner 12.00 30.00
4 Zach LaVine 8.00 20.00
5 Jalen Green 12.00 30.00
6 Ja Morant 75.00 200.00
7 Caleb Martin 4.00 10.00
8 Jalen Williams 20.00 50.00
9 Keegan Murray 6.00 15.00
10 Anthony Edwards 100.00 250.00
11 Chris Paul 20.00 50.00
12 Paul Pierce 20.00 50.00
14 Immanuel Quickley 5.00 12.00
15 Quentin Grimes 5.00 12.00
17 Deandre Ayton 5.00 12.00
19 Christian Wood 4.00 10.00
20 MarJon Beauchamp 4.00 10.00
21 Malaki Branham 4.00 10.00
22 Devin Vassell 6.00 15.00
23 Michael Cooper 5.00 12.00
24 Udonis Haslem 5.00 12.00
25 Rick Barry 6.00 15.00
26 Ben Wallace 6.00 15.00
27 Sam Cassell 4.00 10.00
28 Metta World Peace 5.00 12.00
29 Tim Hardaway 6.00 15.00
30 Keyonte George 30.00 80.00
31 Amen Thompson 25.00 60.00
32 Brandin Podziemski 25.00 60.00
33 Bilal Coulibaly 12.00 30.00
34 Dereck Lively II 10.00 25.00
35 Ricky Council IV 6.00 15.00
36 Trayce Jackson-Davis 6.00 15.00
37 Cason Wallace 10.00 25.00
38 Kobe Bufkin 6.00 15.00
39 Marcus Sasser 8.00 20.00
40 Ausar Thompson 12.00 30.00

2023-24 Panini Mosaic Razzle Dazzle

1 Scoot Henderson 20.00 50.00
2 Stephen Curry 50.00 125.00
3 Nikola Jokic 30.00 80.00
4 Jayson Tatum 25.00 60.00
5 Shai Gilgeous-Alexander 30.00 80.00
6 Giannis Antetokounmpo 30.00 80.00
7 Tyrese Haliburton 12.00 30.00
8 Ausar Thompson 15.00 40.00
9 Victor Wembanyama 200.00 500.00
10 Ja Morant 20.00 50.00
11 Brandon Miller 25.00 60.00
12 LeBron James 50.00 125.00
13 Amen Thompson 30.00 80.00
14 Chet Holmgren 15.00 40.00
15 Luka Doncic 40.00 100.00

2023-24 Panini Mosaic Rookie Autographs Mosaic

*CHOICE: .5X TO 1.25X BASIC
*INTERNATIONAL: .5X TO 1.2X BASIC
*BLUE/49: .6X TO 1.5X BASIC
*WHITE/25: .75X TO 2X BASIC
1 Cason Wallace 12.00 30.00
2 Kris Murray 6.00 15.00
3 Stanley Umude 5.00 12.00
4 Dereck Lively II 12.00 30.00
5 Andre Jackson Jr. 10.00 25.00
6 Ben Sheppard 6.00 15.00
7 GG Jackson II 12.00 30.00
8 Sasha Vezenkov 5.00 12.00
10 Olivier-Maxence Prosper 6.00 15.00
11 Vasilije Micic 6.00 15.00
12 Hunter Tyson 6.00 15.00
13 Jalen Pickett 5.00 12.00
14 Trayce Jackson-Davis 8.00 20.00
15 Keyonte George 30.00 80.00
16 Mouhamed Gueye 6.00 15.00
17 Brice Sensabaugh 10.00 25.00
18 Brandin Podziemski 25.00 60.00
19 Sidy Cissoko 6.00 15.00
20 Dariq Whitehead 8.00 20.00
21 Keyontae Johnson 6.00 15.00
22 Jordan Walsh 6.00 15.00
23 Jaylen Clark 6.00 15.00
24 Ausar Thompson 15.00 40.00
25 Toumani Camara 12.00 30.00
26 Marcus Sasser 10.00 25.00
27 Jalen Wilson 6.00 15.00
28 Kobe Bufkin 8.00 20.00
29 Leonard Miller 6.00 15.00
30 Amari Bailey 6.00 15.00
31 Bilal Coulibaly 15.00 40.00
32 Isaiah Wong 6.00 15.00
33 Maxwell Lewis 5.00 12.00
35 Colby Jones 6.00 15.00
36 Noah Clowney 8.00 20.00
39 Chris Livingston 6.00 15.00
40 Amen Thompson 30.00 80.00

2023-24 Panini Mosaic Rookie Scripts

*GREEN ICE: .5X TO 1.25X BASIC
*GENESIS: 2X TO 5X BASIC
1 Amen Thompson 30.00 80.00
2 Bilal Coulibaly 15.00 40.00
4 Olivier-Maxence Prosper 6.00 15.00
6 Brandin Podziemski 20.00 50.00
7 Jalen Pickett 5.00 12.00
8 Cason Wallace 12.00 30.00
9 Jalen Slawson 6.00 15.00
10 Colby Jones 6.00 15.00
11 Noah Clowney 8.00 20.00
12 Mouhamed Gueye 6.00 15.00
14 Ausar Thompson 15.00 40.00
15 Chris Livingston 6.00 15.00
16 Trayce Jackson-Davis 8.00 20.00
18 Brice Sensabaugh 10.00 25.00
20 Kobe Bufkin 8.00 20.00
22 Marcus Sasser 10.00 25.00
23 Craig Porter Jr. 8.00 20.00
24 Maxwell Lewis 5.00 12.00
25 Keyonte George 20.00 50.00
26 Toumani Camara 12.00 30.00
28 Ricky Council IV 8.00 20.00
29 Vasilije Micic 6.00 15.00
30 Dereck Lively II 12.00 30.00
31 Keyontae Johnson 6.00 15.00
33 GG Jackson II 12.00 30.00
35 Amari Bailey 6.00 15.00
36 Jordan Walsh 6.00 15.00
40 Sasha Vezenkov 5.00 12.00

2023-24 Panini Mosaic Rookie Variations Fast Break

202 Brandon Miller 10.00 25.00
216 Scoot Henderson 8.00 20.00
218 Cason Wallace 5.00 12.00
222 Keyonte George 8.00 20.00
225 Anthony Black 5.00 12.00
226 Ausar Thompson 6.00 15.00
229 Marcus Sasser 4.00 10.00
230 Amen Thompson 12.00 30.00
235 Bilal Coulibaly 6.00 15.00
238 Victor Wembanyama 75.00 200.00
243 Jordan Hawkins 4.00 10.00
245 Brandin Podziemski 8.00 20.00
246 Jaime Jaquez Jr. 4.00 10.00
248 Dereck Lively II 5.00 12.00

2023-24 Panini Mosaic Scripts

*GREEN ICE: .5X TO 1.25X BASIC
*GENESIS: 2X TO 5X BASIC
1 Zeke Nnaji 3.00 8.00
2 Jaden Springer 4.00 10.00
3 Trendon Watford 5.00 12.00
4 Dalano Banton 4.00 10.00
5 Julian Champagnie 5.00 12.00
6 Usman Garuba 4.00 10.00
7 Luka Garza 4.00 10.00
8 Matt Ryan 4.00 10.00
9 Amir Coffey 3.00 8.00
10 Sandro Mamukelashvili 5.00 12.00
11 Ish Smith 4.00 10.00
12 Oshae Brissett 4.00 10.00
13 Keita Bates-Diop 4.00 10.00
14 Ty Jerome 3.00 8.00
15 Isaiah Hartenstein 5.00 12.00
16 JT Thor 4.00 10.00
17 Kessler Edwards 4.00 10.00
18 Skylar Mays 4.00 10.00
19 Jalen McDaniels 4.00 10.00
20 Aaron Wiggins 4.00 10.00
21 Charles Bassey 4.00 10.00
22 Sam Hauser 5.00 12.00

23 Greg Brown III 3.00 8.00
24 Eugene Omoruyi 4.00 10.00
25 Day'Ron Sharpe 4.00 10.00
26 Isaiah Livers 4.00 10.00
27 Corey Kispert 4.00 10.00
28 Jericho Sims 3.00 8.00
29 Miles McBride 5.00 12.00
30 Drew Eubanks 3.00 8.00
31 Daniel Theis 4.00 10.00
32 Jeremiah Robinson-Earl 4.00 10.00
33 Collin Gillespie 5.00 12.00
34 Keon Ellis 4.00 10.00
35 Santi Aldama 4.00 10.00
36 Paul Reed 5.00 12.00
37 Lindy Waters III 5.00 12.00
38 Garrison Mathews 5.00 12.00
39 Thanasis Antetokounmpo 5.00 12.00
40 John Konchar 4.00 10.00
42 Cole Swider 4.00 10.00
43 Brandon Boston Jr. 4.00 10.00
44 David Duke Jr. 3.00 8.00
45 E.J. Liddell 4.00 10.00
46 Christian Koloko 4.00 10.00
47 Max Christie 5.00 12.00
48 Ryan Rollins 5.00 12.00
49 Ousmane Dieng 5.00 12.00
50 Johnny Davis 4.00 10.00
51 Xavier Tillman 5.00 12.00
52 Josh Minott 5.00 12.00
53 Sam Merrill 5.00 12.00
54 Tom Van Arsdale 5.00 12.00
55 Dick Van Arsdale 5.00 12.00
56 Buddy Boeheim 4.00 10.00
57 Dan Majerle 5.00 12.00
58 Moussa Diabate 4.00 10.00
59 Jabari Walker 3.00 8.00
60 Caleb Houstan 5.00 12.00

2023-24 Panini Mosaic Showtime Signatures Mosaic

*CHOICE: .5X TO 1.25X BASIC
*INTERNATIONAL: .5X TO 1.25X BASIC
*BLUE/25-49: .6X TO 1.5X BASIC
*WHITE/15-25: .75X TO 2X BASIC
1 Luka Doncic 200.00 500.00
2 Cade Cunningham 25.00 60.00
3 Zion Williamson 75.00 200.00
4 Domantas Sabonis 12.00 30.00
5 Alperen Sengun 12.00 30.00
6 Chet Holmgren 50.00 120.00
7 Gary Payton 12.00 30.00
8 Tyrese Haliburton 50.00 120.00
9 Kristaps Porzingis 20.00 50.00
10 Keegan Murray 6.00 15.00
11 Shaedon Sharpe 10.00 25.00
12 Brandon Ingram 6.00 15.00
13 Donovan Mitchell 25.00 60.00
14 De'Aaron Fox 20.00 50.00
17 Mark Williams 5.00 12.00
18 Arvydas Sabonis 6.00 15.00
19 John Wall 6.00 15.00
20 Yuta Tabuse 15.00 40.00
21 Grant Hill 20.00 50.00
22 Anfernee Hardaway 30.00 80.00
23 Dennis Rodman 40.00 100.00
24 Rasheed Wallace 12.00 30.00
25 Gilbert Arenas 5.00 12.00

2023-24 Panini Mosaic Stained Glass

1 Ausar Thompson 100.00 250.00
2 Jayson Tatum 125.00 300.00
3 Keyonte George 150.00 400.00
4 Stephen Curry 150.00 400.00
5 Victor Wembanyama 1,500.00 3,000.00
6 LeBron James 150.00 400.00
7 Scoot Henderson 150.00 400.00
8 Zion Williamson 60.00 150.00
9 Luka Doncic 150.00 400.00
10 Shai Gilgeous-Alexander 150.00 400.00
11 Brandon Miller 400.00 800.00
12 Bilal Coulibaly 125.00 300.00
13 Damian Lillard 50.00 120.00
14 Giannis Antetokounmpo 100.00 250.00
15 Amen Thompson 150.00 400.00
16 Brandin Podziemski 150.00 400.00
17 Paolo Banchero 100.00 250.00
18 Ja Morant 100.00 250.00
19 Kevin Durant 75.00 200.00
20 Trae Young 40.00 100.00
21 Marcus Sasser 40.00 100.00
22 Jordan Hawkins 100.00 250.00
23 Nikola Jokic 125.00 300.00
24 Tyrese Haliburton 125.00 300.00
25 Jaime Jaquez Jr. 125.00 300.00

2023-24 Panini Mosaic Stare Masters

1 Luka Doncic 4.00 10.00
2 Ausar Thompson 1.50 4.00
3 Ja Morant 2.00 5.00
4 Shai Gilgeous-Alexander 3.00 8.00
5 Donovan Mitchell 1.25 3.00
6 Jayson Tatum 2.50 6.00
7 Brandon Miller 2.50 6.00
8 Tyrese Haliburton 1.25 3.00
9 Trae Young 1.25 3.00
10 LeBron James 5.00 12.00
11 Nikola Jokic 3.00 8.00
12 Scoot Henderson 2.00 5.00
13 Giannis Antetokounmpo 3.00 8.00
14 Zion Williamson 1.50 4.00
15 Paolo Banchero 1.50 4.00
16 Victor Wembanyama 8.00 20.00
17 Anthony Edwards 3.00 8.00
18 Stephen Curry 5.00 12.00
19 Amen Thompson 3.00 8.00
20 Kevin Durant 2.00 5.00

2023-24 Panini Mosaic Stare Masters Fast Break

*FB: .5X TO 1.2X BASIC
16 Victor Wembanyama 25.00 60.00

2023-24 Panini Mosaic Stare Masters Fast Break Blue

*FB BLUE: 1.5X TO 4X BASIC
STATED PRINT RUN 85 SER.#'d SETS
7 Brandon Miller 25.00 60.00
16 Victor Wembanyama 150.00 400.00

2023-24 Panini Mosaic Stare Masters Mosaic

*MOSAIC: .5X TO 1.2X BASIC
16 Victor Wembanyama 20.00 50.00

2023-24 Panini Mosaic Stare Masters Mosaic Orange

*ORANGE: 2.5X TO 6X BASIC
STATED PRINT RUN 49 SER.#'d SETS
7 Brandon Miller 40.00 100.00
16 Victor Wembanyama 400.00 800.00

2023-24 Panini Mosaic Stare Masters Mosaic Purple

*PURPLE: 1.5X TO 4X BASIC
STATED PRINT RUN 99 SER.#'d SETS
7 Brandon Miller 20.00 50.00
16 Victor Wembanyama 125.00 300.00

2023-24 Panini Mosaic Stare Masters Mosaic Teal

*TEAL: 2X TO 5X BASIC
STATED PRINT RUN 75 SER.#'d SETS
7 Brandon Miller 30.00 80.00
16 Victor Wembanyama 300.00 600.00

2023-24 Panini Mosaic Stare Masters Mosaic White

*WHITE: 4X TO 10X BASIC
STATED PRINT RUN 25 SER.#'d SETS
7 Brandon Miller 60.00 150.00
16 Victor Wembanyama 600.00 1,200.00

2023-24 Panini Mosaic Storm Chasers

1 Ja Morant 6.00 15.00
2 Zach LaVine 3.00 8.00
3 Victor Wembanyama 60.00 150.00
4 Ausar Thompson 5.00 12.00
5 Kyrie Irving 4.00 10.00
6 Nikola Jokic 10.00 25.00
7 Kevin Durant 6.00 15.00
8 Jaime Jaquez Jr. 3.00 8.00
9 Jayson Tatum 8.00 20.00
10 Tyrese Haliburton 4.00 10.00
11 LeBron James 15.00 40.00
12 Giannis Antetokounmpo 10.00 25.00
13 Shai Gilgeous-Alexander 10.00 25.00
14 Brandon Miller 8.00 20.00
15 Jordan Hawkins 3.00 8.00
16 Scoot Henderson 6.00 15.00
17 Amen Thompson 10.00 25.00
18 Anthony Edwards 10.00 25.00
19 Stephen Curry 15.00 40.00
20 Luka Doncic 12.00 30.00

2023-24 Panini Mosaic Thunder Road

1 Kawhi Leonard 1.50 4.00
2 Damian Lillard 1.50 4.00
3 Ja Morant 2.00 5.00
4 Shai Gilgeous-Alexander 3.00 8.00
5 Anthony Edwards 3.00 8.00
6 Giannis Antetokounmpo 3.00 8.00
7 Nikola Jokic 3.00 8.00
8 Victor Wembanyama 8.00 20.00
9 LeBron James 5.00 12.00
10 Zion Williamson 1.50 4.00
11 Trae Young 1.25 3.00
12 Amen Thompson 3.00 8.00
13 Stephen Curry 5.00 12.00
14 Scoot Henderson 2.00 5.00
15 Jayson Tatum 2.50 6.00
16 Ausar Thompson 1.50 4.00
17 Kevin Durant 2.00 5.00
18 Tyrese Haliburton 1.25 3.00
19 Brandon Miller 2.50 6.00
20 Luka Doncic 4.00 10.00

2023-24 Panini Mosaic Thunder Road Mosaic

*MOSAIC: .5X TO 1.2X BASIC
8 Victor Wembanyama 20.00 50.00

2023-24 Panini Mosaic Thunder Road Mosaic Green

*GREEN: .5X TO 1.2X BASIC
8 Victor Wembanyama 25.00 60.00

2023-24 Panini Mosaic Thunder Road Mosaic Orange Fluorescent

*ORANGE FL: 4X TO 10X BASIC
STATED PRINT RUN 25 SER.#'d SETS
8 Victor Wembanyama 600.00 1,200.00
19 Brandon Miller 60.00 150.00

2023-24 Panini Mosaic Thunder Road Mosaic Reactive Blue

*REACTIVE BLUE: 1.5X TO 4X BASIC
STATED PRINT RUN 99 SER.#'d SETS
8 Victor Wembanyama 125.00 300.00
19 Brandon Miller 20.00 50.00

2023-24 Panini Mosaic Thunder Road Mosaic Reactive Yellow

*REACTIVE YELLOW: 1.5X TO 4X BASIC
STATED PRINT RUN 99 SER.#'d SETS
8 Victor Wembanyama 125.00 300.00
19 Brandon Miller 20.00 50.00

2024-25 Panini Mosaic

*GREEN: .6X TO 1.5X BASIC
*MOSAIC: .6X TO 1.5X BASIC
*PREMIUM: .6X TO 1.5X BASIC
*REACTIVE BLUE: .75X TO 2X BASIC
*REACTIVE YELLOW: .75X TO 2X BASIC
*RED: .75X TO 2X BASIC
*FB SILVER: 1X TO 2.5X BASIC
*GREEN ICE: 1X TO 2.5X BASIC
*SILVER: 1X TO 2.5X BASIC
*RED SEISMIC/299: 1.5X TO 4X BASIC
*ORANGE/249: 1.5X TO 4X BASIC
*PRPL FL/249: 1.5X TO 4X BASIC
*BLUE/199: 2X TO 5X BASIC
*PINK/175: 2X TO 5X BASIC
*BLUE SEISMIC/149: 2X TO 5X BASIC
*ICE/125: 2X TO 5X BASIC
*FB RED/99: 2.5X TO 6X BASIC
*PURPLE/99: 2.5X TO 6X BASIC
*FB BLUE/85: 2.5X TO 6X BASIC
*BLUE FL/75: 3X TO 8X BASIC
*BRONZE/75: 3X TO 8X BASIC
*CHOICE FUSION R & Y/75: 3X TO 8X BASIC
*INT RED/75: 3X TO 8X BASIC
*RED FL/75: 3X TO 8X BASIC
*FB PURPLE/50: 4X TO 10X BASIC
*ORANGE ICE/49: 4X TO 10X BASIC
*CHOICE BLUE/45: 4X TO 10X BASIC
1 Paolo Banchero 1.00 2.50
2 Buddy Hield .30 .75
3 Coby White .40 1.00
4 Obi Toppin .30 .75
5 Marcus Smart .40 1.00
6 Bam Adebayo .50 1.25
7 Kawhi Leonard .75 2.00
8 Cameron Thomas .40 1.00
9 Keldon Johnson .30 .75
10 Amen Thompson 1.00 2.50
11 Max Strus .30 .75
12 Isaac Okoro .25 .60
13 Giannis Antetokounmpo 1.50 4.00
14 Paul George .60 1.50
15 Jalen Duren .40 1.00
16 Klay Thompson 1.00 2.50
17 Domantas Sabonis .60 1.50
18 Ochai Agbaji .30 .75
19 Terance Mann .25 .60
20 Mike Conley .30 .75
21 Jaime Jaquez Jr. .40 1.00
22 Terry Rozier III .30 .75
23 Tyrese Maxey .75 2.00
24 Duncan Robinson .30 .75
25 Luguentz Dort .30 .75
26 Jordan Hawkins .30 .75
27 Taurean Prince .25 .60
28 Kentavious Caldwell-Pope .25 .60
29 Bilal Coulibaly .50 1.25
30 Ben Simmons .40 1.00
31 Victor Wembanyama 3.00 8.00
32 Ayo Dosunmu .30 .75
33 Jaylen Brown .60 1.50
34 Spencer Dinwiddie .25 .60
35 Jalen Johnson .50 1.25
36 Anthony Edwards 2.00 5.00
37 Franz Wagner .60 1.50
38 Shai Gilgeous-Alexander 2.00 5.00
39 Anfernee Simons .40 1.00
40 Herbert Jones .30 .75
41 Mikal Bridges .40 1.00
42 James Harden .75 2.00
43 Grant Williams .25 .60
44 Zach LaVine .60 1.50
45 Brook Lopez .30 .75
46 Ausar Thompson .60 1.50
47 Tyler Herro .60 1.50
48 Patrick Williams .30 .75
49 Cason Wallace .50 1.25
50 Harrison Barnes .30 .75
51 Brandon Miller .60 1.50
52 GG Jackson II .40 1.00
53 Jalen Suggs .40 1.00
54 Jeremy Sochan .40 1.00
55 Daniel Gafford .30 .75
56 John Collins .30 .75
57 Keegan Murray .30 .75
58 Robert Williams III .30 .75
59 Chris Paul .60 1.50
60 Naz Reid .40 1.00
61 Shaedon Sharpe .50 1.25
62 Wendell Carter Jr. .30 .75
63 Chet Holmgren .60 1.50
64 Alperen Sengun .60 1.50
65 Dennis Schroder .40 1.00
66 Derrick White .40 1.00
67 Miles Bridges .50 1.25
68 Trey Murphy III .50 1.25
69 Kristaps Porzingis .50 1.25
70 Tari Eason .50 1.25
71 Josh Giddey .50 1.25
72 Desmond Bane .40 1.00
73 Donte DiVincenzo .40 1.00
74 Cade Cunningham 1.00 2.50
75 Jerami Grant .30 .75
76 Anthony Black .50 1.25
77 Scottie Barnes .50 1.25
78 Marcus Sasser .30 .75
79 Saddiq Bey .30 .75
80 Trayce Jackson-Davis .30 .75
81 Kelly Oubre Jr. .30 .75
82 Dejounte Murray .40 1.00
83 Moritz Wagner .30 .75
84 Al Horford .30 .75
85 Tyrese Haliburton .75 2.00
86 De'Andre Hunter .40 1.00
87 Deandre Ayton .30 .75
88 Rui Hachimura .40 1.00
89 Rudy Gobert .40 1.00
90 Aaron Gordon .40 1.00
91 Gary Trent Jr. .30 .75
92 Cole Anthony .40 1.00
93 Isaiah Stewart .30 .75
94 Tyus Jones .25 .60
95 Malaki Branham .30 .75
96 Grayson Allen .30 .75
97 Karl-Anthony Towns .60 1.50
98 Gradey Dick .50 1.25
99 Jaden Hardy .40 1.00
100 Luka Doncic 2.50 6.00
101 Jaden McDaniels .40 1.00
102 Donovan Mitchell .75 2.00
103 Caris LeVert .30 .75
104 Kyle Lowry .40 1.00
105 Brandin Podziemski .50 1.25
106 Nicolas Claxton .30 .75
107 Julius Randle .40 1.00
108 Andrew Nembhard .30 .75
109 Julian Champagnie .30 .75
110 Trae Young .75 2.00
111 DeMar DeRozan .50 1.25
112 Kevin Durant 1.25 3.00
113 Tre Mann .30 .75
114 Bradley Beal .50 1.25
115 Dereck Lively II .40 1.00
116 Keyonte George .50 1.25
117 Nikola Jokic 2.00 5.00
118 Anthony Davis 1.00 2.50
119 Zion Williamson 1.00 2.50
120 Austin Reaves .50 1.25
121 Brandon Ingram .30 .75
122 Isaiah Hartenstein .30 .75
123 OG Anunoby .30 .75
124 De'Aaron Fox .75 2.00
125 Zach Collins .25 .60
126 Andre Drummond .30 .75
127 Malik Monk .40 1.00
128 Michael Porter Jr. .40 1.00
129 T.J. McConnell .30 .75
130 Malik Beasley .30 .75
131 Jalen Green .75 2.00
132 Scotty Pippen Jr. .40 1.00
133 Evan Mobley .60 1.50
134 P.J. Washington Jr. .30 .75
135 Fred VanVleet .40 1.00
136 Josh Hart .30 .75
137 Payton Pritchard .40 1.00
138 Bogdan Bogdanovic .30 .75
139 Dyson Daniels .50 1.25
140 Draymond Green .50 1.25
141 Christian Braun .50 1.25
142 Kyle Kuzma .30 .75
143 Derrick Jones Jr. .25 .60
144 Jabari Smith Jr. .30 .75
145 Pascal Siakam .50 1.25
146 Kris Murray .30 .75
147 Norman Powell .40 1.00
148 Jimmy Butler III .60 1.50
149 Jordan Clarkson .40 1.00
150 Jalen Williams .75 2.00
151 Khris Middleton .30 .75
152 Joel Embiid .60 1.50
153 Myles Turner .30 .75
154 Bennedict Mathurin .50 1.25
155 Damian Lillard 1.00 2.50
156 Devin Vassell .40 1.00
157 Toumani Camara .40 1.00
158 RJ Barrett .50 1.25
159 Jaden Ivey .50 1.25
160 Cameron Johnson .30 .75
161 Jarrett Allen .30 .75
162 Jakob Poeltl .30 .75
163 Stephen Curry 3.00 8.00
164 Dorian Finney-Smith .25 .60
165 Scoot Henderson .50 1.25
166 Collin Sexton .40 1.00
167 Russell Westbrook .60 1.50
168 Nikola Vucevic .30 .75
169 Jonas Valanciunas .30 .75
170 Cam Reddish .25 .60
171 Cam Whitmore .40 1.00
172 Bobby Portis .30 .75
173 Clint Capela .30 .75
174 Tobias Harris .30 .75
175 Andrew Wiggins .50 1.25
176 Jalen Brunson .75 2.00
177 Ivica Zubac .30 .75
178 Jusuf Nurkic .30 .75
179 D'Angelo Russell .40 1.00
180 LeBron James 3.00 8.00
181 Andre Jackson Jr. .30 .75
182 Alex Caruso .40 1.00
183 Dillon Brooks .30 .75
184 Kyrie Irving 1.00 2.50
185 Immanuel Quickley .30 .75
186 Lauri Markkanen .40 1.00
187 Marvin Bagley III .25 .60
188 Jayson Tatum 1.25 3.00
189 Darius Garland .50 1.25
190 LaMelo Ball .75 2.00
191 CJ McCollum .40 1.00
192 Jamal Murray .60 1.50
193 Jonathan Kuminga .50 1.25
194 Peyton Watson .30 .75
195 Ja Morant 1.25 3.00
196 Jrue Holiday .50 1.25
197 Jordan Poole .40 1.00
198 Jaren Jackson Jr. .60 1.50
199 Jose Alvarado .40 1.00
200 Devin Booker 1.00 2.50
201 Jamal Shead RC .75 2.00
202 Johnny Furphy RC .75 2.00
203 Pacome Dadiet RC .75 2.00
204 Ajay Mitchell RC 1.00 2.50
205 Terrence Shannon Jr. RC 1.25 3.00
206 Bub Carrington RC 1.50 4.00
207 Cody Williams RC .75 2.00
208 Tyler Kolek RC 1.00 2.50
209 Yuki Kawamura RC .75 2.00
210 Adem Bona RC .75 2.00
211 Cam Christie RC .75 2.00
212 Yongxi "Jacky" Cui RC 1.25 3.00
213 Zaccharie Risacher RC 2.00 5.00
214 Bronny James Jr. RC 2.00 5.00
215 AJ Johnson RC 1.25 3.00
216 Alexandre Sarr RC 2.00 5.00
217 Jaylon Tyson RC .60 1.50
218 Rob Dillingham RC 1.50 4.00
219 Ron Holland II RC 1.25 3.00
220 Tristen Newton RC .60 1.50
221 Oso Ighodaro RC .75 2.00
222 Isaiah Collier RC 1.25 3.00
223 Matas Buzelis RC 3.00 8.00
224 Dillon Jones RC .60 1.50
225 Tyler Smith RC .75 2.00
226 Bobi Klintman RC .75 2.00
227 Cam Spencer RC .60 1.50
228 Jared McCain RC 2.50 6.00
229 Devin Carter RC .75 2.00
230 Tristan da Silva RC 1.50 4.00
231 Kyle Filipowski RC 1.50 4.00
232 Kel'el Ware RC 1.50 4.00
233 Ryan Dunn RC .75 2.00
234 Ja'Kobe Walter RC .75 2.00
235 Jonathan Mogbo RC 1.00 2.50
236 Stephon Castle RC 4.00 10.00
237 Antonio Reeves RC .60 1.50
238 Dalton Knecht RC 2.00 5.00
239 KJ Simpson Jr. RC .60 1.50
240 Jaylen Wells RC 2.00 5.00
241 Tidjane Salaun RC .60 1.50
242 Nikola Topic RC 2.00 5.00
243 Yves Missi RC 1.50 4.00
244 Harrison Ingram RC .60 1.50
245 Baylor Scheierman RC .75 2.00
246 Donovan Clingan RC 1.50 4.00
247 Kyshawn George RC 1.00 2.50
248 Zach Edey RC 2.00 5.00
249 Reed Sheppard RC 2.00 5.00
250 DaRon Holmes II RC .75 2.00
251 Zach Edey NBA Debut 1.25 3.00
252 Reed Sheppard NBA Debut 1.25 3.00
253 Ja'Kobe Walter NBA Debut .50 1.25
254 Alexandre Sarr NBA Debut 1.25 3.00
255 Yves Missi NBA Debut 1.00 2.50
256 Kyshawn George NBA Debut .60 1.50
257 Matas Buzelis NBA Debut 2.00 5.00
258 Ron Holland II NBA Debut .75 2.00
259 Bub Carrington NBA Debut 1.00 2.50
260 Jaylen Wells NBA Debut 1.25 3.00
261 Donovan Clingan NBA Debut 1.00 2.50
262 Bronny James Jr. NBA Debut 1.25 3.00
263 Jared McCain NBA Debut 1.50 4.00
264 Dalton Knecht NBA Debut 1.25 3.00
265 Yuki Kawamura NBA Debut .50 1.25
266 Tristan da Silva NBA Debut 1.00 2.50
267 Stephon Castle NBA Debut 2.50 6.00
268 Tidjane Salaun NBA Debut .40 1.00
269 Zaccharie Risacher NBA Debut 1.25 3.00
270 Rob Dillingham NBA Debut 1.00 2.50
271 Dalton Knecht City Edition 1.25 3.00
272 Stephen Curry City Edition 3.00 8.00
273 Matas Buzelis City Edition 2.00 5.00
274 Zaccharie Risacher City Edition 1.25 3.00
275 Nikola Jokic City Edition 2.00 5.00
276 Reed Sheppard City Edition 1.25 3.00
277 Jared McCain City Edition 1.50 4.00
278 Alexandre Sarr City Edition 1.25 3.00
279 Anthony Edwards City Edition 2.00 5.00
280 Kevin Durant City Edition 1.25 3.00
281 Ja Morant City Edition 1.25 3.00
282 Giannis Antetokounmpo City Edition 1.50 4.00
283 Paolo Banchero City Edition 1.00 2.50
284 Jalen Brunson City Edition .75 2.00
285 Damian Lillard City Edition 1.00 2.50
286 LeBron James City Edition 3.00 8.00
287 Jayson Tatum City Edition 1.25 3.00
288 Victor Wembanyama City Edition 3.00 8.00
289 Shai Gilgeous-Alexander City Edition 2.00 5.00
290 Stephon Castle City Edition 2.50 6.00
291 Tim Duncan Greats 1.00 2.50
292 Derrick Rose Greats 1.00 2.50
293 Kevin Garnett Greats 1.00 2.50
294 Yao Ming Greats .75 2.00
295 Dirk Nowitzki Greats 1.25 3.00
296 Magic Johnson Greats 1.25 3.00
297 Shaquille O'Neal Greats 1.00 2.50
298 Tracy McGrady Greats .75 2.00
299 Larry Bird Greats 1.25 3.00
300 Dwyane Wade Greats .75 2.00

2024-25 Panini Mosaic Mosaic Choice White

*CHOICE WHITE: 5X TO 12X BASIC
STATED PRINT RUN 35 SER.#'d SETS
236 Stephon Castle 75.00 200.00

2024-25 Panini Mosaic Mosaic Fast Break Blue Camo

*FB BLUE CAMO: 5X TO 12X BASIC
STATED PRINT RUN 35 SER.#'d SETS
236 Stephon Castle 75.00 200.00

2024-25 Panini Mosaic Mosaic Honeycomb

*HONEYCOMB: 6X TO 15X BASIC
236 Stephon Castle 100.00 250.00

2024-25 Panini Mosaic Mosaic International Blue

*INT BLUE: 5X TO 12X BASIC
STATED PRINT RUN 35 SER.#'d SETS
236 Stephon Castle 75.00 200.00

2024-25 Panini Mosaic Mosaic International White

*INT WHITE: 6X TO 15X BASIC
STATED PRINT RUN 25 SER.#'d SETS
236 Stephon Castle 100.00 250.00

2024-25 Panini Mosaic Mosaic Orange Fluorescent

*ORANGE FL: 6X TO 15X BASIC
STATED PRINT RUN 25 SER.#'d SETS
236 Stephon Castle 100.00 250.00

2024-25 Panini Mosaic Mosaic Purple Snakeskin

*PRPL SNAKESKIN: 8X TO 20X BASIC
STATED PRINT RUN 24 SER.#'d SETS
236 Stephon Castle 125.00 300.00

2024-25 Panini Mosaic Mosaic Spectris Blue FOTL

*SPECTRIS BLUE FOTL: 6X TO 15X BASIC
STATED PRINT RUN 25 SER.#'d SETS
236 Stephon Castle 100.00 250.00

2024-25 Panini Mosaic Mosaic White

*WHITE: 6X TO 15X BASIC
STATED PRINT RUN 25 SER.#'d SETS
236 Stephon Castle 100.00 250.00

2024-25 Panini Mosaic Autographs Fast Break

*FB RED/49: .75X TO 2X BASIC
*FB BLUE/25: 1X TO 2.5X BASIC
*FB PINK/15: 1X TO 2.5X BASIC
1 DaRon Holmes II 6.00 15.00
2 Jamal Shead 6.00 15.00
3 Terrence Shannon Jr. 10.00 25.00
4 Bobi Klintman 5.00 12.00
5 Tyler Kolek 8.00 20.00
6 Ja'Kobe Walter 6.00 15.00
7 Cam Spencer 5.00 12.00
8 Jonathan Mogbo 8.00 20.00
9 Anton Watson 4.00 10.00
10 Matas Buzelis 40.00 100.00
11 Enrique Freeman 4.00 10.00
12 Pacome Dadiet 6.00 15.00
13 Yves Missi 12.00 30.00
14 Jaylon Tyson 5.00 12.00
15 Oso Ighodaro 6.00 15.00
16 Baylor Scheierman 6.00 15.00
17 Jaylen Wells 15.00 40.00
18 Zach Edey 15.00 40.00
19 Tristen Newton 5.00 12.00
20 Reed Sheppard 30.00 80.00
21 Dillon Jones 5.00 12.00
22 Ajay Mitchell 8.00 20.00
23 Bub Carrington 12.00 30.00
24 Jared McCain 40.00 100.00
25 Tidjane Salaun 5.00 12.00
26 KJ Simpson Jr. 5.00 12.00
27 Yongxi "Jacky" Cui 10.00 25.00
28 Devin Carter 6.00 15.00
29 Dalton Knecht 15.00 40.00
30 Pelle Larsson 6.00 15.00
31 Cam Christie 6.00 15.00
32 Kyshawn George 8.00 20.00
33 AJ Johnson 10.00 25.00
34 Antonio Reeves 5.00 12.00
35 Adem Bona 6.00 15.00
36 Quinten Post 10.00 25.00
37 Donovan Clingan 12.00 30.00
38 Tristan da Silva 12.00 30.00
39 Johnny Furphy 8.00 20.00
40 Harrison Ingram 5.00 12.00
41 Tracy McGrady 40.00 100.00
42 Chet Holmgren 8.00 20.00
43 Mikal Bridges 5.00 12.00
44 Dereck Lively II 5.00 12.00
45 Amen Thompson 40.00 100.00
46 Cade Cunningham 40.00 100.00
47 Jaden Ivey 6.00 15.00
48 Isiah Thomas 8.00 20.00
49 Paolo Banchero 40.00 100.00
50 Jabari Smith Jr. 5.00 12.00
51 Jalen Duren 5.00 12.00
52 Jalen Suggs 5.00 12.00
53 Anfernee Hardaway 25.00 60.00
54 Keyonte George 6.00 15.00
55 Tyler Herro 8.00 20.00
56 Jamal Crawford 5.00 12.00
57 Ausar Thompson 8.00 20.00
58 Myles Turner 4.00 10.00
59 Josh Giddey 6.00 15.00
60 Lonzo Ball 5.00 12.00
61 Hakeem Olajuwon 40.00 100.00
62 Bennedict Mathurin 6.00 15.00
63 Zach LaVine 8.00 20.00
64 Dominique Wilkins 8.00 20.00
65 Jeremy Lin 40.00 100.00
66 Shawn Kemp 8.00 20.00
67 Damian Lillard 40.00 100.00
68 Kevin Love 4.00 10.00
69 J.J. Barea 4.00 10.00
70 Bob Cousy 40.00 100.00
71 Trae Young 40.00 100.00
72 Pascal Siakam 6.00 15.00
73 B.J. Armstrong 5.00 12.00
74 Magic Johnson 40.00 100.00
75 Charles Barkley 40.00 100.00
76 Jaren Jackson Jr. 8.00 20.00
77 Rick Barry 6.00 15.00
78 Austin Reaves 6.00 15.00
79 Kevin Garnett 40.00 100.00
80 OG Anunoby 4.00 10.00
81 Patrick Ewing 40.00 100.00
82 GG Jackson II 5.00 12.00
83 Ja Morant 50.00 120.00
84 Josh Hart 4.00 10.00
85 Domantas Sabonis 8.00 20.00
86 Dejounte Murray 6.00 15.00
87 Kareem Abdul-Jabbar 50.00 120.00
88 Allen Iverson 50.00 120.00
89 P.J. Washington Jr. 4.00 10.00
90 John Stockton 40.00 100.00
91 Paul Pierce 20.00 50.00
92 Jason Kidd 20.00 50.00
93 Gary Payton 20.00 50.00
94 Shaedon Sharpe 6.00 15.00
95 Tayshaun Prince 6.00 15.00
96 Alperen Sengun 8.00 20.00
97 Jason Terry 5.00 12.00
98 Jermaine O'Neal 4.00 10.00
99 Tim Hardaway 6.00 15.00
100 Amar'e Stoudemire 5.00 12.00

2024-25 Panini Mosaic Autographs Mosaic

*CHOICE: .5X TO 1.2X BASIC
*INT: .5X TO 1.2X BASIC
*BRONZE/75: .6X TO 1.5X BASIC
*BLUE/49: .75X TO 2X BASIC
*WHITE/25: 1X TO 2.5X BASIC
1 Alonzo Mourning 20.00 50.00
2 Dyson Daniels 6.00 15.00
3 Cason Wallace 6.00 15.00
4 Jaden Hardy 5.00 12.00
5 Kevin McHale 8.00 20.00
6 Tyler Herro 8.00 20.00
7 Lonzo Ball 5.00 12.00
8 Jarrett Allen 4.00 10.00
9 Norman Powell 5.00 12.00
10 Joakim Noah 5.00 12.00
11 Nikola Vucevic 4.00 10.00
12 Tyson Chandler 4.00 10.00
13 Marcin Gortat 3.00 8.00
14 Isaiah Thomas 4.00 10.00
15 Derrick Jones Jr. 3.00 8.00
16 Keyonte George 6.00 15.00
17 Jaden Ivey 6.00 15.00
18 Lenny Wilkens 5.00 12.00
19 Zhou Qi 4.00 10.00
20 Ayo Dosunmu 4.00 10.00
21 Carlos Arroyo 3.00 8.00
22 Clint Capela 4.00 10.00
23 Monta Ellis 4.00 10.00
24 Isaiah Joe 4.00 10.00
25 Amen Thompson 40.00 100.00
26 Latrell Sprewell 6.00 15.00
27 Dennis Schroder 5.00 12.00
28 Alex English 6.00 15.00
29 Keith Van Horn 4.00 10.00
30 Trey Murphy III 6.00 15.00
31 Trayce Jackson-Davis 5.00 12.00
32 Ausar Thompson 8.00 20.00
33 Robert Horry 5.00 12.00
34 Jim Paxson 4.00 10.00
35 Michael Redd 4.00 10.00
36 GG Jackson II 5.00 12.00
37 Arvydas Sabonis 5.00 12.00
38 Bruce Brown 4.00 10.00
39 Caris LeVert 4.00 10.00
40 Nick Van Exel 5.00 12.00
41 Jordan Clarkson 5.00 12.00
42 J.J. Barea 4.00 10.00
43 Harrison Barnes 4.00 10.00
44 Domantas Sabonis 8.00 20.00
45 Rasheed Wallace 6.00 15.00
46 Sun Yue 6.00 15.00
47 Bradley Beal 6.00 15.00
48 Ivica Zubac 5.00 12.00
49 Luol Deng 3.00 8.00
50 T.J. McConnell 4.00 10.00
51 Jamario Moon 3.00 8.00
52 Kentavious Caldwell-Pope 3.00 8.00
53 George Hill 4.00 10.00
54 Collin Sexton 5.00 12.00
55 Nicolas Claxton 4.00 10.00
56 Guerschon Yabusele 4.00 10.00
57 Carlos Boozer 4.00 10.00
58 Boris Diaw 4.00 10.00
59 John Paxson 4.00 10.00
60 Lance Stephenson 4.00 10.00

2024-25 Panini Mosaic Bank Shot

*MOSAIC: .6X TO 1.5X BASIC
*FB: 1X TO 2.5X BASIC
*BLUE/199: 2X TO 5X BASIC
*PINK/149: 2X TO 5X BASIC
*FB RED/99: 2.5X TO 6X BASIC
*PURPLE/99: 2.5X TO 6X BASIC
*FB BLUE/85: 2.5X TO 6X BASIC
*BRONZE/75: 3X TO 8X BASIC
*ORANGE/49: 4X TO 10X BASIC
*WHITE/25: 6X TO 15X BASIC
*FB PINK/20: 8X TO 20X BASIC
1 Reed Sheppard 1.25 3.00
2 Donovan Mitchell .75 2.00
3 Zaccharie Risacher 1.25 3.00
4 Stephon Castle 2.50 6.00
5 Kyrie Irving 1.00 2.50
6 Dalton Knecht 1.25 3.00
7 Luka Doncic 2.50 6.00
8 Shai Gilgeous-Alexander 2.00 5.00
9 Damian Lillard 1.00 2.50
10 Ja Morant 1.25 3.00
11 Jayson Tatum 1.25 3.00
12 Bub Carrington 1.00 2.50
13 Trae Young .75 2.00
14 Kevin Durant 1.25 3.00
15 Jared McCain 1.50 4.00
16 Paolo Banchero 1.00 2.50
17 Anthony Edwards 2.00 5.00
18 LeBron James 3.00 8.00
19 Stephen Curry 3.00 8.00
20 Victor Wembanyama 3.00 8.00

2024-25 Panini Mosaic Collage Autographs Mosaic

*INT: .5X TO 1.2X BASIC
*BRONZE/49: .75X TO 2X BASIC
*BLUE/35: .75X TO 2X BASIC
*WHITE/25: 1X TO 2.5X BASIC
1 Jeremy Sochan 5.00 12.00
2 Anfernee Hardaway 20.00 50.00
3 Franz Wagner 8.00 20.00
4 Steve Francis 5.00 12.00
5 Austin Reaves 6.00 15.00
6 Dalton Knecht 15.00 40.00
7 Rafer Alston 4.00 10.00
8 Kristaps Porzingis 6.00 15.00
9 Keegan Murray 4.00 10.00
10 Mikal Bridges 5.00 12.00
11 Michael Finley 5.00 12.00
12 Devin Vassell 6.00 15.00
13 Al Horford 5.00 12.00
14 Chris Mullin 6.00 15.00
15 Larry Johnson 20.00 50.00
16 Jason Richardson 5.00 12.00
17 Miles Bridges 4.00 10.00

18 Yuta Tabuse 6.00 15.00
19 Jrue Holiday 6.00 15.00
20 Metta World Peace 5.00 12.00
21 Grant Hill 20.00 50.00
22 Spud Webb 5.00 12.00
23 Bennedict Mathurin 6.00 15.00
24 Dereck Lively II 5.00 12.00
25 Ajay Mitchell 8.00 20.00
26 Yongxi "Jacky" Cui 10.00 25.00
27 Pacome Dadiet 6.00 15.00
28 Kyshawn George 8.00 20.00
29 Jaylon Tyson 5.00 12.00
30 Jaylen Wells 15.00 40.00
31 Devin Carter 6.00 15.00
32 Zach Edey 15.00 40.00
33 Yves Missi 12.00 30.00
34 Jared McCain 40.00 100.00
35 Matas Buzelis 40.00 100.00

2024-25 Panini Mosaic Color Blast

1 Dalton Knecht 600.00 1,200.00
2 Zaccharie Risacher 800.00 1,500.00
3 Alexandre Sarr 800.00 1,500.00
4 Kevin Durant 500.00 1,000.00
5 Ja Morant 1,000.00 2,000.00
6 Zach Edey 400.00 800.00
7 Damian Lillard 500.00 1,000.00
8 Anthony Edwards 1,500.00 3,000.00
9 Stephen Curry 2,500.00 5,000.00
10 Trae Young 400.00 800.00
11 Luka Doncic 3,000.00 6,000.00
12 Victor Wembanyama 2,000.00 4,000.00
13 Yuki Kawamura 800.00 1,500.00
14 Matas Buzelis 1,000.00 2,000.00
15 Jalen Brunson 1,000.00 2,000.00
16 Stephon Castle 1,500.00 3,000.00
17 Paolo Banchero 1,000.00 2,000.00
18 Giannis Antetokounmpo 1,000.00 2,000.00
19 Shai Gilgeous-Alexander 1,500.00 3,000.00
20 Nikola Jokic 1,000.00 2,000.00
21 Jared McCain 1,250.00 2,500.00
22 LeBron James 2,500.00 5,000.00
23 Jayson Tatum 1,000.00 2,000.00
24 Reed Sheppard 1,000.00 2,000.00

2024-25 Panini Mosaic Colorgraphs

*BRONZE/49: .75X TO 2X BASIC
*BLUE/35: .75X TO 2X BASIC
*WHITE/25: 1X TO 2.5X BASIC
1 Gilbert Arenas 5.00 12.00
2 Cade Cunningham 40.00 100.00
3 Dominique Wilkins 8.00 20.00
4 Magic Johnson 40.00 100.00
5 Carmelo Anthony 40.00 100.00
6 Manu Ginobili 20.00 50.00
7 Ray Allen 20.00 50.00
8 Anthony Davis 20.00 50.00
9 Jeremy Lin 25.00 60.00
10 Alperen Sengun 8.00 20.00
11 LaMarcus Aldridge 5.00 12.00
12 Nikola Jokic 125.00 300.00
13 Anthony Edwards 125.00 300.00
14 Patrick Ewing 40.00 100.00
15 Trae Young 20.00 50.00
16 Chet Holmgren 20.00 50.00
17 Amen Thompson 40.00 100.00
18 Kyrie Irving 40.00 100.00
19 Ausar Thompson 8.00 20.00
20 Paolo Banchero 40.00 100.00

2024-25 Panini Mosaic Elevate

*MOSAIC: .6X TO 1.5X BASIC
*GREEN: .6X TO 1.5X BASIC
*PURPLE FL/175: 2X TO 5X BASIC
*BLUE SEISMIC/149: 2X TO 5X BASIC
*ICE/125: 2X TO 5X BASIC
*REACTIVE BLUE/99: 2.5X TO 6X BASIC
*REACTIVE YELLOW/99: 2.5X TO 6X BASIC
*RED FL/75: 3X TO 8X BASIC
*ORANGE ICE/49: 4X TO 10X BASIC
*BLUE FL/30: 6X TO 15X BASIC
*WHITE FL/30: 6X TO 15X BASIC
*ORANGE FL/25: 6X TO 15X BASIC
1 Ja Morant 1.25 3.00
2 Zion Williamson 1.00 2.50
3 Anthony Edwards 2.00 5.00
4 Jayson Tatum 1.25 3.00
5 Donovan Mitchell .75 2.00
6 Donovan Clingan 1.00 2.50
7 Alexandre Sarr 1.25 3.00
8 Zaccharie Risacher 1.25 3.00
9 Giannis Antetokounmpo 1.50 4.00
10 Paolo Banchero 1.00 2.50
11 Victor Wembanyama 3.00 8.00
12 Zach Edey 1.25 3.00
13 LeBron James 3.00 8.00
14 Matas Buzelis 2.00 5.00
15 Ron Holland II .75 2.00
16 Luka Doncic 2.50 6.00
17 Anthony Davis 1.00 2.50
18 Dalton Knecht 1.25 3.00
19 Tristan da Silva 1.00 2.50
20 Nikola Jokic 2.00 5.00
21 Kevin Durant 1.25 3.00
22 Karl-Anthony Towns .60 1.50
23 Joel Embiid .60 1.50
24 Stephen Curry 3.00 8.00
25 Shai Gilgeous-Alexander 2.00 5.00

2024-25 Panini Mosaic Epic Performers

*MOSAIC: .6X TO 1.5X BASIC
*GREEN: .6X TO 1.5X BASIC
*PURPLE FL/175: 2X TO 5X BASIC
*BLUE SEISMIC/149: 2X TO 5X BASIC
*ICE/125: 2X TO 5X BASIC
*REACTIVE BLUE/99: 2.5X TO 6X BASIC
*REACTIVE YELLOW/99: 2.5X TO 6X BASIC
*RED FL/75: 3X TO 8X BASIC
*ORANGE ICE/49: 4X TO 10X BASIC
*BLUE FL/30: 6X TO 15X BASIC
*WHITE FL/30: 6X TO 15X BASIC
*ORANGE FL/25: 6X TO 15X BASIC
1 Victor Wembanyama 3.00 8.00
2 LeBron James 3.00 8.00
3 Stephen Curry 3.00 8.00
4 Jayson Tatum 1.25 3.00
5 Ja Morant 1.25 3.00
6 Shai Gilgeous-Alexander 2.00 5.00
7 Giannis Antetokounmpo 1.50 4.00
8 Nikola Jokic 2.00 5.00
9 Anthony Edwards 2.00 5.00
10 Luka Doncic 2.50 6.00
11 Zaccharie Risacher 1.25 3.00
12 Alexandre Sarr 1.25 3.00
13 Jared McCain 1.50 4.00
14 Dalton Knecht 1.25 3.00
15 Stephon Castle 2.50 6.00
16 Shaquille O'Neal 1.00 2.50
17 Derrick Rose 1.00 2.50
18 Dirk Nowitzki 1.00 2.50
19 Tim Duncan 1.00 2.50
20 Yao Ming .75 2.00

2024-25 Panini Mosaic Full Capacity

1 Stephen Curry 125.00 300.00
2 Stephon Castle 100.00 250.00
3 Bam Adebayo 20.00 50.00
4 Nikola Jokic 80.00 200.00
5 LeBron James 125.00 300.00
6 Rob Dillingham 40.00 100.00
7 Dalton Knecht 50.00 125.00
8 Tyrese Haliburton 30.00 80.00
9 De'Aaron Fox 30.00 80.00
10 Giannis Antetokounmpo 60.00 150.00
11 Anthony Edwards 80.00 200.00
12 Reed Sheppard 50.00 125.00
13 Devin Booker 40.00 100.00
14 Victor Wembanyama 125.00 300.00
15 Bub Carrington 40.00 100.00
16 Tidjane Salaun 15.00 40.00
17 Shai Gilgeous-Alexander 80.00 200.00
18 Cody Williams 20.00 50.00
19 Damian Lillard 40.00 100.00
20 Zaccharie Risacher 50.00 125.00
21 Ron Holland II 30.00 80.00
22 Luka Doncic 100.00 250.00
23 Tyrese Maxey 30.00 80.00
24 Jayson Tatum 50.00 125.00
25 Jared McCain 60.00 150.00

2024-25 Panini Mosaic Give and Go

*MOSAIC: .6X TO 1.5X BASIC
*GREEN: .6X TO 1.5X BASIC
*PURPLE FL/175: 2X TO 5X BASIC
*BLUE SEISMIC/149: 2X TO 5X BASIC
*ICE/125: 2X TO 5X BASIC
*REACTIVE BLUE/99: 2.5X TO 6X BASIC
*REACTIVE YELLOW/99: 2.5X TO 6X BASIC
*RED FL/75: 3X TO 8X BASIC
*ORANGE ICE/49: 4X TO 10X BASIC
*BLUE FL/30: 6X TO 15X BASIC
*WHITE FL/30: 6X TO 15X BASIC
*ORANGE FL/25: 6X TO 15X BASIC
1 LeBron James 3.00 8.00
2 Shai Gilgeous-Alexander 2.00 5.00
3 Ja Morant 1.25 3.00
4 Luka Doncic 2.50 6.00
5 Jared McCain 1.50 4.00
6 Stephon Castle 2.50 6.00
7 Reed Sheppard 1.25 3.00
8 Trae Young .75 2.00
9 Stephen Curry 3.00 8.00
10 Tyrese Haliburton .75 2.00
11 Jalen Brunson .75 2.00
12 Tyrese Maxey .75 2.00
13 LaMelo Ball .75 2.00
14 Damian Lillard 1.00 2.50
15 Bub Carrington 1.00 2.50

2024-25 Panini Mosaic Heat Check

1 LeBron James 8.00 20.00
2 Victor Wembanyama 8.00 20.00
3 Stephon Castle 6.00 15.00
4 Zaccharie Risacher 3.00 8.00
5 Stephen Curry 8.00 20.00
6 Shai Gilgeous-Alexander 5.00 12.00
7 Jared McCain 4.00 10.00
8 Dalton Knecht 3.00 8.00
9 Kevin Durant 3.00 8.00
10 Luka Doncic 6.00 15.00
11 Reed Sheppard 3.00 8.00
12 LaMelo Ball 2.00 5.00
13 Jayson Tatum 3.00 8.00
14 Anthony Edwards 5.00 12.00
15 Kyrie Irving 2.50 6.00

2024-25 Panini Mosaic Introductions

*MOSAIC: .6X TO 1.5X BASIC
*FB: 1X TO 2.5X BASIC
*BLUE/199: 2X TO 5X BASIC
*PINK/149: 2X TO 5X BASIC
*FB RED/99: 2.5X TO 6X BASIC
*PURPLE/99: 2.5X TO 6X BASIC
*FB BLUE/85: 2.5X TO 6X BASIC
*BRONZE/75: 3X TO 8X BASIC
*ORANGE/49: 4X TO 10X BASIC
*WHITE/25: 6X TO 15X BASIC
*FB PINK/20: 8X TO 20X BASIC
1 Jared McCain 1.50 4.00
2 Alexandre Sarr 1.25 3.00
3 Ja'Kobe Walter .50 1.25
4 Yuki Kawamura .50 1.25
5 Tristan da Silva 1.00 2.50
6 Cody Williams .50 1.25
7 Matas Buzelis 2.00 5.00
8 Bronny James Jr. 1.25 3.00
9 Zaccharie Risacher 1.25 3.00
10 Kyshawn George .60 1.50
11 Donovan Clingan 1.00 2.50
12 Rob Dillingham 1.00 2.50
13 Ron Holland II .75 2.00
14 Reed Sheppard 1.25 3.00
15 Bub Carrington 1.00 2.50
16 Dalton Knecht 1.25 3.00
17 Zach Edey 1.25 3.00
18 Jaylen Wells 1.25 3.00
19 Tidjane Salaun .40 1.00
20 Stephon Castle 2.50 6.00

2024-25 Panini Mosaic Jam Masters

*MOSAIC: .6X TO 1.5X BASIC
*GREEN: .6X TO 1.5X BASIC
*PURPLE FL/175: 2X TO 5X BASIC
*BLUE SEISMIC/149: 2X TO 5X BASIC
*ICE/125: 2X TO 5X BASIC
*REACTIVE BLUE/99: 2.5X TO 6X BASIC
*REACTIVE YELLOW/99: 2.5X TO 6X BASIC
*RED FL/75: 3X TO 8X BASIC
*ORANGE ICE/49: 4X TO 10X BASIC
*BLUE FL/30: 6X TO 15X BASIC
*WHITE FL/30: 6X TO 15X BASIC
*ORANGE FL/25: 6X TO 15X BASIC
1 Zion Williamson 1.00 2.50
2 Anthony Davis 1.00 2.50
3 Jaylen Wells 1.25 3.00
4 Victor Wembanyama 3.00 8.00
5 Donovan Clingan 1.00 2.50
6 Zach Edey 1.25 3.00
7 Bub Carrington 1.00 2.50
8 Zaccharie Risacher 1.25 3.00
9 Donovan Mitchell .75 2.00
10 Anthony Edwards 2.00 5.00
11 Paolo Banchero 1.00 2.50
12 Ja Morant 1.25 3.00
13 Paul George .60 1.50
14 Giannis Antetokounmpo 1.50 4.00
15 Jayson Tatum 1.25 3.00
16 LeBron James 3.00 8.00
17 Matas Buzelis 2.00 5.00
18 Dereck Lively II .40 1.00
19 Jaylen Brown .60 1.50
20 Alexandre Sarr 1.25 3.00

2024-25 Panini Mosaic Micro Mosaic

1 Ron Holland II 125.00 300.00
2 LeBron James 500.00 1,200.00
3 Jayson Tatum 200.00 500.00
4 Shai Gilgeous-Alexander 300.00 800.00
5 Matas Buzelis 300.00 800.00
6 Paolo Banchero 150.00 400.00
7 Victor Wembanyama 500.00 1,200.00
8 Nikola Jokic 300.00 800.00
9 Reed Sheppard 200.00 500.00
10 Kyrie Irving 150.00 400.00
11 Jared McCain 250.00 600.00
12 Bronny James Jr. 200.00 500.00
13 Luka Doncic 400.00 1,000.00
14 Anthony Edwards 300.00 800.00
15 Giannis Antetokounmpo 250.00 600.00
16 Zion Williamson 150.00 400.00
17 Zaccharie Risacher 200.00 500.00
18 Dalton Knecht 200.00 500.00
19 Donovan Clingan 150.00 400.00
20 Kevin Durant 200.00 500.00
21 Stephon Castle 400.00 1,000.00
22 Ja Morant 200.00 500.00
23 Stephen Curry 500.00 1,200.00
24 Alexandre Sarr 200.00 500.00
25 Trae Young 125.00 300.00

2024-25 Panini Mosaic Montage

*MOSAIC: .6X TO 1.5X BASIC
*FB: 1X TO 2.5X BASIC
*BLUE/199: 2X TO 5X BASIC
*PINK/149: 2X TO 5X BASIC
*FB RED/99: 2.5X TO 6X BASIC
*PURPLE/99: 2.5X TO 6X BASIC
*FB BLUE/85: 2.5X TO 6X BASIC
*BRONZE/75: 3X TO 8X BASIC
*ORANGE/49: 4X TO 10X BASIC
*WHITE/25: 6X TO 15X BASIC
*FB PINK/20: 8X TO 20X BASIC
1 Kevin Durant 1.25 3.00
2 Jalen Brunson .75 2.00
3 Nikola Jokic 2.00 5.00
4 Tidjane Salaun .40 1.00
5 Jared McCain 1.50 4.00
6 Donovan Clingan 1.00 2.50
7 Ja Morant 1.25 3.00
8 Zaccharie Risacher 1.25 3.00
9 Donovan Mitchell .75 2.00
10 Tyrese Haliburton .75 2.00
11 Paolo Banchero 1.00 2.50
12 Anthony Edwards 2.00 5.00
13 Jimmy Butler III .60 1.50
14 Damian Lillard 1.00 2.50
15 Stephen Curry 3.00 8.00
16 Reed Sheppard 1.25 3.00
17 Giannis Antetokounmpo 1.50 4.00
18 Shai Gilgeous-Alexander 2.00 5.00
19 LeBron James 3.00 8.00
20 Jaylen Wells 1.25 3.00
21 Stephon Castle 2.50 6.00
22 Trae Young .75 2.00
23 Ron Holland II .75 2.00
24 Zion Williamson 1.00 2.50
25 Victor Wembanyama 3.00 8.00
26 Luka Doncic 2.50 6.00
27 Dalton Knecht 1.25 3.00
28 LaMelo Ball .75 2.00
29 Jayson Tatum 1.25 3.00
30 Alexandre Sarr 1.25 3.00

2024-25 Panini Mosaic NBA Cup

1 Nikola Jokic 10.00 25.00
2 LeBron James 15.00 40.00
3 Bub Carrington 5.00 12.00
4 Kyrie Irving 5.00 12.00
5 Tyrese Maxey 4.00 10.00
6 Dalton Knecht 6.00 15.00
7 Stephon Castle 12.00 30.00
8 Anthony Edwards 10.00 25.00
9 Jaylen Wells 6.00 15.00
10 Zaccharie Risacher 6.00 15.00
11 Damian Lillard 5.00 12.00
12 Ja Morant 6.00 15.00
13 Jared McCain 8.00 20.00
14 Jalen Brunson 4.00 10.00
15 Donovan Mitchell 4.00 10.00
16 Alexandre Sarr 6.00 15.00
17 Reed Sheppard 6.00 15.00
18 Stephen Curry 15.00 40.00
19 Kevin Durant 6.00 15.00
20 Jalen Green 4.00 10.00
21 Shai Gilgeous-Alexander 10.00 25.00
22 Giannis Antetokounmpo 8.00 20.00
23 Jayson Tatum 6.00 15.00
24 Victor Wembanyama 15.00 40.00
25 Trae Young 4.00 10.00

2024-25 Panini Mosaic Notoriety

*MOSAIC: .6X TO 1.5X BASIC
*FB: 1X TO 2.5X BASIC
*BLUE/199: 2X TO 5X BASIC
*PINK/149: 2X TO 5X BASIC
*FB RED/99: 2.5X TO 6X BASIC
*PURPLE/99: 2.5X TO 6X BASIC
*FB BLUE/85: 2.5X TO 6X BASIC
*BRONZE/75: 3X TO 8X BASIC
*ORANGE/49: 4X TO 10X BASIC
*WHITE/25: 6X TO 15X BASIC
*FB PINK/20: 8X TO 20X BASIC
1 Anthony Edwards 2.00 5.00
2 Stephon Castle 2.50 6.00
3 Victor Wembanyama 3.00 8.00
4 Dalton Knecht 1.25 3.00
5 Luka Doncic 2.50 6.00
6 LeBron James 3.00 8.00
7 Shai Gilgeous-Alexander 2.00 5.00
8 Stephen Curry 3.00 8.00
9 Jared McCain 1.50 4.00
10 Zaccharie Risacher 1.25 3.00

2024-25 Panini Mosaic Overdrive

1 Victor Wembanyama 4.00 10.00
2 Luka Doncic 3.00 8.00
3 James Harden 1.00 2.50
4 Reed Sheppard 1.50 4.00
5 Donovan Clingan 1.25 3.00
6 Jared McCain 2.00 5.00
7 Tyrese Haliburton 1.00 2.50
8 Joel Embiid .75 2.00
9 Shai Gilgeous-Alexander 2.50 6.00
10 Rob Dillingham 1.25 3.00
11 Ron Holland II 1.00 2.50
12 Zaccharie Risacher 1.50 4.00
13 Tidjane Salaun .50 1.25
14 Anthony Edwards 2.50 6.00
15 Stephen Curry 4.00 10.00
16 Matas Buzelis 2.50 6.00
17 Nikola Jokic 2.50 6.00
18 Jayson Tatum 1.50 4.00
19 Anthony Davis 1.25 3.00
20 Bronny James Jr. 1.50 4.00
21 LeBron James 4.00 10.00
22 De'Aaron Fox 1.00 2.50
23 Cody Williams .60 1.50
24 Jaylen Brown .75 2.00
25 Chet Holmgren .75 2.00

2024-25 Panini Mosaic Pictographs Mosaic

1 Joe Johnson 4.00 10.00
2 Zach Randolph 4.00 10.00
3 Naz Reid 5.00 12.00
4 P.J. Washington Jr. 4.00 10.00
5 Kyle Korver 4.00 10.00
6 Joe Dumars 6.00 15.00
7 Jonas Valanciunas 4.00 10.00
8 Baron Davis 4.00 10.00
9 Quentin Grimes 5.00 12.00
10 Jared McCain 40.00 100.00
11 Anfernee Simons 5.00 12.00
12 Peja Stojakovic 5.00 12.00
13 Jonathan Kuminga 6.00 15.00
14 Toni Kukoc 6.00 15.00
15 Bobby Portis 4.00 10.00
16 Jalen Johnson 6.00 15.00
17 Tyler Herro 8.00 20.00
18 Doc Rivers 5.00 12.00
19 Matas Buzelis 40.00 100.00
20 Michael Cooper 5.00 12.00
21 Miles McBride 4.00 10.00
22 Andrew Nembhard 4.00 10.00
23 Paolo Banchero 40.00 100.00
24 Bennedict Mathurin 6.00 15.00
25 Marcus Smart 5.00 12.00
26 Rudy Gobert 5.00 12.00
27 Gheorghe Muresan 3.00 8.00
28 Mike Bibby 5.00 12.00
29 Julius Randle 5.00 12.00
30 Terrence Shannon Jr. 10.00 25.00
31 Jonathan Mogbo 8.00 20.00
32 Jamal Shead 6.00 15.00
33 AJ Johnson 10.00 25.00
34 Ja'Kobe Walter 6.00 15.00
35 Tristan da Silva 12.00 30.00
36 Tidjane Salaun 5.00 12.00
37 Donovan Clingan 12.00 30.00
38 Bub Carrington 12.00 30.00
39 Dalton Knecht 15.00 40.00
40 Reed Sheppard 30.00 80.00

2024-25 Panini Mosaic Razzle Dazzle

1 Giannis Antetokounmpo 25.00 60.00
2 Anthony Edwards 30.00 80.00
3 Victor Wembanyama 50.00 125.00
4 Luka Doncic 40.00 100.00
5 Ja Morant 20.00 50.00
6 Zaccharie Risacher 20.00 50.00
7 Stephen Curry 50.00 125.00
8 Jayson Tatum 20.00 50.00
9 Shai Gilgeous-Alexander 30.00 80.00
10 LeBron James 50.00 125.00
11 Dalton Knecht 20.00 50.00
12 Kevin Durant 20.00 50.00
13 Stephon Castle 40.00 100.00
14 Alexandre Sarr 20.00 50.00
15 Jared McCain 25.00 60.00

2024-25 Panini Mosaic Rookie Autographs Mosaic

*CHOICE: .5X TO 1.2X BASIC
*INT: .5X TO 1.2X BASIC
*BRONZE/75: .6X TO 1.5X BASIC
*BLUE/49: .75X TO 2X BASIC
*WHITE/25: 1X TO 2.5X BASIC
1 Yongxi "Jacky" Cui 10.00 25.00
2 Tristan da Silva 12.00 30.00
3 Dalton Knecht 15.00 40.00
4 Bobi Klintman 6.00 15.00
5 Devin Carter 6.00 15.00
6 Ajay Mitchell 8.00 20.00
7 Jared McCain 40.00 100.00
8 Dillon Jones 5.00 12.00
9 Ja'Kobe Walter 6.00 15.00
10 Oso Ighodaro 6.00 15.00
11 Terrence Shannon Jr. 10.00 25.00
12 Reed Sheppard 30.00 80.00
13 Baylor Scheierman 6.00 15.00
14 Adem Bona 6.00 15.00
15 Donovan Clingan 12.00 30.00
16 KJ Simpson Jr. 5.00 12.00
17 Pelle Larsson 6.00 15.00
18 Jaylon Tyson 5.00 12.00
19 Jamal Shead 6.00 15.00
20 Jonathan Mogbo 8.00 20.00
21 Bub Carrington 12.00 30.00
22 Tyler Kolek 8.00 20.00
23 Cam Christie 6.00 15.00
24 Yves Missi 12.00 30.00
25 Antonio Reeves 5.00 12.00
26 Jaylen Wells 15.00 40.00
27 Johnny Furphy 8.00 20.00
28 Harrison Ingram 5.00 12.00
29 DaRon Holmes II 6.00 15.00
30 Tristen Newton 5.00 12.00
31 Tidjane Salaun 5.00 12.00
32 Enrique Freeman 4.00 10.00
33 AJ Johnson 10.00 25.00
34 Cam Spencer 5.00 12.00
35 Quinten Post 10.00 25.00
36 Kyshawn George 8.00 20.00
37 Anton Watson 4.00 10.00
38 Zach Edey 15.00 40.00
39 Pacome Dadiet 6.00 15.00
40 Matas Buzelis 40.00 100.00

2024-25 Panini Mosaic Rookie Jersey Autographs

*CHOICE: .5X TO 1.2X BASIC
*INT: .5X TO 1.2X BASIC
*BRONZE/75: .6X TO 1.5X BASIC
*BLUE/49: .75X TO 2X BASIC
*WHITE/25: 1X TO 2.5X BASIC
1 Matas Buzelis 75.00 200.00
2 Zach Edey 30.00 80.00
3 Tidjane Salaun 10.00 25.00
4 Devin Carter 12.00 30.00
5 Bub Carrington 25.00 60.00
6 Baylor Scheierman 12.00 30.00
7 Jonathan Mogbo 15.00 40.00
8 Johnny Furphy 15.00 40.00
9 Tyler Kolek 15.00 40.00
10 Jaylen Wells 30.00 80.00
11 Donovan Clingan 25.00 60.00
12 Bobi Klintman 12.00 30.00
13 Oso Ighodaro 12.00 30.00
14 Dillon Jones 10.00 25.00
15 Ajay Mitchell 15.00 40.00
16 Dalton Knecht 30.00 80.00
17 Adem Bona 12.00 30.00
18 Terrence Shannon Jr. 20.00 50.00
19 Reed Sheppard 60.00 150.00
20 Jared McCain 75.00 200.00
21 KJ Simpson Jr. 10.00 25.00
22 Pelle Larsson 12.00 30.00
23 Tristan da Silva 25.00 60.00
24 AJ Johnson 20.00 50.00
25 Jamal Shead 12.00 30.00
26 Yongxi "Jacky" Cui 20.00 50.00
27 Cam Christie 12.00 30.00
28 Ja'Kobe Walter 12.00 30.00
29 Antonio Reeves 10.00 25.00
30 Kyshawn George 15.00 40.00
31 Harrison Ingram 10.00 25.00
32 Jaylon Tyson 10.00 25.00
33 Tristen Newton 10.00 25.00
34 Yves Missi 25.00 60.00
35 Cam Spencer 10.00 25.00
36 Enrique Freeman 8.00 20.00
37 Quinten Post 20.00 50.00
38 Anton Watson 8.00 20.00
39 DaRon Holmes II 12.00 30.00
40 Pacome Dadiet 12.00 30.00

2024-25 Panini Mosaic Rookie Scripts

*GREEN ICE: .5X TO 1.2X BASIC
*ORANGE FL/25: .1X TO 2.5X BASIC
1 Trey Alexander 4.00 10.00
2 Kevin McCullar Jr. 5.00 12.00
3 Ulrich Chomche 4.00 10.00
4 Judah Mintz 4.00 10.00
5 Nikola Durisic 6.00 15.00
6 PJ Hall 4.00 10.00
8 Jonathan Mogbo 8.00 20.00
9 Jalen Bridges 4.00 10.00
11 Trentyn Flowers 4.00 10.00
12 Cam Spencer 5.00 12.00
13 Tristen Newton 5.00 12.00
15 Anton Watson 4.00 10.00
16 Jared McCain 40.00 100.00
17 Harrison Ingram 5.00 12.00
18 Cam Christie 6.00 15.00
20 Tidjane Salaun 5.00 12.00
21 Enrique Freeman 4.00 10.00
22 Donovan Clingan 12.00 30.00
23 Antonio Reeves 5.00 12.00
24 Yongxi "Jacky" Cui 10.00 25.00
26 Tristan da Silva 12.00 30.00
27 Devin Carter 6.00 15.00
28 AJ Johnson 10.00 25.00
29 Reed Sheppard 30.00 80.00
30 Kyshawn George 8.00 20.00
31 Jaylon Tyson 5.00 12.00
32 Matas Buzelis 40.00 100.00
34 Yves Missi 12.00 30.00
35 Dillon Jones 5.00 12.00
36 Bub Carrington 12.00 30.00
39 Baylor Scheierman 6.00 15.00
40 Ja'Kobe Walter 6.00 15.00

2024-25 Panini Mosaic Rookie Season Ticket Signatures

*CHOICE: .5X TO 1.2X BASIC
*INT: .5X TO 1.2X BASIC
*BRONZE/75: .6X TO 1.5X BASIC
*BLUE/49: .75X TO 2X BASIC
*WHITE/25: 1X TO 2.5X BASIC
1 Jaylen Wells 15.00 40.00
2 Harrison Ingram 5.00 12.00
3 Tristen Newton 5.00 12.00
4 Antonio Reeves 5.00 12.00
5 Oso Ighodaro 6.00 15.00
6 Bobi Klintman 6.00 15.00
7 Ajay Mitchell 8.00 20.00
8 Cam Christie 6.00 15.00
9 Johnny Furphy 8.00 20.00
10 Baylor Scheierman 6.00 15.00
11 Dillon Jones 5.00 12.00
12 Tyler Kolek 8.00 20.00
13 Quinten Post 10.00 25.00
14 Dalton Knecht 15.00 40.00
15 Jonathan Mogbo 8.00 20.00
16 Cam Spencer 5.00 12.00
17 Pacome Dadiet 6.00 15.00
18 Terrence Shannon Jr. 10.00 25.00
19 Kyshawn George 8.00 20.00
20 Reed Sheppard 30.00 80.00
21 AJ Johnson 10.00 25.00
22 Anton Watson 4.00 10.00
23 Matas Buzelis 40.00 100.00
24 Ja'Kobe Walter 6.00 15.00
25 Enrique Freeman 4.00 10.00
26 Tristan da Silva 12.00 30.00
27 DaRon Holmes II 6.00 15.00
28 Jared McCain 40.00 100.00
29 Donovan Clingan 12.00 30.00
30 Jamal Shead 6.00 15.00
31 Bub Carrington 12.00 30.00
32 Zach Edey 15.00 40.00
33 Yves Missi 12.00 30.00
34 Devin Carter 6.00 15.00
35 Pelle Larsson 6.00 15.00
36 Adem Bona 6.00 15.00
37 Tidjane Salaun 5.00 12.00
38 Yongxi "Jacky" Cui 10.00 25.00
39 Jaylon Tyson 5.00 12.00
40 KJ Simpson Jr. 5.00 12.00

2024-25 Panini Mosaic Rookie Variation Season Ticket Signatures

*CHOICE: .5X TO 1.2X BASIC
*INT: .5X TO 1.2X BASIC
*BRONZE/75: .6X TO 1.5X BASIC
*BLUE/49: .75X TO 2X BASIC
*WHITE/25: 1X TO 2.5X BASIC
1 Jaylen Wells 15.00 40.00
2 Harrison Ingram 5.00 12.00
3 Tristen Newton 5.00 12.00
4 Antonio Reeves 5.00 12.00
5 Oso Ighodaro 6.00 15.00
6 Bobi Klintman 6.00 15.00
7 Ajay Mitchell 8.00 20.00
8 Cam Christie 6.00 15.00
9 Johnny Furphy 8.00 20.00
10 Baylor Scheierman 6.00 15.00
11 Dillon Jones 5.00 12.00
12 Tyler Kolek 8.00 20.00
13 Quinten Post 10.00 25.00
14 Dalton Knecht 15.00 40.00
15 Jonathan Mogbo 8.00 20.00
16 Cam Spencer 5.00 12.00
17 Pacome Dadiet 6.00 15.00
18 Terrence Shannon Jr. 10.00 25.00
19 Kyshawn George 8.00 20.00
20 Reed Sheppard 30.00 80.00
21 AJ Johnson 10.00 25.00
22 Anton Watson 4.00 10.00
23 Matas Buzelis 40.00 100.00
24 Ja'Kobe Walter 6.00 15.00
25 Enrique Freeman 4.00 10.00
26 Tristan da Silva 12.00 30.00
27 DaRon Holmes II 6.00 15.00
28 Jared McCain 40.00 100.00
29 Donovan Clingan 12.00 30.00
30 Jamal Shead 6.00 15.00
31 Bub Carrington 12.00 30.00
32 Zach Edey 15.00 40.00
33 Yves Missi 12.00 30.00
34 Devin Carter 6.00 15.00
35 Pelle Larsson 6.00 15.00
36 Adem Bona 6.00 15.00
37 Tidjane Salaun 5.00 12.00
38 Yongxi "Jacky" Cui 10.00 25.00
39 Jaylon Tyson 5.00 12.00
40 KJ Simpson Jr. 5.00 12.00

2024-25 Panini Mosaic Scripts

*GREEN ICE: .5X TO 1.2X BASIC
*ORANGE FL/25: .1X TO 2.5X BASIC
1 Luke Travers 3.00 8.00
2 A.J. Green 5.00 12.00
3 Micah Potter 3.00 8.00
4 Gabe Vincent 3.00 8.00
5 Brandon Williams 3.00 8.00
6 Tari Eason 5.00 12.00
8 Landry Shamet 3.00 8.00
9 Maxwell Lewis 4.00 10.00
10 Nate Robinson 4.00 10.00
11 Adam Flagler 5.00 12.00
13 Jaylin Williams 4.00 10.00
14 John Konchar 3.00 8.00
15 Colin Castleton 3.00 8.00
16 Dyson Daniels 6.00 15.00
17 Luke Kennard 4.00 10.00
18 Jordan Walsh 4.00 10.00
19 Jarred Vanderbilt 4.00 10.00
20 Jordan Miller 4.00 10.00
22 Day'Ron Sharpe 4.00 10.00
23 Jevon Carter 3.00 8.00
25 Leonard Miller 5.00 12.00
26 Dale Ellis 4.00 10.00
27 Taj Gibson 3.00 8.00
28 Jaylen Nowell 3.00 8.00
29 Daniel Theis 3.00 8.00
32 TyTy Washington Jr. 3.00 8.00
33 Anthony Gill 3.00 8.00
35 Harold Miner 4.00 10.00
36 Justin Champagnie 5.00 12.00
37 Rod Strickland 4.00 10.00
38 Terry Cummings 5.00 12.00
39 Slick Watts 5.00 12.00
40 Carl Landry 3.00 8.00
42 Peyton Watson 4.00 10.00
43 Leonard "Truck" Robinson 4.00 10.00
44 Isaiah Rider 4.00 10.00
47 Jeff Green 4.00 10.00
48 Ziaire Williams 4.00 10.00
49 Marques Johnson 4.00 10.00
50 Fat Lever 4.00 10.00
51 Danny Schayes 3.00 8.00
52 Hunter Tyson 3.00 8.00
53 Alvan Adams 3.00 8.00
54 Andrea Bargnani 3.00 8.00
55 Tyrese Martin 4.00 10.00
56 Quenton Jackson 3.00 8.00
57 Dru Smith 3.00 8.00
58 Liam Robbins 3.00 8.00
59 Jamal Cain 3.00 8.00
60 Jeff Dowtin Jr. 3.00 8.00
61 Sam Perkins 4.00 10.00
62 B.J. Armstrong 5.00 12.00
63 Kenny "Sky" Walker 3.00 8.00
64 Rik Smits 4.00 10.00
65 Mike Miller 3.00 8.00
66 Eddy Curry 3.00 8.00
67 Detlef Schrempf 4.00 10.00
68 Muggsy Bogues 6.00 15.00
69 Quentin Richardson 4.00 10.00
70 Larry Nance 4.00 10.00
71 Jim Paxson 4.00 10.00
72 Wally Szczerbiak 3.00 8.00
73 Garfield Heard 3.00 8.00
74 Ron Harper 5.00 12.00
75 Mahmoud Abdul-Rauf 4.00 10.00
76 Brian Grant 3.00 8.00
77 Gheorghe Muresan 3.00 8.00
78 Jarrett Jack 3.00 8.00
79 Percy Miller 75.00 200.00
80 Drew Gooden 3.00 8.00
81 Dee Brown 4.00 10.00
82 Dennis Scott 4.00 10.00
83 Maurice Cheeks 4.00 10.00
84 Bob McAdoo 6.00 15.00
85 Mark Aguirre 4.00 10.00
86 Cazzie Russell 5.00 12.00
87 Dick Van Arsdale 5.00 12.00
88 Rolando Blackman 4.00 10.00
89 Theo Ratliff 3.00 8.00
90 James Silas 3.00 8.00
91 Brad Miller 3.00 8.00
92 Purvis Short 3.00 8.00
93 Terry Porter 3.00 8.00
94 Pervis Ellison 3.00 8.00
95 Charlie Ward 4.00 10.00
96 Cuttino Mobley 4.00 10.00
97 Michael Olowokandi 4.00 10.00
98 Dell Curry 5.00 12.00
99 Mitch Kupchak 3.00 8.00
100 Tom Chambers 4.00 10.00
101 Sleepy Floyd 4.00 10.00
102 Brian Winters 3.00 8.00
103 Michael Adams 3.00 8.00
104 Tom Gugliotta 3.00 8.00
105 Kendrick Perkins 3.00 8.00
106 Kendall Gill 4.00 10.00
107 Gerald Henderson Sr. 3.00 8.00
108 Herb Williams 3.00 8.00
109 Gerald Wilkins 3.00 8.00
110 Brian Scalabrine 4.00 10.00
113 Bryce McGowens 4.00 10.00
114 Jordan Goodwin 3.00 8.00
115 Collin Gillespie 4.00 10.00
116 De'Anthony Melton 4.00 10.00
117 Moses Moody 5.00 12.00
119 Dorian Finney-Smith 3.00 8.00
120 Duop Reath 4.00 10.00
124 Jae'Sean Tate 4.00 10.00
127 Brandon Boston Jr. 4.00 10.00
128 Malaki Branham 4.00 10.00
129 Mason Plumlee 3.00 8.00
131 Tre Mann 4.00 10.00
132 Chris Duarte 3.00 8.00
134 Moses Brown 3.00 8.00
135 Santi Aldama 4.00 10.00
136 Xavier Tillman 4.00 10.00
137 Luka Garza 4.00 10.00
138 Gary Trent Jr. 4.00 10.00
139 Royce O'Neale 4.00 10.00
140 Gary Harris 3.00 8.00
141 Kevin Porter Jr. 5.00 12.00
142 James Wiseman 3.00 8.00
144 Paul Reed 3.00 8.00
145 Simone Fontecchio 4.00 10.00
146 Dominick Barlow 4.00 10.00
148 Terance Mann 3.00 8.00
149 Pat Connaughton 3.00 8.00
151 Clint Capela 4.00 10.00
152 Kevin Huerter 4.00 10.00
153 Moritz Wagner 4.00 10.00
154 Marvin Bagley III 3.00 8.00
157 Robin Lopez 3.00 8.00

2024-25 Panini Mosaic Stained Glass

1 De'Aaron Fox 50.00 120.00
2 Reed Sheppard 200.00 500.00
3 Bub Carrington 100.00 250.00
4 Nikola Jokic 150.00 400.00
5 Anthony Edwards 300.00 600.00
6 Zaccharie Risacher 200.00 500.00
7 Stephen Curry 500.00 1,000.00
8 James Harden 75.00 200.00
9 Jared McCain 300.00 600.00
10 Jaylen Brown 100.00 250.00
11 Bronny James Jr. 150.00 400.00
12 Jayson Tatum 150.00 400.00
13 Luka Doncic 500.00 1,000.00
14 Jaylen Wells 100.00 250.00
15 Chet Holmgren 100.00 250.00
16 Dalton Knecht 150.00 400.00
17 Shai Gilgeous-Alexander 300.00 600.00
18 Zach Edey 75.00 200.00
19 LeBron James 500.00 1,000.00
20 Anthony Davis 60.00 150.00
21 Victor Wembanyama 400.00 800.00
22 Donovan Clingan 75.00 200.00
23 Ja Morant 125.00 300.00
24 Donovan Mitchell 75.00 200.00
25 Alexandre Sarr 125.00 300.00

2024-25 Panini Mosaic Stare Masters
*MOSAIC: .6X TO 1.5X BASIC
*FB: 1X TO 2.5X BASIC
*BLUE/199: 2X TO 5X BASIC
*PINK/149: 2X TO 5X BASIC
*FB RED/99: 2.5X TO 6X BASIC
*PURPLE/99: 2.5X TO 6X BASIC
*FB BLUE/85: 2.5X TO 6X BASIC
*BRONZE/75: 3X TO 8X BASIC
*ORANGE/49: 4X TO 10X BASIC
*WHITE/25: 6X TO 15X BASIC
*FB PINK/20: 8X TO 20X BASIC
1 Giannis Antetokounmpo 1.50 4.00
2 Shai Gilgeous-Alexander 2.00 5.00
3 Devin Booker 1.00 2.50
4 Stephen Curry 3.00 8.00
5 Ja Morant 1.25 3.00
6 Nikola Jokic 2.00 5.00
7 Luka Doncic 2.50 6.00
8 Zach Edey 1.25 3.00
9 Jared McCain 1.50 4.00
10 Anthony Edwards 2.00 5.00
11 De'Aaron Fox .75 2.00
12 Tyrese Maxey .75 2.00
13 Jayson Tatum 1.25 3.00
14 Alexandre Sarr 1.25 3.00
15 Victor Wembanyama 3.00 8.00
16 Matas Buzelis 2.00 5.00
17 Jalen Brunson .75 2.00
18 LeBron James 3.00 8.00
19 James Harden .75 2.00
20 Zaccharie Risacher 1.25 3.00

2024-25 Panini Mosaic Storm Chasers
1 Paolo Banchero 5.00 12.00
2 Trae Young 4.00 10.00
3 Tyrese Haliburton 4.00 10.00
4 Zion Williamson 5.00 12.00
5 Giannis Antetokounmpo 8.00 20.00
6 Ron Holland II 4.00 10.00
7 Luka Doncic 12.00 30.00
8 Stephen Curry 15.00 40.00
9 Jayson Tatum 6.00 15.00
10 Donovan Clingan 5.00 12.00
11 Dalton Knecht 6.00 15.00
12 Zach Edey 6.00 15.00
13 Victor Wembanyama 15.00 40.00
14 Donovan Mitchell 4.00 10.00
15 Alexandre Sarr 6.00 15.00
16 Shai Gilgeous-Alexander 10.00 25.00
17 Devin Booker 5.00 12.00
18 Zaccharie Risacher 6.00 15.00
19 Jalen Brunson 4.00 10.00
20 LeBron James 15.00 40.00

2024-25 Panini Mosaic Thunder Road
*MOSAIC: .6X TO 1.5X BASIC
*GREEN: .6X TO 1.5X BASIC
*PURPLE FL/175: 2X TO 5X BASIC
*BLUE SEISMIC/149: 2X TO 5X BASIC
*ICE/125: 2X TO 5X BASIC
*REACTIVE BLUE/99: 2.5X TO 6X BASIC
*REACTIVE YELLOW/99: 2.5X TO 6X BASIC
*RED FL/75: 3X TO 8X BASIC
*ORANGE ICE/49: 4X TO 10X BASIC
*BLUE FL/30: 6X TO 15X BASIC
*WHITE FL/30: 6X TO 15X BASIC
*ORANGE FL/25: 6X TO 15X BASIC
1 Luka Doncic 2.50 6.00
2 Kevin Durant 1.25 3.00
3 LeBron James 3.00 8.00
4 Anthony Edwards 2.00 5.00
5 Stephen Curry 3.00 8.00
6 Jayson Tatum 1.25 3.00
7 Shai Gilgeous-Alexander 2.00 5.00
8 Victor Wembanyama 3.00 8.00
9 Giannis Antetokounmpo 1.50 4.00
10 Ja Morant 1.25 3.00
11 Jalen Brunson .75 2.00
12 Tyrese Maxey .75 2.00
13 Nikola Jokic 2.00 5.00
14 Donovan Mitchell .75 2.00
15 Paolo Banchero 1.00 2.50
16 Reed Sheppard 1.25 3.00
17 Jared McCain 1.50 4.00
18 Dalton Knecht 1.25 3.00
19 Alexandre Sarr 1.25 3.00
20 Zaccharie Risacher 1.25 3.00

2024-25 Panini Mosaic Veteran Ticket Signatures
*CHOICE: .5X TO 1.2X BASIC
*INT: .5X TO 1.2X BASIC
*BRONZE/49: .75X TO 2X BASIC
*BLUE/35: .75X TO 2X BASIC
*WHITE/25: 1X TO 2.5X BASIC
1 Charles Barkley 60.00 150.00
2 Giannis Antetokounmpo 125.00 300.00
3 Kareem Abdul-Jabbar 60.00 150.00
4 Kevin Garnett 40.00 100.00
6 Dwyane Wade 40.00 100.00
7 Damian Lillard 40.00 100.00
8 Yao Ming 75.00 200.00
9 Tracy McGrady 60.00 150.00
10 Paolo Banchero 60.00 150.00
11 Chris Bosh 20.00 50.00
12 Zion Williamson 40.00 100.00
13 Trae Young 40.00 100.00
14 Cade Cunningham 40.00 100.00
15 Stephen Curry 400.00 800.00
16 Luka Doncic 800.00 1,500.00
17 Shai Gilgeous-Alexander 200.00 500.00
18 Ja Morant 75.00 200.00
19 Allen Iverson 60.00 150.00
20 Larry Bird 60.00 150.00

2009 Panini National Convention
*BLUE: .6X TO 1.5X BASE HI
*GOLD: .75X TO 2X BASE HI
*RED: .6X TO 1.5X BASE HI
BG Blake Griffin 10.00 25.00
BW Bill Walton OS .60 1.50
DR Derrick Rose 10.00 25.00
HT Hasheem Thabeet 2.00 5.00
KM Kevin McHale OS .60 1.50
LB Larry Bird OS 2.00 5.00
TH Tyler Hansbrough 3.00 8.00

2009 Panini National Convention Autographs
BG Blake Griffin Fabric 125.00 300.00
HT Hasheem Thabeet Fabric 8.00 20.00
OM O.J. Mayo Fabric 10.00 25.00
TH Tyler Hansbrough Fabric 30.00 80.00
BG09 Blake Griffin 40.00 100.00
BG0925 Blake Griffin/25 60.00 150.00
BG0950 Blake Griffin/50 40.00 100.00
TH09 Tyler Hansbrough 20.00 50.00
TH0925 Tyler Hansbrough/25 30.00 80.00
TH0950 Tyler Hansbrough/50 25.00 60.00
NNO Blake Griffin Trade 4.00 10.00
NNO Tyler Hansbrough Trade 2.00 5.00

2011 Panini National Convention VIP
COMPLETE SET (6) 6.00 15.00
*RED: 1.25X TO 3X BASE HI
RED PRINT RUN 25 SER.#'d SETS
VIP 5 AND 6 DO NOT HAVE PARALLELS
VIP1 Kobe Bryant 2.50 6.00
VIP2 Blake Griffin 1.50 4.00
VIP3 John Wall 2.00 5.00
VIP4 Kevin Durant 2.00 5.00
VIP5 Kyrie Irving 4.00 10.00
VIP6 Derrick Williams 1.50 4.00

2012-13 Panini National Treasures
1-100 PRINT RUN 99 SER.#'d SETS
101-200 PRINT RUNS B/WN 25-199 PER
PRIME PATCHES MAY SELL FOR PREMIUM
EXCHANGE DEADLINE 01/31/2015
1 Kobe Bryant 150.00 400.00
2 Marc Gasol 3.00 8.00
3 Tony Parker 5.00 12.00
4 Joe Johnson 2.50 6.00
5 Josh Smith 2.00 5.00
6 Kevin Garnett 8.00 20.00
7 LaMarcus Aldridge 3.00 8.00
8 Ray Allen 5.00 12.00
9 Rajon Rondo 4.00 10.00
10 Raymond Felton 2.00 5.00
11 Luol Deng 2.50 6.00
12 Ben Gordon 2.50 6.00
13 Joakim Noah 2.50 6.00
14 LeBron James 200.00 500.00
15 Anderson Varejao 2.00 5.00
16 Jason Kidd 5.00 12.00
17 Dirk Nowitzki 8.00 20.00
18 Jason Terry 2.50 6.00
19 Carmelo Anthony 5.00 12.00
20 Nene 2.50 6.00
21 Tim Duncan 8.00 20.00
22 Monta Ellis 2.50 6.00
23 Goran Dragic 3.00 8.00
24 Kyle Lowry 3.00 8.00
25 Jameer Nelson 2.00 5.00
26 Nikola Pekovic 2.00 5.00
27 Roy Hibbert 2.50 6.00
28 Jarrett Jack 2.50 6.00
29 Chris Kaman 2.50 6.00
30 Greivis Vasquez 2.00 5.00
31 Pau Gasol 5.00 12.00
32 Mike Conley 2.50 6.00
33 Rudy Gay 3.00 8.00
34 Paul Pierce 5.00 12.00
35 Kevin Durant 20.00 50.00
36 Andrew Bogut 2.50 6.00
37 Ramon Sessions 2.00 5.00
38 Al Jefferson 2.00 5.00
39 Kevin Love 3.00 8.00
40 Ryan Anderson 2.00 5.00
41 Brook Lopez 2.50 6.00
42 Tyson Chandler 2.50 6.00
43 Chris Paul 6.00 15.00
44 Danilo Gallinari 2.00 5.00
45 J.R. Smith 3.00 8.00
46 David Lee 2.50 6.00
47 Dwyane Wade 6.00 15.00
48 Russell Westbrook 5.00 12.00
49 Marcin Gortat 2.00 5.00
50 Dwight Howard 4.00 10.00
51 Andre Iguodala 3.00 8.00
52 Louis Williams 2.50 6.00
53 Grant Hill 5.00 12.00
54 Steve Nash 6.00 15.00
55 Jason Richardson 3.00 8.00
56 Amar'e Stoudemire 3.00 8.00
57 Mario Chalmers 2.50 6.00
58 Nicolas Batum 2.50 6.00
59 Zach Randolph 3.00 8.00
60 Kevin Martin 2.50 6.00
61 Rodney Stuckey 2.00 5.00
62 Manu Ginobili 6.00 15.00
63 Derrick Rose 5.00 12.00
64 Andrea Bargnani 2.00 5.00
65 Chris Bosh 4.00 10.00
66 Jose Calderon 2.00 5.00
67 Kris Humphries 2.00 5.00
68 Shawn Marion 3.00 8.00
69 Carlos Boozer 2.50 6.00
70 Paul Millsap 2.50 6.00
71 Deron Williams 2.50 6.00
72 Caron Butler 2.50 6.00
73 Antawn Jamison 2.50 6.00
74 JaVale McGee 2.50 6.00
75 Nick Young 2.00 5.00
76 Blake Griffin 3.00 8.00
77 Ricky Rubio 2.50 6.00
78 Jrue Holiday 4.00 10.00
79 Ty Lawson 2.00 5.00
80 Jeff Teague 2.00 5.00
81 Darren Collison 2.00 5.00
82 James Harden 6.00 15.00
83 Tyreke Evans 2.50 6.00
84 Jeremy Lin 5.00 12.00
85 Stephen Curry 25.00 60.00
86 DeMar DeRozan 4.00 10.00
87 Brandon Jennings 2.00 5.00
88 Gerald Henderson 2.00 5.00
89 Serge Ibaka 2.50 6.00
90 Wesley Matthews 2.00 5.00
91 John Wall 4.00 10.00
92 Evan Turner 2.00 5.00
93 DeMarcus Cousins 3.00 8.00
94 Greg Monroe 2.00 5.00
95 Gordon Hayward 3.00 8.00
96 Paul George 5.00 12.00
97 Jordan Crawford 2.00 5.00
98 Marcus Thornton 2.00 5.00
99 Danny Granger 2.00 5.00
100 Damian Lillard RC 300.00 600.00
101 K.Irving JSY AU/199 RC 1,500.00 3,000.00
102 D.Will JSY AU/199 RC 15.00 40.00
103 Enes Kanter JSY AU/99 RC 50.00 120.00
104 T.Thompson JSY AU/199 RC 30.00 80.00
105 Jan Vesely JSY AU/99 RC 6.00 15.00
106 B.Biyombo JSY AU/199 RC 25.00 60.00
107 B.Knight JSY AU/199 RC 25.00 60.00
108 K.Walker JSY AU/199 RC 500.00 1,000.00
109 J.Fredette JSY AU/199 RC 20.00 50.00
110 Thomp JSY AU/199 RC 3,000.00 6,000.00
111 Alec Burks JSY AU/199 RC 30.00 80.00
112 Mkieff Morris JSY AU/199 RC 30.00 80.00
113 Mrcus Morris JSY AU/99 RC 30.00 80.00
114 K.Leonard JSY AU/199 RC 3,000.00 6,000.00
115 N.Vucevic JSY AU/99 RC 200.00 500.00
116 I.Shumpert JSY AU/199 RC 8.00 20.00
117 Chris Singleton JSY AU/99 RC 6.00 15.00
118 T.Harris JSY AU/199 RC 75.00 200.00
119 Nolan Smith JSY AU/99 RC 6.00 15.00
120 K.Faried JSY AU/199 RC 30.00 80.00
121 R.Jackson JSY AU/99 RC 30.00 80.00
122 MarShon Brooks JSY AU/199 RC 6.00 15.00
123 Jordan Hamilton JSY AU/99 RC 6.00 15.00
124 Lavoy Allen JSY AU/99 RC 6.00 15.00
125 N.Cole JSY AU/199 RC 15.00 40.00
126 Cory Joseph JSY AU/99 RC 30.00 80.00
127 J.Butler JSY AU/199 RC 1,500.00 4,000.00
128 Ivan Johnson JSY AU/99 RC EXCH 6.00 15.00
129 C.Parsons JSY AU/99 RC 30.00 80.00
130 J.Valanci JSY AU/99 RC 40.00 100.00
131 Gustavo Ayon JSY AU/99 RC 8.00 20.00
132 I.Thomas JSY AU/99 RC 100.00 250.00
133 Chris Copeland JSY AU/99 RC 6.00 15.00
134 Charles Jenkins AU/99 RC 4.00 10.00
135 DeQuan Jones AU/99 RC 4.00 10.00
136 D.Motiejunas AU/99 RC EXCH 5.00 12.00
137 Julyan Stone AU/99 RC 4.00 10.00
138 Malcolm Lee AU/99 RC EXCH 4.00 10.00
139 Jon Leuer AU/99 RC 4.00 10.00
140 E'Twaun Moore AU/99 RC 5.00 12.00
141 Darius Morris AU/99 RC 4.00 10.00
142 Viacheslav Kravtsov AU/99 RC 4.00 10.00
143 Victor Claver AU/99 RC 4.00 10.00
144 Kyle O'Quinn AU/99 RC 5.00 12.00
145 Maurice Harkless AU/99 RC 5.00 12.00
146 Brian Roberts AU/99 RC 4.00 10.00
147 M.Teletovic AU/99 RC EXCH 12.00 30.00
148 Greg Stiemsma AU/99 RC 4.00 10.00
149 DeAndre Liggins AU/99 RC 4.00 10.00
150 Kent Bazemore AU/99 RC 15.00 40.00
151 A.Davis JSY AU/199 RC 3,000.00 6,000.00
152 Kidd-Gilch JSY AU/199 RC 30.00 80.00
153 B.Beal JSY AU/199 RC 400.00 800.00
154 D.Waiters JSY AU/199 RC 60.00 150.00
155 T.Robinson JSY AU/199 RC 6.00 15.00
156 D.Green JSY AU/99 RC 1,500.00 3,000.00
157 H.Barnes JSY AU/199 RC 40.00 100.00
158 T.Ross JSY AU/99 RC 50.00 120.00
159 Drmmnd JSY AU/199 RC 125.00 300.00
160 Austin Rivers JSY AU/199 RC 30.00 80.00
161 M.Leonard JSY AU/99 RC 15.00 40.00
162 Jeremy Lamb JSY AU/99 RC 10.00 25.00
163 K.Marshall JSY AU/99 RC 6.00 15.00
164 J.Henson JSY AU/199 RC 20.00 50.00
165 Kyle Singler JSY AU/99 RC 6.00 15.00
166 Jae Crowder JSY AU/99 RC 40.00 100.00
167 Tyler Zeller JSY AU/99 RC 10.00 25.00
168 T.Jones JSY AU/99 RC 25.00 60.00
169 A.Nicholson JSY AU/99 RC 6.00 15.00
170 E.Fmr JSY AU/99 RC 60.00 150.00
171 J.Sullinger JSY AU/199 RC 20.00 50.00
172 Fab Melo JSY AU/99 RC 6.00 15.00
173 J.Jenkins JSY AU/99 RC 6.00 15.00
174 Jared Cunningham JSY AU/99 RC 6.00 15.00
175 Tony Wroten JSY AU/99 RC 6.00 15.00
176 M.Plumlee JSY AU/99 RC 12.00 30.00
177 Arnett Moultrie AU/99 RC 6.00 15.00
178 Perry Jones JSY AU/99 RC 6.00 15.00
179 M.Teague JSY AU/99 RC 6.00 15.00
180 Festus Ezeli JSY AU/99 RC 25.00 60.00
181 A.Shved JSY AU/25 RC 40.00 100.00
182 Quincy Acy JSY AU/99 RC 6.00 15.00
183 Doron Lamb JSY AU/99 RC 6.00 15.00
184 Jeff Taylor AU/99 RC 4.00 10.00
185 Royce White AU/99 RC EXCH 4.00 10.00
186 Draymond Green AU/99 RC 150.00 300.00
187 Orlando Johnson AU/99 RC 4.00 10.00
188 Quincy Miller AU/99 RC 4.00 10.00
189 Khris Middleton AU/99 RC 150.00 400.00
190 Will Barton AU/99 RC 8.00 20.00
191 Tyshawn Taylor AU/99 RC 4.00 10.00
192 Mike Scott AU/99 RC 15.00 40.00
193 Kim English AU/99 RC 4.00 10.00
194 Darius Miller AU/99 RC 5.00 12.00
195 Kevin Murphy AU/99 RC 4.00 10.00
196 Nando De Colo AU/99 RC 4.00 10.00
197 Tornike Shengelia AU/99 RC 4.00 10.00
198 Bernard James AU/99 RC 4.00 10.00
199 Robert Sacre AU/99 RC 4.00 10.00
200 Lance Thomas AU/99 RC 4.00 10.00
201 D. Lillard JSY AU/99 3,000.00 6,000.00

2012-13 Panini National Treasures Silver
*SILVER: .75X TO 2X BASIC
STATED PRINT RUN 25 SER.#'d SETS

2012-13 Panini National Treasures 11 vs. 12 Signatures
PRINT RUNS B/WN 49-99 COPIES PER
EXCHANGE DEADLINE 01/31/2015
1 K.Irving/A.Davis/49 150.00 300.00
2 Williams/Kidd-Gilchrist/49 6.00 15.00
3 B.Beal/I.Shumpert/49 10.00 25.00
4 Thompson/Waiters/99 8.00 20.00
5 Robinson/Faried/49 6.00 15.00
6 M.Leonard/J.Vesely/99 5.00 12.00
7 B.Biyombo/H.Barnes/49 8.00 20.00
8 B.Knight/T.Ross/99 6.00 15.00
9 Walker/Drummond/49 20.00 50.00
10 J.Fredette/A.Rivers/99 8.00 20.00
11 Thompson/Leonard/99 75.00 200.00
12 A.Burks/C.Copeland/99 5.00 12.00
13 M.Morris/K.Marshall/99 6.00 15.00
14 M.Morris/J.Henson/99 5.00 12.00
15 K.Irving/A.Rivers/49 30.00 80.00
16 E.Kanter/A.Davis/49 40.00 100.00
17 C.Parsons/B.Beal/49 40.00 100.00
18 M.Morris/T.Robinson/49 8.00 20.00
19 B.Knight/A.Davis/49 40.00 100.00
20 K.Walker/J.Lamb/99 10.00 25.00
21 N.Smith/A.Rivers/99 8.00 20.00
22 Kanter/Kidd-Gilchrist/49 5.00 12.00
23 T.Robinson/C.Parsons/49 5.00 12.00
24 Thompson/Barnes/99 12.00 30.00
25 Leonard/Harkless/99 20.00 50.00
26 K.Faried/T.Zeller/49 6.00 15.00
27 T.Harris/J.Sullinger/99 6.00 15.00
28 M.Teague/N.Cole/99 6.00 15.00
29 M.Brooks/J.Jenkins/99 6.00 15.00
30 Q.Acy/N.Vucevic/99 20.00 50.00
31 K.Faried/J.Crowder/49 10.00 25.00
32 C.Parsons/H.Barnes/99 10.00 25.00
33 C.Singleton/B.James/99 6.00 15.00
34 C.Parsons/A.Davis/49 25.00 60.00
35 N.Smith/T.Zeller/99 6.00 15.00
36 D.Green/K.Walker/99 30.00 80.00
37 I.Thomas/T.Ross/99 12.00 30.00
38 M.Morris/R.White/99 5.00 12.00
39 Robinson/Valanciunas/49 10.00 25.00
40 Bazemore/Fredette/49 6.00 15.00
41 E.Kanter/T.Jones/49 8.00 20.00
42 Sullinger/Thompson/49 8.00 20.00
43 A.Shved/E.Moore/49 5.00 12.00
44 Thompson/Ross/49 75.00 200.00
45 D.Williams/A.Shved/49 5.00 12.00
46 A.Burks/T.Ross/99 5.00 12.00
47 N.Smith/M.Plumlee/99 5.00 12.00
48 F.Melo/N.Vucevic/99 6.00 15.00
49 Jackson/Teague/99 6.00 15.00
50 M.Leonard/E.Kanter/99 5.00 12.00
51 B.Knight/D.Lamb/49 6.00 15.00
52 Biyombo/Drummond/49 12.00 30.00
53 Hamilton/Harkless/99 5.00 12.00
54 M.Morris/A.Nicholson/99 5.00 12.00
55 M.Teague/K.Walker/49 10.00 25.00
56 M.Brooks/B.Beal/49 10.00 25.00
57 K.Irving/B.Beal/49 40.00 100.00
58 Knight/Kidd-Gilchrist/49 6.00 15.00
59 Leonard/Sullinger/49 20.00 50.00
60 K.Faried/A.Moultrie/49 8.00 20.00
61 Shumpert/Marshall/49 8.00 20.00
62 Fredette/Robinson/49 8.00 20.00
63 Davis/Thompson/49 40.00 100.00
64 T.Harris/A.Shved/49 15.00 40.00
65 K.Irving/D.Waiters/49 30.00 80.00
66 Drummond/Valanciunas/49 6.00 15.00
67 R.Jackson/K.Marshall/99 5.00 12.00
68 N.Smith/C.Copeland/99 5.00 12.00
69 K.English/B.Knight/49 6.00 15.00
70 L.Allen/Q.Acy/99 5.00 12.00
71 D.Green/J.Fredette/99 10.00 25.00
72 A.Burks/E.Fournier/99 6.00 15.00
73 F.Ezeli/J.Valanciunas/99 5.00 12.00
74 C.Singleton/T.Jones/99 5.00 12.00
75 J.Vesely/J.Henson/99 5.00 12.00
76 M.Brooks/J.Cunningham/99 5.00 12.00
77 B.James/K.Singler/99 6.00 15.00
78 Williams/Robinson/49 5.00 12.00
79 Kidd-Gilchrist/Thompson/49 8.00 20.00
80 Fredette/Fournier/99 6.00 15.00
81 J.Vesely/H.Barnes/49 10.00 25.00
82 Thompson/Bazemore/49 75.00 200.00
83 M.Plumlee/L.Allen/99 5.00 12.00
84 Barton/Jackson/99 10.00 25.00
85 K.Leonard/J.Taylor/49 8.00 20.00
86 I.Thomas/D.Lamb/99 10.00 25.00
87 T.Harris/F.Ezeli/49 6.00 15.00
88 G.Ayon/A.Nicholson/99 5.00 12.00
89 B.Beal/B.Knight/49 10.00 25.00
90 K.Marshall/A.Burks/99 5.00 12.00
91 N.Smith/J.Cunningham/99 5.00 12.00
92 I.Johnson/R.White/99 5.00 12.00
93 T.Shengelia/J.Valanciunas/99 5.00 12.00
94 E.Moore/K.English/99 5.00 12.00
95 J.Hamilton/J.Cunningham/99 5.00 12.00
96 Thompson/Waiters/49 75.00 200.00
97 F.Melo/B.Biyombo/99 5.00 12.00
98 M.Scott/T.Harris/99 6.00 15.00
99 Johnson/Shumpert/49 6.00 15.00
100 K.Faried/D.Green/49 12.00 30.00

2012-13 Panini National Treasures 11 vs. 12 Signatures Gold
*GOLD: .5X TO 1.2X BASE/99
*GOLD: .4X TO 1X BASE/49
STATED PRINT RUN 25 SER.#'d SETS
EXCHANGE DEADLINE 01/31/2015
1 K.Irving/A.Davis 200.00 500.00

2012-13 Panini National Treasures 11 vs. 12 Signatures Silver
*SILVER 49: .5X TO 1.2X BASIC/99
*SILVER 49: .4X TO 1X BASIC/49
*SILVER 25: .6X TO 1.5X BASIC/99
*SILVER 25: .5X TO 1.2X BASIC/49
PRINT RUNS B/WN 25-49 COPIES PER
EXCHANGE DEADLINE 01/31/2015

2012-13 Panini National Treasures ABA Legends Signatures
PRINT RUNS B/WN 25-99 COPIES PER
EXCHANGE DEADLINE 1/31/2015
1 Julius Erving/25 75.00 150.00
2 Louie Dampier/99 EXCH 30.00 60.00
3 Dan Issel/99 6.00 15.00
4 Mel Daniels/75 15.00 40.00
5 George Gervin/75 15.00 40.00
6 Ron Boone/75 EXCH 12.00 30.00
7 Freddie Lewis/75 EXCH 6.00 15.00
8 Rick Barry/75 10.00 25.00
9 George Karl/75 6.00 15.00
10 Jimmy Jones/75 6.00 15.00

2012-13 Panini National Treasures Champions Signatures
ODDS B/WN 25-49 COPIES PER
EXCHANGE DEADLINE 01/31/2015
1 Walt Frazier/49 8.00 20.00
2 Magic Johnson/49 EXCH 75.00 150.00
3 Larry Bird/49 60.00 120.00
4 Julius Erving/25 100.00 200.00
5 Clyde Drexler/25 40.00 80.00
6 John Havlicek/25 40.00 80.00
7 Shaquille O'Neal/25 250.00 400.00
8 Chris Bosh/49 12.00 30.00
9 Mark Aguirre/49 8.00 20.00
10 Rick Barry/49 8.00 20.00
11 Toni Kukoc/49 12.00 30.00
12 Bill Walton/49 60.00 150.00
13 Bob McAdoo/49 12.00 30.00
14 Gail Goodrich/49 5.00 12.00
15 Peja Stojakovic/25 EXCH 30.00 60.00
16 Kobe Bryant/49 2,000.00 4,000.00
17 Willis Reed/49 40.00 100.00
18 Paul Westphal/49 EXCH 10.00 25.00
19 Hakeem Olajuwon/49 20.00 50.00
20 Nate Archibald/49 8.00 20.00
21 Bill Russell/25 500.00 1,000.00
22 Kenny Smith/49 8.00 20.00
23 Glen Rice/49 12.00 30.00
24 Jason Kidd/25 60.00 120.00
25 Jerry West/49 75.00 150.00

2012-13 Panini National Treasures Champions Signatures Combos
ODDS B/WN 15-25 COPIES PER
NO PRICING ON QTY 15
EXCHANGE DEADLINE 01/31/2015
1 J.Kidd/D.Nowitzki/25 125.00 300.00
3 J.Erving/M.Cheeks/25 40.00 100.00
4 S.Pippen/P.Jackson/25 500.00 1,000.00
5 I.Thomas/J.Dumars/25 40.00 100.00
6 T.Parker/D.Robinson/25 50.00 120.00
7 J.Erving/M.Johnson/25 75.00 200.00
8 B.Laimbeer/D.Rodman/25 20.00 50.00
9 B.Pettit/T.Heinsohn/25 20.00 50.00
10 G.Payton/A.Mourning/25 50.00 120.00
11 M.Cooper/B.Scott/25 20.00 50.00
12 D.Nowitzki/L.Bird/25 200.00 500.00
13 Robert Horry/Mario Elie 15.00 40.00
14 Andrew Bynum/Metta World Peace 15.00 40.00
15 R.Hamilton/C.Billups/25 20.00 50.00
16 Cedric Maxwell/Wes Unseld 15.00 40.00
17 P.Westphal/D.Cowens/25 20.00 50.00
18 Robert Parish/Nate Archibald 15.00 40.00
19 B.Armstrong/B.Cartwright/25 30.00 80.00

2012-13 Panini National Treasures Colossal Materials
PRINT RUNS B/WN 25-99 COPIES PER
1 Carmelo Anthony/99 8.00 20.00
2 Carlos Boozer/99 4.00 10.00
3 Rajon Rondo/49 6.00 15.00
4 Serge Ibaka/99 4.00 10.00
5 LeBron James/99 50.00 120.00
6 Ty Lawson/99 3.00 8.00
7 Tony Parker/99 8.00 20.00
8 Dwyane Wade/49 10.00 25.00
9 Kevin Johnson/49 5.00 12.00
10 DeMarcus Cousins/99 5.00 12.00
11 Russell Westbrook/99 6.00 15.00
12 Joakim Noah/49 4.00 10.00
13 Kevin Garnett/49 6.00 15.00
14 Moses Malone/49 8.00 20.00
15 Ricky Rubio/25 4.00 10.00
16 Deron Williams/99 4.00 10.00
17 Michael Cooper/49 5.00 12.00
18 Larry Johnson/49 6.00 15.00
19 John Starks/99 4.00 10.00
20 Chris Webber/49 12.00 30.00

2012-13 Panini National Treasures Colossal Materials Jersey Number Signatures
PRINT RUNS B/WN 10-49 COPIES PER
NO PRICING ON QTY 10
EXCHANGE DEADLINE 1/31/2015
1 Kevin Durant/25 125.00 300.00
2 Kobe Bryant/25 2,000.00 4,000.00
3 Blake Griffin/25 30.00 80.00
4 Vince Carter/25 40.00 100.00
5 D.J. Augustin/49 5.00 12.00
6 Kevin Love/49 20.00 50.00
7 Andre Iguodala/49 12.00 30.00
8 Larry Bird/25 75.00 200.00
9 Kevin Martin/49 8.00 20.00
10 Stephen Curry/49 500.00 1,000.00
11 Jordan Crawford/49 8.00 20.00
12 LaMarcus Aldridge/25 10.00 25.00
13 Tyreke Evans/25 8.00 20.00
14 James Harden/25 60.00 150.00
15 Hakeem Olajuwon/25 30.00 80.00
16 Grant Hill/25 40.00 100.00
18 Al Jefferson/25 10.00 25.00
19 Dikembe Mutombo/25 20.00 50.00
20 Zach Randolph/25 10.00 25.00

2012-13 Panini National Treasures Colossal Materials Jersey Number Signatures Prime
*PRIME: .6X TO 1.5X BASIC
PRINT RUNS B/WN 5-25 COPIES PER
NO PRICING ON QTY 15 OR LESS
EXCHANGE DEADLINE 1/31/2015

2012-13 Panini National Treasures Colossal Materials Jersey Numbers
PRINT RUNS B/WN 49-99 COPIES PER
1 Paul Pierce/49 8.00 20.00
2 Dirk Nowitzki/49 12.00 30.00
3 Rudy Gay/99 5.00 12.00
4 Dennis Rodman/49 15.00 40.00
5 Kobe Bryant/49 125.00 300.00
6 Marcus Thornton/99 3.00 8.00
7 Bill Cartwright/49 4.00 10.00
8 Patrick Ewing/99 8.00 20.00
9 Thaddeus Young/99 3.00 8.00
10 David Lee/99 3.00 8.00
11 Greg Monroe/99 3.00 8.00
12 Karl Malone/49 8.00 20.00
13 Tim Duncan/99 12.00 30.00
14 Jason Terry/99 4.00 10.00
15 Jordan Crawford/49 3.00 8.00
16 Pau Gasol/99 8.00 20.00
17 Artis Gilmore/49 6.00 15.00
18 Steve Nash/99 10.00 25.00
19 Nicolas Batum/49 4.00 10.00
20 Manu Ginobili/99 10.00 25.00

2012-13 Panini National Treasures Colossal Materials Jersey Numbers Prime
*PRIME: .5X TO 1.2X BASIC
PRINT RUNS B/WN 10-25 COPIES PER
NO PRICING ON QTY 15 OR LESS
5 Kobe Bryant/25 150.00 400.00
8 Patrick Ewing/25 20.00 50.00
18 Steve Nash/25 30.00 60.00
20 Manu Ginobili/25 12.00 30.00

2012-13 Panini National Treasures Colossal Materials Prime
*PRIME 25: 1.2X TO 3X BASIC
PRINT RUNS B/WN 10-25 COPIES PER
NO RUBIO PRICING AVAILABLE
5 LeBron James 150.00 400.00
9 Kevin Johnson 40.00 80.00

2012-13 Panini National Treasures Colossal Materials Prime Signatures
*PRIME: 1.2X TO 3X BASIC
PRINT RUNS B/WN 5-25 COPIES PER
NO PRICING ON QTY 10 OR LESS
EXCHANGE DEADLINE 01/31/2015

2012-13 Panini National Treasures Colossal Materials Signatures
ODDS B/WN 10-49 COPIES PER
NO PRICING ON QTY 10 OR LESS
EXCHANGE DEADLINE 01/31/2015
1 Marcin Gortat/49 6.00 15.00
2 Deron Williams/25 15.00 40.00
3 Serge Ibaka/49 12.00 30.00
4 LaMarcus Aldridge/25 12.00 30.00
5 Steve Nash/25 40.00 100.00
6 Alonzo Mourning/25 30.00 80.00
7 Jeff Teague/49 6.00 15.00
8 Luol Deng /49 6.00 15.00
9 Brook Lopez/25 6.00 15.00
10 Mike Conley/49 8.00 20.00
11 Danilo Gallinari/25 10.00 25.00
12 Greg Monroe/49 6.00 15.00
13 Anderson Varejao/49 6.00 15.00
14 Tyreke Evans/25 6.00 15.00
15 Wesley Matthews/49 6.00 15.00
16 Chris Bosh/25 15.00 40.00
18 Jrue Holiday/25 10.00 25.00
20 Dwight Howard/25 30.00 80.00

2012-13 Panini National Treasures Gold Proof Autographs
PRINT RUNS B/WN 10-54 COPIES PER
NO PRICING ON QTY 20 OR LESS
EXCHANGE DEADLINE 1/31/2015
2 Grant Hill/53 EXCH 20.00 50.00
5 Jason Kidd/54 15.00 40.00
9 Kevin Durant/49 EXCH 100.00 250.00
10 Dwyane Wade/49 60.00 150.00
11 Walt Frazier/46 EXCH 8.00 20.00
17 Kevin Durant/49 EXCH 100.00 250.00
19 Mark Aguirre/47 6.00 15.00
25 Blake Griffin/49 EXCH 75.00 200.00

2012-13 Panini National Treasures Jersey Number Autographs
PRINT RUNS B/WN 10-25 COPIES PER
NO PRICING ON QTY 10
EXCHANGE DEADLINE 1/31/2015
101 Kyrie Irving/25 2,000.00 3,000.00
102 Derrick Williams/25 12.00 30.00
103 Enes Kanter/25 75.00 200.00
104 Tristan Thompson/25 75.00 200.00
105 Jan Vesely/25 12.00 30.00
106 Bismack Biyombo/25 20.00 50.00
107 Brandon Knight/25 12.00 30.00
108 Kemba Walker/25 500.00 1,000.00
109 Jimmer Fredette/25 30.00 80.00
110 Klay Thompson/25 4,000.00 8,000.00
111 Alec Burks/25 30.00 80.00
112 Markieff Morris/25 50.00 120.00
113 Marcus Morris/25 50.00 120.00
114 Kawhi Leonard/25 4,000.00 6,000.00
115 Nikola Vucevic/25 500.00 1,000.00
116 Iman Shumpert/25 20.00 50.00
117 Chris Singleton/25 12.00 30.00
118 Tobias Harris/25 125.00 300.00
119 Nolan Smith/25 12.00 30.00
120 Kenneth Faried/25 50.00 120.00
121 Reggie Jackson/25 100.00 250.00
122 MarShon Brooks/25 12.00 30.00
123 Jordan Hamilton/25 12.00 30.00
124 Lavoy Allen/25 12.00 30.00
125 Norris Cole/25 15.00 40.00
126 Cory Joseph/25 20.00 50.00
127 Jimmy Butler/25 600.00 900.00
128 Ivan Johnson/25 12.00 30.00
129 Chandler Parsons/25 30.00 80.00
130 Jonas Valanciunas/25 75.00 200.00
132 Isaiah Thomas/25 60.00 150.00
151 Anthony Davis/25 4,000.00 6,000.00
152 Michael Kidd-Gilchrist/25 50.00 120.00
153 Bradley Beal/25 500.00 800.00
154 Dion Waiters/25 75.00 200.00
155 Thomas Robinson/25 12.00 30.00
156 Draymond Green/25 1,500.00 3,000.00
157 Harrison Barnes/25 125.00 300.00
158 Terrence Ross/25 100.00 250.00
159 Andre Drummond/25 300.00 600.00
160 Austin Rivers/25 75.00 200.00
161 Meyers Leonard/25 20.00 50.00
162 Jeremy Lamb/25 100.00 250.00
163 Kendall Marshall/25 12.00 30.00
164 John Henson/25 15.00 40.00
165 Kyle Singler/25 15.00 40.00
166 Jae Crowder/25 75.00 200.00
167 Tyler Zeller/25 15.00 40.00
168 Terrence Jones/25 12.00 30.00
169 Andrew Nicholson/25 12.00 30.00
170 Evan Fournier/25 60.00 150.00
171 Jared Sullinger/25 12.00 30.00
172 Fab Melo/25 12.00 30.00
173 John Jenkins/25 12.00 30.00
174 Jared Cunningham/25 12.00 30.00
175 Tony Wroten/25 12.00 30.00
176 Miles Plumlee/25 12.00 30.00
177 Arnett Moultrie/25 12.00 30.00
178 Perry Jones/25 12.00 30.00
179 Marquis Teague/25 20.00 50.00
180 Festus Ezeli/25 20.00 50.00
182 Quincy Acy/25 12.00 30.00
183 Doron Lamb/25 12.00 30.00
201 Damian Lillard/25 1,000.00 3,000.00

2012-13 Panini National Treasures Matchups Materials
PRINT RUNS B/WN 25-99 COPIES PER
1 K.Bryant/K.Durant/49 75.00 200.00
2 D.Nowitzki/K.Love/49 12.00 30.00
3 P.Gasol/M.Gasol/99 8.00 20.00
4 D.Rose/J.Wall/49 8.00 20.00
5 R.Rondo/C.Paul/49 10.00 25.00
6 R.Westbrook/R.Rondo/49 8.00 20.00
7 A.Bargnani/B.Lopez/99 4.00 10.00
8 D.Cousins/D.Jordan/49 5.00 12.00
9 S.Ibaka/E.Okafor/49 4.00 10.00
10 R.Felton/M.Conley/99 4.00 10.00
11 J.Holiday/B.Jennings/99 6.00 15.00
12 D.Howard/T.Duncan/99 6.00 15.00
13 L.Deng /A.Iguodala/99 5.00 12.00
14 B.Griffin/J.Smith/49 6.00 15.00
15 S.Nash/J.Kidd/49 10.00 25.00
16 T.Chandler/J.Noah/49 4.00 10.00
17 G.Monroe/R.Hibbert/99 4.00 10.00
18 K.Garnett/D.Nowitzki/49 8.00 20.00
19 R.Westbrook/D.Rose/49 8.00 20.00
20 K.Bryant/D.Wade/99 75.00 200.00
21 K.Durant/L.James/49 15.00 40.00
22 P.Pierce/M.Ginobili/99 10.00 25.00
23 C.Paul/D.Rose/49 10.00 25.00
24 T.Duncan/K.Garnett/49 12.00 30.00
25 B.Griffin/K.Love/49 8.00 20.00
26 T.Parker/R.Rubio/49 8.00 20.00
27 D.Williams/S.Nash/49 10.00 25.00
28 K.Durant/C.Anthony/49 10.00 25.00
29 A.Stoudemire/C.Bosh/99 6.00 15.00
30 K.Bryant/L.James/49 150.00 400.00
31 T.Evans/J.Wall/99 6.00 15.00
32 R.Rubio/S.Nash/49 10.00 25.00
33 D.Williams/D.Wade/49 6.00 15.00
34 C.Boozer/D.West/99 4.00 10.00
35 J.Noah/A.Horford/99 5.00 12.00
36 B.Jennings/J.Johnson/99 4.00 10.00
37 J.Anthony/T.Hansbrough/99 3.00 8.00
38 R.Gay/D.Granger/99 5.00 12.00
39 D.Lee/L.Aldridge/49 5.00 12.00
40 K.Martin/D.DeRozan/99 6.00 15.00
41 R.Allen/J.Harden/49 6.00 15.00
42 V.Carter/D.DeRozan/99 10.00 25.00
43 A.Jefferson/M.Gasol/99 5.00 12.00
44 Z.Randolph/L.Aldridge/49 5.00 12.00
45 P.Pierce/K.Bryant/99 75.00 200.00
46 S.Marion/T.Prince/99 5.00 12.00
47 E.Brand/C.Boozer/99 4.00 10.00
48 D.DeRozan/Mayo/99 6.00 15.00
49 R.Felton/T.Lawson/99 3.00 8.00
50 G.Hayward/T.Booker/99 5.00 12.00
51 P.Pierce/L.James/99 12.00 30.00
52 G.Dragic/B.Udrih/99 5.00 12.00
53 T.Duncan/D.Nowitzki/99 12.00 30.00
54 A.Varejao/C.Andersen/99 4.00 10.00
55 K.Durant/D.Gallinari/49 6.00 15.00
56 J.Erving/D.Wilkins/49 12.00 30.00
57 E.Gordon/D.DeRozan/99 6.00 15.00
58 K.Garnett/P.Gasol/49 6.00 15.00
59 D.Gallinari/A.Bargnani/99 3.00 8.00
60 K.Martin/R.Allen/49 8.00 20.00
61 D.Jordan/C.Frye/99 4.00 10.00
62 J.Holiday/J.Teague/99 6.00 15.00
63 C.Andersen/J.Noah/99 4.00 10.00
64 B.Griffin/D.Cousins/49 6.00 15.00
65 L.Deng /C.Anthony/49 8.00 20.00
66 A.Jamison/V.Carter/49 10.00 25.00
67 M.Williams/T.Hansbrough/99 3.00 8.00
68 S.Battier/Redick/99 5.00 12.00
69 R.Rondo/J.Wall/49 6.00 15.00
70 J.Terry/M.Ginobili/49 10.00 25.00
71 T.Evans/D.Rose/49 12.00 30.00
72 M.Thornton/W.Matthews/25 3.00 8.00
73 G.Hayward/C.Landry/99 5.00 12.00
74 D.Nowitzki/P.Gasol/49 12.00 30.00
75 A.Iguodala/R.Gay/49 5.00 12.00
76 L.Aldridge/C.Bosh/49 6.00 15.00
77 D.Granger/J.Johnson/99 4.00 10.00
78 D.Cousins/D.Favors/49 5.00 12.00
79 R.Anderson/C.Frye/75 3.00 8.00
80 A.Jamison/D.Wright/99 4.00 10.00
81 J.Calderon/R.Rubio/99 6.00 15.00
82 H.Turkoglu/T.Ariza/99 4.00 10.00
83 S.Curry/T.Evans/49 10.00 25.00
84 B.Lopez/R.Lopez/99 4.00 10.00
85 Barea/J.Calderon/99 4.00 10.00
86 M.Peace/P.Pierce/99 8.00 20.00
87 C.Anthony/L.James/49 15.00 40.00
88 A.Stoudemire/D.Howard/49 6.00 15.00
89 B.Lopez/R.Hibbert/49 4.00 10.00
90 D.Howard/K.Garnett/49 6.00 15.00
91 T.Lawson/M.Conley/99 4.00 10.00
92 J.Kidd/G.Hill/49 10.00 25.00
93 M.Malone/H.Olajuwon/25 10.00 25.00
94 Y.Ming/S.Bradley/49 10.00 25.00
95 S.O'Neal /T.Duncan/49 15.00 40.00
96 S.O'Neal /Y.Ming/25 15.00 40.00
97 D.Rodman/K.Malone/25 15.00 40.00
98 D.Robinson/P.Ewing/49 10.00 25.00
99 H.Olajuwon/S.O'Neal /25 15.00 40.00
100 P.Ewing/A.Mourning/49 10.00 25.00

2012-13 Panini National Treasures Matchups Materials Prime
*PRIME: .75X TO 2X BASIC
PRINT RUNS B/WN 5-25 COPIES PER
NO PRICING ON QTY 10 OR LESS
51 P.Pierce/L.James/25 30.00 80.00

2012-13 Panini National Treasures Material Treasures

PRINT RUNS B/WN 10-99 COPIES PER
NO CRAWFORD PRICING AVAILABLE
1 Kobe Bryant/49 75.00 200.00
2 Kyrie Irving/99 12.00 30.00
3 Pau Gasol/49 8.00 20.00
4 Blake Griffin/49 5.00 12.00
5 Chris Paul/49 6.00 15.00
6 Caron Butler/99 4.00 10.00
7 Kevin Durant/49 20.00 50.00
8 Russell Westbrook/49 8.00 20.00
9 James Harden/49 6.00 15.00
10 Serge Ibaka/49 4.00 10.00
11 Derrick Rose/49 8.00 20.00
12 Luol Deng /49 4.00 10.00
13 Joakim Noah/49 4.00 10.00
14 Carlos Boozer/49 4.00 10.00
15 Dirk Nowitzki/49 12.00 30.00
16 Jason Terry/49 4.00 10.00
17 Jeremy Lin/49 8.00 20.00
18 Jason Kidd/49 8.00 20.00
19 Kevin Garnett/49 6.00 15.00
20 Paul Pierce/49 8.00 20.00
21 Rajon Rondo/49 6.00 15.00
22 Ray Allen/49 10.00 25.00
23 Dwight Howard/49 6.00 15.00
24 Hedo Turkoglu/99 4.00 10.00
25 J.J. Redick/99 5.00 12.00
26 Josh Smith/99 3.00 8.00
27 Joe Johnson/49 4.00 10.00
28 Al Horford/49 5.00 12.00
29 Danny Granger/49 3.00 8.00
30 Tyler Hansbrough/99 3.00 8.00
31 Darren Collison/99 3.00 8.00
32 David West/49 4.00 10.00
33 Tim Duncan/49 6.00 15.00
34 Tony Parker/49 8.00 20.00
35 Manu Ginobili/49 10.00 25.00
36 Tiago Splitter/99 3.00 8.00
37 Jrue Holiday/99 6.00 15.00
38 Thaddeus Young/99 3.00 8.00
39 Evan Turner/99 3.00 8.00
40 Elton Brand/99 4.00 10.00
41 John Wall/49 6.00 15.00
42 Andray Blatche/99 3.00 8.00
43 Gordon Hayward/99 5.00 12.00
45 Al Jefferson/99 3.00 8.00
46 Devin Harris/99 3.00 8.00
47 Derrick Favors/99 4.00 10.00
48 Carmelo Anthony/49 8.00 20.00
49 Amar'e Stoudemire/49 5.00 12.00
50 Damian Lillard/99 40.00 100.00
51 Landry Fields/99 3.00 8.00
52 Ricky Rubio/49 4.00 10.00
53 Kevin Love/49 5.00 12.00
54 Wesley Johnson/99 3.00 8.00
55 Luke Ridnour/99 4.00 10.00
56 D.J. Augustin/99 3.00 8.00
57 Tyrus Thomas/99 3.00 8.00
58 Antawn Jamison/99 4.00 10.00
59 Anderson Varejao/99 3.00 8.00
60 Daniel Gibson/99 3.00 8.00
61 Tyreke Evans/49 4.00 10.00
62 Marcus Thornton/49 3.00 8.00
63 DeMarcus Cousins/99 5.00 12.00
64 John Salmons/99 4.00 10.00
65 Dwyane Wade/49 6.00 15.00
66 LeBron James/49 40.00 100.00
67 Chris Bosh/49 6.00 15.00
68 Shane Battier/99 4.00 10.00
69 Marc Gasol/49 5.00 12.00
70 Rudy Gay/49 5.00 12.00
71 Zach Randolph/49 5.00 12.00
72 Mike Conley/99 4.00 10.00
73 Trevor Ariza/99 3.00 8.00
74 Andrea Bargnani/49 3.00 8.00
75 DeMar DeRozan/99 6.00 15.00
76 Stephen Curry/99 20.00 50.00
77 Brandon Jennings/49 3.00 8.00
78 Drew Gooden/99 4.00 10.00
79 Carlos Delfino/99 3.00 8.00
80 Kevin Martin/99 4.00 10.00
81 Luis Scola/99 4.00 10.00
82 Goran Dragic/99 5.00 12.00
83 Channing Frye/99 3.00 8.00
84 Steve Nash/49 10.00 25.00
85 Jared Dudley/49 3.00 8.00
86 Grant Hill/49 8.00 20.00
87 Chris Kaman/99 4.00 10.00
88 Deron Williams/49 4.00 10.00
89 Brook Lopez/49 4.00 10.00
90 Kris Humphries/99 3.00 8.00
91 LaMarcus Aldridge/49 6.00 15.00
92 Carl Landry/99 3.00 8.00
93 Raymond Felton/99 3.00 8.00
94 Ty Lawson/99 3.00 8.00
95 Chris Andersen/99 4.00 10.00
96 Danilo Gallinari/99 3.00 8.00
97 Greg Monroe/49 3.00 8.00
98 Tayshaun Prince/99 5.00 12.00
99 George Hill/99 4.00 10.00
100 David Lee/49 3.00 8.00

2012-13 Panini National Treasures Material Treasures Prime

*PRIME: 1.2X TO 3X BASIC
PRINT RUNS B/WN 5-25 COPIES PER
NO PRICING ON QTY 25 OR LESS
1 Kobe Bryant/25 300.00 600.00
2 Kyrie Irving/25 75.00 150.00
11 Derrick Rose/25 75.00 150.00
13 Joakim Noah/25 15.00 40.00
18 Jason Kidd/25 30.00 80.00
22 Ray Allen/25 40.00 80.00
33 Tim Duncan/25 50.00 120.00
53 Kevin Love/25 40.00 100.00
86 Grant Hill/25 50.00 120.00
91 LaMarcus Aldridge/25 40.00 80.00

2012-13 Panini National Treasures NBA Gear Dual

PRINT RUNS B/WN 25-99 COPIES PER
1 J.J. Hickson/99 3.00 8.00
2 LeBron James/99 40.00 100.00
3 John Wall/99 6.00 15.00
4 Serge Ibaka/99 4.00 10.00
5 Paul Pierce/49 8.00 20.00
6 Jordan Crawford/49 3.00 8.00
7 Dwyane Wade/99 10.00 25.00
8 Derrick Rose/99 8.00 20.00
9 Caron Butler/99 4.00 10.00
10 Brandon Jennings/99 3.00 8.00
11 Andrew Bynum/99 3.00 8.00
12 James Harden/99 10.00 25.00
13 Chris Andersen/99 4.00 10.00
14 Chris Kaman/25 4.00 10.00
15 Dirk Nowitzki/49 8.00 20.00
16 Andrea Bargnani/49 3.00 8.00
17 Mo Williams/99 4.00 10.00
18 Jeremy Lin/99 8.00 20.00
19 Jeff Teague/99 3.00 8.00
20 DeJuan Blair/49 3.00 8.00
21 Pau Gasol/99 8.00 20.00
22 Tyler Hansbrough/99 3.00 8.00
23 Raymond Felton/49 3.00 8.00
24 Russell Westbrook/49 6.00 15.00
25 Kris Humphries/99 3.00 8.00
26 Andre Iguodala/99 5.00 12.00
27 Rodrigue Beaubois/99 3.00 8.00
28 Andre Miller/99 4.00 10.00
29 Al Jefferson/49 3.00 8.00
30 Tim Duncan/99 12.00 30.00
31 David Lee/49 3.00 8.00
32 Jrue Holiday/99 6.00 15.00
33 Dwight Howard/99 6.00 15.00
34 Kevin Durant/99 20.00 50.00
35 DeMar DeRozan/99 6.00 15.00
36 O.J. Mayo/99 3.00 8.00
37 Kevin Martin/99 4.00 10.00
38 Ben Gordon/99 4.00 10.00
39 Vince Carter/49 10.00 25.00
40 Darren Collison/99 3.00 8.00
41 Carmelo Anthony/99 8.00 20.00
42 Rajon Rondo/49 6.00 15.00
43 Al Horford/99 5.00 12.00
44 Greg Monroe/99 3.00 8.00
45 Kevin Garnett/49 12.00 30.00
46 Trevor Ariza/99 3.00 8.00
47 J.J. Barea/99 4.00 10.00
48 Luis Scola/99 4.00 10.00
49 Jason Kidd/49 8.00 20.00
50 Landry Fields/99 3.00 8.00

2012-13 Panini National Treasures NBA Gear Dual Prime

*PRIME: .75X TO 2X BASIC
PRINT RUNS B/WN 5-25 COPIES PER
NO PRICING ON QTY 10 OR LESS
13 Chris Andersen/25 40.00 100.00

2012-13 Panini National Treasures NBA Gear Dual Prime Signatures

*PRIME: .75X TO 2X BASIC
PRINT RUNS B/WN 5-25 COPIES PER
NO PRICING ON QTY 10 OR LESS
EXCHANGE DEADLINE 01/31/2015

2012-13 Panini National Treasures NBA Gear Dual Signatures

PRINT RUNS B/WN 10-99 COPIES PER
NO CHALMERS PRICING AVAILABLE
EXCHANGE DEADLINE 01/31/2015
1 Marcin Gortat/49 6.00 15.00
2 Steve Nash/25 30.00 80.00
3 Ray Allen/25 30.00 80.00
4 Blake Griffin/25 30.00 80.00
5 Tyreke Evans/25 8.00 20.00
6 Chris Kaman/25 6.00 15.00
7 Josh Smith/25 6.00 15.00
8 James Harden/25 40.00 100.00
9 Ben Gordon/25 6.00 15.00
10 Joakim Noah/49 6.00 15.00
11 Marcus Thornton/49 6.00 15.00
12 Mike Conley/25 8.00 20.00
13 Chris Bosh/25 12.00 30.00
14 Evan Turner/25 6.00 15.00
15 Gordon Hayward/99 10.00 25.00
16 Andre Iguodala/25 10.00 25.00
17 Hedo Turkoglu/99 4.00 10.00
18 Vince Carter/25 25.00 60.00
19 Danilo Gallinari/49 6.00 15.00
20 Andre Miller/49 8.00 20.00
21 Devin Harris/25 6.00 15.00
22 Wesley Johnson/99 6.00 15.00
23 Deron Williams/25 8.00 20.00
24 Kobe Bryant/49 1,500.00 3,000.00
25 Kevin Durant/49 75.00 200.00
26 Emeka Okafor/25 6.00 15.00
27 Tyson Chandler/49 8.00 20.00
28 Tony Parker/25 25.00 60.00
30 Kevin Martin/25 6.00 15.00
31 Richard Hamilton/49 10.00 25.00
32 Kevin Love/49 10.00 25.00
33 Al Jefferson/49 6.00 15.00
34 Monta Ellis/49 6.00 15.00
35 Brandon Jennings/49 6.00 15.00
36 Ty Lawson/49 6.00 15.00
37 Trevor Booker/99 6.00 15.00
38 Andrea Bargnani/25 6.00 15.00
39 Jeff Teague/99 6.00 15.00
40 Antawn Jamison/49 6.00 15.00
41 Eric Gordon/25 8.00 20.00
42 Joe Johnson/49 8.00 20.00
43 Carlos Boozer/49 8.00 20.00
44 Anderson Varejao/49 6.00 15.00
45 Derrick Favors/49 6.00 15.00
46 Greg Monroe/49 6.00 15.00
47 J.R. Smith/49 10.00 25.00
48 Zach Randolph/25 10.00 25.00
49 Grant Hill/25 30.00 80.00
50 LaMarcus Aldridge/25 10.00 25.00

2012-13 Panini National Treasures NBA Gear Trios

PRINT RUNS B/WN 49-99 COPIES PER
1 Joakim Noah/99 4.00 10.00
2 LeBron James/49 40.00 100.00
3 Jason Terry/49 4.00 10.00
4 Al Jefferson/99 3.00 8.00
5 Paul Pierce/49 8.00 20.00
6 Tim Duncan/99 12.00 30.00
7 Dwyane Wade/49 10.00 25.00
8 Ty Lawson/99 3.00 8.00
9 Beno Udrih/99 3.00 8.00
10 Kevin Garnett/49 6.00 15.00
11 Andrea Bargnani/99 3.00 8.00
12 DeMar DeRozan/99 6.00 15.00
13 Shawn Marion/49 5.00 12.00
14 Manu Ginobili/49 10.00 25.00
15 Kobe Bryant/49 60.00 150.00
16 Ricky Rubio/49 6.00 15.00
17 Jose Calderon/99 3.00 8.00
18 Zach Randolph/99 5.00 12.00
19 Amar'e Stoudemire/49 5.00 12.00
20 Rudy Gay/99 5.00 12.00
21 Kevin Martin/99 4.00 10.00
22 Danny Granger/99 3.00 8.00
23 Joe Johnson/99 4.00 10.00
24 Russell Westbrook/99 6.00 15.00
25 Evan Turner/99 3.00 8.00

2012-13 Panini National Treasures NBA Gear Trios Prime

*PRIME: X TO X BASIC
PRINT RUNS B/WN 5-25 COPIES PER
NO PRICING ON QTY 10 OR LESS
1 Joakim Noah/25 20.00 50.00
2 LeBron James/25 100.00 200.00
6 Tim Duncan/25 40.00 100.00
7 Dwyane Wade/25 50.00 100.00
10 Kevin Garnett/25 40.00 80.00
14 Manu Ginobili/25 20.00 50.00
15 Kobe Bryant/25 125.00 300.00
24 Russell Westbrook/25 20.00 50.00

2012-13 Panini National Treasures NBA Gear Trios Prime Signatures

*PRIME: .75X TO 2X BASIC
PRINT RUNS B/WN 5-25 COPIES PER
NO PRICING ON QTY 10 OR LESS
EXCHANGE DEADLINE 01/31/2015

2012-13 Panini National Treasures NBA Gear Trios Signatures

PRINT RUNS B/WN 25-99 COPIES PER
EXCHANGE DEADLINE 01/31/2015
1 Greg Monroe/99 6.00 15.00
2 Kobe Bryant/99 1,500.00 3,000.00
3 Tony Parker/49 20.00 50.00
4 Kevin Durant/49 75.00 200.00
5 Chris Bosh/49 12.00 30.00
6 Josh Smith/49 6.00 15.00
7 Blake Griffin/49 20.00 50.00
8 John Wall/25 40.00 100.00
9 Grant Hill/49 30.00 80.00
10 DeMarcus Cousins/49 12.00 30.00
11 Andre Iguodala/49 10.00 25.00
12 Kevin Love/49 10.00 25.00
13 Brook Lopez/49 8.00 20.00
14 Stephen Curry/49 500.00 1,000.00
15 Tyson Chandler/49 8.00 20.00
16 LaMarcus Aldridge/49 10.00 25.00
17 Danny Granger/49 6.00 15.00
18 Zach Randolph/49 10.00 25.00
19 Wesley Matthews/99 6.00 15.00
20 Serge Ibaka/99 8.00 20.00
21 Gordon Hayward/99 10.00 25.00
22 Eric Gordon/49 8.00 20.00
23 Dwight Howard/25 12.00 30.00
24 Al Horford/49 10.00 25.00
25 Metta World Peace/49 8.00 20.00

2012-13 Panini National Treasures Notable Nicknames

PRINT RUNS B/WN 25-99 COPIES PER
EXCHANGE DEADLINE 1/31/2015
1 Kyrie Irving/49 1,500.00 3,000.00
2 Walt Frazier/99 10.00 25.00
3 James Worthy/49 40.00 100.00
4 Robert Horry/99 75.00 200.00
5 Bill Walton/49 75.00 200.00
6 Kobe Bryant/49 2,500.00 5,000.00
7 Clyde Drexler/49 125.00 300.00
8 Anthony Davis/25 3,000.00 6,000.00
9 Nick Van Exel/99 25.00 60.00
10 Anfernee Hardaway/49 400.00 800.00
11 Kenny Smith/99 40.00 100.00
12 Harrison Barnes/49 75.00 200.00
13 Kevin Durant/49 400.00 800.00
14 Toni Kukoc/99 150.00 400.00
15 Cedric Maxwell/99 6.00 15.00
16 Dikembe Mutombo/49 75.00 200.00
17 Kenneth Faried/99 30.00 80.00
18 Julius Erving/25 400.00 800.00
19 Larry Johnson/49 100.00 250.00
20 Marcin Gortat/99 20.00 50.00
21 Dominique Wilkins/49 200.00 500.00
22 Shaquille O'Neal/25 500.00 1,000.00
23 Jerry West/25 300.00 600.00
24 Serge Ibaka/49 EXCH 20.00 50.00
25 Blake Griffin/49 150.00 400.00

2012-13 Panini National Treasures Springfield Bound Signatures

PRINT RUNS B/WN 49-99 COPIES PER
EXCHANGE DEADLINE 1/31/2015
1 Kobe Bryant/49 2,500.00 5,000.00
2 Grant Hill/49 25.00 60.00
3 Vince Carter/99 30.00 80.00
4 Tony Parker/49 20.00 50.00
5 Jason Kidd/49 20.00 50.00
6 Steve Nash/49 30.00 80.00
7 Yao Ming/49 40.00 100.00
8 Chris Bosh/99 EXCH 12.00 30.00
9 Kevin Durant/49 75.00 200.00
10 Dwyane Wade/49 60.00 150.00

2012-13 Panini National Treasures Timeline Materials Custom Names

PRINT RUNS B/WN 25-99 COPIES PER
1 Kevin Durant/49 20.00 50.00
2 Jrue Holiday/99 6.00 15.00
3 Dirk Nowitzki/49 12.00 30.00
4 Emeka Okafor/99 4.00 10.00
5 Andre Iguodala/99 5.00 12.00
6 Deron Williams/99 4.00 10.00
7 Nick Collison/99 3.00 8.00
8 Gordon Hayward/49 5.00 12.00
9 DeMarcus Cousins/49 5.00 12.00
10 Joe Johnson/99 4.00 10.00
11 Kris Humphries/99 3.00 8.00
12 Kevin Garnett/25 12.00 30.00
13 Darren Collison/99 3.00 8.00
14 Tony Parker/49 8.00 20.00
15 Dwight Howard/99 6.00 15.00
16 Damian Lillard/99 40.00 100.00
17 Carlos Boozer/49 4.00 10.00
18 Carmelo Anthony/49 8.00 20.00
19 Russell Westbrook/99 6.00 15.00
20 Metta World Peace/99 4.00 10.00
21 Manu Ginobili/43 10.00 25.00
22 Andrew Bynum/99 3.00 8.00
23 Zach Randolph/99 5.00 12.00
24 Shane Battier/99 4.00 10.00
25 Trevor Booker/99 3.00 8.00

2012-13 Panini National Treasures Timeline Materials Custom Names Prime

21 Manu Ginobili/25 15.00 40.00

2012-13 Panini National Treasures Timeline Materials Custom Names Prime Signatures

*PRIME: .6X TO 1.5X BASIC
PRINT RUNS B/WN 10-25 COPIES PER
NO PRICING ON QTY 10
EXCHANGE DEADLINE 01/31/2015

2012-13 Panini National Treasures Timeline Materials Custom Names Signatures

PRINT RUNS B/WN 25-99 COPIES PER
EXCHANGE DEADLINE 01/31/2015
1 Kevin Durant/49 100.00 200.00
2 LaMarcus Aldridge/49 15.00 40.00
3 Dirk Nowitzki/49 50.00 125.00
4 Emeka Okafor/49 6.00 15.00
5 Andre Iguodala/99 8.00 20.00
6 Tyson Chandler/49 6.00 15.00
7 Michael Kidd-Gilchrist/49 6.00 15.00
8 Gordon Hayward/49 15.00 40.00
9 Derrick Favors/30 8.00 20.00
10 Joe Johnson/99 8.00 20.00
11 Andre Miller/99 6.00 15.00
12 Kobe Bryant/49 1,500.00 3,000.00
13 Richard Hamilton/49 8.00 20.00
14 Julius Erving/25 60.00 150.00
15 Shaquille O'Neal/25 75.00 200.00
16 Anderson Varejao/49 6.00 15.00
17 Zach Randolph/99 8.00 20.00
18 David Robinson/49 30.00 80.00
19 Jerry West/25 40.00 100.00
20 John Stockton/25 40.00 100.00
21 Alex English/49 8.00 20.00
22 Elgin Baylor/25 20.00 50.00
23 Nick Van Exel/25 15.00 40.00
24 Kareem Abdul-Jabbar/25 50.00 125.00
25 Yao Ming/25 40.00 100.00

2012-13 Panini National Treasures Timeline Materials Custom Team Nicknames

PRINT RUNS B/WN 15-99 COPIES PER
NO PRICING ON QTY 15
1 LeBron James/99 40.00 100.00
2 Ben Gordon/99 4.00 10.00
3 Derrick Rose/99 10.00 25.00
4 Russell Westbrook/49 6.00 15.00
5 Kobe Bryant/49 125.00 300.00
6 Antawn Jamison/99 4.00 10.00
7 LaMarcus Aldridge/99 5.00 12.00
8 Pau Gasol/99 8.00 20.00
9 Blake Griffin/49 8.00 20.00
10 Tony Parker/49 8.00 20.00
11 Paul Pierce/49 8.00 20.00
12 Dwyane Wade/49 10.00 25.00
13 Amar'e Stoudemire/99 5.00 12.00
14 Andrea Bargnani/99 3.00 8.00
15 David Lee/49 3.00 8.00
16 Tim Duncan/99 12.00 30.00
17 Eric Gordon/99 4.00 10.00
18 Brook Lopez/99 4.00 10.00
19 Ty Lawson/99 3.00 8.00
20 Josh Smith/99 3.00 8.00
21 David West/99 4.00 10.00
22 Steve Nash/49 10.00 25.00
24 Jeremy Lin/99 8.00 20.00
25 Marc Gasol/99 5.00 12.00

2012-13 Panini National Treasures Timeline Materials Custom Team Nicknames Prime

*PRIME: .75X TO 2X BASIC
PRINT RUNS B/WN 10-25 COPIES PER
NO PRICING ON QTY 15 OR LESS
10 Tony Parker/25 15.00 40.00
16 Tim Duncan/25 25.00 60.00

2012-13 Panini National Treasures Timeline Materials Custom Team Nicknames Prime Signatures

*PRIME: .6X TO 1.5X BASIC
PRINT RUNS B/WN 10-25 COPIES PER
NO PRICING ON QTY 15 OR LESS
EXCHANGE DEADLINE 01/31/2015

2012-13 Panini National Treasures Timeline Materials Custom Team Nicknames Signatures

PRINT RUNS B/WN 49-99 COPIES PER
EXCHANGE DEADLINE 01/31/2015
1 Ray Allen/49 20.00 50.00
2 Ben Gordon/99 6.00 15.00
3 Kyrie Irving/99 200.00 500.00
4 James Harden/49 25.00 60.00
5 Kobe Bryant/49 1,500.00 3,000.00
6 Harrison Barnes/49 15.00 40.00
7 LaMarcus Aldridge/49 8.00 20.00
8 Kevin Love/49 15.00 40.00
9 Blake Griffin/49 15.00 40.00
10 Tony Parker/49 15.00 40.00
11 Jared Sullinger/49 10.00 25.00
12 Mike Conley/99 6.00 15.00
13 DeMarcus Cousins/49 8.00 20.00
14 Ersan Ilyasova/99 6.00 15.00
15 Andre Drummond/49 40.00 100.00
16 Chris Kaman/99 6.00 15.00
17 Deron Williams/49 10.00 25.00
18 Stephen Curry/49 400.00 800.00
19 Al Jefferson/99 6.00 15.00
20 Brandon Jennings/49 8.00 20.00
21 Grant Hill/49 30.00 60.00
22 Raymond Felton/49 6.00 15.00
23 Steve Nash/49 25.00 60.00
24 J.J. Hickson/99 6.00 15.00
25 Chris Bosh/49 15.00 40.00

2013-14 Panini National Treasures

1-100 PRINT RUN 99 SER.#'d SETS
101-200 PRINT RUNS 99 SER.#'d SETS
PRIME PATCHES MAY SELL FOR PREMIUM
EXCHANGE DEADLINE 1/30/2016
1 Jameer Nelson 1.50 4.00
2 Avery Bradley 1.50 4.00
3 Steve Nash 5.00 12.00
4 Josh Smith 1.50 4.00
5 Dirk Nowitzki 6.00 15.00
6 Russell Westbrook 4.00 10.00
7 Al Horford 2.50 6.00
8 DeMar DeRozan 3.00 8.00
9 Chris Paul 5.00 12.00
10 Derrick Favors 1.50 4.00
11 Nikola Vucevic 3.00 8.00
12 Brandon Bass 1.50 4.00
13 Pau Gasol 4.00 10.00
14 Greg Monroe 1.50 4.00
15 Monta Ellis 2.00 5.00
16 Serge Ibaka 2.00 5.00
17 Kyle Korver 2.00 5.00
18 Kyle Lowry 2.50 6.00
19 DeAndre Jordan 2.00 5.00
20 Enes Kanter 2.00 5.00
21 Tony Parker 4.00 10.00
22 Evan Turner 1.50 4.00
23 DeMarcus Cousins 2.50 6.00
24 Andre Drummond 2.50 6.00
25 Vince Carter 5.00 12.00
26 Ty Lawson 1.50 4.00
27 Jeff Teague 1.50 4.00
28 Jonas Valanciunas 2.00 5.00
29 Stephen Curry 100.00 250.00
30 Paul George 4.00 10.00
31 Tim Duncan 6.00 15.00
32 Spencer Hawes 1.50 4.00
33 Isaiah Thomas 2.00 5.00
34 Luol Deng 2.00 5.00
35 Mike Conley 2.50 6.00
36 Kenneth Faried 2.00 5.00
37 John Wall 3.00 8.00
38 Joe Johnson 2.00 5.00
39 Klay Thompson 8.00 20.00
40 Lance Stephenson 2.00 5.00
41 Kawhi Leonard 8.00 20.00
42 Thaddeus Young 1.50 4.00
43 Rudy Gay 2.00 5.00
44 Kyrie Irving 8.00 20.00
45 Zach Randolph 2.00 5.00
46 Nate Robinson 1.50 4.00
47 Bradley Beal 4.00 10.00
48 Kevin Garnett 6.00 15.00
49 David Lee 1.50 4.00
50 Roy Hibbert 1.50 4.00
51 Manu Ginobili 5.00 12.00
52 LaMarcus Aldridge 2.50 6.00
53 LeBron James 100.00 250.00
54 Dion Waiters 1.50 4.00
55 Marc Gasol 2.50 6.00
56 Kevin Love 2.50 6.00
57 Marcin Gortat 1.50 4.00
58 Paul Pierce 4.00 10.00
59 Harrison Barnes 2.50 6.00
60 Danny Granger 2.00 5.00
61 Dwight Howard 3.00 8.00
62 Damian Lillard 8.00 20.00
63 Dwyane Wade 5.00 12.00
64 Brandon Knight 2.00 5.00
65 Anthony Davis 8.00 20.00
66 Nikola Pekovic 1.50 4.00
67 Kemba Walker 2.50 6.00
68 Carmelo Anthony 4.00 10.00
69 Channing Frye 1.50 4.00
70 Derrick Rose 4.00 10.00
71 Jeremy Lin 4.00 10.00
72 Wesley Matthews 1.50 4.00
73 Chris Bosh 3.00 8.00
74 O.J. Mayo 1.50 4.00
75 Eric Gordon 2.00 5.00
76 Kevin Martin 2.00 5.00
77 Gerald Henderson 1.50 4.00
78 Andrea Bargnani 1.50 4.00
79 Goran Dragic 2.50 6.00
80 Joakim Noah 2.00 5.00
81 James Harden 5.00 12.00
82 Nicolas Batum 2.00 5.00
83 Ray Allen 4.00 10.00
84 Larry Sanders 1.50 4.00
85 Jrue Holiday 3.00 8.00
86 Ricky Rubio 2.00 5.00
87 Al Jefferson 1.50 4.00
88 Iman Shumpert 1.50 4.00
89 Gerald Green 2.00 5.00
90 Carlos Boozer 2.00 5.00
91 Chandler Parsons 1.50 4.00
92 Kevin Durant 8.00 20.00
93 Paul Millsap 2.00 5.00
94 Blake Griffin 2.50 6.00
95 Ryan Anderson 1.50 4.00
96 Gordon Hayward 2.00 5.00
97 Arron Afflalo 1.50 4.00
98 Jeff Green 1.50 4.00
99 Kobe Bryant 100.00 250.00
100 Brandon Jennings 1.50 4.00
101 D. Schroder JSY AU RC 75.00 200.00
102 Luigi Datome JSY AU RC 12.00 30.00
103 Solomon Hill JSY AU RC 15.00 40.00
104 Glen Rice Jr. JSY AU RC 12.00 30.00
105 Tony Mitchell JSY AU RC 12.00 30.00
106 Anthony Bennett JSY AU RC 12.00 30.00
107 Cody Zeller JSY AU RC 15.00 40.00
108 CJ McCollum JSY AU RC 150.00 400.00
109 Caldwell-Pope JSY AU RC 20.00 50.00
110 Kelly Olynyk JSY AU RC 15.00 40.00
111 Shane Larkin JSY AU RC 12.00 30.00
112 Rudy Gobert JSY AU RC 150.00 400.00
113 Hardaway Jr. JSY AU RC 25.00 60.00
114 Nate Wolters JSY AU RC 12.00 30.00
115 Jeff Withey JSY AU RC 12.00 30.00
116 Victor Oladipo JSY AU RC 75.00 200.00
117 Alex Len JSY AU RC EXCH 15.00 40.00
118 Ben McLemore JSY AU RC 15.00 40.00
119 Carter-Williams JSY AU RC 15.00 40.00
120 S.Muhammad JSY AU RC 12.00 30.00
121 Dellavedova JSY AU RC 75.00 200.00
122 Tony Snell JSY AU RC 15.00 40.00
123 Andre Roberson JSY AU RC 15.00 40.00
124 Peyton Siva JSY AU RC 12.00 30.00
125 Gorgui Dieng JSY AU RC 15.00 40.00
126 Otto Porter JSY AU RC 20.00 50.00
127 Nerlens Noel JSY AU RC 15.00 40.00
128 Trey Burke JSY AU RC 15.00 40.00
129 Steven Adams JSY AU RC 100.00 250.00
130 Antetokounmpo
JSY AU RC 20,000.00 40,000.00
131 Gal Mekel JSY AU RC 12.00 30.00
132 Mason Plumlee JSY AU RC 15.00 40.00
133 Archie Goodwin JSY AU RC 12.00 30.00
134 Ray McCallum AU RC 4.00 10.00
135 Pero Antic AU RC 4.00 10.00
136 Jamaal Franklin AU RC 4.00 10.00
137 Ryan Kelly AU RC EXCH 4.00 10.00
138 Ricky Ledo AU RC 4.00 10.00
139 Sergey Karasev AU RC EXCH 4.00 10.00
140 Erik Murphy AU RC 4.00 10.00
141 Isaiah Canaan AU RC 4.00 10.00
142 Dwight Buycks AU RC 4.00 10.00
143 Reggie Bullock AU RC 5.00 12.00
144 Ian Clark AU RC 5.00 12.00
145 Nemanja Nedovic AU RC 4.00 10.00
146 Mike Muscala AU RC 6.00 15.00
147 Allen Crabbe AU RC 4.00 10.00
148 Phil Pressey AU RC 4.00 10.00
149 Carrick Felix AU RC 4.00 10.00
150 Vitor Faverani AU RC 4.00 10.00

2013-14 Panini National Treasures Gold

*GOLD 1-100: 1X TO 2.5X BASIC
*GOLD 101-133: .4X TO 1X BASIC
*GOLD 134-150: .5X TO 1.2X BASIC
STATED PRINT RUN 25 SER.#'d SETS
EXCHANGE DEADLINE 1/30/2016

2013-14 Panini National Treasures Air Apparent Materials

STATED PRINT RUN 99 SER.#'d SETS
*PRIME: .75X TO 2X BASIC
1 Marc Gasol 5.00 12.00
2 Kevin Durant 15.00 40.00
3 Evan Turner 3.00 8.00
4 Stephen Curry 75.00 200.00
5 Kawhi Leonard 15.00 40.00
6 Deron Williams 4.00 10.00
7 Dion Waiters 3.00 8.00
8 Andre Drummond 5.00 12.00
9 Kyrie Irving 15.00 40.00
10 Blake Griffin 5.00 12.00
11 Brandon Knight 4.00 10.00
12 Russell Westbrook 8.00 20.00
13 Goran Dragic 4.00 10.00
14 O.J. Mayo 3.00 8.00
15 Derrick Favors 3.00 8.00
16 Al Jefferson 3.00 8.00
17 Nikola Vucevic 6.00 15.00
18 Kenneth Faried 4.00 10.00
19 Brandon Jennings 3.00 8.00
20 Chris Paul 10.00 25.00
21 Larry Sanders 3.00 8.00
22 Damian Lillard 15.00 40.00
23 Monta Ellis 4.00 10.00
24 LaMarcus Aldridge 5.00 12.00
25 Gordon Hayward 4.00 10.00
26 Michael Kidd-Gilchrist 3.00 8.00
27 Iman Shumpert 3.00 8.00
28 James Harden 10.00 25.00
29 Josh Smith 3.00 8.00
30 LeBron James 75.00 200.00
31 Anthony Davis 15.00 40.00
32 John Wall 6.00 15.00
33 DeMarcus Cousins 5.00 12.00
34 Eric Bledsoe 4.00 10.00
35 Enes Kanter 4.00 10.00
36 Jimmy Butler 10.00 25.00
37 Tobias Harris 5.00 12.00
38 Dwight Howard 6.00 15.00
39 Harrison Barnes 5.00 12.00
40 Kevin Love 5.00 12.00
41 Jrue Holiday 6.00 15.00
42 Al Horford 5.00 12.00
43 Isaiah Thomas 4.00 10.00
44 Bradley Beal 8.00 20.00
45 Jeremy Lin 15.00 40.00
46 Kemba Walker 5.00 12.00
47 Maurice Harkless 3.00 8.00
48 Paul George 8.00 20.00
49 Mike Conley 5.00 12.00
50 Ricky Rubio 4.00 10.00

2013-14 Panini National Treasures Career Materials Trios

PRINT RUNS B/WN 49-99 COPIES PER
*PRIME: 1.5X TO 4X BASIC
1 Andre Iguodala/99 8.00 20.00
2 Dan Majerle/99 6.00 15.00
3 Dikembe Mutombo/70 12.00 30.00
4 Dominique Wilkins/99 12.00 30.00
5 Grant Hill/99 12.00 30.00
6 Chris Paul/99 15.00 40.00
7 Kevin Martin/99 6.00 15.00
8 Michael Beasley/95 5.00 12.00
9 Moses Malone/49 12.00 30.00
10 Kiki Vandeweghe/99 6.00 15.00
11 Rashard Lewis/99 6.00 15.00
12 Shaquille O'Neal/49 30.00 80.00
13 Tracy McGrady/49 12.00 30.00
14 Vince Carter/99 15.00 40.00
15 Robert Horry/99 8.00 20.00

2013-14 Panini National Treasures Colossal Materials

PRINT RUNS B/WN 25-99 COPIES PER
1 Klay Thompson/99 40.00 100.00
2 Arron Afflalo/99 3.00 8.00
3 Joakim Noah/75 5.00 12.00
4 Manu Ginobili/75 15.00 40.00
5 Amare Stoudemire/99 5.00 12.00
6 Vinnie Johnson/25 5.00 12.00
7 Rajon Rondo/75 10.00 25.00
8 Tim Duncan/75 15.00 40.00
9 John Wall/99 10.00 25.00
10 Dwight Howard/75 8.00 20.00
11 Chris Paul/75 10.00 25.00
12 Reggie Lewis/49 10.00 25.00
13 Xavier McDaniel/49 4.00 10.00
14 Patrick Ewing/99 12.00 30.00
15 Damian Lillard/99 15.00 40.00
16 LeBron James/75 75.00 200.00
17 Russell Westbrook/99 8.00 20.00
18 Kevin Garnett/99 15.00 40.00
19 Carmelo Anthony/75 12.00 30.00
20 Scottie Pippen/99 15.00 40.00
21 Marc Gasol/75 5.00 12.00
22 Moses Malone/49 12.00 30.00
23 Dennis Johnson/25 10.00 25.00
24 Paul Pierce/99 10.00 25.00
25 Jeremy Lin/75 12.00 30.00

2013-14 Panini National Treasures Colossal Materials Signatures

STATED PRINT RUN 60 SER.#'d SETS
EXCHANGE DEADLINE 1/30/2016
1 James Harden 350.00 700.00
2 Robert Parish 25.00 60.00
3 John Stockton 75.00 200.00
4 Alex English 15.00 40.00
5 Nicolas Batum EXCH 10.00 25.00
6 Kareem Abdul-Jabbar 200.00 500.00
7 Kevin Durant 150.00 400.00
8 Clyde Drexler 40.00 100.00
9 Blake Griffin 30.00 80.00
10 Stephen Curry 1,000.00 2,000.00
11 Dikembe Mutombo 40.00 100.00
12 Scottie Pippen 150.00 400.00
13 Isiah Thomas 40.00 100.00
14 Shaquille O'Neal 200.00 500.00
15 Mark Aguirre 10.00 25.00
16 Tracy McGrady 150.00 400.00
17 Kyrie Irving 125.00 300.00
18 David Robinson 100.00 250.00
19 Anthony Davis 150.00 400.00
20 Magic Johnson 125.00 300.00
21 Kelly Tripucka 10.00 25.00
22 Tyson Chandler 20.00 50.00
23 Tony Parker 75.00 200.00
24 Joe Dumars 20.00 50.00
25 Kobe Bryant 1,500.00 3,000.00

2013-14 Panini National Treasures Game Changers Signatures

STATED PRINT RUN 60 SER.#'d SETS
EXCHANGE DEADLINE 1/30/2016
1 Tracy McGrady 200.00 500.00
2 Stephen Curry 2,000.00 4,000.00
3 Bill Walton 50.00 120.00
4 Kobe Bryant 2,000.00 4,000.00
5 Vince Carter 200.00 500.00
6 Magic Johnson 300.00 600.00
7 Karl Malone 100.00 250.00
8 Anthony Davis 125.00 300.00
9 David Robinson 125.00 300.00
10 Chris Bosh 60.00 150.00
11 Jason Kidd 75.00 200.00
12 James Harden 400.00 800.00
13 Ryan Anderson 8.00 20.00
14 Dwyane Wade 200.00 500.00
15 Larry Bird 300.00 600.00
16 Kevin Durant 200.00 500.00
17 Scottie Pippen 200.00 500.00
18 Grant Hill 100.00 250.00
19 Kevin Love 20.00 50.00
20 Bernard King 25.00 60.00
21 Julius Erving 150.00 400.00
22 Kyrie Irving 125.00 300.00
23 Kareem Abdul-Jabbar 200.00 500.00
24 Carmelo Anthony 200.00 500.00
25 Anfernee Hardaway 125.00 300.00
26 Blake Griffin 20.00 50.00

2013-14 Panini National Treasures International Treasures Signatures

PRINT RUNS B/WN 35-60 COPIES PER
EXCHANGE DEADLINE 1/30/2016
*GOLD: .5X TO 1.2 BASIC
1 Enes Kanter/60 12.00 30.00
2 Tony Parker/35 75.00 200.00
3 Goran Dragic/60 EXCH 12.00 30.00
4 Luol Deng/35 EXCH 12.00 30.00
5 Nikola Vucevic/60 20.00 50.00
6 Manu Ginobili/60 100.00 250.00
7 Kelly Olynyk/60 12.00 30.00
8 Zydrunas Ilgauskas/35 12.00 30.00
9 H.Olajuwon/60 EXCH 125.00 300.00
10 Jonas Valanciunas/60 EXCH 12.00 30.00
11 Rick Fox/35 EXCH 12.00 30.00
12 Toni Kukoc/60 EXCH 30.00 80.00
13 Tiago Splitter/60 EXCH 10.00 25.00
14 Steven Adams/60 20.00 50.00
15 Steve Nash/35 125.00 300.00
16 Yao Ming/35 EXCH 300.00 600.00
17 Anthony Bennett/35 10.00 25.00
18 Detlef Schrempf/60 15.00 40.00
19 G.Antetokounmpo/60 2,000.00 4,000.00
20 Vlade Divac/60 15.00 40.00
21 Andrei Kirilenko/35 15.00 40.00
22 Peja Stojakovic/35 EXCH 30.00 80.00
23 Jonas Jerebko/60 10.00 25.00
24 A.Sabonis/60 EXCH 25.00 60.00
25 A.Bargnani/35 EXCH 10.00 25.00
26 Dennis Schroder/60 30.00 80.00
27 Luc Longley/60 12.00 30.00

2013-14 Panini National Treasures Kobe's All-Rookie Selections Signature Materials
STATED PRINT RUN 99 SER.#'d SETS
*PRIME: .75X TO 2X BASIC
1 Michael Carter-Williams 10.00 25.00
2 Victor Oladipo 20.00 50.00
3 Giannis Antetokounmpo 3,000.00 6,000.00
4 Tim Hardaway Jr. 15.00 40.00
5 C.J. McCollum 30.00 80.00
6 Trey Burke 10.00 25.00
7 Steven Adams 20.00 50.00
8 Ben McLemore 10.00 25.00

2013-14 Panini National Treasures Lasting Legacies Signature Materials
PRINT RUNS B/WN 25-99 COPIES PER
EXCHANGE DEADLINE 1/30/2016
*PRIME: .6X TO 1.5X BASIC
1 Chris Mullin/49 20.00 50.00
2 Joe Dumars/49 20.00 50.00
3 Tom Chambers/99 12.00 30.00
4 Mark Price/99 12.00 30.00
5 Manu Ginobili/49 75.00 200.00
6 Gary Payton/49 60.00 150.00
7 Kevin Love/49 12.00 30.00
8 Bernard King/49 15.00 40.00
9 Isiah Thomas/49 40.00 100.00
10 LaMarcus Aldridge/49 25.00 60.00
11 Kurt Rambis/99 20.00 50.00
12 John Havlicek/49 100.00 250.00
13 Tony Parker/49 75.00 200.00
14 Robert Parish/49 30.00 80.00
15 Hakeem Olajuwon/49 100.00 250.00
16 Kevin McHale/49 60.00 150.00
17 Nick Collison/99 8.00 20.00
18 Toni Kukoc/99 EXCH 30.00 80.00
19 James Worthy/49 40.00 100.00
20 Larry Bird/49 125.00 300.00
21 Bailey Howell/49 12.00 30.00
22 John Stockton/49 75.00 200.00
23 Elgin Baylor/49 75.00 200.00
24 Scottie Pippen/49 150.00 400.00
25 Al Horford/49 12.00 30.00
26 Karl Malone/49 75.00 200.00
27 Kobe Bryant/25 2,000.00 4,000.00
28 Brad Daugherty/99 12.00 30.00
29 Magic Johnson/49 100.00 250.00
30 Kevin Durant/49 150.00 400.00
31 Udonis Haslem/99 10.00 25.00
32 Kareem Abdul-Jabbar/49 125.00 300.00

2013-14 Panini National Treasures Material Treasures
PRINT RUNS B/WN 49-99 COPIES PER
*PRIME: .75X TO 2X BASIC
1 O.J. Mayo/75 2.50 6.00
2 Marc Gasol/99 4.00 10.00
3 Tyson Chandler/99 3.00 8.00
4 Chris Bosh/99 5.00 12.00
5 Robert Parish/75 5.00 12.00
6 Kobe Bryant/99 75.00 200.00
7 Klay Thompson/99 12.00 30.00
8 Al Jefferson/99 2.50 6.00
9 Dwyane Wade/99 8.00 20.00
10 Jimmy Butler/99 8.00 20.00
11 Patrick Ewing/99 6.00 15.00
12 Rajon Rondo/75 5.00 12.00
13 Bradley Beal/99 6.00 15.00
14 Jrue Holiday/99 5.00 12.00
15 Larry Bird/49 15.00 40.00
16 Kevin Durant/99 12.00 30.00
17 Al Horford/99 4.00 10.00
18 Brandon Jennings/99 2.50 6.00
19 Jeremy Lin/75 6.00 15.00
20 Joakim Noah/99 4.00 10.00
21 Paul Pierce/99 6.00 15.00
22 Vinnie Johnson/49 4.00 10.00
23 Paul George/99 6.00 15.00
24 Steve Nash/75 8.00 20.00
25 Kyrie Irving/99 12.00 30.00
26 Magic Johnson/49 15.00 40.00
27 Ricky Pierce/49 3.00 8.00
28 DeMarcus Cousins/99 4.00 10.00
29 Kevin Garnett/99 10.00 25.00
30 Kemba Walker/99 4.00 10.00
31 Scottie Pippen/99 10.00 25.00
32 Xavier McDaniel/99 3.00 8.00
33 Russell Westbrook/99 6.00 15.00
34 Tracy McGrady/99 6.00 15.00
35 Julius Erving/49 10.00 25.00
36 Anthony Davis/99 12.00 30.00
37 Dirk Nowitzki/99 10.00 25.00
38 Dion Waiters/99 2.50 6.00
39 Mark Jackson/49 3.00 8.00
40 Manu Ginobili/75 8.00 20.00
41 Alonzo Mourning/99 6.00 15.00
42 Tim Duncan/75 10.00 25.00
43 Stephen Curry/99 75.00 200.00
44 Amare Stoudemire/99 4.00 10.00
45 Kareem Abdul-Jabbar/49 12.00 30.00
46 Thaddeus Young/49 2.50 6.00
47 Blake Griffin/99 4.00 10.00
48 Doc Rivers/99 3.00 8.00
49 Monta Ellis/99 3.00 8.00
50 Michael Kidd-Gilchrist/99 2.50 6.00
51 Tony Parker/75 6.00 15.00
52 Anfernee Hardaway/49 10.00 25.00
53 Chris Paul/75 8.00 20.00
54 David Robinson/49 8.00 20.00
55 Hakeem Olajuwon/49 8.00 20.00
56 Dikembe Mutombo/49 6.00 15.00
57 Hal Greer/49 3.00 8.00
58 Evan Turner/99 2.50 6.00
59 Pau Gasol/99 6.00 15.00
60 Moses Malone/49 6.00 15.00

2013-14 Panini National Treasures Material Treasures Signatures
PRINT RUNS B/WN 35-99 COPIES PER
EXCHANGE DEADLINE 1/30/2016
*PRIME: .6X TO 1.5X BASIC
1 Josh Smith/49 8.00 20.00
2 Avery Johnson/99 10.00 25.00
3 Larry Johnson/49 40.00 100.00
4 Derrick Favors/99 8.00 20.00
5 Nikola Vucevic/49 15.00 40.00
6 Alex English/49 15.00 40.00
7 Bill Cartwright/49 EXCH 10.00 25.00
8 Jason Kidd/49 40.00 100.00
9 Iman Shumpert/99 8.00 20.00
10 Kawhi Leonard/49 100.00 250.00
11 Buck Williams/99 10.00 25.00
12 Danny Green/99 10.00 25.00
13 Larry Nance/99 10.00 25.00
14 Dikembe Mutombo/49 40.00 100.00
15 Michael Finley/99 12.00 30.00
16 Andre Drummond/49 12.00 30.00
17 Goran Dragic/49 EXCH 10.00 25.00
18 Bob Lanier/49 15.00 40.00
19 Isaiah Thomas/99 10.00 25.00
20 Chris Andersen/49 EXCH 10.00 25.00
21 Paul George/35 100.00 250.00
22 Dennis Rodman/35 100.00 250.00
23 Glen Rice/99 10.00 25.00
24 Enes Kanter/49 10.00 25.00
25 Raymond Felton/99 8.00 20.00
26 Gordon Hayward/49 10.00 25.00
27 Anthony Mason/99 10.00 25.00
28 Brad Daugherty/99 12.00 30.00
29 James Worthy/49 15.00 40.00
30 Grant Hill/49 40.00 100.00
31 LaMarcus Aldridge/49 12.00 30.00
32 Deron Williams/49 EXCH 10.00 25.00
33 Mike Conley/49 12.00 30.00
34 Fat Lever/99 10.00 25.00
35 Serge Ibaka/49 10.00 25.00
36 Bernard King/49 15.00 40.00
37 Harrison Barnes/99 12.00 30.00
38 Brandon Knight/99 10.00 25.00
39 Thabo Sefolosha/99 10.00 25.00
40 Chris Mullin/49 15.00 40.00

2013-14 Panini National Treasures NBA Game Gear Dual
PRINT RUNS B/WN 25-99 COPIES PER
*PRIME/25: .75X TO 2.2X BASIC
1 Dwight Howard/99 6.00 15.00
2 James Harden/99 10.00 25.00
3 Joe Dumars/75 6.00 15.00
4 Michael Cooper/99 5.00 12.00
5 LeBron James/99 75.00 200.00
6 Dwyane Wade/99 10.00 25.00
7 DeMarcus Cousins/99 5.00 12.00
8 Kyrie Irving/99 15.00 40.00
9 Dion Waiters/99 3.00 8.00
10 Charles Oakley/75 5.00 12.00
11 Hakeem Olajuwon/49 10.00 25.00
12 Scottie Pippen/75 12.00 30.00
13 Chris Bosh/99 6.00 15.00
14 Udonis Haslem/99 4.00 10.00
15 Bernard King/49 6.00 15.00
16 Bill Cartwright/49 4.00 10.00
17 Marc Gasol/99 5.00 12.00
18 Serge Ibaka/99 4.00 10.00
19 Dominique Wilkins/49 8.00 20.00
20 Tim Duncan/99 12.00 30.00
21 Tony Parker/99 8.00 20.00
22 Brad Daugherty/75 5.00 12.00
23 Mark Price/49 8.00 20.00
24 Magic Johnson/49 20.00 50.00
25 Roy Hibbert/99 3.00 8.00
26 Ray Allen/99 8.00 20.00
27 Norris Cole/99 3.00 8.00
28 Russell Westbrook/99 8.00 20.00
29 DeAndre Jordan/99 4.00 10.00
30 Jared Sullinger/99 3.00 8.00
31 Jeff Green/99 3.00 8.00
32 Monta Ellis/99 4.00 10.00
33 Blake Griffin/99 5.00 12.00
34 Clyde Drexler/49 8.00 20.00
35 Brandon Knight/99 3.00 8.00
36 Larry Johnson/75 6.00 15.00
37 Anfernee Hardaway/75 12.00 30.00
38 Ty Lawson/99 3.00 8.00
39 Kenneth Faried/99 4.00 10.00
40 Larry Bird/49 20.00 50.00
41 Kobe Bryant/99 75.00 200.00
42 Pau Gasol/99 8.00 20.00
43 Patrick Ewing/75 8.00 20.00
44 Alonzo Mourning/75 8.00 20.00
45 Michael Finley/49 5.00 12.00
46 Chris Paul/99 8.00 20.00
47 Brook Lopez/99 5.00 12.00
48 Deron Williams/99 4.00 10.00
49 Gary Payton/49 8.00 20.00
50 Shawn Kemp/75 8.00 20.00
51 Fat Lever/49 4.00 10.00
52 Kareem Abdul-Jabbar/49 15.00 40.00
53 Kevin Love/99 8.00 20.00
54 Ricky Rubio/99 8.00 20.00
55 David Robinson/75 10.00 25.00
56 Kemba Walker/99 5.00 12.00
57 Gordon Hayward/99 8.00 20.00
58 Enes Kanter/99 3.00 8.00
59 Andre Drummond/99 5.00 12.00
60 Greg Monroe/99 3.00 8.00
61 Kevin McHale/75 8.00 20.00
62 Anthony Davis/99 15.00 40.00
63 Dan Majerle/75 4.00 10.00
64 Karl Malone/49 10.00 25.00
65 Walter Berry/99 3.00 8.00
66 Jayson Williams/99 3.00 8.00
67 Elgin Baylor/25 5.00 12.00
68 Jerry West/25 12.00 30.00
69 Dirk Nowitzki/99 12.00 30.00
70 Tyson Chandler/99 4.00 10.00
71 Jason Kidd/49 8.00 20.00
72 Damian Lillard/99 15.00 40.00
73 LaMarcus Aldridge/99 5.00 12.00
74 Paul George/99 8.00 20.00
75 Carmelo Anthony/99 8.00 20.00
76 Taj Gibson/99 3.00 8.00
77 Joakim Noah/99 5.00 12.00
78 John Wall/99 6.00 15.00
79 Bradley Beal/99 8.00 20.00
80 Stephen Curry/99 75.00 200.00
81 Harrison Barnes/99 5.00 12.00
82 James Worthy/49 6.00 15.00
83 Zach Randolph/99 4.00 10.00
84 Kevin Durant/99 15.00 40.00
85 Shaquille O'Neal/75 20.00 50.00

2013-14 Panini National Treasures NBA Game Gear Signatures
PRINT RUNS B/WN 30-75 COPIES PER
EXCHANGE DEADLINE 1/30/2016
*PRIME: .6X TO 1.5X BASIC
1 Paul George/75 100.00 250.00
2 Deron Williams/49 10.00 25.00
3 Kenyon Martin/75 12.00 30.00
4 Harrison Barnes/49 12.00 30.00
5 Ty Lawson/75 8.00 20.00
6 Kobe Bryant/30 3,000.00 6,000.00
7 Jodie Meeks/75 8.00 20.00
8 Andrew Bogut/75 10.00 25.00
9 Kevin Willis/75 10.00 25.00
10 Charles Oakley/75 12.00 30.00
11 Terry Cummings/75 10.00 25.00
12 Derrick Favors/49 8.00 20.00
13 Stephen Curry/49 1,000.00 2,000.00
14 Iman Shumpert/75 8.00 20.00
15 Udonis Haslem/75 10.00 25.00
16 Kyrie Irving/49 100.00 250.00
17 John Stockton/35 75.00 200.00
18 Anfernee Hardaway/49 100.00 250.00
19 Kurt Rambis/75 12.00 30.00
20 Chris Bosh/49 15.00 40.00
21 Robert Horry/75 12.00 30.00
22 Dikembe Mutombo/75 50.00 120.00
23 Steve Blake/75 8.00 20.00
24 Isaiah Thomas/75 10.00 25.00
25 Vince Carter/49 100.00 250.00
26 Kevin Durant/49 125.00 300.00
27 Anthony Mason/75 10.00 25.00
28 Ricky Pierce/75 10.00 25.00
29 Larry Johnson/75 40.00 100.00
30 Chris Mullin/49 15.00 40.00
31 Robert Parish/75 25.00 60.00
32 Enes Kanter/75 10.00 25.00
33 Lance Stephenson/75 10.00 25.00
34 J.J. Redick/75 12.00 30.00
35 Zach Randolph/49 10.00 25.00
36 Glen Rice/75 10.00 25.00
37 Jordan Hill/49 8.00 20.00
38 Avery Johnson/75 10.00 25.00
39 Larry Nance/75 10.00 25.00
40 Clyde Drexler/49 40.00 100.00
41 Amir Johnson/75 8.00 20.00
42 Fred Brown/75 8.00 20.00
43 Taj Gibson/75 8.00 20.00
44 Jack Sikma/75 12.00 30.00
45 Jared Sullinger/75 8.00 20.00
46 Anthony Davis/35 125.00 300.00
47 Josh Smith/75 8.00 20.00
48 Bernard King/49 15.00 40.00
49 Mark Price/75 10.00 25.00
50 Jared Dudley/75 8.00 20.00
51 Roy Hibbert/75 8.00 20.00
52 Gail Goodrich/75 8.00 20.00
53 Tayshaun Prince/49 12.00 30.00
54 Jalen Rose/75 10.00 25.00
55 Steve Mix/49 8.00 20.00
56 Al Horford/49 12.00 30.00
57 Bill Cartwright/75 10.00 25.00
58 Jrue Holiday/49 15.00 40.00
59 Jonas Valanciunas/75 10.00 25.00
60 Dan Majerle/75 10.00 25.00
61 Scottie Pippen/35 150.00 400.00
62 George Hill/75 10.00 25.00
63 Norm Nixon/75 10.00 25.00
64 James Jones/75 8.00 20.00
65 Bradley Beal/49 20.00 50.00
66 Anderson Varejao/75 8.00 20.00
67 Kawhi Leonard/75 100.00 250.00
68 Ersan Ilyasova/75 8.00 20.00
69 Mike Conley/75 12.00 30.00
70 Danilo Gallinari/75 10.00 25.00
71 Serge Ibaka/75 EXCH 10.00 25.00
72 Goran Dragic/75 10.00 25.00
73 Thabo Sefolosha/75 10.00 25.00
74 Jayson Williams/75 8.00 20.00
75 Fat Lever/75 10.00 25.00
76 Andre Drummond/75 10.00 25.00
77 Brook Lopez/49 12.00 30.00
78 Kelly Tripucka/65 10.00 25.00
79 Nick Collison/75 8.00 20.00
80 Danny Granger/49 8.00 20.00
81 Shane Battier/49 10.00 25.00
82 Gordon Hayward/75 12.00 30.00
83 Tom Chambers/75 12.00 30.00
84 Jeff Green/75 8.00 20.00
85 Joe Dumars/75 15.00 40.00
86 Andre Miller/75 8.00 20.00
87 Kemba Walker/75 EXCH 12.00 30.00
88 Buck Williams/49 10.00 25.00
89 Nick Young/75 8.00 20.00
90 Jose Calderon/75 8.00 20.00
91 Shaquille O'Neal/30 125.00 300.00
92 Greg Monroe/75 8.00 20.00
93 Tracy McGrady/49 100.00 250.00
94 Jeff Malone/35 10.00 25.00
95 Tyson Chandler/49 10.00 25.00
96 Andrei Kirilenko/75 12.00 30.00
97 Kenny Walker/75 8.00 20.00
98 Norris Cole/75 8.00 20.00
99 Nando De Colo/75 8.00 20.00
100 Raymond Felton/75 8.00 20.00

2013-14 Panini National Treasures NBA Greats Signatures
PRINT RUNS B/WN 25-49 COPIES PER
EXCHANGE DEADLINE 1/30/2016
*PRIME: .5X TO 1.2X BASIC
1 Bill Sharman/49 10.00 25.00
2 Jerry West/49 25.00 60.00
3 Gail Goodrich/49 8.00 20.00
4 Tony Parker/49 15.00 40.00
5 Joe Dumars/49 10.00 25.00
6 Clyde Drexler/49 12.00 30.00
7 Spencer Haywood/49 8.00 20.00
8 Rolando Blackman/49 6.00 15.00
9 Walt Frazier/49 12.00 30.00
10 Larry Bird/49 50.00 120.00
11 World B. Free/49 6.00 15.00
12 Earl Monroe/49 12.00 30.00
13 Nate Thurmond/49 8.00 20.00
14 Vince Carter/49 12.00 30.00
15 Walt Bellamy/49 8.00 20.00
16 Jason Kidd/49 12.00 30.00
17 Adrian Dantley/49 8.00 20.00
18 John Stockton/49 25.00 60.00
19 Wayne Embry/49 5.00 12.00
20 Karl Malone/49 25.00 60.00
21 Dirk Nowitzki/49 50.00 120.00
22 Kelly Tripucka/49 6.00 15.00
23 Hal Greer/49 6.00 15.00
24 Wes Unseld/49 10.00 25.00
25 Dave Bing/25 15.00 40.00
26 Dennis Rodman/49 25.00 60.00
27 Jack Sikma/49 8.00 20.00
28 Magic Johnson/49 40.00 100.00
29 Allan Houston/49 8.00 20.00
30 Scottie Pippen/49 40.00 100.00
31 Bill Walton/49 12.00 30.00
32 Steve Nash/49 60.00 150.00
33 Ralph Sampson/49 6.00 15.00
34 Anfernee Hardaway/49 12.00 30.00
35 Michael Finley/49 6.00 15.00
36 Ray Allen/49 20.00 50.00
37 Dan Issel/49 10.00 25.00
38 Julius Erving/49 25.00 60.00
39 Jerry Lucas/49 8.00 20.00
40 Kareem Abdul-Jabbar/49 30.00 80.00

2013-14 Panini National Treasures NBA Materials
PRINT RUNS B/WN 45-99 COPIES PER
*PRIME: .75X TO 2X BASIC
1 Bill Laimbeer/45 4.00 10.00
2 Kevin Garnett/99 5.00 12.00
3 Fred Brown/49 3.00 8.00
4 Kyrie Irving/99 6.00 15.00
5 Larry Nance/49 3.00 8.00
6 Paul George/99 6.00 15.00
7 Bradley Beal/99 6.00 15.00
8 Dwyane Wade/99 6.00 15.00
9 Tyson Chandler/99 3.00 8.00
10 Russell Westbrook/99 5.00 12.00
11 Brad Daugherty/99 4.00 10.00
12 Paul Pierce/99 6.00 15.00
13 Fat Lever/49 3.00 8.00
14 Dirk Nowitzki/99 10.00 25.00
15 Louie Dampier/49 2.50 6.00
16 Blake Griffin/99 5.00 12.00
17 Allen Iverson/49 6.00 15.00
18 Kevin Love/99 4.00 10.00
19 Amare Stoudemire/99 4.00 10.00
20 Damian Lillard/99 6.00 15.00
21 John Starks/49 4.00 10.00
22 Monta Ellis/99 3.00 8.00
23 Grant Hill/49 6.00 15.00
24 Kenneth Faried/99 3.00 8.00
25 Manute Bol/75 10.00 25.00
26 Chris Paul/99 5.00 12.00
27 Alonzo Mourning/49 6.00 15.00
28 Ricky Rubio/99 4.00 10.00
29 Raymond Felton/99 2.50 6.00
30 Tim Duncan/99 5.00 12.00
31 Chris Andersen/99 3.00 8.00
32 Stephen Curry/49 15.00 40.00
33 Jeff Malone/49 3.00 8.00
34 James Harden/99 8.00 20.00
35 Serge Ibaka/99 3.00 8.00
36 Kobe Bryant/99 75.00 200.00
37 Larry Johnson/75 5.00 12.00
38 Anfernee Hardaway/75 10.00 25.00
39 Carmelo Anthony/99 6.00 15.00
40 John Wall/99 5.00 12.00
41 Chris Bosh/99 5.00 12.00
42 O.J. Mayo/99 2.50 6.00
43 Klay Thompson/99 12.00 30.00
44 Dwight Howard/99 5.00 12.00
45 Eric Bledsoe/99 5.00 12.00
46 LeBron James/99 12.00 30.00
47 Bill Cartwright/75 3.00 8.00
48 Kevin Durant/99 8.00 20.00
49 Anthony Mason/49 3.00 8.00
50 Al Horford/99 4.00 10.00

2013-14 Panini National Treasures NBA Rookie Materials
STATED PRINT RUN 99 SER.#'d SETS
1 Peyton Siva 2.50 6.00
2 Trey Burke 3.00 8.00
3 Mason Plumlee 3.00 8.00
4 Dennis Schroder 8.00 20.00
5 Tony Mitchell 2.50 6.00
6 Rudy Gobert 10.00 25.00
7 Kentavious Caldwell-Pope 4.00 10.00
8 Ben McLemore 3.00 8.00
9 Isaiah Canaan 2.50 6.00
10 Steven Adams 6.00 15.00
11 Archie Goodwin 2.50 6.00
12 Luigi Datome 2.50 6.00
13 Anthony Bennett 2.50 6.00
14 Kelly Olynyk 3.00 8.00
15 Tim Hardaway Jr. 5.00 12.00
16 Victor Oladipo 6.00 15.00
17 Michael Carter-Williams 3.00 8.00
18 Tony Snell 3.00 8.00
19 Otto Porter 4.00 10.00
20 Giannis Antetokounmpo 150.00 400.00
21 Solomon Hill 3.00 8.00
22 Cody Zeller 3.00 8.00
23 Shane Larkin 2.50 6.00
24 Nate Wolters 2.50 6.00
25 Alex Len 3.00 8.00
26 Shabazz Muhammad 2.50 6.00
27 Nerlens Noel 3.00 8.00
28 Gal Mekel 2.50 6.00
29 Glen Rice Jr. 2.50 6.00
30 C.J. McCollum 10.00 25.00

2013-14 Panini National Treasures NBA Rookie Materials Prime
*PRIME: 1X TO 2.5X BASIC
STATED PRINT RUN 25 SER.#'d SETS

2013-14 Panini National Treasures Night Moves Signature Materials
PRINT RUNS B/WN 49-99 COPIES PER
EXCHANGE DEADLINE 1/30/2016
*GOLD: .6X TO 1.5X BASIC
1 Clyde Drexler/49 20.00 50.00
2 Larry Bird/49 40.00 100.00
3 Danny Green/99 8.00 20.00
4 Robert Parish/49 10.00 25.00
5 Harrison Barnes/99 10.00 25.00
6 Tom Chambers/99 6.00 15.00
7 Andre Drummond/49 20.00 50.00
8 Jason Kidd/49 12.00 30.00
9 Michael Finley/99 6.00 15.00
10 Kawhi Leonard/49 50.00 120.00
11 Toni Kukoc/99 10.00 25.00
12 Larry Johnson/99 10.00 25.00
13 Fat Lever/99 5.00 12.00
14 Roy Hibbert/49 4.00 10.00
15 Iman Shumpert/99 4.00 10.00
16 Tony Parker/49 20.00 50.00
17 Anfernee Hardaway/49 25.00 60.00
18 Thaddeus Young/75 4.00 10.00
19 Raymond Felton/49 4.00 10.00
20 Kevin Durant/49 50.00 120.00
21 Taj Gibson/99 4.00 10.00
22 Larry Nance/99 6.00 15.00
23 Goran Dragic/49 15.00 40.00
24 Scottie Pippen/49 50.00 120.00
25 Isaiah Thomas/99 5.00 12.00
26 Tracy McGrady/49 20.00 50.00
27 Anthony Davis/49 60.00 120.00
28 Joe Dumars/49 8.00 20.00
29 Bob Lanier/49 8.00 20.00
30 Kevin Love/49 15.00 40.00
31 Carmelo Anthony/49 50.00 120.00
32 Mark Price/99 6.00 15.00
33 Grant Hill/49 20.00 50.00
34 Serge Ibaka/99 5.00 12.00
35 James Harden/49 40.00 100.00
36 Tyson Chandler/49 5.00 12.00
37 Josh Smith/49 4.00 10.00
38 Anthony Mason/99 4.00 10.00
39 Bradley Beal/49 12.00 30.00
40 Kobe Bryant/49 1,500.00 3,000.00
41 Dikembe Mutombo/49 10.00 25.00
42 Mike Conley/49 6.00 15.00
43 Greg Monroe/99 4.00 10.00
44 Shaquille O'Neal/49 75.00 200.00
45 James Jones/99 4.00 10.00
46 Bernard King/49 8.00 20.00
47 Udonis Haslem/99 5.00 12.00
48 Julius Erving/49 40.00 100.00
49 Cedric Maxwell/99 5.00 12.00
50 Enes Kanter/99 5.00 12.00
51 Kurt Rambis/99 6.00 15.00
52 Hakeem Olajuwon/49 20.00 50.00
53 Nick Young/99 4.00 10.00
54 Stephen Curry/49 1,000.00 2,000.00
55 Jared Sullinger/49 4.00 10.00
56 Zach Randolph/49 5.00 12.00
58 Kareem Abdul-Jabbar/49 30.00 80.00
59 Chris Mullin/49 10.00 25.00
60 LaMarcus Aldridge/49 20.00 50.00

2013-14 Panini National Treasures Notable Nicknames
STATED PRINT RUN 49 SER.#'d SETS
EXCHANGE DEADLINE 1/30/2016
1 Andre Iguodala 25.00 60.00
2 Dick Van Arsdale 10.00 25.00
3 Fred Brown 15.00 40.00
4 Josh Smith 15.00 40.00
5 Darrell Griffith 40.00 100.00
6 Tracy McGrady 600.00 1,200.00
7 Nick Van Exel 75.00 200.00
8 Andrei Kirilenko 10.00 25.00
9 Billy Paultz 40.00 100.00
10 Danilo Gallinari 8.00 20.00
11 Robert Parish 40.00 100.00
12 Tom Gugliotta 12.00 30.00
13 Isiah Thomas 125.00 300.00
14 Karl Malone 300.00 600.00
15 Jamaal Wilkes 20.00 50.00
16 Zach Randolph 15.00 40.00
17 Vince Carter 200.00 500.00
18 Sam Perkins 30.00 80.00
19 Dan Majerle 30.00 80.00
20 Andrea Bargnani 6.00 15.00
21 Darryl Dawkins 40.00 100.00
22 Steve Francis 25.00 60.00
23 George Gervin 100.00 250.00
24 Earl Monroe 125.00 300.00
25 John Havlicek 300.00 600.00
26 Goran Dragic 20.00 50.00
27 David Robinson 300.00 600.00
28 Hakeem Olajuwon 300.00 600.00
29 Gus Williams 15.00 40.00
30 Dwyane Wade EXCH 150.00 400.00

2013-14 Panini National Treasures Scripts
STATED PRINT RUN 49 SER.#'d SETS
EXCHANGE DEADLINE 1/30/2016
*GOLD: .5X TO 1.2X BASIC
1 Dolph Schayes 8.00 20.00
2 Ryan Anderson 5.00 12.00
3 Horace Grant 8.00 20.00
4 Tony Parker 40.00 100.00
5 Al Horford 8.00 20.00
6 Cazzie Russell 6.00 15.00
7 Dominique Wilkins 25.00 60.00
8 Bob Love 8.00 20.00
9 Clyde Drexler 40.00 100.00
10 Mike Conley 8.00 20.00
11 Donatas Motiejunas 6.00 15.00
12 Scottie Pippen 150.00 400.00
13 James Worthy 25.00 60.00
14 Tyson Chandler 6.00 15.00
15 Amir Johnson 5.00 12.00
16 Dirk Nowitzki 150.00 400.00
17 Brandon Knight 6.00 15.00
18 Kyle Lowry 8.00 20.00
19 Darrell Griffith 6.00 15.00
20 Nick Collison 5.00 12.00
21 Elgin Baylor 15.00 40.00
22 Steve Francis 6.00 15.00
23 Jared Sullinger 5.00 12.00
24 Vince Carter 125.00 300.00
25 Andre Miller 6.00 15.00
26 Kendrick Perkins 5.00 12.00
27 Chase Budinger 5.00 12.00
28 LaMarcus Aldridge 12.00 30.00
29 Dick Van Arsdale 8.00 20.00
30 Pat Riley 20.00 50.00
31 Gail Goodrich 8.00 20.00
32 Steve Mix 5.00 12.00
33 Jason Terry 6.00 15.00
34 Walt Bellamy 6.00 15.00
35 Anthony Davis 100.00 250.00
36 Karl Malone 25.00 60.00
37 Chris Andersen 12.00 30.00
38 Luol Deng 6.00 15.00
39 Dennis Rodman 60.00 150.00
40 Kevin Durant 125.00 300.00
41 Gus Williams 5.00 12.00
42 Theo Ratliff 5.00 12.00
43 John Hot Rod Williams 5.00 12.00
44 Bill Sharman 20.00 50.00
45 Avery Johnson 6.00 15.00
46 Kevin Love 12.00 30.00
47 Chuck Person 6.00 15.00
48 Maurice Harkless 5.00 12.00
49 Derrick Williams 5.00 12.00
50 Rod Strickland 6.00 15.00

2013-14 Panini National Treasures Signatures
PRINT RUNS B/WN 10-99 COPIES PER
NO PRICING ON QTY 10
EXCHANGE DEADLINE 1/30/2016
SIAD Anthony Davis/49 60.00 150.00
SIAD Andre Drummond/35 20.00 50.00
SIAF Al Horford/35 6.00 15.00
SIAG Artis Gilmore/35 8.00 20.00
SIAH Allan Houston/60 6.00 15.00
SIAH Anfernee Hardaway/35 25.00 60.00
SIAJ Avery Johnson/35 5.00 12.00
SIAJ Amir Johnson/60 4.00 10.00
SIAL Andre Miller/60 5.00 12.00
SIBG Bernard King/35 8.00 20.00
SIBK Brandon Knight/35 5.00 12.00
SIBL Bob Lanier/25 8.00 20.00
SIBR Bill Russell/35 1,500.00 3,000.00
SICA Chris Andersen/35 25.00 60.00
SICB Chris Bosh/35 12.00 30.00
SICB Chase Budinger/60 4.00 10.00
SICD Clyde Drexler/35 20.00 50.00
SICP Chuck Person/60 5.00 12.00
SICR Clifford Robinson/60 15.00 40.00
SICS Cazzie Russell/60 5.00 12.00
SICW Chet Walker/60 5.00 12.00
SIDA Dick Van Arsdale/60 6.00 15.00
SIDD Dale Davis/60 5.00 12.00
SIDE Derrick Williams/25 4.00 10.00
SIDF Derrick Favors/35 4.00 10.00
SIDG Darrell Griffith/60 5.00 12.00
SIDH Dwight Howard/49 10.00 25.00
SIDM Donatas Motiejunas/60 5.00 12.00
SIDN Dirk Nowitzki/49 50.00 120.00
SIDN Danny Manning/35 10.00 25.00
SIDR Dennis Rodman/35 25.00 60.00
SIDR David Robinson/25 20.00 50.00
SIDS Dolph Schayes/35 6.00 15.00
SIDW Dominique Wilkins/35 15.00 40.00
SIEB Elgin Baylor/35 12.00 30.00
SIGG Gail Goodrich/35 6.00 15.00
SIGP Gary Payton/35 20.00 50.00
SIGW Gus Williams/60 4.00 10.00
SIHG Hal Greer/35 6.00 15.00
SIHG Horace Grant/60 10.00 25.00
SIJD Jared Dudley/60 4.00 10.00
SIJH John Havlicek/25 30.00 80.00
SIJI Jack Sikma/60 6.00 15.00
SIJJ Jo Jo White/60 5.00 12.00
SIJK Jason Kidd/35 20.00 50.00
SIJM Jodie Meeks/60 4.00 10.00
SIJP John Thompson/35 15.00 40.00
SIJS John Stockton/35 25.00 60.00
SIJS Jared Sullinger/35 4.00 10.00
SIJT Jason Terry/35 5.00 12.00
SIJW James Worthy/35 15.00 40.00
SIJW John Hot Rod Williams/60 4.00 10.00
SIKA Kareem Abdul-Jabbar/49 30.00 80.00
SIKC K.C. Jones/25 20.00 50.00
SIKI Kyrie Irving/49 50.00 120.00
SIKK Kyle Korver/60 5.00 12.00
SIKL Kevin Love/35 12.00 30.00
SIKL Kyle Lowry/60 8.00 20.00
SIKM Kevin Martin/35 5.00 12.00
SIKM Karl Malone/49 30.00 80.00
SIKP Kendrick Perkins/60 4.00 10.00
SIKT Kelly Tripucka/35 5.00 12.00
SILA LaMarcus Aldridge/35 10.00 25.00
SILB Larry Bird/35 30.00 80.00
SILD Luol Deng/35 6.00 15.00
SIMC Mike Conley/60 5.00 12.00
SIMF Michael Finley/35 10.00 25.00
SIMH Maurice Harkless/60 4.00 10.00
SIMJ Magic Johnson/35 30.00 80.00
SINA Nate Archibald/35 8.00 20.00
SINC Nick Collison/60 4.00 10.00
SIOR Oscar Robertson/25 25.00 60.00
SIPJ Phil Jackson/35 100.00 250.00
SIPR Pat Riley/35 10.00 25.00
SIPS Peja Stojakovic/35 10.00 25.00
SIRA Ryan Anderson/60 4.00 10.00
SIRS Ralph Sampson/35 5.00 12.00
SIRS Rod Strickland/60 5.00 12.00
SIRW Rory Sparrow/60 4.00 10.00
SISB Shane Battier/25 5.00 12.00
SISF Steve Francis/35 5.00 12.00
SISK Steve Kerr/35 12.00 30.00
SISM Steve Mix/60 4.00 10.00
SISP Scottie Pippen/49 50.00 120.00
SISW Scott Wedman/60 5.00 12.00
SITC Tyson Chandler/35 5.00 12.00
SITG Taj Gibson/60 4.00 10.00
SITM Tracy McGrady/35 20.00 50.00
SITP Tony Parker/35 15.00 40.00
SITR Theo Ratliff/60 4.00 10.00
SITV Tom Van Arsdale/60 6.00 15.00
SIVB Vin Baker/60 4.00 10.00
SIVC Vince Carter/35 12.00 30.00
SIWB Walter Berry/60 4.00 10.00
SIWF World B. Free/35 5.00 12.00
SIWF Walt Frazier/35 8.00 20.00
SIZI Zydrunas Ilgauskas/60 5.00 12.00
SIZR Zach Randolph/35 5.00 12.00

2013-14 Panini National Treasures Sneaker Swatches
PRINT RUNS B/WN 2-99 COPIES PER
NO PRICIN ON QTY 10 OR LESS
2 Shawn Marion/75 4.00 10.00
3 Kelly Olynyk/60 10.00 25.00
4 Kevin Garnett/75 6.00 15.00
8 Connie Hawkins/40 6.00 15.00
13 Nate Wolters/99 3.00 8.00
14 Gerald Henderson/99 3.00 8.00
15 Steven Adams/75 8.00 20.00
16 Alonzo Mourning/40 20.00 50.00
18 Shaquille O'Neal/99 12.00 30.00
20 Derrick Rose/65 8.00 20.00
21 C.J. McCollum/60 10.00 25.00
24 David Robinson/20 25.00 60.00
25 Shabazz Muhammad/99 3.00 8.00
26 Larry Johnson/40 20.00 50.00
28 Grant Hill/30 12.00 30.00
29 Dirk Nowitzki/99 10.00 25.00
30 Patrick Ewing/99 10.00 25.00
31 Cody Zeller/99 4.00 10.00
33 Tony Snell/75 8.00 20.00
34 Carmelo Anthony/95 10.00 25.00

2013-14 Panini National Treasures Sneaker Swatches Autographs
PRINT RUNS B/WN 30-60 COPIES PER
EXCHANGE DEADLINE 1/30/2016
1 Jimmer Fredette/49 12.00 30.00
2 Kobe Bryant/39 3,000.00 6,000.00
3 Vince Carter/60 30.00 80.00
4 Ben McLemore/49 10.00 25.00
5 Victor Oladipo/60 60.00 150.00
6 Steven Adams/60 20.00 50.00
7 John Stockton/55 40.00 100.00
8 Shaquille O'Neal/60 125.00 300.00
9 Larry Johnson/60 20.00 50.00
10 Anfernee Hardaway/30 60.00 150.00
11 Deron Williams/49 10.00 25.00
12 Kyrie Irving/49 100.00 200.00
13 Kevin Durant/60 150.00 300.00
14 C.J. McCollum/60 25.00 60.00
15 Tony Snell/60 10.00 25.00
16 Nerlens Noel/60 30.00 80.00
17 Alonzo Mourning/60 30.00 80.00
18 Connie Hawkins/60 15.00 40.00
19 Grant Hill/60 50.00 120.00
20 Jason Kidd/60 30.00 80.00
21 David Robinson/60 50.00 120.00
22 Blake Griffin/60 30.00 80.00
23 Anthony Bennett/49 8.00 20.00
24 Kelly Olynyk/60 10.00 25.00
25 Tim Hardaway Jr./49 30.00 80.00

2013-14 Panini National Treasures Spanning Time Dual Signatures
STATED PRINT RUN 49 SER.#'d SETS
EXCHANGE DEADLINE 1/30/2016
1 D.Williams/J.Kidd 20.00 50.00
2 C.Mullin/H.Barnes 12.00 30.00
3 C.Robinson/L.Aldridge 10.00 25.00
4 M.Daniels/R.Hibbert 10.00 25.00
5 Irving/Price EXCH 90.00 150.00
6 J.West/K.Bryant 1,500.00 3,000.00
7 S.Curry/T.Hardaway 400.00 800.00
8 D.Howard/H.Olajuwon 40.00 80.00
9 A.Mourning/A.Davis 75.00 150.00
10 J.Harden/T.McGrady 30.00 80.00

2013-14 Panini National Treasures Springfield Swatches
PRINT RUNS B/WN 15-99 COPIES PER
*PRIME: .75X TO 2X BASIC
1 Wilt Chamberlain/15 40.00 100.00
2 Scottie Pippen/99 6.00 15.00
3 Isiah Thomas/49 8.00 20.00
4 James Worthy/49 6.00 15.00
5 Adrian Dantley/25 5.00 12.00
6 Kareem Abdul-Jabbar/49 6.00 15.00
7 Julius Erving/49 10.00 25.00
8 Dennis Johnson/49 4.00 10.00
9 Bob Lanier/99 6.00 15.00
10 Pete Maravich/49 25.00 60.00
11 Hakeem Olajuwon/75 10.00 25.00
12 David Robinson/49 6.00 15.00
13 Nate Thurmond/25 8.00 20.00
14 Jamaal Wilkes/49 4.00 10.00
15 Rick Barry/25 6.00 15.00
16 Clyde Drexler/99 8.00 20.00
17 Patrick Ewing/99 8.00 20.00
18 Magic Johnson/49 10.00 25.00
19 Jerry Lucas/25 12.00 30.00
20 Kevin McHale/75 8.00 20.00
21 Dennis Rodman/49 6.00 15.00
22 Robert Parish/49 6.00 15.00
23 Jerry West/25 20.00 50.00
24 Earl Monroe/49 10.00 25.00
25 Elgin Baylor/25 6.00 15.00
26 Joe Dumars/99 6.00 15.00
27 John Havlicek/99 12.00 30.00
28 Bernard King/75 6.00 15.00
29 Karl Malone/49 6.00 15.00
30 George Mikan/49 12.00 30.00
31 Gary Payton/49 8.00 20.00
32 John Stockton/49 6.00 15.00
33 Dominique Wilkins/49 8.00 20.00
34 Arvydas Sabonis/99 6.00 15.00
35 Larry Bird/49 20.00 50.00
36 Alex English/49 6.00 15.00
37 Bailey Howell/49 6.00 15.00
38 Moses Malone/75 8.00 20.00
39 Sam Jones/49 10.00 25.00
40 Chris Mullin/75 6.00 15.00

2013-14 Panini National Treasures Timelines Materials
PRINT RUNS B/WN 49-99 COPIES PER
1 Kobe Bryant/99 100.00 250.00
2 John Stockton/49 10.00 25.00
3 Kevin Love/99 5.00 12.00
4 Karl Malone/49 10.00 25.00
5 Kyrie Irving/99 15.00 40.00
6 Kevin Durant/99 15.00 40.00
7 Dwight Howard/49 6.00 15.00
8 Tim Duncan/49 12.00 30.00

9 Blake Griffin/75 5.00 12.00
10 Ricky Pierce/49 4.00 10.00
11 LeBron James/99 100.00 250.00
12 Tyson Chandler/99 4.00 10.00
13 Ricky Rubio/99 4.00 10.00
14 Tony Parker/49 8.00 20.00
15 Dirk Nowitzki/99 12.00 30.00
16 Russell Westbrook/49 8.00 20.00
17 Paul George/99 8.00 20.00
18 John Wall/99 6.00 15.00
19 Chris Paul/75 10.00 25.00
20 Norm Nixon/49 4.00 10.00
21 Dwyane Wade/99 10.00 25.00
22 Danny Ainge/49 5.00 12.00
23 Carmelo Anthony/75 8.00 20.00
24 Doc Rivers/99 4.00 10.00
25 Kenneth Faried/99 4.00 10.00
26 Damian Lillard/75 15.00 40.00
27 James Harden/99 10.00 25.00
28 Terry Cummings/49 4.00 10.00
29 Shaquille O'Neal/99 20.00 50.00
30 Brad Daugherty/49 5.00 12.00
31 Larry Bird/49 20.00 50.00
32 Magic Johnson/49 20.00 50.00
33 Patrick Ewing/99 8.00 20.00
34 Dikembe Mutombo/99 8.00 20.00
35 Hakeem Olajuwon/49 10.00 25.00
36 Fred Brown/99 4.00 10.00
37 Anthony Davis/99 15.00 40.00
38 Dan Majerle/99 4.00 10.00
39 Mark Price/49 5.00 12.00
40 Xavier McDaniel/99 4.00 10.00

2013-14 Panini National Treasures Timelines Materials Prime

*PRIME: .75X TO 2X BASIC
PRINT RUNS B/WN 10-25 COPIES PER
NO PRICING ON QTY 10
6 Kevin Durant/25 30.00 80.00
11 LeBron James/25 75.00 150.00

2013-14 Panini National Treasures X-Factor Materials

STATED PRINT RUN 99 SER.#'d SETS
*PRIME: .75X TO 2X BASIC
1 James Harden/99 12.00 30.00
2 Mark Jackson/75 4.00 10.00
3 Hakeem Olajuwon/49 15.00 40.00
4 Karl Malone/49 12.00 30.00
5 Jason Kidd/49 12.00 30.00
6 Kevin Garnett/99 20.00 50.00
7 Steve Nash/99 15.00 40.00
8 David Robinson/99 15.00 40.00
9 Pau Gasol/99 10.00 25.00
10 Kyrie Irving/99 15.00 40.00
11 Allen Iverson/49 20.00 50.00
12 LeBron James/75 100.00 250.00
13 Joe Dumars/99 6.00 15.00
14 Kevin Love/99 5.00 12.00
15 Clyde Drexler/99 12.00 30.00
16 Shaquille O'Neal/49 40.00 100.00
17 Patrick Ewing/99 12.00 30.00
18 Kobe Bryant/99 100.00 250.00
19 Dwyane Wade/99 15.00 40.00
20 Anthony Davis/99 20.00 50.00
21 Kareem Abdul-Jabbar/49 40.00 100.00
22 Larry Bird/49 40.00 100.00
23 Magic Johnson/49 40.00 100.00
24 Tim Duncan/99 20.00 50.00
25 Xavier McDaniel/49 4.00 10.00
26 Dirk Nowitzki/99 20.00 50.00
27 Dominique Wilkins/75 12.00 30.00
28 Kevin Durant/99 15.00 40.00
29 Dwight Howard/99 8.00 20.00
30 Blake Griffin/99 8.00 20.00

2014-15 Panini National Treasures

1-100 PRINT RUN 99 SER.#'d SETS
JSY AU RC p/r B/WN 49-99 COPIES PER
134-186 PRINT RUNS 99 SER.#'d SETS
PRIME PATCHES MAY SELL FOR PREMIUM
EXCHANGE DEADLINE 2/5/2017
1 Arron Afflalo 1.25 3.00
2 LaMarcus Aldridge 2.00 5.00
3 Ryan Anderson 1.25 3.00
4 Giannis Antetokounmpo 12.00 30.00
5 Carmelo Anthony 3.00 8.00
6 Bradley Beal 3.00 8.00
7 Patrick Beverley 1.25 3.00
8 Eric Bledsoe 1.50 4.00
9 Carlos Boozer 1.50 4.00
10 Chris Bosh 2.50 6.00
11 Avery Bradley 1.25 3.00
12 Kobe Bryant 100.00 250.00
13 Trey Burke 1.25 3.00
14 Jimmy Butler 3.00 8.00
15 Michael Carter-Williams 1.25 3.00
16 Darren Collison 1.25 3.00
17 Mike Conley 1.50 4.00
18 DeMarcus Cousins 1.50 4.00
19 Stephen Curry 100.00 250.00
20 Anthony Davis 5.00 12.00
21 Luol Deng 1.50 4.00
22 DeMar DeRozan 2.50 6.00
23 Goran Dragic 2.00 5.00
24 Andre Drummond 1.50 4.00
25 Tim Duncan 5.00 12.00
26 Kevin Durant 6.00 15.00
27 Monta Ellis 1.50 4.00
28 Tyreke Evans 1.50 4.00
29 Derrick Favors 1.25 3.00
30 Marc Gasol 2.00 5.00
31 Pau Gasol 3.00 8.00
32 Rudy Gay 2.00 5.00
33 Marcin Gortat 1.25 3.00
34 Draymond Green 2.50 6.00
35 Blake Griffin 2.00 5.00
36 Tim Hardaway Jr. 1.50 4.00
37 James Harden 4.00 10.00
38 Tobias Harris 1.50 4.00
39 Gordon Hayward 1.50 4.00
40 Roy Hibbert 1.50 4.00
41 Jordan Hill 1.25 3.00
42 Jrue Holiday 2.50 6.00
43 Al Horford 2.00 5.00
44 Dwight Howard 2.50 6.00
45 Serge Ibaka 1.50 4.00
46 Andre Iguodala 2.00 5.00
47 Kyrie Irving 4.00 10.00
48 LeBron James 100.00 250.00
49 Al Jefferson 1.25 3.00
50 Brandon Jennings 1.25 3.00
51 Joe Johnson 1.50 4.00
52 Brandon Knight 1.25 3.00
53 Ty Lawson 1.25 3.00
54 Kawhi Leonard 5.00 12.00
55 Damian Lillard 5.00 12.00
56 Brook Lopez 2.00 5.00
57 Kevin Love 2.00 5.00
58 Kyle Lowry 2.50 6.00
59 Wesley Matthews 1.25 3.00
60 O.J. Mayo 1.25 3.00
61 Paul Millsap 1.50 4.00
62 Markieff Morris 1.25 3.00
63 Shabazz Muhammad 1.25 3.00
64 Joakim Noah 2.00 5.00
65 Dirk Nowitzki 5.00 12.00
66 Victor Oladipo 1.50 4.00
67 Tony Parker 3.00 8.00
68 Chris Paul 3.00 8.00
69 Paul Pierce 3.00 8.00
70 Zach Randolph 2.00 5.00
71 J.J. Redick 2.00 5.00
72 Rajon Rondo 2.50 6.00
73 Derrick Rose 4.00 10.00
74 Dennis Schroder 2.00 5.00
75 Luis Scola 1.50 4.00
76 Amar'e Stoudemire 2.00 5.00
77 Jared Sullinger 1.25 3.00
78 Jeff Teague 1.25 3.00
79 Klay Thompson 5.00 12.00
80 Jonas Valanciunas 1.50 4.00
81 Nikola Vucevic 1.50 4.00
82 Dwyane Wade 4.00 10.00
83 Kemba Walker 2.00 5.00
84 John Wall 2.50 6.00
85 Russell Westbrook 3.00 8.00
86 Deron Williams 1.50 4.00
87 Lou Williams 1.50 4.00
88 Tony Wroten 1.25 3.00
89 Thaddeus Young 1.25 3.00
90 Bill Russell 6.00 15.00
91 Jerry West 5.00 12.00
92 Kareem Abdul-Jabbar 6.00 15.00
93 Scottie Pippen 5.00 12.00
94 Pete Maravich 6.00 15.00
95 Wilt Chamberlain 6.00 15.00
96 Karl Malone 4.00 10.00
97 Larry Bird 8.00 20.00
98 Magic Johnson 8.00 20.00
99 Oscar Robertson 4.00 10.00
100 Shaquille O'Neal 8.00 20.00
101 A.Wiggins JSY AU/99 RC 400.00 800.00
102 J.Parker JSY AU/99 RC 15.00 40.00
103 J.Embiid JSY AU/99 RC 3,000.00 6,000.00
104 A.Gordon JSY AU/99 RC 300.00 600.00
105 D.Exum JSY AU/99 RC 20.00 50.00
106 M.Smart JSY AU/99 RC 150.00 400.00
107 J.Randle JSY AU/99 RC 150.00 400.00
108 N.Stauskas JSY AU/99 RC 12.00 30.00
109 N.Vonleh JSY AU/99 RC 12.00 30.00
110 E.Payton JSY AU/99 RC 20.00 50.00
111 D.McDermott JSY AU/99 RC 20.00 50.00
112 Z.LaVine JSY AU/99 RC 1,200.00 2,500.00
113 T. Warren JSY AU/99 RC 20.00 50.00
114 A.Payne JSY AU/99 RC 12.00 30.00
115 J.Young JSY AU/99 RC 12.00 30.00
116 Tyler Ennis JSY AU/99 RC 12.00 30.00
117 Gary Harris JSY AU/99 RC 20.00 50.00
118 B.Caboclo JSY AU/99 RC 15.00 40.00
119 M.McGary JSY AU/99 RC 12.00 30.00
120 J.Adams JSY AU/99 RC 12.00 30.00
121 R.Hood JSY AU/99 RC 15.00 40.00
122 S.Napier JSY AU/99 RC 15.00 40.00
123 P.Hairston JSY AU/99 RC 12.00 30.00
124 N.Mirotic JSY AU/49 RC 20.00 50.00
125 K.Anderson JSY AU/99 RC 20.00 50.00
126 D.Inglis JSY AU/99 RC 12.00 30.00
127 K.McDaniels JSY AU/99 RC 12.00 30.00
128 Joe Harris JSY AU/99 RC 40.00 100.00
129 C.Early JSY AU/99 RC 12.00 30.00
130 L.Galloway JSY AU/49 RC 20.00 50.00
131 J.O'Bryant JSY AU/99 RC 12.00 30.00
132 S.Dinwiddie JSY AU/99 RC 20.00 50.00
133 T. Wear JSY AU/49 RC 12.00 30.00
134 B.Bogdanovic AU RC 15.00 40.00
135 Jusuf Nurkic AU RC 40.00 100.00
136 J.Michael McAdoo AU RC 4.00 10.00
137 K.Papanikolaou AU RC 4.00 10.00
138 Jordan Clarkson AU RC 50.00 120.00
139 Tarik Black AU RC 4.00 10.00
140 Erick Green AU RC 4.00 10.00
141 Markel Brown AU RC 4.00 10.00
142 Dwight Powell AU RC 25.00 60.00
143 C.J. Wilcox AU RC 4.00 10.00
144 Damjan Rudez AU RC 4.00 10.00
145 Cory Jefferson AU RC 4.00 10.00
146 Jarnell Stokes AU RC 4.00 10.00
147 James Ennis AU RC 4.00 10.00
148 Glenn Robinson III AU RC 5.00 12.00
149 Devyn Marble AU RC 4.00 10.00
150 Lucas Nogueira AU RC 4.00 10.00
151 Andrew Wiggins AU 75.00 200.00
152 Jabari Parker AU 5.00 12.00
153 Joel Embiid AU 200.00 500.00
154 Aaron Gordon AU 40.00 100.00
155 Marcus Smart AU 40.00 100.00
156 Julius Randle AU 40.00 100.00
157 Nik Stauskas AU 4.00 10.00
158 Noah Vonleh AU 4.00 10.00
159 Elfrid Payton AU 6.00 15.00
160 D.McDermott AU 6.00 15.00
161 Zach LaVine AU 125.00 300.00
162 T.J. Warren AU 6.00 15.00
163 Adreian Payne AU 4.00 10.00
164 James Young AU 4.00 10.00
165 Tyler Ennis AU 4.00 10.00
166 Gary Harris AU 6.00 15.00
167 Mitch McGary AU 4.00 10.00
168 Jordan Adams AU 4.00 10.00
169 Rodney Hood AU 5.00 12.00
170 Shabazz Napier AU 5.00 12.00
171 P.J. Hairston AU 4.00 10.00
172 C.J. Wilcox AU 4.00 10.00
173 Kyle Anderson AU 6.00 15.00
174 J.Michael McAdoo AU 4.00 10.00
176 Cleanthony Early AU 4.00 10.00
177 Jarnell Stokes AU 4.00 10.00
178 Johnny O'Bryant AU 4.00 10.00
179 Tarik Black AU 4.00 10.00
180 Spencer Dinwiddie AU 6.00 15.00
181 Jerami Grant AU 20.00 50.00
182 Glenn Robinson III AU 5.00 12.00
183 Markel Brown AU 4.00 10.00
184 Dwight Powell AU 25.00 60.00
185 Jordan Clarkson AU 50.00 120.00
186 Russ Smith AU 4.00 10.00

2014-15 Panini National Treasures Blue

*BLUE: .5X TO 1.2X BASIC
STATED PRINT RUN 25 SER.#'d SETS

2014-15 Panini National Treasures Gold

1-100 PRINT RUN 10 SER.#'d SETS
NO PRICING ON 1-100 AVAILABLE
*GOLD 101-133: .6X TO 1.5X BASIC
*GOLD 134-150: .5X TO 1.2X BASIC
101-186 PRINT RUN 25 SER.#'d SETS
EXCHANGE DEADLINE 2/5/2017
104 Aaron Gordon JSY AU 400.00 800.00
185 Jordan Clarkson AU 60.00 150.00

2014-15 Panini National Treasures Air Apparent Jersey Autographs

PRINT RUNS B/WN 25-49 COPIES PER
EXCHANGE DEADLINE 2/5/2017
AAAB Anthony Bennett/49 5.00 12.00
AAAD Anthony Davis/25 75.00 200.00
AAAG Aaron Gordon/49 25.00 60.00
AAAL Alex Len/49 5.00 12.00
AAAW Andrew Wiggins/35 25.00 60.00
AABB Bradley Beal/49 12.00 30.00
AABK Brandon Knight/49 5.00 12.00
AABM Ben McLemore/49 5.00 12.00
AACE Cleanthony Early/49 5.00 12.00
AACJ Cory Jefferson/49 5.00 12.00
AACM C.J. McCollum/49 8.00 20.00
AACZ Cody Zeller/49 5.00 12.00
AADI Damien Inglis/49 5.00 12.00
AADM Donatas Motiejunas/49 5.00 12.00
AAGA G. Antetokounmpo/49 500.00 1,000.00
AAGR Glenn Robinson III/49 6.00 15.00
AAHB Harrison Barnes/49 6.00 15.00
AAJA Jordan Adams/49 5.00 12.00
AAJE Joel Embiid/49 125.00 300.00
AAJG Jerami Grant/49 25.00 60.00
AAJO Johnny O'Bryant/49 5.00 12.00
AAJP Jabari Parker/35 6.00 15.00
AAJR Julius Randle/49 25.00 60.00
AAJS Jarnell Stokes/49 5.00 12.00
AAJV Jonas Valanciunas/35 6.00 15.00
AAJW John Wall/25 10.00 25.00
AAJY James Young/49 5.00 12.00
AAKA Kyle Anderson/49 8.00 20.00
AAKC Kentavious Caldwell-Pope/49 6.00 15.00
AAKI Kyrie Irving/25 75.00 200.00
AAKM K.J. McDaniels/49 5.00 12.00
AALS Lance Stephenson/49 6.00 15.00
AAMC Michael Carter-Williams/49 5.00 12.00
AAMP Mason Plumlee/49 5.00 12.00
AAMS Marcus Smart/49 20.00 50.00
AANN Nerlens Noel/49 5.00 12.00
AANS Nik Stauskas/49 5.00 12.00
AANV Noah Vonleh/49 5.00 12.00
AAOP Otto Porter/49 6.00 15.00
AAPG Paul George/25 60.00 150.00
AARJ Reggie Jackson/49 6.00 15.00
AASD Spencer Dinwiddie/49 8.00 20.00
AASH Solomon Hill/49 5.00 12.00
AASM Shabazz Muhammad/49 5.00 12.00
AATB Trey Burke/49 5.00 12.00
AATH Tim Hardaway Jr./49 6.00 15.00
AATT Tristan Thompson/49 5.00 12.00
AATW T.J. Warren/49 8.00 20.00
AAVO Victor Oladipo/49 6.00 15.00
AAJEN James Ennis/49 5.00 12.00

2014-15 Panini National Treasures Air Apparent Jersey Autographs Prime

*PRIME/25: .6X TO 1.5X
PRINT RUNS B/WN 10-25 COPIES PER
NO PRICING ON QTY 10
EXCHANGE DEADLINE 2/5/2017

2014-15 Panini National Treasures Career Materials Trios

PRINT RUNS B/WN 35-99 COPIES PER
*PRIME: .75X TO 2X BASIC
CMTAJ Al Jefferson/49 2.50 6.00
CMTAM Alonzo Mourning/99 6.00 15.00
CMTCM Cedric Maxwell/35 3.00 8.00
CMTDC Darren Collison/99 2.50 6.00
CMTDH Dwight Howard/99 5.00 12.00
CMTDM Dikembe Mutombo/40 6.00 15.00
CMTDW Dominique Wilkins/99 6.00 15.00
CMTEG Eric Gordon/99 3.00 8.00
CMTJC Jose Calderon/99 2.50 6.00
CMTJF Jimmer Fredette/99 3.00 8.00
CMTJK Jason Kidd/99 6.00 15.00
CMTKG Kevin Garnett/99 10.00 25.00
CMTLS Luis Scola/99 3.00 8.00
CMTPP Paul Pierce/99 6.00 15.00
CMTRG Rudy Gay/99 4.00 10.00

2014-15 Panini National Treasures Clutch Factor Jersey Autographs

PRINT RUNS B/WN 24-75 COPIES PER
EXCHANGE DEADLINE 2/5/2017
CFAD Adrian Dantley/75 8.00 20.00
CFBK Bernard King/35 10.00 25.00
CFBL Bill Laimbeer/75 20.00 50.00
CFCA Chris Andersen/49 20.00 50.00
CFCB Chris Bosh/35 40.00 100.00
CFCD Clyde Drexler/25 60.00 150.00
CFCM Cedric Maxwell/75 6.00 15.00
CFDG Danny Green/75 6.00 15.00
CFDW Dominique Wilkins/49 60.00 150.00
CFEM Earl Monroe/49 20.00 50.00
CFGA G. Antetokounmpo/75 600.00 1,200.00
CFJD Joe Dumars/49 15.00 40.00
CFJE Julius Erving/35 125.00 300.00
CFJW Jerry West/35 75.00 200.00
CFJWO James Worthy/49 40.00 100.00
CFKA Kareem Abdul-Jabbar/24 150.00 400.00
CFKB Kobe Bryant/35 2,500.00 5,000.00
CFKD Kevin Durant/35 200.00 500.00
CFKI Kyrie Irving/35 75.00 200.00
CFKK Kyle Korver/75 12.00 30.00
CFLB Larry Bird/35 150.00 400.00
CFMA Mark Aguirre/75 6.00 15.00
CFRH Robert Horry/75 30.00 80.00
CFRP Robert Parish/49 20.00 50.00
CFSC Stephen Curry/49 1,500.00 3,000.00
CFSE Sean Elliott/75 8.00 20.00
CFTP Tony Parker/49 12.00 30.00

2014-15 Panini National Treasures Clutch Factor Jersey Autographs Prime

*PRIME: .6X TO 1.5X
PRINT RUNS B/WN 5-25 COPIES PER
NO PRICING ON QTY 10 OR LESS
EXCHANGE DEADLINE 2/5/2017
CFKL Kawhi Leonard/25 400.00 800.00

2014-15 Panini National Treasures Colossal Jerseys

STATED PRINT RUN 99 SER.#'d SETS
1 LeBron James 150.00 400.00
2 Kobe Bryant 150.00 400.00
3 Kevin Durant 75.00 200.00
4 Damian Lillard 40.00 100.00
5 Derrick Rose 40.00 100.00
6 Kyrie Irving 20.00 50.00
7 Blake Griffin 5.00 12.00
8 Carmelo Anthony 12.00 30.00
9 Tim Duncan 15.00 40.00
10 John Wall 6.00 15.00
11 Anthony Davis 40.00 100.00
12 Stephen Curry 150.00 400.00
13 Pau Gasol 10.00 25.00
14 James Harden 20.00 50.00
15 Dwyane Wade 20.00 50.00
16 Russell Westbrook 15.00 40.00
17 Marc Gasol 5.00 12.00
18 Kyle Lowry 12.00 30.00
19 Jeff Teague 3.00 8.00
20 Klay Thompson 40.00 100.00
21 Larry Bird 75.00 200.00
22 Karl Malone 40.00 100.00
23 Shaquille O'Neal 75.00 200.00
24 Patrick Ewing 20.00 50.00
25 Hakeem Olajuwon 10.00 25.00

2014-15 Panini National Treasures Colossal Jerseys Signatures

PRINT RUNS B/WN 25-49 COPIES PER
CJSAE Alex English/49 12.00 30.00
CJSAW Antoine Walker/49 8.00 20.00
CJSCD Clyde Drexler/25 60.00 150.00
CJSCM Cedric Maxwell/49 8.00 20.00
CJSCR Clifford Robinson/49 8.00 20.00
CJSDR David Robinson/35 60.00 150.00
CJSEK Enes Kanter/49 8.00 20.00
CJSGR Glen Rice/49 10.00 25.00
CJSHO Hakeem Olajuwon/35 60.00 150.00
CJSJD Joe Dumars/35 12.00 30.00
CJSJE Julius Erving/35 150.00 400.00
CJSJW James Worthy/35 40.00 100.00
CJSKB Kobe Bryant/49 2,000.00 4,000.00
CJSKD Kevin Durant/25 200.00 500.00
CJSKL Kevin Love/35 15.00 40.00
CJSLB Larry Bird/25 200.00 500.00
CJSSC Stephen Curry/35 1,000.00 2,000.00
CJSTH Tim Hardaway/49 12.00 30.00
CJSVC Vince Carter/35 125.00 300.00
CJSZR Zach Randolph/35 15.00 40.00

2014-15 Panini National Treasures Colossal Jerseys Signatures Prime

*PRIME: .75X TO 2X BASIC
PRINT RUNS B/WN 5-25 COPIES PER
NO PRICING ON QTY 10 OR LESS

2014-15 Panini National Treasures Game Changers Autographs

PRINT RUNS B/WN 25-49 COPIES PER
EXCHANGE DEADLINE 2/5/2017
*GOLD: .5X TO 1.2X BASIC p/r 35-49
*GOLD: .4X TO 1X BASIC p/r 25
GCAE Alex English/49 10.00 25.00
GCBK Bernard King/35 10.00 25.00
GCCA Carmelo Anthony/25 100.00 250.00
GCCP Chris Paul/25 200.00 500.00
GCDI Dan Issel/49 10.00 25.00
GCDW Dominique Wilkins/35 60.00 150.00
GCJE Julius Erving/25 125.00 300.00
GCJK Jason Kidd/35 60.00 150.00
GCJW John Wall/35 40.00 100.00
GCKB Kobe Bryant/25 3,000.00 6,000.00
GCKD Kevin Durant/25 200.00 500.00
GCKI Kyrie Irving/35 100.00 250.00
GCKL Kevin Love/35 12.00 30.00
GCKW Kawhi Leonard/35 200.00 500.00
GCLB Larry Bird/25 200.00 500.00
GCLS Latrell Sprewell/35 40.00 100.00
GCMA Mark Aguirre/49 6.00 15.00
GCTC Tyson Chandler/35 15.00 40.00
GCTH Tim Hardaway/49 15.00 40.00
GCWF Walt Frazier/35 40.00 100.00

2014-15 Panini National Treasures Gold Logoman Signatures

STATED PRINT RUN 49 SER.#'d SETS
EXCHANGE DEADLINE 2/5/2017
GLAD Adrian Dantley/49 10.00 25.00
GLAE Alex English/49 15.00 40.00
GLAG Artis Gilmore/49 15.00 40.00
GLAM Alonzo Mourning/49 75.00 200.00
GLAW Antoine Walker/49 10.00 25.00
GLBK Bernard King/49 25.00 60.00
GLBL Bill Laimbeer/49 25.00 60.00
GLCA Chris Andersen/49 20.00 50.00
GLCA Carmelo Anthony/49 75.00 200.00
GLCB Chris Bosh/49 60.00 150.00
GLCD Clyde Drexler/49 75.00 200.00
GLCH Cliff Hagan/49 10.00 25.00
GLDF Derrick Favors/49 6.00 15.00
GLDI Dan Issel/49 12.00 30.00
GLDM Dikembe Mutombo/49 75.00 200.00
GLDW Dominique Wilkins/49 60.00 150.00
GLEK Enes Kanter/49 8.00 20.00
GLGA Giannis Antetokounmpo/49 1,000.00 2,000.00
GLGB Larry Bird/49 10.00 25.00
GLGG George Gervin/49 25.00 60.00
GLGH Gordon Hayward/49 25.00 60.00
GLGH Grant Hill/49 75.00 200.00
GLGP Gary Payton/49 60.00 150.00
GLHW Hakeem Olajuwon/49 75.00 200.00
GLIT Isiah Thomas/49 75.00 200.00
GLJE Julius Erving/49 125.00 300.00
GLJK Jason Kidd/49 60.00 150.00
GLJS John Stockton/49 75.00 200.00
GLJW James Worthy/49 40.00 100.00
GLJW John Wall/49 40.00 100.00
GLKB Kobe Bryant/49 2,000.00 4,000.00
GLKD` 200.00 500.00
GLKI Kyrie Irving/49 75.00 200.00
GLKK Kyle Korver/49 12.00 30.00
GLKL Kawhi Leonard/49 200.00 500.00
GLKLV Kevin Love/49 25.00 60.00
GLKM Karl Malone/49 75.00 200.00
GLKM Kevin McHale/49 75.00 200.00
GLLA LaMarcus Aldridge/49 20.00 50.00
GLLB Larry Bird/49 150.00 400.00
GLLS Latrell Sprewell/49 40.00 100.00
GLLS Lance Stephenson/49 20.00 50.00
GLMF Michael Finley/49 20.00 50.00
GLMG Marcin Gortat/49 6.00 15.00
GLMJ Magic Johnson/49 150.00 400.00
GLMP Mark Price/49 20.00 50.00
GLMT Mychal Thompson/49 8.00 20.00
GLPG Pau Gasol/49 75.00 200.00
GLRB Rolando Blackman/49 8.00 20.00
GLRB Rick Barry/49 30.00 80.00
GLRR Ricky Rubio/49 30.00 80.00
GLRS Rony Seikaly/49 8.00 20.00
GLRT Rudy Tomjanovich/49 10.00 25.00
GLRW Russell Westbrook/49 60.00 150.00
GLSC Stephen Curry/49 1,000.00 2,000.00
GLSO Shaquille O'Neal/49 150.00 400.00
GLTG Taj Gibson/49 6.00 15.00
GLTG Tom Gugliotta/49 6.00 15.00
GLTM Tracy McGrady/49 125.00 300.00
GLTY Thaddeus Young/49 6.00 15.00
GLVC Vince Carter/49 150.00 400.00
GLVD Vlade Divac/49 20.00 50.00
GLWF Walt Frazier/49 40.00 100.00
GLXM Xavier McDaniel/49 8.00 20.00
GLZI Zydrunas Ilgauskas/49 8.00 20.00
GLZR Zach Randolph/49 20.00 50.00

2014-15 Panini National Treasures Kobe's All-Rookie Team Selections Signature Materials

STATED PRINT RUN 99 SER.#'d SETS
EXCHANGE DEADLINE 2/5/2017
KOBEAG Aaron Gordon 15.00 40.00
KOBEAW Andrew Wiggins 75.00 200.00
KOBEDE Dante Exum 5.00 12.00
KOBEDM Doug McDermott 5.00 12.00
KOBEEP Elfrid Payton 5.00 12.00
KOBEGH Gary Harris 5.00 12.00
KOBEJH Joe Harris 5.00 12.00
KOBEJP Jabari Parker 4.00 10.00
KOBEJY James Young 3.00 8.00
KOBEKM K.J. McDaniels 3.00 8.00
KOBEMS Marcus Smart 40.00 100.00
KOBEPH P.J. Hairston 3.00 8.00
KOBERH Rodney Hood 4.00 10.00
KOBESN Shabazz Napier 4.00 10.00
KOBEZL Zach LaVine 100.00 250.00

2014-15 Panini National Treasures Kobe's All-Rookie Team Selections Signature Materials Prime

*PRIME: .75X TO 2X
STATED PRINT RUN 25 SER.#'d SETS
EXCHANGE DEADLINE 2/5/2017

2014-15 Panini National Treasures Lasting Legacies Jersey Autographs

PRINT RUNS B/WN 24-75 COPIES PER
EXCHANGE DEADLINE 2/5/2017
*PRIME: .75X TO 2X BASIC
LLAD Adrian Dantley/49 10.00 25.00
LLAI Allen Iverson/25 75.00 200.00
LLBK Bernard King/35 12.00 30.00
LLCD Clyde Drexler/25 30.00 80.00
LLCM Chris Mullin/35 12.00 30.00
LLDR David Robinson/25 30.00 80.00
LLDW Dominique Wilkins/35 25.00 60.00
LLEB Elgin Baylor/35 20.00 50.00
LLEM Earl Monroe/25 15.00 40.00
LLGH Grant Hill/35 15.00 40.00
LLGP Gary Payton/35 15.00 40.00
LLHO Hakeem Olajuwon/25 30.00 80.00
LLJD Joe Dumars/35 12.00 30.00
LLJW James Worthy/35 15.00 40.00
LLJW Jerry West/25 30.00 80.00
LLKA Kareem Abdul-Jabbar/25 100.00 250.00
LLKM Kevin McHale/35 15.00 40.00
LLLB Larry Bird/25 100.00 250.00
LLMA Mark Aguirre/49 8.00 20.00
LLMF Michael Finley/35 10.00 25.00
LLRB Rick Barry/35 15.00 40.00
LLRH Robert Horry/49 10.00 25.00
LLRP Robert Parish/35 12.00 30.00
LLSO Shaquille O'Neal/25 100.00 250.00
LLNVE Nick Van Exel/35 10.00 25.00

2014-15 Panini National Treasures Material Treasures

STATED PRINT RUN 99 SER.#'d SETS
*PRIME: 1.25X TO 3X BASIC
MTAD Andre Drummond 4.00 10.00
MTAD Anthony Davis 12.00 30.00
MTAI Allen Iverson 12.00 30.00
MTAS Amar'e Stoudemire 5.00 12.00
MTBK Bernard King 6.00 15.00
MTBL Brook Lopez 5.00 12.00
MTCA Chris Andersen 4.00 10.00
MTCP Chandler Parsons 3.00 8.00
MTDC Darren Collison 3.00 8.00
MTDG Danilo Gallinari 3.00 8.00
MTDJ DeAndre Jordan 4.00 10.00
MTDR Derrick Rose 10.00 25.00
MTDW Deron Williams 4.00 10.00
MTDW Dwyane Wade 10.00 25.00
MTGH Gordon Hayward 4.00 10.00
MTGP Gary Payton 8.00 20.00
MTIS Iman Shumpert 3.00 8.00
MTJL Jeremy Lin 10.00 25.00
MTJR J.J. Redick 5.00 12.00
MTJS Josh Smith 3.00 8.00
MTJS John Stockton 10.00 25.00
MTKG Kevin Garnett 12.00 30.00
MTKI Kyrie Irving 10.00 25.00
MTKW Kemba Walker 5.00 12.00
MTLJ Larry Johnson 6.00 15.00
MTMC Michael Carter-Williams 3.00 8.00
MTMC Mario Chalmers 4.00 10.00
MTNB Nicolas Batum 4.00 10.00
MTPM Paul Millsap 4.00 10.00
MTPP Paul Pierce 8.00 20.00
MTRA Ray Allen 8.00 20.00
MTRH Roy Hibbert 4.00 10.00
MTRL Reggie Lewis 5.00 12.00
MTSK Shawn Kemp 8.00 20.00
MTTA Trevor Ariza 3.00 8.00
MTTG Taj Gibson 3.00 8.00
MTTT Tristan Thompson 3.00 8.00
MTTY Thaddeus Young 3.00 8.00
MTWM Wesley Matthews 3.00 8.00

2014-15 Panini National Treasures Material Treasures Signatures

PRINT RUNS B/WN 20-49 COPIES PER
EXCHANGE DEADLINE 2/5/2017
*PRIME: .75X TO 2X BASIC
MTSAA Arron Afflalo/49 5.00 12.00
MTSAB Anthony Bennett/35 5.00 12.00
MTSAH Al Horford/35 8.00 20.00
MTSAL Alex Len/35 5.00 12.00
MTSAV Anderson Varejao/49 5.00 12.00
MTSAW Antoine Walker/49 6.00 15.00
MTSBC Bill Cartwright/49 6.00 15.00
MTSBD Brad Daugherty/49 6.00 15.00
MTSBD Baron Davis/35 8.00 20.00
MTSBG Blake Griffin/25 8.00 20.00
MTSBK Brandon Knight/35 5.00 12.00
MTSBL Bill Laimbeer/49 8.00 20.00
MTSBM Ben McLemore/35 5.00 12.00
MTSBS Byron Scott/35 8.00 20.00
MTSCA Carmelo Anthony/25 60.00 150.00
MTSCB Chris Bosh/25 40.00 100.00
MTSCR Clifford Robinson/49 8.00 20.00
MTSDC Doug Collins/49 8.00 20.00
MTSDG Danilo Gallinari/35 5.00 12.00
MTSDH Dwight Howard/25 40.00 100.00
MTSDM Donatas Motiejunas/49 5.00 12.00
MTSGH George Hill/49 6.00 15.00
MTSHB Harrison Barnes/35 6.00 15.00
MTSJC Jose Calderon/49 5.00 12.00
MTSJS John Stockton/25 60.00 150.00
MTSJS John Starks/49 20.00 50.00
MTSJW John Wall/35 40.00 100.00
MTSKA Kenny Anderson/49 6.00 15.00
MTSKB Kobe Bryant/25 2,000.00 4,000.00
MTSKD Kevin Durant/25 150.00 400.00
MTSKI Kyrie Irving/35 60.00 150.00
MTSKM Karl Malone/20 60.00 150.00
MTSKM Kevin Martin/35 6.00 15.00
MTSKW Kenny Sky Walker/49 5.00 12.00
MTSLL Luc Longley/49 12.00 30.00
MTSLN Larry Nance/49 6.00 15.00
MTSLS Lance Stephenson/49 6.00 15.00
MTSMG Manu Ginobili/35 60.00 150.00
MTSMP Mason Plumlee/49 5.00 12.00
MTSNN Nerlens Noel/35 6.00 15.00
MTSNT Nate Thurmond/49 8.00 20.00
MTSPG Pau Gasol/35 12.00 30.00
MTSPM Patty Mills/49 20.00 50.00
MTSPW Paul Westphal/49 8.00 20.00
MTSRH Roy Hibbert/49 6.00 15.00
MTSRR Ricky Rubio/35 12.00 30.00
MTSSC Stephen Curry/35 800.00 1,500.00
MTSTC Tom Chambers/49 8.00 20.00
MTSTE Tyreke Evans/35 6.00 15.00
MTSTG Taj Gibson/49 5.00 12.00
MTSTH Tim Hardaway Jr./49 6.00 15.00
MTSTL Ty Lawson/35 5.00 12.00
MTSTP Tayshaun Prince/35 8.00 20.00
MTSTT Tristan Thompson/35 5.00 12.00
MTSTY Thaddeus Young/35 5.00 12.00
MTSVD Vlade Divac/49 8.00 20.00
MTSVO Victor Oladipo/35 6.00 15.00
MTSWD Walter Davis/49 6.00 15.00
MTSZI Zydrunas Ilgauskas/49 6.00 15.00
MTSZR Zach Randolph/35 8.00 20.00

2014-15 Panini National Treasures NBA Champions Signatures

STATED PRINT RUN 49 SER.#'d SETS
EXCHANGE DEADLINE 2/5/2017
NBAAG A.C. Green/49 10.00 25.00
NBABS Byron Scott/49 10.00 25.00
NBACD Clyde Drexler/49 75.00 200.00
NBADC Dave Cowens/49 20.00 50.00
NBADR David Robinson/49 100.00 250.00
NBAGP Gary Payton/49 60.00 150.00
NBAGR Glen Rice/49 10.00 25.00
NBAHO Hakeem Olajuwon/49 100.00 250.00
NBAJE Julius Erving/49 125.00 300.00
NBAJW Jo Jo White/49 15.00 40.00
NBAJK Jason Kidd/49 40.00 100.00
NBAKB Kobe Bryant/49 2,500.00 5,000.00
NBAKL Kawhi Leonard/49 200.00 500.00
NBAKM Kevin McHale/49 75.00 200.00
NBALB Larry Bird/49 200.00 500.00
NBAMA Mark Aguirre/49 8.00 20.00
NBAMJ Magic Johnson/49 200.00 500.00
NBARF Rick Fox/49 8.00 20.00
NBARH Robert Horry/49 40.00 100.00
NBASE Sean Elliott/49 10.00 25.00
NBASO Shaquille O'Neal/49 200.00 500.00
NBATP Tony Parker/49 40.00 100.00
NBATS Tiago Splitter/49 6.00 15.00
NBAWF Walt Frazier/49 40.00 100.00

2014-15 Panini National Treasures NBA Game Gear Duals

PRINT RUNS b/wn 25-99 COPIES PER
*PRIME: .75X TO 2X BASIC
GGDN Nene/99 3.00 8.00
GGDAA Arron Afflalo/99 3.00 8.00
GGDAB Avery Bradley/99 3.00 8.00
GGDAD Adrian Dantley/25 10.00 25.00
GGDAI Andre Iguodala/99 5.00 12.00
GGDAJ Al Jefferson/99 3.00 8.00
GGDAM Alonzo Mourning/99 8.00 20.00
GGDAV Anderson Varejao/99 3.00 8.00
GGDBB Bradley Beal/99 8.00 20.00
GGDBG Blake Griffin/99 5.00 12.00
GGDBK Brandon Knight/99 3.00 8.00
GGDBM Ben McLemore/99 3.00 8.00
GGDCA Carmelo Anthony/99 8.00 20.00
GGDCR Clifford Robinson/99 5.00 12.00
GGDDA Danny Ainge/99 5.00 12.00
GGDDC DeMarcus Cousins/99 4.00 10.00
GGDDF Derrick Favors/99 3.00 8.00
GGDDG Draymond Green/99 6.00 15.00
GGDDH Dwight Howard/99 6.00 15.00
GGDDL Damian Lillard/99 12.00 30.00
GGDDM Dan Majerle/99 4.00 10.00
GGDDN Dirk Nowitzki/99 12.00 30.00
GGDDR David Robinson/99 10.00 25.00
GGDDS Detlef Schrempf/99 5.00 12.00
GGDEB Eric Bledsoe/99 4.00 10.00
GGDEI Ersan Ilyasova/99 3.00 8.00
GGDGA G. Antetokounmpo/99 75.00 200.00
GGDGD Goran Dragic/99 5.00 12.00
GGDGH Grant Hill/99 8.00 20.00
GGDHO Hakeem Olajuwon/99 10.00 25.00
GGDIT Isaiah Thomas/99 4.00 10.00
GGDJB Jimmy Butler/99 8.00 20.00
GGDJH Jrue Holiday/99 6.00 15.00
GGDJH James Harden/99 10.00 25.00
GGDJW John Wall/99 6.00 15.00
GGDKB Kobe Bryant/99 75.00 200.00
GGDKC Kentavious Caldwell-Pope/99 4.00 10.00
GGDKD Kevin Duckworth/99 3.00 8.00
GGDKD Kevin Durant/99 15.00 40.00
GGDKF Kenneth Faried/99 3.00 8.00
GGDKK Kyle Korver/99 4.00 10.00
GGDKL Kevin Love/99 5.00 12.00
GGDKL Kawhi Leonard/99 12.00 30.00
GGDKM Karl Malone/99 10.00 25.00
GGDLA LaMarcus Aldridge/99 5.00 12.00
GGDLB Larry Bird/99 20.00 50.00
GGDLD Luol Deng/99 4.00 10.00
GGDLJ LeBron James/99 75.00 200.00
GGDMA Mark Aguirre/99 4.00 10.00
GGDMB Michael Beasley/99 3.00 8.00
GGDMB Manute Bol/99 5.00 12.00
GGDMC Mike Conley/99 4.00 10.00
GGDME Monta Ellis/99 4.00 10.00
GGDMG Marcin Gortat/99 3.00 8.00
GGDMG Manu Ginobili/99 10.00 25.00
GGDNN Nerlens Noel/99 3.00 8.00
GGDNP Nikola Pekovic/99 3.00 8.00
GGDNY Nick Young/99 3.00 8.00
GGDOJ O.J. Mayo/99 3.00 8.00
GGDPE Patrick Ewing/99 8.00 20.00
GGDPG Pau Gasol/99 8.00 20.00
GGDRG Rudy Gay/99 5.00 12.00
GGDRH Robert Horry/99 5.00 12.00
GGDRR Rajon Rondo/99 6.00 15.00
GGDRW Russell Westbrook/99 8.00 20.00
GGDSA Steven Adams/99 6.00 15.00
GGDSB Shawn Bradley/99 3.00 8.00
GGDSB Shane Battier/99 4.00 10.00
GGDSI Serge Ibaka/99 4.00 10.00
GGDSM Shawn Marion/99 4.00 10.00
GGDSN Steve Nash/99 10.00 25.00
GGDSO Shaquille O'Neal/99 20.00 50.00
GGDTA Tony Allen/99 3.00 8.00
GGDTB Trey Burke/99 3.00 8.00
GGDTC Tyson Chandler/99 5.00 12.00
GGDTD Tim Duncan/99 12.00 30.00
GGDTH Tobias Harris/99 4.00 10.00
GGDTL Ty Lawson/99 3.00 8.00
GGDTP Tayshaun Prince/99 5.00 12.00
GGDTP Tony Parker/99 8.00 20.00
GGDTS Tiago Splitter/99 3.00 8.00
GGDTS Thabo Sefolosha/99 3.00 8.00
GGDVO Victor Oladipo/99 4.00 10.00
GGDWD Walter Davis/99 4.00 10.00
GGDZR Zach Randolph/99 5.00 12.00

2014-15 Panini National Treasures NBA Game Gear Signatures

PRINT RUNS B/WN 25-75 COPIES PER
EXCHANGE DEADLINE 2/5/2017
*PRIME: 1.25X TO 3X BASIC
GGSAB Alec Burks/75 8.00 20.00
GGSAD Adrian Dantley/75 10.00 25.00
GGSAE Alex English/75 12.00 30.00
GGSAH Anfernee Hardaway/35 75.00 200.00
GGSAM Alonzo Mourning/35 40.00 100.00
GGSAW Antoine Walker/75 8.00 20.00
GGSBD Brad Daugherty/75 8.00 20.00
GGSBK Bernard King/49 12.00 30.00
GGSBL Bill Laimbeer/75 8.00 20.00
GGSBS Byron Scott/49 10.00 25.00
GGSCA Chris Andersen/49 8.00 20.00
GGSCA Carmelo Anthony/25 100.00 250.00
GGSCB Chris Bosh/25 40.00 100.00
GGSCD Clyde Drexler/25 75.00 200.00
GGSCM Cedric Maxwell/75 8.00 20.00
GGSCP Chris Paul/25 150.00 400.00
GGSCR Clifford Robinson/75 10.00 25.00
GGSDC Doug Collins/49 10.00 25.00
GGSDC DeMarcus Cousins/49 8.00 20.00
GGSDG Danny Green/75 8.00 20.00
GGSDI Dan Issel/49 12.00 30.00
GGSDM Danny Manning/49 8.00 20.00
GGSDM Dan Majerle/75 8.00 20.00

GGSDR David Robinson/35 40.00 100.00
GGSEK Enes Kanter/75 8.00 20.00
GGSGA G. Antetokounmpo/75 500.00 1,000.00
GGSGG George Gervin/49 20.00 50.00
GGSGH Grant Hill/35 40.00 100.00
GGSGP Gary Payton/35 40.00 100.00
GGSGR Glen Rice/75 10.00 25.00
GGSJD Joe Dumars/49 12.00 30.00
GGSJE Julius Erving/25 125.00 300.00
GGSJK Jason Kidd/35 40.00 100.00
GGSJN Joakim Noah/49 10.00 25.00
GGSJS John Stockton/25 75.00 200.00
GGSJS Jack Sikma/75 10.00 25.00
GGSJW John Wall/35 20.00 50.00
GGSJW Jamaal Wilkes/75 10.00 25.00
GGSJWO James Worthy/35 40.00 100.00
GGSKA Abdul-Jabbar/25 200.00 500.00
GGSKA Kenny Anderson/75 8.00 20.00
GGSKB Kobe Bryant/25 2,500.00 5,000.00
GGSKD Kevin Durant/25 200.00 500.00
GGSKI Kyrie Irving/25 75.00 200.00
GGSKL Kevin Love/35 10.00 25.00
GGSKM Karl Malone/25 75.00 200.00
GGSKM Kevin Martin/49 8.00 20.00
GGSKR Kurt Rambis/75 8.00 20.00
GGSKV Kiki Vandeweghe/75 8.00 20.00
GGSKW Kenny Sky Walker/75 6.00 15.00
GGSLB Larry Bird/25 200.00 500.00
GGSLL Luc Longley/49 8.00 20.00
GGSLS Lance Stephenson/60 8.00 20.00
GGSMA Mark Aguirre/75 8.00 20.00
GGSMF Michael Finley/49 10.00 25.00
GGSMG Marcin Gortat/49 6.00 15.00
GGSMJ Magic Johnson/35 150.00 400.00
GGSNC Nick Collison/75 8.00 20.00
GGSNVE Nick Van Exel/75 10.00 25.00
GGSPW Paul Westphal/75 10.00 25.00
GGSRB Rick Barry/49 12.00 30.00
GGSRH Robert Horry/75 10.00 25.00
GGSRP Robert Parish/49 12.00 30.00
GGSRW Russell Westbrook/35 40.00 100.00
GGSSC Stephen Curry/35 800.00 1,500.00
GGSSE Sean Elliott/75 10.00 25.00
GGSSO Shaquille O'Neal/25 200.00 500.00
GGSTC Tyson Chandler/49 10.00 25.00
GGSTC Tom Chambers/75 10.00 25.00
GGSTG Taj Gibson/75 6.00 15.00
GGSTH Tim Hardaway/75 12.00 30.00
GGSTM Tracy McGrady/49 75.00 200.00
GGSTP Tony Parker/25 40.00 100.00
GGSTS Tiago Splitter/75 6.00 15.00
GGSTY Thaddeus Young/75 6.00 15.00
GGSVC Vince Carter/35 75.00 200.00
GGSWD Walter Davis/75 8.00 20.00
GGSXM Xavier McDaniel/75 8.00 20.00
GGSZR Zach Randolph/49 10.00 25.00

2014-15 Panini National Treasures NBA Greats Signatures

PRINT RUNS B/WN 25-75 COPIES PER
EXCHANGE DEADLINE 2/5/2017
*GOLD: .5X TO 1.2X BASIC p/r 35-75
*GOLD: .4X TO 1X BASIC p/r 25
NBGAD Adrian Dantley/75 6.00 15.00
NBGAE Alex English/75 8.00 20.00
NBGAG Artis Gilmore/75 8.00 20.00
NBGAI Allen Iverson/25 75.00 200.00
NBGBK Bernard King/75 8.00 20.00
NBGBR Bill Russell/25 1,000.00 2,000.00
NBGBW Bill Walton/75 10.00 25.00
NBGCM Chris Mullin/75 10.00 25.00
NBGCW Chris Webber/35 75.00 200.00
NBGDI Dan Issel/75 8.00 20.00
NBGDR Dennis Rodman/49 15.00 40.00
NBGDR David Robinson/35 15.00 40.00
NBGDS Dolph Schayes/75 6.00 15.00
NBGDT David Thompson/75 6.00 15.00
NBGEB Elgin Baylor/49 10.00 25.00
NBGEM Earl Monroe/35 10.00 25.00
NBGGG Gail Goodrich/75 6.00 15.00
NBGGG George Gervin/75 8.00 20.00
NBGGM George McGinnis/75 6.00 15.00
NBGGP Gary Payton/49 15.00 40.00
NBGHO Hakeem Olajuwon/35 12.00 30.00
NBGJD Joe Dumars/75 8.00 20.00
NBGJE Julius Erving/25 30.00 80.00
NBGJS John Stockton/25 20.00 50.00
NBGJW James Worthy/49 15.00 40.00
NBGJW Jerry West/25 25.00 60.00
NBGJW Jamaal Wilkes/75 8.00 20.00
NBGKM Kevin McHale/49 10.00 25.00
NBGMA Mark Aguirre/75 5.00 12.00
NBGMD Mel Daniels/75 6.00 15.00
NBGOR Oscar Robertson/25 50.00 120.00
NBGRP Robert Parish/75 8.00 20.00
NBGSM Sarunas Marciulionis/75 6.00 15.00
NBGSM Sidney Moncrief/75 5.00 12.00
NBGSO Shaquille O'Neal/25 75.00 200.00
NBGTS Tom Satch Sanders/75 10.00 25.00
NBGWF Walt Frazier/75 10.00 25.00
NBGWU Wes Unseld/75 8.00 20.00
NBGJJW Jo Jo White/75 8.00 20.00

2014-15 Panini National Treasures NBA Material

STATED PRINT RUN 99 SER.#'d SETS
*PRIME: .75X TO 2X BASIC
NBAAD Andre Drummond 3.00 8.00
NBAAD Anthony Davis 6.00 15.00
NBAAD Adrian Dantley 4.00 10.00
NBABB Bradley Beal 6.00 15.00
NBABG Blake Griffin 4.00 10.00
NBABK Bernard King 5.00 12.00
NBACA Carmelo Anthony 6.00 15.00
NBACP Chris Paul 6.00 15.00
NBADH Dwight Howard 5.00 12.00
NBADJ DeAndre Jordan 3.00 8.00
NBADL Damian Lillard 5.00 12.00
NBADN Dirk Nowitzki 10.00 25.00
NBADR Derrick Rose 8.00 20.00
NBADW Dwyane Wade 5.00 12.00
NBADW Deron Williams 3.00 8.00
NBAGA Giannis Antetokounmpo 25.00 60.00
NBAGH Gordon Hayward 3.00 8.00
NBAGR Glen Rice 4.00 10.00
NBAJB Jimmy Butler 6.00 15.00
NBAJH James Harden 6.00 15.00
NBAJJ Joe Johnson 3.00 8.00
NBAJM Jamal Mashburn 3.00 8.00
NBAJS John Stockton 8.00 20.00
NBAKB Kobe Bryant 75.00 200.00
NBAKD Kevin Durant 6.00 15.00
NBAKK Kyle Korver 3.00 8.00
NBAKL Kevin Love 4.00 10.00
NBAKL Kawhi Leonard 5.00 12.00
NBAKM Karl Malone 6.00 15.00
NBALA LaMarcus Aldridge 4.00 10.00
NBALJ LeBron James 25.00 60.00
NBAME Monta Ellis 3.00 8.00
NBAMG Manu Ginobili 8.00 20.00
NBAMG Marcin Gortat 2.50 6.00
NBANV Nikola Vucevic 3.00 8.00
NBARH Roy Hibbert 3.00 8.00
NBARP Robert Parish 5.00 12.00
NBARR Rajon Rondo 5.00 12.00
NBARS Ralph Sampson 4.00 10.00
NBARW Russell Westbrook 5.00 12.00
NBASK Steve Kerr 4.00 10.00
NBASM Shawn Marion 3.00 8.00
NBASO Shaquille O'Neal 15.00 40.00
NBASP Scottie Pippen 10.00 25.00
NBATB Trey Burke 2.50 6.00
NBATD Tim Duncan 10.00 25.00
NBATP Tony Parker 5.00 12.00
NBAVD Vlade Divac 4.00 10.00
NBAVO Victor Oladipo 3.00 8.00
NBAZR Zach Randolph 4.00 10.00

2014-15 Panini National Treasures NBA Rookie Materials

STATED PRINT RUN 99 SER.#'d SETS
*PRIME: .75X TO 2X BASIC
RMAG Aaron Gordon/99 12.00 30.00
RMAP Adreian Payne/99 2.50 6.00
RMAW Andrew Wiggins/99 20.00 50.00
RMBC Bruno Caboclo/99 5.00 12.00
RMCE Cleanthony Early/99 2.50 6.00
RMCJ Cory Jefferson/99 2.50 6.00
RMCW C.J. Wilcox/99 2.50 6.00
RMDE Dante Exum/99 4.00 10.00
RMDM Doug McDermott/99 4.00 10.00
RMEP Elfrid Payton/99 4.00 10.00
RMGH Gary Harris/99 4.00 10.00
RMGR Glenn Robinson III/99 3.00 8.00
RMJE Joel Embiid/99 6.00 15.00
RMJE James Ennis/99 2.50 6.00
RMJG Jerami Grant/99 12.00 30.00
RMJH Joe Harris/99 4.00 10.00
RMJO Johnny O'Bryant/99 2.50 6.00
RMJP Jabari Parker/99 6.00 15.00
RMJR Julius Randle/99 10.00 25.00
RMJS Jarnell Stokes/99 2.50 6.00
RMJY James Young/99 2.50 6.00
RMKA Kyle Anderson/99 15.00 40.00
RMKM K.J. McDaniels/99 2.50 6.00
RMMM Mitch McGary/99 2.50 6.00
RMMS Marcus Smart/99 10.00 25.00
RMNS Nik Stauskas/99 2.50 6.00
RMNV Noah Vonleh/99 2.50 6.00
RMPH P.J. Hairston/99 2.50 6.00
RMRH Rodney Hood/99 3.00 8.00
RMRS Russ Smith/99 2.50 6.00
RMSD Spencer Dinwiddie/99 4.00 10.00
RMSN Shabazz Napier/99 3.00 8.00
RMTE Tyler Ennis/99 2.50 6.00
RMTW T.J. Warren/99 4.00 10.00
RMZL Zach LaVine/99 15.00 40.00

2014-15 Panini National Treasures Night Moves Jersey Autographs

PRINT RUNS B/WN 23-49 COPIES PER
EXCHANGE DEADLINE 2/5/2017
*PRIME: .75X TO 2X BASIC
NMAA Arron Afflalo/49 4.00 10.00
NMAD Adrian Dantley/49 5.00 12.00
NMAH Al Horford/35 5.00 12.00
NMAI Allen Iverson/25 75.00 150.00
NMAV Anderson Varejao/49 4.00 10.00
NMBC Bill Cartwright/49 5.00 12.00
NMBK Brandon Knight/35 4.00 10.00
NMBM Ben McLemore/35 5.00 12.00
NMBS Byron Scott/35 6.00 15.00
NMCR Clifford Robinson/49 4.00 10.00
NMDG Danilo Gallinari/35 4.00 10.00
NMDN Dirk Nowitzki/25 75.00 200.00
NMDR David Robinson/25 20.00 50.00
NMDW Dwyane Wade/25 50.00 120.00
NMDW Deron Williams/35 4.00 10.00
NMEM Earl Monroe/25 15.00 40.00
NMGD Goran Dragic/30 8.00 20.00
NMGH George Hill/49 5.00 12.00
NMIT Isiah Thomas/35 10.00 25.00
NMJC Jose Calderon/49 3.00 8.00
NMJK Jason Kidd/35 12.00 30.00
NMJS John Starks/49 10.00 25.00
NMJS John Stockton/25 25.00 60.00
NMJV Jonas Valanciunas/23 6.00 15.00
NMKB Kobe Bryant/25 1,500.00 3,000.00
NMKD Kevin Durant/25 60.00 150.00
NMKI Kyrie Irving/25 30.00 80.00
NMKL Kyle Lowry/49 8.00 20.00
NMKL Kawhi Leonard/25 30.00 80.00
NMKL Kevin Love/35 15.00 40.00
NMKM Karl Malone/25 25.00 60.00
NMKM Kevin McHale/35 10.00 25.00
NMKM Kevin Martin/35 5.00 12.00
NMKR Kurt Rambis/49 5.00 12.00
NMKW Kenny Sky Walker/49 5.00 12.00
NMLJ Larry Johnson/35 8.00 20.00
NMLL Luc Longley/49 10.00 25.00
NMLS Lance Stephenson/49 5.00 12.00
NMMC Mike Conley/49 4.00 10.00
NMME Monta Ellis/25 6.00 15.00
NMMF Michael Finley/49 6.00 15.00
NMMG Marcin Gortat/40 6.00 15.00
NMNN Nerlens Noel/35 10.00 25.00
NMNY Nick Young/49 5.00 12.00
NMPG Paul George/25 15.00 40.00
NMPM Patty Mills/49 10.00 25.00
NMPS Peja Stojakovic/35 6.00 15.00
NMRH Roy Hibbert/49 5.00 12.00
NMSB Shane Battier/35 6.00 15.00
NMTC Tom Chambers/49 6.00 15.00
NMTG Taj Gibson/49 4.00 10.00
NMTK Toni Kukoc/49 6.00 15.00
NMTL Ty Lawson/35 4.00 10.00
NMTP Tayshaun Prince/35 5.00 12.00
NMTS Tiago Splitter/35 4.00 10.00
NMTT Tristan Thompson/35 4.00 10.00
NMTY Thaddeus Young/35 4.00 10.00
NMZR Zach Randolph/35 6.00 15.00

2014-15 Panini National Treasures Notable Nicknames

STATED PRINT RUN 49 SER.#'d SETS
EXCHANGE DEADLINE 2/5/2017
NNAG A.C. Green 25.00 60.00
NNAM Alonzo Mourning 30.00 80.00
NNBD Bob Dandridge 15.00 40.00
NNCH Cliff Hagan 15.00 40.00
NNCP Chris Paul 200.00 500.00
NNDM Doug McDermott 30.00 80.00
NNGA Giannis Antetokounmpo 125.00 300.00
NNJK Jason Kidd 150.00 400.00
NNJR Julius Randle 50.00 120.00
NNJS John Salley 12.00 30.00
NNKR Kurt Rambis 12.00 30.00
NNLS Latrell Sprewell 60.00 150.00
NNNS Nik Stauskas 10.00 25.00
NNRS Rony Seikaly 12.00 30.00
NNSC Stephen Curry 500.00 1,000.00
NNSO Shaquille O'Neal 75.00 200.00
NNXM Xavier McDaniel 12.00 30.00
NNZI Zydrunas Ilgauskas 12.00 30.00

2014-15 Panini National Treasures Scripts

PRINT RUNS B/WN 35-75 COPIES PER
EXCHANGE DEADLINE 2/5/2017
*GOLD: .5X TO 1.2X BASIC
SCAG Artis Gilmore/49 8.00 20.00
SCAH Allan Houston/75 6.00 15.00
SCAI Allen Iverson/35 60.00 150.00
SCAJ Avery Johnson/49 5.00 12.00
SCAM Anthony Mason/75 5.00 12.00
SCBD Brad Daugherty/75 5.00 12.00
SCBK Bernard King/49 8.00 20.00
SCBK Brandon Knight/49 4.00 10.00
SCBS Byron Scott/49 6.00 15.00
SCCA Carmelo Anthony/35 20.00 50.00
SCCD Clyde Drexler/35 15.00 40.00
SCCO Charles Oakley/75 6.00 15.00
SCCP Chuck Person/75 5.00 12.00
SCCW Chris Webber/49 60.00 150.00
SCDM Danny Manning/49 5.00 12.00
SCDR David Robinson/49 15.00 40.00
SCDS Dolph Schayes/49 6.00 15.00
SCEJ Eddie Jones/75 6.00 15.00
SCEM Earl Monroe/49 10.00 25.00
SCGG George Gervin/49 8.00 20.00
SCGG Gail Goodrich/49 6.00 15.00
SCGH Grant Hill/49 12.00 30.00
SCGK George Karl/49 6.00 15.00
SCGP Gary Payton/49 10.00 25.00
SCHO Hakeem Olajuwon/49 20.00 50.00
SCJD Joe Dumars/49 8.00 20.00
SCJE Julius Erving/35 30.00 80.00
SCJS John Stockton/35 15.00 40.00
SCJW James Worthy/49 12.00 30.00
SCJW Jerry West/35 25.00 60.00
SCKC Kentavious Caldwell-Pope/49 5.00 12.00
SCKM Kevin Martin/49 5.00 12.00
SCKM Kevin McHale/49 10.00 25.00
SCKR Kurt Rambis/75 5.00 12.00
SCKW Kevin Willis/75 5.00 12.00
SCKW Kenny Sky Walker/75 4.00 10.00
SCMC Michael Carter-Williams/49 4.00 10.00
SCNN Nerlens Noel/49 4.00 10.00
SCOR Oscar Robertson/35 40.00 100.00
SCRF Rick Fox/49 5.00 12.00
SCRP Robert Parish/49 8.00 20.00
SCSS Scott Skiles/75 5.00 12.00
SCTB Trey Burke/49 4.00 10.00
SCTH Tim Hardaway Jr./75 5.00 12.00
SCTS Tom Satch Sanders/75 10.00 25.00
SCVO Victor Oladipo/49 5.00 12.00
SCWD Walter Davis/75 5.00 12.00
SCWF Walt Frazier/49 10.00 25.00
SCWU Wes Unseld/49 8.00 20.00

2014-15 Panini National Treasures Signature Materials

PRINT RUNS B/WN 32-75 COPIES PER
EXCHANGE DEADLINE 2/5/2017
*PRIME: .75X TO 2X BASIC
SMAB Alec Burks/75 6.00 15.00
SMBC Bill Cartwright/75 6.00 15.00
SMBD Brad Daugherty/75 6.00 15.00
SMBL Brook Lopez/49 8.00 20.00
SMBS Byron Scott/49 8.00 20.00
SMCA Carmelo Anthony/35 50.00 120.00
SMCO Charles Oakley/75 8.00 20.00
SMCR Clifford Robinson/75 6.00 15.00
SMDC DeMarcus Cousins/49 6.00 15.00
SMDC Doug Collins/75 8.00 20.00
SMDF Derrick Favors/35 5.00 12.00
SMDG Danilo Gallinari/75 5.00 12.00
SMDM Danny Manning/49 6.00 15.00
SMEK Enes Kanter/75 5.00 12.00
SMGG George Gervin/49 25.00 60.00
SMGH Grant Hill/35 40.00 100.00
SMGH Gordon Hayward/75 6.00 15.00
SMGP Gary Payton/49 40.00 100.00
SMGR Glen Rice/75 8.00 20.00
SMJC Jamal Crawford/75 8.00 20.00
SMJD Jared Dudley/75 5.00 12.00
SMJG Jeff Green/75 6.00 15.00
SMJJ James Jones/75 5.00 12.00
SMJN Joakim Noah/49 8.00 20.00
SMJS John Stockton/35 40.00 100.00
SMJS John Starks/32 30.00 80.00
SMJT Jason Thompson/75 5.00 12.00
SMJW John Wall/49 10.00 25.00
SMKA Kenny Anderson/75 6.00 15.00
SMKL Kevin Love/49 8.00 20.00
SMKM Karl Malone/35 40.00 100.00
SMKM Kevin Martin/49 6.00 15.00
SMKV Kiki Vandeweghe/75 6.00 15.00
SMKW Kenny Sky Walker/75 5.00 12.00
SMMC Mike Conley/75 6.00 15.00
SMMF Michael Finley/49 8.00 20.00
SMMG Marcin Gortat/75 5.00 12.00
SMMK Michael Kidd-Gilchrist/49 5.00 12.00
SMNC Nick Collison/75 6.00 15.00
SMRA Ryan Anderson/50 5.00 12.00
SMRF Randy Foye/75 5.00 12.00
SMRW Russell Westbrook/49 60.00 150.00
SMTC Tyson Chandler/49 8.00 20.00
SMTC Tom Chambers/75 8.00 20.00
SMTG Taj Gibson/75 5.00 12.00
SMTS Tiago Splitter/75 5.00 12.00
SMTY Thaddeus Young/75 5.00 12.00
SMVC Vince Carter/49 60.00 150.00
SMWD Walter Davis/75 6.00 15.00
SMXM Xavier McDaniel/75 6.00 15.00
SMZI Zydrunas Ilgauskas/75 6.00 15.00
SMZR Zach Randolph/49 8.00 20.00
SMKLO Kyle Lowry/75 40.00 100.00

2014-15 Panini National Treasures Signatures

PRINT RUNS B/WN 35-75 COPIES PER
EXCHANGE DEADLINE 2/5/2017
*GOLD: .5X TO 1.2X BASIC
SAD Anthony Davis/49 75.00 200.00
SAE Alex English/75 10.00 25.00
SAG A.C. Green/75 8.00 20.00
SAH Allan Houston/75 8.00 20.00
SBD Bob Dandridge/75 8.00 20.00
SBK Bernard King/49 10.00 25.00
SBR Bill Russell/35 1,000.00 2,000.00
SBS Byron Scott/49 8.00 20.00
SCA Chris Andersen/49 20.00 50.00
SCB Chris Bosh/35 30.00 80.00
SCH Cliff Hagan/49 8.00 20.00
SCM Cedric Maxwell/75 6.00 15.00
SCR Cazzie Russell/75 8.00 20.00
SCR Campy Russell/75 6.00 15.00
SCR Clifford Robinson/75 8.00 20.00
SDB Dee Brown/75 6.00 15.00
SDC Doug Collins/75 8.00 20.00
SDF Derrick Favors/49 5.00 12.00
SDI Dan Issel/75 10.00 25.00
SDR David Robinson/49 40.00 100.00
SDS Dolph Schayes/49 8.00 20.00
SEK Enes Kanter/75 6.00 15.00
SGA Giannis Antetokounmpo/75 500.00 1,000.00
SGG George Gervin/49 20.00 50.00
SGH Gordon Hayward/75 6.00 15.00
SGK George Karl/49 6.00 15.00
SGP Gary Payton/49 40.00 100.00
SIT Isiah Thomas/49 40.00 100.00
SIT Isaiah Thomas/75 6.00 15.00
SJC Jamal Crawford/75 8.00 20.00
SJD Joe Dumars/49 10.00 25.00
SJE Julius Erving/35 125.00 300.00
SJJ Jim Jackson/75 6.00 15.00
SJK Jason Kidd/49 40.00 100.00
SJN Joakim Noah/49 8.00 20.00
SJS John Starks/75 8.00 20.00
SJS Josh Smith/49 8.00 20.00
SJS John Stockton/35 60.00 150.00
SJW Jamaal Wilkes/75 8.00 20.00
SJW Jerome Williams/75 5.00 12.00
SJW John Wall/49 40.00 100.00
SKB Kobe Bryant/49 2,000.00 4,000.00
SKD Kevin Durant/35 200.00 500.00
SKI Kyrie Irving/49 75.00 200.00
SKK Kyle Korver/75 6.00 15.00
SKL Kevin Love/49 12.00 30.00
SKM Karl Malone/35 60.00 150.00
SKM Kevin Martin/49 6.00 15.00
SKR Kurt Rambis/75 6.00 15.00
SKS Kenny Smith/49 6.00 15.00
SKV Kiki Vandeweghe/75 6.00 15.00
SLN Larry Nance/75 6.00 15.00
SLS Lance Stephenson/75 6.00 15.00
SLS Latrell Sprewell/49 30.00 80.00
SMA Mark Aguirre/75 6.00 15.00
SMB Muggsy Bogues/75 20.00 50.00
SMG Marcin Gortat/49 6.00 15.00
SMT Mychal Thompson/75 15.00 40.00
SPG Pau Gasol/49 30.00 80.00
SRB Rick Barry/49 20.00 50.00
SRB Rolando Blackman/75 6.00 15.00
SRH Robert Horry/75 30.00 80.00
SRL Raef LaFrentz/75 5.00 12.00
SRS Rod Strickland/75 6.00 15.00
SRT Rudy Tomjanovich/75 8.00 20.00
SRW Russell Westbrook/49 75.00 200.00
SSB Scott Brooks/75 5.00 12.00
SSC Stephen Curry/49 1,000.00 2,000.00
SSM Sidney Moncrief/75 8.00 20.00
SSO Shaquille O'Neal/35 200.00 500.00
SSS Scott Skiles/75 6.00 15.00
STC Tyson Chandler/49 8.00 20.00
STC Tom Chambers/75 8.00 20.00
STG Tom Gugliotta/75 5.00 12.00
STH Tim Hardaway/75 10.00 25.00
STK Toni Kukoc/75 25.00 60.00
STM Tracy McGrady/49 125.00 300.00
STS Tiago Splitter/75 5.00 12.00
STY Thaddeus Young/75 5.00 12.00
SVC Vince Carter/49 125.00 300.00
SWD Walter Davis/75 6.00 15.00
SWE Wayne Embry/75 6.00 15.00
SXM Xavier McDaniel/75 6.00 15.00
SZI Zydrunas Ilgauskas/75 6.00 15.00
SZR Zach Randolph/49 8.00 20.00
SKLE Kawhi Leonard/49 150.00 400.00

2014-15 Panini National Treasures Sneaker Swatches

PRINT RUNS B/WN 1-49 COPIES PER
NO PRICING ON QTY 17 OR LESS
SSAD Anthony Davis/49 60.00 150.00
SSAI Allen Iverson/49 75.00 200.00
SSAW Andrew Wiggins/13 75.00 200.00
SSDW Dominique Wilkins/49 30.00 80.00
SSGH Grant Hill/20 40.00 100.00
SSGP Gary Payton/49 30.00 80.00
SSHO Hakeem Olajuwon/49 40.00 100.00
SSJE Julius Erving/40 75.00 200.00
SSKM Karl Malone/49 40.00 100.00
SSLJ Larry Johnson/49 30.00 80.00
SSLJ LeBron James/49 500.00 1,000.00
SSMC Michael Carter-Williams/49 4.00 10.00
SSMJ Magic Johnson/49 75.00 200.00
SSMM Moses Malone/49 40.00 100.00
SSRS Ralph Sampson/49 6.00 15.00
SSSC Stephen Curry/45 500.00 1,000.00
SSSK Shawn Kemp/49 40.00 100.00
SSSO Shaquille O'Neal/49 75.00 200.00
SSSP Scottie Pippen/49 60.00 150.00
SSTB Trey Burke/17 4.00 10.00
SSVO Victor Oladipo/31 5.00 12.00

2014-15 Panini National Treasures Sneaker Swatches Autographs

PRINT RUNS B/WN 23-49 COPIES PER
EXCHANGE DEADLINE 2/5/2017
SSAAD Anthony Davis/49 100.00 250.00
SSAAW Andrew Wiggins/35 75.00 200.00
SSACA Carmelo Anthony/43 75.00 200.00
SSADW Dominique Wilkins/49 40.00 100.00
SSAGP Gary Payton/49 40.00 100.00
SSAJD Joe Dumars/49 15.00 40.00
SSAJE Julius Erving/35 125.00 300.00
SSAKB Kobe Bryant/32 1,500.00 3,000.00
SSAKM Karl Malone/49 75.00 200.00
SSALJ Larry Johnson/49 50.00 120.00
SSAMC Michael Carter-Williams/49 6.00 15.00
SSAMJ Magic Johnson/49 125.00 300.00
SSAMK Michael Kidd-Gilchrist/23 6.00 15.00
SSARP Robert Parish/30 20.00 50.00
SSASC Stephen Curry/49 1,500.00 3,000.00
SSASO Shaquille O'Neal/49 200.00 500.00
SSATB Trey Burke/49 6.00 15.00
SSAVO Victor Oladipo/49 25.00 60.00
SSAYM Yao Ming/33 200.00 500.00

2014-15 Panini National Treasures Spanning Time Dual Signatures

PRINT RUNS B/WN 10-49 COPIES PER
NO PRICING ON QTY 10
EXCHANGE DEADLINE 2/5/2017
*GOLD: .5X TO 1.2X BASIC
STAWSN Wiggins/Nash/25 150.00 400.00
STCMKL Maxwell/Leonard/49 100.00 250.00
STCPGP Paul/Payton/25 150.00 400.00
STGHKI Hill/Irving/25 125.00 300.00
STHOAD Olajuwon/Davis/25 150.00 400.00
STLSSC Sprewell/Curry/25 800.00 1,500.00
STMTKT Thompson/Thompson/45 150.00 400.00
STRRJK Rondo/Kidd/25 75.00 200.00
STTHTH Hardaway/Hardaway Jr./49 20.00 50.00

2014-15 Panini National Treasures Springfield Swatches

PRINT RUNS B/WN 35-49 COPIES PER
*PRIME: .75X TO 2X BASIC
SPSAD Adrian Dantley 6.00 15.00
SPSAG Artis Gilmore 8.00 20.00
SPSBK Bernard King 8.00 20.00
SPSDJ Dennis Johnson 6.00 15.00
SPSDM Dikembe Mutombo/35 10.00 25.00
SPSDR David Robinson 12.00 30.00
SPSEB Elgin Baylor 12.00 30.00
SPSEM Earl Monroe 10.00 25.00
SPSGM George Mikan 150.00 400.00
SPSGP Gary Payton 10.00 25.00
SPSHG Hal Greer 6.00 15.00
SPSHO Hakeem Olajuwon 12.00 30.00
SPSIT Isiah Thomas 10.00 25.00
SPSJD Joe Dumars 8.00 20.00
SPSJH John Havlicek 40.00 100.00
SPSJS John Stockton 12.00 30.00
SPSJW James Worthy 10.00 25.00
SPSKA Kareem Abdul-Jabbar 40.00 100.00
SPSKM Karl Malone 12.00 30.00
SPSKM Kevin McHale 10.00 25.00
SPSLB Larry Bird 25.00 60.00
SPSLD Louie Dampier 6.00 15.00
SPSMM Moses Malone 10.00 25.00
SPSNT Nate Thurmond 6.00 15.00
SPSPE Patrick Ewing 10.00 25.00
SPSPM Pete Maravich 75.00 200.00
SPSRB Rick Barry 8.00 20.00
SPSRP Robert Parish 8.00 20.00
SPSRS Ralph Sampson 6.00 15.00
SPSWC Wilt Chamberlain 75.00 200.00

2014-15 Panini National Treasures Timelines

PRINT RUNS B/WN 10-99 COPIES PER
*PRIME: .75X TO 2X BASIC
TAD Anthony Davis/99 12.00 30.00
TAG Aaron Gordon/99 15.00 40.00
TAH Al Horford/99 5.00 12.00
TAI Allen Iverson/99 12.00 30.00
TAW Andrew Wiggins/99 15.00 40.00
TBK Bernard King/99 6.00 15.00
TDE Dante Exum/99 5.00 12.00
TDJ DeAndre Jordan/99 4.00 10.00
TDL Damian Lillard/99 12.00 30.00
TDM Dikembe Mutombo/75 8.00 20.00
TDM Doug McDermott/99 5.00 12.00
TDN Dirk Nowitzki/99 12.00 30.00
TDR Derrick Rose/99 10.00 25.00
TDW Dwyane Wade/99 10.00 25.00
TEP Elfrid Payton/99 5.00 12.00
TGM George Mikan/25 100.00 250.00
TGR Glen Rice/99 5.00 12.00
TJB Jimmy Butler/99 8.00 20.00
TJE Joel Embiid/99 30.00 80.00
TJL Jeremy Lin/99 10.00 25.00
TJM Jamal Mashburn/99 4.00 10.00
TJN Joakim Noah/99 4.00 10.00
TJP Jabari Parker/99 8.00 20.00
TJR Julius Randle/99 15.00 40.00
TJS John Stockton/99 10.00 25.00
TKB Kobe Bryant/99 100.00 250.00
TKG Kevin Garnett/99 12.00 30.00
TKM Karl Malone/99 10.00 25.00
TLJ Larry Johnson/99 6.00 15.00
TMM Mitch McGary/99 3.00 8.00
TMM Moses Malone/99 8.00 20.00
TMS Marcus Smart/99 12.00 30.00
TNS Nik Stauskas/99 3.00 8.00
TPE Patrick Ewing/99 10.00 25.00
TPP Paul Pierce/99 8.00 20.00
TRA Ray Allen/99 8.00 20.00
TRP Robert Parish/99 6.00 15.00
TRS Ralph Sampson/99 5.00 12.00
TSD Spencer Dinwiddie/99 5.00 12.00
TSK Shawn Kemp/99 8.00 20.00
TSK Steve Kerr/99 5.00 12.00
TSN Shabazz Napier/99 4.00 10.00
TSO Shaquille O'Neal/99 20.00 50.00
TSP Scottie Pippen/99 12.00 30.00
TTT Tristan Thompson/99 3.00 8.00
TVD Vlade Divac/99 5.00 12.00
TVJ Vinnie Johnson/49 5.00 12.00
TXM Xavier McDaniel/99 4.00 10.00
TZL Zach LaVine/99 20.00 50.00

2015-16 Panini National Treasures

1-100 PRINT RUN 99 SER.#'d SETS
JSY AU RC p/r B/WN 49-99 COPIES
141-157 PRINT RUN 99 SER.#'d SETS
PRIME PATCHES MAY SELL FOR PREMIUM
EXCHANGE DEADLINE 11/11/2017
1 Kobe Bryant 150.00 400.00
2 Al Horford 2.00 5.00
3 Derrick Favors 1.50 4.00
4 Tim Duncan 5.00 12.00
5 Jusuf Nurkic 1.50 4.00
6 Dwight Howard 2.50 6.00
7 Andre Drummond 2.00 5.00
8 Chris Paul 4.00 10.00
9 DeMar DeRozan 2.50 6.00
10 Julius Randle 2.50 6.00
11 Thaddeus Young 1.25 3.00
12 Tobias Harris 1.50 4.00
13 Andrew Wiggins 2.50 6.00
14 Tony Parker 3.00 8.00
15 Kevin Love 2.00 5.00
16 Trevor Ariza 1.25 3.00
17 Reggie Jackson 1.50 4.00
18 DeAndre Jordan 1.50 4.00
19 Kyle Lowry 2.00 5.00
20 Jordan Clarkson 2.00 5.00
21 Robert Covington 1.50 4.00
22 Victor Oladipo 1.50 4.00
23 Zach LaVine 5.00 12.00
24 Deron Williams 1.50 4.00
25 LeBron James 12.00 30.00
26 Anthony Davis 5.00 12.00
27 Marcus Morris 1.25 3.00
28 Paul Pierce 3.00 8.00
29 Isaiah Thomas 1.50 4.00
30 Chris Bosh 2.50 6.00
31 Nerlens Noel 1.25 3.00
32 Nikola Vucevic 1.50 4.00
33 Ricky Rubio 1.50 4.00
34 Dirk Nowitzki 5.00 12.00
35 Kyrie Irving 4.00 10.00
36 Eric Gordon 1.50 4.00
37 Jabari Parker 1.25 3.00
38 Brandon Knight 1.25 3.00
39 Marcus Smart 2.00 5.00
40 Dwyane Wade 4.00 10.00
41 Isaiah Canaan 1.25 3.00
42 Evan Fournier 1.50 4.00
43 Kevin Garnett 5.00 12.00
44 Zaza Pachulia 1.25 3.00
45 Jimmy Butler 4.00 10.00
46 Ryan Anderson 1.25 3.00
47 Giannis Antetokounmpo 10.00 25.00
48 Tyson Chandler 1.50 4.00
49 Jared Sullinger 1.25 3.00
50 Hassan Whiteside 1.50 4.00
51 Kevin Durant 8.00 20.00
52 Bradley Beal 2.50 6.00
53 Damian Lillard 5.00 12.00
54 Marc Gasol 2.00 5.00
55 Pau Gasol 3.00 8.00
56 Andre Iguodala 2.00 5.00
57 Greg Monroe 1.50 4.00
58 Eric Bledsoe 1.50 4.00
59 Jonas Valanciunas 1.50 4.00
60 Nicolas Batum 1.25 3.00
61 Russell Westbrook 3.00 8.00
62 John Wall 2.50 6.00
63 C.J. McCollum 2.00 5.00
64 Mike Conley 2.00 5.00
65 Derrick Rose 3.00 8.00
66 Enes Kanter 1.25 3.00
67 Stephen Curry 12.00 30.00
68 Rajon Rondo 2.50 6.00
69 Carmelo Anthony 3.00 8.00
70 Kemba Walker 2.00 5.00
71 Serge Ibaka 1.50 4.00
72 Marcin Gortat 1.25 3.00
73 Al-Farouq Aminu 1.25 3.00
74 Zach Randolph 1.25 3.00
75 Paul George 3.00 8.00
76 Marvin Williams 1.25 3.00
77 Draymond Green 2.50 6.00
78 Rudy Gay 2.00 5.00
79 Robin Lopez 1.25 3.00
80 Jeremy Lin 4.00 10.00
81 Rudy Gobert 2.50 6.00
82 Kawhi Leonard 6.00 15.00
83 Danilo Gallinari 1.50 4.00
84 Vince Carter 4.00 10.00
85 George Hill 1.50 4.00
86 Will Barton 1.50 4.00
87 Klay Thompson 5.00 12.00
88 DeMarcus Cousins 2.00 5.00
89 Jose Calderon 1.25 3.00
90 Paul Millsap 1.50 4.00
91 Gordon Hayward 2.00 5.00
92 LaMarcus Aldridge 2.00 5.00
93 Kenneth Faried 1.50 4.00
94 James Harden 4.00 10.00
95 Monta Ellis 1.50 4.00
96 C.J. Miles 1.25 3.00
97 Blake Griffin 2.00 5.00
98 Brook Lopez 2.00 5.00
99 Joe Johnson 1.50 4.00
100 Jeff Teague 1.25 3.00
101 Anthony Towns JSY AU/99 RC 1,500.00 3,000.00
102 D.Russell JSY AU/99 RC 400.00 800.00
103 J.Okafor JSY AU/99 RC 50.00 120.00
104 K.Porzingis JSY AU/99 RC 1,500.00 3,000.00
105 M.Hezonja JSY AU/99 RC 20.00 50.00
106 Cly-Stn JSY AU/99 RC EXCH 20.00 50.00
107 E.Mudiay JSY AU/99 RC EXCH 20.00 50.00
108 S.Johnson JSY AU/99 RC 20.00 50.00
109 Kmnsky JSY AU/99 RC EXCH 20.00 50.00
110 Winslow JSY AU/99 RC EXCH 25.00 60.00
111 M.Turner JSY AU/99 RC 200.00 500.00
112 Trey Lyles JSY AU/99 RC 20.00 50.00
113 D.Booker JSY AU/99 RC 5,000.00 10,000.00
114 C.Payne JSY AU/99 RC 25.00 60.00
115 K.Oubre Jr. JSY AU/99 RC 200.00 500.00
116 T.Rozier JSY AU/99 RC 100.00 250.00
117 J.Anderson JSY AU/99 RC 15.00 40.00
118 S.Dekker JSY AU/99 RC 15.00 40.00
119 J.Grant JSY AU/99 RC 15.00 40.00
120 Delon Wright JSY AU/99 RC 20.00 50.00
121 J.Anderson JSY AU/99 RC 15.00 40.00
122 B.Portis JSY AU/99 RC 100.00 250.00
123 Hlls-Jffrsn JSY AU/99 RC 40.00 100.00
124 T.Jones JSY AU/99 RC 40.00 100.00
125 Jarell Martin JSY AU/99 RC 15.00 40.00
126 L.Nance Jr. JSY AU/49 RC 30.00 80.00
127 R.J. Hunter JSY AU/99 RC 15.00 40.00
128 Chris McCullough JSY AU/99 RC 15.00 40.00
129 K.Looney JSY AU/99 RC 100.00 250.00
130 Montrezl Harrell JSY AU/99 RC 50.00 125.00
131 Jordan Mickey JSY AU/99 RC 15.00 40.00
132 Anthony Brown JSY AU/99 RC 15.00 40.00
133 Rakeem Christmas JSY AU/99 RC 15.00 40.00
134 R.Holmes JSY AU/99 RC 25.00 60.00
135 Pat Connaughton JSY AU/99 RC 40.00 100.00
136 Joe Young JSY AU/99 RC EXCH 15.00 40.00
137 Aaron Harrison JSY AU/49 RC EXCH 20.00 50.00
138 Richardson JSY AU/99 RC 25.00 60.00
139 Walter Tavares JSY AU/99 RC EXCH 15.00 40.00
140 Josh Huestis JSY AU/99 RC 15.00 40.00
141 Branden Dawson AU RC 4.00 10.00
142 T.J. McConnell AU RC EXCH 40.00 100.00
144 Cliff Alexander AU RC EXCH 4.00 10.00
145 Cristiano Felicio AU RC 5.00 12.00
146 Darrun Hilliard AU RC 4.00 10.00
147 Sasha Kaun AU RC 4.00 10.00
148 Duje Dukan AU RC 4.00 10.00
149 Luis Montero AU RC 4.00 10.00
150 J.Simmons AU RC EXCH 5.00 12.00
151 Nemanja Bjelica AU RC 6.00 15.00
152 Nikola Jokic AU RC 6,000.00 12,000.00
153 Norman Powell AU RC 40.00 100.00
154 Salah Mejri AU RC 4.00 10.00
155 Raul Neto AU RC 4.00 10.00
156 Marcelo Huertas AU RC 4.00 10.00
157 Boban Marjanovic AU RC 20.00 50.00

2015-16 Panini National Treasures Silver

*SILVER JSY AU: .5X TO 1.2X BASIC
*SILVER AU: .6X TO 1.5X BASIC
STATED PRINT RUN 25 SER.#'d SETS
EXCHANGE DEADLINE 11/11/2017

2015-16 Panini National Treasures Clutch Factor Jersey Autographs

PRINT RUNS B/WN 25-49 COPIES PER
EXCHANGE DEADLINE 11/11/2017
*PRIME/22-25: .75X TO 2X BASIC
CFAD Anthony Davis/25 40.00 100.00
CFBB Bradley Beal/49 12.00 30.00
CFBK Bernard King/49 8.00 20.00
CFBL Bill Laimbeer/49 6.00 15.00
CFBW Bill Walton/49 60.00 150.00
CFCB Chris Bosh/25 15.00 40.00
CFCL Christian Laettner/49 10.00 25.00
CFDR Dennis Rodman/49 30.00 80.00
CFIT Isiah Thomas/49 12.00 30.00
CFJE Julius Erving/25 40.00 100.00
CFKB Kobe Bryant/25 3,000.00 6,000.00
CFKD Kevin Durant/25 60.00 150.00
CFKI Kyrie Irving/25 40.00 100.00
CFKM Karl Malone/25 20.00 50.00
CFKS Kenny Smith/35 5.00 12.00
CFLB Larry Bird/25 40.00 100.00
CFRA Ray Allen/49 25.00 60.00
CFRA Ryan Anderson/49 4.00 10.00
CFRR Ricky Rubio/49 10.00 25.00
CFSB Shane Battier/49 5.00 12.00
CFSC Stephen Curry/25 600.00 1,200.00
CFSN Steve Nash/49 40.00 100.00
CFTH Tobias Harris/49 5.00 12.00
CFTP Tony Parker/49 15.00 40.00
CFVC Vince Carter/49 20.00 50.00
CFVD Vlade Divac/49 6.00 15.00
CFBDG Brad Daugherty/49 5.00 12.00
CFDGL Danilo Gallinari/49 5.00 12.00
CFDRS David Robinson/49 20.00 50.00
CFJDM Joe Dumars/49 8.00 20.00
CFJST John Stockton/25 25.00 60.00
CFKAJ Kareem Abdul-Jabbar/25 30.00 80.00
CFKVW Kiki VanDeWeghe/49 5.00 12.00
CFRFX Rick Fox/49 5.00 12.00
CFRPS Robert Parish/49 8.00 20.00
CFSKR Steve Kerr/49 12.00 30.00
CFSON Shaquille O'Neal/25 60.00 150.00
CFTHW Tim Hardaway/49 8.00 20.00
CFTKK Toni Kukoc/49 10.00 25.00
CFWBF World B. Free/49 5.00 12.00

2015-16 Panini National Treasures Colossal Jersey Signatures

PRINT RUNS B/WN 12-49 COPIES PER
NO PRICING ON QTY 12
EXCHANGE DEADLINE 11/11/2017
CJAB Anthony Brown/49 6.00 15.00
CJAD Anthony Davis/25 40.00 100.00
CJBG Blake Griffin/25 25.00 60.00
CJCA Carmelo Anthony/25 25.00 60.00
CJDR Dino Radja/35 8.00 20.00
CJEM E. Mudiay/49 EXCH 8.00 20.00
CJFK Frank Kaminsky/49 5.00 12.00
CJGH Gordon Hayward/49 5.00 12.00
CJGP Gary Payton/49 15.00 40.00
CJHO Hakeem Olajuwon/49 20.00 50.00
CJJB Jerryd Bayless/49 4.00 10.00
CJJO Jahlil Okafor/49 8.00 20.00
CJJP Jabari Parker/49 20.00 50.00
CJJR Julius Randle/49 12.00 30.00
CJJW Justise Winslow/49 10.00 25.00
CJJW John Wall/49 20.00 50.00
CJKB Kobe Bryant/25 3,000.00 6,000.00

CJKD Kevin Durant/25 60.00 150.00
CJKI Kyrie Irving/25 40.00 100.00
CJKL Kevon Looney/49 6.00 15.00
CJKL Kevin Love/49 20.00 50.00
CJKM Karl Malone/25 25.00 60.00
CJKP Kristaps Porzingis/49 200.00 500.00
CJMD Matthew Dellavedova/49 12.00 30.00
CJMG Marcin Gortat/49 4.00 10.00
CJMH Mario Hezonja/49 15.00 40.00
CJMT Myles Turner/49 25.00 60.00
CJTM Timofey Mozgov/49 4.00 10.00
CJTP Tony Parker/49 20.00 50.00
CJTR Terry Rozier/49 10.00 25.00
CJADR Andre Drummond/49 12.00 30.00
CJBBD Bojan Bogdanovic/49 5.00 12.00
CJCDX Clyde Drexler/49 20.00 50.00
CJCPN Cameron Payne/49 6.00 15.00
CJCPT Bobby Portis/49 12.00 30.00
CJDBK Devin Booker/49 1,500.00 3,000.00
CJDRS D'Angelo Russell/49 60.00 150.00
CJDWT Delon Wright/49 6.00 15.00
CJJAN Justin Anderson/49 8.00 20.00
CJJDM Joe Dumars/49 8.00 20.00
CJJGR Jerian Grant/49 8.00 20.00
CJJMK Jordan Mickey/49 6.00 15.00
CJKMT Khris Middleton/49 60.00 150.00
CJKOJ Kelly Oubre Jr./49 10.00 25.00
CJKTH Klay Thompson/49 50.00 120.00
CJLGW Langston Galloway/49 4.00 10.00
CJMCL Mike Conley/49 6.00 15.00
CJMJS Mark Jackson/49 5.00 12.00
CJRHJ R. Hollis-Jefferson/49 10.00 25.00
CJRHP Ron Harper/49 6.00 15.00
CJRJH R.J. Hunter/49 5.00 12.00
CJSJS Stanley Johnson/49 15.00 40.00
CJSON Shaquille O'Neal/25 60.00 150.00
CJTHJ Tim Hardaway Jr./49 5.00 12.00
CJTJS Tyus Jones/49 8.00 20.00
CJTJW T.J. Warren/49 6.00 15.00
CJTLS Trey Lyles/49 10.00 25.00
CJWCS Willie Cauley-Stein/49 25.00 60.00
CJZLV Zach LaVine/49 20.00 50.00

2015-16 Panini National Treasures Colossal Jersey Signatures Prime

*PRIME/25: .75X TO 2X BASIC
PRINT RUNS B/WN 9-25 COPIES PER
NO PRICING ON QTY 15 OR LESS
EXCHANGE DEADLINE 11/11/2017
CJKL Kevon Looney/25 75.00 200.00
CJKP Kristaps Porzingis/25 600.00 1,200.00
CJMT Myles Turner/25 250.00 500.00
CJCPT Bobby Portis/25 75.00 200.00
CJDRS D'Angelo Russell/25 400.00 800.00
CJJGR Jerian Grant/25 25.00 60.00
CJKOJ Kelly Oubre Jr./25 60.00 150.00
CJRHJ R. Hollis-Jefferson/25 40.00 100.00
CJSJS Stanley Johnson/25 150.00 300.00
CJTJS Tyus Jones/25 40.00 100.00
CJTLS Trey Lyles/25 150.00 400.00
CJZLV Zach LaVine/25 100.00 200.00

2015-16 Panini National Treasures Colossal Jerseys

PRINT RUNS B/WN 49-99 COPIES PER
1 Andre Iguodala/99 5.00 12.00
2 Paul Millsap/60 3.00 8.00
3 Joakim Noah/99 2.50 6.00
4 Tony Parker/99 6.00 15.00
5 Derrick Rose/49 6.00 15.00
6 Kyrie Irving/99 6.00 15.00
7 Nikola Vucevic/99 3.00 8.00
8 Kyle Korver/60 3.00 8.00
9 Andrew Wiggins/99 5.00 12.00
10 Brook Lopez/99 4.00 10.00
11 Tobias Harris/99 3.00 8.00
12 Greg Monroe/99 3.00 8.00
13 Dirk Nowitzki/99 10.00 25.00
14 Chris Paul/60 8.00 20.00
15 Marcus Smart/99 5.00 12.00
16 LeBron James/49 30.00 80.00
17 Kemba Walker/60 4.00 10.00
18 Ty Lawson/60 2.50 6.00
19 Jimmy Butler/60 8.00 20.00
20 Kyle Lowry/99 4.00 10.00
21 DeAndre Jordan/60 3.00 8.00
22 Nerlens Noel/99 2.50 6.00
23 Tim Duncan/99 10.00 25.00
24 LaMarcus Aldridge/99 4.00 10.00
25 Bojan Bogdanovic/99 3.00 8.00
26 Langston Galloway/99 2.50 6.00
27 Russell Westbrook/60 6.00 15.00
28 Damian Lillard/49 6.00 15.00
29 Manu Ginobili/60 8.00 20.00
30 C.J. McCollum/60 4.00 10.00
31 Jeremy Lin/60 8.00 20.00
32 Victor Oladipo/99 3.00 8.00
33 James Harden/60 8.00 20.00
34 Zach Randolph/99 4.00 10.00
35 Jared Sullinger/99 2.50 6.00

2015-16 Panini National Treasures Colossal Jerseys Prime

*PRIME/20-25: .75X TO 2X BASIC
PRINT RUNS B/WN 5-25 COPIES PER
NO PRICING ON QTY 13 OR LESS
4 Tony Parker/25 25.00 60.00
23 Tim Duncan/25 30.00 80.00
24 LaMarcus Aldridge/25 30.00 80.00
29 Manu Ginobili/25 20.00 50.00

2015-16 Panini National Treasures Game Changers Autographs

PRINT RUNS B/WN 25-49 COPIES PER
EXCHANGE DEADLINE 11/11/2017
GCAD Andre Drummond/49 8.00 20.00
GCAH Anfernee Hardaway/35 30.00 80.00
GCAH Allan Houston/49 5.00 12.00
GCAM Alonzo Mourning/25 20.00 50.00
GCAW Andrew Wiggins/25 20.00 50.00
GCBS Byron Scott/49 5.00 12.00
GCBW Bill Walton/49 40.00 100.00
GCCM Calvin Murphy/49 5.00 12.00
GCDM Dikembe Mutombo/49 12.00 30.00
GCDM Danny Manning/49 5.00 12.00
GCDW Dwyane Wade/25 50.00 120.00
GCEK Enes Kanter/49 4.00 10.00
GCFR Frank Ramsey/49 10.00 25.00
GCJE Julius Erving/25 30.00 80.00
GCJP Jabari Parker/25 20.00 50.00
GCJR Julius Randle/49 10.00 25.00
GCJW James Worthy/49 15.00 40.00
GCKI Kyrie Irving/25 30.00 80.00
GCKL Kevin Love/35 10.00 25.00
GCKM Karl Malone/25 30.00 80.00
GCKR Kurt Rambis/49 5.00 12.00
GCKT Klay Thompson/35 40.00 100.00
GCLB Larry Brown/49 6.00 15.00
GCLW Lenny Wilkens/49 8.00 20.00
GCMC Mike Conley/49 6.00 15.00
GCMR Mitch Richmond/49 8.00 20.00
GCMS Marcus Smart/35 12.00 30.00
GCNA Nate Archibald/49 6.00 15.00
GCRG Rudy Gay/49 8.00 20.00
GCRP Robert Parish/49 8.00 20.00
GCRS Ralph Sampson/49 5.00 12.00
GCSS Satch Sanders/49 12.00 30.00
GCVO Victor Oladipo/35 6.00 15.00
GCWM Wesley Matthews/49 4.00 10.00
GCCAY Carmelo Anthony/25 20.00 50.00
GCDCW Dave Cowens/49 6.00 15.00
GCDMC DeMarre Carroll/49 4.00 10.00
GCDMD Doug McDermott/49 8.00 20.00
GCEHY Elvin Hayes/49 10.00 25.00
GCGAT G. Antetokounmpo/49 60.00 150.00
GCGHW Gordon Hayward/49 6.00 15.00
GCJDM Joe Dumars/49 8.00 20.00
GCJHD Jrue Holiday/49 8.00 20.00
GCJJW Jo Jo White/49 6.00 15.00
GCJKD Jason Kidd/25 12.00 30.00
GCJNK Jusuf Nurkic/49 5.00 12.00
GCKMH Kevin McHale/25 12.00 30.00
GCKSM Kenny Smith/49 5.00 12.00
GCMJS Mark Jackson/49 5.00 12.00
GCNVE Nick Van Exel/49 10.00 25.00
GCTAL Tony Allen/49 4.00 10.00
GCTHS Tobias Harris/49 5.00 12.00
GCTJW T.J. Warren/49 5.00 12.00
GCTMG Tracy McGrady/35 30.00 80.00
GCWCH Wilson Chandler/49 5.00 12.00
GCWFZ Walt Frazier/49 5.00 12.00
GCZLV Zach LaVine/49 15.00 40.00

2015-16 Panini National Treasures Hometown Heroes Autographs

PRINT RUNS B/WN 25-75 COPIES PER
EXCHANGE DEADLINE 11/11/2017
HHAD Anthony Davis/25 40.00 100.00
HHAI Allen Iverson/25 150.00 250.00
HHBG Blake Griffin/25 25.00 60.00
HHCP Chris Paul/25 60.00 150.00
HHDW Dwyane Wade/25 60.00 150.00
HHFR Frank Ramsey/75 12.00 30.00
HHGP Gary Payton/49 15.00 40.00
HHJE Julius Erving/25 30.00 80.00
HHJR Julius Randle/75 10.00 25.00
HHJW Justise Winslow/75 20.00 50.00
HHJW Jerry West/25 25.00 60.00
HHKB Kobe Bryant/25 3,000.00 6,000.00
HHKD Kevin Durant/25 60.00 150.00
HHKI Kyrie Irving/25 30.00 80.00
HHKM Karl Malone/25 20.00 50.00
HHKM Kevin McHale/49 12.00 30.00
HHLB Larry Bird/25 50.00 120.00
HHMC Mike Conley/75 6.00 15.00
HHMR Mitch Richmond/75 8.00 20.00
HHRP Robert Parish/75 8.00 20.00
HHSC Stephen Curry/25 500.00 1,000.00
HHSS Satch Sanders/75 10.00 25.00
HHWF Walt Frazier/75 10.00 25.00
HHAHW Anfernee Hardaway/49 20.00 50.00
HHBKG Bernard King/75 8.00 20.00
HHBWT Bill Walton/75 40.00 100.00
HHCAY Carmelo Anthony/25 20.00 50.00
HHCHG Cliff Hagan/75 6.00 15.00
HHDCR DeMarre Carroll/75 4.00 10.00
HHJJW Jo Jo White/75 6.00 15.00
HHJKD Jason Kidd/49 12.00 30.00
HHKAJ Kareem Abdul-Jabbar/25 40.00 100.00
HHMJS Magic Johnson/25 30.00 80.00
HHMST Marcus Smart/49 8.00 20.00
HHNVE Nick Van Exel/75 8.00 20.00
HHRAL Rafer Alston/75 4.00 10.00
HHSBT Shane Battier/75 5.00 12.00
HHSON S. O'Neal/25 100.00 250.00
HHTMG Tracy McGrady/49 30.00 80.00
HHMJS2 Mark Jackson/75 5.00 12.00

2015-16 Panini National Treasures International Treasures Autographs

PRINT RUNS B/WN 25-75 COPIES PER
EXCHANGE DEADLINE 11/11/2017
ITAW Andrew Wiggins/25 60.00 150.00
ITBB Bojan Bogdanovic/75 6.00 15.00
ITDM Dikembe Mutombo/75 12.00 30.00
ITDW Dominique Wilkins/25 20.00 50.00
ITEK Enes Kanter/75 4.00 10.00
ITEM Emmanuel Mudiay/25 20.00 50.00
ITGA G. Antetokounmpo/75 75.00 200.00
ITJN Jusuf Nurkic/75 12.00 30.00
ITKI Kyrie Irving/25 125.00 250.00
ITKP Kristaps Porzingis/49 100.00 250.00
ITMG Marcin Gortat/75 8.00 20.00
ITMH Mario Hezonja/49 20.00 50.00
ITNB Nemanja Bjelica/75 12.00 30.00
ITNJ Nikola Jokic/75 3,000.00 6,000.00
ITRF Rick Fox/49 5.00 12.00
ITRR Ricky Rubio/25 40.00 100.00
ITSN Steve Nash/25 75.00 200.00
ITTP Tony Parker/25 40.00 100.00
ITWT Walter Tavares/75 4.00 10.00
ITDGL Danilo Gallinari/49 5.00 12.00
ITDRJ Dino Radja/75 12.00 30.00
ITHOW Hakeem Olajuwon/49 20.00 50.00
ITMHT Marcelo Huertas/75 6.00 15.00
ITNMT Nikola Mirotic/75 4.00 10.00
ITRNT Raul Neto/75 4.00 10.00
ITRSK Rony Seikaly/75 5.00 12.00
ITSMC Sarunas Marciulionis/75 8.00 20.00
ITTKK Toni Kukoc/75 15.00 40.00
ITTMZ Timofey Mozgov/75 4.00 10.00
ITVDV Vlade Divac/75 10.00 25.00

2015-16 Panini National Treasures Lasting Legacies Jersey Autographs

PRINT RUNS B/WN 25-49 COPIES PER
EXCHANGE DEADLINE 11/11/2017
*PRIME/25: .75X TO 2X BASIC
LLAD Anthony Davis/25 50.00 120.00
LLAM Alonzo Mourning/25 20.00 50.00
LLBG Blake Griffin/25 20.00 50.00
LLBW Bill Walton/49 60.00 150.00
LLGH Grant Hill/49 20.00 50.00
LLGP Gary Payton/49 20.00 50.00
LLHO Hakeem Olajuwon/25 20.00 50.00
LLJE Julius Erving/25 40.00 100.00
LLJW John Wall/25 20.00 50.00
LLKB Kobe Bryant/25 3,000.00 6,000.00
LLKD Kevin Durant/25 60.00 150.00
LLKI Kyrie Irving/25 30.00 80.00
LLKM Kevin McHale/49 10.00 25.00
LLKM Karl Malone/25 25.00 60.00
LLMJ Mark Jackson/49 5.00 12.00
LLSC Stephen Curry/25 500.00 1,000.00
LLADL Adrian Dantley/49 6.00 15.00
LLBDT Brad Daugherty/49 5.00 12.00
LLCDX Clyde Drexler/25 20.00 50.00
LLDMG Danny Manning/49 5.00 12.00
LLDMT Dikembe Mutombo/49 10.00 25.00
LLDRJ Dino Radja/49 12.00 30.00
LLJDM Joe Dumars/49 8.00 20.00
LLJKD Jason Kidd/49 15.00 40.00
LLMJS Magic Johnson/25 40.00 100.00
LLRAL Rafer Alston/49 5.00 12.00
LLRHP Ron Harper/49 6.00 15.00
LLRSP Ralph Sampson/49 5.00 12.00
LLSON Shaquille O'Neal/25 60.00 150.00
LLWBF World B. Free/49 5.00 12.00

2015-16 Panini National Treasures Material Treasures

1 Arvydas Sabonis/99 4.00 10.00
2 Dirk Nowitzki/75 10.00 25.00
3 Serge Ibaka/75 3.00 8.00
4 Isiah Thomas/49 4.00 10.00
5 Aaron Gordon/75 4.00 10.00
6 Karl Malone/75 6.00 15.00
7 Kevin McHale/75 6.00 15.00
8 C.J. McCollum/75 4.00 10.00
9 Mark Jackson/49 3.00 8.00
10 Danny Green/75 3.00 8.00
11 Ray Allen/75 5.00 12.00
12 Eric Bledsoe/75 3.00 8.00
13 Shaquille O'Neal/75 6.00 15.00
14 Jeff Teague/75 2.50 6.00
15 Alonzo Mourning/99 6.00 15.00
16 Kawhi Leonard/75 12.00 30.00
17 Larry Bird/75 15.00 40.00
18 Chris Andersen/75 3.00 8.00
19 Michael Redd/75 3.00 8.00
20 David Robinson/75 5.00 12.00
21 Reggie Lewis/75 4.00 10.00
22 Gary Payton/75 6.00 15.00
23 Steve Nash/75 6.00 15.00
24 Jimmy Butler/75 8.00 20.00
25 Alonzo Mourning/99 6.00 15.00
26 Kenneth Faried/75 3.00 8.00
27 Chris Bosh/75 5.00 12.00
28 Larry Johnson/75 5.00 12.00
29 Mike Bibby/75 3.00 8.00
30 DeMar DeRozan/75 5.00 12.00
31 Russell Westbrook/75 5.00 12.00
32 Gordon Hayward/75 4.00 10.00
33 Tim Duncan/75 10.00 25.00
34 John Starks/75 4.00 10.00
35 Blake Griffin/75 4.00 10.00
36 Kevin Durant/49 6.00 15.00
37 Manu Ginobili/75 8.00 20.00
38 Clyde Drexler/75 6.00 15.00
39 Moses Malone/75 6.00 15.00
40 DeMarcus Cousins/75 4.00 10.00
41 Scottie Pippen/75 8.00 20.00
42 Grant Hill/75 6.00 15.00
43 Tony Parker/75 6.00 15.00
44 John Stockton/75 5.00 12.00
45 Bradley Beal/75 5.00 12.00
46 Kevin Garnett/75 5.00 12.00
47 Mark Aguirre/75 3.00 8.00
48 Damian Lillard/49 10.00 25.00
49 Patrick Ewing/75 6.00 15.00
50 Dennis Rodman/75 10.00 25.00

2015-16 Panini National Treasures Material Treasures Prime

*PRIME/25: .75X TO 2X BASIC
PRINT RUNS B/WN 10-25 COPIES PER
NO PRICING ON QTY 10
16 Kawhi Leonard/25 20.00 50.00
41 Scottie Pippen/25 25.00 60.00
46 Kevin Garnett/25 20.00 50.00

2015-16 Panini National Treasures Material Treasures Signatures

PRINT RUNS B/WN 25-99 COPIES PER
EXCHANGE DEADLINE 11/11/2017
*PRIME/25: .75X TO 2X BASIC
MTSAH Al Horford/99 6.00 15.00
MTSAI Allen Iverson/99 40.00 100.00
MTSBG Blake Griffin/75 20.00 50.00
MTSBK Bernard King/99 8.00 20.00
MTSBS Byron Scott/90 5.00 12.00
MTSCL Christian Laettner/99 8.00 20.00
MTSCM Chris Mullin/75 12.00 30.00
MTSCW Chris Webber/77 40.00 100.00
MTSDN Dirk Nowitzki/99 60.00 150.00
MTSDR D'Angelo Russell/99 40.00 100.00
MTSDR David Robinson/99 15.00 40.00
MTSDR Dennis Rodman/99 15.00 40.00
MTSEM Emmanuel Mudiay/99 10.00 25.00
MTSGH Grant Hill/99 12.00 30.00
MTSHO Hakeem Olajuwon/99 15.00 40.00
MTSJS John Stockton/85 20.00 50.00
MTSJW Justise Winslow/99 6.00 15.00
MTSJW John Wall/99 20.00 50.00
MTSKA Abdul-Jabbar/30 30.00 80.00
MTSKM Karl Malone/72 20.00 50.00
MTSKP Kristaps Porzingis/99 100.00 250.00
MTSKT Karl-Anthony Towns/99 150.00 300.00
MTSMH Mario Hezonja/99 5.00 12.00
MTSPG Paul George/46 25.00 60.00
MTSRA Ray Allen/99 15.00 40.00
MTSRH Richard Hamilton/76 6.00 15.00
MTSRS Ralph Sampson/99 5.00 12.00
MTSSK Steve Kerr/99 15.00 40.00
MTSSP Scottie Pippen/25 50.00 120.00
MTSTB Trey Burke/99 4.00 10.00
MTSVO Victor Oladipo/99 5.00 12.00
MTSCMU Calvin Murphy/99 5.00 12.00
MTSDMA Danny Manning/99 5.00 12.00

2015-16 Panini National Treasures NBA Game Gear Duals

PRINT RUNS B/WN 45-75 COPIES PER
1 David Robinson/75 8.00 20.00
2 Russell Westbrook/75 6.00 15.00
3 Scottie Pippen/75 10.00 25.00
4 Derrick Rose/49 5.00 12.00
5 World B. Free/49 3.00 8.00
6 Stephen Curry/49 30.00 80.00
7 Rudy Gobert/75 5.00 12.00
8 Blake Griffin/75 4.00 10.00
9 John Stockton/75 5.00 12.00
10 Andrew Wiggins/75 5.00 12.00
11 Dennis Rodman/75 10.00 25.00
12 Damian Lillard/49 6.00 15.00
13 Ben Wallace/75 3.00 8.00
14 Kyrie Irving/75 5.00 12.00
15 Gail Goodrich/49 4.00 10.00
16 James Harden/75 8.00 20.00
17 Rick Fox/75 3.00 8.00
18 Kobe Bryant/75 75.00 200.00
19 Karl Malone/75 6.00 15.00
20 Anthony Davis/75 6.00 15.00
21 Danny Manning/75 3.00 8.00
22 Tim Duncan/75 10.00 25.00
23 Kevin McHale/75 6.00 15.00
24 LeBron James/49 25.00 60.00
25 Moses Malone/75 6.00 15.00
26 Gordon Hayward/75 4.00 10.00
27 Steve Nash/75 6.00 15.00
28 Dwyane Wade/75 6.00 15.00
29 Grant Hill/75 6.00 15.00
30 Carmelo Anthony/75 6.00 15.00
31 Clyde Drexler/75 6.00 15.00
32 John Wall/75 5.00 12.00
33 Larry Bird/75 15.00 40.00
34 Dirk Nowitzki/75 10.00 25.00
35 Gary Payton/75 6.00 15.00
36 Chris Paul/75 5.00 12.00
37 Cazzie Russell/45 3.00 8.00
38 Derrick Favors/75 3.00 8.00
39 Patrick Ewing/75 6.00 15.00
40 Kevin Durant/49 8.00 20.00

2015-16 Panini National Treasures NBA Game Gear Duals Prime

*PRIME/25: .75X TO 2X BASIC
PRINT RUNS B/WN 10-25 COPIES PER
NO PRICING ON QTY 15 OR LESS
18 Kobe Bryant/25 150.00 400.00
22 Tim Duncan/25 20.00 50.00
28 Dwyane Wade/25 20.00 50.00

2015-16 Panini National Treasures NBA Game Gear Signatures

PRINT RUNS B/WN 25-49 COPIES PER
EXCHANGE DEADLINE 11/11/2017
*PRIME/25: .75X TO 2X BASIC
GGAD Anthony Davis/25 40.00 100.00
GGAW Andrew Wiggins/25 40.00 100.00
GGBG Blake Griffin/25 20.00 50.00
GGCP Chris Paul/25 60.00 150.00
GGDW Dwyane Wade/25 40.00 100.00
GGEP Elfrid Payton/49 5.00 12.00
GGGH Gordon Hayward/49 6.00 15.00
GGIT Isaiah Thomas/49 25.00 60.00
GGJH Jrue Holiday/49 8.00 20.00
GGJR Julius Randle/49 12.00 30.00
GGJW John Wall/25 20.00 50.00
GGKB Kobe Bryant/25 3,000.00 6,000.00
GGKD Kevin Durant/25 60.00 150.00
GGKI Kyrie Irving/25 30.00 80.00
GGKL Kevin Love/25 20.00 50.00
GGKL Kawhi Leonard/49 40.00 100.00
GGKT Klay Thompson/49 40.00 100.00
GGMP Mason Plumlee/49 4.00 10.00
GGRA Ryan Anderson/49 4.00 10.00
GGRG Rudy Gay/49 6.00 15.00
GGSC Stephen Curry/25 600.00 1,200.00
GGADR Andre Drummond/49 8.00 20.00
GGAGD Aaron Gordon/49 8.00 20.00
GGBJB Bojan Bogdanovic/49 5.00 12.00
GGCAY Carmelo Anthony/25 25.00 60.00
GGDMC DeMarre Carroll/49 6.00 15.00
GGGAT G. Antetokounmpo/49 40.00 100.00
GGJNK Jusuf Nurkic/49 5.00 12.00
GGJPK Jabari Parker/25 15.00 40.00
GGKFR Kenneth Faried/49 5.00 12.00
GGLGW Langston Galloway/49 4.00 10.00
GGMCL Mike Conley/49 6.00 15.00
GGMGT Marcin Gortat/49 4.00 10.00
GGMST Marcus Smart/49 8.00 20.00
GGNMT Nikola Mirotic/49 8.00 20.00
GGTHJ Tim Hardaway Jr./49 5.00 12.00
GGTJW T.J. Warren/49 6.00 15.00
GGVOD Victor Oladipo/49 5.00 12.00
GGWCH Wilson Chandler/49 5.00 12.00
GGZLV Zach LaVine/49 15.00 40.00

2015-16 Panini National Treasures NBA Game Gear Triples

PRINT RUNS B/WN 25-49 COPIES PER
*PRIME/25: .75X TO 2X BASIC
1 John Wall/49 5.00 12.00
2 Andrew Wiggins/49 5.00 12.00
3 Chris Paul/49 8.00 20.00
4 James Harden/49 8.00 20.00
5 Patrick Ewing/49 6.00 15.00
6 Anthony Davis/49 6.00 15.00
7 LeBron James/25 50.00 120.00
8 Russell Westbrook/49 6.00 15.00
9 Chandler Parsons/49 2.50 6.00
10 Stephen Curry/25 30.00 80.00
11 Dirk Nowitzki/49 10.00 25.00
12 Damian Lillard/25 6.00 15.00
13 Arron Afflalo/49 2.50 6.00
14 Kobe Bryant/49 75.00 200.00
15 Kevin Durant/25 8.00 20.00
16 Tim Duncan/49 10.00 25.00
17 Moses Malone/49 6.00 15.00
18 Derrick Rose/25 6.00 15.00
19 Dwyane Wade/49 5.00 12.00
20 Blake Griffin/49 4.00 10.00

2015-16 Panini National Treasures NBA Greats Signatures

PRINT RUNS B/WN 56-99 COPIES PER
EXCHANGE DEADLINE 11/11/2017
GR8AG Artis Gilmore/99 5.00 12.00
GR8AH Anfernee Hardaway/85 15.00 40.00
GR8BW Bill Walton/99 40.00 100.00
GR8CH Cliff Hagan/99 6.00 15.00
GR8CW Chris Webber/99 30.00 80.00
GR8DB Dave Bing/99 12.00 30.00
GR8EB Elgin Baylor/56 10.00 25.00
GR8EH Elvin Hayes/99 10.00 25.00
GR8FR Frank Ramsey/99 10.00 25.00
GR8GG Gail Goodrich/83 6.00 15.00
GR8HG Hal Greer/99 8.00 20.00
GR8JW Jerry West/99 20.00 50.00
GR8KA K. Abdul-Jabbar/76 25.00 60.00
GR8LW Lenny Wilkens/99 6.00 15.00
GR8OR Oscar Robertson/99 25.00 60.00
GR8SP Scottie Pippen/72 40.00 100.00
GR8WU Wes Unseld/99 6.00 15.00

2015-16 Panini National Treasures NBA Materials

PRINT RUNS B/WN 49-99 COPIES PER
1 Jimmy Butler/99 8.00 20.00
2 Darren Collison/99 2.50 6.00
3 Chris Andersen/99 3.00 8.00
4 Kyle Korver/99 3.00 8.00
5 Tim Duncan/99 10.00 25.00
6 Terrence Ross/99 3.00 8.00
7 Bradley Beal/99 5.00 12.00
8 Kyrie Irving/99 6.00 15.00
9 LaMarcus Aldridge/99 4.00 10.00
10 Derrick Rose/49 5.00 12.00
11 Kenneth Faried/99 3.00 8.00
12 Doug McDermott/99 3.00 8.00
13 Kawhi Leonard/99 5.00 12.00
14 Markieff Morris/99 2.50 6.00
15 Blake Griffin/99 4.00 10.00
16 Trey Burke/99 2.50 6.00
17 Kevin Garnett/99 5.00 12.00
18 John Wall/99 5.00 12.00
19 Dirk Nowitzki/99 10.00 25.00
20 Archie Goodwin/99 2.50 6.00
21 Chris Bosh/99 5.00 12.00
22 Evan Fournier/99 3.00 8.00
23 Jeff Teague/99 2.50 6.00
24 Mo Williams/99 3.00 8.00
25 Manu Ginobili/99 8.00 20.00
26 Zach Randolph/99 4.00 10.00
27 Damian Lillard/49 10.00 25.00
28 Anthony Davis/99 6.00 15.00
29 Serge Ibaka/99 3.00 8.00
30 Boris Diaw/99 3.00 8.00
31 DeMar DeRozan/99 5.00 12.00
32 John Henson/99 2.50 6.00
33 Eric Bledsoe/99 3.00 8.00
34 Otto Porter/99 3.00 8.00
35 DeMarcus Cousins/99 4.00 10.00
36 Kevin Durant/49 8.00 20.00
37 Stephen Curry/49 30.00 80.00
38 Aaron Gordon/99 4.00 10.00
39 Brandon Jennings/99 2.50 6.00
40 Russell Westbrook/99 6.00 15.00
41 Kelly Olynyk/99 2.50 6.00
42 Danny Green/99 3.00 8.00
43 Rodney Hood/99 3.00 8.00
44 Tony Parker/99 6.00 15.00
45 Kobe Bryant/99 60.00 150.00
46 Klay Thompson/99 10.00 25.00
47 C.J. McCollum/99 4.00 10.00
48 Danilo Gallinari/99 3.00 8.00
49 Gordon Hayward/99 4.00 10.00
50 Jordan Clarkson/99 4.00 10.00

2015-16 Panini National Treasures NBA Materials Prime

*PRIME/25: .75X TO 2X BASIC
PRINT RUNS B/WN 5-25 COPIES PER
NO PRICING ON QTY 10
17 Kevin Garnett/25 40.00 100.00
45 Kobe Bryant/25 125.00 300.00

2015-16 Panini National Treasures NBA Rookie Materials

PRINT RUNS B/WN 86-99 COPIES PER
1 Emmanuel Mudiay/99 3.00 8.00
2 Salah Mejri/99 2.50 6.00
3 Cameron Payne/99 4.00 10.00
4 Luis Montero/99 2.50 6.00
5 Marcelo Huertas/99 2.50 6.00
6 Kelly Oubre Jr./99 8.00 20.00
7 Justise Winslow/99 4.00 10.00
8 Cristiano Felicio/99 3.00 8.00
9 Trey Lyles/99 3.00 8.00
10 Nikola Jokic/99 400.00 800.00
11 Frank Kaminsky/99 3.00 8.00
12 Sasha Kaun/99 3.00 8.00
13 Rondae Hollis-Jefferson/99 3.00 8.00
14 Tyus Jones/99 3.00 8.00
15 Jerian Grant/99 2.50 6.00
16 Montrezl Harrell/99 8.00 20.00
17 Kristaps Porzingis/86 15.00 40.00
18 R.J. Hunter/99 2.50 6.00
19 Jahlil Okafor/99 3.00 8.00
20 Raul Neto/99 2.50 6.00
21 Norman Powell/99 5.00 12.00
22 Jonathon Simmons/99 3.00 8.00
23 Cliff Alexander/99 2.50 6.00
24 Nemanja Bjelica/99 4.00 10.00
25 Myles Turner/99 10.00 25.00
26 Stanley Johnson/99 3.00 8.00
27 Bobby Portis/99 6.00 15.00
28 Mario Hezonja/99 3.00 8.00
29 Karl-Anthony Towns/99 12.00 30.00
30 Willie Cauley-Stein/99 3.00 8.00
31 D'Angelo Russell/99 6.00 15.00
32 Pat Connaughton/99 4.00 10.00
33 Terry Rozier/99 10.00 25.00
34 Devin Booker/99 30.00 80.00
35 Justin Anderson/99 2.50 6.00

2015-16 Panini National Treasures NBA Rookie Materials Prime

*PRIME/25: .75X TO 2X BASIC
PRINT RUNS B/WN 10-25 COPIES PER
NO PRICING ON QTY 10

2015-16 Panini National Treasures Night Moves Jersey Autographs

PRINT RUNS B/WN 25-49 COPIES PER
EXCHANGE DEADLINE 11/11/2017
*PRIME/24-25: .75X TO 2X BASIC
NMAD Anthony Davis/25 40.00 100.00
NMAD Andre Drummond/49 10.00 25.00
NMBG Blake Griffin/25 20.00 50.00
NMDR Dino Radja/49 12.00 30.00
NMGH Gordon Hayward/49 6.00 15.00
NMGP Gary Payton/49 10.00 25.00
NMHO Hakeem Olajuwon/25 20.00 50.00
NMJP Jabari Parker/25 15.00 40.00
NMJW John Wall/25 20.00 50.00
NMKB Kobe Bryant/25 2,000.00 4,000.00
NMKD Kevin Durant/25 60.00 150.00
NMKI Kyrie Irving/25 30.00 80.00
NMKL Kevin Love/49 15.00 40.00
NMKM Karl Malone/25 20.00 50.00
NMMJ Mark Jackson/49 5.00 12.00
NMADL Adrian Dantley/49 6.00 15.00
NMBJB Bojan Bogdanovic/49 5.00 12.00
NMCAY Carmelo Anthony/25 25.00 60.00
NMCDX Clyde Drexler/25 20.00 50.00
NMJDM Joe Dumars/49 8.00 20.00
NMJRD Julius Randle/49 10.00 25.00
NMKTM Klay Thompson/49 50.00 120.00
NMLGW Langston Galloway/49 4.00 10.00
NMMCL Mike Conley/49 6.00 15.00
NMMGT Marcin Gortat/49 4.00 10.00
NMRHP Ron Harper/49 6.00 15.00
NMSON Shaquille O'Neal/25 60.00 150.00
NMTHJ Tim Hardaway Jr./49 5.00 12.00
NMTJW T.J. Warren/49 6.00 15.00
NMZLV Zach LaVine/49 15.00 40.00

2015-16 Panini National Treasures Notable Nicknames

STATED PRINT RUN 25 SER.#'d SETS
EXCHANGE DEADLINE 11/11/2017
NNAI Allen Iverson 150.00 400.00
NNFK Frank Kaminsky 25.00 60.00
NNGH Grant Hill 150.00 300.00
NNJW John Wall 250.00 400.00
NNMH Mario Hezonja 30.00 80.00
NNNB Nemanja Bjelica 40.00 100.00
NNRA Ray Allen 75.00 200.00
NNSJ Stanley Johnson 40.00 100.00
NNSN Steve Nash 75.00 200.00
NNDRS D'Angelo Russell 125.00 300.00
NNSON Shaquille O'Neal 150.00 300.00
NNWCS Willie Cauley-Stein 40.00 100.00

2015-16 Panini National Treasures Rookie Jumbo Materials

STATED PRINT RUN 99 SER.#'d SETS
1 Marcelo Huertas 2.50 6.00
2 Jerian Grant 2.50 6.00
3 Myles Turner 10.00 25.00
4 Justin Anderson 2.50 6.00
5 Justise Winslow 4.00 10.00
7 Bobby Portis 6.00 15.00
8 Trey Lyles 3.00 8.00
9 Jahlil Okafor 5.00 12.00
10 Karl-Anthony Towns 12.00 30.00
11 Emmanuel Mudiay 3.00 8.00
12 Frank Kaminsky 3.00 8.00
13 Norman Powell 5.00 12.00
14 D'Angelo Russell 6.00 15.00
15 Cameron Payne 4.00 10.00
16 Rondae Hollis-Jefferson 3.00 8.00
17 Cliff Alexander 2.50 6.00
18 Terry Rozier 10.00 25.00
19 Luis Montero 2.50 6.00
20 Tyus Jones 3.00 8.00
21 Nemanja Bjelica 4.00 10.00
22 Devin Booker 6.00 15.00
23 Kelly Oubre Jr. 8.00 20.00
24 Jarell Martin 2.50 6.00
25 Montrezl Harrell 8.00 20.00
26 Stanley Johnson 3.00 8.00
27 Cristiano Felicio 3.00 8.00
28 Delon Wright 3.00 8.00
29 R.J. Hunter 2.50 6.00
30 Mario Hezonja 3.00 8.00
31 Nikola Jokic 125.00 300.00
32 Anthony Brown 2.50 6.00
33 Raul Neto 2.50 6.00
34 Willie Cauley-Stein 3.00 8.00
35 Pat Connaughton 4.00 10.00

2015-16 Panini National Treasures Rookie Jumbo Materials Prime

*PRIME/25: .75X TO 2X BASIC
PRINT RUNS B/WN 10-25 COPIES PER
NO PRICING ON QTY 15 OR LESS
9 Jahlil Okafor/25 15.00 40.00
11 Emmanuel Mudiay/25 30.00 80.00
14 D'Angelo Russell/25 20.00 50.00
22 Devin Booker/25 20.00 50.00

2015-16 Panini National Treasures Signature Moves

PRINT RUNS B/WN 25-49 COPIES PER
EXCHANGE DEADLINE 11/11/2017
SMAI Allen Iverson 150.00 300.00
SMBG Blake Griffin 20.00 50.00
SMDM Dikembe Mutombo 12.00 30.00
SMDR Dennis Rodman 30.00 80.00
SMDW Dwyane Wade 60.00 150.00
SMDW Dominique Wilkins 12.00 30.00
SMGG George Gervin 15.00 40.00
SMHO Hakeem Olajuwon 20.00 50.00
SMJE Julius Erving 30.00 80.00
SMJS John Stockton 30.00 80.00
SMJW James Worthy 12.00 30.00
SMKB Kobe Bryant 2,000.00 4,000.00
SMKL Kevin Love 15.00 40.00
SMKM Kevin McHale 12.00 30.00
SMMJ Mark Jackson 5.00 12.00
SMRA Ray Allen 50.00 120.00
SMSC Stephen Curry 1,000.00 2,000.00
SMSN Steve Nash 75.00 200.00
SMTP Tony Parker 20.00 50.00
SMWM Wesley Matthews 4.00 10.00
SMWU Wes Unseld 8.00 20.00
SMCAY Carmelo Anthony 20.00 50.00
SMKAJ Kareem Abdul-Jabbar 50.00 120.00
SMKVW Kiki VanDeWeghe 5.00 12.00
SMRBY Rick Barry 12.00 30.00
SMSMC Sarunas Marciulionis 6.00 15.00
SMSON Shaquille O'Neal 75.00 200.00
SMTHW Tim Hardaway 8.00 20.00
SMTMG Tracy McGrady 40.00 100.00
SMMJS2 Magic Johnson 40.00 100.00

2015-16 Panini National Treasures Signatures

PRINT RUNS B/WN 25-75 COPIES PER
EXCHANGE DEADLINE 11/11/2017
SAD Anthony Davis/25 40.00 100.00
SAG Aaron Gordon/49 10.00 25.00
SAH Allan Houston/75 5.00 12.00
SAI Allen Iverson/25 150.00 300.00
SAW Andrew Wiggins/49 12.00 30.00
SBG Blake Griffin/25 20.00 50.00
SBK Bernard King/49 8.00 20.00
SBS Byron Scott/49 5.00 12.00
SCB Chris Bosh/49 8.00 20.00
SCP Chris Paul/25 60.00 150.00
SDH Dwight Howard/25 12.00 30.00
SDM Danny Manning/75 5.00 12.00
SEB Eric Bledsoe/49 6.00 15.00
SEH Elvin Hayes/75 8.00 20.00
SEP Elfrid Payton/75 5.00 12.00
SIT Isaiah Thomas/75 12.00 30.00
SIT Isiah Thomas/75 15.00 40.00
SJE Julius Erving/25 40.00 100.00
SJN Jusuf Nurkic/75 5.00 12.00
SJS Jerry Stackhouse/75 12.00 30.00
SJW Jerry West/25 25.00 60.00
SKB Kobe Bryant/25 3,000.00 6,000.00
SKD Kevin Durant/25 60.00 150.00
SKI Kyrie Irving/25 40.00 100.00
SKL Kevin Love/49 12.00 30.00
SKM Karl Malone/25 25.00 60.00
SKT Klay Thompson/49 60.00 150.00
SLB Larry Brown/49 8.00 20.00
SLW Lenny Wilkens/75 10.00 25.00
SMJ Magic Johnson/25 30.00 80.00
SNA Nate Archibald/75 6.00 15.00
SOR Oscar Robertson/25 40.00 100.00
SRG Rudy Gay/75 6.00 15.00
SRP Robert Parish/75 8.00 20.00
SSC Stephen Curry/25 500.00 1,000.00
SCAY Carmelo Anthony/25 20.00 50.00
SCDX Clyde Drexler/49 12.00 30.00
SCLT Christian Laettner/49 8.00 20.00
SDMD Doug McDermott/75 5.00 12.00
SGAT G. Antetokounmpo/75 125.00 300.00
SKFD Kenneth Faried/75 5.00 12.00
SMCL Mike Conley/75 6.00 15.00
SRSS Ralph Sampson/75 5.00 12.00
SSON Shaquille O'Neal/25 60.00 150.00
STAL Tony Allen/75 4.00 10.00

2015-16 Panini National Treasures Springfield Swatches

PRINT RUNS B/WN 25-49 COPIES PER
*PRIME/20-25: .75X TO 2X BASIC
1 George Mikan/49 15.00 40.00
2 Wilt Chamberlain/49 25.00 60.00
3 Jerry Lucas/49 5.00 12.00
4 Elgin Baylor/49 10.00 25.00
5 Hal Greer/49 6.00 15.00
6 Jerry West/49 10.00 25.00
7 Nate Thurmond/49 5.00 12.00
8 Rick Barry/25 5.00 12.00
9 Pete Maravich/49 20.00 50.00
10 Earl Monroe/49 5.00 12.00
11 Bob Lanier/25 5.00 12.00
12 Julius Erving/49 10.00 25.00
13 Bill Walton/49 6.00 15.00
14 Kareem Abdul-Jabbar/49 8.00 20.00
15 Moses Malone/49 6.00 15.00

2015-16 Panini National Treasures Super Swatches

PRINT RUNS B/WN 45-99 COPIES PER
1 Andrew Wiggins/99 5.00 12.00
2 DeMarcus Cousins/99 4.00 10.00
3 Chris Paul/75 5.00 12.00
4 Kevin Garnett/99 5.00 12.00
5 Jared Sullinger/99 2.50 6.00
6 James Harden/75 8.00 20.00
7 Chris Bosh/99 3.00 8.00
8 Arron Afflalo/99 2.50 6.00
9 Ty Lawson/75 2.50 6.00
10 Avery Bradley/99 2.50 6.00
11 Greg Monroe/99 3.00 8.00
12 Anthony Davis/75 6.00 15.00
13 Dwyane Wade/99 6.00 15.00
14 Hassan Whiteside/99 5.00 12.00
15 Isaiah Thomas/75 3.00 8.00
16 Gordon Hayward/99 4.00 10.00
17 LeBron James/49 25.00 60.00
18 Tyreke Evans/99 3.00 8.00
19 Damian Lillard/49 6.00 15.00
20 Trey Burke/75 2.50 6.00
21 Nerlens Noel/99 2.50 6.00
22 Goran Dragic/99 4.00 10.00
23 Zach Randolph/99 4.00 10.00
24 Markieff Morris/99 2.50 6.00
25 Evan Turner/99 2.50 6.00
26 Al Horford/99 4.00 10.00
27 Joe Johnson/99 3.00 8.00
28 Ryan Anderson/75 2.50 6.00
29 Jeremy Lin/75 6.00 15.00
30 Jimmy Butler/75 8.00 20.00
31 Dirk Nowitzki/99 10.00 25.00
32 Tim Duncan/99 10.00 25.00
33 Rajon Rondo/99 5.00 12.00
34 Manu Ginobili/75 8.00 20.00
35 Nikola Vucevic/99 3.00 8.00

36 Serge Ibaka/99 3.00 8.00
37 DeAndre Jordan/75 3.00 8.00
38 Carmelo Anthony/99 6.00 15.00
39 Brook Lopez/99 4.00 10.00
40 Ricky Rubio/99 3.00 8.00
41 Victor Oladipo/99 3.00 8.00
42 Trevor Ariza/99 2.50 6.00
43 Derrick Rose/45 6.00 15.00
44 Rudy Gobert/99 5.00 12.00
45 Kemba Walker/99 4.00 10.00
46 Andre Iguodala/99 4.00 10.00
47 Wesley Matthews/99 2.50 6.00
48 Nicolas Batum/99 2.50 6.00
49 Kyle Lowry/99 4.00 10.00
50 Deron Williams/99 3.00 8.00
51 Tony Parker/99 6.00 15.00
52 Kenneth Faried/75 3.00 8.00
53 Marcus Smart/99 5.00 12.00
54 Eric Gordon/99 3.00 8.00
55 Russell Westbrook/75 6.00 15.00
56 Kyrie Irving/75 6.00 15.00
57 Kyle Korver/75 3.00 8.00
58 Eric Bledsoe/99 3.00 8.00
59 C.J. McCollum/99 4.00 10.00
60 Jordan Clarkson/99 4.00 10.00
61 Chandler Parsons/99 2.50 6.00
62 Danilo Gallinari/99 3.00 8.00
63 Josh Smith/99 2.50 6.00
64 Draymond Green/99 5.00 12.00
65 Paul Millsap/99 3.00 8.00

2015-16 Panini National Treasures Super Swatches Prime
*PRIME/20-25: .75X TO 2X BASIC
PRINT RUNS B/WN 7-25 COPIES PER
NO PRICING ON QTY 10 OR LESS
4 Kevin Garnett/25 20.00 50.00
32 Tim Duncan/25 20.00 50.00
34 Manu Ginobili/25 15.00 40.00
51 Tony Parker/25 15.00 40.00

2015-16 Panini National Treasures Super Swatches Rookies
PRINT RUNS B/WN 25-99 COPIES PER
1 Tyus Jones/99 3.00 8.00
2 R.J. Hunter/99 2.50 6.00
3 Emmanuel Mudiay/99 3.00 8.00
4 Jonathon Simmons/75 3.00 8.00
5 Justin Anderson/99 2.50 6.00
6 Stanley Johnson/99 3.00 8.00
7 Cristiano Felicio/99 3.00 8.00
8 Karl-Anthony Towns/99 12.00 30.00
9 Frank Kaminsky/99 3.00 8.00
10 Pat Connaughton/99 4.00 10.00
11 Jerian Grant/99 2.50 6.00
12 Jahlil Okafor/99 3.00 8.00
13 Salah Mejri/99 2.50 6.00
14 Cliff Alexander/99 2.50 6.00
15 Marcelo Huertas/75 2.50 6.00
16 Bobby Portis/99 6.00 15.00
17 Trey Lyles/99 3.00 8.00
18 Willie Cauley-Stein/99 3.00 8.00
19 Sasha Kaun/99 2.50 6.00
20 Terry Rozier/99 10.00 25.00
21 Montrezl Harrell/99 8.00 20.00
22 Raul Neto/75 2.50 6.00
23 Cameron Payne/99 4.00 10.00
24 Nemanja Bjelica/99 4.00 10.00
25 Kelly Oubre Jr./99 8.00 20.00
26 Mario Hezonja/99 3.00 8.00
27 Nikola Jokic/99 125.00 300.00
28 D'Angelo Russell/99 6.00 15.00
29 Rondae Hollis-Jefferson/99 3.00 8.00
30 Devin Booker/99 10.00 25.00
31 Kristaps Porzingis/25 15.00 40.00
32 Norman Powell/99 5.00 12.00
33 Luis Montero/99 2.50 6.00
34 Myles Turner/99 10.00 25.00
35 Justise Winslow/99 4.00 10.00

2015-16 Panini National Treasures Super Swatches Rookies Prime
*PRIME/25: .75X TO 2X BASIC
PRINT RUNS B/WN 10-25 COPIES PER
NO PRICING ON QTY 10

2015-16 Panini National Treasures Timelines
PRINT RUNS B/WN 49-99 COPIES PER
*PRIME/25: .75X TO 2X BASIC
1 Chandler Parsons/99 2.50 6.00
2 Tony Parker/99 6.00 15.00
3 Anthony Davis/75 6.00 15.00
4 Russell Westbrook/75 6.00 15.00
5 Deron Williams/99 3.00 8.00
6 Manu Ginobili/75 8.00 20.00
7 Kevin Garnett/99 5.00 12.00
8 Draymond Green/75 5.00 12.00
9 Carmelo Anthony/99 6.00 15.00
10 Kyrie Irving/75 6.00 15.00
11 Jordan Clarkson/99 4.00 10.00
12 Derrick Williams/99 2.50 6.00
13 Goran Dragic/99 4.00 10.00
14 Andrew Wiggins/99 5.00 12.00
15 Kenneth Faried/99 3.00 8.00
16 Dirk Nowitzki/99 10.00 25.00
17 Jared Sullinger/99 2.50 6.00
18 James Harden/75 8.00 20.00
19 Eric Bledsoe/99 3.00 8.00
20 LeBron James/49 30.00 80.00
21 DeMarcus Cousins/99 4.00 10.00
22 Derrick Rose/49 5.00 12.00
23 Tim Duncan/99 10.00 25.00
24 Jimmy Butler/75 8.00 20.00
25 Danilo Gallinari/99 3.00 8.00
26 George Hill/99 3.00 8.00
27 J.R. Smith/99 4.00 10.00
28 Al Horford/99 4.00 10.00
29 Trey Burke/75 2.50 6.00
30 Damian Lillard/49 5.00 12.00

2015-16 Panini National Treasures Treasured Threads
PRINT RUNS B/WN 49-99 COPIES PER
1 Hakeem Olajuwon/99 8.00 20.00
2 Herb Williams/99 2.50 6.00
3 Karl Malone/99 6.00 15.00
4 Danny Manning/99 3.00 8.00
5 Ralph Sampson/99 3.00 8.00
6 Ben Wallace/99 3.00 8.00
7 Louie Dampier/99 4.00 10.00
8 Clifford Robinson/99 3.00 8.00
9 Magic Johnson/49 8.00 20.00
10 Reggie Lewis/99 4.00 10.00
11 Arvydas Sabonis/99 4.00 10.00
12 Alonzo Mourning/99 6.00 15.00
13 Brad Daugherty/99 3.00 8.00
14 Clyde Drexler/99 6.00 15.00
15 Grant Hill/99 6.00 15.00
16 Doc Rivers/99 4.00 10.00
17 Patrick Ewing/99 6.00 15.00
18 Jamal Mashburn/99 3.00 8.00
19 Kenny Smith/99 3.00 8.00
20 Alvan Adams/99 2.50 6.00
21 Dominique Wilkins/49 6.00 15.00
22 Larry Johnson/99 5.00 12.00
23 Derrick Coleman/49 4.00 10.00
24 Scottie Pippen/99 6.00 15.00
25 Bill Laimbeer/99 4.00 10.00
26 Kevin McHale/99 6.00 15.00
27 David Thompson/99 5.00 12.00
28 Ray Allen/99 5.00 12.00
29 Shaquille O'Neal/99 6.00 15.00
30 Vlade Divac/99 4.00 10.00
31 Vinnie Johnson/49 4.00 10.00
32 Dennis Rodman/99 6.00 15.00
33 Kevin Duckworth/99 2.50 6.00
34 Mark Aguirre/99 3.00 8.00
35 Isiah Thomas/49 4.00 10.00
36 Larry Bird/99 8.00 20.00
37 David Robinson/99 5.00 12.00
38 Detlef Schrempf/99 4.00 10.00
39 Mark Price/99 4.00 10.00
40 Allen Iverson/99 6.00 15.00

2015-16 Panini National Treasures Treasured Threads Prime
*PRIME/25: .75X TO 2X BASIC
PRINT RUNS B/WN 5-25 COPIES PER
NO PRICING ON QTY 15 OR LESS
9 Magic Johnson/25 25.00 60.00
24 Scottie Pippen/25 15.00 40.00

2015-16 Panini National Treasures Treasures of the Hall Autographs
PRINT RUNS B/WN 25-49 COPIES PER
EXCHANGE DEADLINE 11/11/2017
THBR Bill Russell/25 1,000.00 2,000.00
THBW Bill Walton/49 40.00 100.00
THDR Dennis Rodman/25 20.00 50.00
THGP Gary Payton/49 15.00 40.00
THJE Julius Erving/25 25.00 60.00
THJW Jerry West/25 20.00 50.00
THKM Karl Malone/25 20.00 50.00
THLB Larry Bird/25 40.00 100.00
THLW Lenny Wilkens/49 10.00 25.00
THMJ Magic Johnson/25 30.00 80.00
THOR Oscar Robertson/25 40.00 100.00
THRB Rick Barry/49 8.00 20.00
THRP Robert Parish/49 8.00 20.00
THWU Wes Unseld/49 10.00 25.00
THAMG Alonzo Mourning/25 20.00 50.00
THCHG Cliff Hagan/49 6.00 15.00
THCMY Calvin Murphy/49 5.00 12.00
THDCW Dave Cowens/49 6.00 15.00
THEHY Elvin Hayes/49 10.00 25.00
THHOW Hakeem Olajuwon/25 15.00 40.00
THJDM Joe Dumars/49 8.00 20.00
THKAJ Kareem Abdul-Jabbar/25 30.00 80.00
THKMH Kevin McHale/25 12.00 30.00
THNAB Nate Archibald/49 8.00 20.00
THRSS Ralph Sampson/49 5.00 12.00

2015-16 Panini National Treasures USA Basketball Autographs
STATED PRINT RUN 25 SER.#'d SETS
EXCHANGE DEADLINE 11/11/2017
1 Kobe Bryant 3,000.00 6,000.00
2 Shaquille O'Neal 400.00 800.00
3 Carmelo Anthony 150.00 400.00
4 Chris Paul 150.00 400.00
5 Dwyane Wade 200.00 500.00
6 Kevin Durant 500.00 1,000.00
7 Allen Iverson 300.00 600.00
8 John Stockton 150.00 400.00
9 Magic Johnson 300.00 600.00
10 Larry Bird 300.00 600.00
11 Karl Malone 150.00 400.00
12 Stephen Curry 1,500.00 3,000.00
13 Anthony Davis 300.00 600.00
14 Jerry West 60.00 150.00
15 Dwight Howard 20.00 50.00
16 Kyrie Irving 100.00 250.00
17 Oscar Robertson 75.00 200.00
18 Alonzo Mourning 40.00 100.00
19 Hakeem Olajuwon 150.00 400.00
20 David Robinson 150.00 400.00
21 Clyde Drexler 150.00 400.00
22 Jason Kidd 100.00 250.00
23 Chris Bosh 75.00 200.00
24 Kevin Love 25.00 60.00
25 Ray Allen 125.00 300.00
26 Vince Carter 125.00 300.00
27 Gary Payton 100.00 250.00
28 Anfernee Hardaway 125.00 300.00
29 Grant Hill 100.00 250.00
30 Larry Brown 40.00 100.00
31 Christian Laettner 75.00 200.00
32 Allan Houston 25.00 60.00
33 Adrian Dantley 50.00 120.00
34 Dan Majerle EXCH 60.00 150.00
35 Mitch Richmond 75.00 200.00

2015-16 Panini National Treasures USA Basketball Jersey Autographs
STATED PRINT RUN 25 SER.#'d SETS
EXCHANGE DEADLINE 11/11/2017
USJAD Andre Drummond 30.00 80.00
USJAM Alonzo Mourning 100.00 250.00
USJBB Bradley Beal 100.00 250.00
USJBG Blake Griffin 75.00 200.00
USJCA Carmelo Anthony 150.00 400.00
USJCB Chris Bosh 75.00 200.00
USJCD Clyde Drexler 150.00 400.00
USJCP Chris Paul 150.00 400.00
USJDH Dwight Howard 75.00 200.00
USJDM Dan Majerle 15.00 40.00
USJDR David Robinson 150.00 400.00
USJDW Dwyane Wade 200.00 500.00
USJDW Dominique Wilkins 125.00 300.00
USJGP Gary Payton 100.00 250.00
USJHO Hakeem Olajuwon 150.00 400.00
USJJK Jason Kidd 100.00 250.00
USJKF Kenneth Faried 12.00 30.00
USJKL Kawhi Leonard 200.00 500.00
USJKM Karl Malone 150.00 400.00
USJKT Klay Thompson 150.00 400.00
USJMJ Magic Johnson 300.00 600.00
USJMP Mason Plumlee 5.00 12.00
USJRA Ray Allen 125.00 300.00
USJRG Rudy Gay 40.00 100.00
USJSO Shaquille O'Neal 400.00 800.00

2016-17 Panini National Treasures
1-100 PRINT RUN 99 SER.#'d SETS
101-150 PRINT RUN 99 SER.#'d SETS
151-200 PRINT RUN B/WN 32-49 COPIES PER
201-206 PRINT RUNS 99 SER.#'d SETS
PRIME PATCHES MAY SELL FOR PREMIUM
EXCHANGE DEADLINE 11/3/2018
1 John Wall 3.00 8.00
2 Dwight Howard 3.00 8.00
3 Dwyane Wade 5.00 12.00
4 Dirk Nowitzki 6.00 15.00
5 Draymond Green 3.00 8.00
6 Myles Turner 2.50 6.00
7 Marc Gasol 2.50 6.00
8 Anthony Davis 8.00 20.00
9 Aaron Gordon 2.50 6.00
10 C.J. McCollum 2.50 6.00
11 Marcin Gortat 1.50 4.00
12 Bradley Beal 3.00 8.00
13 Dennis Schroder 2.50 6.00
14 Nicolas Batum 2.00 5.00
15 Deron Williams 2.00 5.00
16 Kevin Durant 10.00 25.00
17 Paul George 4.00 10.00
18 Mike Conley 2.00 5.00
19 Tim Frazier 1.50 4.00
20 Elfrid Payton 2.00 5.00
21 Damian Lillard 6.00 15.00
22 Otto Porter 2.00 5.00
23 Rudy Gobert 3.00 8.00
24 Paul Millsap 2.00 5.00
25 Jimmy Butler 5.00 12.00
26 Harrison Barnes 2.00 5.00
27 Klay Thompson 6.00 15.00
28 Blake Griffin 2.50 6.00
29 Vince Carter 2.00 5.00
30 Tyreke Evans 2.00 5.00
31 Serge Ibaka 2.00 5.00
32 Evan Turner 1.50 4.00
33 Al Horford 2.50 6.00
34 Gordon Hayward 2.50 6.00
35 Bojan Bogdanovic 2.00 5.00
36 Rajon Rondo 3.00 8.00
37 Emmanuel Mudiay 1.50 4.00
38 Stephen Curry 50.00 120.00
39 Chris Paul 4.00 10.00
40 Giannis Antetokounmpo 12.00 30.00
41 Brandon Jennings 1.50 4.00
42 Joel Embiid 6.00 15.00
43 Kawhi Leonard 6.00 15.00
44 Avery Bradley 1.50 4.00
45 George Hill 2.00 5.00
46 Brook Lopez 2.00 5.00
47 Robin Lopez 1.50 4.00
48 Kenneth Faried 2.00 5.00
49 Eric Gordon 2.00 5.00
50 DeAndre Jordan 2.00 5.00
51 Jabari Parker 1.50 4.00
52 Carmelo Anthony 4.00 10.00
53 Ben Simmons RC 5.00 12.00
54 LaMarcus Aldridge 2.50 6.00
55 Isaiah Thomas 2.00 5.00
56 DeMarcus Cousins 2.00 5.00
57 Jeremy Lin 5.00 12.00
58 J.R. Smith 2.50 6.00
59 Nikola Jokic 12.00 30.00
60 James Harden 5.00 12.00
61 Jamal Crawford 2.50 6.00
62 Matthew Dellavedova 2.00 5.00
63 Kristaps Porzingis 4.00 10.00
64 Robert Covington 2.00 5.00
65 Pau Gasol 4.00 10.00
66 Jae Crowder 1.50 4.00
67 Darren Collison 1.50 4.00
68 Trevor Booker 1.50 4.00
69 Kevin Love 2.50 6.00
70 Andre Drummond 2.50 6.00
71 Patrick Beverley 1.50 4.00
72 D'Angelo Russell 3.00 8.00
73 Andrew Wiggins 3.00 8.00
74 Russell Westbrook 4.00 10.00
75 Devin Booker 10.00 25.00
76 Manu Ginobili 5.00 12.00
77 Goran Dragic 2.50 6.00
78 Ben McLemore 1.50 4.00
79 Frank Kaminsky 1.50 4.00
80 Kyrie Irving 5.00 12.00
81 Reggie Jackson 2.00 5.00
82 Jeff Teague 1.50 4.00
83 Julius Randle 3.00 8.00
84 Karl-Anthony Towns 5.00 12.00
85 Steven Adams 2.00 5.00
86 Eric Bledsoe 2.00 5.00
87 Cory Joseph 1.50 4.00
88 Justise Winslow 2.00 5.00
89 Jonas Valanciunas 2.00 5.00
90 Kemba Walker 2.00 5.00
91 LeBron James 50.00 120.00
92 Tobias Harris 2.50 6.00
93 Monta Ellis 2.00 5.00
94 Lou Williams 2.50 6.00
95 Zach LaVine 5.00 12.00
96 Victor Oladipo 2.00 5.00
97 Tyson Chandler 2.00 5.00
98 DeMar DeRozan 3.00 8.00
99 Josh Richardson 2.00 5.00
100 Kyle Lowry 2.50 6.00
101 Bembry JSY AU/99 RC 40.00 100.00
102 Prince JSY AU/99 RC 30.00 80.00
103 Jackson JSY AU/99 RC 25.00 60.00
104 Brown JSY AU/99 RC 3,000.00 6,000.00
105 LeVert JSY AU/99 RC 60.00 150.00
106 Whitehead JSY AU/99 RC EXCH 25.00 60.00
107 Valentine JSY AU/99 RC EXCH 25.00 60.00
108 Felder JSY AU/99 RC 25.00 60.00
109 A.J. Hammons JSY
AU/99 RC EXCH 25.00 60.00
110 Murray JSY AU/99 RC 1,000.00 2,000.00
111 Hernangomez JSY AU/99 RC 50.00 125.00
112 Beasley JSY AU/99 RC 50.00 125.00
113 Ellenson JSY AU/99 RC 25.00 60.00
114 Michael Gbinije JSY AU/99 RC 25.00 60.00
115 Jones JSY AU/99 RC 25.00 60.00
116 McCaw JSY AU/99 RC 25.00 60.00
117 Chinanu Onuaku JSY AU/99 RC 25.00 60.00
118 Paul Zipser JSY AU/99 RC 25.00 60.00
119 Georges Niang JSY AU/99 RC 40.00 100.00
120 Johnson JSY AU/99 RC EXCH 25.00 60.00
121 Diamond Stone
JSY AU/99 RC EXCH 25.00 60.00
122 Ingram JSY AU/99 RC 600.00 1,200.00
123 Zubac JSY AU/99 RC 60.00 150.00
124 Davis JSY AU/99 RC 25.00 60.00
125 Baldwin IV JSY AU/99 RC 25.00 60.00
126 Brogdon JSY AU/99 RC 80.00 200.00
127 Maker JSY AU/99 RC 30.00 80.00
128 Dunn JSY AU/99 RC 40.00 100.00
129 Hield JSY AU/99 RC 400.00 800.00
130 Diallo JSY AU/99 RC 25.00 60.00
131 Marshall Plumlee JSY AU/99 RC 25.00 60.00
132 Hernangomez JSY AU/99 RC 30.00 80.00
133 Sabonis JSY AU/99 RC 600.00 1,200.00
135 Stephen Zimmerman
JSY AU/99 RC 25.00 60.00
136 Saric JSY AU/99 RC 40.00 100.00
137 Lu-Cabarrot JSY AU/99 RC 40.00 100.00
138 Bender JSY AU/99 RC 25.00 60.00
139 Chriss JSY AU/99 RC 30.00 80.00
140 Ulis JSY AU/99 RC EXCH 30.00 80.00
141 Jake Layman JSY AU/99 RC 30.00 80.00
142 Papagiannis JSY AU/99 RC 25.00 60.00
143 Richardson JSY AU/99 RC EXCH 25.00 60.00
144 Labissiere JSY AU/99 RC 25.00 60.00
146 Murray JSY AU/99 RC 800.00 1,500.00
147 Poeltl JSY AU/99 RC 50.00 120.00
148 Siakam JSY AU/99 RC 500.00 1,000.00
149 Joel Bolomboy JSY AU/99 RC 25.00 60.00
150 Tomas Satoransky JSY AU/99 RC 40.00 100.00
151 DeAndre' Bembry JSY AU/49 20.00 50.00
152 Prince JSY AU/49 15.00 40.00
153 Demetrius Jackson JSY AU/49 12.00 30.00
154 Brown JSY AU/49 2,000.00 4,000.00
155 Caris LeVert JSY AU/49 30.00 80.00
156 Whitehead JSY AU/49 EXCH 12.00 30.00
157 Valentine JSY AU/49 EXCH 12.00 30.00
158 Felder JSY AU/49 12.00 30.00
159 A.J. Hammons JSY AU/49 EXCH 12.00 30.00
160 Murray JSY AU/49 1,000.00 2,000.00
161 Hernangomez JSY AU/49 25.00 60.00
162 Malik Beasley JSY AU/49 25.00 60.00
163 Henry Ellenson JSY AU/49 12.00 30.00
164 Michael Gbinije JSY AU/49 12.00 30.00
165 Jones JSY AU/49 12.00 30.00
166 McCaw JSY AU/49 12.00 30.00
167 Chinanu Onuaku JSY AU/49 12.00 30.00
168 Zipser JSY AU/49 12.00 30.00
169 Georges Niang JSY AU/49 20.00 50.00
170 Johnson JSY AU/49 EXCH 12.00 30.00
171 Stone JSY AU/49 EXCH 12.00 30.00
172 Ingram JSY AU/49 1,000.00 2,000.00
173 Zubac JSY AU/49 30.00 80.00
174 Davis JSY AU/49 12.00 30.00
175 Wade Baldwin IV JSY AU/49 12.00 30.00
176 Brogdon JSY AU/49 40.00 100.00
177 Maker JSY AU/49 15.00 40.00
178 Dunn JSY AU/49 20.00 50.00
179 Hield JSY AU/49 40.00 100.00
180 Cheick Diallo JSY AU/49 12.00 30.00
181 Marshall Plumlee JSY AU/49 12.00 30.00
182 Willy Hernangomez JSY AU/49 15.00 40.00
183 Sabonis JSY AU/49 300.00 600.00
185 Stephen Zimmerman JSY AU/49 12.00 30.00
186 Saric JSY AU/32 20.00 50.00
187 Lu-Cabarrot JSY AU/49 20.00 50.00
188 Bender JSY AU/49 12.00 30.00
189 Chriss JSY AU/49 15.00 40.00
190 Ulis JSY AU/49 EXCH 15.00 40.00
191 Jake Layman JSY AU/49 15.00 40.00
192 Papagiannis JSY AU/49 12.00 30.00
193 Richardson JSY AU/49 12.00 30.00
194 Labissiere JSY AU/49 12.00 30.00
196 Murray JSY AU/49 500.00 1,000.00
197 Poeltl JSY AU/49 25.00 60.00
198 Siakam JSY AU/49 200.00 500.00
199 Joel Bolomboy JSY AU/49 12.00 30.00
200 Tomas Satoransky JSY AU/49 20.00 50.00
201 Jones Jr. AU/99 RC EXCH 5.00 12.00
203 Dorian Finney-Smith AU/99 RC 5.00 12.00
204 Kuzminskas AU/99 RC 4.00 10.00
205 Ron Baker AU/99 RC 4.00 10.00
206 Sheldon McClellan AU/99 RC 4.00 10.00
207 Fred VanVleet AU/99 RC 400.00 800.00
208 Danuel House AU/99 RC 6.00 15.00
209 Malcolm Delaney AU/99 RC 4.00 10.00
210 McGruder AU/99 RC 5.00 12.00

2016-17 Panini National Treasures Bronze
*BRONZE: .6X TO 1.5X BASIC
*BRONZE JSY AU: .5X TO 1.2X BASIC
*BRONZE AU: .5X TO 1.2X BASIC
STATED PRINT RUN 25 SER.#'d SETS
EXCHANGE DEADLINE 11/3/2018

2016-17 Panini National Treasures All-Decade Materials
PRINT RUNS B/WN 15-99 COPIES PER
NO PRICING ON QTY 15
1 Dirk Nowitzki/30 25.00 60.00
2 Kobe Bryant/99 125.00 300.00
3 Tim Duncan/99 15.00 40.00
5 Larry Bird/30 25.00 60.00
6 Magic Johnson/30 25.00 60.00
7 Kareem Abdul-Jabbar/30 25.00 60.00
9 Russell Westbrook/99 8.00 20.00
10 Stephen Curry/30 40.00 100.00
11 Jason Kidd/99 6.00 15.00
12 Shaquille O'Neal/99 25.00 60.00
13 Tony Parker/99 6.00 15.00
14 Kyrie Irving/99 8.00 20.00
15 David Robinson/99 10.00 25.00
16 Karl Malone/99 6.00 15.00
17 Hakeem Olajuwon/30 8.00 20.00
18 Damian Lillard/99 10.00 25.00
19 Vince Carter/99 10.00 25.00

2016-17 Panini National Treasures All-Decade Materials Prime
*PRIME/25: 1X TO 2.5X BASIC
PRINT RUNS B/WN 7-25 COPIES PER
NO PRICING ON QTY 7
3 Tim Duncan/25 60.00 150.00
10 Stephen Curry/25 125.00 300.00

2016-17 Panini National Treasures Century Materials
PRINT RUNS B/WN 30-99 COPIES PER
1 Jimmy Butler/30 8.00 20.00
2 Chris Paul/99 6.00 15.00
3 Kevin Durant/99 20.00 50.00
4 Goran Dragic/99 4.00 10.00
5 Dwight Howard/99 5.00 12.00
6 Dirk Nowitzki/30 15.00 40.00
7 Hassan Whiteside/99 3.00 8.00
8 Devin Booker/99 15.00 40.00
9 Patty Mills/99 4.00 10.00
10 Jahlil Okafor/99 2.50 6.00
11 Michael Kidd-Gilchrist/99 2.50 6.00
12 Blake Griffin/99 4.00 10.00
14 Zach Randolph/30 4.00 10.00
16 Deron Williams/99 3.00 8.00
17 Dennis Schroder/99 4.00 10.00
18 Brandon Knight/99 3.00 8.00
19 LaMarcus Aldridge/99 4.00 10.00
20 Otto Porter/99 3.00 8.00
21 Kemba Walker/99 3.00 8.00
22 Thaddeus Young/99 2.50 6.00
23 Tobias Harris/99 4.00 10.00
24 Vince Carter/99 8.00 20.00
25 Giannis Antetokounmpo/99 20.00 50.00
26 Sasha Vujacic/99 2.50 6.00
27 Alex Len/30 2.50 6.00
28 James Young/99 2.50 6.00
29 Kawhi Leonard/99 10.00 25.00
30 John Wall/99 5.00 12.00
31 Cody Zeller/99 2.50 6.00
32 Paul George/99 6.00 15.00
33 Reggie Jackson/30 3.00 8.00
34 Tony Allen/99 2.50 6.00
35 Jabari Parker/99 2.50 6.00
36 Kristaps Porzingis/99 6.00 15.00
37 Serge Ibaka/99 3.00 8.00
38 Jae Crowder/99 2.50 6.00
39 Rudy Gay/99 4.00 10.00
40 Gordon Hayward/99 4.00 10.00
42 Jeff Teague/30 2.50 6.00
43 Andre Drummond/99 3.00 8.00
44 Mike Conley/99 3.00 8.00
45 Andrew Wiggins/99 5.00 12.00
46 Carmelo Anthony/99 6.00 15.00
47 Elfrid Payton/99 3.00 8.00
48 Al Horford/99 4.00 10.00
49 DeMarcus Cousins/99 3.00 8.00
50 Rodney Hood/99 3.00 8.00
51 Rajon Rondo/99 5.00 12.00
52 James Harden/99 5.00 12.00
53 Marc Gasol/99 4.00 10.00
54 Nikola Jokic/99 20.00 50.00
56 Karl-Anthony Towns/99 8.00 20.00
57 Trevor Booker/99 2.50 6.00
58 Aaron Gordon/99 4.00 10.00
59 Ben McLemore/99 2.50 6.00
60 Joe Johnson/99 4.00 10.00
61 Nikola Mirotic/99 2.50 6.00
62 Patrick Beverley/99 2.50 6.00
63 Julius Randle/99 5.00 12.00
64 Kenneth Faried/99 3.00 8.00
65 Frank Kaminsky/99 2.50 6.00
66 Langston Galloway/99 2.50 6.00
67 Victor Oladipo/99 3.00 8.00
68 Luis Scola/99 3.00 8.00
69 Mason Plumlee/99 2.50 6.00
70 Kyle Lowry/30 4.00 10.00
71 Tristan Thompson/99 3.00 8.00
72 Eric Gordon/99 3.00 8.00
73 Jordan Clarkson/30 4.00 10.00
74 Jusuf Nurkic/99 3.00 8.00
75 Paul Millsap/99 3.00 8.00
76 Anthony Davis/99 12.00 30.00
77 Russell Westbrook/99 8.00 20.00
79 Damian Lillard/99 10.00 25.00
80 Jonas Valanciunas/99 3.00 8.00
81 LeBron James/99 40.00 100.00
82 Stephen Curry/30 40.00 100.00
83 D'Angelo Russell/99 5.00 12.00
84 Emmanuel Mudiay/99 2.50 6.00
85 J.J. Barea/99 3.00 8.00
86 Zach LaVine/99 8.00 20.00
87 Isaiah Thomas/99 3.00 8.00
88 Enes Kanter/99 2.50 6.00
89 C.J. McCollum/99 4.00 10.00
90 Tony Parker/99 6.00 15.00
91 Kyrie Irving/99 8.00 20.00
92 Klay Thompson/99 12.00 30.00
93 J.J. Redick/99 4.00 10.00
94 Wesley Matthews/99 2.50 6.00
95 Kyle Korver/99 3.00 8.00
96 Tyreke Evans/99 3.00 8.00
97 Solomon Hill/99 2.50 6.00
98 Brook Lopez/99 3.00 8.00
99 Eric Bledsoe/99 3.00 8.00
100 Iman Shumpert/99 2.50 6.00

2016-17 Panini National Treasures Century Materials Bronze
*BRONZE: 1X TO 2.5X BASIC
STATED PRINT RUN 25 SER.#'d SETS
81 LeBron James 125.00 300.00
82 Stephen Curry 100.00 250.00

2016-17 Panini National Treasures Clutch Factor Jersey Autographs
PRINT RUNS B/WN 49-75 COPIES PER
EXCHANGE DEADLINE 11/3/2018
1 Carmelo Anthony/49 30.00 80.00
2 Kyrie Irving/49 75.00 200.00
3 Kobe Bryant/49 2,000.00 4,000.00
4 Kevin Durant/49 500.00 1,000.00
5 Stephen Curry/49 800.00 1,500.00
6 Dirk Nowitzki/49 75.00 200.00
7 Ryan Anderson/75 4.00 10.00
8 David Robinson/49 50.00 120.00
9 Elfrid Payton/75 5.00 12.00
10 Karl-Anthony Towns/49 40.00 100.00
11 Andrew Wiggins/49 25.00 60.00
12 Paul Millsap/75 5.00 12.00
13 Larry Bird/49 75.00 200.00
14 Kelly Tripucka/75 4.00 10.00
15 Devin Booker/75 150.00 400.00
16 Myles Turner/75 8.00 20.00
17 C.J. McCollum/75 10.00 25.00
18 Shawn Marion/75 10.00 25.00
19 Kenneth Faried/75 5.00 12.00
20 Julius Erving/49 50.00 120.00
21 Clyde Drexler/49 20.00 50.00
22 Harrison Barnes/75 6.00 15.00
23 DeMar DeRozan/75 20.00 50.00
24 Jabari Parker/49 4.00 10.00
25 Blake Griffin/49 15.00 40.00
26 Damian Lillard/49 75.00 200.00
27 Mitch Richmond/75 12.00 30.00
28 Patrick Ewing/49 50.00 120.00
29 Kevin Love/49 12.00 30.00
30 Tony Parker/49 15.00 40.00
31 Ricky Rubio/49 10.00 25.00
32 Al Horford/75 12.00 30.00
33 Luol Deng/75 5.00 12.00
34 Jeremy Lin/75 40.00 100.00
35 Shaquille O'Neal/49 125.00 300.00
37 Tim Hardaway/75 10.00 25.00
38 Anthony Davis/49 75.00 200.00
39 Rashard Lewis/75 5.00 12.00
40 Kristaps Porzingis/75 25.00 60.00

2016-17 Panini National Treasures Clutch Factor Jersey Autographs Bronze
*BRONZE: .75X TO 2X BASIC
STATED PRINT RUN 25 SER.#'d SETS
EXCHANGE DEADLINE 11/3/2018

2016-17 Panini National Treasures Colossal Jersey Autographs
PRINT RUNS B/WN 49-60 COPIES PER
EXCHANGE DEADLINE 11/3/2018
1 Tim Hardaway/60 10.00 25.00
2 Alonzo Mourning/49 20.00 50.00
3 Julius Erving/49 75.00 200.00
4 Karl Malone/49 40.00 100.00
5 David Robinson/49 50.00 120.00
6 Detlef Schrempf/60 10.00 25.00
8 Kobe Bryant/49 15,000.00 30,000.00
9 Larry Bird/49 150.00 400.00
10 Magic Johnson/49 150.00 400.00
11 Robert Parish/60 12.00 30.00
12 Shaquille O'Neal/49 400.00 800.00
13 Shawn Kemp/60 60.00 150.00
14 Kenny Smith/60 6.00 15.00
15 Dirk Nowitzki/49 150.00 400.00
16 Jeremy Lin/49 75.00 200.00
17 Nicolas Batum/60 5.00 12.00
18 Kevin Love/49 15.00 40.00
19 Langston Galloway/60 4.00 10.00
20 Stephen Curry/49 1,000.00 2,000.00
21 Kyrie Irving/49 60.00 150.00
22 Kevin Durant/49 400.00 800.00
23 Kenneth Faried/60 5.00 12.00
24 Will Barton/60 4.00 10.00
25 Justise Winslow/60 6.00 15.00
26 DeMar DeRozan/60 30.00 80.00
27 Damian Lillard/49 75.00 200.00
28 DeMarre Carroll/60 4.00 10.00
29 Bojan Bogdanovic/60 5.00 12.00
30 Luol Deng/60 5.00 12.00
31 Al Horford/60 12.00 30.00
32 Carmelo Anthony/49 40.00 100.00
33 Chris Paul/49 125.00 300.00
34 Dwyane Wade/49 75.00 200.00
35 Doug McDermott/60 5.00 12.00
36 Mitch Richmond/60 20.00 50.00
37 Alvan Adams/60 5.00 12.00
38 Bernard King/60 12.00 30.00
39 Cedric Maxwell/60 5.00 12.00
40 Patrick Ewing/60 60.00 150.00
41 Kevin McHale/49 20.00 50.00
42 Matthew Dellavedova/60 10.00 25.00
43 Hakeem Olajuwon/49 75.00 200.00
44 Andrew Wiggins/49 20.00 50.00
45 Karl-Anthony Towns/49 40.00 100.00
46 Zach LaVine/60 50.00 120.00
47 Goran Dragic/60 12.00 30.00
48 Gordon Hayward/60 20.00 50.00
49 Blake Griffin/49 15.00 40.00
50 Evan Fournier/60 5.00 12.00
51 Dwight Powell/60 4.00 10.00
52 Reggie Jackson/60 5.00 12.00
53 Tobias Harris/60 6.00 15.00
54 Marc Gasol/49 12.00 30.00
55 Pau Gasol/49 20.00 50.00
56 Mark Price/60 12.00 30.00
57 Jordan Clarkson/60 12.00 30.00
58 Julius Randle/60 30.00 80.00
59 Enes Kanter/60 4.00 10.00
60 Hassan Whiteside/60 5.00 12.00

2016-17 Panini National Treasures Colossal Jersey Autographs Bronze
*BRONZE/22-25: .75X TO 2X BASIC
PRINT RUNS B/WN 18-25 COPIES PER
NO PRICING ON QTY 19 OR LESS
EXCHANGE DEADLINE 11/3/2018
2 Alonzo Mourning/25 75.00 200.00
12 Shaquille O'Neal/25 800.00 1,500.00

2016-17 Panini National Treasures Colossal Materials
PRINT RUNS B/WN 30-60 COPIES PER
1 D'Angelo Russell/60 6.00 15.00
2 Kristaps Porzingis/30 8.00 20.00
3 Kevin Durant/30 20.00 50.00
4 Kawhi Leonard/30 12.00 30.00
5 Rudy Gobert/60 6.00 15.00
6 LaMarcus Aldridge/30 5.00 12.00
7 Emmanuel Mudiay/30 3.00 8.00
8 Jimmy Butler/30 10.00 25.00
10 Russell Westbrook/60 8.00 20.00
11 C.J. McCollum/30 5.00 12.00
12 Zach LaVine/30 10.00 25.00
13 Eric Bledsoe/30 4.00 10.00
14 Kyle Lowry/30 5.00 12.00
15 Derrick Rose/30 8.00 20.00
16 Detlef Schrempf/30 5.00 12.00
17 Karl-Anthony Towns/30 10.00 25.00
18 Carmelo Anthony/30 8.00 20.00
19 DeMarre Carroll/30 3.00 8.00
20 Kyrie Irving/30 10.00 25.00
21 Deron Williams/60 4.00 10.00
23 Tobias Harris/30 5.00 12.00
24 DeMar DeRozan/30 6.00 15.00
25 LeBron James/30 100.00 250.00
26 Damian Lillard/30 12.00 30.00
27 Aaron Gordon/30 5.00 12.00
28 Victor Oladipo/30 4.00 10.00
29 Rudy Gay/30 5.00 12.00
30 Monta Ellis/30 4.00 10.00
31 Dirk Nowitzki/30 12.00 30.00
32 Giannis Antetokounmpo/30 60.00 150.00
33 Tim Frazier/60 3.00 8.00
34 Kobe Bryant/30 125.00 300.00
35 Shabazz Muhammad/30 3.00 8.00
36 Shawn Marion/60 4.00 10.00
37 Jabari Parker/30 3.00 8.00
38 Jrue Holiday/30 6.00 15.00
39 DeMarcus Cousins/30 4.00 10.00
40 Goran Dragic/60 5.00 12.00

2016-17 Panini National Treasures Colossal Materials Prime
*PRIME/21-25: 1X TO 2.5X BASIC
PRINT RUNS B/WN 10-25 COPIES PER
NO PRICING ON QTY 18 OR LESS
4 Kawhi Leonard/25 30.00 80.00

2016-17 Panini National Treasures Colossal Rookie Materials
STATED PRINT RUN 60 SER.#'d SETS
*PRIME/25: 1X TO 2.5X BASIC
1 Jaylen Brown 6.00 15.00
2 Kris Dunn 4.00 10.00
3 Malachi Richardson 2.50 6.00
4 Brice Johnson 2.50 6.00
5 Caris LeVert 6.00 15.00
6 Diamond Stone 2.50 6.00
7 Buddy Hield 5.00 12.00
8 Georgios Papagiannis 2.50 6.00
9 Isaiah Whitehead 2.50 6.00
10 Brandon Ingram 8.00 20.00
11 Cheick Diallo 2.50 6.00
12 Jake Layman 3.00 8.00
14 Denzel Valentine 2.50 6.00
15 Ivica Zubac 6.00 15.00
16 Marquese Chriss 3.00 8.00
17 Chinanu Onuaku 2.50 6.00
18 A.J. Hammons 2.50 6.00
19 Deyonta Davis 2.50 6.00
20 Pascal Siakam 15.00 40.00
21 Tyler Ulis 3.00 8.00
22 Patrick McCaw 2.50 6.00
23 Kay Felder 2.50 6.00
24 Wade Baldwin IV 2.50 6.00
25 Domantas Sabonis 15.00 40.00
26 Dragan Bender 2.50 6.00
27 Damian Jones 2.50 6.00
28 Jamal Murray 75.00 200.00
29 Malcolm Brogdon 8.00 20.00
30 Timothe Luwawu-Cabarrot 4.00 10.00
31 Juan Hernangomez 5.00 12.00
32 Thon Maker 3.00 8.00
33 Stephen Zimmerman 2.50 6.00
34 Dario Saric 4.00 10.00
35 Henry Ellenson 2.50 6.00
36 Malik Beasley 5.00 12.00
37 Demetrius Jackson 2.50 6.00
38 Skal Labissiere 2.50 6.00
39 Dejounte Murray 6.00 15.00
40 Jakob Poeltl 5.00 12.00

2016-17 Panini National Treasures Game Gear
PRINT RUNS B/WN 30-99 COPIES PER
1 James Harden/99 8.00 20.00
2 Russell Westbrook/49 8.00 20.00
3 Stephen Curry/49 20.00 50.00
4 Damian Lillard/99 6.00 15.00
5 Otto Porter/99 3.00 8.00
6 Andrew Wiggins/99 4.00 10.00
7 Giannis Antetokounmpo/99 20.00 50.00
8 Kobe Bryant/99 125.00 300.00
9 Kyrie Irving/99 6.00 15.00
10 Aaron Gordon/99 4.00 10.00
11 Dennis Schroder/99 4.00 10.00
12 Enes Kanter/49 2.50 6.00
13 Mike Conley/99 3.00 8.00
14 Paul Pierce/99 6.00 15.00
15 Bojan Bogdanovic/99 3.00 8.00
16 John Wall/99 5.00 12.00
17 Tony Parker/99 6.00 15.00
18 Marc Gasol/99 4.00 10.00
19 LeBron James/99 30.00 80.00
20 Kawhi Leonard/99 10.00 25.00
21 D'Angelo Russell/99 5.00 12.00
22 Steven Adams/99 3.00 8.00
24 Thomas Robinson/99 2.50 6.00
25 Jason Terry/99 3.00 8.00
26 Bradley Beal/30 5.00 12.00
27 Goran Dragic/99 4.00 10.00
28 Zach Randolph/99 4.00 10.00
29 Jamal Crawford/99 4.00 10.00
30 Manu Ginobili/99 8.00 20.00
31 Brandon Knight/99 2.50 6.00

32 Trevor Booker/99 2.50 6.00
33 Draymond Green/99 5.00 12.00
34 Brook Lopez/99 3.00 8.00
35 Kevin Durant/99 12.00 30.00
36 Paul George/99 6.00 15.00
37 Jabari Parker/99 2.50 6.00
38 Blake Griffin/99 4.00 10.00
39 Adreian Payne/99 2.50 6.00
40 Monta Ellis/99 3.00 8.00

2016-17 Panini National Treasures Game Gear Autographs

PRINT RUNS B/WN 19-49 COPIES PER
NO PRICING ON QTY 19
EXCHANGE DEADLINE 11/3/2018
*PRIME/25: .75X TO 2X BASIC
1 Stanley Johnson/60 4.00 10.00
2 Kristaps Porzingis/75 25.00 60.00
3 Kobe Bryant/25 3,000.00 6,000.00
4 Myles Turner/75 8.00 20.00
5 Justise Winslow/49 6.00 15.00
6 Zach LaVine/75 10.00 25.00
7 Norman Powell/99 6.00 15.00
8 Reggie Jackson/49 5.00 12.00
9 Carmelo Anthony/25 25.00 60.00
10 Kevin Love/25 20.00 50.00
11 Victor Oladipo/25 6.00 15.00
12 Mario Hezonja/70 4.00 10.00
13 C.J. McCollum/99 10.00 25.00
14 Devin Booker/75 150.00 400.00
15 Maurice Harkless/99 4.00 10.00
16 Danny Green/99 6.00 15.00
17 Karl-Anthony Towns/25 40.00 100.00
18 Dennis Rodman/25 20.00 50.00
19 Dan Issel/75 8.00 20.00
20 George Hill/75 5.00 12.00
21 Shaquille O'Neal/25 75.00 200.00
22 Karl Malone/25 25.00 60.00
23 Marques Johnson/75 5.00 12.00
24 Jrue Holiday/99 8.00 20.00
25 Solomon Hill/99 4.00 10.00
26 Magic Johnson/25 40.00 100.00
27 Marcus Camby/49 5.00 12.00
29 Kyrie Irving/25 50.00 120.00
30 John Stockton/25 40.00 100.00

2016-17 Panini National Treasures Game Gear Dual Jersey Autographs

PRINT RUNS B/WN 25-75 COPIES PER
EXCHANGE DEADLINE 11/3/2018
*PRIME/25: .75X TO 2X BASIC
1 Ryan Anderson/49 4.00 10.00
2 George Hill/49 5.00 12.00
3 Myles Turner/49 8.00 20.00
4 Kobe Bryant/25 2,500.00 5,000.00
5 Andrew Wiggins/30 20.00 50.00
6 Langston Galloway/75 4.00 10.00
7 Elfrid Payton/49 5.00 12.00
8 Nikola Vucevic/75 6.00 15.00
9 C.J. McCollum/75 10.00 25.00
10 Evan Turner/49 4.00 10.00
11 Isaiah Thomas/75 8.00 20.00
12 Rondae Hollis-Jefferson/75 4.00 10.00
13 Carmelo Anthony/35 20.00 50.00
14 Kristaps Porzingis/75 25.00 60.00
15 Kenneth Faried/49 5.00 12.00
16 Danilo Gallinari/49 5.00 12.00
18 Dwyane Wade/25 30.00 80.00
19 Blake Griffin/30 12.00 30.00
20 Rashard Lewis/49 5.00 12.00
21 Magic Johnson/35 30.00 80.00
22 Hakeem Olajuwon/35 25.00 60.00
23 Larry Bird/35 50.00 120.00
24 Louie Dampier/49 10.00 25.00
25 Kareem Abdul-Jabbar/35 30.00 80.00

2016-17 Panini National Treasures Game Gear Duals

PRINT RUNS B/WN 49-99 COPIES PER
*PRIME/25: 1X TO 2.5X BASIC
1 Dwight Howard/49 5.00 12.00
2 Kyrie Irving/75 8.00 20.00
3 Dirk Nowitzki/49 10.00 25.00
4 Tristan Thompson/75 3.00 8.00
5 Wesley Matthews/75 2.50 6.00
6 Kemba Walker/49 3.00 8.00
7 J.R. Smith/49 4.00 10.00
8 Michael Kidd-Gilchrist/75 2.50 6.00
9 Deron Williams/75 3.00 8.00
10 Jimmy Butler/75 8.00 20.00
11 Russell Westbrook/49 8.00 20.00
12 James Harden/49 8.00 20.00
13 Rudy Gobert/75 5.00 12.00
14 Jonas Valanciunas/75 3.00 8.00
15 Otto Porter/75 3.00 8.00
16 Carmelo Anthony/49 6.00 15.00
17 LaMarcus Aldridge/75 4.00 10.00
18 Marcus Smart/75 5.00 12.00
19 Kenneth Faried/75 3.00 8.00
20 Kristaps Porzingis/75 6.00 15.00
21 Kawhi Leonard/49 10.00 25.00
22 Evan Turner/75 2.50 6.00
23 Nik Stauskas/75 2.50 6.00
24 Thaddeus Young/49 2.50 6.00
25 Kyle Korver/75 3.00 8.00
26 Isaiah Thomas/49 5.00 12.00
27 Karl-Anthony Towns/49 6.00 15.00
28 Anthony Davis/75 8.00 20.00
29 Elfrid Payton/49 3.00 8.00
30 Nikola Vucevic/75 4.00 10.00

2016-17 Panini National Treasures Game Gear Prime

*PRIME: 1X TO 2.5X BASIC
STATED PRINT RUN 25 SER.#'d SETS
3 Stephen Curry 75.00 200.00
19 LeBron James 75.00 200.00

2016-17 Panini National Treasures Game Gear Triple Jersey Autographs

PRINT RUNS B/WN 25-75 COPIES PER
EXCHANGE DEADLINE 11/3/2018
*PRIME/20-25: .75X TO 2X BASIC
1 Andrew Wiggins/49 15.00 40.00
2 Jabari Parker/49 15.00 40.00
3 Zach LaVine/49 10.00 25.00
4 Khris Middleton/49 20.00 50.00
6 Blake Griffin/35 15.00 40.00
7 Luis Scola/75 5.00 12.00
8 Andre Drummond/49 6.00 15.00
9 Dirk Nowitzki/35 75.00 200.00
10 Tristan Thompson/75 5.00 12.00
11 Michael Carter-Williams/49 4.00 10.00
12 Marcus Camby/75 5.00 12.00
13 Magic Johnson/25 40.00 100.00
14 Shane Battier/75 5.00 12.00
15 Rik Smits/49 10.00 25.00
16 Jason Kidd/49 12.00 30.00
17 Grant Hill/49 15.00 40.00
18 Bill Laimbeer/75 8.00 20.00
19 Brad Daugherty/75 5.00 12.00
20 Kareem Abdul-Jabbar/25 40.00 100.00

2016-17 Panini National Treasures Game Gear Triples

PRINT RUNS B/WN 25-49 COPIES PER
1 Nikola Vucevic/49 4.00 10.00
2 Eric Bledsoe/49 3.00 8.00
3 Kawhi Leonard/49 10.00 25.00
4 Kyle Lowry/49 4.00 10.00
5 Rodney Hood/49 3.00 8.00
6 John Wall/49 5.00 12.00
7 Kyrie Irving/49 8.00 20.00
9 Carmelo Anthony/49 6.00 15.00
10 Jrue Holiday/49 5.00 12.00
11 Russell Westbrook/49 6.00 15.00
12 Isaiah Thomas/49 3.00 8.00
13 Jimmy Butler/49 8.00 20.00
14 Dirk Nowitzki/49 6.00 15.00
15 Emmanuel Mudiay/49 2.50 6.00
16 Stephen Curry/49 20.00 50.00
17 Jeff Teague/49 2.50 6.00
18 George Hill/49 3.00 8.00
19 DeAndre Jordan/49 3.00 8.00
20 Jordan Clarkson/25 4.00 10.00

2016-17 Panini National Treasures Game Gear Triples Prime

*PRIME: 1X TO 2.5X BASIC
STATED PRINT RUN 25 SER.#'d SETS
16 Stephen Curry 100.00 250.00

2016-17 Panini National Treasures Hometown Heroes

PRINT RUNS B/WN 35-75 COPIES PER
EXCHANGE DEADLINE 11/3/2018
*BRONZE/25: .5X TO 1.2X BASIC
1 Carmelo Anthony/35 60.00 150.00
2 Kobe Bryant/35 1,500.00 3,000.00
3 Patrick Ewing/35 150.00 400.00
4 Kevin Durant/35 150.00 400.00
5 Karl Malone/35 30.00 80.00
6 John Stockton/35 30.00 80.00
7 Eddie Jones/75 8.00 20.00
8 Michael Cage/75 6.00 15.00
9 Mark Price/75 10.00 25.00
10 DeMar DeRozan/60 20.00 50.00
11 Jo Jo White/75 8.00 20.00
12 Latrell Sprewell/75 20.00 50.00
13 Gary Payton/35 40.00 100.00
14 Ray Allen/35 40.00 100.00
15 Karl-Anthony Towns/35 40.00 100.00
16 Jeremy Lin/35 30.00 80.00
17 Devin Booker/75 200.00 500.00
18 Anthony Davis/35 75.00 200.00
19 Dwyane Wade/35 60.00 150.00
20 Dante Exum/60 8.00 20.00
21 Al Horford/60 10.00 25.00
22 Khris Middleton/75 10.00 25.00
23 Doug McDermott/75 8.00 20.00
24 Tyler Johnson/75 6.00 15.00
25 Isaiah Thomas/60 30.00 80.00
26 Julius Randle/60 12.00 30.00
27 Aaron Gordon/60 10.00 25.00
28 Jordan Clarkson/75 20.00 50.00
29 Elfrid Payton/75 8.00 20.00
30 Bobby Portis/75 10.00 25.00
31 Larry Bird/35 100.00 250.00
32 Magic Johnson/35 100.00 250.00
33 Shane Battier/60 8.00 20.00
34 Shaquille O'Neal/35 125.00 300.00
35 Gail Goodrich/75 10.00 25.00
36 Alex English/75 8.00 20.00
37 Bernard King/75 12.00 30.00
38 Louie Dampier/75 8.00 20.00
39 Nate Archibald/75 10.00 25.00
40 Dave Cowens/75 8.00 20.00
41 Henry Ellenson/75 6.00 15.00
42 Denzel Valentine/75 6.00 15.00
43 Malachi Richardson/75 6.00 15.00
44 Marquese Chriss/75 8.00 20.00
45 Kris Dunn/60 10.00 25.00
46 Buddy Hield/60 20.00 50.00
47 Jaylen Brown/35 50.00 125.00
48 Isaiah Whitehead/75 6.00 15.00
49 Caris LeVert/75 15.00 40.00
50 Brandon Ingram/35 25.00 60.00

2016-17 Panini National Treasures International Treasures

PRINT RUNS B/WN 49-75 COPIES PER
EXCHANGE DEADLINE 11/3/2018
*BRONZE/25: .5X TO 1.2X BASIC
1 Dragan Bender/75 12.00 30.00
2 Thon Maker/75 12.00 30.00
3 Dario Saric/75 30.00 80.00
4 Juan Hernangomez/75 40.00 100.00
5 T. Luwawu-Cabarrot/75 6.00 15.00
6 Willy Hernangomez/75 12.00 30.00
7 Ivica Zubac/75 25.00 60.00
8 Dirk Nowitzki/49 125.00 300.00
9 Pau Gasol/49 25.00 60.00
10 Ricky Rubio/49 20.00 50.00
11 Marc Gasol/49 20.00 50.00
12 Tony Parker/75 20.00 50.00
13 Dante Exum/75 10.00 25.00
14 Danilo Gallinari/75 5.00 12.00
15 Kristaps Porzingis/75 30.00 80.00
16 Goran Dragic/75 6.00 15.00
17 Mario Hezonja/75 4.00 10.00
18 Marcin Gortat/75 6.00 15.00
19 Yao Ming/75 100.00 250.00
20 Toni Kukoc/75 10.00 25.00
21 Evan Fournier/75 5.00 12.00
22 Bojan Bogdanovic/75 10.00 25.00
23 Clint Capela/75 15.00 40.00
24 Nikola Jokic/75 200.00 500.00
25 Dennis Schroder/75 12.00 30.00
26 Buddy Hield/75 25.00 60.00
27 Jamal Murray/75 100.00 250.00
28 Andrew Wiggins/75 60.00 150.00
29 Dikembe Mutombo/75 40.00 100.00
30 Steve Nash/49 50.00 120.00

2016-17 Panini National Treasures Lasting Legacies Jersey Autographs

PRINT RUNS B/WN 20-99 COPIES PER
EXCHANGE DEADLINE 11/3/2018
*PRIME/25: .75X TO 2X BASIC
1 Tony Parker/20 25.00 60.00
2 Kyrie Irving/20 50.00 120.00
3 Michael Kidd-Gilchrist/75 4.00 10.00
4 Dirk Nowitzki/20 100.00 250.00
5 Andre Drummond/60 6.00 15.00
7 Blake Griffin/20 20.00 50.00
8 Kobe Bryant/20 2,000.00 4,000.00
9 Kevin Durant/20 75.00 200.00
10 Zach Randolph/60 6.00 15.00
11 Anthony Davis/20 50.00 120.00
13 Scottie Pippen/20 40.00 100.00
14 Joe Dumars/60 6.00 15.00
15 Carmelo Anthony/20 25.00 60.00
16 Magic Johnson/20 40.00 100.00
17 Allen Iverson/20 40.00 100.00
18 Shane Battier/99 5.00 12.00
19 Deron Williams/20 6.00 15.00
21 Anfernee Hardaway/20 30.00 80.00
22 Alvan Adams/99 5.00 12.00
23 Tristan Thompson/99 5.00 12.00
24 Udonis Haslem/55 5.00 12.00
25 Mark Aguirre/40 5.00 12.00

2016-17 Panini National Treasures Material Treasures

PRINT RUNS B/WN 30-99 COPIES PER
*BRONZE/25: 1X TO 2.5X BASIC
2 Blake Griffin 4.00 10.00
3 Kawhi Leonard 10.00 25.00
4 Giannis Antetokounmpo 20.00 50.00
5 Kemba Walker 3.00 8.00
6 Chris Paul 6.00 15.00
7 Reggie Jackson 3.00 8.00
8 Andre Drummond 4.00 10.00
9 Paul George 6.00 15.00
10 Jeff Teague 2.50 6.00
11 Otto Porter 3.00 8.00
12 Jimmy Butler 8.00 20.00
13 Andrew Wiggins 4.00 10.00
14 Jabari Parker 2.50 6.00
15 Cody Zeller 2.50 6.00
16 LaMarcus Aldridge 4.00 10.00
17 Kevin Durant 15.00 40.00
18 Tony Allen 2.50 6.00
19 Mike Conley 3.00 8.00
20 John Wall 5.00 12.00
21 Brandon Knight 3.00 8.00
22 Goran Dragic 4.00 10.00
23 Carmelo Anthony 6.00 15.00
24 Kristaps Porzingis 5.00 12.00
25 James Young 2.50 6.00
26 Dennis Schroder 4.00 10.00
27 Dwight Howard 5.00 12.00
28 Serge Ibaka 3.00 8.00
29 Alex Len 2.50 6.00
30 Deron Williams 3.00 8.00
31 Dirk Nowitzki 10.00 25.00
32 Elfrid Payton 3.00 8.00
33 Jae Crowder 2.50 6.00
34 Sasha Vujacic 2.50 6.00
36 Hassan Whiteside 3.00 8.00
37 Rudy Gay 4.00 10.00
38 Vince Carter 8.00 20.00
39 Zach Randolph 4.00 10.00
40 Al Horford 4.00 10.00
41 Devin Booker 15.00 40.00
42 Gordon Hayward 4.00 10.00
43 Tobias Harris 3.00 8.00
45 Patty Mills 4.00 10.00
46 Thaddeus Young 2.50 6.00
47 Michael Kidd-Gilchrist 2.50 6.00
48 Rodney Hood 3.00 8.00
49 DeMarcus Cousins 3.00 8.00
50 Jahlil Okafor 2.50 6.00

2016-17 Panini National Treasures Material Treasures Signatures

PRINT RUNS B/WN 25-99 COPIES PER
EXCHANGE DEADLINE 11/3/2018
*BRONZE/20-25: .75X TO 2X BASIC
1 Mark Aguirre/99 5.00 12.00
2 Cedric Maxwell/99 5.00 12.00
3 Tim Hardaway/99 8.00 20.00
4 Robert Horry/99 6.00 15.00
5 Scottie Pippen/25 40.00 100.00
6 Kiki Vandeweghe/99 5.00 12.00
7 Marcus Camby/99 5.00 12.00
8 Kenny Anderson/99 5.00 12.00
9 Rashard Lewis/99 5.00 12.00
10 Kurt Rambis/99 6.00 15.00
11 Shane Battier/35 5.00 12.00
12 Jeff Malone/99 4.00 10.00
13 Jeff Hornacek/99 5.00 12.00
14 Xavier McDaniel/65 4.00 10.00
15 Chuck Person/99 5.00 12.00
16 Clyde Drexler/25 15.00 40.00
17 Mark Jackson/99 5.00 12.00
18 Anfernee Hardaway/35 25.00 60.00
19 Kareem Abdul-Jabbar/25 40.00 100.00
20 Brad Daugherty/99 5.00 12.00
21 Danny Green/99 6.00 15.00
22 Karl-Anthony Towns/25 50.00 120.00
23 Cody Zeller/35 5.00 12.00
24 Victor Oladipo/35 5.00 12.00
25 Langston Galloway/99 4.00 10.00
26 Larry Bird/25 60.00 150.00
27 Andrew Wiggins/35 10.00 25.00
28 Allen Iverson/25 40.00 100.00
29 Magic Johnson/25 40.00 100.00
30 Karl Malone/25 25.00 60.00
31 Dominique Wilkins/35 12.00 30.00
32 Kyrie Irving/25 50.00 120.00
33 Courtney Lee/99 4.00 10.00
34 C.J. McCollum/35 10.00 25.00
35 Kevin Love/35 15.00 40.00
36 Luis Scola/99 5.00 12.00
37 Allen Crabbe/99 5.00 12.00
38 Jeremy Lin/35 30.00 80.00
39 George Hill/99 5.00 12.00
40 Jeff Teague/99 4.00 10.00

2016-17 Panini National Treasures NBA Greats Signatures

PRINT RUNS B/WN 25-99 COPIES PER
EXCHANGE DEADLINE 11/3/2018
*BRONZE/25: .4X TO 1X BASE p/r 25
*BRONZE/25: .5X TO 1.2X BASE p/r 99
1 Magic Johnson/25 75.00 200.00
2 Kareem Abdul-Jabbar/25 100.00 250.00
3 Elvin Hayes/99 15.00 40.00
4 Calvin Murphy/99 8.00 20.00
5 Oscar Robertson/25 40.00 100.00
6 Karl Malone/25 50.00 120.00
7 Tom Heinsohn/99 25.00 60.00
8 Kobe Bryant/25 1,000.00 2,000.00
9 Alvan Adams/99 10.00 25.00
10 Jeff Hornacek/99 6.00 15.00
11 Mark Aguirre/99 6.00 15.00
12 Mark Price/99 8.00 20.00
13 David Robinson/25 50.00 120.00
14 Nate Archibald/99 8.00 20.00
15 Walt Frazier/99 15.00 40.00
16 Cliff Hagan/99 8.00 20.00
17 Bob Dandridge/99 8.00 20.00
18 Ron Boone/99 6.00 15.00
19 Junior Bridgeman/99 6.00 15.00
20 Kiki Vandeweghe/99 6.00 15.00

2016-17 Panini National Treasures Penmanship

PRINT RUNS B/WN 25-99 COPIES PER
EXCHANGE DEADLINE 11/3/2018
*BRONZE/25: .4X TO 1X BASE p/r 25
*BRONZE/25: .5X TO 1.2X BASE p/r 40-99
1 Kobe Bryant/25 1,000.00 2,000.00
2 Sarunas Marciulionis/99 6.00 15.00
3 Tom "Satch" Sanders/99 6.00 15.00
4 Vin Baker/99 5.00 12.00
5 Spud Webb/99 6.00 15.00
6 Frank Ramsey/99 6.00 15.00
7 World B. Free/99 6.00 15.00
8 Dell Curry/99 6.00 15.00
9 Chuck Person/99 5.00 12.00
10 Larry Brown/40 6.00 15.00
11 Kurt Rambis/99 6.00 15.00
12 Sam Bowie/99 4.00 10.00
13 Michael Cooper/99 6.00 15.00
14 Cedric Ceballos/99 5.00 12.00
15 Marcus Camby/99 6.00 15.00
16 Horace Grant/99 6.00 15.00
17 Dale Davis/99 4.00 10.00
18 Fat Lever/99 6.00 15.00
19 Antoine Carr/99 4.00 10.00
20 Vlade Divac/99 6.00 15.00
21 Sean Elliott/99 5.00 12.00
22 Mark Price/99 6.00 15.00
23 Antoine Walker/99 6.00 15.00
24 Jamal Mashburn/99 5.00 12.00
25 Antonio McDyess/99 5.00 12.00
26 Cody Zeller/40 4.00 10.00
27 Langston Galloway/99 4.00 10.00
28 Mario Hezonja/40 4.00 10.00
29 Danny Green/99 6.00 15.00
30 Cameron Payne/99 6.00 15.00
31 Kurt Thomas/99 4.00 10.00
32 Nikola Mirotic/99 6.00 15.00
33 Karl-Anthony Towns/25 40.00 100.00
34 DeMar DeRozan/40 12.00 30.00
35 Robert Covington/99 5.00 12.00
36 Jonathon Simmons/99 4.00 10.00
37 Jeremy Lin/40 20.00 50.00
38 Adrian Dantley/99 5.00 12.00
39 Allen Crabbe/99 2.50 6.00
40 Kevon Looney/99 6.00 15.00

2016-17 Panini National Treasures Retro Materials

PRINT RUNS B/WN 15-99 COPIES PER
NO PRICING ON QTY 15
1 Shaquille O'Neal/99 12.00 30.00
2 Shaquille O'Neal/30 12.00 30.00
3 Shaquille O'Neal/30 12.00 30.00
4 Dwyane Wade/99 5.00 12.00
5 Kevin Love/99 4.00 10.00
6 Paul Pierce/99 6.00 15.00
7 Paul Pierce/99 6.00 15.00
8 Chris Paul/99 6.00 15.00
9 Al Horford/30 4.00 10.00
10 Tyson Chandler/99 3.00 8.00
11 Tyson Chandler/99 3.00 8.00
12 Pau Gasol/99 6.00 15.00
13 Pau Gasol/99 6.00 15.00
14 Derrick Rose/99 5.00 12.00
15 Dwight Howard/99 5.00 12.00
16 Dwight Howard/99 5.00 12.00
17 Dwight Howard/99 5.00 12.00
18 Vince Carter/30 8.00 20.00
19 Vince Carter/99 8.00 20.00
20 Vince Carter/99 8.00 20.00
21 Luol Deng/99 3.00 8.00
22 Luol Deng/30 3.00 8.00
23 Jeremy Lin/99 8.00 20.00
24 Jeremy Lin/30 8.00 20.00
25 Rajon Rondo/99 5.00 12.00
26 Rajon Rondo/30 5.00 12.00
27 Chris Andersen/99 3.00 8.00
28 Harrison Barnes/99 3.00 8.00
29 Andrew Bogut/99 4.00 10.00
30 Deron Williams/99 3.00 8.00
31 Nene/99 3.00 8.00
32 Nene/99 3.00 8.00
33 Al Jefferson/99 2.50 6.00
34 Chandler Parsons/99 2.50 6.00
35 Chandler Parsons/99 2.50 6.00
36 Joakim Noah/99 2.50 6.00
37 LaMarcus Aldridge/99 4.00 10.00
38 Joe Johnson/99 4.00 10.00
39 Brandon Knight/99 3.00 8.00
40 LeBron James/99 30.00 80.00
41 Tracy McGrady/99 6.00 15.00
42 Grant Hill/30 5.00 12.00
43 Scottie Pippen/30 6.00 15.00
44 Yao Ming/30 6.00 15.00
45 Shane Battier/99 3.00 8.00
46 Patrick Ewing/30 5.00 12.00
47 Magic Johnson/99 8.00 20.00
48 Larry Bird/30 15.00 40.00
49 Kobe Bryant/30 60.00 150.00
50 Julius Erving/30 10.00 25.00

2016-17 Panini National Treasures Retro Materials Bronze

*BRONZE/25: 1X TO 2.5X BASIC
PRINT RUNS B/WN 8-25 COPIES PER
NO PRICING ON QTY 18 OR LESS
40 LeBron James/25 75.00 200.00

2016-17 Panini National Treasures Rookie Dual Materials

STATED PRINT RUN 60 SER.#'d SETS
*BRONZE/25: 1X TO 2.5X BASIC
1 Jaylen Brown 50.00 120.00
2 Kris Dunn 4.00 10.00
3 Malachi Richardson 2.50 6.00
4 Brice Johnson 2.50 6.00
5 Diamond Stone 2.50 6.00
6 Buddy Hield 5.00 12.00
7 Isaiah Whitehead 2.50 6.00
8 Brandon Ingram 8.00 20.00
9 Cheick Diallo 2.50 6.00
10 Dejounte Murray 6.00 15.00
11 Denzel Valentine 2.50 6.00
12 Marquese Chriss 3.00 8.00
13 A.J. Hammons 2.50 6.00
14 Deyonta Davis 2.50 6.00
15 Pascal Siakam 15.00 40.00
16 Patrick McCaw 2.50 6.00
17 Dragan Bender 2.50 6.00
18 Damian Jones 2.50 6.00
19 Jamal Murray 75.00 200.00
20 Timothe Luwawu-Cabarrot 4.00 10.00
21 Juan Hernangomez 5.00 12.00
22 Thon Maker 3.00 8.00
23 Henry Ellenson 2.50 6.00
24 Malik Beasley 5.00 12.00
25 Jakob Poeltl 5.00 12.00

2016-17 Panini National Treasures Rookie Jumbo Materials

PRINT RUNS B/WN 35 COPIES PER
*BRONZE/25: 1X TO 2.5X BASIC
1 Brandon Ingram 8.00 20.00
2 Malik Beasley 5.00 12.00
3 Buddy Hield 5.00 12.00
4 Marquese Chriss 3.00 8.00
5 Jaylen Brown 60.00 150.00
6 Wade Baldwin IV 2.50 6.00
7 Henry Ellenson 2.50 6.00
8 Cheick Diallo 2.50 6.00
9 Tyler Ulis 3.00 8.00
10 Caris LeVert 6.00 15.00
11 Malcolm Brogdon 8.00 20.00
12 Patrick McCaw 2.50 6.00
13 Domantas Sabonis 15.00 40.00
14 Georgios Papagiannis 2.50 6.00
15 Denzel Valentine 2.50 6.00
16 Thon Maker 6.00 15.00
17 Brice Johnson 2.50 6.00
18 Dario Saric 5.00 12.00
19 Skal Labissiere 2.50 6.00
20 Jamal Murray 75.00 200.00
21 Kris Dunn 4.00 10.00
22 Ivica Zubac 6.00 15.00
23 Dragan Bender 2.50 6.00
24 Jakob Poeltl 2.50 6.00
25 Kay Felder 2.50 6.00

2016-17 Panini National Treasures Rookie Materials

STATED PRINT RUN 75 SER.#'d SETS
*BRONZE/25: 1X TO 2.5X BASIC
1 Jaylen Brown 40.00 100.00
2 Kris Dunn 4.00 10.00
3 Malachi Richardson 2.50 6.00
4 Brice Johnson 2.50 6.00
5 Diamond Stone 2.50 6.00
6 Buddy Hield 5.00 12.00
7 Isaiah Whitehead 2.50 6.00
8 Brandon Ingram 8.00 20.00
9 Cheick Diallo 2.50 6.00
10 Dejounte Murray 6.00 15.00
11 Denzel Valentine 2.50 6.00
12 Marquese Chriss 3.00 8.00
13 A.J. Hammons 2.50 6.00
14 Deyonta Davis 2.50 6.00
15 Pascal Siakam 15.00 40.00
16 Patrick McCaw 2.50 6.00
17 Dragan Bender 2.50 6.00
18 Damian Jones 2.50 6.00
19 Jamal Murray 75.00 200.00
20 Timothe Luwawu-Cabarrot 4.00 10.00
21 Juan Hernangomez 5.00 12.00
22 Thon Maker 3.00 8.00
23 Henry Ellenson 2.50 6.00
24 Malik Beasley 5.00 12.00
25 Jakob Poeltl 5.00 12.00

2016-17 Panini National Treasures Rookie Triple Materials

STATED PRINT RUN 49 SER.#'d SETS
*BRONZE/25: 1X TO 2.5X BASIC
1 Jaylen Brown 60.00 150.00
2 Kris Dunn 4.00 10.00
3 Malachi Richardson 2.50 6.00
4 Brice Johnson 2.50 6.00
5 Diamond Stone 2.50 6.00
6 Buddy Hield 5.00 12.00
7 Isaiah Whitehead 2.50 6.00
8 Brandon Ingram 8.00 20.00
9 Cheick Diallo 2.50 6.00
10 Dejounte Murray 6.00 15.00
11 Denzel Valentine 2.50 6.00
12 Marquese Chriss 3.00 8.00
13 A.J. Hammons 2.50 6.00
14 Deyonta Davis 2.50 6.00
15 Pascal Siakam 15.00 40.00
16 Patrick McCaw 2.50 6.00
17 Dragan Bender 2.50 6.00
18 Damian Jones 2.50 6.00
19 Jamal Murray 75.00 200.00
20 Timothe Luwawu-Cabarrot 4.00 10.00
21 Juan Hernangomez 5.00 12.00
22 Thon Maker 3.00 8.00
23 Henry Ellenson 2.50 6.00
24 Malik Beasley 5.00 12.00
25 Jakob Poeltl 5.00 12.00

2016-17 Panini National Treasures Signatures

PRINT RUNS B/WN 35-75 COPIES PER
EXCHANGE DEADLINE 11/3/2018
*BRONZE/25: .5X TO 1.2X BASIC
1 George Gervin/35 15.00 40.00
2 Ben Wallace/75 40.00 100.00
3 Clyde Drexler/35 30.00 80.00
4 Latrell Sprewell/75 12.00 30.00
5 Karl Malone/35 30.00 80.00
6 John Stockton/35 30.00 80.00
7 Walt Frazier/75 20.00 50.00
9 Mark Aguirre/75 8.00 20.00
10 Adrian Dantley/75 10.00 25.00
11 Detlef Schrempf/75 10.00 25.00
12 Gary Payton/35 15.00 40.00
13 Kobe Bryant/35 2,000.00 4,000.00
14 David Robinson/35 60.00 150.00
15 Sean Elliott/75 8.00 20.00
16 Cedric Ceballos/75 8.00 20.00
17 Chauncey Billups/75 12.00 30.00
18 Dan Majerle/75 8.00 20.00
19 Dell Curry/75 10.00 25.00
20 Eddie Jones/75 8.00 20.00
21 Glen Rice/75 10.00 25.00
22 Jo Jo White/75 8.00 20.00
23 Jim Jackson/75 8.00 20.00
24 Bill Laimbeer/75 10.00 25.00
25 Nick Van Exel/75 10.00 25.00
26 Allan Houston/75 10.00 25.00
27 Tom Gugliotta/75 6.00 15.00
28 Larry Brown/49 10.00 25.00
29 Robert Horry/75 10.00 25.00
30 Vin Baker/75 8.00 20.00
31 Jamal Mashburn/75 8.00 20.00
32 Michael Cooper/75 10.00 25.00
33 Kenny Smith/75 8.00 20.00
34 Spud Webb/75 10.00 25.00
35 Grant Hill/35 30.00 80.00
36 Cedric Maxwell/75 8.00 20.00
37 Vlade Divac/75 10.00 25.00
38 Jeff Hornacek/75 8.00 20.00
39 Sidney Moncrief/75 8.00 20.00
40 Horace Grant/75 10.00 25.00
41 Dennis Rodman/35 25.00 60.00
42 Jerry West/35 20.00 50.00
43 David Thompson/75 12.00 30.00
44 Louie Dampier/75 10.00 25.00
45 Bill Russell/35 1,000.00 2,000.00
46 Justise Winslow/75 8.00 20.00
47 Pau Gasol/35 40.00 100.00
48 Jonas Valanciunas/75 8.00 20.00
49 Khris Middleton/75 10.00 25.00
50 Nicolas Batum/75 8.00 20.00
51 Dirk Nowitzki/35 100.00 250.00
52 DeMar DeRozan/49 12.00 30.00
53 Brandon Knight/75 8.00 20.00
54 Chris Paul/35 40.00 100.00
55 Dwyane Wade/35 25.00 60.00
56 Stephen Curry/35 800.00 1,500.00
57 Kevin Durant/35 125.00 300.00
58 Kyrie Irving/35 50.00 120.00
59 Kevin Love/35 10.00 25.00
60 Andrew Wiggins/35 60.00 150.00
61 Tony Parker/35 25.00 60.00
62 Karl-Anthony Towns/35 50.00 120.00
63 Klay Thompson/49 60.00 150.00
64 Tyler Johnson/75 6.00 15.00
65 Allen Crabbe/75 6.00 15.00
66 Clint Capela/75 15.00 40.00
67 Isaiah Thomas/75 15.00 40.00
68 Jordan Clarkson/75 10.00 25.00
69 Marc Gasol/35 20.00 50.00
70 Bojan Bogdanovic/75 8.00 20.00
71 Ryan Anderson/75 8.00 20.00
72 Dwight Powell/75 6.00 15.00
73 Julius Randle/49 12.00 30.00
74 Bobby Portis/75 10.00 25.00
75 Luol Deng/75 8.00 20.00
76 Danilo Gallinari/75 8.00 20.00
77 Elfrid Payton/75 8.00 20.00
78 Blake Griffin/35 15.00 40.00
79 Devin Booker/75 200.00 500.00
80 Evan Fournier/75 8.00 20.00
81 Jeremy Lin/35 40.00 100.00
82 Marcin Gortat/75 6.00 15.00
83 Nikola Vucevic/75 10.00 25.00
84 Nikola Jokic/75 300.00 600.00
85 Jason Terry/75 8.00 20.00
86 Ricky Rubio/35 20.00 50.00
87 Matthew Dellavedova/75 8.00 20.00
88 Kristaps Porzingis/49 40.00 100.00
89 Myles Turner/75 8.00 20.00
90 Carmelo Anthony/35 60.00 150.00

2016-17 Panini National Treasures Treasured Threads

PRINT RUNS B/WN 49-99 COPIES PER
1 Klay Thompson/99 10.00 25.00
2 LeBron James/99 30.00 80.00
3 Jahlil Okafor/49 2.50 6.00
4 Kemba Walker/49 3.00 8.00
5 Kawhi Leonard/49 10.00 25.00
6 Andrew Wiggins/49 6.00 15.00
8 Karl-Anthony Towns/99 6.00 15.00
9 Goran Dragic/99 3.00 8.00
10 Kyrie Irving/49 8.00 20.00
11 Damian Lillard/49 6.00 15.00
12 Devin Booker/99 15.00 40.00
13 Otto Porter/99 3.00 8.00
14 James Young/99 2.50 6.00
15 Rudy Gay/99 4.00 10.00
16 James Harden/99 8.00 20.00
17 Aaron Gordon/99 4.00 10.00
18 Kevin Durant/99 15.00 40.00
19 Tony Parker/49 6.00 15.00
21 Hassan Whiteside/49 3.00 8.00
22 Zach Randolph/49 4.00 10.00
23 Giannis Antetokounmpo/49 20.00 50.00
24 Kristaps Porzingis/49 5.00 12.00
25 DeMarcus Cousins/49 3.00 8.00
26 Kenneth Faried/49 3.00 8.00
27 Chris Paul/99 6.00 15.00
28 Isaiah Thomas/99 5.00 12.00
29 Russell Westbrook/49 8.00 20.00
30 Dirk Nowitzki/49 10.00 25.00
31 Blake Griffin/49 4.00 10.00
32 Tobias Harris/99 4.00 10.00
33 Paul George/49 6.00 15.00
34 Elfrid Payton/49 3.00 8.00
35 Victor Oladipo/49 3.00 8.00
36 Jimmy Butler/49 8.00 20.00
37 Emmanuel Mudiay/49 2.50 6.00
38 Tristan Thompson/99 3.00 8.00
39 Dwight Howard/49 5.00 12.00
40 Michael Kidd-Gilchrist/99 2.50 6.00
41 Vince Carter/99 8.00 20.00
42 John Wall/99 5.00 12.00
43 Carmelo Anthony/49 6.00 15.00
44 Kyle Lowry/49 4.00 10.00
45 D'Angelo Russell/99 5.00 12.00
46 J.J. Redick/49 4.00 10.00
47 Wesley Matthews/99 2.50 6.00
48 Tyreke Evans/99 2.50 6.00
49 Solomon Hill/99 2.50 6.00
50 Brook Lopez/99 3.00 8.00

2016-17 Panini National Treasures Treasured Threads Prime

*PRIME/20-25: 1X TO 2.5X BASIC
PRINT RUNS B/WN 5-25 COPIES PER
NO PRICING ON QTY 5
2 LeBron James/25 75.00 200.00

2016-17 Panini National Treasures Treasures of the Hall Autographs

PRINT RUNS B/WN 49-75 COPIES PER
EXCHANGE DEADLINE 11/3/2018
*BRONZE/25: .5X TO 1.2X BASIC
1 Bill Russell/49 600.00 1,200.00
2 Shaquille O'Neal/49 50.00 120.00
3 Allen Iverson/49 75.00 200.00
4 Scottie Pippen/49 50.00 120.00
5 Karl Malone/49 20.00 50.00
6 Magic Johnson/49 25.00 60.00
7 Larry Bird/49 40.00 100.00
8 Oscar Robertson/49 25.00 60.00
9 Alonzo Mourning/49 20.00 50.00
10 David Robinson/49 20.00 50.00
11 Hakeem Olajuwon/49 15.00 40.00
12 Kevin McHale/49 10.00 25.00
13 Dennis Rodman/49 25.00 60.00
14 Clyde Drexler/49 12.00 30.00
15 Gary Payton/49 10.00 25.00
16 James Worthy/49 15.00 40.00
17 Rick Barry/75 8.00 20.00
18 Bob Lanier/75 8.00 20.00
19 Artis Gilmore/75 8.00 20.00
20 Bernard King/75 8.00 20.00

2016-17 Panini National Treasures Tremendous Treasures

PRINT RUNS B/WN 30-60 COPIES PER
1 James Harden/60 8.00 20.00
2 Karl-Anthony Towns/60 6.00 15.00
3 Nikola Mirotic/60 2.50 6.00
4 Kyle Lowry/60 4.00 10.00
5 Anthony Davis/60 5.00 12.00
6 Russell Westbrook/60 8.00 20.00
7 LeBron James/60 30.00 80.00
8 Stephen Curry/60 20.00 50.00
9 Kyrie Irving/30 8.00 20.00
10 Iman Shumpert/60 2.50 6.00
11 Rajon Rondo/60 5.00 12.00
12 Trevor Booker/60 2.50 6.00
13 Patrick Beverley/60 2.50 6.00
14 Langston Galloway/60 2.50 6.00
15 Tristan Thompson/60 3.00 8.00
16 Paul Millsap/60 3.00 8.00
17 D'Angelo Russell/60 5.00 12.00
18 Isaiah Thomas/60 3.00 8.00
19 Klay Thompson/60 10.00 25.00
20 Eric Bledsoe/60 3.00 8.00
21 Marc Gasol/60 4.00 10.00
22 Aaron Gordon/60 4.00 10.00
23 Julius Randle/60 5.00 12.00
24 Victor Oladipo/60 3.00 8.00
25 Eric Gordon/60 3.00 8.00
27 Emmanuel Mudiay/60 2.50 6.00
28 Enes Kanter/60 2.50 6.00
29 J.J. Redick/60 4.00 10.00
30 Brook Lopez/60 3.00 8.00
31 Nikola Jokic/30 20.00 50.00
32 Ben McLemore/60 2.50 6.00
33 Frank Kaminsky/60 2.50 6.00
34 Luis Scola/60 3.00 8.00
35 Jordan Clarkson/30 4.00 10.00
36 Damian Lillard/60 6.00 15.00
37 J.J. Barea/60 3.00 8.00
38 C.J. McCollum/60 4.00 10.00
39 Wesley Matthews/60 2.50 6.00
40 Solomon Hill/60 2.50 6.00
41 Nicolas Batum/60 3.00 8.00
42 Joe Johnson/60 4.00 10.00
43 Kenneth Faried/60 3.00 8.00
44 Mason Plumlee/60 2.50 6.00
45 Jusuf Nurkic/60 3.00 8.00
46 Jonas Valanciunas/60 3.00 8.00
47 Zach LaVine/60 8.00 20.00
48 Tony Parker/60 6.00 15.00
49 Kyle Korver/60 3.00 8.00
50 Tyreke Evans/60 3.00 8.00

2016-17 Panini National Treasures Tremendous Treasures Bronze

*BRONZE/20-25: 1X TO 2.5X BASIC
PRINT RUNS B/WN 15-25 COPIES PER
NO PRICING ON QTY 15
7 LeBron James/25 125.00 300.00

2017-18 Panini National Treasures

STATED PRINT RUN 99 SER.#'d SETS

PRIME PATCHES MAY SELL FOR PREMIUM
EXCHANGE DEADLINE 11/2/2019
1 Dirk Nowitzki 4.00 10.00
2 Buddy Hield 1.50 4.00
3 Draymond Green 2.00 5.00
4 Rudy Gobert 2.00 5.00
5 Austin Rivers 1.25 3.00
6 Eric Bledsoe 1.25 3.00
7 Dennis Schroder 1.25 3.00
8 Dwight Howard 2.00 5.00
9 Kristaps Porzingis 2.00 5.00
10 Joel Embiid 3.00 8.00
11 Harrison Barnes 1.25 3.00
12 LaMarcus Aldridge 1.50 4.00
13 Kevin Durant 6.00 15.00
14 John Wall 2.00 5.00
15 Kentavious Caldwell-Pope 1.25 3.00
16 Kent Bazemore 1.00 2.50
17 Giannis Antetokounmpo 40.00 100.00
18 Nicolas Batum 1.00 2.50
19 Tim Hardaway Jr. 1.25 3.00
20 JJ Redick 1.50 4.00
21 Jamal Murray 2.50 6.00
22 Kawhi Leonard 4.00 10.00
23 James Harden 3.00 8.00
24 Otto Porter Jr. 1.25 3.00
25 Brandon Ingram 2.00 5.00
26 Khris Middleton 2.00 5.00
27 Taurean Prince 1.00 2.50
28 Zach LaVine 2.50 6.00
29 Enes Kanter 1.25 3.00
30 Devin Booker 4.00 10.00
31 Paul Millsap 1.25 3.00
32 Pau Gasol 2.50 6.00
33 Eric Gordon 1.25 3.00
34 Markieff Morris 1.00 2.50
35 Brook Lopez 1.25 3.00
36 Kyrie Irving 3.00 8.00
37 Jimmy Butler 2.50 6.00
38 Kris Dunn 1.00 2.50
39 Paul George 2.50 6.00
40 TJ Warren 1.25 3.00
41 Nikola Jokic 10.00 25.00
42 Manu Ginobili 3.00 8.00
43 Clint Capela 1.25 3.00
44 Marcin Gortat 1.00 2.50
45 Marc Gasol 1.50 4.00
46 Al Horford 1.50 4.00
47 Andrew Wiggins 2.00 5.00
48 Bobby Portis 1.00 2.50
49 Carmelo Anthony 2.50 6.00
50 Tyson Chandler 1.25 3.00
51 Reggie Jackson 1.25 3.00
52 Kyle Lowry 1.50 4.00
53 Victor Oladipo 1.50 4.00
54 Tobias Harris 1.25 3.00
55 Mike Conley 1.25 3.00
56 Jaylen Brown 4.00 10.00
57 Karl-Anthony Towns 2.50 6.00
58 LeBron James 75.00 200.00
59 Russell Westbrook 2.50 6.00
60 Damian Lillard 4.00 10.00
61 Avery Bradley 1.00 2.50
62 DeMar DeRozan 2.00 5.00
63 Darren Collison 1.00 2.50
64 Steven Adams 1.25 3.00
65 JaMychal Green 1.00 2.50
66 Jeff Teague 1.00 2.50
67 D'Angelo Russell 1.25 3.00
68 Aaron Gordon 1.50 4.00
69 Kevin Love 1.50 4.00
70 CJ McCollum 1.50 4.00
71 Andre Drummond 1.25 3.00
72 Serge Ibaka 1.25 3.00
73 Myles Turner 1.50 4.00
74 Tyreke Evans 1.00 2.50
75 Goran Dragic 1.25 3.00
76 Jrue Holiday 2.00 5.00
77 Rondae Hollis-Jefferson 1.00 2.50
78 Nikola Vucevic 1.25 3.00
79 Dwyane Wade 3.00 8.00
80 Al-Farouq Aminu 1.00 2.50
81 Stephen Curry 12.00 30.00
82 Ricky Rubio 1.25 3.00
83 Chris Paul 2.50 6.00
84 Blake Griffin 1.50 4.00
85 Hassan Whiteside 1.25 3.00
86 Jeremy Lin 2.50 6.00
87 Anthony Davis 4.00 10.00
88 Evan Fournier 1.25 3.00
89 Isaiah Thomas 1.25 3.00
90 Zach Randolph 1.50 4.00
91 Klay Thompson 4.00 10.00
92 Rodney Hood 1.00 2.50
93 DeAndre Jordan 1.25 3.00
94 Bojan Bogdanovic 1.25 3.00
95 Dion Waiters 1.00 2.50
96 DeMarcus Cousins 1.25 3.00
97 Kemba Walker 1.25 3.00
98 Ben Simmons 1.50 4.00
99 Wesley Matthews 1.00 2.50
100 Vince Carter 3.00 8.00
101 Fultz JSY AU RC 80.00 200.00
102 Ball JSY AU RC 500.00 1,000.00
103 Tatum JSY AU RC 10,000.00 20,000.00
104 J.Jcksn JSY AU RC EXCH 40.00 100.00
105 Fox JSY AU RC 1,500.00 3,000.00
106 Isaac JSY AU RC 80.00 200.00
107 Markkanen JSY AU RC 600.00 1,200.00
108 Ntilikina JSY AU RC 40.00 100.00
109 Smith Jr. JSY AU RC 40.00 100.00
110 Z.Collins JSY AU RC 50.00 125.00
111 Monk JSY AU RC 125.00 300.00
112 Kennard JSY AU RC 60.00 150.00
113 Mitchell JSY AU RC 2,500.00 5,000.00
114 Adbyo JSY AU RC EXCH 400.00 800.00
116 Justin Patton JSY AU RC 30.00 80.00
117 D.J. Wilson JSY AU RC 30.00 80.00
118 TJ Leaf JSY AU RC 30.00 80.00
119 J.Collins JSY AU RC 80.00 200.00
120 Giles JSY AU RC 30.00 80.00
121 Ferguson JSY AU RC 30.00 80.00
122 Allen JSY AU RC 80.00 200.00
123 Annby JSY AU RC EXCH 150.00 400.00
124 Tyler Lydon JSY AU RC EXCH 30.00 80.00
125 Caleb Swanigan JSY AU RC 30.00 80.00
126 Kuzma JSY AU RC 300.00 600.00
127 Tony Bradley JSY AU RC 30.00 80.00
128 White JSY AU RC EXCH 125.00 300.00
129 Hart JSY AU RC 150.00 400.00
130 F.Jcksn JSY AU RC 30.00 80.00
131 Davon Reed JSY AU RC 30.00 80.00
132 Wes Iwundu JSY AU RC 30.00 80.00
133 Frank Mason III JSY AU RC 30.00 80.00
134 Ivan Rabb JSY AU RC 30.00 80.00
135 Semi Ojeleye JSY AU RC 40.00 100.00
136 Bell JSY AU RC EXCH 30.00 80.00
137 Jawun Evans JSY AU RC 30.00 80.00
138 Dwayne Bacon JSY AU RC 30.00 80.00
139 Tyler Dorsey JSY AU RC 30.00 80.00
140 Sterling Brown JSY AU RC 30.00 80.00
141 Sindarius Thornwell JSY AU RC 30.00 80.00
142 Ante Zizic JSY AU RC 40.00 100.00
143 Ike Anigbogu JSY AU RC 30.00 80.00
144 Milos Teodosic JSY AU RC 40.00 100.00
145 Damyean Dotson JSY AU RC 40.00 100.00
148 Wayne Selden JSY AU RC 30.00 80.00
149 Zhou Qi JSY AU RC 125.00 300.00
150 Thomas Bryant AU RC 8.00 20.00
151 Brandon Paul AU RC 5.00 12.00
153 Tyler Cavanaugh AU RC 5.00 12.00
154 Alec Peters AU RC 5.00 12.00
155 Abdel Nader AU RC 6.00 15.00
156 Daniel Theis AU RC 10.00 25.00
157 Cedi Osman AU RC 10.00 25.00
158 Johnathan Motley AU RC EXCH 5.00 12.00
159 Dillon Brooks AU RC 30.00 80.00

2017-18 Panini National Treasures Bronze

*BRNZ 1-100: .6X TO 1.5X BASIC
*BRNZ 150-159: .5X TO 1.5X BASIC
STATED PRINT RUN 25 SER.#'d SETS
EXCHANGE DEADLINE 11/2/2019

2017-18 Panini National Treasures All-Decade Materials

PRINT RUNS B/WN 15-99 COPIES PER
NO PRICING ON QTY 15 OR LESS
ADM2 Artis Gilmore/49 5.00 12.00
ADM3 John Havlicek/99 25.00 60.00
4 Dan Issel/49 5.00 12.00
ADM5 Julius Erving/25 10.00 25.00
ADM6 Larry Bird/25 15.00 40.00
ADM7 Magic Johnson/99 15.00 40.00
ADM8 Earl Monroe/99 4.00 10.00
ADM9 Spencer Haywood/25 4.00 10.00
ADM10 Kareem Abdul-Jabbar/25 12.00 30.00
ADM11 Scottie Pippen/99 10.00 25.00
ADM12 Isiah Thomas/49 6.00 15.00
ADM14 Jerry Lucas/49 4.00 10.00
ADM17 Kevin Garnett/99 10.00 25.00
ADM18 Kobe Bryant/99 75.00 200.00
ADM19 Tim Duncan/99 5.00 12.00
ADM20 Dirk Nowitzki/99 10.00 25.00

2017-18 Panini National Treasures All-Decade Memorabilia Signatures

PRINT RUNS B/WN 25-49 COPIES PER
EXCHANGE DEADLINE 11/2/2019
*BRONZE/25: .4X TO 1X BASE p/r 25
*BRONZE/25: .6X TO 1.5X BASE p/r 49
1 Chris Paul/25 60.00 150.00
2 Damian Lillard/25 25.00 60.00
3 Kyrie Irving/25 40.00 100.00
4 Larry Bird/25 40.00 100.00
5 Magic Johnson/25 40.00 100.00
6 Blake Griffin/25 15.00 40.00
7 Giannis Antetokounmpo/25 60.00 150.00
8 Dennis Rodman/49 20.00 50.00
9 Hakeem Olajuwon/25 20.00 50.00
10 Kevin Love/49 12.00 30.00
11 Vince Carter/49 20.00 50.00
12 James Worthy/49 12.00 30.00
13 Dominique Wilkins/49 10.00 25.00
14 Kristaps Porzingis/49 12.00 30.00
15 Dirk Nowitzki/25 40.00 100.00
16 Artis Gilmore/49 8.00 20.00
17 Mitch Richmond/49 8.00 20.00
18 Jamaal Wilkes/49 6.00 15.00
19 Detlef Schrempf/49 10.00 25.00
20 Jack Sikma/49 6.00 15.00

2017-18 Panini National Treasures All-Decade Signatures

PRINT RUNS B/WN 25-49 COPIES PER
EXCHANGE DEADLINE 11/2/2019
*BRONZE/25: .4X TO 1X BASE p/r 25
*BRONZE/25: .5X TO 1.2X BASE p/r 49
1 Artis Gilmore/49 6.00 15.00
2 Bernard King/49 8.00 20.00
3 Clyde Drexler/25 15.00 40.00
4 Dennis Rodman/25 20.00 50.00
5 Larry Bird/25 50.00 120.00
6 George McGinnis/49 4.00 10.00
7 Jerry West/25 30.00 80.00
8 Jo Jo White/49 8.00 20.00
9 Magic Johnson/25 40.00 100.00
10 Ray Allen/25 25.00 60.00
11 Reggie Miller/25 50.00 120.00
12 Shawn Kemp/49 20.00 50.00
13 Walt Frazier/49 10.00 25.00
14 Willis Reed/49 40.00 100.00
15 Manu Ginobili/25 25.00 60.00
16 Chris Paul/25 40.00 100.00
17 Dirk Nowitzki/25 75.00 200.00
18 Giannis Antetokounmpo/25 60.00 150.00
19 Anthony Davis/25 30.00 80.00
20 Kyrie Irving/25 50.00 120.00

2017-18 Panini National Treasures Century Materials

PRINT RUNS B/WN 25-99 COPIES PER
1 Chris Paul/49 5.00 12.00
2 Goran Dragic/49 3.00 8.00
3 Pau Gasol/99 6.00 15.00
4 Kevin Love/49 4.00 10.00
5 Grant Hill/49 6.00 15.00
6 Joel Embiid/49 5.00 12.00
7 Bobby Jackson/99 2.50 6.00
8 Al Horford/99 4.00 10.00
9 Reggie Lewis/99 5.00 12.00
10 Paul Millsap/49 3.00 8.00
11 Dwyane Wade/49 8.00 20.00
12 Brook Lopez/49 3.00 8.00
13 Giannis Antetokounmpo/49 6.00 15.00
14 Vince Carter/99 8.00 20.00
15 Isiah Thomas/49 6.00 15.00
16 Buddy Hield/49 4.00 10.00
17 Buck Williams/99 2.50 6.00
18 Harrison Barnes/99 3.00 8.00
19 Michael Redd/99 3.00 8.00
20 Eric Bledsoe/99 3.00 8.00
21 Kyrie Irving/49 8.00 20.00
22 Marquese Chriss/49 2.50 6.00
23 Karl-Anthony Towns/99 5.00 12.00
24 DeMarcus Cousins/49 3.00 8.00
25 Jermaine O'Neal/99 4.00 10.00
26 Kris Dunn/49 3.00 8.00
27 Clyde Drexler/49 6.00 15.00
28 Dragan Bender/99 2.50 6.00
29 Mike Bibby/99 4.00 10.00
30 Devin Booker/49 5.00 12.00
31 Damian Lillard/49 5.00 12.00
32 Tobias Harris/49 3.00 8.00
33 Andrew Wiggins/49 5.00 12.00
35 Kevin Garnett/99 10.00 25.00
36 Julius Randle/99 4.00 10.00
37 Dennis Rodman/49 10.00 25.00
38 CJ McCollum/49 4.00 10.00
39 Danny Granger/99 2.50 6.00
40 Danilo Gallinari/99 3.00 8.00
41 Dirk Nowitzki/49 10.00 25.00
42 Reggie Jackson/99 3.00 8.00
43 John Wall/49 5.00 12.00
44 LaMarcus Aldridge/99 4.00 10.00
45 Kobe Bryant/99 60.00 150.00
46 Rajon Rondo/49 5.00 12.00
47 Jason Kidd/49 6.00 15.00
48 Jamal Murray/49 6.00 15.00
49 Shawn Marion/99 3.00 8.00
50 Aaron Gordon/99 4.00 10.00
51 Anthony Davis/49 6.00 15.00
52 Elfrid Payton/49 2.50 6.00
53 Jabari Parker/99 2.50 6.00
54 Stephen Curry/49 12.00 30.00
55 Larry Bird/49 15.00 40.00
56 Bradley Beal/99 5.00 12.00
57 Joe Dumars/99 5.00 12.00
58 Klay Thompson/99 10.00 25.00
59 Kevin Durant/99 15.00 40.00
60 Eric Gordon/99 3.00 8.00
61 Blake Griffin/99 4.00 10.00
62 Michael Kidd-Gilchrist/99 2.50 6.00
63 Jimmy Butler/49 6.00 15.00
64 Jeremy Lin/49 6.00 15.00
65 Ray Allen/99 6.00 15.00
66 Mike Conley/99 3.00 8.00
67 John Stockton/25 8.00 20.00
68 Andre Drummond/99 3.00 8.00
69 LeBron James/99 20.00 50.00
70 Nikola Jokic/99 25.00 60.00
71 Derrick Rose/49 6.00 15.00
72 Nikola Mirotic/99 2.50 6.00
73 Marc Gasol/99 4.00 10.00
74 Kristaps Porzingis/99 5.00 12.00
75 Stephen Jackson/99 3.00 8.00
76 DeMar DeRozan/49 5.00 12.00
77 Karl Malone/49 8.00 20.00
78 James Harden/99 8.00 20.00
80 Zach LaVine/49 6.00 15.00
81 Paul George/49 6.00 15.00
82 Nerlens Noel/99 2.50 6.00
83 Ricky Rubio/99 3.00 8.00
84 D'Angelo Russell/49 3.00 8.00
85 Tim Duncan/99 5.00 12.00
86 Tyreke Evans/49 2.50 6.00
87 Kevin McHale/25 5.00 12.00
88 Gordon Hayward/99 3.00 8.00
89 Russell Westbrook/49 6.00 15.00
90 Khris Middleton/99 5.00 12.00
91 Dwight Howard/49 5.00 12.00
92 Victor Oladipo/49 5.00 12.00
93 Brandon Ingram/49 5.00 12.00
94 Marcus Smart/99 4.00 10.00
95 Antawn Jamison/99 3.00 8.00
96 Kemba Walker/99 3.00 8.00
97 Kevin Duckworth/99 2.50 6.00
98 Rodney Hood/99 2.50 6.00
99 Carmelo Anthony/49 6.00 15.00
100 Avery Bradley/49 2.50 6.00

2017-18 Panini National Treasures Century Materials Bronze

*BRONZE/20-25: .75X TO 2X BASIC
PRINT RUNS B/WN 10-25 COPIES PER
NO PRICING ON QTY 15 OR LESS
69 LeBron James/25 100.00 250.00

2017-18 Panini National Treasures Clutch Factor Jersey Autographs

PRINT RUNS B/WN 35-99 COPIES PER
EXCHANGE DEADLINE 11/2/2019
*BRONZE/25: .6X TO 1.5X BASE p/r 35-99
2 Reggie Jackson/99 5.00 12.00
3 Ricky Rubio/49 8.00 20.00
4 Jonathan Isaac/99 25.00 60.00
5 LaMarcus Aldridge/49 10.00 25.00
6 Dennis Smith Jr./99 5.00 12.00
7 CJ McCollum/99 8.00 20.00
8 Willie Cauley-Stein/99 4.00 10.00
9 Rodney Hood/99 4.00 10.00
10 Zach LaVine/99 12.00 30.00
11 Kevin Durant/49 75.00 200.00
12 Detlef Schrempf/99 10.00 25.00
13 Kevin Love/49 12.00 30.00
14 Richard Jefferson/99 5.00 12.00
15 Lonzo Ball/49 60.00 150.00
16 Dario Saric/99 5.00 12.00
17 Harrison Barnes/99 5.00 12.00
18 Malik Monk/99 15.00 40.00
19 Aaron Gordon/99 8.00 20.00
20 Avery Bradley/99 4.00 10.00
22 Victor Oladipo/99 10.00 25.00
23 Markelle Fultz/49 25.00 60.00
24 Rudy Gay/99 5.00 12.00
25 Jayson Tatum/99 150.00 400.00
26 Lance Stephenson/99 5.00 12.00
27 Andre Drummond/99 5.00 12.00
28 Josh Richardson/99 5.00 12.00
29 Eric Gordon/99 5.00 12.00
30 Clint Capela/99 8.00 20.00
31 Kyrie Irving/35 25.00 60.00
32 Gary Harris/99 5.00 12.00
33 Vince Carter/49 20.00 50.00
34 Ryan Anderson/99 4.00 10.00
35 Kristaps Porzingis/99 12.00 30.00
36 Rudy Gobert/99 8.00 20.00
37 Gordon Hayward/99 12.00 30.00
38 Mark Price/99 8.00 20.00
39 Khris Middleton/99 8.00 20.00
40 De'Aaron Fox/99 60.00 150.00
41 Marc Gasol/99 6.00 15.00
42 Jeff Teague/99 4.00 10.00
43 Grant Hill/49 20.00 50.00
44 Artis Gilmore/99 8.00 20.00
45 Mike Conley/99 5.00 12.00
46 Tom Chambers/99 6.00 15.00
47 Mason Plumlee/99 4.00 10.00
48 Omri Casspi/99 4.00 10.00
49 Nikola Jokic/99 300.00 600.00
50 B.J. Armstrong/99 8.00 20.00

2017-18 Panini National Treasures Colossal Jersey Autographs

PRINT RUNS B/WN 35-99 COPIES PER
EXCHANGE DEADLINE 11/2/2019
1 Anthony Davis/35 30.00 80.00
2 Jamaal Wilkes/99 8.00 20.00
3 Markelle Fultz/49 50.00 120.00
4 DeMarre Carroll/99 4.00 10.00
5 Lonzo Ball/49 75.00 200.00
6 Willie Cauley-Stein/99 5.00 12.00
7 Gordon Hayward/99 12.00 30.00
8 Khris Middleton/99 12.00 30.00
9 Allen Iverson/35 50.00 120.00
10 Michael Kidd-Gilchrist/99 4.00 10.00
11 Giannis Antetokounmpo/35 200.00 500.00
12 Gary Harris/99 5.00 12.00
13 Kobe Bryant/49 2,000.00 4,000.00
14 Evan Turner/99 4.00 10.00
15 Jayson Tatum/99 300.00 600.00
16 Thaddeus Young/99 4.00 10.00
17 Rodney Hood/99 4.00 10.00
18 Nikola Jokic/99 200.00 500.00
19 Chris Paul/35 50.00 120.00
20 Ralph Sampson/99 6.00 15.00
21 Andrew Wiggins/35 10.00 25.00
22 Jeff Teague/99 4.00 10.00
23 Dennis Rodman/49 30.00 80.00
24 Dennis Smith Jr./99 5.00 12.00
25 CJ McCollum/99 8.00 20.00
26 Seth Curry/99 6.00 15.00
27 Zach LaVine/99 12.00 30.00
28 Tom Gugliotta/99 4.00 10.00
29 Dwyane Wade/35 25.00 60.00
30 Danny Manning/99 5.00 12.00
31 Karl-Anthony Towns/35 25.00 60.00
32 Glen Rice/99 8.00 20.00
33 Dominique Wilkins/49 12.00 30.00
34 Dario Saric/99 10.00 25.00
35 Harrison Barnes/99 5.00 12.00
36 Tim Hardaway Jr./99 5.00 12.00
37 B.J. Armstrong/99 10.00 25.00
38 Hakeem Olajuwon/35 25.00 60.00
39 Damian Lillard/35 25.00 60.00
40 De'Aaron Fox/99 25.00 60.00
41 Brandon Ingram/49 30.00 80.00
42 Thon Maker/99 4.00 10.00
43 James Worthy/49 12.00 30.00
44 Rudy Gobert/99 6.00 15.00
45 Jack Sikma/99 6.00 15.00
46 Shawn Bradley/99 4.00 10.00
47 Aaron Gordon/99 8.00 20.00
48 Reggie Jackson/99 5.00 12.00
49 Dirk Nowitzki/35 50.00 120.00
50 Ryan Anderson/99 4.00 10.00

2017-18 Panini National Treasures Colossal Jersey Autographs Bronze

*BRONZE: .75X TO 2X BASE p/r 35-99
STATED PRINT RUN 25 SER.#'d SETS
EXCHANGE DEADLINE 11/2/2019
1 Anthony Davis/25 100.00 250.00
5 Lonzo Ball/25 300.00 600.00
11 Giannis Antetokounmpo/25 300.00 600.00
19 Chris Paul/25 75.00 200.00
23 Dennis Rodman/25 100.00 250.00
25 CJ McCollum/25 30.00 80.00
26 Seth Curry/25 15.00 40.00
31 Karl-Anthony Towns/25 60.00 150.00
37 B.J. Armstrong/25 30.00 80.00
41 Brandon Ingram/25 125.00 300.00
49 Dirk Nowitzki/25 500.00 800.00

2017-18 Panini National Treasures Colossal Materials

PRINT RUNS B/WN 47-99 COPIES PER
1 Reggie Jackson/49 3.00 8.00
2 Pau Gasol/99 6.00 15.00
3 Kristaps Porzingis/99 5.00 12.00
4 LeBron James/99 75.00 200.00
5 Harrison Barnes/99 3.00 8.00
6 Damian Lillard/49 10.00 25.00
7 Gordon Hayward/99 3.00 8.00
8 Jimmy Butler/49 6.00 15.00
9 Aaron Gordon/49 4.00 10.00
10 Rajon Rondo/49 5.00 12.00
11 Elfrid Payton/49 2.50 6.00
12 John Wall/49 5.00 12.00
13 Joel Embiid/49 5.00 12.00
15 CJ McCollum/99 4.00 10.00
16 Derrick Rose/49 6.00 15.00
17 Zach LaVine/49 6.00 15.00
18 DeMarcus Cousins/49 3.00 8.00
19 Avery Bradley/49 2.50 6.00
20 Bradley Beal/49 5.00 12.00
21 Nikola Mirotic/99 2.50 6.00
22 Ricky Rubio/99 3.00 8.00
23 Julius Randle/47 4.00 10.00
24 Dwyane Wade/49 8.00 20.00
25 Dragan Bender/49 2.50 6.00
26 Draymond Green/49 5.00 12.00
27 Khris Middleton/49 5.00 12.00
28 Jeremy Lin/49 6.00 15.00
29 Brook Lopez/49 3.00 8.00
30 Al Horford/49 4.00 10.00
31 Victor Oladipo/49 3.00 8.00
32 Vince Carter/99 8.00 20.00
33 Kemba Walker/49 3.00 8.00
34 Carmelo Anthony/49 6.00 15.00
35 Andre Drummond/49 3.00 8.00
36 Andrew Wiggins/49 5.00 12.00
37 Nikola Jokic/99 25.00 60.00
38 Buddy Hield/49 4.00 10.00
39 Michael Kidd-Gilchrist/49 2.50 6.00
40 Blake Griffin/49 4.00 10.00

2017-18 Panini National Treasures Colossal Materials Prime

*PRIME/24-25: 1X TO 2.5X BASIC
PRINT RUNS B/WN 2-25 COPIES PER
NO PRICING ON QTY 10 OR LESS

2017-18 Panini National Treasures Colossal Rookie Materials

STATED PRINT RUN 99 SER.#'d SETS
1 Frank Mason III 2.50 6.00
2 Donovan Mitchell 25.00 60.00
3 Jawun Evans 2.50 6.00
4 D.J. Wilson 2.50 6.00
5 Terrance Ferguson 2.50 6.00
6 Markelle Fultz 6.00 15.00
7 Caleb Swanigan 2.50 6.00
10 Dennis Smith Jr. 3.00 8.00
11 Ivan Rabb 2.50 6.00
12 Bam Adebayo 15.00 40.00
13 Dwayne Bacon 2.50 6.00
14 TJ Leaf 2.50 6.00
15 Jarrett Allen 6.00 15.00
16 Lonzo Ball 8.00 20.00
18 Jonathan Isaac 6.00 15.00
19 Frank Jackson 2.50 6.00
20 Zach Collins 4.00 10.00
21 Semi Ojeleye 3.00 8.00
23 Tyler Dorsey 2.50 6.00
24 John Collins 6.00 15.00
25 OG Anunoby 12.00 30.00
26 Jayson Tatum 200.00 500.00
27 Tony Bradley 2.50 6.00
29 Davon Reed 2.50 6.00
30 Malik Monk 10.00 25.00
31 Jordan Bell 2.50 6.00
32 Justin Patton 2.50 6.00
33 Sterling Brown 2.50 6.00
34 Harry Giles 2.50 6.00
35 Tyler Lydon 2.50 6.00
36 Josh Jackson 3.00 8.00
37 Derrick White 10.00 25.00
38 Frank Ntilikina 3.00 8.00
39 Wes Iwundu 2.50 6.00
40 Luke Kennard 5.00 12.00

2017-18 Panini National Treasures Colossal Rookie Materials Prime

*PRIME: .75X TO 2X BASIC
STATED PRINT RUN 25 SER.#'d SETS
2 Donovan Mitchell 100.00 250.00
8 De'Aaron Fox 40.00 100.00
26 Jayson Tatum 500.00 1,000.00

2017-18 Panini National Treasures Game Gear Dual Relic Autographs

PRINT RUNS B/WN 25-49 COPIES PER
EXCHANGE DEADLINE 11/2/2019
*BRONZE/25: .4X TO 1X BASE p/r 25
*BRONZE/25: .6X TO 1.5X BASE p/r 35-49
1 Kyrie Irving/25 40.00 100.00
2 Rodney Hood/49 4.00 10.00
3 Andrew Wiggins/49 8.00 20.00
4 Nikola Jokic/25 125.00 300.00
5 Ricky Rubio/49 8.00 20.00
6 DeMarre Carroll/25 6.00 15.00
7 Vince Carter/49 20.00 50.00
8 Kristaps Porzingis/35 12.00 30.00
9 Chris Paul/35 25.00 60.00
10 Kemba Walker/25 15.00 40.00
11 Blake Griffin/49 15.00 40.00
12 Eric Bledsoe/25 8.00 20.00
13 Karl-Anthony Towns/49 20.00 50.00
14 Rudy Gay/25 8.00 20.00
15 Brandon Ingram/49 8.00 20.00
16 Evan Turner/35 4.00 10.00
17 D'Angelo Russell/49 12.00 30.00
18 Kawhi Leonard/35 50.00 120.00
19 Damian Lillard/25 25.00 60.00
20 Mike Conley/25 8.00 20.00
21 Giannis Antetokounmpo/49 100.00 250.00
22 Eric Gordon/25 8.00 20.00
23 Marc Gasol/25 10.00 25.00
24 Enes Kanter/25 8.00 20.00
25 Kevin Love/35 10.00 25.00

2017-18 Panini National Treasures Game Gear Dual Relics

PRINT RUNS B/WN 25-99 COPIES PER
1 Otto Porter Jr./99 3.00 8.00
2 Damian Lillard/99 5.00 12.00
3 Bradley Beal/99 5.00 12.00
4 Dwight Howard/99 5.00 12.00
5 Andrew Wiggins/99 5.00 12.00
6 Kevin Durant/99 15.00 40.00
7 Kevin Love/99 4.00 10.00
9 Jeremy Lin/99 6.00 15.00
10 Chris Paul/99 6.00 15.00
11 Rajon Rondo/49 6.00 15.00
12 Dirk Nowitzki/99 10.00 25.00
13 Tyreke Evans/99 2.50 6.00
14 Draymond Green/99 6.00 15.00
15 Jabari Parker/99 2.50 6.00
16 LeBron James/99 20.00 50.00
17 DeMarcus Cousins/49 5.00 12.00
18 Stephen Curry/99 12.00 30.00
19 LaMarcus Aldridge/99 4.00 10.00
20 Carmelo Anthony/99 6.00 15.00
21 Mike Conley/99 3.00 8.00
22 Derrick Rose/99 6.00 15.00
23 Al Horford/99 4.00 10.00
24 Giannis Antetokounmpo/25 12.00 30.00
25 Jimmy Butler/99 6.00 15.00
26 Russell Westbrook/49 6.00 15.00
28 Dwyane Wade/99 8.00 20.00
29 Buddy Hield/99 4.00 10.00
30 Kyrie Irving/49 8.00 20.00

2017-18 Panini National Treasures Game Gear Dual Relics Prime

*PRIME/25: .75X TO 2X BASIC
PRINT RUNS B/WN 6-25 COPIES PER
NO PRICING ON QTY 10 OR LESS
16 LeBron James/25 100.00 250.00

2017-18 Panini National Treasures Game Gear Relic Autographs

PRINT RUNS B/WN 25-49 COPIES PER
EXCHANGE DEADLINE 11/2/2019
*PRIME/25: .4X TO 1X BASE p/r 25
*PRIME/25: .6X TO 1.5X BASE p/r 49
1 Brandon Ingram/49 20.00 50.00
2 Reggie Jackson/49 5.00 12.00
3 D'Angelo Russell/49 12.00 30.00
4 Kemba Walker/49 5.00 12.00
5 Jeff Teague/49 4.00 10.00
6 Eric Bledsoe/49 5.00 12.00
7 Blake Griffin/25 15.00 40.00
8 Aaron Gordon/49 8.00 20.00
9 Karl-Anthony Towns/25 30.00 80.00
10 Michael Kidd-Gilchrist/49 4.00 10.00
11 Kevin Love/49 12.00 30.00
12 Gary Harris/49 5.00 12.00
13 Kristaps Porzingis/49 12.00 30.00
14 Mike Conley/49 5.00 12.00
15 Chris Paul/25 40.00 100.00
16 Eric Gordon/49 5.00 12.00
17 Giannis Antetokounmpo/25 60.00 510.00
18 Avery Bradley/49 4.00 10.00
19 Marc Gasol/25 10.00 25.00
20 Myles Turner/49 6.00 15.00
21 Vince Carter/49 20.00 50.00
22 Kyrie Irving/25 40.00 100.00
23 Kawhi Leonard/25 50.00 120.00
24 Rodney Hood/49 4.00 10.00
25 Damian Lillard/25 25.00 60.00
26 Nikola Jokic/49 150.00 400.00
27 Andrew Wiggins/25 12.00 30.00
28 Elfrid Payton/49 4.00 10.00
29 Ricky Rubio/25 10.00 25.00
30 Nerlens Noel/49 4.00 10.00

2017-18 Panini National Treasures Game Gear Relics

PRINT RUNS B/WN 49-99 COPIES PER
1 Ricky Rubio/99 3.00 8.00
2 Kevin Durant/99 15.00 40.00
4 Dwyane Wade/49 8.00 20.00
5 Marcus Smart/99 4.00 10.00
6 Dirk Nowitzki/99 10.00 25.00
7 Rajon Rondo/49 5.00 12.00
8 Paul George/49 6.00 15.00
9 Kemba Walker/99 3.00 8.00
10 Andrew Wiggins/99 5.00 12.00
11 Kevin Love/49 4.00 10.00
12 LeBron James/99 20.00 50.00
13 D'Angelo Russell/49 3.00 8.00
14 Chris Paul/99 5.00 12.00
15 Buddy Hield/99 4.00 10.00
16 Anthony Davis/49 6.00 15.00
17 Julius Randle/99 4.00 10.00
18 Draymond Green/99 5.00 12.00
19 Tyreke Evans/99 2.50 6.00
20 John Wall/99 5.00 12.00
21 Brandon Ingram/99 5.00 12.00
22 Russell Westbrook/49 6.00 15.00
23 Jeremy Lin/99 6.00 15.00
24 Carmelo Anthony/49 6.00 15.00
25 Joel Embiid/99 5.00 12.00
26 Derrick Rose/99 5.00 12.00
27 Mike Conley/99 3.00 8.00
28 Pau Gasol/99 6.00 15.00
29 DeMar DeRozan/99 5.00 12.00
30 Jabari Parker/99 2.50 6.00
31 DeMarcus Cousins/49 3.00 8.00
33 Kristaps Porzingis/49 5.00 12.00
34 Kyrie Irving/99 8.00 20.00
35 Otto Porter Jr./99 3.00 8.00
36 Blake Griffin/99 4.00 10.00
37 Kawhi Leonard/99 10.00 25.00
38 Giannis Antetokounmpo/49 6.00 15.00
39 Al Horford/99 4.00 10.00
40 Marc Gasol/99 4.00 10.00
41 Vince Carter/99 8.00 20.00
42 Stephen Curry/99 12.00 30.00
43 LaMarcus Aldridge/99 4.00 10.00
44 Damian Lillard/49 5.00 12.00
45 Kris Dunn/49 3.00 8.00
46 Dwight Howard/99 5.00 12.00
47 Bradley Beal/99 5.00 12.00
48 Karl-Anthony Towns/99 5.00 12.00
49 Klay Thompson/99 10.00 25.00
50 Jimmy Butler/49 6.00 15.00

2017-18 Panini National Treasures Game Gear Relics Prime

*PRIME/22-25: .75X TO 2X BASIC
PRINT RUNS B/WN 10-25 COPIES PER
NO PRICING ON QTY 14 OR LESS
12 LeBron James/25 100.00 250.00

2017-18 Panini National Treasures Game Gear Triple Relic Autographs

STATED PRINT RUN 25 SER.#'d SETS
EXCHANGE DEADLINE 11/2/2019
1 Evan Turner/25 6.00 15.00
2 Rudy Gay/25 8.00 20.00
3 Enes Kanter/25 8.00 20.00
4 DeMarre Carroll/25 6.00 15.00
5 Tyus Jones/25 6.00 15.00
6 Malcolm Brogdon/25 8.00 20.00
7 Patrick Beverley/25 6.00 15.00
8 Rudy Gobert/25 12.00 30.00
9 Seth Curry/25 10.00 25.00
10 James Johnson/25 6.00 15.00
11 Chris Paul/25 40.00 100.00
12 Damian Lillard/25 25.00 60.00
13 Kyrie Irving/25 40.00 100.00
14 Blake Griffin/25 15.00 40.00
15 Giannis Antetokounmpo/25 150.00 400.00
16 Andrew Wiggins/25 12.00 30.00
17 Karl-Anthony Towns/25 30.00 80.00
18 Marc Gasol/25 10.00 25.00
19 Ricky Rubio/25 12.00 30.00
20 Brandon Ingram/25 25.00 60.00

2017-18 Panini National Treasures Game Gear Triple Relics

PRINT RUNS B/WN 25-99 COPIES PER
1 Russell Westbrook/49 6.00 15.00
2 Karl-Anthony Towns/99 5.00 12.00
3 Stephen Curry/99 12.00 30.00
4 Marc Gasol/99 4.00 10.00
5 Chris Paul/99 5.00 12.00
6 Brandon Ingram/99 5.00 12.00
7 Kyrie Irving/49 8.00 20.00
8 Anthony Davis/99 6.00 15.00
9 Kevin Durant/99 15.00 40.00
10 Paul George/49 6.00 15.00
12 John Wall/99 5.00 12.00
13 Dwyane Wade/99 8.00 20.00
14 Ricky Rubio/99 3.00 8.00
15 Carmelo Anthony/99 6.00 15.00
16 Vince Carter/99 8.00 20.00
17 Damian Lillard/99 5.00 12.00
18 Blake Griffin/99 4.00 10.00
19 LeBron James/99 20.00 50.00
20 Pau Gasol/99 6.00 15.00

2017-18 Panini National Treasures Game Gear Triple Relics Prime

*PRIME/25: .75X TO 2X BASIC
PRINT RUNS B/WN 5-25 COPIES PER
NO PRICING ON QTY 10 OR LESS
19 LeBron James/25 100.00 250.00

2017-18 Panini National Treasures Hometown Heroes Autographs

PRINT RUNS B/WN 35-99 COPIES PER
EXCHANGE DEADLINE 11/2/2019
*BRONZE/25: .5X TO 1.2X BASE p/r 35-99
1 David Robinson/49 20.00 50.00
2 Richard Jefferson/99 5.00 12.00
3 Jason Kidd/49 15.00 40.00
4 Jason Williams/99 30.00 80.00
5 LaMarcus Aldridge/49 8.00 20.00
6 Artis Gilmore/99 6.00 15.00
7 Kobe Bryant/49 2,000.00 4,000.00
8 Chauncey Billups/99 8.00 20.00
9 Magic Johnson/35 30.00 80.00
10 Dave Cowens/99 6.00 15.00
11 Earl Monroe/49 10.00 25.00
12 Jeff Teague/99 4.00 10.00
13 Markelle Fultz/49 40.00 100.00
14 Marcus Camby/99 5.00 12.00
15 Lonzo Ball/49 60.00 150.00
16 Gordon Hayward/99 12.00 30.00
17 Bill Russell/35 1,000.00 2,000.00
18 Danny Manning/99 5.00 12.00
19 John Stockton/35 25.00 60.00
20 Joe Dumars/99 8.00 20.00
21 Tracy McGrady/49 20.00 50.00
22 Sam Jones/99 20.00 50.00
23 Vince Carter/49 20.00 50.00
24 Spencer Haywood/99 6.00 15.00
25 Rick Barry/99 8.00 20.00
26 Walt Frazier/99 10.00 25.00
27 Shaquille O'Neal/35 40.00 100.00
28 Latrell Sprewell/99 10.00 25.00
29 Kevin Durant/49 60.00 150.00
30 Lenny Wilkens/99 8.00 20.00
31 Kevin Love/49 12.00 30.00
32 Doug McDermott/99 4.00 10.00
33 Gary Payton/49 10.00 25.00
34 Mark Price/99 6.00 15.00
35 Jayson Tatum/99 5,000.00 1,000.00
36 George Gervin/99 8.00 20.00
37 Allen Iverson/35 60.00 150.00
38 Bill Walton/99 8.00 20.00
39 Oscar Robertson/35 30.00 80.00
40 Dennis Smith Jr./99 5.00 12.00
41 Kevin McHale/49 10.00 25.00
42 Cedric Ceballos/99 4.00 10.00
43 Anfernee Hardaway/49 25.00 60.00
44 Dan Issel/99 8.00 20.00
45 Harrison Barnes/99 5.00 12.00
46 Calvin Murphy/99 6.00 15.00
47 Larry Bird/35 40.00 100.00
48 Cliff Hagan/99 8.00 20.00
49 Jerry West/35 25.00 60.00
50 Rudy Gay/99 5.00 12.00

2017-18 Panini National Treasures International Treasures Autographs

PRINT RUNS B/WN 35-99 COPIES PER
EXCHANGE DEADLINE 11/2/2019
*BRONZE/25: .5X TO 1.2X BASE p/r 35-99
1 Dominique Wilkins/49 12.00 30.00
2 Zhou Qi/99 75.00 200.00
3 Felipe Lopez/99 4.00 10.00
4 Dikembe Mutombo/99 12.00 30.00
5 Kyrie Irving/35 40.00 100.00
6 Toni Kukoc/99 10.00 25.00
7 Karl-Anthony Towns/49 25.00 60.00
8 J.J. Barea/99 15.00 40.00
9 Ricky Rubio/49 8.00 20.00
10 Kiki Vandeweghe/99 5.00 12.00
11 Kristaps Porzingis/49 15.00 40.00
12 Bogdan Bogdanovic/99 20.00 50.00
13 Rick Fox/99 5.00 12.00
14 Lauri Markkanen/99 75.00 200.00
15 Dirk Nowitzki/35 60.00 150.00
16 Guerschon Yabusele/99 10.00 25.00
17 Andrew Wiggins/49 20.00 50.00
18 Arvydas Sabonis/99 8.00 20.00
19 Tony Parker/49 20.00 50.00
20 Shawn Bradley/99 5.00 12.00
21 Nikola Jokic/99 300.00 600.00
22 Milos Teodosic/99 10.00 25.00
23 Jonas Valanciunas/99 5.00 12.00
24 Frank Ntilikina/99 12.00 30.00
25 Giannis Antetokounmpo/49 150.00 400.00

26 Omri Casspi/99 4.00 10.00
27 Marc Gasol/49 8.00 20.00
28 Andrei Kirilenko/99 5.00 12.00
29 Nene/99 5.00 12.00
30 Ante Zizic/99 8.00 20.00

2017-18 Panini National Treasures Lasting Legacies Jersey Autographs

PRINT RUNS B/WN 25-49 COPIES PER
EXCHANGE DEADLINE 11/2/2019
*PRIME/25: .4X TO 1X BASE p/r 25
*PRIME/25: .6X TO 1.5X BASE p/r 49
1 Jamaal Wilkes/49 6.00 15.00
2 Giannis Antetokounmpo/25 60.00 150.00
3 Detlef Schrempf/49 10.00 25.00
4 Hakeem Olajuwon/25 20.00 50.00
5 Dominique Wilkins/49 10.00 25.00
6 Chris Paul/25 40.00 100.00
7 Dennis Rodman/49 20.00 50.00
8 Kyrie Irving/25 40.00 100.00
9 Sam Perkins/49 5.00 12.00
10 Magic Johnson/25 40.00 100.00
11 Tom Gugliotta/49 4.00 10.00
12 Andrew Wiggins/25 12.00 30.00
13 Jack Sikma/49 6.00 15.00
14 Marc Gasol/49 6.00 15.00
15 James Worthy/49 12.00 30.00
16 Damian Lillard/25 25.00 60.00
17 B.J. Armstrong/49 8.00 20.00
18 Larry Bird/25 40.00 100.00
19 Mitch Richmond/49 8.00 20.00
20 Blake Griffin/25 15.00 40.00
21 Doug Collins/49 6.00 15.00
22 Karl-Anthony Towns/25 30.00 80.00
23 Shawn Bradley/49 6.00 15.00
24 Vince Carter/49 20.00 50.00
25 Kristaps Porzingis/49 12.00 30.00

2017-18 Panini National Treasures Material Treasures

PRINT RUNS B/WN 49-99 COPIES PER
1 James Harden/99 8.00 20.00
2 Kevin Durant/99 15.00 40.00
3 Jamal Crawford/99 4.00 10.00
4 Anthony Davis/49 6.00 15.00
5 DeMarre Carroll/99 2.50 6.00
6 Jabari Parker/99 2.50 6.00
7 Thaddeus Young/99 2.50 6.00
8 Kristaps Porzingis/49 5.00 12.00
9 DeAndre' Bembry/99 2.50 6.00
10 DeMar DeRozan/99 5.00 12.00
11 Paul Millsap/49 3.00 8.00
13 Gary Harris/99 3.00 8.00
14 Derrick Rose/49 6.00 15.00
15 Evan Turner/99 2.50 6.00
16 Marc Gasol/99 4.00 10.00
17 Marcin Gortat/99 2.50 6.00
18 Marcus Smart/99 5.00 12.00
19 Juan Hernangomez/99 4.00 10.00
20 Kemba Walker/49 3.00 8.00
21 Danilo Gallinari/49 3.00 8.00
22 Carmelo Anthony/49 6.00 15.00
23 Serge Ibaka/99 3.00 8.00
24 Dwight Howard/99 5.00 12.00
25 Patrick Beverley/99 2.50 6.00
26 Brandon Ingram/99 5.00 12.00
27 Bobby Portis/99 2.50 6.00
28 Buddy Hield/99 4.00 10.00
29 Jarell Martin/99 2.50 6.00
30 Harrison Barnes/99 3.00 8.00
31 Nikola Vucevic/99 3.00 8.00
32 Dwyane Wade/49 8.00 20.00
33 Jeff Teague/99 2.50 6.00
34 Giannis Antetokounmpo/49 6.00 15.00
35 Seth Curry/99 4.00 10.00
36 Vince Carter/99 8.00 20.00
37 Steven Adams/99 3.00 8.00
38 Julius Randle/99 4.00 10.00
39 JJ Redick/99 4.00 10.00
40 CJ McCollum/49 4.00 10.00
41 Trevor Ariza/99 2.50 6.00
42 Damian Lillard/49 5.00 12.00
43 Nicolas Batum/99 2.50 6.00
44 Andrew Wiggins/99 5.00 12.00
45 Kyle Lowry/99 4.00 10.00
46 LaMarcus Aldridge/99 4.00 10.00
47 James Johnson/99 2.50 6.00
48 Bradley Beal/99 5.00 12.00
49 Pascal Siakam/99 8.00 20.00
50 Klay Thompson/99 10.00 25.00

2017-18 Panini National Treasures Material Treasures Prime

*PRIME/21-25: .75X TO 2X BASIC
PRINT RUNS B/WN 4-25 COPIES PER
NO PRICING ON QTY 19 OR LESS

2017-18 Panini National Treasures NBA Greats Signatures

PRINT RUNS B/WN 25-49 COPIES PER
EXCHANGE DEADLINE 11/2/2019
*BRONZE/25: .4X TO 1X BASE p/r 25
*BRONZE/25: .5X TO 1.2X BASE p/r 49
1 Robert Parish/49 8.00 20.00
2 Earl Monroe/25 12.00 30.00
3 Al Attles/49 6.00 15.00
4 Dennis Rodman/25 20.00 50.00
5 Willis Reed/49 40.00 100.00
6 Reggie Miller/25 50.00 120.00
7 Artis Gilmore/49 6.00 15.00
8 Jerry West/25 30.00 80.00
9 Walt Frazier/49 10.00 25.00
10 Alonzo Mourning/25 20.00 50.00
11 Bill Walton/49 8.00 20.00
12 Tracy McGrady/25 25.00 60.00
13 Jamaal Wilkes/49 6.00 15.00
14 Dominique Wilkins/49 12.00 30.00
15 Sam Jones/49 20.00 50.00
16 Magic Johnson/25 40.00 100.00
17 Bernard King/49 8.00 20.00
18 Yao Ming/25 40.00 100.00
19 George Gervin/49 8.00 20.00
20 Clyde Drexler/25 15.00 40.00

2017-18 Panini National Treasures Peerless Signatures

PRINT RUNS B/WN 35-99 COPIES PER
EXCHANGE DEADLINE 11/2/2019
*BRONZE/25: .5X TO 1.2X BASE p/r 35-99
1 Alex English/99 8.00 20.00
2 Oscar Robertson/35 30.00 80.00
3 Arvydas Sabonis/99 8.00 20.00
4 Dominique Wilkins/49 12.00 30.00
5 Reggie Miller/35 40.00 100.00
6 Nate Archibald/99 8.00 20.00
7 Ralph Sampson/99 6.00 15.00
8 Bill Russell/35 1,000.00 2,000.00
9 Gail Goodrich/99 6.00 15.00
10 Larry Bird/35 40.00 100.00
11 David Thompson/99 8.00 20.00
12 Earl Monroe/49 10.00 25.00
13 Kobe Bryant/49 2,000.00 4,000.00
14 Walt Frazier/99 10.00 25.00
15 Tracy McGrady/35 20.00 50.00
16 Cliff Hagan/99 8.00 20.00
17 Joe Dumars/99 8.00 20.00
18 Allen Iverson/35 40.00 100.00
19 Dikembe Mutombo/99 12.00 30.00
20 John Stockton/35 25.00 60.00

2017-18 Panini National Treasures Penmanship Autographs

PRINT RUNS B/WN 25-49 COPIES PER
EXCHANGE DEADLINE 11/2/2019
*BRONZE/25: .4X TO 1X BASE p/r 25
*BRONZE/25: .5X TO 1.2X BASE p/r 49
1 Manu Ginobili/25 25.00 60.00
2 Tom Chambers/49 6.00 15.00
3 Caron Butler/49 5.00 12.00
4 Chris Herren/49 5.00 12.00
5 Joe Johnson/49 5.00 12.00
6 Stacey Augmon/49 5.00 12.00
7 Zaza Pachulia/49 4.00 10.00
8 Kenny "Sky" Walker/49 4.00 10.00
9 Magic Johnson/25 40.00 100.00
10 Kristaps Porzingis/49 15.00 40.00
11 D'Angelo Russell/49 5.00 12.00
12 Damon Stoudamire/49 6.00 15.00
13 Rick Fox/49 5.00 12.00
14 Aaron McKie/49 4.00 10.00
15 JR Smith/49 12.00 30.00
16 Terrell Brandon/49 4.00 10.00
17 Freddie Lewis/49 4.00 10.00
18 Stephen Jackson/49 5.00 12.00
19 Jerry West/25 30.00 80.00
20 Eric Snow/49 4.00 10.00
21 Artis Gilmore/49 6.00 15.00
22 Tom Gugliotta/49 4.00 10.00
23 Byron Scott/49 6.00 15.00
24 Jason Williams/49 30.00 80.00
25 Malcolm Brogdon/49 5.00 12.00
26 Shawn Bradley/49 5.00 12.00
27 Jo Jo White/49 8.00 20.00
28 Sam Jones/49 20.00 50.00
29 Clyde Drexler/25 15.00 40.00
30 Sam Cassell/49 8.00 20.00
31 Bernard King/49 8.00 20.00
32 Rolando Blackman/49 8.00 20.00
33 Clint Capela/49 5.00 12.00
34 Bryant Reeves/49 5.00 12.00
35 B.J. Armstrong/49 6.00 15.00
36 Ron Mercer/49 4.00 10.00
37 Elvin Hayes/49 8.00 20.00
38 Purvis Short/49 4.00 10.00
39 Dennis Rodman/25 20.00 50.00
40 Willie Cauley-Stein/49 4.00 10.00

2017-18 Panini National Treasures Retro Materials

PRINT RUNS B/WN 12-99 COPIES PER
NO PRICING ON QTY 15 OR LESS
1 Shaquille O'Neal/49 8.00 20.00
2 Jermaine O'Neal/49 4.00 10.00
4 Juwan Howard/99 3.00 8.00
5 Kevin Duckworth/99 2.50 6.00
7 Michael Redd/49 3.00 8.00
8 Danny Granger/49 2.50 6.00
9 Ray Allen/99 6.00 15.00
10 Herb Williams/99 2.50 6.00
11 Shawn Marion/99 3.00 8.00
12 Joe Dumars/99 5.00 12.00
13 Tree Rollins/49 2.50 6.00
14 Karl Malone/49 8.00 20.00
15 Kevin McHale/25 12.00 30.00
16 Pete Maravich/25 30.00 80.00
17 Mike Bibby/49 4.00 10.00
18 Danny Manning/99 3.00 8.00
19 Reggie Lewis/49 5.00 12.00
20 Grant Hill/99 6.00 15.00
21 Maurice Lucas/49 4.00 10.00
22 Mitch Kupchak/99 3.00 8.00
24 Kelly Tripucka/49 3.00 8.00
26 Alonzo Mourning/49 6.00 15.00
27 Norm Nixon/99 2.50 6.00
28 Dennis Rodman/49 10.00 25.00
29 Reggie Miller/49 10.00 25.00
30 Jalen Rose/99 3.00 8.00
31 Stephen Jackson/99 3.00 8.00
32 John Stockton/25 8.00 20.00
34 Kenny Anderson/99 3.00 8.00
36 Christian Laettner/99 4.00 10.00
37 Patrick Ewing/99 6.00 15.00
38 Doc Rivers/95 4.00 10.00
40 Jason Kidd/49 6.00 15.00
43 World B. Free/49 3.00 8.00
44 Kenny Smith/49 3.00 8.00
45 Manute Bol/49 10.00 25.00
46 Clyde Drexler/49 6.00 15.00
47 Rafer Alston/99 2.50 6.00
48 Dominique Wilkins/49 6.00 15.00
49 Scottie Pippen/49 10.00 25.00
50 Jeff Hornacek/49 3.00 8.00

2017-18 Panini National Treasures Retro Materials Bronze

*BRONZE/20-25: .75X TO 2X BASIC
PRINT RUNS B/WN 4-25 COPIES PER
NO PRICING ON QTY 17 OR LESS
25 Kevin Willis/25 5.00 12.00
39 Rick Mahorn/25 10.00 25.00
41 Steve Mix/25 5.00 12.00

2017-18 Panini National Treasures Rookie Dual Materials

STATED PRINT RUN 99 SER.#'d SETS
1 Frank Ntilikina 3.00 8.00
2 Caleb Swanigan 2.50 6.00
3 Malik Monk 10.00 25.00
4 Bam Adebayo 15.00 40.00
5 Markelle Fultz 6.00 15.00
6 D.J. Wilson 2.50 6.00
7 Josh Jackson 3.00 8.00
8 John Collins 6.00 15.00
9 Jonathan Isaac 6.00 15.00
10 Terrance Ferguson 2.50 6.00
11 Dennis Smith Jr. 3.00 8.00
13 Luke Kennard 5.00 12.00
15 Lonzo Ball 10.00 25.00
16 TJ Leaf 2.50 6.00
18 Harry Giles 2.50 6.00
20 OG Anunoby 12.00 30.00
21 Zach Collins 4.00 10.00
22 Jordan Bell 2.50 6.00
23 Donovan Mitchell 25.00 60.00
24 Justin Patton 2.50 6.00
25 Jayson Tatum 20.00 50.00

2017-18 Panini National Treasures Rookie Dual Materials Bronze

*BRONZE: .75X TO 2X BASIC
STATED PRINT RUN 25 SER.#'d SETS
12 Kyle Kuzma 20.00 50.00
17 De'Aaron Fox 40.00 100.00

2017-18 Panini National Treasures Rookie Jumbo Materials

STATED PRINT RUN 50 SER.#'d SETS
1 Frank Ntilikina 3.00 8.00
2 Caleb Swanigan 2.50 6.00
3 Malik Monk 10.00 25.00
4 Bam Adebayo 15.00 40.00
5 Markelle Fultz 6.00 15.00
6 D.J. Wilson 2.50 6.00
7 Josh Jackson 3.00 8.00
8 John Collins 6.00 15.00
9 Jonathan Isaac 6.00 15.00
10 Terrance Ferguson 2.50 6.00
11 Dennis Smith Jr. 3.00 8.00
13 Luke Kennard 5.00 12.00
15 Lonzo Ball 10.00 25.00
16 TJ Leaf 2.50 6.00
18 Harry Giles 2.50 6.00
20 OG Anunoby 12.00 30.00
21 Zach Collins 4.00 10.00
22 Jordan Bell 2.50 6.00
23 Donovan Mitchell 25.00 60.00
24 Justin Patton 2.50 6.00
25 Jayson Tatum 20.00 50.00

2017-18 Panini National Treasures Rookie Jumbo Materials Bronze

*BRONZE: .75X TO 2X BASIC
STATED PRINT RUN 25 SER.#'d SETS
12 Kyle Kuzma 20.00 50.00
17 De'Aaron Fox 40.00 100.00

2017-18 Panini National Treasures Rookie Materials

STATED PRINT RUN 99 SER.#'d SETS
1 Frank Ntilikina 3.00 8.00
2 Caleb Swanigan 2.50 6.00
3 Malik Monk 10.00 25.00
4 Bam Adebayo 15.00 40.00
5 Markelle Fultz 6.00 15.00
6 D.J. Wilson 2.50 6.00
7 Josh Jackson 3.00 8.00
8 John Collins 6.00 15.00
9 Jonathan Isaac 6.00 15.00
10 Terrance Ferguson 2.50 6.00
11 Dennis Smith Jr. 3.00 8.00
13 Luke Kennard 5.00 12.00
15 Lonzo Ball 10.00 25.00
16 TJ Leaf 2.50 6.00
18 Harry Giles 2.50 6.00
20 OG Anunoby 12.00 30.00
21 Zach Collins 4.00 10.00
22 Jordan Bell 2.50 6.00
23 Donovan Mitchell 25.00 60.00
24 Justin Patton 2.50 6.00
25 Jayson Tatum 20.00 50.00

2017-18 Panini National Treasures Rookie Materials Bronze

*BRONZE: .75X TO 2X BASIC
STATED PRINT RUN 25 SER.#'d SETS
12 Kyle Kuzma 20.00 50.00
17 De'Aaron Fox 40.00 100.00

2017-18 Panini National Treasures Rookie Patch Autographs Horizontal

STATED PRINT RUN 49 SER.#'d SETS
EXCHANGE DEADLINE 11/2/2019
*BRNZ/25: .6X TO 1.5X BASIC
101 Markelle Fultz 40.00 100.00
102 Lonzo Ball 300.00 600.00
103 Jayson Tatum 5,000.00 10,000.00
104 Josh Jackson 20.00 50.00
105 De'Aaron Fox 800.00 1,500.00
106 Jonathan Isaac 40.00 100.00
107 Lauri Markkanen 300.00 600.00
108 Frank Ntilikina 20.00 50.00
109 Dennis Smith Jr. 30.00 80.00
110 Zach Collins 25.00 60.00
111 Malik Monk 60.00 150.00
112 Luke Kennard 30.00 80.00
113 Donovan Mitchell 1,000.00 2,000.00
114 Bam Adebayo 150.00 400.00
115 Justin Patton 15.00 40.00
116 Justin Patton 15.00 40.00
117 D.J. Wilson 15.00 40.00
118 TJ Leaf 15.00 40.00
119 John Collins 40.00 100.00
120 Harry Giles 30.00 80.00
121 Terrance Ferguson 15.00 40.00
122 Jarrett Allen 40.00 100.00
123 OG Anunoby 80.00 200.00
124 Tyler Lydon 15.00 40.00
125 Caleb Swanigan 15.00 40.00
126 Kyle Kuzma 125.00 300.00
127 Tony Bradley 15.00 40.00
128 Derrick White 60.00 150.00
129 Josh Hart 75.00 200.00
130 Frank Jackson 15.00 40.00
131 Davon Reed 15.00 40.00
132 Wes Iwundu 15.00 40.00
133 Frank Mason III 15.00 40.00
134 Ivan Rabb 15.00 40.00
135 Semi Ojeleye 20.00 50.00
136 Jordan Bell 15.00 40.00
137 Jawun Evans 15.00 40.00
138 Dwayne Bacon 15.00 40.00
139 Tyler Dorsey 15.00 40.00
140 Sterling Brown 15.00 40.00
141 Sindarius Thornwell 15.00 40.00
142 Ante Zizic 20.00 50.00
143 Ike Anigbogu 15.00 40.00
144 Milos Teodosic 20.00 50.00
146 Damyean Dotson 20.00 50.00
148 Wayne Selden 15.00 40.00
149 Zhou Qi 60.00 150.00

2017-18 Panini National Treasures Rookie Triple Materials

STATED PRINT RUN 99 SER.#'d SETS
1 Frank Ntilikina 3.00 8.00
2 Caleb Swanigan 2.50 6.00
3 Malik Monk 10.00 25.00
4 Bam Adebayo 15.00 40.00
5 Markelle Fultz 6.00 15.00
6 D.J. Wilson 2.50 6.00
7 Josh Jackson 3.00 8.00
8 John Collins 6.00 15.00
9 Jonathan Isaac 6.00 15.00
10 Terrance Ferguson 2.50 6.00
11 Dennis Smith Jr. 3.00 8.00
13 Luke Kennard 5.00 12.00
15 Lonzo Ball 10.00 25.00
16 TJ Leaf 2.50 6.00
18 Harry Giles 2.50 6.00
20 OG Anunoby 12.00 30.00
21 Zach Collins 4.00 10.00
22 Jordan Bell 2.50 6.00
23 Donovan Mitchell 25.00 60.00
24 Justin Patton 2.50 6.00
25 Jayson Tatum 20.00 50.00

2017-18 Panini National Treasures Rookie Triple Materials Bronze

*BRONZE: .75X TO 2X BASIC
STATED PRINT RUN 25 SER.#'d SETS
12 Kyle Kuzma 20.00 50.00
17 De'Aaron Fox 40.00 100.00
23 Donovan Mitchell 100.00 250.00

2017-18 Panini National Treasures Signatures

PRINT RUNS B/WN 35-99 COPIES PER
EXCHANGE DEADLINE 11/2/2019
*BRONZE/25: .5X TO 1.2X BASE p/r 35-99
1 Anthony Davis/35 40.00 100.00
2 Danny Green/99 5.00 12.00
3 Vince Carter/49 40.00 100.00
4 Toni Kukoc/99 10.00 25.00
5 Rodney Hood/99 4.00 10.00
6 Terrell Brandon/99 4.00 10.00
7 George Gervin/99 12.00 30.00
8 Latrell Sprewell/99 10.00 25.00
9 Kobe Bryant/49 2,000.00 4,000.00
10 Antawn Jamison/99 5.00 12.00
11 Oscar Robertson/35 50.00 120.00
12 Kurt Rambis/99 8.00 20.00
13 Gary Payton/49 20.00 50.00
14 Dan Majerle/99 5.00 12.00
15 Kenny Smith/99 5.00 12.00
16 Mark Price/99 6.00 15.00
17 Zach LaVine/99 20.00 50.00
18 Robert Horry/99 6.00 15.00
19 Shaquille O'Neal/35 100.00 250.00
20 Bryant Reeves/99 4.00 10.00
21 Karl-Anthony Towns/35 25.00 60.00
22 Rudy Gobert/99 8.00 20.00
23 LaMarcus Aldridge/99 8.00 20.00
24 John Starks/99 5.00 12.00
25 Gordon Hayward/99 12.00 30.00
26 Jason Williams/99 60.00 150.00
27 Khris Middleton/99 8.00 20.00
28 Dave Cowens/99 6.00 15.00
29 Allen Iverson/35 60.00 150.00
30 Robert Parish/99 8.00 20.00
31 Marc Gasol/35 8.00 20.00
32 Jose Calderon/99 4.00 10.00
33 Rick Barry/99 8.00 20.00
34 Cedric Maxwell/99 5.00 12.00
35 Nikola Jokic/99 300.00 600.00
36 Bill Laimbeer/99 6.00 15.00
37 Devin Booker/99 200.00 500.00
38 Danny Manning/99 5.00 12.00
39 Dwyane Wade/35 40.00 100.00
40 Victor Oladipo/99 15.00 40.00
41 Earl Monroe/35 10.00 25.00
42 Mark Aguirre/99 5.00 12.00
43 Harrison Barnes/99 5.00 12.00
44 Tim Hardaway/99 8.00 20.00
45 Aaron Gordon/99 6.00 15.00
46 Jamal Mashburn/99 5.00 12.00
47 Nate Archibald/99 8.00 20.00
48 Chauncey Billups/99 20.00 50.00
49 Damian Lillard/35 50.00 120.00
50 Tom Chambers/99 6.00 15.00
51 Tracy McGrady/49 40.00 100.00
52 Lance Stephenson/99 5.00 12.00
53 Richard Hamilton/99 6.00 15.00
54 Isaiah Rider/99 8.00 20.00
55 Walt Frazier/99 10.00 25.00
56 Junior Bridgeman/99 5.00 12.00
57 JJ Redick/99 6.00 15.00
58 Jermaine O'Neal/99 6.00 15.00
59 Dirk Nowitzki/35 60.00 150.00
60 Ben Wallace/99 10.00 25.00
61 Jason Kidd/49 15.00 40.00
62 Jerry Stackhouse/99 10.00 25.00
63 Andre Drummond/99 5.00 12.00
64 Spud Webb/99 5.00 12.00
65 Steve Kerr/99 10.00 25.00
66 Larry Hughes/99 5.00 12.00
67 Reggie Jackson/99 5.00 12.00
68 Bill Walton/99 12.00 30.00
69 Magic Johnson/35 50.00 120.00
70 Louie Dampier/99 6.00 15.00

2017-18 Panini National Treasures Treasured Signatures

PRINT RUNS B/WN 25-50 COPIES PER
EXCHANGE DEADLINE 11/2/2019
1 Rolando Blackman/50 5.00 12.00
2 Kobe Bryant/50 3,000.00 6,000.00
3 Robert Parish/50 8.00 20.00
4 Karl Malone/25 40.00 100.00
5 Latrell Sprewell/50 10.00 25.00
6 Oscar Robertson/25 40.00 100.00
8 Jason Kidd/35 15.00 40.00
9 Derek Harper/50 5.00 12.00
10 Richard Hamilton/50 6.00 15.00
11 Dave Cowens/50 6.00 15.00
12 Bill Russell/25 1,000.00 2,000.00
13 Al Attles/50 6.00 15.00
14 Larry Bird/25 50.00 120.00
15 Robert Horry/50 6.00 15.00
16 David Robinson/25 25.00 60.00
17 Ben Wallace/50 10.00 25.00
18 Gary Payton/35 10.00 25.00
19 Ivica Zubac/50 5.00 12.00
20 Shaun Livingston/50 30.00 80.00
21 Patrick Patterson/50 4.00 10.00
22 Shaquille O'Neal/25 50.00 120.00
23 Antawn Jamison/50 5.00 12.00
24 Magic Johnson/25 40.00 100.00
25 Danny Manning/50 5.00 12.00
26 Dion Waiters/50 10.00 25.00
27 Dikembe Mutombo/50 12.00 30.00
28 Grant Hill/35 15.00 40.00
29 Jason Williams/50 30.00 80.00
30 Walt Frazier/50 10.00 25.00
31 Bill Walton/50 8.00 20.00
32 Allen Iverson/25 50.00 120.00
33 Dan Issel/50 8.00 20.00
34 John Stockton/25 30.00 80.00
35 Chauncey Billups/50 8.00 20.00
36 Tracy McGrady/35 20.00 50.00
37 Glen Rice/50 5.00 12.00
38 Dominique Wilkins/35 12.00 30.00
39 Terrell Brandon/50 4.00 10.00
40 George Gervin/50 8.00 20.00
41 Ralph Sampson/50 6.00 15.00
42 Reggie Miller/25 50.00 120.00
43 Kurt Rambis/50 5.00 12.00
44 Kevin Durant/50 60.00 150.00
45 Jermaine O'Neal/50 6.00 15.00
46 Ray Allen/35 20.00 50.00
47 Michael Cooper/50 10.00 25.00
48 Kemba Walker/50 12.00 30.00
49 Darrell Arthur/50 8.00 20.00
50 Steve Kerr/50 10.00 25.00
51 Bob Dandridge/50 6.00 15.00

2017-18 Panini National Treasures Treasured Threads

PRINT RUNS B/WN 49-99 COPIES PER
TTH1 Blake Griffin/99 4.00 10.00
TTH2 Thon Maker/99 2.50 6.00
TTH3 Jimmy Butler/49 6.00 15.00
4 Allen Crabbe/99 2.50 6.00
TTH5 D'Angelo Russell/49 3.00 8.00
TTH6 Tim Hardaway Jr./99 3.00 8.00
TTH7 Tyreke Evans/99 2.50 6.00
TTH8 Rodney Hood/99 2.50 6.00
TTH9 LeBron James/99 20.00 50.00
TTH10 Rudy Gay/99 3.00 8.00
TTH11 Paul George/49 6.00 15.00
TTH12 Dion Waiters/99 2.50 6.00
TTH13 Ricky Rubio/99 3.00 8.00
TTH14 Jusuf Nurkic/99 3.00 8.00
TTH15 Joel Embiid/49 5.00 12.00
TTH16 Al Jefferson/99 3.00 8.00
TTH17 Al Horford/99 4.00 10.00
TTH18 Devin Booker/99 5.00 12.00
TTH19 Russell Westbrook/49 6.00 15.00
TTH20 Jrue Holiday/99 5.00 12.00
TTH21 Pau Gasol/99 6.00 15.00
TTH22 Willie Cauley-Stein/99 2.50 6.00
TTH23 Kevin Love/99 4.00 10.00
TTH24 Taurean Prince/99 2.50 6.00
TTH25 Kris Dunn/49 3.00 8.00
TTH26 Otto Porter Jr./99 3.00 8.00
TTH27 Dragan Bender/99 2.50 6.00
TTH28 Myles Turner/99 4.00 10.00
TTH29 Chris Paul/49 5.00 12.00
TTH30 DeAndre Jordan/49 3.00 8.00
TTH31 Karl-Anthony Towns/49 5.00 12.00
TTH32 Rudy Gobert/99 5.00 12.00
TTH33 DeMarcus Cousins/49 3.00 8.00
TTH34 Draymond Green/99 5.00 12.00
TTH35 Rajon Rondo/49 5.00 12.00
TTH36 Dennis Schroder/99 3.00 8.00
TTH37 Jamal Murray/99 6.00 15.00
TTH38 Hassan Whiteside/99 3.00 8.00
TTH39 Kyrie Irving/49 8.00 20.00
TTH40 Enes Kanter/99 3.00 8.00
TTH41 John Wall/99 5.00 12.00
TTH42 Dario Saric/49 3.00 8.00
TTH43 Stephen Curry/99 12.00 30.00
TTH44 Markieff Morris/49 2.50 6.00
TTH45 Mike Conley/99 3.00 8.00
TTH46 Willy Hernangomez/99 2.50 6.00
TTH47 Andre Drummond/99 3.00 8.00
TTH48 Ryan Anderson/99 2.50 6.00
TTH49 Dirk Nowitzki/49 10.00 25.00
TTH50 Malcolm Brogdon/99 3.00 8.00

2017-18 Panini National Treasures Treasured Threads Prime

*PRIME/21-25: .75X TO 2X BASIC
PRINT RUNS B/WN 10-25 COPIES PER
NO PRICING ON QTY 16 OR LESS

2017-18 Panini National Treasures Treasures of the Hall Autographs

PRINT RUNS B/WN 35-99 COPIES PER
EXCHANGE DEADLINE 11/2/2019
*BRONZE/25: .5X TO 1.2X BASE p/r 35-99
1 Magic Johnson/35 30.00 80.00
2 Dikembe Mutombo/99 12.00 30.00
3 David Robinson/49 20.00 50.00
4 Alex English/99 8.00 20.00
5 Rick Barry/49 8.00 20.00
6 David Thompson/99 8.00 20.00
7 Dave Cowens/99 6.00 15.00
8 Robert Parish/99 8.00 20.00
9 Shaquille O'Neal/35 60.00 150.00
10 Gail Goodrich/99 6.00 15.00
11 Kareem Abdul-Jabbar/35 40.00 100.00
12 Adrian Dantley/99 6.00 15.00
13 Gary Payton/49 10.00 25.00
14 Bob McAdoo/99 10.00 25.00
15 George Gervin/99 8.00 20.00
16 Tom Heinsohn/99 25.00 60.00
17 Bill Walton/99 8.00 20.00
18 Louie Dampier/99 6.00 15.00
19 Karl Malone/35 30.00 80.00
20 Sam Jones/99 20.00 50.00

2017-18 Panini National Treasures Tremendous Treasures Relics

PRINT RUNS B/WN 49-99 COPIES PER
1 Nikola Vucevic/99 3.00 8.00
2 D'Angelo Russell/49 3.00 8.00
3 Klay Thompson/99 10.00 25.00
4 Kevin Durant/99 15.00 40.00
5 Eric Gordon/49 3.00 8.00
6 Dirk Nowitzki/49 10.00 25.00
7 JJ Redick/49 4.00 10.00
8 Isaiah Thomas/99 3.00 8.00
9 Hassan Whiteside/99 3.00 8.00
10 Anthony Davis/49 6.00 15.00
11 Rudy Gay/49 3.00 8.00
12 Marcus Smart/59 4.00 10.00
13 Jamal Murray/49 6.00 15.00
14 Russell Westbrook/49 6.00 15.00
15 Eric Bledsoe/99 3.00 8.00
16 Dwight Howard/49 5.00 12.00
17 Nerlens Noel/99 2.50 6.00
18 LaMarcus Aldridge/99 4.00 10.00
19 Ryan Anderson/49 2.50 6.00
20 Paul George/49 6.00 15.00
21 Enes Kanter/49 3.00 8.00
22 Kris Dunn/49 3.00 8.00
23 James Harden/99 8.00 20.00
24 Stephen Curry/49 12.00 30.00
25 Danilo Gallinari/49 3.00 8.00
26 Giannis Antetokounmpo/49 6.00 15.00
27 Myles Turner/99 4.00 10.00
28 Otto Porter Jr./49 3.00 8.00
29 DeAndre Jordan/49 3.00 8.00
30 Karl-Anthony Towns/49 5.00 12.00
31 Thon Maker/49 2.50 6.00
32 Kawhi Leonard/99 5.00 12.00
33 Paul Millsap/49 3.00 8.00
34 Chris Paul/49 5.00 12.00
35 Devin Booker/49 5.00 12.00
36 Jabari Parker/49 2.50 6.00
37 Marquese Chriss/49 2.50 6.00
38 Mike Conley/99 3.00 8.00
39 Malcolm Brogdon/49 3.00 8.00
40 Marc Gasol/99 4.00 10.00
41 Rudy Gobert/99 5.00 12.00
42 DeMar DeRozan/49 5.00 12.00
43 Rodney Hood/99 2.50 6.00
44 Kyrie Irving/49 8.00 20.00
45 Goran Dragic/49 3.00 8.00
46 Kevin Love/49 4.00 10.00
47 Tobias Harris/49 3.00 8.00
48 Tyreke Evans/49 2.50 6.00
49 Willie Cauley-Stein/99 2.50 6.00
50 Brandon Ingram/49 5.00 12.00

2017-18 Panini National Treasures Tremendous Treasures Relics Bronze

*BRONZE/20-25: .75X TO 2X BASIC
PRINT RUNS B/WN 10-25 COPIES PER
NO PRICING ON QTY 19 OR LESS

2018-19 Panini National Treasures

STATED PRINT RUN 99 SER.#'d SETS
EXCHANGE DEADLINE 10/26/2020
1 D'Angelo Russell 1.50 4.00
2 Goran Dragic 1.25 3.00
3 Gary Harris 1.25 3.00
4 Dirk Nowitzki 4.00 10.00
5 Giannis Antetokounmpo 8.00 20.00
6 James Harden 3.00 8.00
7 Jordan Clarkson 1.50 4.00
8 Danilo Gallinari 1.25 3.00
9 Kawhi Leonard 4.00 10.00
10 T.J. Warren 1.25 3.00
11 Spencer Dinwiddie 1.25 3.00
12 Bradley Beal 2.00 5.00
13 Damian Lillard 4.00 10.00
14 DeAndre Jordan 1.25 3.00
15 Khris Middleton 1.50 4.00
16 Chris Paul 3.00 8.00
17 Rodney Hood 1.25 3.00
18 Lou Williams 1.25 3.00
19 Serge Ibaka 1.25 3.00
20 Trevor Ariza 1.00 2.50
21 Kristaps Porzingis 2.00 5.00
22 John Wall 2.00 5.00
23 CJ McCollum 1.50 4.00
24 Harrison Barnes 1.25 3.00
25 Eric Bledsoe 1.25 3.00
26 Clint Capela 1.25 3.00
27 Zach LaVine 2.50 6.00
28 LeBron James 25.00 60.00
29 Kyle Lowry 1.50 4.00
30 Kemba Walker 1.25 3.00
31 Tim Hardaway Jr. 1.00 2.50
32 Otto Porter Jr. 1.25 3.00
33 Jusuf Nurkic 1.25 3.00
34 Dennis Smith Jr. 1.00 2.50
35 Victor Oladipo 1.25 3.00
36 Julius Randle 1.50 4.00
37 Jabari Parker 1.00 2.50
38 Kyle Kuzma 1.50 4.00
39 Joel Embiid 4.00 10.00
40 Jeremy Lamb 1.00 2.50
41 Enes Kanter 1.25 3.00
42 John Collins 1.50 4.00
43 Karl-Anthony Towns 2.50 6.00
44 Anthony Davis 4.00 10.00
45 Bojan Bogdanovic 1.25 3.00
46 JJ Redick 1.50 4.00
47 Lauri Markkanen 2.50 6.00
48 Brandon Ingram 1.50 4.00
49 Jimmy Butler 2.50 6.00
50 Tony Parker 2.50 6.00
51 Paul George 2.50 6.00
52 Taurean Prince 1.00 2.50
53 Andrew Wiggins 2.00 5.00
54 Jrue Holiday 2.00 5.00
55 Myles Turner 1.50 4.00
56 Miles Bridges RC 12.00 30.00
57 Stephen Curry 20.00 50.00
58 Lonzo Ball 1.50 4.00
59 Ben Simmons 1.50 4.00
60 Nikola Vucevic 1.25 3.00
61 Russell Westbrook 2.50 6.00
62 Jeremy Lin 2.50 6.00
63 Derrick Rose 3.00 8.00
64 Nikola Mirotic 1.00 2.50
65 Blake Griffin 1.50 4.00
66 Paul Millsap 1.25 3.00
67 Kevin Durant 6.00 15.00
68 Buddy Hield 1.50 4.00
69 Kyrie Irving 4.00 10.00
70 Aaron Gordon 1.50 4.00
71 Steven Adams 1.25 3.00
72 Marc Gasol 1.50 4.00
73 Donovan Mitchell 5.00 12.00
74 DeMar DeRozan 2.00 5.00
75 Reggie Jackson 1.25 3.00
76 Dennis Schroder 1.25 3.00
77 Klay Thompson 4.00 10.00
78 De'Aaron Fox 3.00 8.00
79 Jayson Tatum 6.00 15.00
80 Evan Fournier 1.25 3.00
81 Jamal Murray 3.00 8.00
82 Mike Conley 1.25 3.00
83 Rudy Gobert 2.00 5.00
84 LaMarcus Aldridge 1.50 4.00
85 Andre Drummond 1.25 3.00
86 Montrezl Harrell 1.50 4.00
87 Draymond Green 2.00 5.00
88 Willie Cauley-Stein 1.00 2.50
89 Jaylen Brown 2.50 6.00
90 Josh Richardson 1.25 3.00
91 Nikola Jokic 8.00 20.00
92 Garrett Temple 1.00 2.50
93 Ricky Rubio 1.25 3.00
94 Rudy Gay 1.50 4.00
95 Kevin Love 1.25 3.00
96 Eric Gordon 1.25 3.00
97 Tobias Harris 1.25 3.00
98 Devin Booker 4.00 10.00
99 Caris LeVert 1.50 4.00
100 Dwyane Wade 3.00 8.00
101 Omari Spellman JSY AU RC 30.00 80.00
102 Grayson Allen JSY AU RC 60.00 150.00
103 Trae Young JSY AU RC 10,000.00 20,000.00
104 J.Jackson Jr. JSY AU RC 2,000.00 4,000.00
105 Josh Okogie JSY AU RC 50.00 125.00
106 Aaron Holiday JSY AU RC 50.00 125.00
107 Landry Shamet JSY AU RC 50.00 125.00
108 Collin Sexton JSY AU RC 150.00 400.00
109 M.Porter Jr. JSY AU RC 800.00 1,500.00
110 D.DiVincenzo JSY AU RC 80.00 200.00
112 Hamidou Diallo JSY AU RC 50.00 125.00
113 Troy Brown Jr. JSY AU RC 40.00 100.00
114 Jarred Vanderbilt JSY AU RC 60.00 150.00
115 Keita Bates-Diop JSY AU RC 40.00 100.00
116 ASimons JSY AU RC 600.00 1,200.00
117 LWalker IV JSY AU RC 60.00 150.00
118 Deandre Ayton JSY AU RC 600.00 1,200.00
119 Mikal Bridges JSY AU RC 1,000.00 2,000.00
120 Dzanan Musa JSY AU RC 30.00 80.00
121 SGilgeous-Alexander JSY AU RC 20,000.00 40,000.00
122 Jacob Evans III JSY AU RC 30.00 80.00
123 Wendell Carter Jr. JSY AU RC 80.00 200.00
124 Jerome Robinson JSY AU RC 30.00 80.00
125 Kevin Huerter JSY AU RC 300.00 600.00
126 Bruce Brown JSY AU RC 125.00 300.00
127 LDoncic JSY AU RC 50,000.00 100,000.00
128 De'Anthony Melton JSY AU RC 60.00 150.00
129 Mo Bamba JSY AU RC 50.00 125.00
130 Elie Okobo JSY AU RC 30.00 80.00
131 Svi Mykhailiuk JSY AU RC 40.00 100.00
132 Jalen Brunson JSY AU RC 1,000.00 2,000.00
133 Zhaire Smith JSY AU RC 30.00 80.00
134 Jevon Carter JSY AU RC 50.00 125.00
135 Kevin Knox JSY AU RC 40.00 100.00
136 Chandler Hutchison JSY AU RC EXCH 40.00 100.00
137 MBagley III JSY AU RC 50.00 125.00
138 DGraham JSY AU RC 50.00 125.00
139 Moritz Wagner JSY AU RC 60.00 150.00
140 Gary Trent Jr. JSY AU RC 150.00 400.00
141 Allonzo Trier JSY AU RC 30.00 80.00
143 Chimezie Metu JSY AU RC 40.00 100.00
145 Khyri Thomas JSY AU RC 30.00 80.00
146 KAntetokounmpo JSY AU RC 40.00 100.00
147 Melvin Frazier Jr. JSY AU RC 30.00 80.00
148 MRobinson JSY AU RC EXCH 80.00 200.00
149 Rodions Kurucs JSY AU RC 40.00 100.00
150 Yuta Watanabe JSY AU RC 125.00 300.00
151 Angel Delgado AU RC 5.00 12.00
152 Duncan Robinson AU RC 125.00 300.00
153 George King AU RC 5.00 12.00
154 J.P. Macura AU RC 6.00 15.00
155 Jared Terrell AU RC 5.00 12.00
156 Keenan Evans AU RC 5.00 12.00
157 Shake Milton AU RC EXCH 8.00 20.00
158 Ryan Broekhoff AU RC 8.00 20.00
159 Trevon Bluiett AU RC 5.00 12.00
160 Yante Maten AU RC 5.00 12.00

2018-19 Panini National Treasures Bronze

*BRNZ 1-100: .6X TO 1.5X BASIC
*BRNZ 151-160: .5X TO 1.2X BASIC
1-100 STATED PRINT RUN 39 SER.#'d SETS
151-160 STATED PRINT RUN 25 SER.#'d SETS
EXCHANGE DEADLINE 10/26/2020
159 Trevon Bluiett AU 12.00 30.00

2018-19 Panini National Treasures All-Decade Materials

PRINT RUNS B/WN 49-99 COPIES PER
*PRIME/25: .75X TO 2X BASIC
1 Magic Johnson/99 12.00 30.00
2 Grant Hill/99 5.00 12.00
3 Isiah Thomas/99 5.00 12.00
4 Jason Kidd/99 5.00 12.00
5 Chris Webber/99 4.00 10.00
6 Christian Laettner/99 3.00 8.00
7 Clyde Drexler/99 5.00 12.00
8 Danny Manning/99 2.50 6.00
9 Hakeem Olajuwon/99 4.00 10.00
10 Dominique Wilkins/99 5.00 12.00
11 Glen Rice/99 3.00 8.00
12 Joe Dumars/99 4.00 10.00
13 John Stockton/99 4.00 10.00
14 Karl Malone/99 6.00 15.00
15 Kenny Smith/99 2.50 6.00
16 Kevin Garnett/99 4.00 10.00
17 Kevin McHale/99 5.00 12.00
18 Dikembe Mutombo/99 5.00 12.00
19 Kobe Bryant/99 75.00 200.00
20 Steve Nash/99 6.00 15.00
21 Larry Bird/99 12.00 30.00
22 Mark Aguirre/99 2.50 6.00
23 Mark Jackson/99 2.50 6.00
24 Mitch Richmond/49 4.00 10.00
25 Anfernee Hardaway/99 8.00 20.00
26 Paul Pierce/99 5.00 12.00
27 Robert Parish/99 5.00 12.00
28 Reggie Miller/99 6.00 15.00
29 Tim Duncan/99 4.00 10.00
30 James Worthy/99 5.00 12.00

2018-19 Panini National Treasures All-Decade Materials Prime

*PRIME/25: .75X TO 2X BASIC
PRINT RUNS B/WN 10-25 COPIES PER
NO PRICING ON QTY 15 OR LESS
5 Chris Webber/25 25.00 60.00
11 Glen Rice/25 8.00 20.00
18 Dikembe Mutombo/25 12.00 30.00

2018-19 Panini National Treasures All-Decade Signatures

PRINT RUNS B/WN 25-99 COPIES PER
EXCHANGE DEADLINE 10/26/2020
*BRNZ/25: .5X TO 1.2X p/r 49-99
1 Bob McAdoo/99 8.00 20.00
2 Larry Bird/25 30.00 80.00
3 David Robinson/99 12.00 30.00
4 Nate Archibald/49 8.00 20.00
5 Chris Bosh/99 6.00 15.00
6 Rick Barry/99 8.00 20.00
7 Grant Hill/99 10.00 25.00
8 Jerry West/49 15.00 40.00
9 Adrian Dantley/99 5.00 12.00
10 Kareem Abdul-Jabbar/25 25.00 60.00
11 Clyde Drexler/49 12.00 30.00
12 Louie Dampier/49 6.00 15.00
13 Dennis Rodman/99 15.00 40.00
14 Ray Allen/99 15.00 40.00
15 George Gervin/49 10.00 25.00
16 Tracy McGrady/49 15.00 40.00
17 Hakeem Olajuwon/99 15.00 40.00
18 John Stockton/25 20.00 50.00
19 Allen Iverson/25 25.00 60.00
20 Karl Malone/25 25.00 60.00
21 Dan Issel/49 8.00 20.00
22 Magic Johnson/99 25.00 60.00
23 Dominique Wilkins/49 12.00 30.00
24 Reggie Miller/25 EXCH 40.00 100.00
25 George McGinnis/99 8.00 20.00
26 Walt Frazier/49 10.00 25.00
27 Jason Kidd/99 10.00 25.00
28 Julius Erving/25 25.00 60.00
29 Artis Gilmore/99 8.00 20.00

2018-19 Panini National Treasures All-Decade Signatures Bronze

*BRNZ/25: .5X TO 1.2X p/r 49-99
PRINT RUNS B/WN 15-25 COPIES PER
NO PRICING ON QTY 15 OR LESS
EXCHANGE DEADLINE 10/26/2020
1 Bob McAdoo/25 15.00 40.00
3 David Robinson/25 15.00 40.00
27 Jason Kidd/25 15.00 40.00

2018-19 Panini National Treasures All-NBA Materials

STATED PRINT RUN 99 SER.#'d SETS
*PRIME/25: .75X TO 2X BASIC
1 LeBron James 50.00 120.00
2 DeMar DeRozan 4.00 10.00
3 Paul George 5.00 12.00
4 Goran Dragic 2.50 6.00
5 Stephen Curry 25.00 60.00
6 Joel Embiid 8.00 20.00
7 Kawhi Leonard 8.00 20.00
8 Andre Drummond 2.50 6.00
9 Klay Thompson 8.00 20.00
10 Chris Paul 6.00 15.00
11 Marc Gasol 3.00 8.00
12 Draymond Green 4.00 10.00
13 Rudy Gobert 4.00 10.00
14 James Harden 6.00 15.00
15 Tony Parker 5.00 12.00
16 John Wall 4.00 10.00
17 Kevin Durant 12.00 30.00
18 Anthony Davis 8.00 20.00
19 Kyle Lowry 3.00 8.00
20 Damian Lillard 8.00 20.00
21 Pau Gasol 5.00 12.00
22 Giannis Antetokounmpo 15.00 40.00
23 Russell Westbrook 5.00 12.00
24 Jimmy Butler 5.00 12.00
25 Victor Oladipo 2.50 6.00
26 Karl-Anthony Towns 5.00 12.00
27 Kevin Love 2.50 6.00
28 Blake Griffin 3.00 8.00
29 LaMarcus Aldridge 3.00 8.00
30 DeAndre Jordan 2.50 6.00

2018-19 Panini National Treasures All-NBA Materials Prime

*PRIME/25: .75X TO 2X BASIC
PRINT RUNS B/WN 10-25 COPIES PER
NO PRICING ON QTY 15 OR LESS
3 Paul George/25 12.00 30.00
5 Stephen Curry/25 75.00 200.00
7 Kawhi Leonard/25 25.00 60.00
9 Klay Thompson/25 12.00 30.00
16 John Wall/25 12.00 30.00
17 Kevin Durant/25 20.00 50.00
20 Damian Lillard/25 15.00 40.00
25 Victor Oladipo/25 25.00 60.00
29 LaMarcus Aldridge/25 8.00 20.00

2018-19 Panini National Treasures Biography Materials

STATED PRINT RUN 99 SER.#'d SETS
*PRIME/24-25: .75X TO 2X BASIC
1 Donovan Mitchell 12.00 30.00
2 Mark Aguirre 3.00 8.00
3 Joel Embiid 15.00 40.00
4 Jason Kidd 6.00 15.00
5 Kevin McHale 6.00 15.00
6 Patrick Ewing 6.00 15.00
7 Kyrie Irving 10.00 25.00
8 Dee Brown 3.00 8.00
9 Russell Westbrook 6.00 15.00
10 Toni Kukoc 5.00 12.00
11 Damian Lillard 10.00 25.00
12 A.C. Green 4.00 10.00
13 DeMar DeRozan 12.00 30.00
14 James Worthy 6.00 15.00
15 Robert Parish 6.00 15.00
16 World B. Free 3.00 8.00
17 Kevin Durant 30.00 80.00
18 Tracy McGrady 6.00 15.00
19 Dwyane Wade 8.00 20.00
20 Isiah Thomas 6.00 15.00
21 Kawhi Leonard 10.00 25.00
22 Anfernee Hardaway 10.00 25.00
23 Anthony Davis 10.00 25.00
24 Kareem Abdul-Jabbar 15.00 40.00
25 Dominique Wilkins 6.00 15.00
26 Steve Nash 8.00 20.00
27 Stephen Curry 60.00 150.00
28 Glen Rice 4.00 10.00
29 Ben Simmons 4.00 10.00
30 Steve Kerr 5.00 12.00
31 James Harden 8.00 20.00
32 Stephon Marbury 5.00 12.00
33 Karl-Anthony Towns 6.00 15.00
34 John Stockton 8.00 20.00
35 LeBron James 60.00 150.00
36 Horace Grant 4.00 10.00
37 Giannis Antetokounmpo 30.00 80.00
38 Mark Jackson 3.00 8.00
39 Chris Paul 10.00 25.00
40 Vinnie Johnson 4.00 10.00

2018-19 Panini National Treasures Biography Materials Prime

*PRIME/24-25: .75X TO 2X BASIC
PRINT RUNS B/WN 10-25 COPIES PER
NO PRICING ON QTY 15 OR LESS
7 Kyrie Irving/25 20.00 50.00
12 A.C. Green/25 12.00 30.00
18 Tracy McGrady/25 8.00 20.00
27 Stephen Curry/25 125.00 300.00

2018-19 Panini National Treasures Century Materials

PRINT RUNS B/WN 63-99 COPIES PER
*PRIME/25: .75X TO 2X BASIC
1 Kevin Garnett/99 15.00 40.00
2 Dominique Wilkins/99 6.00 15.00
3 Shawn Marion/99 3.00 8.00
4 Steve Nash/82 12.00 30.00
5 Mark Aguirre/63 3.00 8.00
6 Anfernee Hardaway/99 10.00 25.00
7 James Worthy/99 6.00 15.00
8 Patrick Ewing/99 6.00 15.00
9 Tim Duncan/99 12.00 30.00
10 Robert Parish/99 6.00 15.00
11 Doc Rivers/99 4.00 10.00
12 Isiah Thomas/99 6.00 15.00
13 Steve Kerr/99 5.00 12.00
14 Joe Dumars/99 5.00 12.00
15 John Collins/99 4.00 10.00
16 Kyrie Irving/99 10.00 25.00
17 Rondae Hollis-Jefferson/99 2.50 6.00
18 Tony Parker/99 6.00 15.00
19 Zach LaVine/99 20.00 50.00
20 Kyle Korver/99 3.00 8.00
21 Dirk Nowitzki/99 20.00 50.00
22 Nikola Jokic/99 20.00 50.00
23 Blake Griffin/99 4.00 10.00
24 Stephen Curry/99 60.00 150.00
25 Andre Drummond/99 3.00 8.00
26 Clint Capela/99 3.00 8.00
27 Victor Oladipo/99 3.00 8.00
28 LeBron James/99 60.00 150.00
29 Hassan Whiteside/99 3.00 8.00
30 Khris Middleton/99 4.00 10.00
31 Derrick Rose/99 12.00 30.00
32 Jrue Holiday/99 5.00 12.00
33 Nikola Mirotic/99 2.50 6.00
34 Tim Hardaway Jr./99 2.50 6.00
35 Paul George/99 6.00 15.00
36 Jonathan Isaac/99 4.00 10.00
37 Ben Simmons/99 4.00 10.00
38 Trevor Ariza/99 2.50 6.00
39 CJ McCollum/99 4.00 10.00
40 DeMar DeRozan/99 10.00 25.00

2018-19 Panini National Treasures Century Materials Prime

*PRIME/25: .75X TO 2X BASIC
PRINT RUNS B/WN 3-25 COPIES PER
NO PRICING ON QTY 15 OR LESS
19 Zach LaVine/25 40.00 100.00
21 Dirk Nowitzki/25 40.00 100.00

2018-19 Panini National Treasures Clutch Factor Jersey Signatures

PRINT RUNS B/WN 25-99 COPIES PER
EXCHANGE DEADLINE 10/26/2020
*PRIME/25: .6X TO 1.5X p/r 49-99
1 Allen Iverson/25 125.00 300.00
2 Alex English/99 12.00 30.00
3 Alonzo Mourning/25 60.00 150.00
4 Artis Gilmore/99 15.00 40.00
5 Brent Barry/99 4.00 10.00
6 Charles Barkley/25 EXCH 150.00 400.00
7 Chauncey Billups/99 15.00 40.00
8 Chris Mullin/99 EXCH 20.00 50.00
9 Clifford Robinson/99 12.00 30.00
10 Corey Maggette/99 5.00 12.00
11 Dan Issel/99 8.00 20.00
12 Dikembe Mutombo/99 40.00 100.00
13 Erick Dampier/99 4.00 10.00
14 Gail Goodrich/99 6.00 15.00
15 Herb Williams/99 4.00 10.00
16 Jalen Rose/99 15.00 40.00
17 Jamal Mashburn/99 5.00 12.00
18 Jerry Lucas/99 40.00 100.00
19 Jim Jackson/99 5.00 12.00
20 Joe Dumars/99 15.00 40.00
21 Kareem Abdul-Jabbar/25 150.00 400.00
22 Karl Malone/25 125.00 300.00
23 Keith Van Horn/99 5.00 12.00
24 Kevin Johnson/99 15.00 40.00
25 Kevin McHale/99 EXCH 40.00 100.00
26 Kiki Vandeweghe/99 5.00 12.00
27 Larry Bird/25 200.00 500.00
28 Luc Longley/99 20.00 50.00
29 Magic Johnson/25 40.00 100.00
30 Marcus Camby/99 5.00 12.00
31 Mark Jackson/99 5.00 12.00
32 Mike Bibby/99 6.00 15.00
33 Nick Van Exel/99 EXCH 20.00 50.00
34 Paul Pierce/49 100.00 250.00
35 Rafer Alston/99 5.00 12.00
36 Ralph Sampson/99 5.00 12.00
37 Ray Allen/49 50.00 120.00
38 Rick Barry/68 20.00 50.00
39 Robert Horry/99 20.00 50.00
40 Stephen Jackson/99 5.00 12.00
41 Toni Kukoc/99 20.00 50.00
42 Tracy McGrady/49 60.00 150.00
43 Vlade Divac/99 6.00 15.00
44 Walter Davis/99 6.00 15.00
45 Trae Young/99 1,500.00 3,000.00
46 Deandre Ayton/99 100.00 250.00
47 Luka Doncic/99 3,000.00 6,000.00
48 Kevin Knox/99 EXCH 5.00 12.00
49 Collin Sexton/99 50.00 120.00
50 Marvin Bagley III/99 6.00 15.00

2018-19 Panini National Treasures Clutch Factor Jersey Signatures Prime

*PRIME/25: .75X TO 2X p/r 49-99
PRINT RUNS B/WN 2-25 COPIES PER
NO PRICING ON QTY 15 OR LESS
EXCHANGE DEADLINE 10/26/2020
33 Nick Van Exel/25 EXCH 40.00 100.00

2018-19 Panini National Treasures Colossal Material Autographs

PRINT RUNS B/WN 25-99 COPIES PER
EXCHANGE DEADLINE 10/26/2020
*PRIME/25: .6X TO 1.5X p/r 49-99
1 Isaiah Thomas/99 5.00 12.00
2 Dirk Nowitzki/25 125.00 300.00
3 Grant Hill/99 50.00 120.00
4 Lance Stephenson/99 15.00 40.00
5 Markelle Fultz/99 15.00 40.00
6 Trevor Ariza/99 4.00 10.00
7 Damian Lillard/25 75.00 200.00
8 Zach LaVine/99 60.00 150.00
9 De'Aaron Fox/99 50.00 120.00
10 LaMarcus Aldridge/99 EXCH 25.00 60.00
11 J.J. Barea/99 10.00 25.00
12 Kawhi Leonard/25 100.00 250.00
14 Donovan Mitchell/99 EXCH 75.00 200.00
16 John Collins/99 20.00 50.00
17 Jeremy Lin/99 75.00 200.00
18 Gordon Hayward/99 8.00 20.00
19 Kyrie Irving/25 60.00 150.00
20 Terry Rozier/99 EXCH 20.00 50.00
21 Jayson Tatum/49 125.00 300.00
22 Allen Crabbe/99 4.00 10.00
23 Harrison Barnes/99 5.00 12.00
24 Malik Monk/99 30.00 80.00
25 Nikola Jokic/99 150.00 400.00
26 Gary Harris/99 5.00 12.00
28 Kevin Durant/25 200.00 500.00
29 Gerald Green/99 5.00 12.00
30 Domantas Sabonis/99 30.00 80.00
31 Myles Turner/99 12.00 30.00
32 Lonzo Ball/99 50.00 120.00
33 Brandon Ingram/49 EXCH 40.00 100.00
34 Kyle Kuzma/99 25.00 60.00
35 Dwyane Wade/25 75.00 200.00
36 Giannis Antetokounmpo/25 300.00 600.00
37 Khris Middleton/99 20.00 50.00
38 Karl-Anthony Towns/25 40.00 100.00
40 Nikola Mirotic/99 4.00 10.00
41 Elfrid Payton/99 5.00 12.00
42 Tim Hardaway Jr./99 4.00 10.00
43 Al Horford/99 12.00 30.00
44 JJ Redick/99 10.00 25.00
45 Jose Calderon/99 4.00 10.00
46 Nene/99 4.00 10.00
47 Zaza Pachulia/99 4.00 10.00
48 Kristaps Porzingis/99 25.00 60.00
49 A.C. Green/99 6.00 15.00
50 Kobe Bryant/25 2,500.00 5,000.00

2018-19 Panini National Treasures Colossal Material Autographs Prime

*PRIME/25: .75X TO 2X p/r 49-99
PRINT RUNS B/WN 2-25 COPIES PER
NO PRICING ON QTY 15 OR LESS
EXCHANGE DEADLINE 10/26/2020

2018-19 Panini National Treasures Colossal Materials

STATED PRINT RUN 99 SER.#'d SETS
*PRIME/25: .75X TO 2X BASIC
1 Avery Bradley 2.50 6.00
2 Ben Simmons 4.00 10.00
3 Bradley Beal 5.00 12.00
4 Andrew Wiggins 5.00 12.00
5 Andre Drummond 3.00 8.00
6 Blake Griffin 4.00 10.00
7 Caris LeVert 4.00 10.00
8 D.J. Augustin 2.50 6.00
9 D'Angelo Russell 4.00 10.00
10 Chris Paul 8.00 20.00
11 Danny Green 3.00 8.00
12 Dante Exum 3.00 8.00
13 Dario Saric 3.00 8.00
14 LeBron James 60.00 150.00
15 James Harden 8.00 20.00
16 Dejounte Murray 5.00 12.00
17 DeMar DeRozan 5.00 12.00
18 Jeremy Lin 12.00 30.00
19 Dion Waiters 2.50 6.00
20 Josh Jackson 2.50 6.00
21 Enes Kanter 3.00 8.00
22 Evan Fournier 3.00 8.00
23 Evan Turner 2.50 6.00
24 George Hill 3.00 8.00
25 Gordon Hayward 4.00 10.00
26 Hassan Whiteside 3.00 8.00
27 J.J. Barea 4.00 10.00
28 Jamal Crawford 4.00 10.00
29 Karl-Anthony Towns 6.00 15.00
30 Lauri Markkanen 6.00 15.00

2018-19 Panini National Treasures Colossal Materials Prime

*PRIME/25: .75X TO 2X BASIC
PRINT RUNS B/WN 6-25 COPIES PER
NO PRICING ON QTY 15 OR LESS
12 Dante Exum/25 6.00 15.00

2018-19 Panini National Treasures Colossal Rookie Materials

STATED PRINT RUN 99 SER.#'d SETS
*PRIME: .75X TO 2 BASIC
1 Deandre Ayton 4.00 10.00
2 Marvin Bagley III 4.00 10.00
3 Luka Doncic 200.00 500.00
4 Jaren Jackson Jr. 20.00 50.00
5 Trae Young 100.00 250.00
6 Mo Bamba 4.00 10.00
7 Wendell Carter Jr. 6.00 15.00
8 Collin Sexton 8.00 20.00
9 Kevin Knox 3.00 8.00
10 Mikal Bridges 12.00 30.00
11 Shai Gilgeous-Alexander 25.00 60.00
12 Jerome Robinson 2.50 6.00
13 Michael Porter Jr. 10.00 25.00
14 Troy Brown Jr. 3.00 8.00
15 Zhaire Smith 2.50 6.00
16 Donte DiVincenzo 6.00 15.00
17 Lonnie Walker IV 5.00 12.00
18 Kevin Huerter 5.00 12.00
19 Josh Okogie 4.00 10.00
20 Grayson Allen 5.00 12.00
21 Chandler Hutchison 3.00 8.00
22 Aaron Holiday 4.00 10.00
23 Anfernee Simons 30.00 80.00
24 Moritz Wagner 5.00 12.00
25 Landry Shamet 4.00 10.00
26 Robert Williams III 4.00 10.00
27 Jacob Evans III 2.00 5.00
28 Dzanan Musa 2.00 5.00
29 Omari Spellman 2.00 5.00
30 Elie Okobo 2.00 5.00
31 Jevon Carter 3.00 8.00
32 Jalen Brunson 15.00 40.00
33 Devonte' Graham 3.00 8.00
34 Gary Trent Jr. 3.00 8.00
35 Bruce Brown 4.00 10.00
36 Allonzo Trier 2.00 5.00
37 Keita Bates-Diop 2.50 6.00
38 Svi Mykhailiuk 2.50 6.00
39 Hamidou Diallo 3.00 8.00
40 Kostas Antetokounmpo 2.50 6.00

2018-19 Panini National Treasures Colossal Rookie Materials Prime

*PRIME: .75X TO 2 BASIC
STATED PRINT RUN 25 SER.#'d SETS
1 Deandre Ayton 15.00 40.00
2 Marvin Bagley III 30.00 80.00

2018-19 Panini National Treasures Game Gear Jersey Autographs

PRINT RUNS B/WN 25-99 COPIES PER
EXCHANGE DEADLINE 10/26/2020
*PRIME/25: .6X TO 1.5X p/r 49-99
1 JR Smith/49 12.00 30.00
2 Tony Parker/49 15.00 40.00
3 Myles Turner/49 6.00 15.00
4 Jayson Tatum/99 200.00 500.00
5 Eric Bledsoe/99 5.00 12.00
6 Karl-Anthony Towns/25 30.00 80.00
7 Zach LaVine/49 60.00 150.00
8 Buddy Hield/49 12.00 30.00
10 Kristaps Porzingis/49 12.00 30.00
11 Chris Bosh/99 20.00 50.00
12 Kevin Love/49 8.00 20.00
13 Shaun Livingston/99 5.00 12.00
14 Donovan Mitchell/49 60.00 150.00
15 Al Horford/49 6.00 15.00
16 Dirk Nowitzki/25 125.00 300.00
17 Pascal Siakam/99 20.00 50.00
18 Gordon Hayward/49 8.00 20.00
19 John Collins/49 8.00 20.00
20 Jeremy Lin/49 40.00 100.00
21 Nerlens Noel/99 4.00 10.00
23 Terry Rozier/99 5.00 12.00
24 Joel Embiid/49 125.00 300.00
25 Nikola Mirotic/99 4.00 10.00
26 Damian Lillard/25 60.00 150.00
27 Mike Conley/49 5.00 12.00
28 Khris Middleton/99 12.00 30.00
29 Lauri Markkanen/99 10.00 25.00
30 LaMarcus Aldridge/49 12.00 30.00
31 Elfrid Payton/49 5.00 12.00
32 Tim Hardaway Jr./49 4.00 10.00
33 Reggie Jackson/99 5.00 12.00
34 Andrew Wiggins/99 30.00 80.00
35 Goran Dragic/49 5.00 12.00
36 Kyrie Irving/25 75.00 200.00
38 De'Aaron Fox/49 30.00 80.00
39 Enes Kanter/49 5.00 12.00
40 Lonzo Ball/49 30.00 80.00
41 Trevor Ariza/49 4.00 10.00
43 Gary Harris/99 5.00 12.00
44 Giannis Antetokounmpo/25 200.00 500.00
45 Kyle Kuzma/99 20.00 50.00
46 Dwyane Wade/25 40.00 100.00
47 Harrison Barnes/49 5.00 12.00
48 Nikola Jokic/49 125.00 300.00
50 Isaiah Thomas/49 5.00 12.00

2018-19 Panini National Treasures Game Gear Relics

PRINT RUNS B/WN 50-99 COPIES PER
*PRIME/25: .75X TO 2X BASIC
1 Tracy McGrady/99 6.00 15.00
2 Tim Duncan/99 10.00 25.00
3 Taj Gibson/99 2.50 6.00
4 Rudy Gobert/99 5.00 12.00
5 Rondae Hollis-Jefferson/99 2.50 6.00
6 Robert Parish/99 6.00 15.00
7 Reggie Jackson/99 3.00 8.00
8 Paul Pierce/99 6.00 15.00
9 Pau Gasol/99 6.00 15.00
10 Pascal Siakam/99 6.00 15.00
11 Otto Porter Jr./99 3.00 8.00
12 OG Anunoby/99 4.00 10.00
13 Nikola Vucevic/99 3.00 8.00
14 Nicolas Batum/99 2.50 6.00
15 LaMarcus Aldridge/99 4.00 10.00
16 DeMar DeRozan/99 5.00 12.00
17 Juan Hernangomez/99 4.00 10.00
18 Julius Randle/99 4.00 10.00
19 Jusuf Nurkic/99 3.00 8.00
20 Karl-Anthony Towns/99 6.00 15.00
21 Kawhi Leonard/99 10.00 25.00
22 Kenny Smith/70 3.00 8.00
23 Kevin McHale/99 6.00 15.00
24 Donovan Mitchell/99 12.00 30.00
25 Kurt Rambis/99 3.00 8.00
26 Kyrie Irving/99 10.00 25.00
27 Larry Bird/99 15.00 40.00
28 LeBron James/99 60.00 150.00
29 Lou Williams/99 3.00 8.00
30 Bradley Beal/99 5.00 12.00
31 Mark Jackson/99 3.00 8.00
32 Aaron Gordon/99 4.00 10.00
33 Mark Price/60 4.00 10.00
34 Markieff Morris/99 2.50 6.00
35 Matthew Dellavedova/99 3.00 8.00
36 Mitch Richmond/50 5.00 12.00
37 Nemanja Bjelica/99 2.50 6.00
38 John Wall/99 5.00 12.00
39 John Stockton/99 8.00 20.00
40 Jimmy Butler/99 6.00 15.00

2018-19 Panini National Treasures Hometown Heroes Autographs

PRINT RUNS B/WN 25-99 COPIES PER
EXCHANGE DEADLINE 10/26/2020
*BRNZ/25: .75X TO 2X p/r 49-99
1 Dave Cowens/99 8.00 20.00
2 Charles Barkley/25 EXCH 125.00 300.00
3 Ralph Sampson/99 5.00 12.00
4 Oscar Robertson/25 50.00 120.00
6 Jerry Lucas/99 8.00 20.00
7 Kevin Willis/99 5.00 12.00
8 Artis Gilmore/99 8.00 20.00
9 Damon Stoudamire/99 6.00 15.00
10 Nate Archibald/99 8.00 20.00
11 Joe Dumars/99 8.00 20.00
12 Allen Iverson/25 75.00 200.00
13 Avery Johnson/99 5.00 12.00
14 Isaiah Thomas/49 5.00 12.00
15 Juwan Howard/99 5.00 12.00
16 Walt Frazier/99 15.00 40.00
17 Mark Aguirre/99 5.00 12.00
18 Elvin Hayes/99 8.00 20.00
19 Tom Gugliotta/99 4.00 10.00
20 Kyle Kuzma/99 EXCH 12.00 30.00
21 Myles Turner/99 6.00 15.00
22 Larry Bird/25 125.00 300.00
23 Terry Rozier/99 EXCH 5.00 12.00
25 Bill Cartwright/99 5.00 12.00

2018-19 Panini National Treasures Hometown Heroes Autographs Bronze

*BRNZ/25: .5X TO 1.2X p/r 49-99
PRINT RUNS B/WN 15-25 COPIES PER
EXCHANGE DEADLINE 10/26/2020

2018-19 Panini National Treasures International Treasures Autographs

PRINT RUNS B/WN 25-99 COPIES PER
EXCHANGE DEADLINE 10/26/2020
*BRNZ/25: .6X TO 1.5X p/r 49-99
1 Dirk Nowitzki/25 125.00 300.00
2 Toni Kukoc/99 12.00 30.00
3 Kristaps Porzingis/99 30.00 80.00
4 Jose Calderon/99 4.00 10.00
5 Nikola Jokic/99 200.00 500.00
6 Vlade Divac/99 6.00 15.00
8 Dzanan Musa/99 4.00 10.00
9 Zaza Pachulia/99 4.00 10.00
10 Rodions Kurucs/99 5.00 12.00
11 Giannis Antetokounmpo/49 EXCH 400.00 800.00
12 Ivica Zubac/99 5.00 12.00
13 Luka Doncic/99 5,000.00 10,000.00
15 Nikola Mirotic/99 EXCH 4.00 10.00
16 Zydrunas Ilgauskas/99 5.00 12.00
17 Milos Teodosic/99 4.00 10.00
18 Elie Okobo/99 4.00 10.00
19 Dino Radja/99 4.00 10.00
20 Isaac Bonga/99 5.00 12.00
21 Tony Parker/49 25.00 60.00
22 Arvydas Sabonis/99 15.00 40.00
24 Sarunas Marciulionis/99 6.00 15.00
25 Peja Stojakovic/99 12.00 30.00

2018-19 Panini National Treasures International Treasures Autographs Bronze

*BRNZ/25: .6X TO 1.5X p/r 49-99
PRINT RUNS B/WN 15-25 COPIES PER
EXCHANGE DEADLINE 10/26/2020

2018-19 Panini National Treasures Lasting Legacies Jersey Autographs

PRINT RUNS B/WN 25-99 COPIES PER
EXCHANGE DEADLINE 10/26/2020
*PRIME/25: .6X TO 1.5X p/r 49-99
1 Louie Dampier/49 6.00 15.00
2 Shaquille O'Neal /25 EXCH 125.00 300.00
3 Glen Rice/49 6.00 15.00
4 John Stockton/25 40.00 100.00
5 Mark Aguirre/49 5.00 12.00
6 Paul Pierce/49 25.00 60.00
7 Darrell Griffith/99 5.00 12.00
8 Dominique Wilkins/49 15.00 40.00
9 Mark Price/49 12.00 30.00
10 Kenny Smith/49 5.00 12.00
11 Mark Jackson/49 5.00 12.00
12 Karl Malone/25 60.00 150.00
13 Horace Grant/49 12.00 30.00
14 Kareem Abdul-Jabbar/25 125.00 300.00
15 Mitch Richmond/49 20.00 50.00
16 Tracy McGrady/49 60.00 150.00
17 Dee Brown/49 5.00 12.00
18 James Worthy/49 12.00 30.00
19 Paul Silas/49 5.00 12.00
20 Peja Stojakovic/49 5.00 12.00
21 Rick Fox/49 5.00 12.00
22 Reggie Miller/25 EXCH 100.00 250.00
23 A.C. Green/49 6.00 15.00
24 Magic Johnson/25 125.00 300.00
25 Stephen Jackson/49 5.00 12.00
27 Tony Parker/49 15.00 40.00
28 Christian Laettner/49 12.00 30.00
29 Rafer Alston/99 5.00 12.00
30 Danny Manning/49 5.00 12.00
31 Robert Parish/49 12.00 30.00
32 Larry Bird/25 125.00 300.00
33 Jamaal Wilkes/49 6.00 15.00
34 Grant Hill/99 20.00 50.00
35 Toni Kukoc/49 10.00 25.00
36 Dennis Rodman/99 40.00 100.00
37 Kelly Tripucka/49 4.00 10.00
38 Steve Kerr/49 12.00 30.00
39 Rashard Lewis/99 5.00 12.00
40 Doc Rivers/49 6.00 15.00
41 World B. Free/99 5.00 12.00
42 Dirk Nowitzki/25 125.00 300.00
43 Kurt Rambis/99 5.00 12.00
44 Jason Kidd/49 25.00 60.00
45 Rik Smits/49 EXCH 5.00 12.00
46 Vince Carter/49 40.00 100.00
47 Larry Nance/49 5.00 12.00
48 Artis Gilmore/49 12.00 30.00
49 Walter Davis/49 6.00 15.00
50 Joe Dumars/49 15.00 40.00

2018-19 Panini National Treasures Lasting Legacies Jersey Autographs Prime

*PRIME/25: .6X TO 1.5X p/r 49-99
PRINT RUNS B/WN 10-25 COPIES PER
NO PRICING ON QTY 15 OR LESS
EXCHANGE DEADLINE 10/26/2020
15 Mitch Richmond/25 30.00 80.00

2018-19 Panini National Treasures Material Treasures

PRINT RUNS B/WN 25-99 COPIES PER
*PRIME/25: .75X TO 2X BASIC p/r 99
1 A.C. Green/99 4.00 10.00
2 Aaron Gordon/99 4.00 10.00
3 Al-Farouq Aminu/99 2.50 6.00
4 Allen Crabbe/99 2.50 6.00
5 Andre Roberson/99 2.50 6.00
6 Andrew Wiggins/99 5.00 12.00
7 Anfernee Hardaway/99 10.00 25.00
8 Antawn Jamison/99 3.00 8.00
9 Anthony Davis/99 10.00 25.00
10 Alec Burks/99 2.50 6.00
11 Jaylen Brown/99 6.00 15.00
12 Bobby Portis/99 4.00 10.00
13 DeAndre Jordan/99 3.00 8.00
14 CJ McCollum/99 4.00 10.00
15 Damyean Dotson/99 2.50 6.00
16 Danny Manning/25 6.00 15.00
17 Dee Brown/99 3.00 8.00
18 Derrick Rose/99 8.00 20.00
19 Dominique Wilkins/99 6.00 15.00
20 Jimmy Butler/99 6.00 15.00
21 Julius Randle/99 4.00 10.00
22 Jeff Teague/99 2.50 6.00
23 Joel Embiid/99 10.00 25.00
24 Terrence Ross/99 3.00 8.00
25 Mark Aguirre/99 3.00 8.00
26 Reggie Miller/99 8.00 20.00
27 Vince Carter/99 8.00 20.00
28 Kyle Lowry/99 4.00 10.00
29 Glen Rice/99 4.00 10.00
30 DeMarre Carroll/99 2.50 6.00

2018-19 Panini National Treasures NBA Greats Signatures

PRINT RUNS B/WN 25-99 COPIES PER
EXCHANGE DEADLINE 10/26/2020
*BRNZ/25: .5X TO 1.2X p/r 49-99
1 Nate Archibald/49 8.00 20.00
2 Oscar Robertson/25 25.00 60.00
3 Latrell Sprewell/49 8.00 20.00
4 Grant Hill/99 25.00 60.00
5 Dave Cowens/99 8.00 20.00
6 Tracy McGrady/99 40.00 100.00
7 Jerry Lucas/49 8.00 20.00
8 Karl Malone/49 12.00 30.00
9 Chris Mullin/49 8.00 20.00
10 John Stockton/25 20.00 50.00
11 Peja Stojakovic/49 5.00 12.00
12 Jerry West/49 30.00 80.00
13 Joe Dumars/49 8.00 20.00
14 Jason Kidd/99 15.00 40.00
15 Bill Walton/49 40.00 100.00
16 Dennis Rodman/99 40.00 100.00
17 Walt Frazier/49 12.00 30.00
18 Reggie Miller/25 EXCH 75.00 200.00
19 George Gervin/49 12.00 30.00
20 Julius Erving/25 40.00 100.00
21 Gail Goodrich/49 6.00 15.00
22 Alonzo Mourning/25 20.00 50.00
23 Ralph Sampson/99 5.00 12.00
24 Ray Allen/49 50.00 120.00
25 Robert Parish/99 10.00 25.00
26 Rick Barry/99 8.00 20.00
27 Bernard King/49 6.00 15.00
28 Larry Bird/25 75.00 200.00
29 Elvin Hayes/99 8.00 20.00
30 Kareem Abdul-Jabbar/25 75.00 200.00

2018-19 Panini National Treasures NBA Greats Signatures Bronze

*BRNZ/25: .5X TO 1.2X p/r 49-99
PRINT RUNS B/WN 15-25 COPIES PER
NO PRICING ON QTY 15 OR LESS
EXCHANGE DEADLINE 10/26/2020

2018-19 Panini National Treasures Peerless Signatures

PRINT RUNS B/WN 25-99 COPIES PER
EXCHANGE DEADLINE 10/26/2020
*BRNZ/25: .5X TO 1.2X p/r 49-99
1 Jim Jackson/99 5.00 12.00
2 Bernard King/99 6.00 15.00
3 Rony Seikaly/99 4.00 10.00
4 Doc Rivers/99 6.00 15.00
5 Terry Rozier/99 EXCH 5.00 12.00
6 Kobe Bryant/25 2,000.00 4,000.00
7 Toni Kukoc/99 8.00 20.00
8 Anthony Davis/25 50.00 120.00
9 Bryon Russell/99 4.00 10.00
10 Jeremy Lin/49 60.00 150.00
11 Junior Bridgeman/99 4.00 10.00
12 Nick Van Exel/99 6.00 15.00
13 Sarunas Marciulionis/99 6.00 15.00
14 Gail Goodrich/99 6.00 15.00
15 Trevor Ariza/99 4.00 10.00
16 Kevin Durant/25 100.00 250.00
17 Charlie Scott/99 6.00 15.00
19 Charlie Ward/99 5.00 12.00
20 De'Aaron Fox/99 40.00 100.00
21 Larry Nance/99 5.00 12.00
22 Elvin Hayes/99 EXCH 8.00 20.00
23 Wally Szczerbiak/99 5.00 12.00
24 Jalen Rose/99 5.00 12.00
25 John Collins/99 6.00 15.00
26 Reggie Miller/25 EXCH 75.00 200.00
27 Dan Issel/99 8.00 20.00
28 Ray Allen/99 40.00 100.00
29 Darrell Griffith/99 5.00 12.00
30 Mike Conley/99 5.00 12.00
31 Mark Eaton/99 6.00 15.00
32 Cliff Hagan/99 6.00 15.00
33 Robert Barry/99 4.00 10.00
34 Joe Dumars/99 8.00 20.00
35 Bill Cartwright/99 5.00 12.00
36 Larry Bird/25 75.00 200.00
37 Antonio McDyess/99 5.00 12.00
38 Isaiah Thomas/49 5.00 12.00
39 Derek Harper/99 5.00 12.00
40 Brook Lopez/99 5.00 12.00
41 Rafer Alston/99 5.00 12.00
43 Bryant Reeves/99 4.00 10.00
44 Myles Turner/99 6.00 15.00
45 Kevin Willis/99 5.00 12.00
46 Kyrie Irving/25 50.00 120.00
47 Arvydas Sabonis/99 6.00 15.00
48 Lonzo Ball/49 30.00 80.00
49 Jerome Williams/99 4.00 10.00
50 Artis Gilmore/99 8.00 20.00

2018-19 Panini National Treasures Peerless Signatures Bronze

*BRNZ/25: .5X TO 1.2X p/r 49-99
PRINT RUNS B/WN 15-25 COPIES PER
NO PRICING ON QTY 15 OR LESS
EXCHANGE DEADLINE 10/26/2020
20 De'Aaron Fox/25 50.00 120.00
28 Ray Allen/25 50.00 120.00

2018-19 Panini National Treasures Penmanship Autographs

PRINT RUNS B/WN 25-99 COPIES PER
EXCHANGE DEADLINE 10/26/2020
*BRNZ/25: .5X TO 1.2X p/r 49-99
1 Jayson Tatum/99 100.00 250.00
2 Scott Skiles/99 5.00 12.00
3 Nikola Jokic/99 150.00 400.00
4 Latrell Sprewell/49 8.00 20.00
5 Karl Malone/49 50.00 120.00
6 Kurt Rambis/99 5.00 12.00
7 Damian Lillard/99 40.00 100.00
8 Sarunas Marciulionis/99 6.00 15.00
9 Kareem Abdul-Jabbar/25 75.00 200.00
10 Jerome Williams/99 4.00 10.00
11 Grant Hill/99 25.00 60.00
12 Sean Elliott/99 5.00 12.00
13 Reggie Jackson/99 5.00 12.00
14 Joe Dumars/49 8.00 20.00
15 Reggie Miller/25 EXCH 75.00 200.00
16 Xavier McDaniel/99 5.00 12.00
17 Larry Bird/25 75.00 200.00
18 Mychal Thompson/99 4.00 10.00
19 Jerry West/49 30.00 80.00
20 Rudy Tomjanovich/99 5.00 12.00
21 Kevin Love/99 5.00 12.00
22 Mark Eaton/49 6.00 15.00
23 Serge Ibaka/99 5.00 12.00
24 George McGinnis/99 8.00 20.00
25 Dwyane Wade/99 30.00 80.00
26 Nick Anderson/49 5.00 12.00
27 John Stockton/25 40.00 100.00
28 Clifford Robinson/99 6.00 15.00
29 Andrew Wiggins/99 12.00 30.00
30 Wally Szczerbiak/49 5.00 12.00
31 Dennis Rodman/99 40.00 100.00
32 Kevin Johnson/99 12.00 30.00

33 Gail Goodrich/99 6.00 15.00
34 Glen Rice/99 6.00 15.00
35 Kyrie Irving/49 40.00 100.00
36 Tree Rollins/99 4.00 10.00
37 Julius Erving/25 40.00 100.00
38 Muggsy Bogues/99 20.00 12.00
39 DeMarcus Cousins/99 12.00 30.00
40 Antonio McDyess/99 5.00 12.00

2018-19 Panini National Treasures Penmanship Autographs Bronze

*BRNZ/25: .5X TO 1.2X p/r 49-99
PRINT RUNS B/WN 15-25 COPIES PER
NO PRICING ON QTY 15 OR LESS
EXCHANGE DEADLINE 10/26/2020
11 Grant Hill/25 30.00 80.00

2018-19 Panini National Treasures Retro Materials

PRINT RUNS B/WN 49-99 COPIES PER
*PRIME/25: .75X TO 2X BASIC
1 Luke Walton/99 2.50 6.00
2 Anfernee Hardaway/99 20.00 50.00
3 Patrick Ewing/99 12.00 30.00
4 Christian Laettner/99 4.00 10.00
5 Robert Parish/99 10.00 25.00
6 Dominique Wilkins/99 10.00 25.00
7 Stephen Jackson/99 3.00 8.00
8 Isiah Thomas/99 10.00 25.00
9 Steve Nash/99 12.00 30.00
10 Joe Dumars/99 5.00 12.00
11 Mark Aguirre/99 3.00 8.00
12 Charles Oakley/99 3.00 8.00
13 Reggie Miller/99 15.00 40.00
14 Clyde Drexler/99 10.00 25.00
15 Shaquille O'Neal /99 20.00 50.00
16 Glen Rice/99 4.00 10.00
17 Stephon Marbury/63 12.00 30.00
18 James Worthy/99 10.00 25.00
19 Tim Duncan/99 15.00 40.00
20 Kevin Garnett/99 15.00 40.00
21 Mark Jackson/99 3.00 8.00
22 Chris Webber/99 15.00 40.00
23 Rik Smits/99 3.00 8.00
24 Doc Rivers/99 4.00 10.00
25 Shawn Marion/99 3.00 8.00
26 Grant Hill/99 12.00 30.00
27 Steve Kerr/99 10.00 25.00
28 Jason Kidd/99 12.00 30.00
29 Toni Kukoc/99 12.00 30.00
30 Larry Johnson/99 10.00 25.00

2018-19 Panini National Treasures Retro Materials Prime

*PRIME/25: .75X TO 2X BASIC
PRINT RUNS B/WN 4-25 COPIES PER
NO PRICING ON QTY 17 OR LESS

2018-19 Panini National Treasures Rookie Dual Materials

STATED PRINT RUN 99 SER.#'d SETS
*PRIME: .75X TO 2 BASIC
1 Mo Bamba 4.00 10.00
2 Deandre Ayton 8.00 20.00
3 Josh Okogie 4.00 10.00
4 Luka Doncic 400.00 800.00
5 Hamidou Diallo 4.00 10.00
6 Jaren Jackson Jr. 20.00 50.00
7 Michael Porter Jr. 10.00 25.00
8 Marvin Bagley III 4.00 10.00
9 Troy Brown Jr. 3.00 8.00
10 Kevin Huerter 5.00 12.00
11 Chandler Hutchison 3.00 8.00
12 Trae Young 75.00 200.00
13 Donte DiVincenzo 6.00 15.00
14 Shai Gilgeous-Alexander 100.00 250.00
15 Jalen Brunson 20.00 50.00
16 Landry Shamet 4.00 10.00
17 Jerome Robinson 2.50 6.00
18 Mikal Bridges 12.00 30.00
19 Lonnie Walker IV 5.00 12.00
20 Omari Spellman 2.50 6.00
21 Kevin Knox 3.00 8.00
22 Collin Sexton 8.00 20.00
23 Elie Okobo 2.50 6.00
24 Wendell Carter Jr. 6.00 15.00
25 Grayson Allen 5.00 12.00

2018-19 Panini National Treasures Rookie Dual Materials Prime

*PRIME: .75X TO 2 BASIC
STATED PRINT RUN 25 SER.#'d SETS

2018-19 Panini National Treasures Rookie Jumbo Materials

STATED PRINT RUN 99 SER.#'d SETS
*PRIME: .75X TO 2 BASIC
1 Mo Bamba 4.00 10.00
2 Deandre Ayton 8.00 20.00
3 Josh Okogie 4.00 10.00
4 Luka Doncic 200.00 500.00
5 Hamidou Diallo 4.00 10.00
6 Jaren Jackson Jr. 20.00 50.00
7 Michael Porter Jr. 10.00 25.00
8 Marvin Bagley III 4.00 10.00
9 Troy Brown Jr. 3.00 8.00
10 Kevin Huerter 5.00 12.00
11 Chandler Hutchison 3.00 8.00
12 Trae Young 60.00 150.00
13 Donte DiVincenzo 6.00 15.00
14 Shai Gilgeous-Alexander 30.00 80.00
15 Jalen Brunson 20.00 50.00
16 Landry Shamet 4.00 10.00
17 Jerome Robinson 2.50 6.00
18 Mikal Bridges 12.00 30.00
19 Lonnie Walker IV 5.00 12.00
20 Omari Spellman 2.50 6.00
21 Kevin Knox 3.00 8.00
22 Collin Sexton 8.00 20.00
23 Elie Okobo 2.50 6.00
24 Wendell Carter Jr. 6.00 15.00
25 Grayson Allen 5.00 12.00

2018-19 Panini National Treasures Rookie Jumbo Materials Prime

*PRIME: .75X TO 2 BASIC
STATED PRINT RUN 25 SER.#'d SETS
2 Deandre Ayton 15.00 40.00
4 Luka Doncic 500.00 1,000.00
6 Jaren Jackson Jr. 40.00 100.00
7 Michael Porter Jr. 20.00 50.00
10 Kevin Huerter 10.00 25.00
12 Trae Young 150.00 400.00
14 Shai Gilgeous-Alexander 125.00 300.00

2018-19 Panini National Treasures Rookie Materials

STATED PRINT RUN 99 SER.#'d SETS
*PRIME: .75X TO 2 BASIC
1 Mo Bamba 3.00 8.00
2 Deandre Ayton 12.00 30.00
3 Josh Okogie 3.00 8.00
4 Luka Doncic 400.00 800.00
5 Hamidou Diallo 3.00 8.00
6 Jaren Jackson Jr. 12.00 30.00
7 Michael Porter Jr. 30.00 80.00
8 Marvin Bagley III 3.00 8.00
9 Troy Brown Jr. 2.50 6.00
10 Kevin Huerter 4.00 10.00
11 Chandler Hutchison 2.50 6.00
12 Trae Young 50.00 120.00
13 Donte DiVincenzo 5.00 12.00
14 Shai Gilgeous-Alexander 30.00 80.00
15 Jalen Brunson 15.00 40.00
16 Landry Shamet 3.00 8.00
17 Jerome Robinson 2.00 5.00
18 Mikal Bridges 10.00 25.00
19 Lonnie Walker IV 4.00 10.00
20 Omari Spellman 2.00 5.00
21 Kevin Knox 2.50 6.00
22 Collin Sexton 6.00 15.00
23 Elie Okobo 2.00 5.00
24 Wendell Carter Jr. 5.00 12.00
25 Grayson Allen 4.00 10.00

2018-19 Panini National Treasures Rookie Materials Prime

2 Deandre Ayton 40.00 100.00
7 Michael Porter Jr. 125.00 300.00
12 Trae Young 150.00 400.00
14 Shai Gilgeous-Alexander 125.00 300.00

2018-19 Panini National Treasures Rookie Patch Autographs Horizontal

STATED PRINT RUN 49 SER.#'d SETS
EXCHANGE DEADLINE 10/26/2020
*BRNZ/25: .6X TO 1.5X BASIC
101 Omari Spellman 15.00 40.00
102 Grayson Allen 30.00 80.00
103 Trae Young 5,000.00 10,000.00
104 Jaren Jackson Jr. 1,000.00 2,000.00
105 Josh Okogie 25.00 60.00
106 Aaron Holiday 25.00 60.00
107 Landry Shamet 25.00 60.00
108 Collin Sexton 75.00 200.00
109 Michael Porter Jr. 400.00 800.00
110 Donte DiVincenzo 40.00 100.00
111 Robert Williams III 75.00 200.00
112 Hamidou Diallo 25.00 60.00
113 Troy Brown Jr. 20.00 50.00
114 Jarred Vanderbilt 30.00 80.00
115 Keita Bates-Diop 20.00 50.00
116 Anfernee Simons 300.00 600.00
117 Lonnie Walker IV 30.00 80.00
118 Deandre Ayton 300.00 600.00
119 Mikal Bridges 500.00 1,000.00
120 Dzanan Musa 15.00 40.00
121 Shai Gilgeous-Alexander 10,000.00 20,000.00
122 Jacob Evans III 15.00 40.00
123 Wendell Carter Jr. EXCH 40.00 100.00
124 Jerome Robinson 15.00 40.00
125 Kevin Huerter 125.00 300.00
126 Bruce Brown 60.00 150.00
127 Luka Doncic 250,000.00 50,000.00
128 De'Anthony Melton 30.00 80.00
129 Mo Bamba 25.00 60.00
130 Elie Okobo 15.00 40.00
131 Svi Mykhailiuk 20.00 50.00
132 Jalen Brunson 500.00 1,000.00
133 Zhaire Smith 15.00 40.00
134 Jevon Carter 25.00 60.00
135 Kevin Knox EXCH 20.00 50.00
136 Chandler Hutchison EXCH 20.00 50.00
137 Marvin Bagley III 25.00 60.00
138 Devonte' Graham 25.00 60.00
139 Moritz Wagner 30.00 80.00
140 Gary Trent Jr. 30.00 80.00
141 Allonzo Trier 15.00 40.00
142 Chimezie Metu 20.00 50.00
145 Khyri Thomas 15.00 40.00
146 Kostas Antetokounmpo 20.00 50.00
147 Melvin Frazier Jr. 15.00 40.00
148 Mitchell Robinson EXCH 40.00 100.00
149 Rodions Kurucs 20.00 50.00
150 Yuta Watanabe 60.00 150.00

2018-19 Panini National Treasures Rookie Patch Autographs Horizontal Bronze

*BRNZ/25: .6X TO 1.5X BASIC
STATED PRINT RUN 25 SER.#'d SETS

2018-19 Panini National Treasures Rookie Patch Autographs Limited Edition

STATED PRINT RUN 20 SER.#'d SETS
EXCHANGE DEADLINE 10/26/2020
*LIMITED ED: .6X TO 1.5X BASIC RPA
101 Omari Spellman 125.00 300.00
102 Grayson Allen 300.00 600.00
105 Josh Okogie 200.00 500.00
107 Landry Shamet 400.00 800.00
108 Collin Sexton 1,500.00 3,000.00
111 Robert Williams III 125.00 400.00
117 Lonnie Walker IV 800.00 1,500.00
118 Deandre Ayton 2,000.00 4,000.00
119 Mikal Bridges 300.00 600.00
121 Shai Gilgeous-Alexander 30,000.00 60,000.00
122 Jacob Evans III 75.00 200.00
125 Kevin Huerter 600.00 1,200.00
127 Luka Doncic 40,000.00 80,000.00
134 Jevon Carter 100.00 250.00
136 Chandler Hutchison EXCH 100.00 250.00

2018-19 Panini National Treasures Rookie Triple Materials

STATED PRINT RUN 99 SER.#'d SETS
*PRIME: .75X TO 2 BASIC
1 Mo Bamba 4.00 10.00
2 Deandre Ayton 8.00 20.00
3 Josh Okogie 4.00 10.00
4 Luka Doncic 400.00 800.00
5 Hamidou Diallo 4.00 10.00
6 Jaren Jackson Jr. 20.00 50.00
7 Michael Porter Jr. 10.00 25.00
8 Marvin Bagley III 4.00 10.00
9 Troy Brown Jr. 3.00 8.00
10 Kevin Huerter 5.00 12.00
11 Chandler Hutchison 3.00 8.00
12 Trae Young 75.00 200.00
13 Donte DiVincenzo 6.00 15.00
14 Shai Gilgeous-Alexander 50.00 120.00
15 Jalen Brunson 20.00 50.00
16 Landry Shamet 4.00 10.00
17 Jerome Robinson 2.50 6.00
18 Mikal Bridges 12.00 30.00
19 Lonnie Walker IV 5.00 12.00
20 Omari Spellman 2.50 6.00
21 Kevin Knox 3.00 8.00
22 Collin Sexton 8.00 20.00
23 Elie Okobo 2.50 6.00
24 Wendell Carter Jr. 6.00 15.00
25 Grayson Allen 5.00 12.00

2018-19 Panini National Treasures Rookie Triple Materials Prime

*PRIME: .75X TO 2 BASIC
PRINT RUNS B/WN 9-25 COPIES PER
NO PRICING ON QTY 15 OR LESS

2018-19 Panini National Treasures Signatures

PRINT RUNS B/WN 25-99 COPIES PER
EXCHANGE DEADLINE 10/26/2020
*BRNZ/25: .5X TO 1.2X p/r 49-99
1 Charles Barkley/25 EXCH 100.00 250.00
3 Anthony Davis/25 25.00 60.00
5 JJ Redick/99 6.00 15.00
6 Marcus Camby/99 5.00 12.00
7 Kyle Kuzma/99 EXCH 12.00 30.00
8 Sidney Moncrief/99 4.00 10.00
9 Dave Cowens/99 8.00 20.00
10 Rick Fox/99 5.00 12.00
12 J.J. Barea/99 6.00 15.00
14 Herb Williams/99 4.00 10.00
15 Nikola Jokic/99 150.00 400.00
16 Mark Price/99 6.00 15.00
17 Chris Mullin/99 EXCH 8.00 20.00
18 Tree Rollins/99 4.00 10.00
19 Jermaine O'Neal/99 5.00 12.00
20 Dikembe Mutombo/99 10.00 25.00
21 Allen Iverson/25 75.00 200.00
22 Clifford Robinson/99 6.00 15.00
25 Nate Archibald/99 8.00 20.00
26 Muggsy Bogues/99 6.00 15.00
27 Peja Stojakovic/99 5.00 12.00
28 Vlade Divac/99 6.00 15.00
29 Latrell Sprewell/99 8.00 20.00
30 Juwan Howard/99 5.00 12.00
31 Damian Lillard/25 30.00 80.00
32 Dee Brown/99 5.00 12.00
33 Kareem Abdul-Jabbar/25 75.00 200.00
34 John Salley/99 5.00 12.00
35 Walt Frazier/99 10.00 25.00
36 Rudy Tomjanovich/99 5.00 12.00
37 Danny Manning/99 5.00 12.00
38 Dwyane Wade/25 50.00 120.00
39 Ralph Sampson/99 5.00 12.00
40 Tom Chambers/99 5.00 12.00

2018-19 Panini National Treasures Timeline Materials

PRINT RUNS B/WN 25-99 COPIES PER
*PRIME/25: .75X TO 2X BASIC
1 Kyrie Irving/99 4.00 10.00
2 Stephen Curry/99 25.00 60.00
3 Kevin Durant/99 12.00 30.00
4 LeBron James/99 15.00 40.00
5 Giannis Antetokounmpo/99 15.00 40.00
6 Jayson Tatum/99 4.00 10.00
7 Tony Parker/99 5.00 12.00
8 Kemba Walker/99 2.50 6.00
9 Lauri Markkanen/99 5.00 12.00
10 Kevin Love/99 2.50 6.00
11 DeAndre Jordan/99 2.50 6.00
12 Nikola Jokic/99 15.00 40.00
13 Andre Drummond/99 2.50 6.00
14 Blake Griffin/99 3.00 8.00
15 James Harden/99 4.00 10.00
16 Chris Paul/99 4.00 10.00
17 Lonzo Ball/25 8.00 20.00
18 Dwyane Wade/99 6.00 15.00
19 Karl-Anthony Towns/99 5.00 12.00
20 Andrew Wiggins/99 4.00 10.00
21 Anthony Davis/99 4.00 10.00
22 Kristaps Porzingis/99 4.00 10.00
23 Paul George/99 5.00 12.00
24 Russell Westbrook/99 4.00 10.00
25 Joel Embiid/99 4.00 10.00
26 Ben Simmons/99 3.00 8.00
27 Damian Lillard/99 4.00 10.00
28 LaMarcus Aldridge/99 3.00 8.00
29 Kawhi Leonard/99 10.00 25.00
30 Donovan Mitchell/99 4.00 10.00

2018-19 Panini National Treasures Timeline Materials Prime

*PRIME/25: .75X TO 2X BASIC
PRINT RUNS B/WN 5-25 COPIES PER
NO PRICING ON QTY 15 OR LESS
26 Ben Simmons/25 30.00 80.00

2018-19 Panini National Treasures Treasured Signatures

PRINT RUNS B/WN 25-99 COPIES PER
EXCHANGE DEADLINE 10/26/2020
*BRNZ/25: .5X TO 1.2X p/r 49-99
1 Charlie Scott/99 6.00 15.00
2 Ray Allen/49 40.00 100.00
3 Dan Issel/99 8.00 20.00
4 JJ Redick/99 6.00 15.00
5 Gail Goodrich/99 6.00 15.00
6 Kobe Bryant/25 2,000.00 4,000.00
7 Alex English/99 6.00 15.00
8 Kevin Durant/25 100.00 250.00
9 Jerry Stackhouse/99 8.00 20.00
10 Alonzo Mourning/49 20.00 50.00
11 J.J. Barea/99 6.00 15.00
12 Jeremy Lin/49 75.00 200.00
13 Kelly Oubre Jr./99 6.00 15.00
15 Latrell Sprewell/99 8.00 20.00
17 David Thompson/99 8.00 20.00
18 Magic Johnson/25 75.00 200.00
19 Toni Kukoc/99 8.00 20.00
20 Paul Pierce/49 25.00 60.00
21 Rolando Blackman/99 5.00 12.00
22 Mike Conley/99 5.00 12.00
23 Arvydas Sabonis/99 6.00 15.00
24 Elfrid Payton/99 5.00 12.00
25 John Collins/99 6.00 15.00

2018-19 Panini National Treasures Treasured Threads

STATED PRINT RUN 99 SER.#'d SETS
*PRIME/19-25: 1X TO 2.5X BASIC
1 Ben Simmons 4.00 10.00
2 CJ McCollum 3.00 8.00
3 Courtney Lee 2.00 5.00
4 DeAndre' Bembry 2.00 5.00
5 Devin Booker 4.00 10.00
6 Dirk Nowitzki 8.00 20.00
7 Frank Ntilikina 2.00 5.00
8 Goran Dragic 2.50 6.00
9 Isaiah Thomas 2.50 6.00
10 Jarrett Allen 3.00 8.00
11 Jeremy Lin 5.00 12.00
12 Joe Dumars 4.00 10.00
13 Evan Turner 2.00 5.00
14 Karl Malone 6.00 15.00
15 Kevin Garnett 4.00 10.00
16 Kris Dunn 2.00 5.00
17 Lauri Markkanen 5.00 12.00
18 Markelle Fultz 2.50 6.00
19 Buddy Hield 3.00 8.00
20 Noah Vonleh 2.00 5.00
21 Paul George 5.00 12.00
22 Robert Covington 2.50 6.00
23 Rodney Hood 2.50 6.00
24 Russell Westbrook 4.00 10.00
25 Serge Ibaka 2.50 6.00
26 Steven Adams 2.50 6.00
27 Tyus Jones 2.00 5.00
28 Victor Oladipo 2.50 6.00
29 Wesley Matthews 2.00 5.00
30 Jonathan Isaac 3.00 8.00

2018-19 Panini National Treasures Treasured Threads Prime

*PRIME/19-25: 1X TO 2.5X BASIC
PRINT RUNS B/WN 9-25 COPIES PER
NO PRICING ON QTY 15 OR LESS
1 Ben Simmons/25 25.00 60.00
5 Devin Booker/25 15.00 40.00

2018-19 Panini National Treasures Treasures of the Hall Autographs

PRINT RUNS B/WN 25-99 COPIES PER
EXCHANGE DEADLINE 10/26/2020
*BRNZ/25: .5X TO 1.2X p/r 49-99
1 Karl Malone/25 60.00 150.00
2 Shaquille O'Neal /25 100.00 250.00
3 Magic Johnson/25 100.00 250.00
4 Dave Cowens/99 8.00 20.00
5 Adrian Dantley/99 5.00 12.00
6 Julius Erving/25 EXCH 40.00 100.00
8 George Gervin/99 15.00 40.00
9 Elvin Hayes/99 8.00 20.00
10 Jerry West/25 30.00 80.00
11 Bob Lanier/99 15.00 40.00
12 Larry Bird/25 100.00 250.00
13 Gail Goodrich/99 6.00 15.00
14 Charles Barkley/25 EXCH 100.00 250.00
15 Mitch Richmond/99 15.00 40.00
16 Dennis Rodman/99 40.00 100.00
17 Allen Iverson/25 75.00 200.00
18 Grant Hill/99 25.00 60.00
19 Tracy McGrady/49 50.00 120.00
20 Jason Kidd/49 30.00 80.00
21 Kareem Abdul-Jabbar/25 75.00 200.00
22 Oscar Robertson/25 40.00 100.00
23 Dominique Wilkins/99 12.00 30.00
24 David Robinson/25 40.00 100.00
25 Ray Allen/49 50.00 120.00

2018-19 Panini National Treasures Treasures of the Hall Autographs Bronze

*BRNZ/25: .5X TO 1.2X p/r 49-99
PRINT RUNS B/WN 15-25 COPIES PER
NO PRICING ON QTY 15 OR LESS
EXCHANGE DEADLINE 10/26/2020
18 Grant Hill/25 30.00 80.00

2018-19 Panini National Treasures Tremendous Treasures Relics

PRINT RUNS B/WN 50-99 COPIES PER
*PRIME/25: .75X TO 2X BASIC
1 Jarrett Allen/99 3.00 8.00
2 D'Angelo Russell/99 3.00 8.00
3 Kevin Love/99 2.50 6.00
4 JR Smith/99 3.00 8.00
5 Goran Dragic/99 2.50 6.00
6 Dwyane Wade/99 6.00 15.00
7 Karl-Anthony Towns/99 5.00 12.00
8 Jimmy Butler/99 5.00 12.00
9 Anthony Davis/99 8.00 20.00
10 Elfrid Payton/99 2.50 6.00
11 Aaron Gordon/99 3.00 8.00
12 Nikola Vucevic/99 2.50 6.00
13 Joel Embiid/99 8.00 20.00
14 Markelle Fultz/99 2.50 6.00
15 Damian Lillard/99 8.00 20.00
16 Seth Curry/99 2.50 6.00
17 LaMarcus Aldridge/99 3.00 8.00
18 Pau Gasol/99 5.00 12.00
19 De'Aaron Fox/99 6.00 15.00
20 Devin Booker/99 8.00 20.00
21 Dennis Schroder/99 2.50 6.00
22 Enes Kanter/99 2.50 6.00
23 Giannis Antetokounmpo/99 12.00 30.00
24 Mike Conley/99 2.50 6.00
25 Lonzo Ball/50 3.00 8.00
26 Tobias Harris/99 2.50 6.00
27 Kevin Durant/99 10.00 25.00
28 Gerald Green/99 2.50 6.00
29 Gary Harris/99 2.50 6.00
30 Harrison Barnes/99 2.50 6.00

2018-19 Panini National Treasures Tremendous Treasures Relics Prime

*PRIME/25: .75X TO 2X BASIC
PRINT RUNS B/WN 5-25 COPIES PER
NO PRICING ON QTY 15 OR LESS
8 Jimmy Butler/25 12.00 30.00
9 Anthony Davis/25 25.00 60.00
14 Markelle Fultz/25 10.00 25.00
16 Seth Curry/25 8.00 20.00
19 De'Aaron Fox/25 20.00 50.00
26 Tobias Harris/25 10.00 25.00

2019-20 Panini National Treasures

STATED PRINT RUN 99 SER.#'d SETS
EXCHANGE DEADLINE 12/12/2021
1 Evan Fournier 2.50 6.00
2 Bojan Bogdanovic 2.50 6.00
3 John Collins 3.00 8.00
4 CJ McCollum 3.00 8.00
5 LaMarcus Aldridge 3.00 8.00
6 Andre Drummond 2.50 6.00
7 Anthony Davis 8.00 20.00
8 Jayson Tatum 12.00 30.00
9 Buddy Hield 2.50 6.00
10 Kevin Durant 10.00 25.00
11 Aaron Gordon 3.00 8.00
12 Rudy Gobert 4.00 10.00
13 Jabari Parker 2.00 5.00
14 Carmelo Anthony 5.00 12.00
15 Rudy Gay 2.50 6.00
16 Derrick Rose 6.00 15.00
17 LeBron James 25.00 60.00
18 Jaylen Brown 5.00 12.00
19 De'Aaron Fox 5.00 12.00
20 Kyrie Irving 6.00 15.00
21 Nikola Vucevic 2.50 6.00
22 Mike Conley 2.50 6.00
23 Luka Doncic 20.00 50.00
24 Hassan Whiteside 2.00 5.00
25 Bryn Forbes 2.50 6.00
26 Luke Kennard 2.50 6.00
27 Kyle Kuzma 4.00 10.00
28 Kemba Walker 2.50 6.00
29 Harrison Barnes 2.50 6.00
30 Spencer Dinwiddie 2.50 6.00
31 Devonte' Graham 2.50 6.00
32 Shai Gilgeous-Alexander 15.00 40.00
33 Kristaps Porzingis 4.00 10.00
34 Giannis Antetokounmpo 15.00 40.00
35 Jaren Jackson Jr. 5.00 12.00
36 Zach LaVine 5.00 12.00
37 Kawhi Leonard 8.00 20.00
38 Joel Embiid 6.00 15.00
39 Stephen Curry 25.00 60.00
40 Marcus Morris Sr. 2.00 5.00
41 Terry Rozier 2.50 6.00
42 Chris Paul 6.00 15.00
43 Tim Hardaway Jr. 2.00 5.00
44 Khris Middleton 3.00 8.00
45 Jonas Valanciunas 2.50 6.00
46 Lauri Markkanen 4.00 10.00
47 Paul George 5.00 12.00
48 Ben Simmons 3.00 8.00
49 Klay Thompson 8.00 20.00
50 Julius Randle 4.00 10.00
51 Miles Bridges 3.00 8.00
52 Dennis Schroder 2.50 6.00
53 James Harden 6.00 15.00
54 Eric Bledsoe 2.50 6.00
55 Dillon Brooks 2.50 6.00
56 Wendell Carter Jr. 3.00 8.00
57 Lou Williams 3.00 8.00
58 Tobias Harris 2.50 6.00
59 Draymond Green 4.00 10.00
60 Frank Ntilikina 2.00 5.00
61 John Wall 4.00 10.00
62 Karl-Anthony Towns 5.00 12.00
63 Russell Westbrook 5.00 12.00
64 Malcolm Brogdon 2.50 6.00
65 Brandon Ingram 3.00 8.00
66 Collin Sexton 4.00 10.00
67 Montrezl Harrell 2.50 6.00
68 Pascal Siakam 5.00 12.00
69 D'Angelo Russell 2.50 6.00
70 Jamal Murray 5.00 12.00
71 Bradley Beal 4.00 10.00
72 Andrew Wiggins 4.00 10.00
73 Clint Capela 2.50 6.00
74 Domantas Sabonis 4.00 10.00
75 Jrue Holiday 4.00 10.00
76 Kevin Love 3.00 8.00
77 Devin Booker .75 2.00
78 Kyle Lowry 3.00 8.00
79 Jimmy Butler 6.00 15.00
80 Nikola Jokic 15.00 40.00
81 Isaiah Thomas 2.50 6.00
82 Jeff Teague 2.00 5.00
83 Eric Gordon 2.50 6.00
84 T.J. Warren 2.50 6.00
85 JJ Redick 3.00 8.00
86 Tristan Thompson 2.00 5.00
87 Deandre Ayton 3.00 8.00
88 Fred VanVleet 4.00 10.00
89 Goran Dragic 2.50 6.00
90 Paul Millsap 2.50 6.00
91 Trae Young 8.00 20.00
92 Damian Lillard 8.00 20.00
93 DeMar DeRozan 4.00 10.00
94 Blake Griffin 3.00 8.00
95 Lonzo Ball 3.00 8.00
96 Darius Garland RC 125.00 300.00
97 Ricky Rubio 2.50 6.00
98 Al Horford 3.00 8.00
99 Bam Adebayo 5.00 12.00
100 Donovan Mitchell 6.00 15.00
101 KZ Okpala JSY AU RC 40.00 100.00
102 Cam Reddish JSY AU RC 50.00 125.00
103 Eric Paschall JSY AU RC 40.00 100.00
104 Sekou Doumbouya JSY AU RC 30.00 80.00
105 Isaiah Roby JSY AU RC 40.00 100.00
106 Luka Samanic JSY AU RC 40.00 100.00
107 Darius Bazley JSY AU RC 30.00 80.00
108 Zion Williamson JSY AU RC 10,000.00 20,000.00
109 Mfiondu Kabengele JSY AU RC 40.00 100.00
110 Jarrett Culver JSY AU RC 30.00 80.00
111 Carsen Edwards JSY AU RC 40.00 100.00
112 Cameron Johnson JSY AU RC 125.00 300.00
113 Admiral Schofield JSY AU RC 40.00 100.00
114 Chuma Okeke JSY AU RC 50.00 125.00
115 Ignas Brazdeikis JSY AU RC 40.00 100.00
116 Matisse Thybulle JSY AU RC 60.00 150.00
117 Ty Jerome JSY AU RC 60.00 150.00
118 Ja Morant JSY AU RC 15,000.00 30,000.00
119 Jordan Poole JSY AU RC 1,000.00 2,000.00
120 Coby White JSY AU RC 800.00 1,500.00
121 Bruno Fernando JSY AU RC 40.00 100.00
122 PJ Washington Jr. JSY AU RC 150.00 400.00
123 Jaylen Nowell JSY AU RC 40.00 100.00
124 Nickeil Alexander-Walker JSY AU RC 50.00 125.00
125 Quinndary Weatherspoon JSY AU RC 30.00 80.00
126 Brandon Clarke JSY AU RC 60.00 150.00
127 Nassir Little JSY AU RC 50.00 125.00
128 RJ Barrett JSY AU RC 1,500.00 3,000.00
129 Keldon Johnson JSY AU RC 500.00 1,000.00
130 Jaxson Hayes JSY AU RC 50.00 125.00
131 Cody Martin JSY AU RC 50.00 125.00
132 Tyler Herro JSY AU RC 2,000.00 4,000.00
133 Bol Bol JSY AU RC 125.00 300.00
134 Goga Bitadze JSY AU RC 50.00 125.00
135 Nicolo Melli JSY AU RC 40.00 100.00
136 Grant Williams JSY AU RC 50.00 125.00
137 Dylan Windler JSY AU RC 40.00 100.00
138 De'Andre Hunter JSY AU RC 300.00 600.00
139 Kevin Porter Jr. JSY AU RC 60.00 150.00
140 Rui Hachimura JSY AU RC 500.00 1,000.00
141 Romeo Langford JSY AU RC 30.00 80.00
142 Kyle Guy JSY AU RC 40.00 100.00
143 Nicolas Claxton JSY AU RC 60.00 150.00
144 Tacko Fall JSY AU RC 40.00 100.00
145 Daniel Gafford JSY AU RC 60.00 150.00
146 Alen Smailagic JSY AU RC 30.00 80.00
147 Terence Davis JSY AU RC 50.00 125.00
148 Justin Robinson JSY AU RC 30.00 80.00
149 Terance Mann JSY AU RC 60.00 150.00
150 Kendrick Nunn JSY AU RC 50.00 125.00
151 Talen Horton-Tucker AU RC 6.00 15.00
152 Miye Oni AU RC 4.00 10.00
153 Jordan Bone AU RC 4.00 10.00
154 Brian Bowen II AU RC 4.00 10.00
155 Justin Wright-Foreman AU RC 4.00 10.00
156 Amir Coffey AU RC 6.00 15.00
157 Jaylen Hoard AU RC 4.00 10.00
158 Luguentz Dort AU RC 15.00 40.00
159 Jalen McDaniels AU RC 10.00 25.00
160 Robert Franks AU RC 4.00 10.00

2019-20 Panini National Treasures Bronze

*BRNZ 1-100: .6X TO 1.5X BASIC
*BRNZ 151-160: .5X TO 1.2X BASIC
1-100 STATED PRINT RUN 49 SER.#'d SETS
151-160 STATED PRINT RUN 25 SER.#'d SETS
EXCHANGE DEADLINE 12/12/2021

2019-20 Panini National Treasures All-NBA Materials

STATED PRINT RUN 49-99 SER.#'d SETS
*PRIME/25: .75X TO 2X BASIC
1 Giannis Antetokounmpo/99 20.00 50.00
2 Kevin Love/99 4.00 10.00
3 LaMarcus Aldridge/99 4.00 10.00
4 Chris Paul/49 8.00 20.00
5 Andre Drummond/99 3.00 8.00
6 James Harden/99 8.00 20.00
7 Joel Embiid/99 8.00 20.00
8 Kyle Lowry/99 4.00 10.00
9 Rudy Gobert/99 5.00 12.00
10 Victor Oladipo/99 3.00 8.00
11 Jimmy Butler/49 8.00 20.00
12 Stephen Curry/99 100.00 250.00
13 LeBron James/49 125.00 300.00
14 Damian Lillard/99 10.00 25.00
15 Anthony Davis/49 10.00 25.00
16 Kemba Walker/49 3.00 8.00
17 Karl-Anthony Towns/99 6.00 15.00
18 Kyrie Irving/49 8.00 20.00
19 Blake Griffin/99 4.00 10.00
20 Marc Gasol/49 4.00 10.00
21 Kawhi Leonard/49 10.00 25.00
22 Klay Thompson/99 10.00 25.00
23 Paul George/49 6.00 15.00
24 DeMar DeRozan/99 5.00 12.00
25 DeAndre Jordan/49 3.00 8.00
26 John Wall/99 5.00 12.00
27 Nikola Jokic/99 20.00 50.00
28 Russell Westbrook/49 6.00 15.00
29 Draymond Green/99 5.00 12.00
30 Goran Dragic/99 3.00 8.00

2019-20 Panini National Treasures Apprentice Ink Autographs

STATED PRINT RUN 25-99 SER.#'d SETS
EXCHANGE DEADLINE 12/12/2021
*BRONZE/25: .6X TO 1.5X BASIC
1 Zion Williamson/25 600.00 1,200.00
2 Sekou Doumbouya/99 5.00 12.00
3 Rui Hachimura/49 75.00 200.00
4 Brandon Clarke/99 10.00 25.00
5 Cam Reddish/49 8.00 20.00
6 Luka Samanic/99 6.00 15.00
7 Cameron Johnson/99 25.00 60.00
8 Ty Jerome/99 10.00 25.00
9 Tyler Herro/99 125.00 300.00
10 Matisse Thybulle/99 10.00 25.00
11 Ja Morant/25 1,250.00 2,500.00
12 Chuma Okeke/99 8.00 20.00
13 De'Andre Hunter/49 40.00 100.00
14 Darius Bazley/99 5.00 12.00
15 Coby White/49 75.00 200.00
16 Grant Williams/99 8.00 20.00
17 PJ Washington Jr./99 15.00 40.00
18 Dylan Windler/99 6.00 15.00
19 Romeo Langford/99 5.00 12.00
20 Nassir Little/99 8.00 20.00
21 RJ Barrett/25 100.00 250.00
22 Nickeil Alexander-Walker/99 8.00 20.00
23 Jarrett Culver/49 5.00 12.00
24 Goga Bitadze/99 8.00 20.00
25 Jaxson Hayes/99 8.00 20.00

2019-20 Panini National Treasures Biography Materials

STATED PRINT RUN 49-99 SER.#'d SETS
*PRIME/25: .75X TO 2X BASIC
1 Harrison Barnes/49 2.50 6.00
2 Victor Oladipo/99 2.50 6.00
3 Joel Embiid/99 6.00 15.00
4 Khris Middleton/99 3.00 8.00
5 Aaron Gordon/99 3.00 8.00
6 Malik Monk/99 3.00 8.00
7 Brook Lopez/99 2.50 6.00
8 Paul George/49 5.00 12.00
9 DeMar DeRozan/99 4.00 10.00
10 Steven Adams/99 2.50 6.00
11 Jamal Murray/99 5.00 12.00
12 Wendell Carter Jr./99 3.00 8.00
13 Jordan Clarkson/99 3.00 8.00
14 Kyle Lowry/99 3.00 8.00
15 Andrew Wiggins/99 4.00 10.00
16 Marvin Bagley III/99 2.50 6.00
17 Chris Paul/49 6.00 15.00
18 Rudy Gay/99 2.50 6.00
19 Domantas Sabonis/99 4.00 10.00
20 Terry Rozier/49 2.50 6.00
21 Jarrett Allen/99 3.00 8.00
22 Willie Cauley-Stein/49 2.00 5.00
23 Julius Randle/49 4.00 10.00
24 Lauri Markkanen/99 4.00 10.00
25 Ben Simmons/99 3.00 8.00
26 Miles Bridges/99 3.00 8.00
27 Collin Sexton/99 4.00 10.00
28 Serge Ibaka/99 2.50 6.00
29 Eric Bledsoe/99 2.50 6.00
30 Tobias Harris/49 2.50 6.00
31 Jeff Teague/99 2.00 5.00
32 Zach LaVine/99 5.00 12.00
33 Kemba Walker/49 2.50 6.00
34 Lou Williams/99 3.00 8.00
35 Bojan Bogdanovic/49 2.50 6.00
36 Nikola Jokic/99 15.00 40.00
37 De'Aaron Fox/99 5.00 12.00
38 Shai Gilgeous-Alexander/49 15.00 40.00
39 Gary Harris/99 2.50 6.00
40 Trae Young/99 12.00 30.00

2019-20 Panini National Treasures Century Materials

STATED PRINT RUN 49-99 SER.#'d SETS
*PRIME/25: .75X TO 2X BASIC
1 Devin Booker/99 15.00 40.00
2 Pascal Siakam/99 10.00 25.00
3 Harrison Barnes/49 2.50 6.00
4 Serge Ibaka/99 2.50 6.00
5 Jrue Holiday/99 4.00 10.00
6 Jayson Tatum/99 25.00 60.00
7 Aaron Gordon/99 3.00 8.00
8 Luka Doncic/99 60.00 150.00
9 CJ McCollum/99 3.00 8.00
10 Mike Conley/49 2.50 6.00
11 Domantas Sabonis/99 4.00 10.00
12 Ricky Rubio/49 2.50 6.00
13 Jaylen Brown/99 5.00 12.00
14 Terry Rozier/49 2.50 6.00
15 Julius Randle/49 4.00 10.00
16 Kyle Lowry/99 3.00 8.00
17 Blake Griffin/99 3.00 8.00
18 Malcolm Brogdon/49 2.50 6.00
19 Clint Capela/99 2.50 6.00
20 Montrezl Harrell/49 2.50 6.00
21 Giannis Antetokounmpo/99 30.00 80.00
22 Rudy Gobert/99 4.00 10.00
23 Jeff Teague/99 2.00 5.00
24 Victor Oladipo/99 2.50 6.00
25 Kristaps Porzingis/49 4.00 10.00
26 LaMarcus Aldridge/99 3.00 8.00
27 Bogdan Bogdanovic/99 3.00 8.00
28 Malik Monk/99 3.00 8.00
29 Collin Sexton/99 4.00 10.00
30 Myles Turner/99 3.00 8.00
31 Goran Dragic/49 2.50 6.00
32 Russell Westbrook/49 5.00 12.00
33 Josh Richardson/49 2.00 5.00
34 Zach LaVine/99 5.00 12.00
35 Kyle Kuzma/99 4.00 10.00
36 Lonzo Ball/99 3.00 8.00
37 Bojan Bogdanovic/49 2.50 6.00
38 Markelle Fultz/49 2.50 6.00
39 Derrick Rose/49 6.00 15.00
40 Nikola Jokic/99 15.00 40.00

2019-20 Panini National Treasures Clutch Factor Jersey Signatures

STATED PRINT RUN 25-99 SER.#'d SETS
EXCHANGE DEADLINE 12/12/2021
*PRIME: .75X TO 2X BASIC
1 Zion Williamson/25 2,500.00 5,000.00
2 Ja Morant/25 1,500.00 3,000.00
3 RJ Barrett/25 125.00 300.00
4 Rui Hachimura/49 100.00 250.00
5 De'Andre Hunter/49 50.00 120.00
6 Jarrett Culver/49 5.00 12.00
7 Allen Iverson/25 75.00 200.00
8 Richard Hamilton/49 8.00 20.00
9 Mike Bibby/99 8.00 20.00
10 Paul Pierce/25 40.00 100.00
11 John Stockton/25 60.00 150.00
12 Christian Laettner/49 8.00 20.00
13 Kevin Garnett/25 75.00 200.00
14 Dominique Wilkins/49 15.00 40.00
15 David Robinson/25 40.00 100.00
17 Hakeem Olajuwon/25 40.00 100.00
18 Kyrie Irving/25 60.00 150.00
19 Anthony Davis/25 200.00 500.00
20 Karl-Anthony Towns/25 12.00 30.00
21 Vince Carter/49 60.00 150.00

22 Lauri Markkanen/49 10.00 25.00
24 Khris Middleton/49 8.00 20.00
25 Gordon Hayward/49 6.00 15.00
26 Harrison Barnes/49 6.00 15.00
27 Danilo Gallinari/49 6.00 15.00
28 Wendell Carter Jr./49 8.00 20.00
29 Julius Randle/49 10.00 25.00
30 Rudy Gay/99 6.00 15.00
31 Willie Cauley-Stein/99 5.00 12.00
32 Caris LeVert/99 6.00 15.00
34 Goran Dragic/99 6.00 15.00
35 Al-Farouq Aminu/99 5.00 12.00
37 Ersan Ilyasova/99 5.00 12.00
38 Shaquille O'Neal /25 75.00 200.00
39 Karl Malone/25 15.00 40.00
40 Kareem Abdul-Jabbar/25 40.00 100.00
41 Grant Hill/25 25.00 60.00
42 Kevin Knox II/49 5.00 12.00
43 Tony Parker/49 12.00 30.00
44 Derek Fisher/49 8.00 20.00
45 JJ Redick/49 8.00 20.00
46 Mark Jackson/99 6.00 15.00
47 Danny Manning/99 6.00 15.00
48 Otto Porter Jr./99 5.00 12.00
49 Carlos Boozer/99 6.00 15.00
50 Caron Butler/99 6.00 15.00

2019-20 Panini National Treasures Colossal Material Autographs

PRINT RUNS B/WN 25-99 COPIES PER
EXCHANGE DEADLINE 12/12/2021
*PRIME/25: .6X TO 1.5X p/r 49-99
3 RJ Barrett/25 125.00 300.00
4 Rui Hachimura/49 125.00 300.00
5 De'Andre Hunter/49 60.00 150.00
6 Jarrett Culver/49 4.00 10.00
7 Kyrie Irving/25 75.00 200.00
8 Lonzo Ball/49 30.00 80.00
9 Kristaps Porzingis/49 50.00 120.00
10 Lauri Markkanen/49 8.00 20.00
11 Anthony Davis/25 200.00 500.00
14 Zach LaVine/49 40.00 100.00
15 De'Aaron Fox/49 40.00 100.00
16 Myles Turner/99 6.00 15.00
17 Nikola Jokic/49 200.00 500.00
18 Collin Sexton/99 15.00 40.00
19 Jaren Jackson Jr./49 40.00 100.00
21 Harrison Barnes/49 5.00 12.00
22 PJ Washington Jr./25 40.00 100.00
23 Montrezl Harrell/99 5.00 12.00
24 Jalen Brunson/99 15.00 40.00
25 Rudy Gay/99 5.00 12.00
26 Wendell Carter Jr./49 6.00 15.00
27 Josh Richardson/99 4.00 10.00
28 Harry Giles III/99 4.00 10.00
30 Nikola Vucevic/49 5.00 12.00
31 Khris Middleton/49 15.00 40.00
32 Caris LeVert/99 20.00 50.00
34 Zhaire Smith/99 4.00 10.00
35 Julius Randle/49 8.00 20.00
36 Willie Cauley-Stein/99 4.00 10.00
37 Tyson Chandler/49 5.00 12.00
39 Pascal Siakam/99 20.00 50.00
41 Damian Lillard/25 200.00 500.00
42 Jarrett Allen/99 6.00 15.00
43 Joe Harris/99 5.00 12.00
45 Otto Porter Jr./99 4.00 10.00
46 Dwight Powell/99 4.00 10.00
47 J.J. Barea/49 12.00 30.00
48 Malcolm Brogdon/99 5.00 12.00
50 Mike Conley/49 5.00 12.00

2019-20 Panini National Treasures Colossal Materials

STATED PRINT RUN 25-99 SER.#'d SETS
*PRIME/25: .75X TO 2X BASIC
1 John Collins/99 6.00 15.00
2 Anfernee Simons/49 10.00 25.00
3 Kevin Knox II/99 4.00 10.00
4 Buddy Hield/99 5.00 12.00
5 LeBron James/49 125.00 300.00
6 Deandre Ayton/25 6.00 15.00
7 Miles Bridges/99 6.00 15.00
8 Eric Gordon/99 5.00 12.00
9 Steven Adams/99 5.00 12.00
10 James Harden/99 12.00 30.00
11 Jonas Valanciunas/99 5.00 12.00
12 Anthony Davis/49 15.00 40.00
13 Kevin Love/99 6.00 15.00
14 Caris LeVert/99 6.00 15.00
15 Lou Williams/99 6.00 15.00
16 DeAndre Jordan/49 6.00 15.00
17 Paul Millsap/99 5.00 12.00
18 Fred VanVleet/25 8.00 20.00
19 Trae Young/99 15.00 40.00
20 Jaren Jackson Jr./99 10.00 25.00
21 Jordan Clarkson/99 6.00 15.00
22 Ben Simmons/99 6.00 15.00
23 Khris Middleton/99 6.00 15.00
24 Chris Paul/49 12.00 30.00
25 Michael Porter Jr./49 10.00 25.00
26 DeMar DeRozan/99 8.00 20.00
27 Rudy Gay/25 5.00 12.00
28 Gary Harris/99 5.00 12.00
29 Willie Cauley-Stein/49 4.00 10.00
30 Jarrett Allen/99 6.00 15.00

2019-20 Panini National Treasures Colossal Rookie Materials

STATED PRINT RUN 99 SER.#'d SETS
*PRIME: .75X TO 2 BASIC
1 Grant Williams 6.00 15.00
2 Zion Williamson 100.00 250.00
3 Dylan Windler 5.00 12.00
4 Jarrett Culver 4.00 10.00
5 Kevin Porter Jr 8.00 20.00
6 Cam Reddish 6.00 15.00
7 Cody Martin 6.00 15.00
8 Romeo Langford 4.00 10.00
9 Isaiah Roby 5.00 12.00
10 Goga Bitadze 6.00 15.00
11 Darius Bazley 4.00 10.00
12 Ja Morant 100.00 250.00
13 Mfiondu Kabengele 5.00 12.00
14 Coby White 12.00 30.00
15 KZ Okpala 5.00 12.00
16 Cameron Johnson 10.00 25.00
17 Eric Paschall 5.00 12.00
18 Sekou Doumbouya 4.00 10.00
19 Ignas Brazdeikis 5.00 12.00
20 Luka Samanic 5.00 12.00
21 Ty Jerome 8.00 20.00
22 RJ Barrett 25.00 60.00
23 Jordan Poole 15.00 40.00
24 Jaxson Hayes 6.00 15.00
25 Carsen Edwards 5.00 12.00
26 PJ Washington Jr. 12.00 30.00
27 Admiral Schofield 5.00 12.00
28 Chuma Okeke 6.00 15.00
29 Quinndary Weatherspoon 4.00 10.00
30 Matisse Thybulle 8.00 20.00
31 Nassir Little 8.00 20.00
32 De'Andre Hunter 15.00 40.00
33 Keldon Johnson 12.00 30.00
34 Rui Hachimura 15.00 40.00
35 Bruno Fernando 5.00 12.00
36 Tyler Herro 20.00 50.00
37 Bol Bol 10.00 25.00
38 Nickeil Alexander-Walker 6.00 15.00
39 Kyle Guy 5.00 12.00
40 Brandon Clarke 8.00 20.00

2019-20 Panini National Treasures Colossal Rookie Materials Prime

*PRIME: .75X TO 2 BASIC
STATED PRINT RUN 25 SER.#'d SETS
12 Ja Morant 200.00 500.00
15 KZ Okpala 10.00 25.00
22 RJ Barrett 50.00 120.00
24 Jaxson Hayes 12.00 30.00
28 Chuma Okeke 12.00 30.00
30 Matisse Thybulle 15.00 40.00
33 Keldon Johnson 25.00 60.00

2019-20 Panini National Treasures Definitive Ink Autographs

STATED PRINT RUN 25-49 SER.#'d SETS
EXCHANGE DEADLINE 12/12/2021
1 Carlos Boozer/49 6.00 15.00
3 TJ Leaf/49 5.00 12.00
4 Christian Laettner/35 12.00 30.00
6 Wendell Carter Jr./35 8.00 20.00
7 Kyrie Irving/25 75.00 200.00
8 Charles Barkley/49 125.00 300.00
9 JaVale McGee/49 12.00 30.00
10 Lonzo Ball/35 8.00 20.00
13 Cedi Osman/49 6.00 15.00
14 Walt Frazier/35 12.00 30.00
15 Kevin Durant/25 125.00 300.00
16 Stephen Curry/25 1,000.00 2,000.00
17 Pascal Siakam/49 40.00 100.00
18 Giannis Antetokounmpo/25 400.00 800.00
19 J.J. Barea/49 12.00 30.00
20 Tony Parker/35 30.00 80.00
21 Stephen Jackson/49 5.00 12.00
22 Allen Iverson/25 125.00 300.00
23 Mike Bibby/49 12.00 30.00
24 Danilo Gallinari/35 6.00 15.00
25 Caron Butler/49 6.00 15.00
27 Jason Terry/49 6.00 15.00
28 Karl-Anthony Towns/25 25.00 60.00
29 B.J. Armstrong/49 8.00 20.00
30 Dennis Rodman/35 75.00 200.00
31 Dan Majerle/49 6.00 15.00
32 George Gervin/35 15.00 40.00
33 Shawn Bradley/49 6.00 15.00
34 Chris Mullin/35 10.00 25.00
35 Cuttino Mobley/49 5.00 12.00
36 Rudy Gay/49 6.00 15.00
37 Kevin Johnson/49 8.00 20.00
38 Clyde Drexler/25 40.00 100.00
39 Al-Farouq Aminu/49 5.00 12.00
40 De'Aaron Fox/35 75.00 200.00
41 Tom Heinsohn/49 40.00 100.00
42 Bob Lanier/35 20.00 50.00
43 Jason Richardson/49 8.00 20.00
44 Nick Van Exel/35 12.00 30.00
45 Kevin Garnett/25 150.00 400.00
46 World B. Free/49 6.00 15.00
47 Peja Stojakovic/49 6.00 15.00
48 Paul Pierce/25 60.00 150.00
49 Shaquille O'Neal /25 150.00 400.00
50 Dominique Wilkins/35 40.00 100.00

2019-20 Panini National Treasures Game Gear

PRINT RUNS B/WN 49-99 COPIES PER
*PRIME/25: .75X TO 2X BASIC
1 Brook Lopez/99 2.50 6.00
2 Miles Bridges/99 3.00 8.00
3 DeMar DeRozan/99 4.00 10.00
4 Ricky Rubio/49 2.50 6.00
5 Harrison Barnes/49 2.50 6.00
6 Trae Young/99 15.00 40.00
7 Joel Embiid/99 6.00 15.00
8 Khris Middleton/99 3.00 8.00
9 Aaron Gordon/99 3.00 8.00
10 Luka Doncic/99 75.00 200.00
11 Chris Paul/49 8.00 20.00
12 Myles Turner/99 3.00 8.00
13 Domantas Sabonis/99 4.00 10.00
14 Rudy Gay/49 2.50 6.00
15 Jamal Murray/99 5.00 12.00
16 Wendell Carter Jr./99 3.00 8.00
17 Jordan Clarkson/99 3.00 8.00
18 Kyle Lowry/99 3.00 8.00
19 Andrew Wiggins/99 4.00 10.00
20 Marc Gasol/49 3.00 8.00
21 Collin Sexton/99 4.00 10.00
22 Paul George/49 8.00 20.00
23 Eric Bledsoe/99 2.50 6.00
24 Serge Ibaka/99 2.50 6.00
25 Jarrett Allen/99 3.00 8.00
26 Willie Cauley-Stein/49 2.00 5.00
27 Julius Randle/49 4.00 10.00
28 LeBron James/49 75.00 200.00
29 Ben Simmons/99 8.00 20.00
30 Markelle Fultz/49 2.50 6.00
31 De'Aaron Fox/99 5.00 12.00
32 Paul Millsap/99 2.50 6.00
33 Gary Harris/99 2.50 6.00
34 Steven Adams/99 2.50 6.00
35 Jeff Teague/99 2.00 5.00
36 Zach LaVine/99 5.00 12.00
37 Kemba Walker/49 2.50 6.00
38 Lou Williams/99 3.00 8.00
39 Bojan Bogdanovic/49 2.50 6.00
40 Michael Porter Jr./49 8.00 20.00

2019-20 Panini National Treasures Game Gear Autographs

PRINT RUNS B/WN 25-99 COPIES PER
EXCHANGE DEADLINE 12/12/2021
*PRIME/25: .6X TO 1.5X p/r 49-99
1 Karl-Anthony Towns/25 30.00 80.00
2 Stephen Curry/25 1,000.00 2,000.00
3 Trae Young/49 125.00 300.00
4 Lonzo Ball/49 25.00 60.00
5 Kristaps Porzingis/49 15.00 40.00
6 Lauri Markkanen/49 10.00 25.00
7 Anthony Davis/25 200.00 500.00
8 Aaron Holiday/99 5.00 12.00
9 Giannis Antetokounmpo/25 300.00 600.00
10 Zach LaVine/49 20.00 50.00
11 De'Aaron Fox/49 20.00 50.00
12 Myles Turner/99 6.00 15.00
13 Nikola Jokic/49 200.00 500.00
14 Collin Sexton/99 8.00 20.00
15 Jaren Jackson Jr./99 25.00 60.00
16 Gary Harris/99 5.00 12.00
17 Harrison Barnes/99 5.00 12.00
18 Dwight Howard/25 25.00 60.00
19 Montrezl Harrell/99 5.00 12.00
20 Jalen Brunson/99 15.00 40.00
22 Wendell Carter Jr./99 6.00 15.00
23 Josh Richardson/99 4.00 10.00
24 Harry Giles III/62 4.00 10.00
26 Nikola Vucevic/99 5.00 12.00
27 John Wall/25 12.00 30.00
28 Caris LeVert/99 5.00 12.00
29 Mike Conley/49 5.00 12.00
30 Bam Adebayo/99 20.00 50.00
31 Julius Randle/99 8.00 20.00
32 Willie Cauley-Stein/99 4.00 10.00
33 Tyson Chandler/99 5.00 12.00
34 Fred VanVleet/99 20.00 50.00
35 Pascal Siakam/99 40.00 100.00
36 Enes Kanter/99 6.00 15.00
39 D'Angelo Russell/49 12.00 30.00
40 Wesley Matthews/25 6.00 15.00
41 P.J. Tucker /99 5.00 12.00
42 Terrence Ross/99 6.00 15.00
43 Malcolm Brogdon/99 5.00 12.00
44 Rondae Hollis-Jefferson/49 4.00 10.00
45 Khris Middleton/49 15.00 40.00
46 LaMarcus Aldridge/49 6.00 15.00
47 Gordon Hayward/49 8.00 20.00
48 Deandre Ayton/49 40.00 100.00
49 Michael Porter Jr./37 15.00 40.00
50 Anfernee Simons/99 10.00 25.00

2019-20 Panini National Treasures Game Gear Autographs Prime

*PRIME/25: .6X TO 1.5X p/r 49-99

2019-20 Panini National Treasures Jersey Treasures

STATED PRINT RUN 49-99 SER.#'d SETS
*PRIME/25: .75X TO 2X BASIC
1 Bradley Beal/99 4.00 10.00
2 LaMarcus Aldridge/99 3.00 8.00
3 Donovan Mitchell/99 6.00 15.00
4 Bogdan Bogdanovic/99 3.00 8.00
5 Joel Embiid/99 6.00 15.00
6 John Collins/99 3.00 8.00
7 Luka Doncic/99 75.00 200.00
8 Russell Westbrook/49 5.00 12.00
9 Anthony Davis/49 40.00 100.00
10 Caris LeVert/99 2.50 6.00
11 Brook Lopez/99 2.50 6.00
12 Lonzo Ball/99 8.00 20.00
13 Draymond Green/99 4.00 10.00
14 Brandon Ingram/99 8.00 20.00
15 Jonas Valanciunas/99 2.50 6.00
16 Jordan Clarkson/99 3.00 8.00
17 Malcolm Brogdon/49 2.50 6.00
18 Shai Gilgeous-Alexander/49 12.00 30.00
19 Kyrie Irving/49 8.00 20.00
20 Collin Sexton/99 4.00 10.00
21 CJ McCollum/99 3.00 8.00
22 Marc Gasol/49 3.00 8.00
23 Eric Bledsoe/99 2.50 6.00
24 Clint Capela/99 2.50 6.00
25 Karl-Anthony Towns/99 8.00 20.00
26 Josh Richardson/49 2.00 5.00
27 Mike Conley/49 2.50 6.00
28 Steven Adams/99 2.50 6.00
29 Kawhi Leonard/49 20.00 50.00
30 Deandre Ayton/49 8.00 20.00
31 Chris Paul/49 8.00 20.00
32 Markelle Fultz/49 2.50 6.00
33 Giannis Antetokounmpo/99 30.00 80.00
34 Domantas Sabonis/99 8.00 20.00
35 Kemba Walker/49 2.50 6.00
36 Jrue Holiday/99 4.00 10.00
37 Miles Bridges/99 3.00 8.00
38 Terry Rozier/49 2.50 6.00
39 LeBron James/49 125.00 300.00
40 DeAndre Jordan/49 2.50 6.00
41 Damian Lillard/99 20.00 50.00
42 Marvin Bagley III/99 2.50 6.00
43 Goran Dragic/99 2.50 6.00
44 Eric Gordon/99 2.50 6.00
45 Kevin Love/99 3.00 8.00
46 Kyle Kuzma/99 8.00 20.00
47 Nikola Jokic/99 15.00 40.00
48 Trae Young/99 20.00 50.00
49 Aaron Gordon/99 3.00 8.00
50 Joe Harris/99 2.50 6.00
51 D'Angelo Russell/49 2.50 6.00
52 Michael Porter Jr./49 12.00 30.00
53 Jamal Murray/99 5.00 12.00
54 Gary Harris/99 2.50 6.00
55 Khris Middleton/99 6.00 15.00
56 Malik Monk/99 3.00 8.00
57 Nikola Vucevic/99 2.50 6.00
58 Victor Oladipo/99 2.50 6.00
59 Andre Drummond/99 2.50 6.00
60 Fred VanVleet/99 8.00 20.00
61 De'Aaron Fox/99 10.00 25.00
62 Montrezl Harrell/49 2.50 6.00
63 James Harden/99 6.00 15.00
64 Harrison Barnes/49 2.50 6.00
65 Kristaps Porzingis/49 8.00 20.00
66 Ricky Rubio/49 2.50 6.00
67 Pascal Siakam/99 10.00 25.00
68 Zach LaVine/99 8.00 20.00
69 Andrew Wiggins/99 4.00 10.00
70 Jarrett Allen/99 3.00 8.00
71 DeMar DeRozan/99 4.00 10.00
72 Myles Turner/99 3.00 8.00
73 Jaren Jackson Jr./99 8.00 20.00
74 Hassan Whiteside/99 2.00 5.00
75 Kyle Lowry/99 3.00 8.00
76 Rudy Gay/99 2.50 6.00
77 Paul George/49 8.00 20.00
78 Al Horford/49 3.00 8.00
79 Ben Simmons/99 10.00 25.00
80 Jeff Teague/99 2.00 5.00
81 Derrick Rose/49 6.00 15.00
82 Serge Ibaka/99 2.50 6.00
83 Jayson Tatum/99 20.00 50.00
84 Jabari Parker/99 2.00 5.00
85 Lauri Markkanen/99 4.00 10.00
86 Tobias Harris/49 2.50 6.00
87 Paul Millsap/99 2.50 6.00
88 Anfernee Simons/99 5.00 12.00
89 Blake Griffin/99 3.00 8.00
90 Julius Randle/99 4.00 10.00
91 Devin Booker/99 12.00 30.00
92 Wendell Carter Jr./99 3.00 8.00
93 Jimmy Butler/49 8.00 20.00
94 Jaylen Brown/99 8.00 20.00
95 Lou Williams/99 3.00 8.00
96 Willie Cauley-Stein/49 2.00 5.00
97 Rudy Gobert/99 4.00 10.00
98 Buddy Hield/99 2.50 6.00
99 Bojan Bogdanovic/49 2.50 6.00
100 Kevin Knox II/99 2.00 5.00

2019-20 Panini National Treasures Jersey Treasures Prime

*PRIME/25: .75X TO 2X BASIC
PRINT RUNS B/WN 10-25 COPIES PER
NO PRICING ON QTY 15 OR LESS
33 Giannis Antetokounmpo/25 75.00 200.00

2019-20 Panini National Treasures Lasting Legacies Jersey Autographs

PRINT RUNS B/WN 25-99 COPIES PER
EXCHANGE DEADLINE 12/12/2021
*PRIME/25: .5X TO 1.2X p/r 49-99
1 Wendell Carter Jr./99 6.00 15.00
2 Andrew Wiggins/25 10.00 25.00
3 Caris LeVert/99 5.00 12.00
5 Larry Hughes/99 12.00 30.00
6 D'Angelo Russell/49 15.00 40.00
7 Mike Conley/49 5.00 12.00
9 Christian Laettner/99 8.00 20.00
10 John Stockton/25 40.00 100.00
11 Nerlens Noel/99 4.00 10.00
12 Hakeem Olajuwon/25 40.00 100.00
13 Wesley Matthews/99 4.00 10.00
14 Dennis Rodman/49 60.00 150.00
15 Joe Smith/99 5.00 12.00
16 Kristaps Porzingis/49 8.00 20.00
17 Nikola Jokic/49 200.00 500.00
19 Jaren Jackson Jr./99 20.00 50.00
21 Willie Cauley-Stein/99 4.00 10.00
22 David Robinson/25 40.00 100.00
23 Al-Farouq Aminu/99 4.00 10.00
24 Markelle Fultz/49 12.00 30.00
25 Jack Sikma/99 6.00 15.00
26 De'Aaron Fox/49 50.00 120.00
28 Allen Iverson/25 125.00 300.00
29 Richard Hamilton/99 6.00 15.00
30 Kevin Garnett/25 125.00 300.00
31 Andre Miller/99 5.00 12.00
32 DeMarcus Cousins/25 6.00 15.00
33 Thaddeus Young/99 4.00 10.00
34 Vince Carter/49 75.00 200.00
35 Rashard Lewis/99 5.00 12.00
36 LaMarcus Aldridge/49 6.00 15.00
37 Khris Middleton/49 12.00 30.00
39 Julius Erving/25 20.00 50.00
40 John Wall/25 10.00 25.00
41 Enes Kanter/99 4.00 10.00
42 Jason Kidd/25 12.00 30.00
43 Terrence Ross/99 6.00 15.00
44 Lonzo Ball/49 20.00 50.00
45 Raja Bell/99 5.00 12.00
46 Lauri Markkanen/49 8.00 20.00
47 Zach LaVine/49 12.00 30.00
48 Damian Lillard/25 150.00 400.00
49 Julius Randle/99 8.00 20.00
50 Karl-Anthony Towns/25 12.00 30.00

2019-20 Panini National Treasures Material Treasures

STATED PRINT RUN 49-99 SER.#'d SETS
*PRIME/25: 1X TO 2.5X BASIC
1 Lauri Markkanen/99 4.00 10.00
2 D'Angelo Russell/49 2.50 6.00
3 Montrezl Harrell/49 2.50 6.00
4 Draymond Green/99 4.00 10.00
5 Russell Westbrook/49 8.00 20.00
6 Jabari Parker/99 2.00 5.00
7 Joe Harris/99 2.50 6.00
8 Andre Drummond/99 2.50 6.00
9 Kawhi Leonard/49 25.00 60.00
10 Brandon Ingram/99 8.00 20.00
11 Lonzo Ball/99 15.00 40.00
12 DeAndre Jordan/49 2.50 6.00
13 Nikola Vucevic/99 2.50 6.00
14 Fred VanVleet/99 15.00 40.00
15 Tobias Harris/49 2.50 6.00
16 Jaren Jackson Jr./99 12.00 30.00
17 Jonas Valanciunas/99 2.50 6.00
18 Anthony Davis/49 20.00 50.00
19 Kevin Love/99 3.00 8.00
20 Caris LeVert/99 2.50 6.00
21 Malik Monk/99 3.00 8.00
22 Devin Booker/99 12.00 30.00
23 Pascal Siakam/99 12.00 30.00
24 Goran Dragic/99 2.50 6.00
25 Victor Oladipo/99 2.50 6.00
26 Jayson Tatum/99 20.00 50.00
27 Jrue Holiday/99 4.00 10.00
28 Bogdan Bogdanovic/99 3.00 8.00
29 Kyle Kuzma/99 8.00 20.00
30 Clint Capela/99 2.50 6.00

2019-20 Panini National Treasures National Archives Ink Autographs

PRINT RUNS B/WN 25-49 COPIES PER
EXCHANGE DEADLINE 12/12/2021
1 Horace Grant/49 10.00 25.00
2 Charles Barkley/49 125.00 300.00
3 A.C. Green/49 6.00 15.00
4 Oscar Robertson/25 50.00 120.00
5 Eddie Jones/49 5.00 12.00
6 Chris Bosh/25 15.00 40.00
7 Dino Radja/49 4.00 10.00
8 George Gervin/49 10.00 25.00
9 Erick Dampier/49 4.00 10.00
10 Chauncey Billups/49 10.00 25.00
11 Juwan Howard/49 5.00 12.00
13 Tom Chambers/49 6.00 15.00
14 David Robinson/25 60.00 150.00
15 Mark Price/49 12.00 30.00
16 Tony Parker/35 15.00 40.00
17 Vlade Divac/49 6.00 15.00
18 Robert Parish/49 8.00 20.00
19 Jamal Mashburn/49 6.00 15.00
20 Mark Jackson/49 5.00 12.00
21 Carlos Boozer/49 5.00 12.00
22 Karl Malone/25 50.00 120.00
23 John Starks/49 8.00 20.00
24 Jerry West/25 50.00 120.00
25 Bob Dandridge/49 4.00 10.00
26 Richard Hamilton/35 20.00 50.00
27 Tyronn Lue/49 8.00 20.00
28 Danny Manning/49 5.00 12.00
29 Wally Szczerbiak/49 5.00 12.00
30 Jason Terry/49 5.00 12.00
31 Alvan Adams/49 4.00 10.00
32 Dwyane Wade/25 125.00 300.00
33 Cedric Maxwell/49 5.00 12.00
34 Grant Hill/25 30.00 80.00
35 Cherokee Parks/49 4.00 10.00
37 Maurice Cheeks/49 5.00 12.00
38 Latrell Sprewell/49 8.00 20.00
39 Jason Williams/49 100.00 250.00
40 Elvin Hayes/49 8.00 20.00
41 Kenny Sky Walker/49 5.00 12.00
42 Kevin Garnett/25 150.00 400.00
43 Lionel Hollins/49 4.00 10.00
44 Jason Kidd/25 30.00 80.00
46 Peja Stojakovic/49 12.00 30.00
47 Fat Lever/49 5.00 12.00
48 Avery Johnson/49 4.00 10.00
49 Don Chaney/49 12.00 30.00
50 Michael Cooper/49 6.00 15.00

2019-20 Panini National Treasures NBA Greats Signatures

PRINT RUNS B/WN 25-99 COPIES PER
EXCHANGE DEADLINE 12/12/2021
*BRNZ/25: .5X TO 1.2X p/r 49-99
1 Nate Thurmond/99 5.00 12.00
2 Jamaal Wilkes/99 6.00 15.00
3 Bill Walton/99 40.00 100.00
4 Robert Parish/99 8.00 20.00
5 Kevin Garnett/25 150.00 400.00
6 Michael Cooper/99 6.00 15.00
7 Dennis Rodman/49 50.00 120.00
8 A.C. Green/99 6.00 15.00
9 Chris Mullin/99 6.00 15.00
10 Adrian Dantley/99 6.00 15.00
11 Doc Rivers/99 6.00 15.00
12 Nate McMillan/99 5.00 12.00
13 Latrell Sprewell/99 8.00 20.00
14 Andre Miller/99 5.00 12.00
15 Hakeem Olajuwon/49 20.00 50.00
16 Chuck Person/99 5.00 12.00
17 Christian Laettner/99 8.00 20.00
18 Toni Kukoc/99 10.00 25.00
19 Kenny Smith/99 6.00 15.00
20 John Starks/99 6.00 15.00
21 Chauncey Billups/99 8.00 20.00
22 Tom Satch Sanders/99 6.00 15.00
23 Avery Johnson/99 4.00 10.00
24 Carlos Boozer/99 5.00 12.00
25 Chris Bosh/49 8.00 20.00
26 Greg Anthony/99 4.00 10.00
27 Artis Gilmore/99 8.00 20.00
28 Alvan Adams/99 4.00 10.00
29 Derek Fisher/99 8.00 20.00
30 Sam Cassell/99 5.00 12.00

2019-20 Panini National Treasures Peerless Signatures

PRINT RUNS B/WN 25-99 COPIES PER
EXCHANGE DEADLINE 12/12/2021
*BRNZ/25: .5X TO 1.2X p/r 49-99
1 Giannis Antetokounmpo/25 300.00 600.00
2 Horace Grant/99 10.00 25.00
3 Kevin Garnett/25 150.00 400.00
4 Sam Cassell/99 5.00 12.00
5 Dennis Rodman/49 50.00 120.00
6 John Starks/99 8.00 20.00
7 Sam Jones/49 30.00 80.00
8 Dave Cowens/99 10.00 25.00
9 Charles Barkley/49 100.00 250.00
10 George McGinnis/99 6.00 15.00
11 Allen Iverson/25 75.00 200.00
12 Juwan Howard/99 5.00 12.00
13 Kareem Abdul-Jabbar/25 75.00 200.00
14 Alvan Adams/99 4.00 10.00
15 Elgin Baylor/49 25.00 60.00
16 Tom Heinsohn/99 15.00 40.00
17 Walt Frazier/99 15.00 40.00
18 Lenny Wilkens/99 8.00 20.00
20 B.J. Armstrong/99 8.00 20.00
21 Kyrie Irving/25 30.00 80.00
22 Stephen Jackson/99 8.00 20.00
23 Magic Johnson/25 60.00 150.00
24 Kenny Sky Walker/99 5.00 12.00
25 Dominique Wilkins/49 25.00 60.00
26 Bob McAdoo/99 8.00 20.00
27 Artis Gilmore/49 8.00 20.00
28 Ralph Sampson/99 5.00 12.00
29 Stephen Curry/25 1,000.00 2,000.00
30 Allan Houston/99 5.00 12.00
31 Anthony Davis/25 150.00 400.00
32 Dan Majerle/99 8.00 20.00
33 Clyde Drexler/25 30.00 80.00
34 A.C. Green/49 6.00 15.00
35 James Worthy/49 20.00 50.00
36 Alex English/99 8.00 20.00
37 Chris Mullin/49 12.00 30.00
38 Bill Walton/99 40.00 100.00
39 Shaquille O'Neal /25 75.00 200.00
40 Luke Walton/99 5.00 12.00
41 John Stockton/25 40.00 100.00
42 Toni Kukoc/99 12.00 30.00
43 Kevin McHale/49 12.00 30.00
44 Tom Chambers/99 6.00 15.00
45 Bob Lanier/49 8.00 20.00
46 Cedric Maxwell/99 5.00 12.00
47 Bernard King/49 10.00 25.00
48 Louie Dampier/99 8.00 20.00
49 Kevin Durant/25 125.00 300.00
50 Michael Cooper/99 6.00 15.00

2019-20 Panini National Treasures Penmanship Autographs

PRINT RUNS B/WN 25-99 COPIES PER
EXCHANGE DEADLINE 12/12/2021
*BRNZ/25: .5X TO 1.2X p/r 49-99
2 Ersan Ilyasova/99 4.00 10.00
3 Tyson Chandler/99 5.00 12.00
4 Wendell Carter Jr./99 6.00 15.00
5 John Wall/25 12.00 30.00
6 Malcolm Brogdon/99 5.00 12.00
7 Lonzo Ball/49 20.00 50.00
8 Aaron Holiday/99 5.00 12.00
9 CJ McCollum/49 6.00 15.00
10 Avery Bradley/99 4.00 10.00
11 Khris Middleton/49 12.00 30.00
12 Udonis Haslem/99 4.00 10.00
13 Justin Holiday/99 4.00 10.00
14 Devin Harris/99 4.00 10.00
15 Andrew Wiggins/49 8.00 20.00
16 Otto Porter Jr./99 4.00 10.00
17 Vince Carter/49 75.00 200.00
19 Trae Young/49 100.00 250.00
20 Montrezl Harrell/99 5.00 12.00
21 Zach LaVine/49 12.00 30.00
22 Lou Williams/99 6.00 15.00
23 Rodney Hood/99 5.00 12.00
24 Willie Cauley-Stein/99 4.00 10.00
25 Stephon Marbury/49 15.00 40.00
26 Zhaire Smith/99 4.00 10.00
27 Larry Johnson/49 15.00 40.00
28 Danny Green/99 5.00 12.00
29 Lauri Markkanen/49 8.00 20.00
30 Thaddeus Young/99 4.00 10.00
31 Jaren Jackson Jr./99 20.00 50.00
32 Tim Hardaway Jr./99 4.00 10.00
33 Julius Randle/99 8.00 20.00
34 Pascal Siakam/99 25.00 60.00
35 Markelle Fultz/49 12.00 30.00
36 Goran Dragic/99 5.00 12.00
37 Kristaps Porzingis/49 30.00 80.00
38 Enes Kanter/99 4.00 10.00
39 Deandre Ayton/49 30.00 80.00
40 Luke Kennard/99 5.00 12.00

2019-20 Panini National Treasures Penmanship Autographs Bronze

*BRNZ/25: .5X TO 1.2X p/r 49-99
PRINT RUNS B/WN 15-25 COPIES PER
NO PRICING ON QTY 15 OR LESS
EXCHANGE DEADLINE 12/12/2021
1 Marvin Bagley III/25 6.00 15.00

2019-20 Panini National Treasures Retro Materials

STATED PRINT RUN 70-99 SER.#'d SETS
*PRIME/25: .75X TO 2X BASIC
1 Jack Sikma/99 3.00 8.00
2 Isiah Thomas/99 6.00 15.00
3 Moses Malone/99 8.00 20.00
4 Danny Manning/99 2.50 6.00
5 Jason Richardson/99 3.00 8.00
6 Vlade Divac/99 3.00 8.00
7 Mike Bibby/99 3.00 8.00
8 Steve Nash/99 6.00 15.00
9 Michael Redd/99 2.50 6.00
10 Mitch Richmond/99 8.00 20.00
11 Ricky Pierce/99 2.50 6.00
12 Patrick Ewing/99 5.00 12.00
13 Tracy McGrady/99 6.00 15.00
14 Adrian Dantley/99 3.00 8.00
15 Tony Parker/99 6.00 15.00
16 Ray Allen/99 8.00 20.00
17 Manute Bol/99 20.00 50.00
18 John Stockton/99 6.00 15.00
19 Kevin Johnson/99 3.00 8.00
20 Spud Webb/99 3.00 8.00
21 Charles Barkley/70 12.00 30.00
22 Ralph Sampson/99 2.50 6.00
23 Mark Jackson/99 2.50 6.00
24 Richard Hamilton/99 3.00 8.00
25 Elton Brand/99 2.50 6.00
27 Robert Horry/99 2.50 6.00
28 Anfernee Hardaway/99 12.00 30.00
29 Amar'e Stoudemire/99 2.50 6.00
30 Robert Parish/99 4.00 10.00

2019-20 Panini National Treasures Retro Materials Prime

*PRIME/25: .75X TO 2X BASIC
PRINT RUNS B/WN 10-25 COPIES PER
NO PRICING ON QTY 15 OR LESS
1 Jack Sikma/25 15.00 40.00
2 Isiah Thomas/25 25.00 60.00
3 Moses Malone/25 40.00 100.00
5 Jason Richardson/25 12.00 30.00
6 Vlade Divac/25 15.00 40.00
7 Mike Bibby/25 20.00 50.00
8 Steve Nash/25 25.00 60.00
9 Michael Redd/25 20.00 50.00
10 Mitch Richmond/25 20.00 50.00
12 Patrick Ewing/25 30.00 80.00
14 Adrian Dantley/25 12.00 30.00
16 Ray Allen/25 25.00 60.00
17 Manute Bol/25 50.00 120.00
18 John Stockton/25 25.00 60.00
19 Kevin Johnson/25 25.00 60.00
20 Spud Webb/25 8.00 20.00
24 Richard Hamilton/25 20.00 50.00
25 Elton Brand/25 12.00 30.00
27 Robert Horry/25 15.00 40.00
29 Amar'e Stoudemire/25 15.00 40.00
30 Robert Parish/25 15.00 40.00

2019-20 Panini National Treasures Rookie Dual Materials

STATED PRINT RUN 99 SER.#'d SETS
*PRIME: .75X TO 2 BASIC
1 Jordan Poole 8.00 20.00
2 Bol Bol 20.00 50.00
3 Kevin Porter Jr. 4.00 10.00
4 Grant Williams 3.00 8.00
5 Tyler Herro 40.00 100.00
6 Matisse Thybulle 10.00 25.00
7 Rui Hachimura 25.00 60.00
8 PJ Washington Jr. 8.00 20.00
9 Nickeil Alexander-Walker 8.00 20.00
10 De'Andre Hunter 8.00 20.00
11 Zion Williamson 300.00 600.00
12 Eric Paschall 12.00 30.00
13 Nassir Little 3.00 8.00
14 Jaxson Hayes 8.00 20.00
15 Cameron Johnson 12.00 30.00
16 Romeo Langford 2.00 5.00
17 Coby White 30.00 80.00
18 Cam Reddish 3.00 8.00
19 Sekou Doumbouya 2.00 5.00
20 Ja Morant 150.00 400.00
21 Carsen Edwards 2.50 6.00
22 RJ Barrett 25.00 60.00
23 Darius Bazley 2.00 5.00
24 Jarrett Culver 2.00 5.00
25 Brandon Clarke 15.00 40.00

2019-20 Panini National Treasures Rookie Dual Materials Prime

*PRIME/25: .75X TO 2X BASIC
STATED PRINT RUN 25 SER.#'d SETS
2 Bol Bol 75.00 200.00
3 Kevin Porter Jr. 8.00 20.00
5 Tyler Herro 125.00 300.00
6 Matisse Thybulle 40.00 100.00
7 Rui Hachimura 100.00 250.00
10 De'Andre Hunter 25.00 60.00
11 Zion Williamson 500.00 1,000.00
13 Nassir Little 12.00 30.00
14 Jaxson Hayes 25.00 60.00
17 Coby White 125.00 300.00
19 Sekou Doumbouya 4.00 10.00
20 Ja Morant 350.00 700.00
22 RJ Barrett 100.00 250.00
25 Brandon Clarke 40.00 100.00

2019-20 Panini National Treasures Rookie Jumbo Materials

STATED PRINT RUN 99 SER.#'d SETS
*PRIME: .75X TO 2X BASIC
1 De'Andre Hunter 8.00 20.00
2 Zion Williamson 300.00 600.00
3 Eric Paschall 12.00 30.00
4 Nassir Little 3.00 8.00
5 Jaxson Hayes 8.00 20.00
6 Cameron Johnson 12.00 30.00
7 Romeo Langford 2.00 5.00
8 Coby White 30.00 80.00
9 PJ Washington Jr. 8.00 20.00
10 Sekou Doumbouya 2.00 5.00
11 Ja Morant 150.00 400.00
12 Carsen Edwards 2.50 6.00
13 RJ Barrett 25.00 60.00
14 Darius Bazley 2.00 5.00
15 Jarrett Culver 12.00 30.00
16 Brandon Clarke 15.00 40.00
17 Rui Hachimura 25.00 60.00
18 Nickeil Alexander-Walker 8.00 20.00
19 Cam Reddish 3.00 8.00
20 Jordan Poole 8.00 20.00
21 Bol Bol 20.00 50.00
22 Kevin Porter Jr. 4.00 10.00
23 Grant Williams 3.00 8.00
24 Tyler Herro 25.00 60.00
25 Matisse Thybulle 10.00 25.00

2019-20 Panini National Treasures Rookie Jumbo Materials Prime

*PRIME/25: .75X TO 2X BASIC
STATED PRINT RUN 25 SER.#'d SETS
1 De'Andre Hunter 25.00 60.00
2 Zion Williamson 1,000.00 2,000.00
4 Nassir Little 12.00 30.00
5 Jaxson Hayes 25.00 60.00
8 Coby White 125.00 300.00
10 Sekou Doumbouya 4.00 10.00
11 Ja Morant 400.00 800.00
12 Carsen Edwards 5.00 12.00
13 RJ Barrett 100.00 250.00
16 Brandon Clarke 60.00 150.00
17 Rui Hachimura 100.00 250.00
18 Nickeil Alexander-Walker 15.00 40.00
21 Bol Bol 75.00 200.00
22 Kevin Porter Jr. 8.00 20.00
23 Grant Williams 6.00 15.00
24 Tyler Herro 100.00 250.00
25 Matisse Thybulle 40.00 100.00

2019-20 Panini National Treasures Rookie Materials

STATED PRINT RUN 99 SER.#'d SETS
*PRIME: .75X TO 2 BASIC
1 PJ Washington Jr. 6.00 15.00
2 Cam Reddish 3.00 8.00
3 De'Andre Hunter 3.00 8.00
4 Ja Morant 150.00 400.00
5 Bol Bol 15.00 40.00
6 Eric Paschall 2.50 6.00
7 RJ Barrett 20.00 50.00
8 Grant Williams 3.00 8.00
9 Jaxson Hayes 3.00 8.00
10 Jarrett Culver 2.00 5.00
11 Matisse Thybulle 10.00 25.00
12 Romeo Langford 2.00 5.00

13 Rui Hachimura 15.00 40.00
14 Coby White 25.00 60.00
15 Nickeil Alexander-Walker 3.00 8.00
16 Sekou Doumbouya 2.00 5.00
17 Jordan Poole 8.00 20.00
18 Zion Williamson 300.00 600.00
19 Carsen Edwards 2.50 6.00
20 Kevin Porter Jr. 4.00 10.00
21 Nassir Little 3.00 8.00
23 Tyler Herro 25.00 60.00
24 Cameron Johnson 5.00 12.00
25 Brandon Clarke 15.00 40.00

2019-20 Panini National Treasures Rookie Materials Prime

*PRIME/25: .75X TO 2X BASIC
STATED PRINT RUN 25 SER.#'d SETS
2 Cam Reddish 6.00 15.00
3 De'Andre Hunter 12.00 30.00
4 Ja Morant 400.00 800.00
5 Bol Bol 60.00 150.00
7 RJ Barrett 75.00 200.00
9 Jaxson Hayes 12.00 30.00
13 Rui Hachimura 75.00 200.00
14 Coby White 75.00 200.00
16 Sekou Doumbouya 4.00 10.00
18 Zion Williamson 1,000.00 2,000.00
20 Kevin Porter Jr. 8.00 20.00
23 Tyler Herro 75.00 200.00
24 Cameron Johnson 20.00 50.00
25 Brandon Clarke 40.00 100.00

2019-20 Panini National Treasures Rookie Patch Autographs Horizontal

STATED PRINT RUN 75 SER.#'d SETS
EXCHANGE DEADLINE 12/12/2021
*BRNZE/25: .6X TO 1.5X BASIC
101 KZ Okpala 100.00 250.00
102 Cam Reddish 25.00 60.00
103 Eric Paschall 60.00 150.00
105 Isaiah Roby 40.00 100.00
107 Darius Bazley 15.00 40.00
108 Zion Williamson 15,000.00 20,000.00
109 Mfiondu Kabengele 40.00 100.00
110 Jarrett Culver 100.00 250.00
111 Carsen Edwards 40.00 100.00
112 Cameron Johnson 150.00 400.00
113 Admiral Schofield 75.00 200.00
114 Chuma Okeke 300.00 600.00
115 Ignas Brazdeikis 40.00 100.00
116 Matisse Thybulle 150.00 400.00
117 Ty Jerome 60.00 150.00
118 Ja Morant 5,000.00 8,000.00
119 Jordan Poole 1,250.00 2,500.00
120 Coby White 1,000.00 2,000.00
121 Bruno Fernando 40.00 100.00
122 PJ Washington Jr. 100.00 250.00
123 Jaylen Nowell 40.00 100.00
124 Nickeil Alexander-Walker 150.00 400.00
125 Quinndary Weatherspoon 40.00 100.00
126 Brandon Clarke 400.00 800.00
127 Nassir Little 125.00 300.00
128 RJ Barrett 800.00 1,500.00
129 Keldon Johnson 200.00 500.00
130 Jaxson Hayes 150.00 400.00
131 Cody Martin 75.00 200.00
132 Tyler Herro 1,500.00 3,000.00
133 Bol Bol 800.00 1,500.00
134 Goga Bitadze 60.00 150.00
135 Nicolo Melli 40.00 100.00
136 Grant Williams 75.00 200.00
137 Dylan Windler 75.00 200.00
138 De'Andre Hunter 200.00 500.00
139 Kevin Porter Jr. 30.00 80.00
140 Rui Hachimura 800.00 1,500.00
141 Romeo Langford 15.00 40.00
142 Kyle Guy 75.00 200.00
143 Nicolas Claxton 75.00 200.00
144 Tacko Fall 200.00 500.00
145 Daniel Gafford 60.00 150.00
146 Alen Smailagic 75.00 200.00
147 Terence Davis 400.00 800.00
148 Justin Robinson 40.00 100.00
149 Terance Mann 300.00 600.00
150 Kendrick Nunn 25.00 60.00

2019-20 Panini National Treasures Rookie Triple Materials

STATED PRINT RUN 99 SER.#'d SETS
*PRIME: .75X TO 2 BASIC
1 Rui Hachimura 25.00 60.00
2 PJ Washington Jr. 8.00 20.00
3 Sekou Doumbouya 2.00 5.00
4 Ja Morant 150.00 400.00
5 Carsen Edwards 2.50 6.00
6 RJ Barrett 25.00 60.00
7 Darius Bazley 2.00 5.00
8 Jaxson Hayes 8.00 20.00
9 Cameron Johnson 12.00 30.00
10 Matisse Thybulle 10.00 25.00
11 Coby White 30.00 80.00
12 Cam Reddish 3.00 8.00
13 Jordan Poole 8.00 20.00
14 Bol Bol 20.00 50.00
15 Kevin Porter Jr. 4.00 10.00
16 Grant Williams 3.00 8.00
17 Tyler Herro 25.00 60.00
18 Jarrett Culver 2.00 5.00
19 Brandon Clarke 15.00 40.00
20 Romeo Langford 2.00 5.00
21 Nickeil Alexander-Walker 8.00 20.00
22 De'Andre Hunter 8.00 20.00
23 Zion Williamson 300.00 600.00
24 Eric Paschall 2.50 6.00
25 Nassir Little 3.00 8.00

2019-20 Panini National Treasures Rookie Triple Materials Prime

*PRIME/25: .75X TO 2X BASIC
STATED PRINT RUN 25 SER.#'d SETS
1 Rui Hachimura 100.00 250.00
4 Ja Morant 400.00 800.00
6 RJ Barrett 100.00 250.00
8 Jaxson Hayes 25.00 60.00
10 Matisse Thybulle 40.00 100.00
11 Coby White 125.00 300.00
14 Bol Bol 75.00 200.00
15 Kevin Porter Jr. 8.00 20.00
17 Tyler Herro 100.00 250.00
19 Brandon Clarke 40.00 100.00
22 De'Andre Hunter 25.00 60.00
23 Zion Williamson 1,000.00 2,000.00
25 Nassir Little 12.00 30.00

2019-20 Panini National Treasures Signatures

PRINT RUNS B/WN 25-99 COPIES PER
EXCHANGE DEADLINE 12/12/2021
*BRNZ/25: .5X TO 1.2X p/r 49-99
1 Richard Hamilton/49 8.00 20.00
2 Cody Zeller/99 4.00 10.00
3 Peja Stojakovic/99 8.00 20.00
5 Charles Barkley/49 125.00 300.00
6 Malcolm Brogdon/99 5.00 12.00
7 Giannis Antetokounmpo/25 400.00 800.00
8 Danny Manning/99 5.00 12.00
9 Paul Pierce/25 75.00 200.00
10 Mark Jackson/99 5.00 12.00
12 JaVale McGee/99 5.00 12.00
13 Gary Harris/99 5.00 12.00
14 Collin Sexton/99 10.00 25.00
16 World B. Free/99 5.00 12.00
17 Kyrie Irving/25 40.00 100.00
18 Latrell Sprewell/99 8.00 20.00
19 Grant Hill/25 25.00 60.00
20 George Gervin/99 12.00 30.00
21 Julius Randle/49 8.00 20.00
22 J.J. Barea/99 8.00 20.00
23 Rudy Gay/99 8.00 20.00
24 Myles Turner/99 6.00 15.00
25 Stephen Curry/25 1,000.00 2,000.00
26 Kevin Johnson/99 12.00 30.00
27 Anthony Davis/25 150.00 400.00
28 Avery Johnson/99 4.00 10.00
29 Jason Kidd/25 25.00 60.00
31 Nick Van Exel/49 12.00 30.00
32 Al-Farouq Aminu/99 4.00 10.00
33 Pascal Siakam/99 20.00 50.00
35 Kevin Durant/25 125.00 300.00
36 Jalen Rose/99 8.00 20.00
37 Kevin Garnett/25 150.00 400.00
38 Chauncey Billups/99 8.00 20.00
39 Christian Laettner/49 8.00 20.00
40 Danny Green/99 5.00 12.00

2019-20 Panini National Treasures Timeless Talents Signatures

PRINT RUNS B/WN 25-99 COPIES PER
EXCHANGE DEADLINE 12/12/2021
*BRNZ/25: .5X TO 1.2X p/r 49-99
1 Jerry West/49 25.00 60.00
2 Jerry Stackhouse/99 10.00 25.00
3 Richard Hamilton/99 8.00 20.00
4 Tom Chambers/99 6.00 15.00
5 Peja Stojakovic/99 8.00 20.00
6 Bill Cartwright/99 5.00 12.00
7 Dave Cowens/99 8.00 20.00
8 George Gervin/99 12.00 30.00
10 Horace Grant/99 8.00 20.00
11 James Worthy/49 15.00 40.00
12 Stephen Jackson/99 4.00 10.00
13 Bernard King/99 8.00 20.00
14 Kenny Sky Walker/99 5.00 12.00
15 Jason Terry/99 5.00 12.00
16 Mark Aguirre/99 5.00 12.00
17 Jalen Rose/99 8.00 20.00
18 Nate Archibald/99 6.00 15.00
20 B.J. Armstrong/99 8.00 20.00
21 Jerry Lucas/99 8.00 20.00
22 Alex English/99 8.00 20.00
23 Nick Van Exel/99 10.00 25.00
25 Ralph Sampson/99 5.00 12.00
26 Kurt Rambis/99 10.00 25.00
27 Louie Dampier/99 6.00 15.00
28 Dikembe Mutombo/99 12.00 30.00
29 Jason Kidd/49 20.00 50.00
30 Elvin Hayes/99 8.00 20.00

2019-20 Panini National Treasures Timeless Treasures Materials

STATED PRINT RUN 75-99 SER.#'d SETS
*PRIME/25: .75X TO 2X BASIC
1 Danny Manning/99 2.50 6.00
2 Ralph Sampson/99 2.50 6.00
3 Mike Bibby/99 3.00 8.00
4 Elton Brand/99 2.50 6.00
5 Mitch Richmond/99 3.00 8.00
6 Anfernee Hardaway/99 12.00 30.00
7 Tracy McGrady/99 6.00 15.00
8 Ray Allen/99 5.00 12.00
9 Jack Sikma/99 3.00 8.00
10 Kevin Johnson/99 3.00 8.00
11 Jason Richardson/99 3.00 8.00
12 Mark Jackson/75 2.50 6.00
13 Steve Nash/99 8.00 20.00
14 Larry Bird/99 12.00 30.00
15 Ricky Pierce/99 2.50 6.00
16 Amar'e Stoudemire/99 2.50 6.00
17 Adrian Dantley/99 3.00 8.00
18 Manute Bol/99 20.00 50.00
19 Isiah Thomas/99 8.00 20.00
20 Spud Webb/99 3.00 8.00
21 Vlade Divac/99 3.00 8.00
22 Richard Hamilton/99 3.00 8.00
23 Michael Redd/99 2.50 6.00
24 Robert Horry/99 2.50 6.00
25 Patrick Ewing/99 6.00 15.00
26 Robert Parish/99 4.00 10.00
27 Tony Parker/99 4.00 10.00
28 John Stockton/99 8.00 20.00
29 Moses Malone/99 5.00 12.00
30 Charles Barkley/99 12.00 30.00

2019-20 Panini National Treasures Timeless Treasures Materials Prime

*PRIME/25: .75X TO 2X BASIC
PRINT RUN 25 COPIES PER
3 Mike Bibby 20.00 50.00
5 Mitch Richmond 20.00 50.00
6 Anfernee Hardaway 40.00 100.00
7 Tracy McGrady 40.00 100.00
8 Ray Allen 25.00 60.00
9 Jack Sikma 15.00 40.00
10 Kevin Johnson 20.00 50.00
11 Jason Richardson 12.00 30.00
12 Mark Jackson 8.00 20.00
13 Steve Nash 25.00 60.00
16 Amar'e Stoudemire 15.00 40.00
17 Adrian Dantley 12.00 30.00
18 Manute Bol 50.00 120.00
19 Isiah Thomas 25.00 60.00
20 Spud Webb 8.00 20.00
21 Vlade Divac 15.00 40.00
22 Richard Hamilton 15.00 40.00
23 Michael Redd 15.00 40.00
24 Robert Horry 15.00 40.00
25 Patrick Ewing 30.00 80.00
26 Robert Parish 15.00 40.00
27 Tony Parker 15.00 40.00
28 John Stockton 25.00 60.00
29 Moses Malone 40.00 100.00

2019-20 Panini National Treasures Treasured Signatures

PRINT RUNS B/WN 25-99 COPIES PER
EXCHANGE DEADLINE 12/12/2021
*BRNZ/25: .5X TO 1.2X p/r 49-99
1 Jalen Rose/99 8.00 20.00
2 Paul Pierce/25 60.00 150.00
3 Avery Johnson/99 4.00 10.00
4 Christian Laettner/49 8.00 20.00
5 Elvin Hayes/99 8.00 20.00
6 Nick Van Exel/49 10.00 25.00
7 George Gervin/99 12.00 30.00
8 Karl Malone/25 50.00 120.00
9 World B. Free/99 5.00 12.00
10 David Robinson/25 60.00 150.00
11 Danny Manning/99 5.00 12.00
12 Grant Hill/25 25.00 60.00
13 Chauncey Billups/99 8.00 20.00
14 Richard Hamilton/49 8.00 20.00
15 B.J. Armstrong/99 8.00 20.00
16 Peja Stojakovic/99 8.00 20.00
17 Robert Parish/99 8.00 20.00
18 Oscar Robertson/25 60.00 150.00
19 Kevin Johnson/99 15.00 40.00
20 Jerry West/25 40.00 100.00
21 Latrell Sprewell/99 8.00 20.00
22 Jason Kidd/25 20.00 50.00
23 Mark Jackson/99 5.00 12.00
25 Allan Houston/99 5.00 12.00

2019-20 Panini National Treasures Treasured Threads

STATED PRINT RUN 49-99 SER.#'d SETS
*PRIME/25: 1X TO 2.5X BASIC
1 Al Horford/49 3.00 8.00
2 Karl-Anthony Towns/99 5.00 12.00
3 Bradley Beal/99 4.00 10.00
4 Kyrie Irving/49 6.00 15.00
5 Damian Lillard/99 15.00 40.00
6 Marvin Bagley III/99 2.50 6.00
7 Donovan Mitchell/99 6.00 15.00
8 Rudy Gobert/99 4.00 10.00
9 Hassan Whiteside/99 2.00 5.00
10 Jimmy Butler/45 6.00 15.00
11 Anfernee Simons/99 5.00 12.00
12 Kevin Knox II/99 2.00 5.00
13 Buddy Hield/99 2.50 6.00
14 LaMarcus Aldridge/99 2.50 6.00
15 Deandre Ayton/49 3.00 8.00
16 Mike Conley/49 2.50 6.00
17 Eric Gordon/99 2.50 6.00
18 Shai Gilgeous-Alexander/49 10.00 25.00
19 James Harden/99 6.00 15.00
20 John Collins/99 3.00 8.00
21 Blake Griffin/99 3.00 8.00
22 Kristaps Porzingis/49 4.00 10.00
23 CJ McCollum/99 3.00 8.00
24 Malcolm Brogdon/49 2.50 6.00
25 Derrick Rose/49 6.00 15.00
26 Nikola Jokic/99 15.00 40.00
27 Giannis Antetokounmpo/99 25.00 60.00
28 Terry Rozier/49 2.50 6.00
29 Jaylen Brown/99 5.00 12.00
30 Josh Richardson/49 2.00 5.00

2019-20 Panini National Treasures Treasures of the Hall Autographs

PRINT RUNS B/WN 25-99 COPIES PER
EXCHANGE DEADLINE 12/12/2021
*BRNZ/25: .5X TO 1.2X p/r 49-99
1 Ralph Sampson/99 5.00 12.00
2 Magic Johnson/25 50.00 120.00
3 George McGinnis/99 6.00 15.00
4 Kevin McHale/49 12.00 30.00
5 Alex English/99 8.00 20.00
6 Sam Jones/49 8.00 20.00
7 Bernard King/49 8.00 20.00
8 Karl Malone/25 50.00 120.00
9 Robert Parish/99 8.00 20.00
10 Kareem Abdul-Jabbar/25 60.00 150.00
11 Bill Walton/99 40.00 100.00
12 David Robinson/25 50.00 120.00
13 Elvin Hayes/99 8.00 20.00
14 Elgin Baylor/49 20.00 50.00
15 Adrian Dantley/99 6.00 15.00
16 Artis Gilmore/49 8.00 20.00
17 George Gervin/99 12.00 30.00
18 John Stockton/25 30.00 80.00
19 Lenny Wilkens/99 8.00 20.00
20 Oscar Robertson/25 50.00 120.00
21 Louie Dampier/99 6.00 15.00
22 Jerry West/25 30.00 80.00
23 Bob McAdoo/99 8.00 20.00
24 James Worthy/49 12.00 30.00
25 Arvydas Sabonis/99 6.00 15.00

2019-20 Panini National Treasures Tremendous Treasures Relics

STATED PRINT RUN 49-99 SER.#'d SETS
*PRIME/25: 1X TO 2.5X BASIC
1 Kyrie Irving/49 8.00 20.00
2 Damian Lillard/99 10.00 25.00
3 Marvin Bagley III/99 2.50 6.00
4 Donovan Mitchell/99 6.00 15.00
5 Shai Gilgeous-Alexander/49 8.00 20.00
6 Hassan Whiteside/99 2.00 5.00
7 Jimmy Butler/49 8.00 20.00
8 Al Horford/49 3.00 8.00
9 Karl-Anthony Towns/99 5.00 12.00
10 Bradley Beal/99 4.00 10.00
11 Lauri Markkanen/99 4.00 10.00
12 D'Angelo Russell/49 2.50 6.00
13 Nikola Vucevic/99 2.50 6.00
14 Draymond Green/99 4.00 10.00
15 Tobias Harris/49 2.50 6.00
16 Jabari Parker/99 2.00 5.00
17 Joe Harris/99 2.50 6.00
18 Andre Drummond/99 2.50 6.00
19 Kawhi Leonard/49 15.00 40.00
20 Brandon Ingram/99 6.00 15.00
21 Marc Gasol/49 3.00 8.00
22 De'Aaron Fox/99 8.00 20.00
23 Paul George/49 10.00 25.00
24 Eric Bledsoe/99 2.50 6.00
25 Wendell Carter Jr./99 3.00 8.00
26 Jamal Murray/99 5.00 12.00
27 Joel Embiid/99 6.00 15.00
28 Andrew Wiggins/99 4.00 10.00
29 Kemba Walker/49 6.00 15.00
30 Brook Lopez/99 2.50 6.00

2019-20 Panini National Treasures Validating Marks Autographs

PRINT RUNS B/WN 25-49 COPIES PER
EXCHANGE DEADLINE 12/12/2021
*BRNZ/25: .5X TO 1.2X p/r 49
1 Kristaps Porzingis/49 20.00 50.00
2 Lauri Markkanen/49 8.00 20.00
3 Stephen Curry/25 1,000.00 2,000.00
4 Gordon Hayward/49 20.00 50.00
5 Kyrie Irving/25 40.00 100.00
6 Harrison Barnes/49 5.00 12.00
7 Karl-Anthony Towns/25 20.00 50.00
8 Danilo Gallinari/49 5.00 12.00
9 Lonzo Ball/49 20.00 50.00
10 Wendell Carter Jr./49 6.00 15.00
11 De'Aaron Fox/49 30.00 80.00
13 Kevin Durant/25 150.00 400.00
14 Zach LaVine/49 20.00 50.00
15 Damian Lillard/25 125.00 300.00
16 Jaren Jackson Jr./49 25.00 60.00
17 Al Horford/25 12.00 30.00
18 Tyson Chandler/49 5.00 12.00
19 Vince Carter/49 60.00 150.00
20 Nikola Vucevic/49 5.00 12.00
21 Collin Sexton/49 12.00 30.00
22 Nikola Jokic/49 200.00 500.00
23 Giannis Antetokounmpo/25 400.00 800.00
24 Goran Dragic/49 5.00 12.00
25 Anthony Davis/25 150.00 400.00

2020-21 Panini National Treasures

COMMON CARD (1-100) 1.25 3.00
SEMISTARS 1.50 4.00
UNLISTED STARS 2.00 5.00
COMMON JSY AU RC (101-150) 30.00 80.00
JSY AU RC SEMIS 40.00 100.00
JSY AU RC UNLISTED 50.00 120.00
STATED PRINT RUN 99 SER.#'d SETS
EXCHANGE DEADLINE 2/11/2023
*BRNZ: .6X TO 1.5X BASIC
1 Zach LaVine 3.00 8.00
2 Nikola Jokic 10.00 25.00
3 John Collins 2.00 5.00
4 Andre Drummond 2.00 5.00
5 Giannis Antetokounmpo 10.00 25.00
6 D'Angelo Russell 2.00 5.00
7 Blake Griffin 2.00 5.00
8 Rudy Gobert 2.50 6.00
9 Kristaps Porzingis 2.50 6.00
10 Lauri Markkanen 2.50 6.00
11 Aaron Gordon 2.00 5.00
12 Jayson Tatum 8.00 20.00
13 Keldon Johnson 3.00 8.00
14 Myles Turner 2.00 5.00
15 Dejounte Murray 2.00 5.00
16 Kemba Walker 2.00 5.00
17 Mike Conley 1.50 4.00
18 Brandon Clarke 2.00 5.00
19 Paul George 3.00 8.00
20 Al Horford 2.00 5.00
21 Michael Porter Jr. 2.50 6.00
22 De'Aaron Fox 3.00 8.00
23 Chris Paul 4.00 10.00
24 RJ Barrett 3.00 8.00
25 Lou Williams 2.00 5.00
26 LeBron James 15.00 40.00
27 Darius Bazley 1.25 3.00
28 Fred VanVleet 3.00 8.00
29 Kyrie Irving 4.00 10.00
30 Zion Williamson 6.00 15.00
31 Josh Jackson 1.25 3.00
32 Kyle Lowry 2.50 6.00
33 Kawhi Leonard 5.00 12.00
34 Karl-Anthony Towns 5.00 12.00
35 Russell Westbrook 4.00 10.00
36 Jrue Holiday 2.00 5.00
37 CJ McCollum 2.00 5.00
38 Gordon Hayward 2.00 5.00
39 Tobias Harris 2.00 5.00
40 Trae Young 5.00 12.00
41 Seth Curry 2.00 5.00
42 Jamal Murray 3.00 8.00
43 Darius Garland 3.00 8.00
44 Evan Fournier 1.50 4.00
45 Tim Hardaway Jr. 1.25 3.00
46 LaMarcus Aldridge 2.00 5.00
47 Kyle Kuzma 2.50 6.00
48 Deandre Ayton 2.00 5.00
49 Jimmy Butler 4.00 10.00
50 Lonzo Ball 2.50 6.00
51 Carmelo Anthony 3.00 8.00
52 Jaylen Brown 3.00 8.00
53 Kevin Durant 8.00 20.00
54 De'Andre Hunter 2.00 5.00
55 Tyler Herro 4.00 10.00
56 Coby White 2.50 6.00
57 Shai Gilgeous-Alexander 10.00 25.00
58 Dennis Schroder 2.00 5.00
59 Draymond Green 2.50 6.00
60 Collin Sexton 2.00 5.00
61 Bam Adebayo 3.00 8.00
62 Kelly Oubre Jr. 2.00 5.00
63 Jerami Grant 2.00 5.00
64 Marcus Smart 2.00 5.00
65 Anthony Davis 5.00 12.00
66 Luka Doncic 125.00 300.00
67 Ben Simmons 2.00 5.00
68 Nikola Vucevic 2.00 5.00
69 Bradley Beal 2.50 6.00
70 Dillon Brooks 2.00 5.00
71 Duncan Robinson 2.00 5.00
72 Devin Booker 5.00 12.00
73 DeMar DeRozan 2.50 6.00
74 Damian Lillard 5.00 12.00
75 Joel Embiid 5.00 12.00
76 John Wall 2.50 6.00
77 Buddy Hield 2.00 5.00
78 Stephen Curry 15.00 40.00
79 Patrick Beverley 1.25 3.00
80 Harrison Barnes 1.50 4.00
81 Devonte' Graham 1.50 4.00
82 Julius Randle 2.00 5.00
83 Jordan Clarkson 2.00 5.00
84 Donovan Mitchell 4.00 10.00
85 Khris Middleton 2.50 6.00
86 Ja Morant 6.00 15.00
87 Christian Wood 1.50 4.00
88 Andrew Wiggins 2.50 6.00
89 Pascal Siakam 3.00 8.00
90 James Harden 4.00 10.00
91 Gary Trent Jr. 2.00 5.00
92 Terry Rozier 2.00 5.00
93 Domantas Sabonis 2.50 6.00
94 Rui Hachimura 2.50 6.00
95 Jarrett Culver 1.25 3.00
96 Joe Harris 1.50 4.00
97 Derrick Rose 3.00 8.00
98 Malcolm Brogdon 2.00 5.00
99 Victor Oladipo 1.50 4.00
100 Brandon Ingram 2.50 6.00
101 Xavier Tillman AU JSY RC 50.00 125.00
102 Jae'Sean Tate AU JSY RC 50.00 125.00
103 Tyrese Haliburton AU JSY RC 6,000.00 12,000.00
104 Isaiah Joe AU JSY RC 50.00 125.00
105 Isaac Okoro AU JSY RC 150.00 400.00
106 Theo Maledon AU JSY RC 40.00 100.00
107 Immanuel Quickley AU JSY RC 300.00 600.00
108 CJ Elleby AU JSY RC 40.00 100.00
109 Daniel Oturu AU JSY RC 40.00 100.00
110 Facundo Campazzo AU JSY RC 50.00 125.00
111 Anthony Edwards AU JSY RC 20,000.00 30,000.00
112 Karim Mane AU JSY RC 30.00 80.00
113 Cassius Winston AU JSY RC 40.00 100.00
114 Tyrese Maxey AU JSY RC 5,000.00 10,000.00
115 Precious Achiuwa AU JSY RC 80.00 200.00
116 Jahmi'us Ramsey AU JSY RC 40.00 100.00
117 Zeke Nnaji AU JSY RC 50.00 125.00
118 Devon Dotson AU JSY RC 40.00 100.00
119 Nico Mannion AU JSY RC 40.00 100.00
120 Udoka Azubuike AU JSY RC 50.00 125.00
121 Aleksej Pokusevski AU JSY RC 50.00 125.00
122 RJ Hampton AU JSY RC 40.00 100.00
123 Saddiq Bey AU JSY RC 150.00 400.00
124 James Wiseman AU JSY RC 50.00 125.00
125 Tyrell Terry AU JSY RC 30.00 80.00
126 Jalen Smith AU JSY RC 100.00 250.00
127 Josh Green AU JSY RC 125.00 300.00
128 Onyeka Okongwu AU JSY RC 200.00 500.00
129 Tyler Bey AU JSY RC 40.00 100.00
130 LaMelo Ball AU JSY RC 6,000.00 12,000.00
131 Killian Hayes AU JSY RC 40.00 100.00
132 Saben Lee AU JSY RC 40.00 100.00
133 Robert Woodard II AU JSY RC 40.00 100.00
134 Malachi Flynn AU JSY RC 40.00 100.00
135 Aaron Nesmith AU JSY RC 80.00 200.00
136 Skylar Mays AU JSY RC 40.00 100.00
137 Obi Toppin AU JSY RC 150.00 400.00
138 Deni Avdija AU JSY RC 150.00 400.00
139 Patrick Williams AU JSY RC 150.00 400.00
140 Jordan Nwora AU JSY RC 125.00 300.00
141 Vernon Carey Jr. AU JSY RC 40.00 100.00
142 Devin Vassell AU JSY RC 200.00 500.00
143 Jaden McDaniels AU JSY RC 300.00 600.00
144 Caleb Martin AU JSY RC 75.00 200.00
145 Isaiah Stewart AU JSY RC 80.00 200.00
146 Kira Lewis Jr. AU JSY RC 40.00 100.00
147 Desmond Bane AU JSY RC 2,000.00 4,000.00
148 Payton Pritchard AU JSY RC 150.00 400.00
149 Cole Anthony AU JSY RC 200.00 500.00
150 Tre Jones AU JSY RC 125.00 300.00

2020-21 Panini National Treasures Apprentice Ink

STATED PRINT RUN 25-99 SER.#'d SETS
EXCHANGE DEADLINE 2/11/2023
*BRONZE/25: .75X TO 2X BASIC
1 James Wiseman/25 8.00 20.00
2 Kira Lewis Jr./99 6.00 15.00
3 Vernon Carey Jr./99 6.00 15.00
4 Immanuel Quickley/99 75.00 200.00
5 Patrick Williams/49 100.00 250.00
6 Saddiq Bey/99 75.00 200.00
7 Onyeka Okongwu/49 40.00 100.00
8 RJ Hampton/99 50.00 120.00
9 Devin Vassell/99 50.00 120.00
10 LaMelo Ball/25 1,000.00 2,000.00
11 Jaden McDaniels/99 50.00 120.00
12 Isaac Okoro/49 75.00 200.00
13 Tyrese Haliburton/49 150.00 400.00
14 Malachi Flynn/99 6.00 15.00
15 Cole Anthony/49 100.00 250.00
16 Jahmi'us Ramsey/99 6.00 15.00
17 Obi Toppin/49 75.00 200.00
18 Jordan Nwora/99 30.00 80.00
19 Precious Achiuwa/99 40.00 100.00
20 Deni Avdija/49 60.00 150.00
21 Tyrese Maxey/49 125.00 300.00
22 Payton Pritchard/99 60.00 150.00
23 Killian Hayes/49 75.00 200.00
24 Aaron Nesmith/99 40.00 100.00
25 Anthony Edwards/25 300.00 600.00

2020-21 Panini National Treasures Award-Winning Autographs

COMMON CARD 6.00 15.00
SEMISTARS 8.00 20.00
UNLISTED STARS 10.00 25.00
EXCHANGE DEADLINE 2/11/2023
4 Allen Iverson 200.00 500.00
13 Trae Young 200.00 500.00
15 Kevin Garnett 200.00 500.00
16 Anthony Davis 200.00 500.00
29 Dirk Nowitzki 300.00 600.00
30 Shaquille O'Neal 200.00 500.00

2020-21 Panini National Treasures Biography Materials

STATED PRINT RUN 29-99 SER.#'d SETS
1 Jason Kidd/99 8.00 20.00
2 Tony Parker/99 8.00 20.00
3 Kevin Love/99 4.00 10.00
4 Carmelo Anthony/99 12.00 30.00
5 Kevin Durant/99 20.00 50.00
6 Klay Thompson/99 12.00 30.00
7 Matthew Dellavedova/99 8.00 20.00
8 John Wall/99 5.00 12.00
9 James Harden/35 15.00 40.00
11 Damian Lillard/99 12.00 30.00
12 JJ Redick/99 4.00 10.00
13 LeBron James/99 75.00 200.00
14 Jimmy Butler/99 10.00 25.00
15 Dwyane Wade/99 15.00 40.00
16 John Stockton/99 12.00 30.00
17 Charles Oakley/49 5.00 12.00
18 Russell Westbrook/94 12.00 30.00
19 DeAndre Jordan/80 3.00 8.00
20 Jonathan Isaac/99 8.00 20.00
21 Hakeem Olajuwon/99 12.00 30.00
22 Kristaps Porzingis/99 5.00 12.00
23 Ricky Rubio/99 8.00 20.00
24 Zion Williamson/99 50.00 120.00
25 Tim Duncan/29 15.00 40.00
26 Kyrie Irving/99 15.00 40.00
27 Maurice Cheeks/49 5.00 12.00
28 OG Anunoby/99 4.00 10.00
29 Myles Turner/99 4.00 10.00
30 Nikola Vucevic/99 4.00 10.00
31 Joe Ingles/99 3.00 8.00
32 Karl-Anthony Towns/99 6.00 15.00
33 D'Angelo Russell/43 5.00 12.00
34 Jrue Holiday/56 5.00 12.00
35 Karl Malone/70 8.00 20.00
36 LaMarcus Aldridge/99 4.00 10.00
37 DeMar DeRozan/99 5.00 12.00
38 Rajon Rondo/78 10.00 25.00
39 Tracy McGrady/33 12.00 30.00
40 Paul Pierce/99 6.00 15.00

2020-21 Panini National Treasures Biography Materials Prime

*PRIME: .75X TO 2X BASIC
PRINT RUNS B/WN 3-25 COPIES PER
NO PRICING ON QTY BELOW 20
4 Carmelo Anthony/25 40.00 100.00
5 Kevin Durant/23 60.00 150.00
6 Klay Thompson/25 40.00 100.00
11 Damian Lillard/20 30.00 80.00
15 Dwyane Wade/25 40.00 100.00
18 Russell Westbrook/25 30.00 80.00
25 Tim Duncan/25 60.00 150.00
37 DeMar DeRozan/25 15.00 40.00
40 Paul Pierce/21 15.00 40.00

2020-21 Panini National Treasures Century Materials

COMMON CARD 2.50 6.00
SEMISTARS 3.00 8.00
UNLISTED STARS 4.00 10.00
STATED PRINT RUN 30-99 SER.#'d SETS
*PRIME: .75X TO 2X BASIC
1 Mitchell Robinson/99 4.00 10.00
2 Montrezl Harrell/49 4.00 10.00
3 Elfrid Payton/99 3.00 8.00
4 Jalen Lecque/49 2.50 6.00
5 Marcus Morris Sr./99 2.50 6.00
6 P.J. Dozier/49 3.00 8.00
7 Terance Mann/99 3.00 8.00
8 Kyle Lowry/99 8.00 20.00
9 Spencer Dinwiddie/99 3.00 8.00
10 Serge Ibaka/99 3.00 8.00
11 Naz Reid/49 5.00 12.00
12 Otto Porter Jr./99 2.50 6.00
13 Pascal Siakam/99 6.00 15.00
14 LeBron James/99 75.00 200.00
15 Terry Rozier/99 4.00 10.00
16 Victor Oladipo/99 3.00 8.00
17 Wendell Carter Jr./49 3.00 8.00
18 D.J. Augustin/99 2.50 6.00
19 Grant Williams/49 3.00 8.00
20 James Ennis III/49 2.50 6.00
21 Josh Okogie/99 2.50 6.00
22 Luguentz Dort/49 6.00 15.00
23 Landry Shamet/30 3.00 8.00
24 OG Anunoby/49 4.00 10.00
25 Miles Bridges/49 4.00 10.00
26 Torrey Craig/49 3.00 8.00
27 Mike Muscala/99 3.00 8.00
28 JaMychal Green/99 2.50 6.00
29 Monte Morris/99 2.50 6.00
30 Reggie Jackson/99 3.00 8.00
31 Norman Powell/99 3.00 8.00
32 Michael Porter Jr./99 5.00 12.00
33 Matt Thomas/99 10.00 25.00
34 Marcus Smart/99 4.00 10.00
35 Deandre Ayton/99 4.00 10.00
36 Taj Gibson/99 2.50 6.00
37 Rudy Gobert/99 5.00 12.00
38 Robert Covington/99 3.00 8.00
39 Paul Millsap/99 3.00 8.00
40 Myles Turner/99 4.00 10.00

2020-21 Panini National Treasures Clutch Factor Jersey Signatures

COMMON CARD 5.00 12.00
SEMISTARS 6.00 15.00
UNLISTED STARS 8.00 20.00
STATED PRINT RUN 25-99 SER.#'d SETS
EXCHANGE DEADLINE 2/11/2023
*PRIME: .75X TO 2X BASIC
1 Jayson Tatum/25 300.00 600.00
2 Collin Sexton/49 20.00 50.00
6 RJ Barrett/49 100.00 250.00
7 Zion Williamson/25 500.00 1,000.00
8 Tre Jones/49 125.00 300.00
9 John Stockton/49 75.00 200.00
11 Trae Young/25 400.00 800.00
13 LaMarcus Aldridge/99 12.00 30.00
14 Karl Malone/49 75.00 200.00
15 Kevin Garnett/49 150.00 400.00
17 Rudy Gay/99 12.00 30.00
18 Stephen Curry/25 1,000.00 2,000.00
20 PJ Washington Jr./49 50.00 120.00
21 Jarrett Culver/99 5.00 12.00
23 Anthony Davis/49 200.00 500.00
24 De'Aaron Fox/99 50.00 120.00
25 Jaden McDaniels/49 150.00 400.00
26 Vernon Carey Jr./49 100.00 250.00
27 Kirk Hinrich /49 25.00 60.00
29 Ja Morant/99 400.00 800.00
30 Karl-Anthony Towns/49 50.00 120.00
31 Maxi Kleber/99 6.00 15.00
32 Andrea Bargnani/99 5.00 12.00
33 Kevin Martin/99 6.00 15.00
34 Steven Adams/99 15.00 40.00
35 Jrue Holiday/99 75.00 200.00
36 Brandon Clarke/99 15.00 40.00
37 Domantas Sabonis/48 40.00 100.00
38 Sekou Doumbouya/99 5.00 12.00
40 Kevin Durant/25 400.00 800.00
41 Cole Anthony/49 150.00 400.00
42 Kira Lewis Jr./49 125.00 300.00
43 Devin Vassell/49 125.00 300.00
44 James Wiseman/99 8.00 20.00
45 Anthony Edwards/49 800.00 1,500.00
46 Aaron Nesmith/49 125.00 300.00
47 Obi Toppin/49 150.00 400.00
48 Patrick Williams/49 300.00 600.00
49 Deni Avdija/49 150.00 400.00
NNO LaMelo Ball/49
Missing card number 2,000.00 4,000.00

2020-21 Panini National Treasures Colossal Material Autographs

STATED PRINT RUN 25-99 SER.#'d SETS
EXCHANGE DEADLINE 2/11/2023
*PRIME: .75X TO 2X BASIC
2 Jarrett Jack/99 6.00 15.00
3 Keita Bates-Diop/49 6.00 15.00
7 LaMarcus Aldridge/49 20.00 50.00
9 Chris Kaman/49 6.00 15.00
10 Kevin Martin/49 12.00 30.00
12 Andrea Bargnani/49 6.00 15.00
13 Kevin Garnett/25 200.00 500.00
14 Maxi Kleber/49 8.00 20.00
15 Brandon Clarke/49 25.00 60.00
16 Domantas Sabonis/49 30.00 80.00
20 RJ Hampton/49 8.00 20.00
21 CJ Elleby/49 8.00 20.00
22 Kirk Hinrich /49 15.00 40.00
24 Steven Adams/49 25.00 60.00
25 Zion Williamson/25 1,000.00 2,000.00
26 Karl-Anthony Towns/49 40.00 100.00
27 PJ Washington Jr./49 30.00 80.00
28 Saddiq Bey/49 150.00 400.00
29 Jordan Nwora/49 50.00 120.00
30 Precious Achiuwa/49 50.00 120.00
31 Stephen Curry/25 2,500.00 5,000.00
33 Isaiah Stewart/49 75.00 200.00
37 Josh Green/49 50.00 120.00
38 Trae Young/25 600.00 1,200.00
40 Payton Pritchard/49 125.00 300.00
41 Onyeka Okongwu/49 60.00 150.00
42 Tyrese Haliburton/49 200.00 500.00
43 Tyrese Maxey/49 200.00 500.00
44 Deni Avdija/49 125.00 300.00
45 Isaac Okoro/49 125.00 300.00
46 Obi Toppin/49 100.00 250.00
47 Killian Hayes/49 75.00 200.00
48 James Wiseman/49 10.00 25.00
49 LaMelo Ball/49 2,500.00 5,000.00
50 Anthony Edwards/49 1,500.00 3,000.00

2020-21 Panini National Treasures Colossal Materials

STATED PRINT RUN 25-99 SER.#'d SETS
*PRIME: .75X TO 2X BASIC
1 Karl-Anthony Towns/99 10.00 25.00
2 Otto Porter Jr./99 3.00 8.00
3 Maxi Kleber/99 4.00 10.00
5 Kevin Garnett/99 20.00 50.00
6 Nikola Vucevic/99 8.00 20.00
7 DeAndre Jordan/99 4.00 10.00
8 Myles Turner/99 5.00 12.00
9 Grant Williams/99 4.00 10.00
11 James Harden/99 20.00 50.00
12 Joel Embiid/25 40.00 100.00
13 Bradley Beal/99 10.00 25.00
14 John Wall/99 8.00 20.00
15 Dirk Nowitzki/99 20.00 50.00
16 Mitchell Robinson/99 5.00 12.00
17 Ivica Zubac/99 5.00 12.00
18 Rudy Gobert/99 10.00 25.00
19 Bam Adebayo/99 10.00 25.00
20 Robert Covington/99 4.00 10.00

2020-21 Panini National Treasures Colossal Rookie Materials

STATED PRINT RUN 99 SER.#'d SETS
*PRIME: .75X TO 2 BASIC
1 Tre Jones 6.00 15.00
2 Cole Anthony 20.00 50.00
3 Payton Pritchard 20.00 50.00
4 Desmond Bane 12.00 30.00
5 Kira Lewis Jr. 4.00 10.00
6 Isaiah Stewart 8.00 20.00
7 Caleb Martin 8.00 20.00
8 Jaden McDaniels 12.00 30.00
9 Devin Vassell 12.00 30.00
10 Vernon Carey Jr. 4.00 10.00
11 Jordan Nwora 5.00 12.00
12 Patrick Williams 10.00 25.00
13 Deni Avdija 10.00 25.00
14 Obi Toppin 8.00 20.00

15 Skylar Mays 4.00 10.00
16 Aaron Nesmith 8.00 20.00
17 Malachi Flynn 4.00 10.00
18 Robert Woodard II 4.00 10.00
19 Saben Lee 4.00 10.00
20 Killian Hayes 4.00 10.00
21 LaMelo Ball 150.00 400.00
22 Tyler Bey 4.00 10.00
23 Onyeka Okongwu 8.00 20.00
24 Josh Green 8.00 20.00
25 Jalen Smith 8.00 20.00
26 Tyrell Terry 3.00 8.00
27 James Wiseman 5.00 12.00
28 Saddiq Bey 20.00 50.00
29 RJ Hampton 4.00 10.00
30 Aleksej Pokusevski 5.00 12.00
31 Udoka Azubuike 5.00 12.00
32 Nico Mannion 4.00 10.00
33 Devon Dotson 4.00 10.00
34 Zeke Nnaji 5.00 12.00
35 Jahmi'us Ramsey 4.00 10.00
36 Precious Achiuwa 8.00 20.00
37 Tyrese Maxey 25.00 60.00
38 Cassius Winston 4.00 10.00
39 Karim Mane 3.00 8.00
40 Anthony Edwards 75.00 200.00
41 Facundo Campazzo 5.00 12.00
42 Daniel Oturu 4.00 10.00
43 CJ Elleby 4.00 10.00
44 Immanuel Quickley 10.00 25.00
45 Theo Maledon 4.00 10.00
46 Isaac Okoro 6.00 15.00
47 Isaiah Joe 5.00 12.00
48 Tyrese Haliburton 50.00 120.00
49 Jae'Sean Tate 20.00 50.00
50 Xavier Tillman 5.00 12.00

2020-21 Panini National Treasures Definitive Ink

COMMON CARD 5.00 12.00
SEMISTARS 6.00 15.00
UNLISTED STARS 8.00 20.00
STATED PRINT RUN 25-99 SER.#'d SETS
EXCHANGE DEADLINE 2/11/2023
3 Dwyane Wade/25 125.00 300.00
6 Joe Harris/99 6.00 15.00
7 Karl-Anthony Towns/25 40.00 100.00
8 Jayson Tatum/25 200.00 500.00
9 Detlef Schrempf/49 8.00 20.00
11 Trae Young/49 150.00 400.00
12 Latrell Sprewell/49 12.00 30.00
13 Roy Hibbert/49 5.00 12.00
14 T.J. Ford/49 5.00 12.00
16 Nikola Jokic/49 300.00 600.00
18 Robert Parish/49 20.00 50.00
19 Chris Mullin/49 20.00 50.00
20 Maxi Kleber/49 6.00 15.00
21 RJ Barrett/25 75.00 200.00
22 Dominique Wilkins/49 25.00 60.00
25 Ja Morant/49 200.00 500.00
27 Quinn Cook/49 5.00 12.00
28 Steven Adams/49 20.00 50.00
29 Collin Sexton/49 40.00 100.00
30 Keita Bates-Diop/49 5.00 12.00
35 Kevin Durant/25 200.00 500.00
36 Walt Frazier/49 15.00 40.00
37 Anthony Davis/25 200.00 500.00
38 Elton Brand/49 12.00 30.00
41 Luka Doncic/25 3,000.00 5,000.00
42 Stephen Jackson/49 6.00 15.00
43 Kirk Hinrich /49 15.00 40.00
44 Kendrick Nunn/49 6.00 15.00
45 Dino Radja/49 6.00 15.00
50 Jarrett Culver/49 5.00 12.00

2020-21 Panini National Treasures Game Gear

COMMON CARD 2.50 6.00
SEMISTARS 3.00 8.00
UNLISTED STARS 4.00 10.00
STATED PRINT RUN 99 SER.#'d SETS
1 Rudy Gobert 5.00 12.00
2 Josh Richardson 3.00 8.00
3 Al Horford 4.00 10.00
4 Collin Sexton 12.00 30.00
5 Cam Reddish 8.00 20.00
6 Ja Morant 40.00 100.00
7 Giannis Antetokounmpo 30.00 80.00
8 Anthony Davis 12.00 30.00
9 Luke Kennard 3.00 8.00
11 Jarrett Allen 4.00 10.00
13 Jonas Valanciunas 3.00 8.00
14 Cam Reddish 12.00 30.00
15 Kawhi Leonard 10.00 25.00
16 James Harden 12.00 30.00
17 Jrue Holiday 4.00 10.00
19 Coby White 5.00 12.00
20 Marcus Smart 4.00 10.00
21 Brandon Clarke 4.00 10.00
22 Russell Westbrook 12.00 30.00
23 Khris Middleton 5.00 12.00
24 Lauri Markkanen 5.00 12.00
26 Gary Harris 3.00 8.00
27 Steven Adams 4.00 10.00
28 Victor Oladipo 3.00 8.00
29 Mitchell Robinson 4.00 10.00
30 Blake Griffin 4.00 10.00
31 Kemba Walker 4.00 10.00
32 Cameron Johnson 5.00 12.00
33 Joe Harris 3.00 8.00
34 Zion Williamson 40.00 100.00
35 Lou Williams 4.00 10.00
36 T.J. Warren 3.00 8.00
37 Stephen Curry 60.00 150.00
38 De'Andre Hunter 4.00 10.00
39 Jamal Murray 6.00 15.00
40 Kevin Love 4.00 10.00

2020-21 Panini National Treasures Game Gear Autographs

COMMON CARD 5.00 12.00
SEMISTARS 6.00 15.00
UNLISTED STARS 8.00 20.00
STATED PRINT RUN 14-99 SER.#'d SETS
NO PRICING ON QTY BELOW 20
EXCHANGE DEADLINE 2/11/2023
*PRIME: .75X TO 2X BASIC
1 Dorian Finney-Smith/99 6.00 15.00
2 Jack Sikma/99 8.00 20.00
3 Cam Reddish/99 40.00 100.00
4 Jose Calderon/99 6.00 15.00
6 Michael Porter Jr./49 10.00 25.00
8 Donte DiVincenzo/49 25.00 60.00
9 Bradley Beal/49 40.00 100.00
10 Daniel Gibson/99 5.00 12.00
11 Andrea Bargnani/99 5.00 12.00
12 John Salmons/99 5.00 12.00
13 Roy Hibbert/99 5.00 12.00
14 Maxi Kleber/99 6.00 15.00
15 Jordan Poole/99 30.00 80.00
16 Luka Doncic/25 2,000.00 4,000.00
17 Jarrett Allen/99 8.00 20.00
19 Lauri Markkanen/99 15.00 40.00
20 Ricky Rubio/99 12.00 30.00
21 Doug McDermott/99 6.00 15.00
22 Myles Turner/99 8.00 20.00
23 Kevin Garnett/25 125.00 300.00
24 Mikal Bridges/49 20.00 50.00
25 Shawn Kemp/49 100.00 250.00
26 David Lee/99 5.00 12.00
27 Spencer Dinwiddie/49 6.00 15.00
28 Domantas Sabonis/49 20.00 50.00
29 Kevin Huerter/49 20.00 50.00
30 Anfernee Simons/99 10.00 25.00
31 Jrue Holiday/49 12.00 30.00
32 Daniel Theis/99 6.00 15.00
33 Karl Malone/49 75.00 200.00
34 Jalen Brunson/99 12.00 30.00
35 Derek Fisher/99 12.00 30.00
36 Joe Harris/99 6.00 15.00
37 LaMarcus Aldridge/49 20.00 50.00
38 Wendell Carter Jr./49 15.00 40.00
40 Nikola Vucevic/49 12.00 30.00
41 Robert Parish/49 15.00 40.00
42 Julius Randle/49 40.00 100.00
43 Ja Morant/49 200.00 500.00
45 Jayson Tatum/25 150.00 400.00
46 Larry Bird/25 150.00 400.00
47 Luke Kennard/99 6.00 15.00
48 Nassir Little/99 6.00 15.00
49 Dwyane Wade/49 100.00 250.00
50 Torrey Craig/49 15.00 40.00

2020-21 Panini National Treasures Game Gear Prime

*PRIME/25: .75X TO 2X BASIC
PRINT RUNS B/WN 10-25 COPIES PER
NO PRICING ON QTY 15 OR LESS
15 Kawhi Leonard/25 30.00 80.00
16 James Harden/25 30.00 80.00
22 Russell Westbrook/25 30.00 80.00

2020-21 Panini National Treasures Jersey Treasures

COMMON CARD 2.50 6.00
SEMISTARS 3.00 8.00
UNLISTED STARS 4.00 10.00
STATED PRINT RUN 57-99 SER.#'d SETS
*PRIME: .75X TO 2X BASIC
1 Zion Williamson/99 40.00 100.00
2 Al Horford/99 4.00 10.00
3 Jayson Tatum/99 30.00 80.00
4 Pascal Siakam/99 6.00 15.00
5 T.J. McConnell/99 3.00 8.00
6 Coby White/99 5.00 12.00
7 Kevin Love/99 4.00 10.00
8 LeBron James/99 60.00 150.00
9 Jonas Valanciunas/99 3.00 8.00
10 Mitchell Robinson/99 4.00 10.00
11 Marvin Bagley III/99 3.00 8.00
12 OG Anunoby/99 4.00 10.00
13 Jrue Holiday/99 4.00 10.00
14 Brandon Clarke/99 4.00 10.00
15 Dennis Schroder/99 4.00 10.00
16 Andre Drummond/57 4.00 10.00
17 Lonzo Ball/99 10.00 25.00
18 Victor Oladipo/99 3.00 8.00
19 Danilo Gallinari/99 3.00 8.00
20 Markelle Fultz/99 3.00 8.00
21 Brandon Ingram/99 5.00 12.00
22 Devonte' Graham/99 3.00 8.00
23 Kyle Kuzma/88 5.00 12.00
24 Ricky Rubio/99 4.00 10.00
25 Blake Griffin/99 4.00 10.00
26 Otto Porter Jr./99 2.50 6.00
27 Luguentz Dort/99 6.00 15.00
28 Carmelo Anthony/99 10.00 25.00
29 Rudy Gobert/99 5.00 12.00
30 T.J. Warren/99 3.00 8.00
31 Marcus Morris Sr./99 2.50 6.00
32 Jaren Jackson Jr./99 6.00 15.00
34 D'Angelo Russell/99 4.00 10.00
35 Julius Randle/99 4.00 10.00
36 Devin Booker/99 15.00 40.00
37 Deandre Ayton/99 4.00 10.00
38 Harrison Barnes/99 3.00 8.00
39 Luka Doncic/99 60.00 150.00
40 Norman Powell/99 3.00 8.00
41 Dejounte Murray/99 4.00 10.00
42 Cameron Johnson/99 5.00 12.00
43 RJ Barrett/99 8.00 20.00
44 Paul Millsap/99 3.00 8.00
45 Kristaps Porzingis/99 5.00 12.00
46 Kemba Walker/99 4.00 10.00
47 Eric Bledsoe/99 3.00 8.00
48 Donovan Mitchell/99 12.00 30.00
49 Chris Paul/99 8.00 20.00
50 Caris LeVert/99 4.00 10.00
51 Evan Fournier/99 3.00 8.00
52 Josh Richardson/99 3.00 8.00
53 Trae Young/99 30.00 80.00
54 Marcus Smart/99 4.00 10.00
55 PJ Washington Jr./99 4.00 10.00
56 Zach LaVine/99 12.00 30.00
57 Nikola Vucevic/99 4.00 10.00
58 Tobias Harris/99 4.00 10.00
59 Damian Lillard/99 10.00 25.00
60 Hassan Whiteside/99 3.00 8.00
61 DeMar DeRozan/99 5.00 12.00
62 Buddy Hield/99 4.00 10.00
63 Enes Kanter/99 3.00 8.00
64 Joel Embiid/99 10.00 25.00
65 Aaron Gordon/99 4.00 10.00
66 Jimmy Butler/99 8.00 20.00
67 Darius Bazley/99 2.50 6.00
68 Mike Conley/99 3.00 8.00
69 Steven Adams/99 4.00 10.00
70 Gary Harris/99 3.00 8.00
71 Anthony Davis/99 10.00 25.00
72 CJ McCollum/99 4.00 10.00
74 Bam Adebayo/99 6.00 15.00
75 Andrew Wiggins/99 5.00 12.00
76 Kyrie Irving/99 12.00 30.00
77 John Collins/99 4.00 10.00
78 Shai Gilgeous-Alexander/99 8.00 20.00
79 Myles Turner/99 4.00 10.00
80 Jusuf Nurkic/99 4.00 10.00
81 Monte Morris/99 2.50 6.00
82 Serge Ibaka/99 3.00 8.00
83 Bojan Bogdanovic/99 3.00 8.00
84 Eric Gordon/99 3.00 8.00
85 P.J. Tucker /99 3.00 8.00
86 Kawhi Leonard/99 10.00 25.00
87 Bradley Beal/99 5.00 12.00
88 Lauri Markkanen/99 5.00 12.00
89 Rudy Gay/99 4.00 10.00
90 Patrick Beverley/99 2.50 6.00
91 De'Aaron Fox/99 6.00 15.00
93 Paul George/99 6.00 15.00
94 DeAndre Jordan/99 3.00 8.00
95 George Hill/99 3.00 8.00
96 Joe Ingles/99 3.00 8.00
97 Kyle Lowry/99 5.00 12.00
98 Matisse Thybulle/99 3.00 8.00
99 Landry Shamet/99 3.00 8.00
100 Jarrett Allen/99 4.00 10.00

2020-21 Panini National Treasures Lasting Legacies Jersey Autographs

STATED PRINT RUN 25-99 SER.#'d SETS
EXCHANGE DEADLINE 2/11/2023
1 Jarrett Culver/99 5.00 12.00
2 Dorian Finney-Smith/99 6.00 15.00
3 Jack Sikma/99 8.00 20.00
4 Jose Calderon/99 6.00 15.00
5 Mitch Kupchak/99 5.00 12.00
6 Dominique Wilkins/49 20.00 50.00
7 Marcus Camby/99 12.00 30.00
8 Andrea Bargnani/99 5.00 12.00
9 John Salmons/99 5.00 12.00
10 Roy Hibbert/99 5.00 12.00
11 Mitch Richmond/49 25.00 60.00
12 Isiah Thomas/49 40.00 100.00
13 Robert Horry/99 20.00 50.00
14 Jarrett Allen/99 8.00 20.00
16 Mikal Bridges/99 20.00 50.00
17 Jarrett Jack/99 5.00 12.00
18 Doug McDermott/99 6.00 15.00
19 Myles Turner/99 8.00 20.00
20 Arron Afflalo/99 5.00 12.00
21 David Lee/99 5.00 12.00
22 Spencer Dinwiddie/49 6.00 15.00
23 Elton Brand/49 12.00 30.00
25 Richard Jefferson/99 5.00 12.00
26 Daniel Theis/99 12.00 30.00
27 Wendell Carter Jr./49 6.00 15.00
28 Jonas Valanciunas/99 6.00 15.00
29 Lamar Odom/99 30.00 80.00
30 Larry Nance Jr./99 6.00 15.00
31 Luke Kennard/99 6.00 15.00
32 Ricky Pierce/45 5.00 12.00
33 Torrey Craig/49 12.00 30.00
34 Lonnie Walker IV/99 10.00 25.00
36 Rasheed Wallace/49 60.00 150.00
37 Kawhi Leonard/25 125.00 300.00
38 Bam Adebayo/25 25.00 60.00
39 Derrick White/99 8.00 20.00
40 Harrison Barnes/99 6.00 15.00
41 Furkan Korkmaz/99 6.00 15.00
42 Dwyane Wade/49 75.00 200.00
43 Nassir Little/99 6.00 15.00
44 Al Horford/99 8.00 20.00
45 John Stockton/49 60.00 150.00
46 Matt Bonner/99 5.00 12.00
47 Daniel Gibson/49 5.00 12.00
48 Terry Cummings/99 8.00 20.00

2020-21 Panini National Treasures Lasting Legacies Jersey Autographs Prime

PRINT RUNS B/WN 6-25 COPIES PER
NO PRICING ON QTY BELOW 20
EXCHANGE DEADLINE 2/11/2023
49 Robert Covington/25 20.00 50.00

2020-21 Panini National Treasures Material Treasures

STATED PRINT RUN 99 SER.#'d SETS
*PRIME: .75X TO 2X BASIC
1 Trae Young 15.00 40.00
2 RJ Barrett 6.00 15.00
3 Dennis Schroder 4.00 10.00
4 Nikola Vucevic 4.00 10.00
5 Jayson Tatum 15.00 40.00
6 Devin Booker 15.00 40.00
7 Brandon Clarke 4.00 10.00
8 Damian Lillard 15.00 40.00
9 Giannis Antetokounmpo 25.00 60.00
10 Kyrie Irving 8.00 20.00
11 Brook Lopez 3.00 8.00
12 Nikola Jokic 20.00 50.00
13 LaMarcus Aldridge 4.00 10.00
14 Buddy Hield 4.00 10.00
15 PJ Washington Jr. 4.00 10.00
16 Jarrett Culver 2.50 6.00
17 Domantas Sabonis 5.00 12.00
18 Myles Turner 4.00 10.00
19 Bogdan Bogdanovic 4.00 10.00
20 Zach LaVine 10.00 25.00
21 Joe Ingles 3.00 8.00
22 Blake Griffin 4.00 10.00
24 Donovan Mitchell 8.00 20.00
25 Kyle Lowry 5.00 12.00
26 Collin Sexton 4.00 10.00
27 Marvin Bagley III 3.00 8.00
28 Lonzo Ball 5.00 12.00
29 Bam Adebayo 6.00 15.00
30 Kristaps Porzingis 5.00 12.00

2020-21 Panini National Treasures Material Treasures Prime

PRINT RUNS B/WN 9-25 COPIES PER
NO PRICING ON QTY BELOW 20
5 Jayson Tatum/21 50.00 120.00
6 Devin Booker/25 50.00 120.00
8 Damian Lillard/25 50.00 120.00
9 Giannis Antetokounmpo/25 60.00 150.00
20 Zach LaVine/25 25.00 60.00
24 Donovan Mitchell/25 25.00 60.00
28 Lonzo Ball/25 20.00 50.00

2020-21 Panini National Treasures National Archives Ink

STATED PRINT RUN 25-99 SER.#'d SETS
EXCHANGE DEADLINE 2/11/2023
1 Kevin Garnett/25 125.00 300.00
2 Allan Houston/99 8.00 20.00
3 Dino Radja/49 6.00 15.00
5 Chris Kaman/99 5.00 12.00
7 Isaiah Rider/49 6.00 15.00
8 Roy Hibbert/49 5.00 12.00
9 Jerry Lucas/99 12.00 30.00
10 Rick Barry/49 12.00 30.00
11 Allen Iverson/25 200.00 500.00
12 Kirk Hinrich /99 12.00 30.00
13 David Robinson/49 50.00 120.00
14 Joe Dumars/49 12.00 30.00
15 Bob McAdoo/49 12.00 30.00
17 Calvin Murphy/49 8.00 20.00
18 Derek Fisher/99 8.00 20.00
19 Charles Barkley/25 125.00 300.00
20 Adrian Dantley/99 8.00 20.00
21 Mike Miller/99 6.00 15.00
22 Marcus Camby/99 12.00 30.00
23 Dwyane Wade/25 100.00 250.00
24 Rolando Blackman/99 6.00 15.00
25 Jarrett Jack/49 5.00 12.00
26 Hedo Turkoglu/49 6.00 15.00
27 David Thompson/99 10.00 25.00
28 Kareem Abdul-Jabbar/25 200.00 500.00
29 Kurt Rambis/49 6.00 15.00
30 Fat Lever/99 6.00 15.00
31 Alex English/99 8.00 20.00
32 Maurice Cheeks/49 8.00 20.00
33 Kenny "Sky" Walker/49 6.00 15.00
34 Shaquille O'Neal /25 200.00 500.00
35 Kevin Martin/99 6.00 15.00
36 Lenny Wilkens/49 12.00 30.00
37 Jason Williams/25 75.00 200.00
38 Bill Walton/49 50.00 120.00
39 John Salmons/99 5.00 12.00
40 Gail Goodrich/99 8.00 20.00
41 Spud Webb/99 15.00 40.00
42 Walt Frazier/49 15.00 40.00
43 Elton Brand/49 12.00 30.00
44 Kendall Gill/99 12.00 30.00
45 Nate Archibald/49 10.00 25.00
46 Avery Johnson/99 6.00 15.00
47 George Gervin/49 12.00 30.00
48 Dave Cowens/49 10.00 25.00
49 Stephen Jackson/99 12.00 30.00
50 Grant Hill/49 40.00 100.00

2020-21 Panini National Treasures NBA Greats Signatures

STATED PRINT RUN 25-99 SER.#'d SETS
EXCHANGE DEADLINE 2/11/2023
1 Dominique Wilkins/99 25.00 60.00
2 Fat Lever/99 8.00 20.00
3 Shawn Kemp/99 40.00 100.00
4 Horace Grant/99 8.00 20.00
5 Isiah Thomas/99 40.00 100.00
6 Mark Jackson/99 6.00 15.00
7 Tim Hardaway/99 15.00 40.00
8 Robert Horry/99 20.00 50.00
9 Alex English/99 8.00 20.00
10 Jerry West/99 40.00 100.00
11 Dikembe Mutombo/99 25.00 60.00
12 Gary Payton/99 40.00 100.00
13 Calvin Murphy/99 8.00 20.00
14 Micheal Ray Richardson/99 5.00 12.00
15 Kevin Garnett/25 125.00 300.00
16 Lenny Wilkens/99 8.00 20.00
17 Glen Rice/99 6.00 15.00
18 Karl Malone/49 40.00 100.00
19 Nate Archibald/99 10.00 25.00
20 Rick Barry/99 12.00 30.00
21 Robert Parish/99 12.00 30.00
22 Magic Johnson/49 75.00 200.00
23 Rasheed Wallace/99 60.00 150.00
24 James Worthy/99 12.00 30.00
25 Spencer Haywood/99 8.00 20.00
26 Sarunas Marciulionis/99 8.00 20.00
27 Kenny "Sky" Walker/99 6.00 15.00
28 Mitch Richmond/99 10.00 25.00
29 Detlef Schrempf/99 8.00 20.00
30 Jack Sikma/99 8.00 20.00

2020-21 Panini National Treasures NBA Greats Signatures Bronze

*BRONZE/25: .75X TO 2X BASIC
PRINT RUNS B/WN 25 COPIES PER
EXCHANGE DEADLINE 2/11/2023
15 Kevin Garnett 125.00 300.00

2020-21 Panini National Treasures NBA Materials

STATED PRINT RUN 49-99 SER.#'d SETS
*PRIME: .75X TO 2X BASIC
1 Kyle Kuzma/99 5.00 12.00
2 Deandre Ayton/99 4.00 10.00
3 Jamal Murray/49 6.00 15.00
4 Aaron Gordon/99 4.00 10.00
5 Luka Doncic/99 75.00 200.00
6 Bradley Beal/99 5.00 12.00
7 Kyle Lowry/49 5.00 12.00
8 Nassir Little/49 3.00 8.00
9 Bojan Bogdanovic/99 3.00 8.00
10 Grant Williams/99 3.00 8.00
11 Jordan Clarkson/49 4.00 10.00
12 Victor Oladipo/99 3.00 8.00
13 Paul George/99 10.00 25.00
14 Lauri Markkanen/49 5.00 12.00
15 Mikal Bridges/49 5.00 12.00
16 Kyrie Irving/99 12.00 30.00
17 Fred VanVleet/99 30.00 80.00
18 Marvin Bagley III/99 3.00 8.00
19 Gary Trent Jr./99 4.00 10.00
20 Joel Embiid/75 12.00 30.00
21 John Wall/99 5.00 12.00
22 Otto Porter Jr./99 2.50 6.00
23 De'Aaron Fox/99 8.00 20.00
24 LeBron James/99 75.00 200.00
25 CJ McCollum/99 4.00 10.00
26 James Harden/99 12.00 30.00
27 Trae Young/99 10.00 25.00
28 Kevin Love/99 4.00 10.00
29 Marcus Smart/99 4.00 10.00
30 Vince Carter/99 12.00 30.00

2020-21 Panini National Treasures Peerless Signatures

STATED PRINT RUN 25-99 SER.#'d SETS
EXCHANGE DEADLINE 2/11/2023
1 Allen Iverson/49 125.00 300.00
2 Adrian Dantley/99 8.00 20.00
3 Jason Kidd/49 25.00 60.00
4 Dwyane Wade/25 100.00 250.00
5 Maurice Cheeks/49 8.00 20.00
6 Derek Fisher/75 8.00 20.00
7 Shaquille O'Neal /25 150.00 400.00
9 Fat Lever/99 6.00 15.00
10 Ja Morant/35 300.00 600.00
11 Larry Bird/49 125.00 300.00
12 Rolando Blackman/99 6.00 15.00
13 Kenny "Sky" Walker/75 6.00 15.00
15 Dave Cowens/49 10.00 25.00
17 Magic Johnson/49 125.00 300.00
18 Roy Hibbert/49 5.00 12.00
19 Wally Szczerbiak/99 6.00 15.00
20 John Salmons/75 5.00 12.00
21 Dominique Wilkins/75 30.00 80.00
22 Avery Johnson/49 6.00 15.00
23 Isiah Thomas/99 40.00 100.00
24 John Stockton/49 50.00 120.00
25 Gary Payton/99 30.00 80.00
26 Calvin Murphy/49 8.00 20.00
27 Bernard King/75 10.00 25.00
29 Karl Malone/49 50.00 120.00
30 Allan Houston/75 12.00 30.00
31 Walt Frazier/49 15.00 40.00
32 Kevin Durant/25 300.00 600.00
33 Kareem Abdul-Jabbar/25 200.00 500.00
34 Elton Brand/49 12.00 30.00
36 George Gervin/49 12.00 30.00
37 Kevin Garnett/25 125.00 300.00
38 Joe Dumars/49 12.00 30.00
39 Rick Barry/49 15.00 40.00
41 Hakeem Olajuwon/49 50.00 120.00
42 Bill Russell/25 1,000.00 2,000.00
43 Jonas Valanciunas/49 12.00 30.00
44 Paul Pierce/49 60.00 150.00
45 Sam Cassell/75 6.00 15.00
46 Gail Goodrich/99 8.00 20.00
47 B.J. Armstrong/99 15.00 40.00
49 David Robinson/25 100.00 250.00
50 Charles Barkley/25 150.00 400.00

2020-21 Panini National Treasures Peerless Signatures Bronze

*BRONZE/25: .75X TO 2X BASIC
PRINT RUNS B/WN 15-25 COPIES PER
NO PRICING ON QTY BELOW 20
EXCHANGE DEADLINE 2/11/2023
10 Ja Morant/25 300.00 600.00

2020-21 Panini National Treasures Penmanship

STATED PRINT RUN 25-99 SER.#'d SETS
EXCHANGE DEADLINE 2/11/2023
*BRONZE/25: .75X TO 2X BASIC
1 Thanasis Antetokounmpo/99 50.00 120.00
2 Cam Reddish/99 20.00 50.00
3 Luguentz Dort/99 25.00 60.00
4 Avery Bradley/99 5.00 12.00
5 Otto Porter Jr./99 5.00 12.00
6 Cedi Osman/99 6.00 15.00
7 Donte DiVincenzo/99 12.00 30.00
8 Bradley Beal/49 12.00 30.00
9 Brandon Clarke/99 8.00 20.00
10 Thomas Bryant/99 6.00 15.00
11 Chuma Okeke/99 12.00 30.00
12 Danilo Gallinari/99 6.00 15.00
13 Jarrett Culver/99 5.00 12.00
15 Nickeil Alexander-Walker/99 15.00 40.00
16 Ricky Rubio/99 15.00 40.00
17 Gary Trent Jr./99 12.00 30.00
18 Kawhi Leonard/25 150.00 400.00
19 Collin Sexton/49 8.00 20.00
20 Domantas Sabonis/99 15.00 40.00
21 Gordon Hayward/99 12.00 30.00
23 Wesley Matthews/99 8.00 20.00
24 Lou Williams/99 12.00 30.00
25 Grant Williams/99 6.00 15.00
26 Zach LaVine/99 40.00 100.00
27 Jrue Holiday/99 20.00 50.00
28 Daniel Theis/99 12.00 30.00
29 Bam Adebayo/25 20.00 50.00
30 Matisse Thybulle/99 30.00 80.00
31 Kristaps Porzingis/99 10.00 25.00
32 Derrick White/99 8.00 20.00
33 Malik Beasley/99 6.00 15.00
34 Doug McDermott/99 6.00 15.00
35 Dorian Finney-Smith/99 6.00 15.00
36 De'Andre Hunter/99 8.00 20.00
37 Kelly Oubre Jr./99 12.00 30.00
38 Troy Brown Jr./99 15.00 40.00
39 Michael Porter Jr./99 10.00 25.00
40 Isaac Bonga/99 5.00 12.00

2020-21 Panini National Treasures Retro Materials

STATED PRINT RUN 65-99 SER.#'d SETS
1 Kevin Garnett/99 15.00 40.00
2 Drew Gooden/99 2.50 6.00
3 David Lee/99 2.50 6.00
4 Magic Johnson/99 20.00 50.00
5 Robert Parish/99 5.00 12.00
6 Hakeem Olajuwon/74 8.00 20.00
7 Doc Rivers/99 4.00 10.00
8 Andrea Bargnani/99 2.50 6.00
9 John Stockton/99 8.00 20.00
10 Charles Barkley/65 20.00 50.00
11 Larry Hughes/99 3.00 8.00
12 Matt Bonner/99 2.50 6.00
13 Jose Calderon/99 3.00 8.00
14 Andrei Kirilenko/99 3.00 8.00
15 Julius Erving/99 20.00 50.00
16 Chris Kaman/99 2.50 6.00
17 Chris Webber/99 25.00 60.00
18 Rashard Lewis/99 3.00 8.00
19 Nick Collison/99 3.00 8.00
20 Danny Granger/99 2.50 6.00
21 Kirk Hinrich /99 3.00 8.00
22 Larry Bird/99 20.00 50.00
23 Kenyon Martin/89 4.00 10.00
24 Kareem Abdul-Jabbar/99 30.00 80.00
25 Gerald Wallace/99 3.00 8.00
26 Amar'e Stoudemire/99 4.00 10.00
27 Shawn Bradley/99 3.00 8.00
28 Shaquille O'Neal /99 25.00 60.00
29 Shawn Kemp/99 20.00 50.00
30 Dirk Nowitzki/99 15.00 40.00

2020-21 Panini National Treasures Retro Materials Prime

*PRIME: .75X TO 2X BASIC
PRINT RUNS B/WN 4-25 COPIES PER
NO PRICING ON QTY BELOW 20
9 John Stockton/25 30.00 80.00
22 Larry Bird/25 75.00 200.00
29 Shawn Kemp/25 75.00 200.00

2020-21 Panini National Treasures Rookie Dual Materials

STATED PRINT RUN 99 SER.#'d SETS
1 Cole Anthony 30.00 80.00
2 Payton Pritchard 12.00 30.00
3 Kira Lewis Jr. 4.00 10.00
4 Jaden McDaniels 12.00 30.00
5 Devin Vassell 12.00 30.00
6 Jordan Nwora 5.00 12.00
7 Patrick Williams 10.00 25.00
8 Obi Toppin 8.00 20.00
9 Deni Avdija 10.00 25.00
10 Malachi Flynn 4.00 10.00
11 Killian Hayes 4.00 10.00
12 LaMelo Ball 200.00 500.00
13 Onyeka Okongwu 8.00 20.00
14 Josh Green 8.00 20.00
15 James Wiseman 5.00 12.00
16 Saddiq Bey 8.00 20.00
17 RJ Hampton 4.00 10.00
18 Aleksej Pokusevski 5.00 12.00
19 Precious Achiuwa 8.00 20.00
20 Udoka Azubuike 5.00 12.00
21 Anthony Edwards 75.00 200.00
22 Isaac Okoro 6.00 15.00
23 Immanuel Quickley 10.00 25.00
24 Tyrese Haliburton 50.00 120.00
25 CJ Elleby 4.00 10.00

2020-21 Panini National Treasures Rookie Dual Materials Prime

*PRIME: .75X TO 2X BASIC
PRINT RUN 25 COPIES PER
23 Immanuel Quickley 60.00 150.00
24 Tyrese Haliburton 125.00 300.00

2020-21 Panini National Treasures Rookie Jumbo Materials

STATED PRINT RUN 99 SER.#'d SETS
1 Cole Anthony 30.00 80.00
2 Payton Pritchard 12.00 30.00
3 Kira Lewis Jr. 4.00 10.00
4 Jaden McDaniels 12.00 30.00
5 Devin Vassell 12.00 30.00
6 Jordan Nwora 5.00 12.00
7 Patrick Williams 30.00 80.00
8 Obi Toppin 8.00 20.00
9 Deni Avdija 10.00 25.00
10 Malachi Flynn 4.00 10.00
11 Killian Hayes 4.00 10.00
12 LaMelo Ball 200.00 500.00
13 Onyeka Okongwu 8.00 20.00
14 Josh Green 8.00 20.00
15 James Wiseman 5.00 12.00
16 Saddiq Bey 20.00 50.00
17 RJ Hampton 4.00 10.00
18 Aleksej Pokusevski 5.00 12.00
19 Precious Achiuwa 8.00 20.00
20 Udoka Azubuike 5.00 12.00
21 Anthony Edwards 75.00 200.00
22 Isaac Okoro 6.00 15.00
23 Immanuel Quickley 10.00 25.00
24 Tyrese Haliburton 50.00 120.00
25 CJ Elleby 4.00 10.00

2020-21 Panini National Treasures Rookie Jumbo Materials Prime

*PRIME: .75X TO 2X BASIC
PRINT RUN 25 COPIES PER
2 Payton Pritchard/25 60.00 150.00
7 Patrick Williams/25 75.00 200.00
8 Obi Toppin/25 50.00 120.00
23 Immanuel Quickley/25 60.00 150.00
24 Tyrese Haliburton/25 125.00 300.00

2020-21 Panini National Treasures Rookie Materials

STATED PRINT RUN 99 SER.#'d SETS
1 Cole Anthony 25.00 60.00
2 Payton Pritchard 10.00 25.00
3 Kira Lewis Jr. 3.00 8.00
4 Jaden McDaniels 10.00 25.00
5 Devin Vassell 10.00 25.00
6 Jordan Nwora 4.00 10.00
7 Patrick Williams 25.00 60.00
8 Obi Toppin 6.00 15.00
9 Deni Avdija 8.00 20.00
10 Malachi Flynn 3.00 8.00
11 Killian Hayes 3.00 8.00
12 LaMelo Ball 150.00 400.00
13 Onyeka Okongwu 6.00 15.00
14 Josh Green 6.00 15.00
15 James Wiseman 4.00 10.00
16 Saddiq Bey 15.00 40.00
17 RJ Hampton 3.00 8.00
18 Aleksej Pokusevski 4.00 10.00
19 Precious Achiuwa 6.00 15.00
20 Udoka Azubuike 4.00 10.00
21 Anthony Edwards 60.00 150.00
22 Isaac Okoro 5.00 12.00
23 Immanuel Quickley 8.00 20.00
24 Tyrese Haliburton 40.00 100.00
25 CJ Elleby 3.00 8.00

2020-21 Panini National Treasures Rookie Materials Prime

*PRIME: .75X TO 2X BASIC
PRINT RUN 25 COPIES PER
2 Payton Pritchard 50.00 120.00
7 Patrick Williams 60.00 150.00
8 Obi Toppin 40.00 100.00
23 Immanuel Quickley 50.00 120.00
24 Tyrese Haliburton 100.00 250.00

2020-21 Panini National Treasures Rookie Patch Autographs Gold FOTL

*GOLD FOTL: .5X TO 1.25X BASIC
PRINT RUN 24 COPIES PER
EXCHANGE DEADLINE 2/11/2023

2020-21 Panini National Treasures Rookie Patch Autographs Horizontal

STATED PRINT RUN 54-75 SER.#'d SETS
EXCHANGE DEADLINE 2/11/2023
101 Xavier Tillman/75 30.00 80.00
102 Jae'Sean Tate/54 30.00 80.00
103 Tyrese Haliburton/75 2,000.00 4,000.00
104 Isaiah Joe/75 30.00 80.00
105 Isaac Okoro/75 40.00 100.00
106 Theo Maledon/75 25.00 60.00
107 Immanuel Quickley/75 125.00 300.00
108 CJ Elleby/75 25.00 60.00
109 Daniel Oturu/75 25.00 60.00
110 Facundo Campazzo/75 30.00 80.00
111 Anthony Edwards/75 15,000.00 20,000.00
112 Karim Mane/75 20.00 50.00
113 Cassius Winston/75 25.00 60.00
114 Tyrese Maxey/75 1,000.00 2,000.00
115 Precious Achiuwa/75 50.00 125.00
116 Jahmi'us Ramsey/75 25.00 60.00
117 Zeke Nnaji/75 30.00 80.00
118 Devon Dotson/75 25.00 60.00
119 Nico Mannion/75 25.00 60.00
120 Udoka Azubuike/75 30.00 80.00
121 Aleksej Pokusevski/75 30.00 80.00
122 RJ Hampton/75 25.00 60.00
123 Saddiq Bey/75 50.00 120.00
124 James Wiseman/75 40.00 100.00
125 Tyrell Terry/75 20.00 50.00
126 Jalen Smith/75 50.00 125.00
127 Josh Green/75 50.00 120.00
128 Onyeka Okongwu/75 50.00 120.00
129 Tyler Bey/75 25.00 60.00
130 LaMelo Ball/75 2,000.00 4,000.00
131 Killian Hayes/75 25.00 60.00
132 Saben Lee/75 25.00 60.00
133 Robert Woodard II/75 25.00 60.00
134 Malachi Flynn/75 25.00 60.00
135 Aaron Nesmith/75 50.00 125.00
136 Skylar Mays/75 25.00 60.00
137 Obi Toppin/75 50.00 120.00
138 Deni Avdija/75 60.00 150.00
139 Patrick Williams/75 60.00 150.00
140 Jordan Nwora/75 30.00 80.00
141 Vernon Carey Jr./75 25.00 60.00
142 Devin Vassell/75 200.00 500.00
143 Jaden McDaniels/75 200.00 500.00
144 Caleb Martin/75 50.00 125.00
145 Isaiah Stewart/75 50.00 125.00
146 Kira Lewis Jr./75 25.00 60.00
147 Desmond Bane/75 350.00 700.00
148 Payton Pritchard/75 100.00 250.00
149 Cole Anthony/75 75.00 200.00
150 Tre Jones/75 75.00 200.00

2020-21 Panini National Treasures Rookie Patch Autographs Horizontal Bronze

*BRONZE: .5X TO 1.2X BASIC
PRINT RUN 49 COPIES PER
EXCHANGE DEADLINE 2/11/2023
102 Jae'Sean Tate 40.00 100.00

2020-21 Panini National Treasures Rookie Private Signings Association Version

1 Anthony Edwards 800.00 1,500.00
2 James Wiseman 20.00 50.00
23 Devon Dotson 8.00 20.00
27 Udoka Azubuike 15.00 40.00
30 Desmond Bane 30.00 80.00
41 Jae'Sean Tate 50.00 120.00
49 Cassius Stanley 12.00 30.00

2020-21 Panini National Treasures Rookie Private Signings Icon Version

5 Isaac Okoro 40.00 100.00
23 Devon Dotson 8.00 20.00
27 Udoka Azubuike 15.00 40.00
30 Desmond Bane 30.00 80.00
41 Jae'Sean Tate 50.00 120.00
49 Cassius Stanley 12.00 30.00

2020-21 Panini National Treasures Rookie Triple Materials

STATED PRINT RUN 99 SER.#'d SETS
1 Cole Anthony 30.00 80.00
2 Payton Pritchard 12.00 30.00
3 Kira Lewis Jr. 4.00 10.00
4 Jaden McDaniels 12.00 30.00
5 Devin Vassell 12.00 30.00
6 Jordan Nwora 5.00 12.00
7 Patrick Williams 30.00 80.00
8 Obi Toppin 8.00 20.00
9 Deni Avdija 10.00 25.00
10 Malachi Flynn 4.00 10.00
11 Killian Hayes 4.00 10.00
12 LaMelo Ball 200.00 500.00
13 Onyeka Okongwu 8.00 20.00
14 Josh Green 8.00 20.00
15 James Wiseman 5.00 12.00
16 Saddiq Bey 20.00 50.00
17 RJ Hampton 4.00 10.00
18 Aleksej Pokusevski 5.00 12.00
19 Precious Achiuwa 8.00 20.00
20 Udoka Azubuike 5.00 12.00
21 Anthony Edwards 75.00 200.00

22 Isaac Okoro 6.00 15.00
23 Immanuel Quickley 10.00 25.00
24 Tyrese Haliburton 50.00 120.00
25 CJ Elleby 4.00 10.00

2020-21 Panini National Treasures Rookie Triple Materials Prime

*PRIME: .75X TO 2X BASIC
PRINT RUN 25 COPIES PER
2 Payton Pritchard 60.00 150.00
7 Patrick Williams 75.00 200.00
8 Obi Toppin 50.00 120.00
23 Immanuel Quickley 60.00 150.00
24 Tyrese Haliburton 125.00 300.00

2020-21 Panini National Treasures Signatures

STATED PRINT RUN 25-99 SER.#'d SETS
EXCHANGE DEADLINE 2/11/2023
*BRONZE: .75X TO 2X BASIC
1 Joe Harris/99 6.00 15.00
4 Kendrick Nunn/75 6.00 15.00
5 RJ Barrett/49 30.00 80.00
6 Jarrett Culver/99 5.00 12.00
8 Isaiah Rider/75 15.00 40.00
9 Jayson Tatum/25 200.00 500.00
11 Kevin Durant/25 300.00 600.00
12 Andrea Bargnani/99 5.00 12.00
14 Wendell Carter Jr./99 6.00 15.00
16 Kurt Rambis/49 6.00 15.00
19 Zion Williamson/25 600.00 1,200.00
21 Jason Williams/49 60.00 150.00
24 Thaddeus Young/99 5.00 12.00
25 PJ Washington Jr./99 20.00 50.00
26 Stephen Curry/25 1,000.00 2,000.00
27 Anthony Davis/25 125.00 300.00
28 Trae Young/25 200.00 500.00
29 Rui Hachimura/49 30.00 80.00
30 Buddy Hield/99 12.00 30.00
31 Kevin Garnett/25 150.00 400.00
32 Al Horford/99 12.00 30.00
35 Rick Barry/49 12.00 30.00
37 T.J. Ford/99 5.00 12.00
41 Charles Barkley/25 150.00 400.00
44 LaMarcus Aldridge/75 12.00 30.00
46 Karl-Anthony Towns/49 30.00 80.00
47 Steven Adams/49 12.00 30.00
49 Gordon Hayward/75 20.00 50.00

2020-21 Panini National Treasures Spectra Hall of Fame Signatures

3 Allen Iverson 300.00 600.00
34 Kevin Garnett 200.00 500.00
48 Shaquille O'Neal 300.00 600.00

2020-21 Panini National Treasures Timeless Talents Signatures

STATED PRINT RUN 99 SER.#'d SETS
EXCHANGE DEADLINE 2/11/2023
*BRONZE/25: .75X TO 2X BASIC
1 Hakeem Olajuwon 40.00 100.00
2 Mark Aguirre 6.00 15.00
3 Latrell Sprewell 10.00 25.00
4 Bernard King 10.00 25.00
5 Walt Frazier 12.00 30.00
7 Sam Cassell 6.00 15.00
8 Paul Pierce 30.00 80.00
9 Sam Perkins 6.00 15.00
10 Artis Gilmore 10.00 25.00
11 Danny Manning 6.00 15.00
12 Brent Barry 6.00 15.00
13 Quentin Richardson 5.00 12.00
14 Darius Miles 5.00 12.00
15 Kurt Rambis 6.00 15.00
16 Grant Hill 30.00 80.00
17 Charles Oakley 8.00 20.00
18 Wally Szczerbiak 6.00 15.00
19 Caron Butler 6.00 15.00
20 Fat Lever 8.00 20.00
21 Rod Strickland 6.00 15.00
22 Christian Laettner 12.00 30.00
23 David Lee 5.00 12.00
24 Jason Terry 6.00 15.00
25 Devin Harris 5.00 12.00
26 Tony Delk 6.00 15.00
27 Steve Francis 8.00 20.00
28 Richard Jefferson 5.00 12.00
29 Gail Goodrich 8.00 20.00
30 Clyde Drexler 30.00 80.00

2020-21 Panini National Treasures Timeless Treasures Materials

STATED PRINT RUN 99 SER.#'d SETS
*PRIME: .75X TO 2 BASIC
1 Adrian Dantley 4.00 10.00
2 Dwyane Wade 20.00 50.00
3 Dominique Wilkins 6.00 15.00
4 Calvin Murphy 4.00 10.00
5 Bernard King 5.00 12.00
6 Charles Barkley 25.00 60.00
7 Chris Mullin 8.00 20.00
8 Gary Payton 12.00 30.00
9 Glen Rice 3.00 8.00
10 Hakeem Olajuwon 12.00 30.00
11 Brad Daugherty 3.00 8.00
12 Karl Malone 12.00 30.00
13 Michael Redd 3.00 8.00
14 Mike Bibby 4.00 10.00
15 Allen Iverson 15.00 40.00
16 Ray Allen 8.00 20.00
17 Robert Horry 4.00 10.00
18 Shaquille O'Neal 25.00 60.00
19 Marcus Camby 3.00 8.00
20 Larry Bird 30.00 80.00
21 Kevin McHale 5.00 12.00
22 Anfernee Hardaway 20.00 50.00
23 Jason Kidd 12.00 30.00
24 Jason Richardson 4.00 10.00
25 David Robinson 12.00 30.00
26 John Stockton 12.00 30.00
27 Alonzo Mourning 12.00 30.00
28 Danny Manning 3.00 8.00
29 Clyde Drexler 10.00 25.00
30 Alex English 4.00 10.00

2020-21 Panini National Treasures Timeline Materials

STATED PRINT RUN 30-99 SER.#'d SETS
*PRIME: .75X TO 2 BASIC
1 OG Anunoby/89 10.00 25.00
2 Aaron Gordon/60 5.00 12.00
3 Naz Reid/99 6.00 15.00
4 Paul Millsap/99 4.00 10.00
5 Montrezl Harrell/99 5.00 12.00
6 Andrew Wiggins/99 6.00 15.00
7 Jarrett Allen/99 6.00 15.00
8 DeAndre Jordan/99 4.00 10.00
9 Serge Ibaka/99 4.00 10.00
10 Stanley Johnson/99 3.00 8.00
11 Mitchell Robinson/99 10.00 25.00
12 Ivica Zubac/99 5.00 12.00
13 Danilo Gallinari/99 4.00 10.00
14 Robert Covington/99 4.00 10.00
15 Bojan Bogdanovic/99 4.00 10.00
16 Vince Carter/99 15.00 40.00
17 Miles Bridges/30 5.00 12.00
19 Jonas Valanciunas/49 4.00 10.00
20 Daniel Theis/30 12.00 30.00
21 Elfrid Payton/99 4.00 10.00
22 Josh Okogie/99 4.00 10.00
23 Wendell Carter Jr./49 4.00 10.00
24 Caris LeVert/99 5.00 12.00
25 Steven Adams/99 5.00 12.00
26 Kevin Love/99 5.00 12.00
27 Rudy Gobert/99 8.00 20.00
28 Danny Green/99 4.00 10.00
29 Bam Adebayo/99 10.00 25.00
30 Karl-Anthony Towns/99 10.00 25.00

2020-21 Panini National Treasures Treasured Signatures

STATED PRINT RUN 25-99 SER.#'d SETS
EXCHANGE DEADLINE 2/11/2023
*BRONZE: .75X TO 2X BASIC
1 Mike Bibby/99 8.00 20.00
3 Chauncey Billups/99 15.00 40.00
4 John Stockton/49 75.00 200.00
5 Luka Doncic/49 2,000.00 4,000.00
6 Paul Pierce/49 50.00 120.00
7 Dwyane Wade/49 100.00 250.00
9 Jason Williams/49 60.00 150.00
10 Hakeem Olajuwon/49 75.00 200.00
11 Latrell Sprewell/99 25.00 60.00
12 Hedo Turkoglu/99 6.00 15.00
15 Steve Kerr/99 20.00 50.00
16 Bill Walton/99 40.00 100.00
17 Kendall Gill/49 12.00 30.00
18 Calvin Murphy/99 6.00 15.00
19 Jason Terry/99 6.00 15.00
20 David Robinson/49 75.00 200.00
22 Magic Johnson/49 125.00 300.00
23 Allen Iverson/25 150.00 400.00
24 Robert Parish/99 12.00 30.00
25 Oscar Robertson/25 75.00 200.00

2020-21 Panini National Treasures Treasured Threads

STATED PRINT RUN 49-99 SER.#'d SETS
*PRIME: .75X TO 2 BASIC
1 Joel Embiid/99 12.00 30.00
2 LeBron James/49 75.00 200.00
3 Deandre Ayton/99 5.00 12.00
4 Harrison Barnes/99 4.00 10.00
5 Pascal Siakam/99 8.00 20.00
6 Carmelo Anthony/99 12.00 30.00
7 Rudy Gobert/99 6.00 15.00
8 Mike Conley/99 4.00 10.00
9 Andrew Wiggins/99 10.00 25.00
10 Draymond Green/99 6.00 15.00
11 DeMar DeRozan/99 6.00 15.00
12 CJ McCollum/99 6.00 15.00
13 Shai Gilgeous-Alexander/99 12.00 30.00
14 Tyler Herro/99 10.00 25.00
15 Julius Randle/99 5.00 12.00
16 Darius Bazley/99 3.00 8.00
17 Aaron Gordon/99 5.00 12.00
19 Karl-Anthony Towns/99 8.00 20.00
20 Paul George/99 12.00 30.00
21 Derrick Rose/99 12.00 30.00
22 Stephen Curry/99 75.00 200.00
23 Paul Millsap/99 4.00 10.00
24 Malcolm Brogdon/99 5.00 12.00
25 Rui Hachimura/99 6.00 15.00
26 Bradley Beal/99 6.00 15.00
27 Bojan Bogdanovic/99 4.00 10.00
28 Rudy Gay/99 5.00 12.00
29 Chris Paul/99 10.00 25.00
30 Zion Williamson/49 60.00 150.00

2020-21 Panini National Treasures Treasures of the Hall Autographs

STATED PRINT RUN 35-75 SER.#'d SETS
EXCHANGE DEADLINE 2/11/2023
1 Shaquille O'Neal /35 300.00 600.00
2 Allen Iverson/35 300.00 600.00
3 Joe Dumars/49 12.00 30.00
4 Kareem Abdul-Jabbar/35 200.00 500.00
5 Larry Bird/35 200.00 500.00
6 Hakeem Olajuwon/49 60.00 150.00
7 Lenny Wilkens/75 8.00 20.00
8 Bernard King/75 10.00 25.00
10 Chris Mullin/75 20.00 50.00
11 Walt Frazier/49 12.00 30.00
12 Karl Malone/35 60.00 150.00
13 Alex English/49 8.00 20.00
14 Gary Payton/75 25.00 60.00
15 Nate Archibald/75 10.00 25.00
16 Bob McAdoo/49 20.00 50.00
17 Jason Kidd/49 40.00 100.00
19 George Gervin/75 12.00 30.00
20 Isiah Thomas/75 40.00 100.00
21 Dino Radja/75 6.00 15.00
22 Jerry Lucas/49 12.00 30.00
23 Ray Allen/75 30.00 80.00
25 Grant Hill/75 30.00 80.00

2020-21 Panini National Treasures Treasures of the Hall Autographs Bronze

*BRONZE: .6X TO 1.5X BASIC
PRINT RUN 25 COPIES PER
EXCHANGE DEADLINE 2/11/2023
1 Shaquille O'Neal 300.00 600.00
2 Allen Iverson 300.00 600.00
4 Kareem Abdul-Jabbar 200.00 500.00
5 Larry Bird 200.00 500.00
12 Karl Malone 60.00 150.00

2020-21 Panini National Treasures Tremendous Treasures Relics

STATED PRINT RUN 30-99 SER.#'d SETS
*PRIME: .75X TO 2 BASIC
1 Aaron Gordon/99 5.00 12.00
2 Bojan Bogdanovic/99 4.00 10.00
3 Danny Green/49 4.00 10.00
4 DeAndre Jordan/99 4.00 10.00
6 Eric Bledsoe/38 4.00 10.00
7 Fred VanVleet/99 15.00 40.00
8 Gary Harris/99 4.00 10.00
9 Harrison Barnes/99 4.00 10.00
10 Jabari Parker/99 3.00 8.00
11 Andrew Wiggins/99 10.00 25.00
12 Donovan Mitchell/99 15.00 40.00
13 Chris Paul/99 12.00 30.00
14 Doug McDermott/99 4.00 10.00
15 Jarrett Allen/99 5.00 12.00
16 Joel Embiid/49 12.00 30.00
17 Jordan Clarkson/99 5.00 12.00
18 Josh Okogie/99 4.00 10.00
19 Karl-Anthony Towns/99 8.00 20.00
20 Kevin Knox II/30 3.00 8.00
21 Marvin Bagley III/49 4.00 10.00
22 Stanley Johnson/49 3.00 8.00
23 Lonnie Walker IV/99 5.00 12.00
25 Keita Bates-Diop/99 3.00 8.00
26 CJ McCollum/99 5.00 12.00
27 Caris LeVert/99 5.00 12.00
28 Bradley Beal/99 10.00 25.00
30 Rudy Gobert/99 8.00 20.00

2020-21 Panini National Treasures Validating Marks Autographs

STATED PRINT RUN 25-49 SER.#'d SETS
EXCHANGE DEADLINE 2/11/2023
*BRONZE: .75X TO 2X BASIC
1 Jrue Holiday/49 15.00 40.00
2 Sekou Doumbouya/49 6.00 15.00
3 Gordon Hayward/49 20.00 50.00
4 Collin Sexton/49 10.00 25.00
6 Wendell Carter Jr./49 8.00 20.00
7 Jamal Murray/49 40.00 100.00
8 Brandon Clarke/49 10.00 25.00
9 Anthony Davis/25 125.00 300.00
12 LaMarcus Aldridge/49 10.00 25.00
15 Maxi Kleber/49 8.00 20.00
16 De'Aaron Fox/25 40.00 100.00
17 Domantas Sabonis/49 20.00 50.00
18 Matthew Dellavedova/49 8.00 20.00
20 Stephen Curry/25 1,250.00 2,500.00
24 Rudy Gay/49 10.00 25.00
25 Kevin Durant/25 300.00 600.00

2021-22 Panini National Treasures

COMPLETE SET (150)
COMMON CARD (1-100) 1.25 3.00
SEMISTARS 1.50 4.00
UNLISTED STARS 2.00 5.00
COMMON JSY AU RC (101-150) 30.00 80.00
JSY AU RC SEMIS 40.00 100.00
JSY AU RC UNLISTED 50.00 120.00
STATED PRINT RUN 99 SER.#'d SETS
EXCHANGE DEADLINE 1/20/2024
*75TH ANN/75 (1-100): .5X TO 1.2X BASIC
*75TH ANN/75 (101-150): .4X TO 1X BASIC
*BRNZ RPA/49: .4X TO 1X BASIC
*PINK RPA/25: .5X TO 1.2X BASIC
1 Norman Powell 1.50 4.00
2 Julius Randle 2.50 6.00
3 Kevin Porter Jr. 1.50 4.00
4 Wendell Carter Jr. 2.00 5.00
5 Deandre Ayton 2.00 5.00
6 Kevin Durant 6.00 15.00
7 Jamal Murray 3.00 8.00
8 Tyler Herro 3.00 8.00
9 Karl-Anthony Towns 3.00 8.00
10 Montrezl Harrell 1.50 4.00
11 De'Aaron Fox 3.00 8.00
12 RJ Barrett 3.00 8.00
13 Christian Wood 1.50 4.00
14 Mo Bamba 1.50 4.00
15 Chris Paul 4.00 10.00
16 James Harden 4.00 10.00
17 Nikola Jokic 10.00 25.00
18 Bam Adebayo 3.00 8.00
19 LeBron James 40.00 100.00
20 Miles Bridges 1.50 4.00
21 Harrison Barnes 1.50 4.00
22 Derrick Rose 3.00 8.00
23 John Wall 2.50 6.00
24 Jerami Grant 2.00 5.00
25 Mike Conley 1.50 4.00
26 Kyrie Irving 4.00 10.00
27 Reggie Jackson 1.50 4.00
28 Darius Garland 3.00 8.00
29 Anthony Davis 5.00 12.00
30 LaMelo Ball 5.00 12.00
31 Buddy Hield 1.50 4.00
32 Trae Young 5.00 12.00
33 Jordan Poole 3.00 8.00
34 Saddiq Bey 1.50 4.00
35 Rudy Gobert 2.50 6.00
36 DeMar DeRozan 2.50 6.00
37 Kawhi Leonard 5.00 12.00
38 Jarrett Allen 2.00 5.00
39 Russell Westbrook 3.00 8.00
40 Gordon Hayward 1.50 4.00
41 Shai Gilgeous-Alexander 10.00 25.00
42 John Collins 2.00 5.00
43 Desmond Bane 4.00 10.00
44 Isaiah Stewart 2.00 5.00
45 Donovan Mitchell 4.00 10.00
46 Zach LaVine 3.00 8.00
47 Paul George 3.00 8.00
48 Collin Sexton 2.00 5.00
49 Carmelo Anthony 3.00 8.00
50 Dennis Schroder 2.00 5.00
51 Luguentz Dort 2.00 5.00
52 Clint Capela 2.00 5.00
53 Tyrese Maxey 5.00 12.00
54 Stephen Curry 40.00 100.00
55 Bojan Bogdanovic 1.50 4.00
56 Nikola Vucevic 2.00 5.00
57 Jalen Brunson 4.00 10.00
58 Ben Simmons 2.00 5.00
59 Dejounte Murray 2.00 5.00
60 Jayson Tatum 8.00 20.00
61 Darius Bazley 1.25 3.00
62 Malcolm Brogdon 1.50 4.00
63 Terry Rozier III 1.50 4.00
64 Andrew Wiggins 2.50 6.00
65 Ja Morant 6.00 15.00
66 Giannis Antetokounmpo 10.00 25.00
67 Luka Doncic 40.00 100.00
68 Joel Embiid 5.00 12.00
69 Keldon Johnson 2.50 6.00
70 Jaylen Brown 3.00 8.00
71 Zion Williamson 5.00 12.00
72 Domantas Sabonis 2.50 6.00
73 Kelly Oubre Jr. 2.00 5.00
74 Draymond Green 2.50 6.00
75 Dillon Brooks 2.00 5.00
76 Khris Middleton 2.00 5.00
77 Kristaps Porzingis 2.50 6.00
78 Tobias Harris 1.50 4.00
79 Derrick White 2.00 5.00
80 Fred VanVleet 2.50 6.00
81 Brandon Ingram 2.50 6.00
82 Caris LeVert 1.50 4.00
83 Bobby Portis 1.50 4.00
84 James Wiseman 1.50 4.00
85 Jaren Jackson Jr. 3.00 8.00
86 Jrue Holiday 2.50 6.00
87 D'Angelo Russell 2.00 5.00
88 Rui Hachimura 2.00 5.00
89 Damian Lillard 5.00 12.00
90 OG Anunoby 2.00 5.00
91 Jonas Valanciunas 1.50 4.00
92 Cole Anthony 2.50 6.00
93 Lonzo Ball 2.00 5.00
94 Devin Booker 5.00 12.00
95 Michael Porter Jr. 2.50 6.00
96 Jimmy Butler 3.00 8.00
97 Anthony Edwards 20.00 50.00
98 Bradley Beal 2.50 6.00
99 CJ McCollum 1.50 4.00
100 Pascal Siakam 3.00 8.00
101 Jalen Suggs AU JSY/99 RC 400.00 800.00
103 Kessler Edwards AU JSY/99 RC 50.00 125.00
104 Moses Moody AU JSY/99 RC 300.00 600.00
105 Quentin Grimes AU JSY/99 RC 400.00 800.00
106 Jericho Sims AU JSY/99 RC 60.00 150.00
107 Jalen Green AU JSY/99 RC 3,000.00 6,000.00
108 Bones Hyland AU JSY/99 RC 150.00 400.00
109 Charles Bassey AU JSY/99 RC 50.00 125.00
110 Joshua Primo AU JSY/99 RC 40.00 100.00
111 Scottie Lewis AU JSY/99 RC 40.00 100.00
112 Corey Kispert AU JSY/99 RC 60.00 150.00
113 Cameron Thomas
AU JSY/99 RC 500.00 1,000.00
114 Josh Giddey AU JSY/99 RC 600.00 1,200.00
115 Jason Preston AU JSY/99 RC 40.00 100.00
116 Jaden Springer AU JSY/99 RC 50.00 125.00
117 Chris Duarte AU JSY/99 RC 40.00 100.00
118 Day'Ron Sharpe AU JSY/99 RC 50.00 125.00
119 Jonathan Kuminga
AU JSY/99 RC 1,250.00 2,500.00
120 Isaiah Todd AU JSY/99 RC 40.00 100.00
121 Alperen Sengun
AU JSY/99 RC 1,000.00 2,000.00
122 Santi Aldama AU JSY/99 RC 60.00 150.00
123 Cade Cunningham
AU JSY/99 RC 5,000.00 10,000.00
124 JT Thor AU JSY/99 RC 50.00 125.00
125 Jeremiah Robinson-Earl
AU JSY/99 RC 50.00 125.00
126 Trey Murphy III AU JSY/99 RC 600.00 1,200.00
127 Marko Simonovic AU JSY/99 RC 40.00 100.00
128 Miles McBride AU JSY/99 RC 200.00 500.00
129 Franz Wagner
AU JSY/99 RC 1,000.00 2,000.00
130 Sandro Mamukelashvili
AU JSY/99 RC 60.00 150.00
131 Tre Mann AU JSY/99 RC 80.00 200.00
132 Ayo Dosunmu AU JSY/99 RC 150.00 400.00
133 Scottie Barnes
AU JSY/99 RC 1,500.00 3,000.00
134 Neemias Queta AU JSY/99 RC 50.00 125.00
135 Kai Jones AU JSY/99 RC 40.00 100.00
136 Jared Butler AU JSY/99 RC 50.00 125.00
137 Davion Mitchell AU JSY/99 RC 50.00 125.00
138 Joe Wieskamp AU JSY/99 RC 40.00 100.00
139 Jalen Johnson AU JSY/99 RC 800.00 1,500.00
140 Isaiah Livers AU JSY/99 RC 50.00 125.00
141 Isaiah Jackson AU JSY/99 RC 50.00 125.00
142 Dalano Banton AU JSY/99 RC 60.00 150.00
143 Ziaire Williams AU JSY/99 RC 60.00 150.00
144 Brandon Boston
Jr. AU JSY/99 RC 50.00 125.00
145 Keon Johnson AU JSY/99 RC 50.00 125.00
147 Evan Mobley AU JSY/99 RC 1,000.00 2,000.00
148 Luka Garza AU JSY/99 RC 50.00 125.00
149 Greg Brown III AU JSY/99 RC 40.00 100.00
150 James Bouknight AU JSY/99 RC 40.00 100.00

2021-22 Panini National Treasures Biography Materials

COMMON CARD 2.50 6.00
SEMISTARS 3.00 8.00
UNLISTED STARS 4.00 10.00
STATED PRINT RUN 99 SER.#'d SETS
*PRIME/11-25: 1.25X TO 3X BASIC
1 Kevin Durant 12.00 30.00
2 LaMarcus Aldridge 4.00 10.00
3 DeMar DeRozan 5.00 12.00
4 Carmelo Anthony 6.00 15.00
5 Julius Randle 5.00 12.00
6 Caris LeVert 3.00 8.00
7 Terry Rozier III 3.00 8.00
8 Rajon Rondo 5.00 12.00
9 Chris Paul 8.00 20.00
10 Mike Conley 3.00 8.00
11 Lauri Markkanen 5.00 12.00
12 Derrick Rose 6.00 15.00
13 Goran Dragic 3.00 8.00
14 Andrew Wiggins 5.00 12.00
15 Paul George 6.00 15.00
16 Anthony Davis 10.00 25.00
17 Tobias Harris 3.00 8.00
18 Kawhi Leonard 10.00 25.00
19 Zach LaVine 6.00 15.00
20 Jimmy Butler 6.00 15.00
21 Kemba Walker 4.00 10.00
22 Aaron Gordon 4.00 10.00
23 Steven Adams 3.00 8.00
24 Caron Butler 3.00 8.00
25 Dwight Howard 5.00 12.00
26 John Wall 5.00 12.00
27 LeBron James 60.00 150.00
28 Jason Kidd 6.00 15.00
29 Tim Duncan 10.00 25.00
30 Shawn Marion 3.00 8.00
31 Rudy Gay 4.00 10.00
32 Kyrie Irving 8.00 20.00
33 Russell Westbrook 6.00 15.00
34 Kyle Lowry 4.00 10.00
35 Al Horford 4.00 10.00
36 D'Angelo Russell 4.00 10.00
37 Montrezl Harrell 3.00 8.00
39 James Harden 8.00 20.00
40 Harrison Barnes 3.00 8.00

2021-22 Panini National Treasures Century Materials

COMMON CARD 2.50 6.00
SEMISTARS 3.00 8.00
UNLISTED STARS 4.00 10.00
STATED PRINT RUN 99 SER.#'d SETS
*PRIME/25: 1.25X TO 3X BASIC
1 Domantas Sabonis 5.00 12.00
2 Tobias Harris 3.00 8.00
3 Brandon Ingram 5.00 12.00
4 Lonnie Walker IV 3.00 8.00
5 Donovan Mitchell 8.00 20.00
6 Jaren Jackson Jr. 6.00 15.00
7 Stephen Curry 60.00 150.00
8 Marcus Smart 4.00 10.00
9 Zach LaVine 6.00 15.00
10 Myles Turner 4.00 10.00
11 Kawhi Leonard 10.00 25.00
12 Jae Crowder 2.50 6.00
13 Ben Simmons 4.00 10.00
14 Derrick White 4.00 10.00
15 John Collins 4.00 10.00
16 Tyrese Haliburton 8.00 20.00
17 Zion Williamson 25.00 60.00
18 Jalen Brunson 8.00 20.00
20 RJ Hampton 2.50 6.00
22 Jusuf Nurkic 3.00 8.00
23 Chris Paul 8.00 20.00
25 DeMar DeRozan 5.00 12.00
26 Clint Capela 4.00 10.00
27 Jayson Tatum 15.00 40.00
28 Aaron Gordon 4.00 10.00
29 Nikola Jokic 20.00 50.00
30 Terrence Ross 3.00 8.00
31 Anthony Edwards 30.00 80.00
32 Anfernee Simons 6.00 15.00
33 CJ McCollum 3.00 8.00
35 Jamal Murray 6.00 15.00
36 Cam Reddish 4.00 10.00
37 Kyrie Irving 8.00 20.00
39 Jerami Grant 4.00 10.00

2021-22 Panini National Treasures Clutch Factor Jersey Signatures

COMMON CARD 12.00 30.00
SEMISTARS 15.00 40.00
UNLISTED STARS 20.00 50.00
STATED PRINT RUN 25-49 SER.#'d SETS
*PRIME/25: .6X TO 1.5X BASIC
1 Kristaps Porzingis/25 25.00 60.00
2 JJ Redick/49 20.00 50.00
3 Anthony Davis/25 100.00 250.00
4 Kevin Garnett/49 150.00 400.00
5 Zion Williamson/49 500.00 1,000.00
6 De'Aaron Fox/49 30.00 80.00
7 Luka Doncic/35 800.00 1,500.00
8 James Wiseman/49 15.00 40.00
9 Aleksej Pokusevski/49 15.00 40.00
10 Domantas Sabonis/49 25.00 60.00
12 Saddiq Bey/49 15.00 40.00
13 Rui Hachimura/49 20.00 50.00
15 Nikola Jokic/49 400.00 800.00
16 PJ Washington Jr./49 20.00 50.00
17 Deni Avdija/49 20.00 50.00
18 Onyeka Okongwu/49 20.00 50.00
20 Ja Morant/25 600.00 1,200.00
21 Obi Toppin/25 20.00 50.00
22 Anthony Edwards/25 500.00 1,000.00
23 Larry Johnson/25 75.00 200.00
24 Kevin Durant/49 300.00 600.00
25 Jaren Jackson Jr./49 60.00 150.00
26 Trae Young/49 400.00 800.00
27 Franz Wagner/49 150.00 400.00
28 Allen Iverson/49 200.00 500.00
29 Luis Scola/49 15.00 40.00
30 Stephen Curry/25 1,250.00 2,500.00
31 Vince Carter/49 150.00 400.00
32 Magic Johnson/25 200.00 500.00
34 Julius Randle/25 25.00 60.00
35 Taj Gibson/49 12.00 30.00
36 Wendell Carter Jr./49 20.00 50.00
37 Luka Garza/49 20.00 50.00
38 Larry Bird/49 200.00 500.00
39 Armoni Brooks/49 20.00 50.00
40 Juan Toscano-Anderson/49 20.00 50.00
41 Cade Cunningham/25 500.00 1,000.00
42 Jalen Suggs/49 100.00 250.00
43 Evan Mobley/49 300.00 600.00
44 Moses Moody/49 40.00 100.00
45 Chris Duarte/49 15.00 40.00
46 Jericho Sims/49 25.00 60.00
47 Bones Hyland/49 25.00 60.00
48 Corey Kispert/49 25.00 60.00
49 Miles McBride/49 30.00 80.00
50 Jonathan Kuminga/49 150.00 400.00

2021-22 Panini National Treasures Colossal Materials

COMMON CARD 3.00 8.00
SEMISTARS 4.00 10.00
UNLISTED STARS 5.00 12.00
STATED PRINT RUN 99 SER.#'d SETS
*PRIME/17-25: 1.25X TO 3X BASIC
1 Cameron Johnson 5.00 12.00
2 Saddiq Bey 4.00 10.00
3 Kyle Lowry 5.00 12.00
4 Roy Hibbert 4.00 10.00
5 Karl-Anthony Towns 8.00 20.00
6 Kemba Walker 5.00 12.00
7 Zion Williamson 30.00 80.00
8 Dirk Nowitzki 30.00 80.00
9 Nikola Vucevic 5.00 12.00
10 Nikola Jokic 20.00 50.00
11 CJ McCollum 4.00 10.00
12 Malcolm Brogdon 4.00 10.00
13 Bojan Bogdanovic 4.00 10.00
14 Lamar Odom 5.00 12.00
15 Jamal Crawford 5.00 12.00
16 Kevin Love 5.00 12.00
17 Mitchell Robinson 5.00 12.00
18 Vince Carter 10.00 25.00
19 Deandre Ayton 5.00 12.00
20 Isaiah Stewart 5.00 12.00

2021-22 Panini National Treasures Colossal Rookie Materials

COMMON CARD 3.00 8.00
SEMISTARS 4.00 10.00
UNLISTED STARS 5.00 12.00
STATED PRINT RUN 99 SER.#'d SETS
*PRIME/25: 1.25X TO 3X BASIC
1 Cade Cunningham 40.00 100.00
2 Keon Johnson 5.00 12.00
3 David Johnson 4.00 10.00
4 Neemias Queta 5.00 12.00
5 Greg Brown III 4.00 10.00
6 Scottie Lewis 4.00 10.00
7 Jaden Springer 5.00 12.00
8 Jared Butler 5.00 12.00
9 Aaron Wiggins 6.00 15.00
11 Cameron Thomas 10.00 25.00
12 Luka Garza 5.00 12.00
13 Davion Mitchell 5.00 12.00
14 Quentin Grimes 10.00 25.00
15 Herbert Jones 6.00 15.00
16 Tre Mann 8.00 20.00
17 Jalen Green 25.00 60.00
18 Jason Preston 4.00 10.00
19 Alperen Sengun 15.00 40.00
20 Josh Giddey 15.00 40.00
21 Charles Bassey 5.00 12.00
23 Day'Ron Sharpe 5.00 12.00
24 Sandro Mamukelashvili 6.00 15.00
25 Isaiah Jackson 5.00 12.00
26 Trey Murphy III 15.00 40.00
27 Jalen Johnson 15.00 40.00
28 Jeremiah Robinson-Earl 5.00 12.00
29 Ayo Dosunmu 10.00 25.00
30 Joshua Primo 4.00 10.00
31 Chris Duarte 4.00 10.00
32 Miles McBride 8.00 20.00
33 Evan Mobley 20.00 50.00
34 Santi Aldama 6.00 15.00
37 Jalen Suggs 12.00 30.00
38 Joe Wieskamp 4.00 10.00
39 Bones Hyland 6.00 15.00
40 JT Thor 5.00 12.00
41 Corey Kispert 6.00 15.00
42 Moses Moody 10.00 25.00
43 Franz Wagner 15.00 40.00
44 Scottie Barnes 15.00 40.00
45 Isaiah Todd 4.00 10.00
46 Ziaire Williams 6.00 15.00
47 James Bouknight 4.00 10.00
48 Jonathan Kuminga 15.00 40.00
49 Brandon Boston Jr. 5.00 12.00
50 Kai Jones 4.00 10.00

2021-22 Panini National Treasures Definitive Ink

COMMON CARD 6.00 15.00
SEMISTARS 8.00 20.00
UNLISTED STARS 10.00 25.00
STATED PRINT RUN 49-99 SER.#'d SETS
EXCHANGE DEADLINE 1/20/2024
1 Kwame Brown/49 8.00 20.00
2 Doug Collins/49 8.00 20.00
3 Anthony Davis/49 75.00 200.00
4 Moses Brown/49 6.00 15.00
5 Dirk Nowitzki/49 150.00 400.00
7 Kevin Porter Jr./99 8.00 20.00
8 Dan Issel/99 10.00 25.00
9 Domantas Sabonis/49 12.00 30.00
10 Chauncey Billups/99 12.00 30.00
11 De'Aaron Fox/99 15.00 40.00
12 Mark Aguirre/99 8.00 20.00
13 Bill Walton/99 40.00 100.00
14 Spud Webb/99 10.00 25.00
15 Jason Williams/49 60.00 150.00
16 David Thompson/49 12.00 30.00
17 Jae'Sean Tate/99 10.00 25.00
18 Mychal Thompson/49 8.00 20.00
19 Kristaps Porzingis/49 12.00 30.00
20 T.J. McConnell/49 8.00 20.00
21 Shaquille O'Neal /49 150.00 400.00
23 Bob Dandridge/99 10.00 25.00
24 Tony Parker/99 15.00 40.00
25 Allen Iverson/49 150.00 400.00
26 Mike Conley/49 8.00 20.00
27 Shai Gilgeous-Alexander/99 800.00 1,500.00
30 B.J. Armstrong/99 12.00 30.00
31 Jaren Jackson Jr./49 25.00 60.00
32 Detlef Schrempf/49 10.00 25.00
33 Jonas Valanciunas/49 8.00 20.00
34 Nikola Vucevic/49 10.00 25.00
35 Kendrick Nunn/99 8.00 20.00
37 Bradley Beal/99 12.00 30.00
39 Myles Turner/99 10.00 25.00
40 Ray Allen/49 40.00 100.00
41 Nate Archibald/99 10.00 25.00
43 Charles Barkley/49 150.00 400.00
45 Larry Johnson/49 25.00 60.00
47 Christian Wood/99 8.00 20.00
49 Theo Maledon/99 8.00 20.00
50 RJ Hampton/99 6.00 15.00

2021-22 Panini National Treasures Game Gear

COMMON CARD 2.50 6.00
SEMISTARS 3.00 8.00
UNLISTED STARS 4.00 10.00
STATED PRINT RUN 99 SER.#'d SETS
*PRIME/25: 1.25X TO 3X BASIC
1 Buddy Hield 3.00 8.00
2 Darius Bazley 2.50 6.00
3 Russell Westbrook 6.00 15.00
4 PJ Washington Jr. 4.00 10.00
5 Luka Doncic 40.00 100.00
6 Kevin Porter Jr. 3.00 8.00
7 Ja Morant 40.00 100.00
8 Carmelo Anthony 6.00 15.00
9 Julius Randle 5.00 12.00
10 Malik Beasley 3.00 8.00
11 Fred VanVleet 5.00 12.00
12 Luguentz Dort 4.00 10.00
13 Mikal Bridges 5.00 12.00
15 Giannis Antetokounmpo 40.00 100.00
16 Caris LeVert 3.00 8.00
17 Jimmy Butler 6.00 15.00
18 Steven Adams 3.00 8.00
19 Joel Embiid 10.00 25.00
20 Jonas Valanciunas 3.00 8.00
21 Lonzo Ball 4.00 10.00
22 Cole Anthony 5.00 12.00
23 Rui Hachimura 4.00 10.00
24 Tim Hardaway Jr. 2.50 6.00
25 Jaylen Brown 6.00 15.00
26 Dillon Brooks 4.00 10.00
27 Khris Middleton 4.00 10.00
28 Victor Oladipo 3.00 8.00
29 Devin Booker 20.00 50.00
30 Derrick Rose 6.00 15.00
31 Jarrett Allen 4.00 10.00
32 Wendell Carter Jr. 4.00 10.00
34 Klay Thompson 20.00 50.00
35 James Harden 8.00 20.00
37 Karl-Anthony Towns 6.00 15.00
38 Donte DiVincenzo 4.00 10.00
39 Damian Lillard 10.00 25.00
40 Kemba Walker 4.00 10.00

2021-22 Panini National Treasures Game Gear Autographs

STATED PRINT RUN 25-49 SER.#'d SETS
*PRIME/5-25: .75X TO 2X BASIC
1 Patrick Ewing/74 125.00 300.00
2 Sam Jones/99 40.00 100.00
3 Metta World Peace/99 10.00 25.00
4 Mike Conley/49 8.00 20.00
5 Dominique Wilkins/99 15.00 40.00
6 Hedo Turkoglu/49 8.00 20.00
8 Luke Kennard/49 8.00 20.00
9 Boris Diaw/49 10.00 25.00
10 Fat Lever/49 8.00 20.00
11 Horace Grant/99 10.00 25.00
12 Caron Butler/49 8.00 20.00
13 Spencer Dinwiddie/99 8.00 20.00
14 Shake Milton/49 8.00 20.00
15 Kenyon Martin/49 10.00 25.00
16 Mitch Richmond/49 12.00 30.00
17 Aaron Holiday/49 8.00 20.00
18 Caris LeVert/99 8.00 20.00
19 Udonis Haslem/49 6.00 15.00
20 Lamar Odom/99 10.00 25.00
21 Bernard King/99 12.00 30.00
22 Patty Mills/99 10.00 25.00
23 Obi Toppin/99 10.00 25.00
24 Shawn Kemp/99 30.00 80.00
25 Jamal Crawford/99 10.00 25.00
26 Jaren Jackson Jr./30 40.00 100.00
27 Jerami Grant/49 10.00 25.00
28 Bam Adebayo/25 15.00 40.00
29 Nikola Vucevic/49 10.00 25.00
30 Larry Bird/49 75.00 200.00
31 Joe Dumars/25 12.00 30.00
32 Zion Williamson/25 200.00 500.00
34 J.J. Barea/49 8.00 20.00
35 Robert Parish/99 12.00 30.00
36 Tim Hardaway/99 12.00 30.00
37 Detlef Schrempf/49 10.00 25.00
38 Lonnie Walker IV/99 8.00 20.00
39 Charles Oakley/99 8.00 20.00
40 Mark Jackson/99 8.00 20.00
41 Mike Bibby/49 10.00 25.00
42 Tyrese Haliburton/49 75.00 200.00
43 Kevin Porter Jr./99 8.00 20.00
44 Manu Ginobili/99 60.00 150.00
45 Mark Price/99 10.00 25.00
46 Sam Cassell/99 8.00 20.00
47 Dennis Rodman/99 40.00 100.00
48 P.J. Dozier/99 10.00 25.00
49 Kendrick Nunn/99 8.00 20.00
50 Chuma Okeke/49 10.00 25.00

2021-22 Panini National Treasures Jersey Treasures

COMMON CARD 2.50 6.00
SEMISTARS 3.00 8.00
UNLISTED STARS 4.00 10.00
STATED PRINT RUN 99 SER.#'d SETS
*PRIME/16-25: 1.25X TO 3X BASIC
1 Trae Young 10.00 25.00
2 Jarrett Allen 4.00 10.00
3 Ja Morant 40.00 100.00
4 Anthony Edwards 30.00 80.00
5 Al Horford 4.00 10.00
6 PJ Washington Jr. 4.00 10.00
7 Nikola Vucevic 4.00 10.00
8 Kristaps Porzingis 5.00 12.00
10 John Collins 4.00 10.00
11 Kevin Porter Jr. 3.00 8.00
12 Domantas Sabonis 5.00 12.00
13 Paul George 6.00 15.00
14 Anthony Davis 10.00 25.00
15 Jaylen Brown 6.00 15.00
16 Bam Adebayo 6.00 15.00
17 Jrue Holiday 5.00 12.00
18 Zach LaVine 6.00 15.00
19 Brandon Ingram 5.00 12.00
20 RJ Barrett 6.00 15.00
22 Cole Anthony 5.00 12.00
23 D'Angelo Russell 4.00 10.00
24 Joel Embiid 10.00 25.00

25 Mikal Bridges 5.00 12.00
26 Damian Lillard 10.00 25.00
27 Buddy Hield 3.00 8.00
28 Jaren Jackson Jr. 6.00 15.00
29 Dejounte Murray 4.00 10.00
30 Christian Wood 3.00 8.00
32 Collin Sexton 4.00 10.00
33 Fred VanVleet 5.00 12.00
34 Joe Ingles 3.00 8.00
35 Isaiah Stewart 4.00 10.00
36 Rui Hachimura 4.00 10.00
38 Lonzo Ball 4.00 10.00
41 Aaron Gordon 4.00 10.00
42 Khris Middleton 4.00 10.00
43 Giannis Antetokounmpo 40.00 100.00
44 Jalen Brunson 8.00 20.00
46 Tobias Harris 3.00 8.00
48 Rudy Gobert 5.00 12.00
49 Duncan Robinson 3.00 8.00
51 Gordon Hayward 3.00 8.00
52 Mike Conley 3.00 8.00
53 De'Aaron Fox 6.00 15.00
54 Tyrese Haliburton 8.00 20.00
55 Kemba Walker 4.00 10.00
56 Julius Randle 5.00 12.00
57 LaMelo Ball 30.00 80.00
59 Carmelo Anthony 6.00 15.00
60 Deandre Ayton 4.00 10.00
61 RJ Hampton 2.50 6.00
63 Tim Hardaway Jr. 2.50 6.00
64 Nikola Jokic 20.00 50.00
66 Jonas Valanciunas 3.00 8.00
68 Darius Garland 6.00 15.00
69 Pascal Siakam 6.00 15.00
71 Chris Paul 8.00 20.00
72 Myles Turner 4.00 10.00
73 Luguentz Dort 4.00 10.00
74 Shai Gilgeous-Alexander 20.00 50.00
75 CJ McCollum 3.00 8.00
76 Anfernee Simons 6.00 15.00
77 Kyle Kuzma 5.00 12.00
78 Steven Adams 3.00 8.00
79 Bradley Beal 5.00 12.00
80 Eric Gordon 3.00 8.00
81 Kira Lewis Jr. 2.50 6.00
82 Dillon Brooks 4.00 10.00
83 Zion Williamson 25.00 60.00
84 Michael Porter Jr. 5.00 12.00
85 Blake Griffin 4.00 10.00
86 Kevin Durant 12.00 30.00
87 Terance Mann 4.00 10.00
88 Isaac Okoro 3.00 8.00
89 Clint Capela 4.00 10.00
90 Malik Beasley 3.00 8.00
92 Tyler Herro 6.00 15.00
93 Ben Simmons 4.00 10.00
94 Dennis Schroder 4.00 10.00
96 Harrison Barnes 3.00 8.00
97 James Harden 8.00 20.00
98 Miles Bridges 3.00 8.00
99 Derrick Rose 6.00 15.00
100 Devin Booker 20.00 50.00

2021-22 Panini National Treasures Material Treasures

COMMON CARD 2.50 6.00
SEMISTARS 3.00 8.00
UNLISTED STARS 4.00 10.00
STATED PRINT RUN 99 SER.#'d SETS
*PRIME/13-25: 1.25X TO 3X BASIC
1 Gordon Hayward 3.00 8.00
2 Zach LaVine 6.00 15.00
3 Luguentz Dort 4.00 10.00
5 Giannis Antetokounmpo 40.00 100.00
6 Anthony Davis 10.00 25.00
7 Stephen Curry 60.00 150.00
8 Devin Booker 20.00 50.00
9 Al Horford 4.00 10.00
11 Jalen Brunson 8.00 20.00
12 Christian Laettner 4.00 10.00
13 OG Anunoby 4.00 10.00
14 Victor Oladipo 3.00 8.00
15 LeBron James 60.00 150.00
16 Brandon Ingram 5.00 12.00
17 Jaren Jackson Jr. 6.00 15.00
18 James Harden 8.00 20.00
19 Carmelo Anthony 6.00 15.00
20 Kyrie Irving 8.00 20.00
21 Kemba Walker 4.00 10.00
22 Darrell Armstrong 2.50 6.00
23 RJ Hampton 2.50 6.00
25 Luka Doncic 40.00 100.00
26 Damian Lillard 10.00 25.00
27 Nikola Vucevic 4.00 10.00
28 Joel Embiid 10.00 25.00
29 Derrick Rose 6.00 15.00
30 Pascal Siakam 6.00 15.00

2021-22 Panini National Treasures NBA Greats Signatures

COMMON CARD 6.00 15.00
SEMISTARS 8.00 20.00
UNLISTED STARS 10.00 25.00
STATED PRINT RUN 25-49 SER.#'d SETS
EXCHANGE DEADLINE 1/20/2024
*BRONZE/15-25: .5X TO 1.2X BASIC
1 Dominique Wilkins/25 30.00 80.00
2 Bob Dandridge/49 10.00 25.00
3 Gary Payton/25 40.00 100.00
4 Mark Aguirre/49 8.00 20.00
5 Nate Archibald/49 10.00 25.00
6 Bill Laimbeer/49 15.00 40.00
7 Larry Bird/49 125.00 300.00
8 Dwyane Wade/49 125.00 300.00
9 Tony Allen/49 6.00 15.00
10 Marques Johnson/49 8.00 20.00
11 Cazzie Russell/49 10.00 25.00
13 Rik Smits/49 8.00 20.00
14 Karl Malone/25 50.00 120.00
15 Amar'e Stoudemire/49 10.00 25.00
16 Dirk Nowitzki/25 150.00 400.00
17 George McGinnis/49 10.00 25.00
18 Alex English/49 12.00 30.00
19 Jerry Lucas/49 12.00 30.00
20 Oscar Robertson/49 75.00 200.00
21 Mark Price/49 10.00 25.00
22 Kevin Johnson/49 10.00 25.00
23 Arvydas Sabonis/49 12.00 30.00
24 Spud Webb/49 10.00 25.00
25 Bernard King/49 12.00 30.00
26 Mychal Thompson/49 8.00 20.00
27 David Thompson/49 12.00 30.00
28 Bill Russell/49 400.00 800.00
29 Jalen Rose/49 8.00 20.00
30 Jerry West/25 60.00 150.00

2021-22 Panini National Treasures NBA Materials

COMMON CARD 2.50 6.00
SEMISTARS 3.00 8.00
UNLISTED STARS 4.00 10.00
STATED PRINT RUN 99 SER.#'d SETS
*PRIME/25: 1.25X TO 3X BASIC
1 Saddiq Bey 3.00 8.00
3 Anthony Edwards 30.00 80.00
4 Stephen Curry 60.00 150.00
5 Domantas Sabonis 5.00 12.00
6 Aaron Gordon 4.00 10.00
7 Kevin Durant 12.00 30.00
8 Gary Trent Jr. 3.00 8.00
9 Christian Wood 3.00 8.00
10 Lonnie Walker IV 3.00 8.00
11 Tobias Harris 3.00 8.00
12 LeBron James 60.00 150.00
13 Buddy Hield 3.00 8.00
14 Jamal Murray 6.00 15.00
15 Jaylen Brown 6.00 15.00
17 LaMelo Ball 30.00 80.00
18 Jae Crowder 2.50 6.00
19 Rick Mahorn 3.00 8.00
20 Myles Turner 4.00 10.00
21 James Wiseman 3.00 8.00
22 Luka Doncic 40.00 100.00
23 D'Angelo Russell 4.00 10.00
24 Mikal Bridges 5.00 12.00
25 Jrue Holiday 5.00 12.00
26 De'Andre Hunter 4.00 10.00
27 Paul George 6.00 15.00
29 Josh Jackson 2.50 6.00
30 Reggie Bullock 2.50 6.00

2021-22 Panini National Treasures Notable Nicknames Autographs

2 David Robinson 300.00 600.00
3 Anthony Davis 800.00 1,500.00
6 Larry Bird 500.00 1,000.00
7 Luka Doncic 2,000.00 4,000.00
8 Kevin Garnett 2,000.00 4,000.00
9 Kevin Durant 400.00 800.00
11 Ray Allen 300.00 600.00
13 Vince Carter 2,500.00 5,000.00
15 Dominique Wilkins 400.00 800.00
16 Vince Carter 2,500.00 5,000.00
20 Kevin Garnett 2,000.00 4,000.00
21 Oscar Robertson 200.00 500.00
23 Nikola Jokic 600.00 1,200.00
25 Karl Malone 400.00 800.00

2021-22 Panini National Treasures Peerless Signatures

COMMON CARD 8.00 20.00
SEMISTARS 10.00 25.00
UNLISTED STARS 12.00 30.00
STATED PRINT RUN 25-49 SER.#'d SETS
EXCHANGE DEADLINE 1/20/2024
*BRONZE/15-25: .5X TO 1.2X BASIC
1 James Wiseman/49 10.00 25.00
2 Jordan Nwora/49 12.00 30.00
4 Aleksej Pokusevski/49 20.00 50.00
8 Nikola Vucevic/49 12.00 30.00
10 Jrue Holiday/49 40.00 100.00
12 Bojan Bogdanovic/49 10.00 25.00
13 Bogdan Bogdanovic/49 12.00 30.00
14 Collin Sexton/49 12.00 30.00
16 Mike Conley/49 10.00 25.00
17 Luka Doncic/25 1,000.00 2,000.00
19 Kira Lewis Jr./49 8.00 20.00
20 Clint Capela/49 12.00 30.00
21 Enes Freedom/49 10.00 25.00
22 Onyeka Okongwu/49 12.00 30.00
23 Jaden McDaniels/49 30.00 80.00
25 Myles Turner/49 12.00 30.00
27 Jamal Murray/49 40.00 100.00
28 Bradley Beal/49 40.00 100.00
30 Stephen Curry/49 1,000.00 2,000.00
32 Theo Maledon/49 10.00 25.00
33 Anthony Edwards/49 400.00 800.00
35 Buddy Hield/49 10.00 25.00
37 Anthony Davis/25 125.00 300.00
38 Duncan Robinson/49 10.00 25.00
39 Ivica Zubac/49 10.00 25.00
40 Julius Randle/49 15.00 40.00
41 Brandon Clarke/49 12.00 30.00
43 Lonnie Walker IV/49 10.00 25.00
44 Boban Marjanovic/49 12.00 30.00
45 John Collins/49 12.00 30.00
46 Jonas Valanciunas/49 10.00 25.00
47 CJ McCollum/49 25.00 60.00
48 Shai Gilgeous-Alexander/49 400.00 800.00
49 Joe Harris/49 10.00 25.00
50 Zion Williamson/25 400.00 800.00

2021-22 Panini National Treasures Penmanship

COMMON CARD 8.00 20.00
SEMISTARS 10.00 25.00
UNLISTED STARS 12.00 30.00
STATED PRINT RUN 25-99 SER.#'d SETS
EXCHANGE DEADLINE 1/20/2024
*BRONZE/15-25: .5X TO 1.2X BASIC
1 Anthony Edwards/49 400.00 800.00
2 Jae'Sean Tate/99 12.00 30.00
3 Kevin Porter Jr./49 10.00 25.00
4 T.J. McConnell/49 10.00 25.00
5 Trae Young/25 400.00 800.00
6 Jaden McDaniels/99 30.00 80.00
7 Zion Williamson/25 400.00 800.00
8 Devin Vassell/99 40.00 100.00
10 Bradley Beal/25 40.00 100.00
11 Karl Malone/25 50.00 120.00
12 Onyeka Okongwu/49 12.00 30.00
14 Bill Laimbeer/49 20.00 50.00
15 Dikembe Mutombo/99 20.00 50.00
17 Maxi Kleber/49 10.00 25.00
19 Magic Johnson/49 125.00 300.00
20 Vince Carter/49 150.00 400.00
21 Shaquille O'Neal /25 200.00 500.00
22 Stephen Curry/25 1,000.00 2,000.00
23 Joe Smith/99 10.00 25.00
24 Tony Allen/99 8.00 20.00
25 Devin Harris/49 8.00 20.00
26 Mike Bibby/49 12.00 30.00
28 Allen Iverson/25 200.00 500.00
29 Amar'e Stoudemire/49 20.00 50.00
30 Nikola Jokic/25 300.00 600.00
31 Jordan Nwora/49 12.00 30.00
32 Luka Doncic/25 1,000.00 2,000.00
33 RJ Hampton/49 8.00 20.00
36 Kwame Brown/49 10.00 25.00
37 Kristaps Porzingis/49 15.00 40.00
38 Tyrese Haliburton/49 75.00 200.00
39 Dell Curry/99 12.00 30.00
40 Christian Wood/99 10.00 25.00

2021-22 Panini National Treasures Retro Materials

COMMON CARD 3.00 8.00
SEMISTARS 4.00 10.00
UNLISTED STARS 5.00 12.00
STATED PRINT RUN 99 SER.#'d SETS
*PRIME/25: 1.25X TO 3X BASIC
1 James Worthy 8.00 20.00
2 Caron Butler 4.00 10.00
3 Darrell Armstrong 3.00 8.00
4 Kevin Martin 4.00 10.00
5 Thurl Bailey 4.00 10.00
6 Jamal Crawford 5.00 12.00
7 Clyde Drexler 8.00 20.00
8 Ralph Sampson 5.00 12.00
9 Rick Mahorn 4.00 10.00
10 Slater Martin 5.00 12.00
11 Rony Seikaly 4.00 10.00
12 Carlos Boozer 4.00 10.00
13 Jeff Hornacek 4.00 10.00
14 Al Harrington 4.00 10.00
15 Brad Daugherty 5.00 12.00
16 Dirk Nowitzki 12.00 30.00
17 Amar'e Stoudemire 5.00 12.00
18 Larry Bird 20.00 50.00
19 Garfield Heard 4.00 10.00
20 Robert Parish 6.00 15.00
21 Christian Laettner 5.00 12.00
22 Joakim Noah 4.00 10.00
23 Xavier McDaniel 4.00 10.00
24 Joe Bryant 4.00 10.00
25 Shawn Bradley 4.00 10.00
26 Kevin Garnett 12.00 30.00
27 David Robinson 10.00 25.00
28 Adrian Dantley 5.00 12.00
29 Buck Williams 4.00 10.00
30 Magic Johnson 20.00 50.00

2021-22 Panini National Treasures Rookie Dual Material Autographs

COMMON CARD 12.00 30.00
SEMISTARS 15.00 40.00
UNLISTED STARS 20.00 50.00
STATED PRINT RUN 99 SER.#'d SETS
*PRIME/25: .75X TO 2X BASIC
1 Joshua Primo 15.00 40.00
2 Evan Mobley 80.00 200.00
3 Luka Garza 20.00 50.00
4 Charles Bassey 20.00 50.00
5 Davion Mitchell 20.00 50.00
6 Brandon Boston Jr. 20.00 50.00
7 Scottie Lewis 15.00 40.00
8 Ziaire Williams 25.00 60.00
9 Jason Preston 15.00 40.00
10 Kai Jones 15.00 40.00
11 Scottie Barnes 60.00 150.00
12 JT Thor 20.00 50.00
13 Tre Mann 30.00 80.00
14 Jared Butler 20.00 50.00
15 James Bouknight 15.00 40.00
16 Ayo Dosunmu 40.00 100.00
17 Jalen Johnson 60.00 150.00
18 Jalen Suggs 50.00 125.00
19 Keon Johnson 20.00 50.00
20 Greg Brown III 15.00 40.00
21 Chris Duarte 15.00 40.00
22 Isaiah Jackson 20.00 50.00
23 Cade Cunningham 150.00 400.00
24 Usman Garuba 15.00 40.00
25 Moses Moody 40.00 100.00
26 Isaiah Livers 20.00 50.00
27 Josh Christopher 15.00 40.00
28 Franz Wagner 60.00 150.00
29 Day'Ron Sharpe 20.00 50.00
30 Corey Kispert 25.00 60.00
31 Bones Hyland 25.00 60.00
32 Quentin Grimes 40.00 100.00
33 Josh Giddey 60.00 150.00
34 Jaden Springer 20.00 50.00
35 Alperen Sengun 60.00 150.00
36 Isaiah Todd 15.00 40.00
37 Jonathan Kuminga 60.00 150.00
38 Santi Aldama 25.00 60.00
39 Trey Murphy III 60.00 150.00
40 Jalen Green 100.00 250.00

2021-22 Panini National Treasures Rookie Dual Materials

COMMON CARD 3.00 8.00
SEMISTARS 4.00 10.00
UNLISTED STARS 5.00 12.00
STATED PRINT RUN 99 SER.#'d SETS
*PRIME/25: 1.25X TO 3X BASIC
1 Josh Giddey 15.00 40.00
2 Jeremiah Robinson-Earl 5.00 12.00
3 Corey Kispert 6.00 15.00
4 Jonathan Kuminga 15.00 40.00
5 Jalen Green 25.00 60.00
6 Chris Duarte 4.00 10.00
7 Alperen Sengun 15.00 40.00
8 Cade Cunningham 40.00 100.00
9 Jalen Suggs 12.00 30.00
10 Davion Mitchell 5.00 12.00
11 Bones Hyland 6.00 15.00
12 Jalen Johnson 10.00 25.00
13 Evan Mobley 20.00 50.00
14 Ayo Dosunmu 10.00 25.00
15 Brandon Boston Jr. 5.00 12.00
16 Scottie Barnes 15.00 40.00
17 Joshua Primo 4.00 10.00
18 Moses Moody 10.00 25.00
19 Tre Mann 8.00 20.00
20 Franz Wagner 15.00 40.00
21 Keon Johnson 5.00 12.00
22 Ziaire Williams 6.00 15.00
23 Herbert Jones 6.00 15.00
24 Kai Jones 4.00 10.00
25 James Bouknight 4.00 10.00

2021-22 Panini National Treasures Rookie Jumbo Materials

COMMON CARD 3.00 8.00
SEMISTARS 4.00 10.00
UNLISTED STARS 5.00 12.00
STATED PRINT RUN 99 SER.#'d SETS
*PRIME/25: 1.25X TO 3X BASIC
1 Joshua Primo 4.00 10.00
2 Jalen Suggs 12.00 30.00
3 Davion Mitchell 5.00 12.00
4 Bones Hyland 6.00 15.00
5 Jalen Johnson 15.00 40.00
6 Evan Mobley 20.00 50.00
7 Ayo Dosunmu 10.00 25.00
8 Jalen Green 25.00 60.00
9 Chris Duarte 4.00 10.00
10 James Bouknight 4.00 10.00
11 Cade Cunningham 30.00 80.00
12 Tre Mann 8.00 20.00
13 Franz Wagner 15.00 40.00
14 Keon Johnson 5.00 12.00
15 Ziaire Williams 6.00 15.00
16 Herbert Jones 6.00 15.00
17 Kai Jones 4.00 10.00
18 Brandon Boston Jr. 5.00 12.00
19 Scottie Barnes 15.00 40.00
20 Alperen Sengun 15.00 40.00
21 Moses Moody 10.00 25.00
22 Josh Giddey 15.00 40.00
23 Jeremiah Robinson-Earl 5.00 12.00
24 Corey Kispert 6.00 15.00
25 Jonathan Kuminga 15.00 40.00

2021-22 Panini National Treasures Rookie Materials

COMMON CARD 3.00 8.00
SEMISTARS 4.00 10.00
UNLISTED STARS 5.00 12.00
STATED PRINT RUN 99 SER.#'d SETS
*PRIME/25: 1.25X TO 3X BASIC
1 Jalen Suggs 12.00 30.00
2 Tre Mann 8.00 20.00
3 Josh Giddey 15.00 40.00
4 Bones Hyland 6.00 15.00
5 Keon Johnson 5.00 12.00
6 Corey Kispert 6.00 15.00
7 Evan Mobley 20.00 50.00
8 Herbert Jones 6.00 15.00
9 Jalen Green 25.00 60.00
10 Brandon Boston Jr. 5.00 12.00
11 James Bouknight 4.00 10.00
12 Alperen Sengun 15.00 40.00
13 Joshua Primo 4.00 10.00
14 Cade Cunningham 30.00 80.00
15 Moses Moody 10.00 25.00
16 Davion Mitchell 5.00 12.00
17 Franz Wagner 15.00 40.00
18 Jeremiah Robinson-Earl 5.00 12.00
19 Jalen Johnson 15.00 40.00
20 Ziaire Williams 6.00 15.00
21 Jonathan Kuminga 15.00 40.00
22 Ayo Dosunmu 10.00 25.00
23 Kai Jones 4.00 10.00
24 Chris Duarte 4.00 10.00
25 Scottie Barnes 15.00 40.00

2021-22 Panini National Treasures Rookie Quad Material Autographs

COMMON CARD 12.00 30.00
SEMISTARS 15.00 40.00
UNLISTED STARS 20.00 50.00
STATED PRINT RUN 49-99 SER.#'d SETS
*PRIME/25: .75X TO 2X BASIC
1 Evan Mobley/49 150.00 400.00
2 Jalen Johnson/99 60.00 150.00
3 Jalen Suggs/49 50.00 125.00
4 Davion Mitchell/99 20.00 50.00
5 Cade Cunningham/49 500.00 1,000.00
6 Scottie Barnes/99 125.00 300.00
7 James Bouknight/99 15.00 40.00
8 Jonathan Kuminga/99 125.00 300.00
9 Josh Giddey/99 60.00 150.00
10 Jalen Green/49 300.00 600.00

2021-22 Panini National Treasures Rookie Triple Material Autographs

COMMON CARD 12.00 30.00
SEMISTARS 15.00 40.00
UNLISTED STARS 20.00 50.00
STATED PRINT RUN 49-99 SER.#'d SETS
*PRIME/25: .75X TO 2X BASIC
1 Moses Moody/99 40.00 100.00
2 Tre Mann/99 30.00 80.00
3 Usman Garuba/99 15.00 40.00
4 Kai Jones/99 15.00 40.00
5 Bones Hyland/99 25.00 60.00
6 Day'Ron Sharpe/99 20.00 50.00
7 Santi Aldama/99 25.00 60.00
8 Jason Preston/99 15.00 40.00
9 Isaiah Livers/99 20.00 50.00
10 Cade Cunningham/49 200.00 500.00
11 Jalen Suggs/49 50.00 125.00
12 Ayo Dosunmu/99 50.00 125.00
13 Jalen Green/49 100.00 250.00
14 Jonathan Kuminga/99 60.00 150.00
15 Jared Butler/99 20.00 50.00
16 Miles McBride/99 30.00 80.00
17 Cameron Thomas/99 40.00 100.00
18 Ziaire Williams/99 25.00 60.00
19 Evan Mobley/49 80.00 200.00
20 Franz Wagner/99 60.00 150.00

2021-22 Panini National Treasures Rookie Triple Materials

COMMON CARD 3.00 8.00
SEMISTARS 4.00 10.00
UNLISTED STARS 5.00 12.00
STATED PRINT RUN 99 SER.#'d SETS
*PRIME/25: 1.25X TO 3X BASIC
1 Herbert Jones 6.00 15.00
2 Kai Jones 4.00 10.00
3 James Bouknight 4.00 10.00
4 Cade Cunningham 30.00 80.00
5 Jalen Suggs 12.00 30.00
6 Franz Wagner 15.00 40.00
7 Bones Hyland 6.00 15.00
8 Jalen Johnson 15.00 40.00
9 Corey Kispert 6.00 15.00
10 Jonathan Kuminga 15.00 40.00
11 Jalen Green 25.00 60.00
12 Chris Duarte 4.00 10.00
13 Alperen Sengun 15.00 40.00
14 Moses Moody 10.00 25.00
15 Tre Mann 8.00 20.00
16 Jeremiah Robinson-Earl 5.00 12.00
17 Keon Johnson 5.00 12.00
18 Ziaire Williams 6.00 15.00
19 Evan Mobley 20.00 50.00
20 Ayo Dosunmu 10.00 25.00
21 Brandon Boston Jr. 5.00 12.00
22 Scottie Barnes 15.00 40.00
23 Joshua Primo 4.00 10.00
24 Davion Mitchell 5.00 12.00
25 Josh Giddey 15.00 40.00

2021-22 Panini National Treasures Signatures

COMMON CARD 8.00 20.00
SEMISTARS 10.00 25.00
UNLISTED STARS 12.00 39.00
STATED PRINT RUN 25-49 SER.#'d SETS
EXCHANGE DEADLINE 1/20/2024
*BRONZE/15-25: .5X TO 1.2X BASIC
1 Kenny Sky Walker/49 8.00 20.00
2 Anthony Davis/49 75.00 200.00
3 Christian Wood/25 10.00 25.00
4 Devin Vassell/25 30.00 80.00
5 David Robinson/49 40.00 100.00
6 Raymond Felton/25 8.00 20.00
7 Oscar Robertson/25 60.00 150.00
8 Chauncey Billups/49 20.00 50.00
9 Kevin Durant/49 150.00 400.00
10 Rik Smits/49 10.00 25.00
11 Cazzie Russell/49 12.00 30.00
12 Kevin Johnson/49 20.00 50.00
13 Boban Marjanovic/25 12.00 30.00
14 Deni Avdija/49 12.00 30.00
15 Maurice Cheeks/49 10.00 25.00
16 Bill Russell/49 400.00 800.00
17 Kirk Hinrich /49 12.00 30.00
18 Stephen Jackson/49 10.00 25.00
19 Kira Lewis Jr./49 8.00 20.00
20 Jerry West/25 75.00 200.00
21 Dikembe Mutombo/25 25.00 60.00
23 Ralph Sampson/49 12.00 30.00
24 Corey Kispert/49 15.00 40.00
25 Jalen Johnson/49 40.00 100.00
26 Josh Christopher/49 40.00 100.00
27 Charles Bassey/49 12.00 30.00
28 Rui Hachimura/25 40.00 100.00
29 Spud Webb/25 12.00 30.00
31 Steve Kerr/25 30.00 80.00
33 Theo Maledon/49 10.00 25.00
34 Keon Johnson/49 12.00 30.00
35 Davion Mitchell/49 12.00 30.00
36 Scottie Lewis/49 10.00 25.00
37 Alperen Sengun/49 60.00 150.00
38 Jaden Springer/49 12.00 30.00
39 Toni Kukoc/49 25.00 60.00
40 Luka Doncic/49 800.00 1,500.00
41 Dirk Nowitzki/49 150.00 400.00
42 James Bouknight/49 10.00 25.00
43 Isaiah Todd/49 10.00 25.00
44 Trey Murphy III/49 40.00 100.00
46 Jason Richardson/25 12.00 30.00
47 Mark Aguirre/25 10.00 25.00
48 Jalen Rose/49 10.00 25.00
49 Frank Kaminsky/25 8.00 20.00
50 Anthony Edwards/25 400.00 800.00

2021-22 Panini National Treasures Timeless Talents Signatures

COMMON CARD 8.00 20.00
SEMISTARS 10.00 25.00
UNLISTED STARS 12.00 30.00
STATED PRINT RUN 25-49 SER.#'d SETS
EXCHANGE DEADLINE 1/20/2024
*BRONZE/15-25: .5X TO 1.2X BASIC
1 Gary Payton/49 30.00 80.00
2 Jerry Lucas/49 15.00 40.00
3 Rick Fox/49 12.00 30.00
4 Jason Williams/49 60.00 150.00
6 Jalen Rose/49 10.00 25.00
7 Rick Barry/49 15.00 40.00
8 Jason Kidd/49 40.00 100.00
9 Allen Iverson/25 150.00 400.00
10 Alex English/49 15.00 40.00
11 George McGinnis/49 12.00 30.00
12 Charles Barkley/25 150.00 400.00
13 Carlos Boozer/49 10.00 25.00
14 Clyde Drexler/49 40.00 100.00
15 Robert Horry/49 15.00 40.00
16 Sam Cassell/49 10.00 25.00
17 Kenny Sky Walker/49 8.00 20.00
18 Dirk Nowitzki/25 200.00 500.00
19 Bill Walton/49 20.00 50.00
20 Christian Laettner/49 12.00 30.00
21 Wally Szczerbiak/49 12.00 30.00
22 Kevin Garnett/49 150.00 400.00
23 Elton Brand/49 12.00 30.00
25 Jason Richardson/49 12.00 30.00
27 Dwyane Wade/49 125.00 300.00
28 Kareem Abdul-Jabbar/49 150.00 400.00
29 Richard Hamilton/49 15.00 40.00
30 Steve Kerr/49 25.00 60.00

2021-22 Panini National Treasures Timeless Treasures Materials

STATED PRINT RUN 99 SER.#'d SETS
*PRIME/25: 1.25X TO 3X BASIC
1 Vince Carter 10.00 25.00
2 Jason Kidd 8.00 20.00
3 Isiah Thomas 8.00 20.00
4 Charles Barkley 12.00 30.00
5 Larry Bird 20.00 50.00
6 Roy Hibbert 4.00 10.00
7 Gerald Wallace 4.00 10.00
8 Lamar Odom 5.00 12.00
9 Joakim Noah 4.00 10.00
10 Michael Redd 4.00 10.00
11 Dan Issel 5.00 12.00
12 Elton Brand 5.00 12.00
13 Chris Mullin 6.00 15.00
14 Steve Francis 5.00 12.00
15 Kevin McHale 8.00 20.00
16 Caron Butler 4.00 10.00
17 Larry Johnson 6.00 15.00
18 Magic Johnson 20.00 50.00
19 Richard Hamilton 6.00 15.00
20 Al Harrington 4.00 10.00
21 Adrian Dantley 5.00 12.00
22 David Robinson 10.00 25.00
23 Leandro Barbosa 3.00 8.00
24 Brad Miller 3.00 8.00
25 Robert Parish 6.00 15.00
26 Jamal Crawford 5.00 12.00
27 Alonzo Mourning 8.00 20.00
28 James Worthy 8.00 20.00
29 Dirk Nowitzki 12.00 30.00
30 John Starks 5.00 12.00

2021-22 Panini National Treasures Timeline Materials

COMMON CARD 3.00 8.00
SEMISTARS 4.00 10.00
UNLISTED STARS 5.00 12.00
STATED PRINT RUN 21-99 SER.#'d SETS
*PRIME/25: 1.25X TO 3X BASIC
1 Giannis Antetokounmpo/21 25.00 60.00
2 Bam Adebayo/99 8.00 20.00
3 Stephen Curry/99 60.00 150.00
4 Donovan Mitchell/99 10.00 25.00
5 Tyrese Haliburton/99 10.00 25.00
6 Khris Middleton/99 5.00 12.00
7 Donte DiVincenzo/99 5.00 12.00
8 James Worthy/99 8.00 20.00
9 Kyle Kuzma/99 6.00 15.00
10 Rudy Gobert/99 6.00 15.00
11 LeBron James/99 60.00 150.00
12 Chris Paul/99 10.00 25.00
13 Duncan Robinson/99 4.00 10.00
14 Jayson Tatum/99 20.00 50.00
15 Cam Reddish/99 5.00 12.00
16 Malcolm Brogdon/99 4.00 10.00
17 Jaden McDaniels/99 5.00 12.00
18 Rony Seikaly/99 4.00 10.00
19 Mike Conley/99 4.00 10.00
20 Tim Hardaway Jr./99 3.00 8.00
21 Luka Doncic/99 50.00 120.00
22 Darius Garland/99 8.00 20.00
23 Lonzo Ball/99 5.00 12.00
24 Julius Randle/99 6.00 15.00
25 Darius Bazley/99 3.00 8.00
26 RJ Barrett/99 8.00 20.00
27 Jonas Valanciunas/99 4.00 10.00
28 Buck Williams/99 4.00 10.00
29 Payton Pritchard/99 5.00 12.00
30 Boban Marjanovic/99 5.00 12.00

2021-22 Panini National Treasures Treasured Signatures

COMMON CARD
SEMISTARS
UNLISTED STARS
STATED PRINT RUN 25-49 SER.#'d SETS
EXCHANGE DEADLINE 1/20/2024
*BRONZE/15-25: .5X TO 1.2X BASIC
1 Charles Barkley/25 150.00 400.00
2 Amar'e Stoudemire/49 12.00 30.00
3 Rick Barry/49 15.00 40.00
4 Rick Fox/49 12.00 30.00
5 David Robinson/49 40.00 100.00
6 Dirk Nowitzki/25 200.00 500.00
7 Richard Hamilton/49 15.00 40.00
8 Larry Johnson/49 40.00 100.00
9 Dan Issel/49 12.00 30.00
10 George McGinnis/49 12.00 30.00
11 Kareem Abdul-Jabbar/25 150.00 400.00
12 Christian Laettner/49 12.00 30.00
13 Steve Kerr/49 25.00 60.00
14 Shaquille O'Neal /25 200.00 500.00
15 Bill Russell/25 400.00 800.00
16 Joe Dumars/49 15.00 40.00
17 Jerry West/49 60.00 150.00
18 Derrick Coleman/49 12.00 30.00
19 Vince Carter/25 150.00 400.00
20 Mark Price/49 12.00 30.00
21 Kevin Garnett/49 150.00 400.00
22 Arvydas Sabonis/49 15.00 40.00
23 Louie Dampier/49 12.00 30.00
24 Marques Johnson/49 10.00 25.00
25 Mychal Thompson/49 10.00 25.00

2021-22 Panini National Treasures Treasured Threads

STATED PRINT RUN 99 SER.#'d SETS
*PRIME/25: 1.25X TO 3X BASIC
1 Jamaal Wilkes 5.00 12.00
2 Kevin Porter Jr. 4.00 10.00
4 Giannis Antetokounmpo 25.00 60.00
5 Bradley Beal 6.00 15.00
6 Stephen Curry 60.00 150.00
7 Ja Morant 50.00 120.00
8 Rui Hachimura 5.00 12.00
9 Kyle Lowry 5.00 12.00
10 Derrick White 5.00 12.00
11 Bill Bradley 5.00 12.00
12 Malik Beasley 4.00 10.00
13 Steven Adams 4.00 10.00
14 LeBron James 60.00 150.00
15 Collin Sexton 5.00 12.00
16 Dejounte Murray 5.00 12.00
17 Jimmy Butler 8.00 20.00
18 Anfernee Simons 8.00 20.00
19 Nikola Jokic 25.00 60.00
20 Isaac Okoro 4.00 10.00
21 Grant Williams 5.00 12.00
22 PJ Washington Jr. 5.00 12.00
23 Wendell Carter Jr. 5.00 12.00
24 Luka Doncic 50.00 120.00
25 Deandre Ayton 5.00 12.00
26 Jarrett Allen 5.00 12.00
27 Karl-Anthony Towns 8.00 20.00
28 Clint Capela 5.00 12.00
29 Trae Young 25.00 60.00
30 Joe Ingles 4.00 10.00

2021-22 Panini National Treasures Treasures of the Hall Autographs

COMMON CARD 8.00 20.00
SEMISTARS 10.00 25.00
UNLISTED STARS 12.00 30.00
STATED PRINT RUN 49-99 SER.#'d SETS
EXCHANGE DEADLINE 1/20/2024
*BRONZE/15-25: .5X TO 1.2X BASIC
1 Alex English/99 15.00 40.00
2 Nate Archibald/99 12.00 30.00
3 Louie Dampier/99 12.00 30.00
4 Dikembe Mutombo/99 40.00 100.00
5 David Robinson/49 60.00 150.00
6 Toni Kukoc/49 20.00 50.00
7 Bill Walton/99 60.00 150.00
8 Jerry West/49 60.00 150.00
9 David Thompson/49 15.00 40.00
10 Charles Barkley/49 125.00 300.00
11 Gail Goodrich/99 12.00 30.00
12 Adrian Dantley/99 12.00 30.00
13 Kareem Abdul-Jabbar/99 125.00 300.00
14 Bob Dandridge/49 12.00 30.00
15 Magic Johnson/49 125.00 300.00
16 Elvin Hayes/99 15.00 40.00
17 Rick Barry/99 15.00 40.00
18 Isiah Thomas/99 30.00 80.00
19 Jerry Lucas/99 15.00 40.00
20 Gary Payton/99 40.00 100.00
21 Kevin Garnett/25 200.00 500.00
22 Allen Iverson/49 150.00 400.00
24 Ralph Sampson/99 12.00 30.00
25 Karl Malone/49 60.00 150.00

2021-22 Panini National Treasures Tremendous Treasures Materials

COMMON CARD 4.00 10.00
SEMISTARS 5.00 12.00
UNLISTED STARS 6.00 15.00
STATED PRINT RUN 99 SER.#'d SETS
*PRIME/25: 1.25X TO 3X BASIC
1 Killian Hayes 6.00 15.00
3 Giannis Antetokounmpo 60.00 150.00
4 Ben Simmons 6.00 15.00
5 Stephen Curry 75.00 200.00
6 Fred VanVleet 8.00 20.00
7 Russell Westbrook 10.00 25.00
8 Kristaps Porzingis 8.00 20.00
9 Dillon Brooks 6.00 15.00
10 Davis Bertans 4.00 10.00
11 Marcus Smart 6.00 15.00
12 Terrence Ross 5.00 12.00
13 LeBron James 75.00 200.00
14 CJ McCollum 5.00 12.00
15 DeMar DeRozan 8.00 20.00
16 Jerami Grant 6.00 15.00
17 Bojan Bogdanovic 5.00 12.00
18 Michael Porter Jr. 8.00 20.00
20 Eric Gordon 5.00 12.00
21 Patrick Williams 6.00 15.00
22 Blake Griffin 6.00 15.00
23 Luka Doncic 60.00 150.00
24 De'Aaron Fox 10.00 25.00
25 John Collins 6.00 15.00
26 Kawhi Leonard 15.00 40.00
27 Cole Anthony 8.00 20.00
28 Shai Gilgeous-Alexander 30.00 80.00
29 John Wall 8.00 20.00
30 P.J. Tucker 5.00 12.00

2021-22 Panini National Treasures Triple Autographs

3 Dwyane Wade
Pat Riley
Shaquille O'Neal 1,000.00 2,000.00
4 Luka Doncic
Stephen Curry
Trae Young 4,000.00 8,000.00
6 Jayson Tatum
Larry Bird
Paul Pierce 1,000.00 2,000.00
8 Jamal Murray
Michael Porter Jr.
Nikola Jokic 400.00 800.00
9 Bill Laimbeer
Dennis Rodman
Rick Mahorn 150.00 400.00
10 Cade Cunningham
Luka Doncic
Zion Williamson 4,000.00 8,000.00

2021-22 Panini National Treasures Validating Marks Autographs

COMMON CARD 8.00 20.00
SEMISTARS 10.00 25.00
UNLISTED STARS 12.00 30.00
STATED PRINT RUN 25-49 SER.#'d SETS
EXCHANGE DEADLINE 1/20/2024
*BRONZE/15-25: .5X TO 1.2X BASIC
1 Zion Williamson/25 500.00 1,000.00
2 Bogdan Bogdanovic/49 12.00 30.00
4 Kira Lewis Jr./49 8.00 20.00
5 Kevin Durant/49 150.00 400.00
6 Payton Pritchard/49 20.00 50.00
10 RJ Hampton/49 8.00 20.00
11 Nikola Jokic/25 200.00 500.00
12 Frank Kaminsky/49 8.00 20.00
13 Saddiq Bey/49 10.00 25.00
14 Stephen Curry/49 1,000.00 2,000.00
15 Trae Young/49 150.00 400.00
16 De'Aaron Fox/49 20.00 50.00
17 Juan Toscano-Anderson/49 12.00 30.00

18 Michael Porter Jr./49 15.00 40.00
19 Deni Avdija/49 12.00 30.00
20 Anthony Davis/25 100.00 250.00
23 Wendell Carter Jr./49 12.00 30.00
24 Maxi Kleber/49 10.00 25.00

2022-23 Panini National Treasures

STATED PRINT RUN 99 SER.#'d SETS
*RED/75 (1-100): .5X TO 1.2X BASIC
*RED/75 (101-150): .4X TO 1X BASIC
*BRONZE/49 (101-150): .4X TO 1X BASIC
*PINK/25 (101-150): .5X TO 1.2X BASIC
1 LeBron James 25.00 60.00
2 Alperen Sengun 2.50 6.00
3 Khris Middleton 2.50 6.00
4 Ja Morant 6.00 15.00
5 Damian Lillard 5.00 12.00
6 Dejounte Murray 2.50 6.00
7 Christian Wood 1.25 3.00
8 Chris Paul 4.00 10.00
9 Bam Adebayo 3.00 8.00
10 Devin Booker 5.00 12.00
11 Rudy Gobert 2.50 6.00
12 Aaron Gordon 2.00 5.00
13 Joel Embiid 3.00 8.00
14 Jonathan Kuminga 5.00 12.00
15 Jaren Jackson Jr. 3.00 8.00
16 Kyrie Irving 4.00 10.00
17 Ayo Dosunmu 2.50 6.00
18 Tyrese Maxey 4.00 10.00
19 Collin Sexton 2.50 6.00
20 DeMar DeRozan 2.50 6.00
21 Buddy Hield 2.00 5.00
22 Trae Young 5.00 12.00
23 Ben Simmons 2.00 5.00
24 Domantas Sabonis 2.50 6.00
25 Saddiq Bey 1.50 4.00
26 Tyrese Haliburton 4.00 10.00
27 Lonnie Walker IV 1.50 4.00
28 Terry Rozier III 2.50 6.00
29 Bradley Beal 2.50 6.00
30 James Harden 4.00 10.00
31 John Collins 2.00 5.00
32 Kevin Huerter 2.00 5.00
33 D'Angelo Russell 1.50 4.00
34 Devin Vassell 2.50 6.00
35 Spencer Dinwiddie 1.50 4.00
36 Robert Williams III 1.50 4.00
37 Paul George 3.00 8.00
38 Al Horford 2.00 5.00
39 Kawhi Leonard 5.00 12.00
40 Quentin Grimes 1.50 4.00
41 Tyler Herro 3.00 8.00
42 Kevin Durant 6.00 15.00
43 Giannis Antetokounmpo 10.00 25.00
44 RJ Barrett 3.00 8.00
45 Jordan Clarkson 2.00 5.00
46 Lauri Markkanen 3.00 8.00
47 Scottie Barnes 3.00 8.00
48 Jalen Green 6.00 15.00
49 Darius Garland 3.00 8.00
50 Jamal Murray 3.00 8.00
51 Keldon Johnson 2.50 6.00
52 Dillon Brooks 2.00 5.00
53 Bojan Bogdanovic 2.00 5.00
54 Jimmy Butler 4.00 10.00
55 Kristaps Porzingis 2.50 6.00
56 Tim Hardaway Jr. 1.50 4.00
57 CJ McCollum 2.00 5.00
58 Fred VanVleet 2.50 6.00
59 Evan Mobley 5.00 12.00
60 Bones Hyland 1.50 4.00
61 John Wall 2.50 6.00
62 Shai Gilgeous-Alexander 10.00 25.00
63 Stephen Curry 25.00 60.00
64 Jalen Suggs 2.50 6.00
65 Anthony Davis 5.00 12.00
66 Deandre Ayton 2.00 5.00
67 Trey Murphy III 2.50 6.00
68 Donovan Mitchell 4.00 10.00
69 Zion Williamson 5.00 12.00
70 Desmond Bane 2.50 6.00
71 Jayson Tatum 8.00 20.00
72 Jaylen Brown 4.00 10.00
73 Karl-Anthony Towns 3.00 8.00
74 LaMelo Ball 5.00 12.00
75 Kyle Kuzma 2.50 6.00
76 Jrue Holiday 2.50 6.00
77 Nikola Jokic 10.00 25.00
78 Andrew Wiggins 2.50 6.00
79 Kelly Oubre Jr. 2.00 5.00
80 Luka Doncic 12.00 30.00
81 Michael Porter Jr. 2.50 6.00
82 Russell Westbrook 3.00 8.00
83 Malcolm Brogdon 1.50 4.00
84 Brandon Ingram 2.50 6.00
85 Klay Thompson 5.00 12.00
86 Pascal Siakam 3.00 8.00
87 Franz Wagner 5.00 12.00
88 Julius Randle 2.50 6.00
89 Bol Bol 2.00 5.00
90 Jordan Poole 3.00 8.00
91 Marcus Smart 2.50 6.00
92 Zach LaVine 4.00 10.00
93 Cade Cunningham 6.00 15.00
94 Kevin Porter Jr. 1.50 4.00
95 Jalen Brunson 4.00 10.00
96 Josh Giddey 3.00 8.00
97 De'Aaron Fox 4.00 10.00
98 Jerami Grant 2.50 6.00
99 Anthony Edwards 10.00 25.00
100 Anfernee Simons 2.50 6.00
101 Chet Holmgren AU JSY RC 1,500.00 3,000.00
102 Jalen Williams AU JSY RC 1,500.00 3,000.00
103 AJ Griffin AU JSY RC 40.00 100.00
104 Tari Eason AU JSY RC 200.00 500.00
105 Jalen Duren AU JSY RC 500.00 1,000.00
106 Dalen Terry AU JSY RC 50.00 125.00
107 Ochai Agbaji AU JSY RC 60.00 150.00
108 Jake LaRavia AU JSY RC 50.00 125.00
109 Malaki Branham AU JSY RC 50.00 125.00
110 Paolo Banchero
AU JSY RC 5,000.00 10,000.00
111 Christian Braun AU JSY RC 200.00 500.00
112 David Roddy AU JSY RC 60.00 150.00
113 Walker Kessler AU JSY RC 200.00 500.00
114 MarJon Beauchamp AU JSY RC 50.00 125.00
115 Mark Williams AU JSY RC 200.00 500.00
116 Blake Wesley AU JSY RC 50.00 125.00
117 Nikola Jovic AU JSY RC 400.00 800.00
118 Wendell Moore Jr. AU JSY RC 50.00 125.00
119 Patrick Baldwin Jr. AU JSY RC 50.00 125.00
120 Peyton Watson AU JSY RC 80.00 200.00
121 Jabari Smith Jr. AU JSY RC 400.00 800.00
122 TyTy Washington Jr. AU JSY RC 50.00 125.00
123 Andrew Nembhard AU JSY RC 200.00 500.00
124 Ousmane Dieng AU JSY RC 125.00 300.00
125 Christian Koloko AU JSY RC 50.00 125.00
126 Caleb Houstan AU JSY RC 50.00 125.00
127 Max Christie AU JSY RC 300.00 600.00
128 Kennedy Chandler AU JSY RC 50.00 125.00
129 Jaden Hardy AU JSY RC 125.00 300.00
130 Moussa Diabate AU JSY RC 50.00 125.00
131 Shaedon Sharpe AU JSY RC 600.00 1,200.00
132 Keegan Murray AU JSY RC 300.00 600.00
133 E.J. Liddell AU JSY RC 50.00 125.00
134 Isaiah Mobley AU JSY RC 50.00 125.00
135 Jaylin Williams AU JSY RC 60.00 150.00
136 Johnny Davis AU JSY RC 50.00 125.00
137 Bryce McGowens AU JSY RC 50.00 125.00
138 Trevor Keels AU JSY RC 40.00 100.00
139 Tyrese Martin AU JSY RC 40.00 100.00
140 Bennedict Mathurin AU JSY RC 400.00 800.00
141 Ryan Rollins AU JSY RC 50.00 125.00
142 Jeremy Sochan AU JSY RC 400.00 800.00
143 Josh Minott AU JSY RC 50.00 125.00
144 Vince Williams Jr. AU JSY RC 60.00 150.00
145 Jaden Ivey AU JSY RC 1,000.00 2,000.00
146 Kendall Brown AU JSY RC 40.00 100.00
147 Kenneth Lofton Jr. AU JSY RC 60.00 150.00
148 Dyson Daniels AU JSY RC 300.00 600.00
149 Jabari Walker AU JSY RC 40.00 100.00
150 Scotty Pippen Jr. AU JSY RC 60.00 150.00

2022-23 Panini National Treasures Biography Materials

STATED PRINT RUN 99 SER.#'d SETS
*PRIME/16-25: 1.25X TO 3X BASIC
1 Alec Burks 3.00 8.00
2 Malcolm Brogdon 3.00 8.00
3 Ben Simmons 4.00 10.00
4 Terry Rozier III 5.00 12.00
5 Nikola Vucevic 4.00 10.00
6 Donovan Mitchell 8.00 20.00
7 Tim Hardaway Jr. 3.00 8.00
8 Aaron Gordon 4.00 10.00
10 Andrew Wiggins 5.00 12.00
11 Josh Richardson 3.00 8.00
12 Buddy Hield 4.00 10.00
13 John Wall 5.00 12.00
14 Lonnie Walker IV 3.00 8.00
15 Steven Adams 4.00 10.00
16 Jimmy Butler 8.00 20.00
17 Bobby Portis 4.00 10.00
18 Rudy Gobert 5.00 12.00
19 CJ McCollum 4.00 10.00
20 Julius Randle 5.00 12.00
21 JaVale McGee 3.00 8.00
22 Anthony Davis 10.00 25.00
23 Kristaps Porzingis 5.00 12.00
24 Mike Conley 3.00 8.00
25 Jrue Holiday 5.00 12.00
26 Kevin Huerter 4.00 10.00
27 Malik Monk 4.00 10.00
28 Gary Trent Jr. 4.00 10.00
29 Collin Sexton 5.00 12.00
30 Kyle Kuzma 5.00 12.00
31 Tyrese Haliburton 12.00 30.00
32 Shai Gilgeous-Alexander 20.00 50.00
33 Zach LaVine 8.00 20.00
34 Dejounte Murray 5.00 12.00
35 Kawhi Leonard 10.00 25.00
36 Lauri Markkanen 6.00 15.00
37 Aaron Nesmith 4.00 10.00
38 Danilo Gallinari 3.00 8.00
39 Kemba Walker 4.00 10.00
40 Evan Fournier 3.00 8.00

2022-23 Panini National Treasures Century Materials

STATED PRINT RUN 99 SER.#'d SETS
*PRIME/8-25: 1.25X TO 3X BASIC
1 Giannis Antetokounmpo 20.00 50.00
2 Russell Westbrook 6.00 15.00
3 Zion Williamson 10.00 25.00
4 Pascal Siakam 6.00 15.00
5 Kyrie Irving 8.00 20.00
6 Terry Rozier III 5.00 12.00
7 DeMar DeRozan 5.00 12.00
8 Marvin Bagley III 3.00 8.00
9 Michael Porter Jr. 5.00 12.00
10 Reggie Jackson 3.00 8.00
11 Karl-Anthony Towns 6.00 15.00
12 Seth Curry 3.00 8.00
13 Obi Toppin 4.00 10.00
14 James Harden 8.00 20.00
15 Jerami Grant 5.00 12.00
16 Keldon Johnson 5.00 12.00
17 Fred VanVleet 5.00 12.00
19 Donovan Mitchell 8.00 20.00
20 Steven Adams 4.00 10.00
21 Klay Thompson 10.00 25.00
22 LeBron James 60.00 150.00
23 Tim Hardaway Jr. 3.00 8.00
24 Andre Iguodala 4.00 10.00
25 Bogdan Bogdanovic 4.00 10.00
26 Bones Hyland 3.00 8.00
27 Brook Lopez 4.00 10.00
28 Chris Duarte 3.00 8.00
29 Clint Capela 4.00 10.00
30 Damian Lillard 10.00 25.00
31 John Wall 5.00 12.00
32 Davion Mitchell 3.00 8.00
33 Draymond Green 5.00 12.00
34 Deandre Ayton 4.00 10.00
35 Dennis Schroder 4.00 10.00
36 Derrick Rose 8.00 20.00
37 Victor Oladipo 3.00 8.00
38 Tobias Harris 3.00 8.00
39 Rui Hachimura 4.00 10.00
40 Nikola Vucevic 4.00 10.00

2022-23 Panini National Treasures Clutch Factor Signatures

STATED PRINT RUN 35-49 SER.#'d SETS
*PRIME/5-25: .75X TO 2X BASIC
1 RJ Barrett/49 30.00 80.00
3 Andrew Nembhard/49 40.00 100.00
4 Zach Randolph/49 20.00 50.00
5 Vince Carter/49 200.00 500.00
6 Manu Ginobili/35 100.00 250.00
7 Khris Middleton/49 25.00 60.00
8 Nikola Jokic/35 200.00 500.00
9 Evan Mobley/49 50.00 125.00
10 Luka Doncic/49 600.00 1,200.00
11 Josh Giddey/49 30.00 80.00
13 Tyrese Haliburton/49 150.00 400.00
16 Rudy Gobert/49 25.00 60.00
17 Jayson Tatum/35 200.00 500.00
18 Jaren Jackson Jr./49 30.00 80.00
19 Bradley Beal/49 25.00 60.00
21 Julius Randle/49 25.00 60.00
22 Chris Paul/49 75.00 200.00
24 Obi Toppin/49 20.00 50.00
26 Anthony Edwards/49 200.00 500.00
28 Charles Barkley/35 100.00 250.00
29 Amar'e Stoudemire/49 20.00 50.00
30 Clyde Drexler/35 30.00 80.00
31 Nassir Little/49 20.00 50.00
32 Ray Allen/35 100.00 250.00
33 Anfernee Hardaway/35 100.00 250.00
35 Malaki Branham/49 20.00 50.00
36 Chet Holmgren/49 500.00 1,000.00
37 Paolo Banchero /49 400.00 800.00
38 Isaiah Mobley/49 20.00 50.00
39 Nikola Jovic/49 40.00 100.00
40 Patrick Baldwin Jr./49 20.00 50.00
41 Keegan Murray/49 100.00 250.00
42 Bennedict Mathurin/49 100.00 250.00
43 Jeremy Sochan/49 60.00 150.00
45 Shaedon Sharpe/49 125.00 300.00
46 Dyson Daniels/49 50.00 120.00
47 Jalen Duren/49 60.00 150.00
48 AJ Griffin/49 15.00 40.00
49 Ochai Agbaji/49 25.00 60.00
50 Jabari Smith Jr./49 60.00 150.00

2022-23 Panini National Treasures Colossal Material Autographs

STATED PRINT RUN 25-49 SER.#'d SETS
*PRIME/5-25: .75X TO 2X BASIC
1 Carlos Boozer/49 15.00 40.00
2 Cade Cunningham/25 150.00 400.00
3 Jordan Poole/28 30.00 80.00
4 Karl-Anthony Towns/49 30.00 80.00
5 Stephen Curry/25 1,000.00 2,000.00
6 Deandre Ayton/49 20.00 50.00
7 Khris Middleton/49 25.00 60.00
8 CJ McCollum/49 20.00 50.00
9 Devin Vassell/49 25.00 60.00
10 Dirk Nowitzki/25 300.00 600.00
12 Ayo Dosunmu/49 25.00 60.00
13 Jabari Walker/49 15.00 40.00
14 Caron Butler/49 15.00 40.00
17 Blake Wesley/49 20.00 50.00
18 Rudy Gobert/49 25.00 60.00
20 Jonathan Kuminga/49 50.00 125.00
21 TyTy Washington Jr./49 20.00 50.00
22 Marcus Smart/49 25.00 60.00
25 Caleb Houstan/49 20.00 50.00
26 Bennedict Mathurin/49 100.00 250.00
27 Keegan Murray/49 100.00 250.00
29 Dyson Daniels/49 50.00 125.00
30 AJ Griffin/49 15.00 40.00
31 Walker Kessler/49 40.00 100.00
32 Mark Williams/49 40.00 100.00
33 Paolo Banchero /49 500.00 1,000.00
34 Shaedon Sharpe/49 125.00 300.00
35 Jaden Ivey/49 60.00 150.00
36 Ousmane Dieng/49 25.00 60.00
37 Jaden Hardy/49 100.00 250.00
38 Chet Holmgren/49 500.00 1,000.00
39 Jeremy Sochan/49 60.00 150.00
40 Tari Eason/49 50.00 125.00
41 Jabari Smith Jr./49 60.00 150.00
42 Dalen Terry/49 20.00 50.00
43 Jalen Duren/49 60.00 150.00
44 Jake LaRavia/49 20.00 50.00
45 David Roddy/49 25.00 60.00
46 Christian Braun/49 50.00 125.00
47 Jalen Williams/49 100.00 250.00
48 Christian Koloko/49 20.00 50.00
49 Andrew Nembhard/49 40.00 100.00
50 Ochai Agbaji/49 25.00 60.00

2022-23 Panini National Treasures Colossal Materials

STATED PRINT RUN 99 SER.#'d SETS
*PRIME/5-25: 1.25X TO 3X BASIC
1 Paul George 8.00 20.00
3 Kevin Durant 15.00 40.00
4 Stephen Curry 60.00 150.00
5 Obi Toppin 5.00 12.00
6 Kevin Love 5.00 12.00
7 T.J. Warren 4.00 10.00
8 Karl-Anthony Towns 8.00 20.00
9 De'Aaron Fox 10.00 25.00
10 Rudy Gobert 6.00 15.00
11 Will Barton 3.00 8.00
12 Kyle Kuzma 6.00 15.00
13 Mitchell Robinson 5.00 12.00
14 Saddiq Bey 4.00 10.00
15 Cameron Thomas 8.00 20.00
16 Scottie Barnes 8.00 20.00
17 Josh Giddey 8.00 20.00
18 Franz Wagner 12.00 30.00
19 Reggie Jackson 4.00 10.00
20 Anthony Edwards 25.00 60.00

2022-23 Panini National Treasures Colossal Rookie Materials

STATED PRINT RUN 99 SER.#'d SETS
*PRIME/25: 1.25X TO 3X BASIC
1 Jalen Duren 8.00 20.00
2 E.J. Liddell 2.50 6.00
3 Bryce McGowens 2.50 6.00
4 Kennedy Chandler 2.50 6.00
5 Christian Koloko 2.50 6.00
6 Jeremy Sochan 8.00 20.00
7 Nikola Jovic 5.00 12.00
8 Trevor Keels 2.00 5.00
9 Johnny Davis 2.50 6.00
10 Jaylin Williams 3.00 8.00
11 Tyrese Martin 2.00 5.00
12 Paolo Banchero 40.00 100.00
13 Moussa Diabate 2.50 6.00
14 Shaedon Sharpe 25.00 60.00
15 Jaden Hardy 4.00 10.00
16 Jabari Walker 2.00 5.00
17 Ochai Agbaji 3.00 8.00
18 TyTy Washington Jr. 2.50 6.00
19 Josh Minott 2.50 6.00
20 Jake LaRavia 2.50 6.00
21 Chet Holmgren 40.00 100.00
22 Christian Braun 6.00 15.00
23 MarJon Beauchamp 2.50 6.00
24 Max Christie 6.00 15.00
25 Vince Williams Jr. 3.00 8.00
26 Bennedict Mathurin 8.00 20.00
27 Mark Williams 5.00 12.00
28 Caleb Houstan 2.50 6.00
29 Patrick Baldwin Jr. 2.50 6.00
30 Jabari Smith Jr. 8.00 20.00
31 Simone Fontecchio 2.50 6.00
32 Tari Eason 6.00 15.00
33 Keegan Murray 6.00 15.00
34 Peyton Watson 4.00 10.00
35 Jalen Williams 12.00 30.00
36 Andrew Nembhard 5.00 12.00
37 David Roddy 3.00 8.00
38 Malaki Branham 2.50 6.00
39 Dalen Terry 2.50 6.00
40 Isaiah Mobley 2.50 6.00
41 Wendell Moore Jr. 2.50 6.00
42 Kenneth Lofton Jr. 3.00 8.00
43 Blake Wesley 2.50 6.00
44 AJ Griffin 2.00 5.00
45 Ryan Rollins 2.50 6.00
46 Dyson Daniels 6.00 15.00
47 Kendall Brown 2.00 5.00
48 Walker Kessler 5.00 12.00
49 Jaden Ivey 8.00 20.00
50 Ousmane Dieng 3.00 8.00

2022-23 Panini National Treasures Definitive Ink

STATED PRINT RUN 25-99 SER.#'d SETS
EXCHANGE DEADLINE 5/03/2025
1 James Harden/25 200.00 500.00
2 Cade Cunningham/25 150.00 400.00
4 Bernard King/49 12.00 30.00
6 Larry Bird/25 125.00 300.00
7 Jaren Jackson Jr./49 30.00 80.00
8 Alperen Sengun/99 75.00 200.00
9 Jonathan Kuminga/49 25.00 60.00
10 Ray Allen/49 75.00 200.00
11 Detlef Schrempf/49 10.00 25.00
12 Jalen Brunson/49 40.00 100.00
14 Pat Riley/49 15.00 40.00
15 Isiah Thomas/49 30.00 80.00
16 Derrick White/75 25.00 60.00
18 RJ Barrett/49 15.00 40.00
19 Tony Parker/49 40.00 100.00
20 Stephen Curry/25 1,000.00 2,000.00
21 Allen Iverson/25 150.00 400.00
22 B.J. Armstrong/99 10.00 25.00
23 Jamaal Wilkes/99 10.00 25.00
24 Wally Szczerbiak/99 8.00 20.00
25 Ayo Dosunmu/99 12.00 30.00
26 Rolando Blackman/99 8.00 20.00
28 Rasheed Wallace/49 30.00 80.00
29 Cazzie Russell/99 12.00 30.00
30 Vince Carter/49 150.00 400.00
31 Tyrese Haliburton/49 150.00 400.00
33 Cole Anthony/75 10.00 25.00
34 Artis Gilmore/99 12.00 30.00
36 Chris Paul/25 75.00 200.00
38 Gary Payton/49 25.00 60.00
40 Bradley Beal/49 12.00 30.00
41 Jason Kidd/49 40.00 100.00
42 Lenny Wilkens/49 12.00 30.00
45 Kevin Garnett/49 125.00 300.00
47 Dell Curry/99 10.00 25.00
48 Tim Hardaway Jr./99 8.00 20.00
49 Devin Vassell/75 12.00 30.00
50 Bill Walton/49 60.00 150.00

2022-23 Panini National Treasures Dual Autographs

STATED PRINT RUN 25 SER.#'d SETS
1 Paolo Banchero
Anfernee Hardaway 400.00 800.00
2 Jalen Duren
Jaden Ivey 100.00 250.00
3 Isaiah Mobley
Evan Mobley 60.00 150.00
4 Rudy Gobert
Karl-Anthony Towns 40.00 100.00
5 Rasheed Wallace
Damon Stoudamire 40.00 100.00
6 Jabari Smith Jr.
Hakeem Olajuwon 75.00 200.00
7 Josh Giddey
Chet Holmgren 125.00 300.00
8 Jalen Green
Jabari Smith Jr. 75.00 200.00
9 Bennedict Mathurin
Keegan Murray 100.00 250.00
10 Tyrese Haliburton
Bennedict Mathurin 300.00 600.00
11 Jalen Brunson
RJ Barrett 150.00 400.00
12 Chris Paul
Steve Nash 150.00 400.00
13 CJ McCollum
Brandon Ingram 50.00 120.00
14 Dwyane Wade
Carmelo Anthony 125.00 300.00
15 Jayson Tatum
Paolo Banchero 400.00 800.00
16 Bob Cousy
Larry Bird 200.00 500.00
17 Chet Holmgren
Jalen Suggs 100.00 250.00
18 Pau Gasol
Nikola Jokic 150.00 400.00
19 Jaden Ivey
Cade Cunningham 200.00 500.00
20 Bob Pettit
Lenny Wilkens 40.00 100.00

2022-23 Panini National Treasures Game Gear

STATED PRINT RUN 99 SER.#'d SETS
*PRIME/7-25: 1.25X TO 3X BASIC
1 Tobias Harris 3.00 8.00
2 Jimmy Butler 8.00 20.00
3 Julius Randle 5.00 12.00
4 Isaiah Stewart 3.00 8.00
5 Mitchell Robinson 4.00 10.00
6 Bam Adebayo 6.00 15.00
7 Dennis Schroder 4.00 10.00
8 Shake Milton 3.00 8.00
9 Immanuel Quickley 4.00 10.00
10 Derrick Rose 8.00 20.00
11 Gordon Hayward 3.00 8.00
12 Kyrie Irving 8.00 20.00
13 Kevin Love 4.00 10.00
14 Chris Paul 8.00 20.00
15 LeBron James 60.00 150.00
16 Jayson Tatum 15.00 40.00
17 Luka Doncic 25.00 60.00
18 John Wall 5.00 12.00
19 Anthony Davis 10.00 25.00
20 Ja Morant 12.00 30.00
21 Giannis Antetokounmpo 20.00 50.00
22 Rudy Gobert 5.00 12.00
23 Jonas Valanciunas 3.00 8.00
24 RJ Barrett 6.00 15.00
25 Tyrese Maxey 8.00 20.00
26 Deandre Ayton 4.00 10.00
27 Davion Mitchell 3.00 8.00
28 OG Anunoby 5.00 12.00
29 Mike Conley 3.00 8.00
30 Bradley Beal 5.00 12.00
31 Al Horford 4.00 10.00
32 Georges Niang 3.00 8.00
33 Eric Gordon 3.00 8.00
34 PJ Washington Jr. 4.00 10.00
35 Darius Bazley 2.50 6.00
36 Patrick Williams 4.00 10.00
37 Isaac Okoro 3.00 8.00
38 Jaren Jackson Jr. 6.00 15.00
39 LaMelo Ball 10.00 25.00
40 Jae Crowder 2.50 6.00

2022-23 Panini National Treasures Game Gear Autographs

STATED PRINT RUN 35-99 SER.#'d SETS
*PRIME/5-25: .75X TO 2X BASIC
1 Steve Nash/35 40.00 100.00
2 Dorian Finney-Smith/99 8.00 20.00
3 Rajon Rondo/99 25.00 60.00
4 Elton Brand/99 10.00 25.00
5 Brandon Clarke/99 8.00 20.00
6 Manu Ginobili/35 40.00 100.00
8 Brandon Ingram/75 25.00 60.00
9 Carmelo Anthony/49 60.00 150.00
10 Corey Kispert/99 10.00 25.00
11 Moses Moody/99 12.00 30.00
12 Jordan Clarkson/99 20.00 50.00
13 Lonnie Walker IV/99 8.00 20.00
14 Victor Oladipo/99 8.00 20.00
15 Buddy Hield/99 10.00 25.00
16 Alex English/99 12.00 30.00
18 Seth Curry/99 8.00 20.00
19 Santi Aldama/99 10.00 25.00
20 Reggie Bullock/99 8.00 20.00
22 Luis Scola/99 8.00 20.00
23 B.J. Armstrong/99 10.00 25.00
24 Jason Terry/99 8.00 20.00
27 Gary Payton/49 25.00 60.00
28 Jalen Suggs/49 20.00 50.00
29 Jason Kidd/49 40.00 100.00
30 Cameron Thomas/99 25.00 60.00
32 Horace Grant/49 10.00 25.00
33 Chris Boucher/99 10.00 25.00
35 Bill Laimbeer/99 10.00 25.00
36 Patty Mills/99 10.00 25.00
37 Derrick White/99 15.00 40.00
38 Brook Lopez/99 10.00 25.00
39 Collin Sexton/99 12.00 30.00
40 Royce O'Neale/99 8.00 20.00
42 Tre Mann/99 8.00 20.00
43 Luke Kennard/99 8.00 20.00
44 Juwan Howard/99 10.00 25.00
45 Artis Gilmore/99 12.00 30.00
46 Pat Riley/75 15.00 40.00
47 Earl Monroe/49 15.00 40.00
48 Jalen Rose/99 10.00 25.00
49 Toni Kukoc/99 12.00 30.00
50 Rik Smits/99 8.00 20.00

2022-23 Panini National Treasures Jersey Treasures

STATED PRINT RUN 99 SER.#'d SETS
*PRIME/5-25: 1.25X TO 3X BASIC
1 Immanuel Quickley 4.00 10.00
2 Devin Vassell 5.00 12.00
3 Bradley Beal 5.00 12.00
4 Damian Lillard 10.00 25.00
6 Robert Williams III 3.00 8.00
7 Buddy Hield 4.00 10.00
8 Bam Adebayo 6.00 15.00
9 Tyrese Maxey 8.00 20.00
10 Ayo Dosunmu 5.00 12.00
11 Kyrie Irving 8.00 20.00
12 CJ McCollum 4.00 10.00
13 Shai Gilgeous-Alexander 20.00 50.00
14 Andrew Wiggins 5.00 12.00
15 Zion Williamson 10.00 25.00
16 Jordan Clarkson 4.00 10.00
17 Tim Hardaway Jr. 3.00 8.00
18 Jaylen Brown 8.00 20.00
19 Lonnie Walker IV 3.00 8.00
20 Anfernee Simons 5.00 12.00
21 Scottie Barnes 6.00 15.00
22 Jayson Tatum 15.00 40.00
23 Mikal Bridges 5.00 12.00
24 Kevin Porter Jr. 3.00 8.00
25 Anthony Edwards 20.00 50.00
26 Tyrese Haliburton 8.00 20.00
27 Malcolm Brogdon 3.00 8.00
28 Trey Murphy III 5.00 12.00
29 Quentin Grimes 3.00 8.00
30 Khris Middleton 5.00 12.00
31 Joel Embiid 6.00 15.00
32 Cade Cunningham 12.00 30.00
33 Al Horford 4.00 10.00
34 Ben Simmons 4.00 10.00
36 Darius Garland 6.00 15.00
37 James Harden 8.00 20.00
38 Desmond Bane 5.00 12.00
39 Marcus Smart 5.00 12.00
40 Christian Wood 2.50 6.00
41 Jimmy Butler 8.00 20.00
42 Alperen Sengun 5.00 12.00
43 Saddiq Bey 3.00 8.00
44 Kevin Durant 12.00 30.00
45 Giannis Antetokounmpo 20.00 50.00
47 Spencer Dinwiddie 3.00 8.00
48 Jalen Green 12.00 30.00
49 Dejounte Murray 5.00 12.00
50 DeMar DeRozan 5.00 12.00
51 Aaron Gordon 4.00 10.00
52 Anthony Davis 10.00 25.00
53 Julius Randle 5.00 12.00
54 Dillon Brooks 4.00 10.00
55 Jrue Holiday 5.00 12.00
56 Ja Morant 12.00 30.00
57 Jaren Jackson Jr. 6.00 15.00
58 Kyle Kuzma 5.00 12.00
59 RJ Barrett 6.00 15.00
60 Tyler Herro 6.00 15.00
61 Luka Doncic 25.00 60.00
62 LaMelo Ball 10.00 25.00
63 Fred VanVleet 5.00 12.00
64 D'Angelo Russell 3.00 8.00
65 Jalen Suggs 5.00 12.00
66 Rudy Gobert 5.00 12.00
67 Caris LeVert 3.00 8.00
68 John Collins 4.00 10.00
69 Jonathan Kuminga 10.00 25.00
70 Terry Rozier III 5.00 12.00
71 Brandon Ingram 5.00 12.00
72 Zach LaVine 8.00 20.00
74 Jerami Grant 5.00 12.00
75 Karl-Anthony Towns 6.00 15.00
76 Keldon Johnson 5.00 12.00
77 Davion Mitchell 3.00 8.00
78 John Wall 5.00 12.00
79 Devin Booker 15.00 40.00
80 Bones Hyland 3.00 8.00
81 LeBron James 60.00 150.00
83 Trae Young 10.00 25.00
84 Jalen Brunson 8.00 20.00
85 Pascal Siakam 6.00 15.00
86 Michael Porter Jr. 5.00 12.00
87 Kawhi Leonard 10.00 25.00
88 Stephen Curry 50.00 120.00
89 Chris Paul 8.00 20.00
90 Cole Anthony 4.00 10.00
91 Franz Wagner 10.00 25.00
92 Nikola Jokic 20.00 50.00
93 Klay Thompson 10.00 25.00
94 Paul George 6.00 15.00
95 De'Aaron Fox 8.00 20.00
96 Russell Westbrook 6.00 15.00
97 Evan Mobley 10.00 25.00
98 Jamal Murray 6.00 15.00
99 Deandre Ayton 4.00 10.00
100 Josh Giddey 6.00 15.00

2022-23 Panini National Treasures Lasting Legacies Autograph Jerseys

STATED PRINT RUN 49-99 SER.#'d SETS
*PRIME/2-25: .75X TO 2X BASIC
1 Davion Mitchell/99 8.00 20.00
2 Toni Kukoc/99 12.00 30.00
3 Georges Niang/99 8.00 20.00
5 Christian Laettner/99 10.00 25.00
6 Seth Curry/99 8.00 20.00
7 Stephen Jackson/99 10.00 25.00
9 Robert Williams III/99 8.00 20.00
10 Bill Laimbeer/99 10.00 25.00
11 Arvydas Sabonis/99 12.00 30.00
12 Bill Walton/75 40.00 100.00
13 Carlos Boozer/99 8.00 20.00
14 Buddy Hield/99 10.00 25.00
15 Herbert Jones/99 10.00 25.00
16 Karl-Anthony Towns/49 15.00 40.00
17 Sam Cassell/99 10.00 25.00
18 Nicolas Batum/99 8.00 20.00
19 Carmelo Anthony/49 75.00 200.00
20 Kenyon Martin Jr./99 10.00 25.00
21 Patty Mills/99 10.00 25.00
22 Jason Kidd/49 30.00 80.00
23 Detlef Schrempf/99 10.00 25.00
24 Kevon Looney/99 15.00 40.00
25 Glen Rice/99 10.00 25.00
26 Brandon Ingram/75 25.00 60.00
27 Rajon Rondo/99 25.00 60.00
29 Raymond Felton/99 6.00 15.00
30 Alex English/99 12.00 30.00
31 John Starks/99 15.00 40.00
32 Caron Butler/99 8.00 20.00
33 Hedo Turkoglu/99 10.00 25.00
34 Alvan Adams/99 8.00 20.00
35 Ziaire Williams/99 8.00 20.00
36 Jonathan Kuminga/99 25.00 60.00
38 Lonnie Walker IV/99 8.00 20.00
40 Luis Scola/99 8.00 20.00
41 Isaiah Stewart/99 8.00 20.00
42 Tony Allen/99 6.00 15.00
43 Isaac Okoro/99 8.00 20.00
44 Santi Aldama/99 10.00 25.00
45 Udonis Haslem/99 8.00 20.00
48 Jalen Suggs/75 12.00 30.00
49 Dale Ellis/99 10.00 25.00
50 Jalen Rose/99 10.00 25.00

2022-23 Panini National Treasures Material Treasures

STATED PRINT RUN 99 SER.#'d SETS
*PRIME/5-25: 1.25X TO 3X BASIC
1 Jaylen Brown 8.00 20.00
2 Gordon Hayward 3.00 8.00
4 Shai Gilgeous-Alexander 20.00 50.00
5 Kevin Durant 12.00 30.00
6 Giannis Antetokounmpo 20.00 50.00
7 Jalen Green 12.00 30.00
8 Stephen Curry 50.00 120.00
9 Devin Booker 20.00 50.00
10 Paul George 6.00 15.00
11 Anthony Davis 10.00 25.00
12 Tyler Herro 6.00 15.00
13 LeBron James 60.00 150.00
14 Brandon Ingram 5.00 12.00
15 Ja Morant 12.00 30.00
16 Jordan Clarkson 4.00 10.00
18 Ben Simmons 4.00 10.00
19 Dejounte Murray 5.00 12.00
20 Cole Anthony 4.00 10.00
21 Luka Doncic 25.00 60.00
22 Anfernee Simons 5.00 12.00
23 De'Aaron Fox 8.00 20.00
24 James Harden 8.00 20.00
25 RJ Barrett 6.00 15.00
26 Pascal Siakam 6.00 15.00
28 Michael Porter Jr. 5.00 12.00
29 Rudy Gobert 5.00 12.00
30 Myles Turner 4.00 10.00

2022-23 Panini National Treasures National Archives Ink

STATED PRINT RUN 25-99 SER.#'d SETS
1 Luka Doncic/25 500.00 1,000.00
2 Adrian Dantley/99 10.00 25.00
3 Latrell Sprewell/99 25.00 60.00
5 Khris Middleton/49 12.00 30.00
6 Walt Frazier/49 15.00 40.00
7 Cade Cunningham/49 150.00 400.00
8 Karl-Anthony Towns/49 25.00 60.00
9 Jalen Green/49 100.00 250.00
10 Jalen Suggs/49 20.00 50.00
11 Charles Barkley/25 100.00 250.00
12 Herbert Jones/99 10.00 25.00
13 Bradley Beal/49 12.00 30.00
14 Michael Porter Jr./75 12.00 30.00
15 Dominique Wilkins/25 15.00 40.00
16 Robert Horry/99 10.00 25.00
18 Clyde Drexler/25 30.00 80.00
19 Michael Cooper/99 10.00 25.00
21 Jordan Poole/49 40.00 100.00
22 Deandre Ayton/49 10.00 25.00
24 Rasheed Wallace/49 30.00 80.00
27 Julius Randle/49 12.00 30.00
28 Rudy Gobert/49 12.00 30.00
31 Kevin Garnett/25 125.00 300.00
32 Desmond Bane/75 40.00 100.00
34 James Harden/49 150.00 400.00
35 Joe Dumars/99 12.00 30.00
36 Josh Giddey/99 60.00 150.00
37 Marcus Smart/99 20.00 50.00
38 Shaquille O'Neal /25 150.00 400.00
39 Christian Laettner/75 10.00 25.00
40 Ralph Sampson/49 8.00 20.00
41 Bob Cousy/49 150.00 400.00
42 Hakeem Olajuwon/49 60.00 150.00
43 Dino Radja/99 8.00 20.00
44 Alex English/99 12.00 30.00
46 Chris Mullin/49 12.00 30.00
47 Karl Malone/25 60.00 150.00
48 Kenny ""Sky"" Walker/99 8.00 20.00
49 Mark Aguirre/99 10.00 25.00
50 Nate Archibald/99 12.00 30.00

2022-23 Panini National Treasures NBA Greats Signatures

STATED PRINT RUN 49 SER.#'d SETS
*BRONZE/25: .5X TO 1.2X BASIC
1 Larry Bird 100.00 250.00
2 Paul Pierce 75.00 200.00
3 Clyde Drexler 40.00 100.00
4 Anfernee Hardaway 75.00 200.00
5 Tony Parker 40.00 100.00
6 Gail Goodrich 10.00 25.00
7 Bernard King 12.00 30.00
8 Jerry Stackhouse 12.00 30.00
9 Jason Richardson 10.00 25.00
10 B.J. Armstrong 10.00 25.00
11 John Stockton 50.00 120.00
12 Dominique Wilkins 15.00 40.00
14 Jason Terry 8.00 20.00
15 Bob McAdoo 12.00 30.00
16 Jamaal Wilkes 10.00 25.00
18 Dino Radja 8.00 20.00
19 Detlef Schrempf 10.00 25.00
21 Isiah Thomas 30.00 80.00
22 Mark Price 10.00 25.00
23 Glen Rice 10.00 25.00
24 Jason Kidd 40.00 100.00
25 Joe Dumars 12.00 30.00
26 Wally Szczerbiak 8.00 20.00
27 Charles Barkley 75.00 200.00
28 Lenny Wilkens 12.00 30.00
29 Rolando Blackman 8.00 20.00
30 Grant Hill 40.00 100.00

2022-23 Panini National Treasures NBA Materials

STATED PRINT RUN 99 SER.#'d SETS
*PRIME/5-25: 1.25X TO 3X BASIC
1 Trae Young 10.00 25.00
2 Jayson Tatum 15.00 40.00
3 Kevin Durant 12.00 30.00
4 LaMelo Ball 15.00 40.00
5 James Harden 8.00 20.00
6 Evan Mobley 10.00 25.00
7 Luka Doncic 25.00 60.00
8 Nikola Jokic 20.00 50.00
9 Cade Cunningham 12.00 30.00
10 Stephen Curry 50.00 120.00
11 Jalen Green 12.00 30.00
12 Tyrese Haliburton 8.00 20.00
13 Kawhi Leonard 10.00 25.00
14 LeBron James 60.00 150.00
15 Ja Morant 12.00 30.00
16 Klay Thompson 10.00 25.00
17 Giannis Antetokounmpo 20.00 50.00
18 Anthony Edwards 25.00 60.00
19 Zion Williamson 10.00 25.00
20 RJ Barrett 6.00 15.00
21 Shai Gilgeous-Alexander 20.00 50.00
22 Cole Anthony 4.00 10.00
23 Tyrese Maxey 8.00 20.00

24 Devin Booker 20.00 50.00
25 Anfernee Simons 5.00 12.00
26 De'Aaron Fox 8.00 20.00
27 Keldon Johnson 5.00 12.00
28 Pascal Siakam 6.00 15.00
29 Jordan Clarkson 4.00 10.00
30 Bradley Beal 5.00 12.00

2022-23 Panini National Treasures Notable Nicknames Autographs

STATED PRINT RUN 25 SER.#'d SETS
1 Cade Cunningham 800.00 1,500.00
2 Paul Pierce 600.00 1,200.00
4 Bob Cousy 150.00 400.00
6 Clyde Drexler 40.00 100.00
7 Paul George 200.00 500.00
8 Bradley Beal 40.00 100.00
9 James Harden 200.00 500.00
10 Gary Payton 350.00 700.00

2022-23 Panini National Treasures Peerless Signatures

STATED PRINT RUN 49 SER.#'d SETS
*BRONZE/15-25: .5X TO 1.2X BASIC
1 Rasheed Wallace/49 30.00 80.00
2 Jamal Crawford/99 10.00 25.00
3 Gail Goodrich/99 10.00 25.00
4 Jaren Jackson Jr./75 30.00 80.00
5 Allen Iverson/49 100.00 250.00
6 Alperen Sengun/99 60.00 150.00
7 George McGinnis/99 10.00 25.00
8 Karl-Anthony Towns/49 15.00 40.00
9 Dejounte Murray/49 12.00 30.00
10 Jalen Green/99 75.00 200.00
11 Pau Gasol/49 50.00 120.00
12 Richard Hamilton/99 12.00 30.00
13 Amar'e Stoudemire/49 10.00 25.00
14 Nate Archibald/99 12.00 30.00
15 Austin Reaves/99 100.00 250.00
16 Magic Johnson/99 100.00 250.00
17 Steve Kerr/99 12.00 30.00
18 Karl Malone/49 60.00 150.00
19 Luka Doncic/49 500.00 1,000.00
22 Kenny "Sky" Walker/99 8.00 20.00
23 Walt Frazier/49 15.00 40.00
24 Jason Richardson/99 10.00 25.00
25 Alex English/99 12.00 30.00
26 Stephen Curry/49 800.00 1,500.00
27 Brandon Ingram/99 30.00 80.00
28 Kevin Huerter/99 10.00 25.00
29 Jerry Stackhouse/99 12.00 30.00
30 Ja Morant/25 200.00 500.00
31 Wally Szczerbiak/99 8.00 20.00
32 Dell Curry/49 10.00 25.00
33 Cade Cunningham/49 125.00 300.00
34 Chris Paul/49 75.00 200.00
35 Paul Pierce/49 40.00 100.00
36 Dominique Wilkins/49 20.00 50.00
37 Zach Randolph/99 10.00 25.00
39 Michael Porter Jr./99 12.00 30.00
40 Evan Mobley/99 60.00 150.00
42 Paul George/49 40.00 100.00
43 Jason Terry/99 8.00 20.00
44 Bradley Beal/99 12.00 30.00
45 Devin Vassell/99 25.00 60.00
46 Kelly Oubre Jr./99 10.00 25.00
47 Derrick White/99 20.00 50.00
48 Seth Curry/99 8.00 20.00
50 Chauncey Billups/99 12.00 30.00

2022-23 Panini National Treasures Penmanship Autographs

STATED PRINT RUN 49-99 SER.#'d SETS
*BRONZE/25: .5X TO 1.2X BASIC
1 Rudy Gobert/35 12.00 30.00
2 Jalen Suggs/49 20.00 50.00
3 Khris Middleton/49 12.00 30.00
4 Julius Randle/75 12.00 30.00
5 Carlos Boozer/49 8.00 20.00
8 Gary Harris/49 8.00 20.00
10 RJ Barrett/75 20.00 50.00
12 Anthony Edwards/49 200.00 500.00
13 Ja Morant/49 200.00 500.00
14 Marcus Smart/75 12.00 30.00
15 Desmond Bane/99 40.00 100.00
17 Dejounte Murray/99 12.00 30.00
18 Dwyane Wade/49 125.00 300.00
20 Tim Hardaway/75 20.00 50.00
21 Charles Barkley/49 100.00 250.00
22 Larry Bird/49 100.00 250.00
23 Jamal Crawford/99 10.00 25.00
24 Josh Giddey/99 60.00 150.00
25 Michael Porter Jr./99 12.00 30.00
27 Deandre Ayton/49 10.00 25.00
28 Shawn Kemp/99 40.00 100.00
30 Jalen Brunson/99 50.00 120.00
31 Nassir Little/99 10.00 25.00
34 Tyrese Haliburton/99 125.00 300.00
37 David Thompson/75 12.00 30.00
38 Fat Lever/99 8.00 20.00
39 Manu Ginobili/49 75.00 200.00
40 Grayson Allen/49 10.00 25.00

2022-23 Panini National Treasures Retro Materials

STATED PRINT RUN 40-99 SER.#'d SETS
*PRIME/2-25: 1.25X TO 3X BASIC
2 Alonzo Mourning/99 6.00 15.00
3 Amar'e Stoudemire/99 4.00 10.00
4 Andrew Bogut/99 4.00 10.00
5 Brad Daugherty/99 3.00 8.00
6 Carlos Boozer/99 3.00 8.00
7 Carmelo Anthony/99 6.00 15.00
8 Caron Butler/99 3.00 8.00
9 Christian Laettner/99 4.00 10.00
10 Dale Ellis/99 4.00 10.00
11 Danny Granger/99 3.00 8.00
12 Danny Manning/99 3.00 8.00
13 Dikembe Mutombo/99 6.00 15.00
14 Dirk Nowitzki/99 10.00 25.00
15 Elton Brand/99 4.00 10.00
16 Derrick Rose/99 8.00 20.00
17 Blake Griffin/99 4.00 10.00
18 Tim Duncan/75 10.00 25.00
19 Gordon Hayward/99 3.00 8.00
20 Hedo Turkoglu/40 4.00 10.00
21 James Worthy/99 6.00 15.00
22 Kevin Durant/99 12.00 30.00
23 Kevin Love/99 4.00 10.00
24 Kyrie Irving/99 8.00 20.00
25 LaMarcus Aldridge/99 4.00 10.00
26 LeBron James/99 60.00 150.00
27 Paul George/99 6.00 15.00
29 Dwight Howard/99 5.00 12.00
30 DeMarcus Cousins/99 3.00 8.00

2022-23 Panini National Treasures Rookie Dual Material Autographs

STATED PRINT RUN 99 SER.#'d SETS
*PRIME/25: .75X TO 2X BASIC
1 Paolo Banchero 300.00 600.00
2 Chet Holmgren 500.00 1,000.00
3 Jabari Smith Jr. 60.00 150.00
4 Keegan Murray 50.00 120.00
5 Jaden Ivey 60.00 150.00
6 Bennedict Mathurin 60.00 150.00
7 Shaedon Sharpe 125.00 300.00
8 Dyson Daniels 50.00 125.00
9 Jeremy Sochan 60.00 150.00
11 Ousmane Dieng 25.00 60.00
12 Jalen Williams 100.00 250.00
13 Jalen Duren 60.00 150.00
14 Ochai Agbaji 25.00 60.00
15 Mark Williams 40.00 100.00
16 AJ Griffin 15.00 40.00
17 Tari Eason 50.00 125.00
18 Dalen Terry 20.00 50.00
19 Jake LaRavia 20.00 50.00
20 Malaki Branham 20.00 50.00
21 Christian Braun 50.00 125.00
22 Walker Kessler 40.00 100.00
23 David Roddy 25.00 60.00
24 MarJon Beauchamp 20.00 50.00
25 Blake Wesley 20.00 50.00
26 Wendell Moore Jr. 20.00 50.00
27 Nikola Jovic 40.00 100.00
28 Patrick Baldwin Jr. 20.00 50.00
29 TyTy Washington Jr. 20.00 50.00
30 Peyton Watson 30.00 80.00
31 Andrew Nembhard 40.00 100.00
32 Caleb Houstan 20.00 50.00
33 Christian Koloko 20.00 50.00
34 Max Christie 50.00 125.00
35 Jaden Hardy 30.00 80.00
36 Kennedy Chandler 20.00 50.00
37 Moussa Diabate 20.00 50.00
38 E.J. Liddell 20.00 50.00
39 Trevor Keels 15.00 40.00
40 Isaiah Mobley 20.00 50.00

2022-23 Panini National Treasures Rookie Dual Materials

STATED PRINT RUN 99 SER.#'d SETS
*PRIME/25: 1.25X TO 3X BASIC
1 Dyson Daniels 8.00 20.00
2 Andrew Nembhard 6.00 15.00
3 Paolo Banchero 20.00 50.00
4 Christian Koloko 3.00 8.00
5 Nikola Jovic 6.00 15.00
6 Christian Braun 8.00 20.00
7 Jalen Duren 10.00 25.00
8 Chet Holmgren 15.00 40.00
9 MarJon Beauchamp 3.00 8.00
10 Jaden Hardy 5.00 12.00
11 Tari Eason 8.00 20.00
12 Bennedict Mathurin 10.00 25.00
13 Shaedon Sharpe 12.00 30.00
14 AJ Griffin 2.50 6.00
15 Johnny Davis 3.00 8.00
16 Jabari Smith Jr. 10.00 25.00
17 Walker Kessler 6.00 15.00
18 Jalen Williams 15.00 40.00
19 Ochai Agbaji 4.00 10.00
20 Jake LaRavia 3.00 8.00
21 Ousmane Dieng 4.00 10.00
22 Jeremy Sochan 10.00 25.00
23 Keegan Murray 8.00 20.00
24 Jaden Ivey 10.00 25.00
25 David Roddy 4.00 10.00

2022-23 Panini National Treasures Rookie Jumbo Materials

STATED PRINT RUN 99 SER.#'d SETS
*PRIME/10-25: 1.25X TO 3X BASIC
1 Nikola Jovic 6.00 15.00
2 Paolo Banchero 20.00 50.00
3 Jalen Williams 15.00 40.00
4 Tari Eason 8.00 20.00
5 Jake LaRavia 3.00 8.00
6 AJ Griffin 2.50 6.00
7 Jeremy Sochan 10.00 25.00
8 Jalen Duren 10.00 25.00
9 MarJon Beauchamp 3.00 8.00
10 Bennedict Mathurin 10.00 25.00
11 Jaden Ivey 10.00 25.00
12 Christian Koloko 3.00 8.00
13 Christian Braun 8.00 20.00
14 Dyson Daniels 8.00 20.00
15 Ochai Agbaji 4.00 10.00
16 Johnny Davis 3.00 8.00
17 Chet Holmgren 15.00 40.00
18 Shaedon Sharpe 12.00 30.00
19 Jabari Smith Jr. 10.00 25.00
20 Walker Kessler 6.00 15.00
21 Ousmane Dieng 4.00 10.00
22 Jaden Hardy 5.00 12.00
23 Keegan Murray 8.00 20.00
24 Andrew Nembhard 6.00 15.00
25 David Roddy 4.00 10.00

2022-23 Panini National Treasures Rookie Materials

STATED PRINT RUN 99 SER.#'d SETS
*PRIME/25: 1.25X TO 3X BASIC
1 Paolo Banchero 20.00 50.00
2 Jalen Williams 15.00 40.00
3 Chet Holmgren 15.00 40.00
4 Johnny Davis 3.00 8.00
5 David Roddy 4.00 10.00
6 Walker Kessler 6.00 15.00
7 Christian Koloko 3.00 8.00
8 Christian Braun 8.00 20.00
9 Jeremy Sochan 10.00 25.00
10 Jaden Ivey 10.00 25.00
11 Jalen Duren 10.00 25.00
12 Shaedon Sharpe 12.00 30.00
13 AJ Griffin 2.50 6.00
14 Jaden Hardy 5.00 12.00
15 Dyson Daniels 8.00 20.00
16 MarJon Beauchamp 3.00 8.00
17 Keegan Murray 8.00 20.00
18 Tari Eason 8.00 20.00
19 Andrew Nembhard 6.00 15.00
20 Jabari Smith Jr. 10.00 25.00
21 Bennedict Mathurin 10.00 25.00
22 Nikola Jovic 6.00 15.00
23 Ousmane Dieng 4.00 10.00
24 Jake LaRavia 3.00 8.00
25 Ochai Agbaji 4.00 10.00

2022-23 Panini National Treasures Rookie Quad Material Autographs

STATED PRINT RUN 99 SER.#'d SETS
*PRIME/25: .75X TO 2X BASIC
1 Keegan Murray 60.00 150.00
2 Chet Holmgren 800.00 1,500.00
3 Shaedon Sharpe 150.00 400.00
4 Bennedict Mathurin 80.00 200.00
5 Jaden Ivey 80.00 200.00
6 Jabari Smith Jr. 80.00 200.00
7 Jeremy Sochan 80.00 200.00
9 Dyson Daniels 60.00 150.00
10 Paolo Banchero 500.00 1,200.00

2022-23 Panini National Treasures Rookie Triple Material Autographs

STATED PRINT RUN 99 SER.#'d SETS
*PRIME/25: .75X TO 2X BASIC
1 Johnny Davis 25.00 60.00
2 Chet Holmgren 600.00 1,200.00
3 Dyson Daniels 60.00 150.00
4 Shaedon Sharpe 150.00 400.00
5 Jaden Ivey 80.00 200.00
6 Jeremy Sochan 80.00 200.00
7 Bennedict Mathurin 80.00 200.00
8 Jalen Williams 125.00 300.00
9 Jalen Duren 80.00 200.00
10 Keegan Murray 60.00 150.00
11 Ochai Agbaji 30.00 80.00
12 AJ Griffin 20.00 50.00
13 Dalen Terry 25.00 60.00
14 Paolo Banchero 400.00 800.00
15 Tari Eason 60.00 150.00
16 Ousmane Dieng 30.00 80.00
17 Mark Williams 50.00 125.00
18 Jake LaRavia 25.00 60.00
19 Malaki Branham 25.00 60.00
20 Jabari Smith Jr. 80.00 200.00

2022-23 Panini National Treasures Rookie Triple Materials

STATED PRINT RUN 99 SER.#'d SETS
*PRIME/25: 1.25X TO 3X BASIC
1 Jeremy Sochan 10.00 25.00
2 Christian Braun 8.00 20.00
3 Tari Eason 8.00 20.00
4 Andrew Nembhard 6.00 15.00
5 Jaden Ivey 10.00 25.00
6 Jalen Williams 15.00 40.00
7 Ousmane Dieng 4.00 10.00
8 Jaden Hardy 5.00 12.00
9 Nikola Jovic 6.00 15.00
10 Walker Kessler 6.00 15.00
11 Chet Holmgren 15.00 40.00
12 Christian Koloko 3.00 8.00
13 Ochai Agbaji 4.00 10.00
14 Jake LaRavia 3.00 8.00
15 Keegan Murray 8.00 20.00
16 Shaedon Sharpe 12.00 30.00
17 Paolo Banchero 20.00 50.00
18 Jabari Smith Jr. 10.00 25.00
19 Bennedict Mathurin 10.00 25.00
20 David Roddy 4.00 10.00
21 AJ Griffin 2.50 6.00
22 Johnny Davis 3.00 8.00
23 MarJon Beauchamp 3.00 8.00
24 Jalen Duren 10.00 25.00
25 Dyson Daniels 8.00 20.00

2022-23 Panini National Treasures Signatures

STATED PRINT RUN 49-99 SER.#'d SETS
*BRONZE/15-25: .5X TO 1.2X BASIC
1 Ray Allen/49 75.00 200.00
2 Ja Morant/49 200.00 500.00
3 Ayo Dosunmu/99 12.00 30.00
4 Glen Rice/99 10.00 25.00
5 Jerry Stackhouse/99 12.00 30.00
6 John Stockton/49 30.00 80.00
8 Cole Anthony/99 10.00 25.00
9 David Thompson/99 12.00 30.00
10 Nikola Jokic/49 200.00 500.00
11 Evan Mobley/49 75.00 200.00
12 Dejounte Murray/49 12.00 30.00
13 Herbert Jones/99 10.00 25.00
14 Jonathan Kuminga/75 25.00 60.00
15 Doug Collins/99 10.00 25.00
17 Calvin Murphy/99 10.00 25.00
18 Robert Horry/99 10.00 25.00
19 Steve Kerr/75 12.00 30.00
20 Amar'e Stoudemire/49 10.00 25.00
21 Antawn Jamison/99 10.00 25.00
22 Obi Toppin/99 10.00 25.00
24 Zach Randolph/75 10.00 25.00
25 Seth Curry/99 8.00 20.00
27 Chauncey Billups/99 12.00 30.00
28 Michael Cooper/99 10.00 25.00
29 Grant Hill/49 40.00 100.00
30 CJ McCollum/49 10.00 25.00
31 Ralph Sampson/99 8.00 20.00
32 Bill Walton/49 60.00 150.00
34 Kevin Huerter/99 10.00 25.00
36 Stephen Jackson/99 10.00 25.00
39 Jordan Poole/99 40.00 100.00
40 John Starks/75 10.00 25.00
41 Metta World Peace/49 10.00 25.00
42 Bernard King/99 12.00 30.00
43 Tony Allen/99 6.00 15.00
47 Dino Radja/99 8.00 20.00
48 Isaiah Rider/99 10.00 25.00
49 Luka Doncic/25 600.00 1,200.00
50 Evan Fournier/99 8.00 20.00

2022-23 Panini National Treasures Timeless Talents Signatures

STATED PRINT RUN 49 SER.#'d SETS
*BRONZE/25: .5X TO 1.2X BASIC
1 Manu Ginobili 75.00 200.00
2 Ray Allen 75.00 200.00
3 Pau Gasol 75.00 200.00
4 Walt Frazier 15.00 40.00
5 Jason Kidd 40.00 100.00
6 Kevin Garnett 125.00 300.00
7 Avery Johnson 8.00 20.00
8 Vince Carter 150.00 400.00
9 Grant Hill 40.00 100.00
10 Joe Dumars 12.00 30.00
11 Adrian Dantley 10.00 25.00
12 Elton Brand 10.00 25.00
13 Mychal Thompson 8.00 20.00
14 Dwyane Wade 100.00 250.00
15 Jamal Crawford 10.00 25.00
16 Cazzie Russell 12.00 30.00
17 Latrell Sprewell 25.00 60.00
18 Anfernee Hardaway 75.00 200.00
19 Paul Pierce 60.00 150.00
20 Dirk Nowitzki 150.00 400.00
21 Doug Collins 10.00 25.00
22 Brad Miller 8.00 20.00
23 Chris Mullin 12.00 30.00
24 Allen Iverson 125.00 300.00
25 Dominique Wilkins 20.00 50.00
26 Jason Terry 8.00 20.00
27 Gary Payton 30.00 80.00
30 Mark Price 10.00 25.00

2022-23 Panini National Treasures Timeless Treasures Materials

STATED PRINT RUN 14-99 SER.#'d SETS
*PRIME/5-25: 1.25X TO 3X BASIC
1 Artis Gilmore/66 5.00 12.00
2 B.J. Armstrong/14 4.00 10.00
3 Jamal Crawford/99 4.00 10.00
4 Chris Mullin/99 5.00 12.00
6 Al Harrington/99 3.00 8.00
7 Leandro Barbosa/99 3.00 8.00
8 John Starks/99 4.00 10.00
9 Darrell Armstrong/99 2.50 6.00
10 Kevin Martin/99 3.00 8.00
11 Brad Daugherty/99 3.00 8.00
12 Xavier McDaniel/99 4.00 10.00
13 Shawn Bradley/99 3.00 8.00
14 Toni Kukoc/99 5.00 12.00
15 Danny Granger/99 3.00 8.00
17 Buck Williams/99 4.00 10.00
18 Jeff Hornacek/99 4.00 10.00
19 Dwight Howard/99 5.00 12.00
20 Vince Carter/99 8.00 20.00
21 Rudy Gobert/99 3.00 8.00
22 Paul George/99 6.00 15.00
23 Andrew Wiggins/99 5.00 12.00
24 Derrick Rose/99 8.00 20.00
25 Jimmy Butler/99 8.00 20.00
26 Zach LaVine/99 6.00 15.00
27 Chris Paul/99 8.00 20.00
28 DeAndre Jordan/99 3.00 8.00
30 James Harden/99 8.00 20.00

2022-23 Panini National Treasures Timeline Materials

STATED PRINT RUN 99 SER.#'d SETS
*PRIME/3-25: 1.25X TO 3X BASIC
1 Jaylen Brown 10.00 25.00
2 Kyrie Irving 10.00 25.00
3 Zach LaVine 10.00 25.00
4 Darius Garland 8.00 20.00
5 Dejounte Murray 6.00 15.00
6 Tyler Herro 8.00 20.00
7 Andrew Wiggins 6.00 15.00
8 Alperen Sengun 6.00 15.00
9 Paul George 8.00 20.00
10 Anthony Davis 12.00 30.00
11 Jimmy Butler 10.00 25.00
12 Bam Adebayo 8.00 20.00
13 Deandre Ayton 5.00 12.00
14 Damian Lillard 12.00 30.00
15 Russell Westbrook 8.00 20.00
16 Jalen Brunson 10.00 25.00
17 OG Anunoby 6.00 15.00
18 DeMar DeRozan 8.00 20.00
19 Joel Embiid 8.00 20.00
20 Chris Paul 10.00 25.00
21 Jerami Grant 6.00 15.00
23 Fred VanVleet 6.00 15.00
24 Mike Conley 4.00 10.00
26 Nikola Vucevic 5.00 12.00
27 Jamal Murray 8.00 20.00
28 De'Andre Hunter 5.00 12.00
29 Cam Reddish 4.00 10.00
30 Gordon Hayward 4.00 10.00

2022-23 Panini National Treasures Treasured Moments Autographs

STATED PRINT RUN 49-99 SER.#'d SETS
*BRONZE/25: .5X TO 1.2X BASIC
1 James Harden/49 350.00 700.00
2 Nikola Jokic/49 300.00 600.00
3 Chris Paul/49 100.00 250.00
4 Shaquille O'Neal /49 125.00 300.00
5 Josh Giddey/99 40.00 100.00
6 Magic Johnson/49 100.00 250.00
7 Luka Doncic/49 500.00 1,000.00
8 Ja Morant/49 300.00 600.00
9 Paolo Banchero /99 150.00 400.00
10 Paul George/49 150.00 400.00
11 Robert Horry/99 12.00 30.00
12 Tony Parker/49 75.00 200.00
13 Ray Allen/49 100.00 250.00
14 Stephen Jackson/99 12.00 30.00
15 Jason Richardson/99 12.00 30.00
16 Stephen Curry/49 800.00 1,500.00
17 Cole Anthony/49 12.00 30.00
18 Jayson Tatum/99 200.00 500.00
19 John Stockton/49 75.00 200.00
20 Kevin Garnett/49 150.00 400.00
21 Karl Malone/49 60.00 150.00
22 Isiah Thomas/75 25.00 60.00
23 Paul Pierce/49 75.00 200.00
24 Manu Ginobili/49 150.00 400.00
25 Vince Carter/49 150.00 400.00

2022-23 Panini National Treasures Treasured Signatures

STATED PRINT RUN 49-99 SER.#'d SETS
*BRONZE/25: .5X TO 1.2X BASIC
1 Larry Bird/49 100.00 250.00
1 David Robinson/75
Issued in '23-24 Panini
National Treasures 60.00 150.00
2 Bob McAdoo/99 12.00 30.00
3 Richard Hamilton/75 12.00 30.00
4 Ralph Sampson/99 8.00 20.00
5 Karl Malone/49 50.00 120.00
6 Metta World Peace/75 10.00 25.00
7 Tony Parker/49 40.00 100.00
8 Robert Parish/49 12.00 30.00
9 Calvin Murphy/49 10.00 25.00
10 Peja Stojakovic/49 10.00 25.00
12 Bill Walton/99 40.00 100.00
13 Dirk Nowitzki/49 150.00 400.00
14 Kevin Garnett/49 100.00 250.00
15 Magic Johnson/49 100.00 250.00
16 Jerry West/49 40.00 100.00
17 Lenny Wilkens/49 12.00 30.00
18 Shaquille O'Neal /49 100.00 250.00
19 Gail Goodrich/99 10.00 25.00
20 Dell Curry/99 10.00 25.00
22 Anfernee Hardaway/49 60.00 150.00
23 Nate Archibald/99 12.00 30.00
24 Christian Laettner/99 10.00 25.00
25 Allen Iverson/99 100.00 250.00

2022-23 Panini National Treasures Treasured Threads

STATED PRINT RUN 99 SER.#'d SETS
*PRIME/5-25: 1.25X TO 3X BASIC
1 Karl-Anthony Towns 8.00 20.00
2 Jusuf Nurkic 5.00 12.00
3 Jerami Grant 6.00 15.00
4 LeBron James 60.00 150.00
5 Anthony Davis 12.00 30.00
6 Stephen Curry 60.00 150.00
7 Giannis Antetokounmpo 25.00 60.00
8 Kevin Durant 15.00 40.00
9 Ja Morant 15.00 40.00
10 LaMelo Ball 15.00 40.00
11 Jayson Tatum 20.00 50.00
12 Trae Young 10.00 25.00
13 Zach LaVine 10.00 25.00
14 Evan Mobley 12.00 30.00
15 Luka Doncic 30.00 80.00
16 Nikola Jokic 25.00 60.00
17 Cade Cunningham 15.00 40.00
18 Tyrese Haliburton 10.00 25.00
19 Kawhi Leonard 12.00 30.00
20 Zion Williamson 12.00 30.00
21 Jalen Brunson 10.00 25.00
22 Shai Gilgeous-Alexander 25.00 60.00
23 Joel Embiid 8.00 20.00
24 Devin Booker 12.00 30.00
25 Damian Lillard 12.00 30.00
26 Keldon Johnson 6.00 15.00
27 Scottie Barnes 8.00 20.00
28 Bradley Beal 6.00 15.00
30 James Harden 10.00 25.00

2022-23 Panini National Treasures Tremendous Treasures Relics

STATED PRINT RUN 99 SER.#'d SETS
*PRIME/5-25: 1.25X TO 3X BASIC
1 Jaylen Brown 8.00 20.00
2 Kyle Kuzma 5.00 12.00
3 Trae Young 10.00 25.00
4 Zach LaVine 8.00 20.00
5 Tyrese Maxey 8.00 20.00
6 John Collins 4.00 10.00
7 Ben Simmons 4.00 10.00
8 LaMelo Ball 10.00 25.00
9 Christian Wood 2.50 6.00
10 Spencer Dinwiddie 3.00 8.00
11 Jamal Murray 6.00 15.00
12 Saddiq Bey 3.00 8.00
13 Myles Turner 4.00 10.00
14 Alex Caruso 4.00 10.00
15 Norman Powell 4.00 10.00
16 Kyle Lowry 5.00 12.00
17 Jrue Holiday 5.00 12.00
18 D'Angelo Russell 3.00 8.00
19 Devin Booker 10.00 25.00
21 OG Anunoby 5.00 12.00
22 Mike Conley 3.00 8.00
23 Aaron Gordon 4.00 10.00
24 Collin Sexton 4.00 10.00
25 De'Andre Hunter 4.00 10.00
26 Jarrett Allen 4.00 10.00
27 Mikal Bridges 5.00 12.00
28 Joel Embiid 6.00 15.00
29 Harrison Barnes 3.00 8.00
30 Dillon Brooks 4.00 10.00

2022-23 Panini National Treasures Triple Autographs

1 Josh Giddey
Chet Holmgren
Jalen Williams 350.00 700.00
2 Tim Hardaway
Mitch Richmond
Chris Mullin 200.00 500.00
3 Jabari Smith Jr.
Kevin Porter Jr.
Jalen Green 125.00 300.00
4 Dominique Wilkins
Shawn Kemp
Clyde Drexler 125.00 300.00
5 Julius Randle
Jalen Brunson
RJ Barrett 125.00 300.00
6 Jaden Ivey
Saddiq Bey
Cade Cunningham 125.00 300.00
7 Bennedict Mathurin
Keegan Murray
Shaedon Sharpe 200.00 500.00
8 Jeremy Sochan
Malaki Branham
Blake Wesley 60.00 150.00
9 Kevin Garnett
Latrell Sprewell
Sam Cassell 200.00 500.00
10 Ja Morant
Stephen Curry
Luka Doncic 2,000.00 4,000.00

2022-23 Panini National Treasures Validating Marks Autographs

STATED PRINT RUN 25-99 SER.#'d SETS
*BRONZE/25: .5X TO 1.2X BASIC
1 Pau Gasol/49 40.00 100.00
2 Jaren Jackson Jr./49 30.00 80.00
3 Jayson Tatum/49 150.00 400.00
4 Jason Richardson/99 10.00 25.00
5 Bob Cousy/25 150.00 400.00
8 Tim Hardaway/75 12.00 30.00
9 Peja Stojakovic/99 10.00 25.00
10 Isiah Thomas/49 15.00 40.00
11 James Harden/25 150.00 400.00
13 Ja Morant/49 200.00 500.00
14 Kelly Oubre Jr./99 10.00 25.00
15 Jordan Clarkson/99 15.00 40.00
16 Antawn Jamison/99 10.00 25.00
17 Calvin Murphy/99 10.00 25.00
18 Chauncey Billups/99 12.00 30.00
19 Caron Butler/99 8.00 20.00
20 Grayson Allen/99 10.00 25.00
21 Cole Anthony/99 10.00 25.00
22 RJ Barrett/75 15.00 40.00
23 Tony Parker/49 40.00 100.00
24 Jalen Green/49 50.00 120.00
25 Luka Doncic/25 500.00 1,000.00

2023-24 Panini National Treasures

STATED PRINT RUN 99 SER.#'d SETS
*ORANGE JSY AU RC/75 : .3X TO .75X BASIC
*ORANGE JSY RC/75 : .4X TO 1X BASIC
*BRONZE/49 JSY AU RC: .3X TO .75X BASIC
*BRONZE/RC/75 : .4X TO 1X BASIC
*PINK/25 JSY AU RC: .3X TO .75X BASIC
*PINK JSY RC/25 : .4X TO 1X BASIC
*INTRNTL/33: .75X TO 2X BASIC
*INTRNTL/33 RC: .75X TO 2X BASIC
*INTRNTL/24 JSY AU RC: .3X TO .75X BASIC
1 Evan Mobley 5.00 12.00
2 Jaylen Brown 6.00 15.00
3 Lauri Markkanen 5.00 12.00
4 Nick Smith Jr. 8.00 20.00
5 Rudy Gobert 4.00 10.00
6 Devin Booker 8.00 20.00
7 Jaden Ivey 4.00 10.00
8 Damian Lillard 8.00 20.00
9 Paolo Banchero 8.00 20.00
10 Bam Adebayo 5.00 12.00
11 Buddy Hield 3.00 8.00
12 Jordan Hawkins 10.00 25.00
13 Jordan Poole 5.00 12.00
14 Victor Wembanyama 1,000.00 2,000.00
15 Kevin Durant 10.00 25.00
16 Jeremy Sochan 4.00 10.00
17 Trae Young 6.00 15.00
18 Dejounte Murray 4.00 10.00
19 Fred VanVleet 5.00 12.00
20 Jamal Murray 6.00 15.00
21 Keegan Murray 4.00 10.00
22 Cameron Johnson 3.00 8.00
23 Deandre Ayton 3.00 8.00
24 Terry Rozier III 4.00 10.00
25 Shai Gilgeous-Alexander 15.00 40.00
26 Cameron Thomas 4.00 10.00
27 Keldon Johnson 4.00 10.00
28 Gradey Dick 12.00 30.00
29 Ben Simmons 3.00 8.00
30 Kyrie Irving 6.00 15.00
31 Anthony Davis 8.00 20.00
32 Bennedict Mathurin 5.00 12.00
33 Cade Cunningham 8.00 20.00
34 Austin Reaves 8.00 20.00
35 Tyrese Maxey 6.00 15.00
36 Domantas Sabonis 5.00 12.00
37 Kawhi Leonard 8.00 20.00
38 Aaron Gordon 3.00 8.00
39 Taylor Hendricks 6.00 15.00
40 Alperen Sengun 5.00 12.00
41 De'Aaron Fox 5.00 12.00
42 Jalen Williams 6.00 15.00
43 Karl-Anthony Towns 5.00 12.00
44 Jimmy Butler 5.00 12.00
45 Michael Porter Jr. 4.00 10.00
46 Paul George 5.00 12.00
47 Devin Vassell 4.00 10.00
48 Tyrese Haliburton 6.00 15.00
49 Jarace Walker 12.00 30.00
50 Cam Whitmore 15.00 40.00
51 Anfernee Simons 4.00 10.00
52 CJ McCollum 3.00 8.00
53 Zach LaVine 5.00 12.00
54 Jett Howard 8.00 20.00
55 Shaedon Sharpe 6.00 15.00
56 Stephen Curry 25.00 60.00
57 Jayson Tatum 12.00 30.00
58 OG Anunoby 4.00 10.00
59 Anthony Black 12.00 30.00
60 Kyle Kuzma 4.00 10.00
61 Chet Holmgren 8.00 20.00
62 Julius Randle 4.00 10.00
63 Pascal Siakam 5.00 12.00
64 Luka Doncic 20.00 50.00
65 Jordan Clarkson 3.00 8.00
66 Russell Westbrook 5.00 12.00
67 Jaren Jackson Jr. 5.00 12.00
68 Nikola Jokic 15.00 40.00
69 Jalen Green 5.00 12.00
70 Scottie Barnes 4.00 10.00
71 Darius Garland 5.00 12.00
72 Jalen Brunson 6.00 15.00
73 Kristaps Porzingis 4.00 10.00
74 Khris Middleton 3.00 8.00
75 DeMar DeRozan 5.00 12.00
76 Scoot Henderson 20.00 50.00
77 Mikal Bridges 4.00 10.00
78 Klay Thompson 8.00 20.00
79 Franz Wagner 5.00 12.00
80 Bradley Beal 4.00 10.00
81 RJ Barrett 5.00 12.00
82 James Harden 6.00 15.00
83 Jabari Smith Jr. 5.00 12.00
84 Joel Embiid 8.00 20.00
85 LeBron James 25.00 60.00
86 Zion Williamson 8.00 20.00
87 Brandon Ingram 4.00 10.00
88 Chris Paul 6.00 15.00
89 Jalen Hood-Schifino 6.00 15.00
90 Ja Morant 10.00 25.00
91 Giannis Antetokounmpo 15.00 40.00
92 Desmond Bane 4.00 10.00
93 Anthony Edwards 15.00 40.00
94 Josh Giddey 4.00 10.00
95 Tyler Herro 5.00 12.00
96 LaMelo Ball 8.00 20.00
97 Jrue Holiday 4.00 10.00
98 Jaime Jaquez Jr. 10.00 25.00
99 Donovan Mitchell 6.00 15.00
100 Brandon Miller 25.00 60.00
101 Amen Thompson
JSY AU RC 3,000.00 6,000.00
102 Kris Murray JSY AU RC 60.00 150.00
103 Olivier-Maxence Prosper
JSY AU RC 125.00 300.00
104 Colby Jones JSY AU RC 60.00 150.00
105 Julian Phillips JSY AU RC 60.00 150.00
106 Brandin Podziemski
JSY AU RC 500.00 1,000.00
107 Andre Jackson Jr. JSY AU RC 100.00 250.00
108 Mouhamed Gueye JSY AU RC 60.00 150.00
109 Maxwell Lewis JSY AU RC 50.00 125.00
110 Dariq Whitehead JSY AU RC 80.00 200.00
111 Craig Porter Jr. JSY AU RC 80.00 200.00
112 Hunter Tyson JSY AU RC 60.00 150.00
113 Rayan Rupert JSY AU RC 60.00 150.00
114 Jordan Walsh JSY AU RC 60.00 150.00
115 Noah Clowney JSY AU RC 80.00 200.00
116 Sidy Cissoko JSY AU RC 60.00 150.00
117 GG Jackson II JSY AU RC 800.00 1,500.00
118 Bilal Coulibaly JSY AU RC 500.00 1,000.00
119 Seth Lundy JSY AU RC 50.00 125.00
120 Marcus Sasser JSY AU RC 100.00 250.00
121 Ben Sheppard JSY AU RC 60.00 150.00
122 Jordan Miller JSY AU RC 100.00 250.00
123 Keyontae Johnson JSY AU RC 60.00 150.00
124 Dereck Lively II JSY AU RC 500.00 1,000.00
125 Brice Sensabaugh JSY AU RC 200.00 500.00
126 Julian Strawther JSY AU RC 300.00 600.00
127 Kobe Brown JSY AU RC 60.00 150.00
128 Dru Smith JSY AU RC 50.00 125.00
129 Jalen Pickett JSY AU RC 50.00 125.00
130 Leonard Miller JSY AU RC 60.00 150.00
131 Jalen Wilson JSY AU RC 125.00 300.00
132 Toumani Camara JSY AU RC 200.00 500.00
133 Jaylen Clark JSY AU RC 60.00 150.00
134 Cason Wallace JSY AU RC 500.00 1,000.00
135 Isaiah Wong JSY AU RC 60.00 150.00
136 Trayce Jackson-Davis JSY AU RC 80.00 200.00
137 Ausar Thompson
JSY AU RC 1,000.00 2,000.00
138 Keyonte George JSY AU RC 1,000.00 2,000.00
139 Kobe Bufkin JSY AU RC 200.00 500.00
140 Vasilije Micic JSY AU RC 60.00 150.00
141 Markquis Nowell JSY AU RC 60.00 150.00
142 Sasha Vezenkov JSY AU RC 50.00 125.00
143 Stanley Umude JSY AU RC 50.00 125.00
144 Colin Castleton JSY AU RC 50.00 125.00
145 Leaky Black JSY AU RC 50.00 125.00
146 Oscar Tshiebwe JSY AU RC 80.00 200.00
147 Amari Bailey JSY AU RC 60.00 150.00
148 Adama Sanogo JSY AU RC 60.00 150.00
149 Lester Quinones JSY AU RC 50.00 125.00
150 Chris Livingston JSY AU RC 60.00 150.00
151 Jordan Hawkins JSY RC 30.00 80.00
152 Nick Smith Jr. JSY RC 25.00 60.00
153 Taylor Hendricks JSY RC 20.00 50.00
154 Victor Wembanyama JSY RC 1,500.00 3,000.00
155 Cam Whitmore JSY RC 50.00 120.00
156 Jalen Hood-Schifino JSY RC 20.00 50.00
157 Jaime Jaquez Jr. JSY RC 30.00 80.00
158 Brandon Miller JSY RC 125.00 300.00
159 Anthony Black JSY RC 40.00 100.00
160 Scoot Henderson JSY RC 60.00 150.00
161 Jett Howard JSY RC 25.00 60.00
162 Jarace Walker JSY RC 40.00 100.00
163 Gradey Dick JSY RC 40.00 100.00

2023-24 Panini National Treasures All-NBA Signatures

STATED PRINT RUN 10-49 SER.#'d SETS
NO PRICING ON QTY 10 OR LESS
*BRONZE/15-25: .4X TO 1X BASIC
1 Luka Doncic/25 600.00 1,200.00
2 Chris Paul/25 75.00 200.00
3 Ja Morant/25 400.00 800.00
4 Manu Ginobili/25 75.00 200.00
5 Ben Wallace/25 50.00 120.00
6 Magic Johnson/25 100.00 250.00
7 Russell Westbrook/25 150.00 400.00
8 Clyde Drexler/35 50.00 120.00
9 Kareem Abdul-Jabbar/25 100.00 250.00
10 James Harden/25 200.00 500.00
11 Ray Allen/25 60.00 150.00
12 Tony Parker/35 60.00 150.00
13 Dennis Rodman/35 125.00 300.00
14 Robert Parish/49 25.00 60.00
15 Anthony Davis/25 75.00 200.00
16 Karl Malone/25 60.00 150.00
18 Julius Erving/25 75.00 200.00
19 Pau Gasol/25 75.00 200.00
20 Amar'e Stoudemire/35 40.00 100.00
21 Zach Randolph/49 20.00 50.00
22 Charles Barkley/25 100.00 250.00
23 Shaquille O'Neal/25 150.00 400.00
24 Nikola Jokic/25 200.00 500.00
25 Larry Bird/25 200.00 500.00

2023-24 Panini National Treasures Autographs Dual

1 Ausar Thompson
Amen Thompson/25 150.00 400.00
2 John Wall
Gilbert Arenas/25 50.00 120.00
3 Russell Westbrook
James Harden/25 300.00 600.00
4 Evan Mobley
Jaren Jackson Jr./25 60.00 150.00
5 Keegan Murray
Kris Murray/25 40.00 100.00
7 Cason Wallace
Josh Giddey/25 50.00 120.00
8 Dereck Lively II
Olivier-Maxence Prosper/25 50.00 120.00
9 Dariq Whitehead
Noah Clowney/25 40.00 100.00
10 Bilal Coulibaly
Jordan Poole/25 75.00 200.00
11 Luka Doncic
Kyrie Irving/25 500.00 1,000.00
12 De'Aaron Fox
Donovan Mitchell/25 75.00 200.00
13 Carmelo Anthony
Allen Iverson/15 150.00 400.00
14 Jason Williams
Pau Gasol/25 60.00 150.00
15 Dwyane Wade
Paul Pierce/25 75.00 200.00
16 Keyonte George
Walker Kessler/25 60.00 150.00
17 Cade Cunningham
Ausar Thompson/25 125.00 300.00
18 Jalen Green
Amen Thompson/25 150.00 400.00
19 Dejounte Murray
Kobe Bufkin/25 40.00 100.00
20 Stephen Curry
Chris Paul/25 800.00 1,500.00

2023-24 Panini National Treasures Autographs Triple

1 Rasheed Wallace
Ben Wallace
Chauncey Billups/25 100.00 250.00
2 Jalen Green
Amen Thompson
Jabari Smith Jr./25 125.00 300.00
3 Cade Cunningham
Ausar Thompson
Jaden Ivey/25 100.00 250.00
4 Brandon Ingram
CJ McCollum
Zion Williamson/15 100.00 250.00
5 Anthony Edwards
Cade Cunningham
Paolo Banchero/25 200.00 500.00
6 Dirk Nowitzki
Pau Gasol
Tony Parker/25 150.00 400.00
8 Carmelo Anthony
Paul George
Tracy McGrady/25 150.00 400.00
9 Kyrie Irving
Chris Paul
Stephen Curry/25 1,000.00 2,000.00
10 Tyrese Maxey
De'Aaron Fox
Shai Gilgeous-Alexander/25 400.00 800.00

2023-24 Panini National Treasures Biography Materials

STATED PRINT RUN 99 SER.#'d SETS
*PRIME/5-25: .75X TO 2X BASIC
1 Ben Simmons 4.00 10.00
2 Jrue Holiday 5.00 12.00
3 Deandre Ayton 4.00 10.00
4 Tyrese Haliburton 8.00 20.00
5 LeBron James 50.00 120.00
6 Rudy Gobert 5.00 12.00
7 Julius Randle 5.00 12.00
8 Anthony Davis 10.00 25.00
9 Lauri Markkanen 6.00 15.00
10 Kyrie Irving 8.00 20.00
11 Zach LaVine 6.00 15.00
14 Andrew Wiggins 5.00 12.00
15 DeMar DeRozan 6.00 15.00
17 Kevin Love 4.00 10.00
18 Jimmy Butler 6.00 15.00
19 Gordon Hayward 4.00 10.00
21 Kristaps Porzingis 5.00 12.00
22 CJ McCollum 4.00 10.00
23 Kyle Kuzma 5.00 12.00
24 Kawhi Leonard 10.00 25.00
25 Russell Westbrook 6.00 15.00
26 Cam Reddish 3.00 8.00
27 Brandon Ingram 5.00 12.00
28 Mikal Bridges 5.00 12.00
29 Cameron Johnson 4.00 10.00
30 Fred VanVleet 6.00 15.00
31 Derrick Rose 20.00 50.00
32 Aaron Gordon 4.00 10.00
36 Bradley Beal 5.00 12.00
37 Mike Conley 3.00 8.00
38 Marcus Smart 5.00 12.00

2023-24 Panini National Treasures Century Materials

STATED PRINT RUN 49 SER.#'d SETS
*PRIME/5-25: 1.25X TO 3X BASIC
2 Jaylen Brown 10.00 25.00
3 Mikal Bridges 6.00 15.00
4 Devin Booker 12.00 30.00
5 LeBron James 60.00 150.00
6 Giannis Antetokounmpo 25.00 60.00
7 Damian Lillard 12.00 30.00
8 Bam Adebayo 8.00 20.00
9 OG Anunoby 6.00 15.00
10 Aaron Gordon 5.00 12.00
12 Shai Gilgeous-Alexander 25.00 60.00
14 Joel Embiid 12.00 30.00
16 Jerami Grant 6.00 15.00
17 Klay Thompson 12.00 30.00
18 Clint Capela 4.00 10.00
19 Tobias Harris 5.00 12.00
21 Jayson Tatum 20.00 50.00
23 Tyler Herro 8.00 20.00
24 Scottie Barnes 6.00 15.00
25 Anfernee Simons 6.00 15.00
27 De'Andre Hunter 5.00 12.00
28 Domantas Sabonis 8.00 20.00
31 Trey Murphy III 6.00 15.00
32 Vince Carter 10.00 25.00
33 Tyson Chandler 4.00 10.00
36 Jalen Green 8.00 20.00
38 Keegan Murray 6.00 15.00
39 Jaden Ivey 6.00 15.00

2023-24 Panini National Treasures Clutch Factor Signatures

STATED PRINT RUN 25-49 SER.#'d SETS
*PRIME/4-25: .75X TO 2X BASIC
NO PRICING ON QTY BELOW 25
1 Tyrese Maxey/25 125.00 300.00
2 Damian Lillard/25 125.00 300.00
4 Markelle Fultz/49 15.00 40.00
5 Evan Mobley/25 100.00 250.00
6 Zach LaVine/49 50.00 120.00
7 De'Aaron Fox/25 100.00 250.00
8 Brandon Ingram/25 25.00 60.00
9 Jaren Jackson Jr./25 100.00 250.00
11 Paul George/25 100.00 250.00
12 Donovan Mitchell/25 125.00 300.00
13 Zion Williamson/25 125.00 300.00
14 Jason Terry/25 20.00 50.00
15 Joakim Noah/25 20.00 50.00
16 Gilbert Arenas/15 75.00 200.00
17 Klay Thompson/25 125.00 300.00
21 Desmond Bane/25 50.00 120.00
23 Jordan Poole/25 50.00 120.00
24 Amen Thompson/35 150.00 400.00
25 Ausar Thompson/35 75.00 200.00
26 Cason Wallace/35 40.00 100.00
27 Bilal Coulibaly/35 60.00 150.00
28 Ben Sheppard/49 20.00 50.00
29 Olivier-Maxence Prosper/49 20.00 50.00
30 Kobe Brown/49 20.00 50.00
31 Kris Murray/49 20.00 50.00
33 James Harden/25 200.00 500.00
36 Christian Laettner/49 20.00 50.00
37 Jason Kidd/25 75.00 200.00
38 Paolo Banchero/25 150.00 400.00
39 Keyonte George/25 60.00 150.00
40 GG Jackson II/49 75.00 200.00
41 Brice Sensabaugh/49 30.00 80.00
42 Rayan Rupert/49 20.00 50.00
43 Shai Gilgeous-Alexander/25 600.00 1,200.00
44 Kobe Bufkin/25 25.00 60.00
45 Julian Phillips/49 20.00 50.00
46 Seth Lundy/49 15.00 40.00
47 Julian Strawther/49 25.00 60.00
48 Maxwell Lewis/49 15.00 40.00
50 Bradley Beal/25 25.00 60.00

2023-24 Panini National Treasures Colossal Material Autographs

STATED PRINT RUN 25-49 SER.#'d SETS
*PRIME/5-25: .75X TO 2X BASIC
NO PRICING ON QTY BELOW 25
1 Deandre Ayton/25 20.00 50.00
2 Immanuel Quickley/25 20.00 50.00
3 Jalen Suggs/25 25.00 60.00
4 Jrue Holiday/25 25.00 60.00
5 Devin Vassell/25 25.00 60.00
6 Onyeka Okongwu/49 15.00 40.00
8 Ben Wallace/25 75.00 200.00
9 Christian Braun/49 20.00 50.00
10 Russell Westbrook/25 125.00 300.00
11 Trae Young/25 125.00 300.00
12 Desmond Bane/25 40.00 100.00
13 Obi Toppin/49 20.00 50.00
15 Jabari Smith Jr./25 30.00 80.00
16 Seth Curry/49 20.00 50.00
17 Damian Lillard/25 125.00 300.00
18 Rudy Gobert/25 25.00 60.00
19 Jonas Valanciunas/35 15.00 40.00
20 Jalen Williams/49 125.00 300.00
21 Amen Thompson/25 150.00 400.00
22 Ausar Thompson/25 75.00 200.00
23 Ben Sheppard/49 20.00 50.00
24 Brice Sensabaugh/49 30.00 80.00
25 Kobe Brown/49 20.00 50.00
26 Noah Clowney/49 25.00 60.00
27 GG Jackson II/49 75.00 200.00
28 Keyonte George/49 60.00 150.00
29 Keyontae Johnson/49 20.00 50.00
30 Sasha Vezenkov/49 15.00 40.00
31 Hunter Tyson/49 20.00 50.00
32 Jalen Pickett/49 15.00 40.00
33 Jordan Miller/49 25.00 60.00
34 Andre Jackson Jr./49 30.00 80.00
35 Chris Livingston/49 20.00 50.00
36 Jaylen Clark/49 20.00 50.00
37 Rayan Rupert/49 20.00 50.00
38 Sidy Cissoko/49 20.00 50.00
39 Markquis Nowell/49 20.00 50.00
40 Oscar Tshiebwe/49 25.00 60.00
41 Jalen Wilson/49 20.00 50.00
42 Jordan Walsh/49 20.00 50.00
43 Cason Wallace/35 40.00 100.00
44 Cole Anthony/25 20.00 50.00
45 Dereck Lively II/49 40.00 100.00
46 Kobe Bufkin/25 25.00 60.00
47 Marcus Sasser/49 30.00 80.00
48 Mouhamed Gueye/49 20.00 50.00
49 Colby Jones/49 20.00 50.00
50 Leonard Miller/49 20.00 50.00

2023-24 Panini National Treasures Colossal Materials

STATED PRINT RUN 49-99 SER.#'d SETS
*PRIME/5-25: 1.25X TO 3X BASIC
1 Anfernee Simons/49 6.00 15.00
2 Chris Andersen/99 5.00 12.00
3 LeBron James/99 75.00 200.00
4 Anthony Edwards/99 25.00 60.00
6 Trae Young/99 10.00 25.00
8 Jayson Tatum/99 20.00 50.00
9 Joel Embiid/99 12.00 30.00
11 Bam Adebayo/99 8.00 20.00
12 OG Anunoby/99 6.00 15.00
13 Tobias Harris/99 5.00 12.00
14 Julius Randle/99 6.00 15.00
15 Russell Westbrook/99 8.00 20.00
17 Jakob Poeltl/99 4.00 10.00
19 Cole Anthony/99 5.00 12.00
20 Kyle Kuzma/99 6.00 15.00

2023-24 Panini National Treasures Colossal Rookie Materials

STATED PRINT RUN 99 SER.#'d SETS
*PRIME/25: 1.25X TO 3X BASIC
1 Anthony Black 10.00 25.00
2 Olivier-Maxence Prosper 5.00 12.00
3 Ben Sheppard 5.00 12.00
4 Jett Howard 6.00 15.00
5 Brice Sensabaugh 8.00 20.00
6 Amen Thompson 25.00 60.00
7 Julian Strawther 6.00 15.00
8 Brandon Miller 20.00 50.00
9 Kobe Brown 5.00 12.00
10 Dru Smith 4.00 10.00
11 Jalen Pickett 4.00 10.00
12 Jalen Hood-Schifino 5.00 12.00
13 Leonard Miller 5.00 12.00
14 Kobe Bufkin 6.00 15.00
15 Colby Jones 5.00 12.00
16 Marcus Sasser 8.00 20.00
17 Cam Whitmore 12.00 30.00
18 Julian Phillips 5.00 12.00
19 Ausar Thompson 12.00 30.00
20 Andre Jackson Jr. 8.00 20.00
21 Jaime Jaquez Jr. 8.00 20.00
22 Hunter Tyson 5.00 12.00
23 Jordan Walsh 5.00 12.00
24 Gradey Dick 10.00 25.00
25 Craig Porter Jr. 6.00 15.00
26 Maxwell Lewis 4.00 10.00
27 Victor Wembanyama 150.00 400.00
28 Rayan Rupert 5.00 12.00
29 Sidy Cissoko 5.00 12.00
30 Jarace Walker 10.00 25.00
31 Sasha Vezenkov 4.00 10.00
32 Markquis Nowell 5.00 12.00
33 Toumani Camara 10.00 25.00
34 Jordan Hawkins 8.00 20.00
35 Chris Livingston 5.00 12.00
36 Amari Bailey 5.00 12.00
37 Bilal Coulibaly 12.00 30.00
38 Vasilije Micic 5.00 12.00
39 GG Jackson II 12.00 30.00
40 Nick Smith Jr. 6.00 15.00
41 Emoni Bates 6.00 15.00
42 Isaiah Wong 5.00 12.00
43 Cason Wallace 10.00 25.00
44 Trayce Jackson-Davis 6.00 15.00
45 Scoot Henderson 15.00 40.00
46 Jalen Wilson 5.00 12.00
47 D'Moi Hodge 4.00 10.00
48 Dereck Lively II 10.00 25.00
49 Keyontae Johnson 5.00 12.00
50 Taylor Hendricks 5.00 12.00

2023-24 Panini National Treasures Definitive Ink

STATED PRINT RUN 25-49 SER.#'d SETS
2 Paolo Banchero/25 150.00 400.00
4 Gary Trent Jr./49 12.00 30.00
5 Nick Van Exel/49 12.00 30.00
6 RJ Barrett/49 20.00 50.00
7 Jrue Holiday/25 25.00 60.00
8 Jordan Poole/25 20.00 50.00
9 Amar'e Stoudemire/25 15.00 40.00
10 Cole Anthony/49 12.00 30.00
12 Ayo Dosunmu/49 12.00 30.00
13 Bobby Portis/49 15.00 40.00
14 Ochai Agbaji/49 12.00 30.00
15 Kevin Huerter/49 10.00 25.00
17 Desmond Bane/25 15.00 40.00
18 Anthony Edwards/25 400.00 800.00
20 Dwyane Wade/25 125.00 300.00
21 Jaden Ivey/25 15.00 40.00
22 Jaren Jackson Jr./25 40.00 100.00
23 Onyeka Okongwu/49 10.00 25.00
24 Kerry Kittles/49 10.00 25.00
26 Max Strus/49 12.00 30.00
27 Jonathan Kuminga/49 30.00 80.00
28 Dirk Nowitzki/25 150.00 400.00
29 Bradley Beal/25 15.00 40.00
30 Bojan Bogdanovic/49 12.00 30.00
31 Luka Doncic/25 600.00 1,200.00
32 Toni Kukoc/49 15.00 40.00
33 Immanuel Quickley/49 12.00 30.00
34 Jabari Smith Jr./25 20.00 50.00
35 Rasheed Wallace/25 15.00 40.00
36 Jalen Williams/49 75.00 200.00
37 Khris Middleton/25 12.00 30.00
38 James Wiseman/49 10.00 25.00
39 Chet Holmgren/25 75.00 200.00
43 Carlos Boozer/49 10.00 25.00
46 Michael Cooper/49 12.00 30.00
48 Josh Giddey/25 25.00 60.00
49 De'Aaron Fox/25 60.00 150.00

2023-24 Panini National Treasures Game Gear

STATED PRINT RUN 99 SER.#'d SETS
*PRIME/5-25: .75X TO 2X BASIC
NO PRICING ON QTY 10 OR LESS
1 LeBron James 60.00 150.00
2 Jaylen Brown 8.00 20.00
3 Jimmy Butler 6.00 15.00
4 Cade Cunningham 10.00 25.00
5 Duncan Robinson 4.00 10.00
10 P.J. Washington Jr. 4.00 10.00
11 Quentin Grimes 4.00 10.00
12 Santi Aldama 3.00 8.00
14 Tyler Herro 6.00 15.00
15 Zaire Williams 4.00 10.00
17 Ja Morant 12.00 30.00
18 Devin Booker 10.00 25.00
19 Max Strus 4.00 10.00
20 Tyrese Haliburton 8.00 20.00
21 Mikal Bridges 5.00 12.00
22 Jalen Brunson 8.00 20.00
23 Zion Williamson 10.00 25.00
25 Malik Monk 5.00 12.00
26 Khris Middleton 4.00 10.00
27 Immanuel Quickley 4.00 10.00
29 Tobias Harris 4.00 10.00
30 Kristaps Porzingis 5.00 12.00
31 John Collins 4.00 10.00
34 Obi Toppin 4.00 10.00
35 Josh Hart 4.00 10.00
36 Ayo Dosunmu 4.00 10.00
37 Trey Murphy III 5.00 12.00
39 Keldon Johnson 5.00 12.00

2023-24 Panini National Treasures Material Treasures

STATED PRINT RUN 99 SER.#'d SETS
*PRIME/5-25: .75X TO 2X BASIC
NO PRICING ON QTY 10 OR LESS
1 Jayson Tatum 15.00 40.00
2 LeBron James 60.00 150.00
4 Ja Morant 12.00 30.00
5 Dejounte Murray 5.00 12.00
6 Scottie Barnes 5.00 12.00
8 Stephen Curry 30.00 80.00
10 Cameron Thomas 5.00 12.00
11 Giannis Antetokounmpo 20.00 50.00
12 Evan Mobley 6.00 15.00
13 Bradley Beal 5.00 12.00
14 Joel Embiid 10.00 25.00
15 Anthony Davis 10.00 25.00
16 Jaren Jackson Jr. 6.00 15.00
17 Pascal Siakam 6.00 15.00
18 Brandon Ingram 5.00 12.00
19 De'Aaron Fox 8.00 20.00
20 Austin Reaves 10.00 25.00
21 Chris Paul 8.00 20.00
22 Zach LaVine 6.00 15.00
24 Darius Garland 6.00 15.00
26 Klay Thompson 10.00 25.00
27 Shai Gilgeous-Alexander 40.00 100.00
28 RJ Barrett 6.00 15.00
29 Damian Lillard 10.00 25.00
30 Michael Porter Jr. 5.00 12.00

2023-24 Panini National Treasures National Archives Ink

STATED PRINT RUN 25-49 SER.#'d SETS
1 Karl-Anthony Towns/25 40.00 100.00
2 Damian Lillard/25 125.00 300.00
4 Rasheed Wallace/49 20.00 50.00
5 Tyrese Haliburton/25 200.00 500.00
7 Tari Eason/49 20.00 50.00
8 Evan Mobley/49 40.00 100.00
9 Cade Cunningham/25 75.00 200.00
10 Gilbert Arenas/25 40.00 100.00
11 Jaden Hardy/25 20.00 50.00
12 Shai Gilgeous-Alexander/25 600.00 1,200.00
13 Zion Williamson/25 125.00 300.00
14 Jaren Jackson Jr./25 30.00 80.00
15 Jordan Clarkson/25 15.00 40.00
16 Yao Ming/25 300.00 600.00
17 Bradley Beal/25 20.00 50.00
18 B.J. Armstrong/49 15.00 40.00
19 Seth Curry/49 15.00 40.00
21 Shaedon Sharpe/49 30.00 80.00
22 Chet Holmgren/25 75.00 200.00
23 Markelle Fultz/49 12.00 30.00
24 Peja Stojakovic/49 15.00 40.00
25 Dan Issel/49 20.00 50.00
26 Donovan Mitchell/25 75.00 200.00
27 Klay Thompson/25 125.00 300.00
28 Jason Williams/25 25.00 60.00
29 Pau Gasol/25 60.00 150.00
30 Jalen Williams/25 75.00 200.00
32 Stephen Curry/25 1,000.00 2,000.00
33 Julius Erving/25 75.00 200.00
34 Brandon Ingram/25 20.00 50.00
35 Anfernee Hardaway/25 60.00 150.00
37 Marcus Smart/49 20.00 50.00
38 Bennedict Mathurin/25 25.00 60.00
39 Obi Toppin/49 15.00 40.00
40 Robert Horry/49 15.00 40.00
41 Ivica Zubac/49 15.00 40.00
42 Dale Ellis/49 15.00 40.00
43 Bob Dandridge/49 15.00 40.00
44 Herbert Jones/49 15.00 40.00
47 Nate Archibald/49 20.00 50.00
48 Tim Hardaway/49 20.00 50.00
50 Khris Middleton/25 15.00 40.00

2023-24 Panini National Treasures NBA Greatest Signatures

STATED PRINT RUN 10-49 SER.#'d SETS
NO PRICING ON QTY 10
*BRONZE/15-25: .5X TO 1.2X BASIC
*INTERNTL/18-24: .5X TO 1.2X BASIC
1 Magic Johnson/25 100.00 250.00
2 Isiah Thomas/49 20.00 50.00
3 Charles Barkley/25 100.00 250.00
4 Shaquille O'Neal/25 150.00 400.00
6 Kareem Abdul-Jabbar/25 100.00 250.00
7 Ray Allen/35 60.00 150.00
8 Manu Ginobili/25 75.00 200.00
9 Pau Gasol/25 60.00 150.00
10 Jason Kidd/35 40.00 100.00
11 Jerry West/25 25.00 60.00
12 Allen Iverson/25 125.00 300.00
13 Kevin Garnett/25 125.00 300.00
14 Larry Bird/25 100.00 250.00
15 Karl Malone/25 60.00 150.00
16 Julius Erving/35 60.00 150.00
17 Tony Parker/35 75.00 200.00
18 Clyde Drexler/49 30.00 80.00
19 Ben Wallace/35 50.00 120.00
21 Robert Parish/49 15.00 40.00
22 Alex English/49 15.00 40.00
23 Dwyane Wade/35 100.00 250.00
24 Yao Ming/35 200.00 500.00
25 Grant Hill/49 30.00 80.00
26 Artis Gilmore/49 15.00 40.00
27 Nate Archibald/49 15.00 40.00
28 Bob Pettit/25 15.00 40.00
29 Hakeem Olajuwon/35 60.00 150.00
30 Chauncey Billups/49 30.00 80.00

2023-24 Panini National Treasures NBA Materials

STATED PRINT RUN 99 SER.#'d SETS
*PRIME/5-25: .75X TO 2X BASIC
NO PRICING ON QTY 10 OR LESS
1 Jayson Tatum 15.00 40.00
2 Joel Embiid 10.00 25.00
3 Trae Young 8.00 20.00
4 Jaylen Brown 8.00 20.00
5 LeBron James 60.00 150.00
6 Kawhi Leonard 10.00 25.00
7 Devin Booker 10.00 25.00
8 Giannis Antetokounmpo 20.00 50.00
9 Shai Gilgeous-Alexander 40.00 100.00
10 Luka Doncic 25.00 60.00
15 DeMar DeRozan 6.00 15.00
16 Kyrie Irving 8.00 20.00
17 Jimmy Butler 6.00 15.00
18 Darius Garland 6.00 15.00
19 Stephen Curry 40.00 100.00
20 Pascal Siakam 6.00 15.00
21 Bam Adebayo 6.00 15.00
22 Julius Randle 5.00 12.00
25 Damian Lillard 10.00 25.00
26 De'Andre Hunter 4.00 10.00
27 Tobias Harris 4.00 10.00
28 Mike Conley 3.00 8.00
30 Paul George 6.00 15.00

2023-24 Panini National Treasures Notable Nicknames

3 Donovan Mitchell/25 800.00 1,500.00
4 Carmelo Anthony/25 1,250.00 2,500.00
5 Gilbert Arenas/25 400.00 800.00
7 Jalen Brunson/25 1,000.00 2,000.00
8 Damian Lillard/25 1,500.00 3,000.00
9 De'Aaron Fox/25 400.00 800.00
10 Tyrese Maxey/25 800.00 1,500.00

2023-24 Panini National Treasures Peerless Signatures

STATED PRINT RUN 25-49 SER.#'d SETS
*BRONZE/15-25: .5X TO 1.2X BASIC
1 Brandon Ingram/25 15.00 40.00
2 James Wiseman/49 10.00 25.00
3 Jaden Ivey/35 25.00 60.00
4 Joakim Noah/49 12.00 30.00
5 Karl-Anthony Towns/25 20.00 50.00
9 Hakeem Olajuwon/25 60.00 150.00
10 Jordan Poole/25 20.00 50.00
11 Bennedict Mathurin/49 20.00 50.00
12 Immanuel Quickley/35 12.00 30.00
13 Bobby Portis/49 15.00 40.00
14 Tari Eason/49 15.00 40.00
15 Ben Simmons/49 12.00 30.00
17 Max Strus/49 12.00 30.00
18 Jonathan Kuminga/49 30.00 80.00
19 Bojan Bogdanovic/49 12.00 30.00
22 Christian Braun/49 12.00 30.00
23 Bill Laimbeer/49 12.00 30.00
24 Bob McAdoo/49 15.00 40.00
25 Toni Kukoc/49 15.00 40.00
26 Rick Fox/49 12.00 30.00
27 John Stockton/25 60.00 150.00
28 Devin Vassell/49 15.00 40.00
30 Robert Horry/49 12.00 30.00
31 Zion Williamson/25 125.00 300.00
32 Stephen Jackson/49 10.00 25.00
33 Chet Holmgren/25 100.00 250.00
36 RJ Barrett/49 20.00 50.00
37 Jrue Holiday/35 25.00 60.00
39 Chris Mullin/35 15.00 40.00
40 Metta World Peace/35 12.00 30.00
41 MarJon Beauchamp/49 10.00 25.00
42 Shawn Kemp/49 25.00 60.00
43 Jeff Hornacek/49 10.00 25.00
44 Antoine Walker/49 12.00 30.00
45 Precious Achiuwa/49 10.00 25.00
46 Jonas Valanciunas/49 10.00 25.00
47 Dave Bing/49 15.00 40.00
48 Mark Aguirre/49 10.00 25.00
49 Bob Cousy/25 75.00 200.00
50 Jaden Hardy/25 15.00 40.00

2023-24 Panini National Treasures Penmanship

STATED PRINT RUN 15-49 SER.#'d SETS
*BRONZE/15-25: .5X TO 1.2X BASIC
*INTERNTL/18-24: .5X TO 1.2X BASIC
2 Desmond Bane/49 15.00 40.00
3 Jabari Smith Jr./35 20.00 50.00
4 Jaden Hardy/49 15.00 40.00
5 Jalen Brunson/35 100.00 250.00
6 Karl-Anthony Towns/35 20.00 50.00
7 Marcus Smart/49 15.00 40.00
9 Anthony Edwards/25 400.00 800.00
10 Keegan Murray/49 15.00 40.00
11 Dell Curry/49 12.00 30.00
14 Deandre Ayton/35 12.00 30.00
15 James Wiseman/49 10.00 25.00
16 Devin Vassell/49 15.00 40.00
17 John Starks/49 25.00 60.00
18 Bobby Portis/49 15.00 40.00
19 Tari Eason/49 15.00 40.00
20 Bojan Bogdanovic/49 12.00 30.00
21 Damian Lillard/25 125.00 300.00
22 Jaren Jackson Jr./35 30.00 80.00
23 Cade Cunningham/25 125.00 300.00
24 Jaden Ivey/25 25.00 60.00
26 Tyrese Maxey/49 125.00 300.00
27 Lauri Markkanen/49 20.00 50.00
28 Ochai Agbaji/49 12.00 30.00
29 Jalen Duren/49 15.00 40.00
30 Antawn Jamison/49 12.00 30.00
31 Carmelo Anthony/15 125.00 300.00
32 Larry Bird/25 100.00 250.00
33 Dominique Wilkins/49 20.00 50.00
34 CJ McCollum/25 12.00 30.00
35 Gary Payton/49 20.00 50.00
36 Malaki Branham/49 10.00 25.00
37 Nikola Jovic/49 12.00 30.00
38 Mike Miller/49 10.00 25.00
39 Nick Van Exel/49 12.00 30.00
40 Calvin Murphy/49 12.00 30.00

2023-24 Panini National Treasures Retro Materials

STATED PRINT RUN 25-49 SER.#'d SETS
*PRIME/2-25: 1.25X TO 3X BASIC
NO PRICING ON QTY 10 OR LESS
1 Carmelo Anthony/49 8.00 20.00
2 Tony Parker/49 8.00 20.00
3 Derrick Rose/49 20.00 50.00
6 Dirk Nowitzki/49 12.00 30.00
7 Victor Oladipo/49 4.00 10.00
8 LeBron James/49 40.00 100.00
10 DeMar DeRozan/49 8.00 20.00
11 Nikola Vucevic/49 5.00 12.00
12 Bradley Beal/49 6.00 15.00
14 Ben Simmons/49 5.00 12.00
16 Vince Carter/49 10.00 25.00
19 Steven Adams/49 5.00 12.00
20 Kevin Durant/49 15.00 40.00
21 Russell Westbrook/49 8.00 20.00
22 Paul George/49 8.00 20.00
23 Tim Duncan/25 12.00 30.00
24 Dale Ellis/49 5.00 12.00
25 Andrew Wiggins/49 6.00 15.00
26 LaMarcus Aldridge/49 5.00 12.00
27 D'Angelo Russell/49 5.00 12.00
28 Steve Nash/49 10.00 25.00
29 Jerami Grant/49 6.00 15.00

2023-24 Panini National Treasures Rookie Dual Materials

STATED PRINT RUN 99 SER.#'d SETS
*PRIME/25: 1.25X TO 3X BASIC
1 Jordan Hawkins 8.00 20.00
2 Amari Bailey 5.00 12.00
3 Dereck Lively II 10.00 25.00
4 Anthony Black 10.00 25.00
5 Toumani Camara 10.00 25.00
6 Brandon Miller 20.00 50.00
7 Jaime Jaquez Jr. 8.00 20.00
8 Andre Jackson Jr. 8.00 20.00
9 Keyonte George 15.00 40.00
10 Maxwell Lewis 4.00 10.00
11 Victor Wembanyama 150.00 400.00
12 Scoot Henderson 15.00 40.00
13 Kobe Bufkin 6.00 15.00
14 Amen Thompson 25.00 60.00
15 Brandin Podziemski 15.00 40.00
16 Bilal Coulibaly 12.00 30.00
17 Jett Howard 6.00 15.00
18 Marcus Sasser 8.00 20.00
19 Julian Strawther 6.00 15.00
20 Ausar Thompson 12.00 30.00
21 Colby Jones 5.00 12.00
22 Olivier-Maxence Prosper 5.00 12.00
23 Cam Whitmore 12.00 30.00
24 Gradey Dick 10.00 25.00
25 Cason Wallace 10.00 25.00

2023-24 Panini National Treasures Rookie Dual Materials Autographs

STATED PRINT RUN 99 SER.#'d SETS
*PRIME/25: .75X TO 2X BASIC
1 Amen Thompson 200.00 500.00
2 Kris Murray 20.00 50.00
3 Olivier-Maxence Prosper 20.00 50.00
4 Colby Jones 20.00 50.00
5 Julian Phillips 20.00 50.00
6 Brandin Podziemski 60.00 150.00
7 Andre Jackson Jr. 30.00 80.00
8 Mouhamed Gueye 20.00 50.00
9 Maxwell Lewis 15.00 40.00
10 Dariq Whitehead 25.00 60.00
11 Chris Livingston 20.00 50.00
12 Hunter Tyson 20.00 50.00
13 Rayan Rupert 20.00 50.00
14 Jordan Walsh 20.00 50.00
15 Noah Clowney 25.00 60.00
16 Sidy Cissoko 20.00 50.00
17 GG Jackson II 50.00 125.00
18 Bilal Coulibaly 50.00 125.00
19 Seth Lundy 15.00 40.00
20 Marcus Sasser 30.00 80.00
21 Ben Sheppard 20.00 50.00
22 Jordan Miller 25.00 60.00
23 Keyontae Johnson 20.00 50.00
24 Dereck Lively II 40.00 100.00
25 Brice Sensabaugh 30.00 80.00
26 Julian Strawther 25.00 60.00
27 Kobe Brown 20.00 50.00
28 Oscar Tshiebwe 25.00 60.00
29 Jalen Pickett 15.00 40.00
30 Leonard Miller 20.00 50.00
31 Jalen Wilson 20.00 50.00
32 Toumani Camara 40.00 100.00
33 Jaylen Clark 20.00 50.00
34 Cason Wallace 40.00 100.00
35 Isaiah Wong 20.00 50.00
36 Trayce Jackson-Davis 25.00 60.00
37 Ausar Thompson 50.00 125.00
38 Keyonte George 60.00 150.00
39 Kobe Bufkin 25.00 60.00
40 Sasha Vezenkov 15.00 40.00

2023-24 Panini National Treasures Rookie First Edition Signatures Booklet

1 Amen Thompson 600.00 1,200.00
2 Ausar Thompson 300.00 600.00
3 Cason Wallace 150.00 400.00
4 Bilal Coulibaly 150.00 400.00
5 Kobe Bufkin 60.00 150.00
6 Dereck Lively II 150.00 400.00
7 Keyonte George 200.00 500.00
8 Dariq Whitehead 60.00 150.00
9 Brandin Podziemski 200.00 500.00
10 Kris Murray 60.00 150.00
11 Ben Sheppard 50.00 120.00
12 Marcus Sasser 60.00 150.00

2023-24 Panini National Treasures Rookie Jumbo Jersey Number Booklet Autographs

1 Keyonte George 300.00 600.00
2 Brandin Podziemski 300.00 600.00
3 Kris Murray 75.00 200.00
4 Leonard Miller 60.00 150.00
5 Dereck Lively II 200.00 500.00
6 Dariq Whitehead 75.00 200.00
7 Bilal Coulibaly 200.00 500.00
8 Kobe Bufkin 75.00 200.00
9 Cason Wallace 200.00 500.00
10 Kobe Brown 50.00 120.00
11 Amen Thompson 800.00 1,500.00
12 Olivier-Maxence Prosper 60.00 150.00
13 Brice Sensabaugh 75.00 200.00
14 Ben Sheppard 60.00 150.00
15 Noah Clowney 75.00 200.00
16 Julian Strawther 75.00 200.00
17 Jalen Pickett 40.00 100.00
18 Marcus Sasser 75.00 200.00
19 Julian Phillips 50.00 120.00
20 Ausar Thompson 400.00 800.00
21 Maxwell Lewis 40.00 100.00
22 Craig Porter Jr. 40.00 100.00
23 Colby Jones 40.00 100.00
24 Andre Jackson Jr. 50.00 120.00
25 Hunter Tyson 40.00 100.00
26 Mouhamed Gueye 40.00 100.00
27 Rayan Rupert 50.00 120.00
28 Keyontae Johnson 40.00 100.00
29 Jalen Wilson 50.00 120.00
30 Jordan Walsh 60.00 150.00

2023-24 Panini National Treasures Rookie Jumbo Materials

STATED PRINT RUN 99 SER.#'d SETS
*PRIME/25: 1.25X TO 3X BASIC
1 Olivier-Maxence Prosper 5.00 12.00
2 Maxwell Lewis 4.00 10.00
3 Julian Strawther 6.00 15.00
4 Keyonte George 15.00 40.00
5 Amari Bailey 5.00 12.00
6 Brandin Podziemski 15.00 40.00
7 Victor Wembanyama 150.00 400.00
8 Scoot Henderson 15.00 40.00
9 Amen Thompson 25.00 60.00
10 Colby Jones 5.00 12.00
11 Cam Whitmore 12.00 30.00
12 Andre Jackson Jr. 8.00 20.00
13 Toumani Camara 10.00 25.00
14 Anthony Black 10.00 25.00
15 Cason Wallace 10.00 25.00
16 Marcus Sasser 8.00 20.00
17 Brandon Miller 20.00 50.00
18 Gradey Dick 10.00 25.00
19 Bilal Coulibaly 12.00 30.00
20 Jaime Jaquez Jr. 8.00 20.00
21 Jett Howard 6.00 15.00
22 Ausar Thompson 12.00 30.00
23 Kobe Bufkin 6.00 15.00
24 Jordan Hawkins 8.00 20.00
25 Dereck Lively II 10.00 25.00

2023-24 Panini National Treasures Rookie Materials

STATED PRINT RUN 99 SER.#'d SETS
*PRIME/25: 1.25X TO 3X BASIC
1 Jaime Jaquez Jr. 6.00 15.00
2 Bilal Coulibaly 10.00 25.00
3 Amen Thompson 20.00 50.00
4 Brandin Podziemski 12.00 30.00
5 Julian Strawther 5.00 12.00
6 Dereck Lively II 8.00 20.00
7 Kobe Bufkin 5.00 12.00
8 Cam Whitmore 10.00 25.00
9 Jordan Hawkins 6.00 15.00
10 Olivier-Maxence Prosper 4.00 10.00
11 Maxwell Lewis 3.00 8.00
12 Ausar Thompson 10.00 25.00
13 Amari Bailey 4.00 10.00
14 Brandon Miller 15.00 40.00
15 Colby Jones 4.00 10.00
16 Keyonte George 12.00 30.00
17 Gradey Dick 8.00 20.00
18 Scoot Henderson 12.00 30.00
19 Andre Jackson Jr. 6.00 15.00
20 Anthony Black 8.00 20.00
21 Toumani Camara 8.00 20.00
22 Cason Wallace 8.00 20.00
23 Marcus Sasser 6.00 15.00
24 Jett Howard 5.00 12.00
25 Victor Wembanyama 125.00 300.00

2023-24 Panini National Treasures Rookie Patches '09

STATED PRINT RUN 99 SER.#'d SETS
151 Cam Whitmore JSY 12.00 30.00
152 Jett Howard JSY 6.00 15.00
153 Gradey Dick JSY 10.00 25.00
154 Scoot Henderson JSY 15.00 40.00
155 Jaime Jaquez Jr. JSY 8.00 20.00
156 Taylor Hendricks JSY 5.00 12.00
157 Nick Smith Jr. JSY 6.00 15.00
158 Jalen Hood-Schifino JSY 5.00 12.00
159 Jarace Walker JSY 10.00 25.00
160 Jordan Hawkins JSY 8.00 20.00
161 Anthony Black JSY 10.00 25.00
162 Victor Wembanyama JSY 500.00 1,000.00
163 Brandon Miller JSY 40.00 100.00

2023-24 Panini National Treasures Rookie Quad Materials Autographs

STATED PRINT RUN 99 SER.#'d SETS
*PRIME/25: .75X TO 2X BASIC
*INTNL/24: .75X TO 2X BASIC
1 Ausar Thompson 50.00 125.00
2 Cason Wallace 40.00 100.00
3 Bilal Coulibaly 50.00 125.00
4 Keyonte George 60.00 150.00
5 Amen Thompson 200.00 500.00
6 Dereck Lively II 40.00 100.00
7 Kobe Bufkin 25.00 60.00
8 Dariq Whitehead 25.00 60.00
9 Brandin Podziemski 60.00 150.00
10 Kris Murray 20.00 50.00

2023-24 Panini National Treasures Rookie Triple Materials

STATED PRINT RUN 99 SER.#'d SETS
*PRIME/25: 1.25X TO 3X BASIC
1 Victor Wembanyama 150.00 400.00
2 Jaime Jaquez Jr. 8.00 20.00
3 Cam Whitmore 12.00 30.00
4 Gradey Dick 10.00 25.00
5 Jett Howard 6.00 15.00
6 Cason Wallace 10.00 25.00
7 Amen Thompson 25.00 60.00
8 Anthony Black 10.00 25.00
9 Maxwell Lewis 4.00 10.00
10 Julian Strawther 6.00 15.00
11 Bilal Coulibaly 12.00 30.00
12 Toumani Camara 10.00 25.00
13 Ausar Thompson 12.00 30.00
14 Andre Jackson Jr. 8.00 20.00
15 Keyonte George 15.00 40.00

16 Amari Bailey 5.00 12.00
17 Colby Jones 5.00 12.00
18 Brandon Miller 20.00 50.00
19 Scoot Henderson 15.00 40.00
20 Olivier-Maxence Prosper 5.00 12.00
21 Brandin Podziemski 15.00 40.00
22 Dereck Lively II 10.00 25.00
23 Jordan Hawkins 8.00 20.00
24 Marcus Sasser 8.00 20.00
25 Kobe Bufkin 6.00 15.00

2023-24 Panini National Treasures Rookie Triple Materials Autographs

STATED PRINT RUN 99 SER.#'d SETS
*PRIME/25: .75X TO 2X BASIC
*INTNL/24: .75X TO 2X BASIC
1 Dariq Whitehead 25.00 60.00
2 Keyonte George 60.00 150.00
3 Ben Sheppard 20.00 50.00
4 Kris Murray 20.00 50.00
5 Olivier-Maxence Prosper 20.00 50.00
6 Noah Clowney 25.00 60.00
7 Marcus Sasser 30.00 80.00
8 Brice Sensabaugh 30.00 80.00
9 Kobe Brown 20.00 50.00
10 Ausar Thompson 50.00 125.00
11 Cason Wallace 40.00 100.00
12 Bilal Coulibaly 50.00 125.00
13 Julian Strawther 25.00 60.00
14 Amen Thompson 200.00 500.00
15 Dereck Lively II 40.00 100.00
16 Kobe Bufkin 25.00 60.00
17 Jalen Pickett 15.00 40.00
18 Brandin Podziemski 60.00 150.00
19 Leonard Miller 20.00 50.00
20 Oscar Tshiebwe 25.00 60.00

2023-24 Panini National Treasures Signatures

STATED PRINT RUN 25-49 SER.#'d SETS
1 Josh Giddey/25 15.00 40.00
2 Shaedon Sharpe/35 25.00 60.00
4 Jason Terry/49 12.00 30.00
5 Dominique Wilkins/35 20.00 50.00
6 Marcus Smart/49 15.00 40.00
9 RJ Barrett/49 20.00 50.00
11 Steve Kerr/49 15.00 40.00
12 Cole Anthony/49 12.00 30.00
13 Markelle Fultz/49 10.00 25.00
14 Ayo Dosunmu/49 12.00 30.00
15 Ochai Agbaji/49 12.00 30.00
16 Kevin Huerter/49 10.00 25.00
19 Keegan Murray/49 15.00 40.00
21 Onyeka Okongwu/49 10.00 25.00
23 Herbert Jones/49 12.00 30.00
25 Fat Lever/49 12.00 30.00
26 Dan Issel/49 15.00 40.00
28 Shai Gilgeous-Alexander/25 500.00 1,000.00
29 Wally Szczerbiak/49 10.00 25.00
30 Karl-Anthony Towns/25 20.00 50.00
31 Jaden Hardy/25 15.00 40.00
32 Kevin Garnett/25 75.00 200.00
33 Dwyane Wade/25 75.00 200.00
34 Tyrese Haliburton/25 125.00 300.00
35 Lauri Markkanen/49 20.00 50.00
36 Karl Malone/25 40.00 100.00
37 Magic Johnson/25 75.00 200.00
38 Evan Mobley/25 20.00 50.00
39 Anfernee Hardaway/49 60.00 150.00
40 John Stockton/25 40.00 100.00
42 Jeremy Sochan/49 15.00 40.00
43 Zach LaVine/25 40.00 100.00
44 Rudy Gobert/49 15.00 40.00
45 Rick Barry/35 15.00 40.00
46 Jordan Clarkson/49 12.00 30.00
47 Obi Toppin/49 12.00 30.00
48 Derek Fisher/49 12.00 30.00

2023-24 Panini National Treasures Timeless Talents Signatures

STATED PRINT RUN 25-49 SER.#'d SETS
*BRONZE/25: .5X TO 1.25X BASIC
*INTNL/18-24: .5X TO 1.25X BASIC
1 Steve Nash/25 100.00 250.00
2 Jason Terry/49 12.00 30.00
3 Gilbert Arenas/49 12.00 30.00
4 Grant Hill/49 40.00 100.00
5 Paul Pierce/25 50.00 120.00
6 Isiah Thomas/35 20.00 50.00
7 Steve Kerr/49 15.00 40.00
8 Zach Randolph/49 12.00 30.00
9 Amar'e Stoudemire/35 15.00 40.00
10 Christian Laettner/49 12.00 30.00
11 Jason Williams/49 40.00 100.00
12 B.J. Armstrong/49 12.00 30.00
13 Nick Van Exel/49 12.00 30.00
14 Joakim Noah/49 12.00 30.00
15 Calvin Murphy/49 12.00 30.00
16 Chauncey Billups/49 15.00 40.00
17 Anfernee Hardaway/25 60.00 150.00
18 Alex English/49 15.00 40.00
19 Antawn Jamison/49 12.00 30.00
20 Rolando Blackman/49 10.00 25.00
21 Stephen Jackson/49 10.00 25.00
22 Toni Kukoc/49 15.00 40.00
23 Bob Dandridge/49 12.00 30.00
24 Antoine Walker/49 12.00 30.00
25 Jason Kidd/35 20.00 50.00
26 Dennis Rodman/35 100.00 250.00
27 Maurice Cheeks/49 12.00 30.00
28 Hakeem Olajuwon/25 40.00 100.00

2023-24 Panini National Treasures Timeless Treasures Materials

STATED PRINT RUN 25-99 SER.#'d SETS
*PRIME/10-25: 1.25X TO 3X BASIC
1 Chris Paul 10.00 25.00
2 Rudy Gobert 6.00 15.00
3 LeBron James 60.00 150.00
4 Paul George 8.00 20.00
5 Jimmy Butler 8.00 20.00
6 Andrew Wiggins 6.00 15.00
7 Derrick Rose 8.00 20.00
8 DeAndre Jordan 4.00 10.00
9 Anthony Davis 12.00 30.00
10 Kevin Garnett 12.00 30.00
11 Jrue Holiday 6.00 15.00
12 Kevin Love 5.00 12.00
13 Patrick Beverley 4.00 10.00
14 Jamal Crawford 5.00 12.00
15 Shawn Bradley 4.00 10.00
16 Jeff Hornacek 4.00 10.00
17 Blake Griffin 5.00 12.00
18 Bojan Bogdanovic 5.00 12.00
19 Brandon Roy 6.00 15.00
20 CJ McCollum 5.00 12.00
21 David Robinson 10.00 25.00
23 J.J. Barea 4.00 10.00
24 Juwan Howard 5.00 12.00
25 Larry Bird 20.00 50.00
26 Luol Deng 4.00 10.00
27 Marc Gasol 5.00 12.00
28 Al Harrington 4.00 10.00
29 Paul Pierce 8.00 20.00
30 Zach Randolph 5.00 12.00

2023-24 Panini National Treasures Timeline Materials

STATED PRINT RUN 49-99 SER.#'d SETS
*PRIME/5-25: 1.25X TO 3X BASIC
1 Anfernee Simons/49 6.00 15.00
2 Joel Embiid/99 12.00 30.00
3 Kyle Kuzma/99 6.00 15.00
4 Bradley Beal/99 6.00 15.00
5 Cam Reddish/99 4.00 10.00
6 OG Anunoby/99 6.00 15.00
7 Khris Middleton/99 5.00 12.00
8 Rudy Gobert/99 6.00 15.00
9 John Collins/99 6.00 15.00
10 Scottie Barnes/99 6.00 15.00
11 RJ Barrett/99 8.00 20.00
12 Dejounte Murray/99 6.00 15.00
13 Mikal Bridges/99 6.00 15.00
15 Aaron Gordon/99 5.00 12.00
18 Jalen Suggs/99 6.00 15.00
19 Alperen Sengun/99 8.00 20.00
20 Chris Paul/99 10.00 25.00
23 Tyler Herro/99 8.00 20.00
24 Davion Mitchell/99 4.00 10.00
25 LeBron James/99 60.00 150.00
27 Russell Westbrook/99 8.00 20.00
28 Marcus Smart/99 6.00 15.00
30 Zach LaVine/99 8.00 20.00

2023-24 Panini National Treasures Treasured Metals Silver

1 Amen Thompson 60.00 150.00
2 Victor Wembanyama 400.00 800.00
3 Scoot Henderson 30.00 80.00
4 Ausar Thompson 30.00 80.00
5 Keyonte George 30.00 80.00
6 Bilal Coulibaly 30.00 80.00
7 Brandon Miller 40.00 100.00
8 Jaime Jaquez Jr. 25.00 60.00
9 Anthony Black 25.00 60.00
10 Dereck Lively II 25.00 60.00
11 Jordan Hawkins 20.00 50.00
12 Marcus Sasser 20.00 50.00
13 Cason Wallace 25.00 60.00
14 Nikola Jokic 40.00 100.00
15 Kevin Durant 30.00 80.00
16 Luka Doncic 40.00 100.00
17 Jayson Tatum 30.00 80.00
18 Giannis Antetokounmpo 40.00 100.00
19 Stephen Curry 60.00 150.00
20 LeBron James 60.00 150.00

2023-24 Panini National Treasures Treasured Signatures

STATED PRINT RUN 25-49 SER.#'d SETS
*BRONZE/15-25: .5X TO 1.25X BASIC
*INTNL/18-24: .5X TO 1.25X BASIC
1 Jamal Murray/25 25.00 60.00
3 Deandre Ayton/35 12.00 30.00
4 Jrue Holiday/35 15.00 40.00
5 Bennedict Mathurin/49 20.00 50.00
6 Jalen Williams/35 75.00 200.00
7 Jordan Poole/49 20.00 50.00
8 Jordan Clarkson/49 12.00 30.00
9 Andrew Wiggins/35 15.00 40.00
10 Jerry West/25 25.00 60.00
12 Paolo Banchero/25 200.00 500.00
13 Chris Paul/25 75.00 200.00
14 Shaedon Sharpe/49 25.00 60.00
15 Seth Curry/49 12.00 30.00
16 Tom Chambers/49 12.00 30.00
17 CJ McCollum/25 12.00 30.00
18 Yao Ming/25 200.00 500.00
19 Rasheed Wallace/49 15.00 40.00
21 Shai Gilgeous-Alexander/25 500.00 1,000.00
22 Gary Trent Jr./49 12.00 30.00
25 Bradley Beal/25 15.00 40.00

2023-24 Panini National Treasures Treasured Threads

STATED PRINT RUN 99 SER.#'d SETS
*PRIME/5-25: 1.25X TO 3X BASIC
NO PRICING ON QTY 10 OR LESS
1 Giannis Antetokounmpo 25.00 60.00
2 Jalen Brunson 10.00 25.00
3 Luka Doncic 30.00 80.00
4 Tyrese Maxey 10.00 25.00
5 Bam Adebayo 8.00 20.00
6 LeBron James 60.00 150.00
7 Stephen Curry 60.00 150.00
8 Ja Morant 15.00 40.00
9 Paul George 8.00 20.00
10 DeMar DeRozan 8.00 20.00
12 Nikola Jokic 25.00 60.00
13 Trae Young 10.00 25.00
14 Jayson Tatum 20.00 50.00
19 Marcus Smart 6.00 15.00
21 Rudy Gobert 6.00 15.00
22 Donovan Mitchell 10.00 25.00
23 Franz Wagner 8.00 20.00
25 Fred VanVleet 8.00 20.00
27 Damian Lillard 12.00 30.00
30 Shai Gilgeous-Alexander 25.00 60.00

2023-24 Panini National Treasures Tremendous Treasures Materials

STATED PRINT RUN 49 SER.#'d SETS
*PRIME/4-25: 1.25X TO 3X BASIC
NO PRICING ON QTY 10 OR LESS
1 LeBron James 100.00 250.00
2 DeMar DeRozan 8.00 20.00
3 Joel Embiid 12.00 30.00
6 Jayson Tatum 20.00 50.00
7 Trae Young 10.00 25.00
8 Jimmy Butler 8.00 20.00
9 Kyle Kuzma 6.00 15.00
10 Pascal Siakam 8.00 20.00
13 Khris Middleton 5.00 12.00
15 Rudy Gobert 6.00 15.00
16 Giannis Antetokounmpo 25.00 60.00
19 Klay Thompson 12.00 30.00
21 Darius Garland 8.00 20.00
25 De'Aaron Fox 10.00 25.00
28 Max Strus 5.00 12.00
29 Cameron Thomas 6.00 15.00
30 Payton Pritchard 5.00 12.00

2023-24 Panini National Treasures Viewpoint Signatures

STATED PRINT RUN 25-35 SER.#'d SETS
*BRONZE/15-25: .4X TO 1X BASIC
*INTNL/18-24: .4X TO 1X BASIC
NO PRICING ON QTY 10
1 Nikola Jokic/25 200.00 500.00
2 Zion Williamson/25 125.00 300.00
3 Ja Morant/25 400.00 800.00
4 Luka Doncic/25 800.00 1,500.00
5 Anthony Edwards/25 500.00 1,000.00
6 Paul George/25 100.00 250.00
7 Jamal Murray/25 100.00 250.00
8 De'Aaron Fox/25 150.00 400.00
9 Brandon Ingram/35 60.00 150.00
10 Paolo Banchero/25 300.00 500.00
11 Tyrese Maxey/25 200.00 500.00
12 Stephen Curry/25 1,000.00 2,000.00
13 Amen Thompson/25 300.00 600.00
14 Ausar Thompson/25 150.00 400.00
15 Cason Wallace/35 60.00 150.00
16 Bilal Coulibaly/35 100.00 250.00
17 Carmelo Anthony/25 200.00 500.00
18 Donovan Mitchell/25 125.00 300.00
19 Jalen Brunson/35 150.00 400.00
20 Josh Giddey/25 50.00 120.00
21 James Harden/25 200.00 500.00
22 Tyrese Haliburton/35 150.00 400.00
24 Kevin Garnett/25 125.00 300.00
25 Allen Iverson/25 150.00 400.00

2014-15 Panini Noir

VET PRINT RUN 70 SER.#'d SETS
RC PRINT RUN 99 SER.#'d SETS
JSY AU PRINT RUN 99 SER.#'d SETS
PATCHES MAY SELL FOR PREMIUM
EXCHANGE DEADLINE 3/16/2017
1 Ty Lawson BW 2.50 6.00
2 Al Horford BW 4.00 10.00
3 Kevin Love BW 4.00 10.00
4 Victor Oladipo BW 3.00 8.00
5 Andre Drummond BW 3.00 8.00
6 Rajon Rondo BW 5.00 12.00
7 Kyle Lowry BW 5.00 12.00
8 Julius Erving BW 10.00 25.00
9 Carmelo Anthony BW 6.00 15.00
10 Brandon Knight BW 2.50 6.00
11 Kenneth Faried BW 2.50 6.00
12 Jeff Teague BW 2.50 6.00
13 LeBron James BW 100.00 250.00
14 Nikola Vucevic BW 3.00 8.00
15 Brandon Jennings BW 2.50 6.00
16 Monta Ellis BW 3.00 8.00
17 DeMar DeRozan BW 5.00 12.00
18 Shaquille O'Neal BW 15.00 40.00
19 LaMarcus Aldridge BW 5.00 12.00
20 DeMarcus Cousins BW 3.00 8.00
21 Kevin Garnett BW 10.00 25.00
22 John Wall BW 5.00 12.00
23 Kyrie Irving BW 8.00 20.00
24 Marc Gasol BW 4.00 10.00
25 Stephen Curry BW 40.00 100.00
26 Tim Duncan BW 10.00 25.00
27 Joe Johnson BW 3.00 8.00
28 Patrick Ewing BW 6.00 15.00
29 Damian Lillard BW 10.00 25.00
30 Rudy Gay BW 4.00 10.00
31 Ricky Rubio BW 3.00 8.00
32 Bradley Beal BW 6.00 15.00
33 Giannis Antetokounmpo BW 25.00 60.00
34 Vince Carter BW 8.00 20.00
35 Klay Thompson BW 10.00 25.00
36 Tony Parker BW 6.00 15.00
37 Deron Williams BW 3.00 8.00
38 Pete Maravich BW 12.00 30.00
39 Kevin Durant BW 12.00 30.00
40 Kobe Bryant BW 200.00 500.00
41 Derrick Rose BW 8.00 20.00
42 Chris Bosh BW 5.00 12.00
43 Michael Carter-Williams BW 2.50 6.00
44 Dwight Howard BW 5.00 12.00
45 Blake Griffin BW 4.00 10.00
46 Anthony Davis BW 10.00 25.00
47 Avery Bradley BW 2.50 6.00
48 Scottie Pippen BW 10.00 25.00
49 Russell Westbrook BW 6.00 15.00
50 Steve Nash BW 8.00 20.00
51 Joakim Noah BW 4.00 10.00
52 Dwyane Wade BW 8.00 20.00
53 Paul George BW 6.00 15.00
54 James Harden BW 8.00 20.00
55 Larry Bird BW 15.00 40.00
56 Chris Paul BW 6.00 15.00
57 Jared Sullinger BW 2.50 6.00
58 Jerry West BW 10.00 25.00
59 Gordon Hayward BW 3.00 8.00
60 Jeremy Lin BW 8.00 20.00
61 Jimmy Butler BW 6.00 15.00
62 Al Jefferson BW 2.50 6.00
63 Roy Hibbert BW 3.00 8.00
64 Dirk Nowitzki BW 10.00 25.00
65 Eric Bledsoe BW 3.00 8.00
66 Magic Johnson BW 15.00 40.00
67 Nerlens Noel BW 2.50 6.00
68 Chris Webber BW 5.00 12.00
69 Trey Burke BW 2.50 6.00
70 Allen Iverson BW 10.00 25.00
71 Marcus Smart BW RC 10.00 25.00
72 Bruno Caboclo BW RC 3.00 8.00
73 James Young BW RC 2.50 6.00
74 Bojan Bogdanovic BW RC 4.00 10.00
75 Doug McDermott BW RC 4.00 10.00
76 Julius Randle BW RC 12.00 30.00
77 Aaron Gordon BW RC 12.00 30.00
78 Gary Harris BW RC 4.00 10.00
79 Cleanthony Early BW RC 2.50 6.00
80 Rodney Hood BW RC 3.00 8.00
81 Glenn Robinson III BW RC 3.00 8.00
82 Nikola Mirotic BW RC 4.00 10.00
83 T.J. Warren BW RC 4.00 10.00
84 Joe Ingles BW RC 4.00 10.00
85 Nik Stauskas BW RC 2.50 6.00
86 Dante Exum BW RC 4.00 10.00
87 Shabazz Napier BW RC 3.00 8.00
88 Mitch McGary BW RC 2.50 6.00
89 K.J. McDaniels BW RC 2.50 6.00
90 Joe Harris BW RC 4.00 10.00
91 Noah Vonleh BW RC 2.50 6.00
92 Jusuf Nurkic BW RC 8.00 20.00
93 Andrew Wiggins BW RC 15.00 40.00
94 Jordan Clarkson BW RC 10.00 25.00
95 James Ennis BW RC 2.50 6.00
96 Kyle Anderson BW RC 4.00 10.00
97 Joel Embiid BW RC 75.00 200.00
98 Jabari Parker BW RC 3.00 8.00
99 Elfrid Payton BW RC 4.00 10.00
100 Zach LaVine BW RC 30.00 80.00
101 Ty Lawson CLR 2.50 6.00
102 Al Horford CLR 4.00 10.00
103 Kevin Love CLR 4.00 10.00
104 Victor Oladipo CLR 3.00 8.00
105 Andre Drummond CLR 3.00 8.00
106 Rajon Rondo CLR 5.00 12.00
107 Kyle Lowry CLR 5.00 12.00
108 Julius Erving CLR 10.00 25.00
109 Carmelo Anthony CLR 6.00 15.00
110 Brandon Knight CLR 2.50 6.00
111 Kenneth Faried CLR 2.50 6.00
112 Jeff Teague CLR 2.50 6.00
113 LeBron James CLR 100.00 250.00
114 Nikola Vucevic CLR 3.00 8.00
115 Brandon Jennings CLR 2.50 6.00
116 Monta Ellis CLR 3.00 8.00
117 DeMar DeRozan CLR 5.00 12.00
118 Shaquille O'Neal CLR 15.00 40.00
119 LaMarcus Aldridge CLR 5.00 12.00
120 DeMarcus Cousins CLR 3.00 8.00
121 Kevin Garnett CLR 10.00 25.00
122 John Wall CLR 5.00 12.00
123 Kyrie Irving CLR 8.00 20.00
124 Marc Gasol CLR 4.00 10.00
125 Stephen Curry CLR 40.00 100.00
126 Tim Duncan CLR 10.00 25.00
127 Joe Johnson CLR 3.00 8.00
128 Patrick Ewing CLR 6.00 15.00
129 Damian Lillard CLR 10.00 25.00
130 Rudy Gay CLR 4.00 10.00
131 Ricky Rubio CLR 3.00 8.00
132 Bradley Beal CLR 6.00 15.00
133 Giannis Antetokounmpo CLR 25.00 60.00
134 Vince Carter CLR 8.00 20.00
135 Klay Thompson CLR 10.00 25.00
136 Tony Parker CLR 6.00 15.00
137 Deron Williams CLR 3.00 8.00
138 Pete Maravich CLR 12.00 30.00
139 Kevin Durant CLR 12.00 30.00
140 Kobe Bryant CLR 200.00 500.00
141 Derrick Rose CLR 8.00 20.00
142 Chris Bosh CLR 5.00 12.00
143 Michael Carter-Williams CLR 2.50 6.00
144 Dwight Howard CLR 5.00 12.00
145 Blake Griffin CLR 4.00 10.00
146 Anthony Davis CLR 10.00 25.00
147 Avery Bradley CLR 2.50 6.00
148 Scottie Pippen CLR 10.00 25.00
149 Russell Westbrook CLR 6.00 15.00
150 Steve Nash CLR 8.00 20.00
151 Joakim Noah CLR 4.00 10.00
152 Dwyane Wade CLR 8.00 20.00
153 Paul George CLR 6.00 15.00
154 James Harden CLR 8.00 20.00
155 Larry Bird CLR 15.00 40.00
156 Chris Paul CLR 6.00 15.00
157 Jared Sullinger CLR 2.50 6.00
158 Jerry West CLR 10.00 25.00
159 Gordon Hayward CLR 3.00 8.00
160 Jeremy Lin CLR 8.00 20.00
161 Jimmy Butler CLR 6.00 15.00
162 Al Jefferson CLR 2.50 6.00
163 Roy Hibbert CLR 3.00 8.00
164 Dirk Nowitzki CLR 10.00 25.00
165 Eric Bledsoe CLR 3.00 8.00
166 Magic Johnson CLR 15.00 40.00
167 Nerlens Noel CLR 2.50 6.00
168 Chris Webber CLR 5.00 12.00
169 Trey Burke CLR 2.50 6.00
170 Allen Iverson CLR 10.00 25.00
171 Marcus Smart CLR RC 10.00 25.00
172 Bruno Caboclo CLR RC 3.00 8.00
173 James Young CLR RC 2.50 6.00
174 Bojan Bogdanovic CLR RC 4.00 10.00
175 Doug McDermott CLR RC 4.00 10.00
176 Julius Randle CLR RC 12.00 30.00
177 Aaron Gordon CLR RC 12.00 30.00
178 Gary Harris CLR RC 4.00 10.00
179 Cleanthony Early CLR RC 2.50 6.00
180 Rodney Hood CLR RC 3.00 8.00
181 Glenn Robinson III CLR RC 3.00 8.00
182 Nikola Mirotic CLR RC 4.00 10.00
183 T.J. Warren CLR RC 4.00 10.00
184 Joe Ingles CLR RC 4.00 10.00
185 Nik Stauskas CLR RC 2.50 6.00
186 Dante Exum CLR RC 4.00 10.00
187 Shabazz Napier CLR RC 3.00 8.00
188 Mitch McGary CLR RC 2.50 6.00
189 K.J. McDaniels CLR RC 2.50 6.00
190 Joe Harris CLR RC 4.00 10.00
191 Noah Vonleh CLR RC 2.50 6.00
192 Jusuf Nurkic CLR RC 8.00 20.00
193 Andrew Wiggins CLR RC 15.00 40.00
194 Jordan Clarkson CLR RC 10.00 25.00
195 James Ennis CLR RC 2.50 6.00
196 Kyle Anderson CLR RC 4.00 10.00
197 Joel Embiid CLR RC 75.00 200.00
198 Jabari Parker CLR RC 3.00 8.00
199 Elfrid Payton CLR RC 4.00 10.00
200 Zach LaVine CLR RC 30.00 80.00
201 McDermott BW JSY AU 8.00 20.00
202 Stauskas BW JSY AU 5.00 12.00
203 James Ennis BW JSY AU 5.00 12.00
204 A.Gordon BW JSY AU 20.00 50.00
205 Shabazz Napier BW JSY AU 6.00 15.00
206 Joel Embiid BW JSY AU 300.00 600.00
207 Spencer Dinwiddie BW JSY AU 30.00 80.00
208 K.J. McDaniels BW JSY AU 5.00 12.00
209 Elfrid Payton BW JSY AU 8.00 20.00
210 M.Smart BW JSY AU 20.00 50.00
211 Robinson BW JSY AU 6.00 15.00
212 Noah Vonleh BW JSY AU 5.00 12.00
213 James Young BW JSY AU 5.00 12.00
214 T.J. Warren BW JSY AU 8.00 20.00
215 Wiggins BW JSY AU 60.00 150.00
216 J.Randle BW JSY AU 100.00 250.00
217 Dante Exum BW JSY AU 8.00 20.00
218 Anderson BW JSY AU 8.00 20.00
219 Gary Harris BW JSY AU 8.00 20.00
220 Nurkic BW JSY AU 8.00 20.00
221 Parker BW JSY AU 6.00 15.00
222 R.Hood BW JSY AU 12.00 30.00
223 Joe Harris BW JSY AU 8.00 20.00
224 Zach LaVine BW JSY AU 125.00 300.00
225 Caboclo BW JSY AU 6.00 15.00
226 McDermott CLR JSY AU 8.00 20.00
227 Stauskas CLR JSY AU 5.00 12.00
228 James Ennis CLR JSY AU 5.00 12.00
229 A.Gordon CLR JSY AU 20.00 50.00
230 Shabazz Napier CLR JSY AU 6.00 15.00
231 Joel Embiid CLR JSY AU 300.00 600.00
232 Spencer Dinwiddie CLR JSY AU 8.00 20.00
233 K.J. McDaniels CLR JSY AU 5.00 12.00
234 Elfrid Payton CLR JSY AU 8.00 20.00
235 M.Smart CLR JSY AU 20.00 50.00
236 Robinson CLR JSY AU 6.00 15.00
237 Noah Vonleh CLR JSY AU 5.00 12.00
238 James Young CLR JSY AU 5.00 12.00
239 T.J. Warren CLR JSY AU 8.00 20.00
240 Wiggins CLR JSY AU 60.00 150.00
241 J.Randle CLR JSY AU 100.00 250.00
242 Dante Exum CLR JSY AU 8.00 20.00
243 Anderson CLR JSY AU 8.00 20.00
244 Gary Harris CLR JSY AU 8.00 20.00
246 Parker CLR JSY AU 6.00 15.00
247 R.Hood CLR JSY AU 12.00 30.00
248 Joe Harris CLR JSY AU 8.00 20.00
249 Zach LaVine CLR JSY AU 125.00 300.00
250 Caboclo CLR JSY AU 6.00 15.00

2014-15 Panini Noir China Jerseys

STATED PRINT RUN 99 SER.#'d SETS
PRIME JSY MAY SELL FOR PREMIUM
*PRIME/25: X TO X BASIC
CJAB Andrew Bogut 10.00 25.00
CJAI Andre Iguodala 10.00 25.00
CJCB Corey Brewer 4.00 10.00
CJDG Draymond Green 20.00 50.00
CJDL David Lee 4.00 10.00
CJDM Donatas Motiejunas 4.00 10.00
CJFE Festus Ezeli 4.00 10.00
CJHB Harrison Barnes 10.00 25.00
CJJH James Harden 25.00 60.00
CJJH Justin Holiday 6.00 15.00
CJJS Josh Smith 4.00 10.00
CJJT Jason Terry 10.00 25.00
CJKM K.J. McDaniels 4.00 10.00
CJKT Klay Thompson 20.00 50.00
CJPB Patrick Beverley 4.00 10.00
CJPP Pablo Prigioni 4.00 10.00
CJSC Stephen Curry 50.00 100.00
CJSL Shaun Livingston 10.00 25.00
CJTA Trevor Ariza 4.00 10.00
CJTJ Terrence Jones 4.00 10.00

2014-15 Panini Noir Spotlight Signatures

STATED PRINT RUN 25 SER.#'d SETS
EXCHANGE DEADLINE 3/16/2017
1 Kobe Bryant 10,000.00 20,000.00
2 Kevin Durant 1,000.00 2,000.00
4 Giannis Antetokounmpo 3,000.00 6,000.00
5 Mason Plumlee 20.00 50.00
6 Zach LaVine 500.00 1,000.00
7 Victor Oladipo 50.00 120.00
8 Kenneth Faried 20.00 50.00
9 Anthony Davis 200.00 500.00
10 Nikola Mirotic 75.00 200.00
11 Chris Paul 200.00 500.00
12 Thaddeus Young 20.00 50.00
14 Ty Lawson 20.00 50.00
15 Russell Westbrook EXCH 200.00 500.00
16 Bradley Beal 125.00 300.00
17 Blake Griffin 100.00 250.00
19 Jusuf Nurkic 60.00 150.00
20 Gary Harris 30.00 80.00

2015-16 Panini Noir

VET PRINT RUN 99 SER.#'d SETS
RC PRINT RUN 99 SER.#'d SETS
JSY AU PRINT RUN 99 SER.#'d SETS
PATCHES MAY SELL FOR PREMIUM
EXCHANGE DEADLINE 1/20/2018
1 Kobe Bryant BW 150.00 400.00
2 Kevin Garnett BW 6.00 15.00
3 Anthony Davis BW 6.00 15.00
4 Victor Oladipo BW 2.00 5.00
5 Damian Lillard BW 6.00 15.00
6 DeMar DeRozan BW 5.00 12.00
7 John Wall BW 3.00 8.00
8 Dwyane Wade BW 5.00 12.00
9 Paul George BW 4.00 10.00
10 Stephen Curry BW 20.00 50.00
11 Will Barton BW 1.50 4.00
12 LeBron James BW 12.00 30.00
13 Derrick Rose BW 4.00 10.00
14 Al Horford BW 2.50 6.00
15 Chris Bosh BW 3.00 8.00
16 Khris Middleton BW 3.00 8.00
17 Arron Afflalo BW 1.50 4.00
18 Nikola Vucevic BW 2.00 5.00
19 C.J. McCollum BW 2.50 6.00
20 Tim Duncan BW 6.00 15.00
21 Bradley Beal BW 3.00 8.00
22 Jordan Clarkson BW 2.50 6.00
23 Monta Ellis BW 2.00 5.00
24 Klay Thompson BW 6.00 15.00
25 Danilo Gallinari BW 2.00 5.00
26 Kyrie Irving BW 5.00 12.00
27 Kemba Walker BW 2.50 6.00
28 Jeff Teague BW 1.50 4.00
29 Mike Conley BW 2.50 6.00
30 Jabari Parker BW 1.50 4.00
31 Norris Cole BW 1.50 4.00
32 Russell Westbrook BW 4.00 10.00
33 T.J. Warren BW 2.50 6.00
34 Kawhi Leonard BW 8.00 20.00
35 Gordon Hayward BW 2.50 6.00
36 DeAndre Jordan BW 2.00 5.00
37 Terrence Jones BW 1.50 4.00
38 Draymond Green BW 3.00 8.00
39 Deron Williams BW 2.50 6.00
40 Kevin Love BW 2.50 6.00
41 Jeremy Lin BW 5.00 12.00
42 Kent Bazemore BW 1.50 4.00
43 Marc Gasol BW 2.50 6.00
44 Giannis Antetokounmpo BW 12.00 30.00
45 Zach LaVine BW 6.00 15.00
46 Kevin Durant BW 10.00 25.00
47 Brandon Knight BW 1.50 4.00
48 Rajon Rondo BW 3.00 8.00
49 Alec Burks BW 1.50 4.00
50 Chris Paul BW 5.00 12.00
51 James Harden BW 5.00 12.00
52 Reggie Jackson BW 2.00 5.00
53 J.J. Barea BW 2.00 5.00
54 Pau Gasol BW 4.00 10.00
55 Thaddeus Young BW 1.50 4.00
56 Isaiah Thomas BW 2.00 5.00
57 Lou Williams BW 2.00 5.00
58 Goran Dragic BW 2.50 6.00
59 Andrew Wiggins BW 3.00 8.00
60 Carmelo Anthony BW 4.00 10.00
61 Nerlens Noel BW 1.50 4.00
62 DeMarcus Cousins BW 2.50 6.00
63 Kyle Lowry BW 2.50 6.00
64 Blake Griffin BW 2.50 6.00
65 Dwight Howard BW 3.00 8.00
66 Andre Drummond BW 2.50 6.00
67 Dirk Nowitzki BW 6.00 15.00
68 Jimmy Butler BW 5.00 12.00
69 Brook Lopez BW 2.50 6.00
70 Jae Crowder BW 1.50 4.00
71 Karl-Anthony Towns BW RC 20.00 50.00
72 D'Angelo Russell BW RC 10.00 25.00
73 Jahlil Okafor BW RC 3.00 8.00
74 Emmanuel Mudiay BW RC 3.00 8.00
75 Kristaps Porzingis BW RC 15.00 40.00
76 Mario Hezonja BW RC 3.00 8.00
77 Justise Winslow BW RC 4.00 10.00
78 Willie Cauley-Stein BW RC 3.00 8.00
79 Stanley Johnson BW RC 3.00 8.00
80 Frank Kaminsky BW RC 3.00 8.00
81 Devin Booker BW RC 30.00 80.00
82 Myles Turner BW RC 10.00 25.00
83 Jerian Grant BW RC 2.50 6.00
84 Marcelo Huertas BW RC 2.50 6.00
85 Cameron Payne BW RC 4.00 10.00
86 Delon Wright BW RC 3.00 8.00
87 Sam Dekker BW RC 2.50 6.00
88 Boban Marjanovic BW RC 8.00 20.00
89 Terry Rozier BW RC 10.00 25.00
90 Bobby Portis BW RC 6.00 15.00
91 Jonathon Simmons BW RC 3.00 8.00
92 Rondae Hollis-Jefferson BW RC 3.00 8.00
93 Raul Neto BW RC 2.50 6.00
94 R.J. Hunter BW RC 2.50 6.00
95 Nikola Jokic BW RC 300.00 600.00
96 Nemanja Bjelica BW RC 4.00 10.00
97 Norman Powell BW RC 5.00 12.00
98 Larry Nance Jr. BW RC 5.00 12.00
99 Montrezl Harrell BW RC 8.00 20.00
100 Rashad Vaughn BW RC 2.50 6.00
101 Kobe Bryant CLR 150.00 400.00
102 Kevin Garnett CLR 6.00 15.00
103 Anthony Davis CLR 6.00 15.00
104 Victor Oladipo CLR 2.00 5.00
105 Damian Lillard CLR 6.00 15.00
106 DeMar DeRozan CLR 5.00 12.00
107 John Wall CLR 3.00 8.00
108 Dwyane Wade CLR 5.00 12.00
109 Paul George CLR 4.00 10.00
110 Stephen Curry CLR 20.00 50.00
111 Will Barton CLR 1.50 4.00
112 LeBron James CLR 12.00 30.00
113 Derrick Rose CLR 4.00 10.00
114 Al Horford CLR 2.50 6.00
115 Chris Bosh CLR 3.00 8.00
116 Khris Middleton CLR 3.00 8.00
117 Arron Afflalo CLR 1.50 4.00
118 Nikola Vucevic CLR 2.00 5.00
119 C.J. McCollum CLR 2.50 6.00
120 Tim Duncan CLR 6.00 15.00
121 Bradley Beal CLR 3.00 8.00
122 Jordan Clarkson CLR 2.50 6.00
123 Monta Ellis CLR 2.00 5.00
124 Klay Thompson CLR 6.00 15.00
125 Danilo Gallinari CLR 2.00 5.00
126 Kyrie Irving CLR 5.00 12.00
127 Kemba Walker CLR 2.50 6.00
128 Jeff Teague CLR 1.50 4.00
129 Mike Conley CLR 2.50 6.00
130 Jabari Parker CLR 1.50 4.00
131 Norris Cole CLR 1.50 4.00
132 Russell Westbrook CLR 4.00 10.00
133 T.J. Warren CLR 2.50 6.00
134 Kawhi Leonard CLR 8.00 20.00
135 Gordon Hayward CLR 2.50 6.00
136 DeAndre Jordan CLR 2.00 5.00
137 Terrence Jones CLR 1.50 4.00
138 Draymond Green CLR 3.00 8.00
139 Deron Williams CLR 2.50 6.00
140 Kevin Love CLR 2.50 6.00
141 Jeremy Lin CLR 5.00 12.00
142 Kent Bazemore CLR 1.50 4.00
143 Marc Gasol CLR 2.50 6.00
144 Giannis Antetokounmpo CLR 12.00 30.00
145 Zach LaVine CLR 6.00 15.00
146 Kevin Durant CLR 10.00 25.00
147 Brandon Knight CLR 1.50 4.00
148 Rajon Rondo CLR 3.00 8.00
149 Alec Burks CLR 1.50 4.00
150 Chris Paul CLR 5.00 12.00
151 James Harden CLR 5.00 12.00
152 Reggie Jackson CLR 2.00 5.00
153 J.J. Barea CLR 2.00 5.00
154 Pau Gasol CLR 4.00 10.00
155 Thaddeus Young CLR 1.50 4.00
156 Isaiah Thomas CLR 2.00 5.00
157 Lou Williams CLR 2.00 5.00
158 Goran Dragic CLR 2.50 6.00
159 Andrew Wiggins CLR 3.00 8.00
160 Carmelo Anthony CLR 4.00 10.00
161 Nerlens Noel CLR 1.50 4.00
162 DeMarcus Cousins CLR 2.50 6.00
163 Kyle Lowry CLR 2.50 6.00
164 Blake Griffin CLR 2.50 6.00
165 Dwight Howard CLR 3.00 8.00
166 Andre Drummond CLR 2.50 6.00
167 Dirk Nowitzki CLR 6.00 15.00
168 Jimmy Butler CLR 5.00 12.00
169 Brook Lopez CLR 2.50 6.00
170 Jae Crowder CLR 1.50 4.00
171 Karl-Anthony Towns CLR RC 20.00 50.00
172 D'Angelo Russell CLR RC 10.00 25.00
173 Jahlil Okafor CLR RC 3.00 8.00
174 Emmanuel Mudiay CLR RC 3.00 8.00
175 Kristaps Porzingis CLR RC 15.00 40.00
176 Mario Hezonja CLR RC 3.00 8.00
177 Justise Winslow CLR RC 4.00 10.00
178 Willie Cauley-Stein CLR RC 3.00 8.00
179 Stanley Johnson CLR RC 3.00 8.00
180 Frank Kaminsky CLR RC 3.00 8.00
181 Devin Booker CLR RC 30.00 80.00
182 Myles Turner CLR RC 10.00 25.00
183 Jerian Grant CLR RC 2.50 6.00
184 Marcelo Huertas CLR RC 2.50 6.00
185 Cameron Payne CLR RC 4.00 10.00
186 Delon Wright CLR RC 3.00 8.00
187 Sam Dekker CLR RC 2.50 6.00
188 Boban Marjanovic CLR RC 8.00 20.00
189 Terry Rozier CLR RC 10.00 25.00
190 Bobby Portis CLR RC 6.00 15.00
191 Jonathon Simmons CLR RC 3.00 8.00
192 Rondae Hollis-Jefferson CLR RC 3.00 8.00
193 Raul Neto CLR RC 2.50 6.00
194 R.J. Hunter CLR RC 2.50 6.00
195 Nikola Jokic CLR RC 300.00 600.00
196 Nemanja Bjelica CLR RC 4.00 10.00
197 Norman Powell CLR RC 5.00 12.00
198 Larry Nance Jr. CLR RC 5.00 12.00
199 Montrezl Harrell CLR RC 8.00 20.00
200 Rashad Vaughn CLR RC 2.50 6.00
201 Towns BW JSY AU 150.00 400.00
202 Russell BW JSY AU 50.00 120.00
203 Okafor BW JSY AU 8.00 20.00
204 Mdy BW JSY AU EXCH 8.00 20.00
205 Porzingis BW JSY AU 100.00 250.00
206 Hezonja BW JSY AU 8.00 20.00
207 Winslow BW JSY AU 10.00 25.00
208 Cly-Stn BW JSY AU 8.00 20.00
209 S.Johnson BW JSY AU 8.00 20.00
210 Kaminsky BW JSY AU 8.00 20.00
211 Booker BW JSY AU 300.00 600.00
212 Turner BW JSY AU 25.00 60.00
213 Jerian Grant BW JSY AU 6.00 15.00
214 Marcelo Huertas BW JSY AU 6.00 15.00
215 Cameron Payne BW JSY AU 10.00 25.00
216 Delon Wright BW JSY AU 8.00 20.00
217 Jarell Martin BW JSY AU 6.00 15.00
218 Cristiano Felicio BW JSY AU 8.00 20.00
219 Rozier BW JSY AU 25.00 60.00
220 Rondae Hollis-Jefferson BW JSY AU 8.00 20.00
221 Portis BW JSY AU 15.00 40.00
222 Cliff Alexander BW JSY AU 6.00 15.00
223 Raul Neto BW JSY AU 6.00 15.00
224 R.J. Hunter BW JSY AU 6.00 15.00
225 Jokic BW JSY AU 3,000.00 6,000.00
226 Bjelica BW JSY AU 10.00 25.00
227 Powell BW JSY AU 30.00 80.00
228 Richardson BW JSY AU 10.00 25.00
229 Luis Montero BW JSY AU 6.00 15.00
230 Joe Young BW JSY AU 6.00 15.00
231 Towns CLR JSY AU 150.00 400.00
232 Russell CLR JSY AU 50.00 120.00
233 Okafor CLR JSY AU 8.00 20.00
234 Mdy CLR JSY AU EXCH 8.00 20.00
235 Porzingis CLR JSY AU 75.00 200.00
236 Hezonja CLR JSY AU 8.00 20.00
237 Winslow CLR JSY AU 10.00 25.00
238 Cly-Stn CLR JSY AU 8.00 20.00
239 S.Johnson CLR JSY AU 8.00 20.00
240 Kaminsky CLR JSY AU 8.00 20.00
241 Booker CLR JSY AU 300.00 600.00
242 Turner CLR JSY AU 25.00 60.00
243 Jerian Grant CLR JSY AU 6.00 15.00
244 Marcelo Huertas CLR JSY AU 6.00 15.00
245 Cameron Payne CLR JSY AU 10.00 25.00
246 Delon Wright CLR JSY AU 8.00 20.00
247 Jarell Martin CLR JSY AU 6.00 15.00
248 Cristiano Felicio CLR JSY AU 8.00 20.00
249 Rozier CLR JSY AU 25.00 60.00
250 Rondae Hollis-Jefferson CLR JSY AU 8.00 20.00
251 Portis CLR JSY AU 15.00 40.00
252 Cliff Alexander CLR JSY AU 6.00 15.00
253 Raul Neto CLR JSY AU 6.00 15.00
254 R.J. Hunter CLR JSY AU 6.00 15.00
255 Jokic CLR JSY AU 3,000.00 6,000.00
256 Bjelica CLR JSY AU 10.00 25.00
257 Powell CLR JSY AU 30.00 80.00
258 Richardson CLR JSY AU 10.00 25.00
259 Luis Montero CLR JSY AU 6.00 15.00
260 Joe Young CLR JSY AU 6.00 15.00

2015-16 Panini Noir Acetate Materials Prime

PRINT RUNS B/WN 10-49 COPIES PER
NO PRICING ON QTY 10
ANAB Avery Bradley/49 4.00 10.00
ANAF Arron Afflalo/49 4.00 10.00
ANAH Al Horford/49 6.00 15.00
ANAJ Al Jefferson/49 4.00 10.00
ANAX Alex Len/25 4.00 10.00
ANBB Bojan Bogdanovic/49 5.00 12.00
ANBP Bobby Portis/49 10.00 25.00
ANCP Cameron Payne/49 6.00 15.00

ANDB Devin Booker/25 25.00 60.00
ANDC DeMarcus Cousins/49 6.00 15.00
ANDG Draymond Green/49 8.00 20.00
ANDJ DeAndre Jordan/25 5.00 12.00
ANDR D'Angelo Russell/49 15.00 40.00
ANDW Delon Wright/49 5.00 12.00
ANEF Evan Fournier/49 5.00 12.00
ANEG Eric Gordon/49 5.00 12.00
ANEM Emmanuel Mudiay/49 5.00 12.00
ANET Evan Turner/25 4.00 10.00
ANFK Frank Kaminsky/49 5.00 12.00
ANGH Grant Hill/49 10.00 25.00
ANGN Gary Neal/49 4.00 10.00
ANHO Hakeem Olajuwon/49 8.00 20.00
ANIT Isaiah Thomas/49 6.00 15.00
ANJA Justin Anderson/49 12.00 30.00
ANJB Jimmy Butler/49 10.00 25.00
ANJB Jerryd Bayless/49 4.00 10.00
ANJC Jae Crowder/49 4.00 10.00
ANJG Jerian Grant/25 4.00 10.00
ANJJ Joe Johnson/49 5.00 12.00
ANJJ John Jenkins/49 4.00 10.00
ANJN Joakim Noah/49 4.00 10.00
ANJO John Stockton/49 12.00 30.00
ANJO Jahlil Okafor/49 6.00 15.00
ANJR Josh Richardson/49 6.00 15.00
ANJS Jared Sullinger/49 4.00 10.00
ANJS Jonathon Simmons/49 5.00 12.00
ANJS J.R. Smith/49 6.00 15.00
ANJW John Wall/49 8.00 20.00
ANJW Justise Winslow/49 6.00 15.00
ANKB Kobe Bryant/49 200.00 500.00
ANKD Kevin Durant/49 12.00 30.00
ANKK Kosta Koufos/49 4.00 10.00
ANKL Kevin Love/25 6.00 15.00
ANKM Karl Malone/49 10.00 25.00
ANKM Khris Middleton/49 8.00 20.00
ANKO Kelly Oubre Jr./49 12.00 30.00
ANKP Kristaps Porzingis/49 25.00 60.00
ANKT Karl-Anthony Towns/25 25.00 60.00
ANKT Klay Thompson/49 15.00 40.00
ANKW Kemba Walker/49 6.00 15.00
ANLG Langston Galloway/49 4.00 10.00
ANLJ Larry Johnson/25 8.00 20.00
ANLJ LeBron James/49 50.00 120.00
ANLM Luis Montero/49 4.00 10.00
ANLS Lance Stephenson/49 5.00 12.00
ANMG Manu Ginobili/49 12.00 30.00
ANMG Marcin Gortat/49 4.00 10.00
ANMH Mario Hezonja/49 5.00 12.00
ANMS Marcus Smart/49 8.00 20.00
ANMT Myles Turner/49 15.00 40.00
ANNB Nemanja Bjelica/25 6.00 15.00
ANNJ Nikola Jokic/49 125.00 300.00
ANNN Nerlens Noel/25 4.00 10.00
ANNP Norman Powell/49 8.00 20.00
ANNV Nikola Vucevic/49 5.00 12.00
ANOP Otto Porter/49 5.00 12.00
ANPM Paul Millsap/49 5.00 12.00
ANRC Rakeem Christmas/49 4.00 10.00
ANRG Rudy Gay/49 6.00 15.00
ANRG Rudy Gobert/49 8.00 20.00
ANRH R.J. Hunter/49 4.00 10.00
ANRH Roy Hibbert/49 4.00 10.00
ANRH Richaun Holmes/49 6.00 15.00
ANRH Rodney Hood/49 5.00 12.00
ANRJ Rondae Hollis-Jefferson/49 5.00 12.00
ANRL Robin Lopez/49 4.00 10.00
ANRR Raul Neto/49 4.00 10.00
ANRR Ricky Rubio/25 5.00 12.00
ANRW Russell Westbrook/49 10.00 25.00
ANSC Stephen Curry/49 50.00 120.00
ANSD Sam Dekker/25 4.00 10.00
ANSI Serge Ibaka/49 5.00 12.00
ANSJ Stanley Johnson/25 5.00 12.00
ANSL Shane Larkin/49 4.00 10.00
ANSM Salah Mejri/49 4.00 10.00
ANSO Shaquille O'Neal/49 10.00 25.00
ANSP Scottie Pippen/49 15.00 40.00
ANTD Tim Duncan/49 15.00 40.00
ANTH Tobias Harris/49 5.00 12.00
ANTL Trey Lyles/49 5.00 12.00
ANTM Timofey Mozgov/49 4.00 10.00
ANTP Tony Parker/49 10.00 25.00
ANTR Terry Rozier/49 15.00 40.00
ANTY Thaddeus Young/49 4.00 10.00
ANWCS Willie Cauley-Stein/49 5.00 12.00

2015-16 Panini Noir Autograph Materials Prime Black and White

PRINT RUNS B/WN 10-75 COPIES PER
NO PRICING ON QTY 10
EXCHANGE DEADLINE 1/20/2018
ABAGD Aaron Gordon/49 20.00 50.00
ABAGW Archie Goodwin/39 6.00 15.00
ABBBY Brent Barry/49 6.00 15.00
ABBDT Brad Daugherty/75 8.00 20.00
ABBJB Bojan Bogdanovic/75 8.00 20.00
ABCBO Chris Bosh/25 15.00 40.00
ABCDX Clyde Drexler/25 30.00 80.00
ABCLN Christian Laettner/39 12.00 30.00
ABCMC C.J. McCollum/49 12.00 30.00
ABDMD Doug McDermott/75 8.00 20.00
ABDMG Danny Manning/49 8.00 20.00
ABDRD Dennis Rodman/25 75.00 200.00
ABGHL Grant Hill/49 25.00 60.00
ABGPT Gary Payton/25 25.00 60.00
ABHOW Hakeem Olajuwon/25 40.00 100.00
ABJCD Jose Calderon/25 6.00 15.00
ABJKD Jason Kidd/25 25.00 60.00
ABJVC Jonas Valanciunas/75 8.00 20.00
ABJWL John Wall/25 25.00 60.00
ABKMH Kevin McHale/25 20.00 50.00
ABKOL Kelly Olynyk/75 6.00 15.00
ABMHL Maurice Harkless/75 6.00 15.00
ABMST Marcus Smart/49 12.00 30.00
ABMWL Mo Williams/75 8.00 20.00
ABRAL Ray Allen/25 50.00 120.00
ABRAS Rafer Alston/45 8.00 20.00
ABRRB Ricky Rubio/25 20.00 50.00

2015-16 Panini Noir Autograph Materials Prime Color

PRINT RUNS B/WN 5-75 COPIES PER
NO PRICING ON QTY 10 OR LESS
EXCHANGE DEADLINE 1/20/2018
70 Archie Goodwin/39 6.00 15.00
ACAGD Aaron Gordon/49 10.00 25.00
ACBBY Brent Barry/49 6.00 15.00
ACBDT Brad Daugherty/75 8.00 20.00
ACBJB Bojan Bogdanovic/75 8.00 20.00
ACCBO Chris Bosh/25 15.00 40.00
ACCDX Clyde Drexler/25 30.00 80.00
ACCLN Christian Laettner/49 12.00 30.00
ACCMC C.J. McCollum/49 12.00 30.00
ACDMD Doug McDermott/75 8.00 20.00
ACDMG Danny Manning/49 8.00 20.00
ACDRD Dennis Rodman/25 75.00 200.00
ACGHL Grant Hill/49 25.00 60.00
ACGPY Gary Payton/25 25.00 60.00
ACHOW Hakeem Olajuwon/25 40.00 100.00
ACJCD Jose Calderon/25 6.00 15.00
ACJKD Jason Kidd/25 25.00 60.00
ACJVC Jonas Valanciunas/75 8.00 20.00
ACJWL John Wall/25 25.00 60.00
ACKMH Kevin McHale/25 20.00 50.00
ACKOL Kelly Olynyk/75 6.00 15.00
ACMHL Maurice Harkless/75 6.00 15.00
ACMST Marcus Smart/49 12.00 30.00
ACMWL Mo Williams/75 8.00 20.00
ACRAL Ray Allen/25 50.00 120.00
ACRAT Rafer Alston/45 8.00 20.00
ACRRB Ricky Rubio/25 20.00 50.00

2015-16 Panini Noir Autographs Black and White

PRINT RUNS B/WN 35-60 COPIES PER
EXCHANGE DEADLINE 1/20/2018
*BRONZE/25: .4X TO1X p/r 35
*BRONZE/25: .5X TO1.2X p/r 49-60
NBACG A.C. Green/49 5.00 12.00
NBADR Andre Drummond/49 8.00 20.00
NBADV Anthony Davis/35 30.00 80.00
NBAHF Al Horford/49 5.00 12.00
NBAMG Alonzo Mourning/49 12.00 30.00
NBBGF Blake Griffin/35 20.00 50.00
NBBMA Bob McAdoo/49 6.00 15.00
NBBMJ Boban Marjanovic/60 10.00 25.00
NBBPR Bobby Portis/60 8.00 20.00
NBBWT Bill Walton/49 40.00 100.00
NBCAN Carmelo Anthony/35 25.00 60.00
NBCDX Clyde Drexler/49 10.00 25.00
NBCMB Cuttino Mobley/49 3.00 8.00
NBCPL Chris Paul/35 40.00 100.00
NBCPN Cameron Payne/60 EXCH 5.00 12.00
NBDAR D'Angelo Russell/60 25.00 60.00
NBDBK Devin Booker/60 200.00 500.00
NBDCR DeMarre Carroll 3.00 8.00
NBDGR Danny Green/49 4.00 10.00
NBDHW Dwight Howard/35 10.00 25.00
NBDMD Doug McDermott/49 4.00 10.00
NBDMG Danny Manning/49 4.00 10.00
NBDMJ Dan Majerle/49 5.00 12.00
NBDSD Dennis Schroder/49 8.00 20.00
NBDWD Dwyane Wade/35 20.00 50.00
NBEHS Elvin Hayes/49 8.00 20.00
NBEPT Elfrid Payton/49 4.00 10.00
NBFKA Frank Kaminsky/60 8.00 20.00
NBGAN G. Antetokounmpo/49 75.00 200.00
NBGGR Gail Goodrich/49 5.00 12.00
NBGHW Gordon Hayward/49 5.00 12.00
NBHHK Hersey Hawkins/49 3.00 8.00
NBHOW Hakeem Olajuwon/49 12.00 30.00
NBITM Isaiah Thomas/49 20.00 50.00
NBJDM Joe Dumars/49 6.00 15.00
NBJEV Julius Erving/35 25.00 60.00
NBJGR Jeff Green/49 3.00 8.00
NBJHD Jrue Holiday/49 6.00 15.00
NBJOK Jahlil Okafor/60 10.00 25.00
NBJPK Jabari Parker/49 EXCH 12.00 30.00
NBJRD Julius Randle/49 8.00 20.00
NBJSG Jared Sullinger/49 3.00 8.00
NBJSK John Starks/49 5.00 12.00
NBJWL John Wall/49 15.00 40.00
NBJWS Jerry West/35 20.00 50.00
NBKAT Karl-Anthony Towns/60 75.00 200.00
NBKBR Kobe Bryant/35 5,000.00 10,000.00
NBKDR Kevin Durant/35 50.00 120.00
NBKIV Kyrie Irving/35 30.00 80.00
NBKMH Kevin McHale/49 8.00 20.00
NBKML Karl Malone/35 20.00 50.00
NBKPZ Kristaps Porzingis/60 50.00 120.00
NBLNJ Larry Nance Jr./49 6.00 15.00
NBMGT Marcin Gortat/49 3.00 8.00
NBMHT Marcelo Huertas/49 3.00 8.00
NBMJM Magic Johnson/35 30.00 80.00
NBMRM Mitch Richmond/49 6.00 15.00
NBMST Marcus Smart/49 6.00 15.00
NBMTU Myles Turner/60 10.00 25.00
NBNAB Nate Archibald/49 6.00 15.00
NBNBJ Nemanja Bjelica/49 5.00 12.00
NBNJK Nikola Jokic/49 1,500.00 3,000.00
NBNMT Nikola Mirotic/49 3.00 8.00
NBNPW Norman Powell/49 6.00 15.00
NBPGR Paul George/35 EXCH 30.00 80.00
NBRNT Raul Neto/49 3.00 8.00
NBRPS Robert Parish/49 6.00 15.00
NBRSP Ralph Sampson/49 4.00 10.00
NBSON Shaquille O'Neal /35 40.00 100.00
NBTHW Tim Hardaway Jr./49 4.00 10.00
NBTJW T.J. Warren/49 5.00 12.00
NBVOD Victor Oladipo/49 8.00 20.00
NBWMT Wesley Matthews/49 3.00 8.00
NBWTV Walter Tavares/49 3.00 8.00
NBZLV Zach LaVine/49 20.00 50.00

2015-16 Panini Noir Autographs Color

PRINT RUNS B/WN 35-60 COPIES PER
EXCHANGE DEADLINE 1/20/2018
*BRONZE/25: .4X TO1X p/r 25
*BRONZE/25: .5X TO1.2X p/r 49-60
NCACG A.C. Green/49 5.00 12.00
NCADR Andre Drummond/49 8.00 20.00
NCADV Anthony Davis/25 30.00 80.00
NCAHF Al Horford/49 5.00 12.00
NCAMG Alonzo Mourning/49 12.00 30.00
NCBGF Blake Griffin/25 20.00 50.00
NCBMA Bob McAdoo/49 6.00 15.00
NCBMJ Boban Marjanovic/60 10.00 25.00
NCBPR Bobby Portis/60 8.00 20.00
NCBWT Bill Walton/49 40.00 100.00
NCCAN Carmelo Anthony/25 25.00 60.00
NCCDX Clyde Drexler/49 10.00 25.00
NCCMB Cuttino Mobley/49 3.00 8.00
NCCPL Chris Paul/25 40.00 100.00
NCCPN Cameron Payne/60 EXCH 5.00 12.00
NCDAR D'Angelo Russell/60 25.00 60.00
NCDBK Devin Booker/60 200.00 500.00
NCDCD Doug McDermott/49 4.00 10.00
NCDCR DeMarre Carroll/49 3.00 8.00
NCDGR Danny Green/49 4.00 10.00
NCDHW Dwight Howard/25 10.00 25.00
NCDMG Danny Manning/49 4.00 10.00
NCDMJ Dan Majerle/49 5.00 12.00
NCDSD Dennis Schroder/49 8.00 20.00
NCDWD Dwyane Wade/25 20.00 50.00
NCEHS Elvin Hayes/49 8.00 20.00
NCEPT Elfrid Payton/49 4.00 10.00
NCFKM Frank Kaminsky/60 8.00 20.00
NCGAN G. Antetokounmpo/49 75.00 200.00
NCGGR Gail Goodrich/49 5.00 12.00
NCGHW Gordon Hayward/49 5.00 12.00
NCHHK Hersey Hawkins/49 3.00 8.00
NCHOW Hakeem Olajuwon/49 12.00 30.00
NCITM Isaiah Thomas/49 20.00 50.00
NCJDM Joe Dumars/49 6.00 15.00
NCJEV Julius Erving/25 25.00 60.00
NCJGR Jeff Green/49 3.00 8.00
NCJHD Jrue Holiday/49 6.00 15.00
NCJOK Jahlil Okafor/60 8.00 20.00
NCJPK Jabari Parker/49 EXCH 12.00 30.00
NCJRD Julius Randle/49 8.00 20.00
NCJSG Jared Sullinger/49 3.00 8.00
NCJSK John Starks/49 5.00 12.00
NCJWL John Wall/49 15.00 40.00
NCJWS Jerry West/25 20.00 50.00
NCKAT Karl-Anthony Towns/60 75.00 200.00
NCKBR Kobe Bryant/25 5,000.00 10,000.00
NCKDR Kevin Durant/25 50.00 120.00
NCKIR Kyrie Irving/25 30.00 80.00
NCKMH Kevin McHale/49 8.00 20.00
NCKML Karl Malone/25 20.00 50.00
NCKPZ Kristaps Porzingis/60 50.00 120.00
NCLNJ Larry Nance Jr./49 6.00 15.00
NCMGT Marcin Gortat/49 3.00 8.00
NCMHT Marcelo Huertas/49 3.00 8.00
NCMJS Magic Johnson/25 30.00 80.00
NCMRM Mitch Richmond/49 6.00 15.00
NCMST Marcus Smart/49 6.00 15.00
NCMTU Myles Turner/60 10.00 25.00
NCNAB Nate Archibald/49 6.00 15.00
NCNBJ Nemanja Bjelica/49 5.00 12.00
NCNJK Nikola Jokic/49 1,500.00 3,000.00
NCNMT Nikola Mirotic/49 3.00 8.00
NCNPW Norman Powell/49 6.00 15.00
NCPGG Paul George/25 EXCH 30.00 80.00
NCRNT Raul Neto/49 3.00 8.00
NCRPS Robert Parish/49 6.00 15.00
NCRSP Ralph Sampson/49 4.00 10.00
NCSON Shaquille O'Neal/25 40.00 100.00
NCTHJ Tim Hardaway Jr./49 4.00 10.00
NCTJW T.J. Warren/49 5.00 12.00
NCVOD Victor Oladipo/49 8.00 20.00
NCWMW Wesley Matthews/49 3.00 8.00
NCWTV Walter Tavares/49 3.00 8.00
NCWUN Wes Unseld/49 8.00 20.00
NCZLV Zach LaVine/49 20.00 50.00

2015-16 Panini Noir Jumbo Materials Prime

PRINT RUNS B/WN 10-49 COPIES PER
NO PRICING ON QTY 10
2 Kobe Bryant/25 200.00 500.00
3 Russell Westbrook/49 20.00 50.00
4 Klay Thompson/25 15.00 40.00
6 Jae Crowder/49 4.00 10.00
7 Khris Middleton/49 8.00 20.00
8 LeBron James/25 60.00 150.00
10 Arron Afflalo/49 4.00 10.00
11 Jared Sullinger/25 4.00 10.00
12 Timofey Mozgov/49 4.00 10.00
13 Rodney Hood/49 5.00 12.00
14 Stephen Curry/25 60.00 150.00
15 Robin Lopez/49 4.00 10.00
16 Al Horford/49 6.00 15.00
17 Rudy Gobert/49 8.00 20.00
18 Kemba Walker/49 6.00 15.00
19 Langston Galloway/49 4.00 10.00
20 Paul Millsap/25 5.00 12.00
21 Roy Hibbert/49 4.00 10.00
22 Lance Stephenson/25 5.00 12.00
23 John Jenkins/20 4.00 10.00
24 Kosta Koufos/45 4.00 10.00
25 Thaddeus Young/49 4.00 10.00
27 Draymond Green/25 30.00 80.00
28 Rudy Gay/25 6.00 15.00
29 Shane Larkin/49 4.00 10.00
30 Tim Duncan/49 20.00 50.00
31 Evan Fournier/49 10.00 25.00
32 Serge Ibaka/49 6.00 15.00
34 DeMarcus Cousins/49 6.00 15.00
35 Nikola Vucevic/25 5.00 12.00
37 Tony Parker/49 10.00 25.00
38 Tobias Harris/49 5.00 12.00
39 Manu Ginobili/49 12.00 30.00
41 Kevin Durant/49 12.00 30.00
42 Avery Bradley/49 4.00 10.00
43 John Wall/25 12.00 30.00
46 Marcin Gortat/49 4.00 10.00
47 Eric Gordon/49 5.00 12.00
48 Marcus Smart/49 8.00 20.00
49 Jerryd Bayless/45 4.00 10.00
51 Bojan Bogdanovic/49 5.00 12.00
52 Isaiah Thomas/20 10.00 25.00
53 Otto Porter/49 5.00 12.00
55 Joe Johnson/49 5.00 12.00
58 Grant Hill/49 15.00 40.00
59 John Stockton/25 20.00 50.00
60 Shaquille O'Neal/49 20.00 50.00
62 Patrick Ewing/49 12.00 30.00
63 Karl Malone/25 12.00 30.00
65 Scottie Pippen/25 30.00 80.00

2015-16 Panini Noir Rookie Patches Prime

PRINT RUNS B/WN 8-25 COPIES PER
NO PRICING ON QTY 10 OR LESS
2 Justise Winslow/25 6.00 15.00
3 Bobby Portis/25 10.00 25.00
4 Rondae Hollis-Jefferson/25 5.00 12.00
5 D'Angelo Russell/25 15.00 40.00
6 Willie Cauley-Stein/25 5.00 12.00
8 Cliff Alexander/25 4.00 10.00
9 Terry Rozier/25 15.00 40.00
12 Raul Neto/25 4.00 10.00
13 Cristiano Felicio/25 5.00 12.00
16 R.J. Hunter/25 4.00 10.00
19 Myles Turner/25 15.00 40.00
21 Delon Wright/25 5.00 12.00
22 Mario Hezonja/25 5.00 12.00
23 Jerian Grant/25 4.00 10.00
25 Cameron Payne/25 6.00 15.00
26 Kelly Oubre Jr./25 12.00 30.00
28 Josh Richardson/25 6.00 15.00
29 Luis Montero/25 4.00 10.00
30 Rakeem Christmas/25 4.00 10.00
31 Trey Lyles/25 5.00 12.00
32 Justin Anderson/25 12.00 30.00
33 Salah Mejri/25 4.00 10.00
34 Jonathon Simmons/25 5.00 12.00
35 Richaun Holmes/25 6.00 15.00

2015-16 Panini Noir Spotlight Signatures

PRINT RUNS B/WN 25-99 COPIES PER
EXCHANGE DEADLINE 1/20/2018
SS Kenneth Faried/49 10.00 25.00
SSAW Andrew Wiggins/49 60.00 150.00
SSCP Chris Paul/49 125.00 300.00
SSDB Devin Booker/49 1,000.00 2,000.00
SSDG Danilo Gallinari/49 10.00 25.00
SSEB Eric Bledsoe/49 15.00 40.00
SSEM Mudiay/49 EXCH 10.00 25.00
SSEP Elfrid Payton/49 10.00 25.00
SSGA Giannis/99 EXCH 1,000.00 2,000.00
SSGH Gary Harris/99 30.00 80.00
SSHB Harrison Barnes/25 75.00 200.00
SSKI Kyrie Irving/49 150.00 400.00
SSKL Kevin Love/49 25.00 60.00
SSKT Karl-Anthony Towns/49 400.00 800.00
SSTH Tobias Harris/99 10.00 25.00
SSZL Zach LaVine/99 125.00 300.00

2016-17 Panini Noir

1-200 PRINT RUN 79 SER.#'d SETS
RC PRINT RUN 79 SER.#'d SETS
JSY AU PRINT RUN 99 SER.#'d SETS
PATCHES MAY SELL FOR PREMIUM
231-330 PRINT RUN 25 SER.#'d SETS
EXCHANGE DEADLINE 2/19/2019
1 Kevin Durant BW 30.00 80.00
2 Anthony Davis BW 8.00 20.00
3 Chris Paul BW 4.00 10.00
4 Gordon Hayward BW 2.50 6.00
5 C.J. McCollum BW 2.50 6.00
6 Jimmy Butler BW 5.00 12.00
7 Aaron Gordon BW 2.50 6.00
8 Paul George BW 4.00 10.00
9 Brook Lopez BW 2.00 5.00
10 Carmelo Anthony BW 4.00 10.00
11 Zach LaVine BW 5.00 12.00
12 Andre Drummond BW 2.50 6.00
13 Joel Embiid BW 6.00 15.00
14 Dwight Howard BW 3.00 8.00
15 Zach Randolph BW 2.50 6.00
16 Pau Gasol BW 4.00 10.00
17 Marcus Morris BW 1.50 4.00
18 Robert Covington BW 2.00 5.00
19 LeBron James BW 75.00 200.00
20 Devin Booker BW 30.00 80.00
21 Kemba Walker BW 2.00 5.00
22 Karl-Anthony Towns BW 5.00 12.00
23 Kyle Lowry BW 2.50 6.00
24 Gary Harris BW 2.00 5.00
25 Marc Gasol BW 2.50 6.00
26 Tony Parker BW 4.00 10.00
27 Isaiah Thomas BW 2.00 5.00
28 Tyreke Evans BW 2.00 5.00
29 Jordan Clarkson BW 2.50 6.00
30 John Wall BW 3.00 8.00
31 Dirk Nowitzki BW 6.00 15.00
32 Elfrid Payton BW 2.00 5.00
33 Jeff Teague BW 1.50 4.00
34 DeMar DeRozan BW 3.00 8.00
35 Stephen Curry BW 40.00 100.00
36 Eric Bledsoe BW 2.00 5.00
37 Goran Dragic BW 2.50 6.00
38 James Harden BW 5.00 12.00
39 George Hill BW 2.00 5.00
40 Kyrie Irving BW 5.00 12.00
41 Andrew Wiggins BW 3.00 8.00
42 Blake Griffin BW 2.50 6.00
43 Bradley Beal BW 3.00 8.00
44 Klay Thompson BW 6.00 15.00
45 Kawhi Leonard BW 6.00 15.00
46 Paul Millsap BW 2.00 5.00
47 Derrick Rose BW 4.00 10.00
48 Jabari Parker BW 1.50 4.00
49 Nerlens Noel BW 1.50 4.00
50 Victor Oladipo BW 2.00 5.00
51 D'Angelo Russell BW 3.00 8.00
52 Damian Lillard BW 6.00 15.00
53 Dwyane Wade BW 5.00 12.00
54 Russell Westbrook BW 4.00 10.00
55 Mike Conley BW 2.00 5.00
56 Jeremy Lin BW 5.00 12.00
57 Jahlil Okafor BW 1.50 4.00
58 J.J. Redick BW 2.00 5.00
59 Giannis Antetokounmpo BW 30.00 80.00
60 Nikola Jokic BW 12.00 30.00
61 Kristaps Porzingis BW 4.00 10.00
62 Nicolas Batum BW 2.00 5.00
63 Dion Waiters BW 1.50 4.00
64 Myles Turner BW 2.50 6.00
65 Nick Young BW 1.50 4.00
66 Eric Gordon BW 2.00 5.00
67 Kevin Love BW 2.50 6.00
68 Tobias Harris BW 2.50 6.00
69 Seth Curry BW 2.00 5.00
70 Jae Crowder BW 1.50 4.00
71 Brandon Ingram BW RC 30.00 80.00
72 Ben Simmons BW RC 6.00 15.00
73 Jaylen Brown BW RC 50.00 120.00
74 Jamal Murray BW RC 30.00 80.00
75 Malcolm Brogdon BW RC 6.00 15.00
76 Thon Maker BW RC 2.50 6.00
77 Buddy Hield BW RC 6.00 15.00
78 Dario Saric BW RC 3.00 8.00
79 Denzel Valentine BW RC 2.00 5.00
80 Dragan Bender BW RC 2.00 5.00
81 Domantas Sabonis BW RC 12.00 30.00
82 Willy Hernangomez BW RC 2.50 6.00
83 Marquese Chriss BW RC 2.50 6.00
84 Kris Dunn BW RC 3.00 8.00
85 Jakob Poeltl BW RC 4.00 10.00
86 Skal Labissiere BW RC 2.00 5.00
87 Timothe Luwawu-Cabarrot BW RC 3.00 8.00
88 Yogi Ferrell BW RC 2.50 6.00
89 Malik Beasley BW RC 5.00 12.00
90 Juan Hernangomez BW RC 4.00 10.00
91 Wade Baldwin IV BW RC 2.00 5.00
92 Taurean Prince BW RC 2.50 6.00
93 Patrick McCaw BW RC 2.00 5.00
94 Malachi Richardson BW RC 2.00 5.00
95 Tyler Ulis BW RC 2.50 6.00
96 Pascal Siakam BW RC 12.00 30.00
97 Ivica Zubac BW RC 5.00 12.00
98 Henry Ellenson BW RC 2.00 5.00
99 Deyonta Davis BW RC 2.00 5.00
100 Caris LeVert BW RC 5.00 12.00
101 Brown BW JSY AU 500.00 1,000.00
102 Demetrius Jackson BW JSY AU 5.00 12.00
103 Caris LeVert BW JSY AU 12.00 30.00
104 Valentine BW JSY AU 6.00 15.00
105 Kay Felder BW JSY AU 6.00 15.00
106 Hernangomez BW JSY AU 25.00 60.00
107 Jamal Murray BW JSY AU 300.00 600.00
108 H. Ellenson BW JSY AU 5.00 12.00
109 Isaiah Whitehead BW JSY AU 5.00 12.00
110 Chinanu Onuaku BW JSY AU 5.00 12.00
111 Georges Niang BW JSY AU 8.00 20.00
112 Diamond Stone BW JSY AU 5.00 12.00
113 Brice Johnson BW JSY AU 5.00 12.00
114 Ivica Zubac BW JSY AU 12.00 30.00
115 Ingram BW JSY AU 200.00 500.00
116 Deyonta Davis BW JSY AU 5.00 12.00
117 Wade Baldwin IV BW JSY AU 5.00 12.00
118 Brogdon BW JSY AU 15.00 40.00
119 Thon Maker BW JSY AU 6.00 15.00
120 Kris Dunn BW JSY AU 8.00 20.00
121 Hield BW JSY AU 15.00 40.00
122 Sabonis BW JSY AU 40.00 100.00
123 Stephen Zimmerman BW JSY AU 5.00 12.00
124 Lwwu-Cbrrt BW JSY AU 8.00 20.00
125 Chriss BW JSY AU 6.00 15.00
126 D. Bender BW JSY AU 5.00 12.00
127 Tyler Ulis BW JSY AU 6.00 15.00
128 Labissiere BW JSY AU 5.00 12.00
129 Murray BW JSY AU 200.00 500.00
130 Pascal Siakam BW JSY AU 125.00 300.00
131 Kevin Durant CLR 30.00 80.00
132 Anthony Davis CLR 8.00 20.00
133 Chris Paul CLR 4.00 10.00
134 Gordon Hayward CLR 2.50 6.00
135 C.J. McCollum CLR 2.50 6.00
136 Jimmy Butler CLR 5.00 12.00
137 Aaron Gordon CLR 2.50 6.00
138 Paul George CLR 4.00 10.00
139 Brook Lopez CLR 2.00 5.00
140 Carmelo Anthony CLR 4.00 10.00
141 Zach LaVine CLR 5.00 12.00
142 Andre Drummond CLR 2.50 6.00
143 Joel Embiid CLR 6.00 15.00
144 Dwight Howard CLR 3.00 8.00
145 Zach Randolph CLR 2.50 6.00
146 Pau Gasol CLR 4.00 10.00
147 Marcus Morris CLR 1.50 4.00
148 Robert Covington CLR 2.00 5.00
149 LeBron James CLR 75.00 200.00
150 Devin Booker CLR 30.00 80.00
151 Kemba Walker CLR 2.00 5.00
152 Karl-Anthony Towns CLR 5.00 12.00
153 Kyle Lowry CLR 2.50 6.00
154 Gary Harris CLR 2.00 5.00
155 Marc Gasol CLR 2.50 6.00
156 Tony Parker CLR 4.00 10.00
157 Isaiah Thomas CLR 2.00 5.00
158 Tyreke Evans CLR 2.00 5.00
159 Jordan Clarkson CLR 2.50 6.00
160 John Wall CLR 3.00 8.00
161 Dirk Nowitzki CLR 6.00 15.00
162 Elfrid Payton CLR 2.00 5.00
163 Jeff Teague CLR 1.50 4.00
164 DeMar DeRozan CLR 3.00 8.00
165 Stephen Curry CLR 40.00 100.00
166 Eric Bledsoe CLR 2.00 5.00
167 Goran Dragic CLR 2.50 6.00
168 James Harden CLR 5.00 12.00
169 George Hill CLR 2.00 5.00
170 Kyrie Irving CLR 5.00 12.00
171 Andrew Wiggins CLR 3.00 8.00
172 Blake Griffin CLR 2.50 6.00
173 Bradley Beal CLR 3.00 8.00
174 Klay Thompson CLR 6.00 15.00
175 Kawhi Leonard CLR 6.00 15.00
176 Paul Millsap CLR 2.00 5.00
177 Derrick Rose CLR 4.00 10.00
178 Jabari Parker CLR 1.50 4.00
179 Nerlens Noel CLR 1.50 4.00
180 Victor Oladipo CLR 2.00 5.00
181 D'Angelo Russell CLR 3.00 8.00
182 Damian Lillard CLR 6.00 15.00
183 Dwyane Wade CLR 5.00 12.00
184 Russell Westbrook CLR 4.00 10.00
185 Mike Conley CLR 2.00 5.00
186 Jeremy Lin CLR 5.00 12.00
187 Jahlil Okafor CLR 1.50 4.00
188 J.J. Redick CLR 2.50 6.00
189 G. Antetokounmpo CLR 30.00 80.00
190 Nikola Jokic CLR 12.00 30.00
191 Kristaps Porzingis CLR 4.00 10.00
192 Nicolas Batum CLR 2.00 5.00
193 Dion Waiters CLR 1.50 4.00
194 Myles Turner CLR 2.50 6.00
195 Nick Young CLR 1.50 4.00
196 Eric Gordon CLR 2.00 5.00
197 Kevin Love CLR 2.50 6.00
198 Tobias Harris CLR 2.50 6.00
199 Seth Curry CLR 2.00 5.00
200 Jae Crowder CLR 1.50 4.00
201 Brandon Ingram CLR RC 30.00 80.00
202 Ben Simmons CLR RC 6.00 15.00
203 Jaylen Brown CLR RC 50.00 120.00
204 Jamal Murray CLR RC 30.00 80.00
205 Malcolm Brogdon CLR RC 6.00 15.00
206 Thon Maker CLR RC 2.50 6.00
207 Buddy Hield CLR RC 6.00 15.00
208 Dario Saric CLR RC 3.00 8.00
209 Denzel Valentine CLR RC 2.00 5.00
210 Dragan Bender CLR RC 2.00 5.00
211 Domantas Sabonis CLR RC 12.00 30.00
212 Willy Hernangomez CLR RC 2.50 6.00
213 Marquese Chriss CLR RC 2.50 6.00
214 Kris Dunn CLR RC 3.00 8.00
215 Jakob Poeltl CLR RC 4.00 10.00
216 Skal Labissiere CLR RC 2.00 5.00
217 Timothe Luwawu-Cabarrot CLR RC 3.00 8.00
218 Yogi Ferrell CLR RC 2.50 6.00
219 Malik Beasley CLR RC 4.00 10.00
220 Juan Hernangomez CLR RC 4.00 10.00
221 Wade Baldwin IV CLR RC 2.00 5.00
222 Taurean Prince CLR RC 2.50 6.00
223 Patrick McCaw CLR RC 2.00 5.00
224 Malachi Richardson CLR RC 2.00 5.00
225 Tyler Ulis CLR RC 2.50 6.00
226 Pascal Siakam CLR RC 12.00 30.00
227 Ivica Zubac CLR RC 5.00 12.00
228 Henry Ellenson CLR RC 2.00 5.00
229 Deyonta Davis CLR RC 2.00 5.00
230 Caris LeVert CLR RC 5.00 12.00
231 Kevin Durant MET 40.00 100.00
232 Kyrie Irving MET 20.00 50.00
233 John Wall MET 12.00 30.00
234 Stephen Curry MET 60.00 150.00
235 Russell Westbrook MET 15.00 40.00
236 James Harden MET 20.00 50.00
237 Towns MET 20.00 50.00
238 Carmelo Anthony MET 15.00 40.00
239 Dwyane Wade MET 20.00 50.00
240 Damian Lillard MET 25.00 60.00
241 Jimmy Butler MET 20.00 50.00
242 Anthony Davis MET 30.00 80.00
243 Kawhi Leonard MET 25.00 60.00
244 Blake Griffin MET 10.00 25.00
245 DeMarcus Cousins MET 8.00 20.00
246 LeBron James MET 60.00 150.00
247 Chris Paul MET 15.00 40.00
248 Paul George MET 15.00 40.00
249 DeMar DeRozan MET 12.00 30.00
250 Nikola Jokic MET 50.00 120.00
251 Isaiah Thomas MET 8.00 20.00
252 Rudy Gobert MET 12.00 30.00
253 Kemba Walker MET 8.00 20.00
254 Marc Gasol MET 10.00 25.00
255 Kyle Lowry MET 10.00 25.00
256 Antetokounmpo MET 50.00 120.00
257 Gordon Hayward MET 8.00 20.00
258 Kevin Love MET 10.00 25.00
259 Klay Thompson MET 25.00 60.00
260 Dirk Nowitzki MET 25.00 60.00
261 Brandon Ingram MET 100.00 250.00
262 Ben Simmons MET 20.00 50.00
263 Malcolm Brogdon MET 20.00 50.00
264 Kris Dunn MET 10.00 25.00
265 Marquese Chriss MET 8.00 20.00
266 Buddy Hield MET 20.00 50.00
267 Thon Maker MET 8.00 20.00
268 Jamal Murray MET 50.00 120.00
269 Jaylen Brown MET 150.00 400.00
270 Denzel Valentine MET 6.00 15.00
271 Yogi Ferrell MET 8.00 20.00
272 Dario Saric MET 10.00 25.00
273 Willy Hernangomez MET 8.00 20.00
274 Isaiah Whitehead MET 6.00 15.00
275 Pascal Siakam MET 25.00 60.00
276 Dragan Bender MET 6.00 15.00
277 Patrick McCaw MET 6.00 15.00
278 Mindaugas Kuzminskas MET 6.00 15.00
279 Paul Zipser MET 6.00 15.00
280 Dejounte Murray MET 30.00 80.00
281 Kobe Bryant MET CC 200.00 500.00
282 Ray Allen MET CC 15.00 40.00
283 Tim Duncan MET CC 30.00 80.00
284 O'Neal MET CC 30.00 80.00
285 Allen Iverson MET CC 15.00 40.00
286 Steve Nash MET CC 15.00 40.00
287 David Robinson MET CC 20.00 50.00
288 Larry Bird MET CC 40.00 100.00
289 Magic Johnson MET CC 40.00 100.00
290 Olajuwon MET CC 15.00 40.00
291 Dikembe Mutombo MET CC 15.00 40.00
292 John Stockton MET CC 20.00 50.00
293 Abdul-Jabbar MET CC 30.00 80.00
294 Karl Malone MET CC 15.00 40.00
295 Gary Payton MET CC 25.00 60.00
296 Yao Ming MET CC 25.00 60.00
297 Grant Hill MET CC 15.00 40.00
298 Jason Kidd MET CC 15.00 40.00
299 Julius Erving MET CC 25.00 60.00
300 Scottie Pippen MET CC 20.00 50.00
301 Kobe Bryant MET ENC 200.00 500.00
302 Rudy Tomjanovich MET ENC 8.00 20.00
303 Chamberlain MET ENC 30.00 80.00
304 LeBron James MET ENC 60.00 150.00
305 Dirk Nowitzki MET ENC 25.00 60.00
306 Magic Johnson MET ENC 40.00 100.00
307 Elgin Baylor MET ENC 20.00 50.00
308 Abdul-Jabbar MET ENC 30.00 80.00
309 Tim Duncan MET ENC 30.00 80.00
310 O'Neal MET ENC 30.00 80.00
311 Kobe Bryant MET ENC 200.00 500.00
312 David Robinson MET ENC 20.00 50.00
313 Bill Russell MET ENC 30.00 80.00
314 Allen Iverson MET ENC 15.00 40.00
315 Dwyane Wade MET ENC 20.00 50.00
316 Spud Webb MET ENC 10.00 25.00
317 Larry Bird MET ENC 40.00 100.00
318 John Havlicek MET ENC 25.00 60.00
319 Willis Reed MET ENC 15.00 40.00
320 Grvn/Thmpsn MET ENC 15.00 40.00
321 Stephen Curry MET ART 200.00 500.00
322 LeBron James MET ART 300.00 600.00
323 Kevin Durant MET ART 150.00 300.00
324 Kyrie Irving MET ART 60.00 150.00
325 Westbrook MET ART 50.00 125.00
326 James Harden MET ART 60.00 150.00
327 Anthony Davis MET ART 100.00 250.00
328 Towns MET ART 60.00 150.00
329 Ingram MET ART 125.00 300.00
330 Simmons MET ART 60.00 150.00

2016-17 Panini Noir Autograph Materials Prime Black and White

STATED PRINT RUN 40 SER.#'d SETS
EXCHANGE DEADLINE 2/16/2019
*COLOR/40: .4X TO 1X BASIC
1 Kevin Durant 100.00 250.00
2 Jeremy Lin 50.00 120.00
3 Karl Malone 30.00 80.00
4 Alex English 10.00 25.00
6 Michael Kidd-Gilchrist 5.00 12.00
7 Kyrie Irving 50.00 120.00
8 Evan Turner 5.00 12.00
9 Isaiah Thomas 10.00 25.00
10 Magic Johnson 50.00 120.00
12 Kobe Bryant 5,000.00 10,000.00
14 Kevin Love 12.00 30.00
15 Kenneth Faried 6.00 15.00
16 Vince Carter 40.00 100.00
17 Larry Bird 50.00 120.00
18 Karl-Anthony Towns 50.00 120.00
19 George Hill 6.00 15.00
20 Ryan Anderson 5.00 12.00
21 Jimmy Butler 25.00 60.00
23 Anthony Davis 125.00 300.00
25 Andrew Wiggins 25.00 60.00
26 Jae Crowder 5.00 12.00
27 Luol Deng 6.00 15.00
28 Tobias Harris 8.00 20.00
29 Clint Capela 10.00 25.00
30 John Wall 30.00 80.00
31 Hakeem Olajuwon 25.00 60.00
32 C.J. McCollum 25.00 60.00
33 Bojan Bogdanovic 6.00 15.00
35 Nikola Mirotic 5.00 12.00
36 Myles Turner 12.00 30.00
37 John Stockton 30.00 80.00
38 Grant Hill 30.00 80.00
39 Shaquille O'Neal 60.00 150.00
40 Jordan Clarkson 8.00 20.00

2016-17 Panini Noir Autographs Color

PRINT RUNS B/WN 75-99 COPIES PER
EXCHANGE DEADLINE 2/16/2019
*GOLD/25: .5X TO 1.2X BASIC
1 Paul Millsap/75 6.00 15.00
3 Jae Crowder/75 3.00 8.00
4 Bojan Bogdanovic/99 4.00 10.00
5 Jeremy Lin/75 40.00 100.00
6 Michael Kidd-Gilchrist/75 3.00 8.00
7 Bobby Portis/75 8.00 20.00
8 Michael Carter-Williams/75 3.00 8.00
9 Dwyane Wade/75 25.00 60.00
10 Tristan Thompson/99 4.00 10.00
11 Kevin Love/75 10.00 25.00
12 Kyrie Irving/75 40.00 100.00
13 J.J. Barea/99 15.00 40.00
14 Devin Harris/75 3.00 8.00
15 Justin Anderson/75 3.00 8.00
16 Danilo Gallinari/99 4.00 10.00
17 Kenneth Faried/75 4.00 10.00
18 Tobias Harris/75 5.00 12.00
19 Zaza Pachulia/99 3.00 8.00
20 Kevin Durant/75 125.00 300.00
21 Ryan Anderson/75 3.00 8.00
22 Clint Capela/99 15.00 40.00
23 Myles Turner/75 10.00 25.00
24 Joe Young/99 3.00 8.00
25 Jordan Clarkson/75 25.00 60.00
26 Julius Randle/75 5.00 12.00
27 Luol Deng/99 4.00 10.00
28 Marc Gasol/75 8.00 20.00
29 Zach Randolph/75 5.00 12.00
30 Tyler Johnson/99 5.00 12.00
31 Karl-Anthony Towns/75 60.00 150.00
33 Anthony Davis/75 30.00 80.00
34 Jrue Holiday/99 8.00 20.00
35 Kristaps Porzingis/99 25.00 60.00
36 Justin Holiday/99 4.00 10.00
37 Elfrid Payton/99 6.00 15.00
38 Nikola Vucevic/99 5.00 12.00
39 Alan Williams/99 3.00 8.00
40 Eric Bledsoe/75 4.00 10.00
41 Allen Crabbe/99 3.00 8.00
42 C.J. McCollum/75 12.00 30.00
43 Evan Turner/75 3.00 8.00
44 Pau Gasol/75 8.00 20.00
45 Tony Parker/75 20.00 50.00
46 George Hill/75 4.00 10.00
47 John Wall/75 30.00 80.00
48 Larry Bird/75 75.00 200.00
49 Dennis Rodman/75 40.00 100.00
50 Hakeem Olajuwon/75 20.00 50.00
51 Shaquille O'Neal/75 75.00 200.00
52 Kareem Abdul-Jabbar/75 75.00 200.00
53 Magic Johnson/75 75.00 200.00
54 Jerry West/75 20.00 50.00
55 Alonzo Mourning/75 25.00 60.00
56 Allen Iverson/75 100.00 250.00
57 Bill Walton/75 40.00 100.00
58 George Gervin/75 10.00 25.00
59 Karl Malone/75 25.00 60.00
60 John Stockton/75 20.00 50.00
61 Kobe Bryant/75 4,000.00 8,000.00
62 David Robinson/75 25.00 60.00
63 Grant Hill/75 25.00 60.00
64 Jason Kidd/75 20.00 50.00
65 Ray Allen/75 20.00 50.00
66 Isaiah Thomas/75 20.00 50.00
67 Nikola Mirotic/99 6.00 15.00
68 Giannis Antetokounmpo/75 500.00 1,000.00
69 Reggie Jackson/75 4.00 10.00
70 Marc Gasol/75 10.00 25.00
71 Justise Winslow/99 4.00 10.00
72 Carmelo Anthony/75 25.00 60.00
73 Evan Fournier/75 5.00 12.00
74 Devin Booker/75 200.00 500.00
75 Andrew Wiggins/75 15.00 40.00
76 Marcin Gortat/99 3.00 8.00
77 Dominique Wilkins/75 15.00 40.00
78 Latrell Sprewell/99 6.00 15.00

2016-17 Panini Noir Jumbo Materials

PRINT RUNS B/WN 30-99 COPIES PER
*PRIME/21-25: 1X TO 2.5X BASIC
1 Kevin Durant/99 10.00 25.00

3 Tim Duncan/99 6.00 15.00
4 Carmelo Anthony/99 5.00 12.00
5 Kevin Love/99 3.00 8.00
6 David Robinson/99 6.00 15.00
7 Russell Westbrook/99 6.00 15.00
8 Pau Gasol/99 5.00 12.00
9 Jeremy Lin/99 6.00 15.00
10 DeMarcus Cousins/99 2.50 6.00
11 Kristaps Porzingis/99 5.00 12.00
12 Kawhi Leonard/99 8.00 20.00
13 Blake Griffin/99 3.00 8.00
14 Kevin McHale/40 5.00 12.00
15 Giannis Antetokounmpo/99 15.00 40.00
16 Dennis Rodman/99 6.00 15.00
17 Jimmy Butler/99 6.00 15.00
18 Larry Bird/49 12.00 30.00
19 Joel Embiid/99 8.00 20.00
20 Devin Booker/99 12.00 30.00
21 John Havlicek/30 8.00 20.00
22 Kyrie Irving/99 8.00 20.00
23 Dikembe Mutombo/99 8.00 20.00
24 John Stockton/30 10.00 25.00
25 DeMar DeRozan/99 4.00 10.00
26 Julius Erving/30 8.00 20.00
27 Patrick Ewing/99 4.00 10.00
28 James Worthy/99 4.00 10.00
30 Karl Malone/99 5.00 12.00
31 John Wall/99 4.00 10.00
32 James Harden/99 6.00 15.00
33 Dwyane Wade/99 5.00 12.00
34 Allen Iverson/99 6.00 15.00
35 Karl-Anthony Towns/99 6.00 15.00
36 Clyde Drexler/99 5.00 12.00
37 Myles Turner/75 3.00 8.00
38 Kobe Bryant/99 200.00 500.00
39 Andrew Wiggins/99 4.00 10.00
40 Grant Hill/99 6.00 15.00
41 Paul George/89 5.00 12.00
42 Marc Gasol/99 3.00 8.00
43 D'Angelo Russell/99 4.00 10.00
44 Jason Kidd/99 5.00 12.00
45 Michael Finley/99 3.00 8.00
46 Zach LaVine/99 6.00 15.00
47 Damian Lillard/99 8.00 20.00
48 Jahlil Okafor/99 2.00 5.00
49 Bradley Beal/99 4.00 10.00
50 Tony Parker/99 5.00 12.00
51 Derrick Rose/99 5.00 12.00
52 Anthony Davis/99 10.00 25.00
53 Draymond Green/99 4.00 10.00
54 Chris Paul/99 5.00 12.00
55 Jabari Parker/99 2.00 5.00
56 Ray Allen/99 5.00 12.00
57 Hakeem Olajuwon/99 6.00 15.00
58 Manu Ginobili/99 5.00 12.00
59 Isaiah Thomas/99 2.50 6.00
60 Alex English/99 2.50 6.00
61 Isiah Thomas/99 5.00 12.00
62 Dirk Nowitzki/99 6.00 15.00
63 Bernard King/49 4.00 10.00
64 Gordon Hayward/99 3.00 8.00
65 Dominique Wilkins/99 4.00 10.00
66 Stephen Curry/99 15.00 40.00
67 Joe Dumars/99 3.00 8.00
68 Klay Thompson/99 8.00 20.00
69 Joakim Noah/99 2.00 5.00
70 Dwight Howard/99 4.00 10.00
71 Scottie Pippen/99 6.00 15.00
72 Shaquille O'Neal/48 12.00 30.00
73 Danny Ainge/99 3.00 8.00
74 Harrison Barnes/99 2.50 6.00
75 Magic Johnson/30 12.00 30.00
76 Detlef Schrempf/99 3.00 8.00
77 Mike Conley/99 2.50 6.00
78 Christian Laettner/99 3.00 8.00
79 Zach Randolph/99 3.00 8.00
80 LeBron James/99 15.00 40.00

2016-17 Panini Noir Materials Black and White Prime

1 Dirk Nowitzki/49 10.00 25.00
2 J.J. Barea/49 2.00 5.00
3 Derrick Rose/49 8.00 20.00
4 Joakim Noah/35 2.50 6.00
5 Rondae Hollis-Jefferson/49 2.50 6.00
6 Kawhi Leonard/49 12.00 30.00
7 Manu Ginobili/49 6.00 15.00
8 Tony Parker/49 6.00 15.00
9 Marcus Smart/49 5.00 12.00
10 Avery Bradley/49 2.50 6.00
11 Paul George/49 6.00 15.00
12 Jeff Teague/49 2.50 6.00
13 Willie Cauley-Stein/49 3.00 8.00
14 Rudy Gay/35 4.00 10.00
15 LeBron James/49 30.00 80.00
16 J.R. Smith/49 5.00 12.00
17 Robert Covington/49 3.00 8.00
18 Nerlens Noel/49 2.50 6.00
19 Greg Monroe/49 2.50 6.00
20 John Henson/49 2.50 6.00
21 Nikola Vucevic/49 4.00 10.00
22 Serge Ibaka/49 3.00 8.00
23 Evan Fournier/30 3.00 8.00
24 Tyus Jones/49 2.50 6.00
25 Nemanja Bjelica/49 2.50 6.00
26 Gorgui Dieng/49 2.50 6.00
28 Thabo Sefolosha/25 6.00 15.00
30 Al Horford/49 4.00 10.00
31 Jeremy Lamb/49 2.50 6.00
32 Jimmy Butler/49 5.00 12.00
33 Nikola Mirotic/35 2.50 6.00
34 Richard Jefferson/49 3.00 8.00
35 Danilo Gallinari/49 3.00 8.00
37 Tobias Harris/49 4.00 10.00
39 George Hill/49 3.00 8.00
40 Dwyane Wade/49 10.00 25.00
41 Myles Turner/30 4.00 10.00
42 Julius Randle/25 6.00 15.00
43 Jordan Clarkson/49 5.00 12.00
44 Timofey Mozgov/49 2.50 6.00
45 Marc Gasol/49 4.00 10.00
46 Zach Randolph/49 4.00 10.00
48 Steven Adams/49 8.00 20.00
49 Andre Roberson/49 2.50 6.00
50 Mason Plumlee/49 2.50 6.00
51 Terrence Ross/49 3.00 8.00
52 DeMar DeRozan/49 5.00 12.00
53 Jonas Valanciunas/49 3.00 8.00
54 Alec Burks/49 3.00 8.00
55 Gordon Hayward/49 4.00 10.00
56 Derrick Favors/49 2.50 6.00
57 Bradley Beal/49 5.00 12.00
58 Kelly Oubre Jr./49 5.00 12.00
59 Marcin Gortat/30 2.50 6.00
60 Markieff Morris/35 2.50 6.00
61 Mike Bibby/49 6.00 15.00
62 Danny Ainge/49 4.00 10.00
63 Richard Hamilton/30 3.00 8.00
64 Shawn Marion/49 3.00 8.00
65 Michael Redd/49 3.00 8.00
66 Christian Laettner/49 4.00 10.00
67 Amare Stoudemire/49 5.00 12.00
68 Jason Richardson/49 4.00 10.00
69 Tom Chambers/35 3.00 8.00
70 Kevin Duckworth/49 2.50 6.00

2016-17 Panini Noir Materials Color Prime

*CLR/25-49: .4X TO 1X BASE B/W
PRINT RUNS B/WN 8-49 COPIES PER
NO PRICING ON QTY 15 OR LESS
38 Klay Thompson/35 15.00 40.00

2016-17 Panini Noir Rookie Jumbo Materials

STATED PRINT RUN 99 SER.#'d SETS
*PRIME/25: 1X TO 2.5X BASIC
1 Brandon Ingram 8.00 20.00
2 Jamal Murray 15.00 40.00
3 Kay Felder 2.00 5.00
4 Jaylen Brown 40.00 100.00
5 Jakob Poeltl 4.00 10.00
6 Denzel Valentine 2.00 5.00
7 Buddy Hield 6.00 15.00
8 Kris Dunn 3.00 8.00
9 Dragan Bender 2.00 5.00
10 Malcolm Brogdon 6.00 15.00
11 Tyler Ulis 2.50 6.00
12 Pascal Siakam 12.00 30.00
13 Dejounte Murray 10.00 25.00
14 Thon Maker 2.50 6.00
15 Timothe Luwawu-Cabarrot 3.00 8.00
16 Patrick McCaw 2.00 5.00
17 Willy Hernangomez 2.50 6.00
18 Marquese Chriss 2.50 6.00
19 Wade Baldwin IV 2.00 5.00
20 Domantas Sabonis 12.00 30.00

2016-17 Panini Noir Rookie Materials Black and White Prime

PRINT RUNS B/WN 8-49 COPIES PER
NO PRICING ON QTY 15 OR LESS
*PATCH/20-25: .5X TO 1.2X BASE B/W
1 Demetrius Jackson/99 2.50 6.00
2 Caris LeVert/99 6.00 15.00
3 Denzel Valentine/99 2.50 6.00
4 Kay Felder/99 2.50 6.00
5 A.J. Hammons/99 2.50 6.00
6 Jamal Murray/99 50.00 120.00
7 Juan Hernangomez/99 5.00 12.00
8 Henry Ellenson/61 8.00 20.00
9 Patrick McCaw/99 2.50 6.00
10 Damian Jones/99 2.50 6.00
11 Chinanu Onuaku/76 2.50 6.00
12 Brice Johnson/99 2.50 6.00
13 Diamond Stone/99 2.50 6.00
14 Brandon Ingram/99 10.00 25.00
15 Ivica Zubac/99 6.00 15.00
16 Deyonta Davis/99 2.50 6.00
17 Wade Baldwin IV/99 2.50 6.00
18 Thon Maker/33 15.00 40.00
19 Malcolm Brogdon/99 8.00 20.00
21 Cheick Diallo/99 2.50 6.00
22 Tyler Ulis/99 3.00 8.00
23 Marquese Chriss/35 3.00 8.00
24 Stephen Zimmerman/99 2.50 6.00
26 Skal Labissiere/99 2.50 6.00
27 Malachi Richardson/99 2.50 6.00
28 Dejounte Murray/99 12.00 30.00
29 Isaiah Whitehead/99 2.50 6.00
30 T. Luwawu-Cabarrot/99 4.00 10.00

2016-17 Panini Noir Rookie Materials Color Prime

*CLR/45-99: .4X TO 1X BASE B/W
PRINT RUNS B/WN 45-99 COPIES PER

2016-17 Panini Noir Rookie Patch Autographs Black and White Horizontal

*BW HOR: .5X TO 1.2X BASIC
STATED PRINT RUN 35 SER.#'d SETS
EXCHANGE DEADLINE 2/16/2019

2016-17 Panini Noir Rookie Patch Autographs Color

*CLR: .4X TO 1X BASIC
STATED PRINT RUN 75 SER.#'d SETS
EXCHANGE DEADLINE 2/16/2019

2016-17 Panini Noir Rookie Patch Autographs Color Horizontal

*CLR HOR: .5X TO 1.2X BASIC
STATED PRINT RUN 35 SER.#'d SETS
EXCHANGE DEADLINE 2/16/2019

2016-17 Panini Noir Spotlight Signatures

PRINT RUNS B/WN 75-125 COPIES PER
EXCHANGE DEADLINE 2/16/2019
1 Jamal Murray EXCH 125.00 300.00
2 Dario Saric EXCH 25.00 60.00
3 Joel Embiid/125 300.00 600.00
4 Ricky Rubio/125 40.00 100.00
5 Karl-Anthony Towns/125 75.00 200.00
6 Kobe Bryant/125 5,000.00 10,000.00
7 Kristaps Porzingis/125 100.00 250.00
8 Ray Allen/125 125.00 300.00
9 C.J. McCollum/125 50.00 120.00
10 Damian Lillard EXCH 125.00 300.00
11 Dwyane Wade/125 200.00 500.00
12 Jimmy Butler EXCH 60.00 150.00
13 Tyler Johnson/125 15.00 40.00
14 Dirk Nowitzki/75 1,500.00 3,000.00
15 Malik Beasley/125 20.00 50.00
16 Kevin Durant/125 400.00 800.00
17 Stephen Curry/125 1,000.00 2,000.00
18 Andrew Wiggins/125 40.00 100.00
19 Eric Gordon/125 15.00 40.00
20 Dikembe Mutombo/125 30.00 [illegible]0.00
21 Evan Turner EXCH 10.00 [illegible]5.00
22 Isaiah Thomas EXCH 25.00 [illegible]0.00

2017-18 Panini Noir

1-200 PRINT RUN 79 SER.#'d SETS
RC PRINT RUN 79 SER.#'d SETS
201-300 PRINT RUN 25 SER.#'d SETS
1 Damian Lillard H 6.00 5.00
2 Klay Thompson H 6.00 5.00
3 DeMar DeRozan H 3.00 8.00
4 Blake Griffin H 2.50 6.00
5 Mike Conley H 2.00 5.00
6 Kyrie Irving H 5.00 2.00
7 Karl-Anthony Towns H 4.00 0.00
8 Dwight Howard H 3.00 8.00
9 Paul George H 4.00 0.00
10 Dirk Nowitzki H 6.00 5.00
11 CJ McCollum H 2.50 6.00
12 Kevin Durant H 10.00 25.00
13 Kyle Lowry H 2.50 6.00
14 DeAndre Jordan H 2.00 5.00
15 Goran Dragic H 2.00 5.00
16 Al Horford H 2.50 6.00
17 Anthony Davis H 6.00 15.00
18 Zach LaVine H 4.00 10.00
19 Elfrid Payton H 1.50 4.00
20 Harrison Barnes H 2.00 5.00
21 Zach Randolph H 2.50 6.00
22 Draymond Green H 3.00 8.00
23 Ricky Rubio H 2.00 5.00
24 Lou Williams H 2.00 5.00
25 Hassan Whiteside H 2.00 5.00
26 Dennis Schroder H 2.00 5.00
27 DeMarcus Cousins H 2.00 5.00
28 Kris Dunn H 1.50 4.00
29 Nikola Vucevic H 2.00 5.00
30 Gary Harris H 2.00 5.00
31 Vince Carter H 5.00 12.00
32 Chris Paul H 4.00 10.00
33 Derrick Favors H 1.50 4.00
34 Kentavious Caldwell-Pope H 2.00 5.00
35 Eric Bledsoe H 2.00 5.00
36 Taurean Prince H 1.50 4.00
37 Kristaps Porzingis H 3.00 8.00
38 LeBron James H 20.00 50.00
39 Ben Simmons H 2.50 6.00
40 Nikola Jokic H 15.00 40.00
41 Kawhi Leonard H 6.00 15.00
42 James Harden H 5.00 12.00
43 John Wall H 3.00 8.00
44 Brandon Ingram H 3.00 8.00
45 Giannis Antetokounmpo H 12.00 30.00
46 D'Angelo Russell H 2.00 5.00
47 Enes Kanter H 2.00 5.00
48 Kevin Love H 2.50 6.00
49 Joel Embiid H 6.00 15.00
50 Tobias Harris H 2.00 5.00
51 LaMarcus Aldridge H 2.50 6.00
52 Victor Oladipo H 2.50 6.00
53 Bradley Beal H 3.00 8.00
54 Tyreke Evans H 1.50 4.00
55 Jimmy Butler H 4.00 10.00
56 Rondae Hollis-Jefferson H 1.50 4.00
57 Russell Westbrook H 4.00 10.00
58 Dwyane Wade H 3.00 8.00
59 Devin Booker H 6.00 15.00
60 Andre Drummond H 4.00 10.00
61 Tony Parker H 4.00 10.00
62 Domantas Sabonis H 6.00 15.00
63 Marcin Gortat H 1.50 4.00
64 Marc Gasol H 2.50 6.00
65 Andrew Wiggins H 3.00 8.00
66 Kemba Walker H 2.50 6.00
67 Carmelo Anthony H 4.00 10.00
68 Isaiah Thomas H 2.50 6.00
69 TJ Warren H 2.00 5.00
70 Stephen Curry H 20.00 50.00
71 Malik Monk H RC 10.00 25.00
72 Bam Adebayo H RC 15.00 40.00
73 Zach Collins H RC 4.00 10.00
74 Jarrett Allen H RC 6.00 15.00
75 Lauri Markkanen H RC 15.00 40.00
76 Jordan Bell H RC 2.50 6.00
77 Bogdan Bogdanovic H RC 6.00 15.00
78 Josh Jackson H RC 3.00 8.00
79 Markelle Fultz H RC 6.00 15.00
80 John Collins H RC 6.00 15.00
81 Milos Teodosic H RC 3.00 8.00
82 Jawun Evans H RC 2.00 5.00
83 Kyle Kuzma H RC 10.00 25.00
84 Daniel Theis H RC 3.00 8.00
85 Lonzo Ball H RC 10.00 25.00
86 Frank Mason III H RC 2.50 6.00
87 Dennis Smith Jr. H RC 3.00 8.00
88 OG Anunoby H RC 12.00 30.00
89 Zhou Qi H RC 2.00 5.00
90 Josh Hart H RC 5.00 12.00
91 Jonathan Isaac H RC 5.00 12.00
92 Luke Kennard H RC 5.00 12.00
93 Donovan Mitchell H RC 40.00 100.00
94 Sindarius Thornwell H RC 2.50 6.00
95 Dillon Brooks H RC 8.00 20.00
96 Justin Jackson H RC 2.50 6.00
97 De'Aaron Fox H RC 20.00 50.00
98 Frank Ntilikina H RC 3.00 8.00
99 Jayson Tatum H RC 40.00 100.00
100 Maxi Kleber H RC 4.00 10.00
101 Damian Lillard A 6.00 15.00
102 Klay Thompson A 6.00 15.00
103 DeMar DeRozan A 3.00 8.00
104 Blake Griffin A 2.50 6.00
105 Mike Conley A 2.00 5.00
106 Kyrie Irving A 5.00 12.00
107 Karl-Anthony Towns A 4.00 10.00
108 Dwight Howard A 3.00 8.00
109 Paul George A 4.00 10.00
110 Dirk Nowitzki A 6.00 15.00
111 CJ McCollum A 2.50 6.00
112 Kevin Durant A 10.00 25.00
113 Kyle Lowry A 2.50 6.00
114 DeAndre Jordan A 2.00 5.00
115 Goran Dragic A 2.00 5.00
116 Al Horford A 2.50 6.00
117 Anthony Davis A 6.00 15.00
118 Zach LaVine A 4.00 10.00
119 Elfrid Payton A 1.50 4.00
120 Harrison Barnes A 2.00 5.00
121 Zach Randolph A 2.50 6.00
122 Draymond Green A 3.00 8.00
123 Ricky Rubio A 2.00 5.00
124 Lou Williams A 2.00 5.00
125 Hassan Whiteside A 2.00 5.00
126 Dennis Schroder A 2.00 5.00
127 DeMarcus Cousins A 2.00 5.00
128 Kris Dunn A 1.50 4.00
129 Nikola Vucevic A 2.00 5.00
130 Gary Harris A 2.00 5.00
131 Vince Carter A 5.00 12.00
132 Chris Paul A 4.00 10.00
133 Derrick Favors A 1.50 4.00
134 Kentavious Caldwell-Pope A 2.00 5.00
135 Eric Bledsoe A 2.00 5.00
136 Taurean Prince A 1.50 4.00
137 Kristaps Porzingis A 3.00 8.00
138 LeBron James A 20.00 50.00
139 Ben Simmons A 2.50 6.00
140 Nikola Jokic A 15.00 40.00
141 Kawhi Leonard A 6.00 15.00
142 James Harden A 5.00 12.00
143 John Wall A 3.00 8.00
144 Brandon Ingram A 3.00 8.00
145 Giannis Antetokounmpo A 12.00 30.00
146 D'Angelo Russell A 2.00 5.00
147 Enes Kanter A 2.00 5.00
148 Kevin Love A 2.50 6.00
149 Joel Embiid A 5.00 12.00
150 Tobias Harris A 2.00 5.00
151 LaMarcus Aldridge A 2.50 6.00
152 Victor Oladipo A 2.00 5.00
153 Bradley Beal A 3.00 8.00
154 Tyreke Evans A 1.50 4.00
155 Jimmy Butler A 4.00 10.00
156 Rondae Hollis-Jefferson A 1.50 4.00
157 Russell Westbrook A 4.00 10.00
158 Dwyane Wade A 5.00 12.00
159 Devin Booker A 6.00 15.00
160 Andre Drummond A 4.00 10.00
161 Tony Parker A 4.00 10.00
162 Domantas Sabonis A 5.00 12.00
163 Marcin Gortat A 1.50 4.00
164 Marc Gasol A 2.50 6.00
165 Andrew Wiggins A 3.00 8.00
166 Kemba Walker A 2.50 6.00
167 Carmelo Anthony A 4.00 10.00
168 Isaiah Thomas A 2.50 6.00
169 TJ Warren A 2.00 5.00
170 Stephen Curry A 20.00 50.00
171 Malik Monk A RC 10.00 25.00
172 Bam Adebayo A RC 15.00 40.00
173 Zach Collins A RC 4.00 10.00
174 Jarrett Allen A RC 6.00 15.00
175 Lauri Markkanen A RC 15.00 40.00
176 Jordan Bell A RC 2.50 6.00
177 Bogdan Bogdanovic A RC 6.00 15.00
178 Josh Jackson A RC 3.00 8.00
179 Markelle Fultz A RC 6.00 15.00
180 John Collins A RC 6.00 15.00
181 Milos Teodosic A RC 3.00 8.00
182 Jawun Evans A RC 2.50 6.00
183 Kyle Kuzma A RC 10.00 25.00
184 Daniel Theis A RC 8.00 20.00
185 Lonzo Ball A RC 10.00 25.00
186 Frank Mason III A RC 2.50 6.00
187 Dennis Smith Jr. A RC 10.00 25.00
188 OG Anunoby A RC 12.00 30.00
189 Zhou Qi A RC 5.00 12.00
190 Josh Hart A RC 6.00 15.00
191 Jonathan Isaac A RC 6.00 15.00
192 Luke Kennard A RC 5.00 12.00
193 Donovan Mitchell A RC 40.00 100.00
194 Sindarius Thornwell A RC 2.50 6.00
195 Dillon Brooks A RC 8.00 20.00
196 Justin Jackson A RC 2.00 5.00
197 De'Aaron Fox A RC 20.00 50.00
198 Frank Ntilikina A RC 3.00 8.00
199 Jayson Tatum A RC 40.00 100.00
200 Maxi Kleber A RC 4.00 10.00
201 Damian Lillard MET 20.00 50.00
202 Klay Thompson MET 20.00 50.00
203 DeMar DeRozan MET 10.00 25.00
204 Blake Griffin MET 8.00 20.00
205 Kyrie Irving MET 25.00 60.00
206 Karl-Anthony Towns MET 25.00 60.00
207 Dwight Howard MET 10.00 25.00
208 Paul George MET 12.00 30.00
209 Dirk Nowitzki MET 20.00 50.00
210 Kevin Durant MET 25.00 60.00
211 Anthony Davis MET 20.00 50.00
212 Draymond Green MET 10.00 25.00
213 Chris Paul MET 12.00 30.00
214 Kristaps Porzingis MET 10.00 25.00
215 LeBron James MET 75.00 200.00
216 Ben Simmons MET 8.00 20.00
217 Kawhi Leonard MET 15.00 40.00
218 James Harden MET 15.00 40.00
219 John Wall MET 10.00 25.00
220 Brandon Ingram MET 10.00 25.00
221 Giannis Antetokounmpo MET 25.00 60.00
222 Joel Embiid MET 25.00 60.00
223 Jimmy Butler MET 12.00 30.00
224 Russell Westbrook MET 12.00 30.00
225 DeMarcus Cousins MET 6.00 15.00
226 Devin Booker MET 20.00 50.00
227 Andrew Wiggins MET 10.00 25.00
228 Carmelo Anthony MET 12.00 30.00
229 Isaiah Thomas MET 12.00 30.00
230 Stephen Curry MET 40.00 100.00
231 Malik Monk MET 40.00 100.00
232 Bam Adebayo MET 30.00 80.00
234 Jordan Bell MET 5.00 12.00
235 Bogdan Bogdanovic MET 8.00 20.00
236 Josh Jackson MET 6.00 15.00
237 Markelle Fultz MET 75.00 200.00
238 John Collins MET 20.00 50.00
239 Kyle Kuzma MET 20.00 50.00
240 Lonzo Ball MET 60.00 150.00
241 Dennis Smith Jr. MET 6.00 15.00
242 OG Anunoby MET 25.00 60.00
243 Jonathan Isaac MET 12.00 30.00
244 Luke Kennard MET 10.00 25.00
245 Donovan Mitchell MET 200.00 400.00
246 Dillon Brooks MET 10.00 25.00
247 De'Aaron Fox MET 40.00 100.00
248 Frank Ntilikina MET 12.00 30.00
249 Jayson Tatum MET 200.00 400.00
250 Maxi Kleber MET 8.00 20.00
251 DeAndre Jordan MET FL 6.00 15.00
252 John Wall MET FL 10.00 25.00
253 Klay Thompson MET FL 20.00 50.00
254 Kawhi Leonard MET FL 15.00 40.00
255 Manu Ginobili MET FL 20.00 50.00
256 Elgin Baylor MET FL 20.00 50.00
257 Bill Russell MET FL 25.00 60.00
258 Kobe Bryant MET FL 125.00 300.00
259 DeMar DeRozan MET FL 10.00 25.00
260 John Stockton MET FL 15.00 40.00
261 Reggie Miller MET FL 40.00 100.00
262 John Havlicek MET FL 15.00 40.00
263 Jerry West MET FL 15.00 40.00
264 Russell Westbrook MET FL 25.00 60.00
265 Dirk Nowitzki MET FL 20.00 50.00
266 Stephen Curry MET FL 40.00 100.00
267 Tim Duncan MET FL 30.00 80.00
268 Tony Parker MET FL 12.00 30.00
269 Larry Bird MET FL 30.00 80.00
270 Magic Johnson MET FL 30.00 80.00
271 Gobert/Mitchell 75.00 200.00
272 Abdul-Jabbar/Johnson 30.00 80.00
273 Stockton/Malone 25.00 60.00
274 Ball/Kuzma 20.00 50.00
275 Penny/Shaq 40.00 100.00
276 Tatum/Irving 60.00 150.00
277 Duncan/Robinson 50.00 120.00
278 Paul/Harden 40.00 100.00
279 Durant/Curry 50.00 120.00
280 Wall/Beal 25.00 60.00
281 Love/James 50.00 120.00
282 Rodman/Pippen 40.00 100.00
283 Bryant/O'Neal 200.00 500.00
284 Parish/Bird 30.00 80.00
285 Davis/Cousins 20.00 50.00
286 Smith/Nowitzki 20.00 50.00
287 Olajuwon/Drexler 20.00 50.00
288 Simmons/Embiid 50.00 120.00
289 Wiggins/Towns 25.00 60.00
290 Garnett/Pierce 60.00 150.00
291 Kobe Bryant MET VA 200.00 500.00
292 Kevin Durant MET VA 100.00 250.00
293 Kyrie Irving MET VA 50.00 120.00
294 Stephen Curry MET VA 125.00 300.00
295 Russell Westbrook MET VA 40.00 100.00
296 Charles Barkley MET VA 75.00 200.00
297 Lonzo Ball MET VA 100.00 250.00
298 Kyle Kuzma MET VA 20.00 50.00
299 Donovan Mitchell MET VA 400.00 800.00
300 Jayson Tatum MET VA 400.00 800.00

2017-18 Panini Noir Gold

*GOLD: 1X TO 2.5X BASIC VET
*GOLD RC: .6X TO 1.5X BASIC RC
STATED PRINT RUN 25 SER.#'d SETS
38 LeBron James H 60.00 150.00
39 Ben Simmons H 6.00 15.00
70 Stephen Curry H 50.00 120.00
75 Lauri Markkanen H 40.00 100.00
79 Markelle Fultz H 60.00 150.00
83 Kyle Kuzma H 15.00 40.00
85 Lonzo Ball H 125.00 300.00
89 Zhou Qi H 30.00 80.00
93 Donovan Mitchell H 60.00 150.00
99 Jayson Tatum H 100.00 250.00
138 LeBron James A 60.00 150.00
139 Ben Simmons A 6.00 15.00
170 Stephen Curry A 50.00 120.00
175 Lauri Markkanen A 40.00 100.00
179 Markelle Fultz A 60.00 150.00
183 Kyle Kuzma A 15.00 40.00
185 Lonzo Ball A 125.00 300.00
189 Zhou Qi A 30.00 80.00
193 Donovan Mitchell A 60.00 150.00
199 Jayson Tatum A 100.00 250.00

2017-18 Panini Noir Box Office Memorabilia

STATED PRINT RUN 49 SER.#'d SETS
*PRIME/3-25: .75X TO 2X BASIC
NO PRICING ON QTY 10 OR LESS
1 Russell Westbrook 5.00 12.00
2 Wesley Matthews 2.00 5.00
3 Brandon Ingram 4.00 10.00
4 Wilson Chandler 2.50 6.00
5 CJ McCollum 3.00 8.00
6 Caris LeVert 3.00 8.00
7 Paul Millsap 2.50 6.00
8 Skal Labissiere 2.00 5.00
9 Mario Hezonja 2.00 5.00
10 Jrue Holiday 4.00 10.00
11 Dirk Nowitzki 8.00 20.00
12 Klay Thompson 8.00 20.00
13 Jimmy Butler 5.00 12.00
14 Ricky Rubio 2.50 6.00
15 Rajon Rondo 4.00 10.00
16 Denzel Valentine 2.00 5.00
17 Harrison Barnes 2.50 6.00
18 Al Horford 3.00 8.00
19 Derrick Favors 2.00 5.00
20 Channing Frye 2.00 5.00
21 Blake Griffin 3.00 8.00
22 Darren Collison 2.00 5.00
23 DeMarcus Cousins 2.50 6.00
24 Patrick Beverley 2.00 5.00
25 Kemba Walker 2.50 6.00
26 Chandler Parsons 2.00 5.00
27 Danilo Gallinari 2.50 6.00
28 Zach LaVine 5.00 12.00
29 Tristan Thompson 2.00 5.00
30 Gary Harris 2.50 6.00
31 Kawhi Leonard 8.00 20.00
32 Terrence Ross 2.50 6.00
33 Manu Ginobili 6.00 15.00
34 D.J. Augustin 2.00 5.00
35 Dion Waiters 2.00 5.00
36 John Henson 2.00 5.00
37 Aaron Gordon 3.00 8.00
38 Draymond Green 4.00 10.00
39 Nerlens Noel 2.00 5.00
40 DeAndre Jordan 2.50 6.00
41 Giannis Antetokounmpo 15.00 40.00
42 Danny Green 2.50 6.00
43 Jaylen Brown 8.00 20.00
44 Al-Farouq Aminu 2.00 5.00
45 DeMar DeRozan 4.00 10.00
46 Ed Davis 2.00 5.00
47 Avery Bradley 2.00 5.00
48 Steven Adams 2.50 6.00
49 Reggie Jackson 2.50 6.00
50 Enes Kanter 2.50 6.00
51 Karl-Anthony Towns 5.00 12.00
52 Marvin Williams 2.00 5.00
53 Stephen Curry 40.00 100.00
54 Rudy Gobert 4.00 10.00
55 Jamal Murray 5.00 12.00
56 Patty Mills 3.00 8.00
57 Austin Rivers 2.50 6.00
58 LeBron James 40.00 100.00
59 Myles Turner 3.00 8.00
60 DeMarre Carroll 2.00 5.00

2017-18 Panini Noir Charles Barkley Spotlight Signatures

STATED PRINT RUN 15 SER.#'d SETS
EXCHANGE DEADLINE 02/01/2020
1 Charles Barkley 300.00 600.00
2 Charles Barkley 300.00 600.00
3 Charles Barkley 300.00 600.00
4 Charles Barkley 300.00 600.00
5 Charles Barkley 300.00 600.00
6 Charles Barkley 300.00 600.00
7 Charles Barkley 300.00 600.00
8 Charles Barkley 300.00 600.00
9 Charles Barkley 300.00 600.00
10 Charles Barkley 300.00 600.00

2017-18 Panini Noir Color Autographs

*GOLD/25: .75X TO 2X BASIC
1 Shaquille O'Neal 150.00 400.00
2 Reggie Miller 125.00 300.00
3 Allen Iverson 100.00 250.00
4 Karl Malone 50.00 120.00
5 Magic Johnson 75.00 200.00
6 John Stockton 50.00 120.00
7 Kareem Abdul-Jabbar 100.00 250.00
8 Jerry West 30.00 80.00
9 Alonzo Mourning 30.00 80.00
10 Grant Hill 30.00 80.00
11 Hakeem Olajuwon 50.00 120.00
12 Clyde Drexler 30.00 80.00
13 Tracy McGrady 60.00 150.00
14 Ray Allen 50.00 120.00
15 Jason Kidd 30.00 80.00
16 Eric Snow 6.00 15.00
17 B.J. Armstrong 10.00 25.00
18 Zydrunas Ilgauskas 8.00 20.00
19 Sidney Moncrief 8.00 20.00
20 Rick Fox 8.00 20.00
21 Jack Sikma 10.00 25.00
22 Shareef Abdur-Rahim 8.00 20.00
23 Rolando Blackman 8.00 20.00
24 Bernard King 12.00 30.00
25 Elden Campbell 6.00 15.00
26 Allan Houston 10.00 25.00
27 Mike Bibby 10.00 25.00
28 Sam Cassell 8.00 20.00
29 Ron Mercer 6.00 15.00
30 Derek Harper 8.00 20.00
31 Richard Hamilton 12.00 30.00
32 Damon Stoudamire 10.00 25.00
33 Tom Gugliotta 6.00 15.00
34 Mark Aguirre 8.00 20.00
35 Stephen Jackson 8.00 20.00
36 Bryant Reeves 6.00 15.00
37 Antoine Walker 8.00 20.00
38 Robert Horry 10.00 25.00
39 Artis Gilmore 12.00 30.00
40 Stacey Augmon 8.00 20.00
41 Cedric Ceballos 6.00 15.00
42 Rod Strickland 8.00 20.00
43 Isaiah Rider 8.00 20.00
44 Brian Scalabrine 6.00 15.00
45 Fat Lever 8.00 20.00
46 Walter McCarty 6.00 15.00
47 Shawn Bradley 6.00 15.00
48 Charles Oakley EXCH 8.00 20.00
49 Eddie Jones 6.00 15.00
50 Latrell Sprewell 12.00 30.00

2017-18 Panini Noir Episodic Triple Materials

STATED PRINT RUN 49 SER.#'d SETS
*PRIME/18-25: 1.25X TO 3X BASIC
1 Al Jefferson 5.00 12.00
2 Ray Allen 10.00 25.00
3 Glen Rice 5.00 12.00
4 Vince Carter 20.00 50.00
5 Amar'e Stoudemire 6.00 15.00
6 Kevin Garnett 20.00 50.00
7 Jeremy Lin 20.00 50.00
8 Chris Paul 20.00 50.00
9 Tyson Chandler 5.00 12.00
10 Dwight Howard 8.00 20.00
11 Stephen Jackson 5.00 12.00
12 Jason Kidd 10.00 25.00
13 Joe Smith 5.00 12.00
14 Grant Hill 10.00 25.00
15 Dominique Wilkins 10.00 25.00
16 Shaquille O'Neal 40.00 100.00
17 Rajon Rondo 8.00 20.00
18 Jeff Teague 4.00 10.00
19 Jermaine O'Neal 6.00 15.00
20 Pau Gasol 10.00 25.00

2017-18 Panini Noir Horizontal Spotlight Signatures

STATED PRINT RUN 125 SER.#'d SETS
EXCHANGE DEADLINE 2/1/2020
1 D'Angelo Russell 50.00 120.00
2 Frank Ntilikina EXCH 12.00 30.00
3 Dennis Smith Jr. EXCH 12.00 30.00
4 Lonzo Ball 125.00 300.00
5 Andrew Wiggins 125.00 300.00
6 Devin Booker 300.00 600.00
7 Kobe Bryant 5,000.00 10,000.00
8 Reggie Miller 200.00 500.00
9 Karl Malone 100.00 250.00
10 David Robinson 100.00 250.00
11 Grant Hill 100.00 250.00
12 Hakeem Olajuwon 100.00 250.00
13 Ricky Rubio 50.00 120.00
14 Markelle Fultz 25.00 60.00

2017-18 Panini Noir Icons Memorabilia

PRINT RUNS B/WN 49-99 COPIES PER
1 Scottie Pippen/99 15.00 40.00
2 Kelly Tripucka/99 5.00 12.00
3 Larry Nance/99 5.00 12.00
4 Tim Duncan/99 15.00 40.00
5 Shaquille O'Neal/99 20.00 50.00
6 Larry Bird/99 25.00 60.00
7 Paul Silas/49 6.00 15.00
8 Julius Erving/99 15.00 40.00
9 Jack Sikma/99 6.00 15.00
10 Robert Parish/99 8.00 20.00
11 Christian Laettner/99 6.00 15.00
12 Grant Hill/99 10.00 25.00
13 Kobe Bryant/99 100.00 250.00
14 Charles Oakley/99 5.00 12.00
15 Kevin Johnson/99 6.00 15.00
16 Charlie Scott/99 6.00 15.00
17 Doug Collins/99 6.00 15.00
18 Artis Gilmore/99 8.00 20.00
19 Shawn Bradley/99 4.00 10.00
20 Karl Malone/99 12.00 30.00
21 Dominique Wilkins/99 10.00 25.00
22 Tree Rollins/99 4.00 10.00
23 Stephen Jackson/99 5.00 12.00
24 Chris Webber/99 10.00 25.00
25 Kurt Rambis/99 5.00 12.00
26 Clyde Drexler/99 10.00 25.00
27 Detlef Schrempf/99 6.00 15.00
28 Isiah Thomas/99 10.00 25.00
29 John Salley/99 5.00 12.00
30 Mark Price/99 6.00 15.00
31 Andrei Kirilenko/99 5.00 12.00
32 Reggie Lewis/99 8.00 20.00
33 Paul Pierce/99 10.00 25.00
34 Mitch Kupchak/99 5.00 12.00
35 Kevin Garnett/99 15.00 40.00
36 World B. Free/99 5.00 12.00
37 Sam Perkins/99 5.00 12.00
38 Alonzo Mourning/99 10.00 25.00
39 Tom Gugliotta/99 4.00 10.00
40 Allen Iverson/99 15.00 40.00

2017-18 Panini Noir Jumbo Materials

PRINT RUNS B/WN 35-99 COPIES PER
1 Seth Curry/49 3.00 8.00
2 Kristaps Porzingis/49 4.00 10.00
3 Allen Crabbe/49 2.00 5.00
4 Andre Drummond/49 2.50 6.00
5 Dwight Powell/99 2.00 5.00
6 Brook Lopez/49 2.50 6.00
7 Victor Oladipo/49 2.50 6.00
8 Kevin Durant/49 12.00 30.00
9 Nicolas Batum/49 2.00 5.00
10 John Wall/49 4.00 10.00
11 Lance Stephenson/99 2.50 6.00
12 Buddy Hield/99 3.00 8.00
13 Rondae Hollis-Jefferson/49 2.00 5.00
14 Rodney Hood/99 2.00 5.00
15 Kelly Oubre Jr./99 3.00 8.00
16 Noah Vonleh/99 2.00 5.00
17 Serge Ibaka/99 2.50 6.00
18 Damian Lillard/99 8.00 20.00
19 Stanley Johnson/99 2.00 5.00
20 Marc Gasol/49 3.00 8.00
21 Thaddeus Young/99 2.00 5.00
22 Marcus Smart/49 3.00 8.00
23 J.J. Barea/99 2.50 6.00
24 Nikola Jokic/99 20.00 50.00
25 Spencer Dinwiddie/99 2.50 6.00
26 Michael Kidd-Gilchrist/49 2.50 6.00
27 Kyle Korver/49 2.50 6.00
28 Anthony Davis/49 8.00 20.00
29 Nene/49 2.50 6.00
30 Kevin Love/49 3.00 8.00
31 Courtney Lee/99 2.00 5.00
32 Julius Randle/49 3.00 8.00
33 Udonis Haslem/99 3.00 8.00
34 Eric Bledsoe/49 2.50 6.00
35 Will Barton/99 2.00 5.00
36 Devin Harris/49 2.00 5.00
37 Jeff Teague/49 2.00 5.00
38 Paul George/35 5.00 12.00
39 Thon Maker/49 2.00 5.00
40 Vince Carter/49 6.00 15.00
41 Nikola Vucevic/49 2.50 6.00
42 Khris Middleton/99 4.00 10.00
43 Kyrie Irving/49 6.00 15.00
44 Tyson Chandler/99 2.00 5.00
45 Tyler Johnson/49 2.00 5.00
46 Kenneth Faried/49 2.50 6.00
47 Cody Zeller/99 2.00 5.00
48 Dwight Howard/49 4.00 10.00
49 Evan Turner/49 2.00 5.00
50 Tony Parker/49 5.00 12.00
51 Kyle Lowry/49 3.00 8.00
52 Bradley Beal/99 4.00 10.00
53 Jusuf Nurkic/99 2.50 6.00
54 Emmanuel Mudiay/49 2.00 5.00
55 Maurice Harkless/99 2.00 5.00
56 Shaun Livingston/49 2.50 6.00
57 Jakob Poeltl/99 2.50 6.00
58 Andrew Wiggins/49 4.00 10.00
59 Frank Kaminsky/99 2.00 5.00
60 D'Angelo Russell/49 2.50 6.00

2017-18 Panini Noir New Wave Jerseys

STATED PRINT RUN 49 SER.#'d SETS
*PRIME/18-25: .75X TO 2X BASIC
1 Jayson Tatum 20.00 50.00
2 Luke Kennard 3.00 8.00
3 Harry Giles 1.50 4.00
4 Frank Jackson 1.50 4.00
5 Jonathan Isaac 4.00 10.00
6 Dwayne Bacon 1.50 4.00
7 Donovan Mitchell 15.00 40.00
8 Davon Reed 1.50 4.00
9 Dennis Smith Jr. 2.00 5.00
10 Tony Bradley 1.50 4.00
11 Tyler Lydon 1.50 4.00
12 John Collins 6.00 15.00

13 Semi Ojeleye 2.00 5.00
14 Sterling Brown 1.50 4.00
15 Josh Jackson 2.00 5.00
16 Frank Mason III 1.50 4.00
17 Wes Iwundu 1.50 4.00
18 Jawun Evans 1.50 4.00
19 Jarrett Allen 4.00 10.00
20 Justin Patton 1.50 4.00
21 Josh Hart 4.00 10.00
22 OG Anunoby 8.00 20.00
23 D.J. Wilson 1.50 4.00
24 Caleb Swanigan 1.50 4.00
25 Lauri Markkanen 10.00 25.00
26 Frank Ntilikina 2.00 5.00
27 Terrance Ferguson 1.50 4.00
28 Ivan Rabb 1.50 4.00
29 Derrick White 6.00 15.00
30 Jordan Bell 1.50 4.00
31 Tyler Dorsey 1.50 4.00
32 Lonzo Ball 6.00 15.00
33 TJ Leaf 1.50 4.00
34 Kyle Kuzma 6.00 15.00
35 Markelle Fultz 4.00 10.00
36 De'Aaron Fox 12.00 30.00
37 Malik Monk 6.00 15.00
38 Bam Adebayo 10.00 25.00
39 Sindarius Thornwell 1.50 4.00
40 Zach Collins 2.50 6.00

2017-18 Panini Noir Prime Materials Black and White Autographs

STATED PRINT RUN 20 SER.#'d SETS
EXCHANGE DEADLINE 02/01/2020
1 Taurean Prince 12.00 30.00
2 Kyrie Irving 40.00 100.00
5 Kemba Walker EXCH 6.00 15.00
6 Zach LaVine 15.00 40.00
7 Damian Lillard 30.00 80.00
9 Myles Turner 8.00 20.00
10 Kristaps Porzingis EXCH 30.00 80.00
11 Brandon Ingram EXCH 25.00 60.00
14 Giannis Antetokounmpo 200.00 500.00
15 Avery Bradley 5.00 12.00
16 Rudy Gobert 12.00 30.00
17 Michael Kidd-Gilchrist 5.00 12.00
19 Patrick Beverley 5.00 12.00
20 Trevor Ariza 15.00 40.00
21 Rodney Hood EXCH 5.00 12.00
22 Thaddeus Young 5.00 12.00
24 Enes Kanter 10.00 25.00
25 Blake Griffin 12.00 30.00
26 Tony Parker 25.00 60.00
27 Kevin Love 12.00 30.00
28 Elfrid Payton 5.00 12.00
29 Rudy Gay 6.00 15.00
30 Karl-Anthony Towns 50.00 120.00
31 Dion Waiters 5.00 12.00
32 Gary Harris 6.00 15.00
33 Marc Gasol EXCH 20.00 50.00
34 Jeff Teague EXCH 5.00 12.00
35 Vince Carter 25.00 60.00
36 Nikola Jokic 400.00 800.00
38 Tim Hardaway Jr. 6.00 15.00
40 Harrison Barnes 6.00 15.00

2017-18 Panini Noir Prime Materials Color Autographs

PRINT RUNS B/WN 12-20 COPIES PER
NO PRICING ON QTY 12
EXCHANGE DEADLINE 02/01/2020
1 Taurean Prince/20 12.00 30.00
2 Kyrie Irving/20 40.00 100.00
5 Kemba Walker/20 EXCH 6.00 15.00
6 Zach LaVine/20 15.00 40.00
7 Damian Lillard/20 30.00 80.00
9 Myles Turner/20 8.00 20.00
10 Kristaps Porzingis/20 EXCH 30.00 80.00
11 Brandon Ingram/20 EXCH 25.00 60.00
14 Giannis Antetokounmpo/20 100.00 250.00
15 Avery Bradley/20 5.00 12.00
16 Rudy Gobert/20 12.00 30.00
17 Michael Kidd-Gilchrist/20 5.00 12.00
19 Patrick Beverley/20 5.00 12.00
20 Trevor Ariza/20 15.00 40.00
21 Rodney Hood/20 EXCH 5.00 12.00
22 Thaddeus Young/20 5.00 12.00
24 Enes Kanter/20 10.00 25.00
25 Blake Griffin/20 12.00 30.00
26 Tony Parker/20 25.00 60.00
27 Kevin Love/20 12.00 30.00
28 Elfrid Payton/20 5.00 12.00
29 Rudy Gay/20 6.00 15.00
30 Karl-Anthony Towns/20 50.00 210.00
31 Dion Waiters/20 5.00 12.00
32 Gary Harris/20 6.00 15.00
33 Marc Gasol/20 EXCH 20.00 50.00
34 Jeff Teague/20 EXCH 5.00 12.00
35 Vince Carter/20 25.00 60.00
36 Nikola Jokic/20 400.00 800.00
38 Tim Hardaway Jr./20 6.00 15.00
40 Harrison Barnes/20 6.00 15.00

2017-18 Panini Noir Prime Rookie Patch Autographs Black and White

STATED PRINT RUN 99 SER.#'d SETS
EXHCNAGE DEADLINE 02/01/2020
332 Ante Zizic 5.00 12.00
333 Sindarius Thornwell 4.00 10.00
334 Bam Adebayo 25.00 60.00
335 Frank Mason III 4.00 10.00
337 Tyler Dorsey 4.00 10.00
339 Tyler Lydon 4.00 10.00
340 Derrick White 10.00 25.00
341 Tony Bradley 4.00 10.00
342 Wes Iwundu 4.00 10.00
344 Frank Jackson 4.00 10.00
345 Jawun Evans 4.00 10.00
346 Harry Giles 4.00 10.00
347 Terrance Ferguson 4.00 10.00
348 Semi Ojeleye EXCH 5.00 12.00
349 Sterling Brown 4.00 10.00
350 Lonzo Ball 50.00 120.00
351 Markelle Fultz 50.00 120.00
352 Dennis Smith Jr. EXCH 5.00 12.00
353 Donovan Mitchell 300.00 600.00
354 Jordan Bell EXCH 4.00 10.00
355 Jayson Tatum EXCH 600.00 1,500.00
356 De'Aaron Fox 25.00 60.00
357 Lauri Markkanen 25.00 60.00
358 Frank Ntilikina EXCH 10.00 25.00
359 John Collins 15.00 40.00
360 Kyle Kuzma 15.00 40.00

2017-18 Panini Noir Prime Rookie Patch Autographs Color

STATED PRINT RUN 99 SER.#'d SETS
EXHCNAGE DEADLINE 02/01/2020
332 Ante Zizic 5.00 12.00
333 Sindarius Thornwell 4.00 10.00
334 Bam Adebayo 25.00 60.00
335 Frank Mason III 4.00 10.00
337 Tyler Dorsey 4.00 10.00
339 Tyler Lydon 4.00 10.00
340 Derrick White 10.00 25.00
341 Tony Bradley 4.00 10.00
342 Wes Iwundu 4.00 10.00
344 Frank Jackson 4.00 10.00
345 Jawun Evans 4.00 10.00
346 Harry Giles 4.00 10.00
347 Terrance Ferguson 4.00 10.00
348 Semi Ojeleye EXCH 5.00 12.00
349 Sterling Brown 4.00 10.00
350 Lonzo Ball 50.00 120.00
351 Markelle Fultz 50.00 210.00
352 Dennis Smith Jr. EXCH 5.00 12.00
353 Donovan Mitchell 300.00 600.00
354 Jordan Bell EXCH 4.00 10.00
355 Jayson Tatum EXCH 600.00 1,200.00
356 De'Aaron Fox 25.00 60.00
357 Lauri Markkanen 40.00 100.00
358 Frank Ntilikina EXCH 10.00 25.00
359 John Collins 15.00 40.00
360 Kyle Kuzma 15.00 40.00

2017-18 Panini Noir Rookie Jumbo Materials

STATED PRINT RUN 99 SER.#'d SETS
1 Jonathan Isaac 8.00 20.00
2 Derrick White 6.00 15.00
3 Dennis Smith Jr. 2.00 5.00
4 TJ Leaf 1.50 4.00
5 Semi Ojeleye 2.00 5.00
6 Malik Monk 6.00 15.00
7 Wes Iwundu 1.50 4.00
8 Josh Hart 4.00 10.00
9 Jayson Tatum 60.00 150.00
10 Lauri Markkanen 10.00 25.00
11 Dwayne Bacon 1.50 4.00
12 Jordan Bell 1.50 4.00
13 Tony Bradley 1.50 4.00
14 Kyle Kuzma 6.00 15.00
15 Sterling Brown 1.50 4.00
16 Bam Adebayo 15.00 40.00
17 Jawun Evans 1.50 4.00
18 OG Anunoby 8.00 20.00
19 Luke Kennard 3.00 8.00
20 Frank Ntilikina 2.00 5.00
21 Donovan Mitchell 25.00 60.00
22 Tyler Dorsey 1.50 4.00
23 Tyler Lydon 1.50 4.00
24 Markelle Fultz 4.00 10.00
25 Josh Jackson 2.00 5.00
26 Sindarius Thornwell 1.50 4.00
27 Jarrett Allen 4.00 10.00
28 D.J. Wilson 1.50 4.00
29 Harry Giles 1.50 4.00
30 Terrance Ferguson 1.50 4.00
31 Davon Reed 1.50 4.00
32 Lonzo Ball 15.00 40.00
33 John Collins 4.00 10.00
34 De'Aaron Fox 15.00 40.00
35 Frank Mason III 1.50 4.00
36 Zach Collins 2.50 6.00
37 Justin Patton 1.50 4.00
38 Caleb Swanigan 1.50 4.00
39 Frank Jackson 1.50 4.00
40 Ivan Rabb 1.50 4.00

2017-18 Panini Noir Rookie Patch Autographs Black and White

STATED PRINT RUN 99 SER.#'d SETS
EXHCNAGE DEADLINE 02/01/2020
301 Markelle Fultz 50.00 120.00
302 Lonzo Ball 50.00 120.00
303 Jayson Tatum EXCH 150.00 400.00
304 Josh Jackson 5.00 12.00
305 De'Aaron Fox 25.00 60.00
306 Jonathan Isaac 20.00 50.00
307 Lauri Markkanen 40.00 100.00
308 Frank Ntilikina EXCH 10.00 25.00
309 Dennis Smith Jr. EXCH 5.00 12.00
310 Zach Collins 6.00 15.00
311 Malik Monk 15.00 40.00
312 Luke Kennard 8.00 20.00
313 Donovan Mitchell 300.00 600.00
314 Bam Adebayo 40.00 100.00
315 Justin Patton 4.00 10.00
316 D.J. Wilson 4.00 10.00
317 TJ Leaf 4.00 10.00
318 John Collins 15.00 40.00
319 Harry Giles 4.00 10.00
320 OG Anunoby EXCH 12.00 30.00
321 Kyle Kuzma 15.00 40.00
322 Jordan Bell EXCH 4.00 10.00
324 Ike Anigbogu 4.00 10.00
326 Milos Teodosic 5.00 12.00
327 Semi Ojeleye EXCH 5.00 12.00
328 Dillon Brooks 12.00 30.00
329 Jarrett Allen 10.00 25.00
330 Dwayne Bacon 4.00 10.00

2017-18 Panini Noir Rookie Patch Autographs Color

STATED PRINT RUN 99 SER.#'d SETS
EXHCNAGE DEADLINE 02/01/2020
301 Markelle Fultz 50.00 120.00
302 Lonzo Ball 50.00 120.00
303 Jayson Tatum EXCH 150.00 400.00
304 Josh Jackson 5.00 12.00
305 De'Aaron Fox 25.00 60.00
306 Jonathan Isaac 20.00 50.00
307 Lauri Markkanen 40.00 100.00
308 Frank Ntilikina EXCH 10.00 25.00
309 Dennis Smith Jr. EXCH 5.00 12.00
310 Zach Collins 6.00 15.00
311 Malik Monk 15.00 40.00
312 Luke Kennard 8.00 20.00
313 Donovan Mitchell 300.00 600.00
314 Bam Adebayo 40.00 100.00
315 Justin Patton 4.00 10.00
316 D.J. Wilson 4.00 10.00
317 TJ Leaf 4.00 10.00
318 John Collins 15.00 40.00
319 Harry Giles 4.00 10.00
320 OG Anunoby EXCH 12.00 30.00
321 Kyle Kuzma 15.00 40.00
322 Jordan Bell EXCH 4.00 10.00
324 Ike Anigbogu 4.00 10.00
326 Milos Teodosic 5.00 12.00
327 Semi Ojeleye EXCH 5.00 12.00
328 Dillon Brooks 12.00 30.00
329 Jarrett Allen 10.00 25.00
330 Dwayne Bacon 4.00 10.00

2017-18 Panini Noir Two Shot Rookie Dual Jerseys

STATED PRINT RUN 99 SER.#'d SETS
*PRIME/25: .75X TO 2X BASIC
1 Kuzma/Ball 6.00 15.00
2 Leaf/Ball 6.00 15.00
3 Jonathan Isaac
Wes Iwundu 4.00 10.00
4 Ntilikina/Smith 2.00 5.00
5 Frank Mason III
Harry Giles 1.50 4.00
6 Malik Monk
Luke Kennard 6.00 15.00
7 Frank Jackson
Harry Giles 1.50 4.00
8 Mason/Jackson 2.00 5.00
9 Tyler Dorsey
John Collins 4.00 10.00
10 Fox/Adebayo 3.00 8.00
11 Kuzma/Hart 6.00 15.00
12 Ball/Fultz 6.00 15.00
13 Jackson/Reed 2.00 5.00
14 Fultz/Tatum 8.00 20.00
15 Giles/Fox 3.00 8.00
16 Mitchell/Adebayo 6.00 15.00
17 Luke Kennard
Harry Giles 3.00 8.00
18 Frank Mason III
Wayne Selden 1.50 4.00
19 Tatum/Ojeleye 6.00 15.00
20 Fox/Monk 3.00 8.00
21 Hart/Ball 6.00 15.00
22 Tatum/Jackson 6.00 15.00
23 Caleb Swanigan
Zach Collins 2.50 6.00
24 Tatum/Ball 10.00 25.00
25 Mitchell/Bradley 6.00 15.00
26 Frank Mason III
Wes Iwundu 1.50 4.00
27 Dwayne Bacon
Jonathan Isaac 4.00 10.00
28 Jackson/Selden 2.00 5.00
29 Dwayne Bacon
Malik Monk 6.00 15.00
30 Jordan Bell
Tyler Dorsey 1.50 4.00
31 D.J. Wilson
Sterling Brown 1.50 4.00
32 Isaac/Fox 3.00 8.00
33 Mason/Fox 3.00 8.00
34 Ball/Mitchell 10.00 25.00
35 Frank Jackson
Luke Kennard 3.00 8.00
36 Harry Giles
Tony Bradley 1.50 4.00
37 Ike Anigbogu
TJ Leaf 1.50 4.00
38 Bam Adebayo
Malik Monk 10.00 25.00
39 Sindarius Thornwell
Jawun Evans 1.50 4.00
40 Semi Ojeleye
Sterling Brown 2.00 5.00

2017-18 Panini Noir Vertical Spotlight Signatures

STATED PRINT RUN 125 SER.#'d SETS
EXCHANGE DEADLINE 2/1/2020
1 Nikola Jokic 1,000.00 2,000.00
2 Anthony Davis 125.00 300.00
3 Brandon Ingram EXCH 100.00 250.00
4 Kevin Durant 500.00 1,000.00
5 Lauri Markkanen 75.00 200.00
6 Kyle Kuzma 40.00 100.00
7 Karl-Anthony Towns 125.00 300.00
8 Joel Embiid EXCH 150.00 400.00
9 Jayson Tatum 1,250.00 2,500.00
10 De'Aaron Fox 125.00 300.00
11 Kyrie Irving 200.00 500.00
12 Giannis Antetokounmpo 800.00 1,500.00
13 Isaiah Thomas 25.00 60.00
14 Kristaps Porzingis EXCH 100.00 250.00
15 Shaquille O'Neal 200.00 500.00
16 Blake Griffin 60.00 150.00
17 JJ Redick 50.00 120.00
18 Zach LaVine 125.00 300.00
19 Donovan Mitchell 500.00 1,000.00
20 Jordan Bell EXCH 20.00 50.00
21 Allen Iverson 400.00 800.00
22 Magic Johnson 150.00 400.00
23 Larry Bird 150.00 400.00
24 John Stockton 100.00 250.00
25 Tracy McGrady 125.00 300.00
26 Clyde Drexler 75.00 200.00

2018-19 Panini Noir

1-140 PRINT RUN 85 SER.#'d SETS
RC PRINT RUN 85 SER.#'d SETS
201-300 PRINT RUN 25 SER.#'d SETS
301-380 PRINT RUN 99 SER.#'d SETS
381-400 PRINT RUN 99 SER.#'d SETS
EXCHANGE DEADLINE 12/12/2020
1 Kemba Walker A 2.00 5.00
2 Jrue Holiday A 3.00 8.00
3 Nikola Vucevic A 2.00 5.00
4 Damian Lillard A 6.00 15.00
5 Kawhi Leonard A 6.00 15.00
6 Derrick Rose A 5.00 12.00
7 D'Angelo Russell A 2.50 6.00
8 Danilo Gallinari A 2.00 5.00
9 Bojan Bogdanovic A 2.00 5.00
10 T.J. Warren A 2.00 5.00
11 Jeremy Lamb A 1.50 4.00
12 Julius Randle A 2.50 6.00
13 John Collins A 2.50 6.00
14 CJ McCollum A 2.50 6.00
15 Kyle Lowry A 2.50 6.00
16 Kevin Durant A 10.00 25.00
17 Caris LeVert A 2.50 6.00
18 LeBron James A 20.00 50.00
19 Blake Griffin A 2.50 6.00
20 James Harden A 5.00 12.00
21 Dwyane Wade A 5.00 12.00
22 Harrison Barnes A 2.00 5.00
23 Jeremy Lin A 4.00 10.00
24 Rudy Gobert A 3.00 8.00
25 Ben Simmons A 2.50 6.00
26 Stephen Curry A 20.00 50.00
27 Tim Hardaway Jr. A 1.50 4.00
28 Kyle Kuzma A 2.50 6.00
29 Andre Drummond A 2.00 5.00
30 Chris Paul A 5.00 12.00
31 Josh Richardson A 2.00 5.00
32 DeAndre Jordan A 2.00 5.00
33 Nikola Jokic A 12.00 30.00
34 Donovan Mitchell A 8.00 20.00
35 Joel Embiid A 6.00 15.00
36 Draymond Green A 3.00 8.00
37 Enes Kanter A 2.00 5.00
38 Brandon Ingram A 2.50 6.00
39 Zach LaVine A 4.00 10.00
40 Clint Capela A 2.00 5.00
41 John Wall A 3.00 8.00
42 Dirk Nowitzki A 6.00 15.00
43 Jamal Murray A 5.00 12.00
44 Ricky Rubio A 2.00 5.00
45 Jimmy Butler A 4.00 10.00
46 Klay Thompson A 6.00 15.00
47 Giannis Antetokounmpo A 12.00 30.00
48 Buddy Hield A 2.50 6.00
49 Lauri Markkanen A 4.00 10.00
50 DeMar DeRozan A 3.00 8.00
51 Bradley Beal A 3.00 8.00
52 Mike Conley A 2.00 5.00
53 Russell Westbrook A 4.00 10.00
54 Andrew Wiggins A 3.00 8.00
55 Kyrie Irving A 6.00 15.00
56 DeMarcus Cousins A 2.00 5.00
57 Khris Middleton A 2.50 6.00
58 De'Aaron Fox A 5.00 12.00
59 Kevin Love A 2.00 5.00
60 LaMarcus Aldridge A 2.50 6.00
61 Aaron Gordon A 2.50 6.00
62 Marc Gasol A 2.50 6.00
63 Paul George A 4.00 10.00
64 Karl-Anthony Towns A 4.00 10.00
65 Jayson Tatum A 10.00 25.00
66 Tobias Harris A 2.00 5.00
67 Victor Oladipo A 2.00 5.00
68 Devin Booker A 6.00 15.00
69 Jordan Clarkson A 2.50 6.00
70 Anthony Davis A 6.00 15.00
71 Kemba Walker I 2.00 5.00
72 Jrue Holiday I 3.00 8.00
73 Nikola Vucevic I 2.00 5.00
74 Damian Lillard I 6.00 15.00
75 Kawhi Leonard I 6.00 15.00
76 Derrick Rose I 5.00 12.00
77 D'Angelo Russell I 2.50 6.00
78 Danilo Gallinari I 2.00 5.00
79 Bojan Bogdanovic I 2.00 5.00
80 T.J. Warren I 2.00 5.00
81 Jeremy Lamb I 1.50 4.00
82 Julius Randle I 2.50 6.00
83 John Collins I 2.50 6.00
84 CJ McCollum I 2.50 6.00
85 Kyle Lowry I 2.50 6.00
86 Kevin Durant I 10.00 25.00
87 Caris LeVert I 2.50 6.00
88 LeBron James I 20.00 50.00
89 Blake Griffin I 2.50 6.00
90 James Harden I 5.00 12.00
91 Dwyane Wade I 5.00 12.00
92 Harrison Barnes I 2.00 5.00
93 Jeremy Lin I 4.00 10.00
94 Rudy Gobert I 3.00 8.00
95 Ben Simmons I 2.50 6.00
96 Stephen Curry I 20.00 50.00
97 Tim Hardaway Jr. I 1.50 4.00
98 Kyle Kuzma I 2.50 6.00
99 Andre Drummond I 2.00 5.00
100 Chris Paul I 5.00 12.00
101 Josh Richardson I 2.00 5.00
102 DeAndre Jordan I 2.00 5.00
103 Nikola Jokic I 12.00 30.00
104 Donovan Mitchell I 8.00 20.00
105 Joel Embiid I 6.00 15.00
106 Draymond Green I 3.00 8.00
107 Enes Kanter I 2.00 5.00
108 Brandon Ingram I 2.50 6.00
109 Zach LaVine I 4.00 10.00
110 Clint Capela I 2.00 5.00
111 John Wall I 3.00 8.00
112 Dirk Nowitzki I 6.00 15.00
113 Jamal Murray I 5.00 12.00
114 Ricky Rubio I 2.00 5.00
115 Jimmy Butler I 4.00 10.00
116 Klay Thompson I 6.00 15.00
117 Giannis Antetokounmpo I 12.00 30.00
118 Buddy Hield I 2.50 6.00
119 Lauri Markkanen I 4.00 10.00
120 DeMar DeRozan I 3.00 8.00
121 Bradley Beal I 3.00 8.00
122 Mike Conley I 2.00 5.00
123 Russell Westbrook I 4.00 10.00
124 Andrew Wiggins I 3.00 8.00
125 Kyrie Irving I 6.00 15.00
126 DeMarcus Cousins I 2.00 5.00
127 Khris Middleton I 2.50 6.00
128 De'Aaron Fox I 5.00 12.00
129 Kevin Love I 2.00 5.00
130 LaMarcus Aldridge I 2.50 6.00
131 Aaron Gordon I 2.50 6.00
132 Marc Gasol I 2.50 6.00
133 Paul George I 4.00 10.00
134 Karl-Anthony Towns I 4.00 10.00
135 Jayson Tatum I 10.00 25.00
136 Tobias Harris I 2.00 5.00
137 Victor Oladipo I 2.00 5.00
138 Devin Booker I 6.00 15.00
139 Jordan Clarkson I 2.50 6.00
140 Anthony Davis I 6.00 15.00
141 Jaren Jackson Jr. A RC 20.00 50.00
142 Elie Okobo A RC 2.50 6.00
143 Wendell Carter Jr. A RC 6.00 15.00
144 Hamidou Diallo A RC 4.00 10.00
145 Mikal Bridges A RC 12.00 30.00
146 Grayson Allen A RC 5.00 12.00
147 Kevin Huerter A RC 5.00 12.00
148 Chandler Hutchison A RC 3.00 8.00
149 Deandre Ayton A RC 8.00 20.00
150 Jalen Brunson A RC 20.00 50.00
151 Trae Young A RC 20.00 50.00
152 Mitchell Robinson A RC 6.00 15.00
153 Collin Sexton A RC 8.00 20.00
154 Donte DiVincenzo A RC 6.00 15.00
155 Shai Gilgeous-Alexander A RC 75.00 200.00
156 Troy Brown Jr. A RC 3.00 8.00
157 Landry Shamet A RC 4.00 10.00
158 Josh Okogie A RC 4.00 10.00
159 Marvin Bagley III A RC 4.00 10.00
160 De'Anthony Melton A RC 5.00 12.00
161 Mo Bamba A RC 4.00 10.00
162 Omari Spellman A RC 2.50 6.00
163 Kevin Knox A RC 3.00 8.00
164 Lonnie Walker IV A RC 5.00 12.00
165 Miles Bridges A RC 6.00 15.00
166 Jerome Robinson A RC 2.50 6.00
167 Allonzo Trier A RC 2.50 6.00
168 Bruce Brown A RC 5.00 12.00
169 Luka Doncic A RC 125.00 300.00
170 Rodions Kurucs A RC 3.00 8.00
171 Jaren Jackson Jr. I 20.00 50.00
172 Elie Okobo I 2.50 6.00
173 Wendell Carter Jr. I 6.00 15.00
174 Hamidou Diallo I 4.00 10.00
175 Mikal Bridges I 12.00 30.00
176 Grayson Allen I 5.00 12.00
177 Kevin Huerter I 5.00 12.00
178 Chandler Hutchison I 3.00 8.00
179 Deandre Ayton I 8.00 20.00
180 Jalen Brunson I 20.00 50.00
181 Trae Young I 20.00 50.00
182 Mitchell Robinson I 6.00 15.00
183 Collin Sexton I 8.00 20.00
184 Donte DiVincenzo I 6.00 15.00
185 Shai Gilgeous-Alexander I 75.00 200.00
186 Troy Brown Jr. I 3.00 8.00
187 Landry Shamet I 4.00 10.00
188 Josh Okogie I 4.00 10.00
189 Marvin Bagley III I 4.00 10.00
190 De'Anthony Melton I 5.00 12.00
191 Mo Bamba I 4.00 10.00
192 Omari Spellman I 2.50 6.00
193 Kevin Knox I 3.00 8.00
194 Lonnie Walker IV I 5.00 12.00
195 Miles Bridges I 6.00 15.00
196 Jerome Robinson I 2.50 6.00
197 Allonzo Trier I 2.50 6.00
198 Bruce Brown I 5.00 12.00
199 Luka Doncic I 125.00 300.00
200 Rodions Kurucs I 3.00 8.00
201 Stephen Curry MET 60.00 150.00
202 Giannis Antetokounmpo MET 40.00 100.00
203 Anthony Davis MET 20.00 50.00
204 Kevin Durant MET 30.00 80.00
205 LeBron James MET 75.00 200.00
206 James Harden MET 15.00 40.00
207 Russell Westbrook MET 12.00 30.00
208 Kawhi Leonard MET 20.00 50.00
209 Joel Embiid MET 20.00 50.00
210 Kyrie Irving MET 20.00 50.00
211 Jimmy Butler MET 12.00 30.00
212 Paul George MET 12.00 30.00
213 Damian Lillard MET 20.00 50.00
214 Ben Simmons MET 8.00 20.00
215 Karl-Anthony Towns MET 12.00 30.00
216 Draymond Green MET 10.00 25.00
217 Donovan Mitchell MET 25.00 60.00
218 Nikola Jokic MET 40.00 100.00
219 Bradley Beal MET 10.00 25.00
220 LaMarcus Aldridge MET 8.00 20.00
221 Jayson Tatum MET 30.00 80.00
222 Blake Griffin MET 8.00 20.00
223 Devin Booker MET 20.00 50.00
224 Victor Oladipo MET 6.00 15.00
225 John Wall MET 10.00 25.00
226 Chris Paul MET 15.00 40.00
227 Vince Carter MET 15.00 40.00
228 Dwyane Wade MET 15.00 40.00
229 Klay Thompson MET 20.00 50.00
230 Derrick Rose MET 15.00 40.00
231 Luka Doncic MET 300.00 600.00
232 Jaren Jackson Jr. MET 40.00 100.00
233 Trae Young MET 40.00 100.00
234 Deandre Ayton MET 15.00 40.00
235 Wendell Carter Jr. MET 12.00 30.00
236 Kevin Knox MET 6.00 15.00
237 Shai Gilgeous-Alexander MET 150.00 400.00
238 Marvin Bagley III MET 8.00 20.00
239 Mo Bamba MET 8.00 20.00
240 Kevin Huerter MET 10.00 25.00
241 Miles Bridges MET 12.00 30.00
242 Mikal Bridges MET 25.00 60.00
243 Collin Sexton MET 15.00 40.00
244 Michael Porter Jr. MET 20.00 50.00
245 Robert Williams III MET 10.00 25.00
246 Aaron Holiday MET 8.00 20.00
247 Josh Okogie MET 8.00 20.00
248 Rodions Kurucs MET 6.00 15.00
249 Allonzo Trier MET 5.00 12.00
250 Mitchell Robinson MET 12.00 30.00
251 Charles Barkley FL 15.00 40.00
252 Reggie Miller FL 15.00 40.00
253 Shaquille O'Neal FL 25.00 60.00
254 Kareem Abdul-Jabbar FL 25.00 60.00
255 Allen Iverson FL 20.00 50.00
256 Larry Bird FL 30.00 80.00
257 Magic Johnson FL 30.00 80.00
258 David Robinson FL 15.00 40.00
259 Jerry West FL 15.00 40.00
260 Karl Malone FL 15.00 40.00
261 LeBron James FL 125.00 300.00
262 Dirk Nowitzki FL 20.00 50.00
263 Kevin Garnett FL 20.00 50.00
264 Tim Duncan FL 20.00 50.00
265 Paul Pierce FL 12.00 30.00
266 Jason Kidd FL 12.00 30.00
267 Kobe Bryant FL 125.00 300.00
268 John Stockton FL 15.00 40.00
269 Vince Carter FL 15.00 40.00
270 Robert Parish FL 12.00 30.00
271 LeBron James
Kobe Bryant SS 200.00 500.00
272 Stephen Curry
Kevin Durant SS 40.00 100.00
273 Bill Russell
Wilt Chamberlain SS 40.00 100.00
274 Dirk Nowitzki
Luka Doncic SS 100.00 250.00
275 James Harden
Russell Westbrook SS 15.00 40.00
276 Kareem Abdul-Jabbar
Giannis Antetokounmpo SS 40.00 100.00
277 Ben Simmons
Joel Embiid SS 20.00 50.00
278 Clyde Drexler
Damian Lillard SS 20.00 50.00
279 Anthony Davis
Giannis Antetokounmpo SS 40.00 100.00
280 Klay Thompson
Stephen Curry SS 50.00 120.00
281 Deandre Ayton
Joel Embiid SS 20.00 50.00
282 Trae Young
Stephen Curry SS 50.00 120.00
283 Ben Simmons
Julius Erving SS 20.00 50.00
284 Paul George
Russell Westbrook SS 12.00 30.00
285 LeBron James
Dwyane Wade SS 75.00 200.00
286 Kawhi Leonard
Kyle Lowry SS 20.00 50.00
287 Karl-Anthony Towns
Kevin Garnett SS 20.00 50.00
288 Ray Allen
Reggie Miller SS 15.00 40.00
289 Larry Bird
Magic Johnson SS 30.00 80.00
290 Mike Conley
Jaren Jackson Jr. SS 40.00 100.00
291 Luka Doncic VA 75.00 200.00
292 Kevin Durant VA 40.00 100.00
293 LeBron James VA 150.00 400.00
294 Stephen Curry VA 60.00 150.00
295 Deandre Ayton VA 15.00 40.00
296 Giannis Antetokounmpo VA 50.00 120.00
297 James Harden VA 25.00 60.00
298 Kobe Bryant VA 200.00 500.00
299 Trae Young VA 75.00 200.00
300 Dirk Nowitzki VA 25.00 60.00
301 Deandre Ayton AU JSY BW 40.00 100.00
302 Marvin Bagley III AU JSY BW 20.00 50.00
303 Luka Doncic AU JSY BW 2,500.00 5,000.00
304 Jaren Jackson Jr. AU JSY BW 300.00 600.00
305 Trae Young AU JSY BW 600.00 1,200.00
306 Mo Bamba AU JSY BW 20.00 50.00
307 Wendell Carter Jr. AU JSY BW 30.00 80.00
308 Collin Sexton AU JSY BW 40.00 100.00
309 Kevin Knox AU JSY BW 15.00 40.00
310 Mikal Bridges AU JSY BW 60.00 150.00
311 Shai Gilgeous-Alexander
AU JSY BW 1,000.00 2,000.00
312 Jerome Robinson AU JSY BW 12.00 30.00
313 Michael Porter Jr. AU JSY BW RC 50.00 125.00
314 Troy Brown Jr. AU JSY BW 15.00 40.00
315 Zhaire Smith AU JSY BW RC 12.00 30.00
316 Donte DiVincenzo AU JSY BW 30.00 80.00
317 Lonnie Walker IV AU JSY BW 25.00 60.00
318 Kevin Huerter AU JSY BW 25.00 60.00
319 Josh Okogie AU JSY BW 20.00 50.00
320 Grayson Allen AU JSY BW 25.00 60.00
321 Chandler Hutchison AU JSY BW 15.00 40.00
322 Aaron Holiday AU JSY BW RC 20.00 50.00
323 Anfernee Simons AU JSY BW 60.00 150.00
324 Moritz Wagner AU JSY BW RC 25.00 60.00
325 Landry Shamet AU JSY BW 20.00 50.00
326 Robert Williams III AU JSY BW RC 25.00 60.00
327 Jacob Evans III AU JSY BW 12.00 30.00
328 Dzanan Musa AU JSY BW RC 12.00 30.00
329 Omari Spellman AU JSY BW 12.00 30.00
330 Elie Okobo AU JSY BW 12.00 30.00
331 Jevon Carter AU JSY BW RC 20.00 50.00
332 Jalen Brunson AU JSY BW 200.00 500.00
333 Devonte' Graham AU JSY BW RC 20.00 50.00
334 Gary Trent Jr. AU JSY BW RC 25.00 60.00
335 Hamidou Diallo AU JSY BW 20.00 50.00
336 Svi Mykhailiuk AU JSY BW RC 15.00 40.00
337 Allonzo Trier AU JSY BW 12.00 30.00
338 Mitchell Robinson
AU JSY BW EXCH 30.00 80.00
339 Keita Bates-Diop AU JSY BW RC 15.00 40.00
340 Kostas Antetokounmpo
AU JSY BW 15.00 40.00
341 Deandre Ayton AU JSY C 40.00 100.00
342 Marvin Bagley III AU JSY C 20.00 50.00
343 Luka Doncic AU JSY C 3,000.00 6,000.00
344 Jaren Jackson Jr. AU JSY C 300.00 600.00
345 Trae Young AU JSY C 600.00 1,200.00
346 Mo Bamba AU JSY C 20.00 50.00
347 Wendell Carter Jr. AU JSY C 30.00 80.00
348 Collin Sexton AU JSY C 40.00 100.00
349 Kevin Knox AU JSY C 15.00 40.00
350 Mikal Bridges AU JSY C 60.00 150.00
351 Shai Gilgeous-Alexander
AU JSY C 1,000.00 2,000.00
352 Jerome Robinson AU JSY C 12.00 30.00
353 Michael Porter Jr. AU JSY C 50.00 125.00
354 Troy Brown Jr. AU JSY C 15.00 40.00
355 Zhaire Smith AU JSY C 12.00 30.00
356 Donte DiVincenzo AU JSY C 30.00 80.00
357 Lonnie Walker IV AU JSY C 25.00 60.00
358 Kevin Huerter AU JSY C 25.00 60.00
359 Josh Okogie AU JSY C 20.00 50.00
360 Grayson Allen AU JSY C 25.00 60.00
361 Chandler Hutchison AU JSY C 15.00 40.00
362 Aaron Holiday AU JSY C 20.00 50.00
363 Anfernee Simons AU JSY C 60.00 150.00
364 Moritz Wagner AU JSY C 25.00 60.00
365 Landry Shamet AU JSY C 20.00 50.00
366 Robert Williams III AU JSY C 25.00 60.00
367 Jacob Evans III AU JSY C 12.00 30.00
368 Dzanan Musa AU JSY C 12.00 30.00
369 Omari Spellman AU JSY C 12.00 30.00
370 Elie Okobo AU JSY C 12.00 30.00
371 Jevon Carter AU JSY C 20.00 50.00
372 Jalen Brunson AU JSY C 200.00 500.00
373 Devonte' Graham AU JSY C 20.00 50.00
374 Gary Trent Jr. AU JSY C 25.00 60.00
375 Hamidou Diallo AU JSY C 20.00 50.00
376 Svi Mykhailiuk AU JSY C 15.00 40.00
377 Allonzo Trier AU JSY C 12.00 30.00
378 Mitchell Robinson
AU JSY C EXCH 30.00 80.00
379 Keita Bates-Diop AU JSY C 15.00 40.00
380 Kostas Antetokounmpo AU JSY C 5.00 12.00
381 Rodions Kurucs AU 8.00 20.00
382 Melvin Frazier Jr. AU RC 6.00 15.00
383 Mitchell Robinson AU EXCH 15.00 40.00
384 Bruce Brown AU 12.00 30.00
385 Chimezie Metu AU RC 8.00 20.00
386 J.P. Macura AU RC 8.00 20.00
387 Allonzo Trier AU 6.00 15.00
388 Yuta Watanabe AU RC 20.00 50.00
389 Duncan Robinson AU RC 10.00 25.00
390 Gary Clark AU RC 6.00 15.00
391 Monte Morris AU RC 15.00 40.00
392 Luka Doncic AU 2,000.00 4,000.00
393 Deandre Ayton AU 20.00 50.00
394 Trae Young AU 150.00 400.00
395 Mo Bamba AU 10.00 25.00
396 Kevin Knox AU 8.00 20.00
397 Jacob Evans III AU RC 6.00 15.00
398 Anfernee Simons AU RC 75.00 200.00
399 Khyri Thomas AU RC 6.00 15.00
400 Donte DiVincenzo AU 15.00 40.00

2018-19 Panini Noir 10th Anniversary Signatures

STATED PRINT RUN 49 SER.#'d SETS
EXCHANGE DEADLINE 12/12/2020
1 Charles Barkley 200.00 500.00
2 Kobe Bryant 2,500.00 5,000.00
3 Anthony Davis 150.00 400.00
4 Kyrie Irving 150.00 400.00
5 Allen Iverson 200.00 500.00
6 Donovan Mitchell 125.00 300.00
7 Jayson Tatum 200.00 500.00
8 Shaquille O'Neal 200.00 500.00
9 Larry Bird 200.00 500.00
10 Magic Johnson 200.00 500.00

2018-19 Panini Noir Black and White Autographs

STATED PRINT RUN 99 SER.#'d SETS
EXCHANGE DEADLINE 12/12/2020
1 Gordon Hayward 10.00 25.00
3 Jonas Jerebko 6.00 15.00
4 Kelly Olynyk 6.00 15.00
5 J.J. Barea 10.00 25.00
6 Caris LeVert 10.00 25.00
7 Jordan Bell 6.00 15.00
8 Taurean Prince 6.00 15.00
9 Nemanja Bjelica 6.00 15.00
10 John Collins 10.00 25.00
11 Domantas Sabonis 12.00 30.00
12 LaMarcus Aldridge 10.00 25.00
13 Nikola Jokic 200.00 500.00
14 Josh Hart 8.00 20.00
15 Kevin Love 8.00 20.00
16 Isaiah Thomas 8.00 20.00
18 Myles Turner 10.00 25.00
19 Buddy Hield 10.00 25.00
20 Bruce Bowen 8.00 20.00
21 Jacque Vaughn 6.00 15.00
22 Muggsy Bogues 10.00 25.00
23 Sean Elliott 8.00 20.00
24 Kerry Kittles 6.00 15.00
25 Vlade Divac 10.00 25.00
26 Antonio McDyess 8.00 20.00
27 Bryon Russell 6.00 15.00
28 Brian Scalabrine 6.00 15.00
29 Wally Szczerbiak 8.00 20.00
30 Mike Bibby 10.00 25.00

2018-19 Panini Noir Box Office Memorabilia

STATED PRINT RUN 99 SER.#'d SETS
*PRIME/21-25: .75X TO 2X BASIC
1 Goran Dragic 2.50 6.00
2 CJ McCollum 3.00 8.00
3 Jeremy Lin 5.00 12.00
4 De'Aaron Fox 6.00 15.00
5 Dennis Schroder 2.50 6.00
6 Aaron Gordon 3.00 8.00
7 Dwight Howard 4.00 10.00
8 Anthony Davis 8.00 20.00
9 Enes Kanter 2.50 6.00
10 Bradley Beal 4.00 10.00
11 James Harden 6.00 15.00
12 Clint Capela 2.50 6.00
13 Jimmy Butler 5.00 12.00
14 DeAndre Jordan 2.50 6.00
15 Derrick Rose 6.00 15.00
16 Andre Drummond 2.50 6.00
17 Dwyane Wade 6.00 15.00
18 Ben Simmons 3.00 8.00
19 Eric Gordon 2.50 6.00
20 Buddy Hield 3.00 8.00
21 Jayson Tatum 12.00 30.00
22 Damian Lillard 8.00 20.00
23 Joe Ingles 2.50 6.00
24 DeMar DeRozan 4.00 10.00
25 Donovan Mitchell 10.00 25.00
26 Andrew Wiggins 4.00 10.00
27 Elfrid Payton 2.50 6.00
28 Blake Griffin 3.00 8.00
29 Giannis Antetokounmpo 15.00 40.00
30 Chris Paul 6.00 15.00

2018-19 Panini Noir Color Autographs

STATED PRINT RUN 99 SER.#'d SETS
EXCHANGE DEADLINE 12/12/2020
1 Gordon Hayward 10.00 25.00

3 Jonas Jerebko 6.00 15.00
4 Kelly Olynyk 6.00 15.00
5 J.J. Barea 10.00 25.00
6 Caris LeVert 10.00 25.00
7 Jordan Bell 6.00 15.00
8 Taurean Prince 6.00 15.00
9 Nemanja Bjelica 6.00 15.00
10 John Collins 10.00 25.00
11 Domantas Sabonis 12.00 30.00
12 LaMarcus Aldridge 10.00 25.00
13 Nikola Jokic 200.00 500.00
14 Lonzo Ball 10.00 25.00
15 Kevin Love 8.00 20.00
16 Isaiah Thomas 8.00 20.00
18 Myles Turner 10.00 25.00
19 Buddy Hield 10.00 25.00
20 Bruce Bowen 8.00 20.00
21 Jacque Vaughn 6.00 15.00
22 Muggsy Bogues 10.00 25.00
23 Sean Elliott 8.00 20.00
24 Kerry Kittles 6.00 15.00
25 Vlade Divac 10.00 25.00
26 Antonio McDyess 8.00 20.00
27 Bryon Russell 6.00 15.00
28 Brian Scalabrine 6.00 15.00
29 Wally Szczerbiak 8.00 20.00
30 Mike Bibby 10.00 25.00

2018-19 Panini Noir Dish Night Memorabilia

STATED PRINT RUN 65 SER.#'d SETS
1 Tyreke Evans 2.50 6.00
2 Mark Jackson 3.00 8.00
3 Mike Conley 3.00 8.00
4 Derrick Rose 8.00 20.00
5 Jeremy Lin 6.00 15.00
6 Russell Westbrook 6.00 15.00
7 Tony Parker 6.00 15.00
8 De'Aaron Fox 8.00 20.00
9 Reggie Jackson 3.00 8.00
10 John Wall 5.00 12.00
11 Avery Bradley 2.50 6.00
12 Magic Johnson 15.00 40.00
13 Goran Dragic 3.00 8.00
14 Jrue Holiday 5.00 12.00
15 Kyrie Irving 10.00 25.00
16 Ben Simmons 4.00 10.00
17 Dennis Smith Jr. 2.50 6.00
18 Kyle Lowry 4.00 10.00
19 Stephen Curry 40.00 100.00
20 John Stockton 8.00 20.00
21 Lonzo Ball 4.00 10.00
22 Steve Francis 3.00 8.00
23 Eric Bledsoe 3.00 8.00
24 Tim Hardaway Jr. 2.50 6.00
25 D'Angelo Russell 4.00 10.00
26 Damian Lillard 10.00 25.00
27 Gary Harris 3.00 8.00
28 Ricky Rubio 3.00 8.00
29 Chris Paul 8.00 20.00
30 Danny Ainge 4.00 10.00

2018-19 Panini Noir Elegant Decor Rookie Jerseys

STATED PRINT RUN 65 SER.#'d SETS
1 Mikal Bridges 12.00 30.00
2 Zhaire Smith 2.50 6.00
3 Michael Porter Jr. 10.00 25.00
4 Lonnie Walker IV 5.00 12.00
5 Deandre Ayton 8.00 20.00
6 Grayson Allen 5.00 12.00
7 Jaren Jackson Jr. 20.00 50.00
8 Elie Okobo 2.50 6.00
9 Wendell Carter Jr. 6.00 15.00
10 Devonte' Graham 4.00 10.00
11 Shai Gilgeous-Alexander 60.00 150.00
12 Aaron Holiday 4.00 10.00
13 Troy Brown Jr. 3.00 8.00
14 Kevin Huerter 5.00 12.00
15 Marvin Bagley III 4.00 10.00
16 Landry Shamet 4.00 10.00
17 Trae Young 30.00 80.00
18 Jalen Brunson 20.00 50.00
19 Collin Sexton 8.00 20.00
20 Hamidou Diallo 4.00 10.00
21 Jerome Robinson 2.50 6.00
22 Jacob Evans III 2.50 6.00
23 Donte DiVincenzo 6.00 15.00
24 Josh Okogie 4.00 10.00
25 Luka Doncic 75.00 200.00
26 Omari Spellman 2.50 6.00
27 Mo Bamba 4.00 10.00
28 Jevon Carter 4.00 10.00
29 Kevin Knox 3.00 8.00
30 Bruce Brown 5.00 12.00

2018-19 Panini Noir Horizontal Spotlight Signatures

PRINT RUNS B/WN 49-99 COPIES PER
EXCHANGE DEADLINE 12/12/2020
2 Luka Doncic/99 EXCH 3,000.00 6,000.00
3 Kevin Knox/99 15.00 40.00
4 Collin Sexton/99 75.00 200.00
5 Josh Okogie/99 20.00 50.00
6 Chandler Hutchison/99 15.00 40.00
7 Omari Spellman/99 12.00 30.00
8 Jason Kidd/99 75.00 200.00
9 Ray Allen/99 100.00 250.00
10 Larry Bird/49 150.00 400.00
11 Tracy McGrady/99 150.00 400.00
12 Jayson Tatum/99 400.00 800.00
13 De'Aaron Fox/99 100.00 250.00
14 Zach LaVine/99 100.00 250.00
15 Jason Williams/99 150.00 400.00
16 LaMarcus Aldridge/99 75.00 200.00
17 Paul Pierce/99 100.00 250.00
18 Jarrett Allen/99 25.00 60.00
19 Chris Bosh/99 60.00 150.00
20 Khris Middleton/99 40.00 100.00
21 Nikola Jokic/99 300.00 600.00
22 Danny Manning/99 15.00 40.00
23 David Robinson/99 75.00 200.00
24 Steve Kerr/99 60.00 150.00
25 Dominique Wilkins/99 60.00 150.00

2018-19 Panini Noir Jumbo Material

PRINT RUNS B/WN 49-99 COPIES PER
1 Nerlens Noel/49 2.50 6.00
2 Vince Carter/49 8.00 20.00
3 Nikola Vucevic/49 2.50 6.00
4 D'Angelo Russell/49 4.00 10.00
5 CJ McCollum/49 4.00 10.00
6 Stephen Curry/99 25.00 60.00
7 Buddy Hield/49 4.00 10.00
8 Malcolm Brogdon/49 4.00 10.00
9 Kyle Lowry/49 4.00 10.00
10 Jrue Holiday/49 5.00 12.00
11 Dennis Schroder/49 3.00 8.00
12 John Collins/49 4.00 10.00
13 Joel Embiid/49 10.00 25.00
14 Kevin Love/49 2.50 6.00
15 Evan Turner/49 2.50 6.00
16 Kevin Durant/49 15.00 40.00
17 LaMarcus Aldridge/49 4.00 10.00
18 Khris Middleton/49 4.00 10.00
19 Rudy Gobert/49 4.00 10.00
20 Nikola Mirotic/99 2.00 5.00
21 Russell Westbrook/49 6.00 15.00
22 Jeremy Lin/49 6.00 15.00
23 Markelle Fultz/49 3.00 8.00
24 DeAndre Jordan/49 3.00 8.00
25 Damian Lillard/49 10.00 25.00
26 Goran Dragic/49 3.00 8.00
27 DeMar DeRozan/49 5.00 12.00
28 Karl-Anthony Towns/49 6.00 15.00
29 Joe Ingles/99 2.50 6.00
30 Elfrid Payton/49 3.00 8.00
31 Aaron Gordon/49 4.00 10.00
32 Kyrie Irving/49 10.00 25.00
33 Jimmy Butler/49 6.00 15.00
34 Nikola Jokic/49 20.00 50.00
35 Bogdan Bogdanovic/49 4.00 10.00
36 Dwyane Wade/49 8.00 20.00
37 Pau Gasol/49 6.00 15.00
38 Derrick Rose/99 6.00 15.00
39 Donovan Mitchell/49 12.00 30.00
40 Julius Randle/49 4.00 10.00
41 Jonathan Isaac/49 4.00 10.00
42 Jayson Tatum/49 15.00 40.00
43 Ben Simmons/49 4.00 10.00
44 Paul Millsap/49 3.00 8.00
45 De'Aaron Fox/49 8.00 20.00
46 Hassan Whiteside/49 3.00 8.00
47 Serge Ibaka/99 2.50 6.00
48 Andrew Wiggins/49 5.00 12.00
49 Ricky Rubio/49 3.00 8.00
50 Steven Adams/99 2.50 6.00
51 Terrence Ross/99 2.50 6.00
52 Allen Crabbe/99 2.50 6.00
53 Seth Curry/49 3.00 8.00
54 Jamal Murray/49 8.00 20.00
55 Harry Giles/49 2.50 6.00
56 Giannis Antetokounmpo/49 20.00 50.00
57 Kawhi Leonard/49 10.00 25.00
58 Anthony Davis/49 10.00 25.00
59 George Hill/49 3.00 8.00
60 Paul George/49 6.00 15.00

2018-19 Panini Noir New Wave Jerseys

STATED PRINT RUN 99 SER.#'d SETS
*PRIME: .6X TO 1.5X BASIC
1 Luka Doncic 125.00 300.00
2 Devonte' Graham 3.00 8.00
3 Jevon Carter 3.00 8.00
4 Troy Brown Jr. 2.50 6.00
5 Landry Shamet 3.00 8.00
6 Mikal Bridges 10.00 25.00
7 Collin Sexton 6.00 15.00
8 Lonnie Walker IV 4.00 10.00
9 Jacob Evans III 2.00 5.00
10 Jaren Jackson Jr. 15.00 40.00
11 Omari Spellman 2.00 5.00
12 Shai Gilgeous-Alexander 60.00 150.00
13 Kevin Knox 2.50 6.00
14 Kevin Huerter 4.00 10.00
15 Trae Young 30.00 80.00
16 Zhaire Smith 2.00 5.00
17 Hamidou Diallo 3.00 8.00
18 Deandre Ayton 6.00 15.00
19 Donte DiVincenzo 5.00 12.00
20 Elie Okobo 2.00 5.00
21 Mo Bamba 3.00 8.00
22 Aaron Holiday 3.00 8.00
23 Bruce Brown 4.00 10.00
24 Marvin Bagley III 3.00 8.00
25 Jalen Brunson 15.00 40.00
26 Michael Porter Jr. 8.00 20.00
27 Jerome Robinson 2.00 5.00
28 Grayson Allen 4.00 10.00
29 Josh Okogie 3.00 8.00
30 Wendell Carter Jr. 5.00 12.00

2018-19 Panini Noir Newsreels Jerseys

STATED PRINT RUN 65 SER.#'d SETS
1 Marc Gasol 4.00 10.00
2 Joel Embiid 10.00 25.00
3 Nerlens Noel 2.50 6.00
4 Julius Randle 4.00 10.00
5 Reggie Jackson 3.00 8.00
6 Kevin Durant 15.00 40.00
7 Serge Ibaka 3.00 8.00
8 Kyle Kuzma 4.00 10.00
9 Tony Parker 6.00 15.00
10 Lauri Markkanen 6.00 15.00
11 Markelle Fultz 3.00 8.00
12 John Wall 5.00 12.00
13 Nikola Jokic 20.00 50.00
14 Karl-Anthony Towns 6.00 15.00
15 Ricky Rubio 3.00 8.00
16 Kevin Love 3.00 8.00
17 Stephen Curry 30.00 80.00
18 Kyle Lowry 4.00 10.00
19 Tyreke Evans 2.50 6.00
20 LeBron James 30.00 80.00
21 Mike Conley 3.00 8.00
22 Josh Jackson 2.50 6.00
23 Pau Gasol 6.00 15.00
24 Kawhi Leonard 10.00 25.00
25 Rudy Gobert 5.00 12.00
26 Khris Middleton 4.00 10.00
27 Tim Hardaway Jr. 2.50 6.00
28 Kyrie Irving 10.00 25.00
29 Victor Oladipo 3.00 8.00
30 Lonzo Ball 4.00 10.00
31 Myles Turner 4.00 10.00
32 Jrue Holiday 5.00 12.00
33 Paul George 6.00 15.00
34 Kemba Walker 3.00 8.00
35 Russell Westbrook 6.00 15.00
36 George Hill 3.00 8.00
37 Tobias Harris 3.00 8.00
38 LaMarcus Aldridge 4.00 10.00
39 Zach LaVine 6.00 15.00
40 Lou Williams 3.00 8.00

2018-19 Panini Noir Prime Materials Black and White Autographs

PRINT RUNS B/WN 10-40 COPIES PER
NO PRICING ON QTY 15 OR LESS
EXCHANGE DEADLINE 12/12/2020
2 Gordon Hayward/40 12.00 30.00
4 J.J. Barea/40 12.00 30.00
5 Caris LeVert/40 12.00 30.00
6 Taurean Prince/40 8.00 20.00
7 John Collins/40 12.00 30.00
8 Gary Harris/40 10.00 25.00
9 Karl-Anthony Towns/40 40.00 100.00
15 Tracy McGrady/40 75.00 200.00
16 LaMarcus Aldridge/40 20.00 50.00
17 Nikola Jokic/40 300.00 600.00
18 Kevin Love/40 10.00 25.00
19 De'Aaron Fox/40 50.00 120.00

2018-19 Panini Noir Prime Materials Color Autographs

PRINT RUNS B/WN 10-40 COPIES PER
NO PRICING ON QTY 15 OR LESS
EXCHANGE DEADLINE 12/12/2020
2 Gordon Hayward/40 12.00 30.00
4 J.J. Barea/40 12.00 30.00
5 Caris LeVert/40 12.00 30.00
6 Taurean Prince/40 8.00 20.00
7 John Collins/40 12.00 30.00
8 Gary Harris/40 10.00 25.00
9 Karl-Anthony Towns/40 40.00 100.00
15 Tracy McGrady/40 75.00 200.00
16 LaMarcus Aldridge/40 20.00 50.00
17 Nikola Jokic/40 300.00 600.00
18 Kevin Love/40 10.00 25.00
19 De'Aaron Fox/40 50.00 120.00

2018-19 Panini Noir Reigning Nights Signatures

PRINT RUNS B/WN 25-99 COPIES PER
EXCHANGE DEADLINE 12/12/2020
1 Trae Young/99 500.00 1,000.00
2 Donte DiVincenzo/99 25.00 60.00
3 Luka Doncic/99 2,000.00 4,000.00
4 Allonzo Trier/99 10.00 25.00
5 Mikal Bridges/99 50.00 125.00
6 Troy Brown Jr./99 12.00 30.00
7 Grayson Allen/99 20.00 50.00
8 Aaron Holiday/99 15.00 40.00
9 Landry Shamet/99 15.00 40.00
10 Dzanan Musa/99 10.00 25.00
11 Elie Okobo/99 10.00 25.00
12 Jalen Brunson/25 150.00 400.00
13 Devonte' Graham/99 15.00 40.00
14 Svi Mykhailiuk/99 12.00 30.00
15 Jason Kidd/99 25.00 60.00
16 Ray Allen/99 40.00 100.00
17 Kobe Bryant/99 3,000.00 6,000.00
18 Larry Bird/99 125.00 300.00
19 Gordon Hayward/99 15.00 40.00
20 Kevin Love/99 12.00 30.00
22 Tracy McGrady/99 100.00 250.00
23 Allen Iverson/99 100.00 250.00
24 Jayson Tatum/99 150.00 400.00
25 Buddy Hield/99 15.00 40.00
26 Jason Williams/99 50.00 120.00
27 Antoine Walker/99 12.00 30.00
28 Detlef Schrempf/99 15.00 40.00
29 Jeff Hornacek/99 15.00 40.00
30 Wally Szczerbiak/99 12.00 30.00
31 Rashard Lewis/99 12.00 30.00
32 Dell Curry/99 15.00 40.00
33 Tim Hardaway/99 20.00 50.00
34 Glen Rice/99 20.00 50.00
35 Chauncey Billups/99 20.00 50.00
36 Robert Horry/99 15.00 40.00
37 Mark Jackson/99 12.00 30.00
38 Paul Pierce/99 50.00 120.00
39 Peja Stojakovic/99 12.00 30.00
40 Rick Fox/99 12.00 30.00

2018-19 Panini Noir Rookie Jumbo Material

STATED PRINT RUN 99 SER.#'d SETS
1 Shai Gilgeous-Alexander 60.00 150.00
2 Elie Okobo 2.00 5.00
3 Wendell Carter Jr. 5.00 12.00
4 Jacob Evans III 2.00 5.00
5 Josh Okogie 3.00 8.00
6 Jarred Vanderbilt 4.00 10.00
7 Lonnie Walker IV 4.00 10.00
8 Aaron Holiday 3.00 8.00
9 Mikal Bridges 10.00 25.00
10 Collin Sexton 6.00 15.00
11 Svi Mykhailiuk 5.00 12.00
12 Gary Trent Jr. 4.00 10.00
13 Kevin Huerter 4.00 10.00
14 Jalen Brunson 15.00 40.00
15 Keita Bates-Diop 2.50 6.00
16 Jevon Carter 3.00 8.00
17 Luka Doncic 100.00 250.00
18 Anfernee Simons 10.00 25.00
19 Mo Bamba 3.00 8.00
20 Deandre Ayton 6.00 15.00
21 Trae Young 40.00 100.00
22 Grayson Allen 4.00 10.00
23 Allonzo Trier 2.00 5.00
24 Jaren Jackson Jr. 15.00 40.00
25 Kevin Knox 2.50 6.00
26 Moritz Wagner 4.00 10.00
27 Marvin Bagley III 3.00 8.00
28 Bruce Brown 4.00 10.00
29 Omari Spellman 2.00 5.00
30 Devonte' Graham 3.00 8.00
31 Troy Brown Jr. 2.50 6.00
32 Hamidou Diallo 3.00 8.00
33 Mitchell Robinson 5.00 12.00
34 Jerome Robinson 2.00 5.00
35 Landry Shamet 3.00 8.00
36 Zhaire Smith 2.00 5.00
37 Michael Porter Jr. 8.00 20.00
38 Chandler Hutchison 2.50 6.00
39 Robert Williams III 4.00 10.00
40 Donte DiVincenzo 5.00 12.00

2018-19 Panini Noir Shadow Signatures

PRINT RUNS B/WN 25-99 COPIES PER
EXCHANGE DEADLINE 12/12/2020
1 Deandre Ayton/99 20.00 50.00
2 Jaren Jackson Jr./25 150.00 400.00
3 Wendell Carter Jr./99 15.00 40.00
4 Michael Porter Jr./99 25.00 60.00
5 Grayson Allen/99 12.00 30.00
6 Robert Williams III/99 12.00 30.00
7 Jacob Evans III/99 6.00 15.00
8 Hamidou Diallo/99 10.00 25.00
9 Charles Barkley/99 125.00 300.00
10 Grant Hill/99 40.00 100.00
11 Shaquille O'Neal/99 200.00 500.00
12 Brandon Ingram/99 EXCH 10.00 25.00
13 Magic Johnson/99 125.00 300.00
14 Giannis Antetokounmpo/49 EXCH 200.00 500.00
15 Caris LeVert/99 10.00 25.00
16 Jordan Bell/99 6.00 15.00
17 John Collins/99 10.00 25.00
18 Anthony Davis/49 100.00 250.00
19 Tracy McGrady/99 125.00 300.00
20 Dennis Rodman/99 125.00 300.00
21 Zach LaVine/99 75.00 200.00
22 Ray Allen/99 75.00 200.00
23 David Robinson/99 60.00 150.00
24 Nikola Mirotic/99 6.00 15.00
25 Dominique Wilkins/99 40.00 100.00
26 Luka Doncic/99 1,500.00 3,000.00
27 Trae Young/99 800.00 1,500.00
28 Bruce Brown/99 12.00 30.00
29 Devonte' Graham/99 10.00 25.00
30 Jalen Brunson/25 150.00 400.00

2018-19 Panini Noir Showtime Signatures

PRINT RUNS B/WN 25-99 COPIES PER
EXCHANGE DEADLINE 12/12/2020
1 Mo Bamba/99 12.00 30.00
2 Michael Porter Jr./99 30.00 80.00
3 Zhaire Smith/99 8.00 20.00
4 Josh Okogie/25 12.00 30.00
5 Aaron Holiday/99 12.00 30.00
6 Moritz Wagner/99 15.00 40.00
7 Omari Spellman/99 8.00 20.00
8 Brandon Ingram/99 EXCH 12.00 30.00
9 Giannis Antetokounmpo/49 EXCH 300.00 600.00
10 Lonzo Ball/99 60.00 150.00
12 Myles Turner/99 12.00 30.00
13 Elfrid Payton/99 10.00 25.00
14 Gary Harris/99 10.00 25.00
15 Kyle Kuzma/99 12.00 30.00
16 Pascal Siakam/99 40.00 100.00
17 De'Aaron Fox/99 60.00 150.00
18 Isaiah Thomas/99 10.00 25.00
19 Kevin Durant/99 200.00 500.00
20 Dwyane Wade/99 125.00 300.00
21 Kyrie Irving/99 125.00 300.00
22 Damian Lillard/99 150.00 400.00
23 Karl-Anthony Towns/99 50.00 120.00
24 Zach LaVine/99 75.00 200.00
25 Buddy Hield/99 12.00 30.00
26 Anthony Davis/99 125.00 300.00
27 Donovan Mitchell/99 150.00 400.00
29 Collin Sexton/25 40.00 100.00
30 DeMarcus Cousins/99 100.00 250.00

2018-19 Panini Noir Sneaker Spotlight Autographs

PRINT RUNS B/WN 49-99 COPIES PER
EXCHANGE DEADLINE 12/12/2020
1 Kevin Durant/49 1,500.00 3,000.00
3 Donovan Mitchell/99 600.00 1,200.00
4 Luka Doncic/99 8,000.00 12,000.00
5 Deandre Ayton/99 150.00 400.00
6 Trae Young/99 2,000.00 4,000.00
7 Kyrie Irving/49 200.00 500.00
8 Langston Galloway/99 20.00 50.00
9 Montrezl Harrell/99 75.00 200.00
10 Kyle Kuzma/99 100.00 250.00
11 Lonzo Ball/99 150.00 400.00
12 John Collins/99 75.00 200.00
13 Dwyane Wade/49 400.00 800.00
15 Gary Harris/99 30.00 80.00
16 Damian Lillard/49 600.00 1,200.00
17 Karl-Anthony Towns/49 200.00 500.00
18 Meyers Leonard/99 25.00 60.00
19 LaMarcus Aldridge/99 125.00 300.00
20 Taurean Prince/99 25.00 60.00
21 Brandon Ingram/49 EXCH 125.00 300.00
22 Jerami Grant/99 125.00 300.00
23 Jevon Carter/99 75.00 200.00
24 Kobe Bryant/49 10,000.00 20,000.00
25 Shaquille O'Neal/49 800.00 1,500.00
27 Ray Allen/99 125.00 300.00
28 Jason Kidd/99 100.00 250.00
29 Spencer Dinwiddie/99 75.00 200.00
30 Marvin Bagley III/99 75.00 200.00
31 Mo Bamba/99 75.00 200.00
32 Kevin Knox/99 75.00 200.00
33 Shai Gilgeous-Alexander/99 3,000.00 6,000.00
34 Troy Brown Jr./99 60.00 150.00
35 Jeremy Lin/99 150.00 400.00
36 Grayson Allen/99 75.00 200.00
37 Omari Spellman/99 75.00 200.00
38 Bam Adebayo/99 200.00 500.00
39 Hamidou Diallo/99 125.00 300.00
40 Allonzo Trier/99 20.00 50.00

2018-19 Panini Noir Two Shot Rookie Jerseys

STATED PRINT RUN 99 SER.#'d SETS
*PRIME/25: .6X TO 1.5X BASIC
1 Kevin Huerter
Trae Young 20.00 50.00
2 Deandre Ayton
Elie Okobo 8.00 20.00
3 Kevin Huerter
Omari Spellman 5.00 12.00
4 Simons/Trent Jr. 12.00 30.00
5 Luka Doncic
Jalen Brunson 100.00 250.00
6 Kevin Knox
Shai Gilgeous-Alexander 25.00 60.00
7 Jerome Robinson
Shai Gilgeous-Alexander 40.00 100.00
8 Keita Bates-Diop
Josh Okogie 4.00 10.00
9 Trae Young
Luka Doncic 75.00 200.00
10 Zhaire Smith
Landry Shamet 4.00 10.00
11 Trae Young
Omari Spellman 20.00 50.00
12 Elie Okobo
Mikal Bridges 12.00 30.00
13 Chandler Hutchison
Wendell Carter Jr. 6.00 15.00
14 Marvin Bagley III
Wendell Carter Jr. 6.00 15.00
15 Jarred Vanderbilt
Michael Porter Jr. 10.00 25.00
16 Mikal Bridges
Donte DiVincenzo 12.00 30.00
17 Jaren Jackson Jr.
Jevon Carter 20.00 50.00
18 Allonzo Trier
Kevin Knox 3.00 8.00
19 Deandre Ayton
Marvin Bagley III 8.00 20.00
20 Deandre Ayton
Mikal Bridges 12.00 30.00

2018-19 Panini Noir Vertical Spotlight Signatures

PRINT RUNS B/WN 49-99 COPIES PER
EXCHANGE DEADLINE 12/12/2020
1 Deandre Ayton/99 40.00 100.00
2 Trae Young/99 1,000.00 2,000.00
3 Marvin Bagley III/99 20.00 50.00
4 Troy Brown Jr./99 15.00 40.00
5 Lonnie Walker IV/99 25.00 60.00
6 Grayson Allen/99 25.00 60.00
7 Dzanan Musa/99 12.00 30.00
8 Hamidou Diallo/99 20.00 50.00
9 Grant Hill/99 125.00 300.00
10 Magic Johnson/99 200.00 500.00
11 Dennis Rodman/99 400.00 800.00
12 Giannis Antetokounmpo
99 EXCH 800.00 1,500.00
13 Allen Iverson/49 400.00 800.00
14 Monte Morris/99 30.00 80.00
15 Brian Scalabrine/99 12.00 30.00
17 J.J. Barea/99 20.00 50.00
18 Nikola Mirotic/99 12.00 30.00
19 Damian Lillard/99 400.00 800.00
20 Kyrie Irving/99 200.00 500.00
21 Lonzo Ball/99 20.00 50.00
22 Rick Fox/99 15.00 40.00
23 Glen Rice/99 20.00 50.00
24 Chauncey Billups/99 100.00 250.00
25 Robert Horry/99 40.00 100.00

2019-20 Panini Noir

1 Khris Middleton A 3.00 8.00
2 Bojan Bogdanovic A 2.50 6.00
3 Collin Sexton A 4.00 10.00
4 Kawhi Leonard A 8.00 20.00
5 Joel Embiid A 6.00 15.00
6 Bam Adebayo A 5.00 12.00
7 DeAndre Jordan A 2.50 6.00
8 Nikola Vucevic A 2.50 6.00
9 Donovan Mitchell A 6.00 15.00
10 James Harden A 6.00 15.00
11 Malcolm Brogdon A 2.50 6.00
12 Caris LeVert A 2.50 6.00
13 Zach LaVine A 5.00 12.00
14 Paul George A 5.00 12.00
15 Ben Simmons A 3.00 8.00
16 Terry Rozier A 2.50 6.00
17 Kevin Knox II A 2.00 5.00
18 Aaron Gordon A 3.00 8.00
19 Rudy Gobert A 4.00 10.00
20 Jaren Jackson Jr. A 5.00 12.00
21 Domantas Sabonis A 4.00 10.00
22 Jaylen Brown A 5.00 12.00
23 Lauri Markkanen A 4.00 10.00
24 Stephen Curry A 25.00 60.00
25 Kemba Walker A 2.50 6.00
26 Miles Bridges A 3.00 8.00
27 Marcus Morris Sr. A 2.00 5.00
28 Luka Doncic A 20.00 50.00
29 Damian Lillard A 8.00 20.00
30 Jonas Valanciunas A 2.50 6.00
31 Blake Griffin A 3.00 8.00
32 Goran Dragic A 2.50 6.00
33 Anthony Davis A 8.00 20.00
34 D'Angelo Russell A 2.50 6.00
35 Jayson Tatum A 12.00 30.00
36 John Collins A 3.00 8.00
37 Karl-Anthony Towns A 5.00 12.00
38 Kristaps Porzingis A 4.00 10.00
39 CJ McCollum A 3.00 8.00
40 Brandon Ingram A 3.00 8.00
41 Andre Drummond A 2.50 6.00
42 Fred VanVleet A 4.00 10.00
43 LeBron James A 25.00 60.00
44 De'Aaron Fox A 5.00 12.00
45 Pascal Siakam A 5.00 12.00
46 Trae Young A 8.00 20.00
47 Andrew Wiggins A 4.00 10.00
48 DeMar DeRozan A 4.00 10.00
49 Shai Gilgeous-Alexander A 15.00 40.00
50 Jrue Holiday A 4.00 10.00
51 Derrick Rose A 6.00 15.00
52 Hassan Whiteside A 2.00 5.00
53 Devin Booker A .75 2.00
54 Buddy Hield A 2.50 6.00
55 Kyle Lowry A 3.00 8.00
56 Bradley Beal A 4.00 10.00
57 Jamal Murray A 5.00 12.00
58 LaMarcus Aldridge A 3.00 8.00
59 Chris Paul A 6.00 15.00
60 Tobias Harris A 2.50 6.00
61 Kevin Love A 3.00 8.00
62 Marvin Bagley III A 2.50 6.00
63 Deandre Ayton A 3.00 8.00
64 Jimmy Butler A 6.00 15.00
65 Kyrie Irving A 6.00 15.00
66 Isaiah Thomas A 2.50 6.00
67 Nikola Jokic A 15.00 40.00
68 Russell Westbrook A 5.00 12.00
69 Giannis Antetokounmpo A 15.00 40.00
70 Lou Williams A 3.00 8.00
71 Khris Middleton I 3.00 8.00
72 Bojan Bogdanovic I 2.50 6.00
73 Collin Sexton I 4.00 10.00
74 Kawhi Leonard I 8.00 20.00
75 Joel Embiid I 6.00 15.00
76 Bam Adebayo I 5.00 12.00
77 DeAndre Jordan I 2.50 6.00
78 Nikola Vucevic I 2.50 6.00
79 Donovan Mitchell I 6.00 15.00
80 James Harden I 6.00 15.00
81 Malcolm Brogdon I 2.50 6.00
82 Caris LeVert I 2.50 6.00
83 Zach LaVine I 5.00 12.00
84 Paul George I 5.00 12.00
85 Ben Simmons I 3.00 8.00
86 Terry Rozier I 2.50 6.00
87 Kevin Knox II I 2.00 5.00
88 Aaron Gordon I 3.00 8.00
89 Rudy Gobert I 4.00 10.00
90 Jaren Jackson Jr. I 5.00 12.00
91 Domantas Sabonis I 4.00 10.00
92 Jaylen Brown I 5.00 12.00
93 Lauri Markkanen I 4.00 10.00
94 Stephen Curry I 25.00 60.00
95 Kemba Walker I 2.50 6.00
96 Miles Bridges I 3.00 8.00
97 Marcus Morris Sr. I 2.00 5.00
98 Luka Doncic I 20.00 50.00
99 Damian Lillard I 8.00 20.00
100 Jonas Valanciunas I 2.50 6.00
101 Blake Griffin I 3.00 8.00
102 Goran Dragic I 2.50 6.00
103 Anthony Davis I 8.00 20.00
104 D'Angelo Russell I 2.50 6.00
105 Jayson Tatum I 12.00 30.00
106 John Collins I 3.00 8.00
107 Karl-Anthony Towns I 5.00 12.00
108 Kristaps Porzingis I 4.00 10.00
109 CJ McCollum I 3.00 8.00
110 Brandon Ingram I 3.00 8.00
111 Andre Drummond I 2.50 6.00
112 Fred VanVleet I 4.00 10.00
113 LeBron James I 25.00 60.00
114 De'Aaron Fox I 5.00 12.00
115 Pascal Siakam I 5.00 12.00
116 Trae Young I 8.00 20.00
117 Andrew Wiggins I 4.00 10.00
118 DeMar DeRozan I 4.00 10.00
119 Shai Gilgeous-Alexander I 15.00 40.00
120 Jrue Holiday I 4.00 10.00
121 Derrick Rose I 6.00 15.00
122 Hassan Whiteside I 2.00 5.00
123 Devin Booker I .75 2.00
124 Buddy Hield I 2.50 6.00
125 Kyle Lowry I 3.00 8.00
126 Bradley Beal I 4.00 10.00
127 Jamal Murray I 5.00 12.00
128 LaMarcus Aldridge I 3.00 8.00
129 Chris Paul I 6.00 15.00
130 Tobias Harris I 2.50 6.00
131 Kevin Love I 3.00 8.00
132 Marvin Bagley III I 2.50 6.00
133 Deandre Ayton I 3.00 8.00
134 Jimmy Butler I 6.00 15.00
135 Kyrie Irving I 6.00 15.00
136 Isaiah Thomas I 2.50 6.00
137 Nikola Jokic I 15.00 40.00
138 Russell Westbrook I 5.00 12.00
139 Giannis Antetokounmpo I 15.00 40.00
140 Lou Williams I 3.00 8.00
141 Darius Bazley A RC 3.00 8.00
142 Coby White A RC 10.00 25.00
143 Carsen Edwards A RC 4.00 10.00
145 Admiral Schofield A RC 4.00 10.00
146 Tyler Herro A RC 15.00 40.00
147 Kendrick Nunn A RC 5.00 12.00
148 Zion Williamson A RC 25.00 60.00
149 Kevin Porter Jr. A RC 6.00 15.00
150 De'Andre Hunter A RC 12.00 30.00
151 Nicolo Melli A RC 4.00 10.00
152 Jaxson Hayes A RC 5.00 12.00
153 Nickeil Alexander-Walker A RC 5.00 12.00
154 Cameron Johnson A RC 8.00 20.00
155 Tacko Fall A RC 4.00 10.00
156 Romeo Langford A RC 3.00 8.00
157 Jordan Poole A RC 12.00 30.00
158 Ja Morant A RC 125.00 300.00
159 Grant Williams A RC 5.00 12.00
161 Goga Bitadze A RC 5.00 12.00
162 Rui Hachimura A RC 12.00 30.00
163 Bruno Fernando A RC 4.00 10.00
164 PJ Washington Jr. A RC 10.00 25.00
165 Naz Reid A RC 12.00 30.00
166 Eric Paschall A RC 4.00 10.00
167 Brandon Clarke A RC 6.00 15.00
168 RJ Barrett A RC 12.00 30.00
169 Matisse Thybulle A RC 6.00 15.00
170 Darius Garland A RC 12.00 30.00
171 Darius Bazley I 3.00 8.00
172 Coby White I 10.00 25.00
173 Carsen Edwards I 4.00 10.00
174 Cam Reddish I 5.00 12.00
175 Admiral Schofield I 4.00 10.00
176 Tyler Herro I 15.00 40.00
177 Kendrick Nunn I 5.00 12.00
178 Zion Williamson I 25.00 60.00
179 Kevin Porter Jr. I 6.00 15.00
180 De'Andre Hunter I 12.00 30.00
181 Nicolo Melli I 4.00 10.00
182 Jaxson Hayes I 5.00 12.00
183 Nickeil Alexander-Walker I 5.00 12.00
184 Cameron Johnson I 8.00 20.00
185 Tacko Fall I 4.00 10.00
186 Romeo Langford I 3.00 8.00
187 Jordan Poole I 12.00 30.00
188 Ja Morant I 125.00 300.00
189 Grant Williams I 5.00 12.00
190 Jarrett Culver I 3.00 8.00
191 Goga Bitadze I 5.00 12.00
192 Rui Hachimura I 12.00 30.00
193 Bruno Fernando I 4.00 10.00
194 PJ Washington Jr. I 10.00 25.00
195 Keldon Johnson I 10.00 25.00
196 Eric Paschall I 4.00 10.00
197 Brandon Clarke I 6.00 15.00
198 RJ Barrett I 12.00 30.00
199 Matisse Thybulle I 6.00 15.00
200 Darius Garland I 12.00 30.00
201 Kawhi Leonard MET 30.00 80.00
202 Joel Embiid MET 25.00 60.00
203 Nikola Vucevic MET 10.00 25.00
204 Donovan Mitchell MET 25.00 60.00
205 James Harden MET 25.00 60.00
206 Zach LaVine MET 20.00 50.00
207 Paul George MET 20.00 50.00
208 Ben Simmons MET 12.00 30.00
209 Kemba Walker MET 10.00 25.00
210 Luka Doncic MET 80.00 200.00
211 Damian Lillard MET 30.00 80.00
212 Blake Griffin MET 12.00 30.00
213 Anthony Davis MET 30.00 80.00
214 D'Angelo Russell MET 10.00 25.00
215 Jayson Tatum MET 50.00 125.00
216 Karl-Anthony Towns MET 20.00 50.00
217 CJ McCollum MET 12.00 30.00
218 Andre Drummond MET 10.00 25.00
219 LeBron James MET 100.00 250.00
220 De'Aaron Fox MET 20.00 50.00
221 Pascal Siakam MET 20.00 50.00
222 Trae Young MET 30.00 80.00
223 Shai Gilgeous-Alexander MET 60.00 150.00
224 Derrick Rose MET 25.00 60.00
225 Bradley Beal MET 15.00 40.00
226 Deandre Ayton MET 12.00 30.00
227 Kyrie Irving MET 25.00 60.00
228 Nikola Jokic MET 60.00 150.00
229 Russell Westbrook MET 20.00 50.00
230 Giannis Antetokounmpo MET 60.00 150.00
231 Coby White MET 25.00 60.00
232 Cam Reddish MET 25.00 60.00
233 Tyler Herro MET 40.00 100.00
234 Kendrick Nunn MET 12.00 30.00
235 Zion Williamson MET 60.00 150.00
236 Kevin Porter Jr. MET 15.00 40.00
237 De'Andre Hunter MET 30.00 80.00
238 Jaxson Hayes MET 12.00 30.00
239 Nickeil Alexander-Walker MET 12.00 30.00
240 Cameron Johnson MET 20.00 50.00
241 Romeo Langford MET 8.00 20.00
242 Ja Morant MET 300.00 600.00
243 Jarrett Culver MET 8.00 20.00
244 Rui Hachimura MET 30.00 80.00
245 PJ Washington Jr. MET 25.00 60.00
246 Eric Paschall MET 10.00 25.00
247 Brandon Clarke MET 15.00 40.00
248 RJ Barrett MET 30.00 80.00
249 Matisse Thybulle MET 15.00 40.00
250 Darius Garland MET 30.00 80.00
251 Elgin Baylor FL 25.00 60.00
252 Karl-Anthony Towns FL 20.00 50.00
253 Larry Bird FL 50.00 125.00
254 Luka Doncic FL 80.00 200.00
255 Julius Erving FL 25.00 60.00
256 CJ McCollum FL 12.00 30.00
257 Dirk Nowitzki FL 30.00 80.00
258 Trae Young FL 30.00 80.00
259 Tim Duncan FL 30.00 80.00
260 Damian Lillard FL 30.00 80.00
261 Bill Russell FL 40.00 100.00
262 Nikola Jokic FL 60.00 150.00
263 Magic Johnson FL 40.00 100.00
264 Bradley Beal FL 15.00 40.00
265 Isiah Thomas FL 25.00 60.00
266 Ben Simmons FL 12.00 30.00
267 Allen Iverson FL 30.00 80.00
268 Stephen Curry FL 100.00 250.00
269 John Stockton FL 25.00 60.00
270 Giannis Antetokounmpo FL 60.00 150.00
271 Aaron Gordon
Nikola Vucevic SS 12.00 30.00
272 David Robinson
Tim Duncan SS 30.00 80.00
273 CJ McCollum
Damian Lillard SS 30.00 80.00
274 D'Angelo Russell
Stephen Curry SS 100.00 250.00
275 Kevin Durant
Kyrie Irving SS 40.00 100.00
276 RJ Barrett
Zion Williamson SS 60.00 150.00
277 James Harden
Russell Westbrook SS 25.00 60.00
278 Charles Barkley
Zion Williamson SS 60.00 150.00
279 Anthony Davis
LeBron James SS 100.00 250.00
280 Dirk Nowitzki
Luka Doncic SS 80.00 200.00
281 Deandre Ayton
Devin Booker SS 12.00 30.00
282 Larry Bird
Magic Johnson SS 50.00 125.00
283 Donovan Mitchell
Rudy Gobert SS 25.00 60.00
284 Isiah Thomas
Joe Dumars SS 25.00 60.00
285 Blake Griffin
Derrick Rose SS 25.00 60.00
286 Cam Reddish
Zion Williamson SS 60.00 150.00
287 Kawhi Leonard
Paul George SS 30.00 80.00
288 Cam Reddish
RJ Barrett SS 30.00 80.00
289 Ben Simmons
Joel Embiid SS 25.00 60.00
290 Dwyane Wade
LeBron James SS 100.00 250.00
291 Luka Doncic VA 80.00 200.00
292 Zion Williamson VA 60.00 150.00
293 Ja Morant VA 300.00 600.00
294 RJ Barrett VA 30.00 80.00
295 Kyrie Irving VA 25.00 60.00
296 Giannis Antetokounmpo VA 60.00 150.00

297 Charles Barkley VA 25.00 60.00
298 LeBron James VA 100.00 250.00
299 Kawhi Leonard VA 30.00 80.00
300 Kevin Garnett VA 30.00 80.00
301 Ignas Brazdeikis AU JSY BW 12.00 30.00
302 Grant Williams AU JSY BW 15.00 40.00
303 Keldon Johnson AU JSY BW 30.00 80.00
304 Jaylen Nowell AU JSY BW 12.00 30.00
305 Tremont Waters AU JSY BW 12.00 30.00
306 RJ Barrett AU JSY BW 150.00 400.00
307 Cameron Johnson AU JSY BW 25.00 60.00
308 Bruno Fernando AU JSY BW 12.00 30.00
309 Matisse Thybulle AU JSY BW 20.00 50.00
310 Ty Jerome AU JSY BW 20.00 50.00
311 PJ Washington Jr. AU JSY BW 30.00 80.00
312 Bol Bol AU JSY BW RC 25.00 60.00
313 Dylan Windler AU JSY BW RC 12.00 30.00
314 Ja Morant AU JSY BW 800.00 1,200.00
315 Eric Paschall AU JSY BW 12.00 30.00
316 Tyler Herro AU JSY BW 150.00 400.00
317 Isaiah Roby AU JSY BW 12.00 30.00
318 Rui Hachimura AU JSY BW 40.00 100.00
319 Nassir Little AU JSY BW 15.00 40.00
320 Luka Samanic AU JSY BW 12.00 30.00
322 Admiral Schofield AU JSY BW 12.00 30.00
323 Chuma Okeke AU JSY BW 15.00 40.00
324 Brandon Clarke AU JSY BW 20.00 50.00
325 Goga Bitadze AU JSY BW 15.00 40.00
326 Jaxson Hayes AU JSY BW 15.00 40.00
327 Jordan Poole AU JSY BW 200.00 500.00
328 Zion Williamson AU JSY BW 300.00 600.00
329 Coby White AU JSY BW 75.00 200.00
330 Quinndary Weatherspoon AU JSY BW 10.00 25.00
331 Kevin Porter Jr. AU JSY BW 20.00 50.00
332 Cam Reddish AU JSY BW 15.00 40.00
333 KZ Okpala AU JSY BW 12.00 30.00
334 Cody Martin AU JSY BW 15.00 40.00
335 Jarrett Culver AU JSY BW 10.00 25.00
336 Nickeil Alexander-Walker AU JSY BW 15.00 40.00
337 Carsen Edwards AU JSY BW 12.00 30.00
338 De'Andre Hunter AU JSY BW 40.00 100.00
339 Romeo Langford AU JSY BW 10.00 25.00
340 Mfiondu Kabengele AU JSY BW 12.00 30.00
341 Ignas Brazdeikis AU JSY C 12.00 30.00
342 Grant Williams AU JSY C 15.00 40.00
343 Keldon Johnson AU JSY C 30.00 80.00
344 Jaylen Nowell AU JSY C 12.00 30.00
345 Tremont Waters AU JSY C 12.00 30.00
346 RJ Barrett AU JSY C 150.00 400.00
347 Cameron Johnson AU JSY C 25.00 60.00
348 Bruno Fernando AU JSY C 12.00 30.00
349 Matisse Thybulle AU JSY C 20.00 50.00
350 Ty Jerome AU JSY C 20.00 50.00
351 PJ Washington Jr. AU JSY C 30.00 80.00
352 Bol Bol AU JSY C 25.00 60.00
353 Dylan Windler AU JSY C 12.00 30.00
354 Ja Morant AU JSY C 2,000.00 4,000.00
355 Eric Paschall AU JSY C 12.00 30.00
356 Tyler Herro AU JSY C 150.00 400.00
357 Isaiah Roby AU JSY C 12.00 30.00
358 Rui Hachimura AU JSY C 40.00 100.00
359 Nassir Little AU JSY C 15.00 40.00
360 Luka Samanic AU JSY C 12.00 30.00
362 Admiral Schofield AU JSY C 12.00 30.00
363 Chuma Okeke AU JSY C 15.00 40.00
364 Brandon Clarke AU JSY C 20.00 50.00
365 Goga Bitadze AU JSY C 15.00 40.00
366 Jaxson Hayes AU JSY C 15.00 40.00
367 Jordan Poole AU JSY C 40.00 100.00
368 Zion Williamson AU JSY C 300.00 600.00
369 Coby White AU JSY C 30.00 80.00
370 Quinndary Weatherspoon AU JSY C 10.00 25.00
371 Kevin Porter Jr. AU JSY C 20.00 50.00
372 Cam Reddish AU JSY C 15.00 40.00
373 KZ Okpala AU JSY C 12.00 30.00
374 Cody Martin AU JSY C 15.00 40.00
375 Jarrett Culver AU JSY C 10.00 25.00
376 Nickeil Alexander-Walker AU JSY C 15.00 40.00
377 Carsen Edwards AU JSY C 12.00 30.00
378 De'Andre Hunter AU JSY C 40.00 100.00
379 Romeo Langford AU JSY C 10.00 25.00
380 Mfiondu Kabengele AU JSY C 12.00 30.00
381 Talen Horton-Tucker AU 8.00 20.00
382 Darius Bazley AU 5.00 12.00
383 Nicolas Claxton AU RC 10.00 25.00
384 Jalen Lecque AU 5.00 12.00
385 Luguentz Dort AU 50.00 120.00
386 Tacko Fall AU 6.00 15.00
387 Daniel Gafford AU 10.00 25.00
388 Alen Smailagic AU RC 5.00 12.00
389 Terance Mann AU 10.00 25.00
390 Miye Oni AU 5.00 12.00
391 Jordan Bone AU 5.00 12.00
392 Justin Robinson AU 5.00 12.00
393 Romeo Langford AU 5.00 12.00
394 Jaylen Hoard AU 5.00 12.00
395 Kyle Guy AU 6.00 15.00
396 Ja Morant AU 1,000.00 2,000.00
397 PJ Washington Jr. AU 15.00 40.00
398 Rui Hachimura AU 20.00 50.00
399 RJ Barrett AU 20.00 50.00
400 Isaiah Roby AU 6.00 15.00

2019-20 Panini Noir Holo Silver

148 Zion Williamson A 200.00 500.00
158 Ja Morant A 200.00 500.00
178 Zion Williamson I 200.00 500.00
188 Ja Morant I 200.00 500.00

2019-20 Panini Noir Black and White Autographs

STATED PRINT RUN 25-99 SER.#'d SETS
1 Donovan Mitchell 75.00 200.00
2 Zhaire Smith 6.00 15.00
3 Zach LaVine 100.00 250.00
4 JaVale McGee 8.00 20.00
5 Myles Turner 10.00 25.00
6 Gary Harris 8.00 20.00
7 Cuttino Mobley 6.00 15.00
8 Josh Richardson 6.00 15.00
9 Harrison Barnes 8.00 20.00
10 Toni Kukoc 25.00 60.00
11 Rudy Gay 8.00 20.00
12 Avery Bradley 6.00 15.00
13 Nikola Jokic 200.00 500.00
14 Cherokee Parks 6.00 15.00
16 Lenny Wilkens 12.00 30.00
17 Dan Majerle 8.00 20.00
18 Aaron Holiday 8.00 20.00
19 P.J. Tucker 8.00 20.00
20 Adrian Dantley 10.00 25.00
21 Arvydas Sabonis 10.00 25.00
22 Danny Green 8.00 20.00
23 Jalen Rose 8.00 20.00
24 Horace Grant 10.00 25.00
25 Kyrie Irving 75.00 200.00
26 Lonzo Ball 60.00 150.00
27 Danilo Gallinari 8.00 20.00
28 Thon Maker 6.00 15.00
29 Derek Fisher 20.00 50.00
30 Tom Chambers 10.00 25.00

2019-20 Panini Noir Box Office Memorabilia

*PRIME/23-25: .6X TO 1.5X BASE HI
1 DeMar DeRozan 4.00 10.00
2 Myles Turner 3.00 8.00
3 Giannis Antetokounmpo 15.00 40.00
4 Jayson Tatum 12.00 30.00
5 Aaron Gordon 3.00 8.00
6 Karl-Anthony Towns 5.00 12.00
8 Kyle Lowry 3.00 8.00
9 Collin Sexton 4.00 10.00
10 Malcolm Brogdon 2.50 6.00
11 Devin Booker .75 2.00
12 Nikola Vucevic 2.50 6.00
13 Jamal Murray 5.00 12.00
14 Jimmy Butler 6.00 15.00
15 Andrew Wiggins 4.00 10.00
16 Kemba Walker 2.50 6.00
17 Bradley Beal 4.00 10.00
18 Lauri Markkanen 4.00 10.00
19 D'Angelo Russell 2.50 6.00
20 Marvin Bagley III 2.50 6.00
21 Draymond Green 4.00 10.00
22 Paul George 5.00 12.00
23 Jaren Jackson Jr. 5.00 12.00
24 Jonas Valanciunas 2.50 6.00
25 Anthony Davis 8.00 20.00
26 Khris Middleton 3.00 8.00
27 Caris LeVert 2.50 6.00
28 Lou Williams 3.00 8.00
29 Deandre Ayton 3.00 8.00
30 Mike Conley 2.50 6.00

2019-20 Panini Noir Color Autographs

1 Donovan Mitchell 60.00 150.00
2 Zhaire Smith 3.00 8.00
3 Zach LaVine 12.00 30.00
4 JaVale McGee 4.00 10.00
5 Myles Turner 5.00 12.00
6 Gary Harris 4.00 10.00
7 Cuttino Mobley 3.00 8.00
8 Josh Richardson 3.00 8.00
9 Harrison Barnes 4.00 10.00
10 Toni Kukoc 10.00 25.00
11 Rudy Gay 4.00 10.00
12 Avery Bradley 5.00 12.00
13 Nikola Jokic 200.00 500.00
14 Cherokee Parks 3.00 8.00
15 Julius Randle 6.00 15.00
16 Lenny Wilkens 10.00 25.00
17 Dan Majerle 6.00 15.00
18 Aaron Holiday 4.00 10.00
19 P.J. Tucker 4.00 10.00
20 Adrian Dantley 8.00 20.00
21 Arvydas Sabonis 8.00 20.00
22 Danny Green 4.00 10.00
23 Jalen Rose 4.00 10.00
24 Horace Grant 5.00 12.00
25 Kyrie Irving 60.00 150.00
26 Lonzo Ball 25.00 60.00
27 Danilo Gallinari 4.00 10.00
28 Thon Maker 3.00 8.00
29 Derek Fisher 8.00 20.00
30 Tom Chambers 8.00 20.00

2019-20 Panini Noir Critically Acclaimed Signatures

1 Steve Francis 8.00 20.00
2 Tyler Herro 25.00 60.00
3 Dylan Windler 6.00 15.00
4 Wally Szczerbiak 6.00 15.00
5 Lonzo Ball 8.00 20.00
6 Rondae Hollis-Jefferson 5.00 12.00
7 Darius Bazley 5.00 12.00
8 Shawn Bradley 6.00 15.00
9 Nickeil Alexander-Walker 8.00 20.00
10 Quinn Cook 6.00 15.00
11 Jordan Poole 20.00 50.00
12 J.J. Barea 6.00 15.00
13 Jarrett Culver 5.00 12.00
14 Mike Bibby 8.00 20.00
16 Avery Johnson 5.00 12.00
17 Kyle Guy 6.00 15.00
18 Zion Williamson 150.00 400.00
19 Antoine Walker 6.00 15.00
20 Montrezl Harrell 6.00 15.00
21 Gordon Hayward 6.00 15.00
22 Bruno Fernando 6.00 15.00
23 Cody Martin 8.00 20.00
24 Luka Samanic 6.00 15.00
25 Jaren Jackson Jr. 12.00 30.00
26 Kevin Durant 25.00 60.00
27 Tremont Waters 6.00 15.00
28 Eric Paschall 8.00 20.00
29 Jamal Mashburn 8.00 20.00
30 Giannis Antetokounmpo 200.00 500.00

2019-20 Panini Noir Dish Night Memorabilia

1 D'Angelo Russell 5.00 12.00
2 Mike Conley 5.00 12.00
3 LeBron James 50.00 125.00
4 Eric Bledsoe 5.00 12.00
5 Trae Young 15.00 40.00
6 Dennis Smith Jr. 4.00 10.00
7 Terry Rozier 5.00 12.00
8 Ben Simmons 6.00 15.00
9 Luka Doncic 40.00 100.00
10 De'Aaron Fox 10.00 25.00
11 Russell Westbrook 10.00 25.00
12 Bradley Beal 8.00 20.00
13 James Harden 12.00 30.00
14 Jeff Teague 4.00 10.00
15 Kemba Walker 5.00 12.00
16 Chris Paul 12.00 30.00
17 Zach LaVine 10.00 25.00
18 Ricky Rubio 5.00 12.00
19 Jamal Murray 10.00 25.00
20 Lonnie Walker IV 5.00 12.00
21 Malcolm Brogdon 5.00 12.00
22 Gary Harris 5.00 12.00
23 Goran Dragic 5.00 12.00
24 Lonzo Ball 6.00 15.00
25 Kyrie Irving 12.00 30.00
26 Markelle Fultz 5.00 12.00
27 Collin Sexton 8.00 20.00
28 Damian Lillard 15.00 40.00
29 Derrick Rose 12.00 30.00
30 Kyle Lowry 6.00 15.00

2019-20 Panini Noir Elegant Decor Rookie Jerseys

1 De'Andre Hunter 12.00 30.00
2 Ty Jerome 6.00 15.00
3 Jaxson Hayes 5.00 12.00
4 Mfiondu Kabengele 4.00 10.00
5 Cameron Johnson 8.00 20.00
6 Kevin Porter Jr. 6.00 15.00
7 Romeo Langford 3.00 8.00
8 Goga Bitadze 5.00 12.00
9 Zion Williamson 75.00 200.00
10 Brandon Clarke 6.00 15.00
11 Jarrett Culver 3.00 8.00
12 Nassir Little 5.00 12.00
13 Rui Hachimura 12.00 30.00
14 Jordan Poole 12.00 30.00
15 PJ Washington Jr. 10.00 25.00
16 Carsen Edwards 4.00 10.00
17 Sekou Doumbouya 3.00 8.00
18 Luka Samanic 4.00 10.00
19 Ja Morant 100.00 250.00
20 Grant Williams 5.00 12.00
21 Coby White 10.00 25.00
22 Dylan Windler 4.00 10.00
23 Cam Reddish 5.00 12.00
24 Keldon Johnson 10.00 25.00
25 Tyler Herro 15.00 40.00
26 Bol Bol 8.00 20.00
27 Nickeil Alexander-Walker 5.00 12.00
28 Matisse Thybulle 6.00 15.00
29 RJ Barrett 12.00 30.00
30 Darius Bazley 3.00 8.00

2019-20 Panini Noir Freeze Frame Signatures

1 Kyrie Irving 100.00 250.00
2 Jason Richardson 10.00 25.00
3 Ersan Ilyasova 6.00 15.00
4 Zach LaVine 100.00 250.00
5 Mark Jackson 8.00 20.00
6 Fat Lever 8.00 20.00
7 Michael Cooper 10.00 25.00
8 Kevin Johnson 10.00 25.00
9 Mark Aguirre 8.00 20.00
10 Mike Conley 8.00 20.00
11 Harrison Barnes 8.00 20.00
12 Christian Laettner 10.00 25.00
13 Chris Mullin 40.00 100.00
14 Dell Curry 6.00 15.00
15 Vlade Divac 10.00 25.00
16 Steve Francis 20.00 50.00
17 Elfrid Payton 6.00 15.00
18 Shawn Bradley 6.00 15.00
19 Clyde Drexler 60.00 150.00
20 Nikola Jokic 300.00 600.00
21 Alex English 12.00 30.00
22 Kareem Abdul-Jabbar 200.00 500.00
23 Bill Walton 40.00 100.00
24 Julius Randle 12.00 30.00
25 Latrell Sprewell 40.00 100.00
26 Charles Barkley 125.00 300.00
27 Adrian Dantley 10.00 25.00
28 Wally Szczerbiak 8.00 20.00
29 Wesley Matthews 6.00 15.00
30 Shaquille O'Neal 300.00 600.00
31 Nikola Vucevic 8.00 20.00
32 Giannis Antetokounmpo 500.00 1,000.00
34 John Starks 20.00 50.00
35 Tom Chambers 10.00 25.00
36 Luke Walton 8.00 20.00
37 Avery Bradley 6.00 15.00
38 Quinn Cook 8.00 20.00
39 Gary Harris 8.00 20.00
40 Mark Price 10.00 25.00

2019-20 Panini Noir Horizontal Spotlight Signatures

1 Jason Williams 400.00 700.00
2 Glen Rice 25.00 60.00
3 Eddie Jones 40.00 100.00
4 B.J. Armstrong 25.00 60.00
5 Charles Barkley 200.00 500.00
6 Allen Iverson 400.00 800.00
7 Allan Houston 25.00 60.00
8 Zion Williamson 1,500.00 3,000.00
9 Jaxson Hayes 40.00 100.00
10 Chris Mullin 75.00 200.00
11 Toni Kukoc 60.00 150.00
12 Eric Paschall 15.00 40.00
13 Stephen Jackson 12.00 30.00
14 Clyde Drexler 75.00 200.00
15 Kevin Porter Jr. 25.00 60.00
16 RJ Barrett 200.00 500.00
17 Jarrett Culver 12.00 30.00
18 Bill Walton 60.00 150.00
19 Shaquille O'Neal 400.00 800.00
20 Coby White 75.00 200.00
21 Julius Erving 150.00 400.00
22 Trae Young 400.00 800.00
23 Magic Johnson 300.00 600.00
24 Pascal Siakam 60.00 150.00
25 Stephen Curry 2,000.00 4,000.00

2019-20 Panini Noir Icons Memorabilia

STATED PRINT RUN 99 SER.#'d SETS
1 Tim Duncan 15.00 40.00
2 Kevin Garnett 15.00 40.00
3 Michael Redd 4.00 10.00
4 Dirk Nowitzki 15.00 40.00
5 Dominique Wilkins 8.00 20.00
6 Charles Barkley 15.00 40.00
7 Paul Pierce 8.00 20.00
8 John Stockton 10.00 25.00
9 Ricky Pierce 4.00 10.00
10 David Robinson 12.00 30.00
11 Moses Malone 8.00 20.00
12 Jack Sikma 5.00 12.00
13 Gary Payton 8.00 20.00
14 Christian Laettner 5.00 12.00
15 Amar'e Stoudemire 4.00 10.00
16 Steve Nash 12.00 30.00
17 Danny Manning 4.00 10.00
18 Shawn Marion 4.00 10.00
19 Patrick Ewing 8.00 20.00
20 Larry Bird 15.00 40.00

2019-20 Panini Noir Icons Memorabilia Prime

*PRIME/25: 1X TO 2.5X BASE HI

2019-20 Panini Noir In Focus Signatures

1 Ja Morant 800.00 1,200.00
2 Admiral Schofield 12.00 30.00
3 Isaiah Roby 12.00 30.00
4 Brandon Clarke 20.00 50.00
5 Bruno Fernando 12.00 30.00
6 Cam Reddish 15.00 40.00
7 Cameron Johnson 25.00 60.00
8 Carsen Edwards 12.00 30.00
9 Chuma Okeke 15.00 40.00
10 Coby White 30.00 80.00
11 Cody Martin 15.00 40.00
12 Darius Bazley 10.00 25.00
13 De'Andre Hunter 40.00 100.00
14 Dylan Windler 12.00 30.00
15 Eric Paschall 12.00 30.00
16 Goga Bitadze 15.00 40.00
17 Grant Williams 15.00 40.00
18 Ignas Brazdeikis 12.00 30.00
19 Jarrett Culver 10.00 25.00
20 Jaxson Hayes 15.00 40.00
21 Kevin Porter Jr. 20.00 50.00
22 Jordan Poole 200.00 500.00
23 Keldon Johnson 30.00 80.00
24 Luka Samanic 12.00 30.00
25 Matisse Thybulle 20.00 50.00
26 Mfiondu Kabengele 12.00 30.00
27 Nassir Little 15.00 40.00
28 Nickeil Alexander-Walker 15.00 40.00
29 PJ Washington Jr. 30.00 80.00
30 Sekou Doumbouya 10.00 25.00

2019-20 Panini Noir Jumbo Material

1 Miles Bridges 5.00 12.00
2 Allonzo Trier 3.00 8.00
3 Joel Embiid 10.00 25.00
4 Myles Turner 5.00 12.00
5 John Collins 5.00 12.00
6 Victor Oladipo 4.00 10.00
7 Russell Westbrook 8.00 20.00
8 Enes Kanter 3.00 8.00
9 Goran Dragic 4.00 10.00
10 Karl-Anthony Towns 8.00 20.00
11 Aaron Holiday 4.00 10.00
12 Aaron Gordon 5.00 12.00
13 OG Anunoby 4.00 10.00
14 Steven Adams 4.00 10.00
15 Bogdan Bogdanovic 5.00 12.00
16 Blake Griffin 5.00 12.00
17 DeMarre Carroll 3.00 8.00
18 Derrick Rose 10.00 25.00
19 Kyle Lowry 5.00 12.00
20 Bojan Bogdanovic 4.00 10.00
21 Ersan Ilyasova 3.00 8.00
22 Hassan Whiteside 3.00 8.00
23 Josh Richardson 3.00 8.00
24 Andre Drummond 4.00 10.00
25 Jrue Holiday 6.00 15.00
26 Jarrett Allen 5.00 12.00
27 Bam Adebayo 8.00 20.00
28 Thaddeus Young 3.00 8.00
29 Jamal Murray 8.00 20.00
30 Doug McDermott 3.00 8.00
31 Lauri Markkanen 6.00 15.00
32 Joe Harris 4.00 10.00
33 Harry Giles III 3.00 8.00
34 Markelle Fultz 4.00 10.00
35 Luke Kennard 4.00 10.00
36 Rudy Gobert 6.00 15.00
37 Frank Ntilikina 3.00 8.00
38 Andrew Wiggins 6.00 15.00
39 Willie Cauley-Stein 3.00 8.00
40 Mitchell Robinson 5.00 12.00
41 Spencer Dinwiddie 4.00 10.00
42 Wendell Carter Jr. 5.00 12.00
43 DeAndre' Bembry 3.00 8.00
44 Domantas Sabonis 6.00 15.00
45 Ben Simmons 5.00 12.00
46 John Wall 6.00 15.00
47 Shai Gilgeous-Alexander 25.00 60.00
48 Derrick Favors 3.00 8.00
49 DeAndre Jordan 4.00 10.00
50 Rondae Hollis-Jefferson 3.00 8.00
51 Jonathan Isaac 5.00 12.00
52 Mo Bamba 4.00 10.00
53 Michael Kidd-Gilchrist 3.00 8.00
54 Dennis Schroder 4.00 10.00
55 Troy Brown Jr. 3.00 8.00
56 Dwight Powell 3.00 8.00
58 Paul George 8.00 20.00
59 Eric Bledsoe 4.00 10.00
60 LeBron James 60.00 150.00

2019-20 Panini Noir New Wave Jerseys

STATED PRINT RUN 99 SER.#'d SETS
*PRIME/25: 1X TO 2.5X BASE HI
NW-ZWL Zion Williamson 60.00 150.00
2 Brandon Clarke 6.00 15.00
3 De'Andre Hunter 12.00 30.00
4 Ty Jerome 6.00 15.00
5 Jaxson Hayes 5.00 12.00
6 Mfiondu Kabengele 4.00 10.00
7 Cameron Johnson 8.00 20.00
8 Kevin Porter Jr. 6.00 15.00
9 Romeo Langford 3.00 8.00
10 Goga Bitadze 5.00 12.00
11 Ja Morant 75.00 200.00
12 Grant Williams 5.00 12.00
13 Jarrett Culver 3.00 8.00
14 Nassir Little 5.00 12.00
15 Rui Hachimura 12.00 30.00
16 Jordan Poole 30.00 80.00
17 PJ Washington Jr. 10.00 25.00
18 Carsen Edwards 4.00 10.00
19 Sekou Doumbouya 3.00 8.00
20 Luka Samanic 4.00 10.00
21 RJ Barrett 12.00 30.00
22 Darius Bazley 3.00 8.00
23 Coby White 10.00 25.00
24 Dylan Windler 4.00 10.00
25 Cam Reddish 5.00 12.00
26 Keldon Johnson 10.00 25.00
27 Tyler Herro 15.00 40.00
28 Bol Bol 8.00 20.00
29 Nickeil Alexander-Walker 5.00 12.00
30 Matisse Thybulle 6.00 15.00

2019-20 Panini Noir Newsreels Jerseys

STATED PRINT RUN 65 SER.#'d SETS
1 Wendell Carter Jr. 5.00 12.00
2 Luka Doncic 30.00 80.00
3 Bojan Bogdanovic 4.00 10.00
4 Nikola Jokic 25.00 60.00
5 De'Aaron Fox 8.00 20.00
6 Steven Adams 4.00 10.00
7 Eric Bledsoe 4.00 10.00
8 Jeff Teague 3.00 8.00
9 Rudy Gobert 6.00 15.00
10 Kevin Love 5.00 12.00
11 Andre Drummond 4.00 10.00
12 Markelle Fultz 4.00 10.00
13 Brook Lopez 4.00 10.00
14 Pascal Siakam 8.00 20.00
15 DeAndre Jordan 4.00 10.00
16 Tobias Harris 4.00 10.00
17 Goran Dragic 4.00 10.00
18 Joel Embiid 10.00 25.00
19 Stephen Curry 60.00 150.00
20 Kristaps Porzingis 6.00 15.00
21 Anfernee Simons 8.00 20.00
23 Chris Paul 10.00 25.00
24 Paul Millsap 4.00 10.00
25 Derrick Rose 10.00 25.00
26 Victor Oladipo 4.00 10.00
27 James Harden 10.00 25.00
28 Julius Randle 6.00 15.00
29 Terry Rozier 4.00 10.00
30 Kyrie Irving 10.00 25.00
31 Blake Griffin 5.00 12.00
32 Montrezl Harrell 4.00 10.00
33 Damian Lillard 12.00 30.00
34 Seth Curry 4.00 10.00
35 Donovan Mitchell 10.00 25.00
36 Zach LaVine 8.00 20.00
37 Jarrett Allen 5.00 12.00
38 Kawhi Leonard 12.00 30.00
39 Trae Young 12.00 30.00
40 Lonzo Ball 5.00 12.00

2019-20 Panini Noir Prime Materials Black and White Autographs

2 Derek Fisher 20.00 50.00
3 Zhaire Smith 8.00 20.00
4 Rafer Alston 8.00 20.00
5 Ersan Ilyasova 8.00 20.00
6 Willie Cauley-Stein 8.00 20.00
8 Wendell Carter Jr. 12.00 30.00
9 Al-Farouq Aminu 8.00 20.00
10 Thaddeus Young 8.00 20.00
11 Carlos Boozer 10.00 25.00
13 Enes Kanter 8.00 20.00
14 Harry Giles III 8.00 20.00
15 Christian Laettner 12.00 30.00
16 Richard Hamilton 12.00 30.00
17 Toni Kukoc 15.00 40.00
18 Mike Bibby 12.00 30.00
19 Grant Hill 60.00 150.00

2019-20 Panini Noir Prime Materials Color Autographs

2 Derek Fisher 20.00 50.00
3 Zhaire Smith 8.00 20.00
4 Rafer Alston 8.00 20.00
5 Ersan Ilyasova 8.00 20.00
6 Willie Cauley-Stein 8.00 20.00
8 Wendell Carter Jr. 12.00 30.00
9 Al-Farouq Aminu 8.00 20.00
10 Thaddeus Young 8.00 20.00
11 Carlos Boozer 10.00 25.00
13 Enes Kanter 8.00 20.00
14 Harry Giles III 8.00 20.00
15 Christian Laettner 12.00 30.00
16 Richard Hamilton 12.00 30.00
17 Toni Kukoc 15.00 40.00
18 Mike Bibby 12.00 30.00
19 Grant Hill 60.00 150.00

2019-20 Panini Noir Reigning Nights Signatures

STATED PRINT RUN 25-99 SER.#'d SETS
1 Stephen Curry 2,000.00 4,000.00
2 Nassir Little 12.00 30.00
3 Allan Houston 10.00 25.00
4 Ignas Brazdeikis 12.00 30.00
5 Damian Lillard 125.00 300.00
7 Mark Price 12.00 30.00
8 Luke Walton 10.00 25.00
9 Mark Jackson 10.00 25.00
10 Jason Terry 10.00 25.00
11 Vince Carter 200.00 500.00
12 Jason Kidd 60.00 150.00
13 Jordan Poole 300.00 600.00
14 Wesley Matthews 8.00 20.00
15 Nick Van Exel 25.00 60.00
16 Danny Green 10.00 25.00
17 Goran Dragic 10.00 25.00
18 Dell Curry 8.00 20.00
19 Mike Bibby 20.00 50.00
20 Tony Parker 40.00 100.00
21 Rick Barry 20.00 50.00
22 Derek Fisher 12.00 30.00
23 Shane Battier 10.00 25.00
24 Romeo Langford 8.00 20.00
25 Kenny Smith 10.00 25.00
26 John Starks 20.00 50.00
27 Chris Mullin 40.00 100.00
28 Dan Majerle 10.00 25.00
29 Gordon Hayward 10.00 25.00
30 Jalen Rose 10.00 25.00
31 Peja Stojakovic 20.00 50.00
32 Jamal Mashburn 12.00 30.00
33 Toni Kukoc 25.00 60.00
34 Dylan Windler 10.00 25.00
35 Tyler Herro 150.00 300.00
36 Cameron Johnson 20.00 50.00
37 Carsen Edwards 10.00 25.00
38 Ty Jerome 15.00 40.00
39 Kyle Guy 10.00 25.00
40 Kevin Porter Jr. 12.00 30.00

2019-20 Panini Noir Rookie Jumbo Material

1 KZ Okpala 4.00 10.00
2 Cam Reddish 5.00 12.00
3 Eric Paschall 4.00 10.00
4 Romeo Langford 3.00 8.00
5 Isaiah Roby 4.00 10.00
6 Luka Samanic 4.00 10.00
7 Darius Bazley 3.00 8.00
8 Zion Williamson 25.00 60.00
9 Mfiondu Kabengele 4.00 10.00
10 Jarrett Culver 3.00 8.00
11 Carsen Edwards 4.00 10.00
12 Cameron Johnson 8.00 20.00
13 Admiral Schofield 4.00 10.00
14 Sekou Doumbouya 3.00 8.00
15 Ignas Brazdeikis 4.00 10.00
16 Matisse Thybulle 6.00 15.00
17 Ty Jerome 6.00 15.00
18 Ja Morant 75.00 200.00
19 Jordan Poole 12.00 30.00
20 Coby White 10.00 25.00
21 Bruno Fernando 4.00 10.00
22 PJ Washington Jr. 10.00 25.00
23 Jaylen Nowell 4.00 10.00
24 Nickeil Alexander-Walker 5.00 12.00
25 Quinndary Weatherspoon 3.00 8.00
26 Brandon Clarke 6.00 15.00
27 Nassir Little 5.00 12.00
28 RJ Barrett 12.00 30.00
29 Keldon Johnson 10.00 25.00
30 Jaxson Hayes 5.00 12.00
31 Cody Martin 5.00 12.00
32 Tyler Herro 15.00 40.00
33 Bol Bol 8.00 20.00
34 Goga Bitadze 5.00 12.00
35 Kyle Guy 4.00 10.00
36 Grant Williams 5.00 12.00
37 Dylan Windler 4.00 10.00
38 De'Andre Hunter 12.00 30.00
39 Kevin Porter Jr. 6.00 15.00
40 Rui Hachimura 12.00 30.00

2019-20 Panini Noir Shadow Signatures

STATED PRINT RUN 49-99 SER.#'d SETS
1 Cam Reddish 15.00 40.00
2 RJ Barrett 125.00 300.00
3 Rui Hachimura 50.00 120.00
4 Kendrick Nunn 15.00 40.00
5 Coby White 30.00 80.00
6 Jarrett Culver 10.00 25.00
7 Cameron Johnson 25.00 60.00
8 Brandon Clarke 20.00 50.00
9 Dan Issel 20.00 50.00
10 De'Andre Hunter 40.00 100.00
11 Romeo Langford 10.00 25.00
12 Sekou Doumbouya 10.00 25.00
13 Tremont Waters 12.00 30.00
14 Cody Martin 15.00 40.00
15 Chuma Okeke 15.00 40.00
16 Isaiah Roby 12.00 30.00
17 Lonzo Ball 15.00 40.00
18 Horace Grant 15.00 40.00
19 PJ Washington Jr. 30.00 80.00
20 Ignas Brazdeikis 12.00 30.00
21 Mfiondu Kabengele 12.00 30.00
22 Kareem Abdul-Jabbar 200.00 500.00
23 Keldon Johnson 30.00 80.00
24 Admiral Schofield 12.00 30.00
25 KZ Okpala 12.00 30.00
26 Darius Bazley 10.00 25.00
27 Ty Jerome 20.00 50.00
28 Quinndary Weatherspoon 10.00 25.00
29 LaMarcus Aldridge 15.00 40.00
30 Mark Jackson 12.00 30.00

2019-20 Panini Noir Showtime Signatures

STATED PRINT RUN 25-99 SER.#'d SETS
2 Danny Green 12.00 30.00
3 Dwight Howard 75.00 200.00
4 Josh Hart 12.00 30.00
5 Malcolm Brogdon 12.00 30.00
6 Wendell Carter Jr. 15.00 40.00
7 Jason Richardson 15.00 40.00
8 Pascal Siakam 40.00 100.00
9 Ja Morant 500.00 800.00
10 Grant Hill 100.00 250.00
11 Shaquille O'Neal 150.00 400.00
12 Derek Fisher 25.00 60.00
13 Dennis Rodman 150.00 400.00
14 Mike Conley 12.00 30.00
15 Eddie Jones 12.00 30.00
16 Carlos Boozer 12.00 30.00
17 Jaren Jackson Jr. 40.00 100.00
18 Zhaire Smith 10.00 25.00
19 Chris Bosh 50.00 120.00
20 Paul Pierce 100.00 250.00
21 Willie Cauley-Stein 10.00 25.00
22 De'Aaron Fox 50.00 120.00
23 Chauncey Billups 20.00 50.00
25 Rudy Gay 10.00 25.00
26 Walt Frazier 25.00 60.00
27 Dwyane Wade 100.00 250.00
28 Kevin Durant 300.00 600.00
29 Allen Iverson 200.00 500.00
30 Harry Giles III 10.00 25.00

2019-20 Panini Noir Sneaker Spotlight

STATED PRINT RUN 99 SER.#'d SETS
1 LeBron James 1,000.00 2,000.00
2 Russell Westbrook 150.00 400.00
3 James Harden 150.00 400.00
4 Klay Thompson 200.00 500.00
5 Paul George 150.00 400.00
6 Ben Simmons 150.00 400.00
7 Chris Paul 150.00 400.00
8 LeBron James 1,000.00 2,000.00
9 Stephon Marbury 150.00 400.00
10 Derrick Rose 150.00 400.00

2019-20 Panini Noir Sneaker Spotlight Autographs

STATED PRINT RUN 49-99 SER.#'d SETS
1 Allen Iverson 600.00 1,200.00
2 Vince Carter 500.00 1,000.00
4 Dwyane Wade 500.00 1,000.00
5 Shaquille O'Neal 600.00 1,200.00
6 Richard Hamilton 125.00 300.00
7 Dennis Rodman 500.00 1,000.00
8 Stephen Jackson 125.00 300.00
10 Josh Hart 50.00 125.00
11 Kevin Garnett 600.00 1,200.00
12 Latrell Sprewell 150.00 400.00
13 Paul Pierce 200.00 500.00
14 Chris Bosh 150.00 400.00
15 Carlos Boozer 125.00 300.00
16 Tacko Fall 50.00 120.00
17 Karl Malone 300.00 600.00
18 Gary Payton 150.00 400.00
19 Tacko Fall 50.00 120.00
20 Giannis Antetokounmpo 1,500.00 3,000.00
21 P.J. Tucker 125.00 300.00
22 Damian Lillard 300.00 600.00
23 Montrezl Harrell 100.00 250.00
24 Lauri Markkanen 125.00 300.00
25 Trae Young 600.00 1,200.00
26 Jason Williams 400.00 800.00
27 Zion Williamson 2,000.00 4,000.00
28 Ja Morant 2,500.00 5,000.00
29 RJ Barrett 400.00 800.00
30 Rui Hachimura 200.00 500.00
31 Jason Terry 125.00 300.00
32 Tyler Herro 400.00 800.00
33 Cam Reddish 60.00 150.00
34 Stephen Curry 3,000.00 6,000.00
35 Zach LaVine 500.00 1,000.00
36 Collin Sexton 125.00 300.00
37 Myles Turner 125.00 300.00
38 De'Aaron Fox 300.00 600.00
39 Kyrie Irving 400.00 800.00
40 Mike Bibby 125.00 300.00

2019-20 Panini Noir Two-Shot Rookie Jerseys

STATED PRINT RUN 99 SER.#'d SETS
*PRIME/25: .75X TO 2X BASE HI
1 Admiral Schofield
Grant Williams 5.00 12.00
2 Nickeil Alexander-Walker
Zion Williamson 25.00 60.00
3 Jaylen Nowell
Matisse Thybulle 6.00 15.00
4 Cameron Johnson
Ty Jerome 8.00 20.00
5 Admiral Schofield
Rui Hachimura 12.00 30.00
6 Cam Reddish
De'Andre Hunter 12.00 30.00
7 Brandon Clarke
Rui Hachimura 12.00 30.00
8 Cody Martin
PJ Washington Jr. 10.00 25.00
9 Ignas Brazdeikis
Jordan Poole 12.00 30.00
10 Eric Paschall
Jordan Poole 12.00 30.00
11 De'Andre Hunter
Ty Jerome 12.00 30.00
12 Ignas Brazdeikis
RJ Barrett 12.00 30.00
13 Ja Morant
Zion Williamson 100.00 250.00
14 Keldon Johnson
Luka Samanic 10.00 25.00
15 RJ Barrett
Zion Williamson 25.00 60.00
16 Carsen Edwards
Romeo Langford 4.00 10.00
17 PJ Washington Jr.
Tyler Herro 15.00 40.00
18 Dylan Windler
Kevin Porter Jr. 6.00 15.00
19 Cameron Johnson
Coby White 10.00 25.00
20 Brandon Clarke
Ja Morant 30.00 80.00

2019-20 Panini Noir Two-Shot Rookie Jerseys Prime

*PRIME/25: .6X TO 1.5X BASE HI

2019-20 Panini Noir Vertical Spotlight Signatures

1 Kendrick Nunn 50.00 125.00
2 Cameron Johnson 60.00 150.00
3 Ja Morant 1,500.00 3,000.00
5 Matisse Thybulle 60.00 150.00
6 Vince Carter 400.00 800.00
7 Kevin Garnett 400.00 800.00
8 Zach LaVine 300.00 600.00
9 Dennis Rodman 400.00 800.00
10 Nassir Little 50.00 125.00
11 Montrezl Harrell 40.00 100.00
12 Nickeil Alexander-Walker 50.00 125.00
13 Arvydas Sabonis 50.00 125.00
14 Sekou Doumbouya 30.00 80.00
16 Peja Stojakovic 40.00 100.00
17 Jason Richardson 50.00 125.00
18 Anthony Davis 120.00 300.00
19 Latrell Sprewell 75.00 200.00
20 Gary Payton 75.00 200.00
21 Nick Van Exel 75.00 200.00
22 Brandon Clarke 60.00 150.00
23 Dwyane Wade 300.00 600.00

24 Bill Russell 2,000.00 4,000.00
25 De'Andre Hunter 120.00 300.00

2020-21 Panini Noir

COMMON CARD (1-140) 2.00 5.00
SEMISTARS 2.50 6.00
UNLISTED STARS 3.00 8.00
COM.RC (141-200) 3.00 8.00
RC SEMIS 4.00 10.00
RC UNLSITED 5.00 12.00
COMMON CARD (201-300) 8.00 20.00
SEMISTARS 10.00 25.00
UNLISTED STARS 12.00 30.00
COM. JSY AU (301-380) 10.00 25.00
SEMISTARS 12.00 30.00
UNLISTED STARS 15.00 40.00
COM. AU (381-400) 5.00 12.00
SEMISTARS 6.00 15.00
UNLISTED STARS 8.00 20.00
1 Blake Griffin A 3.00 8.00
2 Carmelo Anthony A 3.00 8.00
3 Terry Rozier A 3.00 8.00
4 Rudy Gobert A 4.00 10.00
5 Trae Young A 8.00 20.00
6 Jaren Jackson Jr. A 5.00 12.00
7 Markelle Fultz A 2.50 6.00
8 De'Aaron Fox A 5.00 12.00
9 Kyle Lowry A 4.00 10.00
10 CJ McCollum A 3.00 8.00
11 Tyler Herro A 6.00 15.00
12 Paul George A 5.00 12.00
13 Chris Paul A 6.00 15.00
14 Karl-Anthony Towns A 5.00 12.00
15 Giannis Antetokounmpo A 15.00 40.00
16 LaMarcus Aldridge A 3.00 8.00
17 Brandon Ingram A 4.00 10.00
18 Domantas Sabonis A 4.00 10.00
19 John Wall A 4.00 10.00
20 Donovan Mitchell A 6.00 15.00
21 Caris LeVert A 3.00 8.00
22 Shai Gilgeous-Alexander A 15.00 40.00
23 Nikola Jokic A 15.00 40.00
24 Zach LaVine A 5.00 12.00
25 DeMar DeRozan A 4.00 10.00
26 Jrue Holiday A 3.00 8.00
27 Zion Williamson A 10.00 25.00
28 Julius Randle A 3.00 8.00
29 Jaylen Brown A 5.00 12.00
30 Pascal Siakam A 5.00 12.00
31 D'Angelo Russell A 3.00 8.00
32 Coby White A 4.00 10.00
33 Joel Embiid A 8.00 20.00
34 Derrick Rose A 5.00 12.00
35 John Collins A 3.00 8.00
36 Damian Lillard A 8.00 20.00
37 LeBron James A 25.00 60.00
38 Dennis Schroder A 3.00 8.00
39 Luguentz Dort A 5.00 12.00
40 RJ Barrett A 5.00 12.00
41 James Harden A 6.00 15.00
42 Nikola Vucevic A 3.00 8.00
43 Ja Morant A 10.00 25.00
44 Kemba Walker A 3.00 8.00
45 Buddy Hield A 3.00 8.00
46 Kevin Love A 3.00 8.00
47 Christian Wood A 2.50 6.00
48 Khris Middleton A 4.00 10.00
49 Deandre Ayton A 3.00 8.00
50 Anthony Davis A 8.00 20.00
51 Jamal Murray A 5.00 12.00
52 Kristaps Porzingis A 4.00 10.00
53 Fred VanVleet A 5.00 12.00
54 Bam Adebayo A 5.00 12.00
55 Kevin Durant A 12.00 30.00
56 Jayson Tatum A 12.00 30.00
57 Russell Westbrook A 6.00 15.00
58 Draymond Green A 4.00 10.00
59 Bradley Beal A 4.00 10.00
60 Luka Doncic A 20.00 50.00
61 Stephen Curry A 25.00 60.00
62 Collin Sexton A 3.00 8.00
63 Jimmy Butler A 6.00 15.00
64 Gordon Hayward A 3.00 8.00
65 Devin Booker A 8.00 20.00
66 Kyrie Irving A 6.00 15.00
67 Ben Simmons A 3.00 8.00
68 Andrew Wiggins A 3.00 8.00
69 Malcolm Brogdon A 3.00 8.00
70 Kawhi Leonard A 8.00 20.00
71 Blake Griffin I 3.00 8.00
72 Carmelo Anthony I 5.00 12.00
73 Terry Rozier I 3.00 8.00
74 Rudy Gobert I 4.00 10.00
75 Trae Young I 8.00 20.00
76 Jaren Jackson Jr. I 5.00 12.00
77 Markelle Fultz I 2.50 6.00
78 De'Aaron Fox I 5.00 12.00
79 Kyle Lowry I 4.00 10.00
80 CJ McCollum I 3.00 8.00
81 Tyler Herro I 6.00 15.00
82 Paul George I 5.00 12.00
83 Chris Paul I 6.00 15.00
84 Karl-Anthony Towns I 5.00 12.00
85 Giannis Antetokounmpo I 15.00 40.00
86 LaMarcus Aldridge I 3.00 8.00
87 Brandon Ingram I 4.00 10.00
88 Domantas Sabonis I 4.00 10.00
89 John Wall I 4.00 10.00
90 Donovan Mitchell I 6.00 15.00
91 Caris LeVert I 3.00 8.00
92 Shai Gilgeous-Alexander I 15.00 40.00
93 Nikola Jokic I 15.00 40.00
94 Zach LaVine I 5.00 12.00
95 DeMar DeRozan I 4.00 10.00
96 Jrue Holiday I 3.00 8.00
97 Zion Williamson I 10.00 25.00
98 Julius Randle I 3.00 8.00
99 Jaylen Brown I 5.00 12.00
100 Pascal Siakam I 5.00 12.00
101 D'Angelo Russell I 3.00 8.00
102 Coby White I 4.00 10.00
103 Joel Embiid I 8.00 20.00
104 Derrick Rose I 5.00 12.00
105 John Collins I 3.00 8.00
106 Damian Lillard I 8.00 20.00
107 LeBron James I 25.00 60.00
108 Dennis Schroder I 3.00 8.00
109 Luguentz Dort I 5.00 12.00
110 RJ Barrett I 5.00 12.00
111 James Harden I 6.00 15.00
112 Nikola Vucevic I 3.00 8.00
113 Ja Morant I 10.00 25.00
114 Kemba Walker I 3.00 8.00
115 Buddy Hield I 3.00 8.00
116 Kevin Love I 3.00 8.00
117 Christian Wood I 2.50 6.00
118 Khris Middleton I 4.00 10.00
119 Deandre Ayton I 3.00 8.00
120 Anthony Davis I 8.00 20.00
121 Jamal Murray I 5.00 12.00
122 Kristaps Porzingis I 4.00 10.00
123 Fred VanVleet I 5.00 12.00
124 Bam Adebayo I 5.00 12.00
125 Kevin Durant I 12.00 30.00
126 Jayson Tatum I 12.00 30.00
127 Russell Westbrook I 6.00 15.00
128 Draymond Green I 4.00 10.00
129 Bradley Beal I 4.00 10.00
130 Luka Doncic I 20.00 50.00
131 Stephen Curry I 25.00 60.00
132 Collin Sexton I 3.00 8.00
133 Jimmy Butler I 6.00 15.00
134 Gordon Hayward I 3.00 8.00
135 Devin Booker I 8.00 20.00
136 Kyrie Irving I 6.00 15.00
137 Ben Simmons I 3.00 8.00
138 Andrew Wiggins I 4.00 10.00
139 Malcolm Brogdon I 3.00 8.00
140 Kawhi Leonard I 8.00 20.00
141 Desmond Bane A RC 12.00 30.00
142 James Wiseman A RC 5.00 12.00
143 Josh Green A RC 8.00 20.00
144 Cole Anthony A RC 10.00 25.00
145 LaMelo Ball A RC 75.00 200.00
146 Aaron Nesmith A RC 8.00 20.00
147 Jalen Smith A RC 8.00 20.00
148 Anthony Edwards A RC 75.00 200.00
149 Precious Achiuwa A RC 8.00 20.00
150 Obi Toppin A RC 8.00 20.00
151 RJ Hampton A RC 4.00 10.00
152 Isaac Okoro A RC 6.00 15.00
153 Udoka Azubuike A RC 5.00 12.00
154 Patrick Williams A RC 10.00 25.00
155 Tyrese Maxey A RC 30.00 80.00
156 Jae'Sean Tate A RC 5.00 12.00
157 Aleksej Pokusevski A RC 5.00 12.00
158 Deni Avdija A RC 10.00 25.00
159 Isaiah Stewart A RC 8.00 20.00
160 Immanuel Quickley A RC 10.00 25.00
161 Jaden McDaniels A RC 12.00 30.00
162 Saddiq Bey A RC 8.00 20.00
163 Onyeka Okongwu A RC 8.00 20.00
164 Kira Lewis Jr. A RC 4.00 10.00
165 Tyrese Haliburton A RC 30.00 80.00
166 Malachi Flynn A RC 4.00 10.00
167 Payton Pritchard A RC 12.00 30.00
168 Killian Hayes A RC 4.00 10.00
169 Devin Vassell A RC 12.00 30.00
170 Zeke Nnaji A RC 5.00 12.00
171 Desmond Bane I 12.00 30.00
172 James Wiseman I 5.00 12.00
173 Josh Green I 8.00 20.00
174 Cole Anthony I 10.00 25.00
175 LaMelo Ball I 75.00 200.00
176 Aaron Nesmith I 8.00 20.00
177 Jalen Smith I 8.00 20.00
178 Anthony Edwards I 75.00 200.00
179 Precious Achiuwa I 8.00 20.00
180 Obi Toppin I 8.00 20.00
181 RJ Hampton I 4.00 10.00
182 Isaac Okoro I 6.00 15.00
183 Udoka Azubuike I 5.00 12.00
184 Patrick Williams I 10.00 25.00
185 Tyrese Maxey I 30.00 80.00
186 Jae'Sean Tate I 5.00 12.00
187 Aleksej Pokusevski I 5.00 12.00
188 Deni Avdija I 10.00 25.00
189 Isaiah Stewart I 8.00 20.00
190 Immanuel Quickley I 10.00 25.00
191 Jaden McDaniels I 12.00 30.00
192 Saddiq Bey I 8.00 20.00
193 Onyeka Okongwu I 8.00 20.00
194 Kira Lewis Jr. I 4.00 10.00
195 Tyrese Haliburton I 30.00 80.00
196 Malachi Flynn I 4.00 10.00
197 Payton Pritchard I 12.00 30.00
198 Killian Hayes I 4.00 10.00
199 Devin Vassell I 12.00 30.00
200 Zeke Nnaji I 5.00 12.00
201 Russell Westbrook MET 25.00 60.00
202 Tyler Herro MET 25.00 60.00
203 Pascal Siakam MET 20.00 50.00
204 Damian Lillard MET 30.00 80.00
205 James Harden MET 25.00 60.00
206 LeBron James MET 100.00 250.00
207 RJ Barrett MET 20.00 50.00
208 Ja Morant MET 40.00 100.00
209 De'Aaron Fox MET 20.00 50.00
210 Karl-Anthony Towns MET 20.00 50.00
211 Zion Williamson MET 40.00 100.00
212 Devin Booker MET 30.00 80.00
213 Luka Doncic MET 80.00 200.00
214 Joel Embiid MET 30.00 80.00
215 Kyrie Irving MET 25.00 60.00
216 Trae Young MET 30.00 80.00
217 Jamal Murray MET 20.00 50.00
218 Nikola Jokic MET 60.00 150.00
219 Bradley Beal MET 15.00 40.00
220 Donovan Mitchell MET 25.00 60.00
221 Jimmy Butler MET 25.00 60.00
222 Chris Paul MET 25.00 60.00
223 Kevin Durant MET 50.00 125.00
224 Jayson Tatum MET 50.00 120.00
225 Paul George MET 20.00 50.00
226 Ben Simmons MET 12.00 30.00
227 Anthony Davis MET 30.00 80.00
228 Giannis Antetokounmpo MET 60.00 150.00
229 Kawhi Leonard MET 30.00 80.00
230 Stephen Curry MET 100.00 250.00
231 Tyrese Haliburton MET 80.00 200.00
232 Payton Pritchard MET 30.00 80.00
233 James Wiseman MET 12.00 30.00
234 Anthony Edwards MET 150.00 400.00
235 Deni Avdija MET 25.00 60.00
236 Obi Toppin MET 20.00 50.00
237 Cole Anthony MET 25.00 60.00
238 Patrick Williams MET 25.00 60.00
239 Killian Hayes MET 10.00 25.00
240 LaMelo Ball MET 150.00 400.00
241 Isaac Okoro MET 15.00 40.00
242 Onyeka Okongwu MET 20.00 50.00
243 Tyrese Maxey MET 60.00 150.00
244 RJ Hampton MET 10.00 25.00
245 Kira Lewis Jr. MET 10.00 25.00
246 Precious Achiuwa MET 20.00 50.00
247 Jalen Smith MET 20.00 50.00
248 Devin Vassell MET 30.00 80.00
249 Aleksej Pokusevski MET 12.00 30.00
250 Isaiah Stewart MET 20.00 50.00
251 Jamal Murray FL 20.00 50.00
252 Paul Pierce FL 20.00 50.00
253 Steve Nash FL 25.00 60.00
254 Shaquille O'Neal FL 50.00 120.00
255 Donovan Mitchell FL 25.00 60.00
256 Zion Williamson FL 40.00 100.00
257 Ja Morant FL 40.00 100.00
258 Vince Carter FL 25.00 60.00
259 James Harden FL 25.00 60.00
260 LeBron James FL 100.00 250.00
261 Jayson Tatum FL 50.00 120.00
262 Jimmy Butler FL 25.00 60.00
263 Kyrie Irving FL 25.00 60.00
264 Kawhi Leonard FL 30.00 80.00
265 Russell Westbrook FL 25.00 60.00
266 Gary Payton FL 20.00 50.00
267 Chris Paul FL 25.00 60.00
268 Dominique Wilkins FL 20.00 50.00
269 Dennis Rodman FL 30.00 80.00
270 RJ Barrett FL 20.00 50.00
271 Dirk Nowitzki
Luka Doncic SS 125.00 300.00
272 Larry Bird
Magic Johnson SS 125.00 300.00
273 LeBron James
Zion Williamson SS 150.00 400.00
274 Anthony Davis
Shaquille O'Neal SS 50.00 120.00
275 Allen Iverson
Ja Morant SS 125.00 300.00
276 Jaylen Brown
Jayson Tatum SS 50.00 120.00
277 Kevin Durant
Kyrie Irving SS 50.00 125.00
278 Kawhi Leonard
Paul George SS 30.00 80.00
279 Anthony Davis
LeBron James SS 125.00 300.00
280 David Robinson
Tim Duncan SS 30.00 80.00
281 James Harden
John Wall SS 25.00 60.00
282 Arvydas Sabonis
Domantas Sabonis SS 15.00 40.00
283 Tracy McGrady
Vince Carter SS 100.00 250.00
284 John Stockton
Karl Malone SS 25.00 60.00
285 Bradley Beal
Russell Westbrook SS 25.00 60.00
286 Chris Paul
Devin Booker SS 30.00 80.00
287 Bill Russell
Kareem Abdul-Jabbar SS 150.00 400.00
288 Charles Barkley
Shaquille O'Neal SS 50.00 120.00
289 Chris Webber
Jason Williams SS 75.00 200.00
290 Stephen Curry
Trae Young SS 125.00 300.00
291 Luka Doncic VA 80.00 200.00
292 James Wiseman VA 12.00 30.00
293 Kevin Durant VA 50.00 125.00
294 Anthony Edwards VA 150.00 400.00
295 Anthony Davis VA 30.00 80.00
296 Damian Lillard VA 30.00 80.00
297 Ben Simmons VA 12.00 30.00
298 LaMelo Ball VA 150.00 400.00
299 Giannis Antetokounmpo VA 60.00 150.00
300 LeBron James VA 150.00 400.00
301 LaMelo Ball AU JSY BW 1,000.00 2,000.00
302 Desmond Bane AU JSY BW 40.00 100.00
303 Precious Achiuwa AU JSY BW 25.00 60.00
304 Tyrell Terry AU JSY BW 10.00 25.00
305 Tyrese Maxey AU JSY BW 200.00 500.00
306 Vernon Carey Jr. AU JSY BW 12.00 30.00
307 Anthony Edwards AU JSY BW 800.00 1,500.00
308 Daniel Oturu AU JSY BW 12.00 30.00
309 Zeke Nnaji AU JSY BW 15.00 40.00
310 Kira Lewis Jr. AU JSY BW 12.00 30.00
311 Jaden McDaniels AU JSY BW 40.00 100.00
312 Aaron Nesmith AU JSY BW 25.00 60.00
313 Tyler Bey AU JSY BW 12.00 30.00
314 Isaac Okoro AU JSY BW 20.00 50.00
315 Killian Hayes AU JSY BW 20.00 50.00
316 Malachi Flynn AU JSY BW 12.00 30.00
317 Cole Anthony AU JSY BW 100.00 250.00
318 RJ Hampton AU JSY BW 12.00 30.00
319 Obi Toppin AU JSY BW 25.00 60.00
320 Theo Maledon AU JSY BW 12.00 30.00
321 Isaiah Stewart AU JSY BW 20.00 50.00
322 Xavier Tillman AU JSY BW 15.00 40.00
323 Deni Avdija AU JSY BW 30.00 80.00
324 Immanuel Quickley AU JSY BW 30.00 80.00
325 Aleksej Pokusevski AU JSY BW 15.00 40.00
326 Robert Woodard II AU JSY BW 12.00 30.00
327 Patrick Williams AU JSY BW 30.00 80.00
328 Tre Jones AU JSY BW 20.00 50.00
329 Josh Green AU JSY BW 25.00 60.00
330 Jalen Smith AU JSY BW 25.00 60.00
331 Payton Pritchard AU JSY BW 40.00 100.00
332 Jordan Nwora AU JSY BW 15.00 40.00
333 Devin Vassell AU JSY BW 40.00 100.00
334 Saddiq Bey AU JSY BW 25.00 60.00
335 Udoka Azubuike AU JSY BW 15.00 40.00
336 Onyeka Okongwu AU JSY BW 25.00 60.00
337 James Wiseman AU JSY BW 15.00 40.00
338 Nico Mannion AU JSY BW 12.00 30.00
339 Tyrese Haliburton AU JSY BW 150.00 400.00
340 CJ Elleby AU JSY BW 12.00 30.00
341 LaMelo Ball AU JSY C 1,000.00 2,000.00
342 Desmond Bane AU JSY C 40.00 100.00
343 Precious Achiuwa AU JSY C 25.00 60.00
344 Tyrell Terry AU JSY C 10.00 25.00
345 Tyrese Maxey AU JSY C 200.00 500.00
346 Vernon Carey Jr. AU JSY C 12.00 30.00
347 Anthony Edwards AU JSY C 800.00 1,500.00
348 Daniel Oturu AU JSY C 12.00 30.00
349 Zeke Nnaji AU JSY C 15.00 40.00
351 Jaden McDaniels AU JSY C 40.00 100.00
352 Aaron Nesmith AU JSY C 25.00 60.00
353 Tyler Bey AU JSY C 12.00 30.00
354 Isaac Okoro AU JSY C 20.00 50.00
355 Killian Hayes AU JSY C 12.00 30.00
356 Malachi Flynn AU JSY C 12.00 30.00
357 Cole Anthony AU JSY C 100.00 250.00
358 RJ Hampton AU JSY C 12.00 30.00
359 Obi Toppin AU JSY C 25.00 60.00
360 Theo Maledon AU JSY C 12.00 30.00
361 Isaiah Stewart AU JSY C 25.00 60.00
362 Xavier Tillman AU JSY C 15.00 40.00
363 Deni Avdija AU JSY C 30.00 80.00
364 Immanuel Quickley AU JSY C 30.00 80.00
0 Aleksej Pokusevski AU JSY C 15.00 40.00
366 Robert Woodard II AU JSY C 12.00 30.00
367 Patrick Williams AU JSY C 30.00 80.00
368 Tre Jones AU JSY C 20.00 50.00
369 Josh Green AU JSY C 25.00 60.00
370 Jalen Smith AU JSY C 25.00 60.00
371 Payton Pritchard AU JSY C 40.00 100.00
372 Jordan Nwora AU JSY C 15.00 40.00
373 Devin Vassell AU JSY C 40.00 100.00
374 Saddiq Bey AU JSY C 25.00 60.00
375 Udoka Azubuike AU JSY C 15.00 40.00
376 Onyeka Okongwu AU JSY C 25.00 60.00
377 James Wiseman AU JSY C 15.00 40.00
378 Nico Mannion AU JSY C 12.00 30.00
379 Tyrese Haliburton AU JSY C 150.00 400.00
380 CJ Elleby AU JSY C 12.00 30.00
381 Killian Hayes AU/49 6.00 15.00
382 Jahmi'us Ramsey AU/99 6.00 15.00
383 Tyrese Haliburton AU/99 125.00 300.00
384 Skylar Mays AU/99 6.00 15.00
385 Cassius Stanley AU/99 6.00 15.00
386 Obi Toppin AU/99 12.00 30.00
387 Grant Riller AU/99 6.00 15.00
388 Tyrese Maxey AU/99 150.00 400.00
389 Saben Lee AU/99 6.00 15.00
390 LaMelo Ball AU/99 800.00 1,500.00
391 Nick Richards AU/99 8.00 20.00
392 Deni Avdija AU/49 15.00 40.00
394 Tyler Bey AU/99 6.00 15.00
395 Anthony Edwards AU/99 600.00 1,200.00
396 Nico Mannion AU/99 6.00 15.00
397 Cole Anthony AU/49 75.00 200.00
398 Udoka Azubuike AU/99 8.00 20.00
399 Onyeka Okongwu AU/99 12.00 30.00
400 James Wiseman AU/49 8.00 20.00

2020-21 Panini Noir Award Winning Autographs

10 Steve Kerr 30.00 80.00
20 Bernard King 15.00 40.00

2020-21 Panini Noir Black and White Autographs

COMMON CARD 6.00 15.00
SEMISTARS 8.00 20.00
UNLISTED STARS 10.00 25.00
STATED PRINT RUN 25-99 SER.#'d SETS
1 Christian Laettner/99 10.00 25.00
2 Willie Cauley-Stein/99 6.00 15.00
3 Allen Iverson/25 200.00 500.00
5 Jarrett Allen/99 20.00 50.00
8 Jaren Jackson Jr./99 25.00 60.00
9 Malcolm Brogdon/99 10.00 25.00
10 Anthony Davis/49 100.00 250.00
11 Spud Webb/99 20.00 50.00
12 Allan Houston/99 15.00 40.00
13 Brook Lopez/99 8.00 20.00
15 Lauri Markkanen/99 12.00 30.00
16 Ja Morant/25 500.00 1,000.00
17 Kristaps Porzingis/49 30.00 80.00
18 Chris Kaman/99 6.00 15.00
19 Vlade Divac/99 8.00 20.00
20 Coby White/49 25.00 60.00
21 Kendrick Nunn/49 8.00 20.00
22 John Collins/99 20.00 50.00
23 Donte DiVincenzo/99 15.00 40.00
24 Marcus Camby/99 20.00 50.00
25 Drew Gooden/99 6.00 15.00
26 Stephen Curry/25 1,500.00 3,000.00
27 Thaddeus Young/99 6.00 15.00
28 Justin Holiday/99 6.00 15.00
29 Matthew Dellavedova/99 8.00 20.00
30 Boris Diaw/99 8.00 20.00
31 Alex English/99 10.00 25.00
32 Ivica Zubac/99 10.00 25.00
33 Avery Bradley/99 6.00 15.00
34 Charles Barkley/25 150.00 400.00
35 Bill Walton/99 40.00 100.00

2020-21 Panini Noir Box Office Memorabilia

COMMON CARD 2.50 6.00
SEMISTARS 3.00 8.00
UNLISTED STARS 4.00 10.00
STATED PRINT RUN 99 SER.#'d SETS
*PRIME/25: 1X TO 2.5X BASE HI
1 LeBron James 50.00 120.00
2 Klay Thompson 12.00 30.00
3 Zach LaVine 12.00 30.00
4 Bam Adebayo 6.00 15.00
5 Tyler Herro 8.00 20.00
6 LaMarcus Aldridge 4.00 10.00
7 Chris Paul 8.00 20.00
8 Kawhi Leonard 10.00 25.00
9 Trae Young 20.00 50.00
10 Ja Morant 30.00 80.00
11 DeMar DeRozan 5.00 12.00
12 Bogdan Bogdanovic 4.00 10.00
14 Giannis Antetokounmpo 30.00 80.00
15 Seth Curry 4.00 10.00
16 Jaylen Brown 6.00 15.00
17 Donte DiVincenzo 4.00 10.00
18 Nassir Little 3.00 8.00
19 CJ McCollum 4.00 10.00
20 Luka Doncic 30.00 80.00
21 Jarrett Culver 2.50 6.00
22 Jordan Poole 6.00 15.00
23 John Wall 5.00 12.00
24 Devin Booker 12.00 30.00
25 Brandon Ingram 5.00 12.00
26 Aaron Gordon 4.00 10.00
27 Victor Oladipo 3.00 8.00
28 Blake Griffin 4.00 10.00
29 Zion Williamson 25.00 60.00
30 Anthony Davis 10.00 25.00

2020-21 Panini Noir Color Autographs

COMMON CARD 6.00 15.00
SEMISTARS 8.00 20.00
UNLISTED STARS 10.00 25.00
STATED PRINT RUN 25-99 SER.#'d SETS
1 Christian Laettner/99 10.00 25.00
2 Willie Cauley-Stein/99 6.00 15.00
3 Allen Iverson/25 200.00 500.00
5 Jarrett Allen/99 20.00 50.00
8 Jaren Jackson Jr./99 25.00 60.00
9 Malcolm Brogdon/99 10.00 25.00
10 Anthony Davis/25 125.00 300.00
11 Spud Webb/99 20.00 50.00
12 Allan Houston/99 15.00 40.00
13 Brook Lopez/99 8.00 20.00
15 Lauri Markkanen/99 12.00 30.00
16 Ja Morant/25 500.00 1,000.00
17 Kristaps Porzingis/49 30.00 80.00
18 Chris Kaman/99 6.00 15.00
19 Vlade Divac/99 8.00 20.00
20 Coby White/49 25.00 60.00
21 Kendrick Nunn/49 8.00 20.00
22 John Collins/99 20.00 50.00
23 Donte DiVincenzo/99 15.00 40.00
24 Marcus Camby/99 20.00 50.00
25 Drew Gooden/99 6.00 15.00
26 Stephen Curry/25 1,500.00 3,000.00
27 Thaddeus Young/99 6.00 15.00
28 Justin Holiday/99 6.00 15.00
29 Matthew Dellavedova/99 8.00 20.00
30 Boris Diaw/99 8.00 20.00
31 Alex English/99 10.00 25.00
32 Ivica Zubac/99 10.00 25.00
33 Avery Bradley/99 6.00 15.00
34 Charles Barkley/25 150.00 400.00
35 Bill Walton/99 40.00 100.00

2020-21 Panini Noir Dish Night Memorabilia

COMMON CARD 3.00 8.00
SEMISTARS 4.00 10.00
UNLISTED STARS 5.00 12.00
STATED PRINT RUN 75 SER.#'d SETS
*PRIME/15-25: 1X TO 2.5X BASE HI
1 Grant Williams 4.00 10.00
2 Myles Turner 5.00 12.00
3 Fred VanVleet 8.00 20.00
4 Dillon Brooks 5.00 12.00
5 Rudy Gobert 6.00 15.00
6 Harry Giles III 3.00 8.00
7 Kevin Love 5.00 12.00
8 Mikal Bridges 6.00 15.00
9 Collin Sexton 5.00 12.00
10 Kyrie Irving 10.00 25.00
11 CJ McCollum 5.00 12.00
12 Mike Conley 4.00 10.00
13 Terry Rozier 5.00 12.00
14 Montrezl Harrell 5.00 12.00
15 De'Aaron Fox 8.00 20.00
16 Luka Doncic 30.00 80.00
17 Trae Young 12.00 30.00
18 LeBron James 50.00 120.00
19 Tyler Herro 10.00 25.00
20 Kemba Walker 5.00 12.00
21 Bam Adebayo 8.00 20.00
22 Coby White 6.00 15.00
23 Marvin Bagley III 4.00 10.00
24 Jamal Murray 8.00 20.00
25 Joel Embiid 12.00 30.00
26 Rui Hachimura 6.00 15.00
27 Seth Curry 5.00 12.00
28 Khris Middleton 6.00 15.00
29 John Collins 5.00 12.00
30 Bojan Bogdanovic 4.00 10.00

2020-21 Panini Noir Elegant Decor Rookie Jerseys

COMMON CARD 3.00 8.00
SEMISTARS 4.00 10.00
UNLISTED STARS 5.00 12.00
STATED PRINT RUN 75 SER.#'d SETS
*PRIME/25: 1X TO 2.5X BASE HI
1 Killian Hayes 4.00 10.00
2 Patrick Williams 10.00 25.00
3 Malachi Flynn 4.00 10.00
5 Precious Achiuwa 8.00 20.00
6 Cole Anthony 10.00 25.00
7 Isaac Okoro 6.00 15.00
8 Anthony Edwards 50.00 120.00
9 Tyrell Terry 3.00 8.00
10 Aaron Nesmith 8.00 20.00
11 Isaiah Stewart 8.00 20.00
12 Saddiq Bey 8.00 20.00
13 Desmond Bane 12.00 30.00
14 Cassius Winston 4.00 10.00
15 Onyeka Okongwu 8.00 20.00
16 Deni Avdija 10.00 25.00
17 Tyrese Haliburton 30.00 80.00
18 Tyrese Maxey 30.00 80.00
19 Tre Jones 6.00 15.00
20 Payton Pritchard 12.00 30.00
21 Immanuel Quickley 10.00 25.00
22 RJ Hampton 4.00 10.00
23 Jalen Smith 8.00 20.00
24 Jordan Nwora 5.00 12.00
25 Devin Vassell 12.00 30.00
26 Theo Maledon 4.00 10.00
27 LaMelo Ball 50.00 120.00
28 Obi Toppin 8.00 20.00
29 James Wiseman 5.00 12.00
30 Josh Green 8.00 20.00

2020-21 Panini Noir Freeze Frame Signatures

COMMON CARD 6.00 15.00
SEMISTARS 8.00 20.00
UNLISTED STARS 10.00 25.00
STATED PRINT RUN 49-99 SER.#'d SETS
1 James Worthy/99 25.00 60.00
2 Walt Frazier/99 20.00 50.00
3 Adrian Dantley/99 10.00 25.00
4 George Gervin/99 20.00 50.00
5 Gail Goodrich/99 10.00 25.00
7 John Stockton/49 100.00 250.00
8 Chris Mullin/99 20.00 50.00
9 RJ Barrett/49 60.00 150.00
10 Nate Archibald/99 12.00 30.00
11 Keita Bates-Diop/49 6.00 15.00
15 Nickeil Alexander-Walker/99 10.00 25.00
17 Calvin Murphy/99 10.00 25.00
18 Dominique Wilkins/99 25.00 60.00
19 Sekou Doumbouya/99 6.00 15.00
20 Kevin Garnett/25 125.00 300.00
21 Andre Miller/99 8.00 20.00
22 Kenyon Martin Jr./49 12.00 30.00
23 Cassius Stanley/49 8.00 20.00
25 Xavier Tillman/49 10.00 25.00
26 Tyler Bey/49 8.00 20.00
27 Skylar Mays/49 8.00 20.00
28 Robert Woodard II/49 8.00 20.00
30 Precious Achiuwa/49 15.00 40.00
31 Cole Anthony/49 50.00 120.00
32 Jordan Nwora/49 10.00 25.00
33 Roy Hibbert/99 6.00 15.00
34 Malachi Flynn/49 8.00 20.00
35 Jahmi'us Ramsey/49 8.00 20.00
36 Boris Diaw/99 8.00 20.00
37 Nico Mannion/49 8.00 20.00
38 Kira Lewis Jr./49 8.00 20.00
39 Josh Green/49 15.00 40.00
40 Jaden McDaniels/49 40.00 100.00

2020-21 Panini Noir Horizontal Spotlight Signatures

COMMON CARD 12.00 30.00
SEMISTARS 15.00 40.00
UNLISTED STARS 20.00 50.00
STATED PRINT RUN 49-99 SER.#'d SETS
1 Nikola Vucevic/99 20.00 50.00
2 Collin Sexton/99 50.00 120.00
3 Larry Bird/49 200.00 500.00
5 Stephen Curry/49 2,000.00 4,000.00
6 Chris Mullin/49 40.00 100.00
7 Tyrese Maxey/99 500.00 1,000.00
9 George Gervin/99 40.00 100.00
11 Trae Young/49 500.00 1,000.00
12 Zion Williamson/49 1,000.00 2,000.00
13 Luka Doncic/49 2,000.00 4,000.00
14 Andre Miller/99 15.00 40.00
15 Cole Anthony/99 150.00 400.00
16 Payton Pritchard/99 75.00 200.00
17 Dwyane Wade/49 150.00 400.00
18 Tobias Harris/99 20.00 50.00
19 Deni Avdija/99 75.00 200.00
20 LaMelo Ball/99 1,500.00 3,000.00
21 Gary Payton/49 125.00 300.00
25 RJ Barrett/49 150.00 400.00

2020-21 Panini Noir Icons Memorabilia

COMMON CARD 3.00 8.00
SEMISTARS 4.00 10.00
UNLISTED STARS 5.00 12.00
STATED PRINT RUN 99 SER.#'d SETS
*PRIME/25: 1X TO 2.5X BASE HI
1 Larry Bird 20.00 50.00
2 Magic Johnson 20.00 50.00
3 Julius Erving 12.00 30.00
4 Kareem Abdul-Jabbar 15.00 40.00
5 David Robinson 10.00 25.00
6 Isiah Thomas 8.00 20.00
7 Mitch Richmond 6.00 15.00
8 Chris Mullin 6.00 15.00
9 Shawn Kemp 8.00 20.00
10 Shaquille O'Neal 20.00 50.00
11 Anfernee Hardaway 12.00 30.00
12 Gary Payton 8.00 20.00
13 Dirk Nowitzki 12.00 30.00
14 Dwyane Wade 10.00 25.00
15 Kevin Garnett 12.00 30.00
16 Ray Allen 8.00 20.00
17 Karl Malone 10.00 25.00
18 John Stockton 10.00 25.00
19 Dennis Rodman 12.00 30.00
20 Tim Duncan 12.00 30.00

2020-21 Panini Noir Jumbo Material

COMMON CARD 3.00 8.00
SEMISTARS 4.00 10.00
UNLISTED STARS 5.00 12.00
STATED PRINT RUN 99 SER.#'d SETS
1 Tim Duncan 12.00 30.00
2 Danny Granger 3.00 8.00
3 Matt Bonner 3.00 8.00
4 Bojan Bogdanovic 4.00 10.00
5 Mitchell Robinson 5.00 12.00
6 Rudy Gobert 6.00 15.00
7 Otto Porter Jr. 3.00 8.00
8 David Lee 3.00 8.00
9 Marcus Smart 5.00 12.00
10 Daniel Theis 4.00 10.00
11 Will Barton 3.00 8.00
12 Steve Nash 10.00 25.00
13 Steven Adams 5.00 12.00
14 Vince Carter 10.00 25.00
15 Kevin Knox II 3.00 8.00
16 D'Angelo Russell 5.00 12.00
17 Nikola Vucevic 5.00 12.00
18 Aaron Gordon 5.00 12.00
19 Karl-Anthony Towns 8.00 20.00
20 Markelle Fultz 4.00 10.00
21 Larry Nance Jr. 4.00 10.00
22 Montrezl Harrell 5.00 12.00
23 Jarrett Allen 5.00 12.00
24 DeAndre Jordan 4.00 10.00
25 Brandon Clarke 5.00 12.00
26 Andrew Wiggins 6.00 15.00
27 Nikola Jokic 25.00 60.00
28 Luka Doncic 50.00 120.00
29 Draymond Green 6.00 15.00
30 Rui Hachimura 6.00 15.00
31 Dirk Nowitzki 12.00 30.00
32 Kevin Love 5.00 12.00
33 Kyle Lowry 6.00 15.00
34 Jarrett Culver 3.00 8.00
35 Jalen Brunson 8.00 20.00
36 Seth Curry 5.00 12.00
37 Norman Powell 4.00 10.00
38 Darius Bazley 3.00 8.00
39 Miles Bridges 5.00 12.00
40 Kyrie Irving 10.00 25.00
41 Spencer Dinwiddie 4.00 10.00
42 Kevin Porter Jr. 4.00 10.00
43 Danny Green 4.00 10.00
44 Julius Randle 5.00 12.00
45 Coby White 6.00 15.00
46 Caris LeVert 5.00 12.00
47 Donovan Mitchell 10.00 25.00
48 Michael Porter Jr. 6.00 15.00
49 Wendell Carter Jr. 4.00 10.00
50 Lauri Markkanen 6.00 15.00
51 Kyle Kuzma 6.00 15.00
52 Sekou Doumbouya 3.00 8.00
53 Khris Middleton 6.00 15.00
54 Anthony Davis 12.00 30.00
55 Bradley Beal 6.00 15.00
56 Myles Turner 5.00 12.00
57 Cameron Johnson 6.00 15.00
58 Gordon Hayward 5.00 12.00
59 Paul George 8.00 20.00
60 John Wall 6.00 15.00

2020-21 Panini Noir New Wave Jerseys

COMMON CARD 3.00 8.00
SEMISTARS 4.00 10.00
UNLISTED STARS 5.00 12.00
STATED PRINT RUN 99 SER.#'d SETS
*PRIME/25: .1X TO 2.5X BASE HI
1 Tyrese Haliburton 30.00 80.00
2 Isaac Okoro 6.00 15.00
3 Theo Maledon 4.00 10.00
4 Immanuel Quickley 10.00 25.00
5 CJ Elleby 4.00 10.00
6 Anthony Edwards 60.00 150.00
8 Cassius Winston 4.00 10.00
9 Tyrese Maxey 30.00 80.00
10 Precious Achiuwa 8.00 20.00
11 Aleksej Pokusevski 5.00 12.00
12 RJ Hampton 4.00 10.00
13 Saddiq Bey 8.00 20.00
14 James Wiseman 5.00 12.00
15 Jalen Smith 8.00 20.00
16 Josh Green 8.00 20.00
17 Onyeka Okongwu 8.00 20.00
18 LaMelo Ball 60.00 150.00
19 Killian Hayes 4.00 10.00
20 Malachi Flynn 4.00 10.00
21 Aaron Nesmith 8.00 20.00
22 Obi Toppin 8.00 20.00
23 Deni Avdija 10.00 25.00
24 Patrick Williams 10.00 25.00
25 Jordan Nwora 5.00 12.00
26 Devin Vassell 12.00 30.00
27 Isaiah Stewart 8.00 20.00
28 Desmond Bane 12.00 30.00
29 Payton Pritchard 12.00 30.00
30 Cole Anthony 10.00 25.00

2020-21 Panini Noir Newsreels Jerseys

COMMON CARD 3.00 8.00
SEMISTARS 4.00 10.00
UNLISTED STARS 5.00 12.00
STATED PRINT RUN 75 SER.#'d SETS
*PRIME/25: 1X TO 2.5X BASE HI
1 Matisse Thybulle 4.00 10.00
2 Jamal Murray 8.00 20.00
3 Nikola Jokic 25.00 60.00
4 Darius Garland 8.00 20.00
5 Jrue Holiday 5.00 12.00
6 Stephen Curry 60.00 150.00
7 Cam Reddish 6.00 15.00
8 James Harden 10.00 25.00
9 Kyle Kuzma 6.00 15.00
10 Chris Paul 10.00 25.00
11 Nikola Vucevic 5.00 12.00
12 Bradley Beal 6.00 15.00
13 Russell Westbrook 10.00 25.00
14 Bam Adebayo 8.00 20.00
15 Joel Embiid 12.00 30.00
16 Blake Griffin 5.00 12.00
17 Damian Lillard 12.00 30.00
18 PJ Washington Jr. 5.00 12.00
19 Aaron Gordon 5.00 12.00
20 Zach LaVine 8.00 20.00
21 DeMar DeRozan 6.00 15.00
22 Ja Morant 15.00 40.00
23 Brandon Ingram 6.00 15.00
24 Shai Gilgeous-Alexander 25.00 60.00
25 RJ Barrett 8.00 20.00
26 Kyrie Irving 10.00 25.00
27 Zion Williamson 15.00 40.00
28 Pascal Siakam 8.00 20.00
29 Anthony Davis 12.00 30.00
30 Giannis Antetokounmpo 25.00 60.00
31 Dirk Nowitzki 12.00 30.00
32 Julius Erving 12.00 30.00
33 Magic Johnson 20.00 50.00
34 Larry Bird 20.00 50.00
35 Hakeem Olajuwon 10.00 25.00
36 Shawn Kemp 8.00 20.00
37 Anfernee Hardaway 12.00 30.00
38 Jason Williams 8.00 20.00
39 Allen Iverson 12.00 30.00
40 Dwyane Wade 10.00 25.00

2020-21 Panini Noir Prime Materials Black and White Autographs

COMMON CARD 8.00 20.00
SEMISTARS 10.00 25.00
UNLISTED STARS 12.00 30.00
STATED PRINT RUN 25-40 SER.#'d SETS
1 Isiah Thomas/40 60.00 150.00
3 Grant Hill/40 60.00 150.00
4 Nikola Vucevic/40 12.00 30.00
5 Karl-Anthony Towns/40 30.00 80.00
6 RJ Barrett/25 20.00 50.00
7 Kevin Garnett/30 150.00 400.00
8 Anthony Davis/25 125.00 300.00
10 Roy Hibbert/40 8.00 20.00

11 Sekou Doumbouya/40	8.00	20.00
13 Maxi Kleber/40	10.00	25.00
14 Ricky Rubio/40	12.00	30.00
15 Kevin Knox II/40	8.00	20.00

2020-21 Panini Noir Prime Materials Color Autographs

COMMON CARD	8.00	20.00
SEMISTARS	10.00	25.00
UNLISTED STARS	12.00	30.00
STATED PRINT RUN 24-40 SER.#'d SETS		
1 Isiah Thomas/40	60.00	150.00
3 Grant Hill/40	60.00	150.00
4 Nikola Vucevic/40	12.00	30.00
5 Karl-Anthony Towns/40	30.00	80.00
6 RJ Barrett/24	20.00	50.00
7 Kevin Garnett/30	150.00	400.00
8 Anthony Davis/25	125.00	300.00
10 Roy Hibbert/40	8.00	20.00
11 Sekou Doumbouya/40	8.00	20.00
13 Maxi Kleber/40	10.00	25.00
14 Ricky Rubio/40	12.00	30.00
15 Kevin Knox II/40	8.00	20.00

2020-21 Panini Noir Reigning Nights Signatures

COMMON CARD	8.00	20.00
SEMISTARS	10.00	25.00
UNLISTED STARS	12.00	30.00
STATED PRINT RUN 25-99 SER.#'d SETS		
1 Kendrick Nunn/99	10.00	25.00
3 Allen Iverson/25	300.00	600.00
5 De'Aaron Fox/49	20.00	50.00
7 Malcolm Brogdon/99	12.00	30.00
9 Allan Houston/99	20.00	50.00
10 Sam Cassell/99	10.00	25.00
11 Trae Young/49	300.00	600.00
12 Ja Morant/25	500.00	1,000.00
13 Paul Pierce/49	75.00	200.00
14 Jayson Tatum/25	200.00	500.00
15 Wally Szczerbiak/99	10.00	25.00
16 Quinn Cook/99	8.00	20.00
17 Rick Barry/99	15.00	40.00
18 Kristaps Porzingis/49	15.00	40.00
19 Nickeil Alexander-Walker/99	12.00	30.00
20 Jordan Poole/99	125.00	300.00
21 Robert Horry/99	12.00	30.00
22 Donte DiVincenzo/49	12.00	30.00
23 Jaylen Nowell/99	10.00	25.00
24 Coby White/49	15.00	40.00
25 Terrence Ross/99	10.00	25.00
26 Steve Kerr/99	30.00	80.00
29 Ray Allen/99	100.00	250.00
30 JJ Redick/99	12.00	30.00
32 Larry Bird/25	150.00	400.00
33 Collin Sexton/99	12.00	30.00
34 Lauri Markkanen/25	15.00	40.00
35 Jarrett Culver/99	8.00	20.00

2020-21 Panini Noir Rookie Jumbo Material

COMMON CARD	3.00	8.00
SEMISTARS	4.00	10.00
UNLISTED STARS	5.00	12.00
STATED PRINT RUN 99 SER.#'d SETS		
1 Xavier Tillman	5.00	12.00
2 Tyrese Haliburton	30.00	80.00
4 Isaac Okoro	6.00	15.00
5 Theo Maledon	4.00	10.00
6 Immanuel Quickley	10.00	25.00
7 CJ Elleby	4.00	10.00
8 Daniel Oturu	4.00	10.00
10 Anthony Edwards	50.00	120.00
12 Cassius Winston	4.00	10.00
13 Tyrese Maxey	30.00	80.00
14 Precious Achiuwa	8.00	20.00
15 Jahmi'us Ramsey	4.00	10.00
16 Nico Mannion	4.00	10.00
17 Aleksej Pokusevski	5.00	12.00
18 RJ Hampton	4.00	10.00
19 Saddiq Bey	8.00	20.00
20 James Wiseman	5.00	12.00
21 Jalen Smith	8.00	20.00
22 Josh Green	8.00	20.00
23 Onyeka Okongwu	8.00	20.00
24 LaMelo Ball	60.00	150.00
25 Killian Hayes	4.00	10.00
26 Saben Lee	4.00	10.00
27 Robert Woodard II	4.00	10.00
28 Malachi Flynn	4.00	10.00
29 Aaron Nesmith	8.00	20.00
30 Skylar Mays	4.00	10.00
31 Obi Toppin	8.00	20.00
32 Deni Avdija	10.00	25.00
33 Patrick Williams	10.00	25.00
34 Jordan Nwora	5.00	12.00
35 Devin Vassell	12.00	30.00
36 Jaden McDaniels	12.00	30.00
37 Isaiah Stewart	8.00	20.00
38 Desmond Bane	12.00	30.00
39 Payton Pritchard	12.00	30.00
40 Cole Anthony	10.00	25.00

2020-21 Panini Noir Rookie Private Signings Association Version

14 Aaron Nesmith	15.00	40.00
22 Zeke Nnaji	12.00	30.00
26 Payton Pritchard	30.00	80.00
34 Theo Maledon	15.00	40.00
50 Grant Riller	6.00	15.00

2020-21 Panini Noir Rookie Private Signings Icon Version

14 Aaron Nesmith	15.00	40.00
22 Zeke Nnaji	12.00	30.00
26 Payton Pritchard	30.00	80.00
34 Theo Maledon	15.00	40.00
50 Grant Riller	6.00	15.00

2020-21 Panini Noir Shadow Signatures

COMMON CARD	10.00	25.00
SEMISTARS	12.00	30.00
UNLISTED STARS	15.00	40.00
STATED PRINT RUN 25-99 SER.#'d SETS		
3 Justin Holiday/49	10.00	25.00
4 Jason Williams/99	100.00	250.00
5 Karl Malone/49	125.00	300.00
6 Bob McAdoo/99	15.00	40.00
7 Kevin Knox II/49	10.00	25.00
8 Rui Hachimura/25	40.00	100.00
9 Dino Radja/99	12.00	30.00
10 Latrell Sprewell/99	40.00	100.00
14 Sekou Doumbouya/99	10.00	25.00
15 Bernard King/99	20.00	50.00
16 Charles Barkley/25	200.00	500.00
17 Wendell Carter Jr./49	12.00	30.00
18 Maxi Kleber/99	12.00	30.00
19 Wally Szczerbiak/99	12.00	30.00
20 Shai Gilgeous-Alexander/99	1,000.00	2,000.00
21 Mike Miller/99	12.00	30.00
22 Hedo Turkoglu/99	12.00	30.00
23 Eric Gordon/99	12.00	30.00
24 Steven Adams/99	15.00	40.00
25 Thaddeus Young/99	10.00	25.00
26 Kurt Rambis/49	12.00	30.00
28 Kendall Gill/99	12.00	30.00
29 John Collins/25	15.00	40.00
30 Stephen Curry/25	2,000.00	4,000.00
31 Spud Webb/99	15.00	40.00
32 Magic Johnson/25	200.00	500.00
33 Chauncey Billups/99	30.00	80.00
34 Al Harrington/99	10.00	25.00
35 Alex English/99	15.00	40.00
36 Marcus Camby/99	12.00	30.00
37 Bill Walton/99	40.00	100.00
38 Vlade Divac/99	12.00	30.00
39 Joe Dumars/99	20.00	50.00
40 Zion Williamson/25	500.00	1,000.00

2020-21 Panini Noir Showtime Signatures

COMMON CARD	10.00	25.00
SEMISTARS	12.00	30.00
UNLISTED STARS	15.00	40.00
STATED PRINT RUN 25-99 SER.#'d SETS		
1 De'Andre Hunter/49	15.00	40.00
3 Steven Adams/49	15.00	40.00
4 Rui Hachimura/25	40.00	100.00
6 Shai Gilgeous-Alexander/25	1,000.00	2,000.00
7 Trae Young/49	300.00	600.00
8 Ricky Rubio/49	15.00	40.00
9 Chauncey Billups/25	20.00	50.00
11 Gordon Hayward/49	15.00	40.00
12 Wendell Carter Jr./49	12.00	30.00
13 Jarrett Culver/49	10.00	25.00
14 Keita Bates-Diop/49	10.00	25.00
15 Jaylen Nowell/49	12.00	30.00
17 Luka Doncic/49	1,000.00	2,000.00
18 Karl Malone/25	125.00	300.00
21 Terrence Ross/49	12.00	30.00
22 Jayson Tatum/25	200.00	500.00
23 Jarrett Jack/49	10.00	25.00
24 Gary Payton/25	40.00	100.00
25 Karl-Anthony Towns/25	40.00	100.00

2020-21 Panini Noir Silver Screen Debut Signatures

COMMON CARD	8.00	20.00
SEMISTARS	10.00	25.00
UNLISTED STARS	12.00	30.00
STATED PRINT RUN 49-99 SER.#'d SETS		
EXCHANGE DEADLINE 12/30/2022		
1 Anthony Edwards/49	400.00	800.00
2 James Wiseman/99	12.00	30.00
3 LaMelo Ball/99	500.00	1,000.00
4 Patrick Williams/99	25.00	60.00
5 Isaac Okoro/99	15.00	40.00
6 Onyeka Okongwu/99	20.00	50.00
7 Killian Hayes/99	10.00	25.00
8 Obi Toppin/99	20.00	50.00
9 Deni Avdija/99	25.00	60.00
10 Jalen Smith/99	20.00	50.00
11 Devin Vassell/99	60.00	150.00
12 Tyrese Haliburton/99	150.00	400.00
13 Kira Lewis Jr./99	10.00	25.00
14 Aaron Nesmith/99	20.00	50.00
15 Cole Anthony/49	75.00	200.00
16 Isaiah Stewart/99	20.00	50.00
17 Aleksej Pokusevski/99	12.00	30.00
18 Josh Green/99	20.00	50.00
19 Saddiq Bey/99	20.00	50.00
20 Precious Achiuwa/99	20.00	50.00
21 Tyrese Maxey/99	125.00	300.00
22 Zeke Nnaji/99	12.00	30.00
23 RJ Hampton/99	10.00	25.00
24 Payton Pritchard/99	30.00	80.00
25 Malachi Flynn/99	10.00	25.00
26 Jaden McDaniels/99	30.00	80.00
27 Desmond Bane/99	75.00	200.00
28 Tyrell Terry/99	8.00	20.00
29 Immanuel Quickley/99	25.00	60.00
30 Vernon Carey Jr./99	10.00	25.00

2020-21 Panini Noir Snapshot Signatures

COMMON CARD	8.00	20.00
SEMISTARS	10.00	25.00
UNLISTED STARS	12.00	30.00
STATED PRINT RUN 49-99 SER.#'d SETS		
1 Kareem Abdul-Jabbar/49	300.00	600.00
2 Jarrett Culver/99	8.00	20.00
3 Paul Pierce/99	100.00	250.00
5 Robert Parish/99	15.00	40.00
6 David Thompson/99	15.00	40.00
7 Tim Hardaway/99	20.00	50.00
8 Dwyane Wade/49	200.00	500.00
9 Jerry Lucas/99	15.00	40.00
10 Rolando Blackman/99	10.00	25.00
11 Jarrett Jack/99	8.00	20.00
12 Matthew Dellavedova/99	10.00	25.00
13 Jordan Poole/99	125.00	300.00
14 Bernard King/99	15.00	40.00
18 Shaquille O'Neal /25	400.00	800.00
19 Kenny "Sky" Walker/99	10.00	25.00
20 Isaiah Rider/99	10.00	25.00
22 Joe Dumars/99	15.00	40.00
23 Kris Humphries/49	8.00	20.00
24 Robert Horry/99	20.00	50.00
25 Rui Hachimura/25	40.00	100.00
26 Rick Barry/99	20.00	50.00
27 Avery Johnson/99	10.00	25.00
28 Christian Laettner/99	12.00	30.00
29 De'Andre Hunter/99	12.00	30.00
30 Bill Russell/25	1,500.00	3,000.00

2020-21 Panini Noir Sneaker Spotlight

COMMON CARD (1-10)	30.00	80.00
SEMISTARS	40.00	100.00
UNLISTED STARS	50.00	120.00
STATED PRINT RUN 99 SER.#'d SETS		
1 Chris Webber	125.00	300.00
2 Carmelo Anthony	200.00	500.00
3 Chris Paul	150.00	400.00
4 Donovan Mitchell	150.00	400.00
5 Tim Duncan	400.00	800.00
6 LeBron James	800.00	1,500.00
7 Luka Doncic	600.00	1,200.00
8 Tracy McGrady	400.00	800.00
9 Stephen Curry	800.00	1,500.00
10 LeBron James	800.00	1,500.00

2020-21 Panini Noir Sneaker Spotlight Signatures

COMMON CARD	40.00	100.00
SEMISTARS	50.00	120.00
UNLISTED STARS	60.00	150.00
STATED PRINT RUN 49-99 SER.#'d SETS		
1 Zion Williamson/99	2,000.00	4,000.00
2 Lonzo Ball/99	150.00	400.00
3 Dwyane Wade/99	500.00	1,000.00
4 Jason Kidd/99	200.00	500.00
5 Allen Iverson/99	600.00	1,200.00
6 John Collins/99	125.00	300.00
7 Jayson Tatum/99	800.00	1,500.00
8 Cam Reddish/99	125.00	300.00
9 Luka Doncic/99	1,000.00	2,000.00
10 Trae Young/99	600.00	1,200.00
11 LaMarcus Aldridge/99	150.00	400.00
12 Ja Morant/99	2,500.00	5,000.00
13 Giannis Antetokounmpo/99	1,000.00	2,000.00
14 Shai Gilgeous-Alexander/99	1,500.00	3,000.00
15 De'Aaron Fox/99	200.00	500.00
16 Joe Harris/99	100.00	250.00
17 Jaren Jackson Jr./99	300.00	600.00
18 RJ Barrett/99	200.00	500.00
19 Latrell Sprewell/99	150.00	400.00
20 Lou Williams/99	150.00	400.00
23 Anthony Davis/99	400.00	800.00
24 P.J. Tucker /99	125.00	300.00
25 Kendrick Nunn/99	50.00	125.00
26 Paul Pierce/99	200.00	500.00
27 PJ Washington Jr./99	125.00	300.00
29 Chauncey Billups/99	150.00	400.00
30 Stephen Curry/99	3,000.00	6,000.00
31 Collin Sexton/99	125.00	300.00
32 Karl Malone/99	300.00	600.00
34 Shaquille O'Neal /99	500.00	1,000.00
35 Kevin Durant/99	1,500.00	3,000.00
36 Lauri Markkanen/99	125.00	300.00
37 Ray Allen/99	300.00	600.00
38 Gary Payton/99	150.00	400.00
39 Karl-Anthony Towns/99	200.00	500.00
40 Dirk Nowitzki/49	1,250.00	2,500.00

2020-21 Panini Noir Two-Shot Rookie Jerseys

COMMON CARD (1-20)	3.00	8.00
SEMISTARS	4.00	10.00
UNLISTED STARS	5.00	12.00
STATED PRINT RUN 99 SER.#'d SETS		
*PRIME/25: .75X TO 2X BASE HI		
1 LaMelo Ball RJ Hampton	30.00	80.00
2 Anthony Edwards Jaden McDaniels	40.00	100.00
3 James Wiseman Nico Mannion	5.00	12.00
4 Killian Hayes Saddiq Bey	8.00	20.00
5 Devin Vassell Tre Jones	12.00	30.00
6 LaMelo Ball Vernon Carey Jr.	30.00	80.00
7 Desmond Bane Xavier Tillman	12.00	30.00
8 Devin Vassell Patrick Williams	12.00	30.00
9 Cole Anthony Kira Lewis Jr.	10.00	25.00
10 Immanuel Quickley Obi Toppin	10.00	25.00
12 Josh Green Tyrell Terry	8.00	20.00
13 Killian Hayes Theo Maledon	4.00	10.00
14 Aleksej Pokusevski Theo Maledon	5.00	12.00
15 Tyrese Haliburton Tyrese Maxey	30.00	80.00
16 Jahmi'us Ramsey Tyrese Haliburton	30.00	80.00
17 Aaron Nesmith Payton Pritchard	12.00	30.00
18 Isaiah Stewart Jaden McDaniels	12.00	30.00
19 Jalen Smith Udoka Azubuike	8.00	20.00

2020-21 Panini Noir Vertical Spotlight Signatures

COMMON CARD (1-24)	12.00	30.00
SEMISTARS	15.00	40.00
UNLISTED STARS	20.00	50.00
STATED PRINT RUN 25-99 SER.#'d SETS		
1 Joe Dumars/49	60.00	150.00
2 Jae'Sean Tate/99	75.00	200.00
3 James Worthy/49	75.00	200.00
4 Obi Toppin/99	100.00	250.00
5 Patrick Williams/99	150.00	400.00
6 Saddiq Bey/99	100.00	250.00
7 Devin Vassell/99	100.00	250.00
8 Eric Gordon/99	15.00	40.00
9 De'Andre Hunter/99	75.00	200.00
10 Grant Hill/99	75.00	200.00
11 Jason Kidd/99	100.00	250.00
12 John Stockton/49	125.00	300.00
13 Charles Barkley/25	150.00	400.00
14 James Wiseman/99	20.00	50.00
15 Isaac Okoro/99	75.00	200.00
16 Isiah Thomas/49	100.00	250.00
18 Hedo Turkoglu/99	20.00	50.00
19 Al Harrington/99	20.00	50.00
20 Anthony Davis/49	125.00	300.00
21 Josh Green/99	75.00	200.00
22 Killian Hayes/99	75.00	200.00
23 Tyrese Haliburton/99	400.00	800.00
24 Anthony Edwards/99	1,000.00	2,000.00
25 Kareem Abdul-Jabbar/49	400.00	800.00

2021-22 Panini Noir

COMMON CARD (1-140)	2.00	5.00
SEMISTARS	2.50	6.00
UNLISTED STARS	3.00	8.00
1-140 PRINT RUN 99 SER.#'d SETS		
COM.RC (141-200)	3.00	8.00
RC SEMIS	4.00	10.00
RC UNLISTED	5.00	12.00
RC PRINT RUN 99 SER.#'d SETS		
COMMON CARD (201-295)	8.00	20.00
SEMISTARS	10.00	25.00
UNLISTED STARS	12.00	30.00
201-295 PRINT RUN 25 SER.#'d SETS		
COM. JSY AU (301-380)	12.00	30.00
SEMISTARS	15.00	40.00
UNLISTED STARS	20.00	50.00
301-380 PRINT RUN 99 SER.#'d SETS		
COM. AU (381-400)	6.00	15.00
SEMISTARS	8.00	20.00
UNLISTED STARS	10.00	25.00
381-400 PRINT RUN 99 SER.#'d SETS		
1 Trae Young A	8.00	20.00
2 Reggie Jackson A	2.50	6.00
3 Dennis Schroder A	3.00	8.00
4 De'Aaron Fox A	5.00	12.00
5 Russell Westbrook A	5.00	12.00
6 Saddiq Bey A	2.50	6.00
7 Draymond Green A	4.00	10.00
8 Zach LaVine A	5.00	12.00
9 Christian Wood A	2.50	6.00
10 Spencer Dinwiddie A	2.50	6.00
11 Kristaps Porzingis A	4.00	10.00
12 Carmelo Anthony A	5.00	12.00
13 RJ Barrett A	5.00	12.00
14 Nikola Vucevic A	3.00	8.00
15 LaMelo Ball A	8.00	20.00
16 Khris Middleton A	3.00	8.00
17 Keldon Johnson A	4.00	10.00
18 Domantas Sabonis A	4.00	10.00
19 Tyrese Maxey A	8.00	20.00
20 Jrue Holiday A	4.00	10.00
21 Paul George A	5.00	12.00
22 Michael Porter Jr. A	4.00	10.00
23 Jayson Tatum A	12.00	30.00
24 Jimmy Butler A	5.00	12.00
25 Chris Paul A	6.00	15.00
26 James Harden A	6.00	15.00
27 Darius Garland A	5.00	12.00
28 Ja Morant A	10.00	25.00
29 Jerami Grant A	3.00	8.00
30 Giannis Antetokounmpo A	15.00	40.00
31 Luguentz Dort A	3.00	8.00
32 Karl-Anthony Towns A	5.00	12.00
33 Damian Lillard A	8.00	20.00
34 DeMar DeRozan A	4.00	10.00
35 Tobias Harris A	2.50	6.00
36 John Collins A	3.00	8.00
37 Jaylen Brown A	5.00	12.00
38 OG Anunoby A	3.00	8.00
39 Julius Randle A	4.00	10.00
40 LeBron James A	25.00	60.00
41 Tyler Herro A	5.00	12.00
42 Bradley Beal A	4.00	10.00
43 Kevin Porter Jr. A	2.50	6.00
44 Anthony Edwards A	15.00	40.00
45 Fred VanVleet A	4.00	10.00
46 Caris LeVert A	2.50	6.00
47 CJ McCollum A	2.50	6.00
48 Luka Doncic A	20.00	50.00
49 Kemba Walker A	3.00	8.00
50 Lonzo Ball A	3.00	8.00
51 Stephen Curry A	20.00	50.00
52 Desmond Bane A	6.00	15.00
53 Aaron Gordon A	3.00	8.00
54 Mike Conley A	2.50	6.00
55 Dejounte Murray A	3.00	8.00
56 Devin Booker A	8.00	20.00
57 Brandon Ingram A	4.00	10.00
58 Collin Sexton A	3.00	8.00
59 Kevin Durant A	10.00	25.00
60 Anthony Davis A	8.00	20.00
61 Kyle Lowry A	3.00	8.00
62 Donovan Mitchell A	6.00	15.00
63 Rudy Gobert A	4.00	10.00
64 Shai Gilgeous-Alexander A	15.00	40.00
65 Nikola Jokic A	15.00	40.00
66 Zion Williamson A	8.00	20.00
67 Miles Bridges A	2.50	6.00
68 Cole Anthony A	4.00	10.00
69 Tyrese Haliburton A	6.00	15.00
70 Joel Embiid A	8.00	20.00
71 Trae Young I	8.00	20.00
72 Reggie Jackson I	2.50	6.00
73 Dennis Schroder I	3.00	8.00
74 De'Aaron Fox I	5.00	12.00
75 Russell Westbrook I	5.00	12.00
76 Saddiq Bey I	2.50	6.00
77 Draymond Green I	4.00	10.00
78 Zach LaVine I	5.00	12.00
79 Christian Wood I	2.50	6.00
80 Spencer Dinwiddie I	2.50	6.00
81 Kristaps Porzingis I	4.00	10.00
82 Carmelo Anthony I	5.00	12.00
83 RJ Barrett I	5.00	12.00
84 Nikola Vucevic I	3.00	8.00
85 LaMelo Ball I	8.00	20.00
86 Khris Middleton I	3.00	8.00
87 Keldon Johnson I	4.00	10.00
88 Domantas Sabonis I	4.00	10.00
89 Tyrese Maxey I	8.00	20.00
90 Jrue Holiday I	4.00	10.00
91 Paul George I	5.00	12.00
92 Michael Porter Jr. I	4.00	10.00
93 Jayson Tatum I	12.00	30.00
94 Jimmy Butler I	5.00	12.00
95 Chris Paul I	6.00	15.00
96 James Harden I	6.00	15.00
97 Darius Garland I	5.00	12.00
98 Ja Morant I	10.00	25.00
99 Jerami Grant I	3.00	8.00
100 Giannis Antetokounmpo I	15.00	40.00
101 Luguentz Dort I	3.00	8.00
102 Karl-Anthony Towns I	5.00	12.00
103 Damian Lillard I	8.00	20.00
104 DeMar DeRozan I	4.00	10.00
105 Tobias Harris I	2.50	6.00
106 John Collins I	3.00	8.00
107 Jaylen Brown I	5.00	12.00
108 OG Anunoby I	3.00	8.00
109 Julius Randle I	4.00	10.00
110 LeBron James I	25.00	60.00
111 Tyler Herro I	5.00	12.00
112 Bradley Beal I	4.00	10.00
113 Kevin Porter Jr. I	2.50	6.00
114 Anthony Edwards I	15.00	40.00
115 Fred VanVleet I	4.00	10.00
116 Caris LeVert I	2.50	6.00
117 CJ McCollum I	2.50	6.00
118 Luka Doncic I	20.00	50.00
119 Kemba Walker I	3.00	8.00
120 Lonzo Ball I	3.00	8.00
121 Stephen Curry I	20.00	50.00
122 Desmond Bane I	6.00	15.00
123 Aaron Gordon I	3.00	8.00
124 Mike Conley I	2.50	6.00
125 Dejounte Murray I	3.00	8.00
126 Devin Booker I	8.00	20.00
127 Brandon Ingram I	4.00	10.00
128 Collin Sexton I	3.00	8.00
129 Kevin Durant I	10.00	25.00
130 Anthony Davis I	8.00	20.00
131 Kyle Lowry I	3.00	8.00
132 Donovan Mitchell I	6.00	15.00
133 Rudy Gobert I	4.00	10.00
134 Shai Gilgeous-Alexander I	15.00	40.00
135 Nikola Jokic I	15.00	40.00
136 Zion Williamson I	8.00	20.00
137 Miles Bridges I	2.50	6.00
138 Cole Anthony I	4.00	10.00
139 Tyrese Haliburton I	6.00	15.00
140 Joel Embiid I	8.00	20.00
141 Scottie Barnes A RC	15.00	40.00
142 Cade Cunningham A RC	30.00	80.00
143 Chris Duarte A RC	4.00	10.00
144 Jalen Green A RC	25.00	60.00
145 Josh Giddey A RC	15.00	40.00
146 Evan Mobley A RC	20.00	50.00
147 Jalen Suggs A RC	12.00	30.00
148 Franz Wagner A RC	15.00	40.00
149 Davion Mitchell A RC	5.00	12.00
150 Alperen Sengun A RC	15.00	40.00
151 Jonathan Kuminga A RC	15.00	40.00
152 Ziaire Williams A RC	6.00	15.00
153 James Bouknight A RC	4.00	10.00
154 Joshua Primo A RC	4.00	10.00
155 Moses Moody A RC	10.00	25.00
156 Corey Kispert A RC	6.00	15.00
157 Trey Murphy III A RC	15.00	40.00
158 Bones Hyland A RC	6.00	15.00
159 Tre Mann A RC	8.00	20.00
160 Kai Jones A RC	4.00	10.00
161 Jalen Johnson A RC	15.00	40.00
162 Jeremiah Robinson-Earl A RC	5.00	12.00
163 Isaiah Jackson A RC	5.00	12.00
164 Usman Garuba A RC	4.00	10.00
165 Josh Christopher A RC	4.00	10.00
166 Herbert Jones A RC	6.00	15.00
167 Ayo Dosunmu A RC	10.00	25.00
168 Day'Ron Sharpe A RC	5.00	12.00
169 Quentin Grimes A RC	10.00	25.00
170 Keon Johnson A RC	5.00	12.00
171 Scottie Barnes I	15.00	40.00
172 Cade Cunningham I	30.00	80.00
173 Chris Duarte I	4.00	10.00
174 Jalen Green I	25.00	60.00
175 Josh Giddey I	15.00	40.00
176 Evan Mobley I	20.00	50.00
177 Jalen Suggs I	12.00	30.00
178 Franz Wagner I	15.00	40.00
179 Davion Mitchell I	5.00	12.00
180 Alperen Sengun I	15.00	40.00
181 Jonathan Kuminga I	15.00	40.00
182 Ziaire Williams I	6.00	15.00
183 James Bouknight I	4.00	10.00
184 Joshua Primo I	4.00	10.00
185 Moses Moody I	10.00	25.00
186 Corey Kispert I	6.00	15.00
187 Trey Murphy III I	15.00	40.00
188 Bones Hyland I	6.00	15.00
189 Tre Mann I	8.00	20.00
190 Kai Jones I	4.00	10.00
191 Jalen Johnson I	15.00	40.00
192 Jeremiah Robinson-Earl I	5.00	12.00
193 Isaiah Jackson I	5.00	12.00
194 Usman Garuba I	4.00	10.00
195 Josh Christopher I	4.00	10.00
196 Herbert Jones I	6.00	15.00
197 Ayo Dosunmu I	10.00	25.00
198 Day'Ron Sharpe I	5.00	12.00
199 Quentin Grimes I	10.00	25.00
200 Keon Johnson I	5.00	12.00
201 Giannis Antetokounmpo MET	60.00	150.00
202 Ja Morant MET	40.00	100.00
203 Anthony Davis MET	30.00	80.00
204 LaMelo Ball MET	30.00	80.00
205 Donovan Mitchell MET	25.00	60.00
206 LeBron James MET	100.00	250.00
207 Kevin Durant MET	40.00	100.00
208 Jayson Tatum MET	50.00	125.00
209 Damian Lillard MET	30.00	80.00
210 Luka Doncic MET	80.00	200.00
211 Trae Young MET	30.00	80.00
212 Devin Booker MET	30.00	80.00
213 James Harden MET	25.00	60.00
214 Paul George MET	20.00	50.00
215 Nikola Jokic MET	60.00	150.00
216 Zach LaVine MET	20.00	50.00
217 Julius Randle MET	15.00	40.00
218 Jimmy Butler MET	20.00	50.00
219 Bradley Beal MET	15.00	40.00
220 Zion Williamson MET	30.00	80.00
221 Russell Westbrook MET	20.00	50.00
222 DeMar DeRozan MET	15.00	40.00
223 Joel Embiid MET	30.00	80.00
224 Chris Paul MET	25.00	60.00
225 Shai Gilgeous-Alexander MET	60.00	150.00
226 De'Aaron Fox MET	20.00	50.00
227 Jaylen Brown MET	20.00	50.00
228 Karl-Anthony Towns MET	20.00	50.00
229 Kyle Lowry MET	12.00	30.00
230 Stephen Curry MET	80.00	200.00
231 Jalen Suggs MET	30.00	80.00
232 Davion Mitchell MET	12.00	30.00
233 Evan Mobley MET	50.00	125.00
234 Cade Cunningham MET	80.00	200.00
235 Jonathan Kuminga MET	40.00	100.00
236 Chris Duarte MET	10.00	25.00
237 Josh Giddey MET	40.00	100.00
238 Jalen Green MET	60.00	150.00
239 Franz Wagner MET	40.00	100.00
240 Scottie Barnes MET	40.00	100.00
241 Joshua Primo MET	10.00	25.00
242 Alperen Sengun MET	40.00	100.00
243 Ziaire Williams MET	15.00	40.00
244 James Bouknight MET	10.00	25.00
245 Moses Moody MET	25.00	60.00
246 Corey Kispert MET	15.00	40.00
247 Trey Murphy III MET	40.00	100.00
248 Tre Mann MET	20.00	50.00
249 Kai Jones MET	10.00	25.00
250 Jalen Johnson MET	40.00	100.00
251 Ja Morant FL	40.00	100.00
252 Stephen Curry FL	80.00	200.00
253 Giannis Antetokounmpo FL	60.00	150.00
254 Russell Westbrook FL	20.00	50.00
255 Luka Doncic FL	80.00	200.00
256 LeBron James FL	100.00	250.00
257 Trae Young FL	30.00	80.00
258 Kevin Durant FL	40.00	100.00
259 Zion Williamson FL	30.00	80.00
260 Donovan Mitchell FL	25.00	60.00
261 LaMelo Ball FL	30.00	80.00
262 Anthony Edwards FL	60.00	150.00
263 Manu Ginobili FL	25.00	60.00
264 Charles Barkley FL	30.00	80.00
265 Kevin Garnett FL	30.00	80.00
266 Dwyane Wade FL	25.00	60.00
267 Tracy McGrady FL	20.00	50.00
268 Zach LaVine FL	20.00	50.00
269 Devin Booker FL	30.00	80.00
270 Kawhi Leonard FL	30.00	80.00
271 LeBron James Stephen Curry SS	100.00	250.00
272 Damian Lillard Trae Young SS	30.00	80.00
273 Ja Morant LaMelo Ball SS	40.00	100.00
274 James Harden Kevin Durant SS	40.00	100.00
275 Donovan Mitchell Jayson Tatum SS	50.00	125.00
276 Vince Carter Zach LaVine SS	25.00	60.00
277 Jalen Green Jalen Suggs SS	60.00	150.00
278 Cade Cunningham Luka Doncic SS	80.00	200.00
279 Evan Mobley Giannis Antetokounmpo SS	60.00	150.00
280 Kawhi Leonard Scottie Barnes SS	40.00	100.00
281 LeBron James VA	100.00	250.00
282 Cade Cunningham VA	80.00	200.00
283 Luka Doncic VA	80.00	200.00
284 Jalen Green VA	60.00	150.00
285 Ja Morant VA	40.00	100.00
286 Jalen Suggs VA	30.00	80.00
287 Stephen Curry VA	80.00	200.00
288 Scottie Barnes VA	40.00	100.00
289 Giannis Antetokounmpo VA	60.00	150.00
290 Evan Mobley VA	50.00	125.00
291 Kevin Durant VA	40.00	100.00
292 Jonathan Kuminga VA	40.00	100.00
293 Damian Lillard VA	30.00	80.00
294 Josh Giddey VA	40.00	100.00
295 Trae Young VA	30.00	80.00
301 James Bouknight AU JSY BW	15.00	40.00
302 Josh Christopher AU JSY BW	15.00	40.00
303 Scottie Lewis AU JSY BW	15.00	40.00
304 Bones Hyland AU JSY BW	25.00	60.00
305 Ayo Dosunmu AU JSY BW	40.00	100.00
306 Alperen Sengun AU JSY BW	60.00	150.00
307 Trey Murphy III AU JSY BW	60.00	150.00
308 Evan Mobley AU JSY BW	80.00	200.00
309 Jaden Springer AU JSY BW	20.00	50.00
310 Day'Ron Sharpe AU JSY BW	20.00	50.00
311 Corey Kispert AU JSY BW	25.00	60.00
312 Ziaire Williams AU JSY BW	25.00	60.00
313 Miles McBride AU JSY BW	30.00	80.00
314 Santi Aldama AU JSY BW	25.00	60.00
315 Usman Garuba AU JSY BW	15.00	40.00
316 Brandon Boston Jr. AU JSY BW	75.00	200.00
317 Cade Cunningham AU JSY BW	600.00	1,200.00
318 Joshua Primo AU JSY BW	15.00	40.00
319 Franz Wagner AU JSY BW	150.00	400.00
320 Luka Garza AU JSY BW	20.00	50.00
321 Scottie Barnes AU JSY BW	500.00	1,000.00
322 Jeremiah Robinson-Earl AU JSY BW	20.00	50.00
323 Josh Giddey AU JSY BW	400.00	800.00
324 Davion Mitchell AU JSY BW	20.00	50.00
325 Charles Bassey AU JSY BW	20.00	50.00
326 Moses Moody AU JSY BW	40.00	100.00
327 Jalen Green AU JSY BW	500.00	1,000.00
328 Jonathan Kuminga AU JSY BW	300.00	600.00
329 Tre Mann AU JSY BW	30.00	80.00
330 Greg Brown III AU JSY BW	15.00	40.00
331 Chris Duarte AU JSY BW	15.00	40.00
332 Jalen Johnson AU JSY BW	60.00	150.00
333 Kai Jones AU JSY BW	15.00	40.00
334 Isaiah Livers AU JSY BW	20.00	50.00
335 Keon Johnson AU JSY BW	20.00	50.00
336 Cameron Thomas AU JSY BW	40.00	100.00
337 Jalen Suggs AU JSY BW	150.00	400.00
338 Isaiah Jackson AU JSY BW	20.00	50.00
339 Quentin Grimes AU JSY BW	40.00	100.00
340 Jared Butler AU JSY BW	20.00	50.00
341 James Bouknight AU JSY BW	15.00	40.00
342 Josh Christopher AU JSY BW	15.00	40.00
343 Scottie Lewis AU JSY BW	15.00	40.00
344 Bones Hyland AU JSY BW	125.00	300.00
345 Ayo Dosunmu AU JSY BW	125.00	300.00
346 Alperen Sengun AU JSY BW	125.00	300.00
347 Trey Murphy III AU JSY BW	60.00	150.00
348 Evan Mobley AU JSY BW	400.00	800.00
349 Jaden Springer AU JSY BW	20.00	50.00
350 Day'Ron Sharpe AU JSY BW	20.00	50.00
351 Corey Kispert AU JSY BW	25.00	60.00
352 Ziaire Williams AU JSY BW	25.00	60.00
353 Miles McBride AU JSY BW	30.00	80.00
354 Santi Aldama AU JSY BW	25.00	60.00
355 Usman Garuba AU JSY BW	15.00	40.00
356 Brandon Boston Jr. AU JSY BW	75.00	200.00
357 Cade Cunningham AU JSY BW	600.00	1,200.00
358 Joshua Primo AU JSY BW	15.00	40.00
359 Franz Wagner AU JSY BW	150.00	400.00
360 Luka Garza AU JSY BW	20.00	50.00
361 Scottie Barnes AU JSY BW	500.00	1,000.00
362 Jeremiah Robinson-Earl AU JSY BW	20.00	50.00
363 Josh Giddey AU JSY BW	400.00	800.00
364 Davion Mitchell AU JSY BW	20.00	50.00
365 Charles Bassey AU JSY BW	20.00	50.00
366 Moses Moody AU JSY BW	150.00	400.00
367 Jalen Green AU JSY BW	500.00	1,000.00
368 Jonathan Kuminga AU JSY BW	300.00	600.00
369 Tre Mann AU JSY BW	30.00	80.00
370 Greg Brown III AU JSY BW	15.00	40.00
371 Chris Duarte AU JSY BW	15.00	40.00
372 Jalen Johnson AU JSY BW	60.00	150.00
373 Kai Jones AU JSY BW	15.00	40.00
374 Isaiah Livers AU JSY BW	20.00	50.00
375 Keon Johnson AU JSY BW	20.00	50.00
376 Cameron Thomas AU JSY BW	40.00	100.00
377 Jalen Suggs AU JSY BW	150.00	400.00
378 Isaiah Jackson AU JSY BW	20.00	50.00
379 Quentin Grimes AU JSY BW	40.00	100.00
380 Jared Butler AU JSY BW	20.00	50.00
381 Evan Mobley AU/99	200.00	500.00
382 Bones Hyland AU/99	75.00	200.00
383 Alperen Sengun AU/99	100.00	250.00
384 Franz Wagner AU/99	100.00	250.00
385 Jalen Suggs AU/99	100.00	250.00
386 Davion Mitchell AU/99	10.00	25.00
387 Greg Brown III AU/99	8.00	20.00
388 Cameron Thomas AU/99	20.00	50.00
389 Josh Giddey AU/99	200.00	500.00
390 Cade Cunningham AU/49	400.00	800.00
391 Moses Moody AU/99	100.00	250.00
392 James Bouknight AU/99	8.00	20.00
393 Kai Jones AU/99	8.00	20.00
394 Brandon Boston Jr. AU/99	10.00	25.00
395 Jonathan Kuminga AU/99	150.00	400.00
396 JT Thor AU/99	10.00	25.00
397 Josh Christopher AU/99	8.00	20.00
398 Trey Murphy III AU/99	30.00	80.00
399 Scottie Barnes AU/49	350.00	700.00
400 Jalen Green AU/49	350.00	700.00

2021-22 Panini Noir Black and White Autographs

COMMON CARD	6.00	15.00
SEMISTARS	8.00	20.00
UNLISTED STARS	10.00	25.00
STATED PRINT RUN 25-99 SER.#'d SETS		
1 Raymond Felton/99	6.00	15.00
2 Kirk Hinrich /99	10.00	25.00
3 Anthony Davis/49	125.00	300.00
4 Mike Conley/49	8.00	20.00
5 David Thompson/99	12.00	30.00
6 Stephen Jackson/99	8.00	20.00
7 Theo Maledon/99	8.00	20.00
8 Rui Hachimura/99	40.00	100.00
9 Alex English/99	12.00	30.00
10 Devin Vassell/99	25.00	60.00
11 Nikola Jokic/49	200.00	500.00
12 Mark Price/99	10.00	25.00
13 Tony Allen/49	6.00	15.00
14 Clint Capela/99	10.00	25.00
15 Mark Aguirre/99	8.00	20.00
16 Talen Horton-Tucker/99	20.00	50.00
18 Steve Kerr/99	40.00	100.00
19 Elton Brand/99	10.00	25.00
20 Ralph Sampson/99	10.00	25.00
21 Mike Bibby/99	25.00	60.00
22 Vince Carter/25	150.00	400.00
23 Toni Kukoc/99	15.00	40.00
24 Drew Gooden/99	8.00	20.00
25 Arvydas Sabonis/99	12.00	30.00
26 Jason Williams/99	75.00	200.00
27 Bill Laimbeer/99	15.00	40.00
28 Nate Archibald/99	10.00	25.00
29 Jordan Nwora/99	10.00	25.00
32 Karl Malone/25	125.00	300.00
33 Frank Kaminsky/99	6.00	15.00
34 Jae'Sean Tate/99	10.00	25.00
35 James Wiseman/49	8.00	20.00

2021-22 Panini Noir Box Office Memorabilia

COMMON CARD	2.00	5.00
SEMISTARS	2.50	6.00
UNLISTED STARS	3.00	8.00
STATED PRINT RUN 99 SER.#'d SETS		
*PRIME/25: 1.25X TO 3X BASE HI		
1 Kevin Durant	10.00	25.00
2 Khris Middleton	3.00	8.00
3 Bam Adebayo	5.00	12.00
4 Joel Embiid	8.00	20.00
5 Paul George	5.00	12.00
6 Trae Young	8.00	20.00
7 Karl-Anthony Towns	5.00	12.00
8 Klay Thompson	8.00	20.00
9 Deandre Ayton	3.00	8.00
10 De'Aaron Fox	5.00	12.00
11 Kristaps Porzingis	4.00	10.00
12 Jaren Jackson Jr.	5.00	12.00
13 Jaylen Brown	5.00	12.00
14 Julius Randle	4.00	10.00
15 DeMar DeRozan	4.00	10.00
16 Seth Curry	2.50	6.00
17 Jerami Grant	3.00	8.00
18 Caris LeVert	2.50	6.00
19 Kevin Love	3.00	8.00
20 Bradley Beal	4.00	10.00
21 Cole Anthony	4.00	10.00
22 LeBron James	40.00	100.00

23 Nikola Vucevic 3.00 8.00
24 Jordan Clarkson 3.00 8.00
25 Dennis Schroder 3.00 8.00
26 Tyler Herro 5.00 12.00
27 Carmelo Anthony 5.00 12.00
28 Damian Lillard 8.00 20.00
29 Aaron Gordon 3.00 8.00
30 Ja Morant 10.00 25.00

2021-22 Panini Noir Color Autographs

COMMON CARD 6.00 15.00
SEMISTARS 8.00 20.00
UNLISTED STARS 10.00 25.00
STATED PRINT RUN 25-99 SER.#'d SETS
1 Raymond Felton/99 6.00 15.00
2 Kirk Hinrich /99 10.00 25.00
3 Anthony Davis/49 125.00 300.00
4 Mike Conley/49 8.00 20.00
5 David Thompson/99 12.00 30.00
6 Stephen Jackson/99 8.00 20.00
7 Theo Maledon/99 8.00 20.00
8 Rui Hachimura/99 40.00 100.00
9 Alex English/99 12.00 30.00
10 Devin Vassell/99 25.00 60.00
11 Nikola Jokic/49 200.00 500.00
12 Mark Price/99 10.00 25.00
13 Tony Allen/49 6.00 15.00
14 Clint Capela/99 10.00 25.00
15 Mark Aguirre/99 8.00 20.00
16 Talen Horton-Tucker/99 20.00 50.00
18 Steve Kerr/99 40.00 100.00
19 Elton Brand/99 10.00 25.00
20 Ralph Sampson/99 10.00 25.00
21 Mike Bibby/99 25.00 60.00
22 Vince Carter/25 150.00 400.00
23 Toni Kukoc/99 15.00 40.00
24 Drew Gooden/99 8.00 20.00
25 Arvydas Sabonis/99 12.00 30.00
26 Jason Williams/99 75.00 200.00
27 Bill Laimbeer/99 15.00 40.00
28 Nate Archibald/99 10.00 25.00
29 Jordan Nwora/99 10.00 25.00
32 Karl Malone/25 125.00 300.00
33 Frank Kaminsky/99 6.00 15.00
34 Jae'Sean Tate/99 10.00 25.00
35 James Wiseman/49 8.00 20.00

2021-22 Panini Noir Dish Night Memorabilia

COMMON CARD 3.00 8.00
SEMISTARS 4.00 10.00
UNLISTED STARS 5.00 12.00
STATED PRINT RUN 75 SER.#'d SETS
*PRIME/25: 1X TO 2.5X BASE HI
1 Tyrese Haliburton 10.00 25.00
2 Isaac Okoro 4.00 10.00
3 Chris Paul 10.00 25.00
4 Dejounte Murray 5.00 12.00
5 Jrue Holiday 6.00 15.00
6 Marcus Smart 5.00 12.00
7 Fred VanVleet 6.00 15.00
8 D'Angelo Russell 5.00 12.00
9 Kyle Lowry 5.00 12.00
10 Russell Westbrook 8.00 20.00
11 Reggie Jackson 4.00 10.00
12 Derrick Rose 8.00 20.00
13 Lonzo Ball 5.00 12.00
14 Immanuel Quickley 5.00 12.00
15 LeBron James 50.00 120.00
16 Malcolm Brogdon 4.00 10.00
17 Ben Simmons 5.00 12.00
18 Jimmy Butler 8.00 20.00
19 Kawhi Leonard 12.00 30.00
20 Terry Rozier III 4.00 10.00
21 Pascal Siakam 8.00 20.00
22 Tobias Harris 4.00 10.00
23 CJ McCollum 4.00 10.00
24 Joe Ingles 4.00 10.00
25 Coby White 5.00 12.00
26 LaMelo Ball 40.00 100.00
27 Draymond Green 6.00 15.00
28 Mike Conley 4.00 10.00
29 Shai Gilgeous-Alexander 25.00 60.00
30 Donovan Mitchell 10.00 25.00

2021-22 Panini Noir Elegant Decor Rookie Jerseys

COMMON CARD 3.00 8.00
SEMISTARS 4.00 10.00
UNLISTED STARS 5.00 12.00
STATED PRINT RUN 75 SER.#'d SETS
*PRIME/25: 1X TO 2.5X BASE HI
1 Bones Hyland 6.00 15.00
2 Austin Reaves 25.00 60.00
3 Trey Murphy III 15.00 40.00
4 Tre Mann 8.00 20.00
5 Kai Jones 4.00 10.00
6 Jalen Johnson 15.00 40.00
7 Cameron Thomas 10.00 25.00
8 Ayo Dosunmu 10.00 25.00
9 Isaiah Jackson 5.00 12.00
10 Quentin Grimes 10.00 25.00
11 Day'Ron Sharpe 5.00 12.00
12 Jeremiah Robinson-Earl 5.00 12.00
13 Jared Butler 5.00 12.00
14 Cade Cunningham 60.00 150.00
15 Jalen Green 40.00 100.00
16 Evan Mobley 20.00 50.00
17 Scottie Barnes 40.00 100.00
18 Jalen Suggs 12.00 30.00
19 Josh Giddey 15.00 40.00
20 Jonathan Kuminga 15.00 40.00
21 Franz Wagner 15.00 40.00
22 Davion Mitchell 5.00 12.00
23 Ziaire Williams 6.00 15.00
24 James Bouknight 4.00 10.00
25 Joshua Primo 4.00 10.00
26 Chris Duarte 4.00 10.00
27 Moses Moody 10.00 25.00
28 Corey Kispert 6.00 15.00
29 Herbert Jones 6.00 15.00
30 Greg Brown III 4.00 10.00

2021-22 Panini Noir Freeze Frame Signatures

COMMON CARD 6.00 15.00
SEMISTARS 8.00 20.00
UNLISTED STARS 10.00 25.00
STATED PRINT RUN 49-99 SER.#'d SETS
3 Hakeem Olajuwon/49 75.00 200.00
4 Justin Holiday/99 6.00 15.00
5 Spud Webb/99 20.00 50.00
6 Eric Gordon/99 8.00 20.00
9 Marques Johnson/99 8.00 20.00
10 Tyrese Haliburton/99 100.00 250.00
11 Maurice Cheeks/99 8.00 20.00
12 Al Horford/99 15.00 40.00
13 Clyde Drexler/99 60.00 150.00
14 Brandon Clarke/99 10.00 25.00
15 Hedo Turkoglu/99 8.00 20.00
16 Lonnie Walker IV/99 8.00 20.00
17 Bill Laimbeer/99 15.00 40.00
18 Mark Aguirre/99 8.00 20.00
19 Trae Young/49 300.00 600.00
20 Kirk Hinrich /99 10.00 25.00
21 Devin Harris/99 6.00 15.00
22 Arvydas Sabonis/99 12.00 30.00
23 Bill Russell/49 600.00 1,200.00
24 Kenny "Sky" Walker/99 6.00 15.00
25 Nikola Jokic/49 150.00 400.00
26 Bob Dandridge/99 10.00 25.00
27 George McGinnis/99 10.00 25.00
28 Xavier Tillman/99 8.00 20.00
29 Charlie Ward/99 8.00 20.00
30 Oscar Robertson/49 75.00 200.00
31 Ja Morant/49 400.00 800.00
32 B.J. Armstrong/99 10.00 25.00
33 James Worthy/99 25.00 60.00
34 Marcus Camby/99 20.00 50.00
35 T.J. Warren/99 6.00 15.00
36 Carlos Boozer/99 8.00 20.00
39 Karl Malone/49 100.00 250.00
40 Alex English/99 12.00 30.00

2021-22 Panini Noir Horizontal Spotlight Signatures

COMMON CARD 12.00 30.00
SEMISTARS 15.00 40.00
UNLISTED STARS 20.00 50.00
STATED PRINT RUN 49-99 SER.#'d SETS
1 Charles Barkley/99 200.00 500.00
2 Alperen Sengun/99 200.00 500.00
3 Anthony Davis/49 200.00 500.00
4 Ben Wallace/99 200.00 500.00
5 Jason Richardson/99 40.00 100.00
7 Jalen Green/99 800.00 1,500.00
8 Bill Walton/99 40.00 100.00
9 Magic Johnson/99 200.00 500.00
10 Zion Williamson/49 800.00 1,500.00
11 Jason Williams/99 200.00 500.00
12 Khris Middleton/49 60.00 150.00
13 Evan Mobley/99 600.00 1,200.00
14 Julius Randle/49 40.00 100.00
15 Tyrese Haliburton/99 200.00 500.00
17 Rui Hachimura/99 125.00 300.00
18 Larry Bird/49 200.00 500.00
19 Scottie Barnes/99 800.00 1,500.00
20 Kevin Garnett/49 200.00 500.00

2021-22 Panini Noir Icons Memorabilia

COMMON CARD 4.00 10.00
SEMISTARS 5.00 12.00
UNLISTED STARS 6.00 15.00
STATED PRINT RUN 75-99 SER.#'d SETS
*PRIME/22-25: 1X TO 2.5X BASE HI
1 Shawn Kemp/99 10.00 25.00
2 Steve Nash/99 12.00 30.00
3 David Robinson/99 12.00 30.00
5 Alonzo Mourning/99 10.00 25.00
6 Paul Pierce/99 10.00 25.00
7 Charles Barkley/99 15.00 40.00
8 Larry Bird/99 20.00 50.00
9 Hakeem Olajuwon/99 12.00 30.00
10 Adrian Dantley/99 6.00 15.00
11 Clyde Drexler/75 10.00 25.00
12 Robert Parish/75 8.00 20.00
13 Tim Hardaway/75 8.00 20.00
14 James Worthy/99 10.00 25.00
15 Karl Malone/99 12.00 30.00
16 Shaquille O'Neal /75 20.00 50.00
17 Jason Kidd/75 10.00 25.00
18 Allen Iverson/99 15.00 40.00
19 Tim Duncan/99 15.00 40.00
20 Vince Carter/99 12.00 30.00

2021-22 Panini Noir Jumbo Material

COMMON CARD 3.00 8.00
SEMISTARS 4.00 10.00
UNLISTED STARS 5.00 12.00
STATED PRINT RUN 99 SER.#'d SETS
1 Gordon Hayward 4.00 10.00
2 Zion Williamson 12.00 30.00
3 Seth Curry 4.00 10.00
4 Jayson Tatum 20.00 50.00
5 Saddiq Bey 4.00 10.00
6 LaMarcus Aldridge 5.00 12.00
7 Cam Reddish 5.00 12.00
8 Nikola Jokic 25.00 60.00
9 Andre Iguodala 5.00 12.00
10 Mikal Bridges 6.00 15.00
11 Rui Hachimura 5.00 12.00
12 Obi Toppin 5.00 12.00
13 Luka Doncic 50.00 120.00
14 De'Andre Hunter 5.00 12.00
15 Jamal Murray 8.00 20.00
16 Andrew Wiggins 6.00 15.00
17 Devin Booker 12.00 30.00
18 Giannis Antetokounmpo 40.00 100.00
19 Tyler Herro 8.00 20.00
20 Malcolm Brogdon 4.00 10.00
21 Andre Drummond 4.00 10.00
22 Carmelo Anthony 8.00 20.00
23 Stephen Curry 75.00 200.00
24 Tyrese Maxey 12.00 30.00
25 Zach LaVine 8.00 20.00
26 Julius Randle 6.00 15.00
27 DeMar DeRozan 6.00 15.00
28 Jalen Brunson 10.00 25.00
29 PJ Washington Jr. 5.00 12.00
30 Matisse Thybulle 4.00 10.00
31 Steven Adams 4.00 10.00
32 Anthony Edwards 40.00 100.00
33 Jerami Grant 5.00 12.00
34 Norman Powell 4.00 10.00
35 Michael Porter Jr. 6.00 15.00
36 Khris Middleton 5.00 12.00
37 Evan Fournier 4.00 10.00
38 Grant Williams 5.00 12.00
39 Payton Pritchard 5.00 12.00
40 Tyrese Haliburton 10.00 25.00
41 Karl-Anthony Towns 8.00 20.00
42 Terrence Ross 4.00 10.00
43 Collin Sexton 5.00 12.00
44 Devonte' Graham 4.00 10.00
45 Jusuf Nurkic 4.00 10.00
46 Kawhi Leonard 12.00 30.00
47 Duncan Robinson 4.00 10.00
48 Harrison Barnes 4.00 10.00
49 Bobby Portis 4.00 10.00
50 Amar'e Stoudemire 5.00 12.00
51 Tim Duncan 12.00 30.00
52 Jamal Crawford 5.00 12.00
53 Michael Redd 4.00 10.00
54 James Wiseman 4.00 10.00
55 Joakim Noah 4.00 10.00
56 Mike Conley 4.00 10.00
57 Metta World Peace 5.00 12.00
58 Kendrick Perkins 4.00 10.00
59 Shai Gilgeous-Alexander 25.00 60.00
60 Cole Anthony 6.00 15.00

2021-22 Panini Noir NBA 75th Autographs

COMMON CARD 20.00 50.00
SEMISTARS 25.00 60.00
UNLISTED STARS 30.00 80.00
STATED PRINT RUN 75 SER.#'d SETS
1 Kareem Abdul-Jabbar 600.00 1,200.00
2 Karl Malone 600.00 1,200.00
3 Charles Barkley 600.00 1,200.00
4 Magic Johnson 600.00 1,200.00
5 Bill Russell 2,000.00 4,000.00
6 Shaquille O'Neal 600.00 1,200.00
7 Dirk Nowitzki 1,000.00 2,000.00
9 Larry Bird 600.00 1,200.00
10 Oscar Robertson 400.00 800.00

2021-22 Panini Noir New Wave Jerseys

COMMON CARD 3.00 8.00
SEMISTARS 4.00 10.00
UNLISTED STARS 5.00 12.00
STATED PRINT RUN 99 SER.#'d SETS
*PRIME/25: .1X TO 2.5X BASE HI
1 Scottie Barnes 30.00 80.00
2 Bones Hyland 6.00 15.00
3 Jalen Suggs 12.00 30.00
4 Josh Giddey 15.00 40.00
5 Franz Wagner 15.00 40.00
6 Cade Cunningham 40.00 100.00
7 Davion Mitchell 5.00 12.00
8 Evan Mobley 20.00 50.00
9 Jalen Green 30.00 80.00
10 Jonathan Kuminga 15.00 40.00
11 James Bouknight 4.00 10.00
12 Ziaire Williams 6.00 15.00
13 Joshua Primo 4.00 10.00
14 Chris Duarte 4.00 10.00
15 Moses Moody 10.00 25.00
16 Luka Garza 5.00 12.00
17 Cameron Thomas 10.00 25.00
18 Trey Murphy III 15.00 40.00
19 Corey Kispert 6.00 15.00
20 Ayo Dosunmu 10.00 25.00
21 Jeremiah Robinson-Earl 5.00 12.00
22 Miles McBride 8.00 20.00
23 Brandon Boston Jr. 5.00 12.00
24 Jaden Springer 5.00 12.00
25 Aaron Wiggins 6.00 15.00
26 Quentin Grimes 10.00 25.00
27 Charles Bassey 5.00 12.00
28 Austin Reaves 25.00 60.00
29 Jalen Johnson 15.00 40.00
30 Isaiah Jackson 5.00 12.00

2021-22 Panini Noir Newsreels Jerseys

COMMON CARD 3.00 8.00
SEMISTARS 4.00 10.00
UNLISTED STARS 5.00 12.00
STATED PRINT RUN 75 SER.#'d SETS
*PRIME/18-25: 1X TO 2.5X BASE HI
1 Luka Doncic 40.00 100.00
2 Giannis Antetokounmpo 25.00 60.00
3 Miles Bridges 4.00 10.00
4 Rudy Gobert 6.00 15.00
5 RJ Barrett 8.00 20.00
6 Luguentz Dort 5.00 12.00
7 Dillon Brooks 5.00 12.00
8 Domantas Sabonis 6.00 15.00
9 OG Anunoby 5.00 12.00
10 Obi Toppin 5.00 12.00
11 Bojan Bogdanovic 4.00 10.00
12 Stephen Curry 60.00 150.00
13 Devin Booker 12.00 30.00
14 Buddy Hield 4.00 10.00
15 Christian Wood 4.00 10.00
16 Zion Williamson 12.00 30.00
17 Devin Vassell 8.00 20.00
18 Zach LaVine 8.00 20.00
19 Kevin Porter Jr. 4.00 10.00
20 Patrick Williams 5.00 12.00
21 Tyrese Maxey 12.00 30.00
22 Isaiah Stewart 5.00 12.00
23 Myles Turner 5.00 12.00
24 Collin Sexton 5.00 12.00
25 Kyle Kuzma 6.00 15.00
26 Mo Bamba 4.00 10.00
27 John Collins 5.00 12.00
28 Anthony Davis 12.00 30.00
29 Kemba Walker 5.00 12.00
30 James Harden 10.00 25.00
31 Dwight Howard 6.00 15.00
32 Dirk Nowitzki 12.00 30.00
33 Manu Ginobili 10.00 25.00
34 Dwyane Wade 15.00 40.00
35 Anfernee Hardaway 12.00 30.00
36 Patrick Ewing 8.00 20.00
37 Sam Cassell 4.00 10.00
38 Chauncey Billups 6.00 15.00
39 Amar'e Stoudemire 5.00 12.00
40 John Stockton 10.00 25.00

2021-22 Panini Noir Prime Materials Black and White Autographs

COMMON CARD 8.00 20.00
SEMISTARS 10.00 25.00
UNLISTED STARS 12.00 30.00
STATED PRINT RUN 15-40 SER.#'d SETS
1 Julius Randle/25 15.00 40.00
2 Elton Brand/40 12.00 30.00
3 Domantas Sabonis/25 40.00 100.00
4 Jamal Crawford/15 12.00 30.00
5 Myles Turner/40 12.00 30.00
7 Luka Doncic/25 1,000.00 2,000.00
8 Joe Harris/40 10.00 25.00
9 Jrue Holiday/25 30.00 80.00
10 Lonnie Walker IV/30 10.00 25.00
11 Trae Young/25 400.00 800.00
12 Tony Allen/25 8.00 20.00
13 Raymond Felton/40 8.00 20.00
14 Nikola Jokic/15 400.00 800.00
15 Mike Conley/40 10.00 25.00

2021-22 Panini Noir Reigning Nights Signatures

COMMON CARD 8.00 20.00
SEMISTARS 10.00 25.00
UNLISTED STARS 12.00 30.00
STATED PRINT RUN 49-99 SER.#'d SETS
1 Jamal Murray/49 40.00 100.00
3 Eric Gordon/99 10.00 25.00
4 Gary Payton/99 40.00 100.00
5 Rick Fox/99 12.00 30.00
7 Luka Doncic/49 1,000.00 2,000.00
8 Larry Bird/49 125.00 300.00
9 Maxi Kleber/99 10.00 25.00
10 Chauncey Billups/99 15.00 40.00
11 Trae Young/49 200.00 500.00
12 Detlef Schrempf/99 12.00 30.00
13 Jerry Lucas/99 15.00 40.00
14 Christian Laettner/99 12.00 30.00
15 Ray Allen/49 75.00 200.00
16 Jason Kidd/49 60.00 150.00
17 Steve Kerr/99 30.00 80.00
18 Joe Harris/99 10.00 25.00
19 Derek Fisher/49 12.00 30.00
20 JJ Redick/99 12.00 30.00
21 Mike Bibby/99 20.00 50.00
22 Kristaps Porzingis/99 15.00 40.00
23 Tyrese Haliburton/49 150.00 400.00
24 T.J. Warren/99 8.00 20.00
25 Khris Middleton/49 12.00 30.00
26 Jordan Nwora/99 12.00 30.00
27 Toni Kukoc/99 15.00 40.00
30 Stephen Curry/49 1,500.00 3,000.00
31 Lonnie Walker IV/99 10.00 25.00
32 Rick Barry/99 15.00 40.00
33 Duncan Robinson/99 10.00 25.00
34 Michael Porter Jr./49 15.00 40.00
35 Dirk Nowitzki/49 200.00 500.00

2021-22 Panini Noir Rookie Jumbo Material

COMMON CARD 3.00 8.00
SEMISTARS 4.00 10.00
UNLISTED STARS 5.00 12.00
STATED PRINT RUN 99 SER.#'d SETS
1 James Bouknight 4.00 10.00
2 Joshua Primo 4.00 10.00
3 Tre Mann 8.00 20.00
4 Isaiah Jackson 5.00 12.00
5 Cade Cunningham 40.00 100.00
6 Jonathan Kuminga 15.00 40.00
7 Ziaire Williams 6.00 15.00
8 Austin Reaves 25.00 60.00
9 Kai Jones 4.00 10.00
10 Evan Mobley 20.00 50.00
11 Quentin Grimes 10.00 25.00
12 Jeremiah Robinson-Earl 5.00 12.00
13 Cameron Thomas 10.00 25.00
14 Ayo Dosunmu 10.00 25.00
15 Davion Mitchell 5.00 12.00
16 Corey Kispert 6.00 15.00
17 Trey Murphy III 15.00 40.00
18 Aaron Wiggins 6.00 15.00
19 Herbert Jones 6.00 15.00
20 Moses Moody 10.00 25.00
21 Jared Butler 5.00 12.00
22 Franz Wagner 15.00 40.00
23 Jalen Johnson 15.00 40.00
24 Bones Hyland 6.00 15.00
25 Jalen Suggs 12.00 30.00
26 Jalen Green 30.00 80.00
27 Day'Ron Sharpe 5.00 12.00
28 Scottie Barnes 30.00 80.00
29 Chris Duarte 4.00 10.00
30 Josh Giddey 15.00 40.00
31 Greg Brown III 4.00 10.00
32 Santi Aldama 6.00 15.00
33 Jaden Springer 5.00 12.00
34 Miles McBride 8.00 20.00
35 Luka Garza 5.00 12.00
36 Joe Wieskamp 4.00 10.00
37 Keon Johnson 5.00 12.00
38 Isaiah Todd 4.00 10.00
39 JT Thor 5.00 12.00
40 Brandon Boston Jr. 5.00 12.00

2021-22 Panini Noir Shadow Signatures

COMMON CARD 10.00 25.00
SEMISTARS 12.00 30.00
UNLISTED STARS 15.00 40.00
STATED PRINT RUN 49-99 SER.#'d SETS
1 Jason Preston/99 12.00 30.00
2 Kai Jones/99 12.00 30.00
3 Devin Vassell/99 75.00 200.00
4 Luka Garza/99 15.00 40.00
5 Jae'Sean Tate/99 15.00 40.00
6 Frank Kaminsky/99 10.00 25.00
7 Luka Doncic/49 1,000.00 2,000.00
8 Clint Capela/99 15.00 40.00
9 Theo Maledon/99 12.00 30.00
10 Cade Cunningham/49 500.00 1,000.00
13 Jeremiah Robinson-Earl/99 15.00 40.00
14 Evan Mobley/49 300.00 600.00
15 Jaren Jackson Jr./49 25.00 60.00
16 James Bouknight/99 12.00 30.00
17 JJ Redick/99 15.00 40.00
18 RJ Hampton/99 10.00 25.00
19 Ricky Rubio/99 15.00 40.00
20 Scottie Barnes/99 350.00 700.00
21 Ivica Zubac/99 15.00 40.00
22 T.J. McConnell/99 12.00 30.00
23 Jalen Suggs/49 150.00 400.00
24 Duncan Robinson/99 12.00 30.00
25 Tre Mann/99 60.00 150.00
26 Miles McBride/99 25.00 60.00
27 Day'Ron Sharpe/99 15.00 40.00
28 Jalen Johnson/99 50.00 125.00
29 Jonathan Kuminga/49 300.00 600.00
30 Aaron Wiggins/99 12.00 30.00
31 Larry Johnson/99 100.00 250.00
32 Josh Giddey/99 300.00 600.00
33 Jared Butler/99 15.00 40.00
35 Jalen Green/49 400.00 800.00
36 Boban Marjanovic/99 15.00 40.00
37 Trae Young/49 200.00 500.00
39 JT Thor/99 15.00 40.00
40 Bones Hyland/99 125.00 300.00

2021-22 Panini Noir Showtime Signatures

COMMON CARD 10.00 25.00
SEMISTARS 12.00 30.00
UNLISTED STARS 15.00 40.00
STATED PRINT RUN 25-99 SER.#'d SETS
1 Jalen Green/49 400.00 800.00
2 Ziaire Williams/49 20.00 50.00
3 Keon Johnson/49 15.00 40.00
4 Chris Duarte/49 12.00 30.00
5 Franz Wagner/49 150.00 400.00
6 Isaiah Jackson/49 15.00 40.00
7 Luka Doncic/25 1,000.00 2,000.00
8 Josh Giddey/49 300.00 600.00
9 Trae Young/25 300.00 600.00
10 Tyrese Haliburton/49 200.00 500.00
11 Evan Mobley/49 300.00 600.00
12 Anthony Davis/49 125.00 300.00
13 Scottie Barnes/49 350.00 700.00
14 Boban Marjanovic/25 15.00 40.00
15 Davion Mitchell/49 15.00 40.00
16 Jalen Johnson/49 50.00 120.00
17 Cameron Thomas/49 30.00 80.00
18 Jalen Suggs/49 150.00 400.00
19 Corey Kispert/49 20.00 50.00
20 James Bouknight/49 12.00 30.00
21 Moses Moody/49 75.00 200.00
22 Kai Jones/49 12.00 30.00
23 Cade Cunningham/49 500.00 1,000.00
24 Alperen Sengun/49 100.00 250.00
25 Jonathan Kuminga/49 300.00 600.00

2021-22 Panini Noir Silver Screen Debut Signatures

COMMON CARD 8.00 20.00
SEMISTARS 10.00 25.00
UNLISTED STARS 12.00 30.00
STATED PRINT RUN 49-99 SER.#'d SETS
EXCHANGE DEADLINE 12/08/2023
1 Evan Mobley/49 300.00 600.00
2 Josh Christopher/99 10.00 25.00
3 Alperen Sengun/99 40.00 100.00
4 Trey Murphy III/99 40.00 100.00
5 Jalen Green/49 300.00 600.00
6 Cameron Thomas/99 25.00 60.00
7 Josh Giddey/49 200.00 500.00
8 Corey Kispert/99 15.00 40.00
9 Bones Hyland/99 15.00 40.00
10 Isaiah Todd/99 10.00 25.00
11 Ziaire Williams/99 15.00 40.00
12 James Bouknight/99 12.00 30.00
13 Davion Mitchell/99 12.00 30.00
14 Keon Johnson/99 12.00 30.00
15 Franz Wagner/99 100.00 250.00
16 Ayo Dosunmu/99 25.00 60.00
17 Jonathan Kuminga/49 200.00 500.00
18 JT Thor/99 12.00 30.00
19 Jared Butler/99 12.00 30.00
20 Chris Duarte/99 10.00 25.00
21 Scottie Barnes/49 300.00 600.00
22 Tre Mann/99 20.00 50.00
23 Austin Reaves/99 60.00 150.00
24 Jeremiah Robinson-Earl/99 12.00 30.00
25 Cade Cunningham/49 300.00 600.00
26 Luka Garza/99 12.00 30.00
28 Greg Brown III/99 10.00 25.00
29 Jason Preston/99 10.00 25.00
30 Jalen Suggs/49 75.00 200.00

2021-22 Panini Noir SLAM! Kicks

1 Dwyane Wade 150.00 400.00
2 Giannis Antetokounmpo 300.00 600.00
3 Allen Iverson 300.00 600.00
4 Kevin Durant 200.00 500.00
5 Donovan Mitchell 125.00 300.00

2021-22 Panini Noir Snapshot Signatures

COMMON CARD 6.00 15.00
SEMISTARS 8.00 20.00
UNLISTED STARS 10.00 25.00
STATED PRINT RUN 49-99 SER.#'d SETS
1 Isaiah Jackson/99 10.00 25.00
2 James Wiseman/99 8.00 20.00
3 Jaden Springer/99 10.00 25.00
4 Taj Gibson/99 6.00 15.00
5 Alex English/99 12.00 30.00
6 Keon Johnson/99 10.00 25.00
7 Isaiah Livers/99 10.00 25.00
8 Andrea Bargnani/99 6.00 15.00
9 Fat Lever/99 8.00 20.00
10 Chris Duarte/49 8.00 20.00
11 Charles Bassey/99 8.00 20.00
12 Luka Doncic/49 1,000.00 2,000.00
13 Ben Wallace/49 60.00 150.00
14 Usman Garuba/99 8.00 20.00
15 Ayo Dosunmu/99 75.00 200.00
16 Aaron Wiggins/99 12.00 30.00
17 Nate Archibald/99 10.00 25.00
18 Kevin Garnett/49 150.00 400.00
19 Alperen Sengun/49 75.00 200.00
21 Ralph Sampson/99 10.00 25.00
22 Charles Barkley/49 150.00 400.00
23 Moses Moody/99 75.00 200.00
24 Brandon Boston Jr./99 10.00 25.00
26 Josh Christopher/99 8.00 20.00
27 David Lee/99 8.00 20.00
28 David Thompson/99 12.00 30.00
29 Marques Johnson/99 8.00 20.00
30 Isaiah Todd/99 8.00 20.00

2021-22 Panini Noir Sneaker Spotlight Signatures

COMMON CARD 40.00 100.00
SEMISTARS 50.00 120.00
UNLISTED STARS 60.00 150.00
STATED PRINT RUN 99 SER.#'d SETS
1 Zion Williamson 1,500.00 3,000.00
2 Ben Wallace 300.00 600.00
3 Allen Iverson 500.00 1,000.00
4 Kevin Garnett 600.00 1,200.00
5 Dennis Rodman 500.00 1,000.00
7 Luka Doncic 2,000.00 4,000.00
8 Rui Hachimura 200.00 500.00
9 Tony Parker 350.00 700.00
10 Jamal Crawford 150.00 400.00
11 Trae Young 600.00 1,200.00
12 Ja Morant 2,000.00 4,000.00
13 Talen Horton-Tucker 100.00 250.00
14 Nikola Jokic 1,000.00 2,000.00
15 Vince Carter 500.00 1,000.00
16 Domantas Sabonis 125.00 300.00
17 Michael Porter Jr. 125.00 300.00
18 Obi Toppin 400.00 800.00
19 Jalen Green 3,000.00 6,000.00
20 Gary Payton 150.00 400.00
23 Anthony Davis 500.00 1,000.00
24 Dirk Nowitzki 1,000.00 2,000.00
25 Cam Reddish 125.00 300.00
26 Jamal Murray 350.00 700.00
27 Julius Randle 125.00 300.00
28 Khris Middleton 150.00 400.00
29 Anthony Edwards 1,500.00 3,000.00
30 Stephen Curry 3,000.00 6,000.00
31 Jalen Rose 125.00 300.00
32 Cade Cunningham 3,000.00 6,000.00
33 Ray Allen 300.00 600.00
34 Shaquille O'Neal 600.00 1,200.00
35 Glen Rice 125.00 300.00
36 James Wiseman 50.00 125.00
37 Jason Richardson 125.00 300.00
40 Tyrese Haliburton 800.00 1,500.00

2021-22 Panini Noir Two-Shot Rookie Jerseys

COMMON CARD (1-20) 3.00 8.00
SEMISTARS 4.00 10.00
UNLISTED STARS 5.00 12.00
STATED PRINT RUN 99 SER.#'d SETS
*PRIME/25: .75X TO 2X BASE HI
1 Cade Cunningham
Jalen Green 75.00 200.00
2 Jonathan Kuminga
Moses Moody 15.00 40.00
3 Franz Wagner
Jalen Suggs 15.00 40.00
4 James Bouknight
Kai Jones 4.00 10.00
5 Herbert Jones
Joshua Primo 6.00 15.00
6 Josh Giddey
Tre Mann 15.00 40.00
7 Davion Mitchell
Jared Butler 5.00 12.00
8 Herbert Jones
Trey Murphy III 6.00 15.00
9 Chris Duarte
Isaiah Jackson 5.00 12.00
10 Jalen Green
Jonathan Kuminga 25.00 60.00
11 Ayo Dosunmu
Davion Mitchell 10.00 25.00
12 Evan Mobley
Scottie Barnes 20.00 50.00
13 Cameron Thomas
Day'Ron Sharpe 10.00 25.00
14 Santi Aldama
Ziaire Williams 6.00 15.00
15 Corey Kispert
Jalen Suggs 12.00 30.00
16 Charles Bassey
Jaden Springer 5.00 12.00
17 Cade Cunningham
Evan Mobley 50.00 120.00
18 Aaron Wiggins
Jeremiah Robinson-Earl 6.00 15.00
19 Brandon Boston Jr.
Keon Johnson 5.00 12.00
20 Miles McBride
Quentin Grimes 10.00 25.00

2021-22 Panini Noir Vertical Spotlight Signatures

COMMON CARD 12.00 30.00
SEMISTARS 15.00 40.00
UNLISTED STARS 20.00 50.00
STATED PRINT RUN 49-99 SER.#'d SETS
1 Anthony Edwards/99 500.00 1,000.00
2 Kareem Abdul-Jabbar/99 300.00 600.00
3 Dennis Rodman/99 300.00 600.00
4 Jalen Suggs/99 200.00 500.00
5 Mark Price/99 20.00 50.00
6 Duncan Robinson/99 15.00 40.00
7 Luka Doncic/99 1,000.00 2,000.00
8 Paul Pierce/99 100.00 250.00
9 CJ McCollum/99 75.00 200.00
10 Ray Allen/99 125.00 300.00
11 Allen Iverson/99 500.00 1,000.00
12 Jonathan Kuminga/99 800.00 1,500.00
13 Kristaps Porzingis/99 50.00 120.00
14 Myles Turner/99 40.00 100.00
15 Jamal Crawford/49 75.00 200.00
16 Collin Sexton/99 60.00 150.00
17 Josh Giddey/99 800.00 1,500.00
18 Vince Carter/99 500.00 1,000.00
19 Cade Cunningham/99 1,000.00 2,000.00
20 Stephen Curry/49 2,000.00 4,000.00

2022-23 Panini Noir

1-140 PRINT RUN 99 SER.#'d SETS
RC PRINT RUN 99 SER.#'d SETS
201-295 PRINT RUN 25 SER.#'d SETS
301-380 PRINT RUN 99 SER.#'d SETS
381-400 PRINT RUN 99 SER.#'d SETS
*HOLO SILVER/49: .5X TO 1.2X BASE
1 Jordan Poole A 5.00 12.00
2 Khris Middleton A 4.00 10.00
3 Cade Cunningham A 10.00 25.00
4 Jayson Tatum A 12.00 30.00
5 Jrue Holiday A 4.00 10.00
6 Karl-Anthony Towns A 5.00 12.00
7 Dejounte Murray A 4.00 10.00
8 Shai Gilgeous-Alexander A 15.00 40.00
9 Anfernee Simons A 4.00 10.00
10 Jamal Murray A 5.00 12.00
11 Klay Thompson A 8.00 20.00
12 Nikola Jokic A 15.00 40.00
13 James Harden A 6.00 15.00
14 De'Aaron Fox A 6.00 15.00
15 Lauri Markkanen A 5.00 12.00
16 Pascal Siakam A 5.00 12.00
17 Zion Williamson A 8.00 20.00
18 Luka Doncic A 20.00 50.00
19 Kevin Durant A 10.00 25.00
20 Kyrie Irving A 6.00 15.00
21 LeBron James A 25.00 60.00
22 Jaren Jackson Jr. A 5.00 12.00
23 Stephen Curry A 25.00 60.00
24 CJ McCollum A 3.00 8.00
25 Buddy Hield A 3.00 8.00
26 Tyrese Haliburton A 6.00 15.00
27 Jalen Green A 10.00 25.00
28 Chris Paul A 6.00 15.00
29 Andrew Wiggins A 4.00 10.00
30 Jaylen Brown A 6.00 15.00
31 Anthony Davis A 8.00 20.00
32 Domantas Sabonis A 4.00 10.00
33 Damian Lillard A 8.00 20.00
34 RJ Barrett A 5.00 12.00
35 Desmond Bane A 4.00 10.00
36 Cole Anthony A 3.00 8.00
37 Rudy Gobert A 4.00 10.00
38 Michael Porter Jr. A 4.00 10.00
39 Kawhi Leonard A 8.00 20.00
40 Paul George A 5.00 12.00
41 Zach LaVine A 6.00 15.00
42 Christian Wood A 2.00 5.00
43 Alperen Sengun A 4.00 10.00
44 Keldon Johnson A 4.00 10.00
45 Brandon Ingram A 4.00 10.00
46 Evan Mobley A 8.00 20.00
47 Darius Garland A 5.00 12.00
48 Tyrese Maxey A 6.00 15.00
49 Giannis Antetokounmpo A 15.00 40.00
50 Tyler Herro A 5.00 12.00
51 DeMar DeRozan A 4.00 10.00
52 Donovan Mitchell A 6.00 15.00
53 Jalen Brunson A 6.00 15.00
54 Josh Giddey A 5.00 12.00
55 Jimmy Butler A 6.00 15.00
56 Fred VanVleet A 4.00 10.00
57 Marcus Smart A 4.00 10.00
58 Joel Embiid A 5.00 12.00
59 Trae Young A 8.00 20.00
60 Kevin Porter Jr. A 2.50 6.00
61 LaMelo Ball A 8.00 20.00
62 Anthony Edwards A 15.00 40.00
63 Julius Randle A 4.00 10.00
64 Franz Wagner A 8.00 20.00
65 Scottie Barnes A 5.00 12.00
66 Ja Morant A 10.00 25.00
67 Russell Westbrook A 5.00 12.00
68 Devin Booker A 8.00 20.00
69 Bradley Beal A 4.00 10.00
70 Jordan Clarkson A 3.00 8.00
71 Jordan Poole I 5.00 12.00
72 Khris Middleton I 4.00 10.00
73 Cade Cunningham I 10.00 25.00
74 Jayson Tatum I 12.00 30.00
75 Jrue Holiday I 4.00 10.00
76 Karl-Anthony Towns I 5.00 12.00
77 Dejounte Murray I 4.00 10.00
78 Shai Gilgeous-Alexander I 15.00 40.00
79 Anfernee Simons I 4.00 10.00
80 Jamal Murray I 5.00 12.00
81 Klay Thompson I 8.00 20.00
82 Nikola Jokic I 15.00 40.00
83 James Harden I 6.00 15.00
84 De'Aaron Fox I 6.00 15.00
85 Lauri Markkanen I 5.00 12.00
86 Pascal Siakam I 5.00 12.00
87 Zion Williamson I 8.00 20.00
88 Luka Doncic I 20.00 50.00
89 Kevin Durant I 10.00 25.00
90 Kyrie Irving I 6.00 15.00
91 LeBron James I 25.00 60.00
92 Jaren Jackson Jr. I 5.00 12.00
93 Stephen Curry I 25.00 60.00
94 CJ McCollum I 3.00 8.00
95 Buddy Hield I 3.00 8.00
96 Tyrese Haliburton I 6.00 15.00
97 Jalen Green I 10.00 25.00
98 Chris Paul I 6.00 15.00
99 Andrew Wiggins I 4.00 10.00
100 Jaylen Brown I 6.00 15.00
101 Anthony Davis I 8.00 20.00
102 Domantas Sabonis I 4.00 10.00
103 Damian Lillard I 8.00 20.00
104 RJ Barrett I 5.00 12.00
105 Desmond Bane I 4.00 10.00
106 Cole Anthony I 3.00 8.00
107 Rudy Gobert I 4.00 10.00
108 Michael Porter Jr. I 4.00 10.00
109 Kawhi Leonard I 8.00 20.00
110 Paul George I 5.00 12.00
111 Zach LaVine I 6.00 15.00
112 Christian Wood I 2.00 5.00
113 Alperen Sengun I 4.00 10.00
114 Keldon Johnson I 4.00 10.00
115 Brandon Ingram I 4.00 10.00
116 Evan Mobley I 8.00 20.00
117 Darius Garland I 5.00 12.00
118 Tyrese Maxey I 6.00 15.00
119 Giannis Antetokounmpo I 15.00 40.00
120 Tyler Herro I 5.00 12.00
121 DeMar DeRozan I 4.00 10.00
122 Donovan Mitchell I 6.00 15.00
123 Jalen Brunson I 6.00 15.00
124 Josh Giddey I 5.00 12.00
125 Jimmy Butler I 6.00 15.00
126 Fred VanVleet I 4.00 10.00
127 Marcus Smart I 4.00 10.00

128 Joel Embiid I 5.00 12.00
129 Trae Young I 8.00 20.00
130 Kevin Porter Jr. I 2.50 6.00
131 LaMelo Ball I 8.00 20.00
132 Anthony Edwards I 15.00 40.00
133 Julius Randle I 4.00 10.00
134 Franz Wagner I 8.00 20.00
135 Scottie Barnes I 5.00 12.00
136 Ja Morant I 10.00 25.00
137 Russell Westbrook I 5.00 12.00
138 Devin Booker I 8.00 20.00
139 Bradley Beal I 4.00 10.00
140 Jordan Clarkson I 3.00 8.00
141 Ousmane Dieng A RC 4.00 10.00
142 Johnny Davis A RC 3.00 8.00
143 Bennedict Mathurin A RC 10.00 25.00
144 Tari Eason A RC 8.00 20.00
145 Jeremy Sochan A RC 10.00 25.00
146 MarJon Beauchamp A RC 3.00 8.00
147 Jalen Williams A RC 15.00 40.00
148 Chet Holmgren A RC 15.00 40.00
149 TyTy Washington Jr. A RC 3.00 8.00
150 Dalen Terry A RC 3.00 8.00
151 Dyson Daniels A RC 8.00 20.00
152 Shaedon Sharpe A RC 12.00 30.00
153 Nikola Jovic A RC 6.00 15.00
154 Christian Braun A RC 8.00 20.00
155 David Roddy A RC 4.00 10.00
156 Paolo Banchero A RC 20.00 50.00
157 Jalen Duren A RC 10.00 25.00
158 Ochai Agbaji A RC 4.00 10.00
159 Patrick Baldwin Jr. A RC 3.00 8.00
160 Jake LaRavia A RC 3.00 8.00
161 Wendell Moore Jr. A RC 3.00 8.00
162 Walker Kessler A RC 6.00 15.00
163 Malaki Branham A RC 3.00 8.00
164 AJ Griffin A RC 2.50 6.00
165 Keegan Murray A RC 8.00 20.00
166 Jabari Smith Jr. A RC 10.00 25.00
167 Jaden Ivey A RC 10.00 25.00
168 Christian Koloko A RC 3.00 8.00
169 Andrew Nembhard A RC 6.00 15.00
170 Moussa Diabate A RC 3.00 8.00
171 Ousmane Dieng I 4.00 10.00
172 Johnny Davis I 3.00 8.00
173 Bennedict Mathurin I 10.00 25.00
174 Tari Eason I 8.00 20.00
175 Jeremy Sochan I 10.00 25.00
176 MarJon Beauchamp I 3.00 8.00
177 Jalen Williams I 15.00 40.00
178 Chet Holmgren I 15.00 40.00
179 TyTy Washington Jr. I 3.00 8.00
180 Dalen Terry I 3.00 8.00
181 Dyson Daniels I 8.00 20.00
182 Shaedon Sharpe I 12.00 30.00
183 Nikola Jovic I 6.00 15.00
184 Christian Braun I 8.00 20.00
185 David Roddy I 4.00 10.00
186 Paolo Banchero I 20.00 50.00
187 Jalen Duren I 10.00 25.00
188 Ochai Agbaji I 4.00 10.00
189 Patrick Baldwin Jr. I 3.00 8.00
190 Jake LaRavia I 3.00 8.00
191 Wendell Moore Jr. I 3.00 8.00
192 Walker Kessler I 6.00 15.00
193 Malaki Branham I 3.00 8.00
194 AJ Griffin I 2.50 6.00
195 Keegan Murray I 8.00 20.00
196 Jabari Smith Jr. I 10.00 25.00
197 Jaden Ivey I 10.00 25.00
198 Christian Koloko I 3.00 8.00
199 Andrew Nembhard I 6.00 15.00
200 Moussa Diabate I 3.00 8.00
201 James Harden MET 25.00 60.00
202 LaMelo Ball MET 30.00 80.00
203 Zion Williamson MET 30.00 80.00
204 Giannis Antetokounmpo MET 60.00 150.00
205 Ja Morant MET 40.00 100.00
206 Luka Doncic MET 80.00 200.00
207 Paul George MET 20.00 50.00
208 Tyrese Haliburton MET 25.00 60.00
209 Shai Gilgeous-Alexander MET 60.00 150.00
210 Damian Lillard MET 30.00 80.00
211 Jalen Brunson MET 25.00 60.00
212 Zach LaVine MET 25.00 60.00
213 Donovan Mitchell MET 25.00 60.00
214 Joel Embiid MET 20.00 50.00
215 Lauri Markkanen MET 20.00 50.00
216 Nikola Jokic MET 60.00 150.00
217 Jalen Green MET 40.00 100.00
218 Stephen Curry MET 100.00 250.00
219 LeBron James MET 100.00 250.00
220 Jaylen Brown MET 25.00 60.00
221 Bradley Beal MET 15.00 40.00
222 Anthony Davis MET 30.00 80.00
223 De'Aaron Fox MET 25.00 60.00
224 Trae Young MET 30.00 80.00
225 Kevin Durant MET 40.00 100.00
226 Kawhi Leonard MET 30.00 80.00
227 Cade Cunningham MET 40.00 100.00
228 Devin Booker MET 30.00 80.00
229 Jayson Tatum MET 50.00 125.00
230 Anthony Edwards MET 60.00 150.00
231 Paolo Banchero MET 80.00 200.00
232 Bennedict Mathurin MET 40.00 100.00
233 Jaden Ivey MET 40.00 100.00
234 Jabari Smith Jr. MET 40.00 100.00
235 Keegan Murray MET 30.00 80.00
236 Jalen Williams MET 60.00 150.00
237 AJ Griffin MET 10.00 25.00
238 Jeremy Sochan MET 40.00 100.00
239 Chet Holmgren MET 125.00 300.00
240 Shaedon Sharpe MET 50.00 125.00
241 Dyson Daniels MET 30.00 80.00
242 Johnny Davis MET 12.00 30.00
243 Ousmane Dieng MET 15.00 40.00
244 Jalen Duren MET 40.00 100.00
245 Ochai Agbaji MET 15.00 40.00
246 Tari Eason MET 30.00 80.00
247 Malaki Branham MET 12.00 30.00
248 Walker Kessler MET 25.00 60.00
249 Christian Koloko MET 12.00 30.00
250 Jaden Hardy MET 20.00 50.00
251 Nikola Jokic FL 60.00 150.00
252 Luka Doncic FL 80.00 200.00
253 Shai Gilgeous-Alexander FL 60.00 150.00
254 Stephen Curry FL 100.00 250.00
255 Ja Morant FL 40.00 100.00
256 LeBron James FL 100.00 250.00
257 Trae Young FL 30.00 80.00
258 Giannis Antetokounmpo FL 60.00 150.00
259 Anthony Edwards FL 60.00 150.00
260 Damian Lillard FL 30.00 80.00
261 Kevin Durant FL 40.00 100.00
262 Zion Williamson FL 30.00 80.00
263 Devin Booker FL 30.00 80.00
264 Jayson Tatum FL 50.00 125.00
265 Jaylen Brown FL 25.00 60.00
266 Anfernee Hardaway FL 30.00 80.00
267 Chris Bosh FL 15.00 40.00
268 Tony Parker FL 20.00 50.00
269 Pau Gasol FL 20.00 50.00
270 Dirk Nowitzki FL 30.00 80.00
271 Paolo Banchero
LeBron James SS 80.00 200.00
272 Damian Lillard
Stephen Curry SS 100.00 250.00
273 Luka Doncic
Giannis Antetokounmpo SS 80.00 200.00
274 Jaden Ivey
Ja Morant SS 40.00 100.00
275 Joel Embiid
James Harden SS 25.00 60.00
276 Darius Garland
Donovan Mitchell SS 25.00 60.00
277 Kevin Durant
Jayson Tatum SS 50.00 125.00
278 Chris Bosh
Jabari Smith Jr. SS 40.00 100.00
279 Bennedict Mathurin
Jaylen Brown SS 40.00 100.00
280 Anfernee Hardaway
Dwyane Wade SS 30.00 80.00
281 Stephen Curry VA 100.00 250.00
282 Zion Williamson VA 30.00 80.00
283 Giannis Antetokounmpo VA 60.00 150.00
284 Kevin Durant VA 40.00 100.00
285 LeBron James VA 100.00 250.00
286 Donovan Mitchell VA 25.00 60.00
287 Luka Doncic VA 80.00 200.00
288 Jayson Tatum VA 50.00 125.00
289 Ja Morant VA 40.00 100.00
290 Nikola Jokic VA 60.00 150.00
291 Paolo Banchero VA 80.00 200.00
292 Jabari Smith Jr. VA 40.00 100.00
293 Keegan Murray VA 30.00 80.00
294 Jaden Ivey VA 40.00 100.00
295 Bennedict Mathurin VA 40.00 100.00
296 Dirk Nowitzki RL 30.00 80.00
297 Dwyane Wade RL 25.00 60.00
298 Larry Bird RL 50.00 125.00
299 Bill Russell RL 40.00 100.00
300 David Robinson RL 25.00 60.00
301 Jalen Duren AU JSY BW 60.00 150.00
302 Dalen Terry AU JSY BW 20.00 50.00
303 Jabari Smith Jr. AU JSY BW 60.00 150.00
304 Jeremy Sochan AU JSY BW 60.00 150.00
305 Kennedy Chandler AU JSY BW RC 20.00 50.00
306 MarJon Beauchamp AU JSY BW 20.00 50.00
307 Christian Koloko AU JSY BW 20.00 50.00
308 Nikola Jovic AU JSY BW 40.00 100.00
309 Blake Wesley AU JSY BW RC 20.00 50.00
310 E.J. Liddell AU JSY BW RC 20.00 50.00
311 Jaden Ivey AU JSY BW 60.00 150.00
312 Max Christie AU JSY BW RC 50.00 125.00
313 Dyson Daniels AU JSY BW 50.00 120.00
314 Ochai Agbaji AU JSY BW 25.00 60.00
316 Patrick Baldwin Jr. AU JSY BW 20.00 50.00
317 Johnny Davis AU JSY BW 20.00 50.00
318 Moussa Diabate AU JSY BW 20.00 50.00
319 Ousmane Dieng AU JSY BW 25.00 60.00
320 Paolo Banchero AU JSY BW 400.00 800.00
321 Jake LaRavia AU JSY BW 20.00 50.00
322 Peyton Watson AU JSY BW RC 30.00 80.00
323 Mark Williams AU JSY BW RC 40.00 100.00
324 Keegan Murray AU JSY BW 50.00 120.00
325 Malaki Branham AU JSY BW 20.00 50.00
327 Andrew Nembhard AU JSY BW 40.00 100.00
328 Walker Kessler AU JSY BW 40.00 100.00
329 Jaden Hardy AU JSY BW 30.00 80.00
330 Shaedon Sharpe AU JSY BW 80.00 200.00
331 Wendell Moore Jr. AU JSY BW 20.00 50.00
332 Jalen Williams AU JSY BW 100.00 250.00
333 Bennedict Mathurin AU JSY BW 60.00 150.00
334 Christian Braun AU JSY BW 50.00 125.00
335 Caleb Houstan AU JSY BW RC 20.00 50.00
336 David Roddy AU JSY BW 25.00 60.00
337 Tari Eason AU JSY BW 50.00 125.00
338 AJ Griffin AU JSY BW 15.00 40.00
339 Chet Holmgren AU JSY BW 300.00 600.00
341 Jalen Duren AU JSY C 60.00 150.00
342 Dalen Terry AU JSY C 20.00 50.00
343 Jabari Smith Jr. AU JSY C 60.00 150.00
344 Jeremy Sochan AU JSY C 60.00 150.00
345 Kennedy Chandler AU JSY C 20.00 50.00
346 MarJon Beauchamp AU JSY C 20.00 50.00
347 Christian Koloko AU JSY C 20.00 50.00
348 Nikola Jovic AU JSY C 40.00 100.00
349 Blake Wesley AU JSY C 20.00 50.00
350 E.J. Liddell AU JSY C 20.00 50.00
351 Jaden Ivey AU JSY C 60.00 150.00
352 Max Christie AU JSY C 50.00 125.00
353 Dyson Daniels AU JSY C 50.00 120.00
354 Ochai Agbaji AU JSY C 25.00 60.00
356 Patrick Baldwin Jr. AU JSY C 20.00 50.00
357 Johnny Davis AU JSY C 20.00 50.00
358 Moussa Diabate AU JSY C 20.00 50.00
359 Ousmane Dieng AU JSY C 25.00 60.00
360 Paolo Banchero AU JSY C 400.00 800.00
361 Jake LaRavia AU JSY C 20.00 50.00
362 Peyton Watson AU JSY C 30.00 80.00
363 Mark Williams AU JSY C 40.00 100.00
364 Keegan Murray AU JSY C 50.00 120.00
365 Malaki Branham AU JSY C 20.00 50.00
366 TyTy Washington Jr. AU JSY C 20.00 50.00
367 Andrew Nembhard AU JSY C 40.00 100.00
368 Walker Kessler AU JSY C 40.00 100.00
369 Jaden Hardy AU JSY C 30.00 80.00
370 Shaedon Sharpe AU JSY C 80.00 200.00
371 Wendell Moore Jr. AU JSY C 20.00 50.00
372 Jalen Williams AU JSY C 100.00 250.00
373 Bennedict Mathurin AU JSY C 60.00 150.00
374 Christian Braun AU JSY C 50.00 125.00
375 Caleb Houstan AU JSY C 20.00 50.00
376 David Roddy AU JSY C 25.00 60.00
377 Tari Eason AU JSY C 50.00 125.00
378 AJ Griffin AU JSY C 15.00 40.00
379 Chet Holmgren AU JSY C 300.00 600.00
381 Jaden Ivey AU 50.00 125.00
382 Shaedon Sharpe AU 60.00 150.00
383 Dyson Daniels AU 40.00 100.00
384 Walker Kessler AU 30.00 80.00
385 Bennedict Mathurin AU 50.00 125.00
386 Jabari Smith Jr. AU 50.00 125.00
387 Max Christie AU 40.00 100.00
388 Ochai Agbaji AU 20.00 50.00
389 AJ Griffin AU 12.00 30.00
390 Paolo Banchero AU 300.00 600.00
391 Dalen Terry AU 15.00 40.00
392 Jalen Williams AU 80.00 200.00
393 Tari Eason AU 40.00 100.00
394 Johnny Davis AU 15.00 40.00
395 Keegan Murray AU 40.00 100.00
396 Jaden Hardy AU 25.00 60.00
397 Christian Koloko AU 15.00 40.00
398 MarJon Beauchamp AU 15.00 40.00
399 Jalen Duren AU 50.00 125.00
400 Chet Holmgren AU 200.00 500.00

2022-23 Panini Noir Autographs Black and White

STATED PRINT RUN 25-99 SER.#'d SETS
1 Jason Terry 8.00 20.00
2 Jamaal Wilkes 10.00 25.00
3 Jason Richardson 10.00 25.00
4 Isaac Okoro 8.00 20.00
5 Tony Parker 50.00 120.00
6 Kenny Sky Walker 8.00 20.00
7 Rudy Gobert 12.00 30.00
8 Herbert Jones 10.00 25.00
10 Kelly Oubre Jr. 10.00 25.00
11 Charles Barkley 100.00 250.00
12 John Stockton 50.00 120.00
13 Jerry West 50.00 120.00
14 RJ Barrett 15.00 40.00
15 B.J. Armstrong 10.00 25.00
16 Jordan Poole 40.00 100.00
17 Luka Doncic 500.00 1,000.00
18 Detlef Schrempf 10.00 25.00
19 Jonathan Kuminga 25.00 60.00
20 Jerry Stackhouse 12.00 30.00
21 Anthony Davis 125.00 300.00
23 Mo Bamba 8.00 20.00
25 Tyrese Haliburton 125.00 300.00
26 Al Horford 10.00 25.00
27 Dino Radja 8.00 20.00
28 Lonnie Walker IV 8.00 20.00
29 Jalen Brunson 40.00 100.00
31 Khris Middleton 12.00 30.00
32 Max Strus 10.00 25.00
33 Larry Bird 100.00 250.00
34 Tim Hardaway Jr. 8.00 20.00
35 Isaiah Rider 10.00 25.00

2022-23 Panini Noir Autographs Color

STATED PRINT RUN 25-99 SER.#'d SETS
1 Jason Terry 8.00 20.00
2 Jamaal Wilkes 10.00 25.00
3 Jason Richardson 10.00 25.00
4 Isaac Okoro 8.00 20.00
5 Tony Parker 50.00 120.00
6 Kenny Sky Walker 8.00 20.00
7 Rudy Gobert 12.00 30.00
8 Herbert Jones 10.00 25.00
10 Kelly Oubre Jr. 10.00 25.00
11 Charles Barkley 100.00 250.00
12 John Stockton 50.00 120.00
13 Jerry West 50.00 120.00
14 RJ Barrett 15.00 40.00
15 B.J. Armstrong 10.00 25.00
16 Jordan Poole 40.00 100.00
17 Luka Doncic 500.00 1,000.00
18 Detlef Schrempf 10.00 25.00
19 Jonathan Kuminga 25.00 60.00
20 Jerry Stackhouse 12.00 30.00
21 Anthony Davis 125.00 300.00
23 Mo Bamba 8.00 20.00
25 Tyrese Haliburton 125.00 300.00
26 Al Horford 10.00 25.00
27 Dino Radja 8.00 20.00
28 Lonnie Walker IV 8.00 20.00
29 Jalen Brunson 40.00 100.00
31 Khris Middleton 12.00 30.00
32 Max Strus 10.00 25.00
33 Larry Bird 100.00 250.00
34 Tim Hardaway Jr. 8.00 20.00
35 Isaiah Rider 10.00 25.00

2022-23 Panini Noir Box Office Memorabilia

STATED PRINT RUN 99 SER.#'d SETS
*PRIME/5-25: 1.25X TO 3X BASE HI
1 Zion Williamson 8.00 20.00
2 LaMelo Ball 8.00 20.00
3 DeMar DeRozan 4.00 10.00
4 Christian Wood 2.00 5.00
5 Jalen Green 10.00 25.00
6 Kawhi Leonard 8.00 20.00
7 Jimmy Butler 6.00 15.00
8 Giannis Antetokounmpo 15.00 40.00
9 Tyrese Maxey 6.00 15.00
10 Devin Booker 8.00 20.00
11 Anfernee Simons 4.00 10.00
12 Domantas Sabonis 4.00 10.00
13 Keldon Johnson 4.00 10.00
14 Pascal Siakam 5.00 12.00
15 Kyle Kuzma 4.00 10.00
16 Nikola Jokic 15.00 40.00
17 Ja Morant 10.00 25.00
18 Cameron Thomas 5.00 12.00
19 Lonzo Ball 3.00 8.00
20 Michael Porter Jr. 4.00 10.00
21 Alperen Sengun 4.00 10.00
22 Anthony Davis 8.00 20.00
23 Brandon Ingram 4.00 10.00
24 Obi Toppin 3.00 8.00
25 Josh Giddey 5.00 12.00
26 Chris Bosh 4.00 10.00
27 Baron Davis 3.00 8.00
28 Tracy McGrady 5.00 12.00
29 Deron Williams 2.50 6.00
30 Tim Duncan 8.00 20.00

2022-23 Panini Noir Casting Call Memorabilia

STATED PRINT RUN 99 SER.#'d SETS
*PRIME/49: .75X TO 2X BASE HI
*PRIME HOLO/25: 1.25X TO 3X BASE HI
1 Keegan Murray 6.00 15.00
2 Paolo Banchero 15.00 40.00
3 Jabari Smith Jr. 8.00 20.00
4 Jaden Ivey 8.00 20.00
5 Bennedict Mathurin 8.00 20.00
6 Shaedon Sharpe 10.00 25.00
7 Dyson Daniels 6.00 15.00
8 Jeremy Sochan 8.00 20.00
9 Jalen Williams 12.00 30.00
10 Jalen Duren 8.00 20.00
11 Ochai Agbaji 3.00 8.00
12 Mark Williams 5.00 12.00
13 AJ Griffin 2.00 5.00
14 Tari Eason 6.00 15.00
15 Jake LaRavia 2.50 6.00
16 Malaki Branham 2.50 6.00
17 Christian Braun 6.00 15.00
18 Walker Kessler 5.00 12.00
19 David Roddy 3.00 8.00
20 MarJon Beauchamp 2.50 6.00
21 Chet Holmgren 12.00 30.00
22 Nikola Jovic 5.00 12.00
23 TyTy Washington Jr. 2.50 6.00
24 Andrew Nembhard 5.00 12.00
25 Caleb Houstan 2.50 6.00
26 Christian Koloko 2.50 6.00
27 Max Christie 6.00 15.00
28 Jaden Hardy 4.00 10.00
29 Kennedy Chandler 2.50 6.00
30 Jaylin Williams 3.00 8.00

2022-23 Panini Noir Elegant Decor Rookie Jerseys

STATED PRINT RUN 99 SER.#'d SETS
*PRIME/49: .75X TO 2X BASE HI
*PRIME HOLO/25: 1.25X TO 3X BASE HI
1 Jaden Ivey 8.00 20.00
2 Paolo Banchero 15.00 40.00
3 Jabari Smith Jr. 8.00 20.00
4 Keegan Murray 6.00 15.00
5 Bennedict Mathurin 8.00 20.00
6 Shaedon Sharpe 10.00 25.00
7 Dyson Daniels 6.00 15.00
8 Jeremy Sochan 8.00 20.00
9 Johnny Davis 2.50 6.00
10 Ousmane Dieng 3.00 8.00
11 Jalen Williams 12.00 30.00
12 Jalen Duren 8.00 20.00
13 Ochai Agbaji 3.00 8.00
14 Mark Williams 5.00 12.00
15 AJ Griffin 2.00 5.00
16 Tari Eason 6.00 15.00
17 Dalen Terry 2.50 6.00
18 Jake LaRavia 2.50 6.00
19 Malaki Branham 2.50 6.00
20 Christian Braun 6.00 15.00
21 Walker Kessler 5.00 12.00
22 Wendell Moore Jr. 2.50 6.00
23 Nikola Jovic 5.00 12.00
24 Patrick Baldwin Jr. 2.50 6.00
25 TyTy Washington Jr. 2.50 6.00
26 Andrew Nembhard 5.00 12.00
27 Christian Koloko 2.50 6.00
28 Chet Holmgren 12.00 30.00
29 Jaden Hardy 4.00 10.00
30 Moussa Diabate 2.50 6.00

2022-23 Panini Noir Freeze Frame Signatures

STATED PRINT RUN 25-99 SER.#'d SETS
*GOLD/15-25: .5X TO 1.2X BASE HI
1 Bill Laimbeer/99 10.00 25.00
2 Lonnie Walker IV/99 8.00 20.00
3 Vince Carter/49 100.00 250.00
4 Larry Bird/49 75.00 200.00
5 Rod Strickland/99 8.00 20.00
6 Nickeil Alexander-Walker/99 8.00 20.00
7 Gary Harris/99 8.00 20.00
9 Dino Radja/99 8.00 20.00
10 Jamaal Wilkes/99 10.00 25.00
11 Harold Miner/99 10.00 25.00
12 Bernard King/99 12.00 30.00
13 Herbert Jones/99 10.00 25.00
15 Bob McAdoo/99 12.00 30.00
16 Lenny Wilkens/99 12.00 30.00
18 Richard Hamilton/99 12.00 30.00
19 Pat Riley/49 15.00 40.00
20 Rudy Gobert/99 12.00 30.00
21 Mike Miller/99 8.00 20.00
22 Kenyon Martin Jr./99 10.00 25.00
23 Devin Vassell/99 12.00 30.00
24 Rolando Blackman/99 8.00 20.00
25 Mark Price/99 10.00 25.00
26 Gail Goodrich/99 10.00 25.00
28 Kevin Huerter/99 10.00 25.00
29 Zach Randolph/99 10.00 25.00
30 Obi Toppin/99 10.00 25.00
31 Juwan Howard/99 10.00 25.00
32 Magic Johnson/25 75.00 200.00
33 George McGinnis/99 10.00 25.00
34 Wally Szczerbiak/99 8.00 20.00
35 Kenny Sky Walker/99 8.00 20.00
37 Peja Stojakovic/99 10.00 25.00
38 Tony Allen/99 6.00 15.00
40 Mark Aguirre/99 10.00 25.00

2022-23 Panini Noir Game Night Jerseys

STATED PRINT RUN 49-99 SER.#'d SETS
*PRIME/5-25: 1.25X TO 3X BASE HI
1 LaMelo Ball/99 10.00 25.00
2 Paul George/99 6.00 15.00
3 Anthony Davis/99 10.00 25.00
4 Deandre Ayton/99 4.00 10.00
5 Joel Embiid/99 6.00 15.00
6 Jaren Jackson Jr./99 6.00 15.00
7 RJ Barrett/99 6.00 15.00
8 Zach LaVine/99 8.00 20.00
9 Jaylen Brown/99 8.00 20.00
10 LeBron James/49 125.00 300.00
11 Jimmy Butler/99 8.00 20.00
12 Giannis Antetokounmpo/99 20.00 50.00
13 Trae Young/99 10.00 25.00
14 Darius Garland/99 6.00 15.00
15 Devin Booker/99 10.00 25.00
16 Damian Lillard/99 10.00 25.00
17 Kawhi Leonard/49 125.00 300.00
18 Klay Thompson/49 10.00 25.00
19 Jalen Brunson/99 8.00 20.00
20 De'Aaron Fox/99 8.00 20.00

2022-23 Panini Noir Horizontal Spotlight Signatures

STATED PRINT RUN 49-99 SER.#'d SETS
1 Jason Kidd/99 75.00 200.00
2 Charles Barkley/25 150.00 400.00
3 Bennedict Mathurin/99 200.00 500.00
4 Vince Carter/99 600.00 1,200.00
5 Anthony Edwards/99 600.00 1,200.00
6 Keegan Murray/99 150.00 400.00
7 Luka Doncic/99 800.00 1,500.00
8 Robert Horry/99 40.00 100.00
9 Jalen Green/49 150.00 400.00
10 RJ Barrett/49 125.00 300.00
11 Anfernee Hardaway/99 125.00 300.00
13 Jaden Ivey/99 150.00 400.00
14 Rasheed Wallace/99 125.00 300.00
16 Ray Allen/99 125.00 300.00
18 Jayson Tatum/49 400.00 800.00
19 Jamal Crawford/99 75.00 200.00
20 Shaedon Sharpe/99 400.00 800.00

2022-23 Panini Noir Jumbo Material

STATED PRINT RUN 99 SER.#'d SETS
1 LeBron James 50.00 120.00
2 Bam Adebayo 5.00 12.00
3 Khris Middleton 4.00 10.00
4 Jonas Valanciunas 2.50 6.00
5 Zion Williamson 8.00 20.00
6 Cole Anthony 3.00 8.00
7 Damian Lillard 8.00 20.00
8 De'Aaron Fox 6.00 15.00
9 Devin Vassell 4.00 10.00
10 OG Anunoby 4.00 10.00
11 Bradley Beal 4.00 10.00
12 Scottie Barnes 5.00 12.00
13 Marcus Smart 4.00 10.00
14 LaMelo Ball 8.00 20.00
15 Devin Booker 8.00 20.00
16 Terry Rozier III 4.00 10.00
17 Tim Hardaway Jr. 2.50 6.00
18 Draymond Green 4.00 10.00
19 Myles Turner 3.00 8.00
20 Norman Powell 3.00 8.00
21 Kyle Lowry 4.00 10.00
22 Victor Oladipo 2.50 6.00
23 Rudy Gobert 4.00 10.00
24 RJ Barrett 5.00 12.00
25 Franz Wagner 8.00 20.00
26 P.J. Tucker 2.50 6.00
27 Tyrese Maxey 12.00 30.00
28 Davion Mitchell 2.50 6.00
29 Spencer Dinwiddie 2.50 6.00
30 Tobias Harris 2.50 6.00
31 Luguentz Dort 3.00 8.00
32 Steven Adams 3.00 8.00
33 Aaron Gordon 3.00 8.00
34 Dennis Schroder 3.00 8.00
35 Josh Green 3.00 8.00
36 Jayson Tatum 12.00 30.00
37 Caris LeVert 2.50 6.00
38 Cade Cunningham 10.00 25.00
39 Stephen Curry 50.00 120.00
40 Giannis Antetokounmpo 15.00 40.00
41 Joel Embiid 5.00 12.00
42 Luka Doncic 30.00 80.00
43 James Harden 6.00 15.00
44 Zach LaVine 6.00 15.00
45 Kawhi Leonard 8.00 20.00
46 Anthony Davis 8.00 20.00
47 Paul George 5.00 12.00
48 Jaylen Brown 6.00 15.00
49 Trae Young 8.00 20.00
50 Anthony Edwards 15.00 40.00
51 Tyrese Haliburton 12.00 30.00
52 Kevin Durant 10.00 25.00
53 Kyrie Irving 6.00 15.00
54 Jimmy Butler 6.00 15.00
55 Lauri Markkanen 5.00 12.00
56 Domantas Sabonis 4.00 10.00
57 Donovan Mitchell 6.00 15.00
58 Jalen Green 10.00 25.00
59 Julius Randle 4.00 10.00
60 Markelle Fultz 2.50 6.00

2022-23 Panini Noir New Wave Jerseys

STATED PRINT RUN 99 SER.#'d SETS
*PRIME/25: 1X TO 2.5X BASE HI
1 Paolo Banchero 15.00 40.00
2 Jabari Smith Jr. 8.00 20.00
3 Keegan Murray 6.00 15.00
4 Jaden Ivey 8.00 20.00
5 Bennedict Mathurin 8.00 20.00
6 Shaedon Sharpe 10.00 25.00
7 Dyson Daniels 6.00 15.00
8 Jeremy Sochan 8.00 20.00
9 Johnny Davis 2.50 6.00
10 Ousmane Dieng 3.00 8.00
11 Jalen Williams 12.00 30.00
12 Jalen Duren 8.00 20.00
13 Ochai Agbaji 3.00 8.00
14 Mark Williams 5.00 12.00
15 AJ Griffin 2.00 5.00
16 Tari Eason 6.00 15.00
17 Chet Holmgren 12.00 30.00
18 Christian Braun 6.00 15.00
19 Walker Kessler 5.00 12.00
20 David Roddy 3.00 8.00
21 MarJon Beauchamp 2.50 6.00
22 Blake Wesley 2.50 6.00
23 Peyton Watson 4.00 10.00
24 Andrew Nembhard 5.00 12.00
25 Caleb Houstan 2.50 6.00
26 Christian Koloko 2.50 6.00
27 Jaylin Williams 3.00 8.00
28 Max Christie 6.00 15.00
29 Jaden Hardy 4.00 10.00
30 Isaiah Mobley 2.50 6.00

2022-23 Panini Noir Newsreels Jerseys

STATED PRINT RUN 75 SER.#'d SETS
*PRIME HOLO/10-25: 1.25X TO 3X BASE HI
1 Ben Simmons 2.50 6.00
2 Zach LaVine 5.00 12.00
3 Jamal Murray 4.00 10.00
4 Klay Thompson 6.00 15.00
5 Paul George 4.00 10.00
6 Tyler Herro 4.00 10.00
7 Jrue Holiday 3.00 8.00
8 Karl-Anthony Towns 4.00 10.00
9 Julius Randle 3.00 8.00
10 Shai Gilgeous-Alexander 12.00 30.00
11 Joel Embiid 4.00 10.00
12 Deandre Ayton 2.50 6.00
13 Jerami Grant 3.00 8.00
14 Fred VanVleet 3.00 8.00
15 Kristaps Porzingis 3.00 8.00
16 Trae Young 6.00 15.00
17 Gordon Hayward 2.00 5.00
18 Darius Garland 4.00 10.00
19 Andrew Wiggins 3.00 8.00
20 Jaren Jackson Jr. 4.00 10.00
21 CJ McCollum 2.50 6.00
22 Jalen Brunson 5.00 12.00
23 Jalen Suggs 3.00 8.00
24 Gilbert Arenas 2.50 6.00
25 Marc Gasol 2.50 6.00
26 Alonzo Mourning 4.00 10.00
27 D'Angelo Russell 2.00 5.00
28 Evan Mobley 6.00 15.00
29 Kyrie Irving 5.00 12.00
30 Kevin Durant 8.00 20.00
31 Chris Paul 5.00 12.00
32 Dejounte Murray 3.00 8.00
33 John Collins 2.50 6.00
34 LeBron James 50.00 120.00
35 Buddy Hield 2.50 6.00
36 Robert Williams III 2.00 5.00
37 Desmond Bane 3.00 8.00
38 Anthony Edwards 12.00 30.00
39 Steve Nash 5.00 12.00
40 Manu Ginobili 5.00 12.00

2022-23 Panini Noir Night Lights Autographs

1 Cade Cunningham 500.00 1,000.00
2 Stephen Curry 1,500.00 3,000.00
5 Anthony Edwards 600.00 1,200.00
10 Ja Morant 600.00 1,200.00

2022-23 Panini Noir Prime Material Autographs Black and White

STATED PRINT RUN 15-40 SER.#'d SETS
1 RJ Barrett 25.00 60.00
2 Isaac Okoro 12.00 30.00
5 Zach Randolph 15.00 40.00
6 Rudy Gobert 20.00 50.00
7 Dwyane Wade 200.00 500.00
8 Lonnie Walker IV 12.00 30.00
10 Jonathan Kuminga 40.00 100.00
11 Luguentz Dort 15.00 40.00
13 Mo Bamba 12.00 30.00
14 Joe Dumars 20.00 50.00
15 Rod Strickland 12.00 30.00

2022-23 Panini Noir Prime Material Autographs Color

STATED PRINT RUN 15-40 SER.#'d SETS
1 RJ Barrett 25.00 60.00
2 Isaac Okoro 12.00 30.00
5 Zach Randolph 15.00 40.00
6 Rudy Gobert 20.00 50.00
7 Dwyane Wade 200.00 500.00
8 Lonnie Walker IV 12.00 30.00
10 Jonathan Kuminga 40.00 100.00
11 Luguentz Dort 15.00 40.00
13 Mo Bamba 12.00 30.00
14 Joe Dumars 20.00 50.00
15 Rod Strickland 12.00 30.00

2022-23 Panini Noir Reel to Reel Dual Memorabilia

STATED PRINT RUN 99 SER.#'d SETS
*PRIME/5-10: 1.5X TO 4X BASE HI
1 Chris Paul
Chris Paul 6.00 15.00
2 Paul George
Paul George 5.00 12.00
3 LeBron James
LeBron James 75.00 200.00
4 Kawhi Leonard
Kawhi Leonard 8.00 20.00
5 Shai Gilgeous-Alexander
Shai Gilgeous-Alexander 12.00 30.00
6 Zach LaVine
Zach LaVine 6.00 15.00
7 Jimmy Butler
Jimmy Butler 6.00 15.00
8 DeMar DeRozan
DeMar DeRozan 4.00 10.00
9 Julius Randle
Julius Randle 4.00 10.00
10 Anthony Davis
Anthony Davis 8.00 20.00
11 Kristaps Porzingis
Kristaps Porzingis 4.00 10.00
12 Domantas Sabonis
Domantas Sabonis 4.00 10.00
13 Carmelo Anthony
Carmelo Anthony 12.00 30.00
14 Dejounte Murray
Dejounte Murray 4.00 10.00
15 Brandon Ingram
Brandon Ingram 4.00 10.00
16 CJ McCollum
CJ McCollum 3.00 8.00
17 Tyrese Haliburton
Tyrese Haliburton 12.00 30.00
18 Jrue Holiday
Jrue Holiday 4.00 10.00
19 Rudy Gobert
Rudy Gobert 4.00 10.00
20 James Harden
James Harden 6.00 15.00

2022-23 Panini Noir Reigning Nights Signatures

STATED PRINT RUN 25-99 SER.#'d SETS
*GOLD/15-25: .5X TO 1.2X BASE HI
1 Derrick White/99 25.00 60.00
2 Chet Holmgren/49 300.00 600.00
3 Ochai Agbaji/99 15.00 40.00
4 Gary Harris/99 10.00 25.00
5 Devin Vassell/99 40.00 100.00
6 David Roddy/99 15.00 40.00
7 Seth Curry/99 10.00 25.00
8 Manu Ginobili/25 100.00 250.00
9 Tim Hardaway Jr./99 10.00 25.00
10 Mike Miller/99 10.00 25.00
11 Khris Middleton/49 15.00 40.00
12 Tyrese Haliburton/49 125.00 300.00
13 Jalen Brunson/99 40.00 100.00
14 Jason Terry/99 10.00 25.00
15 Obi Toppin/99 12.00 30.00
16 Jamal Crawford/99 12.00 30.00
17 Christian Laettner/99 12.00 30.00
18 Nate Archibald/99 15.00 40.00
19 James Harden/25 300.00 600.00
20 Tyrese Martin/99 10.00 25.00
21 Kevin Huerter/99 12.00 30.00
22 Mark Price/99 12.00 30.00
23 Rasheed Wallace/25 50.00 120.00
24 Grant Hill/49 30.00 80.00
25 Richard Hamilton/99 15.00 40.00
26 Adrian Dantley/99 12.00 30.00
27 Wally Szczerbiak/99 10.00 25.00
28 Rick Barry/99 15.00 40.00
29 Caron Butler/99 10.00 25.00
30 Stephen Curry/25 800.00 1,500.00
31 Jordan Poole/49 40.00 100.00
32 Nick Van Exel/99 12.00 30.00
33 Christian Braun/99 50.00 120.00
34 Max Strus/99 12.00 30.00

2022-23 Panini Noir Rookie Jumbo Material

STATED PRINT RUN 99 SER.#'d SETS
1 Chet Holmgren 15.00 40.00
2 Keegan Murray 8.00 20.00
3 Jaden Hardy 5.00 12.00
4 Bennedict Mathurin 10.00 25.00
5 MarJon Beauchamp 3.00 8.00
6 Jalen Duren 10.00 25.00
7 Jabari Smith Jr. 10.00 25.00
8 Jalen Williams 15.00 40.00
9 Walker Kessler 6.00 15.00
10 AJ Griffin 2.50 6.00
11 Paolo Banchero 20.00 50.00
12 Tari Eason 8.00 20.00
13 Jaden Ivey 10.00 25.00
14 Andrew Nembhard 6.00 15.00
15 Malaki Branham 3.00 8.00
16 Shaedon Sharpe 12.00 30.00
17 Dyson Daniels 8.00 20.00
18 David Roddy 4.00 10.00
19 Ochai Agbaji 4.00 10.00
20 Jeremy Sochan 10.00 25.00
21 Christian Braun 8.00 20.00
22 Christian Koloko 3.00 8.00
23 Mark Williams 6.00 15.00
24 Johnny Davis 3.00 8.00
25 Ousmane Dieng 4.00 10.00
26 Jake LaRavia 3.00 8.00
27 Nikola Jovic 6.00 15.00
28 TyTy Washington Jr. 3.00 8.00
29 Wendell Moore Jr. 3.00 8.00
30 Caleb Houstan 3.00 8.00
31 Max Christie 8.00 20.00
32 Moussa Diabate 3.00 8.00
33 Kennedy Chandler 3.00 8.00
34 Patrick Baldwin Jr. 3.00 8.00
35 Blake Wesley 3.00 8.00
36 Isaiah Mobley 3.00 8.00
37 Bryce McGowens 3.00 8.00
38 Dalen Terry 3.00 8.00
39 Peyton Watson 5.00 12.00
40 Jabari Walker 2.50 6.00

2022-23 Panini Noir Shadow Signatures

STATED PRINT RUN 25-99 SER.#'d SETS
*GOLD/25: .5X TO 1.2X BASE HI
1 MarJon Beauchamp/99 15.00 40.00
2 Chet Holmgren/49 300.00 600.00
4 Bill Laimbeer/99 15.00 40.00
5 Jordan Goodwin/99 12.00 30.00
6 Dalen Terry/99 15.00 40.00
7 Kevin Huerter/99 15.00 40.00
8 Kevon Harris/99 12.00 30.00
9 Lindy Waters III/99 12.00 30.00
10 Nikola Jovic/99 30.00 80.00
11 Isaiah Rider/99 15.00 40.00
12 Seth Curry/99 12.00 30.00
13 Glen Rice/99 15.00 40.00
14 Ousmane Dieng/99 20.00 50.00
15 Moussa Diabate/99 15.00 40.00
16 Scotty Pippen Jr./99 20.00 50.00
17 Tyrese Martin/99 12.00 30.00
18 Shai Gilgeous-Alexander/49 800.00 1,500.00
19 Elton Brand/99 15.00 40.00
20 Jerry West/49 50.00 120.00
21 Christian Koloko/99 15.00 40.00
23 Jaylin Williams/99 20.00 50.00
24 Patrick Baldwin Jr./99 15.00 40.00
25 Kennedy Chandler/99 15.00 40.00
26 Harold Miner/99 15.00 40.00
27 Shaedon Sharpe/99 150.00 400.00
28 Wendell Moore Jr./99 15.00 40.00
29 Josh Minott/99 15.00 40.00
30 Juwan Howard/99 15.00 40.00
32 Jalen Williams/99 150.00 400.00
35 TyTy Washington Jr./99 15.00 40.00
36 Jake LaRavia/99 15.00 40.00
38 Max Christie/99 40.00 100.00
39 Ray Allen/25 125.00 300.00
40 Caleb Houstan/99 15.00 40.00

2022-23 Panini Noir Showtime Signatures

STATED PRINT RUN 25-99 SER.#'d SETS

*GOLD/15-25: .5X TO 1.2X BASE HI
1 Keegan Murray/99 100.00 250.00
2 Jalen Duren/49 50.00 125.00
3 Andrew Nembhard/99 30.00 80.00
4 Evan Mobley/25 40.00 100.00
5 Jaden Ivey/25 50.00 125.00
6 Walker Kessler/99 30.00 80.00
7 Kelly Oubre Jr./99 15.00 40.00
8 Ochai Agbaji/99 20.00 50.00
9 Wendell Moore Jr./99 15.00 40.00
10 Paolo Banchero /49 200.00 500.00
11 AJ Griffin/49 12.00 30.00
12 Tari Eason/99 40.00 100.00
13 Nikola Jovic/99 30.00 80.00
14 Bennedict Mathurin/49 100.00 250.00
15 MarJon Beauchamp/99 15.00 40.00
16 Cade Cunningham/25 200.00 500.00
17 Ousmane Dieng/99 20.00 50.00
18 Josh Giddey/99 60.00 150.00
19 Jabari Smith Jr./25 50.00 120.00
20 Jake LaRavia/99 15.00 40.00
21 Jeremy Sochan/99 50.00 125.00
22 Jaden Hardy/49 25.00 60.00
23 Dalen Terry/99 15.00 40.00
24 Jayson Tatum/25 500.00 1,000.00
25 Chet Holmgren/25 400.00 800.00

2022-23 Panini Noir Silver Screen Debut Signatures

STATED PRINT RUN 25-99 SER.#'d SETS
*GOLD/25: .5X TO 1.2X BASE HI
1 Bennedict Mathurin/49 75.00 200.00
2 Christian Braun/99 30.00 80.00
3 TyTy Washington Jr./99 12.00 30.00
4 Nikola Jovic/99 25.00 60.00
5 Dyson Daniels/99 30.00 80.00
6 Keegan Murray/99 75.00 200.00
7 Jaden Ivey/49 40.00 100.00
8 Kennedy Chandler/99 12.00 30.00
9 Mark Williams/99 25.00 60.00
10 Jabari Smith Jr./49 40.00 100.00
11 Blake Wesley/99 12.00 30.00
12 Jordan Goodwin/99 10.00 25.00
13 Dalen Terry/99 12.00 30.00
14 Paolo Banchero /49 150.00 400.00
15 Christian Koloko/99 12.00 30.00
16 Caleb Houstan/99 12.00 30.00
17 Lindy Waters III/99 10.00 25.00
18 Tari Eason/99 30.00 80.00
19 Ochai Agbaji/99 15.00 40.00
20 Andrew Nembhard/99 25.00 60.00
21 Jalen Duren/99 40.00 100.00
22 Jalen Williams/99 60.00 150.00
23 Jake LaRavia/99 12.00 30.00
24 Jaden Hardy/99 20.00 50.00
25 Walker Kessler/99 25.00 60.00
26 Chet Holmgren/49 300.00 600.00
27 AJ Griffin/99 10.00 25.00
28 MarJon Beauchamp/99 12.00 30.00
29 Ousmane Dieng/99 15.00 40.00
30 Wendell Moore Jr./99 12.00 30.00

2022-23 Panini Noir Snapshot Signatures

STATED PRINT RUN 25-99 SER.#'d SETS
*GOLD/15-25: .5X TO 1.2X BASE HI
1 B.J. Armstrong/99 10.00 25.00
2 Isaac Okoro/99 8.00 20.00
3 Artis Gilmore/99 12.00 30.00
4 Joe Dumars/99 12.00 30.00
5 Obi Toppin/99 10.00 25.00
6 Gary Harris/99 8.00 20.00
8 Jason Richardson/49 10.00 25.00
9 Jason Kidd/49 15.00 40.00
10 Bill Laimbeer/99 10.00 25.00
11 George McGinnis/99 10.00 25.00
12 Derrick White/99 15.00 40.00
13 Kenyon Martin Jr./99 10.00 25.00
14 Mark Aguirre/99 10.00 25.00
16 Anthony Edwards/25 200.00 500.00
17 Max Strus/99 10.00 25.00
18 Bob Cousy/25 100.00 250.00
19 Caron Butler/99 8.00 20.00
20 Larry Bird/25 100.00 250.00
21 Wally Szczerbiak/99 8.00 20.00
22 Elton Brand/99 10.00 25.00
23 Christian Laettner/99 10.00 25.00
25 Larry Johnson/99 15.00 40.00
26 Nickeil Alexander-Walker/99 8.00 20.00
27 Jalen Brunson/49 50.00 120.00
28 Carlos Boozer/99 8.00 20.00
29 Kenny Sky Walker/99 8.00 20.00
30 Kelly Oubre Jr./99 10.00 25.00

2022-23 Panini Noir Sneaker Spotlight

STATED PRINT RUN 99 SER.#'d SETS
1 LeBron James 500.00 1,000.00
2 Stephen Curry 500.00 1,000.00
3 LeBron James 500.00 1,000.00
4 Giannis Antetokounmpo 200.00 500.00
5 Ja Morant 300.00 600.00
6 Paul George 200.00 500.00
7 Klay Thompson 200.00 500.00
8 Trae Young 150.00 400.00
9 Damian Lillard 200.00 500.00
10 Zion Williamson 300.00 600.00

2022-23 Panini Noir Sneaker Spotlight Signatures

STATED PRINT RUN 99 SER.#'d SETS
1 Nikola Jokic 800.00 1,500.00
2 Shawn Kemp 200.00 500.00
3 Chris Paul 400.00 800.00
4 Dwyane Wade 400.00 800.00
5 Ja Morant 1,000.00 2,000.00
6 Jalen Suggs 200.00 500.00
7 Luka Doncic 1,500.00 3,000.00
8 Tyrese Haliburton 800.00 1,500.00
9 Cade Cunningham 500.00 1,000.00
10 Shai Gilgeous-Alexander 2,000.00 4,000.00
11 Rasheed Wallace 150.00 400.00
12 CJ McCollum 150.00 400.00
13 James Harden 600.00 1,200.00
14 Jalen Green 400.00 800.00
15 Anthony Davis 350.00 700.00
16 Paolo Banchero 800.00 1,500.00
17 Manu Ginobili 350.00 700.00
18 AJ Griffin 60.00 150.00
19 Jalen Duren 400.00 800.00
21 Dejounte Murray 150.00 400.00
22 Jayson Tatum 1,000.00 2,000.00
23 Anthony Edwards 1,000.00 2,000.00
24 Anfernee Hardaway 600.00 1,200.00
25 Jonathan Kuminga 300.00 600.00
26 Brandon Ingram 300.00 600.00
27 Jaden Ivey 500.00 1,000.00
28 Pau Gasol 500.00 1,000.00
29 Jordan Poole 200.00 500.00
30 Stephen Curry 2,500.00 5,000.00
31 Shaedon Sharpe 600.00 1,200.00
32 Zach Randolph 125.00 300.00
33 Khris Middleton 125.00 300.00
34 Bennedict Mathurin 500.00 1,000.00
35 Deandre Ayton 150.00 400.00
36 Amar'e Stoudemire 125.00 300.00
37 RJ Barrett 200.00 500.00
38 Allen Iverson 500.00 1,000.00
39 Josh Giddey 400.00 800.00
40 Jabari Smith Jr. 500.00 1,000.00

2022-23 Panini Noir Vertical Spotlight Signatures

STATED PRINT RUN 49-99 SER.#'d SETS
1 Grant Hill/99 125.00 300.00
2 Shawn Kemp/99 125.00 300.00
3 Paolo Banchero /99 500.00 1,000.00
4 Antoine Walker/99 20.00 50.00
6 Peja Stojakovic/99 75.00 200.00
7 Christian Braun/99 50.00 125.00
8 Paul Pierce/99 125.00 300.00
9 Nick Van Exel/99 20.00 50.00
10 Manu Ginobili/49 200.00 500.00
11 Jalen Duren/99 125.00 300.00
12 Ja Morant/49 800.00 1,500.00
13 Dyson Daniels/99 50.00 120.00
14 Evan Mobley/49 50.00 125.00
16 Bernard King/99 25.00 60.00
17 Jeremy Sochan/99 150.00 400.00
18 Andrew Nembhard/99 40.00 100.00
19 Caron Butler/99 15.00 40.00
20 Jabari Smith Jr./99 150.00 400.00

2023-24 Panini Noir

1-140 PRINT RUN 99 SER.#'d SETS
RC PRINT RUN 99 SER.#'d SETS 3.00 8.00
201-300 PRINT RUN 25 SER.#'d SETS
301-380 PRINT RUN 99 SER.#'d SETS
381-400 PRINT RUN 99 SER.#'d SETS
*HOLO SILVER/49 (1-200): .6X TO 1.5X BASE
*ROOKIE PATCH AUTO PRIME/25 (301-380): .75X TO 2X BASE
*NOIR GOLD/25 (381-400): .75X TO 2X BASE
1 Mikal Bridges A 4.00 10.00
2 Jayson Tatum A 12.00 30.00
3 Keldon Johnson A 4.00 10.00
4 Desmond Bane A 4.00 10.00
5 Kawhi Leonard A 8.00 20.00
6 Anfernee Simons A 4.00 10.00
7 De'Aaron Fox A 6.00 15.00
8 Kyle Kuzma A 4.00 10.00
9 Kyrie Irving A 6.00 15.00
10 Jalen Williams A 6.00 15.00
11 Shai Gilgeous-Alexander A 15.00 40.00
12 Klay Thompson A 8.00 20.00
13 Keegan Murray A 4.00 10.00
14 Trae Young A 6.00 15.00
15 Jaren Jackson Jr. A 5.00 12.00
16 Chris Paul A 6.00 15.00
17 Nikola Jokic A 15.00 40.00
18 DeMar DeRozan A 5.00 12.00
19 Michael Porter Jr. A 4.00 10.00
20 LeBron James A 25.00 60.00
21 Russell Westbrook A 5.00 12.00
22 Devin Booker A 8.00 20.00
23 Karl-Anthony Towns A 5.00 12.00
24 Zion Williamson A 8.00 20.00
25 LaMelo Ball A 8.00 20.00
26 Bradley Beal A 4.00 10.00
27 Ja Morant A 10.00 25.00
28 Jordan Poole A 5.00 12.00
29 James Harden A 6.00 15.00
30 Jamal Murray A 6.00 15.00
31 Jalen Brunson A 6.00 15.00
32 Giannis Antetokounmpo A 15.00 40.00
33 Anthony Davis A 8.00 20.00
34 Franz Wagner A 5.00 12.00
35 Tyrese Maxey A 6.00 15.00
36 Julius Randle A 4.00 10.00
37 Bam Adebayo A 5.00 12.00
38 Pascal Siakam A 5.00 12.00
39 Joel Embiid A 8.00 20.00
40 Jrue Holiday A 4.00 10.00
41 Paul George A 5.00 12.00
42 Lauri Markkanen A 5.00 12.00
43 Bennedict Mathurin A 5.00 12.00
44 Jimmy Butler A 5.00 12.00
45 Paolo Banchero A 8.00 20.00
46 Chet Holmgren A 8.00 20.00
47 Jalen Green A 5.00 12.00
48 Donovan Mitchell A 6.00 15.00
49 Terry Rozier III A 4.00 10.00
50 Brandon Ingram A 4.00 10.00
51 Damian Lillard A 8.00 20.00
52 Anthony Edwards A 15.00 40.00
53 Alperen Sengun A 5.00 12.00
54 Luka Doncic A 20.00 50.00
55 Domantas Sabonis A 5.00 12.00
56 Fred VanVleet A 4.00 10.00
57 Bojan Bogdanovic A 3.00 8.00
58 Cade Cunningham A 8.00 20.00
59 Shaedon Sharpe A 6.00 15.00
60 Darius Garland A 5.00 12.00
61 Devin Vassell A 4.00 10.00
62 Jordan Clarkson A 3.00 8.00
63 Cameron Thomas A 4.00 10.00
64 Scottie Barnes A 4.00 10.00
65 Stephen Curry A 25.00 60.00
66 Kevin Durant A 10.00 25.00
67 Tyler Herro A 5.00 12.00
68 Tyrese Haliburton A 6.00 15.00
69 Jaylen Brown A 6.00 15.00
70 Zach LaVine A 5.00 12.00
71 Mikal Bridges I 4.00 10.00
72 Jayson Tatum I 12.00 30.00
73 Keldon Johnson I 4.00 10.00
74 Desmond Bane I 4.00 10.00
75 Kawhi Leonard I 8.00 20.00
76 Anfernee Simons I 4.00 10.00
77 De'Aaron Fox I 6.00 15.00
78 Kyle Kuzma I 4.00 10.00
79 Kyrie Irving I 6.00 15.00
80 Jalen Williams I 6.00 15.00
81 Shai Gilgeous-Alexander I 15.00 40.00
82 Klay Thompson I 8.00 20.00
83 Keegan Murray I 4.00 10.00
84 Trae Young I 6.00 15.00
85 Jaren Jackson Jr. I 5.00 12.00
86 Chris Paul I 6.00 15.00
87 Nikola Jokic I 15.00 40.00
88 DeMar DeRozan I 5.00 12.00
89 Michael Porter Jr. I 4.00 10.00
90 LeBron James I 25.00 60.00
91 Russell Westbrook I 5.00 12.00
92 Devin Booker I 8.00 20.00
93 Karl-Anthony Towns I 5.00 12.00
94 Zion Williamson I 8.00 20.00
95 LaMelo Ball I 8.00 20.00
96 Bradley Beal I 4.00 10.00
97 Ja Morant I 10.00 25.00
98 Jordan Poole I 5.00 12.00
99 James Harden I 6.00 15.00
100 Jamal Murray I 6.00 15.00
101 Jalen Brunson I 6.00 15.00
102 Giannis Antetokounmpo I 15.00 40.00
103 Anthony Davis I 8.00 20.00
104 Franz Wagner I 5.00 12.00
105 Tyrese Maxey I 6.00 15.00
106 Julius Randle I 4.00 10.00
107 Bam Adebayo I 5.00 12.00
108 Pascal Siakam I 5.00 12.00
109 Joel Embiid I 8.00 20.00
110 Jrue Holiday I 4.00 10.00
111 Paul George I 5.00 12.00
112 Lauri Markkanen I 5.00 12.00
113 Bennedict Mathurin I 5.00 12.00
114 Jimmy Butler I 5.00 12.00
115 Paolo Banchero I 8.00 20.00
116 Chet Holmgren I 8.00 20.00
117 Jalen Green I 5.00 12.00
118 Donovan Mitchell I 6.00 15.00
119 Terry Rozier III I 4.00 10.00
120 Brandon Ingram I 4.00 10.00
121 Damian Lillard I 8.00 20.00
122 Anthony Edwards I 15.00 40.00
123 Alperen Sengun I 5.00 12.00
124 Luka Doncic I 20.00 50.00
125 Domantas Sabonis I 5.00 12.00
126 Fred VanVleet I 4.00 10.00
127 Bojan Bogdanovic I 3.00 8.00
128 Cade Cunningham I 8.00 20.00
129 Shaedon Sharpe I 6.00 15.00
130 Darius Garland I 5.00 12.00
131 Devin Vassell I 4.00 10.00
132 Jordan Clarkson I 3.00 8.00
133 Cameron Thomas I 4.00 10.00
134 Scottie Barnes I 4.00 10.00
135 Stephen Curry I 25.00 60.00
136 Kevin Durant I 10.00 25.00
137 Tyler Herro I 5.00 12.00
138 Tyrese Haliburton I 6.00 15.00
139 Jaylen Brown I 6.00 15.00
140 Zach LaVine I 5.00 12.00
141 Marcus Sasser A RC 5.00 12.00
142 Jordan Hawkins A RC 5.00 12.00
143 Brandon Miller A RC 12.00 30.00
144 Sasha Vezenkov A RC 2.50 6.00
145 Cason Wallace A RC 6.00 15.00
146 Anthony Black A RC 6.00 15.00
147 Scoot Henderson A RC 10.00 25.00
148 Andre Jackson Jr. A RC 5.00 12.00
149 Victor Wembanyama A RC 75.00 200.00
150 Bilal Coulibaly A RC 8.00 20.00
151 Amari Bailey A RC 3.00 8.00
152 Jarace Walker A RC 6.00 15.00
153 Ausar Thompson A RC 8.00 20.00
154 Brandin Podziemski A RC 10.00 25.00
155 Keyonte George A RC 10.00 25.00
156 Nick Smith Jr. A RC 4.00 10.00
157 Kobe Bufkin A RC 4.00 10.00
158 Amen Thompson A RC 15.00 40.00
159 Jett Howard A RC 4.00 10.00
160 Cam Whitmore A RC 8.00 20.00
161 Vasilije Micic A RC 3.00 8.00
162 Trayce Jackson-Davis A RC 4.00 10.00
163 Toumani Camara A RC 6.00 15.00
164 Kobe Brown A RC 3.00 8.00
165 Kris Murray A RC 3.00 8.00
166 Jaime Jaquez Jr. A RC 5.00 12.00
167 Julian Strawther A RC 4.00 10.00
168 Gradey Dick A RC 6.00 15.00
169 Taylor Hendricks A RC 3.00 8.00
170 Dereck Lively II A RC 6.00 15.00
171 Marcus Sasser I RC 5.00 12.00
172 Jordan Hawkins I RC 5.00 12.00
173 Brandon Miller I RC 12.00 30.00
174 Sasha Vezenkov I RC 2.50 6.00
175 Cason Wallace I RC 6.00 15.00
176 Anthony Black I RC 6.00 15.00
177 Scoot Henderson I RC 10.00 25.00
178 Andre Jackson Jr. I RC 5.00 12.00
179 Victor Wembanyama I RC 75.00 200.00
180 Bilal Coulibaly I RC 8.00 20.00
181 Amari Bailey I RC 3.00 8.00
182 Jarace Walker I RC 6.00 15.00
183 Ausar Thompson I RC 8.00 20.00
184 Brandin Podziemski I RC 10.00 25.00
185 Keyonte George I RC 10.00 25.00
186 Nick Smith Jr. I RC 4.00 10.00
187 Kobe Bufkin I RC 4.00 10.00
188 Amen Thompson I RC 15.00 40.00
189 Jett Howard I RC 4.00 10.00
190 Cam Whitmore I RC 8.00 20.00
191 Vasilije Micic I RC 3.00 8.00
192 Trayce Jackson-Davis I RC 4.00 10.00
193 Toumani Camara I RC 6.00 15.00
194 Kobe Brown I RC 3.00 8.00
195 Kris Murray I RC 3.00 8.00
196 Jaime Jaquez Jr. I RC 5.00 12.00
197 Julian Strawther I RC 4.00 10.00
198 Gradey Dick I RC 6.00 15.00
199 Taylor Hendricks I RC 3.00 8.00
200 Dereck Lively II I RC 6.00 15.00
201 Kyrie Irving MET 25.00 60.00
202 Kevin Durant MET 40.00 100.00
203 Jimmy Butler MET 20.00 50.00
204 Zion Williamson MET 30.00 80.00
205 Luka Doncic MET 80.00 200.00
206 Anthony Davis MET 30.00 80.00
207 Paolo Banchero MET 30.00 80.00
208 Joel Embiid MET 30.00 80.00
209 Cade Cunningham MET 30.00 80.00
210 LaMelo Ball MET 30.00 80.00
211 Kawhi Leonard MET 30.00 80.00
212 Jaylen Brown MET 25.00 60.00
213 Donovan Mitchell MET 25.00 60.00
214 De'Aaron Fox MET 25.00 60.00
215 Stephen Curry MET 100.00 250.00
216 James Harden MET 25.00 60.00
217 Tyrese Haliburton MET 25.00 60.00
218 Chet Holmgren MET 30.00 80.00
219 Nikola Jokic MET 60.00 150.00
220 Giannis Antetokounmpo MET 60.00 150.00
221 Anthony Edwards MET 60.00 150.00
222 Shai Gilgeous-Alexander MET 60.00 150.00
223 Trae Young MET 25.00 60.00
224 LeBron James MET 100.00 250.00
225 Paul George MET 20.00 50.00
226 Jayson Tatum MET 50.00 125.00
227 Tyrese Maxey MET 25.00 60.00
228 Ja Morant MET 40.00 100.00
229 Damian Lillard MET 30.00 80.00
230 Devin Booker MET 30.00 80.00
231 Brandon Miller MET 50.00 120.00
232 Scoot Henderson MET 40.00 100.00
233 Trayce Jackson-Davis MET 15.00 40.00
234 Anthony Black MET 25.00 60.00
235 Gradey Dick MET 25.00 60.00
236 Andre Jackson Jr. MET 20.00 50.00
237 Julian Strawther MET 15.00 40.00
238 Victor Wembanyama MET 300.00 600.00
239 Ausar Thompson MET 30.00 80.00
240 Taylor Hendricks MET 12.00 30.00
241 Brandin Podziemski MET 40.00 100.00
242 Cason Wallace MET 25.00 60.00
243 Jaime Jaquez Jr. MET 20.00 50.00
244 Amen Thompson MET 60.00 150.00
245 Bilal Coulibaly MET 30.00 80.00
246 Keyonte George MET 40.00 100.00
247 Dereck Lively II MET 25.00 60.00
248 Marcus Sasser MET 20.00 50.00
249 Jordan Hawkins MET 20.00 50.00
250 Toumani Camara MET 25.00 60.00
251 Brandon Miller FL 50.00 120.00
252 Victor Wembanyama FL 100.00 250.00
253 Scoot Henderson FL 40.00 100.00
254 Shai Gilgeous-Alexander FL 60.00 150.00
255 Giannis Antetokounmpo FL 60.00 150.00
256 Zion Williamson FL 30.00 80.00
257 Tim Duncan FL 30.00 80.00
258 Nikola Jokic FL 60.00 150.00
259 Ja Morant FL 40.00 100.00
260 Damian Lillard FL 30.00 80.00
261 Luka Doncic FL 80.00 200.00
262 Jayson Tatum FL 50.00 125.00
263 Julius Erving FL 30.00 80.00
264 Kevin Durant FL 40.00 100.00
265 Yao Ming FL 30.00 80.00
266 Stephen Curry FL 100.00 250.00
267 Tyrese Haliburton FL 25.00 60.00
268 Amen Thompson FL 60.00 150.00
269 Ausar Thompson FL 30.00 80.00
270 LeBron James FL 100.00 250.00
271 Stephen Curry MP 100.00 250.00
272 Victor Wembanyama MP 100.00 250.00
273 Luka Doncic MP 80.00 200.00
274 LeBron James MP 100.00 250.00
275 Jayson Tatum MP 50.00 125.00
276 Ja Morant VA 40.00 100.00
277 De'Aaron Fox VA 25.00 60.00
278 Victor Wembanyama VA 300.00 600.00
279 Giannis Antetokounmpo VA 60.00 150.00
280 Tyrese Haliburton VA 25.00 60.00
281 LeBron James VA 100.00 250.00
282 Scoot Henderson VA 40.00 100.00
283 Anthony Davis VA 30.00 80.00
284 Luka Doncic VA 80.00 200.00
285 Donovan Mitchell VA 25.00 60.00
286 Jayson Tatum VA 50.00 125.00
287 Brandon Miller VA 50.00 120.00
288 Stephen Curry VA 100.00 250.00
289 Zion Williamson VA 30.00 80.00
290 Nikola Jokic VA 60.00 150.00
291 LeBron James CA 100.00 250.00
292 Stephen Curry CA 100.00 250.00
293 Giannis Antetokounmpo CA 60.00 150.00
294 Nikola Jokic CA 60.00 150.00
295 Kevin Durant CA 40.00 100.00
296 Luka Doncic CA 80.00 200.00
297 Ja Morant CA 40.00 100.00
298 Dirk Nowitzki CA 30.00 80.00
299 Shaquille O'Neal CA 40.00 100.00
300 Tim Duncan CA 30.00 80.00
301 Kris Murray JSY AU BW 20.00 50.00
302 Amen Thompson JSY AU BW 100.00 250.00
303 Keyonte George JSY AU BW 60.00 150.00
304 Kobe Bufkin JSY AU BW 25.00 60.00
305 Brice Sensabaugh JSY AU BW 30.00 80.00
306 Kobe Brown JSY AU BW 20.00 50.00
307 Julian Strawther JSY AU BW 25.00 60.00
308 Sasha Vezenkov JSY AU BW 15.00 40.00
309 Olivier-Maxence
Prosper JSY AU BW 20.00 50.00
310 Rayan Rupert JSY AU BW RC 20.00 50.00
311 Noah Clowney JSY AU BW 25.00 60.00
312 Ausar Thompson JSY AU BW 50.00 125.00
313 Jalen Wilson JSY AU BW 20.00 50.00
314 Marcus Sasser JSY AU BW 30.00 80.00
315 Ben Sheppard JSY AU BW 20.00 50.00
316 Dereck Lively II JSY AU BW 40.00 100.00
317 Colby Jones JSY AU BW RC 20.00 50.00
318 Leonard Miller JSY AU BW 20.00 50.00
319 Hunter Tyson JSY AU BW RC 20.00 50.00
320 Jordan Walsh JSY AU BW 20.00 50.00
321 Keyontae Johnson JSY AU BW RC 20.00 50.00
322 Jalen Pickett JSY AU BW 20.00 50.00
323 Brandin Podziemski JSY AU BW 60.00 150.00
324 Seth Lundy JSY AU BW RC 15.00 40.00
325 Maxwell Lewis JSY AU BW RC 15.00 40.00
326 GG Jackson II JSY AU BW RC 40.00 100.00
327 Andre Jackson Jr. JSY AU BW 30.00 80.00
328 Julian Phillips JSY AU BW RC 20.00 50.00
329 Bilal Coulibaly JSY AU BW 50.00 125.00
330 Mouhamed Gueye JSY AU BW RC 20.00 50.00
331 Sidy Cissoko JSY AU BW RC 20.00 50.00
332 Toumani Camara JSY AU BW 40.00 100.00
333 Jaylen Clark JSY AU BW RC 20.00 50.00
334 Jalen Slawson JSY AU BW RC 20.00 50.00
335 Cason Wallace JSY AU BW 40.00 100.00
336 Isaiah Wong JSY AU BW RC 20.00 50.00
337 Chris Livingston JSY AU BW RC 20.00 50.00
338 Vasilije Micic JSY AU BW 20.00 50.00
339 Adama Sanogo JSY AU BW RC 20.00 50.00
340 Dariq Whitehead JSY AU BW 25.00 60.00
341 Kris Murray JSY AU CLR 20.00 50.00
342 Amen Thompson JSY AU CLR 100.00 250.00
343 Keyonte George JSY AU CLR 60.00 150.00
344 Kobe Bufkin JSY AU CLR 25.00 60.00
345 Brice Sensabaugh JSY AU CLR 30.00 80.00
346 Kobe Brown JSY AU CLR 20.00 50.00
347 Julian Strawther JSY AU CLR 25.00 60.00
348 Sasha Vezenkov JSY AU CLR 15.00 40.00
349 Olivier-Maxence
Prosper JSY AU CLR 20.00 50.00
350 Rayan Rupert JSY AU CLR RC 20.00 50.00
351 Noah Clowney JSY AU CLR 25.00 60.00
352 Ausar Thompson JSY AU CLR 50.00 125.00
353 Jalen Wilson JSY AU CLR RC 20.00 50.00
354 Marcus Sasser JSY AU CLR 30.00 80.00
355 Ben Sheppard JSY AU CLR 20.00 50.00
356 Dereck Lively II JSY AU CLR 40.00 100.00
357 Colby Jones JSY AU CLR RC 20.00 50.00
358 Leonard Miller JSY AU CLR 20.00 50.00
359 Hunter Tyson JSY AU CLR RC 20.00 50.00
360 Jordan Walsh JSY AU CLR 20.00 50.00
361 Keyontae Johnson JSY AU CLR RC 20.00 50.00
362 Jalen Pickett JSY AU CLR 15.00 40.00
363 Brandin Podziemski JSY AU CLR 60.00 150.00
364 Seth Lundy JSY AU CLR RC 15.00 40.00
365 Maxwell Lewis JSY AU CLR RC 15.00 40.00
366 GG Jackson II JSY AU CLR RC 40.00 100.00
367 Andre Jackson Jr. JSY AU CLR 30.00 80.00
368 Julian Phillips JSY AU CLR RC 20.00 50.00
369 Bilal Coulibaly JSY AU CLR 50.00 125.00
370 Mouhamed Gueye JSY AU CLR RC 20.00 50.00
371 Sidy Cissoko JSY AU CLR RC 20.00 50.00
372 Toumani Camara JSY AU CLR 40.00 100.00
373 Jaylen Clark JSY AU CLR RC 20.00 50.00
374 Jalen Slawson JSY AU CLR RC 20.00 50.00
375 Cason Wallace JSY AU CLR 40.00 100.00
376 Isaiah Wong JSY AU CLR RC 20.00 50.00
377 Chris Livingston JSY AU CLR RC 20.00 50.00
378 Vasilije Micic JSY AU CLR 20.00 50.00
379 Adama Sanogo JSY AU CLR RC 20.00 50.00
380 Dariq Whitehead JSY AU CLR 25.00 60.00
381 Amen Thompson AU 80.00 200.00
382 Ausar Thompson AU 40.00 100.00
383 Bilal Coulibaly AU 40.00 100.00
384 Cason Wallace AU 30.00 80.00
385 Dereck Lively II AU 30.00 80.00
386 Kobe Bufkin AU 20.00 50.00
387 Keyonte George AU 50.00 125.00
388 Brandin Podziemski AU 50.00 125.00
389 Dariq Whitehead AU RC 20.00 50.00
390 Kris Murray AU 15.00 40.00
391 Olivier-Maxence Prosper AU RC 15.00 40.00
392 Marcus Sasser AU 25.00 60.00
393 Ben Sheppard AU RC 15.00 40.00
394 Brice Sensabaugh AU RC 25.00 60.00
395 Julian Strawther AU 15.00 40.00
396 Kobe Brown AU 15.00 40.00
397 Noah Clowney AU RC 20.00 50.00
398 Jalen Pickett AU RC 15.00 40.00
399 Leonard Miller AU RC 15.00 40.00
400 Jordan Walsh AU RC 15.00 40.00

2023-24 Panini Noir Autographs Black and White

STATED PRINT RUN 35-99 SER.#'d SETS
1 Bob Pettit/49 20.00 50.00
2 Ben Wallace/49 40.00 100.00
3 Deandre Ayton/99 12.00 30.00
4 Marcus Smart/99 15.00 40.00
5 Al Horford/99 15.00 40.00
6 Zach Randolph/99 12.00 30.00
7 Ayo Dosunmu/99 12.00 30.00
8 Dale Ellis/99 12.00 30.00
12 Cole Anthony/99 12.00 30.00
13 Toni Kukoc/99 15.00 40.00
15 Hakeem Olajuwon/49 75.00 200.00
16 Kevin McHale/49 20.00 50.00
17 Jordan Poole/49 20.00 50.00
18 Peja Stojakovic/75 12.00 30.00
19 Antoine Walker/99 12.00 30.00
20 Tim Hardaway Jr./99 10.00 25.00
21 Jeff Hornacek/99 10.00 25.00
22 Lenny Wilkens/75 15.00 40.00
23 Gary Payton/49 20.00 50.00
24 James Wiseman/99 10.00 25.00
25 Markelle Fultz/99 10.00 25.00
26 Immanuel Quickley/99 12.00 30.00
27 Brook Lopez/99 10.00 25.00
28 Jason Terry/99 12.00 30.00
29 Rolando Blackman/99 10.00 25.00
30 Caron Butler/99 10.00 25.00
31 Jalen Brunson/35 75.00 200.00
32 Shawn Kemp/49 40.00 100.00
33 Joakim Noah/99 12.00 30.00
34 Bob Dandridge/99 12.00 30.00

2023-24 Panini Noir Autographs Color

STATED PRINT RUN 35-99 SER.#'d SETS
1 Bob Pettit/49 20.00 50.00
2 Ben Wallace/49 40.00 100.00
3 Deandre Ayton/99 12.00 30.00
4 Marcus Smart/99 15.00 40.00
5 Al Horford/99 15.00 40.00
6 Zach Randolph/99 12.00 30.00
7 Ayo Dosunmu/99 12.00 30.00
8 Dale Ellis/99 12.00 30.00
12 Cole Anthony/99 12.00 30.00
13 Toni Kukoc/99 15.00 40.00
15 Hakeem Olajuwon/49 75.00 200.00
16 Kevin McHale/49 20.00 50.00
17 Jordan Poole/49 20.00 50.00
18 Peja Stojakovic/75 12.00 30.00
19 Antoine Walker/99 12.00 30.00
20 Tim Hardaway Jr./99 10.00 25.00
21 Jeff Hornacek/99 10.00 25.00
22 Lenny Wilkens/75 15.00 40.00
23 Gary Payton/49 20.00 50.00
24 James Wiseman/99 10.00 25.00
25 Markelle Fultz/99 10.00 25.00
26 Immanuel Quickley/99 12.00 30.00
27 Brook Lopez/99 10.00 25.00
28 Jason Terry/99 12.00 30.00
29 Rolando Blackman/99 10.00 25.00
30 Caron Butler/99 10.00 25.00
31 Jalen Brunson/35 75.00 200.00
32 Shawn Kemp/49 40.00 100.00
33 Joakim Noah/99 12.00 30.00
34 Bob Dandridge/99 12.00 30.00

2023-24 Panini Noir Box Office Memorabilia

STATED PRINT RUN 99 SER.#'d SETS
*PRIME/3-25: 1.25X TO 3X BASE HI
NO PRICING ON QTY 10 & UNDER
1 LeBron James 40.00 100.00
2 Nikola Jokic 15.00 40.00
3 Giannis Antetokounmpo 15.00 40.00
4 Jayson Tatum 12.00 30.00
5 Trae Young 6.00 15.00
6 Shai Gilgeous-Alexander 15.00 40.00
7 Tyrese Haliburton 6.00 15.00
8 LaMelo Ball 8.00 20.00
9 Ja Morant 10.00 25.00
10 Anthony Edwards 15.00 40.00
11 Brandon Ingram 4.00 10.00
12 Kawhi Leonard 8.00 20.00
13 Jalen Green 5.00 12.00
14 Tyrese Maxey 6.00 15.00
15 Darius Garland 5.00 12.00
16 Jrue Holiday 4.00 10.00
17 Jalen Brunson 6.00 15.00
18 Cameron Thomas 4.00 10.00
19 Devin Vassell 4.00 10.00
20 Jaylen Brown 6.00 15.00
21 Alperen Sengun 5.00 12.00
22 Domantas Sabonis 5.00 12.00
23 Devin Booker 8.00 20.00
24 RJ Barrett 5.00 12.00
25 Fred VanVleet 5.00 12.00
26 Brandon Roy 4.00 10.00
27 Dirk Nowitzki 8.00 20.00
28 Patrick Ewing 5.00 12.00
29 Karl Malone 6.00 15.00
30 Tony Parker 5.00 12.00

2023-24 Panini Noir Casting Call Memorabilia

STATED PRINT RUN 99 SER.#'d SETS
*PRIME/49: .75X TO 2X BASE HI
*PRIME HOLO/25: 1.25X TO 3X BASE HI
1 Jett Howard 4.00 10.00
2 Julian Phillips 3.00 8.00
3 Kobe Brown 3.00 8.00
4 Victor Wembanyama 40.00 100.00
5 Jordan Hawkins 5.00 12.00
6 Amen Thompson 15.00 40.00
7 Dereck Lively II 6.00 15.00
8 Jarace Walker 6.00 15.00
9 Anthony Black 6.00 15.00
10 Bilal Coulibaly 8.00 20.00
11 Toumani Camara 6.00 15.00
12 Cason Wallace 6.00 15.00
13 Nick Smith Jr. 4.00 10.00
14 Colby Jones 3.00 8.00
15 Jaime Jaquez Jr. 5.00 12.00
16 Taylor Hendricks 3.00 8.00
17 Andre Jackson Jr. 5.00 12.00
18 Brandin Podziemski 10.00 25.00
19 Brandon Miller 12.00 30.00
20 Trayce Jackson-Davis 4.00 10.00
21 Amari Bailey 3.00 8.00
22 Marcus Sasser 5.00 12.00
23 Gradey Dick 6.00 15.00
24 Ben Sheppard 3.00 8.00
25 Scoot Henderson 10.00 25.00
26 Keyonte George 10.00 25.00
27 Kobe Bufkin 4.00 10.00
28 Julian Strawther 4.00 10.00
29 Emoni Bates 4.00 10.00
30 Ausar Thompson 8.00 20.00

2023-24 Panini Noir Ceremonial Orange Autographs

1 Dirk Nowitzki/49 300.00 600.00
2 Dwyane Wade/49 150.00 400.00
3 Tony Parker/25 100.00 250.00
4 Pau Gasol/49 100.00 250.00
5 Steve Nash/25 150.00 400.00
6 Paul Pierce/49 125.00 300.00
7 Kevin Garnett/49 125.00 300.00
8 Shaquille O'Neal /49 200.00 500.00
9 Jason Kidd/49 75.00 200.00
10 Tim Duncan/15 1,000.00 2,000.00

2023-24 Panini Noir Elegant Decor Rookie Jerseys

STATED PRINT RUN 99 SER.#'d SETS
*PRIME/49: .75X TO 2X BASE HI
*PRIME HOLO/25: 1.25X TO 3X BASE HI
1 Ausar Thompson 8.00 20.00
2 Kobe Brown 3.00 8.00
3 Jarace Walker 6.00 15.00
4 Trayce Jackson-Davis 4.00 10.00
5 Toumani Camara 6.00 15.00
6 Jalen Pickett 2.50 6.00
7 Taylor Hendricks 3.00 8.00
8 Cam Whitmore 8.00 20.00
9 Jordan Hawkins 5.00 12.00
10 Andre Jackson Jr. 5.00 12.00
11 Marcus Sasser 5.00 12.00
12 Keyonte George 10.00 25.00
13 Jaime Jaquez Jr. 5.00 12.00
14 Cason Wallace 6.00 15.00
15 Ben Sheppard 3.00 8.00
16 Brandon Miller 12.00 30.00
17 Julian Strawther 4.00 10.00
18 Victor Wembanyama 40.00 100.00
19 Dereck Lively II 6.00 15.00
20 Jett Howard 4.00 10.00
21 Amen Thompson 15.00 40.00
22 Amari Bailey 3.00 8.00
23 Bilal Coulibaly 8.00 20.00
24 Nick Smith Jr. 4.00 10.00
25 Brandin Podziemski 10.00 25.00
26 Scoot Henderson 10.00 25.00
27 Gradey Dick 6.00 15.00
28 Anthony Black 6.00 15.00
29 Olivier-Maxence Prosper 3.00 8.00
30 Kris Murray 3.00 8.00

2023-24 Panini Noir Emblazoned Ink

1 De'Aaron Fox/75 150.00 400.00
2 Anthony Edwards/49 800.00 1,500.00
3 Ausar Thompson/49 125.00 300.00
4 Amen Thompson/49 200.00 500.00
5 Cason Wallace/99 125.00 300.00
6 Tyrese Maxey/49 150.00 400.00
7 Paolo Banchero /49 300.00 600.00
8 Jalen Brunson/49 150.00 400.00
9 Donovan Mitchell/49 200.00 500.00
10 Stephen Curry/25 1,500.00 3,000.00
11 Bilal Coulibaly/99 150.00 400.00
12 Michael Porter Jr./99 15.00 40.00
13 Magic Johnson/49 125.00 300.00
14 Tyrese Haliburton/49 150.00 400.00
15 Dereck Lively II/75 125.00 300.00
16 Brice Sensabaugh/99 50.00 120.00
17 Gary Payton/49 100.00 250.00
18 Kris Murray/99 50.00 120.00
19 Kobe Brown/99 50.00 120.00
20 Jordan Walsh/99 50.00 120.00
21 Ja Morant/25 1,000.00 2,000.00
22 Dennis Rodman/49 200.00 500.00
23 Tim Duncan/25 1,000.00 2,000.00
24 CJ McCollum/49 500.00 120.00
25 Amar'e Stoudemire/75 60.00 150.00

2023-24 Panini Noir Freeze Frame Signatures

STATED PRINT RUN 25-99 SER.#'d SETS
*GOLD/25: .5X TO 1.25X BASE HI
1 Amar'e Stoudemire/49 15.00 40.00
2 Alperen Sengun/49 40.00 100.00
3 Robert Parish/99 15.00 40.00
4 Josh Giddey/25 15.00 40.00
5 Immanuel Quickley/99 12.00 30.00
6 Bobby Portis/99 15.00 40.00
7 Chris Mullin/99 15.00 40.00
8 Markelle Fultz/99 10.00 25.00
10 Antawn Jamison/99 12.00 30.00
11 Clyde Drexler/75 30.00 80.00
12 Dave Bing/99 15.00 40.00
13 Mike Bibby/99 12.00 30.00
14 Alonzo Mourning/49 40.00 100.00
15 Desmond Bane/25 15.00 40.00
16 Julius Erving/25 75.00 200.00
17 Alex English/99 15.00 40.00
18 Stephen Jackson/99 10.00 25.00
19 Bob Pettit/49 15.00 40.00
20 Dirk Nowitzki/49 100.00 250.00
22 Christian Braun/99 12.00 30.00
23 Dejounte Murray/75 15.00 40.00
24 Kevin McHale/49 20.00 50.00
25 Jaren Jackson Jr./49 25.00 60.00
26 Jonathan Kuminga/99 30.00 80.00
27 Devin Vassell/99 20.00 50.00
28 Jeremy Sochan/99 15.00 40.00
29 Ochai Agbaji/99 12.00 30.00
30 Dan Issel/99 15.00 40.00
31 Dwyane Wade/25 100.00 250.00
32 Karl Malone/25 60.00 150.00
33 Deandre Ayton/75 12.00 30.00
34 RJ Barrett/49 20.00 50.00
35 Malik Beasley/99 12.00 30.00
36 Herbert Jones/99 12.00 30.00
38 Larry Johnson/99 15.00 40.00
39 Dorian Finney-Smith/99 10.00 25.00
40 Fat Lever/99 12.00 30.00

2023-24 Panini Noir Game Night Jerseys

STATED PRINT RUN 99 SER.#'d SETS
*PRIME/4-25: 1.25X TO 3X BASE HI
NO PRICING ON QTY 20 & UNDER
1 Zach LaVine 5.00 12.00
2 Devin Booker 8.00 20.00
3 Zion Williamson 8.00 20.00
4 Keldon Johnson 4.00 10.00
5 Ja Morant 25.00 60.00
6 LeBron James 40.00 100.00
7 Jimmy Butler 5.00 12.00
8 Jaylen Brown 6.00 15.00
9 Darius Garland 5.00 12.00
10 Damian Lillard 8.00 20.00
11 Shai Gilgeous-Alexander 20.00 50.00
12 Kawhi Leonard 8.00 20.00
13 Jayson Tatum 12.00 30.00
14 Trae Young 6.00 15.00
15 Joel Embiid 8.00 20.00
16 Russell Westbrook 5.00 12.00
17 DeMar DeRozan 5.00 12.00
18 Anfernee Simons 4.00 10.00
19 Fred VanVleet 5.00 12.00
20 Klay Thompson 8.00 20.00

2023-24 Panini Noir Jumbo Material

STATED PRINT RUN 99 SER.#'d SETS
1 Giannis Antetokounmpo 25.00 60.00
2 De'Aaron Fox 10.00 25.00
3 Kyle Kuzma 6.00 15.00
4 Damian Lillard 12.00 30.00
5 Desmond Bane 6.00 15.00
6 Scottie Barnes 6.00 15.00
7 Bam Adebayo 8.00 20.00
8 Anfernee Simons 6.00 15.00
9 Darius Garland 8.00 20.00
10 LaMelo Ball 12.00 30.00
11 Pascal Siakam 8.00 20.00
12 Jimmy Butler 8.00 20.00
13 Kristaps Porzingis 6.00 15.00
14 Bradley Beal 6.00 15.00
15 Jamal Murray 10.00 25.00
16 Domantas Sabonis 8.00 20.00
17 Paul George 8.00 20.00
18 Joel Embiid 12.00 30.00
20 Keldon Johnson 6.00 15.00

2023-24 Panini Noir Jumbo Material

21 Tyrese Maxey 10.00 25.00
22 Michael Porter Jr. 6.00 15.00
23 LeBron James 60.00 150.00
24 Tyrese Haliburton 10.00 25.00
25 Brandon Ingram 6.00 15.00
26 Karl-Anthony Towns 8.00 20.00
27 Khris Middleton 5.00 12.00
28 Cade Cunningham 12.00 30.00
29 Tyler Herro 8.00 20.00
30 Devin Booker 12.00 30.00
31 Draymond Green 6.00 15.00
32 Zach LaVine 8.00 20.00
33 Jordan Poole 8.00 20.00
34 Jrue Holiday 6.00 15.00
35 Jordan Clarkson 5.00 12.00
36 Grant Williams 4.00 10.00
37 Andrew Wiggins 6.00 15.00
38 Jayson Tatum 20.00 50.00
39 Russell Westbrook 8.00 20.00
40 Kawhi Leonard 12.00 30.00
41 Devin Vassell 6.00 15.00
42 Mikal Bridges 6.00 15.00
43 Paolo Banchero 12.00 30.00
44 Kyrie Irving 10.00 25.00
45 Fred VanVleet 8.00 20.00
46 Jalen Brunson 10.00 25.00
47 Bojan Bogdanovic 5.00 12.00
48 Shai Gilgeous-Alexander 25.00 60.00
49 Shaedon Sharpe 10.00 25.00
50 Klay Thompson 12.00 30.00
51 DeMar DeRozan 8.00 20.00
52 Terry Rozier III 6.00 15.00
53 Alperen Sengun 8.00 20.00
54 Franz Wagner 8.00 20.00
55 Cameron Johnson 5.00 12.00
56 Julius Randle 6.00 15.00
57 Lauri Markkanen 8.00 20.00
58 Jaren Jackson Jr. 8.00 20.00
59 Cameron Thomas 6.00 15.00
60 Jaylen Brown 10.00 25.00

2023-24 Panini Noir Midnight Signatures
STATED PRINT RUN 25-99 SER.#'d SETS
*HOLO GOLD/10-25: .5X TO 1.25X BASE HI
NO PRICING ON QTY 10
1 Paul George/49 125.00 300.00
2 Rasheed Wallace/75 60.00 150.00
3 Jason Kidd/49 60.00 150.00
4 Dennis Rodman/75 150.00 400.00
5 Jaren Jackson Jr./99 40.00 100.00
6 Jason Williams/99 75.00 200.00
7 Alperen Sengun/49 75.00 200.00
8 Tony Parker/25 75.00 200.00
10 Charles Barkley/25 125.00 300.00
11 Kevin Garnett/25 125.00 300.00
12 Damian Lillard/49 200.00 500.00
13 Paul Pierce/49 75.00 200.00
14 Anfernee Hardaway/75 100.00 250.00
15 Brandon Roy/25 125.00 300.00
16 Donovan Mitchell/25 125.00 300.00
17 Ausar Thompson/25 100.00 250.00
18 Amen Thompson/25 150.00 400.00
19 Cason Wallace/25 100.00 250.00
20 Bilal Coulibaly/25 100.00 250.00

2023-24 Panini Noir NBA Finals Memorabilia
1 Andre Iguodala/99 25.00 60.00
2 Chris Bosh/85 25.00 60.00
3 Fred VanVleet/90 40.00 100.00
4 Harrison Barnes/30 25.00 60.00
5 Kawhi Leonard/99 40.00 100.00
6 Kawhi Leonard/99 75.00 200.00
7 Kevin Durant/99 40.00 100.00
8 Kevin Love/47 25.00 60.00
9 Klay Thompson/99 40.00 100.00
10 Kyrie Irving/99 40.00 100.00
11 LeBron James/99 200.00 500.00
12 Norman Powell/99 40.00 100.00
13 Tim Duncan/30 50.00 120.00
14 Tony Parker/99 40.00 100.00
16 Andre Iguodala/86 25.00 60.00

2023-24 Panini Noir NBA Finals Memorabilia Prime
17 Manu Ginobili/25 125.00 300.00

2023-24 Panini Noir New Wave Jerseys
STATED PRINT RUN 99 SER.#'d SETS
*PRIME/25: 1.25X TO 3X BASE HI
1 Jaime Jaquez Jr. 5.00 12.00
2 Keyonte George 10.00 25.00
3 Ausar Thompson 8.00 20.00
4 Ben Sheppard 3.00 8.00
5 Noah Clowney 4.00 10.00
6 Jalen Hood-Schifino 3.00 8.00
7 Trayce Jackson-Davis 4.00 10.00
8 Kobe Brown 3.00 8.00
9 Andre Jackson Jr. 5.00 12.00
10 Nick Smith Jr. 4.00 10.00
11 Jarace Walker 6.00 15.00
12 Kris Murray 3.00 8.00
13 Olivier-Maxence Prosper 3.00 8.00
14 Gradey Dick 6.00 15.00
15 Toumani Camara 6.00 15.00
16 Julian Strawther 4.00 10.00
17 Anthony Black 6.00 15.00
18 Victor Wembanyama 40.00 100.00
19 Cason Wallace 6.00 15.00
20 Dereck Lively II 6.00 15.00
21 Marcus Sasser 5.00 12.00
22 Scoot Henderson 10.00 25.00
23 Kobe Bufkin 4.00 10.00
24 Jett Howard 4.00 10.00
25 Brandon Miller 12.00 30.00
26 Brandin Podziemski 10.00 25.00
27 Amen Thompson 15.00 40.00
28 Bilal Coulibaly 8.00 20.00
29 Taylor Hendricks 3.00 8.00
30 Jordan Hawkins 5.00 12.00

2023-24 Panini Noir Night Lights Autographs
1 Charles Barkley 100.00 250.00
2 Dominique Wilkins 50.00 120.00
3 Tyrese Haliburton 200.00 500.00
4 Magic Johnson 125.00 300.00
5 Shai Gilgeous-Alexander 800.00 1,500.00
6 Paolo Banchero 300.00 600.00
7 Chris Paul 200.00 500.00
8 Ja Morant 800.00 1,500.00
9 Allen Iverson 200.00 500.00
10 Karl-Anthony Towns 75.00 200.00

2023-24 Panini Noir Prequel Memorabilia
STATED PRINT RUN 99 SER.#'d SETS
*PRIME/10-25: 1.25X TO 3X BASE HI
1 LeBron James 40.00 100.00
3 Anthony Davis 8.00 20.00
4 Julius Randle 4.00 10.00
5 Kevin Durant 10.00 25.00
6 Damian Lillard 8.00 20.00
7 Russell Westbrook 5.00 12.00
8 Jimmy Butler 5.00 12.00
9 Brandon Ingram 4.00 10.00
10 Bradley Beal 4.00 10.00
11 Deandre Ayton 3.00 8.00
12 Zach LaVine 5.00 12.00
13 Kawhi Leonard 8.00 20.00
14 Donovan Mitchell 6.00 15.00
15 Chris Paul 6.00 15.00
16 Kristaps Porzingis 4.00 10.00
17 D'Angelo Russell 3.00 8.00
18 Kyrie Irving 6.00 15.00
19 Jrue Holiday 4.00 10.00
20 Lauri Markkanen 5.00 12.00

2023-24 Panini Noir Prime Material Autographs Black and White
1 Brandon Ingram/25 25.00 60.00
2 RJ Barrett/25 40.00 100.00
3 De'Aaron Fox/15 100.00 250.00
4 Jaden Hardy/25 25.00 60.00
5 Onyeka Okongwu/49 12.00 30.00
6 Seth Curry/49 15.00 40.00
7 Alperen Sengun/35 75.00 200.00
8 Franz Wagner/49 60.00 150.00
9 Alonzo Mourning/25 100.00 250.00
10 Josh Giddey/15 30.00 80.00
11 Bradley Beal/35 30.00 80.00
12 Larry Bird/25 125.00 300.00
13 Joakim Noah/49 25.00 60.00
14 Zach Randolph/49 25.00 60.00
15 Michael Porter Jr./15 20.00 50.00

2023-24 Panini Noir Prime Material Autographs Color
1 Brandon Ingram/25 25.00 60.00
2 RJ Barrett/25 40.00 100.00
3 De'Aaron Fox/15 100.00 250.00
4 Jaden Hardy/25 25.00 60.00
5 Onyeka Okongwu/49 12.00 30.00
6 Seth Curry/49 15.00 40.00
7 Alperen Sengun/25 75.00 200.00
8 Franz Wagner/49 60.00 150.00
9 Alonzo Mourning/19 100.00 250.00
10 Josh Giddey/15 30.00 80.00
11 Bradley Beal/35 30.00 80.00
12 Larry Bird/25 125.00 300.00
13 Joakim Noah/49 25.00 60.00
14 Zach Randolph/49 25.00 60.00
15 Michael Porter Jr./15 20.00 50.00

2023-24 Panini Noir Reigning Nights Signatures
STATED PRINT RUN 25-99 SER.#'d SETS
*GOLD/25: .5X TO 1.25X BASE HI
1 Jason Terry/99 12.00 30.00
2 Karl-Anthony Towns/49 40.00 100.00
3 RJ Barrett/75 20.00 50.00
4 Max Strus/49 12.00 30.00
5 Jalen Williams/99 100.00 250.00
6 Jordan Poole/75 20.00 50.00
7 Jrue Holiday/99 30.00 80.00
8 Michael Porter Jr./49 15.00 40.00
9 Jordan Clarkson/99 12.00 30.00
11 Derek Fisher/99 12.00 30.00
12 Donte DiVincenzo/99 12.00 30.00
13 Bennedict Mathurin/99 40.00 100.00
14 Dell Curry/99 12.00 30.00
16 Nick Van Exel/99 15.00 40.00
17 Franz Wagner/49 40.00 100.00
18 Manu Ginobili/25 75.00 200.00
19 B.J. Armstrong/99 12.00 30.00
20 Rick Barry/99 15.00 40.00
22 Ray Allen/25 75.00 200.00
23 Kevin Huerter/99 10.00 25.00
24 Dirk Nowitzki/25 150.00 400.00
25 Tony Parker/25 60.00 150.00
26 Steve Kerr/99 15.00 40.00
27 Peja Stojakovic/99 12.00 30.00
28 Lauri Markkanen/99 20.00 50.00
29 Bobby Portis/99 15.00 40.00
30 Mike Bibby/99 12.00 30.00

2023-24 Panini Noir Rookie Jumbo Material
STATED PRINT RUN 99 SER.#'d SETS
1 Nick Smith Jr. 3.00 8.00
2 Olivier-Maxence Prosper 2.50 6.00
3 Anthony Black 5.00 12.00
4 Keyonte George 8.00 20.00
5 Julian Strawther 3.00 8.00
6 Chris Livingston 2.50 6.00
7 Taylor Hendricks 2.50 6.00
8 Scoot Henderson 8.00 20.00
9 Toumani Camara 5.00 12.00
10 Jalen Slawson 2.50 6.00
11 Amen Thompson 12.00 30.00
12 Jordan Hawkins 4.00 10.00
13 Cam Whitmore 6.00 15.00
14 Jaime Jaquez Jr. 4.00 10.00
15 Jarace Walker 5.00 12.00
16 Dereck Lively II 5.00 12.00
17 Ben Sheppard 2.50 6.00
18 Trayce Jackson-Davis 3.00 8.00
19 Kobe Brown 2.50 6.00
20 Amari Bailey 2.50 6.00
21 Cason Wallace 5.00 12.00
22 Bilal Coulibaly 6.00 15.00
23 Jalen Pickett 2.00 5.00
24 Jett Howard 3.00 8.00
25 Ausar Thompson 6.00 15.00
26 Andre Jackson Jr. 4.00 10.00
27 Marcus Sasser 4.00 10.00
28 Victor Wembanyama 60.00 150.00
29 Kris Murray 2.50 6.00
30 Rayan Rupert 2.50 6.00
31 Kobe Bufkin 3.00 8.00
32 Dariq Whitehead 3.00 8.00
33 Brandin Podziemski 8.00 20.00
34 Jordan Miller 3.00 8.00
35 Maxwell Lewis 2.00 5.00
36 Brandon Miller 10.00 25.00
37 Colby Jones 2.50 6.00
38 Gradey Dick 5.00 12.00
39 Emoni Bates 3.00 8.00
40 Julian Phillips 2.50 6.00

2023-24 Panini Noir Screenplay Jerseys
STATED PRINT RUN 49-99 SER.#'d SETS
*PRIME/10-25: 1.25X TO 3X BASE HI
1 Trae Young/99 6.00 15.00
2 Scottie Barnes/99 4.00 10.00
3 De'Aaron Fox/99 6.00 15.00
4 Zion Williamson/99 8.00 20.00
5 Mikal Bridges/99 4.00 10.00
6 Franz Wagner/99 5.00 12.00
7 Kyrie Irving/99 6.00 15.00
8 Paul George/99 5.00 12.00
9 Aaron Gordon/99 3.00 8.00
10 Kyle Kuzma/99 4.00 10.00
11 Karl-Anthony Towns/99 5.00 12.00
12 Jamal Murray/99 6.00 15.00
13 Kawhi Leonard/99 8.00 20.00
14 Jayson Tatum/99 12.00 30.00
15 Donovan Mitchell/99 6.00 15.00
16 Tyrese Haliburton/99 6.00 15.00
17 Evan Mobley/99 5.00 12.00
18 LeBron James/99 40.00 100.00
19 Joel Embiid/99 8.00 20.00
20 Anthony Edwards/99 15.00 40.00
21 Khris Middleton/99 3.00 8.00
22 Jaren Jackson Jr./99 5.00 12.00
23 Kevin Durant/99 10.00 25.00
24 Jaylen Brown/99 6.00 15.00
25 Anthony Davis/99 8.00 20.00
26 Ben Simmons/99 3.00 8.00
27 Terry Rozier III/99 4.00 10.00
28 Giannis Antetokounmpo/99 15.00 40.00
29 Jimmy Butler/99 5.00 12.00
30 LaMelo Ball/99 8.00 20.00
32 Tyler Herro/99 5.00 12.00
33 Josh Giddey/99 4.00 10.00
34 Julius Randle/99 4.00 10.00
35 John Collins/99 3.00 8.00
36 Carmelo Anthony/99 5.00 12.00
37 Patrick Ewing/99 5.00 12.00
38 Tim Duncan/49 15.00 40.00
39 Paul Pierce/99 5.00 12.00
40 Dwyane Wade/99 8.00 20.00

2023-24 Panini Noir Shadow Signatures
STATED PRINT RUN 25-99 SER.#'d SETS
*GOLD/25: .5X TO 1.25X BASE HI
1 Anthony Edwards/49 600.00 1,200.00
2 Ausar Thompson/49 60.00 150.00
3 Amen Thompson/49 125.00 300.00
4 Cason Wallace/49 60.00 150.00
5 Russell Westbrook/25 200.00 500.00
6 Ja Morant/25 500.00 1,000.00
7 Isiah Thomas/49 20.00 50.00
8 Zion Williamson/25 125.00 300.00
9 Tracy McGrady/49 150.00 400.00
10 Shawn Kemp/99 40.00 100.00
11 Jamal Murray/25 100.00 250.00
12 Clyde Drexler/49 40.00 100.00
13 Kobe Bufkin/49 40.00 100.00
14 Noah Clowney/99 15.00 40.00
15 Olivier-Maxence Prosper/99 40.00 100.00
16 Ben Sheppard/99 12.00 30.00
17 Jason Williams/99 75.00 200.00
18 Luka Doncic/25 1,000.00 2,000.00
19 Jaden Ivey/35 75.00 200.00
20 Dennis Rodman/25 150.00 400.00
21 Shaedon Sharpe/49 75.00 200.00
22 Bilal Coulibaly/99 100.00 250.00
23 Keyonte George/75 100.00 250.00
24 Brandin Podziemski/99 60.00 150.00
25 Dereck Lively II/99 75.00 200.00
26 Julian Strawther/99 40.00 100.00
27 Josh Giddey/25 50.00 120.00
28 Desmond Bane/99 30.00 80.00
29 Jordan Clarkson/99 20.00 50.00
30 Marcus Sasser/99 20.00 50.00
31 Dariq Whitehead/75 15.00 40.00
32 GG Jackson II/99 125.00 300.00
33 Ben Wallace/49 40.00 100.00
34 Julius Erving/25 100.00 250.00
35 Derek Fisher/99 12.00 30.00
36 Alex English/99 15.00 40.00
37 Brandon Roy/25 100.00 250.00
38 Brice Sensabaugh/99 20.00 50.00
39 Kobe Brown/99 12.00 30.00
40 Rayan Rupert/99 12.00 30.00

2023-24 Panini Noir Showtime Signatures
1 Dereck Lively II/49 75.00 200.00
2 Ausar Thompson/49 60.00 150.00
3 Amen Thompson/49 125.00 300.00
4 Bilal Coulibaly/99 75.00 200.00
5 Noah Clowney/99 15.00 40.00
6 Kobe Bufkin/75 40.00 100.00
7 Leonard Miller/99 12.00 30.00
8 Mouhamed Gueye/99 12.00 30.00
9 Keyonte George/49 75.00 200.00
10 Cason Wallace/49 60.00 150.00
11 Julian Phillips/99 12.00 30.00
12 Brandin Podziemski/99 60.00 150.00
13 Olivier-Maxence Prosper/99 12.00 30.00
14 Amari Bailey/99 12.00 30.00
15 Rayan Rupert/99 12.00 30.00
16 Kobe Brown/99 12.00 30.00
17 Sidy Cissoko/99 12.00 30.00
18 Chris Livingston/99 12.00 30.00
19 Kris Murray/49 12.00 30.00
20 Jalen Wilson/99 12.00 30.00

2023-24 Panini Noir Silver Screen Debut Signatures
1 Amen Thompson/49 100.00 250.00
2 GG Jackson II/99 50.00 120.00
3 Brandin Podziemski/99 40.00 100.00
4 Bilal Coulibaly/75 60.00 150.00
5 Dariq Whitehead/75 15.00 40.00
6 Rayan Rupert/99 12.00 30.00
7 Maxwell Lewis/99 10.00 25.00
8 Ausar Thompson/49 60.00 150.00
9 Sidy Cissoko/99 12.00 30.00
10 Jordan Walsh/99 12.00 30.00
11 Keyontae Johnson/99 12.00 30.00
12 Kris Murray/75 12.00 30.00
13 Cason Wallace/49 25.00 60.00
14 Hunter Tyson/99 12.00 30.00
15 Kobe Bufkin/99 15.00 40.00
16 Brice Sensabaugh/75 20.00 50.00
17 Kobe Brown/99 12.00 30.00
18 Dereck Lively II/99 25.00 60.00
19 Keyonte George/49 40.00 100.00
20 Noah Clowney/99 15.00 40.00
21 Ben Sheppard/99 12.00 30.00
22 Jalen Pickett/99 10.00 25.00
23 Sasha Vezenkov/99 10.00 25.00
24 Vasilije Micic/99 12.00 30.00
25 Toumani Camara/99 25.00 60.00
26 Olivier-Maxence Prosper/99 12.00 30.00
27 Marcus Sasser/99 20.00 50.00
28 Julian Strawther/99 15.00 40.00
29 Mouhamed Gueye/99 15.00 40.00
30 Trayce Jackson-Davis/99 15.00 40.00

2023-24 Panini Noir Snapshot Signatures
2 Tony Allen/99 8.00 20.00
3 Chauncey Billups/99 15.00 40.00
4 CJ McCollum/49 12.00 30.00
5 Jabari Smith Jr./49 20.00 50.00
6 Bob Dandridge/99 12.00 30.00
7 Franz Wagner/99 40.00 100.00
8 James Wiseman/49 10.00 25.00
9 Karl Malone/25 40.00 100.00
10 Steve Kerr/99 15.00 40.00
11 Jaden Ivey/25 40.00 100.00
12 Dominique Wilkins/49 20.00 50.00
13 Brook Lopez/99 10.00 25.00
14 Anfernee Hardaway/49 60.00 150.00
15 Calvin Murphy/99 12.00 30.00
16 Nate Archibald/99 15.00 40.00
17 Lauri Markkanen/99 20.00 50.00
18 Artis Gilmore/99 15.00 40.00
19 Onyeka Okongwu/99 10.00 25.00
20 Nikola Jokic/25 200.00 500.00
23 Jalen Williams/99 75.00 200.00
24 Jalen Duren/49 15.00 40.00
25 Isiah Thomas/99 20.00 50.00
27 Marcus Smart/75 15.00 40.00
28 Cole Anthony/75 12.00 30.00
29 Al Horford/99 12.00 30.00
30 Charles Oakley/99 12.00 30.00

2023-24 Panini Noir Sneaker Spotlight
1 Victor Wembanyama 1,000.00 2,000.00
2 Scoot Henderson 125.00 300.00
3 Brandon Miller 300.00 600.00
4 Anthony Black 100.00 250.00
5 Gradey Dick 100.00 250.00
6 Jordan Hawkins 75.00 200.00
7 Cam Whitmore 100.00 250.00
8 Jett Howard 75.00 200.00
9 Devin Booker 100.00 250.00
10 Giannis Antetokounmpo 100.00 250.00
11 Joel Embiid 100.00 250.00
12 LeBron James 300.00 600.00
13 Kevin Durant 125.00 300.00
14 DeMar DeRozan 100.00 250.00
15 Jayson Tatum 100.00 250.00

2023-24 Panini Noir Sneaker Spotlight Signatures
1 Donovan Mitchell/99 500.00 1,000.00
2 Russell Westbrook/99 500.00 1,000.00
3 Stephen Curry/75 2,000.00 4,000.00
4 Gilbert Arenas/99 200.00 500.00
5 Rasheed Wallace/99 150.00 400.00
6 Klay Thompson/75 500.00 1,000.00
7 Manu Ginobili/99 300.00 600.00
8 Damian Lillard/99 400.00 800.00
9 De'Aaron Fox/99 400.00 800.00
11 Amen Thompson/99 600.00 1,200.00
12 Luka Doncic/99 1,500.00 3,000.00
13 Brandin Podziemski/99 400.00 800.00
14 Chris Paul/75 500.00 1,000.00
15 Paul Pierce/99 200.00 500.00
16 Pau Gasol/99 300.00 600.00
17 Domantas Sabonis/99 200.00 500.00
18 Nikola Jokic/99 500.00 1,000.00
19 Bilal Coulibaly/99 400.00 800.00
20 Tracy McGrady/75 1,000.00 2,000.00
21 Jaren Jackson Jr./99 200.00 500.00
22 Cade Cunningham/75 500.00 1,000.00
23 Carmelo Anthony/99 1,000.00 2,000.00
24 Paul George/99 500.00 1,000.00
25 Zach LaVine/99 300.00 600.00
26 Ben Wallace/99 150.00 400.00
27 Jonathan Kuminga/99 300.00 800.00
28 Yao Ming/99 1,500.00 3,000.00
29 Ausar Thompson/99 400.00 800.00
30 Karl-Anthony Towns/99 400.00 800.00
31 Zion Williamson/75 500.00 1,000.00
32 Josh Giddey/99 200.00 500.00
33 Cason Wallace/99 400.00 800.00
34 Keyonte George/99 500.00 1,000.00
35 Yuta Watanabe/99 125.00 300.00
36 Tony Parker/99 200.00 500.00
37 Ja Morant/99 1,000.00 2,000.00
38 Jaden Ivey/99 200.00 500.00
39 Ben Simmons/99 200.00 500.00
40 Dirk Nowitzki/99 600.00 1,200.00
41 Jaden Hardy/99 150.00 400.00
42 Anthony Davis/99 500.00 1,000.00
43 Tyrese Maxey/99 800.00 1,500.00
44 Brandon Roy/49 300.00 600.00
45 James Harden/99 600.00 1,200.00
46 Alonzo Mourning/99 300.00 600.00
47 Ray Allen/99 300.00 600.00
48 Dejounte Murray/99 200.00 500.00
49 Steve Nash/99 300.00 600.00
50 Keldon Johnson/99 125.00 300.00

2023-24 Panini Noir Spotlight
1 LeBron James 75.00 200.00
2 Jayson Tatum 40.00 100.00
3 Devin Booker 30.00 80.00
4 Giannis Antetokounmpo 40.00 100.00
5 Joel Embiid 20.00 50.00
6 Wilt Chamberlain 25.00 60.00
7 Drazen Petrovic 20.00 50.00
8 Pete Maravich 20.00 50.00
9 Patrick Ewing 20.00 50.00
10 Vince Carter 40.00 100.00
11 Damian Lillard 25.00 60.00
12 Cam Whitmore 25.00 60.00
13 Jaime Jaquez Jr. 25.00 60.00
14 Victor Wembanyama 200.00 500.00
15 Jordan Hawkins 20.00 50.00
16 Gradey Dick 25.00 60.00
17 Anthony Black 25.00 60.00
18 Jarace Walker 20.00 50.00
19 Brandon Miller 100.00 250.00
20 Scoot Henderson 40.00 100.00

2023-24 Panini Noir Spotlight Signatures Horizontal
1 Ausar Thompson/99 200.00 500.00
2 Luka Doncic/75 1,000.00 2,000.00
3 Tyrese Haliburton/99 400.00 800.00
4 Jamal Murray/99 125.00 300.00
5 Jalen Brunson/99 150.00 400.00
6 Bilal Coulibaly/99 200.00 500.00
7 Julius Erving/99 125.00 300.00
8 Julian Strawther/99 75.00 200.00
9 Kareem Abdul-Jabbar/99 150.00 400.00
10 Larry Bird/75 200.00 500.00
11 Dariq Whitehead/99 60.00 150.00
12 Kobe Bufkin/99 125.00 300.00
13 Anthony Edwards/75 1,000.00 2,000.00
14 Alonzo Mourning/99 125.00 300.00
15 Shai Gilgeous-Alexander/99 1,500.00 3,000.00
16 Tyrese Maxey/99 500.00 1,000.00
17 Noah Clowney/99 125.00 300.00
18 Jrue Holiday/99 125.00 300.00
19 Desmond Bane/99 100.00 250.00
20 Carmelo Anthony/49 500.00 1,000.00

2023-24 Panini Noir Spotlight Signatures Vertical
1 Amen Thompson/99 400.00 800.00
SSVNKG Nikola Jokic/75 400.00 800.00
3 James Harden/75 400.00 800.00
4 Paolo Banchero /49 400.00 800.00
5 Cason Wallace/99 150.00 400.00
6 Alperen Sengun/99 150.00 400.00
7 Dereck Lively II/99 200.00 500.00
8 Hakeem Olajuwon/99 150.00 400.00
9 Josh Giddey/99 100.00 250.00
11 Keyonte George/99 200.00 500.00
12 Anfernee Hardaway/99 150.00 400.00
13 Russell Westbrook/99 200.00 500.00
14 Allen Iverson/99 300.00 600.00
15 Brandin Podziemski/99 150.00 400.00
17 Yao Ming/99 1,000.00 2,000.00
18 Manu Ginobili/99 150.00 400.00
19 Kris Murray/99 50.00 120.00
20 Tracy McGrady/75 400.00 800.00

2023-24 Panini Noir Stars and Stripes Gear
1 Allen Iverson/99 20.00 50.00
2 Dwyane Wade/99 10.00 25.00
3 Carmelo Anthony/99 8.00 20.00
4 Chris Paul/99 10.00 25.00
5 Clyde Drexler/99 8.00 20.00
6 David Robinson/99 10.00 25.00
7 Jason Kidd/99 8.00 20.00
8 Dominique Wilkins/99 8.00 20.00
9 Magic Johnson/15 20.00 50.00
10 Larry Bird/99 20.00 50.00

2023-24 Panini Noir Stars and Stripes Gear Autographs
1 Carmelo Anthony 150.00 400.00
2 Dwyane Wade 150.00 400.00
3 Larry Bird 125.00 300.00
4 Magic Johnson 125.00 300.00
5 Ray Allen 125.00 300.00
6 Allen Iverson 150.00 400.00
7 Chris Paul 125.00 300.00
8 Karl Malone 100.00 250.00
9 Kevin Garnett 125.00 300.00
10 Shaquille O'Neal 150.00 400.00

2019-20 Panini Obsidian
1 Luka Doncic 20.00 50.00
2 Damian Lillard 8.00 20.00
3 Stephen Curry 25.00 60.00
4 Fred VanVleet 4.00 10.00
5 Kawhi Leonard 8.00 20.00
6 Goran Dragic 2.50 6.00
7 Trae Young 8.00 20.00
8 Jrue Holiday 4.00 10.00
9 Terry Rozier 2.50 6.00
10 Evan Fournier 2.50 6.00
11 Kristaps Porzingis 4.00 10.00
12 CJ McCollum 3.00 8.00
13 Klay Thompson 8.00 20.00
14 Kyle Lowry 3.00 8.00
15 Lou Williams 3.00 8.00
16 Jimmy Butler 6.00 15.00
17 Jabari Parker 2.00 5.00
18 Lonzo Ball 3.00 8.00
19 Devonte' Graham 2.50 6.00
20 Aaron Gordon 3.00 8.00
21 Tim Hardaway Jr. 2.00 5.00
22 Anfernee Simons 5.00 12.00
23 D'Angelo Russell 2.50 6.00
24 Pascal Siakam 5.00 12.00
25 Paul George 5.00 12.00
26 Bam Adebayo 5.00 12.00
27 John Collins 3.00 8.00
28 JJ Redick 3.00 8.00
29 Miles Bridges 3.00 8.00
30 Nikola Vucevic 2.50 6.00
31 Seth Curry 2.50 6.00
32 Hassan Whiteside 2.00 5.00
33 Draymond Green 4.00 10.00
34 Marc Gasol 3.00 8.00
35 Montrezl Harrell 2.50 6.00
36 Justise Winslow 2.00 5.00
37 Vince Carter 6.00 15.00
38 Brandon Ingram 3.00 8.00
39 Cody Zeller 2.00 5.00
40 Jonathan Isaac 3.00 8.00
41 J.J. Barea 2.50 6.00
42 Carmelo Anthony 5.00 12.00
43 Willie Cauley-Stein 2.00 5.00
44 Norman Powell 2.50 6.00
45 Patrick Beverley 2.50 6.00
46 Meyers Leonard 2.00 5.00
47 Kevin Huerter 3.00 8.00
48 Derrick Favors 2.00 5.00
49 Malik Monk 3.00 8.00
50 D.J. Augustin 2.00 5.00
51 Jamal Murray 5.00 12.00
52 De'Aaron Fox 5.00 12.00
53 Russell Westbrook 5.00 12.00
54 Donovan Mitchell 6.00 15.00
55 LeBron James 25.00 60.00
56 Eric Bledsoe 2.50 6.00
57 Kemba Walker 2.50 6.00
58 Marcus Morris Sr. 2.00 5.00
59 Zach LaVine 5.00 12.00
60 Ben Simmons 3.00 8.00
61 Gary Harris 2.50 6.00
62 Buddy Hield 2.50 6.00
63 James Harden 6.00 15.00
64 Rudy Gobert 4.00 10.00
65 Anthony Davis 8.00 20.00
66 Khris Middleton 3.00 8.00
67 Marcus Smart 2.50 6.00
68 Frank Ntilikina 2.00 5.00
69 Kris Dunn 2.00 5.00
70 Josh Richardson 2.00 5.00
71 Will Barton 2.00 5.00
72 Bogdan Bogdanovic 3.00 8.00
73 P.J. Tucker 2.50 6.00
74 Mike Conley 2.50 6.00
75 Rajon Rondo 4.00 10.00
76 Giannis Antetokounmpo 15.00 40.00
77 Jaylen Brown 5.00 12.00
78 Julius Randle 4.00 10.00
79 Wendell Carter Jr. 3.00 8.00
80 Tobias Harris 2.50 6.00
81 Paul Millsap 2.50 6.00
82 Harrison Barnes 2.50 6.00
83 Clint Capela 2.50 6.00
84 Bojan Bogdanovic 2.50 6.00
85 Dwight Howard 4.00 10.00
86 Brook Lopez 2.50 6.00
87 Jayson Tatum 12.00 30.00
88 Taj Gibson 2.00 5.00
89 Lauri Markkanen 4.00 10.00
90 Al Horford 3.00 8.00
91 Nikola Jokic 15.00 40.00
92 Marvin Bagley III 2.50 6.00
93 Eric Gordon 2.50 6.00
94 Joe Ingles 2.50 6.00
95 Kyle Kuzma 4.00 10.00
96 Donte DiVincenzo 2.50 6.00
97 Gordon Hayward 2.50 6.00
98 Mitchell Robinson 3.00 8.00
99 Otto Porter Jr. 2.00 5.00
100 Joel Embiid 6.00 15.00
101 Derrick Rose 6.00 15.00
102 DeMar DeRozan 4.00 10.00
103 Malcolm Brogdon 2.50 6.00
104 John Wall 4.00 10.00
105 Dillon Brooks 2.50 6.00
106 Jeff Teague 2.00 5.00
107 Kevin Durant 10.00 25.00
108 Chris Paul 6.00 15.00
109 Collin Sexton 4.00 10.00
110 Ricky Rubio 2.50 6.00
111 Luke Kennard 2.50 6.00
112 Dejounte Murray 3.00 8.00
113 Victor Oladipo 2.50 6.00
114 Alex Caruso 3.00 8.00
115 Jae Crowder 2.00 5.00
116 Andrew Wiggins 4.00 10.00
117 Kyrie Irving 6.00 15.00
118 Shai Gilgeous-Alexander 15.00 40.00
119 Cedi Osman 2.50 6.00
120 Deandre Ayton 3.00 8.00
121 Blake Griffin 3.00 8.00
122 LaMarcus Aldridge 3.00 8.00
123 T.J. Warren 2.50 6.00
124 Bradley Beal 4.00 10.00
125 Jaren Jackson Jr. 5.00 12.00
126 Karl-Anthony Towns 5.00 12.00
127 Spencer Dinwiddie 2.50 6.00
128 Danilo Gallinari 2.50 6.00
129 Kevin Love 3.00 8.00
130 Devin Booker .75 2.00
131 Andre Drummond 2.50 6.00
132 Rudy Gay 2.50 6.00
133 Myles Turner 3.00 8.00
134 Thomas Bryant 2.50 6.00
135 Jonas Valanciunas 2.50 6.00
136 Robert Covington 2.00 5.00
137 Jarrett Allen 3.00 8.00
138 Dennis Schroder 2.50 6.00
139 Tristan Thompson 2.00 5.00
140 Kelly Oubre Jr. 2.50 6.00
141 Reggie Jackson 2.50 6.00
142 Patty Mills 3.00 8.00
143 Domantas Sabonis 4.00 10.00
144 Troy Brown Jr. 2.00 5.00
145 Grayson Allen 3.00 8.00
146 Josh Okogie 2.00 5.00
147 DeAndre Jordan 2.50 6.00
148 Steven Adams 2.50 6.00
149 Jordan Clarkson 3.00 8.00
150 Dario Saric 2.50 6.00
151 Cameron Johnson RC 5.00 12.00
152 Tremont Waters RC 2.50 6.00
153 Nickeil Alexander-Walker RC 3.00 8.00
154 Nicolo Melli RC 2.50 6.00
155 Grant Williams RC 3.00 8.00
156 Mfiondu Kabengele RC 2.50 6.00
157 Zion Williamson RC 60.00 150.00
158 Carsen Edwards RC 5.00 12.00
159 Jarrett Culver RC 4.00 10.00
160 Jaylen Nowell RC 5.00 12.00
161 PJ Washington Jr. RC 12.00 30.00
162 Kyle Guy RC 5.00 12.00
163 Goga Bitadze RC 6.00 15.00
164 Daniel Gafford RC 8.00 20.00
165 Darius Bazley RC 4.00 10.00
166 Jordan Poole RC 15.00 40.00
167 Ja Morant RC 125.00 300.00
168 Bruno Fernando RC 5.00 12.00
169 Coby White RC 12.00 30.00
170 Bol Bol RC 10.00 25.00
171 Tyler Herro RC 20.00 50.00
172 Kendrick Nunn RC 6.00 15.00
173 Luka Samanic RC 5.00 12.00
174 Tacko Fall RC 5.00 12.00
175 Ty Jerome RC 8.00 20.00
176 Keldon Johnson RC 12.00 30.00
177 RJ Barrett RC 15.00 40.00
178 Cody Martin RC 6.00 15.00
179 Jaxson Hayes RC 6.00 15.00
180 Isaiah Roby RC 5.00 12.00
181 Romeo Langford RC 4.00 10.00
182 Ky Bowman RC 5.00 12.00
183 Matisse Thybulle RC 8.00 20.00
184 Terance Mann RC 8.00 20.00
185 Nassir Little RC 6.00 15.00
186 Kevin Porter Jr. RC 8.00 20.00
187 De'Andre Hunter RC 15.00 40.00
188 Eric Paschall RC 5.00 12.00
189 Rui Hachimura RC 15.00 40.00
190 Ignas Brazdeikis RC 5.00 12.00
191 Sekou Doumbouya RC 4.00 10.00
192 Terence Davis RC 6.00 15.00
193 Brandon Clarke RC 8.00 20.00
194 Luguentz Dort RC 15.00 40.00
195 Dylan Windler RC 5.00 12.00
196 KZ Okpala RC 5.00 12.00
197 Darius Garland RC 15.00 40.00
198 Admiral Schofield RC 5.00 12.00
199 Cam Reddish RC 6.00 15.00
200 Quinndary Weatherspoon RC 4.00 10.00
201 Eric Paschall JSY AU/99 8.00 20.00
202 Tremont Waters JSY AU/99 8.00 20.00
203 Ja Morant JSY AU/99 600.00 1,200.00
204 Nicolo Melli JSY AU/99 8.00 20.00
205 Admiral Schofield JSY AU/99 8.00 20.00
206 KZ Okpala JSY AU/99 8.00 20.00
207 Cam Reddish JSY AU/99 10.00 25.00
208 Nassir Little JSY AU/99 10.00 25.00
209 Coby White JSY AU/99 20.00 50.00
210 RJ Barrett JSY AU/99 25.00 60.00
211 Goga Bitadze JSY AU/99 10.00 25.00
212 Ty Jerome JSY AU/99 12.00 30.00
213 Jarrett Culver JSY AU/99 6.00 15.00
214 Keldon Johnson JSY AU/99 20.00 50.00
215 Bol Bol JSY AU/99 15.00 40.00
216 Luka Samanic JSY AU/99 8.00 20.00
217 Cameron Johnson JSY AU/99 15.00 40.00
218 Nickeil Alexander-Walker JSY AU/99 10.00 25.00
219 Cody Martin JSY AU/99 10.00 25.00
220 Tacko Fall JSY AU/99 8.00 20.00
221 Grant Williams JSY AU/99 10.00 25.00
222 Tyler Herro JSY AU/99 75.00 200.00
224 Kevin Porter Jr. JSY AU/99 12.00 30.00
225 Brandon Clarke JSY AU/99 12.00 30.00
226 Matisse Thybulle JSY AU/99 12.00 30.00
227 Carsen Edwards JSY AU/99 8.00 20.00
228 PJ Washington Jr. JSY AU/99 20.00 50.00
229 Darius Bazley JSY AU/99 6.00 15.00
230 Rui Hachimura JSY AU/49 25.00 60.00
231 Kendrick Nunn JSY AU/99 10.00 25.00
232 Zion Williamson JSY AU/75 300.00 800.00
233 Jaylen Nowell JSY AU/99 8.00 20.00
234 Kyle Guy JSY AU/99 8.00 20.00
235 Bruno Fernando JSY AU/99 8.00 20.00
236 Mfiondu Kabengele JSY AU/99 8.00 20.00
237 Chuma Okeke JSY AU/99 10.00 25.00
238 Quinndary Weatherspoon JSY AU/99 6.00 15.00
239 De'Andre Hunter JSY AU/99 25.00 60.00
240 Sekou Doumbouya JSY AU/99 6.00 15.00
241 Isaiah Roby JSY AU/99 8.00 20.00
242 Dylan Windler JSY AU/99 8.00 20.00

2019-20 Panini Obsidian Electric Etch Green
*VET.GREEN/25: 1.25X TO 3X BASE HI
*RC.GREEN/25: 1X TO 2.5X BASE HI
*RC.GREEN.AUTO/25: 1.25X TO 3X BASE HI
1 Luka Doncic/25 125.00 300.00
55 LeBron James/25 125.00 300.00
157 Zion Williamson/25 400.00 800.00
167 Ja Morant/25 400.00 800.00
203 Ja Morant JSY AU/25 600.00 1,000.00

2019-20 Panini Obsidian Electric Etch Orange
*VET.ORANGE/75: .8X TO 2X BASE HI
*RC.ORANGE/75: .6X TO 1.5X BASE HI
*RC.ORANGE.AUTO/75: .8X TO 2X BASE HI
1 Luka Doncic/50 80.00 200.00
157 Zion Williamson/50 200.00 500.00
167 Ja Morant/50 200.00 500.00
203 Ja Morant JSY AU/50 400.00 700.00
232 Zion Williamson JSY AU/25 1,000.00 2,000.00

2019-20 Panini Obsidian Electric Etch Purple
*VET.PURPLE/75: .8X TO 2X BASE HI
*RC.PURPLE/75: .6X TO 1.5X BASE HI
*RC.PURPLE.AUTO/75: .8X TO 2X BASE HI
1 Luka Doncic/75 80.00 200.00
55 LeBron James/75 80.00 200.00
157 Zion Williamson/75 200.00 500.00
167 Ja Morant/75 200.00 500.00
203 Ja Morant JSY AU/75 400.00 700.00
232 Zion Williamson JSY AU/50 1,000.00 2,000.00

2019-20 Panini Obsidian Atomic
1 Derrick Rose 6.00 15.00
2 Shai Gilgeous-Alexander 25.00 60.00
3 Damian Lillard 12.00 30.00
4 Devin Booker 1.25 3.00
5 LeBron James 80.00 200.00
6 D'Angelo Russell 4.00 10.00
7 Joel Embiid 10.00 25.00
8 De'Aaron Fox 8.00 20.00
9 Ben Simmons 5.00 12.00

10 Nikola Jokic 25.00 60.00
11 Trae Young 12.00 30.00
12 Kevin Durant 15.00 40.00
13 Karl-Anthony Towns 8.00 20.00
14 Kemba Walker 4.00 10.00
15 Stephen Curry 40.00 100.00
16 DeMar DeRozan 6.00 15.00
17 James Harden 10.00 25.00
18 Deandre Ayton 5.00 12.00
19 Luka Doncic 80.00 200.00
20 Nikola Vucevic 4.00 10.00
21 Bradley Beal 6.00 15.00
22 Klay Thompson 12.00 30.00
23 Donovan Mitchell 10.00 25.00
24 Zach LaVine 8.00 20.00
25 Kyrie Irving 10.00 25.00
26 Jayson Tatum 20.00 50.00
27 Russell Westbrook 8.00 20.00
28 Andre Drummond 4.00 10.00
29 Paul George 8.00 20.00
30 Blake Griffin 5.00 12.00
31 Anthony Davis 12.00 30.00
32 John Wall 6.00 15.00
33 Pascal Siakam 8.00 20.00
34 CJ McCollum 5.00 12.00
35 Giannis Antetokounmpo 25.00 60.00
36 Kyle Lowry 5.00 12.00
37 Jimmy Butler 10.00 25.00
38 Jamal Murray 8.00 20.00
39 Kawhi Leonard 12.00 30.00
40 Chris Paul 10.00 25.00

2019-20 Panini Obsidian Atomic Electric Green

*GREEN/25: 1X TO 2.5X BASE HI
5 LeBron James 125.00 300.00
19 Luka Doncic 125.00 300.00

2019-20 Panini Obsidian Atomic Electric Orange

*ORANGE/35: .6X TO 1.5X BASE HI
5 LeBron James 100.00 250.00
19 Luka Doncic 100.00 250.00

2019-20 Panini Obsidian Atomic Electric Purple

*PURPLE/50: .6X TO 1.5X BASE HI
5 LeBron James 100.00 250.00
19 Luka Doncic 100.00 250.00

2019-20 Panini Obsidian Galaxy Autographs

1 Richard Hamilton/49 10.00 25.00
2 Detlef Schrempf/99 8.00 20.00
3 Pascal Siakam/49 15.00 40.00
4 Bogdan Bogdanovic/99 10.00 25.00
5 Charles Barkley/25 80.00 200.00
6 Mike Miller/99 8.00 20.00
7 Karl-Anthony Towns/35 15.00 40.00
8 Dale Ellis/99 8.00 20.00
9 CJ McCollum/49 10.00 25.00
10 Ricky Davis/99 8.00 20.00
11 Bernard King/49 12.00 30.00
12 Kenyon Martin/99 8.00 20.00
13 Shawn Kemp/60 15.00 40.00
14 Luke Kennard/99 8.00 20.00
15 John Stockton/35 30.00 80.00
16 DeShawn Stevenson/99 6.00 15.00
17 Andrew Wiggins/60 12.00 30.00
18 Bruce Brown/99 10.00 25.00
19 Lauri Markkanen/49 12.00 30.00
20 James Johnson/99 6.00 15.00
21 Derek Fisher/60 10.00 25.00
22 Meyers Leonard/99 6.00 15.00
23 Joe Harris/60 8.00 20.00
24 Vin Baker/99 8.00 20.00
25 Julius Erving/35 40.00 100.00
26 Sterling Brown/99 6.00 15.00
27 Jerry West/60 15.00 40.00
28 Mike Scott/99 6.00 15.00
29 Steve Kerr/49 12.00 30.00
30 Larry Nance Jr./99 8.00 20.00
31 Calvin Murphy/49 10.00 25.00
32 Shawn Bradley/99 6.00 15.00
33 Michael Cooper/60 10.00 25.00
34 M.L. Carr/99 10.00 25.00
35 Anthony Davis/35 125.00 300.00
36 Jevon Carter/99 6.00 15.00
37 Jayson Tatum/35 125.00 300.00
38 Torrey Craig/99 6.00 15.00
39 Kevin Knox II/49 6.00 15.00
40 Devonte' Graham/99 8.00 20.00
41 Robert Parish/60 12.00 30.00
42 Alex Caruso/99 20.00 50.00
43 Nate McMillan/99 8.00 20.00
44 Jack Sikma/99 10.00 25.00
45 John Wall/35 12.00 30.00
46 Malik Beasley/99 8.00 20.00
47 Dennis Rodman/60 25.00 60.00
48 Matt Bonner/99 8.00 20.00
49 Harrison Barnes/40 8.00 20.00
50 Devean George/99 8.00 20.00

2019-20 Panini Obsidian Galaxy Autographs Electric Etch Green

*GREEN/25: .6X TO 1.5X BASE HI
13 Shawn Kemp 40.00 100.00
15 John Stockton 40.00 100.00
25 Julius Erving 50.00 125.00
35 Anthony Davis 125.00 300.00
37 Jayson Tatum 125.00 300.00
47 Dennis Rodman 80.00 200.00

2019-20 Panini Obsidian Galaxy Autographs Electric Etch Orange

*ORANGE/30-50: .6X TO 1.5X BASE HI
13 Shawn Kemp/35 30.00 80.00
42 Alex Caruso/50 30.00 80.00
47 Dennis Rodman/35 40.00 100.00

2019-20 Panini Obsidian Galaxy Autographs Electric Etch Purple

*PURPLE/49-75: .4X TO 1X BASE HI
13 Shawn Kemp/49 30.00 80.00
42 Alex Caruso/75 30.00 80.00
47 Dennis Rodman/49 40.00 100.00

2019-20 Panini Obsidian Jersey Autographs

*PURPLE/75: X TO X BASE HI
*ORANGE/50: .6 TO 1.5X BASE HI
1 Bogdan Bogdanovic/99 10.00 25.00
2 D'Angelo Russell/49 8.00 20.00
3 Josh Richardson/99 6.00 15.00
4 Jrue Holiday/49 12.00 30.00
5 Anfernee Simons/99 20.00 50.00
6 Eric Gordon/49 8.00 20.00
7 Mo Bamba/99 8.00 20.00
8 Damian Lillard/35 80.00 200.00
9 Domantas Sabonis/99 12.00 30.00
10 Trae Young/35 200.00 500.00
12 CJ McCollum/49 10.00 25.00
13 Jalen Brunson/99 25.00 60.00
14 Al Horford/49 10.00 25.00
15 Aaron Holiday/99 8.00 20.00
16 Otto Porter Jr./49 6.00 15.00
17 Terrence Ross/99 10.00 25.00
18 Andrew Wiggins/35 12.00 30.00

2019-20 Panini Obsidian Jersey Autographs Electric Etch Green

*GREEN/25: .6X TO 1.5X BASE HI
5 Anfernee Simons 30.00 80.00
8 Damian Lillard 100.00 250.00

2019-20 Panini Obsidian Lightning Strike Signatures

*PURPLE/49-75: .4X TO 1X BASE HI
*ORANGE/35-50: 1X TO 1.5X BASE HI
1 David Robinson/35 20.00 50.00
2 Gerald Henderson Sr./99 6.00 15.00
3 D'Angelo Russell/60 8.00 20.00
4 Kevin Huerter/99 10.00 25.00
5 Jrue Holiday/60 12.00 30.00
6 Kyle Kuzma/49 12.00 30.00
7 Charles Barkley/35 60.00 150.00
8 Nate Thurmond/45 8.00 20.00
9 Oscar Robertson/35 25.00 60.00
10 Jason Richardson/60 10.00 25.00
11 Jason Kidd/35 15.00 40.00
12 Mark Aguirre/99 8.00 20.00
13 Stephon Marbury/60 12.00 30.00
14 Rodney Hood/99 8.00 20.00
15 Buddy Hield/49 8.00 20.00
16 JJ Redick/60 10.00 25.00
17 Giannis Antetokounmpo/35 125.00 300.00
18 Kevin Johnson/49 10.00 25.00
19 Kawhi Leonard/35 125.00 300.00
20 Bam Adebayo/60 15.00 40.00
21 Paul Pierce/35 15.00 40.00
22 Rolando Blackman/99 8.00 20.00
23 Deandre Ayton/30 40.00 100.00
24 Jarrett Jack/99 6.00 15.00
25 Walt Frazier/49 15.00 40.00
26 Julius Randle/49 12.00 30.00
27 Kareem Abdul-Jabbar/35 60.00 150.00
28 Dave Cowens/49 12.00 30.00
29 Magic Johnson/35 60.00 150.00
30 Jarrett Allen/60 10.00 25.00

2019-20 Panini Obsidian Lightning Strike Signatures Electric Etch Green

*GREEN/25: .6X TO 1.5X BASE HI
7 Charles Barkley 60.00 150.00
17 Giannis Antetokounmpo 125.00 300.00
19 Kawhi Leonard 125.00 300.00
27 Kareem Abdul-Jabbar 60.00 125.00
29 Magic Johnson 60.00 150.00

2019-20 Panini Obsidian Matrix Autographs

1 Tony Parker/35 12.00 30.00
2 Luke Kennard/99 8.00 20.00
3 Buddy Hield/49 8.00 20.00
4 Anfernee Simons/99 15.00 40.00
5 Kenny Smith/49 8.00 20.00
6 Calvin Murphy/60 8.00 20.00
7 Charles Barkley/25 75.00 200.00
8 Jason Richardson/60 10.00 25.00
9 David Robinson/35 20.00 50.00
10 Greg Anthony/49 6.00 15.00
11 CJ McCollum/49 10.00 25.00
12 Rolando Blackman/99 8.00 20.00
13 Al Horford/60 8.00 20.00
14 Vin Baker/99 8.00 20.00
15 Julius Randle/49 12.00 30.00
16 Nate Thurmond/44 8.00 20.00
17 Giannis Antetokounmpo/35 200.00 500.00
18 Mo Bamba/60 8.00 20.00
19 Chris Bosh/35 12.00 30.00
20 Mark Aguirre/99 8.00 20.00
21 Stephon Marbury/60 12.00 30.00
22 Mike Miller/99 8.00 20.00
23 Christian Laettner/49 10.00 25.00
24 DeShawn Stevenson/99 6.00 15.00
25 Eric Gordon/60 8.00 20.00
26 Latrell Sprewell/60 12.00 30.00
27 Stephen Curry/25 500.00 1,000.00
28 Joe Harris/60 8.00 20.00
29 Shake Milton/99 6.00 15.00
30 Derrick Coleman/99 8.00 20.00
31 Nikola Jokic/49 125.00 300.00
32 Jarrett Jack/99 6.00 15.00
33 Dwight Howard/60 12.00 30.00
34 Arron Afflalo/99 6.00 15.00
35 George Gervin/49 15.00 40.00
36 Ralph Sampson/49 8.00 20.00
37 Kevin Durant/25 200.00 500.00
38 Michael Cooper/60 10.00 25.00
39 Markelle Fultz/35 8.00 20.00
40 Charles Oakley/99 8.00 20.00
41 Harrison Barnes/40 8.00 20.00
42 Craig Ehlo/99 6.00 15.00
43 Walt Frazier/49 15.00 40.00
44 Gheorghe Muresan/99 12.00 30.00
45 Brook Lopez/60 8.00 20.00
46 Bill Walton/60 40.00 100.00
47 Andrew Wiggins/60 12.00 30.00
48 Bam Adebayo/60 30.00 80.00
49 D'Angelo Russell/35 8.00 20.00
50 Patrick Beverley/99 8.00 20.00

2019-20 Panini Obsidian Matrix Autographs Electric Etch Green

*GREEN/25: .8X TO 1.5X BASE HI
17 Giannis Antetokounmpo 300.00 600.00
31 Nikola Jokic 200.00 500.00
48 Bam Adebayo 50.00 125.00

2019-20 Panini Obsidian Matrix Autographs Electric Etch Orange

*ORANGE/30-50: .8X TO 1.5X BASE HI
48 Bam Adebayo/35 40.00 100.00

2019-20 Panini Obsidian Matrix Autographs Electric Etch Purple

*PURPLE/40-75: .4X TO 1X BASE HI
48 Bam Adebayo/49 30.00 80.00

2019-20 Panini Obsidian Onyx Autographs

*PURPLE/49-75: .4X TO 1X BASE HI
*ORANGE/30-50: .6X TO 1.5X BASE HI
1 Allen Iverson/35 60.00 150.00
2 Domantas Sabonis/75 12.00 30.00
3 Clyde Drexler/35 15.00 40.00
4 Charles Oakley/99 8.00 20.00
5 De'Aaron Fox/49 15.00 40.00
6 Craig Ehlo/99 6.00 15.00
7 Christian Laettner/60 10.00 25.00
8 Eric Gordon/60 8.00 20.00
9 Stephen Curry/25 500.00 1,000.00
10 Rick Fox/60 8.00 20.00
11 Larry Bird/35 40.00 100.00
12 Thaddeus Young/60 6.00 15.00
13 Chris Bosh/35 12.00 30.00
14 Josh Richardson/99 6.00 15.00
15 James Worthy/49 15.00 40.00
16 Arron Afflalo/99 6.00 15.00
17 Artis Gilmore/49 12.00 30.00
18 George Gervin/49 15.00 40.00
19 Giannis Antetokounmpo/25 200.00 400.00
20 Latrell Sprewell/60 12.00 30.00
21 Trae Young/35 75.00 200.00
22 Derrick Coleman/99 8.00 20.00
23 Tony Parker/35 12.00 30.00
24 Bonzi Wells/99 8.00 20.00
25 Al Horford/60 10.00 25.00
26 T.J. Ford/99 8.00 20.00
27 Chris Mullin/49 12.00 30.00
28 Larry Johnson/60 12.00 30.00
29 Kevin Durant/25 30.00 80.00
30 Mo Bamba/60 8.00 20.00

2019-20 Panini Obsidian Onyx Autographs Electric Etch Green

*ORANGE/25: .6X TO 1.5X BASE HI
1 Allen Iverson 60.00 150.00
21 Trae Young 100.00 250.00

2019-20 Panini Obsidian Pitch Black

*PURPLE/50: .5X TO 1.25X BASE HI
*ORANGE/35: .8X TO 2X BASE HI
*GREEN/25: .8X TO 2X BASE HI
1 Joel Embiid 12.00 30.00
2 Blake Griffin 6.00 15.00
3 Nikola Jokic 30.00 80.00
4 CJ McCollum 6.00 15.00
5 Kemba Walker 5.00 12.00
6 Jimmy Butler 12.00 30.00
7 Luka Doncic 40.00 100.00
8 Zach LaVine 10.00 25.00
9 Damian Lillard 15.00 40.00
10 Russell Westbrook 10.00 25.00
11 De'Aaron Fox 10.00 25.00
12 Anthony Davis 15.00 40.00
13 Trae Young 15.00 40.00
14 Giannis Antetokounmpo 30.00 80.00
15 Stephen Curry 50.00 120.00
16 Jamal Murray 10.00 25.00
17 Bradley Beal 8.00 20.00
18 Kyrie Irving 12.00 30.00
19 Devin Booker 1.50 4.00
20 Andre Drummond 5.00 12.00
21 Ben Simmons 6.00 15.00
22 Pascal Siakam 10.00 25.00
23 Karl-Anthony Towns 10.00 25.00
24 Kyle Lowry 6.00 15.00
25 James Harden 12.00 30.00
26 Kawhi Leonard 15.00 40.00
27 Donovan Mitchell 12.00 30.00
28 Jayson Tatum 25.00 60.00
29 LeBron James 50.00 125.00
30 Paul George 10.00 25.00

2019-20 Panini Obsidian Rookie Autographs

1 Nicolo Melli/99 12.00 30.00
2 PJ Washington Jr./99 30.00 80.00
3 Tacko Fall/99 12.00 30.00
4 Brandon Clarke/99 UER 20.00 50.00
5 Kyle Guy/99 UER 12.00 30.00
6 Carsen Edwards/99 12.00 30.00
7 Admiral Schofield/99 12.00 30.00
8 Zion Williamson/75 500.00 1,000.00
9 Talen Horton-Tucker/99 15.00 40.00
10 Cam Reddish/99 15.00 40.00
11 Kevin Porter Jr./99 20.00 50.00
12 Tyler Herro/99 75.00 200.00
13 Nicolas Claxton/99 20.00 50.00
14 Chuma Okeke/99 15.00 40.00
15 Terance Mann/99 20.00 50.00
16 Goga Bitadze/99 15.00 40.00
17 Bruno Fernando/99 12.00 30.00
18 Ja Morant/99 600.00 1,200.00
19 Dylan Windler/99 12.00 30.00
21 KZ Okpala/99 12.00 30.00
22 Matisse Thybulle/99 20.00 50.00
23 Cody Martin/99 8.00 20.00
24 Darius Bazley/99 10.00 25.00
25 Jaylen Nowell/99 12.00 30.00
26 Keldon Johnson/99 30.00 80.00
27 Grant Williams/99 15.00 40.00
28 RJ Barrett/99 40.00 100.00
29 Eric Paschall/99 12.00 30.00
30 Bol Bol/99 25.00 60.00
31 Mfiondu Kabengele/99 12.00 30.00
32 Nassir Little/99 15.00 40.00
33 Isaiah Roby/99 12.00 30.00
34 Nickeil Alexander-Walker/99 15.00 40.00
35 Quinndary Weatherspoon/99 10.00 25.00
36 Luka Samanic/99 12.00 30.00
37 Ty Jerome/99 20.00 50.00
38 Rui Hachimura/49 40.00 100.00
39 Kendrick Nunn/99 15.00 40.00
40 Cameron Johnson/99 25.00 60.00

2019-20 Panini Obsidian Rookie Autographs Electric Etch Green

*GREEN/15-25: .8X TO 1.5X BASE HI
12 Tyler Herro/25 150.00 400.00
18 Ja Morant/25 1,000.00 2,000.00

2019-20 Panini Obsidian Rookie Autographs Electric Etch Orange

*ORANGE/25-50: .6X TO 1.5X BASE HI
8 Zion Williamson/25 800.00 1,500.00
12 Tyler Herro/50 125.00 300.00
18 Ja Morant/50 800.00 1,500.00

2019-20 Panini Obsidian Rookie Autographs Electric Etch Purple

*PURPLE/40-75: .6X TO 1.5X BASE HI
18 Ja Morant/75 800.00 1,500.00

2019-20 Panini Obsidian Tunnel Vision

*ORANGE/35: .6X TO 1.5X BASE HI
*GREEN/25: .8X TO 2X BASE HI
1 Nikola Jokic 30.00 80.00
2 Ben Simmons 6.00 15.00
3 Jimmy Butler 12.00 30.00
4 James Harden 12.00 30.00
5 Damian Lillard 15.00 40.00
6 LeBron James 50.00 125.00
7 Anthony Davis 15.00 40.00
8 Giannis Antetokounmpo 30.00 80.00
9 Joel Embiid 12.00 30.00
10 Kyrie Irving 12.00 30.00
11 CJ McCollum 6.00 15.00
12 Pascal Siakam 10.00 25.00
13 Luka Doncic 40.00 100.00
14 Kawhi Leonard 15.00 40.00
15 Russell Westbrook 10.00 25.00
16 Paul George 10.00 25.00
17 Trae Young 15.00 40.00
18 Bradley Beal 8.00 20.00
19 Blake Griffin 6.00 15.00
20 Devin Booker 1.50 4.00
21 Kemba Walker 5.00 12.00
22 Karl-Anthony Towns 10.00 25.00
23 Zach LaVine 10.00 25.00
24 Donovan Mitchell 12.00 30.00
25 De'Aaron Fox 10.00 25.00

2019-20 Panini Obsidian Tunnel Vision Electric Etch Purple

*PURPLE/50: .6X TO 1.5X BASE HI
6 LeBron James 80.00 200.00
13 Luka Doncic 80.00 200.00

2019-20 Panini Obsidian Vitreous

*GREEN/25: .8X TO 2X BASE HI
1 LeBron James 50.00 125.00
2 Giannis Antetokounmpo 30.00 80.00
3 Luka Doncic 40.00 100.00
4 James Harden 12.00 30.00
5 Kawhi Leonard 15.00 40.00

2019-20 Panini Obsidian Vitreous Electric Etch Orange

*ORANGE/35: .6X TO 1.5X BASE HI
1 LeBron James 125.00 300.00
3 Luka Doncic 125.00 300.00

2019-20 Panini Obsidian Vitreous Electric Etch Purple

*PURPLE/50: .6X TO 1.5X BASE HI
1 LeBron James 100.00 250.00
3 Luka Doncic 125.00 300.00

2019-20 Panini Obsidian Volcanic Signatures Electric Etch Green

*GREEN/25: X TO X BASE HI
1 Kevin Garnett 125.00 300.00
19 Dwyane Wade 40.00 100.00
39 Damian Lillard 100.00 250.00

2021-22 Panini Obsidian

COMMON CARD (1-150) .75 2.00
SEMISTARS 1.00 2.50
UNLISTED STARS 1.25 3.00
COMMON ROOKIE (151-200) 1.50 4.00
ROOKIE SEMISTARS 2.00 5.00
ROOKIE UNL.STARS 2.50 6.00
COMMON ROOKIE (201-240) 8.00 20.00
ROOKIE SEMISTARS 10.00 25.00
ROOKIE UNL.STARS 12.00 30.00
ROOKIE PRINT RUN 99 SER.#'d SETS
1 LaMelo Ball 3.00 8.00
2 Kawhi Leonard 3.00 8.00
3 Anthony Davis 3.00 8.00
4 Karl-Anthony Towns 2.00 5.00
5 Shai Gilgeous-Alexander 6.00 15.00
6 LeBron James 10.00 25.00
7 Kevin Durant 4.00 10.00
8 Bradley Beal 1.50 4.00
9 Jayson Tatum 5.00 12.00
10 Dejounte Murray 1.25 3.00
11 Trae Young 3.00 8.00
12 Ja Morant 4.00 10.00
13 James Harden 2.50 6.00
14 Kevin Porter Jr. 1.00 2.50
15 Nikola Jokic 6.00 15.00
16 Tobias Harris 1.00 2.50
17 Jerami Grant 1.25 3.00
18 Will Barton .75 2.00
19 Zach LaVine 2.00 5.00
20 Kyle Lowry 1.25 3.00
21 Kevin Love 1.25 3.00
22 Buddy Hield 1.00 2.50
23 Jaylen Brown 2.00 5.00
24 Domantas Sabonis 1.50 4.00
25 Deandre Ayton 1.25 3.00
26 Lauri Markkanen 1.50 4.00
27 Evan Fournier 1.00 2.50
28 John Collins 1.25 3.00
29 Rudy Gobert 1.50 4.00
30 Stephen Curry 8.00 20.00
31 Devin Vassell 2.00 5.00
32 Collin Sexton 1.25 3.00
33 Jonas Valanciunas 1.00 2.50
34 Giannis Antetokounmpo 6.00 15.00
35 Fred VanVleet 1.50 4.00
36 Mike Conley 1.00 2.50
37 Mikal Bridges 1.50 4.00
38 Derrick Rose 2.00 5.00
39 Jae'Sean Tate 1.25 3.00
40 Klay Thompson 3.00 8.00
41 DeMar DeRozan 1.50 4.00
42 De'Andre Hunter 1.25 3.00
43 Bam Adebayo 2.00 5.00
44 Ben Simmons 1.25 3.00
45 Mo Bamba 1.00 2.50
46 Luguentz Dort 1.25 3.00
47 Terry Rozier III 1.00 2.50
48 Paul George 2.00 5.00
49 Damian Lillard 3.00 8.00
50 Andrew Wiggins 1.50 4.00
51 Bogdan Bogdanovic 1.25 3.00
52 Blake Griffin 1.25 3.00
53 Saddiq Bey 1.00 2.50
54 Bojan Bogdanovic 1.00 2.50
55 Tyrese Maxey 3.00 8.00
56 Tyler Herro 2.00 5.00
57 Caris LeVert 1.00 2.50
58 Jrue Holiday 1.50 4.00
59 Kelly Oubre Jr. 1.25 3.00
60 Isaiah Stewart 1.25 3.00
61 Jaren Jackson Jr. 2.00 5.00
62 Jordan Clarkson 1.25 3.00
63 Duncan Robinson 1.00 2.50
64 Christian Wood 1.00 2.50
65 RJ Barrett 2.00 5.00
66 Clint Capela 1.25 3.00
67 Aaron Gordon 1.25 3.00
68 Norman Powell 1.00 2.50
69 Jimmy Butler 2.00 5.00
70 Jordan Poole 2.00 5.00
71 Seth Curry 1.00 2.50
72 Zion Williamson 3.00 8.00
73 Darius Garland 2.00 5.00
74 De'Aaron Fox 2.00 5.00
75 Kentavious Caldwell-Pope .75 2.00
76 Desmond Bane 2.50 6.00
77 Luka Doncic 8.00 20.00
78 CJ McCollum 1.00 2.50
79 Malcolm Brogdon 1.00 2.50
80 Dillon Brooks 1.25 3.00
81 LaMarcus Aldridge 1.25 3.00
82 Reggie Jackson 1.00 2.50
83 Gary Trent Jr. 1.00 2.50
84 Russell Westbrook 2.00 5.00
85 Devin Booker 3.00 8.00
86 Gordon Hayward 1.00 2.50
87 Pascal Siakam 2.00 5.00
88 Jalen Brunson 2.50 6.00
89 Patrick Beverley .75 2.00
90 Bobby Portis 1.00 2.50
91 Anthony Edwards 6.00 15.00
92 Alex Caruso 1.25 3.00
93 Draymond Green 1.50 4.00
94 Michael Porter Jr. 1.50 4.00
95 Kyle Kuzma 1.50 4.00
96 Myles Turner 1.25 3.00
97 Keldon Johnson 1.50 4.00
98 Dennis Schroder 1.25 3.00
99 Tim Hardaway Jr. .75 2.00
100 Jarrett Allen 1.25 3.00
101 Tyrese Haliburton 2.50 6.00
102 Kemba Walker 1.25 3.00
103 Wendell Carter Jr. 1.25 3.00
104 Carmelo Anthony 2.00 5.00
105 Anfernee Simons 2.00 5.00
106 Dorian Finney-Smith .75 2.00
107 Brandon Ingram 1.50 4.00
108 Marcus Smart 1.25 3.00
109 Steven Adams 1.00 2.50
110 D'Angelo Russell 1.25 3.00
111 Spencer Dinwiddie 1.00 2.50
112 Lance Stephenson 1.00 2.50
113 Joel Embiid 3.00 8.00
114 Montrezl Harrell 1.00 2.50
115 Lonzo Ball 1.25 3.00
116 Cole Anthony 1.50 4.00
117 OG Anunoby 1.25 3.00
118 Harrison Barnes 1.00 2.50
119 Robert Covington .75 2.00
120 Chris Paul 2.50 6.00
121 Julius Randle 1.50 4.00
122 Nikola Vucevic 1.25 3.00
123 Jamal Murray 2.00 5.00
124 Khris Middleton 1.25 3.00
125 Kyrie Irving 2.50 6.00
126 Donovan Mitchell 2.50 6.00
127 Malik Beasley 1.00 2.50
128 Devonte' Graham 1.00 2.50
129 Kristaps Porzingis 1.50 4.00
130 Cameron Johnson 1.50 4.00
131 Dirk Nowitzki 3.00 8.00
132 Tim Duncan 3.00 8.00
133 Magic Johnson 4.00 10.00
134 Larry Bird 4.00 10.00
135 Vince Carter 2.50 6.00
136 Charles Barkley 3.00 8.00
137 Shaquille O'Neal 4.00 10.00
138 Allen Iverson 3.00 8.00
139 Kevin Garnett 3.00 8.00
140 Dwyane Wade 2.50 6.00
141 Kareem Abdul-Jabbar 4.00 10.00
142 Isiah Thomas 2.00 5.00
143 Dominique Wilkins 2.00 5.00
144 Karl Malone 2.50 6.00
145 Steve Nash 2.50 6.00
146 Dennis Rodman 3.00 8.00
147 Hakeem Olajuwon 2.50 6.00
148 Ray Allen 2.00 5.00
149 David Robinson 2.50 6.00
150 Clyde Drexler 2.00 5.00
151 Cade Cunningham RC 15.00 40.00
152 Jalen Green RC 12.00 30.00
153 Evan Mobley RC 10.00 25.00
154 Scottie Barnes RC 8.00 20.00
155 Jalen Suggs RC 6.00 15.00
156 Josh Giddey RC 8.00 20.00
157 Jonathan Kuminga RC 8.00 20.00
158 Franz Wagner RC 8.00 20.00
159 Davion Mitchell RC 2.50 6.00
160 Ziaire Williams RC 3.00 8.00
161 James Bouknight RC 2.00 5.00
162 Joshua Primo RC 2.00 5.00
163 Chris Duarte RC 2.00 5.00
164 Moses Moody RC 5.00 12.00
165 Corey Kispert RC 3.00 8.00
166 Alperen Sengun RC 8.00 20.00
167 Bones Hyland RC 3.00 8.00
168 Ayo Dosunmu RC 5.00 12.00
169 Isaiah Jackson RC 2.50 6.00
170 Austin Reaves RC 12.00 30.00
171 Cameron Thomas RC 5.00 12.00
172 Trey Murphy III RC 8.00 20.00
173 Tre Mann RC 4.00 10.00
174 Josh Christopher RC 2.00 5.00
175 Day'Ron Sharpe RC 2.50 6.00
176 Brandon Boston Jr. RC 2.50 6.00
177 Dalano Banton RC 3.00 8.00
178 Herbert Jones RC 3.00 8.00
179 Miles McBride RC 4.00 10.00
180 Jared Butler RC 2.50 6.00
181 Jeremiah Robinson-Earl RC 2.50 6.00
182 Juan Toscano-Anderson RC 2.50 6.00
183 Luka Garza RC 2.50 6.00
184 Kessler Edwards RC 2.50 6.00
185 Kai Jones RC 2.00 5.00
186 Jalen Johnson RC 8.00 20.00
187 Keon Johnson RC 2.50 6.00
188 Usman Garuba RC 2.00 5.00
189 Quentin Grimes RC 5.00 12.00
190 Omer Yurtseven RC 2.50 6.00
191 Aaron Wiggins RC 3.00 8.00
192 Jaden Springer RC 2.50 6.00
193 Santi Aldama RC 3.00 8.00
194 Sandro Mamukelashvili RC 3.00 8.00
195 Greg Brown III RC 2.00 5.00
196 Jericho Sims RC 3.00 8.00
197 Charles Bassey RC 2.50 6.00
198 Joe Wieskamp RC 2.00 5.00
199 JT Thor RC 2.50 6.00
200 David Duke Jr. RC 2.50 6.00
201 Scottie Barnes AU JSY/99 75.00 200.00
202 Austin Reaves AU JSY/99 60.00 150.00
203 Charles Bassey AU JSY/99 12.00 30.00
204 Franz Wagner AU JSY/99 40.00 100.00
205 Jeremiah Robinson-Earl AU JSY/99 12.00 30.00
206 Jared Butler AU JSY/99 12.00 30.00
207 Cade Cunningham AU JSY/99 125.00 300.00
208 Kessler Edwards AU JSY/99 12.00 30.00
209 Greg Brown III AU JSY/99 10.00 25.00
210 Scottie Lewis AU JSY/99 10.00 25.00
211 Ayo Dosunmu AU JSY/99 25.00 60.00
212 Trey Murphy III AU JSY/99 40.00 100.00
213 James Bouknight AU JSY/99 10.00 25.00
214 Kai Jones AU JSY/99 10.00 25.00
215 Jonathan Kuminga AU JSY/99 40.00 100.00
216 Jaden Springer AU JSY/99 12.00 30.00
217 Aaron Wiggins AU JSY/99 15.00 40.00
218 Chris Duarte AU JSY/99 10.00 25.00
219 Jalen Johnson AU JSY/99 40.00 100.00
220 Joshua Primo AU JSY/99 10.00 25.00
221 Bones Hyland AU JSY/49 15.00 40.00
222 Miles McBride AU JSY/99 20.00 50.00
223 Evan Mobley AU JSY/99 75.00 200.00
224 Keon Johnson AU JSY/49 12.00 30.00
225 Davion Mitchell AU JSY/99 12.00 30.00
226 Quentin Grimes AU JSY/99 25.00 60.00
227 Brandon Boston Jr. AU JSY/99 12.00 30.00
228 Herbert Jones AU JSY/99 15.00 40.00
229 Tre Mann AU JSY/99 20.00 50.00
230 Moses Moody AU JSY/99 25.00 60.00
231 Cameron Thomas AU JSY/99 25.00 60.00
232 JT Thor AU JSY/99 12.00 30.00
233 Jalen Green AU JSY/99 125.00 300.00
234 Isaiah Jackson AU JSY/99 12.00 30.00
235 Ziaire Williams AU JSY/99 15.00 40.00
236 Santi Aldama AU JSY/99 15.00 40.00
237 Jalen Suggs AU JSY/99 30.00 80.00
238 Day'Ron Sharpe AU JSY/99 12.00 30.00
239 Corey Kispert AU JSY/99 15.00 40.00
240 Josh Giddey AU JSY/99 40.00 100.00

2021-22 Panini Obsidian Galaxy Autographs

COMMON CARD 4.00 10.00
SEMISTARS 5.00 12.00
UNLISTED STARS 6.00 15.00
STATED PRINT RUN 49-149 SER.#'d SETS
*PURPLE/49-75: .5X TO 1.2X BASE HI
*ORANGE/25-50: .6X TO 1.5X BASE HI
*GREEN/15-25: .75X TO 2X BASE HI
1 Rajon Rondo/99 12.00 30.00
2 Devin Vassell/149 10.00 25.00
3 Luc Longley/149 5.00 12.00
4 T.J. McConnell/149 5.00 12.00
5 Latrell Sprewell/149 10.00 25.00
6 Zeke Nnaji/149 5.00 12.00
7 RJ Barrett/75 10.00 25.00
8 Robert Williams III/149 15.00 40.00
9 De'Aaron Fox/75 20.00 50.00
10 Robert Horry/149 6.00 15.00
11 Steve Francis/149 6.00 15.00
12 Luis Scola/149 5.00 12.00
13 Jason Williams/99 30.00 80.00
14 Bobby Portis/149 5.00 12.00
15 Robert Parish/99 8.00 20.00
16 Onyeka Okongwu/149 6.00 15.00
17 Bruce Brown/149 5.00 12.00
18 Jamal Murray/99 20.00 50.00
19 Avery Johnson/149 5.00 12.00
20 Duncan Robinson/149 5.00 12.00
21 Deni Avdija/149 6.00 15.00
22 Cameron Payne/149 6.00 15.00
23 Dennis Rodman/99 40.00 100.00
24 Spencer Dinwiddie/149 5.00 12.00
25 Al Horford/149 6.00 15.00
26 Jrue Holiday/99 8.00 20.00
27 Coby White/99 6.00 15.00
28 Kenyon Martin Jr./149 6.00 15.00
29 Isiah Thomas/99 15.00 40.00
30 Dwyane Wade/49 50.00 120.00
32 Stephen Curry/49 500.00 1,000.00
33 Carlos Boozer/149 5.00 12.00
34 Furkan Korkmaz/149 5.00 12.00
35 Rudy Gobert/149 8.00 20.00
36 Anthony Edwards/75 125.00 300.00
37 Bogdan Bogdanovic/149 6.00 15.00
38 Kevin Garnett/75 50.00 120.00
39 Brad Daugherty/149 6.00 15.00
40 Roy Hibbert/149 5.00 12.00
41 Evan Fournier/149 5.00 12.00
43 Rick Fox/149 6.00 15.00
44 Mitch Richmond/149 8.00 20.00
45 Rolando Blackman/149 5.00 12.00
46 Calvin Murphy/149 6.00 15.00
47 Bojan Bogdanovic/149 5.00 12.00
48 Dell Curry/149 6.00 15.00
49 Manu Ginobili/99 40.00 100.00
50 Max Strus/149 6.00 15.00

2021-22 Panini Obsidian Lightning Strike Signatures

COMMON CARD 4.00 10.00
SEMISTARS 5.00 12.00
UNLISTED STARS 6.00 15.00
STATED PRINT RUN 49-99 SER.#'d SETS
*PURPLE/35-75: .5X TO 1.2X BASE HI
*ORANGE/25-50: .6X TO 1.5X BASE HI
*GREEN/15-25: .75X TO 2X BASE HI
1 Jae'Sean Tate/99 6.00 15.00
2 Kenny Sky Walker/99 4.00 10.00
3 David Robinson/49 25.00 60.00
4 Mitch Richmond/99 8.00 20.00
5 Coby White/75 6.00 15.00
8 Kristaps Porzingis/99 8.00 20.00
9 Rick Barry/99 8.00 20.00
10 Kelly Oubre Jr./99 6.00 15.00
12 Nickeil Alexander-Walker/99 5.00 12.00
13 Tyrese Haliburton/75 40.00 100.00
14 Kevin Huerter/99 5.00 12.00
16 T.J. Warren/99 4.00 10.00
17 Wally Szczerbiak/99 5.00 12.00
18 Hakeem Olajuwon/49 30.00 80.00
19 Steve Kerr/75 8.00 20.00
20 Will Barton/99 4.00 10.00
21 John Collins/75 6.00 15.00
22 Karl-Anthony Towns/49 10.00 25.00
23 Tony Parker/75 25.00 60.00
24 Monte Morris/99 5.00 12.00
25 Danilo Gallinari/99 5.00 12.00
26 Rick Fox/99 6.00 15.00
29 Nate Archibald/99 6.00 15.00
30 Doug McDermott/99 5.00 12.00

2023-24 Panini Obsidian

ROOKIE AU JSY PRINT RUN 99 SER.#'d SETS
*ELECTRIC ETCH INTR: .75X TO 2X BASIC
*EE RED FLOOD: .75X TO 2X BASIC
*EE RED FLOOD AU JSY RC: .4X TO 1X BASIC
*EE PINK PULSAR: 1.25X TO 3X BASIC
*EE ORANGE FLOOD/99: 1.25X TO 3X BASIC
*EE ORANGE FLOOD AU JSY RC/75: .5X TO 1.2X BASIC
*EE REGGAE FLOOD/75: 1.5X TO 4X BASIC
*EE PURPLE FLOOD/49: 2X TO 5X BASIC
*EE PURPLE FLOOD AU JSY RC/49:X .6 TO 1.5X BASIC
*EE BLUE/30: 2.5X TO 6X BASIC
*EE BLUE FOTL AU JSY RC/27: .75X TO 2X BASIC
*EE GREEN/25: 3X TO 8X BASIC
*EE GREEN AU JSY RC/25: .75X TO 2X BASIC
*EE GREEN FLOOD/25: 3X TO 8X BASIC
*EE GREEN FLOOD AU JSY RC/20: .75X TO 2X BASIC
1 Dirk Nowitzki 2.00 5.00
2 Scoot Henderson 5.00 12.00
3 Fred VanVleet 1.25 3.00
4 Immanuel Quickley .75 2.00
5 Kyle Lowry 1.00 2.50
6 OG Anunoby 1.00 2.50
7 Paolo Banchero 2.00 5.00
8 Jaden Hardy 1.00 2.50
9 Victor Wembanyama 100.00 250.00
10 Shaquille O'Neal 2.50 6.00
11 Derrick White 1.00 2.50
12 John Collins .75 2.00
13 Magic Johnson 3.00 8.00
14 Brook Lopez .60 1.50
15 LeBron James 6.00 15.00
16 Bruce Brown .75 2.00
17 Kyle Kuzma 1.00 2.50
18 Dennis Schroder .75 2.00
19 Dariq Whitehead 2.00 5.00
20 Desmond Bane 1.00 2.50
21 Jalen Suggs 1.00 2.50
22 Jaren Jackson Jr. 1.25 3.00
23 Jamal Murray 1.50 4.00
24 Miles Bridges .75 2.00
25 Charles Barkley 2.00 5.00
26 Kelly Oubre Jr. .75 2.00
27 D'Angelo Russell .75 2.00
28 Jaime Jaquez Jr. 2.50 6.00
29 Joel Embiid 2.00 5.00
30 Chet Holmgren 2.00 5.00
31 Tyrese Maxey 1.50 4.00
32 Lauri Markkanen 1.25 3.00
33 Cam Whitmore 4.00 10.00
34 Jalen Johnson 1.00 2.50
35 Keyonte George 5.00 12.00
36 Gordon Hayward .75 2.00
37 Ben Sheppard 1.50 4.00
38 Julian Phillips 1.50 4.00
39 Kevin Garnett 2.00 5.00
40 Bogdan Bogdanovic .75 2.00
41 Coby White .75 2.00
42 Dwyane Wade 1.50 4.00
43 Jimmy Butler 1.25 3.00
44 Damian Lillard 2.00 5.00
45 Stephen Curry 6.00 15.00
46 Domantas Sabonis 1.25 3.00
47 Kris Murray 1.50 4.00
48 Grayson Allen .75 2.00
49 Nikola Jokic 4.00 10.00
50 Trayce Jackson-Davis 2.00 5.00
51 Terry Rozier III 1.00 2.50
52 Ivica Zubac .75 2.00
53 Jalen Green 1.25 3.00
54 Deandre Ayton .75 2.00
55 Jarrett Allen .75 2.00
56 Kristaps Porzingis 1.00 2.50
57 Khris Middleton .75 2.00
58 Ausar Thompson 4.00 10.00
59 Darius Garland 1.25 3.00
60 Chris Livingston 1.50 4.00
61 Julius Erving 2.00 5.00
62 Karl-Anthony Towns 1.25 3.00
63 Tari Eason 1.00 2.50
64 Anthony Davis 2.00 5.00
65 Cameron Johnson .75 2.00
66 Andre Jackson Jr. 2.50 6.00

67 Larry Bird 3.00 8.00
68 Noah Clowney 2.00 5.00
69 Pascal Siakam 1.25 3.00
70 Markelle Fultz .60 1.50
71 Jalen Hood-Schifino 1.50 4.00
72 Bam Adebayo 1.25 3.00
73 Josh Giddey 1.00 2.50
74 Evan Mobley 1.25 3.00
75 Andrew Wiggins 1.00 2.50
76 Franz Wagner 1.25 3.00
77 Jalen Williams 1.50 4.00
78 Paul George 1.25 3.00
79 Gradey Dick 3.00 8.00
80 Allen Iverson 2.00 5.00
81 Alperen Sengun 1.25 3.00
82 Maxwell Lewis 1.25 3.00
83 Olivier-Maxence Prosper 1.50 4.00
84 Kareem Abdul-Jabbar 2.50 6.00
85 Grant Williams .60 1.50
86 Duncan Robinson .75 2.00
87 Amari Bailey 1.50 4.00
88 Draymond Green 1.00 2.50
89 GG Jackson II 8.00 20.00
90 Craig Porter Jr. 2.00 5.00
91 Sasha Vezenkov 1.25 3.00
92 Jonas Valanciunas .60 1.50
93 Jordan Hawkins 2.50 6.00
94 Donovan Mitchell 1.50 4.00
95 Brandin Podziemski 5.00 12.00
96 Chris Paul 1.50 4.00
97 Michael Porter Jr. 1.00 2.50
98 Taylor Hendricks 1.50 4.00
99 Jaylen Brown 1.50 4.00
100 Bennedict Mathurin 1.25 3.00
101 Jalen Pickett 1.25 3.00
102 Derrick Rose 1.25 3.00
103 Isaiah Stewart .75 2.00
104 Zach LaVine 1.25 3.00
105 Tyler Herro 1.25 3.00
106 DeMar DeRozan 1.25 3.00
107 Anfernee Simons 1.00 2.50
108 Nikola Vucevic .75 2.00
109 Tony Parker 1.25 3.00
110 Karl Malone 1.50 4.00
111 Naz Reid .75 2.00
112 Brandon Miller 12.00 30.00
113 Jayson Tatum 3.00 8.00
114 Devin Booker 2.00 5.00
115 Austin Reaves 2.00 5.00
116 De'Andre Hunter .75 2.00
117 Jalen Slawson 1.50 4.00
118 Keegan Murray 1.00 2.50
119 Rudy Gobert 1.00 2.50
120 Dereck Lively II 3.00 8.00
121 Harrison Barnes .60 1.50
122 David Robinson 1.50 4.00
123 Dillon Brooks .75 2.00
124 Julius Randle 1.00 2.50
125 Buddy Hield .75 2.00
126 James Harden 1.50 4.00
127 Zion Williamson 2.00 5.00
128 Jordan Clarkson .75 2.00
129 Dejounte Murray 1.00 2.50
130 Rayan Rupert 1.50 4.00
131 Kyrie Irving 1.50 4.00
132 Tim Duncan 2.00 5.00
133 Bobby Portis 1.00 2.50
134 Hakeem Olajuwon 1.50 4.00
135 Emoni Bates 2.00 5.00
136 Mikal Bridges 1.00 2.50
137 Tobias Harris .75 2.00
138 Marcus Smart 1.00 2.50
139 Luka Doncic 5.00 12.00
140 Trae Young 1.50 4.00
141 Cade Cunningham 2.00 5.00
142 Tracy McGrady 1.25 3.00
143 Devin Vassell 1.00 2.50
144 Julian Strawther 2.00 5.00
145 Keldon Johnson 1.00 2.50
146 Jett Howard 2.00 5.00
147 Kawhi Leonard 2.00 5.00
148 Klay Thompson 2.00 5.00
149 Shaedon Sharpe 1.50 4.00
150 Anthony Black 3.00 8.00
151 Jabari Smith Jr. 1.25 3.00
152 Jalen Brunson 1.50 4.00
153 Giannis Antetokounmpo 4.00 10.00
154 Leonard Miller 1.50 4.00
155 Brandon Ingram 1.00 2.50
156 Marcus Sasser 2.50 6.00
157 Vasilije Micic 1.50 4.00
158 De'Aaron Fox 1.50 4.00
159 Kobe Bufkin 2.00 5.00
160 Shai Gilgeous-Alexander 4.00 10.00
161 Tyrese Haliburton 1.50 4.00
162 Bilal Coulibaly 4.00 10.00
163 Bojan Bogdanovic .75 2.00
164 Russell Westbrook 1.25 3.00
165 Jrue Holiday 1.00 2.50
166 Vince Carter 1.50 4.00
167 Ja Morant 2.50 6.00
168 Anthony Edwards 4.00 10.00
169 Jerami Grant 1.00 2.50
170 Jeremy Sochan 1.00 2.50
171 Myles Turner .75 2.00
172 Kevin Durant 2.50 6.00
173 Scottie Barnes 1.00 2.50
174 Sidy Cissoko 1.50 4.00
175 Colby Jones 1.50 4.00
176 Aaron Gordon .75 2.00
177 LaMelo Ball 2.00 5.00
178 RJ Barrett 1.25 3.00
179 Amen Thompson 8.00 20.00
180 Bradley Beal 1.00 2.50
181 Cameron Thomas 1.00 2.50
182 Toumani Camara 3.00 8.00
183 Hunter Tyson 1.50 4.00
184 Jaden Ivey 1.00 2.50
185 Kobe Brown 1.50 4.00
186 Yao Ming 2.00 5.00
187 Jarace Walker 3.00 8.00
188 Cason Wallace 3.00 8.00
189 Trey Murphy III 1.00 2.50
190 Carmelo Anthony 1.25 3.00
191 Nick Smith Jr. 2.00 5.00
192 Ben Simmons .75 2.00
193 Jalen Duren 1.00 2.50
194 Jaylen Clark 1.50 4.00
195 Mark Williams .75 2.00
196 Jordan Poole 1.25 3.00
197 Jalen Wilson 1.50 4.00
198 CJ McCollum .75 2.00
199 Tim Hardaway Jr. .60 1.50
200 Brandon Roy 1.00 2.50
201 Sasha Vezenkov JSY AU RC 8.00 20.00
202 Julian Strawther JSY AU RC 12.00 30.00
203 Marcus Sasser JSY AU RC 15.00 40.00
204 Amari Bailey JSY AU RC 10.00 25.00
205 Ben Sheppard JSY AU RC 10.00 25.00
206 Dariq Whitehead JSY AU RC 12.00 30.00
207 Brice Sensabaugh JSY AU RC 15.00 40.00
208 Jalen Pickett JSY AU RC 8.00 20.00
209 Vasilije Micic JSY AU RC 10.00 25.00
210 Leonard Miller JSY AU RC 10.00 25.00
211 Colby Jones JSY AU RC 10.00 25.00
212 Kris Murray JSY AU RC 10.00 25.00
213 Andre Jackson Jr. JSY AU RC 15.00 40.00
214 Olivier-Maxence
Prosper JSY AU RC 10.00 25.00
215 Bilal Coulibaly JSY AU RC 25.00 60.00
216 Hunter Tyson JSY AU RC 10.00 25.00
217 Cason Wallace JSY AU RC 20.00 50.00
218 Kobe Brown JSY AU RC 10.00 25.00
219 Jordan Walsh JSY AU RC 10.00 25.00
220 Ausar Thompson JSY AU RC 25.00 60.00
221 Maxwell Lewis JSY AU RC 8.00 20.00
222 Rayan Rupert JSY AU RC 10.00 25.00
223 Brandin Podziemski JSY AU RC 30.00 80.00
224 GG Jackson II JSY AU RC 20.00 50.00
225 Sidy Cissoko JSY AU RC 10.00 25.00
226 Noah Clowney JSY AU RC 12.00 30.00
227 Isaiah Wong JSY AU RC 10.00 25.00
228 Jaylen Clark JSY AU RC 10.00 25.00
229 Dereck Lively II JSY AU RC 20.00 50.00
230 Keyontae Johnson JSY AU RC 10.00 25.00
231 Trayce Jackson-Davis JSY AU RC 12.00 30.00
232 Jalen Wilson JSY AU RC 10.00 25.00
233 Kobe Bufkin JSY AU RC 12.00 30.00
234 Mouhamed Gueye JSY AU RC 10.00 25.00
235 Toumani Camara JSY AU RC 20.00 50.00
236 Keyonte George JSY AU RC 30.00 80.00
237 Markquis Nowell JSY AU RC 10.00 25.00
238 Julian Phillips JSY AU RC 10.00 25.00
239 Seth Lundy JSY AU RC 8.00 20.00
240 Amen Thompson JSY AU RC 50.00 120.00

2023-24 Panini Obsidian Black Color Blast

1 Tyrese Haliburton 400.00 800.00
2 Shai Gilgeous-Alexander 500.00 1,000.00
3 Victor Wembanyama 4,000.00 8,000.00
4 Nikola Jokic 400.00 800.00
5 Paolo Banchero 400.00 800.00
6 Brandon Miller 1,000.00 2,000.00
7 LeBron James 1,250.00 2,500.00
8 Scoot Henderson 500.00 1,000.00
9 Keyonte George 500.00 1,000.00
10 Jaime Jaquez Jr. 500.00 1,000.00
11 Jordan Hawkins 125.00 300.00
12 Damian Lillard 300.00 600.00
13 Trae Young 300.00 600.00
14 Ja Morant 500.00 1,000.00
15 Ausar Thompson 300.00 600.00
16 Bilal Coulibaly 200.00 500.00
17 Jayson Tatum 400.00 800.00
18 Giannis Antetokounmpo 400.00 800.00
19 Anthony Edwards 800.00 1,500.00
20 Brandin Podziemski 350.00 700.00
21 Kevin Durant 300.00 600.00
22 Cason Wallace 200.00 500.00
23 Stephen Curry 1,000.00 2,000.00
24 Luka Doncic 600.00 1,200.00
25 Amen Thompson 300.00 600.00

2023-24 Panini Obsidian Cutting Edge Memorabilia

STATED PRINT RUN 249 SER.#'d SETS
*ORANGE FLOOD/99: .5 TO 1.2X BASE HI
*PURPLE FLOOD/49: .6 TO 1.5X BASE HI
*GREEN/25: 1 TO 2.5X BASE HI
1 Kristaps Porzingis 3.00 8.00
2 De'Aaron Fox 5.00 12.00
3 LaMelo Ball 6.00 15.00
4 LeBron James 40.00 100.00
5 Kevin Durant 8.00 20.00
6 Pascal Siakam 4.00 10.00
7 Jamal Murray 5.00 12.00
8 Desmond Bane 3.00 8.00
9 Donovan Mitchell 5.00 12.00
10 Anthony Edwards 12.00 30.00
11 Jordan Poole 4.00 10.00
12 Paul George 4.00 10.00
13 Giannis Antetokounmpo 12.00 30.00
14 Joel Embiid 6.00 15.00
15 Kyrie Irving 5.00 12.00
16 RJ Barrett 4.00 10.00
17 Kawhi Leonard 6.00 15.00
18 Julius Randle 3.00 8.00
19 Jayson Tatum 10.00 25.00
20 Trae Young 5.00 12.00

2023-24 Panini Obsidian Eclipse Materials

STATED PRINT RUN 249 SER.#'d SETS
*ORANGE FLOOD/99: .5XTO 1.2X BASE HI
*PURPLE FLOOD/49: .6X TO 1.5X BASE HI
1 Dereck Lively II 4.00 10.00
2 Julian Strawther 2.50 6.00
3 Marcus Sasser 3.00 8.00
4 Jaime Jaquez Jr. 3.00 8.00
5 Brandon Miller 12.00 30.00
6 Jarace Walker 4.00 10.00
7 Amen Thompson 10.00 25.00
8 Victor Wembanyama 60.00 150.00
9 Brandin Podziemski 6.00 15.00
10 Andre Jackson Jr. 3.00 8.00
11 Kobe Brown 2.00 5.00
12 Amari Bailey 2.00 5.00
13 Vasilije Micic 2.00 5.00
14 Sasha Vezenkov 1.50 4.00
15 Scoot Henderson 6.00 15.00
16 Nick Smith Jr. 2.50 6.00
17 Cason Wallace 4.00 10.00
18 Taylor Hendricks 2.00 5.00
19 Cam Whitmore 5.00 12.00
20 Jalen Wilson 2.00 5.00
21 Keyonte George 6.00 15.00
22 Bilal Coulibaly 5.00 12.00
23 Jordan Hawkins 3.00 8.00
24 Trayce Jackson-Davis 2.50 6.00
25 Olivier-Maxence Prosper 2.00 5.00
26 Toumani Camara 4.00 10.00
27 Chris Livingston 2.00 5.00
28 Gradey Dick 4.00 10.00
29 Anthony Black 4.00 10.00
30 Ausar Thompson 5.00 12.00

2023-24 Panini Obsidian Eclipse Materials Green

*GREEN: 1X TO 2.5X BASE HI
STATED PRINT RUN 25 SER.#'d SETS
5 Brandon Miller 40.00 100.00
8 Victor Wembanyama 300.00 600.00

2023-24 Panini Obsidian Equinox

STATED PRINT RUN 99 SER.#'d SETS
*ORANGE FLOOD/75: .5 TO 1.2X BASE HI
*REGGAE FLOOD/60: .6 TO 1.5X BASE HI
*PURPLE FLOOD/49: .6 TO 1.5X BASE HI
*GREEN/25: .75 TO 2X BASE HI
*GREEN FLOOD/25: .75 TO 2X BASE HI
1 Paolo Banchero 8.00 20.00
2 Zion Williamson 8.00 20.00
3 Marcus Sasser 5.00 12.00
4 Paul George 5.00 12.00
5 Ja Morant 10.00 25.00
6 Jordan Hawkins 5.00 12.00
7 Anthony Black 6.00 15.00
8 Anthony Edwards 15.00 40.00
9 Victor Wembanyama 100.00 250.00
10 Stephen Curry 25.00 60.00
11 Gradey Dick 6.00 15.00
12 Devin Booker 8.00 20.00
13 Brandin Podziemski 10.00 25.00
14 Dereck Lively II 6.00 15.00
15 Anthony Davis 8.00 20.00
16 Nikola Jokic 15.00 40.00
17 Jayson Tatum 12.00 30.00
18 Scoot Henderson 10.00 25.00
19 Giannis Antetokounmpo 15.00 40.00
20 Cason Wallace 6.00 15.00
21 Damian Lillard 8.00 20.00
22 Jalen Brunson 6.00 15.00
23 Donovan Mitchell 6.00 15.00
24 Ausar Thompson 8.00 20.00
25 Kevin Durant 10.00 25.00
26 LeBron James 25.00 60.00
27 DeMar DeRozan 5.00 12.00
28 Bilal Coulibaly 8.00 20.00
29 Kyrie Irving 6.00 15.00
30 Cade Cunningham 8.00 20.00
31 Tyrese Haliburton 6.00 15.00
32 Luka Doncic 20.00 50.00
33 Amen Thompson 15.00 40.00
34 Keyonte George 10.00 25.00
35 Brandon Miller 12.00 30.00
36 Shai Gilgeous-Alexander 15.00 40.00
37 Trae Young 6.00 15.00
38 Joel Embiid 8.00 20.00
39 Jaime Jaquez Jr. 5.00 12.00
40 Kawhi Leonard 8.00 20.00

2023-24 Panini Obsidian Equinox Gear

COMMON CARD 2.00 5.00
SEMISTARS 2.50 6.00
UNLISTED STARS 3.00 8.00
STATED PRINT RUN 249 SER.#'d SETS
*ORANGE FLOOD/99: .5XTO 1.2X BASE HI
*PURPLE FLOOD/49: .6X TO 1.5X BASE HI
1 Scoot Henderson 10.00 25.00
2 DeMar DeRozan 5.00 12.00
3 Khris Middleton 3.00 8.00
4 Scottie Barnes 4.00 10.00
6 Amen Thompson 15.00 40.00
7 Brandon Miller 12.00 30.00
8 Terry Rozier III 4.00 10.00
9 Bilal Coulibaly 8.00 20.00
10 Jordan Hawkins 5.00 12.00
11 Darius Garland 5.00 12.00
12 Dereck Lively II 6.00 15.00
13 Jaime Jaquez Jr. 5.00 12.00
14 Jimmy Butler 5.00 12.00
15 Victor Wembanyama 100.00 250.00
16 Jaylen Brown 6.00 15.00
17 Keyonte George 10.00 25.00
18 Immanuel Quickley 3.00 8.00
19 Cameron Thomas 4.00 10.00
20 Ausar Thompson 8.00 20.00

2023-24 Panini Obsidian Equinox Gear Green

*GREEN: .75X TO 2X BASE HI
STATED PRINT RUN 25 SER.#'d SETS
15 Victor Wembanyama 300.00 600.00

2023-24 Panini Obsidian Galaxy Ink

STATED PRINT RUN 49-149 SER.#'d SETS
*ORANGE FLOOD/75: .5XTO 1.2X BASE HI
*PURPLE FLOOD/49: .6X TO 1.5X BASE HI
1 Luka Doncic/49 350.00 700.00
2 Julian Champagnie/149 6.00 15.00
3 Day'Ron Sharpe/149 5.00 12.00
4 Evan Fournier/149 5.00 12.00
5 Sam Cassell/99 5.00 12.00
6 Glen Rice/99 6.00 15.00
7 Yuta Tabuse/99 8.00 20.00
8 Zach LaVine/75 10.00 25.00
9 Ben Simmons/99 10.00 25.00
10 Jonas Valanciunas/99 5.00 12.00
11 Josh Green/99 5.00 12.00
12 Scottie Barnes/99 15.00 40.00
13 Moses Moody/99 8.00 20.00
15 Lenny Wilkens/99 8.00 20.00
16 Josh Giddey/99 8.00 20.00
17 Corey Kispert/149 5.00 12.00
18 Isaiah Hartenstein/149 6.00 15.00
19 Jabari Smith Jr./75 10.00 25.00
20 D'Angelo Russell/99 6.00 15.00
21 Monte Morris/149 6.00 15.00
22 Amir Coffey/149 4.00 10.00
23 Ayo Dosunmu/99 6.00 15.00
24 Jalen McDaniels/149 5.00 12.00
25 Larry Nance Jr./149 4.00 10.00
26 Payton Pritchard/149 6.00 15.00
27 Carlos Boozer/99 5.00 12.00
28 Gabe Vincent/149 6.00 15.00
29 Chris Duarte/149 5.00 12.00
30 Max Christie/149 6.00 15.00
31 Allan Houston/149 6.00 15.00
32 Mark Williams/149 6.00 15.00
33 Justin Holiday/149 5.00 12.00
35 Nate Archibald/99 8.00 20.00
36 Zeke Nnaji/149 4.00 10.00
37 Isaiah Joe/149 6.00 15.00
38 Dee Brown/149 5.00 12.00
39 Kevon Looney/149 6.00 15.00
40 Doug McDermott/149 5.00 12.00
41 Taj Gibson/149 4.00 10.00
42 Kelly Olynyk/149 4.00 10.00
43 Quentin Grimes/99 6.00 15.00
44 Harold Miner/149 6.00 15.00
45 Royce O'Neale/149 5.00 12.00
46 Max Strus/149 O 2X BASE HI
STATED PRINT RUN 25 SER.#'d SETS
1 Luka Doncic 400.00 800.00

2023-24 Panini Obsidian Hotspot

STATED PRINT RUN 99 SER.#'d SETS
*ORANGE FLOOD/75: .5 TO 1.2X BASE HI
*REGGAE FLOOD/60: .6 TO 1.5X BASE HI
*PURPLE FLOOD/49: .6 TO 1.5X BASE HI
*GREEN/25: .75 TO 2X BASE HI
*GREEN FLOOD/25: .75 TO 2X BASE HI
1 Shai Gilgeous-Alexander 15.00 40.00
2 Kevin Durant 10.00 25.00
3 Damian Lillard 8.00 20.00
4 Donovan Mitchell 6.00 15.00
5 Trae Young 6.00 15.00
6 Scoot Henderson 10.00 25.00
7 Ausar Thompson 8.00 20.00
8 Nikola Jokic 15.00 40.00
9 Amen Thompson 15.00 40.00
10 Ja Morant 10.00 25.00
11 Tyrese Haliburton 6.00 15.00
12 LeBron James 25.00 60.00
13 Brandon Miller 12.00 30.00
14 Giannis Antetokounmpo 15.00 40.00
15 Kyrie Irving 6.00 15.00
16 Anthony Edwards 15.00 40.00
17 Luka Doncic 20.00 50.00
18 Victor Wembanyama 100.00 250.00
19 Stephen Curry 25.00 60.00
20 Jayson Tatum 12.00 30.00

2023-24 Panini Obsidian Magmatic Signatures

STATED PRINT RUN 49-149 SER.#'d SETS
*ORANGE FLOOD/75: .5XTO 1.2X BASE HI
*PURPLE FLOOD/49: .6X TO 1.5X BASE HI
1 Ja Morant/49 100.00 250.00
2 Domantas Sabonis/99 10.00 25.00
3 Stephen Curry/49 350.00 700.00
4 Grant Williams/99 5.00 12.00
5 Arvydas Sabonis/99 8.00 20.00
6 Bruce Bowen/149 5.00 12.00
8 Clint Capela/99 5.00 12.00
9 Tre Mann/149 6.00 15.00
10 Josh Hart/99 6.00 15.00
11 Peja Stojakovic/99 6.00 15.00
12 Donte DiVincenzo/149 6.00 15.00
13 Isaiah Livers/149 5.00 12.00
14 Tyrese Maxey/99 25.00 60.00
15 Jeremy Sochan/99 8.00 20.00
16 Alperen Sengun/99 15.00 40.00
17 Lonnie Walker IV/99 6.00 15.00
19 Jalen McDaniels/149 5.00 12.00
20 Justin Champagnie/99 5.00 12.00
21 Bennedict Mathurin/99 10.00 25.00
22 Walker Kessler/99 6.00 15.00
23 Isaac Okoro/149 5.00 12.00
24 Aaron Wiggins/149 5.00 12.00
25 Jeff Hornacek/149 5.00 12.00
26 Nikola Jovic/149 6.00 15.00
27 Norman Powell/149 6.00 15.00
28 Daniel Gafford/149 6.00 15.00
29 Robin Lopez/149 5.00 12.00
30 Torrey Craig/149 5.00 12.00
31 Max Christie/149 6.00 15.00
33 Chris Boucher/149 5.00 12.00
34 Matt Ryan/149 6.00 15.00
35 Xavier Tillman/149 6.00 15.00
36 Jason Terry/99 6.00 15.00
37 Moritz Wagner/149 6.00 15.00
38 Adrian Dantley/149 6.00 15.00
39 Austin Reaves/149 15.00 40.00
40 Chuma Okeke/149 5.00 12.00
41 Kelly Olynyk/149 5.00 12.00
42 Kerry Kittles/149 5.00 12.00
43 Caleb Martin/149 5.00 12.00
44 Udonis Haslem/99 6.00 15.00
45 Dante Exum/149 5.00 12.00
46 Bill Laimbeer/149 6.00 15.00
47 Drew Eubanks/149 4.00 10.00
48 Patty Mills/99 6.00 15.00
49 Usman Garuba/149 5.00 12.00
50 Ziaire Williams/149 6.00 15.00

2023-24 Panini Obsidian Magmatic Signatures Electric Etch Green

*GREEN: .75X TO 2X BASE HI
STATED PRINT RUN 25 SER.#'d SETS
1 Ja Morant 125.00 300.00
3 Stephen Curry 400.00 800.00

2023-24 Panini Obsidian Matrix Material Autographs

STATED PRINT RUN 49-99 SER.#'d SETS
*RED FLOOD: .4XTO 1X BASE HI
*ORANGE FLOOD/35-75: .5XTO 1.2X BASE HI
*PURPLE FLOOD/25-49: .6X TO 1.5X BASE HI
*GREEN/25: .75X TO 2X BASE HI
1 Anfernee Simons/75 10.00 25.00
2 Keldon Johnson/75 10.00 25.00
3 Franz Wagner/75 12.00 30.00
4 Bogdan Bogdanovic/99 8.00 20.00
5 Quentin Grimes/99 8.00 20.00
6 Brook Lopez/99 6.00 15.00
7 Dejounte Murray/75 10.00 25.00
8 Davion Mitchell/99 6.00 15.00
9 Cameron Thomas/99 10.00 25.00
10 Jalen Suggs/49 10.00 25.00
11 Chris Paul/49 15.00 40.00
12 Jalen Green/75 12.00 30.00
13 CJ McCollum/75 8.00 20.00
16 Trey Murphy III/99 10.00 25.00
17 Jonathan Isaac/99 6.00 15.00
18 Nikola Vucevic/75 8.00 20.00
19 Anthony Davis/49 60.00 150.00
20 Russell Westbrook/49 60.00 150.00

2023-24 Panini Obsidian Matrix Material Autographs Electric Etch Green Flood

*GREEN FLOOD: .75X TO 2X BASE HI
STATED PRINT RUN 20 SER.#'d SETS
19 Anthony Davis 100.00 250.00
20 Russell Westbrook 100.00 250.00

2023-24 Panini Obsidian Orbital

STATED PRINT RUN 99 SER.#'d SETS
*ORANGE FLOOD/75: .5 TO 1.2X BASE HI
*REGGAE FLOOD/60: .6 TO 1.5X BASE HI
*PURPLE FLOOD/49: .6 TO 1.5X BASE HI
*GREEN/25: .75 TO 2X BASE HI
*GREEN FLOOD/25: .75 TO 2X BASE HI
1 LaMelo Ball 8.00 20.00
2 Tyrese Haliburton 6.00 15.00
3 Scoot Henderson 10.00 25.00
4 Amen Thompson 15.00 40.00
5 LeBron James 25.00 60.00
6 Ja Morant 10.00 25.00
7 Jaylen Brown 6.00 15.00
8 Brandin Podziemski 10.00 25.00
9 Dereck Lively II 6.00 15.00
10 Jaime Jaquez Jr. 5.00 12.00
11 Giannis Antetokounmpo 15.00 40.00
12 Zion Williamson 8.00 20.00
13 Zach LaVine 5.00 12.00
14 Chet Holmgren 8.00 20.00
15 Tyrese Maxey 6.00 15.00
16 Keyonte George 10.00 25.00
17 Jimmy Butler 5.00 12.00
18 Victor Wembanyama 125.00 300.00
19 De'Aaron Fox 6.00 15.00
20 Joel Embiid 8.00 20.00
21 Stephen Curry 25.00 60.00
22 Jayson Tatum 12.00 30.00
23 Nikola Jokic 15.00 40.00
24 Jordan Hawkins 5.00 12.00
25 Anthony Edwards 15.00 40.00
26 Brandon Miller 12.00 30.00
27 Shai Gilgeous-Alexander 15.00 40.00
28 James Harden 6.00 15.00
29 Luka Doncic 20.00 50.00
30 Ausar Thompson 8.00 20.00

2023-24 Panini Obsidian Rookie Eruption Autographs

STATED PRINT RUN 75-99 SER.#'d SETS
*ORANGE FLOOD/49: .5XTO 1.2X BASE HI
*PURPLE FLOOD/49: .6X TO 1.5X BASE HI
*GREEN/25: .75X TO 2X BASE HI
1 Ausar Thompson/75 15.00 40.00
2 Maxwell Lewis/99 5.00 12.00
3 Toumani Camara/99 12.00 30.00
4 Kobe Bufkin/99 8.00 20.00
5 Colby Jones/99 6.00 15.00
6 Trayce Jackson-Davis/99 8.00 20.00
7 Marcus Sasser/99 10.00 25.00
8 Amari Bailey/99 6.00 15.00
9 Olivier-Maxence Prosper/99 6.00 15.00
10 Bilal Coulibaly/99 15.00 40.00
11 Keyonte George/75 20.00 50.00
12 Jalen Wilson/99 6.00 15.00
13 Julian Phillips/99 6.00 15.00
14 Amen Thompson/75 30.00 80.00
15 Ricky Council IV/99 8.00 20.00
16 Keyontae Johnson/99 6.00 15.00
17 Dereck Lively II/75 12.00 30.00
18 Hunter Tyson/99 6.00 15.00
19 Cason Wallace/75 12.00 30.00
20 GG Jackson II/75 12.00 30.00
21 Brandin Podziemski/75 20.00 50.00
22 Rayan Rupert/99 6.00 15.00
23 Brice Sensabaugh/99 10.00 25.00
24 Jordan Walsh/99 6.00 15.00
25 Vasilije Micic/99 6.00 15.00
26 Kris Murray/99 6.00 15.00
27 Duop Reath/99 6.00 15.00
28 Chris Livingston/99 6.00 15.00
29 Andre Jackson Jr./99 10.00 25.00
30 Sasha Vezenkov/99 5.00 12.00

2023-24 Panini Obsidian Rookie Jersey Ink

STATED PRINT RUN 75-99 SER.#'d SETS
*RED FLOOD: .5XTO 1.2X BASE HI
*ORANGE FLOOD/75: .5XTO 1.2X BASE HI
*PURPLE FLOOD/49: .6X TO 1.5X BASE HI
*BLUE FOTL/27: .75X TO 2X BASE HI
*GREEN/25: .75X TO 2X BASE HI
1 Jordan Walsh/99 8.00 20.00
2 Colby Jones/99 8.00 20.00
3 Noah Clowney/99 10.00 25.00
4 Dereck Lively II/99 15.00 40.00
5 Mouhamed Gueye/99 8.00 20.00
6 Amen Thompson/99 40.00 100.00
7 Leonard Miller/99 8.00 20.00
8 Markquis Nowell/99 8.00 20.00
9 Sidy Cissoko/99 8.00 20.00
10 Keyontae Johnson/99 8.00 20.00
11 Kris Murray/99 8.00 20.00
12 Jalen Pickett/99 8.00 20.00
13 Maxwell Lewis/99 6.00 15.00
14 Kobe Brown/99 8.00 20.00
15 Keyonte George/99 25.00 60.00
16 Ausar Thompson/99 20.00 50.00
17 Dariq Whitehead/99 10.00 25.00
18 Julian Strawther/75 10.00 25.00
19 Trayce Jackson-Davis/99 10.00 25.00
20 Jaylen Clark/99 8.00 20.00
21 Olivier-Maxence Prosper/99 8.00 20.00
22 Isaiah Wong/99 8.00 20.00
23 Amari Bailey/99 8.00 20.00
24 Vasilije Micic/99 8.00 20.00
25 Kobe Bufkin/99 10.00 25.00
26 Ben Sheppard/99 8.00 20.00
27 Marcus Sasser/99 12.00 30.00
28 Jalen Wilson/99 8.00 20.00
29 Bilal Coulibaly/99 20.00 50.00
30 Cason Wallace/99 15.00 40.00
31 Hunter Tyson/99 8.00 20.00
32 Brandin Podziemski/99 25.00 60.00
33 GG Jackson II/99 15.00 40.00
34 Rayan Rupert/99 8.00 20.00
35 Brice Sensabaugh/99 12.00 30.00
36 Julian Phillips/99 8.00 20.00
37 Seth Lundy/99 6.00 15.00
38 Andre Jackson Jr./99 12.00 30.00
39 Sasha Vezenkov/99 6.00 15.00
40 Toumani Camara/99 15.00 40.00

2023-24 Panini Obsidian Supernova

STATED PRINT RUN 99 SER.#'d SETS
*ORANGE FLOOD/75: .5 TO 1.2X BASE HI
*REGGAE FLOOD/60: .6 TO 1.5X BASE HI
*PURPLE FLOOD/49: .6 TO 1.5X BASE HI
1 Ausar Thompson 8.00 20.00
2 Ja Morant 10.00 25.00
3 Jayson Tatum 12.00 30.00
4 Nikola Jokic 15.00 40.00
5 Victor Wembanyama 125.00 300.00
6 Brandon Miller 12.00 30.00
7 Scoot Henderson 10.00 25.00
8 LeBron James 25.00 60.00
9 Stephen Curry 25.00 60.00
10 Luka Doncic 20.00 50.00

2023-24 Panini Obsidian Supernova Electric Etch Green

*GREEN: .75X TO 2X BASE HI
STATED PRINT RUN 25 SER.#'d SETS
5 Victor Wembanyama 400.00 800.00

2023-24 Panini Obsidian Supernova Electric Etch Green Flood

*GREEN FLOOD: .75X TO 2X BASE HI
STATED PRINT RUN 25 SER.#'d SETS
5 Victor Wembanyama 400.00 800.00

2023-24 Panini Obsidian Twilight Signatures

STATED PRINT RUN 49-149 SER.#'d SETS
*ORANGE FLOOD/75: .5XTO 1.2X BASE HI
1 Zion Williamson/30 75.00 200.00
2 Nicolas Batum/99 4.00 10.00
3 Rudy Gobert/99 8.00 20.00
4 Jalen Johnson/99 8.00 20.00
5 Spud Webb/149 6.00 15.00
6 T.J. McConnell/99 6.00 15.00
8 Metta World Peace/99 6.00 15.00
9 John Wall/99 8.00 20.00
10 Paolo Banchero /49 60.00 150.00
11 Donovan Mitchell/49 40.00 100.00
12 Cameron Thomas/99 8.00 20.00
13 Isaiah Livers/149 5.00 12.00
14 Oshae Brissett/149 5.00 12.00
15 Yuta Watanabe/99 8.00 20.00
16 Nikola Jokic/30 125.00 300.00
17 Simone Fontecchio/149 6.00 15.00
18 Shaedon Sharpe/99 20.00 50.00
19 Jalen Williams/99 20.00 50.00
20 Fred VanVleet/99 10.00 25.00
22 Sam Merrill/149 6.00 15.00
23 Isaiah Joe/149 6.00 15.00
24 Tyus Jones/99 5.00 12.00
25 Anthony Edwards/49 150.00 400.00
28 Drew Eubanks/149 4.00 10.00
29 David Roddy/99 5.00 12.00

2023-24 Panini Obsidian Twilight Signatures Electric Etch Green

*GREEN: .75X TO 2X BASE HI
STATED PRINT RUN 25 SER.#'d SETS
1 Zion Williamson 75.00 200.00
10 Paolo Banchero 75.00 200.00
11 Donovan Mitchell 50.00 120.00
16 Nikola Jokic 125.00 300.00
25 Anthony Edwards 200.00 500.00

2023-24 Panini Obsidian Twilight Signatures Electric Etch Purple Flood

*PURPLE FLOOD: .6X TO 1.5X BASE HI
STATED PRINT RUN 35-49 SER.#'d SETS
10 Paolo Banchero 75.00 200.00
25 Anthony Edwards 200.00 500.00

2023-24 Panini Obsidian Unbreakable Memorabilia

STATED PRINT RUN 149-249 SER.#'d SETS
*ORANGE FLOOD/99: .5XTO 1.2X BASE HI
*PURPLE FLOOD/49: .6X TO 1.5X BASE HI
1 Taylor Hendricks/249 2.50 6.00
2 Cam Whitmore/249 6.00 15.00
3 Jett Howard/249 3.00 8.00
4 Vasilije Micic/149 2.50 6.00
5 Keyonte George/249 8.00 20.00
6 Jordan Hawkins/249 4.00 10.00
7 Kobe Bufkin/249 3.00 8.00
8 Victor Wembanyama/249 75.00 200.00
9 Jarace Walker/249 5.00 12.00
10 Ausar Thompson/249 6.00 15.00
11 Bilal Coulibaly/249 6.00 15.00
12 Scoot Henderson/249 8.00 20.00
13 Brandon Miller/249 15.00 40.00
14 Dereck Lively II/249 5.00 12.00
15 Gradey Dick/249 5.00 12.00
16 Trayce Jackson-Davis/249 3.00 8.00
17 Marcus Sasser/249 4.00 10.00
18 Amen Thompson/249 12.00 30.00
19 Sasha Vezenkov/149 2.00 5.00
20 Jalen Pickett/149 2.00 5.00
21 Anthony Black/249 5.00 12.00
22 Cason Wallace/249 5.00 12.00
23 Andre Jackson Jr./249 4.00 10.00
24 Jalen Slawson/149 2.50 6.00
25 Toumani Camara/249 5.00 12.00
26 Julian Strawther/249 3.00 8.00
27 Jaime Jaquez Jr./249 4.00 10.00
28 Nick Smith Jr./149 3.00 8.00
29 Brandin Podziemski/249 8.00 20.00
30 Olivier-Maxence Prosper/149 2.50 6.00

2023-24 Panini Obsidian Unbreakable Memorabilia Green

*GREEN: 1X TO 2.5X BASE HI
STATED PRINT RUN 25 SER.#'d SETS
8 Victor Wembanyama 300.00 600.00
13 Brandon Miller 50.00 120.00

2023-24 Panini Obsidian Vitreous

1 Giannis Antetokounmpo 30.00 80.00
2 Amen Thompson 30.00 80.00
3 Trae Young 12.00 30.00
4 Scoot Henderson 20.00 50.00
5 Ja Morant 20.00 50.00
6 Shai Gilgeous-Alexander 30.00 80.00
7 Stephen Curry 50.00 125.00
8 Nikola Jokic 30.00 80.00
9 Luka Doncic 40.00 100.00
10 Ausar Thompson 15.00 40.00
11 Jayson Tatum 25.00 60.00
12 Victor Wembanyama 400.00 800.00
13 LeBron James 50.00 125.00
14 Tyrese Haliburton 12.00 30.00
15 Brandon Miller 125.00 300.00

2023-24 Panini Obsidian Volcanic Signatures

STATED PRINT RUN 75-149 SER.#'d SETS
*ORANGE FLOOD/75: .5XTO 1.2X BASE HI
1 MarJon Beauchamp/99 5.00 12.00
2 Chet Holmgren/75 60.00 150.00
3 Latrell Sprewell/99 8.00 20.00
4 Moritz Wagner/99 6.00 15.00
5 Matt Ryan/149 5.00 12.00
6 Kristaps Porzingis/99 20.00 50.00
7 Gabe Vincent/99 6.00 15.00
8 Jusuf Nurkic/99 6.00 15.00
9 Aaron Wiggins/149 5.00 12.00
10 Luke Kennard/99 5.00 12.00
11 Dante Exum/99 5.00 12.00
12 Luka Garza/149 5.00 12.00
13 Jarred Vanderbilt/99 5.00 12.00
14 Mike Bibby/99 6.00 15.00
15 Malik Beasley/99 6.00 15.00
16 Cazzie Russell/99 6.00 15.00
17 Juan Toscano-Anderson/99 5.00 12.00
18 De'Aaron Fox/75 25.00 60.00
19 Jaden Hardy/99 8.00 20.00
20 Jericho Sims/149 4.00 10.00
21 Wally Szczerbiak/99 5.00 12.00
22 Devonte' Graham/99 5.00 12.00
23 Tim Hardaway/99 8.00 20.00
24 Ish Smith/99 5.00 12.00
25 Caleb Martin/99 5.00 12.00
26 Cade Cunningham/75 40.00 100.00
27 Keegan Murray/99 8.00 20.00
28 Jaden Ivey/75 8.00 20.00
29 JT Thor/149 5.00 12.00
30 Ziaire Williams/99 6.00 15.00
31 Monte Morris/99 6.00 15.00
32 Thanasis Antetokounmpo/99 6.00 15.00
33 Amir Coffey/149 4.00 10.00
34 Isaiah Hartenstein/149 6.00 15.00
35 Sam Merrill/149 6.00 15.00
36 Tyus Jones/99 5.00 12.00
37 Usman Garuba/99 5.00 12.00
38 Santi Aldama/149 5.00 12.00
39 Tari Eason/99 8.00 20.00
40 Christian Braun/149 6.00 15.00

2023-24 Panini Obsidian Volcanic Signatures Electric Etch Green

*GREEN: .75X TO 2X BASE HI
STATED PRINT RUN 25 SER.#'d SETS
2 Chet Holmgren 100.00 250.00
18 De'Aaron Fox 40.00 100.00
26 Cade Cunningham 60.00 150.00

2023-24 Panini Obsidian Volcanic Signatures Electric Etch Purple Flood

*PURPLE FLOOD: .6X TO 1.5X BASE HI
STATED PRINT RUN 49 SER.#'d SETS
2 Chet Holmgren 75.00 200.00
18 De'Aaron Fox 30.00 80.00

2023-24 Panini Obsidian Volcanix

1 Ausar Thompson 15.00 40.00
2 Jaime Jaquez Jr. 10.00 25.00
3 Donovan Mitchell 12.00 30.00
4 Damian Lillard 15.00 40.00
5 Marcus Sasser 10.00 25.00
6 Brandon Miller 75.00 200.00
7 Dereck Lively II 12.00 30.00
8 Tyrese Haliburton 12.00 30.00
9 Gradey Dick 12.00 30.00
10 Amen Thompson 30.00 80.00
11 Tyrese Maxey 12.00 30.00
12 Anthony Black 12.00 30.00
13 Bilal Coulibaly 15.00 40.00
14 Stephen Curry 50.00 125.00
15 Trae Young 12.00 30.00
16 Paolo Banchero 15.00 40.00
17 Kevin Durant 20.00 50.00
18 Jordan Hawkins 10.00 25.00
19 Shai Gilgeous-Alexander 30.00 80.00
20 Keyonte George 20.00 50.00
21 LeBron James 50.00 125.00
22 De'Aaron Fox 12.00 30.00
23 Scoot Henderson 20.00 50.00
24 Anthony Davis 15.00 40.00
25 Jayson Tatum 25.00 60.00
26 Nikola Jokic 30.00 80.00
27 Giannis Antetokounmpo 30.00 80.00
28 Zion Williamson 15.00 40.00
29 Anthony Edwards 30.00 80.00
30 Brandin Podziemski 20.00 50.00
31 Luka Doncic 40.00 100.00
32 Ja Morant 20.00 50.00
33 Cason Wallace 12.00 30.00
34 Victor Wembanyama 400.00 800.00
35 Chet Holmgren 15.00 40.00

2019-20 Panini One and One

COMPLETE SET (180)
STATED PRINT RUN 99 SER.#'d SETS
*BLUE/25: .75X TO 2X BASIC
*PURPLE/20: .75X TO 2X BASIC
*RED/15: .75X TO 2X BASIC
1 Goran Dragic 6.00 15.00
2 Trae Young 20.00 50.00

3 Jrue Holiday 10.00 25.00
4 Terry Rozier 6.00 15.00
5 Nikola Vucevic 6.00 15.00
6 Tim Hardaway Jr. 5.00 12.00
7 CJ McCollum 8.00 20.00
8 Russell Westbrook 12.00 30.00
9 Kyle Lowry 8.00 20.00
10 Montrezl Harrell 6.00 15.00
11 Giannis Antetokounmpo 40.00 100.00
12 John Collins 8.00 20.00
13 Julius Randle 10.00 25.00
14 Miles Bridges 8.00 20.00
15 Ben Simmons 8.00 20.00
16 Nikola Jokic 40.00 100.00
17 Carmelo Anthony 12.00 30.00
18 James Harden 15.00 40.00
19 Pascal Siakam 12.00 30.00
20 LeBron James 60.00 150.00
21 Khris Middleton 8.00 20.00
22 Vince Carter 15.00 40.00
23 Kevin Knox II 5.00 12.00
24 Zach LaVine 12.00 30.00
25 Josh Richardson 5.00 12.00
26 Jamal Murray 12.00 30.00
27 Hassan Whiteside 5.00 12.00
28 Eric Gordon 6.00 15.00
29 Marc Gasol 8.00 20.00
30 Anthony Davis 20.00 50.00
31 Brook Lopez 6.00 15.00
32 Jayson Tatum 30.00 80.00
33 Elfrid Payton 5.00 12.00
34 Lauri Markkanen 10.00 25.00
35 Tobias Harris 6.00 15.00
36 Gary Harris 6.00 15.00
37 De'Aaron Fox 12.00 30.00
38 Malcolm Brogdon 6.00 15.00
39 Donovan Mitchell 15.00 40.00
40 Kyle Kuzma 10.00 25.00
41 Eric Bledsoe 6.00 15.00
42 Kemba Walker 6.00 15.00
43 Chris Paul 15.00 40.00
44 Wendell Carter Jr. 8.00 20.00
45 Al Horford 8.00 20.00
46 Blake Griffin 8.00 20.00
47 Buddy Hield 6.00 15.00
48 Victor Oladipo 6.00 15.00
49 Joe Ingles 6.00 15.00
50 Dwight Howard 10.00 25.00
51 Karl-Anthony Towns 12.00 30.00
52 Jaylen Brown 12.00 30.00
53 Shai Gilgeous-Alexander 40.00 100.00
54 Andre Drummond 6.00 15.00
55 Joel Embiid 15.00 40.00
56 Derrick Rose 15.00 40.00
57 Marvin Bagley III 6.00 15.00
58 Domantas Sabonis 10.00 25.00
59 Bojan Bogdanovic 6.00 15.00
60 Dillon Brooks 6.00 15.00
61 D'Angelo Russell 6.00 15.00
62 Kevin Durant 25.00 60.00
63 Danilo Gallinari 6.00 15.00
64 Collin Sexton 10.00 25.00
65 Ricky Rubio 6.00 15.00
66 Luke Kennard 6.00 15.00
67 DeMar DeRozan 10.00 25.00
68 T.J. Warren 6.00 15.00
69 Rudy Gobert 10.00 25.00
70 Jaren Jackson Jr. 12.00 30.00
71 Lonzo Ball 8.00 20.00
72 Kyrie Irving 15.00 40.00
73 Steven Adams 6.00 15.00
74 Kevin Love 8.00 20.00
75 Devin Booker 2.00 5.00
76 Stephen Curry 60.00 150.00
77 LaMarcus Aldridge 8.00 20.00
78 Kawhi Leonard 20.00 50.00
79 John Wall 10.00 25.00
80 Jonas Valanciunas 6.00 15.00
81 JJ Redick 8.00 20.00
82 Spencer Dinwiddie 6.00 15.00
83 Markelle Fultz 6.00 15.00
84 Luka Doncic 50.00 125.00
85 Deandre Ayton 8.00 20.00
86 Andrew Wiggins 10.00 25.00
87 Dejounte Murray 8.00 20.00
88 Paul George 12.00 30.00
89 Bradley Beal 10.00 25.00
90 Jimmy Butler 15.00 40.00
91 Brandon Ingram 8.00 20.00
92 Devonte' Graham 6.00 15.00
93 Aaron Gordon 8.00 20.00
94 Kristaps Porzingis 10.00 25.00
95 Damian Lillard 20.00 50.00
96 Draymond Green 10.00 25.00
97 Fred VanVleet 10.00 25.00
98 Lou Williams 8.00 20.00
99 Thomas Bryant 6.00 15.00
100 Bam Adebayo 12.00 30.00
101 Cameron Johnson RC 12.00 30.00
102 Tremont Waters RC 6.00 15.00
103 Nickeil Alexander-Walker RC 8.00 20.00
104 Nicolo Melli RC 6.00 15.00
105 Grant Williams RC 8.00 20.00
106 Mfiondu Kabengele RC 6.00 15.00
107 Zion Williamson RC 75.00 200.00
108 Carsen Edwards RC 6.00 15.00
109 Jarrett Culver RC 5.00 12.00
110 Jaylen Nowell RC 6.00 15.00
111 PJ Washington Jr. RC 15.00 40.00
112 Kyle Guy RC 6.00 15.00
113 Goga Bitadze RC 8.00 20.00
114 Ky Bowman RC 6.00 15.00
115 Darius Bazley RC 5.00 12.00
116 Jordan Poole RC 20.00 50.00
117 Darius Garland RC 20.00 50.00
118 Bruno Fernando RC 6.00 15.00
119 Coby White RC 15.00 40.00
120 Bol Bol RC 12.00 30.00
121 Tyler Herro RC 25.00 60.00
122 Tacko Fall RC 6.00 15.00
123 Luka Samanic RC 6.00 15.00
124 Luguentz Dort RC 20.00 50.00
125 Ty Jerome RC 10.00 25.00
126 Keldon Johnson RC 15.00 40.00
127 Ja Morant RC 100.00 250.00
128 Cody Martin RC 8.00 20.00
129 Jaxson Hayes RC 8.00 20.00
130 Isaiah Roby RC 6.00 15.00
131 Romeo Langford RC 5.00 12.00
132 Kendrick Nunn RC 8.00 20.00
133 Matisse Thybulle RC 10.00 25.00
134 Daniel Gafford RC 10.00 25.00
135 Nassir Little RC 8.00 20.00
136 Kevin Porter Jr. RC 10.00 25.00
137 RJ Barrett RC 20.00 50.00
138 Eric Paschall RC 6.00 15.00
139 Rui Hachimura RC 20.00 50.00
140 Ignas Brazdeikis RC 6.00 15.00
141 Sekou Doumbouya RC 5.00 12.00
142 Terence Davis II RC 8.00 20.00
143 Brandon Clarke RC 10.00 25.00
144 Nicolas Claxton RC 10.00 25.00
145 Dylan Windler RC 6.00 15.00
146 KZ Okpala RC 6.00 15.00
147 De'Andre Hunter RC 20.00 50.00
148 Admiral Schofield RC 6.00 15.00
149 Cam Reddish RC 15.00 40.00
150 Quinndary Weatherspoon RC 5.00 12.00
151 Tim Duncan 20.00 50.00
152 Steve Nash 15.00 40.00
153 Manute Bol 10.00 25.00
154 Paul Pierce 12.00 30.00
155 Yao Ming 20.00 50.00
156 Chris Webber 10.00 25.00
157 Julius Erving 20.00 50.00
158 Anfernee Hardaway 20.00 50.00
159 Wilt Chamberlain 30.00 80.00
160 Stephon Marbury 10.00 25.00
161 Reggie Lewis 8.00 20.00
162 Shaquille O'Neal 30.00 80.00
163 Darryl Dawkins 8.00 20.00
164 Scottie Pippen 20.00 50.00
165 Larry Bird 30.00 80.00
166 Kareem Abdul-Jabbar 25.00 60.00
167 Patrick Ewing 12.00 30.00
168 Allen Iverson 20.00 50.00
169 Pete Maravich 20.00 50.00
170 Tracy McGrady 12.00 30.00
171 Moses Malone 12.00 30.00
172 Gary Payton 12.00 30.00
173 Drazen Petrovic 10.00 25.00
174 Bill Russell 25.00 60.00
175 Bill Bradley 10.00 25.00
176 Karl Malone 15.00 40.00
177 Kevin Garnett 20.00 50.00
178 Jason Kidd 12.00 30.00
179 Dennis Johnson 10.00 25.00
180 Alonzo Mourning 12.00 30.00

2019-20 Panini One and One Downtown

COMPLETE SET (20)
1 Ben Simmons 60.00 150.00
2 LeBron James 1,000.00 2,000.00
3 Trae Young 300.00 600.00
4 Stephen Curry 1,250.00 2,500.00
5 James Harden 300.00 600.00
6 Zion Williamson 600.00 1,200.00
7 Kawhi Leonard 300.00 600.00
8 RJ Barrett 150.00 400.00
9 Kyrie Irving 300.00 600.00
10 Tyler Herro 300.00 600.00
11 Coby White 150.00 400.00
12 Giannis Antetokounmpo 400.00 800.00
13 Nikola Jokic 500.00 1,000.00
14 Jayson Tatum 600.00 1,200.00
15 Luka Doncic 1,000.00 2,000.00
16 Ja Morant 1,000.00 2,000.00
17 Anthony Davis 200.00 500.00
18 Rui Hachimura 150.00 400.00
19 Russell Westbrook 200.00 500.00
20 Kendrick Nunn 50.00 120.00

2019-20 Panini One and One Dual Jersey Autographs

COMPLETE SET (19)
STATED PRINT RUN 25-99 SER.#'d SETS
*BLUE/49: .5X TO 1.2X BASIC
*PURPLE/35: .6X TO 1.5X BASIC
*RED/13-25: .75X TO 2X BASIC
1 Kristaps Porzingis/99 25.00 60.00
2 Charles Barkley/25 150.00 400.00
3 Lauri Markkanen/99 50.00 120.00
4 Giannis Antetokounmpo/25 300.00 600.00
5 Zach LaVine/99 100.00 250.00
6 Anthony Davis/25 150.00 400.00
7 Andrew Wiggins/99 75.00 200.00
8 Karl-Anthony Towns/25 75.00 200.00
10 Hakeem Olajuwon/49 75.00 200.00
11 De'Aaron Fox/99 100.00 250.00
12 Stephen Curry/25 1,500.00 3,000.00
13 Mike Conley/99 12.00 30.00
14 Damian Lillard/25 150.00 400.00
15 Jaren Jackson Jr./99 100.00 250.00
16 Magic Johnson/25 200.00 500.00
17 Shai Gilgeous-Alexander/99 400.00 800.00
18 Trae Young/49 300.00 600.00
19 Jason Williams/99 50.00 120.00
20 David Robinson/49 75.00 200.00

2019-20 Panini One and One First-Team Signatures

COMPLETE SET (40)
STATED PRINT RUN 25-99 SER.#'d SETS
*BLUE/49: .5X TO 1.2X BASIC
*PURPLE/35: .6X TO 1.5X BASIC
*RED/25: .75X TO 2X BASIC
1 Charles Barkley/25 125.00 300.00
2 Jerry West/99 60.00 150.00
3 Bill Russell/25 300.00 600.00
4 Dominique Wilkins/99 20.00 50.00
5 Dwyane Wade/25 150.00 400.00
6 Walt Frazier/99 20.00 50.00
7 John Stockton/25 75.00 200.00
8 Elvin Hayes/99 15.00 40.00
9 Kevin Garnett/25 150.00 400.00
10 Hakeem Olajuwon/49 60.00 150.00
11 Stephen Curry/25 600.00 1,200.00
12 Kevin McHale/99 20.00 50.00
13 Giannis Antetokounmpo/25 400.00 800.00
14 Nikola Jokic/99 200.00 500.00
15 Damian Lillard/25 125.00 300.00
16 Bernard King/99 15.00 40.00
17 David Thompson/99 12.00 30.00
18 Latrell Sprewell/99 15.00 40.00
19 Kareem Abdul-Jabbar/25 150.00 400.00
20 Clyde Drexler/99 40.00 100.00
21 Shaquille O'Neal /25 200.00 500.00
22 Elgin Baylor/99 60.00 150.00
23 Allen Iverson/25 200.00 500.00
24 Rick Barry/99 15.00 40.00
25 Larry Bird/25 150.00 400.00
26 Chris Mullin/99 15.00 40.00
27 Julius Erving/25 125.00 300.00
28 Bill Walton/99 50.00 120.00
29 Oscar Robertson/25 75.00 200.00
30 Grant Hill/99 50.00 120.00
31 Kevin Durant/25 125.00 300.00
32 Gary Payton/99 40.00 100.00
33 Karl Malone/25 125.00 300.00
34 Dwight Howard/99 40.00 100.00
35 Anthony Davis/25 100.00 250.00
36 George Gervin/99 20.00 50.00
37 Magic Johnson/25 150.00 400.00
38 Bob McAdoo/99 15.00 40.00
39 David Robinson/49 60.00 150.00
40 Jason Kidd/99 40.00 100.00

2019-20 Panini One and One Jersey Autographs

COMPLETE SET (19)
STATED PRINT RUN 25-99 SER.#'d SETS
*BLUE/49: .5X TO 1.2X BASIC
*PURPLE/35: .6X TO 1.5X BASIC
*RED/13-25: .75X TO 2X BASIC
1 Zach LaVine/99 75.00 200.00
2 Anthony Davis/25 125.00 300.00
3 Andrew Wiggins/99 60.00 150.00
4 Karl-Anthony Towns/25 60.00 150.00
6 Hakeem Olajuwon/49 60.00 150.00
7 Kristaps Porzingis/99 20.00 50.00
8 Charles Barkley/25 125.00 300.00
9 Lauri Markkanen/99 40.00 100.00
10 Giannis Antetokounmpo/25 200.00 500.00
11 Jaren Jackson Jr./99 75.00 200.00
12 Magic Johnson/25 150.00 400.00
13 Shai Gilgeous-Alexander/99 400.00 800.00
14 Trae Young/99 200.00 500.00
15 Jason Williams/99 40.00 100.00
16 David Robinson/49 60.00 150.00
17 De'Aaron Fox/99 75.00 200.00
18 Stephen Curry/25 2,000.00 4,000.00
19 Mike Conley/99 10.00 25.00
20 Damian Lillard/25 125.00 300.00

2019-20 Panini One and One Premium Rookie Jersey Autographs

COMPLETE SET (20)
STATED PRINT RUN 75-99 SER.#'d SETS
*BLUE/49: .5X TO 1.2X BASIC
*PURPLE/35: .6X TO 1.5X BASIC
*RED/25: .75X TO 2X BASIC
1 Cam Reddish/99 10.00 25.00
2 Brandon Clarke/99 12.00 30.00
3 Carsen Edwards/99 8.00 20.00
4 Cameron Johnson/99 15.00 40.00
5 De'Andre Hunter/99 25.00 60.00
6 Coby White/99 20.00 50.00
7 Ja Morant/99 400.00 800.00
8 Eric Paschall/99 8.00 20.00
9 Jaxson Hayes/99 10.00 25.00
10 Jarrett Culver/99 6.00 15.00
11 PJ Washington Jr./99 20.00 50.00
12 Nickeil Alexander-Walker/99 10.00 25.00
13 Tacko Fall/99 8.00 20.00
14 RJ Barrett/99 25.00 60.00
15 Darius Bazley/99 6.00 15.00
16 Rui Hachimura/75 25.00 60.00
17 Zion Williamson/99 300.00 600.00
18 Tyler Herro/99 50.00 120.00
19 Matisse Thybulle/99 12.00 30.00
20 Kendrick Nunn/99 10.00 25.00

2019-20 Panini One and One Rookie Autographs

COMPLETE SET (20)
STATED PRINT RUN 99 SER.#'d SETS
*BLUE/49: .5X TO 1.2X BASIC
*PURPLE/35: .6X TO 1.5X BASIC
*RED/25: .75X TO 2X BASIC
1 Ja Morant 300.00 600.00
2 Eric Paschall 6.00 15.00
3 Jaxson Hayes 8.00 20.00
4 Jarrett Culver 5.00 12.00
5 Cam Reddish 8.00 20.00
6 Brandon Clarke 10.00 25.00
7 Carsen Edwards 6.00 15.00
8 Cameron Johnson 12.00 30.00
9 De'Andre Hunter 20.00 50.00
10 Coby White 15.00 40.00
11 Zion Williamson 150.00 400.00
12 Tyler Herro 40.00 100.00
13 Matisse Thybulle 10.00 25.00
14 Kendrick Nunn 8.00 20.00
15 PJ Washington Jr. 15.00 40.00
16 Nickeil Alexander-Walker 8.00 20.00
17 Bol Bol 12.00 30.00
18 RJ Barrett 20.00 50.00
19 Darius Bazley 5.00 12.00
20 Tacko Fall 6.00 15.00

2019-20 Panini One and One Rookie Dual Jersey Autographs

COMPLETE SET (25)
STATED PRINT RUN 75-99 SER.#'d SETS
*BLUE/49: .5X TO 1.2X BASIC
*PURPLE/35: .6X TO 1.5X BASIC
*RED/25: .75X TO 2X BASIC
1 Carsen Edwards/99 10.00 25.00
2 Cameron Johnson/99 25.00 60.00
3 De'Andre Hunter/99 30.00 80.00
4 Coby White/99 25.00 60.00
5 Ja Morant/99 500.00 1,000.00
6 Eric Paschall/99 10.00 25.00
7 Jaxson Hayes/99 12.00 30.00
8 Jarrett Culver/99 8.00 20.00
9 Cam Reddish/99 12.00 30.00
10 Brandon Clarke/99 15.00 40.00
11 Goga Bitadze/99 8.00 20.00
12 RJ Barrett/99 30.00 80.00
13 Darius Bazley/99 8.00 20.00
14 Rui Hachimura/75 30.00 80.00
15 Zion Williamson/99 400.00 800.00
16 Tyler Herro/99 60.00 150.00
17 Matisse Thybulle/99 15.00 40.00
18 Kendrick Nunn/99 12.00 30.00
19 PJ Washington Jr./99 25.00 60.00
20 Nickeil Alexander-Walker/99 12.00 30.00
21 Kevin Porter Jr./99 15.00 40.00
22 Tacko Fall/99 10.00 25.00
23 Naz Reid/99 30.00 80.00
24 Bol Bol/99 20.00 50.00
25 Grant Williams/99 12.00 30.00

2019-20 Panini One and One Rookie Jersey Autographs

COMPLETE SET (25)
STATED PRINT RUN 75-99 SER.#'d SETS
*BLUE/49: .5X TO 1.2X BASIC
*PURPLE/35: .6X TO 1.5X BASIC
*RED/25: .75X TO 2X BASIC
1 Cameron Johnson/99 15.00 40.00
2 RJ Barrett/99 25.00 60.00
3 Coby White/99 20.00 50.00
4 Rui Hachimura/75 25.00 60.00
5 Eric Paschall/99 8.00 20.00
6 Tyler Herro/99 50.00 120.00
7 Jarrett Culver/99 6.00 15.00
8 Kendrick Nunn/99 10.00 25.00
9 Brandon Clarke/99 12.00 30.00
10 Nickeil Alexander-Walker/99 8.00 20.00
11 Carsen Edwards/99 8.00 20.00
12 Goga Bitadze/99 10.00 25.00
13 De'Andre Hunter/99 25.00 60.00
14 Darius Bazley/99 6.00 15.00
15 Ja Morant/99 400.00 800.00
16 Zion Williamson/99 300.00 600.00
17 Jaxson Hayes/99 10.00 25.00
18 Matisse Thybulle/99 12.00 30.00
19 Cam Reddish/99 10.00 25.00
20 PJ Washington Jr./99 20.00 50.00
21 Kevin Porter Jr./99 12.00 30.00
22 Tacko Fall/99 8.00 20.00
23 Naz Reid/99 25.00 60.00
24 Bol Bol/99 15.00 40.00
25 Grant Williams/99 10.00 25.00

2019-20 Panini One and One Timeless Moments Autographs

COMPLETE SET (30)
*BLUE/49: .5X TO 1.2X BASIC
*PURPLE/35: .6X TO 1.5X BASIC
*RED/25: .75X TO 2X BASIC
2 Zach LaVine/99 150.00 400.00
4 Trae Young/49 600.00 1,200.00
5 Grant Hill/99 100.00 250.00
7 Vince Carter/99 1,000.00 2,000.00
11 Ray Allen/99 800.00 1,500.00
12 Chris Bosh/99 100.00 250.00
13 Stephen Curry/25 3,000.00 6,000.00
14 Tony Parker/99 150.00 400.00
15 Dirk Nowitzki/49 800.00 1,500.00
16 Dominique Wilkins/99 150.00 400.00
18 Clyde Drexler/99 150.00 400.00
20 Dennis Rodman/99 1,500.00 3,000.00
22 Nikola Jokic/99 300.00 600.00
25 Kevin Durant/49 600.00 1,200.00
26 Jason Kidd/99 150.00 400.00
27 Paul Pierce/99 150.00 400.00
28 Giannis Antetokounmpo/25 1,500.00 3,000.00
29 Kawhi Leonard/49 1,250.00 2,500.00

2020-21 Panini One and One

COMPLETE SET (180)
STATED PRINT RUN 99 SER.#'d SETS
*BLUE/30: .75X TO 2X BASIC
*PURPLE/25: .75X TO 2X BASIC
1 Kawhi Leonard 20.00 50.00
2 Carmelo Anthony 12.00 30.00
3 Lauri Markkanen 10.00 25.00
4 Evan Fournier 6.00 15.00
5 Buddy Hield 8.00 20.00
6 Derrick Rose 12.00 30.00
7 Dennis Schroder 8.00 20.00
8 Gary Trent Jr. 8.00 20.00
9 Kendrick Nunn 6.00 15.00
10 Giannis Antetokounmpo 40.00 100.00
11 Andre Drummond 6.00 15.00
12 RJ Barrett 12.00 30.00
13 Tobias Harris 8.00 20.00
14 Keldon Johnson 12.00 30.00
15 Michael Porter Jr. 10.00 25.00
16 LeBron James 60.00 150.00
17 Bam Adebayo 12.00 30.00
18 John Collins 8.00 20.00
19 Jrue Holiday 8.00 20.00
20 DeMar DeRozan 10.00 25.00
21 James Harden 15.00 40.00
22 Myles Turner 8.00 20.00
23 Domantas Sabonis 10.00 25.00
24 Devin Booker 20.00 50.00
25 Joel Embiid 15.00 40.00
26 CJ McCollum 8.00 20.00
27 Deandre Ayton 8.00 20.00
28 Nikola Jokic 40.00 100.00
29 Donovan Mitchell 15.00 40.00
30 Zion Williamson 25.00 60.00
31 Ricky Rubio 8.00 20.00
32 Collin Sexton 8.00 20.00
33 Gordon Hayward 8.00 20.00
34 Stephen Curry 60.00 150.00
35 Josh Jackson 5.00 12.00
36 Kevin Durant 30.00 80.00
37 Malcolm Brogdon 8.00 20.00
38 Kelly Oubre Jr. 8.00 20.00
39 Karl-Anthony Towns 12.00 30.00
40 Andrew Wiggins 10.00 25.00
41 Russell Westbrook 15.00 40.00
42 Aaron Gordon 8.00 20.00
43 Paul George 12.00 30.00
44 Tyler Herro 15.00 40.00
45 Luguentz Dort 12.00 30.00
46 Darius Garland 12.00 30.00
47 Terry Rozier 8.00 20.00
48 Damian Lillard 20.00 50.00
49 Lonzo Ball 10.00 25.00
50 Caris LeVert 8.00 20.00
51 Jaylen Brown 12.00 30.00
52 Chris Paul 15.00 40.00
53 De'Andre Hunter 8.00 20.00
54 Jayson Tatum 30.00 80.00
55 Markelle Fultz 6.00 15.00
56 Devonte' Graham 6.00 15.00
57 Chuma Okeke 8.00 20.00
58 Draymond Green 10.00 25.00
59 Brandon Ingram 10.00 25.00
60 Kyle Lowry 10.00 25.00
61 Victor Oladipo 6.00 15.00
62 Fred VanVleet 12.00 30.00
63 Zach LaVine 12.00 30.00
64 Luka Doncic 50.00 125.00
65 D'Angelo Russell 8.00 20.00
66 Trae Young 20.00 50.00
67 Kristaps Porzingis 10.00 25.00
68 Kevin Porter Jr. 6.00 15.00
69 Blake Griffin 8.00 20.00
70 Rui Hachimura 10.00 25.00
71 Bradley Beal 10.00 25.00
72 Dejounte Murray 8.00 20.00
73 Nikola Vucevic 8.00 20.00
74 Harrison Barnes 6.00 15.00
75 Jordan Clarkson 8.00 20.00
76 Anthony Davis 20.00 50.00
77 Jimmy Butler 15.00 40.00
78 De'Aaron Fox 12.00 30.00
79 Shai Gilgeous-Alexander 40.00 100.00
80 Clint Capela 6.00 15.00
81 Kemba Walker 8.00 20.00
82 Ben Simmons 8.00 20.00
83 Christian Wood 6.00 15.00
84 Julius Randle 8.00 20.00
85 Jalen Brunson 12.00 30.00
86 Pascal Siakam 12.00 30.00
87 John Wall 10.00 25.00
88 Kyrie Irving 15.00 40.00
89 Mike Conley 6.00 15.00
90 Jerami Grant 8.00 20.00
91 Jarrett Allen 8.00 20.00
92 Norman Powell 8.00 20.00
93 Rudy Gobert 10.00 25.00
94 Rajon Rondo 8.00 20.00
95 Ja Morant 25.00 60.00
96 Jamal Murray 12.00 30.00
97 Khris Middleton 10.00 25.00
98 Jaren Jackson Jr. 12.00 30.00
99 Dillon Brooks 8.00 20.00
100 Wendell Carter Jr. 6.00 15.00
101 Killian Hayes RC 6.00 15.00
102 Precious Achiuwa RC 12.00 30.00
103 Facundo Campazzo RC 8.00 20.00
104 LaMelo Ball RC 100.00 250.00
105 Malachi Flynn RC 6.00 15.00
106 Isaiah Joe RC 8.00 20.00
107 Saben Lee RC 6.00 15.00
108 Tyrese Haliburton RC 150.00 400.00
109 Obi Toppin RC 12.00 30.00
110 Kenyon Martin Jr. RC 10.00 25.00
111 Udoka Azubuike RC 8.00 20.00
112 Josh Green RC 12.00 30.00
113 Saddiq Bey RC 12.00 30.00
114 Tyrese Maxey RC 60.00 150.00
115 Jalen Smith RC 12.00 30.00
116 Zeke Nnaji RC 8.00 20.00
117 Isaac Okoro RC 10.00 25.00
118 Desmond Bane RC 20.00 50.00
119 Nico Mannion RC 6.00 15.00
120 Theo Maledon RC 6.00 15.00
121 Cole Anthony RC 15.00 40.00
122 Payton Pritchard RC 20.00 50.00
123 CJ Elleby RC 6.00 15.00
124 Jordan Nwora RC 8.00 20.00
125 Isaiah Stewart RC 12.00 30.00
126 Aleksej Pokusevski RC 8.00 20.00
127 Paul Reed RC 8.00 20.00
128 Devin Vassell RC 20.00 50.00
129 Lamar Stevens RC 8.00 20.00
130 James Wiseman RC 12.00 30.00
131 Onyeka Okongwu RC 12.00 30.00
132 RJ Hampton RC 6.00 15.00
133 Jaden McDaniels RC 20.00 50.00
134 Xavier Tillman RC 8.00 20.00
135 Cassius Stanley RC 6.00 15.00
136 Naji Marshall RC 6.00 15.00
137 Sam Merrill RC 10.00 25.00
138 Anthony Edwards RC 150.00 400.00
139 Deni Avdija RC 15.00 40.00
140 Mason Jones RC 5.00 12.00
141 Patrick Williams RC 15.00 40.00
142 Immanuel Quickley RC 15.00 40.00
143 Kira Lewis Jr. RC 6.00 15.00
144 Aaron Nesmith RC 12.00 30.00
145 Jae'Sean Tate RC 8.00 20.00
146 Moses Brown RC 5.00 12.00
147 Tre Jones RC 10.00 25.00
148 Nathan Knight RC 6.00 15.00
149 Reggie Perry RC 6.00 15.00
150 Robert Woodard II RC 6.00 15.00
151 Dirk Nowitzki 20.00 50.00
152 Tracy McGrady 12.00 30.00
153 John Stockton 12.00 30.00
154 Charles Barkley 20.00 50.00
155 Kevin Garnett 20.00 50.00
156 Ray Allen 12.00 30.00
157 Shaquille O'Neal 30.00 80.00
158 Vince Carter 15.00 40.00
159 Magic Johnson 30.00 80.00
160 David Robinson 15.00 40.00
161 Dennis Rodman 20.00 50.00
162 Ben Wallace 10.00 25.00
163 Dominique Wilkins 12.00 30.00
164 George Gervin 12.00 30.00
165 Hakeem Olajuwon 15.00 40.00
166 Oscar Robertson 20.00 50.00
167 Bill Walton 12.00 30.00
168 Dikembe Mutombo 12.00 30.00
169 Clyde Drexler 12.00 30.00
170 Kareem Abdul-Jabbar 25.00 60.00
171 Jerry West 15.00 40.00
172 Walt Frazier 12.00 30.00
173 Dwyane Wade 15.00 40.00
174 Amar'e Stoudemire 8.00 20.00
175 James Worthy 12.00 30.00
176 Jason Kidd 12.00 30.00
177 Isiah Thomas 12.00 30.00
178 Shawn Kemp 12.00 30.00
179 Pete Maravich 20.00 50.00
180 Tony Parker 12.00 30.00

2020-21 Panini One and One Downtown

COMPLETE SET (20)
1 Zion Williamson 300.00 600.00
2 Luka Doncic 1,000.00 2,000.00
3 LeBron James 1,250.00 2,500.00
4 LaMelo Ball 800.00 1,500.00
5 Anthony Edwards 1,250.00 2,500.00
6 Kevin Durant 300.00 600.00
7 Stephen Curry 1,250.00 2,500.00
8 Trae Young 300.00 600.00
9 Giannis Antetokounmpo 500.00 1,000.00
10 James Harden 300.00 600.00
11 Ja Morant 800.00 1,500.00
12 Jayson Tatum 600.00 1,200.00
13 Jamal Murray 300.00 600.00
14 James Wiseman 25.00 60.00
15 Kawhi Leonard 200.00 500.00
16 Joel Embiid 150.00 400.00
17 Tyrese Haliburton 1,000.00 2,000.00
18 Jimmy Butler 200.00 500.00
19 Donovan Mitchell 200.00 500.00
20 Damian Lillard 200.00 500.00

2020-21 Panini One and One Dual Jersey Autographs

COMPLETE SET (18)
STATED PRINT RUN 25-99 SER.#'d SETS
*BLUE/35: .5X TO 1.2X BASIC
*PURPLE/25: .6X TO 1.5X BASIC
*RED/15: .75X TO 2X BASIC
2 Karl-Anthony Towns/49 50.00 120.00
3 Lauri Markkanen/99 40.00 100.00
4 Paul Pierce/49 60.00 150.00
5 Clyde Drexler/49 40.00 100.00
6 LaMarcus Aldridge/49 15.00 40.00
7 Stephen Curry/25 1,000.00 2,000.00
8 Steven Adams/49 15.00 40.00
10 Nikola Jokic/49 150.00 400.00
11 Cam Reddish/99 20.00 50.00
12 John Stockton/49 50.00 120.00
13 Robert Parish/99 20.00 50.00
14 Charles Barkley/49 125.00 300.00
15 Kareem Abdul-Jabbar/49 125.00 300.00
16 Kevin Garnett/49 125.00 300.00
17 Dwyane Wade/49 125.00 300.00
18 Domantas Sabonis/99 20.00 50.00
19 CJ McCollum/99 15.00 40.00
20 Khris Middleton/49 20.00 50.00

2020-21 Panini One and One First Team Signatures

COMPLETE SET (38)
STATED PRINT RUN 25-99 SER.#'d SETS
*BLUE/35-49: .5X TO 1.2X BASIC
*PURPLE/25: .6X TO 1.5X BASIC
*RED/15-20: .75X TO 2X BASIC
1 Kevin Garnett/49 150.00 400.00
2 Anfernee Hardaway/75 75.00 200.00
3 Allen Iverson/25 200.00 500.00
4 Jason Kidd/75 40.00 100.00
5 Gary Payton/75 40.00 100.00
6 Hakeem Olajuwon/75 50.00 120.00
7 David Robinson/75 50.00 120.00
8 Charles Barkley/25 125.00 300.00
9 Chris Mullin/75 15.00 40.00
10 Bill Walton/99 20.00 50.00
11 Nate Archibald/99 15.00 40.00
12 Rick Barry/99 15.00 40.00
13 David Thompson/99 15.00 40.00
14 Clyde Drexler/75 40.00 100.00
15 Nikola Jokic/49 150.00 400.00
16 Shaquille O'Neal/49 150.00 400.00
17 Luka Doncic/25 1,000.00 2,000.00
18 Dominique Wilkins/75 20.00 50.00
19 Kareem Abdul-Jabbar/25 150.00 400.00
20 Isiah Thomas/75 40.00 100.00
21 Jerry Lucas/75 15.00 40.00
22 Bill Russell/25 300.00 600.00
23 Larry Bird/49 125.00 300.00
25 Jerry West/75 60.00 150.00
26 Mark Price/99 12.00 30.00
27 Elvin Hayes/99 15.00 40.00
28 Latrell Sprewell/75 15.00 40.00
29 Bernard King/99 15.00 40.00
30 Stephen Curry/25 1,000.00 2,000.00
31 John Stockton/49 60.00 150.00
32 Karl Malone/49 75.00 200.00
33 Grant Hill/99 40.00 100.00
34 Oscar Robertson/49 60.00 150.00
36 Gail Goodrich/99 12.00 30.00
37 Walt Frazier/99 20.00 50.00
38 George Gervin/99 20.00 50.00
39 Magic Johnson/49 125.00 300.00
40 Dwyane Wade/49 125.00 300.00

2020-21 Panini One and One Jersey Autographs

COMPLETE SET (18)
STATED PRINT RUN 49-99 SER.#'d SETS
*BLUE/35: .5X TO 1.2X BASIC
*PURPLE/15-35: .6X TO 1.5X BASIC
*RED/15: .75X TO 2X BASIC
1 Trae Young/49 200.00 500.00
3 PJ Washington Jr./99 12.00 30.00
4 Tony Parker/49 50.00 120.00
6 Luka Doncic/49 800.00 1,500.00
7 Ja Morant/49 400.00 800.00
8 RJ Barrett/49 40.00 100.00
9 Joe Harris/49 10.00 25.00
10 Lonnie Walker IV/49 12.00 30.00
11 John Collins/99 12.00 30.00
12 Shai Gilgeous-Alexander/99 500.00 1,000.00
13 Wendell Carter Jr./99 10.00 25.00
14 Malcolm Brogdon/99 12.00 30.00
15 Karl-Anthony Towns/49 40.00 100.00
16 Steven Adams/49 12.00 30.00
17 T.J. Warren/99 10.00 25.00
18 Khris Middleton/49 15.00 40.00
19 CJ McCollum/49 12.00 30.00
20 Jamal Murray/99 60.00 150.00

2020-21 Panini One and One Rookie Autographs

COMPLETE SET (20)
STATED PRINT RUN 99 SER.#'d SETS
*BLUE/49: .5X TO 1.2X BASIC
*PURPLE/35: .6X TO 1.5X BASIC
*RED/25: .75X TO 2X BASIC
1 Josh Green 20.00 50.00
2 Facundo Campazzo 12.00 30.00
3 Saddiq Bey 20.00 50.00
4 Theo Maledon 10.00 25.00
5 Anthony Edwards 500.00 1,000.00
6 Tyrese Maxey 125.00 300.00
7 Payton Pritchard 30.00 80.00
8 Deni Avdija 25.00 60.00
9 Desmond Bane 60.00 150.00
10 Obi Toppin 20.00 50.00
11 Patrick Williams 25.00 60.00
12 Tyrese Haliburton 200.00 500.00
13 Cole Anthony 25.00 60.00
14 Isaac Okoro 15.00 40.00
15 LaMelo Ball 200.00 500.00
16 Devin Vassell 30.00 80.00
17 Killian Hayes 10.00 25.00
18 James Wiseman 12.00 30.00
19 Immanuel Quickley 25.00 60.00
20 Jae'Sean Tate 12.00 30.00

2020-21 Panini One and One Rookie Dual Jersey Autographs

COMPLETE SET (25)
STATED PRINT RUN 99 SER.#'d SETS
*BLUE/49: .5X TO 1.2X BASIC
*PURPLE/35: .6X TO 1.5X BASIC
*RED/25: .75X TO 2X BASIC
1 LaMelo Ball 300.00 600.00
2 Isaiah Stewart 25.00 60.00
3 Precious Achiuwa 25.00 60.00
4 Tyrese Maxey 150.00 400.00
5 Jordan Nwora 15.00 40.00
6 Devin Vassell 40.00 100.00
7 Tyrese Haliburton 300.00 600.00
8 Onyeka Okongwu 25.00 60.00
9 Isaac Okoro 20.00 50.00
10 Josh Green 25.00 60.00
11 Immanuel Quickley 30.00 80.00
12 Saddiq Bey 25.00 60.00
13 Anthony Edwards 600.00 1,200.00
14 Facundo Campazzo 15.00 40.00
15 Malachi Flynn 12.00 30.00
16 Obi Toppin 25.00 60.00
17 Cole Anthony 30.00 80.00
18 Payton Pritchard 40.00 100.00
19 Killian Hayes 12.00 30.00
20 Patrick Williams 30.00 80.00
21 RJ Hampton 12.00 30.00
22 Theo Maledon 12.00 30.00
23 Desmond Bane 75.00 200.00
24 Deni Avdija 30.00 80.00
25 James Wiseman 15.00 40.00

2020-21 Panini One and One Rookie Jersey Autographs

COMPLETE SET (25)
STATED PRINT RUN 99 SER.#'d SETS
*BLUE/49: .5X TO 1.2X BASIC
*PURPLE/35: .6X TO 1.5X BASIC
*RED/25: .75X TO 2X BASIC
1 Tyrese Haliburton 200.00 500.00
2 Deni Avdija 25.00 60.00
3 Immanuel Quickley 25.00 60.00
4 Devin Vassell 30.00 80.00
5 Killian Hayes 10.00 25.00
6 Cole Anthony 25.00 60.00
7 Onyeka Okongwu 20.00 50.00
8 Jaden McDaniels 30.00 80.00
9 LaMelo Ball 200.00 500.00
10 Jordan Nwora 12.00 30.00
11 Isaac Okoro 15.00 40.00
12 Jalen Smith 20.00 50.00
13 Saddiq Bey 20.00 50.00
14 Patrick Williams 25.00 60.00
15 RJ Hampton 10.00 25.00
16 Payton Pritchard 30.00 80.00
17 Anthony Edwards 500.00 1,000.00
18 Aaron Nesmith 20.00 50.00
19 Kira Lewis Jr. 10.00 25.00
20 Obi Toppin 20.00 50.00
21 Desmond Bane 60.00 150.00
22 Theo Maledon 10.00 25.00
23 Tyrese Maxey 125.00 300.00
24 Precious Achiuwa 20.00 50.00
25 James Wiseman 12.00 30.00

2020-21 Panini One and One Rookie Jersey Autographs Prime

COMPLETE SET (20)
STATED PRINT RUN 99 SER.#'d SETS
*BLUE/49: .5X TO 1.2X BASIC
*PURPLE/35: .6X TO 1.5X BASIC
*RED/25: .75X TO 2X BASIC
1 Tyrese Haliburton 300.00 600.00
2 James Wiseman 15.00 40.00
3 Deni Avdija 30.00 80.00
4 Saddiq Bey 25.00 60.00
5 Immanuel Quickley 30.00 80.00
6 Anthony Edwards 600.00 1,200.00
7 Cole Anthony 30.00 80.00
8 Tyrese Maxey 150.00 400.00
9 Isaac Okoro 20.00 50.00
10 Killian Hayes 12.00 30.00
11 LaMelo Ball 300.00 600.00
12 RJ Hampton 12.00 30.00
13 Desmond Bane 75.00 200.00
14 Kira Lewis Jr. 12.00 30.00
15 Patrick Williams 30.00 80.00
16 Onyeka Okongwu 25.00 60.00
17 Payton Pritchard 40.00 100.00
18 Theo Maledon 12.00 30.00
19 Precious Achiuwa 25.00 60.00
20 Obi Toppin 25.00 60.00

2020-21 Panini One and One Timeless Moments Autographs

COMPLETE SET (29)
STATED PRINT RUN 25-99 SER.#'d SETS
*BLUE/25-49: .5X TO 1.2X BASIC
*PURPLE/15-25: .6X TO 1.5X BASIC

*RED/15-20: .75X TO 2X BASIC
2 Magic Johnson/49 125.00 300.00
3 Kevin Garnett/49 400.00 800.00
6 Jerry West/49 150.00 400.00
7 Ray Allen/49 125.00 300.00
9 Oscar Robertson/49 100.00 250.00
11 RJ Barrett/49 75.00 200.00
14 Collin Sexton/99 60.00 150.00
16 Shaquille O'Neal/25 800.00 1,500.00
19 Paul Pierce/49 150.00 400.00
20 Coby White/75 60.00 150.00
25 Ben Wallace/75 100.00 250.00
26 Kareem Abdul-Jabbar/49 200.00 500.00
27 Karl Malone/49 125.00 300.00
29 Tony Parker/75 125.00 300.00
30 Luka Doncic/49 1,000.00 2,000.00

2022-23 Panini One and One

STATED PRINT RUN 99 SER.#'d SETS
*BLUE/40: .5X TO 1.2X BASIC
*PURPLE/25: .6X TO 1.5X BASIC
*RED/15: .75X TO 2X BASIC
1 Bojan Bogdanovic 5.00 12.00
2 Jaylen Brown 10.00 25.00
3 Julius Randle 6.00 15.00
4 Pascal Siakam 8.00 20.00
5 Jayson Tatum 20.00 50.00
6 Scottie Barnes 8.00 20.00
7 Cameron Johnson 4.00 10.00
8 Donovan Mitchell 10.00 25.00
9 Mikal Bridges 6.00 15.00
10 Cade Cunningham 15.00 40.00
11 Fred VanVleet 6.00 15.00
12 Cameron Thomas 8.00 20.00
13 Buddy Hield 5.00 12.00
14 RJ Barrett 8.00 20.00
15 Darius Garland 8.00 20.00
16 Spencer Dinwiddie 4.00 10.00
17 Jalen Brunson 10.00 25.00
18 DeMar DeRozan 6.00 15.00
19 Joel Embiid 8.00 20.00
20 James Harden 10.00 25.00
21 Evan Mobley 12.00 30.00
22 Marcus Smart 6.00 15.00
23 Tyrese Haliburton 10.00 25.00
24 Zach LaVine 10.00 25.00
25 Tyrese Maxey 10.00 25.00
26 Michael Porter Jr. 6.00 15.00
27 Khris Middleton 6.00 15.00
28 Dejounte Murray 6.00 15.00
29 Saddiq Bey 4.00 10.00
30 Rudy Gobert 6.00 15.00
31 Bradley Beal 6.00 15.00
32 Jrue Holiday 6.00 15.00
33 Trae Young 12.00 30.00
34 Tyler Herro 8.00 20.00
35 Markelle Fultz 4.00 10.00
36 Jamal Murray 8.00 20.00
37 Anthony Edwards 25.00 60.00
38 Bam Adebayo 8.00 20.00
39 Franz Wagner 12.00 30.00
40 Malcolm Brogdon 4.00 10.00
41 Kristaps Porzingis 6.00 15.00
42 Giannis Antetokounmpo 25.00 60.00
43 Kyle Kuzma 6.00 15.00
44 Cole Anthony 5.00 12.00
45 LaMelo Ball 12.00 30.00
46 Nikola Jokic 25.00 60.00
47 Jimmy Butler 10.00 25.00
48 Karl-Anthony Towns 8.00 20.00
49 PJ Washington Jr. 5.00 12.00
50 Terry Rozier III 6.00 15.00
51 Paul George 8.00 20.00
52 Harrison Barnes 4.00 10.00
53 Anthony Davis 12.00 30.00
54 Klay Thompson 12.00 30.00
55 Deandre Ayton 5.00 12.00
56 Kyrie Irving 10.00 25.00
57 Chris Paul 10.00 25.00
58 Anfernee Simons 6.00 15.00
59 Jordan Poole 8.00 20.00
60 Domantas Sabonis 6.00 15.00
61 Kawhi Leonard 12.00 30.00
62 Lauri Markkanen 8.00 20.00
63 D'Angelo Russell 4.00 10.00
64 LeBron James 40.00 100.00
65 Jordan Clarkson 5.00 12.00
66 Luka Doncic 30.00 80.00
67 De'Aaron Fox 10.00 25.00
68 Damian Lillard 12.00 30.00
69 Cam Reddish 4.00 10.00
70 Russell Westbrook 8.00 20.00
71 Devin Booker 12.00 30.00
72 Kevin Durant 15.00 40.00
73 Shai Gilgeous-Alexander 25.00 60.00
74 Josh Giddey 8.00 20.00
75 Stephen Curry 40.00 100.00
76 De'Anthony Melton 4.00 10.00
77 Norman Powell 5.00 12.00
78 Devonte' Graham 4.00 10.00
79 Jalen Green 15.00 40.00
80 Jonathan Kuminga 12.00 30.00
81 Jaden McDaniels 5.00 12.00
82 Devin Vassell 6.00 15.00
83 Jaren Jackson Jr. 8.00 20.00
84 Christian Wood 3.00 8.00
85 Zion Williamson 12.00 30.00
86 De'Andre Hunter 5.00 12.00
87 Derrick White 5.00 12.00
88 Brandon Ingram 6.00 15.00
89 Desmond Bane 6.00 15.00
90 Keldon Johnson 6.00 15.00
91 CJ McCollum 5.00 12.00
92 Aaron Gordon 5.00 12.00
93 Trey Murphy III 6.00 15.00
94 Josh Hart 5.00 12.00
95 Alperen Sengun 6.00 15.00
96 Josh Green 5.00 12.00
97 Ja Morant 15.00 40.00
98 Malik Beasley 4.00 10.00
99 Kevin Porter Jr. 4.00 10.00
100 Jerami Grant 6.00 15.00
101 Jaden Ivey RC 15.00 40.00
102 Kenneth Lofton Jr. RC 6.00 15.00
103 MarJon Beauchamp RC 5.00 12.00
104 Scotty Pippen Jr. RC 6.00 15.00
105 Jalen Williams RC 25.00 60.00
106 TyTy Washington Jr. RC 5.00 12.00
107 Dalen Terry RC 5.00 12.00
108 Isaiah Mobley RC 5.00 12.00
109 AJ Griffin RC 4.00 10.00
110 Kennedy Chandler RC 5.00 12.00
111 Dyson Daniels RC 12.00 30.00
112 Max Christie RC 12.00 30.00
113 Johnny Davis RC 5.00 12.00
114 Caleb Houstan RC 5.00 12.00
115 David Roddy RC 6.00 15.00
116 Tyrese Martin RC 4.00 10.00
117 Peyton Watson RC 8.00 20.00
118 Ryan Rollins RC 5.00 12.00
119 Wendell Moore Jr. RC 5.00 12.00
120 Bryce McGowens RC 5.00 12.00
121 Bennedict Mathurin RC 15.00 40.00
122 Jeremy Sochan RC 15.00 40.00
123 Malaki Branham RC 5.00 12.00
124 Walker Kessler RC 10.00 25.00
125 Ousmane Dieng RC 6.00 15.00
126 Shaedon Sharpe RC 20.00 50.00
127 Jordan Goodwin RC 4.00 10.00
128 Mark Williams RC 10.00 25.00
129 Kendall Brown RC 4.00 10.00
130 Jabari Smith Jr. RC 15.00 40.00
131 Moussa Diabate RC 5.00 12.00
132 Ochai Agbaji RC 6.00 15.00
133 Vince Williams Jr. RC 6.00 15.00
134 Andrew Nembhard RC 10.00 25.00
135 Jaden Hardy RC 8.00 20.00
136 Jake LaRavia RC 5.00 12.00
137 Simone Fontecchio RC 5.00 12.00
138 Keegan Murray RC 12.00 30.00
139 Jalen Duren RC 15.00 40.00
140 Nikola Jovic RC 10.00 25.00
141 Christian Braun RC 12.00 30.00
142 Patrick Baldwin Jr. RC 5.00 12.00
143 Jabari Walker RC 4.00 10.00
144 Josh Minott RC 5.00 12.00
145 Chet Holmgren RC 75.00 200.00
146 Paolo Banchero RC 100.00 250.00
147 Tari Eason RC 12.00 30.00
148 Jaylin Williams RC 6.00 15.00
149 Christian Koloko RC 5.00 12.00
150 Blake Wesley RC 5.00 12.00
151 Dirk Nowitzki 12.00 30.00
152 Pau Gasol 8.00 20.00
153 Tony Parker 8.00 20.00
154 Dwyane Wade 10.00 25.00
155 Shaquille O'Neal 20.00 50.00
156 Charles Barkley 12.00 30.00
157 Allen Iverson 12.00 30.00
158 Tracy McGrady 8.00 20.00
160 Anfernee Hardaway 12.00 30.00
161 Jason Williams 8.00 20.00
162 Tim Duncan 12.00 30.00
163 Vince Carter 10.00 25.00
164 Kareem Abdul-Jabbar 15.00 40.00
165 Dennis Rodman 12.00 30.00
166 Larry Bird 20.00 50.00
167 Paul Pierce 8.00 20.00
168 Kevin Garnett 12.00 30.00
169 Chris Bosh 6.00 15.00
170 Hakeem Olajuwon 10.00 25.00
171 Yao Ming 12.00 30.00
172 John Stockton 10.00 25.00
173 Dominique Wilkins 8.00 20.00
174 Steve Nash 10.00 25.00
175 Patrick Ewing 8.00 20.00
176 Jason Kidd 8.00 20.00
177 Clyde Drexler 8.00 20.00
178 Pete Maravich 12.00 30.00
179 Karl Malone 10.00 25.00
180 Shawn Kemp 8.00 20.00

2022-23 Panini One and One Downtown

1 Ja Morant 500.00 1,000.00
2 Jayson Tatum 600.00 1,200.00
3 Luka Doncic 1,000.00 2,000.00
4 Stephen Curry 1,000.00 2,000.00
5 Giannis Antetokounmpo 500.00 1,000.00
6 LeBron James 1,000.00 2,000.00
7 Kevin Durant 500.00 1,000.00
8 Zion Williamson 400.00 800.00
9 Trae Young 400.00 800.00
10 Nikola Jokic 500.00 1,000.00
11 Donovan Mitchell 300.00 600.00
12 Damian Lillard 400.00 800.00
13 Jalen Williams 600.00 1,200.00
14 Shaedon Sharpe 600.00 1,200.00
15 Bennedict Mathurin 500.00 1,000.00
16 Jaden Ivey 400.00 800.00
17 Keegan Murray 600.00 1,200.00
18 Jabari Smith Jr. 500.00 1,000.00
19 Paolo Banchero 1,000.00 2,000.00
20 Chet Holmgren 1,500.00 3,000.00

2022-23 Panini One and One Jersey Autographs

STATED PRINT RUN 25-99 SER.#'d SETS
*BLUE/35-49: .5X TO 1.2X BASIC
*PURPLE/15-35: .6X TO 1.5X BASIC
*RED/13-25: .75X TO 2X BASIC
1 RJ Barrett/75 25.00 60.00
2 Cade Cunningham/49 125.00 300.00
3 Rudy Gobert/99 15.00 40.00
4 Obi Toppin/99 12.00 30.00
5 Stephen Curry/25 1,000.00 2,000.00
6 Saddiq Bey/99 10.00 25.00
7 Luka Doncic/49 500.00 1,000.00
8 Jonathan Kuminga/99 30.00 80.00
9 Jordan Poole/99 25.00 60.00
10 Jaren Jackson Jr./99 75.00 200.00
12 Ja Morant/25 200.00 500.00
13 Jalen Green/49 75.00 200.00
15 Joe Dumars/75 15.00 40.00
16 Christian Laettner/99 12.00 30.00
17 Evan Mobley/75 30.00 80.00
18 Anthony Edwards/49 200.00 500.00
19 Devin Vassell/99 20.00 50.00
21 Magic Johnson/49 100.00 250.00
22 Paul Pierce/75 60.00 150.00
23 Nikola Jokic/25 400.00 800.00
24 Tyrese Haliburton/99 125.00 300.00
25 Jalen Suggs/49 15.00 40.00

2022-23 Panini One and One Jumbo Jersey Autographs

STATED PRINT RUN 25-99 SER.#'d SETS
*BLUE/35-49: .5X TO 1.2X BASIC
*PURPLE/25-35: .6X TO 1.5X BASIC
*RED/13-25: .75X TO 2X BASIC
1 RJ Barrett/99 25.00 60.00
2 Cade Cunningham/49 125.00 300.00
3 Jordan Poole/99 25.00 60.00
4 Rudy Gobert/99 15.00 40.00
5 Ja Morant/25 200.00 500.00
6 Jalen Green/49 75.00 200.00
7 Luka Doncic/25 500.00 1,000.00
8 Jonathan Kuminga/99 30.00 80.00
10 Saddiq Bey/99 10.00 25.00
11 Tyrese Haliburton/75 125.00 300.00
12 CJ McCollum/75 12.00 30.00
13 Larry Bird/49 100.00 250.00
14 Devin Vassell/75 20.00 50.00
15 Gary Payton/75 40.00 100.00
16 Jaren Jackson Jr./99 75.00 200.00
17 Stephen Curry/25 1,000.00 2,000.00
18 Evan Mobley/99 30.00 80.00
19 Jalen Suggs/49 15.00 40.00

2022-23 Panini One and One Prime Rookie Jersey Autographs

STATED PRINT RUN 99 SER.#'d SETS
*BLUE/49: .5X TO 1.2X BASIC
*PURPLE/35: .6X TO 1.5X BASIC
*RED/25: .75X TO 2X BASIC
1 Andrew Nembhard 30.00 80.00
2 Dyson Daniels 40.00 100.00
3 Walker Kessler 30.00 80.00
4 David Roddy 20.00 50.00
5 Keegan Murray 100.00 250.00
6 Dalen Terry 15.00 40.00
7 Christian Braun 40.00 100.00
8 Christian Koloko 15.00 40.00
9 AJ Griffin 12.00 30.00
10 TyTy Washington Jr. 15.00 40.00
11 Johnny Davis 15.00 40.00
12 Jabari Smith Jr. 100.00 250.00
13 Chet Holmgren 350.00 700.00
14 Tari Eason 40.00 100.00
15 Jeremy Sochan 50.00 125.00
16 Jaden Hardy 25.00 60.00
17 Nikola Jovic 30.00 80.00
18 Shaedon Sharpe 100.00 250.00
19 Jalen Duren 50.00 125.00
20 Kennedy Chandler 15.00 40.00
21 Paolo Banchero 300.00 600.00
22 Ochai Agbaji 20.00 50.00
23 Bennedict Mathurin 75.00 200.00
24 Jalen Williams 100.00 250.00
25 Jaden Ivey 50.00 125.00

2022-23 Panini One and One Rookie Autographs

STATED PRINT RUN 99 SER.#'d SETS
*BLUE/49: .5X TO 1.2X BASIC
*PURPLE/35: .6X TO 1.5X BASIC
*RED/15-25: .75X TO 2X BASIC
1 Jabari Smith Jr. 40.00 100.00
2 Keegan Murray 30.00 80.00
3 Nikola Jovic 25.00 60.00
4 Jaden Ivey 40.00 100.00
5 Bennedict Mathurin 40.00 100.00
6 Jalen Williams 60.00 150.00
7 Jalen Duren 40.00 100.00
8 Paolo Banchero 150.00 400.00
9 Ousmane Dieng 15.00 40.00
10 Christian Koloko 12.00 30.00
11 Malaki Branham 12.00 30.00
12 Andrew Nembhard 25.00 60.00
13 Walker Kessler 25.00 60.00
14 Jaden Hardy 20.00 50.00
15 Shaedon Sharpe 50.00 125.00
16 Tari Eason 30.00 80.00
17 Jeremy Sochan 40.00 100.00
18 Chet Holmgren 300.00 600.00
19 AJ Griffin 10.00 25.00
20 Dyson Daniels 30.00 80.00

2022-23 Panini One and One Rookie Jersey Autographs

STATED PRINT RUN 99 SER.#'d SETS
*BLUE/49: .5X TO 1.2X BASIC
*PURPLE/35: .6X TO 1.5X BASIC
*RED/25: .75X TO 2X BASIC
1 Keegan Murray 30.00 80.00
2 Andrew Nembhard 25.00 60.00
3 Jeremy Sochan 40.00 100.00
4 Jalen Williams 60.00 150.00
5 Malaki Branham 12.00 30.00
6 Bennedict Mathurin 40.00 100.00
7 Shaedon Sharpe 50.00 125.00
8 Paolo Banchero 150.00 400.00
9 Jaden Hardy 20.00 50.00
10 Tari Eason 30.00 80.00
11 Jabari Smith Jr. 40.00 100.00
12 Dyson Daniels 30.00 80.00
13 Ousmane Dieng 15.00 40.00
14 Nikola Jovic 25.00 60.00
15 Chet Holmgren 200.00 500.00
16 Walker Kessler 25.00 60.00
17 AJ Griffin 10.00 25.00
18 Jaden Ivey 30.00 80.00
19 Christian Koloko 12.00 30.00
20 Jalen Duren 40.00 100.00

2022-23 Panini One and One Rookie Jumbo Jersey Autographs

STATED PRINT RUN 99 SER.#'d SETS
*BLUE/49: .5X TO 1.2X BASIC
*PURPLE/35: .6X TO 1.5X BASIC
*RED/25: .75X TO 2X BASIC
1 Jeremy Sochan 40.00 100.00
2 Keegan Murray 30.00 80.00
3 Malaki Branham 12.00 30.00
4 Nikola Jovic 25.00 60.00
5 Tari Eason 30.00 80.00
6 Jaden Ivey 40.00 100.00
7 Jaden Hardy 20.00 50.00
8 Jabari Smith Jr. 40.00 100.00
9 Chet Holmgren 200.00 500.00
10 Shaedon Sharpe 50.00 125.00
11 Christian Koloko 12.00 30.00
12 Paolo Banchero 150.00 400.00
13 Dyson Daniels 30.00 80.00
14 Walker Kessler 25.00 60.00
15 Ousmane Dieng 15.00 40.00
16 Jalen Duren 40.00 100.00
17 AJ Griffin 10.00 25.00
18 Jalen Williams 60.00 150.00
19 Bennedict Mathurin 40.00 100.00
20 Andrew Nembhard 25.00 60.00
21 Ochai Agbaji 15.00 40.00
22 Johnny Davis 12.00 30.00
23 TyTy Washington Jr. 12.00 30.00
24 Kennedy Chandler 12.00 30.00
25 MarJon Beauchamp 12.00 30.00

2022-23 Panini One and One Team Titans Signatures

STATED PRINT RUN 49-99 SER.#'d SETS
*BLUE/35-49: .5X TO 1.2X BASIC
*PURPLE/25-35: .6X TO 1.5X BASIC
*RED/25: .75X TO 2X BASIC
1 Khris Middleton/99 15.00 40.00
2 Jalen Duren/99 40.00 100.00
3 Deandre Ayton/99 12.00 30.00
4 Jaden Ivey/75 60.00 150.00
5 Ochai Agbaji/99 15.00 40.00
6 Jabari Smith Jr./75 60.00 150.00
7 Paul Pierce/99 40.00 100.00
8 Dominique Wilkins/99 20.00 50.00
9 AJ Griffin/99 10.00 25.00
10 RJ Barrett/49 20.00 50.00
11 Rasheed Wallace/49 30.00 80.00
12 Jalen Green/75 60.00 150.00
13 Shawn Kemp/99 40.00 100.00
14 Paolo Banchero/75 150.00 400.00
15 Dyson Daniels/99 30.00 80.00
16 Andrew Nembhard/99 25.00 60.00
17 Jason Williams/99 40.00 100.00
18 Lauri Markkanen/99 20.00 50.00
19 Anfernee Hardaway/99 75.00 200.00
20 Keegan Murray/99 75.00 200.00
21 Kevin Garnett/49 100.00 250.00
22 Ousmane Dieng/99 15.00 40.00
23 Allen Iverson/49 125.00 300.00
24 Bennedict Mathurin/99 75.00 200.00
25 Shaedon Sharpe/99 75.00 200.00
26 Tony Parker/99 40.00 100.00
27 Magic Johnson/49 100.00 250.00
28 TyTy Washington Jr./99 12.00 30.00
29 Jalen Williams/99 75.00 200.00
30 Larry Bird/49 100.00 250.00
31 Jason Kidd/99 40.00 100.00
32 Grant Hill/99 40.00 100.00
33 Pat Riley/99 20.00 50.00
34 Ray Allen/99 40.00 100.00
35 Kennedy Chandler/99 12.00 30.00

2022-23 Panini One and One Timeless Moments

1 LeBron James 400.00 800.00
2 Stephen Curry 400.00 800.00
3 Kyrie Irving 300.00 600.00
4 Giannis Antetokounmpo 200.00 500.00
5 LeBron James 400.00 800.00

2022-23 Panini One and One Timeless Moments Autographs

STATED PRINT RUN 49-99 SER.#'d SETS
*BLUE/35-49: .5X TO 1.2X BASIC
*PURPLE/25-35: .6X TO 1.5X BASIC
*RED/15-25: .75X TO 2X BASIC
1 Bob Cousy/49 150.00 400.00
2 Stephen Curry/49 4,000.00 8,000.00
3 Kevin Garnett/49 500.00 1,000.00
4 James Harden/49 1,000.00 2,000.00
5 Obi Toppin/99 100.00 250.00
6 Magic Johnson/49 200.00 500.00
7 Luka Doncic/49 1,250.00 2,500.00
8 Anthony Edwards/49 1,000.00 2,000.00
9 Allen Iverson/49 500.00 1,000.00
10 Anthony Davis/49 350.00 700.00
11 Nikola Jokic/49 500.00 1,000.00
12 Jayson Tatum/49 500.00 1,000.00
13 Karl Malone/49 125.00 300.00
14 John Stockton/49 125.00 300.00
15 Larry Bird/49 300.00 600.00
16 Dirk Nowitzki/49 600.00 1,200.00
17 Rasheed Wallace/49 300.00 600.00
18 Ja Morant/49 800.00 1,500.00
19 Deandre Ayton/49 60.00 150.00
20 Paul George/49 600.00 1,200.00
21 Paolo Banchero /49 800.00 1,500.00
22 Manu Ginobili/75 200.00 500.00
23 Khris Middleton/99 125.00 300.00
25 Pau Gasol/49 200.00 500.00

2023-24 Panini One and One

STATED PRINT RUN 99 SER.#'d SETS
*BLUE/35: .5X TO 1.2X BASIC
*PURPLE/25-35: .6X TO 1.5X BASIC
*RED/15: .75X TO 2X BASIC
1 Deandre Ayton 5.00 12.00
2 Jalen Johnson 6.00 15.00
3 Jalen Suggs 6.00 15.00
4 Paul George 8.00 20.00
5 Evan Mobley 8.00 20.00
6 Mark Williams 5.00 12.00
7 Damian Lillard 12.00 30.00
8 Jordan Poole 8.00 20.00
9 Marvin Bagley III 4.00 10.00
10 Joel Embiid 12.00 30.00
11 Jrue Holiday 6.00 15.00
12 Trae Young 10.00 25.00
13 Nikola Jokic 25.00 60.00
14 Anthony Edwards 25.00 60.00
15 Desmond Bane 6.00 15.00
16 Karl-Anthony Towns 8.00 20.00
17 Rudy Gobert 6.00 15.00
18 Stephen Curry 40.00 100.00
19 Tyler Herro 8.00 20.00
20 Zion Williamson 12.00 30.00
21 LaMelo Ball 12.00 30.00
22 Tyrese Maxey 10.00 25.00
23 Domantas Sabonis 8.00 20.00
24 OG Anunoby 6.00 15.00
25 Coby White 5.00 12.00
26 Terry Rozier III 6.00 15.00
27 Klay Thompson 12.00 30.00
28 Jaylen Brown 10.00 25.00
29 Kristaps Porzingis 6.00 15.00
30 Jalen Brunson 10.00 25.00
31 Lauri Markkanen 8.00 20.00
32 De'Aaron Fox 10.00 25.00
33 Austin Reaves 12.00 30.00
34 Immanuel Quickley 5.00 12.00
35 Kawhi Leonard 12.00 30.00
36 Michael Porter Jr. 6.00 15.00
37 RJ Barrett 8.00 20.00
38 Chet Holmgren 12.00 30.00
39 Shai Gilgeous-Alexander 25.00 60.00
40 Jaden Ivey 6.00 15.00
41 Shaedon Sharpe 10.00 25.00
42 CJ McCollum 5.00 12.00
43 Kyrie Irving 10.00 25.00
44 Mikal Bridges 6.00 15.00
45 Anthony Davis 12.00 30.00
46 Alperen Sengun 8.00 20.00
47 Jordan Clarkson 5.00 12.00
48 Jalen Williams 10.00 25.00
49 Jalen Green 8.00 20.00
50 Jerami Grant 6.00 15.00
51 Jaren Jackson Jr. 8.00 20.00
52 Tim Hardaway Jr. 4.00 10.00
53 Rui Hachimura 5.00 12.00
54 Aaron Gordon 5.00 12.00
55 Kevin Durant 15.00 40.00
56 Jabari Smith Jr. 8.00 20.00
57 Brandon Ingram 6.00 15.00
58 Bradley Beal 6.00 15.00
59 Derrick Rose 8.00 20.00
60 Fred VanVleet 8.00 20.00
61 Julius Randle 6.00 15.00
62 Jalen Duren 6.00 15.00
63 Franz Wagner 8.00 20.00
64 John Collins 5.00 12.00
65 Bam Adebayo 8.00 20.00
66 P.J. Washington Jr. 5.00 12.00
67 Dejounte Murray 6.00 15.00
68 Devin Vassell 6.00 15.00
69 Jayson Tatum 20.00 50.00
70 Giannis Antetokounmpo 25.00 60.00
71 Cameron Thomas 6.00 15.00
72 Pascal Siakam 8.00 20.00
73 Josh Giddey 6.00 15.00
74 James Harden 10.00 25.00
75 Tyrese Haliburton 10.00 25.00
76 Kyle Kuzma 6.00 15.00
77 Paolo Banchero 12.00 30.00
78 Russell Westbrook 8.00 20.00
79 Ja Morant 15.00 40.00
80 Jimmy Butler 8.00 20.00
81 DeMar DeRozan 8.00 20.00
82 Tobias Harris 5.00 12.00
83 Bennedict Mathurin 8.00 20.00
84 Jonathan Kuminga 12.00 30.00
85 Scottie Barnes 6.00 15.00
86 Zach LaVine 8.00 20.00
87 LeBron James 40.00 100.00
88 Donovan Mitchell 10.00 25.00
89 Cade Cunningham 12.00 30.00
90 Chris Paul 10.00 25.00
91 Jeremy Sochan 6.00 15.00
92 Keegan Murray 6.00 15.00
93 Anfernee Simons 6.00 15.00
94 Cameron Johnson 5.00 12.00
95 Khris Middleton 5.00 12.00
96 Jamal Murray 10.00 25.00
97 Luka Doncic 30.00 80.00
98 Devin Booker 12.00 30.00
99 Keldon Johnson 6.00 15.00
100 Darius Garland 8.00 20.00
101 Jaime Jaquez Jr. RC 8.00 20.00
102 Gradey Dick RC 10.00 25.00
103 Seth Lundy RC 4.00 10.00
104 Julian Phillips RC 5.00 12.00
105 Jett Howard RC 6.00 15.00
106 Nick Smith Jr. RC 6.00 15.00
107 Scoot Henderson RC 15.00 40.00
108 Toumani Camara RC 10.00 25.00
109 Kobe Brown RC 5.00 12.00
110 Colby Jones RC 5.00 12.00
111 Kris Murray RC 5.00 12.00
112 Jalen Pickett RC 4.00 10.00
113 Noah Clowney RC 6.00 15.00
114 Jordan Hawkins RC 8.00 20.00
115 Maxwell Lewis RC 4.00 10.00
116 Marcus Sasser RC 8.00 20.00
117 Sasha Vezenkov RC 4.00 10.00
118 Bilal Coulibaly RC 12.00 30.00
119 Emoni Bates RC 6.00 15.00
120 Brandin Podziemski RC 15.00 40.00
121 Ausar Thompson RC 12.00 30.00
122 Victor Wembanyama RC 600.00 1,200.00
123 Amari Bailey RC 5.00 12.00
124 Keyonte George RC 15.00 40.00
125 Brice Sensabaugh RC 8.00 20.00
126 Kobe Bufkin RC 6.00 15.00
127 Jarace Walker RC 10.00 25.00
128 Taylor Hendricks RC 5.00 12.00
129 Leonard Miller RC 5.00 12.00
130 Ben Sheppard RC 5.00 12.00
131 Olivier-Maxence Prosper RC 5.00 12.00
132 Andre Jackson Jr. RC 8.00 20.00
133 Jalen Wilson RC 5.00 12.00
134 Vasilije Micic RC 5.00 12.00
135 Rayan Rupert RC 5.00 12.00
136 Hunter Tyson RC 5.00 12.00
137 Brandon Miller RC 40.00 100.00
138 Jalen Hood-Schifino RC 5.00 12.00
139 Julian Strawther RC 6.00 15.00
140 Dariq Whitehead RC 6.00 15.00
141 Craig Porter Jr. RC 6.00 15.00
142 Keyontae Johnson RC 5.00 12.00
143 Amen Thompson RC 40.00 100.00
144 Trayce Jackson-Davis RC 6.00 15.00
145 Dereck Lively II RC 10.00 25.00
146 Anthony Black RC 10.00 25.00
147 Cason Wallace RC 10.00 25.00
148 Cam Whitmore RC 12.00 30.00
149 Duop Reath RC 5.00 12.00
150 GG Jackson II RC 10.00 25.00
151 Karl Malone 10.00 25.00
152 Chris Bosh 6.00 15.00
153 Bob Pettit 6.00 15.00
154 Carmelo Anthony 8.00 20.00
155 Charles Barkley 12.00 30.00
156 Anfernee Hardaway 12.00 30.00
157 Ray Allen 8.00 20.00
158 Pete Maravich 12.00 30.00
159 Dwyane Wade 10.00 25.00
160 Brandon Roy 6.00 15.00
161 Pau Gasol 8.00 20.00
162 Wilt Chamberlain 15.00 40.00
163 Julius Erving 12.00 30.00
164 Mahmoud Abdul-Rauf 4.00 10.00
165 Hakeem Olajuwon 10.00 25.00
166 John Stockton 10.00 25.00
167 Tracy McGrady 8.00 20.00
168 George Gervin 8.00 20.00
169 Gilbert Arenas 5.00 12.00
170 Amar'e Stoudemire 6.00 15.00
171 Yuta Tabuse 5.00 12.00
172 Yao Ming 12.00 30.00
173 Zach Randolph 5.00 12.00
174 Jason Kidd 8.00 20.00
175 Steve Nash 10.00 25.00
176 Jason Williams 8.00 20.00
177 Paul Pierce 8.00 20.00
178 Magic Johnson 20.00 50.00
179 Peja Stojakovic 5.00 12.00
180 Gary Payton 8.00 20.00
181 Manu Ginobili 10.00 25.00
182 Kareem Abdul-Jabbar 15.00 40.00
183 Tony Parker 8.00 20.00
184 Jerry Stackhouse 5.00 12.00
185 Shawn Kemp 8.00 20.00
186 Vince Carter 10.00 25.00
187 Clyde Drexler 8.00 20.00
188 Antawn Jamison 5.00 12.00
189 David Robinson 10.00 25.00
190 Patrick Ewing 8.00 20.00
191 Dennis Rodman 12.00 30.00
192 Kevin Garnett 12.00 30.00
193 Shaquille O'Neal 15.00 40.00
194 Larry Bird 20.00 50.00
195 Allen Iverson 12.00 30.00
196 Alonzo Mourning 8.00 20.00
197 Tim Duncan 12.00 30.00
198 Dirk Nowitzki 12.00 30.00
199 Isiah Thomas 8.00 20.00
200 Dominique Wilkins 8.00 20.00

2023-24 Panini One and One Day One Signatures

STATED PRINT RUN 25-99 SER.#'d SETS
*RED/25: .5X TO 1.2X BASIC
1 Jason Kidd/49 40.00 100.00
2 Kevin Garnett/49 100.00 250.00
4 Zion Williamson/35 75.00 200.00
5 Cade Cunningham/49 75.00 200.00
6 Rudy Gobert/75 15.00 40.00
7 Myles Turner/75 12.00 30.00
8 Jordan Walsh/99 12.00 30.00
10 Tim Hardaway/99 25.00 60.00
12 Desmond Bane/49 25.00 60.00
13 Kristaps Porzingis/49 25.00 60.00
14 Dennis Rodman/49 125.00 300.00
15 Ray Allen/49 60.00 150.00
16 Amar'e Stoudemire/75 20.00 50.00
17 Paul George/25 75.00 200.00
18 Sasha Vezenkov/99 10.00 25.00
19 Vasilije Micic/99 12.00 30.00
20 Keyonte George/99 50.00 120.00
21 Brandin Podziemski/49 40.00 100.00
22 Amen Thompson/35 75.00 200.00
23 Ausar Thompson/35 75.00 200.00
24 Dereck Lively II/49 30.00 80.00
25 Chris Paul/49 75.00 200.00

2023-24 Panini One and One Downtown

1 Ja Morant 500.00 1,000.00
2 Brandin Podziemski 400.00 800.00
3 Trae Young 300.00 600.00
4 Shai Gilgeous-Alexander 1,250.00 2,500.00
5 Anthony Edwards 800.00 1,500.00
6 Tyrese Haliburton 500.00 1,000.00
7 Jayson Tatum 800.00 1,500.00
8 Nikola Jokic 800.00 1,500.00
9 Dereck Lively II 200.00 500.00
10 Anthony Black 300.00 600.00
11 Brandon Miller 1,000.00 2,000.00
12 Giannis Antetokounmpo 500.00 1,000.00
13 Scoot Henderson 400.00 800.00
14 Amen Thompson 1,000.00 2,000.00
15 Jaime Jaquez Jr. 200.00 500.00
16 Stephen Curry 1,250.00 2,500.00
17 LeBron James 1,250.00 2,500.00
18 Keyonte George 400.00 800.00
19 Jordan Hawkins 200.00 500.00
20 Zion Williamson 300.00 600.00
21 Kevin Durant 500.00 1,000.00
22 Victor Wembanyama 3,000.00 6,000.00
23 Jalen Brunson 800.00 1,500.00
24 Ausar Thompson 800.00 1,500.00
25 Luka Doncic 1,250.00 2,500.00

2023-24 Panini One and One Downtown Variations

1 Nikola Jokic 800.00 1,500.00
2 Shai Gilgeous-Alexander 1,250.00 2,500.00
3 Luka Doncic 1,250.00 2,500.00
4 Yao Ming 800.00 1,500.00
5 Stephen Curry 1,250.00 2,500.00
6 Victor Wembanyama 3,000.00 6,000.00
7 Giannis Antetokounmpo 500.00 1,000.00
8 LeBron James 1,250.00 2,500.00
9 Bilal Coulibaly 400.00 800.00
10 Dirk Nowitzki 500.00 1,000.00

2023-24 Panini One and One Jersey Autographs

STATED PRINT RUN 49-99 SER.#'d SETS
*BLUE/25-49: .5X TO 1.2X BASIC
*PURPLE/35: .5X TO 1.2X BASIC
*RED/13-25: .6X TO 1.5X BASIC
1 Karl-Anthony Towns/75 30.00 80.00
2 Jaren Jackson Jr./99 125.00 300.00
3 Brandon Ingram/99 25.00 60.00
5 Aaron Gordon/99 20.00 50.00
7 Andrew Wiggins/99 40.00 100.00
9 Brook Lopez/99 15.00 40.00
10 RJ Barrett/75 30.00 80.00
11 Tyrese Maxey/49 125.00 300.00
12 CJ McCollum/75 20.00 50.00
13 Jordan Poole/75 30.00 80.00
14 Rudy Gobert/75 25.00 60.00
15 Jordan Clarkson/99 20.00 50.00
16 Cole Anthony/75 20.00 50.00
18 Alperen Sengun/49 60.00 150.00
19 Myles Turner/99 20.00 50.00
20 Ben Simmons/49 20.00 50.00

2023-24 Panini One and One Jumbo Jersey Autographs

STATED PRINT RUN 75-99 SER.#'d SETS
*BLUE/49: .5X TO 1.2X BASIC
*PURPLE/35: .5X TO 1.2X BASIC
*RED/15-25: .6X TO 1.5X BASIC
1 Domantas Sabonis/75 30.00 80.00
2 Bogdan Bogdanovic/99 20.00 50.00
4 Clint Capela/99 15.00 40.00
6 Jonas Valanciunas/99 15.00 40.00
7 Franz Wagner/99 60.00 150.00
8 Marcus Smart/99 25.00 60.00
9 Al Horford/99 20.00 50.00
10 Immanuel Quickley/99 20.00 50.00
11 Jordan Poole/75 30.00 80.00

2023-24 Panini One and One Number Ones

STATED PRINT RUN 49 SER.#'d SETS
*RED/25: .5X TO 1.2X BASIC
1 Shaquille O'Neal 150.00 400.00
2 Cade Cunningham 125.00 300.00
3 Allen Iverson 125.00 300.00
4 Anthony Edwards 300.00 600.00
5 Paolo Banchero 150.00 400.00
6 Anthony Davis 75.00 200.00
7 David Robinson 60.00 150.00
8 Magic Johnson 75.00 200.00
9 Kareem Abdul-Jabbar 100.00 250.00
10 Yao Ming 300.00 600.00

2023-24 Panini One and One Once Upon a Time Signatures

STATED PRINT RUN 49-75 SER.#'d SETS
*RED/25: .5X TO 1.2X BASIC
1 Larry Bird/49 150.00 400.00
2 Karl Malone/49 50.00 120.00
3 Isiah Thomas/75 25.00 60.00
4 Pau Gasol/49 75.00 200.00
5 Ray Allen/49 75.00 200.00
6 Kevin McHale/75 25.00 60.00
7 Bob Pettit/49 25.00 60.00
8 Anfernee Hardaway/75 75.00 200.00
9 Dennis Rodman/49 125.00 300.00
10 Dominique Wilkins/75 25.00 60.00

2023-24 Panini One and One Precision Rookie Jersey Autographs

STATED PRINT RUN 75-99 SER.#'d SETS
*BLUE/49: .5X TO 1.2X BASIC
*PURPLE/35: .5X TO 1.2X BASIC
*RED/25: .6X TO 1.5X BASIC
1 Dereck Lively II/75 40.00 100.00
2 Bilal Coulibaly/75 50.00 125.00
3 Kobe Bufkin/99 25.00 60.00
4 Ausar Thompson/75 50.00 125.00
5 Marcus Sasser/99 30.00 80.00
6 Kobe Brown/99 20.00 50.00
7 Kris Murray/99 20.00 50.00
8 Cason Wallace/75 40.00 100.00
9 Trayce Jackson-Davis/99 25.00 60.00
10 Toumani Camara/99 40.00 100.00
11 Andre Jackson Jr./99 30.00 80.00
12 Ben Sheppard/99 20.00 50.00
13 Keyonte George/75 60.00 150.00
14 Brice Sensabaugh/99 30.00 80.00
15 Sasha Vezenkov/99 15.00 40.00
16 Julian Strawther/99 25.00 60.00
17 Julian Phillips/99 20.00 50.00
18 Olivier-Maxence Prosper/99 20.00 50.00
19 Noah Clowney/99 25.00 60.00
20 Amen Thompson/75 150.00 400.00

2023-24 Panini One and One Presenting Autographs

STATED PRINT RUN 25-99 SER.#'d SETS
*RED/25: .5X TO 1.2X BASIC
2 Ben Simmons/25 12.00 30.00
3 Lauri Markkanen/49 20.00 50.00
5 Desmond Bane/49 15.00 40.00
6 CJ McCollum/49 12.00 30.00
7 Hakeem Olajuwon/49 60.00 150.00
8 Ben Wallace/49 40.00 100.00
9 Kristaps Porzingis/75 40.00 100.00
10 Cason Wallace/49 25.00 60.00
11 Chauncey Billups/75 40.00 100.00
12 Rasheed Wallace/49 40.00 100.00
13 Clyde Drexler/49 40.00 100.00
14 Jrue Holiday/49 40.00 100.00
16 Domantas Sabonis/49 20.00 50.00
17 Manu Ginobili/35 60.00 150.00
18 Al Horford/75 12.00 30.00
19 Jordan Clarkson/75 12.00 30.00
20 Peja Stojakovic/99 12.00 30.00
21 Joe Dumars/99 15.00 40.00
22 Arvydas Sabonis/99 15.00 40.00
24 Immanuel Quickley/99 12.00 30.00
25 Marcus Smart/75 15.00 40.00
27 Dereck Lively II/25 50.00 120.00
28 Amen Thompson/25 125.00 300.00
29 Ausar Thompson/25 75.00 200.00
30 Keyonte George/25 75.00 200.00

2023-24 Panini One and One Prolific Signatures

STATED PRINT RUN 35-49 SER.#'d SETS
*RED/25: .5X TO 1.2X BASIC
1 Charles Barkley/35 100.00 250.00
2 Dirk Nowitzki/35 200.00 500.00
3 Bob Cousy/35 100.00 250.00
4 Tony Parker/49 40.00 100.00
5 John Stockton/49 100.00 250.00
6 Julius Erving/49 100.00 250.00
7 Karl Malone/49 50.00 120.00
8 Pau Gasol/49 75.00 200.00
9 Isiah Thomas/49 25.00 60.00
10 Jason Kidd/49 40.00 100.00

2023-24 Panini One and One Rookie Autographs
STATED PRINT RUN 99 SER.#'d SETS
*BLUE/49: .5X TO 1.2X BASIC
*PURPLE/35: .5X TO 1.2X BASIC
*RED/25: .6X TO 1.5X BASIC
1 Olivier-Maxence Prosper 10.00 25.00
2 Marcus Sasser 15.00 40.00
3 Kobe Brown 10.00 25.00
4 Maxwell Lewis 8.00 20.00
5 Brice Sensabaugh 15.00 40.00
6 Jordan Walsh 10.00 25.00
7 Noah Clowney 12.00 30.00
8 Amen Thompson 125.00 300.00
9 Andre Jackson Jr. 15.00 40.00
10 Cason Wallace 20.00 50.00
11 Rayan Rupert 10.00 25.00
12 Vasilije Micic 10.00 25.00
13 Kris Murray 12.00 30.00
14 Ausar Thompson 40.00 100.00
15 Bilal Coulibaly 25.00 60.00
16 Kobe Bufkin 12.00 30.00
17 Jalen Pickett 8.00 20.00
18 Julian Strawther 12.00 30.00
20 Ben Sheppard 10.00 25.00
21 Dereck Lively II 40.00 100.00
22 Brandin Podziemski 30.00 80.00
23 Toumani Camara 20.00 50.00

2023-24 Panini One and One Rookie Exclusive
2 Amen Thompson 40.00 100.00
3 Ausar Thompson 12.00 30.00
4 Bilal Coulibaly 12.00 30.00
5 Keyonte George 15.00 40.00
6 Brandin Podziemski 15.00 40.00

2023-24 Panini One and One Rookie Jersey Autographs
STATED PRINT RUN 75-99 SER.#'d SETS
*BLUE/49: .5X TO 1.2X BASIC
*PURPLE/35: .5X TO 1.2X BASIC
*RED/25: .6X TO 1.5X BASIC
1 Cason Wallace/99 40.00 100.00
2 Amen Thompson/75 150.00 400.00
3 Brandin Podziemski/99 60.00 150.00
4 Kris Murray/99 25.00 60.00
5 Keyonte George/75 60.00 150.00
6 Brice Sensabaugh/99 30.00 80.00
7 Dereck Lively II/99 50.00 125.00
8 Bilal Coulibaly/75 50.00 125.00
9 Kobe Bufkin/99 25.00 60.00
10 Ausar Thompson/75 50.00 125.00
11 Marcus Sasser/99 30.00 80.00
12 Kobe Brown/99 20.00 50.00
13 Sasha Vezenkov/99 15.00 40.00
14 Julian Strawther/99 25.00 60.00
16 Vasilije Micic/99 20.00 50.00
17 Olivier-Maxence Prosper/99 20.00 50.00
18 Noah Clowney/99 25.00 60.00
19 Toumani Camara/99 40.00 100.00
20 Andre Jackson Jr./99 30.00 80.00

2023-24 Panini One and One Rookie Jumbo Jersey Autographs
STATED PRINT RUN 75-99 SER.#'d SETS
*BLUE/49: .5X TO 1.2X BASIC
*PURPLE/35: .5X TO 1.2X BASIC
*RED/25: .6X TO 1.5X BASIC
1 Brice Sensabaugh/99 30.00 80.00
2 Dereck Lively II/99 50.00 125.00
3 Bilal Coulibaly/99 50.00 125.00
4 Kobe Bufkin/99 25.00 60.00
5 Ausar Thompson/75 50.00 125.00
6 Julian Strawther/99 25.00 60.00
8 Vasilije Micic/99 20.00 50.00
9 Olivier-Maxence Prosper/99 20.00 50.00
10 Marcus Sasser/99 30.00 80.00
11 Kobe Brown/99 20.00 50.00
12 Sasha Vezenkov/99 15.00 40.00
13 Noah Clowney/99 25.00 60.00
14 Toumani Camara/99 40.00 100.00
15 Andre Jackson Jr./99 30.00 80.00
16 Cason Wallace/99 40.00 100.00
17 Amen Thompson/75 150.00 400.00
18 Brandin Podziemski/75 60.00 150.00
19 Kris Murray/99 25.00 60.00
20 Keyonte George/99 60.00 150.00

2023-24 Panini One and One The Oneders Signatures
STATED PRINT RUN 15-99 SER.#'d SETS
*BLUE/35-49: .5X TO 1.2X BASIC
*PURPLE/35: .5X TO 1.2X BASIC
*RED/25: .5X TO 1.2X BASIC P/R 35-49
*RED/25: .6X TO 1.5X BASIC P/R 75-99
1 Luka Doncic/35 500.00 1,000.00
2 Ja Morant/35 300.00 600.00
3 Klay Thompson/49 125.00 300.00
4 Donovan Mitchell/49 100.00 250.00
5 Nikola Jokic/49 200.00 500.00
6 Anthony Davis/25 100.00 250.00
7 Carmelo Anthony/49 100.00 250.00
8 Magic Johnson/49 100.00 250.00
9 Yao Ming/35 300.00 600.00
10 Tony Parker/75 60.00 150.00
11 Tyrese Haliburton/49 125.00 300.00
12 Jalen Brunson/75 100.00 250.00
13 Shai Gilgeous-Alexander/75 400.00 800.00
14 Fred VanVleet/75 20.00 50.00
15 Tyrese Maxey/75 100.00 250.00
17 Russell Westbrook/35 125.00 300.00
18 Charles Barkley/35 100.00 250.00
19 Anthony Edwards/49 300.00 600.00
20 Josh Giddey/99 30.00 80.00
21 Alperen Sengun/99 40.00 100.00
22 Kareem Abdul-Jabbar/49 100.00 250.00
23 Chris Bosh/49 50.00 120.00
24 David Robinson/49 60.00 150.00
26 James Harden/75 150.00 400.00
27 Zach LaVine/75 60.00 150.00
28 Stephen Curry/49 800.00 1,500.00
29 Paul Pierce/75 75.00 200.00
30 Kobe Bufkin/99 20.00 50.00
31 De'Aaron Fox/75 100.00 250.00
32 Tracy McGrady/49 150.00 400.00
33 Zion Williamson/49 100.00 250.00
34 Bilal Coulibaly/99 60.00 150.00
35 Cason Wallace/99 40.00 100.00
36 Brandin Podziemski/99 40.00 100.00
37 Dereck Lively II/99 40.00 100.00
38 Ausar Thompson/75 60.00 150.00
39 Amen Thompson/75 125.00 300.00
40 Keyonte George/99 60.00 150.00
41 Dirk Nowitzki/49 200.00 500.00
42 Kevin Garnett/49 125.00 300.00
43 Dwyane Wade/49 125.00 300.00
44 Cade Cunningham/49 125.00 300.00
45 Steve Nash/49 100.00 250.00

2023-24 Panini One and One Timeless Moments
1 Victor Wembanyama 1,000.00 2,000.00
2 Jayson Tatum 100.00 250.00
3 LeBron James 400.00 800.00
4 LeBron James 400.00 800.00
5 LeBron James 400.00 800.00

2023-24 Panini One and One Timeless Moments Autographs
STATED PRINT RUN 25-99 SER.#'d SETS
*BLUE/35-49: .5X TO 1.2X BASIC
*PURPLE/35: .4X TO 1X BASIC P/R 49
*PURPLE/35: .5X TO 1.2X BASIC P/R 75-99
*RED/25: .5X TO 1.2X BASIC P/R 35-49
*RED/25: .6X TO 1.5X BASIC P/R 75-99
1 Chris Bosh/49 150.00 400.00
2 Alonzo Mourning/99 125.00 300.00
3 Zach LaVine/49 1,000.00 2,000.00
5 Julius Erving/49 200.00 500.00
6 Aaron Gordon/75 600.00 1,200.00
7 Tracy McGrady/49 1,250.00 2,500.00
8 Allen Iverson/49 1,000.00 2,000.00
9 Ausar Thompson/49 300.00 600.00
10 Nikola Jokic/49 600.00 1,200.00
11 Keyonte George/75 300.00 600.00
12 De'Aaron Fox/75 300.00 600.00
13 Anthony Edwards/49 1,250.00 2,500.00
14 Ja Morant/49 1,250.00 2,500.00
15 Giannis Antetokounmpo/49 1,000.00 2,000.00
16 Donovan Mitchell/49 400.00 800.00
17 Russell Westbrook/49 600.00 1,200.00
18 Carmelo Anthony/75 600.00 1,200.00
19 Chet Holmgren/75 600.00 1,200.00
20 Paolo Banchero /49 800.00 1,500.00
21 Luka Doncic/49 1,000.00 2,000.00
22 Tim Duncan/25 2,000.00 4,000.00
23 Yao Ming/35 1,250.00 2,500.00
24 Chris Paul/49 300.00 600.00
25 Stephen Curry/49 3,000.00 6,000.00
26 Manu Ginobili/75 300.00 600.00
27 Patrick Ewing/49 300.00 600.00
28 Dereck Lively II/49 300.00 600.00
29 Shaquille O'Neal /49 500.00 1,000.00
30 Shai Gilgeous-Alexander/49 2,000.00 4,000.00

2017-18 Panini Opulence
STATED PRINT RUN 79 SER.#'d SETS
EXCHANGE DEADLINE 03/21/2020
1 Markelle Fultz RC 5.00 12.00
2 Ricky Rubio 1.50 4.00
3 Bojan Bogdanovic 1.50 4.00
4 Giannis Antetokounmpo 10.00 25.00
5 Joel Embiid 4.00 10.00
6 DeMar DeRozan 2.50 6.00
7 Nikola Jokic 12.00 30.00
8 Chris Paul 3.00 8.00
9 Josh Richardson 1.50 4.00
10 Paul George 3.00 8.00
11 Jusuf Nurkic 1.50 4.00
12 D'Angelo Russell 1.50 4.00
13 Goran Dragic 1.50 4.00
14 Russell Westbrook 3.00 8.00
15 Myles Turner 2.00 5.00
16 TJ Warren 1.50 4.00
17 Lonzo Ball RC 8.00 20.00
18 Lou Williams 1.50 4.00
19 Pau Gasol 3.00 8.00
20 Andrew Wiggins 2.50 6.00
21 Damian Lillard 5.00 12.00
22 Blake Griffin 2.00 5.00
23 Rudy Gobert 2.50 6.00
24 CJ McCollum 2.00 5.00
25 Kentavious Caldwell-Pope 1.50 4.00
26 Jayson Tatum RC 150.00 400.00
27 Jaylen Brown 5.00 12.00
28 Al Horford 2.00 5.00
29 Bradley Beal 2.50 6.00
30 Tyreke Evans 1.25 3.00
31 DeAndre Jordan 1.50 4.00
32 Jrue Holiday 2.50 6.00
33 James Harden 4.00 10.00
34 Brandon Ingram 2.50 6.00
35 Stephen Curry 15.00 40.00
36 Dirk Nowitzki 5.00 12.00
37 Donovan Mitchell RC 20.00 50.00
38 Tim Hardaway Jr. 1.50 4.00
39 Nicolas Batum 1.25 3.00
40 Spencer Dinwiddie 1.50 4.00
41 Trevor Ariza 1.25 3.00
42 LaMarcus Aldridge 2.00 5.00
43 Victor Oladipo 1.50 4.00
44 Nikola Vucevic 1.50 4.00
45 Dion Waiters 1.25 3.00
46 Kyle Lowry 2.00 5.00
47 Serge Ibaka 1.50 4.00
48 Kris Dunn 1.25 3.00
49 Jimmy Butler 3.00 8.00
50 Marc Gasol 2.00 5.00
51 Courtney Lee 1.25 3.00
52 Devin Booker 5.00 12.00
53 Julius Randle 2.00 5.00
54 Ben Simmons 2.00 5.00
55 Kristaps Porzingis 2.50 6.00
56 Gary Harris 1.50 4.00
57 Klay Thompson 5.00 12.00
58 Eric Bledsoe 1.50 4.00
59 Mike Conley 1.50 4.00
60 Kyle Kuzma RC 8.00 20.00
61 Reggie Jackson 1.50 4.00
62 Otto Porter Jr. 1.50 4.00
63 Tobias Harris 1.50 4.00
64 LeBron James 15.00 40.00
65 Carmelo Anthony 3.00 8.00
66 Kemba Walker 1.50 4.00
67 Will Barton 1.25 3.00
68 Eric Gordon 1.50 4.00
69 Marcin Gortat 1.25 3.00
70 DeMarre Carroll 1.25 3.00
71 Harrison Barnes 1.50 4.00
72 Isaiah Thomas 1.50 4.00
73 Jamal Murray 3.00 8.00
74 Josh Jackson RC 2.50 6.00
75 Dwight Howard 2.50 6.00
76 Dennis Smith Jr. RC 2.50 6.00
77 Elfrid Payton 1.25 3.00
78 Kawhi Leonard 5.00 12.00
79 Kevin Love 2.00 5.00
80 Karl-Anthony Towns 3.00 8.00
81 Anthony Davis 5.00 12.00
82 De'Aaron Fox RC 15.00 40.00
83 Zach LaVine 3.00 8.00
84 DeMarcus Cousins 1.50 4.00
85 Enes Kanter 1.50 4.00
86 JJ Redick 2.00 5.00
87 Aaron Gordon 2.00 5.00
88 Rondae Hollis-Jefferson 1.25 3.00
89 Kevin Durant 8.00 20.00
90 Dario Saric 1.50 4.00
91 John Wall 2.50 6.00
92 Khris Middleton 2.50 6.00
93 Kyrie Irving 4.00 10.00
94 Andre Drummond 1.50 4.00
95 Bam Adebayo RC 12.00 30.00
96 Jordan Clarkson 2.00 5.00
97 Hassan Whiteside 1.50 4.00
98 Draymond Green 2.50 6.00
99 Dennis Schroder 1.50 4.00
100 John Collins RC 5.00 12.00
101 Dennis Smith Jr. AU 8.00 20.00
102 Dillon Brooks AU RC 20.00 50.00
103 Josh Jackson AU 8.00 20.00
104 Frank Mason III AU RC 6.00 15.00
105 Lonzo Ball AU 25.00 60.00
106 Zach Collins AU RC 10.00 25.00
107 OG Anunoby AU RC 30.00 80.00
108 John Collins AU 15.00 40.00
109 Lauri Markkanen AU RC 40.00 100.00
110 Maxi Kleber AU RC 10.00 25.00
112 Bogdan Bogdanovic AU RC 15.00 40.00
113 Malik Monk AU RC 25.00 60.00
114 Jonathan Isaac AU RC 15.00 40.00
115 Donovan Mitchell AU 100.00 250.00
116 De'Aaron Fox AU 50.00 120.00
117 Markelle Fultz AU 15.00 40.00
118 Kyle Kuzma AU 25.00 60.00
119 Frank Ntilikina AU RC 8.00 20.00
120 Zhou Qi AU RC 40.00 100.00
121 Terrance Ferguson AU RC 6.00 15.00
122 Milos Teodosic AU RC 8.00 20.00
123 Luke Kennard AU RC 12.00 30.00
124 Bam Adebayo AU 40.00 100.00
125 Jayson Tatum AU 400.00 800.00
126 Dwayne Bacon JSY AU RC 10.00 25.00
127 De'Aaron Fox JSY AU 100.00 250.00
128 Luke Kennard JSY AU 20.00 50.00
129 TJ Leaf JSY AU RC 10.00 25.00
130 Lonzo Ball JSY AU 40.00 100.00
131 Justin Patton JSY AU RC 10.00 25.00
132 Kyle Kuzma JSY AU 40.00 100.00
133 Terrance Ferguson JSY AU 10.00 25.00
134 Frank Ntilikina JSY AU 12.00 30.00
135 Josh Jackson JSY AU 12.00 30.00
136 Frank Mason III JSY AU 10.00 25.00
137 Harry Giles JSY AU RC 10.00 25.00
138 Donovan Mitchell JSY AU 125.00 300.00
139 Bam Adebayo JSY AU 60.00 150.00
140 Markelle Fultz JSY AU 25.00 60.00
141 Wes Iwundu JSY AU RC 10.00 25.00
142 Dennis Smith Jr. JSY AU EXCH 12.00 30.00
143 Malik Monk JSY AU 40.00 100.00
144 Jonathan Isaac JSY AU 25.00 60.00
145 Semi Ojeleye JSY AU RC 12.00 30.00
146 Jayson Tatum JSY AU 600.00 1,200.00
147 Caleb Swanigan JSY AU RC 10.00 25.00
148 Lauri Markkanen JSY AU 60.00 150.00
149 Dillon Brooks JSY AU 30.00 80.00

2017-18 Panini Opulence Silver
*SLVR 1-100: .6X TO 1.5X BASIC
*SLVR 1-100 RC: .6X TO 1.5X BASIC
*SLVR 101-125: .5X TO 1.2X BASIC
*SLVR 126-149: .5X TO 1.2X BASIC
STATED PRINT RUN 25 SER.#'d SETS
EXCHANGE DEADLINE 03/21/2020

2017-18 Panini Opulence Championship Hall Signatures
STATED PRINT RUNS B/TW 25-49 SER.#'d SETS
EXCHANGE DEADLINE 03/21/2020
*SILVER/25: .5X TO 1.2X
1 Robert Horry/49 12.00 30.00
2 Clyde Drexler/35 40.00 100.00
3 Joe Dumars/49 15.00 40.00
4 Jason Kidd/35 40.00 100.00
5 James Worthy/35 15.00 40.00
6 Shaquille O'Neal/35 125.00 300.00
7 Steve Kerr/49 15.00 40.00
8 Jerry West/35 40.00 100.00
9 Frank Ramsey/49 12.00 30.00
10 David Robinson/35 60.00 150.00
11 Chauncey Billups/49 15.00 40.00
12 Kevin Love/35 12.00 30.00
13 Kobe Bryant/35 1,500.00 3,000.00
14 Dennis Rodman/35 30.00 80.00
15 Sam Jones/49 15.00 40.00
16 Magic Johnson/35 125.00 300.00
17 Elvin Hayes/49 15.00 40.00
18 Alonzo Mourning/35 40.00 100.00
19 Rick Fox/49 10.00 25.00
20 Hakeem Olajuwon/35 60.00 150.00
22 Ray Allen/35 60.00 150.00
23 Stephen Curry/25 1,000.00 2,000.00
24 Tony Parker/35 40.00 100.00
25 Richard Hamilton/49 15.00 40.00

2017-18 Panini Opulence Gold Metal Autographs
STATED PRINT RUNS 20 SER.#'d SETS
EXCHANGE DEADLINE 03/21/2020
1 Chris Paul 100.00 250.00
2 Dwyane Wade 100.00 250.00
3 Harrison Barnes 20.00 50.00
4 Kevin Durant 200.00 500.00
5 Kyrie Irving 125.00 300.00
6 Larry Bird 150.00 400.00
7 Alonzo Mourning 75.00 200.00
8 Shaquille O'Neal 150.00 400.00
9 Kevin Love 25.00 60.00
10 Jason Kidd 100.00 250.00
11 Tim Hardaway 40.00 100.00
12 Vince Carter 150.00 400.00
13 Clyde Drexler 100.00 250.00
14 David Robinson 100.00 250.00
16 Magic Johnson 125.00 300.00
17 Kobe Bryant 2,500.00 5,000.00

2017-18 Panini Opulence Gold Records Signatures
STATED PRINT RUNS B/TW 25-49 SER.#'d SETS
EXCHANGE DEADLINE 03/21/2020
*SILVER/25: .5X TO 1.2X
1 Robert Parish/49 15.00 40.00
2 Dirk Nowitzki/35 125.00 300.00
3 Stephen Curry/25 1,000.00 2,000.00
4 Hakeem Olajuwon/35 60.00 150.00
5 Kareem Abdul-Jabbar/35 100.00 250.00
6 Alonzo Mourning/35 40.00 100.00
7 Kobe Bryant/35 1,500.00 3,000.00
8 Bill Russell/25 400.00 800.00
9 Marc Gasol/35 EXCH 12.00 30.00
10 A.C. Green/49 12.00 30.00
11 Shawn Bradley/49 8.00 20.00
12 Dominique Wilkins/35 20.00 50.00
13 Steve Kerr/49 15.00 40.00
15 Karl Malone/25 50.00 120.00
16 Anthony Davis/35 50.00 120.00
17 Alex English/49 15.00 40.00
18 Walt Frazier/49 20.00 50.00
19 Ray Allen/35 60.00 150.00
20 Dennis Rodman/35 100.00 250.00
21 John Stockton/25 50.00 120.00
22 George Gervin/49 20.00 50.00
23 Tracy McGrady/35 100.00 250.00
24 Jason Kidd/35 40.00 100.00
25 Kevin Love/35 12.00 30.00
26 Ben Wallace/49 EXCH 30.00 80.00
27 Magic Johnson/25 125.00 300.00
28 Clyde Drexler/35 40.00 100.00
29 Reggie Miller/25 125.00 300.00
30 Dikembe Mutombo/49 40.00 100.00

2017-18 Panini Opulence Golden Autographed Memorabilia
PRINT RUNS B/WN 25-49 COPIES PER
EXCHANGE DEADLINE 03/21/2020
*SILVER/25: .5X TO 1.2X p/r 49
*SILVER/5-25: .4X TO 1X p/r 25
1 Rudy Gobert/49 15.00 40.00
2 Eric Gordon/49 10.00 25.00
3 Harrison Barnes/49 10.00 25.00
4 Andre Drummond/49 10.00 25.00
5 Aaron Gordon/49 12.00 30.00
6 Khris Middleton/49 15.00 40.00
7 Anthony Davis/25 60.00 150.00
8 Jeff Teague/49 8.00 20.00
9 Gordon Hayward/25 12.00 30.00
10 Dwight Powell/49 8.00 20.00
11 Blake Griffin/25 15.00 40.00
13 Brook Lopez/49 10.00 25.00
14 Reggie Jackson/49 10.00 25.00
15 Kevin Love/25 15.00 40.00
16 Evan Turner/49 8.00 20.00
17 LaMarcus Aldridge/25 15.00 40.00
18 Chris Paul/25 50.00 120.00
20 Avery Bradley/49 8.00 20.00
21 Vince Carter/25 125.00 300.00
22 Willie Cauley-Stein/49 8.00 20.00
23 Rodney Hood/49 8.00 20.00
24 Thaddeus Young/49 8.00 20.00
25 Malcolm Brogdon/49 10.00 25.00
26 Ricky Rubio/25 12.00 30.00
27 Michael Kidd-Gilchrist/49 8.00 20.00
28 Serge Ibaka/49 10.00 25.00
29 Kemba Walker/49 10.00 25.00
30 Mike Conley/49 10.00 25.00
31 Patrick Beverley/49 8.00 20.00
32 Seth Curry/49 12.00 30.00
33 Derrick Favors/49 8.00 20.00
34 Enes Kanter/49 10.00 25.00
35 Nerlens Noel/49 8.00 20.00
36 Eric Bledsoe/49 10.00 25.00
37 Marcus Smart/49 12.00 30.00
38 Trevor Ariza/49 8.00 20.00
39 Elfrid Payton/49 8.00 20.00
40 CJ McCollum/25 15.00 40.00

2017-18 Panini Opulence Golden Ink
STATED PRINT RUNS 20 SER.#'d SETS
EXCHANGE DEADLINE 03/21/2020
1 Jonathan Isaac 40.00 100.00
2 Kristaps Porzingis 30.00 80.00
3 Luke Kennard 30.00 80.00
4 Rick Fox 20.00 50.00
5 Bogdan Bogdanovic 40.00 100.00
6 Kyrie Irving 100.00 250.00
7 Nikola Jokic 300.00 600.00
8 Karl-Anthony Towns 40.00 100.00
9 Lonzo Ball 60.00 150.00
10 Tony Parker 40.00 100.00
11 Frank Ntilikina 20.00 50.00
12 LaMarcus Aldridge 25.00 60.00
13 Donovan Mitchell 150.00 400.00
14 Bam Adebayo 100.00 250.00
15 Lauri Markkanen 100.00 250.00
16 Damian Lillard 125.00 300.00
17 Al Horford 25.00 60.00
18 Brandon Ingram 30.00 80.00
19 Josh Jackson 20.00 50.00
20 Isaiah Thomas 20.00 50.00
21 Dennis Smith Jr. 20.00 50.00
22 Gordon Hayward 20.00 50.00
23 Kyle Kuzma 60.00 150.00
24 Robert Horry 25.00 60.00
25 Zhou Qi 50.00 120.00
26 Blake Griffin 25.00 60.00
27 Myles Turner 25.00 60.00
28 Anfernee Hardaway 100.00 250.00
30 Jeremy Lin 75.00 200.00
31 Malik Monk EXCH 60.00 150.00
32 Richard Hamilton 30.00 80.00
34 Milos Teodosic 20.00 50.00
35 Terrance Ferguson 15.00 40.00
36 Giannis Antetokounmpo 150.00 400.00
37 Markelle Fultz 40.00 100.00
38 Vince Carter 125.00 300.00
39 De'Aaron Fox 150.00 400.00
40 Grant Hill 100.00 250.00

2017-18 Panini Opulence Identifying Ink
STATED PRINT RUNS B/TWN 25-35 SER.#'d SETS
EXCHANGE DEADLINE 03/21/2020
*SILVER/25: .4X TO 1.2X BASIC
1 Gordon Hayward/35 10.00 25.00
2 Charles Barkley/25 150.00 400.00
3 Artis Gilmore/35 15.00 40.00
5 Ivica Zubac/35 10.00 25.00
6 Jerry West/35 30.00 80.00
7 Sam Cassell/35 10.00 25.00
8 Brandon Ingram/35 15.00 40.00
9 Lance Stephenson/35 10.00 25.00
10 Isaiah Thomas/35 10.00 25.00
11 Kemba Walker/35 10.00 25.00
12 Kobe Bryant/35 1,000.00 2,000.00
13 Nikola Jokic/35 200.00 500.00
14 Kyrie Irving/25 100.00 250.00
15 Stephen Jackson/35 10.00 25.00
16 Alonzo Mourning/35 40.00 100.00
17 Tom Chambers/35 12.00 30.00
18 Dennis Rodman/35 100.00 250.00
19 Willie Cauley-Stein/35 8.00 20.00
20 Jeremy Lin/35 25.00 60.00
21 Richard Hamilton/35 15.00 40.00
22 Allen Iverson/25 125.00 300.00
23 George Gervin/35 20.00 50.00
24 Magic Johnson/25 100.00 250.00
25 Patrick Beverley/35 8.00 20.00
26 David Robinson/35 40.00 100.00
27 Mark Aguirre/35 10.00 25.00
28 Vince Carter/35 100.00 250.00
29 Avery Johnson/35 10.00 25.00
30 Kristaps Porzingis/35 15.00 40.00

2017-18 Panini Opulence NBA Finals Booklet
PRINT RUN B/WN 18-26 COPIES PER
2 Kevin Love 50.00 120.00
3 Tristan Thompson 20.00 50.00
5 JR Smith 25.00 60.00
6 Kyle Korver 75.00 200.00
7 Iman Shumpert 20.00 50.00
8 Richard Jefferson 25.00 60.00
9 Channing Frye 20.00 50.00
10 Kevin Durant 500.00 1,000.00
11 Draymond Green 75.00 200.00
12 Zaza Pachulia 20.00 50.00
13 Klay Thompson 400.00 800.00
14 Stephen Curry 600.00 1,200.00
15 Andre Iguodala 100.00 250.00
16 Shaun Livingston 50.00 120.00
17 Ian Clark 20.00 50.00
18 Patrick McCaw 20.00 50.00
19 James Michael McAdoo 25.00 60.00
20 JaVale McGee 50.00 120.00

2017-18 Panini Opulence Opulent Autographs
PRINT RUNS B/WN 34-49 COPIES PER
EXCHANGE DEADLINE 03/21/2020
1 David Robinson/35 40.00 100.00
2 Terrence Ross/49 10.00 25.00
3 Jeremy Lin/35 75.00 200.00
4 Marques Johnson/49 10.00 25.00
5 Artis Gilmore/49 15.00 40.00
6 Adrian Dantley/49 12.00 30.00
7 Avery Bradley/49 8.00 20.00
8 Chauncey Billups/49 15.00 40.00
9 Allen Iverson/35 100.00 250.00
10 Enes Kanter/49 10.00 25.00
11 Brandon Ingram/35 15.00 40.00
12 Jerami Grant/49 10.00 25.00
13 Kristaps Porzingis/35 15.00 40.00
14 D.J. Augustin/49 8.00 20.00
15 Nikola Jokic/49 200.00 500.00
16 Matthew Dellavedova/49 10.00 25.00
17 Myles Turner/49 12.00 30.00
18 Justise Winslow/49 8.00 20.00
19 Kyrie Irving/35 100.00 250.00
20 Allan Houston/49 12.00 30.00
21 Dennis Rodman/35 100.00 250.00
22 Thaddeus Young/49 8.00 20.00
23 Gordon Hayward/49 10.00 25.00
24 Mitch Richmond/49 15.00 40.00
25 George Gervin/49 20.00 50.00
26 Domantas Sabonis/49 25.00 60.00
27 Jrue Holiday/49 15.00 40.00
28 Emmanuel Mudiay/49 8.00 20.00
29 Magic Johnson/35 100.00 250.00
30 Alex English/49 15.00 40.00
31 Vince Carter/35 100.00 250.00
32 Marvin Williams/49 8.00 20.00
33 Kemba Walker/49 10.00 25.00
34 Seth Curry/49 12.00 30.00
35 Al Horford/49 12.00 30.00
36 Kobe Bryant/35 1,000.00 2,000.00
37 Rick Fox/49 10.00 25.00
38 Shaun Livingston/49 10.00 25.00
39 Jerry West/35 40.00 100.00
40 Zaza Pachulia/49 8.00 20.00
41 Isaiah Thomas/35 10.00 25.00
42 Kenny "Sky" Walker/49 8.00 20.00
43 Richard Hamilton/49 15.00 40.00
44 Jamaal Wilkes/49 12.00 30.00
45 Calvin Murphy/49 12.00 30.00
46 Kevin Durant/35 100.00 250.00
47 Elfrid Payton/49 8.00 20.00
48 Iman Shumpert/49 8.00 20.00
49 Alonzo Mourning/35 20.00 50.00
50 Patrick Patterson/49 8.00 20.00

2017-18 Panini Opulence Opulent Scripts
STATED PRINT RUNS B/TWN 25-35 SER.#'d SETS
EXCHANGE DEADLINE 03/21/2020
*SILVER: .4X TO 1X BASIC
1 Elvin Hayes/35 20.00 50.00
2 Shaquille O'Neal/25 125.00 300.00
3 Jermaine O'Neal/35 15.00 40.00
4 Giannis Antetokounmpo/35 125.00 300.00
5 Clint Capela/35 12.00 30.00
6 Anfernee Hardaway/35 60.00 150.00
7 Malcolm Brogdon/35 12.00 30.00
8 James Worthy/35 20.00 50.00
9 Danny Green/35 12.00 30.00
10 Rodney Hood/35 10.00 25.00
11 Derrick Favors/35 10.00 25.00
12 Reggie Miller/25 125.00 300.00
13 Robert Horry/35 15.00 40.00
14 Karl-Anthony Towns/35 25.00 60.00
15 Nerlens Noel/35 10.00 25.00
16 Tony Parker/35 25.00 60.00
17 B.J. Armstrong/35 15.00 40.00
18 Sam Jones/35 20.00 50.00
19 Evan Turner/35 10.00 25.00
20 Tyson Chandler/35 12.00 30.00
21 Trevor Ariza/35 12.00 30.00
22 Damian Lillard/25 100.00 250.00
23 Michael Kidd-Gilchrist/35 10.00 25.00
24 Hakeem Olajuwon/35 60.00 150.00
25 Channing Frye/35 10.00 25.00
26 Gary Payton/35 25.00 60.00
27 Antawn Jamison/35 12.00 30.00
28 Dion Waiters/35 10.00 25.00
29 Tony Allen/35 10.00 25.00
30 Kentavious Caldwell-Pope/35 12.00 30.00
31 Reggie Jackson/35 12.00 30.00
32 Blake Griffin/35 15.00 40.00
33 Joe Johnson/35 12.00 30.00
34 Clyde Drexler/35 25.00 60.00
35 Cody Zeller/35 10.00 25.00
36 Grant Hill/35 40.00 100.00
37 Nene/35 12.00 30.00
38 Bernard King/35 20.00 50.00
39 Courtney Lee/35 10.00 25.00
40 Eric Bledsoe/35 12.00 30.00

2017-18 Panini Opulence Precious Swatch Signatures
STATED PRINT RUNS B/TW 25-49 SER.#'d SETS
EXCHANGE DEADLINE 03/21/2020
*SILVER/25: .5X TO 1.2X p/r 49
*SILVER/25: .4X TO 1X p/r 25
1 Brandon Ingram/25 25.00 60.00
2 Kemba Walker/49 12.00 30.00
3 Kristaps Porzingis/25 25.00 60.00
4 Mark Price/49 15.00 40.00
5 Marcus Smart/49 15.00 40.00
6 Grant Hill/25 40.00 100.00
7 Al Horford/49 15.00 40.00
8 Allen Iverson/25 125.00 300.00
9 Nikola Jokic/49 300.00 600.00
10 Magic Johnson/25 100.00 250.00
11 Marc Gasol/25 EXCH 20.00 50.00
12 Mike Conley/49 12.00 30.00
13 Gordon Hayward/49 12.00 30.00
14 Enes Kanter/49 12.00 30.00
15 Trevor Ariza/49 10.00 25.00
16 David Robinson/25 60.00 150.00
17 Myles Turner/49 15.00 40.00
18 Shaquille O'Neal/25 125.00 300.00
19 Jeremy Lin/25 75.00 200.00
20 Hakeem Olajuwon/25 60.00 150.00
21 Isaiah Thomas/25 15.00 40.00
22 Patrick Beverley/49 10.00 25.00
23 Damian Lillard/25 100.00 250.00
24 Nerlens Noel/49 10.00 25.00
25 Elfrid Payton/49 10.00 25.00
26 Tony Parker/25 30.00 80.00
27 Jrue Holiday/49 20.00 50.00
28 Larry Bird/25 125.00 300.00
29 Giannis Antetokounmpo/25 150.00 400.00
30 Serge Ibaka/49 12.00 30.00
31 Karl-Anthony Towns/25 25.00 60.00
33 Kyrie Irving/25 125.00 300.00
34 Eric Bledsoe/49 12.00 30.00
35 CJ McCollum/25 20.00 50.00

2017-18 Panini Opulence Rookie Patch Autographs Booklets
STATED PRINT RUNS 25 SER.#'d SETS
EXCHANGE DEADLINE 03/21/2020
1 Lonzo Ball 300.00 600.00
2 Donovan Mitchell 800.00 1,500.00
3 Jayson Tatum 1,500.00 3,000.00
4 Kyle Kuzma 125.00 300.00
5 Markelle Fultz 125.00 300.00
6 Lauri Markkanen 200.00 500.00
7 Frank Ntilikina 40.00 100.00
8 Dennis Smith Jr. 40.00 100.00
10 De'Aaron Fox 300.00 600.00
11 Josh Jackson 40.00 100.00
12 Malik Monk 125.00 300.00
13 Luke Kennard 75.00 200.00
14 Frank Mason III 30.00 80.00
15 Jonathan Isaac 80.00 200.00
16 Bam Adebayo 200.00 500.00
17 Justin Patton 30.00 80.00
18 Caleb Swanigan 30.00 80.00
19 Derrick White 125.00 300.00
20 Semi Ojeleye 40.00 100.00
21 John Collins 80.00 200.00

2017-18 Panini Opulence Vintage Gold Signatures
STATED PRINT RUNS 20 SER.#'d SETS
EXCHANGE DEADLINE 03/21/2020
1 Shaquille O'Neal 125.00 300.00
2 Allen Iverson 100.00 250.00
3 Reggie Miller 100.00 250.00
4 Karl Malone 75.00 200.00
5 Magic Johnson 125.00 300.00
6 John Stockton 75.00 200.00
7 Jerry West 75.00 200.00
8 Alonzo Mourning 40.00 100.00
9 David Robinson 75.00 200.00
10 Hakeem Olajuwon 75.00 200.00
11 Paul Silas 15.00 40.00
12 Clyde Drexler 75.00 200.00
13 Dennis Rodman 100.00 250.00
14 Gary Payton 25.00 60.00
15 James Worthy 25.00 60.00
16 Sam Jones 20.00 50.00
17 Bernard King 20.00 50.00
18 Artis Gilmore 20.00 50.00
19 George Gervin 25.00 60.00
20 Calvin Murphy 15.00 40.00
21 Nate Archibald 20.00 50.00
22 Elvin Hayes 20.00 50.00
23 Lenny Wilkens 20.00 50.00
24 Kobe Bryant 1,500.00 3,000.00
25 Ralph Sampson 15.00 40.00
26 Charles Barkley 125.00 300.00
27 Bill Walton 40.00 100.00
28 Joe Dumars 20.00 50.00
29 David Thompson 20.00 50.00
30 Bob McAdoo 20.00 50.00
32 Jamaal Wilkes 15.00 40.00
33 Adrian Dantley 15.00 40.00
34 Alex English 20.00 50.00
35 Tracy McGrady 100.00 250.00
36 Rick Barry 20.00 50.00
37 Walt Frazier 25.00 60.00
38 Dave Cowens 25.00 60.00
39 Louie Dampier 15.00 40.00
40 Robert Parish 20.00 50.00

2019-20 Panini Opulence
1 RJ Barrett RC 15.00 40.00
2 John Wall 8.00 20.00
3 Jaren Jackson Jr. 10.00 25.00
4 Klay Thompson 15.00 40.00
5 Kendrick Nunn RC 6.00 15.00
6 Carsen Edwards RC 5.00 12.00
7 Coby White RC 12.00 30.00
8 Vince Carter 12.00 30.00
9 Nikola Vucevic 5.00 12.00
10 Jaylen Brown 10.00 25.00
11 Kevin Porter Jr. 8.00 20.00
12 Donovan Mitchell 12.00 30.00
13 Devonte' Graham 5.00 12.00
14 Kyrie Irving 12.00 30.00
15 Zion Williamson RC 200.00 500.00
16 Buddy Hield 5.00 12.00
17 Nickeil Alexander-Walker RC 6.00 15.00
18 Kristaps Porzingis 8.00 20.00
19 Kevin Durant 20.00 50.00
20 Tyler Herro RC 20.00 50.00
21 Jayson Tatum 25.00 60.00
22 Devin Booker 1.50 4.00
23 Khris Middleton 6.00 15.00
24 De'Andre Hunter RC 15.00 40.00
25 Ben Simmons 6.00 15.00
26 Paul George 10.00 25.00
27 Terence Davis RC 6.00 15.00
28 Rudy Gobert 8.00 20.00
29 Keldon Johnson 12.00 30.00
30 Sekou Doumbouya RC 4.00 10.00
31 Derrick Rose 12.00 30.00
32 Bol Bol RC 10.00 25.00
33 Ja Morant RC 300.00 600.00
34 LaMarcus Aldridge 6.00 15.00
35 Tacko Fall RC 5.00 12.00
36 Lauri Markkanen 8.00 20.00
37 Nikola Jokic 30.00 80.00
38 Jrue Holiday 8.00 20.00
39 Romeo Langford RC 4.00 10.00
40 Zach LaVine 10.00 25.00
41 Giannis Antetokounmpo 30.00 80.00
42 CJ McCollum 6.00 15.00
43 Elfrid Payton 4.00 10.00
44 Kevin Love 6.00 15.00
45 Kemba Walker 5.00 12.00
46 Andrew Wiggins 8.00 20.00
47 Bam Adebayo 10.00 25.00
48 Goga Bitadze 6.00 15.00
49 Nassir Little 6.00 15.00
50 Damian Lillard 15.00 40.00
51 Kawhi Leonard 15.00 40.00
52 Michael Porter Jr. 10.00 25.00
53 Luka Samanic RC 5.00 12.00
54 Blake Griffin 6.00 15.00
55 Chris Paul 12.00 30.00
56 Julius Randle 8.00 20.00
57 Shai Gilgeous-Alexander 30.00 80.00
58 Jarrett Culver RC 4.00 10.00
59 Aaron Gordon 6.00 15.00
60 Joel Embiid 12.00 30.00
61 Fred VanVleet 8.00 20.00
62 Victor Oladipo 5.00 12.00
63 DeMar DeRozan 8.00 20.00
64 Deandre Ayton 6.00 15.00
65 Pascal Siakam 10.00 25.00
66 Carmelo Anthony 10.00 25.00
67 Jamal Murray 10.00 25.00
68 Karl-Anthony Towns 10.00 25.00
69 Nicolo Melli 5.00 12.00
70 Luka Doncic 125.00 300.00
71 Andre Drummond 5.00 12.00
72 Brandon Ingram 6.00 15.00
73 De'Aaron Fox 10.00 25.00
74 Draymond Green 8.00 20.00
75 Matisse Thybulle 8.00 20.00
76 Domantas Sabonis 8.00 20.00
77 Bruno Fernando 5.00 12.00
78 Bradley Beal 8.00 20.00
79 Jimmy Butler 12.00 30.00
80 Stephen Curry 50.00 125.00
81 Ty Jerome 8.00 20.00
82 Rui Hachimura RC 15.00 40.00
83 Brandon Clarke RC 8.00 20.00
84 John Collins 6.00 15.00
85 LeBron James 150.00 400.00
86 Eric Paschall RC 5.00 12.00
87 Kyle Lowry 6.00 15.00
88 Cameron Johnson RC 10.00 25.00
89 James Harden 12.00 30.00
90 Jaxson Hayes RC 6.00 15.00
91 Terry Rozier 5.00 12.00
92 Grant Williams RC 6.00 15.00
93 Cam Reddish RC 6.00 15.00
94 PJ Washington Jr. RC 12.00 30.00
95 Russell Westbrook 10.00 25.00
96 Trae Young 15.00 40.00
97 Dillon Brooks 5.00 12.00
98 D'Angelo Russell 5.00 12.00

99 Jordan Poole RC 15.00 40.00
100 Anthony Davis 15.00 40.00
112 Tyler Herro JSY AU EXCH 150.00 400.00
RPABCL Brandon Clarke JSY AU 60.00 150.00
RPACBW Coby White JSY AU 100.00 250.00
RPACEW Carsen Edwards JSY AU 40.00 100.00
RPACJN Cameron Johnson JSY AU 80.00 200.00
RPACRD Cam Reddish JSY AU 50.00 125.00
RPADHT De'Andre Hunter JSY AU 125.00 300.00
RPAEPS Eric Paschall JSY AU 40.00 100.00
RPAGWL Grant Williams JSY AU 50.00 125.00
RPAJCV Jarrett Culver JSY AU 30.00 80.00
RPAJMT Ja Morant JSY AU 1,000.00 2,000.00
RPAJPL Jordan Poole JSY AU 125.00 300.00
RPAJXH Jaxson Hayes JSY AU 50.00 125.00
RPAKDN Kendrick Nunn JSY AU 50.00 125.00
RPALSM Luka Samanic JSY AU 40.00 100.00
RPANAW Nickeil Alexander-Walker JSY AU 50.00 125.00
RPAPJW PJ Washington Jr. JSY AU 100.00 250.00
RPARHM Rui Hachimura JSY AU RC 125.00 300.00
RPARJB RJ Barrett JSY AU 125.00 300.00
RPARLF Romeo Langford JSY AU 30.00 80.00
RPASKD Sekou Doumbouya JSY AU 30.00 80.00
RPATDV Terence Davis JSY AU 50.00 125.00
RPATFL Tacko Fall JSY AU 40.00 100.00
RPAZWL Zion Williamson JSY AU 800.00 1,500.00

2019-20 Panini Opulence 24K Autographs

1 Allen Iverson 150.00 300.00
2 Ray Allen 30.00 80.00
3 Artis Gilmore 20.00 50.00
4 Jerry West 60.00 150.00
5 Rick Barry 20.00 50.00
6 Vince Carter 150.00 300.00
7 Alex English 20.00 50.00
8 Kevin Garnett 200.00 350.00
9 Paul Pierce 30.00 80.00
10 George Gervin 25.00 60.00
11 Dominique Wilkins 25.00 60.00
12 Oscar Robertson 40.00 100.00
13 Hakeem Olajuwon 30.00 80.00
14 Elvin Hayes 20.00 50.00
15 Dan Issel 20.00 50.00
16 Julius Erving 60.00 150.00
17 Karl Malone 30.00 80.00
18 Kareem Abdul-Jabbar 60.00 150.00

2019-20 Panini Opulence All-Star Booklet

1 Anthony Davis 40.00 100.00
2 Blake Griffin 15.00 40.00
3 Bradley Beal 20.00 50.00
4 D'Angelo Russell 12.00 30.00
5 Damian Lillard 60.00 150.00
6 Kawhi Leonard 40.00 100.00
7 Kemba Walker 12.00 30.00
8 Khris Middleton 15.00 40.00
9 Kyle Lowry 15.00 40.00
10 LaMarcus Aldridge 15.00 40.00
11 Nikola Vucevic 12.00 30.00
12 Russell Westbrook 25.00 60.00

2019-20 Panini Opulence City of Gold Signatures

1 Trae Young 100.00 250.00
2 Karl-Anthony Towns 25.00 60.00
3 Tyler Herro 300.00 500.00
4 Anthony Davis 40.00 100.00
5 Kristaps Porzingis 20.00 50.00
6 Domantas Sabonis 20.00 50.00
8 Zach LaVine 25.00 60.00
9 Bogdan Bogdanovic 15.00 40.00
10 De'Andre Hunter 40.00 100.00
11 Jarrett Culver 10.00 25.00
12 Coby White 30.00 80.00
13 Gary Harris 12.00 30.00
14 Giannis Antetokounmpo 80.00 200.00
15 PJ Washington Jr. 30.00 80.00
16 Ja Morant 500.00 700.00
17 RJ Barrett 40.00 100.00
18 Cam Reddish 15.00 40.00
19 Kendrick Nunn 15.00 40.00
20 Lauri Markkanen 20.00 50.00
21 Brandon Clarke 20.00 50.00
22 Nikola Jokic 200.00 500.00
23 Cameron Johnson 25.00 60.00
24 Rui Hachimura 40.00 100.00
25 Eric Paschall 12.00 30.00

2019-20 Panini Opulence City of Gold Signatures Gold

*GOLD/25: .6X TO 1.5X BASE HI
3 Tyler Herro 400.00 800.00
16 Ja Morant 600.00 1,000.00

2019-20 Panini Opulence Gilded Signatures

2 Al Harrington 15.00 40.00
3 Josh Hart 12.00 30.00
4 Charles Oakley 12.00 30.00
5 TJ Leaf 10.00 25.00
7 Mike Conley 12.00 30.00
8 Charles Barkley 60.00 150.00
9 Gary Harris 12.00 30.00
10 Giannis Antetokounmpo 300.00 500.00
11 Stephen Curry 1,000.00 2,000.00
12 Kevin Knox II 10.00 25.00
13 Kurt Rambis 12.00 30.00
14 Julius Erving 60.00 150.00
15 Bob McAdoo 20.00 50.00
16 Chris Boucher 15.00 40.00
17 Shai Gilgeous-Alexander 200.00 500.00
18 Allen Iverson 100.00 250.00
19 David Robinson 30.00 80.00
20 Rolando Blackman 12.00 30.00
21 Lonzo Ball 15.00 40.00
22 Lauri Markkanen 20.00 50.00
23 Christian Laettner 15.00 40.00
24 Keita Bates-Diop 10.00 25.00
27 Joe Harris 12.00 30.00
28 Kevin Garnett 40.00 100.00
29 Jason Kidd 25.00 60.00
30 Horace Grant 15.00 40.00
31 Dwyane Wade 60.00 150.00
33 Harrison Barnes 12.00 30.00

2019-20 Panini Opulence Gold Medal Autographs

1 Adrian Dantley 20.00 50.00
2 Jerry West 30.00 80.00
3 Oscar Robertson 50.00 120.00
4 Chris Mullin 25.00 60.00
6 David Robinson 40.00 100.00
7 Kevin Durant 100.00 250.00
8 Anthony Davis 50.00 120.00
9 Karl Malone 40.00 100.00
10 John Stockton 40.00 100.00
11 Magic Johnson 60.00 150.00
12 Gary Payton 30.00 80.00
14 Vince Carter 40.00 100.00
15 Kevin Garnett 100.00 250.00
17 Jason Kidd 30.00 80.00
18 Charles Barkley 60.00 150.00

2019-20 Panini Opulence Gold Medal Autographs Gold

*GOLD/25: .6X TO 1.5X BASE HI
15 Kevin Garnett 150.00 300.00
18 Charles Barkley 80.00 200.00

2019-20 Panini Opulence Gold Medal Jersey Autographs

STATED PRINT RUN 79 SER.#'d SETS
1 David Robinson 50.00 125.00
2 Gary Payton 40.00 100.00
3 Hakeem Olajuwon 50.00 125.00
4 Harrison Barnes 20.00 50.00
5 Karl Malone 50.00 125.00
7 Kevin Durant 80.00 200.00
8 Kevin Garnett 100.00 250.00
10 Ray Allen 50.00 125.00

2019-20 Panini Opulence Golden Autographed Memorabilia

1 Charles Barkley 50.00 125.00
2 Dwyane Wade 50.00 125.00
3 Gary Payton 40.00 100.00
4 Hakeem Olajuwon 50.00 125.00
6 Jason Kidd 40.00 100.00
7 John Stockton 50.00 125.00
8 Kareem Abdul-Jabbar 80.00 200.00
9 Karl Malone 50.00 125.00
10 Kevin Garnett 60.00 150.00
11 Kevin Johnson 25.00 60.00
12 David Robinson 50.00 125.00
13 Larry Bird 100.00 250.00
14 Magic Johnson 80.00 200.00
15 Mark Aguirre 20.00 50.00
16 Mike Bibby 25.00 60.00
17 Paul Pierce 40.00 100.00
18 Ray Allen 40.00 100.00
19 Richard Hamilton 25.00 60.00
20 Robert Parish 30.00 80.00
21 Jason Richardson 25.00 60.00
23 Vlade Divac 25.00 60.00
24 Steve Francis 25.00 60.00
25 Isaiah Rider 20.00 50.00
26 Spud Webb 25.00 60.00
27 Jack Sikma 25.00 60.00
28 Danny Granger 25.00 60.00
30 Julius Erving 60.00 150.00

2019-20 Panini Opulence Golden Rookie Graphs

*GOLD/25: .6X TO 1.5X BASE HI
STATED PRINT RUN 25 SER.#'d SETS
1 Cody Martin 25.00 60.00
2 Mfiondu Kabengele 12.00 30.00
3 Jordan Poole 40.00 100.00
4 Kevin Porter Jr. 20.00 50.00
5 Carsen Edwards 12.00 30.00
6 Bruno Fernando 12.00 30.00
7 Eric Paschall 12.00 30.00
8 Bol Bol 25.00 60.00
9 Talen Horton-Tucker 15.00 40.00
10 Luka Samanic 12.00 30.00
11 Goga Bitadze 15.00 40.00
12 Matisse Thybulle 20.00 50.00
13 Brandon Clarke 20.00 50.00
14 Grant Williams 15.00 40.00
15 Nicolas Claxton 20.00 50.00
16 Ty Jerome 20.00 50.00
17 Nassir Little 15.00 40.00
18 Dylan Windler 12.00 30.00
19 Keldon Johnson 30.00 80.00
20 Isaiah Roby 12.00 30.00
21 Kendrick Nunn 15.00 40.00
22 Terence Davis 15.00 40.00
23 Chuma Okeke 15.00 40.00
24 Nickeil Alexander-Walker 15.00 40.00
25 Sekou Doumbouya 10.00 25.00

2019-20 Panini Opulence Golden Vintage Autographs

1 Mike Bibby 15.00 40.00
2 Isaiah Rider 12.00 30.00
3 Spud Webb 15.00 40.00
4 Jack Sikma 15.00 40.00
5 Danny Granger 10.00 25.00
6 Vlade Divac 15.00 40.00
8 Fat Lever 12.00 30.00
9 Kurt Rambis 12.00 30.00
10 Bob McAdoo 20.00 50.00
11 Rolando Blackman 12.00 30.00
12 Christian Laettner 15.00 40.00
13 Horace Grant 15.00 40.00
14 Steve Francis 15.00 40.00
15 Richard Hamilton 15.00 40.00
16 Ralph Sampson 12.00 30.00
17 A.C. Green 15.00 40.00
18 Kevin Johnson 15.00 40.00
19 Stephen Jackson 10.00 25.00
20 Mark Aguirre 12.00 30.00
21 Elvin Hayes 20.00 50.00
22 Rick Fox 12.00 30.00
23 Toni Kukoc 20.00 50.00
24 Andre Miller 12.00 30.00
25 Chris Mullin 20.00 50.00
26 Chauncey Billups 20.00 50.00
27 Walt Frazier 25.00 60.00
28 Mark Price 15.00 40.00
29 Steve Kerr 20.00 50.00
30 Shawn Bradley 10.00 25.00
31 Charles Barkley 100.00 250.00
32 Bill Russell 1,000.00 2,000.00

2019-20 Panini Opulence Golden Vintage Autographs Gold

*GOLD/25: X TO X BASE HI
31 Charles Barkley 125.00 300.00
32 Bill Russell 1,250.00 2,500.00

2019-20 Panini Opulence Luxurious Autographs

STATED PRINT RUN 49 SER.#'d SETS
3 Ivica Zubac 12.00 30.00
4 Trevor Ariza 10.00 25.00
5 Al Horford 15.00 40.00
6 Eric Gordon 12.00 30.00
8 Jrue Holiday 20.00 50.00
9 Caris LeVert 12.00 30.00
10 Mo Bamba 12.00 30.00
11 Dennis Rodman 60.00 150.00
12 JJ Redick 15.00 40.00
14 Oscar Robertson 30.00 80.00
15 J.J. Barea 12.00 30.00
16 Vince Carter 150.00 300.00
17 Gary Payton 25.00 60.00
18 Richard Hamilton 15.00 40.00
19 Ralph Sampson 12.00 30.00
20 Jalen Brunson 40.00 100.00
21 Clyde Drexler 25.00 60.00
22 Karl Malone 30.00 80.00
23 A.C. Green 15.00 40.00
24 Kevin Johnson 15.00 40.00
25 Stephen Jackson 10.00 25.00
26 Mark Aguirre 12.00 30.00
27 Elvin Hayes 20.00 50.00
28 Rick Fox 12.00 30.00
29 Toni Kukoc 20.00 50.00
30 Kareem Abdul-Jabbar 60.00 150.00
31 Matt Bonner 12.00 30.00
32 Kevin Martin 10.00 25.00
34 T.J. Ford 12.00 30.00

2019-20 Panini Opulence Magnificent Autographs

STATED PRINT RUN 49 SER.#'d SETS
1 Trae Young 100.00 250.00
2 Giannis Antetokounmpo 80.00 200.00
3 Karl-Anthony Towns 25.00 60.00
4 Stephen Curry 1,000.00 2,000.00
5 Zhaire Smith 10.00 25.00
6 Larry Bird 60.00 150.00
7 Steve Francis 15.00 40.00
9 Anthony Davis 40.00 100.00
10 Kristaps Porzingis 20.00 50.00
11 Jarrett Allen 15.00 40.00
12 Mike Bibby 15.00 40.00
13 Isaiah Rider 12.00 30.00
14 Spud Webb 15.00 40.00
15 Jack Sikma 15.00 40.00
16 Danny Granger 10.00 25.00
17 Domantas Sabonis 20.00 50.00
18 Allonzo Trier 10.00 25.00
20 Jason Richardson 15.00 40.00
21 Bobby Portis 10.00 25.00
22 Al Harrington 15.00 40.00
24 Drew Gooden 10.00 25.00
26 Harry Giles III 10.00 25.00
27 Zach LaVine 60.00 150.00
29 Charles Barkley 30.00 80.00
30 Bogdan Bogdanovic 15.00 40.00
31 Matthew Dellavedova 12.00 30.00
32 Vlade Divac 15.00 40.00
33 Myles Turner 15.00 40.00

2019-20 Panini Opulence Nouveau Riche Patch Autographs

1 Zion Williamson 2,000.00 3,500.00
2 Ja Morant 700.00 1,000.00
3 RJ Barrett 400.00 600.00
4 Jarrett Culver 25.00 60.00
5 Coby White 80.00 200.00
6 Jaxson Hayes 40.00 100.00
7 Rui Hachimura 300.00 600.00
8 Cam Reddish 40.00 100.00
9 Cameron Johnson 60.00 150.00
10 PJ Washington Jr. 60.00 150.00
11 Tyler Herro 500.00 700.00
12 Romeo Langford 25.00 60.00
13 Sekou Doumbouya 25.00 60.00
14 Chuma Okeke 40.00 100.00
15 Nickeil Alexander-Walker 40.00 100.00
16 Goga Bitadze 40.00 100.00
17 Luka Samanic 30.00 80.00
18 Matisse Thybulle 50.00 120.00
19 Brandon Clarke 50.00 120.00
20 Grant Williams 40.00 100.00
21 KZ Okpala 30.00 80.00
22 Ty Jerome 50.00 120.00
23 Nassir Little 40.00 100.00
24 Dylan Windler 40.00 100.00
25 Mfiondu Kabengele 30.00 80.00

2019-20 Panini Opulence Nouveau Riche Signatures

2 Mfiondu Kabengele 15.00 40.00
3 Jordan Poole 50.00 120.00
4 Kevin Porter Jr. 25.00 60.00
5 Carsen Edwards 15.00 40.00
6 Bruno Fernando 15.00 40.00
7 Eric Paschall 15.00 40.00
8 Bol Bol 30.00 80.00
9 Talen Horton-Tucker 20.00 50.00
10 Luka Samanic 15.00 40.00
11 Goga Bitadze 20.00 50.00
12 Matisse Thybulle 25.00 60.00
13 Brandon Clarke 25.00 60.00
14 Grant Williams 20.00 50.00
15 KZ Okpala 15.00 40.00
16 Ty Jerome 25.00 60.00
17 Nassir Little 20.00 50.00
18 Dylan Windler 20.00 50.00
19 Keldon Johnson 40.00 100.00
20 Isaiah Roby 15.00 40.00
21 Kendrick Nunn 20.00 50.00
22 Terence Davis 20.00 50.00
23 Chuma Okeke 20.00 50.00
24 Nickeil Alexander-Walker 20.00 50.00
25 Sekou Doumbouya 12.00 30.00

2019-20 Panini Opulence Opulent Autographs

*GOLD/25: .6X TO 1.5X BASE HI
STATED PRINT RUN 25 SER.#'d SETS
1 Zhaire Smith 10.00 25.00
2 Kristaps Porzingis 20.00 50.00
3 Jarrett Allen 15.00 40.00
4 Allonzo Trier 10.00 25.00
5 Lonzo Ball 15.00 40.00
7 Domantas Sabonis 20.00 50.00
8 Bobby Portis 10.00 25.00
9 Chris Boucher 15.00 40.00
11 Zach LaVine 25.00 60.00
12 Bogdan Bogdanovic 15.00 40.00
13 Matthew Dellavedova 12.00 30.00
14 Myles Turner 15.00 40.00
16 Josh Hart 12.00 30.00
17 Nemanja Bjelica 10.00 25.00
18 Mike Conley 12.00 30.00
19 Gary Harris 12.00 30.00
20 Kevin Knox II 10.00 25.00
21 Shai Gilgeous-Alexander 300.00 600.00
22 Lauri Markkanen 20.00 50.00
23 Keita Bates-Diop 10.00 25.00
24 Joe Harris 12.00 30.00

2019-20 Panini Opulence Opulent Scripts

1 Mike Bibby 15.00 40.00
2 Isaiah Rider 12.00 30.00
3 Spud Webb 15.00 40.00
4 Jack Sikma 15.00 40.00
5 Danny Granger 10.00 25.00
6 Vlade Divac 15.00 40.00
8 Fat Lever 12.00 30.00
9 Kurt Rambis 12.00 30.00
10 Bob McAdoo 20.00 50.00
11 Rolando Blackman 12.00 30.00
12 Christian Laettner 15.00 40.00
13 Horace Grant 15.00 40.00
14 Jason Richardson 15.00 40.00
15 Richard Hamilton 15.00 40.00
16 Ralph Sampson 12.00 30.00
17 A.C. Green 15.00 40.00
18 Kevin Johnson 15.00 40.00
19 Stephen Jackson 10.00 25.00
20 Mark Aguirre 12.00 30.00
21 Elvin Hayes 20.00 50.00
22 Rick Fox 12.00 30.00
23 Toni Kukoc 20.00 50.00
24 Andre Miller 12.00 30.00
25 Chris Mullin 20.00 50.00
26 Chauncey Billups 20.00 50.00
27 Walt Frazier 25.00 60.00
28 Mark Price 15.00 40.00
29 Steve Kerr 20.00 50.00
30 Shawn Bradley 10.00 25.00
31 Charles Oakley 12.00 30.00
32 Jamal Mashburn 15.00 40.00

2019-20 Panini Opulence Precious Swatch Signatures

1 Trae Young 100.00 250.00
2 Karl-Anthony Towns 30.00 80.00
3 Stephen Curry 1,000.00 2,000.00
4 Anthony Davis 50.00 120.00
5 Domantas Sabonis 25.00 60.00
7 Zach LaVine 30.00 80.00
8 Myles Turner 20.00 50.00
10 Giannis Antetokounmpo 100.00 250.00
11 Shai Gilgeous-Alexander 500.00 1,000.00
12 Lauri Markkanen 25.00 60.00
14 Lonzo Ball 20.00 50.00
15 Al Horford 20.00 50.00
16 Jrue Holiday 25.00 60.00
17 Caris LeVert 15.00 40.00
18 Mike Conley 15.00 40.00
19 Aaron Holiday 15.00 40.00
20 JJ Redick 20.00 50.00
21 Eric Gordon 15.00 40.00
22 Joe Harris 15.00 40.00
23 Harrison Barnes 15.00 40.00
24 A.C. Green 20.00 50.00
25 Adrian Dantley 20.00 50.00
26 Andre Miller 15.00 40.00
27 Arvydas Sabonis 20.00 50.00
28 Bernard King 25.00 60.00
29 Charles Barkley 40.00 100.00
30 Christian Laettner 20.00 50.00
31 Dan Majerle 15.00 40.00
32 Danny Manning 15.00 40.00
33 David Robinson 40.00 100.00
34 Dirk Nowitzki 60.00 150.00
35 Dominique Wilkins 30.00 80.00

2019-20 Panini Opulence Rookie Octo Signature Booklet

1 Coby White
De'Andre Hunter
Ja Morant
Jaxson Hayes
Rui Hachimura
RJ Barrett
Zion Williamson
Jarrett Culver
Jaxson Hayes 4,000.00 6,000.00

2019-20 Panini Opulence Rookie Patches Booklet

1 Zion Williamson 150.00 400.00
2 Ja Morant 200.00 500.00
3 RJ Barrett 80.00 200.00
4 De'Andre Hunter 80.00 200.00
5 Jarrett Culver 20.00 50.00
6 Coby White 60.00 150.00
7 Jaxson Hayes 30.00 80.00
8 Rui Hachimura 80.00 200.00
9 Cam Reddish 30.00 80.00
10 Cameron Johnson 50.00 120.00
11 PJ Washington Jr. 60.00 150.00
12 Tyler Herro 100.00 250.00
13 Romeo Langford 20.00 50.00
14 Brandon Clarke 40.00 100.00
15 Jordan Poole 80.00 200.00
16 Carsen Edwards 25.00 60.00
17 Eric Paschall 25.00 60.00
18 Kendrick Nunn 30.00 80.00
19 Terence Davis 30.00 80.00
20 Tacko Fall 25.00 60.00
21 Nickeil Alexander-Walker 30.00 80.00
22 Luka Samanic 25.00 60.00
23 Grant Williams 30.00 80.00
24 Sekou Doumbouya 20.00 50.00

2019-20 Panini Origins

EXCHANGE DEADLINE 6/18/21
1 Tyler Herro RC 15.00 40.00
2 Luka Samanic RC 1.25 3.00
3 Paul George 1.50 4.00
4 D'Angelo Russell .75 2.00
5 Stephen Curry 8.00 20.00
6 Mfiondu Kabengele RC 1.25 3.00
7 Bruno Fernando RC 1.25 3.00
8 Trae Young 2.50 6.00
9 Deandre Ayton 1.00 2.50
10 Keldon Johnson RC 3.00 8.00
11 Coby White RC 3.00 8.00
12 Quinndary Weatherspoon RC 1.00 2.50
13 Carsen Edwards RC 1.25 3.00
14 Kyle Lowry 1.00 2.50
15 Zion Williamson RC 12.00 30.00
16 Giannis Antetokounmpo 5.00 12.00
17 Karl-Anthony Towns 1.50 4.00
18 DeMar DeRozan 1.25 3.00
19 Joel Embiid 2.00 5.00
20 Goga Bitadze RC 1.50 4.00
21 Jimmy Butler 2.00 5.00
22 RJ Barrett RC 4.00 10.00
23 Devin Booker .25 .60
24 KZ Okpala RC 1.25 3.00
25 De'Aaron Fox 1.50 4.00
26 Bradley Beal 1.25 3.00
27 Nassir Little RC 1.50 4.00
28 Bol Bol RC 2.50 6.00
29 Klay Thompson 2.50 6.00
30 Jordan Poole RC 4.00 10.00
31 Jayson Tatum 4.00 10.00
32 Isaiah Roby RC 1.25 3.00
33 Tremont Waters RC 1.25 3.00
34 Eric Paschall RC 1.25 3.00
35 Kemba Walker .75 2.00
36 Cam Reddish RC 1.50 4.00
37 Nickeil Alexander-Walker RC 1.50 4.00
38 Zach LaVine 1.50 4.00
39 Kyrie Irving 2.00 5.00
40 Miles Bridges 1.00 2.50
41 Darius Bazley .60 1.50
42 James Harden 2.00 5.00
43 Lonzo Ball 1.00 2.50
44 Matisse Thybulle RC 2.00 5.00
45 Jaren Jackson Jr. 1.50 4.00
46 Ty Jerome RC 2.00 5.00
47 De'Andre Hunter RC 4.00 10.00
48 Kevin Durant 3.00 8.00
49 Pascal Siakam 1.50 4.00
50 Victor Oladipo .75 2.00
51 Kyle Guy .75 2.00
52 Romeo Langford RC 1.00 2.50
53 Kristaps Porzingis 1.25 3.00
54 John Wall 1.25 3.00
55 Luka Doncic 6.00 15.00
56 Nikola Jokic 5.00 12.00
57 Dylan Windler RC 1.25 3.00
58 Nikola Vucevic .75 2.00
59 Kawhi Leonard 2.50 6.00
60 Donovan Mitchell 2.00 5.00
61 Chris Paul 2.00 5.00
62 Anthony Davis 2.50 6.00
63 Kevin Love 1.00 2.50
64 Rudy Gobert 1.25 3.00
65 Cameron Johnson RC 2.50 6.00
66 Brandon Clarke RC 2.00 5.00
67 Ben Simmons 1.00 2.50
68 Aaron Gordon 1.00 2.50
69 Dennis Smith Jr. .60 1.50
70 Ja Morant RC 10.00 25.00
71 Brandon Ingram 1.00 2.50
72 CJ McCollum 1.00 2.50
73 Jarrett Culver RC 1.00 2.50
74 Damian Lillard 2.50 6.00
75 Admiral Schofield RC 1.25 3.00
76 Jaxson Hayes RC 1.50 4.00
77 Ignas Brazdeikis RC 1.25 3.00
78 Cody Martin RC 1.50 4.00
79 Julius Randle 1.25 3.00
80 PJ Washington Jr. RC 3.00 8.00
81 Blake Griffin 1.00 2.50
82 Rui Hachimura RC 4.00 10.00
83 LeBron James 8.00 20.00
84 Talen Horton-Tucker 1.00 2.50
85 Sekou Doumbouya RC 1.00 2.50
86 Jaylen Nowell RC 1.25 3.00
87 Kevin Porter Jr. RC 2.00 5.00
88 Darius Garland 2.50 6.00
89 Russell Westbrook 1.50 4.00
90 Grant Williams RC 1.50 4.00
101 Jarrett Culver AU 3.00 8.00
102 Carsen Edwards AU 4.00 10.00
103 Cam Reddish AU 5.00 12.00
104 Admiral Schofield AU 4.00 10.00
105 Romeo Langford AU 3.00 8.00
106 Ignas Brazdeikis AU 4.00 10.00
107 Goga Bitadze AU 5.00 12.00
108 Ty Jerome AU 6.00 15.00
109 Zion Williamson AU 400.00 800.00
110 Jordan Poole AU 12.00 30.00
111 Coby White AU 20.00 50.00
112 Bruno Fernando AU 4.00 10.00
113 Cameron Johnson AU 8.00 20.00
114 Jaylen Nowell AU 8.00 20.00
115 Sekou Doumbouya AU 3.00 8.00
116 Quinndary Weatherspoon AU 3.00 8.00
117 Luka Samanic AU 4.00 10.00
118 Nassir Little AU 5.00 12.00
119 Ja Morant AU 125.00 300.00
120 Keldon Johnson AU 10.00 25.00
121 Jaxson Hayes AU 8.00 20.00
122 Cody Martin AU 5.00 12.00
123 PJ Washington Jr. AU 10.00 25.00
124 Bol Bol AU 10.00 25.00
125 Chuma Okeke AU RC 8.00 20.00
126 Tremont Waters AU 4.00 10.00
127 Brandon Clarke AU 15.00 40.00
128 Dylan Windler AU 4.00 10.00
129 RJ Barrett AU 30.00 80.00
130 Kevin Porter Jr. AU 6.00 15.00
131 Rui Hachimura AU 40.00 100.00
132 Eric Paschall AU 4.00 10.00
133 Tyler Herro AU 30.00 80.00
134 Isaiah Roby AU 4.00 10.00
135 Nickeil Alexander-Walker AU 5.00 12.00
136 Matisse Thybulle AU 12.00 30.00
137 Grant Williams AU 6.00 15.00
138 Mfiondu Kabengele AU 4.00 10.00
139 De'Andre Hunter AU 12.00 30.00
140 KZ Okpala AU 4.00 10.00
141 Goga Bitadze JSY AU 6.00 15.00
142 Ty Jerome JSY AU 8.00 20.00
143 Zion Williamson JSY AU 300.00 600.00
144 Jordan Poole JSY AU 15.00 40.00
145 Jarrett Culver JSY AU 4.00 10.00
146 Carsen Edwards JSY AU 5.00 12.00
147 Cam Reddish JSY AU 6.00 15.00
148 Admiral Schofield JSY AU 5.00 12.00
149 Romeo Langford JSY AU 4.00 10.00
150 Ignas Brazdeikis JSY AU 5.00 12.00
151 Luka Samanic JSY AU 5.00 12.00
152 Nassir Little JSY AU 6.00 15.00
153 Ja Morant JSY AU 75.00 200.00
154 Keldon Johnson JSY AU 12.00 30.00
155 Coby White JSY AU 12.00 30.00
156 Bruno Fernando JSY AU 5.00 12.00
157 Cameron Johnson JSY AU 10.00 25.00
158 Jaylen Nowell JSY AU 5.00 12.00
159 Sekou Doumbouya JSY AU 4.00 10.00
160 Quinndary Weatherspoon JSY AU 4.00 10.00
161 Brandon Clarke JSY AU 8.00 20.00
162 Dylan Windler JSY AU 5.00 12.00
163 RJ Barrett JSY AU 30.00 80.00
164 Kevin Porter Jr. JSY AU 8.00 20.00
165 Jaxson Hayes JSY AU EXCH 10.00 25.00
166 Cody Martin JSY AU 6.00 15.00
167 PJ Washington Jr. JSY AU 12.00 30.00
168 Bol Bol JSY AU 10.00 25.00
169 Chuma Okeke JSY AU 6.00 15.00
170 Tremont Waters JSY AU 5.00 12.00
171 Grant Williams JSY AU 6.00 15.00
172 Mfiondu Kabengele JSY AU 5.00 12.00
173 De'Andre Hunter JSY AU 15.00 40.00
174 KZ Okpala JSY AU 5.00 12.00
175 Rui Hachimura JSY AU 30.00 80.00
176 Eric Paschall JSY AU 5.00 12.00
177 Tyler Herro JSY AU EXCH 40.00 100.00
178 Isaiah Roby JSY AU 5.00 12.00
179 Nickeil Alexander-Walker JSY AU 6.00 15.00
180 Matisse Thybulle JSY AU 10.00 25.00

2019-20 Panini Origins Blue

*BLUE: 1X TO 2.5X BASIC
*BLUE RC: .6X TO 1.5X BASIC
*BLUE JSY AU RC: .6X TO 1.5X BASIC
1-90 STATED PRINT 99 SER. #'d SETS
JSY AU RC STATED PRINT 49 SER. #'d SETS
EXCHANGE DEADLINE 6/18/21
1 Tyler Herro 25.00 60.00
15 Zion Williamson 50.00 120.00
55 Luka Doncic 20.00 50.00
70 Ja Morant 30.00 80.00
82 Rui Hachimura 10.00 25.00
83 LeBron James 60.00 150.00
164 Kevin Porter Jr. JSY AU 12.00 30.00

2019-20 Panini Origins Orange

*ORANGE: 1X TO 2.5X BASIC
*ORANGE RC: .6X TO 1.5X BASIC
STATED PRINT 75 SER. #'d SETS
1 Tyler Herro 25.00 60.00
15 Zion Williamson 50.00 120.00
55 Luka Doncic 20.00 50.00
70 Ja Morant 30.00 80.00
82 Rui Hachimura 10.00 25.00
83 LeBron James 60.00 150.00

2019-20 Panini Origins Pink

*PINK: 1.5X TO 4X BASIC
*PINK RC: 1X TO 2.5X BASIC
STATED PRINT 35 SER. #'d SETS
1 Tyler Herro 40.00 100.00
15 Zion Williamson 75.00 200.00
55 Luka Doncic 30.00 80.00
70 Ja Morant 50.00 120.00
82 Rui Hachimura 15.00 40.00
83 LeBron James 125.00 300.00

2019-20 Panini Origins Purple

*PURPLE: 2X TO 5X BASIC
*PURPLE RC: 1.2X TO 3X BASIC
*PURPLE AU RC: .6X TO 1.5X BASIC
1-90 STATED PRINT 21 SER. #'d SETS
AU RC STATED PRINT 49 SER. #'d SETS
EXCHANGE DEADLINE 6/18/21
1 Tyler Herro 60.00 150.00
15 Zion Williamson 125.00 300.00
55 Luka Doncic 100.00 250.00
70 Ja Morant 75.00 200.00
82 Rui Hachimura 20.00 50.00
83 LeBron James 150.00 400.00
105 Romeo Langford AU 5.00 12.00
109 Zion Williamson AU 500.00 1,000.00
111 Coby White AU 40.00 100.00
119 Ja Morant AU 250.00 500.00
129 RJ Barrett AU 75.00 200.00
130 Kevin Porter Jr. AU 10.00 25.00
131 Rui Hachimura AU 75.00 200.00
133 Tyler Herro AU 60.00 150.00

2019-20 Panini Origins Red

*RED: .75X TO 2X BASIC
*RED RC: .5X TO 1.2X BASIC
*RED AU RC: .8X TO 2X BASIC
*RED JSY AU RC: .5X TO 1.2X BASIC
AU RC STATED PRINT 25 SER. #'d SETS
JSY AU RC STATED PRINT 99 SER. #'d SETS
EXCHANGE DEADLINE 6/18/21
15 Zion Williamson 20.00 50.00
70 Ja Morant 15.00 40.00
82 Rui Hachimura 8.00 20.00
108 Ty Jerome AU 10.00 25.00
109 Zion Williamson AU 600.00 1,200.00
111 Coby White AU 50.00 120.00
119 Ja Morant AU 300.00 600.00
125 Chuma Okeke AU 20.00 50.00
129 RJ Barrett AU 100.00 250.00
130 Kevin Porter Jr. AU 12.00 30.00
131 Rui Hachimura AU 100.00 250.00
133 Tyler Herro AU 75.00 200.00
134 Isaiah Roby AU 20.00 50.00
137 Grant Williams AU 15.00 40.00

2019-20 Panini Origins Turquoise

*TURQUOISE: 2X TO 5X BASIC
*TURQUOISE RC: 1.2X TO 3X BASIC
*TURQUOISE JSY AU RC: .8X TO 2X BASIC
STATED PRINT 25 SER. #'d SETS
EXCHANGE DEADLINE 6/18/21
1 Tyler Herro 60.00 150.00
15 Zion Williamson 125.00 300.00
55 Luka Doncic 100.00 250.00
70 Ja Morant 75.00 200.00
82 Rui Hachimura 20.00 50.00
83 LeBron James 150.00 400.00
143 Zion Williamson JSY AU 600.00 1,200.00
147 Cam Reddish JSY AU 12.00 30.00
153 Ja Morant JSY AU 250.00 500.00
157 Cameron Johnson JSY AU 30.00 80.00
161 Brandon Clarke JSY AU 30.00 80.00
164 Kevin Porter Jr. JSY AU 15.00 40.00
180 Matisse Thybulle JSY AU 50.00 120.00

2019-20 Panini Origins Autographs

EXCHANGE DEADLINE 6/18/2021
*RED/25: .6X TO 1.5X BASIC
1 Kobe Bryant EXCH 1,000.00 2,000.00
2 Kevin Durant 75.00 200.00
3 Shaquille O'Neal EXCH 75.00 200.00
4 Karl Malone 40.00 100.00
5 Damian Lillard 40.00 100.00
6 Karl-Anthony Towns 10.00 25.00
7 Kevin Garnett 100.00 250.00
8 Jerry West 40.00 100.00
9 Hakeem Olajuwon 40.00 100.00
10 Grant Hill 12.00 30.00
11 Pat Riley 10.00 25.00
12 Elgin Baylor 10.00 25.00
13 DeAndre Jordan 4.00 10.00
14 Nikola Vucevic 4.00 10.00
15 Malcolm Brogdon 4.00 10.00
16 Robert Horry 8.00 20.00
17 Glen Rice 4.00 10.00
18 Charles Barkley 30.00 80.00
19 Kurt Rambis 4.00 10.00
20 Derek Fisher 5.00 12.00

2019-20 Panini Origins Autographs Red

16 Robert Horry 15.00 40.00
17 Glen Rice 12.00 30.00

2019-20 Panini Origins Memorabilia

*RED/49: .5X TO 1.2X BASIC
*BLUE/35: .5X TO 1.2X BASIC
*TURQUOISE/25: .6X TO 1.5X BASIC
1 Kevin Garnett 8.00 20.00
2 Serge Ibaka 2.50 6.00
3 Andre Drummond 2.50 6.00
4 Kevin Love 3.00 8.00
5 Kobe Bryant 25.00 60.00
6 Rudy Gobert 4.00 10.00
7 Eric Gordon 2.50 6.00
8 Caris LeVert 2.50 6.00
9 Taj Gibson 2.00 5.00
10 Steven Adams 2.50 6.00
11 Allen Crabbe 2.00 5.00
12 Karl-Anthony Towns 5.00 12.00
13 LeBron James 40.00 100.00
14 John Wall 4.00 10.00
15 Larry Bird 12.00 30.00
16 Rondae Hollis-Jefferson 2.00 5.00
17 Harrison Barnes 2.50 6.00
18 Jarrett Allen 3.00 8.00
19 CJ McCollum 3.00 8.00
20 Buddy Hield 2.50 6.00
21 Wesley Matthews 2.00 5.00
22 Andrew Wiggins 4.00 10.00
23 J.J. Barea 2.50 6.00
24 Enes Kanter 2.00 5.00
25 Nikola Jokic 15.00 40.00
26 Jimmy Butler 6.00 15.00
27 Blake Griffin 3.00 8.00
28 Joe Harris 2.50 6.00
29 Kristaps Porzingis 4.00 10.00
30 De'Aaron Fox 5.00 12.00
31 DeMarre Carroll 2.00 5.00
32 Dirk Nowitzki 6.00 15.00
33 Aaron Gordon 3.00 8.00
34 Shaquille O'Neal 12.00 30.00
35 Grant Hill 5.00 12.00
36 Roy Hibbert 2.50 6.00
37 Victor Oladipo 2.50 6.00
38 Dennis Schroder 2.50 6.00
39 Nikola Vucevic 2.50 6.00
40 Kyle Lowry 3.00 8.00

2019-20 Panini Origins Memorabilia Blue

*BLUE/35: .5X TO 1.2X BASIC
STATED PRINT RUN 35 SER. #'d SETS
13 LeBron James 60.00 150.00
35 Grant Hill 8.00 20.00

2019-20 Panini Origins Memorabilia Red

*RED/49: .5X TO 1.2X BASIC
STATED PRINT RUN 49 SER. #'d SETS
13 LeBron James 50.00 120.00
35 Grant Hill 8.00 20.00

2019-20 Panini Origins Memorabilia Turquoise

*TURQUOISE/25: .6X TO 1.5X BASIC
STATED PRINT RUN 25 SER. #'d SETS
13 LeBron James 100.00 250.00

2019-20 Panini Origins Origins Autographs Silver Ink

STATED PRINT RUN 49 SER. #'d SET
EXCHANGE DEADLINE 6/18/2021

1 Zion Williamson 500.00 1,000.00
2 Jordan Poole 8.00 20.00
3 Jarrett Culver 5.00 12.00
5 Cam Reddish 8.00 20.00
6 Admiral Schofield 15.00 40.00
7 Romeo Langford 5.00 12.00
8 Ignas Brazdeikis 6.00 15.00
9 Goga Bitadze 8.00 20.00
10 Ty Jerome 10.00 25.00
11 Ja Morant 300.00 600.00
12 Keldon Johnson 15.00 40.00
13 Coby White 40.00 100.00
14 Bruno Fernando 8.00 20.00
15 Cameron Johnson 12.00 30.00
16 Jaylen Nowell 6.00 15.00
17 Sekou Doumbouya 5.00 12.00
18 Quinndary Weatherspoon 5.00 12.00
19 Luka Samanic 6.00 15.00
20 Nassir Little 8.00 20.00
21 RJ Barrett 60.00 150.00
22 Kevin Porter Jr. 10.00 25.00
23 Jaxson Hayes 8.00 20.00
24 Cody Martin 8.00 20.00
26 Bol Bol 12.00 30.00
27 Chuma Okeke 8.00 20.00
28 Tremont Waters 12.00 30.00
29 Brandon Clarke 25.00 60.00
30 Dylan Windler 6.00 15.00
31 De'Andre Hunter 20.00 50.00
32 KZ Okpala 6.00 15.00
33 Rui Hachimura 125.00 300.00
35 Tyler Herro 75.00 200.00
36 Isaiah Roby 6.00 15.00
37 Nickeil Alexander-Walker 12.00 30.00
38 Matisse Thybulle 30.00 80.00
39 Grant Williams 12.00 30.00
40 Mfiondu Kabengele 6.00 15.00

2019-20 Panini Origins Rookie Jumbo Jerseys

*RED/49: .5X TO 1.2X BASIC
*BLUE/35: .5X TO 1.2X BASIC
*TURQUOISE/25: .6X TO 1.5X BASIC
1 Cam Reddish 3.00 8.00
2 Romeo Langford 2.00 5.00
3 Zion Williamson 15.00 40.00
4 Jarrett Culver 2.00 5.00
5 Cameron Johnson 5.00 12.00
6 Sekou Doumbouya 2.00 5.00
7 Ja Morant 40.00 100.00
8 Coby White 6.00 15.00
9 PJ Washington Jr. 6.00 15.00
10 Bol Bol 5.00 12.00
11 Chuma Okeke 3.00 8.00
12 RJ Barrett 8.00 20.00
13 Kevin Porter Jr. 4.00 10.00
14 Jaxson Hayes 3.00 8.00
15 Tyler Herro 10.00 25.00
16 Nickeil Alexander-Walker 3.00 8.00
17 Matisse Thybulle 4.00 10.00
18 De'Andre Hunter 8.00 20.00
19 KZ Okpala 2.50 6.00
20 Rui Hachimura 8.00 20.00

2019-20 Panini Origins Rookie Jumbo Jerseys Blue

*BLUE/35: .5X TO 1.2X BASIC
STATED PRINT RUN 35 SER. #'d SETS
7 Ja Morant 100.00 250.00

2019-20 Panini Origins Rookie Jumbo Jerseys Red

*RED/49: .5X TO 1.2X BASIC
STATED PRINT RUN 49 SER. #'d SETS
7 Ja Morant 75.00 200.00

2019-20 Panini Origins Rookie Jumbo Jerseys Turquoise

*TURQUOISE/25: .6X TO 1.5X BASIC
STATED PRINT RUN 25 SER. #'d SETS
7 Ja Morant 125.00 300.00

2020-21 Panini Origins

1 Rudy Gobert 1.25 3.00
2 Lonzo Ball 1.25 3.00
3 Chris Paul 2.00 5.00
4 Blake Griffin 1.00 2.50
5 Collin Sexton 1.00 2.50
6 Kawhi Leonard 2.50 6.00
7 Draymond Green 1.25 3.00
8 Rui Hachimura 1.25 3.00
9 Jamal Murray 1.50 4.00
10 PJ Washington Jr. 1.00 2.50
11 Michael Porter Jr. 1.25 3.00
12 CJ McCollum 1.00 2.50
13 De'Andre Hunter 1.00 2.50
14 Pascal Siakam 1.50 4.00
15 Damian Lillard 2.50 6.00
16 Joel Embiid 2.50 6.00
17 Jimmy Butler 2.00 5.00
18 Zach LaVine 1.50 4.00
19 Donovan Mitchell 2.00 5.00
20 Khris Middleton 1.25 3.00
21 Devin Booker 2.50 6.00
22 T.J. Warren .75 2.00
23 Kevin Durant 4.00 10.00
24 Bradley Beal 1.25 3.00
25 Ben Simmons 1.00 2.50
26 Jaylen Brown 1.50 4.00
27 Victor Oladipo .75 2.00
28 Derrick Rose 1.50 4.00
29 Kyle Kuzma 1.25 3.00
30 Paul George 1.50 4.00
31 Kristaps Porzingis 1.25 3.00
32 James Harden 2.00 5.00
33 Shai Gilgeous-Alexander 5.00 12.00
34 Deandre Ayton 1.00 2.50
35 Karl-Anthony Towns 1.50 4.00
36 Ja Morant 3.00 8.00
37 DeMar DeRozan 1.25 3.00
38 Markelle Fultz .75 2.00
39 Lauri Markkanen 1.25 3.00
40 D'Angelo Russell 1.00 2.50
41 Brandon Ingram 1.25 3.00
42 Jaren Jackson Jr. 1.50 4.00
43 Nikola Vucevic 1.00 2.50
44 Stephen Curry 8.00 20.00
45 Anthony Davis 2.50 6.00
46 Devonte' Graham .75 2.00
47 Kyrie Irving 2.00 5.00
48 Kemba Walker 1.00 2.50
49 Kyle Lowry 1.25 3.00
50 De'Aaron Fox 1.50 4.00
51 Bam Adebayo 1.50 4.00
52 Klay Thompson 2.50 6.00
53 Fred VanVleet 1.50 4.00
54 Jayson Tatum 4.00 10.00
55 Trae Young 2.50 6.00
56 Giannis Antetokounmpo 5.00 12.00
57 RJ Barrett 1.50 4.00
58 Domantas Sabonis 1.25 3.00
59 Luka Doncic 6.00 15.00
60 Coby White 1.25 3.00
61 Russell Westbrook 2.00 5.00
62 Julius Randle 1.00 2.50
63 LaMarcus Aldridge 1.00 2.50
64 Bogdan Bogdanovic 1.00 2.50
65 Tyler Herro 2.00 5.00
66 LeBron James 8.00 20.00
67 Kevin Love 1.00 2.50
68 Carmelo Anthony 1.50 4.00
69 Zion Williamson 3.00 8.00
70 Nikola Jokic 5.00 12.00
71 Anthony Edwards RC 30.00 80.00
72 James Wiseman RC 1.50 4.00
73 LaMelo Ball RC 10.00 25.00
74 Patrick Williams RC 3.00 8.00
75 Isaac Okoro RC 2.00 5.00
76 Onyeka Okongwu RC 2.50 6.00
77 Killian Hayes RC 1.25 3.00
78 Obi Toppin RC 2.50 6.00
79 Deni Avdija RC 3.00 8.00
80 Jalen Smith RC 2.50 6.00
81 Devin Vassell RC 4.00 10.00
82 Tyrese Haliburton RC 12.00 30.00
83 Kira Lewis Jr. RC 1.25 3.00
84 Aaron Nesmith RC 2.50 6.00
85 Cole Anthony RC 3.00 8.00
86 Isaiah Stewart RC 2.50 6.00
87 Aleksej Pokusevski RC 1.50 4.00
88 Josh Green RC 2.50 6.00
89 Saddiq Bey RC 2.50 6.00
90 Precious Achiuwa RC 2.50 6.00

2020-21 Panini Origins Blue

STATED PRINT RUN 99 SER. #'d SETS
32 James Harden 8.00 20.00
44 Stephen Curry 15.00 40.00
59 Luka Doncic 60.00 150.00
66 LeBron James 60.00 150.00
71 Anthony Edwards 125.00 300.00
73 LaMelo Ball 150.00 400.00
81 Devin Vassell 12.00 30.00
85 Cole Anthony 20.00 50.00

2020-21 Panini Origins Orange

STATED PRINT RUN 75 SER. #'d SETS
32 James Harden 8.00 20.00
44 Stephen Curry 15.00 40.00
59 Luka Doncic 60.00 150.00
66 LeBron James 60.00 150.00
71 Anthony Edwards 125.00 300.00
73 LaMelo Ball 150.00 400.00
81 Devin Vassell 12.00 30.00
85 Cole Anthony 15.00 40.00

2020-21 Panini Origins Pink

STATED PRINT RUN 60 SER. #'d SETS
59 Luka Doncic 75.00 200.00
66 LeBron James 75.00 200.00
71 Anthony Edwards 150.00 400.00
73 LaMelo Ball 200.00 500.00
85 Cole Anthony 20.00 50.00

2020-21 Panini Origins Purple

STATED PRINT RUN 21 SER. #'d SETS
32 James Harden 15.00 40.00
44 Stephen Curry 30.00 80.00
59 Luka Doncic 125.00 300.00
66 LeBron James 125.00 300.00
71 Anthony Edwards 300.00 600.00
73 LaMelo Ball 400.00 800.00
81 Devin Vassell 25.00 60.00
85 Cole Anthony 30.00 80.00

2020-21 Panini Origins Red

66 LeBron James 25.00 60.00

2020-21 Panini Origins Turquoise

STATED PRINT 25 SER. #'d SETS
32 James Harden 15.00 40.00
44 Stephen Curry 30.00 80.00
59 Luka Doncic 125.00 300.00
66 LeBron James 125.00 300.00
71 Anthony Edwards 300.00 600.00
73 LaMelo Ball 400.00 800.00
81 Devin Vassell 25.00 60.00
85 Cole Anthony 30.00 80.00

2020-21 Panini Origins Legendary Autographs

STATED PRINT RUN 49 SER. #'d SETS
EXCHANGE DEADLINE 10/14/2022
*RED/25: .6X TO 1.5X BASIC
1 Karl Malone 50.00 120.00
2 Ray Allen 50.00 120.00
3 Larry Bird 100.00 250.00
4 Paul Pierce 40.00 100.00
5 John Stockton 40.00 100.00
6 Kevin Garnett 100.00 250.00
7 Charles Barkley 100.00 250.00
8 Oscar Robertson 75.00 200.00
9 Bill Russell 500.00 1,000.00
10 Hakeem Olajuwon 75.00 200.00
11 Dwyane Wade 75.00 200.00
12 Jason Kidd 25.00 60.00
13 Magic Johnson 100.00 250.00
14 Grant Hill 30.00 80.00
15 Julius Erving 100.00 250.00
16 Kareem Abdul-Jabbar 100.00 250.00
17 Shaquille O'Neal 125.00 300.00
18 Jerry West 40.00 100.00
19 Allen Iverson 125.00 300.00
20 David Robinson 40.00 100.00

2020-21 Panini Origins Memorabilia

STATED PRINT RUN 99 SER. #'d SETS
1 Rudy Gobert 5.00 2.00
2 Julius Randle 4.00 0.00
3 Marcus Smart 4.00 0.00
4 Jamal Murray 6.00 15.00
5 Bam Adebayo 6.00 15.00
6 Devin Booker 10.00 25.00
7 Khris Middleton 5.00 12.00
8 Shai Gilgeous-Alexander 20.00 50.00
9 CJ McCollum 4.00 10.00
10 Kyle Lowry 5.00 12.00
12 Blake Griffin 4.00 10.00
13 Aaron Gordon 4.00 10.00
14 John Wall 5.00 12.00
15 DeMar DeRozan 5.00 12.00
16 Kawhi Leonard 10.00 25.00
17 Trae Young 10.00 25.00
18 Seth Curry 4.00 10.00
19 Caris LeVert 4.00 10.00
20 LeBron James 40.00 00.00

2020-21 Panini Origins Memorabilia Blue

*BLUE: .5X TO 1.2X BASIC
STATED PRINT RUN 35 SER. #'d SETS
20 LeBron James 75.00 200.00

2020-21 Panini Origins Memorabilia Red

*RED: .5X TO 1.2X BASIC
STATED PRINT RUN 49 SER. #'d SETS
20 LeBron James 60.00 150.00

2020-21 Panini Origins Memorabilia Turquoise

*TURQUOISE: .5X TO 1.5X BASIC
STATED PRINT RUN 25 SER. #'d SETS
20 LeBron James 100.00 250.00

2020-21 Panini Origins Origins Autographs Silver Ink

STATED PRINT RUN 99 SER. #'d SETS
EXCHANGE DEADLINE 10/14/2022
1 Nico Mannion 30.00 80.00
2 Jordan Nwora 40.00 100.00
3 Tre Jones 12.00 30.00
4 Robert Woodard II 8.00 20.00
5 Tyler Bey 8.00 20.00
6 Xavier Tillman 20.00 50.00
7 Theo Maledon 60.00 150.00
8 Daniel Oturu 8.00 20.00
9 Vernon Carey Jr. 25.00 60.00
10 Tyrell Terry 6.00 15.00
11 Desmond Bane 50.00 120.00
12 Malachi Flynn 8.00 20.00
13 Jaden McDaniels 50.00 120.00
14 Udoka Azubuike 10.00 25.00
15 Payton Pritchard 60.00 150.00
16 Immanuel Quickley 100.00 250.00
17 RJ Hampton 8.00 20.00
18 Elijah Hughes 8.00 20.00
19 Zeke Nnaji 10.00 25.00
20 Tyrese Maxey 100.00 250.00
21 Precious Achiuwa 60.00 150.00
22 Saddiq Bey 60.00 150.00
23 Josh Green 30.00 80.00
24 Aleksej Pokusevski 10.00 25.00
25 Isaiah Stewart 150.00 400.00
26 Cole Anthony 75.00 200.00
27 Aaron Nesmith 60.00 150.00
28 Kira Lewis Jr. 40.00 100.00
29 Tyrese Haliburton 150.00 400.00
30 Devin Vassell 60.00 150.00
31 Jalen Smith 15.00 40.00
32 Deni Avdija 75.00 200.00
33 Obi Toppin 75.00 200.00
34 Killian Hayes 75.00 200.00
35 Onyeka Okongwu 40.00 100.00
36 Isaac Okoro 75.00 200.00
37 Patrick Williams 150.00 400.00
38 LaMelo Ball 600.00 1,200.00
39 James Wiseman 10.00 25.00
40 Anthony Edwards 400.00 800.00

2020-21 Panini Origins Rookie Autographs

EXCHANGE DEADLINE 10/14/2022
*RED/99: .5X TO 1.25X BASIC
*BLUE/49: .6X TO 1.5X BASIC
*PURPLE/49: .6X TO 1.5X BASIC
1 Anthony Edwards 300.00 600.00
2 James Wiseman 5.00 12.00
3 LaMelo Ball 60.00 150.00
4 Patrick Williams 10.00 25.00
5 Isaac Okoro 6.00 15.00
6 Onyeka Okongwu 8.00 20.00
7 Killian Hayes 4.00 10.00
8 Obi Toppin 8.00 20.00
9 Deni Avdija 10.00 25.00
10 Jalen Smith 8.00 20.00
11 Devin Vassell 12.00 30.00
12 Tyrese Haliburton 100.00 250.00
13 Kira Lewis Jr. 4.00 10.00
14 Aaron Nesmith 8.00 20.00
15 Cole Anthony 10.00 25.00
16 Isaiah Stewart 8.00 20.00
17 Aleksej Pokusevski 5.00 12.00
18 Josh Green 8.00 20.00
19 Saddiq Bey 8.00 20.00
20 Precious Achiuwa 8.00 20.00
21 Tyrese Maxey 60.00 150.00
22 Zeke Nnaji 5.00 12.00
23 Elijah Hughes 4.00 10.00
24 RJ Hampton 4.00 10.00
25 Immanuel Quickley 10.00 25.00
26 Payton Pritchard 12.00 30.00
27 Udoka Azubuike 5.00 12.00
28 Jaden McDaniels 12.00 30.00
29 Malachi Flynn 4.00 10.00
30 Desmond Bane 12.00 30.00
31 Tyrell Terry 3.00 8.00
32 Vernon Carey Jr. 4.00 10.00
33 Daniel Oturu 4.00 10.00
34 Theo Maledon 4.00 10.00
35 Xavier Tillman 5.00 12.00
36 Tyler Bey 4.00 10.00
37 Robert Woodard II 4.00 10.00
38 Tre Jones 6.00 15.00
39 Jordan Nwora 5.00 12.00
40 Nico Mannion 4.00 10.00

2020-21 Panini Origins Rookie Jersey Autographs

STATED PRINT RUN 99 SER. #'d SETS
EXCHANGE DEADLINE 10/14/2022
*RED/75: .5X TO 1.25X BASIC
*BLUE/49: .6X TO 1.5X BASIC
*TURQUOISE/25: .75X TO 2X BASIC
1 Anthony Edwards 300.00 600.00
2 Jordan Nwora 6.00 15.00
3 Patrick Williams 12.00 30.00
4 Tre Jones 8.00 20.00
5 Robert Woodard II 5.00 12.00
6 Killian Hayes 5.00 12.00
7 Jalen Smith 10.00 25.00
8 Xavier Tillman 6.00 15.00
9 Theo Maledon 5.00 12.00
10 Kira Lewis Jr. 5.00 12.00
11 Isaiah Stewart 10.00 25.00
12 Saddiq Bey 10.00 25.00
13 Vernon Carey Jr. 5.00 12.00
14 Tyrese Maxey 60.00 150.00
15 Tyrell Terry 4.00 10.00
16 RJ Hampton 5.00 12.00
17 Malachi Flynn 5.00 12.00
18 Udoka Azubuike 6.00 15.00
19 Payton Pritchard 15.00 40.00
20 Immanuel Quickley 12.00 30.00
21 CJ Elleby 5.00 12.00
22 Zeke Nnaji 6.00 15.00
23 Precious Achiuwa 10.00 25.00
24 Jaden McDaniels 25.00 60.00
25 Josh Green 10.00 25.00
26 Aleksej Pokusevski 6.00 15.00
27 Desmond Bane 15.00 40.00
28 Cole Anthony 12.00 30.00
29 Aaron Nesmith 10.00 25.00
30 Daniel Oturu 5.00 12.00
31 Tyrese Haliburton 100.00 250.00
32 Devin Vassell 15.00 40.00
33 Tyler Bey 5.00 12.00
34 Deni Avdija 12.00 30.00
35 Obi Toppin 10.00 25.00
36 Nico Mannion 5.00 12.00
37 Onyeka Okongwu 10.00 25.00
38 Isaac Okoro 8.00 20.00
39 LaMelo Ball 75.00 200.00
40 James Wiseman 6.00 15.00

2020-21 Panini Origins Rookie Jumbo Jerseys

STATED PRINT RUN 99 SER. #'d SETS
*RED/49: .5X TO 1.2X BASIC
*BLUE/49: .5X TO 1.2X BASIC
*TURQUOISE/25: .6X TO 1.5X BASIC
1 Robert Woodard II 2.50 6.00
2 Deni Avdija 6.00 15.00
3 Obi Toppin 5.00 12.00
4 Jalen Smith 5.00 12.00
5 Malachi Flynn 2.50 6.00
6 Theo Maledon 2.50 6.00
7 CJ Elleby 2.50 6.00
8 Isaiah Stewart 5.00 12.00
9 Anthony Edwards 60.00 150.00
10 Isaac Okoro 4.00 10.00
11 Daniel Oturu 2.50 6.00
12 Patrick Williams 6.00 15.00
13 Vernon Carey Jr. 2.50 6.00
14 Desmond Bane 8.00 20.00
15 Tyrell Terry 2.00 5.00
16 Jaden McDaniels 5.00 12.00
17 RJ Hampton 2.50 6.00
18 Udoka Azubuike 3.00 8.00
19 Tre Jones 4.00 10.00
20 Payton Pritchard 5.00 12.00
21 Immanuel Quickley 6.00 15.00
22 Zeke Nnaji 3.00 8.00
23 Precious Achiuwa 5.00 12.00
24 Killian Hayes 2.50 6.00
25 Saddiq Bey 5.00 12.00
26 Jordan Nwora 3.00 8.00
27 Josh Green 5.00 12.00
28 Aleksej Pokusevski 3.00 8.00
29 Xavier Tillman 3.00 8.00
30 Cole Anthony 6.00 15.00
31 Aaron Nesmith 5.00 12.00
32 Tyrese Haliburton 20.00 50.00
33 Devin Vassell 8.00 20.00
35 Tyrese Maxey 20.00 50.00
36 Nico Mannion 2.50 6.00
37 Onyeka Okongwu 5.00 12.00
38 LaMelo Ball 125.00 300.00
39 Kira Lewis Jr. 2.50 6.00
40 James Wiseman 3.00 8.00

2021-22 Panini Origins

COMMON CARD (1-90) .60 1.50
SEMISTARS .75 2.00
UNLISTED STARS 1.00 2.50
COMMON RC (1-90) .60 1.50
RC SEMIS .75 2.00
RC UNLISTED 1.00 2.50
*RED: .6X TO 1.5X BASIC
*VAR: .75X TO 2X BASIC
*BLUE/99: 1.5X TO 4X BASIC
*ORANGE/75: 1.5X TO 4X BASIC
*PINK/60: 2X TO 5X BASIC
*TURQUOISE/25: 4X TO 10X BASIC
1 Zion Williamson 2.50 6.00
2 LaMelo Ball 12.00 30.00
3 Bradley Beal 1.25 3.00
4 Russell Westbrook 1.50 4.00
5 Kawhi Leonard 2.50 6.00
6 LeBron James 12.00 30.00
7 Kevin Durant 3.00 8.00
8 Damian Lillard 2.50 6.00
9 Zach LaVine 1.50 4.00
10 Luka Doncic 12.00 30.00
11 Kyrie Irving 2.00 5.00
12 Paul George 1.50 4.00
13 James Harden 2.00 5.00
14 Karl-Anthony Towns 1.50 4.00
15 Nikola Jokic 5.00 12.00
16 Anthony Edwards 5.00 12.00
17 Devin Booker 2.50 6.00
18 De'Aaron Fox 1.50 4.00
19 Trae Young 2.50 6.00
20 Jayson Tatum 4.00 10.00
21 Joel Embiid 2.50 6.00
22 Khris Middleton 1.00 2.50
23 Anthony Davis 2.50 6.00
24 Chris Paul 2.00 5.00
25 Jaylen Brown 1.50 4.00
26 Rudy Gobert 1.25 3.00
27 Jamal Murray 1.50 4.00
28 Collin Sexton 1.00 2.50
29 John Wall 1.25 3.00
30 Stephen Curry 10.00 25.00
31 Tyrese Haliburton 2.00 5.00
32 Nikola Vucevic 1.00 2.50
33 Julius Randle 1.25 3.00
34 Giannis Antetokounmpo 5.00 12.00
35 Domantas Sabonis 1.25 3.00
36 Shai Gilgeous-Alexander 5.00 12.00
37 DeMar DeRozan 1.25 3.00
38 Pascal Siakam 1.50 4.00
39 Kristaps Porzingis 1.25 3.00
40 Ben Simmons 1.00 2.50
41 Jerami Grant 1.00 2.50
42 Brandon Ingram 1.25 3.00
43 Jimmy Butler 1.50 4.00
44 Cole Anthony 1.00 2.50
45 Donovan Mitchell 2.00 5.00
46 Bam Adebayo 1.50 4.00
47 Ja Morant 3.00 8.00
48 Dejounte Murray 1.00 2.50
49 Klay Thompson 2.50 6.00
50 Kemba Walker 1.00 2.50
51 Cade Cunningham RC 6.00 15.00
52 Jalen Green RC 5.00 12.00
53 Evan Mobley RC 4.00 10.00
54 Scottie Barnes RC 3.00 8.00
55 Jalen Suggs RC 2.50 6.00
56 Josh Giddey RC 3.00 8.00
57 Jonathan Kuminga RC 3.00 8.00
58 Franz Wagner RC 3.00 8.00
59 Davion Mitchell RC 1.00 2.50
60 Ziaire Williams RC 1.25 3.00
61 James Bouknight RC .75 2.00
62 Joshua Primo RC .75 2.00
63 Chris Duarte RC .75 2.00
64 Moses Moody RC 2.00 5.00
65 Corey Kispert RC 1.25 3.00
66 Alperen Sengun RC 3.00 8.00
67 Trey Murphy III RC 3.00 8.00
68 Tre Mann RC 1.50 4.00
69 Kai Jones RC .75 2.00
70 Jalen Johnson RC 3.00 8.00
71 Keon Johnson RC 1.00 2.50
72 Isaiah Jackson RC 1.00 2.50
73 Usman Garuba RC .75 2.00
74 Josh Christopher RC .75 2.00
75 Quentin Grimes RC 2.00 5.00
76 Bones Hyland RC 1.25 3.00
77 Cameron Thomas RC 2.00 5.00
78 Jaden Springer RC 1.00 2.50
79 Day'Ron Sharpe RC 1.00 2.50
80 Santi Aldama RC 1.25 3.00
81 Jeremiah Robinson-Earl RC 1.00 2.50
82 Miles McBride RC 1.50 4.00
83 Ayo Dosunmu RC 2.00 5.00
84 Jared Butler RC 1.00 2.50
85 Isaiah Livers RC 1.00 2.50
86 Greg Brown III RC .75 2.00
87 Brandon Boston Jr. RC 1.00 2.50
88 Luka Garza RC 1.00 2.50
89 Charles Bassey RC 1.00 2.50
90 Scottie Lewis RC .75 2.00

2021-22 Panini Origins Award-Winning Autographs

COMMON CARD 4.00 10.00
SEMISTARS 5.00 12.00
UNLISTED STARS 6.00 15.00
EXCHANGE DEADLINE 9/9/2023
1 Dennis Rodman 75.00 200.00
3 Bill Walton 30.00 80.00
6 Dominique Wilkins 40.00 100.00
9 Karl Malone 60.00 150.00
41 Spud Webb 15.00 40.00
43 Isiah Thomas 60.00 150.00
44 Kevin Durant 400.00 800.00
45 Vince Carter 400.00 800.00

2021-22 Panini Origins Big Bang

COMMON CARD 6.00 15.00
SEMISTARS 8.00 20.00
UNLISTED STARS 10.00 25.00
1 Luka Doncic 200.00 500.00
2 LeBron James 200.00 500.00
3 Giannis Antetokounmpo 125.00 300.00
4 Stephen Curry 150.00 400.00
5 Trae Young 75.00 200.00
6 Damian Lillard 60.00 150.00
7 Anthony Davis 60.00 150.00
8 Bradley Beal 30.00 80.00
9 Ja Morant 200.00 500.00
10 LaMelo Ball 200.00 500.00
11 Jayson Tatum 125.00 300.00
12 Kawhi Leonard 40.00 100.00
13 Zion Williamson 125.00 300.00
14 Kevin Durant 125.00 300.00
15 James Harden 40.00 100.00
16 Nikola Jokic 60.00 150.00
17 Joel Embiid 60.00 150.00
18 Donovan Mitchell 50.00 120.00
19 Devin Booker 75.00 200.00
20 Zach LaVine 60.00 150.00
21 Jalen Green 150.00 400.00
22 Evan Mobley 150.00 400.00
23 Cade Cunningham 200.00 500.00
24 Jalen Suggs 75.00 200.00
25 Scottie Barnes 150.00 400.00

2021-22 Panini Origins Legendary Autographs

COMMON CARD 6.00 15.00
SEMISTARS 8.00 20.00
UNLISTED STARS 10.00 25.00
EXCHANGE DEADLINE 9/9/2023
*RED/25: .6X TO 1.5X BASIC
1 Charles Barkley 100.00 250.00
2 Jason Williams 60.00 150.00
3 Larry Bird 100.00 250.00
4 Ben Wallace 60.00 150.00
5 Nikola Jokic 125.00 300.00
6 Luka Doncic 600.00 1,200.00
7 Robert Parish 20.00 50.00
8 Bill Russell 500.00 1,000.00
9 Ray Allen 60.00 150.00
10 Jason Kidd 60.00 150.00
11 Bill Walton 30.00 80.00
12 Ja Morant 400.00 800.00
14 Anfernee Hardaway 125.00 300.00
16 Trae Young 200.00 500.00
17 Steve Kerr 20.00 50.00
18 Oscar Robertson 60.00 150.00
19 Tony Parker 60.00 150.00
20 Shaquille O'Neal 125.00 300.00

2021-22 Panini Origins Origins Autographs Silver Ink

COMMON CARD 6.00 15.00
SEMISTARS 8.00 20.00
UNLISTED STARS 10.00 25.00
EXCHANGE DEADLINE 9/9/2023
1 Cade Cunningham/49 800.00 1,500.00
2 Jalen Green/49 500.00 1,000.00
3 Evan Mobley/49 500.00 1,000.00
4 Scottie Barnes/99 500.00 1,000.00
5 Jalen Suggs/49 125.00 300.00
6 Josh Giddey/99 300.00 600.00
7 Jonathan Kuminga/99 300.00 600.00
8 Franz Wagner/99 150.00 400.00
9 Davion Mitchell/99 75.00 200.00
10 Ziaire Williams/99 40.00 100.00
11 James Bouknight/99 8.00 20.00
12 Joshua Primo/99 8.00 20.00
13 Chris Duarte/99 60.00 150.00
14 Moses Moody/99 60.00 150.00
15 Corey Kispert/99 25.00 60.00
16 Alperen Sengun/99 125.00 300.00
17 Trey Murphy III/99 30.00 80.00
18 Tre Mann/99 75.00 200.00
19 Kai Jones/99 8.00 20.00
20 Jalen Johnson/99 30.00 80.00
21 Keon Johnson/99 10.00 25.00
22 Isaiah Jackson/99 10.00 25.00
23 Usman Garuba/99 8.00 20.00
24 Josh Christopher/99 40.00 100.00
25 Quentin Grimes/99 20.00 50.00
27 Cameron Thomas/99 20.00 50.00
28 Jaden Springer/99 10.00 25.00
29 Day'Ron Sharpe/99 10.00 25.00
30 Santi Aldama/99 12.00 30.00
31 Jeremiah Robinson-Earl/99 10.00 25.00
32 Miles McBride/99 15.00 40.00
33 Ayo Dosunmu/99 100.00 250.00
34 Jared Butler/99 10.00 25.00
35 Isaiah Livers/99 10.00 25.00
36 Greg Brown III/99 8.00 20.00
37 Luka Garza/99 10.00 25.00
38 Charles Bassey/99 10.00 25.00
39 Scottie Lewis/99 8.00 20.00
40 Brandon Boston Jr./99 30.00 80.00

2021-22 Panini Origins Origins Memorabilia

COMMON CARD 3.00 8.00
SEMISTARS 4.00 10.00
UNLISTED STARS 5.00 12.00
*RED/49: .5X TO 1.2X BASIC
*BLUE/35: .6X TO 1.5X BASIC
*TURQUOISE/25: .75X TO 2X BASIC
1 Jimmy Butler 6.00 15.00
2 Jaylen Brown 6.00 15.00
3 LeBron James 75.00 200.00
4 Donovan Mitchell 8.00 20.00
5 Bradley Beal 5.00 12.00
6 Zion Williamson 10.00 25.00
7 Zach LaVine 6.00 15.00
8 Karl-Anthony Towns 6.00 15.00
9 De'Aaron Fox 6.00 15.00
10 Collin Sexton 4.00 10.00
11 Pascal Siakam 6.00 15.00
12 Jrue Holiday 5.00 12.00
13 Trae Young 10.00 25.00
14 Chris Paul 8.00 20.00
15 Ben Simmons 4.00 10.00
16 Malcolm Brogdon 3.00 8.00
17 Kawhi Leonard 10.00 25.00
18 Damian Lillard 10.00 25.00
19 Kristaps Porzingis 5.00 12.00
20 Shai Gilgeous-Alexander 20.00 50.00

2021-22 Panini Origins Origins Stories

COMMON CARD 6.00 15.00
SEMISTARS 8.00 20.00
UNLISTED STARS 10.00 25.00
1 LeBron James 150.00 400.00
2 Carmelo Anthony 40.00 100.00
3 Anthony Davis 60.00 150.00
4 Stephen Curry 125.00 300.00
5 Kyrie Irving 60.00 150.00
6 Jimmy Butler 40.00 100.00
7 Kevin Durant 125.00 300.00
8 James Harden 40.00 100.00
9 Russell Westbrook 40.00 100.00
10 Kawhi Leonard 60.00 150.00
11 Chris Paul 30.00 80.00
12 John Wall 30.00 80.00
13 Julius Randle 25.00 60.00
14 Kemba Walker 25.00 60.00
15 Kristaps Porzingis 30.00 80.00
16 DeMar DeRozan 40.00 100.00
17 Zach LaVine 60.00 150.00
18 Blake Griffin 25.00 60.00
19 Giannis Antetokounmpo 100.00 250.00
20 Paul George 40.00 100.00
21 Dwight Howard 40.00 100.00
22 Rajon Rondo 25.00 60.00
23 Derrick Rose 40.00 100.00
24 Lonzo Ball 40.00 100.00
25 LaMarcus Aldridge 30.00 80.00
26 Shaquille O'Neal 75.00 200.00
27 Jason Kidd 40.00 100.00
28 Kevin Garnett 75.00 200.00
29 Tracy McGrady 50.00 120.00
30 Charles Barkley 75.00 200.00

2021-22 Panini Origins Rookie Autographs

COMMON CARD 4.00 10.00
SEMISTARS 5.00 12.00
UNLISTED STARS 6.00 15.00
EXCHANGE DEADLINE 9/9/2023
*RED/99: .5X TO 1.2X BASIC
*PURPLE FOTL/49: .6X TO 1.5X BASIC
*BLUE/35: .6X TO 1.5X BASIC
*PINK/25: .75X TO 2X BASIC
1 Cade Cunningham 400.00 800.00
2 Jalen Green 300.00 600.00
3 Evan Mobley 200.00 500.00
4 Scottie Barnes 200.00 500.00
5 Jalen Suggs 75.00 200.00
6 Josh Giddey 150.00 400.00
7 Jonathan Kuminga 150.00 400.00
8 Franz Wagner 100.00 250.00
9 Davion Mitchell 50.00 120.00
10 Ziaire Williams 8.00 20.00
11 James Bouknight 5.00 12.00
12 Joshua Primo 5.00 12.00
13 Chris Duarte 40.00 100.00
14 Moses Moody 40.00 100.00
15 Corey Kispert 15.00 40.00
16 Alperen Sengun 75.00 200.00
17 Trey Murphy III 20.00 50.00
18 Tre Mann 30.00 80.00
19 Kai Jones 5.00 12.00
20 Jalen Johnson 20.00 50.00
21 Keon Johnson 6.00 15.00
22 Isaiah Jackson 6.00 15.00
23 Usman Garuba 6.00 15.00
24 Josh Christopher 20.00 50.00
25 Quentin Grimes 12.00 30.00
27 Cameron Thomas 12.00 30.00
28 Jaden Springer 6.00 15.00
29 Day'Ron Sharpe 6.00 15.00
30 Santi Aldama 8.00 20.00
31 Jeremiah Robinson-Earl 6.00 15.00
32 Miles McBride 10.00 25.00
33 Ayo Dosunmu 60.00 150.00
34 Jared Butler 6.00 15.00
35 Isaiah Livers 6.00 15.00
36 Greg Brown III 5.00 12.00
37 Luka Garza 6.00 15.00
38 Charles Bassey 6.00 15.00
39 Scottie Lewis 5.00 12.00
40 Brandon Boston Jr. 20.00 50.00

2021-22 Panini Origins Rookie Jersey Autographs

COMMON CARD 4.00 10.00
SEMISTARS 5.00 12.00
UNLISTED STARS 6.00 15.00
EXCHANGE DEADLINE 9/9/2023
*RED/75: .5X TO 1.25X BASIC
*BLUE/49: .6X TO 1.5X BASIC
*TURQUOISE/25: .75X TO 2X BASIC
1 Cade Cunningham 400.00 800.00
2 Jalen Green 300.00 600.00
3 Evan Mobley 300.00 600.00
4 Scottie Barnes 300.00 600.00
5 Jalen Suggs 75.00 200.00
6 Josh Giddey 150.00 400.00
7 Jonathan Kuminga 150.00 400.00
8 Franz Wagner 100.00 250.00
9 Davion Mitchell 50.00 120.00
10 Ziaire Williams 8.00 20.00
11 James Bouknight 5.00 12.00
12 Joshua Primo 5.00 12.00
13 Chris Duarte 40.00 100.00
14 Moses Moody 40.00 100.00
15 Corey Kispert 15.00 40.00
16 Alperen Sengun 75.00 200.00
17 Trey Murphy III 20.00 50.00
18 Tre Mann 40.00 100.00
19 Kai Jones 5.00 12.00
20 Jalen Johnson 20.00 50.00
21 Keon Johnson 6.00 15.00
22 Isaiah Jackson 6.00 15.00
23 Usman Garuba 5.00 12.00
24 Josh Christopher 20.00 50.00
25 Quentin Grimes 12.00 30.00
26 Bones Hyland 8.00 20.00
27 Cameron Thomas 12.00 30.00
28 Jaden Springer 6.00 15.00
29 Day'Ron Sharpe 6.00 15.00
30 Santi Aldama 8.00 20.00
31 Jeremiah Robinson-Earl 6.00 15.00
32 Miles McBride 10.00 25.00
33 Ayo Dosunmu 60.00 150.00
34 Jared Butler 6.00 15.00
35 Isaiah Livers 6.00 15.00
36 Greg Brown III 5.00 12.00
37 Luka Garza 6.00 15.00
38 Charles Bassey 6.00 15.00
39 Scottie Lewis 5.00 12.00
40 Brandon Boston Jr. 20.00 50.00

2021-22 Panini Origins Rookie Jumbo Jerseys

COMMON CARD 1.50 4.00
SEMISTARS 2.00 5.00
UNLISTED STARS 2.50 6.00
*RED/49: .6X TO 1.5X BASIC
*BLUE/35: .6X TO 1.5X BASIC
*TURQUOISE/25: .75X TO 2X BASIC
1 Cade Cunningham 15.00 40.00
2 Jalen Green 12.00 30.00
3 Evan Mobley 10.00 25.00
4 Scottie Barnes 8.00 20.00
5 Jalen Suggs 6.00 15.00
6 Josh Giddey 8.00 20.00
7 Jonathan Kuminga 8.00 20.00
8 Franz Wagner 8.00 20.00
9 Davion Mitchell 2.50 6.00
10 Ziaire Williams 3.00 8.00
11 James Bouknight 2.00 5.00

12 Joshua Primo 2.00 5.00
13 Chris Duarte 2.00 5.00
14 Moses Moody 5.00 12.00
15 Corey Kispert 3.00 8.00
16 Alperen Sengun 8.00 20.00
17 Trey Murphy III 8.00 20.00
18 Tre Mann 4.00 10.00
20 Jalen Johnson 8.00 20.00
21 Keon Johnson 2.50 6.00
22 Isaiah Jackson 2.50 6.00
23 Usman Garuba 2.00 5.00
24 Josh Christopher 2.00 5.00
25 Quentin Grimes 5.00 12.00
26 Bones Hyland 3.00 8.00
27 Cameron Thomas 5.00 12.00
28 Jaden Springer 2.50 6.00
29 Day'Ron Sharpe 2.50 6.00
30 Santi Aldama 3.00 8.00
31 Jeremiah Robinson-Earl 2.50 6.00
32 Miles McBride 4.00 10.00
33 Ayo Dosunmu 5.00 12.00
34 Jared Butler 2.50 6.00
35 Isaiah Livers 2.50 6.00
36 Greg Brown III 2.00 5.00
37 Scottie Lewis 2.00 5.00
38 Luka Garza 2.50 6.00
39 Charles Bassey 2.50 6.00
40 Brandon Boston Jr. 2.50 6.00

2022-23 Panini Origins

COMMON CARD (1-100) .60 1.50
SEMISTARS .75 2.00
UNLISTED STARS 1.00 2.50
COMMON RC (1-100) .60 1.50
RC SEMIS .75 2.00
RC UNLISTED 1.00 2.50
*RED: .6X TO 1.5X BASIC
*WHITE: .6X TO 1.5X BASIC
*BASKETBALL: 1.25X TO 3X BASIC
*KNIGHT: 1.25X TO 3X BASIC
*MAROON/115: 1.5X TO 4X BASIC
*BLUE/99: 1.5X TO 4X BASIC
*ORANGE/75: 1.5X TO 4X BASIC
*PINK/60: 2X TO 5X BASIC
*NEON GREEN/49: 2.5X TO 6X BASIC
*TURQUOISE/25: 4X TO 10X BASIC
1 De'Aaron Fox 2.00 5.00
2 Bennedict Mathurin RC 3.00 8.00
3 Giannis Antetokounmpo 5.00 12.00
4 Ben Simmons 1.00 2.50
5 Isaiah Mobley RC 1.00 2.50
6 Spencer Dinwiddie .75 2.00
7 Johnny Davis RC 1.00 2.50
8 Kyrie Irving 2.00 5.00
9 Scottie Barnes 1.50 4.00
10 Max Christie RC 2.50 6.00
11 Jaden Ivey RC 3.00 8.00
12 Chris Paul 2.00 5.00
13 Christian Wood .60 1.50
14 Peyton Watson RC 1.50 4.00
15 Dyson Daniels RC 2.50 6.00
16 Anthony Davis 2.50 6.00
17 Damian Lillard 2.50 6.00
18 Andrew Nembhard RC 2.00 5.00
19 Jeremy Sochan RC 3.00 8.00
20 Saddiq Bey .75 2.00
21 Anthony Edwards 5.00 12.00
22 RJ Barrett 1.50 4.00
23 Jayson Tatum 4.00 10.00
24 Trae Young 2.50 6.00
25 Jalen Duren RC 3.00 8.00
26 Ja Morant 3.00 8.00
27 Jalen Suggs 1.25 3.00
28 Patrick Baldwin Jr. RC 1.00 2.50
29 Jalen Green 3.00 8.00
30 Malaki Branham RC 1.00 2.50
31 Andrew Wiggins 1.25 3.00
32 Donovan Mitchell 2.00 5.00
33 Jordan Poole 1.50 4.00
34 Shai Gilgeous-Alexander 5.00 12.00
35 Mike Conley .75 2.00
36 Russell Westbrook 1.50 4.00
37 Shaedon Sharpe RC 4.00 10.00
38 Brandon Ingram 1.25 3.00
39 Caleb Houstan RC 1.00 2.50
40 Paolo Banchero RC 6.00 15.00
41 Bradley Beal 1.25 3.00
42 Tari Eason RC 2.50 6.00
43 Wendell Moore Jr. RC 1.00 2.50
44 Christian Koloko RC 1.00 2.50
45 Karl-Anthony Towns 1.50 4.00
46 Jimmy Butler 2.00 5.00
47 Tyler Herro 1.50 4.00
48 Paul George 1.50 4.00
49 Cade Cunningham 3.00 8.00
50 Walker Kessler RC 2.00 5.00
51 LaMelo Ball 2.50 6.00
52 LeBron James 8.00 20.00
53 Nikola Jokic 5.00 12.00
54 Josh Giddey 1.50 4.00
55 Kevin Durant 3.00 8.00
56 Tyrese Haliburton 2.00 5.00
57 Jabari Smith Jr. RC 3.00 8.00
58 Cole Anthony 1.00 2.50
59 Mark Williams RC 2.00 5.00
60 Klay Thompson 2.50 6.00
61 James Harden 2.00 5.00
62 Darius Garland 1.50 4.00
63 Dalen Terry RC 1.00 2.50
64 Luka Doncic 6.00 15.00
65 Keegan Murray RC 2.50 6.00
66 Ochai Agbaji RC 1.25 3.00
67 Keldon Johnson 1.25 3.00
68 Trevor Keels RC .75 2.00
69 Rudy Gobert 1.25 3.00
70 Davion Mitchell .75 2.00
71 Nikola Jovic RC 2.00 5.00
72 Jake LaRavia RC 1.00 2.50
73 David Roddy RC 1.25 3.00
74 Zion Williamson 2.50 6.00
75 Chet Holmgren RC 5.00 12.00
76 Joel Embiid 1.50 4.00
77 Blake Wesley RC 1.00 2.50
78 Jalen Williams RC 5.00 12.00
79 Stephen Curry 8.00 20.00
80 Christian Braun RC 2.50 6.00
81 Jamal Murray 1.50 4.00
82 Devin Booker 2.50 6.00
83 DeMar DeRozan 1.25 3.00
84 Moussa Diabate RC 1.00 2.50
85 Zach LaVine 2.00 5.00
86 Evan Mobley 2.50 6.00
87 Fred VanVleet 1.25 3.00
88 Kennedy Chandler RC 1.00 2.50
89 Jaylen Brown 2.00 5.00
90 Khris Middleton 1.25 3.00
91 Kawhi Leonard 2.50 6.00
92 TyTy Washington Jr. RC 1.00 2.50
93 AJ Griffin RC .75 2.00
94 MarJon Beauchamp RC 1.00 2.50
95 Ousmane Dieng RC 1.25 3.00
96 Dejounte Murray 1.25 3.00
97 E.J. Liddell RC 1.00 2.50
98 Jaren Jackson Jr. 1.50 4.00
99 Jaden Hardy RC 1.50 4.00
100 Anfernee Simons 1.25 3.00

2022-23 Panini Origins Big Bang

1 Trae Young 60.00 150.00
2 Ja Morant 60.00 150.00
3 LeBron James 300.00 600.00
4 Jayson Tatum 125.00 300.00
5 Stephen Curry 200.00 500.00
6 LaMelo Ball 60.00 150.00
7 Zion Williamson 60.00 150.00
8 Kevin Durant 60.00 150.00
9 Anthony Edwards 75.00 200.00
10 Luka Doncic 150.00 400.00
11 Giannis Antetokounmpo 150.00 400.00
12 Paolo Banchero 200.00 500.00
13 Chet Holmgren 150.00 400.00
14 Jabari Smith Jr. 75.00 200.00
15 Jaden Ivey 125.00 300.00

2022-23 Panini Origins Catapults

COMMON CARD .60 1.50
SEMISTARS .75 2.00
UNLISTED STARS 1.00 2.50
*PINK/99: 1.5X TO 4X BASIC
*TURQUOISE/25: 3X TO 8X BASIC
1 Jaylen Brown 2.00 5.00
2 Anthony Davis 2.50 6.00
3 Joel Embiid 1.50 4.00
4 Dwyane Wade 2.00 5.00
5 Vince Carter 2.00 5.00
6 Dominique Wilkins 1.50 4.00
7 DeMar DeRozan 1.25 3.00
8 Dejounte Murray 1.25 3.00
9 Shaquille O'Neal 4.00 10.00
10 LeBron James 8.00 20.00
11 Jayson Tatum 4.00 10.00
12 Zach LaVine 2.00 5.00
13 Donovan Mitchell 2.00 5.00
14 Jalen Green 3.00 8.00
15 Kevin Durant 3.00 8.00
16 Anthony Edwards 5.00 12.00
17 Russell Westbrook 1.50 4.00
18 Ja Morant 3.00 8.00
19 Paul George 1.50 4.00
20 Bam Adebayo 1.50 4.00
21 Zion Williamson 2.50 6.00
22 Shawn Kemp 1.50 4.00
23 Kawhi Leonard 2.50 6.00
24 Giannis Antetokounmpo 5.00 12.00
25 Jimmy Butler 2.00 5.00

2022-23 Panini Origins Dawn

COMMON CARD .60 1.50
SEMISTARS .75 2.00
UNLISTED STARS 1.00 2.50
*RED/75: 2X TO 5X BASIC
1 Evan Mobley 2.50 6.00
2 Shaedon Sharpe 4.00 10.00
3 Jonathan Kuminga 2.50 6.00
4 Ochai Agbaji 1.25 3.00
5 Bennedict Mathurin 3.00 8.00
6 Dalen Terry 1.00 2.50
7 Paolo Banchero 6.00 15.00
8 Jeremy Sochan 3.00 8.00
9 Johnny Davis 1.00 2.50
10 Jabari Smith Jr. 3.00 8.00
11 Christian Braun 2.50 6.00
12 Jalen Williams 5.00 12.00
13 Jalen Green 3.00 8.00
14 Keegan Murray 2.50 6.00
15 Jake LaRavia 1.00 2.50
16 Chet Holmgren 5.00 12.00
17 Ousmane Dieng 1.25 3.00
18 AJ Griffin .75 2.00
19 Dyson Daniels 2.50 6.00
20 Cade Cunningham 3.00 8.00
21 Jaden Ivey 3.00 8.00
22 Malaki Branham 1.00 2.50
23 Nikola Jovic 2.00 5.00
24 Wendell Moore Jr. 1.00 2.50
25 Scottie Barnes 1.50 4.00

2022-23 Panini Origins Elevation Signatures

COMMON CARD 5.00 12.00
SEMISTARS 6.00 15.00
UNLISTED STARS 8.00 20.00
STATED PRINT RUN 99 SER.#'d SETS
*TURQUOISE: .4X TO 1X BASIC
1 Malaki Branham 8.00 20.00
2 Walker Kessler 15.00 40.00
3 Andrew Nembhard 15.00 40.00
4 TyTy Washington Jr. 8.00 20.00
5 Trevor Keels 6.00 15.00
6 Moussa Diabate 8.00 20.00
7 Nikola Jovic 15.00 40.00
8 Blake Wesley 8.00 20.00
9 Jalen Williams 75.00 200.00
10 Max Christie 20.00 50.00
11 MarJon Beauchamp 8.00 20.00
12 Chet Holmgren 150.00 400.00
13 Ousmane Dieng 10.00 25.00
14 Jeremy Sochan 75.00 200.00
15 Jake LaRavia 8.00 20.00
16 Tari Eason 20.00 50.00
17 Keegan Murray 40.00 100.00
18 Jaden Ivey 125.00 300.00
19 Kennedy Chandler 8.00 20.00
20 Ochai Agbaji 10.00 25.00
21 Patrick Baldwin Jr. 8.00 20.00
22 Wendell Moore Jr. 8.00 20.00
23 Jaden Hardy 40.00 100.00
24 Christian Koloko 8.00 20.00
25 David Roddy 10.00 25.00
26 Christian Braun 20.00 50.00
27 Shaedon Sharpe 125.00 300.00
28 Peyton Watson 12.00 30.00
29 AJ Griffin 6.00 15.00
30 E.J. Liddell 8.00 20.00
31 Dyson Daniels 20.00 50.00
32 Bennedict Mathurin 100.00 250.00
33 Mark Williams 15.00 40.00
34 Jalen Duren 40.00 100.00
35 Jabari Smith Jr. 75.00 200.00
36 Paolo Banchero 300.00 600.00
37 Caleb Houstan 8.00 20.00
38 Johnny Davis 8.00 20.00
39 Isaiah Mobley 8.00 20.00
40 Dalen Terry 8.00 20.00

2022-23 Panini Origins Euphoria

COMMON CARD 1.25 3.00
SEMISTARS 1.50 4.00
UNLISTED STARS 2.00 5.00
*PINK/99: 1X TO 2.5X BASIC
*TURQUOISE/25: 2.5X TO 6X BASIC
1 Jayson Tatum 8.00 20.00
2 Ja Morant 6.00 15.00
3 Anthony Edwards 10.00 25.00
4 LaMelo Ball 5.00 12.00
5 Kawhi Leonard 5.00 12.00
6 Luka Doncic 12.00 30.00
7 Zion Williamson 5.00 12.00
8 Giannis Antetokounmpo 10.00 25.00
9 Stephen Curry 15.00 40.00
10 LeBron James 15.00 40.00
11 Trae Young 5.00 12.00
12 James Harden 4.00 10.00
13 Damian Lillard 5.00 12.00
14 Donovan Mitchell 4.00 10.00
15 Kevin Durant 6.00 15.00
16 Jaylen Brown 4.00 10.00
17 Anthony Davis 5.00 12.00
18 Jonathan Kuminga 5.00 12.00
19 Jalen Green 6.00 15.00
20 Cade Cunningham 6.00 15.00
21 Shaquille O'Neal 8.00 20.00
22 Dirk Nowitzki 5.00 12.00
23 Larry Bird 8.00 20.00
24 Allen Iverson 5.00 12.00
25 Magic Johnson 8.00 20.00

2022-23 Panini Origins Originals

COMMON CARD .60 1.50
SEMISTARS .75 2.00
UNLISTED STARS 1.00 2.50
*RED/75: 2X TO 5X BASIC
1 Johnny Davis 1.00 2.50
2 Bennedict Mathurin 3.00 8.00
3 Keegan Murray 2.50 6.00
4 Blake Wesley 1.00 2.50
5 Malaki Branham 1.00 2.50
6 Ousmane Dieng 1.25 3.00
7 Jalen Williams 5.00 12.00
8 Ochai Agbaji 1.25 3.00
9 AJ Griffin .75 2.00
10 Chet Holmgren 5.00 12.00
11 Jabari Smith Jr. 3.00 8.00
12 Christian Braun 2.50 6.00
13 Jalen Duren 3.00 8.00
14 Paolo Banchero 6.00 15.00
15 Shaedon Sharpe 4.00 10.00
16 Jaden Ivey 3.00 8.00
17 MarJon Beauchamp 1.00 2.50
18 TyTy Washington Jr. 1.00 2.50
19 Jake LaRavia 1.00 2.50
20 Jeremy Sochan 3.00 8.00
21 Dyson Daniels 2.50 6.00
22 Tari Eason 2.50 6.00
23 Jaden Hardy 1.50 4.00
24 Dalen Terry 1.00 2.50
25 Nikola Jovic 2.00 5.00

2022-23 Panini Origins Origins Memorabilia

COMMON CARD 2.00 5.00
SEMISTARS 2.50 6.00
UNLISTED STARS 3.00 8.00
*RED/49: .6X TO 1.5X BASIC
*BLUE/35: .6X TO 1.5X BASIC
*TURQUOISE/25: .75X TO 2X BASIC
1 LeBron James 40.00 100.00
2 Shai Gilgeous-Alexander 15.00 40.00
3 Damian Lillard 8.00 20.00
4 Kawhi Leonard 8.00 20.00
5 Trae Young 8.00 20.00
6 Pascal Siakam 5.00 12.00
7 Zach LaVine 6.00 15.00
8 Donovan Mitchell 6.00 15.00
9 Bradley Beal 4.00 10.00
10 Jimmy Butler 6.00 15.00
11 Jaylen Brown 6.00 15.00
12 Devin Booker 8.00 20.00
13 Brandon Ingram 4.00 10.00
14 Ben Simmons 3.00 8.00
15 Russell Westbrook 5.00 12.00
16 Jamal Murray 5.00 12.00
17 Giannis Antetokounmpo 15.00 40.00
18 Andrew Wiggins 4.00 10.00
19 Joel Embiid 5.00 12.00
20 LaMelo Ball 8.00 20.00

2022-23 Panini Origins Photo Variations

2 Bennedict Mathurin 6.00 15.00
11 Jaden Ivey 6.00 15.00
26 Ja Morant 6.00 15.00
37 Shaedon Sharpe 8.00 20.00
40 Paolo Banchero 12.00 30.00
52 LeBron James 15.00 40.00
57 Jabari Smith Jr. 6.00 15.00
64 Luka Doncic 12.00 30.00
75 Chet Holmgren 10.00 25.00
79 Stephen Curry 15.00 40.00

2022-23 Panini Origins Rookie Autographs

COMMON CARD 5.00 12.00
SEMISTARS 6.00 15.00
UNLISTED STARS 8.00 20.00
*TURQUOISE: .4X TO 1X BASIC
*RED/99: .4X TO 1X BASIC
*PURPLE FOTL/40: .5X TO 1.25X BASIC
*BLUE/35: .5X TO 1.25X BASIC
*PINK/25: .6X TO 1.5X BASIC
1 TyTy Washington Jr. 8.00 20.00
2 Jeremy Sochan 75.00 200.00
3 Christian Koloko 8.00 20.00
4 Jalen Duren 40.00 100.00
5 Moussa Diabate 8.00 20.00
6 Tari Eason 20.00 50.00
7 Christian Braun 20.00 50.00
8 Paolo Banchero 300.00 600.00
9 Blake Wesley 8.00 20.00
10 Jaden Ivey 125.00 300.00
11 Peyton Watson 12.00 30.00
12 Johnny Davis 8.00 20.00
13 Max Christie 20.00 50.00
14 Ochai Agbaji 60.00 150.00
15 E.J. Liddell 8.00 20.00
16 Dalen Terry 8.00 20.00
17 Walker Kessler 75.00 200.00
18 Chet Holmgren 150.00 400.00
19 Wendell Moore Jr. 8.00 20.00
20 Bennedict Mathurin 100.00 250.00
21 Andrew Nembhard 15.00 40.00
22 Ousmane Dieng 10.00 25.00
23 Jaden Hardy 40.00 100.00
24 Mark Williams 15.00 40.00
25 Trevor Keels 6.00 15.00
26 Jake LaRavia 8.00 20.00
27 David Roddy 10.00 25.00
28 Jabari Smith Jr. 75.00 200.00
29 Nikola Jovic 15.00 40.00
30 Keegan Murray 125.00 300.00
31 Shaedon Sharpe 125.00 300.00
32 Caleb Houstan 8.00 20.00
33 Jalen Williams 75.00 200.00
34 Kennedy Chandler 8.00 20.00
35 AJ Griffin 6.00 15.00
36 Isaiah Mobley 8.00 20.00
37 Malaki Branham 8.00 20.00
38 MarJon Beauchamp 8.00 20.00
39 Patrick Baldwin Jr. 8.00 20.00
40 Dyson Daniels 20.00 50.00

2022-23 Panini Origins Rookie Jersey Autographs

COMMON CARD 5.00 12.00
SEMISTARS 6.00 15.00
UNLISTED STARS 8.00 20.00
*RED/49: .5X TO 1.2X BASIC
*BLUE/25: .6X TO 1.5X BASIC
1 Moussa Diabate 8.00 20.00
2 Nikola Jovic 15.00 40.00
3 Blake Wesley 8.00 20.00
4 Jalen Williams 60.00 150.00
5 Max Christie 20.00 50.00
6 Malaki Branham 8.00 20.00
7 Walker Kessler 15.00 40.00
8 Andrew Nembhard 15.00 40.00
9 TyTy Washington Jr. 8.00 20.00
10 Trevor Keels 6.00 15.00
11 Tari Eason 20.00 50.00
12 Keegan Murray 20.00 50.00
13 Jaden Ivey 25.00 60.00
14 Kennedy Chandler 8.00 20.00
15 Ochai Agbaji 10.00 25.00
16 MarJon Beauchamp 8.00 20.00
17 Chet Holmgren 125.00 300.00
18 Ousmane Dieng 10.00 25.00
19 Jeremy Sochan 25.00 60.00
20 Jake LaRavia 8.00 20.00
21 Christian Braun 20.00 50.00
22 Shaedon Sharpe 30.00 80.00
23 Peyton Watson 12.00 30.00
24 AJ Griffin 6.00 15.00
25 E.J. Liddell 8.00 20.00
26 Patrick Baldwin Jr. 8.00 20.00
27 Wendell Moore Jr. 8.00 20.00
28 Jaden Hardy 12.00 30.00
29 Christian Koloko 8.00 20.00
30 David Roddy 10.00 25.00
31 Paolo Banchero 125.00 300.00
32 Caleb Houstan 8.00 20.00
33 Johnny Davis 8.00 20.00
34 Isaiah Mobley 8.00 20.00
35 Dalen Terry 8.00 20.00
36 Dyson Daniels 20.00 50.00
37 Bennedict Mathurin 25.00 60.00
38 Mark Williams 15.00 40.00
39 Jalen Duren 25.00 60.00
40 Jabari Smith Jr. 25.00 60.00

2022-23 Panini Origins Rookie Jumbo Jerseys

COMMON CARD 1.50 4.00
SEMISTARS 2.00 5.00
UNLISTED STARS 2.50 6.00
*RED/49: .6X TO 1.5X BASIC
*BLUE/35: .6X TO 1.5X BASIC
*TURQUOISE/25: .75X TO 2X BASIC
1 Kennedy Chandler 2.50 6.00
2 Max Christie 6.00 15.00
3 Mark Williams 5.00 12.00
4 Wendell Moore Jr. 2.50 6.00
5 Keegan Murray 6.00 15.00
6 Jalen Duren 8.00 20.00
7 Blake Wesley 2.50 6.00
8 Chet Holmgren 12.00 30.00
9 Johnny Davis 2.50 6.00
10 Malaki Branham 2.50 6.00
11 Patrick Baldwin Jr. 2.50 6.00
12 David Roddy 3.00 8.00
13 Christian Braun 6.00 15.00
14 Caleb Houstan 2.50 6.00
15 E.J. Liddell 2.50 6.00
16 Dyson Daniels 6.00 15.00
17 Nikola Jovic 5.00 12.00
18 Jeremy Sochan 8.00 20.00
19 Jabari Smith Jr. 8.00 20.00
20 Trevor Keels 2.00 5.00
21 Jaden Hardy 4.00 10.00
22 Jalen Williams 12.00 30.00
23 Ousmane Dieng 3.00 8.00
24 Tari Eason 6.00 15.00
25 Peyton Watson 4.00 10.00
26 Isaiah Mobley 2.50 6.00
27 Christian Koloko 2.50 6.00
28 MarJon Beauchamp 2.50 6.00
29 Walker Kessler 5.00 12.00
30 Jalen Ivey 8.00 20.00
31 Paolo Banchero 15.00 40.00
32 AJ Griffin 2.00 5.00
33 Bennedict Mathurin 8.00 20.00
34 Ochai Agbaji 3.00 8.00
35 Moussa Diabate 2.50 6.00
36 Andrew Nembhard 5.00 12.00
37 TyTy Washington Jr. 2.50 6.00
38 Shaedon Sharpe 10.00 25.00
39 Dalen Terry 2.50 6.00
40 Jake LaRavia 2.50 6.00

2022-23 Panini Origins Snake Eyes

1 Luka Doncic 350.00 700.00
2 LaMelo Ball 200.00 500.00
3 Jayson Tatum 300.00 600.00
4 Zion Williamson 200.00 500.00
5 Anthony Edwards 300.00 600.00
6 LeBron James 500.00 1,000.00
7 Giannis Antetokounmpo 300.00 600.00
8 Trae Young 150.00 400.00
9 Ja Morant 200.00 500.00
10 Stephen Curry 400.00 800.00

2022-23 Panini Origins Taking the Leap

COMMON CARD .75 2.00
SEMISTARS 1.00 2.50
UNLISTED STARS 1.25 3.00
*PINK/99: 1.5X TO 4X BASIC
*TURQUOISE/25: 3X TO 8X BASIC
1 Malaki Branham 1.25 3.00
2 Shaedon Sharpe 5.00 12.00
3 Paolo Banchero 8.00 20.00
4 Blake Wesley 1.25 3.00
5 Dyson Daniels 3.00 8.00
6 Jake LaRavia 1.25 3.00
7 AJ Griffin 1.00 2.50
8 Nikola Jovic 2.50 6.00
9 Chet Holmgren 6.00 15.00
10 Dalen Terry 1.25 3.00
11 Jalen Williams 6.00 15.00
12 Johnny Davis 1.25 3.00
13 Jalen Duren 4.00 10.00
14 Tari Eason 3.00 8.00
15 Ousmane Dieng 1.50 4.00
16 Patrick Baldwin Jr. 1.25 3.00
17 Bennedict Mathurin 4.00 10.00
18 Wendell Moore Jr. 1.25 3.00
19 Jaden Ivey 4.00 10.00
20 Christian Braun 3.00 8.00
21 Jabari Smith Jr. 4.00 10.00
22 Keegan Murray 3.00 8.00
23 Jeremy Sochan 4.00 10.00
24 Mark Williams 2.50 6.00
25 Ochai Agbaji 1.50 4.00

2022-23 Panini Origins Team Origins

COMMON CARD .60 1.50
SEMISTARS .75 2.00
UNLISTED STARS 1.00 2.50
*RED/75: 1.25X TO 3X BASIC
1 Kawhi Leonard 2.50 6.00
2 James Harden 2.00 5.00
3 Zach LaVine 2.00 5.00
4 LeBron James 8.00 20.00
5 Devin Booker 2.50 6.00
6 Tyrese Haliburton 2.00 5.00
7 Damian Lillard 2.50 6.00
8 Evan Mobley 2.50 6.00
9 Jalen Green 3.00 8.00
10 Trae Young 2.50 6.00
11 Luka Doncic 6.00 15.00
12 Jayson Tatum 4.00 10.00
13 Ja Morant 3.00 8.00
14 Anthony Edwards 5.00 12.00
15 Nikola Jokic 5.00 12.00
16 Cade Cunningham 3.00 8.00
17 LaMelo Ball 2.50 6.00
18 Donovan Mitchell 2.00 5.00
19 Jimmy Butler 2.00 5.00
20 Josh Giddey 1.50 4.00
21 Zion Williamson 2.50 6.00
22 Stephen Curry 8.00 20.00
23 Bradley Beal 1.25 3.00
24 Kevin Durant 3.00 8.00
25 Giannis Antetokounmpo 5.00 12.00

2022-23 Panini Origins Tiger Eyes

1 LeBron James 300.00 600.00
2 Luka Doncic 200.00 500.00
3 Stephen Curry 300.00 600.00
4 Giannis Antetokounmpo 125.00 300.00
5 Ja Morant 150.00 400.00
6 Anthony Edwards 200.00 500.00
7 LaMelo Ball 125.00 300.00
8 Zion Williamson 125.00 300.00
9 Jayson Tatum 150.00 400.00
10 Trae Young 125.00 300.00
11 Kevin Durant 125.00 300.00
12 James Harden 125.00 300.00
13 Kawhi Leonard 125.00 300.00
14 Nikola Jokic 200.00 500.00
15 Devin Booker 125.00 300.00

2022-23 Panini Origins Universal Autographs

COMMON CARD 4.00 10.00
SEMISTARS 5.00 12.00
UNLISTED STARS 6.00 15.00
*TURQUOISE: .4X TO 1X BASIC
*RED/49: .5X TO 1.2X BASIC
*PINK/25: .6X TO 1.5X BASIC
1 Rick Fox 6.00 15.00
2 Shai Gilgeous-Alexander 400.00 800.00
3 CJ McCollum 6.00 15.00
4 Stephen Curry 800.00 1,500.00
5 Tony Parker 25.00 60.00
6 Jayson Tatum 125.00 300.00
7 Al Horford 12.00 30.00
8 Jerry West 30.00 80.00
9 Victor Oladipo 5.00 12.00
10 Jason Kidd 25.00 60.00
11 Jerry Stackhouse 8.00 20.00
12 Grant Hill 25.00 60.00
13 Julius Randle 8.00 20.00
14 Chris Paul 40.00 100.00
15 Duncan Robinson 20.00 50.00
16 John Stockton 30.00 80.00
17 Jordan Clarkson 20.00 50.00
18 Karl-Anthony Towns 20.00 50.00
19 Luka Doncic 500.00 1,000.00
20 RJ Barrett 15.00 40.00

2023-24 Panini Origins

*RED: .6X TO 1.5X BASIC
*MAROON/115: 1.5X TO 4X BASIC
*BASKETBALL: 2X TO 5X BASIC
*BLUE/99: 2X TO 5X BASIC
*TESSELLATED: 2.5X TO 6X BASIC
*ORANGE/75: 2.5X TO 6X BASIC
*PINK/60: 2.5X TO 6X BASIC
*NEON STRIPES/49: 3X TO 8X BASIC
*NEON GREEN/25: 4X TO 10X BASIC
*TURQUOISE/25: 4X TO 10X BASIC
1 Shaedon Sharpe 1.00 2.50
2 Darius Garland .75 2.00
3 Jaylen Brown 1.00 2.50
4 Hunter Tyson RC 1.00 2.50
5 Stephen Curry 4.00 10.00
6 Chris Paul 1.00 2.50
7 Julius Randle .60 1.50
8 Keegan Murray .75 2.00
9 Tyrese Maxey 1.00 2.50
10 Jayson Tatum 2.50 6.00
11 Lauri Markkanen .75 2.00
12 LeBron James 4.00 10.00
13 Anthony Davis 1.50 4.00
14 Devin Booker 1.25 3.00
15 De'Aaron Fox 1.00 2.50
16 Taylor Hendricks RC 1.50 4.00
17 Scoot Henderson RC 3.00 8.00
18 Paolo Banchero 1.50 4.00
19 Zach LaVine .75 2.00
20 Maxwell Lewis RC .75 2.00
21 Chet Holmgren 1.50 4.00
22 Nikola Jokic 2.50 6.00
23 Shai Gilgeous-Alexander 2.50 6.00
24 Brandin Podziemski RC 3.00 8.00
25 Jordan Walsh RC 1.50 4.00
26 Cam Whitmore RC 2.50 6.00
27 Kevin Durant 1.50 4.00
28 Dereck Lively II RC 3.00 8.00
29 Amari Bailey RC 1.00 2.50
30 Mikal Bridges .75 2.00
31 Leonard Miller RC 1.00 2.50
32 Bradley Beal .60 1.50
33 Jaime Jaquez Jr. RC 1.50 4.00
34 Anthony Black RC 2.50 6.00
35 Trae Young 1.25 3.00
36 Bam Adebayo .75 2.00
37 Joel Embiid 1.50 4.00
38 James Nnaji RC 1.00 2.50
39 Jalen Brunson 1.00 2.50
40 Damian Lillard 1.25 3.00
41 Zion Williamson 1.25 3.00
42 Paul George .75 2.00
43 Giannis Antetokounmpo 3.00 8.00
44 James Harden 1.00 2.50
45 Kawhi Leonard 1.25 3.00
46 Tyrese Haliburton 1.00 2.50
47 Marcus Sasser RC 2.00 5.00
48 Nick Smith Jr. RC 1.25 3.00
49 GG Jackson II RC 3.00 8.00
50 Julian Strawther RC 1.25 3.00
51 Colby Jones RC 1.25 3.00
52 Jaden Ivey .60 1.50
53 Jalen Williams 1.00 2.50
54 Rayan Rupert RC 1.00 2.50
55 Jalen Green 1.25 3.00
56 Austin Reaves 1.25 3.00
57 Jabari Smith Jr. 1.00 2.50
58 Kris Murray RC 1.25 3.00
59 Anthony Edwards 2.50 6.00
60 Brice Sensabaugh RC 1.50 4.00
61 Bennedict Mathurin .75 2.00
62 Scottie Barnes .75 2.00
63 Noah Clowney RC 1.25 3.00
64 Jalen Wilson RC 1.00 2.50
65 Jordan Poole .75 2.00
66 Kobe Brown RC 1.00 2.50
67 Jalen Pickett RC 1.00 2.50
68 Pascal Siakam .75 2.00
69 Julian Phillips RC 1.00 2.50
70 Bilal Coulibaly RC 2.50 6.00
71 Tristan Vukcevic RC 1.00 2.50
72 Cade Cunningham 1.25 3.00
73 Ja Morant 1.50 4.00
74 Kyle Kuzma .60 1.50
75 Ausar Thompson RC 3.00 8.00
76 DeMar DeRozan .75 2.00
77 Ben Sheppard RC 1.00 2.50
78 Kobe Bufkin RC 1.25 3.00
79 Andre Jackson Jr. RC 1.50 4.00
80 Keyonte George RC 3.00 8.00
81 Jett Howard RC 1.25 3.00
82 Jarace Walker RC 2.00 5.00
83 Keyontae Johnson RC 1.00 2.50
84 Gradey Dick RC 2.00 5.00
85 Kyrie Irving 1.00 2.50
86 Victor Wembanyama RC 15.00 40.00
87 Dejounte Murray .60 1.50
88 Cason Wallace RC 2.50 6.00
89 Brandon Miller RC 4.00 10.00
90 Luka Doncic 3.00 8.00
91 Olivier-Maxence Prosper RC 1.00 2.50
92 Jalen Hood-Schifino RC 1.25 3.00
93 Jimmy Butler 1.00 2.50
94 Jamal Murray 1.00 2.50
95 Karl-Anthony Towns .75 2.00
96 LaMelo Ball 1.25 3.00
97 Donovan Mitchell 1.00 2.50
98 Dariq Whitehead RC 1.25 3.00
99 Amen Thompson RC 5.00 12.00
100 Jordan Hawkins RC 2.00 5.00

2023-24 Panini Origins Catapults

*PINK/99: 1.5X TO 4X BASIC
*TURQUOISE/25: 2.5X TO 6X BASIC
1 Amen Thompson 5.00 12.00
2 Ausar Thompson 2.50 6.00
3 Victor Wembanyama 30.00 80.00
4 Scoot Henderson 3.00 8.00
5 Brandon Miller 4.00 10.00
6 Bilal Coulibaly 2.50 6.00
7 Anthony Black 2.50 6.00
8 Jarace Walker 2.00 5.00
9 Taylor Hendricks 1.00 2.50
10 Jordan Hawkins 1.50 4.00
11 Cason Wallace 2.00 5.00
12 Jett Howard 1.25 3.00
13 Zion Williamson 2.50 6.00
14 LeBron James 8.00 20.00
15 Donovan Mitchell 2.00 5.00
16 Giannis Antetokounmpo 6.00 15.00
17 Luka Doncic 6.00 15.00
18 Jayson Tatum 4.00 10.00
19 Ja Morant 3.00 8.00
20 Anthony Edwards 5.00 12.00
21 Joel Embiid 2.50 6.00
22 LaMelo Ball 2.00 5.00
23 Cade Cunningham 2.50 6.00
24 Zach LaVine 1.50 4.00
25 Paul George 1.50 4.00

2023-24 Panini Origins Cosmic Storm

*RED/75: 1.5X TO 4X BASIC
1 LeBron James 12.00 30.00
2 Giannis Antetokounmpo 8.00 20.00
3 Shai Gilgeous-Alexander 8.00 20.00
4 Stephen Curry 12.00 30.00
5 Donovan Mitchell 3.00 8.00
6 Trae Young 3.00 8.00
7 Ja Morant 5.00 12.00
8 Luka Doncic 10.00 25.00
9 Jayson Tatum 6.00 15.00
10 Nikola Jokic 8.00 20.00
11 Kevin Durant 5.00 12.00
12 De'Aaron Fox 3.00 8.00
13 Anthony Edwards 8.00 20.00
14 Victor Wembanyama 50.00 120.00
15 Amen Thompson 8.00 20.00
16 Scoot Henderson 5.00 12.00
17 Taylor Hendricks 1.50 4.00
18 Cason Wallace 3.00 8.00
19 Brandon Miller 6.00 15.00
20 Cam Whitmore 4.00 10.00
21 Keyonte George 5.00 12.00
22 Anthony Black 4.00 10.00
23 Jarace Walker 3.00 8.00
24 Bilal Coulibaly 4.00 10.00
25 Ausar Thompson 4.00 10.00

2023-24 Panini Origins Dawn

*RED/75: 1.5X TO 4X BASIC
1 Brice Sensabaugh 2.50 6.00
2 Anthony Black 3.00 8.00
3 Rayan Rupert 1.50 4.00
4 Jarace Walker 3.00 8.00
5 Taylor Hendricks 1.50 4.00
6 GG Jackson II 3.00 8.00
7 Jett Howard 2.00 5.00
8 Dariq Whitehead 2.00 5.00
9 Gradey Dick 3.00 8.00
10 Tristan Vukcevic 1.50 4.00
11 Brandin Podziemski 5.00 12.00
12 Ben Sheppard 1.50 4.00
13 Scoot Henderson 5.00 12.00
14 Bilal Coulibaly 4.00 10.00
15 Brandon Miller 6.00 15.00
16 Cam Whitmore 4.00 10.00
17 Nick Smith Jr. 2.00 5.00
18 Jordan Hawkins 2.50 6.00
19 Jaime Jaquez Jr. 2.50 6.00
20 Jalen Hood-Schifino 1.50 4.00
21 Amen Thompson 8.00 20.00
22 Ausar Thompson 4.00 10.00
23 Keyonte George 5.00 12.00
24 Kobe Bufkin 2.00 5.00
25 Victor Wembanyama 50.00 120.00

2023-24 Panini Origins Elevation Signatures

STATED PRINT RUN 49-150 SER.#'d SETS
*RED/25-49: .5X TO 1.2X BASIC
*PINK/15-25: .6X TO 1.5X BASIC
1 Dariq Whitehead/99 12.00 30.00
2 Marcus Sasser/150 15.00 40.00
3 Olivier-Maxence Prosper/99 10.00 25.00
4 Julian Phillips/150 10.00 25.00
5 Bilal Coulibaly/99 25.00 60.00
7 Andre Jackson Jr./150 15.00 40.00
8 Kobe Bufkin/99 12.00 30.00
10 Cason Wallace/99 20.00 50.00
11 GG Jackson II/99 20.00 50.00
12 Brice Sensabaugh/99 15.00 40.00
13 Julius Erving/49 60.00 150.00
15 Kobe Brown/150 10.00 25.00
16 Amen Thompson/99 50.00 120.00
17 Jalen Wilson/150 10.00 25.00
18 Ausar Thompson/99 25.00 60.00
20 Jordan Walsh/150 10.00 25.00
21 Shawn Kemp/99 30.00 80.00
22 Trayce Jackson-Davis/150 12.00 30.00
23 Rayan Rupert/150 10.00 25.00
24 Colby Jones/150 10.00 25.00
25 Brandin Podziemski/150 30.00 80.00
26 James Nnaji/150 8.00 20.00
27 Keyontae Johnson/150 10.00 25.00
28 Ben Sheppard/150 10.00 25.00
29 Maxwell Lewis/150 8.00 20.00
30 Kris Murray/150 10.00 25.00
31 Jalen Pickett/150 8.00 20.00
32 Dereck Lively II/99 20.00 50.00
33 Anthony Edwards/49 300.00 600.00
34 Toumani Camara/150 20.00 50.00
35 Donovan Mitchell/49 60.00 150.00
36 Ben Wallace/99 25.00 60.00
37 Noah Clowney/150 12.00 30.00
40 Keyonte George/99 30.00 80.00

2023-24 Panini Origins Euphoria
*PINK/99: 1.5X TO 4X BASIC
*TURQUOISE/25: 2.5X TO 6X BASIC
1 Victor Wembanyama 40.00 100.00
2 Bilal Coulibaly 2.50 6.00
3 Scoot Henderson 3.00 8.00
4 Ausar Thompson 2.50 6.00
5 Brandon Miller 4.00 10.00
6 Amen Thompson 5.00 12.00
7 Cam Whitmore 2.50 6.00
8 Gradey Dick 2.00 5.00
9 Jalen Hood-Schifino 1.00 2.50
10 Jaime Jaquez Jr. 1.50 4.00
11 Nick Smith Jr. 1.25 3.00
12 Keyonte George 3.00 8.00
13 Damian Lillard 2.50 6.00
14 Trae Young 2.00 5.00
15 Luka Doncic 6.00 15.00
16 Kawhi Leonard 2.50 6.00
17 Giannis Antetokounmpo 6.00 15.00
18 Ja Morant 3.00 8.00
19 Jaylen Brown 2.00 5.00
20 Stephen Curry 8.00 20.00
21 Kevin Durant 3.00 8.00
22 Shai Gilgeous-Alexander 5.00 12.00
23 LeBron James 8.00 20.00
24 James Harden 2.00 5.00
25 Nikola Jokic 4.00 10.00

2023-24 Panini Origins Nucleus
*PINK/99: 1.5X TO 4X BASIC
*TURQUOISE/25: 2.5X TO 6X BASIC
1 Jaylen Brown
Jayson Tatum
Kristaps Porzingis 5.00 12.00
2 Luka Doncic
Dereck Lively II
Kyrie Irving 12.00 30.00
3 Tobias Harris
Tyrese Maxey
Joel Embiid 3.00 8.00
4 Alperen Sengun
Amen Thompson
Cam Whitmore 6.00 15.00
5 Jaren Jackson Jr.
Desmond Bane
Ja Morant 4.00 10.00
6 Cade Cunningham
Jaden Ivey
Ausar Thompson 3.00 8.00
7 Jordan Hawkins
Zion Williamson
Brandon Ingram 3.00 8.00
8 Jeremy Sochan
Victor Wembanyama
Keldon Johnson 30.00 80.00
9 LaMelo Ball
Nick Smith Jr.
Brandon Miller 5.00 12.00
10 Anfernee Simons
Scoot Henderson
Shaedon Sharpe 4.00 10.00
11 Paolo Banchero
Anthony Black
Jett Howard 4.00 10.00
12 Jarace Walker
Tyrese Haliburton
Bennedict Mathurin 2.50 6.00
13 Cason Wallace
Chet Holmgren
Shai Gilgeous-Alexander 6.00 15.00
14 Trae Young
Dejounte Murray
Kobe Bufkin 2.50 6.00
15 Lauri Markkanen
Taylor Hendricks
Keyonte George 4.00 10.00
16 Austin Reaves
LeBron James
Anthony Davis 10.00 25.00
17 Jimmy Butler
Bam Adebayo
Jaime Jaquez Jr. 2.00 5.00
18 Klay Thompson
Stephen Curry
Chris Paul 10.00 25.00
19 Giannis Antetokounmpo
Khris Middleton
Damian Lillard 8.00 20.00
20 Nikola Jokic
Jamal Murray
Michael Porter Jr. 5.00 12.00
21 Rudy Gobert
Anthony Edwards
Karl-Anthony Towns 6.00 15.00
22 Paul George
Russell Westbrook
Kawhi Leonard 3.00 8.00
23 Kevin Durant
Bradley Beal
Devin Booker 4.00 10.00
24 Manu Ginobili
Tony Parker
Tim Duncan 2.50 6.00
25 Ray Allen
Sam Cassell
Paul Pierce 2.00 5.00

2023-24 Panini Origins Originals
*RED/75: 1.5X TO 4X BASIC
1 Scoot Henderson 5.00 12.00
2 Taylor Hendricks 1.50 4.00
3 Amen Thompson 8.00 20.00
4 Cason Wallace 3.00 8.00
5 Brandon Miller 6.00 15.00
6 Jett Howard 2.00 5.00
7 Bilal Coulibaly 4.00 10.00
8 Dereck Lively II 3.00 8.00
9 Anthony Black 4.00 10.00
10 Gradey Dick 3.00 8.00
11 Ausar Thompson 4.00 10.00
12 Jarace Walker 3.00 8.00
13 Victor Wembanyama 50.00 120.00
14 Kobe Bufkin 2.00 5.00
15 Keyonte George 5.00 12.00
16 Nick Smith Jr. 2.00 5.00
17 Jalen Hood-Schifino 1.50 4.00
18 Jaime Jaquez Jr. 2.50 6.00
19 Cam Whitmore 4.00 10.00
20 Brandin Podziemski 4.00 10.00
21 Noah Clowney 2.00 5.00
22 Dariq Whitehead 2.00 5.00
23 Kris Murray 1.50 4.00
24 Olivier-Maxence Prosper 1.50 4.00
25 Jordan Hawkins 2.50 6.00

2023-24 Panini Origins Origins Memorabilia
*RED/49: .6X TO 1.5X BASIC
*TURQUOISE/25: .75X TO 2X BASIC
1 Anthony Davis 8.00 20.00
2 Damian Lillard 8.00 20.00
3 Jimmy Butler 5.00 12.00
4 De'Aaron Fox 6.00 15.00
5 Julius Randle 4.00 10.00
6 Bam Adebayo 5.00 12.00
7 Mikal Bridges 4.00 10.00
8 Joel Embiid 8.00 20.00
9 Giannis Antetokounmpo 15.00 40.00
10 Tyrese Maxey 6.00 15.00
11 Karl-Anthony Towns 5.00 12.00
12 Devin Booker 8.00 20.00
13 LeBron James 40.00 100.00
14 Kawhi Leonard 8.00 20.00
15 DeMar DeRozan 4.00 10.00
16 Jaylen Brown 6.00 15.00
17 Zach LaVine 5.00 12.00
18 Kyrie Irving 6.00 15.00
19 Trae Young 6.00 15.00
20 Jalen Green 5.00 12.00

2023-24 Panini Origins Photo Variations
5 Stephen Curry 15.00 40.00
10 Jayson Tatum 8.00 20.00
12 LeBron James 15.00 40.00
17 Scoot Henderson 6.00 15.00
22 Nikola Jokic 8.00 20.00
34 Anthony Black 5.00 12.00
70 Bilal Coulibaly 5.00 12.00
75 Ausar Thompson 5.00 12.00
84 Gradey Dick 4.00 10.00
86 Victor Wembanyama 60.00 150.00
88 Cason Wallace 4.00 10.00
89 Brandon Miller 8.00 20.00
90 Luka Doncic 12.00 30.00
99 Amen Thompson 10.00 25.00
100 Jordan Hawkins 3.00 8.00

2023-24 Panini Origins Rookie Autographs
*RED/99: .5X TO 1.2X BASIC
*BLUE/49: .6X TO 1.5X BASIC
*PINK/25: .75X TO 2X BASIC
2 Amen Thompson 40.00 100.00
3 Bilal Coulibaly 20.00 50.00
5 GG Jackson II 15.00 40.00
6 Cason Wallace 15.00 40.00
7 Dariq Whitehead 10.00 25.00
8 Ben Sheppard 8.00 20.00
9 Maxwell Lewis 6.00 15.00
10 Ausar Thompson 20.00 50.00
11 Sidy Cissoko 8.00 20.00
13 Kobe Brown 6.00 15.00
14 Mouhamed Gueye 6.00 15.00
15 Julian Phillips 8.00 20.00
16 Keyontae Johnson 8.00 20.00
17 Mike Miles Jr. 6.00 15.00
18 Colby Jones 8.00 20.00
19 Marcus Sasser 12.00 30.00
20 Seth Lundy 6.00 15.00
21 Brandin Podziemski 20.00 50.00
22 Olivier-Maxence Prosper 8.00 20.00
23 Jalen Wilson 8.00 20.00
24 Rayan Rupert 8.00 20.00
25 Jordan Walsh 8.00 20.00
26 Markquis Nowell 8.00 20.00
27 Dereck Lively II 15.00 40.00
28 Trayce Jackson-Davis 10.00 25.00
29 Hunter Tyson 8.00 20.00
30 Andre Jackson Jr. 12.00 30.00
31 Keyonte George 25.00 60.00
32 Kobe Bufkin 10.00 25.00
33 James Nnaji 8.00 20.00
34 Brice Sensabaugh 10.00 25.00
35 Jaylen Clark 6.00 15.00
36 Jalen Pickett 6.00 15.00
37 Kris Murray 8.00 20.00
38 Toumani Camara 15.00 40.00
39 Noah Clowney 8.00 20.00

2023-24 Panini Origins Rookie Jersey Autographs
*RED/99: .5X TO 1.2X BASIC
*BLUE/49: .6X TO 1.5X BASIC
1 Amen Thompson 40.00 100.00
2 Ausar Thompson 20.00 50.00
3 Keyonte George 25.00 60.00
4 Bilal Coulibaly 20.00 50.00
5 Cason Wallace 15.00 40.00
6 Dereck Lively II 15.00 40.00
7 Kobe Bufkin 10.00 25.00
8 Brandin Podziemski 25.00 60.00
9 Noah Clowney 10.00 25.00
10 Dariq Whitehead 10.00 25.00
11 Kris Murray 8.00 20.00
12 Olivier-Maxence Prosper 8.00 20.00
13 Marcus Sasser 12.00 30.00
14 Julian Strawther 10.00 25.00
15 Ben Sheppard 8.00 20.00
16 Brice Sensabaugh 12.00 30.00
17 Kobe Brown 8.00 20.00
18 James Nnaji 6.00 15.00
19 Jalen Pickett 6.00 15.00
21 Colby Jones 8.00 20.00
22 Maxwell Lewis 6.00 15.00
23 Tristan Vukcevic 8.00 20.00
24 Rayan Rupert 8.00 20.00
25 Sidy Cissoko 8.00 20.00
26 GG Jackson II 15.00 40.00
28 Mike Miles Jr. 6.00 15.00
29 Keyontae Johnson 8.00 20.00
30 Jalen Wilson 8.00 20.00
32 Jalen Slawson 8.00 20.00
33 Isaiah Wong 8.00 20.00
34 Trayce Jackson-Davis 10.00 25.00
35 Toumani Camara 15.00 40.00
36 Jordan Walsh 8.00 20.00
37 Chris Livingston 8.00 20.00
38 Markquis Nowell 8.00 20.00
39 Andre Jackson Jr. 12.00 30.00
40 Hunter Tyson 8.00 20.00

2023-24 Panini Origins Rookie Jumbo Jerseys
*RED/49: .75X TO 2X BASIC
1 Nick Smith Jr. 3.00 8.00
2 Maxwell Lewis 2.00 5.00
3 Olivier-Maxence Prosper 2.50 6.00
4 Dariq Whitehead 3.00 8.00
5 GG Jackson II 5.00 12.00
6 Ausar Thompson 6.00 15.00
7 Kobe Brown 2.50 6.00
8 Amen Thompson 12.00 30.00
9 Jalen Pickett 2.00 5.00
10 Jett Howard 3.00 8.00
11 Cason Wallace 5.00 12.00
12 Cam Whitmore 6.00 15.00
13 Kobe Bufkin 3.00 8.00
14 Bilal Coulibaly 6.00 15.00
15 Jordan Hawkins 4.00 10.00
16 Gradey Dick 5.00 12.00
17 Jarace Walker 5.00 12.00
18 Scoot Henderson 8.00 20.00
19 Kris Murray 2.50 6.00
20 Andre Jackson Jr. 4.00 10.00
21 Brice Sensabaugh 4.00 10.00
22 James Nnaji 2.00 5.00
23 Brandin Podziemski 8.00 20.00
24 Jordan Walsh 2.50 6.00
25 Marcus Sasser 4.00 10.00
26 Julian Phillips 2.50 6.00
27 Colby Jones 2.50 6.00
28 Keyonte George 8.00 20.00
29 Victor Wembanyama 60.00 150.00
30 Brandon Miller 10.00 25.00
31 Ben Sheppard 2.50 6.00
32 Leonard Miller 2.50 6.00
33 Anthony Black 5.00 12.00
34 Taylor Hendricks 2.50 6.00
35 Noah Clowney 3.00 8.00
36 Dereck Lively II 5.00 12.00
37 Jaime Jaquez Jr. 4.00 10.00
38 Jalen Hood-Schifino 2.50 6.00
39 Julian Strawther 3.00 8.00
40 Hunter Tyson 2.50 6.00

2023-24 Panini Origins Roots of Greatness
1 Kyrie Irving
Luka Doncic 10.00 25.00
2 Anthony Davis
LeBron James 12.00 30.00
3 Jaylen Brown
Jayson Tatum 6.00 15.00
4 Darius Garland
Donovan Mitchell 3.00 8.00
5 Stephen Curry
Klay Thompson 12.00 30.00
6 Karl-Anthony Towns
Anthony Edwards 8.00 20.00
7 Shai Gilgeous-Alexander
Chet Holmgren 8.00 20.00
8 Alperen Sengun
Jabari Smith Jr. 2.50 6.00
9 Zach LaVine
DeMar DeRozan 2.50 6.00
10 Devin Booker
Kevin Durant 5.00 12.00
11 Brandon Ingram
Zion Williamson 4.00 10.00
12 Joel Embiid
Tyrese Maxey 4.00 10.00
13 Damian Lillard
Giannis Antetokounmpo 10.00 25.00
14 Jimmy Butler
Bam Adebayo 2.50 6.00
15 Tyrese Haliburton
Bennedict Mathurin 3.00 8.00
16 Trae Young
Dejounte Murray 3.00 8.00
17 Paul George
Kawhi Leonard 4.00 10.00
18 Ja Morant
Jaren Jackson Jr. 5.00 12.00
19 De'Aaron Fox
Domantas Sabonis 3.00 8.00
20 Jalen Brunson
Julius Randle 3.00 8.00
21 Manu Ginobili
Tim Duncan 3.00 8.00
22 Carmelo Anthony
Allen Iverson 4.00 10.00
23 Yao Ming
Tracy McGrady 4.00 10.00
24 Steve Nash
Dirk Nowitzki 4.00 10.00
25 Shaquille O'Neal
Anfernee Hardaway 5.00 12.00

2023-24 Panini Origins Snake Eyes
1 Victor Wembanyama 1,500.00 3,000.00
2 Scoot Henderson 125.00 300.00
3 LeBron James 350.00 700.00
4 Stephen Curry 350.00 700.00
5 Ausar Thompson 100.00 250.00
6 Ja Morant 200.00 500.00
7 Luka Doncic 350.00 700.00
8 Brandon Miller 200.00 500.00
9 Jayson Tatum 150.00 400.00
10 Amen Thompson 100.00 250.00

2023-24 Panini Origins Taking the Leap
*PINK/99: 1.5X TO 4X BASIC
1 Jalen Hood-Schifino 1.00 2.50
2 Jaime Jaquez Jr. 1.50 4.00
3 Cam Whitmore 2.50 6.00
4 Gradey Dick 2.00 5.00
5 Dereck Lively II 2.00 5.00
6 Jett Howard 1.50 4.00
7 Keyonte George 3.00 8.00
8 Noah Clowney 1.25 3.00
9 Amen Thompson 5.00 12.00
10 Olivier-Maxence Prosper 1.00 2.50
11 Jordan Hawkins 1.50 4.00
12 Kobe Bufkin 1.25 3.00
13 Dariq Whitehead 1.25 3.00
14 Cason Wallace 2.00 5.00
15 Brandin Podziemski 2.50 6.00
16 Taylor Hendricks 1.00 2.50
17 Kris Murray 1.00 2.50
18 Ausar Thompson 2.50 6.00
19 Victor Wembanyama 30.00 80.00
20 Anthony Black 2.50 6.00
21 Jarace Walker 2.00 5.00
22 Bilal Coulibaly 2.50 6.00
23 Brandon Miller 4.00 10.00
24 Scoot Henderson 3.00 8.00
25 Nick Smith Jr. 1.25 3.00

2023-24 Panini Origins Taking the Leap Turquoise
*TURQUOISE: 2.5X TO 6X BASIC
STATED PRINT RUN 25 SER. #'d SETS
19 Victor Wembanyama 350.00 700.00

2023-24 Panini Origins Tiger Eyes
1 Scoot Henderson 125.00 300.00
2 LeBron James 350.00 700.00
3 Brandon Miller 200.00 500.00
4 Giannis Antetokounmpo 150.00 400.00
5 Ausar Thompson 100.00 250.00
6 Stephen Curry 350.00 700.00
7 Jayson Tatum 150.00 400.00
8 Victor Wembanyama 1,500.00 3,000.00
9 Luka Doncic 350.00 700.00
10 Amen Thompson 100.00 250.00

2023-24 Panini Origins Universal Autographs
STATED PRINT RUN 30 SER.#'d SETS
*RED/25: .4X TO 1X BASIC
1 Manu Ginobili 60.00 150.00
2 Anfernee Hardaway 75.00 200.00
3 Josh Giddey 25.00 60.00
4 Pau Gasol 40.00 100.00
5 Stephen Curry 600.00 1,200.00
7 Jason Williams 60.00 150.00
8 Lauri Markkanen 20.00 50.00
9 Luka Doncic 400.00 800.00
10 Alperen Sengun 40.00 100.00
11 Zach Randolph 12.00 30.00
12 Jaren Jackson Jr. 40.00 100.00
13 Deandre Ayton 12.00 30.00
14 Jordan Clarkson 15.00 40.00
15 Amar'e Stoudemire 15.00 40.00
16 Jalen Brunson 100.00 250.00
17 Nikola Jokic 150.00 400.00
18 Dennis Rodman 100.00 250.00
19 Marcus Smart 12.00 30.00
20 Zion Williamson 100.00 250.00

2024-25 Panini Origins
*VARIATION: .6X TO 1.5X BASIC
*RED/299: 1.25X TO 3X BASIC
*MAROON/115: 1.5X TO 4X BASIC
*BLUE/99: 1.5X TO 4X BASIC
*BASKETBALLS: 2X TO 5X BASIC
*ORANGE/75: 2X TO 5X BASIC
*PINK/60: 2X TO 5X BASIC
*WHITE/60: 2X TO 5X BASIC
*TESSELLATED: 2.5X TO 6X BASIC
*NEON STRIPES/49: 2.5X TO 6X BASIC
*NEON GREEN/25: 3X TO 8X BASIC
*TURQUOISE/25: 3X TO 8X BASIC
*PURPLE FOTL/22: 3X TO 8X BASIC
1 Anthony Davis 1.00 2.50
2 Devin Booker 1.00 2.50
3 Deandre Ayton .30 .75
4 Paolo Banchero 1.00 2.50
5 Immanuel Quickley .30 .75
6 Coby White .40 1.00
7 Chris Paul .60 1.50
8 Anthony Edwards 2.00 5.00
9 Mikal Bridges .40 1.00
10 Scottie Barnes .50 1.25
11 Jordan Poole .40 1.00
12 Zach LaVine .60 1.50
13 LaMelo Ball .75 2.00
14 Dejounte Murray .40 1.00
15 Zion Williamson 1.00 2.50
16 De'Aaron Fox .75 2.00
17 Lauri Markkanen .40 1.00
18 Luka Doncic 2.50 6.00
19 Alperen Sengun .60 1.50
20 Franz Wagner .60 1.50
21 Kyle Kuzma .30 .75
22 Tyrese Maxey .75 2.00
23 Desmond Bane .40 1.00
24 Cameron Thomas .40 1.00
25 Jaden Ivey .50 1.25
26 Darius Garland .50 1.25
27 Donovan Mitchell .75 2.00
28 James Harden .75 2.00
29 Jamal Murray .60 1.50
30 Kevin Durant 1.25 3.00
31 Harrison Barnes .30 .75
32 Draymond Green .50 1.25
33 Keyonte George .50 1.25
34 Klay Thompson 1.00 2.50
35 LeBron James 3.00 8.00
36 Trae Young .75 2.00
37 Jayson Tatum 1.25 3.00
38 Victor Wembanyama 3.00 8.00
39 Brandon Ingram .40 1.00
40 Joel Embiid .60 1.50
41 Paul George .60 1.50
42 Kyrie Irving 1.00 2.50
43 Karl-Anthony Towns .60 1.50
44 Pascal Siakam .50 1.25
45 Damian Lillard 1.00 2.50
46 Brandon Miller .60 1.50
47 Giannis Antetokounmpo 1.50 4.00
48 Jalen Johnson .50 1.25
49 RJ Barrett .50 1.25
50 Jalen Green .75 2.00
51 Bam Adebayo .50 1.25
52 Jimmy Butler III .60 1.50
53 DeMar DeRozan .50 1.25
54 Stephen Curry 3.00 8.00
55 Jaylen Brown .60 1.50
56 Julius Randle .40 1.00
57 Jalen Brunson .75 2.00
58 Kristaps Porzingis .50 1.25
59 Shai Gilgeous-Alexander 2.00 5.00
60 Cade Cunningham 1.00 2.50
61 Cameron Johnson .30 .75
62 Ja Morant 1.25 3.00
63 Domantas Sabonis .60 1.50
64 Jalen Williams .75 2.00
65 Chet Holmgren .60 1.50
66 Nikola Jokic 2.00 5.00
67 Jaren Jackson Jr. .60 1.50
68 Anfernee Simons .40 1.00
69 Kawhi Leonard .75 2.00
70 Tyrese Haliburton .75 2.00
71 Jaylon Tyson RC .75 2.00
72 Yves Missi RC 2.00 5.00
73 Alexandre Sarr RC 2.50 6.00
74 Bub Carrington RC 2.00 5.00
75 Stephon Castle RC 5.00 12.00
76 Rob Dillingham RC 2.00 5.00
77 Kyshawn George RC 1.25 3.00
78 Jared McCain RC 3.00 8.00
79 Cody Williams RC 1.00 2.50
80 Baylor Scheierman RC 1.00 2.50
81 Kel'el Ware RC 2.00 5.00
82 Reed Sheppard RC 2.50 6.00
83 Isaiah Collier RC 1.50 4.00
84 AJ Johnson RC 1.50 4.00
85 Pacome Dadiet RC 1.00 2.50
86 Matas Buzelis RC 4.00 10.00
87 Donovan Clingan RC 2.00 5.00
88 Nikola Topic RC 2.50 6.00
89 Ron Holland II RC 1.50 4.00
90 Ja'Kobe Walter RC 1.00 2.50
91 Tristan da Silva RC 2.00 5.00
92 Terrence Shannon Jr. RC 1.50 4.00
93 Dillon Jones RC .75 2.00
94 Zaccharie Risacher RC 2.50 6.00
95 Tidjane Salaun RC .75 2.00
96 Dalton Knecht RC 2.50 6.00
97 Jaylen Wells RC 2.50 6.00
98 Bronny James Jr. RC 2.50 6.00
99 Devin Carter RC 1.00 2.50
100 Zach Edey RC 2.50 6.00

2024-25 Panini Origins Big Bang
1 Stephen Curry 60.00 150.00
2 Victor Wembanyama 60.00 150.00
3 Cody Williams 10.00 25.00
4 Bub Carrington 20.00 50.00
5 Jayson Tatum 25.00 60.00
6 Giannis Antetokounmpo 30.00 80.00
7 LeBron James 60.00 150.00
8 Luka Doncic 50.00 125.00
9 Paolo Banchero 20.00 50.00
10 Trae Young 15.00 40.00
11 Rob Dillingham 20.00 50.00
12 Kevin Durant 25.00 60.00
13 Ja Morant 25.00 60.00
14 Ron Holland II 15.00 40.00
15 Nikola Jokic 40.00 100.00

2024-25 Panini Origins Black Snake Eyes
1 Jayson Tatum 200.00 500.00
2 Anthony Edwards 300.00 600.00
3 Luka Doncic 300.00 600.00
4 Alexandre Sarr 150.00 400.00
5 LeBron James 400.00 800.00
6 Stephen Curry 400.00 800.00
7 Victor Wembanyama 400.00 800.00
8 Dalton Knecht 125.00 300.00
9 Matas Buzelis 150.00 400.00
10 Reed Sheppard 150.00 400.00

2024-25 Panini Origins Blue Moon Signatures
STATED PRINT RUN 25 SER.#'d SETS
1 Al Horford 20.00 50.00
1 Jaden Ivey 25.00 60.00
2 Jalen Johnson 25.00 60.00
3 Khris Middleton 20.00 50.00
3 Pau Gasol 50.00 120.00
4 RJ Barrett 25.00 60.00
4 Keegan Murray 15.00 40.00
5 Trae Young 75.00 200.00
8 Cade Cunningham 125.00 300.00
9 Jalen Duren 20.00 50.00
10 Ausar Thompson 30.00 80.00
11 GG Jackson II 20.00 50.00
12 Keyonte George 25.00 60.00
13 Rudy Gobert 20.00 50.00
14 Trayce Jackson-Davis 20.00 50.00
15 Aaron Gordon 20.00 50.00
17 CJ McCollum 15.00 40.00
20 Gary Payton 30.00 80.00
21 Donte DiVincenzo 20.00 50.00
22 Bennedict Mathurin 25.00 60.00
23 Zach LaVine 40.00 100.00
24 Clint Capela 15.00 40.00
25 Zach Randolph 15.00 40.00
26 Bobby Portis 15.00 40.00
29 Jermaine O'Neal 15.00 40.00
30 Robert Horry 20.00 50.00
31 Arvydas Sabonis 20.00 50.00
32 Yuta Tabuse 25.00 60.00
34 Muggsy Bogues 25.00 60.00

2024-25 Panini Origins Constellations Signatures
STATED PRINT RUN 25 SER.#'d SETS
1 Shaquille O'Neal 150.00 400.00
1 Franz Wagner 30.00 80.00
2 Fred VanVleet 20.00 50.00
3 Jeremy Lin 75.00 200.00
5 Jamal Crawford 20.00 50.00
6 Jabari Smith Jr. 20.00 50.00
7 Michael Porter Jr. 20.00 50.00
8 Jalen Duren 20.00 50.00
9 Amen Thompson 100.00 250.00
10 Bogdan Bogdanovic 15.00 40.00
12 Metta World Peace 20.00 50.00
13 Desmond Bane 20.00 50.00
14 Gabe Vincent 12.00 30.00
15 De'Aaron Fox 60.00 150.00
16 Bradley Beal 25.00 60.00
18 Isiah Thomas 30.00 80.00
19 Deandre Ayton 15.00 40.00
21 Josh Giddey 40.00 100.00
22 Devin Vassell 25.00 60.00
23 Bennedict Mathurin 25.00 60.00
24 Tayshaun Prince 25.00 60.00
26 Yuta Watanabe 20.00 50.00
27 Jonas Valanciunas 15.00 40.00
28 Joe Dumars 25.00 60.00
29 Jakob Poeltl 15.00 40.00
30 Josh Hart 15.00 40.00
33 Jarred Vanderbilt 15.00 40.00
35 Zydrunas Ilgauskas 15.00 40.00

2024-25 Panini Origins Cosmic Storm
*RED/75: 1.5X TO 4X BASIC
*TURQUOISE/25: 2.5X TO 6X BASIC
1 Ja Morant 2.50 6.00
2 Trae Young 1.50 4.00
3 Kyrie Irving 2.00 5.00
4 Giannis Antetokounmpo 3.00 8.00
5 Paolo Banchero 2.00 5.00
6 Dalton Knecht 2.50 6.00
7 Stephon Castle 5.00 12.00
8 Zion Williamson 2.00 5.00
9 Reed Sheppard 2.50 6.00
10 Zaccharie Risacher 2.50 6.00
11 Jayson Tatum 2.50 6.00
12 Nikola Jokic 4.00 10.00
13 Anthony Edwards 4.00 10.00
14 LeBron James 6.00 15.00
15 Victor Wembanyama 6.00 15.00
16 Damian Lillard 2.00 5.00
17 Bronny James Jr. 2.50 6.00
18 Luka Doncic 5.00 12.00
19 Devin Booker 2.00 5.00
20 Donovan Clingan 2.00 5.00
21 Alexandre Sarr 2.50 6.00
22 Kevin Durant 2.50 6.00
23 Tyrese Haliburton 1.50 4.00
24 Stephen Curry 6.00 15.00
25 Shai Gilgeous-Alexander 4.00 10.00

2024-25 Panini Origins Dawn
*RED/75: 1.5X TO 4X BASIC
*TURQUOISE/25: 2.5X TO 6X BASIC
1 Jared McCain 3.00 8.00
2 Devin Carter 1.00 2.50
3 Jaylen Wells 2.50 6.00
4 Isaiah Collier 1.50 4.00
5 Zach Edey 2.50 6.00
6 Matas Buzelis 4.00 10.00
7 Stephon Castle 5.00 12.00
8 Pacome Dadiet 1.00 2.50
9 Kyshawn George 1.25 3.00
10 Tyler Kolek 1.25 3.00
11 Donovan Clingan 2.00 5.00
12 Bronny James Jr. 2.50 6.00
13 Cody Williams 1.00 2.50
14 Alexandre Sarr 2.50 6.00
15 Tidjane Salaun .75 2.00
16 Bub Carrington 2.00 5.00
17 Zaccharie Risacher 2.50 6.00
18 Dalton Knecht 2.50 6.00
19 Ja'Kobe Walter 1.00 2.50
20 Terrence Shannon Jr. 1.50 4.00
21 Tristan da Silva 2.00 5.00
22 Rob Dillingham 2.00 5.00
23 Reed Sheppard 2.50 6.00
24 Yves Missi 2.00 5.00
25 Ron Holland II 1.50 4.00

2024-25 Panini Origins Dual Signatures Purple FOTL
STATED PRINT RUN 18 SER.#'d SETS
1 Donovan Mitchell
De'Aaron Fox 150.00 400.00
2 Rasheed Wallace
Ben Wallace 150.00 400.00
3 Dirk Nowitzki
Jason Kidd 200.00 500.00
4 Amar'e Stoudemire
Steve Nash 200.00 500.00
5 Alonzo Mourning
Tim Hardaway 125.00 300.00
6 Zach Edey
Tidjane Salaun 75.00 200.00
7 Reed Sheppard
Matas Buzelis 150.00 400.00
8 Devin Carter
Bub Carrington 125.00 300.00
9 Ja'Kobe Walter
Dalton Knecht 125.00 300.00
10 Donovan Clingan
Zach Edey 125.00 300.00

2024-25 Panini Origins Elevation Signatures
PRINT RUNS B/WN 25-175 COPIES PER
*RED/49: .6X TO 1.5X p/r 125-175
*RED/49: .5X TO 1.2X p/r 75
*PINK/15-25: .75X TO 2X p/r 125-175
*PINK/15-25: .6X TO 1.5X p/r 75
*PINK/15-25: .5X TO 1.2X p/r 49
*PINK/15-25: .4X TO 1X p/r 25
1 Matas Buzelis/75 60.00 150.00
1 Pacome Dadiet 12.00 30.00
2 Dalton Knecht/75 40.00 100.00
3 Ja'Kobe Walter/75 15.00 40.00
4 Bub Carrington/75 30.00 80.00
5 Reed Sheppard/75 40.00 100.00
6 Tristan da Silva/125 25.00 60.00
7 Yves Missi/150 25.00 60.00
8 Zach Edey/125 30.00 80.00
9 Jared McCain/75 50.00 125.00
10 Tidjane Salaun/125 10.00 25.00
11 Devin Carter/150 12.00 30.00
12 Jaylon Tyson/150 10.00 25.00
13 Donovan Clingan/75 30.00 80.00
14 Tristen Newton/175 10.00 25.00
15 AJ Johnson/150 20.00 50.00
16 Kyshawn George/150 15.00 40.00
19 Jonathan Mogbo/175 15.00 40.00
20 Tyler Kolek/150 15.00 40.00
21 Johnny Furphy/150 15.00 40.00
22 Cam Christie/175 12.00 30.00
23 Ajay Mitchell/175 15.00 40.00
24 Jaylen Wells/175 30.00 80.00
25 Oso Ighodaro/175 12.00 30.00
26 Adem Bona/150 12.00 30.00
27 KJ Simpson Jr./175 10.00 25.00
28 Pelle Larsson/175 12.00 30.00
29 Jamal Shead/175 12.00 30.00
30 Antonio Reeves/175 10.00 25.00
31 Tyrese Maxey/49 30.00 80.00
32 Lauri Markkanen/49 15.00 40.00
33 John Stockton/25 40.00 100.00
34 Ja Morant/25 400.00 800.00
35 Anfernee Simons/49 15.00 40.00
36 Shawn Kemp/49 25.00 60.00
37 Zach LaVine/25 30.00 80.00
38 Shai Gilgeous-Alexander/25 500.00 1,000.00
39 Paolo Banchero /49 125.00 300.00
40 Magic Johnson/25 125.00 300.00

2024-25 Panini Origins Euphoria
*MAROON/115: 1.25X TO 3X BASIC
*PINK/99: 1.5X TO 4X BASIC
*TURQUOISE/25: 2.5X TO 6X BASIC
1 Dalton Knecht 2.50 6.00
2 Jaylen Brown 1.25 3.00
3 Tyrese Haliburton 1.50 4.00
4 Paolo Banchero 2.00 5.00
5 Anthony Edwards 4.00 10.00
6 Stephen Curry 6.00 15.00
7 Ja Morant 2.50 6.00
8 Nikola Jokic 4.00 10.00
9 Damian Lillard 2.00 5.00
10 Shai Gilgeous-Alexander 4.00 10.00
11 Alexandre Sarr 2.50 6.00
12 Stephon Castle 5.00 12.00
13 Trae Young 1.50 4.00
14 Zaccharie Risacher 2.50 6.00
15 Jayson Tatum 2.50 6.00
16 Kevin Durant 2.50 6.00
17 Anthony Davis 2.00 5.00
18 Donovan Clingan 2.00 5.00
19 Luka Doncic 5.00 12.00
20 LeBron James 6.00 15.00
21 Reed Sheppard 2.50 6.00
22 Giannis Antetokounmpo 3.00 8.00
23 Matas Buzelis 4.00 10.00
24 Bronny James Jr. 2.50 6.00
25 Victor Wembanyama 6.00 15.00

2024-25 Panini Origins Meteor Shower
*MAROON/115: 1.25X TO 3X BASIC
*PINK/99: 1.5X TO 4X BASIC
*TURQUOISE/25: 2.5X TO 6X BASIC
1 Shai Gilgeous-Alexander 4.00 10.00
2 Zaccharie Risacher 2.50 6.00
3 Luka Doncic 5.00 12.00
4 Stephen Curry 6.00 15.00
5 De'Aaron Fox 1.50 4.00
6 Reed Sheppard 2.50 6.00
7 Jalen Brunson 1.50 4.00
8 Kevin Durant 2.50 6.00
9 Anthony Edwards 4.00 10.00
10 Alexandre Sarr 2.50 6.00
11 Donovan Mitchell 1.50 4.00
12 Dalton Knecht 2.50 6.00
13 Tyrese Maxey 1.50 4.00
14 Nikola Jokic 4.00 10.00
15 Devin Booker 2.00 5.00
16 Victor Wembanyama 6.00 15.00
17 Ron Holland II 1.50 4.00
18 Kyrie Irving 2.00 5.00
19 Rob Dillingham 2.00 5.00
20 LeBron James 6.00 15.00
21 Jayson Tatum 2.50 6.00
22 Giannis Antetokounmpo 3.00 8.00
23 Zion Williamson 2.00 5.00
24 Bronny James Jr. 2.50 6.00
25 Donovan Clingan 2.00 5.00

2024-25 Panini Origins Nucleus
*MAROON/115: 1.25X TO 3X BASIC
*PINK/99: 1.5X TO 4X BASIC
*TURQUOISE/25: 2.5X TO 6X BASIC
1 Joel Embiid
Paul George
Tyrese Maxey 1.50 4.00
2 Donovan Clingan
Anfernee Simons
Deandre Ayton 2.00 5.00
3 Giannis Antetokounmpo
Khris Middleton
Damian Lillard 3.00 8.00
4 Matas Buzelis
Zach LaVine
Coby White 4.00 10.00
5 Kristaps Porzingis
Jaylen Brown
Jayson Tatum 2.50 6.00
6 Jaren Jackson Jr.
Zach Edey
Ja Morant 2.50 6.00
7 Trae Young
Zaccharie Risacher
Jalen Johnson 2.50 6.00
8 Tyler Herro
Bam Adebayo
Jimmy Butler III 1.25 3.00
9 Domantas Sabonis
De'Aaron Fox
DeMar DeRozan 1.50 4.00
10 Karl-Anthony Towns
Mikal Bridges
Jalen Brunson 1.50 4.00
11 Anthony Davis
LeBron James
Bronny James Jr. 6.00 15.00
12 Paolo Banchero
Tristan da Silva
Franz Wagner 2.00 5.00
13 Kyrie Irving
Luka Doncic
Klay Thompson 5.00 12.00
14 Nikola Jokic
Jamal Murray
Michael Porter Jr. 4.00 10.00
15 Dejounte Murray
Zion Williamson
Brandon Ingram 2.00 5.00
16 Jalen Green
Reed Sheppard
Alperen Sengun 2.50 6.00
17 Victor Wembanyama

Chris Paul
Stephon Castle 6.00 15.00
18 Kevin Durant
Bradley Beal
Devin Booker 2.50 6.00
19 Jalen Williams
Shai Gilgeous-Alexander
Chet Holmgren 4.00 10.00
20 Jordan Poole
Alexandre Sarr
Bub Carrington 2.50 6.00
21 Rob Dillingham
Anthony Edwards
Julius Randle 4.00 10.00
22 Tim Duncan
Victor Wembanyama
David Robinson 6.00 15.00
23 Chris Bosh
Dwyane Wade
LeBron James 6.00 15.00
24 Russell Westbrook
James Harden
Kevin Durant 2.50 6.00
25 Klay Thompson
Stephen Curry
Kevin Durant 6.00 15.00

2024-25 Panini Origins Origin Stories

1 DeMar DeRozan 1.00 2.50
2 De'Aaron Fox 1.50 4.00
3 Jalen Brunson 1.50 4.00
4 Stephen Curry 6.00 15.00
5 Luka Doncic 5.00 12.00
6 Kevin Durant 2.50 6.00
7 Jimmy Butler III 1.25 3.00
8 Paul George 1.25 3.00
9 Damian Lillard 2.00 5.00
10 Zach LaVine 1.25 3.00
11 James Harden 1.50 4.00
12 Zion Williamson 2.00 5.00
13 Anthony Edwards 4.00 10.00
14 Kyrie Irving 2.00 5.00
15 Joel Embiid 1.25 3.00
16 LeBron James 6.00 15.00
17 Julius Randle .75 2.00
18 Ja Morant 2.50 6.00
19 Jayson Tatum 2.50 6.00
20 Trae Young 1.50 4.00
21 Victor Wembanyama 6.00 15.00
22 Kawhi Leonard 1.50 4.00
23 Tyrese Haliburton 1.50 4.00
24 Nikola Jokic 4.00 10.00
25 Anthony Davis 2.00 5.00

2024-25 Panini Origins Originals

*RED/75: 1.5X TO 4X BASIC
*TURQUOISE/25: 2.5X TO 6X BASIC
1 Tristan da Silva 2.00 5.00
2 Zaccharie Risacher 2.50 6.00
3 Matas Buzelis 4.00 10.00
4 Tidjane Salaun .75 2.00
5 Dillon Jones .75 2.00
6 Stephon Castle 5.00 12.00
7 Ron Holland II 1.50 4.00
8 Reed Sheppard 2.50 6.00
9 Jared McCain 3.00 8.00
10 Bub Carrington 2.00 5.00
11 Nikola Topic 2.50 6.00
12 Alexandre Sarr 2.50 6.00
13 Ryan Dunn 1.00 2.50
14 Dalton Knecht 2.50 6.00
15 Donovan Clingan 2.00 5.00
16 Rob Dillingham 2.00 5.00
17 AJ Johnson 1.50 4.00
18 Kel'el Ware 2.00 5.00
19 Bronny James Jr. 2.50 6.00
20 Baylor Scheierman 1.00 2.50
21 Ja'Kobe Walter 1.00 2.50
22 Jaylon Tyson .75 2.00
23 Johnny Furphy 1.25 3.00
24 Zach Edey 2.50 6.00
25 Cody Williams 1.00 2.50

2024-25 Panini Origins Origination Memorabilia

*RED/49: .6X TO 1.5X BASIC
*PINK/25: .75X TO 2X BASIC
1 Jayson Tatum 10.00 25.00
2 Joel Embiid 5.00 12.00
3 Devin Booker 8.00 20.00
4 LeBron James 25.00 60.00
5 Kawhi Leonard 6.00 15.00
6 Victor Wembanyama 25.00 60.00
7 Jaylen Brown 5.00 12.00
8 Jimmy Butler III 5.00 12.00
9 Klay Thompson 8.00 20.00
10 Stephon Castle 20.00 50.00
11 Rob Dillingham 8.00 20.00
12 DeMar DeRozan 4.00 10.00
13 Derrick Rose 8.00 20.00
14 Reed Sheppard 10.00 25.00
15 Ron Holland II 6.00 15.00
16 Matas Buzelis 15.00 40.00
17 Cody Williams 4.00 10.00
18 Bronny James Jr. 10.00 25.00
19 Alexandre Sarr 10.00 25.00
20 Zaccharie Risacher 10.00 25.00

2024-25 Panini Origins Provenance Autographs

STATED PRINT RUN 15-25 SER.#'d SETS
*PURPLE FOTL/18: .4X TO 1X BASE
1 Russell Westbrook/15 75.00 200.00
2 Anthony Davis/15 75.00 200.00
3 Carmelo Anthony/15 100.00 250.00
4 Paul George/15 100.00 250.00
5 Donovan Mitchell/15 75.00 200.00
6 Ben Simmons/25 20.00 50.00
7 Tracy McGrady/15 125.00 300.00
8 Ray Allen/25 75.00 200.00
9 Paul Pierce/25 50.00 120.00
10 Shai Gilgeous-Alexander/15 500.00 1,000.00
11 Grant Hill/25 30.00 80.00
12 Kristaps Porzingis/25 25.00 60.00
13 DeMarcus Cousins/25 15.00 40.00
14 Tony Parker/25 30.00 80.00
15 Dwyane Wade/15 75.00 200.00
16 Kevin Garnett/25 100.00 250.00
17 Brandon Roy/25 30.00 80.00
18 Giannis Antetokounmpo/15 300.00 600.00
19 Luka Doncic/15 400.00 1,000.00
20 Stephen Curry/15 800.00 1,500.00

2024-25 Panini Origins Rookie Autographs

*RED/99: .4X TO 1X BASE
*BLUE/49: .6X TO 1.5X BASE
*PINK/25: .75X TO 2X BASE
*PURPLE FOTL/13-18: .75X TO 2X BASE
1 Quinten Post 20.00 50.00
2 Reed Sheppard 30.00 80.00
2 Pacome Dadiet 12.00 30.00
2 Jared McCain 40.00 100.00
3 DaRon Holmes II 12.00 30.00
4 Terrence Shannon Jr. 20.00 50.00
5 Tyler Kolek 15.00 40.00
6 Johnny Furphy 15.00 40.00
7 Bobi Klintman 12.00 30.00
8 Dalton Knecht 30.00 80.00
9 Oso Ighodaro 12.00 30.00
10 Jaylen Wells 30.00 80.00
11 Tidjane Salaun 10.00 25.00
12 Adem Bona 12.00 30.00
13 KJ Simpson Jr. 10.00 25.00
15 Tristan da Silva 25.00 60.00
16 Pelle Larsson 12.00 30.00
17 Jamal Shead 12.00 30.00
18 Donovan Clingan 25.00 60.00
19 AJ Johnson 20.00 50.00
20 Cam Christie 12.00 30.00
21 Harrison Ingram 10.00 25.00
22 Ja'Kobe Walter 12.00 30.00
23 Tristen Newton 10.00 25.00
24 Ajay Mitchell 15.00 40.00
25 Zach Edey 30.00 80.00
26 Melvin Ajinca 8.00 20.00
27 Jonathan Mogbo 15.00 40.00
28 Kyshawn George 15.00 40.00
29 Kevin McCullar Jr. 10.00 25.00
30 Matas Buzelis 50.00 125.00
31 Dillon Jones 10.00 25.00
32 Jalen Bridges 8.00 20.00
33 Jaylon Tyson 10.00 25.00
34 Trey Alexander 8.00 20.00
35 Devin Carter 12.00 30.00
37 Yves Missi 25.00 60.00
39 Trentyn Flowers 8.00 20.00
40 Bub Carrington 25.00 60.00

2024-25 Panini Origins Rookie Jersey Autographs

*RED/99: .5X TO 1.2X BASIC
*BLUE/49: .6X TO 1.5X BASIC
*TESSELLATED: .75X TO 2X BASIC
*PINK/25: .75X TO 2X BASIC
*PURPLE FOTL/18: .75X TO 2X BASIC
1 Antonio Reeves 8.00 20.00
2 Enrique Freeman 6.00 15.00
3 Judah Mintz 6.00 15.00
4 Anton Watson 6.00 15.00
5 Armando Bacot 6.00 15.00
6 Keshad Johnson 6.00 15.00
7 PJ Hall 6.00 15.00
8 Matas Buzelis 40.00 100.00
9 Devin Carter 10.00 25.00
10 Bub Carrington 20.00 50.00
11 Jared McCain 30.00 80.00
12 Dalton Knecht 25.00 60.00
13 Tristan da Silva 20.00 50.00
14 Ja'Kobe Walter 10.00 25.00
15 Jaylon Tyson 8.00 20.00
16 Jaylen Wells 25.00 60.00
17 Tyler Kolek 12.00 30.00
19 Oso Ighodaro 10.00 25.00
20 Adem Bona 10.00 25.00
21 Tidjane Salaun 8.00 20.00
22 Donovan Clingan 20.00 50.00
23 Zach Edey 25.00 60.00
24 Yves Missi 20.00 50.00
25 KJ Simpson Jr. 8.00 20.00
26 Pelle Larsson 10.00 25.00
27 Jamal Shead 10.00 25.00
28 Bobi Klintman 10.00 25.00
29 Cam Christie 10.00 25.00
30 Tristen Newton 8.00 20.00
31 Ariel Hukporti 6.00 15.00
32 Ajay Mitchell 12.00 30.00
33 Ulrich Chomche 6.00 15.00
34 DaRon Holmes II 10.00 25.00
35 AJ Johnson 15.00 40.00
36 Kyshawn George 12.00 30.00
37 Pacome Dadiet 10.00 25.00
38 Baylor Scheierman 10.00 25.00
39 Jonathan Mogbo 12.00 30.00
40 Reed Sheppard 25.00 60.00

2024-25 Panini Origins Rookie Jumbo Jerseys

*RED/49: .6X TO 1.5X BASIC
*PINK/25: .75X TO 2X BASIC
1 Rob Dillingham 5.00 12.00
2 Kel'el Ware 5.00 12.00
3 Reed Sheppard 6.00 15.00
4 Cody Williams 2.50 6.00
5 Tidjane Salaun 2.00 5.00
6 Jared McCain 8.00 20.00
7 Zaccharie Risacher 6.00 15.00
8 Dalton Knecht 6.00 15.00
9 Donovan Clingan 5.00 12.00
10 Bronny James Jr. 6.00 15.00
11 Zach Edey 6.00 15.00
12 Nikola Topic 6.00 15.00
13 Tristan da Silva 5.00 12.00
14 Matas Buzelis 10.00 25.00
15 Isaiah Collier 4.00 10.00
16 Alexandre Sarr 6.00 15.00
17 Ja'Kobe Walter 2.50 6.00
18 Bub Carrington 4.00 10.00
19 Stephon Castle 12.00 30.00
20 Ron Holland II 8.00 20.00

2024-25 Panini Origins Saber Tooth Tiger Eyes

1 Stephon Castle 300.00 600.00
2 Donovan Clingan 125.00 300.00
3 LeBron James 400.00 800.00
4 Stephen Curry 400.00 800.00
5 Shai Gilgeous-Alexander 300.00 600.00
6 Jayson Tatum 200.00 500.00
7 Victor Wembanyama 400.00 800.00
8 Zaccharie Risacher 125.00 300.00
9 Luka Doncic 300.00 600.00
10 Bronny James Jr. 125.00 300.00

2024-25 Panini Origins Snake Eyes

1 Jayson Tatum 200.00 500.00
2 Anthony Edwards 300.00 600.00
3 Luka Doncic 300.00 600.00
4 Alexandre Sarr 150.00 400.00
5 LeBron James 400.00 800.00
6 Stephen Curry 400.00 800.00
7 Victor Wembanyama 400.00 800.00
8 Dalton Knecht 125.00 300.00
9 Matas Buzelis 150.00 400.00
10 Reed Sheppard 150.00 400.00

2024-25 Panini Origins Taking the Leap

*MAROON/115: 1.25X TO 3X BASIC
*PINK/99: 1.5X TO 4X BASIC
*TURQUOISE/25: 2.5X TO 6X BASIC
1 Zaccharie Risacher 2.50 6.00
2 Stephon Castle 5.00 12.00
3 Terrence Shannon Jr. 1.50 4.00
4 Jaylon Tyson .75 2.00
5 Alexandre Sarr 2.50 6.00
6 Devin Carter 1.00 2.50
7 Nikola Topic 2.50 6.00
8 Ron Holland II 1.50 4.00
9 Jared McCain 3.00 8.00
10 Dalton Knecht 2.50 6.00
11 Yves Missi 2.00 5.00
12 Bub Carrington 2.00 5.00
13 Tristan da Silva 2.00 5.00
14 Reed Sheppard 2.50 6.00
15 Kyshawn George 1.25 3.00
16 Bronny James Jr. 2.50 6.00
17 Tidjane Salaun .75 2.00
18 Donovan Clingan 2.00 5.00
19 Cody Williams 1.00 2.50
20 Matas Buzelis 4.00 10.00
21 AJ Johnson 1.50 4.00
22 Kel'el Ware 2.00 5.00
23 Rob Dillingham 2.00 5.00
24 Zach Edey 2.50 6.00
25 Ja'Kobe Walter 1.00 2.50

2024-25 Panini Origins Tiger Eyes

1 Stephon Castle 300.00 600.00
2 Donovan Clingan 125.00 300.00
3 LeBron James 400.00 800.00
4 Stephen Curry 400.00 800.00
5 Shai Gilgeous-Alexander 300.00 600.00
6 Jayson Tatum 200.00 500.00
7 Victor Wembanyama 400.00 800.00
8 Zaccharie Risacher 125.00 300.00
9 Luka Doncic 300.00 600.00
10 Bronny James Jr. 125.00 300.00

2024-25 Panini Origins Universal Autographs

STATED PRINT RUN 30 SER.#'d SETS
*TESSELLATED: .4X TO 1X BASE
*RED/25: .4X TO 1X BASE
*PURPLE FOTL/18: .4X TO 1X BASE
1 Chet Holmgren 100.00 250.00
2 Trae Young 75.00 200.00
3 Larry Bird 125.00 300.00
4 Nikola Jokic 200.00 500.00
7 Gilbert Arenas 20.00 50.00
8 Julius Erving 75.00 200.00
9 David Robinson 50.00 120.00
10 Carmelo Anthony 125.00 300.00
11 Alperen Sengun 30.00 80.00
12 Stephen Curry 800.00 1,500.00
13 Anthony Davis 75.00 200.00
14 Hakeem Olajuwon 60.00 150.00
15 Yao Ming 150.00 400.00
16 Anthony Edwards 300.00 600.00
17 Dominique Wilkins 30.00 80.00
18 Manu Ginobili 60.00 150.00
19 Paolo Banchero 125.00 300.00
20 Allen Iverson 100.00 250.00

2023 Panini Origins WNBA

*RED: .5X TO 1.2X BASIC
*RAINBOW: 1.5X TO 4X BASIC
*BLUE/75: 2X TO 5X BASIC
*TEAL/35: 2.5X TO 6X BASIC
1 Kahleah Copper 1.25 3.00
2 Isabelle Harrison .75 2.00
3 Michaela Onyenwere .75 2.00
4 Crystal Dangerfield .75 2.00
5 Lexie Brown .75 2.00
6 Sophie Cunningham 2.00 5.00
7 Dearica Hamby 1.00 2.50
8 Courtney Vandersloot 1.25 3.00
9 Shakira Austin .75 2.00
10 Nneka Ogwumike 1.25 3.00
11 Jasmine Thomas .75 2.00
12 Brianna Turner .75 2.00
13 Karlie Samuelson 1.00 2.50
14 Aerial Powers .75 2.00
15 Jewell Loyd 1.25 3.00
16 Betnijah Laney .75 2.00
17 Breanna Stewart 3.00 8.00
18 Dana Evans .75 2.00
19 Veronica Burton .75 2.00
20 Kelsey Plum 2.00 5.00
21 Kelsey Mitchell 1.50 4.00
22 Ariel Atkins 1.00 2.50
23 Tiffany Mitchell 1.00 2.50
24 Napheesa Collier 1.50 4.00
25 Erica Wheeler .75 2.00
26 Marine Johannes 2.00 5.00
27 Alanna Smith .75 2.00
28 Ari McDonald .75 2.00
29 Kalani Brown .75 2.00
30 Brittney Sykes 1.25 3.00
31 Stefanie Dolson .75 2.00
32 A'ja Wilson 3.00 8.00
33 Natasha Howard 1.00 2.50
34 Elizabeth Williams .75 2.00
35 DiJonai Carrington 1.00 2.50
36 Jordin Canada 1.00 2.50
37 Chiney Ogwumike .75 2.00
38 Diamond DeShields .75 2.00
39 Sydney Colson .75 2.00
40 Rebekah Gardner .75 2.00
41 Sabrina Ionescu 3.00 8.00
42 DeWanna Bonner 1.00 2.50
43 Jackie Young 1.25 3.00
44 Brittney Griner 2.50 6.00
45 Satou Sabally 1.50 4.00
46 Natasha Cloud 1.00 2.50
47 Alysha Clark .75 2.00
48 NaLyssa Smith 1.00 2.50
49 Jonquel Jones 1.50 4.00
50 Moriah Jefferson .75 2.00
51 Chelsea Gray 1.00 2.50
52 Kayla McBride .75 2.00
53 Rhyne Howard 1.25 3.00
54 Katie Lou Samuelson 1.25 3.00
55 Cheyenne Parker .75 2.00
56 Kia Nurse .75 2.00
57 Ezi Magbegor 1.00 2.50
58 Kayla Thornton .75 2.00
59 Diana Taurasi 3.00 8.00
60 Brionna Jones 1.00 2.50
61 Alyssa Thomas 1.25 3.00
62 Asia Durr .75 2.00
63 Allisha Gray 1.00 2.50
64 Rebecca Allen .75 2.00
65 Lexie Hull 1.50 4.00
66 Marina Mabrey 1.00 2.50
67 Courtney Williams .75 2.00
68 Tiffany Hayes .75 2.00
69 Naz Hillmon .75 2.00
70 Candace Parker 3.00 8.00
71 Odyssey Sims .75 2.00
72 Arike Ogunbowale 1.25 3.00
73 Kristy Wallace .75 2.00
74 Elena Delle Donne 2.50 6.00
75 Skylar Diggins-Smith 1.25 3.00
76 Nyara Sabally .75 2.00
77 Sylvia Fowles 1.00 2.50
78 Sue Bird 3.00 8.00
79 Tamika Catchings 2.50 6.00
80 Becky Hammon 2.00 5.00
81 Lauren Jackson 2.00 5.00
82 Sheryl Swoopes 1.25 3.00
83 Cynthia Cooper-Dyke 1.25 3.00
84 Katie Smith 1.00 2.50
85 Maya Moore 2.00 5.00
86 Jackie Stiles 1.25 3.00
87 Lisa Leslie 2.00 5.00
88 Aliyah Boston RC 6.00 15.00
89 Diamond Miller 1.25 3.00
90 Maddy Siegrist 2.00 5.00
91 Stephanie Soares 1.00 2.50
92 Lou Lopez Senechal 1.25 3.00
93 Haley Jones 1.00 2.50
94 Grace Berger 1.00 2.50
95 Laeticia Amihere 1.50 4.00
96 Jordan Horston 1.50 4.00
97 Zia Cooke 1.50 4.00
98 Abby Meyers 1.00 2.50
99 Kadi Sissoko 1.00 2.50
100 Ivana Dojkic 1.00 2.50

2023 Panini Origins WNBA Aficionado

1 Nneka Ogwumike 1.50 4.00
2 Maya Moore 2.50 6.00
3 Becky Hammon 2.50 6.00
4 Diana Taurasi 4.00 10.00
5 Alyssa Thomas 1.50 4.00
6 Sheryl Swoopes 1.50 4.00
7 Cynthia Cooper-Dyke 1.50 4.00
8 Cheryl Ford 1.50 4.00
9 Elena Delle Donne 3.00 8.00
10 Candace Parker 4.00 10.00
11 Lisa Leslie 2.50 6.00
12 Ruth Riley 1.50 4.00
13 Jonquel Jones 2.00 5.00
14 Jackie Stiles 1.50 4.00
15 Chelsea Gray 1.25 3.00
16 Tamika Catchings 3.00 8.00
17 Katie Smith 1.25 3.00
18 Sue Bird 4.00 10.00
19 Sylvia Fowles 1.25 3.00
20 Jewell Loyd 1.50 4.00

2023 Panini Origins WNBA Art Nouveau Memorabilia

*RED/49: .5X TO 1.2X BASIC
*BLUE/25: 1.25X TO 3X BASIC
1 Arike Ogunbowale 3.00 8.00
2 Napheesa Collier 4.00 10.00
3 Kelsey Mitchell 4.00 10.00
4 Sabrina Ionescu 8.00 20.00
5 Aliyah Boston 8.00 20.00
6 Chelsea Gray 2.50 6.00
7 Azura Stevens 2.50 6.00
8 Sophie Cunningham 5.00 12.00
9 Sue Bird 8.00 20.00
10 Haley Jones 2.00 5.00
11 Elena Delle Donne 6.00 15.00
12 Kelsey Plum 5.00 12.00
13 Courtney Vandersloot 3.00 8.00
14 Alyssa Thomas 3.00 8.00
15 Jordin Canada 2.50 6.00
16 Candace Parker 8.00 20.00
17 Brittney Griner 6.00 15.00
18 Jewell Loyd 3.00 8.00
19 A'ja Wilson 8.00 20.00
20 Rhyne Howard 3.00 8.00
21 Nneka Ogwumike 3.00 8.00
22 DeWanna Bonner 2.50 6.00
23 Breanna Stewart 8.00 20.00
24 NaLyssa Smith 2.50 6.00
25 Dearica Hamby 2.50 6.00
26 Tiffany Hayes 2.00 5.00
27 Shey Peddy 2.00 5.00
28 Allisha Gray 2.50 6.00
29 Diana Taurasi 8.00 20.00
30 Diamond Miller 2.50 6.00
31 Skylar Diggins-Smith 3.00 8.00
32 Satou Sabally 4.00 10.00
33 Jonquel Jones 4.00 10.00
34 Natasha Howard 2.50 6.00
35 Ezi Magbegor 2.50 6.00

2023 Panini Origins WNBA Blank Slate

1 Sabrina Ionescu 125.00 300.00
2 Sue Bird 60.00 150.00
3 Maya Moore 40.00 100.00
4 Candace Parker 60.00 150.00
5 Breanna Stewart 60.00 150.00

2023 Panini Origins WNBA Drip

1 Lexie Brown 2.00 5.00
2 Kelsey Plum 5.00 12.00
3 Skylar Diggins-Smith 3.00 8.00
4 Natasha Cloud 2.50 6.00
5 A'ja Wilson 8.00 20.00
6 Sophie Cunningham 5.00 12.00
7 Tiffany Mitchell 2.50 6.00
8 Satou Sabally 4.00 10.00
9 DiJonai Carrington 2.50 6.00
10 Isabelle Harrison 2.00 5.00

2023 Panini Origins WNBA Jersey Autographs

*RED/49: .5X TO 1.2X BASIC
*BLUE/25: .6X TO 1.5X BASIC
1 Breanna Stewart 30.00 80.00
2 Satou Sabally 15.00 40.00
7 Arike Ogunbowale 12.00 30.00
8 Haley Jones 8.00 20.00
11 Jonquel Jones 15.00 40.00
12 Sabrina Ionescu 60.00 150.00
15 A'ja Wilson 75.00 200.00
16 Jewell Loyd 12.00 30.00
17 Elena Delle Donne 25.00 60.00
19 Kelsey Mitchell 40.00 100.00
22 Chelsea Gray 10.00 25.00
27 Nneka Ogwumike 12.00 30.00
29 Courtney Vandersloot 12.00 30.00
30 DeWanna Bonner 10.00 25.00

2023 Panini Origins WNBA Jumbo Jerseys

*BLUE/25: 1.25X TO 3X BASIC
1 Sue Bird 8.00 20.00
2 Haley Jones 2.00 5.00
3 Elena Delle Donne 6.00 15.00
4 Kelsey Plum 5.00 12.00
5 Courtney Vandersloot 3.00 8.00
6 Alyssa Thomas 3.00 8.00
7 Jordin Canada 2.50 6.00
9 Azura Stevens 2.50 6.00
10 Sophie Cunningham 5.00 12.00
12 Rhyne Howard 3.00 8.00
13 Skylar Diggins-Smith 3.00 8.00
15 Breanna Stewart 8.00 20.00
16 NaLyssa Smith 2.50 6.00
17 Dearica Hamby 2.50 6.00
18 Candace Parker 8.00 20.00
19 Brittney Griner 6.00 15.00
20 Jewell Loyd 3.00 8.00
21 Diana Taurasi 8.00 20.00
22 Diamond Miller 2.50 6.00
23 Nneka Ogwumike 3.00 8.00
24 Satou Sabally 4.00 10.00
25 Jonquel Jones 4.00 10.00
26 Natasha Howard 2.50 6.00
27 Ezi Magbegor 2.50 6.00
28 Tiffany Hayes 2.00 5.00
29 Shey Peddy 2.00 5.00
30 Allisha Gray 2.50 6.00
31 Arike Ogunbowale 3.00 8.00
32 Napheesa Collier 4.00 10.00
33 Kelsey Mitchell 4.00 10.00
34 Sabrina Ionescu 8.00 20.00
35 Aliyah Boston 8.00 20.00

2023 Panini Origins WNBA Legacy Signatures

*RED/49: .5X TO 1.2X BASIC
*BLUE/25: .6X TO 1.5X BASIC
1 Diana Taurasi 20.00 50.00
2 Sheryl Swoopes 8.00 20.00
3 Maya Moore 12.00 30.00
4 Lauren Jackson 12.00 30.00
5 Elena Delle Donne 15.00 40.00
6 Tamika Catchings 15.00 40.00
7 Becky Hammon 12.00 30.00
8 Lisa Leslie 12.00 30.00
9 Sue Bird 20.00 50.00
10 Nykesha Sales 5.00 12.00
11 Cynthia Cooper-Dyke 8.00 20.00
12 Deanna Nolan 5.00 12.00
13 Brittney Griner 15.00 40.00
14 Tina Charles 6.00 15.00
15 Sylvia Fowles 6.00 15.00

2023 Panini Origins WNBA Origins Autographs

*RED/49: .5X TO 1.2X BASIC
*BLUE/25: .6X TO 1.5X BASIC
1 Breanna Stewart 20.00 50.00
2 Diana Taurasi 20.00 50.00
3 Arike Ogunbowale 8.00 20.00
4 Elena Delle Donne 15.00 40.00
5 Kelsey Mitchell 25.00 60.00
6 Sue Bird 20.00 50.00
8 Deanna Nolan 5.00 12.00
9 Diamond Miller 6.00 15.00
10 Sylvia Fowles 6.00 15.00
11 Jackie Young 8.00 20.00
12 Sheryl Swoopes 8.00 20.00
13 A'ja Wilson 20.00 50.00
14 Tamika Catchings 15.00 40.00
15 Betnijah Laney 5.00 12.00
16 Nykesha Sales 5.00 12.00
18 Brittney Griner 15.00 40.00
19 Haley Jones 5.00 12.00
20 Azura Stevens 6.00 15.00
21 Skylar Diggins-Smith 8.00 20.00
22 Maya Moore 12.00 30.00
23 Jonquel Jones 10.00 25.00
24 Becky Hammon 12.00 30.00
25 Courtney Williams 5.00 12.00
26 Cynthia Cooper-Dyke 8.00 20.00
28 Tina Charles 6.00 15.00
30 Courtney Vandersloot 8.00 20.00
31 Rhyne Howard 8.00 20.00
32 Lauren Jackson 12.00 30.00
33 Becky Hammon 12.00 30.00
34 Lisa Leslie 12.00 30.00
35 Brionna Jones 6.00 15.00

2023 Panini Origins WNBA Roots of Greatness

1 Candace Parker
A'ja Wilson 8.00 20.00
2 Arike Ogunbowale
Maddy Siegrist 4.00 10.00
3 Sophie Cunningham
Diana Taurasi 8.00 20.00
4 Aliyah Boston
Kelsey Mitchell 8.00 20.00
5 Cheyenne Parker
Rhyne Howard 3.00 8.00
6 Sabrina Ionescu
Breanna Stewart 8.00 20.00
7 Jordan Horston
Jewell Loyd 3.00 8.00
8 Elena Delle Donne
Shakira Austin 6.00 15.00

2023 Panini Origins WNBA Splitting Image

1 Jonquel Jones
Breanna Stewart 4.00 10.00
2 Rhyne Howard
Allisha Gray 1.50 4.00
3 Natasha Cloud
Ariel Atkins 1.25 3.00
4 Courtney Vandersloot
Sabrina Ionescu 4.00 10.00
5 Diamond DeShields
Arike Ogunbowale 1.50 4.00
6 DeWanna Bonner
Alyssa Thomas 1.50 4.00
7 Aliyah Boston
NaLyssa Smith 4.00 10.00
8 Jackie Young
Kelsey Plum 2.50 6.00
9 Kayla McBride
Tiffany Mitchell 1.25 3.00
10 Lexie Brown
Jordin Canada 1.25 3.00
11 Chiney Ogwumike
Nneka Ogwumike 1.50 4.00
12 Kahleah Copper
Marina Mabrey 1.50 4.00
13 Katie Lou Samuelson
Karlie Samuelson 1.50 4.00
14 Erica Wheeler
Kelsey Mitchell 2.00 5.00
15 Satou Sabally
Natasha Howard 2.00 5.00

2023 Panini Origins WNBA Team Origins

1 Lauren Jackson 2.50 6.00
2 Candace Parker 4.00 10.00
3 Becky Hammon 2.50 6.00
4 Sheryl Swoopes 1.50 4.00
5 Breanna Stewart 4.00 10.00
6 Diana Taurasi 4.00 10.00
7 Sue Bird 4.00 10.00
8 Maya Moore 2.50 6.00
9 Sylvia Fowles 1.25 3.00
10 A'ja Wilson 4.00 10.00
11 Jackie Stiles 1.50 4.00
12 Elena Delle Donne 3.00 8.00

2023 Panini Origins WNBA Tiger Eyes

1 Diana Taurasi 40.00 100.00
2 A'ja Wilson 60.00 150.00
3 Elena Delle Donne 40.00 100.00
4 Breanna Stewart 50.00 120.00
5 Sabrina Ionescu 60.00 150.00
6 Brittney Griner 30.00 80.00
7 Lisa Leslie 25.00 60.00
8 Sheryl Swoopes 25.00 60.00
9 Becky Hammon 30.00 80.00
10 Aliyah Boston 50.00 120.00

2023 Panini Origins WNBA Universal Autographs

*RED/49: .5X TO 1.2X BASIC
*BLUE/25: .6X TO 1.5X BASIC
1 Becky Hammon 12.00 30.00
2 Courtney Williams 5.00 12.00
3 Nykesha Sales 5.00 12.00
5 Brittney Griner 15.00 40.00
6 Jackie Young 8.00 20.00
7 Diana Taurasi 20.00 50.00
8 Arike Ogunbowale 8.00 20.00
9 Lauren Jackson 12.00 30.00
11 Lisa Leslie 12.00 30.00
12 Brionna Jones 6.00 15.00
13 Cynthia Cooper-Dyke 8.00 20.00
14 Diamond Miller 6.00 15.00
15 Tina Charles 6.00 15.00
16 Skylar Diggins-Smith 8.00 20.00
17 Sheryl Swoopes 8.00 20.00
18 Jonquel Jones 10.00 25.00
19 Elena Delle Donne 15.00 40.00
20 Kelsey Mitchell 25.00 60.00
21 Sue Bird 20.00 50.00
23 Deanna Nolan 5.00 12.00
24 Haley Jones 5.00 12.00
25 Sylvia Fowles 6.00 15.00
26 Rhyne Howard 8.00 20.00
27 Maya Moore 12.00 30.00
28 A'ja Wilson 20.00 50.00
29 Tamika Catchings 15.00 40.00
30 Betnijah Laney 5.00 12.00
31 Azura Stevens 6.00 15.00
33 Courtney Vandersloot 8.00 20.00
35 Breanna Stewart 20.00 50.00

2023 Panini Origins WNBA Water Color

1 Cheryl Ford 1.50 4.00
2 Jewell Loyd 1.50 4.00
3 Chelsea Gray 1.25 3.00
4 Sheryl Swoopes 1.50 4.00
5 Lisa Leslie 2.50 6.00
6 Elena Delle Donne 3.00 8.00
7 Becky Hammon 2.50 6.00
8 Nneka Ogwumike 1.50 4.00
9 Katie Smith 1.25 3.00
10 Diana Taurasi 4.00 10.00
11 Maya Moore 2.50 6.00
12 Ruth Riley 1.50 4.00
13 Sue Bird 4.00 10.00
14 Sylvia Fowles 1.25 3.00
15 Candace Parker 4.00 10.00
16 Angel McCoughtry 1.25 3.00
17 Arike Ogunbowale 1.50 4.00
18 Brittney Griner 3.00 8.00
19 Tamika Catchings 3.00 8.00
20 Alyssa Thomas 1.50 4.00

2023 Panini Origins WNBA Works in Progress

1 Aliyah Boston 4.00 10.00
2 Diamond Miller 1.25 3.00
3 Zia Cooke 1.25 3.00
4 Rhyne Howard 1.50 4.00
5 Jordan Horston 1.50 4.00
6 NaLyssa Smith 1.25 3.00
7 Naz Hillmon 1.00 2.50
8 Veronica Burton 1.00 2.50
9 Maddy Siegrist 2.00 5.00
10 Rebekah Gardner 1.00 2.50
11 Shakira Austin 1.00 2.50
12 Laeticia Amihere 1.50 4.00
13 Dana Evans 1.00 2.50
14 Lexie Hull 2.00 5.00
15 Haley Jones 1.00 2.50

2024 Panini Origins WNBA

*RED/99: .5X TO 1.2X BASIC
*BLUE/75: 6X TO 1.5X BASIC
*TEAL/49: .75X TO 2X BASIC
*SWIRL: 1.25X TO 3X BASIC
*PURPLE/25: 1.25X TO 3X BASIC
1 Lauren Jackson 1.50 4.00
2 Stefanie Dolson .75 2.00
3 Aari McDonald .75 2.00
4 Jordin Canada .75 2.00
5 Courtney Vandersloot 1.00 2.50
6 Dearica Hamby 1.00 2.50
7 Cheyenne Parker-Tyus .60 1.50
8 Kelsey Plum 2.50 6.00
9 Betnijah Laney-Hamilton .75 2.00
10 Brionna Jones 1.00 2.50
11 Lexie Hull 1.50 4.00
12 Kalani Brown .60 1.50
13 Caitlin Clark RC 100.00 250.00
14 Dawn Staley 1.50 4.00
15 Lisa Leslie 1.50 4.00
16 Breanna Stewart 3.00 8.00
17 Lou Lopez Senechal .60 1.50
18 Tina Charles 1.00 2.50
19 Kamilla Cardoso RC 6.00 15.00
20 Skylar Diggins-Smith 1.25 3.00
21 Satou Sabally 1.25 3.00
22 Aerial Powers .60 1.50
23 DeWanna Bonner 1.25 3.00
24 Brittney Sykes .75 2.00
25 DiDi Richards .60 1.50
26 Julie Vanloo RC 1.50 4.00
27 Nneka Ogwumike 1.00 2.50
28 Jordan Horston .75 2.00
29 Napheesa Collier 2.50 6.00
30 Diana Taurasi 2.50 6.00
31 Maddy Siegrist .75 2.00
32 Marine Johannes 1.25 3.00
33 Ezi Magbegor 1.00 2.50
34 A'ja Wilson 3.00 8.00
35 Kahleah Copper 1.25 3.00
36 Angel Reese RC 10.00 25.00
37 Natasha Howard 1.00 2.50
38 Sophie Cunningham 2.00 5.00
39 Rhyne Howard 1.25 3.00
40 Arike Ogunbowale 1.50 4.00
41 Rae Burrell .60 1.50
42 Diamond DeShields .75 2.00
43 Sabrina Ionescu 2.50 6.00
44 Katie Lou Samuelson 1.25 3.00
45 Haley Jones .60 1.50
46 Kia Nurse .75 2.00
47 Diamond Miller .75 2.00
48 Jonquel Jones 1.50 4.00
49 Jackie Young 1.50 4.00
50 Natasha Cloud 1.00 2.50
51 Kate Martin RC 20.00 50.00
52 Kelsey Mitchell 2.00 5.00
53 Ariel Atkins 1.00 2.50
54 NaLyssa Smith .60 1.50
55 Erica Wheeler 1.00 2.50
56 Kayla McBride 1.00 2.50
57 Sue Bird 2.50 6.00
58 Zia Cooke .60 1.50
59 Isabelle Harrison .75 2.00
60 Alyssa Thomas 1.25 3.00
61 Courtney Williams 1.25 3.00
62 Dorka Juhasz 1.25 3.00
63 Aaliyah Edwards RC 1.50 4.00
64 Maya Moore 1.50 4.00
65 Karlie Samuelson .75 2.00
66 Shakira Austin .75 2.00
67 Chelsea Gray .75 2.00
68 Cameron Brink RC 10.00 25.00
69 Alysha Clark .75 2.00
70 Dana Evans .75 2.00
71 Elena Delle Donne 1.50 4.00
72 Sydney Colson .75 2.00
73 Sheryl Swoopes 1.25 3.00
74 Rickea Jackson RC 6.00 15.00
75 Chennedy Carter .60 1.50
76 Cynthia Cooper-Dyke 1.25 3.00
77 Jewell Loyd 1.25 3.00
78 Brittney Griner 2.00 5.00
79 Grace Berger .75 2.00
80 Allisha Gray 1.00 2.50
81 Tamika Catchings 1.25 3.00
82 Stephanie Soares .60 1.50
83 Aliyah Boston 2.50 6.00

84 Jacy Sheldon RC 2.50 6.00
85 Marina Mabrey 1.00 2.50
86 Lexie Brown 1.00 2.50
87 DiJonai Carrington 1.00 2.50
88 Nancy Lieberman 1.25 3.00
89 Tiffany Mitchell .60 1.50
90 Crystal Dangerfield .60 1.50
91 Alissa Pili RC 1.50 4.00
92 Nika Muhl RC 3.00 8.00
93 Celeste Taylor RC 1.50 4.00
94 Azura Stevens .60 1.50
95 Marquesha Davis RC 1.25 3.00
96 Kysre Gondrezick .75 2.00
97 Dyaisha Fair RC 1.25 3.00
98 Jaelyn Brown RC 1.25 3.00
99 Tyasha Harris .75 2.00
100 Moriah Jefferson .60 1.50

2024 Panini Origins WNBA Art Nouveau Memorabilia

*RED/49: .6X TO 1.5X BASIC
*BLUE/25: 1X TO 2.5X BASIC
1 Alyssa Thomas 3.00 8.00
2 Maddy Siegrist 2.00 5.00
3 Kalani Brown 1.50 4.00
4 Dearica Hamby 2.50 6.00
5 Nika Muhl 5.00 12.00
6 Nyara Sabally 2.00 5.00
7 Courtney Vandersloot 2.50 6.00
8 Nneka Ogwumike 2.50 6.00
9 Jordin Canada 2.00 5.00
10 Cameron Brink 20.00 50.00
11 Celeste Taylor 2.50 6.00
12 Satou Sabally 3.00 8.00
13 Aaliyah Edwards 2.50 6.00
14 Jewell Loyd 3.00 8.00
15 Dyaisha Fair 2.00 5.00
16 Marquesha Davis 2.00 5.00
17 Dorka Juhasz 3.00 8.00
18 Lexie Hull 15.00 40.00
19 Diamond Miller 2.00 5.00
20 Elena Delle Donne 4.00 10.00
21 Jacy Sheldon 4.00 10.00
22 Caitlin Clark 125.00 300.00
23 Angel Reese 20.00 50.00
24 Kelsey Plum 15.00 40.00
25 Kahleah Copper 3.00 8.00
26 Erica Wheeler 2.50 6.00
27 Dana Evans 2.00 5.00
28 Karlie Samuelson 2.00 5.00
29 Sabrina Ionescu 15.00 40.00
30 Lexie Brown 2.50 6.00

2024 Panini Origins WNBA Blank Slate

1 Caitlin Clark 1,000.00 2,000.00
2 Cameron Brink 125.00 300.00
3 Angel Reese 125.00 300.00
4 Kamilla Cardoso 60.00 150.00
5 Aliyah Boston 60.00 150.00
6 A'ja Wilson 60.00 150.00
7 Satou Sabally 60.00 150.00
8 Sabrina Ionescu 60.00 150.00
9 Kelsey Plum 75.00 200.00
10 Breanna Stewart 60.00 150.00

2024 Panini Origins WNBA Drip

*TEAL/49: 1.25X TO 3X BASIC
1 Kahleah Copper 5.00 12.00
2 Arike Ogunbowale 6.00 15.00
3 Natasha Cloud 4.00 10.00
4 Nika Muhl 8.00 20.00
5 Jewell Loyd 5.00 12.00
6 Satou Sabally 5.00 12.00
7 Sophie Cunningham 8.00 20.00
8 Isabelle Harrison 3.00 8.00
9 Skylar Diggins-Smith 5.00 12.00
10 Kelsey Plum 15.00 40.00
11 Angel Reese 10.00 25.00
12 Lexie Brown 4.00 10.00
13 Cameron Brink 25.00 60.00
14 DiJonai Carrington 4.00 10.00
15 A'ja Wilson 12.00 30.00

2024 Panini Origins WNBA Dual Autographs

STATED PRINT RUN 25 SER.#'d SETS
1 Cameron Brink
Rickea Jackson 150.00 400.00
2 Angel Reese
Kamilla Cardoso 150.00 400.00
3 Courtney Vandersloot
Marine Johannes 30.00 80.00
4 Diamond Miller
Alissa Pili 25.00 60.00
5 Skylar Diggins-Smith
Jewell Loyd 30.00 80.00
6 Breanna Stewart
Sue Bird 150.00 400.00
7 Cynthia Cooper-Dyke
Sheryl Swoopes 30.00 80.00
8 Natasha Cloud
Sophie Cunningham 100.00 250.00
9 Maya Moore
Caitlin Clark 1,000.00 2,000.00
10 DeWanna Bonner
DiJonai Carrington 30.00 80.00
11 Sue Bird
Nika Muhl 60.00 150.00
12 Arike Ogunbowale
Jacy Sheldon 40.00 100.00
13 Caitlin Clark
Aliyah Boston 1,250.00 2,500.00
14 Diana Taurasi
Brittney Griner 60.00 150.00
15 Jackie Young
A'ja Wilson 125.00 300.00

2024 Panini Origins WNBA Euphoria

*TEAL/49: 2.5X TO 6X BASIC
1 Sophie Cunningham 2.50 6.00
2 Satou Sabally 1.50 4.00
3 Jewell Loyd 1.50 4.00
4 Kelsey Plum 3.00 8.00
5 Sheryl Swoopes 1.50 4.00
6 Sabrina Ionescu 3.00 8.00
7 Diamond Miller 1.00 2.50
8 A'ja Wilson 4.00 10.00
9 Lexie Brown 1.25 3.00
10 Maya Moore 2.00 5.00
11 Brittney Griner 2.50 6.00
12 Arike Ogunbowale 2.00 5.00
13 Lisa Leslie 2.00 5.00
14 Aliyah Boston 3.00 8.00
15 Sue Bird 3.00 8.00

2024 Panini Origins WNBA Jersey Autographs

*RED/49: .5X TO 1.2X BASIC
*BLUE/25: .6X TO 1.5X BASIC
1 Natasha Cloud 10.00 25.00
2 Angel Reese 60.00 150.00
3 Jackie Young 15.00 40.00
4 Diamond Miller 8.00 20.00
5 Caitlin Clark 1,500.00 3,000.00
6 Cameron Brink 60.00 150.00
7 Kamilla Cardoso 15.00 40.00
8 Sophie Cunningham 75.00 200.00
9 Arike Ogunbowale 15.00 40.00
10 Breanna Stewart 30.00 80.00
11 Aliyah Boston 25.00 60.00
12 Elena Delle Donne 15.00 40.00
13 Alissa Pili 10.00 25.00
14 Sue Bird 25.00 60.00
15 Marine Johannes 12.00 30.00
16 A'ja Wilson 40.00 100.00
17 Nika Muhl 20.00 50.00
18 DeWanna Bonner 12.00 30.00
19 Rickea Jackson 20.00 50.00
20 Jacy Sheldon 15.00 40.00

2024 Panini Origins WNBA Jumbo Jerseys

*RED/49: .5X TO 1.2X BASIC
*BLUE/25: .6X TO 1.5X BASIC
1 Angel Reese 8.00 20.00
2 Dorka Juhasz 4.00 10.00
3 Sabrina Ionescu 8.00 20.00
4 Cameron Brink 20.00 50.00
5 Caitlin Clark 150.00 400.00
6 Diana Taurasi 8.00 20.00
7 Satou Sabally 4.00 10.00
8 Natasha Cloud 3.00 8.00
9 A'ja Wilson 10.00 25.00
10 Kamilla Cardoso 5.00 12.00
11 Haley Jones 2.00 5.00
12 DiJonai Carrington 3.00 8.00
13 Jacy Sheldon 5.00 12.00
14 Jonquel Jones 5.00 12.00
15 Dyaisha Fair 2.50 6.00
16 Marine Johannes 4.00 10.00
17 Kate Martin 25.00 60.00
18 Nika Muhl 6.00 15.00
19 Rhyne Howard 4.00 10.00
20 Sophie Cunningham 6.00 15.00
21 Katie Lou Samuelson 4.00 10.00
22 Sue Bird 8.00 20.00
23 Kelsey Plum 8.00 20.00
24 Jewell Loyd 4.00 10.00
25 Rickea Jackson 6.00 15.00
26 Arike Ogunbowale 5.00 12.00
27 Aaliyah Edwards 3.00 8.00
28 Alissa Pili 3.00 8.00
29 Marquesha Davis 2.50 6.00
30 Aliyah Boston 8.00 20.00

2024 Panini Origins WNBA Legacy Signatures

*RED/99: .5X TO 1.2X BASIC
*RED/49: .6X TO 1.5X BASIC
*BLUE/25: .75X TO 2X BASIC
1 Lisa Leslie 10.00 25.00
2 Diana Taurasi 15.00 40.00
4 Sheryl Swoopes 8.00 20.00
5 Sue Bird 15.00 40.00
6 Cynthia Cooper-Dyke 8.00 20.00
7 Tamika Catchings 8.00 20.00
8 Dawn Staley 10.00 25.00
9 Kristi Toliver 6.00 15.00
10 Shey Peddy 5.00 12.00
11 Nancy Lieberman 8.00 20.00
12 Ticha Penicheiro 6.00 15.00
13 Cheryl Miller 10.00 25.00
14 Maya Moore 10.00 25.00
15 Katie Douglas 6.00 15.00

2024 Panini Origins WNBA Origin Stories

*TEAL/49: 2.5X TO 6X BASIC
1 Skylar Diggins-Smith 1.50 4.00
2 Courtney Vandersloot 1.25 3.00
3 Erica Wheeler 1.25 3.00
4 Jewell Loyd 1.50 4.00
5 Maya Moore 2.00 5.00
6 Sue Bird 3.00 8.00
7 Tina Charles 1.25 3.00
8 Lisa Leslie 2.00 5.00
9 Breanna Stewart 4.00 10.00
10 Napheesa Collier 3.00 8.00
11 Brittney Griner 2.50 6.00
12 Elena Delle Donne 2.00 5.00
13 Kelsey Plum 3.00 8.00
14 A'ja Wilson 4.00 10.00
15 Diana Taurasi 3.00 8.00

2024 Panini Origins WNBA Origins Autographs

*RED/99: .5X TO 1.2X BASIC
*RED/49: .6X TO 1.5X BASIC
*BLUE/25: .75X TO 2X BASIC
1 A'ja Wilson 40.00 100.00
2 Maddy Siegrist 5.00 12.00
3 Dawn Staley 10.00 25.00
4 Aliyah Boston 15.00 40.00
5 Jordin Canada 5.00 12.00
6 Rickea Jackson 12.00 30.00
7 Natasha Cloud 6.00 15.00
8 Angel Reese 60.00 150.00
9 DiJonai Carrington 6.00 15.00
10 Aaliyah Edwards 6.00 15.00
12 Jacy Sheldon 10.00 25.00
13 Breanna Stewart 20.00 50.00
14 Jackie Young 10.00 25.00
15 Nika Muhl 20.00 50.00
16 Grace Berger 12.00 30.00

17 Kamilla Cardoso 10.00 25.00
18 Marine Johannes 8.00 20.00
19 Alissa Pili 6.00 15.00
20 DeWanna Bonner 8.00 20.00
21 Arike Ogunbowale 10.00 25.00
22 Caitlin Clark 1,000.00 2,000.00
23 Maya Moore 10.00 25.00
24 Diana Taurasi 15.00 40.00
25 Napheesa Collier 30.00 80.00
26 Elena Delle Donne 10.00 25.00
27 Brittney Griner 12.00 30.00
28 Alysha Clark 5.00 12.00
29 Jewell Loyd 8.00 20.00
30 Cameron Brink 60.00 150.00

2024 Panini Origins WNBA Prototypes

*TEAL/49: 1.5X TO 4X BASIC
1 Caitlin Clark 100.00 250.00
2 Cameron Brink 25.00 60.00
3 Kamilla Cardoso 3.00 8.00
4 Rickea Jackson 4.00 10.00
5 Jacy Sheldon 3.00 8.00
6 Aaliyah Edwards 2.00 5.00
7 Angel Reese 5.00 12.00
8 Nika Muhl 4.00 10.00
9 Kate Martin 20.00 50.00
10 Alissa Pili 2.00 5.00

2024 Panini Origins WNBA Roots of Greatness

*TEAL/49: 1.5X TO 4X BASIC
1 Napheesa Collier
Diamond Miller 2.50 6.00
2 Jackie Young
Chelsea Gray 1.50 4.00
3 Jacy Sheldon
Arike Ogunbowale 1.50 4.00
4 Diana Taurasi
Sophie Cunningham 2.50 6.00
5 A'ja Wilson
Kate Martin 8.00 20.00
6 Caitlin Clark
Erica Wheeler 30.00 80.00
7 Aaliyah Edwards
Elena Delle Donne 1.50 4.00
8 Rickea Jackson
Zia Cooke 2.00 5.00
9 DiJonai Carrington
DeWanna Bonner 1.25 3.00
10 Sabrina Ionescu
Breanna Stewart 3.00 8.00
11 Jordan Horston
Jewell Loyd 1.25 3.00
12 Haley Jones
Rhyne Howard .60 1.50
13 Maddy Siegrist
Satou Sabally 1.25 3.00
14 Angel Reese
Diamond DeShields 2.50 6.00
15 Aliyah Boston
NaLyssa Smith 2.50 6.00

2024 Panini Origins WNBA Sneaker Spotlight

1 Sheryl Swoopes 50.00 120.00
2 Breanna Stewart 60.00 150.00
3 Jewell Loyd 40.00 100.00
4 Arike Ogunbowale 40.00 100.00
5 Sabrina Ionescu 100.00 250.00

2024 Panini Origins WNBA Splitting Image

*TEAL/49: 1.5X TO 4X BASIC
1 Jonquel Jones
Breanna Stewart 3.00 8.00
2 Jaelyn Brown
Arike Ogunbowale 1.50 4.00
3 Natisha Hiedeman
Courtney Williams 1.00 2.50
4 Elena Delle Donne
Aaliyah Edwards 1.50 4.00
5 A'ja Wilson
Alysha Clark 3.00 8.00
6 Diana Taurasi
Natasha Cloud 2.50 6.00
7 Caitlin Clark
Kelsey Mitchell 30.00 80.00
8 Jackie Young
Kelsey Plum 2.50 6.00
9 Zia Cooke
Lexie Brown 1.00 2.50
10 Jewell Loyd
Skylar Diggins-Smith 1.25 3.00
11 Sophie Cunningham
Kahleah Copper 2.00 5.00
12 Sabrina Ionescu
Marine Johannes 2.50 6.00
13 Diamond DeShields
Dana Evans .75 2.00
14 Allisha Gray
Rhyne Howard 1.00 2.50
15 Alyssa Thomas
DeWanna Bonner 1.25 3.00

2024 Panini Origins WNBA Team Origins

*TEAL/49: 1.5X TO 4X BASIC
1 Ticha Penicheiro 1.00 2.50
2 Diana Taurasi 2.50 6.00
3 Tamika Catchings 1.25 3.00
4 Maya Moore 1.50 4.00
5 Lauren Jackson 1.50 4.00
6 Arike Ogunbowale 1.50 4.00
7 Dawn Staley 1.50 4.00
8 Sue Bird 2.50 6.00
9 Napheesa Collier 2.50 6.00
10 Lisa Leslie 1.50 4.00
11 A'ja Wilson 3.00 8.00
12 Elena Delle Donne 1.50 4.00
13 Brittney Griner 2.00 5.00
14 Sheryl Swoopes 1.25 3.00
15 DeWanna Bonner 1.25 3.00

2024 Panini Origins WNBA Tiger Eyes

1 Diana Taurasi 40.00 100.00
2 Aliyah Boston 40.00 100.00
3 Rickea Jackson 75.00 200.00
4 Caitlin Clark 1,000.00 2,000.00

5 Angel Reese 75.00 200.00
6 Nika Muhl 75.00 200.00
7 Cameron Brink 125.00 300.00
8 Sabrina Ionescu 75.00 200.00
9 Breanna Stewart 40.00 100.00
10 Brittney Griner 30.00 80.00

2024 Panini Origins WNBA Triple Autographs

STATED PRINT RUN 25 SER.#'d SETS
1 Arike Ogunbowale
Jacy Sheldon
Maddy Siegrist 50.00 120.00
2 Diana Taurasi
Natasha Cloud
Brittney Griner 75.00 200.00
3 A'ja Wilson
Jackie Young
Chelsea Gray 100.00 250.00
4 Caitlin Clark
Aliyah Boston
Kelsey Mitchell 1,500.00 3,000.00
5 Skylar Diggins-Smith
Nika Muhl
Jewell Loyd 125.00 300.00

2024 Panini Origins WNBA Universal Autographs

*RED/99: .5X TO 1.2X BASIC
*RED/49: .6X TO 1.5X BASIC
*BLUE/25: .75X TO 2X BASIC
1 Tamika Catchings 8.00 20.00
2 Lisa Leslie 10.00 25.00
3 Dana Evans 5.00 12.00
4 Zia Cooke 4.00 10.00
5 Natasha Howard 6.00 15.00
6 Cameron Brink 60.00 150.00
7 Erica Wheeler 6.00 15.00
8 Kalani Brown 4.00 10.00
9 Sophie Cunningham 60.00 150.00
10 Cynthia Cooper-Dyke 8.00 20.00
11 Brionna Jones 6.00 15.00
12 Alissa Pili 6.00 15.00
13 Marine Johannes 8.00 20.00
14 Kelsey Mitchell 12.00 30.00
15 Aliyah Boston 15.00 40.00
16 Kamilla Cardoso 10.00 25.00
17 Crystal Dangerfield 4.00 10.00
18 Alysha Clark 5.00 12.00
19 Caitlin Clark 1,000.00 2,000.00
20 Allisha Gray 6.00 15.00
21 Courtney Vandersloot 6.00 15.00
22 Lexie Hull 50.00 120.00
23 Nancy Lieberman 8.00 20.00
24 Jacy Sheldon 10.00 25.00
25 Rickea Jackson 12.00 30.00
26 Skylar Diggins-Smith 8.00 20.00
27 Chelsea Gray 5.00 12.00
28 Angel Reese 60.00 150.00
29 Sheryl Swoopes 8.00 20.00
30 Tina Charles 6.00 15.00

2011-12 Panini Past and Present

COMPLETE SET (200) 20.00 50.00
1 LaMarcus Aldridge .40 1.00
2 Ray Allen .60 1.50
3 Chris Andersen .30 .75
4 Carmelo Anthony .60 1.50
5 Shane Battier .30 .75
6 Eric Bledsoe .40 1.00
7 Carlos Boozer .30 .75
8 Chris Bosh .50 1.25
9 Elton Brand .40 1.00
10 Andrew Bynum .25 .60
11 Vince Carter .75 2.00
12 Tyson Chandler .30 .75
13 Darren Collison .25 .60
14 Mike Conley .30 .75
15 Stephen Curry 3.00 8.00
16 Baron Davis .30 .75
17 Brandon Bass .25 .60
18 Luol Deng .30 .75
19 DeMar DeRozan .50 1.25
20 Tim Duncan 1.00 2.50
21 Kevin Durant 1.50 4.00
22 Monta Ellis .30 .75
23 Raymond Felton .25 .60
24 Derek Fisher .40 1.00
25 Kevin Garnett 1.00 2.50
26 Marc Gasol .40 1.00
27 Pau Gasol .60 1.50
28 Manu Ginobili .75 2.00
29 Marcin Gortat .25 .60
30 Danny Granger .30 .75
31 Blake Griffin .40 1.00
32 James Harden .75 2.00
33 Devin Harris .25 .60
34 Roy Hibbert .30 .75
35 George Hill .30 .75
36 Grant Hill .60 1.50
37 Dwight Howard .50 1.25
38 Serge Ibaka .30 .75
39 Andre Iguodala .40 1.00
40 LeBron James 3.00 8.00
41 Al Jefferson .25 .60
42 Brandon Jennings .25 .60
43 Joe Johnson .30 .75
44 DeAndre Jordan .30 .75
45 Jason Kidd .60 1.50
46 Ty Lawson .25 .60
47 Brook Lopez .40 1.00
48 Kevin Love .40 1.00
49 Shawn Marion .40 1.00
50 Wesley Matthews .25 .60
51 Tracy McGrady .75 2.00
52 Greg Monroe .25 .60
53 Steve Nash .75 2.00
54 Nene .30 .75
55 Joakim Noah .40 1.00
56 Dirk Nowitzki 1.00 2.50
57 Chris Paul .75 2.00
58 Tony Parker .50 1.25
59 Paul Pierce .60 1.50
60 Jason Richardson .40 1.00
61 Rajon Rondo .50 1.25
62 Ricky Rubio .40 1.00
63 Josh Smith .25 .60
64 Tiago Splitter .25 .60
65 Amare Stoudemire .40 1.00
66 Jason Terry .30 .75
67 Hedo Turkoglu .30 .75
68 Evan Turner .25 .60
69 Ekpe Udoh .25 .60
70 Dwyane Wade .75 2.00
71 David West .30 .75
72 Russell Westbrook .60 1.50
73 Deron Williams .30 .75
74 Jeremy Lin .75 2.00
75 Thaddeus Young .25 .60
76 Elgin Baylor .60 1.50
77 Larry Bird 1.50 4.00
78 Julius Erving 1.00 2.50
79 Patrick Ewing .60 1.50
80 George Gervin .60 1.50
81 John Havlicek .75 2.00
82 Magic Johnson 1.50 4.00
83 Sam Jones .50 1.25
84 Karl Malone .75 2.00
85 Pete Maravich .75 2.00
86 George Mikan 1.25 3.00
87 Hakeem Olajuwon .75 2.00
88 Shaquille O'Neal 1.50 4.00
89 Scottie Pippen 1.00 2.50
90 Willis Reed .60 1.50
91 Oscar Robertson .75 2.00
92 David Robinson .75 2.00
93 Bill Russell 1.25 3.00
94 John Stockton .75 2.00
95 Isiah Thomas .60 1.50
96 David Thompson .40 1.00
97 Wes Unseld .60 1.50
98 Bill Walton .60 1.50
99 Jerry West .75 2.00
100 James Worthy .60 1.50
101 Carmelo Anthony .60 1.50
102 Ray Allen .60 1.50
103 Shane Battier .30 .75
104 Andrea Bargnani .25 .60
105 Michael Beasley .25 .60
106 Chauncey Billups .50 1.25
107 Andrew Bogut .30 .75
108 Carlos Boozer .30 .75
109 Chris Bosh .50 1.25
110 Elton Brand .40 1.00
111 Kobe Bryant 3.00 8.00
112 Tyson Chandler .30 .75
113 DeMarcus Cousins .40 1.00
114 Stephen Curry 3.00 8.00
115 Baron Davis .30 .75
116 Luol Deng .30 .75
117 Tim Duncan 1.00 2.50
118 Kevin Durant 1.50 4.00
119 Monta Ellis .30 .75
120 Tyreke Evans .30 .75
121 Kevin Garnett 1.00 2.50
122 Pau Gasol .60 1.50
123 Rudy Gay .40 1.00
124 Eric Gordon .30 .75
125 Danny Granger .30 .75
126 Blake Griffin .40 1.00
127 Richard Hamilton .50 1.25
128 Roy Hibbert .30 .75
129 Tyler Hansbrough .25 .60
130 James Harden .75 2.00
131 Devin Harris .25 .60
132 Grant Hill .60 1.50
133 Al Horford .40 1.00
134 Dwight Howard .50 1.25
135 Serge Ibaka .30 .75
136 Andre Iguodala .40 1.00
137 LeBron James 3.00 8.00
138 Stephen Jackson .30 .75
139 Al Jefferson .25 .60
140 Joe Johnson .30 .75
141 Jason Kidd .60 1.50
142 Ty Lawson .25 .60
143 David Lee .25 .60
144 Brook Lopez .40 1.00
145 Kevin Love .40 1.00
146 Kyle Lowry .40 1.00
147 Shawn Marion .40 1.00
148 Kevin Martin .30 .75
149 Andre Miller .30 .75
150 Paul Millsap .30 .75
151 Steve Nash .75 2.00
152 Jameer Nelson .25 .60
153 Nene .30 .75
154 Joakim Noah .40 1.00
155 Dirk Nowitzki 1.00 2.50
156 Lamar Odom .30 .75
157 Emeka Okafor .30 .75
158 Chris Paul .75 2.00
159 Paul Pierce .60 1.50
160 Zach Randolph .30 .75
161 Rajon Rondo .50 1.25
162 Derrick Rose .60 1.50
163 Luis Scola .30 .75
164 Josh Smith .25 .60
165 Amare Stoudemire .40 1.00
166 Rodney Stuckey .25 .60
167 Jeff Teague .25 .60
168 Jason Terry .30 .75
169 Hedo Turkoglu .30 .75
170 Dwyane Wade .75 2.00
171 John Wall .50 1.25
172 Gerald Wallace .30 .75
173 Russell Westbrook .60 1.50
174 Deron Williams .30 .75
175 Jeremy Lin .75 2.00
176 Nate Archibald .50 1.25
177 B.J. Armstrong .40 1.00
178 Elgin Baylor .60 1.50
179 Rick Barry .50 1.25
180 Walt Bellamy .40 1.00
181 Bill Cartwright .30 .75
182 Tom Chambers .40 1.00
183 Bob Cousy .60 1.50
184 Dave DeBusschere .40 1.00
185 Walt Frazier .60 1.50
186 Harry Gallatin .40 1.00
187 Artis Gilmore .50 1.25
188 Phil Jackson .50 1.25
189 K.C. Jones .40 1.00
190 Mitch Kupchak .40 1.00
191 Clyde Lovellette .40 1.00
192 Jerry Lucas .40 1.00
193 Moses Malone .60 1.50
194 Gail Goodrich .40 1.00
195 Vern Mikkelsen .40 1.00
196 Bob Pettit .50 1.25
197 Robert Parish .50 1.25
198 Wes Unseld .60 1.50
199 Jo Jo White .30 .75
200 Lenny Wilkens .40 1.00

2011-12 Panini Past and Present 2011 Draft Pick Redemptions Autographs

XRCA Isaiah Thomas 6.00 15.00
XRCB Shelvin Mack 3.00 8.00
XRCC Alec Burks 5.00 12.00
XRCD Lavoy Allen 4.00 10.00
XRCE MarShon Brooks 4.00 10.00
XRCF Josh Harrellson 3.00 8.00
XRCG Klay Thompson 25.00 60.00
XRCH Brandon Knight 4.00 10.00
XRCI Kemba Walker 15.00 40.00
XRCJ Chris Singleton 3.00 8.00
XRCK Markieff Morris 5.00 12.00
XRCL Marcus Morris 5.00 12.00
XRCM Gustavo Ayon 3.00 8.00
XRCN Kawhi Leonard 50.00 120.00
XRCO Kyrie Irving 30.00 80.00
XRCP Justin Harper 3.00 8.00
XRCQ JaJuan Johnson 3.00 8.00
XRCR Jan Vesely 3.00 8.00
XRCS Kenneth Faried 5.00 12.00
XRCT Norris Cole 4.00 10.00
XRCU Jeremy Tyler 3.00 8.00
XRCV Charles Jenkins 3.00 8.00
XRCW Enes Kanter 5.00 12.00
XRCX Nolan Smith 3.00 8.00
XRCY Jimmy Butler 20.00 50.00
XRCZ Chandler Parsons 4.00 10.00
XRCAA Cory Joseph 4.00 10.00
XRCBB Bismack Biyombo 4.00 10.00
XRCCC Tristan Thompson 5.00 12.00
XRCDD Tobias Harris 8.00 20.00
XRCEE Reggie Jackson 4.00 10.00
XRCFF Iman Shumpert 5.00 12.00
XRCGG Derrick Williams 3.00 8.00
XRCHH Jimmer Fredette 5.00 12.00
XRCII Jordan Hamilton 3.00 8.00

2011-12 Panini Past and Present 2012 Draft Pick Redemptions

1 Anthony Davis 20.00 50.00
2 Michael Kidd-Gilchrist 2.50 6.00
3 Bradley Beal 5.00 12.00
4 Dion Waiters 2.50 6.00
5 Thomas Robinson 1.50 4.00
6 Damian Lillard 15.00 40.00
7 Harrison Barnes 6.00 15.00
8 Terrence Ross 2.50 6.00
9 Andre Drummond 8.00 20.00
10 Austin Rivers 3.00 8.00
11 Meyers Leonard 2.00 5.00
12 Jeremy Lamb 2.50 6.00
13 Kendall Marshall 1.50 4.00
14 John Henson 2.50 6.00
15 Maurice Harkless 2.50 6.00
16 Royce White 1.50 4.00
17 Tyler Zeller 2.00 5.00
18 Terrence Jones 2.00 5.00
19 Andrew Nicholson 1.50 4.00
20 Evan Fournier 2.50 6.00
21 Jared Sullinger 2.00 5.00
22 Fab Melo 1.50 4.00
23 John Jenkins 1.50 4.00
24 Jared Cunningham 1.50 4.00
25 Tony Wroten 1.50 4.00
26 Miles Plumlee 2.00 5.00
27 Arnett Moultrie 2.00 5.00
28 Perry Jones 1.50 4.00
29 Marquis Teague 1.50 4.00
30 Festus Ezeli 2.00 5.00
NNO COMPLETE SET EXCH 200.00 400.00

2011-12 Panini Past and Present Autographs

5 Shane Battier 5.00 12.00
6 Eric Bledsoe 5.00 12.00
12 Tyson Chandler 4.00 10.00
14 Mike Conley 4.00 10.00
16 Baron Davis 6.00 15.00
21 Kevin Durant 100.00 250.00
31 Blake Griffin 12.00 30.00
32 James Harden 40.00 100.00
34 Roy Hibbert 4.00 10.00
36 Grant Hill 75.00 200.00
38 Serge Ibaka 4.00 10.00
42 Brandon Jennings 3.00 8.00
47 Brook Lopez 5.00 12.00
48 Kevin Love 10.00 25.00
52 Greg Monroe 3.00 8.00
53 Steve Nash 60.00 150.00
56 Dirk Nowitzki 100.00 250.00
57 Chris Paul EXCH 60.00 150.00
61 Rajon Rondo 15.00 40.00
65 Amare Stoudemire 6.00 15.00
68 Evan Turner 3.00 8.00
72 Russell Westbrook 50.00 120.00
73 Deron Williams 4.00 10.00
74 Jeremy Lin 100.00 250.00
76 Elgin Baylor 30.00 80.00
80 George Gervin 15.00 40.00
81 John Havlicek 75.00 200.00
82 Magic Johnson 100.00 250.00
83 Sam Jones 12.00 30.00
87 Hakeem Olajuwon 30.00 80.00
91 Oscar Robertson 30.00 80.00
93 Bill Russell 400.00 800.00
95 Isiah Thomas 20.00 50.00
96 David Thompson 5.00 12.00
97 Wes Unseld 10.00 25.00
98 Bill Walton 10.00 25.00
99 Jerry West 30.00 80.00
100 James Worthy 20.00 50.00
103 Shane Battier 5.00 12.00
107 Andrew Bogut 4.00 10.00
111 Kobe Bryant 800.00 1,500.00
112 Tyson Chandler 4.00 10.00
113 DeMarcus Cousins 12.00 30.00
114 Stephen Curry 500.00 1,000.00
115 Baron Davis 6.00 15.00
118 Kevin Durant EXCH 100.00 250.00
126 Blake Griffin 12.00 30.00
127 Richard Hamilton 8.00 20.00
130 James Harden 40.00 100.00
133 Al Horford 5.00 12.00
135 Serge Ibaka 4.00 10.00
144 Brook Lopez 5.00 12.00
145 Kevin Love 10.00 25.00
151 Steve Nash 60.00 150.00
155 Dirk Nowitzki 100.00 250.00
157 Emeka Okafor 4.00 10.00
158 Chris Paul EXCH 60.00 150.00
161 Rajon Rondo 12.00 30.00
162 Derrick Rose EXCH 50.00 120.00
163 Luis Scola 4.00 10.00
165 Amare Stoudemire 6.00 15.00
167 Jeff Teague 3.00 8.00
173 Russell Westbrook 50.00 120.00
175 Jeremy Lin 100.00 250.00
176 Nate Archibald 8.00 20.00
177 B.J. Armstrong 8.00 20.00
178 Elgin Baylor 30.00 80.00
179 Rick Barry 12.00 30.00
180 Walt Bellamy 12.00 30.00
182 Tom Chambers 5.00 12.00
185 Walt Frazier 20.00 50.00
186 Harry Gallatin 10.00 25.00
187 Artis Gilmore 8.00 20.00
188 Phil Jackson 300.00 600.00
189 K.C. Jones 15.00 40.00
191 Clyde Lovellette 8.00 20.00
194 Gail Goodrich 8.00 20.00
196 Bob Pettit 15.00 40.00
197 Robert Parish 8.00 20.00
198 Wes Unseld 8.00 20.00
200 Lenny Wilkens 8.00 20.00

2011-12 Panini Past and Present Bread for Energy

COMPLETE SET (50) 25.00 60.00
1 Carmelo Anthony 1.25 3.00
2 Leandro Barbosa .60 1.50
3 J.J. Barea .75 2.00
4 Andrea Bargnani .50 1.25
5 Andray Blatche .50 1.25
6 Ronnie Brewer .50 1.25
7 Carlos Boozer .60 1.50
8 Mario Chalmers .60 1.50
9 Darren Collison .50 1.25
10 Stephen Curry 6.00 15.00
11 DeMar DeRozan 1.00 2.50
12 Kevin Durant 3.00 8.00
13 Tyreke Evans .60 1.50
14 Raymond Felton .50 1.25
15 Landry Fields .50 1.25
16 Danilo Gallinari .60 1.50
17 Kevin Garnett 2.00 5.00
18 Marc Gasol .75 2.00
19 Pau Gasol 1.25 3.00
20 Taj Gibson .60 1.50
21 Manu Ginobili 1.50 4.00
22 Devin Harris .50 1.25
23 Gordon Hayward .75 2.00
24 Grant Hill 1.25 3.00
25 Jrue Holiday 1.00 2.50
26 Al Horford .75 2.00
27 Dwight Howard 1.00 2.50
28 Stephen Jackson .60 1.50
29 Amir Johnson .50 1.25
30 Carl Landry .50 1.25
31 David Lee .50 1.25
32 Rashard Lewis .60 1.50
33 Corey Maggette .60 1.50
34 Tracy McGrady 1.50 4.00
35 Joakim Noah .75 2.00
36 Lamar Odom .60 1.50
37 Mehmet Okur .50 1.25
38 Tony Parker 1.00 2.50
39 J.J. Redick .75 2.00
40 Luke Ridnour .60 1.50
41 Rajon Rondo 1.00 2.50
42 Derrick Rose 1.25 3.00
43 Jason Terry .60 1.50
44 Dwyane Wade 1.50 4.00
45 John Wall 1.00 2.50
46 Hakim Warrick .50 1.25
47 David West .60 1.50
48 Russell Westbrook 1.25 3.00
49 Deron Williams .60 1.50
50 Anderson Varejao .50 1.25

2011-12 Panini Past and Present Bread for Health

COMPLETE SET (50) 30.00 80.00
1 LaMarcus Aldridge .75 2.00
2 Ray Allen 1.25 3.00
3 Chauncey Billups 1.00 2.50
4 Andrew Bogut .60 1.50
5 Chris Bosh 1.00 2.50
6 Elton Brand .75 2.00
7 Kobe Bryant 6.00 15.00
8 Chase Budinger .50 1.25
9 Andrew Bynum .50 1.25
10 Jose Calderon .50 1.25
11 Tyson Chandler .60 1.50
12 DeMarcus Cousins .75 2.00
13 Jamal Crawford .75 2.00
14 Luol Deng .60 1.50
15 Tim Duncan 2.00 5.00
16 Monta Ellis .60 1.50
17 Derek Fisher .75 2.00
18 Rudy Gay .75 2.00
19 Drew Gooden .60 1.50
20 Ben Gordon .60 1.50
21 Danny Granger .60 1.50
22 Blake Griffin .75 2.00
23 James Harden 1.50 4.00
24 Kris Humphries .50 1.25
25 Andre Iguodala .75 2.00
26 Chris Kaman .60 1.50
27 Jason Kidd 1.25 3.00
28 Jarrett Jack .60 1.50
29 LeBron James 6.00 15.00
30 Antawn Jamison .60 1.50

31 Al Jefferson .50 1.25
32 Brandon Jennings .50 1.25
33 Joe Johnson .60 1.50
34 Brook Lopez .75 2.00
35 Kevin Love .75 2.00
36 Kevin Martin .60 1.50
37 JaVale McGee .60 1.50
38 Andre Miller .60 1.50
39 Greg Monroe .50 1.25
40 Steve Nash 1.50 4.00
41 Gary Neal .50 1.25
42 Dirk Nowitzki 2.00 5.00
43 Paul Pierce 1.25 3.00
44 Tayshaun Prince .75 2.00
45 Zach Randolph .60 1.50
46 Brandon Rush .50 1.25
47 Amare Stoudemire .75 2.00
48 Rodney Stuckey .50 1.25
49 Evan Turner .50 1.25
50 D.J. White .50 1.25

2011-12 Panini Past and Present Bread for Life

COMPLETE SET (50) 75.00 150.00
1 Elgin Baylor 2.50 6.00
2 Larry Bird 6.00 15.00
3 Wilt Chamberlain 5.00 12.00
4 Phil Chenier 1.00 2.50
5 Maurice Cheeks 1.25 3.00
6 Clyde Drexler 2.50 6.00
7 Dale Ellis 1.25 3.00
8 Sean Elliott 1.25 3.00
9 Julius Erving 4.00 10.00
10 Patrick Ewing 6.00 15.00
11 Harry Gallatin 1.50 4.00
12 A.C. Green 1.50 4.00
13 Anfernee Hardaway 4.00 10.00
14 Ron Harper 1.50 4.00
15 Hersey Hawkins 1.25 3.00
16 Robert Horry 1.50 4.00
17 Mark Jackson 1.25 3.00
18 Magic Johnson 6.00 15.00
19 Dave Cowens 2.00 5.00
20 Bill Laimbeer 1.50 4.00
21 Dan Majerle 1.50 4.00
22 Karl Malone 3.00 8.00
23 Pete Maravich 3.00 8.00
24 Bob McAdoo 2.00 5.00
25 George Mikan 5.00 12.00
26 Alonzo Mourning 6.00 15.00
27 Dikembe Mutombo 2.00 5.00
28 Charles Oakley 1.50 4.00
29 Hakeem Olajuwon 3.00 8.00
30 Shaquille O'Neal 6.00 15.00
31 Robert Parish 2.00 5.00
32 Gary Payton 2.00 5.00
33 Scottie Pippen 4.00 10.00
34 Sam Perkins 1.00 2.50
35 Terry Porter 1.25 3.00
36 Mark Price 1.50 4.00
37 Glen Rice 1.50 4.00
38 Arnie Risen 1.50 4.00
39 Dennis Rodman 4.00 10.00
40 Tree Rollins 1.00 2.50
41 Bill Russell 5.00 12.00
42 Jack Sikma 1.50 4.00
43 Kenny Smith 1.25 3.00
44 Dolph Schayes 1.50 4.00
45 Paul Silas 1.50 4.00
46 Isiah Thomas 2.50 6.00
47 Chet Walker 1.25 3.00
48 Dominique Wilkins 2.50 6.00
49 Lenny Wilkens 1.50 4.00
50 Kevin Willis 1.25 3.00

2011-12 Panini Past and Present Breakout

COMPLETE SET (30) 15.00 40.00
1 Blake Griffin .75 2.00
2 John Wall 1.00 2.50
3 DeMarcus Cousins .75 2.00
4 Stephen Curry 6.00 15.00
5 Brandon Jennings .50 1.25
6 Taj Gibson .60 1.50
7 Tyler Hansbrough .50 1.25
8 Tyreke Evans .60 1.50
9 Brook Lopez .75 2.00
10 Eric Gordon .60 1.50
11 Andrew Bynum .50 1.25
12 Derrick Rose 1.25 3.00
13 Russell Westbrook 1.25 3.00
14 Kevin Love .75 2.00
15 DeJuan Blair .50 1.25
16 James Harden 1.50 4.00
17 Jrue Holiday 1.00 2.50
18 Wesley Matthews .50 1.25
19 Derrick Favors .60 1.50
20 Landry Fields .50 1.25
21 Greg Monroe .50 1.25
22 Jeremy Lin 1.50 4.00
23 Serge Ibaka .60 1.50
24 Eric Bledsoe .75 2.00
25 DeMar DeRozan 1.00 2.50
26 Gordon Hayward .75 2.00
27 Danilo Gallinari .60 1.50
28 Michael Beasley .50 1.25
29 O.J. Mayo .50 1.25
30 Ricky Rubio .75 2.00

2011-12 Panini Past and Present Breakout Autographs

1 Blake Griffin 12.00 30.00
3 DeMarcus Cousins 15.00 40.00
4 Stephen Curry 300.00 600.00
6 Taj Gibson 4.00 10.00
8 Tyreke Evans 4.00 10.00
9 Brook Lopez 5.00 12.00
10 Eric Gordon 4.00 10.00
12 Derrick Rose EXCH 20.00 50.00
13 Russell Westbrook 60.00 150.00
14 Kevin Love 10.00 25.00
15 DeJuan Blair 3.00 8.00
16 James Harden EXCH 40.00 100.00
17 Jrue Holiday 6.00 15.00
18 Wesley Matthews 3.00 8.00
19 Derrick Favors 4.00 10.00
20 Landry Fields 3.00 8.00
21 Greg Monroe 3.00 8.00
22 Jeremy Lin 100.00 250.00
23 Serge Ibaka 4.00 10.00
24 Eric Bledsoe 5.00 12.00
25 DeMar DeRozan 20.00 50.00
26 Gordon Hayward 6.00 15.00
27 Danilo Gallinari 4.00 10.00
28 Michael Beasley 3.00 8.00

2011-12 Panini Past and Present Changing Times

COMPLETE SET (30) 20.00 50.00
1 Bill Russell 2.50 6.00
2 Oscar Robertson 1.50 4.00
3 Dolph Schayes .75 2.00
4 Al Attles .60 1.50
5 Bob Cousy 1.25 3.00
6 Lenny Wilkens .75 2.00
7 Harry Gallatin .75 2.00
8 George Mikan 2.50 6.00
9 Clyde Lovellette .75 2.00
10 Julius Erving 2.00 5.00
11 George Gervin 1.25 3.00
12 Dan Issel 1.00 2.50
13 David Thompson .75 2.00
14 Artis Gilmore 1.00 2.50
15 Spencer Haywood .75 2.00
16 Connie Hawkins .75 2.00
17 Mel Daniels .75 2.00
18 Billy Cunningham .75 2.00
19 George McGinnis .75 2.00
20 Bobby Jones .60 1.50
21 Kobe Bryant 6.00 15.00
22 Blake Griffin .75 2.00
23 Kevin Durant 3.00 8.00
24 Chris Paul 1.50 4.00
25 LeBron James 6.00 15.00
26 Dirk Nowitzki 2.00 5.00
27 Derrick Rose 1.25 3.00
28 Kevin Love .75 2.00
29 Marc Gasol .75 2.00
30 Monta Ellis .60 1.50

2011-12 Panini Past and Present Elusive Ink Autographs

AA Anthony Avent 3.00 8.00
AC Archie Clark 5.00 12.00
AH Allan Houston 5.00 12.00
AJ Avery Johnson 4.00 10.00
AM Anthony Mason 8.00 20.00
BA B.J. Armstrong 8.00 20.00
BB Brent Barry 4.00 10.00
BD Brad Davis 3.00 8.00
BE Bob Elliott 4.00 10.00
BG Brian Grant 4.00 10.00
BL Bob Love 5.00 12.00
BO Bo Outlaw 3.00 8.00
BR Bryant Reeves 4.00 10.00
BS Bob Sura 3.00 8.00
BW Bill Wennington 8.00 20.00
BW Buck Williams 4.00 10.00
CC Cedric Ceballos 4.00 10.00
CO Charles Oakley 5.00 12.00
DB Dee Brown 4.00 10.00
DC Dell Curry 5.00 12.00
DF Danny Ferry 4.00 10.00
DM Danny Manning 4.00 10.00
GM Gheorghe Muresan 4.00 10.00
HD Hubert Davis 4.00 10.00
HH Hersey Hawkins 4.00 10.00
JM Jamal Mashburn 4.00 10.00
JP John Paxson 8.00 20.00
JS John Starks 5.00 12.00
JS John Salley 4.00 10.00
KA Kenny Anderson 4.00 10.00
KK Kerry Kittles 4.00 10.00
KS Kenny Smith 4.00 10.00
KW Kevin Willis 4.00 10.00
LF Lawrence Funderburke 3.00 8.00
LL Luc Longley 10.00 25.00
LN Larry Nance 4.00 10.00
LS LaBradford Smith 3.00 8.00
LW Luther Wright 3.00 8.00
MA Mark Aguirre 5.00 12.00
MB Muggsy Bogues 10.00 25.00
ME Mario Elie 4.00 10.00
MF Michael Finley 5.00 12.00
MJ Major Jones 4.00 10.00
MR Marv Roberts 4.00 10.00
MW Morlon Wiley 3.00 8.00
NA Nick Anderson 4.00 10.00
OB Otis Birdsong 4.00 10.00
RB Ron Brewer 4.00 10.00
RC Rex Chapman 4.00 10.00
RM Rick Mahorn 4.00 10.00
RS Rod Strickland 4.00 10.00
RS Rory Sparrow 3.00 8.00
RT Reggie Theus 4.00 10.00
SA Stacey Augmon 4.00 10.00
SE Sean Elliott 4.00 10.00
SF Sleepy Floyd 5.00 12.00
SK Steve Kerr 10.00 25.00
SM Scooter McCray 3.00 8.00
SP Scot Pollard 4.00 10.00
TB Thurl Bailey 4.00 10.00
TG Tom Gugliotta 4.00 10.00
TH Tim Hardaway 10.00 25.00
VB Vin Baker 4.00 10.00
WB Willie Burton 3.00 8.00
VDN Vinny Del Negro 4.00 10.00

2011-12 Panini Past and Present Fireworks

COMPLETE SET (20) 25.00 60.00
1 Kevin Durant 5.00 12.00
2 LeBron James 10.00 25.00
3 Kobe Bryant 10.00 25.00
4 Dwyane Wade 2.50 6.00
5 Dwight Howard 1.50 4.00
6 Blake Griffin 1.25 3.00
7 Dirk Nowitzki 3.00 8.00
8 Derrick Rose 2.00 5.00
9 Carmelo Anthony 2.00 5.00
10 Amare Stoudemire 1.25 3.00
11 Monta Ellis 1.00 2.50
12 Kevin Garnett 3.00 8.00
13 Kevin Love 1.25 3.00
14 John Wall 1.50 4.00
15 Russell Westbrook 2.00 5.00
16 Rajon Rondo 1.50 4.00
17 Josh Smith .75 2.00
18 Jeremy Lin 2.50 6.00
19 Chris Paul 2.50 6.00
20 Tyreke Evans 1.00 2.50

2011-12 Panini Past and Present Gamers Jerseys

1 Amare Stoudemire 4.00 10.00
2 Al Jefferson 2.50 6.00
3 Allan Houston 5.00 12.00
4 Al Horford 4.00 10.00
5 Allen Iverson 12.00 30.00
6 Alonzo Mourning 6.00 15.00
7 Andre Iguodala 4.00 10.00
8 Avery Bradley 4.00 10.00
9 Darren Collison 2.50 6.00
10 Ben Wallace 5.00 12.00
11 Beno Udrih 2.50 6.00
12 Ed Davis 2.50 6.00
13 Blake Griffin 4.00 10.00
14 Bobby Jackson 2.50 6.00
15 Brandon Jennings 2.50 6.00
16 Brendan Haywood 2.50 6.00
17 Brook Lopez 4.00 10.00
18 Carlos Boozer 3.00 8.00
19 Grant Hill 8.00 20.00
20 Charles Oakley 4.00 10.00
21 Charlie Villanueva 2.50 6.00
22 Chris Andersen 3.00 8.00
23 Chris Bosh 5.00 12.00
24 Chris Webber 10.00 25.00
25 Cole Aldrich 2.50 6.00
26 Danny Granger 3.00 8.00
27 DeMar DeRozan 5.00 12.00
28 Damion James 2.50 6.00
29 Daniel Orton 2.50 6.00
30 Danny Manning 3.00 8.00
31 Patrick Ewing 12.00 30.00
32 Derrick Favors 3.00 8.00
33 Ekpe Udoh 2.50 6.00
34 Evan Turner 2.50 6.00
35 Greg Monroe 2.50 6.00
36 Hassan Whiteside 3.00 8.00
37 J.J. Redick 4.00 10.00
38 James Anderson 2.50 6.00
39 Jason Richardson 4.00 10.00
40 Jermaine O'Neal 4.00 10.00
41 Joe Johnson 3.00 8.00
42 John Wall 5.00 12.00
43 John Stockton 8.00 20.00
44 David Robinson 8.00 20.00
45 Kevin Durant 5.00 12.00
46 Kevin Garnett 10.00 25.00
47 Kevin Love 4.00 10.00
48 Gary Neal 2.50 6.00
49 Kobe Bryant 30.00 80.00
50 Lance Stephenson 3.00 8.00
51 Larry Johnson 8.00 20.00
52 Lazar Hayward 2.50 6.00
53 LeBron James 12.00 30.00
54 Landry Fields 2.50 6.00
55 Luke Walton 2.50 6.00
56 Manu Ginobili 8.00 20.00
57 Marcus Camby 3.00 8.00
58 Mario Chalmers 3.00 8.00
59 Marvin Williams 2.50 6.00
60 Mo Williams 3.00 8.00
61 Marc Gasol 4.00 10.00
62 Eric Bledsoe 4.00 10.00
63 Patrick Patterson 2.50 6.00
64 Paul George 6.00 15.00
65 Pau Gasol 6.00 15.00
66 Paul Pierce 8.00 20.00
67 Peja Stojakovic 6.00 15.00
68 Quincy Pondexter 2.50 6.00
69 Raja Bell 3.00 8.00
70 Rajon Rondo 5.00 12.00
71 Ray Allen 8.00 20.00
72 Hedo Turkoglu 3.00 8.00
73 Jeff Teague 2.50 6.00
74 Ramon Sessions 2.50 6.00
75 Reggie Miller 15.00 40.00
76 Robert Parish 5.00 12.00
77 Robin Lopez 2.50 6.00
78 Rodrigue Beaubois 2.50 6.00
79 Stephen Curry 12.00 30.00
80 Ron Harper 4.00 10.00
81 Roy Hibbert 3.00 8.00
82 Rudy Gay 4.00 10.00
83 Russell Westbrook 6.00 15.00
84 Steve Nash 8.00 20.00
85 LaMarcus Aldridge 4.00 10.00
86 Jalen Rose 3.00 8.00
87 Spencer Hawes 2.50 6.00
88 Andrew Bogut 2.50 6.00
89 Tim Duncan 10.00 25.00
90 Toney Douglas 2.50 6.00
91 Tony Parker 5.00 12.00
92 Trevor Booker 2.50 6.00
93 Ty Lawson 2.50 6.00
94 Tyrus Thomas 2.50 6.00
95 Udonis Haslem 3.00 8.00
96 Terrence Williams 2.50 6.00
97 Yao Ming 8.00 20.00
98 Zach Randolph 3.00 8.00
99 Jrue Holiday 5.00 12.00
100 Derrick Rose 6.00 15.00

2011-12 Panini Past and Present Gamers Jerseys Prime

*PRIME: 2.5X TO 6X BASE HI
STATED PRINT RUN ONE TO 25 SETS
62 Eric Bledsoe/15 30.00 80.00

2011-12 Panini Past and Present Modern Marks Autographs

1 Kobe Bryant 800.00 1,500.00
2 Blake Griffin 40.00 100.00
3 Kevin Durant 150.00 400.00
4 Derrick Rose 100.00 250.00
5 Chris Paul 100.00 250.00
6 Kevin Love 20.00 50.00
7 LaMarcus Aldridge 30.00 80.00
8 Stephen Curry 800.00 1,500.00
9 Marc Gasol 50.00 125.00
10 Andrew Bogut 20.00 50.00

2011-12 Panini Past and Present Raining 3's

COMPLETE SET (20) 20.00 50.00
1 Dirk Nowitzki 2.50 6.00
2 Joe Johnson .75 2.00
3 Carmelo Anthony 1.50 4.00
4 Vince Carter 2.00 5.00
5 Paul Pierce 1.50 4.00
6 Kobe Bryant 8.00 20.00
7 Kevin Durant 4.00 10.00
8 Jason Terry .75 2.00
9 LeBron James 8.00 20.00
10 Jeremy Lin 2.00 5.00
11 Derrick Rose 1.50 4.00
12 Jason Richardson 1.00 2.50
13 Ray Allen 1.50 4.00
14 Steve Nash 2.00 5.00
15 Larry Bird 4.00 10.00
16 Robert Horry 1.00 2.50
17 Allen Iverson 2.00 5.00
18 Dan Majerle 1.00 2.50
19 Chris Mullin 1.25 3.00
20 John Stockton 2.00 5.00

2011-12 Panini Past and Present Variations

1 Ray Allen 5.00 12.00
2 Carmelo Anthony 5.00 12.00
3 Chris Bosh 4.00 10.00
4 Kobe Bryant 25.00 60.00
5 Vince Carter 6.00 15.00
6 Baron Davis 2.50 6.00
7 Tim Duncan 8.00 20.00
8 Kevin Durant 12.00 30.00
9 Kevin Garnett 8.00 20.00
10 Blake Griffin 3.00 8.00
11 Grant Hill 6.00 15.00
12 Dwight Howard 4.00 10.00
13 LeBron James 25.00 60.00
14 DeAndre Jordan 2.50 6.00
15 Jason Kidd 5.00 12.00
16 Kevin Love 3.00 8.00
17 Steve Nash 4.00 10.00
18 Dirk Nowitzki 8.00 20.00
19 Chris Paul 6.00 15.00
20 Paul Pierce 5.00 12.00
21 Rajon Rondo 4.00 10.00
22 Amare Stoudemire 3.00 8.00
23 Dwyane Wade 6.00 15.00
24 Deron Williams 2.50 6.00
25 Metta World Peace 4.00 10.00
26 Larry Bird 8.00 20.00
27 Julius Erving 8.00 20.00
28 Patrick Ewing 6.00 15.00
29 George Gervin 5.00 12.00
30 Magic Johnson 12.00 30.00
31 Karl Malone 6.00 15.00
32 Pete Maravich 6.00 15.00
33 George Mikan 10.00 25.00
34 Shaquille O'Neal 12.00 30.00
35 Scottie Pippen 8.00 20.00
36 Oscar Robertson 6.00 15.00
37 David Robinson 6.00 15.00
38 Bill Russell 10.00 25.00
39 John Stockton 6.00 15.00
40 Isiah Thomas 5.00 12.00
41 David Thompson 3.00 8.00
42 Bill Walton 5.00 12.00
43 Jerry West 6.00 15.00
44 Bob Cousy 5.00 12.00
45 Dave DeBusschere 3.00 8.00
46 Artis Gilmore 4.00 10.00
47 Phil Jackson 4.00 10.00
48 Moses Malone 5.00 12.00
49 Robert Parish 4.00 10.00
50 Wes Unseld 5.00 12.00

2012-13 Panini Past and Present

COMPLETE SET (250) 75.00 200.00
1 Shawn Marion .40 1.00
2 David West .30 .75
3 Amare Stoudemire .40 1.00
4 Pau Gasol .60 1.50
5 Carmelo Anthony .60 1.50
6 LeBron James 3.00 8.00
7 Dirk Nowitzki 1.00 2.50
8 Jeremy Lin .60 1.50
9 Tim Duncan 1.00 2.50
10 Samuel Dalembert .25 .60
11 Paul Pierce .60 1.50
12 DeJuan Blair .25 .60
13 Spencer Hawes .25 .60
14 Rasheed Wallace .50 1.25
15 Luc Mbah a Moute .25 .60
16 Tyreke Evans .30 .75
17 John Wall .50 1.25
18 Kevin Garnett 1.00 2.50
19 Derrick Rose .60 1.50
20 Ty Lawson .25 .60
21 Marcus Thornton .25 .60
22 James Harden .75 2.00
23 David Lee .25 .60
24 Elton Brand .30 .75
25 Damon Stoudamire .40 1.00
26 Magic Johnson 1.25 3.00
27 Cedric Ceballos .30 .75
28 Larry Bird 1.25 3.00
29 John Thompson .40 1.00
30 Glen Rice .30 .75
31 Drazen Petrovic .40 1.00
32 Manute Bol .40 1.00
33 Vlade Divac .40 1.00
34 Clyde Drexler .60 1.50
35 Brandon Jennings .40 1.00
36 Tony Parker .60 1.50
37 Mo Williams .30 .75
38 Evan Turner .25 .60
39 Steve Blake .25 .60
40 Glen Davis .25 .60
41 Chris Andersen .30 .75
42 Larry Sanders .25 .60
43 Robin Lopez .25 .60
44 Manu Ginobili .75 2.00
45 Leandro Barbosa .40 1.00
46 Jrue Holiday .50 1.25
47 Stephen Jackson .30 .75
48 Paul Millsap .30 .75
49 Jerry Stackhouse .30 .75
50 Dwight Howard .50 1.25
51 Greg Monroe .50 1.25
52 Gordon Hayward .40 1.00
53 Paul George .60 1.50
54 George Hill .30 .75
55 Blake Griffin .40 1.00
56 Kyle Lowry .40 1.00
57 Raymond Felton .25 .60
58 Kevin Durant 1.50 4.00
59 Steve Nash .75 2.00
60 Gerald Wallace .30 .75
61 Kevin Love .40 1.00
62 Jodie Meeks .25 .60
63 Andrew Bogut .30 .75
64 Vince Carter .75 2.00
65 Chris Bosh .50 1.25
66 Grant Hill .60 1.50
67 Mike Conley .30 .75
68 Ricky Rubio .30 .75
69 Carlos Boozer .30 .75
70 Kobe Bryant 3.00 8.00
71 Chris Kaman .30 .75
72 Ronnie Brewer .25 .60
73 Corey Brewer .25 .60
74 Rashard Lewis .40 1.00
75 Danny Granger .25 .60
76 Dwyane Wade .75 2.00
77 Caron Butler .30 .75
78 Goran Dragic .40 1.00
79 Rajon Rondo .50 1.25
80 JaVale McGee .30 .75
81 Shane Battier .30 .75
82 Tony Allen .25 .60
83 Antawn Jamison .30 .75
84 Brook Lopez .30 .75
85 Josh Smith .25 .60
86 Brent Barry .25 .60
87 Byron Scott .30 .75
88 Vernon Maxwell .25 .60
89 Reggie Theus .30 .75
90 Chris Mullin .50 1.25
91 Bobby Jackson .25 .60
92 Larry Nance .30 .75
93 Michael Cooper .40 1.00
94 Toni Kukoc .40 1.00
95 Robert Horry .40 1.00
96 Larry Johnson .50 1.25
97 Connie Hawkins .40 1.00
98 Darryl Dawkins .25 .60
99 Bailey Howell .40 1.00
100 George Gervin .60 1.50
101 Doc Rivers .40 1.00
102 Rod Strickland .25 .60
103 Mitch Richmond .40 1.00
104 Jamal Mashburn .30 .75
105 Bernard King .50 1.25
106 Fat Lever .30 .75
107 Sidney Moncrief .25 .60
108 Dell Curry .25 .60
109 Dominique Wilkins .50 1.25
110 Nate Archibald .50 1.25
111 Alex English .50 1.25
112 John Stockton .75 2.00
113 Tom Heinsohn .40 1.00
114 Kareem Abdul-Jabbar 1.25 3.00
115 Antoine Walker .30 .75
116 Hal Greer .50 1.25
117 Alonzo Mourning .60 1.50
118 Gary Payton .50 1.25
119 David Robinson .60 1.50
120 Hakeem Olajuwon .75 2.00
121 Moses Malone .60 1.50
122 Wes Unseld .50 1.25
123 Shaquille O'Neal 1.25 3.00
124 Dikembe Mutombo .60 1.50
125 Anfernee Hardaway 1.00 2.50
126 Chris Paul .75 2.00
127 Mario Chalmers .30 .75
128 Joakim Noah .30 .75
129 Eric Bledsoe .30 .75
130 Joe Johnson .30 .75
131 Tyson Chandler .30 .75
132 Anderson Varejao .25 .60
133 Metta World Peace .30 .75
134 J.J. Hickson .25 .60
135 Deron Williams .30 .75
136 Taj Gibson .30 .75
137 Kris Humphries .25 .60
138 Jason Richardson .40 1.00
139 Roy Hibbert .30 .75
140 Ersan Ilyasova .25 .60
141 Eric Gordon .30 .75
142 Tyler Hansbrough .25 .60
143 Ryan Anderson .25 .60
144 Stephen Curry 3.00 8.00
145 Chase Budinger .25 .60
146 Hedo Turkoglu .30 .75
147 Tiago Splitter .25 .60
148 Al-Farouq Aminu .25 .60
149 Ben Gordon .30 .75
150 James Anderson .25 .60
151 Pablo Prigioni RC .40 1.00
152 Will Barton RC .75 2.00
153 Greg Stiemsma RC .40 1.00
154 Lavoy Allen RC .40 1.00
155 Tyshawn Taylor RC .40 1.00
156 Festus Ezeli RC .40 1.00
157 Lance Thomas RC .40 1.00
158 Tyler Zeller RC .40 1.00
159 Fab Melo RC .40 1.00
160 Kyrie Irving RC 4.00 10.00
161 Tyler Honeycutt RC .40 1.00
162 Evan Fournier RC .60 1.50
163 Kyle Singler RC .60 1.50
164 Tristan Thompson RC .60 1.50
165 E'Twaun Moore RC .60 1.50
166 Kyle O'Quinn RC .50 1.25
167 Tornike Shengelia RC .40 1.00
168 Enes Kanter RC .60 1.50
169 Mirza Teletovic RC .50 1.25
170 Tony Wroten RC .40 1.00
171 Draymond Green RC 2.50 6.00
172 Klay Thompson RC 5.00 12.00
173 Tobias Harris RC 1.25 3.00
174 Doron Lamb RC .40 1.00
175 Kim English RC .40 1.00
176 Thomas Robinson RC .40 1.00
177 Donatas Motiejunas RC .50 1.25
178 Khris Middleton RC 2.00 5.00
179 Terrence Ross RC 1.00 2.50
180 Dion Waiters RC .50 1.25
181 Kent Bazemore RC .60 1.50
182 Terrence Jones RC .40 1.00
183 Derrick Williams RC .40 1.00
184 Kenneth Faried RC .50 1.25
185 Victor Claver RC .40 1.00
186 DeQuan Jones RC .40 1.00
187 Kendall Marshall RC .40 1.00
188 Royce White RC .40 1.00
189 Darius Morris RC .40 1.00
190 Kemba Walker RC 1.50 4.00
191 Robert Sacre RC .40 1.00
192 DeAndre Liggins RC .40 1.00
193 Kawhi Leonard RC 6.00 15.00
194 Reggie Jackson RC .60 1.50
195 Harrison Barnes RC .75 2.00
196 Julyan Stone RC .40 1.00
197 Quincy Miller RC .40 1.00
198 Cory Joseph RC .50 1.25
199 Jeff Taylor RC .40 1.00
200 Quincy Acy RC .40 1.00
201 Chris Singleton RC .40 1.00
202 Jordan Hamilton RC .40 1.00
203 Perry Jones RC .40 1.00
204 Chris Copeland RC .40 1.00
205 Jonas Valanciunas RC .75 2.00
206 Orlando Johnson RC .40 1.00
207 Charles Jenkins RC .40 1.00
208 John Jenkins RC .40 1.00
209 Norris Cole RC .40 1.00
210 Chandler Parsons RC .50 1.25
211 John Henson RC .50 1.25
212 Nolan Smith RC .40 1.00
213 Brian Roberts RC .40 1.00
214 Jimmy Butler RC 4.00 10.00
215 Nikola Vucevic RC 1.50 4.00
216 Brandon Knight RC .50 1.25
217 Jimmer Fredette RC .60 1.50
218 Nando De Colo RC .40 1.00
219 Bradley Beal RC 3.00 8.00
220 Jeremy Pargo RC .40 1.00
221 Maurice Harkless RC .50 1.25
222 Bismack Biyombo RC .50 1.25
223 Jeremy Lamb RC .60 1.50
224 Miles Plumlee RC .40 1.00
225 Bernard James RC .40 1.00
226 Jared Sullinger RC .40 1.00
227 Mike Scott RC .50 1.25
228 Ben Hansbrough RC .40 1.00
229 Jared Cunningham RC .40 1.00
230 Michael Kidd-Gilchrist RC .50 1.25
231 Austin Rivers RC .60 1.50
232 Jan Vesely RC .40 1.00
233 Meyers Leonard RC .50 1.25
234 Arnett Moultrie RC .40 1.00
235 Jae Crowder RC .75 2.00
236 MarShon Brooks RC .40 1.00
237 Anthony Davis RC 8.00 20.00
238 Ivan Johnson RC .40 1.00
239 Marquis Teague RC .40 1.00
240 Andrew Nicholson RC .40 1.00
241 Isaiah Thomas RC .75 2.00
242 Markieff Morris RC .60 1.50
243 Andre Drummond RC 1.00 2.50
244 Iman Shumpert RC .50 1.25
245 Marcus Morris RC .60 1.50
246 Alec Burks RC .60 1.50
247 Gustavo Ayon RC .40 1.00
248 Malcolm Lee RC .40 1.00
249 Damian Lillard RC 8.00 20.00
250 Alexey Shved RC .40 1.00

2012-13 Panini Past and Present Variations

COMMON CARD 1.00 2.50
SEMISTARS 1.25 3.00
UNLISTED STARS 1.50 4.00
1 Kevin Love 1.50 4.00
2 Kevin Durant 6.00 15.00
3 Dwyane Wade 3.00 8.00
4 Rudy Gay 1.50 4.00
5 Derrick Rose 2.50 6.00
6 Steve Nash 3.00 8.00
7 LeBron James 12.00 30.00
8 Kobe Bryant 12.00 30.00
9 Blake Griffin 1.50 4.00
10 Chris Paul 3.00 8.00
11 Carmelo Anthony 2.50 6.00
12 Deron Williams 1.25 3.00
13 Stephen Curry 12.00 30.00
14 LaMarcus Aldridge 1.50 4.00
15 James Harden 3.00 8.00
16 Jrue Holiday 2.00 5.00
17 Jeremy Lin 2.50 6.00
18 Vince Carter 3.00 8.00
19 Rajon Rondo 2.00 5.00
20 Ray Allen 2.50 6.00
21 Eric Gordon 1.25 3.00
22 Kyrie Irving 10.00 25.00
23 Bradley Beal 8.00 20.00
24 Anthony Davis 12.00 30.00
25 Damian Lillard 10.00 25.00
26 Shaquille O'Neal 5.00 12.00
27 Larry Bird 5.00 12.00
28 Mitch Richmond 1.50 4.00
29 Moses Malone 2.50 6.00
30 George Gervin 2.50 6.00
31 Magic Johnson 5.00 12.00
32 Larry Johnson 2.00 5.00
33 Kareem Abdul-Jabbar 5.00 12.00
34 Julius Erving 4.00 10.00
35 John Stockton 3.00 8.00
36 Joe Dumars 2.00 5.00
37 Dominique Wilkins 2.00 5.00
38 Hakeem Olajuwon 3.00 8.00
39 Gary Payton 2.00 5.00
40 Alonzo Mourning 2.50 6.00
41 Drazen Petrovic 1.50 4.00
42 Dikembe Mutombo 2.50 6.00
43 Clyde Drexler 2.50 6.00
44 Chris Mullin 2.00 5.00
45 Charles Oakley 1.50 4.00
46 Anfernee Hardaway 4.00 10.00
47 Nate Archibald 2.00 5.00
48 Fat Lever 1.25 3.00
49 Alex English 2.00 5.00
50 Connie Hawkins 1.50 4.00

2012-13 Panini Past and Present Championship Banners

COMPLETE SET (25) 20.00 50.00
APPX.ODDS 1:10 HOBBY
1 Tim Duncan 2.50 6.00
2 Dirk Nowitzki 2.50 6.00
3 Kobe Bryant 8.00 20.00
4 Hakeem Olajuwon 2.00 5.00
5 Scottie Pippen 2.50 6.00
6 Isiah Thomas 2.00 5.00
7 Dwyane Wade 2.00 5.00
8 Larry Bird 3.00 8.00
9 Robert Horry 1.00 2.50
10 Dennis Rodman 2.50 6.00
11 Shaquille O'Neal 3.00 8.00
12 Manu Ginobili 2.00 5.00
13 Moses Malone 1.50 4.00
14 Kareem Abdul-Jabbar 3.00 8.00
15 Kenny Smith .75 2.00
16 Tony Parker 1.50 4.00
17 LeBron James 8.00 20.00
18 Joe Dumars 1.25 3.00
19 Bill Russell 3.00 8.00
20 Magic Johnson 3.00 8.00
21 Chris Bosh 1.25 3.00
22 David Robinson 1.50 4.00
23 Luc Longley .75 2.00
24 James Worthy 1.50 4.00
25 Paul Pierce 1.50 4.00

2012-13 Panini Past and Present Dual Jerseys

1 T.Lawson/R.Felton/99 3.00 8.00
2 A.Bargnani/D.Nowitzki/99 12.00 30.00
3 M.Gasol/P.Gasol/99 8.00 20.00
4 V.Carter/K.Bryant/99 10.00 25.00
5 T.Hansbrough/S.Hawes/99 3.00 8.00
6 G.Hill/J.Calderon/99 4.00 10.00
7 G.Monroe/A.Mourning/99 8.00 20.00
8 S.Pippen/P.Pierce/99 12.00 30.00
9 C.Drexler/A.Iguodala/99 8.00 20.00
10 J.Smith/T.Evans/99 5.00 12.00
11 B.Wallace/M.Camby/99 5.00 12.00
12 D.Robinson/K.Garnett/49 12.00 30.00
13 J.Smith/T.Thomas/99 3.00 8.00
14 K.Irving/D.Rose/99 15.00 40.00
15 T.Thompson/C.Bosh/99 6.00 15.00
16 B.Griffin/K.Malone/49 8.00 20.00
17 L.James/K.Bryant/49 25.00 60.00
18 L.Johnson/D.Favors/49 12.00 30.00
19 T.Duncan/P.Ewing/49 12.00 30.00
20 I.Thomas/C.Paul/49 6.00 15.00

2012-13 Panini Past and Present Dual Jerseys Prime

*PRIME: .75X TO 2X BASIC
STATED PRINT RUN 25 SER.#'d SETS

2012-13 Panini Past and Present Elusive Ink

EXCHANGE DEADLINE 11/01/2014
1 Rick Fox 4.00 10.00
2 Fat Lever 4.00 10.00
3 Luc Longley 4.00 10.00
4 Jack Sikma 4.00 10.00
5 B.J. Armstrong 5.00 12.00
6 Willis Reed 40.00 100.00
7 Will Perdue 3.00 8.00
8 Dana Barros 3.00 8.00
9 Ray Williams 3.00 8.00
11 George McGinnis 5.00 12.00
12 Horace Grant 5.00 12.00
14 Glen Rice 4.00 10.00
15 Bob Dandridge 3.00 8.00
16 Tom Gugliotta 3.00 8.00
17 Rod Strickland 3.00 8.00
19 Doug Christie 3.00 8.00
20 Jeff Malone 3.00 8.00
21 Jim Jackson 4.00 10.00
22 Jo Jo White 4.00 10.00
23 Cazzie Russell 4.00 10.00
24 Nate McMillan 3.00 8.00
25 Sam Cassell 4.00 10.00
26 Spud Webb 4.00 10.00
27 Scott Skiles 4.00 10.00
28 Paul Silas 5.00 12.00
29 Brad Daugherty 4.00 10.00
30 Terry Porter 4.00 10.00
31 Christian Laettner 5.00 12.00
32 Charles Oakley 5.00 12.00
33 Vlade Divac 5.00 12.00
34 Herb Williams 3.00 8.00
35 Kendall Gill 3.00 8.00
37 Isaiah Rider 8.00 20.00
39 Jay Williams 3.00 8.00

2012-13 Panini Past and Present Gamers Jerseys

NO PRICING DUE TO LACK OF MARKET INFO
1 Dwyane Wade 5.00 12.00
2 Kevin Durant 8.00 20.00
3 Dirk Nowitzki 8.00 20.00
4 Tayshaun Prince 3.00 8.00
5 Derrick Williams 2.00 5.00
6 Zach Randolph 3.00 8.00
7 Gordon Hayward 3.00 8.00
8 Kevin Love 3.00 8.00
9 Rodney Stuckey 2.00 5.00
10 Arron Afflalo 2.00 5.00
11 Calvin Murphy 2.50 6.00
12 Dominique Wilkins 5.00 12.00
13 Bill Laimbeer 4.00 10.00
14 Alvan Adams 2.00 5.00
15 Larry Johnson 6.00 15.00
16 Hakeem Olajuwon 6.00 15.00
17 Karl Malone 6.00 15.00
18 James Worthy 8.00 20.00
19 Tyreke Evans 2.50 6.00
20 Metta World Peace 2.50 6.00
21 LaMarcus Aldridge 3.00 8.00
22 Andrea Bargnani 2.50 6.00
23 Tim Duncan 8.00 20.00
24 Kobe Bryant 10.00 25.00
25 David Lee 2.00 5.00
26 Glen Davis 2.00 5.00
27 Marc Gasol 3.00 8.00
28 Amare Stoudemire 3.00 8.00
29 John Wall 4.00 10.00
30 Derrick Favors 2.50 6.00

2012-13 Panini Past and Present Hall Marks Autographs

EXCHANGE DEADLINE 11/01/2014
1 Larry Bird 75.00 150.00

2 Magic Johnson 30.00 80.00
3 David Robinson 20.00 50.00
4 Dennis Rodman 40.00 80.00
5 Scottie Pippen 40.00 100.00
6 Hakeem Olajuwon 15.00 40.00
7 James Worthy 12.00 30.00
8 Bob McAdoo EXCH 6.00 15.00
9 Alex English 8.00 20.00
12 Nate Archibald 12.00 30.00
13 David Thompson 6.00 15.00
14 Kareem Abdul-Jabbar 30.00 80.00
17 Julius Erving 30.00 80.00
18 Bill Sharman 6.00 15.00
20 Clyde Drexler 15.00 40.00

2012-13 Panini Past and Present Headbands

COMPLETE SET (25) 20.00 50.00
APPX.THREE PER HOBBY BOX
1 Isaiah Thomas 1.25 3.00
2 Zach Randolph 1.00 2.50
3 Corey Brewer .60 1.50
4 Vince Carter 2.00 5.00
5 Ronnie Brewer .60 1.50
6 Gerald Wallace .75 2.00
7 Dwight Howard 1.25 3.00
8 Paul Pierce 1.50 4.00
9 Anderson Varejao .60 1.50
10 Josh Smith .60 1.50
11 Rasheed Wallace 1.25 3.00
12 LeBron James 8.00 20.00
13 Jared Dudley .60 1.50
14 DeMarcus Cousins 1.00 2.50
15 Ty Lawson .60 1.50
16 Carmelo Anthony 1.50 4.00
17 Chris Andersen .75 2.00
18 Jason Terry .75 2.00
19 Stephen Jackson .75 2.00
20 Drew Gooden .75 2.00
21 Daniel Gibson .60 1.50
22 Michael Beasley .60 1.50
23 Reggie Evans .60 1.50
24 Dirk Nowitzki 2.50 6.00
25 Corey Maggette .75 2.00

2012-13 Panini Past and Present Modern Marks Autographs

EXCHANGE DEADLINE 11/01/2014
1 Kobe Bryant 400.00 800.00
2 Kevin Durant 60.00 150.00
3 Blake Griffin 15.00 40.00
4 Andre Iguodala 5.00 12.00
5 Ben Gordon 4.00 10.00
6 Carl Landry 3.00 8.00
7 Carlos Boozer EXCH 4.00 10.00
8 Chris Bosh 6.00 15.00
9 David Lee 3.00 8.00
12 Deron Williams 4.00 10.00
13 Eric Gordon 4.00 10.00
14 Gordon Hayward 10.00 25.00
15 Grant Hill 25.00 60.00
16 James Harden 30.00 80.00
17 JaVale McGee EXCH 4.00 10.00
18 Joakim Noah 4.00 10.00
19 Joe Johnson 4.00 10.00
20 Kendrick Perkins 3.00 8.00
21 Kevin Love 10.00 25.00
22 Kevin Martin 4.00 10.00
23 Stephen Curry EXCH 500.00 1,000.00
24 Stephen Jackson EXCH 4.00 10.00
25 Steve Nash 40.00 100.00
26 Steve Novak 3.00 8.00
27 Tony Parker 15.00 40.00
28 Vince Carter EXCH 40.00 100.00
29 Zach Randolph 5.00 12.00
30 Artis Gilmore 12.00 30.00
31 Dolph Schayes 10.00 25.00
32 Elvin Hayes 10.00 25.00
33 Don Nelson 15.00 40.00
35 Kelly Tripucka 4.00 10.00
36 Kyrie Irving 50.00 120.00
37 Anthony Davis 200.00 500.00
38 Kawhi Leonard 60.00 150.00
39 Michael Kidd-Gilchrist 4.00 10.00
40 Dion Waiters EXCH 4.00 10.00

2012-13 Panini Past and Present Raining 3's

COMPLETE SET (15) 15.00 40.00
APPX.ODDS 1:10 HOBBY
1 Joe Johnson .75 2.00
2 Jason Terry .75 2.00
3 Carmelo Anthony 1.50 4.00
4 Damian Lillard 6.00 15.00
5 Ryan Anderson .60 1.50
6 Kevin Martin .60 1.50
7 Klay Thompson 6.00 15.00
8 Randy Foye .60 1.50
9 Kobe Bryant 8.00 20.00
10 Steve Novak .60 1.50
11 Chandler Parsons .75 2.00
12 O.J. Mayo .60 1.50
13 Stephen Curry 8.00 20.00
14 James Harden 2.00 5.00
15 Nicolas Batum .60 1.50

2012-13 Panini Past and Present Rise N Shine

ONE PER HOBBY PACK
1 James Harden 1.50 4.00
2 Alexey Shved .50 1.25
3 Dwight Howard 1.00 2.50
4 Blake Griffin .75 2.00
5 Kendrick Perkins .50 1.25
6 Avery Bradley .50 1.25
7 DeMar DeRozan 1.00 2.50
8 Bradley Beal 4.00 10.00
9 Evan Turner .50 1.25
10 Kevin Durant 3.00 8.00
11 Dirk Nowitzki 2.00 5.00
12 Kawhi Leonard 20.00 50.00
13 Goran Dragic .75 2.00
14 Alonzo Gee .50 1.25
15 Andre Iguodala .75 2.00
16 Damian Lillard 8.00 20.00
17 David Lee .50 1.25
18 Chris Paul 1.50 4.00
19 Brandon Jennings .50 1.25
20 JaVale McGee .60 1.50
21 Andre Drummond 1.25 3.00
22 Kevin Garnett 2.00 5.00
23 John Wall 1.00 2.50
24 Derrick Rose 1.25 3.00
25 Marreese Speights .50 1.25
26 George Hill .60 1.50
27 Mike Conley .60 1.50
28 Brandon Knight .60 1.50
29 Amare Stoudemire .75 2.00
30 Kevin Love .75 2.00
31 Jodie Meeks .50 1.25
32 Joakim Noah .60 1.50
33 Manu Ginobili 1.50 4.00
34 Jae Crowder 1.00 2.50
35 Paul George 1.25 3.00
36 Al-Farouq Aminu .50 1.25
37 Anderson Varejao .50 1.25
38 Rudy Gay .75 2.00
39 O.J. Mayo .50 1.25
40 Isaiah Thomas 1.00 2.50
41 Jrue Holiday 1.00 2.50
42 Deron Williams .60 1.50
43 Harrison Barnes 1.00 2.50
44 Chandler Parsons .60 1.50
45 Michael Kidd-Gilchrist .60 1.50
46 Carmelo Anthony 1.25 3.00
47 Jonas Valanciunas 1.00 2.50
48 Jeremy Lin 1.25 3.00
49 DeAndre Jordan .60 1.50
50 Dwyane Wade 1.50 4.00
51 Ricky Rubio .60 1.50
52 Ben Gordon .60 1.50
53 Paul Pierce 1.25 3.00
54 Al Jefferson .50 1.25
55 Thomas Robinson .50 1.25
56 Iman Shumpert .60 1.50
57 Rajon Rondo 1.00 2.50
58 Eric Bledsoe .60 1.50
59 Greg Monroe .50 1.25
60 Kobe Bryant 6.00 15.00
61 Al Horford .75 2.00
62 Kemba Walker 2.00 5.00
63 LeBron James 6.00 15.00
64 Anthony Davis 12.00 30.00
65 Mario Chalmers .60 1.50
66 Austin Rivers .75 2.00
67 J.R. Smith .75 2.00
68 Kevin Martin .60 1.50
69 Gerald Wallace .60 1.50
70 Russell Westbrook 1.25 3.00
71 Josh Smith .50 1.25
72 Kenneth Faried .60 1.50
73 LaMarcus Aldridge .75 2.00
74 Derrick Favors .60 1.50
75 Omer Asik .50 1.25
76 Roy Hibbert .60 1.50
77 Ty Lawson .50 1.25
78 Gordon Hayward .75 2.00
79 Larry Sanders .50 1.25
80 Marcin Gortat .50 1.25
81 Stephen Curry 6.00 15.00
82 Brook Lopez .60 1.50
83 Mo Williams .60 1.50
84 Nick Young .50 1.25
85 Serge Ibaka .60 1.50
86 Zach Randolph .75 2.00
87 Taj Gibson .50 1.25
88 Ray Allen 1.25 3.00
89 Eric Gordon .60 1.50
90 Jameer Nelson .50 1.25
91 Dion Waiters .60 1.50
92 Thaddeus Young .50 1.25
93 Nicolas Batum .60 1.50
94 Greivis Vasquez .50 1.25
95 Shawn Marion .75 2.00
96 Nikola Vucevic 2.00 5.00
97 Metta World Peace .60 1.50
98 Tony Parker 1.25 3.00
99 Kyrie Irving 5.00 12.00
100 Jared Sullinger .50 1.25

2012-13 Panini Past and Present Shattered

APPX.ODDS 1:10 HOBBY
1 Dominique Wilkins 1.25 3.00
2 Josh Smith .60 1.50
3 Kevin Garnett 2.50 6.00
4 Gerald Wallace .75 2.00
5 Byron Mullens .60 1.50
6 Michael Kidd-Gilchrist .75 2.00
7 Steve Francis .75 2.00
8 Derrick Rose 1.50 4.00
9 Joakim Noah .75 2.00
10 Brandon Bass .60 1.50
11 Taj Gibson .60 1.50
12 Alonzo Gee .60 1.50
13 Anderson Varejao .60 1.50
14 Dion Waiters .75 2.00
15 Vince Carter 2.00 5.00
16 Andre Iguodala 1.00 2.50
17 Corey Brewer .60 1.50
18 JaVale McGee .75 2.00
19 David Lee .60 1.50
20 Harrison Barnes 1.25 3.00
21 James Harden 2.00 5.00
22 Gerald Green .75 2.00
23 Paul George 1.50 4.00
24 Blake Griffin 1.00 2.50
25 DeAndre Jordan .75 2.00
26 Dwight Howard 1.25 3.00
27 Kobe Bryant 8.00 20.00
28 Rudy Gay 1.00 2.50
29 Dwyane Wade 2.00 5.00
30 LeBron James 8.00 20.00
31 Larry Sanders .60 1.50
32 Anthony Davis 8.00 20.00
33 Amare Stoudemire 1.00 2.50
34 Tyson Chandler .75 2.00
35 Kevin Durant 4.00 10.00
36 Russell Westbrook 1.50 4.00
37 Serge Ibaka .75 2.00
38 Darryl Dawkins .60 1.50
39 Shawn Marion 1.00 2.50
40 Julius Erving 2.50 6.00
41 Shannon Brown .60 1.50
42 Clyde Drexler 1.50 4.00
43 LaMarcus Aldridge 1.00 2.50
44 Will Barton 1.25 3.00
45 George Gervin 1.50 4.00
46 Shawn Kemp 1.50 4.00
47 DeMar DeRozan 1.25 3.00
48 J.R. Smith 1.00 2.50
49 Shaquille O'Neal 3.00 8.00
50 Bradley Beal 5.00 12.00

2012-13 Panini Past and Present Shattered Black

APPX.ODDS 1:20 HOBBY
1 Dominique Wilkins 1.50 4.00
2 Josh Smith .75 2.00
3 Kevin Garnett 3.00 8.00
4 Gerald Wallace 1.00 2.50
5 Byron Mullens .75 2.00
6 Michael Kidd-Gilchrist 1.00 2.50
7 Steve Francis 1.00 2.50
8 Derrick Rose 2.00 5.00
9 Joakim Noah 1.00 2.50
10 Brandon Bass .75 2.00
11 Taj Gibson .75 2.00
12 Alonzo Gee .75 2.00
13 Anderson Varejao .75 2.00
14 Dion Waiters 1.00 2.50
15 Vince Carter 2.50 6.00
16 Andre Iguodala 1.25 3.00
17 Corey Brewer .75 2.00
18 JaVale McGee 1.00 2.50
19 David Lee .75 2.00
20 Harrison Barnes 1.50 4.00
21 James Harden 2.50 6.00
22 Gerald Green 1.00 2.50
23 Paul George 2.00 5.00
24 Blake Griffin 1.25 3.00
25 DeAndre Jordan 1.00 2.50
26 Dwight Howard 1.50 4.00
27 Kobe Bryant 10.00 25.00
28 Rudy Gay 1.25 3.00
29 Dwyane Wade 2.50 6.00
30 LeBron James 10.00 25.00
31 Larry Sanders .75 2.00
32 Anthony Davis 10.00 25.00
33 Amare Stoudemire 1.25 3.00
34 Tyson Chandler 1.00 2.50
35 Kevin Durant 5.00 12.00
36 Russell Westbrook 2.00 5.00
37 Serge Ibaka 1.00 2.50
38 Darryl Dawkins .75 2.00
39 Shawn Marion 1.25 3.00
40 Julius Erving 3.00 8.00
41 Shannon Brown .75 2.00
42 Clyde Drexler 2.00 5.00
43 LaMarcus Aldridge 1.25 3.00
44 Will Barton 1.50 4.00
45 George Gervin 2.00 5.00
46 Shawn Kemp 2.00 5.00
47 DeMar DeRozan 1.50 4.00
48 J.R. Smith 1.25 3.00
49 Shaquille O'Neal 4.00 10.00
50 Bradley Beal 6.00 15.00

2012-13 Panini Past and Present Signatures

EXCHANGE DEADLINE 11/01/2014
51 Greg Monroe 3.00 8.00
52 Gordon Hayward 6.00 15.00
54 George Hill 4.00 10.00
55 Blake Griffin EXCH 12.00 30.00
56 Kyle Lowry 5.00 12.00
57 Raymond Felton 3.00 8.00
58 Kevin Durant 60.00 150.00
59 Steve Nash 40.00 100.00
60 Gerald Wallace 4.00 10.00
61 Kevin Love 12.00 30.00
62 Jodie Meeks 3.00 8.00
63 Andrew Bogut 4.00 10.00
64 Vince Carter 12.00 30.00
65 Chris Bosh 6.00 15.00
66 Grant Hill 12.00 30.00
67 Mike Conley 6.00 15.00
68 Ricky Rubio 10.00 25.00
69 Carlos Boozer 4.00 10.00
70 Kobe Bryant 400.00 800.00
71 Chris Kaman 4.00 10.00
72 Ronnie Brewer 3.00 8.00
73 Corey Brewer 3.00 8.00
74 Rashard Lewis 5.00 12.00
75 Danny Granger 3.00 8.00
76 Dwyane Wade 30.00 80.00
77 Caron Butler 4.00 10.00
78 Goran Dragic 8.00 20.00
80 JaVale McGee 4.00 10.00
81 Shane Battier 4.00 10.00
82 Tony Allen 3.00 8.00
83 Antawn Jamison 4.00 10.00
84 Brook Lopez 4.00 10.00
85 Josh Smith 3.00 8.00
86 Brent Barry 3.00 8.00
87 Byron Scott 4.00 10.00
88 Vernon Maxwell 3.00 8.00
89 Reggie Theus 4.00 10.00
90 Chris Mullin 6.00 15.00
91 Bobby Jackson 3.00 8.00
92 Larry Nance 4.00 10.00
93 Michael Cooper 5.00 12.00
94 Toni Kukoc 8.00 20.00
95 Robert Horry 5.00 12.00
96 Larry Johnson 4.00 10.00
97 Connie Hawkins 8.00 20.00
98 Darryl Dawkins 3.00 8.00
100 George Gervin 6.00 15.00
101 Doc Rivers 5.00 12.00
102 Rod Strickland 3.00 8.00
103 Mitch Richmond EXCH 12.00 30.00
104 Jamal Mashburn 4.00 10.00
105 Bernard King 6.00 15.00
106 Fat Lever 4.00 10.00
107 Sidney Moncrief [illegible] 8.00
108 Dell Curry [illegible] 8.00
109 Dominique Wilkins 12.00 30.00
110 Nate Archibald [illegible] 15.00
111 Alex English [illegible] 15.00
113 Tom Heinsohn 25.00 60.00
115 Antoine Walker 4.00 10.00
116 Gail Hill 6.00 15.00
117 Alonzo Mourning 8.00 20.00
119 David Robinson 12.00 30.00
120 Hakeem Olajuwon 20.00 50.00
122 Wes Unseld 10.00 25.00
124 Dikembe Mutombo 10.00 25.00
125 Anfernee Hardaway 12.00 30.00
127 Mario Chalmers 4.00 10.00
128 Joakim Noah 4.00 10.00
129 Eric Bledsoe 4.00 10.00
130 Joe Johnson 4.00 10.00
131 Tyson Chandler 4.00 10.00
132 Anderson Varejao 3.00 8.00
133 Metta World Peace 4.00 10.00
134 J.J. Hickson 3.00 8.00
135 Deron Williams 4.00 10.00
136 Taj Gibson 3.00 8.00
137 Kris Humphries 3.00 8.00
138 Jason Richardson 5.00 12.00
139 Roy Hibbert 4.00 10.00
140 Ersan Ilyasova 3.00 8.00
141 Eric Gordon 4.00 10.00
142 Tyler Hansbrough 3.00 8.00
143 Ryan Anderson 3.00 8.00
144 Stephen Curry 400.00 800.00
145 Chase Budinger 3.00 8.00
146 Hedo Turkoglu 4.00 10.00
147 Tiago Splitter 3.00 8.00
148 Al-Farouq Aminu 3.00 8.00
149 Ben Gordon 4.00 10.00
150 James Anderson 3.00 8.00
152 Will Barton 6.00 15.00
153 Greg Stiemsma 3.00 8.00
154 Lavoy Allen 3.00 8.00
155 Tyshawn Taylor 3.00 8.00
156 Festus Ezeli 3.00 8.00
157 Lance Thomas 3.00 8.00
158 Tyler Zeller 3.00 8.00
159 Fab Melo EXCH 3.00 8.00
160 Kyrie Irving 40.00 100.00
161 Tyler Honeycutt 3.00 8.00
162 Evan Fournier 5.00 12.00
163 Kyle Singler 3.00 8.00
164 Tristan Thompson 5.00 12.00
165 E'Twaun Moore 4.00 10.00
166 Kyle O'Quinn 4.00 10.00
167 Tornike Shengelia 3.00 8.00
168 Enes Kanter 5.00 12.00
169 Mirza Teletovic 4.00 10.00
170 Tony Wroten 3.00 8.00
171 Draymond Green 40.00 100.00
172 Klay Thompson 75.00 200.00
173 Tobias Harris 8.00 20.00
174 Doron Lamb 3.00 8.00
175 Kim English 3.00 8.00
176 Thomas Robinson 3.00 8.00
177 Donatas Motiejunas 4.00 10.00
178 Kris Middleton 15.00 40.00
179 Terrence Ross 8.00 20.00
180 Dion Waiters EXCH 4.00 10.00
181 Kent Bazemore 5.00 12.00
182 Terrence Jones 3.00 8.00
183 Derrick Williams 3.00 8.00
184 Kenneth Faried 4.00 10.00
185 Victor Claver 3.00 8.00
186 DeQuan Jones 3.00 8.00
187 Kendall Marshall 3.00 8.00
188 Royce White 3.00 8.00
189 Darius Morris 4.00 10.00
190 Kemba Walker 12.00 30.00
191 Robert Sacre 3.00 8.00
192 DeAndre Liggins 3.00 8.00
193 Kawhi Leonard 125.00 300.00
194 Reggie Jackson 5.00 12.00
195 Harrison Barnes 6.00 15.00
196 Julyan Stone 3.00 8.00
197 Quincy Miller 3.00 8.00
198 Cory Joseph 4.00 10.00
199 Jeff Taylor 3.00 8.00
200 Quincy Acy 3.00 8.00
201 Chris Singleton 3.00 8.00
202 Jordan Hamilton 3.00 8.00
203 Perry Jones 3.00 8.00
204 Chris Copeland 3.00 8.00
205 Jonas Valanciunas 6.00 15.00
206 Orlando Johnson 3.00 8.00
207 Charles Jenkins 3.00 8.00
208 John Jenkins 3.00 8.00
209 Norris Cole 3.00 8.00
210 Chandler Parsons 4.00 10.00
211 John Henson 4.00 10.00
212 Nolan Smith 3.00 8.00
213 Brian Roberts 3.00 8.00
214 Jimmy Butler 40.00 100.00
215 Nikola Vucevic 12.00 30.00
216 Brandon Knight 4.00 10.00
217 Jimmer Fredette 5.00 12.00
218 Nando De Colo 3.00 8.00
219 Bradley Beal 25.00 60.00
220 Jeremy Pargo 3.00 8.00
221 Maurice Harkless 4.00 10.00
222 Bismack Biyombo 4.00 10.00
223 Jeremy Lamb 5.00 12.00
224 Miles Plumlee 3.00 8.00
225 Bernard James 3.00 8.00
226 Jared Sullinger 3.00 8.00
227 Mike Scott 4.00 10.00
228 Ben Hansbrough 3.00 8.00
229 Jared Cunningham 3.00 8.00
230 Michael Kidd-Gilchrist 4.00 10.00
231 Austin Rivers 5.00 12.00
232 Jan Vesely 3.00 8.00
233 Meyers Leonard 4.00 10.00
234 Arnett Moultrie 3.00 8.00
235 Jae Crowder 6.00 15.00
236 MarShon Brooks 3.00 8.00
237 Anthony Davis 75.00 200.00
238 Ivan Johnson 3.00 8.00
239 Marquis Teague 3.00 8.00
240 Andrew Nicholson 3.00 8.00
241 Isaiah Thomas 6.00 15.00
242 Markieff Morris 5.00 12.00
243 Andre Drummond 8.00 20.00
244 Iman Shumpert 4.00 10.00
245 Marcus Morris 5.00 12.00
246 Alec Burks 5.00 12.00
247 Gustavo Ayon 3.00 8.00
248 Malcolm Lee 3.00 8.00
250 Alexey Shved 3.00 8.00

2012-13 Panini Past and Present Treads

COMPLETE SET (35) 20.00 50.00
APPX.ODDS 1:4 HOBBY
1 Chris Paul 1.50 4.00
2 Monta Ellis .60 1.50
3 Dwight Howard 1.00 2.50
4 Harrison Barnes 1.00 2.50
5 Kevin Durant 3.00 8.00
6 LeBron James 6.00 15.00
7 Paul George 1.25 3.00
8 Kevin Love .75 2.00
9 Vince Carter 1.50 4.00
10 Tim Duncan 2.00 5.00
11 Ricky Rubio .60 1.50
12 Rudy Gay .75 2.00
13 Paul Pierce 1.25 3.00
14 John Wall 1.00 2.50
15 Dirk Nowitzki 2.00 5.00
16 David Lee .60 1.50
17 Blake Griffin .75 2.00
18 Russell Westbrook 1.25 3.00
19 Michael Kidd-Gilchrist .60 1.50
20 Rajon Rondo 1.00 2.50
21 Dwyane Wade 1.50 4.00
22 Andre Iguodala .75 2.00
23 Anthony Davis 6.00 15.00
24 Kobe Bryant 6.00 15.00
25 Tyreke Evans .60 1.50
26 Brandon Knight .60 1.50
27 O.J. Mayo .50 1.25
28 Deron Williams .60 1.50
29 Derrick Rose 1.25 3.00
30 Carmelo Anthony 1.25 3.00
31 DeMar DeRozan 1.00 2.50
32 Kyrie Irving 5.00 12.00
33 Kevin Garnett 2.00 5.00
34 Damian Lillard 8.00 20.00
35 James Harden 1.50 4.00

2023-24 Panini Phoenix

1 Kevin Durant 1.25 3.00
2 Jason Kidd .60 1.50
3 Karl Malone .75 2.00
4 Mikal Bridges .50 1.25
5 Naz Reid .40 1.00
6 Larry Bird 1.50 4.00
7 Immanuel Quickley .40 1.00
8 Allen Iverson 1.00 2.50
9 Marcus Smart .50 1.25
10 John Stockton .75 2.00
11 Zion Williamson 1.00 2.50
12 Tyus Jones .30 .75
13 Taurean Prince .25 .60
14 Jaden Hardy .50 1.25
15 Gordon Hayward .40 1.00
16 Jerami Grant .50 1.25
17 Norman Powell .40 1.00
18 Jerry West .75 2.00
19 Jaden McDaniels .40 1.00
20 Josh Giddey .50 1.25
21 Coby White .40 1.00
22 Isaac Okoro .30 .75
23 Tim Hardaway Jr. .30 .75
24 Jeremy Sochan .50 1.25
25 Jrue Holiday .50 1.25
26 Jose Alvarado .40 1.00
27 Gary Payton .60 1.50
28 Reggie Jackson .25 .60
29 Shaedon Sharpe .75 2.00
30 Pascal Siakam .60 1.50
31 Derrick Rose .60 1.50
32 Chris Paul .75 2.00
33 Rasheed Wallace .50 1.25
34 Wilt Chamberlain 1.25 3.00
35 Ja Morant 1.25 3.00
36 Marvin Bagley III .30 .75
37 Dyson Daniels .50 1.25
38 Malik Monk .50 1.25
39 Tre Mann .40 1.00
40 Malcolm Brogdon .40 1.00
41 Shaquille O'Neal 1.25 3.00
42 Walker Kessler .40 1.00
43 Dwyane Wade .75 2.00
44 Jalen Suggs .50 1.25
45 Pete Maravich 1.00 2.50
46 Miles Bridges .40 1.00
47 Paul Pierce .60 1.50
48 Mike Conley .30 .75
49 Manu Ginobili .75 2.00
50 Peyton Watson .40 1.00
51 Austin Reaves 1.00 2.50
52 Kareem Abdul-Jabbar 1.25 3.00
53 Tobias Harris .40 1.00
54 Yao Ming 1.00 2.50
55 Bennedict Mathurin .60 1.50
56 Dennis Schroder .40 1.00
57 Devin Booker 1.00 2.50
58 Jalen Green .60 1.50
59 Jamal Murray .75 2.00
60 Tim Duncan 1.00 2.50
61 Steve Nash .75 2.00
62 Nikola Vucevic .40 1.00
63 Grant Hill .60 1.50
64 Brandon Roy .50 1.25
65 Kevin Love .40 1.00
66 Dirk Nowitzki 1.00 2.50
67 Michael Porter Jr. .50 1.25
68 Carmelo Anthony .60 1.50
69 Bol Bol .40 1.00
70 Kyle Lowry .50 1.25
71 Zach Collins .30 .75
72 OG Anunoby .50 1.25
73 Jarrett Allen .40 1.00
74 RJ Barrett .60 1.50
75 CJ McCollum .40 1.00
76 Bruce Brown .40 1.00
77 Jaylen Brown .75 2.00
78 Derrick White .50 1.25
79 Damian Lillard 1.00 2.50
80 Magic Johnson 1.50 4.00
81 MarJon Beauchamp .30 .75
82 Chet Holmgren 1.00 2.50
83 Jordan Clarkson .40 1.00
84 Zach LaVine .60 1.50
85 Duncan Robinson .40 1.00
86 Rudy Gobert .50 1.25
87 Gary Trent Jr. .40 1.00
88 Jermaine O'Neal .40 1.00
89 Domantas Sabonis .60 1.50
90 De'Aaron Fox .75 2.00
91 Al Horford .40 1.00
92 Tracy McGrady .60 1.50
93 Alonzo Mourning .60 1.50
94 Shai Gilgeous-Alexander 2.00 5.00
95 Evan Mobley .60 1.50
96 Kawhi Leonard 1.00 2.50
97 Toni Kukoc .50 1.25
98 Jerry Stackhouse .40 1.00
99 Tyrese Haliburton .75 2.00
100 Vince Williams Jr. .40 1.00
101 Julius Randle .50 1.25
102 Lauri Markkanen .60 1.50
103 Bam Adebayo .60 1.50
104 Deni Avdija .40 1.00
105 Ben Simmons .40 1.00
106 Bradley Beal .50 1.25
107 Rui Hachimura .40 1.00
108 DeMar DeRozan .60 1.50
109 Gilbert Arenas .40 1.00
110 Alex Caruso .40 1.00
111 Saddiq Bey .40 1.00
112 Jonathan Kuminga 1.00 2.50
113 Patrick Williams .30 .75
114 Tyrese Maxey .75 2.00
115 Patrick Beverley .30 .75
116 Eric Gordon .30 .75
117 Terry Rozier III .50 1.25
118 Trey Murphy III .50 1.25
119 Kyrie Irving .75 2.00
120 Keegan Murray .50 1.25
121 Wendell Carter Jr. .40 1.00
122 Kelly Oubre Jr. .40 1.00
123 Charles Barkley 1.00 2.50
124 Kelly Olynyk .25 .60
125 Aaron Gordon .40 1.00
126 Markelle Fultz .30 .75
127 Dillon Brooks .40 1.00
128 Kyle Kuzma .50 1.25
129 Brandon Ingram .50 1.25
130 Onyeka Okongwu .30 .75
131 P.J. Washington Jr. .40 1.00
132 Fred VanVleet .60 1.50
133 Pau Gasol .60 1.50
134 Isaiah Stewart .40 1.00
135 De'Anthony Melton .40 1.00
136 D'Angelo Russell .40 1.00
137 Josh Hart .40 1.00
138 Clint Capela .30 .75
139 Luguentz Dort .40 1.00
140 LaMelo Ball 1.00 2.50
141 Andrew Wiggins .50 1.25
142 Dennis Rodman 1.00 2.50
143 Tari Eason .50 1.25
144 Jalen Johnson .50 1.25
145 Jayson Tatum 1.50 4.00
146 Donovan Mitchell .75 2.00
147 Mark Williams .40 1.00
148 Jaden Ivey .50 1.25
149 Gary Harris .30 .75
150 Collin Sexton .50 1.25
151 Jordan Poole .60 1.50
152 Kristaps Porzingis .50 1.25
153 Malaki Branham .30 .75
154 Precious Achiuwa .30 .75
155 Kevin Garnett 1.00 2.50
156 Trae Young .75 2.00
157 Luka Doncic 2.50 6.00
158 Buddy Hield .40 1.00
159 Anfernee Hardaway 1.00 2.50
160 David Robinson .75 2.00
161 Josh Green .30 .75
162 Ayo Dosunmu .40 1.00
163 Cam Reddish .30 .75
164 Klay Thompson 1.00 2.50
165 Karl-Anthony Towns .60 1.50
166 John Collins .40 1.00
167 Grayson Allen .40 1.00
168 Devin Vassell .50 1.25
169 Nikola Jokic 2.00 5.00
170 Paolo Banchero 1.00 2.50
171 Caleb Martin .30 .75
172 Russell Westbrook .60 1.50
173 Spencer Dinwiddie .30 .75
174 Stephen Curry 3.00 8.00
175 Malik Beasley .40 1.00
176 Giannis Antetokounmpo 2.00 5.00
177 Anfernee Simons .50 1.25
178 Jalen Williams .75 2.00
179 Herbert Jones .40 1.00
180 Zach Randolph .40 1.00
181 Patrick Ewing .60 1.50
182 Alperen Sengun .60 1.50
183 Myles Turner .40 1.00
184 Darius Garland .60 1.50
185 Chris Bosh .50 1.25
186 Jimmy Butler .60 1.50
187 Obi Toppin .40 1.00
188 Andre Drummond .30 .75
189 James Harden .75 2.00
190 Quentin Grimes .40 1.00
191 Jonas Valanciunas .30 .75
192 Cameron Thomas .50 1.25
193 Kevin Huerter .30 .75
194 Keldon Johnson .50 1.25
195 Andrew Nembhard .40 1.00
196 Jaren Jackson Jr. .60 1.50
197 Hakeem Olajuwon .75 2.00
198 Jakob Poeltl .30 .75
199 Khris Middleton .40 1.00
200 Ivica Zubac .40 1.00
201 Joel Embiid 1.00 2.50
202 Paul George .60 1.50
203 Tony Parker .60 1.50
204 De'Andre Hunter .40 1.00
205 Kevon Looney .40 1.00
206 Caris LeVert .40 1.00
207 Dejounte Murray .50 1.25
208 Daniel Gafford .40 1.00
209 Franz Wagner .60 1.50
210 Nicolas Batum .25 .60
211 LeBron James 3.00 8.00
212 Dominique Wilkins .60 1.50
213 Brook Lopez .30 .75
214 Cole Anthony .40 1.00
215 Moritz Wagner .40 1.00
216 Cameron Johnson .40 1.00
217 Bob Pettit .50 1.25
218 Max Strus .40 1.00
219 Nicolas Claxton .40 1.00
220 Yuta Tabuse .40 1.00
221 Ray Allen .60 1.50
222 Vince Carter .75 2.00
223 Dorian Finney-Smith .30 .75
224 Jabari Smith Jr. .60 1.50
225 Jason Williams .60 1.50
226 Evan Fournier .30 .75
227 Anthony Edwards 2.00 5.00
228 Desmond Bane .50 1.25
229 Bogdan Bogdanovic .40 1.00
230 Scottie Barnes .50 1.25
231 Tim Hardaway .50 1.25
232 Tre Jones .40 1.00
233 Jalen Duren .50 1.25
234 Grant Williams .30 .75
235 Isiah Thomas .60 1.50
236 Cade Cunningham 1.00 2.50
237 Shawn Kemp .60 1.50
238 Tyler Herro .60 1.50
239 Bojan Bogdanovic .40 1.00
240 Clyde Drexler .60 1.50
241 Draymond Green .50 1.25
242 Jalen Brunson .75 2.00
243 Bobby Portis .50 1.25
244 Julius Erving 1.00 2.50
245 Harrison Barnes .30 .75
246 Deandre Ayton .40 1.00
247 Terance Mann .30 .75
248 Anthony Davis 1.00 2.50
249 Ochai Agbaji .40 1.00
250 Donte DiVincenzo .40 1.00
251 Amari Bailey RC .60 1.50
252 Jett Howard RC .75 2.00
253 Ben Sheppard RC .60 1.50
254 Jordan Hawkins RC 1.00 2.50
255 Nick Smith Jr. RC .75 2.00
256 Victor Wembanyama RC 8.00 20.00
257 Kobe Brown RC .60 1.50
258 Olivier-Maxence Prosper RC .60 1.50
259 Leonard Miller RC .60 1.50
260 Jalen Hood-Schifino RC .60 1.50
261 Dariq Whitehead RC .75 2.00
262 Hunter Tyson RC .60 1.50
263 Marcus Sasser RC 1.00 2.50
264 Taylor Hendricks RC .60 1.50
265 Chris Livingston RC .60 1.50
266 GG Jackson II RC 1.25 3.00
267 Kris Murray RC .60 1.50
268 Jalen Pickett RC .50 1.25
269 Toumani Camara RC 1.25 3.00
270 Keyontae Johnson RC .60 1.50
271 Rayan Rupert RC .60 1.50
272 Jordan Walsh RC .60 1.50
273 Brandon Miller RC 2.50 6.00
274 Sasha Vezenkov RC .50 1.25
275 Julian Phillips RC .60 1.50
276 Jalen Wilson RC .60 1.50
277 Colby Jones RC .60 1.50
278 Anthony Black RC 1.25 3.00
279 Andre Jackson Jr. RC 1.00 2.50
280 Jaime Jaquez Jr. RC 1.00 2.50
281 Duop Reath RC .60 1.50
282 Gradey Dick RC 1.25 3.00
283 Julian Strawther RC .75 2.00
284 Kobe Bufkin RC .75 2.00
285 Bilal Coulibaly RC 1.50 4.00
286 Noah Clowney RC .75 2.00
287 Emoni Bates RC .75 2.00
288 Trayce Jackson-Davis RC .75 2.00
289 Brice Sensabaugh RC 1.00 2.50
290 Dereck Lively II RC 1.25 3.00
291 Cason Wallace RC 1.25 3.00
292 Ausar Thompson RC 1.50 4.00
293 Jarace Walker RC 1.25 3.00
294 Cam Whitmore RC 1.50 4.00
295 Brandin Podziemski RC 2.00 5.00
296 Keyonte George RC 2.00 5.00
297 Vasilije Micic RC .60 1.50
298 Scoot Henderson RC 2.00 5.00
299 Maxwell Lewis RC .50 1.25
300 Amen Thompson RC 3.00 8.00

2023-24 Panini Phoenix Blue

*BLUE: 5X TO 12X BASIC
STATED PRINT RUN 35 SER.#'d SETS
256 Victor Wembanyama 400.00 800.00

2023-24 Panini Phoenix Blue Ice

*BLUE ICE: 1X TO 2.5X BASIC
256 Victor Wembanyama 30.00 80.00

2023-24 Panini Phoenix Blue Lazer

*BLUE LAZER: 1.5X TO 4X BASIC
STATED PRINT RUN 275 SER.#'d SETS
256 Victor Wembanyama 100.00 250.00

2023-24 Panini Phoenix Bronze Lazer

*BRONZE LAZER: 4X TO 10X BASIC
STATED PRINT RUN 49 SER.#'d SETS
256 Victor Wembanyama 300.00 600.00

2023-24 Panini Phoenix Dream Weaver

*DREAM WEAVER: 3X TO 8X BASIC
256 Victor Wembanyama 300.00 600.00

2023-24 Panini Phoenix Green Ice

*GREEN ICE: 2.5X TO 6X BASIC
STATED PRINT RUN 149 SER.#'d SETS
256 Victor Wembanyama 150.00 400.00

2023-24 Panini Phoenix Green Lazer

*GREEN LAZER: 2X TO 5X BASIC
STATED PRINT RUN 175 SER.#'d SETS
256 Victor Wembanyama 125.00 300.00

2023-24 Panini Phoenix Heiroglyphs

*HEIROGLYPHS(1-250): 10X TO 25X BASIC
*HEIROGLYPHS(250-300): 6X TO 15X BASIC
256 Victor Wembanyama 500.00 1,000.00

2023-24 Panini Phoenix International Blue

*INT BLUE: 5X TO 12X BASIC
STATED PRINT RUN 35 SER.#'d SETS
256 Victor Wembanyama 400.00 800.00

2023-24 Panini Phoenix International Fire and Ice

*INT FIRE & ICE: 6X TO 15X BASIC
STATED PRINT RUN 25 SER.#'d SETS
256 Victor Wembanyama 600.00 1,200.00

2023-24 Panini Phoenix International Red
*INTER RED: 3X TO 8X BASIC
STATED PRINT RUN 75 SER.#'d SETS
256 Victor Wembanyama 200.00 500.00

2023-24 Panini Phoenix Lava
*LAVE: 3X TO 8X BASIC
STATED PRINT RUN 75 SER.#'d SETS
256 Victor Wembanyama 200.00 500.00

2023-24 Panini Phoenix Maroon Ice
*MAROON ICE: 1.5X TO 4X BASIC
STATED PRINT RUN 275 SER.#'d SETS
256 Victor Wembanyama 100.00 250.00

2023-24 Panini Phoenix Orange
*ORANGE: 3X TO 8X BASIC
STATED PRINT RUN 99 SER.#'d SETS
256 Victor Wembanyama 200.00 500.00

2023-24 Panini Phoenix Orange Ice
*ORANGE ICE: 1.5X TO 4X BASIC
STATED PRINT RUN 249 SER.#'d SETS
256 Victor Wembanyama 125.00 300.00

2023-24 Panini Phoenix Pink Ice
*PINK ICE: 6X TO 15X BASIC
STATED PRINT RUN 25 SER.#'d SETS
256 Victor Wembanyama 600.00 1,200.00

2023-24 Panini Phoenix Purple Ice
*PURPLE ICE: 6X TO 15X BASIC
STATED PRINT RUN 25 SER.#'d SETS
256 Victor Wembanyama 600.00 1,200.00

2023-24 Panini Phoenix Red
*RED: 1.5X TO 4X BASIC
STATED PRINT RUN 199 SER.#'d SETS
256 Victor Wembanyama 125.00 300.00

2023-24 Panini Phoenix Red Ice
*RED ICE: 1X TO 2.5X BASIC
256 Victor Wembanyama 30.00 80.00

2023-24 Panini Phoenix Seismic
*SEISMIC: 2.5X TO 6X BASIC
STATED PRINT RUN 125 SER.#'d SETS
256 Victor Wembanyama 150.00 400.00

2023-24 Panini Phoenix Teal Lazer
*TEAL LAZER: 1X TO 2.5X BASIC
256 Victor Wembanyama 50.00 120.00

2023-24 Panini Phoenix White Ice
*WHITE ICE: 2.5X TO 6X BASIC
STATED PRINT RUN 125 SER.#'d SETS
256 Victor Wembanyama 150.00 400.00

2023-24 Panini Phoenix White Lazer
*WHITE LAZER: 2.5X TO 6X BASIC
STATED PRINT RUN 150 SER.#'d SETS
256 Victor Wembanyama 150.00 400.00

2023-24 Panini Phoenix Yellow
*YELLOW: 4X TO 10X BASIC
STATED PRINT RUN 49 SER.#'d SETS
256 Victor Wembanyama 300.00 600.00

2023-24 Panini Phoenix Yellow Ice
*YELLOW ICE: 2X TO 5X BASIC
STATED PRINT RUN 175 SER.#'d SETS
256 Victor Wembanyama 125.00 300.00

2021-22 Panini PhotoGenic
COM CARD (1-100) .40 1.00
SEMISTARS .50 1.25
UNLISTED STARS .60 1.50
COMMON RC (101-140) .75 2.00
RC SEMIS 1.00 2.50
RC UNLISTED 1.25 3.00
*SILVER: .75X TO 2X BASIC
1 Trae Young 1.50 4.00
2 Luka Doncic 4.00 10.00
3 Stephen Curry 4.00 10.00
4 LeBron James 5.00 12.00
5 Keldon Johnson .75 2.00
6 Kevin Durant 2.00 5.00
7 Jimmy Butler 1.00 2.50
8 Nikola Jokic 3.00 8.00
9 Donovan Mitchell 1.25 3.00
10 Paul George 1.00 2.50
11 RJ Barrett 1.00 2.50
12 Ja Morant 2.00 5.00
13 Zion Williamson 1.50 4.00
14 Jayson Tatum 2.50 6.00
15 LaMelo Ball 1.50 4.00
16 DeMar DeRozan .75 2.00
17 Darius Garland 1.00 2.50
18 Jerami Grant .60 1.50
19 Christian Wood .50 1.25
20 Tyrese Haliburton 1.25 3.00
21 Giannis Antetokounmpo 3.00 8.00
22 Karl-Anthony Towns 1.00 2.50
23 Shai Gilgeous-Alexander 3.00 8.00
24 Cole Anthony .75 2.00
25 Joel Embiid 1.50 4.00
26 Devin Booker 1.50 4.00
27 Damian Lillard 1.50 4.00
28 De'Aaron Fox 1.00 2.50
29 Fred VanVleet .75 2.00
30 Bradley Beal .75 2.00
31 Anthony Davis 1.50 4.00
32 CJ McCollum .50 1.25
33 Miles Bridges .50 1.25
34 De'Andre Hunter .60 1.50
35 Khris Middleton .60 1.50
36 Kawhi Leonard 1.50 4.00
37 Chris Paul 1.25 3.00
38 Caris LeVert .50 1.25
39 Domantas Sabonis .75 2.00
40 Klay Thompson 1.50 4.00
41 James Harden 1.25 3.00
42 Anfernee Hardaway 1.50 4.00
43 Hakeem Olajuwon 1.25 3.00
44 Clyde Drexler 1.00 2.50
45 Allen Iverson 1.50 4.00
46 Tim Duncan 1.50 4.00
47 Rudy Gobert .75 2.00
48 Desmond Bane 1.25 3.00
49 Kyle Kuzma .75 2.00
50 Jaylen Brown 1.00 2.50
51 Dennis Rodman 6.00 15.00
52 Dwyane Wade 1.25 3.00
53 Dirk Nowitzki 1.50 4.00
54 Isiah Thomas 1.00 2.50
55 Aaron Gordon .60 1.50
56 Buddy Hield .50 1.25
57 Anthony Edwards 3.00 8.00
58 Vince Carter 1.25 3.00
59 Luguentz Dort .60 1.50
60 Patrick Ewing 1.00 2.50
61 Kristaps Porzingis .75 2.00
62 Karl Malone 1.25 3.00
63 Pascal Siakam 1.00 2.50
64 Dejounte Murray .60 1.50
65 Jason Williams .75 2.00
66 Anfernee Simons 1.00 2.50
67 Deandre Ayton .60 1.50
68 Ben Simmons .60 1.50
69 Wendell Carter Jr. .60 1.50
70 Julius Randle .75 2.00
71 Brandon Ingram .75 2.00
72 Kevin Garnett 1.50 4.00
73 Bobby Portis .50 1.25
74 Tyler Herro 1.00 2.50
75 Dillon Brooks .60 1.50
76 Russell Westbrook 1.00 2.50
77 Norman Powell .50 1.25
78 Malcolm Brogdon .50 1.25
79 Kevin Porter Jr. .50 1.25
80 Draymond Green .75 2.00
81 Saddiq Bey .50 1.25
82 Dikembe Mutombo .75 2.00
83 Spencer Dinwiddie .50 1.25
84 Collin Sexton .60 1.50
85 Zach LaVine 1.00 2.50
86 Gordon Hayward .50 1.25
87 Kyrie Irving 1.25 3.00
88 Larry Bird 2.00 5.00
89 Dominique Wilkins 1.00 2.50
90 Magic Johnson 2.00 5.00
91 Charles Barkley 1.50 4.00
92 David Robinson 1.25 3.00
93 Shaquille O'Neal 2.00 5.00
94 Lonzo Ball .60 1.50
95 Bam Adebayo 1.00 2.50
96 Ray Allen 1.00 2.50
97 Gary Payton 1.00 2.50
98 Steve Nash 1.25 3.00
99 John Stockton 1.25 3.00
100 Shawn Kemp 1.00 2.50
101 Cade Cunningham RC 15.00 40.00
102 James Bouknight RC 1.00 2.50
103 Chris Duarte RC 1.00 2.50
104 Josh Giddey RC 10.00 25.00
105 Jalen Green RC 12.00 30.00
106 Isaiah Jackson RC 1.25 3.00
107 Jalen Johnson RC 4.00 10.00
108 Corey Kispert RC 1.50 4.00
109 Jonathan Kuminga RC 4.00 10.00
110 Davion Mitchell RC 1.25 3.00
111 Evan Mobley RC 10.00 25.00
112 Moses Moody RC 2.50 6.00
113 Jalen Suggs RC 3.00 8.00
114 Cameron Thomas RC 2.50 6.00
115 Franz Wagner RC 4.00 10.00
116 Scottie Barnes RC 12.00 30.00
117 Alperen Sengun RC 4.00 10.00
118 Ziaire Williams RC 1.50 4.00
119 Kai Jones RC 1.00 2.50
120 Keon Johnson RC 1.25 3.00
121 Joshua Primo RC 1.00 2.50
122 Trey Murphy III RC 4.00 10.00
123 Tre Mann RC 2.00 5.00
124 Usman Garuba RC 1.00 2.50
125 Josh Christopher RC 1.00 2.50
126 Quentin Grimes RC 2.50 6.00
127 Bones Hyland RC 1.50 4.00
128 Jaden Springer RC 1.25 3.00
129 Day'Ron Sharpe RC 1.25 3.00
130 Santi Aldama RC 1.50 4.00
131 Jeremiah Robinson-Earl RC 1.25 3.00
132 Herbert Jones RC 1.50 4.00
133 Miles McBride RC 2.00 5.00
134 JT Thor RC 1.25 3.00
135 Ayo Dosunmu RC 2.50 6.00
136 Kessler Edwards RC 1.25 3.00
137 Austin Reaves RC 10.00 25.00
138 Brandon Boston Jr. RC 1.25 3.00
139 Dalano Banton RC 1.50 4.00
140 Duane Washington Jr. RC 1.25 3.00

2023-24 Panini Phoenix Archetype
1 Scoot Henderson 30.00 80.00
2 Anthony Edwards 50.00 125.00
3 Kyrie Irving 20.00 50.00
4 Tyrese Haliburton 20.00 50.00
5 Jayson Tatum 40.00 100.00
6 Stephen Curry 80.00 200.00
7 Trae Young 20.00 50.00
8 Giannis Antetokounmpo 50.00 125.00
9 Ja Morant 30.00 80.00
10 Jalen Brunson 20.00 50.00
11 Luka Doncic 60.00 150.00
12 Brandin Podziemski 30.00 80.00
13 Victor Wembanyama 300.00 600.00
14 Kawhi Leonard 25.00 60.00
15 Nikola Jokic 50.00 125.00
16 Chet Holmgren 25.00 60.00
17 Damian Lillard 25.00 60.00
18 Ausar Thompson 25.00 60.00
19 Devin Booker 25.00 60.00
20 Brandon Miller 40.00 100.00
21 LeBron James 80.00 200.00
22 Amen Thompson 50.00 120.00
23 Tyrese Maxey 20.00 50.00
24 Shai Gilgeous-Alexander 50.00 120.00
25 Zion Williamson 25.00 60.00

2023-24 Panini Phoenix Ascension Autographs
STATED PRINT RUN BTWN 49-99 SER.#'d SETS
*PURPLE/35-75: .5X TO 1.2X BASIC
*ORANGE/49: .6X TO 1.5X BASIC
*YELLOW/25-35: .75X TO 2X p/r 99
*YELLOW/25-35: .6X TO 1.5X p/r 75
*YELLOW/25-35: .5X TO 1.2X p/r 49
*BLUE/15-25: .75X TO 2X p/r 99
*BLUE/15-25: .6X TO 1.5X p/r 75
*BLUE/15-25: .5X TO 1.2X p/r 49
1 Franz Wagner/99 10.00 25.00
2 Anfernee Simons/99 8.00 20.00
3 Jabari Smith Jr./99 10.00 25.00
4 Dominique Wilkins/99 10.00 25.00
5 Jarrett Allen/99 6.00 15.00
6 Dwyane Wade/49 40.00 100.00
7 Desmond Bane/99 8.00 20.00
8 Peja Stojakovic/99 6.00 15.00
9 Pau Gasol/49 15.00 40.00
10 Bernard King/99 8.00 20.00
11 Magic Johnson/49 50.00 120.00
12 Cade Cunningham/49 25.00 60.00
13 Payton Pritchard/99 6.00 15.00
14 Shaedon Sharpe/75 15.00 40.00
15 Alex Caruso/75 8.00 20.00
16 Stephen Jackson/99 5.00 12.00
17 Mike Bibby/99 6.00 15.00
18 Walker Kessler/99 6.00 15.00
19 David Robinson/49 20.00 50.00
20 Moritz Wagner/99 6.00 15.00
22 Cameron Thomas/99 8.00 20.00
23 Steve Nash/49 40.00 100.00
24 Landry Shamet/99 4.00 10.00
25 Rasheed Wallace/99 15.00 40.00

2023-24 Panini Phoenix Autographs
*GREEN: .5X TO 1.2X BASIC
*WHITE LAZER/99: .5X TO 1.2X BASIC
*WHITE LAZER/15: .75X TO 2X BASIC
*WHITE ICE/49: .6X TO 1.5X BASIC
*WHITE ICE/15: .75X TO 2X BASIC
1 Dante Exum 4.00 10.00
2 Gary Harris 4.00 10.00
3 Jock Landale 4.00 10.00
4 Kendall Brown 3.00 8.00
5 Ziaire Williams 5.00 12.00
6 Tony Delk 4.00 10.00
7 Keon Ellis 4.00 10.00
8 Bilal Coulibaly 12.00 30.00
9 Delon Wright 3.00 8.00
11 Blake Wesley 3.00 8.00
12 Mark Aguirre 4.00 10.00
13 Terry Cummings 5.00 12.00
14 Cade Cunningham 20.00 50.00
15 Jeff Malone 4.00 10.00
16 Greg Anthony 4.00 10.00
17 Kirk Hinrich 4.00 10.00
18 Day'Ron Sharpe 4.00 10.00
19 Paolo Banchero 40.00 100.00
20 Vince Williams Jr. 5.00 12.00
21 Amir Coffey 3.00 8.00
22 Derek Harper 4.00 10.00
23 Keyonte George 15.00 40.00
24 A.J. Green 4.00 10.00
25 Paul Pressey 4.00 10.00
26 M.L. Carr 4.00 10.00
27 Micheal Ray Richardson 4.00 10.00
28 Swen Nater 4.00 10.00
29 Kiki Vandeweghe 4.00 10.00
30 Sleepy Floyd 4.00 10.00
31 David Wesley 4.00 10.00
32 Vit Krejci 6.00 15.00
33 Trevelin Queen 3.00 8.00
34 Colby Jones 5.00 12.00
35 Jordan Walsh 5.00 12.00
36 Ricky Davis 4.00 10.00
37 Tristan Vukcevic 5.00 12.00
38 James Nnaji 4.00 10.00
39 Tosan Evbuomwan 4.00 10.00
40 Chris Livingston 5.00 12.00

2023-24 Panini Phoenix Calligraphy
STATED PRINT RUN BTWN 49-99 SER.#'d SETS
*PURPLE/35-75: .5X TO 1.2X BASIC
*ORANGE/35-49: .6X TO 1.5X BASIC p/r 99
*ORANGE/35-49: .5X TO 1.2X BASIC p/r 75
*ORANGE/35-49: .5X TO 1.2X BASIC p/r 49
*YELLOW/25-35: .75X TO 2X p/r 99
*YELLOW/25-35: .6X TO 1.5X p/r 75
*YELLOW/25-35: .5X TO 1.2X p/r 49
*BLUE/15-25: .75X TO 2X p/r 99
*BLUE/15-25: .6X TO 1.5X p/r 75
*BLUE/15-25: .5X TO 1.2X p/r 49
1 Patrick Ewing/75 50.00 120.00
2 Cade Cunningham/75 25.00 60.00
3 Kareem Abdul-Jabbar/49 75.00 200.00
4 Kevin Garnett/49 60.00 150.00
5 Paolo Banchero/49 60.00 150.00
6 Manu Ginobili/49 30.00 80.00
7 Amar'e Stoudemire/75 10.00 25.00
8 Scottie Barnes/75 10.00 25.00
9 Alperen Sengun/75 12.00 30.00
10 Carmelo Anthony/49 60.00 150.00
11 Charles Barkley/49 60.00 150.00
13 Evan Mobley/99 10.00 25.00
14 Tyrese Maxey/75 40.00 100.00
15 Josh Giddey/75 10.00 25.00
16 Jerry West/49 30.00 80.00
17 Julius Randle/75 10.00 25.00
18 Chet Holmgren/75 40.00 100.00
19 Grant Hill/75 20.00 50.00
20 John Stockton/75 40.00 100.00
21 Paul Pierce/75 30.00 80.00
22 Jason Kidd/75 25.00 60.00
23 Russell Westbrook/49 60.00 150.00
24 Stephen Curry/49 300.00 600.00
25 Luka Doncic/49 300.00 600.00
26 Trae Young/49 40.00 100.00
27 Anthony Davis/75 40.00 100.00
28 Chris Paul/49 25.00 60.00
29 Shai Gilgeous-Alexander/49 150.00 400.00
30 Alonzo Mourning/49 30.00 80.00
31 Bradley Beal/49 12.00 30.00
32 Ja Morant/49 125.00 300.00
33 Giannis Antetokounmpo/49 200.00 500.00
34 Donovan Mitchell/75 25.00 60.00
35 Tracy McGrady/75 60.00 150.00

2023-24 Panini Phoenix Color Burst
*COLOR BURST: 2X TO 5X BASIC
256 Victor Wembanyama 150.00 400.00

2023-24 Panini Phoenix Court of the Kings
*SILVER: .75X TO 2X BASIC
1 Tyrese Haliburton .75 2.00
2 Tim Duncan 1.00 2.50
3 Ja Morant 1.25 3.00
4 Shaquille O'Neal 1.25 3.00
5 Jaime Jaquez Jr. .60 1.50
6 Keyonte George 1.25 3.00
7 Kareem Abdul-Jabbar 1.25 3.00
8 Nikola Jokic 2.00 5.00
9 Ausar Thompson 1.00 2.50
10 Brandon Miller 1.50 4.00
11 Dirk Nowitzki 1.00 2.50
12 Shai Gilgeous-Alexander 2.00 5.00
13 Scoot Henderson 1.25 3.00
14 Anthony Black .75 2.00
15 Vince Carter .75 2.00
16 LeBron James 3.00 8.00
17 Brandin Podziemski 1.25 3.00
18 Giannis Antetokounmpo 2.00 5.00
19 Luka Doncic 2.50 6.00
20 Jayson Tatum 1.50 4.00
21 Stephen Curry 3.00 8.00
22 Dereck Lively II .75 2.00
23 Victor Wembanyama 10.00 25.00
24 Amen Thompson 2.00 5.00
25 Anthony Edwards 2.00 5.00

2023-24 Panini Phoenix Court of the Kings Blue
*BLUE: 4X TO 10X BASIC
STATED PRINT RUN 25 SER.#'d SETS
23 Victor Wembanyama 150.00 400.00

2023-24 Panini Phoenix Court of the Kings Orange
*ORANGE: 3X TO 8X BASIC
STATED PRINT RUN 49 SER.#'d SETS
23 Victor Wembanyama 125.00 300.00

2023-24 Panini Phoenix Court of the Kings Pink
*PINK: 2.5X TO 6X BASIC
STATED PRINT RUN 99 SER.#'d SETS
23 Victor Wembanyama 100.00 250.00

2023-24 Panini Phoenix Court of the Kings Purple
*PURPLE: 2.5X TO 6X BASIC
STATED PRINT RUN 75 SER.#'d SETS
23 Victor Wembanyama 100.00 250.00

2023-24 Panini Phoenix Court of the Kings Red
*RED: 2X TO 5X BASIC
STATED PRINT RUN 125 SER.#'d SETS
23 Victor Wembanyama 75.00 200.00

2023-24 Panini Phoenix Court of the Kings Yellow
*YELLOW: 3X TO 8X BASIC
STATED PRINT RUN 35 SER.#'d SETS
23 Victor Wembanyama 125.00 300.00

2023-24 Panini Phoenix Crusade
*SILVER: .75X TO 2X BASIC
1 Giannis Antetokounmpo 3.00 8.00
2 Shai Gilgeous-Alexander 3.00 8.00
3 Victor Wembanyama 10.00 25.00
4 Ausar Thompson 1.50 4.00
5 Brandin Podziemski 2.00 5.00
6 Luka Doncic 4.00 10.00
7 Jordan Hawkins 1.00 2.50
8 Kevin Durant 2.00 5.00
9 LeBron James 5.00 12.00
10 Joel Embiid 1.50 4.00
11 Jalen Brunson 1.25 3.00
12 Cason Wallace 1.25 3.00
13 Anthony Edwards 3.00 8.00
14 Donovan Mitchell 1.25 3.00
15 Paolo Banchero 1.50 4.00
16 Jaime Jaquez Jr. 1.00 2.50
17 Amen Thompson 3.00 8.00
18 Brandon Miller 2.50 6.00
19 Tyrese Haliburton 1.25 3.00
20 Keyonte George 2.00 5.00
21 Ja Morant 2.00 5.00
22 Nikola Jokic 3.00 8.00
23 Scoot Henderson 2.00 5.00
24 Jayson Tatum 2.50 6.00
25 Stephen Curry 5.00 12.00

2023-24 Panini Phoenix Crusade Blue
*BLUE: 3X TO 8X BASIC
STATED PRINT RUN 25 SER.#'d SETS
3 Victor Wembanyama 200.00 500.00

2023-24 Panini Phoenix Crusade International Red
*INT RED: 2X TO 5X BASIC
STATED PRINT RUN 75 SER.#'d SETS
3 Victor Wembanyama 125.00 300.00

2023-24 Panini Phoenix Crusade Orange
*ORANGE: 2.5X TO 6X BASIC
STATED PRINT RUN 49 SER.#'d SETS
3 Victor Wembanyama 150.00 400.00

2023-24 Panini Phoenix Crusade Phoenix White Ice
*WHITE ICE: 1.5X TO 4X BASIC
STATED PRINT RUN 125 SER.#'d SETS
3 Victor Wembanyama 100.00 250.00

2023-24 Panini Phoenix Crusade Phoenix White Lazer
*WHITE LAZER: 1.5X TO 4X BASIC
STATED PRINT RUN 150 SER.#'d SETS
3 Victor Wembanyama 100.00 250.00

2023-24 Panini Phoenix Crusade Pink
*PINK: 2X TO 5X BASIC
STATED PRINT RUN 99 SER.#'d SETS
3 Victor Wembanyama 125.00 300.00

2023-24 Panini Phoenix Crusade Purple
*PURPLE: 2X TO 5X BASIC
STATED PRINT RUN 75 SER.#'d SETS
3 Victor Wembanyama 125.00 300.00

2023-24 Panini Phoenix Crusade Red
*RED: 1.5X TO 4X BASIC
STATED PRINT RUN 125 SER.#'d SETS
3 Victor Wembanyama 100.00 250.00

2023-24 Panini Phoenix Crusade Yellow
*YELLOW: 3X TO 8X BASIC
STATED PRINT RUN 35 SER.#'d SETS
3 Victor Wembanyama 200.00 500.00

2023-24 Panini Phoenix Crusade Signatures
*GREEN: .5X TO 1.2X BASIC
*WHITE LAZER/99: .5X TO 1.2X BASIC
*WHITE LAZER/15: .75X TO 2X BASIC
*WHITE ICE/49: .6X TO 1.5X BASIC
*WHITE ICE/15: .75X TO 2X BASIC
1 Dalano Banton 4.00 10.00
2 Cole Swider 4.00 10.00
3 Mark Williams 5.00 12.00
4 Amen Thompson 30.00 80.00
5 Ausar Thompson 25.00 60.00
6 Jason Preston 3.00 8.00
7 Trendon Watford 5.00 12.00
8 Cason Wallace 10.00 25.00
9 Luc Longley 5.00 12.00
10 Brent Barry 4.00 10.00
11 Boban Marjanovic 5.00 12.00
12 Roy Hibbert 4.00 10.00
13 Gerald Henderson Sr. 3.00 8.00
14 Jim Paxson 5.00 12.00
15 Dereck Lively II 10.00 25.00
16 Jim Jackson 4.00 10.00
17 Muggsy Bogues 10.00 25.00
18 Devin Harris 3.00 8.00
19 Buddy Boeheim 4.00 10.00
20 Goran Dragic 4.00 10.00
21 Johnny Juzang 3.00 8.00
22 Wally Szczerbiak 4.00 10.00
23 Jeff Malone 4.00 10.00
24 Xavier Tillman 5.00 12.00
25 Lester Quinones 4.00 10.00
26 Jevon Carter 4.00 10.00
27 Alondes Williams 3.00 8.00
28 MarJon Beauchamp 4.00 10.00
29 Nikola Jovic 5.00 12.00
30 Julian Champagnie 5.00 12.00
31 Dale Ellis 5.00 12.00
32 Xavier McDaniel 5.00 12.00
33 David Duke Jr. 3.00 8.00
34 Derrick Coleman 5.00 12.00
35 Chet Holmgren 30.00 80.00
36 Ricky Pierce 4.00 10.00
37 Vin Baker 4.00 10.00
38 Theo Ratliff 4.00 10.00
39 Terence Davis II 3.00 8.00
41 Isaiah Wong 5.00 12.00
42 Naji Marshall 5.00 12.00
43 Paul Reed 5.00 12.00
44 Terquavion Smith 5.00 12.00
45 Craig Porter Jr. 6.00 15.00
47 Oscar Tshiebwe 6.00 15.00
48 Jalen Slawson 5.00 12.00
49 Leaky Black 4.00 10.00
50 Ricky Council IV 6.00 15.00

2023-24 Panini Phoenix Dual Rookie Jersey Autographs
STATED PRINT RUN 49 SER.#'d SETS
*BLUE: .5X TO 1.2X BASIC
2 Ausar Thompson
Amen Thompson 75.00 200.00
3 Brandin Podziemski
Trayce Jackson-Davis 75.00 200.00
4 Cason Wallace
Keyonte George 50.00 120.00
5 Kris Murray
Duop Reath 20.00 50.00

2023-24 Panini Phoenix Fade To Black
*SILVER: .75X TO 2X BASIC
1 Jalen Brunson .75 2.00
2 Jaime Jaquez Jr. .60 1.50
3 LeBron James 3.00 8.00
4 Anthony Black .75 2.00
5 Shai Gilgeous-Alexander 2.00 5.00
6 Scoot Henderson 1.25 3.00
7 Brandin Podziemski 1.25 3.00
8 Brandon Miller 1.50 4.00
9 Ausar Thompson 1.00 2.50
10 Jayson Tatum 1.50 4.00
11 Victor Wembanyama 6.00 15.00
12 Tyrese Haliburton .75 2.00
13 Kevin Durant 1.25 3.00
14 Zion Williamson 1.00 2.50
15 Ja Morant 1.25 3.00
16 Trae Young .75 2.00
17 Keyonte George 1.25 3.00
18 Luka Doncic 2.50 6.00
19 Anthony Edwards 2.00 5.00
20 Nikola Jokic 2.00 5.00
21 Amen Thompson 2.00 5.00
22 Stephen Curry 3.00 8.00
23 Giannis Antetokounmpo 2.00 5.00
24 Jordan Hawkins .60 1.50
25 Damian Lillard 1.00 2.50

2023-24 Panini Phoenix Fade To Black Blue Ice
*BLUE ICE: .75X TO 2X BASIC
11 Victor Wembanyama 30.00 80.00

2023-24 Panini Phoenix Fade To Black Blue Lazer
*BLUE LAZER: 1.5X TO 4X BASIC
STATED PRINT RUN 275 SER.#'d SETS
11 Victor Wembanyama 60.00 150.00

2023-24 Panini Phoenix Fade To Black Bronze Lazer
*BRONZE LAZER: 4X TO 10X BASIC
STATED PRINT RUN 49 SER.#'d SETS
11 Victor Wembanyama 150.00 400.00

2023-24 Panini Phoenix Fade To Black Green Ice
*GREEN ICE: 2X TO 5X BASIC
STATED PRINT RUN 149 SER.#'d SETS
11 Victor Wembanyama 75.00 200.00

2023-24 Panini Phoenix Fade To Black Green Lazer
*GREEN LAZER: 2X TO 5X BASIC
STATED PRINT RUN 175 SER.#'d SETS
11 Victor Wembanyama 75.00 200.00

2023-24 Panini Phoenix Fade To Black Maroon Ice
*MAROON ICE: 1.5X TO 4X BASIC
STATED PRINT RUN 275 SER.#'d SETS
11 Victor Wembanyama 60.00 150.00

2023-24 Panini Phoenix Fade To Black Phoenix Orange Ice
*ORANGE ICE: 1.5X TO 4X BASIC
STATED PRINT RUN 249 SER.#'d SETS
11 Victor Wembanyama 60.00 150.00

2023-24 Panini Phoenix Fade To Black Phoenix Pink Ice
*PINK ICE: 5X TO 12X BASIC
STATED PRINT RUN 25 SER.#'d SETS
11 Victor Wembanyama 200.00 500.00

2023-24 Panini Phoenix Fade To Black Phoenix Purple Ice
*PURPLE ICE: 5X TO 12X BASIC
STATED PRINT RUN 25 SER.#'d SETS
11 Victor Wembanyama 200.00 500.00

2023-24 Panini Phoenix Fade To Black Phoenix Red Ice
*RED ICE: .75X TO 2X BASIC
11 Victor Wembanyama 30.00 80.00

2023-24 Panini Phoenix Fade To Black Phoenix Teal Lazer
*TEAL LAZER: .75X TO 2X BASIC
11 Victor Wembanyama 30.00 80.00

2023-24 Panini Phoenix Fade To Black Phoenix White Ice
*WHITE ICE: 2.5X TO 6X BASIC
STATED PRINT RUN 125 SER.#'d SETS
11 Victor Wembanyama 100.00 250.00

2023-24 Panini Phoenix Fade To Black Phoenix White Lazer
*WHITE LAZER: 2X TO 5X BASIC
STATED PRINT RUN 150 SER.#'d SETS
11 Victor Wembanyama 75.00 200.00

2023-24 Panini Phoenix Fade To Black Phoenix Yellow Ice
*YELLOW ICE: 2X TO 5X BASIC
STATED PRINT RUN 175 SER.#'d SETS
11 Victor Wembanyama 75.00 200.00

2023-24 Panini Phoenix Fire and Ice
*FIRE & ICE: 6X TO 15X BASIC
STATED PRINT RUN 25 SER.#'d SETS
256 Victor Wembanyama 600.00 1,200.00

2023-24 Panini Phoenix Fire Fabrics
*PURPLE/99: .5X TO 1.2X BASIC
*ORANGE/75: .6X TO 1.5X BASIC
*YELLOW/49: .75X TO 2X BASIC
*BLUE/25: 1X TO 2.5X BASIC
1 Davion Mitchell 1.50 4.00
2 Terry Rozier III 2.50 6.00
3 Bones Hyland 1.50 4.00
4 Cameron Johnson 2.00 5.00
5 Tobias Harris 2.00 5.00
6 Scottie Barnes 2.50 6.00
7 Darius Garland 3.00 8.00
8 Jalen Green 3.00 8.00
9 Tyler Herro 3.00 8.00
10 Giannis Antetokounmpo 10.00 25.00
11 OG Anunoby 2.50 6.00
12 Pascal Siakam 3.00 8.00
13 Bam Adebayo 3.00 8.00
14 Gordon Hayward 2.00 5.00
15 Kawhi Leonard 5.00 12.00
16 Ayo Dosunmu 2.00 5.00
18 Evan Mobley 3.00 8.00
19 Kevin Durant 6.00 15.00
20 Jimmy Butler 3.00 8.00
21 Kyrie Irving 4.00 10.00
22 LeBron James 30.00 80.00
23 Devin Booker 5.00 12.00
24 Joel Embiid 5.00 12.00
25 Jayson Tatum 8.00 20.00

2023-24 Panini Phoenix Fire Forged
*SILVER: .75X TO 2X BASIC
1 De'Aaron Fox .75 2.00
2 Trae Young .75 2.00
3 Chet Holmgren 1.00 2.50
4 Nikola Jokic 2.00 5.00
5 Tyrese Maxey .75 2.00
6 LeBron James 3.00 8.00
7 Damian Lillard 1.00 2.50
8 Tyrese Haliburton .75 2.00
9 Anthony Davis 1.00 2.50
10 Kevin Durant 1.25 3.00
11 Donovan Mitchell .75 2.00
12 Stephen Curry 3.00 8.00
13 Cade Cunningham 1.00 2.50
14 Paolo Banchero 1.00 2.50
15 Giannis Antetokounmpo 2.00 5.00
16 Paul George .60 1.50
17 Anthony Edwards 2.00 5.00
18 Victor Wembanyama 10.00 25.00
19 Shai Gilgeous-Alexander 2.00 5.00
20 Jayson Tatum 1.50 4.00
21 Devin Booker 1.00 2.50
22 Zion Williamson 1.00 2.50
23 Ja Morant 1.25 3.00
24 Luka Doncic 2.50 6.00
25 Jalen Brunson .75 2.00

2023-24 Panini Phoenix Fire Forged Blue
*BLUE: 4X TO 10X BASIC
STATED PRINT RUN 25 SER.#'d SETS
18 Victor Wembanyama 150.00 400.00

2023-24 Panini Phoenix Fire Forged Orange
*ORANGE: 3X TO 8X BASIC
STATED PRINT RUN 49 SER.#'d SETS
18 Victor Wembanyama 125.00 300.00

2023-24 Panini Phoenix Fire Forged Pink
*PINK: 2.5X TO 6X BASIC
STATED PRINT RUN 99 SER.#'d SETS
18 Victor Wembanyama 100.00 250.00

2023-24 Panini Phoenix Fire Forged Purple
*PURPLE: 2.5X TO 6X BASIC
STATED PRINT RUN 75 SER.#'d SETS
18 Victor Wembanyama 100.00 250.00

2023-24 Panini Phoenix Fire Forged Red
*RED: 2X TO 5X BASIC
STATED PRINT RUN 125 SER.#'d SETS
18 Victor Wembanyama 75.00 200.00

2023-24 Panini Phoenix Fire Forged Yellow
*YELLOW: 3X TO 8X BASIC
STATED PRINT RUN 35 SER.#'d SETS
18 Victor Wembanyama 125.00 300.00

2023-24 Panini Phoenix Fuego Autographs
STATED PRINT RUN BTWN 49-99 SER.#'d SETS
*PURPLE/49-75: .5X TO 1.2X BASIC
*ORANGE/49: .6X TO 1.5X BASIC
*YELLOW/35: .75X TO 2X p/r 99
*YELLOW/35: .6X TO 1.5X p/r 75
*YELLOW/35: .5X TO 1.2X p/r 49
*BLUE/25: .75X TO 2X p/r 99
*BLUE/25: .6X TO 1.5X p/r 75
*BLUE/25: .5X TO 1.2X p/r 49
1 Donte DiVincenzo/99 12.00 30.00
2 Cameron Thomas/99 8.00 20.00
3 Keldon Johnson/99 8.00 20.00
4 Jalen Duren/99 8.00 20.00
5 Jalen Suggs/99 8.00 20.00
6 Jaden Hardy/75 10.00 25.00
7 Larry Bird/49 60.00 150.00
8 De'Aaron Fox/49 25.00 60.00
9 Gail Goodrich/99 6.00 15.00
10 Jason Terry/99 6.00 15.00
11 Clyde Drexler/75 20.00 50.00
12 Jermaine O'Neal/99 6.00 15.00
14 Corey Kispert/99 5.00 12.00
15 Dell Curry/99 6.00 15.00
16 Tim Hardaway/99 5.00 12.00
17 Ray Allen/75 30.00 80.00
18 Latrell Sprewell/99 8.00 20.00
20 Santi Aldama/99 5.00 12.00
21 Andre Drummond/99 5.00 12.00
22 Dennis Rodman/75 40.00 100.00
23 Rick Barry/99 8.00 20.00
24 Jeremy Lin/99 60.00 150.00
25 Ben Wallace/99 8.00 20.00

2023-24 Panini Phoenix Genies
1 Anthony Davis 25.00 60.00
2 Ausar Thompson 25.00 60.00
3 Chet Holmgren 25.00 60.00
4 Giannis Antetokounmpo 50.00 125.00
5 Paolo Banchero 25.00 60.00
6 Jayson Tatum 40.00 100.00
7 Zion Williamson 25.00 60.00
8 Jaime Jaquez Jr. 15.00 40.00
9 LeBron James 80.00 200.00
10 Amen Thompson 50.00 120.00
11 Victor Wembanyama 300.00 600.00
12 Kevin Durant 30.00 80.00
13 Luka Doncic 60.00 150.00
14 Donovan Mitchell 20.00 50.00
15 Anthony Edwards 50.00 125.00
16 Damian Lillard 25.00 60.00
17 Shai Gilgeous-Alexander 50.00 120.00
18 Scoot Henderson 30.00 80.00
19 Trae Young 20.00 50.00
20 Tyrese Haliburton 20.00 50.00
21 Nikola Jokic 50.00 125.00
22 Ja Morant 30.00 80.00
23 Stephen Curry 80.00 200.00
24 Brandon Miller 40.00 100.00
25 Kyrie Irving 20.00 50.00

2023-24 Panini Phoenix Hall of Fame Autographs
*GREEN: .5X TO 1.2X BASIC
*WHITE LAZER/99: .5X TO 1.2X BASIC
*WHITE LAZER/15: .75X TO 2X BASIC
*WHITE ICE/49: .6X TO 1.5X BASIC
*WHITE ICE/15: .75X TO 2X BASIC
1 Jerry West 30.00 80.00
2 Jack Sikma 5.00 12.00
3 Kareem Abdul-Jabbar 60.00 150.00
4 Calvin Murphy 5.00 12.00
5 Jamaal Wilkes 5.00 12.00
6 Louie Dampier 5.00 12.00
7 Arvydas Sabonis 6.00 15.00
8 Ralph Sampson 5.00 12.00
9 Sarunas Marciulionis 6.00 15.00
10 Spencer Haywood 6.00 15.00

2023-24 Panini Phoenix Honored Signatures
*PURPLE/35-75: .5X TO 1.2X BASIC
*ORANGE/49: .6X TO 1.5X p/r 99
*ORANGE/49: .4X TO 1X p/r 49
*INT RED/49: .6X TO 1.5X p/r 99
*INT RED/25: .75X TO 2X p/r 99
*INT RED/25: .5X TO 1.2X p/r 49
*YELLOW/35: .75X TO 2X p/r 99
*YELLOW/25-35: .5X TO 1.2X p/r 49
*BLUE/25: .75X TO 2X p/r 99
*BLUE/25: .5X TO 1.2X p/r 49
1 Rudy Gobert 8.00 20.00
2 Lauri Markkanen 10.00 25.00
3 Ben Simmons 6.00 15.00
4 Andrew Wiggins 8.00 20.00
5 Kevin McHale 10.00 25.00
6 CJ McCollum 6.00 15.00
7 Isiah Thomas 10.00 25.00
8 Hakeem Olajuwon 25.00 60.00
9 Jaren Jackson Jr. 15.00 40.00
10 Nikola Jokic 100.00 250.00

2023-24 Panini Phoenix Inferno Etchings Signatures
STATED PRINT RUN BTWN 49-99 SER.#'d SETS
*PURPLE/49-75: .5X TO 1.2X BASIC
*ORANGE/49: .6X TO 1.5X BASIC p/r 99
*ORANGE/49: .5X TO 1.2X BASIC p/r 75
*ORANGE/35: .5X TO 1.2X BASIC p/r 49
*YELLOW/35: .75X TO 2X p/r 99
*YELLOW/35: .6X TO 1.5X p/r 75
*YELLOW/25: .5X TO 1.2X p/r 49
*BLUE/25: .75X TO 2X p/r 99
*BLUE/25: .6X TO 1.5X p/r 75
1 Jonathan Kuminga/99 15.00 40.00
2 Jalen Johnson/99 8.00 20.00
3 Shaedon Sharpe/75 15.00 40.00
4 Aaron Gordon/99 6.00 15.00
5 Domantas Sabonis/75 12.00 30.00
6 Isaac Okoro/99 5.00 12.00
7 Gary Payton/75 12.00 30.00
8 Allan Houston/99 6.00 15.00

9 Caleb Martin/99 5.00 12.00
10 Chris Bosh/49 12.00 30.00
11 De'Anthony Melton/99 6.00 15.00
12 Keegan Murray/99 8.00 20.00
13 Jalen Green/75 12.00 30.00
14 Shawn Kemp/99 10.00 25.00
15 Kenyon Martin/99 5.00 12.00
16 Anfernee Hardaway/75 20.00 50.00
17 Aaron Nesmith/99 6.00 15.00
18 Tayshaun Prince/99 6.00 15.00
19 Glen Rice/99 6.00 15.00
20 Nicolas Claxton/99 6.00 15.00

2023-24 Panini Phoenix Instant Phenom

*SILVER: .75X TO 2X BASIC
1 GG Jackson II 1.25 3.00
2 Jaime Jaquez Jr. 1.00 2.50
3 Anthony Black 1.25 3.00
4 Ausar Thompson 1.50 4.00
5 Keyonte George 2.00 5.00
6 Julian Strawther 1.25 3.00
7 Cason Wallace 1.25 3.00
8 Noah Clowney .75 2.00
9 Toumani Camara 1.25 3.00
10 Scoot Henderson 2.00 5.00
11 Olivier-Maxence Prosper .60 1.50
12 Jarace Walker 1.25 3.00
13 Victor Wembanyama 5.00 12.00
14 Jordan Hawkins 1.00 2.50
15 Bilal Coulibaly 1.50 4.00
16 Taylor Hendricks .60 1.50
17 Cam Whitmore 1.50 4.00
18 Marcus Sasser 1.00 2.50
19 Dereck Lively II 1.25 3.00
20 Nick Smith Jr. .75 2.00
21 Brandin Podziemski 2.00 5.00
22 Amen Thompson 3.00 8.00
23 Gradey Dick 1.25 3.00
24 Brandon Miller 2.50 6.00
25 Kobe Bufkin .75 2.00

2023-24 Panini Phoenix Instant Phenom Phoenix Blue Ice

*BLUE ICE: .75X TO 2X BASIC
13 Victor Wembanyama 30.00 80.00

2023-24 Panini Phoenix Instant Phenom Phoenix Blue Lazer

*BLUE LAZER: 1.5X TO 4X BASIC
STATED PRINT RUN 275 SER.#'d SETS
13 Victor Wembanyama 60.00 150.00

2023-24 Panini Phoenix Instant Phenom Phoenix Bronze Lazer

*BRONZE LAZER: 4X TO 10X BASIC
STATED PRINT RUN 49 SER.#'d SETS
13 Victor Wembanyama 150.00 400.00

2023-24 Panini Phoenix Instant Phenom Phoenix Green Ice

*GREEN ICE: 2X TO 5X BASIC
STATED PRINT RUN 149 SER.#'d SETS
13 Victor Wembanyama 75.00 200.00

2023-24 Panini Phoenix Instant Phenom Phoenix Green Lazer

*GREEN LAZER: 2X TO 5X BASIC
STATED PRINT RUN 175 SER.#'d SETS
13 Victor Wembanyama 75.00 200.00

2023-24 Panini Phoenix Instant Phenom Phoenix Maroon Ice

*MAROON ICE: 1.5X TO 4X BASIC
STATED PRINT RUN 275 SER.#'d SETS
13 Victor Wembanyama 60.00 150.00

2023-24 Panini Phoenix Instant Phenom Phoenix Orange Ice

*ORANGE ICE: 1.5X TO 4X BASIC
STATED PRINT RUN 249 SER.#'d SETS
13 Victor Wembanyama 60.00 150.00

2023-24 Panini Phoenix Instant Phenom Phoenix Pink Ice

*PINK ICE: 5X TO 12X BASIC
STATED PRINT RUN 25 SER.#'d SETS
13 Victor Wembanyama 200.00 500.00

2023-24 Panini Phoenix Instant Phenom Phoenix Purple Ice

*PURPLE ICE: 5X TO 12X BASIC
STATED PRINT RUN 25 SER.#'d SETS
13 Victor Wembanyama 200.00 500.00

2023-24 Panini Phoenix Instant Phenom Phoenix Red Ice

*RED ICE: .75X TO 2X BASIC
13 Victor Wembanyama 30.00 80.00

2023-24 Panini Phoenix Instant Phenom Phoenix Teal Lazer

*TEAL LAZER: .75X TO 2X BASIC
13 Victor Wembanyama 30.00 80.00

2023-24 Panini Phoenix Instant Phenom Phoenix White Ice

*WHITE ICE: 2.5X TO 6X BASIC
STATED PRINT RUN 125 SER.#'d SETS
13 Victor Wembanyama 100.00 250.00

2023-24 Panini Phoenix Instant Phenom Phoenix White Lazer

*WHITE LAZER: 2X TO 5X BASIC
STATED PRINT RUN 150 SER.#'d SETS
13 Victor Wembanyama 75.00 200.00

2023-24 Panini Phoenix Instant Phenom Phoenix Yellow Ice

*YELLOW ICE: 2X TO 5X BASIC
STATED PRINT RUN 175 SER.#'d SETS
13 Victor Wembanyama 75.00 200.00

2023-24 Panini Phoenix Metropolis

1 Shai Gilgeous-Alexander 50.00 120.00
2 Nikola Jokic 50.00 125.00
3 Luka Doncic 60.00 150.00
4 Tyrese Haliburton 20.00 50.00
5 Victor Wembanyama 300.00 600.00
6 Jayson Tatum 40.00 100.00
7 LeBron James 80.00 200.00
8 Ja Morant 30.00 80.00
9 Giannis Antetokounmpo 50.00 125.00
10 Stephen Curry 80.00 200.00

2023-24 Panini Phoenix Mystique

*SILVER: .75X TO 2X BASIC
1 Jordan Hawkins .60 1.50
2 Luka Doncic 2.50 6.00
3 Bilal Coulibaly 1.00 2.50
4 Nikola Jokic 2.00 5.00
5 Giannis Antetokounmpo 2.00 5.00
6 Amen Thompson 2.00 5.00
7 Magic Johnson 1.50 4.00
8 Allen Iverson 1.00 2.50
9 Charles Barkley 1.00 2.50
10 Stephen Curry 3.00 8.00
11 Yao Ming 1.00 2.50
12 Dwyane Wade .75 2.00
13 Brandon Miller 1.50 4.00
14 LeBron James 3.00 8.00
15 Ausar Thompson 1.00 2.50
16 Victor Wembanyama 10.00 25.00
17 Scoot Henderson 1.25 3.00
18 Jaime Jaquez Jr. .60 1.50
19 Jayson Tatum 1.50 4.00
20 Keyonte George 1.25 3.00
21 Shai Gilgeous-Alexander 2.00 5.00
22 Kevin Garnett 1.00 2.50
23 Tracy McGrady .60 1.50
24 Larry Bird 1.50 4.00
25 Cason Wallace .75 2.00

2023-24 Panini Phoenix Mystique Blue

*BLUE: 4X TO 10X BASIC
STATED PRINT RUN 25 SER.#'d SETS
16 Victor Wembanyama 150.00 400.00

2023-24 Panini Phoenix Mystique Orange

*ORANGE: 3X TO 8X BASIC
STATED PRINT RUN 49 SER.#'d SETS
16 Victor Wembanyama 125.00 300.00

2023-24 Panini Phoenix Mystique Purple

*PURPLE: 2.5X TO 6X BASIC
STATED PRINT RUN 75 SER.#'d SETS
16 Victor Wembanyama 100.00 250.00

2023-24 Panini Phoenix Mystique Red

*RED: 2X TO 5X BASIC
STATED PRINT RUN 125 SER.#'d SETS
16 Victor Wembanyama 75.00 200.00

2023-24 Panini Phoenix Mystique Yellow

*YELLOW: 3X TO 8X BASIC
STATED PRINT RUN 35 SER.#'d SETS
16 Victor Wembanyama 125.00 300.00

2023-24 Panini Phoenix Mythical Autographs

STATED PRINT RUN BTWN 49-99 SER.#'d SETS
*PURPLE/35-75: .5X TO 1.2X BASIC
*ORANGE/49: .6X TO 1.5X BASIC
*INT RED/49: .6X TO 1.5X p/r 99
*INT RED/49: .5X TO 1.2X p/r 75
*INT RED/25: .5X TO 1.2X p/r 49
*YELLOW/25-35: .75X TO 2X p/r 99
*YELLOW/25-35: .6X TO 1.5X p/r 75
*YELLOW/25-35: .5X TO 1.2X p/r 49
*BLUE/25: .75X TO 2X p/r 99
*BLUE/25: .6X TO 1.5X p/r 75
*BLUE/25: .5X TO 1.2X p/r 49
2 Ayo Dosunmu/99 6.00 15.00
3 Austin Reaves/99 15.00 40.00
4 Myles Turner/99 6.00 15.00
5 Gilbert Arenas/99 6.00 15.00
6 D'Angelo Russell/99 6.00 15.00
7 James Worthy/49 15.00 40.00
8 Joe Dumars/99 8.00 20.00
9 Anthony Edwards/49 150.00 400.00
10 Corey Kispert/99 5.00 12.00
11 Yuta Watanabe/99 6.00 15.00
12 Nate Archibald/99 8.00 20.00
13 Adrian Dantley/99 6.00 15.00
14 Spud Webb/99 6.00 15.00
15 Bob Cousy/49 100.00 250.00
16 David Thompson/99 8.00 20.00
18 Chet Holmgren/49 60.00 150.00
19 Johnny Davis/99 5.00 12.00
20 Grant Williams/99 5.00 12.00
21 Christian Braun/99 6.00 15.00
22 Alvan Adams/99 5.00 12.00
23 Malik Beasley/99 6.00 15.00
24 Jaden Hardy/75 10.00 25.00
25 Charlie Scott/99 6.00 15.00
26 Nick Anderson/99 6.00 15.00
27 Jerry West/49 30.00 80.00
28 Tony Allen/99 4.00 10.00
29 Tony Parker/75 12.00 30.00
30 Bob Dandridge/99 6.00 15.00

2023-24 Panini Phoenix Operation Detonation

*SILVER: .75X TO 2X BASIC
1 Tyrese Haliburton .75 2.00
2 Brandon Miller 1.50 4.00
3 Shai Gilgeous-Alexander 2.00 5.00
4 Victor Wembanyama 6.00 15.00
5 Trae Young .75 2.00
6 Chet Holmgren 1.00 2.50
7 Ausar Thompson 1.00 2.50
8 LeBron James 3.00 8.00
9 Scoot Henderson 1.25 3.00
10 Jayson Tatum 1.50 4.00
11 Keyonte George 1.25 3.00
12 Anthony Edwards 2.00 5.00
13 Bilal Coulibaly 1.00 2.50
14 Kevin Durant 1.25 3.00
15 James Harden .75 2.00
16 Zion Williamson 1.00 2.50
17 Stephen Curry 3.00 8.00
18 Damian Lillard 1.00 2.50
19 Dereck Lively II .75 2.00
20 Giannis Antetokounmpo 2.00 5.00
21 Amen Thompson 2.00 5.00
22 Luka Doncic 2.50 6.00
23 Anthony Black .75 2.00
24 Jaime Jaquez Jr. .60 1.50
25 Nikola Jokic 2.00 5.00

2023-24 Panini Phoenix Operation Detonation Blue

*BLUE: 4X TO 10X BASIC
STATED PRINT RUN 25 SER.#'d SETS
4 Victor Wembanyama 150.00 400.00

2023-24 Panini Phoenix Operation Detonation International Blue

*INT BLUE: 3X TO 8X BASIC
STATED PRINT RUN 35 SER.#'d SETS
4 Victor Wembanyama 125.00 300.00

2023-24 Panini Phoenix Operation Detonation International Red

*INT RED: 2.5X TO 6X BASIC
STATED PRINT RUN 75 SER.#'d SETS
4 Victor Wembanyama 100.00 250.00

2023-24 Panini Phoenix Operation Detonation Orange

*ORANGE: 3X TO 8X BASIC
STATED PRINT RUN 49 SER.#'d SETS
4 Victor Wembanyama 125.00 300.00

2023-24 Panini Phoenix Operation Detonation Pink

*PINK: 2.5X TO 6X BASIC
STATED PRINT RUN 99 SER.#'d SETS
4 Victor Wembanyama 100.00 250.00

2023-24 Panini Phoenix Operation Detonation Purple

*PURPLE: 2.5X TO 6X BASIC
STATED PRINT RUN 75 SER.#'d SETS
4 Victor Wembanyama 100.00 250.00

2023-24 Panini Phoenix Operation Detonation Red

*RED: 2X TO 5X BASIC
STATED PRINT RUN 125 SER.#'d SETS
4 Victor Wembanyama 75.00 200.00

2023-24 Panini Phoenix Operation Detonation Yellow

*YELLOW: 3X TO 8X BASIC
STATED PRINT RUN 35 SER.#'d SETS
4 Victor Wembanyama 125.00 300.00

2023-24 Panini Phoenix Paragon

1 Donovan Mitchell 1.00 2.50
2 Stephen Curry 4.00 10.00
3 Luka Doncic 3.00 8.00
4 Devin Booker 1.25 3.00
5 Paul George .75 2.00
6 Nikola Jokic 2.50 6.00
7 Jayson Tatum 2.00 5.00
8 Tyrese Maxey 1.00 2.50
9 Anthony Edwards 2.50 6.00
10 Giannis Antetokounmpo 2.50 6.00
11 Jimmy Butler .75 2.00
12 Shai Gilgeous-Alexander 2.50 6.00
13 Victor Wembanyama 4.00 10.00
14 LeBron James 4.00 10.00
15 Zach LaVine .75 2.00
16 Joel Embiid 1.25 3.00
17 Kevin Durant 1.50 4.00
18 Kyrie Irving 1.00 2.50
19 De'Aaron Fox 1.00 2.50
20 Jalen Brunson 1.00 2.50
21 Chet Holmgren 1.25 3.00
22 Ja Morant 1.50 4.00
23 Paolo Banchero 1.25 3.00
24 Trae Young 1.00 2.50
25 Tyrese Haliburton 1.00 2.50

2023-24 Panini Phoenix Paragon Phoenix Blue Ice

*BLUE ICE: .75X TO 2X BASIC
13 Victor Wembanyama 30.00 80.00

2023-24 Panini Phoenix Paragon Phoenix Blue Lazer

*BLUE LAZER: 1.5X TO 4X BASIC
STATED PRINT RUN 275 SER.#'d SETS
13 Victor Wembanyama 60.00 150.00

2023-24 Panini Phoenix Paragon Phoenix Bronze Lazer

*BRONZE LAZER: 4X TO 10X BASIC
STATED PRINT RUN 49 SER.#'d SETS
13 Victor Wembanyama 150.00 400.00

2023-24 Panini Phoenix Paragon Phoenix Green Ice

*GREEN ICE: 2X TO 5X BASIC
STATED PRINT RUN 149 SER.#'d SETS
13 Victor Wembanyama 75.00 200.00

2023-24 Panini Phoenix Paragon Phoenix Green Lazer

*GREEN LAZER: 2X TO 5X BASIC
STATED PRINT RUN 175 SER.#'d SETS
13 Victor Wembanyama 75.00 200.00

2023-24 Panini Phoenix Paragon Phoenix Maroon Ice

*MAROON ICE: 1.5X TO 4X BASIC
STATED PRINT RUN 275 SER.#'d SETS
13 Victor Wembanyama 60.00 150.00

2023-24 Panini Phoenix Paragon Phoenix Orange Ice

*ORANGE ICE: 1.5X TO 4X BASIC
STATED PRINT RUN 249 SER.#'d SETS
13 Victor Wembanyama 60.00 150.00

2023-24 Panini Phoenix Paragon Phoenix Pink Ice

*PINK ICE: 5X TO 12X BASIC
STATED PRINT RUN 25 SER.#'d SETS
13 Victor Wembanyama 200.00 500.00

2023-24 Panini Phoenix Paragon Phoenix Purple Ice

*PURPLE ICE: 5X TO 12X BASIC
STATED PRINT RUN 25 SER.#'d SETS
13 Victor Wembanyama 200.00 500.00

2023-24 Panini Phoenix Paragon Phoenix Red Ice

*RED ICE: .75X TO 2X BASIC
13 Victor Wembanyama 30.00 80.00

2023-24 Panini Phoenix Paragon Phoenix White Ice

*WHITE ICE: 2.5X TO 6X BASIC
STATED PRINT RUN 125 SER.#'d SETS
13 Victor Wembanyama 100.00 250.00

2023-24 Panini Phoenix Paragon Phoenix White Lazer

*WHITE LAZER: 2X TO 5X BASIC
STATED PRINT RUN 150 SER.#'d SETS
13 Victor Wembanyama 75.00 200.00

2023-24 Panini Phoenix Paragon Phoenix Yellow Ice

*YELLOW ICE: 2X TO 5X BASIC
STATED PRINT RUN 175 SER.#'d SETS
13 Victor Wembanyama 75.00 200.00

2023-24 Panini Phoenix Paragon Silver

*SILVER: .75X TO 2X BASIC
13 Victor Wembanyama 30.00 80.00

2023-24 Panini Phoenix Pyro

1 Luka Doncic 4.00 10.00
2 Kawhi Leonard 1.50 4.00
3 Anthony Edwards 3.00 8.00
4 Jalen Brunson 1.25 3.00
5 Victor Wembanyama 15.00 40.00
6 Stephen Curry 5.00 12.00
7 Anthony Davis 1.50 4.00
8 Damian Lillard 1.50 4.00
9 Paolo Banchero 1.50 4.00
10 De'Aaron Fox 1.25 3.00
11 Jayson Tatum 2.50 6.00
12 Scoot Henderson 2.00 5.00
13 Tyrese Maxey 1.25 3.00
14 Shai Gilgeous-Alexander 3.00 8.00
15 Devin Booker 1.50 4.00
16 LeBron James 5.00 12.00
17 Brandon Miller 2.50 6.00
18 Ausar Thompson 1.50 4.00
19 Giannis Antetokounmpo 3.00 8.00
20 Jaylen Brown 1.25 3.00
21 Amen Thompson 3.00 8.00
22 Kyrie Irving 1.25 3.00
23 Nikola Jokic 3.00 8.00
24 Zion Williamson 1.50 4.00
25 Trae Young 1.25 3.00

2023-24 Panini Phoenix Pyro Blue

*BLUE: 2.5X TO 6X BASIC
STATED PRINT RUN 25 SER.#'d SETS
5 Victor Wembanyama 150.00 400.00

2023-24 Panini Phoenix Pyro International Blue

*INT BLUE: 2.5X TO 6X BASIC
STATED PRINT RUN 35 SER.#'d SETS
5 Victor Wembanyama 150.00 400.00

2023-24 Panini Phoenix Pyro International Red

*INT RED: 1.5X TO 4X BASIC
STATED PRINT RUN 75 SER.#'d SETS
5 Victor Wembanyama 100.00 250.00

2023-24 Panini Phoenix Pyro Orange

*ORANGE: 2X TO 5X BASIC
STATED PRINT RUN 49 SER.#'d SETS
5 Victor Wembanyama 125.00 300.00

2023-24 Panini Phoenix Pyro Pink

*PINK: 1.25X TO 3X BASIC
STATED PRINT RUN 99 SER.#'d SETS
5 Victor Wembanyama 75.00 200.00

2023-24 Panini Phoenix Pyro Purple

*PURPLE: 1.5X TO 4X BASIC
STATED PRINT RUN 75 SER.#'d SETS
5 Victor Wembanyama 100.00 250.00

2023-24 Panini Phoenix Pyro Red

*RED: 1.25X TO 3X BASIC
STATED PRINT RUN 125 SER.#'d SETS
5 Victor Wembanyama 75.00 200.00

2023-24 Panini Phoenix Pyro Yellow

*YELLOW: 2.5X TO 6X BASIC
STATED PRINT RUN 35 SER.#'d SETS
5 Victor Wembanyama 150.00 400.00

2023-24 Panini Phoenix Rookie Autographs

STATED PRINT RUN 99 SER.#'d SETS
*PURPLE/75: .5X TO 1.2X BASIC
*ORANGE/49: .6X TO 1.5X BASIC
*YELLOW/35: .75X TO 2X BASIC
*BLUE/25: .75X TO 2X BASIC
1 Bilal Coulibaly 15.00 40.00
2 Amen Thompson 30.00 80.00
3 Keyonte George 20.00 50.00
4 GG Jackson II 12.00 30.00
5 Toumani Camara 12.00 30.00
6 Andre Jackson Jr. 10.00 25.00
7 Brandin Podziemski 20.00 50.00
8 Vasilije Micic 6.00 15.00
9 Marcus Sasser 10.00 25.00
10 Olivier-Maxence Prosper 6.00 15.00
11 Kobe Bufkin 8.00 20.00
12 Dariq Whitehead 8.00 20.00
13 Cason Wallace 12.00 30.00
14 Duop Reath 6.00 15.00
15 Julian Phillips 6.00 15.00
16 Ben Sheppard 6.00 15.00
17 Maxwell Lewis 5.00 12.00
18 Jalen Wilson 6.00 15.00
19 Sasha Vezenkov 5.00 12.00
20 Kris Murray 6.00 15.00
21 Rayan Rupert 6.00 15.00
22 Trayce Jackson-Davis 8.00 20.00
23 Hunter Tyson 6.00 15.00
24 Dereck Lively II 12.00 30.00
25 Ausar Thompson 15.00 40.00

2023-24 Panini Phoenix Rookie Jersey Autographs

STATED PRINT RUN 199 SER.#'d SETS
*PURPLE/99: .5X TO 1.2X BASIC
*ORANGE/49: .6X TO 1.5X BASIC
*YELLOW/35: .75X TO 2X BASIC
*BLUE/25: .75X TO 2X BASIC
1 Andre Jackson Jr. 10.00 25.00
2 Marcus Sasser 10.00 25.00
3 Mouhamed Gueye 6.00 15.00
4 Seth Lundy 5.00 12.00
5 Jalen Wilson 6.00 15.00
6 Ausar Thompson 15.00 40.00
7 Jalen Slawson 6.00 15.00
8 Sasha Vezenkov 5.00 12.00
9 Jordan Walsh 6.00 15.00
10 Brandin Podziemski 20.00 50.00
11 Olivier-Maxence Prosper 6.00 15.00
12 Keyontae Johnson 6.00 15.00
13 Kobe Bufkin 8.00 20.00
14 Kobe Brown 6.00 15.00
15 Dariq Whitehead 8.00 20.00
16 Duop Reath 6.00 15.00
17 Noah Clowney 8.00 20.00
18 Toumani Camara 12.00 30.00
19 Maxwell Lewis 5.00 12.00
20 Leonard Miller 6.00 15.00
21 Dereck Lively II 12.00 30.00
22 Julian Strawther 8.00 20.00
23 Brice Sensabaugh 10.00 25.00
24 Colby Jones 6.00 15.00
25 Cason Wallace 12.00 30.00
26 Trayce Jackson-Davis 8.00 20.00
27 GG Jackson II 12.00 30.00
28 Sidy Cissoko 6.00 15.00
29 Jaylen Clark 6.00 15.00
30 Rayan Rupert 6.00 15.00
31 Hunter Tyson 6.00 15.00
32 Amen Thompson 30.00 80.00
33 Julian Phillips 6.00 15.00
34 Bilal Coulibaly 15.00 40.00
35 Kris Murray 6.00 15.00
36 Jalen Pickett 5.00 12.00
37 Keyonte George 20.00 50.00
38 Isaiah Wong 6.00 15.00
39 Jordan Miller 8.00 20.00
40 Ben Sheppard 6.00 15.00

2023-24 Panini Phoenix Rookie Jumbo Memorabilia

*PURPLE/99: .5X TO 1.2X BASIC
*ORANGE/75: .6X TO 1.5X BASIC
*YELLOW/49: .75X TO 2X BASIC
*BLUE/25: 1X TO 2.5X BASIC
1 Amen Thompson 10.00 25.00
2 Victor Wembanyama 60.00 150.00
3 Scoot Henderson 6.00 15.00
4 Kris Murray 2.00 5.00
5 Dereck Lively II 4.00 10.00
6 Ausar Thompson 5.00 12.00
7 Jordan Hawkins 3.00 8.00
8 Jaime Jaquez Jr. 3.00 8.00
9 Brandin Podziemski 6.00 15.00
10 Brandon Miller 8.00 20.00
11 Anthony Black 4.00 10.00
12 Cason Wallace 4.00 10.00
13 Gradey Dick 4.00 10.00
14 Cam Whitmore 5.00 12.00
15 Marcus Sasser 3.00 8.00
16 Bilal Coulibaly 5.00 12.00
17 Sasha Vezenkov 1.50 4.00
18 Taylor Hendricks 2.00 5.00
19 Trayce Jackson-Davis 2.50 6.00
20 Toumani Camara 4.00 10.00
21 Dariq Whitehead 2.50 6.00
22 Olivier-Maxence Prosper 2.00 5.00
23 Jarace Walker 4.00 10.00
24 Vasilije Micic 2.00 5.00
25 GG Jackson II 4.00 10.00

2023-24 Panini Phoenix Rookie Memorabilia

*PURPLE/99: .5X TO 1.2X BASIC
*ORANGE/75: .6X TO 1.5X BASIC
*YELLOW/49: .75X TO 2X BASIC
*BLUE/25: 1X TO 2.5X BASIC
1 GG Jackson II 4.00 10.00
2 Julian Strawther 2.50 6.00
3 Jarace Walker 4.00 10.00
4 Maxwell Lewis 1.50 4.00
5 Nick Smith Jr. 2.50 6.00
6 Toumani Camara 4.00 10.00
7 Trayce Jackson-Davis 2.50 6.00
8 Kobe Bufkin 2.50 6.00
9 Jett Howard 2.50 6.00
10 Bilal Coulibaly 5.00 12.00
11 Emoni Bates 2.50 6.00
12 Brice Sensabaugh 3.00 8.00
13 Jordan Walsh 2.00 5.00
14 Cason Wallace 4.00 10.00
15 Anthony Black 4.00 10.00
16 Brandon Miller 8.00 20.00
17 Brandin Podziemski 6.00 15.00
18 Jaime Jaquez Jr. 3.00 8.00
19 Jordan Hawkins 3.00 8.00
20 Ausar Thompson 5.00 12.00
21 Dereck Lively II 4.00 10.00
22 Jalen Hood-Schifino 2.00 5.00
23 Scoot Henderson 6.00 15.00
24 Victor Wembanyama 60.00 150.00
25 Amen Thompson 10.00 25.00

2023-24 Panini Phoenix Rookie Rising Blue

*BLUE: 2.5X TO 6X BASIC
STATED PRINT RUN 25 SER.#'d SETS

2023-24 Panini Phoenix Rookie Rising International Blue

*INT BLUE: 2.5X TO 6X BASIC
STATED PRINT RUN 35 SER.#'d SETS
13 Victor Wembanyama 150.00 400.00

2023-24 Panini Phoenix Rookie Rising International Red

*INT RED: 1.5X TO 4X BASIC
STATED PRINT RUN 75 SER.#'d SETS
13 Victor Wembanyama 100.00 250.00

2023-24 Panini Phoenix Rookie Rising Orange

*ORANGE: 2X TO 5X BASIC
STATED PRINT RUN 49 SER.#'d SETS
13 Victor Wembanyama 125.00 300.00

2023-24 Panini Phoenix Rookie Rising Pink

*PINK: 1.5X TO 4X BASIC
STATED PRINT RUN 99 SER.#'d SETS
13 Victor Wembanyama 100.00 250.00

2023-24 Panini Phoenix Rookie Rising Purple

*PURPLE: 1.5X TO 4X BASIC
STATED PRINT RUN 75 SER.#'d SETS
13 Victor Wembanyama 100.00 250.00

2023-24 Panini Phoenix Rookie Rising Red

*RED: 1.25X TO 3X BASIC
STATED PRINT RUN 125 SER.#'d SETS
13 Victor Wembanyama 75.00 200.00

2023-24 Panini Phoenix Rookie Rising Yellow

*YELLOW: 2.5X TO 6X BASIC
STATED PRINT RUN 35 SER.#'d SETS
13 Victor Wembanyama 150.00 400.00

2023-24 Panini Phoenix Rookie Signs

STATED PRINT RUN 199 SER.#'d SETS
*PURPLE/75: .5X TO 1.2X BASIC
*INT RED/49: .6X TO 1.5X BASIC
*ORANGE/49: .6X TO 1.5X BASIC
*YELLOW/35: .75X TO 2X BASIC
*BLUE/25: .75X TO 2X BASIC
1 Ausar Thompson 15.00 40.00
2 Duop Reath 6.00 15.00
5 Dereck Lively II 12.00 30.00
6 Cason Wallace 12.00 30.00
7 Trayce Jackson-Davis 8.00 20.00
8 Marcus Sasser 10.00 25.00
9 Keyonte George 20.00 50.00
10 Amen Thompson 30.00 80.00
11 Bilal Coulibaly 15.00 40.00
12 Jordan Walsh 6.00 15.00
13 Tristan Vukcevic 6.00 15.00
14 GG Jackson II 12.00 30.00
15 Vasilije Micic 6.00 15.00
16 Olivier-Maxence Prosper 6.00 15.00
18 Noah Clowney 8.00 20.00
19 Maxwell Lewis 5.00 12.00
20 Andre Jackson Jr. 10.00 25.00
21 Brice Sensabaugh 10.00 25.00
22 Kris Murray 6.00 15.00
23 Julian Phillips 6.00 15.00
24 Toumani Camara 12.00 30.00
25 Oscar Tshiebwe 8.00 20.00
26 Rayan Rupert 6.00 15.00
27 Leonard Miller 6.00 15.00
28 Colby Jones 6.00 15.00
29 Isaiah Wong 6.00 15.00
30 Brandin Podziemski 20.00 50.00

2023-24 Panini Phoenix Shooting Stars

1 Nikola Jokic 50.00 125.00
2 Victor Wembanyama 200.00 500.00
3 Ja Morant 30.00 80.00
4 Trae Young 20.00 50.00
5 Amen Thompson 50.00 120.00
6 Shai Gilgeous-Alexander 50.00 120.00
7 Luka Doncic 60.00 150.00
8 Damian Lillard 25.00 60.00
9 Anthony Edwards 50.00 125.00
10 De'Aaron Fox 20.00 50.00
11 Tyrese Haliburton 20.00 50.00
12 Giannis Antetokounmpo 50.00 125.00
13 Brandon Miller 40.00 100.00
14 Scoot Henderson 30.00 80.00
15 Donovan Mitchell 20.00 50.00
16 Tyrese Maxey 20.00 50.00
17 Stephen Curry 80.00 200.00
18 Paolo Banchero 25.00 60.00
19 Zion Williamson 25.00 60.00
20 LeBron James 80.00 200.00
21 James Harden 20.00 50.00
22 Jayson Tatum 40.00 100.00
23 Devin Booker 25.00 60.00
24 Ausar Thompson 25.00 60.00
25 Kevin Durant 30.00 80.00

2023-24 Panini Phoenix Stellar Signatures

STATED PRINT RUN BTWN 49-99 SER.#'d SETS
*PURPLE/25-75: .5X TO 1.2X BASIC
*ORANGE/49: .6X TO 1.5X BASIC
*YELLOW/35: .75X TO 2X p/r 99
*YELLOW/35: .6X TO 1.5X p/r 75
*YELLOW/35: .5X TO 1.2X p/r 49
*BLUE/15-25: .75X TO 2X p/r 99
*BLUE/15-25: .6X TO 1.5X p/r 75
*BLUE/15-25: .5X TO 1.2X p/r 49
1 Jalen Green/75 12.00 30.00
2 Alex Caruso/99 6.00 15.00
3 Kristaps Porzingis/99 8.00 20.00
4 Dejounte Murray/99 8.00 20.00
5 Jamal Crawford/99 6.00 15.00
6 Jeremy Sochan/99 8.00 20.00
7 Chris Mullin/99 8.00 20.00
8 Clint Capela/99 5.00 12.00
9 Khris Middleton/99 6.00 15.00
10 Zach Randolph/99 6.00 15.00
11 Josh Hart/99 6.00 15.00
12 Jaden Ivey/99 8.00 20.00
13 Deandre Ayton/99 6.00 15.00
14 De'Aaron Fox/49 20.00 50.00
15 Metta World Peace/99 6.00 15.00
16 Jonas Valanciunas/99 5.00 12.00
17 Luke Kennard/99 5.00 12.00
18 Elton Brand/99 5.00 12.00
19 Danny Granger/99 5.00 12.00
21 Dirk Nowitzki/49 75.00 200.00
22 Bob Pettit/49 12.00 30.00
23 Walt Frazier/75 12.00 30.00
25 Julius Erving/49 40.00 100.00
26 Mahmoud Abdul-Rauf/99 5.00 12.00
27 Paolo Banchero /49 60.00 150.00
28 Jose Alvarado/99 6.00 15.00
29 Moses Moody/99 8.00 20.00
30 Norman Powell/99 6.00 15.00

2023-24 Panini Phoenix Temple Men

1 Kevin Durant 1.50 4.00
2 LeBron James 4.00 10.00
3 DeMar DeRozan .75 2.00
4 Jayson Tatum 2.00 5.00
5 Damian Lillard 1.25 3.00
6 Zion Williamson 1.25 3.00
7 Victor Wembanyama 4.00 10.00
8 Tyrese Haliburton 1.00 2.50
9 Cade Cunningham 1.25 3.00
10 Paolo Banchero 1.25 3.00
11 Donovan Mitchell 1.00 2.50
12 Kawhi Leonard 1.25 3.00
13 Luka Doncic 3.00 8.00
14 Joel Embiid 1.25 3.00
15 Nikola Jokic 2.50 6.00
16 Stephen Curry 4.00 10.00
17 Devin Booker 1.25 3.00
18 Giannis Antetokounmpo 2.50 6.00
19 Domantas Sabonis .75 2.00
20 Jaylen Brown 1.00 2.50
21 Chet Holmgren 1.25 3.00
22 Shai Gilgeous-Alexander 2.50 6.00
23 Scottie Barnes .60 1.50
24 Lauri Markkanen .75 2.00
25 Anthony Davis 1.25 3.00

2023-24 Panini Phoenix Temple Men Phoenix Blue Ice

*BLUE ICE: .75X TO 2X BASIC
7 Victor Wembanyama 30.00 80.00

2023-24 Panini Phoenix Temple Men Phoenix Blue Lazer

*BLUE LAZER: 1.5X TO 4X BASIC
STATED PRINT RUN 275 SER.#'d SETS
7 Victor Wembanyama 60.00 150.00

2023-24 Panini Phoenix Temple Men Phoenix Bronze Lazer

*BRONZE LAZER: 4X TO 10X BASIC
STATED PRINT RUN 49 SER.#'d SETS
7 Victor Wembanyama 150.00 400.00

2023-24 Panini Phoenix Temple Men Phoenix Green Ice

*GREEN ICE: 2X TO 5X BASIC
STATED PRINT RUN 149 SER.#'d SETS
7 Victor Wembanyama 75.00 200.00

2023-24 Panini Phoenix Temple Men Phoenix Green Lazer

*GREEN LAZER: 2X TO 5X BASIC
STATED PRINT RUN 175 SER.#'d SETS
7 Victor Wembanyama 75.00 200.00

2023-24 Panini Phoenix Temple Men Phoenix Maroon Ice

*MAROON ICE: 1.5X TO 4X BASIC
STATED PRINT RUN 275 SER.#'d SETS
7 Victor Wembanyama 60.00 150.00

2023-24 Panini Phoenix Temple Men Phoenix Orange Ice

*ORANGE ICE: 1.5X TO 4X BASIC
STATED PRINT RUN 249 SER.#'d SETS
7 Victor Wembanyama 60.00 150.00

2023-24 Panini Phoenix Temple Men Phoenix Pink Ice

*PINK ICE: 5X TO 12X BASIC
STATED PRINT RUN 25 SER.#'d SETS
7 Victor Wembanyama 200.00 500.00

2023-24 Panini Phoenix Temple Men Phoenix Purple Ice

*PURPLE ICE: 5X TO 12X BASIC
STATED PRINT RUN 25 SER.#'d SETS
7 Victor Wembanyama 200.00 500.00

2023-24 Panini Phoenix Temple Men Phoenix Red Ice

*RED ICE: .75X TO 2X BASIC
7 Victor Wembanyama 30.00 80.00

2023-24 Panini Phoenix Temple Men Phoenix Teal Lazer

*TEAL LAZER: .75X TO 2X BASIC
7 Victor Wembanyama 30.00 80.00

2023-24 Panini Phoenix Temple Men Phoenix White Ice

*WHITE ICE: 2.5X TO 6X BASIC
STATED PRINT RUN 125 SER.#'d SETS
7 Victor Wembanyama 100.00 250.00

2023-24 Panini Phoenix Temple Men Phoenix White Lazer

*WHITE LAZER: 2X TO 5X BASIC
STATED PRINT RUN 150 SER.#'d SETS
7 Victor Wembanyama 75.00 200.00

2023-24 Panini Phoenix Temple Men Phoenix Yellow Ice

*YELLOW ICE: 2X TO 5X BASIC
STATED PRINT RUN 175 SER.#'d SETS
7 Victor Wembanyama 75.00 200.00

2023-24 Panini Phoenix Temple Men Silver

*SILVER: .75X TO 2X BASIC
7 Victor Wembanyama 30.00 80.00

2023-24 Panini Phoenix Thrillers

1 Keyonte George 2.00 5.00
2 Victor Wembanyama 15.00 40.00
3 Stephen Curry 5.00 12.00
4 Ausar Thompson 1.50 4.00
5 Nikola Jokic 3.00 8.00
6 Dereck Lively II 1.25 3.00
7 Paolo Banchero 1.50 4.00
8 Brandon Miller 2.50 6.00
9 Anthony Edwards 3.00 8.00
10 Scoot Henderson 2.00 5.00
11 Jayson Tatum 2.50 6.00
12 Jaime Jaquez Jr. 1.00 2.50
13 Luka Doncic 4.00 10.00
14 Shai Gilgeous-Alexander 3.00 8.00
15 LeBron James 5.00 12.00
16 Damian Lillard 1.50 4.00
17 Chet Holmgren 1.50 4.00
18 Trae Young 1.50 4.00
19 Giannis Antetokounmpo 3.00 8.00
20 Ja Morant 2.00 5.00
21 Tyrese Haliburton 1.25 3.00
22 Zion Williamson 1.50 4.00
23 Kevin Durant 2.00 5.00
24 Amen Thompson 3.00 8.00
25 Brandin Podziemski 2.00 5.00

2023-24 Panini Phoenix Thrillers Blue

*BLUE: 2.5X TO 6X BASIC
STATED PRINT RUN 25 SER.#'d SETS
2 Victor Wembanyama 150.00 400.00

2023-24 Panini Phoenix Thrillers Orange

*ORANGE: 2X TO 5X BASIC
STATED PRINT RUN 49 SER.#'d SETS
2 Victor Wembanyama 125.00 300.00

2023-24 Panini Phoenix Thrillers Pink

*PINK: 1.25X TO 3X BASIC
STATED PRINT RUN 99 SER.#'d SETS
2 Victor Wembanyama 75.00 200.00

2023-24 Panini Phoenix Thrillers Purple

*PURPLE: 1.5X TO 4X BASIC
STATED PRINT RUN 75 SER.#'d SETS
2 Victor Wembanyama 100.00 250.00

2023-24 Panini Phoenix Thrillers Red

*RED: 1.25X TO 3X BASIC
STATED PRINT RUN 125 SER.#'d SETS
2 Victor Wembanyama 75.00 200.00

2023-24 Panini Phoenix Thrillers Yellow
*YELLOW: 2.5X TO 6X BASIC
STATED PRINT RUN 35 SER.#'d SETS
2 Victor Wembanyama 150.00 400.00

2023-24 Panini Phoenix Veteran Materials
*PURPLE/99: .5X TO 1.2X BASIC
*ORANGE/75: .6X TO 1.5X BASIC
*YELLOW/49: .75X TO 2X BASIC
*BLUE/25: 1X TO 2.5X BASIC
1 Jayson Tatum 10.00 25.00
2 Joel Embiid 6.00 15.00
3 Devin Booker 6.00 15.00
4 LeBron James 40.00 100.00
5 Kyrie Irving 5.00 12.00
6 Jimmy Butler 4.00 10.00
7 Kevin Durant 8.00 20.00
8 Damian Lillard 6.00 15.00
9 Trae Young 5.00 12.00
10 DeMar DeRozan 4.00 10.00
11 Kawhi Leonard 6.00 15.00
12 Mikal Bridges 3.00 8.00
13 Bam Adebayo 4.00 10.00
14 Pascal Siakam 4.00 10.00
15 LaMelo Ball 6.00 15.00
16 Kyle Kuzma 3.00 8.00
17 Tyler Herro 4.00 10.00
18 Jalen Green 4.00 10.00
19 Darius Garland 4.00 10.00
20 Scottie Barnes 3.00 8.00
21 Tobias Harris 2.50 6.00
22 Jaylen Brown 5.00 12.00
23 Bradley Beal 3.00 8.00
24 John Collins 2.50 6.00
25 Miles Bridges 2.50 6.00

2021-22 Panini PhotoGenic Diamond Anniversary
*DIAMOND ANN(1-100): 6X TO 15X BASIC
*DIAMOND ANN(101-140): 4X TO 10X BASIC
STATED PRINT RUN 75 SER. #'D SETS
2 Luka Doncic 75.00 200.00
3 Stephen Curry 200.00 500.00
4 LeBron James 350.00 700.00
101 Cade Cunningham 300.00 600.00
104 Josh Giddey 150.00 400.00
105 Jalen Green 300.00 600.00
109 Jonathan Kuminga 100.00 250.00
111 Evan Mobley 150.00 400.00
113 Jalen Suggs 75.00 200.00
115 Franz Wagner 75.00 200.00
116 Scottie Barnes 200.00 500.00

2021-22 Panini PhotoGenic Championship First Night
COMMON CARD .75 2.00
SEMISTARS 1.00 2.50
UNLISTED STARS 1.25 3.00
1 Cade Cunningham 10.00 25.00
2 Anthony Edwards 6.00 15.00
3 Zion Williamson 3.00 8.00
4 Deandre Ayton 1.25 3.00
5 Ben Simmons 1.25 3.00
6 Karl-Anthony Towns 2.00 5.00
7 Anthony Davis 3.00 8.00
8 Kyrie Irving 2.50 6.00
9 Blake Griffin 1.25 3.00
10 Derrick Rose 2.00 5.00
11 LeBron James 10.00 25.00
12 Tim Duncan 3.00 8.00
13 Allen Iverson 3.00 8.00
14 Shaquille O'Neal 4.00 10.00

2021-22 Panini PhotoGenic Dual Autographs
1 Luka Doncic
Trae Young 2,000.00 4,000.00
2 Larry Bird
Magic Johnson 500.00 1,000.00
5 Anthony Edwards
Karl-Anthony Towns 500.00 1,000.00
7 Jonathan Kuminga
Moses Moody 200.00 500.00
8 Manu Ginobili
Tony Parker 300.00 600.00
9 Cade Cunningham
Jalen Green 1,000.00 2,000.00
10 Anthony Davis
Evan Mobley 200.00 500.00

2021-22 Panini PhotoGenic Pregame
COMMON CARD .75 2.00
SEMISTARS 1.00 2.50
UNLISTED STARS 1.25 3.00
1 LeBron James 10.00 25.00
2 Stephen Curry 8.00 20.00
3 LaMelo Ball 3.00 8.00
4 Giannis Antetokounmpo 6.00 15.00
5 Luka Doncic 8.00 20.00
6 James Harden 2.50 6.00
7 Karl-Anthony Towns 2.00 5.00
8 Devin Booker 3.00 8.00
9 Donovan Mitchell 2.50 6.00
10 Darius Garland 2.00 5.00
11 Jayson Tatum 5.00 12.00
12 Ja Morant 4.00 10.00

2021-22 Panini PhotoGenic Respect
COMMON CARD .75 2.00
SEMISTARS 1.00 2.50
UNLISTED STARS 1.25 3.00
1 Luka Doncic
Zion Williamson 8.00 20.00
2 LaMelo Ball
LeBron James 10.00 25.00
3 Dwyane Wade
Giannis Antetokounmpo 6.00 15.00
4 Bill Russell
Shaquille O'Neal 4.00 10.00
5 Ja Morant
Stephen Curry 8.00 20.00

2021-22 Panini PhotoGenic Rookie Autographs
COMMON CARD 4.00 10.00
SEMISTARS 5.00 12.00
UNLISTED STARS 6.00 15.00
EXCHANGE DEADLINE 12/20/2023
1 Day'Ron Sharpe 6.00 15.00
2 Davion Mitchell 6.00 15.00
3 Ayo Dosunmu 12.00 30.00
4 Chris Duarte 5.00 12.00
5 Brandon Boston Jr. 6.00 15.00
6 Trey Murphy III 20.00 50.00
7 Keon Johnson 6.00 15.00
8 Cade Cunningham 300.00 600.00
9 Quentin Grimes 12.00 30.00
10 Jalen Suggs 40.00 100.00
11 Santi Aldama 8.00 20.00
12 Ziaire Williams 8.00 20.00
13 Jared Butler 6.00 15.00
14 Moses Moody 40.00 100.00
15 Luka Garza 6.00 15.00
16 Tre Mann 10.00 25.00
17 Isaiah Jackson 6.00 15.00
18 Jalen Green 200.00 500.00
19 Bones Hyland 30.00 80.00
20 Josh Giddey 100.00 250.00
21 Jeremiah Robinson-Earl 6.00 15.00
22 James Bouknight 5.00 12.00
23 Isaiah Livers 6.00 15.00
24 Corey Kispert 8.00 20.00
25 Charles Bassey 6.00 15.00
26 Kai Jones 5.00 12.00
27 Usman Garuba 5.00 12.00
28 Evan Mobley 100.00 250.00
29 Cameron Thomas 12.00 30.00
30 Jonathan Kuminga 100.00 250.00
31 Miles McBride 10.00 25.00
32 Joshua Primo 5.00 12.00
33 Austin Reaves 25.00 60.00
34 Alperen Sengun 40.00 100.00
35 Scottie Lewis 5.00 12.00
36 Jalen Johnson 20.00 50.00
37 Josh Christopher 5.00 12.00
38 Scottie Barnes 200.00 500.00
39 Jaden Springer 6.00 15.00
40 Franz Wagner 50.00 120.00

2021-22 Panini PhotoGenic Rookie Focus
COMMON CARD .75 2.00
SEMISTARS 1.00 2.50
UNLISTED STARS 1.25 3.00
1 Evan Mobley 12.00 30.00
2 Jalen Suggs 3.00 8.00
3 Josh Giddey 12.00 30.00
4 Jalen Green 15.00 40.00
5 Cade Cunningham 20.00 50.00
6 Davion Mitchell 1.25 3.00
7 Scottie Barnes 15.00 40.00
8 Franz Wagner 4.00 10.00
9 Chris Duarte 1.00 2.50
10 Bones Hyland 1.50 4.00

2021-22 Panini PhotoGenic Rookies in Motion
COMMON CARD .75 2.00
SEMISTARS 1.00 2.50
UNLISTED STARS 1.25 3.00
1 Cade Cunningham 8.00 20.00
2 Jalen Green 6.00 15.00
3 Evan Mobley 5.00 12.00
4 Scottie Barnes 4.00 10.00
5 Alperen Sengun 4.00 10.00
6 Davion Mitchell 1.25 3.00
7 Franz Wagner 4.00 10.00
8 Josh Giddey 4.00 10.00
9 Joshua Primo 1.00 2.50
10 Herbert Jones 1.50 4.00
11 Jalen Suggs 3.00 8.00
12 Chris Duarte 1.00 2.50
13 Ayo Dosunmu 2.50 6.00
14 Bones Hyland 1.50 4.00
15 Ziaire Williams 1.50 4.00

2021-22 Panini PhotoGenic Shoe Game
1 Luka Doncic 800.00 1,500.00
2 LeBron James 1,000.00 2,000.00
3 Giannis Antetokounmpo 600.00 1,200.00
4 Russell Westbrook 200.00 500.00
5 LaMelo Ball 400.00 800.00
6 Kevin Durant 400.00 800.00
7 Trae Young 400.00 800.00
8 Stephen Curry 800.00 1,500.00
9 Kyrie Irving 300.00 600.00
10 P.J. Tucker 150.00 400.00

2021-22 Panini PhotoGenic With Authority
COMMON CARD 1.00 2.50
SEMISTARS 1.25 3.00
UNLISTED STARS 1.50 4.00
1 LeBron James 12.00 30.00
2 Giannis Antetokounmpo 8.00 20.00
3 Zion Williamson 4.00 10.00
4 Jalen Green 8.00 20.00
5 Evan Mobley 6.00 15.00
6 Joel Embiid 4.00 10.00
7 Anthony Edwards 8.00 20.00
8 Ja Morant 5.00 12.00

2023-24 Panini PhotoGenic
*SILVER/99 (1-150): 3X TO 8X BASIC
*DIAMOND/75 (1-150): 4X TO 10X BASIC
*WEDGES/49 (1-150): 5X TO 12X BASIC
*MAZE/25 (1-150): 8X TO 20X BASIC
1 Brandon Ingram .60 1.50
2 Jarrett Allen .50 1.25
3 Bam Adebayo .75 2.00
4 Isaiah Stewart .50 1.25
5 Herbert Jones .50 1.25
6 Jaylen Brown 1.00 2.50
7 Paolo Banchero 1.25 3.00
8 Bradley Beal .60 1.50
9 Stephen Curry 4.00 10.00
10 Cameron Johnson .50 1.25
11 OG Anunoby .60 1.50
12 DeMar DeRozan .75 2.00
13 Nikola Jokic 2.50 6.00
14 Domantas Sabonis .75 2.00
15 De'Aaron Fox 1.00 2.50
16 Buddy Hield .50 1.25
17 Jalen Green .75 2.00
18 Marcus Smart .60 1.50
19 Cole Anthony .50 1.25
20 Trae Young 1.00 2.50
21 Jamal Murray 1.00 2.50
22 Keegan Murray .60 1.50
23 Anthony Davis 1.25 3.00
24 John Collins .50 1.25
25 Donovan Mitchell 1.00 2.50
26 Karl-Anthony Towns .75 2.00
27 Klay Thompson 1.25 3.00
28 Kawhi Leonard 1.25 3.00
29 Tim Hardaway Jr. .40 1.00
30 Andrew Wiggins .60 1.50
31 Kyrie Irving 1.00 2.50
32 Mikal Bridges .60 1.50
33 Keldon Johnson .60 1.50
34 Immanuel Quickley .50 1.25
35 Darius Garland .75 2.00
36 Anthony Edwards 2.50 6.00
37 Miles Bridges .50 1.25
38 Alperen Sengun .75 2.00
39 Jalen Williams 1.00 2.50
40 Desmond Bane .60 1.50
41 LeBron James 4.00 10.00
42 Walker Kessler .50 1.25
43 Chris Paul 1.00 2.50
44 Terry Rozier III .60 1.50
45 Shai Gilgeous-Alexander 2.50 6.00
46 Lauri Markkanen .75 2.00
47 CJ McCollum .50 1.25
48 Tyler Herro .75 2.00
49 Ben Simmons .50 1.25
50 Jaden Ivey .60 1.50
51 Nikola Vucevic .50 1.25
52 Anfernee Simons .60 1.50
53 D'Angelo Russell .50 1.25
54 Fred VanVleet .75 2.00
55 Grant Williams .40 1.00
56 Draymond Green .60 1.50
57 Myles Turner .50 1.25
58 De'Andre Hunter .50 1.25
59 Shaedon Sharpe 1.00 2.50
60 Kelly Oubre Jr. .50 1.25
61 Scottie Barnes .60 1.50
62 Bogdan Bogdanovic .50 1.25
63 Chet Holmgren 1.25 3.00
64 Brook Lopez .40 1.00
65 Devin Booker 1.25 3.00
66 LaMelo Ball 1.25 3.00
67 James Harden 1.00 2.50
68 Damian Lillard 1.25 3.00
69 Jayson Tatum 2.00 5.00
70 Cade Cunningham 1.25 3.00
71 Ja Morant 1.50 4.00
72 Franz Wagner .75 2.00
73 Austin Reaves 1.25 3.00
74 Deandre Ayton .50 1.25
75 Naz Reid .50 1.25
76 RJ Barrett .75 2.00
77 Jaren Jackson Jr. .75 2.00
78 Giannis Antetokounmpo 2.50 6.00
79 Jeremy Sochan .60 1.50
80 Jerami Grant .60 1.50
81 Kyle Kuzma .60 1.50
82 Paul George .75 2.00
83 Julius Randle .60 1.50
84 Kristaps Porzingis .60 1.50
85 Dejounte Murray .60 1.50
86 Michael Porter Jr. .60 1.50
87 Tobias Harris .50 1.25
88 Khris Middleton .50 1.25
89 Kevin Durant 1.50 4.00
90 Tyrese Haliburton 1.00 2.50
91 Pascal Siakam .75 2.00
92 Jimmy Butler .75 2.00
93 Rudy Gobert .60 1.50
94 Bennedict Mathurin .75 2.00
95 Joel Embiid 1.25 3.00
96 Dennis Schroder .50 1.25
97 Zach LaVine .75 2.00
98 Jrue Holiday .60 1.50
99 Josh Giddey .60 1.50
100 Devin Vassell .60 1.50
101 Aaron Gordon .50 1.25
102 Russell Westbrook .75 2.00
103 Jordan Clarkson .50 1.25
104 Evan Mobley .75 2.00
105 Luka Doncic 3.00 8.00
106 Tyrese Maxey 1.00 2.50
107 Mark Williams .50 1.25
108 Cameron Thomas .60 1.50
109 Jordan Poole .75 2.00
110 Kevin Huerter .40 1.00
111 Zion Williamson 1.25 3.00
112 Jalen Suggs .60 1.50
113 Jabari Smith Jr. .75 2.00
114 Jalen Brunson 1.00 2.50
115 Charles Barkley 1.25 3.00
116 Carmelo Anthony .75 2.00
117 Magic Johnson 2.00 5.00
118 Shaquille O'Neal 1.50 4.00
119 Dennis Rodman 1.25 3.00
120 Julius Erving 1.25 3.00
121 Jason Kidd .75 2.00
122 Karl Malone 1.00 2.50
123 Pete Maravich 1.25 3.00
124 Dwyane Wade 1.00 2.50
125 Anfernee Hardaway 1.25 3.00
126 Tim Duncan 1.25 3.00
127 Pau Gasol .75 2.00
128 Shawn Kemp .75 2.00
129 Ray Allen .75 2.00
130 Yao Ming 1.25 3.00
131 Jason Williams .75 2.00
132 Vince Carter 1.00 2.50
133 John Stockton 1.00 2.50
134 Tony Parker .75 2.00
135 Patrick Ewing .75 2.00
136 Allen Iverson 1.25 3.00
137 Clyde Drexler .75 2.00
138 Gary Payton .75 2.00
139 Hakeem Olajuwon 1.00 2.50
140 Kevin Garnett 1.25 3.00
141 David Robinson 1.00 2.50
142 Brandon Roy .60 1.50
143 Larry Bird 2.00 5.00
144 Steve Nash 1.00 2.50
145 Tracy McGrady .75 2.00
146 Dirk Nowitzki 1.25 3.00
147 Yuta Tabuse .50 1.25
148 Paul Pierce .75 2.00
149 Kareem Abdul-Jabbar 1.50 4.00
150 Manu Ginobili 1.00 2.50
151 Hunter Tyson RC 1.00 2.50
152 Rayan Rupert RC 1.00 2.50
153 Kobe Brown RC 1.00 2.50
154 Jalen Slawson RC 1.00 2.50
155 Jordan Miller RC 1.25 3.00
156 Cason Wallace RC 2.00 5.00
157 Jaime Jaquez Jr. RC 1.50 4.00
158 Emoni Bates RC 1.25 3.00
159 Toumani Camara RC 2.00 5.00
160 Amen Thompson RC 5.00 12.00
161 Sidy Cissoko RC 1.00 2.50
162 Mouhamed Gueye RC 1.00 2.50
163 Julian Phillips RC 1.00 2.50
164 Dereck Lively II RC 2.00 5.00
165 Ausar Thompson RC 2.50 6.00
166 Keyontae Johnson RC 1.00 2.50
167 Chris Livingston RC 1.00 2.50
168 Cam Whitmore RC 2.50 6.00
169 Julian Strawther RC 1.25 3.00
170 Jalen Wilson RC 1.00 2.50
171 Olivier-Maxence Prosper RC 1.00 2.50
172 Maxwell Lewis RC .75 2.00
173 Ben Sheppard RC 1.00 2.50
174 Jordan Hawkins RC 1.50 4.00
175 Keyonte George RC 3.00 8.00
176 Jalen Pickett RC .75 2.00
177 Anthony Black RC 2.00 5.00
178 Nick Smith Jr. RC 1.25 3.00
179 Scoot Henderson RC 3.00 8.00
180 Andre Jackson Jr. RC 1.50 4.00
181 Kobe Bufkin RC 1.25 3.00
182 Leonard Miller RC 1.00 2.50
183 Brandon Miller RC 4.00 10.00
184 Kris Murray RC 1.00 2.50
185 Jett Howard RC 1.25 3.00
186 Colby Jones RC 1.00 2.50
187 Brandin Podziemski RC 3.00 8.00
188 Noah Clowney RC 1.25 3.00
189 Trayce Jackson-Davis RC 1.25 3.00
190 Amari Bailey RC 1.00 2.50
191 Taylor Hendricks RC 1.00 2.50
192 Jarace Walker RC 2.00 5.00
193 Marcus Sasser RC 1.50 4.00
194 Dariq Whitehead RC 1.25 3.00
195 Bilal Coulibaly RC 2.50 6.00
196 Brice Sensabaugh RC 1.50 4.00
197 Gradey Dick RC 2.00 5.00
198 GG Jackson II RC 2.00 5.00
199 Jalen Hood-Schifino RC 1.00 2.50
200 Victor Wembanyama RC 30.00 80.00

2023-24 Panini PhotoGenic Diamond
*DIAMOND RC (151-200): 2X TO 5X BASIC
STATED PRINT RUN 75 SER. #'D SETS
200 Victor Wembanyama 300.00 600.00

2023-24 Panini PhotoGenic Maze
*MAZE RC (151-200): 4X TO 10X BASIC
STATED PRINT RUN 25 SER. #'D SETS
200 Victor Wembanyama 500.00 1,000.00

2023-24 Panini PhotoGenic Silver
*SILVER RC (151-200): 1.5X TO 4X BASIC
STATED PRINT RUN 99 SER. #'D SETS
200 Victor Wembanyama 200.00 500.00

2023-24 Panini PhotoGenic Wedges
*WEDGES RC (151-200): 2.5X TO 6X BASIC
STATED PRINT RUN 49 SER. #'D SETS
200 Victor Wembanyama 350.00 700.00

2023-24 Panini PhotoGenic All-Star
*DIAMOND/75: 2X TO 5X BASIC
*MAZE/25: 4X TO 10X BASIC
1 Giannis Antetokounmpo 5.00 12.00
2 Shai Gilgeous-Alexander 5.00 12.00
3 Jayson Tatum 4.00 10.00
4 Joel Embiid 2.50 6.00
5 Lauri Markkanen 1.50 4.00
6 Nikola Jokic 5.00 12.00
7 Kyrie Irving 2.00 5.00
8 Luka Doncic 6.00 15.00
9 Tyrese Haliburton 2.00 5.00
10 Anthony Edwards 5.00 12.00
11 LeBron James 8.00 20.00
12 Donovan Mitchell 2.00 5.00
13 De'Aaron Fox 2.00 5.00
14 Damian Lillard 2.50 6.00
15 Ja Morant 3.00 8.00

2023-24 Panini PhotoGenic Burst Rate Signatures
*DIAMOND/50-75: .5X TO 1.2X BASIC
*MAZE/25: .75X TO 2X BASIC
1 Tyrese Maxey 40.00 100.00
2 Keldon Johnson 8.00 20.00
3 Franz Wagner 10.00 25.00
4 Devin Vassell 8.00 20.00
5 Stephen Curry 350.00 700.00
6 Luka Doncic 350.00 700.00
7 Desmond Bane 8.00 20.00
8 Kristaps Porzingis 20.00 50.00
9 Zach LaVine 10.00 25.00
10 Bradley Beal 8.00 20.00
11 Brandon Ingram 8.00 20.00
12 Lauri Markkanen 10.00 25.00
13 Cameron Thomas 8.00 20.00
14 Jalen Brunson 40.00 100.00
15 Anthony Edwards 125.00 300.00

2023-24 Panini PhotoGenic Championship Feels
*DIAMOND/75: 1.25X TO 3X BASIC
*MAZE/25: 2X TO 5X BASIC
1 Nikola Jokic 10.00 25.00
2 Jamal Murray 4.00 10.00
3 Stephen Curry 15.00 40.00
4 LeBron James 15.00 40.00
5 Giannis Antetokounmpo 10.00 25.00
6 Kevin Durant 6.00 15.00
7 Kyrie Irving 4.00 10.00
8 Tim Duncan 5.00 12.00
9 Dirk Nowitzki 5.00 12.00
10 Shaquille O'Neal 6.00 15.00

2023-24 Panini PhotoGenic Dual Autographs
1 Tracy McGrady
Amen Thompson 100.00 250.00
2 Cade Cunningham
Ausar Thompson 100.00 250.00
3 Domantas Sabonis
De'Aaron Fox 100.00 250.00
4 Allen Iverson
Tyrese Maxey 300.00 600.00
5 John Stockton
Tyrese Haliburton 100.00 250.00
6 Anthony Edwards
Kevin Garnett 400.00 800.00
7 Chris Bosh
Dwyane Wade 100.00 250.00
8 Russell Westbrook
Cason Wallace 100.00 250.00
9 Tony Parker
Manu Ginobili 100.00 250.00
10 RJ Barrett
Immanuel Quickley 25.00 60.00

2023-24 Panini PhotoGenic First Night
1 Tracy McGrady 1.50 4.00
2 Jayson Tatum 4.00 10.00
3 Keyonte George 3.00 8.00
4 Luka Doncic 6.00 15.00
5 LeBron James 8.00 20.00
6 Brandon Miller 4.00 10.00
7 Allen Iverson 2.50 6.00
8 Stephen Curry 8.00 20.00
9 Jordan Hawkins 1.50 4.00
10 Amen Thompson 5.00 12.00
11 Jaime Jaquez Jr. 1.50 4.00
12 Nikola Jokic 5.00 12.00
13 Victor Wembanyama 20.00 50.00
14 Scoot Henderson 3.00 8.00
15 Ausar Thompson 2.50 6.00

2023-24 Panini PhotoGenic First Night Diamond
*DIAMOND: 2X TO 5X BASIC
STATED PRINT RUN 75 SER. #'D SETS
13 Victor Wembanyama 150.00 400.00

2023-24 Panini PhotoGenic First Night Maze
*MAZE: 4X TO 10X BASIC
STATED PRINT RUN 25 SER. #'D SETS
13 Victor Wembanyama 400.00 800.00

2023-24 Panini PhotoGenic Mirrored
1 Cam Whitmore 25.00 60.00
2 Anthony Black 20.00 50.00
3 Victor Wembanyama 400.00 800.00
4 Ausar Thompson 25.00 60.00
5 Taylor Hendricks 10.00 25.00
6 Cason Wallace 20.00 50.00
7 Bilal Coulibaly 25.00 60.00
8 Jaime Jaquez Jr. 15.00 40.00
9 Brandin Podziemski 30.00 80.00
10 Marcus Sasser 15.00 40.00
11 Kobe Bufkin 12.00 30.00
12 Brandon Miller 40.00 100.00
13 Gradey Dick 20.00 50.00
14 Scoot Henderson 30.00 80.00
15 Jordan Hawkins 15.00 40.00
16 Keyonte George 30.00 80.00
17 Dereck Lively II 20.00 50.00
18 Amen Thompson 50.00 120.00
19 Andre Jackson Jr. 15.00 40.00

2023-24 Panini PhotoGenic Progressions
1 Shai Gilgeous-Alexander 10.00 25.00
2 Steve Nash 4.00 10.00
3 Kyrie Irving 4.00 10.00
4 Damian Lillard 5.00 12.00
5 Tracy McGrady 3.00 8.00
6 Tyrese Haliburton 4.00 10.00
7 Anthony Davis 5.00 12.00
8 Carmelo Anthony 3.00 8.00
9 Kevin Durant 6.00 15.00
10 LeBron James 15.00 40.00

2023-24 Panini PhotoGenic Progressions Diamond
*DIAMOND: 1.25X TO 3X BASIC
STATED PRINT RUN 75 SER. #'D SETS
10 LeBron James 75.00 200.00

2023-24 Panini PhotoGenic Progressions Maze
*MAZE: 2X TO 5X BASIC
STATED PRINT RUN 25 SER. #'D SETS
10 LeBron James 125.00 300.00

2023-24 Panini PhotoGenic Ritual
1 LeBron James 15.00 40.00
2 Stephen Curry 15.00 40.00
3 Luka Doncic 12.00 30.00
4 Kevin Garnett 12.00 30.00
5 Dwyane Wade 8.00 20.00

2023-24 Panini PhotoGenic Ritual Diamond
*DIAMOND: 1.25X TO 3X BASIC
STATED PRINT RUN 75 SER. #'D SETS
1 LeBron James 75.00 200.00
4 Kevin Garnett 40.00 100.00

2023-24 Panini PhotoGenic Ritual Maze
*MAZE: 2X TO 5X BASIC
STATED PRINT RUN 25 SER. #'D SETS
1 LeBron James 125.00 300.00

2023-24 Panini PhotoGenic Rookie Autographs
*DIAMOND/75: .5X TO 1.2X BASIC
*MAZE/25: .75X TO 2X BASIC
1 Oscar Tshiebwe 8.00 20.00
2 Olivier-Maxence Prosper 6.00 15.00
3 Duop Reath 6.00 15.00
4 Ausar Thompson 40.00 100.00
5 Bilal Coulibaly 15.00 40.00
6 Keyonte George 40.00 100.00
7 Isaiah Wong 6.00 15.00
9 Brandin Podziemski 40.00 100.00
10 Rayan Rupert 6.00 15.00
11 Vasilije Micic 6.00 15.00
12 Chris Livingston 6.00 15.00
13 Mouhamed Gueye 6.00 15.00
14 Craig Porter Jr. 8.00 20.00
15 Kris Murray 6.00 15.00
16 Trayce Jackson-Davis 8.00 20.00
18 Maxwell Lewis 5.00 12.00
19 Kobe Brown 6.00 15.00
21 Amen Thompson 40.00 100.00
22 Sasha Vezenkov 5.00 12.00
23 Colby Jones 6.00 15.00
25 Dereck Lively II 12.00 30.00
26 Jordan Miller 8.00 20.00
27 Leonard Miller 6.00 15.00
28 Jalen Slawson 6.00 15.00
29 Julian Phillips 6.00 15.00
30 Cason Wallace 12.00 30.00
31 Jalen Wilson 6.00 15.00
32 Colin Castleton 5.00 12.00
33 Stanley Umude 5.00 12.00
34 Amari Bailey 6.00 15.00
35 Lester Quinones 5.00 12.00
36 AJ Lawson 5.00 12.00
37 Jordan Walsh 6.00 15.00
38 Kobe Bufkin 8.00 20.00
39 Brice Sensabaugh 10.00 25.00
40 Jaylen Clark 6.00 15.00

2023-24 Panini PhotoGenic Rookie Focus
1 Dereck Lively II 2.00 5.00
2 Brandon Miller 4.00 10.00
3 Cam Whitmore 2.50 6.00
4 Brandin Podziemski 3.00 8.00
5 Keyonte George 3.00 8.00
6 Ausar Thompson 2.50 6.00
7 Amen Thompson 5.00 12.00
8 Scoot Henderson 3.00 8.00
9 Jarace Walker 2.00 5.00
10 Jaime Jaquez Jr. 1.50 4.00
11 Victor Wembanyama 20.00 50.00
12 Anthony Black 2.00 5.00
13 Cason Wallace 2.00 5.00
14 Bilal Coulibaly 2.50 6.00
15 Jordan Hawkins 1.50 4.00

2023-24 Panini PhotoGenic Rookie Focus Diamond
*DIAMOND: 2X TO 5X BASIC
STATED PRINT RUN 75 SER. #'D SETS
2 Brandon Miller 40.00 100.00
11 Victor Wembanyama 150.00 400.00

2023-24 Panini PhotoGenic Rookie Focus Maze
*MAZE: 4X TO 10X BASIC
STATED PRINT RUN 25 SER. #'D SETS
2 Brandon Miller 75.00 200.00
11 Victor Wembanyama 400.00 800.00

2023-24 Panini PhotoGenic Rookies In Motion
1 Victor Wembanyama 20.00 50.00
2 Brandin Podziemski 3.00 8.00
3 Jaime Jaquez Jr. 1.50 4.00
4 Anthony Black 2.00 5.00
5 Keyonte George 3.00 8.00
6 Scoot Henderson 3.00 8.00
7 Gradey Dick 2.00 5.00
8 Cason Wallace 2.00 5.00
9 Bilal Coulibaly 2.50 6.00
10 Marcus Sasser 1.50 4.00
11 Amen Thompson 5.00 12.00
12 Brandon Miller 4.00 10.00
13 Ausar Thompson 2.50 6.00
14 Jordan Hawkins 1.50 4.00
15 Dereck Lively II 2.00 5.00

2023-24 Panini PhotoGenic Rookies In Motion Diamond
*DIAMOND: 2X TO 5X BASIC
STATED PRINT RUN 75 SER. #'D SETS
1 Victor Wembanyama 150.00 400.00
12 Brandon Miller 40.00 100.00

2023-24 Panini PhotoGenic Rookies In Motion Maze
*MAZE: 4X TO 10X BASIC
STATED PRINT RUN 25 SER. #'D SETS
1 Victor Wembanyama 400.00 800.00
12 Brandon Miller 75.00 200.00

2023-24 Panini PhotoGenic The Shoe Game
1 Jayson Tatum 150.00 400.00
2 Victor Wembanyama 800.00 1,500.00
3 LeBron James 400.00 800.00
4 Luka Doncic 300.00 600.00
5 Stephen Curry 400.00 800.00

2023-24 Panini PhotoGenic Unforgettable
1 Luka Doncic 12.00 30.00
2 Stephen Curry 15.00 40.00
3 LeBron James 15.00 40.00
4 Nikola Jokic 10.00 25.00
5 Tim Duncan 8.00 20.00

2023-24 Panini PhotoGenic Unforgettable Diamond
*DIAMOND: 1.25X TO 3X BASIC
STATED PRINT RUN 75 SER. #'D SETS
3 LeBron James 75.00 200.00

2023-24 Panini PhotoGenic Unforgettable Maze
*MAZE: 2X TO 5X BASIC
STATED PRINT RUN 25 SER. #'D SETS
3 LeBron James 125.00 300.00

2023-24 Panini PhotoGenic Veteran Autographs
*DIAMOND/50-75: .5X TO 1.2X BASIC
*MAZE/25: .75X TO 2X BASIC
2 Brook Lopez 5.00 12.00
3 Ayo Dosunmu 6.00 15.00
4 Lonnie Walker IV 6.00 15.00
5 Dennis Schroder 6.00 15.00
8 Jalen Johnson 8.00 20.00
9 Yuta Watanabe 6.00 15.00
11 Alperen Sengun 10.00 25.00
12 Al Horford 6.00 15.00
13 Marcus Smart 8.00 20.00
14 Deandre Ayton 6.00 15.00
15 Rudy Gobert 8.00 20.00
16 Fred VanVleet 10.00 25.00
17 Lauri Markkanen 10.00 25.00
18 CJ McCollum 6.00 15.00
19 Brandon Ingram 8.00 20.00
20 Jalen Duren 8.00 20.00
21 Rui Hachimura 30.00 80.00
22 Dejounte Murray 8.00 20.00
23 Keegan Murray 8.00 20.00
24 Derrick White 8.00 20.00
25 Clint Capela 5.00 12.00
28 Jarred Vanderbilt 5.00 12.00
29 Malik Monk 8.00 20.00
30 Bruce Brown 6.00 15.00
31 Dante Exum 5.00 12.00
32 Max Christie 6.00 15.00
33 Jalen McDaniels 5.00 12.00
34 Zach LaVine 15.00 40.00
35 Jrue Holiday 25.00 60.00

2023-24 Panini PhotoGenic With Authority
1 Jayson Tatum 4.00 10.00
2 Zion Williamson 2.50 6.00
3 Amen Thompson 5.00 12.00
4 Ausar Thompson 2.50 6.00
5 Brandon Miller 4.00 10.00
6 Giannis Antetokounmpo 5.00 12.00
7 Luka Doncic 6.00 15.00
8 Ja Morant 3.00 8.00
9 Victor Wembanyama 20.00 50.00
10 LeBron James 8.00 20.00

2023-24 Panini PhotoGenic With Authority Diamond
*DIAMOND: 2X TO 5X BASIC
STATED PRINT RUN 75 SER. #'D SETS
5 Brandon Miller 40.00 100.00
9 Victor Wembanyama 150.00 400.00

2023-24 Panini PhotoGenic With Authority Maze
*MAZE: 4X TO 10X BASIC
STATED PRINT RUN 25 SER. #'D SETS
5 Brandon Miller 75.00 200.00
9 Victor Wembanyama 400.00 800.00

2022-23 Panini Player of the Day
COMPLETE SET (100)
1 Anthony Davis 1.00 2.50
2 Andrew Wiggins .50 1.25
3 Anthony Edwards 2.00 5.00
4 Bam Adebayo .60 1.50
5 Bradley Beal .50 1.25
6 Cade Cunningham 1.25 3.00
7 Chris Paul .75 2.00
8 Collin Sexton .50 1.25
9 Damian Lillard 1.00 2.50
10 De'Aaron Fox .75 2.00
11 Dejounte Murray .50 1.25
12 DeMar Derozan .50 1.25
13 Devin Booker 1.00 2.50
14 Domantas Sabonis .50 1.25
15 Donovan Mitchell .75 2.00
16 Fred VanVleet .50 1.25
17 Giannis Antetokounmpo 2.00 5.00
18 Ja Morant 1.25 3.00
19 Jalen Brunson .75 2.00
20 Jalen Green 1.25 3.00
21 Jamal Murray .60 1.50
22 James Harden .75 2.00
23 Jarrett Allen .40 1.00
24 Jaylen Brown .75 2.00
25 Jayson Tatum 1.50 4.00
26 Jimmy Butler .75 2.00
27 Joel Embiid .60 1.50
28 Julius Randle .50 1.25
29 Karl-Anthony Towns .60 1.50
30 Kawhi Leonard 1.00 2.50
31 Keldon Johnson .50 1.25
32 Kevin Durant 1.25 3.00
33 Khris Middleton .50 1.25
34 Klay Thompson 1.00 2.50
35 Lamelo Ball 1.00 2.50
36 Lauri Markkanen .60 1.50
37 LeBron James 3.00 8.00
38 Luka Doncic 2.50 6.00
39 Nikola Jokic 2.00 5.00
40 Nikola Vucevic .40 1.00
41 Pascal Siakam .60 1.50
42 Paul George .60 1.50
43 Rudy Gobert .50 1.25
44 Scottie Barnes .60 1.50
45 Shai Gilgeous-Alexander 2.00 5.00
46 Stephen Curry 3.00 8.00
47 Trae Young 1.00 2.50
48 Tyrese Haliburton .75 2.00
49 Zach Lavine .75 2.00
50 Zion Williamson 1.00 2.50
51 Paolo Banchero 2.50 6.00
52 Chet Holmgren 2.00 5.00
53 David Robinson .75 2.00
54 Vince Carter .75 2.00
55 Jason Kidd .60 1.50
56 Patrick Ewing .60 1.50
57 Magic Johnson 1.50 4.00
58 Ray Allen .60 1.50
59 Dominique Wilkins .60 1.50
60 Tracy McGrady .60 1.50
61 Allen Iverson 1.00 2.50
62 Kevin Garnett 1.00 2.50
63 Gary Payton .60 1.50
64 Karl Malone .75 2.00
65 Chris Webber .50 1.25
66 Amar'e Stoudemire .40 1.00
67 Hakeem Olajuwon .75 2.00
68 Dennis Rodman 1.00 2.50
69 John Stockton .75 2.00
70 Tim Duncan 1.00 2.50
71 Dwyane Wade .75 2.00
72 Chris Mullin .50 1.25
73 Shaquille O'Neal 1.50 4.00
74 Dirk Nowitzki 1.00 2.50
75 Charles Barkley 1.00 2.50
76 Grant Hill .60 1.50
77 Shawn Kemp .60 1.50
78 Larry Johnson .50 1.25
79 Larry Bird 1.50 4.00
80 Jason Williams .60 1.50
81 Paolo Banchero 2.50 6.00
82 Chet Holmgren 2.00 5.00
83 Jabari Smith 1.25 3.00
84 Keegan Murray 1.00 2.50
85 Jaden Ivey 1.25 3.00
86 Bennedict Mathurin 1.25 3.00
87 Shaedon Sharpe 1.50 4.00
88 Dyson Daniels 1.00 2.50
89 Jeremy Sochan 1.25 3.00
90 Johnny Davis .40 1.00

91 Ousmane Dieng .50 1.25
92 Jalen Duren 1.25 3.00
93 Tari Eason 1.00 2.50
94 Jake Laravia .40 1.00
95 Christian Koloko .40 1.00
96 Jalen Williams 2.00 5.00
97 David Roddy .50 1.25
98 Andrew Nembhard .75 2.00
99 Christian Braun 1.00 2.50
100 Nikola Jovic .75 2.00

2022-23 Panini Player of the Day Blue

COMPLETE SET (100)
STATED PRINT RUN 50 SER.#'d SETS 2.00 5.00
1 Anthony Davis 4.00 10.00
2 Andrew Wiggins 2.00 5.00
3 Anthony Edwards 8.00 20.00
4 Bam Adebayo 2.50 6.00
5 Bradley Beal 2.00 5.00
6 Cade Cunningham 5.00 12.00
7 Chris Paul 3.00 8.00
8 Collin Sexton 2.00 5.00
9 Damian Lillard 4.00 10.00
10 De'Aaron Fox 3.00 8.00
11 Dejounte Murray 2.00 5.00
12 DeMar Derozan 2.00 5.00
13 Devin Booker 4.00 10.00
14 Domantas Sabonis 2.00 5.00
15 Donovan Mitchell 3.00 8.00
16 Fred VanVleet 2.00 5.00
17 Giannis Antetokounmpo 8.00 20.00
18 Ja Morant 5.00 12.00
19 Jalen Brunson 3.00 8.00
20 Jalen Green 5.00 12.00
21 Jamal Murray 2.50 6.00
22 James Harden 3.00 8.00
23 Jarrett Allen 1.50 4.00
24 Jaylen Brown 3.00 8.00
25 Jayson Tatum 6.00 15.00
26 Jimmy Butler 3.00 8.00
27 Joel Embiid 2.50 6.00
28 Julius Randle 2.00 5.00
29 Karl-Anthony Towns 2.50 6.00
30 Kawhi Leonard 4.00 10.00
31 Keldon Johnson 2.00 5.00
32 Kevin Durant 5.00 12.00
33 Khris Middleton 2.00 5.00
34 Klay Thompson 4.00 10.00
35 Lamelo Ball 4.00 10.00
36 Lauri Markkanen 2.50 6.00
37 LeBron James 12.00 30.00
38 Luka Doncic 10.00 25.00
39 Nikola Jokic 8.00 20.00
40 Nikola Vucevic 1.50 4.00
41 Pascal Siakam 2.50 6.00
42 Paul George 2.50 6.00
43 Rudy Gobert 2.00 5.00
44 Scottie Barnes 2.50 6.00
45 Shai Gilgeous-Alexander 8.00 20.00
46 Stephen Curry 12.00 30.00
47 Trae Young 4.00 10.00
48 Tyrese Haliburton 3.00 8.00
49 Zach Lavine 3.00 8.00
50 Zion Williamson 4.00 10.00
51 Paolo Banchero 20.00 50.00
52 Chet Holmgren 8.00 20.00
53 David Robinson 3.00 8.00
54 Vince Carter 3.00 8.00
55 Jason Kidd 2.50 6.00
56 Patrick Ewing 2.50 6.00
57 Magic Johnson 6.00 15.00
58 Ray Allen 2.50 6.00
59 Dominique Wilkins 2.50 6.00
60 Tracy McGrady 2.50 6.00
61 Allen Iverson 4.00 10.00
62 Kevin Garnett 4.00 10.00
63 Gary Payton 2.50 6.00
64 Karl Malone 3.00 8.00
65 Chris Webber 2.00 5.00
66 Amar'e Stoudemire 1.50 4.00
67 Hakeem Olajuwon 3.00 8.00
68 Dennis Rodman 4.00 10.00
69 John Stockton 3.00 8.00
70 Tim Duncan 4.00 10.00
71 Dwyane Wade 3.00 8.00
72 Chris Mullin 2.00 5.00
73 Shaquille O'Neal 6.00 15.00
74 Dirk Nowitzki 4.00 10.00
75 Charles Barkley 4.00 10.00
76 Grant Hill 2.50 6.00
77 Shawn Kemp 2.50 6.00
78 Larry Johnson 2.00 5.00
79 Larry Bird 6.00 15.00
80 Jason Williams 2.50 6.00
81 Paolo Banchero 20.00 50.00
82 Chet Holmgren 8.00 20.00
83 Jabari Smith 5.00 12.00
84 Keegan Murray 4.00 10.00
85 Jaden Ivey 5.00 12.00
86 Bennedict Mathurin 5.00 12.00
87 Shaedon Sharpe 6.00 15.00
88 Dyson Daniels 4.00 10.00
89 Jeremy Sochan 5.00 12.00
90 Johnny Davis 1.50 4.00
91 Ousmane Dieng 2.00 5.00
92 Jalen Duren 5.00 12.00
93 Tari Eason 4.00 10.00
94 Jake Laravia 1.50 4.00
95 Christian Koloko 1.50 4.00
96 Jalen Williams 8.00 20.00
97 David Roddy 2.00 5.00
98 Andrew Nembhard 3.00 8.00
99 Christian Braun 4.00 10.00
100 Nikola Jovic 3.00 8.00

2022-23 Panini Player of the Day Holo

COMPLETE SET (100)
1 Anthony Davis 2.00 5.00
2 Andrew Wiggins 1.00 2.50
3 Anthony Edwards 4.00 10.00
4 Bam Adebayo 1.25 3.00
5 Bradley Beal 1.00 2.50
6 Cade Cunningham 2.50 6.00
7 Chris Paul 1.50 4.00
8 Collin Sexton 1.00 2.50
9 Damian Lillard 2.00 5.00
10 De'Aaron Fox 1.50 4.00
11 Dejounte Murray 1.00 2.50
12 DeMar Derozan 1.00 2.50
13 Devin Booker 2.00 5.00
14 Domantas Sabonis 1.00 2.50
15 Donovan Mitchell 1.50 4.00
16 Fred VanVleet 1.00 2.50
17 Giannis Antetokounmpo 4.00 10.00
18 Ja Morant 2.50 6.00
19 Jalen Brunson 1.50 4.00
20 Jalen Green 2.50 6.00
21 Jamal Murray 1.25 3.00
22 James Harden 1.50 4.00
23 Jarrett Allen .75 2.00
24 Jaylen Brown 1.50 4.00
25 Jayson Tatum 3.00 8.00
26 Jimmy Butler 1.50 4.00
27 Joel Embiid 1.25 3.00
28 Julius Randle 1.00 2.50
29 Karl-Anthony Towns 1.25 3.00
30 Kawhi Leonard 2.00 5.00
31 Keldon Johnson 1.00 2.50
32 Kevin Durant 2.50 6.00
33 Khris Middleton 1.00 2.50
34 Klay Thompson 2.00 5.00
35 Lamelo Ball 2.00 5.00
36 Lauri Markkanen 1.25 3.00
37 LeBron James 6.00 15.00
38 Luka Doncic 5.00 12.00
39 Nikola Jokic 4.00 10.00
40 Nikola Vucevic .75 2.00
41 Pascal Siakam 1.25 3.00
42 Paul George 1.25 3.00
43 Rudy Gobert 1.00 2.50
44 Scottie Barnes 1.25 3.00
45 Shai Gilgeous-Alexander 4.00 10.00
46 Stephen Curry 6.00 15.00
47 Trae Young 2.00 5.00
48 Tyrese Haliburton 1.50 4.00
49 Zach Lavine 1.50 4.00
50 Zion Williamson 2.00 5.00
51 Paolo Banchero 5.00 12.00
52 Chet Holmgren 4.00 10.00
53 David Robinson 1.50 4.00
54 Vince Carter 1.50 4.00
55 Jason Kidd 1.25 3.00
56 Patrick Ewing 1.25 3.00
57 Magic Johnson 3.00 8.00
58 Ray Allen 1.25 3.00
59 Dominique Wilkins 1.25 3.00
60 Tracy McGrady 1.25 3.00
61 Allen Iverson 2.00 5.00
62 Kevin Garnett 2.00 5.00
63 Gary Payton 1.25 3.00
64 Karl Malone 1.50 4.00
65 Chris Webber 1.00 2.50
66 Amar'e Stoudemire .75 2.00
67 Hakeem Olajuwon 1.50 4.00
68 Dennis Rodman 2.00 5.00
69 John Stockton 1.50 4.00
70 Tim Duncan 2.00 5.00
71 Dwyane Wade 1.50 4.00
72 Chris Mullin 1.00 2.50
73 Shaquille O'Neal 3.00 8.00
74 Dirk Nowitzki 2.00 5.00
75 Charles Barkley 2.00 5.00
76 Grant Hill 1.25 3.00
77 Shawn Kemp 1.25 3.00
78 Larry Johnson 1.00 2.50
79 Larry Bird 3.00 8.00
80 Jason Williams 1.25 3.00
81 Paolo Banchero 5.00 12.00
82 Chet Holmgren 4.00 10.00
83 Jabari Smith 2.50 6.00
84 Keegan Murray 2.00 5.00
85 Jaden Ivey 2.50 6.00
86 Bennedict Mathurin 2.50 6.00
87 Shaedon Sharpe 3.00 8.00
88 Dyson Daniels 2.00 5.00
89 Jeremy Sochan 2.50 6.00
90 Johnny Davis .75 2.00
91 Ousmane Dieng 1.00 2.50
92 Jalen Duren 2.50 6.00
93 Tari Eason 2.00 5.00
94 Jake Laravia .75 2.00
95 Christian Koloko .75 2.00
96 Jalen Williams 4.00 10.00
97 David Roddy 1.00 2.50
98 Andrew Nembhard 1.50 4.00
99 Christian Braun 2.00 5.00
100 Nikola Jovic 1.50 4.00

2022-23 Panini Player of the Day Orange

COMPLETE SET (100)
STATED PRINT RUN 199 SER.#'d SETS
1 Anthony Davis 2.50 6.00
2 Andrew Wiggins 1.25 3.00
3 Anthony Edwards 5.00 12.00
4 Bam Adebayo 1.50 4.00
5 Bradley Beal 1.25 3.00
6 Cade Cunningham 3.00 8.00
7 Chris Paul 2.00 5.00
8 Collin Sexton 1.25 3.00
9 Damian Lillard 2.50 6.00
10 De'Aaron Fox 2.00 5.00
11 Dejounte Murray 1.25 3.00
12 DeMar Derozan 1.25 3.00
13 Devin Booker 2.50 6.00
14 Domantas Sabonis 1.25 3.00
15 Donovan Mitchell 2.00 5.00
16 Fred VanVleet 1.25 3.00
17 Giannis Antetokounmpo 5.00 12.00
18 Ja Morant 3.00 8.00
19 Jalen Brunson 2.00 5.00
20 Jalen Green 3.00 8.00
21 Jamal Murray 1.50 4.00
22 James Harden 2.00 5.00
23 Jarrett Allen 1.00 2.50
24 Jaylen Brown 2.00 5.00
25 Jayson Tatum 4.00 10.00
26 Jimmy Butler 2.00 5.00
27 Joel Embiid 1.50 4.00
28 Julius Randle 1.25 3.00
29 Karl-Anthony Towns 1.50 4.00
30 Kawhi Leonard 2.50 6.00
31 Keldon Johnson 1.25 3.00
32 Kevin Durant 3.00 8.00
33 Khris Middleton 1.25 3.00
34 Klay Thompson 2.50 6.00
35 Lamelo Ball 2.50 6.00
36 Lauri Markkanen 1.50 4.00
37 LeBron James 8.00 20.00
38 Luka Doncic 6.00 15.00
39 Nikola Jokic 5.00 12.00
40 Nikola Vucevic 1.00 2.50
41 Pascal Siakam 1.50 4.00
42 Paul George 1.50 4.00
43 Rudy Gobert 1.25 3.00
44 Scottie Barnes 1.50 4.00
45 Shai Gilgeous-Alexander 5.00 12.00
46 Stephen Curry 8.00 20.00
47 Trae Young 2.50 6.00
48 Tyrese Haliburton 2.00 5.00
49 Zach Lavine 2.00 5.00
50 Zion Williamson 2.50 6.00
51 Paolo Banchero 12.00 30.00
52 Chet Holmgren 5.00 12.00
53 David Robinson 2.00 5.00
54 Vince Carter 2.00 5.00
55 Jason Kidd 1.50 4.00
56 Patrick Ewing 1.50 4.00
57 Magic Johnson 4.00 10.00
58 Ray Allen 1.50 4.00
59 Dominique Wilkins 1.50 4.00
60 Tracy McGrady 1.50 4.00
61 Allen Iverson 2.50 6.00
62 Kevin Garnett 2.50 6.00
63 Gary Payton 1.50 4.00
64 Karl Malone 2.00 5.00
65 Chris Webber 1.25 3.00
66 Amar'e Stoudemire 1.00 2.50
67 Hakeem Olajuwon 2.00 5.00
68 Dennis Rodman 2.50 6.00
69 John Stockton 2.00 5.00
70 Tim Duncan 2.50 6.00
71 Dwyane Wade 2.00 5.00
72 Chris Mullin 1.25 3.00
73 Shaquille O'Neal 4.00 10.00
74 Dirk Nowitzki 2.50 6.00
75 Charles Barkley 2.50 6.00
76 Grant Hill 1.50 4.00
77 Shawn Kemp 1.50 4.00
78 Larry Johnson 1.25 3.00
79 Larry Bird 4.00 10.00
80 Jason Williams 1.50 4.00
81 Paolo Banchero 12.00 30.00
82 Chet Holmgren 5.00 12.00
83 Jabari Smith 3.00 8.00
84 Keegan Murray 2.50 6.00
85 Jaden Ivey 3.00 8.00
86 Bennedict Mathurin 3.00 8.00
87 Shaedon Sharpe 4.00 10.00
88 Dyson Daniels 2.50 6.00
89 Jeremy Sochan 3.00 8.00
90 Johnny Davis 1.00 2.50
91 Ousmane Dieng 1.25 3.00
92 Jalen Duren 3.00 8.00
93 Tari Eason 2.50 6.00
94 Jake Laravia 1.00 2.50
95 Christian Koloko 1.00 2.50
96 Jalen Williams 5.00 12.00
97 David Roddy 1.25 3.00
98 Andrew Nembhard 2.00 5.00
99 Christian Braun 2.50 6.00
100 Nikola Jovic 2.00 5.00

2022-23 Panini Player of the Day Red

COMPLETE SET (100)
STATED PRINT RUN 99 SER.#'d SETS
1 Anthony Davis 3.00 8.00
2 Andrew Wiggins 1.50 4.00
3 Anthony Edwards 6.00 15.00
4 Bam Adebayo 2.00 5.00
5 Bradley Beal 1.50 4.00
6 Cade Cunningham 4.00 10.00
7 Chris Paul 2.50 6.00
8 Collin Sexton 1.50 4.00
9 Damian Lillard 3.00 8.00
10 De'Aaron Fox 2.50 6.00
11 Dejounte Murray 1.50 4.00
12 DeMar Derozan 1.50 4.00
13 Devin Booker 3.00 8.00
14 Domantas Sabonis 1.50 4.00
15 Donovan Mitchell 2.50 6.00
16 Fred VanVleet 1.50 4.00
17 Giannis Antetokounmpo 6.00 15.00
18 Ja Morant 4.00 10.00
19 Jalen Brunson 2.50 6.00
20 Jalen Green 4.00 10.00
21 Jamal Murray 2.00 5.00
22 James Harden 2.50 6.00
23 Jarrett Allen 1.25 3.00
24 Jaylen Brown 2.50 6.00
25 Jayson Tatum 5.00 12.00
26 Jimmy Butler 2.50 6.00
27 Joel Embiid 2.00 5.00
28 Julius Randle 1.50 4.00
29 Karl-Anthony Towns 2.00 5.00
30 Kawhi Leonard 3.00 8.00
31 Keldon Johnson 1.50 4.00
32 Kevin Durant 4.00 10.00
33 Khris Middleton 1.50 4.00
34 Klay Thompson 3.00 8.00
35 Lamelo Ball 3.00 8.00
36 Lauri Markkanen 2.00 5.00
37 LeBron James 10.00 25.00
38 Luka Doncic 8.00 20.00
39 Nikola Jokic 6.00 15.00
40 Nikola Vucevic 1.25 3.00
41 Pascal Siakam 2.00 5.00
42 Paul George 2.00 5.00
43 Rudy Gobert 1.50 4.00
44 Scottie Barnes 2.00 5.00
45 Shai Gilgeous-Alexander 6.00 15.00
46 Stephen Curry 10.00 25.00
47 Trae Young 3.00 8.00
48 Tyrese Haliburton 2.50 6.00
49 Zach Lavine 2.50 6.00
50 Zion Williamson 3.00 8.00
51 Paolo Banchero 15.00 40.00
52 Chet Holmgren 6.00 15.00
53 David Robinson 2.50 6.00
54 Vince Carter 2.50 6.00
55 Jason Kidd 2.00 5.00
56 Patrick Ewing 2.00 5.00
57 Magic Johnson 5.00 12.00
58 Ray Allen 2.00 5.00
59 Dominique Wilkins 2.00 5.00
60 Tracy McGrady 2.00 5.00
61 Allen Iverson 3.00 8.00
62 Kevin Garnett 3.00 8.00
63 Gary Payton 2.00 5.00
64 Karl Malone 2.50 6.00
65 Chris Webber 1.50 4.00
66 Amar'e Stoudemire 1.25 3.00
67 Hakeem Olajuwon 2.50 6.00
68 Dennis Rodman 3.00 8.00
69 John Stockton 2.50 6.00
70 Tim Duncan 3.00 8.00
71 Dwyane Wade 2.50 6.00
72 Chris Mullin 1.50 4.00
73 Shaquille O'Neal 5.00 12.00
74 Dirk Nowitzki 3.00 8.00
75 Charles Barkley 3.00 8.00
76 Grant Hill 2.00 5.00
77 Shawn Kemp 2.00 5.00
78 Larry Johnson 1.50 4.00
79 Larry Bird 5.00 12.00
80 Jason Williams 2.00 5.00
81 Paolo Banchero 15.00 40.00
82 Chet Holmgren 6.00 15.00
83 Jabari Smith 4.00 10.00
84 Keegan Murray 3.00 8.00
85 Jaden Ivey 4.00 10.00
86 Bennedict Mathurin 4.00 10.00
87 Shaedon Sharpe 5.00 12.00
88 Dyson Daniels 3.00 8.00
89 Jeremy Sochan 4.00 10.00
90 Johnny Davis 1.25 3.00
91 Ousmane Dieng 1.50 4.00
92 Jalen Duren 4.00 10.00
93 Tari Eason 3.00 8.00
94 Jake Laravia 1.25 3.00
95 Christian Koloko 1.25 3.00
96 Jalen Williams 6.00 15.00
97 David Roddy 1.50 4.00
98 Andrew Nembhard 2.50 6.00
99 Christian Braun 3.00 8.00
100 Nikola Jovic 2.50 6.00

2022-23 Panini Player of the Day Silver

COMPLETE SET (100)
STATED PRINT RUN 499 SER.#'d SETS
1 Anthony Davis 2.00 5.00
2 Andrew Wiggins 1.00 2.50
3 Anthony Edwards 4.00 10.00
4 Bam Adebayo 1.25 3.00
5 Bradley Beal 1.00 2.50
6 Cade Cunningham 2.50 6.00
7 Chris Paul 1.50 4.00
8 Collin Sexton 1.00 2.50
9 Damian Lillard 2.00 5.00
10 De'Aaron Fox 1.50 4.00
11 Dejounte Murray 1.00 2.50
12 DeMar Derozan 1.00 2.50
13 Devin Booker 2.00 5.00
14 Domantas Sabonis 1.00 2.50
15 Donovan Mitchell 1.50 4.00
16 Fred VanVleet 1.00 2.50
17 Giannis Antetokounmpo 4.00 10.00
18 Ja Morant 2.50 6.00
19 Jalen Brunson 1.50 4.00
20 Jalen Green 2.50 6.00
21 Jamal Murray 1.25 3.00
22 James Harden 1.50 4.00
23 Jarrett Allen .75 2.00
24 Jaylen Brown 1.50 4.00
25 Jayson Tatum 3.00 8.00
26 Jimmy Butler 1.50 4.00
27 Joel Embiid 1.25 3.00
28 Julius Randle 1.00 2.50
29 Karl-Anthony Towns 1.25 3.00
30 Kawhi Leonard 2.00 5.00
31 Keldon Johnson 1.00 2.50
32 Kevin Durant 2.50 6.00
33 Khris Middleton 1.00 2.50
34 Klay Thompson 2.00 5.00
35 Lamelo Ball 2.00 5.00
36 Lauri Markkanen 1.25 3.00
37 LeBron James 6.00 15.00
38 Luka Doncic 5.00 12.00
39 Nikola Jokic 4.00 10.00
40 Nikola Vucevic .75 2.00
41 Pascal Siakam 1.25 3.00
42 Paul George 1.25 3.00
43 Rudy Gobert 1.00 2.50
44 Scottie Barnes 1.25 3.00
45 Shai Gilgeous-Alexander 4.00 10.00
46 Stephen Curry 6.00 15.00
47 Trae Young 2.00 5.00
48 Tyrese Haliburton 1.50 4.00
49 Zach Lavine 1.50 4.00
50 Zion Williamson 2.00 5.00
51 Paolo Banchero 5.00 12.00
52 Chet Holmgren 4.00 10.00
53 David Robinson 1.50 4.00
54 Vince Carter 1.50 4.00
55 Jason Kidd 1.25 3.00
56 Patrick Ewing 1.25 3.00
57 Magic Johnson 3.00 8.00
58 Ray Allen 1.25 3.00
59 Dominique Wilkins 1.25 3.00
60 Tracy McGrady 1.25 3.00
61 Allen Iverson 2.00 5.00
62 Kevin Garnett 2.00 5.00
63 Gary Payton 1.25 3.00
64 Karl Malone 1.50 4.00
65 Chris Webber 1.00 2.50
66 Amar'e Stoudemire .75 2.00
67 Hakeem Olajuwon 1.50 4.00
68 Dennis Rodman 2.00 5.00
69 John Stockton 1.50 4.00
70 Tim Duncan 2.00 5.00
71 Dwyane Wade 1.50 4.00
72 Chris Mullin 1.00 2.50
73 Shaquille O'Neal 3.00 8.00
74 Dirk Nowitzki 2.00 5.00
75 Charles Barkley 2.00 5.00
76 Grant Hill 1.25 3.00
77 Shawn Kemp 1.25 3.00
78 Larry Johnson 1.00 2.50
79 Larry Bird 3.00 8.00
80 Jason Williams 1.25 3.00
81 Paolo Banchero 5.00 12.00
82 Chet Holmgren 4.00 10.00
83 Jabari Smith 2.50 6.00
84 Keegan Murray 2.00 5.00
85 Jaden Ivey 2.50 6.00
86 Bennedict Mathurin 2.50 6.00
87 Shaedon Sharpe 3.00 8.00
88 Dyson Daniels 2.00 5.00
89 Jeremy Sochan 2.50 6.00
90 Johnny Davis .75 2.00
91 Ousmane Dieng 1.00 2.50
92 Jalen Duren 2.50 6.00
93 Tari Eason 2.00 5.00
94 Jake Laravia .75 2.00
95 Christian Koloko .75 2.00
96 Jalen Williams 4.00 10.00
97 David Roddy 1.00 2.50
98 Andrew Nembhard 1.50 4.00
99 Christian Braun 2.00 5.00
100 Nikola Jovic 1.50 4.00

2011-12 Panini Preferred

PS PRINT RUN 10 TO 99 SER.#'d SETS
PC PRINT RUN 15 TO 74 SER.#'d SETS
SL PRINT RUN 5 TO 99 SER.#'d SETS
CR PRINT RUN 24 TO 99 SER.#'d SETS
PS STANDS FOR PREFERRED SIGNATURES
PC STANDS FOR PANINIS CHOICE
SL STANDS FOR SILHOUETTE
CR STANDS FOR CROWN ROYALE
1 Walt Bellamy PS/25 AU 5.00 12.00
2 Adrian Dantley PS/74 AU 4.00 10.00
3 Al Thornton PS/74 AU 4.00 10.00
4 Alex English PS/74 AU 4.00 10.00
5 Alonzo Mourning PS/25 AU 20.00 50.00
6 Andre Iguodala PS/25 AU 5.00 12.00
7 Andre Miller PS/49 AU 4.00 10.00
8 Andrea Bargnani PS/25 AU 6.00 15.00
9 Andrei Kirilenko PS/25 AU 8.00 20.00
10 Artis Gilmore PS/25 AU 8.00 20.00
11 Bailey Howell PS/74 AU 5.00 12.00
12 Bernard King PS/74 AU 6.00 15.00
13 Bill Cartwright PS/74 AU 6.00 15.00
14 Bill Laimbeer PS/74 AU 4.00 10.00
16 Bill Walton PS/25 AU 10.00 25.00
18 Bob Dandridge PS/74 AU 4.00 10.00
19 Bob McAdoo PS/74 AU 10.00 25.00
20 Brandon Jennings PS/25 AU 10.00 25.00
21 Byron Scott PS/49 AU 6.00 15.00
22 Calvin Murphy PS/25 AU 5.00 12.00
23 Campy Russell PS/74 AU 4.00 10.00
24 Cazzie Russell PS/74 AU 4.00 10.00
25 Cedric Maxwell PS/74 AU 4.00 10.00
26 Charles Oakley PS/74 AU 10.00 25.00
27 Chris Ford PS/74 AU 4.00 10.00
28 Chris Mullin PS/74 AU 10.00 25.00
30 Christian Laettner PS/25 AU 6.00 15.00
31 Clyde Lovellette PS/25 AU 6.00 15.00
32 Connie Hawkins PS/74 AU 8.00 20.00
33 Dan Issel PS/74 AU 5.00 12.00
34 Dan Majerle PS/74 AU 5.00 12.00
35 Darrell Griffith PS/74 AU 4.00 10.00
36 Darren Collison PS/74 AU 4.00 10.00
37 Darryl Dawkins PS/74 AU 5.00 12.00
38 Dave Cowens PS/49 AU 5.00 12.00
40 David Thompson PS/74 AU 4.00 10.00
41 DeMar DeRozan PS/25 AU 40.00 100.00
44 Detlef Schrempf PS/74 AU 8.00 20.00
45 D.Mutombo PS/74 AU 15.00 40.00
46 Dirk Nowitzki PS/15 AU 75.00 200.00
47 Elgin Baylor PS/20 AU 12.00 30.00
48 Elvin Hayes PS/49 AU 5.00 12.00
49 Eric Gordon PS/49 AU 5.00 12.00
50 Frank Ramsey PS/74 AU 6.00 15.00
51 Gail Goodrich PS/25 AU 8.00 20.00
52 George Gervin PS/25 AU 10.00 25.00
53 George McGinnis PS/74 AU 4.00 10.00
54 Grant Hill PS/15 AU 75.00 200.00
55 Hakeem Olajuwon PS/15 AU 30.00 80.00
56 Isiah Thomas PS/25 AU 10.00 25.00
57 James Harden PS/25 AU 30.00 80.00
58 James Worthy PS/15 AU 25.00 60.00
59 Jeff Hornacek PS/74 AU 5.00 12.00
61 Jrue Holiday PS/49 AU 8.00 20.00
65 Kiki Vandeweghe PS/74 AU 4.00 10.00
66 Kobe Bryant PS/49 AU 125.00 300.00
68 Lenny Wilkens PS/25 AU 8.00 20.00
69 Luol Deng PS/25 AU 10.00 25.00
71 Mark Aguirre PS/74 AU 4.00 10.00
72 Mark Eaton PS/74 AU 4.00 10.00
73 Mark Price PS/74 AU 6.00 15.00
74 Maurice Cheeks PS/74 AU 4.00 10.00
75 Michael Cage PS/74 AU 4.00 10.00
76 M.Richmond PS/74 AU 8.00 20.00
77 Monta Ellis PS/49 AU 8.00 20.00
78 Nate Archibald PS/25 AU 8.00 20.00
79 Nate Thurmond PS/25 AU 8.00 20.00
82 Paul Westphal PS/74 AU 4.00 10.00
83 Ralph Sampson PS/74 AU 5.00 12.00
84 Robert Horry PS/49 AU 8.00 20.00
85 Robert Parish PS/25 AU 8.00 20.00
86 Rolando Blackman PS/74 AU 4.00 10.00
87 Sam Perkins PS/74 AU 4.00 10.00
88 Spencer Haywood PS/74 AU 4.00 10.00
89 Stephen Curry PS/49 AU 500.00 1,000.00
90 Stephen Jackson PS/74 AU 4.00 10.00
91 Steve Smith PS/74 AU 4.00 10.00
92 Tom Heinsohn PS/74 AU 15.00 40.00
93 D.Wilkins PS/25 AU 12.00 30.00
94 Toney Douglas PS/74 AU 4.00 10.00
95 Toni Kukoc PS/74 AU 6.00 15.00
96 Ty Lawson PS/49 AU 4.00 10.00
97 Walt Frazier PS/25 AU 10.00 25.00
98 Zach Randolph PS/25 AU 8.00 20.00
99 Xavier McDaniel PS/74 AU 4.00 10.00
100 World B. Free PS/25 AU 6.00 15.00
101 Walt Bellamy PC/25 AU 6.00 15.00
102 Adrian Dantley PC/74 AU 5.00 12.00
103 A.Thornton PC/74 AU EXCH 5.00 12.00
104 Alex English PC/74 AU 5.00 12.00
105 A.Mourning PC/25 AU 60.00 150.00
106 Andre Iguodala PC/25 AU 6.00 15.00
107 Andre Miller PC/49 AU 5.00 12.00
108 Andrea Bargnani PC/25 AU 6.00 15.00
110 Artis Gilmore PC/25 AU 10.00 25.00
111 Bailey Howell PC/74 AU 5.00 12.00
112 Bernard King PC/74 AU 6.00 15.00
113 Bill Cartwright PC/74 AU 6.00 15.00
114 Bill Laimbeer PC/74 AU 6.00 15.00
115 Bill Russell PC/15 AU 1,000.00 2,000.00
116 Bill Walton PC/25 AU 6.00 15.00
117 Blake Griffin PC/25 AU 20.00 50.00
118 Bob Dandridge PC/74 AU 5.00 12.00
119 Bob McAdoo PC/74 AU 6.00 15.00
120 B.Jennings PC/25 AU 5.00 12.00
121 Byron Scott PC/74 AU 5.00 12.00
122 Calvin Murphy PC/25 AU 6.00 15.00
123 Campy Russell PC/74 AU 5.00 12.00
124 Cazzie Russell PC/74 AU 5.00 12.00
125 Cedric Maxwell PC/74 AU 5.00 12.00
126 Charles Oakley PC/74 AU 8.00 20.00
127 Chris Ford PC/74 AU 5.00 12.00
128 Chris Mullin PC/74 AU 10.00 25.00
129 Chris Paul PC/25 AU 75.00 200.00
130 Christian Laettner PC/25 AU 8.00 20.00
131 Clyde Lovellette PC/25 AU 6.00 15.00
132 Connie Hawkins PC/74 AU 8.00 20.00
133 Dan Issel PC/74 AU 5.00 12.00
134 Dan Majerle PC/74 AU 6.00 15.00
135 Darrell Griffith PC/74 AU 5.00 12.00
136 Darren Collison PC/74 AU 6.00 15.00
137 Darryl Dawkins PC/74 AU 5.00 12.00
138 Dave Cowens PC/25 AU 10.00 25.00
139 David Robinson PC/25 AU 50.00 125.00
140 David Thompson PC/74 AU 6.00 15.00
141 DeMar DeRozan PC/25 AU 40.00 100.00
142 Dennis Rodman PC/25 AU 30.00 80.00
143 Derrick Rose PC/20 AU 50.00 120.00
144 Detlef Schrempf PC/74 AU 8.00 20.00
145 D.Mutombo PC/74 AU 10.00 25.00
146 Elgin Baylor PC/25 AU 12.00 30.00
147 Elvin Hayes PC/25 AU 6.00 15.00
148 Eric Gordon PC/25 AU 8.00 20.00
149 Frank Ramsey PC/74 AU 6.00 15.00
150 Gail Goodrich PC/25 AU 8.00 20.00
151 George Gervin PC/25 AU 15.00 40.00
152 George McGinnis PC/74 AU 5.00 12.00
153 Grant Hill PC/25 AU 60.00 150.00
154 H.Olajuwon PC/25 AU 30.00 80.00
155 Isiah Thomas PC/25 AU 12.00 30.00
156 James Harden PC/25 AU 40.00 100.00
157 James Worthy PC/25 AU 15.00 40.00
158 Jeff Hornacek PC/74 AU 6.00 15.00
159 John Stockton PC/15 AU 50.00 120.00
160 Jrue Holiday PC/74 AU 8.00 20.00
161 Julius Erving PC/15 AU 50.00 125.00
162 K.Abdul-Jabbar PC/15 AU 50.00 100.00
163 Kevin Durant PC/25 AU 75.00 200.00
164 K.Vandeweghe PC/74 AU EXCH 5.00 12.00
165 Kobe Bryant PC/49 AU 150.00 400.00
166 Larry Bird PC/15 AU 100.00 250.00
167 Lenny Wilkens PC/25 AU 10.00 25.00
168 Luol Deng PC/25 AU 12.00 30.00
169 Magic Johnson PC/15 AU 75.00 200.00
170 Mark Aguirre PC/74 AU 5.00 12.00
171 Mark Eaton PC/74 AU 5.00 12.00
172 Mark Price PC/74 AU 12.00 30.00
173 Maurice Cheeks PC/74 AU 5.00 12.00
174 Michael Cage PC/74 AU 5.00 12.00
175 M.Richmond PC/74 AU 10.00 25.00
176 Monta Ellis PC/49 AU 5.00 12.00
177 Nate Archibald PC/25 AU 12.00 30.00
178 Nate Thurmond PC/25 AU 10.00 25.00
179 Oscar Robertson PC/25 AU 50.00 125.00
180 Pat Riley PC/25 AU 15.00 40.00
181 Paul Westphal PC/74 AU 5.00 12.00
182 Ralph Sampson PC/74 AU 6.00 15.00
183 Robert Horry PC/74 AU 8.00 20.00
184 Robert Parish PC/25 AU 10.00 25.00
185 R.Blackman PC/74 AU 6.00 15.00
186 Sam Perkins PC/74 AU 8.00 20.00
187 Spencer Haywood PC/74 AU 5.00 12.00
188 Stephen Curry PC/74 AU 600.00 1,200.00
189 Stephen Jackson PC/74 AU 5.00 12.00
190 Steve Nash PC/20 AU 20.00 50.00
191 Steve Smith PC/74 AU 5.00 12.00
192 Tom Heinsohn PC/74 AU 8.00 20.00
193 D.Wilkins PC/25 AU 15.00 40.00
194 Toney Douglas PC/74 AU 5.00 12.00
195 Toni Kukoc PC/49 AU 15.00 40.00
196 Ty Lawson PC/49 AU 5.00 12.00
197 Walt Frazier PC/25 AU 10.00 25.00
198 Zach Randolph PC/25 AU 10.00 25.00
199 Xavier McDaniel PC/74 AU 5.00 12.00
200 World B. Free PC/25 AU 8.00 20.00
201 Al Jefferson SL/25 JSY AU 6.00 15.00
202 Thornton SL/49 JSY AU EXCH 6.00 15.00
203 Alex English SL/49 JSY AU 10.00 25.00
204 A.Mourning SL/25 JSY AU 50.00 125.00
205 A.Iguodala SL/49 JSY AU 8.00 20.00
206 A.Bargnani SL/49 JSY AU 6.00 15.00
208 A.Gilmore SL/25 JSY AU 20.00 50.00
210 Ben Gordon SL/25 JSY AU 12.00 30.00
211 Bernard King SL/24 JSY AU 15.00 40.00
212 B.Griffin SL/25 JSY AU 75.00 200.00
213 B.Jennings SL/49 JSY AU 6.00 15.00
214 C.Oakley SL/99 JSY AU 15.00 40.00
215 Chris Paul SL/25 JSY AU 100.00 250.00
216 C.Drexler SL/25 JSY AU 50.00 120.00
217 Dan Issel SL/49 JSY AU 6.00 15.00
218 D.Griffith SL/49 JSY AU 10.00 25.00
220 D.DeRozan SL/49 JSY AU 40.00 100.00
223 D.Schrempf SL/99 JSY AU 12.00 30.00
224 D.Mutombo SL/49 JSY AU 25.00 60.00
226 Grant Hill SL/25 JSY AU 125.00 250.00
227 H.Olajuwon SL/25 JSY AU 75.00 150.00
228 Isiah Thomas SL/25 JSY AU 30.00 80.00
229 J.Worthy SL/25 JSY AU 50.00 125.00
230 Jason Kidd SL/20 JSY AU 50.00 125.00
234 Kevin Love SL/25 JSY AU 25.00 60.00
235 Vandeweghe SL/99 JSY AU 8.00 20.00
236 K.Bryant SL/49 JSY AU 300.00 600.00
237 Luol Deng SL/49 JSY AU 6.00 15.00
238 Mark Aguirre SL/49 JSY AU 6.00 15.00
239 Mark Eaton SL/99 JSY AU 10.00 25.00
240 M.Cheeks SL/49 JSY AU 10.00 25.00
241 M.Cage SL/99 JSY AU 10.00 25.00
242 M.Richmond SL/25 JSY AU 40.00 80.00
243 Monta Ellis SL/49 JSY AU 6.00 15.00
246 R.Parish SL/49 JSY AU 15.00 40.00
247 S.Curry SL/99 JSY AU 600.00 1,200.00
248 D.Wilkins SL/25 JSY AU 30.00 80.00
249 Toni Kukoc SL/49 JSY AU 30.00 80.00
250 Ty Lawson SL/49 JSY AU 6.00 15.00
251 Artis Gilmore CR/25 AU 10.00 25.00
252 Bill Walton CR/25 AU 10.00 25.00
253 Dan Issel CR/25 AU 8.00 20.00
254 Darryl Dawkins CR/25 AU 6.00 15.00
255 Dave Cowens CR/25 AU 10.00 25.00
256 David Thompson CR/25 AU 8.00 20.00
257 Elgin Baylor CR/25 AU 15.00 40.00
258 George Gervin CR/25 AU 12.00 30.00
259 Oscar Robertson CR/25 AU 40.00 100.00
260 Walt Frazier CR/24 AU 10.00 25.00
261 Cole Aldrich CR/99 AU 3.00 8.00
262 Al-Farouq Aminu CR/99 AU 3.00 8.00
263 James Anderson CR/99 AU 3.00 8.00
264 Luke Babbitt CR/99 AU 3.00 8.00
265 Eric Bledsoe CR/99 AU 10.00 25.00
266 Trevor Booker CR/99 AU 3.00 8.00
267 Craig Brackins CR/99 AU 3.00 8.00
268 Avery Bradley CR/99 AU 6.00 15.00
269 D.Cousins CR/49 AU 20.00 50.00
270 Jordan Crawford CR/99 AU 3.00 8.00
271 Ed Davis CR/99 AU 3.00 8.00
272 Derrick Favors CR/49 AU 8.00 20.00
273 Landry Fields CR/99 AU 3.00 8.00
274 Paul George CR/99 AU 75.00 200.00
275 Luke Harangody CR/99 AU 3.00 8.00
276 Gordon Hayward CR/99 AU 6.00 15.00
277 Lazar Hayward CR/99 AU 3.00 8.00
278 Xavier Henry CR/99 AU 3.00 8.00
279 Wesley Johnson CR/49 AU 3.00 8.00
280 Greg Monroe CR/99 AU 3.00 8.00
281 Daniel Orton CR/99 AU 3.00 8.00
282 Patrick Patterson CR/99 AU 3.00 8.00
284 Gary Neal CR/99 AU 3.00 8.00
285 Devin Ebanks CR/99 AU 3.00 8.00
286 Evan Turner CR/49 AU 3.00 8.00
287 Ekpe Udoh CR/98 AU 3.00 8.00
288 Greivis Vasquez CR/99 AU 3.00 8.00
289 John Wall CR/49 AU 50.00 125.00
290 Elliot Williams CR/99 AU 3.00 8.00
291 Cole Aldrich PS/99 AU 3.00 8.00
292 Al-Farouq Aminu PS/99 AU 3.00 8.00
293 James Anderson PS/99 AU 3.00 8.00
294 Luke Babbitt PS/99 AU 3.00 8.00
295 Eric Bledsoe PS/99 AU 6.00 15.00
296 Trevor Booker PS/99 AU 3.00 8.00
297 Craig Brackins PS/99 AU 3.00 8.00
298 Avery Bradley PS/99 AU 3.00 8.00
299 D.Cousins PS/49 AU 12.00 30.00
300 Jordan Crawford PS/99 AU 3.00 8.00
301 Ed Davis PS/99 AU 3.00 8.00
302 Derrick Favors PS/49 AU 6.00 15.00
303 Landry Fields PS/99 AU 3.00 8.00
304 Paul George PS/99 AU 25.00 60.00
305 Luke Harangody PS/99 AU 3.00 8.00
306 Gordon Hayward PS/99 AU 6.00 15.00
307 L.Hayward PS/99 AU EXCH 3.00 8.00
308 Xavier Henry PS/99 AU 3.00 8.00
309 Wesley Johnson PS/49 AU 3.00 8.00
310 Greg Monroe PS/99 AU 3.00 8.00
311 Daniel Orton PS/99 AU 3.00 8.00
312 Patrick Patterson PS/99 AU 3.00 8.00
313 Andy Rautins PS/99 AU 3.00 8.00
314 Gary Neal PS/99 AU 3.00 8.00
315 Devin Ebanks PS/99 AU 3.00 8.00
316 Evan Turner PS/49 AU 3.00 8.00
317 Ekpe Udoh PS/99 AU 3.00 8.00
318 Greivis Vasquez PS/99 AU 3.00 8.00
319 John Wall PS/49 AU 40.00 100.00
320 Elliot Williams PS/99 AU 3.00 8.00
321 Cole Aldrich SL/99 JSY AU 6.00 15.00
322 A.Aminu SL/99 JSY AU 6.00 15.00
323 J.Anderson SL/99 JSY AU 6.00 15.00
324 Luke Babbitt SL/99 JSY AU 6.00 15.00
325 Eric Bledsoe SL/99 JSY AU 12.00 30.00
326 Trevor Booker SL/99 JSY AU 6.00 15.00
327 Craig Brackins SL/99 JSY AU 6.00 15.00
328 Avery Bradley SL/99 JSY AU 6.00 15.00
329 D.Cousins SL/49 JSY AU 30.00 80.00
330 Jo.Crawford SL/99 JSY AU 6.00 15.00
331 Ed Davis SL/99 JSY AU 6.00 15.00
332 D.Favors SL/49 JSY AU 8.00 20.00
333 Landry Fields SL/99 JSY AU 6.00 15.00
334 Paul George SL/99 JSY AU 40.00 100.00
335 L.Harangody SL/99 JSY AU 6.00 15.00
336 G.Hayward SL/99 JSY AU 15.00 40.00
337 L.Hayward SL/99 JSY AU 6.00 15.00
338 Xavier Henry SL/99 JSY AU 6.00 15.00
339 W.Johnson SL/49 JSY AU 6.00 15.00
340 Greg Monroe SL/99 JSY AU 6.00 15.00
341 Daniel Orton SL/99 JSY AU 6.00 15.00
342 P.Patterson SL/99 JSY AU 6.00 15.00
344 Gary Neal SL/99 JSY AU 6.00 15.00
345 Devin Ebanks SL/99 JSY AU 6.00 15.00
346 Evan Turner SL/49 JSY AU 6.00 15.00
347 Ekpe Udoh SL/99 JSY AU 6.00 15.00
348 G.Vasquez SL/99 JSY AU 6.00 15.00
349 John Wall SL/49 JSY AU 60.00 150.00
350 Elliot Williams SL/99 JSY AU 6.00 15.00

2011-12 Panini Preferred Blue

*BLUE: .5X TO 1.25X HI COLUMN
PS STATED PRINT RUN 5 TO 49 SETS
PC STATED PRINT RUN 6 TO 50 SER.#'d SETS
84 Robert Horry PS/25 AU 12.00 30.00
86 Rolando Blackman PS/25 AU 8.00 20.00
95 Toni Kukoc PS/25 AU 10.00 25.00
106 Andre Iguodala PC/20 AU 6.00 15.00
108 Andrea Bargnani PC/20 AU 6.00 15.00
110 Artis Gilmore PC/20 AU 10.00 25.00
119 Bob McAdoo PC/50 AU 10.00 25.00
138 Dave Cowens PC/20 AU 10.00 25.00
139 David Robinson PC/15 AU 50.00 125.00
140 David Thompson PC/50 AU 6.00 15.00
142 Dennis Rodman PC/25 AU 30.00 80.00
143 Derrick Rose PC/15 AU 60.00 150.00
150 Gail Goodrich PC/20 AU 8.00 20.00
151 George Gervin PC/20 AU 15.00 40.00
153 Grant Hill PC/15 AU 75.00 150.00
154 H.Olajuwon PC/15 AU 30.00 80.00
158 Jeff Hornacek PC/50 AU 8.00 20.00
165 Kobe Bryant PC/50 AU 200.00 500.00
177 Nate Archibald PC/20 AU 12.00 30.00
179 Oscar Robertson PC/15 AU 50.00 125.00
180 Pat Riley PC/15 AU 15.00 40.00
184 Robert Parish PC/20 AU 10.00 25.00
185 R.Blackman PC/35 AU 8.00 20.00
190 Steve Nash PC/15 AU 30.00 80.00
197 Walt Frazier PC/20 AU 10.00 25.00
199 Xavier McDaniel PC/35 AU 8.00 20.00

2011-12 Panini Preferred Emerald
*EMERALD: .4X TO 1X HI COLUMN
PS STATED PRINT RUN 2 TO 75 SER.#'d SETS
PC STATED PRINT RUN 2 TO 5 SER.#'d SETS
299 D.Cousins PS/25 AU 15.00 40.00
302 Derrick Favors PS/25 AU 8.00 20.00
309 Wesley Johnson PS/25 AU 8.00 20.00
319 John Wall PS/25 AU 40.00 100.00

2011-12 Panini Preferred Gold
*GOLD: .5X TO 1.25X HI COLUMN
PC STATED PRINT RUN 5 TO 10 SER.#'d SETS
CR STATED PRINT RUN 10 TO 25 SER.#'d SETS
265 Eric Bledsoe CR/25 AU 15.00 40.00
268 Avery Bradley CR/25 AU 12.00 30.00
276 Gordon Hayward CR/25 AU 12.00 30.00

2011-12 Panini Preferred Silhouettes Prime
STATED PRINT RUN ONE TO 25 SER.#'d SETS
202 Al Thornton/15 EXCH 25.00 60.00
203 Alex English/25 75.00 200.00
205 Andre Iguodala/15 75.00 200.00
213 Brandon Jennings/25 25.00 60.00
214 Charles Oakley/25 50.00 125.00
218 Darrell Griffith/25 50.00 120.00
224 Dikembe Mutombo/25 125.00 300.00
235 Kiki Vandeweghe/25 30.00 80.00
237 Luol Deng/25 25.00 60.00
238 Mark Aguirre/25 25.00 60.00
239 Mark Eaton/15 25.00 60.00
240 Maurice Cheeks/25 75.00 200.00
241 Michael Cage/25 25.00 60.00
242 Mitch Richmond/25 75.00 200.00
243 Monta Ellis/15 30.00 80.00
247 Stephen Curry/25 3,000.00 6,000.00
249 Toni Kukoc/25 150.00 400.00
250 Ty Lawson/25 25.00 60.00
321 Cole Aldrich/25 25.00 60.00
322 Al-Farouq Aminu/25 25.00 60.00
323 James Anderson/25 25.00 60.00
326 Trevor Booker/25 25.00 60.00
329 DeMarcus Cousins/25 75.00 200.00
332 Derrick Favors/25 30.00 80.00
333 Landry Fields/25 25.00 60.00
336 Gordon Hayward/25 75.00 200.00
337 Lazar Hayward/24 25.00 60.00
338 Xavier Henry/20 25.00 60.00
340 Greg Monroe/25 25.00 60.00
341 Daniel Orton/25 25.00 60.00
344 Gary Neal/25 25.00 60.00
345 Devin Ebanks/25 25.00 60.00
346 Evan Turner/25 25.00 60.00
347 Ekpe Udoh/25 25.00 60.00
349 John Wall/25 150.00 400.00
350 Elliot Williams/25 25.00 60.00

2011-12 Panini Preferred Silver
*SILVER: .5X TO 1.25X HI COLUMN
STATED PRINT RUN 5 TO 25 SER.#'d SETS
104 Alex English PC/25 AU 8.00 20.00
106 Andre Iguodala PC/15 AU 10.00 25.00
108 Andrea Bargnani PC/15 AU 10.00 25.00
110 Artis Gilmore PC/15 AU 10.00 25.00
112 Bernard King PC/25 AU 10.00 25.00
126 Charles Oakley PC/25 AU 12.00 30.00
145 D.Mutombo PC/25 AU 15.00 40.00
151 George Gervin PC/15 AU 15.00 40.00
155 Isiah Thomas PC/15 AU 20.00 50.00
156 James Harden PC/15 AU 30.00 80.00
160 Jrue Holiday PC/25 AU 12.00 30.00
175 Mitch Richmond PC/25 AU 15.00 40.00
183 Robert Horry PC/25 AU 12.00 30.00
184 Robert Parish PC/15 AU 10.00 25.00
195 Toni Kukoc PC/25 AU 25.00 60.00

2011-12 Panini Preferred All-Star Memorabilia
STATED PRINT RUN 50 TO 199 SER.#'d SETS
1 AI/DR/RR/JK/CP/SN/TP/99 15.00 40.00
2 BG/DW/KD/CA/DN/LJ/DR/199 25.00 60.00
3 RL/XM/DS/GP/SK/RA/KD/79 15.00 40.00
4 LJ/DW/DW/MW/JH/CA/CK/199 15.00 40.00
5 AM/RA/KG/GH/LJ/DR/AH/50 15.00 40.00
6 CM/JS/KM/SP/CL/CD/LB/50 25.00 60.00
7 PE/LB/CD/CM/MJ/KM/JS/50 30.00 80.00
8 CO/EM/LJ/MJ/PE/JS/AS/199 15.00 40.00
9 KB/JO/VC/PP/KG/TM/AI/99 25.00 60.00
10 KJ/MM/SO/KB/DR/HO/KM/50 30.00 80.00

2011-12 Panini Preferred All-Star Memorabilia Prime
STATED PRINT RUN 10 TO 25 SER.#'d SETS
1 AI/DR/RR/JK/CP/SN/TP/25 100.00 200.00
2 BG/DW/KD/CA/DN/LJ/DR/25 150.00 300.00
4 LJ/DW/DW/MW/JH/CA/CK/25 100.00 200.00
5 AM/RA/KG/GH/LJ/DR/AH/25 100.00 200.00
8 CO/EM/LJ/MJ/PE/JS/AS/25 75.00 150.00
9 KB/JO/VC/PP/KG/TM/AI/25 75.00 150.00
10 KJ/MM/SO/KB/DR/HO/KM/25 100.00 200.00

2011-12 Panini Preferred Assists Memorabilia
STATED PRINT RUN 50 TO 199 SER.#'d SETS
1 JS/IT/GP/MJ/MJ/JK/SN/99 20.00 50.00
2 JK/SN/TP/CP/DW/RR/DR/199 12.00 30.00
3 KB/LB/RR/DF/MJ/NV/GP/50 40.00 100.00
4 CB/SC/RW/DW/AM/MW/DR/199 50.00 120.00
5 DR/CB/ME/RR/RW/CP/SC/199 50.00 120.00
6 JS/MP/IT/KJ/MJ/MJ/LB/50 15.00 40.00

2011-12 Panini Preferred Assists Memorabilia Prime
STATED PRINT RUN 5 TO 25 SER.#'d SETS
1 JS/IT/GP/MJ/MJ/JK/SN/25 100.00 250.00
2 JK/SN/TP/CP/DW/RR/DR/25 30.00 80.00
4 CB/SC/RW/DW/AM/MW/DR/25 150.00 400.00
5 DR/CB/ME/RR/RW/CP/SC/25 150.00 400.00

2011-12 Panini Preferred Centers Memorabilia
STATED PRINT RUN 99 TO 199 SER.#'d SETS
1 AB/MG/AV/MG/AB/TM/199 10.00 25.00
2 AS/AB/MO/PG/KL/EO/199 10.00 25.00
3 EO/CA/MC/TC/DH/GO/199 10.00 25.00
4 BC/DR/HO/DM/ME/MB/99 15.00 40.00

2011-12 Panini Preferred Centers Memorabilia Prime
STATED PRINT RUN 10 TO 25 SER.#'d SETS
1 AB/MG/AV/MG/AB/TM/25 30.00 80.00
2 AS/AB/MO/PG/KL/EO/25 30.00 80.00
3 EO/CA/MC/TC/DH/GO/25 40.00 100.00

2011-12 Panini Preferred Decades Memorabilia
STATED PRINT RUN 10 TO 199 SER.#'d SETS
2 BL/CM/KM/JW/KV/MC/MA/DJ/25 20.00 50.00
3 PE/MJ/ME/KV/IT/JD/LB/DA/25 30.00 80.00
4 AM/DM/CM/DR/PE/MJ/MP/JS/99 15.00 40.00
5 DM/MR/MJ/LJ/PE/RH/KM/DS/99 12.00 30.00
6 AI/AM/RA/BW/KJ/SK/NV/LJ/199 20.00 50.00
7 KB/SP/AH/AI/TM/PP/VC/SN/199 20.00 50.00
8 CA/MG/TP/PG/DH/JJ/YM/LJ/199 12.00 30.00

2011-12 Panini Preferred Defense Memorabilia
STATED PRINT RUN 25 TO 199 SER.#'d SETS
1 PE/RP/DR/MB/KA/DM/HO/50 15.00 40.00
2 SO/KA/PE/WC/DR/AM/YM/25 50.00 120.00
3 JS/BW/CA/EO/TT/TC/AK/199 10.00 25.00
4 JE/KM/PE/SH/MJ/MC/JS/25 25.00 60.00
5 TP/RB/RR/ME/SB/RA/MB/199 10.00 25.00
6 AM/TP/CP/JK/JS/IT/GP/50 12.00 30.00

2011-12 Panini Preferred Forwards Memorabilia
STATED PRINT RUN 125 TO 199 SETS
1 BG/DN/TM/PP/KD/TD/CB/125 25.00 60.00
2 GM/PG/LS/PP/AA/LH/LF/199 10.00 25.00
3 CB/ED/DC/EU/DE/DJ/ET/199 10.00 25.00
4 JN/AI/LA/HT/LO/LD/CA/199 10.00 25.00
5 CM/CP/DC/GR/DS/KW/LJ/125 10.00 25.00
6 KM/SP/KV/DC/TC/CD/DW/125 15.00 40.00

2011-12 Panini Preferred Forwards Memorabilia Prime
STATED PRINT RUN 15 TO 25 SER.#'d SETS
1 BG/DN/TM/PP/KD/TD/CB/25 40.00 100.00
4 JN/AI/LA/HT/LO/LD/CA/25 30.00 80.00
5 CM/CP/DC/GR/DS/KW/LJ/15 75.00 150.00
6 KM/SP/KV/DC/TC/CD/DW/25 125.00 250.00

2011-12 Panini Preferred Inducted Memorabilia
STATED PRINT RUN 50 TO 99 SER.#'d SETS
1 CM/DW/CD/DR/IT/JS/HO/PE/99 20.00 50.00
2 LB/PE/KM/KA/WC/DR/DW/JE/50 50.00 120.00
3 JE/LB/MM/RP/DR/KA/JD/MJ/50 40.00 100.00
4 KM/SP/JD/JS/JW/KM/CM/AE/99 20.00 50.00

2011-12 Panini Preferred Legends Memorabilia
STATED PRINT RUN 50 TO 150 SER.#'d SETS
1 GM/SO/KA/EB/MJ/WC/50 50.00 120.00
2 SO/PE/DM/HO/KA/DR/150 20.00 50.00
3 KM/DR/IT/JS/PE/SP/150 20.00 50.00
4 LB/MJ/IT/KA/JE/CD/50 40.00 100.00
5 DA/SO/RP/LB/KM/SJ/50 30.00 80.00
6 AE/PE/KM/RP/MM/BK/150 12.00 30.00

2011-12 Panini Preferred Rebound Memorabilia
STATED PRINT RUN 199 SER.#'d SETS
1 AM/PE/KM/HO/DR/SO/DR 12.00 30.00
2 AS/KD/DH/KL/DN/KG/LJ 15.00 40.00
3 CB/LD/ZR/AJ/DL/MO/CB 10.00 25.00
4 SD/AB/CK/MC/JN/ZI/MG 10.00 25.00
5 NH/LD/AV/KL/TC/DG/SB 10.00 25.00
6 BM/TJ/LA/GO/PM/DW/UH 10.00 25.00

2011-12 Panini Preferred Rebound Memorabilia Prime
STATED PRINT RUN 10 TO 25 SER.#'d SETS
1 AM/PE/KM/HO/DR/SO/DR/25 50.00 120.00
2 AS/KD/DH/KL/DN/KG/LJ/25 90.00 150.00
4 SD/AB/CK/MC/JN/ZI/MG/25 40.00 80.00
5 NH/LD/AV/KL/TC/DG/SB/25 25.00 50.00
6 BM/TJ/LA/GO/PM/DW/UH/25 30.00 60.00

2011-12 Panini Preferred Rookies Memorabilia
STATED PRINT RUN 99 SER.#'d SETS
1 JC/JW/ET/GM/DC/LF 12.00 30.00
2 JW/AR/DC/LS/ET/DF 10.00 25.00
3 EB/JW/ET/EU/DC/LH 10.00 25.00
4 JW/CA/EU/JA/JC/DE 10.00 25.00
5 CB/JW/DP/DC/JL/GN 15.00 40.00
6 JW/DJ/EU/QP/GH/ET 12.00 30.00
7 WJ/JW/GH/QP/EU/LS 10.00 25.00
8 JW/LF/EU/QP/GH/JC 12.00 30.00

2011-12 Panini Preferred Rookies Memorabilia Prime
STATED PRINT RUN 25 SER.#'d SETS
1 JC/JW/ET/GM/DC/LF 25.00 60.00
2 JW/AR/DC/LS/ET/DF 25.00 60.00
3 EB/JW/ET/EU/DC/LH 25.00 60.00
4 JW/CA/EU/JA/JC/DE 25.00 60.00
5 CB/JW/DP/DC/JL/GN 60.00 150.00
6 JW/DJ/EU/QP/GH/ET 25.00 60.00
7 WJ/JW/GH/QP/EU/LS 60.00 150.00
8 JW/LF/EU/QP/GH/JC 25.00 60.00

2011-12 Panini Preferred Slam Dunk Memorabilia
STATED PRINT RUN 99 TO 199 SER.#'d SETS
1 KB/SO/KG/TM/VC/GH/DR/CW/125 40.00 100.00
2 SP/CD/GH/KG/SO/DW/SK/LJ/125 12.00 30.00
3 JE/BG/DW/KB/LJ/VC/DW/CD/99 20.00 50.00
4 BG/AI/RW/TY/JM/TG/DD/SI/199 12.00 30.00
5 YM/TD/LA/AS/DH/PG/KG/SO/125 15.00 40.00
6 KD/JE/KB/DW/LJ/DW/VC/BG/125 20.00 50.00
7 NR/RW/TC/RG/JR/JS/CA/CA/199 12.00 30.00
8 JE/DW/TY/CD/BG/SI/DD/LJ/99 25.00 60.00

2011-12 Panini Preferred Slam Dunk Memorabilia Prime
STATED PRINT RUN 25 SER.#'d SETS
1 KB/SO/KG/TM/VC/GH/DR/CW 125.00 300.00
2 SP/CD/GH/KG/SO/DW/SK/LJ 100.00 250.00
3 JE/BG/DW/KB/LJ/VC/DW/CD 75.00 150.00
4 BG/AI/RW/TY/JM/TG/DD/SI 30.00 80.00
5 YM/TD/LA/AS/DH/PG/KG/SO 100.00 250.00
6 KD/JE/KB/DW/LJ/DW/VC/BG 125.00 250.00
7 NR/RW/TC/RG/JR/JS/CA/CA 30.00 80.00
8 JE/DW/TY/CD/BG/SI/DD/LJ 75.00 200.00

2012-13 Panini Preferred
PC PRINT RUN 20 TO 99 SER.#'d SETS
PS PRINT RUN 20 TO 74 SER.#'d SETS
SL PRINT RUN 8 TO 99 SER.#'d SETS
CR PRINT RUN 25 TO 99 SER.#'d SETS
PS STANDS FOR PREFERRED SIGNATURES
PC STANDS FOR PANINIS CHOICE
SL STANDS FOR SILHOUETTE
CR STANDS FOR CROWN ROYALE
NO PRICING ON QTY 15 OR LESS
EXCHANGE DEADLINE 10/24/2014
1 Al Jefferson PC AU/25 EXCH 5.00 12.00
2 A.Bynum PC AU/25 EXCH 5.00 12.00
3 Anfernee Hardaway PC AU/35 25.00 60.00
4 Antawn Jamison PC AU/50 5.00 12.00
5 Anthony Mason PC AU/74 5.00 12.00
6 Bailey Howell PC AU/74 6.00 15.00
7 Bernard King PC AU/74 8.00 20.00
8 Bill Cartwright PC AU/74 EXCH 5.00 12.00
9 Bill Laimbeer PC AU/74 8.00 20.00
10 Bill Russell PC AU/25 1,000.00 2,000.00
11 H.Grant PC AU/74 6.00 15.00
12 Bill Walton PC AU/35 12.00 30.00
13 B.Griffin PC AU/74 EXCH 30.00 80.00
14 Bob McAdoo PC AU/74 5.00 12.00
15 Byron Scott PC AU/25 6.00 15.00
16 Brandon Jennings PC AU/25 5.00 12.00
17 Brandon Rush PC AU/74 EXCH 4.00 10.00
18 Brook Lopez PC AU/35 6.00 15.00
19 Carl Landry PC AU/50 4.00 10.00
20 Chase Budinger PC AU/74 4.00 10.00
21 Chris Bosh PC AU/25 10.00 25.00
22 Chris Paul PC AU/35 EXCH 40.00 100.00
23 Clyde Drexler PC AU/35 12.00 30.00
24 Clyde Lovellette PC AU/25 10.00 25.00
25 Danny Granger PC AU/25 5.00 12.00
26 Darryl Dawkins PC AU/74 4.00 10.00
27 John Paxson PC AU/74 5.00 12.00
28 David Robinson PC AU/50 20.00 50.00
29 Ray Allen PC AU/35 EXCH 20.00 50.00
30 D.Cousins PC AU/25 8.00 20.00
31 Dennis Rodman PC AU/35 20.00 50.00
32 Deron Williams PC AU/50 5.00 12.00
33 Dolph Schayes PC AU/25 10.00 25.00
34 Derrick Favors PC AU/25 6.00 15.00
35 Anderson Varejao PC AU/74 4.00 10.00
36 Doc Rivers PC AU/25 8.00 20.00
37 Kyle Lowry PC AU/74 6.00 15.00
39 Rodney Stuckey PC AU/74 4.00 10.00
40 Gary Payton PC AU/35 10.00 25.00
41 Glen Rice PC AU/74 5.00 12.00
42 G.Hayward PC AU/74 6.00 15.00
43 Grant Hill PC AU/74 25.00 60.00
44 Greg Monroe PC AU/74 4.00 10.00
45 J.Harden PC AU/74 EXCH 30.00 80.00
46 Jason Kidd PC AU/35 12.00 30.00
47 Jerry West PC AU/25 20.00 50.00
48 Joe Johnson PC AU/25 6.00 15.00
49 John Starks PC AU/74 5.00 12.00
50 J.Stockton PC AU/25 EXCH 30.00 80.00
51 Jordan Crawford PC AU/74 EXCH 4.00 10.00
52 Jose Calderon PC AU/50 4.00 10.00
53 Julius Erving PC AU/25 40.00 100.00
54 K.Abdul-Jabbar PC AU/25 40.00 100.00
55 Kenny Anderson PC AU/74 5.00 12.00
56 Kevin Durant PC AU/50 60.00 150.00
57 Kevin Love PC AU/50 6.00 15.00
58 Kobe Bryant PC AU/74 500.00 1,000.00
59 L.Aldridge PC AU/50 6.00 15.00
60 Landry Fields PC AU/74 4.00 10.00
61 Larry Bird PC AU/25 50.00 120.00
62 L.Johnson PC AU/74 EXCH 8.00 20.00
63 R.Horry PC AU/74 EXCH 6.00 15.00
64 Magic Johnson PC AU/25 40.00 100.00
65 Marcin Gortat PC AU/74 4.00 10.00
66 Mario Chalmers PC AU/74 5.00 12.00
67 Mark Jackson PC AU/35 6.00 15.00
68 Marreese Speights PC AU/74 EXCH 4.00 10.00
69 Michael Finley PC AU/25 8.00 20.00
70 Muggsy Bogues PC AU/74 6.00 15.00
71 Nazr Mohammed PC AU/74 EXCH 4.00 10.00
72 Nick Collison PC AU/74 4.00 10.00
74 Nick Young PC AU/74 4.00 10.00
76 J.Crawford PC AU/50 EXCH 6.00 15.00
77 P.George PC AU/74 EXCH 20.00 50.00
78 Rashard Lewis PC AU/74 EXCH 6.00 15.00
79 Raymond Felton PC AU/50 4.00 10.00
80 Rick Fox PC AU/25 EXCH 6.00 15.00
81 Robert Parish PC AU/25 12.00 30.00
82 R.Beaubois PC AU/74 4.00 10.00
83 Ronnie Brewer PC AU/74 4.00 10.00
84 Ronny Turiaf PC AU/74 4.00 10.00
85 Roy Hibbert PC AU/74 5.00 12.00
86 Sam Perkins PC AU/74 5.00 12.00
87 Scottie Pippen PC AU/35 100.00 250.00
88 Serge Ibaka PC AU/74 5.00 12.00
89 Shane Battier PC AU/25 6.00 15.00
90 Spud Webb PC AU/74 6.00 15.00
92 Thabo Sefolosha PC AU/50 4.00 10.00
93 Tim Hardaway PC AU/74 8.00 20.00
94 Satch Sanders PC AU/74 6.00 15.00
95 Toni Kukoc PC AU/74 6.00 15.00
96 Tony Parker PC AU/35 12.00 30.00
97 Tyreke Evans PC AU/25 6.00 15.00
100 Z.Ilgauskas PC AU/74 6.00 15.00
101 Adrian Dantley PS AU/74 5.00 12.00
102 Alex English PS AU/25 8.00 20.00
103 Al-Farouq Aminu PS AU/74 4.00 10.00
104 Alonzo Mourning PS AU/50 20.00 50.00
108 Bailey Howell PS AU/74 6.00 15.00
109 Bernard King PS AU/74 8.00 20.00
111 B.Griffin PS AU/74 EXCH 20.00 50.00
112 Bob Love PS AU/74 4.00 10.00
113 Bob Love PS AU/74 6.00 15.00
116 Campy Russell PS AU/74 4.00 10.00
118 Cazzie Russell PS AU/74 5.00 12.00
119 Charles Oakley PS AU/74 5.00 12.00
121 Chris Mullin PS AU/74 8.00 20.00
122 Connie Hawkins PS AU/74 6.00 15.00
123 Corey Brewer PS AU/74 4.00 10.00
124 Dan Issel PS AU/74 6.00 15.00
125 D.Majerle PS AU/74 5.00 12.00
126 Danny Green PS AU/74 6.00 15.00
128 Darren Collison PS AU/50 4.00 10.00
130 David Lee PS AU/25 5.00 12.00
131 David Thompson PS AU/74 6.00 15.00
132 Jim Jackson PS AU/74 5.00 12.00
133 Ersan Ilyasova PS AU/74 4.00 10.00
134 John Starks PS AU/74 5.00 12.00
135 Goran Dragic PS AU/74 12.00 30.00
137 Deron Williams PS AU/35 6.00 15.00
138 Detlef Schrempf PS AU/74 5.00 12.00
139 Dikembe Mutombo PS AU/50 10.00 25.00
140 D.Wilkins PS AU/25 20.00 50.00
141 Anderson Varejao PS AU/74 4.00 10.00
142 Ekpe Udoh PS AU/74 4.00 10.00
144 Eric Bledsoe PS AU/74 EXCH 5.00 12.00
146 Fat Lever PS AU/74 5.00 12.00
147 Kurt Rambis PS AU/74 6.00 15.00
149 George Gervin PS AU/25 12.00 30.00
150 George McGinnis PS AU/74 6.00 15.00
152 H.Olajuwon PS AU/25 25.00 60.00
153 Isiah Thomas PS AU/35 15.00 40.00
154 Jamaal Tinsley PS AU/74 4.00 10.00
155 J.Worthy PS AU/50 10.00 25.00
156 Jarrett Jack PS AU/74 5.00 12.00
158 Jason Richardson PS AU/50 6.00 15.00
159 Jeff Green PS AU/50 4.00 10.00
159 Jeff Hornacek PS AU/74 5.00 12.00
160 Jeff Teague PS AU/74 4.00 10.00
161 Jerry West PS AU/25 30.00 80.00
162 Joel Anthony PS AU/74 4.00 10.00
163 Cedric Maxwell PS AU/74 4.00 10.00
164 George Hill PS AU/74 5.00 12.00
165 K.Abdul-Jabbar PS AU/25 40.00 100.00
166 Kevin Durant PS AU/74 60.00 120.00
167 Kevin Love PS AU/50 6.00 15.00
168 Kobe Bryant PS AU/74 400.00 800.00
169 Kris Humphries PS AU/74 4.00 10.00
170 Kyle Korver PS AU/50 5.00 12.00
171 Larry Bird PS AU/25 50.00 120.00
172 Luc Mbah a Moute PS AU/74 4.00 10.00
174 L.Deng PS AU/25 EXCH 20.00 50.00
175 Magic Johnson PS AU/25 30.00 80.00
176 Marcus Thornton PS AU/74 4.00 10.00
177 Mark Aguirre PS AU/50 5.00 12.00
178 Mark Eaton PS AU/74 5.00 12.00
179 Mark Price PS AU/74 6.00 15.00
180 Maurice Cheeks PS AU/74 5.00 12.00
181 Ryan Anderson PS AU/74 4.00 10.00
182 Mitch Richmond PS AU/74 6.00 15.00
183 Monta Ellis PS AU/25 6.00 15.00
184 Nate Archibald PS AU/25 10.00 25.00
185 N.Thurmond PS AU/25 EXCH 8.00 20.00
186 Paul Westphal PS AU/73 6.00 15.00
187 R.Sampson PS AU/74 5.00 12.00
188 Rolando Blackman PS AU/74 5.00 12.00
189 Spencer Haywood PS AU/74 6.00 15.00
190 Stephen Curry PS AU/50 400.00 800.00
191 Steve Kerr PS AU/35 8.00 20.00
192 Steve Nash PS AU/25 20.00 50.00
193 Steve Smith PS AU/74 5.00 12.00
194 Taj Gibson PS AU/74 4.00 10.00
195 Tom Heinsohn PS AU/50 6.00 15.00
196 Tony Allen PS AU/25 6.00 15.00
197 Vince Carter PS AU/35 15.00 40.00
200 World B. Free PS AU/25 6.00 15.00
201 Glen Rice SL JSY AU/49 15.00 40.00
204 B.Griffin SL JSY AU/25 EXCH 20.00 50.00
205 H.Olajuwon SL JSY AU/25 75.00 150.00
206 J.Stockton SL JSY AU/25 40.00 100.00
208 Tony Parker SL JSY AU/49 20.00 50.00
209 R.Parish SL JSY AU/49 10.00 25.00
210 D.Rbnsn SL JSY AU/49 20.00 50.00
212 K.Bryant SL JSY AU/49 800.00 1,500.00
213 Ron Harper SL JSY AU/25 40.00 80.00
214 Tayshaun Prince SL JSY AU/49 6.00 15.00
215 A.Mourning SL JSY AU/49 40.00 100.00
216 Jalen Rose SL JSY AU/25 10.00 25.00
217 Joe Dumars SL JSY AU/49 8.00 20.00
218 D.Wilkins SL JSY AU/49 15.00 40.00
219 Raymond Felton SL JSY AU/49 8.00 20.00
220 Mark Price SL JSY AU/25 50.00 120.00
223 J.Hornacek SL JSY AU/25 12.00 30.00
224 Jose Calderon SL JSY AU/49 6.00 15.00
226 K.McHale SL JSY AU/25 EXCH 30.00 60.00
229 L.Aldridge SL JSY AU/49 15.00 40.00
230 Taj Gibson SL JSY AU/49 10.00 25.00
231 D.Manning SL JSY AU/25 10.00 25.00
233 Alex English SL JSY AU/25 12.00 30.00
235 H.Turkoglu SL JSY AU/49 6.00 15.00
236 Mark Jackson SL JSY AU/25 15.00 40.00
237 Luol Deng SL JSY AU/25 8.00 20.00
238 Kevin Love SL JSY AU/49 12.00 30.00
239 Derrick Favors SL JSY AU/25 12.00 30.00
240 Mark Aguirre SL JSY AU/25 8.00 20.00
241 E.Monroe SL JSY AU/25 EXCH 30.00 80.00
242 Bill Laimbeer SL JSY AU/25 10.00 25.00
243 C.Person SL JSY AU/25 EXCH 12.00 30.00
244 David Lee SL JSY AU/49 12.00 30.00
245 Maurice Cheeks SL JSY AU/29 8.00 20.00
246 Toni Kukoc SL JSY AU/49 15.00 40.00
247 Nick Van Exel SL JSY AU/49 30.00 60.00
248 Jamaal Wilkes SL JSY AU/25 20.00 50.00
251 Tyler Hansbrough SL JSY AU/49 8.00 20.00
252 Zach Randolph SL JSY AU/49 15.00 40.00
253 Cedric Maxwell SL JSY AU/29 15.00 40.00
255 Ty Lawson SL JSY AU/49 8.00 20.00
259 George Hill SL JSY AU/49 12.00 30.00
260 Steve Smith SL JSY AU/25 8.00 20.00
261 Yao Ming SL JSY AU/49 40.00 100.00
262 Tiago Splitter SL JSY AU/49 10.00 25.00
264 Mike Conley SL JSY AU/25 12.00 30.00
265 Joe Johnson SL JSY AU/49 8.00 20.00
266 Chris Bosh SL JSY AU/49 12.00 30.00
268 Gerald Wallace SL JSY AU/49 15.00 40.00
269 Marcus Camby SL JSY AU/49 10.00 25.00
270 Al-Farouq Aminu SL JSY AU/49 8.00 20.00
273 Ray Allen SL JSY AU/49 40.00 80.00
274 Carl Landry SL JSY AU/49 6.00 15.00
275 Chris Kaman SL JSY AU/49 8.00 20.00
276 Clyde Drexler SL JSY AU/25 90.00 150.00
277 Anderson Varejao SL JSY AU/49 8.00 20.00
278 C.Paul SL JSY AU/49 EXCH 60.00 150.00
279 D.Cousins SL JSY AU/49 10.00 25.00
280 Gary Neal SL JSY AU/49 EXCH 8.00 20.00
281 K.Lewis SL JSY AU/49 EXCH 5.00 12.00
282 Kevin Martin SL JSY AU/49 8.00 20.00
283 Grant Hill SL JSY AU/49 50.00 120.00
284 Artis Gilmore SL JSY AU/25 15.00 40.00
285 Sean Elliott SL JSY AU/49 15.00 40.00
286 A.Jamison SL JSY AU/49 6.00 15.00
287 Tyreke Evans SL JSY AU/49 10.00 25.00
288 A.Iguodala SL JSY AU/49 8.00 20.00
289 E.Gordon SL JSY AU/49 EXCH 6.00 15.00
290 Serge Ibaka SL JSY AU/49 30.00 60.00
291 Darren Collison SL JSY AU/49 5.00 12.00
292 Devin Harris SL JSY AU/45 5.00 12.00
293 E.Bledsoe SL JSY AU/49 EXCH 12.00 30.00
294 Dm.Williams SL JSY AU/25 20.00 50.00
296 J.Nelson SL JSY AU/49 EXCH 8.00 20.00
297 Wesley Matthews SL JSY AU/49 8.00 20.00
298 L.Johnson SL JSY AU/49 30.00 80.00
299 S.Curry SL JSY AU/49 1,500.00 3,000.00
300 Brandon Jennings SL JSY AU/49 8.00 20.00
301 Will Barton SL JSY AU/99 6.00 15.00
302 Royce White SL JSY AU/99 5.00 12.00
303 Ter.Jones SL JSY AU/99 6.00 15.00
304 T.Robinson SL JSY AU/99 5.00 12.00
305 Tobias Harris SL JSY AU/99 12.00 30.00
306 Tyler Zeller SL JSY AU/99 6.00 15.00
307 Quincy Miller SL JSY AU/99 5.00 12.00
308 Kim English SL JSY AU/99 5.00 12.00
309 K.Middleton SL JSY AU/99 8.00 20.00
310 K.Faried SL JSY AU/99 8.00 20.00
311 K.Marshall SL JSY AU/99 5.00 12.00
312 J.Sullinger SL JSY AU/99 5.00 12.00
313 Jared Cunningham SL JSY AU/99 5.00 12.00
314 Perry Jones SL JSY AU/99 5.00 12.00
315 Orlando Johnson SL JSY AU/99 5.00 12.00
316 Norris Cole SL JSY AU/99 6.00 15.00
317 Kris Joseph SL JSY AU/99 5.00 12.00
318 K.Walker SL JSY AU/99 75.00 200.00
319 K.Leonard SL JSY AU/99 150.00 400.00
320 John Henson SL JSY AU/99 8.00 20.00
321 Jimmy Butler SL JSY AU/99 40.00 100.00
322 J.Fredette SL JSY AU/99 8.00 20.00
323 J.Lamb SL JSY AU/99 EXCH 12.00 30.00
324 B.James SL JSY AU/99 EXCH 6.00 15.00
325 A.Davis SL JSY AU/99 800.00 1,500.00
326 Andrew Nicholson SL JSY AU/99 8.00 20.00
327 Kyrie Irving SL JSY AU/99 100.00 250.00
328 Marquis Teague SL JSY AU/99 6.00 15.00
329 MarShon Brooks SL JSY AU/99 8.00 20.00
330 Meyers Leonard SL JSY AU/99 6.00 15.00
331 Kidd-Gilch SL JSY AU/99 12.00 30.00
332 Mike Scott SL JSY AU/99 5.00 12.00
333 Doron Lamb SL JSY AU/99 6.00 15.00
334 M.Harkless SL JSY AU/99 12.00 30.00
335 R.Jackson SL JSY AU/99 12.00 30.00
336 Robert Sacre SL JSY AU/99 5.00 12.00
337 Markieff Morris SL JSY AU/99 6.00 15.00
338 Lavoy Allen SL JSY AU/99 5.00 12.00
339 Lance Thomas SL JSY AU/99 5.00 12.00
340 Josh Selby SL JSY AU/99 5.00 12.00
341 Josh Harrellson
SL JSY AU/99 EXCH 5.00 12.00
342 Jordan Hamilton SL JSY AU/99 5.00 12.00
343 J.Valanciunas SL JSY AU/99 12.00 30.00
344 John Jenkins SL JSY AU/99 6.00 15.00
345 Jan Vesely SL JSY AU/99 5.00 12.00
346 Jae Crowder SL JSY AU/99 6.00 15.00
347 Ivan Johnson SL JSY AU/99 5.00 12.00
348 H.Barnes SL JSY AU/99 20.00 50.00
349 Evan Fournier SL JSY AU/99 8.00 20.00
350 E'Twaun Moore SL JSY AU/99 6.00 15.00
351 Enes Kanter SL JSY AU/99 15.00 40.00
352 D.Green SL JSY AU/99 125.00 300.00
353 Marcus Morris SL JSY AU/99 6.00 15.00
354 Dion Waiters SL JSY AU/99 12.00 30.00
355 Derrick Williams SL JSY AU/99 6.00 15.00
356 Darius Morris SL JSY AU/99 6.00 15.00
357 Brandon Knight SL JSY AU/99 6.00 15.00
358 Bradley Beal SL JSY AU/99 30.00 80.00
359 B.Biyombo SL JSY AU/99 8.00 20.00
360 N.Vucevic SL JSY AU/99 60.00 150.00
361 A.Drummond SL JSY AU/99 50.00 120.00
362 Alec Burks SL JSY AU/99 10.00 25.00
363 Tony Wroten SL JSY AU/99 12.00 30.00
364 T.Thompson SL JSY AU/99 10.00 25.00
365 Kyle Singler SL JSY AU/99 8.00 20.00
366 Darius Johnson-
Odom SL JSY AU/99 EXCH 5.00 12.00
367 A.Rivers SL JSY AU/99 EXCH 10.00 25.00
368 Arnett Moultrie SL JSY AU/99 5.00 12.00
369 Kyle O'Quinn SL JSY AU/99 5.00 12.00
370 Miles Plumlee SL JSY AU/99 5.00 12.00
371 T.Ross SL JSY AU/99 EXCH 10.00 25.00
372 Quincy Acy SL JSY AU/99 6.00 15.00
373 Iman Shumpert SL JSY AU/99 5.00 12.00
374 Charles Jenkins SL JSY AU/99 5.00 12.00
375 C.Parsons SL JSY AU/99 6.00 15.00
376 Tyler Honeycutt SL JSY AU/99 5.00 12.00
377 Nolan Smith SL JSY AU/99 5.00 12.00
378 Cory Joseph SL JSY AU/99 8.00 20.00
379 Festus Ezeli SL JSY AU/99 6.00 15.00
380 I.Thomas SL JSY AU/99 25.00 60.00
381 Jeremy Pargo SL JSY AU/99 5.00 12.00
382 Will Barton CR AU/99 8.00 20.00
383 Royce White CR AU/99 4.00 10.00
384 Brian Roberts CR AU/99 4.00 10.00
385 Terrence Jones CR AU/99 4.00 10.00
386 Thomas Robinson CR AU/79 4.00 10.00
387 Tobias Harris CR AU/99 12.00 30.00
388 Tyler Zeller CR AU/99 4.00 10.00
389 Quincy Miller CR AU/99 EXCH 4.00 10.00
390 Kim English CR AU/99 4.00 10.00
391 Khris Middleton CR AU/99 20.00 50.00
392 Kenneth Faried CR AU/99 5.00 12.00
393 Kendall Marshall CR AU/99 4.00 10.00
394 Jared Sullinger CR AU/99 4.00 10.00
395 Jared Cunningham CR AU/99 4.00 10.00
396 Perry Jones CR AU/99 4.00 10.00
397 Orlando Johnson CR AU/99 4.00 10.00
398 Norris Cole CR AU/99 4.00 10.00
399 Kris Joseph CR AU/99 4.00 10.00
400 Kemba Walker CR AU/49 20.00 50.00
401 Kawhi Leonard CR AU/99 125.00 300.00
402 John Henson CR AU/99 5.00 12.00
403 Jimmy Butler CR AU/99 20.00 50.00
404 Jimmer Fredette CR AU/99 6.00 15.00
405 Jeremy Lamb CR AU/99 EXCH 6.00 15.00
406 Bernard James CR AU/99 4.00 10.00
407 Anthony Davis CR AU/25 400.00 800.00
408 Andrew Nicholson CR AU/99 4.00 10.00
409 Kyrie Irving CR AU/79 75.00 200.00
410 Marquis Teague CR AU/99 4.00 10.00
411 MarShon Brooks CR AU/99 4.00 10.00
412 Meyers Leonard CR AU/99 5.00 12.00
413 M.Kidd-Gilchrist CR AU/49 5.00 12.00
414 Mike Scott CR AU/99 5.00 12.00
415 Doron Lamb CR AU/99 4.00 10.00
416 Maurice Harkless CR AU/99 5.00 12.00
417 Reggie Jackson CR AU/99 6.00 15.00
418 Robert Sacre CR AU/99 4.00 10.00
419 Markieff Morris CR AU/79 6.00 15.00
420 Chris Copeland CR AU/99 4.00 10.00
421 Lavoy Allen CR AU/99 4.00 10.00
422 Lance Thomas CR AU/99 4.00 10.00
423 Josh Selby CR AU/99 4.00 10.00
424 Josh Harrellson CR AU/99 EXCH 4.00 10.00
425 Jordan Hamilton CR AU/99 4.00 10.00
426 Jonas Valanciunas CR AU/99 8.00 20.00
427 John Jenkins CR AU/99 4.00 10.00
428 Jan Vesely CR AU/99 4.00 10.00
429 Jae Crowder CR AU/99 8.00 20.00
430 Ivan Johnson CR AU/99 4.00 10.00
431 Harrison Barnes CR AU/49 15.00 40.00
432 Fab Melo CR AU/99 4.00 10.00
433 Evan Fournier CR AU/99 6.00 15.00
434 E'Twaun Moore CR AU/99 5.00 12.00
435 Enes Kanter CR AU/99 6.00 15.00
436 Draymond Green CR AU/99 20.00 50.00
437 Marcus Morris CR AU/79 6.00 15.00
438 Dion Waiters CR AU/99 5.00 12.00
439 Derrick Williams CR AU/99 4.00 10.00
440 Darius Morris CR AU/99 5.00 12.00
441 Brandon Knight CR AU/99 5.00 12.00
442 Bradley Beal CR AU/99 30.00 80.00
443 Bismack Biyombo CR AU/99 5.00 12.00
444 Nikola Vucevic CR AU/99 15.00 40.00
445 DeQuan Jones CR AU/99 4.00 10.00
446 A.Drummond CR AU/99 20.00 50.00
447 Alec Burks CR AU/99 6.00 15.00
448 Tony Wroten CR AU/49 4.00 10.00
449 Tristan Thompson CR AU/99 6.00 15.00
450 Kyle Singler CR AU/99 4.00 10.00
451 Darius Johnson-
Odom CR AU/99 EXCH 4.00 10.00
452 A.Rivers CR AU/79 EXCH 6.00 15.00
453 Arnett Moultrie CR AU/99 4.00 10.00
454 Kyle O'Quinn CR AU/99 5.00 12.00
455 T.Ross CR AU/99 EXCH 10.00 25.00
456 Quincy Acy CR AU/99 4.00 10.00
457 Iman Shumpert CR AU/99 5.00 12.00
458 Charles Jenkins CR AU/99 4.00 10.00
459 Chandler Parsons CR AU/99 5.00 12.00
460 Tyler Honeycutt CR AU/99 4.00 10.00
461 Nolan Smith CR AU/99 4.00 10.00
462 Cory Joseph CR AU/99 5.00 12.00
463 Festus Ezeli CR AU/99 4.00 10.00
464 Isaiah Thomas CR AU/99 12.00 30.00
465 Jeremy Pargo CR AU/99 4.00 10.00
466 Jeremy Tyler CR AU/99 4.00 10.00
467 Kevin Murphy CR AU/99 4.00 10.00
468 Darius Miller CR AU/99 EXCH 5.00 12.00
469 DeAndre Liggins CR AU/99 EXCH 4.00 10.00
470 Greg Stiemsma CR AU/99 4.00 10.00
471 Gustavo Ayon CR AU/99 4.00 10.00
472 Jeff Taylor CR AU/99 4.00 10.00
473 Jon Leuer CR AU/99 4.00 10.00
474 Nando De Colo CR AU/99 4.00 10.00
475 Maalik Wayns CR AU/99 EXCH 5.00 12.00
476 Malcolm Lee CR AU/99 4.00 10.00
477 Trey Thompkins CR AU/99 4.00 10.00
478 Tyshawn Taylor CR AU/99 EXCH 4.00 10.00
479 Chris Singleton CR AU/99 EXCH 4.00 10.00
480 Kent Bazemore CR AU/99 6.00 15.00
481 Miles Plumlee CR AU/99 EXCH 4.00 10.00
482 Will Barton PC AU/99 8.00 20.00
483 Royce White PC AU/99 4.00 10.00
484 Chris Copeland PC AU/99 4.00 10.00
485 Terrence Jones PC AU/99 4.00 10.00
486 Thomas Robinson PC AU/74 4.00 10.00
487 Tobias Harris PC AU/99 12.00 30.00
488 Tyler Zeller PC AU/99 4.00 10.00
489 Quincy Miller PC AU/99 EXCH 4.00 10.00
490 Kim English PC AU/99 4.00 10.00
491 Khris Middleton PC AU/99 20.00 50.00
492 Kenneth Faried PC AU/99 5.00 12.00
493 Kendall Marshall PC AU/99 4.00 10.00
494 Jared Sullinger PC AU/74 4.00 10.00
495 Jared Cunningham PC AU/99 4.00 10.00
496 Perry Jones PC AU/99 4.00 10.00
497 Orlando Johnson PC AU/99 4.00 10.00
498 Norris Cole PC AU/99 4.00 10.00
499 DeQuan Jones PC AU/99 4.00 10.00
500 Kemba Walker PC AU/49 20.00 50.00
501 Kawhi Leonard PC AU/99 125.00 300.00
502 John Henson PC AU/99 5.00 12.00
503 Jimmy Butler PC AU/99 25.00 60.00
504 Jimmer Fredette PC AU/99 6.00 15.00
505 Jeremy Lamb PC AU/99 EXCH 6.00 15.00
506 Bernard James PC AU/99 4.00 10.00
507 Anthony Davis PC AU/25 400.00 800.00
508 Andrew Nicholson PC AU/99 4.00 10.00
509 Kyrie Irving PC AU/25 100.00 250.00
510 Marquis Teague PC AU/99 4.00 10.00
511 MarShon Brooks PC AU/99 4.00 10.00
512 Meyers Leonard PC AU/99 5.00 12.00
513 M.Kidd-Gilchrist PC AU/25 6.00 15.00
514 Mike Scott PC AU/99 5.00 12.00
515 Doron Lamb PC AU/99 4.00 10.00
516 Maurice Harkless PC AU/99 5.00 12.00
517 Reggie Jackson PC AU/99 6.00 15.00
518 Robert Sacre PC AU/99 4.00 10.00
519 Markieff Morris PC AU/99 6.00 15.00
520 Lavoy Allen PC AU/99 4.00 10.00
521 Lance Thomas PC AU/99 4.00 10.00
522 Josh Selby PC AU/99 4.00 10.00
523 Josh Harrellson PC AU/99 EXCH 4.00 10.00
524 Jordan Hamilton PC AU/99 4.00 10.00
525 Jonas Valanciunas PC AU/99 8.00 20.00
526 John Jenkins PC AU/99 4.00 10.00
527 Jan Vesely PC AU/99 4.00 10.00
528 Jae Crowder PC AU/99 8.00 20.00
529 Ivan Johnson PC AU/99 4.00 10.00
530 Harrison Barnes PC AU/74 8.00 20.00
531 Nando De Colo PC AU/99 4.00 10.00
532 Evan Fournier PC AU/99 6.00 15.00
533 E'Twaun Moore PC AU/99 5.00 12.00
534 Enes Kanter PC AU/99 6.00 15.00
535 Draymond Green PC AU/99 30.00 80.00
536 Marcus Morris PC AU/99 6.00 15.00
537 Dion Waiters PC AU/99 5.00 12.00
538 Derrick Williams PC AU/74 4.00 10.00
539 Darius Morris PC AU/99 5.00 12.00
540 Brandon Knight PC AU/99 5.00 12.00
541 Bradley Beal PC AU/99 30.00 80.00
542 Bismack Biyombo PC AU/99 5.00 12.00
543 Nikola Vucevic PC AU/99 30.00 80.00
544 Kris Joseph PC AU/99 4.00 10.00
545 A.Drummond PC AU/74 20.00 50.00
546 Alec Burks PC AU/99 6.00 15.00
547 Tony Wroten PC AU/99 4.00 10.00
548 Tristan Thompson PC AU/99 6.00 15.00
549 Kyle Singler PC AU/99 4.00 10.00
550 Darius Johnson-
Odom PC AU/99 EXCH 4.00 10.00
551 Austin Rivers PC AU/99 EXCH 6.00 15.00
552 Arnett Moultrie PC AU/99 4.00 10.00
553 Kyle O'Quinn PC AU/99 5.00 12.00
554 Terrence Ross PC AU/99 EXCH 10.00 25.00
555 Quincy Acy PC AU/99 4.00 10.00
556 Iman Shumpert PC AU/99 5.00 12.00
557 Charles Jenkins PC AU/99 4.00 10.00
558 Chandler Parsons PC AU/99 5.00 12.00
559 Tyler Honeycutt PC AU/99 4.00 10.00
560 Nolan Smith PC AU/99 4.00 10.00
561 Cory Joseph PC AU/99 5.00 12.00
562 Festus Ezeli PC AU/99 4.00 10.00
563 Isaiah Thomas PC AU/99 12.00 30.00
564 Jeremy Pargo PC AU/99 4.00 10.00
565 Jeremy Tyler PC AU/99 4.00 10.00
566 Kevin Murphy PC AU/99 4.00 10.00
567 Darius Miller PC AU/99 EXCH 5.00 12.00
568 DeAndre Liggins PC AU/99 EXCH 4.00 10.00
569 Greg Stiemsma PC AU/99 4.00 10.00
570 Gustavo Ayon PC AU/99 4.00 10.00
571 Jeff Taylor PC AU/99 4.00 10.00
572 Jon Leuer PC AU/99 4.00 10.00
573 Brian Roberts PC AU/99 4.00 10.00
574 Maalik Wayns PC AU/99 EXCH 5.00 12.00
575 Malcolm Lee PC AU/99 4.00 10.00
576 Trey Thompkins PC AU/99 4.00 10.00
577 Tyshawn Taylor PC AU/99 EXCH 4.00 10.00
578 Chris Singleton PC AU/99 EXCH 4.00 10.00
579 Kent Bazemore PC AU/99 6.00 15.00
580 Miles Plumlee PC AU/99 EXCH 4.00 10.00
581 Fab Melo PC AU/99 4.00 10.00
582 D.Lillard CR JSY AU/99 75.00 200.00

2012-13 Panini Preferred Blue
*BLUE: .5X TO 1.2X BASIC
PRINT RUNS BW/N 15-49 COPIES PER
NO PRICING ON QTY 20 OR LESS
EXCHANGE DEADLINE 10/24/2014
543 Nikola Vucevic PC AU/49 40.00 100.00

2012-13 Panini Preferred 50 Greats Memorabilia
PRINT RUNS B/WN 129-149 COPIES PER
1 G/S/P/E/D/R/O/M/129 15.00 40.00
2 M/O/D/E/T/R/S/P/149 15.00 40.00

2012-13 Panini Preferred All World Memorabilia
STATED PRINT RUN 199 SER.#'d SETS
1 K/V/D/H/B/R/D/G 10.00 25.00
2 G/M/O/M/B/S/G/T 12.00 30.00
3 T/U/B/K/C/N/G/P 12.00 30.00

2012-13 Panini Preferred Awards Memorabilia
STATED PRINT RUN 199 SER.#'d SETS
1 Jam/Ros/Bry/Now/Nash/Garn 20.00 50.00
2 Irv/Grif/Evan/Ros/Dur/Roy 10.00 25.00
3 Hard/Terry/Ginoi/Jack/McH/Kuk 10.00 25.00
4 Wal/How/Gar/Metta/Chan/Mut 10.00 25.00

2012-13 Panini Preferred Boston Memorabilia
PRINT RUNS B/WN 129-149 COPIES PER
1 John/Ron/Pier/Bird/McH/Sul/129 20.00 50.00
2 Gart/Pie/McH/Par/Sul/Ron/199 12.00 30.00

2012-13 Panini Preferred Bryant Memorabilia
STATED PRINT RUN 199 SER.#'d SET
1 Kobe Bryant 30.00 80.00

2012-13 Panini Preferred Buckets Memorabilia
STATED PRINT RUN 199 SER.#'d SETS
1 Har/Bry/Cur/Wes/Pau/Jam/Pie 15.00 40.00
2 Wall/Will/Wes/Ros/Joh/May/Thom 30.00 80.00
3 Thom/Col/Fred/Pri/Sto/All/Gino 30.00 80.00
4 Bry/Thom/Dur/Now/Gino/Ros/Lov 60.00 150.00
5 Gino/Fel/Wal/Wad/Ros/Wall/Cur 10.00 25.00

2012-13 Panini Preferred Celtics Memorabilia
PRINT RUNS B/WN 25-149 COPIES PER
1 Pie/Gar/RonSul/Mel/Ter/Gre/149 12.00 30.00
2 McH/Bir/Par/How/Cha/Pie/Gar/25 12.00 30.00

2012-13 Panini Preferred Center Memorabilia
STATED PRINT RUN 199 SER.#'d SETS
1 Bog/Haw/How/Ola/Rob/O'Ne 10.00 25.00
2 Haw/Kan/Wal/Min/Jef/Spl 15.00 40.00

2012-13 Panini Preferred Champs Memorabilia
STATED PRINT RUN 199 SER.#'d SETS
1 Jon/Jam/Wad/Bos/Col/Has 10.00 25.00
2 Now/Bea/Cha/Kid/But/Mar 10.00 25.00
3 Bry/Gas/Wor/Pea/Byn/Fis/Wal 15.00 40.00

2012-13 Panini Preferred Chicago Memorabilia
PRINT RUNS B/WN 179-199 COPIES PER
1 Har/KukPar/Ros/Noa/Den/Boo/179 15.00 40.00
2 But/Noa/Ros/Gib/Den/Hin/Boo/199 12.00 30.00

2012-13 Panini Preferred Clutch Memorabilia
STATED PRINT RUN 199 SER.#'d SETS
1 Cur/Law/Bry/Bil/Pau/Ron 12.00 30.00
2 Bry/Pau/All/Har/Jen/Eva 12.00 30.00

2012-13 Panini Preferred Decades Memorabilia
PRINT RUNS B/WN 10-199 COPIES PER
2 1970s 20.00 50.00
3 1980s 8.00 20.00
4 1990s 12.00 30.00
5 2000s 12.00 30.00

2012-13 Panini Preferred Defense Memorabilia
STATED PRINT RUN 199 SER.#'d SETS
1 How/Wal/Rod/Dun/Gar/Far/Ran 12.50 30.00
2 Bos/Wad/Ros/Par/Pau/Ron/Metta 12.50 30.00
3 Ola/Mut/Mou/Rod/Rob/How/Cam 12.50 30.00

2012-13 Panini Preferred Detroit Memorabilia
STATED PRINT RUN 199 SER.#'d SETS
1 Dru/Mon/Pri/Mid/Eng/Sin/Stu 10.00 25.00
2 Tri/Kni/Pri/Dru/Mon/Tho/Wal 8.00 20.00
3 Kni/Sin/Wal/Pri/Dru/Tho/Mon 10.00 25.00

2012-13 Panini Preferred Diesel Memorabilia
STATED PRINT RUN 199 SER.#'d SETS
1 Shaquille O'Neal 15.00 40.00

2012-13 Panini Preferred Draft Memorabilia
STATED PRINT RUN 199 SER.#'d SETS
1 Ive/All/Cam/Bry/Nas/Fis/Ilg 15.00 40.00

2 Jam/Ant/Bos/Wad/Kam/Wes/Hin 15.00 40.00
3 Wal/Fav/Cou/Cur/Jen/Law/Tea 10.00 25.00
4 How/Jef/Den/Igu/Smi/Mar/Nel 10.00 25.00
5 Bog/Pau/Wil/Fel/Byn/Gra/Lee 10.00 25.00

2012-13 Panini Preferred Duncan Memorabilia
STATED PRINT RUN 199 SER.#'d SETS
1 Tim Duncan 15.00 40.00

2012-13 Panini Preferred Finals Memorabilia
STATED PRINT RUN 199 SER.#'d SETS
1 Gar/Pie/Ron/Bry/Odo/Gas 15.00 40.00
2 Gin/Dun/Par/Var/Jam/Ilg 15.00 40.00
3 Har/Wes/Dur/Jam/Wad/Bos 15.00 40.00

2012-13 Panini Preferred Forward Memorabilia
STATED PRINT RUN 199 SER.#'d SETS
1 Chas/Ell/Tur/Mul/Pie/Hil/Dur 10.00 25.00
2 Web/Mal/Gar/Dun/Lov/Ald/Lee 15.00 40.00
3 Fav/Dun/Ald/You/Now/Ran/Booz 12.00 30.00
4 Now/Far/Dur/Pip/Jam/Ant/Hil 15.00 40.00

2012-13 Panini Preferred Inducted Memorabilia
PRINT RUNS B/WN 10-129 COPIES PER
1 Dr/Mu/Ro/Pi/Ma/Ro/St/Pa/99 15.00 40.00
2 Ew/Ol/Du/Wi/Dr/Th/Mu/Mc/129 8.00 20.00
4 En/Is/Mo/Ew/Dr/Ge/Ol/Ma/79 15.00 40.00

2012-13 Panini Preferred Knicks Memorabilia
STATED PRINT RUN 199 SER.#'d SETS
1 Ewi/Sto/Kid/Ant/Car/Cam 10.00 25.00
2 Fel/Smi/Cam/CopNov/Ant 12.00 30.00
3 Che/Mon/Ant/Ewi/Sto/Fel 12.50 30.00

2012-13 Panini Preferred Lakers Memorabilia
PRINT RUNS B/WN 129-199 COPIES PER
1 Mo/Sa/Jo/Od/Ga/Pe/Br/199 12.00 30.00
2 Va/Br/Jo/O'N/Pe/Ga/199 12.00 30.00
3 Co/Br/Va/Jo/Pe/O'N/129 15.00 40.00

2012-13 Panini Preferred LeBron Memorabilia
STATED PRINT RUN 199 SER.#'d SETS
1 LeBron James 40.00 100.00

2012-13 Panini Preferred Legends Memorabilia
PRINT RUNS B/WN 10-199 COPIES PER
1 An/Ro/Ri/Sm/Ja/Ho/Sc/199 12.00 30.00
2 Mo/We/O'N/Mu/Ew/Jo/Ma/129 10.00 25.00
4 Ca/Ch/Pr/La/Ha/Wi/Le/99 10.00 25.00

2012-13 Panini Preferred London Memorabilia
STATED PRINT RUN 199 SER.#'d SETS
1 Will/Jam/Har/Bry/Lov/Dur 20.00 50.00

2012-13 Panini Preferred Lottery Memorabilia
STATED PRINT RUN 199 SER.#'d SETS
1 Au/Ro/Be/Lo/Ma/Go/We 12.00 30.00
2 Du/Ho/Co/No/Yo/Gr/Ha 10.00 25.00
3 Gr/Ha/Ev/Cu/De/Je/Ha 12.00 30.00
4 Wa/Fa/Co/Mo/Am/Ha/Tu 10.00 25.00
5 Da/Ki/Wa/Li/Ba/Dr/Ri 10.00 25.00

2012-13 Panini Preferred Match Up Memorabilia
STATED PRINT RUN 199 SER.#'d SETS
1 Dr/Ga/Al/Gr/Je/No/Ro 8.00 20.00
2 Bo/Le/Lo/Co/Du/Ho/Ga 8.00 20.00

2012-13 Panini Preferred New York Memorabilia
STATED PRINT RUN 199 SER.#'d SETS
1 An/Sh/St/Fe/Ca/Co/No 10.00 25.00
2 Ch/Ew/St/Mo/Ma/Ca/Ja 10.00 25.00
3 An/Ja/Ch/Sh/Mo/St/Ki 12.50 30.00

2012-13 Panini Preferred Pistons Memorabilia
PRINT RUNS B/WN 99-129 COPIES PER
1 Ho/Ma/Pr/Dr/Kn/Mo/Ag/99 10.00 25.00
2 Th/Tr/Wa/Ag/La/Ma/Du/129 10.00 25.00

2012-13 Panini Preferred Rebound Memorabilia
STATED PRINT RUN 199 SER.#'d SETS
1 Le/Ra/Ho/Gr/Lo/Ro/Du 10.00 25.00
2 Ro/Gr/O'N/Wa/No/Il/Mu 10.00 25.00
3 Mo/Ma/Ka/Br/Du/O'N/Ol 10.00 25.00

2012-13 Panini Preferred Repeat Memorabilia
STATED PRINT RUN 199 SER.#'d SETS
1 Pip/Kuk/Dre/Ola/Bry/Fis 10.00 25.00
2 O'N/Ola/Coo/Rod/Tho/Wal 12.50 30.00

2012-13 Panini Preferred Rivals Memorabilia
STATED PRINT RUN 199 SER.#'d SETS
1 BOS-MIA 20.00 50.00
3 OKC-LAL 12.00 30.00

2012-13 Panini Preferred Rookie Memorabilia
STATED PRINT RUN 249 SER.#'d SETS
1 Da/Be/Ki/Wa/Ro/Li 12.00 30.00
2 Ir/Le/Wa/Li/Ba/Da 12.00 30.00
3 Va/Le/Ro/Da/Ka/Dr 12.00 30.00
4 Le/Pa/Wil/Ba/Fa/Ki 10.00 25.00
5 Wa/Ir/Kn/Be/Li/Wa 12.00 30.00
6 Fo/Ka/Va/Bi/Ve/Vu 8.00 20.00
7 Kn/Te/Mi/Da/Ki/Jo 10.00 25.00
8 Ma/Ba/He/Ir/Ri/Pl 10.00 25.00
9 Ir/Wi/Ka/Th/Va/Ve 10.00 25.00
10 Da/Ki/Be/Ir/Wil/Ka 12.00 30.00

2012-13 Panini Preferred Silhouettes Prime
*SIL.PRIME: .8X TO 2X BASE HI
STATED PRINT RUN B/WN 1-25 COPIES PER
NO PRICING ON QTY 15 OR LESS
208 Tony Parker/25 100.00 200.00
229 LaMarcus Aldridge/25 100.00 200.00
230 Taj Gibson/25 40.00 100.00
235 Hedo Turkoglu/25 30.00 80.00
265 Joe Johnson/20 40.00 100.00
281 Rashard Lewis/25 25.00 60.00
285 Sean Elliott/25 25.00 60.00
291 Darren Collison/25 15.00 40.00
292 Devin Harris/25 15.00 40.00
301 Will Barton/25 30.00 80.00
305 Tobias Harris/25 60.00 150.00
309 Khris Middleton/25 30.00 80.00
310 Kenneth Faried/25 30.00 80.00
318 Kemba Walker/25 200.00 500.00
319 Kawhi Leonard/25 1,000.00 3,000.00
320 John Henson/24 40.00 100.00
321 Jimmy Butler/25 200.00 500.00
322 Jimmer Fredette/25 30.00 80.00
323 Jeremy Lamb/25 20.00 50.00
325 Anthony Davis/25 6,000.00 12,000.00
326 Andrew Nicholson/25 50.00 120.00
327 Kyrie Irving/25 800.00 1,200.00
328 Marquis Teague/25 20.00 50.00
329 MarShon Brooks/25 25.00 60.00
331 Michael Kidd-Gilchrist/25 40.00 100.00
332 Mike Scott/25 40.00 100.00
334 Maurice Harkless/25 75.00 200.00
335 Reggie Jackson/25 75.00 150.00
337 Markieff Morris/25 30.00 80.00
339 Lance Thomas/25 12.00 30.00
346 Jae Crowder/25 25.00 60.00
348 Harrison Barnes/25 75.00 200.00
349 Evan Fournier/25 75.00 150.00
350 E'Twaun Moore/25 20.00 50.00
351 Enes Kanter/25 50.00 120.00
352 Draymond Green/25 400.00 800.00
353 Marcus Morris/25 20.00 50.00
354 Dion Waiters/25 25.00 60.00
357 Brandon Knight/25 50.00 120.00
358 Bradley Beal/25 250.00 500.00
359 Bismack Biyombo/25 25.00 60.00
360 Nikola Vucevic/25 300.00 600.00
361 Andre Drummond/25 125.00 300.00
362 Alec Burks/25 50.00 120.00
363 Tony Wroten/25 40.00 100.00
364 Tristan Thompson/25 75.00 150.00
366 Darius Johnson-Odom/25 12.00 30.00
367 Austin Rivers/25 100.00 200.00
368 Arnett Moultrie/25 12.00 30.00
369 Kyle O'Quinn/25 15.00 40.00
370 Miles Plumlee/25 25.00 60.00
371 Terrence Ross/25 40.00 100.00
377 Nolan Smith/25 40.00 100.00
582 Damian Lillard/25 300.00 600.00

2012-13 Panini Preferred Slam Dunk Memorabilia
STATED PRINT RUN 199 SER.#'d SETS
1 De/Ig/Ca/Ja/Wi/Gr/Dr/Ho 12.00 30.00
2 Ri/Ig/Br/Ja/St/Ke/Ca/De 15.00 40.00

2012-13 Panini Preferred Steals Memorabilia
STATED PRINT RUN 199 SER.#'d SETS
1 Con/Smi/Gra/Jam/Igu/Pau 12.50 30.00
2 Rub/Kidd/Ron/Hill/Jen/Smi 10.00 25.00

2012-13 Panini Preferred Veteran Memorabilia
STATED PRINT RUN 199 SER.#'d SETS
1 Pr/Du/Pa/Ga/Ga/Wa/Ro 12.00 30.00
2 Ga/Pi/Gi/Ro/Ha/Gi/Sa 12.00 30.00
3 G/St/Br/Du/Ho/Gr/Bo 12.00 30.00
4 Lo/Du/No/Th/Yo/Fr/Da 20.00 50.00
5 Ne/Ud/Al/Ro/Fe/Ki/Pa 12.00 30.00

2013-14 Panini Preferred
PRINT RUNS B/WN 20-99 COPIES PER
EXCHANGE DEADLINE 1/23/2016
1 Larry Johnson PC AU/25 15.00 40.00
2 Vinny Del Negro PC AU/25 8.00 20.00
3 Phil Chenier PC AU/74 5.00 12.00
4 Marques Johnson PC AU/60 6.00 15.00
5 Brian Grant PC AU/74 4.00 10.00
6 Christian Laettner PC AU/25 12.00 30.00
7 Jay Williams PC AU/35 6.00 15.00
8 Michael Cooper PC AU/74 8.00 20.00
9 Billy Paultz PC AU/74 8.00 20.00
10 Bob McAdoo PC AU/60 6.00 15.00
11 Avery Johnson PC AU/25 10.00 25.00
12 Tom Gugliotta PC AU/60 6.00 15.00
13 Antoine Walker PC AU/74 6.00 15.00
14 Michael Finley PC AU/35 10.00 25.00
15 Raef LaFrentz PC AU/74 5.00 12.00
16 George Karl PC AU/25 12.00 30.00
17 Jerry West PC AU/20 50.00 120.00
18 Clyde Drexler PC AU/20 40.00 100.00
19 Eddie Johnson PC AU/74 5.00 12.00
20 Dana Barros PC AU/74 5.00 12.00
21 Kelly Tripucka PC AU/25 10.00 25.00
22 Len Elmore PC AU/74 6.00 15.00
23 Chris Mullin PC AU/25 15.00 40.00
24 Kenny Anderson PC AU/74 6.00 15.00
25 Clifford Robinson PC AU/74 8.00 20.00
26 Peja Stojakovic PC AU/25 10.00 25.00
27 Lindsey Hunter PC AU/74 5.00 12.00
28 Danny Manning PC AU/25 10.00 25.00
29 World B. Free PC AU/25 10.00 25.00
30 Tracy McGrady PC AU/20 100.00 250.00
31 Jalen Rose PC AU/25 10.00 25.00
32 Muggsy Bogues PC AU/74 8.00 20.00
33 Fat Lever PC AU/74 6.00 15.00
34 Cedric Maxwell PC AU/74 6.00 15.00
35 Darrell Griffith PC AU/74 6.00 15.00
36 Darryl Dawkins PC AU/60 6.00 15.00
37 Bobby Jones PC AU/74 10.00 25.00
38 Bill Willoughby PC AU/74 8.00 20.00
39 Dale Davis PC AU/74 6.00 15.00
40 B.J. Armstrong PC AU/25 12.00 30.00
41 George Gervin PC AU/25 20.00 50.00
42 Travis Best PC AU/74 5.00 12.00
43 Scottie Pippen PC AU/25 125.00 300.00
44 Wayne Embry PC AU/60 5.00 12.00
45 Kenny Smith PC AU/60 6.00 15.00
46 Jamaal Wilkes PC AU/60 6.00 15.00
47 Julius Erving PC AU/20 100.00 250.00
48 Joe Dumars PC AU/25 15.00 40.00
49 Dan Issel PC AU/74 10.00 25.00
50 Terry Cummings PC AU/74 6.00 15.00
51 P.J. Tucker PC AU/74 8.00 20.00
52 Nick Young PC AU/25 8.00 20.00
53 Carlos Boozer PC AU/25 10.00 25.00
54 Arron Afflalo PC AU/25 8.00 20.00
55 Kevin Martin PC AU/25 10.00 25.00
56 Marcin Gortat PC AU/25 8.00 20.00
57 Jrue Holiday PC AU/25 30.00 80.00
58 Al-Farouq Aminu PC AU/60 5.00 12.00
59 Andrew Bogut PC AU/25 20.00 50.00
60 Boris Diaw PC AU/35 25.00 60.00
61 D.J. Augustin PC AU/35 6.00 15.00
62 Marcus Thornton PC AU/35 6.00 15.00
63 Shaquille O'Neal PC AU/20 125.00 300.00
64 Tobias Harris PC AU/35 10.00 25.00
65 Nikola Vucevic PC AU/35 12.00 30.00
66 Marreese Speights PC AU/74 5.00 12.00
67 Josh Smith PC AU/35 8.00 20.00
68 Jimmer Fredette PC AU/35 10.00 25.00
69 LaMarcus Aldridge PC AU/25 12.00 30.00
70 Tyler Zeller PC AU/60 5.00 12.00
71 Taj Gibson PC AU/35 6.00 15.00
72 Lavoy Allen PC AU/74 5.00 12.00
73 Kevin Durant PC AU/49 100.00 250.00
74 Jared Dudley PC AU/25 8.00 20.00
75 Roy Hibbert PC AU/25 8.00 20.00
76 Eric Maynor PC AU/74 5.00 12.00
77 Tony Wroten PC AU/74 5.00 12.00
78 Mike Conley PC AU/25 12.00 30.00
79 Tayshaun Prince PC AU/25 12.00 30.00
80 Brandan Wright PC AU/60 5.00 12.00
81 Danny Green PC AU/25 10.00 25.00
82 Khris Middleton PC AU/74 15.00 40.00
83 Courtney Lee PC AU/74 5.00 12.00
84 Kyrie Irving PC AU/25 100.00 250.00
85 Jonas Valanciunas PC AU/35 8.00 20.00
86 Kemba Walker PC AU/25 12.00 30.00
87 Quincy Acy PC AU/74 5.00 12.00
88 Patrick Beverley PC AU/74 5.00 12.00
89 Hollis Thompson PC AU/74 5.00 12.00
90 Danilo Gallinari PC AU/25 10.00 25.00
91 Trevor Booker PC AU/74 5.00 12.00
92 Andre Drummond PC AU/25 12.00 30.00
93 Andrew Nicholson PC AU/60 5.00 12.00
94 Andrea Bargnani PC AU/25 8.00 20.00
95 John Wall PC AU/20 15.00 40.00
96 Eric Gordon PC AU/25 10.00 25.00
97 Bradley Beal PC AU/25 20.00 50.00
98 Ty Lawson PC AU/25 8.00 20.00
99 Tiago Splitter PC AU/25 8.00 20.00
100 Kendall Marshall PC AU/49 6.00 15.00
101 Andre Roberson PC AU/99 5.00 12.00
102 Rudy Gobert PC AU/75 20.00 50.00
103 MCW PC AU/49 8.00 20.00
104 Miroslav Raduljica PC AU/99 5.00 12.00
105 Tony Snell PC AU/49 8.00 20.00
106 Vitor Faverani PC AU/99 5.00 12.00
107 Gal Mekel PC AU/75 5.00 12.00
108 Jeff Withey PC AU/99 5.00 12.00
109 Nemanja Nedovic PC AU/75 5.00 12.00
110 Robert Covington PC AU/99 5.00 12.00
111 Ian Clark PC AU/99 6.00 15.00
112 Ryan Kelly PC AU/99 5.00 12.00
113 Trey Burke PC AU/35 8.00 20.00
114 Peyton Siva PC AU/99 5.00 12.00
115 Ricky Ledo PC AU/75 5.00 12.00
116 Antetokounmpo PC AU/99 400.00 800.00
117 Kentavious Caldwell-
Pope PC AU/35 10.00 25.00
118 Erik Murphy PC AU/99 5.00 12.00
119 Archie Goodwin PC AU/99 5.00 12.00
120 Matthew Dellavedova PC AU/99 8.00 20.00
121 Nate Wolters PC AU/99 5.00 12.00
122 Ben McLemore PC AU/35 8.00 20.00
123 Toure Murry PC AU/99 5.00 12.00
124 Anthony Bennett PC AU/35 6.00 15.00
125 Ray McCallum PC AU/99 5.00 12.00
126 Carrick Felix PC AU/75 5.00 12.00
127 Glen Rice Jr. PC AU/49 6.00 15.00
128 Allen Crabbe PC AU/75 6.00 15.00
129 Otto Porter PC AU/35 10.00 25.00
130 Victor Oladipo PC AU/49 15.00 40.00
131 Dennis Schroder PC AU/75 15.00 40.00
132 Solomon Hill PC AU/99 6.00 15.00
133 Lorenzo Brown PC AU/99 5.00 12.00
134 Kelly Olynyk PC AU/60 6.00 15.00
135 Tim Hardaway Jr. PC AU/49 12.00 30.00
136 Alex Len PC AU/35 8.00 20.00
137 Shane Larkin PC AU/35 8.00 20.00
138 Pero Antic PC AU/75 5.00 12.00
139 Mason Plumlee PC AU/75 6.00 15.00
140 Nerlens Noel PC AU/35 8.00 20.00
141 Kyle Singler CR AU/25 6.00 15.00
142 Alan Anderson CR AU/25 5.00 12.00
143 Andrei Kirilenko CR AU/20 12.00 30.00
144 Evan Fournier CR AU/99 6.00 15.00
145 Patrick Beverley CR AU/99 5.00 12.00
146 Andre Iguodala CR AU/20 20.00 50.00
147 Kobe Bryant CR AU/25 1,000.00 2,000.00
148 Reggie Jackson CR AU/25 10.00 25.00
149 Chris Singleton CR AU/99 5.00 12.00
150 Victor Claver CR AU/99 5.00 12.00
151 Alexey Shved CR AU/49 6.00 15.00
152 Tony Wroten CR AU/49 6.00 15.00
153 Bradley Beal CR AU/20 20.00 50.00
154 Wesley Matthews CR AU/25 8.00 20.00
155 P.J. Tucker CR AU/99 5.00 12.00
156 Richard Jefferson CR AU/20 10.00 25.00
157 Will Barton CR AU/99 5.00 12.00
158 Jared Sullinger CR AU/20 8.00 20.00
160 Khris Middleton CR AU/99 15.00 40.00
161 Raymond Felton CR AU/20 8.00 20.00
162 Kawhi Leonard CR AU/25 75.00 200.00
163 Jared Dudley CR AU/25 8.00 20.00
164 Keith Bogans CR AU/49 5.00 12.00
165 Kevin Martin CR AU/20 10.00 25.00
166 Timofey Mozgov CR AU/99 5.00 12.00
167 Trevor Booker CR AU/99 5.00 12.00
168 Jason Thompson CR AU/25 6.00 15.00
169 John Salmons CR AU/99 6.00 15.00
170 Brandon Knight CR AU/20 10.00 25.00
171 Jonas Jerebko CR AU/99 5.00 12.00
172 Arron Afflalo CR AU/20 8.00 20.00
173 D.J. Augustin CR AU/49 6.00 15.00
174 Brian Roberts CR AU/99 5.00 12.00
175 Goran Dragic CR AU/99 10.00 25.00
176 Lavoy Allen CR AU/75 5.00 12.00
177 Marcin Gortat CR AU/25 8.00 20.00
178 MarShon Brooks CR AU/99 5.00 12.00
179 Tiago Splitter CR AU/25 8.00 20.00
180 Ersan Ilyasova CR AU/25 8.00 20.00
181 Jason Maxiell CR AU/99 5.00 12.00
182 Antawn Jamison CR AU/20 10.00 25.00
183 Chris Copeland CR AU/99 5.00 12.00
184 Brandon Bass CR AU/20 8.00 20.00
185 Randy Foye CR AU/25 8.00 20.00
186 Chris Andersen CR AU/20 10.00 25.00
187 Xavier Henry CR AU/25 8.00 20.00
188 Jason Terry CR AU/20 10.00 25.00
189 Ryan Anderson CR AU/25 8.00 20.00
190 Amir Johnson CR AU/99 5.00 12.00
191 H.Olajuwon PC AU/20 40.00 100.00
192 David Robinson CR AU/20 40.00 100.00
193 Steve Smith CR AU/99 6.00 15.00
194 Walt Frazier CR AU/20 20.00 50.00
195 Jerry Lucas CR AU/25 8.00 20.00
196 Robert Parish CR AU/20 15.00 40.00
197 Dan Issel CR AU/99 6.00 15.00
198 Dennis Rodman CR AU/20 100.00 250.00
199 Toni Kukoc CR AU/25 15.00 40.00
200 Nate Archibald CR AU/20 15.00 40.00
201 Larry Bird CR AU/20 100.00 250.00
202 Gary Payton CR AU/20 20.00 50.00
203 Christian Laettner CR AU/20 12.00 30.00
204 Dale Davis CR AU/99 6.00 15.00
205 Theo Ratliff CR AU/99 5.00 12.00
206 Phil Chenier CR AU/99 5.00 12.00
207 Campy Russell CR AU/99 5.00 12.00
208 Bill Walton CR AU/25 40.00 100.00
209 Danny Manning CR AU/20 10.00 25.00
210 Mark Price CR AU/99 8.00 20.00
211 Len Elmore CR AU/99 6.00 15.00
212 Scott Wedman CR AU/99 6.00 15.00
213 Fat Lever CR AU/99 6.00 15.00
214 Kevin Willis CR AU/25 10.00 25.00
215 Bob McAdoo CR AU/25 15.00 40.00
216 Rory Sparrow CR AU/99 5.00 12.00
217 Cazzie Russell CR AU/99 6.00 15.00
218 Nick Van Exel CR AU/20 12.00 30.00
219 Jack Sikma CR AU/99 8.00 20.00
220 Tyronn Lue CR AU/99 5.00 12.00
221 Connie Hawkins CR AU/20 15.00 40.00
222 Clyde Drexler CR AU/20 40.00 100.00
223 Michael Finley CR AU/20 12.00 30.00
224 Jerry West CR AU/20 40.00 100.00
225 Raef LaFrentz CR AU/99 5.00 12.00
226 Cedric Ceballos CR AU/99 5.00 12.00
227 S. O'Neal CR AU/20 125.00 300.00
228 Kendall Gill CR AU/99 8.00 20.00
229 Nick Anderson CR AU/99 6.00 15.00
230 Scott Skiles CR AU/99 6.00 15.00
231 Jo Jo White CR AU/99 6.00 15.00
232 Mario Elie CR AU/99 6.00 15.00
233 John Salley CR AU/99 5.00 12.00
234 Glen Rice CR AU/25 10.00 25.00
235 Bill Laimbeer CR AU/99 8.00 20.00
236 Maurice Cheeks CR AU/99 6.00 15.00
237 Horace Grant CR AU/25 8.00 20.00
238 Robert Horry CR AU/25 12.00 30.00
239 Terry Porter CR AU/99 8.00 20.00
240 Arvydas Sabonis CR AU/99 10.00 25.00
241 Nemanja Nedovic CR AU/75 5.00 12.00
242 Phil Pressey CR AU/75 5.00 12.00
243 Anthony Bennett CR AU/25 8.00 20.00
244 C.J. McCollum CR AU/35 30.00 80.00
245 Trey Burke CR AU/49 8.00 20.00
246 Antetokounmpo CR AU/49 400.00 800.00
247 Ian Clark CR AU/75 6.00 15.00
248 Archie Goodwin CR AU/75 5.00 12.00
249 Ryan Kelly CR AU/75 5.00 12.00
250 Alex Len CR AU/25 10.00 25.00
251 Victor Oladipo CR AU/49 15.00 40.00
252 Dwight Buycks CR AU/99 5.00 12.00
253 Andre Roberson CR AU/75 6.00 15.00
254 MCW CR AU/49 8.00 20.00
255 Isaiah Canaan CR AU/75 5.00 12.00
256 Gorgui Dieng CR AU/75 6.00 15.00
257 Tony Mitchell CR AU/75 5.00 12.00
258 Allen Crabbe CR AU/75 5.00 12.00
259 Otto Porter CR AU/25 12.00 30.00
260 Carrick Felix CR AU/75 5.00 12.00
261 Tim Hardaway Jr. CR AU/60 10.00 25.00
262 Jamaal Franklin CR AU/75 5.00 12.00
263 Toure Murry CR AU/75 5.00 12.00
264 M.Dellavedova CR AU/25 8.00 20.00
265 S.Muhammad CR AU/25 8.00 20.00
266 Tony Snell CR AU/49 8.00 20.00
267 Rudy Gobert CR AU/75 20.00 50.00
268 Reggie Bullock CR AU/75 6.00 15.00
269 Luigi Datome CR AU/75 5.00 12.00
270 Miroslav Raduljica CR AU/75 5.00 12.00
271 Gal Mekel CR AU/75 5.00 12.00
272 Ricky Ledo CR AU/75 5.00 12.00
273 Peyton Siva CR AU/75 5.00 12.00
274 Lorenzo Brown CR AU/75 5.00 12.00
275 Cody Zeller CR AU/25 10.00 25.00
276 Erik Murphy CR AU/75 5.00 12.00
277 Solomon Hill CR AU/75 6.00 15.00
278 Robert Covington CR AU/75 8.00 20.00
279 Glen Rice Jr. CR AU/75 5.00 12.00
280 Steven Adams CR AU/49 15.00 40.00
281 Tim Hardaway Jr. RR AU/60 10.00 25.00
282 Vitor Faverani RR AU/99 5.00 12.00
283 Kelly Olynyk RR AU/35 8.00 20.00
284 S.Muhammad RR AU/35 8.00 20.00
285 Trey Burke RR AU/35 8.00 20.00
286 MCW RR AU/99 6.00 15.00
287 Steven Adams RR AU/49 15.00 40.00
288 Phil Pressey RR AU/99 5.00 12.00
289 Otto Porter RR AU/25 12.00 30.00
290 Victor Oladipo RR AU/49 15.00 40.00
291 Ben McLemore RR AU/25 10.00 25.00
292 Nate Wolters RR AU/25 5.00 12.00
293 Alex Len RR AU/25 10.00 25.00
294 Tony Snell RR AU/60 6.00 15.00
295 Dwight Buycks RR AU/99 5.00 12.00
296 Pero Antic RR AU/99 5.00 12.00
297 Nerlens Noel RR AU/25 10.00 25.00
298 Mason Plumlee RR AU/99 6.00 15.00
299 Shane Larkin RR AU/99 5.00 12.00
300 Gorgui Dieng RR AU/99 6.00 15.00
301 Karl Malone SL JSY AU/35 75.00 200.00
302 D.Robinson SL JSY AU/35 75.00 200.00
303 Brad Daugherty SL JSY AU/49 10.00 25.00
304 Anthony Mason SL JSY AU/99 8.00 20.00
305 Fred Brown SL JSY AU/49 8.00 20.00
306 Chris Mullin SL JSY AU/35 12.00 30.00
307 Grant Hill SL JSY AU/35 40.00 100.00
308 S.O'Neal SL JSY AU/35 150.00 400.00
309 L.Johnson SL JSY AU/35 40.00 100.00
310 Dan Majerle SL JSY AU/35 12.00 30.00
311 John Starks SL JSY AU/35 40.00 100.00
312 Norm Nixon SL JSY AU/49 8.00 20.00
313 D.Wilkins SL JSY AU/25 40.00 100.00
314 Doc Rivers SL JSY AU/35 8.00 20.00
315 A.Johnson SL JSY AU/35 8.00 20.00
316 Scott Wedman SL JSY AU/49 8.00 20.00
317 Steve Mix SL JSY AU/49 6.00 15.00
318 Gary Payton SL JSY AU/25 50.00 120.00
319 Cedric Maxwell SL JSY AU/49 8.00 20.00
320 B.Cartwright SL JSY AU/35 8.00 20.00
321 A.Hardaway SL JSY AU/35 75.00 200.00
322 Mark Jackson SL JSY AU/35 8.00 20.00
323 Kiki Vandeweghe SL JSY AU/49 8.00 20.00
324 Rick Barry SL JSY AU/35 15.00 40.00
325 Jeff Malone SL JSY AU/49 8.00 20.00
326 M.Johnson SL JSY AU/35 300.00 600.00
327 Abdul-Jabbar SL JSY AU/35 300.00 600.00
328 Julius Erving SL JSY AU/35 300.00 600.00
329 Xavier McDaniel SL JSY AU/49 8.00 20.00
330 D.Mutombo SL JSY AU/35 40.00 100.00
331 H.Barnes SL JSY AU/35 10.00 25.00
332 Tiago Splitter SL JSY AU/35 6.00 15.00
333 J.Valanciunas SL JSY AU/35 8.00 20.00
334 Nicolas Batum SL JSY AU/35 8.00 20.00
335 Danny Green SL JSY AU/49 8.00 20.00
336 Tyson Chandler SL JSY AU/35 8.00 20.00
337 Raymond Felton SL JSY AU/35 6.00 15.00
338 Kendrick Perkins SL JSY AU/35 6.00 15.00
339 K.Durant SL JSY AU/35 300.00 600.00
340 Reggie Jackson SL JSY AU/35 8.00 20.00
341 Ryan Anderson SL JSY AU/35 6.00 15.00
342 G.Hayward SL JSY AU/35 8.00 20.00
343 A.Davis SL JSY AU/35 60.00 150.00
344 Jrue Holiday SL JSY AU/35 40.00 100.00
345 Kevin Love SL JSY AU/25 12.00 30.00
346 Ersan Ilyasova SL JSY AU/35 6.00 15.00
347 Lance Stephenson SL JSY AU/49 8.00 20.00
348 L.Aldridge SL JSY AU/35 10.00 25.00
349 C.Andersen SL JSY AU/35 8.00 20.00
350 Kobe Bryant SL JSY AU/35 2,000.00 4,000.00
351 Nick Young SL JSY AU/35 6.00 15.00
352 Blake Griffin SL JSY AU/25 12.00 30.00
353 Steve Nash SL JSY AU/35 75.00 200.00
354 Bernard King SL JSY AU/35 12.00 30.00
355 J.Harden SL JSY AU/35 100.00 250.00
356 A.Iguodala SL JSY AU/35 25.00 60.00
357 S.Curry SL JSY AU/35 1,000.00 2,000.00
358 Kyrie Irving SL JSY AU/35 300.00 600.00
359 A.Drummond SL JSY AU/35 10.00 25.00
360 Josh Smith SL JSY AU/35 6.00 15.00
361 J.Calderon SL JSY AU/35 6.00 15.00
362 Jeff Green SL JSY AU/35 6.00 15.00
363 Andrew Bogut SL JSY AU/35 8.00 20.00
364 Bradley Beal SL JSY AU/35 15.00 40.00
365 Z.Randolph SL JSY AU/35 8.00 20.00
366 Gal Mekel SL JSY AU/99 5.00 12.00
367 Kelly Olynyk SL JSY AU/60 6.00 15.00
368 V.Oladipo SL JSY AU/75 12.00 30.00
369 MCW SL JSY/75 6.00 15.00
370 Alex Len SL JSY AU/49 8.00 20.00
371 A.Goodwin SL JSY AU/99 5.00 12.00
372 A.Bennett SL JSY AU/49 8.00 20.00
373 Ricky Ledo SL JSY AU/99 5.00 12.00
374 Tony Snell SL JSY AU/99 6.00 15.00
375 Hardaway Jr. SL JSY AU/60 10.00 25.00
376 Solomon Hill SL JSY AU/99 6.00 15.00
377 Nerlens Noel SL JSY AU/75 6.00 15.00
378 Trey Burke SL JSY AU/75 6.00 15.00
379 Erik Murphy SL JSY AU/99 5.00 12.00
380 G.Anttknmpo SL JSY AU/99 2,000.00 4,000.00
381 Jeff Withey SL JSY AU/99 5.00 12.00
382 D.Schroder SL JSY AU/99 25.00 60.00
383 Shane Larkin SL JSY AU/60 5.00 12.00
384 Nate Wolters SL JSY AU/99 5.00 12.00
385 Ryan Kelly SL JSY AU/99 5.00 12.00
386 Dellavedova SL JSY AU/99 8.00 20.00
387 Allen Crabbe SL JSY AU/99 5.00 12.00
388 Carrick Felix SL JSY AU/99 5.00 12.00
389 Jamaal Franklin SL JSY AU/99 5.00 12.00
390 Peyton Siva SL JSY AU/99 5.00 12.00
391 Cody Zeller SL JSY AU/49 8.00 20.00
392 Tony Mitchell SL JSY AU/99 5.00 12.00
393 M.Plumlee SL JSY AU/60 6.00 15.00
394 Caldwell-Pope SL JSY AU/49 10.00 25.00
395 S.Muhammad SL JSY AU/49 6.00 15.00
396 B.McLemore SL JSY AU/49 8.00 20.00
397 C.McCollum SL JSY AU/49 25.00 60.00
398 S.Adams SL JSY AU/99 12.00 30.00
399 Otto Porter SL JSY AU/49 10.00 25.00
400 Luigi Datome SL JSY AU/99 5.00 12.00
401 Goran Dragic NP AU/20 10.00 25.00
402 Carlos Boozer NP AU/20 10.00 25.00
403 Kevin Durant NP AU/25 125.00 300.00
404 Shane Battier NP AU/20 10.00 25.00
405 Anthony Davis NP AU/20 100.00 250.00
406 Udonis Haslem NP AU/99 6.00 15.00
407 Joakim Noah NP AU/20 12.00 30.00
408 Eric Gordon NP AU/20 10.00 25.00
409 Xavier Henry NP AU/25 8.00 20.00
410 Steve Blake NP AU/99 5.00 12.00
411 Harrison Barnes NP AU/20 12.00 30.00
412 Kobe Bryant NP AU/25 1,000.00 2,000.00
413 Brandon Knight NP AU/20 10.00 25.00
414 Kyrie Irving NP AU/20 100.00 250.00
415 Ty Lawson NP AU/20 8.00 20.00
416 DeAndre Jordan NP AU/20 10.00 25.00
417 Brandon Bass NP AU/20 8.00 20.00
418 Marcin Gortat NP AU/20 8.00 20.00
419 Gordon Hayward NP AU/20 10.00 25.00
420 LaMarcus Aldridge NP AU/20 12.00 30.00
421 Andre Drummond NP AU/20 12.00 30.00
422 George Hill NP AU/20 10.00 25.00
423 Tyson Chandler NP AU/20 10.00 25.00
424 Kemba Walker NP AU/20 12.00 30.00
425 Roy Hibbert NP AU/20 8.00 20.00
426 Deron Williams NP AU/20 10.00 25.00
427 Andrea Bargnani NP AU/20 8.00 20.00
428 Tony Parker NP AU/20 50.00 120.00
429 Wesley Matthews NP AU/20 8.00 20.00
430 J.R. Smith NP AU/20 12.00 30.00
431 Brook Lopez NP AU/20 12.00 30.00
432 Iman Shumpert NP AU/99 5.00 12.00
433 Kendrick Perkins NP AU/20 8.00 20.00
434 John Henson NP AU/20 8.00 20.00
435 James Harden NP AU/20 100.00 250.00
436 Robert Sacre NP AU/99 5.00 12.00
437 Marvin Williams NP AU/99 5.00 12.00
438 Mirza Teletovic NP AU/99 5.00 12.00
439 Tobias Harris NP AU/20 12.00 30.00
440 Jared Sullinger NP AU/20 8.00 20.00
441 Spencer Hawes NP AU/99 5.00 12.00
442 Nicolas Batum NP AU/99 6.00 15.00
443 Jared Dudley NP AU/20 8.00 20.00
444 J.J. Redick NP AU/20 20.00 50.00
445 Kendall Marshall NP AU/35 6.00 15.00
446 Robin Lopez NP AU/49 6.00 15.00
447 Maurice Harkless NP AU/20 8.00 20.00
448 Isaiah Thomas NP AU/99 6.00 15.00
449 Eric Maynor NP AU/99 5.00 12.00
450 Nick Young NP AU/20 8.00 20.00
451 Tim Hardaway NP AU/99 10.00 25.00
452 Shaquille O'Neal NP AU/20 125.00 300.00
453 Will Perdue NP AU/99 5.00 12.00
454 Magic Johnson NP AU/20 125.00 300.00
455 Bill Walton NP AU/20 40.00 100.00
456 Sam Perkins NP AU/20 6.00 15.00
457 Gary Payton NP AU/20 40.00 100.00
458 Connie Hawkins NP AU/20 15.00 40.00
459 Scottie Pippen NP AU/20 100.00 250.00
460 Norm Nixon NP AU/60 6.00 15.00
461 Darrell Griffith NP AU/99 6.00 15.00
462 Grant Hill NP AU/20 40.00 100.00
463 Nate Archibald NP AU/20 15.00 40.00
464 Rory Sparrow NP AU/99 5.00 12.00
465 Nick Collison NP AU/99 5.00 12.00
466 Julius Erving NP AU/25 100.00 250.00
467 Vernon Maxwell NP AU/99 6.00 15.00
468 Mark Jackson NP AU/20 10.00 25.00
469 Larry Bird NP AU/20 125.00 300.00
470 Rolando Blackman NP AU/99 6.00 15.00
471 Muggsy Bogues NP AU/99 8.00 20.00
472 Spud Webb NP AU/99 8.00 20.00
473 Mark Aguirre NP AU/99 6.00 15.00
474 Isiah Thomas NP AU/20 50.00 120.00
475 Sidney Moncrief NP AU/99 8.00 20.00
476 Zydrunas Ilgauskas NP AU/99 6.00 15.00
477 B.J. Armstrong NP AU/20 12.00 30.00
478 George McGinnis NP AU/20 12.00 30.00
479 Marques Johnson NP AU/99 6.00 15.00
480 Bob Dandridge NP AU/99 6.00 15.00
481 Bobby Jones NP AU/99 10.00 25.00
482 Buck Williams NP AU/99 6.00 15.00
483 Bruce Bowen NP AU/99 6.00 15.00
484 Allan Houston NP AU/20 12.00 30.00
485 Derrick Coleman NP AU/20 12.00 30.00
486 Vin Baker NP AU/99 5.00 12.00
487 Lindsey Hunter NP AU/99 5.00 12.00
488 Jay Williams NP AU/20 8.00 20.00
489 Larry Nance NP AU/99 6.00 15.00
490 Michael Cage NP AU/99 5.00 12.00
491 Fred Brown NP AU/99 6.00 15.00
492 Brent Barry NP AU/20 8.00 20.00
493 Byron Scott NP AU/20 12.00 30.00
494 Alex English NP AU/20 15.00 40.00
495 George Gervin NP AU/20 25.00 60.00
496 Karl Malone NP AU/20 60.00 150.00
497 Cedric Ceballos NP AU/75 5.00 12.00
498 Wes Unseld NP AU/20 15.00 40.00
499 Gail Goodrich NP AU/20 12.00 30.00
500 Walt Frazier NP AU/20 20.00 50.00
501 Kendall Gill PS AU/99 8.00 20.00
502 Jerry Lucas PS AU/20 12.00 30.00
503 Rick Barry PS AU/20 15.00 40.00
504 Abdul-Jabbar PS AU/20 125.00 300.00
505 Larry Johnson PS AU/25 15.00 40.00
506 M.Abdul-Rauf PS AU/99 5.00 12.00
507 Robert Parish PS AU/20 15.00 40.00
508 Joe Dumars PS AU/20 15.00 40.00
509 Isiah Thomas PS AU/20 20.00 50.00
510 Nate Thurmond PS AU/20 12.00 30.00
511 Scottie Pippen PS AU/20 100.00 250.00
512 Mark Aguirre PS AU/99 6.00 15.00
513 Adrian Dantley PS AU/35 10.00 25.00
514 Rex Chapman PS AU/99 8.00 20.00
515 H.Olajuwon PS AU/20 40.00 100.00
516 Alex English PS AU/35 12.00 30.00
517 Dee Brown PS AU/99 6.00 15.00
518 Tom Heinsohn PS AU/25 40.00 100.00
519 Thaddeus Young PS AU/99 5.00 12.00
520 D.Wilkins PS AU/20 25.00 60.00
521 Steve Mix PS AU/99 5.00 12.00
522 Adrian Smith PS AU/99 5.00 12.00
523 George Karl PS AU/20 12.00 30.00
524 Jon McGlocklin PS AU/75 6.00 15.00
525 Byron Scott PS AU/20 12.00 30.00
526 Tracy McGrady PS AU/20 100.00 250.00
527 Bernard King PS AU/20 15.00 40.00
528 John Lucas PS AU/35 8.00 20.00
529 Luc Longley PS AU/49 8.00 20.00
530 Jerome Williams PS AU/99 5.00 12.00
531 Antonio Davis PS AU/99 6.00 15.00
532 Jack Sikma PS AU/99 8.00 20.00
533 Charlie Scott PS AU/99 8.00 20.00
534 Jalen Rose PS AU/25 10.00 25.00
535 Tom Chambers PS AU/35 10.00 25.00
536 D.Mutombo PS AU/25 40.00 100.00
537 Tom Van Arsdale PS AU/99 8.00 20.00
538 Gail Goodrich PS AU/20 12.00 30.00
539 Walt Frazier PS AU/20 20.00 50.00
540 Dick Van Arsdale PS AU/99 8.00 20.00
541 Rolando Blackman PS AU/99 6.00 15.00
542 Anthony Mason PS AU/99 6.00 15.00
543 Grant Hill PS AU/20 40.00 100.00
544 Spud Webb PS AU/99 8.00 20.00
545 Doug Christie PS AU/75 5.00 12.00
546 A.Hardaway PS AU/20 100.00 250.00
547 Robert Horry PS AU/25 12.00 30.00
548 Billy Paultz PS AU/99 8.00 20.00
549 Brian Grant PS AU/99 6.00 15.00
550 Mark Price PS AU/99 8.00 20.00
551 Isaiah Thomas PS AU/99 6.00 15.00
552 Travis Outlaw PS AU/99 5.00 12.00
553 Kyle Lowry PS AU/25 12.00 30.00
554 Zach Randolph PS AU/20 10.00 25.00
555 Alan Anderson PS AU/35 6.00 15.00
556 Greg Stiemsma PS AU/99 5.00 12.00
557 Patrick Patterson PS AU/99 5.00 12.00
558 Tyler Zeller PS AU/35 6.00 15.00
559 C.J. Watson PS AU/99 5.00 12.00
560 James Jones PS AU/99 5.00 12.00
561 Courtney Lee PS AU/25 8.00 20.00
562 Andrew Nicholson PS AU/75 5.00 12.00
563 Shelvin Mack PS AU/99 5.00 12.00
564 Udonis Haslem PS AU/99 6.00 15.00
565 Nick Collison PS AU/99 5.00 12.00
566 Gordon Hayward PS AU/35 8.00 20.00
567 Gerald Henderson PS AU/35 6.00 15.00
568 Lance Stephenson PS AU/75 6.00 15.00
569 Quincy Acy PS AU/99 5.00 12.00
570 Kevin Love PS AU/20 12.00 30.00
571 Jeff Green PS AU/25 8.00 20.00
572 Goran Dragic PS AU/25 10.00 25.00
573 Jeff Teague PS AU/35 6.00 15.00
574 Bernard James PS AU/99 5.00 12.00
575 Al-Farouq Aminu PS AU/35 6.00 15.00
576 DeAndre Jordan PS AU/25 10.00 25.00
577 Greg Monroe PS AU/35 6.00 15.00
578 Danny Green PS AU/25 8.00 20.00
579 Kenyon Martin PS AU/99 8.00 20.00
580 Kyle Korver PS AU/25 10.00 25.00
581 Tristan Thompson PS AU/20 8.00 20.00
582 Robin Lopez PS AU/49 6.00 15.00
583 Mike Conley PS AU/25 12.00 30.00
584 Taj Gibson PS AU/35 6.00 15.00
585 Andre Miller PS AU/25 10.00 25.00
586 Amir Johnson PS AU/99 5.00 12.00
587 Reggie Jackson PS AU/35 8.00 20.00
588 J.R. Smith PS AU/25 12.00 30.00
589 Greg Oden PS AU/99 5.00 12.00
590 Brian Roberts PS AU/99 5.00 12.00
591 Timofey Mozgov PS AU/99 5.00 12.00
592 Joakim Noah PS AU/20 12.00 30.00
593 Ersan Ilyasova PS AU/35 6.00 15.00
594 DeMarre Carroll PS AU/99 5.00 12.00
595 Jason Smith PS AU/99 5.00 12.00
596 Boris Diaw PS AU/25 10.00 25.00
597 Marvin Williams PS AU/99 5.00 12.00
598 Harrison Barnes PS AU/20 12.00 30.00
599 Jose Calderon PS AU/25 8.00 20.00
600 Jodie Meeks PS AU/99 5.00 12.00

2013-14 Panini Preferred Blue
*BLUE p/r 49: .4X TO 1X p/r 60-99
*BLUE p/r 35: .5X TO 1.2X p/r 49-99
*BLUE p/r 25: .6X TO 1.5X p/r 49-60
*BLUE p/r 25: .5X TO 1.2X p/r 35
*BLUE p/r 20: .4X TO 1X p/r 25
PRINT RUN B/WN 15-49 COPIES PER
NO PRICING ON QTY 15
EXCHANGE DEADLINE 1/23/2016
82 Khris Middleton PC AU/49 10.00 25.00

2013-14 Panini Preferred Purple
*PURPLE p/r 25: .6X TO 1.5X p/r 49-99
*PURPLE p/r 25: .5X TO 1.2X p/r 35
*PURPLE p/r 25: .4X TO 1X p/r 25
PRINT RUN B/WN 10-25 COPIES PER
NO PRICING ON QTY 15 OR LESS
EXCHANGE DEADLINE 1/23/2016
82 Khris Middleton PC AU/25 15.00 40.00
116 G.Anttknmpo PC AU/25 500.00 1,000.00
246 Giannis Antetokounmpo
CR AU/25 500.00 1,000.00
529 Luc Longley PS AU/25 10.00 25.00

2013-14 Panini Preferred Silhouettes Prime
*PRIME ROOKIES: 2.5X TO 6X BASIC
PRINT RUNS B/WN 10-25 COPIES PER
NO PRICING ON QTY 10
EXCHANGE DEADLINE 1/23/2016
301 Karl Malone/25 400.00 800.00
303 Brad Daugherty/25 40.00 100.00
304 Anthony Mason/25 50.00 120.00
305 Fred Brown/25 30.00 80.00
306 Chris Mullin/25 75.00 200.00
307 Grant Hill/25 150.00 400.00
308 Shaquille O'Neal/25 500.00 1,000.00
309 Larry Johnson/25 125.00 300.00
310 Dan Majerle/25 30.00 80.00
311 John Starks/25 150.00 400.00
312 Norm Nixon/25 30.00 80.00
315 Avery Johnson/25 30.00 80.00
316 Scott Wedman/25 30.00 80.00
317 Steve Mix/25 25.00 60.00
319 Cedric Maxwell/25 25.00 60.00
320 Bill Cartwright/25 30.00 80.00
321 Anfernee Hardaway/25 300.00 600.00
322 Mark Jackson/25 30.00 80.00
323 Kiki Vandeweghe/25 30.00 80.00
325 Jeff Malone/25 30.00 80.00
326 Magic Johnson/25 1,000.00 2,000.00
327 Kareem Abdul-Jabbar/25 1,000.00 2,000.00
328 Julius Erving/25 1,000.00 2,000.00
329 Xavier McDaniel/25 30.00 80.00
330 Dikembe Mutombo/25 100.00 200.00
331 Harrison Barnes/25 60.00 150.00
332 Tiago Splitter/25 25.00 60.00
335 Danny Green/25 75.00 200.00
336 Tyson Chandler/25 30.00 80.00
337 Raymond Felton/25 25.00 60.00
338 Kendrick Perkins/25 25.00 60.00
339 Kevin Durant/25 1,000.00 2,000.00
340 Reggie Jackson/25 40.00 100.00
341 Ryan Anderson/25 25.00 60.00
342 Gordon Hayward/25 30.00 80.00
343 Anthony Davis/25 200.00 500.00
344 Jrue Holiday/25 50.00 120.00
346 Ersan Ilyasova/25 25.00 60.00
348 LaMarcus Aldridge/25 100.00 250.00
349 Chris Andersen/25 100.00 250.00
351 Nick Young/25 60.00 150.00
353 Steve Nash/25 300.00 600.00
354 Bernard King/25 50.00 120.00
355 James Harden/25 400.00 800.00
356 Andre Iguodala/25 40.00 100.00
357 Stephen Curry/25 3,000.00 6,000.00
358 Kyrie Irving/25 400.00 800.00
359 Andre Drummond/25 40.00 100.00
360 Josh Smith/25 25.00 60.00
361 Jose Calderon/25 25.00 60.00
364 Bradley Beal/25 125.00 300.00
365 Zach Randolph/25 30.00 80.00
366 Gal Mekel/25 20.00 50.00
367 Kelly Olynyk/25 25.00 60.00
368 Victor Oladipo/25 150.00 400.00
369 Michael Carter-Williams/25 25.00 60.00
370 Alex Len/25 25.00 60.00
371 Archie Goodwin/25 20.00 50.00
372 Anthony Bennett/25 20.00 50.00
373 Ricky Ledo/25 20.00 50.00
374 Tony Snell/25 25.00 60.00
375 Tim Hardaway Jr./25 40.00 100.00
376 Solomon Hill/25 25.00 60.00
377 Nerlens Noel/25 25.00 60.00
378 Trey Burke/25 25.00 60.00
379 Erik Murphy/25 20.00 50.00
380 G.Antetokounmpo/25 10,000.00 15,000.00
381 Jeff Withey/25 20.00 50.00
382 Dennis Schroder/25 75.00 200.00
383 Shane Larkin/25 20.00 50.00

384 Nate Wolters/25 20.00 50.00
385 Ryan Kelly/25 20.00 50.00
386 Matthew Dellavedova/25 30.00 80.00
387 Allen Crabbe/25 20.00 50.00
388 Carrick Felix/25 20.00 50.00
389 Jamaal Franklin/25 20.00 50.00
390 Peyton Siva/25 20.00 50.00
391 Cody Zeller/25 25.00 60.00
392 Tony Mitchell/25 20.00 50.00
393 Mason Plumlee/25 25.00 60.00
394 Kentavious Caldwell-Pope/25 30.00 80.00
395 Shabazz Muhammad/25 20.00 50.00
396 Ben McLemore/25 25.00 60.00
397 C.J. McCollum/25 400.00 800.00
398 Steven Adams/25 125.00 300.00
399 Otto Porter/25 30.00 80.00
400 Luigi Datome/25 20.00 50.00

2013-14 Panini Preferred Cavaliers Memorabilia

STATED PRINT RUN 199 SER.#'d SETS
*PRIME: 1.2X TO 3X BASIC
1 Be/Ma/Ir/Ze/Da/Na/Pr/Th 75.00 200.00

2013-14 Panini Preferred Celtics Memorabilia

PRINT RUNS B/WN 99-199 COPIES PER
*PRIME: 1.2X TO 3X BASIC
1 Bi/Mc/Br/Jo/Su/Ro/Pa/199 60.00 150.00
2 Ho/Mc/Pa/Ju/Bi/Le/Mc/99 75.00 200.00

2013-14 Panini Preferred Clippers Memorabilia

STATED PRINT RUN 199 SER.#'d SETS
*PRIME: 1.2X TO 3X BASIC
1 Gr/Pa/Jo/Wi/Ri/Hi/Cr/Ha 30.00 80.00
2 Pa/Du/Ba/Bu/Gr/Jo/Re/Cr 30.00 80.00

2013-14 Panini Preferred Decades Memorabilia

PRINT RUNS BW/N 99-199 COPIES PER
*PRIME: 1.2X TO 3X BASIC
1 Du/Mc/Iv/No/Br/O'N/Ca/199 125.00 300.00
2 Ew/Pi/Ke/Dr/Ro/St/Ma/99 75.00 200.00
3 En/Th/Bi/Jo/Ma/Ab/Pa/99 75.00 200.00
4 Da/An/Ha/Du/Ir/Ja/Ho/199 125.00 300.00

2013-14 Panini Preferred Europe Memorabilia

STATED PRINT RUN 199 SER.#'d SETS
1 Ba/Da/Ga/Ca/Ga/Ru 20.00 50.00
2 Dr/Vu/St/Ku/Te/Ne 20.00 50.00
3 Di/Sc/Sc/Ba/Pa/No 40.00 100.00
4 Sa/De/Se/Il/Go/Ka 20.00 50.00

2013-14 Panini Preferred Europe Memorabilia Prime

*PRIME: 1.2X TO 3X BASIC
STATED PRINT RUN 25 SER.#'d SETS

2013-14 Panini Preferred Finals Memorabilia

STATED PRINT RUN 99 SER.#'d SETS
*PRIME/10-25: 1.2X TO 3X BASIC
NO PRICING ON QTY 10
1 Chris Andersen 8.00 20.00
2 Chris Bosh 12.00 30.00
3 Dwyane Wade 20.00 50.00
4 LeBron James 300.00 600.00
5 Mario Chalmers 8.00 20.00
6 Ray Allen 15.00 40.00
7 Danny Green 8.00 20.00
8 Kawhi Leonard 30.00 80.00
9 Manu Ginobili 20.00 50.00
10 Tim Duncan 25.00 60.00
11 Tony Parker 15.00 40.00
12 Tracy McGrady 15.00 40.00

2013-14 Panini Preferred Finals Memorabilia Prime

*PRIME: 1.2X TO 3X BASIC
STATED PRINT RUN 25 SER.#'d SETS
3 Dwyane Wade 100.00 250.00
6 Ray Allen 75.00 200.00
8 Kawhi Leonard 100.00 250.00
9 Manu Ginobili 100.00 250.00
10 Tim Duncan 125.00 300.00
11 Tony Parker 75.00 200.00

2013-14 Panini Preferred Houston Memorabilia

STATED PRINT RUN 199 SER.#'d SETS
*PRIME/25: 1.2X TO 3X BASIC
1 Ha/Ca/Be/Jo/Pa/Ho/Li 40.00 100.00
2 Mu/Ha/Li/Ho/Mc/Ba/Dr 40.00 100.00
3 Mu/Ho/Jo/As/Jo/Ol/Mi 40.00 100.00

2013-14 Panini Preferred Jumbo Book Memorabilia

STATED PRINT RUN 149 SER.#'d SETS
1 Kobe Bryant 125.00 300.00
2 LeBron James 125.00 300.00
3 Tim Duncan 25.00 60.00
4 Kevin Love 10.00 25.00
5 Carmelo Anthony 15.00 40.00
6 Dirk Nowitzki 25.00 60.00
7 Kevin Durant 30.00 80.00
8 Anthony Davis 30.00 80.00
9 Paul George 15.00 40.00
10 Shaquille O'Neal 40.00 100.00
11 Grant Hill 15.00 40.00
12 David Robinson 20.00 50.00

2013-14 Panini Preferred Jumbo Book Memorabilia Prime

*PRIME: 1.2X TO 3X BASIC
PRINT RUNS B/WN 10-25 COPIES PER
NO PRICING ON QTY 10
2 LeBron James/25 1,000.00 2,000.00

2013-14 Panini Preferred Knicks Memorabilia

STATED PRINT RUN 199 SER.#'d SETS
*PRIME/25: 1.2X TO 3X BASIC
1 Sh/Fe/Ch/St/An/Pr 40.00 100.00
2 Oa/Ew/St/An/Jo/Ch 40.00 100.00
3 St/Ew/Ma/Oa/Va/Ja 40.00 100.00
4 Ki/An/St/Va/Fe/Sm 40.00 100.00

2013-14 Panini Preferred Lake Show Memorabilia

*PRIME/25: 1.2X TO 3X BASIC
1 Hi/Br/Yo/Na/Me/Fa/Ga/He/199 75.00 200.00
2 We/Ab/Ri/O'N/Na/Wo/Br/Co/49 125.00 300.00

2013-14 Panini Preferred One on One Rivalry Memorabilia

PRINT RUNS B/WN 99-199 COPIES PER
*PRIME/10-25: 1.2X TO 3X BASIC
NO PRICING ON QTY 10
1 D.Robinson/H.Olajuwon/199 20.00 50.00
2 H.Olajuwon/P.Ewing/199 20.00 50.00
3 J.Erving/L.Bird/99 40.00 100.00
4 K.Bryant/T.McGrady/199 80.00 200.00
5 T.Duncan/S.O'Neal/199 40.00 100.00
6 C.Paul/D.Williams/199 20.00 50.00
7 K.Durant/L.James/199 75.00 200.00
8 L.Bird/M.Johnson/99 75.00 200.00
9 MCW/V.Oladipo/199 15.00 40.00
10 B.McLemore/T.Burke/199 8.00 20.00
11 K.Durant/C.Anthony/199 30.00 80.00
12 P.Pierce/L.James/199 75.00 200.00
13 T.Chambers/K.Malone/199 20.00 50.00
14 M.Jackson/J.Stockton/199 20.00 50.00
15 A.English/B.King/199 12.00 30.00
16 D.Nowitzki/T.Duncan/199 25.00 60.00
17 M.Gasol/P.Gasol/199 15.00 40.00
18 C.Bosh/J.Noah/199 12.00 30.00

2013-14 Panini Preferred Rookie Memorabilia

COMMON CARD 10.00 25.00
STATED PRINT RUN 249 SER.#'d SETS
*PRIME/25: 1.2X TO 3X BASIC
1 Len/Bennett/Zeller
Noel/Porter/Oladipo 10.00 25.00
2 McCollum/McLemore/Caldwell-Pope/Carter-
Williams/Adams/Burke 10.00 25.00
3 McLemore/Withey/Burke
Zeller/Hardaway/Oladipo 10.00 25.00
4 McCollum/Hardaway/Oladipo/McLemore
Carter-Williams/Burke 10.00 25.00
5 Adams/Len/Zeller
Olynyk/Plumlee/Noel 10.00 25.00
6 Len/Adams/Bennett/Schroder
Mekel/Antetokounmpo 40.00 100.00
7 Porter/Muhammad/Hill
Antetokounmpo/Bullock/Snell 40.00 100.00
8 Gian/Carter-Willi/Adam/Bur/Oly/Ola 40.00 100.00

2013-14 Panini Preferred Rookie Rotation Memorabilia

STATED PRINT RUN 249 SER.#'d SETS
*PRIME/25: 1.2X TO 3X BASIC
1 Michael Carter-Williams 3.00 8.00
2 Ben McLemore 3.00 8.00
3 Shabazz Muhammad 2.50 6.00
4 Victor Oladipo 6.00 15.00
5 Otto Porter 4.00 10.00
6 Trey Burke 3.00 8.00
7 C.J. McCollum 10.00 25.00
8 Giannis Antetokounmpo 125.00 300.00
9 Steven Adams 6.00 15.00
10 Tim Hardaway Jr. 5.00 12.00
11 Anthony Bennett 2.50 6.00
12 Kelly Olynyk 3.00 8.00

2013-14 Panini Preferred Two on Two Rivalry Memorabilia

PRINT RUNS B/WN 49-199 COPIES PER
*PRIME/5-25 1.2X TO 3X BASIC
NO PRICING ON QTY 15 OR LESS
1 Wad/Hib/Jam/Geo/199 80.00 200.00
2 Dur/Par/Iba/Dun/199 30.00 80.00
3 Sto/Dre/Ola/Mal/199 20.00 50.00
4 Mou/Mas/Joh/Ewi/49 15.00 40.00
5 Lai/Bir/Par/Mah/149 40.00 100.00
6 Dum/Joh/Joh/Abd/99 40.00 100.00
7 Byn/Gar/Bry/Pie/199 80.00 200.00
8 Dun/Sto/Gin/Nas/199 25.00 60.00
9 Mut/Gin/Dun/McG/199 25.00 60.00
10 Var/Jam/But/Jam/99 80.00 200.00
11 Sto/Kuk/Mal/Pip/99 25.00 60.00
12 Ola/Wor/Abd/Sam/49 30.00 80.00
13 Ant/Wil/Gar/Cha/199 25.00 60.00
14 Gri/Bry/Gas/Jor/199 80.00 200.00
15 Dau/Pri/Pip/Kuk/199 25.00 60.00
16 Ant/Jam/Gas/Gas/199 80.00 200.00
17 Dre/Pay/Ola/Ken/199 20.00 50.00

2013-14 Panini Preferred USA Memorabilia

PRINT RUNS BW/N 99-199 COPIES PER
*PRIME/25: 1.2X TO 3X BASIC
1 Mu/Dr/Ma/Jo/Bi/Pi/99 60.00 150.00
2 Ho/O'N/Mo/Ro/Ga/Ja/199 60.00 150.00
3 La/Wi/Du/Ja/An/Pa/199 60.00 150.00
4 Be/Du/Dr/Co/Ha/Cu/199 40.00 100.00

2013-14 Panini Preferred Warriors Memorabilia

PRINT RUNS BW/N 49-199 COPIES PER
*PRIME/25: 1.2X TO 3X BASIC
1 Ig/Bo/Ba/O'N/Th/Cu/Le/Gr/199 75.00 200.00
2 Ig/Mu/Th/Ba/Ba/Th/Cu/Fr/49 75.00 200.00

2014-15 Panini Preferred

AU PRINT RUNS B/WN 25-99 COPIES PER
SL JSY AU PRINT RUN B/WN 35-99 COPIES PER
OVERALL ODDS THREE AU PER BOX
EXCHANGE DEADLINE 12/17/2016
1 Aaron Gordon RB AU/99 25.00 60.00
2 Andrew Wiggins RB AU/35 75.00 200.00
3 Elfrid Payton RB AU/35 8.00 20.00
4 James Ennis RB AU/99 4.00 10.00
5 Bojan Bogdanovic RB AU/99 6.00 15.00
6 Damjan Rudez RB AU/99 4.00 10.00
8 Zoran Dragic RB AU/99 4.00 10.00
9 Jordan Clarkson RB AU/99 15.00 40.00
10 T.J. Warren RB AU/99 6.00 15.00
12 Nikola Mirotic RB AU/99 6.00 15.00
13 Doug McDermott RB AU/99 8.00 20.00
14 Spencer Dinwiddie RB AU/99 5.00 12.00
16 K.J. McDaniels RB AU/99 4.00 10.00
17 Jerami Grant RB AU/99 20.00 50.00
18 Travis Wear RB AU/99 4.00 10.00
19 Shabazz Napier RB AU/99 5.00 12.00
20 Jabari Parker RB AU/35 6.00 15.00
21 Johnny O'Bryant RB AU/99 4.00 10.00
22 Cory Jefferson RB AU/99 4.00 10.00
23 Devyn Marble RB AU/99 4.00 10.00
24 Russ Smith RB AU/99 4.00 10.00
25 Jarnell Stokes RB AU/99 4.00 10.00
26 Lucas Nogueira RB AU/99 4.00 10.00
27 Gary Harris RB AU/35 8.00 20.00
28 Jusuf Nurkic RB AU/99 15.00 40.00
29 Erick Green RB AU/99 4.00 10.00
30 Glenn Robinson III RB AU/35 6.00 15.00
31 Rodney Hood RB AU/99 6.00 15.00
32 Bruno Caboclo RB AU/35 6.00 15.00
33 Marcus Smart RB AU/35 20.00 50.00
34 James Young RB AU/35 5.00 12.00
35 Dante Exum RB AU/35 8.00 20.00
36 Kevin Durant RB AU/35 75.00 200.00
37 Kobe Bryant RB AU/35 100.00 250.00
38 Kyrie Irving RB AU/35 50.00 120.00
39 Carmelo Anthony RB AU/35 20.00 50.00
41 Victor Oladipo RB AU/35 6.00 15.00
43 Michael Kidd-Gilchrist RB AU/25 5.00 12.00
44 Otto Porter RB AU/25 6.00 15.00
45 Bradley Beal RB AU/25 10.00 25.00
46 John Wall RB AU/35 30.00 80.00
47 Kelly Olynyk RB AU/99 4.00 10.00
48 Tyler Zeller RB AU/99 4.00 10.00
49 Harrison Barnes RB AU/25 6.00 15.00
50 Stephen Curry RB AU/35 500.00 1,000.00
51 Carl Landry RB AU/35 5.00 12.00
52 Ben McLemore RB AU/25 5.00 12.00
53 Blake Griffin RB AU/25 25.00 60.00
54 Goran Dragic RB AU/25 8.00 20.00
55 Ty Lawson RB AU/25 5.00 12.00
56 LaMarcus Aldridge RB AU/25 12.00 30.00
57 Udonis Haslem RB AU/35 6.00 15.00
60 Steven Adams RB AU/99 8.00 20.00
61 Giannis Antetokounmpo RB AU/99 75.00 200.00
62 Tim Hardaway Jr. RB AU/99 5.00 12.00
63 Jason Terry RB AU/25 6.00 15.00
64 Josh Smith RB AU/25 5.00 12.00
66 Mason Plumlee RB AU/99 4.00 10.00
67 Anthony Davis RB AU/35 50.00 120.00
68 Brook Lopez RB AU/25 8.00 20.00
69 Rudy Gobert RB AU/99 10.00 25.00
71 Marques Johnson RB AU/99 5.00 12.00
72 Rudy Tomjanovich RB AU/75 6.00 15.00
73 Scott Brooks RB AU/25 5.00 12.00
74 Mark Price RB AU/99 6.00 15.00
75 Zydrunas Ilgauskas RB AU/99 5.00 12.00
76 Clifford Robinson RB AU/99 6.00 15.00
77 Terry Porter RB AU/99 4.00 10.00
78 Dikembe Mutombo RB AU/25 12.00 30.00
79 Rod Strickland RB AU/99 5.00 12.00
80 Cedric Maxwell RB AU/99 5.00 12.00
81 Mark Aguirre RB AU/99 5.00 12.00
82 Adrian Dantley RB AU/99 6.00 15.00
83 Alex English RB AU/99 8.00 20.00
84 Horace Grant RB AU/25 12.00 30.00
85 Fat Lever RB AU/60 6.00 15.00
87 Ron Harper RB AU/99 6.00 15.00
88 Michael Finley RB AU/25 8.00 20.00
91 Hakeem Olajuwon RB AU/25 15.00 40.00
92 Magic Johnson RB AU/35 30.00 80.00
93 James Worthy RB AU/25 12.00 30.00
94 Steve Nash RB AU/25 20.00 50.00
95 George Gervin RB AU/25 12.00 30.00
96 Bill Walton RB AU/25 12.00 30.00
97 Gary Payton RB AU/25 12.00 30.00
98 Clyde Drexler RB AU/25 12.00 30.00
100 Scott Skiles RB AU/99 5.00 12.00
101 Tim Hardaway Jr. CR AU/75 5.00 12.00
102 Bill Cartwright CR AU/35 6.00 15.00
103 Ty Lawson CR AU/35 5.00 12.00
104 Steve Nash CR AU/35 40.00 100.00
105 Eddie Jones CR AU/75 6.00 15.00
107 Don Nelson CR AU/35 12.00 30.00
108 Alonzo Mourning CR AU/35 20.00 50.00
109 Jeff Malone CR AU/75 4.00 10.00
111 George Gervin CR AU/35 12.00 30.00
112 Tracy McGrady CR AU/35 25.00 60.00
113 Jim Jackson CR AU/75 5.00 12.00
114 Kurt Rambis CR AU/35 6.00 15.00
115 Mark Jackson CR AU/35 6.00 15.00
116 Kevin Love CR AU/35 12.00 30.00
118 Mark Aguirre CR AU/35 6.00 15.00
119 Nate Archibald CR AU/35 10.00 25.00
120 Michael Kidd-Gilchrist CR AU/35 5.00 12.00
121 Mateen Cleaves CR AU/75 4.00 10.00
122 Chase Budinger CR AU/35 5.00 12.00
123 Ralph Sampson CR AU/35 8.00 20.00
124 Grant Hill CR AU/35 20.00 50.00
125 Maurice Cheeks CR AU/75 5.00 12.00
126 Courtney Lee CR AU/35 5.00 12.00
127 Avery Johnson CR AU/35 6.00 15.00
128 Victor Oladipo CR AU/35 6.00 15.00
129 Sean Elliott CR AU/75 6.00 15.00
130 Jonas Valanciunas CR AU/35 6.00 15.00
131 Kyle Korver CR AU/35 6.00 15.00
132 Rick Barry CR AU/35 10.00 25.00
133 Antoine Walker CR AU/75 5.00 12.00
134 Robert Horry CR AU/35 10.00 25.00
135 J.R. Smith CR AU/35 8.00 20.00
136 Zach Randolph CR AU/35 8.00 20.00
137 Spencer Hawes CR AU/75 4.00 10.00
138 Reggie Jackson CR AU/35 6.00 15.00
141 Thaddeus Young CR AU/75 4.00 10.00
142 Jamaal Wilkes CR AU/35 8.00 20.00
143 D. Mutombo CR AU/35 12.00 30.00
145 Timofey Mozgov CR AU/75 6.00 15.00
146 George McGinnis CR AU/35 5.00 12.00
147 Jose Calderon CR AU/35 5.00 12.00
148 Byron Scott CR AU/35 8.00 20.00
149 Bill Laimbeer CR AU/75 8.00 20.00
150 G.Antetokounmpo CR AU/75 60.00 150.00
151 Richard Jefferson CR AU/35 6.00 15.00
152 L. Aldridge CR AU/35 12.00 30.00
153 Dee Brown CR AU/75 5.00 12.00
154 C.J. Watson CR AU/75 4.00 10.00
155 Glen Rice CR AU/35 8.00 20.00
156 Isiah Thomas CR AU/35 10.00 25.00
157 Jack Sikma CR AU/75 6.00 15.00
158 Adrian Smith CR AU/75 5.00 12.00
159 Tiago Splitter CR AU/35 5.00 12.00
160 Walt Frazier CR AU/35 10.00 25.00
161 Larry Nance CR AU/75 5.00 12.00
162 Darryl Dawkins CR AU/75 6.00 15.00
163 Marcin Gortat CR AU/35 10.00 25.00
164 Michael Finley CR AU/35 8.00 20.00
165 Ron Harper CR AU/75 6.00 15.00
167 Toni Kukoc CR AU/35 10.00 25.00
169 Evan Fournier CR AU/75 4.00 10.00
170 Mychal Thompson CR AU/75 5.00 12.00
173 John Starks CR AU/75 5.00 12.00
174 DeMarre Carroll CR AU/75 6.00 15.00
176 Rick Fox CR AU/35 6.00 15.00
177 Troy Daniels CR AU/75 4.00 10.00
178 Alec Burks CR AU/75 5.00 12.00
180 Joe Dumars CR AU/35 10.00 25.00
181 Mirza Teletovic CR AU/75 4.00 10.00
182 Arvydas Sabonis CR AU/75 8.00 20.00
184 Jerry Lucas CR AU/35 10.00 25.00
185 P.J. Tucker CR AU/75 5.00 12.00
187 Tobias Harris CR AU/35 6.00 15.00
188 Dolph Schayes CR AU/35 8.00 20.00
190 Zydrunas Ilgauskas CR AU/75 5.00 12.00
191 Lance Stephenson CR AU/35 6.00 15.00
192 Kevin Martin CR AU/35 6.00 15.00
193 Solomon Hill CR AU/75 4.00 10.00
194 Walter Davis CR AU/75 5.00 12.00
195 Tom Chambers CR AU/35 8.00 20.00
196 Shabazz Muhammad CR AU/35 5.00 12.00
197 Phil Pressey CR AU/75 4.00 10.00
198 Norm Nixon CR AU/75 5.00 12.00
199 Satch Sanders CR AU/35 12.00 30.00
200 Tristan Thompson CR AU/35 5.00 12.00
201 Jabari Parker CR AU/49 RC 5.00 12.00
202 A. Wiggins CR AU/49 RC 40.00 100.00
203 Joel Embiid CR AU/49 RC 60.00 150.00
204 Marcus Smart CR AU/49 RC 15.00 40.00
205 Dante Exum CR AU/49 RC 6.00 15.00
206 Julius Randle CR AU/49 RC 15.00 40.00
207 Aaron Gordon CR AU/49 RC 20.00 50.00
208 Noah Vonleh CR AU/49 RC 4.00 10.00
209 Tyler Ennis CR AU/49 RC 4.00 10.00
211 Elfrid Payton CR AU/49 RC 6.00 15.00
212 Doug McDermott CR AU/49 RC 6.00 15.00
213 James Young CR AU/49 RC 4.00 10.00
214 Jusuf Nurkic CR AU/49 RC 12.00 30.00
215 Zach LaVine CR AU/49 RC 15.00 40.00
216 Glenn Robinson III CR AU/49 RC 5.00 12.00
217 Bojan Bogdanovic CR AU/49 RC 6.00 15.00
218 Damjan Rudez CR AU/49 RC 4.00 10.00
220 Jordan Adams CR AU/49 RC 4.00 10.00
221 Bruno Caboclo CR AU/49 RC 5.00 12.00
224 Markel Brown CR AU/49 RC 4.00 10.00
225 Lucas Nogueira CR AU/49 RC 4.00 10.00
227 Joe Harris CR AU/49 RC 6.00 15.00
228 Devyn Marble CR AU/49 RC 4.00 10.00
229 Johnny O'Bryant CR AU/49 RC 4.00 10.00
230 J. Clarkson CR AU/49 RC 10.00 25.00
231 Erick Green CR AU/49 RC 4.00 10.00
232 James Ennis CR AU/49 RC 4.00 10.00
233 Nikola Mirotic CR AU/49 RC 15.00 40.00
234 K. Bryant SL JSY AU/35 200.00 500.00
236 C. Anthony SL JSY AU/35 40.00 100.00
237 Kevin Durant SL JSY AU/35 60.00 150.00
238 J. Stockton SL JSY AU/35 30.00 80.00
239 Blake Griffin SL JSY AU/35 25.00 60.00
240 Kyrie Irving SL JSY AU/35 50.00 120.00
241 D. Robinson SL JSY AU/35 20.00 50.00
242 John Wall SL JSY AU/35 20.00 50.00
244 C.Drexler SL JSY AU/35 25.00 60.00
245 H. Olajuwon SL JSY AU/35 20.00 50.00
246 Jason Kidd SL JSY AU/35 20.00 50.00
247 Kevin Love SL JSY AU/35 20.00 50.00
248 Tony Parker SL JSY AU/35 25.00 60.00
249 Michael Kidd-
Gilchrist SL JSY AU/35 6.00 15.00
250 Steph Curry SL JSY AU/35 500.00 1,000.00
251 Chris Andersen SL JSY AU/35 8.00 20.00
254 Tyreke Evans SL JSY AU/35 8.00 20.00
255 Tyson Chandler SL JSY AU/35 10.00 25.00
256 Matthew Dellavedova SL JSY AU/35 8.00 20.00
258 Brent Barry SL JSY AU/35 6.00 15.00
259 Andre Drummond SL JSY AU/35 8.00 20.00
260 Isiah Thomas SL JSY AU/35 15.00 40.00
261 L. Aldridge SL JSY AU/35 20.00 50.00
263 Tobias Harris SL JSY AU/60 6.00 15.00
264 Goran Dragic SL JSY AU/35 10.00 25.00
266 Grant Hill SL JSY AU/35 25.00 60.00
267 Kemba Walker SL JSY AU/35 10.00 25.00
268 Tristan Thompson SL JSY AU/35 6.00 15.00
269 D. Mutombo SL JSY AU/60 12.00 30.00
270 Kenneth Faried SL JSY AU/60 5.00 12.00
271 Carl Landry SL JSY AU/60 5.00 12.00
272 D. Schroder SL JSY AU/60 8.00 20.00
273 Wesley Matthews SL JSY AU/60 5.00 12.00
274 Clifford Robinson SL JSY AU/60 8.00 20.00
276 Robert Horry SL JSY AU/60 8.00 20.00
277 Marques Johnson SL JSY AU/60 6.00 15.00
279 Danny Manning SL JSY AU/60 6.00 15.00
280 Dan Majerle SL JSY AU/60 6.00 15.00
281 Alan Anderson SL JSY AU/60 5.00 12.00
282 Maurice Harkless SL JSY AU/60 5.00 12.00
283 Adrian Dantley SL JSY AU/60 8.00 20.00
284 Nick Young SL JSY AU/60 5.00 12.00
285 Luis Scola SL JSY AU/35 8.00 20.00
286 Archie Goodwin SL JSY AU/60 5.00 12.00
287 Steven Adams SL JSY AU/60 10.00 25.00
289 Timofey Mozgov SL JSY AU/60 5.00 12.00
290 Walter Davis SL JSY AU/60 6.00 15.00
291 Evan Fournier SL JSY AU/60 5.00 12.00
293 Mason Plumlee SL JSY AU/60 5.00 12.00
294 Mirza Teletovic SL JSY AU/60 5.00 12.00
295 G. Hayward SL JSY AU/60 12.00 30.00
296 A. Gordon SL JSY AU/99 RC 60.00 150.00
297 Wiggins SL JSY AU/99 RC 40.00 100.00
298 E. Payton SL JSY AU/99 RC 20.00 50.00
299 James Ennis SL JSY AU/99 RC 5.00 12.00
300 Russ Smith SL JSY AU/99 RC 5.00 12.00
301 Jarnell Stokes SL JSY AU/99 RC 5.00 12.00
303 M. Smart SL JSY AU/99 RC 10.00 25.00
304 Tyler Ennis SL JSY AU/99 RC 5.00 12.00
305 TJ Warren SL JSY AU/99 RC 40.00 100.00
307 Bruno Caboclo SL JSY AU/99 RC 6.00 15.00
308 McDermott SL JSY AU/99 RC 8.00 20.00
309 Spencer Dinwiddie
SL JSY AU/99 RC 8.00 20.00
310 Embiid SL JSY AU/99 RC 200.00 400.00
311 K.J. McDaniels SL JSY AU/99 RC 5.00 12.00
312 Jerami Grant SL JSY AU/99 RC 25.00 60.00
314 Shabazz Napier SL JSY AU/99 RC 6.00 15.00
315 J. Parker SL JSY AU/99 RC 6.00 15.00
316 Johnny O'Bryant SL JSY AU/99 RC 5.00 12.00
318 Damien Inglis SL JSY AU/99 RC 5.00 12.00
319 James Young SL JSY AU/99 RC 5.00 12.00
320 D.Exum SL JSY AU/99 RC 8.00 20.00
321 Jordan Adams SL JSY AU/99 RC 5.00 12.00
322 Gary Harris SL JSY AU/99 RC 8.00 20.00
323 R.Hood SL JSY AU/99 RC 10.00 25.00
324 Glenn Robinson III
SL JSY AU/99 RC 6.00 15.00
325 J. Randle SL JSY AU/99 RC 20.00 50.00
326 Joe Harris SL JSY AU/99 RC 8.00 20.00
327 Noah Vonleh SL JSY AU/99 RC 5.00 12.00
329 Adreian Payne SL JSY AU/99 RC 5.00 12.00
330 Cory Jefferson SL JSY AU/99 RC 5.00 12.00
331 Markel Brown SL JSY AU/99 RC 5.00 12.00
332 C.J. Wilcox SL JSY AU/99 RC 5.00 12.00
333 Z. LaVine SL JSY AU/99 RC 40.00 100.00
334 A. Wiggins DD AU/49 75.00 200.00
335 Dante Exum DD AU/49 6.00 15.00
336 Jabari Parker DD AU/49 5.00 12.00
337 Marcus Smart DD AU/49 15.00 40.00
338 Shabazz Napier DD AU/49 5.00 12.00
340 Spencer Dinwiddie DD AU/49 6.00 15.00
341 Erick Green DD AU/49 4.00 10.00
342 Jordan Clarkson DD AU/49 20.00 50.00
343 Julius Randle DD AU/49 15.00 40.00
344 Aaron Gordon DD AU/49 20.00 50.00
345 James Ennis DD AU/49 4.00 10.00
346 Zach LaVine DD AU/49 15.00 40.00
347 Gary Harris DD AU/49 6.00 15.00
348 Jusuf Nurkic DD AU/49 12.00 30.00
350 Rodney Hood DD AU/49 5.00 12.00
351 Bojan Bogdanovic DD AU/49 6.00 15.00
352 Nikola Mirotic DD AU/49 25.00 60.00
353 Glenn Robinson III DD AU/49 5.00 12.00
354 Travis Wear DD AU/49 4.00 10.00
355 Devyn Marble DD AU/49 4.00 10.00
356 Elfrid Payton DD AU/49 6.00 15.00
358 Joe Harris DD AU/49 6.00 15.00
359 K.J. McDaniels DD AU/49 4.00 10.00
360 Bruno Caboclo DD AU/49 5.00 12.00
361 C.J. Wilcox DD AU/49 4.00 10.00
362 Jarnell Stokes DD AU/49 4.00 10.00
363 Cory Jefferson DD AU/49 4.00 10.00
364 Noah Vonleh DD AU/49 4.00 10.00
365 Tyler Ennis DD AU/49 4.00 10.00
366 Doug McDermott DD AU/49 6.00 15.00
367 Jabari Parker RR AU/49 RC 5.00 12.00
368 A. Wiggins RR AU/49 RC 50.00 120.00
369 Joel Embiid RR AU/49 RC 100.00 250.00
370 Marcus Smart RR AU/49 RC 15.00 40.00
371 Dante Exum RR AU/49 RC 6.00 15.00
372 Julius Randle RR AU/49 RC 15.00 40.00
373 Aaron Gordon RR AU/49 RC 20.00 50.00
374 Noah Vonleh RR AU/49 RC 4.00 10.00
375 Tyler Ennis RR AU/49 RC 4.00 10.00
377 Elfrid Payton RR AU/49 RC 6.00 15.00
378 T.J. Warren RR AU/49 RC 6.00 15.00
379 C.J. Wilcox RR AU/49 RC 4.00 10.00
380 Zach LaVine RR AU/49 RC 15.00 40.00
381 Adreian Payne RR AU/49 RC 4.00 10.00
382 Damjan Rudez RR AU/49 RC 4.00 10.00
383 Jordan Adams RR AU/49 RC 4.00 10.00
384 Jarnell Stokes RR AU/49 RC 4.00 10.00
385 Shabazz Napier RR AU/49 RC 5.00 12.00
386 Damien Inglis RR AU/49 RC 4.00 10.00
388 Devyn Marble RR AU/49 RC 4.00 10.00
389 Travis Wear RR AU/49 RC 4.00 10.00
390 N. Mirotic RR AU/49 RC 20.00 50.00
391 Markel Brown RR AU/49 RC 4.00 10.00
394 J. Clarkson RR AU/49 RC 15.00 40.00
395 Joe Harris RR AU/49 RC 6.00 15.00
396 Bojan Bogdanovic RR AU/49 RC 6.00 15.00
397 Rodney Hood RR AU/49 RC 5.00 12.00
398 Zoran Dragic RR AU/49 RC 5.00 12.00
399 James Young RR AU/49 RC 4.00 10.00
401 Chris Andersen PS AU/30 12.00 30.00
402 Goran Dragic PS AU/30 8.00 20.00
404 Victor Oladipo PS AU/30 6.00 15.00
405 Mark Aguirre PS AU/75 6.00 15.00
406 Phil Pressey PS AU/30 5.00 12.00
407 Alec Burks PS AU/75 5.00 12.00
408 J.R. Smith PS AU/30 8.00 20.00
409 Anthony Davis PS AU/30 50.00 120.00
410 Mason Plumlee PS AU/35 5.00 12.00
411 Tristan Thompson PS AU/30 5.00 12.00
412 Steve Nash PS AU/30 40.00 100.00
413 Dan Issel PS AU/35 10.00 25.00
414 Tim Hardaway PS AU/75 8.00 20.00
415 Kendall Gill PS AU/35 8.00 20.00
416 Gus Williams PS AU/35 8.00 20.00
417 Thaddeus Young PS AU/35 5.00 12.00
419 Andrew Nicholson PS AU/75 4.00 10.00
421 Enes Kanter PS AU/75 4.00 10.00
423 Derrick Williams PS AU/30 5.00 12.00
424 Derrick Favors PS AU/75 5.00 12.00
425 Rod Strickland PS AU/75 5.00 12.00
427 Steve Smith PS AU/75 5.00 12.00
428 Rick Mahorn PS AU/75 5.00 12.00
429 Phil Chenier PS AU/75 5.00 12.00
430 Paul Westphal PS AU/75 6.00 15.00
431 Mychal Thompson PS AU/75 5.00 12.00
433 Kiki Vandeweghe PS AU/75 5.00 12.00
434 Keith Van Horn PS AU/75 5.00 12.00
435 Eddie Jones PS AU/75 6.00 15.00
436 Doug Collins PS AU/75 6.00 15.00
437 Tom Van Arsdale PS AU/75 5.00 12.00
438 Charlie Scott PS AU/75 6.00 15.00
439 Brian Grant PS AU/75 5.00 12.00
441 Bob Dandridge PS AU/75 6.00 15.00
442 Tom Gugliotta PS AU/75 4.00 10.00
443 Wayne Embry PS AU/30 6.00 15.00
444 John Starks PS AU/75 6.00 15.00
445 Robert Horry PS AU/30 8.00 20.00
446 Alonzo Mourning PS AU/30 25.00 60.00
447 Latrell Sprewell PS AU/30 30.00 80.00
448 Bill Walton PS AU/30 12.00 30.00
449 Grant Hill PS AU/30 20.00 50.00
450 Tracy McGrady PS AU/30 30.00 80.00
451 Zach Randolph PS AU/30 8.00 20.00
452 Josh Smith PS AU/30 5.00 12.00
453 Stephen Curry PS AU/30 500.00 1,000.00
454 Kawhi Leonard PS AU/30 60.00 150.00
455 Tobias Harris PS AU/30 6.00 15.00
456 Kenneth Faried PS AU/30 5.00 12.00
459 Iman Shumpert PS AU/30 5.00 12.00
461 Lance Stephenson PS AU/30 6.00 15.00
463 Reggie Jackson PS AU/30 6.00 15.00
465 Nick Collison PS AU/75 5.00 12.00
468 Tyler Zeller PS AU/75 4.00 10.00
469 Maurice Harkless PS AU/75 4.00 10.00
470 Walt Frazier PS AU/30 10.00 25.00
472 Dolph Schayes PS AU/30 8.00 20.00
473 Don Nelson PS AU/30 12.00 30.00
474 George Gervin PS AU/30 12.00 30.00
475 Hal Greer PS AU/30 8.00 20.00
476 James Worthy PS AU/30 12.00 30.00
477 Robert Parish PS AU/30 10.00 25.00
478 Alex English PS AU/30 10.00 25.00
479 David Thompson PS AU/30 8.00 20.00
480 Jason Kidd PS AU/30 15.00 40.00
481 Gary Payton PS AU/30 15.00 40.00
482 Christian Laettner PS AU/30 8.00 20.00
483 Brent Barry PS AU/30 5.00 12.00
484 Michael Finley PS AU/30 12.00 30.00
485 Dave Cowens PS AU/30 10.00 25.00
486 Horace Grant PS AU/30 15.00 40.00
487 Jalen Rose PS AU/30 6.00 15.00
488 Scott Brooks PS AU/30 5.00 12.00
489 Rudy Tomjanovich PS AU/75 6.00 15.00
490 Kevin Love PS AU/30 12.00 30.00
491 Tony Parker PS AU/30 12.00 30.00
492 Muggsy Bogues PS AU/75 8.00 20.00
493 Kenny Smith PS AU/30 6.00 15.00
494 C.Anthony PS AU/30 25.00 60.00
495 Michael Kidd-Gilchrist PS AU/30 5.00 12.00
496 Harrison Barnes PS AU/30 6.00 15.00
497 Tyson Chandler PS AU/30 10.00 25.00
498 John Wall PS AU/30 25.00 60.00
499 Bradley Beal PS AU/30 12.00 30.00
500 Kobe Bryant U AU/50 150.00 400.00
501 Kevin Durant U AU/50 60.00 150.00
502 Kyrie Irving U AU/50 25.00 60.00
503 Anthony Davis U AU/50 75.00 150.00
504 Bradley Beal U AU/50 10.00 25.00
505 John Wall U AU/50 20.00 50.00
506 Tony Parker U AU/50 15.00 40.00
507 Iman Shumpert U AU/50 4.00 10.00
509 Marcin Gortat U AU/50 4.00 10.00
510 Danny Green U AU/50 5.00 12.00
511 Gordon Hayward U AU/50 5.00 12.00
512 Jonas Valanciunas U AU/50 5.00 12.00
514 Lance Stephenson U AU/50 5.00 12.00
515 Reggie Jackson U AU/50 5.00 12.00
517 Corey Brewer U AU/50 4.00 10.00
518 G. Antetokounmpo U AU/50 50.00 120.00
519 Steven Adams U AU/50 8.00 20.00
520 Spencer Hawes U AU/50 4.00 10.00
521 Thaddeus Young U AU/50 4.00 10.00
522 Kelly Olynyk U AU/50 4.00 10.00
524 Lavoy Allen U AU/50 4.00 10.00
525 Gorgui Dieng U AU/50 4.00 10.00
526 Ryan Kelly U AU/50 4.00 10.00
527 Kent Bazemore U AU/50 5.00 12.00
528 P.J. Tucker U AU/50 5.00 12.00
529 Troy Daniels U AU/50 4.00 10.00
530 Mason Plumlee U AU/50 4.00 10.00
531 Enes Kanter U AU/50 5.00 12.00
532 Tobias Harris U AU/50 5.00 12.00
533 Latrell Sprewell U AU/50 25.00 60.00
534 Larry Bird U AU/50 50.00 120.00
535 Magic Johnson U AU/50 30.00 80.00
536 Abdul-Jabbar U AU/50 30.00 80.00
537 Isiah Thomas U AU/50 10.00 25.00
538 Gary Payton U AU/50 10.00 25.00
539 Rick Barry U AU/50 8.00 20.00
540 Alex English U AU/50 8.00 20.00
541 Joe Dumars U AU/50 8.00 20.00
542 George Gervin U AU/50 10.00 25.00
543 Bill Laimbeer U AU/50 6.00 15.00
544 Antoine Walker U AU/50 5.00 12.00
545 Bob McAdoo U AU/50 10.00 25.00
546 Allan Houston U AU/50 6.00 15.00
547 D. Mutombo U AU/50 10.00 25.00
548 Eddie Jones U AU/50 8.00 20.00
550 Jeff Hornacek U AU/50 5.00 12.00
551 Jim Jackson U AU/50 5.00 12.00
552 Muggsy Bogues U AU/50 8.00 20.00
553 Scott Skiles U AU/50 5.00 12.00
554 David Robinson U AU/50 20.00 50.00
555 Tim Hardaway U AU/50 8.00 20.00
556 Kenny Smith U AU/50 5.00 12.00
557 Sidney Moncrief U AU/50 6.00 15.00
558 Mark Aguirre U AU/50 5.00 12.00
559 Adrian Dantley U AU/50 6.00 15.00
560 Jo Jo White U AU/50 6.00 15.00
561 John Salley U AU/50 10.00 25.00
562 Mark Price U AU/50 6.00 15.00
563 Bobby Jones U AU/50 5.00 12.00
564 Doug Collins U AU/50 6.00 15.00
565 Dick Van Arsdale U AU/50 6.00 15.00
566 Aaron Gordon U AU/50 RC 20.00 50.00
567 A. Wiggins U AU/50 RC 60.00 150.00
568 Elfrid Payton U AU/50 RC 6.00 15.00
569 James Ennis U AU/50 RC 4.00 10.00
570 Russ Smith U AU/50 RC 4.00 10.00
572 Marcus Smart U AU/50 RC 15.00 40.00
573 Tyler Ennis U AU/50 RC 4.00 10.00
574 Zoran Dragic U AU/50 RC 5.00 12.00
576 Bruno Caboclo U AU/50 RC 5.00 12.00
577 Doug McDermott U AU/50 RC 6.00 15.00
578 Spencer Dinwiddie U AU/50 RC 6.00 15.00
579 Joel Embiid U AU/50 RC 100.00 250.00
580 K.J. McDaniels U AU/50 RC 4.00 10.00
582 Shabazz Napier U AU/50 RC 5.00 12.00
583 Jabari Parker U AU/50 RC 5.00 12.00
585 Damien Inglis U AU/50 RC 4.00 10.00
586 James Young U AU/50 RC 4.00 10.00
587 Dante Exum U AU/50 RC 6.00 15.00
588 Jordan Adams U AU/50 RC 4.00 10.00
589 Gary Harris U AU/50 RC 6.00 15.00
590 Rodney Hood U AU/50 RC 6.00 15.00
591 Erick Green U AU/50 RC 4.00 10.00
592 Julius Randle U AU/50 RC 15.00 40.00
593 Joe Harris U AU/50 RC 6.00 15.00
594 Noah Vonleh U AU/50 RC 4.00 10.00
596 Adreian Payne U AU/50 RC 4.00 10.00
597 Cory Jefferson U AU/50 RC 4.00 10.00
598 Markel Brown U AU/50 RC 4.00 10.00
599 Zach LaVine U AU/50 RC 20.00 50.00

2014-15 Panini Preferred Purple

*PURPLE: .5X TO 1.2X BASE p/r 49-99
*PURPLE: .4X TO 1X BASE p/r 25-35
OVERALL ODDS THREE AU PER BOX
STATED PRINT RUN 20 SER.#'d SETS
EXCHANGE DEADLINE 12/17/2016

2014-15 Panini Preferred Silhouettes Prime

*SL PRIME: 2.5X TO 6X BASE p/r 60-99
*SL PRIME: 2X TO 5X BASE p/r 25-35
OVERALL ODDS THREE AU PER BOX
PRINT RUNS B/WN 5-25 COPIES PER
NO PRICING ON QTY 15 OR LESS
EXCHANGE DEADLINE 12/17/2016
234 Kobe Bryant/25 1,000.00 3,000.00
238 John Stockton/25 200.00 500.00
239 Blake Griffin/25 150.00 300.00
244 Clyde Drexler/25 75.00 200.00
250 Stephen Curry/25 2,000.00 4,000.00
266 Grant Hill/25 100.00 250.00
296 Aaron Gordon/25 400.00 800.00
297 Andrew Wiggins/25 300.00 600.00
298 Elfrid Payton/25 150.00 400.00
303 Marcus Smart/25 75.00 200.00
305 T.J. Warren/25 300.00 600.00
309 Spencer Dinwiddie/25 60.00 150.00
310 Joel Embiid/25 800.00 1,500.00
320 Dante Exum/25 40.00 100.00
322 Gary Harris/25 125.00 300.00
325 Julius Randle/25 150.00 400.00
333 Zach LaVine/25 400.00 800.00

2014-15 Panini Preferred '14 NBA Finals Game 2 Memorabilia

OVERALL MEM ODDS ONE PER BOX
STATED PRINT RUN 99 SER.#'d SETS
1 Tim Duncan 15.00 40.00
2 Tony Parker 12.00 30.00
3 Kawhi Leonard 15.00 40.00
4 Tiago Splitter 4.00 10.00
5 Danny Green 6.00 15.00
6 Manu Ginobili 8.00 20.00
7 Patty Mills 12.00 30.00
8 Boris Diaw 5.00 12.00
9 Chris Bosh 8.00 20.00
10 Dwyane Wade 8.00 20.00
11 Ray Allen 10.00 25.00
12 Chris Andersen 5.00 12.00
13 Mario Chalmers 5.00 12.00
14 Norris Cole 4.00 10.00
15 Rashard Lewis 5.00 12.00
16 James Jones 4.00 10.00

2014-15 Panini Preferred '14 NBA Finals Game 2 Memorabilia Prime

*PRIME: 2.5X TO 6X BASIC
OVERALL MEM ODDS ONE PER BOX
STATED PRINT RUN 25 SER.#'d SETS
PRICING IS FOR BASIC PATCH CARDS
1 Tim Duncan 250.00 600.00
2 Tony Parker 250.00 600.00
3 Kawhi Leonard 200.00 500.00
6 Manu Ginobili 125.00 300.00

2014-15 Panini Preferred Champs Memorabilia

OVERALL MEM ODDS ONE PER BOX
STATED PRINT RUN 99 SER.#'d SETS
1 Tony Parker 12.00 30.00
2 LeBron James 30.00 80.00
3 Dirk Nowitzki 8.00 20.00
4 Dwyane Wade 10.00 25.00
5 Paul Pierce 8.00 20.00
6 Chris Bosh 6.00 15.00
7 Tim Duncan 25.00 60.00
8 Tayshaun Prince 5.00 12.00
9 Tyson Chandler 5.00 12.00
10 Shaquille O'Neal 15.00 40.00
11 David Robinson 20.00 50.00
12 Hakeem Olajuwon 12.00 30.00

2014-15 Panini Preferred Crazy Eights Memorabilia

OVERALL MEM ODDS ONE PER BOX
STATED PRINT RUN 99 SER.#'d SETS
*PRIME/25: 1.5X TO 4X BASIC
1 R/B/N/H/D/G/G/S 12.00 30.00
2 V/L/I/J/D/M/M/T 20.00 50.00
3 D/G/L/G/B/M/D/P 20.00 50.00
4 I/B/L/G/B/T/S/C 30.00 80.00
5 A/B/W/E/D/C/N/H 8.00 20.00
6 W/D/G/M/P/R/M/L 15.00 40.00
7 B/W/S/G/W/N/P/P 10.00 25.00
8 R/L/D/C/J/W/I/A 12.00 30.00

2014-15 Panini Preferred Playbook Rookie Memorabilia

OVERALL MEM ODDS ONE PER BOX
STATED PRINT RUN 99 SER.#'d SETS
1 Marcus Smart 12.00 30.00
2 Gary Harris 5.00 12.00
3 Noah Vonleh 3.00 8.00
4 Jabari Parker 12.00 30.00
5 Shabazz Napier 4.00 10.00
6 Aaron Gordon 15.00 40.00
7 Joe Harris 5.00 12.00
8 Bruno Caboclo 4.00 10.00
9 Julius Randle 15.00 40.00
10 Doug McDermott 5.00 12.00
11 Nik Stauskas 3.00 8.00
12 Jerami Grant 15.00 40.00
13 Rodney Hood 4.00 10.00
14 James Young 3.00 8.00
15 Zach LaVine 20.00 50.00
16 Andrew Wiggins 12.00 30.00
17 Joel Embiid 20.00 50.00
18 Dante Exum 5.00 12.00
19 T.J. Warren 5.00 12.00
20 Elfrid Payton 5.00 12.00
21 Adreian Payne 3.00 8.00
22 James Ennis 3.00 8.00
23 Kyle Anderson 5.00 12.00
24 Mitch McGary 3.00 8.00
25 Cleanthony Early 3.00 8.00
26 P.J. Hairston 3.00 8.00

2014-15 Panini Preferred Playbook Rookie Memorabilia Prime

*PRIME: 1.5X TO 4X BASIC
OVERALL MEM ODDS ONE PER BOX
STATED PRINT RUN 25 SER.#'d SETS
PRICING IS FOR BASIC PATCH CARDS
15 Zach LaVine 60.00 150.00

2014-15 Panini Preferred Playbook Veteran Memorabilia

OVERALL MEM ODDS ONE PER BOX
STATED PRINT RUN 99 SER.#'d SETS
1 Kobe Bryant 25.00 60.00
2 Chris Bosh 6.00 15.00
3 Kevin Love 10.00 25.00
4 Pau Gasol 8.00 20.00
5 Blake Griffin 5.00 12.00
6 Dirk Nowitzki 10.00 25.00
7 Jimmy Butler 10.00 25.00
8 Dwyane Wade 10.00 25.00
9 Victor Oladipo 4.00 10.00
10 Ricky Rubio 4.00 10.00

2014-15 Panini Preferred Stat Line Memorabilia

OVERALL MEM ODDS ONE PER BOX
STATED PRINT RUN 99 SER.#'d SETS
1 Ricky Rubio 3.00 8.00
2 Klay Thompson 10.00 25.00
3 Kobe Bryant 30.00 80.00
4 Andrew Bogut 3.00 8.00
5 Deron Williams 3.00 8.00
6 Tyreke Evans 3.00 8.00
7 Kyrie Irving 8.00 20.00
8 Anthony Davis 10.00 25.00
9 Joe Johnson 3.00 8.00
10 Dwyane Wade 8.00 20.00
11 Dwight Howard 5.00 12.00
12 Stephen Curry 15.00 40.00
13 James Harden 6.00 15.00
14 Chris Paul 6.00 15.00
15 LaMarcus Aldridge 4.00 10.00
16 Bradley Beal 6.00 15.00
17 Ty Lawson 2.50 6.00
18 John Wall 5.00 12.00
19 Kyle Korver 3.00 8.00
20 DeMarcus Cousins 3.00 8.00

2014-15 Panini Preferred Stat Line Memorabilia Prime

*PRIME: 2.5X TO 6X BASIC
OVERALL MEM ODDS ONE PER BOX
STATED PRINT RUN 25 SER.#'d SETS
PRICING IS FOR BASIC PATCH CARDS
2 Klay Thompson 60.00 150.00
3 Kobe Bryant 150.00 400.00
4 Andrew Bogut 30.00 80.00

2014-15 Panini Preferred Swish Memorabilia

OVERALL MEM ODDS ONE PER BOX
STATED PRINT RUN 99 SER.#'d SETS
1 Kobe Bryant 40.00 100.00
2 Kevin Durant 15.00 40.00
3 Stephen Curry 40.00 100.00
4 Dirk Nowitzki 15.00 40.00
5 James Harden 12.00 30.00
6 Bradley Beal 6.00 15.00

2014-15 Panini Preferred Swish Memorabilia Prime

*PRIME: 2X TO 5X BASIC
OVERALL MEM ODDS ONE PER BOX
STATED PRINT RUN 25 SER.#'d SETS
PRICING IS FOR BASIC PATCH CARDS
1 Kobe Bryant 250.00 400.00
3 Stephen Curry 150.00 400.00

2014-15 Panini Preferred Trending Upward Memorabilia

OVERALL MEM ODDS ONE PER BOX
STATED PRINT RUN 199 SER.#'d SETS
*PRIME/25: .75X TO 2X BASIC
1 Gn/Ws/Em/Pr/Ed/Sl 12.00 30.00
2 Gn/Pn/Es/Vh/Hn/Nr 6.00 15.00
3 Jn/Yg/Gl/Ed/St/Bn 12.00 30.00
4 Ws/Em/Hs/My/Hd/Le 8.00 20.00
5 Em/Pn/St/Nr/De/Le 8.00 20.00
6 Ws/Hs/Yg/Hs/Ss/Le 8.00 20.00
7 Gn/Jn/D'B/Re/My/Vh 6.00 15.00
8 Co/Ey/Mt/Pr/An/Hd 2.00 5.00
9 Ws/Co/Em/Ed/Ss/Es 12.00 30.00
10 Mt/Pn/Re/Ss/Vh/Le 8.00 20.00

2014-15 Panini Preferred VS 1 on 1 Memorabilia

OVERALL MEM ODDS ONE PER BOX
PRINT RUNS B/WN 25-99 COPIES PER
*PRIME/20-25: 2.5X TO 6X BASIC
1 A.Horford/M.Gasol/49 4.00 10.00
2 D.Rose/S.Curry/99 30.00 80.00
3 D.Rose/R.Rondo/99 8.00 20.00
4 K.Love/L.Aldridge/99 4.00 10.00
5 K.Irving/R.Westbrook/99 8.00 20.00
6 B.Lopez/D.Cousins/99 4.00 10.00
7 A.Jefferson/N.Noel/49 2.50 6.00
8 T.Harris/Z.Randolph/49 4.00 10.00
9 B.Griffin/L.James/99 30.00 80.00
10 C.Paul/T.Lawson/49 6.00 15.00
11 D.Jordan/T.Duncan/99 8.00 20.00
12 D.Green/L.James/99 20.00 50.00
13 B.McLemore/M.Ellis/49 3.00 8.00
14 C.Andersen/D.Williams/49 3.00 8.00
15 L.Aldridge/T.Duncan/99 12.00 30.00
16 K.Durant/R.Gay/99 6.00 15.00
17 J.Johnson/P.Pierce/99 6.00 15.00
18 K.Durant/L.James/99 20.00 50.00
19 L.Bird/M.Johnson/25 50.00 120.00
20 I.Thomas/K.McHale/25 10.00 25.00
21 K.McHale/R.Sampson/25 10.00 25.00
22 D.Mutombo/S.O'Neal/25 20.00 50.00
23 A.Iverson/K.Bryant/49 30.00 80.00
24 D.Lee/N.Noel/49 2.50 6.00
25 D.Williams/D.Wade/99 8.00 20.00
26 D.Jordan/V.Oladipo/99 3.00 8.00
27 L.Scola/P.Millsap/49 3.00 8.00
28 C.Parsons/T.Hardaway Jr./49 3.00 8.00

2015-16 Panini Preferred

SL JSY AU PRINT RUN B/WN 21-99 COPIES PER
AU PRINT RUNS B/WN 40-99 COPIES PER
EXCHANGE DEADLINE 2/17/2018
1 Porzingis SL JSY AU/99 RC 75.00 200.00
2 Cauley-Stein SL JSY AU/99 RC 12.00 30.00
3 Portis SL JSY AU/99 RC 10.00 25.00
4 Richardson SL JSY AU/99 RC 6.00 15.00
5 Marcelo Huertas SL JSY AU/99 RC 4.00 10.00
7 R.J. Hunter SL JSY AU/99 RC EXCH 4.00 10.00
8 Payne SL JSY AU/99 RC 6.00 15.00
9 Anderson SL JSY AU/99 RC 4.00 10.00
10 Hezonja SL JSY AU/99 RC 5.00 12.00
11 Richaun Holmes SL JSY AU/99 RC 6.00 15.00
12 Hollis-Jefferson SL JSY AU/99 RC 5.00 12.00
13 Russell SL JSY AU/99 RC EXCH 40.00 100.00
14 Winslow SL JSY AU/99 RC 15.00 40.00
15 Turner SL JSY AU/99 RC 20.00 50.00
16 Anthony Brown SL JSY AU/99 RC 4.00 10.00
17 Luis Montero SL JSY AU/99 RC 8.00 20.00
18 Delon Wright SL JSY AU/99 RC 5.00 12.00
19 Towns SL JSY AU/99 RC 100.00 250.00
20 Nemanja Bjelica SL JSY AU/99 RC 6.00 15.00
21 Salah Mejri SL JSY AU/99 RC 4.00 10.00
22 Powell SL JSY AU/99 RC 8.00 20.00
23 Booker SL JSY AU/99 RC 400.00 800.00
24 Oubre Jr. SL JSY AU/99 RC 8.00 20.00
25 Jokic SL JSY AU/99 RC 800.00 1,500.00
26 Johnson SL JSY AU/99 RC 5.00 12.00
27 Kevon Looney SL JSY AU/99 RC 12.00 30.00
28 Mudiay SL JSY AU/99 RC 5.00 12.00
29 Rozier SL JSY AU/99 RC 20.00 50.00
30 Montrezl Harrell SL JSY AU/99 RC 40.00 100.00
31 Frank Kaminsky SL JSY AU/99 RC 5.00 12.00
32 Lyles SL JSY AU/99 RC 12.00 30.00
33 Okafor SL JSY AU/99 RC 5.00 12.00
34 Jerian Grant SL JSY AU/99 RC 4.00 10.00
35 Joe Young SL JSY AU/99 RC 4.00 10.00
36 Simmons SL JSY AU/99 RC 5.00 12.00
37 Jordan Mickey SL JSY AU/99 RC 4.00 10.00
38 Bryant SL JSY AU/40 500.00 1,000.00
39 Durant SL JSY AU/40 75.00 200.00
40 Irving SL JSY AU/40 40.00 100.00
41 Love SL JSY AU/40 20.00 50.00
42 Wall SL JSY AU/40 20.00 50.00
43 Davis SL JSY AU/40 50.00 120.00
44 Wiggins SL JSY AU/49 30.00 80.00
45 Parker SL JSY AU/40 20.00 50.00
46 Randle SL JSY AU/60 8.00 20.00
47 Marcus Smart SL JSY AU/40 10.00 25.00
48 LaVine SL JSY AU/75 25.00 60.00
49 Robin Lopez SL JSY AU/75 EXCH 4.00 10.00
50 Johnson SL JSY AU/40 40.00 100.00
51 Khris Middleton SL JSY AU/75 8.00 20.00
52 Giannis SL JSY AU/75 40.00 100.00
53 Marcin Gortat SL JSY AU/75 5.00 12.00
54 Evan Fournier SL JSY AU/75 5.00 12.00
55 Eric Gordon SL JSY AU/60 5.00 12.00
56 Donatas Motiejunas SL JSY AU/75 4.00 10.00
57 Olajuwon SL JSY AU/40 25.00 60.00
58 Griffin SL JSY AU/40 25.00 60.00
59 Tobias Harris SL JSY AU/75 5.00 12.00
60 Bojan Bogdanovic SL JSY AU/75 5.00 12.00
61 George SL JSY AU/40 EXCH 25.00 60.00
62 Drexler SL JSY AU/40 15.00 40.00
63 Gary Harris SL JSY AU/75 5.00 12.00
64 Nene SL JSY AU/75 5.00 12.00
65 Brook Lopez SL JSY AU/60 EXCH 6.00 15.00
66 Bosh SL JSY AU/40 12.00 30.00
67 Mourning SL JSY AU/40 15.00 40.00
68 Jonas Valanciunas SL JSY AU/75 5.00 12.00
69 Gary Neal SL JSY AU/75 4.00 10.00
70 Batum SL JSY AU/75 4.00 10.00
71 Whiteside SL JSY AU/60 5.00 12.00
72 Stockton SL JSY AU/40 30.00 80.00
73 Oladipo SL JSY AU/40 10.00 25.00
74 Wesley Matthews SL JSY AU/75 4.00 10.00
75 Walker SL JSY AU/60 10.00 25.00
76 Nikola Vucevic SL JSY AU/75 5.00 12.00
77 Hill SL JSY AU/40 25.00 60.00
78 Payton SL JSY AU/60 10.00 25.00
79 Rudy Gay SL JSY AU/75 EXCH 6.00 15.00
80 Gasol SL JSY AU/40 15.00 40.00
81 Gordon SL JSY AU/60 12.00 30.00
82 Starks SL JSY AU/75 6.00 15.00
83 Mo Williams SL JSY AU/55 5.00 12.00
84 Horford SL JSY AU/75 6.00 15.00
85 Nikola Mirotic SL JSY AU/75 EXCH 4.00 10.00
86 DeMarre Carroll SL JSY AU/60 4.00 10.00
87 Allen SL JSY AU/40 30.00 80.00
88 Smith SL JSY AU/75 15.00 40.00
89 Hayward SL JSY AU/75 12.00 30.00
90 Dellavedova SL JSY AU/75 10.00 25.00
91 Brandon Knight SL JSY AU/60 4.00 10.00
92 Kerr SL JSY AU/21 20.00 50.00
93 Timofey Mozgov SL JSY AU/75 4.00 10.00
94 Doug McDermott SL JSY AU/75 5.00 12.00
95 Zaza Pachulia SL JSY AU/75 4.00 10.00
96 Alec Burks SL JSY AU/75 4.00 10.00
97 Kidd SL JSY AU/40 12.00 30.00
98 Jeff Teague SL JSY AU/50 EXCH 4.00 10.00
99 Bird SL JSY AU/40 40.00 100.00
100 Howard SL JSY AU/40 15.00 40.00
101 Kobe Bryant AU/40 500.00 1,000.00
102 Kevin Durant AU/40 50.00 120.00
103 Kyrie Irving AU/40 40.00 100.00
104 Gordon Hayward AU/60 12.00 30.00
105 John Wall AU/40 15.00 40.00
106 Anthony Davis AU/40 30.00 80.00
107 Andrew Wiggins AU/40 20.00 50.00
108 Jabari Parker AU/40 12.00 30.00
109 Julius Randle AU/60 12.00 30.00
110 Marcus Smart AU/45 10.00 25.00
111 Zach LaVine AU/99 8.00 20.00
112 Marcin Gortat AU/60 4.00 10.00
113 Blake Griffin AU/40 20.00 50.00
114 Gary Harris AU/99 5.00 12.00
115 Jonas Valanciunas AU/60 5.00 12.00
116 Victor Oladipo AU/45 6.00 15.00
117 Bill Laimbeer AU/99 6.00 15.00
118 Sam Dekker AU/99 4.00 10.00
119 Emmanuel Mudiay AU/45 6.00 15.00
120 Kemba Walker AU/60 8.00 20.00
121 Kristaps Porzingis AU/60 40.00 100.00
122 Donatas Motiejunas AU/99 4.00 10.00
123 Rashad Vaughn AU/99 4.00 10.00
124 Jonathon Simmons AU/99 5.00 12.00
125 Al Horford AU/60 6.00 15.00
126 Jahlil Okafor AU/45 6.00 15.00
127 Jusuf Nurkic AU/99 5.00 12.00
128 Jerian Grant AU/99 4.00 10.00
129 Boban Marjanovic AU/99 12.00 30.00
130 Chris Bosh AU/40 10.00 25.00
131 Alec Burks AU/99 4.00 10.00
132 Norman Powell AU/99 8.00 20.00
134 Nikola Jokic AU/99 800.00 1,500.00
135 Marcelo Huertas AU/99 4.00 10.00
136 Joe Ingles AU/99 6.00 15.00
137 Cameron Payne AU/99 5.00 12.00
138 Richaun Holmes AU/99 6.00 15.00
139 Festus Ezeli AU/99 4.00 10.00
140 Julius Erving AU/40 30.00 80.00
141 Klay Thompson AU/45 20.00 50.00
142 Matthew Dellavedova AU/99 5.00 12.00
143 Magic Johnson AU/40 25.00 60.00
144 D'Angelo Russell AU/45 20.00 50.00
145 Pau Gasol AU/40 10.00 25.00
146 Devin Booker AU/99 150.00 400.00
147 Rudy Gay AU/60 6.00 15.00
148 Eric Bledsoe AU/60 5.00 12.00
149 Paul Millsap AU/60 5.00 12.00
150 Mario Hezonja AU/60 5.00 12.00
151 Hardaway CR AU/40 25.00 60.00
152 Hill CR AU/40 12.00 30.00
153 Kidd CR AU/40 15.00 40.00
154 Bryant CR AU/40 500.00 1,000.00
155 Durant CR AU/40 50.00 120.00
156 Irving CR AU/40 40.00 100.00
157 Love CR AU/40 8.00 20.00
158 Wiggins CR AU/40 30.00 80.00
159 Davis CR AU/40 30.00 80.00
160 Griffin CR AU/40 15.00 40.00
161 Marcus Smart CR AU/40 10.00 25.00
162 Julius Randle CR AU/49 10.00 25.00
163 Parker CR AU/40 15.00 40.00
164 Walt Frazier CR AU/85 12.00 30.00
165 Heinsohn CR AU/85 15.00 40.00
166 Isiah Thomas CR AU/49 8.00 20.00
167 Stockton CR AU/40 20.00 50.00
168 Byron Scott CR AU/85 5.00 12.00
169 Robert Horry CR AU/85 5.00 12.00
170 Wall CR AU/40 15.00 40.00
171 Hayward CR AU/85 8.00 20.00
172 Thomas CR AU/85 25.00 60.00
173 Nikola Mirotic CR AU/49 5.00 12.00
174 Gary Harris CR AU/85 5.00 12.00
175 Norris Cole CR AU/85 4.00 10.00
176 LaVine CR AU/85 15.00 40.00
177 Brandon Knight CR AU/85 4.00 10.00
178 Schroder CR AU/85 10.00 25.00
179 Archibald CR AU/40 8.00 20.00
180 Ralph Sampson CR AU/85 5.00 12.00
182 Trey Lyles CR AU/85 5.00 12.00
183 Cauley-Stein CR AU/85 5.00 12.00
184 Anthony Brown CR AU/85 4.00 10.00
185 Cameron Payne CR AU/85 6.00 15.00
186 Russell CR AU/85 25.00 60.00
187 Sasha Kaun CR AU/85 4.00 10.00
188 Booker CR AU/85 150.00 400.00
189 Mudiay CR AU/85 5.00 12.00
190 Frank Kaminsky CR AU/85 5.00 12.00
191 Okafor CR AU/85 20.00 50.00
192 Jerian Grant CR AU/85 4.00 10.00
193 Jokic CR AU/85 800.00 1,500.00
194 Simmons CR AU/85 5.00 12.00
195 Walter Tavares CR AU/85 4.00 10.00
196 Nemanja Bjelica CR AU/85 6.00 15.00
197 Anderson CR AU/85 8.00 20.00
198 Winslow CR AU/85 12.00 30.00
199 Towns CR AU/85 75.00 200.00
200 Porzingis CR AU/85 40.00 100.00
201 Kobe Bryant UP AU 500.00 1,000.00
202 Kevin Durant UP AU 60.00 150.00
203 Anthony Davis UP AU 50.00 120.00
204 Blake Griffin UP AU 20.00 50.00
205 Kyrie Irving UP AU 40.00 100.00
206 Pau Gasol UP AU 12.00 30.00
207 Andrew Wiggins UP AU 40.00 100.00
208 John Wall UP AU 12.00 30.00
209 Jabari Parker UP AU 15.00 40.00
210 Andre Drummond UP AU 12.00 30.00
211 Kevin Love UP AU 10.00 25.00
212 Chris Bosh UP AU 8.00 20.00
213 Al Horford UP AU 8.00 20.00
214 Klay Thompson UP AU 30.00 80.00
215 Victor Oladipo UP AU 8.00 20.00
216 Eric Bledsoe UP AU 5.00 12.00
217 Brandon Knight UP AU 4.00 10.00
218 Donatas Motiejunas UP AU 4.00 10.00
219 Jason Terry UP AU 4.00 10.00
220 Dennis Schroder UP AU 6.00 15.00
221 Kemba Walker UP AU 10.00 25.00
223 Paul George UP AU 20.00 50.00
224 Julius Randle UP AU 10.00 25.00
225 Jeff Teague UP AU 4.00 10.00
226 Evan Fournier UP AU 8.00 20.00
227 Norris Cole UP AU 4.00 10.00
228 G. Antetokounmpo UP AU 100.00 250.00
229 Jonas Valanciunas UP AU 8.00 20.00
230 T.J. Warren UP AU 6.00 15.00
231 Doug McDermott UP AU 5.00 12.00
232 Wesley Matthews UP AU 4.00 10.00
233 Timofey Mozgov UP AU 4.00 10.00
234 J.R. Smith UP AU 15.00 40.00
235 Marcus Smart UP AU 8.00 20.00
236 Nikola Vucevic UP AU 5.00 12.00
237 Grant Hill UP AU 15.00 40.00
238 Ray Allen UP AU 20.00 50.00
239 Hakeem Olajuwon UP AU 15.00 40.00
240 Larry Bird UP AU 40.00 100.00
241 John Stockton UP AU 30.00 80.00
242 John Starks UP AU 6.00 15.00
243 David Robinson UP AU 20.00 50.00
244 Bill Walton UP AU 25.00 60.00
245 Tom Heinsohn UP AU 25.00 60.00
246 Isiah Thomas UP AU 15.00 40.00
247 Dennis Rodman UP AU 40.00 100.00
248 Walt Frazier UP AU 10.00 25.00
249 Nate Archibald UP AU 6.00 15.00
250 Clyde Drexler UP AU 20.00 50.00
251 Julius Erving UP AU 40.00 100.00
252 Magic Johnson UP AU 30.00 80.00
253 Anfernee Hardaway UP AU 15.00 40.00
254 Tracy McGrady UP AU 25.00 60.00
255 Damon Stoudamire UP AU 6.00 15.00
256 Bobby Jones UP AU 5.00 12.00
257 Robert Horry UP AU 5.00 12.00
258 Shaquille O'Neal UP AU 60.00 150.00
259 Allan Houston UP AU 5.00 12.00
260 Marques Johnson UP AU 5.00 12.00
261 Cedric Ceballos UP AU 4.00 10.00
262 Eddie Jones UP AU 6.00 15.00
263 Cuttino Mobley UP AU 4.00 10.00
264 Bill Laimbeer UP AU 6.00 15.00
265 Jason Kidd UP AU 12.00 30.00
266 Bobby Portis UP AU 10.00 25.00
267 Cameron Payne UP AU 6.00 15.00
268 D'Angelo Russell UP AU 25.00 60.00
269 Delon Wright UP AU 5.00 12.00
270 Devin Booker UP AU 300.00 600.00
271 Emmanuel Mudiay UP AU 5.00 12.00
272 Frank Kaminsky UP AU 5.00 12.00
273 Jahlil Okafor UP AU 5.00 12.00
274 Jerian Grant UP AU 4.00 10.00
275 Joe Young UP AU 4.00 10.00
276 Jonathon Simmons UP AU 5.00 12.00
277 Jordan Mickey UP AU 4.00 10.00
278 Josh Richardson UP AU 12.00 30.00
279 Justin Anderson UP AU 4.00 10.00
280 Justise Winslow UP AU 6.00 15.00
281 Karl-Anthony Towns UP AU 75.00 200.00
282 Kelly Oubre Jr. UP AU 20.00 50.00
283 Kristaps Porzingis UP AU 60.00 150.00
284 Marcelo Huertas UP AU 4.00 10.00
285 Mario Hezonja UP AU 5.00 12.00
286 Myles Turner UP AU 10.00 25.00
287 Nemanja Bjelica UP AU 6.00 15.00
288 Nikola Jokic UP AU 1,000.00 2,000.00
290 Richaun Holmes UP AU 6.00 15.00
291 Kevon Looney UP AU 12.00 30.00
292 Walter Tavares UP AU 4.00 10.00
293 Stanley Johnson UP AU 5.00 12.00
294 Terry Rozier UP AU 12.00 30.00
295 Trey Lyles UP AU 5.00 12.00
296 Willie Cauley-Stein UP AU 12.00 30.00
297 Anthony Brown UP AU 4.00 10.00
298 Sam Dekker UP AU 4.00 10.00
299 Luis Montero UP AU 4.00 10.00
300 Norman Powell UP AU 8.00 20.00

2015-16 Panini Preferred Autographs Purple

*PURPLE: .5X TO 1.2X BASE p/r 50-99
*PURPLE: .4X TO 1.X BASE p/r 40-49
PRINT RUNS B/WN 25-49 COPIES PER
EXCHANGE DEADLINE 2/17/2018

2015-16 Panini Preferred Silhouettes Prime

*SL PRIME: 2X TO 5X BASE p/r 50-99
*SL PRIME: 1.5X TO 4X BASE p/r 21-49
PRINT RUNS B/WN 5-25 COPIES PER
NO PRICING ON QTY 19 OR LESS
EXCHANGE DEADLINE 2/17/2018
1 Porzingis SL JSY AU/25 600.00 1,200.00
19 Towns SL JSY AU/25 800.00 1,500.00
23 Devin Booker SL JSY AU/25 2,000.00 4,000.00
26 Stanley Johnson SL JSY AU/25 75.00 200.00
38 Kobe Bryant SL JSY AU/25 1,500.00 3,000.00
39 Kevin Durant SL JSY AU/25 400.00 800.00
50 M. Johnson SL JSY AU/25 300.00 600.00
52 Antetokounmpo SL JSY AU/25 300.00 600.00

2015-16 Panini Preferred '15 NBA Finals

STATED PRINT RUN 99 SER.#'d SETS
1 Stephen Curry 40.00 100.00
2 Andre Iguodala 10.00 25.00
3 Klay Thompson 15.00 40.00
4 Harrison Barnes 5.00 12.00
5 Andrew Bogut 5.00 12.00
6 Leandro Barbosa 4.00 10.00
7 Draymond Green 12.00 30.00
8 Festus Ezeli 4.00 10.00
9 Shaun Livingston 8.00 20.00
10 Marreese Speights 4.00 10.00
11 Iman Shumpert 8.00 20.00
12 J.R. Smith 15.00 40.00
13 Timofey Mozgov 4.00 10.00
14 Joe Harris 5.00 12.00
15 Kendrick Perkins 4.00 10.00
16 Tristan Thompson 10.00 25.00
17 Matthew Dellavedova 12.00 30.00
18 Mike Miller 5.00 12.00
19 James Jones 4.00 10.00
20 LeBron James 40.00 100.00

2015-16 Panini Preferred '15 NBA Finals Prime

*PRIME: 2X TO 5X BASIC
PRINT RUNS B/WN 19-25 COPIES PER
NO PRICING ON QTY 19
1 Stephen Curry/25 400.00 800.00
2 Andre Iguodala/23 100.00 250.00
3 Klay Thompson/23 200.00 400.00
4 Harrison Barnes/25 50.00 120.00
5 Andrew Bogut/25 75.00 200.00
6 Leandro Barbosa/25 20.00 50.00
7 Draymond Green/25 75.00 200.00
8 Festus Ezeli/25 50.00 120.00
10 Marreese Speights/23 75.00 200.00
20 LeBron James/25 200.00 500.00

2015-16 Panini Preferred Board Members

PRINT RUNS B/WN 75-149 COPIES PER
1 Tristan Thompson/149 2.50 6.00
2 Dwight Howard/149 5.00 12.00
3 DeMarcus Cousins/149 4.00 10.00
4 Andre Drummond/149 4.00 10.00
5 DeAndre Jordan/149 3.00 8.00
6 Greg Monroe/149 3.00 8.00
7 Andrew Bogut/149 3.00 8.00
8 Nikola Vucevic/149 3.00 8.00
9 Joakim Noah/149 2.50 6.00
10 Marc Gasol/149 4.00 10.00
11 Shaquille O'Neal/75 10.00 25.00
12 Hakeem Olajuwon/75 6.00 15.00
13 Karl Malone/75 6.00 15.00
14 Tim Duncan/149 10.00 25.00
15 Patrick Ewing/75 6.00 15.00
16 Robert Parish/75 5.00 12.00

2015-16 Panini Preferred Crazy Eights

STATED PRINT RUN 149 SER.#'d SETS
1 Hawks 5.00 12.00
2 Cavaliers 40.00 100.00
3 Mavericks 12.00 30.00
4 Warriors 25.00 60.00
5 Rockets 10.00 25.00
6 Clippers 10.00 25.00
7 Knicks 10.00 25.00
8 Thunder 10.00 25.00
9 Spurs 15.00 40.00
11 Celtics 6.00 15.00
12 Magic 5.00 12.00
13 Lakers 40.00 100.00
14 Nets 5.00 12.00

2015-16 Panini Preferred Dual Memorabilia

STATED PRINT RUN 199 SER.#'d SETS
1 L.James/S.Curry 50.00 120.00
2 R.Jackson/A.Drummond 4.00 10.00
3 R.Westbrook/J.Harden 8.00 20.00
4 D.Lillard/C.McCollum 6.00 15.00
5 D.Cousins/R.Rondo 5.00 12.00
6 K.Lowry/D.DeRozan 5.00 12.00
7 R.Gobert/D.Favors 5.00 12.00
8 I.Thomas/J.Sullinger 3.00 8.00
9 J.Butler/D.Rose 8.00 20.00
10 D.Williams/C.Parsons 3.00 8.00

2015-16 Panini Preferred Playbook Rookie Jumbo

PRINT RUNS B/WN 10-199 COPIES PER
NO PRICING ON QTY 10
2 Bobby Portis/199 6.00 15.00
3 Cameron Payne/199 4.00 10.00
4 Chris McCullough/199 2.50 6.00
5 Devin Booker/199 8.00 20.00
6 Emmanuel Mudiay/199 3.00 8.00
7 Frank Kaminsky/199 3.00 8.00
8 Jarell Martin/199 2.50 6.00
9 Joe Young/199 2.50 6.00
10 Jonathon Simmons/49 3.00 8.00
11 Josh Richardson/199 4.00 10.00
12 Justin Anderson/199 2.50 6.00
13 Kelly Oubre Jr./199 8.00 20.00
14 Kevon Looney/199 8.00 20.00
15 Myles Turner/125 10.00 25.00
16 R.J. Hunter/199 2.50 6.00
17 Rakeem Christmas/199 2.50 6.00
18 Rondae Hollis-Jefferson/199 3.00 8.00
19 Sasha Kaun/199 2.50 6.00
20 Terry Rozier/199 10.00 25.00
21 Trey Lyles/199 3.00 8.00
22 Anthony Brown/199 2.50 6.00
23 Jahlil Okafor/199 5.00 12.00
24 Jerian Grant/199 2.50 6.00
25 Willie Cauley-Stein/199 3.00 8.00
26 Tyus Jones/199 3.00 8.00

2015-16 Panini Preferred Playbook Veteran Jumbo

STATED PRINT RUN 99 SER.#'d SETS
1 Monta Ellis 3.00 8.00
2 Kobe Bryant 30.00 80.00
3 Derrick Rose 6.00 15.00
4 DeMarcus Cousins 4.00 10.00
5 Dwyane Wade 8.00 20.00
6 Marc Gasol 4.00 10.00
7 Giannis Antetokounmpo 20.00 50.00
8 Andre Iguodala 4.00 10.00
9 Tim Duncan 10.00 25.00
10 John Wall 5.00 12.00

2015-16 Panini Preferred Quads Relics

PRINT RUNS B/WN 49-149 COPIES PER
1 Pistons/149 8.00 20.00
2 Blazers/149 6.00 15.00
3 Lowry/DeRozan/Carroll
Valanciunas/149 6.00 15.00
4 Del/Exu/Mil/Bog/149 8.00 20.00
5 Irv/Bra/Bat/Hil/149 8.00 20.00
6 Wig/Oly/Nic/Tho/149 6.00 15.00
7 Noel/Canaan/Stauskas/Covington/149 4.00 10.00
8 Batum/Fournier/Gobert/Diaw/149 6.00 15.00
9 Gas/Gas/Cal/Rub/149 10.00 25.00
10 Cavaliers/149 40.00 100.00
11 Joh/Bir/Erv/Mal/49 20.00 50.00
12 Jam/Dav/Wig/Wal/149 12.00 30.00

2015-16 Panini Preferred Stat Line Memorabilia

STATED PRINT RUN 149 SER.#'d SETS
1 Damian Lillard 10.00 25.00
2 Thaddeus Young 2.50 6.00
3 Dirk Nowitzki 10.00 25.00
4 Tim Duncan 10.00 25.00
5 Rudy Gobert 5.00 12.00
6 Gordon Hayward 4.00 10.00
7 Nikola Vucevic 3.00 8.00
8 Russell Westbrook 6.00 15.00
9 Anthony Davis 10.00 25.00
10 Julius Randle 5.00 12.00
11 James Harden 8.00 20.00
12 Danilo Gallinari 3.00 8.00
13 Klay Thompson 10.00 25.00
14 Kenneth Faried 3.00 8.00
15 Dwyane Wade 5.00 12.00
16 Marc Gasol 4.00 10.00
17 Kemba Walker 4.00 10.00
18 John Wall 5.00 12.00
19 Paul George 6.00 15.00
20 Zach Randolph 4.00 10.00
21 Dwight Howard 5.00 12.00
22 DeMarcus Cousins 4.00 10.00
23 Kevin Love 4.00 10.00
24 LeBron James 30.00 80.00
25 C.J. McCollum 4.00 10.00
26 Rajon Rondo 5.00 12.00

2015-16 Panini Preferred Stat Line Memorabilia Prime

*PRIME: 1.5X TO 4X BASIC
STATED PRINT RUN 25 SER.#'d SETS
3 Dirk Nowitzki 40.00 100.00
4 Tim Duncan 40.00 100.00
18 John Wall 30.00 80.00
19 Paul George 40.00 100.00

2015-16 Panini Preferred Trending Upward

STATED PRINT RUN 199 SER.#'d SETS
1 Twns/Bkr/Cly-Stn/Lyls 8.00 20.00
2 Okfr/Trnr/Prts/Kmnsky 5.00 12.00
3 Mdy/Rssll/Bkr/Pyne 6.00 15.00
4 Okfr/Wnslw/Grnt/Rzr 5.00 12.00
5 Jhnsn/Wrght/Hlls-Jffrsn/Yng 3.00 8.00
6 Rssll/Brwn/Hrts/Nnce Jr. 6.00 15.00
8 Oubre Jr./Alexander/Kaminsky/Dekker 8.00 20.00
9 Hunter/Mickey/Winslow/Richardson 4.00 10.00
10 Cly-Stn/Prts/Mrtn/Rchrdsn 6.00 15.00

2015-16 Panini Preferred Triple Memorabilia

STATED PRINT RUN 99 SER.#'d SETS
1 Duncan/Ginobili/Parker 12.00 30.00
2 Cousins/Gay/Rondo 6.00 15.00
3 James/Irving/Love 25.00 60.00
4 Paul/Jordan/Griffin 8.00 20.00
5 Wall/Beal/Porter 6.00 15.00
6 Smart/Sullinger/Thomas 6.00 15.00
7 Davis/Irving/Wiggins 12.00 30.00
8 Okafor/Winslow/Jones 6.00 15.00
9 Towns/Russell/Okafor 10.00 25.00
10 Towns/Booker/Lyles 12.00 30.00

2015-16 Panini Preferred VS One on One Relics

STATED PRINT RUN 99 SER.#'d SETS
1 K.Towns/K.Porzingis 15.00 40.00
2 A.Horford/S.Ibaka 5.00 12.00
3 J.Randle/E.Payton 6.00 15.00
4 L.Aldridge/A.Davis 8.00 20.00
5 K.Walker/J.Clarkson 5.00 12.00
6 K.Durant/K.Bryant 40.00 100.00
7 J.Teague/T.Parker 6.00 15.00
8 P.George/L.James 12.00 30.00
9 C.Bosh/P.George 8.00 20.00
10 D.Green/J.Clarkson 6.00 15.00
11 T.Lyles/K.Towns 8.00 20.00
12 C.Anthony/K.Bryant 12.00 30.00
13 P.Gasol/A.Len 8.00 20.00
14 C.McCollum/M.Carter-Williams 5.00 12.00
15 D.Rose/D.Nowitzki 12.00 30.00
16 V.Oladipo/D.DeRozan 6.00 15.00
17 K.Faried/H.Barnes 4.00 10.00
18 R.Westbrook/K.Bryant 40.00 100.00

2016-17 Panini Preferred

SL JSY AU PRINT RUN B/WN 35-99 COPIES PER
AU PRINT RUNS B/WN 35-99 COPIES PER
EXCHANGE DEADLINE 2/28/2019
1 J.Brown SL JSY AU/99 RC 150.00 400.00
2 J.Murray SL JSY AU/99 RC 75.00 200.00
3 P.McCaw SL JSY AU/99 RC 4.00 10.00
4 Brice Johnson SL JSY AU/99 RC 4.00 10.00
5 Wade Baldwin IV SL JSY AU/99 RC 4.00 10.00
6 C.Diallo SL JSY AU/99 RC 4.00 10.00
7 D.Saric SL JSY AU/99 RC 6.00 15.00
8 Tyler Ulis SL JSY AU/99 RC 5.00 12.00
9 M.Richardson SL JSY AU/99 RC 4.00 10.00
10 J.Hrnngmz SL JSY AU/99 RC 25.00 60.00
11 Demetrius Jackson SL JSY AU/99 RC 4.00 10.00
12 Malik Beasley SL JSY AU/99 RC 8.00 20.00
13 Chinanu Onuaku SL JSY AU/99 RC 4.00 10.00
14 I.Zubac SL JSY AU/99 RC 10.00 25.00
15 M.Brogdon SL JSY AU/99 RC 12.00 30.00
16 B.Hield SL JSY AU/99 RC 12.00 30.00
17 T.Satoransky SL JSY AU/99 RC 6.00 15.00
18 J.Layman SL JSY AU/99 RC 5.00 12.00
19 D.Murray SL JSY AU/99 RC 100.00 250.00
20 AJ Hammons SL JSY AU/99 RC 4.00 10.00
21 Caris LeVert SL JSY AU/99 RC 10.00 25.00
22 H.Ellenson SL JSY AU/99 RC 4.00 10.00
23 Georges Niang SL JSY AU/99 RC 6.00 15.00
24 B.Ingram SL JSY AU/99 RC 50.00 120.00
25 T.Maker SL JSY AU/99 RC 5.00 12.00
26 D.Sabonis SL JSY AU/99 RC 25.00 60.00
27 M.Chriss SL JSY AU/99 RC 5.00 12.00
28 S.Labissiere SL JSY AU/99 RC 4.00 10.00
29 J.Poeltl SL JSY AU/99 RC 8.00 20.00
30 Kay Felder SL JSY AU/99 RC 4.00 10.00
31 Isaiah Whitehead SL JSY AU/99 RC 4.00 10.00
32 Damian Jones SL JSY AU/99 RC 4.00 10.00
33 Diamond Stone SL JSY AU/99 RC 4.00 10.00
34 Deyonta Davis SL JSY AU/99 RC 4.00 10.00
35 K.Dunn SL JSY AU/99 RC 10.00 25.00
36 Stephen Zimmerman
SL JSY AU/99 RC 4.00 10.00
37 D.Bender SL JSY AU/99 RC 4.00 10.00
38 Papagiannis SL JSY AU/99 RC 4.00 10.00
39 Pascal Siakam SL JSY AU/99 RC 15.00 40.00
40 Denzel Valentine SL JSY AU/99 RC 4.00 10.00
42 Michael Carter-Williams
SL JSY AU/60 4.00 10.00
43 J.Butler SL JSY AU/35 15.00 40.00
44 Z.LaVine SL JSY AU/60 10.00 25.00
45 P.Millsap SL JSY AU/75 5.00 12.00
46 M.Turner SL JSY AU/60 10.00 25.00
47 D.Booker SL JSY AU/60 125.00 300.00
48 D.Mutombo SL JSY AU/60 12.00 30.00
49 T.Hardaway SL JSY AU/47 12.00 30.00
51 Jordan Clarkson SL JSY AU/75 6.00 15.00
53 Evan Turner SL JSY AU/75 4.00 10.00
54 I.Thomas SL JSY AU/49 6.00 15.00
57 R.Miller SL JSY AU/75 125.00 300.00
58 Kenny Smith SL JSY AU/60 5.00 12.00
59 Jae Crowder SL JSY AU/75 4.00 10.00
60 Marc Gasol SL JSY AU/35 12.00 30.00
62 Mario Hezonja SL JSY AU/75 4.00 10.00
64 Michael Kidd-Gilchrist SL JSY AU/60 4.00 10.00
66 Allen Crabbe SL JSY AU/75 4.00 10.00
67 Toni Kukoc SL JSY AU/45 15.00 40.00
68 Justin Anderson SL JSY AU/60 4.00 10.00
71 Porzingis SL JSY AU/49 30.00 80.00
73 Artis Gilmore SL JSY AU/60 6.00 15.00
74 Marcus Camby SL JSY AU/60 6.00 15.00
77 Mark Price SL JSY AU/38 15.00 40.00
78 Rafer Alston SL JSY AU/60 6.00 15.00
80 Jrue Holiday SL JSY AU/75 8.00 20.00
81 Ray Allen SL JSY AU/35 30.00 80.00
82 Goran Dragic SL JSY AU/75 6.00 15.00
83 H.Barnes SL JSY AU/75 5.00 12.00
85 Langston Galloway SL JSY AU/60 4.00 10.00
86 Tony Parker SL JSY AU/35 12.00 30.00
87 D.Russell SL JSY AU/75 8.00 20.00
90 A.Davis SL JSY AU/35 30.00 80.00
91 K.Durant SL JSY AU/35 75.00 200.00
94 Tobias Harris SL JSY AU/75 6.00 15.00
96 George Hill SL JSY AU/60 6.00 15.00
99 Kurt Thomas SL JSY AU/60 10.00 25.00
100 Ryan Anderson SL JSY AU/60 4.00 10.00
101 Kenneth Faried AU/35 5.00 12.00
102 Dennis Scott AU/99 3.00 8.00
103 Kidd-Gilchrist AU/35 8.00 20.00
104 Nikola Mirotic AU/35 6.00 15.00
105 Zach LaVine AU/35 15.00 40.00
106 Kyrie Irving AU/35 30.00 80.00
107 Tristan Thompson AU/35 5.00 12.00
108 Kristaps Porzingis AU/35 25.00 60.00
109 J.J. Barea AU/99 10.00 25.00
110 Clint Capela AU/75 5.00 12.00
111 Vlade Divac AU/99 5.00 12.00
112 Ryan Anderson AU/35 4.00 10.00
113 Cedric Ceballos AU/99 6.00 15.00
114 Hersey Hawkins AU/99 3.00 8.00
115 KATowns AU/35 30.00 80.00
117 Langston Galloway AU/99 3.00 8.00
118 Anthony Davis AU/35 40.00 100.00
119 Elfrid Payton AU/35 5.00 12.00
120 Devin Booker AU/35 125.00 300.00
121 Allen Crabbe AU/99 3.00 8.00
122 C.J. McCollum AU/35 10.00 25.00
124 Danilo Gallinari AU/35 5.00 12.00
125 Jonas Valanciunas AU/35 5.00 12.00
127 Shawn Kemp AU/35 25.00 60.00
128 Latrell Sprewell AU/35 15.00 40.00
129 Dan Majerle AU/49 6.00 15.00
130 Bob McAdoo AU/99 6.00 15.00
131 Jim Chones AU/99 3.00 8.00
132 Larry Nance Jr. AU/99 3.00 8.00
133 Abdul-Jabbar AU/35 30.00 80.00
134 Magic Johnson AU/35 40.00 100.00
135 Chauncey Billups AU/35 8.00 20.00
136 Rod Strickland AU/99 3.00 8.00
137 Kurt Rambis AU/99 5.00 12.00
138 Rick Fox AU/35 5.00 12.00
139 Kurt Thomas AU/99 3.00 8.00
140 Marcus Camby AU/99 6.00 15.00
141 Alex English CR AU/99 4.00 10.00
142 Isaiah Thomas CR AU/35 15.00 40.00
143 Jae Crowder CR AU/99 3.00 8.00
144 Kenny ""Sky"" Walker CR AU/49 4.00 10.00
145 Jeff Hornacek CR AU/99 4.00 10.00
146 Chauncey Billups CR AU/35 8.00 20.00
148 Kyrie Irving CR AU/35 30.00 80.00
149 Kenneth Faried CR AU/35 5.00 12.00
150 Justin Anderson CR AU/99 3.00 8.00
151 Robert Horry CR AU/35 6.00 15.00
152 Reggie Jackson CR AU/60 4.00 10.00
153 Kevin Durant CR AU/35 60.00 150.00
154 Junior Bridgeman CR AU/99 4.00 10.00
155 Clint Capela CR AU/75 10.00 25.00
156 Myles Turner CR AU/99 10.00 25.00
157 Tyler Johnson CR AU/60 3.00 8.00
160 KATowns CR AU/35 30.00 80.00
161 Zach LaVine CR AU/35 15.00 40.00
162 Sidney Moncrief CR AU/99 4.00 10.00
163 Porzingis CR AU/35 25.00 60.00
164 Nikola Vucevic CR AU/35 6.00 15.00
165 Zaza Pachulia CR AU/99 3.00 8.00
166 Joel Embiid CR AU/35 125.00 300.00
167 Michael Cooper CR AU/99 5.00 12.00
168 George Hill CR AU/35 6.00 15.00
169 Langston Galloway CR AU/35 4.00 10.00
170 Larry Bird CR AU/35 40.00 100.00
171 Magic Johnson CR AU/35 40.00 100.00
172 Jalen Rose CR AU/35 5.00 12.00
173 D.Stoudamire CR AU/99 6.00 15.00
174 Cedric Maxwell CR AU/99 4.00 10.00
177 Kiki VanDeWeghe CR AU/99 4.00 10.00
178 Bill Laimbeer CR AU/99 5.00 12.00
179 Latrell Sprewell CR AU/35 15.00 40.00
181 Dario Saric PC AU/75 12.00 30.00
182 Kris Dunn PC AU/35 6.00 15.00
183 Jamal Murray PC AU/35 150.00 400.00
184 M.Brogdon PC AU/99 12.00 30.00
185 B.Ingram PC AU/35 60.00 150.00
186 Kenneth Faried PC AU/35 5.00 12.00
187 Magic Johnson PC AU/35 40.00 100.00
188 Shawn Kemp PC AU/75 20.00 50.00
189 Larry Bird PC AU/35 40.00 100.00
190 Wade Baldwin IV PC AU/99 3.00 8.00
191 Walter Berry PC AU/99 3.00 8.00
192 Devin Booker PC AU/35 125.00 300.00
193 Joel Embiid PC AU/35 125.00 300.00
194 A.Wiggins PC AU/35 20.00 50.00
195 KATowns PC AU/35 30.00 80.00
196 Kyrie Irving PC AU/35 30.00 80.00
197 Jimmy Butler PC AU/35 15.00 40.00
199 Kevin Durant PC AU/35 60.00 150.00
200 Kobe Bryant PC AU/35 600.00 1,200.00
201 Alex English UP AU/50 5.00 12.00
202 Jalen Rose UP AU/50 5.00 12.00
204 Zach Randolph UP AU/50 8.00 20.00
206 Anthony Davis UP AU/50 40.00 100.00
207 Artis Gilmore UP AU/50 8.00 20.00
208 Bill Laimbeer UP AU/50 6.00 15.00
209 Demetrius Jackson UP AU/50 4.00 10.00
210 Bob McAdoo UP AU/50 8.00 20.00
211 C.J. McCollum UP AU/50 10.00 25.00
212 Michael Cooper UP AU/50 6.00 15.00
213 Cedric Ceballos UP AU/50 8.00 20.00
214 Cedric Maxwell UP AU/50 5.00 12.00
215 Rodney McGruder UP AU/50 5.00 12.00
216 Larry Nance Jr. UP AU/50 10.00 25.00
217 D.Murray UP AU/50 100.00 250.00
218 Dan Majerle UP AU/50 6.00 15.00
219 Dennis Scott UP AU/50 4.00 10.00
220 Devin Booker UP AU/50 125.00 300.00
221 Elfrid Payton UP AU/50 5.00 12.00
222 Paul Millsap UP AU/50 5.00 12.00
223 Evan Turner UP AU/50 4.00 10.00
224 Goran Dragic UP AU/50 6.00 15.00
225 George Hill UP AU/50 6.00 15.00
226 Grant Hill UP AU/50 25.00 60.00
227 Hersey Hawkins UP AU/50 4.00 10.00
228 Isaiah Thomas UP AU/50 20.00 50.00
229 K.""Sky"" Walker UP AU/50 8.00 20.00
230 Jae Crowder UP AU/50 4.00 10.00
231 Jeff Hornacek UP AU/50 5.00 12.00
232 Danilo Gallinari UP AU/50 5.00 12.00
233 Jim Chones UP AU/50 4.00 10.00
235 Julius Randle UP AU/50 12.00 30.00
236 Joel Embiid UP AU/50 100.00 250.00
237 Thon Maker UP AU/50 5.00 12.00
238 Jonas Valanciunas UP AU/50 5.00 12.00
240 Juan Hernangomez UP AU/50 25.00 60.00
241 Junior Bridgeman UP AU/50 5.00 12.00
242 Justin Anderson UP AU/50 4.00 10.00
243 Abdul-Jabbar UP AU/50 30.00 80.00
244 KATowns UP AU/50 30.00 80.00
245 Kenny Smith UP AU/50 5.00 12.00
246 Kevin Durant UP AU/50 60.00 150.00
247 Rod Strickland UP AU/50 4.00 10.00
248 Kiki VanDeWeghe UP AU/50 5.00 12.00
249 Porzingis UP AU/50 25.00 60.00
250 Kurt Rambis UP AU/50 6.00 15.00
251 Kurt Thomas UP AU/50 4.00 10.00
252 Marc Gasol UP AU/50 12.00 30.00
254 D.Mutombo UP AU/50 15.00 40.00
255 Latrell Sprewell UP AU/50 15.00 40.00
257 Kobe Bryant UP AU/50 500.00 1,000.00
258 Marcus Camby UP AU/50 8.00 20.00
261 Shawn Kemp UP AU/50 30.00 80.00
262 Walter Berry UP AU/50 4.00 10.00
263 Nikola Mirotic UP AU/50 6.00 15.00
264 Brice Johnson UP AU/50 4.00 10.00
265 Rick Fox UP AU/50 5.00 12.00
266 Myles Turner UP AU/50 12.00 30.00
267 Ryan Anderson UP AU/50 4.00 10.00
268 Sidney Moncrief UP AU/50 5.00 12.00
271 Tristan Thompson UP AU/50 5.00 12.00
272 Tyler Johnson UP AU/50 4.00 10.00
273 Vlade Divac UP AU/50 6.00 15.00
275 Nikola Vucevic UP AU/50 6.00 15.00
277 Kay Felder UP AU/50 4.00 10.00

278 Dorian Finney-Smith UP AU/50 5.00 12.00
279 Malik Beasley UP AU/50 10.00 25.00
280 Jamal Murray UP AU/50 30.00 80.00
282 Kyle Wiltjer UP AU/50 6.00 15.00
283 Diamond Stone UP AU/50 4.00 10.00
284 B.Ingram UP AU/50 60.00 150.00
285 Wade Baldwin IV UP AU/50 4.00 10.00
286 Troy Williams UP AU/50 RC 8.00 20.00
287 M.Brogdon UP AU/50 15.00 40.00
288 Buddy Hield UP AU/50 20.00 50.00
289 W.Hernangomez UP AU/50 8.00 20.00
290 Ron Baker UP AU/50 4.00 10.00
291 Domantas Sabonis UP AU/50 25.00 60.00
292 Dario Saric UP AU/50 15.00 40.00
293 M.Chriss UP AU/50 5.00 12.00
294 Tyler Ulis UP AU/50 5.00 12.00
296 Jake Layman UP AU/50 5.00 12.00
297 Pascal Siakam UP AU/50 25.00 60.00
298 Jakob Poeltl UP AU/50 8.00 20.00
299 Tomas Satoransky UP AU/50 6.00 15.00

2016-17 Panini Preferred Autographs Blue

*BLUE/25: .6X TO 1.5X p/r 60-99
*BLUE/25: .5X TO 1.2X p/r 35-50
PRINT RUNS B/WN 15-25 COPIES PER
NO PRICING ON QTY 15
EXCHANGE DEADLINE 2/28/2019

2016-17 Panini Preferred Autographs Purple

*PURPLE/49: .5X TO 1.2X p/r 60-99
*PURPLE/49: .4X TO 1X p/r 35-50
*PURPLE/25: .6X TO 1.5X p/r 60-99
*PURPLE/25: .5X TO 1.2X p/r 35-50
PRINT RUNS B/WN 25-49 COPIES PER
EXCHANGE DEADLINE 2/28/2019

2016-17 Panini Preferred Crown Royale Autographs Blue

*BLUE/25: .6X TO 1.5X p/r 60-99
*BLUE/25: .5X TO 1.2X p/r 35-50
PRINT RUNS B/WN 15-25 COPIES PER
NO PRICING ON QTY 15
EXCHANGE DEADLINE 2/28/2019

2016-17 Panini Preferred Crown Royale Autographs Purple

*PURPLE/35-49: .5X TO 1.2X p/r 60-99
*PURPLE/35-49: .4X TO 1X p/r 35-50
*PURPLE/25: .5X TO 1.2X p/r 35-50
PRINT RUNS B/WN 25-49 COPIES PER
EXCHANGE DEADLINE 2/28/2019

2016-17 Panini Preferred Panini's Choice Autographs Blue

*BLUE/25: .6X TO 1.5X p/r 60-99
PRINT RUNS B/WN 15-25 COPIES PER
NO PRICING ON QTY 15
EXCHANGE DEADLINE 2/28/2019

2016-17 Panini Preferred Panini's Choice Autographs Purple

*PURPLE/49: .5X TO 1.2X p/r 60-99
*PURPLE/25: .5X TO 1.2X p/r 35-50
PRINT RUNS B/WN 25-49 COPIES PER
EXCHANGE DEADLINE 2/28/2019

2016-17 Panini Preferred Silhouettes Prime

*SL PRIME: 1.5X TO 4X BASE p/r 50-99
*SL PRIME: 1.2X TO 3X BASE p/r 35-49
PRINT RUNS B/WN 3-25 COPIES PER
NO PRICING ON QTY 15 OR LESS
EXCHANGE DEADLINE 2/28/2019
1 Jaylen Brown JSY AU/25 1,500.00 3,000.00
2 Jamal Murray JSY AU/25 500.00 1,000.00
19 D.Murray JSY AU/25 800.00 1,500.00
24 B.Ingram JSY AU/25 300.00 600.00
35 Kris Dunn JSY AU/25 100.00 250.00
39 Pascal Siakam JSY AU/25 150.00 400.00

2016-17 Panini Preferred '16 NBA Finals Memorabilia

PRINT RUNS B/WN 3-99 COPIES PER
NO PRICING ON QTY 13 OR LESS
1 Channing Frye/99 8.00 20.00
2 Dahntay Jones/86 10.00 25.00
3 Iman Shumpert/76 10.00 25.00
4 J.R. Smith/99 12.00 30.00
5 James Jones/99 4.00 10.00
6 Kevin Love/99 15.00 40.00
8 LeBron James/31 150.00 400.00
9 Mo Williams/99 5.00 12.00
10 Richard Jefferson/99 5.00 12.00
11 Tristan Thompson/99 12.00 30.00
12 Andrew Bogut/99 6.00 15.00
13 Brandon Rush/99 4.00 10.00
15 Festus Ezeli/99 4.00 10.00
16 Ian Clark/99 6.00 15.00
17 Klay Thompson/99 15.00 40.00
18 Leandro Barbosa/99 4.00 10.00
19 Marreese Speights/99 4.00 10.00

2016-17 Panini Preferred Board Members Memorabilia

STATED PRINT RUN 99 SER.#'d SETS
1 Al Horford 4.00 10.00
2 DeAndre Jordan 3.00 8.00
3 Myles Turner 6.00 15.00
4 Bobby Portis 4.00 10.00
5 Nene 3.00 8.00
6 Andre Drummond 4.00 10.00
7 Dirk Nowitzki 10.00 25.00
8 Cody Zeller 2.50 6.00
9 Brook Lopez 3.00 8.00
10 Alexis Ajinca 5.00 12.00
11 DeMarcus Cousins 3.00 8.00
12 Mason Plumlee 2.50 6.00
13 Jahlil Okafor 2.50 6.00
14 Nerlens Noel 2.50 6.00
15 Nikola Vucevic 4.00 10.00
16 Derrick Favors 2.50 6.00

2016-17 Panini Preferred Crazy Eights Memorabilia

STATED PRINT RUN 149 SER.#'d SETS
1 Wizards 6.00 15.00
2 Timberwolves 10.00 25.00
3 Nuggets 25.00 60.00
4 Cavaliers 25.00 60.00
5 Hornets 4.00 10.00
6 Celtics 25.00 60.00
7 Raptors 10.00 25.00
8 Kings 10.00 25.00
9 Trail Blazers 12.00 30.00
10 Suns 15.00 40.00
11 Thunder 8.00 20.00
12 Knicks 6.00 15.00
13 Pelicans 6.00 15.00
14 Rockets 10.00 25.00

2016-17 Panini Preferred Dual Memorabilia

STATED PRINT RUN 99 SER.#'d SETS
1 Randle/Russell 5.00 12.00
2 Conley/Randolph 4.00 10.00
3 Henson/Monroe 2.50 6.00
4 Chriss/Ulis 3.00 8.00
5 Lillard/McCollum 6.00 15.00
6 Beal/Porter 5.00 12.00
7 Hayward/Favors 4.00 10.00
8 Cauley-Stein/Collison 3.00 8.00
9 George/James 12.00 30.00
10 Durant/Westbrook 12.00 30.00

2016-17 Panini Preferred Playbook Jumbo Memorabilia

STATED PRINT RUN 99 SER.#'d SETS
1 Richard Jefferson 3.00 8.00
2 Thaddeus Young 2.50 6.00
3 Dirk Nowitzki 10.00 25.00
4 Rondae Hollis-Jefferson 2.50 6.00
5 LeBron James 30.00 80.00
6 Shawn Marion 3.00 8.00
7 Evan Fournier 3.00 8.00
8 David Robinson 8.00 20.00
9 Tim Duncan 8.00 20.00
10 Shabazz Muhammad 2.50 6.00
11 Joe Smith 3.00 8.00
12 Derrick Rose 6.00 15.00
13 Joakim Noah 2.50 6.00
14 Steven Adams 5.00 12.00
15 Chandler Parsons 2.50 6.00
16 Nemanja Bjelica 2.50 6.00
17 Deron Williams 3.00 8.00
18 Alec Burks 3.00 8.00
19 Carmelo Anthony 6.00 15.00
20 Nicolas Batum 3.00 8.00
21 Manu Ginobili 6.00 15.00
22 Andrew Wiggins 5.00 12.00
23 Wilson Chandler 3.00 8.00
24 Ricky Rubio 3.00 8.00
25 Rudy Gay 4.00 10.00
26 Mason Plumlee 2.50 6.00
27 Brandon Knight 3.00 8.00
28 Noah Vonleh 2.50 6.00
29 Timofey Mozgov 2.50 6.00
31 Victor Oladipo 3.00 8.00
32 Damian Lillard 10.00 25.00
33 Courtney Lee 2.50 6.00
34 Serge Ibaka 3.00 8.00
35 Monta Ellis 3.00 8.00
36 Russell Westbrook 15.00 40.00

2016-17 Panini Preferred Quads Memorabilia

STATED PRINT RUN 149 SER.#'d SETS
1 Jms/Crry/Hrdn/Dmt 30.00 80.00
2 Nwtzki/Anthny/Wall/Wade 6.00 15.00
3 Wggns/Twns/Rbo/Lvne 10.00 25.00
4 Love/Beal/Przngs/Dvs 15.00 40.00
5 O'Nl/Brnt/Hill/Drxlr 25.00 60.00
6 Wall/Irvng/Crry/Llrd 25.00 60.00
7 Lwry/Wlkr/Paul/Wstbrk 8.00 20.00
8 Gnns/Jms/Thms/Btlr 40.00 100.00
9 Grge/Hywrd/Jkc/Hrdn 25.00 60.00
10 Twns/Przngs/Bkr/Rssll 20.00 50.00
12 Nwtzki/Gnns/Dvs/Btlr 25.00 60.00

2016-17 Panini Preferred Rookie Playbook Memorabilia

STATED PRINT RUN 99 SER.#'d SETS
1 Malcolm Brogdon 6.00 15.00
2 Patrick McCaw 3.00 8.00
3 Brandon Ingram 12.00 30.00
4 Dragan Bender 3.00 8.00
5 Tyler Ulis 4.00 10.00
6 Domantas Sabonis 20.00 50.00
7 Jaylen Brown 12.00 30.00
8 Pascal Siakam 20.00 50.00
9 Henry Ellenson 3.00 8.00
10 Demetrius Jackson 3.00 8.00
11 Kay Felder 3.00 8.00
12 AJ Hammons 3.00 8.00
13 Chinanu Onuaku 3.00 8.00
14 Wade Baldwin IV 3.00 8.00
15 Juan Hernangomez 6.00 15.00
16 Mindaugas Kuzminskas 3.00 8.00
17 Denzel Valentine 3.00 8.00
18 Isaiah Whitehead 3.00 8.00
19 Dejounte Murray 15.00 40.00
20 Malachi Richardson 3.00 8.00
21 Stephen Zimmerman 3.00 8.00
22 Malik Beasley 6.00 15.00
23 Paul Zipser 3.00 8.00
24 Georges Niang 5.00 12.00
25 Ivica Zubac 8.00 20.00
26 Willy Hernangomez 4.00 10.00
27 Cheick Diallo 3.00 8.00
28 Deyonta Davis 3.00 8.00
29 Marquese Chriss 4.00 10.00
30 Michael Gbinije 3.00 8.00
31 Diamond Stone 3.00 8.00
32 Brice Johnson 3.00 8.00
33 Georgios Papagiannis 3.00 8.00
34 Joel Bolomboy 3.00 8.00
35 Skal Labissiere 5.00 12.00
36 Tomas Satoransky 5.00 12.00

2016-17 Panini Preferred Stat Line Memorabilia

PRINT RUNS B/WN 125-149 COPIES PER
1 Avery Bradley/149 2.50 6.00
2 Kyrie Irving/149 8.00 20.00
3 Kevin Love/149 4.00 10.00
4 Kentavious Caldwell-Pope/149 3.00 8.00
5 Andre Drummond/149 4.00 10.00
6 Tobias Harris/149 4.00 10.00
7 DeAndre Jordan/149 3.00 8.00
8 Blake Griffin/149 4.00 10.00
9 Mike Conley/149 3.00 8.00
10 Marc Gasol/125 4.00 10.00
11 Hassan Whiteside/149 3.00 8.00
12 Anthony Davis/149 6.00 15.00
13 Derrick Rose/149 6.00 15.00
14 Steven Adams/149 5.00 12.00
15 Russell Westbrook/149 8.00 20.00
16 Joel Embiid/149 5.00 12.00
17 Jahlil Okafor/149 2.50 6.00
18 DeMar DeRozan/149 5.00 12.00
19 Jonas Valanciunas/149 3.00 8.00
20 Markieff Morris/149 2.50 6.00
21 Dwyane Wade/149 5.00 12.00
22 LeBron James/149 12.00 30.00
23 Stephen Curry/149 12.00 30.00
24 Goran Dragic/149 4.00 10.00
25 Dion Waiters/149 2.50 6.00
26 Hassan Whiteside/149 3.00 8.00

2016-17 Panini Preferred Stat Line Memorabilia Prime

*PRIME: 1.5X TO 4X BASIC
PRINT RUNS B/WN 15-25 COPIES PER
NO PRICING ON QTY 15 OR LESS
22 LeBron James/25 75.00 200.00

2016-17 Panini Preferred Trending Upward Memorabilia

STATED PRINT RUN 149 SER.#'d SETS
*PRIME/25: 1.5X TO 4X BASIC
1 Brgdn/Dunn/Mkr/Hld 10.00 25.00
2 Ingrm/Brwn/Mkr/Hld 10.00 25.00
3 Ingrm/Stne/Ulis/Dllo 8.00 20.00
4 Brwn/Pggnns/Vlntne/Dvs 6.00 15.00
5 Brgdn/McCw/Jns/Jhnsn 8.00 20.00
6 Dunn/Bldwn/Rchrdsn/Mrry 12.00 30.00
7 Mrry/Lwwu-Cbrrt/Hrnngmz/Ellnsn 20.00 50.00
8 Bndr/McCw/Jhnsn/Prnce 3.00 8.00
9 Poeltl/Felder/Hammons/Jackson 5.00 12.00
10 LeVert/Whitehead
Onuaku/Zimmerman 6.00 15.00

2016-17 Panini Preferred Triple Memorabilia

STATED PRINT RUN 99 SER.#'d SETS
1 Gllnri/Chndlr/Hrrs 12.00 30.00
3 Irvng/Jms/Love 25.00 60.00
4 Btlr/Wade/Rndo 10.00 25.00
5 Walker/Lamb/Zeller 4.00 10.00
6 Horford/Bradley/Smart 5.00 12.00
7 Howard/Hardaway/Schroder 5.00 12.00
8 Crry/Thmpsn/Grn 40.00 100.00
9 DRzn/Lwry/Vlncns 6.00 15.00
10 Lnrd/Gsl/Aldrdge 15.00 40.00

2016-17 Panini Preferred VS One on One Memorabilia

STATED PRINT RUN 99 SER.#'d SETS
1 K.Towns/K.Porzingis 10.00 25.00
2 L.James/C.Anthony 30.00 80.00
3 P.George/R.Jackson 8.00 20.00
4 S.Curry/R.Westbrook 40.00 100.00
5 H.Barnes/D.Rose 8.00 20.00
6 Antknmpo/Turner 12.00 30.00
7 Julius Randle/Al Horford 6.00 15.00
8 J.Wall/D.Schroder 6.00 15.00
9 Thompson/Turner 5.00 12.00
10 J.Parker/A.Gordon 10.00 25.00
11 J.Brown/B.Ingram 15.00 40.00
12 DeRozan/K.Irving 10.00 25.00
13 Zubac/Hrnngmz 8.00 20.00
14 Gobert/Lowry 6.00 15.00
15 Eric Bledsoe/Elfrid Payton 4.00 10.00
16 Gasol/Adams 6.00 15.00
17 Rudy Gay/Andre Drummond 5.00 12.00
18 Hassan Whiteside/Brook Lopez 4.00 10.00

2011 Panini Private Signings CS Exchange

AE Alex English 6.00 15.00
BWL Bill Walton 8.00 20.00
CON Connie Hawkins 6.00 15.00

2012-13 Panini Prizm

COMPLETE SET (300) 400.00 800.00
1 LeBron James 30.00 80.00
2 Paul Pierce 1.25 3.00
3 Jrue Holiday 1.00 2.50
4 Dwight Howard 1.00 2.50
5 Danny Granger .50 1.25
6 Elton Brand .60 1.50
7 Deron Williams .60 1.50
8 Omer Asik .50 1.25
9 Devin Harris .50 1.25
10 DeMarcus Cousins .75 2.00
11 Arron Afflalo .50 1.25
12 Kirk Hinrich .60 1.50
13 LaMarcus Aldridge .75 2.00
14 Thabo Sefolosha .50 1.25
15 Amare Stoudemire .75 2.00
16 Andris Biedrins .50 1.25
17 Tayshaun Prince .75 2.00
18 Al-Farouq Aminu .50 1.25
19 Chris Paul 1.50 4.00
20 Andrea Bargnani .50 1.25
21 Martell Webster .50 1.25
22 John Wall 1.00 2.50
23 Matt Bonner .50 1.25
24 Kobe Bryant 20.00 50.00
25 Paul Millsap .60 1.50
26 Brendan Haywood .50 1.25
27 DeAndre Jordan .60 1.50
28 Andre Iguodala .75 2.00
29 Nicolas Batum .60 1.50
30 Paul George 1.25 3.00
31 Mike Conley .60 1.50
32 Blake Griffin .75 2.00
33 Kevin Garnett 2.00 5.00
34 Jeremy Lin 1.25 3.00
35 Kevin Durant 3.00 8.00
36 Vince Carter 1.50 4.00
37 Ray Allen 1.25 3.00
38 Marco Belinelli .50 1.25
39 Corey Brewer .50 1.25
40 Glen Davis .50 1.25
41 Tyson Chandler .60 1.50
42 Eric Gordon .60 1.50
43 Andrew Bogut .60 1.50
44 Tyreke Evans .60 1.50
45 Pau Gasol 1.25 3.00
46 Jose Calderon .50 1.25
47 Russell Westbrook 1.25 3.00
48 Ricky Rubio .60 1.50
49 Stephen Jackson .60 1.50
50 Jeff Teague .50 1.25
51 Marc Gasol .75 2.00
52 Hollis Thompson RC .50 1.25
53 Carlos Boozer .60 1.50
54 Grant Hill 1.25 3.00
55 Al Jefferson .50 1.25
56 Evan Turner .50 1.25
57 Kendrick Perkins .50 1.25
58 Ramon Sessions .50 1.25
59 Danilo Gallinari .50 1.25
60 DeMar Derozan 1.00 2.50
61 Ryan Anderson .50 1.25
62 Brandon Bass .50 1.25
63 Dirk Nowitzki 2.00 5.00
64 Roy Hibbert .60 1.50
65 Emeka Okafor .60 1.50
66 Channing Frye .50 1.25
67 Wesley Matthews .50 1.25
68 Corey Maggette .60 1.50
69 Serge Ibaka .60 1.50
70 Luke Ridnour .60 1.50
71 Carmelo Anthony 1.25 3.00
72 Stephen Curry 30.00 80.00
73 Luol Deng .60 1.50
74 J.J. Redick .75 2.00
75 Avery Bradley .50 1.25
76 Rudy Gay .75 2.00
77 Dwyane Wade 1.50 4.00
78 Thaddeus Young .50 1.25
79 Brandon Jennings .50 1.25
80 Manu Ginobili 1.50 4.00
81 Jason Kidd 1.25 3.00
82 Kevin Martin .60 1.50
83 Andrew Bynum .50 1.25
84 Kyle Lowry .75 2.00
85 Gordon Hayward .75 2.00
86 Al Harrington .60 1.50
87 Gerald Wallace .60 1.50
88 Antawn Jamison .60 1.50
89 Caron Butler .60 1.50
90 Anderson Varejao .60 1.50
91 Nene .60 1.50
92 David Lee .50 1.25
93 Shane Battier .60 1.50
94 Jason Thompson .50 1.25
95 James Harden 1.50 4.00
96 Tyrus Thomas .50 1.25
97 J.J. Barea .60 1.50
98 Tyler Hansbrough .50 1.25
99 J.J. Hickson .50 1.25
100 Louis Williams .60 1.50
101 Tim Duncan 2.00 5.00
102 Chris Kaman .60 1.50
103 Jodie Meeks .50 1.25
104 Ty Lawson .50 1.25
105 Derrick Favors .60 1.50
106 Luis Scola .60 1.50
107 Rajon Rondo 1.00 2.50
108 Hedo Turkoglu .60 1.50
109 Rodney Stuckey .50 1.25
110 Zach Randolph .75 2.00
111 Steve Novak .50 1.25
112 Jon Brockman .50 1.25
113 Steve Nash 1.50 4.00
114 Joakim Noah .60 1.50
115 Chase Budinger .50 1.25
116 Chris Bosh 1.00 2.50
117 Brook Lopez .60 1.50
118 Jordan Crawford .50 1.25
119 Luc Mbah a Moute .50 1.25
120 Tony Parker 1.25 3.00
121 Daniel Gibson .50 1.25
122 Chauncey Billups 1.00 2.50
123 Brandon Rush .50 1.25
124 Shawn Marion .75 2.00
125 Al Horford .75 2.00
126 Raja Bell .60 1.50
127 Daequan Cook .50 1.25
128 Goran Dragic .75 2.00
129 Ben Gordon .60 1.50
130 Andre Miller .60 1.50
131 Jason Richardson .75 2.00
132 Udonis Haslem .60 1.50
133 Jason Terry .60 1.50
134 Nick Collison .60 1.50
135 Kevin Love .75 2.00
136 Marreese Speights .50 1.25
137 Toney Douglas .50 1.25
138 Charlie Villanueva .50 1.25
139 Tiago Splitter .60 1.50
140 George Hill .60 1.50
141 Marcin Gortat .50 1.25
142 Raymond Felton .50 1.25
143 O.J. Mayo .50 1.25
144 Ersan Ilyasova .50 1.25
145 Derrick Rose 1.25 3.00
146 Trevor Ariza .50 1.25
147 Metta World Peace .60 1.50
148 Mario Chalmers .60 1.50
149 Joe Johnson .60 1.50
150 Josh Smith .50 1.25
151 Wilt Chamberlain 2.50 6.00
152 Pete Maravich 1.50 4.00
153 Bill Russell 2.50 6.00
154 Oscar Robertson 1.50 4.00
155 Hakeem Olajuwon 1.50 4.00
156 Julius Erving 2.00 5.00
157 Dennis Rodman 2.00 5.00
158 Maurice Cheeks .60 1.50
159 Kareem Abdul-Jabbar 2.50 6.00
160 Anfernee Hardaway 2.00 5.00
161 David Thompson .75 2.00
162 Horace Grant .75 2.00
163 Larry Bird 2.50 6.00
164 Rolando Blackman .60 1.50
165 Larry Johnson 1.00 2.50
166 Shaquille O'Neal 2.50 6.00
167 Derrick Coleman .75 2.00
168 Karl Malone 1.25 3.00
169 Moses Malone 1.25 3.00
170 Mark Aguirre .60 1.50
171 Rudy Tomjanovich 1.00 2.50
172 Jerry West 1.50 4.00
173 George Mikan 2.50 6.00
174 Kelly Tripucka .60 1.50
175 David Robinson 1.25 3.00
176 Scottie Pippen 2.00 5.00
177 Danny Manning .60 1.50
178 Elgin Baylor 2.00 5.00
179 Charles Oakley .75 2.00
180 Sam Jones 1.00 2.50
181 Magic Johnson 2.50 6.00
182 Isiah Thomas 1.50 4.00
183 Bill Laimbeer 1.00 2.50
184 Patrick Ewing 1.25 3.00
185 Chris Mullin 1.00 2.50
186 John Stockton 1.50 4.00
187 Allen Iverson 1.25 3.00
188 Dominique Wilkins 1.00 2.50
189 Tim Hardaway 1.00 2.50
190 Zydrunas Ilgauskas .60 1.50
191 George Gervin 1.25 3.00
192 Toni Kukoc .75 2.00
193 James Worthy 1.25 3.00
194 Vlade Divac .75 2.00
195 Terry Porter .60 1.50
196 Bill Walton 1.25 3.00
197 Shawn Kemp 1.25 3.00
198 Yao Ming 1.50 4.00
199 Dikembe Mutombo 1.25 3.00
200 Alonzo Mourning 1.25 3.00
201 Kyrie Irving RC 25.00 60.00
202 MarShon Brooks RC .50 1.25
203 Klay Thompson RC 25.00 60.00
204 Alec Burks RC .75 2.00
205 Jimmy Butler RC 15.00 40.00
206 Norris Cole RC .50 1.25
207 Brandon Knight RC .60 1.50
208 Kenneth Faried RC .60 1.50
209 Kawhi Leonard RC 30.00 80.00
210 Reggie Jackson RC .75 2.00
211 Jordan Hamilton RC .50 1.25
212 Jimmer Fredette RC .75 2.00
213 Bismack Biyombo RC .60 1.50
214 Enes Kanter RC .75 2.00
215 Marcus Morris RC .75 2.00
216 Chandler Parsons RC .60 1.50
217 Iman Shumpert RC .60 1.50
218 Markieff Morris RC .75 2.00
219 Tobias Harris RC 1.50 4.00
220 Chris Singleton RC .50 1.25
221 Nolan Smith RC .50 1.25
222 Isaiah Thomas RC 1.00 2.50
223 Tristan Thompson RC .75 2.00
224 Jan Vesely RC .60 1.50
225 Kemba Walker RC 2.00 5.00
226 Derrick Williams RC .50 1.25
227 Cory Joseph RC .60 1.50
228 JaJuan Johnson RC .50 1.25
229 Justin Harper RC .50 1.25
230 Shelvin Mack RC .60 1.50
231 Gustavo Ayon RC .50 1.25
232 Charles Jenkins RC .50 1.25
233 Jeremy Tyler RC .50 1.25
234 Kyle Singler RC .50 1.25
235 Lavoy Allen RC .50 1.25
236 Anthony Davis RC 30.00 80.00
237 Michael Kidd-Gilchrist RC .60 1.50
238 Bradley Beal RC 4.00 10.00
239 Terrence Ross RC 1.25 3.00
240 Austin Rivers RC .75 2.00
241 Jeremy Lamb RC .75 2.00
242 Dion Waiters RC .60 1.50
243 Darius Morris RC .60 1.50
244 Thomas Robinson RC .50 1.25
245 Damian Lillard RC 25.00 60.00
246 Harrison Barnes RC 1.00 2.50
247 Andre Drummond RC 1.25 3.00
248 Meyers Leonard RC .60 1.50
249 Kendall Marshall RC .50 1.25
250 John Jenkins RC .50 1.25
251 John Henson RC .60 1.50
252 E'Twaun Moore RC .60 1.50
253 Royce White RC .50 1.25
254 Tyler Zeller RC .50 1.25
255 Terrence Jones RC .50 1.25
256 Andrew Nicholson RC .50 1.25
257 Evan Fournier RC .75 2.00
258 Jared Sullinger RC .60 1.50
259 Fab Melo RC .50 1.25
260 Jared Cunningham RC .50 1.25
261 Festus Ezeli RC .50 1.25
262 Tony Wroten RC .50 1.25
263 Miles Plumlee RC .50 1.25
264 Marquis Teague RC .50 1.25
265 Perry Jones RC .50 1.25
266 Arnett Moultrie RC .50 1.25
267 Nikola Vucevic RC 2.00 5.00
268 Donald Sloan RC .50 1.25
269 Jon Leuer RC .50 1.25
270 John Shurna RC .50 1.25
271 Andrew Goudelock RC .50 1.25
272 Lance Thomas RC .50 1.25
273 Cory Higgins RC .50 1.25
274 Elliot Williams .30 .75
275 Terrel Harris RC .50 1.25
276 Malcolm Lee RC .50 1.25
277 Jeff Taylor RC .50 1.25
278 Jae Crowder RC 1.00 2.50
279 Orlando Johnson RC .50 1.25
280 Jonas Valanciunas RC 1.00 2.50
281 Bernard James RC .50 1.25
282 Draymond Green RC 15.00 40.00
283 Quincy Acy RC .50 1.25
284 Quincy Miller RC .50 1.25
285 Khris Middleton RC 2.50 6.00
286 Will Barton RC 1.00 2.50
287 Tyshawn Taylor RC .50 1.25
288 Doron Lamb RC .50 1.25
289 Josh Selby RC .50 1.25
290 Kim English RC .50 1.25
291 Scott Machado RC .50 1.25
292 Kris Joseph RC .50 1.25
293 Julyan Stone RC .50 1.25
294 DeAndre Liggins RC .50 1.25
295 Robert Sacre RC .50 1.25
296 Darrell Arthur .30 .75
297 Kyle O'Quinn RC .60 1.50
298 Darius Miller RC .60 1.50
299 Darius Johnson-Odom RC .50 1.25
300 Greg Stiemsma RC .50 1.25

2012-13 Panini Prizm Prizms

*VETS: 6X TO 15X BASE HI
*RETIRED: 6X TO 15X BASE HI
*ROOKIES: 6X TO 15X BASE HI
1 LeBron James 2,500.00 5,000.00
2 Paul Pierce 50.00 120.00
3 Jrue Holiday 40.00 100.00
4 Dwight Howard 25.00 60.00
19 Chris Paul 100.00 250.00
22 John Wall 20.00 50.00
24 Kobe Bryant 1,000.00 2,000.00
30 Paul George 100.00 250.00
31 Mike Conley 15.00 40.00
32 Blake Griffin 20.00 50.00
33 Kevin Garnett 75.00 200.00
34 Jeremy Lin 60.00 150.00
35 Kevin Durant 125.00 300.00
36 Vince Carter 75.00 200.00
37 Ray Allen 40.00 100.00
47 Russell Westbrook 75.00 200.00
54 Grant Hill 30.00 80.00
60 DeMar Derozan 40.00 100.00
63 Dirk Nowitzki 75.00 200.00
71 Carmelo Anthony 60.00 150.00
72 Stephen Curry 600.00 1,200.00
74 J.J. Redick 12.00 30.00
77 Dwyane Wade 75.00 200.00
80 Manu Ginobili 40.00 100.00
81 Jason Kidd 30.00 80.00
84 Kyle Lowry 25.00 60.00
95 James Harden 100.00 250.00
101 Tim Duncan 75.00 200.00
107 Rajon Rondo 25.00 60.00
110 Zach Randolph 12.00 30.00
113 Steve Nash 60.00 150.00
116 Chris Bosh 25.00 60.00
120 Tony Parker 25.00 60.00
145 Derrick Rose 40.00 100.00
151 Wilt Chamberlain 75.00 200.00
152 Pete Maravich 75.00 200.00
153 Bill Russell 100.00 250.00
154 Oscar Robertson 75.00 200.00
155 Hakeem Olajuwon 60.00 150.00
156 Julius Erving 60.00 150.00
157 Dennis Rodman 60.00 150.00
159 Kareem Abdul-Jabbar 75.00 200.00
160 Anfernee Hardaway 60.00 150.00
163 Larry Bird 75.00 200.00
165 Larry Johnson 25.00 60.00
166 Shaquille O'Neal 75.00 200.00
168 Karl Malone 40.00 100.00
172 Jerry West 60.00 150.00
175 David Robinson 40.00 100.00
176 Scottie Pippen 60.00 150.00
181 Magic Johnson 75.00 200.00
182 Isiah Thomas 40.00 100.00
184 Patrick Ewing 40.00 100.00
185 Chris Mullin 15.00 40.00
186 John Stockton 40.00 100.00
187 Allen Iverson 75.00 200.00
188 Dominique Wilkins 40.00 100.00
192 Toni Kukoc 20.00 50.00
197 Shawn Kemp 40.00 100.00
198 Yao Ming 100.00 250.00
200 Alonzo Mourning 20.00 50.00
201 Kyrie Irving 300.00 600.00
203 Klay Thompson 300.00 600.00
205 Jimmy Butler 300.00 600.00
209 Kawhi Leonard 600.00 1,200.00
236 Anthony Davis 400.00 800.00
238 Bradley Beal 125.00 300.00
245 Damian Lillard 300.00 600.00
282 Draymond Green 150.00 400.00

2012-13 Panini Prizm Prizms Green

*VETS: 6X TO 15X BASE HI
*RETIRED: 6X TO 15X BASE HI
*ROOKIES: 6X TO 15X BASE HI
1 LeBron James 1,500.00 3,000.00
2 Paul Pierce 40.00 100.00
3 Jrue Holiday 40.00 100.00
4 Dwight Howard 20.00 50.00
19 Chris Paul 60.00 150.00
24 Kobe Bryant 600.00 1,200.00
30 Paul George 60.00 150.00
33 Kevin Garnett 125.00 300.00
35 Kevin Durant 125.00 300.00
36 Vince Carter 50.00 120.00
37 Ray Allen 25.00 60.00
47 Russell Westbrook 50.00 120.00
54 Grant Hill 20.00 50.00
60 DeMar Derozan 25.00 60.00
63 Dirk Nowitzki 60.00 150.00
71 Carmelo Anthony 75.00 200.00
72 Stephen Curry 1,000.00 2,000.00
77 Dwyane Wade 50.00 120.00
80 Manu Ginobili 25.00 60.00
81 Jason Kidd 30.00 80.00
84 Kyle Lowry 25.00 60.00
95 James Harden 60.00 150.00
101 Tim Duncan 50.00 120.00
107 Rajon Rondo 15.00 40.00
113 Steve Nash 40.00 100.00
116 Chris Bosh 20.00 50.00
120 Tony Parker 15.00 40.00
125 Al Horford 25.00 60.00
145 Derrick Rose 25.00 60.00
151 Wilt Chamberlain 75.00 200.00
152 Pete Maravich 75.00 200.00
153 Bill Russell 125.00 300.00
154 Oscar Robertson 75.00 200.00
155 Hakeem Olajuwon 75.00 200.00
156 Julius Erving 40.00 100.00
157 Dennis Rodman 75.00 200.00
159 Kareem Abdul-Jabbar 75.00 200.00
160 Anfernee Hardaway 40.00 100.00
163 Larry Bird 75.00 200.00
166 Shaquille O'Neal 100.00 250.00
168 Karl Malone 30.00 80.00
169 Moses Malone 30.00 80.00
172 Jerry West 60.00 150.00
175 David Robinson 25.00 60.00
176 Scottie Pippen 40.00 100.00
181 Magic Johnson 75.00 200.00
182 Isiah Thomas 25.00 60.00
184 Patrick Ewing 25.00 60.00
186 John Stockton 25.00 60.00
187 Allen Iverson 50.00 120.00
188 Dominique Wilkins 25.00 60.00
192 Toni Kukoc 12.00 30.00
197 Shawn Kemp 25.00 60.00
198 Yao Ming 125.00 300.00
200 Alonzo Mourning 12.00 30.00
201 Kyrie Irving 150.00 400.00
203 Klay Thompson 300.00 600.00
205 Jimmy Butler 200.00 500.00
209 Kawhi Leonard 500.00 1,000.00
236 Anthony Davis 300.00 600.00
238 Bradley Beal 75.00 200.00
245 Damian Lillard 300.00 600.00
282 Draymond Green 100.00 250.00

2012-13 Panini Prizm Autographs

1 Kobe Bryant 3,000.00 6,000.00
2 Kevin Durant 500.00 1,200.00
3 Blake Griffin 15.00 40.00
4 Kyrie Irving 300.00 600.00
5 Anthony Davis 500.00 1,000.00
6 Michael Kidd-Gilchrist 3.00 8.00
7 Brandon Knight 3.00 8.00
8 Alex English 5.00 12.00
9 World B. Free 6.00 15.00
10 Kenneth Faried 3.00 8.00
11 Iman Shumpert 3.00 8.00
12 MarShon Brooks 2.50 6.00
13 Austin Rivers 4.00 10.00
14 Meyers Leonard 3.00 8.00
15 Clyde Lovellette 5.00 12.00
16 Gary Payton 15.00 40.00
17 George McGinnis 4.00 10.00
18 Kendall Marshall 2.50 6.00
19 John Starks 3.00 8.00
20 Terrence Ross 6.00 15.00
21 Bernard James 2.50 6.00
22 Reggie Jackson 4.00 10.00
23 Sean Elliott 5.00 12.00
24 Tyler Honeycutt 2.50 6.00
25 Jonas Valanciunas 5.00 12.00
26 Jared Sullinger 2.50 6.00
27 Kenny Anderson 3.00 8.00
28 Marco Belinelli 3.00 8.00
29 Michael Finley 4.00 10.00
30 Peja Stojakovic 5.00 12.00
31 Rex Chapman 3.00 8.00
32 Reggie Theus 3.00 8.00
33 Robert Sacre 2.50 6.00
34 Sidney Moncrief 2.50 6.00
35 Tristan Thompson 4.00 10.00
36 Jimmer Fredette 4.00 10.00
37 Steve Kerr 8.00 20.00
38 Tom Chambers 4.00 10.00
39 Terry Porter 3.00 8.00
40 Nikola Vucevic 25.00 60.00
41 Kemba Walker 75.00 200.00
42 Lance Thomas 2.50 6.00
43 Vlade Divac 4.00 10.00
44 Tyler Zeller 2.50 6.00
45 Zydrunas Ilgauskas 5.00 12.00
46 Tony Wroten 2.50 6.00
47 Ivan Johnson 2.50 6.00
48 Jan Vesely 2.50 6.00
49 Jared Cunningham 2.50 6.00
50 Jeff Hornacek 3.00 8.00
51 Justin Hamilton 2.50 6.00
52 Will Barton 5.00 12.00
53 Kurt Rambis 4.00 10.00
54 Kareem Abdul-Jabbar 30.00 80.00
55 Miles Plumlee 2.50 6.00
56 Lenny Wilkens 6.00 15.00
57 Fab Melo 2.50 6.00
58 Kevin Willis 3.00 8.00
59 Kim English 2.50 6.00
60 Harry Gallatin 4.00 10.00
61 Quincy Miller 2.50 6.00
62 Ralph Sampson 3.00 8.00
63 Thomas Robinson 2.50 6.00
64 Walker Berry 2.50 6.00
65 Nate Archibald 5.00 12.00
66 Lavoy Allen 2.50 6.00
67 Quincy Acy 2.50 6.00
68 John Henson 3.00 8.00
69 Alec Burks 4.00 10.00
70 Allan Houston 6.00 15.00
71 Andrew Goudelock EXCH 2.50 6.00
72 Andrew Nicholson 2.50 6.00
73 Chandler Parsons 3.00 8.00
74 Larry Johnson 15.00 40.00
75 Mike Scott 3.00 8.00
76 DeAndre Liggins 2.50 6.00
77 Norris Cole 2.50 6.00
78 Perry Jones 2.50 6.00
79 Rolando Blackman 3.00 8.00
80 Royce White 2.50 6.00
81 Shelvin Mack 2.50 6.00
82 Terrence Jones 2.50 6.00
83 Tyshawn Taylor 2.50 6.00
84 Evan Fournier 4.00 10.00
85 Charles Jenkins 2.50 6.00
86 Darius Johnson-Odom 2.50 6.00
87 Greg Stiemsma 2.50 6.00
88 Arnett Moultrie 2.50 6.00
89 Bradley Beal 25.00 60.00
90 Jeremy Lamb 4.00 10.00
91 Marquis Teague 2.50 6.00
92 Jeff Taylor 2.50 6.00
93 Festus Ezeli 2.50 6.00
94 Jae Crowder 12.00 30.00
95 Draymond Green 75.00 200.00
96 Dion Waiters 3.00 8.00
97 Chris Singleton 2.50 6.00
98 Jimmy Butler 150.00 400.00
99 Malcolm Lee 2.50 6.00
100 E'Twaun Moore 2.50 6.00

2012-13 Panini Prizm Autographs Prizms

*PRIZMS: 1X TO 2.5X BASE HI
STATED PRINT RUN 25 SER.#'d SETS
1 Kobe Bryant 10,000.00 20,000.00
8 Alex English 20.00 50.00
16 Gary Payton 30.00 80.00
54 Kareem Abdul-Jabbar 50.00 120.00
95 Draymond Green 200.00 500.00

2012-13 Panini Prizm Downtown Bound

COMPLETE SET (25) 40.00 100.00
*PRIZMS: 1.25X TO 3X HI COLUMN
*PRIZMS GREEN: 2.5X TO 6X HI COLUMN
1 Ray Allen 2.00 5.00
2 Dirk Nowitzki 6.00 15.00
3 Steve Novak .75 2.00

4 Steve Nash 6.00 15.00
5 Kevin Durant 12.00 30.00
6 Kobe Bryant 15.00 40.00
7 Stephen Curry 15.00 40.00
8 Dwyane Wade 6.00 15.00
9 LeBron James 20.00 50.00
10 Jeremy Lin 2.00 5.00
11 Brandon Jennings .75 2.00
12 Kevin Love 1.25 3.00
13 Kyrie Irving 20.00 50.00
14 Chris Paul 5.00 12.00
15 Mario Chalmers 1.00 2.50
16 Ryan Anderson .75 2.00
17 Shane Battier 1.00 2.50
18 Paul Pierce 2.00 5.00
19 James Harden 6.00 15.00
20 Joe Johnson 1.00 2.50
21 Russell Westbrook 6.00 15.00
22 Deron Williams 1.00 2.50
23 Danny Granger .75 2.00
24 Klay Thompson 20.00 50.00
25 Brandon Rush .75 2.00

2012-13 Panini Prizm Downtown Bound Prizms

*PRIZMS: 2.5X TO 6X BASE HI
1 Ray Allen 10.00 25.00
2 Dirk Nowitzki 12.00 30.00
4 Steve Nash 20.00 50.00
5 Kevin Durant 75.00 200.00
6 Kobe Bryant 300.00 600.00
7 Stephen Curry 125.00 300.00
8 Dwyane Wade 30.00 80.00
9 LeBron James 300.00 600.00
10 Jeremy Lin 12.00 30.00
13 Kyrie Irving 60.00 150.00
19 James Harden 60.00 150.00
21 Russell Westbrook 40.00 100.00

2012-13 Panini Prizm Downtown Bound Prizms Green

*PRIZMS GREEN: 2X TO 5X BASE HI
6 Kobe Bryant 50.00 120.00
7 Stephen Curry 50.00 120.00
14 Chris Paul 15.00 40.00

2012-13 Panini Prizm Finalists

COMPLETE SET (38) 60.00 150.00
*PRIZMS: 1X TO 2.5X HI COLUMN
*PRIZMS GREEN: 2.5X TO 6X HI COLUMN
1 Bill Russell 4.00 10.00
2 Bill Laimbeer 1.50 4.00
3 Kareem Abdul-Jabbar 4.00 10.00
4 Scottie Pippen 6.00 15.00
5 Kobe Bryant 30.00 80.00
6 LeBron James 60.00 150.00
7 Dwyane Wade 2.50 6.00
8 Tim Duncan 3.00 8.00
9 David Robinson 2.00 5.00
10 Shaquille O'Neal 4.00 10.00
11 Robert Horry 1.25 3.00
12 Magic Johnson 4.00 10.00
13 Larry Bird 4.00 10.00
14 Dennis Rodman 6.00 15.00
15 Derek Fisher 1.00 2.50
16 Robert Parish 2.00 5.00
17 Kurt Rambis 1.25 3.00
18 Chris Bosh 1.50 4.00
19 Dirk Nowitzki 3.00 8.00
20 Jason Kidd 2.00 5.00
21 Tyson Chandler 1.00 2.50
22 Mario Chalmers 1.00 2.50
23 Tony Parker 2.00 5.00
24 Chauncey Billups 1.50 4.00
25 Hakeem Olajuwon 2.50 6.00
26 Isiah Thomas 2.50 6.00
27 Joe Dumars 1.50 4.00
28 James Worthy 2.00 5.00
29 Toni Kukoc 1.25 3.00
30 Rajon Rondo 1.50 4.00
31 Paul Pierce 2.00 5.00
32 Kevin Garnett 3.00 8.00
33 Ray Allen 2.00 5.00
34 Manu Ginobili 2.50 6.00
35 Clyde Drexler 2.00 5.00
36 Pau Gasol 2.00 5.00
37 Jason Terry 1.00 2.50
38 Michael Finley 1.25 3.00

2012-13 Panini Prizm Finalists Prizms Green

6 LeBron James 75.00 200.00

2012-13 Panini Prizm Most Valuable Players

COMPLETE SET (25) 60.00 150.00
*PRIZMS: 1X TO 2.5X HI COLUMN
1 LeBron James 60.00 150.00
2 Derrick Rose 2.00 5.00
3 Kobe Bryant 25.00 60.00
4 Dirk Nowitzki 3.00 8.00
5 Steve Nash 2.50 6.00
6 Kevin Garnett 3.00 8.00
7 Tim Duncan 3.00 8.00
8 Allen Iverson 2.00 5.00
9 Shaquille O'Neal 4.00 10.00
10 Karl Malone 2.00 5.00
11 David Robinson 2.00 5.00
12 Hakeem Olajuwon 2.50 6.00
13 Magic Johnson 4.00 10.00
14 Larry Bird 4.00 10.00
15 Moses Malone 2.00 5.00
16 Julius Erving 3.00 8.00
17 Kareem Abdul-Jabbar 4.00 10.00
18 Bill Walton 2.00 5.00
19 Bob McAdoo 1.00 2.50
20 Dave Cowens 2.00 5.00
21 Willis Reed 2.00 5.00
22 Wes Unseld 1.50 4.00
23 Wilt Chamberlain 4.00 10.00
24 Bill Russell 4.00 10.00
25 Oscar Robertson 2.50 6.00

2012-13 Panini Prizm Most Valuable Players Prizms

*PRIZMS: 1.25X TO 3X BASE HI
1 LeBron James 300.00 600.00
3 Kobe Bryant 150.00 400.00
4 Dirk Nowitzki 30.00 80.00
6 Kevin Garnett 12.00 30.00
7 Tim Duncan 12.00 30.00
8 Allen Iverson 15.00 40.00
13 Magic Johnson 15.00 40.00
17 Kareem Abdul-Jabbar 10.00 25.00

2012-13 Panini Prizm Most Valuable Players Prizms Green

*PRIZMS GREEN: 3X TO 8X BASE HI
1 LeBron James 150.00 400.00
3 Kobe Bryant 75.00 200.00

2012-13 Panini Prizm USA Basketball

COMPLETE SET (12) 200.00 500.00
1 Tyson Chandler 2.50 6.00
2 Kevin Durant 25.00 60.00
3 LeBron James 60.00 150.00
4 Russell Westbrook 15.00 40.00
5 Deron Williams 2.50 6.00
6 Andre Iguodala 3.00 8.00
7 Kobe Bryant 60.00 150.00
8 Kevin Love 12.00 30.00
9 James Harden 15.00 40.00
10 Chris Paul 20.00 50.00
11 Anthony Davis 40.00 100.00
12 Carmelo Anthony 20.00 50.00

2012-13 Panini Prizm USA Basketball Prizms

*PRIZMS: 1.25X TO 3X BASE HI
1 Tyson Chandler 40.00 100.00
2 Kevin Durant 500.00 1,000.00
3 LeBron James 1,000.00 2,000.00
4 Russell Westbrook 125.00 300.00
7 Kobe Bryant 600.00 1,200.00
9 James Harden 200.00 500.00
10 Chris Paul 150.00 400.00
12 Carmelo Anthony 125.00 300.00

2012-13 Panini Prizm USA Basketball Prizms Green

*PRIZMS GREEN: 1.2X TO 3X BASE HI
2 Kevin Durant 125.00 300.00
3 LeBron James 800.00 1,500.00
4 Russell Westbrook 75.00 200.00
5 Deron Williams 10.00 25.00
6 Andre Iguodala 12.00 30.00
7 Kobe Bryant 300.00 600.00
8 Kevin Love 40.00 100.00
9 James Harden 100.00 250.00
10 Chris Paul 100.00 250.00

2013-14 Panini Prizm

COMPLETE SET (297) 800.00 1,500.00
1 Kobe Bryant 8.00 20.00
2 Zach Randolph .40 1.00
3 Larry Sanders .30 .75
4 Anthony Davis 1.50 4.00
5 J.R. Smith .50 1.25
6 Carl Landry .30 .75
7 Jamal Crawford .50 1.25
8 Paul George .75 2.00
9 Harrison Barnes .50 1.25
10 Nate Robinson .30 .75
11 Monta Ellis .40 1.00
12 Taj Gibson .40 1.00
13 Ben Gordon .40 1.00
14 Rajon Rondo .60 1.50
15 Jeff Teague .30 .75
16 Gordon Hayward .60 1.50
17 DeMar DeRozan .60 1.50
18 Jimmer Fredette .50 1.25
19 Damian Lillard 1.50 4.00
20 Spencer Hawes .30 .75
21 Arron Afflalo .30 .75
22 Nick Young .30 .75
23 Chris Bosh .60 1.50
24 Ersan Ilyasova .30 .75
25 Austin Rivers .30 .75
26 Kenyon Martin .50 1.25
27 Eric Maynor .30 .75
28 Jared Dudley .30 .75
29 Lance Stephenson .40 1.00
30 Draymond Green .75 2.00
31 J.J. Hickson .30 .75
32 Samuel Dalembert .30 .75
33 Luol Deng .40 1.00
34 Al Jefferson .30 .75
35 Jeff Green .30 .75
36 Al Horford .50 1.25
37 Marvin Williams .30 .75
38 Tracy McGrady .75 2.00
39 Jason Thompson .30 .75
40 Markieff Morris .30 .75
41 Lavoy Allen .30 .75
42 Andrew Nicholson .30 .75
43 Pau Gasol .75 2.00
44 Dwyane Wade 1.00 2.50
45 O.J. Mayo .30 .75
46 Jason Smith .30 .75
47 Metta World Peace .40 1.00
48 Paul Millsap .40 1.00
49 J.J. Redick .50 1.25
50 Danny Granger .30 .75
51 David Lee .30 .75
52 JaVale McGee .40 1.00
53 Dirk Nowitzki 1.25 3.00
54 Joakim Noah .50 1.25
55 Paul Pierce .75 2.00
56 Jared Sullinger .30 .75
57 Trevor Ariza .30 .75
58 Enes Kanter .40 1.00
59 Tony Parker .75 2.00
60 Greivis Vasquez .30 .75
61 Marcus Morris .40 1.00
62 Jason Richardson .50 1.25
63 Thabo Sefolosha .40 1.00
64 Steve Blake .30 .75
65 LeBron James 8.00 20.00
66 John Henson .30 .75
67 Jrue Holiday .60 1.50
68 Raymond Felton .30 .75
69 Kevin Seraphin .30 .75
70 DeAndre Jordan .40 1.00
71 Jeremy Lin .75 2.00
72 Andre Iguodala .50 1.25
73 Ty Lawson .30 .75
74 Tyler Zeller .30 .75
75 Jimmy Butler 1.00 2.50
76 Kevin Garnett 1.25 3.00
77 Gerald Wallace .40 1.00
78 Nene .40 1.00
79 Derrick Favors .30 .75
80 Tim Duncan 1.25 3.00
81 DeMarcus Cousins .50 1.25
82 Marcin Gortat .30 .75
83 Evan Turner .30 .75
84 Serge Ibaka .40 1.00
85 Steve Nash 1.00 2.50
86 Norris Cole .30 .75
87 Kevin Love .50 1.25
88 Ryan Anderson .30 .75
89 Tyson Chandler .40 1.00
90 Martell Webster .30 .75
91 Chris Paul 1.00 2.50
92 James Harden 1.00 2.50
93 Chauncey Billups .60 1.50
94 Kenneth Faried .40 1.00
95 Dion Waiters .30 .75
96 Derrick Rose .75 2.00
97 Joe Johnson .40 1.00
98 Brandon Bass .30 .75
99 John Wall .60 1.50
100 Tyler Hansbrough .30 .75
101 Tiago Splitter .30 .75
102 Thomas Robinson .30 .75
103 Kendall Marshall .30 .75
104 Tobias Harris .50 1.25
105 Russell Westbrook .75 2.00
106 Robert Sacre .30 .75
107 Shane Battier .40 1.00
108 Kevin Martin .40 1.00
109 Tyreke Evans .40 1.00
110 Francisco Garcia .30 .75
111 Ryan Hollins .30 .75
112 Blake Griffin .50 1.25
113 Dwight Howard .60 1.50
114 Rodney Stuckey .30 .75
115 Evan Fournier .40 1.00
116 Tristan Thompson .30 .75
117 Carlos Boozer .40 1.00
118 Jason Terry .40 1.00
119 Avery Bradley .30 .75
120 Emeka Okafor .40 1.00
121 Terrence Ross .40 1.00
122 Manu Ginobili 1.00 2.50
123 Wesley Matthews .30 .75
124 Goran Dragic .40 1.00
125 Nikola Vucevic .60 1.50
126 Ronnie Brewer .30 .75
127 Marc Gasol .50 1.25
128 Udonis Haslem .40 1.00
129 Ricky Rubio .40 1.00
130 Eric Gordon .40 1.00
131 Marcus Camby .40 1.00
132 Arnett Moultrie .30 .75
133 George Hill .40 1.00
134 Chandler Parsons .30 .75
135 Josh Smith .30 .75
136 Andre Miller .40 1.00
137 Kyrie Irving 1.50 4.00
138 Michael Kidd-Gilchrist .30 .75
139 Deron Williams .40 1.00
140 Louis Williams .40 1.00
141 Bradley Beal .75 2.00
142 Rudy Gay .40 1.00
143 Kawhi Leonard 1.50 4.00
144 Nicolas Batum .40 1.00
145 Eric Bledsoe .40 1.00
146 Maurice Harkless .30 .75
147 Kevin Durant 1.50 4.00
148 Mike Conley .50 1.25
149 Ray Allen .75 2.00
150 Alexey Shved .30 .75
151 Amar'e Stoudemire .50 1.25
152 Bismack Biyombo .30 .75
153 Andrei Kirilenko .50 1.25
154 David West .40 1.00
155 Aaron Brooks .30 .75
156 Greg Monroe .30 .75
157 Jae Crowder .30 .75
158 Andrew Bynum .30 .75
159 Kemba Walker .50 1.25
160 Brook Lopez .50 1.25
161 Kyle Korver .40 1.00
162 Alec Burks .30 .75
163 Kyle Lowry .50 1.25
164 Danny Green .30 .75
165 Meyers Leonard .30 .75
166 Caron Butler .40 1.00
167 Jameer Nelson .30 .75
168 Kendrick Perkins .30 .75
169 Tayshaun Prince .50 1.25
170 Brandon Knight .40 1.00
171 Chase Budinger .30 .75
172 Carmelo Anthony .75 2.00
173 Mike Miller .40 1.00
174 Andray Blatche .30 .75
175 Chris Copeland .30 .75
176 Stephen Curry 10.00 25.00
177 Brandon Jennings .30 .75
178 Vince Carter 1.00 2.50
179 Anderson Varejao .30 .75
180 Gerald Henderson .30 .75
181 MarShon Brooks .30 .75
182 John Jenkins .30 .75
183 Jeremy Evans .30 .75
184 Jonas Valanciunas .40 1.00
185 Marcus Thornton .30 .75
186 LaMarcus Aldridge .50 1.25
187 Thaddeus Young .30 .75
188 Glen Davis .30 .75
189 Jeremy Lamb .30 .75
190 Tony Allen .30 .75
191 Carlos Delfino .30 .75
192 Corey Brewer .30 .75
193 Iman Shumpert .30 .75
194 Tony Wroten .30 .75
195 C.J. Miles .30 .75
196 Roy Hibbert .30 .75
197 Klay Thompson 1.50 4.00
198 Andre Drummond .50 1.25
199 Shawn Marion .50 1.25
200 Kirk Hinrich .30 .75
201 John Stockton 1.00 2.50
202 Pete Maravich .75 2.00
203 Rolando Blackman .40 1.00
204 Shaquille O'Neal 2.00 5.00
205 Larry Johnson .60 1.50
206 Sean Elliott .50 1.25
207 Dan Majerle .40 1.00
208 Vlade Divac .50 1.25
209 Yao Ming 1.00 2.50
210 Rick Fox .40 1.00
211 Norm Nixon .40 1.00
212 Oscar Robertson .75 2.00
213 Ron Harper .50 1.25
214 Allen Iverson 1.00 2.50
215 Gary Payton .75 2.00
216 Joe Dumars .60 1.50
217 Detlef Schrempf .50 1.25
218 Jack Sikma .50 1.25
219 Dennis Rodman 1.25 3.00
220 John Havlicek 1.25 3.00
221 Julius Erving 1.25 3.00
222 Phil Jackson .60 1.50
223 Scottie Pippen 1.25 3.00
224 Dennis Johnson .40 1.00
225 Nick Van Exel .50 1.25
226 David Robinson 1.00 2.50
227 Robert Horry .50 1.25
228 Sam Perkins .40 1.00
229 Moses Malone .75 2.00
230 Dave DeBusschere .50 1.25
231 Kareem Abdul-Jabbar 1.50 4.00
232 Larry Bird 2.00 5.00
233 Clyde Drexler .75 2.00
234 Shawn Kemp .75 2.00
235 Nate Archibald .60 1.50
236 Isiah Thomas .60 1.50
237 Manute Bol .50 1.25
238 Adrian Dantley .50 1.25
239 Jerry West 1.25 3.00
240 George Gervin .75 2.00
241 Karl Malone 1.00 2.50
242 Magic Johnson 2.00 5.00
243 Dominique Wilkins .75 2.00
244 Alonzo Mourning .75 2.00
245 Grant Hill .75 2.00
246 Tim Hardaway .60 1.50
247 Muggsy Bogues .50 1.25
248 Mark Jackson .40 1.00
249 Lucius Allen .50 1.25
250 Bernard King .60 1.50
251 Walt Frazier .75 2.00
252 James Worthy .60 1.50
253 Anfernee Hardaway 1.25 3.00
254 Hakeem Olajuwon 1.00 2.50
255 Jason Kidd .75 2.00
256 Chris Mullin .60 1.50
257 Wilt Chamberlain 1.50 4.00
258 Glen Rice .40 1.00
259 B.J. Armstrong .50 1.25
260 Bill Russell 1.50 4.00
261 Shabazz Muhammad RC .50 1.25
262 Alex Len RC .60 1.50
263 Ben McLemore RC .60 1.50
264 Cody Zeller RC .60 1.50
265 M.Carter-Williams RC .60 1.50
266 Glen Rice Jr. RC .50 1.25
267 Archie Goodwin RC .50 1.25
268 Nate Wolters RC .50 1.25
269 Jamaal Franklin RC .50 1.25
270 Reggie Bullock RC .60 1.50
271 Anthony Bennett RC .50 1.25
272 Kelly Olynyk RC .60 1.50
273 Tony Mitchell RC .50 1.25
274 Isaiah Canaan RC .50 1.25
275 Carrick Felix RC .50 1.25
276 Victor Oladipo RC 1.25 3.00
277 Solomon Hill RC .60 1.50
278 Ricky Ledo RC .60 1.50
279 Shane Larkin RC .50 1.25
280 Ryan Kelly RC .50 1.25
281 Otto Porter RC .75 2.00
282 Trey Burke RC .60 1.50
283 C.J. McCollum RC 2.00 5.00
284 Kentavious Caldwell-Pope RC .75 2.00
285 Nerlens Noel RC .60 1.50
286 Dennis Schroder RC 1.50 4.00
287 Tim Hardaway Jr. RC .60 1.50
288 Mason Plumlee RC .60 1.50
289 Peyton Siva RC .50 1.25
290 G.Antetokounmpo RC 100.00 250.00
291 Steven Adams RC 1.25 3.00
292 Tony Snell RC .60 1.50
293 Ray McCallum RC .50 1.25
294 Gorgui Dieng RC .60 1.50
295 Allen Crabbe RC .50 1.25
296 Jeff Withey RC .50 1.25
297 Gal Mekel RC .50 1.25

2013-14 Panini Prizm Prizms

*PRIZM VET: 3X TO 8X BASIC
*PRIZM RC: 1X TO 2.5X BASIC
1 Kobe Bryant 200.00 500.00
4 Anthony Davis 125.00 300.00
8 Paul George 40.00 100.00
19 Damian Lillard 400.00 800.00
44 Dwyane Wade 40.00 100.00
53 Dirk Nowitzki 15.00 40.00
65 LeBron James 1,000.00 2,000.00
80 Tim Duncan 6.00 15.00
92 James Harden 125.00 300.00
105 Russell Westbrook 15.00 40.00
137 Kyrie Irving 10.00 25.00
141 Bradley Beal 60.00 150.00
143 Kawhi Leonard 300.00 600.00
147 Kevin Durant 200.00 500.00
164 Danny Green 10.00 25.00
176 Stephen Curry 200.00 500.00
197 Klay Thompson 12.00 30.00
204 Shaquille O'Neal 10.00 25.00
209 Yao Ming 10.00 25.00
214 Allen Iverson 10.00 25.00
253 Anfernee Hardaway 12.00 30.00
262 Alex Len 6.00 15.00
276 Victor Oladipo 100.00 250.00
281 Otto Porter 8.00 20.00
282 Trey Burke 15.00 40.00
283 C.J. McCollum 125.00 300.00
284 Kentavious Caldwell-Pope 8.00 20.00
285 Nerlens Noel 10.00 25.00
286 Dennis Schroder 75.00 200.00
287 Tim Hardaway Jr. 15.00 40.00
290 Giannis Antetokounmpo 2,000.00 4,000.00
291 Steven Adams 40.00 100.00
295 Allen Crabbe 6.00 15.00

2013-14 Panini Prizm Prizms Blue

*BLUE VET: 3X TO 8X BASIC
*BLUE RC: 2X TO 5X BASIC
1 Kobe Bryant 200.00 500.00
4 Anthony Davis 75.00 200.00
19 Damian Lillard 200.00 500.00
44 Dwyane Wade 20.00 50.00
53 Dirk Nowitzki 25.00 60.00
65 LeBron James 200.00 500.00
92 James Harden 25.00 60.00
141 Bradley Beal 50.00 120.00
143 Kawhi Leonard 150.00 400.00
147 Kevin Durant 200.00 500.00
176 Stephen Curry 200.00 500.00
197 Klay Thompson 20.00 50.00
253 Anfernee Hardaway 12.00 30.00
276 Victor Oladipo 30.00 80.00
281 Otto Porter 10.00 25.00
283 C.J. McCollum 100.00 250.00
286 Dennis Schroder 60.00 150.00
287 Tim Hardaway Jr. 10.00 25.00
290 Giannis Antetokounmpo 3,000.00 6,000.00
291 Steven Adams 12.00 30.00

2013-14 Panini Prizm Prizms Green

*GREEN VET: 2.5X TO 6X BASIC
*GREEN RC: 1.5X TO 4X BASIC
1 Kobe Bryant 150.00 400.00
4 Anthony Davis 75.00 200.00
19 Damian Lillard 75.00 200.00
65 LeBron James 200.00 500.00
92 James Harden 25.00 60.00
105 Russell Westbrook 8.00 20.00
141 Bradley Beal 40.00 100.00
143 Kawhi Leonard 150.00 400.00
147 Kevin Durant 100.00 250.00
159 Kemba Walker 12.00 30.00
176 Stephen Curry 75.00 200.00
197 Klay Thompson 15.00 40.00
253 Anfernee Hardaway 10.00 25.00
276 Victor Oladipo 30.00 80.00
283 C.J. McCollum 75.00 200.00
286 Dennis Schroder 40.00 100.00
287 Tim Hardaway Jr. 8.00 20.00
290 Giannis Antetokounmpo 2,000.00 4,000.00
291 Steven Adams 12.00 30.00

2013-14 Panini Prizm Prizms Light Blue Die Cut

*LT.BLUE VET: 2.5X TO 6X BASIC
*LT.BLUE RC: 1.5X TO 4X BASIC
STATED PRINT RUN 199 SER.#'d SETS
4 Anthony Davis 30.00 80.00
19 Damian Lillard 100.00 250.00
65 LeBron James 125.00 300.00
92 James Harden 10.00 25.00
141 Bradley Beal 30.00 80.00
143 Kawhi Leonard 125.00 300.00
147 Kevin Durant 40.00 100.00
176 Stephen Curry 60.00 150.00
197 Klay Thompson 6.00 15.00
276 Victor Oladipo 25.00 60.00
281 Otto Porter 10.00 25.00
283 C.J. McCollum 100.00 250.00
286 Dennis Schroder 60.00 150.00
287 Tim Hardaway Jr. 15.00 40.00
290 Giannis Antetokounmpo 500.00 1,000.00
291 Steven Adams 6.00 15.00

2013-14 Panini Prizm Prizms Orange

*ORANGE VET: 4X TO 10X BASIC
*ORANGE RC: 2.5X TO 6X BASIC
STATED PRINT RUN 60 SER.#'d SETS
1 Kobe Bryant 300.00 600.00
4 Anthony Davis 125.00 300.00
19 Damian Lillard 500.00 1,000.00
65 LeBron James 300.00 600.00
92 James Harden 15.00 40.00
141 Bradley Beal 60.00 150.00
143 Kawhi Leonard 400.00 800.00
147 Kevin Durant 300.00 600.00
159 Kemba Walker 12.00 30.00
176 Stephen Curry 300.00 600.00
197 Klay Thompson 15.00 40.00
253 Anfernee Hardaway 15.00 40.00
276 Victor Oladipo 100.00 250.00
281 Otto Porter 30.00 80.00
283 C.J. McCollum 200.00 500.00
286 Dennis Schroder 100.00 250.00
287 Tim Hardaway Jr. 50.00 120.00
290 Giannis Antetokounmpo 500.00 1,000.00
291 Steven Adams 20.00 50.00

2013-14 Panini Prizm Prizms Purple Die Cut

*PURPLE VET: 5X TO 12X BASIC
*PURPLE RC: 3X TO 8X BASIC
STATED PRINT RUN 49 SER.#'d SETS
1 Kobe Bryant 300.00 600.00
4 Anthony Davis 125.00 300.00
19 Damian Lillard 300.00 600.00
65 LeBron James 300.00 600.00
92 James Harden 20.00 50.00
141 Bradley Beal 60.00 150.00
143 Kawhi Leonard 20.00 50.00
147 Kevin Durant 300.00 600.00
176 Stephen Curry 300.00 600.00
197 Klay Thompson 20.00 50.00
276 Victor Oladipo 75.00 200.00
281 Otto Porter 40.00 100.00
283 C.J. McCollum 125.00 300.00
286 Dennis Schroder 100.00 250.00
287 Tim Hardaway Jr. 40.00 100.00
290 Giannis Antetokounmpo 800.00 1,500.00
291 Steven Adams 20.00 50.00

2013-14 Panini Prizm Prizms Red

*RED VET: 3X TO 8X BASIC
*RED RC: 2X TO 5X BASIC
1 Kobe Bryant 200.00 500.00
4 Anthony Davis 75.00 200.00
19 Damian Lillard 200.00 500.00
44 Dwyane Wade 20.00 50.00
65 LeBron James 150.00 400.00
92 James Harden 25.00 60.00
141 Bradley Beal 50.00 120.00
143 Kawhi Leonard 150.00 400.00
147 Kevin Durant 200.00 500.00
176 Stephen Curry 200.00 500.00
197 Klay Thompson 15.00 40.00
253 Anfernee Hardaway 12.00 30.00
276 Victor Oladipo 30.00 80.00
281 Otto Porter 8.00 20.00
283 C.J. McCollum 100.00 250.00
286 Dennis Schroder 60.00 150.00
290 Giannis Antetokounmpo 3,000.00 6,000.00
291 Steven Adams 12.00 30.00

2013-14 Panini Prizm Prizms Red White and Blue Mosaic

*RWB VET: 2.5X TO 6X BASIC
*RWB RC: 1.5X TO 4X BASIC
4 Anthony Davis 50.00 120.00
19 Damian Lillard 60.00 150.00
65 LeBron James 100.00 250.00
92 James Harden 10.00 25.00
141 Bradley Beal 15.00 40.00
143 Kawhi Leonard 75.00 200.00
147 Kevin Durant 40.00 100.00
176 Stephen Curry 50.00 120.00
197 Klay Thompson 12.00 30.00
276 Victor Oladipo 30.00 80.00
283 C.J. McCollum 50.00 120.00
286 Dennis Schroder 40.00 100.00
290 Giannis Antetokounmpo 1,500.00 3,000.00
291 Steven Adams 10.00 25.00

2013-14 Panini Prizm Autographs

EXCHANGE DEADLINE 6/18/2015
*PRIZM/25: .75X TO 2X BASIC
1 Otto Porter 5.00 12.00
2 Erik Murphy 3.00 8.00
3 Ryan Kelly 3.00 8.00
4 Kentavious Caldwell-Pope 5.00 12.00
5 Ricky Ledo 3.00 8.00
6 C.J. McCollum 12.00 30.00
7 Michael Carter-Williams 4.00 10.00
8 Anthony Bennett 3.00 8.00
9 Andre Roberson 4.00 10.00
10 Alex Len 4.00 10.00
11 Trey Burke 4.00 10.00
12 Tony Snell 4.00 10.00
13 Victor Oladipo 8.00 20.00
14 Cody Zeller 4.00 10.00
15 Allen Crabbe 3.00 8.00
16 Peyton Siva 3.00 8.00
17 Tim Hardaway Jr. 6.00 15.00
18 Solomon Hill 4.00 10.00
19 Jamaal Franklin 3.00 8.00
20 Jeff Withey 3.00 8.00
21 Ben McLemore 4.00 10.00
22 Steven Adams 20.00 50.00
23 Isaiah Canaan 3.00 8.00
24 Nate Wolters 3.00 8.00
25 Archie Goodwin 3.00 8.00
26 Kelly Olynyk 4.00 10.00
27 Shane Larkin 3.00 8.00
28 Shabazz Muhammad 3.00 8.00
29 Ray McCallum 3.00 8.00
30 Nerlens Noel 4.00 10.00
31 Glen Rice Jr. 3.00 8.00
32 Mason Plumlee 4.00 10.00
33 Giannis Antetokounmpo 1,000.00 2,000.00
34 Elias Harris 3.00 8.00
35 Gorgui Dieng 4.00 10.00
36 Dennis Schroder 10.00 25.00
37 Nemanja Nedovic 3.00 8.00
38 Matthew Dellavedova 5.00 12.00
39 Phil Pressey 3.00 8.00
40 Carrick Felix 3.00 8.00
41 Rudy Gobert 40.00 100.00
42 Ian Clark 4.00 10.00
43 Miroslav Raduljica 3.00 8.00
44 C.J. Leslie 3.00 8.00
45 Gal Mekel 3.00 8.00
46 Nick Anderson 4.00 10.00
47 Marcus Camby 4.00 10.00
48 Dee Brown 4.00 10.00
49 Bobby Jones 6.00 15.00
50 Damian Lillard 75.00 200.00
51 Vince Carter 40.00 100.00
52 Kenny Walker 4.00 10.00
53 Tom Chambers 5.00 12.00
54 Tony Parker 8.00 20.00
55 Stephen Curry 500.00 1,000.00
56 Steve Smith 4.00 10.00
57 Larry Johnson 12.00 30.00
58 Darrell Griffith 4.00 10.00
59 Magic Johnson 40.00 100.00
60 Larry Bird 60.00 150.00
61 Bill Russell 300.00 600.00
62 Blake Griffin 15.00 40.00
63 Lance Thomas 3.00 8.00
64 Kenny Smith 4.00 10.00
65 Mark Aguirre 4.00 10.00
66 Dominique Wilkins 12.00 30.00
67 Deron Williams 4.00 10.00
68 David Robinson 20.00 50.00
69 Harrison Barnes 5.00 12.00
70 Steve Nash 40.00 100.00
71 Jerry West 20.00 50.00
72 Kawhi Leonard 60.00 150.00
73 Kenyon Martin 5.00 12.00
74 Ersan Ilyasova 3.00 8.00
75 Tobias Harris 5.00 12.00
76 Chris Andersen 10.00 25.00
77 Kenneth Faried 4.00 10.00
78 Norm Nixon 4.00 10.00
79 Rick Barry 6.00 15.00
80 Iman Shumpert 3.00 8.00
81 Bernard King 6.00 15.00
82 Nicolas Batum 4.00 10.00
83 LaMarcus Aldridge 12.00 30.00
84 Sean Elliott 5.00 12.00
85 Isiah Thomas 12.00 30.00
86 Jannero Pargo 4.00 10.00
87 Micheal Ray Richardson 4.00 10.00
88 Gail Goodrich 5.00 12.00
89 Michael Finley 5.00 12.00
90 Charlie Scott 5.00 12.00
91 Bill Sharman 25.00 60.00
92 Rory Sparrow 3.00 8.00
93 Wes Unseld 6.00 15.00
94 Ronnie Brewer 3.00 8.00
95 Jamaal Wilkes 3.00 8.00
96 Kendall Marshall 3.00 8.00
97 John Lucas III 3.00 8.00
98 Nate Archibald 8.00 20.00
99 Scottie Pippen 50.00 120.00
100 Raymond Felton 3.00 8.00
101 Byron Scott 5.00 12.00
102 Bill Laimbeer 5.00 12.00
103 J.R. Smith 5.00 12.00
104 J.J. Redick 12.00 30.00
105 Connie Hawkins 6.00 15.00
106 A.C. Green 5.00 12.00
107 Jim Jackson 3.00 8.00
108 Tyson Chandler 4.00 10.00
109 Joe Johnson 4.00 10.00
110 Herb Williams 3.00 8.00
111 Dick Barnett 15.00 40.00
112 Jeff Teague 3.00 8.00
113 Jason Terry 4.00 10.00
114 Rajon Rondo 12.00 30.00
115 Kurt Rambis 5.00 12.00
116 Jason Kidd 12.00 30.00
117 Fred Jones 3.00 8.00
118 Larry Nance 4.00 10.00
119 Danny Green 4.00 10.00
120 Paul Westphal 5.00 12.00
121 Andrea Bargnani 3.00 8.00
122 Danilo Gallinari 4.00 10.00
123 Tiago Splitter 3.00 8.00
124 Dean Meminger 5.00 12.00
125 Kendall Gill 5.00 12.00
126 Alexey Shved 3.00 8.00
127 Dikembe Mutombo 12.00 30.00
128 George Gervin 12.00 30.00
129 Grant Hill 15.00 40.00
130 David West 4.00 10.00
131 Gary Payton 12.00 30.00
132 Josh Smith 3.00 8.00
133 Horace Grant 8.00 20.00
134 Jeff Green 3.00 8.00
135 Ryan Anderson 3.00 8.00
136 Kyle Lowry 5.00 12.00
137 Andre Drummond 5.00 12.00
138 Mark Jackson 4.00 10.00
139 Brandon Roy 5.00 12.00
140 Kobe Bryant 800.00 1,500.00
141 Kyrie Irving 40.00 100.00
142 Kevin Durant 75.00 200.00
143 Karl Malone 30.00 80.00
144 Kareem Abdul-Jabbar 50.00 120.00
145 Derrick Williams 3.00 8.00
146 Rex Chapman 5.00 12.00
147 Bradley Beal 10.00 25.00
148 Kenny Anderson 4.00 10.00
149 Kevin Willis 4.00 10.00
150 Bismack Biyombo 3.00 8.00
151 Marvin Williams 3.00 8.00
152 Ricky Davis 4.00 10.00
153 Jared Sullinger 3.00 8.00
154 Maurice Cheeks 4.00 10.00
155 Boris Diaw 4.00 10.00
156 Robert Parish 10.00 25.00
157 Jared Dudley 3.00 8.00
158 B.J. Armstrong 5.00 12.00
159 Brandon Knight 4.00 10.00
160 Michael Curry 3.00 8.00
161 Zach Randolph 4.00 10.00
162 Anfernee Hardaway 20.00 50.00
163 Kiki Vandeweghe 4.00 10.00
164 Jrue Holiday 15.00 40.00
165 Darryl Dawkins 4.00 10.00
166 Brandon Bass 3.00 8.00
167 Peja Stojakovic 4.00 10.00
168 Draymond Green 30.00 80.00
169 Jack Sikma 5.00 12.00
170 Greg Stiemsma 3.00 8.00
171 Alonzo Mourning 15.00 40.00
172 Sam Cassell 4.00 10.00
173 Dennis Rodman 50.00 120.00
174 Marcin Gortat 3.00 8.00
175 Goran Dragic 4.00 10.00
176 Jeff Ayres 3.00 8.00
177 Al-Farouq Aminu 3.00 8.00
178 Elgin Baylor 15.00 40.00
179 Allan Houston 5.00 12.00
180 Jason Smith 3.00 8.00
181 Luis Scola 4.00 10.00
182 Joe Dumars 6.00 15.00
183 World B. Free 4.00 10.00
184 DeMarre Carroll 3.00 8.00
185 John Salley 4.00 10.00
186 Michael Cage 3.00 8.00
187 Andrei Kirilenko 5.00 12.00
188 Theo Ratliff 3.00 8.00
189 Vinny Del Negro 3.00 8.00
190 John Lucas 4.00 10.00
191 Sleepy Floyd 4.00 10.00
192 Elvin Hayes 8.00 20.00
193 Tariq Abdul-Wahad 3.00 8.00
194 Reggie Theus 4.00 10.00
195 Bill Walton 15.00 40.00
196 P.J. Tucker 5.00 12.00
197 Keith Bogans 3.00 8.00
198 Dwight Howard 12.00 30.00
199 Nick Van Exel 10.00 25.00
200 James Harden EXCH 75.00 200.00

2013-14 Panini Prizm Autographs Prizms Blue

*BLUE p/r 75-99: .5X TO 1.2X BASIC
*BLUE p/r 49-50: .6X TO 1.5X BASIC
*BLUE p/r 25: .75X TO 2X BASIC
PRINT RUNS B/WN 5-99 COPIES PER
NO PRICING ON QTY 10 OR LESS
EXCHANGE DEADLINE 6/18/2015

2013-14 Panini Prizm Autographs Prizms Red

*RED p/r 75-99: .5X TO 1.2X BASIC
*RED p/r 49-50: .6X TO 1.5X BASIC
*RED p/r 25: .75X TO 2X BASIC
PRINT RUNS B/WN 5-99 COPIES PER
NO PRICING ON QTY 10 OR LESS
EXCHANGE DEADLINE 6/18/2015

2013-14 Panini Prizm BK HRX

COMPLETE SET (24) 6.00 15.00
1 Alex Len .40 1.00
2 Anthony Bennett .30 .75
3 Archie Goodwin .30 .75
4 Ben McLemore .40 1.00
5 C.J. McCollum 1.25 3.00
6 Cody Zeller .40 1.00

7 Erik Murphy .30 .75
8 Glen Rice Jr. .30 .75
9 Isaiah Canaan .30 .75
10 Jamaal Franklin .30 .75
11 Kelly Olynyk .40 1.00
12 Kentavious Caldwell-Pope .50 1.25
13 Mason Plumlee .40 1.00
14 Michael Carter-Williams .40 1.00
15 Nerlens Noel .40 1.00
16 Otto Porter .50 1.25
17 Ricky Ledo .30 .75
18 Ryan Kelly .30 .75
19 Shabazz Muhammad .30 .75
20 Shane Larkin .40 1.00
21 Solomon Hill .40 1.00
22 Tim Hardaway Jr. .60 1.50
23 Trey Burke .40 1.00
24 Victor Oladipo .75 2.00

2013-14 Panini Prizm Brilliance

1 Tony Parker 1.25 3.00
2 Steve Nash 1.50 4.00
3 Jeremy Lin 1.25 3.00
4 Joe Johnson .60 1.50
5 Paul George 1.25 3.00
6 Ty Lawson .50 1.25
7 LeBron James 10.00 25.00
8 Kevin Durant 2.50 6.00
9 Kobe Bryant 6.00 15.00
10 Kyrie Irving 2.50 6.00
11 Tyson Chandler .60 1.50
12 Marc Gasol .75 2.00
13 Chandler Parsons .50 1.25
14 Kawhi Leonard 2.50 6.00
15 Joakim Noah .75 2.00
16 Ricky Rubio .60 1.50
17 Danny Green .60 1.50
18 Jimmy Butler 1.50 4.00
19 Dion Waiters .50 1.25
20 Paul Pierce 1.25 3.00
21 Chris Andersen .60 1.50
22 Iman Shumpert .50 1.25
23 Rudy Gay .60 1.50
24 Chris Bosh 1.00 2.50
25 Kevin Garnett 2.00 5.00

2013-14 Panini Prizm Brilliance Prizms

*PRIZM: .75X TO 2X BASIC
7 LeBron James 150.00 400.00
8 Kevin Durant 40.00 100.00
9 Kobe Bryant 75.00 200.00
14 Kawhi Leonard 50.00 120.00

2013-14 Panini Prizm Brilliance Prizms Blue

*BLUE: 1.2X TO 3X BASIC
7 LeBron James 200.00 500.00
9 Kobe Bryant 125.00 300.00
14 Kawhi Leonard 30.00 80.00

2013-14 Panini Prizm Brilliance Prizms Green

*GREEN: 1.2X TO 3X BASIC
7 LeBron James 125.00 300.00
8 Kevin Durant 15.00 40.00
9 Kobe Bryant 60.00 150.00
14 Kawhi Leonard 30.00 80.00

2013-14 Panini Prizm Brilliance Prizms Light Blue Die Cut

*LT BLUE: 1.5X TO 4X BASIC
STATED PRINT RUN 199 SER.#'d SETS
7 LeBron James 150.00 400.00
9 Kobe Bryant 60.00 150.00
14 Kawhi Leonard 25.00 60.00

2013-14 Panini Prizm Brilliance Prizms Orange

*ORANGE: 2X TO 5X BASIC
STATED PRINT RUN 60 SER.#'d SETS
3 Jeremy Lin 8.00 20.00
7 LeBron James 400.00 800.00
8 Kevin Durant 20.00 50.00
9 Kobe Bryant 75.00 200.00
14 Kawhi Leonard 75.00 200.00

2013-14 Panini Prizm Brilliance Prizms Purple Die Cut

*PURPLE: 2.5X TO 6X BASIC
STATED PRINT RUN 49 SER.#'d SETS
7 LeBron James 400.00 800.00
9 Kobe Bryant 75.00 200.00
14 Kawhi Leonard 100.00 250.00

2013-14 Panini Prizm Brilliance Prizms Red

*RED: 1.2X TO 3X BASIC
7 LeBron James 200.00 500.00
9 Kobe Bryant 125.00 300.00
14 Kawhi Leonard 30.00 80.00

2013-14 Panini Prizm Dominance

*PRIZM: .75X TO 2X BASIC
*GREEN: 1.2X TO 3X BASIC
*LT BLUE: 1.5X TO 4X BASIC
*ORANGE: 2X TO 5X BASIC
1 LeBron James 8.00 20.00
2 Carmelo Anthony 1.25 3.00
3 Kevin Durant 2.50 6.00
4 Chris Paul 1.50 4.00
5 James Harden 1.50 4.00
6 Kevin Love .75 2.00
7 Kyrie Irving 2.50 6.00
8 Tim Duncan 2.00 5.00
9 Derrick Rose 1.25 3.00
10 Dwight Howard 1.00 2.50
11 Blake Griffin .75 2.00
12 Rajon Rondo 1.00 2.50
13 Stephen Curry 6.00 15.00
14 Damian Lillard 2.50 6.00
15 Deron Williams .60 1.50
16 Kenneth Faried .60 1.50
17 Harrison Barnes .75 2.00
18 Bradley Beal 1.25 3.00
19 Dwyane Wade 1.50 4.00
20 Russell Westbrook 1.25 3.00
21 Vince Carter 1.50 4.00
22 Brook Lopez .75 2.00
23 Dirk Nowitzki 2.00 5.00
24 Kobe Bryant 6.00 15.00
25 Anthony Davis 2.50 6.00

2013-14 Panini Prizm Dominance Prizms

1 LeBron James 100.00 250.00
3 Kevin Durant 12.00 30.00
13 Stephen Curry 12.00 30.00
24 Kobe Bryant 60.00 150.00
25 Anthony Davis 60.00 150.00

2013-14 Panini Prizm Dominance Prizms Green

*GREEN: 1.2X TO 3X BASIC
1 LeBron James 60.00 150.00
13 Stephen Curry 20.00 50.00
25 Anthony Davis 15.00 40.00

2013-14 Panini Prizm Dominance Prizms Light Blue Die Cut

*LT BLUE: 1.5X TO 4X BASIC
STATED PRINT RUN 199 SER.#'d SETS
1 LeBron James 75.00 200.00
13 Stephen Curry 20.00 50.00
24 Kobe Bryant 50.00 120.00
25 Anthony Davis 20.00 50.00

2013-14 Panini Prizm Dominance Prizms Purple Die Cut

*PURPLE: 2.5X TO 6X BASIC
STATED PRINT RUN 60 SER.#'d SETS
1 LeBron James 125.00 300.00
24 Kobe Bryant 40.00 100.00
25 Anthony Davis 40.00 100.00

2013-14 Panini Prizm Guard Duty

*GREEN 1.25X TO 3X BASIC
*PRIZM: 1.5X TO 4X BASIC
*LT BLUE: 1.5X TO 4X BASIC
*ORANGE: 2X TO 5X BASIC
*PURPLE: 2.5X TO 6X BASIC
1 Chris Paul 1.50 4.00
2 Kyrie Irving 2.50 6.00
3 Russell Westbrook 1.25 3.00
4 Damian Lillard 2.50 6.00
5 John Wall 1.00 2.50
6 James Harden 1.50 4.00
7 Derrick Rose 1.25 3.00
8 Ricky Rubio .60 1.50
9 Stephen Curry 6.00 15.00
10 Steve Nash 1.50 4.00
11 Dwyane Wade 1.50 4.00
12 Tony Parker 1.25 3.00
13 Jeremy Lin 1.25 3.00
14 Rajon Rondo 1.00 2.50
15 Kobe Bryant 6.00 15.00

2013-14 Panini Prizm Guard Duty Prizms Blue

*BLUE: 1.5X TO 4X BASIC
6 James Harden 20.00 50.00
9 Stephen Curry 30.00 80.00

2013-14 Panini Prizm Guard Duty Prizms Green

*GREEN: 1.25X TO 3X BASIC
9 Stephen Curry 20.00 50.00

2013-14 Panini Prizm Hall Monitors

*PRIZM: .75X TO 2X BASIC
*BLUE: 1X TO 2.5X BASIC
*GREEN: .75X TO 2X BASIC
*LT BLUE: 1.5X TO 4X BASIC
*ORANGE: 2X TO 5X BASIC
*PURPLE: 2.5X TO 6X BASIC
*RED: .75X TO 2X BASIC
1 Gary Payton 1.25 3.00
2 Scottie Pippen 2.00 5.00
3 Bill Russell 2.50 6.00
4 Karl Malone 1.50 4.00
5 Arvydas Sabonis 1.00 2.50
6 John Stockton 1.50 4.00
7 David Robinson 1.50 4.00
8 Patrick Ewing 1.25 3.00
9 Magic Johnson 3.00 8.00
10 Drazen Petrovic 1.00 2.50
11 Moses Malone 1.25 3.00
12 Pete Maravich 1.25 3.00
13 Wilt Chamberlain 2.50 6.00
14 George Mikan 2.50 6.00
15 Jerry West 2.00 5.00
16 Oscar Robertson 1.25 3.00
17 Earl Monroe 1.25 3.00
18 Bill Walton 1.25 3.00
19 John Havlicek 2.00 5.00
20 Elgin Baylor .75 2.00
21 Julius Erving 2.00 5.00
22 Wes Unseld 1.00 2.50
23 Hakeem Olajuwon 1.50 4.00
24 Larry Bird 3.00 8.00
25 Kareem Abdul-Jabbar 2.50 6.00

2013-14 Panini Prizm Post Season

1 Tyson Chandler .60 1.50
2 Marc Gasol .75 2.00
3 Pau Gasol 1.25 3.00
4 Dwight Howard 1.00 2.50
5 Joakim Noah .75 2.00
6 Marcin Gortat .50 1.25
7 Roy Hibbert .50 1.25
8 Blake Griffin .75 2.00
9 Tim Duncan 2.00 5.00
10 Andre Drummond .75 2.00

2013-14 Panini Prizm Post Season Prizms

*PRIZM: .75X TO 2X BASIC

2013-14 Panini Prizm Post Season Prizms Light Blue Die Cut

*LT BLUE: 1.5X TO 4X BASIC
STATED PRINT RUN 199 SER.#'d SETS

2013-14 Panini Prizm Post Season Prizms Orange

*ORANGE: 2X TO 5X BASIC
STATED PRINT RUN 60 SER.#'d SETS

2013-14 Panini Prizm Post Season Prizms Purple Die Cut

*PURPLE: 2.5X TO 6X BASIC
STATED PRINT RUN 49 SER.#'d SETS

2014-15 Panini Prizm

COMPLETE SET (300) 125.00 300.00
*BLUE GRN MOSAIC VET: 1.5X TO 4X BASIC
*BLUE GRN MOSAIC RC: 1X TO 2.5X BASIC
*GREEN: 1.5X TO 4X BASIC
*GREEN: 1X TO 2.5X BASIC
*RWB PLUSAR VET: 1.5X TO 4X BASIC
*RWB PULSAR RC: 1X TO 2.5X BASIC
*YLLW RED MOSAIC VET: 1.5X TO 4X BASIC
*YLLW RED MOSAIC RC: 1X TO 2.5X BASIC
1 Damian Lillard 1.00 2.50
2 Randy Foye .25 .60
3 Enes Kanter .30 .75
4 Terrence Ross .30 .75
5 Jamal Crawford .40 1.00
6 Jordan Hill .25 .60
7 Al Horford .40 1.00
8 Kyle Lowry .50 1.25
9 Blake Griffin .40 1.00
10 Nene .30 .75
11 Danilo Gallinari .25 .60
12 Mario Chalmers .30 .75
13 Eric Bledsoe .30 .75
14 Thaddeus Young .25 .60
15 Jameer Nelson .25 .60
16 Jose Calderon .25 .60
17 Al Jefferson .25 .60
18 Kyrie Irving .75 2.00
19 Bradley Beal .60 1.50
20 Nerlens Noel .25 .60
21 David West .30 .75
22 Ricky Rubio .30 .75
23 Eric Gordon .30 .75
24 Tiago Splitter .25 .60
25 James Harden .75 2.00
26 Josh Smith .25 .60
27 Alex Len .25 .60
28 LaMarcus Aldridge .40 1.00
29 Brandon Bass .25 .60
30 Nick Collison .30 .75
31 David Lee .25 .60
32 Roy Hibbert .30 .75
33 Ersan Ilyasova .25 .60
34 Tim Duncan 1.00 2.50
35 Jared Sullinger .25 .60
36 Jrue Holiday .50 1.25
37 Amar'e Stoudemire .40 1.00
38 Lance Stephenson .30 .75
39 Brandon Jennings .25 .60
40 Nick Young .25 .60
41 DeAndre Jordan .30 .75
42 Rudy Gay .40 1.00
43 George Hill .30 .75
44 Tim Hardaway Jr. .30 .75
45 Jason Terry .30 .75
46 Kawhi Leonard 1.00 2.50
47 Amir Johnson .25 .60
48 LeBron James 8.00 20.00
49 Brandon Knight .25 .60
50 Nicolas Batum .30 .75
51 DeMar DeRozan .50 1.25
52 Russell Westbrook .60 1.50
53 Gerald Green .30 .75
54 Tobias Harris .30 .75
55 JaVale McGee .30 .75
56 Kemba Walker .40 1.00
57 Anderson Varejao .25 .60
58 Brook Lopez .40 1.00
59 Luol Deng .30 .75
60 Nikola Vucevic .30 .75
61 DeMarcus Cousins .30 .75
62 Ryan Anderson .25 .60
63 Gerald Henderson .25 .60
64 Tony Parker .60 1.50
65 Jeff Green .30 .75
66 Kenneth Faried .25 .60
67 Andre Drummond .30 .75
68 Manu Ginobili .75 2.00
69 C.J. McCollum .40 1.00
70 Nikola Pekovic .25 .60
71 Dennis Schroder .40 1.00
72 Serge Ibaka .30 .75
73 Giannis Antetokounmpo 2.50 6.00
74 Trey Burke .25 .60
75 Jeff Teague .25 .60
76 Kentavious Caldwell-Pope .30 .75
77 Andre Iguodala .40 1.00
78 Marc Gasol .40 1.00
79 Carlos Boozer .30 .75
80 Norris Cole .25 .60
81 Deron Williams .30 .75
82 Shawn Marion .30 .75
83 Goran Dragic .40 1.00
84 Tristan Thompson .25 .60
85 Jeremy Lin .75 2.00
86 Kevin Durant 1.25 3.00
87 Andrew Bogut .30 .75
88 Marcin Gortat .25 .60
89 Carmelo Anthony .60 1.50
90 O.J. Mayo .25 .60
91 Derrick Favors .25 .60
92 Stephen Curry 8.00 20.00
93 Gordon Hayward .30 .75
94 Ty Lawson .25 .60
95 Jimmy Butler .60 1.50
96 Kevin Garnett 1.00 2.50
97 Anthony Bennett .25 .60
98 Marco Belinelli .25 .60
99 Chandler Parsons .25 .60
100 Otto Porter .30 .75
101 Derrick Rose .75 2.00
102 Steve Nash .75 2.00
103 Greg Monroe .25 .60
104 Tyreke Evans .30 .75
105 Joakim Noah .40 1.00
106 Kevin Love .40 1.00
107 Anthony Davis 1.00 2.50
108 Matt Barnes .30 .75
109 Channing Frye .25 .60
110 Pau Gasol .60 1.50
111 Dion Waiters .25 .60
112 Steven Adams .50 1.25
113 Harrison Barnes .30 .75
114 Tyson Chandler .40 1.00
115 Jodie Meeks .25 .60
116 Kevin Martin .30 .75
117 Archie Goodwin .25 .60
118 Michael Carter-Williams .25 .60
119 Chris Bosh .50 1.25
120 Paul George .60 1.50
121 Dirk Nowitzki 1.00 2.50
122 Zach Randolph .40 1.00
123 Isaiah Thomas .30 .75
124 Victor Oladipo .30 .75
125 Joe Johnson .30 .75
126 Klay Thompson 1.00 2.50
127 Arron Afflalo .25 .60
128 Mike Conley .30 .75
129 Chris Paul .60 1.50
130 Paul Millsap .30 .75
131 Dwight Howard .50 1.25
132 Taj Gibson .25 .60
133 J.J. Redick .40 1.00
134 Vince Carter .75 2.00
135 John Wall .50 1.25
136 Kobe Bryant 8.00 20.00
137 Avery Bradley .25 .60
138 Monta Ellis .30 .75
139 Cody Zeller .25 .60
140 Paul Pierce .60 1.50
141 Dwyane Wade .75 2.00
142 Tayshaun Prince .40 1.00
143 J.R. Smith .40 1.00
144 Wesley Matthews .25 .60
145 Jonas Valanciunas .30 .75
146 Kyle Korver .30 .75
147 Ben McLemore .25 .60
148 Michael Kidd-Gilchrist .25 .60
149 Corey Brewer .25 .60
150 Rajon Rondo .50 1.25
151 Adrian Dantley .40 1.00
152 Swen Nater .25 .60
153 Hakeem Olajuwon .75 2.00
154 John Stockton .75 2.00
155 Latrell Sprewell .50 1.25
156 Avery Johnson .30 .75
157 Sam Jones .40 1.00
158 George Mikan 1.25 3.00
159 Rick Barry .50 1.25
160 Dikembe Mutombo .60 1.50
161 Tim Hardaway .50 1.25
162 Isiah Thomas .60 1.50
163 Julius Erving 1.00 2.50
164 Alex English .50 1.25
165 Louie Dampier .40 1.00
166 Baron Davis .40 1.00
167 Moses Malone .60 1.50
168 Clifford Robinson .40 1.00
169 Robert Horry .40 1.00
170 Dominique Wilkins .60 1.50
171 Tom Chambers .40 1.00
172 James Worthy .60 1.50
173 Kareem Abdul-Jabbar 1.25 3.00
174 Allan Houston .40 1.00
175 Magic Johnson 1.50 4.00
176 Bernard King .50 1.25
177 Mychal Thompson .30 .75
178 Clyde Drexler .60 1.50
179 Robert Parish .50 1.25
180 Drazen Petrovic .50 1.25
181 Toni Kukoc .50 1.25
182 Jason Kidd .60 1.50
183 Karl Malone .75 2.00
184 Allen Iverson 1.00 2.50
185 Mahmoud Abdul-Rauf .30 .75
186 Bill Laimbeer .40 1.00
187 Oscar Robertson .75 2.00
188 Rudy Tomjanovich .40 1.00
189 Eddie Jones .40 1.00
190 Tracy McGrady .60 1.50
191 Jeff Hornacek .30 .75
192 Kenny Smith .30 .75
193 Alonzo Mourning .60 1.50
194 Mark Aguirre .30 .75
195 Bill Russell 1.25 3.00
196 Patrick Ewing .60 1.50
197 Damon Stoudamire .30 .75
198 Elgin Baylor .75 2.00
199 Sam Perkins .30 .75
200 Vlade Divac .40 1.00
201 Jerry Sloan .40 1.00
202 Kevin McHale .60 1.50
203 Anfernee Hardaway 1.00 2.50
204 Mark Jackson .30 .75
205 Bill Walton .60 1.50
206 Paul Silas .40 1.00
207 Danny Manning .30 .75
208 Sarunas Marciulionis .40 1.00
209 Gary Payton .60 1.50
210 Walt Frazier .60 1.50
211 Jerry West 1.00 2.50
212 Kevin Willis .30 .75
213 Antoine Walker .30 .75
214 Mark Price .40 1.00
215 Bob Cousy .75 2.00
216 Peja Stojakovic .30 .75
217 Dave Cowens .50 1.25
218 Scottie Pippen 1.00 2.50
219 George Gervin .60 1.50
220 Wilt Chamberlain 1.25 3.00
221 Joe Dumars .50 1.25
222 Kurt Rambis .30 .75
223 Artis Gilmore .50 1.25
224 Maurice Cheeks .30 .75
225 Bob Love .40 1.00
226 Pete Maravich 1.25 3.00
227 David Robinson .75 2.00
228 Shaquille O'Neal 1.50 4.00
229 Gheorghe Muresan .25 .60
230 John Havlicek .75 2.00
231 Xavier McDaniel .30 .75
232 Larry Bird 1.50 4.00
233 Michael Cooper .40 1.00
234 Arvydas Sabonis .50 1.25
235 Byron Scott .40 1.00
236 Phil Jackson .60 1.50
237 Dennis Rodman 1.00 2.50
238 Shawn Kemp .60 1.50
239 Glen Rice .40 1.00
240 Yao Ming 1.00 2.50
241 John Starks .40 1.00
242 Larry Johnson .50 1.25
243 Michael Finley .40 1.00
244 Chris Mullin .50 1.25
245 Ralph Sampson .40 1.00
246 Detlef Schrempf .40 1.00
247 Spud Webb .40 1.00
248 Grant Hill .60 1.50
249 Craig Ehlo .25 .60
250 Austin Carr .40 1.00
251 Andrew Wiggins RC 2.00 5.00
252 Jabari Parker RC .50 1.25
253 Joel Embiid RC 8.00 20.00
254 Aaron Gordon RC 2.00 5.00
255 Dante Exum RC .60 1.50
256 Marcus Smart RC 1.50 4.00
257 Julius Randle RC 2.00 5.00
258 Nik Stauskas RC .40 1.00
259 Noah Vonleh RC .40 1.00
260 Elfrid Payton RC .60 1.50
261 Doug McDermott RC .60 1.50
262 Zach LaVine RC 2.50 6.00
263 T.J. Warren RC .60 1.50
264 Adreian Payne RC .40 1.00
265 James Young RC .40 1.00
266 Tyler Ennis RC .40 1.00
267 Gary Harris RC .60 1.50
268 Mitch McGary RC .40 1.00
269 Jordan Adams RC .40 1.00
270 Rodney Hood RC .50 1.25
271 Shabazz Napier RC .50 1.25
272 P.J. Hairston RC .40 1.00
273 C.J. Wilcox RC .40 1.00
274 James Ennis RC .40 1.00
275 Kyle Anderson RC .60 1.50
276 Joe Harris RC .60 1.50
277 Cleanthony Early RC .40 1.00
278 Jarnell Stokes RC .40 1.00
279 Johnny O'Bryant RC .40 1.00
280 Jusuf Nurkic RC 1.25 3.00
281 Spencer Dinwiddie RC .60 1.50
282 Jerami Grant RC 2.00 5.00
283 Glenn Robinson III RC .50 1.25
284 Nick Johnson RC .40 1.00
285 Markel Brown RC .40 1.00
286 Dwight Powell RC .50 1.25
287 Jordan Clarkson RC 1.50 4.00
288 Russ Smith RC .40 1.00
289 Erick Green RC .40 1.00
290 Patric Young RC .40 1.00
291 Will Cherry RC .40 1.00
292 Devyn Marble RC .40 1.00
293 Bojan Bogdanovic RC .60 1.50
294 Damjan Rudez RC .40 1.00
295 Cory Jefferson RC .40 1.00
296 James Michael McAdoo RC .40 1.00
297 Cameron Bairstow RC .40 1.00
298 Bruno Caboclo RC .50 1.25
299 Damien Inglis RC .40 1.00
300 Nikola Mirotic RC .60 1.50

2014-15 Panini Prizm Prizms

*PRIZM VET: 2.5X TO 6X BASIC
*PRIZM RC: 1.5X TO 4X BASIC
253 Joel Embiid 100.00 250.00

2014-15 Panini Prizm Prizms Blue

*PRIZM BLUE VET: 6X TO 15X BASIC
*PRIZM BLUE RC: 4X TO 10X BASIC
STATED PRINT RUN 99 SER.#'d SETS
48 LeBron James 125.00 300.00
92 Stephen Curry 125.00 300.00
136 Kobe Bryant 125.00 300.00
253 Joel Embiid 150.00 400.00

2014-15 Panini Prizm Prizms Blue Mojo

*BLUE MOJO VET: 2.5X TO 6X BASIC
*BLUE MOJO RC: 1.5X TO 4X BASIC
253 Joel Embiid 100.00 250.00

2014-15 Panini Prizm Prizms Blue Wave

*BLUE WAVE VET: 4X TO 10X BASIC
*BLUE WAVE RC: 2.5X TO 6X BASIC
48 LeBron James 75.00 200.00
92 Stephen Curry 75.00 200.00
136 Kobe Bryant 75.00 200.00
253 Joel Embiid 100.00 250.00

2014-15 Panini Prizm Prizms Light Blue

*LGHT BLUE VET: 8X TO 20X BASIC
*LGHT BLUE RC: 5X TO 12X BASIC
STATED PRINT RUN 49 SER.#'d SETS
48 LeBron James 150.00 400.00
92 Stephen Curry 150.00 400.00
136 Kobe Bryant 150.00 400.00
253 Joel Embiid 200.00 500.00

2014-15 Panini Prizm Prizms Orange Die Cut

*PRIZM ORNG VET: 4X TO 10X BASIC
*PRIZM ORNG RC: 2.5X TO 6X BASIC
STATED PRINT RUN 139 SER.#'d SETS
48 LeBron James 75.00 200.00
92 Stephen Curry 75.00 200.00
136 Kobe Bryant 75.00 200.00
253 Joel Embiid 100.00 250.00

2014-15 Panini Prizm Prizms Purple Die Cut

*PRIZM PRPLE VET: 4X TO 10X BASIC
*PRIZM PRPLE RC: 2.5X TO 6X BASIC
STATED PRINT RUN 139 SER.#'d SETS
92 Stephen Curry 75.00 200.00
136 Kobe Bryant 75.00 200.00
253 Joel Embiid 100.00 250.00

2014-15 Panini Prizm Prizms Red

*PRIZMS RED VET: 8X TO 20X BASIC
*PRIZMS RED RC: 5X TO 12X BASIC
STATED PRINT RUN 49 SER.#'d SETS
48 LeBron James 150.00 400.00
92 Stephen Curry 150.00 400.00
136 Kobe Bryant 150.00 400.00
253 Joel Embiid 200.00 500.00

2014-15 Panini Prizm Prizms Red Pulsar

*PRIZMS RED VET: 10X TO 25X BASIC
*PRIZMS RED RC: 6X TO 15X BASIC
STATED PRINT RUN 25 SER.#'d SETS
48 LeBron James 200.00 500.00
92 Stephen Curry 200.00 500.00
136 Kobe Bryant 200.00 500.00
253 Joel Embiid 300.00 600.00

2014-15 Panini Prizm Autographs Green

1 Nerlens Noel 3.00 8.00
2 Brandan Wright 3.00 8.00
3 Trey Burke 3.00 8.00
4 Gorgui Dieng 3.00 8.00
5 Kobe Bryant 800.00 1,500.00
6 John Thompson 8.00 20.00
7 Kevin McHale 12.00 30.00
8 Bill Walton 20.00 50.00
9 Victor Oladipo 4.00 10.00
10 David Thompson 5.00 12.00
11 Joe Johnson 4.00 10.00
12 Bill Willoughby 3.00 8.00
13 Brent Barry 3.00 8.00
14 Tim Hardaway Jr. 4.00 10.00
15 Kevin Durant 75.00 200.00
16 Tony Allen 3.00 8.00
17 Hakeem Olajuwon 40.00 100.00
18 Glen Rice 5.00 12.00
19 Cody Zeller 3.00 8.00
20 Steven Adams 6.00 15.00
21 Kentavious Caldwell-Pope 4.00 10.00
23 James Harden 40.00 100.00
24 Jae Crowder 3.00 8.00
25 Dwyane Wade 60.00 150.00
26 Kelly Tripucka 4.00 10.00
27 Jason Kidd 20.00 50.00
28 JaVale McGee 4.00 10.00
29 Otto Porter 4.00 10.00
30 Phil Chenier 4.00 10.00
31 Michael Finley 5.00 12.00
32 Kenny Anderson 4.00 10.00
33 Shabazz Muhammad 3.00 8.00
35 Karl Malone 30.00 80.00
36 Nate Archibald 6.00 15.00
37 Kevin Love 5.00 12.00
38 Ralph Sampson 5.00 12.00
39 Alex Len 3.00 8.00
40 Brook Lopez 5.00 12.00
41 Nate Thurmond 5.00 12.00
42 Otis Birdsong 4.00 10.00
43 Jason Terry 4.00 10.00
44 Carrick Felix 3.00 8.00
45 Kyrie Irving 30.00 80.00
46 Steve Kerr 12.00 30.00
47 Anthony Bennett 3.00 8.00
48 Kevin Willis 4.00 10.00
49 Derrick Williams 3.00 8.00
50 Jim Jackson 4.00 10.00
51 Monta Ellis 4.00 10.00
52 Michael Cooper 5.00 12.00
53 Gail Goodrich 5.00 12.00
54 Matthew Dellavedova 4.00 10.00
55 John Havlicek 60.00 150.00
56 Jared Sullinger 3.00 8.00
57 Gary Payton 25.00 60.00
58 Kurt Rambis 4.00 10.00
59 Stephen Curry 600.00 1,200.00
60 Ron Harper 5.00 12.00
61 C.J. McCollum 5.00 12.00
62 Dennis Schroder 5.00 12.00
63 Elvin Hayes 8.00 20.00
64 Phil Pressey 3.00 8.00
65 John Wall 15.00 40.00
66 Peja Stojakovic 4.00 10.00
67 Dominique Wilkins 20.00 50.00
68 Reggie Jackson 4.00 10.00
69 Ben McLemore 3.00 8.00
70 Pearl Washington 5.00 12.00
71 Michael Carter-Williams 3.00 8.00
72 Vitor Faverani 3.00 8.00
73 Jerry Lucas 6.00 15.00
74 Troy Daniels 3.00 8.00
75 Earl Monroe 12.00 30.00
76 Jabari Parker 4.00 10.00
77 Andrew Wiggins 15.00 40.00
78 Julius Randle 15.00 40.00
79 Joel Embiid 125.00 300.00
80 Marcus Smart 12.00 30.00
81 Dante Exum 5.00 12.00
82 Aaron Gordon 15.00 40.00
83 Noah Vonleh 3.00 8.00
84 Gary Harris 5.00 12.00
85 Tyler Ennis 3.00 8.00
86 Nik Stauskas 3.00 8.00
87 Doug McDermott 5.00 12.00
88 Bruno Caboclo 3.00 8.00
89 James Young 3.00 8.00
90 Zach LaVine 20.00 50.00
91 Spencer Dinwiddie 5.00 12.00
92 Mitch McGary 3.00 8.00
93 Rodney Hood 4.00 10.00
94 Cleanthony Early 3.00 8.00
95 Shabazz Napier 4.00 10.00
96 Kyle Anderson 5.00 12.00
97 Adreian Payne 3.00 8.00
98 Elfrid Payton 5.00 12.00
99 T.J. Warren 5.00 12.00
100 C.J. Wilcox 3.00 8.00

2014-15 Panini Prizm Autographs Prizms Purple Pulsar

*PURPLE PULSAR: .6X TO 1.5X BASE HI
PRINT RUNS B/WN 15-49 COPIES PER
NO PRICING ON QTY 15 OR LESS

2014-15 Panini Prizm Autographs Prizms Red Pulsar

*RED p/r 49-149: .5X TO 1.2X GREEN
*RED p/r 25-35: .6X TO 1.5X GREEN
PRINT RUNS B/WN 25-149 COPIES PER
22 Udonis Haslem/99 5.00 12.00

2014-15 Panini Prizm Fireworks

1 Blake Griffin 1.25 3.00
2 Kobe Bryant 25.00 60.00
3 Damian Lillard 3.00 8.00
4 LeBron James 25.00 60.00
5 Dirk Nowitzki 3.00 8.00
6 Tony Parker 2.00 5.00
7 James Harden 2.50 6.00
8 Kevin Durant 4.00 10.00
9 Anthony Davis 3.00 8.00
10 Kevin Love 1.25 3.00
11 Chris Paul 2.00 5.00
12 Kyrie Irving 2.50 6.00
13 Derrick Rose 2.50 6.00
14 Russell Westbrook 2.00 5.00
15 Dwyane Wade 2.50 6.00

2014-15 Panini Prizm Freshman Phenoms

COMPLETE SET (10) 10.00 25.00
1 Andrew Wiggins 3.00 8.00
2 Jabari Parker .75 2.00
3 Joel Embiid 6.00 15.00
4 Aaron Gordon 3.00 8.00
5 Dante Exum 1.00 2.50
6 Marcus Smart 2.50 6.00
7 Julius Randle 3.00 8.00
8 Elfrid Payton 1.00 2.50
9 Doug McDermott 1.00 2.50
10 Shabazz Napier .75 2.00

2014-15 Panini Prizm Jerseys Prizms Blue Mojo

1 Blake Griffin 4.00 10.00
2 Matt Barnes 3.00 8.00
3 David Lee 2.50 6.00
4 Raymond Felton 2.50 6.00
5 Rashard Lewis 3.00 8.00
6 Udonis Haslem 3.00 8.00
7 James Jones 2.50 6.00
8 Jeremy Lamb 2.50 6.00
9 Al Horford 4.00 10.00
10 Kendrick Perkins 2.50 6.00
11 Boris Diaw 3.00 8.00
12 Zach Randolph 4.00 10.00
13 David Robinson 8.00 20.00
14 Reggie Jackson 3.00 8.00
15 Gary Payton 6.00 15.00
16 Kevin Durant 12.00 30.00
17 Jared Sullinger 2.50 6.00
18 Jimmy Butler 6.00 15.00
19 Amar'e Stoudemire 4.00 10.00
20 Kevin Garnett 10.00 25.00
21 Carlos Boozer 3.00 8.00
22 Mirza Teletovic 2.50 6.00
23 DeAndre Jordan 3.00 8.00
24 Scottie Pippen 10.00 25.00
25 Grant Hill 6.00 15.00
26 Kyrie Irving 8.00 20.00
27 Jason Kidd 6.00 15.00
28 Jodie Meeks 2.50 6.00
29 Carmelo Anthony 6.00 15.00
30 Kevin Love 4.00 10.00
31 Chandler Parsons 2.50 6.00
32 Norris Cole 2.50 6.00
33 DeMar DeRozan 5.00 12.00
34 Shaquille O'Neal 15.00 40.00
35 Greg Monroe 2.50 6.00
36 Chris Kaman 3.00 8.00
37 Jason Terry 3.00 8.00
38 Joe Johnson 3.00 8.00
39 Andre Iguodala 4.00 10.00
40 Kirk Hinrich 3.00 8.00
41 Chris Bosh 5.00 12.00
42 Patrick Ewing 6.00 15.00
43 Deron Williams 3.00 8.00
44 Taj Gibson 2.50 6.00
45 Harrison Barnes 3.00 8.00
46 Patty Mills 4.00 10.00
47 JaVale McGee 3.00 8.00
48 Jordan Hill 2.50 6.00
49 Andrea Bargnani 2.50 6.00
50 Kobe Bryant 30.00 80.00
51 Clyde Drexler 6.00 15.00
52 Pau Gasol 6.00 15.00
53 Dikembe Mutombo 6.00 15.00
54 Thabo Sefolosha 2.50 6.00
55 J.R. Smith 4.00 10.00
56 Evan Fournier 2.50 6.00
57 Luol Deng 3.00 8.00
58 Kawhi Leonard 10.00 25.00
59 Andrew Bogut 3.00 8.00
60 Marco Belinelli 2.50 6.00
61 Darren Collison 2.50 6.00
62 Paul Pierce 6.00 15.00
63 Dirk Nowitzki 10.00 25.00
64 Tyson Chandler 4.00 10.00
65 Jamal Crawford 4.00 10.00
66 Andrew Wiggins 12.00 30.00
67 Jabari Parker 3.00 8.00
68 Joel Embiid 25.00 60.00
69 Aaron Gordon 12.00 30.00
70 Dante Exum 4.00 10.00
71 Marcus Smart 10.00 25.00
72 Julius Randle 12.00 30.00
73 Nik Stauskas 2.50 6.00
74 Noah Vonleh 2.50 6.00
75 Elfrid Payton 4.00 10.00
76 Doug McDermott 4.00 10.00
77 Zach LaVine 15.00 40.00
78 T.J. Warren 4.00 10.00
79 Adreian Payne 2.50 6.00
80 James Young 2.50 6.00
81 Tyler Ennis 2.50 6.00
82 Gary Harris 4.00 10.00
83 Bruno Caboclo 3.00 8.00
84 Mitch McGary 2.50 6.00
85 Jordan Adams 2.50 6.00
86 Rodney Hood 3.00 8.00
87 Shabazz Napier 3.00 8.00
88 P.J. Hairston 2.50 6.00
89 C.J. Wilcox 2.50 6.00
90 Cory Jefferson 2.50 6.00
91 Kyle Anderson 4.00 10.00
92 K.J. McDaniels 2.50 6.00
93 Joe Harris 4.00 10.00
94 Cleanthony Early 2.50 6.00
95 Jarnell Stokes 2.50 6.00
96 James Ennis 2.50 6.00
97 Spencer Dinwiddie 4.00 10.00
98 Glenn Robinson III 3.00 8.00
99 Russ Smith 2.50 6.00
100 Markel Brown 2.50 6.00

2014-15 Panini Prizm Photo Variations

*GREEN/25: 2.5X TO 6X BASIC
1 Dirk Nowitzki 4.00 10.00
2 Russell Westbrook 2.50 6.00
3 Dwyane Wade 3.00 8.00
4 Tim Duncan 4.00 10.00
5 Anthony Davis 4.00 10.00
6 Kevin Durant 5.00 12.00
7 Carmelo Anthony 2.50 6.00
8 Kobe Bryant 30.00 80.00
9 Damian Lillard 4.00 10.00
10 LeBron James 30.00 80.00
11 Dwight Howard 2.00 5.00
12 Stephen Curry 30.00 80.00
13 James Harden 3.00 8.00
14 Tony Parker 2.50 6.00

15 Blake Griffin 1.50 4.00
16 Kevin Love 1.50 4.00
17 Chris Paul 2.50 6.00
18 Kyrie Irving 3.00 8.00
19 Derrick Rose 3.00 8.00
20 Paul George 2.50 6.00
21 Wilt Chamberlain 5.00 12.00
22 Karl Malone 3.00 8.00
23 Bill Russell 5.00 12.00
24 Kareem Abdul-Jabbar 5.00 12.00
25 Larry Bird 6.00 15.00
26 Magic Johnson 6.00 15.00
27 Scottie Pippen 4.00 10.00
28 David Robinson 3.00 8.00
29 Julius Erving 4.00 10.00
30 Pete Maravich 5.00 12.00
31 Andrew Wiggins 5.00 12.00
32 Jabari Parker 1.25 3.00
33 Joel Embiid 20.00 50.00
34 Aaron Gordon 5.00 12.00
35 Dante Exum 1.50 4.00
36 Marcus Smart 4.00 10.00
37 Julius Randle 5.00 12.00
38 Nik Stauskas 1.00 2.50
39 Noah Vonleh 1.00 2.50
40 Elfrid Payton 1.50 4.00
41 Doug McDermott 1.50 4.00
42 Zach LaVine 6.00 15.00
43 T.J. Warren 1.50 4.00
44 Adreian Payne 1.00 2.50
45 James Young 1.00 2.50
46 Tyler Ennis 1.00 2.50
47 Gary Harris 1.50 4.00
48 Bruno Caboclo 1.25 3.00
49 Mitch McGary 1.00 2.50
50 Shabazz Napier 1.25 3.00

2014-15 Panini Prizm Representatives

COMPLETE SET (20) 20.00 50.00
*GREEN MOJO/25: 4X TO 10X BASE HI
1 Kevin Durant 3.00 8.00
2 Kevin Love 1.00 2.50
3 Tony Parker 1.50 4.00
4 Anthony Davis 2.50 6.00
5 Andrei Kirilenko .75 2.00
6 Chris Paul 1.50 4.00
7 Ricky Rubio .75 2.00
8 Russell Westbrook 1.50 4.00
9 LeBron James 12.00 30.00
10 Kobe Bryant 12.00 30.00
11 Dwyane Wade 2.00 5.00
12 Carmelo Anthony 1.50 4.00
13 Manu Ginobili 2.00 5.00
14 James Harden 2.00 5.00
15 Marc Gasol 1.00 2.50
16 Magic Johnson 4.00 10.00
17 Larry Bird 4.00 10.00
18 Scottie Pippen 2.50 6.00
19 Patrick Ewing 1.50 4.00
20 Karl Malone 2.00 5.00

2014-15 Panini Prizm Rookie Autographs Prizms

PRINT RUNS B/WN 249-499 COPIES PER
*RED/199: .5X TO 1.2X BASIC
*PURPLE/99: .6X TO 1.5X BASIC
1 Jabari Parker/249 4.00 10.00
2 Andrew Wiggins/249 15.00 40.00
3 Joel Embiid/249 150.00 400.00
4 Marcus Smart/299 12.00 30.00
5 Julius Randle/299 15.00 40.00
6 Dante Exum/299 5.00 12.00
7 Aaron Gordon/349 15.00 40.00
8 Noah Vonleh/349 3.00 8.00
9 Tyler Ennis/349 3.00 8.00
10 Nik Stauskas/349 3.00 8.00
11 Elfrid Payton/399 5.00 12.00
13 Doug McDermott/449 5.00 12.00
14 James Young/449 3.00 8.00
15 Gary Harris/449 5.00 12.00
16 Zach LaVine/449 20.00 50.00
17 Glenn Robinson III/449 4.00 10.00
18 Adreian Payne/449 3.00 8.00
19 C.J. Wilcox/449 3.00 8.00
20 Mitch McGary/449 3.00 8.00
21 Shabazz Napier/449 4.00 10.00
22 Jordan Adams/449 3.00 8.00
23 Devyn Marble/499 3.00 8.00
24 Spencer Dinwiddie/449 5.00 12.00
25 Bruno Caboclo/499 4.00 10.00
26 Kyle Anderson/499 5.00 12.00
27 Rodney Hood/499 4.00 10.00
28 P.J. Hairston/499 3.00 8.00
29 Cleanthony Early/499 3.00 8.00
30 Jerami Grant/499 15.00 40.00
31 James Ennis/499 3.00 8.00
32 Jordan Clarkson/499 12.00 30.00
33 Johnny O'Bryant/499 3.00 8.00
34 K.J. McDaniels/499 3.00 8.00
35 Dwight Powell/499 4.00 10.00
36 Markel Brown/499 3.00 8.00
37 Cory Jefferson/499 3.00 8.00
38 Joe Harris/499 5.00 12.00
39 Russ Smith/499 3.00 8.00
40 Lucas Nogueira/499 3.00 8.00

2014-15 Panini Prizm Superstars

*GREEN MOJO/25: 5X TO 12X BASIC
1 LeBron James 12.00 30.00
2 Kobe Bryant 12.00 30.00
3 Kevin Durant 3.00 8.00
4 Kyrie Irving 2.00 5.00
5 Anthony Davis 2.50 6.00

2015-16 Panini Prizm

*RWB: 1X TO 2.5X BASE
*RWB RC: .6X TO 1.5X BASE
*FLASH: 1X TO 2.5X BASE
*GREEN: 1.2X TO 3X BASE
*ORNGE WAVE: 1.2X TO 3X BASE
*SILVER: 2X TO 5X BASE
*RUBY/399: 2X TO 5X BASE
*LIGHT BLUE/199: 2.5X TO 6X BASE
*PURPLE/99: 3X TO 8X BASIC
*ORANGE/65: 4X TO 10X BASIC
1 DeMarcus Cousins .40 1.00
2 Marvin Williams .25 .60
3 John Wall .50 1.25
4 Vince Carter .75 2.00
5 Donatas Motiejunas .25 .60
6 Kevin Garnett 1.00 2.50
7 Aron Baynes .25 .60
8 Tim Hardaway Jr. .30 .75
9 Nik Stauskas .25 .60
10 Michael Kidd-Gilchrist .25 .60
11 Darren Collison .25 .60
12 Al Jefferson .25 .60
13 Marcin Gortat .25 .60
14 Mike Conley .40 1.00
15 Patrick Beverley .25 .60
16 Shabazz Muhammad .25 .60
17 Jae Crowder .25 .60
18 Tiago Splitter .25 .60
19 Jason Thompson .25 .60
20 Jeremy Lin .75 2.00
21 Omri Casspi .25 .60
22 Jordan Hill .25 .60
23 Bradley Beal .50 1.25
24 Zach Randolph .40 1.00
25 Josh Smith .25 .60
26 Arron Afflalo .25 .60
27 Cody Zeller .25 .60
28 Al Horford .40 1.00
29 Tony Wroten .25 .60
30 Deron Williams .30 .75
31 David West .25 .60
32 Chase Budinger .25 .60
33 Nene .30 .75
34 Marc Gasol .40 1.00
35 Jason Terry .30 .75
36 Robin Lopez .25 .60
37 Boris Diaw .30 .75
38 Kyle Korver .30 .75
39 Nerlens Noel .25 .60
40 Wesley Matthews .25 .60
41 LaMarcus Aldridge .40 1.00
42 Solomon Hill .25 .60
43 Rasual Butler .25 .60
44 Courtney Lee .25 .60
45 Tyreke Evans .30 .75
46 Derrick Williams .25 .60
47 John Henson .25 .60
48 Paul Millsap .30 .75
49 Robert Covington .30 .75
50 Dirk Nowitzki 1.00 2.50
51 Tim Duncan 1.00 2.50
52 Rodney Stuckey .25 .60
53 Otto Porter .30 .75
54 Gerald Green .30 .75
55 Anthony Davis 1.00 2.50
56 Carmelo Anthony .60 1.50
57 Kelly Olynyk .25 .60
58 Jeff Teague .25 .60
59 Wesley Johnson .25 .60
60 Chandler Parsons .30 .75
61 Tony Parker .60 1.50
62 Paul George .60 1.50
63 Kris Humphries .25 .60
64 Dwyane Wade .75 2.00
65 Eric Gordon .30 .75
66 Langston Galloway .25 .60
67 Amare Stoudemire .40 1.00
68 Dennis Schroder .30 .75
69 Tyson Chandler .30 .75
70 Devin Harris .25 .60
71 Manu Ginobili .75 2.00
72 C.J. Miles .25 .60
73 Ty Lawson .25 .60
74 Chris Bosh .50 1.25
75 Omer Asik .25 .60
76 Jose Calderon .25 .60
77 Tyler Hansbrough .25 .60
78 David Lee .25 .60
79 Eric Bledsoe .30 .75
80 J.J. Barea .30 .75
81 Kawhi Leonard 1.25 3.00
82 Lance Stephenson .30 .75
83 Wilson Chandler .30 .75
84 Luol Deng .30 .75
85 Ryan Anderson .25 .60
86 Quincy Acy .25 .60
87 Aaron Brooks .25 .60
88 Amir Johnson .25 .60
89 Brandon Knight .25 .60
90 Zaza Pachulia .25 .60
91 Danny Green .30 .75
92 Paul Pierce .60 1.50
93 Kenneth Faried .30 .75
94 Hassan Whiteside .30 .75
95 Jrue Holiday .50 1.25
96 Kevin Durant 1.50 4.00
97 Kosta Koufos .25 .60
98 Avery Bradley .25 .60
99 Markieff Morris .25 .60
100 Ersan Ilyasova .25 .60
101 DeMarre Carroll .25 .60
102 Chris Paul .75 2.00
103 Danilo Gallinari .30 .75
104 Mario Chalmers .30 .75
105 Quincy Pondexter .25 .60
106 Russell Westbrook .60 1.50
107 Alexis Ajinca .25 .60
108 Tyler Zeller .25 .60
109 P.J. Tucker .25 .60
110 Marcus Morris .25 .60
111 Luis Scola .30 .75
112 Blake Griffin .40 1.00
113 J.J. Hickson .25 .60
114 Chris Andersen .30 .75
115 Kyrie Irving .75 2.00
116 Serge Ibaka .30 .75
117 Tarik Black .25 .60
118 Evan Turner .25 .60
119 Alex Len .25 .60
120 Kentavious Caldwell-Pope .25 .60
121 Kyle Lowry .40 1.00
122 DeAndre Jordan .30 .75
123 Jusuf Nurkic .30 .75
124 Greg Monroe .30 .75
125 LeBron James 3.00 8.00
126 Dion Waiters .25 .60
127 Lavoy Allen .25 .60
128 Jared Sullinger .25 .60
129 T.J. Warren .40 1.00
130 Jodie Meeks .25 .60
131 Patrick Patterson .25 .60
132 J.J. Redick .40 1.00
133 Randy Foye .25 .60
134 Greivis Vasquez .25 .60
135 Kevin Love .40 1.00
136 Andre Roberson .25 .60
137 Leandro Barbosa .25 .60
138 Marcus Smart .50 1.25
139 Mason Plumlee .25 .60
140 Andre Drummond .40 1.00
141 DeMar DeRozan .50 1.25
142 Jamal Crawford .40 1.00
143 Pau Gasol .60 1.50
144 Giannis Antetokounmpo 2.00 5.00
145 Tristan Thompson .25 .60
146 Steven Adams .30 .75
147 Alan Anderson .25 .60
148 Wayne Ellington .25 .60
149 Gerald Henderson .25 .60
150 Brandon Jennings .25 .60
151 Jonas Valanciunas .30 .75
152 Brandon Bass .25 .60
153 Jimmy Butler .75 2.00
154 Khris Middleton .50 1.25
155 J.R. Smith .40 1.00
156 Anthony Morrow .25 .60
157 Thabo Sefolosha .25 .60
158 Shane Larkin .25 .60
159 Noah Vonleh .25 .60
160 Reggie Jackson .30 .75
161 Terrence Ross .30 .75
162 Roy Hibbert .30 .75
163 Joakim Noah .25 .60
164 Jabari Parker .25 .60
165 Matthew Dellavedova .30 .75
166 Aaron Gordon .40 1.00
167 Jarrett Jack .30 .75
168 Thomas Robinson .25 .60
169 Al-Farouq Aminu .25 .60
170 Stephen Curry 3.00 8.00
171 Gordon Hayward .40 1.00
172 Lou Williams .30 .75
173 Derrick Rose .60 1.50
174 O.J. Mayo .25 .60
175 Timofey Mozgov .25 .60
176 Elfrid Payton .30 .75
177 Hollis Thompson .25 .60
178 Joe Johnson .30 .75
179 Damian Lillard 1.00 2.50
180 Klay Thompson 1.00 2.50
181 Trey Burke .30 .75
182 Kobe Bryant 3.00 8.00
183 Mike Dunleavy .25 .60
184 Michael Carter-Williams .25 .60
185 Ed Davis .25 .60
186 Tobias Harris .30 .75
187 Tayshaun Prince .30 .75
188 Brook Lopez .40 1.00
189 Chris Kaman .25 .60
190 Draymond Green .50 1.25
191 Derrick Favors .30 .75
192 Julius Randle .50 1.25
193 Taj Gibson .25 .60
194 Andrew Wiggins .50 1.25
195 Cory Joseph .25 .60
196 Nikola Vucevic .30 .75
197 Nick Collison .25 .60
198 Markel Brown .25 .60
199 C.J. McCollum .40 1.00
200 Andre Iguodala .40 1.00
201 Dante Exum .30 .75
202 Jordan Clarkson .40 1.00
203 Nikola Mirotic .25 .60
204 Zach LaVine 1.00 2.50
205 Tony Allen .25 .60
206 Victor Oladipo .30 .75
207 Tony Snell .25 .60
208 Bojan Bogdanovic .30 .75
209 Rajon Rondo .50 1.25
210 Andrew Bogut .30 .75
211 Rudy Gobert .50 1.25
212 Nick Young .25 .60
213 James Harden .75 2.00
214 Gorgui Dieng .25 .60
215 Jared Dudley .25 .60
216 Channing Frye .25 .60
217 Caron Butler .30 .75
218 Spencer Hawes .25 .60
219 Marco Belinelli .25 .60
220 Shaun Livingston .30 .75
221 Trevor Booker .25 .60
222 Matt Barnes .25 .60
223 Dwight Howard .50 1.25
224 Ricky Rubio .30 .75
225 James Johnson .25 .60
226 Evan Fournier .25 .60
227 Jameer Nelson .25 .60
228 Nicolas Batum .25 .60
229 Ben McLemore .25 .60
230 Marreese Speights .25 .60
231 Rodney Hood .30 .75
232 Brandan Wright .25 .60
233 Trevor Ariza .25 .60
234 Kevin Martin .25 .60
235 Bismack Biyombo .25 .60
236 Carl Landry .25 .60
237 Joe Ingles .30 .75
238 Kemba Walker .40 1.00
239 Rudy Gay .40 1.00
240 Monta Ellis .30 .75
241 Patrick Ewing .60 1.50
242 Scottie Pippen 1.00 2.50
243 Alonzo Mourning .60 1.50
244 Tracy McGrady .60 1.50
245 Dennis Rodman 1.00 2.50
246 Steve Nash .60 1.50
247 Hakeem Olajuwon .75 2.00
248 Magic Johnson 1.50 4.00
249 Kevin McHale .60 1.50
250 Chauncey Billups .50 1.25
251 Drazen Petrovic .40 1.00
252 Tim Hardaway .50 1.25
253 Anfernee Hardaway 1.00 2.50
254 Latrell Sprewell .50 1.25
255 Dikembe Mutombo .60 1.50
256 Robert Horry .40 1.00
257 Isiah Thomas .60 1.50
258 Jason Williams .40 1.00
259 Karl Malone .60 1.50
260 Moses Malone .60 1.50
261 Larry Bird 1.50 4.00
262 Yao Ming 1.00 2.50
263 Antonio McDyess .30 .75
264 Robert Parish .50 1.25
265 Mike Bibby .30 .75
266 Dino Radja .25 .60
267 Jason Kidd .60 1.50
268 Sam Bowie .25 .60
269 Steve Francis .40 1.00
270 Shawn Kemp .60 1.50
271 Jerry Stackhouse .40 1.00
272 Rick Fox .30 .75
273 Chris Mullin .50 1.25
274 Darryl Dawkins .25 .60
275 Dominique Wilkins .60 1.50
276 Michael Finley .40 1.00
277 John Stockton .75 2.00
278 James Worthy .60 1.50
279 Mark Eaton .40 1.00
280 Jalen Rose .30 .75
281 Rony Seikaly .30 .75
282 Richard Hamilton .40 1.00
283 Clyde Drexler .60 1.50
284 Shaquille O'Neal 1.25 3.00
285 Gary Payton .60 1.50
286 Allen Iverson 1.00 2.50
287 Vlade Divac .40 1.00
288 Julius Erving 1.00 2.50
289 Shareef Abdur-Rahim .30 .75
290 Rik Smits .30 .75
291 Joe Dumars .50 1.25
292 Clifford Robinson .40 1.00
293 David Robinson .75 2.00
294 Mark Jackson .30 .75
295 Grant Hill .60 1.50
296 Michael Redd .30 .75
297 Kareem Abdul-Jabbar 1.25 3.00
298 Eddie Jones .40 1.00
299 Dan Majerle .40 1.00
300 Maurice Cheeks .30 .75
301 Jarell Martin RC .50 1.25
302 Larry Nance Jr. RC 1.00 2.50
303 Justin Anderson RC .50 1.25
304 Anthony Brown RC .50 1.25
305 Joe Young RC .50 1.25
306 Jerian Grant RC .50 1.25
307 Ryan Boatright RC .50 1.25
308 Devin Booker RC 20.00 50.00
309 Kelly Oubre Jr. RC 1.50 4.00
310 Delon Wright RC .50 1.25
311 R.J. Hunter RC .50 1.25
312 Cameron Payne RC .75 2.00
313 Rakeem Christmas RC .50 1.25
314 Frank Kaminsky RC .60 1.50
315 Dakari Johnson RC .60 1.50
316 Emmanuel Mudiay RC .60 1.50
317 Josh Richardson RC .75 2.00
318 Raul Neto RC .50 1.25
319 Aaron Harrison RC .60 1.50
320 Stanley Johnson RC .60 1.50
321 Chris McCullough RC .50 1.25
322 D'Angelo Russell RC 2.00 5.00
323 Richaun Holmes RC .75 2.00
324 Tyus Jones RC .60 1.50
325 Tyler Harvey RC .50 1.25
326 Bobby Portis RC 1.25 3.00
327 Terran Petteway RC .50 1.25
328 Karl-Anthony Towns RC 8.00 20.00
329 Jahlil Okafor RC .60 1.50
330 Rondae Hollis-Jefferson RC .60 1.50
331 Montrezl Harrell RC 1.50 4.00
332 Rashad Vaughn RC .50 1.25
333 Pat Connaughton RC .75 2.00
334 Trey Lyles RC .60 1.50
335 Nikola Jokic RC 125.00 300.00
336 Justise Winslow RC .75 2.00
337 Norman Powell RC 1.00 2.50
338 Terry Rozier RC 2.00 5.00
339 Sam Dekker RC .50 1.25
340 Myles Turner RC 2.00 5.00
341 Jordan Mickey RC .60 1.50
342 Mario Hezonja RC .60 1.50
343 Andrew Harrison RC .60 1.50
344 Walter Tavares RC .50 1.25
345 Darrun Hilliard RC .50 1.25
346 Kevon Looney RC 1.50 4.00
347 Branden Dawson RC .50 1.25
348 Kristaps Porzingis RC 6.00 15.00
349 Willie Cauley-Stein RC .60 1.50
350 Nemanja Bjelica RC .75 2.00
351 Carmelo Anthony AS .60 1.50
352 LeBron James AS 3.00 8.00
353 Pau Gasol AS .60 1.50
354 John Wall AS .50 1.25
355 Kyle Lowry AS .40 1.00
356 Chris Bosh AS .50 1.25
357 Jimmy Butler AS .75 2.00
358 Al Horford AS .40 1.00
359 Kyrie Irving AS .75 2.00
360 Kyle Korver AS .30 .75
361 Paul Millsap AS .30 .75
362 Jeff Teague AS .25 .60
363 Marc Gasol AS .40 1.00
364 Stephen Curry AS 3.00 8.00
365 LaMarcus Aldridge AS .40 1.00
366 DeMarcus Cousins AS .40 1.00
367 Tim Duncan AS 1.00 2.50
368 Kevin Durant AS 1.50 4.00
369 James Harden AS .75 2.00
370 Damian Lillard AS 1.00 2.50
371 Dirk Nowitzki AS 1.00 2.50
372 Chris Paul AS .75 2.00
373 Klay Thompson AS 1.00 2.50
374 Russell Westbrook AS .60 1.50
375 LeBron James ANBA 3.00 8.00
376 Anthony Davis ANBA 1.00 2.50
377 Stephen Curry ANBA 3.00 8.00
378 James Harden ANBA .75 2.00
379 Marc Gasol ANBA .40 1.00
380 LaMarcus Aldridge ANBA .40 1.00
381 DeMarcus Cousins ANBA .40 1.00
382 Russell Westbrook ANBA .60 1.50
383 Chris Paul ANBA .75 2.00
384 Pau Gasol ANBA .60 1.50
385 Blake Griffin ANBA .40 1.00
386 Tim Duncan ANBA 1.00 2.50
387 Kyrie Irving ANBA .75 2.00
388 Klay Thompson ANBA 1.00 2.50
389 DeAndre Jordan ANBA .30 .75
390 Kawhi Leonard ANBA 1.25 3.00
391 Draymond Green ANBA .50 1.25
392 Tony Allen ANBA .25 .60
393 DeAndre Jordan ANBA .30 .75
394 Chris Paul ANBA .75 2.00
395 Anthony Davis ANBA 1.00 2.50
396 Jimmy Butler ANBA .75 2.00
397 Andrew Bogut ANBA .30 .75
398 John Wall ANBA .50 1.25
399 Tim Duncan ANBA 1.00 2.50
400 Stephen Curry MVP 6.00 15.00

2015-16 Panini Prizm Prizms Green

*GREEN: 1.2X TO 3X BASE

2015-16 Panini Prizm Prizms Light Blue

*BLUE/199: 2.5X TO 6X BASIC
STATED PRINT RUN 199 SER.#'d SETS

2015-16 Panini Prizm Prizms Mojo

*MOJO: 10X TO 25X BASIC
STATED PRINT RUN 25 SER.#'d SETS
125 LeBron James 300.00 600.00
144 Giannis Antetokounmpo 125.00 300.00
170 Stephen Curry 300.00 600.00
182 Kobe Bryant 200.00 500.00
308 Devin Booker 1,500.00 3,000.00
335 Nikola Jokic 5,000.00 10,000.00
346 Kevon Looney 75.00 200.00
352 LeBron James AS 125.00 300.00
375 LeBron James ANBA 125.00 300.00
400 Stephen Curry MVP 300.00 600.00

2015-16 Panini Prizm Autographs

OVERALL AU ODDS 1:20 HOBBY
EXCHANGE DEADLINE 5/16/2017
1 Otto Porter 3.00 8.00
2 Shabazz Muhammad 2.50 6.00
3 Cody Zeller 2.50 6.00
4 Jerami Grant 4.00 10.00
5 Dante Exum 3.00 8.00
6 Jarrell Stokes 2.50 6.00
7 Langston Galloway 2.50 6.00
8 Bojan Bogdanovic 3.00 8.00
9 C.J. McCollum 10.00 25.00
10 Robert Covington 3.00 8.00
11 Chucky Brown 2.50 6.00
12 Ben McLemore 2.50 6.00
13 Trey Burke 2.50 6.00
14 Alex Len 2.50 6.00
15 Mike Muscala 2.50 6.00
16 Victor Oladipo 8.00 20.00
17 Nerlens Noel 2.50 6.00
18 Robert Sacre 2.50 6.00
19 Michael Carter-Williams 2.50 6.00
20 Kentavious Caldwell-Pope 3.00 8.00
21 Jabari Brown 2.50 6.00
22 Andre Roberson 2.50 6.00
23 Matthew Dellavedova 3.00 8.00
24 Carl Landry 2.50 6.00
25 Mason Plumlee 2.50 6.00
26 Al-Farouq Aminu 2.50 6.00
27 Allen Iverson 60.00 150.00
28 Alan Anderson 2.50 6.00
29 Maurice Harkless 2.50 6.00
30 Brandon Knight 2.50 6.00
31 Cliff Hagan 4.00 10.00
32 Artis Gilmore 5.00 12.00
33 Robert Parish 5.00 12.00
34 Gail Goodrich 4.00 10.00
35 Joe Dumars 5.00 12.00
36 Don Nelson 10.00 25.00
37 Dave Cowens 5.00 12.00
38 Dominique Wilkins 12.00 30.00
39 Raef LaFrentz 2.50 6.00
40 Terry Cummings 3.00 8.00
41 Larry Brown 4.00 10.00
42 Scott Brooks 2.50 6.00
43 Chuck Person 3.00 8.00
44 Mitch Richmond 5.00 12.00
45 Jerry Stackhouse 4.00 10.00
46 Damon Stoudamire 4.00 10.00
47 Dino Radja 2.50 6.00
48 Jeff Malone 2.50 6.00
49 Bobby Jones 3.00 8.00
50 Vernon Maxwell 2.50 6.00
51 Kurt Rambis 3.00 8.00
52 Michael Cage 2.50 6.00
53 John Lucas 3.00 8.00
54 Muggsy Bogues 12.00 30.00
55 Kenny Walker 2.50 6.00
56 Marques Johnson 3.00 8.00
57 Peja Stojakovic 3.00 8.00
58 Vinny Del Negro 3.00 8.00
59 Jabari Parker 3.00 8.00
60 Julius Randle 5.00 12.00
61 Christian Laettner 3.00 8.00
62 Tom Chambers 3.00 8.00
63 Scott Skiles 3.00 8.00
64 Rik Smits 3.00 8.00
65 Steve Mix 2.50 6.00
66 Bill Cartwright 3.00 8.00
67 Adrian Smith 2.50 6.00
68 Sean Elliott 3.00 8.00
69 Keith Van Horn 3.00 8.00
70 George Karl 4.00 10.00
71 Allan Houston 3.00 8.00
72 Noah Vonleh 2.50 6.00
73 Dennis Rodman 40.00 100.00
74 Antoine Walker 3.00 8.00
75 Tracy McGrady 100.00 250.00
76 Nick Van Exel 4.00 10.00
77 Brent Barry 2.50 6.00
78 Aaron Gordon 4.00 10.00
79 Baron Davis 3.00 8.00
80 Kobe Bryant 800.00 1,500.00
81 Kevin Durant 100.00 250.00
82 Kyrie Irving 50.00 120.00
83 Ricky Rubio 8.00 20.00
84 Anthony Davis 40.00 100.00
85 Andrew Wiggins 15.00 40.00
86 Justin Anderson 2.50 6.00
87 Montrezl Harrell 8.00 20.00
88 Devin Booker 500.00 1,000.00
89 Sam Dekker 2.50 6.00
90 Willie Cauley-Stein 3.00 8.00
91 Karl-Anthony Towns 75.00 200.00
92 Jahlil Okafor 3.00 8.00
93 Bobby Portis 6.00 15.00
94 Jerian Grant 2.50 6.00
95 Myles Turner 10.00 25.00
96 Justise Winslow 4.00 10.00
97 Jordan Mickey 2.50 6.00
98 Kristaps Porzingis 15.00 40.00
99 Emmanuel Mudiay 3.00 8.00
100 D'Angelo Russell 20.00 50.00

2015-16 Panini Prizm Autographs Prizms Orange

*ORANGE: .5X TO 1.2X BASIC
OVERALL AU ODDS 1:20 HOBBY
STATED PRINT RUN 65 SER.#'d SETS
EXCHANGE DEADLINE 5/16/2017
88 Devin Booker 1,000.00 2,000.00
91 Karl-Anthony Towns 125.00 300.00

2015-16 Panini Prizm Emergent

STATED ODDS 1:17 HOBBY
*GREEN: 1.25X TO 3X BASIC
*SILVER: 2X TO 5X BASIC
1 Jerian Grant .50 1.25
2 Emmanuel Mudiay .60 1.50
3 Bobby Portis 1.25 3.00
4 Justise Winslow .75 2.00
5 Joe Young .50 1.25
6 Devin Booker 6.00 15.00
7 Raul Neto .50 1.25
8 Karl-Anthony Towns 3.00 8.00
9 Terry Rozier 2.00 5.00
10 Kristaps Porzingis 3.00 8.00
11 Delon Wright .60 1.50
12 Stanley Johnson .60 1.50
13 Rondae Hollis-Jefferson .60 1.50
14 Myles Turner 2.00 5.00
15 Nemanja Bjelica .75 2.00
16 Larry Nance Jr. 1.00 2.50
17 Cameron Payne .75 2.00
18 D'Angelo Russell 2.00 5.00
19 Rashad Vaughn .50 1.25
20 Mario Hezonja .60 1.50
21 Justin Anderson .50 1.25
22 Frank Kaminsky .60 1.50
23 Tyus Jones .60 1.50
24 Trey Lyles .60 1.50
25 Walter Tavares .50 1.25
26 Kelly Oubre Jr. 1.50 4.00
27 Kevon Looney 1.50 4.00
28 Jahlil Okafor .60 1.50
29 Sam Dekker .50 1.25
30 Willie Cauley-Stein .60 1.50

2015-16 Panini Prizm Fireworks

STATED ODDS 1:15 HOBBY
*GREEN: 1.25X TO 3X BASIC
*SILVER: 2X TO 5X BASIC
1 Andre Iguodala .75 2.00
2 Russell Westbrook 1.25 3.00
3 Stephen Curry 6.00 15.00
4 Mike Conley .75 2.00
5 James Harden 1.50 4.00
6 Jabari Parker .50 1.25
7 Kyrie Irving 1.50 4.00
8 Joakim Noah .50 1.25
9 LeBron James 6.00 15.00
10 Kobe Bryant 6.00 15.00
11 Tim Duncan 2.00 5.00
12 Kyle Lowry .75 2.00
13 Dwight Howard 1.00 2.50
14 Goran Dragic .75 2.00
15 Dirk Nowitzki 2.00 5.00
16 Klay Thompson 2.00 5.00
17 Chris Bosh 1.00 2.50
18 Damian Lillard 2.00 5.00
19 Kevin Durant 3.00 8.00
20 DeMarcus Cousins .75 2.00
21 Anthony Davis 2.00 5.00
22 Blake Griffin 1.50 4.00
23 John Wall 1.00 2.50
24 DeAndre Jordan .60 1.50
25 Tony Parker 1.25 3.00
26 Bradley Beal 1.00 2.50
27 Dwyane Wade 1.50 4.00
28 Derrick Rose 1.25 3.00
29 Chris Paul 1.50 4.00
30 Kawhi Leonard 2.50 6.00
31 Kevin Love 1.00 2.50
32 Andrew Wiggins 1.00 2.50
33 Carmelo Anthony 1.25 3.00
34 Manu Ginobili 1.25 3.00
35 Marc Gasol .75 2.00

2015-16 Panini Prizm Point Men

STATED ODDS 1:33 HOBBY
*GREEN: 1.25X TO 3X BASIC
*SILVER: 2X TO 5X BASIC
1 John Wall 1.00 2.50
2 Anfernee Hardaway 2.00 5.00
3 Stephen Curry 6.00 15.00
4 Steve Nash 1.25 3.00
5 Isiah Thomas .75 2.00
6 Damon Stoudamire .75 2.00
7 Magic Johnson 3.00 8.00
8 John Stockton 1.50 4.00
9 Derrick Rose 1.25 3.00
10 Russell Westbrook 1.25 3.00
11 Kyrie Irving 1.50 4.00
12 Allen Iverson 2.00 5.00
13 Jason Kidd 1.25 3.00
14 Tony Parker 1.25 3.00
15 Chris Paul 1.50 4.00

2015-16 Panini Prizm Rookie Autographs

OVERALL AU ODDS 1:20 HOBBY
EXCHANGE DEADLINE 5/16/2017
RSAB Anthony Brown 2.50 6.00
RSAH Aaron Harrison 3.00 8.00
RSAH Andrew Harrison 3.00 8.00
RSBD Branden Dawson 2.50 6.00
RSBP Bobby Portis 6.00 15.00
RSCM Chris McCullough 2.50 6.00
RSCP Cameron Payne 4.00 10.00
RSDB Devin Booker 200.00 500.00
RSDH Darrun Hilliard 2.50 6.00
RSDJ Dakari Johnson 2.50 6.00
RSDR D'Angelo Russell 25.00 60.00
RSDW Delon Wright 3.00 8.00
RSEM Emmanuel Mudiay 3.00 8.00
RSFK Frank Kaminsky 3.00 8.00
RSJA Justin Anderson 2.50 6.00
RSJG Jerian Grant 2.50 6.00
RSJM Jarell Martin 2.50 6.00
RSJM Jordan Mickey 2.50 6.00
RSJO Jahlil Okafor 3.00 8.00
RSJR Josh Richardson 4.00 10.00
RSJW Justise Winslow 4.00 10.00
RSJY Joe Young 2.50 6.00
RSKL Kevon Looney 8.00 20.00
RSKO Kelly Oubre Jr. 8.00 20.00
RSKP Kristaps Porzingis 50.00 120.00
RSKT Karl-Anthony Towns 50.00 120.00
RSLN Larry Nance Jr. 10.00 25.00
RSMH Mario Hezonja 3.00 8.00
RSMH Montrezl Harrell 6.00 15.00
RSMT Myles Turner 8.00 20.00
RSNP Norman Powell 5.00 12.00
RSPC Pat Connaughton 4.00 10.00
RSRC Rakeem Christmas 2.50 6.00
RSRH Rondae Hollis-Jefferson 3.00 8.00
RSRH Richaun Holmes 4.00 10.00
RSRH R.J. Hunter 2.50 6.00
RSRV Rashad Vaughn 2.50 6.00
RSSD Sam Dekker 2.50 6.00
RSSJ Stanley Johnson 3.00 8.00
RSTH Tyler Harvey 2.50 6.00
RSTJ Tyus Jones 6.00 15.00
RSTL Trey Lyles 3.00 8.00
RSTR Terry Rozier 20.00 50.00
RSWC Willie Cauley-Stein 3.00 8.00

2015-16 Panini Prizm Rookie Autographs Prizms

*PRIZMS: .6X TO 1.5X BASIC
OVERALL AU ODDS 1:20 HOBBY
STATED PRINT RUN 25 SER.#'d SETS
EXCHANGE DEADLINE 5/16/2017
RSDB Devin Booker 500.00 1,000.00
RSKP Kristaps Porzingis 100.00 250.00
RSKT Karl-Anthony Towns 125.00 300.00

2015-16 Panini Prizm USA Basketball

STATED ODDS 1:25 HOBBY
1 Russell Westbrook 1.50 4.00
2 Rudy Gay 1.00 2.50
3 Chris Paul 2.00 5.00
4 Kyrie Irving 2.00 5.00
5 Kevin Love 1.00 2.50
6 DeMarcus Cousins 1.00 2.50
7 Derrick Rose 1.50 4.00
8 Anthony Davis 2.50 6.00
9 Kevin Durant 4.00 10.00
10 Andre Drummond 1.00 2.50
11 Kobe Bryant 15.00 40.00
12 James Harden 2.00 5.00
13 Carmelo Anthony 1.50 4.00
14 Mason Plumlee .60 1.50
15 Andre Iguodala 1.00 2.50
16 Stephen Curry 8.00 20.00
17 Klay Thompson 2.50 6.00
18 DeMar DeRozan 1.25 3.00
19 LeBron James 15.00 40.00
20 Kenneth Faried .75 2.00

2015-16 Panini Prizm Veteran Autographs

OVERALL AU ODDS 1:20 HOBBY
STATED PRINT RUN 150 SER.#'d SETS
EXCHANGE DEADLINE 5/16/2017
*PRIZMS/25: .6X TO 1.5X BASIC
1 Kobe Bryant 1,000.00 2,000.00
2 Kevin Durant 75.00 200.00
3 Kyrie Irving 40.00 100.00
4 Dwyane Wade 60.00 150.00
7 Carmelo Anthony 100.00 250.00
8 Andrew Wiggins 15.00 40.00
9 Bradley Beal EXCH 20.00 50.00
10 Blake Griffin 25.00 60.00
11 Tony Parker 20.00 50.00
12 Klay Thompson 50.00 120.00
13 Jabari Parker 6.00 15.00
14 Anthony Davis 60.00 150.00
15 Kawhi Leonard EXCH 100.00 250.00

2016-17 Panini Prizm

1 Ben Simmons RC 1.50 4.00
2 Dario Saric RC .75 2.00
3 T. Luwawu-Cabarrot RC .75 2.00
4 Joel Embiid 1.00 2.50
5 T.J. McConnell .30 .75
6 Robert Covington .30 .75
7 Nerlens Noel .25 .60
8 Jahlil Okafor .25 .60
9 Jerami Grant .40 1.00
10 Nik Stauskas .25 .60
11 Jabari Parker .25 .60
12 Khris Middleton .40 1.00
13 Giannis Antetokounmpo 2.00 5.00
14 Thon Maker RC .60 1.50
15 Greg Monroe .25 .60
16 Matthew Dellavedova .30 .75
17 Malcolm Brogdon RC 1.50 4.00
18 John Henson .25 .60
19 Michael Carter-Williams .25 .60
20 Rashad Vaughn .25 .60
21 Jimmy Butler .75 2.00
22 Bobby Portis .40 1.00
23 Denzel Valentine RC .50 1.25
24 Dwyane Wade .75 2.00
25 Rajon Rondo .50 1.25
26 Robin Lopez .25 .60
27 Jerian Grant .25 .60
28 Doug McDermott .30 .75
29 Nikola Mirotic .25 .60
30 Taj Gibson .25 .60
31 LeBron James 3.00 8.00
32 Kyrie Irving .75 2.00
33 Kay Felder RC .50 1.25
34 Kevin Love .40 1.00
35 Richard Jefferson .30 .75
36 Tristan Thompson .30 .75
37 Iman Shumpert .25 .60
38 Channing Frye .25 .60
39 J.R. Smith .40 1.00

40 Mo Williams .30 .75
41 Al Horford .40 1.00
42 Isaiah Thomas .30 .75
43 Avery Bradley .25 .60
44 Jaylen Brown RC 12.00 30.00
45 Jae Crowder .25 .60
46 Marcus Smart .50 1.25
47 Kelly Olynyk .25 .60
48 Ben Bentil RC .50 1.25
49 Terry Rozier .40 1.00
50 Jordan Mickey .25 .60
51 Chris Paul .60 1.50
52 Blake Griffin .40 1.00
53 DeAndre Jordan .30 .75
54 J.J. Redick .40 1.00
55 Diamond Stone RC .50 1.25
56 Brice Johnson RC .50 1.25
57 Jamal Crawford .40 1.00
58 Paul Pierce .60 1.50
59 Marreese Speights .25 .60
60 Brandon Bass .25 .60
61 Mike Conley .30 .75
62 Chandler Parsons .25 .60
63 Marc Gasol .40 1.00
64 Zach Randolph .40 1.00
65 Vince Carter .75 2.00
66 Brandan Wright .25 .60
67 Tony Allen .25 .60
68 Wade Baldwin IV RC .50 1.25
69 Deyonta Davis RC .50 1.25
70 James Ennis .25 .60
71 Dwight Howard .50 1.25
72 Dennis Schroder .40 1.00
73 Paul Millsap .30 .75
74 Kyle Korver .30 .75
75 Kent Bazemore .25 .60
76 Kris Humphries .25 .60
77 DeAndre' Bembry RC .75 2.00
78 Taurean Prince RC .60 1.50
79 Thabo Sefolosha .25 .60
80 Jarrett Jack .30 .75
81 Hassan Whiteside .30 .75
82 Justise Winslow .30 .75
83 Josh Richardson .30 .75
84 Goran Dragic .40 1.00
85 Tyler Johnson .25 .60
86 Chris Bosh .50 1.25
87 Dion Waiters .25 .60
88 Derrick Williams .25 .60
89 Udonis Haslem .30 .75
90 Wayne Ellington .25 .60
91 Kemba Walker .30 .75
92 Nicolas Batum .30 .75
93 Frank Kaminsky .25 .60
94 Marvin Williams .25 .60
95 Roy Hibbert .30 .75
96 Michael Kidd-Gilchrist .25 .60
97 Jeremy Lamb .25 .60
98 Aaron Harrison .25 .60
99 Marco Belinelli .25 .60
100 Ramon Sessions .25 .60
101 Gordon Hayward .40 1.00
102 Rudy Gobert .50 1.25
103 Derrick Favors .25 .60
104 Dante Exum .30 .75
105 Joe Johnson .40 1.00
106 George Hill .30 .75
107 Boris Diaw .30 .75
108 Trey Lyles .30 .75
109 Alec Burks .30 .75
110 Rodney Hood .30 .75
111 DeMarcus Cousins .30 .75
112 Rudy Gay .40 1.00
113 Georgios Papagiannis RC .50 1.25
114 Skal Labissiere RC .50 1.25
115 Malachi Richardson RC .50 1.25
116 Ben McLemore .25 .60
117 Willie Cauley-Stein .25 .60
118 Matt Barnes .25 .60
119 Arron Afflalo .25 .60
120 Omri Casspi .25 .60
121 Carmelo Anthony .60 1.50
122 Derrick Rose .60 1.50
123 Joakim Noah .25 .60
124 Kristaps Porzingis .60 1.50
125 Courtney Lee .25 .60
126 Brandon Jennings .25 .60
127 Lance Thomas .25 .60
128 Justin Holiday RC .60 1.50
129 Marshall Plumlee RC .50 1.25
130 Kyle O'Quinn .25 .60
131 Brandon Ingram RC 2.00 5.00
132 D'Angelo Russell .50 1.25
133 Timofey Mozgov .25 .60
134 Jordan Clarkson .40 1.00
135 Julius Randle .50 1.25
136 Ivica Zubac RC 1.25 3.00
137 Luol Deng .30 .75
138 Jose Calderon .25 .60
139 Marcelo Huertas .25 .60
140 Lou Williams .40 1.00
141 Serge Ibaka .30 .75
142 Nikola Vucevic .40 1.00
143 Aaron Gordon .40 1.00
144 Evan Fournier .30 .75
145 Bismack Biyombo .25 .60
146 Elfrid Payton .30 .75
147 Mario Hezonja .25 .60
148 Stephen Zimmerman RC .50 1.25
149 Jeff Green .25 .60
150 D.J. Augustin .25 .60
151 Dirk Nowitzki 1.00 2.50
152 Harrison Barnes .30 .75
153 Andrew Bogut .40 1.00
154 Deron Williams .30 .75
155 Justin Anderson .25 .60
156 J.J. Barea .30 .75
157 Seth Curry .25 .60
158 Salah Mejri .25 .60
159 A.J. Hammons RC .50 1.25
160 Dwight Powell .25 .60
161 Jeremy Lin .75 2.00
162 Isaiah Whitehead RC .50 1.25
163 Brook Lopez .30 .75
164 Bojan Bogdanovic .30 .75
165 Caris LeVert RC 1.25 3.00
166 Chris McCullough .25 .60
167 Trevor Booker .25 .60
168 Rondae Hollis-Jefferson .25 .60
169 Sean Kilpatrick RC .50 1.25
170 Anthony Bennett .25 .60
171 Danilo Gallinari .30 .75
172 Kenneth Faried .30 .75
173 Emmanuel Mudiay .25 .60
174 Nikola Jokic 6.00 15.00
175 Jamal Murray RC 6.00 15.00
176 Wilson Chandler .30 .75
177 Jusuf Nurkic .30 .75
178 Gary Harris .30 .75
179 Will Barton .25 .60
180 Darrell Arthur .25 .60
181 Paul George .60 1.50
182 Jeff Teague .25 .60
183 Monta Ellis .30 .75
184 Al Jefferson .25 .60
185 Thaddeus Young .25 .60
186 Myles Turner .40 1.00
187 Georges Niang RC .75 2.00
188 Joe Young .25 .60
189 Rodney Stuckey .25 .60
190 C.J. Miles .25 .60
191 Anthony Davis 1.25 3.00
192 Buddy Hield RC 1.50 4.00
193 Tyreke Evans .30 .75
194 Jrue Holiday .50 1.25
195 Omer Asik .25 .60
196 Cheick Diallo RC .50 1.25
197 Terrence Jones .25 .60
198 Alonzo Gee .25 .60
199 Tim Frazier RC .50 1.25
200 Langston Galloway .25 .60
201 Andre Drummond .40 1.00
202 Reggie Jackson .30 .75
203 Kentavious Caldwell-Pope .30 .75
204 Marcus Morris .25 .60
205 Henry Ellenson RC .50 1.25
206 Boban Marjanovic .30 .75
207 Ish Smith .25 .60
208 Tobias Harris .40 1.00
209 Michael Gbinije .25 .60
210 Jon Leuer .25 .60
211 DeMar DeRozan .50 1.25
212 Kyle Lowry .40 1.00
213 Jonas Valanciunas .30 .75
214 Jared Sullinger .25 .60
215 DeMarre Carroll .25 .60
216 Jakob Poeltl RC 1.00 2.50
217 Norman Powell .40 1.00
218 Cory Joseph .25 .60
219 Patrick Patterson .25 .60
220 Pascal Siakam RC 3.00 8.00
221 James Harden .75 2.00
222 Michael Beasley .25 .60
223 Patrick Beverley .25 .60
224 Gary Payton II RC 1.25 3.00
225 Eric Gordon .30 .75
226 Ryan Anderson .25 .60
227 Nene .30 .75
228 Trevor Ariza .25 .60
229 Sam Dekker .25 .60
230 Clint Capela .30 .75
231 Kawhi Leonard 1.00 2.50
232 Pau Gasol .60 1.50
233 Tony Parker .60 1.50
234 Manu Ginobili .75 2.00
235 LaMarcus Aldridge .40 1.00
236 Dejounte Murray RC 2.50 6.00
237 Danny Green .30 .75
238 Kyle Anderson .25 .60
239 Jonathon Simmons .25 .60
240 Patty Mills .40 1.00
241 Devin Booker 1.50 4.00
242 Dragan Bender RC .50 1.25
243 Marquese Chriss RC .60 1.50
244 Eric Bledsoe .30 .75
245 Brandon Knight .30 .75
246 Tyler Ulis RC .60 1.50
247 Tyson Chandler .25 .60
248 Leandro Barbosa .25 .60
249 T.J. Warren .30 .75
250 Alex Len .25 .60
251 Russell Westbrook .60 1.50
252 Steven Adams .30 .75
253 Victor Oladipo .30 .75
254 Enes Kanter .25 .60
255 Domantas Sabonis RC 3.00 8.00
256 Andre Roberson .25 .60
257 Cameron Payne .40 1.00
258 Ersan Ilyasova .25 .60
259 Mitch McGary .25 .60
260 Anthony Morrow .25 .60
261 Ricky Rubio .30 .75
262 Karl-Anthony Towns .75 2.00
263 Andrew Wiggins .50 1.25
264 Kevin Garnett 1.00 2.50
265 Zach LaVine .30 .75
266 Kris Dunn RC .75 2.00
267 Nikola Pekovic .25 .60
268 Gorgui Dieng .25 .60
269 Cole Aldrich .25 .60
270 Shabazz Muhammad .25 .60
271 Damian Lillard 1.00 2.50
272 Allen Crabbe .25 .60
273 C.J. McCollum .40 1.00
274 Evan Turner .25 .60
275 Festus Ezeli .25 .60
276 Mason Plumlee .25 .60
277 Meyers Leonard .25 .60
278 Al-Farouq Aminu .25 .60
279 Jake Layman RC .60 1.50
280 Ed Davis .25 .60
281 Stephen Curry 3.00 8.00
282 Kevin Durant 1.50 4.00
283 Klay Thompson 1.00 2.50
284 Draymond Green .50 1.25
285 Andre Iguodala .40 1.00
286 Anderson Varejao .25 .60
287 Shaun Livingston .25 .60
288 David West .30 .75
289 Zaza Pachulia .25 .60
290 Patrick McCaw RC .50 1.25
291 John Wall .50 1.25
292 Bradley Beal .50 1.25
293 Marcin Gortat .25 .60
294 Kelly Oubre Jr. .50 1.25
295 Trey Burke .25 .60
296 Markieff Morris .25 .60
297 Ian Mahinmi .25 .60
298 Otto Porter .30 .75
299 Andrew Nicholson .25 .60
300 Jason Smith .25 .60

2016-17 Panini Prizm Prizms Blue Wave

*BLUE WAVE: 1.5X TO 4X BASIC
*BLUE WAVE RC: 1.5X TO 4X BASIC
STATED PRINT RUN 99 SER.#'d SETS
31 LeBron James 125.00 300.00
44 Jaylen Brown 125.00 300.00
131 Brandon Ingram 40.00 100.00
174 Nikola Jokic 50.00 120.00
175 Jamal Murray 60.00 150.00
192 Buddy Hield 10.00 25.00
231 Kawhi Leonard 40.00 100.00
236 Dejounte Murray 30.00 80.00
255 Domantas Sabonis 25.00 60.00
281 Stephen Curry 40.00 100.00

2016-17 Panini Prizm Prizms Green

*GREEN: 1X TO 2.5X BASIC
*GREEN RC: 1X TO 2.5X BASIC
44 Jaylen Brown 100.00 250.00
174 Nikola Jokic 15.00 40.00
175 Jamal Murray 40.00 100.00
192 Buddy Hield 8.00 20.00

2016-17 Panini Prizm Prizms Mojo

*MOJO: 5X TO 12X BASIC
*MOJO RC: .5X TO 12X BASIC
STATED PRINT RUN 25 SER.#'d SETS
13 Giannis Antetokounmpo 150.00 400.00
31 LeBron James 300.00 600.00
44 Jaylen Brown 600.00 1,200.00
131 Brandon Ingram 150.00 400.00
174 Nikola Jokic 125.00 300.00
175 Jamal Murray 300.00 600.00
192 Buddy Hield 40.00 100.00
236 Dejounte Murray 125.00 300.00
255 Domantas Sabonis 100.00 250.00
281 Stephen Curry 125.00 300.00
282 Kevin Durant 100.00 250.00

2016-17 Panini Prizm Prizms Orange

*ORANGE: 1.5X TO 4X BASIC
*ORANGE RC: 1.5X TO 4X BASIC
STATED PRINT RUN 49 SER.#'d SETS
13 Giannis Antetokounmpo 50.00 120.00
31 LeBron James 125.00 300.00
44 Jaylen Brown 200.00 500.00
131 Brandon Ingram 50.00 120.00
174 Nikola Jokic 50.00 120.00
175 Jamal Murray 75.00 200.00
192 Buddy Hield 12.00 30.00
236 Dejounte Murray 40.00 100.00
255 Domantas Sabonis 30.00 80.00
281 Stephen Curry 40.00 100.00

2016-17 Panini Prizm Prizms Orange Wave

*ORANGE WAVE: 5X TO 12X BASIC
*ORANGE WAVE RC: .5X TO 12X BASIC
STATED PRINT RUN 25 SER.#'d SETS
13 Giannis Antetokounmpo 150.00 400.00
31 LeBron James 300.00 600.00
44 Jaylen Brown 600.00 1,200.00
131 Brandon Ingram 150.00 400.00
174 Nikola Jokic 125.00 300.00
175 Jamal Murray 300.00 600.00
192 Buddy Hield 40.00 100.00
231 Kawhi Leonard 125.00 300.00
236 Dejounte Murray 125.00 300.00
243 Marquese Chriss 20.00 50.00
255 Domantas Sabonis 100.00 250.00
281 Stephen Curry 125.00 300.00
282 Kevin Durant 20.00 50.00

2016-17 Panini Prizm Prizms Purple

*PURPLE: 1.2X TO 3X BASIC
*PURPLE RC: 1.2X TO 3X BASIC
STATED PRINT RUN 75 SER.#'d SETS
13 Giannis Antetokounmpo 50.00 120.00
31 LeBron James 125.00 300.00
44 Jaylen Brown 150.00 400.00
131 Brandon Ingram 40.00 100.00
174 Nikola Jokic 40.00 100.00
175 Jamal Murray 60.00 150.00
192 Buddy Hield 10.00 25.00
231 Kawhi Leonard 40.00 100.00
236 Dejounte Murray 30.00 80.00
255 Domantas Sabonis 25.00 60.00
281 Stephen Curry 30.00 80.00

2016-17 Panini Prizm Prizms Ruby Wave

*RUBY WAVE: 1X TO 2.5X BASIC
*RUBY WAVE RC: 1X TO 2.5X BASIC
44 Jaylen Brown 60.00 150.00
174 Nikola Jokic 15.00 40.00
175 Jamal Murray 40.00 100.00
192 Buddy Hield 8.00 20.00

2016-17 Panini Prizm Prizms Silver

*SILVER: 1.5X TO 4X BASIC
*SILVER RC: 1.5X TO 4X BASIC
174 Nikola Jokic 30.00 80.00
192 Buddy Hield 12.00 30.00

2016-17 Panini Prizm Prizms Starburst

*STARBURST: 1.5X TO 4X BASIC
*STARBURST RC: .75X TO 2X BASIC
44 Jaylen Brown 50.00 120.00
174 Nikola Jokic 25.00 60.00

2016-17 Panini Prizm Prizms Teal Wave

*TEAL WAVE: 5X TO 12X BASIC
*TEAL WAVE RC: .5X TO 12X BASIC
STATED PRINT RUN 25 SER.#'d SETS
13 Giannis Antetokounmpo 150.00 400.00
31 LeBron James 300.00 600.00
44 Jaylen Brown 600.00 1,200.00
131 Brandon Ingram 150.00 400.00
174 Nikola Jokic 125.00 300.00
175 Jamal Murray 300.00 600.00
192 Buddy Hield 40.00 100.00
231 Kawhi Leonard 125.00 300.00
236 Dejounte Murray 125.00 300.00
255 Domantas Sabonis 100.00 250.00
281 Stephen Curry 125.00 300.00

2016-17 Panini Prizm All Day

*GREEN: .5X TO 1.2X BASIC
*SILVER: .5X TO 1.2X BASIC
*RUBY: .5X TO 1.2X BASIC
*BLUE/99: .6X TO 1.5X BASIC
*PURPLE/75: .75X TO 2X BASIC
*ORANGE/49: 1X TO 2.5X BASIC
*MOJO/25: 1.5X TO 4X BASIC
*ORNG WAVE/25: 1.5X TO 4X BASIC
*TEAL WAVE/25: 1.5X TO 4X BASIC
1 Kyrie Irving 1.25 3.00
2 Carmelo Anthony 1.00 2.50
3 Khris Middleton .60 1.50
4 J.J. Redick .60 1.50
5 Kyle Korver .50 1.25
6 Evan Fournier .50 1.25
7 Dirk Nowitzki 1.50 4.00
8 Paul George 1.00 2.50
9 James Harden 1.25 3.00
10 Devin Booker 2.50 6.00
11 C.J. McCollum .60 1.50
12 Klay Thompson 1.50 4.00
13 Stephen Curry 5.00 12.00
14 John Wall .75 2.00
15 Bradley Beal .75 2.00

2016-17 Panini Prizm Autographs

*ORANGE/25: .6X TO 1.5X BASIC
1 Brandon Ingram 150.00 400.00
2 Anthony Bennett 3.00 8.00
3 Cody Zeller 3.00 8.00
4 C.J. McCollum 10.00 25.00
5 Lamar Patterson 3.00 8.00
6 James Ennis 3.00 8.00
7 Dwight Powell 3.00 8.00
8 Ray McCallum 3.00 8.00
9 T.J. McConnell 4.00 10.00
10 Walter Tavares 3.00 8.00
11 Allen Crabbe 3.00 8.00
12 Reggie Jackson 4.00 10.00
13 Aaron Harrison 3.00 8.00
14 Kevon Looney 5.00 12.00
15 Tristan Thompson 4.00 10.00
16 Jeff Withey 3.00 8.00
17 Jonas Valanciunas 4.00 10.00
18 Deron Williams 4.00 10.00
19 Seth Curry 4.00 10.00
20 Rashad Vaughn 3.00 8.00
21 Andrew Nicholson 3.00 8.00
22 Jusuf Nurkic 4.00 10.00
23 Matthew Dellavedova 4.00 10.00
25 Courtney Lee 3.00 8.00
26 Devin Harris 3.00 8.00
27 James Johnson 3.00 8.00
28 Kelly Olynyk 3.00 8.00
30 Michael Kidd-Gilchrist 3.00 8.00
31 Alex Len 3.00 8.00
32 E'Twaun Moore 3.00 8.00
33 Justin Hamilton 3.00 8.00
34 Ian Clark 3.00 8.00
35 Josh Huestis 3.00 8.00
36 Frank Kaminsky 5.00 12.00
37 Kelly Oubre Jr. 6.00 15.00
38 Kristaps Porzingis 25.00 60.00
39 Cameron Payne 5.00 12.00
40 Tobias Harris 5.00 12.00
41 Bobby Portis 5.00 12.00
42 Luol Deng 4.00 10.00
43 Willie Cauley-Stein 4.00 10.00
44 Devin Booker 125.00 300.00
45 Zach Randolph 5.00 12.00
46 Nikola Vucevic 5.00 12.00
48 Larry Nance Jr. 3.00 8.00
51 Bill Willoughby 4.00 10.00
52 Vin Baker 4.00 10.00
53 Brian Grant 4.00 10.00
54 Zydrunas Ilgauskas 4.00 10.00
55 Mark Price 6.00 15.00
56 Dan Majerle 4.00 10.00
57 Shane Battier 4.00 10.00
58 Dan Issel 6.00 15.00
59 Cedric Ceballos 4.00 10.00
60 Jim Jackson 4.00 10.00
61 Glen Rice 5.00 12.00
62 Jamal Mashburn 5.00 12.00
63 Dell Curry 5.00 12.00
64 Artis Gilmore 6.00 15.00
65 Brent Barry 3.00 8.00
66 Kurt Rambis 5.00 12.00
67 Vlade Divac 5.00 12.00
68 Dikembe Mutombo 8.00 20.00
69 Toni Kukoc 5.00 12.00
70 Spud Webb 5.00 12.00
71 Jalen Rose 4.00 10.00
72 Tim Hardaway 6.00 15.00
73 Cedric Maxwell 4.00 10.00
74 Josh Richardson 4.00 10.00
75 Jordan Mickey 3.00 8.00
76 Raul Neto 3.00 8.00
77 Justin Anderson 3.00 8.00
78 Nikola Jokic 125.00 300.00
79 Malachi Richardson 3.00 8.00
80 Rondae Hollis-Jefferson 3.00 6.00
81 Kent Bazemore 3.00 8.00
82 Jae Crowder 3.00 8.00
83 Donatas Motiejunas 3.00 8.00
84 Festus Ezeli 3.00 8.00
85 Trey Lyles 4.00 10.00
86 Patrick Patterson 3.00 8.00
87 Jaylen Brown 150.00 400.00
88 Dragan Bender 3.00 8.00
89 Kris Dunn 5.00 12.00
90 Buddy Hield 10.00 25.00
91 Jamal Murray 150.00 400.00
92 Marquese Chriss 4.00 10.00
93 Jakob Poeltl 6.00 15.00
94 Thon Maker 4.00 10.00
95 Domantas Sabonis 60.00 150.00
96 Taurean Prince 4.00 10.00
97 Denzel Valentine 3.00 8.00
98 Wade Baldwin IV 3.00 8.00
99 Henry Ellenson 3.00 8.00
100 Dejounte Murray 100.00 250.00

2016-17 Panini Prizm Autographs Prizms Orange

*ORANGE: .6X TO 1.5X BASIC
78 Nikola Jokic 200.00 500.00
87 Jaylen Brown 400.00 800.00
90 Buddy Hield 25.00 60.00
95 Domantas Sabonis 200.00 500.00

2016-17 Panini Prizm Explosion

*GREEN: .5X TO 1.2X BASIC
*SILVER: .5X TO 1.2X BASIC
*RUBY: .5X TO 1.2X BASIC
*BLUE/99: .6X TO 1.5X BASIC
*PURPLE/75: .75X TO 2X BASIC
*ORANGE/49: 1X TO 2.5X BASIC
*MOJO/25: 1.5X TO 4X BASIC
*ORNG WAVE/25: 1.5X TO 4X BASIC
*TEAL WAVE/25: 1.5X TO 4X BASIC
1 LeBron James 5.00 12.00
2 Kyrie Irving 1.25 3.00
3 Paul George 1.00 2.50
4 James Harden 1.25 3.00
5 Jimmy Butler 1.25 3.00
6 Carmelo Anthony 1.00 2.50
7 Karl-Anthony Towns 1.25 3.00
8 Chris Paul 1.00 2.50
9 Klay Thompson 1.50 4.00
10 Anthony Davis 2.00 5.00
11 Dirk Nowitzki 1.50 4.00
12 DeMar DeRozan .75 2.00
13 Kawhi Leonard 1.50 4.00
14 LaMarcus Aldridge .60 1.50
15 Russell Westbrook 1.00 2.50
16 Blake Griffin .60 1.50
17 Stephen Curry 5.00 12.00
18 Andrew Wiggins .75 2.00
19 Damian Lillard 1.50 4.00
20 John Wall .75 2.00

2016-17 Panini Prizm First Step

*GREEN: .5X TO 1.2X BASIC
*SILVER: .5X TO 1.2X BASIC
*RUBY: .5X TO 1.2X BASIC
*BLUE/99: .6X TO 1.5X BASIC
*PURPLE/75: .75X TO 2X BASIC
*ORANGE/49: 1X TO 2.5X BASIC
*MOJO/25: 1.5X TO 4X BASIC
*ORNG WAVE/25: 1.5X TO 4X BASIC
*TEAL WAVE/25: 1.5X TO 4X BASIC
1 Damian Lillard 1.50 4.00
2 Tony Parker 1.00 2.50
3 Reggie Jackson .50 1.25
4 Stephen Curry 5.00 12.00
5 John Wall .75 2.00
6 LeBron James 5.00 12.00
7 Russell Westbrook 1.00 2.50
8 Isaiah Thomas .50 1.25
9 Andrew Wiggins .75 2.00
10 James Harden 1.25 3.00

2016-17 Panini Prizm First Step Prizms Blue Wave

*BLUE WAVE: .75X TO 2X BASIC
6 LeBron James 8.00 20.00

2016-17 Panini Prizm First Step Prizms Mojo

*MOJO: 1.5X TO 4X BASIC
4 Stephen Curry 20.00 50.00
6 LeBron James 25.00 60.00

2016-17 Panini Prizm First Step Prizms Orange

*ORANGE:1X TO 2.5X BASIC
6 LeBron James 20.00 50.00

2016-17 Panini Prizm First Step Prizms Orange Wave

*ORANGE WAVE: 1.5X TO 4X BASIC
6 LeBron James 40.00 100.00

2016-17 Panini Prizm First Step Prizms Purple

*PURPLE: .75X TO 2X BASIC
6 LeBron James 10.00 25.00

2016-17 Panini Prizm First Step Prizms Silver

*SILVER: .6X TO 1.5X BASIC
6 LeBron James 5.00 12.00

2016-17 Panini Prizm First Step Prizms Teal Wave

*TEAL WAVE: 1.5X TO 4X BASIC
6 LeBron James 30.00 80.00

2016-17 Panini Prizm Go Hard or Go Home

*GREEN: .5X TO 1.2X BASIC
*SILVER: .5X TO 1.2X BASIC
*RUBY: .5X TO 1.2X BASIC
*BLUE/99: .6X TO 1.5X BASIC
*PURPLE/75: .75X TO 2X BASIC
*ORANGE/49: 1X TO 2.5X BASIC
*MOJO/25: 1.5X TO 4X BASIC
*ORNG WAVE/25: 1.5X TO 4X BASIC
*TEAL WAVE/25: 1.5X TO 4X BASIC
1 John Wall .75 2.00
2 Damian Lillard 1.50 4.00
3 Anthony Davis 2.00 5.00
4 LeBron James 5.00 12.00
5 Jahlil Okafor .40 1.00
6 Giannis Antetokounmpo 3.00 8.00
7 Jimmy Butler 1.25 3.00
8 Mike Conley .50 1.25
9 Kyrie Irving 1.25 3.00
10 Isaiah Thomas .50 1.25
11 Chris Paul 1.00 2.50
12 Justise Winslow .50 1.25
13 Kemba Walker .50 1.25
14 Gordon Hayward .60 1.50
15 DeMarcus Cousins .50 1.25
16 Carmelo Anthony 1.00 2.50
17 Jordan Clarkson .60 1.50
18 Manu Ginobili 1.25 3.00
19 Emmanuel Mudiay .40 1.00
20 Jeff Teague .40 1.00
21 Reggie Jackson .50 1.25
22 DeMar DeRozan .75 2.00
23 James Harden 1.25 3.00
24 Tony Parker 1.00 2.50
25 Brandon Knight .50 1.25
26 Ricky Rubio .50 1.25
27 Draymond Green .75 2.00
28 Bradley Beal .75 2.00
29 Elfrid Payton .50 1.25
30 Eric Bledsoe .50 1.25

2016-17 Panini Prizm Go Hard or Go Home Prizms Orange Wave

*ORANGE WAVE: 1.5X TO 4X BASIC
4 LeBron James 20.00 50.00

2016-17 Panini Prizm Mosaic

COMPLETE SET (100) 125.00 300.00
1 Aaron Gordon .75 2.00
2 Al Horford .75 2.00
3 Andre Drummond .75 2.00
4 Andrew Wiggins 1.00 2.50
5 Anthony Davis 2.50 6.00
6 Ben Simmons 2.50 6.00
7 Blake Griffin .75 2.00
8 Brandon Ingram 3.00 8.00
9 Brook Lopez .60 1.50
10 Buddy Hield 2.50 6.00
11 C.J. McCollum .75 2.00
12 Carmelo Anthony 1.25 3.00
13 Chris Paul 1.25 3.00
14 Damian Lillard 2.00 5.00
15 Dario Saric 1.25 3.00
16 DeAndre Jordan .60 1.50
17 D'Angelo Russell 1.00 2.50
18 DeMar DeRozan 1.00 2.50
19 DeMarcus Cousins .60 1.50
20 Denzel Valentine .75 2.00
21 Derrick Favors .50 1.25
22 Derrick Rose 1.25 3.00
23 Devin Booker 3.00 8.00
24 Dirk Nowitzki 2.00 5.00
25 Domantas Sabonis 5.00 12.00
26 Dragan Bender .75 2.00
27 Dwight Howard 1.00 2.50
28 Dwyane Wade 1.50 4.00
29 Emmanuel Mudiay .50 1.25
30 Eric Bledsoe .60 1.50
31 Eric Gordon .60 1.50
32 Evan Fournier .60 1.50
33 Giannis Antetokounmpo 4.00 10.00
34 Goran Dragic .75 2.00
35 Gordon Hayward .75 2.00
36 Harrison Barnes .60 1.50
37 Hassan Whiteside .60 1.50
38 Henry Ellenson .75 2.00
39 Isaiah Thomas .60 1.50
40 Jabari Parker .50 1.25
41 Jakob Poeltl 1.50 4.00
42 Jamal Murray 25.00 60.00
43 James Harden 1.50 4.00
44 Jeremy Lin 1.50 4.00
45 Jaylen Brown 25.00 60.00
46 Jimmy Butler 1.50 4.00
47 Joel Embiid 2.00 5.00
48 John Wall 1.00 2.50
49 Juan Hernangomez 1.50 4.00
50 Julius Randle 1.00 2.50
51 Karl-Anthony Towns 1.50 4.00
52 Kawhi Leonard 2.00 5.00
53 Kay Felder .75 2.00
54 Kemba Walker .60 1.50
55 Kenneth Faried .60 1.50
56 Kevin Durant 3.00 8.00
57 Kevin Love .75 2.00
58 Klay Thompson 2.00 5.00
59 Kris Dunn 1.25 3.00
60 Kristaps Porzingis 1.25 3.00
61 Kyle Lowry .75 2.00
62 Kyrie Irving 1.50 4.00
63 LaMarcus Aldridge .75 2.00
64 LeBron James 20.00 50.00
65 Malcolm Brogdon 2.50 6.00
66 Malik Beasley 1.50 4.00
67 Marc Gasol .75 2.00
68 Marquese Chriss 1.00 2.50
69 Mike Conley .60 1.50
70 Myles Turner .75 2.00
71 Nicolas Batum .60 1.50
72 Pascal Siakam 5.00 12.00
73 Patrick McCaw .75 2.00
74 Pau Gasol 1.25 3.00
75 Paul George 1.25 3.00
76 Paul Millsap .60 1.50
77 Reggie Jackson .60 1.50
78 Rudy Gay .75 2.00
79 Rudy Gobert 1.00 2.50
80 Russell Westbrook 1.25 3.00
81 Stephen Curry 6.00 15.00
82 Thon Maker 1.00 2.50
83 Tyler Ulis 1.00 2.50
84 Vince Carter 1.50 4.00
85 Zach LaVine 1.50 4.00
86 Tristan Thompson .60 1.50
87 Victor Oladipo .60 1.50
88 Nikola Vucevic .75 2.00
89 Bradley Beal 1.00 2.50
90 J.J. Redick .75 2.00
91 Jordan Clarkson .75 2.00
92 Wilson Chandler .60 1.50
93 Marcin Gortat .50 1.25
94 Nikola Mirotic .50 1.25
95 Taurean Prince 1.00 2.50
96 Rajon Rondo 1.00 2.50
97 Jeff Teague .50 1.25
98 Sergio Rodriguez .50 1.25
99 Wade Baldwin IV .75 2.00
100 Jonas Valanciunas .60 1.50

2016-17 Panini Prizm Mosaic Blue

*BLUE: .6X TO 1.5X BASIC
*BLUE RC: .6X TO 1.5X BASIC RC

2016-17 Panini Prizm Mosaic Camo

*CAMO: 2X TO 5X BASIC
*CAMO RC: 2X TO 5X BASIC RC
STATED PRINT RUN 25 SER.#'d SETS
8 Brandon Ingram 75.00 200.00
10 Buddy Hield 30.00 80.00
15 Dario Saric 20.00 50.00
20 Denzel Valentine 15.00 40.00
25 Domantas Sabonis 200.00 500.00
41 Jakob Poeltl 10.00 25.00
42 Jamal Murray 400.00 800.00
45 Jaylen Brown 300.00 600.00
47 Joel Embiid 20.00 50.00
52 Kawhi Leonard 20.00 50.00
64 LeBron James 400.00 800.00
65 Malcolm Brogdon 20.00 50.00
66 Malik Beasley 8.00 20.00
72 Pascal Siakam 200.00 500.00
81 Stephen Curry 20.00 50.00
95 Taurean Prince 10.00 25.00

2016-17 Panini Prizm Mosaic Red

COMPLETE SET (100) 100.00 250.00
*RED: .6X TO 1.5X BASIC
*RED RC: .6X TO 1.5X BASIC RC

2016-17 Panini Prizm Mosaic Autographs

5 Anthony Davis 50.00 120.00
7 Blake Griffin 6.00 15.00
8 Brandon Ingram 40.00 100.00
10 Buddy Hield 12.00 30.00
15 Dario Saric 6.00 15.00
20 Denzel Valentine 4.00 10.00
24 Dirk Nowitzki 100.00 250.00
25 Domantas Sabonis 100.00 250.00
28 Dwyane Wade 20.00 50.00
38 Henry Ellenson 4.00 10.00
42 Jamal Murray 100.00 250.00
45 Jaylen Brown 150.00 400.00
49 Juan Hernangomez 8.00 20.00
51 Karl-Anthony Towns 12.00 30.00
53 Kay Felder 4.00 10.00
59 Kris Dunn 6.00 15.00
62 Kyrie Irving 30.00 80.00
65 Malcolm Brogdon 12.00 30.00
66 Malik Beasley 8.00 20.00
72 Pascal Siakam 30.00 80.00
73 Patrick McCaw 4.00 10.00
81 Stephen Curry 500.00 1,000.00
82 Thon Maker 5.00 12.00
83 Tyler Ulis 5.00 12.00
95 Taurean Prince 5.00 12.00
99 Wade Baldwin IV 4.00 10.00

2016-17 Panini Prizm Rookie Jerseys

*GREEN: .5X TO 1.2X BASIC
2 Brandon Ingram 8.00 20.00
3 Jaylen Brown 15.00 40.00
4 Dragan Bender 2.00 5.00
5 Kris Dunn 3.00 8.00
6 Buddy Hield 6.00 15.00
7 Jamal Murray 15.00 40.00
8 Marquese Chriss 2.50 6.00
9 Jakob Poeltl 4.00 10.00
10 Thon Maker 2.50 6.00
11 Taurean Prince 2.50 6.00
12 Georgios Papagiannis 2.00 5.00
13 Denzel Valentine 2.00 5.00
14 Juan Hernangomez 4.00 10.00
15 Wade Baldwin IV 2.00 5.00
16 Henry Ellenson 2.00 5.00
17 Malik Beasley 4.00 10.00
18 Caris LeVert 5.00 12.00
19 DeAndre' Bembry 3.00 8.00
20 Malachi Richardson 2.00 5.00
21 T. Luwawu-Cabarrot 3.00 8.00
22 Brice Johnson 2.00 5.00
23 Pascal Siakam 12.00 30.00
24 Skal Labissiere 2.00 5.00
25 Dejounte Murray 10.00 25.00
26 Damian Jones 2.00 5.00
27 Deyonta Davis 2.00 5.00
28 Cheick Diallo 2.00 5.00
29 Tyler Ulis 2.50 6.00
30 Patrick McCaw 2.00 5.00
31 Malcolm Brogdon 6.00 15.00
32 Isaiah Whitehead 2.00 5.00
33 Demetrius Jackson 2.00 5.00
34 Kay Felder 2.00 5.00
35 Gary Payton II 6.00 15.00
36 Diamond Stone 2.00 5.00
37 Ivica Zubac 5.00 12.00
38 Chinanu Onuaku 2.00 5.00
39 Stephen Zimmerman 2.00 5.00
40 A.J. Hammons 2.00 5.00
42 Brandon Ingram 8.00 20.00
43 Jaylen Brown 15.00 40.00
44 Dragan Bender 2.00 5.00
45 Kris Dunn 3.00 8.00
46 Buddy Hield 6.00 15.00
47 Jamal Murray 15.00 40.00
48 Marquese Chriss 2.50 6.00
49 Jakob Poeltl 4.00 10.00
50 Thon Maker 2.50 6.00
51 Taurean Prince 2.50 6.00
52 Georgios Papagiannis 2.00 5.00
53 Denzel Valentine 2.00 5.00
54 Juan Hernangomez 4.00 10.00
55 Wade Baldwin IV 2.00 5.00
56 Henry Ellenson 2.00 5.00
57 Malik Beasley 4.00 10.00
58 Caris LeVert 5.00 12.00
59 DeAndre' Bembry 3.00 8.00
60 Malachi Richardson 2.00 5.00
61 T. Luwawu-Cabarrot 3.00 8.00
62 Brice Johnson 2.00 5.00
63 Pascal Siakam 12.00 30.00
64 Skal Labissiere 2.00 5.00
65 Dejounte Murray 10.00 25.00
66 Damian Jones 2.00 5.00
67 Deyonta Davis 2.00 5.00
68 Cheick Diallo 2.00 5.00
69 Tyler Ulis 2.50 6.00
70 Patrick McCaw 2.00 5.00
71 Malcolm Brogdon 6.00 15.00
72 Isaiah Whitehead 2.00 5.00
73 Demetrius Jackson 2.00 5.00
74 Kay Felder 2.00 5.00
75 Gary Payton II 6.00 15.00
76 Diamond Stone 2.00 5.00
77 Ivica Zubac 5.00 12.00
78 Chinanu Onuaku 2.00 5.00
79 Stephen Zimmerman 2.00 5.00
80 A.J. Hammons 2.00 5.00
82 Brandon Ingram 8.00 20.00
83 Jaylen Brown 15.00 40.00
84 Dragan Bender 2.00 5.00
85 Kris Dunn 3.00 8.00

86 Buddy Hield 6.00 15.00
87 Jamal Murray 15.00 40.00
88 Marquese Chriss 2.50 6.00
89 Jakob Poeltl 4.00 10.00
90 Thon Maker 2.50 6.00
91 Taurean Prince 2.50 6.00
92 Georgios Papagiannis 2.00 5.00
93 Denzel Valentine 2.00 5.00
94 Juan Hernangomez 4.00 10.00
95 Wade Baldwin IV 2.00 5.00
96 Henry Ellenson 2.00 5.00
97 Malik Beasley 4.00 10.00
98 Caris LeVert 5.00 12.00
99 DeAndre' Bembry 3.00 8.00
100 Malachi Richardson 2.00 5.00

2016-17 Panini Prizm Rookie Jerseys Prizms Orange Wave

2 Brandon Ingram 60.00 150.00
3 Jaylen Brown 75.00 200.00
35 Gary Payton II 50.00 120.00
42 Brandon Ingram 60.00 150.00
43 Jaylen Brown 75.00 200.00
75 Gary Payton II 50.00 120.00
82 Brandon Ingram 60.00 150.00
83 Jaylen Brown 75.00 200.00

2016-17 Panini Prizm Rookie Jerseys Prizms Silver

*SILVER: .6X TO 1.5X BASIC
35 Gary Payton II 12.00 30.00
75 Gary Payton II 12.00 30.00

2016-17 Panini Prizm Rookie Signatures

*BLUE/49: .5X TO 1.2X BASIC
1 Brandon Ingram 50.00 120.00
2 Jaylen Brown 150.00 400.00
3 Dragan Bender 3.00 8.00
4 Kris Dunn 5.00 12.00
5 Buddy Hield 10.00 25.00
6 Jamal Murray 60.00 150.00
7 Marquese Chriss 4.00 10.00
8 Jakob Poeltl 6.00 15.00
9 Thon Maker 4.00 10.00
10 Domantas Sabonis 40.00 100.00
11 Taurean Prince 4.00 10.00
12 Georgios Papagiannis 3.00 8.00
13 Denzel Valentine 3.00 8.00
14 Juan Hernangomez 6.00 15.00
15 Wade Baldwin IV 3.00 8.00
16 Henry Ellenson 3.00 8.00
17 Malik Beasley 6.00 15.00
18 Caris LeVert 8.00 20.00
19 DeAndre' Bembry 5.00 12.00
20 Malachi Richardson 3.00 8.00
21 T. Luwawu-Cabarrot 5.00 12.00
22 Brice Johnson 3.00 8.00
23 Pascal Siakam 30.00 80.00
24 Skal Labissiere 3.00 8.00
25 Dejounte Murray 75.00 200.00
26 Damian Jones 3.00 8.00
27 Deyonta Davis 3.00 8.00
28 Ivica Zubac 8.00 20.00
29 Cheick Diallo 3.00 8.00
30 Tyler Ulis 4.00 10.00
31 Malcolm Brogdon 10.00 25.00
32 Chinanu Onuaku 3.00 8.00
33 Patrick McCaw 3.00 8.00
34 Diamond Stone 3.00 8.00
35 Stephen Zimmerman 3.00 8.00
36 Dario Saric 5.00 12.00
37 Isaiah Whitehead 3.00 8.00
38 Demetrius Jackson 3.00 8.00
39 A.J. Hammons 3.00 8.00
40 Jake Layman 4.00 10.00
41 Georges Niang 5.00 12.00
42 Kay Felder 3.00 8.00
43 Gary Payton II 25.00 60.00
44 Isaiah Cousins 3.00 8.00
45 Ben Bentil 3.00 8.00
46 Ron Baker 3.00 8.00
47 Joel Bolomboy 3.00 8.00
48 Daniel Hamilton 3.00 8.00
49 Sheldon McClellan 3.00 8.00
50 Zach Auguste 3.00 8.00

2016-17 Panini Prizm Rookie Signatures Prizms Blue

*BLUE: .5X TO 1.2X BASIC
2 Jaylen Brown 300.00 600.00

2016-17 Panini Prizm Sky's the Limit

*GREEN: .5X TO 1.2X BASIC
*SILVER: .6X TO 1.5X BASIC
*RUBY: .5X TO 1.2X BASIC
*BLUE/99: .6X TO 1.5X BASIC
*PURPLE/75: .75X TO 2X BASIC
*ORANGE/49: 1X TO 2.5X BASIC
*MOJO/25: 1.5X TO 4X BASIC
*ORNG WAVE/25: 1.5X TO 4X BASIC
*TEAL WAVE/25: 1.5X TO 4X BASIC
1 Zach LaVine 1.25 3.00
2 Andre Drummond .60 1.50
3 Aaron Gordon .60 1.50
4 LeBron James 5.00 12.00
5 Vince Carter 1.25 3.00
6 Will Barton .40 1.00
7 Giannis Antetokounmpo 3.00 8.00
8 Terrence Ross .50 1.25
9 John Wall .75 2.00
10 DeAndre Jordan .50 1.25
11 Andre Iguodala .60 1.50
12 Russell Westbrook 1.00 2.50
13 Blake Griffin .60 1.50
14 Andrew Wiggins .75 2.00
15 Julius Randle .75 2.00
16 Mason Plumlee .40 1.00
17 Victor Oladipo .60 1.50
18 Paul George 1.00 2.50
19 Damian Lillard 1.50 4.00
20 Eric Bledsoe .50 1.25
21 Justise Winslow .50 1.25
22 Kristaps Porzingis 1.00 2.50
23 Kenneth Faried .50 1.25
24 Stanley Johnson .40 1.00
25 Anthony Davis 2.00 5.00

2016-17 Panini Prizm Sky's the Limit Prizms Mojo

*MOJO: 1.5X TO 4X BASIC
4 LeBron James 40.00 100.00
7 Giannis Antetokounmpo 30.00 80.00

2016-17 Panini Prizm Veteran Signatures

*BLUE/49: .5X TO 1.2X BASIC
1 Kevin Durant 125.00 300.00
2 Andrew Wiggins 15.00 40.00
3 Kobe Bryant 600.00 1,200.00
4 Anthony Davis 60.00 150.00
5 Karl-Anthony Towns 30.00 80.00
6 Kristaps Porzingis 25.00 60.00
8 Justise Winslow 4.00 10.00
10 Klay Thompson 60.00 150.00
11 Kyrie Irving 60.00 150.00
12 D'Angelo Russell 12.00 30.00
13 Dirk Nowitzki 75.00 200.00
14 Draymond Green 15.00 40.00
15 Bobby Portis 5.00 12.00
16 Isaiah Thomas 4.00 10.00
17 Vince Carter 60.00 150.00
18 Reggie Jackson 4.00 10.00
19 Tony Parker 25.00 60.00
21 Hassan Whiteside 4.00 10.00
22 Danilo Gallinari 4.00 10.00
23 Mario Hezonja 3.00 8.00
24 Wesley Matthews 3.00 8.00
26 Tony Allen 3.00 8.00
28 Boban Marjanovic 4.00 10.00
30 Emmanuel Mudiay 3.00 8.00
31 Jonas Valanciunas 4.00 10.00
32 Andrew Bogut 3.00 8.00
33 Dwyane Wade/150 40.00 100.00
34 John Wall 10.00 25.00
35 C.J. McCollum 8.00 20.00
36 Anthony Bennett 3.00 8.00
37 Cody Zeller 3.00 8.00
38 Dwight Powell 3.00 8.00
39 E'Twaun Moore 3.00 8.00
40 Ian Clark 3.00 8.00
41 James Ennis 3.00 8.00
42 Ray McCallum 3.00 8.00
43 T.J. McConnell 4.00 10.00
44 Alex Len 3.00 8.00
45 Allen Crabbe 3.00 8.00
46 Aaron Harrison 3.00 8.00
47 Tristan Thompson 4.00 10.00
48 Lamar Patterson 3.00 8.00
50 Victor Oladipo 4.00 10.00

2017-18 Panini Prizm

COMPLETE SET (300) 75.00 200.00
1 Markelle Fultz RC 1.50 4.00
2 Joel Embiid 1.00 2.50
3 Dario Saric .40 1.00
4 Furkan Korkmaz RC 1.00 2.50
5 T.J. McConnell .40 1.00
6 Jahlil Okafor .30 .75
7 JJ Redick .50 1.25
8 Robert Covington .30 .75
9 Ben Simmons .50 1.25
10 Brett Brown CO .30 .75
11 Jaylen Brown 1.25 3.00
12 Isaiah Thomas .40 1.00
13 Marcus Smart .50 1.25
14 Al Horford .50 1.25
15 Gordon Hayward .50 1.25
16 Jayson Tatum RC 20.00 50.00
17 Semi Ojeleye RC .75 2.00
18 Terry Rozier .40 1.00
19 Ante Zizic RC .75 2.00
20 Brad Stevens CO .40 1.00
21 Buddy Hield .50 1.25
22 Skal Labissiere .30 .75
23 George Hill .40 1.00
24 De'Aaron Fox RC 5.00 12.00
25 Vince Carter 1.00 2.50
26 Frank Mason III RC .60 1.50
27 Justin Jackson RC .60 1.50
28 Harry Giles RC .60 1.50
29 Willie Cauley-Stein .40 1.00
30 Dave Joerger CO .30 .75
31 DeMar DeRozan .60 1.50
32 Kyle Lowry .50 1.25
33 Jonas Valanciunas .40 1.00
34 Pascal Siakam 1.00 2.50
35 Jakob Poeltl .40 1.00
36 Serge Ibaka .40 1.00
37 Norman Powell .50 1.25
38 OG Anunoby RC 3.00 8.00
39 Lucas Nogueira .30 .75
40 Dwane Casey CO .30 .75
41 Stephen Curry 4.00 10.00
42 Klay Thompson 1.25 3.00
43 Andre Iguodala .50 1.25
44 Kevin Durant 2.00 5.00
45 Patrick McCaw .30 .75
46 Draymond Green .60 1.50
47 Jordan Bell RC .60 1.50
48 David West .30 .75
49 Shaun Livingston .30 .75
50 Steve Kerr CO .60 1.50
51 Bam Adebayo RC 4.00 10.00
52 Okaro White .30 .75
53 Goran Dragic .30 .75
54 Dion Waiters .30 .75
55 Hassan Whiteside .40 1.00
56 Tyler Johnson .30 .75
57 Justise Winslow .30 .75
58 Kelly Olynyk .30 .75
59 James Johnson .30 .75
60 Erik Spoelstra CO .50 1.25
61 Josh Jackson RC .75 2.00
62 Eric Bledsoe .40 1.00
63 Devin Booker 1.25 3.00
64 T.J. Warren .40 1.00
65 Marquese Chriss .30 .75
66 Dragan Bender .30 .75
67 Tyler Ulis .30 .75
68 Davon Reed RC .60 1.50
69 Tyson Chandler .40 1.00
70 Earl Watson CO .30 .75
71 Elfrid Payton .30 .75
72 Aaron Gordon .50 1.25
73 Jonathan Isaac RC 1.50 4.00
74 Wesley Iwundu RC .60 1.50
75 Bismack Biyombo .30 .75
76 Evan Fournier .40 1.00
77 Terrence Ross .40 1.00
78 Nikola Vucevic .40 1.00
79 Jonathon Simmons .30 .75
80 Frank Vogel CO .30 .75
81 Andrew Wiggins .60 1.50
82 Karl-Anthony Towns .75 2.00
83 Jeff Teague .30 .75
84 Jimmy Butler .75 2.00
85 Justin Patton RC .60 1.50
86 Jamal Crawford .50 1.25
87 Nemanja Bjelica .30 .75
88 Gorgui Dieng .30 .75
89 Tyus Jones .30 .75
90 Tom Thibodeau CO .40 1.00
91 Dirk Nowitzki 1.25 3.00
92 Dwight Powell .30 .75
93 Harrison Barnes .40 1.00
94 J.J. Barea .40 1.00
95 Wesley Matthews .30 .75
96 Seth Curry .50 1.25
97 Yogi Ferrell .30 .75
98 Dorian Finney-Smith .30 .75
99 Dennis Smith Jr. RC .75 2.00
100 Rick Carlisle CO .40 1.00
101 Dennis Schroder .40 1.00
102 Ersan Ilyasova .30 .75
103 Taurean Prince .30 .75
104 Mike Muscala .30 .75
105 Malcolm Delaney .30 .75
106 Marco Belinelli .30 .75
107 Tyler Dorsey RC .60 1.50
108 Kent Bazemore .30 .75
109 John Collins RC 1.50 4.00
110 Mike Budenholzer CO .40 1.00
111 Rodney Hood .30 .75
112 Dante Exum .30 .75
113 Joe Ingles .40 1.00
114 Rudy Gobert .60 1.50
115 Derrick Favors .30 .75
116 Joe Johnson .40 1.00
117 Donovan Mitchell RC 8.00 20.00
118 Tony Bradley RC .60 1.50
119 Ricky Rubio .40 1.00
120 Quin Snyder CO .40 1.00
121 Anthony Davis 1.25 3.00
122 Jrue Holiday .60 1.50
123 DeMarcus Cousins .40 1.00
124 Rajon Rondo .60 1.50
125 Frank Jackson RC .60 1.50
126 Cheick Diallo .30 .75
127 Solomon Hill .30 .75
128 E'Twaun Moore .30 .75
129 Omer Asik .30 .75
130 Alvin Gentry CO .30 .75
131 John Wall .60 1.50
132 Bradley Beal .60 1.50
133 Otto Porter Jr. .40 1.00
134 Marcin Gortat .30 .75
135 Markieff Morris .30 .75
136 Kelly Oubre Jr. .50 1.25
137 Tomas Satoransky .40 1.00
138 Ian Mahinmi .30 .75
139 Jason Smith .30 .75
140 Scott Brooks CO .30 .75
141 Damian Lillard 1.25 3.00
142 C.J. McCollum .50 1.25
143 Allen Crabbe .30 .75
144 Zach Collins RC 1.00 2.50
145 Caleb Swanigan RC .60 1.50
146 Maurice Harkless .30 .75
147 Ed Davis .30 .75
148 Evan Turner .30 .75
149 Jusuf Nurkic .40 1.00
150 Terry Stotts CO .30 .75
151 Jeremy Lin .75 2.00
152 D'Angelo Russell .40 1.00
153 Rondae Hollis-Jefferson .30 .75
154 Jarrett Allen RC 1.50 4.00
155 DeMarre Carroll .30 .75
156 Timofey Mozgov .30 .75
157 Caris LeVert .50 1.25
158 Sean Kilpatrick .30 .75
159 Trevor Booker .30 .75
160 Kenny Atkinson CO .30 .75
161 Emmanuel Mudiay .30 .75
162 Wilson Chandler .40 1.00
163 Paul Millsap .40 1.00
164 Trey Lyles .30 .75
165 Gary Harris .40 1.00
166 Nikola Jokic 3.00 8.00
167 Jamal Murray .75 2.00
168 Tyler Lydon RC .60 1.50
169 Jameer Nelson .30 .75
170 Michael Malone CO .50 1.25
171 Luke Kennard RC 1.25 3.00
172 Andre Drummond .40 1.00
173 Avery Bradley .30 .75
174 Reggie Jackson .40 1.00
175 Ish Smith .30 .75
176 Stanley Johnson .30 .75
177 Reggie Bullock .30 .75
178 Jon Leuer .30 .75
179 Tobias Harris .40 1.00
180 Stan Van Gundy CO .30 .75
181 D.J. Wilson RC .60 1.50
182 Giannis Antetokounmpo 2.50 6.00
183 Tony Snell .30 .75
184 Thon Maker .30 .75
185 Malcolm Brogdon .40 1.00
186 Greg Monroe .30 .75
187 Jabari Parker .30 .75
188 Sterling Brown RC .60 1.50
189 Matthew Dellavedova .40 1.00
190 Jason Kidd CO .75 2.00
191 LeBron James 4.00 10.00
192 Kyrie Irving 1.00 2.50
193 Kevin Love .50 1.25
194 Tristan Thompson .30 .75
195 Derrick Rose .75 2.00
196 Jae Crowder .30 .75
197 Iman Shumpert .30 .75
198 J.R. Smith .40 1.00
199 Kyle Korver .40 1.00
200 Tyronn Lue CO .50 1.25
201 Mike Conley .40 1.00
202 Ivan Rabb RC .60 1.50
203 Ben McLemore .30 .75
204 Marc Gasol .50 1.25
205 Wayne Selden Jr. RC .60 1.50
206 Chandler Parsons .30 .75
207 Tyreke Evans .30 .75
208 Deyonta Davis .30 .75
209 Wade Baldwin IV .30 .75
210 David Fizdale CO .30 .75
211 Blake Griffin .50 1.25
212 Patrick Beverley .30 .75
213 Wesley Johnson .30 .75
214 DeAndre Jordan .40 1.00
215 Sindarius Thornwell RC .60 1.50
216 Jawun Evans RC .60 1.50
217 Danilo Gallinari .40 1.00
218 Lou Williams .40 1.00
219 Austin Rivers .40 1.00
220 Doc Rivers CO .50 1.25
221 Victor Oladipo .40 1.00
222 Cory Joseph .30 .75
223 Bojan Bogdanovic .40 1.00
224 Myles Turner .50 1.25
225 T.J. Leaf RC .60 1.50
226 Ike Anigbogu RC .60 1.50
227 Edmond Sumner RC 1.00 2.50
228 Domantas Sabonis 1.00 2.50
229 Darren Collison .30 .75
230 Nate McMillan CO .30 .75
231 Kemba Walker .40 1.00
232 Dwight Howard .60 1.50
233 Malik Monk RC 2.50 6.00
234 Dwayne Bacon RC .60 1.50
235 Michael Carter-Williams .30 .75
236 Nicolas Batum .30 .75
237 Michael Kidd-Gilchrist .30 .75
238 Marvin Williams .30 .75
239 Treveon Graham RC .75 2.00
240 Steve Clifford CO .30 .75
241 Dwyane Wade 1.00 2.50
242 Kris Dunn .30 .75
243 Cristiano Felicio .30 .75
244 Zach LaVine .75 2.00
245 Bobby Portis .30 .75
246 Denzel Valentine .30 .75
247 Lauri Markkanen RC 4.00 10.00
248 Nikola Mirotic .30 .75
249 Robin Lopez .30 .75
250 Fred Hoiberg CO .30 .75
251 James Harden 1.00 2.50
252 Chris Paul .75 2.00
253 Nene .40 1.00
254 Eric Gordon .40 1.00
255 Ryan Anderson .30 .75
256 Chinanu Onuaku .30 .75
257 Trevor Ariza .30 .75
258 Clint Capela .60 1.50
259 Troy Williams RC .60 1.50
260 Mike D'Antoni CO .40 1.00
261 Russell Westbrook .75 2.00
262 Enes Kanter .40 1.00
263 Steven Adams .40 1.00
264 Paul George .75 2.00
265 Doug McDermott .40 1.00
266 Jerami Grant .40 1.00
267 Terrance Ferguson RC .60 1.50
268 Andre Roberson .30 .75
269 Raymond Felton .30 .75
270 Billy Donovan CO .60 1.50
271 Kristaps Porzingis .60 1.50
272 Damyean Dotson RC .75 2.00
273 Tim Hardaway Jr. .40 1.00
274 Courtney Lee .30 .75
275 Frank Ntilikina RC .75 2.00
276 Willy Hernangomez .30 .75
277 Mindaugas Kuzminskas .30 .75
278 Lance Thomas .30 .75
279 Carmelo Anthony .75 2.00
280 Jeff Hornacek CO .40 1.00
281 Thomas Bryant RC 1.00 2.50
282 Josh Hart RC 1.50 4.00
283 Kyle Kuzma RC 2.50 6.00
284 Brandon Ingram .60 1.50
285 Brook Lopez .40 1.00
286 Jordan Clarkson .50 1.25
287 Julius Randle .50 1.25
288 Larry Nance Jr. .40 1.00
289 Lonzo Ball RC 2.50 6.00
290 Luke Walton CO .30 .75
291 Tony Parker .75 2.00
292 Patty Mills .50 1.25
293 Kawhi Leonard 1.25 3.00
294 Dejounte Murray .50 1.25
295 Pau Gasol .75 2.00
296 Rudy Gay .40 1.00
297 Manu Ginobili 1.00 2.50
298 Derrick White RC 2.50 6.00
299 Danny Green .40 1.00
300 Gregg Popovich CO 2.50 6.00

2017-18 Panini Prizm Prizms Blue

*PRIZM.BLUE: 3X TO 8X BASIC
*PRIZM.BLUE RC: 3X TO 8X BASIC RC
STATED PRINT RUN 199 SER.#'d SETS
16 Jayson Tatum 400.00 800.00
24 De'Aaron Fox 60.00 150.00
117 Donovan Mitchell 100.00 250.00
300 Gregg Popovich CO 30.00 80.00

2017-18 Panini Prizm Prizms Blue Ice

*PRIZM.BLUE ICE: 5X TO 12X BASIC
*PRIZM.BLUE ICE RC: 5X TO 12X BASIC RC
STATED PRINT RUN 99 SER.#'d SETS
16 Jayson Tatum 800.00 1,500.00
24 De'Aaron Fox 150.00 400.00
117 Donovan Mitchell 150.00 400.00
300 Gregg Popovich CO 50.00 120.00

2017-18 Panini Prizm Prizms Green

*PRIZM.GREEN: 1X TO 2.5X BASIC
16 Jayson Tatum 400.00 800.00
24 De'Aaron Fox 20.00 50.00
117 Donovan Mitchell 30.00 80.00
300 Gregg Popovich CO 3.00 8.00

2017-18 Panini Prizm Prizms Green Pulsar

*GREEN PULSAR: 8X TO 20X BASIC
*GREEN PULSAR RC: 8X TO 20X BASIC RC
STATED PRINT RUN 25 SER.#'d SETS
16 Jayson Tatum 1,500.00 3,000.00
24 De'Aaron Fox 300.00 600.00
117 Donovan Mitchell 300.00 600.00
300 Gregg Popovich CO 100.00 250.00

2017-18 Panini Prizm Prizms Hyper

*HYPER: 1.5X TO 4X BASIC
16 Jayson Tatum 150.00 400.00
24 De'Aaron Fox 30.00 80.00
117 Donovan Mitchell 50.00 120.00
300 Gregg Popovich CO 10.00 25.00

2017-18 Panini Prizm Prizms Mojo

*PRIZM.MOJO: 10X TO 25X BASIC
*PRIZM.MOJO RC: 10X TO 25X BASIC RC
STATED PRINT RUN 25 SER.#'d SETS
16 Jayson Tatum 2,000.00 4,000.00
24 De'Aaron Fox 400.00 800.00
117 Donovan Mitchell 400.00 800.00
300 Gregg Popovich CO 100.00 250.00

2017-18 Panini Prizm Prizms Orange

*PRIZM.ORANGE: 6X TO 15X BASIC
*PRIZM.ORANGE RC: 6X TO 15X BASIC RC
STATED PRINT RUN 49 SER.#'d SETS
16 Jayson Tatum 1,000.00 2,000.00
24 De'Aaron Fox 200.00 500.00
117 Donovan Mitchell 200.00 500.00
300 Gregg Popovich CO 60.00 150.00

2017-18 Panini Prizm Prizms Pink Pulsar

*PINK PULSAR: 6X TO 15X BASIC
*PINK PULSAR RC: 6X TO 15X BASIC RC
STATED PRINT RUN 42 SER.#'d SETS
16 Jayson Tatum 1,000.00 2,000.00
24 De'Aaron Fox 200.00 500.00
117 Donovan Mitchell 200.00 500.00
300 Gregg Popovich CO 60.00 150.00

2017-18 Panini Prizm Prizms Purple

*PRIZM.PURPLE: 5X TO 12X BASIC
*PRIZM.PURPLE RC: 5X TO 12X BASIC RC
STATED PRINT RUN 75 SER.#'d SETS
16 Jayson Tatum 800.00 1,500.00
24 De'Aaron Fox 150.00 400.00
117 Donovan Mitchell 150.00 400.00
300 Gregg Popovich CO 50.00 120.00

2017-18 Panini Prizm Prizms Red Pulsar

*RED PULSAR: 8X TO 20X BASIC
*RED PULSAR RC: 8X TO 20X BASIC RC
STATED PRINT RUN 25 SER.#'d SETS
16 Jayson Tatum 1,500.00 3,000.00
24 De'Aaron Fox 300.00 600.00
117 Donovan Mitchell 300.00 600.00
300 Gregg Popovich CO 100.00 250.00

2017-18 Panini Prizm Prizms Red White and Blue

*RWB: .6X TO 1.5X BASIC
*RWB RC: .5X TO 1.5X BASIC RC
16 Jayson Tatum 60.00 150.00
51 Bam Adebayo 10.00 25.00
117 Donovan Mitchell 20.00 50.00
300 Gregg Popovich CO 6.00 15.00

2017-18 Panini Prizm Prizms Ruby Wave

*PRIZM.RUBY: .75X TO 2X BASIC
*PRIZM.RUBY RC: 2X TO 5X BASIC RC
16 Jayson Tatum 125.00 300.00
24 De'Aaron Fox 25.00 60.00
117 Donovan Mitchell 40.00 100.00
300 Gregg Popovich CO 8.00 20.00

2017-18 Panini Prizm Prizms Silver

*SILVER: 1.5X TO 4X BASIC
*SILVER RC: 1.5X TO 4X BASIC RC
16 Jayson Tatum 150.00 400.00
117 Donovan Mitchell 50.00 120.00
300 Gregg Popovich CO 10.00 25.00

2017-18 Panini Prizm Prizms Fast Break

*PRIZM FB: 1.25X TO 3X BASIC
16 Jayson Tatum 125.00 300.00
24 De'Aaron Fox 25.00 60.00
117 Donovan Mitchell 40.00 100.00
300 Gregg Popovich CO 8.00 20.00

2017-18 Panini Prizm Prizms Fast Break Blue

*FB BLUE: 2.5X TO 6X BASIC
STATED PRINT RUN 175 SER.#'d SETS
16 Jayson Tatum 300.00 600.00
24 De'Aaron Fox 50.00 120.00
117 Donovan Mitchell 75.00 200.00
300 Gregg Popovich CO 25.00 60.00

2017-18 Panini Prizm Prizms Fast Break Bronze

*FB BRONZE: 10X TO 25X BASIC
*FB BRONZE RC: 10X TO 25X BASIC RC
STATED PRINT RUN 20 SER.#'d SETS
16 Jayson Tatum 2,000.00 4,000.00
24 De'Aaron Fox 400.00 800.00
117 Donovan Mitchell 400.00 800.00
300 Gregg Popovich CO 100.00 250.00

2017-18 Panini Prizm Prizms Fast Break Pink

*FB PINK: 6X TO 15X BASIC
*FB PINK RC: 6X TO 15X BASIC RC
STATED PRINT RUN 50 SER.#'d SETS
16 Jayson Tatum 1,000.00 2,000.00
24 De'Aaron Fox 200.00 500.00
117 Donovan Mitchell 200.00 500.00
300 Gregg Popovich CO 60.00 150.00

2017-18 Panini Prizm Prizms Fast Break Purple

*FB PURPLE: 5X TO 12X BASIC
*FB PURPLE RC: 5X TO 12X BASIC RC
STATED PRINT RUN 75 SER.#'d SETS
16 Jayson Tatum 600.00 1,200.00
24 De'Aaron Fox 150.00 400.00
117 Donovan Mitchell 300.00 600.00
300 Gregg Popovich CO 50.00 120.00

2017-18 Panini Prizm Prizms Fast Break Red

*FB RED: 4X TO 10X BASIC
*FB RED RC: 4X TO 10X BASIC RC
STATED PRINT RUN 125 SER.#'d SETS
16 Jayson Tatum 600.00 1,200.00
24 De'Aaron Fox 75.00 200.00
117 Donovan Mitchell 125.00 300.00
300 Gregg Popovich CO 40.00 100.00

2017-18 Panini Prizm Mosaic

1 Karl-Anthony Towns 1.25 3.00
2 Harry Giles RC 1.00 2.50
3 Josh Hart RC 2.50 6.00
4 Blake Griffin .75 2.00
5 Donovan Mitchell RC 25.00 60.00
6 Goran Dragic .60 1.50
7 Caleb Swanigan RC 1.00 2.50
8 Joel Embiid 1.50 4.00
9 Lauri Markkanen RC 6.00 15.00
10 D.J. Wilson RC 1.00 2.50
11 Terrance Ferguson RC 1.00 2.50
12 Kevin Love .75 2.00
13 Dennis Schroder .60 1.50
14 Klay Thompson 2.00 5.00
15 Kawhi Leonard 2.00 5.00
16 Dwight Howard 1.00 2.50
17 Bradley Beal 1.00 2.50
18 Tyler Lydon RC 1.00 2.50
19 Elfrid Payton .50 1.25
20 Jayson Tatum RC 50.00 120.00
21 Jimmy Butler 1.25 3.00
22 Willie Cauley-Stein .50 1.25
23 Kyle Kuzma RC 4.00 10.00
24 DeAndre Jordan .60 1.50
25 Tony Bradley RC 1.00 2.50
26 Hassan Whiteside .60 1.50
27 Jeremy Lin 1.25 3.00
28 Dario Saric .60 1.50
29 James Harden 1.50 4.00
30 Giannis Antetokounmpo 4.00 10.00
31 Kristaps Porzingis 1.00 2.50
32 Derrick Rose 1.25 3.00
33 Kent Bazemore .50 1.25
34 Kevin Durant 3.00 8.00
35 Pau Gasol 1.25 3.00
36 Malik Monk RC 4.00 10.00
37 Damian Lillard 2.00 5.00
38 Luke Kennard RC 2.00 5.00
39 Aaron Gordon .75 2.00
40 De'Aaron Fox RC 8.00 20.00
41 Justin Patton RC 1.00 2.50
42 DeMar DeRozan 1.00 2.50
43 Brandon Ingram 1.00 2.50
44 Victor Oladipo .60 1.50
45 Ricky Rubio .60 1.50
46 Josh Jackson RC 1.25 3.00
47 D'Angelo Russell .60 1.50
48 Ben Simmons .75 2.00
49 Chris Paul 1.25 3.00
50 Malcolm Brogdon .60 1.50
51 Frank Ntilikina RC 1.25 3.00
52 Mike Conley .60 1.50
53 John Collins RC 2.50 6.00
54 Draymond Green 1.00 2.50
55 Derrick White RC 4.00 10.00
56 Dwyane Wade 1.50 4.00
57 CJ McCollum .75 2.00
58 Andre Drummond .60 1.50
59 Jonathan Isaac RC 2.50 6.00
60 Vince Carter 1.50 4.00
61 Dirk Nowitzki 2.00 5.00
62 Kyle Lowry .75 2.00
63 Julius Randle .75 2.00
64 Myles Turner .75 2.00
65 Anthony Davis 2.00 5.00
66 Eric Bledsoe .60 1.50
67 Jarrett Allen RC 2.50 6.00
68 Isaiah Thomas .60 1.50
69 Russell Westbrook 1.25 3.00
70 Jabari Parker .50 1.25
71 Harrison Barnes .60 1.50
72 OG Anunoby RC 5.00 12.00
73 Lonzo Ball RC 4.00 10.00
74 TJ Leaf RC 1.00 2.50
75 DeMarcus Cousins .75 2.00
76 Devin Booker 2.00 5.00
77 Paul Millsap .60 1.50
78 Al Horford .75 2.00
79 Enes Kanter .60 1.50
80 LeBron James 30.00 80.00
81 Andrew Wiggins 1.00 2.50
82 Justin Jackson RC 1.00 2.50
83 Carmelo Anthony 1.25 3.00
84 Marc Gasol .75 2.00
85 Rudy Gobert 1.00 2.50
86 Bam Adebayo RC 25.00 60.00
87 Zach Collins RC 1.50 4.00
88 Markelle Fultz RC 2.50 6.00
89 Zach LaVine 1.25 3.00
90 Reggie Jackson .60 1.50
91 Dennis Smith Jr. RC 1.25 3.00
92 Stephen Curry 6.00 15.00
93 Tony Parker 1.25 3.00
94 Kemba Walker .60 1.50
95 John Wall 1.00 2.50
96 Nikola Vucevic .60 1.50
97 Nikola Jokic 5.00 12.00
98 Gordon Hayward .60 1.50
99 Paul George .60 1.50
100 Kyrie Irving 1.50 4.00

2017-18 Panini Prizm Mosaic Blue

*BLUE VET: .75X TO 2X BASIC
*BLUE RK: .75X TO 2X BASIC

2017-18 Panini Prizm Mosaic Camo

*CAMO VET: 2X TO 5X BASIC
*CAMO RK: 4X TO 10X BASIC
STATED PRINT RUN 25 SER.#'d SETS
80 LeBron James 200.00 500.00
86 Bam Adebayo 400.00 800.00

2017-18 Panini Prizm Mosaic Green

*GREEN VET: .75X TO 2X BASIC
*GREEN RK: .75X TO 2X BASIC

2017-18 Panini Prizm Mosaic Orange

*ORANGE VET: 1X TO 2.5X BASIC
*ORANGE RK: 1X TO 2.5X BASIC

2017-18 Panini Prizm Mosaic Purple

*PURPLE VET: 1X TO 2.5X BASIC
*PURPLE RK: 2X TO 5X BASIC
STATED PRINT RUN 99 SER.#'d SETS
80 LeBron James 100.00 250.00

2017-18 Panini Prizm Mosaic Red

*RED VET: .75X TO 2X BASIC
*RED RK: .75X TO 2X BASIC

2017-18 Panini Prizm Mosaic Autographs

PRINT RUNS B/WN 49-99 COPIES PER
EXCHANGE DEADLINE 9/14/2019
1 Ricky Rubio/99 6.00 15.00
2 Kyle Kuzma/99 12.00 30.00
3 Isaiah Thomas/99 6.00 15.00
4 Bam Adebayo/99 150.00 400.00
5 Kevin Durant/49 EXCH 125.00 300.00
6 Markelle Fultz/99 50.00 120.00
7 Damian Lillard/99 60.00 150.00
8 Josh Jackson/99 4.00 10.00
9 Karl-Anthony Towns/99 20.00 50.00
10 Lauri Markkanen/99 40.00 100.00
11 Kevin Love/99 10.00 25.00
12 Malik Monk/99 40.00 100.00
13 Larry Bird/99 60.00 150.00
14 Kobe Bryant/49 EXCH 3,000.00 6,000.00
15 Kyrie Irving/99 30.00 80.00
16 Lonzo Ball/99 150.00 400.00
17 Magic Johnson/99 60.00 150.00
18 De'Aaron Fox/99 75.00 200.00
19 Andrew Wiggins/99 15.00 40.00
20 Frank Ntilikina/99 4.00 10.00
21 Vince Carter/99 30.00 80.00
22 Luke Kennard/99 8.00 20.00
23 Anthony Davis/99 50.00 120.00
24 Shaquille O'Neal/49 50.00 120.00
25 Chris Paul/49 75.00 200.00
26 Jayson Tatum/99 500.00 1,000.00
27 G.Antetokounmpo/99 EXCH 150.00 400.00
28 Jonathan Isaac/99 60.00 150.00
29 Marc Gasol/99 6.00 15.00
30 Dennis Smith Jr./99 4.00 10.00
31 Tony Parker/99 12.00 30.00
32 Donovan Mitchell/99 150.00 400.00
A-RGM Reggie Miller/49 60.00 150.00

2017-18 Panini Prizm Mosaic Autographs Camo

*CAMO: .5X TO 1.2X BASIC
STATED PRINT RUN 25 SER.#'d SETS
EXCHANGE DEADLINE 9/14/2019
4 Bam Adebayo 400.00 800.00
5 Kevin Durant EXCH 200.00 500.00
26 Jayson Tatum 1,500.00 3,000.00
32 Donovan Mitchell 500.00 1,000.00

2017-18 Panini Prizm Autographs

1 Markelle Fultz 40.00 100.00
2 Joel Embiid 30.00 80.00
3 Dario Saric 4.00 10.00
5 T.J. McConnell 4.00 10.00
6 Jahlil Okafor 3.00 8.00
7 JJ Redick 5.00 12.00
8 Robert Covington 3.00 8.00
11 Jaylen Brown 40.00 100.00
12 Isaiah Thomas 4.00 10.00
13 Marcus Smart 5.00 12.00
14 Al Horford 5.00 12.00
15 Gordon Hayward 4.00 10.00
16 Jayson Tatum 400.00 800.00
17 Semi Ojeleye 4.00 10.00
19 Ante Zizic 4.00 10.00
21 Buddy Hield 5.00 12.00
23 George Hill 4.00 10.00
24 De'Aaron Fox 60.00 150.00
25 Vince Carter 50.00 120.00
26 Frank Mason III 3.00 8.00
27 Justin Jackson 3.00 8.00
28 Harry Giles 3.00 8.00
29 Willie Cauley-Stein 3.00 8.00
32 Kyle Lowry 5.00 12.00
33 Jonas Valanciunas 4.00 10.00
34 Pascal Siakam 15.00 40.00
35 Jakob Poeltl 4.00 10.00
37 Norman Powell 5.00 12.00
38 OG Anunoby 15.00 40.00
42 Klay Thompson 40.00 100.00
47 Jordan Bell 3.00 8.00
48 David West 12.00 30.00
50 Steve Kerr 15.00 40.00
53 Goran Dragic 10.00 25.00
57 Justise Winslow 3.00 8.00
58 Kelly Olynyk 3.00 8.00
62 Eric Bledsoe 4.00 10.00
63 Devin Booker 75.00 200.00
64 T.J. Warren 4.00 10.00
66 Dragan Bender 3.00 8.00
67 Tyler Ulis 3.00 8.00
68 Davon Reed 3.00 8.00
69 Tyson Chandler 4.00 10.00
71 Elfrid Payton 3.00 8.00
73 Jonathan Isaac 40.00 100.00
74 Wesley Iwundu 3.00 8.00
75 Bismack Biyombo 3.00 8.00
76 Evan Fournier 4.00 10.00
78 Nikola Vucevic 4.00 10.00
81 Andrew Wiggins 12.00 30.00
83 Jeff Teague 3.00 8.00
85 Justin Patton 3.00 8.00
87 Nemanja Bjelica 3.00 8.00
89 Tyus Jones 3.00 8.00
92 Dwight Powell 3.00 8.00
93 Harrison Barnes 4.00 10.00
95 Wesley Matthews 3.00 8.00
96 Seth Curry 5.00 12.00
97 Yogi Ferrell 3.00 8.00
98 Dorian Finney-Smith 3.00 8.00
103 Taurean Prince 3.00 8.00
104 Mike Muscala 3.00 8.00
106 Marco Belinelli 3.00 8.00
107 Tyler Dorsey 3.00 8.00
108 Kent Bazemore 3.00 8.00
109 John Collins 8.00 20.00

112 Dante Exum 3.00 8.00
115 Derrick Favors 3.00 8.00
116 Joe Johnson 4.00 10.00
117 Donovan Mitchell 125.00 300.00
118 Tony Bradley 3.00 8.00
125 Frank Jackson 3.00 8.00
126 Cheick Diallo 3.00 8.00
127 Solomon Hill 3.00 8.00
128 E'Twaun Moore 3.00 8.00
133 Otto Porter Jr. 4.00 10.00
134 Marcin Gortat 3.00 8.00
137 Tomas Satoransky 4.00 10.00
139 Jason Smith 3.00 8.00
140 Scott Brooks 3.00 8.00
142 C.J. McCollum 5.00 12.00
143 Allen Crabbe 3.00 8.00
144 Zach Collins 5.00 12.00
145 Caleb Swanigan 3.00 8.00
146 Maurice Harkless 3.00 8.00
147 Ed Davis 3.00 8.00
149 Jusuf Nurkic 12.00 30.00
152 D'Angelo Russell 4.00 10.00
153 Rondae Hollis-Jefferson 3.00 8.00
154 Jarrett Allen 40.00 100.00
155 DeMarre Carroll 3.00 8.00
156 Timofey Mozgov 3.00 8.00
157 Caris LeVert 5.00 12.00
158 Sean Kilpatrick 3.00 8.00
159 Trevor Booker 3.00 8.00
162 Wilson Chandler 4.00 10.00
164 Trey Lyles 3.00 8.00
165 Gary Harris 4.00 10.00
166 Nikola Jokic 125.00 300.00
167 Jamal Murray 10.00 25.00
168 Tyler Lydon 3.00 8.00
169 Jameer Nelson 3.00 8.00
171 Luke Kennard 6.00 15.00
172 Andre Drummond 4.00 10.00
174 Reggie Jackson 4.00 10.00
177 Reggie Bullock 3.00 8.00
178 Jon Leuer 3.00 8.00
182 Giannis Antetokounmpo 200.00 500.00
183 Tony Snell 3.00 8.00
184 Thon Maker 3.00 8.00
185 Malcolm Brogdon 4.00 10.00
186 Greg Monroe 3.00 8.00
188 Sterling Brown 3.00 8.00
189 Matthew Dellavedova 4.00 10.00
190 Jason Kidd 12.00 30.00
193 Kevin Love 5.00 12.00
194 Tristan Thompson 3.00 8.00
197 Iman Shumpert 3.00 8.00
199 Kyle Korver 4.00 10.00
200 Tyronn Lue 5.00 12.00
201 Mike Conley 4.00 10.00
202 Ivan Rabb 3.00 8.00
203 Ben McLemore 3.00 8.00
205 Wayne Selden Jr. 3.00 8.00
208 Deyonta Davis 3.00 8.00
212 Patrick Beverley 3.00 8.00
213 Wesley Johnson 3.00 8.00
215 Sindarius Thornwell 3.00 8.00
216 Jawun Evans 3.00 8.00
217 Danilo Gallinari 4.00 10.00
219 Austin Rivers 4.00 10.00
225 T.J. Leaf 3.00 8.00
226 Ike Anigbogu 3.00 8.00
227 Edmond Sumner 5.00 12.00
228 Domantas Sabonis 10.00 25.00
229 Darren Collison 3.00 8.00
233 Malik Monk 15.00 40.00
234 Dwayne Bacon 3.00 8.00
235 Michael Carter-Williams 3.00 8.00
236 Nicolas Batum 3.00 8.00
238 Marvin Williams 3.00 8.00
239 Treveon Graham 4.00 10.00
242 Kris Dunn 3.00 8.00
245 Bobby Portis 3.00 8.00
246 Denzel Valentine 3.00 8.00
247 Lauri Markkanen 40.00 100.00
254 Eric Gordon 4.00 10.00
255 Ryan Anderson 3.00 8.00
256 Chinanu Onuaku 3.00 8.00
263 Steven Adams 4.00 10.00
269 Raymond Felton 3.00 8.00
272 Damyean Dotson 4.00 10.00
273 Tim Hardaway Jr. 6.00 15.00
274 Courtney Lee 3.00 8.00
275 Frank Ntilikina 4.00 10.00
276 Willy Hernangomez 3.00 8.00
278 Lance Thomas 3.00 8.00
281 Thomas Bryant 5.00 12.00
282 Josh Hart 20.00 50.00
284 Brandon Ingram 75.00 200.00
285 Brook Lopez 4.00 10.00
286 Jordan Clarkson 12.00 30.00
287 Julius Randle 5.00 12.00
288 Larry Nance Jr. 4.00 10.00
289 Lonzo Ball 40.00 100.00
291 Tony Parker 20.00 50.00
292 Patty Mills 5.00 12.00
297 Manu Ginobili 40.00 100.00
298 Derrick White 12.00 30.00
299 Danny Green 4.00 10.00

2017-18 Panini Prizm Emergent

*GREEN: .75X TO 2X BASIC
*HYPER: 1X TO 2.5X BASIC
*FAST BREAK: 1.25X TO 3X BASIC
*SILVER: 1.25X TO 3X BASIC
*MOJO/25: 8X TO 20X BASIC
1 Markelle Fultz 1.00 2.50
2 Lonzo Ball 1.50 4.00
3 Jayson Tatum 8.00 20.00
4 Josh Jackson .50 1.25
5 De'Aaron Fox 3.00 8.00
6 Jonathan Isaac 1.00 2.50
7 Lauri Markkanen 2.50 6.00
8 Frank Ntilikina .50 1.25
9 Dennis Smith Jr. .50 1.25
10 Zach Collins .60 1.50
11 Malik Monk 1.50 4.00
12 Luke Kennard .75 2.00
13 Donovan Mitchell 4.00 10.00
14 Bam Adebayo 2.50 6.00
15 Justin Jackson .40 1.00
16 Justin Patton .40 1.00
17 D.J. Wilson .40 1.00
18 T.J. Leaf .40 1.00
19 John Collins 1.00 2.50
20 Harry Giles .40 1.00
21 Terrance Ferguson .40 1.00
22 OG Anunoby 2.00 5.00
23 Kyle Kuzma 1.50 4.00
24 Josh Hart 1.00 2.50
25 Derrick White 1.50 4.00

2017-18 Panini Prizm Fundamentals

*GREEN: .5X TO 1.2X BASIC
*HYPER: .5X TO 1.2X BASIC
*FAST BREAK: .6X TO 1.5X BASIC
*SILVER: .6X TO 1.5X BASIC
*MOJO/25: 2X TO 5X BASIC
1 Tim Duncan 1.50 4.00
2 Kobe Bryant 5.00 12.00
3 Hakeem Olajuwon 1.25 3.00
4 John Stockton 1.25 3.00
5 Gary Payton 1.00 2.50
6 Wes Unseld .60 1.50
7 Larry Bird 2.50 6.00
8 Rick Barry .75 2.00
9 Alonzo Mourning 1.00 2.50
10 Patrick Ewing 1.00 2.50
11 Dirk Nowitzki 1.50 4.00
12 Andre Drummond .50 1.25
13 Isaiah Thomas .50 1.25
14 Devin Booker 1.50 4.00
15 Klay Thompson 1.50 4.00
16 Stephen Curry 5.00 12.00
17 Karl-Anthony Towns 1.00 2.50
18 Kristaps Porzingis .75 2.00
19 Al Horford .60 1.50
20 Bradley Beal .75 2.00
21 DeMarcus Cousins .50 1.25
22 John Wall .75 2.00
23 Anthony Davis 1.50 4.00
24 Kyle Lowry .60 1.50
25 Kevin Durant 2.50 6.00
26 Damian Lillard 1.50 4.00
27 Mike Conley .50 1.25
28 Russell Westbrook 1.00 2.50
29 Rudy Gobert .75 2.00
30 Kemba Walker .50 1.25
31 Jeremy Lin .60 1.50
32 Giannis Antetokounmpo 3.00 8.00
33 C.J. McCollum .60 1.50
34 Buddy Hield .60 1.50
35 DeAndre Jordan .50 1.25
36 Wesley Matthews .50 1.25
37 Kawhi Leonard 1.50 4.00
38 James Harden 1.25 3.00
39 Steven Adams .50 1.25
40 Myles Turner .60 1.50
41 Marcin Gortat .40 1.00
42 Goran Dragic .50 1.25
43 Andrew Wiggins .75 2.00
44 Dennis Schroder .50 1.25
45 Carmelo Anthony 1.00 2.50
46 Kyrie Irving 1.25 3.00
47 Tony Parker 1.00 2.50
48 Harrison Barnes .50 1.25
49 Nikola Vucevic .50 1.25
50 Nikola Jokic 4.00 10.00

2017-18 Panini Prizm Fundamentals Prizms Mojo

*MOJO: 2X TO 5X BASIC
32 Giannis Antetokounmpo 20.00 50.00

2017-18 Panini Prizm Get Hyped!

*GREEN: .5X TO 1.2X BASIC
*HYPER: .5X TO 1.2X BASIC
*FAST BREAK: .6X TO 1.5X BASIC
*SILVER: .6X TO 1.5X BASIC
*MOJO/25: 2X TO 5X BASIC
1 John Wall .75 2.00
2 Willy Hernangomez .40 1.00
3 Carmelo Anthony 1.00 2.50
4 Joel Embiid 1.25 3.00
5 James Harden 1.25 3.00
6 Stephen Curry 5.00 12.00
7 Draymond Green .75 2.00
8 LeBron James 5.00 12.00
9 Russell Westbrook 1.00 2.50
10 Isaiah Thomas .50 1.25
11 Patty Mills .60 1.50
12 Manu Ginobili 1.25 3.00
13 Kyrie Irving 1.25 3.00
14 Jonas Valanciunas .50 1.25
15 Jusuf Nurkic .50 1.25
16 Giannis Antetokounmpo 3.00 8.00
17 Buddy Hield .60 1.50
18 Myles Turner .60 1.50
19 Kemba Walker .50 1.25
20 Marcin Gortat .40 1.00
21 Dirk Nowitzki 1.50 4.00
22 Damian Lillard 1.50 4.00
23 Hassan Whiteside .50 1.25
24 Bradley Beal .75 2.00
25 Karl-Anthony Towns 1.00 2.50

2017-18 Panini Prizm Get Hyped! Prizms Mojo

8 LeBron James 50.00 120.00

2017-18 Panini Prizm Luck of the Lottery

1 Markelle Fultz 1.50 4.00
2 Lonzo Ball 2.50 6.00
3 Jayson Tatum 15.00 40.00
4 Josh Jackson .75 2.00
5 De'Aaron Fox 5.00 12.00
6 Jonathan Isaac 1.50 4.00
7 Lauri Markkanen 4.00 10.00
8 Frank Ntilikina .75 2.00
9 Dennis Smith Jr. .75 2.00
10 Zach Collins 1.00 2.50
11 Malik Monk 2.50 6.00
12 Luke Kennard 1.25 3.00
13 Donovan Mitchell 6.00 15.00
14 Bam Adebayo 4.00 10.00

2017-18 Panini Prizm Luck of the Lottery Prizms Hyper

*HYPER: 1.5X TO 4X BASIC
3 Jayson Tatum 75.00 200.00

2017-18 Panini Prizm Luck of the Lottery Prizms Mojo

3 Jayson Tatum 400.00 800.00

2017-18 Panini Prizm Luck of the Lottery Prizms Silver

*SILVER: 1.5X TO 4X BASIC
3 Jayson Tatum 75.00 200.00

2017-18 Panini Prizm Rookie Signatures

1 Markelle Fultz 12.00 30.00
2 Lonzo Ball 40.00 100.00
3 Jayson Tatum 150.00 400.00
4 De'Aaron Fox 40.00 100.00
5 Jonathan Isaac 12.00 30.00
6 Lauri Markkanen 40.00 100.00
7 Frank Ntilikina 4.00 10.00
8 Dennis Smith Jr. 4.00 10.00
9 Zach Collins 5.00 12.00
10 Malik Monk 15.00 40.00
11 Luke Kennard 6.00 15.00
12 Donovan Mitchell 100.00 250.00
13 Bam Adebayo 40.00 100.00
14 Justin Jackson 3.00 8.00
15 Justin Patton 3.00 8.00
16 D.J. Wilson 3.00 8.00
17 T.J. Leaf 3.00 8.00
18 John Collins 8.00 20.00
19 Harry Giles 3.00 8.00
21 Jarrett Allen 15.00 40.00
22 OG Anunoby 15.00 40.00
23 Tyler Lydon 3.00 8.00
25 Derrick White 12.00 30.00
26 Josh Hart 8.00 20.00
27 Frank Jackson 3.00 8.00
28 Wesley Iwundu 3.00 8.00
29 Frank Mason III 3.00 8.00
30 Jordan Bell 3.00 8.00
RSKK Kyle Kuzma 12.00 30.00

2017-18 Panini Prizm Rookie Signatures Prizms Mojo

*MOJO: 1.25X TO 3X BASIC
STATED PRINT RUN 25 SER.#'d SETS
1 Markelle Fultz 75.00 200.00
3 Jayson Tatum 1,500.00 3,000.00
RSKK Kyle Kuzma 40.00 100.00

2017-18 Panini Prizm Sensational Signatures

1 Markelle Fultz 8.00 20.00
2 Lonzo Ball 40.00 100.00
3 Jayson Tatum 150.00 400.00
4 De'Aaron Fox 40.00 100.00
5 Jonathan Isaac 12.00 30.00
6 Lauri Markkanen 20.00 50.00
7 Frank Ntilikina 4.00 10.00
8 Zach Collins 5.00 12.00
9 Malik Monk 12.00 30.00
10 Luke Kennard 6.00 15.00

2017-18 Panini Prizm Sensational Swatches

1 Markelle Fultz 5.00 12.00
2 Lonzo Ball 8.00 20.00
3 Jayson Tatum 25.00 60.00
4 De'Aaron Fox 15.00 40.00
5 Jonathan Isaac 5.00 12.00
6 Sindarius Thornwell 2.00 5.00
7 Frank Ntilikina 2.50 6.00
8 Dennis Smith Jr. 2.50 6.00
9 Zach Collins 3.00 8.00
10 Malik Monk 8.00 20.00
11 Luke Kennard 4.00 10.00
12 Donovan Mitchell 20.00 50.00
13 Bam Adebayo 12.00 30.00
14 Tony Bradley 2.00 5.00
15 Ivan Rabb 2.00 5.00
16 D.J. Wilson 2.00 5.00
17 T.J. Leaf 2.00 5.00
18 John Collins 5.00 12.00
19 Harry Giles 2.00 5.00
20 Terrance Ferguson 2.00 5.00
21 Jarrett Allen 5.00 12.00
22 OG Anunoby 10.00 25.00
23 Tyler Lydon 2.00 5.00
24 Kyle Kuzma 8.00 20.00
25 Derrick White 8.00 20.00
26 Josh Hart 5.00 12.00
27 Frank Jackson 2.00 5.00
28 Wesley Iwundu 2.00 5.00
29 Frank Mason III 2.00 5.00
30 Jordan Bell 2.00 5.00
31 Tyler Dorsey 2.00 5.00
32 Jawun Evans 2.00 5.00
33 Davon Reed 2.00 5.00
34 Sterling Brown 2.00 5.00
35 Semi Ojeleye 2.50 6.00
36 Ante Zizic 2.50 6.00
37 Caleb Swanigan 2.00 5.00
38 Josh Jackson 2.50 6.00
39 Justin Patton 2.00 5.00
40 Dwayne Bacon 2.00 5.00
41 Alec Burks 2.00 5.00
42 Al-Farouq Aminu 2.00 5.00
43 Andrew Wiggins 4.00 10.00
44 Blake Griffin 3.00 8.00
45 Bradley Beal 4.00 10.00
46 Brook Lopez 2.50 6.00
47 C.J. McCollum 3.00 8.00
48 Carmelo Anthony 5.00 12.00
49 Clyde Drexler 5.00 12.00
50 Danilo Gallinari 2.50 6.00
51 Dante Exum 2.00 5.00
52 DeAndre Jordan 2.50 6.00
53 Derrick Favors 2.00 5.00
54 Dirk Nowitzki 8.00 20.00
55 Emmanuel Mudiay 2.00 5.00
56 Evan Turner 2.00 5.00
57 Gary Harris 2.50 6.00
58 Gordon Hayward 2.50 6.00
59 Gorgui Dieng 2.00 5.00
60 Grant Hill 5.00 12.00
61 Jameer Nelson 2.00 5.00
62 JJ Redick 3.00 8.00
63 Joe Ingles 2.50 6.00
64 John Wall 4.00 10.00
65 Juan Hernangomez 3.00 8.00
66 Kenneth Faried 2.50 6.00
67 Kevin Garnett 8.00 20.00
68 Kevin Love 3.00 8.00
69 Kobe Bryant 60.00 150.00
70 Kris Dunn 2.00 5.00
71 Kristaps Porzingis 4.00 10.00
72 Kyrie Irving 6.00 15.00
73 LeBron James 40.00 100.00
74 Marcin Gortat 2.00 5.00
75 Nemanja Bjelica 2.00 5.00
76 Nikola Jokic 20.00 50.00
77 Noah Vonleh 2.00 5.00
78 Ricky Rubio 2.50 6.00
79 Rodney Hood 2.00 5.00
80 Scottie Pippen 8.00 20.00
81 Shaquille O'Neal 10.00 25.00
82 Shawn Marion 2.50 6.00
83 Steven Adams 2.50 6.00
84 Shabazz Muhammad 2.00 5.00
85 Tyreke Evans 2.00 5.00
86 Will Barton 2.00 5.00
87 Wilson Chandler 2.50 6.00
88 Zach LaVine 5.00 12.00
89 Karl-Anthony Towns 5.00 12.00
90 Rudy Gobert 4.00 10.00

2017-18 Panini Prizm Signatures

*MOJO/25: 1.25X TO 3X BASIC
1 Marcus Smart 4.00 10.00
2 E'Twaun Moore 2.50 6.00
3 Chinanu Onuaku 2.50 6.00
4 Edy Tavares 2.50 6.00
5 Joel Bolomboy 2.50 6.00
6 Frank Kaminsky 2.50 6.00
7 Justin Anderson 2.50 6.00
8 Yogi Ferrell 2.50 6.00
9 Sean Kilpatrick 2.50 6.00
10 Taurean Prince 2.50 6.00
11 Salah Mejri 2.50 6.00
12 Cody Zeller 2.50 6.00
13 Tony Snell 2.50 6.00
14 Ian Clark 2.50 6.00
15 Trey Lyles 2.50 6.00
16 Cheick Diallo 2.50 6.00
17 Mario Hezonja 2.50 6.00
18 Tim Hardaway Jr. 3.00 8.00
19 Larry Nance Jr. 3.00 8.00
20 Willy Hernangomez 2.50 6.00
21 Malcolm Delaney 2.50 6.00
22 Emmanuel Mudiay 2.50 6.00
23 Nemanja Bjelica 2.50 6.00
24 Mirza Teletovic 2.50 6.00
25 Georgios Papagiannis 2.50 6.00
26 Demetrius Jackson 2.50 6.00
27 C.J. McCollum 4.00 10.00
28 DeMarre Carroll 2.50 6.00
29 Deyonta Davis 2.50 6.00
30 Evan Turner 2.50 6.00
31 Richaun Holmes 2.50 6.00
32 Kobe Bryant 1,000.00 2,000.00
33 Harrison Barnes 3.00 8.00
34 Reggie Miller 75.00 200.00
35 Kevin Durant 125.00 300.00
36 Ivica Zubac 3.00 8.00
37 Julius Randle 4.00 10.00
38 Nikola Jokic 100.00 250.00
39 Karl-Anthony Towns 20.00 50.00
40 Jabari Parker 2.50 6.00
41 Pau Gasol 12.00 30.00
42 J.J. Barea 8.00 20.00
43 Kyrie Irving 75.00 200.00
44 Damian Lillard 75.00 200.00
46 Malcolm Brogdon 3.00 8.00
47 Giannis Antetokounmpo 200.00 500.00
48 Andrew Wiggins 20.00 50.00
49 Shaquille O'Neal 125.00 300.00
50 Allen Iverson 100.00 250.00
51 Mike Muscala 2.50 6.00
52 Dwight Powell 2.50 6.00
53 Pat Connaughton 2.50 6.00
54 Chris McCullough 2.50 6.00
55 Tim Quarterman 2.50 6.00
56 Jon Leuer 2.50 6.00

2018-19 Panini Prizm

COMPLETE SET (300) 125.00 300.00
1 Brandon Knight .25 .60
2 Dirk Nowitzki 1.00 2.50
3 Rudy Gay .40 1.00
4 De'Anthony Melton RC 1.00 2.50
5 Charles Barkley .75 2.00
6 LeBron James 3.00 8.00
7 Ersan Ilyasova .25 .60
8 Jeremy Lin .60 1.50
9 Hamidou Diallo RC .75 2.00
10 Tony Parker .60 1.50
11 Devin Booker 1.00 2.50
12 DeAndre Jordan .30 .75
13 Pau Gasol .60 1.50
14 Vincent Edwards RC .50 1.25
15 Kobe Bryant 3.00 8.00
16 Kyle Kuzma .40 1.00
17 John Henson .25 .60
18 Kent Bazemore .25 .60
19 Billy Preston .25 .60
20 Nicolas Batum .25 .60
21 TJ Warren .25 .60
22 Kostas Antetokounmpo RC .60 1.50
23 Patty Mills .40 1.00
24 Chris Paul .75 2.00
25 Bill Russell 1.25 3.00
26 Brandon Ingram .40 1.00
27 Thon Maker .25 .60
28 DeAndre' Bembry .25 .60
29 Kevin Hervey RC .50 1.25
30 Michael Kidd-Gilchrist .25 .60
31 Josh Jackson .25 .60
32 Michael Porter Jr. RC 2.00 5.00
33 Kyle Lowry .40 1.00
34 James Harden .75 2.00
35 Shaquille O'Neal 1.25 3.00
36 Rajon Rondo .50 1.25
37 Josh Okogie RC .75 2.00
38 Taurean Prince .25 .60
39 Russell Westbrook .60 1.50
40 Marvin Williams .25 .60
41 Trevor Ariza .25 .60
42 Jarred Vanderbilt RC 1.00 2.50
43 Danny Green .30 .75
44 Michael Carter-Williams .25 .60
45 Allen Iverson 1.00 2.50
46 Josh Hart .30 .75
47 Keita Bates-Diop RC .60 1.50
48 John Collins .40 1.00
49 Paul George .60 1.50
50 Malik Monk .40 1.00
51 Dragan Bender .25 .60
52 Isaiah Thomas .30 .75
53 Kawhi Leonard 1.00 2.50
54 Eric Gordon .30 .75
55 Reggie Miller .75 2.00
56 Kentavious Caldwell-Pope .25 .60
57 Jeff Teague .25 .60
58 Dewayne Dedmon .25 .60
59 Carmelo Anthony .60 1.50
60 Frank Kaminsky .25 .60
61 Anfernee Simons RC 2.50 6.00
62 Jamal Murray .75 2.00
63 OG Anunoby .40 1.00
64 Ryan Anderson .25 .60
65 Scottie Pippen 1.00 2.50
66 Jaren Jackson Jr. RC 2.00 5.00
67 Jimmy Butler .60 1.50
68 Kevin Huerter RC 1.00 2.50
69 Steven Adams .60 1.50
70 Chandler Hutchison RC .60 1.50
71 Gary Trent Jr. RC 1.00 2.50
72 Gary Harris .30 .75
73 Serge Ibaka .30 .75
74 Clint Capela .30 .75
75 Karl Malone .75 2.00
76 Jevon Carter RC .75 2.00
77 Derrick Rose .75 2.00
78 Trae Young RC 4.00 10.00
79 Nerlens Noel .25 .60
80 Wendell Carter Jr. RC 1.25 3.00
81 Damian Lillard 1.00 2.50
82 Paul Millsap .30 .75
83 Pascal Siakam .60 1.50
84 Gerald Green .30 .75
85 Larry Bird 1.50 4.00
86 Mike Conley .30 .75
87 Andrew Wiggins .50 1.25
88 Omari Spellman RC .50 1.25
89 Jerami Grant .40 1.00
90 Kris Dunn .25 .60
91 CJ McCollum .40 1.00
92 Nikola Jokic 2.00 5.00
93 Jonas Valanciunas .40 1.00
94 Tyreke Evans .25 .60
95 Julius Erving 1.00 2.50
96 MarShon Brooks .25 .60
97 Taj Gibson .25 .60
98 Kyrie Irving 1.00 2.50
99 Mo Bamba RC .75 2.00
100 Zach LaVine .60 1.50
101 Evan Turner .25 .60
102 Will Barton .25 .60
103 Fred VanVleet .50 1.25
104 Darren Collison .25 .60
105 Patrick Ewing .60 1.50
106 Dillon Brooks .40 1.00
107 Karl-Anthony Towns .60 1.50
108 Jaylen Brown .60 1.50
109 Melvin Frazier Jr. RC .50 1.25
110 Lauri Markkanen .60 1.50
111 Al-Farouq Aminu .25 .60
112 Trey Lyles .25 .60
113 Delon Wright .25 .60
114 Aaron Holiday RC .75 2.00
115 Kareem Abdul-Jabbar 1.25 3.00
116 Chandler Parsons .25 .60
117 Gorgui Dieng .25 .60
118 Jayson Tatum 1.50 4.00
119 Justin Jackson RC .50 1.25
120 Robin Lopez .25 .60
121 Jusuf Nurkic .30 .75
122 Khyri Thomas RC .50 1.25
123 Grayson Allen RC 1.00 2.50
124 TJ Leaf .25 .60
125 Oscar Robertson .75 2.00
126 JaMychal Green .25 .60
127 Elfrid Payton .30 .75
128 Al Horford .40 1.00
129 D.J. Augustin .25 .60
130 Jabari Parker .25 .60
131 Seth Curry .25 .60
132 Bruce Brown RC 1.00 2.50
133 Ricky Rubio .30 .75
134 Victor Oladipo .30 .75
135 Yao Ming 1.00 2.50
136 Marc Gasol .40 1.00
137 Jrue Holiday .50 1.25
138 Robert Williams III RC .50 1.25
139 Evan Fournier .30 .75
140 Bobby Portis .40 1.00
141 Zach Collins .30 .75
142 Reggie Jackson .30 .75
143 Donovan Mitchell 1.25 3.00
144 Bojan Bogdanovic .30 .75
145 Jerry West .75 2.00
146 Yuta Watanabe RC .75 2.00
147 E'Twaun Moore .25 .60
148 Terry Rozier .30 .75
149 Terrence Ross .30 .75
150 Justin Holiday .25 .60
151 De'Aaron Fox .75 2.00
152 Luke Kennard .30 .75
153 Joe Ingles .30 .75
154 Thaddeus Young .25 .60
155 Steve Nash .75 2.00
156 Goran Dragic .30 .75
157 Nikola Mirotic .25 .60
158 Gordon Hayward .40 1.00
159 Aaron Gordon .40 1.00
160 George Hill .30 .75
161 Bogdan Bogdanovic .40 1.00
162 Stanley Johnson .25 .60
163 Dante Exum .30 .75
164 Myles Turner .40 1.00
165 Chris Webber .50 1.25
166 Dion Waiters .25 .60
167 Julius Randle .40 1.00
168 Marcus Morris .25 .60
169 Nikola Vucevic .40 1.00
170 Collin Sexton RC 1.50 4.00
171 Buddy Hield .40 1.00
172 Blake Griffin .40 1.00
173 Derrick Favors .25 .60
174 Domantas Sabonis .50 1.25
175 Paul Pierce .60 1.50
176 Josh Richardson .30 .75
177 Anthony Davis 1.00 2.50
178 Marcus Smart .40 1.00
179 Jonathan Isaac .40 1.00
180 JR Smith .40 1.00
181 Marvin Bagley III RC .75 2.00
182 Andre Drummond .30 .75
183 Jae Crowder .25 .60
184 Shai Gilgeous-Alexander RC 15.00 40.00
185 John Stockton .75 2.00
186 James Johnson .25 .60
187 Emeka Okafor .30 .75
188 Rodions Kurucs RC .60 1.50
189 Zhaire Smith RC .50 1.25
190 Jordan Clarkson .40 1.00
191 Justin Jackson .25 .60
192 Zaza Pachulia .25 .60
193 Rudy Gobert .50 1.25
194 Jerome Robinson RC .50 1.25
195 David Robinson .75 2.00
196 Hassan Whiteside .30 .75
197 Solomon Hill .25 .60
198 Dzanan Musa RC .50 1.25
199 Landry Shamet RC .75 2.00
200 Kyle Korver .30 .75
201 Harry Giles .25 .60
202 Ish Smith .25 .60
203 Alec Burks .25 .60
204 Patrick Beverley .25 .60
205 Wilt Chamberlain 1.25 3.00
206 Dwyane Wade .75 2.00
207 Ian Clark .25 .60
208 Spencer Dinwiddie .30 .75
209 Allonzo Trier RC .50 1.25
210 Larry Nance Jr. .25 .60
211 Zach Randolph .30 .75
212 Jacob Evans III RC .50 1.25
213 Troy Brown Jr. RC .60 1.50
214 Milos Teodosic .25 .60
215 Baron Davis .30 .75
216 Tyler Johnson .25 .60
217 Kevin Knox RC .60 1.50
218 DeMarre Carroll .25 .60
219 Ben Simmons .40 1.00
220 Channing Frye .25 .60
221 Willie Cauley-Stein .25 .60
222 Stephen Curry 3.00 8.00
223 John Wall .50 1.25
224 Lou Williams .30 .75
225 Tim Duncan 1.00 2.50
226 Bam Adebayo .60 1.50
227 Mitchell Robinson RC 1.25 3.00
228 Jarrett Allen .40 1.00
229 Markelle Fultz .30 .75
230 Kevin Love .30 .75
231 Frank Mason III .25 .60
232 Quinn Cook .30 .75
233 Bradley Beal .50 1.25
234 Avery Bradley .25 .60
235 Kevin Garnett 1.00 2.50
236 Kelly Olynyk .25 .60
237 Tim Hardaway Jr. .25 .60
238 Rondae Hollis-Jefferson .25 .60
239 JJ Redick .40 1.00
240 Tristan Thompson .25 .60
241 Chimezie Metu RC .60 1.50
242 Klay Thompson 1.00 2.50
243 Austin Rivers .30 .75
244 Tobias Harris .30 .75
245 Dennis Johnson .40 1.00
246 Donte DiVincenzo RC 1.25 3.00
247 Frank Ntilikina .25 .60
248 D'Angelo Russell .40 1.00
249 Wilson Chandler .25 .60
250 Jalen Brunson RC 6.00 15.00
251 Lonnie Walker IV RC 1.00 2.50
252 Kevin Durant 1.50 4.00
253 Otto Porter Jr. .30 .75
254 Danilo Gallinari .30 .75
255 Pete Maravich 1.00 2.50
256 Eric Bledsoe .30 .75
257 Mario Hezonja .25 .60
258 Allen Crabbe .25 .60
259 Joel Embiid 1.00 2.50
260 Dennis Smith Jr. .25 .60
261 Dejounte Murray .50 1.25
262 Andre Iguodala .30 .75
263 Kelly Oubre Jr. .40 1.00
264 Marcin Gortat .25 .60
265 Stephon Marbury .50 1.25
266 Matthew Dellavedova .25 .60
267 Kristaps Porzingis .50 1.25
268 Shabazz Napier .25 .60
269 Robert Covington .30 .75
270 J.J. Barea .40 1.00
271 DeMar DeRozan .50 1.25
272 Draymond Green .50 1.25
273 Markieff Morris .25 .60
274 Svi Mykhailiuk RC .60 1.50
275 Drazen Petrovic .50 1.25
276 Malcolm Brogdon .40 1.00
277 Enes Kanter .30 .75
278 Miles Bridges RC 1.25 3.00
279 Deandre Ayton RC 1.50 4.00
280 Luka Doncic RC 50.00 120.00
281 Manu Ginobili .75 2.00
282 DeMarcus Cousins .30 .75
283 Jeff Green .25 .60
284 Moritz Wagner RC 1.00 2.50
285 George Mikan .75 2.00
286 Khris Middleton .40 1.00
287 Trey Burke .25 .60
288 Devonte' Graham RC .75 2.00
289 Mikal Bridges RC 2.50 6.00
290 Wesley Matthews .25 .60
291 LaMarcus Aldridge .40 1.00
292 Jordan Bell .25 .60
293 Dwight Howard .50 1.25
294 Lonzo Ball .40 1.00
295 Amar'e Stoudemire .40 1.00
296 Giannis Antetokounmpo 2.00 5.00
297 Courtney Lee .25 .60
298 Kemba Walker .30 .75
299 Elie Okobo RC .50 1.25
300 Harrison Barnes .30 .75

2018-19 Panini Prizm Prizms Blue

*BLUE: 3X TO 8X BASIC
*BLUE RC: 3X TO 8X BASIC RC
STATED PRINT RUN 199 SER.#'d SETS
15 Kobe Bryant 150.00 400.00
66 Jaren Jackson Jr. 40.00 100.00
78 Trae Young 125.00 300.00
184 Shai Gilgeous-Alexander 1,000.00 2,000.00
250 Jalen Brunson 200.00 500.00
280 Luka Doncic 4,000.00 8,000.00

2018-19 Panini Prizm Prizms Blue Ice

*BLUE ICE: 5X TO 12X BASIC
*BLUE ICE RC: 5X TO 12X BASIC RC
STATED PRINT RUN 99 SER.#'d SETS
15 Kobe Bryant 200.00 500.00
66 Jaren Jackson Jr. 60.00 150.00
78 Trae Young 200.00 500.00
184 Shai Gilgeous-Alexander 1,500.00 3,000.00
250 Jalen Brunson 300.00 600.00
280 Luka Doncic 5,000.00 10,000.00

2018-19 Panini Prizm Prizms Choice Blue Yellow and Green

*BYG: 1.25X TO 3X BASIC
*BYG RC: 1.5X TO 4X BASIC RC
78 Trae Young 50.00 120.00
184 Shai Gilgeous-Alexander 150.00 400.00
250 Jalen Brunson 100.00 250.00
280 Luka Doncic 500.00 1,000.00

2018-19 Panini Prizm Prizms Choice Red

*CH RED: 4X TO 10X BASIC
*CH RED RC: 5X TO 12X BASIC RC
STATED PRINT RUN 88 SER.#'d SETS
6 LeBron James 125.00 300.00
15 Kobe Bryant 125.00 300.00
61 Anfernee Simons 100.00 250.00
66 Jaren Jackson Jr. 75.00 200.00
78 Trae Young 200.00 500.00
184 Shai Gilgeous-Alexander 1,000.00 2,000.00
222 Stephen Curry 75.00 200.00
250 Jalen Brunson 125.00 300.00
280 Luka Doncic 2,500.00 5,000.00

2018-19 Panini Prizm Prizms Fast Break

*FB: 1.5X TO 4X BASIC
*FB RC: 1.5X TO 4X BASIC RC
15 Kobe Bryant 20.00 50.00
184 Shai Gilgeous-Alexander 75.00 200.00
250 Jalen Brunson 20.00 50.00

2018-19 Panini Prizm Prizms Fast Break Blue

*FB BLUE: 2.5X TO 6X BASIC
*FB BLUE RC: 2.5X TO 6X BASIC RC
STATED PRINT RUN 175 SER.#'d SETS
15 Kobe Bryant 125.00 300.00
66 Jaren Jackson Jr. 30.00 80.00
78 Trae Young 100.00 250.00
184 Shai Gilgeous-Alexander 800.00 1,500.00
250 Jalen Brunson 150.00 400.00
280 Luka Doncic 1,500.00 3,000.00

2018-19 Panini Prizm Prizms Fast Break Bronze

*FB BRONZE: 10X TO 25X BASIC
*FB BRONZE RC: 12X TO 30X BASIC RC
STATED PRINT RUN 20 SER.#'d SETS
6 LeBron James 400.00 800.00
15 Kobe Bryant 400.00 800.00
61 Anfernee Simons 300.00 800.00
66 Jaren Jackson Jr. 200.00 500.00
78 Trae Young 600.00 1,200.00
184 Shai Gilgeous-Alexander 2,500.00 5,000.00
222 Stephen Curry 200.00 500.00
250 Jalen Brunson 400.00 800.00
280 Luka Doncic 8,000.00 15,000.00

2018-19 Panini Prizm Prizms Fast Break Pink

*FB PINK: 5X TO 12X BASIC
*FB PINK RC: 6X TO 15X BASIC RC
STATED PRINT RUN 50 SER.#'d SETS
6 LeBron James 150.00 400.00
15 Kobe Bryant 150.00 400.00
61 Anfernee Simons 125.00 300.00
66 Jaren Jackson Jr. 100.00 250.00
78 Trae Young 300.00 600.00
184 Shai Gilgeous-Alexander 1,250.00 2,500.00
222 Stephen Curry 100.00 250.00
250 Jalen Brunson 150.00 400.00
280 Luka Doncic 3,000.00 6,000.00

2018-19 Panini Prizm Prizms Fast Break Purple

*FB PURPLE: 4X TO 10X BASIC
*FB PURPLE RC: 5X TO 12X BASIC RC
STATED PRINT RUN 75 SER.#'d SETS
6 LeBron James 125.00 300.00
15 Kobe Bryant 125.00 300.00
61 Anfernee Simons 100.00 250.00
66 Jaren Jackson Jr. 75.00 200.00
78 Trae Young 200.00 500.00
184 Shai Gilgeous-Alexander 1,000.00 2,000.00
222 Stephen Curry 75.00 200.00
250 Jalen Brunson 125.00 300.00
280 Luka Doncic 2,500.00 5,000.00

2018-19 Panini Prizm Prizms Fast Break Red

*FB RED: 3X TO 8X BASIC
*FB RED RC: 3X TO 8X BASIC RC
STATED PRINT RUN 125 SER.#'d SETS
6 LeBron James 75.00 200.00
15 Kobe Bryant 200.00 500.00
78 Trae Young 100.00 250.00
184 Shai Gilgeous-Alexander 300.00 600.00
250 Jalen Brunson 150.00 400.00
280 Luka Doncic 1,500.00 3,000.00

2018-19 Panini Prizm Prizms Green

*GREEN: 1.25X TO 3X BASIC
*GREEN RC: 1.25X TO 3X BASIC RC
15 Kobe Bryant 20.00 50.00
250 Jalen Brunson 20.00 50.00

2018-19 Panini Prizm Prizms Green Pulsar

*GREEN PULSAR: 8X TO 20X BASIC
*GREEN PULSAR RC: 10X TO 25X BASIC RC
STATED PRINT RUN 25 SER.#'d SETS

6 LeBron James 300.00 600.00
15 Kobe Bryant 300.00 600.00
61 Anfernee Simons 200.00 500.00
66 Jaren Jackson Jr. 150.00 400.00
78 Trae Young 500.00 1,000.00
184 Shai Gilgeous-Alexander 2,000.00 4,000.00
222 Stephen Curry 150.00 400.00
250 Jalen Brunson 300.00 600.00
280 Luka Doncic 5,000.00 10,000.00

2018-19 Panini Prizm Prizms Hyper
*HYPER: 1.2X TO 3X BASIC
*HYPER RC: 1.2X TO 3X BASIC RC
15 Kobe Bryant 20.00 50.00
184 Shai Gilgeous-Alexander 75.00 200.00
250 Jalen Brunson 20.00 50.00

2018-19 Panini Prizm Prizms Mojo
*MOJO: 8X TO 20X BASIC
*MOJO RC: 10X TO 25X BASIC RC
STATED PRINT RUN 25 SER.#'d SETS
6 LeBron James 300.00 600.00
15 Kobe Bryant 300.00 600.00
61 Anfernee Simons 200.00 500.00
66 Jaren Jackson Jr. 150.00 400.00
78 Trae Young 500.00 1,000.00
184 Shai Gilgeous-Alexander 2,000.00 4,000.00
222 Stephen Curry 150.00 400.00
250 Jalen Brunson 300.00 600.00
280 Luka Doncic 6,000.00 12,000.00

2018-19 Panini Prizm Prizms Orange
*ORANGE: 5X TO 12X BASIC
*ORANGE RC: 6X TO 15X BASIC RC
STATED PRINT RUN 49 SER.#'d SETS
6 LeBron James 150.00 400.00
15 Kobe Bryant 150.00 400.00
61 Anfernee Simons 125.00 300.00
66 Jaren Jackson Jr. 100.00 250.00
78 Trae Young 300.00 600.00
184 Shai Gilgeous-Alexander 1,250.00 2,500.00
222 Stephen Curry 100.00 250.00
250 Jalen Brunson 150.00 400.00
280 Luka Doncic 3,000.00 6,000.00

2018-19 Panini Prizm Prizms Pink Ice
*PINK ICE: .75X TO 2X BASIC
*PINK ICE RC: 1.2X TO 3X BASIC RC
184 Shai Gilgeous-Alexander 75.00 200.00

2018-19 Panini Prizm Prizms Pink Pulsar
*PINK PULSAR: 6X TO 15X BASIC
*PINK PULSAR RC: 8X TO 20X BASIC RC
STATED PRINT RUN 42 SER.#'d SETS
6 LeBron James 100.00 250.00
15 Kobe Bryant 200.00 500.00
61 Anfernee Simons 150.00 400.00
66 Jaren Jackson Jr. 125.00 300.00
78 Trae Young 400.00 800.00
184 Shai Gilgeous-Alexander 1,500.00 3,000.00
222 Stephen Curry 125.00 300.00
250 Jalen Brunson 200.00 500.00
280 Luka Doncic 4,000.00 8,000.00

2018-19 Panini Prizm Prizms Purple
*PURPLE: 4X TO 10X BASIC
*PURPLE RC: 5X TO 12X BASIC RC
STATED PRINT RUN 75 SER.#'d SETS
6 LeBron James 125.00 300.00
15 Kobe Bryant 125.00 300.00
61 Anfernee Simons 100.00 250.00
66 Jaren Jackson Jr. 75.00 200.00
78 Trae Young 200.00 500.00
184 Shai Gilgeous-Alexander 1,000.00 2,000.00
222 Stephen Curry 75.00 200.00
250 Jalen Brunson 125.00 300.00
280 Luka Doncic 2,500.00 5,000.00

2018-19 Panini Prizm Prizms Purple Ice
*PURPLE ICE: 3X TO 8X BASIC
*PURPLE ICE RC: 3X TO 8X BASIC RC
STATED PRINT RUN 149 SER.#'d SETS
6 LeBron James 75.00 200.00
15 Kobe Bryant 300.00 600.00
78 Trae Young 100.00 250.00
184 Shai Gilgeous-Alexander 300.00 600.00
250 Jalen Brunson 150.00 400.00
280 Luka Doncic 1,500.00 3,000.00

2018-19 Panini Prizm Prizms Purple Pulsar
*PURPLE PULSAR: 6X TO 15X BASIC
*PURPLE PULSAR RC: 8X TO 20X BASIC RC
STATED PRINT RUN 35 SER.#'d SETS
6 LeBron James 200.00 500.00
15 Kobe Bryant 200.00 500.00
61 Anfernee Simons 150.00 400.00
66 Jaren Jackson Jr. 125.00 300.00
78 Trae Young 400.00 800.00
184 Shai Gilgeous-Alexander 1,500.00 3,000.00
222 Stephen Curry 125.00 300.00
250 Jalen Brunson 200.00 500.00
280 Luka Doncic 4,000.00 8,000.00

2018-19 Panini Prizm Prizms Purple Wave
*PURPLE WAVE: 2X TO 5X BASIC
*PURPLE WAVE ICE RC: 2X TO 5X BASIC RC
15 Kobe Bryant 60.00 150.00
184 Shai Gilgeous-Alexander 125.00 300.00
250 Jalen Brunson 40.00 100.00
280 Luka Doncic 300.00 600.00

2018-19 Panini Prizm Prizms Red
*RED: 2.5X TO 6X BASIC
*RED RC: 2.5X TO 6X BASIC RC
STATED PRINT RUN 299 SER.#'d SETS
15 Kobe Bryant 75.00 200.00
78 Trae Young 125.00 300.00
184 Shai Gilgeous-Alexander 300.00 600.00
250 Jalen Brunson 75.00 200.00
280 Luka Doncic 1,000.00 2,000.00

2018-19 Panini Prizm Prizms Red Ice
*RED ICE: 1.2X TO 3X BASIC
*RED ICE RC: 1.2X TO 3X BASIC RC
15 Kobe Bryant 20.00 50.00
184 Shai Gilgeous-Alexander 60.00 150.00

2018-19 Panini Prizm Prizms Red White and Blue
*RWB: 1.25X TO 3X BASIC
*RWB RC: 1.25X TO 3X BASIC RC
15 Kobe Bryant 20.00 50.00
250 Jalen Brunson 20.00 50.00

2018-19 Panini Prizm Prizms Ruby Wave
*RUBY WAVE: 1.5X TO 4X BASIC
*RUBY WAVE RC: 1.5X TO 4X BASIC RC
15 Kobe Bryant 25.00 60.00
184 Shai Gilgeous-Alexander 75.00 200.00
250 Jalen Brunson 25.00 60.00

2018-19 Panini Prizm Prizms Silver
*SILVER: 1.2X TO 3X BASIC
*SILVER RC: 1.5X TO 4X BASIC RC
15 Kobe Bryant 15.00 40.00
184 Shai Gilgeous-Alexander 125.00 300.00
250 Jalen Brunson 25.00 60.00

2018-19 Panini Prizm All Day
*FAST BREAK: .75X TO 2X BASIC
*HYPER: .75X TO 2X BASIC
*SILVER: .75X TO 2X BASIC
1 Joel Embiid 1.25 3.00
2 Dwyane Wade 1.00 2.50
3 Ben Simmons .50 1.25
4 Victor Oladipo .40 1.00
5 Paul George .75 2.00
6 Dirk Nowitzki 1.25 3.00
7 Chris Paul 1.00 2.50
8 Kyle Kuzma .50 1.25
9 Russell Westbrook .75 2.00
10 LeBron James 4.00 10.00
11 James Harden 1.00 2.50
12 Stephen Curry 4.00 10.00
13 Kyrie Irving 1.25 3.00
14 Kevin Durant 2.00 5.00
15 Jayson Tatum 2.00 5.00
16 Kristaps Porzingis .60 1.50
17 Donovan Mitchell 1.50 4.00
18 Giannis Antetokounmpo 2.50 6.00
19 Blake Griffin .50 1.25
20 Anthony Davis 1.25 3.00
21 John Wall .60 1.50
22 DeMar DeRozan .60 1.50
23 Lauri Markkanen .75 2.00
24 Karl-Anthony Towns .75 2.00
25 Damian Lillard 1.25 3.00

2018-19 Panini Prizm All Day Prizms Mojo
*MOJO: 4X TO 10X BASIC
STATED PRINT RUN 25 SER.#'d SETS
10 LeBron James 100.00 250.00

2018-19 Panini Prizm Dominance
*GREEN: .6X TO 1.5X BASIC
*SILVER: .75X TO 2X BASIC
1 Reggie Miller 1.00 2.50
2 Magic Johnson 2.00 5.00
3 Paul Pierce .75 2.00
4 Shaquille O'Neal 1.50 4.00
5 Oscar Robertson 1.00 2.50
6 Kobe Bryant 5.00 12.00
7 Kareem Abdul-Jabbar 1.50 4.00
8 Clyde Drexler .75 2.00
9 Kevin Durant 2.00 5.00
10 Walt Frazier .75 2.00
11 Steve Nash 1.00 2.50
12 Karl Malone 1.00 2.50
13 Jason Kidd .75 2.00
14 Robert Parish .75 2.00
15 John Stockton 1.00 2.50
16 Larry Bird 2.00 5.00
17 Julius Erving 1.25 3.00
18 Stephen Curry 4.00 10.00
19 Allen Iverson 1.25 3.00
20 George Gervin .75 2.00
21 Dirk Nowitzki 1.25 3.00
22 Hakeem Olajuwon .60 1.50
23 Dwyane Wade 1.00 2.50
24 Scottie Pippen 1.25 3.00
25 Bill Walton .75 2.00
26 Wilt Chamberlain 1.50 4.00
27 Tim Duncan 1.25 3.00
28 Patrick Ewing .75 2.00
29 LeBron James 4.00 10.00
30 John Havlicek .75 2.00

2018-19 Panini Prizm Emergent
1 Deandre Ayton 1.50 4.00
2 Marvin Bagley III .75 2.00
3 Luka Doncic 15.00 40.00
4 Jaren Jackson Jr. 4.00 10.00
5 Trae Young 6.00 15.00
6 Mo Bamba .75 2.00
7 Wendell Carter Jr. 1.25 3.00
8 Collin Sexton 1.50 4.00
9 Kevin Knox .60 1.50
10 Mikal Bridges 2.50 6.00
11 Shai Gilgeous-Alexander 5.00 12.00
12 Miles Bridges 1.25 3.00
13 Jerome Robinson .50 1.25
14 Michael Porter Jr. 2.00 5.00
15 Troy Brown Jr. .60 1.50
16 Zhaire Smith .50 1.25
17 Donte DiVincenzo 1.25 3.00
18 Lonnie Walker IV 1.00 2.50
19 Kevin Huerter 1.00 2.50
20 Josh Okogie .75 2.00
21 Grayson Allen 1.00 2.50
22 Chandler Hutchison .60 1.50
23 Aaron Holiday .75 2.00
24 Anfernee Simons 2.50 6.00
25 Moritz Wagner 1.00 2.50

2018-19 Panini Prizm Emergent Prizms Green
*GREEN: .6X TO 1.5X BASIC
3 Luka Doncic 30.00 80.00

2018-19 Panini Prizm Emergent Prizms Silver
*SILVER: .75X TO 2X BASIC
3 Luka Doncic 40.00 100.00

2018-19 Panini Prizm Fast Break Autographs
COMMON CARD 4.00 10.00
SEMISTARS 5.00 12.00
UNLISTED STARS 6.00 15.00
EXCHANGE DEADLINE 5/21/2020
1 Kobe Bryant 800.00 1,500.00
3 Julius Erving 60.00 150.00
5 Andrew Wiggins 20.00 50.00
7 Dominique Wilkins 20.00 50.00
11 Charles Barkley 100.00 250.00
13 Kyrie Irving 60.00 150.00
15 Joel Embiid 60.00 150.00
16 Bogdan Bogdanovic 12.00 30.00
21 Kevin Durant 125.00 300.00
23 Dwyane Wade 75.00 200.00
25 Magic Johnson 100.00 250.00
28 Tim Hardaway 12.00 30.00
31 David Robinson 40.00 100.00
33 Kareem Abdul-Jabbar 100.00 250.00
35 Kevin McHale 20.00 50.00
39 Dave Cowens 12.00 30.00
40 Dikembe Mutombo 30.00 80.00
41 Reggie Miller 100.00 250.00
43 Oscar Robertson 60.00 150.00
47 Zach LaVine 50.00 120.00
48 Kevin Johnson 12.00 30.00
50 Cody Zeller 4.00 10.00
51 John Stockton 40.00 100.00
53 Tracy McGrady 60.00 150.00
54 Domantas Sabonis 15.00 40.00
55 Kristaps Porzingis 12.00 30.00

2018-19 Panini Prizm Fast Break Rookie Autographs
EXCHANGE DEADLINE 5/21/2020
1 Deandre Ayton 12.00 30.00
2 Marvin Bagley III 6.00 15.00
3 Luka Doncic 1,500.00 3,000.00
4 Jaren Jackson Jr. 150.00 400.00
5 Trae Young 200.00 500.00
6 Mo Bamba 6.00 15.00
7 Wendell Carter Jr. 10.00 25.00
8 Collin Sexton 12.00 30.00
9 Kevin Knox 5.00 12.00
10 Mikal Bridges 20.00 50.00
11 Shai Gilgeous-Alexander 600.00 1,200.00
12 Mitchell Robinson 10.00 25.00
13 Jerome Robinson 4.00 10.00
14 Michael Porter Jr. 15.00 40.00
15 Troy Brown Jr. 5.00 12.00
16 Zhaire Smith 4.00 10.00
17 Donte DiVincenzo 10.00 25.00
18 Lonnie Walker IV 8.00 20.00
19 Kevin Huerter 8.00 20.00
20 Josh Okogie 6.00 15.00
21 Grayson Allen 8.00 20.00
22 Chandler Hutchison 5.00 12.00
23 Aaron Holiday 6.00 15.00
24 Anfernee Simons 20.00 50.00
25 Moritz Wagner 8.00 20.00
26 Landry Shamet 6.00 15.00
27 Robert Williams III 8.00 20.00
28 Jacob Evans III 4.00 10.00
29 Dzanan Musa 4.00 10.00
30 Omari Spellman 4.00 10.00
31 Elie Okobo 4.00 10.00
32 Jevon Carter 6.00 15.00
33 Devonte' Graham 6.00 15.00
34 Jarred Vanderbilt 8.00 20.00
35 Keita Bates-Diop 5.00 12.00
36 Bruce Brown 8.00 20.00
37 De'Anthony Melton 8.00 20.00
38 Hamidou Diallo 6.00 15.00
39 Jalen Brunson 200.00 500.00
40 Gary Trent Jr. 8.00 20.00

2018-19 Panini Prizm Fireworks
*HYPER: .5X TO 1.2X BASIC
*FAST BREAK: .6X TO 1.5X BASIC
*SILVER: .6X TO 1.5X BASIC
1 Dennis Smith Jr. .30 .75
2 Russell Westbrook .75 2.00
3 Blake Griffin .50 1.25
4 Joel Embiid 1.25 3.00
5 James Harden 1.00 2.50
6 John Wall .60 1.50
7 Lonzo Ball .50 1.25
8 Dwyane Wade 1.00 2.50
9 Kyrie Irving 1.25 3.00
10 Andrew Wiggins .60 1.50
11 Lauri Markkanen .75 2.00
12 Paul George .75 2.00
13 Kevin Durant 2.00 5.00
14 Damian Lillard 1.25 3.00
15 Chris Paul 1.00 2.50
16 Donovan Mitchell 1.50 4.00
17 Kyle Kuzma .50 1.25
18 Giannis Antetokounmpo 2.50 6.00
19 LeBron James 4.00 10.00
20 Anthony Davis 1.25 3.00
21 Nikola Jokic 2.50 6.00
22 Ben Simmons .50 1.25
23 Stephen Curry 4.00 10.00
24 DeMar DeRozan .60 1.50
25 Victor Oladipo .40 1.00
26 Jayson Tatum 2.00 5.00
27 Marc Gasol .50 1.25
28 Karl-Anthony Towns .75 2.00
29 Dirk Nowitzki 1.25 3.00
30 Kristaps Porzingis .60 1.50

2018-19 Panini Prizm Fireworks Prizms Mojo
*MOJO: 4X TO 10X BASIC
STATED PRINT RUN 25 SER.#'d SETS
19 LeBron James 100.00 250.00
23 Stephen Curry 30.00 80.00

2018-19 Panini Prizm Freshman Phenoms
1 Moritz Wagner 1.00 2.50
2 Anfernee Simons 2.50 6.00
3 Aaron Holiday .75 2.00
4 Chandler Hutchison .60 1.50
5 Grayson Allen 1.00 2.50
6 Josh Okogie .75 2.00
7 Kevin Huerter 1.00 2.50
8 Lonnie Walker IV 1.00 2.50
9 Donte DiVincenzo 1.25 3.00
10 Zhaire Smith .50 1.25
11 Troy Brown Jr. .60 1.50
12 Michael Porter Jr. 2.00 5.00
13 Jerome Robinson .50 1.25
14 Miles Bridges 1.25 3.00
15 Shai Gilgeous-Alexander 5.00 12.00
16 Mikal Bridges 2.50 6.00
17 Kevin Knox .60 1.50
18 Collin Sexton 1.50 4.00
19 Wendell Carter Jr. 1.25 3.00
20 Mo Bamba .75 2.00
21 Trae Young 6.00 15.00
22 Jaren Jackson Jr. 4.00 10.00
23 Luka Doncic 15.00 40.00
24 Marvin Bagley III .75 2.00
25 Deandre Ayton 1.50 4.00

2018-19 Panini Prizm Freshman Phenoms Prizms Green
*GREEN: .6X TO 1.5X BASIC
23 Luka Doncic 30.00 80.00

2018-19 Panini Prizm Freshman Phenoms Prizms Silver
*SILVER: .75X TO 2X BASIC
23 Luka Doncic 40.00 100.00

2018-19 Panini Prizm Get Hyped!
*GREEN: .6X TO 1.5X BASIC
*SILVER: .75X TO 2X BASIC
1 Russell Westbrook .75 2.00
2 Stephen Curry 4.00 10.00
3 Kristaps Porzingis .60 1.50
4 LeBron James 4.00 10.00
5 Joel Embiid 1.25 3.00
6 Kevin Durant 2.00 5.00
7 James Harden 1.00 2.50
8 Giannis Antetokounmpo 2.50 6.00
9 Ben Simmons .50 1.25
10 Kyrie Irving 1.25 3.00

2018-19 Panini Prizm Go Hard or Go Home
*FAST BREAK: .75X TO 2X BASIC
*HYPER: .75X TO 2X BASIC
*SILVER: .75X TO 2X BASIC
1 Anthony Davis 1.25 3.00
2 LeBron James 4.00 10.00
3 Stephen Curry 4.00 10.00
4 Karl-Anthony Towns .75 2.00
5 Kevin Durant 2.00 5.00
6 Joel Embiid 1.25 3.00
7 Kristaps Porzingis .60 1.50
8 Ben Simmons .50 1.25
9 Giannis Antetokounmpo 2.50 6.00
10 Chris Paul 1.00 2.50
11 DeMar DeRozan .60 1.50
12 James Harden 1.00 2.50
13 Damian Lillard 1.25 3.00
14 Kyrie Irving 1.25 3.00
15 Dwyane Wade 1.00 2.50
16 Jayson Tatum 2.00 5.00
17 Donovan Mitchell 1.50 4.00
18 Dirk Nowitzki 1.25 3.00
19 Blake Griffin .50 1.25
20 Russell Westbrook .75 2.00

2018-19 Panini Prizm Go Hard or Go Home Prizms Mojo
*MOJO: 4X TO 10X BASIC
STATED PRINT RUN 25 SER.#'d SETS
2 LeBron James 100.00 250.00

2018-19 Panini Prizm Hall Monitors
*GREEN: .6X TO 1.5X BASIC
*SILVER: .75X TO 2X BASIC
1 Magic Johnson 2.00 5.00
2 Larry Bird 2.00 5.00
3 Charles Barkley 1.00 2.50
4 Bill Russell 1.50 4.00
5 Karl Malone 1.00 2.50
6 Shaquille O'Neal 1.50 4.00
7 John Stockton 1.00 2.50
8 Allen Iverson 1.25 3.00
9 Kareem Abdul-Jabbar 1.50 4.00
10 Reggie Miller 1.00 2.50

2018-19 Panini Prizm Luck of the Lottery
1 Deandre Ayton 1.00 2.50
2 Marvin Bagley III .50 1.25
3 Luka Doncic 25.00 60.00
4 Jaren Jackson Jr. 2.50 6.00
5 Trae Young 2.50 6.00
6 Mo Bamba .50 1.25
7 Wendell Carter Jr. .75 2.00
8 Collin Sexton 1.00 2.50
9 Kevin Knox .40 1.00
10 Mikal Bridges 1.50 4.00
11 Shai Gilgeous-Alexander 10.00 25.00
12 Miles Bridges .75 2.00
13 Jerome Robinson .30 .75
14 Michael Porter Jr. 1.25 3.00
15 Lottery Class 5.00 12.00

2018-19 Panini Prizm Luck of the Lottery Prizms Fast Break
*FAST BREAK: 1.25X TO 3X BASIC
11 Shai Gilgeous-Alexander 40.00 100.00

2018-19 Panini Prizm Luck of the Lottery Prizms Hyper
*HYPER: 1.25X TO 3X BASIC
11 Shai Gilgeous-Alexander 40.00 100.00

2018-19 Panini Prizm Luck of the Lottery Prizms Mojo
*MOJO: 15X TO 40X BASIC
STATED PRINT RUN 25 SER.#'d SETS
11 Shai Gilgeous-Alexander 800.00 1,500.00

2018-19 Panini Prizm Luck of the Lottery Prizms Silver
SILVER: .6X TO 1.5X BASIC
1 Shai Gilgeous-Alexander 60.00 150.00

2018-19 Panini Prizm Mosaic Blue
*BLUE: .75X TO 2X BASIC
68 Luka Doncic 400.00 800.00

2018-19 Panini Prizm Mosaic Autographs
EXCHANGE DEADLINE 11/29/2020
1 Anthony Davis 75.00 200.00
2 Charles Barkley 75.00 200.00
3 Collin Sexton 20.00 50.00
4 Damian Lillard EXCH 75.00 200.00
5 Deandre Ayton 20.00 50.00
6 Dirk Nowitzki EXCH 100.00 250.00
7 Donovan Mitchell 60.00 150.00
8 Donte DiVincenzo 20.00 50.00
9 Giannis Antetokounmpo 300.00 600.00
10 Grayson Allen 12.00 30.00
11 Jayson Tatum 150.00 400.00
12 Jerome Robinson 6.00 15.00
14 Karl-Anthony Towns 15.00 40.00
15 Kevin Durant 100.00 250.00
16 Kevin Huerter 12.00 30.00
17 Kevin Knox 8.00 20.00
18 Kobe Bryant 1,500.00 3,000.00
19 Kristaps Porzingis 20.00 50.00
20 Kyrie Irving 60.00 150.00
21 Lauri Markkanen 15.00 40.00
22 Luka Doncic 1,500.00 3,000.00
23 Marvin Bagley III 10.00 25.00
24 Michael Porter Jr. 25.00 60.00
25 Mikal Bridges 30.00 80.00
26 Mo Bamba 10.00 25.00
27 Nikola Jokic 150.00 400.00
28 Shai Gilgeous-Alexander 300.00 600.00
29 Shaquille O'Neal 100.00 250.00
31 Trae Young 125.00 300.00
32 Wendell Carter Jr. 15.00 40.00
33 Zach LaVine 15.00 40.00

2018-19 Panini Prizm Mosaic
*GREEN: .75X TO 2X BASIC
*RED: .75X TO 2X BASIC
*ORANGE/99: 1.5X TO 4X BASIC
*PURPLE/49: 2X TO 5X BASIC
*CAMO/25: 3X TO 8X BASIC
1 Aaron Gordon .75 2.00
2 Andre Drummond .60 1.50
3 Andrew Wiggins 1.00 2.50
4 Anthony Davis 2.00 5.00
5 Ben Simmons .75 2.00
6 Blake Griffin .75 2.00
7 Bradley Beal 1.00 2.50
8 Buddy Hield .75 2.00
9 Caris LeVert .75 2.00
10 Chris Paul 1.50 4.00
11 CJ McCollum .75 2.00
12 Clint Capela .60 1.50
13 Collin Sexton RC 3.00 8.00
14 Damian Lillard 2.00 5.00
15 D'Angelo Russell .75 2.00
16 Danilo Gallinari .60 1.50
17 De'Aaron Fox 1.50 4.00
18 Deandre Ayton RC 3.00 8.00
19 DeMar DeRozan 1.00 2.50
20 DeMarcus Cousins .60 1.50
21 Dennis Smith Jr. .50 1.25
22 Derrick Rose 1.50 4.00
23 Devin Booker 2.00 5.00
24 Dirk Nowitzki 2.00 5.00
25 Donovan Mitchell 2.50 6.00
26 Donte DiVincenzo RC 2.50 6.00
27 Draymond Green 1.00 2.50
28 Dwyane Wade 1.50 4.00
29 Enes Kanter .60 1.50
30 Giannis Antetokounmpo 4.00 10.00
31 Goran Dragic .60 1.50
32 Gordon Hayward .75 2.00
33 Grayson Allen RC 2.00 5.00
34 Hassan Whiteside .60 1.50
35 Jamal Murray 1.50 4.00
36 James Harden 1.50 4.00
37 Jaren Jackson Jr. RC 8.00 20.00
38 Jarrett Allen .75 2.00
39 Jayson Tatum 3.00 8.00
40 Allonzo Trier RC 1.00 2.50
41 Jimmy Butler 1.25 3.00
42 Joe Ingles .60 1.50
43 Joel Embiid 2.00 5.00
44 John Collins .75 2.00
45 John Wall 1.00 2.50
46 Josh Jackson .50 1.25
47 Josh Okogie RC 1.50 4.00
48 Jrue Holiday .60 1.50
49 Jusuf Nurkic .60 1.50
50 Karl-Anthony Towns 1.25 3.00
51 Kawhi Leonard 2.00 5.00
52 Kemba Walker .60 1.50
53 Kevin Durant 3.00 8.00
54 Kevin Huerter RC 2.00 5.00
55 Kevin Knox RC 1.25 3.00
56 Kevin Love .60 1.50
57 Klay Thompson 2.00 5.00
58 Kristaps Porzingis 1.00 2.50
59 Kyle Kuzma .75 2.00
60 Kyle Lowry .75 2.00
61 Kyrie Irving 2.00 5.00
62 LaMarcus Aldridge .75 2.00
63 Landry Shamet RC 1.50 4.00
64 Lauri Markkanen 1.25 3.00
65 LeBron James 6.00 15.00
66 Lonnie Walker IV RC 2.00 5.00
67 Lonzo Ball .75 2.00
68 Luka Doncic RC 60.00 150.00
69 Malcolm Brogdon .75 2.00
70 Marc Gasol .75 2.00
71 Marvin Bagley III RC 1.50 4.00
72 Michael Kidd-Gilchrist .50 1.25
73 Michael Porter Jr. RC 4.00 10.00
74 Mikal Bridges RC 5.00 12.00
75 Mike Conley .60 1.50
76 Miles Bridges RC 2.50 6.00
77 Mo Bamba RC 1.50 4.00
78 Montrezl Harrell .75 2.00
79 Myles Turner .75 2.00
80 Nikola Jokic 4.00 10.00
81 Nikola Mirotic .50 1.25
82 Otto Porter Jr. .60 1.50
83 Pascal Siakam 1.25 3.00
84 Pau Gasol 1.25 3.00
85 Paul George 1.25 3.00
86 Paul Millsap .60 1.50
87 Rudy Gobert 1.00 2.50
88 Russell Westbrook 1.25 3.00
89 Shai Gilgeous-Alexander RC 30.00 80.00
90 Stephen Curry 6.00 15.00
91 Steven Adams .60 1.50
92 Tim Hardaway Jr. .50 1.25
93 Trae Young RC 8.00 20.00
94 Tristan Thompson .50 1.25
95 Troy Brown Jr. RC 1.25 3.00
96 Victor Oladipo .60 1.50
97 Vince Carter 1.50 4.00
98 Wendell Carter Jr. RC 2.50 6.00
99 Zach LaVine 1.25 3.00
100 Zhaire Smith RC 1.00 2.50

2018-19 Panini Prizm Rookie Signatures
EXCHANGE DEADLINE 5/21/2020
1 Deandre Ayton 40.00 100.00
2 Marvin Bagley III 4.00 10.00
3 Luka Doncic 1,500.00 3,000.00
4 Jaren Jackson Jr. 75.00 200.00
5 Trae Young 300.00 600.00
6 Mo Bamba 10.00 25.00
7 Wendell Carter Jr. EXCH 12.00 30.00
8 Collin Sexton 25.00 60.00
9 Kevin Knox 3.00 8.00
10 Mikal Bridges 20.00 50.00
11 Shai Gilgeous-Alexander 400.00 800.00
14 Michael Porter Jr. 40.00 100.00
15 Troy Brown Jr. 3.00 8.00
16 Zhaire Smith 2.50 6.00
17 Donte DiVincenzo 6.00 15.00
18 Lonnie Walker IV 12.00 30.00
19 Kevin Huerter 5.00 12.00
20 Josh Okogie 8.00 20.00
21 Rodions Kurucs 3.00 8.00
22 Chandler Hutchison 3.00 8.00
23 Aaron Holiday 4.00 10.00
24 Anfernee Simons 40.00 100.00
25 Moritz Wagner 5.00 12.00
26 Landry Shamet 4.00 10.00
27 Robert Williams III 15.00 40.00
28 Jacob Evans III 2.50 6.00
29 Dzanan Musa 2.50 6.00
30 Omari Spellman 2.50 6.00
31 Elie Okobo 2.50 6.00
33 Devonte' Graham 4.00 10.00
34 Khyri Thomas 2.50 6.00
35 Keita Bates-Diop 3.00 8.00
36 Bruce Brown 5.00 12.00
37 De'Anthony Melton 5.00 12.00
38 Hamidou Diallo 4.00 10.00
39 Kostas Antetokounmpo 3.00 8.00
40 Melvin Frazier Jr. 2.50 6.00

2018-19 Panini Prizm Rookie Signatures Prizms Choice
*CHOICE: .5X TO 1.2X BASIC
EXCHANGE DEADLINE 5/21/2020
12 Mitchell Robinson 20.00 50.00
13 Jerome Robinson 3.00 8.00
32 Jevon Carter 5.00 12.00

2018-19 Panini Prizm Rookie Signatures Prizms Mojo
*MOJO: 2X TO 5X BASIC
STATED PRINT RUN 25 SER.#'d SETS
EXCHANGE DEADLINE 5/21/2020
3 Luka Doncic 10,000.00 20,000.00
4 Jaren Jackson Jr. 500.00 1,000.00
5 Trae Young 1,500.00 3,000.00
6 Mo Bamba 60.00 150.00
7 Wendell Carter Jr. EXCH 75.00 200.00
10 Mikal Bridges 125.00 300.00
24 Anfernee Simons 400.00 800.00
32 Jevon Carter 20.00 50.00

2018-19 Panini Prizm Rookie Signatures Prizms Silver
*SILVER: .6X TO 1.5X BASIC
EXCHANGE DEADLINE 5/21/2020
3 Luka Doncic 3,000.00 6,000.00
24 Anfernee Simons 75.00 200.00

2018-19 Panini Prizm Sensational Signatures
EXCHANGE DEADLINE 5/21/2020
1 Stephen Curry 500.00 1,000.00
2 Bogdan Bogdanovic 10.00 25.00
3 Tracy McGrady 75.00 200.00
4 Bob Lanier 5.00 12.00
5 Goran Dragic 3.00 8.00
6 Courtney Lee 2.50 6.00
7 Matthew Dellavedova 3.00 8.00
8 Reggie Miller EXCH 75.00 200.00
9 Kevin McHale 12.00 30.00
10 Buddy Hield 4.00 10.00
11 Dave Cowens 5.00 12.00
12 Ivica Zubac 3.00 8.00
13 Caris LeVert 4.00 10.00
14 Dwyane Wade 20.00 50.00
15 Jason Kidd 12.00 30.00
16 Dion Waiters 2.50 6.00
17 Emmanuel Mudiay 2.50 6.00
18 Jerami Grant 4.00 10.00
20 Damian Lillard 25.00 60.00
21 Anfernee Hardaway 60.00 150.00
22 Harrison Barnes 3.00 8.00
23 Justise Winslow 3.00 8.00
24 Seth Curry 3.00 8.00
26 Kyrie Irving EXCH 15.00 40.00
27 Tony Parker 12.00 30.00
28 Khris Middleton 4.00 10.00
29 Mark Jackson 3.00 8.00
30 TJ Warren 2.50 6.00
31 Jose Calderon 2.50 6.00
32 Larry Bird 75.00 200.00
33 Isaiah Thomas 3.00 8.00
34 Steve Kerr 15.00 40.00
36 Zach Collins 3.00 8.00
38 Julius Erving 25.00 60.00
39 Dominique Wilkins 15.00 40.00
40 Zach LaVine 25.00 60.00
41 Myles Turner 4.00 10.00
42 Domantas Sabonis 12.00 30.00
43 Rik Smits 3.00 8.00
44 Kareem Abdul-Jabbar 75.00 200.00
45 Kristaps Porzingis 8.00 20.00
46 Brook Lopez 3.00 8.00
47 JR Smith 12.00 30.00
48 Guerschon Yabusele 2.50 6.00
49 Tim Hardaway 5.00 12.00
50 Donovan Mitchell 60.00 150.00
51 Gordon Hayward 6.00 15.00
52 Bernard King 4.00 10.00
53 Dikembe Mutombo 12.00 30.00
54 Aaron McKie 2.50 6.00
56 Jayson Tatum EXCH 100.00 250.00
57 Rick Barry 10.00 25.00
58 Kenny Smith 3.00 8.00
59 Patrick Patterson 2.50 6.00
60 Amir Johnson 2.50 6.00
61 Deandre Ayton 40.00 100.00
62 Marvin Bagley III 4.00 10.00
63 Luka Doncic 1,500.00 3,000.00
64 Jaren Jackson Jr. 75.00 200.00
65 Trae Young 300.00 600.00
66 Mo Bamba 10.00 25.00
67 Wendell Carter Jr. 12.00 30.00
68 Collin Sexton 25.00 60.00
69 Kevin Knox 3.00 8.00
70 Mikal Bridges 20.00 50.00
71 Shai Gilgeous-Alexander 400.00 800.00
72 Svi Mykhailiuk 3.00 8.00
74 Michael Porter Jr. 40.00 100.00
75 Troy Brown Jr. 3.00 8.00
76 Zhaire Smith 2.50 6.00
77 Donte DiVincenzo 6.00 15.00
78 Lonnie Walker IV 12.00 30.00
79 Kevin Huerter 8.00 20.00
80 Josh Okogie 8.00 20.00
81 Grayson Allen 10.00 25.00
82 Chandler Hutchison 3.00 8.00
83 Aaron Holiday 4.00 10.00
84 Anfernee Simons 40.00 100.00
85 Moritz Wagner 5.00 12.00
86 Landry Shamet 4.00 10.00
87 Robert Williams III 15.00 40.00
88 Jacob Evans III 2.50 6.00
89 Dzanan Musa 2.50 6.00
90 Omari Spellman 2.50 6.00
91 Elie Okobo 2.50 6.00
93 Jalen Brunson 20.00 50.00
94 Devonte' Graham 4.00 10.00
95 Gary Trent Jr. 20.00 50.00
96 Jarred Vanderbilt 5.00 12.00
97 Keita Bates-Diop 3.00 8.00
98 Bruce Brown 5.00 12.00
99 De'Anthony Melton 5.00 12.00
100 Hamidou Diallo 4.00 10.00

2018-19 Panini Prizm Sensational Signatures Prizms Choice
*CHOICE: .5X TO 1.2X BASIC
EXCHANGE DEADLINE 5/21/2020
1 Stephen Curry 800.00 1,500.00
19 Ed Davis 3.00 8.00
25 John Henson 3.00 8.00
35 Milos Teodosic 3.00 8.00
37 Omri Casspi 3.00 8.00
55 Tim Hardaway Jr. 3.00 8.00
73 Jerome Robinson 3.00 8.00
92 Jevon Carter 5.00 12.00

2018-19 Panini Prizm Sensational Signatures Prizms Mojo
*MOJO: 1.25X TO 3X BASIC
STATED PRINT RUN 25 SER.#'d SETS
EXCHANGE DEADLINE 5/21/2020
19 Ed Davis 8.00 20.00
25 John Henson 8.00 20.00
37 Omri Casspi 8.00 20.00
40 Zach LaVine 100.00 250.00
55 Tim Hardaway Jr. 8.00 20.00
56 Jayson Tatum EXCH 400.00 800.00
61 Deandre Ayton 150.00 400.00
63 Luka Doncic 10,000.00 20,000.00
65 Trae Young 1,500.00 3,000.00
66 Mo Bamba 60.00 150.00
67 Wendell Carter Jr. 60.00 150.00
68 Collin Sexton 75.00 200.00
70 Mikal Bridges 125.00 300.00
71 Shai Gilgeous-Alexander 1,500.00 3,000.00
73 Jerome Robinson 15.00 40.00
84 Anfernee Simons 300.00 600.00
92 Jevon Carter 15.00 40.00

2018-19 Panini Prizm Sensational Swatches
1 Shaquille O'Neal 6.00 15.00
2 Draymond Green 2.50 6.00
3 Rondae Hollis-Jefferson 1.25 3.00
4 Courtney Lee 1.25 3.00
5 Andrew Wiggins 2.50 6.00
6 Damian Lillard 5.00 12.00
7 Derrick Favors 1.25 3.00
8 Amar'e Stoudemire 2.00 5.00
9 Wesley Matthews 1.25 3.00
10 Ray Allen 2.50 6.00
11 CJ McCollum 2.00 5.00
12 Seth Curry 1.50 4.00
13 Harrison Barnes 1.50 4.00
14 Hakeem Olajuwon 2.50 6.00
15 Karl-Anthony Towns 3.00 8.00
16 Nicolas Batum 1.25 3.00
17 Kevin Garnett 5.00 12.00
18 Shawn Marion 1.50 4.00
19 Kobe Bryant 6.00 15.00
20 Jason Kidd 3.00 8.00
21 Grant Hill 3.00 8.00
22 DeMar DeRozan 2.50 6.00
23 Blake Griffin 2.00 5.00
24 Elfrid Payton 1.50 4.00
25 Jimmy Butler 3.00 8.00
26 JR Smith 2.00 5.00
27 Chris Paul 4.00 10.00
28 Tristan Thompson 1.25 3.00
29 Kristaps Porzingis 2.50 6.00
30 Ryan Anderson 1.25 3.00
31 Nikola Jokic 10.00 25.00
32 Allen Iverson 5.00 12.00
33 Scottie Pippen 5.00 12.00
34 David Robinson 4.00 10.00
35 Rudy Gobert 2.50 6.00
36 John Wall 2.50 6.00
37 Markieff Morris 1.25 3.00
38 Dwyane Wade 4.00 10.00
39 Paul Pierce 3.00 8.00
40 Tim Hardaway Jr. 1.25 3.00
41 Nerlens Noel 1.25 3.00
42 Andre Drummond 1.50 4.00
43 Clyde Drexler 3.00 8.00
44 Dwight Powell 1.25 3.00
45 Dirk Nowitzki 5.00 12.00
46 Klay Thompson 5.00 12.00
47 DeAndre Jordan 1.50 4.00
48 Bradley Beal 2.50 6.00
49 Shaquille O'Neal 6.00 15.00
50 Karl Malone 4.00 10.00
51 Aaron Gordon 2.00 5.00

52 Willie Cauley-Stein 1.25 3.00
53 Larry Bird 8.00 20.00
54 Anthony Davis 5.00 12.00
55 Kevin Love 1.50 4.00
56 Kenneth Faried 1.50 4.00
57 Derrick Rose 4.00 10.00
58 Kenny Anderson 1.50 4.00
59 LeBron James 15.00 40.00
60 Marcin Gortat 1.25 3.00
61 Aaron Holiday 2.00 5.00
62 Anfernee Simons 6.00 15.00
63 Bruce Brown 2.50 6.00
64 Chandler Hutchison 1.50 4.00
65 Collin Sexton 4.00 10.00
66 Deandre Ayton 5.00 12.00
67 De'Anthony Melton 2.50 6.00
68 Devonte' Graham 2.00 5.00
69 Donte DiVincenzo 3.00 8.00
70 Dzanan Musa 1.25 3.00
71 Elie Okobo 1.25 3.00
72 Gary Trent Jr. 2.50 6.00
73 Grayson Allen 2.50 6.00
74 Hamidou Diallo 2.00 5.00
75 Jacob Evans III 1.25 3.00
76 Jalen Brunson 10.00 25.00
77 Jaren Jackson Jr. 10.00 25.00
78 Pau Gasol 3.00 8.00
79 Jerome Robinson 1.25 3.00
80 Christian Laettner 2.00 5.00
81 Josh Okogie 2.00 5.00
82 Keita Bates-Diop 1.50 4.00
83 Kevin Huerter 2.50 6.00
84 Kevin Knox 1.50 4.00
85 Landry Shamet 2.00 5.00
86 Lonnie Walker IV 2.50 6.00
87 Luka Doncic 10.00 25.00
88 Marvin Bagley III 3.00 8.00
89 Michael Porter Jr. 5.00 12.00
90 Mikal Bridges 6.00 15.00
91 Mo Bamba 2.00 5.00
92 Maurice Harkless 1.25 3.00
93 Omari Spellman 1.25 3.00
94 Robert Williams III 2.50 6.00
95 Shai Gilgeous-Alexander 12.00 30.00
96 Svi Mykhailiuk 1.50 4.00
97 Trae Young 4.00 10.00
98 Troy Brown Jr. 1.50 4.00
99 Wendell Carter Jr. 3.00 8.00
100 Jermaine O'Neal 1.50 4.00

2018-19 Panini Prizm Signatures

EXCHANGE DEADLINE 5/21/2020
1 Rick Barry 10.00 25.00
2 Langston Galloway 2.50 6.00
3 Bob Dandridge 3.00 8.00
4 Brook Lopez 3.00 8.00
5 Justise Winslow 3.00 8.00
6 Charles Barkley 125.00 300.00
7 Thon Maker 2.50 6.00
8 Kyrie Irving EXCH 15.00 40.00
9 Allen Crabbe 2.50 6.00
10 Kevin McHale 12.00 30.00
11 Andrei Kirilenko 3.00 8.00
12 Bob Lanier 5.00 12.00
13 Purvis Short 2.50 6.00
14 Kenny Smith 3.00 8.00
15 Jrue Holiday 12.00 30.00
16 Kobe Bryant EXCH 1,000.00 2,000.00
17 Terrence Ross 3.00 8.00
18 John Stockton 25.00 60.00
19 Bismack Biyombo 2.50 6.00
20 Jason Kidd 12.00 30.00
21 Dino Radja 2.50 6.00
24 Nikola Mirotic 2.50 6.00
25 World B. Free 3.00 8.00
26 Stephen Curry 500.00 1,000.00
27 Luke Walton 2.50 6.00
28 Julius Erving 25.00 60.00
29 Trey Lyles 2.50 6.00
30 Anfernee Hardaway 60.00 150.00
31 Hersey Hawkins 2.50 6.00
33 Eric Snow 2.50 6.00
34 Goran Dragic 3.00 8.00
35 JR Smith 4.00 10.00
S-KDR Kevin Durant 150.00 400.00
37 Nene 3.00 8.00
38 Kareem Abdul-Jabbar 75.00 200.00
39 Charlie Scott 4.00 10.00
40 Kristaps Porzingis 8.00 20.00
41 P.J. Brown 2.50 6.00
43 Quentin Richardson 3.00 8.00
44 Jason Terry 3.00 8.00
45 Glen Rice 4.00 10.00
46 Andrew Wiggins 12.00 30.00
47 Zaza Pachulia 2.50 6.00
48 Joel Embiid EXCH 50.00 120.00
49 Jonas Jerebko 2.50 6.00
50 Dominique Wilkins 12.00 30.00
51 Michael Adams 2.50 6.00
52 Zach LaVine 30.00 80.00
53 Darius Miles 2.50 6.00
54 Mark Jackson 3.00 8.00
55 Cody Zeller 2.50 6.00
56 Reggie Miller EXCH 75.00 200.00
57 Malcolm Brogdon 4.00 10.00
58 Tracy McGrady 75.00 200.00
59 Wade Baldwin IV 2.50 6.00

2018-19 Panini Prizm Signatures Prizms Choice

*CHOICE: .5X TO 1.2X BASIC
EXCHANGE DEADLINE 5/21/2020
16 Kobe Bryant EXCH 1,500.00 3,000.00
23 Dell Curry 5.00 12.00
26 Stephen Curry 800.00 1,500.00

2018-19 Panini Prizm Signatures Prizms Mojo

*SILVER: 1.25X TO 3X BASIC
STATED PRINT RUN 25 SER.#'d SETS
EXCHANGE DEADLINE 5/21/2020
16 Kobe Bryant EXCH 5,000.00 10,000.00
23 Dell Curry 12.00 30.00
26 Stephen Curry 1,500.00 3,000.00
S-KDR Kevin Durant 300.00 600.00
48 Joel Embiid EXCH 125.00 300.00

2018-19 Panini Prizm Signatures Prizms Silver

*SILVER: .6X TO 1.5X BASIC
EXCHANGE DEADLINE 5/21/2020
16 Kobe Bryant EXCH 2,000.00 4,000.00
23 Dell Curry 6.00 15.00
26 Stephen Curry 1,000.00 2,000.00

2018-19 Panini Prizm That's Savage!

*FAST BREAK: .75X TO 2X BASIC
*HYPER: .75X TO 2X BASIC
*SILVER: .75X TO 2X BASIC
1 DeAndre Jordan .40 1.00
2 LeBron James 4.00 10.00
3 Anthony Davis 1.25 3.00
4 Blake Griffin .50 1.25
5 Kevin Durant 2.00 5.00
6 Donovan Mitchell 1.50 4.00
7 Zach LaVine .75 2.00
8 Giannis Antetokounmpo 2.50 6.00
9 Aaron Gordon .50 1.25
10 Russell Westbrook .75 2.00

2018-19 Panini Prizm That's Savage! Prizms Mojo

*MOJO: 4X TO 10X BASIC
STATED PRINT RUN 25 SER.#'d SETS
2 LeBron James 100.00 250.00

2019-20 Panini Prizm

1 Kevin Garnett 1.00 2.50
2 Charles Barkley .75 2.00
3 Dennis Rodman 1.00 2.50
4 Hakeem Olajuwon .75 2.00
5 Jason Kidd .60 1.50
6 Allen Iverson 1.00 2.50
7 Yao Ming 1.00 2.50
8 Kobe Bryant 3.00 8.00
9 David Robinson .75 2.00
10 Scottie Pippen 1.00 2.50
11 Shaquille O'Neal 1.50 4.00
12 Anfernee Hardaway 1.00 2.50
13 Patrick Ewing .60 1.50
14 Shawn Kemp .60 1.50
15 Larry Johnson .50 1.25
16 Larry Bird 1.50 4.00
17 Pete Maravich 1.00 2.50
18 Wilt Chamberlain 1.50 4.00
19 Karl Malone .75 2.00
20 Kareem Abdul-Jabbar 1.25 3.00
21 Bill Russell 1.25 3.00
22 Ray Allen .60 1.50
23 Clyde Drexler .60 1.50
24 Grant Hill .60 1.50
25 Magic Johnson 1.25 3.00
26 Tracy McGrady .60 1.50
27 Alonzo Mourning .60 1.50
28 Steve Nash .75 2.00
29 Paul Pierce .60 1.50
30 Isiah Thomas .75 2.00
31 Trae Young 1.00 2.50
32 John Collins .40 1.00
33 Vince Carter .75 2.00
34 Kevin Huerter .40 1.00
35 Kent Bazemore .25 .60
36 JJ Redick .40 1.00
37 Dewayne Dedmon .25 .60
38 Alex Len .25 .60
39 Jayson Tatum 1.50 4.00
40 Jaylen Brown .60 1.50
41 Marcus Smart .30 .75
42 Gordon Hayward .30 .75
43 Terry Rozier .30 .75
44 Terrence Ross .40 1.00
45 Tobias Harris .30 .75
46 Marcus Morris .25 .60
47 Jarrett Allen .40 1.00
48 Spencer Dinwiddie .30 .75
49 Joe Harris .30 .75
50 Caris LeVert .30 .75
51 Zhaire Smith .25 .60
52 Rodions Kurucs .40 1.00
53 Mike Scott .25 .60
54 Kemba Walker .30 .75
55 Miles Bridges .40 1.00
56 Michael Kidd-Gilchrist .25 .60
57 Nicolas Batum .25 .60
58 Bismack Biyombo .25 .60
59 Dwayne Bacon .25 .60
60 Danny Green .30 .75
61 Zach LaVine .60 1.50
62 Kris Dunn .25 .60
63 Lauri Markkanen .50 1.25
64 Otto Porter Jr. .25 .60
65 Wendell Carter Jr. .40 1.00
66 Denzel Valentine .25 .60
67 Devin Booker .10 .25
68 Kevin Love .40 1.00
69 Jordan Clarkson .40 1.00
70 Matthew Dellavedova .30 .75
71 Deandre Ayton .40 1.00
72 Tristan Thompson .25 .60
73 Larry Nance Jr. .30 .75
74 Collin Sexton .50 1.25
75 Luka Doncic 2.50 6.00
76 Kristaps Porzingis .50 1.25
77 Tim Hardaway Jr. .25 .60
78 Jalen Brunson 1.00 2.50
79 Courtney Lee .25 .60
80 Justin Jackson .25 .60
81 Dwight Powell .25 .60
82 DeMarre Carroll .25 .60
83 Jamal Murray .60 1.50
84 Nikola Jokic 2.00 5.00
85 Will Barton .25 .60
86 Malik Beasley .30 .75
87 Torrey Craig .25 .60
88 Michael Porter Jr. .60 1.50
89 Gary Harris .30 .75
90 Josh Jackson .25 .60
91 Blake Griffin .40 1.00
92 Andre Drummond .30 .75
93 Luke Kennard .30 .75
94 Langston Galloway .25 .60
95 Reggie Jackson .30 .75
96 Thon Maker .25 .60
97 Bruce Brown .40 1.00
98 Stephen Curry 3.00 8.00
99 Mikal Bridges .60 1.50
100 Tyler Johnson .25 .60
101 Draymond Green .50 1.25
102 Andre Iguodala .30 .75
103 DeMarcus Cousins .30 .75
104 Kevon Looney .25 .60
105 Quinn Cook .30 .75
106 Alfonzo McKinnie .25 .60
107 James Harden .75 2.00
108 Kelly Oubre Jr. .30 .75
109 Eric Gordon .30 .75
110 Clint Capela .30 .75
111 P.J. Tucker .30 .75
112 Damian Lillard 1.00 2.50
113 CJ McCollum .40 1.00
114 Victor Oladipo .30 .75
115 Aaron Holiday .30 .75
116 Zach Collins .25 .60
117 Meyers Leonard .25 .60
118 Jusuf Nurkic .30 .75
119 Evan Turner .25 .60
120 De'Aaron Fox .60 1.50
121 Marvin Bagley III .30 .75
122 Shai Gilgeous-Alexander 2.00 5.00
123 Danilo Gallinari .30 .75
124 Montrezl Harrell .30 .75
125 Landry Shamet .30 .75
126 Lou Williams .40 1.00
127 Buddy Hield .30 .75
128 Harry Giles .25 .60
129 LeBron James 3.00 8.00
130 Kyle Kuzma .50 1.25
131 Bogdan Bogdanovic .40 1.00
132 Willie Cauley-Stein .25 .60
133 LaMarcus Aldridge .40 1.00
134 DeMar DeRozan .50 1.25
135 Rudy Gay .30 .75
136 Jaren Jackson Jr. .60 1.50
137 Avery Bradley .25 .60
138 Dejounte Murray .40 1.00
139 Lonnie Walker IV .30 .75
140 Chandler Parsons .25 .60
141 Derrick White .40 1.00
142 Kyle Anderson .25 .60
143 Bruno Caboclo .25 .60
144 Bam Adebayo .60 1.50
145 Goran Dragic .30 .75
146 Kelly Olynyk .25 .60
147 Josh Richardson .25 .60
148 Dion Waiters .25 .60
149 Kawhi Leonard 1.00 2.50
150 Derrick Jones Jr. .25 .60
151 Hassan Whiteside .25 .60
152 Giannis Antetokounmpo 2.00 5.00
153 Marc Gasol .40 1.00
154 Serge Ibaka .30 .75
155 Kyle Lowry .40 1.00
156 Pascal Siakam .60 1.50
157 Fred VanVleet .50 1.25
158 Ersan Ilyasova .25 .60
159 Norman Powell .30 .75
160 Andrew Wiggins .50 1.25
161 Karl-Anthony Towns .60 1.50
162 Gorgui Dieng .25 .60
163 Josh Okogie .30 .75
164 Donovan Mitchell .75 2.00
165 Jeff Teague .25 .60
166 Robert Covington .25 .60
167 Ricky Rubio .30 .75
168 Rudy Gobert .50 1.25
169 Derrick Favors .25 .60
170 Jrue Holiday .50 1.25
171 Jahlil Okafor .25 .60
172 Julius Randle .50 1.25
173 Joe Ingles .30 .75
174 E'Twaun Moore .25 .60
175 Kevin Knox II .25 .60
176 Emmanuel Mudiay .25 .60
177 Frank Ntilikina .25 .60
178 Mitchell Robinson .40 1.00
179 Dennis Smith Jr. .25 .60
180 Allonzo Trier .25 .60
181 John Wall .50 1.25
182 Russell Westbrook .60 1.50
183 Steven Adams .30 .75
184 Hamidou Diallo .30 .75
185 Paul George .60 1.50
186 Dennis Schroder .30 .75
187 Andre Roberson .25 .60
188 Terrance Ferguson .25 .60
189 Bradley Beal .50 1.25
190 Aaron Gordon .40 1.00
191 Mo Bamba .30 .75
192 Evan Fournier .30 .75
193 Markelle Fultz .30 .75
194 Jonathan Isaac .40 1.00
195 Thomas Bryant .30 .75
196 Troy Brown Jr. .25 .60
197 D.J. Augustin .25 .60
198 Ben Simmons .40 1.00
199 Joel Embiid .75 2.00
200 Allen Crabbe .25 .60
201 Kyrie Irving .75 2.00
202 Al Horford .40 1.00
203 Taurean Prince .25 .60
204 D'Angelo Russell .30 .75
205 Malik Monk .40 1.00
206 Robin Lopez .25 .60
207 John Henson .25 .60
208 Isaiah Thomas .30 .75
209 Klay Thompson 1.00 2.50
210 Kevin Durant 1.25 3.00
211 Chris Paul .75 2.00
212 Enes Kanter .25 .60
213 Austin Rivers .25 .60
214 Wesley Matthews .25 .60
215 Domantas Sabonis .50 1.25
216 Myles Turner .40 1.00
217 Thaddeus Young .25 .60
218 Bojan Bogdanovic .30 .75
219 Mario Hezonja .25 .60
220 Ivica Zubac .30 .75
221 Wilson Chandler .25 .60
222 Anthony Davis 1.00 2.50
223 Rajon Rondo .50 1.25
224 Kentavious Caldwell-Pope .30 .75
225 JaVale McGee .30 .75
226 Seth Curry .30 .75
227 Jae Crowder .25 .60
228 T.J. Warren .30 .75
229 Jonas Valanciunas .30 .75
230 Justise Winslow .25 .60
231 Eric Bledsoe .30 .75
232 Malcolm Brogdon .30 .75
233 Pau Gasol .60 1.50
234 Brook Lopez .30 .75
235 Khris Middleton .40 1.00
236 Trevor Ariza .25 .60
237 Derrick Rose .75 2.00
238 Jabari Parker .25 .60
239 Lonzo Ball .40 1.00
240 Josh Hart .30 .75
241 Brandon Ingram .40 1.00
242 Elfrid Payton .25 .60
243 DeAndre Jordan .30 .75
244 Mike Conley .30 .75
245 Markieff Morris .25 .60
246 Jimmy Butler .75 2.00
247 Nikola Vucevic .30 .75
248 Zion Williamson RC 4.00 10.00
249 Ja Morant RC 5.00 12.00
250 RJ Barrett RC 2.00 5.00
251 De'Andre Hunter RC 2.00 5.00
252 Jarrett Culver RC .50 1.25
253 Coby White RC 1.50 4.00
254 Jaxson Hayes RC .75 2.00
255 Rui Hachimura RC 2.00 5.00
256 Cam Reddish RC .75 2.00
257 Cameron Johnson RC 1.25 3.00
258 PJ Washington Jr. RC 1.50 4.00
259 Tyler Herro RC 2.50 6.00
260 Romeo Langford RC .50 1.25
261 Sekou Doumbouya RC .50 1.25
262 Chuma Okeke RC .75 2.00
263 Nickeil Alexander-Walker RC .75 2.00
264 Goga Bitadze RC .75 2.00
265 Luka Samanic RC .60 1.50
266 Brandon Clarke RC 1.00 2.50
267 Grant Williams RC .75 2.00
268 Ty Jerome RC 1.00 2.50
269 Nassir Little RC .75 2.00
270 Dylan Windler RC .60 1.50
271 Mfiondu Kabengele RC .60 1.50
272 Jordan Poole RC 2.00 5.00
273 Keldon Johnson RC 1.50 4.00
274 Kevin Porter Jr. RC 1.00 2.50
275 KZ Okpala RC .60 1.50
276 Carsen Edwards RC .60 1.50
277 Bruno Fernando RC .60 1.50
278 Cody Martin RC .75 2.00
279 Eric Paschall RC .60 1.50
280 Admiral Schofield RC .60 1.50
281 Jaylen Nowell RC .60 1.50
282 Bol Bol RC 1.25 3.00
283 Isaiah Roby RC .60 1.50
284 Ignas Brazdeikis RC .60 1.50
285 Quinndary Weatherspoon RC .50 1.25
286 Tremont Waters RC .60 1.50
287 Kyle Guy RC .60 1.50
288 Darius Garland RC 2.00 5.00
289 Darius Bazley RC .50 1.25
290 Matisse Thybulle RC 1.00 2.50
291 Jordan Bone RC .50 1.25
292 Nicolas Claxton RC 1.00 2.50
293 Jaylen Hands RC .50 1.25
294 Daniel Gafford RC 1.00 2.50
295 Justin James RC .50 1.25
296 Terance Mann RC 1.00 2.50
297 Jalen McDaniels RC 1.25 3.00
298 Deividas Sirvydis RC .50 1.25
299 Alen Smailagic RC .50 1.25
300 Miye Oni RC .50 1.25

2019-20 Panini Prizm Prizms Blue

*BLUE: 4X TO 10X BASIC
*BLUE RC: 4X TO 10X BASIC RC
STATED PRINT RUN 199 SER.#'d SETS
8 Kobe Bryant 75.00 200.00
248 Zion Williamson 300.00 600.00
249 Ja Morant 500.00 1,000.00

2019-20 Panini Prizm Prizms Blue Ice

*BLUE ICE: 5X TO 12X BASIC
*BLUE ICE RC: 5X TO 12X BASIC RC
STATED PRINT RUN 99 SER.#'d SETS
8 Kobe Bryant 100.00 250.00
248 Zion Williamson 400.00 800.00
249 Ja Morant 600.00 1,200.00

2019-20 Panini Prizm Prizms Choice Blue Yellow and Green

*BYG: 2.5X TO 6X BASIC RC
8 Kobe Bryant 75.00 200.00
248 Zion Williamson 40.00 100.00
249 Ja Morant 100.00 250.00

2019-20 Panini Prizm Prizms Choice Red

*CH RED: 5X TO 12X BASIC
*CH RED RC: 5X TO 12X BASIC RC
STATED PRINT RUN 88 SER.#'d SETS
8 Kobe Bryant 100.00 250.00
248 Zion Williamson 400.00 800.00
249 Ja Morant 600.00 1,200.00

2019-20 Panini Prizm Prizms Fast Break

*FB: 1.25X TO 3X BASIC
*FB RC: 1.25X TO 3X BASIC RC
8 Kobe Bryant 25.00 60.00
248 Zion Williamson 25.00 60.00
249 Ja Morant 50.00 120.00

2019-20 Panini Prizm Prizms Fast Break Blue

*BLUE: 4X TO 10X BASIC
*BLUE RC: 4X TO 10X BASIC RC
STATED PRINT RUN 175 SER.#'d SETS
8 Kobe Bryant 75.00 200.00
248 Zion Williamson 300.00 600.00
249 Ja Morant 500.00 1,000.00

2019-20 Panini Prizm Prizms Fast Break Bronze

*FB BRONZE: 10X TO 25X BASIC
*FB BRONZE RC: 10X TO 25X BASIC RC
STATED PRINT RUN 20 SER.#'d SETS
8 Kobe Bryant 200.00 500.00
98 Stephen Curry 150.00 400.00
129 LeBron James 150.00 400.00
248 Zion Williamson 600.00 1,200.00
249 Ja Morant 1,250.00 2,500.00

2019-20 Panini Prizm Prizms Fast Break Pink

*FB PINK: 6X TO 15X BASIC
*FB PINK RC: 6X TO 15X BASIC RC
STATED PRINT RUN 50 SER.#'d SETS
8 Kobe Bryant 150.00 400.00
248 Zion Williamson 500.00 1,000.00
249 Ja Morant 800.00 1,500.00

2019-20 Panini Prizm Prizms Fast Break Purple

*FB PURPLE: 5X TO 12X BASIC
*FB PURPLE RC: 5X TO 12X BASIC RC
STATED PRINT RUN 75 SER.#'d SETS
8 Kobe Bryant 100.00 250.00
248 Zion Williamson 400.00 800.00
249 Ja Morant 600.00 1,200.00

2019-20 Panini Prizm Prizms Fast Break Red

*FB RED: 4X TO 10X BASIC
*FB RED RC: 4X TO 10X BASIC RC
STATED PRINT RUN 125 SER.#'d SETS
8 Kobe Bryant 75.00 200.00
248 Zion Williamson 300.00 600.00
249 Ja Morant 500.00 1,000.00

2019-20 Panini Prizm Prizms Green

*GREEN: 1X TO 2.5X BASIC
*GREEN RC: 1X TO 2.5X BASIC RC
8 Kobe Bryant 20.00 50.00
249 Ja Morant 25.00 60.00

2019-20 Panini Prizm Prizms Green Ice

*GREEN ICE: 2X TO 5X BASIC
*GREEN ICE RC: 2X TO 5X BASIC RC
8 Kobe Bryant 125.00 300.00
248 Zion Williamson 40.00 100.00
249 Ja Morant 75.00 200.00

2019-20 Panini Prizm Prizms Green Pulsar

*GREEN PULSAR: 4X TO 10X BASIC
*GREEN PULSAR RC: 10X TO 25X BASIC RC
STATED PRINT RUN 25 SER.#'d SETS
6 Allen Iverson 25.00 60.00
7 Yao Ming 20.00 50.00
8 Kobe Bryant 600.00 1,200.00
14 Shawn Kemp 20.00 50.00
22 Ray Allen 12.00 30.00
23 Clyde Drexler 12.00 30.00
24 Grant Hill 15.00 40.00
28 Steve Nash 20.00 50.00
31 Trae Young 20.00 50.00
75 Luka Doncic 600.00 1,200.00
88 Michael Porter Jr. 150.00 400.00
98 Stephen Curry 75.00 200.00
107 James Harden 25.00 60.00
122 Shai Gilgeous-Alexander 20.00 50.00
129 LeBron James 800.00 1,500.00
149 Kawhi Leonard 20.00 50.00
152 Giannis Antetokounmpo 150.00 400.00
161 Karl-Anthony Towns 15.00 40.00
198 Ben Simmons 20.00 50.00
210 Kevin Durant 20.00 50.00
248 Zion Williamson 600.00 1,200.00
249 Ja Morant 1,250.00 2,500.00
250 RJ Barrett 800.00 1,600.00
251 De'Andre Hunter 800.00 1,600.00
253 Coby White 200.00 500.00
254 Jaxson Hayes 75.00 200.00
255 Rui Hachimura 300.00 800.00
258 PJ Washington Jr. 100.00 250.00
259 Tyler Herro 1,500.00 3,000.00
262 Chuma Okeke 60.00 150.00
263 Nickeil Alexander-Walker 125.00 300.00
272 Jordan Poole 1,000.00 2,000.00
273 Keldon Johnson 600.00 1,200.00
274 Kevin Porter Jr. 25.00 60.00
288 Darius Garland 500.00 1,000.00

2019-20 Panini Prizm Prizms Hyper

*HYPER: 1.5X TO 4X BASIC
*HYPER RC: 1.5X TO 4X BASIC RC
8 Kobe Bryant 15.00 40.00
248 Zion Williamson 30.00 80.00
249 Ja Morant 60.00 150.00

2019-20 Panini Prizm Prizms Mojo

*MOJO: 12X TO 30X BASIC
*MOJO RC: 12X TO 30X BASIC RC
STATED PRINT RUN 25 SER.#'d SETS
8 Kobe Bryant 300.00 600.00
98 Stephen Curry 200.00 500.00
129 LeBron James 200.00 500.00
248 Zion Williamson 800.00 1,500.00
249 Ja Morant 1,500.00 3,000.00

2019-20 Panini Prizm Prizms Orange

*ORANGE: 6X TO 15X BASIC
*ORANGE RC: 6X TO 15X BASIC RC
STATED PRINT RUN 49 SER.#'d SETS
8 Kobe Bryant 150.00 400.00
248 Zion Williamson 500.00 1,000.00
249 Ja Morant 800.00 1,500.00

2019-20 Panini Prizm Prizms Orange Ice

*ORANGE ICE: 1X TO 2.5X BASIC
*ORANGE ICE RC: 1.5X TO 4X BASIC RC
8 Kobe Bryant 40.00 100.00
248 Zion Williamson 30.00 80.00
249 Ja Morant 60.00 150.00

2019-20 Panini Prizm Prizms Pink Ice

*PINK ICE: 1.25X TO 3X BASIC
*PINK ICE RC: 1.2X TO 3X BASIC RC
8 Kobe Bryant 25.00 60.00
248 Zion Williamson 25.00 60.00
249 Ja Morant 50.00 120.00

2019-20 Panini Prizm Prizms Pink Pulsar

*PINK PULSAR: 6X TO 15X BASIC
*PINK PULSAR RC: 6X TO 15X BASIC RC
STATED PRINT RUN 42 SER.#'d SETS
8 Kobe Bryant 125.00 300.00
248 Zion Williamson 500.00 1,000.00
249 Ja Morant 800.00 1,500.00

2019-20 Panini Prizm Prizms Premium Green Shimmer

*PREM GRN SHM: 12X TO 30X BASIC
*PREM GRN SHM RC: 12X TO 30X BASE RC
STATED PRINT RUN 25 SER.#'d SETS
8 Kobe Bryant 300.00 600.00
98 Stephen Curry 200.00 500.00
129 LeBron James 200.00 500.00
248 Zion Williamson 800.00 1,500.00
249 Ja Morant 1,500.00 3,000.00

2019-20 Panini Prizm Prizms Purple

*PURPLE: 4X TO 10X BASIC
*PURPLE RC: 4X TO 10X BASIC RC
STATED PRINT RUN 75 SER.#'d SETS
8 Kobe Bryant 200.00 500.00
248 Zion Williamson 75.00 200.00
249 Ja Morant 150.00 400.00

2019-20 Panini Prizm Prizms Purple Ice

*PURPLE ICE: 2.5X TO 6X BASIC
*PURPLE ICE RC: 2.5X TO 6X BASIC RC
STATED PRINT RUN 149 SER.#'d SETS
8 Kobe Bryant 125.00 300.00
248 Zion Williamson 50.00 120.00
249 Ja Morant 100.00 250.00

2019-20 Panini Prizm Prizms Purple Pulsar

*PURPLE PULSAR: 8X TO 20X BASIC
*PURPLE PULSAR RC: 8X TO 20X BASIC RC
STATED PRINT RUN 35 SER.#'d SETS
8 Kobe Bryant 500.00 1,000.00
98 Stephen Curry 125.00 300.00
129 LeBron James 125.00 300.00
248 Zion Williamson 500.00 1,000.00
249 Ja Morant 1,000.00 2,000.00

2019-20 Panini Prizm Prizms Purple Wave

*PURPLE WAVE: 1.2X TO 3X BASIC
*PURPLE WAVE RC: 1.2X TO 3X BASIC RC
8 Kobe Bryant 60.00 150.00
248 Zion Williamson 25.00 60.00
249 Ja Morant 50.00 120.00

2019-20 Panini Prizm Prizms Red

*RED: 2.5X TO 6X BASIC
*RED RC: 2.5X TO 6X BASIC RC
STATED PRINT RUN 299 SER.#'d SETS
8 Kobe Bryant 60.00 150.00
248 Zion Williamson 100.00 250.00
249 Ja Morant 200.00 500.00

2019-20 Panini Prizm Prizms Red Ice

*RED ICE: 1.25X TO 3X BASIC
*RED ICE RC: 1.2X TO 3X BASIC RC
8 Kobe Bryant 25.00 60.00
248 Zion Williamson 25.00 60.00
249 Ja Morant 50.00 120.00

2019-20 Panini Prizm Prizms Red White and Blue

*RWB: .75X TO 2X BASIC
*RWB RC: .75X TO 2X BASIC RC
8 Kobe Bryant 12.00 30.00
249 Ja Morant 20.00 50.00

2019-20 Panini Prizm Prizms Ruby Wave

*RUBY WAVE: 1.25X TO 3X BASIC
*RUBY WAVE RC: 1.25X TO 3X BASIC RC
8 Kobe Bryant 25.00 60.00
248 Zion Williamson 25.00 60.00
249 Ja Morant 50.00 120.00

2019-20 Panini Prizm Prizms Silver

*SILVER: 1.25X TO 3X BASIC
*SILVER RC: 1.25X TO 3X BASIC RC
8 Kobe Bryant 15.00 40.00
248 Zion Williamson 30.00 80.00
249 Ja Morant 40.00 100.00

2019-20 Panini Prizm Dominance

*GREEN: .6X TO 1.5X BASIC
*SILVER: .75X TO 2X BASIC
1 Andre Drummond .40 1.00
2 Anthony Davis 1.25 3.00
3 Ben Simmons .50 1.25
4 Blake Griffin .50 1.25
5 Bradley Beal .60 1.50
6 Damian Lillard 1.25 3.00
7 De'Aaron Fox .75 2.00
8 Devin Booker .12 .30
9 Donovan Mitchell 1.00 2.50
10 Giannis Antetokounmpo 2.50 6.00
11 Jamal Murray .75 2.00
12 James Harden 1.00 2.50
13 Jayson Tatum 2.00 5.00
14 Joel Embiid 1.00 2.50
15 Karl-Anthony Towns .75 2.00
16 Kawhi Leonard 1.25 3.00
17 Klay Thompson 1.25 3.00
18 Kyle Kuzma .60 1.50
19 Kyrie Irving 1.00 2.50
20 Luka Doncic 3.00 8.00
21 Nikola Jokic 2.50 6.00
22 Paul George .75 2.00
23 Russell Westbrook .75 2.00
24 Stephen Curry 4.00 10.00
25 Trae Young 1.25 3.00

2019-20 Panini Prizm Emergent

*GREEN: .75X TO 2X BASIC
*SILVER: 1.25X TO 3X BASIC
1 Coby White 1.25 3.00
2 Nassir Little .60 1.50
3 Cam Reddish .60 1.50
4 Jordan Poole 1.50 4.00
5 Tyler Herro 2.00 5.00
6 Chuma Okeke .60 1.50
7 Zion Williamson 3.00 8.00
8 Luka Samanic .50 1.25
9 De'Andre Hunter 1.50 4.00
10 Grant Williams .60 1.50
11 Jaxson Hayes .60 1.50
12 Dylan Windler .50 1.25
13 Cameron Johnson 1.00 2.50
14 Keldon Johnson 1.25 3.00
15 Romeo Langford .40 1.00
16 Nickeil Alexander-Walker .60 1.50
17 Ja Morant 4.00 10.00
18 Matisse Thybulle .75 2.00
19 Darius Garland 1.50 4.00
20 Darius Bazley .40 1.00
21 Rui Hachimura 1.50 4.00
22 Mfiondu Kabengele .50 1.25
23 PJ Washington Jr. 1.25 3.00
24 Kevin Porter Jr. .75 2.00
25 Sekou Doumbouya .40 1.00
26 Goga Bitadze .60 1.50
27 RJ Barrett 1.50 4.00
28 Brandon Clarke .75 2.00
29 Jarrett Culver .40 1.00
30 Ty Jerome .75 2.00

2019-20 Panini Prizm Far Out!

1 Stephen Curry 4.00 10.00
2 LeBron James 4.00 10.00
3 James Harden 1.00 2.50
4 Russell Westbrook .75 2.00
5 Kevin Durant 1.50 4.00
6 Larry Bird 2.00 5.00
7 Anthony Davis 1.25 3.00
8 Magic Johnson 1.50 4.00
9 Giannis Antetokounmpo 2.50 6.00
10 Julius Erving 1.25 3.00
11 Jimmy Butler 1.00 2.50
12 Shaquille O'Neal 2.00 5.00
13 Kawhi Leonard 1.25 3.00
14 Dirk Nowitzki 1.25 3.00
15 Damian Lillard 1.25 3.00
16 Charles Barkley 1.00 2.50
17 Kyrie Irving 1.00 2.50
18 Allen Iverson 1.25 3.00
19 Klay Thompson 1.25 3.00
20 Khris Middleton .50 1.25
21 Luka Doncic 3.00 8.00
22 Jayson Tatum 2.00 5.00
23 Lauri Markkanen .60 1.50
24 Zion Williamson 2.50 6.00
25 RJ Barrett 1.25 3.00

2019-20 Panini Prizm Far Out! Fast Break

*FAST BREAK: .6X TO 1.5X BASIC

2019-20 Panini Prizm Far Out! Prizms Hyper

*HYPER: .5X TO 1.2X BASIC

2019-20 Panini Prizm Far Out! Prizms Mojo

*MOJO: 6X TO 15X BASIC
STATED PRINT RUN 25 SER.#'d SETS
1 Stephen Curry 60.00 150.00
2 LeBron James 60.00 150.00
9 Giannis Antetokounmpo 40.00 100.00
13 Kawhi Leonard 20.00 50.00
18 Allen Iverson 20.00 50.00
21 Luka Doncic 50.00 120.00
24 Zion Williamson 40.00 100.00

2019-20 Panini Prizm Far Out! Prizms Silver

*SILVER: .6X TO 1.5X BASIC

2019-20 Panini Prizm Fast Break Autographs

EXCHANGE DEADLINE 6/4/2021
1 Karl Malone 20.00 50.00
2 Tyus Jones 2.50 6.00
3 Grant Hill 12.00 30.00
4 Jamal Mashburn 4.00 10.00
5 Nikola Jokic EXCH 125.00 300.00
6 Quinn Cook 3.00 8.00
7 Elfrid Payton 2.50 6.00
8 Montrezl Harrell 3.00 8.00
9 Charles Barkley EXCH 50.00 120.00
10 John Starks 4.00 10.00
11 Damian Lillard 30.00 80.00
12 Aron Baynes 2.50 6.00
13 Paul Pierce 15.00 40.00
14 Justin Holiday 2.50 6.00
15 Zach LaVine 10.00 25.00
16 Tariq Abdul-Wahad 2.50 6.00
17 Latrell Sprewell 5.00 12.00
18 J.J. Barea 3.00 8.00
19 Kobe Bryant EXCH 1,000.00 2,000.00
20 Nate McMillan 3.00 8.00
21 John Stockton 10.00 25.00
22 Caron Butler 3.00 8.00
23 Markelle Fultz 8.00 20.00
24 Kenny Anderson 3.00 8.00
25 Harrison Barnes 3.00 8.00
26 Xavier McDaniel 3.00 8.00
27 Michael Kidd-Gilchrist 2.50 6.00
28 Mario Hezonja 2.50 6.00
29 Allen Iverson 30.00 80.00
30 Tom Chambers 4.00 10.00
31 Oscar Robertson 20.00 50.00
32 Dennis Scott EXCH 2.50 6.00
33 Vince Carter 15.00 40.00
34 Bob Dandridge 2.50 6.00
35 Danilo Gallinari 3.00 8.00
36 Ricky Davis 3.00 8.00
37 Pascal Siakam 8.00 20.00
38 Thaddeus Young 2.50 6.00
39 Dwyane Wade 20.00 50.00
40 Cedric Maxwell 3.00 8.00
41 Magic Johnson 25.00 60.00
42 Dino Radja 2.50 6.00
43 Trae Young 100.00 250.00
44 Mark Price 4.00 10.00
45 Julius Randle 5.00 12.00
46 Keita Bates-Diop 2.50 6.00
47 Cam Reynolds 2.50 6.00
48 Adrian Dantley 4.00 10.00
49 Anthony Davis EXCH 25.00 60.00
50 Noah Vonleh 2.50 6.00
51 Joe Harris 3.00 8.00
52 Fat Lever 3.00 8.00
53 James Worthy 10.00 25.00
54 Mychal Thompson 2.50 6.00
55 Wendell Carter Jr. 4.00 10.00
56 Isaac Bonga 3.00 8.00
57 Danny Green 3.00 8.00
58 Dan Majerle 3.00 8.00
59 Kareem Abdul-Jabbar 30.00 80.00
60 Robert Covington 2.50 6.00

2019-20 Panini Prizm Fast Break Rookie Autographs

1 Jarrett Culver 2.50 6.00
2 Isaiah Roby 5.00 12.00

Card	Low	High
3 Chuma Okeke	8.00	20.00
4 Cameron Johnson	6.00	15.00
5 Ignas Brazdeikis	3.00	8.00
6 Goga Bitadze	4.00	10.00
7 Brandon Clarke	12.00	30.00
8 Admiral Schofield	3.00	8.00
FR-DAH De'Andre Hunter	12.00	30.00
10 Coby White	20.00	50.00
11 Keldon Johnson	5.00	12.00
12 Jaylen Nowell	3.00	8.00
13 Quinndary Weatherspoon	2.50	6.00
14 Nickeil Alexander-Walker	4.00	10.00
15 Zion Williamson	600.00	1,200.00
16 Ty Jerome	5.00	12.00
17 Luka Samanic	3.00	8.00
18 Kyle Guy	15.00	40.00
19 Rui Hachimura	40.00	100.00
20 RJ Barrett	40.00	100.00
21 Bruno Fernando	3.00	8.00
22 Bol Bol	8.00	20.00
23 Dylan Windler	3.00	8.00
24 Cody Martin	4.00	10.00
25 Jaxson Hayes	10.00	25.00
26 Ja Morant	200.00	500.00
27 Carsen Edwards	3.00	8.00
28 Cam Reddish	4.00	10.00
29 Grant Williams	4.00	10.00
30 Eric Paschall	3.00	8.00
31 Mfiondu Kabengele	3.00	8.00
32 KZ Okpala	3.00	8.00
33 Sekou Doumbouya	2.50	6.00
34 Romeo Langford	2.50	6.00
35 Kevin Porter Jr.	5.00	12.00
36 Jordan Poole	5.00	12.00
37 PJ Washington Jr.	8.00	20.00
38 Nassir Little	5.00	12.00
39 Tyler Herro	30.00	80.00
40 Tremont Waters	4.00	10.00

2019-20 Panini Prizm Fearless

*HYPER: .5X TO 1.2X BASIC
*FAST BREAK: .6X TO 1.5X BASIC
*SILVER: .6X TO 1.5X BASIC

Card	Low	High
1 Kyrie Irving	1.00	2.50
2 Allen Iverson	1.25	3.00
3 LeBron James	4.00	10.00
4 Russell Westbrook	.75	2.00
5 James Harden	1.00	2.50
6 Steve Nash	1.00	2.50
7 Giannis Antetokounmpo	2.50	6.00
8 John Starks	.50	1.25
9 Steve Francis	.50	1.25
10 Vince Carter	1.00	2.50
11 Magic Johnson	1.50	4.00
12 Kobe Bryant	4.00	10.00
13 Tracy McGrady	.75	2.00
14 Kevin Garnett	1.25	3.00
15 Dominique Wilkins	.75	2.00
16 Clyde Drexler	.75	2.00
17 Julius Erving	1.25	3.00
18 Shawn Kemp	.75	2.00
19 Shaquille O'Neal	2.00	5.00
20 Derrick Rose	1.00	2.50

2019-20 Panini Prizm Fearless Prizms Mojo

*MOJO: 6X TO 15X BASIC
STATED PRINT RUN 25 SER.#'d SETS

2019-20 Panini Prizm Fireworks

Card	Low	High
1 Kevin Durant	1.50	4.00
2 LeBron James	4.00	10.00
3 Stephen Curry	4.00	10.00
4 Giannis Antetokounmpo	2.50	6.00
5 James Harden	1.00	2.50
6 Russell Westbrook	.75	2.00
7 Anthony Davis	1.25	3.00
8 Kawhi Leonard	1.25	3.00
9 Kyrie Irving	1.00	2.50
10 Paul George	.75	2.00
11 Damian Lillard	1.25	3.00
12 Klay Thompson	1.25	3.00
13 Chris Paul	1.00	2.50
14 Jimmy Butler	1.00	2.50
15 Joel Embiid	1.00	2.50
16 John Wall	.60	1.50
17 Ben Simmons	.50	1.25
18 Nikola Jokic	2.50	6.00
19 Kyle Lowry	.50	1.25
20 Kristaps Porzingis	.60	1.50
21 Karl-Anthony Towns	.75	2.00
22 Luka Doncic	3.00	8.00
23 Donovan Mitchell	1.00	2.50
24 Devin Booker	.12	.30
25 Trae Young	1.25	3.00
26 Zion Williamson	2.50	6.00
27 RJ Barrett	1.25	3.00
28 Ja Morant	3.00	8.00
29 Rui Hachimura	1.25	3.00
30 Jarrett Culver	.30	.75

2019-20 Panini Prizm Fireworks Fast Break

*FAST BREAK: .75X TO 2X BASIC

2019-20 Panini Prizm Fireworks Prizms Hyper

*HYPER: .75X TO 2X BASIC

2019-20 Panini Prizm Fireworks Prizms Mojo

*MOJO: 4X TO 10X BASIC
STATED PRINT RUN 25 SER.#'d SETS

2019-20 Panini Prizm Fireworks Prizms Silver

*SILVER: .75X TO 2X BASIC

2019-20 Panini Prizm Get Hyped!

*GREEN: .5X TO 1.2X BASIC
*SILVER: .6X TO 1.5X BASIC

Card	Low	High
1 Karl-Anthony Towns	.75	2.00
2 LeBron James	4.00	10.00
3 Giannis Antetokounmpo	2.50	6.00
4 Stephen Curry	4.00	10.00
5 James Harden	1.00	2.50
6 Luka Doncic	3.00	8.00
7 Devin Booker	.12	.30
8 Damian Lillard	1.25	3.00
9 Ben Simmons	.50	1.25
10 Donovan Mitchell	1.00	2.50

2019-20 Panini Prizm Instant Impact

Card	Low	High
1 Tyler Herro	1.50	4.00
2 Zion Williamson	2.50	6.00
3 Chuma Okeke	.50	1.25
4 De'Andre Hunter	1.25	3.00
5 Luka Samanic	.40	1.00
6 Coby White	1.00	2.50
7 Grant Williams	.50	1.25
8 Rui Hachimura	1.25	3.00
9 Ty Jerome	.60	1.50
10 Cameron Johnson	.75	2.00
11 Romeo Langford	.30	.75
12 Ja Morant	3.00	8.00
13 Nickeil Alexander-Walker	.50	1.25
14 Darius Garland	1.25	3.00
15 Matisse Thybulle	.60	1.50
16 Jaxson Hayes	.50	1.25
17 Darius Bazley	.30	.75
18 Cam Reddish	.50	1.25
19 Nassir Little	.50	1.25
20 PJ Washington Jr.	1.00	2.50
21 Sekou Doumbouya	.30	.75
22 RJ Barrett	1.25	3.00
23 Goga Bitadze	.50	1.25
24 Jarrett Culver	.30	.75
25 Brandon Clarke	.60	1.50

2019-20 Panini Prizm Instant Impact Prims Green

*GREEN: .6X TO 1.5X BASIC

2019-20 Panini Prizm Instant Impact Prizms Silver

*SILVER: .6X TO 1.5X BASIC

Card	Low	High
2 Zion Williamson	5.00	12.00
12 Ja Morant	6.00	15.00

2019-20 Panini Prizm Luck of the Lottery

*MOJO/25: 15X TO 40X BASIC

Card	Low	High
1 Zion Williamson	8.00	20.00
2 Ja Morant	4.00	10.00
3 RJ Barrett	1.50	4.00
4 De'Andre Hunter	1.50	4.00
5 Darius Garland	1.50	4.00
6 Jarrett Culver	.40	1.00
7 Coby White	1.25	3.00
8 Jaxson Hayes	.60	1.50
9 Rui Hachimura	1.50	4.00
10 Cam Reddish	.60	1.50
11 Cameron Johnson	1.00	2.50
12 PJ Washington Jr.	1.25	3.00
13 Tyler Herro	8.00	20.00
14 Romeo Langford	.40	1.00
15 Lottery Group Photo	3.00	8.00

2019-20 Panini Prizm Luck of the Lottery Fast Break

*FAST BREAK: .75X TO 2X BASIC

Card	Low	High
1 Zion Williamson	25.00	60.00
13 Tyler Herro	20.00	50.00

2019-20 Panini Prizm Luck of the Lottery Prizms Hyper

*HYPER: .6X TO 1.5X BASIC

Card	Low	High
1 Zion Williamson	20.00	50.00
13 Tyler Herro	20.00	50.00

2019-20 Panini Prizm Luck of the Lottery Prizms Silver

*SILVER: .75X TO 2X BASIC

Card	Low	High
1 Zion Williamson	25.00	60.00
13 Tyler Herro	20.00	50.00

2019-20 Panini Prizm NBA Finalists

*GREEN: .6X TO 1.5X BASIC
*SILVER: .75X TO 2X BASIC

Card	Low	High
1 Kawhi Leonard	1.25	3.00
2 Kevin Durant	1.50	4.00
3 LeBron James	4.00	10.00
4 Kareem Abdul-Jabbar	1.50	4.00
5 Tim Duncan	1.25	3.00
6 Stephen Curry	4.00	10.00
7 Magic Johnson	1.50	4.00
8 Larry Bird	2.00	5.00
9 Kobe Bryant	4.00	10.00
10 Hakeem Olajuwon	1.00	2.50

2019-20 Panini Prizm Penmanship

EXCHANGE DEADLINE 6/4/2021

Card	Low	High
1 Aron Baynes	2.50	6.00
2 Jakob Poeltl	2.50	6.00
3 Mark Jackson	3.00	8.00
4 Quinn Buckner	2.50	6.00
5 Luke Walton	3.00	8.00
6 Seth Curry	3.00	8.00
8 Kurt Thomas	2.50	6.00
9 Kevin McHale	8.00	20.00
10 Wally Szczerbiak	3.00	8.00
12 Cam Reynolds	2.50	6.00
13 Otto Porter Jr.	2.50	6.00
14 Rick Mahorn	3.00	8.00
15 Terrence Ross	4.00	10.00
16 Cedi Osman	3.00	8.00
18 Luc Longley	3.00	8.00
19 Tony Parker	5.00	12.00
20 Antonio Daniels	2.50	6.00
21 Derek Fisher	4.00	10.00
22 Kelly Tripucka	3.00	8.00
23 World B. Free	3.00	8.00
24 Stromile Swift	2.50	6.00
25 A.C. Green	4.00	10.00
27 Jerry West	20.00	50.00
28 Micheal Ray Richardson	4.00	10.00
PM-DAF De'Aaron Fox	30.00	80.00
30 Bruce Bowen	4.00	10.00
31 Nikola Vucevic	3.00	8.00
32 Kyle O'Quinn	2.50	6.00
33 Channing Frye	2.50	6.00
34 Will Perdue	2.50	6.00
35 Bob McAdoo	5.00	12.00
36 Rik Smits	3.00	8.00
37 Hakeem Olajuwon	30.00	80.00
38 Quentin Richardson	2.50	6.00
39 James Worthy	10.00	25.00
40 Darius Miles	4.00	10.00
41 Danny Manning	3.00	8.00
42 M.L. Carr	4.00	10.00
43 Mo Bamba	3.00	8.00
44 Devonte' Graham	8.00	20.00
45 Ivica Zubac	3.00	8.00
46 Dan Issel	5.00	12.00
48 Reggie Bullock	2.50	6.00
49 DeAndre Jordan	3.00	8.00
50 Dewayne Dedmon	2.50	6.00
51 Jason Terry	3.00	8.00
52 Mike Scott	2.50	6.00
55 Kurt Rambis	3.00	8.00
56 Keith Van Horn	3.00	8.00
57 Josh Jackson	2.50	6.00
58 Shawn Bradley	2.50	6.00
59 Dennis Rodman	40.00	100.00
60 Eddie Jones	5.00	12.00

2019-20 Panini Prizm Penmanship Prizms Orange Ice

*ORANGE ICE: 5X TO 1.2X BASIC
EXCHANGE DEADLINE 6/4/2021

Card	Low	High
11 Steve Kerr	8.00	20.00

2019-20 Panini Prizm Penmanship Prizms Silver

*SILVER: 5X TO 1.2X BASIC
EXCHANGE DEADLINE 6/4/2021

Card	Low	High
11 Steve Kerr	8.00	20.00

2019-20 Panini Prizm Rookie Penmanship

*ORANGE ICE: .6X TO 1.5X BASIC
*SILVER: .6X TO 1.5X BASIC

Card	Low	High
1 Brandon Clarke	5.00	12.00
2 Admiral Schofield	3.00	8.00
3 Garrison Mathews	4.00	10.00
4 Jared Harper	3.00	8.00
5 Jarrett Culver	2.50	6.00
6 Isaiah Roby	3.00	8.00
7 Louis King	3.00	8.00
8 Cameron Johnson	6.00	15.00
9 Jalen Lecque	2.50	6.00
10 Goga Bitadze	4.00	10.00
11 Luka Samanic	3.00	8.00
12 Kyle Guy	3.00	8.00
13 Josh Reaves	2.50	6.00
14 RJ Barrett	10.00	25.00
15 Keldon Johnson	8.00	20.00
16 Jaylen Nowell	3.00	8.00
17 Quinndary Weatherspoon	2.50	6.00
18 Nickeil Alexander-Walker	4.00	10.00
19 Zion Williamson	150.00	400.00
20 Ty Jerome	5.00	12.00
21 Carsen Edwards	3.00	8.00
22 Cam Reddish	4.00	10.00
23 Grant Williams	4.00	10.00
24 Darius Bazley	2.50	6.00
25 Bruno Fernando	3.00	8.00
26 Justin Wright-Foreman	2.50	6.00
27 Dylan Windler	2.50	6.00
28 Cody Martin	4.00	10.00
29 Jaxson Hayes	4.00	10.00
30 Ja Morant	150.00	400.00
31 PJ Washington Jr.	8.00	20.00
32 Nassir Little	4.00	10.00
33 Tyler Herro	20.00	50.00
34 Max Strus	5.00	12.00
35 Mfiondu Kabengele	3.00	8.00
36 Matisse Thybulle	5.00	12.00
37 Ky Bowman	3.00	8.00
38 Jarrell Brantley	2.50	6.00
39 Kevin Porter Jr.	5.00	12.00
40 Brian Bowen II	2.50	6.00

2019-20 Panini Prizm Rookie Signatures

*BLUE SHIMMER: .6X TO 1.5X BASIC
*CHOICE: .6X TO 1.5X BASIC
*SILVER: .6X TO 1.5X BASIC
*GREEN SHIMMER/25: .75X TO 2X BASIC
*MOJO/25: .75X TO 2X BASIC

Card	Low	High
1 Admiral Schofield	4.00	10.00
2 Kyle Guy	4.00	10.00
3 Cam Reddish	5.00	12.00
4 Nassir Little	5.00	12.00
5 Coby White	10.00	25.00
6 RJ Barrett	12.00	30.00
7 Eric Paschall	4.00	10.00
8 Tremont Waters	4.00	10.00
9 Isaiah Roby	4.00	10.00
10 Jaylen Nowell	4.00	10.00
11 Bol Bol	8.00	20.00
12 KZ Okpala	4.00	10.00
13 Cameron Johnson	8.00	20.00
14 Nickeil Alexander-Walker	5.00	12.00
15 Cody Martin	5.00	12.00
16 Romeo Langford	3.00	8.00
17 Goga Bitadze	5.00	12.00
18 Ty Jerome	6.00	15.00
19 Ja Morant	150.00	400.00
20 Jordan Poole	12.00	30.00
21 Brandon Clarke	6.00	15.00
22 Luka Samanic	4.00	10.00
23 Carsen Edwards	4.00	10.00
24 PJ Washington Jr.	10.00	25.00
25 De'Andre Hunter	12.00	30.00
26 Rui Hachimura	12.00	30.00
27 Grant Williams	5.00	12.00
28 Tyler Herro	20.00	50.00
29 Jarrett Culver	3.00	8.00
30 Keldon Johnson	10.00	25.00
31 Bruno Fernando	4.00	10.00
32 Mfiondu Kabengele	4.00	10.00
33 Chuma Okeke	5.00	12.00
34 Quinndary Weatherspoon	3.00	8.00
35 Dylan Windler	4.00	10.00
36 Sekou Doumbouya	3.00	8.00
37 Ignas Brazdeikis	4.00	10.00
38 Zion Williamson	150.00	400.00
39 Jaxson Hayes	5.00	12.00
40 Kevin Porter Jr.	6.00	15.00

2019-20 Panini Prizm Rookie Variations

*FB: .6X TO 1.5X BASIC

Card	Low	High
248 Zion Williamson	20.00	50.00
249 Ja Morant	20.00	50.00
250 RJ Barrett	2.50	6.00
251 De'Andre Hunter	2.50	6.00
252 Jarrett Culver	.60	1.50
253 Coby White	2.00	5.00
254 Jaxson Hayes	1.00	2.50
255 Rui Hachimura	2.50	6.00
256 Cam Reddish	1.50	4.00
257 Cameron Johnson	1.50	4.00
258 PJ Washington Jr.	2.00	5.00
259 Tyler Herro	3.00	8.00
260 Romeo Langford	.60	1.50
288 Darius Garland	2.50	6.00

2019-20 Panini Prizm Sensational Signatures

EXCHANGE DEADLINE 6/4/2021
*BLUE SHIMMER: 6X TO 1.5X BASIC
*CHOICE: .6X TO 1.5X BASIC
*SILVER: .6X TO 1.5X BASIC
*GREEN SHMR/25: .75X TO 2X BASIC
*MOJO/25: .75X TO 2X BASIC

Card	Low	High
1 Clyde Drexler	12.00	30.00
2 Grant Williams	5.00	12.00
3 Dennis Rodman	20.00	50.00
4 Isaiah Roby	4.00	10.00
5 Nerlens Noel	3.00	8.00
6 Marial Shayok	3.00	8.00
7 Cameron Johnson	8.00	20.00
8 Cam Reynolds	3.00	8.00
9 Charles Barkley EXCH	60.00	150.00
10 Devean George	4.00	10.00
12 Ty Jerome	6.00	15.00
13 Sam Jones	6.00	15.00
14 Kyle Guy	4.00	10.00
15 Willie Cauley-Stein	3.00	8.00
16 Jaylen Hoard	3.00	8.00
17 PJ Washington Jr.	10.00	25.00
19 Kobe Bryant EXCH	1,000.00	2,000.00
20 Doug Christie	4.00	10.00
21 Kevin Love	5.00	12.00
22 Dylan Windler	4.00	10.00
23 Cam Reddish	5.00	12.00
24 Luguentz Dort	12.00	30.00
25 Caris LeVert	4.00	10.00
26 Gary Clark	3.00	8.00
27 Alvan Adams	3.00	8.00
28 TJ Leaf	3.00	8.00
29 Kevin Durant EXCH	100.00	250.00
30 Jack Marin	3.00	8.00
31 Rui Hachimura	12.00	30.00
32 Eric Paschall	4.00	10.00
33 Jarrett Culver	3.00	8.00
34 Daniel Gafford	6.00	15.00
35 George McGinnis	5.00	12.00
36 Naz Reid	12.00	30.00
37 Ersan Ilyasova	3.00	8.00
38 Brandon Clarke	6.00	15.00
39 Chris Paul	40.00	100.00
40 Jared Dudley	3.00	8.00
41 Pat Riley	12.00	30.00
42 Dewan Hernandez	3.00	8.00
43 Bernard King	6.00	15.00
44 Deividas Sirvydis	3.00	8.00
45 Jaxson Hayes	5.00	12.00
46 Justin Jackson	3.00	8.00
47 Kevin Willis	3.00	8.00
48 Chuma Okeke	5.00	12.00
49 Larry Bird	75.00	200.00
50 Carsen Edwards	4.00	10.00
51 Kristaps Porzingis	20.00	50.00
52 Kevin Porter Jr.	6.00	15.00
53 Coby White	10.00	25.00
54 Jalen McDaniels	8.00	20.00
55 Carlos Boozer	4.00	10.00
56 Zach Norvell Jr.	4.00	10.00
57 Sam Cassell	4.00	10.00
58 Nickeil Alexander-Walker	5.00	12.00
59 Kevin Garnett	40.00	100.00
60 Goga Bitadze	5.00	12.00
61 Dominique Wilkins	12.00	30.00
62 KZ Okpala	4.00	10.00
63 Danny Green	4.00	10.00
64 Justin James	3.00	8.00
65 Juwan Howard	4.00	10.00
66 Alen Smailagic	3.00	8.00
67 Tyrone Wallace	3.00	8.00
68 Sekou Doumbouya	3.00	8.00
69 Ja Morant	150.00	400.00
70 Keldon Johnson	10.00	25.00
71 Mike Conley	4.00	10.00
72 Mfiondu Kabengele	4.00	10.00
73 Collin Sexton	6.00	15.00
74 Nicolas Claxton	6.00	15.00
75 Montrezl Harrell	4.00	10.00
76 Jaylen Hands	3.00	8.00
77 Tyler Herro	20.00	50.00
78 Antonio Blakeney	3.00	8.00
79 Magic Johnson	40.00	100.00
81 De'Andre Hunter	12.00	30.00
82 Cody Martin	5.00	12.00
83 Jalen Rose	4.00	10.00
84 Jaylen Nowell	4.00	10.00
85 Wesley Matthews	3.00	8.00
86 Jordan Bone	3.00	8.00
87 Nassir Little	5.00	12.00
88 Brad Davis	3.00	8.00
89 RJ Barrett	12.00	30.00
90 Admiral Schofield	4.00	10.00
91 Rick Barry	6.00	15.00
92 Miye Oni	3.00	8.00
93 Malcolm Brogdon	4.00	10.00
94 Talen Horton-Tucker	5.00	12.00
95 Bol Bol	8.00	20.00
96 Terance Mann	6.00	15.00
97 Romeo Langford	3.00	8.00
98 Dana Barros	3.00	8.00
99 David Robinson	20.00	50.00
100 Bruno Fernando	4.00	10.00

2019-20 Panini Prizm Sensational Swatches

*ORNGE ICE: .6X TO 1.5X BASE
*GRN ICE/56: 1.25X TO 3X BASE

Card	Low	High
1 Zion Williamson	12.00	30.00
2 Ja Morant	15.00	40.00
3 RJ Barrett	6.00	15.00
4 De'Andre Hunter	6.00	15.00
5 Jarrett Culver	1.50	4.00
6 Coby White	5.00	12.00
7 Jaxson Hayes	2.50	6.00
8 Rui Hachimura	6.00	15.00
9 Cam Reddish	2.50	6.00
10 Cameron Johnson	4.00	10.00
11 PJ Washington Jr.	5.00	12.00
12 Tyler Herro	8.00	20.00
13 Romeo Langford	1.50	4.00
14 Sekou Doumbouya	1.50	4.00
15 Chuma Okeke	2.50	6.00
16 Nickeil Alexander-Walker	2.50	6.00
17 Goga Bitadze	2.50	6.00
18 Luka Samanic	2.00	5.00
19 Brandon Clarke	3.00	8.00
20 Grant Williams	2.50	6.00
21 Ty Jerome	3.00	8.00
22 Nassir Little	2.50	6.00
23 Dylan Windler	2.00	5.00
24 Mfiondu Kabengele	2.00	5.00
25 Jordan Poole	6.00	15.00
26 Keldon Johnson	5.00	12.00
27 Kevin Porter Jr.	3.00	8.00
28 KZ Okpala	2.00	5.00
29 Carsen Edwards	2.00	5.00
30 Bruno Fernando	2.00	5.00
31 Cody Martin	2.50	6.00
32 Eric Paschall	2.00	5.00
33 Admiral Schofield	2.00	5.00
34 Jaylen Nowell	2.00	5.00
35 Bol Bol	4.00	10.00
36 Isaiah Roby	2.00	5.00
37 Ignas Brazdeikis	2.00	5.00
38 Quinndary Weatherspoon	1.50	4.00
39 Tremont Waters	2.00	5.00
40 Matisse Thybulle	3.00	8.00
41 Dirk Nowitzki	6.00	15.00
42 Karl-Anthony Towns	4.00	10.00
43 Andrew Wiggins	3.00	8.00
44 Kevin Love	2.50	6.00
45 Darius Bazley	1.50	4.00
46 DeAndre Jordan	2.00	5.00
47 Jarrett Allen	2.50	6.00
48 Ricky Rubio	2.00	5.00
49 Enes Kanter	1.50	4.00
50 Bradley Beal	3.00	8.00
51 Rondae Hollis-Jefferson	1.50	4.00
52 Pau Gasol	4.00	10.00
53 Tyus Jones	1.50	4.00
54 Kyrie Irving	5.00	12.00
55 Nicolas Batum	1.50	4.00
56 Rudy Gobert	3.00	8.00
57 Thaddeus Young	1.50	4.00
58 Jimmy Butler	5.00	12.00
59 John Wall	3.00	8.00
60 Eric Gordon	2.00	5.00
61 Harrison Barnes	2.00	5.00
62 Evan Turner	1.50	4.00
63 Joe Harris	2.00	5.00
64 Derrick Rose	5.00	12.00
65 Gorgui Dieng	1.50	4.00
66 Allen Crabbe	1.50	4.00
67 DeMarre Carroll	1.50	4.00
68 CJ McCollum	2.50	6.00
69 Kristaps Porzingis	3.00	8.00
70 Kevin Garnett	6.00	15.00
71 Andre Drummond	2.00	5.00
72 Victor Oladipo	2.00	5.00
73 LeBron James	40.00	100.00
74 Paul Millsap	2.00	5.00
75 Kobe Bryant	60.00	150.00
76 Anthony Davis	6.00	15.00
77 Goran Dragic	2.00	5.00
78 Nikola Vucevic	2.00	5.00
79 Kevin Durant	8.00	20.00
80 Steven Adams	2.00	5.00
81 Dwight Powell	1.50	4.00
82 Dennis Smith Jr.	1.50	4.00
83 Dario Saric	2.00	5.00
84 LaMarcus Aldridge	2.50	6.00
85 Aaron Gordon	2.50	6.00
86 Jeff Teague	1.50	4.00
87 Deandre Ayton	2.50	6.00
88 Caris LeVert	2.00	5.00
89 Hassan Whiteside	1.50	4.00
90 Otto Porter Jr.	1.50	4.00
91 Klay Thompson	6.00	15.00
92 Chris Paul	5.00	12.00
93 Stephen Curry	40.00	100.00
94 Wendell Carter Jr.	2.50	6.00
95 Dwyane Wade	5.00	12.00
96 Kyle Lowry	2.50	6.00
97 Kevin Knox II	1.50	4.00
98 Myles Turner	2.50	6.00
99 Nikola Jokic	12.00	30.00
100 James Harden	5.00	12.00

2019-20 Panini Prizm Signatures

EXCHANGE DEADLINE 6/4/2021
*CHOICE: .6X TO 1.5X BASIC
*SILVER: .6X TO 1.5X BASIC
*BLUE SHIMMER: .6X TO 1.5X BASIC
*GREEN SHIMMER/25: .75X TO 2X BASIC
*MOJO/25: .75X TO 2X BASIC

Card	Low	High
1 Lionel Hollins	3.00	8.00
2 Tyson Chandler	4.00	10.00
3 Yogi Ferrell	3.00	8.00
3 Dennis Rodman	20.00	50.00
4 Hakeem Olajuwon	20.00	50.00
4 Rudy Gay	4.00	10.00
5 Thon Maker	3.00	8.00
6 Allen Iverson	75.00	200.00
6 Charles Barkley EXCH	75.00	200.00
8 Karl-Anthony Towns	12.00	30.00
9 David Robinson	20.00	50.00
9 Derrick Jones Jr.	3.00	8.00
11 Maurice Cheeks	4.00	10.00
12 Nick Van Exel	5.00	12.00
13 Moritz Wagner	3.00	8.00
13 Patrick Ewing	75.00	200.00
14 Allonzo Trier	3.00	8.00
15 Alex English	6.00	15.00
15 Larry Johnson	12.00	30.00
16 Kobe Bryant EXCH	1,000.00	2,000.00
17 P.J. Tucker	4.00	10.00
18 Andrew Wiggins	6.00	15.00
19 Don Chaney	5.00	12.00
20 Cam Reynolds	3.00	8.00
20 Kareem Abdul-Jabbar	60.00	150.00
21 Otis Birdsong	5.00	12.00
22 Ray Allen	20.00	50.00
22 Avery Bradley	3.00	8.00
23 Clyde Drexler	12.00	30.00
23 Rodions Kurucs	5.00	12.00
24 Grant Hill	12.00	30.00
24 Enes Kanter	3.00	8.00
25 Dario Saric	4.00	10.00
25 Magic Johnson	40.00	100.00
26 Shaquille O'Neal EXCH	100.00	250.00
27 Rondae Hollis-Jefferson	3.00	8.00
28 Chris Bosh	6.00	15.00
30 Lauri Markkanen	6.00	15.00
31 Raja Bell	4.00	10.00
31 Trae Young	75.00	200.00
32 Gary Harris	4.00	10.00
32 John Collins	5.00	12.00
33 Yuta Watanabe	5.00	12.00
34 Al-Farouq Aminu	3.00	8.00
35 Kenny Walker	4.00	10.00
36 Magic Johnson	40.00	100.00
36 JJ Redick	5.00	12.00
37 Dewayne Dedmon	3.00	8.00
37 Antoine Walker	4.00	10.00
38 Alex Len	3.00	8.00
38 Jason Kidd	10.00	25.00
39 James Ennis	3.00	8.00
39 Jayson Tatum EXCH	75.00	200.00
40 Alex Len	3.00	8.00
41 Marcus Smart	4.00	10.00
41 Royce O'Neale	3.00	8.00
42 Lenny Wilkens	6.00	15.00
43 Terry Rozier	4.00	10.00
43 Robert Williams III	3.00	8.00
44 Terrence Ross	5.00	12.00
44 Josh Hart	4.00	10.00
45 Rudy Gobert	6.00	15.00
45 Tobias Harris	4.00	10.00
47 Arvydas Sabonis	5.00	12.00
47 Jarrett Allen	5.00	12.00
48 Spencer Dinwiddie	4.00	10.00
48 Ray Allen	20.00	50.00
49 Justin Jackson	3.00	8.00
49 Joe Harris	4.00	10.00
50 Bob Lanier	6.00	15.00
51 Tyronn Lue	3.00	8.00
51 Zhaire Smith	3.00	8.00
52 Rodions Kurucs	5.00	12.00
52 Myles Turner	5.00	12.00
53 Mike Scott	3.00	8.00
53 Kenrich Williams	4.00	10.00
54 Michael Cooper	5.00	12.00
55 Toni Kukoc	6.00	15.00
56 Michael Kidd-Gilchrist	3.00	8.00
58 Elgin Baylor	20.00	50.00
59 Kiki Vandeweghe	4.00	10.00
59 Dwayne Bacon	3.00	8.00
60 Danny Green	4.00	10.00
60 Jaren Jackson Jr.	12.00	30.00
61 Zach LaVine	12.00	30.00
62 Kris Dunn	3.00	8.00
63 Lauri Markkanen	6.00	15.00
64 Otto Porter Jr.	3.00	8.00
65 Wendell Carter Jr.	5.00	12.00
66 Denzel Valentine	3.00	8.00
69 Jordan Clarkson	5.00	12.00
70 Matthew Dellavedova	4.00	10.00
71 Deandre Ayton	5.00	12.00
73 Larry Nance Jr.	4.00	10.00
75 Luka Doncic	500.00	1,000.00
78 Jalen Brunson	60.00	150.00
79 Courtney Lee	3.00	8.00
81 Dwight Powell	3.00	8.00
82 DeMarre Carroll	3.00	8.00
85 Will Barton	3.00	8.00
86 Malik Beasley	4.00	10.00
87 Torrey Craig	3.00	8.00
88 Michael Porter Jr.	8.00	20.00
89 Gary Harris	4.00	10.00
90 Josh Jackson	3.00	8.00
91 Blake Griffin	5.00	12.00
93 Luke Kennard	4.00	10.00
94 Langston Galloway	3.00	8.00
95 Reggie Jackson	4.00	10.00
96 Thon Maker	3.00	8.00
99 Mikal Bridges	8.00	20.00
100 Tyler Johnson	3.00	8.00
103 DeMarcus Cousins	4.00	10.00
104 Kevon Looney	3.00	8.00
105 Quinn Cook	4.00	10.00
106 Alfonzo McKinnie	3.00	8.00
108 Kelly Oubre Jr.	4.00	10.00
111 P.J. Tucker	4.00	10.00
113 CJ McCollum	5.00	12.00
114 Victor Oladipo	4.00	10.00
115 Aaron Holiday	4.00	10.00
116 Zach Collins	3.00	8.00
117 Meyers Leonard	3.00	8.00
119 Evan Turner	3.00	8.00
120 De'Aaron Fox	20.00	50.00
123 Danilo Gallinari	4.00	10.00
124 Montrezl Harrell	4.00	10.00
126 Lou Williams	5.00	12.00
131 Bogdan Bogdanovic	5.00	12.00
132 Willie Cauley-Stein	3.00	8.00
133 LaMarcus Aldridge	5.00	12.00
135 Rudy Gay	4.00	10.00
137 Avery Bradley	3.00	8.00
141 Derrick White	5.00	12.00
142 Kyle Anderson	3.00	8.00
144 Bam Adebayo	8.00	20.00
146 Kelly Olynyk	3.00	8.00
147 Josh Richardson	3.00	8.00
154 Serge Ibaka	4.00	10.00
156 Pascal Siakam	8.00	20.00
158 Ersan Ilyasova	3.00	8.00
159 Norman Powell	4.00	10.00
160 Andrew Wiggins	6.00	15.00
162 Gorgui Dieng	3.00	8.00
163 Josh Okogie	4.00	10.00
165 Jeff Teague	3.00	8.00
166 Robert Covington	3.00	8.00
167 Ricky Rubio	4.00	10.00
168 Rudy Gobert	6.00	15.00
169 Derrick Favors	3.00	8.00
172 Julius Randle	6.00	15.00
174 E'Twaun Moore	3.00	8.00
175 Kevin Knox II	3.00	8.00
177 Frank Ntilikina	3.00	8.00
178 Mitchell Robinson	5.00	12.00
180 Allonzo Trier	3.00	8.00
183 Steven Adams	4.00	10.00
184 Hamidou Diallo	4.00	10.00
188 Terrance Ferguson	3.00	8.00
191 Mo Bamba	4.00	10.00
192 Evan Fournier	4.00	10.00
193 Markelle Fultz	4.00	10.00
194 Jonathan Isaac	5.00	12.00
195 Thomas Bryant	4.00	10.00
196 Troy Brown Jr.	3.00	8.00
197 D.J. Augustin	3.00	8.00
200 Allen Crabbe	3.00	8.00
201 Kyrie Irving EXCH	40.00	100.00
202 Al Horford	5.00	12.00
203 Taurean Prince	3.00	8.00
204 D'Angelo Russell	4.00	10.00
206 Robin Lopez	3.00	8.00
207 John Henson	3.00	8.00
208 Isaiah Thomas	4.00	10.00
213 Austin Rivers	3.00	8.00
214 Wesley Matthews	3.00	8.00
215 Domantas Sabonis	6.00	15.00
216 Myles Turner	5.00	12.00
217 Thaddeus Young	3.00	8.00
218 Bojan Bogdanovic	4.00	10.00
219 Mario Hezonja	3.00	8.00
220 Ivica Zubac	4.00	10.00
224 Kentavious Caldwell-Pope	4.00	10.00
225 JaVale McGee	4.00	10.00
226 Seth Curry	4.00	10.00
227 Jae Crowder	3.00	8.00
229 Jonas Valanciunas	4.00	10.00
230 Justise Winslow	3.00	8.00
231 Eric Bledsoe	4.00	10.00
232 Malcolm Brogdon	4.00	10.00
233 Pau Gasol	15.00	40.00
235 Khris Middleton	5.00	12.00
236 Trevor Ariza	3.00	8.00
239 Lonzo Ball	5.00	12.00
240 Josh Hart	4.00	10.00
242 Elfrid Payton	3.00	8.00
244 Mike Conley	4.00	10.00
247 Nikola Vucevic	4.00	10.00
248 Zion Williamson	150.00	400.00
249 Ja Morant	150.00	400.00
250 RJ Barrett	12.00	30.00
251 De'Andre Hunter	12.00	30.00
253 Coby White	10.00	25.00
255 Rui Hachimura	12.00	30.00
256 Cam Reddish	5.00	12.00
257 Cameron Johnson	8.00	20.00
258 PJ Washington Jr.	10.00	25.00
259 Tyler Herro	15.00	40.00
261 Sekou Doumbouya	3.00	8.00
262 Chuma Okeke	5.00	12.00
264 Goga Bitadze	5.00	12.00
266 Brandon Clarke	6.00	15.00
267 Grant Williams	5.00	12.00
268 Ty Jerome	6.00	15.00
269 Nassir Little	5.00	12.00
270 Dylan Windler	4.00	10.00
271 Mfiondu Kabengele	4.00	10.00
272 Jordan Poole	12.00	30.00
273 Keldon Johnson	10.00	25.00
274 Kevin Porter Jr.	6.00	15.00
275 KZ Okpala	4.00	10.00
276 Carsen Edwards	4.00	10.00
277 Bruno Fernando	4.00	10.00
278 Cody Martin	5.00	12.00
279 Eric Paschall	4.00	10.00
280 Admiral Schofield	4.00	10.00
282 Bol Bol	8.00	20.00
283 Isaiah Roby	4.00	10.00
284 Ignas Brazdeikis	4.00	10.00
285 Quinndary Weatherspoon	3.00	8.00
286 Tremont Waters	4.00	10.00
287 Kyle Guy	4.00	10.00
289 Darius Bazley	3.00	8.00
290 Matisse Thybulle	6.00	15.00
291 Jordan Bone	3.00	8.00
292 Nicolas Claxton	6.00	15.00
293 Jaylen Hands	3.00	8.00
294 Daniel Gafford	6.00	15.00
296 Terance Mann	6.00	15.00
297 Jalen McDaniels	8.00	20.00
298 Deividas Sirvydis	3.00	8.00
299 Alen Smailagic	3.00	8.00
300 Miye Oni	3.00	8.00

2019-20 Panini Prizm Widescreen

*HYPER: .6X TO 1.5X BASIC
*FAST BREAK: .6X TO 1.5X BASIC
*SILVER: .75X TO 2X BASIC
*MOJO/25: 6X TO 15X BASIC

Card	Low	High
1 Kobe Bryant	4.00	10.00
2 James Harden	1.00	2.50
3 Stephen Curry	4.00	10.00
4 Giannis Antetokounmpo	2.50	6.00
5 Kyrie Irving	1.00	2.50
6 Damian Lillard	1.25	3.00
7 Kawhi Leonard	1.25	3.00
8 Shaquille O'Neal	2.00	5.00
9 Russell Westbrook	.75	2.00
10 Anthony Davis	1.25	3.00

2020-21 Panini Prizm

Card	Low	High
COMMON CARD (1-250)	.25	.60
SEMISTARS	.30	.75
UNLISTED STARS	.40	1.00
COMMON RC (251-300)	.50	1.25
RC SEMIS	.60	1.50
RC UNLISTED	.75	2.00
1 LeBron James	5.00	12.00
2 Jeff Green	.25	.60
3 Coby White	.50	1.25
4 Rudy Gay	.40	1.00
5 Deandre Ayton	.40	1.00
6 Zach Collins	.30	.75
7 Torrey Craig	.30	.75
8 Robert Covington	.30	.75
9 Nikola Vucevic	.40	1.00
10 Alex Caruso	.40	1.00
11 DeAndre' Bembry	.25	.60
12 Spencer Dinwiddie	.30	.75
13 De'Aaron Fox	.60	1.50
14 Paul George	.60	1.50
15 Malik Monk	.40	1.00
16 Gary Harris	.30	.75
17 Eric Bledsoe	.30	.75
18 Kristaps Porzingis	.50	1.25
19 Allen Iverson	1.00	2.50
20 Jaxson Hayes	.30	.75
21 Tyus Jones	.30	.75
22 Josh Hart	.30	.75
23 Domantas Sabonis	.50	1.25

24 Anfernee Simons .50 1.25
25 Elfrid Payton .30 .75
26 De'Anthony Melton .30 .75
27 Bogdan Bogdanovic .40 1.00
28 John Collins .40 1.00
29 Brook Lopez .30 .75
30 Tim Duncan 1.00 2.50
31 Luguentz Dort .60 1.50
32 Luka Doncic 2.50 6.00
33 Terrence Ross .30 .75
34 Kevon Looney .30 .75
35 Robert Williams III .30 .75
36 Buddy Hield .40 1.00
37 Ish Smith .25 .60
38 De'Andre Hunter .40 1.00
39 Dwayne Bacon .25 .60
40 Ersan Ilyasova .25 .60
41 Landry Shamet .30 .75
42 Jeff Teague .25 .60
43 Doug McDermott .30 .75
44 Paul Millsap .30 .75
45 Joe Harris .30 .75
46 Cameron Johnson .50 1.25
47 Gordon Hayward .40 1.00
48 Kevin Porter Jr. .30 .75
49 Aron Baynes .25 .60
50 Donte DiVincenzo .40 1.00
51 Eric Gordon .30 .75
52 Tim Hardaway Jr. .25 .60
53 Rudy Gobert .50 1.25
54 Julius Randle .40 1.00
55 Derrick Jones Jr. .30 .75
56 John Wall .50 1.25
57 Matthew Dellavedova .30 .75
58 Sekou Doumbouya .25 .60
59 Frank Kaminsky .25 .60
60 Terry Rozier .40 1.00
61 Danilo Gallinari .30 .75
62 Blake Griffin .40 1.00
63 Dorian Finney-Smith .30 .75
64 Trae Young 1.00 2.50
65 Bismack Biyombo .25 .60
66 Patty Mills .40 1.00
67 Donovan Mitchell .75 2.00
68 Cody Zeller .25 .60
69 Clint Capela .30 .75
70 Dillon Brooks .40 1.00
71 Eric Paschall .30 .75
72 Bojan Bogdanovic .30 .75
73 Devonte' Graham .30 .75
74 Aaron Holiday .30 .75
75 Jrue Holiday .40 1.00
76 Thomas Bryant .30 .75
77 Kentavious Caldwell-Pope .30 .75
78 Malcolm Brogdon .40 1.00
79 Will Barton .25 .60
80 Danuel House Jr. .30 .75
81 Kevin Durant 1.50 4.00
82 T.J. Warren .30 .75
83 Dwight Powell .25 .60
84 J.J. Barea .30 .75
85 George Hill .30 .75
86 Michael Porter Jr. .50 1.25
87 Klay Thompson 1.00 2.50
88 Royce O'Neale .25 .60
89 Tristan Thompson .25 .60
90 Reggie Bullock .25 .60
91 Jusuf Nurkic .40 1.00
92 Khris Middleton .50 1.25
93 Chris Paul .75 2.00
94 Harrison Barnes .30 .75
95 D'Angelo Russell .40 1.00
96 Jeremy Lamb .25 .60
97 Marcus Smart .40 1.00
98 Davis Bertans .30 .75
99 Montrezl Harrell .40 1.00
100 Victor Oladipo .30 .75
101 Kris Dunn .25 .60
102 Malik Beasley .30 .75
103 Kyle Lowry .50 1.25
104 LaMarcus Aldridge .40 1.00
105 PJ Washington Jr. .40 1.00
106 Josh Jackson .25 .60
107 Kevin Huerter .30 .75
108 Nerlens Noel .25 .60
109 Anthony Davis 1.00 2.50
110 Steven Adams .40 1.00
111 Giannis Antetokounmpo 2.00 5.00
112 James Harden .75 2.00
113 Frank Ntilikina .25 .60
114 Nikola Jokic 2.00 5.00
115 Ja Morant 1.25 3.00
116 Lauri Markkanen .50 1.25
117 Vince Carter .75 2.00
118 Shai Gilgeous-Alexander 2.00 5.00
119 Jayson Tatum 1.50 4.00
120 Anfernee Hardaway 1.00 2.50
121 Daniel Theis .30 .75
122 Kemba Walker .40 1.00
123 Draymond Green .50 1.25
124 Jamal Murray .60 1.50
125 Ben Simmons .40 1.00
126 Jaren Jackson Jr. .60 1.50
127 Troy Brown Jr. .30 .75
128 Dennis Schroder .40 1.00
129 Tony Snell .25 .60
130 DeAndre Jordan .30 .75
131 Shake Milton .30 .75
132 Andrew Wiggins .50 1.25
133 Derrick Favors .30 .75
134 Pascal Siakam .60 1.50
135 Jordan Clarkson .40 1.00
136 Josh Richardson .30 .75
137 Jimmy Butler .75 2.00
138 Bam Adebayo .60 1.50
139 Kyrie Irving .75 2.00
140 Patrick Beverley .25 .60
141 Joel Embiid 1.00 2.50
142 Lonnie Walker IV .40 1.00
143 Jerami Grant .40 1.00
144 Jarrett Allen .40 1.00
145 Brandon Ingram .50 1.25
146 Jae Crowder .25 .60
147 Jordan Poole .60 1.50
148 Aaron Gordon .40 1.00
149 Danny Green .30 .75
150 Taurean Prince .25 .60
151 Lou Williams .40 1.00
152 Al Horford .40 1.00
153 Dejounte Murray .40 1.00
154 Carmelo Anthony .60 1.50
155 Josh Okogie .30 .75
156 Otto Porter Jr. .25 .60
157 Norman Powell .30 .75
158 Hassan Whiteside .30 .75
159 Stephen Curry 3.00 8.00
160 Furkan Korkmaz .30 .75
161 D.J. Augustin .25 .60
162 Caris LeVert .40 1.00
163 Kevin Knox II .25 .60
164 Darius Bazley .25 .60
165 Thaddeus Young .25 .60
166 Dennis Rodman 1.00 2.50
167 Karl-Anthony Towns .60 1.50
168 Wesley Matthews .25 .60
169 Cam Reddish .50 1.25
170 Mitchell Robinson .40 1.00
171 Mo Bamba .40 1.00
172 Marvin Bagley III .30 .75
173 Damian Lillard 1.00 2.50
174 Derrick White .40 1.00
175 Dwight Howard .50 1.25
176 Emmanuel Mudiay .25 .60
177 Marquese Chriss .25 .60
178 Miles Bridges .40 1.00
179 Goran Dragic .40 1.00
180 Dirk Nowitzki 1.00 2.50
181 Duncan Robinson .40 1.00
182 Austin Rivers .30 .75
183 Tomas Satoransky .25 .60
184 JJ Redick .40 1.00
185 Zion Williamson 1.25 3.00
186 Maxi Kleber .30 .75
187 Kevin Garnett 1.00 2.50
188 Jonas Valanciunas .30 .75
189 Jaylen Brown .60 1.50
190 Nemanja Bjelica .25 .60
191 Larry Nance Jr. .30 .75
192 Juancho Hernangomez .40 1.00
193 Shabazz Napier .25 .60
194 Seth Curry .40 1.00
195 Dwyane Wade .75 2.00
196 Ivica Zubac .40 1.00
197 Terence Davis II .40 1.00
198 Mike Conley .30 .75
199 Marcus Morris Sr. .25 .60
200 Matisse Thybulle .30 .75
201 Luke Kennard .30 .75
202 Tobias Harris .40 1.00
203 Rodney Hood .25 .60
204 Mikal Bridges .50 1.25
205 DeMarre Carroll .25 .60
206 Marc Gasol .40 1.00
207 Shaquille O'Neal 1.50 4.00
208 Kelly Oubre Jr. .40 1.00
209 Kawhi Leonard 1.00 2.50
210 DeMar DeRozan .50 1.25
211 OG Anunoby .40 1.00
212 Enes Kanter .30 .75
213 Kendrick Nunn .30 .75
214 Devin Booker 1.00 2.50
215 Fred VanVleet .60 1.50
216 Evan Fournier .30 .75
217 Christian Wood .30 .75
218 Tyler Herro .75 2.00
219 Magic Johnson 1.50 4.00
220 Jabari Parker .25 .60
221 Bobby Portis .40 1.00
222 Andre Drummond .40 1.00
223 Wendell Carter Jr. .30 .75
224 Lonzo Ball .50 1.25
225 Collin Sexton .40 1.00
226 Darius Garland .60 1.50
227 Langston Galloway .25 .60
228 Brandon Clarke .40 1.00
229 Markelle Fultz .30 .75
230 Bradley Beal .50 1.25
231 Derrick Rose .60 1.50
232 Bryn Forbes .30 .75
233 Harry Giles III .25 .60
234 Zach LaVine .60 1.50
235 Ricky Rubio .40 1.00
236 CJ McCollum .40 1.00
237 Avery Bradley .25 .60
238 Jarrett Culver .25 .60
239 Bruce Brown .30 .75
240 Myles Turner .40 1.00
241 RJ Barrett .60 1.50
242 Kevin Love .40 1.00
243 Joe Ingles .30 .75
244 Kyle Kuzma .50 1.25
245 Jake Layman .25 .60
246 Serge Ibaka .30 .75
247 James Johnson .25 .60
248 Russell Westbrook .75 2.00
249 Rui Hachimura .50 1.25
250 Jonathan Isaac .40 1.00
251 Tyler Bey RC .60 1.50
252 Devin Vassell RC 2.00 5.00
253 Nick Richards RC .75 2.00
254 Isaiah Stewart RC 1.25 3.00
255 Skylar Mays RC .60 1.50
256 Tyrese Maxey RC 5.00 12.00
257 Payton Pritchard RC 2.00 5.00
258 Anthony Edwards RC 15.00 40.00
259 Tyrell Terry RC .50 1.25
260 Onyeka Okongwu RC 1.25 3.00
261 Saben Lee RC .60 1.50
262 Tyrese Haliburton RC 5.00 12.00
263 Jahmi'us Ramsey RC .60 1.50
264 Aleksej Pokusevski RC .75 2.00
265 Kenyon Martin Jr. RC 1.00 2.50
266 Zeke Nnaji RC .75 2.00
267 Udoka Azubuike RC .75 2.00
268 James Wiseman RC 1.25 3.00
269 Vernon Carey Jr. RC .60 1.50
270 Killian Hayes RC .60 1.50
271 Elijah Hughes RC .60 1.50
272 Kira Lewis Jr. RC .60 1.50
273 Jordan Nwora RC .75 2.00
274 Josh Green RC 1.25 3.00
275 Cassius Winston RC .60 1.50
276 Caleb Martin RC 1.25 3.00
277 Jaden McDaniels RC 2.00 5.00
278 LaMelo Ball RC 6.00 15.00
279 Daniel Oturu RC .60 1.50
280 Obi Toppin RC 1.25 3.00
281 Robert Woodard II RC .60 1.50
282 Aaron Nesmith RC 1.25 3.00
283 CJ Elleby RC .60 1.50
284 Saddiq Bey RC 1.25 3.00
285 Cassius Stanley RC .60 1.50
286 RJ Hampton RC .60 1.50
287 Malachi Flynn RC .60 1.50
288 Patrick Williams RC 1.50 4.00
289 Theo Maledon RC .60 1.50
290 Deni Avdija RC 1.50 4.00
291 Tre Jones RC 1.00 2.50
292 Cole Anthony RC 1.50 4.00
293 Nico Mannion RC .60 1.50
294 Precious Achiuwa RC 1.25 3.00
295 Grant Riller RC .60 1.50
296 Immanuel Quickley RC 1.50 4.00
297 Desmond Bane RC 2.00 5.00
299 Xavier Tillman RC .75 2.00
300 Jalen Smith RC 1.25 3.00

2020-21 Panini Prizm Prizms Blue

*BLUE: 5X TO 12X BASIC
*BLUE RC: 5X TO 12X BASIC RC
STATED PRINT RUN 199 SER.#'d SETS
1 LeBron James 400.00 800.00
159 Stephen Curry 60.00 150.00
256 Tyrese Maxey 200.00 500.00
258 Anthony Edwards 1,250.00 2,500.00
262 Tyrese Haliburton 300.00 600.00
278 LaMelo Ball 150.00 400.00

2020-21 Panini Prizm Prizms Blue Ice

*BLUE ICE: 5X TO 12X BASIC
*BLUE ICE RC: 5X TO 12X BASIC RC
STATED PRINT RUN 125 SER.#'d SETS
1 LeBron James 800.00 1,500.00
159 Stephen Curry 60.00 150.00
256 Tyrese Maxey 200.00 500.00
258 Anthony Edwards 1,250.00 2,500.00
262 Tyrese Haliburton 300.00 600.00
278 LaMelo Ball 150.00 400.00

2020-21 Panini Prizm Prizms Blue Shimmer

*BLUE SHIMMER: 8X TO 20X BASIC
*BLUE SHIMMER RC: 8X TO 20X BASIC RC
STATED PRINT RUN 35 SER.#'d SETS
1 LeBron James 1,000.00 2,000.00
159 Stephen Curry 100.00 250.00
256 Tyrese Maxey 400.00 800.00
258 Anthony Edwards 2,000.00 4,000.00
262 Tyrese Haliburton 500.00 1,000.00
278 LaMelo Ball 300.00 600.00

2020-21 Panini Prizm Prizms Blue Wave

*BLUE WAVE: 2.5X TO 6X BASIC
1 LeBron James 100.00 250.00
258 Anthony Edwards 200.00 500.00
278 LaMelo Ball 40.00 100.00

2020-21 Panini Prizm Prizms Choice Blue

*CHOICE BLUE: 6X TO 15X BASIC
*CHOICE BLUE RC: 6X TO 15X BASIC RC
STATED PRINT RUN 49 SER.#'d SETS
1 LeBron James 500.00 1,000.00
159 Stephen Curry 75.00 200.00
256 Tyrese Maxey 300.00 600.00
258 Anthony Edwards 1,500.00 3,000.00
262 Tyrese Haliburton 400.00 800.00
278 LaMelo Ball 200.00 500.00

2020-21 Panini Prizm Prizms Choice Blue Yellow and Green

*BYG: 2.5X TO 6X BASIC
1 LeBron James 150.00 400.00
54 Julius Randle 12.00 30.00
258 Anthony Edwards 125.00 300.00
262 Tyrese Haliburton 40.00 100.00

2020-21 Panini Prizm Prizms Choice Red

*CHOICE RED: 5X TO 12X BASIC
*CHOICE RED RC: 5X TO 12X BASIC RC
STATED PRINT RUN 88 SER.#'d SETS
1 LeBron James 400.00 800.00
159 Stephen Curry 60.00 150.00
256 Tyrese Maxey 200.00 500.00
258 Anthony Edwards 1,250.00 2,500.00
262 Tyrese Haliburton 300.00 600.00
278 LaMelo Ball 150.00 400.00

2020-21 Panini Prizm Prizms Fast Break

*FB: 2X TO 5X BASIC RC
1 LeBron James 75.00 200.00
258 Anthony Edwards 150.00 400.00
278 LaMelo Ball 30.00 80.00

2020-21 Panini Prizm Prizms Fast Break Blue

*FB BLUE: 4X TO 10X BASIC
STATED PRINT RUN 175 SER.#'d SETS
1 LeBron James 200.00 500.00
159 Stephen Curry 50.00 120.00
256 Tyrese Maxey 150.00 400.00
258 Anthony Edwards 1,000.00 2,000.00
262 Tyrese Haliburton 200.00 500.00
278 LaMelo Ball 125.00 300.00

2020-21 Panini Prizm Prizms Fast Break Bronze

*FB BRONZE: 10X TO 25X BASIC
STATED PRINT RUN 20 SER.#'d SETS
1 LeBron James 1,500.00 3,000.00
159 Stephen Curry 125.00 300.00
256 Tyrese Maxey 500.00 1,000.00
258 Anthony Edwards 2,500.00 5,000.00
262 Tyrese Haliburton 600.00 1,200.00
278 LaMelo Ball 400.00 800.00

2020-21 Panini Prizm Prizms Fast Break Pink

*FB PINK: 6X TO 15X BASIC
STATED PRINT RUN 50 SER.#'d SETS
1 LeBron James 500.00 1,000.00
159 Stephen Curry 75.00 200.00
256 Tyrese Maxey 300.00 600.00
258 Anthony Edwards 1,500.00 3,000.00
262 Tyrese Haliburton 400.00 800.00
278 LaMelo Ball 200.00 500.00

2020-21 Panini Prizm Prizms Fast Break Purple

*FB PURPLE: 5X TO 12X BASIC
STATED PRINT RUN 75 SER.#'d SETS
1 LeBron James 400.00 800.00
159 Stephen Curry 60.00 150.00
256 Tyrese Maxey 200.00 500.00
258 Anthony Edwards 1,250.00 2,500.00
262 Tyrese Haliburton 300.00 600.00
278 LaMelo Ball 150.00 400.00

2020-21 Panini Prizm Prizms Fast Break Red

*FB RED: 4X TO 10X BASIC
STATED PRINT RUN 125 SER.#'d SETS
1 LeBron James 300.00 600.00
159 Stephen Curry 50.00 120.00
256 Tyrese Maxey 150.00 400.00
258 Anthony Edwards 1,000.00 2,000.00
262 Tyrese Haliburton 200.00 500.00
278 LaMelo Ball 125.00 300.00

2020-21 Panini Prizm Prizms Gold Wave

*GOLD WAVE: 5X TO 12X BASIC
*GOLD WAVE RC: 8X TO 20X BASIC RC
1 LeBron James 400.00 800.00
159 Stephen Curry 60.00 150.00
256 Tyrese Maxey 150.00 400.00
258 Anthony Edwards 600.00 1,200.00
262 Tyrese Haliburton 150.00 400.00
278 LaMelo Ball 150.00 400.00

2020-21 Panini Prizm Prizms Green

*GREEN: 1X TO 2.5X BASIC
*GREEN RC: 1X TO 2.5X BASIC RC
1 LeBron James 40.00 100.00
258 Anthony Edwards 75.00 200.00
278 LaMelo Ball 15.00 40.00

2020-21 Panini Prizm Prizms Green Ice

*GREEN ICE: 3X TO 8X BASIC
1 LeBron James 200.00 500.00
258 Anthony Edwards 300.00 600.00
278 LaMelo Ball 50.00 120.00

2020-21 Panini Prizm Prizms Green Pulsar

*GREEN PULSAR: 10X TO 25X BASIC
*GREEN PULSAR RC: 10X TO 25X BASIC RC
STATED PRINT RUN 25 SER.#'d SETS
1 LeBron James 1,500.00 3,000.00
159 Stephen Curry 125.00 300.00
256 Tyrese Maxey 500.00 1,000.00
258 Anthony Edwards 2,500.00 5,000.00
262 Tyrese Haliburton 600.00 1,200.00
278 LaMelo Ball 400.00 800.00

2020-21 Panini Prizm Prizms Hyper

*HYPER: 2X TO 5X BASIC
*HYPER RC: 2X TO 5X BASIC RC
1 LeBron James 75.00 200.00
258 Anthony Edwards 150.00 400.00
278 LaMelo Ball 30.00 80.00

2020-21 Panini Prizm Prizms Mojo

*MOJO: 10X TO 25X BASIC
*MOJO RC: 10X TO 25X BASIC RC
STATED PRINT RUN 25 SER.#'d SETS
1 LeBron James 1,500.00 3,000.00
159 Stephen Curry 125.00 300.00
256 Tyrese Maxey 500.00 1,000.00
258 Anthony Edwards 2,500.00 5,000.00
262 Tyrese Haliburton 600.00 1,200.00
278 LaMelo Ball 400.00 800.00

2020-21 Panini Prizm Prizms Orange

*ORANGE: 6X TO 15X BASIC
*ORANGE RC: 6X TO 15X BASIC RC
STATED PRINT RUN 49 SER.#'d SETS
1 LeBron James 500.00 1,000.00
159 Stephen Curry 75.00 200.00
256 Tyrese Maxey 300.00 600.00
258 Anthony Edwards 1,500.00 3,000.00
262 Tyrese Haliburton 400.00 800.00
278 LaMelo Ball 200.00 500.00

2020-21 Panini Prizm Prizms Orange Ice

*ORANGE ICE: 1.5X TO 4X BASIC
*ORANGE ICE RC: 1.5X TO 4X BASIC RC
1 LeBron James 75.00 200.00
258 Anthony Edwards 150.00 400.00
278 LaMelo Ball 30.00 80.00

2020-21 Panini Prizm Prizms Orange Wave

*ORANGE WAVE: 6X TO 15X BASIC
*ORANGE WAVE RC: 6X TO 15X BASIC RC
STATED PRINT RUN 60 SER.#'d SETS
1 LeBron James 500.00 1,000.00
159 Stephen Curry 75.00 200.00
256 Tyrese Maxey 300.00 600.00
258 Anthony Edwards 1,500.00 3,000.00
262 Tyrese Haliburton 400.00 800.00
278 LaMelo Ball 200.00 500.00

2020-21 Panini Prizm Prizms Pink Ice

*PINK ICE: 1.25X TO 3X BASIC
*PINK ICE RC: 1.2X TO 3X BASIC RC
1 LeBron James 60.00 150.00
258 Anthony Edwards 125.00 300.00
278 LaMelo Ball 25.00 60.00

2020-21 Panini Prizm Prizms Pink Pulsar

*PINK PULSAR: 6X TO 15X BASIC
*PINK PULSAR RC: 6X TO 15X BASIC RC
STATED PRINT RUN 42 SER.#'d SETS
1 LeBron James 500.00 1,000.00
159 Stephen Curry 75.00 200.00
256 Tyrese Maxey 300.00 600.00
258 Anthony Edwards 1,500.00 3,000.00
262 Tyrese Haliburton 400.00 800.00
278 LaMelo Ball 200.00 500.00

2020-21 Panini Prizm Prizms Purple

*PURPLE: 5X TO 12X BASIC
*PURPLE RC: 5X TO 12X BASIC RC
STATED PRINT RUN 99 SER.#'d SETS
1 LeBron James 400.00 800.00
159 Stephen Curry 60.00 150.00
256 Tyrese Maxey 200.00 500.00
258 Anthony Edwards 1,250.00 2,500.00
262 Tyrese Haliburton 300.00 600.00
278 LaMelo Ball 150.00 400.00

2020-21 Panini Prizm Prizms Purple Ice

*PURPLE ICE: 4X TO 10X BASIC
STATED PRINT RUN 175 SER.#'d SETS
1 LeBron James 300.00 600.00
159 Stephen Curry 50.00 120.00
256 Tyrese Maxey 150.00 400.00
258 Anthony Edwards 1,000.00 2,000.00
262 Tyrese Haliburton 200.00 500.00
278 LaMelo Ball 125.00 300.00

2020-21 Panini Prizm Prizms Purple Pulsar

*PURPLE PULSAR: 8X TO 20X BASIC
*PURPLE PULSAR RC: 8X TO 20X BASIC RC
STATED PRINT RUN 35 SER.#'d SETS
1 LeBron James 1,000.00 2,000.00
159 Stephen Curry 100.00 250.00
256 Tyrese Maxey 400.00 800.00
258 Anthony Edwards 2,000.00 4,000.00
262 Tyrese Haliburton 500.00 1,000.00
278 LaMelo Ball 300.00 600.00

2020-21 Panini Prizm Prizms Purple Wave

*PURPLE WAVE: 2X TO 5X BASIC
*PURPLE WAVE RC: 2X TO 5X BASIC RC
1 LeBron James 75.00 200.00
258 Anthony Edwards 150.00 400.00
278 LaMelo Ball 30.00 80.00

2020-21 Panini Prizm Prizms Red

*RED: 3X TO 8X BASIC
STATED PRINT RUN 299 SER.#'d SETS
1 LeBron James 150.00 400.00
256 Tyrese Maxey 75.00 200.00
258 Anthony Edwards 400.00 800.00
278 LaMelo Ball 60.00 150.00

2020-21 Panini Prizm Prizms Red Ice

*RED ICE: 1.5X TO 4X BASIC
1 LeBron James 60.00 150.00
258 Anthony Edwards 125.00 300.00
278 LaMelo Ball 25.00 60.00

2020-21 Panini Prizm Prizms Red White and Blue

*RWB: .75X TO 2X BASIC
*RWB RC: .75X TO 2X BASIC RC
1 LeBron James 30.00 80.00
258 Anthony Edwards 60.00 150.00
278 LaMelo Ball 12.00 30.00

2020-21 Panini Prizm Prizms Ruby Wave

*RUBY WAVE: 1.25X TO 3X BASIC
1 LeBron James 50.00 120.00
258 Anthony Edwards 100.00 250.00
278 LaMelo Ball 20.00 50.00

2020-21 Panini Prizm Prizms Silver

*SILVER: 2X TO 5X BASIC
*SILVER RC: 2X TO 5X BASIC RC
1 LeBron James 75.00 200.00
258 Anthony Edwards 125.00 300.00
262 Tyrese Haliburton 40.00 100.00
278 LaMelo Ball 30.00 80.00

2020-21 Panini Prizm Dominance

COMMON CARD .30 .75
SEMISTARS .40 1.00
UNLISTED STARS .50 1.25
*GREEN: .5X TO 1.5X BASIC
*SILVER: .75X TO 2X BASIC
1 Anthony Davis 1.25 3.00
2 Ben Simmons .50 1.25
3 Bradley Beal .60 1.50
4 Ja Morant 1.50 4.00
5 Devin Booker 1.25 3.00
6 Donovan Mitchell 1.00 2.50
7 Giannis Antetokounmpo 2.50 6.00
8 James Harden 1.00 2.50
9 Jayson Tatum 2.00 5.00
10 Jimmy Butler 1.00 2.50
11 Joel Embiid 1.25 3.00
12 Kawhi Leonard 1.25 3.00
13 Kemba Walker .50 1.25
14 Kevin Durant 2.00 5.00
15 Zion Williamson 1.50 4.00
16 Kyrie Irving 1.00 2.50
17 LeBron James 4.00 10.00
18 Luka Doncic 3.00 8.00
19 Nikola Jokic 2.50 6.00
20 Pascal Siakam .75 2.00
21 Paul George .75 2.00
22 Rudy Gobert .60 1.50
23 Russell Westbrook 1.00 2.50
24 Stephen Curry 4.00 10.00
25 Trae Young 1.25 3.00

2020-21 Panini Prizm Downtown Bound

COMMON CARD .40 1.00
SEMISTARS .50 1.25
UNLISTED STARS .60 1.50
*FAST BREAK: .75X TO 2X BASIC
*HYPER: .75X TO 2X BASIC
*SILVER: 1.25X TO 3X BASIC
1 Kyle Lowry .75 2.00
2 Donovan Mitchell 1.25 3.00
3 Paul George 1.00 2.50
4 Chris Paul 1.25 3.00
5 Bradley Beal .75 2.00
6 Jayson Tatum 2.50 6.00
7 Devin Booker 1.50 4.00
8 Trae Young 1.50 4.00
9 Stephen Curry 5.00 12.00
10 Kemba Walker .60 1.50
11 Jimmy Butler 1.25 3.00
12 Damian Lillard 1.50 4.00
13 Luka Doncic 4.00 10.00
14 Kawhi Leonard 1.50 4.00
15 Anthony Davis 1.50 4.00
16 James Harden 1.25 3.00
17 Russell Westbrook 1.25 3.00
18 LeBron James 5.00 12.00
19 Giannis Antetokounmpo 3.00 8.00
20 Buddy Hield .60 1.50
21 Ja Morant 2.00 5.00
22 Jamal Murray 1.00 2.50
23 Kyrie Irving 1.25 3.00
24 RJ Barrett 1.00 2.50
25 Zion Williamson 2.00 5.00

2020-21 Panini Prizm Downtown Bound Prizms Mojo

*MOJO: 5X TO 12X BASIC
STATED PRINT RUN 25 SER.#'d SETS
9 Stephen Curry 100.00 250.00
13 Luka Doncic 100.00 250.00
18 LeBron James 100.00 250.00
21 Ja Morant 75.00 200.00
25 Zion Williamson 60.00 150.00

2020-21 Panini Prizm Emergent

COMMON CARD .30 .75
SEMISTARS .40 1.00
UNLISTED STARS .50 1.25
*GREEN: .75X TO 2X BASIC
*SILVER: 1.25X TO 3X BASIC
1 Kira Lewis Jr. .40 1.00
2 Isaiah Stewart .75 2.00
3 Anthony Edwards 4.00 10.00
4 Saddiq Bey .75 2.00
5 Patrick Williams 1.00 2.50
6 Zeke Nnaji .50 1.25
7 Killian Hayes .40 1.00
8 Immanuel Quickley 1.00 2.50
9 Jalen Smith .75 2.00
10 Jaden McDaniels 1.25 3.00
11 Aaron Nesmith .75 2.00
12 Aleksej Pokusevski .50 1.25
13 James Wiseman .50 1.25
14 Precious Achiuwa .75 2.00
15 Isaac Okoro .60 1.50
16 Malachi Flynn .40 1.00
17 Obi Toppin .75 2.00
18 Payton Pritchard 1.25 3.00
19 Devin Vassell 1.25 3.00
20 Malachi Flynn .40 1.00
21 Cole Anthony 1.00 2.50
22 Josh Green .75 2.00
23 LaMelo Ball 3.00 8.00
24 Tyrese Maxey 3.00 8.00
25 Onyeka Okongwu .75 2.00
26 RJ Hampton .40 1.00
27 Deni Avdija 1.00 2.50
28 Udoka Azubuike .50 1.25
29 Tyrese Haliburton 3.00 8.00
30 Desmond Bane 1.25 3.00

2020-21 Panini Prizm Fast Break Autographs

COMMON CARD 2.50 6.00
SEMISTARS 3.00 8.00
UNLISTED STARS 4.00 10.00
EXCHANGE DEADLINE 9/30/22
1 Torrey Craig 3.00 8.00
2 Keita Bates-Diop 2.50 6.00
3 Markelle Fultz 8.00 20.00
4 Anderson Varejao 2.50 6.00
5 Kelly Oubre Jr. 4.00 10.00
6 James Ennis 2.50 6.00
7 Jeff Mullins 3.00 8.00
8 Dale Ellis 3.00 8.00
9 Devonte' Graham 3.00 8.00
10 Spencer Dinwiddie 3.00 8.00
11 Donovan Mitchell 50.00 120.00
12 Magic Johnson 60.00 150.00
13 Patrick Beverley 2.50 6.00
14 Sterling Brown 2.50 6.00
15 Karl-Anthony Towns 15.00 40.00
16 Spud Webb 4.00 10.00
17 Tom Heinsohn 25.00 60.00
18 Hakeem Olajuwon 40.00 100.00
19 Brian Scalabrine 2.50 6.00
20 De'Andre Hunter 4.00 10.00
21 Quinn Cook 2.50 6.00
22 Al Horford 4.00 10.00
24 Juwan Howard 3.00 8.00
25 James Johnson 2.50 6.00
26 Brook Lopez 3.00 8.00
27 Bol Bol 4.00 10.00
28 Larry Bird 60.00 150.00
29 Norman Powell 3.00 8.00
30 Thomas Bryant 3.00 8.00
31 Reggie Bullock 3.00 8.00
33 Josh Richardson 3.00 8.00
34 Dino Radja 3.00 8.00
35 De'Aaron Fox 40.00 100.00
36 Talen Horton-Tucker 20.00 50.00
37 Walt Frazier 20.00 50.00
38 Sam Cassell 3.00 8.00
39 Thaddeus Young 2.50 6.00
40 Nikola Vucevic 4.00 10.00
41 Roy Hibbert 2.50 6.00
42 Tim Hardaway 2.50 6.00
43 RJ Barrett 12.00 30.00
44 Gary Harris 3.00 8.00
45 Tyronn Lue 4.00 10.00
47 Ivica Zubac 4.00 10.00
49 Dominique Wilkins 15.00 40.00
50 Tyus Jones 3.00 8.00
51 JJ Redick 4.00 10.00
52 Jarrett Culver 2.50 6.00
53 Jerry West 30.00 80.00
54 David Robinson 30.00 80.00
55 Pascal Siakam 6.00 15.00
56 Vlade Divac 3.00 8.00
57 Rudy Gay 4.00 10.00
58 Mike Miller 3.00 8.00
59 Jack Sikma 4.00 10.00
60 Ray Allen 25.00 60.00

2020-21 Panini Prizm Fast Break Rookie Autographs

COMMON CARD 2.50 6.00
SEMISTARS 3.00 8.00
UNLISTED STARS 4.00 10.00
1 Daniel Oturu 10.00 25.00
3 Robert Woodard II 3.00 8.00
5 Cole Anthony 40.00 100.00
6 Kira Lewis Jr. 25.00 60.00
7 Onyeka Okongwu 25.00 60.00
10 Jalen Smith 6.00 15.00
11 Theo Maledon 20.00 50.00
12 Precious Achiuwa 25.00 60.00
13 Tre Jones 5.00 12.00
14 Payton Pritchard 60.00 150.00
15 Josh Green 6.00 15.00
16 Isaiah Stewart 20.00 50.00
17 RJ Hampton 3.00 8.00
18 Zeke Nnaji 12.00 30.00
19 Desmond Bane 30.00 80.00
20 Jaden McDaniels 30.00 80.00
21 Xavier Tillman 15.00 40.00
22 Isaac Okoro 40.00 100.00
23 Jordan Nwora 25.00 60.00
27 Deni Avdija 40.00 100.00
28 Killian Hayes 40.00 100.00
29 Tyrell Terry 2.50 6.00
30 Aaron Nesmith 6.00 15.00
31 Tyler Bey 3.00 8.00
32 Devon Dotson 3.00 8.00
33 Nico Mannion 3.00 8.00
34 Malachi Flynn 3.00 8.00
35 Tyrese Maxey 40.00 100.00
36 Saddiq Bey 40.00 100.00
37 Udoka Azubuike 4.00 10.00
39 Vernon Carey Jr. 3.00 8.00
40 Aleksej Pokusevski 4.00 10.00

2020-21 Panini Prizm Fearless

COMMON CARD .40 1.00
SEMISTARS .50 1.25
UNLISTED STARS .60 1.50
*FAST BREAK: .75X TO 2X BASIC
*HYPER: .75X TO 2X BASIC
*SILVER: 1.25X TO 3X BASIC
1 Stephon Marbury .75 2.00
2 Gary Payton 1.00 2.50
3 Tim Duncan 1.50 4.00
4 Larry Bird 2.50 6.00
5 Shaquille O'Neal 2.50 6.00
6 LeBron James 5.00 12.00
7 Zion Williamson 2.00 5.00
8 Jason Williams 1.00 2.50
9 Kyrie Irving 1.25 3.00
10 Scottie Pippen 1.25 3.00
11 Steve Nash 1.25 3.00
12 Paul Pierce 1.00 2.50
13 Ja Morant 2.00 5.00
14 Anthony Davis 1.50 4.00
15 Giannis Antetokounmpo 3.00 8.00
16 Dwyane Wade 1.25 3.00
17 Dirk Nowitzki 1.50 4.00
18 Kevin Garnett 1.50 4.00
19 Dennis Rodman 1.50 4.00
20 Allen Iverson 1.50 4.00

2020-21 Panini Prizm Fearless Prizms Mojo

*MOJO: 5X TO 12X BASIC
STATED PRINT RUN 25 SER.#'d SETS
6 LeBron James 100.00 250.00
7 Zion Williamson 60.00 150.00
13 Ja Morant 75.00 200.00

2020-21 Panini Prizm Fireworks Prizms Hyper

*HYPER: .75X TO 2X BASIC

2020-21 Panini Prizm Fireworks Prizms Mojo

*MOJO: 5X TO 12X BASIC
STATED PRINT RUN 25 SER.#'d SETS
1 Stephen Curry 100.00 250.00
2 Ja Morant 75.00 200.00
14 Luka Doncic 100.00 250.00
29 LeBron James 100.00 250.00
30 Zion Williamson 60.00 150.00

2020-21 Panini Prizm Fireworks Prizms Silver

*SILVER: 1.25X TO 3X BASIC

2020-21 Panini Prizm Instant Impact

COMMON CARD .30 .75
SEMISTARS .40 1.00
UNLISTED STARS .50 1.25
1 Anthony Edwards 8.00 20.00
2 Aaron Nesmith .75 2.00
3 Patrick Williams 1.00 2.50
4 Aleksej Pokusevski .50 1.25
5 Killian Hayes .40 1.00
6 Precious Achiuwa .75 2.00
7 Jalen Smith .75 2.00
8 Zeke Nnaji .50 1.25
9 Tyrese Haliburton 5.00 12.00
10 RJ Hampton .40 1.00
11 James Wiseman .50 1.25
12 Cole Anthony 1.00 2.50
13 Isaac Okoro .60 1.50
14 Josh Green .75 2.00
15 Obi Toppin .75 2.00
16 Tyrese Maxey 3.00 8.00
17 Devin Vassell 1.25 3.00
18 Malachi Flynn .40 1.00
19 Kira Lewis Jr. .40 1.00
20 Immanuel Quickley 1.00 2.50
21 LaMelo Ball 12.00 30.00
22 Isaiah Stewart .75 2.00
23 Onyeka Okongwu .75 2.00
24 Saddiq Bey .75 2.00
25 Deni Avdija 1.00 2.50

2020-21 Panini Prizm Instant Impact Prizms Green

*GREEN: .75X TO 2X BASIC
1 Anthony Edwards 25.00 60.00
3 Patrick Williams 6.00 15.00
9 Tyrese Haliburton 10.00 25.00
10 RJ Hampton .75 2.00
15 Obi Toppin 6.00 15.00
20 Immanuel Quickley 8.00 20.00
21 LaMelo Ball 40.00 100.00
22 Isaiah Stewart 6.00 15.00
24 Saddiq Bey 6.00 15.00

2020-21 Panini Prizm Instant Impact Prizms Silver

*SILVER: 1.25X TO 3X BASIC
1 Anthony Edwards 30.00 80.00
3 Patrick Williams 8.00 20.00
9 Tyrese Haliburton 12.00 30.00
10 RJ Hampton 1.25 3.00
15 Obi Toppin 8.00 20.00
20 Immanuel Quickley 10.00 5.00

21 LaMelo Ball 60.00 150.00
22 Isaiah Stewart 8.00 20.00
24 Saddiq Bey 8.00 20.00

2020-21 Panini Prizm Penmanship

COMMON CARD 2.50 6.00
SEMISTARS 3.00 8.00
UNLISTED STARS 4.00 10.00
*ORANGE ICE: .6X TO 1.5X BASIC
*SILVER: .6X TO 1.5X BASIC
1 Tyler Herro 50.00 120.00
2 Isaiah Hartenstein 2.50 6.00
3 Monte Morris 2.50 6.00
4 Skal Labissiere 2.50 6.00
5 Frank Jackson 2.50 6.00
6 Damian Jones 2.50 6.00
7 Jaren Jackson Jr. 15.00 40.00
8 Ricky Davis 3.00 8.00
9 Larry Nance Jr. 3.00 8.00
10 Meyers Leonard 2.50 6.00
11 Karl-Anthony Towns 12.00 30.00
12 Hamidou Diallo 3.00 8.00
13 Alex Caruso 20.00 50.00
14 Ron Harper 8.00 20.00
15 Danuel House Jr. 3.00 8.00
16 Chris Kaman 2.50 6.00
17 Cedi Osman 3.00 8.00
18 Dennis Rodman 40.00 100.00
19 Otis Birdsong 3.00 8.00
20 DeAndre' Bembry 2.50 6.00
21 Trae Young 75.00 200.00
22 Naz Reid 5.00 12.00
23 Dylan Windler 2.50 6.00
24 Anthony Davis 75.00 200.00
25 Chris Clemons 2.50 6.00
26 Justin James 2.50 6.00
27 Archie Clark 3.00 8.00
28 Joe Dumars 5.00 12.00
30 Grant Hill 25.00 60.00
31 Desmond Mason 3.00 8.00
32 Jonah Bolden 2.50 6.00
34 Ben McLemore 2.50 6.00
35 Magic Johnson 60.00 150.00
36 Karl Malone 30.00 80.00
37 Paul Pierce 40.00 100.00
38 Mason Plumlee 2.50 6.00
39 Geoff Petrie 3.00 8.00
40 Miye Oni 2.50 6.00
41 Ja Morant 150.00 400.00
42 Alen Smailagic 2.50 6.00
43 Amir Coffey 2.50 6.00
44 Slick Watts 3.00 8.00
45 Kevon Looney 3.00 8.00
46 Stephon Marbury 12.00 30.00
47 Dominique Wilkins 15.00 40.00
48 Mikal Bridges 10.00 25.00
49 Jonas Valanciunas 3.00 8.00
50 Jevon Carter 3.00 8.00

2020-21 Panini Prizm Prizm Flashback

COMMON CARD .60 1.50
SEMISTARS .75 2.00
UNLISTED STARS 1.00 2.50
1 James Harden 5.00 12.00
2 Kawhi Leonard 6.00 15.00
3 Luka Doncic 20.00 50.00
4 Kevin Durant 8.00 20.00
5 Anthony Davis 8.00 20.00
6 LeBron James 25.00 60.00
7 Ja Morant 15.00 40.00
8 Zion Williamson 25.00 60.00
9 Jayson Tatum 8.00 20.00
10 Stephen Curry 15.00 40.00
11 Damian Lillard 6.00 15.00
12 Kyrie Irving 6.00 15.00
13 Trae Young 6.00 15.00
14 Russell Westbrook 5.00 12.00
15 Giannis Antetokounmpo 8.00 20.00

2020-21 Panini Prizm Prizm Flashback Prizms Hyper

*HYPER: 1.2X TO 3X BASIC
1 James Harden 30.00 80.00
2 Kawhi Leonard 40.00 100.00
3 Luka Doncic 150.00 400.00
4 Kevin Durant 40.00 100.00
5 Anthony Davis 40.00 100.00
6 LeBron James 300.00 600.00
7 Ja Morant 75.00 200.00
8 Zion Williamson 200.00 500.00
9 Jayson Tatum 40.00 100.00
10 Stephen Curry 100.00 250.00
11 Damian Lillard 40.00 100.00
12 Kyrie Irving 40.00 100.00
13 Trae Young 30.00 80.00
14 Russell Westbrook 25.00 60.00
15 Giannis Antetokounmpo 50.00 120.00

2020-21 Panini Prizm Prizm Flashback Prizms Mojo

*MOJO: 4X TO 10X BASIC
STATED PRINT RUN 25 SER.#'d SETS
2 Kawhi Leonard 800.00 1,500.00
4 Kevin Durant 1,000.00 2,000.00
5 Anthony Davis 1,000.00 2,000.00
9 Jayson Tatum 800.00 1,500.00
10 Stephen Curry 2,000.00 4,000.00
11 Damian Lillard 800.00 1,500.00
12 Kyrie Irving 800.00 1,500.00
13 Trae Young 800.00 1,500.00
14 Russell Westbrook 400.00 800.00
15 Giannis Antetokounmpo 800.00 1,500.00

2020-21 Panini Prizm Prizm Flashback Prizms Silver

*SILVER: 1.5X TO 4X BASIC
1 James Harden 50.00 120.00
2 Kawhi Leonard 50.00 120.00
3 Luka Doncic 200.00 500.00
4 Kevin Durant 60.00 150.00
5 Anthony Davis 60.00 150.00
6 LeBron James 500.00 1,000.00
7 Ja Morant 100.00 250.00
8 Zion Williamson 300.00 600.00
9 Jayson Tatum 50.00 120.00
10 Stephen Curry 200.00 500.00
11 Damian Lillard 50.00 120.00
12 Kyrie Irving 50.00 120.00
13 Trae Young 40.00 100.00
14 Russell Westbrook 30.00 80.00
15 Giannis Antetokounmpo 60.00 150.00

2020-21 Panini Prizm Rookie Penmanship

COMMON CARD 3.00 8.00
SEMISTARS 4.00 10.00
UNLISTED STARS 5.00 12.00
*BLUE WAVE: .6X TO 1.5X BASIC
*ORANGE ICE: .6X TO 1.5X BASIC
*SILVER: .6X TO 1.5X BASIC
1 Saben Lee 4.00 10.00
2 Aleksej Pokusevski 5.00 12.00
3 Caleb Martin 8.00 20.00
4 Daniel Oturu 4.00 10.00
5 Tyrese Haliburton 100.00 250.00
6 Kenyon Martin Jr. 6.00 15.00
7 Jaden McDaniels 12.00 30.00
8 Obi Toppin 8.00 20.00
9 Jahmi'us Ramsey 4.00 10.00
10 LaMelo Ball 125.00 300.00
11 Tre Jones 6.00 15.00
12 Precious Achiuwa 8.00 20.00
13 Tyler Bey 4.00 10.00
14 Isaiah Stewart 8.00 20.00
15 Cole Anthony 10.00 25.00
16 Grant Riller 4.00 10.00
17 Devin Vassell 12.00 30.00
18 Skylar Mays 4.00 10.00
19 Nico Mannion 4.00 10.00
20 Nick Richards 5.00 12.00
21 Zeke Nnaji 5.00 12.00
22 Vernon Carey Jr. 4.00 10.00
23 Robert Woodard II 4.00 10.00
24 Saddiq Bey 8.00 20.00
25 Udoka Azubuike 5.00 12.00
26 Killian Hayes 4.00 10.00
27 Aaron Nesmith 8.00 20.00
28 Cassius Stanley 4.00 10.00
29 James Wiseman 5.00 12.00
30 CJ Elleby 4.00 10.00
31 Immanuel Quickley 10.00 25.00
32 Xavier Tillman 4.00 10.00
33 Tyrese Maxey 60.00 150.00
34 Tyrell Terry 3.00 8.00
35 Desmond Bane 12.00 30.00
36 Jalen Smith 8.00 20.00
37 Payton Pritchard 12.00 30.00
38 Onyeka Okongwu 8.00 20.00
39 Isaac Okoro 6.00 15.00
40 Anthony Edwards 300.00 600.00
41 Elijah Hughes 4.00 10.00
42 Josh Green 8.00 20.00
43 RJ Hampton 4.00 10.00
44 Theo Maledon 4.00 10.00
45 Kira Lewis Jr. 4.00 10.00
46 Cassius Winston 4.00 10.00
47 Malachi Flynn 4.00 10.00
48 Deni Avdija 10.00 25.00
49 Jordan Nwora 5.00 12.00
50 Patrick Williams 10.00 25.00

2020-21 Panini Prizm Rookie Signatures

COMMON CARD 3.00 8.00
SEMISTARS 4.00 10.00
UNLISTED STARS 5.00 10.00
*CHOICE: .5X TO 1.2X BASIC
*SILVER: .6X TO 1.5X BASIC
*MOJO: 1.25X TO 3X BASIC
1 Saben Lee 4.00 10.00
2 Tre Jones 6.00 15.00
3 Zeke Nnaji 5.00 12.00
4 Immanuel Quickley 10.00 25.00
5 Elijah Hughes 4.00 10.00
6 Caleb Martin 8.00 20.00
7 Tyler Bey 4.00 10.00
8 Robert Woodard II 4.00 10.00
9 Tyrese Maxey 60.00 150.00
10 RJ Hampton 4.00 10.00
11 Tyrese Haliburton 100.00 250.00
12 Cole Anthony 10.00 25.00
13 Udoka Azubuike 5.00 12.00
14 Desmond Bane 12.00 30.00
15 Kira Lewis Jr. 4.00 10.00
16 Jaden McDaniels 12.00 30.00
17 Devin Vassell 12.00 30.00
18 Aaron Nesmith 8.00 20.00
19 Payton Pritchard 12.00 30.00
20 Malachi Flynn 4.00 10.00
21 Jahmi'us Ramsey 4.00 10.00
22 Nico Mannion 4.00 10.00
23 James Wiseman 5.00 12.00
24 Isaac Okoro 6.00 15.00
25 Jordan Nwora 5.00 12.00
26 LaMelo Ball 125.00 300.00
27 Nick Richards 5.00 12.00
28 CJ Elleby 4.00 10.00
29 Anthony Edwards 300.00 600.00
30 Patrick Williams 10.00 25.00
31 Aleksej Pokusevski 5.00 12.00
32 Precious Achiuwa 8.00 20.00
33 Vernon Carey Jr. 4.00 10.00
34 Xavier Tillman 5.00 12.00
35 Josh Green 8.00 20.00
36 Daniel Oturu 4.00 10.00
37 Isaiah Stewart 8.00 20.00
38 Saddiq Bey 8.00 20.00
39 Tyrell Terry 3.00 8.00
40 Theo Maledon 4.00 10.00
41 Kenyon Martin Jr. 6.00 15.00
42 Grant Riller 4.00 10.00
43 Killian Hayes 4.00 10.00
44 Jalen Smith 8.00 20.00
45 Cassius Winston 4.00 10.00
46 Obi Toppin 8.00 20.00
47 Skylar Mays 4.00 10.00
48 Cassius Stanley 4.00 10.00
49 Onyeka Okongwu 8.00 20.00
50 Deni Avdija 10.00 25.00

2020-21 Panini Prizm Sensational Signatures

COMMON CARD 3.00 8.00
SEMISTARS 4.00 10.00
UNLISTED STARS 5.00 12.00
EXCHANGE DEADLINE 9/30/2022
*CHOICE: .5X TO 1.2X BASIC
*SILVER: .6X TO 1.5X BASIC
*MOJO/25: 1.25X TO 3X BASIC
1 Anthony Davis 50.00 120.00
2 Charles Barkley 60.00 150.00
3 Boban Marjanovic 4.00 10.00
4 Mike Miller 4.00 10.00
5 Bradley Beal 12.00 30.00
6 Shake Milton 4.00 10.00
7 Markelle Fultz 4.00 10.00
8 Jack Sikma 5.00 12.00
9 Anfernee Simons 6.00 15.00
10 Tobias Harris 5.00 12.00
11 Anderson Varejao 3.00 8.00
12 Donte DiVincenzo 5.00 12.00
13 Dwyane Wade 50.00 120.00
14 Justin James 3.00 8.00
15 Caron Butler 4.00 10.00
16 Zach Collins 4.00 10.00
17 Patrick Beverley 3.00 8.00
18 Jerry West 25.00 60.00
19 Jaxson Hayes 4.00 10.00
20 Xavier McDaniel 4.00 10.00
21 Kevin Garnett 40.00 100.00
22 Jevon Carter 4.00 10.00
23 Donovan Mitchell 40.00 100.00
24 Doug McDermott 4.00 10.00
25 Kevin Huerter 4.00 10.00
26 Dale Ellis 4.00 10.00
27 John Collins 5.00 12.00
28 David Lee 3.00 8.00
29 Matt Bonner 3.00 8.00
30 Calvin Murphy 5.00 12.00
31 Gordon Hayward 5.00 12.00
32 Jarrett Allen 5.00 12.00
33 Justin Holiday 3.00 8.00
34 Robert Horry 12.00 30.00
35 Harold Miner 4.00 10.00
36 LaMarcus Aldridge 5.00 12.00
37 Larry Bird 75.00 200.00
38 Jamal Mashburn 4.00 10.00
39 Thon Maker 3.00 8.00
40 Magic Johnson 40.00 100.00
41 Dino Radja 4.00 10.00
42 RJ Barrett 8.00 20.00
43 P.J. Tucker 4.00 10.00
44 Jason Terry 4.00 10.00
45 Ky Bowman 3.00 8.00
46 Maxi Kleber 4.00 10.00
47 Jayson Tatum 125.00 300.00
48 Joe Harris 4.00 10.00
49 Jason Williams 25.00 60.00
50 Shawn Kemp 25.00 60.00
51 Jae'Sean Tate 5.00 12.00
52 Daniel Oturu 4.00 10.00
53 Tyrese Haliburton 100.00 250.00
54 Kenyon Martin Jr. 6.00 15.00
55 Jaden McDaniels 12.00 30.00
56 Obi Toppin 8.00 20.00
57 Jahmi'us Ramsey 4.00 10.00
58 LaMelo Ball 125.00 300.00
59 Saben Lee 4.00 10.00
60 Aleksej Pokusevski 5.00 12.00
61 Tyler Bey 4.00 10.00
62 Isaiah Stewart 8.00 20.00
63 Cole Anthony 10.00 25.00
64 Grant Riller 4.00 10.00
65 Devin Vassell 12.00 30.00
66 Skylar Mays 4.00 10.00
67 Nico Mannion 4.00 10.00
68 Nick Richards 5.00 12.00
69 Tre Jones 6.00 15.00
70 Precious Achiuwa 8.00 20.00
71 Robert Woodard II 4.00 10.00
72 Saddiq Bey 8.00 20.00
73 Udoka Azubuike 5.00 12.00
74 Killian Hayes 4.00 10.00
75 Aaron Nesmith 8.00 20.00
76 Cassius Stanley 4.00 10.00
77 James Wiseman 5.00 12.00
78 CJ Elleby 4.00 10.00
79 Zeke Nnaji 5.00 12.00
80 Vernon Carey Jr. 4.00 10.00
81 Tyrese Maxey 60.00 150.00
82 Tyrell Terry 3.00 8.00
83 Desmond Bane 12.00 30.00
84 Jalen Smith 8.00 20.00
85 Payton Pritchard 12.00 30.00
86 Onyeka Okongwu 8.00 20.00
87 Isaac Okoro 6.00 15.00
88 Anthony Edwards 300.00 600.00
89 Immanuel Quickley 10.00 25.00
90 Xavier Tillman 5.00 12.00
91 RJ Hampton 4.00 10.00
92 Theo Maledon 4.00 10.00
93 Kira Lewis Jr. 4.00 10.00
94 Cassius Winston 4.00 10.00
95 Malachi Flynn 4.00 10.00
96 Deni Avdija 10.00 25.00
97 Jordan Nwora 5.00 12.00
98 Patrick Williams 10.00 25.00
99 Elijah Hughes 4.00 10.00
100 Josh Green 8.00 20.00

2020-21 Panini Prizm Sensational Swatches

COMMON CARD 2.00 5.00
SEMISTARS 2.50 6.00
UNLISTED STARS 3.00 8.00
*ORANGE ICE: .5X TO 1.2X BASIC
*GRN ICE/56: 1.25X TO 3X BASE
1 Miles Bridges 3.00 8.00
2 Karl-Anthony Towns 5.00 12.00
3 Nikola Vucevic 3.00 8.00
4 Michael Redd 2.50 6.00
5 Paul Pierce 5.00 12.00
6 Chris Bosh 3.00 8.00
7 Amar'e Stoudemire 3.00 8.00
8 Xavier McDaniel 2.50 6.00
9 Tracy McGrady 5.00 12.00
10 Nikola Jokic 15.00 40.00
11 Elton Brand 3.00 8.00
12 Dirk Nowitzki 8.00 20.00
13 Clyde Drexler 5.00 12.00
14 Shaquille O'Neal 12.00 30.00
15 Paul Millsap 2.50 6.00
16 Anthony Davis 8.00 20.00
17 Tristan Thompson 2.00 5.00
18 Aaron Gordon 3.00 8.00
19 Richard Jefferson 2.00 5.00
20 Mo Bamba 3.00 8.00
21 Dikembe Mutombo 5.00 12.00
22 Jonathan Isaac 3.00 8.00
23 Kristaps Porzingis 4.00 10.00
24 Kyle Kuzma 4.00 10.00
25 Luka Doncic 20.00 50.00
26 Terrence Ross 2.50 6.00
27 Kawhi Leonard 8.00 20.00
28 Serge Ibaka 2.50 6.00
29 Boban Marjanovic 2.50 6.00
30 Jarrett Allen 3.00 8.00
31 Rudy Gobert 4.00 10.00
32 Andre Drummond 3.00 8.00
33 Thomas Bryant 2.50 6.00
34 LeBron James 40.00 100.00
35 Spencer Dinwiddie 2.50 6.00
36 Mitchell Robinson 3.00 8.00
37 Patrick Ewing 4.00 10.00
38 DeAndre' Bembry 2.00 5.00
39 Joe Ingles 2.50 6.00
40 Brook Lopez 2.50 6.00
41 Kevin Love 3.00 8.00
42 Robert Covington 2.50 6.00
43 Andrew Wiggins 4.00 10.00
44 LaMarcus Aldridge 3.00 8.00
45 Zach Collins 2.50 6.00
46 Pascal Siakam 5.00 12.00
47 Keita Bates-Diop 2.00 5.00
48 Andrea Bargnani 2.00 5.00
49 Ben Simmons 3.00 8.00
50 Jusuf Nurkic 3.00 8.00
51 Draymond Green 4.00 10.00
52 Grant Hill 5.00 12.00
53 Jamal Murray 5.00 12.00
54 David Robinson 6.00 15.00
55 Aaron Holiday 2.50 6.00
56 Allonzo Trier 2.00 5.00
57 Andre Miller 2.50 6.00
58 Blake Griffin 3.00 8.00
59 Bradley Beal 4.00 10.00
60 Buddy Hield 3.00 8.00
61 Carlos Boozer 2.50 6.00
62 CJ McCollum 3.00 8.00
63 Clint Capela 3.00 8.00
64 Collin Sexton 3.00 8.00
65 Damian Lillard 8.00 20.00
66 Danny Granger 2.00 5.00
67 DeMar DeRozan 4.00 10.00
68 Deron Williams 2.50 6.00
69 Devin Booker 8.00 20.00
70 Domantas Sabonis 4.00 10.00
71 Donovan Mitchell 6.00 15.00
72 Doug McDermott 2.50 6.00
73 Dwight Powell 2.00 5.00
74 Eric Bledsoe 2.50 6.00
75 Eric Gordon 2.50 6.00
76 Frank Ntilikina 2.00 5.00
77 Gary Harris 2.50 6.00
78 Giannis Antetokounmpo 15.00 40.00
79 Hakeem Olajuwon 6.00 15.00
80 J.J. Barea 2.50 6.00
81 Jaren Jackson Jr. 5.00 12.00
82 Jaylen Brown 5.00 12.00
83 Jayson Tatum 12.00 30.00
84 Jermaine O'Neal 2.50 6.00
85 Joe Harris 2.50 6.00
86 Joel Embiid 8.00 20.00
87 John Collins 3.00 8.00
88 John Wall 4.00 10.00
89 Jrue Holiday 3.00 8.00
90 Karl Malone 6.00 15.00
91 Kevin Knox II 2.00 5.00
92 Khris Middleton 4.00 10.00
93 Kyle Lowry 4.00 10.00
94 Larry Bird 12.00 30.00
95 Lauri Markkanen 4.00 10.00
96 Lonnie Walker IV 3.00 8.00
97 Malik Monk 3.00 8.00
98 Matthew Dellavedova 2.50 6.00
99 Michael Kidd-Gilchrist 2.00 5.00
100 Mike Bibby 3.00 8.00

2020-21 Panini Prizm Signatures

COMMON CARD 2.50 6.00
SEMISTARS 3.00 8.00
UNLISTED STARS 4.00 10.00
EXCHANGE DEADLINE 9/30/2022
*CHOICE: .6X TO 1.5X BASIC
*SILVER: .6X TO 1.5X BASIC
1 Torrey Craig 3.00 8.00
2 Markelle Fultz 8.00 20.00
3 Kelly Oubre Jr. 8.00 20.00
4 Jeff Malone 2.50 6.00
5 Zhaire Smith 2.50 6.00
6 Devonte' Graham 3.00 8.00
7 Donovan Mitchell 60.00 150.00
8 Justin Holiday 2.50 6.00
9 Kenny Walker 2.50 6.00
10 Robert Horry 12.00 30.00
11 Jerry West 30.00 80.00
12 Brian Scalabrine 2.50 6.00
13 Jaylen Hoard 2.50 6.00
14 Coby White 25.00 60.00
15 Terry Cummings 4.00 10.00
16 Zion Williamson 300.00 600.00
17 Darius Miles 2.50 6.00
18 John Collins 8.00 20.00
19 Tyler Herro 75.00 200.00
20 Shawn Kemp 25.00 60.00
21 Daniel Gafford 3.00 8.00
22 Patty Mills 10.00 25.00
23 Darius Bazley 12.00 30.00
24 Zach Collins 3.00 8.00
25 Ray Allen 40.00 100.00
26 Wesley Matthews 2.50 6.00
27 Deron Williams 3.00 8.00
28 Steve Kerr 12.00 30.00
29 Andrew Wiggins 10.00 25.00
30 Dirk Nowitzki 75.00 200.00
31 Kristaps Porzingis 12.00 30.00
32 Ja Morant 300.00 600.00
33 Stephen Curry 1,000.00 2,000.00
34 Goga Bitadze 2.50 6.00
35 Royce O'Neale 2.50 6.00
36 Damian Lillard 60.00 150.00
37 Tobias Harris 4.00 10.00
38 Bill Walton 25.00 60.00
39 Harry Giles III 2.50 6.00
40 Tacko Fall 8.00 20.00
41 Ish Smith 2.50 6.00
44 Dennis Rodman 40.00 100.00
45 Dorian Finney-Smith 3.00 8.00
46 Kent Benson 2.50 6.00
47 RJ Barrett 50.00 120.00
48 Justin James 2.50 6.00
49 Dave Bing 12.00 30.00
50 Trae Young 75.00 200.00

2020-21 Panini Prizm Signatures Prizms Mojo

*MOJO: 75X TO 2X BASIC
STATED PRINT RUN 25 SER.#'d SETS
EXCHANGE DEADLINE 9/30/2022
20 Shawn Kemp 60.00 150.00
34 Goga Bitadze 20.00 50.00
44 Dennis Rodman 125.00 300.00

2020-21 Panini Prizm Sophomore Stars

COMMON CARD .30 .75
SEMISTARS .40 1.00
UNLISTED STARS .50 1.25
*GREEN: .5X TO 1.5X BASIC
*SILVER: .75X TO 2X BASIC
1 Rui Hachimura .60 1.50
2 Tyler Herro 1.00 2.50
3 Zion Williamson 1.50 4.00
4 Darius Garland .75 2.00
5 Coby White .60 1.50
6 Cam Reddish .60 1.50
7 RJ Barrett .75 2.00
8 PJ Washington Jr. .50 1.25
9 Kendrick Nunn .40 1.00
10 Ja Morant 1.50 4.00

2020-21 Panini Prizm USA Basketball

COMMON CARD .30 .75
SEMISTARS .40 1.00
UNLISTED STARS .50 1.25
*GREEN: .5X TO 1.5X BASIC
*SILVER: .75X TO 2X BASIC
1 Allen Iverson 1.25 3.00
2 Charles Barkley 1.25 3.00
3 Kevin Durant 2.00 5.00
4 Kevin Garnett 1.25 3.00
5 David Robinson 1.00 2.50
6 Clyde Drexler .75 2.00
7 Magic Johnson 2.00 5.00
8 Anthony Davis 1.25 3.00
9 Dwyane Wade 1.00 2.50
10 Stephen Curry 4.00 10.00

2020-21 Panini Prizm Variations

COMMON CARD 1.25 3.00
SEMISTARS 1.50 4.00
UNLISTED STARS 2.00 5.00
252 Devin Vassell 5.00 12.00
258 Anthony Edwards 30.00 80.00
260 Onyeka Okongwu 3.00 8.00
262 Tyrese Haliburton 12.00 30.00
268 James Wiseman 2.00 5.00
270 Killian Hayes 1.50 4.00
272 Kira Lewis Jr. 1.50 4.00
278 LaMelo Ball 12.00 30.00
280 Obi Toppin 3.00 8.00
282 Aaron Nesmith 3.00 8.00
288 Patrick Williams 4.00 10.00
290 Deni Avdija 4.00 10.00
298 Isaac Okoro 2.50 6.00
300 Jalen Smith 3.00 8.00

2020-21 Panini Prizm Variations Fast Break

*FB: 1.25X TO 3X BASIC

2020-21 Panini Prizm Widescreen

COMMON CARD .40 1.00
SEMISTARS .50 1.25
UNLISTED STARS .60 1.50
*FAST BREAK: .75X TO 2X BASIC
*HYPER: .75X TO 2X BASIC
*SILVER: 1.25X TO 3X BASIC
1 LeBron James 5.00 12.00
2 Kawhi Leonard 1.50 4.00
3 Stephen Curry 5.00 12.00
4 Zion Williamson 2.00 5.00
5 Anthony Davis 1.50 4.00
6 Ja Morant 2.00 5.00
7 Trae Young 1.50 4.00
8 James Harden 1.25 3.00
9 Giannis Antetokounmpo 3.00 8.00
10 Luka Doncic 4.00 10.00

2020-21 Panini Prizm Widescreen Prizms Mojo

*MOJO: 5X TO 12X BASIC
STATED PRINT RUN 25 SER.#'d SETS
1 LeBron James 100.00 250.00
2 Kawhi Leonard 20.00 50.00
3 Stephen Curry 100.00 250.00
4 Zion Williamson 75.00 200.00
5 Anthony Davis 20.00 50.00
6 Ja Morant 100.00 250.00
7 Trae Young 20.00 50.00
8 James Harden 15.00 40.00
9 Giannis Antetokounmpo 60.00 150.00
10 Luka Doncic 100.00 250.00

2020-21 Panini Prizm Widescreen Prizms Silver

*SILVER: 1.25X TO 3X BASIC

2021-22 Panini Prizm

COMMON CARD .30 .75
SEMISTARS .40 1.00
UNLISTED STARS .50 1.25
COMMON RC .60 1.50
RC SEMIS .75 2.00
RC UNLISTED 1.00 2.50
*GREEN: .75X TO 2X BASIC
*RWB: .75X TO 2X BASIC
*FCTY SET SILVER WAVE: 1X TO 2.5X BASIC
*ICE: 1.25X TO 3X BASIC
*RUBY WAVE: 1.25X TO 3X BASIC
*HYPER: 1.5X TO 4X BASIC
BLUE WAVE: 1.5X TO 4X BASIC
*FAST BREAK: 1.5X TO 4X BASIC
*SILVER: 2X TO 5X BASIC
*GREEN ICE: 2X TO 5X BASIC
*PRM FACTORY SET/150: 2X TO 5X BASIC
*CHOICE BYG: 2.5X TO 6X BASIC
*75TH ANNV: 3X TO 8X BASIC
1 Giannis Antetokounmpo 2.00 5.00
2 DeAndre Jordan .30 .75
3 Daniel Theis .30 .75
4 Deandre Ayton .40 1.00
5 Andre Drummond .30 .75
6 Patrick Williams .40 1.00
7 Thomas Bryant .25 .60
8 Jrue Holiday .50 1.25
9 Brandon Ingram .50 1.25
10 Eric Bledsoe .30 .75
11 Carmelo Anthony .60 1.50
12 Jaden McDaniels .40 1.00
13 Jayson Tatum 1.50 4.00
14 Marcus Morris Sr. .25 .60
15 Nickeil Alexander-Walker .30 .75
16 Monte Morris .30 .75
17 Payton Pritchard .40 1.00
18 Serge Ibaka .30 .75
19 Derrick White .40 1.00
20 Dennis Schroder .40 1.00
21 Cam Reddish .40 1.00
22 CJ McCollum .30 .75
23 Davis Bertans .25 .60
24 Victor Oladipo .30 .75
25 Patrick Beverley .25 .60
26 Trae Young 1.00 2.50
27 Mikal Bridges .50 1.25
28 Tyrese Maxey 1.00 2.50
29 Hassan Whiteside .30 .75
30 Danny Green .30 .75
31 Kyle Lowry .40 1.00
32 Nikola Jokic 2.00 5.00
33 Bryn Forbes .30 .75
34 Robin Lopez .25 .60
35 Jaren Jackson Jr. .60 1.50
36 Lonnie Walker IV .30 .75
37 Anthony Edwards 2.00 5.00
38 Nicolas Claxton .40 1.00
39 Precious Achiuwa .40 1.00
40 Doug McDermott .30 .75
41 Jaylen Nowell .25 .60
42 Mo Bamba .30 .75
43 Marcus Smart .40 1.00
44 James Harden .75 2.00
45 Bradley Beal .50 1.25
46 Paul Millsap .30 .75
47 Maxi Kleber .30 .75
48 Josh Hart .30 .75
49 John Collins .40 1.00
50 Royce O'Neale .30 .75
51 Enes Freedom .30 .75
52 D'Angelo Russell .40 1.00
53 Anthony Davis 1.00 2.50
54 Facundo Campazzo .40 1.00
55 Russell Westbrook .60 1.50
56 Malik Monk .40 1.00
57 Delon Wright .25 .60
58 Shake Milton .30 .75
59 Jae Crowder .25 .60
60 Cedi Osman .30 .75
61 James Wiseman .30 .75
62 Jonas Valanciunas .30 .75
63 Kira Lewis Jr. .25 .60
64 Harrison Barnes .30 .75
65 Alec Burks .25 .60
66 Dario Saric .25 .60
67 Bojan Bogdanovic .30 .75
68 John Wall .50 1.25
69 Lonzo Ball .40 1.00
70 Tim Hardaway Jr. .25 .60
71 Kawhi Leonard 1.00 2.50
72 Donovan Mitchell .75 2.00
73 De'Andre Hunter .40 1.00
74 Kristaps Porzingis .50 1.25
75 Onyeka Okongwu .40 1.00
76 Jerami Grant .40 1.00
77 Brandon Clarke .40 1.00
78 PJ Washington Jr. .40 1.00
79 Deni Avdija .40 1.00
80 Jordan Nwora .40 1.00
81 Duncan Robinson .30 .75
82 Derrick Rose .60 1.50
83 Alex Caruso .40 1.00
84 Kevin Porter Jr. .30 .75
85 Julius Randle .50 1.25
86 Lauri Markkanen .50 1.25
87 Bobby Portis .30 .75
88 Donte DiVincenzo .40 1.00
89 Chris Paul .75 2.00
90 T.J. Warren .25 .60
91 LeBron James 3.00 8.00
92 Klay Thompson 1.00 2.50
93 Jae'Sean Tate .40 1.00
94 Aaron Nesmith .40 1.00
95 Joe Harris .30 .75
96 Ricky Rubio .40 1.00
97 Jaylen Brown .60 1.50
98 Malik Beasley .30 .75
99 Kyrie Irving .75 2.00
100 Nikola Vucevic .40 1.00
101 Killian Hayes .40 1.00
102 Jamal Murray .60 1.50
103 Kelly Oubre Jr. .40 1.00
104 Rajon Rondo .50 1.25
105 Xavier Tillman .30 .75
106 Gordon Hayward .30 .75
107 Zach LaVine .60 1.50
108 Zion Williamson 1.00 2.50
109 Avery Bradley .25 .60
110 Jalen Smith .40 1.00
111 Malachi Flynn .25 .60
112 Christian Wood .30 .75
113 DeMar DeRozan .50 1.25
114 Luguentz Dort .40 1.00
115 Kevin Love .40 1.00
116 Damian Lillard 1.00 2.50
117 Mike Conley .30 .75
118 Thaddeus Young .25 .60
119 Norman Powell .30 .75
120 Kevin Durant 1.25 3.00
121 Cole Anthony .50 1.25
122 Kemba Walker .40 1.00
123 Draymond Green .50 1.25
124 Derrick Favors .25 .60
125 Daniel Gafford .30 .75
126 Larry Nance Jr. .30 .75
127 Jordan Clarkson .40 1.00
128 Khris Middleton .40 1.00
129 Immanuel Quickley .40 1.00
130 Devin Vassell .60 1.50
131 Gary Trent Jr. .30 .75
132 Miles Bridges .30 .75
133 Isaiah Roby .25 .60
134 Brook Lopez .30 .75
135 Malcolm Brogdon .30 .75
136 Marvin Bagley III .30 .75
137 Montrezl Harrell .30 .75
138 Oshae Brissett .30 .75
139 Terence Davis II .30 .75
140 Hamidou Diallo .30 .75
141 Obi Toppin .40 1.00
142 Talen Horton-Tucker .40 1.00
143 Coby White .40 1.00
144 Jalen Brunson .75 2.00
145 Tobias Harris .30 .75
146 Chuma Okeke .40 1.00
147 Caris LeVert .30 .75
148 De'Aaron Fox .60 1.50
149 Bogdan Bogdanovic .40 1.00
150 Kelly Olynyk .25 .60
151 Patty Mills .40 1.00
152 Terry Rozier III .30 .75
153 Evan Fournier .30 .75
154 Stephen Curry 2.50 6.00
155 Andrew Wiggins .50 1.25
156 Kyle Kuzma .50 1.25
157 Karl-Anthony Towns .60 1.50
158 Isaiah Stewart .40 1.00
159 Taurean Prince .25 .60
160 Wendell Carter Jr. .40 1.00
161 Josh Richardson .30 .75
162 Robert Williams III .40 1.00
163 Markelle Fultz .25 .60
164 Michael Porter Jr. .50 1.25
165 Austin Reaves RC 4.00 10.00
166 Marko Simonovic RC .60 1.50
167 Boban Marjanovic .40 1.00
168 Anfernee Simons .60 1.50
169 Eric Gordon .30 .75
170 Richaun Holmes .25 .60
171 Jusuf Nurkic .30 .75
172 Dwight Howard .50 1.25
173 Moses Brown .25 .60
174 Pascal Siakam .60 1.50
175 Myles Turner .40 1.00
176 Joel Embiid 1.00 2.50
177 Danilo Gallinari .30 .75
178 Blake Griffin .40 1.00
179 Theo Maledon .30 .75
180 Reggie Bullock .25 .60
181 Joe Ingles .30 .75
182 Chris Boucher .40 1.00
183 Domantas Sabonis .50 1.25
184 Devonte' Graham .30 .75
185 LaMelo Ball 1.00 2.50
186 Cameron Johnson .40 1.00
187 Clint Capela .40 1.00
188 Justin Holiday .25 .60
189 Terrence Ross .30 .75
190 Josh Jackson .25 .60
191 Naji Marshall .30 .75
192 Buddy Hield .30 .75
193 Saddiq Bey .30 .75
194 Ja Morant 1.25 3.00
195 Bismack Biyombo .25 .60
196 Tyrese Haliburton .75 2.00
197 Dwayne Bacon .25 .60
198 Seth Curry .30 .75
199 Ben Simmons .40 1.00
200 Nicolas Batum .30 .75
201 RJ Barrett .60 1.50
202 Dillon Brooks .40 1.00
203 Devin Booker 1.00 2.50
204 Goran Dragic .30 .75
205 Saben Lee .30 .75
206 OG Anunoby .40 1.00
207 RJ Hampton .25 .60
208 Dorian Finney-Smith .25 .60
209 Jarrett Allen .40 1.00
210 Keldon Johnson .50 1.25
211 Kyle Anderson .25 .60
212 Isaac Okoro .30 .75
213 Reggie Jackson .30 .75
214 Ty Jerome .30 .75
215 Desmond Bane .75 2.00
216 Kendrick Nunn .30 .75
217 Aaron Gordon .40 1.00
218 Markus Howard .40 1.00
219 Al-Farouq Aminu .25 .60
220 Paul George .60 1.50
221 Mason Plumlee .25 .60
222 Jordan Poole .60 1.50
223 Luka Doncic 2.50 6.00
224 Nerlens Noel .25 .60
225 Aleksej Pokusevski .30 .75
226 Darius Garland .60 1.50
227 Tyler Herro .60 1.50
228 Bam Adebayo .60 1.50
229 Naz Reid .40 1.00
230 Bruce Brown .30 .75
231 Dejounte Murray .40 1.00
232 Fred VanVleet .50 1.25
233 Robert Covington .25 .60
234 Rui Hachimura .40 1.00
235 Kenyon Martin Jr. .40 1.00
236 Jimmy Butler .60 1.50
237 Darius Bazley .25 .60
238 Shai Gilgeous-Alexander 2.00 5.00
239 Rudy Gobert .50 1.25
240 Collin Sexton .40 1.00
241 Rudy Gay .40 1.00
242 David Robinson .75 2.00
243 Paul Pierce .60 1.50
244 Jason Kidd .60 1.50
245 Patrick Ewing .60 1.50
246 Vince Carter .75 2.00
247 Toni Kukoc .50 1.25
248 Magic Johnson 1.25 3.00
249 Ben Wallace .50 1.25
250 Jermaine O'Neal .30 .75
251 Ray Allen .60 1.50
252 Dominique Wilkins .60 1.50
253 Tracy McGrady .60 1.50
254 Bill Russell 1.25 3.00
255 Allen Iverson 1.00 2.50
256 Kevin Garnett 1.00 2.50

257 Gary Payton .60 1.50
258 Rasheed Wallace .50 1.25
259 Karl Malone .75 2.00
260 Wilt Chamberlain 1.25 3.00
261 Pete Maravich 1.00 2.50
262 Amar'e Stoudemire .40 1.00
263 Chris Webber .50 1.25
264 Steve Nash .75 2.00
265 Hakeem Olajuwon .75 2.00
266 Jason Williams .50 1.25
267 John Stockton .75 2.00
268 Tim Duncan 1.00 2.50
269 Dwyane Wade .75 2.00
270 Alonzo Mourning .60 1.50
271 Ayo Dosunmu RC 1.50 4.00
272 JT Thor RC .75 2.00
273 Wang Zhi-zhi .40 1.00
274 Tre Mann RC 1.25 3.00
275 Corey Kispert RC 1.00 2.50
276 Santi Aldama RC 1.00 2.50
277 Stephon Marbury .50 1.25
278 David Johnson RC .60 1.50
279 Reggie Lewis .40 1.00
280 Sharife Cooper RC .60 1.50
281 Day'Ron Sharpe RC .75 2.00
282 Cade Cunningham RC 5.00 12.00
283 Miles McBride RC 1.25 3.00
284 Kessler Edwards RC .75 2.00
285 Quentin Grimes RC 1.50 4.00
286 Aaron Wiggins RC 1.00 2.50
287 Scottie Lewis RC .60 1.50
288 Trey Murphy III RC 2.50 6.00
289 Dirk Nowitzki 1.00 2.50
290 Jared Butler RC .75 2.00
291 Greg Brown III RC .60 1.50
292 Drazen Petrovic .50 1.25
293 Sandro Mamukelashvili RC 1.00 2.50
294 Anfernee Hardaway 1.00 2.50
295 Juan Toscano-Anderson RC .75 2.00
296 Isaiah Livers RC .75 2.00
297 Cameron Thomas RC 1.50 4.00
298 Joshua Primo RC .60 1.50
299 Isaiah Todd RC .60 1.50
300 Marcus Zegarowski RC .60 1.50
301 Josh Giddey RC 2.50 6.00
302 Bones Hyland RC 1.00 2.50
303 Luka Garza RC .75 2.00
304 Charles Bassey RC .75 2.00
305 Jalen Johnson RC 2.50 6.00
306 Jalen Green RC 4.00 10.00
307 Jonathan Kuminga RC 2.50 6.00
308 Moses Moody RC 1.50 4.00
309 Isaiah Jackson RC .75 2.00
310 Franz Wagner RC 2.50 6.00
311 James Bouknight RC .60 1.50
312 Davion Mitchell RC .75 2.00
313 Ziaire Williams RC 1.00 2.50
314 Jalen Suggs RC 2.00 5.00
315 Chris Duarte RC .60 1.50
316 Neemias Queta RC .75 2.00
317 Jaden Springer RC .75 2.00
318 Alperen Sengun RC 2.50 6.00
319 Jeremiah Robinson-Earl RC .75 2.00
320 Scottie Barnes RC 2.50 6.00
321 Usman Garuba RC .60 1.50
322 Joe Wieskamp RC .60 1.50
323 Kai Jones RC .60 1.50
324 Josh Christopher RC .60 1.50
325 Evan Mobley RC 3.00 8.00
326 Keon Johnson RC .75 2.00
327 Jason Preston RC .60 1.50
328 Dalano Banton RC 1.00 2.50
329 Herbert Jones RC 1.00 2.50
330 Brandon Boston Jr. RC .75 2.00

2021-22 Panini Prizm Prizms Blue

COMPLETE SET (330)
*BLUE: 4X TO 10X BASIC
STATED PRINT RUN 199 SER.#'d SETS
282 Cade Cunningham 150.00 400.00
306 Jalen Green 75.00 200.00

2021-22 Panini Prizm Prizms Blue Ice

*BLUE ICE: 4X TO 10X BASIC
*BLUE ICE RC: 4X TO 10X BASIC RC
STATED PRINT RUN 125 SER.#'d SETS
282 Cade Cunningham 150.00 400.00
306 Jalen Green 75.00 200.00

2021-22 Panini Prizm Prizms Blue Shimmer

COMPLETE SET (330)
*BLUE SHIMMER: 8X TO 20X BASIC
STATED PRINT RUN 30 SER.#'d SETS
282 Cade Cunningham 400.00 800.00
306 Jalen Green 150.00 400.00

2021-22 Panini Prizm Prizms Choice Blue

COMPLETE SET (330)
*CHOICE BLUE: 6X TO 15X BASIC
STATED PRINT RUN 39 SER.#'d SETS
282 Cade Cunningham 300.00 600.00
306 Jalen Green 125.00 300.00

2021-22 Panini Prizm Prizms Choice Red

*CHOICE RED: 5X TO 12X BASIC
STATED PRINT RUN 88 SER.#'d SETS
282 Cade Cunningham 200.00 500.00
306 Jalen Green 100.00 250.00

2021-22 Panini Prizm Prizms Factory Set Purple Hyper

COMPLETE SET (330)
*FACTORY SET HYPER PRPL: 3X TO 8X BASIC
165 Austin Reaves 50.00 120.00
282 Cade Cunningham 125.00 300.00
301 Josh Giddey 75.00 200.00
306 Jalen Green 100.00 250.00
307 Jonathan Kuminga 60.00 150.00
310 Franz Wagner 60.00 150.00
318 Alperen Sengun 40.00 100.00
320 Scottie Barnes 60.00 150.00
325 Evan Mobley 60.00 150.00

2021-22 Panini Prizm Prizms Fast Break Blue

*FB BLUE: 4X TO 10X BASIC
*FB BLUE RC: 4X TO 10X BASIC RC
STATED PRINT RUN 150 SER.#'d SETS
282 Cade Cunningham 150.00 400.00
306 Jalen Green 75.00 200.00

2021-22 Panini Prizm Prizms Fast Break Bronze

COMPLETE SET (330)
*FB BRONZE: 12X TO 30X BASIC
STATED PRINT RUN 20 SER.#'d SETS
282 Cade Cunningham 800.00 1,500.00
306 Jalen Green 300.00 600.00

2021-22 Panini Prizm Prizms Fast Break Pink

COMPLETE SET (330)
*FB PINK: 5X TO 12X BASIC
STATED PRINT RUN 50 SER.#'d SETS
282 Cade Cunningham 200.00 500.00
306 Jalen Green 100.00 250.00

2021-22 Panini Prizm Prizms Fast Break Purple

COMPLETE SET (330)
*FB PURPLE: 5X TO 12X BASIC
STATED PRINT RUN 75 SER.#'d SETS
282 Cade Cunningham 200.00 500.00
306 Jalen Green 100.00 250.00

2021-22 Panini Prizm Prizms Fast Break Red

*FB RED: 5X TO 12X BASIC
*FB RED RC: 5X TO 12X BASIC RC
STATED PRINT RUN 100 SER.#'d SETS
282 Cade Cunningham 200.00 500.00
306 Jalen Green 100.00 250.00

2021-22 Panini Prizm Prizms Green Pulsar

COMPLETE SET (330)
*GREEN PULSAR: 12X TO 30X BASIC
STATED PRINT RUN 25 SER.#'d SETS
282 Cade Cunningham 800.00 1,500.00
306 Jalen Green 300.00 600.00

2021-22 Panini Prizm Prizms Mojo

COMPLETE SET (330)
*MOJO: 12X TO 30X BASIC
STATED PRINT RUN 25 SER.#'d SETS
282 Cade Cunningham 800.00 1,500.00
306 Jalen Green 300.00 600.00

2021-22 Panini Prizm Prizms NBA 75th Anniversary Diamond

COMPLETE SET (330)
*NBA 75TH ANN DMD: 8X TO 20X BASIC
STATED PRINT RUN 75 SER.#'d SETS
282 Cade Cunningham 400.00 800.00
306 Jalen Green 150.00 400.00

2021-22 Panini Prizm Prizms Orange

COMPLETE SET (330)
*ORANGE: 6X TO 15X BASIC
STATED PRINT RUN 49 SER.#'d SETS
282 Cade Cunningham 300.00 600.00
306 Jalen Green 125.00 300.00

2021-22 Panini Prizm Prizms Orange Ice

COMPLETE SET (330)
*ORANGE ICE: .75X TO 2X BASIC
282 Cade Cunningham 30.00 80.00

2021-22 Panini Prizm Prizms Orange Wave

COMPLETE SET (330)
*ORANGE WAVE: 5X TO 12X BASIC
STATED PRINT RUN 60 SER.#'d SETS
282 Cade Cunningham 200.00 500.00
306 Jalen Green 100.00 250.00

2021-22 Panini Prizm Prizms Pink Ice

*PINK ICE: 1.25X TO 3X BASIC
282 Cade Cunningham 20.00 50.00
301 Josh Giddey 10.00 25.00
306 Jalen Green 15.00 40.00
320 Scottie Barnes 10.00 25.00
325 Evan Mobley 12.00 30.00

2021-22 Panini Prizm Prizms Pink Pulsar

COMPLETE SET (330)
*PINK PULSAR: 6X TO 15X BASIC
STATED PRINT RUN 42 SER.#'d SETS
282 Cade Cunningham 300.00 600.00
306 Jalen Green 125.00 300.00

2021-22 Panini Prizm Prizms Premium Factory Set

*PRM FACTORY SET: 2X TO 5X BASIC
STATED PRINT RUN 150 SER.#'d SETS
282 Cade Cunningham 150.00 400.00
306 Jalen Green 75.00 200.00

2021-22 Panini Prizm Prizms Pulsar

*PULSAR: .75X TO 2X BASIC
282 Cade Cunningham 40.00 100.00
301 Josh Giddey 20.00 50.00
306 Jalen Green 40.00 100.00
320 Scottie Barnes 20.00 50.00
325 Evan Mobley 20.00 50.00

2021-22 Panini Prizm Prizms Purple

*PURPLE: 5X TO 12X BASIC
STATED PRINT RUN 99 SER.#'d SETS
282 Cade Cunningham 200.00 500.00
306 Jalen Green 100.00 250.00

2021-22 Panini Prizm Prizms Purple Ice

COMPLETE SET (330)
*PURPLE ICE: 4X TO 10X BASIC
*PURPLE ICE RC: 4X TO 10X BASIC RC
STATED PRINT RUN 149 SER.#'d SETS
282 Cade Cunningham 150.00 400.00
306 Jalen Green 75.00 200.00

2021-22 Panini Prizm Prizms Purple Pulsar

COMPLETE SET (330)
*PURPLE PULSAR: 6X TO 15X BASIC
STATED PRINT RUN 35 SER.#'d SETS
282 Cade Cunningham 300.00 600.00
306 Jalen Green 125.00 300.00

2021-22 Panini Prizm Prizms Purple Wave

*PURPLE WAVE: 1.5X TO 4X BASIC
*PURPLE WAVE RC: 1.5X TO 4X BASIC RC
282 Cade Cunningham 75.00 200.00
306 Jalen Green 50.00 120.00

2021-22 Panini Prizm Prizms Red

*RED: 3X TO 8X BASIC
*RED RC: 3X TO 8X BASIC RC
STATED PRINT RUN 299 SER.#'d SETS
282 Cade Cunningham 125.00 300.00
306 Jalen Green 60.00 150.00

2021-22 Panini Prizm Dominance

COMPLETE SET (25)
*GREEN: .75X TO 2X BASIC
*GREEN WAVE: .75X TO 2X BASIC
*SILVER: 1.25X TO 3X BASIC
1 Bam Adebayo .75 2.00
2 James Harden 1.00 2.50
3 Devin Booker 1.25 3.00
4 Kevin Durant 1.50 4.00
5 Jayson Tatum 2.00 5.00
6 LeBron James 4.00 10.00
7 Paul George .75 2.00
8 Chris Paul 1.00 2.50
9 Karl-Anthony Towns .75 2.00
10 Luka Doncic 3.00 8.00
11 Donovan Mitchell 1.00 2.50
12 Giannis Antetokounmpo 2.50 6.00
13 Bradley Beal .60 1.50
14 Stephen Curry 3.00 8.00
15 Kyrie Irving 1.00 2.50
16 Nikola Jokic 2.50 6.00
17 Zion Williamson 1.25 3.00
18 Damian Lillard 1.25 3.00
19 Jrue Holiday .60 1.50
20 Anthony Davis 1.25 3.00
21 Julius Randle .60 1.50
22 Kawhi Leonard 1.25 3.00
23 Rudy Gobert .60 1.50
24 Joel Embiid 1.25 3.00
25 Jimmy Butler .75 2.00

2021-22 Panini Prizm Emergent

COMMON CARD .40 1.00
SEMISTARS .50 1.25
UNLISTED STARS .60 1.50
*GREEN: .75X TO 2X BASIC
*GREEN WAVE: 1.25X TO 3X BASIC
*SILVER: 1.25X TO 3X BASIC
1 Kai Jones .50 1.25
2 Isaiah Jackson .60 1.50
3 Trey Murphy III 2.00 5.00
4 Cameron Thomas 1.25 3.00
5 Jonathan Kuminga 2.00 5.00
6 Keon Johnson .60 1.50
7 Josh Giddey 2.00 5.00
8 James Bouknight .50 1.25
9 Evan Mobley 2.50 6.00
10 Corey Kispert .75 2.00
11 Bones Hyland .75 2.00
12 Jalen Suggs 1.50 4.00
13 Scottie Barnes 2.00 5.00
14 Chris Duarte .50 1.25
15 Jalen Green 3.00 8.00
16 Moses Moody 1.25 3.00
17 Joshua Primo .50 1.25
18 Jalen Johnson 2.00 5.00
19 Quentin Grimes 1.25 3.00
20 Ziaire Williams .75 2.00
21 Tre Mann 1.00 2.50
22 Cade Cunningham 4.00 10.00
23 Franz Wagner 2.00 5.00
24 Josh Christopher .50 1.25
25 Davion Mitchell .60 1.50
26 Jaden Springer .60 1.50
27 Day'Ron Sharpe .60 1.50
28 Alperen Sengun 2.00 5.00
29 Usman Garuba .50 1.25
30 Isaiah Todd .50 1.25

2021-22 Panini Prizm Fast Break Autographs

COMPLETE SET (59)
1 Trae Young 60.00 150.00
2 Fat Lever 5.00 12.00
3 Metta World Peace 6.00 15.00
4 Micheal Ray Richardson 5.00 12.00
5 Jason Williams 25.00 60.00
6 John Stockton 25.00 60.00
7 Darius Bazley 4.00 10.00
8 Kelly Olynyk 4.00 10.00
9 Luka Doncic 400.00 800.00
10 T.J. McConnell 5.00 12.00
11 Nikola Jokic 150.00 400.00
12 Hedo Turkoglu 5.00 12.00
13 Ben Wallace 25.00 60.00
14 Spencer Haywood 6.00 15.00
15 Spencer Dinwiddie 6.00 15.00
16 Magic Johnson 75.00 200.00
17 George McGinnis 6.00 15.00
18 Kenny "Sky" Walker 4.00 10.00
19 Anthony Davis 60.00 150.00
20 Dan Issel 6.00 15.00
21 Vince Carter 75.00 200.00
22 Jack Sikma 6.00 15.00
23 Danilo Gallinari 5.00 12.00
24 Spud Webb 6.00 15.00
25 Chauncey Billups 12.00 30.00
26 Oscar Robertson 30.00 80.00
27 Jarrett Allen 6.00 15.00
28 Mark Aguirre 5.00 12.00
29 Kevin Durant 125.00 300.00
30 Nerlens Noel 4.00 10.00
31 Caron Butler 5.00 12.00
32 Mario Chalmers 5.00 12.00
33 Domantas Sabonis 12.00 30.00
34 Charles Barkley 100.00 250.00
35 Kendrick Nunn 5.00 12.00
36 Kareem Abdul-Jabbar 100.00 250.00
37 Talen Horton-Tucker 6.00 15.00
38 Stephen Jackson 5.00 12.00
39 Larry Bird 100.00 250.00
40 Dennis Rodman 40.00 100.00
41 Raymond Felton 4.00 10.00
42 Mark Eaton 6.00 15.00
43 Eric Bledsoe 5.00 12.00
44 Shaquille O'Neal 125.00 300.00
46 David Robinson 30.00 80.00
47 Tony Allen 4.00 10.00
48 Drew Gooden 5.00 12.00
49 Anthony Edwards 200.00 500.00
50 Arvydas Sabonis 12.00 30.00
51 James Worthy 12.00 30.00
52 Mark Price 6.00 15.00
53 PJ Washington Jr. 6.00 15.00
54 Allen Iverson 100.00 250.00
55 Louie Dampier 6.00 15.00
56 Hakeem Olajuwon 30.00 80.00
57 Ron Harper 10.00 25.00
58 Grant Williams 6.00 15.00
59 Rui Hachimura 20.00 50.00
60 Steve Kerr 12.00 30.00

2021-22 Panini Prizm Fast Break Rookie Autographs

COMPLETE SET (39)
1 Scottie Lewis 5.00 12.00
2 Charles Bassey 6.00 15.00
3 Luka Garza 6.00 15.00
4 Brandon Boston Jr. 6.00 15.00
5 Greg Brown III 5.00 12.00
6 Isaiah Livers 6.00 15.00
7 Jared Butler 6.00 15.00
8 Ayo Dosunmu 12.00 30.00
9 Miles McBride 10.00 25.00
10 Jeremiah Robinson-Earl 6.00 15.00
11 Santi Aldama 8.00 20.00
12 Day'Ron Sharpe 6.00 15.00
13 Jaden Springer 6.00 15.00
14 Cameron Thomas 30.00 80.00
15 Bones Hyland 8.00 20.00
16 Quentin Grimes 12.00 30.00
17 Josh Christopher 5.00 12.00
18 Jason Preston 5.00 12.00
19 Isaiah Jackson 6.00 15.00
20 Keon Johnson 6.00 15.00
21 Jalen Johnson 20.00 50.00
22 Kai Jones 5.00 12.00
23 Tre Mann 10.00 25.00
24 Trey Murphy III 20.00 50.00
25 Herbert Jones 8.00 20.00
26 Corey Kispert 8.00 20.00
27 Moses Moody 20.00 50.00
28 Chris Duarte 5.00 12.00
29 Joshua Primo 5.00 12.00
31 Ziaire Williams 8.00 20.00
32 Davion Mitchell 6.00 15.00
33 Franz Wagner 20.00 50.00
34 Jonathan Kuminga 20.00 50.00
35 Josh Giddey 20.00 50.00
36 Jalen Suggs 15.00 40.00
37 Scottie Barnes 20.00 50.00
38 Evan Mobley 25.00 60.00
39 Jalen Green 75.00 200.00
40 Cade Cunningham 100.00 250.00

2021-22 Panini Prizm Fearless

COMPLETE SET (20)
*FAST BREAK: .75X TO 2X BASIC
*HYPER: .75X TO 2X BASIC
*SILVER: .75X TO 2X BASIC
*MOJO/25: 8X TO 20X BASIC
1 Zion Williamson 1.25 3.00
2 Kevin Durant 1.50 4.00
3 Anfernee Hardaway 1.25 3.00
4 Anthony Davis 1.25 3.00
5 Bradley Beal .60 1.50
6 LeBron James 4.00 10.00
7 Stephen Curry 3.00 8.00
8 Giannis Antetokounmpo 2.50 6.00
9 Ja Morant 1.50 4.00
10 Luka Doncic 3.00 8.00
11 LaMelo Ball 1.25 3.00
12 Devin Booker 1.25 3.00
13 Damian Lillard 1.25 3.00
14 James Harden 1.00 2.50
15 Anthony Edwards 2.50 6.00
16 Chris Webber .60 1.50
17 Ben Wallace .60 1.50
18 Shaquille O'Neal 1.50 4.00
19 Charles Barkley 1.25 3.00
20 Trae Young 1.25 3.00

2021-22 Panini Prizm Fireworks

COMMON CARD .30 .75
SEMISTARS .40 1.00
UNLISTED STARS .50 1.25
*FAST BREAK: .75X TO 2X BASIC
*HYPER: .75X TO 2X BASIC
*SILVER: .75X TO 2X BASIC
*MOJO/25: 8X TO 20X BASIC
1 LeBron James 4.00 10.00
2 Stephen Curry 3.00 8.00
3 Giannis Antetokounmpo 2.50 6.00
4 Luka Doncic 3.00 8.00
5 Nikola Jokic 2.50 6.00
6 Zion Williamson 1.25 3.00
7 Kawhi Leonard 1.25 3.00
8 Kevin Durant 1.50 4.00
9 Bradley Beal .60 1.50
10 Donovan Mitchell 1.00 2.50
11 Damian Lillard 1.25 3.00
12 LaMelo Ball 1.25 3.00
13 Joel Embiid 1.25 3.00
14 James Harden 1.00 2.50
15 Jayson Tatum 2.00 5.00
16 Anthony Davis 1.25 3.00
17 Julius Randle .60 1.50
18 Russell Westbrook .75 2.00
19 Devin Booker 1.25 3.00
20 Zach LaVine .75 2.00
21 Ben Simmons .50 1.25
22 Paul George .75 2.00
23 Anthony Edwards 2.50 6.00
24 Ja Morant 1.50 4.00
25 Trae Young 1.25 3.00

2021-22 Panini Prizm Flashback Signatures

COMMON CARD 4.00 10.00
SEMISTARS 5.00 12.00
UNLISTED STARS 6.00 15.00
EXCHANGE DEADLINE 1/08/2024
*SILVER: .6X TO 1.5X BASIC
*MOJO/25: 1.25X TO 3X BASIC
1 Kevin Durant 125.00 300.00
2 CJ McCollum 20.00 50.00
3 Damian Lillard 100.00 250.00
4 Khris Middleton 15.00 40.00
5 Stephen Curry 500.00 1,000.00
6 Karl-Anthony Towns 30.00 80.00
7 Luka Doncic 400.00 800.00
8 Trae Young 125.00 300.00
9 Zion Williamson 350.00 700.00
10 Nikola Jokic 125.00 300.00
11 Anthony Davis 60.00 150.00
12 Jamal Murray 40.00 100.00
13 Ja Morant 350.00 700.00
14 De'Aaron Fox 25.00 60.00
15 Rui Hachimura 20.00 50.00

2021-22 Panini Prizm Global Reach

COMMON CARD .30 .75
SEMISTARS .40 1.00
UNLISTED STARS .50 1.20
*GREEN: .75X TO 2X BASIC
*SILVER: .75X TO 2X BASIC
*GREEN WAVE: 1.25X TO 3X BASIC
1 Giannis Antetokounmpo 2.50 6.00
2 Joel Embiid 1.25 3.00
3 Nikola Jokic 2.50 6.00
4 Luka Doncic 3.00 8.00
5 Ben Simmons .50 1.25
6 Rui Hachimura .50 1.25
7 Pascal Siakam .75 2.00
8 Deni Avdija .50 1.25
9 Rudy Gobert .60 1.50
10 Domantas Sabonis .60 1.50

2021-22 Panini Prizm Instant Impact

COMMON CARD .50 1.25
SEMISTARS .60 1.50
UNLISTED STARS .75 2.00
*GREEN: .75X TO 2X BASIC
*GREEN WAVE: 1.25X TO 3X BASIC
*SILVER: 1.25X TO 3X BASIC
1 Cade Cunningham 5.00 12.00
2 Cameron Thomas 1.50 4.00
3 Ziaire Williams 1.00 2.50
4 Josh Giddey 2.50 6.00
5 Keon Johnson .75 2.00
6 Bones Hyland 1.00 2.50
7 Jonathan Kuminga 2.50 6.00
8 James Bouknight .60 1.50
9 Isaiah Jackson .75 2.00
10 Evan Mobley 3.00 8.00
11 Josh Christopher .60 1.50
12 Joshua Primo .60 1.50
13 Franz Wagner 2.50 6.00
14 Corey Kispert 1.00 2.50
15 Tre Mann 1.25 3.00
16 Scottie Barnes 2.50 6.00
17 Chris Duarte .60 1.50
18 Trey Murphy III 2.50 6.00
19 Davion Mitchell .75 2.00
20 Kai Jones .60 1.50
21 Quentin Grimes 1.50 4.00
22 Jalen Suggs 2.00 5.00
23 Jalen Johnson 2.50 6.00
24 Moses Moody 1.50 4.00
25 Jalen Green 4.00 10.00

2021-22 Panini Prizm Mindset

COMMON CARD .40 1.00
SEMISTARS .50 1.25
UNLISTED STARS .60 1.50
*FAST BREAK: .75X TO 2X BASIC
*HYPER .75X TO 2X BASIC
*SILVER .75X TO 2X BASIC
1 Damian Lillard 1.50 4.00
2 Russell Westbrook 1.00 2.50
3 LeBron James 5.00 12.00
4 Luka Doncic 4.00 10.00
5 James Harden 1.25 3.00
6 Chris Paul 1.25 3.00
7 Zion Williamson 1.50 4.00
8 Giannis Antetokounmpo 3.00 8.00
9 Stephen Curry 4.00 10.00
10 Kevin Durant 2.00 5.00
11 Donovan Mitchell 1.25 3.00
12 Trae Young 1.50 4.00
13 Jayson Tatum 2.50 6.00
14 Kawhi Leonard 1.50 4.00
15 Julius Randle .75 2.00

2021-22 Panini Prizm Mindset Prizms Mojo

*MOJO: 5X TO 12X BASIC
STATED PRINT RUN 25 SER.#'d SETS
3 LeBron James 100.00 250.00
4 Luka Doncic 100.00 250.00
7 Zion Williamson 60.00 150.00
9 Stephen Curry 100.00 250.00

2021-22 Panini Prizm NBA 75th Logo

COMMON CARD 2.00 5.00
SEMISTARS 2.50 6.00
UNLISTED STARS 3.00 8.00
1 LeBron James 25.00 60.00
2 Ja Morant 10.00 25.00
3 Trae Young 8.00 20.00
4 Larry Bird 10.00 25.00
5 Kevin Durant 10.00 25.00
6 Damian Lillard 8.00 20.00
7 Shaquille O'Neal 10.00 25.00
8 Dirk Nowitzki 8.00 20.00
9 Donovan Mitchell 6.00 15.00
10 Allen Iverson 8.00 20.00
11 Karl Malone 6.00 15.00
12 Luka Doncic 20.00 50.00
13 Zion Williamson 8.00 20.00
14 Stephen Curry 20.00 50.00
15 Magic Johnson 10.00 25.00
16 Giannis Antetokounmpo 15.00 40.00
17 James Harden 6.00 15.00
18 Charles Barkley 8.00 20.00
19 Tim Duncan 8.00 20.00
20 Jayson Tatum 12.00 30.00
21 Dwyane Wade 6.00 15.00
22 Kevin Garnett 8.00 20.00

2021-22 Panini Prizm Prizmatic

COMMON CARD .40 1.00
SEMISTARS .50 1.25
UNLISTED STARS .60 1.50
*FAST BREAK: .75X TO 2X BASIC
*HYPER .75X TO 2X BASIC
*SILVER .75X TO 2X BASIC
1 LaMelo Ball 1.50 4.00
2 Joel Embiid 1.50 4.00
3 James Harden 1.25 3.00
4 Jayson Tatum 2.50 6.00
5 Zion Williamson 1.50 4.00
6 Kawhi Leonard 1.50 4.00
7 Damian Lillard 1.50 4.00
8 Donovan Mitchell 1.25 3.00
9 Bradley Beal .75 2.00
10 Kevin Durant 2.00 5.00
11 Zach LaVine 1.00 2.50
12 Ben Simmons .60 1.50
13 Paul George 1.00 2.50
14 Ja Morant 2.00 5.00
15 Kyrie Irving 1.25 3.00
16 Jaylen Brown 1.00 2.50
17 Trae Young 1.50 4.00
18 Chris Paul 1.25 3.00
19 Anthony Edwards 3.00 8.00
20 Devin Booker 1.50 4.00
21 Anthony Davis 1.50 4.00
22 Julius Randle .75 2.00
23 Russell Westbrook 1.00 2.50
24 De'Aaron Fox 1.00 2.50
25 LeBron James 5.00 12.00
26 Stephen Curry 4.00 10.00
27 Luka Doncic 4.00 10.00
28 Nikola Jokic 3.00 8.00
29 Giannis Antetokounmpo 3.00 8.00
30 James Wiseman .50 1.25

2021-22 Panini Prizm Prizmatic Prizms Mojo

*MOJO: 6X TO 15X BASIC
STATED PRINT RUN 25 SER.#'d SETS
1 LaMelo Ball 125.00 300.00
2 Joel Embiid 50.00 120.00
4 Jayson Tatum 125.00 300.00
5 Zion Williamson 125.00 300.00
6 Kawhi Leonard 50.00 120.00
7 Damian Lillard 40.00 100.00
8 Donovan Mitchell 40.00 100.00
10 Kevin Durant 60.00 150.00
14 Ja Morant 150.00 400.00
16 Jaylen Brown 30.00 80.00
17 Trae Young 75.00 200.00
19 Anthony Edwards 125.00 300.00
20 Devin Booker 50.00 120.00
25 LeBron James 200.00 500.00
26 Stephen Curry 200.00 500.00
27 Luka Doncic 200.00 500.00
28 Nikola Jokic 40.00 100.00
29 Giannis Antetokounmpo 150.00 400.00

2021-22 Panini Prizm Rookie Penmanship

COMMON CARD 3.00 8.00
SEMISTARS 4.00 10.00
UNLISTED STARS 5.00 12.00
EXCHANGE DEADLINE 1/08/2024
*ORANGE ICE: .6X TO 1.5X BASIC
*SILVER: .6X TO 1.5X BASIC
1 Cade Cunningham 300.00 600.00
2 Jalen Green 200.00 500.00
3 Evan Mobley 150.00 400.00
4 Scottie Barnes 200.00 500.00
5 Jalen Suggs 50.00 120.00
6 Josh Giddey 150.00 400.00
7 Jonathan Kuminga 100.00 1,250.00
8 Franz Wagner 40.00 100.00
9 Davion Mitchell 5.00 12.00
10 Ziaire Williams 6.00 15.00
12 Joshua Primo 4.00 10.00
13 Chris Duarte 4.00 10.00
14 Moses Moody 40.00 100.00
15 Corey Kispert 6.00 15.00
16 Jericho Sims 6.00 15.00
17 Trey Murphy III 15.00 40.00
18 Tre Mann 8.00 20.00
19 Kai Jones 4.00 10.00
20 Brandon Boston Jr. 5.00 12.00
21 Jared Butler 5.00 12.00
22 Isaiah Jackson 5.00 12.00
23 Joel Ayayi 4.00 10.00
24 Josh Christopher 4.00 10.00
25 Quentin Grimes 10.00 25.00
26 Bones Hyland 40.00 100.00
27 Keon Johnson 5.00 12.00
28 Jaden Springer 5.00 12.00
29 Day'Ron Sharpe 5.00 12.00
30 Santi Aldama 6.00 15.00
31 Jeremiah Robinson-Earl 5.00 12.00
32 Sandro Mamukelashvili 6.00 15.00
33 JaQuori McLaughlin 3.00 8.00
34 RaiQuan Gray 4.00 10.00
35 Isaiah Livers 5.00 12.00
36 Greg Brown III 4.00 10.00
37 Aaron Henry 3.00 8.00
38 Luka Garza 5.00 12.00
39 Charles Bassey 5.00 12.00
40 Scottie Lewis 4.00 10.00
41 Jason Preston 4.00 10.00
42 Herbert Jones 6.00 15.00
43 RJ Nembhard 3.00 8.00
44 Joe Wieskamp 4.00 10.00
45 Kessler Edwards 5.00 12.00
46 Aaron Wiggins 6.00 15.00
47 Neemias Queta 5.00 12.00
48 Marcus Zegarowski 4.00 10.00
49 David Johnson 4.00 10.00
50 Trendon Watford 6.00 15.00

2021-22 Panini Prizm Rookie Signatures

COMMON CARD 3.00 8.00
SEMISTARS 4.00 10.00
UNLISTED STARS 5.00 12.00
EXCHANGE DEADLINE 1/08/2024
*SILVER: .5X TO 1.2X BASIC
*BLUE WAVE: .5X TO 1.2X BASIC
*CHOICE: .5X TO 1.2X BASIC
*MOJO/25: 1X TO 2.5X BASIC
1 Cade Cunningham 125.00 300.00
2 Jalen Green 125.00 300.00
3 Evan Mobley 75.00 200.00
4 Scottie Barnes 75.00 200.00
5 Jalen Suggs 30.00 80.00
6 Josh Giddey 75.00 200.00
7 Jonathan Kuminga 40.00 100.00
8 Franz Wagner 75.00 200.00
9 Davion Mitchell 5.00 12.00
10 Ziaire Williams 6.00 15.00
11 James Bouknight 4.00 10.00
12 Joshua Primo 4.00 10.00
13 Chris Duarte 4.00 10.00
14 Moses Moody 10.00 25.00
15 Corey Kispert 6.00 15.00
16 Alperen Sengun 40.00 100.00
17 Trey Murphy III 30.00 80.00
18 Tre Mann 8.00 20.00
19 Kai Jones 4.00 10.00
20 Jalen Johnson 15.00 40.00
21 Keon Johnson 5.00 12.00
22 Isaiah Jackson 5.00 12.00
23 Joel Ayayi 4.00 10.00
24 Josh Christopher 4.00 10.00
25 Quentin Grimes 10.00 25.00
26 Bones Hyland 6.00 15.00
27 Cameron Thomas 25.00 60.00
28 Jaden Springer 5.00 12.00
29 Day'Ron Sharpe 5.00 12.00
30 Santi Aldama 6.00 15.00
31 Jeremiah Robinson-Earl 5.00 12.00
32 Miles McBride 8.00 20.00
33 Ayo Dosunmu 10.00 25.00
34 Jared Butler 5.00 12.00
35 Isaiah Livers 5.00 12.00
36 Greg Brown III 4.00 10.00
37 Brandon Boston Jr. 5.00 12.00
38 Luka Garza 5.00 12.00
39 Charles Bassey 5.00 12.00
40 Scottie Lewis 4.00 10.00
41 Jason Preston 4.00 10.00
42 Herbert Jones 6.00 15.00
43 JT Thor 5.00 12.00
44 Joe Wieskamp 4.00 10.00
45 Kessler Edwards 5.00 12.00
46 Aaron Wiggins 6.00 15.00
47 Neemias Queta 5.00 12.00
48 Marcus Zegarowski 4.00 10.00
49 David Johnson 4.00 10.00
50 Trendon Watford 6.00 15.00

2021-22 Panini Prizm Rookie Variations

COMMON CARD .50 1.25
SEMISTARS .60 1.50
UNLISTED STARS .75 2.00
*FB: .75X TO 2X BASIC
*SILVER: .75X TO 2X BASIC
282 Cade Cunningham 5.00 12.00
298 Joshua Primo .60 1.50
301 Josh Giddey 2.50 6.00
306 Jalen Green 4.00 10.00
307 Jonathan Kuminga 2.50 6.00
308 Moses Moody 1.50 4.00
310 Franz Wagner 2.50 6.00
311 James Bouknight .60 1.50
312 Davion Mitchell .75 2.00
313 Ziaire Williams 1.00 2.50
314 Jalen Suggs 2.00 5.00
315 Chris Duarte .60 1.50
320 Scottie Barnes 2.50 6.00
325 Evan Mobley 3.00 8.00

2021-22 Panini Prizm Sensational Signatures

COMMON CARD 3.00 8.00
SEMISTARS 4.00 10.00
UNLISTED STARS 5.00 12.00
EXCHANGE DEADLINE 1/08/2024
*SILVER: .6X TO 1.5X BASIC
*MOJO/25: 1,25X TO 3X BASIC
1 Darius Bazley 3.00 8.00
2 Lauri Markkanen 6.00 15.00
3 Luguentz Dort 5.00 12.00
4 Coby White 5.00 12.00
5 Duncan Robinson 4.00 10.00
6 Luka Doncic 400.00 800.00
7 JJ Redick 5.00 12.00
8 Karl-Anthony Towns 20.00 50.00
9 T.J. Warren 3.00 8.00
10 Jamal Murray 20.00 50.00
11 Anfernee Simons 10.00 25.00
12 Tony Allen 3.00 8.00
13 Zach Collins 3.00 8.00
14 Tony Parker 20.00 50.00
15 Eric Gordon 4.00 10.00
16 Anthony Davis 50.00 120.00
17 Michael Porter Jr. 6.00 15.00
18 Rui Hachimura 15.00 40.00
19 Brandon Clarke 5.00 12.00
20 De'Aaron Fox 15.00 40.00
21 Bobby Portis 4.00 10.00
22 Metta World Peace 5.00 12.00
23 Mason Plumlee 3.00 8.00
24 Jerry Lucas 6.00 15.00
25 Ricky Rubio 5.00 12.00
26 Damian Lillard 60.00 150.00
27 Montrezl Harrell 4.00 10.00
28 Trae Young 125.00 300.00
29 Avery Bradley 3.00 8.00
30 Lonzo Ball 12.00 30.00
31 Tom Gugliotta 4.00 10.00
32 Julius Randle 6.00 15.00
33 Aron Baynes 3.00 8.00
34 Cam Reddish 5.00 12.00
35 Domantas Sabonis 6.00 15.00
36 Ja Morant 300.00 600.00
37 Myles Turner 5.00 12.00
38 Nikola Jokic 75.00 200.00
39 Clint Capela 5.00 12.00
40 Khris Middleton 5.00 12.00
41 Ersan Ilyasova 3.00 8.00
42 Buddy Hield 4.00 10.00
43 Ben McLemore 3.00 8.00
44 Danilo Gallinari 4.00 10.00
45 Eric Bledsoe 4.00 10.00
46 Jayson Tatum 125.00 300.00
47 PJ Washington Jr. 5.00 12.00
48 CJ McCollum 4.00 10.00
49 Joe Harris 4.00 10.00
50 De'Andre Hunter 5.00 12.00
51 Cade Cunningham 300.00 600.00
52 Jalen Green 200.00 500.00
53 Evan Mobley 150.00 400.00
54 Scottie Barnes 200.00 500.00
55 Jalen Suggs 50.00 120.00
56 Josh Giddey 150.00 400.00
57 Jonathan Kuminga 100.00 250.00
58 Franz Wagner 40.00 100.00
59 Davion Mitchell 5.00 12.00

60 Ziaire Williams 6.00 15.00
61 James Bouknight 4.00 10.00
62 Joshua Primo 4.00 10.00
63 Chris Duarte 4.00 10.00
64 Moses Moody 40.00 100.00
65 Corey Kispert 6.00 15.00
66 Luka Garza 5.00 12.00
67 Trey Murphy III 15.00 40.00
68 Tre Mann 8.00 20.00
69 Kai Jones 4.00 10.00
70 Jalen Johnson 15.00 40.00
71 Keon Johnson 5.00 12.00
72 Isaiah Jackson 5.00 12.00
73 Brandon Boston Jr. 5.00 12.00
74 Josh Christopher 4.00 10.00
75 Quentin Grimes 10.00 25.00
76 Bones Hyland 40.00 100.00
77 Cameron Thomas 25.00 60.00
78 Jaden Springer 5.00 12.00
79 Day'Ron Sharpe 5.00 12.00
80 Santi Aldama 6.00 15.00
81 Jeremiah Robinson-Earl 5.00 12.00
82 Miles McBride 8.00 20.00
83 Ayo Dosunmu 30.00 80.00
84 Jared Butler 5.00 12.00
85 Isaiah Livers 5.00 12.00

2021-22 Panini Prizm Sensational Swatches

COMMON CARD 1.50 4.00
SEMISTARS 2.00 5.00
UNLISTED STARS 2.50 6.00
*ORANGE ICE: .75X TO 2X BASIC
1 Buddy Hield 2.00 5.00
2 Will Barton 1.50 4.00
3 Marcus Camby 2.00 5.00
4 Jonas Valanciunas 2.00 5.00
5 Kyle Lowry 2.50 6.00
6 Walter Davis 2.00 5.00
7 J.J. Barea 2.00 5.00
8 Kevin Love 2.50 6.00
9 Nikola Jokic 12.00 30.00
10 Bojan Bogdanovic 2.00 5.00
11 Donovan Mitchell 5.00 12.00
12 Brook Lopez 2.00 5.00
13 Pascal Siakam 4.00 10.00
14 Carlos Boozer 2.00 5.00
15 Kevin Durant 8.00 20.00
16 Alvan Adams 2.00 5.00
17 Udonis Haslem 1.50 4.00
18 Vince Carter 5.00 12.00
19 Khris Middleton 2.50 6.00
20 Al Horford 2.50 6.00
21 Stephen Curry 25.00 60.00
22 Jarrett Allen 2.50 6.00
23 CJ McCollum 2.00 5.00
24 Lamar Odom 2.50 6.00
25 Julius Randle 3.00 8.00
26 Karl-Anthony Towns 4.00 10.00
27 Zion Williamson 6.00 15.00
28 Kyrie Irving 5.00 12.00
29 Jamal Murray 4.00 10.00
30 Jusuf Nurkic 2.00 5.00
31 Maxi Kleber 2.00 5.00
32 D'Angelo Russell 2.50 6.00
33 Giannis Antetokounmpo 12.00 30.00
34 Kawhi Leonard 6.00 15.00
35 Luka Doncic 20.00 50.00
36 Rudy Gobert 3.00 8.00
37 Aaron Gordon 2.50 6.00
38 Roy Hibbert 2.00 5.00
39 Trae Young 6.00 15.00
40 David Lee 2.00 5.00
41 De'Aaron Fox 4.00 10.00
42 Chris Kaman 1.50 4.00
43 Markelle Fultz 1.50 4.00
44 Anthony Davis 6.00 15.00
45 Joakim Noah 2.00 5.00
46 Ricky Rubio 2.00 5.00
47 DeMar DeRozan 3.00 8.00
48 Mike Miller 2.00 5.00
49 Josh Richardson 2.00 5.00
50 Myles Turner 2.50 6.00
51 Collin Sexton 2.50 6.00
52 Paul Pierce 4.00 10.00
53 Draymond Green 3.00 8.00
54 Steven Adams 2.00 5.00
55 Mike Conley 2.00 5.00
56 Paul George 4.00 10.00
57 Mario Chalmers 2.00 5.00
58 Kristaps Porzingis 3.00 8.00
59 Brandon Clarke 2.50 6.00
60 Nikola Vucevic 2.50 6.00
61 Cade Cunningham 20.00 50.00
62 Jalen Green 15.00 40.00
63 Evan Mobley 10.00 25.00
64 Scottie Barnes 8.00 20.00
65 Jalen Suggs 6.00 15.00
66 Josh Giddey 8.00 20.00
67 Jonathan Kuminga 8.00 20.00
68 Franz Wagner 8.00 20.00
69 Davion Mitchell 2.50 6.00
70 Ziaire Williams 3.00 8.00
71 James Bouknight 2.00 5.00
72 Joshua Primo 2.00 5.00
73 Chris Duarte 2.00 5.00
74 Moses Moody 5.00 12.00
75 Corey Kispert 3.00 8.00
76 Alperen Sengun 8.00 20.00
77 Trey Murphy III 8.00 20.00
78 Tre Mann 4.00 10.00
79 Kai Jones 2.00 5.00
80 Jalen Johnson 8.00 20.00
81 Keon Johnson 2.50 6.00
82 Isaiah Jackson 2.50 6.00
83 Usman Garuba 2.00 5.00
84 Josh Christopher 2.00 5.00
85 Quentin Grimes 5.00 12.00
86 Bones Hyland 3.00 8.00
87 Cameron Thomas 5.00 12.00
88 Jaden Springer 2.50 6.00
89 Day'Ron Sharpe 2.50 6.00
90 Santi Aldama 3.00 8.00
91 Jeremiah Robinson-Earl 2.50 6.00
92 Miles McBride 4.00 10.00
93 Ayo Dosunmu 5.00 12.00
94 Jared Butler 2.50 6.00
95 Isaiah Livers 2.50 6.00
96 Greg Brown III 2.00 5.00
97 Brandon Boston Jr. 2.50 6.00
98 Luka Garza 2.50 6.00
99 Charles Bassey 2.50 6.00
100 Scottie Lewis 2.00 5.00

2021-22 Panini Prizm Signatures

COMMON CARD 3.00 8.00
SEMISTARS 4.00 10.00
UNLISTED STARS 5.00 12.00
EXCHANGE DEADLINE 1/08/2024
*CHOICE: .6X TO 1.5X BASIC
*SILVER: .6X TO 1.5X BASIC
*MOJO/25: 1.25X TO 3X BASIC
1 Ben Wallace 30.00 80.00
2 Charles Barkley 75.00 200.00
3 Richard Hamilton 6.00 15.00
4 Larry Bird 75.00 200.00
5 Rick Fox 5.00 12.00
6 Kareem Abdul-Jabbar 100.00 250.00
7 Clint Capela 5.00 12.00
8 Anfernee Hardaway 40.00 100.00
9 Lamar Odom 5.00 12.00
10 Lauri Markkanen 6.00 15.00
11 Christian Laettner 5.00 12.00
12 Shaquille O'Neal 100.00 250.00
13 Kenny Smith 4.00 10.00
14 John Stockton 30.00 80.00
15 Elvin Hayes 6.00 15.00
16 Anthony Edwards 150.00 400.00
17 Mark Jackson 4.00 10.00
18 Nikola Jokic 75.00 200.00
19 Andrea Bargnani 3.00 8.00
20 James Worthy 8.00 20.00
21 Artis Gilmore 6.00 15.00
22 Allen Iverson 75.00 200.00
23 JJ Redick 5.00 12.00
24 Luka Doncic 400.00 800.00
25 Danny Manning 4.00 10.00
26 Jason Kidd 20.00 50.00
27 Wang Zhi-zhi 60.00 150.00
28 Dennis Rodman 40.00 100.00
29 B.J. Armstrong 5.00 12.00
30 Metta World Peace 5.00 12.00
31 Eric Gordon 4.00 10.00
32 Kevin Garnett 50.00 120.00
33 Michael Porter Jr. 6.00 15.00
34 Magic Johnson 75.00 200.00
35 Alex Caruso 5.00 12.00
36 Trae Young 125.00 300.00
37 Cade Cunningham 4.00 10.00
38 Vince Carter 50.00 120.00
39 Elton Brand 5.00 12.00
40 Julius Randle 6.00 15.00
41 Ricky Rubio 5.00 12.00
42 Dwyane Wade 60.00 150.00
43 Montrezl Harrell 4.00 10.00
44 Oscar Robertson 40.00 100.00
45 Avery Bradley 3.00 8.00
46 Rasheed Wallace 20.00 50.00
47 Darius Bazley 3.00 8.00
48 Khris Middleton 5.00 12.00
49 Harold Miner 5.00 12.00

2021-22 Panini Prizm USA Basketball

COMMON CARD .40 1.00
SEMISTARS .50 1.25
UNLISTED STARS .60 1.50
*GREEN: .75X TO 2X BASIC
*GREEN WAVE: 1.25X TO 3X BASIC
*SILVER: 1.25X TO 3X BASIC
1 Jayson Tatum 2.50 6.00
2 Kevin Durant 2.00 5.00
3 Anthony Davis 1.50 4.00
4 Dwyane Wade 1.25 3.00
5 Khris Middleton .60 1.50
6 Vince Carter 1.25 3.00
7 Kevin Garnett 1.50 4.00
8 Jrue Holiday .75 2.00
9 Charles Barkley 1.50 4.00
10 Shaquille O'Neal 2.00 5.00

2021-22 Panini Prizm Widescreen

COMMON CARD .40 1.00
SEMISTARS .50 1.25
UNLISTED STARS .60 1.50
*FAST BREAK: .75X TO 2X BASIC
*HYPER: .75X TO 2X BASIC
*SILVER: 1.25X TO 3X BASIC
1 Luka Doncic 4.00 10.00
2 Stephen Curry 4.00 10.00
3 Giannis Antetokounmpo 3.00 8.00
4 Zion Williamson 1.50 4.00
5 Kevin Durant 2.00 5.00
6 Damian Lillard 1.50 4.00
7 Donovan Mitchell 1.25 3.00
8 Nikola Jokic 3.00 8.00
9 LaMelo Ball 1.50 4.00
10 LeBron James 5.00 12.00

2021-22 Panini Prizm Widescreen Prizms Mojo

*MOJO: 5X TO 12X BASIC
STATED PRINT RUN 25 SER.#'d SETS
1 Luka Doncic 100.00 250.00
2 Stephen Curry 125.00 300.00
3 Giannis Antetokounmpo 60.00 150.00
4 Zion Williamson COR
Card #'d/25 60.00 150.00
5 Kevin Durant 25.00 60.00
6 Damian Lillard 20.00 50.00
7 Donovan Mitchell 15.00 40.00
9 LaMelo Ball 100.00 250.00
10 LeBron James 125.00 300.00

2022-23 Panini Prizm

COMPLETE SET (300)
*RED WHITE & BLUE: 1X TO 2.5X BASIC
*GREEN: 1.25X TO 3X BASIC
*PINK ICE: 1.5X TO 4X BASIC
*RED ICE: 1.5X TO 4X BASIC
*RUBY WAVE: 1.5X TO 4X BASIC
*FAST BREAK: 2X TO 5X BASIC
*GREEN WAVE: 2X TO 5X BASIC
*ICE: 2X TO 5X BASIC
*PULSAR: 2X TO 5X BASIC
1 Robert Williams III .30 .75
2 Jaylen Brown .75 2.00
3 Marcus Smart .50 1.25
4 Al Horford .40 1.00
5 Kyrie Irving .75 2.00
6 Malcolm Brogdon .30 .75
7 Julius Randle .50 1.25
8 Evan Fournier .30 .75
9 Obi Toppin .40 1.00
10 Kevin Durant 1.25 3.00
11 Jalen Brunson .75 2.00
12 Derrick White .40 1.00
13 Ben Simmons .40 1.00
14 RJ Barrett .60 1.50
15 Quentin Grimes .30 .75
16 Cam Reddish .30 .75
17 Jayson Tatum 1.50 4.00
18 Patty Mills .40 1.00
19 Seth Curry .30 .75
20 Cameron Thomas .60 1.50
21 Tyrese Maxey .75 2.00
22 OG Anunoby .50 1.25
23 Jeff Green .25 .60
24 Georges Niang .30 .75
25 Scottie Barnes .60 1.50
26 Fred VanVleet .50 1.25
27 Bones Hyland .30 .75
28 Michael Porter Jr. .50 1.25
29 Pascal Siakam .60 1.50
30 Chris Boucher .40 1.00
31 Tobias Harris .30 .75
32 Jamal Murray .60 1.50
33 Kentavious Caldwell-Pope .30 .75
34 Joel Embiid .60 1.50
35 James Harden .75 2.00
36 De'Anthony Melton .30 .75
37 Precious Achiuwa .40 1.00
38 Gary Trent .40 1.00
39 Nikola Jokic 2.00 5.00
40 Bruce Brown .40 1.00
41 Aaron Gordon .40 1.00
42 P.J. Tucker .30 .75
43 D'Angelo Russell .30 .75
44 Bojan Bogdanovic .40 1.00
45 Mike Conley .30 .75
46 Anfernee Simons .50 1.25
47 Rudy Gay .40 1.00
48 Josh Hart .40 1.00
49 Drew Eubanks .25 .60
50 Gary Payton II .30 .75
51 Darius Bazley .25 .60
52 Aleksej Pokusevski .40 1.00
53 Jaden McDaniels .40 1.00
54 Jordan Clarkson .40 1.00
55 Luguentz Dort .40 1.00
56 Anthony Edwards 2.00 5.00
57 Austin Rivers .25 .60
58 Jerami Grant .50 1.25
59 Talen Horton-Tucker .30 .75
60 Malik Beasley .30 .75
61 Josh Giddey .60 1.50
62 Damian Lillard 1.00 2.50
63 Jusuf Nurkic .40 1.00
64 Shai Gilgeous-Alexander 2.00 5.00
65 Aaron Wiggins .30 .75
66 Donovan Mitchell .75 2.00
67 Rudy Gobert .50 1.25
68 Karl-Anthony Towns .60 1.50
69 Tre Mann .30 .75
70 Jaylen Nowell .40 1.00
71 Coby White .30 .75
72 DeMar DeRozan .50 1.25
73 Marvin Bagley III .30 .75
74 Lauri Markkanen .60 1.50
75 Darius Garland .60 1.50
76 Jarrett Allen .40 1.00
77 Caris LeVert .30 .75
78 Isaac Okoro .30 .75
79 Ayo Dosunmu .50 1.25
80 Nikola Vucevic .40 1.00
81 Evan Mobley 1.00 2.50
82 Hamidou Diallo .30 .75
83 Alex Caruso .40 1.00
84 Saddiq Bey .30 .75
85 Frank Jackson .25 .60
86 Kemba Walker .40 1.00
87 Collin Sexton .50 1.25
88 Lonzo Ball .40 1.00
89 Cade Cunningham 1.25 3.00
90 Kevin Love .40 1.00
91 Alec Burks .30 .75
92 Zach LaVine .75 2.00
93 Tyrese Haliburton .75 2.00
94 Brook Lopez .40 1.00
95 Buddy Hield .40 1.00
96 Giannis Antetokounmpo 2.00 5.00
97 Pat Connaughton .30 .75
98 Grayson Allen .40 1.00
99 Chris Duarte .30 .75
100 James Wiseman .30 .75
101 Stephen Curry 3.00 8.00
102 Jordan Poole .60 1.50
103 Moses Moody .50 1.25
104 Jonathan Kuminga 1.00 2.50
105 Bobby Portis .40 1.00
106 Daniel Theis .30 .75
107 Joe Ingles .30 .75
108 Myles Turner .40 1.00
109 Jalen Smith .40 1.00
110 Draymond Green .50 1.25
111 Aaron Nesmith .40 1.00
112 Khris Middleton .50 1.25
113 Jrue Holiday .50 1.25
114 Andrew Wiggins .50 1.25
115 Klay Thompson 1.00 2.50
116 Reggie Jackson .30 .75
117 Chris Paul .75 2.00
118 De'Aaron Fox .75 2.00
119 Jason Preston .30 .75
120 Mikal Bridges .50 1.25
121 Neemias Queta .30 .75
122 Anthony Davis 1.00 2.50
123 Austin Reaves 1.00 2.50
124 Kevin Huerter .40 1.00
125 John Wall .50 1.25
126 Cameron Johnson .30 .75
127 Jae Crowder .25 .60
128 Kawhi Leonard 1.00 2.50
129 Cameron Payne .30 .75
130 Marcus Morris Sr. .25 .60
131 Harrison Barnes .30 .75
132 Norman Powell .40 1.00
133 Russell Westbrook .60 1.50
134 LeBron James 3.00 8.00
135 Deandre Ayton .40 1.00
136 Davion Mitchell .30 .75
137 Terance Mann .30 .75
138 Paul George .60 1.50
139 Patrick Beverley .25 .60
140 Devin Booker 1.00 2.50
141 Luke Kennard .30 .75
142 Malik Monk .40 1.00
143 Domantas Sabonis .50 1.25
144 Carmelo Anthony .60 1.50
145 Kendrick Nunn .30 .75
146 Dejounte Murray .50 1.25
147 Kyle Lowry .50 1.25
148 Gordon Hayward .30 .75
149 Jimmy Butler .75 2.00
150 LaMelo Ball 1.00 2.50
151 Justin Holiday .25 .60
152 John Collins .40 1.00
153 Terry Rozier III .50 1.25
154 De'Andre Hunter .40 1.00
155 Bam Adebayo .60 1.50
156 Cody Martin .30 .75
157 Lou Williams .40 1.00
158 Bogdan Bogdanovic .40 1.00
159 Kelly Oubre Jr. .40 1.00
160 PJ Washington Jr. .40 1.00
161 Max Strus .40 1.00
162 Clint Capela .40 1.00
163 Onyeka Okongwu .40 1.00
164 Trae Young 1.00 2.50
165 Montrezl Harrell .40 1.00
166 Tyler Herro .60 1.50
167 Victor Oladipo .30 .75
168 Duncan Robinson .40 1.00
169 Jonathan Isaac .40 1.00
170 Deni Avdija .40 1.00
171 Monte Morris .25 .60
172 Kyle Kuzma .50 1.25
173 Corey Kispert .40 1.00
174 Markelle Fultz .30 .75
175 Kevin Porter Jr. .30 .75
176 Bradley Beal .50 1.25
177 RJ Hampton .30 .75
178 Alperen Sengun .50 1.25
179 Reggie Bullock .30 .75
180 Cole Anthony .40 1.00
181 Jalen Green 1.25 3.00
182 Franz Wagner 1.00 2.50
183 Kenyon Martin Jr. .40 1.00
184 Jalen Suggs .50 1.25
185 Dennis Schroder .40 1.00
186 Eric Gordon .30 .75
187 Dwight Powell .25 .60
188 Garrison Mathews .40 1.00
189 Davis Bertans .25 .60
190 Rui Hachimura .40 1.00
191 Kristaps Porzingis .50 1.25
192 Christian Wood .25 .60
193 Tim Hardaway Jr. .30 .75
194 Will Barton .25 .60
195 Wendell Carter Jr. .40 1.00
196 Luka Doncic 2.50 6.00
197 Dorian Finney-Smith .30 .75
198 Jae'Sean Tate .25 .60
199 Spencer Dinwiddie .30 .75
200 Ja Morant 1.25 3.00
201 Herbert Jones .40 1.00
202 CJ McCollum .40 1.00
203 Danny Green .30 .75
204 Brandon Clarke .30 .75
205 Dillon Brooks .40 1.00
206 Jaren Jackson Jr. .60 1.50
207 Devin Vassell .50 1.25
208 Brandon Ingram .50 1.25
209 Tre Jones .40 1.00
210 Doug McDermott .25 .60
211 Keldon Johnson .50 1.25
212 Tyus Jones .30 .75
213 Josh Richardson .30 .75
214 Zion Williamson 1.00 2.50
215 Trey Murphy III .50 1.25
216 Isaiah Roby .25 .60
217 Desmond Bane .50 1.25
218 Devonte' Graham .30 .75
219 Jonas Valanciunas .30 .75
220 T.J. Warren .30 .75
221 Wendell Moore Jr. RC .75 2.00
222 Bryce McGowens RC .75 2.00
223 Christian Braun RC 2.00 5.00
224 Ousmane Dieng RC 1.00 2.50
225 Kendall Brown RC .60 1.50
226 Jaden Hardy RC 1.25 3.00
227 Andrew Nembhard RC 1.50 4.00
228 Jabari Smith Jr. RC 2.50 6.00
229 Ryan Rollins RC .75 2.00
230 Malaki Branham RC .75 2.00
231 Johnny Davis RC .75 2.00
232 Scotty Pippen Jr. RC 1.00 2.50
233 Dyson Daniels RC 2.00 5.00
234 Walker Kessler RC 1.50 4.00
235 Kennedy Chandler RC .75 2.00
236 Nikola Jokic RC 1.50 4.00
237 Jabari Walker RC .60 1.50
238 Josh Minott RC .75 2.00
239 Jalen Duren RC 2.50 6.00
240 Dalen Terry RC .75 2.00
241 Tyrese Martin RC .60 1.50
242 Patrick Baldwin Jr. RC .75 2.00
243 TyTy Washington Jr. RC .75 2.00
244 Jake LaRavia RC .75 2.00
245 Keegan Murray RC 2.00 5.00
246 Jalen Williams RC 4.00 10.00
247 Jaylin Williams RC 1.00 2.50
248 AJ Griffin RC .60 1.50
249 Paolo Banchero RC 5.00 12.00
250 Shaedon Sharpe RC 3.00 8.00
251 E.J. Liddell RC .75 2.00
252 Isaiah Mobley RC .75 2.00
253 Kenneth Lofton Jr. RC 1.00 2.50
254 Bennedict Mathurin RC 2.50 6.00
255 Vince Williams Jr. RC 1.00 2.50
256 Jaden Ivey RC 2.50 6.00
257 Mark Williams RC 1.50 4.00
258 Tari Eason RC 2.00 5.00
259 Peyton Watson RC 1.25 3.00
260 Trevor Keels RC .60 1.50
261 David Roddy RC 1.00 2.50
262 Moussa Diabate RC .75 2.00
263 Jeremy Sochan RC 2.50 6.00
264 Blake Wesley RC .75 2.00
265 Christian Koloko RC .75 2.00
266 Chet Holmgren RC 4.00 10.00
267 Ochai Agbaji RC 1.00 2.50
268 MarJon Beauchamp RC .75 2.00
269 Caleb Houstan RC .75 2.00
270 Max Christie RC 2.00 5.00
271 David Robinson .75 2.00
272 Paul Pierce .60 1.50
273 Jason Kidd .60 1.50
274 Vince Carter .75 2.00
275 Patrick Ewing .60 1.50
276 Magic Johnson 1.50 4.00
277 Ben Wallace .50 1.25
278 Ray Allen .60 1.50
279 Dominique Wilkins .60 1.50
280 Tracy McGrady .60 1.50
281 Allen Iverson 1.00 2.50
282 Kevin Garnett 1.00 2.50
283 Gary Payton .60 1.50
284 Karl Malone .75 2.00
285 Wilt Chamberlain 1.25 3.00
286 Pete Maravich 1.00 2.50
287 Amar'e Stoudemire .40 1.00
288 Chris Webber .50 1.25
289 Steve Nash .75 2.00
290 Hakeem Olajuwon .75 2.00
291 Dennis Rodman 1.00 2.50
292 John Stockton .75 2.00
293 Tim Duncan 1.00 2.50
294 Dwyane Wade .75 2.00
295 Chris Mullin .50 1.25
296 Manu Ginobili .75 2.00
297 Shaquille O'Neal 1.50 4.00
298 Dirk Nowitzki 1.00 2.50
299 Tony Parker .60 1.50
300 Charles Barkley 1.00 2.50

2022-23 Panini Prizm Prizm Blue Sparkle

COMPLETE SET (300)
*BLUE SPARKLE: 5X TO 12X BASIC
STATED PRINT RUN 144 SER.#'d SETS
249 Paolo Banchero 200.00 500.00
266 Chet Holmgren 125.00 300.00

2022-23 Panini Prizm Prizm Gold Sparkle

COMPLETE SET (300)
*GOLD SPARKLE: 15X TO 40X BASIC
STATED PRINT RUN 24 SER.#'d SETS
249 Paolo Banchero 1,000.00 2,000.00
266 Chet Holmgren 600.00 1,200.00

2022-23 Panini Prizm Prizm Red Sparkle

COMPLETE SET (300)
*RED SPARKLE: 3X TO 8X BASIC
249 Paolo Banchero 75.00 200.00
266 Chet Holmgren 60.00 150.00

2022-23 Panini Prizm Prizms Blue

COMPLETE SET (300)
*BLUE: 5X TO 12X BASIC
STATED PRINT RUN 199 SER.#'d SETS
249 Paolo Banchero 300.00 600.00
266 Chet Holmgren 125.00 300.00

2022-23 Panini Prizm Prizms Blue Ice

COMPLETE SET (300)
*BLUE ICE: 6X TO 15X BASIC
STATED PRINT RUN 125 SER.#'d SETS
249 Paolo Banchero 400.00 800.00
266 Chet Holmgren 200.00 500.00

2022-23 Panini Prizm Prizms Blue Shimmer FOTL

COMPLETE SET (300)
*BLUE SHIMMER: 8X TO 20X BASIC
STATED PRINT RUN 35 SER.#'d SETS
249 Paolo Banchero 500.00 1,000.00
266 Chet Holmgren 300.00 600.00

2022-23 Panini Prizm Prizms Blue Wave

COMPLETE SET (300)
*BLUE WAVE: 2X TO 5X BASIC
249 Paolo Banchero 40.00 100.00

2022-23 Panini Prizm Prizms Choice Blue

COMPLETE SET (300)
*CHOICE BLUE: 6X TO 15X BASIC
STATED PRINT RUN 49 SER.#'d SETS
249 Paolo Banchero 400.00 800.00
266 Chet Holmgren 200.00 500.00

2022-23 Panini Prizm Prizms Choice Blue Yellow and Green

*CHOICE BL YLLW GRN: 2.5X TO 6X BASIC
249 Paolo Banchero 60.00 150.00

2022-23 Panini Prizm Prizms Choice Purple

COMPLETE SET (300)
*CHOICE PURPLE: 15X TO 40X BASIC
STATED PRINT RUN 20 SER.#'d SETS
249 Paolo Banchero 1,000.00 2,000.00
266 Chet Holmgren 600.00 1,200.00

2022-23 Panini Prizm Prizms Choice Red

COMPLETE SET (300)
*CHOICE RED: 5X TO 12X BASIC
STATED PRINT RUN 88 SER.#'d SETS
249 Paolo Banchero 300.00 600.00
266 Chet Holmgren 150.00 400.00

2022-23 Panini Prizm Prizms Fast Break Blue

COMPLETE SET (300)
*FB BLUE: 5X TO 12X BASIC
STATED PRINT RUN 150 SER.#'d SETS
249 Paolo Banchero 150.00 400.00
266 Chet Holmgren 75.00 200.00

2022-23 Panini Prizm Prizms Fast Break Bronze

COMPLETE SET (300)
*FB BRONZE: 15X TO 40X BASIC
STATED PRINT RUN 20 SER.#'d SETS
249 Paolo Banchero 1,000.00 2,000.00
266 Chet Holmgren 600.00 1,200.00

2022-23 Panini Prizm Prizms Fast Break Pink

COMPLETE SET (300)
*FB PINK: 6X TO 15X BASIC
STATED PRINT RUN 50 SER.#'d SETS
249 Paolo Banchero 400.00 800.00
266 Chet Holmgren 200.00 500.00

2022-23 Panini Prizm Prizms Fast Break Purple

COMPLETE SET (300)
*FB PURPLE: 5X TO 12X BASIC
STATED PRINT RUN 75 SER.#'d SETS
249 Paolo Banchero 300.00 600.00
266 Chet Holmgren 150.00 400.00

2022-23 Panini Prizm Prizms Fast Break Red

COMPLETE SET (300)
*FB RED: 5X TO 12X BASIC
STATED PRINT RUN 100 SER.#'d SETS
249 Paolo Banchero 300.00 600.00
266 Chet Holmgren 150.00 400.00

2022-23 Panini Prizm Prizms Green Ice

COMPLETE SET (300)
*GREEN ICE: 2X TO 5X BASIC
249 Paolo Banchero 60.00 150.00
266 Chet Holmgren 50.00 120.00

2022-23 Panini Prizm Prizms Green Pulsar

COMPLETE SET (300)
*GREEN PULSAR: 15X TO 40X BASIC
STATED PRINT RUN 25 SER.#'d SETS
249 Paolo Banchero 1,000.00 2,000.00
266 Chet Holmgren 600.00 1,200.00

2022-23 Panini Prizm Prizms Hyper

*HYPER: 1.5X TO 4X BASIC
249 Paolo Banchero 40.00 100.00

2022-23 Panini Prizm Prizms Mojo

COMPLETE SET (300)
*MOJO: 15X TO 40X BASIC
STATED PRINT RUN 25 SER.#'d SETS
249 Paolo Banchero 1,000.00 2,000.00
266 Chet Holmgren 600.00 1,200.00

2022-23 Panini Prizm Prizms Orange

COMPLETE SET (300)
*ORANGE: 8X TO 20X BASIC
STATED PRINT RUN 49 SER.#'d SETS
249 Paolo Banchero 500.00 1,000.00
266 Chet Holmgren 300.00 600.00

2022-23 Panini Prizm Prizms Orange Wave

COMPLETE SET (300)
*ORANGE WAVE: 6X TO 15X BASIC
STATED PRINT RUN 60 SER.#'d SETS
249 Paolo Banchero 400.00 800.00
266 Chet Holmgren 200.00 500.00

2022-23 Panini Prizm Prizms Pink Pulsar

COMPLETE SET (300)
*PINK PULSAR: 8X TO 20X BASIC
STATED PRINT RUN 42 SER.#'d SETS
249 Paolo Banchero 500.00 1,000.00
266 Chet Holmgren 300.00 600.00

2022-23 Panini Prizm Prizms Premium Factory Set

COMPLETE SET (300)
*PRM FACTORY SET: 2.5X TO 6X BASIC
STATED PRINT RUN 150 SER.#'d SETS
249 Paolo Banchero 100.00 250.00
266 Chet Holmgren 60.00 150.00

2022-23 Panini Prizm Prizms Purple

COMPLETE SET (300)
*PURPLE: 6X TO 15X BASIC
STATED PRINT RUN 99 SER.#'d SETS
249 Paolo Banchero 400.00 800.00
266 Chet Holmgren 200.00 500.00

2022-23 Panini Prizm Prizms Purple Ice

COMPLETE SET (300)
*PURPLE ICE: 5X TO 12X BASIC
STATED PRINT RUN 149 SER.#'d SETS
249 Paolo Banchero 200.00 500.00
266 Chet Holmgren 125.00 300.00

2022-23 Panini Prizm Prizms Purple Pulsar

COMPLETE SET (300)
PURPLE PULSAR: 8X TO 20X BASIC
STATED PRINT RUN 35 SER.#'d SETS
249 Paolo Banchero 500.00 1,000.00
266 Chet Holmgren 300.00 600.00

2022-23 Panini Prizm Prizms Red

COMPLETE SET (300)
*RED: 4X TO 10X BASIC
STATED PRINT RUN 299 SER. #'D SETS
249 Paolo Banchero 100.00 250.00

2022-23 Panini Prizm Prizms Red Power

COMPLETE SET (300)
*RED POWER: 5X TO 12X BASIC
STATED PRINT RUN 75 SER.#'d SETS
249 Paolo Banchero 300.00 600.00
266 Chet Holmgren 150.00 400.00

2022-23 Panini Prizm Prizms Silver

*SILVER: 2X TO 5X BASIC
246 Jalen Williams 25.00 60.00
249 Paolo Banchero 50.00 120.00

2022-23 Panini Prizm Champion Signatures

COMPLETE SET (10)
*SILVER: .5X TO 1.2X BASIC
1 Kareem Abdul-Jabbar 75.00 200.00
2 Kevin Garnett 75.00 200.00
3 Stephen Curry 1,500.00 3,000.00
4 Manu Ginobili 75.00 200.00
5 Bob Cousy 125.00 300.00
6 Hakeem Olajuwon 40.00 100.00
7 Dirk Nowitzki 125.00 300.00
8 Kyrie Irving 75.00 200.00
9 Larry Bird 75.00 200.00
10 Dwyane Wade 75.00 200.00

2022-23 Panini Prizm Champion Signatures Prizms Mojo

COMPLETE SET (10)
*MOJO: .75X TO 2X BASIC
STATED PRINT RUN 25 SER.#'d SETS
3 Stephen Curry 4,000.00 8,000.00

2022-23 Panini Prizm Dominance

COMPLETE SET (25)
*GREEN: .75X TO 2X BASIC
*SILVER: .75X TO 2X BASIC
1 Kyrie Irving 1.00 2.50
2 Devin Booker 1.25 3.00
3 Luka Doncic 3.00 8.00
4 Kevin Durant 1.50 4.00
5 Ja Morant 1.50 4.00
6 Zach LaVine 1.00 2.50
7 Cade Cunningham 1.50 4.00
8 Anthony Davis 1.25 3.00
9 Scottie Barnes .75 2.00
10 Nikola Jokic 2.50 6.00
11 Jayson Tatum 2.00 5.00
12 Joel Embiid .75 2.00
13 Bradley Beal .60 1.50
14 Donovan Mitchell 1.00 2.50
15 Zion Williamson 1.25 3.00
16 Damian Lillard 1.25 3.00
17 Anthony Edwards 2.50 6.00
18 DeMar DeRozan .60 1.50
19 Trae Young 1.25 3.00
20 Kawhi Leonard 1.25 3.00
21 Giannis Antetokounmpo 2.50 6.00
22 LaMelo Ball 1.25 3.00
23 Stephen Curry 4.00 10.00
24 LeBron James 4.00 10.00
25 James Harden 1.00 2.50

2022-23 Panini Prizm Emergent

COMPLETE SET (30)
*GREEN: .75X TO 2X BASIC
*SILVER: 1.25X TO 3X BASIC
1 Patrick Baldwin Jr. .60 1.50
2 Andrew Nembhard 1.25 3.00
3 MarJon Beauchamp .60 1.50
4 Dyson Daniels 1.50 4.00
5 Tari Eason 1.50 4.00
6 AJ Griffin .50 1.25
7 Jeremy Sochan 2.00 5.00
8 Keegan Murray 1.50 4.00
9 Ochai Agbaji .75 2.00
10 Jaden Ivey 2.00 5.00
11 Jaden Hardy 1.00 2.50
12 Jalen Williams 3.00 8.00
13 Johnny Davis .60 1.50
14 Ousmane Dieng .75 2.00
15 Shaedon Sharpe 2.50 6.00
16 Chet Holmgren 3.00 8.00
17 Nikola Jovic 1.25 3.00
18 TyTy Washington Jr. .60 1.50
19 Peyton Watson 1.00 2.50
20 Jalen Duren 2.00 5.00
21 Christian Braun 1.50 4.00
22 Bennedict Mathurin 2.00 5.00
23 Wendell Moore Jr. .60 1.50
24 Mark Williams 1.25 3.00
25 Paolo Banchero 4.00 10.00
26 Jabari Smith Jr. 2.00 5.00
27 Jake LaRavia .60 1.50
28 Malaki Branham .60 1.50
29 Dalen Terry .60 1.50
30 Blake Wesley .60 1.50

2022-23 Panini Prizm Fast Break Autographs

COMPLETE SET (60)
1 Jordan Clarkson 6.00 15.00
2 Mark Price 6.00 15.00
3 Cade Cunningham 75.00 200.00
4 Detlef Schrempf 6.00 15.00
5 Malik Monk 6.00 15.00
6 RJ Barrett 10.00 25.00
7 Marcus Smart 8.00 20.00
8 Jason Kidd 20.00 50.00
9 Jamal Crawford 6.00 15.00
10 Shawn Kemp 20.00 50.00
11 Caris LeVert 5.00 12.00
12 Glen Rice 6.00 15.00
13 Manu Ginobili 40.00 100.00
14 Duncan Robinson 6.00 15.00
15 Ziaire Williams 5.00 12.00
16 Grant Hill 20.00 50.00
17 Collin Sexton 8.00 20.00
18 Christian Wood 4.00 10.00
19 Al Horford 6.00 15.00
20 Lenny Wilkens 8.00 20.00
21 Jonathan Kuminga 15.00 40.00
22 Jaren Jackson Jr. 20.00 50.00
23 Ray Allen 40.00 100.00
24 John Stockton 40.00 100.00
25 Bernard King 8.00 20.00
26 Dejounte Murray 8.00 20.00
27 Gail Goodrich 6.00 15.00
28 Keldon Johnson 8.00 20.00
29 Jerry Stackhouse 8.00 20.00
30 Tyrese Haliburton 20.00 50.00
31 Jason Richardson 6.00 15.00
32 Tony Parker 20.00 50.00
33 Evan Mobley 15.00 40.00
34 Bob McAdoo 8.00 20.00
35 B.J. Armstrong 6.00 15.00
36 De'Aaron Fox 20.00 50.00
37 Adrian Dantley 6.00 15.00
38 Jamaal Wilkes 6.00 15.00
39 Ja Morant 125.00 300.00
40 Michael Porter Jr. 8.00 20.00
41 Juwan Howard 6.00 15.00
42 Wally Szczerbiak 5.00 12.00
43 Luka Doncic 400.00 800.00
44 Luguentz Dort 6.00 15.00
45 Jerry West 25.00 60.00
46 Luc Longley 6.00 15.00
47 Jalen Green 75.00 200.00
48 Paul Pierce 25.00 60.00
49 Jason Terry 5.00 12.00
50 Karl-Anthony Towns 10.00 25.00
51 Chris Paul 40.00 100.00

52 Walt Frazier 10.00 25.00
53 Jayson Tatum 150.00 400.00
54 Rik Smits 5.00 12.00
55 Brook Lopez 6.00 15.00
56 Joe Dumars 8.00 20.00
57 Jalen Suggs 8.00 20.00
58 Payton Pritchard 6.00 15.00
59 Lonnie Walker IV 5.00 12.00
60 Jeff Hornacek 6.00 15.00

2022-23 Panini Prizm Fast Break Rookie Autographs

COMPLETE SET (40)
1 Andrew Nembhard 12.00 30.00
2 Jalen Duren 20.00 50.00
3 Jabari Smith Jr. 20.00 50.00
4 Ousmane Dieng 8.00 20.00
5 Kennedy Chandler 6.00 15.00
6 AJ Griffin 5.00 12.00
7 Tari Eason 15.00 40.00
8 Christian Koloko 6.00 15.00
9 Keegan Murray 15.00 40.00
10 TyTy Washington Jr. 6.00 15.00
11 Jalen Williams 30.00 80.00
12 Wendell Moore Jr. 6.00 15.00
13 Trevor Keels 5.00 12.00
14 Johnny Davis 6.00 15.00
15 Jeremy Sochan 20.00 50.00
16 Mark Williams 12.00 30.00
17 Nikola Jovic 12.00 30.00
18 Walker Kessler 12.00 30.00
19 Chet Holmgren 30.00 80.00
20 MarJon Beauchamp 6.00 15.00
21 Kenneth Lofton Jr. 8.00 20.00
22 Jake LaRavia 6.00 15.00
23 Bennedict Mathurin 20.00 50.00
24 Malaki Branham 6.00 15.00
25 Isaiah Mobley 6.00 15.00
26 Paolo Banchero 40.00 100.00
27 Caleb Houstan 6.00 15.00
28 Dalen Terry 6.00 15.00
29 Christian Braun 15.00 40.00
30 Dyson Daniels 15.00 40.00
31 Mac McClung 15.00 40.00
32 Moussa Diabate 6.00 15.00
33 Jaden Ivey 20.00 50.00
34 Shaedon Sharpe 75.00 200.00
35 Collin Gillespie 6.00 15.00
36 Max Christie 15.00 40.00
37 Blake Wesley 6.00 15.00
38 David Roddy 8.00 20.00
39 Ochai Agbaji 8.00 20.00
40 Jaden Hardy 10.00 25.00

2022-23 Panini Prizm Fearless

COMPLETE SET (21)
*FAST BREAK: .75X TO 2X BASIC
*SILVER: .75X TO 2X BASIC
*MOJO/25: 6X TO 15X BASIC
1 Giannis Antetokounmpo 2.50 6.00
2 Charles Barkley 1.25 3.00
3 Allen Iverson 1.25 3.00
4 Donovan Mitchell 1.00 2.50
5 LaMelo Ball 1.25 3.00
6 Kawhi Leonard 1.25 3.00
7 Kevin Durant 1.50 4.00
8 Ja Morant 1.50 4.00
9 Dirk Nowitzki 1.25 3.00
10 Anthony Edwards 2.50 6.00
11 Jayson Tatum 2.00 5.00
12 Trae Young 1.25 3.00
13 Luka Doncic 3.00 8.00
14 Shaquille O'Neal 2.00 5.00
15 Stephen Curry 4.00 10.00
16 Manu Ginobili 1.00 2.50
17 Damian Lillard 1.25 3.00
18 LeBron James 4.00 10.00
19 Zion Williamson 1.25 3.00
20 Nikola Jokic 2.50 6.00
21 James Harden 1.00 2.50

2022-23 Panini Prizm Fireworks

COMPLETE SET (25)
*FAST BREAK: .75X TO 2X BASIC
*SILVER: 1X TO 2.5X BASIC
*MOJO/25: 6X TO 15X BASIC
1 LaMelo Ball 1.00 2.50
2 Kyrie Irving .75 2.00
3 Damian Lillard 1.00 2.50
4 Zach LaVine .75 2.00
5 Jayson Tatum 1.50 4.00
6 Devin Booker 1.00 2.50
7 Ja Morant 1.25 3.00
8 Zion Williamson 1.00 2.50
9 Kevin Durant 1.25 3.00
10 LeBron James 3.00 8.00
11 Chris Paul .75 2.00
12 Anthony Davis 1.00 2.50
13 Giannis Antetokounmpo 2.00 5.00
14 Anthony Edwards 2.00 5.00
15 Joel Embiid .60 1.50
16 Kawhi Leonard 1.00 2.50
17 James Harden .75 2.00
18 Nikola Jokic 2.00 5.00
19 Stephen Curry 3.00 8.00
20 Cade Cunningham 1.25 3.00
21 Trae Young 1.00 2.50
22 Julius Randle .50 1.25
23 Donovan Mitchell .75 2.00
24 Luka Doncic 2.50 6.00
25 Bradley Beal .50 1.25

2022-23 Panini Prizm Global Reach

COMPLETE SET (10)
*GREEN: .75X TO 2X BASIC
*SILVER: .75X TO 2X BASIC
1 Nikola Jokic 2.50 6.00
2 Rudy Gobert .60 1.50
3 Giannis Antetokounmpo 2.50 6.00
4 Pascal Siakam .75 2.00
5 Andrew Wiggins .60 1.50
6 Shai Gilgeous-Alexander 2.50 6.00
7 Joel Embiid .75 2.00
8 Ben Simmons .50 1.25
9 Domantas Sabonis .60 1.50
10 Luka Doncic 3.00 8.00

2022-23 Panini Prizm Instant Impact

COMPLETE SET (25)
*GREEN: .75X TO 2X BASIC
*SILVER: 1.25X TO 3X BASIC
1 Paolo Banchero 4.00 10.00
2 Chet Holmgren 3.00 8.00
3 Jabari Smith Jr. 2.00 5.00
4 Keegan Murray 1.50 4.00
5 AJ Griffin .50 1.25
6 Dalen Terry .60 1.50
7 Nikola Jovic 1.25 3.00
8 Christian Braun 1.50 4.00
9 Tari Eason 1.50 4.00
10 Jalen Duren 2.00 5.00
11 Jalen Williams 3.00 8.00
12 Malaki Branham .60 1.50
13 Johnny Davis .60 1.50
14 Shaedon Sharpe 2.50 6.00
15 Ousmane Dieng .75 2.00
16 Jaden Hardy 1.00 2.50
17 Jake LaRavia .60 1.50
18 Mark Williams 1.25 3.00
19 Bennedict Mathurin 2.00 5.00
20 Wendell Moore Jr. .60 1.50
21 Dyson Daniels 1.50 4.00
22 Ochai Agbaji .75 2.00
23 MarJon Beauchamp .60 1.50
24 Jeremy Sochan 2.00 5.00
25 Jaden Ivey 2.00 5.00

2022-23 Panini Prizm Luck of the Lottery

COMPLETE SET (14)
*FAST BREAK: .75X TO 2X BASIC
*SILVER: .75X TO 2X BASIC
*MOJO/25: 10X TO 25X BASIC
1 Jalen Williams 2.50 6.00
2 Ousmane Dieng .60 1.50
3 Ochai Agbaji .60 1.50
4 Jeremy Sochan 1.50 4.00
5 Jaden Ivey 1.50 4.00
6 Dyson Daniels 1.25 3.00
7 Jabari Smith Jr. 1.50 4.00
8 Bennedict Mathurin 1.50 4.00
9 Keegan Murray 1.25 3.00
10 Shaedon Sharpe 2.00 5.00
11 Paolo Banchero 3.00 8.00
12 Johnny Davis .50 1.25
13 Chet Holmgren 2.50 6.00
14 Jalen Duren 1.50 4.00

2022-23 Panini Prizm Penmanship

COMPLETE SET (50)
*SILVER: .5X TO 1.2X BASIC
1 Frank Ntilikina 3.00 8.00
2 Nerlens Noel 3.00 8.00
3 Roy Hibbert 4.00 10.00
4 Chuma Okeke 5.00 12.00
5 Kenyon Martin 5.00 12.00
6 Will Barton 3.00 8.00
7 Fred Brown 4.00 10.00
8 Harold Miner 5.00 12.00
9 Swen Nater 5.00 12.00
10 Aaron Nesmith 5.00 12.00
11 Danny Green 4.00 10.00
12 Jared Sullinger 3.00 8.00
13 Jarred Vanderbilt 4.00 10.00
14 Lenny Wilkens 6.00 15.00
15 Kwame Brown 4.00 10.00
16 Kendrick Perkins 3.00 8.00
17 Max Strus 5.00 12.00
18 Mehmet Okur 3.00 8.00
19 Royce O'Neale 4.00 10.00
20 Luke Kennard 4.00 10.00
21 Alton Lister 3.00 8.00
22 Ty Jerome 4.00 10.00
23 Gerald Henderson Sr. 3.00 8.00
24 Greg Anthony 4.00 10.00
25 Jaden Springer 4.00 10.00
26 Ja Morant 125.00 300.00
27 Xavier McDaniel 5.00 12.00
28 Ricky Davis 4.00 10.00
29 Vernon Carey Jr. 5.00 12.00
30 De'Anthony Melton 4.00 10.00
31 Rick Mahorn 4.00 10.00
32 Doug McDermott 3.00 8.00
33 Kiki Vandeweghe 4.00 10.00
34 Adam Morrison 4.00 10.00
35 Kelly Olynyk 4.00 10.00
36 Tony Delk 4.00 10.00
37 Brian Scalabrine 3.00 8.00
38 Jalen Green 25.00 60.00
39 Frank Kaminsky 4.00 10.00
40 Terence Davis II 4.00 10.00
41 Kyle Anderson 4.00 10.00
42 Zeke Nnaji 4.00 10.00
43 Herb Williams 3.00 8.00
44 Damian Jones 3.00 8.00
45 Dee Brown 4.00 10.00
46 Terance Mann 4.00 10.00
47 Morris Peterson 4.00 10.00
48 Luka Doncic 200.00 500.00
49 Brent Barry 4.00 10.00
50 Usman Garuba 3.00 8.00

2022-23 Panini Prizm Prizmatic

COMPLETE SET (30)
*FAST BREAK: 1X TO 2.5X BASIC
*SILVER 1X TO 2.5X BASIC
*MOJO/25 8X TO 20X BASIC
1 Kyrie Irving 1.00 2.50
2 Scottie Barnes .75 2.00
3 Donovan Mitchell 1.00 2.50
4 Jayson Tatum 2.00 5.00
5 Giannis Antetokounmpo 2.50 6.00
6 Zach LaVine 1.00 2.50
7 Kawhi Leonard 1.25 3.00
8 Cade Cunningham 1.50 4.00
9 LeBron James 4.00 10.00
10 Trae Young 1.25 3.00
11 James Harden 1.00 2.50
12 DeMar DeRozan .60 1.50
13 Ja Morant 1.50 4.00
14 Paul George .75 2.00
15 Zion Williamson 1.25 3.00
16 Luka Doncic 3.00 8.00
17 Anthony Davis 1.25 3.00
18 Devin Booker 1.25 3.00
19 Joel Embiid .75 2.00
20 Kevin Durant 1.50 4.00
21 Bradley Beal .60 1.50
22 Stephen Curry 4.00 10.00
23 Jalen Green 1.50 4.00
24 Anthony Edwards 2.50 6.00
25 Nikola Jokic 2.50 6.00
26 LaMelo Ball 1.25 3.00
27 Evan Mobley 1.25 3.00
28 Jaylen Brown 1.00 2.50
29 Darius Garland .75 2.00
30 Damian Lillard 1.25 3.00

2022-23 Panini Prizm Rookie Penmanship

COMPLETE SET (49)
*SILVER: .5X TO 1.2X BASIC
1 Johnny Juzang 6.00 15.00
2 Trevor Keels 4.00 10.00
3 Jabari Walker 4.00 10.00
4 Jabari Smith Jr. 40.00 100.00
5 MarJon Beauchamp 5.00 12.00
6 E.J. Liddell 5.00 12.00
7 Ron Harper Jr. 6.00 15.00
8 Blake Wesley 5.00 12.00
9 David Roddy 6.00 15.00
10 Isaiah Mobley 5.00 12.00
11 Christian Braun 12.00 30.00
12 Justin Lewis 5.00 12.00
13 Bennedict Mathurin 40.00 100.00
14 Walker Kessler 10.00 25.00
15 Alondes Williams 5.00 12.00
16 Julian Champagnie 6.00 15.00
17 Jaden Ivey 40.00 100.00
18 Bryce McGowens 5.00 12.00
19 Shaedon Sharpe 60.00 150.00
20 Dalen Terry 5.00 12.00
21 Caleb Houstan 5.00 12.00
22 A.J. Green 25.00 60.00
23 Jaylin Williams 6.00 15.00
24 Kenneth Lofton Jr. 6.00 15.00
25 Chet Holmgren 125.00 300.00
26 Cole Swider 6.00 15.00
27 Scotty Pippen Jr. 6.00 15.00
28 Jaden Hardy 25.00 60.00
29 Christian Koloko 5.00 12.00
30 Jalen Williams 40.00 100.00
31 Tyrese Martin 4.00 10.00
32 Josh Minott 5.00 12.00
33 Ousmane Dieng 6.00 15.00
34 Kevon Harris 4.00 10.00
35 Jake LaRavia 6.00 15.00
36 Max Christie 25.00 60.00
37 Jalen Duren 25.00 60.00
38 Mark Williams 10.00 25.00
40 TyTy Washington Jr. 5.00 12.00
41 Collin Gillespie 5.00 12.00
42 Keon Ellis 5.00 12.00
43 Johnny Davis 5.00 12.00
44 Kennedy Chandler 5.00 12.00
45 Vince Williams Jr. 6.00 15.00
46 Keegan Murray 40.00 100.00
47 Kendall Brown 4.00 10.00
48 Ochai Agbaji 6.00 15.00
49 Paolo Banchero 150.00 400.00
50 Ryan Rollins 5.00 12.00

2022-23 Panini Prizm Rookie Signatures

COMPLETE SET (50)
*BLUE WAVE: .5X TO 1.2X BASIC
*CHOICE: .5X TO 1.2X BASIC
*SILVER: .5X TO 1.2X BASIC
1 Paolo Banchero 150.00 400.00
2 Jalen Duren 25.00 60.00
3 Malaki Branham 5.00 12.00
4 David Roddy 6.00 15.00
5 Cole Swider 6.00 15.00
6 Shaedon Sharpe 60.00 150.00
7 AJ Griffin 4.00 10.00
8 Christian Braun 12.00 30.00
9 Jalen Williams 40.00 100.00
10 Walker Kessler 10.00 25.00
11 Kendall Brown 4.00 10.00
12 Kennedy Chandler 5.00 12.00
13 Chet Holmgren 125.00 300.00
14 Peyton Watson 8.00 20.00
15 Tari Eason 12.00 30.00
16 Bryce McGowens 5.00 12.00
17 Patrick Baldwin Jr. 5.00 12.00
18 Dyson Daniels 12.00 30.00
19 MarJon Beauchamp 5.00 12.00
20 Dalen Terry 5.00 12.00
21 Blake Wesley 5.00 12.00
22 Jaylin Williams 5.00 12.00
23 Keegan Murray 40.00 100.00
24 Wendell Moore Jr. 5.00 12.00
25 E.J. Liddell 5.00 12.00
26 Ochai Agbaji 6.00 15.00
27 Vince Williams Jr. 6.00 15.00
28 Trevor Keels 4.00 10.00
29 Jeremy Sochan 40.00 100.00
30 TyTy Washington Jr. 5.00 12.00
31 Max Christie 12.00 30.00
32 Mac McClung 12.00 30.00
33 Jaden Ivey 40.00 100.00
34 Nikola Jovic 10.00 25.00
35 Jake LaRavia 5.00 12.00
36 Jaden Hardy 25.00 60.00
37 Ousmane Dieng 6.00 15.00
38 Kenneth Lofton Jr. 6.00 15.00
39 Moussa Diabate 5.00 12.00
40 Andrew Nembhard 10.00 25.00
41 Bennedict Mathurin 40.00 100.00
42 Isaiah Mobley 5.00 12.00
43 Josh Minott 5.00 12.00
44 Caleb Houstan 5.00 12.00
45 Johnny Davis 5.00 12.00
46 Tyrese Martin 4.00 10.00
47 Christian Koloko 5.00 12.00
48 Jabari Walker 4.00 10.00
49 Mark Williams 10.00 25.00
50 Jabari Smith Jr. 40.00 100.00

2022-23 Panini Prizm Rookie Signatures Prizms Mojo

COMPLETE SET (50)
*MOJO: 1.25X TO 3X BASIC
STATED PRINT RUN 25 SER.#'d SETS
1 Paolo Banchero 1,000.00 2,000.00
6 Shaedon Sharpe 350.00 700.00
9 Jalen Williams 200.00 500.00
13 Chet Holmgren 800.00 1,500.00
23 Keegan Murray 200.00 500.00
29 Jeremy Sochan 200.00 500.00
33 Jaden Ivey 200.00 500.00
36 Jaden Hardy 100.00 250.00
41 Bennedict Mathurin 200.00 500.00
50 Jabari Smith Jr. 200.00 500.00

2022-23 Panini Prizm Rookie Variation Fast Break

COMPLETE SET (14)
*FAST BREAK: .75X TO 2X BASIC
224 Ousmane Dieng 2.50 6.00
228 Jabari Smith Jr. 6.00 15.00
231 Johnny Davis 2.00 5.00
233 Dyson Daniels 5.00 12.00
245 Keegan Murray 5.00 12.00
246 Jalen Williams 10.00 25.00
248 AJ Griffin 1.50 4.00
249 Paolo Banchero 12.00 30.00
250 Shaedon Sharpe 8.00 20.00
254 Bennedict Mathurin 6.00 15.00
256 Jaden Ivey 6.00 15.00
263 Jeremy Sochan 6.00 15.00
266 Chet Holmgren 10.00 25.00
267 Ochai Agbaji 2.50 6.00

2022-23 Panini Prizm Sensational Signatures

COMPLETE SET (89)
*CHOICE: .5X TO 1.2X BASIC
*SILVER: .5X TO 1.2X BASIC
1 Jason Williams 20.00 50.00
2 Pau Gasol 30.00 80.00
3 Allen Iverson 50.00 120.00
4 Dave Bing 6.00 15.00
6 Adrian Dantley 5.00 12.00
7 Clark Kellogg 4.00 10.00
8 Antawn Jamison 5.00 12.00
9 Gary Payton II 4.00 10.00
10 Carmelo Anthony 75.00 200.00
11 Kelly Olynyk 4.00 10.00
12 Mark Price 5.00 12.00
13 Scottie Barnes 8.00 20.00
14 Jerry West 30.00 80.00
15 Doug McDermott 3.00 8.00
16 David Wesley 4.00 10.00
17 Ray Allen 25.00 60.00
18 Anthony Edwards 75.00 200.00
19 De'Anthony Melton 4.00 10.00
20 Charlie Ward 5.00 12.00
21 Luka Doncic 200.00 500.00
22 Reggie Jackson 4.00 10.00
23 Chuma Okeke 5.00 12.00
24 Shawn Kemp 8.00 20.00
25 Josh Christopher 3.00 8.00
26 Ja Morant 125.00 300.00
27 Roy Hibbert 4.00 10.00
28 Jonathan Kuminga 12.00 30.00
29 Jalen Green 25.00 60.00
30 Kevin Garnett 50.00 120.00
31 Willie Green 5.00 12.00
32 Chris Paul 40.00 100.00
33 Dwyane Wade 40.00 100.00
34 Jalen Johnson 6.00 15.00
35 Jason Terry 4.00 10.00
36 Jeff Hornacek 5.00 12.00
37 Fred Brown 4.00 10.00
38 Wally Szczerbiak 4.00 10.00
39 John Stockton 30.00 80.00
40 Ziaire Williams 4.00 10.00
41 Eddy Curry 4.00 10.00
42 Paul Pierce 20.00 50.00
43 Jarred Vanderbilt 4.00 10.00
44 Udoka Azubuike 5.00 12.00
45 Jayson Tatum 75.00 200.00
46 Moses Moody 6.00 15.00
47 Isaiah Livers 4.00 10.00
48 RJ Barrett 8.00 20.00
49 Dejounte Murray 6.00 15.00
50 Jabari Smith Jr. 40.00 100.00
51 Moussa Diabate 5.00 12.00
52 Scotty Pippen Jr. 6.00 15.00
53 Collin Gillespie 5.00 12.00
54 Justin Lewis 5.00 12.00
55 Andrew Nembhard 10.00 25.00
56 Keegan Murray 40.00 100.00
57 Ron Harper Jr. 6.00 15.00
58 Austin Reaves 60.00 150.00
59 Julian Champagnie 6.00 15.00
60 Paolo Banchero 150.00 400.00
61 Ryan Rollins 5.00 12.00
62 Alondes Williams 5.00 12.00
63 Bennedict Mathurin 40.00 100.00
64 Peyton Watson 8.00 20.00
65 Wendell Moore Jr. 5.00 12.00
66 Kevon Harris 4.00 10.00
67 Mac McClung 12.00 30.00
68 Jalen Duren 15.00 40.00
69 Dereon Seabron 4.00 10.00
70 Patrick Baldwin Jr. 5.00 12.00
71 Shaedon Sharpe 60.00 150.00
72 Grant Hill 20.00 50.00
73 Johnny Davis 5.00 12.00
74 Jaden Hardy 8.00 20.00
75 Chet Holmgren 125.00 300.00
76 Jeremy Sochan 40.00 100.00
77 Nikola Jovic 10.00 25.00
78 Malaki Branham 5.00 12.00
79 Ochai Agbaji 6.00 15.00
80 Jalen Williams 40.00 100.00
81 Dyson Daniels 12.00 30.00
82 Jaden Ivey 40.00 100.00
83 Keon Ellis 5.00 12.00
84 Johnny Juzang 6.00 15.00
85 AJ Griffin 4.00 10.00
86 Jaylin Williams 6.00 15.00
87 TyTy Washington Jr. 5.00 12.00
88 Walker Kessler 10.00 25.00
89 Tari Eason 12.00 30.00
90 Max Christie 12.00 30.00

2022-23 Panini Prizm Sensational Signatures Prizms Mojo

COMPLETE SET (90)
*MOJO: 1.25X TO 3X BASIC
STATED PRINT RUN 25 SER.#'d SETS
50 Jabari Smith Jr. 200.00 500.00
56 Keegan Murray 200.00 500.00
60 Paolo Banchero 1,000.00 2,000.00
63 Bennedict Mathurin 200.00 500.00
71 Shaedon Sharpe 350.00 700.00
75 Chet Holmgren 800.00 1,500.00
76 Jeremy Sochan 200.00 500.00
80 Jalen Williams 200.00 500.00
82 Jaden Ivey 200.00 500.00

2022-23 Panini Prizm Signatures

COMPLETE SET (49)
*CHOICE: .5X TO 1.2X BASIC
*SILVER: .5X TO 1.2X BASIC
*MOJO/25: 1X TO 2.5X BASIC
1 Jason Kidd 15.00 40.00
2 Cade Cunningham 50.00 120.00
3 Dan Issel 6.00 15.00
5 Moses Moody 6.00 15.00
6 B.J. Armstrong 5.00 12.00
7 Jason Richardson 5.00 12.00
8 Jerry Stackhouse 6.00 15.00
9 Calvin Murphy 5.00 12.00
10 Detlef Schrempf 5.00 12.00
11 Manu Ginobili 40.00 100.00
12 Joe Dumars 6.00 15.00
13 Jamal Crawford 5.00 12.00
14 Vince Carter 60.00 150.00
15 Dell Curry 5.00 12.00
16 Evan Mobley 12.00 30.00
17 Jaren Jackson Jr. 30.00 80.00
18 Jaden McDaniels 5.00 12.00
19 Alperen Sengun 15.00 40.00
20 RJ Barrett 8.00 20.00
21 Luka Doncic 300.00 600.00
22 Jordan Clarkson 12.00 30.00
23 Grant Hill 15.00 40.00
24 Bernard King 6.00 15.00
25 Christian Wood 3.00 8.00
26 Jalen Johnson 6.00 15.00
27 Rick Fox 5.00 12.00
28 Ayo Dosunmu 6.00 15.00
29 Sam Cassell 5.00 12.00
30 Stephen Curry 500.00 1,000.00
31 Tim Hardaway Jr. 4.00 10.00
32 Marcus Smart 6.00 15.00
33 Jalen Suggs 6.00 15.00
34 Mychal Thompson 4.00 10.00
35 Tyrese Haliburton 25.00 60.00
36 Ja Morant 100.00 250.00
37 Shawn Kemp 12.00 30.00
38 Bob McAdoo 6.00 15.00
39 Josh Christopher 3.00 8.00
40 Aleksej Pokusevski 5.00 12.00
41 Juan Toscano-Anderson 5.00 12.00
42 Brad Daugherty 4.00 10.00
43 Larry Johnson 10.00 25.00
44 Tre Mann 4.00 10.00
45 Collin Sexton 6.00 15.00
46 Josh Giddey 30.00 80.00
47 Reggie Jackson 4.00 10.00
48 Brook Lopez 5.00 12.00
49 Jonathan Kuminga 12.00 30.00
50 Pat Riley 12.00 30.00

2022-23 Panini Prizm USA Basketball

COMPLETE SET (10)
*GREEN: .75X TO 2X BASIC
*SILVER: .75X TO 2X BASIC
1 Jayson Tatum 2.00 5.00
2 Chris Paul 1.00 2.50
3 Kevin Durant 1.50 4.00
4 Larry Bird 2.00 5.00
5 David Robinson 1.00 2.50
6 Tim Hardaway .60 1.50
7 Magic Johnson 2.00 5.00
8 Kyrie Irving 1.00 2.50
9 Shaquille O'Neal 2.00 5.00
10 Stephen Curry 4.00 10.00

2022-23 Panini Prizm Widescreen

COMPLETE SET (10)
*FAST BREAK: .75X TO 2X BASIC
*SILVER: .75X TO 2X BASIC
*MOJO/25: 5X TO 12X BASIC
1 Jayson Tatum 2.00 5.00
2 LeBron James 4.00 10.00
3 LaMelo Ball 1.25 3.00
4 Stephen Curry 4.00 10.00
5 Ja Morant 1.50 4.00
6 Zion Williamson 1.25 3.00
7 Giannis Antetokounmpo 2.50 6.00
8 Luka Doncic 3.00 8.00
9 Kevin Durant 1.50 4.00
10 Damian Lillard 1.25 3.00

2023-24 Panini Prizm

1 Franz Wagner .60 1.50
2 Jayson Tatum 1.50 4.00
3 Trae Young .75 2.00
4 Kawhi Leonard 1.00 2.50
5 Kevin Durant 1.25 3.00
6 De'Aaron Fox .75 2.00
7 Keegan Murray .50 1.25
8 Kristaps Porzingis .50 1.25
9 Jalen Brunson .75 2.00
10 Malcolm Brogdon .40 1.00
11 Cade Cunningham 1.00 2.50
12 Aaron Gordon .40 1.00
13 Collin Sexton .50 1.25
14 Bennedict Mathurin .60 1.50
15 Tyrese Maxey .75 2.00
16 Cole Anthony .40 1.00
17 Nikola Jokic 2.00 5.00
18 Julius Randle .50 1.25
19 Jalen Williams .75 2.00
20 Alperen Sengun .60 1.50
21 Jaden Hardy .50 1.25
22 Kyrie Irving .75 2.00
23 Bogdan Bogdanovic .40 1.00
24 Scottie Barnes .50 1.25
25 Kyle Kuzma .50 1.25
26 Ben Simmons .40 1.00
27 Zion Williamson 1.00 2.50
28 Tari Eason .50 1.25
29 Jalen Green .60 1.50
30 Pascal Siakam .60 1.50
31 Jaylen Brown .75 2.00
32 Tyler Herro .60 1.50
33 Immanuel Quickley .40 1.00
34 Myles Turner .40 1.00
35 Damian Lillard 1.00 2.50
36 DeMar DeRozan .60 1.50
37 Jamal Murray .75 2.00
38 Johnny Davis .30 .75
39 Russell Westbrook .60 1.50
40 Kyle Lowry .50 1.25
41 LaMelo Ball 1.00 2.50
42 Rui Hachimura .40 1.00
43 Donovan Mitchell .75 2.00
44 Bojan Bogdanovic .40 1.00
45 Domantas Sabonis .60 1.50
46 Mikal Bridges .50 1.25
47 Kevin Love .40 1.00
48 Jonathan Kuminga 1.00 2.50
49 Jabari Smith Jr. .60 1.50
50 Josh Giddey .50 1.25
51 Jordan Poole .60 1.50
52 Jaden Ivey .50 1.25
53 Deandre Ayton .40 1.00
54 John Collins .40 1.00
55 Evan Mobley .60 1.50
56 Bones Hyland .30 .75
57 Mike Conley .30 .75
58 Devin Booker 1.00 2.50
59 Rudy Gobert .50 1.25
60 Khris Middleton .40 1.00
61 Jaren Jackson Jr. .60 1.50
62 Marcus Smart .50 1.25
63 LeBron James 3.00 8.00
64 Bradley Beal .50 1.25
65 Jordan Clarkson .40 1.00
66 Bam Adebayo .60 1.50
67 Bruce Brown .40 1.00
68 Dillon Brooks .40 1.00
69 Tim Hardaway Jr. .30 .75
70 Jerami Grant .50 1.25
71 Malik Monk .50 1.25
72 Zach LaVine .60 1.50
73 Joel Embiid 1.00 2.50
74 Jalen Suggs .50 1.25
75 Draymond Green .50 1.25
76 Austin Reaves 1.00 2.50
77 Buddy Hield .40 1.00
78 Karl-Anthony Towns .60 1.50
79 Kenneth Lofton Jr. .40 1.00
80 Kentavious Caldwell-Pope .30 .75
81 Darius Garland .60 1.50
82 Keldon Johnson .50 1.25
83 Andrew Wiggins .50 1.25
84 Spencer Dinwiddie .30 .75
85 Shai Gilgeous-Alexander 2.00 5.00
86 James Wiseman .30 .75
87 Nikola Vucevic .40 1.00
88 Tobias Harris .40 1.00
89 Brandon Ingram .50 1.25
90 Terry Rozier III .40 1.00
91 OG Anunoby .50 1.25
92 Ochai Agbaji .40 1.00
93 Lauri Markkanen .60 1.50
94 Anthony Davis 1.00 2.50
95 Devin Vassell .50 1.25
96 Ja Morant 1.25 3.00
97 Fred VanVleet .60 1.50
98 James Harden .75 2.00
99 Chris Paul .75 2.00
100 Paolo Banchero 1.00 2.50
101 Paul George .60 1.50
102 Tyrese Haliburton .75 2.00
103 Giannis Antetokounmpo 2.00 5.00
104 Shaedon Sharpe .75 2.00
105 Desmond Bane .50 1.25
106 Anfernee Simons .50 1.25
107 Jrue Holiday .50 1.25
108 Anthony Edwards 2.00 5.00
109 Klay Thompson 1.00 2.50
110 Luka Doncic 2.50 6.00
111 D'Angelo Russell .40 1.00
112 Dejounte Murray .50 1.25
113 Cameron Thomas .50 1.25
114 CJ McCollum .40 1.00
115 Chet Holmgren 1.00 2.50
116 Michael Porter Jr. .50 1.25
117 PJ Washington Jr. .40 1.00
118 Jimmy Butler .60 1.50
119 Stephen Curry 3.00 8.00
120 Walker Kessler .40 1.00
121 Nikola Jovic .40 1.00
122 Jeremy Sochan .50 1.25
123 Max Christie .40 1.00
124 Julian Champagnie .40 1.00
125 Julian Phillips RC .75 2.00
126 Tristan Vukcevic RC .75 2.00
127 Keyonte George RC 2.50 6.00
128 Jalen Wilson RC .75 2.00
129 Cam Whitmore RC 2.00 5.00
130 Jordan Hawkins RC 1.25 3.00
131 Andre Jackson Jr. RC 1.25 3.00
132 Jett Howard RC 1.00 2.50
133 Julian Strawther RC 1.00 2.50
134 Gradey Dick RC 1.50 4.00
135 Nick Smith Jr. RC 1.00 2.50
136 Victor Wembanyama RC 15.00 40.00
137 Jaime Jaquez Jr. RC 1.25 3.00
138 Seth Lundy RC .60 1.50
139 Cason Wallace RC 1.50 4.00
140 Rayan Rupert RC .75 2.00
141 Scoot Henderson RC 2.50 6.00
142 Kris Murray RC .75 2.00
143 Maxwell Lewis RC .60 1.50
144 Kobe Brown RC .75 2.00
145 Jalen Hood-Schifino RC .75 2.00
146 Olivier-Maxence Prosper RC .75 2.00
147 Brandin Podziemski RC 2.50 6.00
148 Trayce Jackson-Davis RC 1.00 2.50
149 Jalen Slawson RC .75 2.00
150 Amen Thompson RC 4.00 10.00
151 Kobe Bufkin RC 1.00 2.50
152 Brandon Miller RC 3.00 8.00
153 Bilal Coulibaly RC 2.00 5.00
154 Isaiah Wong RC .75 2.00
155 Leonard Miller RC .75 2.00
156 Chris Livingston RC .75 2.00
157 Mouhamed Gueye RC .75 2.00
158 Jordan Walsh RC .75 2.00
159 James Nnaji RC .60 1.50
160 Colby Jones RC .75 2.00
161 Taylor Hendricks RC .75 2.00
162 Amari Bailey RC .75 2.00
163 Dereck Lively II RC 1.50 4.00
164 Toumani Camara RC 1.50 4.00
165 Noah Clowney RC 1.00 2.50
166 Jaylen Clark RC .75 2.00
167 Jalen Pickett RC .60 1.50
168 Jarace Walker RC 1.50 4.00
169 Emoni Bates RC 1.00 2.50
170 Anthony Black RC 1.50 4.00
171 Hunter Tyson RC .75 2.00
172 Ben Sheppard RC .75 2.00
173 Sidy Cissoko RC .75 2.00
174 Marcus Sasser RC 1.25 3.00
175 Dariq Whitehead RC 1.00 2.50
176 Keyontae Johnson RC .75 2.00
177 Brice Sensabaugh RC 1.25 3.00
178 Ausar Thompson RC 2.00 5.00
179 GG Jackson II RC 1.50 4.00
180 Charles Barkley 1.00 2.50
181 Shaquille O'Neal 1.25 3.00
182 Dwyane Wade .75 2.00
183 Kevin Garnett 1.00 2.50
184 Allen Iverson 1.00 2.50
185 Magic Johnson 1.50 4.00
186 Carmelo Anthony .60 1.50
187 Dirk Nowitzki 1.00 2.50
188 Patrick Ewing .60 1.50
189 Larry Bird 1.50 4.00
190 Manu Ginobili .75 2.00
191 Hakeem Olajuwon .75 2.00
192 Ray Allen .60 1.50
193 Paul Pierce .60 1.50
194 Jason Kidd .60 1.50
195 Vince Carter .75 2.00
196 Tracy McGrady .60 1.50
197 Jason Williams .60 1.50
198 John Stockton .75 2.00
199 Yao Ming 1.00 2.50
200 Steve Nash .75 2.00
201 Josh Green .30 .75
202 Jarred Vanderbilt .30 .75
203 Kevin Knox II .25 .60
204 Naz Reid .40 1.00
205 Steven Adams .40 1.00
206 Talen Horton-Tucker .30 .75
207 De'Andre Hunter .30 .75
208 Duncan Robinson .40 1.00
209 Robert Williams III .40 1.00
210 Jalen Duren .50 1.25
211 Andrew Nembhard .40 1.00
212 Richaun Holmes .25 .60
213 Saddiq Bey .40 1.00
214 Jaylin Williams .40 1.00
215 Shake Milton .30 .75
216 Joe Harris .30 .75
217 Ousmane Dieng .40 1.00
218 Nickeil Alexander-Walker .25 .60
219 Seth Curry .40 1.00
220 Dyson Daniels .50 1.25
221 Harrison Barnes .30 .75
222 Cameron Johnson .40 1.00
223 Eric Gordon .30 .75
224 Robert Covington .30 .75
225 Gabe Vincent .40 1.00
226 Grayson Allen .40 1.00
227 Davion Mitchell .40 1.00
228 Moses Moody .50 1.25
229 Derrick White .50 1.25
230 Cam Reddish .40 1.00
231 Lonnie Walker IV .30 .75
232 Tre Jones .30 .75
233 Devonte' Graham .30 .75
234 Marvin Bagley III .30 .75
235 Reggie Jackson .25 .60
236 Al Horford .40 1.00
237 Malik Beasley .40 1.00
238 Jaden McDaniels .40 1.00
239 Coby White .40 1.00
240 Kevin Huerter .30 .75
241 Kenyon Martin Jr. .40 1.00
242 Gary Payton II .30 .75
243 Gary Trent Jr. .40 1.00
244 Jose Alvarado .40 1.00
245 Christian Wood .30 .75
246 Victor Oladipo .30 .75
247 Peyton Watson .40 1.00
248 Jarrett Allen .40 1.00
249 Obi Toppin .40 1.00
250 Herbert Jones .40 1.00
251 Gordon Hayward .40 1.00
252 Markelle Fultz .30 .75
253 Caris LeVert .40 1.00
254 Luguentz Dort .40 1.00
255 Bol Bol .40 1.00
256 Andre Drummond .30 .75
257 Kelly Oubre Jr. .40 1.00
258 Mac McClung .50 1.25
259 MarJon Beauchamp .30 .75
260 Josh Hart .40 1.00
261 Deni Avdija .40 1.00
262 Nicolas Batum .25 .60
263 RJ Barrett .60 1.50
264 Grant Williams .30 .75
265 Dennis Schroder .40 1.00
266 AJ Griffin .30 .75
267 David Roddy .30 .75
268 Patrick Beverley .30 .75
269 Matisse Thybulle .30 .75
270 Malaki Branham .30 .75
271 DeAndre Jordan .30 .75
272 Derrick Rose .60 1.50
273 Max Strus .40 1.00
274 Norman Powell .40 1.00
275 Ayo Dosunmu .40 1.00
276 Caleb Martin .30 .75
277 Jusuf Nurkic .40 1.00
278 Austin Rivers .25 .60
279 Wendell Carter Jr. .40 1.00
280 Donte DiVincenzo .40 1.00
281 Aleksandar Vezenkov RC .60 1.50
282 Filip Petrusev RC .75 2.00
283 Azuolas Tubelis RC .60 1.50
284 Leaky Black RC .60 1.50
285 Yuta Watanabe .40 1.00
286 Adama Sanogo RC .75 2.00
287 Colin Castleton RC .60 1.50
288 Jonathan Isaac .30 .75

289 Jonas Valanciunas .30 .75
290 Onyeka Okongwu .30 .75
291 Jalen McDaniels .30 .75
292 Oscar Tshiebwe RC 1.00 2.50
293 Joey Hauser RC .60 1.50
294 Ricky Council IV RC 1.00 2.50
295 Mike Miles Jr. RC .60 1.50
296 Joe Ingles .30 .75
297 Vasilije Micic RC .75 2.00
298 D'Moi Hodge RC .60 1.50
299 Sir'Jabari Rice RC .60 1.50
300 Markquis Nowell RC .75 2.00

2023-24 Panini Prizm Prizms Blue
*BLUE: 5X TO 12X BASIC
STATED PRINT RUN 199 SER.#'d SETS
127 Keyonte George 60.00 150.00
136 Victor Wembanyama 1,500.00 3,000.00
141 Scoot Henderson 60.00 150.00
147 Brandin Podziemski 60.00 150.00
148 Trayce Jackson-Davis 50.00 120.00
150 Amen Thompson 60.00 150.00
152 Brandon Miller 150.00 400.00
179 GG Jackson II 125.00 300.00

2023-24 Panini Prizm Prizms Blue Ice
*BLUE ICE: 6X TO 15X BASIC
STATED PRINT RUN 125 SER.#'d SETS
127 Keyonte George 75.00 200.00
136 Victor Wembanyama 2,000.00 4,000.00
141 Scoot Henderson 75.00 200.00
147 Brandin Podziemski 75.00 200.00
148 Trayce Jackson-Davis 60.00 150.00
150 Amen Thompson 75.00 200.00
152 Brandon Miller 200.00 500.00
179 GG Jackson II 150.00 400.00

2023-24 Panini Prizm Prizms Blue Seismic
*BLUE SEISMIC: 6X TO 15X BASIC
STATED PRINT RUN 99 SER.#'d SETS
127 Keyonte George 75.00 200.00
136 Victor Wembanyama 2,000.00 4,000.00
141 Scoot Henderson 75.00 200.00
147 Brandin Podziemski 75.00 200.00
148 Trayce Jackson-Davis 60.00 150.00
150 Amen Thompson 75.00 200.00
152 Brandon Miller 200.00 500.00
179 GG Jackson II 150.00 400.00

2023-24 Panini Prizm Prizms Blue Shimmer FOTL
*BLUE SHMR FOTL: 10X TO 25X BASIC
STATED PRINT RUN 35 SER.#'d SETS
127 Keyonte George 200.00 500.00
136 Victor Wembanyama 3,000.00 6,000.00
141 Scoot Henderson 125.00 300.00
147 Brandin Podziemski 125.00 300.00
148 Trayce Jackson-Davis 100.00 250.00
150 Amen Thompson 125.00 300.00
152 Brandon Miller 400.00 800.00
179 GG Jackson II 300.00 600.00

2023-24 Panini Prizm Prizms Blue Sparkle
*BLUE SPRKL: 5X TO 12X BASIC
STATED PRINT RUN 144 SER.#'d SETS
127 Keyonte George 60.00 150.00
136 Victor Wembanyama 1,500.00 3,000.00
141 Scoot Henderson 60.00 150.00
147 Brandin Podziemski 60.00 150.00
148 Trayce Jackson-Davis 50.00 120.00
150 Amen Thompson 60.00 150.00
152 Brandon Miller 150.00 400.00
179 GG Jackson II 125.00 300.00

2023-24 Panini Prizm Prizms Choice Blue
*CHOICE BLUE: 8X TO 20X BASIC
STATED PRINT RUN 49 SER.#'d SETS
127 Keyonte George 125.00 300.00
136 Victor Wembanyama 2,500.00 5,000.00
150 Amen Thompson 150.00 400.00
152 Brandon Miller 200.00 500.00

2023-24 Panini Prizm Prizms Choice Blue Yellow and Green
*CHOICE BLU YLW GRN: 2X TO 5X BASIC
127 Keyonte George 30.00 80.00
136 Victor Wembanyama 300.00 600.00
147 Brandin Podziemski 30.00 80.00
148 Trayce Jackson-Davis 20.00 50.00
150 Amen Thompson 20.00 50.00
152 Brandon Miller 75.00 200.00
178 Ausar Thompson 20.00 50.00
179 GG Jackson II 30.00 80.00

2023-24 Panini Prizm Prizms Choice Red
*CHOICE RED: 6X TO 15X BASIC
STATED PRINT RUN 88 SER.#'d SETS
127 Keyonte George 75.00 200.00
136 Victor Wembanyama 2,000.00 4,000.00
141 Scoot Henderson 75.00 200.00
147 Brandin Podziemski 75.00 200.00
148 Trayce Jackson-Davis 60.00 150.00
150 Amen Thompson 75.00 200.00
152 Brandon Miller 200.00 500.00
179 GG Jackson II 150.00 400.00

2023-24 Panini Prizm Prizms Fast Break
*FAST BREAK: 1.5X TO 4X BASIC
136 Victor Wembanyama 150.00 400.00
150 Amen Thompson 20.00 50.00
152 Brandon Miller 20.00 50.00

2023-24 Panini Prizm Prizms Fast Break Blue
*FB BLUE: 5X TO 12X BASIC
STATED PRINT RUN 150 SER.#'d SETS
127 Keyonte George 60.00 150.00
136 Victor Wembanyama 1,500.00 3,000.00
141 Scoot Henderson 60.00 150.00
147 Brandin Podziemski 60.00 150.00
148 Trayce Jackson-Davis 50.00 120.00
150 Amen Thompson 60.00 150.00
152 Brandon Miller 150.00 400.00
179 GG Jackson II 125.00 300.00

2023-24 Panini Prizm Prizms Fast Break Pink
*FB PINK: 8X TO 20X BASIC
STATED PRINT RUN 50 SER.#'d SETS
127 Keyonte George 125.00 300.00
136 Victor Wembanyama 2,500.00 5,000.00
141 Scoot Henderson 100.00 250.00
147 Brandin Podziemski 100.00 250.00
148 Trayce Jackson-Davis 75.00 200.00
150 Amen Thompson 100.00 250.00
152 Brandon Miller 300.00 600.00
179 GG Jackson II 200.00 500.00

2023-24 Panini Prizm Prizms Fast Break Purple
*FB PURPLE: 6X TO 15X BASIC
STATED PRINT RUN 75 SER.#'d SETS
127 Keyonte George 75.00 200.00
136 Victor Wembanyama 2,000.00 4,000.00
141 Scoot Henderson 75.00 200.00
147 Brandin Podziemski 75.00 200.00
148 Trayce Jackson-Davis 60.00 150.00
150 Amen Thompson 75.00 200.00
152 Brandon Miller 200.00 500.00
179 GG Jackson II 150.00 400.00

2023-24 Panini Prizm Prizms Fast Break Red
*FB RED: 6X TO 15X BASIC
STATED PRINT RUN 100 SER.#'d SETS
127 Keyonte George 75.00 200.00
136 Victor Wembanyama 2,000.00 4,000.00
141 Scoot Henderson 75.00 200.00
147 Brandin Podziemski 75.00 200.00
148 Trayce Jackson-Davis 60.00 150.00
150 Amen Thompson 75.00 200.00
152 Brandon Miller 200.00 500.00
179 GG Jackson II 150.00 400.00

2023-24 Panini Prizm Prizms Glitter
*GLITTER: 15X TO 40X BASIC
63 LeBron James 200.00 500.00
119 Stephen Curry 200.00 500.00
127 Keyonte George 400.00 800.00
130 Jordan Hawkins 200.00 500.00
134 Gradey Dick 200.00 500.00
136 Victor Wembanyama 6,000.00 12,000.00
139 Cason Wallace 200.00 500.00
141 Scoot Henderson 200.00 500.00
147 Brandin Podziemski 200.00 500.00
148 Trayce Jackson-Davis 150.00 400.00
150 Amen Thompson 300.00 600.00
152 Brandon Miller 600.00 1,200.00
153 Bilal Coulibaly 125.00 300.00
178 Ausar Thompson 200.00 500.00
179 GG Jackson II 400.00 800.00

2023-24 Panini Prizm Prizms Gold Sparkle
*GOLD SPARKLE: 15X TO 40X BASIC
STATED PRINT RUN 25 SER.#'d SETS
127 Keyonte George 400.00 800.00
130 Jordan Hawkins 200.00 500.00
134 Gradey Dick 200.00 500.00
136 Victor Wembanyama 6,000.00 12,000.00
139 Cason Wallace 200.00 500.00
141 Scoot Henderson 200.00 500.00
147 Brandin Podziemski 200.00 500.00
148 Trayce Jackson-Davis 150.00 400.00
150 Amen Thompson 400.00 800.00
152 Brandon Miller 600.00 1,200.00
153 Bilal Coulibaly 150.00 400.00
178 Ausar Thompson 300.00 600.00
179 GG Jackson II 500.00 1,000.00

2023-24 Panini Prizm Prizms Green
*GREEN: 1X TO 2.5X BASIC
136 Victor Wembanyama 75.00 200.00

2023-24 Panini Prizm Prizms Green Pulsar
*GREEN PULSAR: 12X TO 30X BASIC
STATED PRINT RUN 25 SER.#'d SETS
127 Keyonte George 300.00 600.00
130 Jordan Hawkins 150.00 400.00
134 Gradey Dick 150.00 400.00
136 Victor Wembanyama 5,000.00 10,000.00
139 Cason Wallace 150.00 400.00
141 Scoot Henderson 150.00 400.00
147 Brandin Podziemski 150.00 400.00
148 Trayce Jackson-Davis 125.00 300.00
150 Amen Thompson 300.00 600.00
152 Brandon Miller 500.00 1,000.00
153 Bilal Coulibaly 125.00 300.00
178 Ausar Thompson 200.00 500.00
179 GG Jackson II 400.00 800.00

2023-24 Panini Prizm Prizms Green Wave
GREEN WAVE: 1.25X TO 3X BASIC
136 Victor Wembanyama 100.00 250.00

2023-24 Panini Prizm Prizms Hyper
*HYPER: 1.25X TO 3X BASIC
136 Victor Wembanyama 125.00 300.00
150 Amen Thompson 15.00 40.00

2023-24 Panini Prizm Prizms Ice
*ICE: 1.25X TO 3X BASIC
127 Keyonte George 8.00 20.00
136 Victor Wembanyama 100.00 250.00
147 Brandin Podziemski 15.00 40.00
148 Trayce Jackson-Davis 12.00 30.00
152 Brandon Miller 25.00 60.00
179 GG Jackson II 12.00 30.00

2023-24 Panini Prizm Prizms Mojo
*MOJO: 15X TO 40X BASIC
STATED PRINT RUN 25 SER.#'d SETS
63 LeBron James 200.00 500.00
119 Stephen Curry 200.00 500.00
127 Keyonte George 400.00 800.00
130 Jordan Hawkins 150.00 400.00
134 Gradey Dick 200.00 500.00
136 Victor Wembanyama 6,000.00 12,000.00
139 Cason Wallace 100.00 250.00
141 Scoot Henderson 200.00 500.00
147 Brandin Podziemski 150.00 400.00
148 Trayce Jackson-Davis 150.00 400.00
150 Amen Thompson 400.00 800.00
152 Brandon Miller 600.00 1,200.00
153 Bilal Coulibaly 150.00 400.00
178 Ausar Thompson 200.00 500.00
179 GG Jackson II 400.00 800.00

2023-24 Panini Prizm Prizms Multi Wave
*MULTI WAVE: 6X TO 15X BASIC
STATED PRINT RUN 88 SER.#'d SETS
127 Keyonte George 75.00 200.00
136 Victor Wembanyama 2,000.00 4,000.00
141 Scoot Henderson 75.00 200.00
147 Brandin Podziemski 75.00 200.00
148 Trayce Jackson-Davis 60.00 150.00
150 Amen Thompson 75.00 200.00
152 Brandon Miller 200.00 500.00
179 GG Jackson II 150.00 400.00

2023-24 Panini Prizm Prizms Orange
*ORANGE: 8X TO 20X BASIC
STATED PRINT RUN 49 SER.#'d SETS
127 Keyonte George 125.00 300.00
136 Victor Wembanyama 2,500.00 5,000.00
141 Scoot Henderson 100.00 250.00
147 Brandin Podziemski 100.00 250.00
148 Trayce Jackson-Davis 75.00 200.00
150 Amen Thompson 100.00 250.00
152 Brandon Miller 300.00 600.00
179 GG Jackson II 200.00 500.00

2023-24 Panini Prizm Prizms Orange Ice
*ORANGE ICE: 1.25X TO 3X BASIC
136 Victor Wembanyama 100.00 250.00
150 Amen Thompson 15.00 40.00

2023-24 Panini Prizm Prizms Orange Wave
*ORANGE WAVE: 8X TO 20X BASIC
STATED PRINT RUN 60 SER.#'d SETS
127 Keyonte George 125.00 300.00
136 Victor Wembanyama 2,500.00 5,000.00
141 Scoot Henderson 100.00 250.00
147 Brandin Podziemski 100.00 250.00
148 Trayce Jackson-Davis 75.00 200.00
150 Amen Thompson 100.00 250.00
152 Brandon Miller 300.00 600.00
179 GG Jackson II 200.00 500.00

2023-24 Panini Prizm Prizms Pink Ice
*PINK ICE: 1.25X TO 3X BASIC
136 Victor Wembanyama 100.00 250.00
147 Brandin Podziemski 15.00 40.00
148 Trayce Jackson-Davis 12.00 30.00
150 Amen Thompson 12.00 30.00
152 Brandon Miller 25.00 60.00
179 GG Jackson II 15.00 40.00

2023-24 Panini Prizm Prizms Pink Pulsar
*PINK PULSAR: 8X TO 20X BASIC
STATED PRINT RUN 42 SER.#'d SETS
127 Keyonte George 150.00 400.00
136 Victor Wembanyama 2,500.00 5,000.00
141 Scoot Henderson 100.00 250.00
147 Brandin Podziemski 100.00 250.00
148 Trayce Jackson-Davis 75.00 200.00
150 Amen Thompson 150.00 400.00
152 Brandon Miller 300.00 600.00
179 GG Jackson II 200.00 500.00

2023-24 Panini Prizm Prizms Premium Factory Set
*PREMIUM FAC SET: 5X TO 12X BASIC
STATED PRINT RUN 150 SER.#'d SETS
127 Keyonte George 60.00 150.00
136 Victor Wembanyama 1,500.00 3,000.00
141 Scoot Henderson 60.00 150.00
147 Brandin Podziemski 60.00 150.00
148 Trayce Jackson-Davis 50.00 120.00
150 Amen Thompson 60.00 150.00
152 Brandon Miller 150.00 400.00
179 GG Jackson II 125.00 300.00

2023-24 Panini Prizm Prizms Pulsar
*PULSAR 1.25X TO 3X BASIC
127 Keyonte George 20.00 50.00
136 Victor Wembanyama 125.00 300.00
147 Brandin Podziemski 20.00 50.00
148 Trayce Jackson-Davis 12.00 30.00
150 Amen Thompson 12.00 30.00
152 Brandon Miller 50.00 120.00
178 Ausar Thompson 12.00 30.00
179 GG Jackson II 20.00 50.00

2023-24 Panini Prizm Prizms Purple
*PURPLE: 6X TO 15X BASIC
STATED PRINT RUN 99 SER.#'d SETS
127 Keyonte George 75.00 200.00
136 Victor Wembanyama 2,000.00 4,000.00
141 Scoot Henderson 75.00 200.00
147 Brandin Podziemski 75.00 200.00
148 Trayce Jackson-Davis 60.00 150.00
150 Amen Thompson 75.00 200.00
152 Brandon Miller 200.00 500.00
179 GG Jackson II 150.00 400.00

2023-24 Panini Prizm Prizms Purple Ice
*PURPLE ICE: 5X TO 12X BASIC
STATED PRINT RUN 149 SER.#'d SETS
127 Keyonte George 60.00 150.00
136 Victor Wembanyama 1,500.00 3,000.00
141 Scoot Henderson 60.00 150.00
147 Brandin Podziemski 60.00 150.00
148 Trayce Jackson-Davis 50.00 120.00
150 Amen Thompson 60.00 150.00
152 Brandon Miller 150.00 400.00
179 GG Jackson II 125.00 300.00

2023-24 Panini Prizm Prizms Purple Pulsar
*PURPLE PULSAR: 10X TO 25X BASIC
STATED PRINT RUN 35 SER.#'d SETS
127 Keyonte George 200.00 500.00
136 Victor Wembanyama 3,000.00 6,000.00
141 Scoot Henderson 125.00 300.00
147 Brandin Podziemski 125.00 300.00
148 Trayce Jackson-Davis 100.00 250.00
150 Amen Thompson 200.00 500.00
152 Brandon Miller 400.00 800.00
179 GG Jackson II 300.00 600.00

2023-24 Panini Prizm Prizms Red
*RED: 3X TO 8X BASIC
STATED PRINT RUN 299 SER. #'D SETS
127 Keyonte George 40.00 100.00
136 Victor Wembanyama 1,000.00 2,000.00
141 Scoot Henderson 40.00 100.00
147 Brandin Podziemski 40.00 100.00
148 Trayce Jackson-Davis 30.00 80.00
150 Amen Thompson 40.00 100.00
152 Brandon Miller 100.00 250.00
179 GG Jackson II 75.00 200.00

2023-24 Panini Prizm Prizms Red Ice
*RED ICE: 1.25X TO 3X BASIC
136 Victor Wembanyama 125.00 300.00
147 Brandin Podziemski 15.00 40.00
148 Trayce Jackson-Davis 12.00 30.00
150 Amen Thompson 12.00 30.00
152 Brandon Miller 25.00 60.00
179 GG Jackson II 15.00 40.00

2023-24 Panini Prizm Prizms Red Power
*RED POWER: 6X TO 15X BASIC
STATED PRINT RUN 75 SER.#'d SETS
127 Keyonte George 75.00 200.00
136 Victor Wembanyama 2,000.00 4,000.00
141 Scoot Henderson 75.00 200.00
147 Brandin Podziemski 75.00 200.00
148 Trayce Jackson-Davis 60.00 150.00
150 Amen Thompson 75.00 200.00
152 Brandon Miller 200.00 500.00
179 GG Jackson II 150.00 400.00

2023-24 Panini Prizm Prizms Red Seismic
*RED SEISMIC: 3X TO 8X BASIC
STATED PRINT RUN 299 SER.#'d SETS
127 Keyonte George 40.00 100.00
136 Victor Wembanyama 1,000.00 2,000.00
141 Scoot Henderson 40.00 100.00
147 Brandin Podziemski 40.00 100.00
148 Trayce Jackson-Davis 30.00 80.00
150 Amen Thompson 30.00 80.00
152 Brandon Miller 100.00 250.00
179 GG Jackson II 75.00 200.00

2023-24 Panini Prizm Prizms Red White and Blue
*RED WHITE & BLUE: .75X TO 2X BASIC
136 Victor Wembanyama 50.00 120.00

2023-24 Panini Prizm Prizms Ruby Wave
*RUBY WAVE: 1.5X TO 4X BASIC
136 Victor Wembanyama 150.00 400.00
147 Brandin Podziemski 20.00 50.00
148 Trayce Jackson-Davis 15.00 40.00
150 Amen Thompson 20.00 50.00
152 Brandon Miller 30.00 80.00
179 GG Jackson II 20.00 50.00

2023-24 Panini Prizm Prizms Silver
*SILVER: 1.5X TO 4X BASIC
136 Victor Wembanyama 150.00 400.00
150 Amen Thompson 30.00 80.00
152 Brandon Miller 30.00 80.00

2023-24 Panini Prizm Prizms Teal Ice
*TEAL ICE: 4X TO 10X BASIC
STATED PRINT RUN 225 SER.#'d SETS
127 Keyonte George 50.00 120.00
136 Victor Wembanyama 1,250.00 2,500.00
141 Scoot Henderson 50.00 120.00
147 Brandin Podziemski 50.00 120.00
148 Trayce Jackson-Davis 40.00 100.00
150 Amen Thompson 50.00 120.00
152 Brandon Miller 125.00 300.00
179 GG Jackson II 100.00 250.00

2023-24 Panini Prizm Prizms White
*WHITE: 5X TO 12X BASIC
STATED PRINT RUN 175 SER.#'d SETS
127 Keyonte George 60.00 150.00
136 Victor Wembanyama 1,500.00 3,000.00
141 Scoot Henderson 60.00 150.00
147 Brandin Podziemski 60.00 150.00
148 Trayce Jackson-Davis 50.00 120.00
150 Amen Thompson 60.00 150.00
152 Brandon Miller 150.00 400.00
179 GG Jackson II 125.00 300.00

2023-24 Panini Prizm Prizms White Ice
*WHITE ICE: 10X TO 25X BASIC
STATED PRINT RUN 35 SER.#'d SETS
127 Keyonte George 200.00 500.00
136 Victor Wembanyama 3,000.00 6,000.00
141 Scoot Henderson 125.00 300.00
147 Brandin Podziemski 125.00 300.00
148 Trayce Jackson-Davis 100.00 250.00
150 Amen Thompson 200.00 500.00
152 Brandon Miller 400.00 800.00
179 GG Jackson II 300.00 600.00

2023-24 Panini Prizm Prizms White Wave
*WHITE WAVE: 10X TO 25X BASIC
STATED PRINT RUN 38 SER.#'d SETS
127 Keyonte George 200.00 500.00
136 Victor Wembanyama 4,000.00 8,000.00
141 Scoot Henderson 125.00 300.00
147 Brandin Podziemski 125.00 300.00
148 Trayce Jackson-Davis 100.00 250.00
150 Amen Thompson 200.00 500.00
152 Brandon Miller 400.00 800.00
179 GG Jackson II 300.00 600.00

2023-24 Panini Prizm Deep Space Prizms Green
*GREEN: .6X TO 1.5X BASIC
1 Victor Wembanyama 25.00 60.00

2023-24 Panini Prizm Deep Space Prizms Silver
*SILVER: .75X TO 2X BASIC
1 Victor Wembanyama 30.00 80.00

2023-24 Panini Prizm Dominance
*GREEN: .6X TO 1.5X BASIC
*SILVER: .75X TO 2X BASIC
1 Ja Morant 1.25 3.00
2 Luka Doncic 2.50 6.00
3 LeBron James 3.00 8.00
4 Damian Lillard 1.00 2.50
5 Donovan Mitchell .75 2.00
6 Jayson Tatum 1.50 4.00
7 Giannis Antetokounmpo 2.00 5.00
8 Kyrie Irving .75 2.00
9 Kevin Durant 1.25 3.00
10 Nikola Jokic 2.00 5.00
11 Devin Booker 1.00 2.50
12 Bradley Beal .50 1.25
13 DeMar DeRozan .60 1.50
14 Trae Young .75 2.00
15 Anthony Edwards 2.00 5.00
16 Zion Williamson 1.00 2.50
17 De'Aaron Fox .75 2.00
18 Kawhi Leonard 1.00 2.50
19 Stephen Curry 3.00 8.00
20 Joel Embiid 1.00 2.50
21 James Harden .75 2.00
22 Shai Gilgeous-Alexander 2.00 5.00
23 Lauri Markkanen .60 1.50
24 Jamal Murray .75 2.00
25 Anthony Davis 1.00 2.50

2023-24 Panini Prizm Emergent
*GREEN: 1X TO 2.5X BASIC
1 Marcus Sasser .60 1.50
2 Keyonte George 1.25 3.00
3 Anthony Black .75 2.00
4 Bilal Coulibaly 1.00 2.50
5 Jett Howard .50 1.25
6 Brice Sensabaugh .60 1.50
7 Ausar Thompson 1.00 2.50
8 Noah Clowney .50 1.25
9 Kobe Bufkin .50 1.25
10 Nick Smith Jr. .50 1.25
11 Kris Murray .40 1.00
12 Victor Wembanyama 8.00 20.00
13 Amen Thompson 2.00 5.00
14 Ben Sheppard .40 1.00
15 Jalen Hood-Schifino .40 1.00
16 Scoot Henderson 1.25 3.00
17 Brandon Miller 1.50 4.00
18 Kobe Brown .40 1.00
19 Jordan Hawkins .60 1.50
20 Dariq Whitehead .50 1.25
21 Julian Strawther .50 1.25
22 Gradey Dick .75 2.00
23 Jaime Jaquez Jr. .60 1.50
24 Brandin Podziemski 1.25 3.00
25 Jarace Walker .75 2.00
26 Dereck Lively II .75 2.00
27 Cam Whitmore 1.00 2.50
28 Olivier-Maxence Prosper .40 1.00
29 Cason Wallace .75 2.00
30 Taylor Hendricks .40 1.00

2023-24 Panini Prizm Emergent Prizms Silver
*SILVER: 1.25X TO 3X BASIC
12 Victor Wembanyama 30.00 80.00

2023-24 Panini Prizm Fireworks
*BLUE WAVE: .75X TO 2X BASIC
*FAST BREAK: .75X TO 2X BASIC
*SILVER: 1X TO 2.5X BASIC
*MOJO/25: 6X TO 15X BASIC
1 DeMar DeRozan .60 1.50
2 Tyrese Haliburton .75 2.00
3 LeBron James 3.00 8.00
4 Jalen Brunson .75 2.00
5 Stephen Curry 3.00 8.00
6 Tyrese Maxey .75 2.00
7 Luka Doncic 2.50 6.00
8 Ja Morant 1.25 3.00
9 Kyrie Irving .75 2.00
10 Zion Williamson 1.00 2.50
11 Anthony Edwards 2.00 5.00
12 LaMelo Ball 1.00 2.50
13 Joel Embiid 1.00 2.50
14 Damian Lillard 1.00 2.50
15 De'Aaron Fox .75 2.00
16 Shai Gilgeous-Alexander 2.00 5.00
17 Jayson Tatum 1.50 4.00
18 Donovan Mitchell .75 2.00
19 Giannis Antetokounmpo 2.00 5.00
20 Trae Young .75 2.00
21 Jalen Green .60 1.50
22 Nikola Jokic 2.00 5.00
23 Lauri Markkanen .60 1.50
24 Kevin Durant 1.25 3.00
25 Jamal Murray .75 2.00

2023-24 Panini Prizm Franchise Favorites Signatures
*SILVER: .5X TO 1.2X BASIC
*RED/99: .5X TO 1.2X BASIC
*BLUE/49: .6X TO 1.5X BASIC
*MOJO/25: .75X TO 2X BASIC
1 Stephen Curry 400.00 800.00
2 Shaquille O'Neal 60.00 150.00
3 Larry Bird 60.00 150.00
4 Hakeem Olajuwon 25.00 60.00
5 Clyde Drexler 20.00 50.00
6 Allen Iverson 50.00 120.00
7 Julius Erving 50.00 120.00
8 Dwyane Wade 30.00 80.00
9 Karl Malone 25.00 60.00
10 Kareem Abdul-Jabbar 60.00 150.00

2023-24 Panini Prizm Global Reach Prizms Green
*GREEN: .6X TO 1.5X BASIC
2 Victor Wembanyama 25.00 60.00

2023-24 Panini Prizm Global Reach Prizms Silver
*SILVER: .75X TO 2X BASIC
2 Victor Wembanyama 30.00 80.00

2023-24 Panini Prizm Instant Impact Prizms Green
*GREEN: .75X TO 2X BASIC
3 Victor Wembanyama 40.00 100.00

2023-24 Panini Prizm Instant Impact Prizms Silver
*SILVER: 1X TO 2.5X BASIC
3 Victor Wembanyama 50.00 120.00

2023-24 Panini Prizm Kaleidoscopic
*BLUE WAVE: 1X TO 2.5X BASIC
*FAST BREAK: 1X TO 2.5X BASIC
*SILVER: 1.25X TO 3X BASIC
*MOJO/25: 8X TO 20X BASIC
1 Jayson Tatum 2.50 6.00
2 LeBron James 5.00 12.00
3 Luka Doncic 4.00 10.00
4 Giannis Antetokounmpo 3.00 8.00
5 Ja Morant 2.00 5.00
6 Kyrie Irving 1.25 3.00
7 Kevin Durant 2.00 5.00
8 Nikola Jokic 3.00 8.00
9 Joel Embiid 1.50 4.00
10 Damian Lillard 1.50 4.00
11 Donovan Mitchell 1.25 3.00
12 Devin Booker 1.50 4.00
13 Shai Gilgeous-Alexander 3.00 8.00
14 Anthony Edwards 3.00 8.00
15 James Harden 1.25 3.00
16 Zion Williamson 1.50 4.00
17 LaMelo Ball 1.50 4.00
18 Trae Young 1.25 3.00
19 Kawhi Leonard 1.50 4.00
20 Paul George 1.00 2.50
21 Stephen Curry 5.00 12.00
22 Zach LaVine 1.00 2.50
23 Bradley Beal .75 2.00
24 Julius Randle .75 2.00
25 Cade Cunningham 1.50 4.00
26 Jaylen Brown 1.25 3.00
27 Darius Garland 1.00 2.50
28 Anthony Davis 1.50 4.00
29 De'Aaron Fox 1.25 3.00
30 Jimmy Butler 1.00 2.50

2023-24 Panini Prizm Luck of the Lottery Prizms Blue Wave
*BLUE WAVE: .75X TO 2X BASIC
7 Victor Wembanyama 40.00 100.00

2023-24 Panini Prizm Luck of the Lottery Prizms Fast Break
*FAST BREAK: .75X TO 2X BASIC
7 Victor Wembanyama 40.00 100.00

2023-24 Panini Prizm Luck of the Lottery Prizms Mojo
*MOJO/25: 10X TO 25X BASIC
7 Victor Wembanyama 1,500.00 3,000.00
13 Brandon Miller 200.00 500.00
14 Scoot Henderson 75.00 200.00

2023-24 Panini Prizm Luck of the Lottery Prizms Silver
*SILVER: .75X TO 2X BASIC
7 Victor Wembanyama 40.00 100.00

2023-24 Panini Prizm Penmanship
*SILVER: .5X TO 1.2X BASIC
1 Stephen Jackson 4.00 10.00
3 Tyrese Martin 4.00 10.00
4 Willie Green 5.00 12.00
5 Ron Harper Jr. 4.00 10.00
7 Scotty Pippen Jr. 5.00 12.00
9 Rolando Blackman 4.00 10.00
10 Juan Toscano-Anderson 4.00 10.00
12 Daniel Gafford 5.00 12.00
13 Bobby Portis 6.00 15.00
14 Herbert Jones 5.00 12.00
15 Mario Chalmers 4.00 10.00
17 Dale Ellis 5.00 12.00
18 Collin Gillespie 5.00 12.00
19 Dennis Scott 4.00 10.00
20 Tim Hardaway Jr. 4.00 10.00
21 Max Strus 5.00 12.00
22 B.J. Armstrong 5.00 12.00
24 Jalen McDaniels 4.00 10.00
25 Bill Laimbeer 5.00 12.00
26 Jaylin Williams 5.00 12.00
27 Dan Issel 6.00 15.00
28 Kendrick Perkins 3.00 8.00
29 MarJon Beauchamp 4.00 10.00
30 Bruce Brown 5.00 12.00
31 Darius Days 3.00 8.00
32 Jose Alvarado 5.00 12.00
34 Maurice Cheeks 5.00 12.00
35 Rashard Lewis 5.00 12.00
36 Kendall Brown 3.00 8.00
37 Keon Ellis 4.00 10.00
38 Josh Minott 5.00 12.00
39 Bryce McGowens 5.00 12.00
41 Jabari Walker 3.00 8.00
43 Justin Lewis 4.00 10.00
44 Kenneth Lofton Jr. 5.00 12.00
45 Mason Plumlee 4.00 10.00
46 Boban Marjanovic 5.00 12.00
47 Rod Strickland 5.00 12.00
48 Vince Williams Jr. 5.00 12.00
49 Tari Eason 6.00 15.00
50 Seth Curry 5.00 12.00

2023-24 Panini Prizm Prizmania
1 Dirk Nowitzki 400.00 800.00
2 Stephen Curry 1,500.00 3,000.00
3 Allen Iverson 300.00 600.00
4 Giannis Antetokounmpo 600.00 1,200.00
6 Luka Doncic 1,500.00 3,000.00
7 Trae Young 200.00 500.00
8 Anthony Edwards 800.00 1,500.00
9 Nikola Jokic 600.00 1,200.00
11 Victor Wembanyama 6,000.00 12,000.00
12 Scoot Henderson 800.00 1,500.00
13 Bilal Coulibaly 350.00 700.00
14 Keyonte George 600.00 1,200.00
15 Cason Wallace 400.00 800.00
16 Cam Whitmore 400.00 800.00
17 Brandon Miller 1,000.00 2,000.00
18 Anthony Black 350.00 700.00
19 Amen Thompson 500.00 1,000.00
20 Ausar Thompson 400.00 800.00

2023-24 Panini Prizm Rookie Penmanship
*SILVER: .5X TO 1.2X BASIC
1 Jaylen Clark 5.00 12.00
5 Colby Jones 5.00 12.00
6 Rayan Rupert 5.00 12.00
8 Kobe Brown 5.00 12.00
10 Bilal Coulibaly 40.00 100.00
12 Jordan Walsh 12.00 30.00
13 Filip Petrusev 5.00 12.00
14 Brandin Podziemski 75.00 200.00
15 Cason Wallace 15.00 40.00
16 Adama Sanogo 5.00 12.00
17 Joey Hauser 4.00 10.00
18 Chris Livingston 5.00 12.00
20 Mouhamed Gueye 5.00 12.00
21 Azuolas Tubelis 4.00 10.00
22 Kris Murray 5.00 12.00
23 Ausar Thompson 40.00 100.00
24 Markquis Nowell 5.00 12.00
25 Dariq Whitehead 6.00 15.00
26 Sir'Jabari Rice 4.00 10.00
27 Oscar Tshiebwe 10.00 25.00
28 Ricky Council IV 6.00 15.00
29 Keyonte George 40.00 100.00
30 Maxwell Lewis 4.00 10.00
31 Keyontae Johnson 5.00 12.00
32 Julian Strawther 6.00 15.00
34 Isaiah Wong 5.00 12.00
35 Noah Clowney 6.00 15.00
36 Jalen Wilson 5.00 12.00
37 GG Jackson II 40.00 100.00
38 Marcus Sasser 8.00 20.00
39 James Nnaji 4.00 10.00
40 Colin Castleton 4.00 10.00
41 Amen Thompson 40.00 100.00
42 Brice Sensabaugh 8.00 20.00
43 Kobe Bufkin 6.00 15.00
44 Sidy Cissoko 5.00 12.00
45 Toumani Camara 10.00 25.00
46 Olivier-Maxence Prosper 5.00 12.00
48 Omari Moore 4.00 10.00
49 Terquavion Smith 5.00 12.00

2023-24 Panini Prizm Rookie Signatures
*BLUE WAVE: .5X TO 1.2X BASIC
*SILVER: .5X TO 1.2X BASIC
*RED/99: .5X TO 1.2X BASIC
*CHOICE/88: .5X TO 1.2X BASIC
*BLUE/49: .6X TO 1.5X BASIC
*CHOICE BLUE/49: .6X TO 1.5X BASIC
*MOJO/25: .75X TO 2X BASIC
1 Bilal Coulibaly 40.00 100.00
2 Filip Petrusev 5.00 12.00
3 Ausar Thompson 40.00 100.00
4 Mike Miles Jr. 4.00 10.00
5 Amen Thompson 25.00 60.00
6 Tristan Vukcevic 5.00 12.00
7 Rayan Rupert 5.00 12.00
8 Jordan Miller 6.00 15.00
9 Omari Moore 4.00 10.00
10 Isaiah Wong 5.00 12.00
11 Kris Murray 5.00 12.00
12 Kobe Bufkin 6.00 15.00
13 GG Jackson II 10.00 25.00
14 James Nnaji 4.00 10.00
15 Marcus Sasser 8.00 20.00
16 Hunter Tyson 5.00 12.00
17 Ben Sheppard 5.00 12.00
18 Keyontae Johnson 5.00 12.00
19 Dariq Whitehead 6.00 15.00
20 Leonard Miller 5.00 12.00
21 Keyonte George 40.00 100.00
22 D'Moi Hodge 4.00 10.00
23 Markquis Nowell 5.00 12.00
24 Jalen Slawson 5.00 12.00
25 Adama Sanogo 5.00 12.00
26 Olivier-Maxence Prosper 5.00 12.00
27 Colby Jones 5.00 12.00
28 Julian Strawther 6.00 15.00
29 Jordan Walsh 12.00 30.00
30 Jalen Pickett 4.00 10.00
31 Jaylen Clark 5.00 12.00
32 Azuolas Tubelis 4.00 10.00
33 Julian Phillips 5.00 12.00
34 Dereck Lively II 10.00 25.00
35 Jalen Wilson 5.00 12.00
36 Andre Jackson Jr. 8.00 20.00
37 Trayce Jackson-Davis 6.00 15.00
38 Kobe Brown 5.00 12.00
39 Cason Wallace 20.00 50.00
40 Sir'Jabari Rice 4.00 10.00
41 Colin Castleton 4.00 10.00
42 Brandin Podziemski 75.00 200.00
43 Noah Clowney 6.00 15.00
44 Brice Sensabaugh 8.00 20.00
45 Maxwell Lewis 4.00 10.00
46 Seth Lundy 4.00 10.00
47 Mouhamed Gueye 5.00 12.00
48 Chris Livingston 5.00 12.00
49 Toumani Camara 10.00 25.00
50 Sidy Cissoko 5.00 12.00

2023-24 Panini Prizm Rookie Variations
127 Keyonte George 3.00 8.00
129 Cam Whitmore 2.50 6.00
130 Jordan Hawkins 1.50 4.00
132 Jett Howard 1.25 3.00
134 Gradey Dick 2.00 5.00
136 Victor Wembanyama 30.00 80.00
137 Jaime Jaquez Jr. 1.50 4.00
139 Cason Wallace 2.00 5.00
141 Scoot Henderson 3.00 8.00
145 Jalen Hood-Schifino 1.00 2.50
147 Brandin Podziemski 3.00 8.00
150 Amen Thompson 5.00 12.00
151 Kobe Bufkin 1.25 3.00
152 Brandon Miller 4.00 10.00
153 Bilal Coulibaly 2.50 6.00
161 Taylor Hendricks 1.00 2.50
163 Dereck Lively II 2.00 5.00
168 Jarace Walker 2.00 5.00
170 Anthony Black 2.00 5.00
178 Ausar Thompson 2.50 6.00

2023-24 Panini Prizm Rookie Variations Fast Break
*FB: 1X TO 2.5X BASIC
136 Victor Wembanyama 150.00 400.00

2023-24 Panini Prizm Signatures
*BLUE WAVE: .5X TO 1.2X BASIC
*SILVER: .5X TO 1.2X BASIC
*RED/99: .5X TO 1.2X BASIC
*CHOICE/88: .5X TO 1.2X BASIC
*BLUE/49: .6X TO 1.5X BASIC
*CHOICE BLUE/35-49: .6X TO 1.5X BASIC
*MOJO/25: .75X TO 2X BASIC
1 Ayo Dosunmu 5.00 12.00
2 Kenyon Martin Jr. 5.00 12.00
3 Nikola Jokic 100.00 250.00
4 Evan Mobley 8.00 20.00
5 Cameron Payne 4.00 10.00
6 Bennedict Mathurin 8.00 20.00
7 James Worthy 8.00 20.00
8 James Harden 75.00 200.00
9 Tom Chambers 5.00 12.00

10 Bradley Beal 6.00 15.00
11 Steve Kerr 6.00 15.00
12 Austin Reaves 25.00 60.00
13 Bojan Bogdanovic 5.00 12.00
14 Nikola Vucevic 5.00 12.00
15 Ochai Agbaji 5.00 12.00
16 Josh Giddey 6.00 15.00
17 Michael Porter Jr. 6.00 15.00
18 Max Strus 5.00 12.00
19 Malik Monk 6.00 15.00
20 Jerry Stackhouse 5.00 12.00
21 Austin Rivers 3.00 8.00
22 Jaren Jackson Jr. 12.00 30.00
23 Robert Parish 6.00 15.00
24 Donovan Mitchell 40.00 100.00
25 Lauri Markkanen 8.00 20.00
26 Richard Hamilton 6.00 15.00
27 Jaden Hardy 6.00 15.00
28 Anthony Edwards 100.00 250.00
29 Chauncey Billups 6.00 15.00
30 Caron Butler 4.00 10.00
31 Jeremy Sochan 6.00 15.00
32 Steve Francis 5.00 12.00
33 Detlef Schrempf 4.00 10.00
34 Mario Chalmers 4.00 10.00
35 Andrew Nembhard 5.00 12.00
36 David Thompson 6.00 15.00
37 Deandre Ayton 5.00 12.00
38 Immanuel Quickley 5.00 12.00
39 Alperen Sengun 20.00 50.00
40 Cade Cunningham 40.00 100.00
41 Nikola Jovic 5.00 12.00
42 Gary Trent Jr. 5.00 12.00
43 Rui Hachimura 40.00 100.00
44 Larry Johnson 12.00 30.00
45 Onyeka Okongwu 4.00 10.00
46 Malcolm Brogdon 5.00 12.00
47 Bob McAdoo 6.00 15.00
48 Bruce Brown 5.00 12.00
49 Peja Stojakovic 5.00 12.00
50 Walker Kessler 5.00 12.00

2024-25 Panini Prizm

*RC VAR: .4X TO 1X BASIC
1 Dejounte Murray .40 1.00
2 Jamal Murray .60 1.50
3 Jordan Clarkson .40 1.00
4 Jalen Suggs .40 1.00
5 Deandre Ayton .30 .75
6 Andrew Nembhard .30 .75
7 Keegan Murray .30 .75
8 Devin Booker 1.00 2.50
9 Kelly Oubre Jr. .30 .75
10 Zion Williamson 1.00 2.50
11 Obi Toppin .30 .75
12 Tari Eason .40 1.00
13 Deni Avdija .40 1.00
14 Rui Hachimura .40 1.00
15 Mikal Bridges .40 1.00
16 Scottie Barnes .50 1.25
17 Chet Holmgren .60 1.50
18 Andre Drummond .30 .75
19 Andrew Wiggins .50 1.25
20 Jalen Duren .40 1.00
21 Marcus Sasser .30 .75
22 Aaron Nesmith .30 .75
23 Jeremy Sochan .40 1.00
24 Keldon Johnson .30 .75
25 Devin Vassell .50 1.25
26 Austin Reaves .50 1.25
27 Max Strus .30 .75
28 Joel Embiid .60 1.50
29 Michael Porter Jr. .40 1.00
30 LaMelo Ball .75 2.00
31 Grant Williams .25 .60
32 Taylor Hendricks .40 1.00
33 Gary Trent Jr. .30 .75
34 Derrick Jones Jr. .25 .60
35 Jae Crowder .25 .60
36 Bilal Coulibaly .50 1.25
37 Kyle Anderson .25 .60
38 Nicolas Claxton .30 .75
39 Ivica Zubac .40 1.00
40 Bennedict Mathurin .50 1.25
41 Cade Cunningham 1.00 2.50
42 Precious Achiuwa .30 .75
43 Miles Bridges .30 .75
44 Saddiq Bey .30 .75
45 Anfernee Simons .40 1.00
46 Payton Pritchard .40 1.00
47 De'Andre Hunter .40 1.00
48 Jordan Hawkins .30 .75
49 D'Angelo Russell .30 .75
50 Paul George .60 1.50
51 Donte DiVincenzo .40 1.00
52 Andre Jackson Jr. .30 .75
53 Derrick Rose 1.00 2.50
54 Bradley Beal .50 1.25
55 Harrison Barnes .30 .75
56 Mark Williams .30 .75
57 Julius Randle .40 1.00
58 De'Aaron Fox .75 2.00
59 Marcus Smart .40 1.00
60 Cam Reddish .25 .60
61 Tre Jones .30 .75
62 Pascal Siakam .50 1.25
63 Kentavious Caldwell-Pope .25 .60
64 Ja Morant 1.25 3.00
65 Jalen Williams .75 2.00
66 Derrick White .40 1.00
67 Caleb Martin .25 .60
68 Patrick Williams .30 .75
69 Terance Mann .25 .60
70 Coby White .40 1.00
71 Caris LeVert .30 .75
72 Grayson Allen .30 .75
73 Cole Anthony .40 1.00
74 Brook Lopez .30 .75
75 Lonzo Ball .40 1.00
76 Jonas Valanciunas .30 .75
77 Jabari Smith Jr. .40 1.00
78 Immanuel Quickley .30 .75
79 Wendell Carter Jr. .30 .75
80 Bol Bol .25 .60
81 Brandin Podziemski .50 1.25
82 Ben Simmons .40 1.00
83 Alex Caruso .40 1.00
84 Trae Young .75 2.00
85 Giannis Antetokounmpo 1.50 4.00
86 Domantas Sabonis .60 1.50
87 Keyonte George .50 1.25
88 Vasilije Micic .40 1.00
89 Luka Doncic 2.50 6.00
90 Damian Lillard 1.00 2.50
91 Cameron Thomas .40 1.00
92 Julian Strawther .40 1.00
93 Malik Monk .40 1.00
94 Scoot Henderson .50 1.25
95 Scotty Pippen Jr. .40 1.00
96 Tyrese Maxey .75 2.00
97 Bam Adebayo .50 1.25
98 Tyler Herro .60 1.50
99 Tyrese Haliburton .75 2.00
100 Anthony Edwards 2.00 5.00
101 RJ Barrett .50 1.25
102 Jalen Green .75 2.00
103 Jayson Tatum 1.25 3.00
104 Jonathan Kuminga .50 1.25
105 Bogdan Bogdanovic .30 .75
106 Isaiah Stewart .30 .75
107 Klay Thompson 1.00 2.50
108 Dorian Finney-Smith .25 .60
109 Brandon Miller .60 1.50
110 Cam Whitmore .40 1.00
111 Kyrie Irving 1.00 2.50
112 Josh Giddey .50 1.25
113 Shai Gilgeous-Alexander 2.00 5.00
114 Kristaps Porzingis .50 1.25
115 Myles Turner .30 .75
116 Moritz Wagner .30 .75
117 DeMar DeRozan .50 1.25
118 Amen Thompson 1.00 2.50
119 Luguentz Dort .30 .75
120 Jalen Johnson .50 1.25
121 Ayo Dosunmu .30 .75
122 Dyson Daniels .50 1.25
123 Herbert Jones .30 .75
124 Daniel Gafford .30 .75
125 Desmond Bane .40 1.00
126 Robert Williams III .30 .75
127 Jusuf Nurkic .30 .75
128 Jaden Hardy .40 1.00
129 Nikola Jokic 2.00 5.00
130 LeBron James 3.00 8.00
131 Draymond Green .50 1.25
132 Chris Paul .60 1.50
133 Peyton Watson .30 .75
134 Stephen Curry 3.00 8.00
135 Nickeil Alexander-Walker .25 .60
136 Taurean Prince .25 .60
137 Mike Conley .30 .75
138 Jaime Jaquez Jr. .40 1.00
139 Jaylen Brown .60 1.50
140 Jaren Jackson Jr. .60 1.50
141 Karl-Anthony Towns .60 1.50
142 Terry Rozier III .30 .75
143 Franz Wagner .60 1.50
144 Shaedon Sharpe .50 1.25
145 Marvin Bagley III .25 .60
146 Darius Garland .50 1.25
147 Ausar Thompson .60 1.50
148 Evan Mobley .60 1.50
149 OG Anunoby .30 .75
150 Kyle Kuzma .30 .75
151 Collin Sexton .40 1.00
152 Kelly Olynyk .25 .60
153 Khris Middleton .40 1.00
154 Isaiah Hartenstein .30 .75
155 Donovan Mitchell .75 2.00
156 Mitchell Robinson .30 .75
157 Russell Westbrook .60 1.50
158 Julian Champagnie .30 .75
159 Rudy Gobert .40 1.00
160 CJ McCollum .30 .75
161 Clint Capela .30 .75
162 Reggie Jackson .25 .60
163 Isaac Okoro .25 .60
164 Jimmy Butler .60 1.50
165 Kevin Huerter .30 .75
166 Kobe Bufkin .30 .75
167 Jose Alvarado .30 .75
168 Aaron Gordon .40 1.00
169 Jarrett Allen .30 .75
170 Fred VanVleet .40 1.00
171 Jrue Holiday .50 1.25
172 Victor Wembanyama 3.00 8.00
173 Trey Murphy III .50 1.25
174 P.J. Washington Jr. .30 .75
175 Jaden McDaniels .40 1.00
176 Naz Reid .40 1.00
177 Nicolas Batum .25 .60
178 Tobias Harris .30 .75
179 Tre Mann .30 .75
180 Eric Gordon .30 .75
181 James Harden .75 2.00
182 Brandon Ingram .40 1.00
183 Paolo Banchero 1.00 2.50
184 Jordan Poole .40 1.00
185 Nick Smith Jr. .30 .75
186 Lauri Markkanen .40 1.00
187 Kevin Durant 1.25 3.00
188 Trayce Jackson-Davis .40 1.00
189 Kawhi Leonard .75 2.00
190 Duncan Robinson .30 .75
191 T.J. McConnell .30 .75
192 Zach LaVine .60 1.50
193 Al Horford .40 1.00
194 Jaden Ivey .50 1.25
195 Anthony Davis 1.00 2.50
196 Josh Hart .30 .75
197 Zach Collins .25 .60
198 Jakob Poeltl .30 .75
199 Markelle Fultz .25 .60
200 Buddy Hield .30 .75
201 Alperen Sengun .60 1.50
202 Cameron Johnson .30 .75
203 Norman Powell .40 1.00
204 Jerami Grant .30 .75
205 Gradey Dick .50 1.25
206 Bobby Portis .30 .75
207 Tyus Jones .25 .60
208 GG Jackson II .40 1.00
209 Malaki Branham .30 .75
210 Kyle Lowry .40 1.00
211 Malik Beasley .30 .75
212 Cason Wallace .50 1.25
213 Dillon Brooks .30 .75
214 Dereck Lively II .40 1.00
215 Toumani Camara .40 1.00
216 Nikola Vucevic .30 .75
217 Jalen Brunson .75 2.00
218 Dennis Schroder .40 1.00
219 Anthony Black .50 1.25
220 John Collins .30 .75
221 Donovan Clingan RC 2.00 5.00
222 Jared McCain RC 3.00 8.00
223 Ja'Kobe Walter RC 1.00 2.50
224 Terrence Shannon Jr. RC 1.50 4.00
225 Tyler Kolek RC 1.25 3.00
226 Ajay Mitchell RC 1.25 3.00
227 Isaiah Collier RC 1.50 4.00
228 Jaylon Tyson RC .75 2.00
229 Nikola Durisic RC 1.00 2.50
230 Nikola Topic RC 2.50 6.00
231 Devin Carter RC 1.00 2.50
232 Cody Williams RC 1.00 2.50
233 Yves Missi RC 2.00 5.00
234 Stephon Castle RC 5.00 12.00
235 DaRon Holmes II RC 1.00 2.50
236 Baylor Scheierman RC 1.00 2.50
237 Johnny Furphy RC 1.25 3.00
238 Dalton Knecht RC 2.50 6.00
239 Jaylen Wells RC 2.50 6.00
240 Dillon Jones RC .75 2.00
241 Jamal Shead RC 1.00 2.50
242 Cam Christie RC 1.00 2.50
243 Bronny James Jr. RC 2.50 6.00
244 Bub Carrington RC 2.00 5.00
245 Oso Ighodaro RC 1.00 2.50
246 Cam Spencer RC .75 2.00
247 KJ Simpson Jr. RC .75 2.00
248 Kel'el Ware RC 2.00 5.00
249 Zach Edey RC 2.50 6.00
250 Rob Dillingham RC 2.00 5.00
251 AJ Johnson RC 1.50 4.00
252 Matas Buzelis RC 4.00 10.00
253 Antonio Reeves RC .75 2.00
254 Harrison Ingram RC .75 2.00
255 Melvin Ajinca RC .60 1.50
256 Tristan da Silva RC 2.00 5.00
257 Kyshawn George RC 1.25 3.00
258 Ryan Dunn RC 1.00 2.50
259 Pacome Dadiet RC 1.00 2.50
260 Jonathan Mogbo RC 1.25 3.00
261 Tristen Newton RC .75 2.00
262 Tidjane Salaun RC .75 2.00
263 Kyle Filipowski RC 2.00 5.00
264 Alexandre Sarr RC 2.50 6.00
265 Zaccharie Risacher RC 2.50 6.00
266 Bobi Klintman RC 1.00 2.50
267 Adem Bona RC 1.00 2.50
268 Reed Sheppard RC 2.50 6.00
269 Ron Holland II RC 1.50 4.00
270 Tyler Smith RC 1.00 2.50
271 Brandon Roy .60 1.50
272 Dirk Nowitzki 1.00 2.50
273 Tracy McGrady .75 2.00
274 Anfernee Hardaway 1.00 2.50
275 Gilbert Arenas .40 1.00
276 Dwyane Wade .75 2.00
277 Dennis Rodman 1.00 2.50
278 Pete Maravich 1.00 2.50
279 Kareem Abdul-Jabbar 1.25 3.00
280 Charles Barkley 1.00 2.50
281 Pau Gasol .60 1.50
282 Dominique Wilkins .60 1.50
283 Kevin Garnett 1.00 2.50
284 Yao Ming .75 2.00
285 Carmelo Anthony .60 1.50
286 Gary Payton .60 1.50
287 Jason Williams .60 1.50
288 David Robinson .75 2.00
289 Karl Malone .75 2.00
290 Shaquille O'Neal 1.00 2.50
291 Allen Iverson 1.00 2.50
292 Julius Erving 1.00 2.50
293 Rasheed Wallace .50 1.25
294 Magic Johnson 1.25 3.00
295 Vince Carter .75 2.00
296 Hakeem Olajuwon .75 2.00
297 Tim Duncan 1.00 2.50
298 Steve Nash .75 2.00
299 Larry Bird 1.25 3.00
300 Ray Allen .60 1.50

2024-25 Panini Prizm Prizms Basketball

*BASKETBALL: 4X TO 10X BASIC
STATED PRINT RUN 225 SER. #'D SETS
130 LeBron James 100.00 250.00
234 Stephon Castle 150.00 400.00

2024-25 Panini Prizm Prizms Blue

*BLUE: 5X TO 12X BASIC
STATED PRINT RUN 199 SER. #'D SETS
130 LeBron James 125.00 300.00
234 Stephon Castle 200.00 500.00

2024-25 Panini Prizm Prizms Blue Ice

*BLUE ICE: 6X TO 15X BASIC
STATED PRINT RUN 125 SER. #'D SETS
130 LeBron James 150.00 400.00
234 Stephon Castle 300.00 600.00

2024-25 Panini Prizm Prizms Blue Pulsar

*BLUE PULSAR: 8X TO 20X BASIC
STATED PRINT RUN 99 SER. #'D SETS
130 LeBron James 200.00 500.00
234 Stephon Castle 400.00 800.00

2024-25 Panini Prizm Prizms Blue Seismic

*BLUE SEISMIC: 8X TO 20X BASIC
STATED PRINT RUN 99 SER. #'D SETS
130 LeBron James 200.00 500.00
234 Stephon Castle 400.00 800.00

2024-25 Panini Prizm Prizms Blue Shimmer FOTL

*BLUE SHMR FOTL: 10X TO 25X BASIC
STATED PRINT RUN 35 SER. #'D SETS
130 LeBron James 300.00 600.00
234 Stephon Castle 500.00 1,000.00

2024-25 Panini Prizm Prizms Blue Sparkle

*BLUE SPARKLE: 6X TO 15X BASIC
STATED PRINT RUN 144 SER. #'D SETS
130 LeBron James 150.00 400.00
234 Stephon Castle 300.00 600.00

2024-25 Panini Prizm Prizms Blue Wave

*BLUE WAVE: 6X TO 15X BASIC
STATED PRINT RUN 125 SER. #'D SETS
130 LeBron James 150.00 400.00
234 Stephon Castle 300.00 600.00

2024-25 Panini Prizm Prizms Choice Blue

*CHOICE BLUE: 10X TO 25X BASIC
STATED PRINT RUN 49 SER.#'d SETS
130 LeBron James 300.00 600.00
234 Stephon Castle 500.00 1,000.00

2024-25 Panini Prizm Prizms Choice Blue Yellow and Green

*CHOICE BLUE YLW GRN: 2X TO 5X BASIC
130 LeBron James 40.00 100.00
234 Stephon Castle 60.00 150.00

2024-25 Panini Prizm Prizms Choice Cherry Blossom

*CHOICE CHERRY BLOSSOM: 12X TO 30X BASIC
STATED PRINT RUN 20 SER.#'d SETS
130 LeBron James 400.00 800.00
234 Stephon Castle 600.00 1,200.00

2024-25 Panini Prizm Prizms Choice Cherry Blossum

*CHOICE CHERRY BLOSSUM: 12X TO 30X BASIC
STATED PRINT RUN 20 SER.#'d SETS

2024-25 Panini Prizm Prizms Choice Red

*CHOICE RED: 8X TO 20X BASIC
STATED PRINT RUN 88 SER.#'d SETS
130 LeBron James 200.00 500.00
234 Stephon Castle 400.00 800.00

2024-25 Panini Prizm Prizms Dragon Year

*DRAGON YEAR: 8X TO 20X BASIC
STATED PRINT RUN 88 SER.#'d SETS
130 LeBron James 200.00 500.00
234 Stephon Castle 400.00 800.00

2024-25 Panini Prizm Prizms Fast Break

*FAST BREAK: 1.5X TO 4X BASIC
234 Stephon Castle 50.00 120.00

2024-25 Panini Prizm Prizms Fast Break Blue

*FB BLUE: 6X TO 15X BASIC
STATED PRINT RUN 150 SER.#'d SETS
130 LeBron James 150.00 400.00
234 Stephon Castle 300.00 600.00

2024-25 Panini Prizm Prizms Fast Break Bronze

*FB BRONZE: 12X TO 30X BASIC
STATED PRINT RUN 20 SER.#'d SETS
130 LeBron James 400.00 800.00
234 Stephon Castle 600.00 1,200.00

2024-25 Panini Prizm Prizms Fast Break Orange

*FB ORANGE: 6X TO 15X BASIC
STATED PRINT RUN 125 SER.#'d SETS
130 LeBron James 150.00 400.00
234 Stephon Castle 300.00 600.00

2024-25 Panini Prizm Prizms Fast Break Pink

*FB PINK: 10X TO 25X BASIC
STATED PRINT RUN 50 SER.#'d SETS
130 LeBron James 300.00 600.00
234 Stephon Castle 500.00 1,000.00

2024-25 Panini Prizm Prizms Fast Break Purple

*FB PURPLE: 8X TO 20X BASIC
STATED PRINT RUN 75 SER.#'d SETS
130 LeBron James 200.00 500.00
234 Stephon Castle 400.00 800.00

2024-25 Panini Prizm Prizms Fast Break Red

*FB RED: 8X TO 20X BASIC
STATED PRINT RUN 100 SER.#'d SETS
130 LeBron James 200.00 500.00
234 Stephon Castle 400.00 800.00

2024-25 Panini Prizm Prizms Gold Sparkle

*GOLD SPARKLE: 12X TO 30X BASIC
STATED PRINT RUN 24 SER.#'d SETS
130 LeBron James 400.00 800.00
234 Stephon Castle 600.00 1,200.00

2024-25 Panini Prizm Prizms Green

*GREEN: 1X TO 2.5X BASIC
234 Stephon Castle 20.00 50.00

2024-25 Panini Prizm Prizms Green Ice

*GREEN ICE: 2X TO 5X BASIC
234 Stephon Castle 60.00 150.00

2024-25 Panini Prizm Prizms Green Pulsar

*GREEN PULSAR: 12X TO 30X BASIC
STATED PRINT RUN 25 SER.#'d SETS
130 LeBron James 400.00 800.00
234 Stephon Castle 600.00 1,200.00

2024-25 Panini Prizm Prizms Green Wave

*GREEN WAVE: 1.25X TO 3X BASIC
234 Stephon Castle 25.00 60.00

2024-25 Panini Prizm Prizms Hyper

*HYPER: 1.25X TO 3X BASIC
234 Stephon Castle 25.00 60.00

2024-25 Panini Prizm Prizms Ice

*ICE: 1.25X TO 3X BASIC
234 Stephon Castle 25.00 60.00

2024-25 Panini Prizm Prizms Jade Dragon Scale

*JADE DRAGON SCALE: 10X TO 25X BASIC
STATED PRINT RUN 48 SER.#'d SETS
130 LeBron James 300.00 600.00
234 Stephon Castle 500.00 1,000.00

2024-25 Panini Prizm Prizms Mojo

*MOJO: 12X TO 30X BASIC
STATED PRINT RUN 25 SER.#'d SETS
130 LeBron James 400.00 800.00
234 Stephon Castle 600.00 1,200.00

2024-25 Panini Prizm Prizms Multi Wave

*MULTI WAVE: 8X TO 20X BASIC
STATED PRINT RUN 88 SER.#'d SETS
130 LeBron James 200.00 500.00
234 Stephon Castle 400.00 800.00

2024-25 Panini Prizm Prizms Orange

*ORANGE: 10X TO 25X BASIC
STATED PRINT RUN 49 SER.#'d SETS
130 LeBron James 300.00 600.00
234 Stephon Castle 500.00 1,000.00

2024-25 Panini Prizm Prizms Orange Seismic

*ORANGE SEISMIC: 5X TO 12X BASIC
STATED PRINT RUN 199 SER.#'d SETS
130 LeBron James 125.00 300.00
234 Stephon Castle 200.00 500.00

2024-25 Panini Prizm Prizms Orange Wave

*ORANGE WAVE: 8X TO 20X BASIC
STATED PRINT RUN 60 SER.#'d SETS
130 LeBron James 200.00 500.00
234 Stephon Castle 400.00 800.00

2024-25 Panini Prizm Prizms Pink

*PINK: 4X TO 10X BASIC
STATED PRINT RUN 249 SER. #'D SETS
130 LeBron James 100.00 250.00
234 Stephon Castle 150.00 400.00

2024-25 Panini Prizm Prizms Pink Ice

*PINK ICE: 1X TO 2.5X BASIC
234 Stephon Castle 20.00 50.00

2024-25 Panini Prizm Prizms Pink Pulsar

*PINK PULSAR: 10X TO 25X BASIC
STATED PRINT RUN 42 SER.#'d SETS
130 LeBron James 300.00 600.00
234 Stephon Castle 500.00 1,000.00

2024-25 Panini Prizm Prizms Premium Factory Set

*PREMIUM FACTORY SET: 6X TO 15X BASIC
STATED PRINT RUN 150 SER.#'d SETS
130 LeBron James 150.00 400.00
234 Stephon Castle 300.00 600.00

2024-25 Panini Prizm Prizms Pulsar

*PULSAR 1.25X TO 3X BASIC
234 Stephon Castle 25.00 60.00

2024-25 Panini Prizm Prizms Purple

*PURPLE: 8X TO 20X BASIC
STATED PRINT RUN 99 SER.#'d SETS
130 LeBron James 200.00 500.00
234 Stephon Castle 400.00 800.00

2024-25 Panini Prizm Prizms Purple Ice

*PURPLE ICE: 6X TO 15X BASIC
STATED PRINT RUN 149 SER.#'d SETS
130 LeBron James 150.00 400.00
234 Stephon Castle 300.00 600.00

2024-25 Panini Prizm Prizms Purple Pulsar

*PURPLE PULSAR: 10X TO 25X BASIC
STATED PRINT RUN 35 SER.#'d SETS
130 LeBron James 300.00 600.00
234 Stephon Castle 500.00 1,000.00

2024-25 Panini Prizm Prizms Red

*RED: 3X TO 8X BASIC
STATED PRINT RUN 299 SER. #'D SETS
130 LeBron James 75.00 200.00
234 Stephon Castle 125.00 300.00
252 Matas Buzelis 100.00 250.00

2024-25 Panini Prizm Prizms Red Ice

*RED ICE: 1.25X TO 3X BASIC
234 Stephon Castle 25.00 60.00

2024-25 Panini Prizm Prizms Red Lazer

*RED LAZER: 10X TO 25X BASIC
STATED PRINT RUN 35 SER.#'d SETS
130 LeBron James 300.00 600.00
234 Stephon Castle 500.00 1,000.00

2024-25 Panini Prizm Prizms Red Power

*RED POWER: 8X TO 20X BASIC
STATED PRINT RUN 75 SER.#'d SETS
130 LeBron James 200.00 500.00
234 Stephon Castle 400.00 800.00

2024-25 Panini Prizm Prizms Red Pulsar

*RED PULSAR: 8X TO 20X BASIC
STATED PRINT RUN 75 SER.#'d SETS
130 LeBron James 200.00 500.00
234 Stephon Castle 400.00 800.00

2024-25 Panini Prizm Prizms Red Seismic

*RED SEISMIC: 3X TO 8X BASIC
STATED PRINT RUN 299 SER. #'D SETS
130 LeBron James 75.00 200.00
234 Stephon Castle 125.00 300.00
252 Matas Buzelis 100.00 250.00

2024-25 Panini Prizm Prizms Red White and Blue

*RED WHITE & BLUE: 1.25X TO 3X BASIC
234 Stephon Castle 25.00 60.00

2024-25 Panini Prizm Prizms Ruby Wave

*RUBY WAVE: 1.25X TO 3X BASIC
234 Stephon Castle 25.00 60.00

2024-25 Panini Prizm Prizms Silver

*SILVER: 1.5X TO 4X BASIC
234 Stephon Castle 30.00 80.00

2024-25 Panini Prizm Prizms Skewed

*SKEWED: 4X TO 10X BASIC
STATED PRINT RUN 249 SER. #'D SETS
130 LeBron James 100.00 250.00
234 Stephon Castle 150.00 400.00

2024-25 Panini Prizm Prizms Teal Ice

*TEAL ICE: 4X TO 10X BASIC
STATED PRINT RUN 225 SER. #'D SETS
130 LeBron James 100.00 250.00
234 Stephon Castle 150.00 400.00

2024-25 Panini Prizm Prizms White

*WHITE: 6X TO 15X BASIC
STATED PRINT RUN 175 SER. #'D SETS
130 LeBron James 150.00 400.00
234 Stephon Castle 300.00 600.00

2024-25 Panini Prizm Prizms White Ice

*WHITE ICE: 10X TO 25X BASIC
STATED PRINT RUN 35 SER.#'d SETS
130 LeBron James 300.00 600.00
234 Stephon Castle 500.00 1,000.00

2024-25 Panini Prizm Prizms White Lazer

*WHITE LAZER: 4X TO 10X BASIC
STATED PRINT RUN 275 SER. #'D SETS
130 LeBron James 100.00 250.00
234 Stephon Castle 150.00 400.00

2024-25 Panini Prizm Prizms White Wave

*WHITE WAVE: 10X TO 25X BASIC
STATED PRINT RUN 38 SER.#'d SETS
129 Nikola Jokic 50.00 125.00
130 LeBron James 300.00 600.00
234 Stephon Castle 500.00 1,000.00

2024-25 Panini Prizm Deep Space

*GREEN: .6X TO 1.5X BASIC
*SILVER: .6X TO 1.5X BASIC
*BLUE PULSAR/99: 3X TO 8X BASIC
*RED PULSAR/75: 4X TO 10X BASIC
*PINK PULSAR/42: 5X TO 12X BASIC
*PURPLE PULSAR/35: 6X TO 15X BASIC
*GREEN PULSAR/25: 8X TO 20X BASIC
1 Nikola Jokic 2.00 5.00
2 Victor Wembanyama 3.00 8.00
3 Anthony Edwards 2.00 5.00
4 Luka Doncic 2.50 6.00
5 LeBron James 3.00 8.00
6 Reed Sheppard 1.25 3.00
7 Jayson Tatum 1.25 3.00
8 Zaccharie Risacher 1.25 3.00
9 Alexandre Sarr 1.25 3.00
10 Stephen Curry 3.00 8.00

2024-25 Panini Prizm Dominance

*GREEN: .6X TO 1.5X BASIC
*SILVER: .6X TO 1.5X BASIC
*BLUE PULSAR/99: 3X TO 8X BASIC
*RED PULSAR/75: 4X TO 10X BASIC
*PINK PULSAR/42: 5X TO 12X BASIC
*PURPLE PULSAR/35: 6X TO 15X BASIC
*GREEN PULSAR/25: 8X TO 20X BASIC
1 Damian Lillard 1.00 2.50
2 Nikola Jokic 2.00 5.00
3 Kevin Durant 1.25 3.00
4 Giannis Antetokounmpo 1.50 4.00
5 Kyrie Irving 1.00 2.50
6 Jaylen Brown .60 1.50
7 Victor Wembanyama 3.00 8.00
8 James Harden .75 2.00
9 Anthony Edwards 2.00 5.00
10 Joel Embiid .60 1.50
11 Shai Gilgeous-Alexander 2.00 5.00
12 Luka Doncic 2.50 6.00
13 Jayson Tatum 1.25 3.00
14 LeBron James 3.00 8.00
15 Ja Morant 1.25 3.00
16 Tyrese Haliburton .75 2.00
17 Jalen Brunson .75 2.00
18 Kawhi Leonard .75 2.00
19 Paolo Banchero 1.00 2.50
20 Trae Young .75 2.00
21 Stephen Curry 3.00 8.00
22 Zion Williamson 1.00 2.50
23 Donovan Mitchell .75 2.00
24 Tyrese Maxey .75 2.00
25 Anthony Davis 1.00 2.50

2024-25 Panini Prizm Emergent

*GREEN: .6X TO 1.5X BASIC
*SILVER: .6X TO 1.5X BASIC
*BLUE PULSAR/99: 3X TO 8X BASIC
*RED PULSAR/75: 4X TO 10X BASIC
*PINK PULSAR/42: 5X TO 12X BASIC
*PURPLE PULSAR/35: 6X TO 15X BASIC
*GREEN PULSAR/25: 8X TO 20X BASIC
1 Isaiah Collier 1.00 2.50
2 Kel'el Ware 1.25 3.00
3 Kyshawn George .75 2.00
4 Ron Holland II 1.00 2.50
5 Tidjane Salaun .50 1.25
6 Zaccharie Risacher 1.50 4.00
7 Matas Buzelis 2.50 6.00
8 Bronny James Jr. 1.50 4.00
9 Devin Carter .60 1.50
10 Dalton Knecht 1.50 4.00
11 Dillon Jones .50 1.25
12 Cody Williams .60 1.50
13 Donovan Clingan 1.25 3.00
14 Alexandre Sarr 1.50 4.00
15 AJ Johnson 1.00 2.50
16 Zach Edey 1.50 4.00
17 Terrence Shannon Jr. 1.00 2.50
18 Nikola Topic 1.50 4.00
19 Jared McCain 2.00 5.00
20 Bub Carrington 1.25 3.00
21 Yves Missi 1.25 3.00
22 Ryan Dunn .60 1.50
23 Tristan da Silva 1.25 3.00
24 Rob Dillingham 1.25 3.00
25 Jaylon Tyson .60 1.50
26 Reed Sheppard 1.50 4.00
27 Ja'Kobe Walter .60 1.50
28 Pacome Dadiet .60 1.50
29 Stephon Castle 3.00 8.00
30 DaRon Holmes II .60 1.50

2024-25 Panini Prizm Fast Break Autographs

*RED/99: .5X TO 1.2X BASIC
*BLUE/49: .6X TO 1.5X BASIC
1 Cason Wallace 10.00 25.00
2 Cade Cunningham 50.00 120.00
3 Paolo Banchero 40.00 100.00
5 Jaden Hardy 8.00 20.00
6 Jalen Duren 8.00 20.00
7 Chet Holmgren 40.00 100.00
8 Ben Simmons 8.00 20.00
9 Jalen Green 15.00 40.00
10 Keegan Murray 6.00 15.00
11 Bennedict Mathurin 10.00 25.00
12 Jabari Smith Jr. 8.00 20.00
13 Brandon Roy 20.00 50.00
14 Tyrese Maxey 40.00 100.00
15 Quentin Grimes 8.00 20.00
16 Shaedon Sharpe 10.00 25.00
17 Cameron Thomas 8.00 20.00
19 Amen Thompson 20.00 50.00
20 Ausar Thompson 12.00 30.00
21 Jaden Ivey 10.00 25.00
22 Damian Lillard 50.00 120.00
23 Tracy McGrady 50.00 120.00
24 Tony Parker 12.00 30.00
25 Gilbert Arenas 8.00 20.00
26 George Hill 6.00 15.00
27 Jason Terry 8.00 20.00
28 Stephen Jackson 6.00 15.00
29 Mike Bibby 8.00 20.00
30 John Stockton 15.00 40.00
31 Kareem Abdul-Jabbar 60.00 150.00
32 Jayson Tatum 100.00 250.00
33 Chris Paul 40.00 100.00
34 Donovan Mitchell 40.00 100.00
35 Yao Ming 75.00 200.00
36 Rudy Gobert 8.00 20.00
37 Gary Payton 12.00 30.00
38 Jakob Poeltl 6.00 15.00
39 Mark Williams 6.00 15.00
40 Walker Kessler 6.00 15.00
41 Paul George 40.00 100.00
42 Shai Gilgeous-Alexander 300.00 600.00
43 Bradley Beal 10.00 25.00
44 Patrick Ewing 50.00 120.00
45 Hakeem Olajuwon 15.00 40.00
46 Keyonte George 10.00 25.00
47 Nikola Vucevic 6.00 15.00
48 Shaquille O'Neal 50.00 120.00
49 Giannis Antetokounmpo 100.00 250.00
50 LaMarcus Aldridge 8.00 20.00
51 CJ McCollum 6.00 15.00
52 Chris Bosh 10.00 25.00
53 Lauri Markkanen 8.00 20.00
54 Clyde Drexler 12.00 30.00
55 Pat Riley 12.00 30.00
56 James Worthy 12.00 30.00
57 Fred VanVleet 8.00 20.00
58 Pau Gasol 12.00 30.00
59 Oscar Robertson 20.00 50.00
60 Karl Malone 15.00 40.00

2024-25 Panini Prizm Fast Break Rookie Autographs

*RED/75-99: .5X TO 1.2X BASIC
*BLUE/49: .6X TO 1.5X BASIC
1 Dalton Knecht 40.00 100.00
2 Donovan Clingan 20.00 50.00
3 Tidjane Salaun 8.00 20.00
4 Reed Sheppard 50.00 120.00
5 Matas Buzelis 60.00 150.00
6 Zach Edey 25.00 60.00
7 Devin Carter 10.00 25.00
8 Bub Carrington 20.00 50.00
9 Jared McCain 30.00 80.00
10 Baylor Scheierman 10.00 25.00
11 Terrence Shannon Jr. 15.00 40.00
12 Dillon Jones 8.00 20.00
13 Pacome Dadiet 10.00 25.00
14 Kyshawn George 12.00 30.00
15 AJ Johnson 15.00 40.00
16 DaRon Holmes II 10.00 25.00
17 Yves Missi 20.00 50.00
18 Jaylon Tyson 8.00 20.00
19 Ja'Kobe Walter 8.00 20.00
20 Tristan da Silva 20.00 50.00
21 Jonathan Mogbo 12.00 30.00
22 Tyler Kolek 12.00 30.00
23 Johnny Furphy 12.00 30.00
24 Bobi Klintman 10.00 25.00
25 Ajay Mitchell 12.00 30.00
26 Jaylen Wells 25.00 60.00
27 Adem Bona 10.00 25.00
28 KJ Simpson Jr. 8.00 20.00
29 Nikola Durisic 10.00 25.00
30 Pelle Larsson 10.00 25.00
31 Jamal Shead 10.00 25.00
32 Cam Christie 10.00 25.00
33 Antonio Reeves 8.00 20.00
34 Harrison Ingram 8.00 20.00
35 Tristen Newton 8.00 20.00
37 Quinten Post 12.00 30.00
38 Cam Spencer 8.00 20.00
39 Anton Watson 6.00 15.00
40 Oso Ighodaro 10.00 25.00

2024-25 Panini Prizm Fireworks

*FAST BREAK: .6X TO 1.5X BASIC
*SILVER: .6X TO 1.5X BASIC
*BLUE WAVE/175: 2.5X TO 6X BASIC
*BLUE ICE/125: 3X TO 8X BASIC
*ORANGE/49: 5X TO 12X BASIC
*MOJO/25: 8X TO 20X BASIC
*WHITE WAVE/25: 8X TO 20X BASIC
1 Luka Doncic 3.00 8.00
2 Victor Wembanyama 4.00 10.00
3 Trae Young 1.00 2.50
4 Giannis Antetokounmpo 2.00 5.00
5 Paolo Banchero 1.25 3.00
6 Zaccharie Risacher 1.50 4.00
7 Tidjane Salaun .50 1.25
8 Damian Lillard 1.25 3.00
9 Donovan Clingan 1.25 3.00
10 James Harden 1.00 2.50
11 Nikola Jokic 2.50 6.00
12 Jayson Tatum 1.50 4.00
13 Stephon Castle 3.00 8.00
14 Bronny James Jr. 2.00 5.00

15 Reed Sheppard 1.50 4.00
16 Jimmy Butler .75 2.00
17 Tyrese Maxey 1.00 2.50
18 Cody Williams .60 1.50
19 LeBron James 4.00 10.00
20 Stephen Curry 4.00 10.00
21 Alexandre Sarr 1.50 4.00
22 Shai Gilgeous-Alexander 2.50 6.00
23 De'Aaron Fox 1.00 2.50
24 Ja Morant 1.50 4.00
25 Anthony Edwards 2.50 6.00

2024-25 Panini Prizm Fractal

*FAST BREAK: .6X TO 1.5X BASIC
*SILVER: .6X TO 1.5X BASIC
*BLUE WAVE/175: 2.5X TO 6X BASIC
*BLUE ICE/125: 3X TO 8X BASIC
*ORANGE/49: 5X TO 12X BASIC
*MOJO/25: 8X TO 20X BASIC
*WHITE WAVE/25: 8X TO 20X BASIC
1 Shai Gilgeous-Alexander 2.50 6.00
2 Reed Sheppard 1.50 4.00
3 LeBron James 4.00 10.00
4 Luka Doncic 3.00 8.00
5 Anthony Edwards 2.50 6.00
6 Alexandre Sarr 1.50 4.00
7 Stephen Curry 4.00 10.00
8 Zaccharie Risacher 1.50 4.00
9 Jayson Tatum 1.50 4.00
10 Victor Wembanyama 4.00 10.00

2024-25 Panini Prizm Global Reach

*GREEN: .6X TO 1.5X BASIC
*SILVER: .6X TO 1.5X BASIC
*BLUE PULSAR/99: 3X TO 8X BASIC
*RED PULSAR/75: 4X TO 10X BASIC
*PINK PULSAR/42: 5X TO 12X BASIC
*PURPLE PULSAR/35: 6X TO 15X BASIC
*GREEN PULSAR/25: 8X TO 20X BASIC
1 Alperen Sengun .60 1.50
2 Nikola Jokic 2.00 5.00
3 Tidjane Salaun .40 1.00
4 Giannis Antetokounmpo 1.50 4.00
5 Kristaps Porzingis .50 1.25
6 Shai Gilgeous-Alexander 2.00 5.00
7 Zaccharie Risacher 1.25 3.00
8 Luka Doncic 2.50 6.00
9 Victor Wembanyama 3.00 8.00
10 Alexandre Sarr 1.25 3.00

2024-25 Panini Prizm Groovy

1 Stephon Castle 125.00 300.00
2 Shai Gilgeous-Alexander 50.00 125.00
3 LeBron James 125.00 300.00
4 Kevin Durant 30.00 80.00
5 Damian Lillard 25.00 60.00
6 Zaccharie Risacher 75.00 200.00
7 Jimmy Butler 15.00 40.00
8 Alexandre Sarr 75.00 200.00
9 Jared McCain 60.00 150.00
10 Dalton Knecht 75.00 200.00
11 Zion Williamson 25.00 60.00
12 Trae Young 20.00 50.00
13 Ron Holland II 40.00 100.00
14 Stephen Curry 125.00 300.00
15 Tyrese Maxey 20.00 50.00
16 Joel Embiid 15.00 40.00
17 Tyrese Haliburton 20.00 50.00
18 Kawhi Leonard 20.00 50.00
19 Luka Doncic 60.00 150.00
20 Donovan Clingan 25.00 60.00
21 Nikola Jokic 50.00 125.00
22 Anthony Edwards 50.00 125.00
23 Giannis Antetokounmpo 40.00 100.00
24 Matas Buzelis 75.00 200.00
25 Jalen Brunson 20.00 50.00
26 Reed Sheppard 50.00 120.00
27 Ja Morant 30.00 80.00
28 Victor Wembanyama 125.00 300.00
29 Bronny James Jr. 40.00 100.00
30 Jayson Tatum 30.00 80.00

2024-25 Panini Prizm Instant Impact

*GREEN: .6X TO 1.5X BASIC
*SILVER: .6X TO 1.5X BASIC
*BLUE PULSAR/99: 3X TO 8X BASIC
*RED PULSAR/75: 4X TO 10X BASIC
*PINK PULSAR/42: 5X TO 12X BASIC
*PURPLE PULSAR/35: 6X TO 15X BASIC
*GREEN PULSAR/25: 8X TO 20X BASIC
1 Alexandre Sarr 1.50 4.00
2 Cody Williams .60 1.50
3 Nikola Topic 1.50 4.00
4 Stephon Castle 3.00 8.00
5 Dalton Knecht 1.50 4.00
6 Yves Missi 1.25 3.00
7 Bronny James Jr. 2.00 5.00
8 Rob Dillingham 1.25 3.00
9 Jaylon Tyson .50 1.25
10 Jared McCain 2.00 5.00
11 AJ Johnson 1.00 2.50
12 DaRon Holmes II .60 1.50
13 Ron Holland II 1.00 2.50
14 Matas Buzelis 2.50 6.00
15 Donovan Clingan 1.25 3.00
16 Kel'el Ware 1.25 3.00
17 Bub Carrington 1.25 3.00
18 Ja'Kobe Walter .60 1.50
19 Kyshawn George .75 2.00
20 Tristan da Silva 1.25 3.00
21 Zaccharie Risacher 1.50 4.00
22 Tidjane Salaun .50 1.25
23 Devin Carter .60 1.50
24 Reed Sheppard 1.50 4.00
25 Zach Edey 1.50 4.00

2024-25 Panini Prizm Kaleidoscopic

*FAST BREAK: .6X TO 1.5X BASIC
*SILVER: .6X TO 1.5X BASIC
*BLUE WAVE/175: 2.5X TO 6X BASIC
*BLUE ICE/125: 3X TO 8X BASIC
*ORANGE/49: 5X TO 12X BASIC
*MOJO/25: 8X TO 20X BASIC
*WHITE WAVE/25: 8X TO 20X BASIC
1 Anthony Edwards 2.50 6.00
2 Trae Young 1.00 2.50
3 Brandon Miller .75 2.00
4 Tyrese Haliburton 1.00 2.50
5 Rob Dillingham 1.25 3.00
6 Devin Booker 1.25 3.00
7 Zaccharie Risacher 1.50 4.00
8 Jayson Tatum 1.50 4.00
9 Jalen Brunson 1.00 2.50
10 Jaylen Brown .75 2.00
11 Giannis Antetokounmpo 2.00 5.00
12 Stephen Curry 4.00 10.00
13 Kevin Durant 1.50 4.00
14 Luka Doncic 3.00 8.00
15 Chet Holmgren .75 2.00
16 Dalton Knecht 1.50 4.00
17 Bronny James Jr. 2.00 5.00
18 Donovan Clingan 1.25 3.00
19 Stephon Castle 3.00 8.00
20 Victor Wembanyama 4.00 10.00
21 Zion Williamson 1.25 3.00
22 Ja Morant 1.50 4.00
23 Ron Holland II 1.00 2.50
24 Reed Sheppard 1.50 4.00
25 Shai Gilgeous-Alexander 2.50 6.00
26 Alexandre Sarr 1.50 4.00
27 Matas Buzelis 2.50 6.00
28 Damian Lillard 1.25 3.00
29 LeBron James 4.00 10.00
30 Nikola Jokic 2.50 6.00

2024-25 Panini Prizm Luck of the Lottery

*FAST BREAK: .6X TO 1.5X BASIC
*SILVER: .6X TO 1.5X BASIC
*BLUE WAVE/175: 2.5X TO 6X BASIC
*BLUE ICE/125: 3X TO 8X BASIC
*ORANGE/49: 5X TO 12X BASIC
*MOJO/25: 8X TO 20X BASIC
*WHITE WAVE/25: 8X TO 20X BASIC
1 Reed Sheppard 2.50 6.00
2 Bub Carrington 2.00 5.00
3 Zach Edey 2.50 6.00
4 Ron Holland II 1.50 4.00
5 Nikola Topic 2.50 6.00
6 Alexandre Sarr 2.50 6.00
7 Cody Williams 1.00 2.50
8 Matas Buzelis 4.00 10.00
9 Donovan Clingan 2.50 6.00
10 Zaccharie Risacher 2.50 6.00
11 Devin Carter 1.00 2.50
12 Stephon Castle 5.00 12.00
13 Tidjane Salaun .75 2.00
14 Rob Dillingham 2.00 5.00

2024-25 Panini Prizm Manga

1 Matas Buzelis 1,000.00 2,000.00
2 Isaiah Collier 500.00 1,000.00
3 Bronny James Jr. 1,000.00 2,000.00
4 Stephen Curry 4,000.00 8,000.00
5 Giannis Antetokounmpo 1,500.00 3,000.00
6 Zaccharie Risacher 800.00 1,500.00
7 Anthony Edwards 1,500.00 3,000.00
8 Kevin Durant 800.00 1,500.00
9 Victor Wembanyama 3,000.00 6,000.00
10 Donovan Clingan 800.00 1,500.00
11 Tidjane Salaun 400.00 800.00
12 LeBron James 4,000.00 8,000.00
13 Nikola Topic 800.00 1,500.00
14 Rob Dillingham 800.00 1,500.00
15 Stephon Castle 2,500.00 5,000.00
16 Nikola Jokic 1,500.00 3,000.00
17 Dalton Knecht 800.00 1,500.00
18 Shai Gilgeous-Alexander 2,000.00 4,000.00
19 Luka Doncic 2,000.00 4,000.00
20 Alexandre Sarr 800.00 1,500.00

2024-25 Panini Prizm Penmanship

*SILVER: .5X TO 1.2X BASIC
1 Brandon Boston Jr. 4.00 10.00
2 Kendall Brown 4.00 10.00
3 Charles Bassey 4.00 10.00
4 Johnny Juzang 4.00 10.00
5 Alondes Williams 4.00 10.00
6 Tristan Vukcevic 5.00 12.00
7 Dalano Banton 5.00 12.00
8 Julian Champagnie 4.00 10.00
9 Josh Christopher 3.00 8.00
10 Buddy Boeheim 4.00 10.00
11 Bryce McGowens 4.00 10.00
12 Jordan Miller 4.00 10.00
13 Sandro Mamukelashvili 6.00 15.00
14 Garrett Temple 4.00 10.00
15 Collin Gillespie 4.00 10.00
16 Adam Flagler 5.00 12.00
17 Pete Nance 3.00 8.00
18 Jason Preston 3.00 8.00
19 David Duke Jr. 3.00 8.00
20 Mouhamed Gueye 5.00 12.00
21 Jay Huff 4.00 10.00
22 Wendell Moore Jr. 4.00 10.00
23 Cole Swider 4.00 10.00
24 Eugene Omoruyi 4.00 10.00
25 Jake LaRavia 4.00 10.00
26 Jabari Walker 3.00 8.00
27 Tosan Evbuomwan 3.00 8.00
28 Lindy Waters III 4.00 10.00
29 Trevelin Queen 4.00 10.00
30 Herb Williams 3.00 8.00
31 Jalen Suggs 5.00 12.00
32 Cason Wallace 6.00 15.00
33 Mark Williams 4.00 10.00
35 Jaden Hardy 5.00 12.00
36 Cade Cunningham 40.00 100.00
37 Jabari Smith Jr. 5.00 12.00
38 Jalen Duren 5.00 12.00
39 Paolo Banchero 40.00 100.00
40 Willie Anderson 3.00 8.00
41 Doug Collins 4.00 10.00
42 Daniel Gibson 3.00 8.00
43 Jeff Ruland 4.00 10.00
44 Dana Barros 5.00 12.00
45 LaSalle Thompson 3.00 8.00
46 Rick Mahorn 4.00 10.00
47 Johnny Moore 5.00 12.00
48 James Edwards 4.00 10.00
49 Lucius Allen 4.00 10.00
50 Jay Humphries 4.00 10.00

2024-25 Panini Prizm Prizmania

1 Ja Morant 600.00 1,200.00
2 Bronny James Jr. 500.00 1,000.00
3 Stephen Curry 1,250.00 2,500.00
4 Alexandre Sarr 600.00 1,200.00
5 Kevin Durant 500.00 1,000.00
6 Dalton Knecht 500.00 1,000.00
7 Luka Doncic 600.00 1,200.00
8 Victor Wembanyama 1,500.00 3,000.00
9 Reed Sheppard 600.00 1,200.00
10 Paolo Banchero 500.00 1,000.00
11 Nikola Jokic 500.00 1,000.00
12 Anthony Edwards 800.00 1,500.00
13 Stephon Castle 1,000.00 2,000.00
14 Donovan Clingan 500.00 1,000.00
15 LeBron James 1,250.00 2,500.00
16 Jayson Tatum 500.00 1,000.00
17 Matas Buzelis 500.00 1,000.00
18 Giannis Antetokounmpo 500.00 1,000.00
19 Shai Gilgeous-Alexander 600.00 1,200.00
20 Zaccharie Risacher 500.00 1,000.00

2024-25 Panini Prizm Prizmatrix Signatures

*SILVER: .5X TO 1.2X BASIC
*BLUE/49: .6X TO 1.5X BASIC
*BLUE SHIMMER/25: .75X TO 2X BASIC
*MOJO/25: .75X TO 2X BASIC
1 Shai Gilgeous-Alexander 300.00 600.00
2 Stephen Curry 400.00 800.00
3 Anthony Edwards 125.00 300.00
4 Kevin Durant 75.00 200.00
5 Luka Doncic 300.00 600.00
6 Ja Morant 100.00 250.00
7 Dwyane Wade 50.00 120.00
8 Carmelo Anthony 40.00 100.00
9 Larry Bird 100.00 250.00
10 David Robinson 40.00 100.00

2024-25 Panini Prizm Rookie Penmanship

*SILVER: .5X TO 1.2X BASIC
1 Jaylen Wells 20.00 50.00
2 Kyshawn George 10.00 25.00
3 Judah Mintz 5.00 12.00
4 Oso Ighodaro 8.00 20.00
5 Baylor Scheierman 8.00 20.00
6 Tidjane Salaun 6.00 15.00
7 Keshad Johnson 5.00 12.00
8 Yves Missi 15.00 40.00
10 Cam Spencer 6.00 15.00
12 Kevin McCullar Jr. 6.00 15.00
14 Anton Watson 5.00 12.00
15 Ajay Mitchell 10.00 25.00
16 Johnny Furphy 10.00 25.00
20 Ja'Kobe Walter 8.00 20.00
21 Ariel Hukporti 5.00 12.00
22 Matas Buzelis 50.00 120.00
23 Reed Sheppard 40.00 100.00
24 Quinten Post 10.00 25.00
25 Zach Edey 20.00 50.00
26 Jared McCain 25.00 60.00
29 PJ Hall 5.00 12.00
30 Pacome Dadiet 8.00 20.00
31 Dalton Knecht 30.00 80.00
33 Devin Carter 8.00 20.00
35 Ulrich Chomche 5.00 12.00
36 Bobi Klintman 8.00 20.00
37 Cam Christie 8.00 20.00
38 Adem Bona 8.00 20.00
39 Dillon Jones 6.00 15.00
40 Tristan da Silva 15.00 40.00
41 Bub Carrington 15.00 40.00
42 Armando Bacot 5.00 12.00
43 AJ Johnson 12.00 30.00
44 Harrison Ingram 6.00 15.00
45 Terrence Shannon Jr. 12.00 30.00
46 Trey Alexander 5.00 12.00
47 Tristen Newton 6.00 15.00
48 Nikola Durisic 8.00 20.00
49 Donovan Clingan 15.00 40.00
50 Tyler Kolek 10.00 25.00

2024-25 Panini Prizm Rookie Signatures

*BLUE WAVE: .5X TO 1.2X BASIC
*CHOICE: .5X TO 1.2X BASIC
*DRAGON YEAR: .5X TO 1.2X BASIC
*SILVER: .5X TO 1.2X BASIC
*RED/99: .5X TO 1.2X BASIC
*BLUE/49: .6X TO 1.5X BASIC
*CHOICE BLUE/49: .6X TO 1.5X BASIC
*BLUE SHMR FOTL/25: .75X TO 2X BASIC
*MOJO/25: .75X TO 2X BASIC
1 Matas Buzelis 60.00 150.00
2 Bobi Klintman 10.00 25.00
3 Bub Carrington 20.00 50.00
4 Kyshawn George 12.00 30.00
5 Tidjane Salaun 8.00 20.00
6 Reed Sheppard 50.00 120.00
7 Pacome Dadiet 10.00 25.00
8 Dillon Jones 8.00 20.00
9 Terrence Shannon Jr. 15.00 40.00
10 Donovan Clingan 20.00 50.00
11 Baylor Scheierman 10.00 25.00
12 Jonathan Mogbo 12.00 30.00
13 Tyler Kolek 12.00 30.00
14 Johnny Furphy 12.00 30.00
15 Devin Carter 10.00 25.00
16 Ajay Mitchell 12.00 30.00
17 Jaylen Wells 25.00 60.00
18 Oso Ighodaro 10.00 25.00
19 Ja'Kobe Walter 10.00 25.00
20 Pelle Larsson 10.00 25.00
21 Jamal Shead 10.00 25.00
22 Zach Edey 25.00 60.00
23 Cam Christie 10.00 25.00
24 Antonio Reeves 8.00 20.00
25 Kevin McCullar Jr. 8.00 20.00
26 Jared McCain 30.00 80.00
27 Ulrich Chomche 6.00 15.00
28 DaRon Holmes II 10.00 25.00
29 Ariel Hukporti 6.00 15.00
30 Trey Alexander 6.00 15.00
31 Dalton Knecht 40.00 100.00
32 Trentyn Flowers 6.00 15.00
33 Judah Mintz 6.00 15.00
34 Tristan da Silva 20.00 50.00
35 Armando Bacot 6.00 15.00
36 PJ Hall 6.00 15.00
37 Jalen Bridges 6.00 15.00
38 Adem Bona 8.00 20.00
39 KJ Simpson Jr. 6.00 15.00
40 Nikola Durisic 10.00 25.00
41 Jaylon Tyson 8.00 20.00
42 Yves Missi 20.00 50.00
43 Tristen Newton 8.00 20.00
45 Quinten Post 12.00 30.00
46 Cam Spencer 8.00 20.00
47 Harrison Ingram 8.00 20.00
48 Anton Watson 6.00 15.00
49 Keshad Johnson 6.00 15.00
50 AJ Johnson 15.00 40.00

2024-25 Panini Prizm Sensational Signatures

*BLUE WAVE: .5X TO 1.2X BASIC
*CHOICE: .5X TO 1.2X BASIC
*DRAGON YEAR: .5X TO 1.2X BASIC
*SILVER: .5X TO 1.2X BASIC
*RED/99: .5X TO 1.2X BASIC
*BLUE/49: .6X TO 1.5X BASIC
*CHOICE BLUE/49: .6X TO 1.5X BASIC
*BLUE SHMR FOTL/25: .75X TO 2X BASIC
*MOJO/25: .75X TO 2X BASIC
1 Paolo Banchero 40.00 100.00
2 Jalen Suggs 6.00 15.00
3 Jalen Duren 6.00 15.00
4 Chet Holmgren 40.00 100.00
5 Jamal Shead 8.00 20.00
6 Anfernee Simons 6.00 15.00
7 Bennedict Mathurin 8.00 20.00
8 Jaylen Wells 20.00 50.00
9 Kevin McCullar Jr. 6.00 15.00
10 Donovan Clingan 15.00 40.00
11 Jabari Smith Jr. 6.00 15.00
12 Oso Ighodaro 8.00 20.00
13 Ulrich Chomche 6.00 15.00
14 Jaylon Tyson 6.00 15.00
15 Armando Bacot 5.00 12.00
16 Yves Missi 15.00 40.00
17 Jalen Johnson 8.00 20.00
18 AJ Johnson 12.00 30.00
19 Josh Hart 5.00 12.00
20 Kyshawn George 10.00 25.00
21 DeMarcus Cousins 5.00 12.00
22 Ausar Thompson 10.00 25.00
23 De'Aaron Fox 12.00 30.00
24 Khris Middleton 6.00 15.00
25 Dejounte Murray 6.00 15.00
26 Trentyn Flowers 5.00 12.00
27 Andrew Wiggins 8.00 20.00
28 Zach Edey 20.00 50.00
29 Deandre Ayton 5.00 12.00
30 Julius Randle 6.00 15.00
31 Pelle Larsson 5.00 12.00
32 Judah Mintz 5.00 12.00
33 Dalton Knecht 40.00 100.00
34 Tristan da Silva 15.00 40.00
35 Josh Giddey 8.00 20.00
36 Bub Carrington 15.00 40.00
37 Jared McCain 25.00 60.00
38 Devin Carter 8.00 20.00
39 Pacome Dadiet 8.00 20.00
40 Cam Christie 8.00 20.00
41 Baylor Scheierman 8.00 20.00
42 Tyler Kolek 10.00 25.00
43 Johnny Furphy 10.00 25.00
44 Tidjane Salaun 6.00 15.00
45 Ariel Hukporti 5.00 12.00
46 GG Jackson II 6.00 15.00
47 Trayce Jackson-Davis 6.00 15.00
48 Dillon Jones 6.00 15.00
49 Ajay Mitchell 10.00 25.00
50 Alperen Sengun 10.00 25.00
51 Adem Bona 8.00 20.00
52 Anton Watson 5.00 12.00
53 KJ Simpson Jr. 6.00 15.00
54 Klay Thompson 40.00 100.00
55 Kevin Garnett 40.00 100.00
56 Julius Erving 60.00 150.00
57 Matas Buzelis 60.00 150.00
58 Brandon Ingram 6.00 15.00
59 Rasheed Wallace 8.00 20.00
60 Reed Sheppard 40.00 100.00
61 Andrew Nembhard 5.00 12.00
62 Trey Alexander 5.00 12.00
63 Domantas Sabonis 10.00 25.00
64 Antonio Reeves 6.00 15.00
65 Harrison Ingram 6.00 15.00
66 Bobi Klintman 8.00 20.00
67 Tristen Newton 6.00 15.00
68 Ja'Kobe Walter 8.00 20.00
69 Peja Stojakovic 6.00 15.00
71 Quinten Post 10.00 25.00
72 Cam Spencer 6.00 15.00
73 DaRon Holmes II 8.00 20.00
74 Keshad Johnson 5.00 12.00
75 Jonathan Mogbo 10.00 25.00
76 Terrence Shannon Jr. 12.00 30.00
77 Jalen Bridges 5.00 12.00
78 Jeremy Lin 40.00 100.00
79 Yuta Tabuse 8.00 20.00
80 PJ Hall 5.00 12.00
81 Joe Dumars 8.00 20.00
82 Tayshaun Prince 8.00 20.00
83 Metta World Peace 6.00 15.00
84 Chris Mullin 8.00 20.00
85 Isiah Thomas 10.00 25.00
86 Nikola Durisic 8.00 20.00
87 Jason Kidd 10.00 25.00
88 Manu Ginobili 20.00 50.00
89 Grant Hill 10.00 25.00
90 Alonzo Mourning 10.00 25.00

2024-25 Panini Prizm Signatures

*BLUE WAVE: .5X TO 1.2X BASIC
*CHOICE: .5X TO 1.2X BASIC
*DRAGON YEAR: .5X TO 1.2X BASIC
*SILVER: .5X TO 1.2X BASIC
*RED/99: .5X TO 1.2X BASIC
*BLUE/49: .6X TO 1.5X BASIC
*CHOICE BLUE/49: .6X TO 1.5X BASIC
*BLUE SHMR FOTL/25: .75X TO 2X BASIC
*MOJO/25: .75X TO 2X BASIC
1 Cason Wallace 8.00 20.00
2 Cade Cunningham 40.00 100.00
3 Jaden Hardy 6.00 15.00
4 Ben Simmons 6.00 15.00
5 Kristaps Porzingis 8.00 20.00
6 Johnny Davis 5.00 12.00
7 Shaedon Sharpe 8.00 20.00
8 Nikola Jovic 6.00 15.00
9 Jose Alvarado 5.00 12.00
10 Bones Hyland 5.00 12.00
11 Jonathan Kuminga 8.00 20.00
12 Franz Wagner 10.00 25.00
13 Yuta Tabuse 8.00 20.00
14 Steven Adams 5.00 12.00
15 Marvin Bagley III 4.00 10.00
16 Jonathan Isaac 5.00 12.00
17 Bruce Brown 5.00 12.00
18 Myles Turner 5.00 12.00
19 Grant Williams 4.00 10.00
20 David Roddy 5.00 12.00
21 Amen Thompson 30.00 80.00
22 Anthony Davis 40.00 100.00
23 Evan Mobley 10.00 25.00
24 Jaden Ivey 8.00 20.00
25 Trae Young 12.00 30.00
26 Russell Westbrook 60.00 150.00
27 Keegan Murray 5.00 12.00
28 Steve Kerr 8.00 20.00
29 Aaron Gordon 6.00 15.00
30 Ben Wallace 8.00 20.00
31 Ivica Zubac 6.00 15.00
32 Larry Johnson 8.00 20.00
33 Jermaine O'Neal 5.00 12.00
34 Carlos Boozer 5.00 12.00
35 Tim Hardaway 8.00 20.00
36 T.J. McConnell 5.00 12.00
37 Magic Johnson 40.00 100.00
38 Ray Allen 20.00 50.00
39 Rick Fox 5.00 12.00
40 Sun Yue 15.00 40.00
41 Shawn Kemp 10.00 25.00
42 Zach Randolph 5.00 12.00
43 Christian Laettner 6.00 15.00
44 Doc Rivers 6.00 15.00
45 Jamal Crawford 6.00 15.00
46 Rick Barry 8.00 20.00
47 Anfernee Hardaway 20.00 50.00
48 Paul Pierce 10.00 25.00
49 John Stockton 20.00 50.00
50 Cole Anthony 6.00 15.00

2024-25 Panini Prizm Sublime

1 Dalton Knecht 40.00 100.00
2 Shai Gilgeous-Alexander 60.00 150.00
3 Devin Booker 30.00 80.00
4 Nikola Jokic 60.00 150.00
5 Jaylen Brown 20.00 50.00
6 Dereck Lively II 12.00 30.00
7 Tidjane Salaun 12.00 30.00
8 Luka Doncic 80.00 200.00
9 Giannis Antetokounmpo 50.00 125.00
10 Stephen Curry 100.00 250.00
11 Alexandre Sarr 40.00 100.00
12 Chet Holmgren 20.00 50.00
13 Donovan Mitchell 25.00 60.00
14 Reed Sheppard 40.00 100.00
15 Paolo Banchero 30.00 80.00
16 Bronny James Jr. 50.00 125.00
17 Zaccharie Risacher 40.00 100.00
18 James Harden 25.00 60.00
19 Kyrie Irving 30.00 80.00
20 De'Aaron Fox 25.00 60.00
21 Anthony Edwards 60.00 150.00
22 LeBron James 100.00 250.00
23 Anthony Davis 30.00 80.00
24 Rob Dillingham 30.00 80.00
25 Victor Wembanyama 100.00 250.00
26 Cody Williams 15.00 40.00
27 Stephon Castle 80.00 200.00
28 Ja Morant 40.00 100.00
29 Jayson Tatum 40.00 100.00
30 Donovan Clingan 30.00 80.00

2024-25 Panini Prizm Talismen

*FAST BREAK: .6X TO 1.5X BASIC
*SILVER: .6X TO 1.5X BASIC
*BLUE WAVE/175: 2.5X TO 6X BASIC
*BLUE ICE/125: 3X TO 8X BASIC
*ORANGE/49: 5X TO 12X BASIC
*MOJO/25: 8X TO 20X BASIC
*WHITE WAVE/25: 8X TO 20X BASIC
1 Kyrie Irving 1.00 2.50
2 Reed Sheppard 1.25 3.00
3 Donovan Mitchell .75 2.00
4 Ja Morant 1.25 3.00
5 LeBron James 3.00 8.00
6 Anthony Davis 1.00 2.50
7 Nikola Jokic 2.00 5.00
8 Zaccharie Risacher 1.25 3.00
9 Jayson Tatum 1.25 3.00
10 Victor Wembanyama 3.00 8.00
11 Kevin Durant 1.25 3.00
12 Giannis Antetokounmpo 1.50 4.00
13 Luka Doncic 2.50 6.00
14 Stephon Castle 2.50 6.00
15 Dalton Knecht 1.25 3.00
16 Anthony Edwards 2.00 5.00
17 Alexandre Sarr 1.25 3.00
18 Kawhi Leonard .75 2.00
19 Shai Gilgeous-Alexander 2.00 5.00
20 Stephen Curry 3.00 8.00
21 Zach Edey 1.25 3.00

2023-24 Panini Prizm Deca

1 Fred VanVleet .60 1.50
2 Luka Doncic 2.50 6.00
3 Tim Hardaway Jr. .30 .75
4 Alex Caruso .40 1.00
5 Josh Green .30 .75
6 Toumani Camara RC 1.50 4.00
7 Jermaine O'Neal .40 1.00
8 Bojan Bogdanovic .40 1.00
9 De'Anthony Melton .40 1.00
10 Zach LaVine .60 1.50
11 Buddy Hield .40 1.00
12 Ben Simmons .40 1.00
13 Chris Bosh .50 1.25
14 Zion Williamson 1.00 2.50
15 Maxwell Lewis RC .60 1.50
16 Dyson Daniels .50 1.25
17 Moritz Wagner .40 1.00
18 Desmond Bane .50 1.25
19 Isaiah Stewart .40 1.00
20 Dorian Finney-Smith .30 .75
21 Steven Adams .40 1.00
22 Corey Kispert .30 .75
23 Harrison Barnes .30 .75
24 Malik Monk .50 1.25
25 Cameron Thomas .50 1.25
26 Anfernee Simons .50 1.25
27 Evan Fournier .30 .75
28 Gary Payton .60 1.50
29 Ochai Agbaji .40 1.00
30 Darius Garland .60 1.50
31 Miles Bridges .40 1.00
32 Vince Carter .75 2.00
33 Malcolm Brogdon .40 1.00
34 Austin Reaves 1.00 2.50
35 Nikola Jokic 2.00 5.00
36 Wendell Carter Jr. .40 1.00
37 Kevin Durant 1.25 3.00
38 Clyde Drexler .60 1.50
39 Jonathan Kuminga 1.00 2.50
40 Obi Toppin .40 1.00
41 Bobby Portis .50 1.25
42 Aaron Gordon .40 1.00
43 Vince Williams Jr. .40 1.00
44 MarJon Beauchamp .30 .75
45 Dennis Schroder .40 1.00
46 Allen Iverson 1.00 2.50
47 Kevin Love .40 1.00
48 Mike Conley .30 .75
49 Chris Paul .75 2.00
50 Jaren Jackson Jr. .60 1.50
51 Donte DiVincenzo .40 1.00
52 Anthony Davis 1.00 2.50
53 Steve Nash .75 2.00
54 P.J. Washington Jr. .40 1.00
55 Walker Kessler .40 1.00
56 Spencer Dinwiddie .30 .75
57 Deni Avdija .40 1.00
58 Tre Jones .40 1.00
59 Kyle Lowry .50 1.25
60 Jabari Smith Jr. .60 1.50
61 Naz Reid .40 1.00
62 Jusuf Nurkic .40 1.00
63 Anthony Edwards 2.00 5.00
64 Paul Pierce .60 1.50
65 Draymond Green .50 1.25
66 Nick Smith Jr. RC 1.00 2.50
67 Magic Johnson 1.50 4.00
68 Jalen Green .60 1.50
69 Patrick Williams .30 .75
70 Kelly Olynyk .25 .60
71 Saddiq Bey .40 1.00
72 Dillon Brooks .40 1.00
73 Rayan Rupert RC .75 2.00
74 Tim Duncan 1.00 2.50
75 Mikal Bridges .50 1.25
76 Bam Adebayo .60 1.50
77 Keldon Johnson .50 1.25
78 Quentin Grimes .40 1.00
79 Peyton Watson .40 1.00
80 Chris Livingston RC .75 2.00
81 Immanuel Quickley .40 1.00
82 Marcus Smart .50 1.25
83 Bruce Brown .40 1.00
84 Isiah Thomas .60 1.50
85 Luguentz Dort .40 1.00
86 Paul George .60 1.50
87 Tyrese Maxey .75 2.00
88 Michael Porter Jr. .50 1.25
89 Devin Vassell .50 1.25
90 Jeremy Lin .60 1.50
91 Patrick Ewing .60 1.50
92 Andrew Nembhard .40 1.00
93 De'Aaron Fox .75 2.00
94 Rasheed Wallace .50 1.25
95 Andre Drummond .30 .75
96 Dereck Lively II RC 1.50 4.00
97 Jaden Hardy .50 1.25
98 LaMelo Ball 1.00 2.50
99 Onyeka Okongwu .30 .75
100 Ben Sheppard RC .75 2.00
101 Ray Allen .60 1.50
102 Noah Clowney RC 1.00 2.50
103 Brandon Ingram .50 1.25
104 Kevin Huerter .30 .75
105 Caris LeVert .40 1.00
106 Anthony Black RC 1.50 4.00
107 Jalen Brunson .75 2.00
108 David Robinson .75 2.00
109 Trae Young .75 2.00
110 Shai Gilgeous-Alexander 2.00 5.00
111 Tim Hardaway .50 1.25
112 Yao Ming 1.00 2.50
113 Tre Mann .40 1.00
114 John Stockton .75 2.00
115 Keyontae Johnson RC .75 2.00
116 Victor Wembanyama RC 20.00 50.00
117 Jerami Grant .50 1.25
118 DeMar DeRozan .60 1.50
119 Jaden McDaniels .40 1.00
120 Giannis Antetokounmpo 2.00 5.00
121 John Collins .40 1.00
122 Alperen Sengun .60 1.50
123 Rudy Gobert .50 1.25
124 RJ Barrett .60 1.50
125 Craig Porter Jr. .50 1.25
126 Jamal Murray .75 2.00
127 De'Andre Hunter .40 1.00
128 Dominique Wilkins .60 1.50
129 Jaime Jaquez Jr. RC 1.25 3.00
130 Malik Beasley .40 1.00
131 Brice Sensabaugh RC 1.25 3.00
132 Hakeem Olajuwon .75 2.00
133 Jalen Johnson .50 1.25
134 Marcus Sasser RC 1.25 3.00
135 Jordan Clarkson .40 1.00
136 Ausar Thompson RC 2.00 5.00
137 Kevon Looney .40 1.00
138 Kareem Abdul-Jabbar 1.25 3.00
139 Caleb Martin .30 .75
140 Ja Morant 1.25 3.00
141 Jordan Poole .60 1.50
142 Andrew Wiggins .50 1.25
143 Precious Achiuwa .30 .75
144 Stephen Curry 3.00 8.00
145 LeBron James 3.00 8.00
146 Cason Wallace RC 1.50 4.00
147 Damian Lillard 1.00 2.50
148 Chet Holmgren 1.00 2.50
149 Reggie Jackson .25 .60
150 Charles Barkley .75 2.00
151 Wilt Chamberlain 1.25 3.00
152 Jalen Duren .50 1.25
153 Jakob Poeltl .30 .75
154 Bradley Beal .50 1.25
155 Jason Kidd .60 1.50
156 Derrick White .50 1.25
157 Kobe Bufkin RC 1.00 2.50
158 Larry Bird 1.50 4.00
159 Gilbert Arenas .40 1.00
160 Gradey Dick RC 1.50 4.00
161 Colby Jones RC .75 2.00
162 Kristaps Porzingis .50 1.25
163 Evan Mobley .60 1.50
164 Tony Parker .60 1.50
165 Olivier-Maxence Prosper RC .75 2.00
166 Tyus Jones .30 .75
167 Karl Malone .75 2.00
168 D'Angelo Russell .40 1.00
169 Dariq Whitehead RC 1.00 2.50
170 Jrue Holiday .50 1.25
171 Kris Murray RC .75 2.00
172 Nicolas Batum .25 .60
173 Jett Howard RC 1.00 2.50
174 Scottie Barnes .50 1.25
175 Vasilije Micic RC .75 2.00
176 Cole Anthony .40 1.00
177 Bilal Coulibaly RC 2.00 5.00
178 Jason Williams .60 1.50
179 Keyonte George RC 2.50 6.00
180 Dwyane Wade .75 2.00
181 Brandon Roy .50 1.25
182 Bob Pettit .50 1.25
183 Ivica Zubac .40 1.00
184 Jeremy Sochan .50 1.25
185 Andre Jackson Jr. RC 1.25 3.00
186 Russell Westbrook .60 1.50
187 Pete Maravich 1.00 2.50
188 Julius Randle .50 1.25
189 Jayson Tatum 1.50 4.00
190 Ayo Dosunmu .40 1.00
191 Tobias Harris .40 1.00
192 Yuta Tabuse .40 1.00
193 Collin Sexton .50 1.25
194 Karl-Anthony Towns .60 1.50
195 Dejounte Murray .50 1.25
196 Kelly Oubre Jr. .40 1.00
197 Brandin Podziemski RC 2.50 6.00
198 Jordan Hawkins RC 1.25 3.00
199 Norman Powell .40 1.00
200 Josh Hart .40 1.00
201 Jarace Walker RC 1.50 4.00
202 Markelle Fultz .30 .75
203 Jalen Hood-Schifino RC .75 2.00
204 Seth Lundy RC .50 1.25
205 Brandon Miller RC 3.00 8.00
206 Manu Ginobili .75 2.00
207 Bennedict Mathurin .60 1.50
208 Marvin Bagley III .30 .75
209 Tyler Herro .60 1.50
210 Bogdan Bogdanovic .40 1.00
211 Terry Rozier III .50 1.25
212 Coby White .40 1.00
213 Scoot Henderson 1.25 3.00
214 Kevin Garnett 1.00 2.50
215 Lauri Markkanen .60 1.50
216 Bol Bol .40 1.00
217 Brook Lopez .30 .75
218 Alonzo Mourning .60 1.50
219 Julius Erving 1.00 2.50
220 Max Strus .40 1.00
221 Patrick Beverley .30 .75
222 Jalen Wilson RC .75 2.00
223 Jose Alvarado .40 1.00
224 Keegan Murray .50 1.25
225 Jalen Pickett RC .60 1.50
226 OG Anunoby .50 1.25
227 Khris Middleton .40 1.00
228 Franz Wagner .60 1.50
229 Cam Reddish .30 .75
230 Grant Williams .30 .75
231 Pascal Siakam .60 1.50
232 Anfernee Simons .60 1.50
233 Pau Gasol .60 1.50
234 Kyle Kuzma .50 1.25
235 Malaki Branham .30 .75
236 Duncan Robinson .40 1.00
237 Cameron Johnson .40 1.00
238 Joel Embiid 1.00 2.50
239 Trayce Jackson-Davis RC 1.00 2.50
240 Sasha Vezenkov .30 .75
241 Gary Harris .30 .75
242 Nikola Vucevic .40 1.00
243 Tracy McGrady .60 1.50
244 James Harden .75 2.00
245 Domantas Sabonis .60 1.50
246 Gordon Hayward .40 1.00
247 Tyrese Haliburton .75 2.00
248 Dirk Nowitzki 1.00 2.50
249 Shawn Kemp .60 1.50
250 Klay Thompson 1.00 2.50
251 Jimmy Butler .60 1.50
252 Herbert Jones .40 1.00
253 Kyrie Irving .75 2.00
254 GG Jackson II RC 1.50 4.00
255 Zach Collins .30 .75
256 Donovan Mitchell .75 2.00
257 Jaden Ivey .50 1.25
258 Eric Gordon .30 .75
259 Nicolas Claxton .40 1.00
260 Grayson Allen .40 1.00
261 CJ McCollum .40 1.00
262 Mark Williams .40 1.00
263 Clint Capela .30 .75
264 Paolo Banchero 1.00 2.50
265 Dennis Rodman 1.00 2.50
266 Emoni Bates RC 1.00 2.50
267 Jonas Valanciunas .30 .75
268 Rui Hachimura .40 1.00
269 Jarrett Allen .40 1.00
270 Myles Turner .30 .75
271 Trey Murphy III .50 1.25
272 Gary Trent Jr. .40 1.00
273 Duop Reath .40 1.00
274 Jalen Suggs .50 1.25
275 Derrick Rose .60 1.50
276 Hunter Tyson RC .75 2.00
277 Julian Phillips RC .75 2.00

278 Kawhi Leonard 1.00 2.50
279 Devin Booker 1.00 2.50
280 Daniel Gafford .40 1.00
281 Shaquille O'Neal 1.25 3.00
282 Jaylen Brown .75 2.00
283 Al Horford .40 1.00
284 Jerry West .75 2.00
285 Zach Randolph .40 1.00
286 Shaedon Sharpe .75 2.00
287 Carmelo Anthony .60 1.50
288 Taurean Prince .25 .60
289 Tari Eason .50 1.25
290 Cam Whitmore RC 2.00 5.00
291 Cade Cunningham 1.00 2.50
292 Kobe Brown RC .75 2.00
293 Jalen Williams .75 2.00
294 Amen Thompson RC 4.00 10.00
295 Grant Hill .60 1.50
296 Amari Bailey RC .75 2.00
297 Deandre Ayton .40 1.00
298 Julian Strawther RC 1.00 2.50
299 Josh Giddey .50 1.25
300 Taylor Hendricks RC .75 2.00

2023-24 Panini Prizm Deca Prizms Blue

*BLUE: 3X TO 8X BASIC
STATED PRINT RUN 149 SER.#'d SETS
116 Victor Wembanyama 600.00 1,200.00
144 Stephen Curry 60.00 150.00
145 LeBron James 60.00 150.00
205 Brandon Miller 100.00 250.00

2023-24 Panini Prizm Deca Prizms Mojo

*MOJO: 10X TO 25X BASIC
STATED PRINT RUN 25 SER.#'d SETS
116 Victor Wembanyama 2,500.00 5,000.00
144 Stephen Curry 300.00 600.00
145 LeBron James 300.00 600.00
205 Brandon Miller 500.00 1,000.00

2023-24 Panini Prizm Deca Prizms Orange

*ORANGE: 5X TO 12X BASIC
STATED PRINT RUN 49 SER.#'d SETS
116 Victor Wembanyama 1,250.00 2,500.00
144 Stephen Curry 125.00 300.00
145 LeBron James 125.00 300.00
205 Brandon Miller 200.00 500.00

2023-24 Panini Prizm Deca Prizms Purple

*PURPLE: 4X TO 10X BASIC
STATED PRINT RUN 99 SER.#'d SETS
116 Victor Wembanyama 800.00 1,500.00
144 Stephen Curry 75.00 200.00
145 LeBron James 75.00 200.00
205 Brandon Miller 125.00 300.00

2023-24 Panini Prizm Deca Prizms Red

*RED: 2.5X TO 6X BASIC
STATED PRINT RUN 199 SER.#'d SETS
116 Victor Wembanyama 500.00 1,000.00
144 Stephen Curry 50.00 120.00
145 LeBron James 50.00 120.00
205 Brandon Miller 75.00 200.00

2023-24 Panini Prizm Deca Prizms Silver

*SILVER: 2X TO 5X BASIC
116 Victor Wembanyama 400.00 800.00
144 Stephen Curry 40.00 100.00
145 LeBron James 40.00 100.00
205 Brandon Miller 60.00 150.00

2023-24 Panini Prizm Deca Brilliance

*SILVER: 1.25X TO 3X BASIC
1 Brandon Miller 2.50 6.00
2 Kevin Durant 2.00 5.00
3 Zion Williamson 1.50 4.00
4 Luka Doncic 4.00 10.00
5 Amen Thompson 3.00 8.00
6 Jayson Tatum 2.50 6.00
7 Anthony Edwards 3.00 8.00
8 Stephen Curry 5.00 12.00
9 Scoot Henderson 2.00 5.00
10 Chet Holmgren 1.50 4.00
11 Yao Ming 1.50 4.00
12 Shai Gilgeous-Alexander 3.00 8.00
13 LeBron James 5.00 12.00
14 Paolo Banchero 1.50 4.00
15 Ausar Thompson 1.50 4.00
16 Tyrese Haliburton 1.25 3.00
17 Victor Wembanyama 10.00 25.00
18 Nikola Jokic 3.00 8.00
19 Julius Erving 1.50 4.00
20 Giannis Antetokounmpo 3.00 8.00

2023-24 Panini Prizm Deca Brilliance Prizms Mojo

*MOJO: 8X TO 20X BASIC
STATED PRINT RUN 25 SER.#'d SETS
17 Victor Wembanyama 400.00 800.00

2023-24 Panini Prizm Deca Decade Dominance

*SILVER: 1.25X TO 3X BASIC
*MOJO/25: 8X TO 20X BASIC
1 Dirk Nowitzki 1.50 4.00
2 Damian Lillard 1.50 4.00
3 Vince Carter 1.25 3.00
4 Anthony Davis 1.50 4.00
5 Karl Malone 1.25 3.00
6 Kevin Durant 2.00 5.00
7 LeBron James 5.00 12.00
8 Julius Erving 1.50 4.00
9 Allen Iverson 1.50 4.00
10 Giannis Antetokounmpo 3.00 8.00
11 Chris Paul 1.25 3.00
12 Klay Thompson 1.50 4.00
13 Stephen Curry 5.00 12.00
14 Charles Barkley 1.50 4.00
15 Paul George 1.00 2.50
16 Larry Bird 2.50 6.00
17 Magic Johnson 2.50 6.00
18 David Robinson 1.25 3.00
19 Shaquille O'Neal 2.00 5.00
20 James Harden 1.25 3.00
21 Russell Westbrook 1.00 2.50
22 Tony Parker 1.00 2.50
23 Ben Wallace .75 2.00
24 Tim Duncan 1.50 4.00
25 Hakeem Olajuwon 1.25 3.00

2023-24 Panini Prizm Deca Downtown Bound

*SILVER: 1.25X TO 3X BASIC
1 Stephen Curry 5.00 12.00
2 James Harden 1.25 3.00
3 Ja Morant 2.00 5.00
4 Klay Thompson 1.50 4.00
5 Kevin Durant 2.00 5.00
6 Steve Nash 1.25 3.00
7 Larry Bird 2.50 6.00
8 Victor Wembanyama 10.00 25.00
9 Devin Booker 1.50 4.00
10 Trae Young 1.25 3.00
11 Donovan Mitchell 1.25 3.00
12 Tyrese Haliburton 1.25 3.00
13 Luka Doncic 4.00 10.00
14 Brandon Miller 2.50 6.00
15 Jayson Tatum 2.50 6.00
16 Shai Gilgeous-Alexander 3.00 8.00
17 LeBron James 5.00 12.00
18 Ray Allen 1.00 2.50
19 Kyrie Irving 1.25 3.00
20 Dirk Nowitzki 1.50 4.00
21 Damian Lillard 1.50 4.00
22 Anthony Edwards 3.00 8.00
23 Jalen Brunson 1.25 3.00
24 Carmelo Anthony 1.00 2.50
25 Scoot Henderson 2.00 5.00

2023-24 Panini Prizm Deca Downtown Bound Prizms Mojo

*MOJO: 8X TO 20X BASIC
STATED PRINT RUN 25 SER.#'d SETS
8 Victor Wembanyama 400.00 800.00

2023-24 Panini Prizm Deca Finalists

*SILVER: 1.25X TO 3X BASIC
*MOJO/25: 8X TO 20X BASIC
1 Dwyane Wade 1.25 3.00
2 Nikola Jokic 3.00 8.00
3 Anthony Davis 1.50 4.00
4 Kyrie Irving 1.25 3.00
5 Kawhi Leonard 1.50 4.00
6 Giannis Antetokounmpo 3.00 8.00
7 Larry Bird 2.50 6.00
8 Dirk Nowitzki 1.50 4.00
9 Pau Gasol 1.00 2.50
10 Klay Thompson 1.50 4.00
11 Stephen Curry 5.00 12.00
12 Kareem Abdul-Jabbar 2.00 5.00
13 LeBron James 5.00 12.00
14 Kevin Durant 2.00 5.00
15 Tim Duncan 1.50 4.00

2023-24 Panini Prizm Deca Most Valuable Players

*SILVER: 1.25X TO 3X BASIC
*MOJO/25: 8X TO 20X BASIC
1 Julius Erving 1.50 4.00
2 Shaquille O'Neal 2.00 5.00
3 Nikola Jokic 3.00 8.00
4 Stephen Curry 5.00 12.00
5 Steve Nash 1.25 3.00
6 Kevin Garnett 1.50 4.00
7 Magic Johnson 2.50 6.00
8 LeBron James 5.00 12.00
9 Russell Westbrook 1.00 2.50
10 Derrick Rose 1.00 2.50
11 Tim Duncan 1.50 4.00
12 Kevin Durant 2.00 5.00
13 Joel Embiid 1.50 4.00
14 James Harden 1.25 3.00
15 Giannis Antetokounmpo 3.00 8.00

2023-24 Panini Prizm Deca Signatures

*SILVER: .5X TO 1.2X BASIC
*BLUE/49: .6X TO 1.5X BASIC
*GRN SHMR/15-25: .75X TO 2X BASIC
*MOJO/15-25: .75X TO 2X BASIC
1 Luka Doncic 400.00 800.00
2 Stephen Curry 500.00 1,000.00
3 Trae Young 40.00 100.00
4 Russell Westbrook 40.00 100.00
5 Chet Holmgren 40.00 100.00
6 Cade Cunningham 60.00 150.00
7 Paolo Banchero 75.00 200.00
8 Anthony Davis 40.00 100.00
9 Klay Thompson 40.00 100.00
10 Chris Paul 25.00 60.00
11 Ja Morant 75.00 200.00
12 Anthony Edwards 150.00 400.00
13 Zach LaVine 10.00 25.00
14 Brandon Ingram 8.00 20.00
15 Jalen Green 40.00 100.00
16 RJ Barrett 10.00 25.00
17 Kristaps Porzingis 20.00 50.00
18 Jeremy Sochan 8.00 20.00
19 Keegan Murray 8.00 20.00
20 Shaedon Sharpe 12.00 30.00
21 Josh Giddey 8.00 20.00
22 Alperen Sengun 20.00 50.00
23 Shaquille O'Neal 75.00 200.00
24 Dyson Daniels 8.00 20.00
25 Tari Eason 8.00 20.00
26 Mark Williams 6.00 15.00
27 Austin Reaves 15.00 40.00
28 Jose Alvarado 6.00 15.00
29 Jalen McDaniels 5.00 12.00
30 David Roddy 5.00 12.00
31 Wendell Moore Jr. 5.00 12.00
32 Malaki Branham 5.00 12.00
33 MarJon Beauchamp 5.00 12.00
34 Vince Williams Jr. 6.00 15.00
35 Jabari Walker 4.00 10.00
36 Amen Thompson 40.00 100.00
37 Ausar Thompson 15.00 40.00
38 Cason Wallace 12.00 30.00
39 Dereck Lively II 12.00 30.00
40 Kobe Bufkin 8.00 20.00
41 Brandin Podziemski 20.00 50.00
42 GG Jackson II 12.00 30.00
43 Trayce Jackson-Davis 8.00 20.00
44 Brice Sensabaugh 10.00 25.00
45 Dariq Whitehead 8.00 20.00
46 Amari Bailey 6.00 15.00
47 Chris Livingston 6.00 15.00
48 Olivier-Maxence Prosper 6.00 15.00
49 Ricky Council IV 8.00 20.00
50 Hunter Tyson 6.00 15.00
51 Jalen Pickett 5.00 12.00
52 Keyonte George 20.00 50.00
53 Kobe Brown 6.00 15.00
54 Oscar Tshiebwe 8.00 20.00
55 Julian Strawther 8.00 20.00
56 Leonard Miller 6.00 15.00
57 Duop Reath 6.00 15.00
58 Kris Murray 6.00 15.00
59 Ben Sheppard 6.00 15.00
60 Toumani Camara 12.00 30.00
61 Bilal Coulibaly 15.00 40.00
63 Colby Jones 6.00 15.00
64 Andre Jackson Jr. 10.00 25.00
65 Noah Clowney 8.00 20.00
66 Julian Phillips 6.00 15.00
67 Maxwell Lewis 5.00 12.00
68 Jordan Walsh 6.00 15.00
69 Vasilije Micic 6.00 15.00
70 Jalen Wilson 6.00 15.00
71 Marcus Sasser 10.00 25.00
72 Jordan Miller 8.00 20.00
74 Sasha Vezenkov 5.00 12.00
75 Keyontae Johnson 6.00 15.00
76 Charles Barkley 75.00 200.00
77 Dirk Nowitzki 75.00 200.00
78 Allen Iverson 75.00 200.00
79 Dwyane Wade 60.00 150.00
80 Karl Malone 25.00 60.00
81 Carmelo Anthony 60.00 150.00
82 Kevin Garnett 60.00 150.00
83 Kareem Abdul-Jabbar 75.00 200.00
84 Steve Nash 40.00 100.00
85 Ray Allen 30.00 80.00
86 Pau Gasol 25.00 60.00
87 Manu Ginobili 25.00 60.00
88 Paul Pierce 30.00 80.00
89 Jason Kidd 30.00 80.00
90 Tony Parker 20.00 50.00
91 Rasheed Wallace 12.00 30.00
92 Anfernee Hardaway 40.00 100.00
93 Dennis Rodman 40.00 100.00
94 Dominique Wilkins 10.00 25.00
95 John Wall 8.00 20.00
96 Jeremy Lin 60.00 150.00
97 Amar'e Stoudemire 8.00 20.00
98 Jamal Crawford 6.00 15.00
99 Peja Stojakovic 6.00 15.00
100 Jerry Stackhouse 6.00 15.00

2019-20 Panini Prizm Draft Picks

*PRIZMS GREEN: .75X TO 2X BASIC
*PRIZMS SILVER: 1X TO 2.5X BASIC
*PRIZMS GRN YLLW/249: 1.25X TO 3X BASIC
*PRIZMS RED: 1.25X TO 3X BASIC
*PRIZMS RWB/99: 2X TO 5X BASIC
1 Zion Williamson 2.00 5.00
2 Ja Morant 2.50 6.00
3 RJ Barrett 1.00 2.50
4 De'Andre Hunter 1.00 2.50
5 Rui Hachimura CR 1.00 2.50
6 Darius Garland 1.00 2.50
7 Jarrett Culver .25 .60
8 Coby White .75 2.00
9 Jaxson Hayes .40 1.00
10 Rui Hachimura 1.00 2.50
11 Ja Morant CR 2.50 6.00
12 Cam Reddish .40 1.00
13 Cameron Johnson .60 1.50
14 PJ Washington Jr. .75 2.00
15 Tyler Herro 1.25 3.00
16 Romeo Langford .25 .60
17 Chuma Okeke .40 1.00
18 Nickeil Alexander-Walker .40 1.00
19 Matisse Thybulle .50 1.25
20 Brandon Clarke .50 1.25
21 Grant Williams .40 1.00
22 Grant Williams AA .40 1.00
23 Darius Garland CR 1.00 2.50
24 Ty Jerome .50 1.25
25 Nassir Little .40 1.00
26 Dylan Windler .30 .75
27 Mfiondu Kabengele .30 .75
28 Jordan Poole 1.00 2.50
29 Keldon Johnson .75 2.00
30 Kevin Porter Jr. .50 1.25
31 Nicolas Claxton .50 1.25
32 Cameron Johnson CR .60 1.50
33 KZ Okpala .30 .75
34 Carsen Edwards .30 .75
35 Bruno Fernando .30 .75
36 Cody Martin .40 1.00
37 Chuma Okeke CR .40 1.00
38 Daniel Gafford .50 1.25
39 Justin James .25 .60
40 Eric Paschall .30 .75
41 Admiral Schofield .30 .75
42 Jaylen Nowell .30 .75
43 Cam Reddish CR .40 1.00
44 Ja Morant AA 2.50 6.00
45 Bol Bol .60 1.50
46 Isaiah Roby .30 .75
47 Talen Horton-Tucker .40 1.00
48 Ignas Brazdeikis .30 .75
49 Terance Mann .50 1.25
50 Quinndary Weatherspoon .25 .60
51 Zion Williamson CR 2.00 5.00
52 Jarrell Brantley .25 .60
53 Tremont Waters .30 .75
54 Jalen McDaniels .60 1.50
55 Justin Wright-Foreman .25 .60
56 Marial Shayok .25 .60
57 Kyle Guy .30 .75
58 Jaylen Hands .25 .60
59 Jordan Bone .25 .60
60 Miye Oni .25 .60
61 Coby White CR .75 2.00
62 RJ Barrett AA 1.00 2.50
63 Dewan Hernandez .25 .60
64 Zion Williamson 2.00 5.00
65 Ja Morant 2.50 6.00
66 RJ Barrett 1.00 2.50
67 De'Andre Hunter 1.00 2.50
68 Darius Garland 1.00 2.50
69 Jarrett Culver .25 .60
70 Coby White .75 2.00
71 Jaxson Hayes .40 1.00
72 RJ Barrett CR 1.00 2.50
73 Rui Hachimura 1.00 2.50
74 Cam Reddish .40 1.00
75 Tyler Herro CR 1.25 3.00
76 Cameron Johnson .60 1.50
77 PJ Washington Jr. .75 2.00
78 De'Andre Hunter CR 1.00 2.50
79 Tyler Herro 1.25 3.00
80 Romeo Langford .25 .60
81 Chuma Okeke .40 1.00
82 Nickeil Alexander-Walker .40 1.00
83 Jarrett Culver CR .25 .60
84 Rui Hachimura AA 1.00 2.50
85 Matisse Thybulle .50 1.25
86 Brandon Clarke .50 1.25
87 Grant Williams .40 1.00
88 Ty Jerome .50 1.25
89 Jaxson Hayes CR .40 1.00
90 Nassir Little .40 1.00
91 Mfiondu Kabengele .30 .75
92 Jordan Poole 1.00 2.50
93 Keldon Johnson .75 2.00
94 Kevin Porter Jr. .50 1.25
95 PJ Washington Jr. CR .75 2.00
96 Nicolas Claxton .50 1.25
97 KZ Okpala .30 .75
98 Carsen Edwards .30 .75
99 Romeo Langford CR .25 .60
100 Zion Williamson AA 2.00 5.00

2019-20 Panini Prizm Draft Picks Prizms Camo

*PRIZMS CAMO: 8X TO 20X BASIC
STATED PRINT RUN 25 SER.#'d SETS

2019-20 Panini Prizm Draft Picks Prizms Mojo

*PRIZMS MOJO: 4X TO 10X BASIC
STATED PRINT RUN 49 SER.#'d SETS

2019-20 Panini Prizm Draft Picks Autographs Prizms

EXCHANGE DEADLINE 4/16/2021
*PRIZM BLUE: .5X TO 1.2X
*PRIZM RED: .5X TO 1.2X
*PRIZM GREEN: .6X TO 1.5X
*PRZM PRPLE GRN/125-199: .5X TO 1.2X
*PRZM NEON ORNG/125-149: .5X TO 1.2X
*PRIZM NEON GRN/125: .5X TO 1.2X
*PRIZM NEON ORNG/100: .6X TO 1.5X
*PRIZM NEON GRN/25: .75X TO 2X
*PRIZM RWB/99: .6X TO 1.5X
*PRIZM HYPER/75: .6X TO 1.5X
*PRIZM MOJO/49: .6X TO 1.5X
*PRIZM CAR.BLUE/30: .75X TO 2X
*PRIZM CAMO/25: .75X TO 2X
*PRIZM ORNG PLSR/20: .75X TO 2X
1 Zion Williamson 125.00 300.00
2 Ja Morant 125.00 300.00
4 De'Andre Hunter 10.00 25.00
5 Jared Harper 3.00 8.00
6 Jarrett Culver 2.50 6.00
7 Coby White 8.00 20.00
8 Jaxson Hayes 4.00 10.00
9 Rui Hachimura 10.00 25.00
10 Cam Reddish 4.00 10.00
11 Cameron Johnson 6.00 15.00
12 PJ Washington Jr. 8.00 20.00
13 Tyler Herro 12.00 30.00
14 Romeo Langford 2.50 6.00
15 Sekou Doumbouya 2.50 6.00
16 Chuma Okeke 4.00 10.00
17 Nickeil Alexander-Walker 4.00 10.00
18 Goga Bitadze 4.00 10.00
19 Luka Samanic 3.00 8.00
20 Matisse Thybulle 5.00 12.00
21 Brandon Clarke 5.00 12.00
22 Grant Williams 4.00 10.00
23 Darius Bazley 2.50 6.00
24 Ty Jerome 5.00 12.00
25 Nassir Little 5.00 12.00
26 Dylan Windler 3.00 8.00
27 Mfiondu Kabengele 3.00 8.00
28 Jordan Poole 10.00 25.00
29 Keldon Johnson 8.00 20.00
30 Kevin Porter Jr. 8.00 20.00
31 Nicolas Claxton 5.00 12.00
32 KZ Okpala 3.00 8.00
33 Carsen Edwards 3.00 8.00
34 Bruno Fernando 3.00 8.00
35 Kyle Alexander 2.50 6.00
36 Cody Martin 4.00 10.00
37 Deividas Sirvydis 2.50 6.00
38 Daniel Gafford 5.00 12.00
39 Alen Smailagic 2.50 6.00
40 Justin James 2.50 6.00
41 Eric Paschall 3.00 8.00
42 Admiral Schofield 3.00 8.00
43 Jaylen Nowell 3.00 8.00
44 Bol Bol 6.00 15.00
45 Isaiah Roby 3.00 8.00
46 Talen Horton-Tucker 4.00 10.00
47 Ignas Brazdeikis 3.00 8.00
48 Terance Mann 5.00 12.00
49 Quinndary Weatherspoon 2.50 6.00
50 Jarrell Brantley 2.50 6.00
51 Tremont Waters 3.00 8.00
52 Jalen McDaniels 6.00 15.00
53 Justin Wright-Foreman 2.50 6.00
54 Marial Shayok 2.50 6.00
55 Kyle Guy 3.00 8.00
56 Jaylen Hands 2.50 6.00
57 Jordan Bone 2.50 6.00
58 Miye Oni 2.50 6.00
59 Dewan Hernandez 2.50 6.00
60 Josh Perkins 2.50 6.00
61 Zion Williamson 125.00 300.00
62 Ja Morant 125.00 300.00
63 RJ Barrett 10.00 25.00
64 De'Andre Hunter 10.00 25.00
65 Jarrett Culver 2.50 6.00
66 Coby White 8.00 20.00
67 Jaxson Hayes 4.00 10.00
68 Rui Hachimura 10.00 25.00
69 Cam Reddish 4.00 10.00
70 Cameron Johnson 6.00 15.00
71 PJ Washington Jr. 8.00 20.00
72 Tyler Herro 12.00 30.00
73 Romeo Langford 2.50 6.00
74 Jontay Porter 2.50 6.00
75 Luguentz Dort 10.00 25.00
76 Zach Norvell Jr. 3.00 8.00
77 Dedric Lawson 2.50 6.00
78 Shamorie Ponds 2.50 6.00
80 Jaylen Hoard 2.50 6.00
81 James Palmer 2.50 6.00
82 Simi Shittu 2.50 6.00
83 Kris Wilkes 2.50 6.00
84 Robert Franks 2.50 6.00
85 Sagaba Konate 2.50 6.00
86 Max Strus 5.00 12.00
87 Ky Bowman 3.00 8.00
88 Tyler Cook 2.50 6.00
89 Kaleb Johnson 2.50 6.00
90 Bennie Boatwright 2.50 6.00
91 Aric Holman 2.50 6.00
92 Luke Maye 3.00 8.00
93 Justin Robinson 2.50 6.00
94 DaQuan Jeffries 2.50 6.00
95 Moses Brown 4.00 10.00
96 Oshae Brissett 3.00 8.00
97 Tyus Battle 2.50 6.00
98 Ethan Happ 2.50 6.00
99 Tacko Fall 3.00 8.00
100 Jalen Lecque 2.50 6.00
101 Terence Davis 4.00 10.00
102 Louis King 3.00 8.00
103 Charles Matthews 4.00 10.00
104 Zylan Cheatham 2.50 6.00
105 Kerwin Roach 2.50 6.00
106 Fletcher Magee 2.50 6.00
107 Phil Booth 2.50 6.00
108 Garrison Mathews 4.00 10.00
109 Corey Davis Jr. 2.50 6.00
110 Nick Ward 2.50 6.00
111 Juwan Morgan 2.50 6.00
112 Marques Bolden 2.50 6.00
113 Dean Wade 3.00 8.00
114 Josh Reaves 2.50 6.00
115 Lindell Wigginton 2.50 6.00
116 Matt McQuaid 2.50 6.00
117 Chris Clemons 2.50 6.00
118 William McDowell-White 2.50 6.00
119 Brian Bowen II 2.50 6.00
120 Amir Coffey 4.00 10.00
121 Devontae Cacok 2.50 6.00
122 John Konchar 4.00 10.00
123 Jeremiah Martin 3.00 8.00
124 Dererk Pardon 2.50 6.00
125 Lamar Peters 2.50 6.00
126 Aubrey Dawkins 2.50 6.00
127 Vic Law 2.50 6.00

2019-20 Panini Prizm Draft Picks College Ties Autographs Prizms

EXCHANGE DEADLINE 4/16/2021
*ORNGE PLSR/20: .6X TO 1.5X
1 R.Barrett/Zion 150.00 400.00
2 D.Hunter/T.Jerome 25.00 60.00
3 C.Johnson/C.White 20.00 50.00
4 B.Clarke/R.Hachimura 25.00 60.00
5 P.Washington Jr./T.Herro 30.00 80.00
6 A.Schofield/G.Williams 10.00 25.00
7 J.Nowell/M.Thybulle 12.00 30.00
8 M.Kabengele/T.Mann 12.00 30.00
9 I.Brazdeikis/J.Poole 25.00 60.00

2019-20 Panini Prizm Draft Picks Prizms Color Blast

1 Zion Williamson 300.00 600.00
2 Ja Morant 300.00 600.00
3 RJ Barrett 100.00 250.00
4 De'Andre Hunter 60.00 150.00
5 Darius Garland 75.00 200.00
6 Jarrett Culver 30.00 80.00
7 Coby White 40.00 100.00
8 Jaxson Hayes 40.00 100.00
9 Rui Hachimura 75.00 200.00
10 Cam Reddish 60.00 150.00
11 Cameron Johnson 60.00 150.00
12 PJ Washington Jr. 40.00 100.00
13 Tyler Herro 125.00 300.00
14 Romeo Langford 15.00 40.00
15 Nassir Little 30.00 80.00
16 Chuma Okeke 40.00 100.00
17 Nickeil Alexander-Walker 40.00 100.00
18 Grant Williams 40.00 100.00
19 Brandon Clarke 60.00 150.00
20 Matisse Thybulle 60.00 150.00

2020-21 Panini Prizm Draft Picks

*GREEN: .6X TO 1.5X BASIC
*PINK ICE: .75X TO 2X BASIC
*RWB: .75X TO 2X BASIC
*PURPLE WAVE: 1X TO 2.5X BASIC
*RED ICE: 1X TO 2.5X BASIC
*RUBY WAVE: 1X TO 2.5X BASIC
*FAST BREAK: 1.2X TO 3X BASIC
*HYPER: 1.2X TO 3X BASIC
*SILVER: 1.2X TO 3X BASIC
*BYG: 1.5X TO 4X BASIC
*RED/299: 1.5X TO 4X BASIC
*BLUE/199: 2X TO 5X BASIC
*FB BLUE/175: 2X TO 5X BASIC
*PURPLE ICE/149: 2X TO 5X BASIC
*FB RED/125: 2.5X TO 6X BASIC
*BLUE ICE/99: 2.5X TO 6X BASIC
*CHOICE RED/88: 2.5X TO 6X BASIC
*PURPLE/75: 2.5X TO 6X BASIC
*FB PURPLE/49: 4X TO 10X BASIC
*ORANGE PULSAR/49: 4X TO 10X BASIC
*GREEN PULSAR/25: 8X TO 20X BASIC
*MOJO/25: 8X TO 20X BASIC
*FB PINK/25: 8X TO 20X BASIC
1 Anthony Edwards 4.00 10.00
2 James Wiseman .50 1.25
3 LaMelo Ball 3.00 8.00
4 Isaac Okoro .60 1.50
5 Onyeka Okongwu .75 2.00
6 Deni Avdija 1.00 2.50
7 Obi Toppin .75 2.00
8 Precious Achiuwa .75 2.00
9 Cole Anthony .75 2.00
10 Tyrese Haliburton 3.00 8.00
11 Jaden McDaniels 1.25 3.00
12 Killian Hayes .40 1.00
13 RJ Hampton .40 1.00
14 Tyrese Maxey 3.00 8.00
15 Aaron Nesmith .75 2.00
16 Devin Vassell 1.25 3.00
17 Theo Maledon .40 1.00
18 Nico Mannion .40 1.00
19 Saddiq Bey .75 2.00
20 Patrick Williams 1.00 2.50
21 Josh Green .75 2.00
22 Xavier Tillman .50 1.25
23 Robert Woodard II .40 1.00
24 Kira Lewis Jr. .40 1.00
25 Jahmi'us Ramsey .40 1.00
26 Isaiah Stewart .75 2.00
27 Vernon Carey Jr. .40 1.00
28 Cassius Stanley .40 1.00
29 Cassius Winston .40 1.00
30 Jalen Smith .75 2.00
31 Udoka Azubuike .50 1.25
32 Devon Dotson .40 1.00
33 Daniel Oturu .40 1.00
34 Zeke Nnaji .50 1.25
35 Tyler Bey .40 1.00
36 Payton Pritchard 1.25 3.00
37 Tre Jones .60 1.50
38 Jordan Nwora .50 1.25
39 Ashton Hagans .50 1.25
40 Markus Howard .50 1.25
41 Anthony Edwards 4.00 10.00
42 James Wiseman .50 1.25
43 LaMelo Ball 3.00 8.00
44 Isaac Okoro .60 1.50
45 Onyeka Okongwu .75 2.00
46 Deni Avdija 1.00 2.50
47 Obi Toppin .75 2.00
48 Precious Achiuwa .75 2.00
49 Cole Anthony 1.00 2.50
50 Tyrese Haliburton 3.00 8.00
51 Jaden McDaniels 1.25 3.00
52 Killian Hayes .40 1.00
53 RJ Hampton .40 1.00
54 Tyrese Maxey 3.00 8.00
55 Aaron Nesmith .75 2.00
56 Devin Vassell 1.25 3.00
57 Theo Maledon .40 1.00
58 Nico Mannion .40 1.00
59 Saddiq Bey .75 2.00
60 Patrick Williams 1.00 2.50
61 Josh Green .75 2.00
62 Xavier Tillman .50 1.25
63 Robert Woodard II .40 1.00
64 Kira Lewis Jr. .40 1.00
65 Jahmi'us Ramsey .40 1.00
66 Isaiah Stewart .75 2.00
67 Vernon Carey Jr. .40 1.00
68 Cassius Stanley .40 1.00
69 Cassius Winston .40 1.00
70 Jalen Smith .75 2.00
71 Udoka Azubuike .50 1.25
72 Devon Dotson .40 1.00
73 Daniel Oturu .40 1.00
74 Zeke Nnaji .50 1.25
75 Tyler Bey .40 1.00
76 Payton Pritchard 1.25 3.00
77 Tre Jones .60 1.50
78 Jordan Nwora .50 1.25
79 Ashton Hagans .50 1.25
80 Markus Howard .50 1.25
81 Anthony Edwards CR 4.00 10.00
82 James Wiseman CR .50 1.25
83 LaMelo Ball CR 3.00 8.00
84 Isaac Okoro CR .60 1.50
85 Onyeka Okongwu CR .75 2.00
86 Deni Avdija CR 1.00 2.50
87 Obi Toppin CR .75 2.00
88 Precious Achiuwa CR .75 2.00
89 Cole Anthony CR 1.00 2.50
90 Tyrese Haliburton CR 3.00 8.00
91 Jaden McDaniels CR 1.25 3.00
92 Killian Hayes CR .40 1.00
93 RJ Hampton CR .40 1.00
94 Tyrese Maxey CR 3.00 8.00
95 Aaron Nesmith CR .75 2.00
96 Killian Hayes GP .40 1.00
97 James Wiseman GP .50 1.25
98 LaMelo Ball GP 3.00 8.00
99 RJ Hampton GP .40 1.00
100 Deni Avdija GP 1.00 2.50

2020-21 Panini Prizm Draft Picks Color Blast

1 Anthony Edwards 600.00 1,200.00
2 James Wiseman 40.00 100.00
4 Isaac Okoro 100.00 250.00
5 Onyeka Okongwu 75.00 200.00
6 Deni Avdija 200.00 500.00
7 Obi Toppin 200.00 500.00
8 Precious Achiuwa 100.00 250.00
9 Cole Anthony 200.00 500.00
10 Tyrese Haliburton 300.00 600.00

2020-21 Panini Prizm Draft Picks Downtown

1 James Wiseman 25.00 60.00
2 LaMelo Ball 150.00 400.00
3 Cole Anthony 50.00 125.00
4 Anthony Edwards 200.00 500.00
5 Zion Williamson 80.00 200.00
6 Nico Mannion 20.00 50.00
7 Tyrese Maxey 150.00 400.00
8 Ja Morant 80.00 200.00
9 Jaden McDaniels 60.00 150.00
10 Theo Maledon 20.00 50.00
11 Onyeka Okongwu 40.00 100.00
12 RJ Hampton 20.00 50.00
13 Tyrese Haliburton 150.00 400.00
14 Precious Achiuwa 40.00 100.00
15 Isaac Okoro 30.00 80.00
16 Killian Hayes 20.00 50.00
17 Rui Hachimura 30.00 80.00
18 Obi Toppin 40.00 100.00
19 Josh Green 40.00 100.00
20 Tyler Herro 50.00 125.00

2020-21 Panini Prizm Draft Picks Prospect Autographs

EXCHANGE DEADLINE 5/4/2022
*FAST BREAK: .5X TO 1.25X BASIC
*GREEN: .5X TO 1.25X BASIC
*HYPER: .5X TO 1.25X BASIC
*PINK ICE: .5X TO 1.25X BASIC
*RED ICE: .5X TO 1.25X BASIC
*RED/199: .6X TO 1.5X BASIC
*BLUE/149: .6X TO 1.5X BASIC
*SILVER: .6X TO 1.5X BASIC
*PURPLE ICE/99: .75X TO 2X BASIC
*CHOICE RED/88: .75X TO 2X BASIC
*BLUE ICE/75: .75X TO 2X BASIC
*ORANGE PULSAR/49: 1X TO 2.5X BASIC
*GREEN PULSAR/25: 1.5X TO 4X BASIC
*MOJO/25: 1.5X TO 4X BASIC
*FB PINK/25: 1.5X TO 4X BASIC
1 Anthony Edwards 100.00 250.00
2 James Wiseman 5.00 12.00
3 LaMelo Ball 75.00 200.00
4 Isaac Okoro 6.00 15.00
5 Onyeka Okongwu 8.00 20.00
6 Deni Avdija 10.00 25.00
7 Obi Toppin 8.00 20.00
8 Precious Achiuwa 8.00 20.00
9 Cole Anthony 10.00 25.00
10 Tyrese Haliburton 60.00 150.00
11 Jaden McDaniels 12.00 30.00
12 Killian Hayes 4.00 10.00
13 RJ Hampton 4.00 10.00
14 Tyrese Maxey 60.00 150.00
15 Aaron Nesmith 8.00 20.00
16 Devin Vassell 12.00 30.00
17 Theo Maledon 4.00 10.00
18 Nico Mannion 4.00 10.00
19 Saddiq Bey 8.00 20.00
20 Patrick Williams 10.00 25.00
21 Josh Green 8.00 20.00
22 Josh Hall 3.00 8.00
23 Robert Woodard II 4.00 10.00
24 Kira Lewis Jr. 4.00 10.00
25 Jahmi'us Ramsey 4.00 10.00
26 Isaiah Stewart 8.00 20.00
27 Vernon Carey Jr. 4.00 10.00
28 Aleksej Pokusevski 5.00 12.00
29 Lamine Diane 3.00 8.00
30 Jalen Smith 8.00 20.00
31 Udoka Azubuike 5.00 12.00
32 Devon Dotson 4.00 10.00
33 Daniel Oturu 4.00 10.00
34 Zeke Nnaji 5.00 12.00
35 Tyler Bey 4.00 10.00
36 Payton Pritchard 12.00 30.00
37 Tre Jones 6.00 15.00
38 Jordan Nwora 5.00 12.00
39 Quinton Rose 3.00 8.00
40 Javin DeLaurier 3.00 8.00
41 Brandon Robinson 3.00 8.00
42 Malachi Flynn 4.00 10.00
43 Grant Riller 4.00 10.00
44 Skylar Mays 4.00 10.00
45 Elijah Hughes 4.00 10.00
46 Cassius Stanley 4.00 10.00
47 Reggie Perry 4.00 10.00
48 Xavier Tillman 5.00 12.00
49 Paul Reed 5.00 12.00
50 Kenyon Martin Jr. 6.00 15.00
51 Ashton Hagans 5.00 12.00
52 Killian Tillie 5.00 12.00
53 Paul Eboua 3.00 8.00
54 Rayshaun Hammonds 3.00 8.00
55 Saben Lee 4.00 10.00
56 Immanuel Quickley 10.00 25.00
57 Desmond Bane 12.00 30.00
58 Markus Howard 5.00 12.00
59 Mason Jones 3.00 8.00
60 CJ Elleby 4.00 10.00
61 Alpha Diallo 3.00 8.00
62 Omer Yurtseven 12.00 30.00
63 Ryan Woolridge 3.00 8.00
64 EJ Montgomery 3.00 8.00
65 Mamadi Diakite 4.00 10.00
66 Jake Toolson 3.00 8.00
67 Kerry Blackshear Jr. 3.00 8.00
68 Lamar Stevens 5.00 12.00
69 Mustapha Heron 3.00 8.00
70 Myles Powell 6.00 15.00
71 Yoeli Childs 4.00 10.00
72 Nathan Knight 4.00 10.00
73 John Mooney 3.00 8.00
74 Josh Nebo 3.00 8.00
75 Kristian Doolittle 3.00 8.00
76 Tyrique Jones 3.00 8.00
77 Tres Tinkle 3.00 8.00
78 Naji Marshall 4.00 10.00
79 Jordan Bowden 3.00 8.00
80 Pat Spencer 3.00 8.00
81 Tyrell Terry 3.00 8.00
82 Gytis Masiulis 3.00 8.00
83 Sam Merrill 6.00 15.00
84 Anthony Lamb 4.00 10.00
85 Trent Forrest 5.00 12.00
86 Braxton Key 3.00 8.00
87 Dwayne Sutton 3.00 8.00
88 DJ Vasiljevic 3.00 8.00
89 Caleb Homesley 3.00 8.00
90 Uros Trifunovic 3.00 8.00

2021-22 Panini Prizm Draft Picks

*GREEN: .6X TO 1.5X BASIC
*PURPLE WAVE: .75X TO 2X BASIC
*RED ICE: .75X TO 2X BASIC
*BLUE CIRCLES: .75X TO 2X BASIC
*RUBY WAVE: 1X TO 2.5X BASIC
*RWB: .75X TO 2X BASIC
*HYPER: 1X TO 2.5X BASIC
*SILVER: 1X TO 2.5X BASIC
*RED/299: 1.25X TO 3X BASIC
*BLUE WAVE/249: 1.25X TO 3X BASIC
*BLUE/199: 1.5X TO 4X BASIC
*PURPLE ICE/149: 1.5X TO 4X BASIC
*BLUE ICE/99: 2X TO 5X BASIC
*CHOICE RED/88: 2X TO 5X BASIC
*ORANGE WAVE/75: 2.5X TO 6X BASIC
*PURPLE/75: 2.5X TO 6X BASIC
*PURPLE CIRCLES/50: 3X TO 8X BASIC
*ORANGE PULSAR/49: 3X TO 8X BASIC
*MOJO/25: 5X TO 12X BASIC
1 Cade Cunningham 2.50 6.00
2 Evan Mobley 1.50 4.00
3 Jalen Suggs 1.00 2.50
4 Jalen Green 2.00 5.00
5 Jonathan Kuminga 1.25 3.00

6 Scottie Barnes 1.25 3.00
7 Keon Johnson .40 1.00
8 Corey Kispert .50 1.25
9 Franz Wagner 1.25 3.00
10 Jalen Johnson 1.25 3.00
11 Moses Moody .75 2.00
12 James Bouknight .30 .75
13 Davion Mitchell .40 1.00
14 Kai Jones .30 .75
15 Ziaire Williams .50 1.25
16 Isaiah Jackson .40 1.00
17 Josh Giddey 1.25 3.00
18 Cameron Thomas .75 2.00
19 Jaden Springer .40 1.00
20 Ayo Dosunmu .75 2.00
21 Tre Mann .60 1.50
22 Josh Christopher .30 .75
23 Chris Duarte .30 .75
24 Brandon Boston Jr. .40 1.00
25 Day'Ron Sharpe .40 1.00
26 Sharife Cooper .30 .75
27 Greg Brown III .30 .75
28 JT Thor .40 1.00
29 Joel Ayayi .30 .75
30 Jared Butler .40 1.00
31 Jaren Jackson Jr. .60 1.50
32 Miles McBride .60 1.50
33 Herbert Jones .50 1.25
34 Matt Hurt .40 1.00
35 Coby White .40 1.00
36 Isiah Thomas .60 1.50
37 Tyrese Haliburton .75 2.00
38 David Johnson .30 .75
39 Mac McClung .75 2.00
40 Trey Murphy III 1.25 3.00
41 Usman Garuba .30 .75
42 Alperen Sengun 1.25 3.00
43 Jeremiah Robinson-Earl .40 1.00
44 David Duke Jr. .40 1.00
45 Charles Bassey .40 1.00
46 Quentin Grimes .75 2.00
47 Patrick Williams .40 1.00
48 Aaron Henry .25 .60
49 Austin Reaves 2.00 5.00
50 Joshua Primo .30 .75
51 Luka Garza .40 1.00
52 Kevin Durant 1.25 3.00
53 James Harden .75 2.00
54 Russell Westbrook .60 1.50
55 Kevin Love .40 1.00
56 Stephen Curry 2.50 6.00
57 Kawhi Leonard 1.00 2.50
58 Anthony Davis 1.00 2.50
59 Joel Embiid 1.00 2.50
60 Bradley Beal .50 1.25
61 Jayson Tatum 1.50 4.00
62 Kyrie Irving .75 2.00
63 Zion Williamson 1.00 2.50
64 Ja Morant 1.25 3.00
65 Anthony Edwards 2.00 5.00
66 Jimmy Butler .60 1.50
67 Karl-Anthony Towns .60 1.50
68 Chris Paul .75 2.00
69 Paul George .60 1.50
70 Devin Booker 1.00 2.50
71 Ben Simmons .40 1.00
72 De'Aaron Fox .60 1.50
73 Draymond Green .50 1.25
74 Malcolm Brogdon .30 .75
75 Julius Randle .50 1.25
76 Alex Caruso .40 1.00
77 Jamal Murray .60 1.50
78 Trae Young 1.00 2.50
79 Jaylen Brown .60 1.50
80 Zach LaVine .60 1.50
81 Donovan Mitchell .75 2.00
82 Klay Thompson 1.00 2.50
83 Damian Lillard 1.00 2.50
84 Shaquille O'Neal 1.25 3.00
85 Allen Iverson 1.00 2.50
86 Magic Johnson 1.25 3.00
87 John Stockton .75 2.00
88 Anfernee Hardaway 1.00 2.50
89 Paul Pierce .60 1.50
90 Grant Hill .60 1.50
91 Ray Allen .60 1.50
92 Andre Drummond .30 .75
93 Dominique Wilkins .60 1.50
94 John Collins .40 1.00
95 RJ Barrett .60 1.50
96 JJ Redick .40 1.00
97 Rajon Rondo .50 1.25
98 Michael Porter Jr. .50 1.25
99 Gordon Hayward .30 .75
100 Jerry West .75 2.00

2021-22 Panini Prizm Draft Picks Brilliance

COMMON CARD .25 .60
SEMISTARS .30 .75
UNLISTED STARS .40 1.00
*HYPER: .6X TO 1.5X BASIC
*CIRCLES: .75X TO 2X BASIC
*SILVER: .75X TO 2X BASIC
*ORANGE WAVE/75: 2.5X TO 6X BASIC
*GREEN PULSAR/25: 5X TO 12X BASIC
*MOJO/25: 5X TO 12X BASIC
1 Cade Cunningham 2.50 6.00
2 Evan Mobley 1.50 4.00
3 Jalen Suggs 1.00 2.50
4 Scottie Barnes 1.25 3.00
5 Keon Johnson .40 1.00
6 Chris Duarte .30 .75
7 Brandon Boston Jr. .40 1.00
8 Greg Brown III .30 .75
9 Jalen Green 2.00 5.00
10 Joel Ayayi .30 .75
11 Herbert Jones .50 1.25
12 Matt Hurt .40 1.00
13 Jonathan Kuminga 1.25 3.00
14 Joel Embiid 1.00 2.50
15 Ben Simmons .40 1.00
16 Trae Young 1.00 2.50
17 Tyler Herro .60 1.50
18 Russell Westbrook .60 1.50
19 Bradley Beal .50 1.25
20 Zion Williamson 1.00 2.50

2021-22 Panini Prizm Draft Picks College Penmanship

COMMON CARD 2.50 6.00
SEMISTARS 3.00 8.00
UNLISTED STARS 4.00 10.00
*HYPER: .5X TO 1.25X BASIC
*RED ICE: .5X TO 1.25X BASIC
*SILVER: .6X TO 1.5X BASIC
*RED/199: .6X TO 1.5X BASIC
*RED/49: 1X TO 2.5X BASIC
*BLUE/149: .6X TO 1.5X BASIC
*BLUE/45: 1X TO 2.5X BASIC
*PURPLE ICE/99: .75X TO 2X BASIC
*PURPLE ICE/29: 1.25X TO 3X BASIC
*CHOICE RED/88: .75X TO 2X BASIC
*BLUE ICE/75: .75X TO 2X BASIC
*BLUE ICE/29: 1.25X TO 3X BASIC
*PURPLE CIRCLES/50: 1X TO 2.5X BASIC
*ORANGE PULSAR/49: 1X TO 2.5X BASIC
*GREEN PULSAR/25: 1.25X TO 3X BASIC
*MOJO/25: 1.25X TO 3X BASIC
*PINK CIRCLES/20: 1.25X TO 3X BASIC
2 Aaron Wiggins 5.00 12.00
6 David Johnson 3.00 8.00
9 Dejon Jarreau 2.50 6.00
10 Colbey Ross 2.50 6.00
11 D'Mitrik Trice 2.50 6.00
12 Mitch Ballock 3.00 8.00
13 Moses Wright 3.00 8.00
14 Eugene Omoruyi 3.00 8.00
15 Ryan Daly 2.50 6.00
16 Javion Hamlet 2.50 6.00
17 Jay Huff 3.00 8.00
18 Jeremiah Robinson-Earl 4.00 10.00
19 Hasahn French 3.00 8.00
20 Jamorko Pickett 3.00 8.00
21 Joe Wieskamp 3.00 8.00
22 Jordan Burns 2.50 6.00
23 Justin Champagnie 3.00 8.00
24 Justin Smith 3.00 8.00
25 Kessler Edwards 4.00 10.00
26 Joshua Primo 3.00 8.00
27 Luka Garza 4.00 10.00
28 Manny Camper 3.00 8.00
29 Marek Dolezaj 3.00 8.00
30 Duane Washington Jr. 4.00 10.00
31 Jason Preston 3.00 8.00
32 Neemias Queta 4.00 10.00
33 RaiQuan Gray 3.00 8.00
34 RJ Nembhard 2.50 6.00
35 Santi Aldama 5.00 12.00
36 AJ Lawson 3.00 8.00
37 Trendon Watford 5.00 12.00
38 Trey Murphy III 12.00 30.00
39 Yves Pons 3.00 8.00
40 Cade Cunningham 25.00 60.00
41 Evan Mobley 15.00 40.00
42 Jalen Suggs 10.00 25.00
43 Scottie Barnes 12.00 30.00
44 Keon Johnson 4.00 10.00
45 Corey Kispert 5.00 12.00
46 Franz Wagner 12.00 30.00
47 Jalen Johnson 12.00 30.00
48 Moses Moody 8.00 20.00
49 James Bouknight 3.00 8.00
50 Davion Mitchell 4.00 10.00
51 Kai Jones 3.00 8.00
52 Ziaire Williams 5.00 12.00
53 Isaiah Jackson 4.00 10.00
54 Cameron Thomas 8.00 20.00
55 Jaden Springer 4.00 10.00
56 Ayo Dosunmu 8.00 20.00

2021-22 Panini Prizm Draft Picks Colorblast

COMMON CARD 12.00 30.00
SEMISTARS 15.00 40.00
UNLISTED STARS 20.00 50.00
1 Cade Cunningham 200.00 500.00
2 Evan Mobley 150.00 400.00
3 Jalen Suggs 125.00 300.00
4 Jalen Green 150.00 400.00
5 Jonathan Kuminga 150.00 400.00
6 Scottie Barnes 150.00 400.00
7 Keon Johnson 60.00 150.00
8 Corey Kispert 75.00 200.00
9 Franz Wagner 150.00 400.00
10 Jalen Johnson 100.00 250.00
11 James Harden 100.00 250.00
12 Trae Young 125.00 300.00
13 Kevin Durant 125.00 300.00
14 Devin Booker 125.00 300.00
15 Kyrie Irving 125.00 300.00

2021-22 Panini Prizm Draft Picks Draft Picks Autographs

COMMON CARD 2.50 6.00
SEMISTARS 3.00 8.00
UNLISTED STARS 4.00 10.00
*HYPER: .5X TO 1.25X BASIC
*RED ICE: .5X TO 1.25X BASIC
*RED/199: .6X TO 1.5X BASIC
*BLUE/149: .6X TO 1.5X BASIC
*SILVER: .6X TO 1.5X BASIC
*PURPLE ICE/99: .75X TO 2X BASIC
*BLUE ICE/75: .75X TO 2X BASIC
*ORANGE PULSAR/49: 1X TO 2.5X BASIC
*PURPLE CIRCLES/30: 1.25X TO 3X BASIC
*GREEN PULSAR/25: 1.25X TO 3X BASIC
*MOJO/25: 1.25X TO 3X BASIC
*PINK CIRCLES/20: 1.25X TO 3X BASIC
1 Sandro Mamukelashvili 5.00 12.00
2 DJ Steward 3.00 8.00
3 DJ Stewart Jr. 2.50 6.00
4 Matt Mitchell 2.50 6.00
5 John Petty Jr. 3.00 8.00
6 Sam Hauser 10.00 25.00
7 Marcus Garrett 3.00 8.00
8 Scottie Lewis 3.00 8.00
9 MJ Walker 3.00 8.00
10 Mac McClung 8.00 20.00
11 Mark Vital 2.50 6.00
12 MaCio Teague 2.50 6.00
13 Mike Smith 2.50 6.00
14 Matt Coleman III 2.50 6.00
15 Aamir Simms 2.50 6.00
16 Tahj Eaddy 2.50 6.00
17 Cameron Krutwig 3.00 8.00
18 Joshua Langford 2.50 6.00
19 Loren Cristian Jackson 2.50 6.00
20 Troy Baxter Jr. 2.50 6.00
21 Ethan Thompson 2.50 6.00
22 Jalen Tate 2.50 6.00
23 McKinley Wright IV 2.50 6.00
24 JaQuori McLaughlin 2.50 6.00
25 Justin Turner 2.50 6.00
26 Chandler Vaudrin 2.50 6.00
27 Terrell Gomez 2.50 6.00
28 LJ Figueroa 2.50 6.00
30 Nojel Eastern 2.50 6.00
31 Aleem Ford 2.50 6.00
32 Giorgi Bezhanishvili 2.50 6.00
33 Damien Jefferson 2.50 6.00
34 Jordan Schakel 2.50 6.00
36 Marcus Burk 2.50 6.00
37 Brandon Rachal 2.50 6.00
38 Isaiah Miller 2.50 6.00
39 Juwan Durham 2.50 6.00
40 Jalen Crutcher 2.50 6.00
41 Justin Gorham 2.50 6.00
42 Ariel Hukporti 2.50 6.00
43 D.J. Funderburk 2.50 6.00
44 Vrenz Bleijenbergh 2.50 6.00
45 Derrick Alston Jr. 2.50 6.00
46 Johnny Wang 2.50 6.00
47 Elyjah Goss 2.50 6.00
48 Balsa Koprivica 2.50 6.00
49 Amar Sylla 2.50 6.00
50 Derek Culver 2.50 6.00
51 Feron Hunt 2.50 6.00

2021-22 Panini Prizm Draft Picks Fireworks

COMMON CARD .25 .60
SEMISTARS .30 .75
UNLISTED STARS .40 1.00
*HYPER: .6X TO 1.5X BASIC
*SILVER: .6X TO 1.5X BASIC
*CIRCLES: .75X TO 2X BASIC
*ORANGE WAVE/75: 2.5X TO 6X BASIC
*GREEN PULSAR/25: 5X TO 12X BASIC
*MOJO/25: 5X TO 12X BASIC
1 Cade Cunningham 2.50 6.00
2 Evan Mobley 1.50 4.00
3 Jalen Suggs 1.00 2.50
4 Scottie Barnes 1.25 3.00
5 Keon Johnson .40 1.00
6 Corey Kispert .50 1.25
7 Franz Wagner 1.25 3.00
8 Jalen Johnson 1.25 3.00
9 Moses Moody .75 2.00
10 James Bouknight .30 .75
11 Davion Mitchell .40 1.00
12 Kai Jones .30 .75
13 Ziaire Williams .50 1.25
14 Usman Garuba .30 .75
15 Alperen Sengun 1.25 3.00
16 Kevin Durant 1.25 3.00
17 James Harden .75 2.00
18 Kyrie Irving .75 2.00
19 Jayson Tatum 1.50 4.00
20 Stephen Curry 2.50 6.00

2021-22 Panini Prizm Draft Picks Flashback

*HYPER: .6X TO 1.5X BASIC
*SILVER: .6X TO 1.5X BASIC
*CIRCLES: .75X TO 2X BASIC
*ORANGE WAVE/75: 2.5X TO 6X BASIC
*GREEN PULSAR/25: 5X TO 12X BASIC
*MOJO/25: 5X TO 12X BASIC
*PINK CIRCLES/20: 5X TO 12X BASIC
1 Cade Cunningham 2.50 6.00
2 Evan Mobley 1.50 4.00
3 Jalen Suggs 1.00 2.50
4 Jalen Green 2.00 5.00
5 Jonathan Kuminga 1.25 3.00
6 Scottie Barnes 1.25 3.00
7 Keon Johnson .40 1.00
8 Corey Kispert .50 1.25
9 Franz Wagner 1.25 3.00
10 Jalen Johnson 1.25 3.00
11 Vince Carter .75 2.00
12 Dwyane Wade .75 2.00
13 Larry Bird 1.25 3.00
14 Shaquille O'Neal 1.25 3.00
15 Magic Johnson 1.25 3.00
16 Jason Kidd .60 1.50
17 Anfernee Hardaway 1.00 2.50
18 Paul Pierce .60 1.50
19 Grant Hill .60 1.50
20 Jerry West .75 2.00

2021-22 Panini Prizm Draft Picks Instant Impact

COMMON CARD .25 .60
SEMISTARS .30 .75
UNLISTED STARS .40 1.00
*HYPER: .6X TO 1.5X BASIC
*SILVER: .6X TO 1.5X BASIC
*CIRCLES: .75X TO 2X BASIC
*ORANGE WAVE/75: 2.5X TO 6X BASIC
*GREEN PULSAR/25: 5X TO 12X BASIC
*MOJO/25: 5X TO 12X BASIC
*PINK CIRCLES/20: 5X TO 12X BASIC
1 Cade Cunningham 2.50 6.00
2 Evan Mobley 1.50 4.00
3 Jalen Suggs 1.00 2.50
4 Scottie Barnes 1.25 3.00
5 Keon Johnson .40 1.00
6 Corey Kispert .50 1.25
7 Franz Wagner 1.25 3.00
8 Jalen Johnson 1.25 3.00
9 Moses Moody .75 2.00
10 James Bouknight .30 .75
11 Davion Mitchell .40 1.00
12 Kai Jones .30 .75
13 Ziaire Williams .50 1.25
14 Usman Garuba .30 .75
15 Alperen Sengun 1.25 3.00
16 Jalen Green 2.00 5.00
17 Jonathan Kuminga 1.25 3.00
18 Isaiah Jackson .40 1.00
19 Josh Giddey 1.25 3.00
20 Cameron Thomas .75 2.00

2021-22 Panini Prizm Draft Picks On Campus

1 Cade Cunningham 50.00 125.00
2 Evan Mobley 30.00 80.00
3 Jalen Suggs 20.00 50.00
4 Keon Johnson 8.00 20.00
5 Scottie Barnes 25.00 60.00
6 Franz Wagner 25.00 60.00
7 Jalen Johnson 25.00 60.00
8 Moses Moody 15.00 40.00
9 James Bouknight 6.00 15.00
10 Davion Mitchell 8.00 20.00
11 Kai Jones 6.00 15.00
12 Ziaire Williams 10.00 25.00
13 James Harden 15.00 40.00
14 Stephen Curry 50.00 120.00
15 Joel Embiid 20.00 50.00
16 Anthony Davis 20.00 50.00
17 Kawhi Leonard 20.00 50.00
18 Bradley Beal 10.00 25.00
19 Russell Westbrook 12.00 30.00
20 Jimmy Butler 12.00 30.00

2021-22 Panini Prizm Draft Picks Sensational Signatures

COMMON CARD 2.50 6.00
SEMISTARS 3.00 8.00
UNLISTED STARS 4.00 10.00
*GREEN: .5X TO 1.25X BASIC
*HYPER: .5X TO 1.25X BASIC
*RED ICE: .5X TO 1.25X BASIC
*SILVER: .6X TO 1.5X BASIC
*RED/199: .6X TO 1.5X BASIC
*RED/49: 1X TO 2.5X BASIC
*BLUE/149: .6X TO 1.5X BASIC
*BLUE/45: 1X TO 2.5X BASIC
*PURPLE ICE/99: .75X TO 2X BASIC
*PURPLE ICE/29: 1.25X TO 3X BASIC
*CHOICE RED/88: .75X TO 2X BASIC
*BLUE ICE/75: .75X TO 2X BASIC
*BLUE ICE/29: 1.25X TO 3X BASIC
*PURPLE CIRCLES/50: 1X TO 2.5X BASIC
*ORANGE PULSAR/49: 1X TO 2.5X BASIC
*GREEN PULSAR/25: 1.25X TO 3X BASIC
*MOJO/25: 1.25X TO 3X BASIC
*PINK CIRCLES/20: 1.25X TO 3X BASIC
1 Cade Cunningham 25.00 60.00
2 Evan Mobley 15.00 40.00
3 Jalen Suggs 10.00 25.00
4 Jalen Green 20.00 50.00
5 Jonathan Kuminga 12.00 30.00
6 Scottie Barnes 12.00 30.00
7 Keon Johnson 4.00 10.00
8 Corey Kispert 5.00 12.00
9 Franz Wagner 12.00 30.00
10 Jalen Johnson 12.00 30.00
11 Moses Moody 8.00 20.00
12 James Bouknight 3.00 8.00
13 Davion Mitchell 4.00 10.00
14 Kai Jones 3.00 8.00
15 Ziaire Williams 5.00 12.00
16 Usman Garuba 3.00 8.00
17 Alperen Sengun 12.00 30.00
18 Isaiah Jackson 4.00 10.00
19 Josh Giddey 12.00 30.00
20 Cameron Thomas 8.00 20.00
21 Jaden Springer 4.00 10.00
22 Ayo Dosunmu 8.00 20.00
23 Tre Mann 6.00 15.00
24 Josh Christopher 3.00 8.00
25 Chris Duarte 3.00 8.00
26 Brandon Boston Jr. 4.00 10.00
27 Day'Ron Sharpe 4.00 10.00
28 Filip Petrusev 3.00 8.00
30 Charles Bassey 4.00 10.00
32 Greg Brown III 3.00 8.00
34 Joel Ayayi 3.00 8.00
35 Jared Butler 4.00 10.00
37 Bones Hyland 5.00 12.00
38 Miles McBride 6.00 15.00
39 Quentin Grimes 8.00 20.00
40 Herbert Jones 5.00 12.00
41 Matt Hurt 4.00 10.00
45 Austin Reaves 20.00 50.00
47 David Duke Jr. 4.00 10.00
49 Isaiah Livers 4.00 10.00
50 Luka Garza 4.00 10.00
51 Mac McClung 8.00 20.00
53 Aaron Wiggins 5.00 12.00
54 Santi Aldama 5.00 12.00
55 Justin Champagnie 3.00 8.00
56 Sandro Mamukelashvili 3.00 8.00
57 DJ Stewart Jr. 2.50 6.00
58 Marcus Zegarowski 3.00 8.00

2021-22 Panini Prizm Draft Picks Stained Glass

COMMON CARD 6.00 15.00
SEMISTARS 8.00 20.00
UNLISTED STARS 10.00 25.00
1 Cade Cunningham 60.00 150.00
2 Evan Mobley 40.00 100.00
3 Jalen Suggs 25.00 60.00
4 Jalen Green 50.00 120.00
5 Jonathan Kuminga 30.00 80.00
6 Scottie Barnes 30.00 80.00
7 Keon Johnson 10.00 25.00
8 Moses Moody 20.00 50.00
9 James Bouknight 8.00 20.00
10 Davion Mitchell 10.00 25.00
11 Zion Williamson 25.00 60.00
12 Chris Paul 20.00 50.00
13 Anthony Davis 25.00 60.00
14 Stephen Curry 60.00 150.00
15 Joel Embiid 25.00 60.00

2021-22 Panini Prizm Draft Picks Variations

COMMON CARD .30 .75
SEMISTARS .40 1.00
UNLISTED STARS .50 1.25
*RWB: .75X TO 2X BASIC
*RED ICE: 1X TO 2.5X BASIC
*RUBY WAVE: 1X TO 2.5X BASIC
PRIZMS HYPER: 1.2X TO 3X BASIC
PRIZMS PURPLE WAVE: 1.2X TO 3X BASIC
PRIZMS SILVER: 1.2X TO 3X BASIC
*RED/299: 1.5X TO 4X BASIC
*BLUE WAVE/249: 1.5X TO 4X BASIC
*BLUE/199: 1.5X TO 4X BASIC
*PURPLE ICE/149: 2X TO 5X BASIC
*BLUE ICE/99: 2.5X TO 6X BASIC
*CHOICE RED/88: 2.5X TO 6X BASIC
*ORANGE WAVE/75: 3X TO 8X BASIC
*PURPLE/75: 3X TO 8X BASIC
*PURPLE CIRCLES/50: 4X TO 10X BASIC
*ORANGE PULSAR: 4X TO 10X BASIC
*GREEN PULSAR/25: 5X TO 12X BASIC
*MOJO/25: 5X TO 12X BASIC
1 Cade Cunningham 3.00 8.00
2 Evan Mobley 2.00 5.00
3 Jalen Suggs 1.25 3.00
4 Jalen Green 2.50 6.00
5 Jonathan Kuminga 1.50 4.00
6 Scottie Barnes 1.50 4.00
7 Keon Johnson .50 1.25
8 Corey Kispert .60 1.50
9 Franz Wagner 1.50 4.00
10 Jalen Johnson 1.50 4.00
11 Moses Moody 1.00 2.50
12 James Bouknight .40 1.00
13 Davion Mitchell .50 1.25
14 Kai Jones .40 1.00
15 Ziaire Williams .60 1.50
16 Isaiah Jackson .50 1.25
17 Josh Giddey 1.50 4.00
18 Cameron Thomas 1.00 2.50
19 Jaden Springer .50 1.25
20 Ayo Dosunmu 1.00 2.50
21 Tre Mann .75 2.00
22 Josh Christopher .40 1.00
23 Chris Duarte .40 1.00
24 Brandon Boston Jr. .50 1.25
25 Day'Ron Sharpe .50 1.25

2021-22 Panini Prizm Draft Picks Widescreen

*HYPER: .6X TO 1.5X BASIC
*SILVER: .6X TO 1.5X BASIC
*ORANGE WAVE/75: 2.5X TO 6X BASIC
*GREEN PULSAR/25: 5X TO 12X BASIC
*MOJO/25: 5X TO 12X BASIC
*PINK CIRCLES/20: 5X TO 12X BASIC
1 Cade Cunningham 2.50 6.00
2 Evan Mobley 1.50 4.00
3 Jalen Suggs 1.00 2.50
4 Scottie Barnes 1.25 3.00
5 Keon Johnson .40 1.00
6 David Johnson .30 .75
7 Jalen Green 2.00 5.00
8 Jaden Springer .40 1.00
9 Ayo Dosunmu .75 2.00
10 Tre Mann .60 1.50
11 Josh Christopher .30 .75
12 Chris Duarte .30 .75
13 Brandon Boston Jr. .40 1.00
14 Day'Ron Sharpe .40 1.00
15 Sharife Cooper .30 .75
16 Derrick Rose .60 1.50
17 Anthony Davis 1.00 2.50
18 Kawhi Leonard 1.00 2.50
19 Kevin Durant 1.25 3.00
20 Michael Porter Jr. .50 1.25

2023-24 Panini Prizm Draft Picks

*VARIATIONS: .4X TO 1X BASIC
*GREEN: 1X TO 2.5X BASIC
*GREEN WAVE: 1.25X TO 3X BASIC
*PURPLE WAVE: 1.25X TO 3X BASIC
*SILVER: 1.25X TO 3X BASIC
*CHOICE BLUE YLW & GRN:1.5X TO 4X BASIC
*RED ICE: 1.5X TO 4X BASIC
*RED/299: 2X TO 5X BASIC
1 Ricky Council IV .60 1.50
2 Victor Wembanyama 4.00 10.00
3 James Nnaji .40 1.00
4 Amen Thompson 2.50 6.00
5 Markquis Nowell .50 1.25
6 Jaylen Clark .60 1.50
7 Trayce Jackson-Davis .60 1.50
8 Adama Sanogo .50 1.25
9 Colby Jones .50 1.25
10 Terquavion Smith .50 1.25
11 Tosan Evbuomwan .40 1.00
12 Cason Wallace 1.00 2.50
13 Matas Buzelis 1.25 3.00
14 KJ Evans .60 1.50
15 Aaron Bradshaw .60 1.50
16 David Singleton .50 1.25
17 Ausar Thompson 1.25 3.00
18 Leaky Black .40 1.00
19 Taylor Hendricks .50 1.25
20 Brice Sensabaugh .75 2.00
21 Adam Flagler .50 1.25
22 Kobe Bufkin .60 1.50
23 Omaha Biliew .50 1.25
24 Scoot Henderson 1.50 4.00
25 Dariq Whitehead .60 1.50
26 Justin Edwards .75 2.00
27 Ja'Kobe Walter .60 1.50
28 KJ Williams .50 1.25
29 Tyger Campbell .50 1.25
30 Marcus Sasser .75 2.00
31 Gabe Kalscheur .40 1.00
32 Jalen Pickett .40 1.00
33 Jarace Walker 1.00 2.50
34 Ben Sheppard .50 1.25
35 Dillon Mitchell .50 1.25
36 Kendric Davis .50 1.25
37 Timmy Allen .50 1.25
38 Tristan Vukcevic .50 1.25
39 Mojave King .50 1.25
40 Sidy Cissoko .50 1.25
41 Desmond Cambridge Jr. .50 1.25
42 Jordan Hawkins .75 2.00
43 Jared McCain 1.50 4.00
44 Olivier-Maxence Prosper .50 1.25
45 Colin Castleton .40 1.00
46 Seth Lundy .40 1.00
47 Keyonte George 1.50 4.00
48 Donovan Clingan 1.25 3.00
49 Kris Murray .50 1.25
50 Nick Smith Jr. .60 1.50
51 Jayson Tatum 1.25 3.00
52 Joel Embiid .75 2.00
53 Stephen Curry 2.50 6.00
54 Trae Young .60 1.50
55 Russell Westbrook .50 1.25
56 Jimmy Butler .50 1.25
57 Ja Morant 1.00 2.50
58 Paul George .50 1.25
59 Zach LaVine .50 1.25
60 Kawhi Leonard .75 2.00
61 DeMar DeRozan .50 1.25
62 Scottie Barnes .40 1.00
63 Brandon Miller 2.00 5.00
64 Bradley Beal .40 1.00
65 Cade Cunningham .75 2.00
66 Donovan Mitchell .60 1.50
67 Jaylen Brown .60 1.50
68 Anthony Black 1.00 2.50
69 Evan Mobley .50 1.25
70 Kevin Durant 1.00 2.50
71 Chris Paul .60 1.50
72 Kyrie Irving .60 1.50
73 Zion Williamson .75 2.00
74 Paolo Banchero .75 2.00
75 Jaden Ivey .40 1.00
76 Chet Holmgren .75 2.00
77 Allen Iverson .75 2.00
78 Isiah Thomas .50 1.25
79 Magic Johnson 1.25 3.00
80 Hakeem Olajuwon .60 1.50
81 Jerry West .60 1.50
82 Benedict Mathurin .50 1.25
83 Dell Curry .30 .75
84 Gradey Dick 1.00 2.50
85 Charles Barkley .75 2.00
86 Tre Johnson 1.25 3.00
87 Jalen Brunson .60 1.50
88 Jalen Williams .60 1.50
89 Damian Lillard .75 2.00
90 Desmond Bane .40 1.00
91 Clyde Drexler .50 1.25
92 Shaquille O'Neal 1.00 2.50
93 Karl Malone .60 1.50
94 Jeremy Sochan .40 1.00
95 Larry Bird 1.25 3.00
96 Patrick Ewing .50 1.25
97 Bilal Coulibaly 1.25 3.00
98 Cam Whitmore 1.25 3.00
99 Dwyane Wade .60 1.50
100 Keegan Murray .40 1.00

2023-24 Panini Prizm Draft Picks Prizms Blue

*BLUE:2.5X TO 6X BASIC
STATED PRINT RUN 199 SER.#'d SETS
2 Victor Wembanyama 300.00 600.00

2023-24 Panini Prizm Draft Picks Prizms Blue Ice

*BLUE ICE:2.5X TO 6X BASIC
STATED PRINT RUN 99 SER.#'d SETS
2 Victor Wembanyama 400.00 800.00

2023-24 Panini Prizm Draft Picks Prizms Blue Wave

*BLUE WAVE:2X TO 5X BASIC
STATED PRINT RUN 249 SER.#'d SETS
2 Victor Wembanyama 200.00 500.00

2023-24 Panini Prizm Draft Picks Prizms Choice Red

*CHOICE RED:2.5X TO 6X BASIC
STATED PRINT RUN 88 SER.#'d SETS
2 Victor Wembanyama 150.00 400.00

2023-24 Panini Prizm Draft Picks Prizms Green Pulsar

*GREEN PULSAR: 5X TO 12X BASIC
STATED PRINT RUN 25 SER.#'d SETS
2 Victor Wembanyama 600.00 1,200.00
17 Ausar Thompson 50.00 120.00
24 Scoot Henderson 40.00 100.00

2023-24 Panini Prizm Draft Picks Prizms Mojo

*MOJO: 5X TO 12X BASIC
STATED PRINT RUN 25 SER.#'d SETS
2 Victor Wembanyama 600.00 1,200.00
17 Ausar Thompson 50.00 120.00
24 Scoot Henderson 40.00 100.00

2023-24 Panini Prizm Draft Picks Prizms Orange Pulsar

*ORANGE PULSAR: 3X TO 8X BASIC
STATED PRINT RUN 49 SER.#'d SETS
2 Victor Wembanyama 400.00 800.00

2023-24 Panini Prizm Draft Picks Prizms Purple

*PURPLE: 3X TO 8X BASIC
STATED PRINT RUN 75 SER.#'d SETS
2 Victor Wembanyama 300.00 600.00
17 Ausar Thompson 30.00 80.00
24 Scoot Henderson 25.00 60.00

2023-24 Panini Prizm Draft Picks Prizms Purple Ice

*PURPLE ICE: 2X TO 5X BASIC
STATED PRINT RUN 149 SER.#'d SETS
2 Victor Wembanyama 150.00 400.00

2023-24 Panini Prizm Draft Picks Autographs

*GREEN: .5X TO 1.2X BASIC
*HYPER: .5X TO 1.2X BASIC
*SILVER: .5X TO 1.2X BASIC
*RED/149: .5X TO 1.2X BASIC
*BLUE/99-125: .5X TO 1.2X BASIC
*PURPLE ICE/75-99: .6X TO 1.5X BASIC
*BLUE ICE/49-75: .6X TO 1.5X BASIC
*ORANGE PULSAR/35-49: .75X TO 2X BASIC
*CHOICE RED/40: .75X TO 2X BASIC
*GREEN PULSAR/25: 1X TO 2.5X BASIC
*MOJO/25: 1X TO 2.5X BASIC
1 Colin Castleton 4.00 10.00
2 Leaky Black 4.00 10.00
3 KJ Williams 5.00 12.00
4 Amen Thompson 25.00 60.00
5 David Singleton 5.00 12.00
6 Trayce Jackson-Davis 6.00 15.00
7 Markquis Nowell 5.00 12.00
8 Jalen Pickett 4.00 10.00
9 Colby Jones 5.00 12.00
10 Mojave King 5.00 12.00
11 James Nnaji 4.00 10.00
12 Tristan Vukcevic 5.00 12.00
13 Sidy Cissoko 5.00 12.00
14 Dariq Whitehead 6.00 15.00
15 Julian Strawther 6.00 15.00
16 Omaha Biliew 5.00 12.00
17 Timmy Allen 5.00 12.00
18 Seth Lundy 4.00 10.00
19 Tosan Evbuomwan 4.00 10.00
20 Adama Sanogo 5.00 12.00
21 Ben Sheppard 5.00 12.00
22 Keyonte George 15.00 40.00
23 Adam Flagler 5.00 12.00
24 Kobe Brown 5.00 12.00
25 Azuolas Tubelis 4.00 10.00
26 Justin Edwards 8.00 20.00
27 Kris Murray 5.00 12.00
28 Dexter Dennis 4.00 10.00
29 Olivier-Maxence Prosper 5.00 12.00
30 Aaron Bradshaw 6.00 15.00
31 Ricky Council IV 6.00 15.00
32 Marcus Sasser 8.00 20.00
33 Joey Hauser 4.00 10.00
34 Kendric Davis 5.00 12.00
35 Terquavion Smith 5.00 12.00
36 Andre Jackson Jr. 8.00 20.00
37 Kobe Bufkin 6.00 15.00
38 Gabe Kalscheur 4.00 10.00
39 Brandin Podziemski 15.00 40.00
40 Keyontae Johnson 5.00 12.00
41 Grant Sherfield 4.00 10.00
42 Bilal Coulibaly 12.00 30.00
43 Ausar Thompson 12.00 30.00
44 Jalen Slawson 5.00 12.00
45 Sir'Jabari Rice 4.00 10.00
46 Desmond Cambridge Jr. 5.00 12.00
47 Jaylen Clark 5.00 12.00
48 Cason Wallace 10.00 25.00
49 Tyger Campbell 5.00 12.00
50 Dereck Lively II 10.00 25.00
51 Mike Miles Jr. 4.00 10.00
52 Matas Buzelis 12.00 30.00
53 KJ Evans 5.00 12.00
54 Ja'Kobe Walter 6.00 15.00
55 Mark Price 5.00 12.00
56 Jose Alvarado 5.00 12.00
57 Dell Curry 5.00 12.00
58 Fat Lever 5.00 12.00
59 Doug McDermott 4.00 10.00
60 Landers Nolley 3.00 8.00
62 Caleb Martin 4.00 10.00
64 Tre Johnson 12.00 30.00
65 Julian Phillips 5.00 12.00
66 Scotty Pippen Jr. 5.00 12.00
67 Kevon Looney 5.00 12.00
68 Isaiah Wong 5.00 12.00
69 Mo Bamba 4.00 10.00
70 Kelly Oubre Jr. 5.00 12.00
71 Bobby Portis 6.00 15.00
72 Maxwell Lewis 4.00 10.00
73 Onyeka Okongwu 4.00 10.00
74 Leonard Miller 5.00 12.00
75 Jordan Walsh 5.00 12.00
76 Max Strus 5.00 12.00
77 Jalen Wilson 5.00 12.00
78 Herbert Jones 5.00 12.00

2023-24 Panini Prizm Draft Picks Black Colorblast

2 Anthony Black 100.00 250.00
3 Brandon Miller 125.00 300.00
4 Cam Whitmore 100.00 250.00
5 Gradey Dick 75.00 200.00
6 Jordan Hawkins 125.00 300.00
7 Nick Smith Jr. 100.00 250.00
8 Scoot Henderson 150.00 400.00
9 Taylor Hendricks 75.00 200.00
10 Amen Thompson 150.00 400.00
11 Ausar Thompson 200.00 500.00
12 Keyonte George 125.00 300.00
14 Stephen Curry 200.00 500.00
15 Ja Morant 150.00 400.00

2023-24 Panini Prizm Draft Picks Brilliance

COMPLETE SET (20)
*GREEN WAVE: 1.25X TO 3X BASIC
*HYPER: 1.25X TO 3X BASIC
*RED ICE: 1.25X TO 3X BASIC
*SILVER: 1.25X TO 3X BASIC
1 Victor Wembanyama 10.00 25.00
2 Taylor Hendricks .50 1.25
3 Scoot Henderson 1.50 4.00
4 Nick Smith Jr. .60 1.50
5 Jordan Hawkins .75 2.00
6 Colby Jones .50 1.25
7 Gradey Dick 1.00 2.50
8 Cam Whitmore 1.25 3.00
9 Brandon Miller 2.00 5.00
10 Anthony Black 1.00 2.50
11 Amen Thompson 2.50 6.00
12 Ausar Thompson 1.25 3.00
13 Kris Murray .50 1.25
14 Keyonte George 1.50 4.00
15 Markquis Nowell .50 1.25
16 James Harden 1.00 2.50
17 Chris Paul 1.00 2.50
18 Stephen Curry 4.00 10.00
19 Jaylen Brown 1.00 2.50
20 Matas Buzelis 1.25 3.00

2023-24 Panini Prizm Draft Picks Brilliance Prizms Green Pulsar

*GREEN PULSAR: 5X TO 12X BASIC
STATED PRINT RUN 25 SER.#'d SETS
1 Victor Wembanyama 300.00 600.00
3 Scoot Henderson 40.00 100.00
12 Ausar Thompson 40.00 100.00

2023-24 Panini Prizm Draft Picks Brilliance Prizms Mojo

*MOJO: 5X TO 12X BASIC
STATED PRINT RUN 25 SER.#'d SETS
1 Victor Wembanyama 300.00 600.00
3 Scoot Henderson 40.00 100.00

2023-24 Panini Prizm Draft Picks College Penmanship Signatures

*GREEN: .5X TO 1.2X BASIC
*HYPER: .5X TO 1.2X BASIC
*SILVER: .5X TO 1.2X BASIC
*RED/99-199: .5X TO 1.2X BASIC
*BLUE/125-149: .5X TO 1.2X BASIC
*PURPLE ICE/75-99: .6X TO 1.5X BASIC
*BLUE ICE/49-75: .6X TO 1.5X BASIC
*ORANGE PULSAR/49: .75X TO 2X BASIC
*CHOICE RED/40: .75X TO 2X BASIC

*GREEN PULSAR/25: 1X TO 2.5X BASIC
*MOJO/25: 1X TO 2.5X BASIC
1 Grant Sherfield 4.00 10.00
2 Kris Murray 5.00 12.00
3 Omaha Biliew 5.00 12.00
4 Sir'Jabari Rice 4.00 10.00
5 Colin Castleton 4.00 10.00
6 Trayce Jackson-Davis 6.00 15.00
7 Ricky Council IV 6.00 15.00
8 Mouhamed Gueye 5.00 12.00
9 Keyonte George 15.00 40.00
10 Joey Hauser 4.00 10.00
11 Aaron Bradshaw 6.00 15.00
12 Keyontae Johnson 5.00 12.00
13 Ja'Kobe Walter 6.00 15.00
14 Marcus Sasser 8.00 20.00
15 Tosan Evbuomwan 4.00 10.00
16 Timmy Allen 5.00 12.00
17 Seth Lundy 4.00 10.00
18 Kobe Bufkin 6.00 15.00
19 Brice Sensabaugh 8.00 20.00
20 GG Jackson II 10.00 25.00
21 Dariq Whitehead 6.00 15.00
22 Desmond Cambridge Jr. 5.00 12.00
23 Jalen Slawson 5.00 12.00
24 Adam Flagler 5.00 12.00
25 Donovan Clingan 12.00 30.00
26 David Singleton 5.00 12.00
27 Adama Sanogo 5.00 12.00
28 Azuolas Tubelis 4.00 10.00
29 Leaky Black 4.00 10.00
30 Terquavion Smith 5.00 12.00
31 Jaylen Clark 5.00 12.00
32 Jalen Wilson 5.00 12.00
33 Dereck Lively II 10.00 25.00
34 Maxwell Lewis 4.00 10.00
35 KJ Williams 5.00 12.00
36 KJ Evans 5.00 12.00
37 Gabe Kalscheur 4.00 10.00
38 Markquis Nowell 5.00 12.00
39 Justin Edwards 8.00 20.00
40 Jared McCain 15.00 40.00
41 Jalen Pickett 4.00 10.00
42 Kendric Davis 5.00 12.00
43 Dillon Mitchell 5.00 12.00
44 Julian Phillips 5.00 12.00
45 Dexter Dennis 4.00 10.00
46 Liam Robbins 4.00 10.00
47 Cason Wallace 10.00 25.00
48 Noah Clowney 6.00 15.00
49 Tyger Campbell 5.00 12.00
50 Pete Nance 4.00 10.00

2023-24 Panini Prizm Draft Picks Color Wheel
1 Victor Wembanyama 1,000.00 2,000.00
2 Anthony Black 75.00 200.00
3 Brandon Miller 75.00 200.00
4 Cam Whitmore 30.00 80.00
5 Gradey Dick 40.00 100.00
6 Jordan Hawkins 75.00 200.00
7 Nick Smith Jr. 40.00 100.00
8 Amen Thompson 75.00 200.00
9 Ausar Thompson 100.00 250.00
10 Scoot Henderson 125.00 300.00

2023-24 Panini Prizm Draft Picks Colorblast
2 Anthony Black 100.00 250.00
3 Brandon Miller 125.00 300.00
4 Cam Whitmore 100.00 250.00
5 Gradey Dick 75.00 200.00
6 Jordan Hawkins 125.00 300.00
7 Nick Smith Jr. 100.00 250.00
8 Scoot Henderson 150.00 400.00
9 Taylor Hendricks 75.00 200.00
10 Amen Thompson 150.00 400.00
11 Ausar Thompson 200.00 500.00
12 Keyonte George 125.00 300.00
13 Jett Howard 75.00 200.00
14 Ja Morant 150.00 400.00
15 Stephen Curry 200.00 500.00

2023-24 Panini Prizm Draft Picks Fearless
COMPLETE SET (20)
*GREEN WAVE: 1.25X TO 3X BASIC
*HYPER: 1.25X TO 3X BASIC
*RED ICE: 1.25X TO 3X BASIC
*SILVER: 1.25X TO 3X BASIC
1 Victor Wembanyama 10.00 25.00
2 Taylor Hendricks .50 1.25
3 Scoot Henderson 1.50 4.00
4 Nick Smith Jr. .60 1.50
5 Jordan Hawkins .75 2.00
6 James Nnaji .40 1.00
7 Gradey Dick 1.00 2.50
8 Cam Whitmore 1.25 3.00
9 Brandon Miller 2.00 5.00
10 Anthony Black 1.00 2.50
11 Amen Thompson 2.50 6.00
12 Ausar Thompson 1.25 3.00
13 Sidy Cissoko .50 1.25
14 Keyonte George 1.50 4.00
15 Kobe Bufkin .60 1.50
16 Kyrie Irving 1.00 2.50
17 Stephen Curry 4.00 10.00
18 Zion Williamson 1.25 3.00
19 Jayson Tatum 2.00 5.00
20 Ja Morant 1.50 4.00

2023-24 Panini Prizm Draft Picks Fearless Prizms Green Pulsar
*GREEN PULSAR: 5X TO 12X BASIC
STATED PRINT RUN 25 SER.#'d SETS
1 Victor Wembanyama 300.00 600.00
3 Scoot Henderson 40.00 100.00
12 Ausar Thompson 40.00 100.00

2023-24 Panini Prizm Draft Picks Fearless Prizms Mojo
*MOJO: 5X TO 12X BASIC
STATED PRINT RUN 25 SER.#'d SETS
1 Victor Wembanyama 300.00 600.00
3 Scoot Henderson 40.00 100.00
12 Ausar Thompson 40.00 100.00

2023-24 Panini Prizm Draft Picks Fireworks
COMPLETE SET (20)
*GREEN WAVE: 1.25X TO 3X BASIC
*HYPER: 1.25X TO 3X BASIC
*RED ICE: 1.25X TO 3X BASIC
*SILVER: 1.25X TO 3X BASIC
1 Victor Wembanyama 10.00 25.00
2 Taylor Hendricks .50 1.25
3 Scoot Henderson 1.50 4.00
4 Nick Smith Jr. .60 1.50
5 Jordan Hawkins .75 2.00
6 Jett Howard .60 1.50
7 Gradey Dick 1.00 2.50
8 Cam Whitmore 1.25 3.00
9 Brandon Miller 2.00 5.00
10 Anthony Black 1.00 2.50
11 Amen Thompson 2.50 6.00
12 Ausar Thompson 1.25 3.00
13 Dariq Whitehead .60 1.50
14 Keyonte George 1.50 4.00
15 Dereck Lively II 1.00 2.50
16 Stephen Curry 4.00 10.00
17 Kevin Durant 1.50 4.00
18 Ja Morant 1.50 4.00
19 Trae Young 1.00 2.50
20 Jayson Tatum 2.00 5.00

2023-24 Panini Prizm Draft Picks Fireworks Prizms Green Pulsar
*GREEN PULSAR: 5X TO 12X BASIC
STATED PRINT RUN 25 SER.#'d SETS
1 Victor Wembanyama 300.00 600.00
3 Scoot Henderson 40.00 100.00
12 Ausar Thompson 40.00 100.00

2023-24 Panini Prizm Draft Picks Fireworks Prizms Mojo
*MOJO: 5X TO 12X BASIC
STATED PRINT RUN 25 SER.#'d SETS
1 Victor Wembanyama 300.00 600.00
3 Scoot Henderson 40.00 100.00
12 Ausar Thompson 40.00 100.00

2023-24 Panini Prizm Draft Picks Legacy Signatures
*GREEN: .5X TO 1.2X BASIC
*HYPER: .5X TO 1.2X BASIC
*SILVER: .5X TO 1.2X BASIC
*RED/149: .5X TO 1.2X BASIC
*BLUE/125: .5X TO 1.2X BASIC
*PURPLE ICE/99: .6X TO 1.5X BASIC
*BLUE ICE/75: .6X TO 1.5X BASIC
*ORANGE PULSAR/49: .75X TO 2X BASIC
*CHOICE RED/40: .75X TO 2X BASIC
*GREEN PULSAR/25: 1X TO 2.5X BASIC
*MOJO/25: 1X TO 2.5X BASIC
1 Mario Chalmers 3.00 8.00
2 Christian Laettner 4.00 10.00
3 Corey Kispert 3.00 8.00
4 Ayo Dosunmu 4.00 10.00
5 Bob McAdoo 5.00 12.00
6 John Lucas 3.00 8.00
7 Rick Fox 4.00 10.00
8 Steve Francis 4.00 10.00
9 David Thompson 5.00 12.00
10 Antawn Jamison 4.00 10.00
11 Juwan Howard 4.00 10.00
12 Richard Hamilton 5.00 12.00
13 Larry Johnson 8.00 20.00
14 Luka Garza 3.00 8.00
15 Daniel Gibson 2.50 6.00
16 Cazzie Russell 4.00 10.00
17 Glen Rice 4.00 10.00
18 Ty Jerome 2.50 6.00
19 Adam Morrison 4.00 10.00
21 Christian Braun 4.00 10.00
22 Jalen Suggs 5.00 12.00

2023-24 Panini Prizm Draft Picks Manga
1 Amen Thompson 40.00 100.00
2 Ausar Thompson 60.00 150.00
3 Victor Wembanyama 800.00 1,500.00
4 Anthony Black 40.00 100.00
5 Keyonte George 50.00 120.00
6 Nick Smith Jr. 25.00 60.00
7 Jayson Tatum 75.00 200.00
8 Stephen Curry 100.00 250.00
9 Cam Whitmore 30.00 80.00
10 Gradey Dick 40.00 100.00
11 Jordan Hawkins 50.00 120.00
12 Brandon Miller 75.00 200.00
13 Brice Sensabaugh 30.00 80.00
14 Scoot Henderson 100.00 250.00
15 Taylor Hendricks 25.00 60.00

2023-24 Panini Prizm Draft Picks National Pride
1 Tristan Vukcevic 1.00 2.50
2 Victor Wembanyama 75.00 200.00
3 Joel Embiid 2.50 6.00
4 Hakeem Olajuwon 2.00 5.00
5 Nikola Jokic 5.00 12.00
6 Manu Ginobili 2.00 5.00
7 Stephen Curry 8.00 20.00
8 Luka Doncic 6.00 15.00
9 Pau Gasol 1.50 4.00
10 Dirk Nowitzki 2.50 6.00
11 Josh Giddey 1.25 3.00
12 Andrew Wiggins 1.25 3.00
13 Giannis Antetokounmpo 5.00 12.00
14 Tony Parker 1.50 4.00
15 Bilal Coulibaly 2.50 6.00

2023-24 Panini Prizm Draft Picks Prizm Break
COMPLETE SET (20)
*GREEN WAVE: 1.25X TO 3X BASIC
*HYPER: 1.25X TO 3X BASIC
*RED ICE: 1.25X TO 3X BASIC
*SILVER: 1.25X TO 3X BASIC
1 Victor Wembanyama 10.00 25.00
2 Taylor Hendricks .50 1.25
3 Nick Smith Jr. .60 1.50
4 Jordan Hawkins .75 2.00
5 Olivier-Maxence Prosper .50 1.25
6 Gradey Dick 1.00 2.50
7 Cam Whitmore 1.25 3.00
8 Brandon Miller 2.00 5.00
9 Anthony Black 1.00 2.50
10 Amen Thompson 2.50 6.00
11 Ausar Thompson 1.25 3.00
12 Kendric Davis .50 1.25
13 Keyonte George 1.50 4.00
14 Tristan Vukcevic .50 1.25
15 Kevin Durant 1.50 4.00
16 Ja Morant 1.50 4.00
17 Jimmy Butler .75 2.00
18 Russell Westbrook .75 2.00
19 Donovan Mitchell 1.00 2.50
20 Scoot Henderson 1.50 4.00

2023-24 Panini Prizm Draft Picks Prizm Break Prizms Green Pulsar
*GREEN PULSAR: 5X TO 12X BASIC
STATED PRINT RUN 25 SER.#'d SETS
1 Victor Wembanyama 300.00 600.00
11 Ausar Thompson 40.00 100.00
20 Scoot Henderson 40.00 100.00

2023-24 Panini Prizm Draft Picks Prizm Break Prizms Mojo
*MOJO: 5X TO 12X BASIC
STATED PRINT RUN 25 SER.#'d SETS
1 Victor Wembanyama 300.00 600.00
11 Ausar Thompson 40.00 100.00
20 Scoot Henderson 40.00 100.00

2023-24 Panini Prizm Draft Picks Rated Prospect
*GREEN: 1X TO 2.5X BASIC
*HYPER: 1.25X TO 3X BASIC
*PURPLE WAVE: 1.25X TO 3X BASIC
*SILVER: 1.25X TO 3X BASIC
*CHOICE BLUE YLW & GRN: 1.5X TO 4X BASIC
*BLUE/199: 2.5X TO 6X BASIC
*PURPLE ICE/149: 2X TO 5X BASIC
*BLUE ICE/99: 2.5X TO 6X BASIC
*CHOICE RED/88: 2.5X TO 6X BASIC
*PURPLE/75: 3X TO 8X BASIC
*ORANGE PULSAR/49: 3X TO 8X BASIC
*GREEN PULSAR/25: 5X TO 12X BASIC
*MOJO/25: 5X TO 12X BASIC
1 Omaha Biliew .50 1.25
2 Jared McCain 1.50 4.00
3 Matas Buzelis 1.25 3.00
4 KJ Evans .50 1.25
5 Ja'Kobe Walter .60 1.50
6 Dillon Mitchell .50 1.25
7 Aaron Bradshaw .60 1.50
8 Donovan Clingan 1.25 3.00

2023-24 Panini Prizm Draft Picks Sensational Signatures
*GREEN: .5X TO 1.2X BASIC
*HYPER: .5X TO 1.2X BASIC
*SILVER: .5X TO 1.2X BASIC
*RED/99-199: .5X TO 1.2X BASIC
*BLUE/125-149: .5X TO 1.2X BASIC
*PURPLE ICE/75-99: .6X TO 1.5X BASIC
*BLUE ICE/49-75: .6X TO 1.5X BASIC
*ORANGE PULSAR/49: .75X TO 2X BASIC
*CHOICE RED/40: .75X TO 2X BASIC
*GREEN PULSAR/25: 1X TO 2.5X BASIC
*MOJO/25: 1X TO 2.5X BASIC
1 Chris Livingston 5.00 12.00
2 Jazian Gortman 4.00 10.00
3 Tyger Campbell 5.00 12.00
4 David Singleton 5.00 12.00
5 Joey Hauser 4.00 10.00
6 Kobe Brown 5.00 12.00
7 Olivier-Maxence Prosper 5.00 12.00
8 Ausar Thompson 12.00 30.00
9 Brice Sensabaugh 8.00 20.00
10 James Nnaji 4.00 10.00
11 Adama Sanogo 5.00 12.00
12 Tristan Vukcevic 5.00 12.00
13 Jordan Walsh 5.00 12.00
14 Aaron Bradshaw 6.00 15.00
15 Adam Flagler 5.00 12.00
16 KJ Williams 5.00 12.00
17 Ben Sheppard 5.00 12.00
18 Hunter Tyson 5.00 12.00
19 Liam Robbins 4.00 10.00
20 Dexter Dennis 4.00 10.00
21 Azuolas Tubelis 4.00 10.00
22 Donovan Clingan 12.00 30.00
23 Kendric Davis 5.00 12.00
24 Tosan Evbuomwan 4.00 10.00
25 Mojave King 5.00 12.00
26 Colin Castleton 4.00 10.00
27 Amen Thompson 25.00 60.00
28 Leonard Miller 5.00 12.00
29 Julian Strawther 6.00 15.00
30 Terquavion Smith 5.00 12.00
31 Timmy Allen 5.00 12.00
32 Toumani Camara 10.00 25.00
33 Justin Edwards 8.00 20.00
34 Leaky Black 4.00 10.00
35 Keyonte George 15.00 40.00
36 Markquis Nowell 5.00 12.00
37 Gabe Kalscheur 4.00 10.00
38 Desmond Cambridge Jr. 5.00 12.00
39 Jared McCain 15.00 40.00
40 Ricky Council IV 6.00 15.00
41 Sidy Cissoko 5.00 12.00
42 Bilal Coulibaly 12.00 30.00
43 Isaiah Wong 5.00 12.00
44 GG Jackson II 10.00 25.00
45 Matas Buzelis 12.00 30.00
46 Ja'Kobe Walter 6.00 15.00
47 Dillon Mitchell 5.00 12.00
48 Grant Sherfield 4.00 10.00
49 Sir'Jabari Rice 4.00 10.00
50 Omaha Biliew 5.00 12.00

2023-24 Panini Prizm Draft Picks Stained Glass
1 Victor Wembanyama 600.00 1,200.00
2 Anthony Black 20.00 50.00
3 Brandon Miller 50.00 120.00
4 Cam Whitmore 15.00 40.00
5 Gradey Dick 40.00 100.00
6 Jordan Hawkins 50.00 120.00
7 Nick Smith Jr. 15.00 40.00
8 Scoot Henderson 60.00 150.00
9 Taylor Hendricks 15.00 40.00
10 Amen Thompson 40.00 100.00
11 Ausar Thompson 40.00 100.00
12 Keyonte George 40.00 100.00
13 Dariq Whitehead 15.00 40.00
14 Stephen Curry 60.00 150.00
15 Trae Young 25.00 60.00

2023-24 Panini Prizm Draft Picks Widescreen
COMPLETE SET (20)
*GREEN WAVE: 1.25X TO 3X BASIC
*HYPER: 1.25X TO 3X BASIC
*RED ICE: 1.25X TO 3X BASIC
*SILVER: 1.25X TO 3X BASIC
1 Victor Wembanyama 20.00 50.00
2 Taylor Hendricks .50 1.25
3 Scoot Henderson 1.50 4.00
4 Nick Smith Jr. .60 1.50
5 Jordan Hawkins .75 2.00
6 Trayce Jackson-Davis .60 1.50
7 Gradey Dick 1.00 2.50
8 Cam Whitmore 1.25 3.00
9 Brandon Miller 2.00 5.00
10 Anthony Black 1.00 2.50
11 Amen Thompson 2.50 6.00
12 Ausar Thompson 1.25 3.00
13 Brice Sensabaugh .75 2.00
14 Keyonte George 1.50 4.00
15 Dillon Mitchell .50 1.25
16 Joel Embiid 1.25 3.00
17 Donovan Mitchell 1.00 2.50
18 Kawhi Leonard 1.25 3.00
19 Cade Cunningham 1.25 3.00
20 Jimmy Butler .75 2.00

2023-24 Panini Prizm Draft Picks Widescreen Prizms Green Pulsar
*GREEN PULSAR: 5X TO 12X BASIC
STATED PRINT RUN 25 SER.#'d SETS
1 Victor Wembanyama 400.00 800.00
3 Scoot Henderson 40.00 100.00
12 Ausar Thompson 40.00 100.00

2023-24 Panini Prizm Draft Picks Widescreen Prizms Mojo
*MOJO: 5X TO 12X BASIC
STATED PRINT RUN 25 SER.#'d SETS
1 Victor Wembanyama 400.00 800.00
3 Scoot Henderson 40.00 100.00
12 Ausar Thompson 40.00 100.00

2024-25 Panini Prizm Draft Picks
*GREEN: 1.25X TO 3X BASIC
*HYPER: 1.25X TO 3X BASIC
*PURPLE WAVE: 1.25X TO 3X BASIC
*RED ICE: 1.25X TO 3X BASIC
*SILVER: 1.25X TO 3X BASIC
*GREEN WAVE: 1.5X TO 4X BASIC
*ORANGE ICE: 1.5X TO 4X BASIC
*RED WAVE: 1.5X TO 4X BASIC
1 Zach Edey 1.25 3.00
2 Isaiah Collier .75 2.00
3 Aaliyah Edwards .40 1.00
4 Cam Christie .50 1.25
5 Ryan Dunn .50 1.25
6 Rob Dillingham 1.00 2.50
7 Tyler Kolek .60 1.50
8 Ron Holland II .75 2.00
9 Ja'Kobe Walter .50 1.25
10 Nikola Topic 1.25 3.00
11 Isaiah Thomas .60 1.50
12 Buddy Hield .30 .75
13 Ray Allen .60 1.50
14 Dillon Jones .40 1.00
15 Nika Muhl .60 1.50
16 Pelle Larsson .50 1.25
17 Stephon Castle 2.50 6.00
18 Oso Ighodaro .50 1.25
19 Kevin McCullar Jr. .40 1.00
20 Patrick Ewing .60 1.50
21 Reed Sheppard 1.25 3.00
22 Jalen Brunson .75 2.00
23 Magic Johnson 1.25 3.00
24 Kel'el Ware 1.00 2.50
25 Justin Edwards .60 1.50
26 Keisei Tominaga .60 1.50
27 Devin Carter .50 1.25
28 Kyle Filipowski 1.00 2.50
29 Ja Morant 1.25 3.00
30 Jonathan Mogbo .60 1.50
31 Jaylen Wells 1.25 3.00
32 Jack Gohlke .30 .75
33 Allen Iverson 1.00 2.50
34 Bobi Klintman .50 1.25
35 Jared McCain 1.50 4.00
36 Juan Nunez .40 1.00
37 Ajay Mitchell .60 1.50
38 Angel Reese 1.25 3.00
39 Charles Barkley 1.00 2.50
40 Austin Reaves .50 1.25
41 James Harden .75 2.00
42 Kevin Durant 1.25 3.00
43 Terrence Shannon Jr. .75 2.00
44 Rickea Jackson .60 1.50
45 Jacy Sheldon .60 1.50
46 Jamal Shead .50 1.25
47 Russell Westbrook .60 1.50
48 Melvin Ajinca .30 .75
49 Trae Young .75 2.00
50 Dalton Knecht 1.25 3.00
51 Tristen Newton .40 1.00
52 Alexandre Sarr 1.25 3.00
53 Chris Paul .60 1.50
54 Yves Missi 1.00 2.50
55 PJ Hall .30 .75
56 Jalen Bridges .30 .75
57 Caitlin Clark 4.00 10.00
58 Sue Bird 1.00 2.50
59 Kamilla Cardoso .60 1.50
60 Adem Bona .50 1.25
61 Tristan da Silva 1.00 2.50
62 Kate Martin 1.00 2.50
63 Tim Duncan 1.00 2.50
64 DeMar DeRozan .50 1.25
65 Tyrese Haliburton .75 2.00
66 Keshad Johnson .30 .75
67 Matas Buzelis 2.00 5.00
68 Baylor Scheierman .50 1.25
69 Zaccharie Risacher 1.25 3.00
70 DaRon Holmes II .50 1.25
71 Kyshawn George .60 1.50
72 Enrique Freeman .30 .75
73 Quinten Post .75 2.00
74 Gordon Hayward .30 .75
75 Donovan Mitchell .75 2.00
76 Anton Watson .30 .75
77 Stephen Curry 3.00 8.00
78 Ariel Hukporti .30 .75
79 Armando Bacot .30 .75
80 Cody Williams .50 1.25
81 Pacome Dadiet .50 1.25
82 Tidjane Salaun .40 1.00
83 Reece Beekman .40 1.00
84 Harrison Ingram .40 1.00
85 Trey Alexander .30 .75
86 Bronny James Jr. 1.50 4.00
87 Kawhi Leonard .75 2.00
88 Bub Carrington 1.00 2.50
89 Cameron Brink 2.00 5.00
90 AJ Johnson .60 1.50
91 Johnny Furphy .60 1.50
92 Jaylon Tyson .50 1.25
93 KJ Simpson Jr. .40 1.00
94 Cam Spencer .40 1.00
95 Donovan Clingan 1.00 2.50
96 Marquesha Davis .40 1.00
97 DJ Burns .40 1.00
98 Richard Hamilton .50 1.25
99 Victor Wembanyama 3.00 8.00
100 Antonio Reeves .40 1.00

2024-25 Panini Prizm Draft Picks Prizms Blue
*BLUE: 2.5X TO 6X BASIC
STATED PRINT RUN 199 SER.#'d SETS
57 Caitlin Clark 40.00 100.00

2024-25 Panini Prizm Draft Picks Prizms Blue Ice
*BLUE ICE: 3X TO 8X BASIC
STATED PRINT RUN 99 SER.#'d SETS
57 Caitlin Clark 75.00 200.00

2024-25 Panini Prizm Draft Picks Prizms Blue Pulsar
*BLUE PULSAR: 3X TO 8X BASIC
STATED PRINT RUN 99 SER.#'d SETS
57 Caitlin Clark 75.00 200.00

2024-25 Panini Prizm Draft Picks Prizms Blue Seismic
*BLUE SEISMIC: 2.5X TO 6X BASIC
STATED PRINT RUN 149 SER.#'d SETS
57 Caitlin Clark 60.00 150.00

2024-25 Panini Prizm Draft Picks Prizms Blue Shimmer FOTL
*BLUE SHMR FOTL: 6X TO 15X BASIC
STATED PRINT RUN 19 SER.#'d SETS
57 Caitlin Clark 200.00 500.00

2024-25 Panini Prizm Draft Picks Prizms Blue Wave
*BLUE WAVE: 2X TO 5X BASIC
STATED PRINT RUN 249 SER.#'d SETS
57 Caitlin Clark 30.00 80.00

2024-25 Panini Prizm Draft Picks Prizms Green Pulsar
*GREEN PULSAR: 6X TO 15X BASIC
STATED PRINT RUN 25 SER.#'d SETS
57 Caitlin Clark 200.00 500.00

2024-25 Panini Prizm Draft Picks Prizms Mojo
*MOJO: 6X TO 15X BASIC
STATED PRINT RUN 25 SER.#'d SETS
57 Caitlin Clark 200.00 500.00

2024-25 Panini Prizm Draft Picks Prizms Orange Pulsar
*ORANGE PULSAR: 4X TO 10X BASIC
STATED PRINT RUN 49 SER.#'d SETS
57 Caitlin Clark 100.00 250.00

2024-25 Panini Prizm Draft Picks Prizms Purple
*PURPLE: 3X TO 8X BASIC
STATED PRINT RUN 75 SER.#'d SETS
57 Caitlin Clark 75.00 200.00

2024-25 Panini Prizm Draft Picks Prizms Purple Ice
*PURPLE ICE: 2.5X TO 6X BASIC
STATED PRINT RUN 149 SER.#'d SETS
57 Caitlin Clark 60.00 150.00

2024-25 Panini Prizm Draft Picks Prizms Purple Pulsar
*PURPLE PULSAR: 4X TO 10X BASIC
STATED PRINT RUN 55 SER.#'d SETS
57 Caitlin Clark 100.00 250.00

2024-25 Panini Prizm Draft Picks Prizms Red Pulsar
*RED PULSAR: 2X TO 5X BASIC
STATED PRINT RUN 299 SER.#'d SETS
57 Caitlin Clark 30.00 80.00

2024-25 Panini Prizm Draft Picks Prizms Red Scope
*RED SCOPE: 3X TO 8X BASIC
STATED PRINT RUN 88 SER.#'d SETS
57 Caitlin Clark 75.00 200.00

2024-25 Panini Prizm Draft Picks Prizms Red Seismic
*RED SEISMIC: 2.5X TO 6X BASIC
STATED PRINT RUN 225 SER.#'d SETS
57 Caitlin Clark 40.00 100.00

2024-25 Panini Prizm Draft Picks All-American
*GREEN: 1.25X TO 3X BASIC
*HYPER: 1.25X TO 3X BASIC
*PURPLE WAVE: 1.25X TO 3X BASIC
*RED ICE: 1.25X TO 3X BASIC
*SILVER: 1.25X TO 3X BASIC
*GREEN WAVE: 1.5X TO 4X BASIC
*ORANGE ICE: 1.5X TO 4X BASIC
*RED WAVE: 1.5X TO 4X BASIC
1 Hunter Dickinson .40 1.00
2 Trae Young .75 2.00
3 Kamilla Cardoso .60 1.50
4 Brandon Roy .60 1.50
5 Kevin Durant 1.25 3.00
6 Angel Reese 1.25 3.00
7 Jalen Brunson .75 2.00
8 Jaime Jaquez Jr. .40 1.00
9 Tristen Newton .40 1.00
10 Cameron Brink 2.00 5.00
11 Baylor Scheierman .50 1.25
12 DaRon Holmes II .50 1.25
13 Stephen Curry 3.00 8.00
14 Ja Morant 1.25 3.00
15 Zach Edey 1.25 3.00
16 Jacy Sheldon .60 1.50
17 Jamal Shead .50 1.25
18 Allen Iverson 1.00 2.50
19 Keegan Murray .30 .75
20 Kyle Filipowski 1.00 2.50
21 Chris Paul .60 1.50
22 Tyler Kolek .60 1.50
23 Caitlin Clark 4.00 10.00
24 Terrence Shannon Jr. .75 2.00
25 Tim Duncan 1.00 2.50
26 Luka Garza .30 .75
27 Ray Allen .60 1.50
28 Magic Johnson 1.50 4.00
29 Trayce Jackson-Davis .40 1.00
30 Dalton Knecht 1.25 3.00

2024-25 Panini Prizm Draft Picks All-American Prizms Blue
*BLUE: 2.5X TO 6X BASIC
STATED PRINT RUN 199 SER.#'d SETS
23 Caitlin Clark 40.00 100.00

2024-25 Panini Prizm Draft Picks All-American Prizms Blue Ice
*BLUE ICE: 3X TO 8X BASIC
STATED PRINT RUN 99 SER.#'d SETS
23 Caitlin Clark 75.00 200.00

2024-25 Panini Prizm Draft Picks All-American Prizms Blue Pulsar
*BLUE PULSAR: 3X TO 8X BASIC
STATED PRINT RUN 99 SER.#'d SETS
23 Caitlin Clark 75.00 200.00

2024-25 Panini Prizm Draft Picks All-American Prizms Blue Seismic
*BLUE SEISMIC: 2.5X TO 6X BASIC
STATED PRINT RUN 149 SER.#'d SETS
23 Caitlin Clark 60.00 150.00

2024-25 Panini Prizm Draft Picks All-American Prizms Blue Shimmer FOTL
*BLUE SHMR FOTL: 6X TO 15X BASIC
STATED PRINT RUN 19 SER.#'d SETS
23 Caitlin Clark 200.00 500.00

2024-25 Panini Prizm Draft Picks All-American Prizms Blue Wave
*BLUE WAVE: 2X TO 5X BASIC
STATED PRINT RUN 249 SER.#'d SETS
23 Caitlin Clark 30.00 80.00

2024-25 Panini Prizm Draft Picks All-American Prizms Green Pulsar
*GREEN PULSAR: 6X TO 15X BASIC
STATED PRINT RUN 25 SER.#'d SETS
23 Caitlin Clark 200.00 500.00

2024-25 Panini Prizm Draft Picks All-American Prizms Mojo
*MOJO: 6X TO 15X BASIC
STATED PRINT RUN 25 SER.#'d SETS
23 Caitlin Clark 200.00 500.00

2024-25 Panini Prizm Draft Picks All-American Prizms Orange Pulsar
*ORANGE PULSAR: 4X TO 10X BASIC
STATED PRINT RUN 49 SER.#'d SETS
23 Caitlin Clark 100.00 250.00

2024-25 Panini Prizm Draft Picks All-American Prizms Purple
*PURPLE: 3X TO 8X BASIC
STATED PRINT RUN 75 SER.#'d SETS
23 Caitlin Clark 75.00 200.00

2024-25 Panini Prizm Draft Picks All-American Prizms Purple Ice
*PURPLE ICE: 2.5X TO 6X BASIC
STATED PRINT RUN 149 SER.#'d SETS
23 Caitlin Clark 60.00 150.00

2024-25 Panini Prizm Draft Picks All-American Prizms Purple Pulsar
*PURPLE PULSAR: 4X TO 10X BASIC
STATED PRINT RUN 55 SER.#'d SETS
23 Caitlin Clark 100.00 250.00

2024-25 Panini Prizm Draft Picks All-American Prizms Red Pulsar
*RED PULSAR: 2X TO 5X BASIC
STATED PRINT RUN 299 SER.#'d SETS
23 Caitlin Clark 30.00 80.00

2024-25 Panini Prizm Draft Picks All-American Prizms Red Scope
*RED SCOPE: 3X TO 8X BASIC
STATED PRINT RUN 88 SER.#'d SETS
23 Caitlin Clark 75.00 200.00

2024-25 Panini Prizm Draft Picks All-American Prizms Red Seismic
*RED SEISMIC: 2.5X TO 6X BASIC
STATED PRINT RUN 225 SER.#'d SETS
23 Caitlin Clark 40.00 100.00

2024-25 Panini Prizm Draft Picks Black Colorblast
1 Kevin Durant 75.00 200.00
2 Bronny James Jr. 100.00 250.00
3 Reed Sheppard 125.00 300.00
4 Donovan Clingan 50.00 120.00
5 Caitlin Clark 500.00 1,000.00
6 Dalton Knecht 125.00 300.00
7 Ja Morant 100.00 250.00
8 Jared McCain 60.00 150.00
9 Stephen Curry 150.00 400.00
10 Trae Young 60.00 150.00
11 Angel Reese 100.00 250.00
12 Cameron Brink 150.00 400.00
13 Ja'Kobe Walter 30.00 80.00
14 Stephon Castle 125.00 300.00
15 Cody Williams 30.00 80.00

2024-25 Panini Prizm Draft Picks Brilliance
*HYPER: 1.25X TO 3X BASIC
*SILVER: 1.25X TO 3X BASIC
1 Tidjane Salaun .40 1.00
2 Caitlin Clark 4.00 10.00
3 Nikola Topic 1.25 3.00
4 Stephon Castle 2.00 5.00
5 Zaccharie Risacher 1.00 2.50
6 Bub Carrington 1.00 2.50
7 Ja'Kobe Walter .50 1.25
8 Kyle Filipowski 1.00 2.50
9 Dalton Knecht 1.25 3.00
10 Stephen Curry 3.00 8.00
11 Ja Morant 1.25 3.00
12 Angel Reese 1.25 3.00
13 Donovan Clingan 1.00 2.50
14 Matas Buzelis 2.00 5.00
15 Alexandre Sarr 1.25 3.00
16 Donovan Mitchell .75 2.00
17 Cameron Brink 2.00 5.00
18 Allen Iverson 1.00 2.50
19 Tim Duncan 1.00 2.50
20 Cody Williams .50 1.25

2024-25 Panini Prizm Draft Picks Brilliance Prizms Mojo
*MOJO: 10X TO 25X BASIC
STATED PRINT RUN 25 SER.#'d SETS
2 Caitlin Clark 200.00 500.00

2024-25 Panini Prizm Draft Picks Brilliance Prizms Wave
*WAVE: 4X TO 10X BASIC
STATED PRINT RUN 99 SER.#'d SETS
2 Caitlin Clark 75.00 200.00

2024-25 Panini Prizm Draft Picks Campus Favorites Signatures
*HYPER: .5X TO 1.25X BASIC
*SILVER: .5X TO 1.25X BASIC
*BLUE/149: .5X TO 1.25X BASIC
*PURPLE ICE/99: .5X TO 1.25X BASIC
*BLUE ICE/75: .5X TO 1.25X BASIC
*ORANGE PULSAR/49: .6X TO 1.5X BASIC
*MOJO/25: .75X TO 2X BASIC
1 Kevin McCullar Jr. 5.00 12.00
2 Trae Young 20.00 50.00
3 Zach Edey 15.00 40.00
4 Jamal Shead 6.00 15.00
5 Daniel Gibson 3.00 8.00
6 Jared McCain 20.00 50.00
7 Jaylon Tyson 6.00 15.00
8 Vernon Carey Jr. 4.00 10.00
9 Alondes Williams 4.00 10.00
10 Leaky Black 4.00 10.00
11 Jose Alvarado 4.00 10.00
12 Johnny Juzang 4.00 10.00
13 Keisei Tominaga 8.00 20.00
14 Christian Braun 6.00 15.00
15 Luke Kennard 4.00 10.00
16 Naji Marshall 5.00 12.00
17 Bones Hyland 4.00 10.00
19 Theo Pinson 3.00 8.00
20 Frank Kaminsky 4.00 10.00
21 Milos Uzan 4.00 10.00
22 Tristen Newton 5.00 12.00
23 Aidan Mahaney 3.00 8.00
24 Hunter Dickinson 5.00 12.00
25 Armando Bacot 4.00 10.00

2024-25 Panini Prizm Draft Picks Campus Legends
*GREEN: 1.25X TO 3X BASIC
*HYPER: 1.25X TO 3X BASIC
*PURPLE WAVE: 1.25X TO 3X BASIC
*RED ICE: 1.25X TO 3X BASIC
*SILVER: 1.25X TO 3X BASIC
*GREEN WAVE: 1.5X TO 4X BASIC
*ORANGE ICE: 1.5X TO 4X BASIC
*RED WAVE: 1.5X TO 4X BASIC
1 Tim Duncan 1.00 2.50
2 Stephen Curry 3.00 8.00
3 Kevin Durant 1.25 3.00
4 Angel Reese 1.25 3.00
5 Caitlin Clark 4.00 10.00
6 Jared McCain 1.50 4.00
7 Trae Young .75 2.00
8 Zach Edey 1.25 3.00
9 Donovan Clingan 1.00 2.50
10 Ja Morant 1.25 3.00

2024-25 Panini Prizm Draft Picks Campus Legends Prizms Blue Ice
*BLUE ICE: 3X TO 8X BASIC
STATED PRINT RUN 99 SER.#'d SETS
5 Caitlin Clark 75.00 200.00

2024-25 Panini Prizm Draft Picks Campus Legends Prizms Blue Pulsar
*BLUE PULSAR: 3X TO 8X BASIC
STATED PRINT RUN 99 SER.#'d SETS
5 Caitlin Clark 75.00 200.00

2024-25 Panini Prizm Draft Picks Campus Legends Prizms Blue Shimmer FOTL
*BLUE SHMR FOTL: 6X TO 15X BASIC
STATED PRINT RUN 19 SER.#'d SETS
5 Caitlin Clark 200.00 500.00

2024-25 Panini Prizm Draft Picks Campus Legends Prizms Green Pulsar
*GREEN PULSAR: 6X TO 15X BASIC
STATED PRINT RUN 25 SER.#'d SETS
5 Caitlin Clark 200.00 500.00

2024-25 Panini Prizm Draft Picks Campus Legends Prizms Mojo
*MOJO: 6X TO 15X BASIC
STATED PRINT RUN 25 SER.#'d SETS
5 Caitlin Clark 200.00 500.00

2024-25 Panini Prizm Draft Picks Campus Legends Prizms Orange Pulsar
*ORANGE PULSAR: 4X TO 10X BASIC
STATED PRINT RUN 49 SER.#'d SETS
5 Caitlin Clark 100.00 250.00

2024-25 Panini Prizm Draft Picks Campus Legends Prizms Purple
*PURPLE: 3X TO 8X BASIC
STATED PRINT RUN 75 SER.#'d SETS
5 Caitlin Clark 75.00 200.00

2024-25 Panini Prizm Draft Picks Campus Legends Prizms Purple Pulsar
*PURPLE PULSAR: 4X TO 10X BASIC
STATED PRINT RUN 55 SER.#'d SETS
5 Caitlin Clark 100.00 250.00

2024-25 Panini Prizm Draft Picks Campus Legends Prizms Red Pulsar
*RED PULSAR: 2X TO 5X BASIC
5 Caitlin Clark 30.00 80.00

2024-25 Panini Prizm Draft Picks Campus Legends Prizms Red Scope
*RED SCOPE: 3X TO 8X BASIC
STATED PRINT RUN 88 SER.#'d SETS
5 Caitlin Clark 75.00 200.00

2024-25 Panini Prizm Draft Picks Color Wheel
1 Tidjane Salaun 20.00 50.00
2 Angel Reese 75.00 200.00
3 Stephon Castle 75.00 200.00
4 Donovan Clingan 25.00 60.00
5 Matas Buzelis 60.00 150.00
6 Caitlin Clark 600.00 1,200.00
7 Dalton Knecht 40.00 100.00
8 Alexandre Sarr 25.00 60.00
9 Zaccharie Risacher 25.00 60.00
10 Cody Williams 20.00 50.00

2024-25 Panini Prizm Draft Picks Colorblast
1 Matas Buzelis 60.00 150.00
2 Rob Dillingham 75.00 200.00
3 Stephon Castle 125.00 300.00
4 Caitlin Clark 1,000.00 2,000.00
5 Zach Edey 75.00 200.00
6 Zaccharie Risacher 60.00 150.00
7 Angel Reese 100.00 250.00
8 Tim Duncan 100.00 250.00
9 Allen Iverson 125.00 300.00
10 Alexandre Sarr 60.00 150.00
11 Ja'Kobe Walter 30.00 80.00
12 Ron Holland II 40.00 100.00
13 Bronny James Jr. 100.00 250.00
14 Cody Williams 30.00 80.00
15 Cameron Brink 150.00 400.00

2024-25 Panini Prizm Draft Picks Deep Space
*ICE: 1.25X TO 3X BASIC
*SILVER: 1.25X TO 3X BASIC
1 Tyler Kolek .60 1.50
2 Reed Sheppard 1.25 3.00
3 Ron Holland II .75 2.00
4 Zach Edey 1.25 3.00
5 Nikola Topic 1.25 3.00
6 Jared McCain 1.50 4.00
7 Matas Buzelis 2.00 5.00
8 Caitlin Clark 4.00 10.00
9 Tidjane Salaun .40 1.00
10 Donovan Mitchell .75 2.00
11 Ja'Kobe Walter .50 1.25
12 Zaccharie Risacher 1.00 2.50
13 Angel Reese 1.25 3.00
14 Ja Morant 1.25 3.00
15 Stephon Castle 2.00 5.00
16 Rob Dillingham 1.00 2.50
17 Dalton Knecht 1.25 3.00
18 Donovan Clingan 1.00 2.50
19 Bronny James Jr. 1.50 4.00
20 Cody Williams .50 1.25
21 Bub Carrington 1.00 2.50
22 Kevin Durant 1.25 3.00
23 Alexandre Sarr 1.25 3.00
24 Tim Duncan 1.00 2.50
25 Kyle Filipowski 1.00 2.50

2024-25 Panini Prizm Draft Picks Deep Space Prizms Green Pulsar
*GREEN PULSAR: 10X TO 25X BASIC
STATED PRINT RUN 25 SER.#'d SETS
8 Caitlin Clark 200.00 500.00

2024-25 Panini Prizm Draft Picks Deep Space Prizms Purple Pulsar
*PURPLE PULSAR: 6X TO 15X BASIC
STATED PRINT RUN 55 SER.#'d SETS
8 Caitlin Clark 125.00 300.00

2024-25 Panini Prizm Draft Picks Dominance
*GREEN: 1.25X TO 3X BASIC
*SILVER: 1.25X TO 3X BASIC
*BLUE PULSAR/99: 4X TO 10X BASIC
*RED PULSAR/75: 4X TO 10X BASIC
*PINK PULSAR/42: 5X TO 12X BASIC
*PURPLE PULSAR/35: 4X TO 15X BASIC
*GREEN PULSAR/25: 10X TO 25X BASIC
1 Damian Lillard 1.00 2.50
2 Nikola Jokic 2.00 5.00
3 Kevin Durant 1.25 3.00
4 Giannis Antetokounmpo 1.50 4.00
5 Kyrie Irving 1.00 2.50
6 Jaylen Brown .60 1.50
7 Victor Wembanyama 3.00 8.00
8 James Harden .75 2.00
9 Anthony Edwards 2.00 5.00
10 Joel Embiid .60 1.50
11 Shai Gilgeous-Alexander 1.50 4.00
12 Luka Doncic 2.50 6.00
13 Jayson Tatum 1.25 3.00
14 LeBron James 3.00 8.00
15 Ja Morant 1.25 3.00
16 Tyrese Haliburton .75 2.00
17 Jalen Brunson .75 2.00
18 Kawhi Leonard .75 2.00
19 Paolo Banchero 1.00 2.50
20 Trae Young .75 2.00
21 Stephen Curry 3.00 8.00
22 Zion Williamson 1.00 2.50
23 Donovan Mitchell .75 2.00
24 Tyrese Maxey .75 2.00
25 Anthony Davis 1.00 2.50

2024-25 Panini Prizm Draft Picks Draft Picks Autographs
*HYPER: .5X TO 1.25X BASIC
*SILVER: .5X TO 1.25X BASIC
*BLUE/149: .5X TO 1.25X BASIC
*PURPLE ICE/99: .5X TO 1.25X BASIC
*BLUE ICE/75: .5X TO 1.25X BASIC
*ORANGE PULSAR/49: .6X TO 1.5X BASIC
*MOJO/25: .75X TO 2X BASIC
1 Matas Buzelis 25.00 60.00
2 Omaha Biliew 4.00 10.00
3 Dalton Knecht 15.00 40.00
4 Ajay Mitchell 8.00 20.00
5 Ja'Kobe Walter 6.00 15.00
6 Jalen Bridges 4.00 10.00
7 Bub Carrington 12.00 30.00
8 DaRon Holmes II 6.00 15.00
9 Devin Carter 6.00 15.00
10 Donovan Clingan 12.00 30.00
11 Harrison Ingram 5.00 12.00
12 Ariel Hukporti 4.00 10.00
13 Judah Mintz 4.00 10.00
14 Reed Sheppard 15.00 40.00
15 Terrance Arceneaux 4.00 10.00
16 Tristen Newton 5.00 12.00
17 Ugonna Onyenso 4.00 10.00
18 Zach Edey 15.00 40.00
19 Tyler Kolek 8.00 20.00
20 Cam Spencer 5.00 12.00
21 Adem Bona 6.00 15.00
22 Baylor Scheierman 6.00 15.00
23 Jamal Shead 6.00 15.00
24 Jared McCain 20.00 50.00
25 Keshad Johnson 4.00 10.00
26 KJ Simpson Jr. 5.00 12.00
27 Oso Ighodaro 6.00 15.00
28 Payton Sandfort 4.00 10.00
29 Pelle Larsson 5.00 12.00
30 PJ Hall 4.00 10.00
31 Tristan da Silva 12.00 30.00
32 Trey Alexander 4.00 10.00
34 Jonathan Mogbo 8.00 20.00
35 Terrence Shannon Jr. 10.00 25.00
36 Bobi Klintman 6.00 15.00
37 Kevin McCullar Jr. 5.00 12.00
38 Trevon Brazile 5.00 12.00
39 Caitlin Clark 500.00 1,000.00
40 Angel Reese 15.00 40.00
41 Cameron Brink 50.00 120.00
42 AJ Johnson 8.00 20.00
43 Garwey Dual 4.00 10.00
44 Tidjane Salaun 5.00 12.00
45 Kyshawn George 8.00 20.00
46 Jaylon Tyson 6.00 15.00
47 Jack Gohlke 4.00 10.00
48 Johnny Furphy 8.00 20.00
49 Yves Missi 12.00 30.00
50 Dillon Jones 5.00 12.00

2024-25 Panini Prizm Draft Picks Fearless
*ICE: 1.25X TO 3X BASIC
*SILVER: 1.25X TO 3X BASIC
1 Trae Young .75 2.00
2 Donovan Mitchell .75 2.00
3 Bronny James Jr. 1.50 4.00
4 Tidjane Salaun .40 1.00
5 Cody Williams .50 1.25
6 Zach Edey 1.25 3.00
7 Rob Dillingham 1.00 2.50
8 Jared McCain 1.50 4.00
9 Kel'el Ware 1.00 2.50
10 Tristan da Silva 1.00 2.50
11 Zaccharie Risacher 1.00 2.50
12 Nikola Topic 1.25 3.00
13 Magic Johnson 1.50 4.00
14 Matas Buzelis 2.00 5.00
15 Kyshawn George .60 1.50
16 Alexandre Sarr 1.25 3.00
17 Allen Iverson 1.00 2.50
18 Ron Holland II .75 2.00
19 Stephen Curry 3.00 8.00
20 Reed Sheppard 1.25 3.00
21 Angel Reese 1.25 3.00
22 Dalton Knecht 1.25 3.00
23 Donovan Clingan 1.00 2.50
24 Caitlin Clark 4.00 10.00
25 Stephon Castle 2.00 5.00

2024-25 Panini Prizm Draft Picks Fearless Prizms Green Pulsar
*GREEN PULSAR: 10X TO 25X BASIC
STATED PRINT RUN 25 SER.#'d SETS
24 Caitlin Clark 200.00 500.00

2024-25 Panini Prizm Draft Picks Fearless Prizms Purple Pulsar
*PURPLE PULSAR: 6X TO 15X BASIC
STATED PRINT RUN 55 SER.#'d SETS
24 Caitlin Clark 125.00 300.00

2024-25 Panini Prizm Draft Picks Fireworks
*HYPER: 1.25X TO 3X BASIC
*SILVER: 1.25X TO 3X BASIC
1 Dalton Knecht 1.25 3.00
2 Cameron Brink 2.00 5.00
3 Ja'Kobe Walter .50 1.25
4 Angel Reese 1.25 3.00
5 Stephen Curry 3.00 8.00
6 Trae Young .75 2.00
7 Jared McCain 1.50 4.00
8 Matas Buzelis 2.00 5.00
9 Ron Holland II .75 2.00
10 Devin Carter .50 1.25
11 Tyler Kolek .60 1.50
12 Alexandre Sarr 1.25 3.00
13 Zaccharie Risacher 1.00 2.50
14 Donovan Clingan 1.00 2.50
15 Caitlin Clark 4.00 10.00
16 Cody Williams .50 1.25
17 Reed Sheppard 1.25 3.00
18 Ja Morant 1.25 3.00
19 Stephon Castle 2.00 5.00
20 Kevin Durant 1.25 3.00

2024-25 Panini Prizm Draft Picks Fireworks Prizms Mojo
*MOJO: 10X TO 25X BASIC
STATED PRINT RUN 25 SER.#'d SETS
15 Caitlin Clark 200.00 500.00

2024-25 Panini Prizm Draft Picks Fireworks Prizms Wave
*WAVE: 4X TO 10X BASIC
STATED PRINT RUN 99 SER.#'d SETS
15 Caitlin Clark 75.00 200.00

2024-25 Panini Prizm Draft Picks High Voltage
1 Stephen Curry 40.00 100.00
2 Cody Williams 6.00 15.00
3 Cameron Brink 25.00 60.00
4 Caitlin Clark 150.00 400.00
5 Nikola Topic 15.00 40.00
6 Devin Carter 6.00 15.00
7 Dalton Knecht 15.00 40.00
8 Alexandre Sarr 15.00 40.00
9 Angel Reese 15.00 40.00
10 Kevin Durant 15.00 40.00
11 Ron Holland II 10.00 25.00
12 Stephon Castle 25.00 60.00
13 Donovan Clingan 12.00 30.00
14 Tidjane Salaun 5.00 12.00
15 Zaccharie Risacher 12.00 30.00

2024-25 Panini Prizm Draft Picks Kaleidoscopic
*HYPER: 1.25X TO 3X BASIC
*SILVER: 1.25X TO 3X BASIC
*WAVE/99: 4X TO 10X BASIC
*MOJO/25: 6X TO 15X BASIC
1 Stephon Castle 3.00 8.00
2 Jared McCain 2.50 6.00
3 Stephen Curry 5.00 12.00
4 Matas Buzelis 3.00 8.00
5 Ja Morant 2.00 5.00
6 Allen Iverson 1.50 4.00
7 Rob Dillingham 1.50 4.00
8 Bronny James Jr. 2.50 6.00
9 Kevin Durant 2.00 5.00
10 Zach Edey 2.00 5.00
11 Alexandre Sarr 2.00 5.00
12 Cameron Brink 3.00 8.00
13 Donovan Clingan 1.50 4.00
14 Trae Young 1.25 3.00
15 Reed Sheppard 2.00 5.00
16 Zaccharie Risacher 1.50 4.00
17 Caitlin Clark 15.00 40.00
18 Cody Williams .75 2.00
19 Dalton Knecht 2.00 5.00
20 Angel Reese 2.00 5.00

2024-25 Panini Prizm Draft Picks Legacy Signatures
*HYPER: .5X TO 1.25X BASIC
*SILVER: .5X TO 1.25X BASIC
*BLUE/35-149: .5X TO 1.25X BASIC
*PURPLE ICE/99: .5X TO 1.25X BASIC
*BLUE ICE/25-75: .5X TO 1.25X BASIC
*ORANGE PULSAR/49: .6X TO 1.5X BASIC
*MOJO/15-25: .75X TO 2X BASIC
1 Magic Johnson 40.00 100.00
2 Kareem Abdul-Jabbar 50.00 120.00
3 David Thompson 6.00 15.00
4 Jalen Suggs 5.00 12.00
5 Luka Garza 4.00 10.00
6 Ty Jerome 5.00 12.00
7 Calvin Murphy 4.00 10.00
8 Christian Laettner 5.00 12.00
11 Jared Butler 4.00 10.00
12 Raymond Felton 3.00 8.00
13 Kyle Anderson 3.00 8.00
14 Cade Cunningham 40.00 100.00
15 Kirk Hinrich 5.00 12.00
16 Dana Barros 5.00 12.00
17 Kenyon Martin 5.00 12.00
18 Larry Johnson 10.00 25.00
19 Harold Miner 4.00 10.00
20 Sam Hauser 4.00 10.00
21 Austin Carr 4.00 10.00
22 Tony Delk 5.00 12.00
23 Bobby Knight 60.00 150.00
24 Paige Bueckers 100.00 250.00
25 Ja Morant 60.00 150.00

2024-25 Panini Prizm Draft Picks Manga
1 Zaccharie Risacher 50.00 125.00
2 Isaiah Collier 40.00 100.00
3 Dalton Knecht 75.00 200.00
4 Donovan Clingan 50.00 125.00
5 Ja Morant 60.00 150.00
6 Stephon Castle 100.00 250.00
7 Cody Williams 25.00 60.00
8 Caitlin Clark 800.00 1,500.00
9 Tim Duncan 75.00 200.00
10 Matas Buzelis 100.00 250.00
11 Reed Sheppard 60.00 150.00
12 Angel Reese 60.00 150.00
13 Nikola Topic 60.00 150.00
14 Stephen Curry 150.00 400.00
15 Bronny James Jr. 80.00 200.00

2024-25 Panini Prizm Draft Picks Net Marvels
1 Zach Edey 30.00 80.00
2 Bub Carrington 25.00 60.00
3 Caitlin Clark 200.00 500.00
4 Stephon Castle 50.00 125.00
5 Alexandre Sarr 30.00 80.00
6 Donovan Clingan 25.00 60.00
7 Zaccharie Risacher 25.00 60.00
8 Cody Williams 12.00 30.00
9 Angel Reese 30.00 80.00
10 Stephen Curry 80.00 200.00
11 Dalton Knecht 30.00 80.00
12 Nikola Topic 30.00 80.00
13 Reed Sheppard 30.00 80.00
14 Matas Buzelis 50.00 120.00
15 Kevin Durant 30.00 80.00

2024-25 Panini Prizm Draft Picks New Recruits
*ICE: 1.25X TO 3X BASIC
*SILVER: 1.25X TO 3X BASIC
1 Kamilla Cardoso .60 1.50
2 Bronny James Jr. 1.50 4.00
3 Ron Holland II .75 2.00
4 Alexandre Sarr 1.25 3.00
5 Cameron Brink 2.00 5.00
6 Stephon Castle 2.00 5.00
7 Tidjane Salaun .40 1.00
8 Jared McCain 1.50 4.00
9 Bub Carrington 1.00 2.50
10 Ja'Kobe Walter .50 1.25
11 Kel'el Ware 1.00 2.50
12 Isaiah Collier .75 2.00
13 Reed Sheppard 1.25 3.00
14 Caitlin Clark 4.00 10.00
15 Donovan Clingan 1.00 2.50
16 Nikola Topic 1.25 3.00
17 Dalton Knecht 1.25 3.00
18 Rob Dillingham 1.00 2.50
19 Devin Carter .50 1.25
20 Tristan da Silva 1.00 2.50
21 Zaccharie Risacher 1.00 2.50
22 Cody Williams 1.00 2.50
23 Matas Buzelis 2.00 5.00
24 Angel Reese 1.25 3.00
25 Zach Edey 1.25 3.00

2024-25 Panini Prizm Draft Picks New Recruits Prizms Green Pulsar
*GREEN PULSAR: 10X TO 25X BASIC
STATED PRINT RUN 25 SER.#'d SETS
14 Caitlin Clark 200.00 500.00

2024-25 Panini Prizm Draft Picks New Recruits Prizms Purple Pulsar
*PURPLE PULSAR: 6X TO 15X BASIC
STATED PRINT RUN 55 SER.#'d SETS
14 Caitlin Clark 125.00 300.00

2024-25 Panini Prizm Draft Picks Penmanship Signatures
*HYPER: .5X TO 1.25X BASIC
*SILVER: .5X TO 1.25X BASIC
*BLUE/149: .5X TO 1.25X BASIC
*PURPLE ICE/99: .5X TO 1.25X BASIC
*BLUE ICE/75: .5X TO 1.25X BASIC
*ORANGE PULSAR/49: .6X TO 1.5X BASIC
*MOJO/25: .75X TO 2X BASIC
1 Elmarko Jackson 5.00 12.00
2 Garwey Dual 4.00 10.00
3 Ariel Hukporti 4.00 10.00
4 Johni Broome 25.00 60.00
5 KJ Evans 4.00 10.00
6 Milos Uzan 4.00 10.00
7 Solo Ball 6.00 15.00
8 Terrance Arceneaux 4.00 10.00
9 Reece Beekman 5.00 12.00
10 Carter Bryant 6.00 15.00
11 Jamari Phillips 5.00 12.00
12 Paige Bueckers 100.00 250.00
13 VJ Edgecombe 20.00 50.00
14 Omaha Biliew 4.00 10.00
15 Aidan Mahaney 3.00 8.00
16 Ben Simmons 5.00 12.00
17 Keisei Tominaga 8.00 20.00
18 Moses Moody 5.00 12.00
19 DJ Burns 6.00 15.00
20 Walker Kessler 4.00 10.00
21 Davion Mitchell 4.00 10.00
22 Jeremy Sochan 5.00 12.00
23 Tristan da Silva 12.00 30.00
24 Devin Carter 6.00 15.00
25 Ja'Kobe Walter 6.00 15.00
26 Terrence Shannon Jr. 10.00 25.00
27 Cam Spencer 5.00 12.00
28 Bobi Klintman 6.00 15.00
29 Pelle Larsson 5.00 12.00
30 Kyshawn George 8.00 20.00
31 Harrison Ingram 5.00 12.00
32 Payton Sandfort 4.00 10.00
33 DaRon Holmes II 6.00 15.00
34 PJ Hall 4.00 10.00
35 Baylor Scheierman 6.00 15.00
36 Ugonna Onyenso 4.00 10.00
37 Judah Mintz 4.00 10.00
38 Trey Alexander 4.00 10.00
39 Trevon Brazile 5.00 12.00
40 Johnny Furphy 8.00 20.00
41 AJ Johnson 8.00 20.00
42 Tyran Stokes 12.00 30.00
43 Alijah Arenas 12.00 30.00
44 Zoom Diallo 8.00 20.00
45 Tahaad Pettiford 8.00 20.00
46 Mercy Miller 6.00 15.00
47 Ian Jackson 6.00 15.00
48 Keshad Johnson 4.00 10.00
49 Matas Buzelis 25.00 60.00
50 Donovan Clingan 12.00 30.00

2024-25 Panini Prizm Draft Picks Prizm Break
*HYPER: 1.25X TO 3X BASIC
*SILVER: 1.25X TO 3X BASIC
1 Chris Paul .60 1.50
2 Ja'Kobe Walter .50 1.25
3 Rob Dillingham 1.00 2.50
4 Ron Holland II .75 2.00
5 Alexandre Sarr 1.25 3.00
6 Zaccharie Risacher 1.00 2.50
7 Kyle Filipowski 1.00 2.50
8 Donovan Clingan 1.00 2.50
9 Dalton Knecht 1.25 3.00
10 Ja Morant 1.25 3.00
11 Magic Johnson 1.50 4.00
12 Jared McCain 1.50 4.00
13 Caitlin Clark 4.00 10.00
14 Angel Reese 1.25 3.00
15 Stephon Castle 2.00 5.00
16 Cody Williams .50 1.25
17 Stephen Curry 3.00 8.00
18 Matas Buzelis 2.00 5.00
19 Trae Young .75 2.00
20 Bronny James Jr. 1.50 4.00

2024-25 Panini Prizm Draft Picks Prizm Break Prizms Mojo
*MOJO: 10X TO 25X BASIC
STATED PRINT RUN 25 SER.#'d SETS
13 Caitlin Clark 200.00 500.00

2024-25 Panini Prizm Draft Picks Prizm Break Prizms Wave
*WAVE: 4X TO 10X BASIC
STATED PRINT RUN 99 SER.#'d SETS
13 Caitlin Clark 75.00 200.00

2024-25 Panini Prizm Draft Picks Rated Prospect Prizms Blue
*BLUE: 2.5X TO 6X BASIC
STATED PRINT RUN 199 SER.#'d SETS
2 Paige Bueckers 50.00 120.00

2024-25 Panini Prizm Draft Picks Rated Prospect Prizms Blue Ice
*BLUE ICE: 3X TO 8X BASIC
STATED PRINT RUN 99 SER.#'d SETS
2 Paige Bueckers 60.00 150.00

2024-25 Panini Prizm Draft Picks Rated Prospect Prizms Blue Pulsar
*BLUE PULSAR: 3X TO 8X BASIC
STATED PRINT RUN 99 SER.#'d SETS
2 Paige Bueckers 60.00 150.00

2024-25 Panini Prizm Draft Picks Rated Prospect Prizms Blue Seismic
*BLUE SEISMIC: 2.5X TO 6X BASIC
STATED PRINT RUN 149 SER.#'d SETS
2 Paige Bueckers 50.00 120.00

2024-25 Panini Prizm Draft Picks Rated Prospect Prizms Blue Shimmer FOTL
*BLUE SHMR FOTL: 6X TO 15X BASIC
STATED PRINT RUN 19 SER.#'d SETS
2 Paige Bueckers 100.00 250.00

2024-25 Panini Prizm Draft Picks Rated Prospect Prizms Blue Wave
*BLUE WAVE: 2X TO 5X BASIC
STATED PRINT RUN 249 SER.#'d SETS
2 Paige Bueckers 40.00 100.00

2024-25 Panini Prizm Draft Picks Rated Prospect Prizms Green Pulsar
*GREEN PULSAR: 6X TO 15X BASIC
STATED PRINT RUN 25 SER.#'d SETS
2 Paige Bueckers 100.00 250.00

2024-25 Panini Prizm Draft Picks Rated Prospect Prizms Mojo
*MOJO: 6X TO 15X BASIC
STATED PRINT RUN 25 SER.#'d SETS
2 Paige Bueckers 100.00 250.00

2024-25 Panini Prizm Draft Picks Rated Prospect Prizms Orange Pulsar
*ORANGE PULSAR: 4X TO 10X BASIC
STATED PRINT RUN 49 SER.#'d SETS
2 Paige Bueckers 75.00 200.00

2024-25 Panini Prizm Draft Picks Rated Prospect Prizms Purple
*PURPLE: 3X TO 8X BASIC
STATED PRINT RUN 75 SER.#'d SETS
2 Paige Bueckers 60.00 150.00

2024-25 Panini Prizm Draft Picks Rated Prospect Prizms Purple Ice
*PURPLE ICE: 2.5X TO 6X BASIC
STATED PRINT RUN 149 SER.#'d SETS
2 Paige Bueckers 50.00 120.00

2024-25 Panini Prizm Draft Picks Rated Prospect Prizms Purple Pulsar
*PURPLE PULSAR: 4X TO 10X BASIC
STATED PRINT RUN 55 SER.#'d SETS
2 Paige Bueckers 75.00 200.00

2024-25 Panini Prizm Draft Picks Rated Prospect Prizms Red Pulsar
*RED PULSAR: 2X TO 5X BASIC
STATED PRINT RUN 299 SER.#'d SETS
2 Paige Bueckers 40.00 100.00

2024-25 Panini Prizm Draft Picks Rated Prospect Prizms Red Scope
*RED SCOPE: 3X TO 8X BASIC
STATED PRINT RUN 88 SER.#'d SETS
2 Paige Bueckers 60.00 150.00

2024-25 Panini Prizm Draft Picks Rated Prospect Prizms Red Seismic
*RED SEISMIC: 2.5X TO 6X BASIC
STATED PRINT RUN 225 SER.#'d SETS
2 Paige Bueckers 50.00 120.00

2024-25 Panini Prizm Draft Picks Sensational Signatures
*HYPER: .5X TO 1.25X BASIC
*SILVER: .5X TO 1.25X BASIC
*BLUE/99-149: .5X TO 1.25X BASIC
*PURPLE ICE/99: .5X TO 1.25X BASIC
*BLUE ICE/75: .5X TO 1.25X BASIC
*ORANGE PULSAR/49: .6X TO 1.5X BASIC
*MOJO/25: .75X TO 2X BASIC
1 KJ Evans 4.00 10.00
2 Matas Buzelis 25.00 60.00
3 Ajay Mitchell 8.00 20.00
4 Armando Bacot 4.00 10.00
5 Bub Carrington 12.00 30.00
6 Donovan Clingan 12.00 30.00
7 Mark Mitchell 4.00 10.00
8 Solo Ball 5.00 12.00
9 Ugonna Onyenso 4.00 10.00
10 Jerry Easter II 4.00 10.00
11 Tre Johnson 20.00 50.00
12 Elliot Cadeau 5.00 12.00
13 Caitlin Clark 500.00 1,000.00
14 Hunter Dickinson 5.00 12.00
15 Tyran Stokes 12.00 30.00
16 Dink Pate 6.00 15.00
17 Mercy Miller 6.00 15.00
18 Garwey Dual 4.00 10.00
19 Tahaad Pettiford 8.00 20.00
20 Zoom Diallo 8.00 20.00
21 Gabe Cupps 4.00 10.00
22 Alijah Arenas 12.00 30.00
23 Mac McClung 8.00 20.00
24 Jack Gohlke 4.00 10.00
25 Keegan Murray 4.00 10.00
26 Ian Jackson 6.00 15.00
27 Johnny Davis 4.00 10.00
28 Paolo Banchero 40.00 100.00
29 Christian Braun 6.00 15.00
30 Reed Sheppard 15.00 40.00
31 Dalton Knecht 15.00 40.00
32 Tidjane Salaun 5.00 12.00
33 KJ Simpson Jr. 5.00 12.00
34 Oso Ighodaro 6.00 15.00
35 Antonio Reeves 5.00 12.00
36 Adem Bona 6.00 15.00
37 Tyler Kolek 8.00 20.00
38 Yves Missi 12.00 30.00
39 Johni Broome 25.00 60.00
41 Elmarko Jackson 5.00 12.00
42 DJ Burns 5.00 12.00
43 Breanna Stewart 20.00 50.00
46 Elena Delle Donne 10.00 25.00
47 Cason Wallace 6.00 15.00
49 Jalen Bridges 4.00 10.00
50 Trey Jemison 4.00 10.00

2024-25 Panini Prizm Draft Picks Signatures
*RED SCOPE/88: .5X TO 1.25X BASIC
*GREEN PULSAR/25: .75X TO 2X BASIC
1 Luka Garza 4.00 10.00
2 David Duke Jr. 3.00 8.00
3 Justin Champagnie 5.00 12.00
4 Jason Preston 3.00 8.00
5 Johnny Juzang 4.00 10.00
6 Charles Bassey 4.00 10.00
7 Jose Alvarado 4.00 10.00
8 Malaki Branham 4.00 10.00
9 RJ Nembhard 3.00 8.00
10 Collin Gillespie 4.00 10.00
11 Ziaire Williams 4.00 10.00
12 Blake Wesley 3.00 8.00
13 Jericho Sims 4.00 10.00
14 Garwey Dual 4.00 10.00
15 AJ Lawson 3.00 8.00
16 Harold Miner 4.00 10.00
17 Tyrese Martin 4.00 10.00
18 Jared Butler 4.00 10.00
19 Jay Huff 4.00 10.00
20 Jake LaRavia 4.00 10.00
21 Trendon Watford 4.00 10.00
22 Desmond Cambridge Jr. 3.00 8.00
23 Zach Edey 15.00 40.00
24 Jared McCain 20.00 50.00
25 Tre Johnson 10.00 25.00
26 David Roddy 4.00 10.00
27 Nerlens Noel 3.00 8.00
28 Adam Flagler 5.00 12.00
29 Bobi Klintman 6.00 15.00
30 Baylor Scheierman 6.00 15.00
31 Kevin McCullar Jr. 5.00 12.00
32 Alijah Arenas 12.00 30.00
33 Elliot Cadeau 5.00 12.00
34 Jerry Easter II 4.00 10.00
35 Carter Bryant 6.00 15.00
36 Dink Pate 6.00 15.00
37 Jamari Phillips 5.00 12.00
38 Paige Bueckers 100.00 250.00
39 Mercy Miller 6.00 15.00
40 Reece Beekman 5.00 12.00
41 Tahaad Pettiford 8.00 20.00
42 VJ Edgecombe 20.00 50.00
44 Ian Jackson 6.00 15.00
45 Tyran Stokes 12.00 30.00
46 Wendell Moore Jr. 4.00 10.00
47 Tidjane Salaun 5.00 12.00
48 AJ Johnson 10.00 25.00
49 Greg Brown III 3.00 8.00
50 Buddy Boeheim 4.00 10.00

2024-25 Panini Prizm Draft Picks Signing Day Signatures
*RED SCOPE/88: .5X TO 1.25X BASIC
*GREEN PULSAR/25: .75X TO 2X BASIC
1 Mark Mitchell 4.00 10.00
2 Garwey Dual 4.00 10.00
3 Armando Bacot 4.00 10.00
4 Enrique Freeman 4.00 10.00
5 Jalen Bridges 4.00 10.00
6 Keshad Johnson 4.00 10.00
7 Tristen Newton 5.00 12.00
8 Ugonna Onyenso 4.00 10.00
9 Milos Uzan 6.00 15.00
10 Terrance Arceneaux 4.00 10.00
11 Solo Ball 5.00 12.00
12 Donovan Clingan 12.00 30.00
13 Ja'Kobe Walter 6.00 15.00
14 Matas Buzelis 25.00 60.00
15 Dalton Knecht 15.00 40.00
16 Caitlin Clark 500.00 1,000.00
17 Trey Alexander 4.00 10.00
18 Reed Sheppard 15.00 40.00
19 Devin Carter 6.00 15.00
20 Tristan da Silva 12.00 30.00
21 Aidan Mahaney 3.00 8.00
22 Hunter Dickinson 5.00 12.00
23 Reece Beekman 5.00 12.00
24 Cam Spencer 5.00 12.00
25 Tyler Kolek 8.00 20.00
27 Anton Watson 4.00 10.00
28 KJ Evans 4.00 10.00
29 Judah Mintz 4.00 10.00
30 Omaha Biliew 4.00 10.00
31 Dillon Jones 5.00 12.00
32 Kyshawn George 8.00 20.00
33 Johnny Furphy 8.00 20.00
34 Jonathan Mogbo 8.00 20.00
35 Jamal Shead 6.00 15.00
36 KJ Simpson Jr. 5.00 12.00
37 Oso Ighodaro 6.00 15.00
38 Pelle Larsson 5.00 12.00
39 Terrence Shannon Jr. 10.00 25.00
40 Quinten Post 6.00 15.00
41 Bub Carrington 12.00 30.00
42 PJ Hall 4.00 10.00
43 Adem Bona 6.00 15.00
44 Ajay Mitchell 8.00 20.00
45 DaRon Holmes II 6.00 15.00
46 Harrison Ingram 5.00 12.00
49 Trevon Brazile 5.00 12.00
50 Yves Missi 12.00 30.00

2024-25 Panini Prizm Draft Picks Stained Glass
1 Caitlin Clark 200.00 500.00
2 Stephen Curry 80.00 200.00
3 Reed Sheppard 30.00 80.00
4 Dalton Knecht 30.00 80.00
5 Ja'Kobe Walter 12.00 30.00
6 Trae Young 20.00 50.00
7 Bronny James Jr. 40.00 100.00
8 Cody Williams 12.00 30.00
9 Zaccharie Risacher 25.00 60.00
10 Alexandre Sarr 30.00 80.00
11 Stephon Castle 50.00 125.00
12 Kamilla Cardoso 15.00 40.00
13 Angel Reese 30.00 80.00
14 Matas Buzelis 50.00 120.00
15 Donovan Clingan 25.00 60.00

2024-25 Panini Prizm Draft Picks Student Orientation
*ICE: 1.25X TO 3X BASIC
*SILVER: 1.25X TO 3X BASIC
1 Ron Holland II .75 2.00
2 Kyle Filipowski 1.00 2.50
3 Cameron Brink 2.00 5.00
4 Kamilla Cardoso .60 1.50
5 Rob Dillingham 1.00 2.50
6 Tidjane Salaun .40 1.00
7 Dalton Knecht 1.25 3.00
8 Devin Carter .50 1.25
9 Matas Buzelis 2.00 5.00
10 Donovan Clingan 1.00 2.50
11 Tyler Kolek .60 1.50
12 Bronny James Jr. 1.50 4.00
13 Stephon Castle 2.00 5.00
14 Isaiah Collier .75 2.00
15 Zach Edey 1.25 3.00
16 Zaccharie Risacher 1.00 2.50
17 Alexandre Sarr 1.25 3.00
18 Angel Reese 1.25 3.00
19 Reed Sheppard 1.25 3.00
20 Jared McCain 1.50 4.00
21 Ja'Kobe Walter .50 1.25
22 Caitlin Clark 4.00 10.00
23 Cody Williams .50 1.25
24 Johnny Furphy .60 1.50
25 Yves Missi 1.00 2.50

2024-25 Panini Prizm Draft Picks Student Orientation Prizms Green Pulsar
*GREEN PULSAR: 10X TO 25X BASIC
STATED PRINT RUN 25 SER.#'d SETS
22 Caitlin Clark 200.00 500.00

2024-25 Panini Prizm Draft Picks Student Orientation Prizms Purple Pulsar
*PURPLE PULSAR: 6X TO 15X BASIC
STATED PRINT RUN 55 SER.#'d SETS
22 Caitlin Clark 125.00 300.00

2024-25 Panini Prizm Draft Picks Variation
*GREEN: 1.25X TO 3X BASIC
*HYPER: 1.25X TO 3X BASIC
*PURPLE WAVE: 1.25X TO 3X BASIC
*RED ICE: 1.25X TO 3X BASIC
*SILVER: 1.25X TO 3X BASIC
*GREEN WAVE: 1.5X TO 4X BASIC
*ORANGE ICE: 1.5X TO 4X BASIC
*RED WAVE: 1.5X TO 4X BASIC

2024-25 Panini Prizm Draft Picks Variation Prizms Blue
*BLUE: 2.5X TO 6X BASIC
STATED PRINT RUN 199 SER.#'d SETS
57 Caitlin Clark 40.00 100.00

2024-25 Panini Prizm Draft Picks Variation Prizms Blue Ice
*BLUE ICE: 3X TO 8X BASIC
STATED PRINT RUN 99 SER.#'d SETS
57 Caitlin Clark 75.00 200.00

2024-25 Panini Prizm Draft Picks Variation Prizms Blue Pulsar
*BLUE PULSAR: 3X TO 8X BASIC
STATED PRINT RUN 99 SER.#'d SETS
57 Caitlin Clark 75.00 200.00

2024-25 Panini Prizm Draft Picks Variation Prizms Blue Seismic
*BLUE SEISMIC: 2.5X TO 6X BASIC
STATED PRINT RUN 149 SER.#'d SETS
57 Caitlin Clark 60.00 150.00

2024-25 Panini Prizm Draft Picks Variation Prizms Blue Shimmer FOTL
*BLUE SHMR FOTL: 6X TO 15X BASIC
STATED PRINT RUN 19 SER.#'d SETS
57 Caitlin Clark 200.00 500.00

2024-25 Panini Prizm Draft Picks Variation Prizms Blue Wave
*BLUE WAVE: 2X TO 5X BASIC
STATED PRINT RUN 249 SER.#'d SETS
57 Caitlin Clark 30.00 80.00

2024-25 Panini Prizm Draft Picks Variation Prizms Green Pulsar
*GREEN PULSAR: 6X TO 15X BASIC
STATED PRINT RUN 25 SER.#'d SETS
57 Caitlin Clark 200.00 500.00

2024-25 Panini Prizm Draft Picks Variation Prizms Mojo
*MOJO: 6X TO 15X BASIC
STATED PRINT RUN 25 SER.#'d SETS
57 Caitlin Clark 200.00 500.00

2024-25 Panini Prizm Draft Picks Variation Prizms Orange Pulsar
*ORANGE PULSAR: 4X TO 10X BASIC
STATED PRINT RUN 49 SER.#'d SETS
57 Caitlin Clark 100.00 250.00

2024-25 Panini Prizm Draft Picks Variation Prizms Purple
*PURPLE: 3X TO 8X BASIC
STATED PRINT RUN 75 SER.#'d SETS
57 Caitlin Clark 75.00 200.00

2024-25 Panini Prizm Draft Picks Variation Prizms Purple Ice
*PURPLE ICE: 2.5X TO 6X BASIC
STATED PRINT RUN 149 SER.#'d SETS
57 Caitlin Clark 60.00 150.00

2024-25 Panini Prizm Draft Picks Variation Prizms Purple Pulsar
*PURPLE PULSAR: 4X TO 10X BASIC
STATED PRINT RUN 55 SER.#'d SETS
57 Caitlin Clark 100.00 250.00

2024-25 Panini Prizm Draft Picks Variation Prizms Red Pulsar
*RED PULSAR: 2X TO 5X BASIC
STATED PRINT RUN 299 SER.#'d SETS
57 Caitlin Clark 30.00 80.00

2024-25 Panini Prizm Draft Picks Variation Prizms Red Scope
*RED SCOPE: 3X TO 8X BASIC
STATED PRINT RUN 88 SER.#'d SETS
57 Caitlin Clark 75.00 200.00

2024-25 Panini Prizm Draft Picks Variation Prizms Red Seismic
*RED SEISMIC: 2.5X TO 6X BASIC
STATED PRINT RUN 225 SER.#'d SETS
57 Caitlin Clark 40.00 100.00

2024-25 Panini Prizm Draft Picks Widescreen
*HYPER: 1.25X TO 3X BASIC
*SILVER: 1.25X TO 3X BASIC
1 Donovan Clingan 1.00 2.50
2 Kamilla Cardoso .60 1.50
3 Nikola Topic 1.25 3.00
4 Alexandre Sarr 1.25 3.00
5 Magic Johnson 1.50 4.00
6 Caitlin Clark 4.00 10.00
7 Zach Edey 1.25 3.00
8 Stephon Castle 2.00 5.00
9 Jalen Brunson .75 2.00
10 Cody Williams .50 1.25
11 Trae Young .75 2.00

12 Ja'Kobe Walter .50 1.25
13 Angel Reese 1.25 3.00
14 Dalton Knecht 1.25 3.00
15 Patrick Ewing .60 1.50
16 Tidjane Salaun .40 1.00
17 Zaccharie Risacher 1.00 2.50
18 Yves Missi 1.00 2.50
19 Matas Buzelis 2.00 5.00
20 Stephon Curry 3.00 8.00

2024-25 Panini Prizm Draft Picks Widescreen Prizms Mojo
*MOJO: 10X TO 25X BASIC
STATED PRINT RUN 25 SER.#'d SETS
6 Caitlin Clark 200.00 500.00

2024-25 Panini Prizm Draft Picks Widescreen Prizms Wave
*WAVE: 4X TO 10X BASIC
STATED PRINT RUN 99 SER.#'d SETS
6 Caitlin Clark 75.00 200.00

2023-24 Panini Prizm Monopoly
*PURPLE: .6X TO 1.5X BASIC
1 Nikola Jokic 2.00 5.00
2 Aaron Gordon .40 1.00
3 Jamal Murray .75 2.00
4 Trae Young .75 2.00
5 Dejounte Murray .50 1.25
6 Kobe Bufkin RC 1.00 2.50
7 Jayson Tatum 1.50 4.00
8 Jaylen Brown .75 2.00
9 Robert Williams III .40 1.00
10 Mikal Bridges .50 1.25
11 Spencer Dinwiddie .30 .75
12 Noah Clowney RC 1.00 2.50
13 LaMelo Ball 1.00 2.50
14 Nick Smith Jr. RC 1.00 2.50
15 Brandon Miller RC 3.00 8.00
16 DeMar DeRozan .60 1.50
17 Zach Lavine .60 1.50
18 Nikola Vucevic .40 1.00
19 Donovan Mitchell .75 2.00
20 Evan Mobley .60 1.50
21 Darius Garland .60 1.50
22 Luka Doncic 2.50 6.00
23 Kyrie Irving .75 2.00
24 Dereck Lively II RC 1.50 4.00
25 Cade Cunningham 1.00 2.50
26 Jaden Ivey .50 1.25
27 Ausar Thompson RC 2.00 5.00
28 Stephen Curry 3.00 8.00
29 Klay Thompson 1.00 2.50
30 Jonathan Kuminga 1.00 2.50
31 Cam Whitmore RC 2.00 5.00
32 Jabari Smith Jr. .60 1.50
33 Amen Thompson RC 4.00 10.00
34 Tyrese Haliburton .75 2.00
35 Bennedict Mathurin .60 1.50
36 Jarace Walker RC 1.50 4.00
37 Kawhi Leonard 1.00 2.50
38 Russell Westbrook .60 1.50
39 Paul George .60 1.50
40 LeBron James 3.00 8.00
41 Anthony Davis 1.00 2.50
42 Austin Reaves 1.00 2.50
43 Jaren Jackson Jr. .60 1.50
44 Ja Morant 1.25 3.00
45 Desmond Bane .50 1.25
46 Jimmy Butler .60 1.50
47 Bam Adebayo .60 1.50
48 Jaime Jaquez Jr. RC 1.25 3.00
49 Giannis Antetokounmpo 2.00 5.00
50 Khris Middleton .40 1.00
51 Jrue Holiday .50 1.25
52 Anthony Edwards 2.00 5.00
53 Karl-Anthony Towns .60 1.50
54 Rudy Gobert .50 1.25
55 Zion Williamson 1.00 2.50
56 Jordan Hawkins RC 1.25 3.00
57 Brandon Ingram .50 1.25
58 Julius Randle .50 1.25
59 Jalen Brunson .75 2.00
60 Immanuel Quickley .40 1.00
61 Shai Gilgeous-Alexander 2.00 5.00
62 Chet Holmgren 1.00 2.50
63 Cason Wallace RC 1.50 4.00
64 Paolo Banchero 1.00 2.50
65 Jett Howard RC 1.00 2.50
66 Anthony Black RC 1.50 4.00
67 James Harden .75 2.00
68 Tyrese Maxey .75 2.00
69 Joel Embiid 1.00 2.50
70 Kevin Durant 1.25 3.00
71 Bradley Beal .50 1.25
72 Devin Booker 1.00 2.50
73 Damian Lillard 1.00 2.50
74 Anfernee Simons .50 1.25
75 Scoot Henderson RC 2.50 6.00
76 De'Aaron Fox .75 2.00
77 Domantas Sabonis .60 1.50
78 Keegan Murray .50 1.25
79 Keldon Johnson .50 1.25
80 Devin Vassell .50 1.25
81 Victor Wembanyama RC 6.00 15.00
82 Pascal Siakam .60 1.50
83 OG Anunoby .50 1.25
84 Gradey Dick RC 1.50 4.00
85 Lauri Markkanen .60 1.50
86 Taylor Hendricks RC .75 2.00
87 Keyonte George RC 2.50 6.00
88 Jordan Poole .60 1.50
89 Kyle Kuzma .50 1.25
90 Bilal Coulibaly RC 2.00 5.00

2023-24 Panini Prizm Monopoly Brown
*BROWN: 2X TO 5X BASIC
STATED PRINT RUN 249 SER.#'d SETS
81 Victor Wembanyama 100.00 250.00

2023-24 Panini Prizm Monopoly Deal
*DEAL: 4X TO 10X BASIC
81 Victor Wembanyama 200.00 500.00

2023-24 Panini Prizm Monopoly Dice
*DICE: 3X TO 8X BASIC
81 Victor Wembanyama 150.00 400.00

2023-24 Panini Prizm Monopoly Free Parking
*FREE PARKING: 1.5X TO 4X BASIC
81 Victor Wembanyama 75.00 200.00

2023-24 Panini Prizm Monopoly Go
*GO: 4X TO 10X BASIC
15 Brandon Miller 60.00 150.00
81 Victor Wembanyama 200.00 500.00

2023-24 Panini Prizm Monopoly Gold
*GOLD: 6X TO 15X BASIC
STATED PRINT RUN 49 SER.#'d SETS
81 Victor Wembanyama 400.00 800.00

2023-24 Panini Prizm Monopoly Gold Millionaire Shimmer
*GOLD MILLIONAIRE SHIMMER: 4X TO 10X BASIC
STATED PRINT RUN 500 SER.#'d SETS
81 Victor Wembanyama 200.00 500.00

2023-24 Panini Prizm Monopoly Green
*GREEN: 8X TO 20X BASIC
STATED PRINT RUN 24 SER.#'d SETS
81 Victor Wembanyama 500.00 1,000.00

2023-24 Panini Prizm Monopoly Green Millionaire Shimmer
*GREEN MILLIONAIRE SHMR: 10X TO 25X BASIC
STATED PRINT RUN 20 SER.#'d SETS
81 Victor Wembanyama 600.00 1,200.00

2023-24 Panini Prizm Monopoly Light Blue
*LIGHT BLUE: 2.5X TO 6X BASIC
STATED PRINT RUN 199 SER.#'d SETS
81 Victor Wembanyama 125.00 300.00

2023-24 Panini Prizm Monopoly Monopoly Man Black and White
*MONOPOLY MAN B & W: 2X TO 5X BASIC
81 Victor Wembanyama 200.00 500.00

2023-24 Panini Prizm Monopoly Monopoly Red
*MONOPOLY RED: 2X TO 5X BASIC
81 Victor Wembanyama 75.00 200.00

2023-24 Panini Prizm Monopoly Orange
*ORANGE: 2.5X TO 6X BASIC
STATED PRINT RUN 124 SER.#'d SETS
81 Victor Wembanyama 150.00 400.00

2023-24 Panini Prizm Monopoly Pink
*PINK: 2.5X TO 6X BASIC
STATED PRINT RUN 149 SER.#'d SETS
81 Victor Wembanyama 150.00 400.00

2023-24 Panini Prizm Monopoly Purple Millionaire Shimmer
*PURPLE MILLIONAIRE SHIMMER: 5X TO 12X BASIC
STATED PRINT RUN 50 SER.#'d SETS
81 Victor Wembanyama 300.00 600.00

2023-24 Panini Prizm Monopoly Question Mark
*QUESTION MARK: 8X TO 20X BASIC
STATED PRINT RUN 25 SER.#'d SETS
81 Victor Wembanyama 500.00 1,000.00

2023-24 Panini Prizm Monopoly Red
*RED: 4X TO 10X BASIC
STATED PRINT RUN 99 SER.#'d SETS
81 Victor Wembanyama 200.00 500.00

2023-24 Panini Prizm Monopoly Red Millionaire Shimmer
*RED MILLIONAIRE SHIMMER: 4X TO 10X BASIC
STATED PRINT RUN 100 SER.#'d SETS
81 Victor Wembanyama 150.00 400.00

2023-24 Panini Prizm Monopoly Silver
*SILVER: 1X TO 2.5X BASIC
81 Victor Wembanyama 20.00 50.00

2023-24 Panini Prizm Monopoly Tiger Stripe Boadwalk Blue
*TIGER STRP BRDWLK BLUE: 10X TO 25X BASIC
81 Victor Wembanyama 600.00 1,200.00

2024-25 Panini Prizm Monopoly
*RED: .6X TO 1.5X BASIC
*SILVER: .75X TO 2X BASIC
*FREE PARKING: 1.25X TO 3X BASIC
*MILLIONAIRE CLUB/1499: 1.5X TO 4X BASIC
*GO: 2X TO 5X BASIC
*MONOPOLY MAN B & W: 2X TO 5X BASIC
*BROWN/299: 2X TO 5X BASIC
*LIGHT BLUE/249: 2X TO 5X BASIC
*DICE: 2.5X TO 6X BASIC
*PINK/199: 2.5X TO 6X BASIC
*ORANGE/149: 2.5X TO 6X BASIC
*QUESTION MARK: 3X TO 8X BASIC
*GOLD MILLIONAIRE SHMR/500: 4X TO 10X BASIC
*RED MILLIONAIRE SHMR/100: 4X TO 10X BASIC
*PURPLE/91: 4X TO 10X BASIC
*PRPL MILLIONAIRE SHMR/50: 6X TO 15X BASIC
*GOLD/49: 6X TO 15X BASIC
*GREEN/35: 6X TO 15X BASIC
*DEAL/25: 8X TO 20X BASIC
*GREEN MILLIONAIRE SHMR/20: 8X TO 20X BASIC
*TIGER STRIPE BOARDWALK BLUE: 10X TO 25X BASIC
1 Joel Embiid .60 1.50
2 Tyrese Maxey .75 2.00
3 Jared McCain RC 3.00 8.00
4 Deandre Ayton .30 .75
5 Scoot Henderson .50 1.25
6 Donovan Clingan RC 2.00 5.00
7 Giannis Antetokounmpo 1.50 4.00
8 Damian Lillard 1.00 2.50
9 Khris Middleton .40 1.00
10 Zach Lavine .60 1.50
11 Coby White .40 1.00
12 Matas Buzelis RC 4.00 10.00
13 Donovan Mitchell .75 2.00
14 Darius Garland .50 1.25
15 Jaylon Tyson RC .75 2.00
16 Jayson Tatum 1.25 3.00
17 Jaylen Brown .60 1.50
18 Kristaps Porzingis .50 1.25
19 Kawhi Leonard .75 2.00
20 James Harden .75 2.00
21 Ivica Zubac .40 1.00
22 Ja Morant 1.25 3.00
23 Jaren Jackson Jr. .60 1.50
24 Zach Edey RC 2.50 6.00
25 Trae Young .75 2.00
26 Jalen Johnson .50 1.25
27 Zaccharie Risacher RC 2.50 6.00
28 Jimmy Butler III .60 1.50
29 Bam Adebayo .50 1.25
30 Kel'el Ware RC 2.00 5.00
31 LaMelo Ball .75 2.00
32 Brandon Miller .60 1.50
33 Tidjane Salaun RC .75 2.00
34 Lauri Markkanen .40 1.00
35 Cody Williams RC 1.00 2.50
36 Isaiah Collier RC 1.50 4.00
37 De'Aaron Fox .75 2.00
38 DeMar DeRozan .50 1.25
39 Devin Carter RC 1.00 2.50
40 Jalen Brunson .75 2.00
41 Julius Randle .40 1.00
42 Mikal Bridges .40 1.00
43 LeBron James 3.00 8.00
44 Anthony Davis 1.00 2.50
45 Bronny James Jr. RC 2.50 6.00
46 Paolo Banchero 1.00 2.50
47 Franz Wagner .60 1.50
48 Tristan da Silva RC 2.00 5.00
49 Luka Doncic 2.50 6.00
50 Kyrie Irving 1.00 2.50
51 Klay Thompson 1.00 2.50
52 Cameron Thomas .40 1.00
53 Cameron Johnson .30 .75
54 Nicolas Claxton .30 .75
55 Nikola Jokic 2.00 5.00
56 Michael Porter Jr. .40 1.00
57 Jamal Murray .60 1.50
58 Tyrese Haliburton .75 2.00
59 Pascal Siakam .50 1.25
60 Johnny Furphy RC 1.25 3.00
61 Zion Williamson .60 1.50
62 Brandon Ingram .40 1.00
63 Dejounte Murray .40 1.00
64 Cade Cunningham 1.00 2.50
65 Jaden Ivey .50 1.25
66 Ron Holland II RC 1.50 4.00
67 Scottie Barnes .50 1.25
68 RJ Barrett .50 1.25
69 Ja'Kobe Walter RC 1.00 2.50
70 Alperen Sengun .60 1.50
71 Jalen Green .75 2.00
72 Reed Sheppard RC 2.50 6.00
73 Victor Wembanyama 3.00 8.00
74 Devin Vassell .50 1.25
75 Stephon Castle RC 5.00 12.00
76 Kevin Durant 1.25 3.00
77 Devin Booker 1.00 2.50
78 Bradley Beal .50 1.25
79 Shai Gilgeous-Alexander 2.00 5.00
80 Chet Holmgren .60 1.50
81 Jalen Williams .75 2.00
82 Draymond Green .50 1.25
83 Stephen Curry 3.00 8.00
84 Jonathan Kuminga .50 1.25
85 Jordan Poole .40 1.00
86 Alexandre Sarr RC 2.50 6.00
87 Bub Carrington RC 2.00 5.00
88 Anthony Edwards 2.00 5.00
89 Karl-Anthony Towns .60 1.50
90 Rob Dillingham RC 2.00 5.00

2024-25 Panini Prizm Monopoly Free Parking
*FREE PARKING: 1.5X TO 4X BASIC
0 Luka Doncic 75.00 200.00

2024-25 Panini Prizm Monopoly Legends
*RED: .6X TO 1.5X BASIC
*SILVER: .75X TO 2X BASIC
*FREE PARKING: 1.25X TO 3X BASIC
*MILLIONAIRE CLUB/1499: 1.5X TO 4X BASIC
*GO: 2X TO 5X BASIC
*MONOPOLY MAN B & W: 2X TO 5X BASIC
*BROWN/299: 2X TO 5X BASIC
*LIGHT BLUE/249: 2X TO 5X BASIC
*DICE: 2.5X TO 6X BASIC
*PINK/199: 2.5X TO 6X BASIC
*ORANGE/149: 2.5X TO 6X BASIC
*QUESTION MARK: 3X TO 8X BASIC
*GOLD MILLIONAIRE SHMR/500: 4X TO 10X BASIC
*RED MILLIONAIRE SHMR/100: 4X TO 10X BASIC
*PURPLE/91: 4X TO 10X BASIC
*PRPL MILLIONAIRE SHMR/50: 6X TO 15X BASIC
*GOLD/49: 6X TO 15X BASIC
*GREEN/35: 6X TO 15X BASIC
*DEAL/25: 8X TO 20X BASIC
*GREEN MILLIONAIRE SHMR/20: 8X TO 20X BASIC
*TIGER STRIPE BOARDWALK BLUE: 10X TO 25X BASIC
LEG1 Allen Iverson 1.00 2.50
LEG2 Shaquille O'Neal 1.00 2.50
LEG3 Larry Bird 1.25 3.00
LEG4 Magic Johnson 1.25 3.00
LEG5 Tim Duncan 1.00 2.50
LEG6 Charles Barkley 1.00 2.50
LEG7 Dennis Rodman 1.00 2.50
LEG8 Patrick Ewing .60 1.50
LEG9 Yao Ming .75 2.00
LEG10 Dwyane Wade .75 2.00

2024-25 Panini Prizm Monopoly Black Money Blast
BMB1 Giannis Antetokounmpo 200.00 500.00
BMB2 Jayson Tatum 200.00 500.00
BMB3 LeBron James 500.00 1,000.00
BMB4 Luka Doncic 300.00 600.00
BMB5 Nikola Jokic 300.00 600.00
BMB6 Victor Wembanyama 500.00 1,000.00
BMB7 Shai Gilgeous-Alexander 300.00 600.00
BMB8 Stephen Curry 500.00 1,000.00
BMB9 Anthony Edwards 300.00 600.00
BMB10 Reed Sheppard 200.00 500.00
BMB11 Zach Edey 150.00 300.00
BMB12 Matas Buzelis 300.00 600.00
BMB13 Donovan Clingan 100.00 250.00
BMB14 Zaccharie Risacher 200.00 500.00
BMB15 Alexandre Sarr 150.00 400.00
BMB16 Stephon Castle 400.00 800.00
BMB17 Ron Holland II 125.00 300.00
BMB18 Mr. Monopoly 125.00 300.00
BMB19 Scottie 125.00 300.00
BMB20 T-Rex 125.00 300.00
SSXXX Luka Doncic 1,000.00 2,000.00

2024-25 Panini Prizm Monopoly Millionaire Black
B1 Joel Embiid 50.00 120.00
B2 Giannis Antetokounmpo 100.00 250.00
B3 Donovan Mitchell 60.00 150.00
B4 Jayson Tatum 75.00 200.00
B5 Jaylen Brown 60.00 150.00
B6 LaMelo Ball 60.00 150.00
B7 Jalen Brunson 100.00 250.00
B8 LeBron James 200.00 500.00
B9 Paolo Banchero 75.00 200.00
B10 Luka Doncic 125.00 300.00
B11 Nikola Jokic 125.00 300.00
B12 Tyrese Haliburton 75.00 200.00
B13 Victor Wembanyama 300.00 600.00
B14 Kevin Durant 60.00 150.00
B15 Devin Booker 60.00 150.00
B16 Shai Gilgeous-Alexander 150.00 400.00
B17 Chet Holmgren 60.00 150.00
B18 Stephen Curry 200.00 500.00
B19 Anthony Edwards 125.00 300.00
B20 Reed Sheppard 75.00 200.00
B21 Zach Edey 75.00 200.00
B22 Matas Buzelis 100.00 250.00
B23 Donovan Clingan 60.00 150.00
B24 Zaccharie Risacher 100.00 250.00
B25 Alexandre Sarr 75.00 200.00
B26 Stephon Castle 150.00 400.00
B27 Ron Holland II 60.00 150.00
B28 Mr. Monopoly 100.00 250.00
B29 Scottie 100.00 250.00
B30 T-Rex 125.00 300.00

2024-25 Panini Prizm Monopoly Millionaire White
W1 Giannis Antetokounmpo 100.00 250.00
W2 Tyrese Maxey 75.00 200.00
W3 Karl-Anthony Towns 60.00 150.00
W4 Kawhi Leonard 60.00 150.00
W5 Jaylen Brown 60.00 150.00
W6 Brandon Miller 50.00 120.00
W7 Allen Iverson 60.00 150.00
W8 LeBron James 200.00 500.00
W9 Zion Williamson 60.00 150.00
W10 Luka Doncic 125.00 300.00
W11 Nikola Jokic 125.00 300.00
W12 Kyrie Irving 60.00 150.00
W13 Victor Wembanyama 300.00 600.00
W14 Damian Lillard 60.00 150.00
W15 Ja Morant 75.00 200.00
W16 Shai Gilgeous-Alexander 150.00 400.00
W17 Jimmy Butler III 60.00 150.00
W18 Stephen Curry 200.00 500.00
W19 Anthony Edwards 125.00 300.00
W20 Reed Sheppard 75.00 200.00
W21 Zach Edey 75.00 200.00
W22 Matas Buzelis 100.00 250.00
W23 Donovan Clingan 60.00 150.00
W24 Zaccharie Risacher 100.00 250.00
W25 Alexandre Sarr 75.00 200.00
W26 Stephon Castle 150.00 400.00
W27 Jared McCain 75.00 200.00
W28 Mr. Monopoly 100.00 250.00
W29 Scottie 100.00 250.00
W30 T-Rex 125.00 300.00
SSXXX Luka Doncic 400.00 800.00

2024-25 Panini Prizm Monopoly Starter Deck
S1 Luka Doncic 2.50 6.00
S2 Nikola Jokic 2.00 5.00
S3 Anthony Edwards 2.00 5.00
S4 Stephen Curry 3.00 8.00
S5 Giannis Antetokounmpo 1.50 4.00
S6 Shai Gilgeous-Alexander 2.00 5.00
S7 Jaylen Brown .60 1.50
S8 Reed Sheppard 2.50 6.00

2024-25 Panini Prizm Monopoly White Money Blast
WMB1 Giannis Antetokounmpo 200.00 500.00
WMB2 Jayson Tatum 200.00 500.00
WMB4 Luka Doncic 300.00 600.00
WMB5 Nikola Jokic 300.00 600.00
WMB6 Victor Wembanyama 500.00 1,000.00
WMB7 Shai Gilgeous-Alexander 300.00 600.00
WMB8 Stephen Curry 500.00 1,000.00
WMB9 Anthony Edwards 300.00 600.00
WMB3 LeBron James 500.00 1,000.00
WMB10 Reed Sheppard 200.00 500.00
WMB11 Zach Edey 150.00 400.00
WMB12 Matas Buzelis 300.00 600.00
WMB13 Donovan Clingan 100.00 250.00
WMB14 Zaccharie Risacher 200.00 500.00
WMB15 Alexandre Sarr 150.00 400.00
WMB16 Stephon Castle 400.00 800.00
WMB17 Ron Holland II 125.00 300.00
WMB19 Scottie 125.00 300.00
WMB20 T-Rex 125.00 300.00
WWB18 Mr. Monopoly 125.00 300.00

2020 Panini Prizm WNBA
*GREEN: 1X TO 2.5X BASIC
*RUBY WAVE: 1X TO 2.5X BASIC
*HYPER: 1.2X TO 3X BASIC
*ICE: 1.5X TO 4X BASIC
*SILVER: 1.5X TO 4X BASIC
*RED/275: 2.5X TO 6X BASIC
*GREEN ICE: 4X TO 10X BASIC
1 Napheesa Collier 1.50 4.00
2 Briann January .50 1.25
3 Sami Whitcomb .60 1.50
4 Chiney Ogwumike .50 1.25
5 Teaira McCowan .50 1.25
6 Elena Delle Donne 1.50 4.00
7 Jasmine Thomas .50 1.25
8 Aerial Powers .60 1.50
9 Kelsey Plum 1.25 3.00
10 Angel McCoughtry .60 1.50
11 Natalie Achonwa .50 1.25
12 Brianna Turner .75 2.00
13 Seimone Augustus .50 1.25
14 Courtney Vandersloot 1.00 2.50
15 Tierra Ruffin-Pratt .50 1.25
16 Elizabeth Williams .50 1.25
17 Jessica Breland .40 1.00
18 A'ja Wilson 2.50 6.00
19 Kia Nurse .60 1.50
20 Ariel Atkins .50 1.25
21 Natasha Cloud .50 1.25
22 Reshanda Gray .50 1.25
23 Shekinna Stricklen .50 1.25
24 Courtney Williams .50 1.25
25 Tiffany Hayes .50 1.25
26 Emma Meesseman .60 1.50
27 Jewell Loyd .60 1.50
28 Temi Fagbenle .75 2.00
29 Kristi Toliver .60 1.50
30 Arike Ogunbowale .75 2.00
31 Natasha Howard .60 1.50
32 Brittney Griner 2.00 5.00
33 Skylar Diggins-Smith 1.50 4.00
34 Damiris Dantas .50 1.25
35 Tiffany Mitchell .60 1.50
36 Erica Wheeler .50 1.25
37 Jonquel Jones .50 1.25
38 Alex Bentley .50 1.25
39 LaToya Sanders .50 1.25
40 Asia Durr .50 1.25
41 Nneka Ogwumike .60 1.50
42 Brittney Sykes 1.00 2.50
43 Stefanie Dolson .50 1.25
44 Danielle Robinson .50 1.25
45 Tina Charles 1.00 2.50
46 Essence Carson .50 1.25
47 Jordin Canada .60 1.50
48 Allie Quigley .60 1.50
49 Layshia Clarendon .50 1.25
50 Astou Ndour .50 1.25
51 Odyssey Sims .50 1.25
52 Candace Parker 1.50 4.00
53 Sue Bird 2.00 5.00
54 Dearica Hamby .60 1.50
55 Yvonne Turner .50 1.25
56 Glory Johnson .50 1.25
57 Katie Lou Samuelson 1.25 3.00
58 Allisha Gray .50 1.25
59 Leilani Mitchell .50 1.25
60 Betnijah Laney .50 1.25
61 Lexie Brown .50 1.25
62 Candice Dupree .50 1.25
63 Sylvia Fowles .60 1.50
64 DeWanna Bonner .60 1.50
65 Sydney Wiese .50 1.25
66 Isabelle Harrison .50 1.25
67 Kayla McBride .60 1.50
68 Alysha Clark .50 1.25
69 Liz Cambage .50 1.25
70 Breanna Stewart 2.00 5.00
71 Renee Montgomery .50 1.25
72 Chelsea Gray .50 1.25
73 Tamera Young .50 1.25
74 Diamond DeShields .50 1.25
75 Mercedes Russell .50 1.25
76 Jackie Young .50 1.25
77 Kayla Thornton .50 1.25
78 Alyssa Thomas .50 1.25
79 Monique Billings .50 1.25
80 Bria Hartley .50 1.25
81 Riquna Williams .50 1.25
82 Cheyenne Parker .50 1.25
83 Alanna Smith .75 2.00
84 Diana Taurasi 1.50 4.00
85 Bria Holmes .50 1.25
86 Jantel Lavender .50 1.25
87 Kelsey Mitchell 1.00 2.50
88 Amanda Zahui B. .50 1.25
89 Sabrina Ionescu RC 15.00 40.00
90 Satou Sabally RC 4.00 10.00
91 Lauren Cox RC .75 2.00
92 Chennedy Carter RC 1.25 3.00
93 Bella Alarie RC .75 2.00
94 Mikiah Herbert Harrigan RC 1.00 2.50
95 Tyasha Harris RC 1.00 2.50
96 Ruthy Hebard RC .75 2.00
97 Megan Walker RC .75 2.00
98 Jocelyn Willoughby RC .75 2.00
99 Kitija Laksa RC .75 2.00
100 Jazmine Jones RC .75 2.00

2020 Panini Prizm WNBA Prizms Blue
*BLUE: 2.5X TO 6X BASIC
STATED PRINT RUN 149 SER.#'d SETS
18 A'ja Wilson 15.00 40.00
33 Skylar Diggins-Smith 25.00 60.00
52 Candace Parker 15.00 40.00
53 Sue Bird 15.00 40.00
70 Breanna Stewart 25.00 60.00
84 Diana Taurasi 15.00 40.00

2020 Panini Prizm WNBA Prizms Green Pulsar
*GREEN PULSAR: 10X TO 25X BASIC
STATED PRINT RUN 25 SER.#'d SETS
53 Sue Bird 75.00 200.00
70 Breanna Stewart 75.00 200.00
84 Diana Taurasi 60.00 150.00

2020 Panini Prizm WNBA Prizms Mojo
*MOJO: 10X TO 25X BASIC
STATED PRINT RUN 25 SER.#'d SETS
53 Sue Bird 75.00 200.00
70 Breanna Stewart 75.00 200.00
84 Diana Taurasi 60.00 150.00

2020 Panini Prizm WNBA Prizms Orange
*ORANGE: 5X TO 12X BASIC
STATED PRINT RUN 65 SER.#'d SETS

2020 Panini Prizm WNBA Prizms Purple
*PURPLE: 3X TO 8X BASIC
STATED PRINT RUN 125 SER.#'d SETS
6 Elena Delle Donne 25.00 60.00
33 Skylar Diggins-Smith 30.00 80.00
52 Candace Parker 25.00 60.00
53 Sue Bird 50.00 120.00
70 Breanna Stewart 50.00 120.00
84 Diana Taurasi 20.00 50.00

2020 Panini Prizm WNBA Dominance
*GREEN: .75X TO 2X BASIC
*GREEN ICE: .75X TO 2X BASIC
1 Brittney Griner 2.00 5.00
2 Elena Delle Donne 1.50 4.00
3 Arike Ogunbowale .75 2.00
4 Liz Cambage .50 1.25
5 Nneka Ogwumike .60 1.50
6 Breanna Stewart 2.00 5.00
7 Odyssey Sims .50 1.25
8 Sue Bird 2.00 5.00
9 Natasha Howard .60 1.50
10 Diana Taurasi 1.50 4.00
11 Skylar Diggins-Smith 1.50 4.00
12 A'ja Wilson 2.50 6.00
13 Diamond DeShields .50 1.25
14 Candace Parker 1.50 4.00
15 Tina Charles 1.00 2.50

2020 Panini Prizm WNBA Dominance Prizms Green Pulsar
*GREEN PULSAR: 4X TO 10X BASIC
STATED PRINT RUN 25 SER.#'d SETS
6 Breanna Stewart 30.00 80.00
8 Sue Bird 30.00 80.00
10 Diana Taurasi 25.00 60.00
11 Skylar Diggins-Smith 30.00 80.00
14 Candace Parker 25.00 60.00

2020 Panini Prizm WNBA Dominance Prizms Mojo
*MOJO: 4X TO 10X BASIC
STATED PRINT RUN 25 SER.#'d SETS
6 Breanna Stewart 30.00 80.00
8 Sue Bird 30.00 80.00
10 Diana Taurasi 25.00 60.00
11 Skylar Diggins-Smith 30.00 80.00
14 Candace Parker 25.00 60.00

2020 Panini Prizm WNBA Emergent
*GREEN: .75X TO 2X BASIC
*GREEN ICE: .75X TO 2X BASIC
1 Jonquel Jones .50 1.25
2 Arike Ogunbowale .75 2.00
3 Liz Cambage .50 1.25
4 A'ja Wilson 2.50 6.00
5 Nneka Ogwumike .60 1.50
6 Diamond DeShields .50 1.25
7 Chelsea Gray .50 1.25
8 Breanna Stewart 2.00 5.00
9 Odyssey Sims .50 1.25
10 Natasha Howard .60 1.50

2020 Panini Prizm WNBA Emergent Prizms Green Pulsar
*GREEN PULSAR: 4X TO 10X BASIC
STATED PRINT RUN 25 SER.#'d SETS
8 Breanna Stewart 40.00 100.00

2020 Panini Prizm WNBA Emergent Prizms Mojo
*MOJO: 4X TO 10X BASIC
STATED PRINT RUN 25 SER.#'d SETS
8 Breanna Stewart 40.00 100.00

2020 Panini Prizm WNBA Far Out
*GREEN: .75X TO 2X BASIC
*GREEN ICE: .75X TO 2X BASIC
1 Arike Ogunbowale .75 2.00
2 Diamond DeShields .50 1.25
3 Nneka Ogwumike .60 1.50
4 Candace Parker 1.50 4.00
5 Chelsea Gray .50 1.25
6 Breanna Stewart 2.00 5.00
7 Sue Bird 2.00 5.00
8 Natasha Howard .60 1.50
9 Jonquel Jones .50 1.25
10 Skylar Diggins-Smith 1.50 4.00

2020 Panini Prizm WNBA Far Out Prizms Green Pulsar
*GREEN PULSAR: 4X TO 10X BASIC
STATED PRINT RUN 25 SER.#'d SETS
4 Candace Parker 20.00 50.00
6 Breanna Stewart 40.00 100.00
7 Sue Bird 30.00 80.00
10 Skylar Diggins-Smith 30.00 80.00

2020 Panini Prizm WNBA Far Out Prizms Mojo
*MOJO: 4X TO 10X BASIC
STATED PRINT RUN 25 SER.#'d SETS
4 Candace Parker 20.00 50.00
6 Breanna Stewart 40.00 100.00
7 Sue Bird 30.00 80.00
10 Skylar Diggins-Smith 30.00 80.00

2020 Panini Prizm WNBA Fearless
*GREEN: .75X TO 2X BASIC
*GREEN ICE: .75X TO 2X BASIC
1 Liz Cambage .50 1.25
2 Nneka Ogwumike .60 1.50
3 Candice Dupree .50 1.25
4 Chelsea Gray .50 1.25
5 Odyssey Sims .50 1.25
6 Sue Bird 2.00 5.00
7 Brittney Griner 2.00 5.00
8 Jonquel Jones .50 1.25
9 Elena Delle Donne 1.50 4.00
10 Arike Ogunbowale .75 2.00
11 A'ja Wilson 2.50 6.00
12 Diamond DeShields .50 1.25
13 Tiffany Hayes .50 1.25
14 Candace Parker 1.50 4.00
15 Tina Charles 1.00 2.50
16 Breanna Stewart 2.00 5.00
17 Sylvia Fowles .60 1.50
18 Natasha Howard .60 1.50
19 Diana Taurasi 1.50 4.00
20 Skylar Diggins-Smith 1.50 4.00

2020 Panini Prizm WNBA Fearless Prizms Green Pulsar
*GREEN PULSAR: 4X TO 10X BASIC
STATED PRINT RUN 25 SER.#'d SETS
3 Candice Dupree 15.00 40.00
6 Sue Bird 40.00 100.00
10 Arike Ogunbowale 12.00 30.00
12 Diamond DeShields 12.00 30.00
14 Candace Parker 25.00 60.00
16 Breanna Stewart 40.00 100.00
19 Diana Taurasi 25.00 60.00
20 Skylar Diggins-Smith 30.00 80.00

2020 Panini Prizm WNBA Fearless Prizms Mojo
*MOJO: 4X TO 10X BASIC
STATED PRINT RUN 25 SER.#'d SETS
3 Candice Dupree 15.00 40.00
6 Sue Bird 40.00 100.00
10 Arike Ogunbowale 12.00 30.00
12 Diamond DeShields 12.00 30.00
14 Candace Parker 25.00 60.00
16 Breanna Stewart 40.00 100.00
19 Diana Taurasi 25.00 60.00
20 Skylar Diggins-Smith 30.00 80.00

2020 Panini Prizm WNBA Fireworks
*GREEN: .75X TO 2X BASIC
*GREEN ICE: .75X TO 2X BASIC
1 Diamond DeShields .50 1.25
2 A'ja Wilson 2.50 6.00
3 Candace Parker 1.50 4.00
4 Tiffany Hayes .50 1.25
5 Breanna Stewart 2.00 5.00
6 Tina Charles 1.00 2.50
7 Natasha Howard .60 1.50
8 Sylvia Fowles .60 1.50
9 Skylar Diggins-Smith 1.50 4.00
10 Diana Taurasi 1.50 4.00
11 Nneka Ogwumike .60 1.50
12 Liz Cambage .50 1.25
13 Chelsea Gray .50 1.25
14 Candice Dupree .50 1.25
15 Sue Bird 2.00 5.00
16 Odyssey Sims .50 1.25
17 Jonquel Jones .50 1.25
18 Brittney Griner 2.00 5.00
19 Arike Ogunbowale .75 2.00
20 Elena Delle Donne 1.50 4.00

2020 Panini Prizm WNBA Fireworks Prizms Green Pulsar
*GREEN PULSAR: 4X TO 10X BASIC
STATED PRINT RUN 25 SER.#'d SETS
3 Candace Parker 25.00 60.00
5 Breanna Stewart 40.00 100.00
8 Sylvia Fowles 12.00 30.00
9 Skylar Diggins-Smith 30.00 80.00
15 Sue Bird 30.00 80.00
20 Elena Delle Donne 25.00 60.00

2020 Panini Prizm WNBA Fireworks Prizms Mojo
*MOJO: 4X TO 10X BASIC
STATED PRINT RUN 25 SER.#'d SETS
3 Candace Parker 25.00 60.00
5 Breanna Stewart 40.00 100.00
8 Sylvia Fowles 12.00 30.00
9 Skylar Diggins-Smith 30.00 80.00
15 Sue Bird 30.00 80.00
20 Elena Delle Donne 25.00 60.00

2020 Panini Prizm WNBA Get Hyped
*GREEN: .75X TO 2X BASIC
*GREEN ICE: .75X TO 2X BASIC
1 Liz Cambage .50 1.25
2 Candace Parker 1.50 4.00
3 Candice Dupree .50 1.25
4 Breanna Stewart 2.00 5.00
5 Sue Bird 2.00 5.00
6 Diana Taurasi 1.50 4.00
7 Elena Delle Donne 1.50 4.00
8 Skylar Diggins-Smith 1.50 4.00
9 A'ja Wilson 2.50 6.00
10 Courtney Vandersloot 1.00 2.50
11 Nneka Ogwumike .60 1.50
12 Tina Charles 1.00 2.50
13 Chelsea Gray .50 1.25
14 Natasha Howard .60 1.50
15 Brittney Griner 2.00 5.00

2020 Panini Prizm WNBA Get Hyped Prizms Green Pulsar
*GREEN PULSAR: 4X TO 10X BASIC
STATED PRINT RUN 25 SER.#'d SETS
2 Candace Parker 25.00 60.00
4 Breanna Stewart 40.00 100.00
5 Sue Bird 30.00 80.00
6 Diana Taurasi 20.00 50.00
8 Skylar Diggins-Smith 30.00 80.00

2020 Panini Prizm WNBA Get Hyped Prizms Mojo
*MOJO: 4X TO 10X BASIC
STATED PRINT RUN 25 SER.#'d SETS
2 Candace Parker 25.00 60.00
4 Breanna Stewart 40.00 100.00
5 Sue Bird 30.00 80.00
6 Diana Taurasi 20.00 50.00
8 Skylar Diggins-Smith 30.00 80.00

2020 Panini Prizm WNBA Signatures
*GREEN: .5X TO 1.2X BASIC
*GREEN ICE: .6X TO 1.5X BASIC
*SILVER: .6X TO 1.5X BASIC
1 Jackie Young 4.00 10.00
2 Cynthia Cooper-Dyke 12.00 30.00
3 Chiney Ogwumike 4.00 10.00
4 A'ja Wilson 30.00 80.00
5 Alana Beard 4.00 10.00
6 Nneka Ogwumike 5.00 12.00
7 Seimone Augustus 4.00 10.00
8 Sylvia Fowles 5.00 12.00
9 Tina Charles 8.00 20.00
10 Angel McCoughtry 5.00 12.00
11 Candice Dupree 4.00 10.00
12 Cappie Pondexter 4.00 10.00
13 Chelsea Gray 4.00 10.00
14 Courtney Vandersloot 8.00 20.00
15 DeWanna Bonner 5.00 12.00
16 Jewell Loyd 5.00 12.00
17 Kayla McBride 5.00 12.00
18 Kristi Toliver 4.00 10.00
19 Rebekkah Brunson 4.00 10.00
20 Becky Hammon 15.00 40.00
21 Elena Delle Donne 25.00 60.00
22 Liz Cambage 8.00 20.00
23 Brittney Griner 15.00 40.00
24 Cheryl Miller 15.00 40.00
25 Maya Moore 40.00 100.00
26 Skylar Diggins-Smith 15.00 40.00
27 Breanna Stewart 100.00 250.00
28 Candace Parker 20.00 50.00
29 Diana Taurasi 60.00 150.00
30 Sue Bird 100.00 250.00
31 Lisa Leslie 20.00 50.00
32 Nancy Lieberman 6.00 15.00

33 Allie Quigley 4.00 10.00
34 Kia Nurse 8.00 20.00
35 Sheryl Swoopes 12.00 30.00
36 Natasha Howard 5.00 12.00
37 Dearica Hamby 5.00 12.00
38 Lynette Woodard 5.00 12.00
39 Dawn Staley 5.00 12.00
40 Napheesa Collier 15.00 40.00
41 Teresa Weatherspoon 6.00 15.00
42 Yolanda Griffith 6.00 15.00
43 Lauren Jackson 8.00 20.00
44 Tina Thompson 8.00 20.00
45 Sabrina Ionescu 150.00 400.00
46 Satou Sabally 20.00 50.00
47 Lauren Cox 4.00 10.00

2020 Panini Prizm WNBA Signatures Prizms Mojo

*MOJO: 1.25X TO 3X BASIC
STATED PRINT RUN 25 SER.#'d SETS
1 Jackie Young 30.00 80.00
8 Sylvia Fowles 25.00 60.00
11 Candice Dupree 25.00 60.00
18 Kristi Toliver 20.00 50.00
27 Breanna Stewart 350.00 700.00
30 Sue Bird 350.00 700.00
35 Sheryl Swoopes 75.00 200.00
43 Lauren Jackson 75.00 200.00
45 Sabrina Ionescu 800.00 1,500.00
46 Satou Sabally 100.00 250.00

2020 Panini Prizm WNBA Widescreen

*GREEN: .75X TO 2X BASIC
*GREEN ICE: .75X TO 2X BASIC
1 Elena Delle Donne 1.50 4.00
2 A'ja Wilson 2.50 6.00
3 Liz Cambage .50 1.25
4 Tiffany Hayes .50 1.25
5 Candice Dupree .50 1.25
6 Tina Charles 1.00 2.50
7 Odyssey Sims .50 1.25
8 Sylvia Fowles .60 1.50
9 Brittney Griner 2.00 5.00
10 Diana Taurasi 1.50 4.00

2020 Panini Prizm WNBA Widescreen Prizms Green Pulsar

*GREEN PULSAR: 4X TO 10X BASIC
STATED PRINT RUN 25 SER.#'d SETS
1 Elena Delle Donne 40.00 100.00
5 Candice Dupree 12.00 30.00
10 Diana Taurasi 25.00 60.00

2020 Panini Prizm WNBA Widescreen Prizms Mojo

*MOJO: 4X TO 10X BASIC
STATED PRINT RUN 25 SER.#'d SETS
1 Elena Delle Donne 40.00 100.00
5 Candice Dupree 12.00 30.00
10 Diana Taurasi 25.00 60.00

2021 Panini Prizm WNBA

*GREEN: 1.25X TO 3X BASIC
*RUBY WAVE: 1.25X TO 3X BASIC
*HYPER: 1.5X TO 4X BASIC
*ICE: 1.5X TO 4X BASIC
*SILVER: 1.5X TO 4X BASIC
*GREEN ICE: 2.5X TO 6X BASIC
*RED/299: 2.5X TO 6X BASIC
*BLUE/149: 3X TO 8X BASIC
*PREMIUM BOX SET/99: 4X TO 10X BASIC
*PURPLE/99: 4X TO 10X BASIC
*ORANGE/50: 6X TO 15X BASIC
*GREEN PULSAR/25: 12X TO 30X BASIC
*MOJO/25: 12X TO 30X BASIC
*25TH ANN/25: 15X TO 40X BASIC
1 Lauren Cox .50 1.25
2 Jewell Loyd .60 1.50
3 Leilani Mitchell .40 1.00
4 Ezi Magbegor .50 1.25
5 Monique Billings .40 1.00
6 Courtney Williams .50 1.25
7 Victoria Vivians .40 1.00
8 Brionna Jones .50 1.25
9 Moriah Jefferson .30 .75
10 Courtney Vandersloot .60 1.50
11 Kia Nurse .50 1.25
12 Kelsey Mitchell 1.00 2.50
13 A'ja Wilson 1.50 4.00
14 Jocelyn Willoughby .40 1.00
15 Marina Mabrey RC .75 2.00
16 Bridget Carleton .60 1.50
17 Allie Quigley .60 1.50
18 Briann January .30 .75
19 Sylvia Fowles .50 1.25
20 Layshia Clarendon .40 1.00
21 Natasha Howard .50 1.25
22 Isabelle Harrison .40 1.00
23 Bria Holmes .40 1.00
24 Jordin Canada .50 1.25
25 Brianna Turner .40 1.00
26 Aerial Powers .40 1.00
27 Jasmine Thomas .40 1.00
28 Diana Taurasi 1.25 3.00
29 Jonquel Jones .60 1.50
30 Napheesa Collier 1.25 3.00
31 Brittney Griner 1.00 2.50
32 Natasha Cloud .50 1.25
33 Ariel Atkins .50 1.25
34 Elizabeth Williams .40 1.00
35 Shekinna Stricklen .40 1.00
36 Candice Dupree .40 1.00
37 Jantel Lavender .40 1.00
38 Riquna Williams .40 1.00
39 Sabrina Ionescu 1.50 4.00
40 Myisha Hines-Allen .40 1.00
41 Crystal Dangerfield .40 1.00
42 Alyssa Thomas .60 1.50
43 Dearica Hamby .60 1.50
44 Angel McCoughtry .50 1.25
45 Erica Wheeler .40 1.00
46 Amanda Zahui B. .40 1.00
47 Jackie Young .60 1.50
48 Allisha Gray .50 1.25
49 Chennedy Carter .40 1.00
50 Kahleah Copper .60 1.50
51 Betnijah Laney .50 1.25
52 Alanna Smith .50 1.25
53 DeWanna Bonner .60 1.50
54 Emma Meesseman .50 1.25
55 Chiney Ogwumike .40 1.00
56 Kristi Toliver .40 1.00
57 Teaira McCowan .30 .75
58 Stefanie Dolson .40 1.00
59 Nia Coffey .40 1.00
60 Kelsey Plum 1.00 2.50
61 Kayla McBride .50 1.25
62 Tianna Hawkins .30 .75
63 Danielle Robinson .40 1.00
64 Skylar Diggins-Smith .75 2.00
65 Sue Bird 1.50 4.00
66 Kylee Shook .40 1.00
67 Katie Lou Samuelson .60 1.50
68 Brittney Sykes .60 1.50
69 Chelsea Gray .50 1.25
70 Satou Sabally .75 2.00
71 Tina Charles .75 2.00
72 Diamond DeShields .40 1.00
73 Sami Whitcomb .40 1.00
74 Tiffany Mitchell .50 1.25
75 Nneka Ogwumike .50 1.25
76 Candace Parker 1.25 3.00
77 Liz Cambage .50 1.25
78 Damiris Dantas .50 1.25
79 Arike Ogunbowale .75 2.00
80 Odyssey Sims .40 1.00
81 Elena Delle Donne 1.00 2.50
82 Sophie Cunningham RC 15.00 40.00
83 Kayla Thornton .40 1.00
84 Ruthy Hebard .30 .75
85 Breanna Stewart 1.50 4.00
86 Epiphanny Prince .40 1.00
87 Tiffany Hayes .40 1.00
88 Kia Vaughn .40 1.00
89 Charli Collier RC .75 2.00
90 Awak Kuier RC .75 2.00
91 Aari McDonald RC 1.25 3.00
92 Kysre Gondrezick RC .75 2.00
93 Chelsea Dungee RC .60 1.50
94 Michaela Onyenwere RC 1.00 2.50
95 Jasmine Walker RC .60 1.50
96 Shyla Heal RC .60 1.50
97 Rennia Davis RC .60 1.50
98 Stephanie Watts RC .60 1.50
99 Aaliyah Wilson RC .60 1.50
100 Iliana Rupert RC .75 2.00

2021 Panini Prizm WNBA Color Blast

1 A'ja Wilson 200.00 500.00
2 Liz Cambage 125.00 300.00
3 Arike Ogunbowale 150.00 400.00
4 Sue Bird 200.00 500.00
5 Diana Taurasi 200.00 500.00
6 Elena Delle Donne 150.00 400.00
7 Brittney Griner 150.00 400.00
8 Crystal Dangerfield 125.00 300.00
9 Breanna Stewart 200.00 500.00
10 Sabrina Ionescu 200.00 500.00

2021 Panini Prizm WNBA Dominance

*GREEN: .6X TO 1.5X BASIC
*GREEN ICE: 1.5X TO 4X BASIC
*GREEN PULSAR/25: 5X TO 12X BASIC
*MOJO/25: 5X TO 12X BASIC
1 Breanna Stewart 2.00 5.00
2 Jewell Loyd .75 2.00
3 Arike Ogunbowale 1.00 2.50
4 Candace Parker 1.50 4.00
5 Diana Taurasi 1.50 4.00
6 Sabrina Ionescu 2.00 5.00
7 Nneka Ogwumike .60 1.50
8 Sue Bird 2.00 5.00
9 Brittney Griner 1.25 3.00
10 Elena Delle Donne 1.25 3.00
11 A'ja Wilson 2.00 5.00
12 Satou Sabally 1.00 2.50
13 Crystal Dangerfield .50 1.25
14 Skylar Diggins-Smith 1.00 2.50
15 Liz Cambage .60 1.50

2021 Panini Prizm WNBA Emergent

*GREEN: .6X TO 1.5X BASIC
*GREEN ICE: 1.5X TO 4X BASIC
*GREEN PULSAR/25: 5X TO 12X BASIC
*MOJO/25: 5X TO 12X BASIC
1 Satou Sabally 1.00 2.50
2 Chiney Ogwumike .50 1.25
3 A'ja Wilson 2.00 5.00
4 Chennedy Carter .50 1.25
5 Erica Wheeler .50 1.25
6 Arike Ogunbowale 1.00 2.50
7 Crystal Dangerfield .50 1.25
8 Jewell Loyd .75 2.00
9 Breanna Stewart 2.00 5.00
10 Sabrina Ionescu 2.00 5.00

2021 Panini Prizm WNBA Far Out

*GREEN: .6X TO 1.5X BASIC
*GREEN ICE: 1.5X TO 4X BASIC
*GREEN PULSAR/25: 5X TO 12X BASIC
*MOJO/25: 5X TO 12X BASIC
1 Elena Delle Donne 1.25 3.00
2 A'ja Wilson 2.00 5.00
3 Brittney Griner 1.25 3.00
4 Liz Cambage .60 1.50
5 Crystal Dangerfield .50 1.25
6 Arike Ogunbowale 1.00 2.50
7 Breanna Stewart 2.00 5.00
8 Sue Bird 2.00 5.00
9 Sabrina Ionescu 2.00 5.00
10 Diana Taurasi 1.50 4.00

2021 Panini Prizm WNBA Fearless

*GREEN: .6X TO 1.5X BASIC
*GREEN ICE: 1.5X TO 4X BASIC
*GREEN PULSAR/25: 5X TO 12X BASIC
*MOJO/25: 5X TO 12X BASIC
1 Nneka Ogwumike .60 1.50
2 Satou Sabally 1.00 2.50
3 Chiney Ogwumike .50 1.25
4 A'ja Wilson 2.00 5.00
5 Liz Cambage .60 1.50
6 Chennedy Carter .50 1.25
7 Kelsey Mitchell 1.25 3.00
8 Candace Parker 1.50 4.00
9 Erica Wheeler .50 1.25
10 Arike Ogunbowale 1.00 2.50
11 Sue Bird 2.00 5.00
12 Diana Taurasi 1.50 4.00
13 Elena Delle Donne 1.25 3.00
14 Brittney Griner 1.25 3.00
15 Skylar Diggins-Smith 1.00 2.50
16 Crystal Dangerfield .50 1.25
17 Jewell Loyd .75 2.00
18 Sylvia Fowles .60 1.50
19 Breanna Stewart 2.00 5.00
20 Sabrina Ionescu 2.00 5.00

2021 Panini Prizm WNBA Fireworks

*GREEN: .6X TO 1.5X BASIC
*GREEN ICE: 1.5X TO 4X BASIC
*GREEN PULSAR/25: 5X TO 12X BASIC
*MOJO/25: 5X TO 12X BASIC
1 Chennedy Carter .50 1.25
2 Crystal Dangerfield .50 1.25
3 Candace Parker 1.50 4.00
4 Sylvia Fowles .60 1.50
5 Arike Ogunbowale 1.00 2.50
6 Sabrina Ionescu 2.00 5.00
7 Satou Sabally 1.00 2.50
8 Diana Taurasi 1.50 4.00
9 A'ja Wilson 2.00 5.00
10 Brittney Griner 1.25 3.00
11 Liz Cambage .60 1.50
12 Skylar Diggins-Smith 1.00 2.50
13 Kelsey Mitchell 1.25 3.00
14 Jewell Loyd .75 2.00
15 Erica Wheeler .50 1.25
16 Breanna Stewart 2.00 5.00
17 Nneka Ogwumike .60 1.50
18 Sue Bird 2.00 5.00
19 Chiney Ogwumike .50 1.25
20 Elena Delle Donne 1.25 3.00

2021 Panini Prizm WNBA Get Hyped

*GREEN: .6X TO 1.5X BASIC
*GREEN ICE: 1.5X TO 4X BASIC
*GREEN PULSAR/25: 5X TO 12X BASIC
*MOJO/25: 5X TO 12X BASIC
1 Breanna Stewart 2.00 5.00
2 Arike Ogunbowale 1.00 2.50
3 Diana Taurasi 1.50 4.00
4 Nneka Ogwumike .60 1.50
5 Brittney Griner 1.25 3.00
6 A'ja Wilson 2.00 5.00
7 Crystal Dangerfield .50 1.25
8 Liz Cambage .60 1.50
9 Jewell Loyd .75 2.00
10 Candace Parker 1.50 4.00
11 Sabrina Ionescu 2.00 5.00
12 Sue Bird 2.00 5.00
13 Elena Delle Donne 1.25 3.00
14 Satou Sabally 1.00 2.50
15 Skylar Diggins-Smith 1.00 2.50

2021 Panini Prizm WNBA Signatures

*GREEN: .5X TO 1.2X BASIC
*SILVER: .5X TO 1.2X BASIC
*GREEN PULSAR: .6X TO 1.5X BASIC
*MOJO/25: 1,25X TO 3X BASIC
1 A'ja Wilson 40.00 100.00
2 Allie Quigley 5.00 12.00
3 Alyssa Thomas 8.00 20.00
4 Angel McCoughtry 6.00 15.00
5 Arike Ogunbowale 10.00 25.00
6 Becky Hammon 20.00 50.00
7 Betnijah Laney 6.00 15.00
8 Breanna Stewart 40.00 100.00
9 Brittney Griner 12.00 30.00
10 Candace Parker 30.00 80.00
11 Chennedy Carter 5.00 12.00
12 Cheryl Ford 5.00 12.00
13 Chiney Ogwumike 5.00 12.00
14 Crystal Dangerfield 5.00 12.00
15 Cynthia Cooper-Dyke 10.00 25.00
16 Dearica Hamby 8.00 20.00
17 Diamond DeShields 5.00 12.00
18 Diana Taurasi 15.00 40.00
19 Elena Delle Donne 12.00 30.00
20 Erica Wheeler 5.00 12.00
21 Jackie Young 8.00 20.00
22 Kayla McBride 6.00 15.00
23 Kelsey Mitchell 12.00 30.00
24 Kia Nurse 6.00 15.00
25 Lauren Jackson 15.00 40.00
26 Lisa Leslie 12.00 30.00
27 Liz Cambage 6.00 15.00
28 Myisha Hines-Allen 5.00 12.00
29 Napheesa Collier 30.00 80.00
30 Nneka Ogwumike 6.00 15.00
31 Odyssey Sims 5.00 12.00
32 Sabrina Ionescu 50.00 120.00
33 Sheryl Swoopes 10.00 25.00
34 Skylar Diggins-Smith 10.00 25.00
35 Sue Bird 20.00 50.00
36 Tiffany Hayes 5.00 12.00
37 Tina Charles 10.00 25.00
38 Charli Collier 6.00 15.00
39 Awak Kuier 6.00 15.00
40 Aari McDonald 10.00 25.00

2021 Panini Prizm WNBA Widescreen

*GREEN: .6X TO 1.5X BASIC
*GREEN ICE: 1.5X TO 4X BASIC
*GREEN PULSAR/25: 5X TO 12X BASIC
*MOJO/25: 5X TO 12X BASIC
1 Arike Ogunbowale 1.00 2.50
2 Crystal Dangerfield .50 1.25
3 Breanna Stewart 2.00 5.00
4 Elena Delle Donne 1.25 3.00
5 Sue Bird 2.00 5.00
6 A'ja Wilson 2.00 5.00
7 Sabrina Ionescu 2.00 5.00
8 Brittney Griner 1.25 3.00
9 Diana Taurasi 1.50 4.00
10 Liz Cambage .60 1.50

2022 Panini Prizm WNBA

COMMON CARD .30 .75
SEMISTARS .40 1.00
UNLISTED STARS .50 1.25
COMMON RC .50 1.25
RC SEMIS .60 1.50
RC UNLISTED .75 2.00
*GREEN: 1X TO 2.5X BASIC
*HYPER: 1.25X TO 3X BASIC
*RUBY WAVE: 1.25X TO 3X BASIC
*SILVER: 1.25X TO 3X BASIC
*ICE: 1.5X TO 4X BASIC
*GREEN ICE: 2.5X TO 6X BASIC
*RED/199: 2.5X TO 6X BASIC
*BLUE/149: 2.5X TO 6X BASIC
*PREMIUM BOX SET/99: 3X TO 8X BASIC
*PURPLE/99: 3X TO 8X BASIC
*ORANGE/49: 4X TO 10X BASIC
1 Awak Kuier .50 1.25
2 Moriah Jefferson .40 1.00
3 Candace Parker 1.50 4.00
4 Ruthy Hebard .40 1.00
5 Danielle Robinson .50 1.25
6 Diana Taurasi 1.50 4.00
7 Jackie Young 1.00 2.50
8 Nneka Ogwumike .75 2.00
9 Alaina Coates .50 1.25
10 Lauren Jackson 1.25 3.00
11 Azura Stevens .50 1.25
12 Myisha Hines-Allen .60 1.50
13 Tina Krajisnik .75 2.00
14 Sabrina Ionescu 2.00 5.00
15 Dearica Hamby .50 1.25
16 Chamique Holdsclaw 1.00 2.50
17 Jantel Lavender .50 1.25
18 Katie Lou Samuelson .75 2.00
19 Aari McDonald .60 1.50
20 Rui Machida 1.25 3.00
21 Beatrice Mompremier .50 1.25
22 Napheesa Collier 1.50 4.00
23 Cappie Pondexter .50 1.25
24 Sami Whitcomb .60 1.50
25 Nina Milic 1.00 2.50
26 Sylvia Fowles .60 1.50
27 Jasmine Thomas .50 1.25
28 Katie Smith 1.00 2.50
29 Aerial Powers .50 1.25
30 Lauren Jackson 1.25 3.00
31 Becky Hammon 2.00 5.00
32 Natalie Achonwa .50 1.25
33 Charli Collier .50 1.25
34 Satou Sabally 1.00 2.50
35 DeWanna Bonner .60 1.50
36 Tamika Catchings 1.25 3.00
37 Jasmine Walker .50 1.25
38 Kayla McBride .60 1.50
39 A'ja Wilson 2.00 5.00
40 Cynthia Cooper-Dyke 1.25 3.00
41 Jasmine Dickey .75 2.00
42 Natasha Cloud .50 1.25
43 Sparkle Taylor .50 1.25
44 Seimone Augustus .50 1.25
45 Diamond DeShields .50 1.25
46 Teaira McCowan .50 1.25
47 Amy Atwell .75 2.00
48 Kayla Thornton .50 1.25
49 Alanna Smith .50 1.25
50 Lindsay Whalen 1.00 2.50
51 Joyner Holmes .50 1.25
52 Natasha Howard .60 1.50
53 Chelsea Gray .60 1.50
54 Shatori Walker-Kimbrough .50 1.25
55 Diana Taurasi 1.50 4.00
56 Theresa Plaisance .50 1.25
57 Lexie Brown .50 1.25
58 Kelsey Mitchell 1.00 2.50
59 Allie Quigley .50 1.25
60 Lisa Leslie 1.50 4.00
61 Betnijah Laney .75 2.00
62 Sheryl Swoopes 2.00 5.00
63 Sydney Colson .50 1.25
64 Maya Moore 1.50 4.00
65 DiDi Richards .60 1.50
66 Tianna Hawkins .50 1.25
67 Jessica Shepard .60 1.50
68 Kelsey Plum 1.25 3.00
69 Allisha Gray .50 1.25
70 Liz Cambage .60 1.50
71 Kristy Wallace .75 2.00
72 Natisha Hiedeman .75 2.00
73 Chennedy Carter .60 1.50
74 Anneli Maley .75 2.00
75 DiJonai Carrington 1.00 2.50
76 Ticha Penicheiro .75 2.00
77 Jewell Loyd .75 2.00
78 Kennedy Burke .50 1.25
79 Alysha Clark .50 1.25
80 Gabby Williams .50 1.25
81 Breanna Stewart 2.00 5.00
82 Nia Coffey .50 1.25
83 Cheyenne Parker .50 1.25
84 Sheryl Swoopes 2.00 5.00
85 Elena Delle Donne 1.50 4.00
86 Tiffany Hayes .50 1.25
87 Yvonne Turner .50 1.25
88 Kia Nurse .50 1.25
89 Alyssa Thomas .50 1.25
90 Marina Mabrey .60 1.50
91 Bria Hartley .50 1.25
92 Nneka Ogwumike .75 2.00
93 Chiney Ogwumike .50 1.25
94 Shey Peddy .50 1.25
95 Elizabeth Williams .50 1.25
96 Tiffany Mitchell .60 1.50
97 Jonquel Jones .75 2.00
98 Kia Vaughn .50 1.25
99 Jocelyn Willoughby .50 1.25
100 Maya Moore 1.50 4.00
101 Briann January .50 1.25
102 Odyssey Sims .50 1.25
103 Courtney Vandersloot 1.00 2.50
104 Skylar Diggins-Smith 1.50 4.00
105 Aisha Sheppard .50 1.25
106 Tina Charles 1.00 2.50
107 Jordin Canada .50 1.25
108 Kiah Stokes .50 1.25
109 Angel McCoughtry .60 1.50
110 Megan Gustafson .50 1.25
111 Brianna Turner .75 2.00
112 Rachel Banham .50 1.25
113 Courtney Williams .50 1.25
114 Sophie Cunningham 1.25 3.00
115 Epiphanny Prince .50 1.25
116 Chamique Holdsclaw 1.00 2.50
117 Julie Allemand .50 1.25
118 Kristi Toliver .50 1.25
119 Han Xu .75 2.00
120 Megan Walker .50 1.25
121 Bridget Carleton .50 1.25
122 Rebecca Allen .60 1.50
123 Emma Meesseman .60 1.50
124 Stefanie Dolson .50 1.25
125 Tamika Catchings 1.25 3.00
126 Tyasha Harris .50 1.25
127 Kaela Davis .50 1.25
128 A'ja Wilson 2.00 5.00
129 Ariel Atkins .50 1.25
130 Mercedes Russell .50 1.25
131 Brionna Jones .60 1.50
132 Elena Delle Donne 1.50 4.00
133 Crystal Dangerfield .60 1.50
134 Stephanie Jones .50 1.25
135 Erica Wheeler .50 1.25
136 Victoria Vivians .50 1.25
137 Kahleah Copper .50 1.25
138 Rebekah Gardner .60 1.50
139 Arike Ogunbowale .60 1.50
140 Michaela Onyenwere .60 1.50
141 Brittney Griner 2.00 5.00
142 Reshanda Gray .50 1.25
143 Cynthia Cooper-Dyke 1.25 3.00
144 Stephanie Talbot .50 1.25
145 Ezi Magbegor .50 1.25
146 Yolanda Griffith 1.00 2.50
147 Kaila Charles .50 1.25
148 Sam Thomas .50 1.25
149 Dana Evans .75 2.00
150 Monique Billings .50 1.25
151 Brittney Sykes 1.00 2.50
152 Riquna Williams .50 1.25
153 Damiris Dantas .50 1.25
154 Sue Bird 2.00 5.00
155 Isabelle Harrison .50 1.25
156 Seimone Augustus W25 .50 1.25
157 Sue Bird W25 2.00 5.00
158 Tamika Catchings W25 1.25 3.00
159 Tina Charles W25 1.00 2.50
160 Cynthia Cooper-Dyke W25 1.25 3.00
161 Elena Delle Donne W25 1.50 4.00
162 Sylvia Fowles W25 .60 1.50
163 Yolanda Griffith W25 1.00 2.50
164 Brittney Griner W25 2.00 5.00
165 Becky Hammon W25 2.00 5.00
166 Lauren Jackson W25 1.25 3.00
167 Lisa Leslie W25 1.50 4.00
168 Angel McCoughtry W25 .60 1.50
169 Maya Moore W25 1.50 4.00
170 Nneka Ogwumike W25 .75 2.00
171 Candace Parker W25 1.50 4.00
172 Ticha Penicheiro W25 .75 2.00
173 Cappie Pondexter W25 .50 1.25
174 Katie Smith W25 1.00 2.50
175 Breanna Stewart W25 2.00 5.00
176 Sheryl Swoopes W25 2.00 5.00
177 Diana Taurasi W25 1.50 4.00
178 Lindsay Whalen W25 1.00 2.50
179 Becky Hammon 2.00 5.00
180 Evina Westbrook .50 1.25
181 Rhyne Howard 3.00 8.00
182 NaLyssa Smith 2.50 6.00
183 Shakira Austin 2.00 5.00
184 Emily Engstler 2.00 5.00
185 Nyara Sabally 1.50 4.00
186 Lexie Hull RC 12.00 30.00
187 Veronica Burton RC 1.50 4.00
188 Asia Durr .75 2.00
189 Rae Burrell 1.50 4.00
190 Queen Egbo 1.50 4.00
191 Kierstan Bell 1.50 4.00
192 Nia Clouden 1.50 4.00
193 Lorela Cubaj 1.50 4.00
194 Lisa Leslie 1.50 4.00
195 Naz Hillmon 1.00 2.50
196 Kristine Anigwe .50 1.25
197 Candace Parker 1.50 4.00
198 Olivia Nelson-Ododa 1.00 2.50
199 Destanni Henderson 1.00 2.50
200 Tina Charles 1.00 2.50

2022 Panini Prizm WNBA Prizms Green Pulsar

*GREEN PULSAR: 6X TO 15X BASIC
STATED PRINT RUN 25 SER.#'d SETS
181 Rhyne Howard 75.00 200.00

2022 Panini Prizm WNBA Prizms Mojo

*MOJO: 6X TO 15X BASIC
STATED PRINT RUN 25 SER.#'d SETS
181 Rhyne Howard 75.00 200.00

2022 Panini Prizm WNBA Color Blast

1 Skylar Diggins-Smith 200.00 500.00
2 Sue Bird 200.00 500.00
3 Brittney Griner 200.00 500.00
4 Elena Delle Donne 125.00 300.00
5 Sabrina Ionescu 300.00 600.00
6 Breanna Stewart 300.00 600.00
7 Becky Hammon 200.00 500.00
8 Diana Taurasi 200.00 500.00
9 Lisa Leslie 125.00 300.00
10 Candace Parker 200.00 500.00

2022 Panini Prizm WNBA Dominance

COMMON CARD .40 1.00
SEMISTARS .50 1.25
UNLISTED STARS .60 1.50
*GREEN: .5X TO 1.2X BASIC
*GREEN ICE: 1.25X TO 3X BASIC
*GREEN PULSAR/25: 3X TO 8X BASIC
*MOJO/25: 3X TO 8X BASIC
1 Cynthia Cooper-Dyke 1.50 4.00
2 Elena Delle Donne 2.00 5.00
3 Sheryl Swoopes 2.50 6.00
4 Skylar Diggins-Smith 2.00 5.00
5 Sue Bird 2.50 6.00
6 Jonquel Jones 1.00 2.50
7 Sabrina Ionescu 2.50 6.00
8 Candace Parker 2.00 5.00
9 Lisa Leslie 2.00 5.00
10 Diana Taurasi 2.00 5.00
11 Becky Hammon 2.50 6.00
12 Brittney Griner 2.50 6.00
13 Maya Moore 2.00 5.00
14 A'ja Wilson 2.50 6.00
15 Breanna Stewart 2.50 6.00

2022 Panini Prizm WNBA Emergent

COMMON CARD .40 1.00
SEMISTARS .50 1.25
UNLISTED STARS .60 1.50
*GREEN: .5X TO 1.2X BASIC
*GREEN ICE: 1.25X TO 3X BASIC
*GREEN PULSAR/25: 3X TO 8X BASIC
*MOJO/25: 3X TO 8X BASIC
1 Napheesa Collier 2.00 5.00
2 Jackie Young 1.25 3.00
3 Arike Ogunbowale .75 2.00
4 Sabrina Ionescu 2.50 6.00
5 Ariel Atkins .60 1.50
6 Michaela Onyenwere .75 2.00
7 Brionna Jones .75 2.00
8 Kelsey Mitchell 1.25 3.00
9 A'ja Wilson 2.50 6.00
10 Myisha Hines-Allen .75 2.00

2022 Panini Prizm WNBA Far Out

COMMON CARD .40 1.00
SEMISTARS .50 1.25
UNLISTED STARS .60 1.50
*GREEN: .5X TO 1.2X BASIC
*GREEN ICE: 1.25X TO 3X BASIC
*GREEN PULSAR/25: 3X TO 8X BASIC
*MOJO/25: 3X TO 8X BASIC
1 Skylar Diggins-Smith 2.00 5.00
2 Sabrina Ionescu 2.50 6.00
3 Arike Ogunbowale .75 2.00
4 Diana Taurasi 2.00 5.00
5 Napheesa Collier 2.00 5.00
6 Nneka Ogwumike 1.00 2.50
7 Brittney Griner 2.50 6.00
8 Sue Bird 2.50 6.00
9 Liz Cambage .75 2.00
10 Breanna Stewart 2.50 6.00
11 Jonquel Jones 1.00 2.50
12 Candace Parker 2.00 5.00
13 Chiney Ogwumike .60 1.50
14 Elena Delle Donne 2.00 5.00
15 Jewell Loyd 1.00 2.50

2022 Panini Prizm WNBA Fearless

COMMON CARD .40 1.00
SEMISTARS .50 1.25
UNLISTED STARS .60 1.50
*GREEN: .5X TO 1.2X BASIC
*GREEN ICE: 1.25X TO 3X BASIC
*GREEN PULSAR/25: 3X TO 8X BASIC
*MOJO/25: 3X TO 8X BASIC
1 Liz Cambage .75 2.00
2 A'ja Wilson 2.50 6.00
3 Sue Bird 2.50 6.00
4 Tina Charles 1.25 3.00
5 Sabrina Ionescu 2.50 6.00
6 Satou Sabally 1.25 3.00
7 Diana Taurasi 2.00 5.00
8 Erica Wheeler .60 1.50
9 Brittney Griner 2.50 6.00
10 Jewell Loyd 1.00 2.50
11 Skylar Diggins-Smith 2.00 5.00
12 Jonquel Jones 1.00 2.50
13 Breanna Stewart 2.50 6.00
14 Arike Ogunbowale .75 2.00
15 Candace Parker 2.00 5.00

2022 Panini Prizm WNBA Fireworks

COMMON CARD .40 1.00
SEMISTARS .50 1.25
UNLISTED STARS .60 1.50
*GREEN: .5X TO 1.2X BASIC
*GREEN ICE: 1.25X TO 3X BASIC
*GREEN PULSAR/25: 3X TO 8X BASIC
*MOJO/25: 3X TO 8X BASIC
1 Diana Taurasi 2.00 5.00
2 Erica Wheeler .60 1.50
3 Liz Cambage .75 2.00
4 Tina Charles 1.25 3.00
5 Sue Bird 2.50 6.00
6 Chiney Ogwumike .60 1.50
7 Sabrina Ionescu 2.50 6.00
8 Satou Sabally 1.25 3.00
9 Candace Parker 2.00 5.00
10 Napheesa Collier 2.00 5.00
11 Nneka Ogwumike 1.00 2.50
12 Jewell Loyd 1.00 2.50
13 A'ja Wilson 2.50 6.00
14 Kelsey Mitchell 1.25 3.00
15 Breanna Stewart 2.50 6.00

2022 Panini Prizm WNBA Get Hyped

COMMON CARD .40 1.00
SEMISTARS .50 1.25
UNLISTED STARS .60 1.50
*GREEN: .5X TO 1.2X BASIC
*GREEN ICE: 1.25X TO 3X BASIC
*GREEN PULSAR/25: 3X TO 8X BASIC
*MOJO/25: 3X TO 8X BASIC
1 Skylar Diggins-Smith 2.00 5.00
2 Breanna Stewart 2.50 6.00
3 Tina Charles 1.25 3.00
4 Candace Parker 2.00 5.00
5 Kelsey Mitchell 1.25 3.00
6 Elena Delle Donne 2.00 5.00
7 Satou Sabally 1.25 3.00
8 Nneka Ogwumike 1.00 2.50
9 Brittney Griner 2.50 6.00
10 Sue Bird 2.50 6.00
11 Jonquel Jones 1.00 2.50
12 Sabrina Ionescu 2.50 6.00
13 Arike Ogunbowale .75 2.00
14 Diana Taurasi 2.00 5.00
15 Chiney Ogwumike .60 1.50

2022 Panini Prizm WNBA Signatures

COMMON CARD 3.00 8.00
SEMISTARS 4.00 10.00
UNLISTED STARS 5.00 12.00
*GREEN: .5X TO 1.2X BASIC
*SILVER: .6X TO 1.5X BASIC
*GREEN ICE: .6X TO 1.5X BASIC
*GREEN PULSAR/25: 1.25X TO 3X BASIC
*MOJO/25: 1.25X TO 3X BASIC
1 Sue Bird 40.00 100.00
2 DeWanna Bonner 6.00 15.00
3 Jewell Loyd 8.00 20.00
4 A'ja Wilson 20.00 50.00
5 Kelsey Mitchell 10.00 25.00
6 Betnijah Laney 8.00 20.00
7 Maya Moore 15.00 40.00
8 Natasha Howard 6.00 15.00
9 Satou Sabally 10.00 25.00
10 Courtney Vandersloot 10.00 25.00
11 Lexie Hull 40.00 100.00
12 Diana Taurasi 15.00 40.00
13 Jonquel Jones 8.00 20.00
14 Nyara Sabally 10.00 25.00
15 Lisa Leslie 15.00 40.00
16 Breanna Stewart 40.00 100.00
17 Napheesa Collier 30.00 80.00
18 Chelsea Gray 5.00 12.00
19 Sheryl Swoopes 20.00 50.00
20 Courtney Williams 5.00 12.00
21 Alana Beard 5.00 12.00
22 Elena Delle Donne 15.00 40.00
23 Kahleah Copper 5.00 12.00
24 Arike Ogunbowale 6.00 15.00
25 Liz Cambage 6.00 15.00
26 Brionna Jones 6.00 15.00
27 Nneka Ogwumike 8.00 20.00
28 Chiney Ogwumike 5.00 12.00
29 Skylar Diggins-Smith 15.00 40.00
30 Cynthia Cooper-Dyke 12.00 30.00
31 Dearica Hamby 5.00 12.00
32 Erica Wheeler 5.00 12.00
33 Kayla McBride 6.00 15.00
34 Becky Hammon 20.00 50.00
35 Emily Engstler 12.00 30.00
36 Chamique Holdsclaw 10.00 25.00
37 Sabrina Ionescu 40.00 100.00
38 Rhyne Howard 40.00 100.00
39 NaLyssa Smith 15.00 40.00

2022 Panini Prizm WNBA W25 Prizms Signatures

COMMON CARD 4.00 10.00
SEMISTARS 5.00 12.00
UNLISTED STARS 6.00 15.00
156 Seimone Augustus 6.00 15.00
157 Sue Bird 40.00 100.00
158 Tamika Catchings 15.00 40.00
160 Cynthia Cooper-Dyke 15.00 40.00
161 Elena Delle Donne 20.00 50.00
162 Sylvia Fowles 8.00 20.00
163 Yolanda Griffith 12.00 30.00
165 Becky Hammon 25.00 60.00
166 Lauren Jackson 15.00 40.00
167 Lisa Leslie 20.00 50.00
168 Angel McCoughtry 8.00 20.00
169 Maya Moore 20.00 50.00
170 Nneka Ogwumike 10.00 25.00
172 Ticha Penicheiro 10.00 25.00
173 Cappie Pondexter 6.00 15.00
174 Katie Smith 12.00 30.00
175 Breanna Stewart 40.00 100.00
176 Sheryl Swoopes 25.00 60.00
177 Diana Taurasi 20.00 50.00
178 Lindsay Whalen 12.00 30.00

2022 Panini Prizm WNBA Widescreen

COMMON CARD .40 1.00
SEMISTARS .50 1.25
UNLISTED STARS .60 1.50
*GREEN: .5X TO 1.2X BASIC
*GREEN ICE: 1.25X TO 3X BASIC
*GREEN PULSAR/25: 3X TO 8X BASIC
*MOJO/25: 3X TO 8X BASIC
1 Sue Bird 2.50 6.00
2 Jonquel Jones 1.00 2.50
3 Sabrina Ionescu 2.50 6.00
4 Kelsey Mitchell 1.25 3.00
5 Diana Taurasi 2.00 5.00
6 Napheesa Collier 2.00 5.00
7 Nneka Ogwumike 1.00 2.50
8 Brittney Griner 2.50 6.00
9 Arike Ogunbowale .75 2.00
10 Skylar Diggins-Smith 2.00 5.00
11 Breanna Stewart 2.50 6.00
12 A'ja Wilson 2.50 6.00
13 Candace Parker 2.00 5.00
14 Chiney Ogwumike .60 1.50
15 Elena Delle Donne 2.00 5.00

2023 Panini Prizm WNBA

*GREEN: .6X TO 1.5X BASIC
*HYPER: .75X TO 2X BASIC
*ICE: .75X TO 2X BASIC
*SILVER: .75X TO 2X BASIC
*BLUE WAVE: 1X TO 2.5X BASIC
*RUBY WAVE: 1X TO 2.5X BASIC
*RED/199: 1.5X TO 4X BASIC
*BLUE/175: 2X TO 5X BASIC
*PURPLE/149: 2X TO 5X BASIC
*ORANGE/99: 2.5X TO 6X BASIC
*PREMIUM BOX SET/99: 2.5X TO 6X BASIC
1 DiJonai Carrington .50 1.25
2 Sophie Cunningham 1.00 2.50
3 Jasmine Thomas .40 1.00
4 Kelsey Plum 1.00 2.50
5 Aari McDonald .40 1.00
6 Marine Johannes 1.00 2.50
7 Betnijah Laney .40 1.00
8 Naz Hillmon .40 1.00
9 Courtney Vandersloot .60 1.50
10 Robyn Parks RC .75 2.00
11 Elena Delle Donne 1.25 3.00
12 Stefanie Dolson .40 1.00
13 Asia Durr .40 1.00
14 Kia Nurse .40 1.00
15 Aerial Powers .40 1.00
16 Maya Caldwell .40 1.00
17 Breanna Stewart 1.50 4.00
18 Nia Clouden .40 1.00
19 Courtney Williams .40 1.00
20 Rebecca Allen .40 1.00
21 Elizabeth Williams .40 1.00
22 Kalani Brown .40 1.00
23 Nia Coffey .40 1.00
24 Alanna Smith .60 1.50
25 A'ja Wilson 1.50 4.00
26 Lindsay Allen .40 1.00

27 Brianna Turner .40 1.00
28 Nikolina Milic .40 1.00
29 Crystal Dangerfield .40 1.00
30 Ruth Riley .60 1.50
31 Sami Whitcomb .40 1.00
32 Sue Bird 1.50 4.00
33 Jessica Shepard .40 1.00
34 Kiah Stokes .40 1.00
35 Allie Quigley .40 1.00
36 Maya Moore 1.00 2.50
37 Bridget Carleton .40 1.00
38 Nneka Ogwumike .60 1.50
39 Cynthia Cooper-Dyke .60 1.50
40 Ruthie Bolton .50 1.25
41 Emma Meesseman .50 1.25
42 Dulcy Fankam Mendjiadeu RC 1.00 2.50
43 Jewell Loyd .60 1.50
44 Kristi Toliver .40 1.00
45 Allisha Gray .50 1.25
46 Megan Gustafson .50 1.25
47 Brionna Jones .50 1.25
48 Nykesha Sales .40 1.00
49 Jocelyn Willoughby .40 1.00
50 Sabrina Ionescu 1.50 4.00
51 Evina Westbrook .40 1.00
52 Teaira McCowan .40 1.00
53 Jonquel Jones .75 2.00
54 Kristy Wallace .40 1.00
55 Alysha Clark .40 1.00
56 Michaela Onyenwere .40 1.00
57 Brittney Griner 1.25 3.00
58 Cayla George .40 1.00
59 Dana Evans .40 1.00
60 Satou Sabally .75 2.00
61 Erica Wheeler .40 1.00
62 Monique Billings .40 1.00
63 Jordin Canada .50 1.25
64 Lauren Jackson 1.00 2.50
65 Alyssa Thomas .60 1.50
66 Karlie Samuelson .50 1.25
67 Brittney Sykes .60 1.50
68 Olivia Nelson-Ododa .40 1.00
69 Danielle Robinson .40 1.00
70 Shakira Austin .40 1.00
71 Ezi Magbegor .50 1.25
72 Tiffany Hayes .40 1.00
73 Kahleah Copper .60 1.50
74 Layshia Clarendon .40 1.00
75 Angel McCoughtry .50 1.25
76 Moriah Jefferson .40 1.00
77 Candace Parker 1.50 4.00
78 Queen Egbo .40 1.00
79 Deanna Nolan .40 1.00
80 Shannon Johnson .40 1.00
81 Mercedes Russell .40 1.00
82 Tiffany Mitchell .50 1.25
83 Katie Douglas .40 1.00
84 Lexie Brown .40 1.00
85 Ariel Atkins .50 1.25
86 Myisha Hines-Allen .40 1.00
87 Chelsea Gray .50 1.25
88 Rachel Banham .40 1.00
89 Dearica Hamby .50 1.25
90 Shatori Walker-Kimbrough .40 1.00
91 Han Xu .40 1.00
92 Tina Charles .50 1.25
93 Katie Lou Samuelson .60 1.50
94 Lexie Hull .75 2.00
95 Arike Ogunbowale .60 1.50
96 NaLyssa Smith .50 1.25
97 Sydney Colson .40 1.00
98 Rebekah Gardner .40 1.00
99 Joyner Holmes .40 1.00
100 Sheryl Swoopes .60 1.50
101 Isabelle Harrison .40 1.00
102 Tyasha Harris .40 1.00
103 Kayla McBride .40 1.00
104 Arella Guirantes .40 1.00
105 Awak Kuier .40 1.00
106 Natasha Cloud .50 1.25
107 Cheryl Ford .60 1.50
108 Yvonne Turner .40 1.00
109 DeWanna Bonner .50 1.25
110 Shey Peddy .40 1.00
111 Jackie Stiles .60 1.50
112 Veronica Burton .40 1.00
113 Kayla Thornton .40 1.00
114 Lisa Leslie 1.00 2.50
115 Azura Stevens .50 1.25
116 Natasha Howard .50 1.25
117 Cheyenne Parker .40 1.00
118 Rhyne Howard .60 1.50
119 Diamond DeShields .40 1.00
120 Sika Kone RC .75 2.00
121 Jackie Young .60 1.50
122 Victoria Vivians .40 1.00
123 Kelsey Mitchell .75 2.00
124 Marina Mabrey .50 1.25
125 Becky Hammon 1.00 2.50
126 Natisha Hiedeman .40 1.00
127 Chiney Ogwumike .40 1.00
128 Riquna Williams .40 1.00
129 Diana Taurasi 1.50 4.00
130 Skylar Diggins-Smith .60 1.50
131 Jade Melbourne RC .75 2.00
132 Li Meng RC 1.00 2.50
133 Aliyah Boston RC 6.00 15.00
134 Diamond Miller RC 1.00 2.50
135 Maddy Siegrist RC 1.50 4.00
136 Stephanie Soares RC .75 2.00
137 Lou Lopez Senechal RC 1.00 2.50
138 Haley Jones RC .75 2.00
139 Grace Berger RC .75 2.00
140 Laeticia Amihere RC 1.25 3.00
141 Jordan Horston RC 1.25 3.00
142 Zia Cooke RC 1.00 2.50
143 Abby Meyers RC .75 2.00
144 Kadi Sissoko RC .75 2.00
145 Taylor Mikesell RC 1.00 2.50
146 Leigha Brown RC .75 2.00
147 Dorka Juhasz RC 1.25 3.00
148 Ashley Joens RC .75 2.00
149 Taylor Soule RC .75 2.00
150 Ivana Dojkic RC .75 2.00

2023 Panini Prizm WNBA Prizms Green Pulsar
*GREEN PULSAR: 6X TO 15X BASIC
STATED PRINT RUN 25 SER.#'d SETS
133 Aliyah Boston 75.00 200.00

2023 Panini Prizm WNBA Prizms Mojo
*MOJO: 6X TO 15X BASIC
STATED PRINT RUN 25 SER.#'d SETS
133 Aliyah Boston 75.00 200.00

2023 Panini Prizm WNBA Prizms Teal
*TEAL: 4X TO 10X BASIC
STATED PRINT RUN 49 SER.#'d SETS
133 Aliyah Boston 50.00 120.00

2023 Panini Prizm WNBA All Out
*GREEN: .6X TO 1.5X BASIC
*GREEN PULSAR/25: 4X TO 10X BASIC
*MOJO/25: 4X TO 10X BASIC
1 A'ja Wilson 2.00 5.00
2 Courtney Vandersloot .75 2.00
3 Arike Ogunbowale .75 2.00
4 Brionna Jones .60 1.50
5 Breanna Stewart 2.00 5.00
6 Aerial Powers .50 1.25
7 Jewell Loyd .75 2.00
8 Dearica Hamby .60 1.50
9 Kelsey Plum 1.25 3.00
10 Chelsea Gray .60 1.50
11 Brittney Griner 1.50 4.00
12 Sylvia Fowles .60 1.50
13 Alyssa Thomas .75 2.00
14 Nneka Ogwumike .75 2.00
15 Ariel Atkins .60 1.50

2023 Panini Prizm WNBA Color Blast
1 Candace Parker 125.00 300.00
2 Brittney Griner 125.00 300.00
3 Breanna Stewart 200.00 500.00
4 Sue Bird 300.00 600.00
5 Skylar Diggins-Smith 200.00 500.00
6 Diana Taurasi 200.00 500.00
7 Kelsey Plum 200.00 500.00
8 Sheryl Swoopes 125.00 300.00
9 Sabrina Ionescu 300.00 600.00
10 Cynthia Cooper-Dyke 125.00 300.00

2023 Panini Prizm WNBA Fearless
*GREEN: .6X TO 1.5X BASIC
*GREEN PULSAR/25: 4X TO 10X BASIC
*MOJO/25: 4X TO 10X BASIC
1 Brionna Jones .60 1.50
2 Sabrina Ionescu 2.00 5.00
3 Courtney Vandersloot .75 2.00
4 Rhyne Howard .75 2.00
5 Jessica Shepard .50 1.25
6 Kahleah Copper .75 2.00
7 Natasha Howard .60 1.50
8 Skylar Diggins-Smith .75 2.00
9 Chelsea Gray .60 1.50
10 Sue Bird 2.00 5.00
11 Dearica Hamby .60 1.50
12 Tina Charles .60 1.50
13 Jackie Young .75 2.00
14 Jonquel Jones 1.00 2.50
15 Jordin Canada .60 1.50

2023 Panini Prizm WNBA Fireworks
*GREEN: .6X TO 1.5X BASIC
*GREEN PULSAR/25: 4X TO 10X BASIC
*MOJO/25: 4X TO 10X BASIC
1 Kelsey Mitchell 1.00 2.50
2 Tina Charles .60 1.50
3 NaLyssa Smith .60 1.50
4 Chelsea Gray .60 1.50
5 Dearica Hamby .60 1.50
6 Candace Parker 2.00 5.00
7 Jackie Young .75 2.00
8 Diana Taurasi 2.00 5.00
9 Jordin Canada .60 1.50
10 Elena Delle Donne 1.50 4.00
11 Alyssa Thomas .75 2.00
12 Skylar Diggins-Smith .75 2.00
13 Ariel Atkins .60 1.50
14 Sue Bird 2.00 5.00
15 Jessica Shepard .50 1.25

2023 Panini Prizm WNBA Get Hyped
*GREEN: .6X TO 1.5X BASIC
*GREEN PULSAR/25: 4X TO 10X BASIC
*MOJO/25: 4X TO 10X BASIC
1 Jewell Loyd .75 2.00
2 Alyssa Thomas .75 2.00
3 Kelsey Plum 1.25 3.00
4 Ariel Atkins .60 1.50
5 Brittney Griner 1.50 4.00
6 Kahleah Copper .75 2.00
7 A'ja Wilson 2.00 5.00
8 Natasha Howard .60 1.50
9 Arike Ogunbowale .75 2.00
10 Kelsey Mitchell 1.00 2.50
11 Breanna Stewart 2.00 5.00
12 NaLyssa Smith .60 1.50
13 Nneka Ogwumike .75 2.00
14 Natasha Cloud .60 1.50
15 Sylvia Fowles .60 1.50

2023 Panini Prizm WNBA Hall Monitors
*GREEN: .6X TO 1.5X BASIC
*GREEN PULSAR/25: 4X TO 10X BASIC
*MOJO/25: 4X TO 10X BASIC
1 Cynthia Cooper-Dyke .75 2.00
2 Lisa Leslie 1.25 3.00
3 Sheryl Swoopes .75 2.00
4 Lauren Jackson 1.25 3.00
5 Becky Hammon 1.25 3.00
6 Ruth Riley .75 2.00
7 Ruthie Bolton .60 1.50
8 Jackie Stiles .75 2.00
9 Tamika Catchings 1.50 4.00
10 Katie Smith .60 1.50

2023 Panini Prizm WNBA Signatures
*GREEN: .5X TO 1.2X BASIC
*SILVER: .5X TO 1.2X BASIC
*RED/99: .6X TO 1.5X BASIC
*BLUE/49: .75X TO 2X BASIC
*GREEN PULSAR/25: 1.25X TO 3X BASIC
*MOJO/25: 1.25X TO 3X BASIC
1 Tamika Catchings 12.00 30.00
2 Becky Hammon 10.00 25.00
3 Maya Moore 10.00 25.00
4 A'ja Wilson 15.00 40.00
5 Jackie Stiles 6.00 15.00
6 Chiney Ogwumike 4.00 10.00
7 Angel McCoughtry 5.00 12.00
8 Jonquel Jones 8.00 20.00
9 Katie Douglas 4.00 10.00
10 Skylar Diggins-Smith 6.00 15.00
11 Katie Smith 5.00 12.00
12 Cynthia Cooper-Dyke 6.00 15.00
13 Sheryl Swoopes 6.00 15.00
14 Arike Ogunbowale 6.00 15.00
15 Jordin Canada 5.00 12.00
16 Diana Taurasi 15.00 40.00
17 Cheryl Ford 6.00 15.00
18 Nneka Ogwumike 6.00 15.00
19 Sylvia Fowles 5.00 12.00
20 Sue Bird 15.00 40.00
21 Ruth Riley 6.00 15.00
22 Lauren Jackson 10.00 25.00
23 Allisha Gray 5.00 12.00
24 Breanna Stewart 15.00 40.00
25 Shannon Johnson 4.00 10.00
26 Elena Delle Donne 12.00 30.00
27 Dearica Hamby 5.00 12.00
28 Rhyne Howard 6.00 15.00
30 Tina Charles 5.00 12.00
31 Ruthie Bolton 5.00 12.00
32 Lisa Leslie 10.00 25.00
33 Azura Stevens 5.00 12.00
34 Brittney Griner 12.00 30.00
35 Sophie Cunningham 60.00 150.00
36 Jackie Young 6.00 15.00
37 Jewell Loyd 6.00 15.00
39 Diamond Miller 5.00 12.00
40 Haley Jones 4.00 10.00

2023 Panini Prizm WNBA Top Tier
*GREEN: .6X TO 1.5X BASIC
*GREEN PULSAR/25: 4X TO 10X BASIC
*MOJO/25: 4X TO 10X BASIC
1 Kelsey Plum 1.25 3.00
2 Elena Delle Donne 1.50 4.00
3 Brittney Griner 1.50 4.00
4 Jonquel Jones 1.00 2.50
5 Rhyne Howard .75 2.00
6 A'ja Wilson 2.00 5.00
7 Sabrina Ionescu 2.00 5.00
8 Arike Ogunbowale .75 2.00
9 Skylar Diggins-Smith .75 2.00
10 Breanna Stewart 2.00 5.00
11 Sue Bird 2.00 5.00
12 Candace Parker 2.00 5.00
13 Tina Charles .60 1.50
14 Diana Taurasi 2.00 5.00
15 Jewell Loyd .75 2.00

2023 Panini Prizm WNBA Widescreen
*GREEN: .6X TO 1.5X BASIC
*GREEN PULSAR/25: 4X TO 10X BASIC
*MOJO/25: 4X TO 10X BASIC
1 Nneka Ogwumike .75 2.00
2 Sabrina Ionescu 2.00 5.00
3 Sylvia Fowles .60 1.50
4 Candace Parker 2.00 5.00
5 Natasha Cloud .60 1.50
6 Diana Taurasi 2.00 5.00
7 Teaira McCowan .50 1.25
8 Elena Delle Donne 1.50 4.00
9 Aerial Powers .50 1.25
10 Jackie Young .75 2.00
11 Jordin Canada .60 1.50
12 Jonquel Jones 1.00 2.50
13 Kahleah Copper .75 2.00
14 Rhyne Howard .75 2.00
15 Natasha Howard .60 1.50

2024 Panini Prizm Monopoly WNBA
1 Veronica Burton .30 .75
2 Kamilla Cardoso RC 1.50 4.00
3 Shakira Austin .40 1.00
4 Nika Muhl RC 2.00 5.00
5 Ariel Atkins .50 1.25
6 Allisha Gray .50 1.25
7 Alysha Clark .40 1.00
8 Ezi Magbegor .50 1.25
9 Diamond Miller .40 1.00
10 Courtney Williams .50 1.25
11 Natasha Cloud .50 1.25
12 Lauren Jackson .50 1.25
13 Aaliyah Edwards RC 1.00 2.50
14 Ruthie Bolton .40 1.00
15 Jaelyn Brown RC .40 1.00
16 Kia Nurse .40 1.00
17 DiJonai Carrington .50 1.25
18 Rebecca Allen .60 1.50
19 Monique Billings .30 .75
20 Charisma Osborne RC .75 2.00
21 Cheyenne Parker-Tyus .30 .75
22 Sevgi Uzun RC .75 2.00
23 Sydney Colson .40 1.00
24 Tyasha Harris .40 1.00
25 Dorka Juhasz .60 1.50
26 Temi Fagbenle .40 1.00
27 Nancy Lieberman .60 1.50
28 NaLyssa Smith .30 .75
29 Marina Mabrey .50 1.25
30 Ari McDonald .40 1.00
31 Betnijah Laney-Hamilton .40 1.00
32 Nyara Sabally .40 1.00
33 Karlie Samuelson .40 1.00
34 Julie Vanloo RC 1.00 2.50
35 Katie Lou Samuelson .60 1.50
36 Isabelle Harrison .40 1.00
37 Sophie Cunningham 1.00 2.50
38 Brittney Sykes .40 1.00
39 Cameron Brink RC 4.00 10.00
40 Kate Martin RC 2.50 6.00
41 Lexie Brown .50 1.25
42 Marquesha Davis RC .75 2.00
43 Haley Jones .30 .75
44 Erica Wheeler .30 .75
45 Jonquel Jones .75 2.00
46 Mercedes Russell .25 .60
47 Kalani Brown .30 .75
48 Aerial Powers .30 .75
49 Natasha Howard .50 1.25
50 Cynthia Cooper-Dyke .60 1.50
51 Brionna Jones .50 1.25
52 Chennedy Carter .30 .75
53 Courtney Vandersloot .50 1.25
54 Nneka Ogwumike .50 1.25
55 Dana Evans .40 1.00
56 Jordin Canada .40 1.00
57 Layshia Clarendon .30 .75
58 Kahleah Copper .60 1.50
59 Maddy Siegrist .40 1.00
60 Diamond DeShields .40 1.00
61 Kayla McBride .50 1.25
62 Natisha Hiedeman .40 1.00
63 Rickea Jackson RC 2.00 5.00
64 Jordan Horston .40 1.00
65 Caitlin Clark RC 6.00 15.00
66 Celeste Taylor RC 1.00 2.50
67 Jacy Sheldon RC 1.50 4.00
68 Angel Reese RC 2.50 6.00
69 Zia Cooke .30 .75
70 Lexie Hull .75 2.00
71 Tina Charles .50 1.25
72 Alissa Pili RC 1.00 2.50

2024 Panini Prizm Monopoly WNBA Brown
*BROWN: 1.25X TO 3X BASIC
STATED PRINT RUN 249 SER.#'d SETS
65 Caitlin Clark 75.00 200.00

2024 Panini Prizm Monopoly WNBA Dice
*DICE: 1.5X TO 4X BASIC
65 Caitlin Clark 100.00 250.00

2024 Panini Prizm Monopoly WNBA Free Parking
*FREE PARKING: 1.5X TO 4X BASIC
65 Caitlin Clark 100.00 250.00

2024 Panini Prizm Monopoly WNBA Go
*GO: 1.5X TO 4X BASIC
65 Caitlin Clark 100.00 250.00

2024 Panini Prizm Monopoly WNBA Gold
*GOLD: 5X TO 12X BASIC
STATED PRINT RUN 49 SER.#'d SETS
65 Caitlin Clark 500.00 1,000.00

2024 Panini Prizm Monopoly WNBA Green
*GREEN: 8X TO 20X BASIC
STATED PRINT RUN 24 SER.#'d SETS
65 Caitlin Clark 800.00 1,500.00

2024 Panini Prizm Monopoly WNBA Light Blue
*LIGHT BLUE: 1.25X TO 3X BASIC
STATED PRINT RUN 199 SER.#'d SETS
65 Caitlin Clark 75.00 200.00

2024 Panini Prizm Monopoly WNBA Millionaire Club
*MILLIONAIRE CLUB: 1X TO 2.5X BASIC
65 Caitlin Clark 50.00 120.00

2024 Panini Prizm Monopoly WNBA Millionaire Shimmer Gold
*MILLIONAIRE SHM GOLD: 2X TO 5X BASIC
STATED PRINT RUN 500 SER.#'d SETS
65 Caitlin Clark 125.00 300.00

2024 Panini Prizm Monopoly WNBA Millionaire Shimmer Green
*MILLIONAIRE SHM GRN: 8X TO 20X BASIC
STATED PRINT RUN 20 SER.#'d SETS
65 Caitlin Clark 800.00 1,500.00

2024 Panini Prizm Monopoly WNBA Millionaire Shimmer Purple
*MILLIONAIRE SHM PRPL: 4X TO 10X BASIC
STATED PRINT RUN 50 SER.#'d SETS
65 Caitlin Clark 400.00 800.00

2024 Panini Prizm Monopoly WNBA Millionaire Shimmer Red
*MILLIONAIRE SHM RED: 2.5X TO 6X BASIC
STATED PRINT RUN 100 SER.#'d SETS
65 Caitlin Clark 200.00 500.00

2024 Panini Prizm Monopoly WNBA Monopoly Man Black and White
*MONOPOLY MAN B & W: 5X TO 12X BASIC
65 Caitlin Clark 500.00 1,000.00

2024 Panini Prizm Monopoly WNBA Orange
*ORANGE: 2X TO 5X BASIC
STATED PRINT RUN 124 SER.#'d SETS
65 Caitlin Clark 125.00 300.00

2024 Panini Prizm Monopoly WNBA Pink
*PINK: 1.5X TO 4X BASIC
STATED PRINT RUN 149 SER.#'d SETS
65 Caitlin Clark 100.00 250.00

2024 Panini Prizm Monopoly WNBA Prizms Silver
*SILVER: 1X TO 2.5X BASIC
65 Caitlin Clark 25.00 60.00

2024 Panini Prizm Monopoly WNBA Purple
*PURPLE: 1.25X TO 3X BASIC
65 Caitlin Clark 75.00 200.00

2024 Panini Prizm Monopoly WNBA Question Mark
*QUESTION MARK: 8X TO 20X BASIC
STATED PRINT RUN 25 SER.#'d SETS
65 Caitlin Clark 800.00 1,500.00

2024 Panini Prizm Monopoly WNBA Red
*RED: 2.5X TO 6X BASIC
STATED PRINT RUN 100 SER.#'d SETS
65 Caitlin Clark 200.00 500.00

2024 Panini Prizm Monopoly WNBA Insert
WNBA1 Dawn Staley .75 2.00
WNBA2 Kelsey Plum 1.25 3.00
WNBA3 A'ja Wilson 1.50 4.00
WNBA4 Breanna Stewart 1.50 4.00
WNBA5 Skylar Diggins-Smith .60 1.50
WNBA6 Cameron Brink 4.00 10.00
WNBA7 DeWanna Bonner .60 1.50
WNBA8 Satou Sabally .60 1.50
WNBA9 Napheesa Collier 1.25 3.00
WNBA10 Alyssa Thomas .60 1.50
WNBA11 Rhyne Howard .60 1.50
WNBA12 Chelsea Gray .40 1.00
WNBA13 Lisa Leslie .75 2.00
WNBA14 Arike Ogunbowale .75 2.00
WNBA15 Jackie Young .75 2.00
WNBA16 Angel Reese 2.50 6.00
WNBA17 Aliyah Boston 1.25 3.00
WNBA18 Sabrina Ionescu 1.25 3.00
WNBA19 Sue Bird 1.25 3.00
WNBA20 Diana Taurasi 1.25 3.00
WNBA21 Sheryl Swoopes .60 1.50
WNBA22 Brittney Griner 1.00 2.50
WNBA23 Dearica Hamby .50 1.25
WNBA24 Jewell Loyd .60 1.50
WNBA25 Rickea Jackson 2.00 5.00
WNBA26 Nika Muhl 2.00 5.00
WNBA27 Caitlin Clark 6.00 15.00
WNBA28 Kelsey Mitchell 1.00 2.50

2024 Panini Prizm Monopoly WNBA Insert Brown
*BROWN: 1.25X TO 3X BASIC
STATED PRINT RUN 249 SER.#'d SETS
WNBA27 Caitlin Clark 75.00 200.00

2024 Panini Prizm Monopoly WNBA Insert Dice
*DICE: 1.5X TO 4X BASIC
WNBA27 Caitlin Clark 100.00 250.00

2024 Panini Prizm Monopoly WNBA Insert Free Parking
*FREE PARKING: 1.5X TO 4X BASIC
WNBA27 Caitlin Clark 100.00 250.00

2024 Panini Prizm Monopoly WNBA Insert Go
*GO: 1.5X TO 4X BASIC
WNBA27 Caitlin Clark 100.00 250.00

2024 Panini Prizm Monopoly WNBA Insert Gold
*GOLD: 5X TO 12X BASIC
STATED PRINT RUN 49 SER.#'d SETS
WNBA27 Caitlin Clark 500.00 1,000.00

2024 Panini Prizm Monopoly WNBA Insert Green
*GREEN: 8X TO 20X BASIC
STATED PRINT RUN 24 SER.#'d SETS
WNBA27 Caitlin Clark 800.00 1,500.00

2024 Panini Prizm Monopoly WNBA Insert Light Blue
*LIGHT BLUE: 1.25X TO 3X BASIC
STATED PRINT RUN 199 SER.#'d SETS
WNBA27 Caitlin Clark 75.00 200.00

2024 Panini Prizm Monopoly WNBA Insert Millionaire Club
*MILLIONAIRE CLUB: 1X TO 2.5X BASIC
WNBA27 Caitlin Clark 50.00 120.00

2024 Panini Prizm Monopoly WNBA Insert Millionaire Shimmer Gold
*MILLIONAIRE SHM GOLD: 2X TO 5X BASIC
STATED PRINT RUN 500 SER.#'d SETS
WNBA27 Caitlin Clark 125.00 300.00

2024 Panini Prizm Monopoly WNBA Insert Millionaire Shimmer Green
*GREEN: 8X TO 20X BASIC
STATED PRINT RUN 24 SER.#'d SETS
WNBA27 Caitlin Clark 800.00 1,500.00

2024 Panini Prizm Monopoly WNBA Insert Millionaire Shimmer Purple
*MILLIONAIRE SHM PRPL: 4X TO 10X BASIC
STATED PRINT RUN 50 SER.#'d SETS
WNBA27 Caitlin Clark 400.00 800.00

2024 Panini Prizm Monopoly WNBA Insert Millionaire Shimmer Red
*MILLIONAIRE SHM RED: 2.5X TO 6X BASIC
STATED PRINT RUN 100 SER.#'d SETS
WNBA27 Caitlin Clark 200.00 500.00

2024 Panini Prizm Monopoly WNBA Insert Monopoly Man Black and White
*MONOPOLY MAN B & W: 5X TO 12X BASIC
WNBA27 Caitlin Clark 500.00 1,000.00

2024 Panini Prizm Monopoly WNBA Insert Orange
*ORANGE: 2X TO 5X BASIC
STATED PRINT RUN 124 SER.#'d SETS
WNBA27 Caitlin Clark 125.00 300.00

2024 Panini Prizm Monopoly WNBA Insert Pink
*PINK: 1.5X TO 4X BASIC
STATED PRINT RUN 149 SER.#'d SETS
WNBA27 Caitlin Clark 100.00 250.00

2024 Panini Prizm Monopoly WNBA Insert Prizms Silver
*SILVER: 1X TO 2.5X BASIC
WNBA27 Caitlin Clark 25.00 60.00

2024 Panini Prizm Monopoly WNBA Insert Purple
*PURPLE: 1.25X TO 3X BASIC
WNBA27 Caitlin Clark 75.00 200.00

2024 Panini Prizm Monopoly WNBA Insert Question Mark
*QUESTION MARK: 8X TO 20X BASIC
STATED PRINT RUN 25 SER.#'d SETS
WNBA27 Caitlin Clark 1,000.00 2,000.00

2024 Panini Prizm Monopoly WNBA Insert Red
*RED: 2.5X TO 6X BASIC
STATED PRINT RUN 100 SER.#'d SETS

2024 Panini Prizm Monopoly WNBA Millionaire Black
B1 Cameron Brink 200.00 500.00
B2 Angel Reese 150.00 400.00
B3 Kelsey Plum 75.00 200.00
B4 A'ja Wilson 125.00 300.00
B5 Aliyah Boston 100.00 250.00
B6 Caitlin Clark 800.00 1,500.00
B7 Sabrina Ionescu 125.00 300.00
B8 Scottie 125.00 300.00

2024 Panini Prizm Monopoly WNBA Millionaire White
W1 Cameron Brink 200.00 500.00
W2 Brittney Griner 75.00 200.00
W3 A'ja Wilson 125.00 300.00
W4 Caitlin Clark 800.00 1,500.00
W5 Napheesa Collier 100.00 250.00
W6 Angel Reese 150.00 400.00
W7 T-Rex 125.00 300.00
W8 Sabrina Ionescu 125.00 300.00

2024 Panini Prizm Monopoly WNBA Money Blast Black
BMB1 Rickea Jackson 150.00 400.00
BMB2 Cameron Brink 300.00 600.00
BMB3 Sabrina Ionescu 150.00 400.00
BMB4 A'ja Wilson 125.00 300.00
BMB5 T-Rex 125.00 300.00
BMB6 Caitlin Clark 1,500.00 3,000.00
BMB7 Angel Reese 200.00 500.00
BMB8 Kelsey Plum 125.00 300.00
BMB9 Diana Taurasi 75.00 200.00
BMB10 Nika Muhl 150.00 400.00

2024 Panini Prizm Monopoly WNBA Money Blast White
WMB1 Cameron Brink 300.00 600.00
WMB2 Angel Reese 200.00 500.00
WMB3 Scottie 125.00 300.00
WMB4 Jacy Sheldon 125.00 300.00
WMB5 Jewell Loyd 100.00 250.00
WMB6 A'ja Wilson 125.00 300.00
WMB7 Caitlin Clark 1,500.00 3,000.00
WMB8 Breanna Stewart 125.00 300.00
WMB9 Arike Ogunbowale 100.00 250.00
WMB10 Kamilla Cardoso 125.00 300.00

2024 Panini Prizm WNBA
1 Jackie Young .75 2.00
2 Haley Jones .30 .75
3 Aliyah Boston 1.25 3.00
4 Jacy Sheldon RC 1.50 4.00
5 Betnijah Laney-Hamilton .40 1.00
6 Isabelle Harrison .40 1.00
7 Elena Delle Donne .75 2.00
8 Diamond DeShields .40 1.00
9 Joyner Holmes .30 .75
10 Angel Reese RC 2.50 6.00
11 Natasha Cloud .50 1.25
12 Kristi Toliver .50 1.25
13 Kayla McBride .50 1.25
14 Jonquel Jones .75 2.00
15 Ruthie Bolton .40 1.00
16 Lexie Hull .75 2.00
17 Sabrina Ionescu 1.25 3.00
18 Natisha Hiedeman .40 1.00
19 Dearica Hamby .50 1.25
20 Myisha Hines-Allen .30 .75
21 Cynthia Cooper-Dyke .60 1.50
22 Caitlin Clark RC 15.00 40.00
23 Li Yueru .50 1.25
24 Elizabeth Williams .30 .75
25 Rachel Banham .30 .75
26 Napheesa Collier 1.25 3.00
27 Brionna Jones .50 1.25
28 Arike Ogunbowale .75 2.00
29 Kalani Brown .30 .75
30 Leonie Fiebich RC 1.25 3.00
31 Jaelyn Brown RC .75 2.00
32 Cappie Pondexter .30 .75
33 Jaylyn Sherrod RC .75 2.00
34 Stefanie Dolson .40 1.00
35 Veronica Burton .30 .75
36 Tina Charles .50 1.25
37 Aerial Powers .30 .75
38 Maya Caldwell .30 .75
39 Rhyne Howard .60 1.50
40 Tamika Catchings .60 1.50
41 Marine Johannes .60 1.50
42 Julie Vanloo RC 1.00 2.50
43 Satou Sabally .60 1.50
44 Alyssa Thomas .60 1.50
45 Marquesha Davis RC .75 2.00
46 Zia Cooke .30 .75
47 Stephanie Soares .30 .75
48 Celeste Taylor RC 1.00 2.50
49 Jewell Loyd .60 1.50
50 Ezi Magbegor .50 1.25
51 Sug Sutton .30 .75
52 Nneka Ogwumike .50 1.25
53 Courtney Vandersloot .50 1.25
54 Laeticia Amihere .40 1.00
55 Gabby Williams .60 1.50
56 Ariel Atkins .50 1.25
57 Tiffany Mitchell .40 1.00
58 Diana Taurasi 1.25 3.00
59 Cheryl Ford .30 .75
60 Rickea Jackson RC 2.00 5.00
61 Erica Wheeler .50 1.25
62 Rae Burrell .30 .75
63 Diamond Miller .40 1.00
64 Kelsey Mitchell 1.00 2.50
65 Charisma Osborne RC .75 2.00
66 Chennedy Carter .30 .75
67 Emily Engstler .40 1.00
68 Jade Melbourne .30 .75
69 Victoria Vivians .30 .75
70 Aaliyah Edwards RC 1.00 2.50
71 Nia Coffey .30 .75
72 Dana Evans .40 1.00
73 Sydney Colson .40 1.00
74 Sheryl Swoopes .60 1.50
75 Nika Muhl RC 2.00 5.00
76 Skylar Diggins-Smith .60 1.50
77 Kelsey Plum 1.25 3.00
78 Megan Gustafson .40 1.00
79 Courtney Williams .50 1.25
80 Brittney Sykes .40 1.00
81 Tiffany Hayes .30 .75
82 Karlie Samuelson .30 .75
83 Alissa Pili RC 1.00 2.50
84 Chelsea Gray .40 1.00
85 Alanna Beard .30 .75
86 A'ja Wilson 1.50 4.00
87 Nyara Sabally .40 1.00
88 Sami Whitcomb .30 .75
89 Grace Berger .40 1.00
90 Kayla Thornton .40 1.00
91 Jordin Canada .40 1.00
92 Sevgi Uzun RC .75 2.00
93 Kamilla Cardoso RC 1.50 4.00
94 Maddy Siegrist .40 1.00
95 Olivia Epoupa RC .75 2.00
96 Allisha Gray .50 1.25
97 Ari McDonald .40 1.00
98 Lisa Leslie .75 2.00
99 Breanna Stewart 1.50 4.00
100 Ruth Riley .50 1.25
101 Alysha Clark .40 1.00
102 Tyasha Harris .40 1.00
103 Jordan Horston .40 1.00
104 Ivana Dojkic .50 1.25
105 Teaira McCowan .30 .75
106 Dawn Staley .75 2.00
107 Lindsay Allen .30 .75
108 Lauren Jackson .75 2.00
109 Mercedes Russell .25 .60
110 Lexie Brown .50 1.25
111 Alanna Smith .60 1.50
112 Sue Bird 1.25 3.00
113 Brittney Griner 1.00 2.50
114 Cheyenne Parker-Tyus .30 .75
115 Kahleah Copper .60 1.50
116 DeWanna Bonner .60 1.50
117 Sophie Cunningham 1.00 2.50
118 DiJonai Carrington .50 1.25
119 Katie Douglas .50 1.25
120 Monique Billings .30 .75
121 Lou Lopez Senechal .30 .75
122 Kiah Stokes .40 1.00
123 Dorka Juhasz .60 1.50
124 Rebecca Allen .60 1.50
125 Cheryl Miller .75 2.00
126 Kate Martin RC 2.50 6.00
127 Cameron Brink RC 4.00 10.00
128 Katie Lou Samuelson .60 1.50
129 Kia Nurse .40 1.00
130 Natasha Howard .50 1.25
131 Moriah Jefferson .30 .75
132 Marina Mabrey .50 1.25
133 Kristy Wallace .30 .75
134 Shakira Austin .40 1.00
135 Ticha Penicheiro .50 1.25
136 Temi Fagbenle .40 1.00
137 NaLyssa Smith .30 .75
138 Bridget Carleton .50 1.25
139 Nancy Lieberman .60 1.50
140 Elizabeth Kitley RC 1.00 2.50
141 Jacy Sheldon 1.50 4.00
142 Aaliyah Edwards 1.00 2.50
143 Cameron Brink 4.00 10.00
144 Rickea Jackson 2.00 5.00
145 Caitlin Clark 15.00 40.00
146 Nika Muhl 2.00 5.00
147 Angel Reese 2.50 6.00
148 Kate Martin 2.50 6.00
149 Kamilla Cardoso 1.50 4.00
150 Alissa Pili 1.00 2.50

2024 Panini Prizm WNBA Prizms Black Velocity
*BLACK VELOCITY: 8X TO 20X BASIC
STATED PRINT RUN 39 SER. #'D SETS
22 Caitlin Clark 2,000.00 4,000.00
127 Cameron Brink 125.00 300.00
143 Cameron Brink 125.00 300.00
145 Caitlin Clark 2,000.00 4,000.00

2024 Panini Prizm WNBA Prizms Blue
*BLUE: 3X TO 8X BASIC
STATED PRINT RUN 199 SER. #'D SETS
22 Caitlin Clark 400.00 800.00
145 Caitlin Clark 400.00 800.00

2024 Panini Prizm WNBA Prizms Blue Pulsar
*BLUE PULSAR: 3X TO 8X BASIC
STATED PRINT RUN 199 SER. #'D SETS
22 Caitlin Clark 400.00 800.00
145 Caitlin Clark 400.00 800.00

2024 Panini Prizm WNBA Prizms Blue Velocity
*BLUE VELOCITY: .75X TO 2X BASIC
22 Caitlin Clark 60.00 150.00
145 Caitlin Clark 60.00 150.00

2024 Panini Prizm WNBA Prizms Cherry Blossom FOTL
*CHERRY BLOSSOM FOTL: 10X TO 25X BASIC
STATED PRINT RUN 20 SER. #'D SETS
22 Caitlin Clark 2,500.00 5,000.00
127 Cameron Brink 150.00 400.00
143 Cameron Brink 150.00 400.00
145 Caitlin Clark 2,500.00 5,000.00

2024 Panini Prizm WNBA Prizms Green
*GREEN: .75X TO 2X BASIC
22 Caitlin Clark 50.00 120.00
145 Caitlin Clark 50.00 120.00

2024 Panini Prizm WNBA Prizms Green Pulsar
*GREEN PULSAR: 10X TO 25X BASIC
STATED PRINT RUN 25 SER. #'D SETS
22 Caitlin Clark 2,500.00 5,000.00
127 Cameron Brink 150.00 400.00
143 Cameron Brink 150.00 400.00
145 Caitlin Clark 2,500.00 5,000.00

2024 Panini Prizm WNBA Prizms Ice
*ICE: .75X TO 2X BASIC
22 Caitlin Clark 50.00 120.00
145 Caitlin Clark 50.00 120.00

2024 Panini Prizm WNBA Prizms Mojo
*MOJO: 10X TO 25X BASIC
STATED PRINT RUN 25 SER. #'D SETS
22 Caitlin Clark 2,500.00 5,000.00
127 Cameron Brink 150.00 400.00
143 Cameron Brink 150.00 400.00
145 Caitlin Clark 2,500.00 5,000.00

2024 Panini Prizm WNBA Prizms Orange
*ORANGE: 4X TO 10X BASIC
STATED PRINT RUN 99 SER. #'D SETS
22 Caitlin Clark 600.00 1,200.00
127 Cameron Brink 60.00 150.00
143 Cameron Brink 60.00 150.00
145 Caitlin Clark 600.00 1,200.00

2024 Panini Prizm WNBA Prizms Orange Ice
*ORANGE ICE: .75X TO 2X BASIC
22 Caitlin Clark 60.00 150.00
145 Caitlin Clark 60.00 150.00

2024 Panini Prizm WNBA Prizms Orange Velocity
*ORANGE VELOCITY: .75X TO 2X BASIC
22 Caitlin Clark 60.00 150.00
145 Caitlin Clark 60.00 150.00

2024 Panini Prizm WNBA Prizms Pink Velocity
*PINK VELOCITY: 5X TO 12X BASIC
STATED PRINT RUN 79 SER. #'D SETS
22 Caitlin Clark 800.00 1,500.00
127 Cameron Brink 75.00 200.00
143 Cameron Brink 75.00 200.00
145 Caitlin Clark 800.00 1,500.00

2024 Panini Prizm WNBA Prizms Premium Box Set
*PRM BOX SET: 4X TO 10X BASIC
STATED PRINT RUN 99 SER. #'D SETS
22 Caitlin Clark 500.00 1,000.00
127 Cameron Brink 60.00 150.00
143 Cameron Brink 60.00 150.00
145 Caitlin Clark 500.00 1,000.00

2024 Panini Prizm WNBA Prizms Pulsar
*PULSAR: 2X TO 5X BASIC
STATED PRINT RUN 499 SER. #'D SETS
145 Caitlin Clark 200.00 500.00

2024 Panini Prizm WNBA Prizms Purple
*PURPLE: 4X TO 10X BASIC
STATED PRINT RUN 149 SER. #'D SETS
22 Caitlin Clark 500.00 1,000.00
127 Cameron Brink 60.00 150.00
143 Cameron Brink 60.00 150.00
145 Caitlin Clark 500.00 1,000.00

2024 Panini Prizm WNBA Prizms Red
*RED: 2.5X TO 6X BASIC
STATED PRINT RUN 299 SER. #'D SETS
22 Caitlin Clark 300.00 600.00
145 Caitlin Clark 300.00 600.00

2024 Panini Prizm WNBA Prizms Red Pulsar
*RED PULSAR: 2.5X TO 6X BASIC
STATED PRINT RUN 299 SER. #'D SETS
22 Caitlin Clark 300.00 600.00
145 Caitlin Clark 300.00 600.00

2024 Panini Prizm WNBA Prizms Silver
*SILVER: 1.5X TO 4X BASIC
22 Caitlin Clark 200.00 500.00
145 Caitlin Clark 125.00 300.00

2024 Panini Prizm WNBA Prizms Teal
*TEAL: 6X TO 15X BASIC
STATED PRINT RUN 49 SER. #'D SETS
22 Caitlin Clark 1,000.00 2,000.00
127 Cameron Brink 100.00 250.00
143 Cameron Brink 100.00 250.00
145 Caitlin Clark 1,000.00 2,000.00

2024 Panini Prizm WNBA Prizms White Ice
*WHITE ICE: 8X TO 20X BASIC
STATED PRINT RUN 35 SER. #'D SETS
22 Caitlin Clark 2,000.00 4,000.00
127 Cameron Brink 125.00 300.00
143 Cameron Brink 125.00 300.00
145 Caitlin Clark 2,000.00 4,000.00

2024 Panini Prizm WNBA Prizms WNBA Logo
*WNBA LOGO: 1.5X TO 4X BASIC
22 Caitlin Clark 125.00 300.00
145 Caitlin Clark 125.00 300.00

2024 Panini Prizm WNBA Clark-Mania!
1 Caitlin Clark 2,000.00 4,000.00

2024 Panini Prizm WNBA Color Blast
1 Napheesa Collier 150.00 400.00
2 Sabrina Ionescu 150.00 400.00
3 Kamilla Cardoso 150.00 400.00
4 Rickea Jackson 150.00 400.00
5 Cameron Brink 500.00 1,000.00
6 A'ja Wilson 150.00 400.00
7 Angel Reese 400.00 800.00
8 Caitlin Clark 2,000.00 4,000.00
9 Arike Ogunbowale 100.00 250.00
10 Breanna Stewart 150.00 400.00

2024 Panini Prizm WNBA Fearless
1 NaLyssa Smith .40 1.00
2 Kayla McBride .60 1.50
3 Alysha Clark .50 1.25
4 Betnijah Laney-Hamilton .50 1.25
5 Kahleah Copper .75 2.00
6 Dearica Hamby .60 1.50
7 Alyssa Thomas .75 2.00
8 Jonquel Jones 1.00 2.50
9 Chelsea Gray .50 1.25
10 Caitlin Clark 10.00 25.00
11 Marina Mabrey .60 1.50
12 Diana Taurasi 1.50 4.00
13 Aerial Powers .40 1.00
14 Nneka Ogwumike .60 1.50
15 Brittney Sykes .50 1.25

2024 Panini Prizm WNBA Fearless Prizms Blue
*BLUE: 5X TO 12X BASIC
STATED PRINT RUN 49 SER. #'D SETS
10 Caitlin Clark 300.00 600.00

2024 Panini Prizm WNBA Fearless Prizms Blue Pulsar
*BLUE PULSAR: 2.5X TO 6X BASIC
STATED PRINT RUN 199 SER. #'D SETS
10 Caitlin Clark 125.00 300.00

2024 Panini Prizm WNBA Fearless Prizms Green
*GREEN: .6X TO 1.5X BASIC
10 Caitlin Clark 30.00 80.00

2024 Panini Prizm WNBA Fearless Prizms Green Pulsar
*GREEN PULSAR: 6X TO 15X BASIC
STATED PRINT RUN 25 SER. #'D SETS
10 Caitlin Clark 400.00 800.00

2024 Panini Prizm WNBA Fearless Prizms Mojo
*MOJO: 6X TO 15X BASIC
STATED PRINT RUN 25 SER. #'D SETS
10 Caitlin Clark 400.00 800.00

2024 Panini Prizm WNBA Fearless Prizms Orange Pulsar
*ORANGE PULSAR: 4X TO 10X BASIC
STATED PRINT RUN 75 SER. #'D SETS
10 Caitlin Clark 200.00 500.00

2024 Panini Prizm WNBA Fearless Prizms Red
*RED: 3X TO 8X BASIC
STATED PRINT RUN 99 SER. #'D SETS
10 Caitlin Clark 150.00 400.00

2024 Panini Prizm WNBA Fireworks
1 Zia Cooke .40 1.00
2 A'ja Wilson 2.00 5.00
3 Ariel Atkins .60 1.50
4 Kamilla Cardoso 1.00 2.50
5 DiJonai Carrington .60 1.50
6 Allisha Gray .60 1.50
7 Courtney Williams .60 1.50
8 Jewell Loyd .75 2.00
9 Sophie Cunningham 1.25 3.00
10 Maddy Siegrist .50 1.25
11 Sabrina Ionescu 1.50 4.00
12 Haley Jones .40 1.00
13 Caitlin Clark 10.00 25.00
14 Ezi Magbegor .60 1.50
15 Aliyah Boston 1.50 4.00

2024 Panini Prizm WNBA Fireworks Prizms Blue
*BLUE: 5X TO 12X BASIC
STATED PRINT RUN 49 SER. #'D SETS
13 Caitlin Clark 300.00 600.00

2024 Panini Prizm WNBA Fireworks Prizms Blue Pulsar
*BLUE PULSAR: 2.5X TO 6X BASIC
STATED PRINT RUN 199 SER. #'D SETS
13 Caitlin Clark 125.00 300.00

2024 Panini Prizm WNBA Fireworks Prizms Green
*GREEN: .6X TO 1.5X BASIC
13 Caitlin Clark 30.00 80.00

2024 Panini Prizm WNBA Fireworks Prizms Green Pulsar
*GREEN PULSAR: 6X TO 15X BASIC
STATED PRINT RUN 25 SER. #'D SETS
13 Caitlin Clark 500.00 1,000.00

2024 Panini Prizm WNBA Fireworks Prizms Mojo
*MOJO: 6X TO 15X BASIC
STATED PRINT RUN 25 SER. #'D SETS
13 Caitlin Clark 500.00 1,000.00

2024 Panini Prizm WNBA Fireworks Prizms Orange Pulsar
*ORANGE PULSAR: 4X TO 10X BASIC
STATED PRINT RUN 75 SER. #'D SETS
13 Caitlin Clark 200.00 500.00

2024 Panini Prizm WNBA Fireworks Prizms Red
*RED: 3X TO 8X BASIC
STATED PRINT RUN 99 SER. #'D SETS
13 Caitlin Clark 150.00 400.00

2024 Panini Prizm WNBA Fractal
1 Caitlin Clark 20.00 50.00
2 Diamond Miller .50 1.25
3 Aaliyah Edwards .60 1.50
4 Kelsey Mitchell 1.25 3.00
5 Cameron Brink 4.00 10.00
6 Kate Martin 1.50 4.00
7 Kayla Thornton .50 1.25
8 Courtney Vandersloot .60 1.50
9 Brionna Jones .60 1.50
10 Kia Nurse .50 1.25
11 Skylar Diggins-Smith .75 2.00
12 Natasha Cloud .60 1.50
13 Natasha Howard .60 1.50
14 Elizabeth Williams .40 1.00
15 Tina Charles .60 1.50

2024 Panini Prizm WNBA Fractal Prizms Blue
*BLUE: 5X TO 12X BASIC
STATED PRINT RUN 49 SER. #'D SETS
1 Caitlin Clark 400.00 800.00
5 Cameron Brink 60.00 150.00

2024 Panini Prizm WNBA Fractal Prizms Blue Pulsar
*BLUE PULSAR: 2.5X TO 6X BASIC
STATED PRINT RUN 199 SER. #'D SETS
1 Caitlin Clark 150.00 400.00
5 Cameron Brink 30.00 80.00

2024 Panini Prizm WNBA Fractal Prizms Green
*GREEN: .6X TO 1.5X BASIC
1 Caitlin Clark 50.00 120.00

2024 Panini Prizm WNBA Fractal Prizms Green Pulsar
*GREEN PULSAR: 6X TO 15X BASIC
STATED PRINT RUN 25 SER. #'D SETS
1 Caitlin Clark 500.00 1,000.00
5 Cameron Brink 75.00 200.00

2024 Panini Prizm WNBA Fractal Prizms Mojo
*MOJO: 6X TO 15X BASIC
STATED PRINT RUN 25 SER. #'D SETS
1 Caitlin Clark 500.00 1,000.00
5 Cameron Brink 75.00 200.00

2024 Panini Prizm WNBA Fractal Prizms Orange Pulsar
*ORANGE PULSAR: 4X TO 10X BASIC
STATED PRINT RUN 75 SER. #'D SETS
1 Caitlin Clark 300.00 600.00
5 Cameron Brink 50.00 120.00

2024 Panini Prizm WNBA Fractal Prizms Red
*RED: 3X TO 8X BASIC
STATED PRINT RUN 99 SER. #'D SETS
1 Caitlin Clark 200.00 500.00
5 Cameron Brink 40.00 100.00

2024 Panini Prizm WNBA Groovy
1 Shakira Austin .50 1.25
2 Jacy Sheldon 1.00 2.50
3 Lexie Hull 1.00 2.50
4 Dorka Juhasz .75 2.00
5 Natasha Cloud .60 1.50
6 Jackie Young 1.00 2.50
7 Cameron Brink 4.00 10.00
8 Dana Evans .50 1.25
9 Rhyne Howard .75 2.00
10 Skylar Diggins-Smith .75 2.00
11 Veronica Burton .40 1.00
12 Angel Reese 1.50 4.00
13 Caitlin Clark 12.00 30.00
14 Rickea Jackson 1.25 3.00
15 Marine Johannes .75 2.00

2024 Panini Prizm WNBA Groovy Prizms Blue
*BLUE: 5X TO 12X BASIC
STATED PRINT RUN 49 SER. #'D SETS
7 Cameron Brink 60.00 150.00
13 Caitlin Clark 400.00 800.00

2024 Panini Prizm WNBA Groovy Prizms Blue Pulsar
*BLUE PULSAR: 2.5X TO 6X BASIC
STATED PRINT RUN 199 SER. #'D SETS
7 Cameron Brink 30.00 80.00
13 Caitlin Clark 150.00 400.00

2024 Panini Prizm WNBA Groovy Prizms Green
*GREEN: .6X TO 1.5X BASIC
13 Caitlin Clark 50.00 120.00

2024 Panini Prizm WNBA Groovy Prizms Green Pulsar
*GREEN PULSAR: 6X TO 15X BASIC
STATED PRINT RUN 25 SER. #'D SETS
7 Cameron Brink 75.00 200.00
13 Caitlin Clark 500.00 1,000.00

2024 Panini Prizm WNBA Groovy Prizms Mojo
*MOJO: 6X TO 15X BASIC
STATED PRINT RUN 25 SER. #'D SETS
7 Cameron Brink 75.00 200.00
13 Caitlin Clark 500.00 1,000.00

2024 Panini Prizm WNBA Groovy Prizms Orange Pulsar
*ORANGE PULSAR: 4X TO 10X BASIC
STATED PRINT RUN 75 SER. #'D SETS
7 Cameron Brink 50.00 120.00
13 Caitlin Clark 300.00 600.00

2024 Panini Prizm WNBA Groovy Prizms Red
*RED: 3X TO 8X BASIC
STATED PRINT RUN 99 SER. #'D SETS
7 Cameron Brink 40.00 100.00
13 Caitlin Clark 200.00 500.00

2024 Panini Prizm WNBA Kaleidoscopic
1 Angel Reese 1.50 4.00
2 Nika Muhl 1.25 3.00
3 Jacy Sheldon 1.00 2.50
4 Kamilla Cardoso 1.00 2.50
5 Kelsey Plum 1.50 4.00
6 Aaliyah Edwards .60 1.50
7 DeWanna Bonner .75 2.00
8 Brittney Griner 1.25 3.00
9 Caitlin Clark 15.00 40.00
10 Marquesha Davis .50 1.25
11 Satou Sabally .75 2.00
12 Rickea Jackson 1.25 3.00
13 Alissa Pili .60 1.50
14 Cameron Brink 4.00 10.00
15 Sabrina Ionescu 1.50 4.00

2024 Panini Prizm WNBA Kaleidoscopic Prizms Blue
*BLUE: 5X TO 12X BASIC
STATED PRINT RUN 49 SER. #'D SETS
9 Caitlin Clark 400.00 800.00
14 Cameron Brink 60.00 150.00

2024 Panini Prizm WNBA Kaleidoscopic Prizms Blue Pulsar
*BLUE PULSAR: 2.5X TO 6X BASIC
STATED PRINT RUN 199 SER. #'D SETS
9 Caitlin Clark 150.00 400.00
14 Cameron Brink 30.00 80.00

2024 Panini Prizm WNBA Kaleidoscopic Prizms Green
*GREEN: .6X TO 1.5X BASIC
9 Caitlin Clark 50.00 120.00

2024 Panini Prizm WNBA Kaleidoscopic Prizms Green Pulsar
*GREEN PULSAR: 6X TO 15X BASIC
STATED PRINT RUN 25 SER. #'D SETS
9 Caitlin Clark 500.00 1,000.00
14 Cameron Brink 75.00 200.00

2024 Panini Prizm WNBA Kaleidoscopic Prizms Mojo
*MOJO: 6X TO 15X BASIC
STATED PRINT RUN 25 SER. #'D SETS
9 Caitlin Clark 500.00 1,000.00
14 Cameron Brink 75.00 200.00

2024 Panini Prizm WNBA Kaleidoscopic Prizms Orange Pulsar
*ORANGE PULSAR: 4X TO 10X BASIC
STATED PRINT RUN 75 SER. #'D SETS
9 Caitlin Clark 300.00 600.00
14 Cameron Brink 50.00 120.00

2024 Panini Prizm WNBA Kaleidoscopic Prizms Red
*RED: 3X TO 8X BASIC
STATED PRINT RUN 99 SER. #'D SETS
9 Caitlin Clark 200.00 500.00
14 Cameron Brink 40.00 100.00

2024 Panini Prizm WNBA Pioneers
*GREEN: .6X TO 1.5X BASIC
*BLUE PULSAR/199: 2.5X TO 6X BASIC
*RED/99: 3X TO 8X BASIC
*ORANGE PULSAR/75: 4X TO 10X BASIC
*BLUE/49: 5X TO 12X BASIC
*GREEN PULSAR/25: 6X TO 15X BASIC
*MOJO/25: 6X TO 15X BASIC
1 Dawn Staley 1.00 2.50
2 Lauren Jackson 1.00 2.50
3 Nancy Lieberman .75 2.00
4 Sheryl Swoopes .75 2.00
5 Yolanda Griffith .50 1.25
6 Ruthie Bolton .50 1.25
7 Tamika Catchings .75 2.00
8 Cynthia Cooper-Dyke .75 2.00
9 Ruth Riley .60 1.50
10 Ticha Penicheiro .60 1.50

2024 Panini Prizm WNBA Signatures
*GREEN: .5X TO 1.2X BASIC
*RED/99: .5X TO 1.2X BASIC
*BLUE/75: .6X TO 1.5X BASIC
*PURPLE/49: .6X TO 1.5X BASIC
*TEAL/35: .75X TO 2X BASIC
*GREEN PULSAR/25: .75X TO 2X BASIC
*MOJO/25: .75X TO 2X BASIC
1 DiJonai Carrington 6.00 15.00
2 Sheryl Swoopes 8.00 20.00
3 Erica Wheeler 6.00 15.00
5 Natasha Cloud 6.00 15.00
6 Katie Douglas 6.00 15.00
7 Gabby Williams 8.00 20.00
9 Nyara Sabally 5.00 12.00
11 Rickea Jackson 40.00 100.00
13 Diana Taurasi 15.00 40.00
14 Cameron Brink 75.00 200.00
15 Betnijah Laney-Hamilton 5.00 12.00
16 Kamilla Cardoso 10.00 25.00
17 Lou Lopez Senechal 4.00 10.00
18 Courtney Williams 6.00 15.00
19 Jackie Young 10.00 25.00
20 Alysha Clark 5.00 12.00
24 Caitlin Clark 1,000.00 2,000.00
25 A'ja Wilson 20.00 50.00
26 Alana Beard 4.00 10.00
27 Breanna Stewart 20.00 50.00
28 Nneka Ogwumike 6.00 15.00
29 Brittney Sykes 5.00 12.00
30 Jacy Sheldon 10.00 25.00
32 Zia Cooke 4.00 10.00
35 Angel Reese 60.00 150.00
36 Jordin Canada 5.00 12.00
37 Marina Mabrey 6.00 15.00
39 Sophie Cunningham 30.00 80.00

2024 Panini Prizm WNBA Throwback Signatures
*GREEN: .5X TO 1.2X BASIC
*RED/99: .5X TO 1.2X BASIC
*BLUE/75: .6X TO 1.5X BASIC
*PURPLE/49: .6X TO 1.5X BASIC
*TEAL/35: .75X TO 2X BASIC
*GREEN PULSAR/25: .75X TO 2X BASIC
*MOJO/25: .75X TO 2X BASIC
1 Kelsey Mitchell 12.00 30.00
3 Allisha Gray 6.00 15.00
4 Chelsea Gray 5.00 12.00
5 Rickea Jackson 40.00 100.00
6 Brionna Jones 6.00 15.00
7 Jacy Sheldon 10.00 25.00
9 DeWanna Bonner 8.00 20.00
10 Brittney Griner 12.00 30.00
11 Cheryl Ford 4.00 10.00
12 Elena Delle Donne 10.00 25.00
13 Lexie Hull 40.00 100.00
14 Natasha Howard 6.00 15.00
15 Ruthie Bolton 5.00 12.00
16 Ticha Penicheiro 6.00 15.00
17 Courtney Vandersloot 6.00 15.00
18 Jewell Loyd 8.00 20.00
19 Tamika Catchings 8.00 20.00
20 Angel McCoughtry 5.00 12.00
21 Lisa Leslie 10.00 25.00
22 Lauren Jackson 10.00 25.00
23 Marine Johannes 8.00 20.00
24 Sydney Colson 5.00 12.00
25 Cameron Brink 75.00 200.00
26 Caitlin Clark 1,000.00 2,000.00
27 Angel Reese 60.00 150.00
28 Maya Moore 10.00 25.00
29 Yolanda Griffith 5.00 12.00
30 Tina Charles 6.00 15.00
31 Diamond Miller 5.00 12.00
32 Dana Evans 5.00 12.00
33 Napheesa Collier 30.00 80.00
34 Teresa Edwards 6.00 15.00
35 Cynthia Cooper-Dyke 8.00 20.00
36 Shey Peddy 5.00 12.00
37 Chiney Ogwumike 6.00 15.00
38 Aliyah Boston 15.00 40.00
39 Sue Bird 15.00 40.00

2024 Panini Prizm WNBA Top Tier
*GREEN: .6X TO 1.5X BASIC
*BLUE PULSAR/199: 2.5X TO 6X BASIC
*RED/99: 3X TO 8X BASIC
*ORANGE PULSAR/75: 4X TO 10X BASIC
*BLUE/49: 5X TO 12X BASIC
*GREEN PULSAR/25: 6X TO 15X BASIC
*MOJO/25: 6X TO 15X BASIC
1 A'ja Wilson 2.00 5.00
2 Kelsey Mitchell 1.25 3.00
3 DeWanna Bonner .75 2.00
4 Kahleah Copper .75 2.00
5 Arike Ogunbowale 1.00 2.50
6 Jewell Loyd .75 2.00
7 Breanna Stewart 2.00 5.00
8 Marina Mabrey .60 1.50
9 Napheesa Collier 1.50 4.00
10 Ariel Atkins .60 1.50
11 Rhyne Howard .75 2.00
12 Brittney Griner 1.25 3.00
13 Alyssa Thomas .75 2.00
14 Sabrina Ionescu 1.50 4.00
15 Aliyah Boston 1.50 4.00

2020-21 Panini Recon
COMMON CARD (1-200) .25 .60
SEMISTARS .30 .75
UNLISTED STARS .40 1.00
COMMON RC (1-200) .50 1.25
RC SEMIS .60 1.50
RC UNLISTED .75 2.00
*HOLO PINK: .6X TO 1.5X BASIC
*HOLO: .6X TO 1.5X BASIC
*HOLO BRONZE: .6X TO 1.5X BASIC
*HOLO RED/199: 1.5X TO 4X BASIC
*HOLO BLUE/99: 2.5X TO 6X BASIC
*HOLO PURPLE/49: 2.5X TO 6X BASIC
1 Eric Paschall .30 .75
2 Kendrick Nunn .30 .75
3 Bobby Portis .40 1.00
4 Ja Morant 1.25 3.00
5 Zach LaVine .60 1.50
6 Kristaps Porzingis .50 1.25
7 Nikola Vucevic .40 1.00
8 Clint Capela .30 .75
9 Reggie Perry RC .60 1.50
10 Deni Avdija RC 1.50 4.00
11 Eric Bledsoe .30 .75
12 Cole Anthony RC 1.50 4.00
13 Keldon Johnson .60 1.50
14 Donovan Mitchell .75 2.00
16 Elfrid Payton .30 .75
17 Myles Turner .40 1.00
18 Jayson Tatum 1.50 4.00
19 Robert Covington .30 .75
20 Lamar Stevens RC .75 2.00
21 Damian Lillard 1.00 2.50
22 Thaddeus Young .25 .60
23 Derrick Rose .60 1.50
24 Serge Ibaka .30 .75
25 James Wiseman RC .75 2.00
26 Luka Doncic 2.50 6.00
27 Stephen Curry 3.00 8.00
28 Vernon Carey Jr. RC .60 1.50
29 CJ Elleby RC .60 1.50
30 Pascal Siakam .60 1.50
31 Dillon Brooks .40 1.00
32 Andrew Wiggins .50 1.25
33 Dennis Smith Jr. .25 .60
34 Rudy Gobert .50 1.25
35 Shai Gilgeous-Alexander 2.00 5.00
36 Jalen Smith RC 1.25 3.00
37 Markelle Fultz .30 .75
38 Immanuel Quickley RC 1.50 4.00
39 Tyrese Maxey RC 5.00 12.00
40 Tyrese Haliburton RC 5.00 12.00
41 Aaron Nesmith RC 1.25 3.00
42 Kevin Durant 1.50 4.00
43 Jaden McDaniels RC 2.00 5.00
44 Patrick Beverley .25 .60
45 Devin Vassell RC 2.00 5.00
46 Joe Ingles .30 .75
47 De'Andre Hunter .40 1.00
48 Joe Harris .30 .75
49 Shake Milton .30 .75
50 Fred VanVleet .60 1.50
51 Josh Richardson .30 .75
52 Marvin Bagley III .30 .75
53 Jarrett Culver .25 .60
54 Chris Paul .75 2.00
55 Isaiah Joe RC .75 2.00
56 Lauri Markkanen .50 1.25
57 James Harden .75 2.00
58 Kyle Lowry .50 1.25
59 Jamal Murray .60 1.50
60 Mason Jones RC .50 1.25
61 Robert Woodard II RC .60 1.50
62 Karl-Anthony Towns .60 1.50
63 Domantas Sabonis .50 1.25
64 Jaylen Brown .60 1.50
65 Saben Lee RC .60 1.50
66 Josh Jackson .25 .60
67 Devin Booker 1.00 2.50
68 Devon Dotson RC .60 1.50
69 John Wall .50 1.25
70 Andre Drummond .40 1.00
71 Trae Young 1.00 2.50
72 Evan Fournier .30 .75
73 Julius Randle .40 1.00
74 Thomas Bryant .30 .75
75 Paul Millsap .30 .75
76 Kelly Oubre Jr. .40 1.00
77 Danny Green .30 .75
78 Josh Green RC 1.25 3.00
79 Cassius Stanley RC .60 1.50
80 Harrison Barnes .30 .75
81 Jerami Grant .40 1.00
82 Jrue Holiday .40 1.00
83 Xavier Tillman RC .75 2.00
84 Lonzo Ball .50 1.25
85 Jalen Brunson .60 1.50
86 Draymond Green .50 1.25
87 DeMar DeRozan .50 1.25
88 Sam Merrill RC 1.00 2.50
89 Zeke Nnaji RC .75 2.00
90 Collin Sexton .40 1.00
91 Tyrell Terry RC .50 1.25
92 Terrence Ross .30 .75
93 Kawhi Leonard 1.00 2.50
94 LeBron James 3.00 8.00
95 Danilo Gallinari .30 .75
96 Enes Kanter .30 .75
97 Tim Hardaway Jr. .25 .60
98 PJ Washington Jr. .40 1.00
99 Isaiah Stewart RC 1.25 3.00
100 Patrick Williams RC 1.50 4.00
101 Theo Maledon RC .60 1.50
102 LaMelo Ball RC 5.00 12.00
103 Alex Caruso .40 1.00
104 Jarrett Allen .40 1.00
105 Malcolm Brogdon .40 1.00
106 Isaac Okoro RC 1.00 2.50
107 Kemba Walker .40 1.00
108 Seth Curry .40 1.00
109 Victor Oladipo .30 .75
110 D'Angelo Russell .40 1.00
111 Ben Simmons .40 1.00
112 Michael Porter Jr. .50 1.25
113 Marcus Smart .40 1.00
114 Jordan Clarkson .40 1.00
115 Caris LeVert .40 1.00
116 Tristan Thompson .25 .60
117 Duncan Robinson .40 1.00
118 Jimmy Butler .75 2.00
119 Lonnie Walker IV .40 1.00
120 CJ McCollum .40 1.00
121 Jonas Valanciunas .30 .75
122 Darius Garland .60 1.50
123 Jordan Nwora RC .75 2.00
124 Montrezl Harrell .40 1.00
125 Anthony Edwards RC 6.00 15.00
126 Ricky Rubio .40 1.00
127 Desmond Bane RC 2.00 5.00
128 Brandon Ingram .50 1.25
129 Kyrie Irving .75 2.00
130 Mikal Bridges .50 1.25
131 Gary Trent Jr. .40 1.00
132 Goran Dragic .40 1.00
133 Delon Wright .25 .60
134 Bojan Bogdanovic .30 .75
135 Khris Middleton .50 1.25
136 Saddiq Bey RC 1.25 3.00
137 Terry Rozier .40 1.00
138 Paul Reed RC .75 2.00
139 Wendell Carter Jr. .30 .75
140 Coby White .50 1.25
141 OG Anunoby .40 1.00
142 Onyeka Okongwu RC 1.25 3.00
143 Kyle Kuzma .50 1.25
144 Deandre Ayton .40 1.00
145 Tobias Harris .40 1.00
146 Tyler Herro .75 2.00
147 Carmelo Anthony .60 1.50
148 Kenyon Martin Jr. RC 1.00 2.50
149 Jae Crowder .25 .60
150 RJ Hampton RC .60 1.50
151 Rui Hachimura .50 1.25
152 RJ Barrett .60 1.50
153 Daniel Theis .30 .75
154 Maxi Kleber .30 .75
155 Christian Wood .30 .75
156 Aleksej Pokusevski RC .75 2.00
157 Facundo Campazzo RC .75 2.00
158 Kevin Porter Jr. .30 .75
159 Buddy Hield .40 1.00
160 LaMarcus Aldridge .40 1.00
161 Dennis Schroder .40 1.00
162 Brandon Clarke .40 1.00
163 Joel Embiid 1.00 2.50
164 Anthony Davis 1.00 2.50
165 Killian Hayes RC .60 1.50
166 Obi Toppin RC 1.25 3.00
167 Tre Jones RC 1.00 2.50
168 Kira Lewis Jr. RC .60 1.50
169 Devonte' Graham .30 .75
170 Jae'Sean Tate RC .75 2.00
171 Cam Reddish .50 1.25
172 Precious Achiuwa RC 1.25 3.00
173 Mike Conley .30 .75
174 Bradley Beal .50 1.25
175 Payton Pritchard RC 2.00 5.00
176 Lou Williams .40 1.00
177 Russell Westbrook .75 2.00
178 Al Horford .40 1.00
179 Luguentz Dort .60 1.50
180 Dejounte Murray .40 1.00
181 Giannis Antetokounmpo 2.00 5.00
182 De'Aaron Fox .60 1.50
183 Paul George .60 1.50
184 Skylar Mays RC .60 1.50
185 Darius Bazley .25 .60
186 Malachi Flynn RC .60 1.50
187 John Collins .40 1.00
188 Nikola Jokic 2.00 5.00
189 Blake Griffin .40 1.00
190 Zion Williamson 1.25 3.00
191 Norman Powell .30 .75
192 Donte DiVincenzo .40 1.00
193 Gordon Hayward .40 1.00
194 Malik Monk .40 1.00
195 Rudy Gay .40 1.00
196 Udoka Azubuike RC .75 2.00
197 Bam Adebayo .60 1.50
198 Aaron Gordon .40 1.00
199 Eric Gordon .30 .75
200 Kevin Love .40 1.00

2020-21 Panini Recon Holo Orange FOTL
*HOLO ORANGE FOTL: 4X TO 10X BASIC
STATED PRINT RUN 25 COPIES PER
26 Luka Doncic 60.00 150.00
27 Stephen Curry 60.00 150.00
94 LeBron James 60.00 150.00
102 LaMelo Ball 150.00 400.00
125 Anthony Edwards 150.00 400.00

2020-21 Panini Recon Eyes on the Prize
COMMON CARD .40 1.00
SEMISTARS .50 1.25
UNLISTED STARS .60 1.50
*RED/199: 1.5X TO 4X BASIC
*BLUE/99: 2X TO 5X BASIC
*PURPLE/49: 3X TO 8X BASIC
1 Stephen Curry 5.00 12.00
2 Kawhi Leonard 1.50 4.00
3 Kyrie Irving 1.25 3.00
4 LeBron James 5.00 12.00
5 Tim Duncan 1.50 4.00
6 Dirk Nowitzki 1.50 4.00
7 Anthony Davis 1.50 4.00
8 Dwyane Wade 1.25 3.00
9 Shaquille O'Neal 2.50 6.00
10 Klay Thompson 1.50 4.00
11 Magic Johnson 2.50 6.00
12 Kevin Garnett 1.50 4.00
13 Chauncey Billups .75 2.00
14 Kevin Durant 2.50 6.00
15 Paul Pierce 1.00 2.50
16 LeBron James 5.00 12.00
17 Hakeem Olajuwon 1.25 3.00
18 Tony Parker 1.00 2.50
19 Jason Kidd 1.00 2.50
20 Dennis Rodman 1.50 4.00

2020-21 Panini Recon Future Legends
COMMON CARD .50 1.25
SEMISTARS .60 1.50
UNLISTED STARS .75 2.00
*RED/199: 1.5X TO 4X BASIC
*BLUE/99: 2X TO 5X BASIC
*PURPLE/49: 3X TO 8X BASIC
1 Anthony Edwards 8.00 20.00
2 Zion Williamson 2.50 6.00
3 Tyler Herro 1.50 4.00
4 Tyrese Haliburton 5.00 12.00
5 Ja Morant 2.50 6.00
6 RJ Barrett 1.25 3.00
7 Luka Doncic 5.00 12.00
8 Trae Young 2.00 5.00
9 Collin Sexton .75 2.00
10 LaMelo Ball 8.00 20.00
11 Shai Gilgeous-Alexander 4.00 10.00
12 Michael Porter Jr. 1.00 2.50
13 Coby White 1.00 2.50
14 Keldon Johnson 1.25 3.00
15 James Wiseman .75 2.00
16 Immanuel Quickley 1.50 4.00
17 Deandre Ayton .75 2.00
18 Rui Hachimura 1.00 2.50
19 De'Andre Hunter .75 2.00
20 Patrick Williams 1.50 4.00
21 Saddiq Bey 1.25 3.00
22 Donovan Mitchell 1.50 4.00
23 Jayson Tatum 3.00 8.00
24 Deni Avdija 1.50 4.00
25 De'Aaron Fox 1.25 3.00

2020-21 Panini Recon Glorified Signatures
COMMON CARD 3.00 8.00
SEMISTARS 4.00 10.00
UNLISTED STARS 5.00 12.00
EXCHANGE DEADLINE 4/27/2023
*RED/49-99: .5X TO 1.2X BASIC
*BLUE/25-49: .6X TO 1.5X BASIC
1 Joakim Noah 4.00 10.00
2 Calvin Natt 4.00 10.00
3 Quentin Richardson 3.00 8.00
4 Alex Caruso 12.00 30.00
5 Otis Birdsong 4.00 10.00
6 Ben McLemore 3.00 8.00
7 Tony Delk 4.00 10.00
8 Clint Capela 4.00 10.00
9 Luguentz Dort 8.00 20.00
10 Kenny Smith 4.00 10.00
11 Myles Turner 5.00 12.00
12 Duncan Robinson 5.00 12.00
13 Troy Brown Jr. 4.00 10.00
14 Anfernee Simons 12.00 30.00
15 Josh Hart 4.00 10.00
16 Mason Plumlee 3.00 8.00
17 Luke Kennard 4.00 10.00
18 Zach Collins 4.00 10.00
19 Sam Perkins 4.00 10.00
20 Tony Parker 12.00 30.00
21 Devin Harris 3.00 8.00
22 Anfernee Hardaway 30.00 80.00
26 Eric Bledsoe 4.00 10.00
27 Grant Hill 20.00 50.00
28 Jamal Murray 25.00 60.00
29 Lamar Odom 5.00 12.00
30 John Shumate 4.00 10.00
31 Glen Rice 4.00 10.00
32 Jaylen Nowell 4.00 10.00
33 Rudy Gay 5.00 12.00
34 Gerald Henderson 3.00 8.00
35 Ersan Ilyasova 3.00 8.00
36 Nikola Jokic 125.00 300.00
37 Christian Laettner 5.00 12.00
38 Malcolm Brogdon 5.00 12.00
39 Fat Lever 5.00 12.00
40 Frank Jackson 3.00 8.00
41 Jason Kidd 15.00 40.00
42 Nerlens Noel 3.00 8.00
43 Nassir Little 4.00 10.00
44 James Ennis III 3.00 8.00
45 Garfield Heard 4.00 10.00
46 Khris Middleton 6.00 15.00
47 Steven Adams 5.00 12.00
48 Coby White 6.00 15.00
49 Jason Richardson 5.00 12.00
50 Spencer Dinwiddie 4.00 10.00
51 De'Andre Hunter 5.00 12.00
52 Chauncey Billups 6.00 15.00
53 Ja Morant 200.00 500.00
54 Mikal Bridges 6.00 15.00
55 Mike Bibby 5.00 12.00
56 Reggie Bullock 4.00 10.00
57 Carsen Edwards 4.00 10.00
58 Rick Mahorn 4.00 10.00
59 Daniel Gafford 4.00 10.00
60 Carlos Boozer 4.00 10.00

2020-21 Panini Recon Maneuvers
COMMON CARD .40 1.00
SEMISTARS .50 1.25
UNLISTED STARS .60 1.50
*RED/199: 1.5X TO 4X BASIC
*BLUE/99: 2X TO 5X BASIC
*PURPLE/49: 3X TO 8X BASIC
1 James Harden 1.25 3.00
2 Ja Morant 2.00 5.00
3 LeBron James 5.00 12.00
4 Zion Williamson 2.00 5.00
5 Devin Booker 1.50 4.00
6 Russell Westbrook 1.25 3.00
7 Luka Doncic 4.00 10.00
8 Giannis Antetokounmpo 3.00 8.00
9 Donovan Mitchell 1.25 3.00
10 Jayson Tatum 2.50 6.00
11 Kawhi Leonard 1.50 4.00
12 Zach LaVine 1.00 2.50
13 Jamal Murray 1.00 2.50
14 Trae Young 1.50 4.00
15 Kyrie Irving 1.25 3.00
16 Ben Simmons .60 1.50
17 De'Aaron Fox 1.00 2.50
18 Paul George 1.00 2.50
19 Stephen Curry 5.00 12.00
20 Kevin Durant 2.50 6.00
21 Bradley Beal .75 2.00
22 Damian Lillard 1.50 4.00
23 Jaylen Brown 1.00 2.50
24 Chris Paul 1.25 3.00
25 Shai Gilgeous-Alexander 3.00 8.00

2020-21 Panini Recon Recon Signatures
COMMON CARD 3.00 8.00
SEMISTARS 4.00 10.00
UNLISTED STARS 5.00 12.00

EXCHANGE DEADLINE 4/27/2023
1 Anthony Davis 60.00 150.00
2 Nerlens Noel 3.00 8.00
3 Spud Webb 5.00 12.00
4 PJ Washington Jr. 5.00 12.00
5 James Ennis III 3.00 8.00
6 Langston Galloway 3.00 8.00
7 Monte Morris 3.00 8.00
8 Andre Drummond 5.00 12.00
10 Jim Jackson 4.00 10.00
12 Toni Kukoc 8.00 20.00
13 Anfernee Simons 12.00 30.00
14 Jalen Brunson 8.00 20.00
15 Mark Price 5.00 12.00
16 Shaquille O'Neal 75.00 200.00
17 Lauri Markkanen 6.00 15.00
21 Thaddeus Young 3.00 8.00
22 Dwyane Wade 50.00 120.00
23 Jakob Poeltl 4.00 10.00
24 JJ Redick 5.00 12.00
25 Darius Bazley 3.00 8.00
27 Bruce Brown 4.00 10.00
28 Jarrett Culver 3.00 8.00
29 Montrezl Harrell 5.00 12.00
30 Joakim Noah 4.00 10.00
31 Julius Randle 5.00 12.00
32 John Salley 4.00 10.00
33 Robert Williams III 4.00 10.00
35 Joe Harris 4.00 10.00
36 Eric Gordon 4.00 10.00
37 Sam Cassell 4.00 10.00
38 Nikola Vucevic 5.00 12.00
39 Malcolm Brogdon 5.00 12.00
40 David Lee 3.00 8.00
41 Ivica Zubac 5.00 12.00
42 Bryn Forbes 4.00 10.00
43 Magic Johnson 60.00 150.00
44 Maxi Kleber 4.00 10.00
45 Lonnie Walker IV 5.00 12.00
46 T.J. Warren 4.00 10.00
47 Danilo Gallinari 4.00 10.00
48 Al Horford 5.00 12.00
49 Brad Wanamaker 3.00 8.00
50 Dee Brown 4.00 10.00
51 Kelly Olynyk 3.00 8.00
52 Jrue Holiday 5.00 12.00
53 CJ McCollum 5.00 12.00
54 Boban Marjanovic 4.00 10.00
55 Luka Doncic 400.00 800.00
56 Allen Iverson 60.00 150.00
57 Jarrett Allen 5.00 12.00
58 Trae Young 75.00 200.00
59 Naz Reid 6.00 15.00
60 Xavier McDaniel 4.00 10.00

2020-21 Panini Recon Recon Signatures Blue

*BLUE: .6X TO 1.5X BASIC
STATED PRINT RUN 25-49 COPIES PER
34 RJ Barrett/25 15.00 40.00

2020-21 Panini Recon Recon Signatures Red

*RED: .5X TO 1.2X BASIC
STATED PRINT RUN 49-99 COPIES PER
11 Talen Horton-Tucker/99 15.00 40.00
34 RJ Barrett/49 12.00 30.00

2020-21 Panini Recon Rock the Rim

COMMON CARD .40 1.00
SEMISTARS .50 1.25
UNLISTED STARS .60 1.50
*RED/199: 1.5X TO 4X BASIC
*BLUE/99: 2X TO 5X BASIC
*PURPLE/49: 3X TO 8X BASIC
1 Zion Williamson 2.00 5.00
2 Zach LaVine 1.00 2.50
3 Giannis Antetokounmpo 3.00 8.00
4 Donovan Mitchell 1.25 3.00
5 Paul George 1.00 2.50
6 LeBron James 5.00 12.00
7 Russell Westbrook 1.25 3.00
8 Anthony Edwards 8.00 20.00
9 Ben Simmons .60 1.50
10 Ja Morant 2.00 5.00
11 Anthony Davis 1.50 4.00
12 Victor Oladipo .50 1.25
13 DeMar DeRozan .75 2.00
14 John Wall .75 2.00
15 Kevin Durant 2.50 6.00
16 Bam Adebayo 1.00 2.50
17 Jayson Tatum 2.50 6.00
18 Kawhi Leonard 1.50 4.00
19 Joel Embiid 1.50 4.00
20 Bradley Beal .75 2.00
21 Pascal Siakam 1.00 2.50
22 Obi Toppin 1.00 2.50
23 Aaron Gordon .60 1.50
24 James Wiseman .60 1.50
25 Blake Griffin .60 1.50

2020-21 Panini Recon Rookie Recon

COMMON CARD .50 1.25
SEMISTARS .60 1.50
UNLISTED STARS .75 2.00
*RED/199: 1.5X TO 4X BASIC
*BLUE/99: 2X TO 5X BASIC
*PURPLE/49: 3X TO 8X BASIC
1 LaMelo Ball 12.00 30.00
2 Udoka Azubuike .75 2.00
3 Zeke Nnaji .75 2.00
4 Kenyon Martin Jr. 1.00 2.50
5 James Wiseman .75 2.00
6 Tyrese Haliburton 5.00 12.00
7 Obi Toppin 1.25 3.00
8 Jordan Nwora .75 2.00
9 Xavier Tillman .75 2.00
10 Deni Avdija 1.50 4.00
11 Immanuel Quickley 1.50 4.00
12 Tyrese Maxey 5.00 12.00
13 Patrick Williams 1.50 4.00
14 Payton Pritchard 2.00 5.00
15 Cole Anthony 1.50 4.00
16 Isaac Okoro 1.00 2.50
17 Aaron Nesmith 1.25 3.00
18 Onyeka Okongwu 1.25 3.00
19 Saddiq Bey 1.25 3.00
20 Jae'Sean Tate .75 2.00
21 Facundo Campazzo .75 2.00
22 Killian Hayes .60 1.50
23 RJ Hampton .60 1.50
24 Precious Achiuwa 1.25 3.00
25 Devin Vassell 2.00 5.00
26 Kira Lewis Jr. .60 1.50
27 Desmond Bane 2.00 5.00
28 Isaiah Joe .75 2.00
29 Nico Mannion .60 1.50
30 Saben Lee .60 1.50
31 Aleksej Pokusevski .75 2.00
32 Malachi Flynn .60 1.50
33 Theo Maledon .60 1.50
34 Tre Jones 1.00 2.50
35 Vernon Carey Jr. .60 1.50
36 Jaden McDaniels 2.00 5.00
37 Josh Green 1.25 3.00
38 Isaiah Stewart 1.25 3.00
39 Jalen Smith 1.25 3.00
40 Anthony Edwards 8.00 20.00

2020-21 Panini Recon Rookie Review

COMMON CARD .50 1.25
SEMISTARS .60 1.50
UNLISTED STARS .75 2.00
*RED/199: 1.5X TO 4X BASIC
*BLUE/99: 2X TO 5X BASIC
*PURPLE/49: 3X TO 8X BASIC
1 Derrick Rose 1.25 3.00
2 Carmelo Anthony 1.25 3.00
3 Kevin Durant 3.00 8.00
4 Kyrie Irving 1.50 4.00
5 Anthony Davis 2.00 5.00
6 James Harden 1.50 4.00
7 Chris Paul 1.50 4.00
8 LeBron James 6.00 15.00
9 Jimmy Butler 1.50 4.00
10 Paul George 1.25 3.00
11 Russell Westbrook 1.50 4.00
12 Kawhi Leonard 2.00 5.00
13 Zach LaVine 1.25 3.00
14 Julius Randle .75 2.00
15 Brandon Ingram 1.00 2.50
16 Blake Griffin .75 2.00
17 DeMar DeRozan 1.00 2.50
18 Kristaps Porzingis 1.00 2.50
19 John Wall 1.00 2.50
20 Giannis Antetokounmpo 4.00 10.00
21 Stephen Curry 6.00 15.00
22 Damian Lillard 2.00 5.00
23 Gordon Hayward .75 2.00
24 Kyle Lowry 1.00 2.50
25 Kemba Walker .75 2.00

2020-21 Panini Recon Scouting Reports

COMMON CARD .50 1.25
SEMISTARS .60 1.50
UNLISTED STARS .75 2.00
*RED/199: 1.5X TO 4X BASIC
*BLUE/99: 2X TO 5X BASIC
*PURPLE/49: 3X TO 8X BASIC
1 LaMelo Ball 15.00 40.00
2 James Wiseman .75 2.00
3 Anthony Edwards 10.00 25.00
4 Tyrese Haliburton 5.00 12.00
5 Obi Toppin 1.25 3.00
6 Deni Avdija 1.50 4.00
7 Immanuel Quickley 1.50 4.00
8 Tyrese Maxey 5.00 12.00
9 Patrick Williams 1.50 4.00
10 Payton Pritchard 2.00 5.00
11 Cole Anthony 1.50 4.00
12 Isaac Okoro 1.00 2.50
13 Aaron Nesmith 1.25 3.00
14 Onyeka Okongwu 1.25 3.00
15 Saddiq Bey 1.25 3.00
16 Jae'Sean Tate .75 2.00
17 Facundo Campazzo .75 2.00
18 Killian Hayes .60 1.50
19 RJ Hampton .60 1.50
20 Precious Achiuwa 1.25 3.00
21 Devin Vassell 2.00 5.00
22 Kira Lewis Jr. .60 1.50
23 Desmond Bane 2.00 5.00
24 Xavier Tillman .75 2.00
25 Nico Mannion .60 1.50
26 Saben Lee .60 1.50
27 Aleksej Pokusevski .75 2.00
28 Jalen Smith 1.25 3.00
29 Theo Maledon .60 1.50
30 Isaiah Stewart 1.25 3.00

2020-21 Panini Recon Sky's the Limit

COMMON CARD .50 1.25
SEMISTARS .60 1.50
UNLISTED STARS .75 2.00
*RED/199: 1.5X TO 4X BASIC
*BLUE/99: 2X TO 5X BASIC
*PURPLE/49: 3X TO 8X BASIC
1 Luka Doncic 10.00 25.00
2 LeBron James 10.00 25.00
3 Stephen Curry 8.00 20.00
4 Kevin Durant 3.00 8.00
5 Zion Williamson 2.50 6.00
6 Damian Lillard 2.00 5.00
7 Giannis Antetokounmpo 4.00 10.00
8 Kawhi Leonard 2.00 5.00
9 Nikola Jokic 4.00 10.00
10 Donovan Mitchell 1.50 4.00

2020-21 Panini Recon True Potential Signatures

COMMON CARD 4.00 10.00
SEMISTARS 5.00 12.00
UNLISTED STARS 6.00 15.00
EXCHANGE DEADLINE 4/27/2023
*RED/49-99: .5X TO 1.2X BASIC
*BLUE/25-49: .6X TO 1.5X BASIC
1 Moses Brown 4.00 10.00
2 Jay Scrubb 6.00 15.00
3 Gabe Vincent 10.00 25.00
4 Caleb Martin 10.00 25.00
5 Markus Howard 6.00 15.00
6 Jae'Sean Tate 6.00 15.00
7 Ty-Shon Alexander 5.00 12.00
8 Onyeka Okongwu 10.00 25.00
9 Isaac Okoro 8.00 20.00
10 Desmond Bane 15.00 40.00
11 Payton Pritchard 15.00 40.00
12 Obi Toppin 10.00 25.00
13 Tyrese Haliburton 50.00 120.00
14 Tyrese Maxey 50.00 120.00
15 Anthony Edwards 200.00 500.00
16 Killian Tillie 6.00 15.00
17 Trent Forrest 6.00 15.00
18 Reggie Perry 5.00 12.00
19 Saben Lee 5.00 12.00
20 Paul Reed 6.00 15.00
21 Isaiah Joe 6.00 15.00
22 James Wiseman 6.00 15.00
23 Mason Jones 4.00 10.00
24 Deni Avdija 12.00 30.00
25 Sam Merrill 8.00 20.00
26 Facundo Campazzo 6.00 15.00
27 Jalen Harris 4.00 10.00
28 Nathan Knight 5.00 12.00
29 Cole Anthony 50.00 120.00
30 Aaron Nesmith 10.00 25.00
31 Theo Maledon 5.00 12.00
32 Cassius Winston 5.00 12.00
33 Vernon Carey Jr. 5.00 12.00
34 Saddiq Bey 10.00 25.00
35 Patrick Williams 12.00 30.00
36 Mamadi Diakite 5.00 12.00
37 Ashton Hagans 6.00 15.00
38 Karim Mane 4.00 10.00
39 Devon Dotson 5.00 12.00
40 Lamar Stevens 6.00 15.00

2021-22 Panini Recon

COMMON CARD (1-200) .25 .60
SEMISTARS .30 .75
UNLISTED STARS .40 1.00
COMMON RC (201-250) .50 1.25
RC SEMIS .60 1.50
RC UNLISTED .75 2.00
*HOLO: .6X TO 1.5X BASIC
*HOLO PINK: .6X TO 1.5X BASIC
1 LaMelo Ball 1.00 2.50
2 Kawhi Leonard 1.00 2.50
3 Anthony Davis 1.00 2.50
4 Karl-Anthony Towns .60 1.50
5 Shai Gilgeous-Alexander 2.00 5.00
6 LeBron James 3.00 8.00
7 Kevin Durant 1.25 3.00
8 Bradley Beal .50 1.25
9 Jayson Tatum 1.50 4.00
10 Dejounte Murray .40 1.00
11 Trae Young 1.00 2.50
12 Ja Morant 1.25 3.00
13 James Harden .75 2.00
14 Devonte' Graham .30 .75
15 Nikola Jokic 2.00 5.00
16 Kevin Porter Jr. .30 .75
17 Tobias Harris .30 .75
18 Jerami Grant .40 1.00
19 Will Barton .25 .60
20 Zach LaVine .60 1.50
21 Kyle Lowry .40 1.00
22 Kevin Love .40 1.00
23 Buddy Hield .30 .75
24 Jaylen Brown .60 1.50
25 Domantas Sabonis .50 1.25
26 Deandre Ayton .40 1.00
27 Lauri Markkanen .50 1.25
28 Evan Fournier .30 .75
29 John Collins .40 1.00
30 Stephen Curry 2.50 6.00
31 Rudy Gobert .50 1.25
32 Devin Vassell .50 1.25
33 Collin Sexton .40 1.00
34 Giannis Antetokounmpo 2.00 5.00
35 Jonas Valanciunas .30 .75
36 Fred VanVleet .50 1.25
37 Mike Conley .30 .75
38 Mikal Bridges .50 1.25
39 Miles Bridges .30 .75
40 Derrick Rose .60 1.50
41 Jae'Sean Tate .40 1.00
42 Klay Thompson 1.00 2.50
43 DeMar DeRozan .50 1.25
44 De'Andre Hunter .40 1.00
45 Bam Adebayo .60 1.50
46 Ben Simmons .40 1.00
47 Mo Bamba .30 .75
48 Luguentz Dort .40 1.00
49 Terry Rozier III .30 .75
50 Paul George .60 1.50
51 Damian Lillard 1.00 2.50
52 Andrew Wiggins .50 1.25
53 Bogdan Bogdanovic .40 1.00
54 Blake Griffin .40 1.00
55 Saddiq Bey .30 .75
56 Bojan Bogdanovic .30 .75
57 Tyrese Maxey 1.00 2.50
58 Tyler Herro .60 1.50
59 Caris LeVert .30 .75
60 Jrue Holiday .50 1.25
61 Kelly Oubre Jr. .40 1.00
62 Isaiah Stewart .30 .75
63 Jaren Jackson Jr. .60 1.50
64 Jordan Clarkson .40 1.00
65 Duncan Robinson .40 1.00
66 Cameron Johnson .40 1.00
67 Christian Wood .30 .75
68 RJ Barrett .60 1.50
69 Clint Capela .40 1.00
70 Aaron Gordon .40 1.00
71 Norman Powell .40 1.00
72 Jimmy Butler .60 1.50
73 Jordan Poole .60 1.50
74 Seth Curry .30 .75
75 Zion Williamson 1.00 2.50
76 Darius Garland .60 1.50
77 Luka Doncic 2.50 6.00
78 Kristaps Porzingis .50 1.25
79 De'Aaron Fox .50 1.25
80 Kentavious Caldwell-Pope .25 .60
81 Desmond Bane .75 2.00
82 CJ McCollum .40 1.00
83 Malcolm Brogdon .30 .75
84 Dillon Brooks .40 1.00
85 LaMarcus Aldridge .40 1.00
86 Reggie Jackson .30 .75
87 Grayson Allen .40 1.00
88 Gary Trent Jr. .30 .75
89 Russell Westbrook .60 1.50
90 Devin Booker 1.00 2.50
91 Gordon Hayward .30 .75
92 Pascal Siakam .60 1.50
93 Jalen Brunson .75 2.00
94 Patrick Beverley .25 .60
95 Bobby Portis .30 .75
96 Anthony Edwards 2.00 5.00
97 Alex Caruso .40 1.00
98 Draymond Green .50 1.25
99 Michael Porter Jr. .50 1.25
100 Kyle Kuzma .50 1.25
101 Myles Turner .40 1.00
102 Keldon Johnson .50 1.25
103 Dennis Schroder .40 1.00
104 Tim Hardaway Jr. .25 .60
105 Jarrett Allen .40 1.00
106 Tyrese Haliburton .75 2.00
107 Kemba Walker .40 1.00
108 Wendell Carter Jr. .40 1.00
109 Derrick White .40 1.00
110 Carmelo Anthony .60 1.50
111 Anfernee Simons .60 1.50
112 Dorian Finney-Smith .25 .60
113 Brandon Ingram .50 1.25
114 Marcus Smart .40 1.00
115 Steven Adams .30 .75
116 D'Angelo Russell .40 1.00
117 Spencer Dinwiddie .30 .75
118 Lance Stephenson .30 .75
119 Joel Embiid 1.00 2.50
120 Montrezl Harrell .30 .75
121 Lonzo Ball .40 1.00
122 Cole Anthony .50 1.25
123 OG Anunoby .40 1.00
124 Harrison Barnes .30 .75
125 Robert Covington .25 .60
126 Chris Paul .75 2.00
127 Julius Randle .50 1.25
128 Nikola Vucevic .40 1.00
129 Jamal Murray .60 1.50
130 Khris Middleton .40 1.00
131 Kyrie Irving .75 2.00
132 Donovan Mitchell .75 2.00
133 Malik Beasley .30 .75
134 Maxi Kleber .30 .75
135 Richaun Holmes .25 .60
136 Immanuel Quickley .40 1.00
137 Obi Toppin .40 1.00
138 Matisse Thybulle .30 .75
139 Danny Green .30 .75
140 Jusuf Nurkic .30 .75
141 Josh Hart .30 .75
142 Patrick Williams .40 1.00
143 Coby White .40 1.00
144 Rui Hachimura .40 1.00
145 Al Horford .30 .75
146 Darius Bazley .25 .60
147 Brandon Clarke .40 1.00
148 Jakob Poeltl .30 .75
149 Precious Achiuwa .40 1.00
150 Luke Kennard .30 .75
151 Deni Avdija .40 1.00
152 Markelle Fultz .25 .60
153 Marvin Bagley III .30 .75
154 Monte Morris .30 .75
155 Doug McDermott .30 .75
156 Talen Horton-Tucker .40 1.00
157 Eric Gordon .30 .75
158 Jaden McDaniels .40 1.00
159 Rudy Gay .40 1.00
160 P.J. Tucker .30 .75
161 Chris Boucher .40 1.00
162 DeMarcus Cousins .30 .75
163 Kelly Olynyk .25 .60
164 Robert Williams III .40 1.00
165 RJ Hampton .25 .60
166 Malik Monk .40 1.00
167 Terance Mann .40 1.00
168 Dwight Howard .50 1.25
169 Patty Mills .40 1.00
170 Kevin Huerter .30 .75
171 Cam Reddish .40 1.00
172 Josh Richardson .30 .75
173 Eric Bledsoe .30 .75
174 Hassan Whiteside .30 .75
175 Davis Bertans .25 .60
176 Oshae Brissett .30 .75
177 Chuma Okeke .40 1.00
178 Raul Neto .25 .60
179 Pat Connaughton .30 .75
180 Mitchell Robinson .40 1.00
181 Tim Duncan 1.00 2.50
182 Dirk Nowitzki 1.00 2.50
183 Kevin Garnett 1.00 2.50
184 Charles Barkley 1.00 2.50
185 Shaquille O'Neal 1.25 3.00
186 Isiah Thomas .60 1.50
187 Hakeem Olajuwon .75 2.00
188 Gary Payton .60 1.50
189 Allen Iverson 1.00 2.50
190 Clyde Drexler .60 1.50
191 Karl Malone .75 2.00
192 Jason Kidd .60 1.50
193 Dennis Rodman 1.00 2.50
194 Larry Bird 1.25 3.00
195 Magic Johnson 1.25 3.00
196 Paul Pierce .60 1.50
197 Steve Nash .75 2.00
198 Dwyane Wade .75 2.00
199 Ray Allen .60 1.50
200 David Robinson .75 2.00
201 Jonathan Kuminga RC 2.50 6.00
202 Cade Cunningham RC 5.00 12.00
203 Scottie Barnes RC 2.50 6.00
204 Cameron Thomas RC 1.50 4.00
205 Josh Giddey RC 2.50 6.00
206 Davion Mitchell RC .75 2.00
207 James Bouknight RC .60 1.50
208 Jalen Green RC 4.00 10.00
209 Jalen Suggs RC 2.00 5.00
210 Franz Wagner RC 2.50 6.00
211 Herbert Jones RC 1.00 2.50
212 Evan Mobley RC 3.00 8.00
213 Ayo Dosunmu RC 1.50 4.00
214 Joshua Primo RC .60 1.50
215 Austin Reaves RC 4.00 10.00
216 Tre Mann RC 1.25 3.00
217 Trey Murphy III RC 2.50 6.00
218 Ziaire Williams RC 1.00 2.50
219 Quentin Grimes RC 1.50 4.00
220 Bones Hyland RC 1.00 2.50
221 Corey Kispert RC 1.00 2.50
222 Moses Moody RC 1.50 4.00
223 Josh Christopher RC .60 1.50
224 Jeremiah Robinson-Earl RC .75 2.00
225 Day'Ron Sharpe RC .75 2.00
226 Alperen Sengun RC 2.50 6.00
227 Greg Brown III RC .60 1.50
228 Brandon Boston Jr. RC .75 2.00
229 Dalano Banton RC 1.00 2.50
230 Luka Garza RC .75 2.00
231 Jared Butler RC .75 2.00
232 Kai Jones RC .60 1.50
233 Jalen Johnson RC 2.50 6.00
234 Usman Garuba RC .60 1.50
235 Santi Aldama RC 1.00 2.50
236 Keon Johnson RC .75 2.00
237 Omer Yurtseven RC .75 2.00
238 Aaron Wiggins RC 1.00 2.50
239 Kessler Edwards RC .75 2.00
240 Jose Alvarado RC 2.00 5.00
241 Sandro Mamukelashvili RC 1.00 2.50
242 Miles McBride RC 1.25 3.00
243 Duane Washington Jr. RC .75 2.00
244 Joe Wieskamp RC .60 1.50
245 Charles Bassey RC .75 2.00
246 JT Thor RC .75 2.00
247 Juan Toscano-Anderson RC .75 2.00
248 Jock Landale RC 1.25 3.00
249 Jaden Springer RC .75 2.00
250 Jericho Sims RC 1.00 2.50

2021-22 Panini Recon Holo Blue

*HOLO BLUE: 2.5X TO 6X BASIC
STATED PRINT RUN 99 COPIES PER
202 Cade Cunningham 40.00 100.00

2021-22 Panini Recon Holo Bronze

*HOLO BRONZE: 1.25X TO 3X BASIC
STATED PRINT RUN 299 COPIES PER
202 Cade Cunningham 20.00 50.00

2021-22 Panini Recon Holo Purple

*HOLO PURPLE: 3X TO 8X BASIC
STATED PRINT RUN 49 COPIES PER
202 Cade Cunningham 50.00 120.00

2021-22 Panini Recon Holo Red

*HOLO RED: 1.5X TO 4X BASIC
STATED PRINT RUN 199 COPIES PER
202 Cade Cunningham 25.00 60.00

2021-22 Panini Recon All Systems Go

COMMON CARD .50 1.25
SEMISTARS .60 1.50
UNLISTED STARS .75 2.00
1 James Harden 1.50 4.00
2 Cade Cunningham 5.00 12.00
3 Kawhi Leonard 2.00 5.00
4 Donovan Mitchell 1.50 4.00
5 LaMelo Ball 2.00 5.00
6 LeBron James 6.00 15.00
7 Kevin Durant 2.50 6.00
8 Josh Giddey 2.50 6.00
9 Dejounte Murray .75 2.00
10 Jalen Green 4.00 10.00
11 Evan Mobley 3.00 8.00
12 Ja Morant 2.50 6.00
13 Giannis Antetokounmpo 4.00 10.00
14 Trae Young 2.00 5.00
15 Jimmy Butler 1.25 3.00
16 Scottie Barnes 2.50 6.00
17 Damian Lillard 2.00 5.00
18 Luka Doncic 5.00 12.00
19 Stephen Curry 5.00 12.00
20 Jayson Tatum 3.00 8.00

2021-22 Panini Recon Called to Excellence Signatures

COMMON CARD 5.00 12.00
SEMISTARS 6.00 15.00
UNLISTED STARS 8.00 20.00
STATED PRINT RUN 25-75 SER.#'d SETS
EXCHANGE DEADLINE 01/29/2024
*RED/49: .5X TO 1.2X BASIC
*BLUE/35: .5X TO 1.2X BASIC
*PURPLE/25: .6X TO 1.5X BASIC
1 John Stockton/25 40.00 100.00
2 CJ McCollum/75 6.00 15.00
3 Anthony Edwards/49 150.00 400.00
4 Dominique Wilkins/75 12.00 30.00
5 Allen Iverson/35 100.00 250.00
6 Elvin Hayes/75 10.00 25.00
7 Karl-Anthony Towns/49 20.00 50.00
8 Isiah Thomas/75 20.00 50.00
9 Luka Doncic/49 400.00 800.00
10 David Robinson/35 30.00 80.00
11 Jerry West/35 30.00 80.00
12 Anthony Davis/35 30.00 80.00
13 Shai Gilgeous-Alexander/75 200.00 500.00
14 RJ Barrett/75 20.00 50.00
15 Chris Paul/35 60.00 150.00
16 Karl Malone/25 40.00 100.00
17 Kevin Garnett/35 60.00 150.00
18 Jason Williams/75 30.00 80.00
19 Dwyane Wade/25 60.00 150.00
20 Jayson Tatum/25 125.00 300.00
21 De'Aaron Fox/75 12.00 30.00
22 Stephen Curry/35 500.00 1,000.00
23 Clyde Drexler/75 25.00 60.00
24 Bradley Beal/49 10.00 25.00
25 Hakeem Olajuwon/49 30.00 80.00
26 Tony Parker/75 12.00 30.00
27 Jamal Murray/75 12.00 30.00
28 Robert Parish/75 10.00 25.00
29 Rick Barry/75 20.00 50.00
30 Amar'e Stoudemire/75 8.00 20.00

2021-22 Panini Recon Claim to Fame Signatures

COMMON CARD 4.00 10.00
SEMISTARS 5.00 12.00
UNLISTED STARS 6.00 15.00
STATED PRINT RUN 75-249 SER.#'d SETS
EXCHANGE DEADLINE 01/29/2024
*RED/49-99: .5X TO 1.2X BASIC
*BLUE/35-49: .6X TO 1.5X BASIC
*PURPLE/25: .75X TO 2X BASIC
1 Larry Johnson/99 20.00 50.00
2 Tim Hardaway/249 8.00 20.00
3 Jalen Rose/99 5.00 12.00
4 Rick Barry/75 8.00 20.00
5 Jerry West/49 30.00 80.00
6 Latrell Sprewell/99 6.00 15.00
7 Jason Williams/99 25.00 60.00
8 Steve Kerr/75 8.00 20.00
9 Artis Gilmore/99 8.00 20.00
10 Mehmet Okur/249 4.00 10.00
11 Mitch Richmond/149 8.00 20.00
12 Calvin Murphy/99 6.00 15.00
13 Robert Horry/99 6.00 15.00
14 Mark Jackson/99 5.00 12.00
15 Alex English/99 8.00 20.00
16 Jason Richardson/249 6.00 15.00
17 Steve Francis/99 6.00 15.00
18 Hedo Turkoglu/149 5.00 12.00
19 Xavier McDaniel/249 5.00 12.00
20 Andrew Bogut/99 6.00 15.00
21 Mike Bibby/249 6.00 15.00
22 Mychal Thompson/249 5.00 12.00
23 Detlef Schrempf/199 6.00 15.00
24 Sam Perkins/249 5.00 12.00
25 Dave Bing/99 8.00 20.00
26 Manu Ginobili/75 60.00 150.00
27 Dominique Wilkins/75 12.00 30.00
28 Chauncey Billups/99 8.00 20.00
29 Elton Brand/149 6.00 15.00
30 David Thompson/99 8.00 20.00

2021-22 Panini Recon Closing Statements

COMMON CARD 1.25 3.00
SEMISTARS 1.50 4.00
UNLISTED STARS 2.00 5.00
1 Ja Morant 15.00 40.00
2 Trae Young 5.00 12.00
3 Stephen Curry 20.00 50.00
4 Kevin Durant 6.00 15.00
5 Giannis Antetokounmpo 10.00 25.00
6 LeBron James 20.00 50.00
7 Joel Embiid 5.00 12.00
8 Luka Doncic 20.00 50.00

2021-22 Panini Recon Destined for Greatness Signatures

COMMON CARD 4.00 10.00
SEMISTARS 5.00 12.00
UNLISTED STARS 6.00 15.00
EXCHANGE DEADLINE 01/29/2024
*RED/49-99: .5X TO 1.2X BASIC
*BLUE/35-49: .6X TO 1.5X BASIC
*PURPLE/25: .75X TO 2X BASIC
1 Kevin Huerter 5.00 12.00
2 Aleksej Pokusevski 5.00 12.00
3 Coby White 6.00 15.00
4 Zeke Nnaji 5.00 12.00
5 Jae'Sean Tate 6.00 15.00
6 Chris Duarte 5.00 12.00
7 Keon Johnson 6.00 15.00
8 Jeremiah Robinson-Earl 6.00 15.00
9 Anthony Edwards 100.00 250.00
10 Max Strus 6.00 15.00
11 Franz Wagner 20.00 50.00
12 Duane Washington Jr. 6.00 15.00
13 Nassir Little 6.00 15.00
14 James Bouknight 5.00 12.00
15 Ayo Dosunmu 12.00 30.00
16 Scottie Barnes 20.00 50.00
17 RJ Hampton 4.00 10.00
18 Robert Williams III 6.00 15.00
19 Jaren Jackson Jr. 10.00 25.00
20 Kevin Porter Jr. 5.00 12.00

2021-22 Panini Recon Future Legends

COMMON CARD .50 1.25
SEMISTARS .60 1.50
UNLISTED STARS .75 2.00
1 LaMelo Ball 2.00 5.00
2 Cade Cunningham 5.00 12.00
3 Tyrese Maxey 2.00 5.00
4 Tyrese Haliburton 1.50 4.00
5 Jalen Green 4.00 10.00
6 Ja Morant 2.50 6.00
7 Evan Mobley 3.00 8.00
8 Desmond Bane 1.50 4.00
9 Cole Anthony 1.00 2.50
10 Jalen Suggs 2.00 5.00
11 Scottie Barnes 2.50 6.00
12 Anthony Edwards 4.00 10.00
13 Saddiq Bey .60 1.50
14 Darius Garland 1.25 3.00
15 Zion Williamson 2.00 5.00
16 Tyler Herro 1.25 3.00
17 Josh Giddey 2.50 6.00
18 Jonathan Kuminga 2.50 6.00
19 Franz Wagner 2.50 6.00
20 Luka Doncic 5.00 12.00
21 Jaren Jackson Jr. 1.25 3.00
22 Deandre Ayton .75 2.00
23 Ayo Dosunmu 1.50 4.00
24 Cameron Thomas 1.50 4.00
25 Shai Gilgeous-Alexander 4.00 10.00

2021-22 Panini Recon Glorified Signatures

COMMON CARD 4.00 10.00
SEMISTARS 5.00 12.00
UNLISTED STARS 6.00 15.00
STATED PRINT RUN 75-249 SER.#'d SETS
EXCHANGE DEADLINE 01/29/2024
*RED/49-99: .5X TO 1.2X BASIC
*BLUE/35-49: .6X TO 1.5X BASIC
*PURPLE/25: .75X TO 2X BASIC
1 Malik Monk/99 6.00 15.00
2 Wendell Carter Jr./75 6.00 15.00
3 Grayson Allen/199 6.00 15.00
4 Joe Harris/99 5.00 12.00
5 Chris Boucher/99 6.00 15.00
6 Brandon Clarke/99 6.00 15.00
7 Myles Turner/99 6.00 15.00
8 Robert Williams III/99 6.00 15.00
9 Will Barton/199 4.00 10.00
10 Max Strus/249 6.00 15.00
11 Kristaps Porzingis/75 8.00 20.00
12 Kevin Huerter/249 5.00 12.00
13 Josh Hart/99 5.00 12.00
14 Monte Morris/199 5.00 12.00
15 Kyle Anderson/199 4.00 10.00
16 Joe Ingles/99 5.00 12.00
17 Keldon Johnson/99 8.00 20.00
18 RJ Hampton/99 4.00 10.00
19 Taj Gibson/99 4.00 10.00
20 Karl-Anthony Towns/75 20.00 50.00
21 Theo Maledon/99 5.00 12.00
22 Rudy Gobert/75 8.00 20.00
23 Devin Vassell/99 10.00 25.00
24 Aleksej Pokusevski/99 5.00 12.00
25 Jae'Sean Tate/99 6.00 15.00
26 Tim Hardaway Jr./199 4.00 10.00
27 Bobby Portis/99 5.00 12.00
28 Bojan Bogdanovic/99 5.00 12.00
29 Christian Wood/99 5.00 12.00
30 Danilo Gallinari/75 5.00 12.00
31 Daniel Theis/249 5.00 12.00
32 Landry Shamet/249 5.00 12.00
33 Bogdan Bogdanovic/99 6.00 15.00
34 Terance Mann/99 6.00 15.00
35 Rajon Rondo/75 8.00 20.00
36 T.J. McConnell/249 5.00 12.00
37 Tyrese Haliburton/99 20.00 50.00
38 Kevin Huerter/99 5.00 12.00
39 Kenyon Martin Jr./249 6.00 15.00
40 Pat Connaughton/99 5.00 12.00

2021-22 Panini Recon Hall Hopefuls

COMMON CARD .50 1.25
SEMISTARS .60 1.50
UNLISTED STARS .75 2.00
1 Stephen Curry 5.00 12.00
2 James Harden 1.50 4.00
3 Chris Paul 1.50 4.00
4 Anthony Davis 2.00 5.00
5 Damian Lillard 2.00 5.00
6 LeBron James 6.00 15.00
7 Kevin Durant 2.50 6.00
8 Giannis Antetokounmpo 4.00 10.00
9 Carmelo Anthony 1.25 3.00
10 Russell Westbrook 1.25 3.00
11 Kawhi Leonard 2.00 5.00
12 Klay Thompson 2.00 5.00
13 Kyrie Irving 1.50 4.00
14 Derrick Rose 1.25 3.00
15 Paul George 1.25 3.00

2021-22 Panini Recon Maneuvers

COMMON CARD .50 1.25
SEMISTARS .60 1.50
UNLISTED STARS .75 2.00
1 Cade Cunningham 5.00 12.00
2 LaMelo Ball 2.00 5.00
3 Jalen Green 4.00 10.00
4 Chris Paul 1.50 4.00
5 Donovan Mitchell 1.50 4.00
6 LeBron James 6.00 15.00
7 Luka Doncic 5.00 12.00
8 Josh Giddey 2.50 6.00
9 Stephen Curry 5.00 12.00
10 Kyrie Irving 1.50 4.00
11 Trae Young 2.00 5.00
12 Ja Morant 2.50 6.00
13 Nikola Jokic 4.00 10.00
14 Dejounte Murray .75 2.00
15 Darius Garland 1.25 3.00
16 James Harden 1.50 4.00
17 Russell Westbrook 1.25 3.00
18 Scottie Barnes 2.50 6.00
19 De'Aaron Fox 1.25 3.00
20 Tyrese Haliburton 1.50 4.00
21 Jason Kidd 1.25 3.00
22 Magic Johnson 2.50 6.00
23 John Stockton 1.50 4.00
24 Allen Iverson 2.00 5.00
25 Steve Nash 1.00 2.50

2021-22 Panini Recon Panini All-Pro Team

COMMON CARD .50 1.25
SEMISTARS .60 1.50
UNLISTED STARS .75 2.00
1 Luka Doncic 5.00 12.00
2 Stephen Curry 5.00 12.00
3 Giannis Antetokounmpo 4.00 10.00
4 Nikola Jokic 4.00 10.00
5 Joel Embiid 2.00 5.00
6 LeBron James 6.00 15.00
7 Kevin Durant 2.50 6.00
8 Trae Young 2.00 5.00
9 DeMar DeRozan 1.00 2.50
10 Devin Booker 2.00 5.00
11 Jayson Tatum 3.00 8.00
12 Ja Morant 2.50 6.00

2021-22 Panini Recon Rock the Rim

COMMON CARD .50 1.25
SEMISTARS .60 1.50
UNLISTED STARS .75 2.00
1 Jalen Green 4.00 10.00
2 Anthony Edwards 4.00 10.00
3 Zach LaVine 1.25 3.00
4 Obi Toppin .75 2.00
5 Giannis Antetokounmpo 4.00 10.00
6 LeBron James 6.00 15.00
7 Donovan Mitchell 1.50 4.00
8 Zion Williamson 2.00 5.00
9 Jonathan Kuminga 2.50 6.00
10 Russell Westbrook 1.25 3.00
11 Joel Embiid 2.00 5.00
12 Ja Morant 2.50 6.00
13 Cole Anthony 1.00 2.50
14 Aaron Gordon .75 2.00
15 Evan Mobley 3.00 8.00
16 John Collins .75 2.00
17 Miles Bridges .60 1.50
18 Jayson Tatum 3.00 8.00
19 Paul George 1.25 3.00
20 DeMar DeRozan 1.00 2.50
21 Anfernee Simons 1.25 3.00
22 Jason Richardson .75 2.00
23 Shaquille O'Neal 2.50 6.00
24 Dominique Wilkins 1.25 3.00
25 Vince Carter 1.50 4.00

2021-22 Panini Recon Rookie Jersey Autographs

COMMON CARD 6.00 15.00
SEMISTARS 8.00 20.00
UNLISTED STARS 10.00 25.00
STATED PRINT RUN 75-99 SER.#'d SETS
EXCHANGE DEADLINE 01/29/2024
1 Austin Reaves/99 75.00 200.00
2 Evan Mobley/75 40.00 100.00
3 Chris Duarte/99 8.00 20.00
4 Moses Moody/75 20.00 50.00
5 Aaron Wiggins/99 12.00 30.00
6 Cameron Thomas/99 20.00 50.00
7 Jonathan Kuminga/75 30.00 80.00
8 Keon Johnson/75 10.00 25.00
9 Trey Murphy III/99 30.00 80.00
10 Davion Mitchell/75 10.00 25.00
11 JT Thor/99 10.00 25.00
12 Jaden Springer/99 10.00 25.00
13 Scottie Barnes/75 30.00 80.00
14 Herbert Jones/99 12.00 30.00
15 Ziaire Williams/75 12.00 30.00
16 Tre Mann/99 15.00 40.00
17 Jeremiah Robinson-Earl/99 10.00 25.00
18 Luka Garza/99 10.00 25.00
19 Josh Giddey/99 30.00 80.00
20 Bones Hyland/99 12.00 30.00
21 Miles McBride/99 15.00 40.00
22 Joshua Primo/99 8.00 20.00
23 Isaiah Jackson/75 10.00 25.00
24 Jalen Johnson/75 30.00 80.00
25 Cade Cunningham/75 100.00 250.00
26 Jared Butler/99 10.00 25.00
27 Greg Brown III/99 8.00 20.00
28 Jason Preston/99 8.00 20.00
29 Franz Wagner/75 30.00 80.00
30 Scottie Lewis/99 8.00 20.00
31 Charles Bassey/99 10.00 25.00
32 Corey Kispert/75 12.00 30.00
33 Jalen Suggs/75 25.00 60.00
34 Ayo Dosunmu/99 20.00 50.00
35 Santi Aldama/99 12.00 30.00
36 James Bouknight/75 8.00 20.00
37 Brandon Boston Jr./99 10.00 25.00
38 Quentin Grimes/99 20.00 50.00
39 Kai Jones/75 8.00 20.00
40 Jalen Green/75 50.00 125.00

2021-22 Panini Recon Rookie Recon

COMMON CARD .60 1.50
SEMISTARS .75 2.00
UNLISTED STARS 1.00 2.50
1 Cade Cunningham 6.00 15.00
2 Jalen Green 5.00 12.00
3 Evan Mobley 4.00 10.00
4 Scottie Barnes 3.00 8.00
5 Jalen Suggs 2.50 6.00
6 Josh Giddey 3.00 8.00
7 Jonathan Kuminga 3.00 8.00
8 Franz Wagner 3.00 8.00
9 Davion Mitchell 1.00 2.50
10 Ziaire Williams 1.25 3.00
11 Ayo Dosunmu 2.00 5.00
12 Cameron Thomas 2.00 5.00
13 Chris Duarte .75 2.00
14 Bones Hyland 1.25 3.00
15 James Bouknight .75 2.00
16 Alperen Sengun 3.00 8.00
17 Joshua Primo .75 2.00
18 Tre Mann 1.50 4.00
19 Herbert Jones 1.25 3.00
20 Moses Moody 2.00 5.00
21 Corey Kispert 1.25 3.00
22 Quentin Grimes 2.00 5.00
23 Austin Reaves 5.00 12.00
24 Isaiah Jackson 1.00 2.50
25 Josh Christopher .75 2.00

2021-22 Panini Recon Rookie Recon Signatures

COMMON CARD 4.00 10.00
SEMISTARS 5.00 12.00
UNLISTED STARS 6.00 15.00
EXCHANGE DEADLINE 01/29/2024
*RED/49-99: .5X TO 1.2X BASIC
*BLUE/35-49: .6X TO 1.5X BASIC
*PURPLE/25: .75X TO 2X BASIC
1 Aaron Wiggins 8.00 20.00
2 Duane Washington Jr. 6.00 15.00
3 Josh Christopher 5.00 12.00
4 Isaiah Livers 6.00 15.00
5 Jose Alvarado 15.00 40.00
6 Neemias Queta 6.00 15.00
7 Jalen Johnson 20.00 50.00
8 Kai Jones 5.00 12.00
9 Miles McBride 10.00 25.00
10 Day'Ron Sharpe 6.00 15.00
11 Juan Toscano-Anderson 6.00 15.00
12 Jericho Sims 8.00 20.00
13 Jalen Suggs 30.00 80.00
14 Sandro Mamukelashvili 8.00 20.00
15 Alperen Sengun 20.00 50.00
16 Trey Murphy III 20.00 50.00
17 Davion Mitchell 6.00 15.00
18 David Duke Jr. 6.00 15.00
19 JT Thor 6.00 15.00
20 Cade Cunningham 200.00 500.00
21 Isaiah Jackson 6.00 15.00
22 Jason Preston 5.00 12.00
23 Charles Bassey 6.00 15.00
24 Armoni Brooks 6.00 15.00
25 Jalen Green 125.00 300.00
26 Herbert Jones 8.00 20.00
27 Ziaire Williams 8.00 20.00
28 Isaiah Todd 5.00 12.00
29 Cameron Thomas 12.00 30.00
30 Ayo Dosunmu 12.00 30.00
31 Jaden Springer 6.00 15.00
32 Quentin Grimes 12.00 30.00
33 Scottie Barnes 125.00 300.00
34 Trendon Watford 8.00 20.00
35 Josh Giddey 75.00 200.00
36 James Bouknight 5.00 12.00
37 Jonathan Kuminga 75.00 200.00
38 Joe Wieskamp 5.00 12.00
39 Evan Mobley 100.00 250.00
40 Usman Garuba 5.00 12.00

2021-22 Panini Recon Rookie Review

COMMON CARD .75 2.00
SEMISTARS 1.00 2.50
UNLISTED STARS 1.25 3.00
1 Giannis Antetokounmpo 6.00 15.00
2 Klay Thompson 3.00 8.00
3 James Harden 2.50 6.00
4 DeMar DeRozan 1.50 4.00
5 Dwight Howard 1.50 4.00
6 LeBron James 10.00 25.00
7 Kevin Durant 4.00 10.00
8 Ben Simmons 1.25 3.00
9 Andrew Wiggins 1.50 4.00
10 Karl-Anthony Towns 2.00 5.00
11 Joel Embiid 3.00 8.00
12 Stephen Curry 8.00 20.00
13 Kawhi Leonard 3.00 8.00
14 Anthony Davis 3.00 8.00
15 Nikola Jokic 6.00 15.00

2021-22 Panini Recon Sky's the Limit

COMMON CARD 1.25 3.00
SEMISTARS 1.50 4.00
UNLISTED STARS 2.00 5.00
1 Luka Doncic 20.00 50.00
2 Ja Morant 15.00 40.00
3 Trae Young 5.00 12.00
4 Giannis Antetokounmpo 10.00 25.00
5 Kevin Durant 6.00 15.00
6 LeBron James 20.00 50.00
7 Stephen Curry 20.00 50.00
8 Cade Cunningham 30.00 80.00
9 Evan Mobley 8.00 20.00
10 Josh Giddey 6.00 15.00

2021-22 Panini Recon Top of the Charts

COMMON CARD .50 1.25
SEMISTARS .60 1.50
UNLISTED STARS .75 2.00
1 Josh Giddey 2.50 6.00
2 Russell Westbrook 1.25 3.00
3 Ja Morant 2.50 6.00
4 Dejounte Murray .75 2.00
5 LeBron James 6.00 15.00
6 Klay Thompson 2.00 5.00
7 Devin Booker 2.00 5.00
8 Stephen Curry 5.00 12.00
9 Luka Doncic 5.00 12.00
10 James Harden 1.50 4.00
11 Trae Young 2.00 5.00
12 Kevin Durant 2.50 6.00
13 Chris Paul 1.50 4.00
14 John Stockton 1.50 4.00
15 Dirk Nowitzki 2.00 5.00
16 Magic Johnson 2.50 6.00
17 Kareem Abdul-Jabbar 2.50 6.00
18 Vince Carter 1.50 4.00
19 Donovan Mitchell 1.50 4.00
20 Damian Lillard 2.00 5.00

2021-22 Panini Recon True Potential Signatures

COMMON CARD 4.00 10.00
SEMISTARS 5.00 12.00
UNLISTED STARS 6.00 15.00
EXCHANGE DEADLINE 01/29/2024
*RED/49-99: .5X TO 1.2X BASIC
*BLUE/35-49: .6X TO 1.5X BASIC
*PURPLE/25: .75X TO 2X BASIC
1 Jalen Green 30.00 80.00
2 Kessler Edwards 6.00 15.00
3 Jock Landale 10.00 25.00
4 Armoni Brooks 6.00 15.00
5 Luka Garza 6.00 15.00
6 Dalano Banton 8.00 20.00
7 Aaron Wiggins 8.00 20.00
8 Jason Preston 5.00 12.00
9 Day'Ron Sharpe 6.00 15.00
10 Trendon Watford 8.00 20.00
11 Cameron Thomas 12.00 30.00
12 Neemias Queta 6.00 15.00
13 Scottie Lewis 5.00 12.00
14 David Duke Jr. 6.00 15.00
15 Miles McBride 10.00 25.00
16 Isaiah Todd 5.00 12.00
17 Tre Mann 10.00 25.00
18 Usman Garuba 5.00 12.00
19 Kai Jones 5.00 12.00
20 Cade Cunningham 75.00 200.00
21 Jared Butler 6.00 15.00
22 JT Thor 6.00 15.00
23 Isaiah Livers 6.00 15.00
24 Evan Mobley 25.00 60.00
25 Josh Giddey 20.00 50.00
26 Jonathan Kuminga 20.00 50.00
27 Keon Johnson 6.00 15.00
28 Alperen Sengun 20.00 50.00
29 Jalen Suggs 15.00 40.00
30 Joshua Primo 5.00 12.00
31 Sam Hauser 15.00 40.00
32 Austin Reaves 50.00 120.00
33 Moses Moody 12.00 30.00
34 Joe Wieskamp 5.00 12.00
35 Corey Kispert 8.00 20.00
36 Isaiah Jackson 6.00 15.00
37 Sandro Mamukelashvili 8.00 20.00
38 Josh Christopher 5.00 12.00
39 Herbert Jones 8.00 20.00
40 Bones Hyland 8.00 20.00

2022-23 Panini Recon

COMMON CARD (1-200) .25 .60
SEMISTARS .30 .75
UNLISTED STARS .40 1.00
COMMON RC (201-250) .50 1.25
RC SEMIS .60 1.50
RC UNLISTED .75 2.00
*HOLO: .6X TO 1.5X BASIC
*HOLO BRONZE/299: 1.25X TO 3X BASIC
*HOLO RED/199: 1.5X TO 4X BASIC
*HOLO BLUE/99: 2X TO 5X BASIC
*HOLO PURPLE/49: 2.5X TO 6X BASIC
1 Chris Paul .75 2.00
2 Donovan Mitchell .75 2.00
3 Bojan Bogdanovic .40 1.00
4 Kyrie Irving .75 2.00
5 Mikal Bridges .50 1.25
6 RJ Barrett .60 1.50
7 Josh Green .40 1.00
8 Jaylen Nowell .40 1.00
9 Pascal Siakam .60 1.50
10 Michael Porter Jr. .50 1.25
11 Desmond Bane .50 1.25
12 Tim Hardaway Jr. .30 .75
13 Gary Trent Jr. .40 1.00
14 Franz Wagner 1.00 2.50
15 James Harden .75 2.00
16 Cade Cunningham 1.25 3.00
17 Jonathan Kuminga 1.00 2.50
18 Tyrese Maxey .75 2.00
19 Klay Thompson 1.00 2.50
20 Grayson Allen .40 1.00
21 Cameron Payne .30 .75
22 Marcus Smart .50 1.25
23 Domantas Sabonis .50 1.25
24 Jae'Sean Tate .25 .60
25 Norman Powell .40 1.00
26 Christian Wood .25 .60
27 Nikola Jokic 2.00 5.00
28 Royce O'Neale .30 .75
29 PJ Washington Jr. .40 1.00
30 CJ McCollum .40 1.00
31 Darius Garland .60 1.50
32 Eric Gordon .30 .75
33 Mike Conley .30 .75
34 Gordon Hayward .30 .75
35 Dennis Schroder .40 1.00
36 Josh Hart .40 1.00
37 Kevin Durant 1.25 3.00
38 Deandre Ayton .40 1.00
39 Kristaps Porzingis .50 1.25
40 Jarrett Allen .40 1.00
41 Ivica Zubac .40 1.00
42 Keldon Johnson .50 1.25
43 Kyle Lowry .50 1.25
44 Evan Mobley 1.00 2.50
45 Saddiq Bey .30 .75
46 Marcus Morris Sr. .25 .60
47 Joel Embiid .60 1.50
48 Alperen Sengun .50 1.25
49 Zach LaVine .75 2.00
50 Nikola Vucevic .40 1.00
51 Onyeka Okongwu .40 1.00
52 Josh Giddey .60 1.50
53 Chris Duarte .30 .75
54 Immanuel Quickley .40 1.00
55 Harrison Barnes .30 .75
56 Alec Burks .30 .75
57 Julius Randle .50 1.25
58 Kyle Kuzma .50 1.25
59 Brandon Clarke .30 .75
60 Donte DiVincenzo .40 1.00
61 Al Horford .40 1.00
62 Aaron Nesmith .40 1.00
63 Bradley Beal .50 1.25
64 Nicolas Claxton .40 1.00
65 Killian Hayes .25 .60
66 Karl-Anthony Towns .60 1.50
67 Rui Hachimura .40 1.00
68 Kentavious Caldwell-Pope .30 .75
69 Anthony Edwards 2.00 5.00
70 Damian Lillard 1.00 2.50
71 Jakob Poeltl .30 .75
72 Tre Jones .40 1.00
73 Trae Young 1.00 2.50
74 Scottie Barnes .60 1.50
75 Shai Gilgeous-Alexander 2.00 5.00
76 Patrick Williams .40 1.00
77 Bones Hyland .30 .75
78 Alex Caruso .40 1.00
79 Fred VanVleet .50 1.25
80 Doug McDermott .25 .60
81 P.J. Tucker .30 .75
82 Derrick White .40 1.00
83 Jordan Clarkson .40 1.00
84 Trey Murphy III .50 1.25
85 Malcolm Brogdon .30 .75
86 Josh Richardson .30 .75
87 Spencer Dinwiddie .30 .75
88 Kawhi Leonard 1.00 2.50
89 De'Aaron Fox .75 2.00
90 Bruce Brown .40 1.00
91 Deni Avdija .40 1.00
92 Davion Mitchell .30 .75
93 Tyler Herro .60 1.50
94 Bam Adebayo .60 1.50
95 LeBron James 3.00 8.00
96 Lonzo Ball .40 1.00
97 Robert Williams III .40 1.00
98 Lauri Markkanen .60 1.50
99 Devin Booker 1.00 2.50
100 Coby White .30 .75
101 Jerami Grant .50 1.25
102 Myles Turner .40 1.00
103 Jamal Murray .60 1.50
104 Grant Williams .30 .75
105 Jalen McDaniels .40 1.00
106 Isaac Okoro .30 .75
107 D'Angelo Russell .30 .75
108 Malik Monk .40 1.00
109 Anthony Davis 1.00 2.50
110 Terry Rozier III .50 1.25
111 Kenyon Martin Jr. .40 1.00
112 Brandon Ingram .50 1.25
113 Wendell Carter Jr. .40 1.00
114 Devin Vassell .50 1.25
115 Caris LeVert .30 .75
116 Bol Bol .40 1.00
117 Jimmy Butler .75 2.00
118 Cameron Thomas .60 1.50
119 Jalen Brunson .75 2.00
120 Clint Capela .40 1.00
121 Cameron Johnson .30 .75
122 Luguentz Dort .40 1.00
123 Caleb Martin .40 1.00
124 Jrue Holiday .50 1.25
125 DeMar DeRozan .50 1.25
126 Bogdan Bogdanovic .40 1.00
127 Tobias Harris .30 .75
128 Russell Westbrook .60 1.50
129 Anfernee Simons .50 1.25
130 OG Anunoby .50 1.25
131 Kevin Huerter .40 1.00
132 Tyrese Haliburton .75 2.00
133 Reggie Jackson .30 .75
134 Khris Middleton .50 1.25
135 Rudy Gobert .50 1.25
136 Dejounte Murray .50 1.25
137 John Collins .40 1.00
138 Jaylen Brown .75 2.00
139 Ja Morant 1.25 3.00
140 Corey Kispert .40 1.00
141 Quentin Grimes .30 .75
142 Kevin Porter Jr. .30 .75
143 Zion Williamson 1.00 2.50
144 Luke Kennard .30 .75
145 Kelly Oubre Jr. .40 1.00
146 Jose Alvarado .40 1.00
147 Buddy Hield .40 1.00
148 Isaiah Stewart .30 .75
149 Derrick Rose .75 2.00
150 Tre Mann .30 .75
151 Jusuf Nurkic .40 1.00
152 Collin Sexton .50 1.25
153 Santi Aldama .40 1.00
154 LaMelo Ball 1.00 2.50
155 Herbert Jones .40 1.00
156 Reggie Bullock .30 .75
157 Ayo Dosunmu .50 1.25
158 Jeremiah Robinson-Earl .30 .75
159 Dorian Finney-Smith .30 .75
160 Aleksej Pokusevski .40 1.00
161 Jalen Green 1.25 3.00
162 Jaden McDaniels .40 1.00
163 Kelly Olynyk .30 .75
164 Mitchell Robinson .30 .75
165 Jonas Valanciunas .30 .75
166 Chris Boucher .40 1.00
167 Andrew Wiggins .50 1.25
168 Max Strus .40 1.00
169 Brook Lopez .40 1.00
170 Dillon Brooks .40 1.00
171 Larry Nance Jr. .40 1.00
172 Bobby Portis .40 1.00
173 John Wall .50 1.25
174 Paul George .60 1.50
175 Jalen Smith .40 1.00
176 Malik Beasley .30 .75
177 Jayson Tatum 1.50 4.00
178 Cam Reddish .30 .75
179 De'Anthony Melton .30 .75
180 Cole Anthony .40 1.00
181 Lonnie Walker IV .30 .75
182 Giannis Antetokounmpo 2.00 5.00
183 Jarred Vanderbilt .30 .75
184 Jalen Suggs .50 1.25
185 Monte Morris .25 .60
186 De'Andre Hunter .40 1.00
187 Luka Doncic 2.50 6.00
188 Stephen Curry 3.00 8.00
189 Ben Simmons .40 1.00
190 Aaron Gordon .40 1.00
191 Draymond Green .50 1.25
192 Moritz Wagner .30 .75
193 Shake Milton .30 .75
194 Kevin Love .40 1.00
195 Joe Harris .30 .75
196 Tyus Jones .30 .75
197 Austin Reaves 1.00 2.50
198 Jaren Jackson Jr. .60 1.50
199 Jordan Poole .60 1.50
200 Markelle Fultz .30 .75
201 Paolo Banchero RC 5.00 12.00
202 Keegan Murray RC 2.00 5.00
203 Jaden Ivey RC 2.50 6.00
204 Jaden Hardy RC 1.25 3.00
205 Patrick Baldwin Jr. RC .75 2.00
206 Max Christie RC 2.00 5.00
207 Isaiah Mobley RC .75 2.00
208 David Roddy RC 1.00 2.50
209 Ryan Rollins RC .75 2.00
210 Wendell Moore Jr. RC .75 2.00
211 AJ Griffin RC .60 1.50
212 Simone Fontecchio RC .75 2.00
213 Mark Williams RC 1.50 4.00
214 Nikola Jovic RC 1.50 4.00
215 Jabari Smith Jr. RC 2.50 6.00
216 Christian Koloko RC .75 2.00
217 TyTy Washington Jr. RC .75 2.00
218 Caleb Houstan RC .75 2.00
219 Bryce McGowens RC .75 2.00
220 Johnny Davis RC .75 2.00
221 Jaylin Williams RC 1.00 2.50
222 Walker Kessler RC 1.50 4.00
223 Jake LaRavia RC .75 2.00
224 MarJon Beauchamp RC .75 2.00
225 Ousmane Dieng RC 1.00 2.50
226 Kendall Brown RC .60 1.50
227 Chet Holmgren RC 4.00 10.00
228 Trevor Keels RC .60 1.50
229 E.J. Liddell RC .75 2.00
230 Andrew Nembhard RC 1.50 4.00
231 Tyrese Martin RC .60 1.50
232 Moussa Diabate RC .75 2.00
233 Bennedict Mathurin RC 2.50 6.00
234 Jalen Duren RC 2.50 6.00
235 Kenneth Lofton Jr. RC 1.00 2.50
236 Kennedy Chandler RC .75 2.00
237 Jalen Williams RC 4.00 10.00
238 Ochai Agbaji RC 1.00 2.50
239 Peyton Watson RC 1.25 3.00
240 Shaedon Sharpe RC 3.00 8.00
241 Tari Eason RC 2.00 5.00
242 Dyson Daniels RC 2.00 5.00
243 Malaki Branham RC .75 2.00
244 Christian Braun RC 2.00 5.00
245 Dalen Terry RC .75 2.00
246 Vince Williams Jr. RC 1.00 2.50
247 Jeremy Sochan RC 2.50 6.00
248 Jabari Walker RC .60 1.50
249 Josh Minott RC .75 2.00
250 Blake Wesley RC .75 2.00

2022-23 Panini Recon All Systems Go

1 Ja Morant 2.50 6.00
2 Jayson Tatum 3.00 8.00
3 Donovan Mitchell 1.50 4.00
4 Trae Young 2.00 5.00
5 Jaylen Brown 1.50 4.00
6 Anthony Edwards 4.00 10.00
7 Zion Williamson 2.00 5.00
8 LaMelo Ball 2.00 5.00
9 Paolo Banchero 5.00 12.00
10 Stephen Curry 6.00 15.00
11 Luka Doncic 5.00 12.00
12 LeBron James 6.00 15.00
13 Devin Booker 2.00 5.00
14 Jabari Smith Jr. 2.50 6.00
15 Kevin Durant 2.50 6.00
16 Jaden Ivey 2.50 6.00
17 Shai Gilgeous-Alexander 4.00 10.00
18 Keegan Murray 2.00 5.00
19 Giannis Antetokounmpo 4.00 10.00
20 Bennedict Mathurin 2.50 6.00

2022-23 Panini Recon Called to Excellence Signatures

COMMON CARD 4.00 10.00
SEMISTARS 5.00 12.00
UNLISTED STARS 6.00 15.00
STATED PRINT RUN 75-149 SER.#'d SETS
*RED/75-99: .4X TO 1X BASIC
*BLUE/49: .5X TO 1.2X BASIC
*PURPLE/25: .6X TO 1.5X BASIC
1 Kevon Looney/149 6.00 15.00
2 Malcolm Brogdon/75 5.00 12.00
3 Kelly Oubre Jr./99 6.00 15.00
4 Max Strus/149 6.00 15.00
5 Derrick White/99 8.00 20.00
6 Goran Dragic/99 5.00 12.00
7 Anthony Edwards/75 100.00 250.00
8 Udonis Haslem/125 5.00 12.00
9 Bobby Portis/99 6.00 15.00
10 Thomas Bryant/125 5.00 12.00
11 Moses Moody/99 8.00 20.00
12 Jose Alvarado/149 6.00 15.00
13 Nerlens Noel/149 4.00 10.00
14 Lonnie Walker IV/99 5.00 12.00
15 De'Anthony Melton/149 5.00 12.00
16 Cam Reddish/99 5.00 12.00
17 Franz Wagner/99 15.00 40.00
18 Aleksej Pokusevski/125 6.00 15.00
19 Tim Hardaway Jr./99 5.00 12.00
20 Kevin Huerter/125 6.00 15.00
21 Rudy Gobert/99 8.00 20.00
22 Jonas Valanciunas/99 5.00 12.00
23 Grant Williams/149 5.00 12.00
24 Jordan Clarkson/99 12.00 30.00
25 Brook Lopez/99 6.00 15.00
26 Ayo Dosunmu/125 8.00 20.00
27 Caleb Martin/149 6.00 15.00
28 Landry Shamet/149 4.00 10.00
29 Wendell Carter Jr./99 6.00 15.00
30 Dejounte Murray/75 12.00 30.00

2022-23 Panini Recon Claim to Fame Signatures

COMMON CARD 4.00 10.00
SEMISTARS 5.00 12.00
UNLISTED STARS 6.00 15.00
STATED PRINT RUN 75-149 SER.#'d SETS
*RED/75-99: .4X TO 1X BASIC
*BLUE/49: .5X TO 1.2X BASIC
*PURPLE/25: .6X TO 1.5X BASIC
1 Peja Stojakovic/75 6.00 15.00
2 Toni Kukoc/99 8.00 20.00
3 Allen Iverson/75 75.00 200.00
4 Gary Payton/75 20.00 50.00
5 Metta World Peace/75 6.00 15.00
6 Jamal Crawford/75 6.00 15.00
7 Zach Randolph/99 6.00 15.00
8 Glen Rice/99 6.00 15.00
9 Tony Allen/125 4.00 10.00
10 Dale Ellis/125 6.00 15.00
11 Bill Laimbeer/125 6.00 15.00
12 Kenyon Martin/125 6.00 15.00
13 Dennis Scott/125 5.00 12.00
14 Hedo Turkoglu/125 6.00 15.00
15 Mitch Richmond/125 8.00 20.00
16 Stephen Jackson/125 6.00 15.00
17 Fat Lever/149 5.00 12.00
18 Roy Hibbert/149 5.00 12.00
19 Doug Collins/149 6.00 15.00
20 Tim Hardaway/149 8.00 20.00
21 Dikembe Mutombo/99 15.00 40.00
22 Lenny Wilkens/99 8.00 20.00
23 George McGinnis/99 6.00 15.00
24 Anfernee Hardaway/75 40.00 100.00
25 Detlef Schrempf/149 6.00 15.00
26 Greg Anthony/149 5.00 12.00
27 Jalen Rose/99 6.00 15.00
28 Bob Dandridge/99 6.00 15.00
29 Dino Radja/149 5.00 12.00
30 Dan Issel/149 8.00 20.00

2022-23 Panini Recon Destined for Greatness Signatures

COMMON CARD 4.00 10.00
SEMISTARS 5.00 12.00
UNLISTED STARS 6.00 15.00
STATED PRINT RUN 75-149 SER.#'d SETS
*RED/49-99: .4X TO 1X BASIC
*BLUE/49: .5X TO 1.2X BASIC
*PURPLE/25: .6X TO 1.5X BASIC
1 Chris Duarte/125 5.00 12.00
2 Trey Murphy III/125 8.00 20.00
3 Tyrese Haliburton/75 60.00 150.00
4 Jonathan Kuminga/75 15.00 40.00
5 Scottie Barnes/75 25.00 60.00
6 Josh Giddey/75 25.00 60.00
7 Kenyon Martin Jr./125 6.00 15.00
8 Juan Toscano-Anderson/125 4.00 10.00
9 Jordan Poole/75 25.00 60.00
10 Bones Hyland/149 5.00 12.00
11 Obi Toppin/75 6.00 15.00
12 Isaac Okoro/125 5.00 12.00
13 Devin Vassell/99 8.00 20.00
14 Desmond Bane/75 8.00 20.00
15 RJ Barrett/75 10.00 25.00
16 Alperen Sengun/125 8.00 20.00
17 Herbert Jones/149 6.00 15.00
18 Austin Reaves/149 25.00 60.00
19 Davion Mitchell/75 5.00 12.00
20 Jalen Green/75 40.00 100.00

2022-23 Panini Recon Fleet Feet

1 Josh Giddey 1.00 2.50
2 LaMelo Ball 1.50 4.00
3 Anthony Edwards 3.00 8.00
4 Donovan Mitchell 1.25 3.00
5 Russell Westbrook 1.00 2.50
6 Jalen Suggs .75 2.00
7 Tyrese Maxey 1.25 3.00
8 Tyrese Haliburton 1.25 3.00
9 Darius Garland 1.00 2.50
10 De'Aaron Fox 1.25 3.00
11 Bennedict Mathurin 2.00 5.00
12 Damian Lillard 1.50 4.00
13 Jaden Ivey 2.00 5.00
14 Shaedon Sharpe 2.50 6.00
15 Chris Paul 1.25 3.00
16 Stephen Curry 5.00 12.00
17 Zion Williamson 1.50 4.00
18 Trae Young 1.50 4.00
19 Jalen Green 2.00 5.00
20 Ja Morant 2.00 5.00

2022-23 Panini Recon Future Legends

1 Jaden Ivey 2.50 6.00
2 Bennedict Mathurin 2.50 6.00
3 Paolo Banchero 5.00 12.00
4 Dyson Daniels 2.00 5.00
5 Johnny Davis .75 2.00
6 AJ Griffin .60 1.50
7 Jabari Smith Jr. 2.50 6.00
8 Shaedon Sharpe 3.00 8.00
9 Ousmane Dieng 1.00 2.50
10 Jeremy Sochan 2.50 6.00
11 Ochai Agbaji 1.00 2.50
12 Jalen Williams 4.00 10.00
13 Keegan Murray 2.00 5.00
14 Jalen Duren 2.50 6.00
15 Chet Holmgren 4.00 10.00
16 Cade Cunningham 2.50 6.00
17 Jalen Green 2.50 6.00
18 Evan Mobley 2.00 5.00
19 Scottie Barnes 1.25 3.00
20 Jalen Suggs 1.00 2.50
21 Josh Giddey 1.25 3.00
22 Anthony Edwards 4.00 10.00
23 LaMelo Ball 2.00 5.00
24 Tyrese Haliburton 1.50 4.00
25 Tyrese Maxey 1.50 4.00

2022-23 Panini Recon Glorified Signatures

COMMON CARD 4.00 10.00
SEMISTARS 5.00 12.00
UNLISTED STARS 6.00 15.00
STATED PRINT RUN 75-149 SER.#'d SETS
*RED/75-99: .4X TO 1X BASIC
*BLUE/49: .5X TO 1.2X BASIC
*PURPLE/25: .6X TO 1.5X BASIC
1 Danny Green/125 5.00 12.00
2 Luke Kennard/125 5.00 12.00
3 Brandon Clarke/99 5.00 12.00
4 RJ Hampton/125 5.00 12.00
5 Josh Hart/149 6.00 15.00
6 Brandon Ingram/75 8.00 20.00
7 Khris Middleton/75 8.00 20.00
8 Aaron Nesmith/125 6.00 15.00
9 Doug McDermott/125 4.00 10.00
10 Corey Kispert/125 6.00 15.00
11 Isaiah Stewart/125 5.00 12.00
12 Trey Murphy III/125 8.00 20.00
13 Ja Morant/75 125.00 300.00
14 Cameron Payne/125 5.00 12.00
15 Gary Harris/125 5.00 12.00
16 Luka Doncic/75 200.00 500.00
17 Gail Goodrich/99 6.00 15.00
18 Onyeka Okongwu/99 6.00 15.00
19 Pau Gasol/75 15.00 40.00
20 Jack Sikma/125 8.00 20.00
21 Chris Duarte/149 5.00 12.00
22 Royce O'Neale/125 5.00 12.00
23 Joe Ingles/125 5.00 12.00
24 Pat Connaughton/99 5.00 12.00
25 Richard Hamilton/99 8.00 20.00
26 Santi Aldama/149 6.00 15.00
27 Anfernee Simons/99 8.00 20.00
28 Victor Oladipo/99 5.00 12.00
29 Chauncey Billups/99 8.00 20.00
30 Luguentz Dort/99 6.00 15.00
31 Adrian Dantley/125 6.00 15.00
32 Kyle Anderson/125 5.00 12.00
33 Calvin Murphy/99 6.00 15.00
34 Mo Bamba/99 5.00 12.00
35 Torrey Craig/125 4.00 10.00
36 Jaylen Nowell/125 6.00 15.00
37 Caron Butler/99 5.00 12.00
38 Alex Caruso/99 12.00 30.00
39 Mason Plumlee/99 5.00 12.00
40 Jamaal Wilkes/99 6.00 15.00

2022-23 Panini Recon Rock the Rim

COMMON CARD .50 1.25
SEMISTARS .60 1.50
UNLISTED STARS .75 2.00
1 LeBron James 6.00 15.00
2 Paolo Banchero 5.00 12.00
3 Aaron Gordon .75 2.00
4 Jaylen Brown 1.50 4.00
5 Jalen Duren 2.50 6.00
6 Jayson Tatum 3.00 8.00
7 Giannis Antetokounmpo 4.00 10.00
8 Anthony Davis 2.00 5.00
9 Jalen Green 2.50 6.00
10 Lauri Markkanen 1.25 3.00
11 John Collins .75 2.00
12 Donovan Mitchell 1.50 4.00
13 Zion Williamson 2.00 5.00
14 Paul George 1.25 3.00
15 Jabari Smith Jr. 2.50 6.00
16 Jaden Ivey 2.50 6.00
17 Jarrett Allen .75 2.00
18 Bennedict Mathurin 2.50 6.00
19 Zach LaVine 1.50 4.00
20 Ja Morant 2.50 6.00
21 Bam Adebayo 1.25 3.00
22 Kenyon Martin Jr. .75 2.00
23 Joel Embiid 1.25 3.00
24 Anthony Edwards 4.00 10.00
25 Russell Westbrook 1.25 3.00

2022-23 Panini Recon Rookie Jersey Autographs

COMMON CARD 8.00 20.00
SEMISTARS 10.00 25.00
UNLISTED STARS 12.00 30.00
STATED PRINT RUN 75-99 SER.#'d SETS
1 Dyson Daniels/75 30.00 80.00
2 Jaden Ivey/75 75.00 200.00
3 Christian Braun/99 30.00 80.00
4 Blake Wesley/99 12.00 30.00
5 Ochai Agbaji/99 15.00 40.00
6 Jalen Duren/75 40.00 100.00
7 Andrew Nembhard/99 25.00 60.00
8 Shaedon Sharpe/75 100.00 250.00
9 Keegan Murray/75 100.00 250.00
10 Jalen Williams/99 60.00 150.00
11 Walker Kessler/99 25.00 60.00
12 Ousmane Dieng/99 15.00 40.00
13 AJ Griffin/75 10.00 25.00
14 David Roddy/99 15.00 40.00
15 Tari Eason/99 30.00 80.00
16 Jake LaRavia/99 12.00 30.00
17 Chet Holmgren/75 150.00 400.00
18 TyTy Washington Jr./99 12.00 30.00
19 Jeremy Sochan/99 40.00 100.00
20 Nikola Jovic/99 25.00 60.00
21 Malaki Branham/99 12.00 30.00
22 Jabari Smith Jr./75 40.00 100.00
23 Wendell Moore Jr./99 12.00 30.00
24 Johnny Davis/75 12.00 30.00
25 Mark Williams/99 25.00 60.00
26 Bennedict Mathurin/75 40.00 100.00
27 Jaden Hardy/75 20.00 50.00
28 Dalen Terry/99 12.00 30.00
29 MarJon Beauchamp/99 12.00 30.00
30 Christian Koloko/99 12.00 30.00
31 Paolo Banchero /75 200.00 500.00

2022-23 Panini Recon Rookie Recon

1 Jaden Ivey 2.50 6.00
2 Dalen Terry .75 2.00
3 Jalen Duren 2.50 6.00
4 Chet Holmgren 4.00 10.00
5 Jeremy Sochan 2.50 6.00
6 Tari Eason 2.00 5.00
7 Christian Braun 2.00 5.00
8 Jalen Williams 4.00 10.00
9 David Roddy 1.00 2.50
10 Jake LaRavia .75 2.00
11 Bennedict Mathurin 2.50 6.00
12 MarJon Beauchamp .75 2.00
13 Shaedon Sharpe 3.00 8.00
14 Ousmane Dieng 1.00 2.50
15 Walker Kessler 1.50 4.00
16 Dyson Daniels 2.00 5.00
17 Blake Wesley .75 2.00
18 Malaki Branham .75 2.00
19 Johnny Davis .75 2.00
20 Mark Williams 1.50 4.00
21 AJ Griffin .60 1.50
22 Paolo Banchero 5.00 12.00
23 Keegan Murray 2.00 5.00
24 Ochai Agbaji 1.00 2.50
25 Jabari Smith Jr. 2.50 6.00

2022-23 Panini Recon Rookie Recon Signatures

COMMON CARD 4.00 10.00
SEMISTARS 5.00 12.00
UNLISTED STARS 6.00 15.00
STATED PRINT RUN 75-149 SER.#'d SETS
*RED/49-99: .5X TO 1.2X BASIC
*BLUE/35-49: .5X TO 1.2X BASIC
*PURPLE/25: .6X TO 1.5X BASIC
1 Jabari Smith Jr./75 40.00 100.00
2 Keegan Murray/75 40.00 100.00
3 Matt Ryan/149 6.00 15.00
4 Dyson Daniels/99 15.00 40.00
5 Bennedict Mathurin/75 40.00 100.00
6 Ousmane Dieng/99 8.00 20.00
7 Ochai Agbaji/99 8.00 20.00
8 Paolo Banchero /75 125.00 300.00
9 Mark Williams/99 12.00 30.00
10 Vince Williams Jr./149 8.00 20.00
11 Dalen Terry/125 6.00 15.00
12 Alondes Williams/149 6.00 15.00
13 Walker Kessler/125 12.00 30.00
14 David Roddy/125 8.00 20.00
15 TyTy Washington Jr./99 6.00 15.00
16 Blake Wesley/125 6.00 15.00
17 Jaden Ivey/75 20.00 50.00
18 Andrew Nembhard/149 12.00 30.00
19 Max Christie/99 15.00 40.00
20 Jeremy Sochan/99 20.00 50.00
21 Caleb Houstan/149 6.00 15.00
22 Moussa Diabate/149 6.00 15.00
23 Jalen Williams/99 30.00 80.00
24 Christian Koloko/149 6.00 15.00
25 Jabari Walker/149 5.00 12.00
26 Jordan Hall/149 5.00 12.00
27 Malaki Branham/149 6.00 15.00
28 Chet Holmgren/75 125.00 300.00
29 Kevon Harris/149 5.00 12.00
30 MarJon Beauchamp/125 6.00 15.00
31 Trevor Keels/149 5.00 12.00
32 Isaiah Mobley/149 6.00 15.00
33 Dereon Seabron/149 5.00 12.00
34 Jaylin Williams/99 8.00 20.00
35 Josh Minott/149 6.00 15.00
36 Scotty Pippen Jr./149 8.00 20.00
37 Nikola Jovic/125 12.00 30.00
38 Tyrese Martin/149 5.00 12.00
39 Bryce McGowens/125 6.00 15.00
40 Wendell Moore Jr./125 6.00 15.00

2022-23 Panini Recon Rookie Review

1 LeBron James 10.00 25.00
2 Giannis Antetokounmpo 6.00 15.00
3 Jayson Tatum 5.00 12.00
4 Stephen Curry 10.00 25.00
5 Nikola Jokic 6.00 15.00
6 Kawhi Leonard 3.00 8.00
7 Chris Paul 2.50 6.00
8 James Harden 2.50 6.00
9 Kevin Durant 4.00 10.00
10 Shai Gilgeous-Alexander 6.00 15.00
11 Jaylen Brown 2.50 6.00
12 Julius Randle 1.50 4.00
13 Donovan Mitchell 2.50 6.00
14 Luka Doncic 8.00 20.00
15 Dejounte Murray 1.50 4.00

2022-23 Panini Recon Sky's the Limit

1 Giannis Antetokounmpo 6.00 15.00
2 Zion Williamson 3.00 8.00
3 Paolo Banchero 8.00 20.00
4 Jaden Ivey 4.00 10.00
5 Luka Doncic 8.00 20.00
6 Stephen Curry 10.00 25.00
7 Bennedict Mathurin 4.00 10.00
8 LeBron James 10.00 25.00
9 Jayson Tatum 5.00 12.00
10 Ja Morant 4.00 10.00

2022-23 Panini Recon Sophomore Acetate Autographs

COMMON CARD 5.00 12.00
SEMISTARS 6.00 15.00
UNLISTED STARS 8.00 20.00
STATED PRINT RUN 48 SER.#'d SETS
1 Cade Cunningham/48 75.00 200.00
2 Josh Giddey/48 75.00 200.00
3 Jonathan Kuminga/48 40.00 100.00
4 Evan Mobley/48 50.00 120.00
5 Jalen Suggs/48 20.00 50.00
6 Quentin Grimes/48 6.00 15.00
7 Scottie Barnes/48 40.00 100.00
8 Ayo Dosunmu/48 10.00 25.00
9 Franz Wagner/48 50.00 120.00
10 Trey Murphy III/48 10.00 25.00
11 Herbert Jones/48 8.00 20.00
12 Bones Hyland/48 6.00 15.00
13 Alperen Sengun/48 20.00 50.00
14 Jalen Green/48 75.00 200.00
15 Tre Mann/48 6.00 15.00
16 Davion Mitchell/48 6.00 15.00
17 Moses Moody/48 10.00 25.00
18 Santi Aldama/48 8.00 20.00
19 Ziaire Williams/48 6.00 15.00
20 Jalen Johnson/48 10.00 25.00
21 Josh Christopher/48 5.00 12.00
22 Cameron Thomas/48 20.00 50.00
23 Isaiah Jackson/48 8.00 20.00
24 James Bouknight/48 5.00 12.00
25 Chris Duarte/48 6.00 15.00
26 Jeremiah Robinson-Earl/48 6.00 15.00
27 Keon Johnson/48 5.00 12.00
28 Miles McBride/48 8.00 20.00
30 Corey Kispert/37 8.00 20.00
31 Isaiah Livers/48 8.00 20.00
32 Greg Brown III/48 5.00 12.00
33 Brandon Boston Jr./48 5.00 12.00
34 JT Thor/48 8.00 20.00
35 Aaron Wiggins/48 6.00 15.00
36 Usman Garuba/48 5.00 12.00
37 Charles Bassey/48 8.00 20.00
38 Day'Ron Sharpe/48 6.00 15.00
39 Sandro Mamukelashvili/48 8.00 20.00
40 Jason Preston/48 6.00 15.00

2022-23 Panini Recon Top of the Charts

1 Fred VanVleet 1.00 2.50
2 Stephen Curry 6.00 15.00
3 Rudy Gobert 1.00 2.50
4 Giannis Antetokounmpo 4.00 10.00
5 DeMar DeRozan 1.00 2.50
6 Cade Cunningham 2.50 6.00
7 Chris Paul 1.50 4.00
8 Jayson Tatum 3.00 8.00
9 Luka Doncic 5.00 12.00
10 Anthony Edwards 4.00 10.00
11 Jaren Jackson Jr. 1.25 3.00
12 LeBron James 6.00 15.00
13 Devin Booker 2.00 5.00
14 Damian Lillard 2.00 5.00
15 Klay Thompson 2.00 5.00
16 Nikola Jokic 4.00 10.00
17 John Stockton 1.50 4.00
18 Hakeem Olajuwon 1.50 4.00
19 Dirk Nowitzki 2.00 5.00
20 Allen Iverson 2.00 5.00

2022-23 Panini Recon True Potential Signatures

COMMON CARD
SEMISTARS
UNLISTED STARS
STATED PRINT RUN 75-149 SER.#'d SETS
*RED/49-99: .5X TO 1.2X BASIC
*BLUE/35-49: .5X TO 1.2X BASIC
*PURPLE/25: .6X TO 1.5X BASIC
1 Paolo Banchero /75 125.00 300.00
2 Jaden Ivey/75 40.00 100.00
3 Shaedon Sharpe/75 60.00 150.00
4 Jeremy Sochan/99 20.00 50.00
5 Keegan Murray/75 40.00 100.00
6 Tari Eason/99 15.00 40.00
7 Dyson Daniels/99 15.00 40.00
8 A.J. Green/149 40.00 100.00
9 Dalen Terry/149 6.00 15.00
10 Jabari Smith Jr./75 40.00 100.00
11 David Roddy/125 8.00 20.00
12 Christian Braun/125 15.00 40.00
13 Kenneth Lofton Jr./149 8.00 20.00
14 MarJon Beauchamp/125 6.00 15.00
15 Jamal Cain/149 6.00 15.00
16 Malaki Branham/99 6.00 15.00
17 Patrick Baldwin Jr./125 6.00 15.00
18 Jordan Goodwin/149 5.00 12.00
19 Ryan Rollins/149 6.00 15.00
20 AJ Griffin/75 5.00 12.00
21 Ron Harper Jr./149 8.00 20.00
22 Max Christie/149 15.00 40.00
23 Kendall Brown/149 5.00 12.00
24 Andrew Nembhard/149 12.00 30.00
25 Caleb Houstan/149 6.00 15.00
26 Julian Champagnie/149 15.00 40.00
27 Jabari Walker/149 5.00 12.00
28 Kennedy Chandler/125 6.00 15.00
29 Daishen Nix/149 6.00 15.00
30 Josh Minott/149 6.00 15.00
31 Christian Koloko/149 6.00 15.00
32 Peyton Watson/149 10.00 25.00
33 Jalen Duren/75 20.00 50.00
34 Isaiah Mobley/149 6.00 15.00
35 Trevor Keels/149 5.00 12.00
36 Walker Kessler/99 12.00 30.00
37 Nikola Jovic/125 12.00 30.00
38 Johnny Davis/75 6.00 15.00
39 Jalen Williams/99 30.00 80.00
40 Bennedict Mathurin/75 40.00 100.00

2022-23 Panini Recon Vector

1 LeBron James 10.00 25.00
2 Giannis Antetokounmpo 6.00 15.00
3 Jayson Tatum 5.00 12.00
4 Zion Williamson 3.00 8.00
5 Stephen Curry 10.00 25.00
6 Kevin Durant 4.00 10.00
7 Luka Doncic 8.00 20.00
8 Ja Morant 4.00 10.00
9 LaMelo Ball 3.00 8.00
10 Nikola Jokic 6.00 15.00
11 Devin Booker 3.00 8.00
12 Anthony Edwards 6.00 15.00
13 Donovan Mitchell 2.50 6.00
14 Trae Young 3.00 8.00
15 Cade Cunningham 4.00 10.00
16 Shai Gilgeous-Alexander 6.00 15.00
17 Damian Lillard 3.00 8.00
18 James Harden 2.50 6.00
19 Kawhi Leonard 3.00 8.00
20 Paolo Banchero 8.00 20.00
21 Chet Holmgren 6.00 15.00
22 Jabari Smith Jr. 4.00 10.00
23 Keegan Murray 3.00 8.00
24 Jaden Ivey 4.00 10.00
25 Bennedict Mathurin 4.00 10.00

2022-23 Panini Recon World Travelers

1 Rudy Gobert 1.25 3.00
2 Josh Giddey 1.50 4.00
3 Al Horford 1.00 2.50
4 Joel Embiid 1.50 4.00
5 Pascal Siakam 1.50 4.00
6 Luka Doncic 6.00 15.00
7 Rui Hachimura 15.00 40.00
8 Alperen Sengun 1.25 3.00
9 Franz Wagner 2.50 6.00
10 Giannis Antetokounmpo 5.00 12.00
11 Kristaps Porzingis 1.25 3.00
12 Nikola Jokic 5.00 12.00
13 Lauri Markkanen 4.00 10.00
14 Bojan Bogdanovic 1.00 2.50
15 Shai Gilgeous-Alexander 5.00 12.00

2023-24 Panini Recon

*HOLO: .6X TO 1.5X BASIC
1 Dennis Schroder .40 1.00
2 Cameron Johnson .40 1.00
3 Draymond Green .50 1.25
4 Donovan Mitchell .75 2.00
5 Matisse Thybulle .30 .75
6 Cam Reddish .30 .75
7 Harrison Barnes .30 .75
8 Nikola Vucevic .40 1.00
9 David Roddy .30 .75
10 Moritz Wagner .40 1.00
11 Dejounte Murray .50 1.25
12 Tim Hardaway Jr. .30 .75
13 Aaron Gordon .40 1.00
14 Terance Mann .30 .75
15 Spencer Dinwiddie .30 .75
16 Malaki Branham .30 .75
17 Julius Randle .50 1.25
18 Jimmy Butler .60 1.50
19 Ben Simmons .40 1.00
20 De'Aaron Fox .75 2.00
21 Landry Shamet .25 .60
22 Isaiah Joe .40 1.00
23 Paolo Banchero 1.00 2.50
24 Alex Caruso .40 1.00
25 Fred VanVleet .60 1.50
26 Kyrie Irving .75 2.00
27 Gary Payton II .30 .75
28 Cameron Thomas .50 1.25
29 Jakob Poeltl .30 .75
30 Domantas Sabonis .60 1.50
31 Zion Williamson 1.00 2.50
32 Jaden Hardy .50 1.25
33 Bradley Beal .50 1.25
34 Mitchell Robinson .40 1.00
35 Josh Richardson .25 .60
36 Zach LaVine .60 1.50
37 Josh Hart .40 1.00
38 Pascal Siakam .60 1.50
39 Trey Murphy III .50 1.25
40 Jonathan Kuminga 1.00 2.50
41 Terry Rozier III .50 1.25
42 Luguentz Dort .40 1.00
43 Jalen Johnson .50 1.25
44 Lonnie Walker IV .40 1.00
45 Norman Powell .40 1.00
46 Tyrese Haliburton .75 2.00
47 Josh Giddey .50 1.25
48 Tyler Herro .60 1.50
49 Ivica Zubac .40 1.00
50 Jaylen Brown .75 2.00
51 Jerami Grant .50 1.25
52 Grant Williams .30 .75
53 Cade Cunningham 1.00 2.50
54 Mikal Bridges .50 1.25
55 Kentavious Caldwell-Pope .30 .75
56 Buddy Hield .40 1.00
57 Andrew Wiggins .50 1.25
58 MarJon Beauchamp .30 .75
59 Zach Collins .30 .75
60 Kyle Anderson .30 .75
61 Khris Middleton .40 1.00
62 Malik Beasley .40 1.00
63 Ja Morant 1.25 3.00
64 Caleb Martin .30 .75
65 Derrick White .50 1.25
66 Darius Garland .60 1.50
67 Max Christie .40 1.00
68 Gordon Hayward .40 1.00
69 Karl-Anthony Towns .60 1.50
70 Nikola Jokic 2.00 5.00
71 Russell Westbrook .60 1.50
72 OG Anunoby .50 1.25
73 D'Angelo Russell .40 1.00
74 Jrue Holiday .50 1.25
75 Alperen Sengun .60 1.50
76 Immanuel Quickley .40 1.00
77 Kevin Love .40 1.00
78 Anthony Davis 1.00 2.50
79 Talen Horton-Tucker .30 .75
80 Tyus Jones .30 .75
81 Bogdan Bogdanovic .40 1.00
82 Kyle Lowry .50 1.25
83 Jalen Williams .75 2.00
84 James Wiseman .30 .75
85 Saddiq Bey .40 1.00
86 LeBron James 3.00 8.00
87 Danilo Gallinari .30 .75
88 Max Strus .40 1.00
89 Wendell Carter Jr. .40 1.00
90 Grayson Allen .40 1.00
91 Jaden Ivey .50 1.25
92 Shaedon Sharpe .75 2.00
93 Miles Bridges .40 1.00
94 Patrick Beverley .30 .75
95 Naz Reid .40 1.00
96 Reggie Jackson .25 .60
97 Bobby Portis .50 1.25
98 Kyle Kuzma .50 1.25
99 Joel Embiid 1.00 2.50
100 Keldon Johnson .50 1.25
101 Paul George .60 1.50
102 Eric Gordon .30 .75
103 Markelle Fultz .30 .75
104 Derrick Rose .60 1.50
105 Anfernee Simons .50 1.25
106 Jalen Green .60 1.50
107 Jalen Suggs .50 1.25
108 Jusuf Nurkic .40 1.00
109 Malik Monk .50 1.25
110 Bam Adebayo .60 1.50
111 Jonas Valanciunas .30 .75
112 Klay Thompson 1.00 2.50
113 Dorian Finney-Smith .30 .75
114 Giannis Antetokounmpo 2.00 5.00
115 Obi Toppin .40 1.00
116 Marvin Bagley III .30 .75
117 Tobias Harris .40 1.00
118 Brandon Ingram .50 1.25
119 Marcus Smart .50 1.25
120 Deandre Ayton .40 1.00
121 Rudy Gobert .50 1.25
122 Onyeka Okongwu .30 .75
123 Trae Young .75 2.00
124 Daniel Gafford .40 1.00
125 Desmond Bane .50 1.25
126 Lauri Markkanen .60 1.50
127 Derrick Jones Jr. .30 .75
128 Malcolm Brogdon .40 1.00
129 Nicolas Claxton .40 1.00
130 Jordan Poole .60 1.50
131 Jalen Duren .50 1.25
132 Austin Reaves 1.00 2.50
133 Isaiah Stewart .40 1.00
134 Patrick Williams .30 .75
135 Jaden McDaniels .40 1.00
136 Duncan Robinson .40 1.00
137 Kenyon Martin Jr. .40 1.00
138 Kawhi Leonard 1.00 2.50
139 Jamal Murray .75 2.00
140 RJ Barrett .60 1.50
141 Bruce Brown .40 1.00
142 Coby White .40 1.00
143 Damian Lillard 1.00 2.50
144 Luka Doncic 2.50 6.00
145 Kevon Looney .40 1.00
146 Dyson Daniels .50 1.25
147 Chris Paul .60 1.50
148 Stephen Curry 3.00 8.00
149 Bennedict Mathurin .60 1.50
150 PJ Washington Jr. .40 1.00
151 Franz Wagner .60 1.50
152 Anthony Edwards 2.00 5.00
153 Caris LeVert .40 1.00
154 Jarrett Allen .40 1.00
155 Jabari Smith Jr. .60 1.50
156 Tyrese Maxey .75 2.00
157 Clint Capela .30 .75
158 Ziaire Williams .40 1.00
159 Mike Conley .30 .75
160 Gabe Vincent .40 1.00
161 James Harden .75 2.00
162 DeMar DeRozan .60 1.50
163 Jordan Clarkson .40 1.00
164 Tari Eason .50 1.25
165 John Collins .40 1.00
166 Gary Trent Jr. .40 1.00
167 Chet Holmgren 1.00 2.50
168 Jalen Brunson .75 2.00
169 Brook Lopez .30 .75
170 Michael Porter Jr. .50 1.25
171 Kevin Durant 1.25 3.00
172 De'Andre Hunter .40 1.00
173 Jayson Tatum 1.50 4.00
174 Walker Kessler .40 1.00
175 Dillon Brooks .40 1.00
176 Devin Booker 1.00 2.50
177 Myles Turner .40 1.00
178 Shai Gilgeous-Alexander 2.00 5.00
179 Kevin Huerter .30 .75
180 DeAndre Jordan .30 .75
181 CJ McCollum .40 1.00
182 Collin Sexton .50 1.25
183 Rui Hachimura .40 1.00
184 Kelly Oubre Jr. .40 1.00
185 LaMelo Ball 1.00 2.50
186 Evan Mobley .60 1.50
187 Mark Williams .40 1.00
188 Devin Vassell .50 1.25
189 Kristaps Porzingis .50 1.25
190 Tre Jones .40 1.00
191 Bones Hyland .30 .75
192 Jeremy Sochan .50 1.25
193 Scottie Barnes .50 1.25
194 Herbert Jones .40 1.00
195 Keegan Murray .50 1.25
196 Cole Anthony .40 1.00
197 Deni Avdija .40 1.00
198 Jaren Jackson Jr. .60 1.50
199 Al Horford .40 1.00
200 De'Anthony Melton .40 1.00
201 Julian Strawther RC 1.00 2.50
202 Brandin Podziemski RC 2.50 6.00
203 Jalen Pickett RC .60 1.50
204 Julian Phillips RC .75 2.00
205 Trayce Jackson-Davis RC 1.00 2.50
206 Dariq Whitehead RC 1.00 2.50
207 Taylor Hendricks RC .75 2.00
208 Ben Sheppard RC .75 2.00
209 Marcus Sasser RC 1.25 3.00
210 Colby Jones RC .75 2.00
211 Gradey Dick RC 1.50 4.00
212 Kobe Bufkin RC 1.00 2.50
213 Noah Clowney RC 1.00 2.50
214 Vasilije Micic RC .75 2.00
215 Keyontae Johnson RC .75 2.00
216 Nick Smith Jr. RC 1.00 2.50
217 Mouhamed Gueye RC .75 2.00
218 Chris Livingston RC .75 2.00
219 Maxwell Lewis RC .60 1.50
220 Toumani Camara RC 1.50 4.00
221 Dereck Lively II RC 1.50 4.00
222 Emoni Bates RC 1.00 2.50
223 Kobe Brown RC .75 2.00
224 Jett Howard RC 1.00 2.50
225 Victor Wembanyama RC 15.00 40.00
226 Leonard Miller RC .75 2.00
227 Rayan Rupert RC .75 2.00
228 Sasha Vezenkov RC .60 1.50
229 Jordan Hawkins RC 1.25 3.00
230 Andre Jackson Jr. RC 1.25 3.00
231 Hunter Tyson RC .75 2.00
232 Jarace Walker RC 1.50 4.00
233 Brandon Miller RC 3.00 8.00
234 Amen Thompson RC 4.00 10.00
235 Brice Sensabaugh RC 1.25 3.00
236 Bilal Coulibaly RC 2.00 5.00
237 Keyonte George RC 2.50 6.00
238 GG Jackson II RC 1.50 4.00
239 Jalen Hood-Schifino RC .75 2.00
240 Cam Whitmore RC 2.00 5.00
241 Jaime Jaquez Jr. RC 1.25 3.00
242 Ausar Thompson RC 2.00 5.00
243 Anthony Black RC 1.50 4.00
244 Cason Wallace RC 1.50 4.00
245 Kris Murray RC .75 2.00
246 Scoot Henderson RC 2.50 6.00
247 Jordan Miller RC 1.00 2.50
248 Amari Bailey RC .75 2.00
249 Jalen Slawson RC .75 2.00
250 Olivier-Maxence Prosper RC .75 2.00

2023-24 Panini Recon Holo Blue

*HOLO BLUE: 2X TO 5X BASIC
STATED PRINT RUN 99 SER.#'d SETS
225 Victor Wembanyama 125.00 300.00

2023-24 Panini Recon Holo Bronze

*HOLO BRONZE: 1.25X TO 3X BASIC
STATED PRINT RUN 299 SER.#'d SETS
225 Victor Wembanyama 75.00 200.00

2023-24 Panini Recon Holo Effect

*HOLO EFFECT: 2.5X TO 6X BASIC
STATED PRINT RUN 49 SER.#'d SETS
225 Victor Wembanyama 150.00 400.00

2023-24 Panini Recon Holo Purple

*HOLO PURPLE: 2X TO 5X BASIC
STATED PRINT RUN 75 SER.#'d SETS
225 Victor Wembanyama 125.00 300.00

2023-24 Panini Recon Holo Red

*HOLO RED: 1.5X TO 4X BASIC
STATED PRINT RUN 199 SER.#'d SETS
225 Victor Wembanyama 100.00 250.00

2023-24 Panini Recon Archetype Signatures

*RED/75: .5X TO 1.2X BASIC
*BLUE/49: .6X TO 1.5X BASIC
*PURPLE/25: .75X TO 2X BASIC
1 Max Christie 5.00 12.00
2 Christian Braun 5.00 12.00
3 Ziaire Williams 5.00 12.00
4 Jalen Johnson 6.00 15.00
5 Arvydas Sabonis 6.00 15.00
6 Evan Fournier 4.00 10.00
7 Spud Webb 5.00 12.00
8 Bruce Bowen 4.00 10.00
9 Kenny Anderson 4.00 10.00
10 Xavier Tillman 5.00 12.00
11 Cameron Payne 4.00 10.00
12 Luol Deng 4.00 10.00
13 Dennis Schroder 5.00 12.00
14 Kentavious Caldwell-Pope 4.00 10.00
15 Sandro Mamukelashvili 5.00 12.00
16 Jalen McDaniels 4.00 10.00
17 Jaden Springer 4.00 10.00
18 Larry Nance Jr. 3.00 8.00
19 Bones Hyland 4.00 10.00
20 Georges Niang 3.00 8.00
21 Daniel Gafford 12.00 30.00
22 Dalano Banton 4.00 10.00
23 Tyus Jones 4.00 10.00
24 Mark Williams 5.00 12.00
25 Sam Hauser 5.00 12.00
26 Jerry Stackhouse 5.00 12.00
27 Luke Kennard 4.00 10.00
28 Aaron Wiggins 4.00 10.00
29 Jalen Green 20.00 50.00
30 Ja Morant 75.00 200.00

2023-24 Panini Recon Contours

1 LaMelo Ball 40.00 100.00
2 Stephen Curry 125.00 300.00
3 Ja Morant 75.00 200.00
4 De'Aaron Fox 40.00 100.00
5 Kyrie Irving 60.00 150.00
6 Victor Wembanyama 500.00 1,000.00
7 Scoot Henderson 50.00 120.00
8 Jaylen Brown 50.00 120.00
9 Donovan Mitchell 40.00 100.00
10 Joel Embiid 40.00 100.00
11 Anthony Edwards 75.00 200.00
12 Amen Thompson 50.00 120.00
13 Damian Lillard 50.00 120.00
14 LeBron James 125.00 300.00
15 Zion Williamson 40.00 100.00
16 Luka Doncic 100.00 250.00
17 Shai Gilgeous-Alexander 50.00 120.00
18 Kevin Durant 50.00 120.00
19 Paolo Banchero 40.00 100.00
20 Nikola Jokic 75.00 200.00
21 Jayson Tatum 60.00 150.00
22 Trae Young 40.00 100.00
23 Giannis Antetokounmpo 60.00 150.00
24 Ausar Thompson 50.00 120.00
25 Brandon Miller 75.00 200.00

2023-24 Panini Recon Fleet Feet

*PURPLE/75: 1.5X TO 4X BASIC
*EFFECT/25: 2.5X TO 6X BASIC
1 Anthony Edwards 3.00 8.00
2 Russell Westbrook 1.00 2.50
3 Chris Paul 1.25 3.00
4 Damian Lillard 1.50 4.00
5 Jrue Holiday .75 2.00
6 Tyrese Haliburton 1.25 3.00
7 Jamal Murray 1.25 3.00
8 Cameron Thomas .75 2.00
9 Trae Young 1.25 3.00
10 Stephen Curry 5.00 12.00
11 Ja Morant 2.00 5.00
12 De'Aaron Fox 1.25 3.00
13 Tyrese Maxey 1.25 3.00
14 Tyler Herro 1.00 2.50
15 Donovan Mitchell 1.25 3.00
16 Kyrie Irving 1.25 3.00
17 Paul George 1.00 2.50
18 Luka Doncic 4.00 10.00
19 LaMelo Ball 1.50 4.00
20 Shai Gilgeous-Alexander 3.00 8.00

2023-24 Panini Recon Future Legends

1 Marcus Sasser 1.25 3.00
2 Jalen Williams 1.50 4.00
3 Ausar Thompson 2.00 5.00
4 Cade Cunningham 2.00 5.00
5 Jaime Jaquez Jr. 1.25 3.00
6 Brandon Miller 3.00 8.00
7 Tyrese Maxey 1.50 4.00
8 Scottie Barnes 1.00 2.50
9 Dereck Lively II 1.50 4.00
10 Bennedict Mathurin 1.25 3.00
11 Brandin Podziemski 2.50 6.00
12 Chet Holmgren 2.00 5.00
13 Gradey Dick 1.50 4.00
14 Victor Wembanyama 15.00 40.00
15 Scoot Henderson 2.50 6.00
16 Anthony Black 1.50 4.00
17 Keyonte George 2.50 6.00
18 Amen Thompson 4.00 10.00
19 Jaden Ivey 1.00 2.50
20 Jordan Hawkins 1.25 3.00
21 Bilal Coulibaly 2.00 5.00
22 Paolo Banchero 2.00 5.00
23 Tyrese Haliburton 1.50 4.00
24 Cason Wallace 1.50 4.00
25 Shaedon Sharpe 1.50 4.00

2023-24 Panini Recon Future Legends Effect

*EFFECT: 2.5X TO 6X BASIC
STATED PRINT RUN 25 SER.#'d SETS
14 Victor Wembanyama 300.00 600.00

2023-24 Panini Recon Future Legends Purple

*PURPLE: 1.5X TO 4X BASIC
STATED PRINT RUN 75 SER.#'d SETS
14 Victor Wembanyama 150.00 400.00

2023-24 Panini Recon Fuzion

1 Jayson Tatum 60.00 150.00
2 Zion Williamson 40.00 100.00
3 Brandon Miller 75.00 200.00
4 Stephen Curry 150.00 400.00
5 Ausar Thompson 50.00 120.00
6 Shai Gilgeous-Alexander 50.00 120.00
7 Scoot Henderson 50.00 120.00
8 Luka Doncic 100.00 250.00
9 Amen Thompson 50.00 120.00
10 Victor Wembanyama 500.00 1,000.00
11 Damian Lillard 40.00 100.00
12 LeBron James 150.00 400.00
13 Giannis Antetokounmpo 75.00 200.00
14 Nikola Jokic 75.00 200.00
15 Anthony Edwards 125.00 300.00

2023-24 Panini Recon Glorified Signatures

STATED PRINT RUN 25-149 SER.#'d SETS
*RED/99: .5X TO 1.2X BASIC
*BLUE/75: .5X TO 1.2X BASIC
*PURPLE/49: .6X TO 1.5X BASIC
1 Stephen Curry/25 350.00 700.00
2 Trey Murphy III/149 6.00 15.00
3 Kenyon Martin/149 5.00 12.00
4 Boban Marjanovic/149 5.00 12.00
5 Kerry Kittles/149 4.00 10.00
6 Cameron Thomas/149 6.00 15.00
7 Isaiah Joe/149 5.00 12.00
8 Malik Beasley/149 5.00 12.00
9 Gabe Vincent/149 5.00 12.00
10 Dillon Brooks/149 5.00 12.00
11 Moritz Wagner/149 5.00 12.00
12 T.J. McConnell/149 5.00 12.00
13 Franz Wagner/149 8.00 20.00
14 Luka Doncic/25 350.00 700.00
15 Caleb Martin/149 4.00 10.00
16 Jalen McDaniels/149 4.00 10.00
17 Patty Mills/149 5.00 12.00
18 Josh Green/149 4.00 10.00
19 Dante Exum/149 4.00 10.00
20 Dee Brown/149 4.00 10.00

2023-24 Panini Recon Novice Patch Autographs

STATED PRINT RUN 99 SER.#'d SETS
*RED/49-75: .5X TO 1.2X BASIC
*BLUE/35-49: .6X TO 1.5X BASIC
*PURPLE/25: .75X TO 2X BASIC
*PINK FOTL/18: .75X TO 2X BASIC
1 Jalen Wilson 10.00 25.00
2 Olivier-Maxence Prosper 10.00 25.00
3 Julian Phillips 10.00 25.00
4 Andre Jackson Jr. 15.00 40.00
5 Mouhamed Gueye 10.00 25.00
6 Maxwell Lewis 8.00 20.00
7 Kobe Bufkin 12.00 30.00
8 Noah Clowney 12.00 30.00
9 Amen Thompson 50.00 120.00
10 Keyonte George 30.00 80.00
11 Cason Wallace 20.00 50.00
12 Dariq Whitehead 12.00 30.00
13 Jalen Pickett 8.00 20.00
14 Hunter Tyson 10.00 25.00
16 Colby Jones 10.00 25.00
17 Dereck Lively II 20.00 50.00
18 GG Jackson II 20.00 50.00
19 Vasilije Micic 10.00 25.00
20 Toumani Camara 20.00 50.00
22 Bilal Coulibaly 25.00 60.00
23 Sasha Vezenkov 8.00 20.00
24 Jordan Walsh 10.00 25.00
25 Marcus Sasser 15.00 40.00
26 Kobe Brown 10.00 25.00
27 Kris Murray 10.00 25.00
28 Julian Strawther 12.00 30.00
29 Ausar Thompson 25.00 60.00
30 Brandin Podziemski 30.00 80.00

2023-24 Panini Recon Rock the Rim

1 Paolo Banchero 2.00 5.00
2 Kawhi Leonard 2.00 5.00
3 Anthony Edwards 4.00 10.00
4 Amen Thompson 4.00 10.00
5 Aaron Gordon .75 2.00
6 Russell Westbrook 1.25 3.00
7 Ausar Thompson 2.00 5.00
8 Ja Morant 2.50 6.00
9 Chet Holmgren 2.00 5.00
10 Donovan Mitchell 1.50 4.00
11 Nikola Jokic 4.00 10.00
12 Anthony Davis 2.00 5.00
13 Kevin Durant 2.50 6.00
14 Giannis Antetokounmpo 4.00 10.00
15 Jayson Tatum 3.00 8.00
16 LeBron James 6.00 15.00
17 Brandon Miller 3.00 8.00
18 Victor Wembanyama 15.00 40.00
19 Zach LaVine 1.25 3.00
20 Scoot Henderson 2.50 6.00
21 Zion Williamson 2.00 5.00
22 Jaylen Brown 1.50 4.00
23 Joel Embiid 2.00 5.00
24 Lauri Markkanen 1.25 3.00
25 Luka Doncic 5.00 12.00

2023-24 Panini Recon Rock the Rim Effect

*EFFECT: 2.5X TO 6X BASIC
STATED PRINT RUN 25 SER.#'d SETS
18 Victor Wembanyama 300.00 600.00

2023-24 Panini Recon Rock the Rim Purple

*PURPLE: 1.5X TO 4X BASIC
STATED PRINT RUN 75 SER.#'d SETS
18 Victor Wembanyama 150.00 400.00

2023-24 Panini Recon Rookie Jersey Autographs

STATED PRINT RUN 75-99 SER.#'d SETS
*PINK FOTL/18: .75X TO 2X BASIC
1 Julian Phillips/99 10.00 25.00
2 Dereck Lively II/99 20.00 50.00
3 Bilal Coulibaly/99 25.00 60.00
4 Dariq Whitehead/99 12.00 30.00
5 Amen Thompson/75 50.00 120.00
6 Noah Clowney/99 12.00 30.00
7 Brandin Podziemski/99 30.00 80.00
8 Ausar Thompson/75 25.00 60.00
9 Marcus Sasser/99 15.00 40.00
10 Kris Murray/99 10.00 25.00
11 Olivier-Maxence Prosper/99 10.00 25.00
12 Cason Wallace/99 20.00 50.00
13 Keyonte George/99 30.00 80.00
14 Kobe Bufkin/99 12.00 30.00
15 Brice Sensabaugh/99 15.00 40.00
17 Julian Strawther/99 12.00 30.00
18 Amari Bailey/99 10.00 25.00
19 GG Jackson II/99 20.00 50.00
20 Vasilije Micic/99 10.00 25.00
21 Rayan Rupert/99 10.00 25.00
23 Sasha Vezenkov/99 8.00 20.00
24 Colby Jones/99 10.00 25.00
25 Andre Jackson Jr./99 15.00 40.00
26 Hunter Tyson/99 10.00 25.00
27 Jordan Walsh/99 10.00 25.00
28 Maxwell Lewis/99 8.00 20.00
29 Jalen Wilson/99 10.00 25.00
30 Toumani Camara/99 20.00 50.00

2023-24 Panini Recon Rookie Portraits

*PURPLE/75: 1.5X TO 4X BASIC
*EFFECT/25: 2.5X TO 6X BASIC
1 Cason Wallace 2.00 5.00
2 Taylor Hendricks 1.00 2.50
3 Toumani Camara 2.00 5.00
4 Jaime Jaquez Jr. 1.50 4.00
5 Brandin Podziemski 3.00 8.00
6 Anthony Black 2.00 5.00
7 Keyonte George 3.00 8.00
8 Dereck Lively II 2.00 5.00
9 Scoot Henderson 3.00 8.00
10 Amen Thompson 5.00 12.00
11 Brandon Miller 4.00 10.00
12 Bilal Coulibaly 2.50 6.00
13 Ausar Thompson 2.50 6.00
14 Marcus Sasser 1.50 4.00
15 Gradey Dick 2.00 5.00
16 Kobe Bufkin 1.25 3.00
17 Cam Whitmore 2.50 6.00
18 Jordan Hawkins 1.50 4.00
19 Julian Strawther 1.25 3.00
20 Victor Wembanyama 40.00 100.00

2023-24 Panini Recon Rookie Recon

1 Jarace Walker 1.50 4.00
2 Jalen Pickett .60 1.50
3 Julian Strawther 1.00 2.50
4 Ausar Thompson 2.00 5.00
5 Cam Whitmore 2.00 5.00
6 Trayce Jackson-Davis 1.00 2.50
7 Brandon Miller 3.00 8.00
8 Brandin Podziemski 2.50 6.00
9 Taylor Hendricks .75 2.00
10 Dereck Lively II 1.50 4.00
11 Gradey Dick 1.50 4.00
12 Cason Wallace 1.50 4.00
13 Amen Thompson 4.00 10.00
14 Victor Wembanyama 15.00 40.00
15 Kobe Bufkin 1.00 2.50
16 Bilal Coulibaly 2.00 5.00
17 Keyonte George 2.50 6.00
18 Toumani Camara 1.50 4.00
19 Jordan Hawkins 1.25 3.00
20 Scoot Henderson 2.50 6.00
21 Ben Sheppard .75 2.00
22 Anthony Black 1.50 4.00
23 Marcus Sasser 1.25 3.00
24 Jaime Jaquez Jr. 1.25 3.00
25 Colby Jones .75 2.00

2023-24 Panini Recon Rookie Recon Signatures

COMMON CARD 3.00 8.00
SEMISTARS 4.00 10.00
UNLISTED STARS 5.00 12.00
STATED PRINT RUN 125-149 SER.#'d SETS
*RED/99: .5X TO 1.2X BASIC
*BLUE/75: .5X TO 1.2X BASIC
*PURPLE/49: .6X TO 1.5X BASIC
*EFFECT/25: .75X TO 2X BASIC
1 Bilal Coulibaly/125 12.00 30.00
2 Sasha Vezenkov/149 4.00 10.00
3 Brandin Podziemski/125 15.00 40.00
4 Trayce Jackson-Davis/149 6.00 15.00
5 Jordan Walsh/149 5.00 12.00
6 Kris Murray/149 5.00 12.00
7 Kobe Brown/149 5.00 12.00
9 Jordan Miller/149 6.00 15.00
10 Stanley Umude/149 4.00 10.00
11 Isaiah Wong/149 5.00 12.00
12 Amen Thompson/125 25.00 60.00
13 Ausar Thompson/125 12.00 30.00
14 Keyonte George/125 15.00 40.00
15 Cason Wallace/125 10.00 25.00
16 Dereck Lively II/125 10.00 25.00
17 Craig Porter Jr./149 6.00 15.00
18 Oscar Tshiebwe/149 6.00 15.00
19 Colin Castleton/149 4.00 10.00
20 Markquis Nowell/149 5.00 12.00
21 Mouhamed Gueye/149 5.00 12.00
22 Dru Smith/149 4.00 10.00
23 Toumani Camara/149 10.00 25.00
24 Lester Quinones/149 4.00 10.00
25 Jalen Slawson/149 5.00 12.00
26 AJ Lawson/149 4.00 10.00
27 Leonard Miller/149 5.00 12.00
28 Olivier-Maxence Prosper/149 5.00 12.00
29 Andre Jackson Jr./149 8.00 20.00
30 Colby Jones/149 5.00 12.00
31 Jaylen Clark/149 5.00 12.00
32 Chris Livingston/149 5.00 12.00
33 Kobe Bufkin/125 6.00 15.00
35 Julian Phillips/149 5.00 12.00
36 Brice Sensabaugh/149 8.00 20.00
37 Amari Bailey/149 5.00 12.00
38 Rayan Rupert/149 5.00 12.00
39 Jalen Wilson/149 5.00 12.00
40 Vasilije Micic/149 5.00 12.00

2023-24 Panini Recon Rookie Review

*PURPLE/75: 1.5X TO 4X BASIC
*EFFECT/25: 2.5X TO 6X BASIC
1 LeBron James 6.00 15.00
2 Kyrie Irving 1.50 4.00
3 Tim Duncan 2.00 5.00
4 Damian Lillard 2.00 5.00
5 Ja Morant 2.50 6.00
6 Chris Paul 1.50 4.00
7 Luka Doncic 5.00 12.00
8 Derrick Rose 1.25 3.00
9 Brandon Roy 1.00 2.50
10 Paolo Banchero 2.00 5.00
11 LaMelo Ball 2.00 5.00
12 Kevin Durant 2.50 6.00
13 Vince Carter 1.50 4.00
14 Allen Iverson 2.00 5.00
15 Shaquille O'Neal 2.50 6.00

2023-24 Panini Recon Seasoned Pro Autographs

STATED PRINT RUN 35-99 SER.#'d SETS
*BLUE/49: .5X TO 1.2X BASIC
*PURPLE/25: .6X TO 1.5X BASIC
1 Alperen Sengun/75 12.00 30.00
2 Cameron Thomas/99 10.00 25.00
3 Keldon Johnson/75 10.00 25.00
4 Moses Moody/99 10.00 25.00
5 Josh Giddey/75 10.00 25.00
6 Zach LaVine/35 30.00 80.00
7 Malaki Branham/99 6.00 15.00
8 Terance Mann/99 6.00 15.00
10 Ziaire Williams/75 8.00 20.00
11 Walker Kessler/75 8.00 20.00
12 Scottie Barnes/75 10.00 25.00
14 Day'Ron Sharpe/99 6.00 15.00
15 Davion Mitchell/75 6.00 15.00
16 Brook Lopez/75 6.00 15.00
17 Immanuel Quickley/75 8.00 20.00
18 Bruce Brown/75 8.00 20.00
19 Jonas Valanciunas/75 6.00 15.00
20 JT Thor/99 6.00 15.00
22 Quentin Grimes/75 8.00 20.00
23 Payton Pritchard/99 8.00 20.00
24 Ayo Dosunmu/75 8.00 20.00
25 Isaac Okoro/75 6.00 15.00
26 Christian Wood/75 6.00 15.00
28 Corey Kispert/99 6.00 15.00
29 Miles McBride/99 8.00 20.00
30 Jarred Vanderbilt/75 6.00 15.00
31 Dorian Finney-Smith/99 6.00 15.00
32 Isaiah Stewart/75 8.00 20.00
33 Donte DiVincenzo/75 8.00 20.00
34 Nicolas Batum/99 5.00 12.00
35 Norman Powell/99 8.00 20.00
36 David Roddy/99 6.00 15.00
37 Nikola Jovic/99 8.00 20.00
38 TyTy Washington Jr./99 6.00 15.00
39 Peyton Watson/75 8.00 20.00
40 Bones Hyland/75 6.00 15.00

2023-24 Panini Recon Sky's the Limit

1 Giannis Antetokounmpo 4.00 10.00
2 Brandon Miller 3.00 8.00
3 LeBron James 6.00 15.00
4 Ja Morant 2.50 6.00
5 Jayson Tatum 3.00 8.00
6 Luka Doncic 5.00 12.00
7 Tyrese Haliburton 1.50 4.00
8 Nikola Jokic 4.00 10.00
9 Victor Wembanyama 15.00 40.00
10 Stephen Curry 6.00 15.00

2023-24 Panini Recon Sky's the Limit Effect
*EFFECT: 2.5X TO 6X BASIC
STATED PRINT RUN 25 SER.#'d SETS
9 Victor Wembanyama 300.00 600.00

2023-24 Panini Recon Sky's the Limit Purple
*PURPLE: 1.5X TO 4X BASIC
STATED PRINT RUN 75 SER.#'d SETS
9 Victor Wembanyama 150.00 400.00

2023-24 Panini Recon Sophomore Acetate Autographs
STATED PRINT RUN 48 SER.#'d SETS
1 Paolo Banchero 75.00 200.00
2 Jabari Smith Jr. 15.00 40.00
3 Jaden Ivey 12.00 30.00
4 Jaden Hardy 12.00 30.00
5 Jalen Duren 12.00 30.00
6 Shaedon Sharpe 20.00 50.00
7 Bennedict Mathurin 15.00 40.00
8 Keegan Murray 12.00 30.00
9 Jalen Williams 20.00 50.00
10 Max Christie 10.00 25.00
11 Walker Kessler 10.00 25.00
12 Jeremy Sochan 12.00 30.00
14 Ousmane Dieng 10.00 25.00
15 Mark Williams 10.00 25.00
16 Nikola Jovic 10.00 25.00
17 Christian Braun 10.00 25.00
18 Peyton Watson 10.00 25.00
19 David Roddy 8.00 20.00
20 Dalen Terry 10.00 25.00
21 Malaki Branham 8.00 20.00
22 AJ Griffin 8.00 20.00
23 Ochai Agbaji 10.00 25.00
24 Tari Eason 12.00 30.00
25 Jake LaRavia 8.00 20.00
26 Wendell Moore Jr. 8.00 20.00
27 E.J. Liddell 8.00 20.00
28 MarJon Beauchamp 8.00 20.00
29 Andrew Nembhard 10.00 25.00
31 Moussa Diabate 8.00 20.00
35 Christian Koloko 8.00 20.00
36 Caleb Houstan 10.00 25.00
39 Isaiah Mobley 6.00 15.00

2023-24 Panini Recon The Mighty
1 Ausar Thompson 2.00 5.00
2 Brandon Miller 3.00 8.00
3 Shai Gilgeous-Alexander 4.00 10.00
4 Donovan Mitchell 1.50 4.00
5 Tyrese Haliburton 1.50 4.00
6 Kevin Durant 2.50 6.00
7 LeBron James 6.00 15.00
8 Jayson Tatum 3.00 8.00
9 Amen Thompson 4.00 10.00
10 Scoot Henderson 2.50 6.00
11 Damian Lillard 2.00 5.00
12 Nikola Jokic 4.00 10.00
13 Stephen Curry 6.00 15.00
14 Ja Morant 2.50 6.00
15 Victor Wembanyama 20.00 50.00
16 Giannis Antetokounmpo 4.00 10.00
17 Zion Williamson 2.00 5.00
18 Joel Embiid 2.00 5.00
19 Luka Doncic 5.00 12.00
20 Anthony Davis 2.00 5.00

2023-24 Panini Recon The Mighty Effect
*EFFECT: 2.5X TO 6X BASIC
STATED PRINT RUN 25 SER.#'d SETS
15 Victor Wembanyama 300.00 600.00

2023-24 Panini Recon The Mighty Purple
*PURPLE: 1.5X TO 4X BASIC
STATED PRINT RUN 75 SER.#'d SETS
15 Victor Wembanyama 150.00 400.00

2023-24 Panini Recon True Potential Signatures
STATED PRINT RUN 125-149 SER.#'d SETS
*RED/99: .5X TO 1.2X BASIC
*BLUE/49-75: .6X TO 1.5X BASIC
*PURPLE/35-49: .6X TO 1.5X BASIC
*EFFECT/25: .75X TO 2X BASIC
1 Bilal Coulibaly/125 12.00 30.00
2 Jalen Wilson/149 5.00 12.00
3 Amen Thompson/125 25.00 60.00
4 Jalen Pickett/149 4.00 10.00
5 D'Moi Hodge/149 4.00 10.00
6 Javon Freeman-Liberty/149 4.00 10.00
7 Craig Porter Jr./149 6.00 15.00
8 Jamaree Bouyea/149 4.00 10.00
9 Jordan Miller/149 6.00 15.00
12 Chris Livingston/149 5.00 12.00
13 Trayce Jackson-Davis/149 6.00 15.00
14 Julian Strawther/149 6.00 15.00
15 Cason Wallace/125 10.00 25.00
16 Ausar Thompson/125 12.00 30.00
17 Isaiah Wong/149 5.00 12.00
18 Jaylen Clark/149 5.00 12.00
19 Lester Quinones/149 4.00 10.00
20 Charles Bediako/149 4.00 10.00
21 Colin Castleton/149 4.00 10.00
22 Mouhamed Gueye/149 5.00 12.00
23 Kobe Brown/149 5.00 12.00
24 Hunter Tyson/149 5.00 12.00
25 Colby Jones/149 5.00 12.00
26 Dereck Lively II/125 10.00 25.00
27 Noah Clowney/149 6.00 15.00
29 Julian Phillips/149 5.00 12.00
30 Marcus Sasser/149 8.00 20.00
32 Stanley Umude/149 4.00 10.00
33 Oscar Tshiebwe/149 6.00 15.00
34 AJ Lawson/149 4.00 10.00
35 Dru Smith/149 4.00 10.00
36 Kobe Bufkin/125 6.00 15.00
37 Brandin Podziemski/125 15.00 40.00
38 Keyonte George/125 15.00 40.00
39 Jalen Slawson/149 5.00 12.00
40 Markquis Nowell/149 5.00 12.00

2023-24 Panini Recon Vector
1 Shai Gilgeous-Alexander 5.00 12.00
2 Tyrese Haliburton 2.00 5.00
3 Luka Doncic 6.00 15.00
4 Ausar Thompson 2.50 6.00
5 Joel Embiid 2.50 6.00
6 Kevin Durant 3.00 8.00
7 Tyrese Maxey 2.00 5.00
8 LaMelo Ball 2.50 6.00
9 Jordan Hawkins 1.50 4.00
10 Nikola Jokic 5.00 12.00
11 Brandon Miller 4.00 10.00
12 Trae Young 2.00 5.00
13 Damian Lillard 2.50 6.00
14 Amen Thompson 5.00 12.00
15 Jayson Tatum 4.00 10.00
16 Ja Morant 3.00 8.00
17 LeBron James 8.00 20.00
18 Scoot Henderson 3.00 8.00
19 Giannis Antetokounmpo 5.00 12.00
20 Zion Williamson 2.50 6.00
21 Stephen Curry 8.00 20.00
22 Victor Wembanyama 25.00 60.00
23 Jimmy Butler 1.50 4.00
24 Anthony Edwards 5.00 12.00
25 Jaime Jaquez Jr. 1.50 4.00

2023-24 Panini Recon Vector Effect
*EFFECT: 2.5X TO 6X BASIC
STATED PRINT RUN 25 SER.#'d SETS
22 Victor Wembanyama 300.00 600.00

2023-24 Panini Recon Vector Purple
*PURPLE: 1.5X TO 4X BASIC
STATED PRINT RUN 75 SER.#'d SETS
22 Victor Wembanyama 150.00 400.00

2023-24 Panini Recon World Travelers
1 Shai Gilgeous-Alexander 5.00 12.00
2 Luka Doncic 6.00 15.00
3 Victor Wembanyama 25.00 60.00
4 Kristaps Porzingis 1.25 3.00
5 Domantas Sabonis 1.50 4.00
6 Giannis Antetokounmpo 5.00 12.00
7 OG Anunoby 1.25 3.00
8 Jamal Murray 2.00 5.00
9 Franz Wagner 1.50 4.00
10 Ben Simmons 1.00 2.50
11 Joel Embiid 2.50 6.00
12 Lauri Markkanen 1.50 4.00
13 Deandre Ayton 1.00 2.50
14 Alperen Sengun 1.50 4.00
15 Nikola Jokic 5.00 12.00

2023-24 Panini Recon World Travelers Effect
*EFFECT: 2.5X TO 6X BASIC
STATED PRINT RUN 25 SER.#'d SETS

2023-24 Panini Recon World Travelers Purple
*PURPLE: 1.5X TO 4X BASIC
STATED PRINT RUN 75 SER.#'d SETS
3 Victor Wembanyama 150.00 400.00

2015-16 Panini Revolution
1 John Wall .50 1.25
2 DeMarcus Cousins .40 1.00
3 Elfrid Payton .30 .75
4 Kevin Garnett 1.00 2.50
5 Mike Conley .40 1.00
6 James Harden .75 2.00
7 Chandler Parsons .25 .60
8 Jeremy Lamb .25 .60
9 Bradley Beal .50 1.25
10 Jeff Teague .25 .60
11 Rajon Rondo .50 1.25
12 Tobias Harris .30 .75
13 Ricky Rubio .30 .75
14 Zach Randolph .40 1.00
15 Terrence Jones .25 .60
16 Deron Williams .30 .75
17 Jeremy Lin .75 2.00
18 Marcin Gortat .25 .60
19 Rudy Gay .40 1.00
20 Victor Oladipo .30 .75
21 Zach LaVine 1.00 2.50
22 Jordan Clarkson .40 1.00
23 Draymond Green .50 1.25
24 Dirk Nowitzki 1.00 2.50
25 Kemba Walker .40 1.00
26 Gordon Hayward .40 1.00
27 C.J. McCollum .40 1.00
28 Kevin Durant 1.50 4.00
29 Giannis Antetokounmpo 2.00 5.00
30 Julius Randle .50 1.25
31 Harrison Barnes .30 .75
32 John Jenkins .25 .60
33 Nicolas Batum .25 .60
34 Rodney Hood .30 .75
35 Damian Lillard 1.00 2.50
36 Russell Westbrook .60 1.50
37 Greg Monroe .30 .75
38 Kobe Bryant 8.00 20.00
39 Klay Thompson 1.00 2.50
40 Kevin Love .40 1.00
41 Bojan Bogdanovic .30 .75
42 Rudy Gobert .50 1.25
43 Meyers Leonard .25 .60
44 Serge Ibaka .30 .75
45 Jabari Parker .25 .60
46 Blake Griffin .40 1.00
47 Stephen Curry 3.00 8.00
48 Kyrie Irving .75 2.00
49 Brook Lopez .40 1.00
50 DeMar DeRozan .50 1.25
51 Brandon Knight .25 .60
52 Arron Afflalo .25 .60
53 Michael Carter-Williams .25 .60
54 Chris Paul .75 2.00
55 Andre Drummond .40 1.00
56 LeBron James 3.00 8.00
57 Joe Johnson .30 .75
58 Jonas Valanciunas .30 .75
59 Eric Bledsoe .30 .75
60 Carmelo Anthony .60 1.50
61 Chris Andersen .30 .75
62 DeAndre Jordan .30 .75
63 Kentavious Caldwell-Pope .30 .75
64 Matthew Dellavedova .30 .75
65 Avery Bradley .25 .60
66 Kyle Lowry .40 1.00
67 T.J. Warren .40 1.00
68 Robin Lopez .25 .60
69 Chris Bosh .50 1.25
70 George Hill .30 .75
71 Reggie Jackson .30 .75
72 Derrick Rose .60 1.50
73 Evan Turner .25 .60
74 Kawhi Leonard 1.25 3.00
75 Isaiah Canaan .25 .60
76 Anthony Davis 1.00 2.50
77 Dwyane Wade .75 2.00
78 Monta Ellis .30 .75
79 Gary Harris .30 .75
80 Jimmy Butler .75 2.00
81 Marcus Smart .50 1.25
82 Manu Ginobili .75 2.00
83 Nerlens Noel .25 .60
84 Jrue Holiday .50 1.25
85 Goran Dragic .40 1.00
86 Paul George .60 1.50
87 Kenneth Faried .30 .75
88 Nikola Mirotic .25 .60
89 Al Horford .40 1.00
90 Tim Duncan 1.00 2.50
91 Nik Stauskas .25 .60
92 Tyreke Evans .30 .75
93 Marc Gasol .40 1.00
94 Dwight Howard .50 1.25
95 Danilo Gallinari .30 .75
96 Pau Gasol .60 1.50
97 Dennis Schroder .40 1.00
98 Tony Parker .60 1.50
99 Aaron Gordon .40 1.00
100 Andrew Wiggins .50 1.25
101 D'Angelo Russell RC 1.50 4.00
102 Devin Booker RC 40.00 100.00
103 Josh Richardson RC .60 1.50
104 Myles Turner RC 1.50 4.00
105 R.J. Hunter RC .40 1.00
106 Aaron Harrison RC .50 1.25
107 Duje Dukan RC .40 1.00
108 Justin Anderson RC .40 1.00
109 Nemanja Bjelica RC .60 1.50
110 Rondae Hollis-Jefferson RC .50 1.25
111 Anthony Brown RC .40 1.00
112 Emmanuel Mudiay RC .50 1.25
113 Justise Winslow RC .60 1.50
114 Nikola Jokic RC 75.00 200.00
115 Marcelo Huertas RC .40 1.00
116 Boban Marjanovic RC 1.25 3.00
117 Frank Kaminsky RC .50 1.25
118 Karl-Anthony Towns RC 2.50 6.00
119 Norman Powell RC .75 2.00
120 Sam Dekker RC .40 1.00
121 Bobby Portis RC 1.00 2.50
122 Jahlil Okafor RC .50 1.25
123 Kelly Oubre Jr. RC 1.25 3.00
124 Pat Connaughton RC .60 1.50
125 Stanley Johnson RC .50 1.25
126 T.J. McConnell RC 1.50 4.00
127 Jarell Martin RC .40 1.00
128 Kevon Looney RC 1.25 3.00
129 Josh Huestis RC .40 1.00
130 Terry Rozier RC 1.50 4.00
131 Branden Dawson RC .40 1.00
132 Jerian Grant RC .40 1.00
133 Kristaps Porzingis RC 2.50 6.00
134 Rakeem Christmas RC .40 1.00
135 Trey Lyles RC .50 1.25
136 Cameron Payne RC .60 1.50
137 Joe Young RC .40 1.00
138 Larry Nance Jr. RC .75 2.00
139 Rashad Vaughn RC .40 1.00
140 Tyus Jones RC .50 1.25
141 Chris McCullough RC .40 1.00
142 Jonathon Simmons RC .50 1.25
143 Mario Hezonja RC .50 1.25
144 Raul Neto RC .40 1.00
145 Walter Tavares RC .40 1.00
146 Delon Wright RC .50 1.25
147 Jordan Mickey RC .40 1.00
148 Montrezl Harrell RC 1.25 3.00
149 Richaun Holmes RC .60 1.50
150 Willie Cauley-Stein RC .50 1.25

2015-16 Panini Revolution Angular
*ANG 1-100: 1X TO 2.5X BASIC
*ANG 101-150: .6X TO 1.5X BASIC
STATED ODDS 1:12 PACKS

2015-16 Panini Revolution Cosmic
*COS 1-100: 2.5X TO 6X BASIC
*COS 101-150: 1.5X TO 4X BASIC
STATED PRINT RUN 100 SER.#'d SETS
133 Kristaps Porzingis 12.00 30.00

2015-16 Panini Revolution Futura
*FUT 1-100: 5X TO 12X BASIC
*FUT 101-150: 3X TO 8X BASIC
STATED PRINT RUN 25 SER.#'d SETS
28 Kevin Durant 20.00 50.00
38 Kobe Bryant 125.00 300.00
56 LeBron James 40.00 100.00
101 D'Angelo Russell 25.00 60.00
114 Nikola Jokic 1,000.00 2,000.00
118 Karl-Anthony Towns 75.00 200.00
133 Kristaps Porzingis 75.00 200.00

2015-16 Panini Revolution Infinite
*INF 1-100: .75X TO 2X BASIC
*INF 101-150: .5X TO 1.2X BASIC
STATED ODDS 1:6 PACKS

2015-16 Panini Revolution Nova
*NOVA 1-100: .75X TO 2X BASIC
*NOVA 101-150: .5X TO 1.2X BASIC
STATED ODDS 1:6 PACKS

2015-16 Panini Revolution Sunburst
*SUN 1-100: 2.5X TO 6X BASIC
*SUN 101-150: 1.5X TO 4X BASIC
STATED PRINT RUN 75 SER.#'d SETS
118 Karl-Anthony Towns 30.00 80.00
133 Kristaps Porzingis 30.00 80.00

2015-16 Panini Revolution Autographs
STATED ODDS 1:69 PACKS
EXCHANGE DEADLINE 9/23/2017
1 Kobe Bryant 300.00 600.00
2 Kevin Durant 60.00 150.00
3 Kyrie Irving 40.00 100.00
4 Blake Griffin EXCH 20.00 50.00
5 Anthony Davis 60.00 150.00
6 Kevin Love 15.00 40.00
7 Dwyane Wade 125.00 250.00
8 Julius Randle 15.00 40.00
10 John Wall 40.00 100.00
11 Carmelo Anthony 25.00 60.00
12 Zach LaVine 30.00 80.00
13 Andrew Wiggins 25.00 60.00
14 Victor Oladipo 12.00 30.00
16 Tony Parker 30.00 80.00
17 Harrison Barnes 12.00 30.00
18 Kenneth Faried 12.00 30.00
19 Elfrid Payton 12.00 30.00
20 Jabari Parker 25.00 60.00
21 Chris Paul 50.00 120.00
22 Bradley Beal 25.00 60.00
24 Hakeem Olajuwon 20.00 50.00
25 Isiah Thomas 20.00 50.00
26 Grant Hill 20.00 50.00
27 Anfernee Hardaway 30.00 80.00
28 Alonzo Mourning 20.00 50.00
29 Dennis Rodman 40.00 100.00
30 Tracy McGrady 40.00 100.00
31 Jason Kidd 25.00 60.00
32 Gary Payton 20.00 50.00

2015-16 Panini Revolution Icons
STATED ODDS 1:10 PACKS
*COSMIC/100: 1.2X TO 3X BASIC
1 Larry Bird 4.00 10.00
2 Magic Johnson 4.00 10.00
3 Wilt Chamberlain 4.00 10.00
4 Pete Maravich 2.50 6.00
5 Julius Erving 2.50 6.00
6 Gary Payton 1.50 4.00
7 Hakeem Olajuwon 2.00 5.00
8 Dominique Wilkins 1.50 4.00
9 Shaquille O'Neal 3.00 8.00
10 Scottie Pippen 2.50 6.00
11 Bob Cousy 1.50 4.00
12 Bill Russell 3.00 8.00
13 John Stockton 2.00 5.00
14 Karl Malone 1.50 4.00
15 David Robinson 2.00 5.00
16 Oscar Robertson 2.50 6.00
17 Kareem Abdul-Jabbar 3.00 8.00
18 Steve Nash 1.50 4.00
19 Grant Hill 1.50 4.00
20 Patrick Ewing 1.50 4.00
21 Alonzo Mourning 1.50 4.00
22 Allen Iverson 2.50 6.00
23 Yao Ming 2.50 6.00
24 Clyde Drexler 1.50 4.00
25 Jason Kidd 1.50 4.00
26 Walt Frazier 1.50 4.00
27 Dikembe Mutombo 1.50 4.00
28 Shawn Kemp 1.50 4.00
29 Dennis Rodman 2.50 6.00
30 Jerry West 1.50 4.00
31 Chris Mullin 1.25 3.00
32 Nate Archibald 1.25 3.00
33 Tracy McGrady 1.50 4.00

2015-16 Panini Revolution New Wave
STATED ODDS 1:4 PACKS
*COSMIC/100: 2X TO 5X BASIC
1 Zach LaVine 1.50 4.00
2 Elfrid Payton .50 1.25
3 Kyle Anderson .40 1.00
4 Victor Oladipo .50 1.25
5 Dennis Schroder .60 1.50
6 Kentavious Caldwell-Pope .50 1.25
7 T.J. Warren .60 1.50
8 C.J. McCollum .60 1.50
9 Kawhi Leonard 2.00 5.00
10 Rodney Hood .50 1.25
11 Bruno Caboclo .40 1.00
12 Jusuf Nurkic .50 1.25
13 Reggie Jackson .50 1.25
14 Bradley Beal .75 2.00
15 Julius Randle .75 2.00
16 Otto Porter .50 1.25
17 Bojan Bogdanovic .50 1.25
18 Jordan Clarkson .60 1.50
19 Nikola Mirotic .40 1.00
20 Archie Goodwin .40 1.00
21 Nikola Jokic 60.00 150.00
22 Nerlens Noel .40 1.00
23 Anthony Davis 1.50 4.00
24 Jabari Parker .40 1.00
25 Michael Carter-Williams .40 1.00
26 Andrew Wiggins .75 2.00
27 Harrison Barnes .50 1.25
28 Marcus Smart .75 2.00
29 Aaron Gordon .60 1.50
30 Gary Harris .50 1.25

2015-16 Panini Revolution Rookie Autographs
STATED ODDS 1:55 PACKS
EXCHANGE DEADLINE 9/23/2017
1 Karl-Anthony Towns 125.00 300.00
2 Jahlil Okafor 6.00 15.00
3 Myles Turner 20.00 50.00
5 Justise Winslow 8.00 20.00
6 Jerian Grant 5.00 12.00
7 Kristaps Porzingis 75.00 200.00
8 Mario Hezonja 6.00 15.00
9 Nemanja Bjelica 8.00 20.00
10 Emmanuel Mudiay 6.00 15.00
11 Willie Cauley-Stein 6.00 15.00
12 Delon Wright 6.00 15.00
13 Bobby Portis 12.00 30.00
14 Sam Dekker 5.00 12.00
15 Devin Booker 300.00 600.00
16 D'Angelo Russell 20.00 50.00
17 Trey Lyles 6.00 15.00
18 Frank Kaminsky 6.00 15.00

2015-16 Panini Revolution Rookie Revolution
STATED ODDS 1:10 PACKS
1 Willie Cauley-Stein .75 2.00
2 Rashad Vaughn .60 1.50
3 Karl-Anthony Towns 4.00 10.00
4 Emmanuel Mudiay .75 2.00
5 Tyus Jones .75 2.00
6 Nemanja Bjelica 1.00 2.50
7 Justise Winslow 1.00 2.50
8 Devin Booker 30.00 80.00
9 Trey Lyles .75 2.00
10 Myles Turner 2.50 6.00
11 Justin Anderson .60 1.50
12 Delon Wright .75 2.00
13 Terry Rozier 2.50 6.00
14 Mario Hezonja .75 2.00
15 Josh Richardson 1.00 2.50
16 D'Angelo Russell 2.50 6.00
17 Stanley Johnson .75 2.00
18 Kristaps Porzingis 4.00 10.00
19 Jerian Grant .60 1.50
20 Cameron Payne 1.00 2.50
21 Sam Dekker .60 1.50
22 Jahlil Okafor .75 2.00
23 Bobby Portis 1.50 4.00
24 R.J. Hunter .60 1.50
25 Kelly Oubre Jr. 2.00 5.00

2015-16 Panini Revolution Showstoppers
STATED ODDS 1:64 PACKS
*COSMIC/100: 1.2X TO 3X BASIC
1 Stephen Curry 15.00 40.00
2 Russell Westbrook 3.00 8.00
3 LeBron James 15.00 40.00
4 Tim Duncan 5.00 12.00
5 Kobe Bryant 15.00 40.00
6 Kevin Durant 8.00 20.00
7 James Harden 4.00 10.00
8 Dirk Nowitzki 5.00 12.00
9 Kyrie Irving 4.00 10.00
10 Derrick Rose 3.00 8.00
11 Damian Lillard 5.00 12.00
12 Chris Paul 4.00 10.00

2016-17 Panini Revolution
1 Steven Adams .30 .75
2 LaMarcus Aldridge .40 1.00
3 Ryan Anderson .25 .60
4 Giannis Antetokounmpo 2.00 5.00
5 Carmelo Anthony .60 1.50
6 Trevor Ariza .25 .60
7 Harrison Barnes .30 .75
8 Nicolas Batum .30 .75
9 Bradley Beal .50 1.25
10 Eric Bledsoe .30 .75
11 Devin Booker 1.50 4.00
12 Justise Winslow .30 .75
13 Jimmy Butler .75 2.00
14 Kentavious Caldwell-Pope .30 .75
15 Willie Cauley-Stein .30 .75
16 Jordan Clarkson .40 1.00
17 Darren Collison .25 .60
18 Mike Conley .30 .75
19 DeMarcus Cousins .30 .75
20 Stephen Curry 3.00 8.00
21 Anthony Davis 1.25 3.00
22 DeMar DeRozan .50 1.25
23 Goran Dragic .40 1.00
24 Andre Drummond .40 1.00
25 Kevin Durant 1.50 4.00
26 Monta Ellis .30 .75
27 Tyreke Evans .30 .75
28 Kenneth Faried .30 .75
29 Derrick Favors .25 .60
30 Evan Fournier .30 .75
31 Marc Gasol .40 1.00
32 Pau Gasol .60 1.50
33 Paul George .60 1.50
34 Rudy Gobert .50 1.25
35 Aaron Gordon .40 1.00
36 Eric Gordon .30 .75
37 Marcin Gortat .25 .60
38 Draymond Green .50 1.25
39 Blake Griffin .40 1.00
40 James Harden .75 2.00
41 Gordon Hayward .40 1.00
42 Jrue Holiday .50 1.25
43 Al Horford .40 1.00
44 Dwight Howard .50 1.25
45 Kyrie Irving .75 2.00
46 LeBron James 3.00 8.00
47 Stanley Johnson .25 .60
48 Nikola Jokic 2.00 5.00
49 DeAndre Jordan .30 .75
50 Michael Kidd-Gilchrist .25 .60
51 Brandon Knight .30 .75
52 Zach LaVine .75 2.00
53 Kawhi Leonard 1.00 2.50
54 Damian Lillard 1.00 2.50
55 Jeremy Lin .75 2.00
56 Brook Lopez .30 .75
57 Kevin Love .40 1.00
58 Kyle Lowry .40 1.00
59 C.J. McCollum .40 1.00
60 T.J. McConnell .30 .75
61 Paul Millsap .30 .75
62 Nikola Mirotic .25 .60
63 Greg Monroe .25 .60
64 Emmanuel Mudiay .25 .60
65 Joakim Noah .25 .60
66 Nerlens Noel .25 .60
67 Dirk Nowitzki 1.00 2.50
68 Jahlil Okafor .25 .60
69 Victor Oladipo .30 .75
70 Jabari Parker .25 .60
71 Tony Parker .60 1.50
72 Chandler Parsons .25 .60
73 Chris Paul .60 1.50
74 Kristaps Porzingis .60 1.50
75 Julius Randle .50 1.25
76 Zach Randolph .40 1.00
77 J.J. Redick .40 1.00
78 Rajon Rondo .50 1.25
79 Derrick Rose .60 1.50
80 Ricky Rubio .30 .75
81 D'Angelo Russell .50 1.25
82 Dennis Schroder .40 1.00
83 Luis Scola .30 .75
84 Marcus Smart .50 1.25
85 Jared Sullinger .25 .60
86 Isaiah Thomas .30 .75
87 Klay Thompson 1.00 2.50
88 Tristan Thompson .30 .75
89 Karl-Anthony Towns .75 2.00
90 Myles Turner .40 1.00
91 Jonas Valanciunas .30 .75
92 Noah Vonleh .25 .60
93 Nikola Vucevic .40 1.00
94 Dwyane Wade .75 2.00
95 Kemba Walker .30 .75
96 John Wall .50 1.25
97 Russell Westbrook .60 1.50
98 Hassan Whiteside .30 .75
99 Andrew Wiggins .50 1.25
100 Deron Williams .30 .75
101 Wade Baldwin IV RC .40 1.00
102 Malik Beasley RC .75 2.00
103 DeAndre' Bembry RC .60 1.50
104 Dragan Bender RC .40 1.00
105 Joel Bolomboy RC .40 1.00
106 Malcolm Brogdon RC 1.25 3.00
107 Jaylen Brown RC 10.00 25.00
108 Marquese Chriss RC .50 1.25
109 Deyonta Davis RC .40 1.00
110 Cheick Diallo RC .40 1.00
111 Kris Dunn RC .60 1.50
112 Henry Ellenson RC .40 1.00
113 Kay Felder RC .40 1.00
114 Michael Gbinije RC .40 1.00
115 A.J. Hammons RC .40 1.00
116 Willy Hernangomez RC .50 1.25
117 Buddy Hield RC 1.25 3.00
118 Brandon Ingram RC 1.50 4.00
119 Demetrius Jackson RC .40 1.00
120 Brice Johnson RC .40 1.00
121 Damian Jones RC .40 1.00
122 Mindaugas Kuzminskas RC .40 1.00
123 Skal Labissiere RC .40 1.00
124 Jake Layman RC .50 1.25
125 Caris LeVert RC 1.00 2.50
126 T. Luwawu-Cabarrot RC .60 1.50
127 Thon Maker RC .50 1.25
128 Patrick McCaw RC .40 1.00
129 Dejounte Murray RC 2.00 5.00
130 Jamal Murray RC 8.00 20.00
131 Georges Niang RC .60 1.50
132 Chinanu Onuaku RC .40 1.00
133 Georgios Papagiannis RC .40 1.00
134 Ron Baker RC .40 1.00
135 Marshall Plumlee RC .40 1.00
136 Jakob Poeltl RC .75 2.00
137 Taurean Prince RC .50 1.25
138 Malachi Richardson RC .40 1.00
139 Domantas Sabonis RC 2.50 6.00
140 Dario Saric RC .60 1.50
141 Tomas Satoransky RC .60 1.50
142 Pascal Siakam RC 2.50 6.00
143 Ben Simmons RC 1.25 3.00
144 Diamond Stone RC .40 1.00
145 Tyler Ulis RC .50 1.25
146 Denzel Valentine RC .40 1.00
147 Isaiah Whitehead RC .40 1.00
148 Stephen Zimmerman RC .40 1.00
149 Paul Zipser RC .40 1.00
150 Ivica Zubac RC 1.00 2.50

2016-17 Panini Revolution Astro
*ASTRO: .75X TO 2X BASIC
*ASTRO RC: .75X TO 2X BASIC RC

2016-17 Panini Revolution Futura
*FUTURA: 5X TO 12X BASIC
*FUTURA RC: 5X TO 12X BASIC RC
STATED PRINT RUN 25 SER.#'d SETS

2016-17 Panini Revolution Infinite
*INFINITE: 1X TO 2.5X BASIC
*INFINITE RC: 1X TO 2.5X BASIC RC

2016-17 Panini Revolution Autographs
*FUTURA/25: .6X TO 1.5X BASIC
1 Anthony Davis 30.00 80.00
2 Kobe Bryant 500.00 1,000.00
3 Kyrie Irving 30.00 80.00
4 Kevin Durant 75.00 200.00
6 Vince Carter 30.00 80.00
8 Kevin Love 6.00 15.00
9 Kristaps Porzingis 30.00 80.00
12 Justise Winslow 5.00 12.00
13 Andrew Wiggins 15.00 40.00
14 Myles Turner 6.00 15.00
15 Karl-Anthony Towns 25.00 60.00
16 Hassan Whiteside 5.00 12.00
17 Reggie Jackson 5.00 12.00
18 Nikola Jokic 150.00 400.00
19 Zach LaVine 8.00 20.00
20 Josh Richardson 5.00 12.00
21 James Worthy 12.00 30.00
22 Gary Payton 10.00 25.00
24 Grant Hill 20.00 50.00
25 Ray Allen 30.00 80.00
26 David Robinson 30.00 80.00
27 Patrick Ewing 100.00 250.00
28 John Stockton 25.00 60.00
29 Allen Iverson 100.00 250.00
30 Larry Bird 50.00 120.00
31 Magic Johnson 30.00 80.00
33 Karl Malone 25.00 60.00
34 Dennis Rodman 25.00 60.00
35 Shaquille O'Neal 50.00 120.00

2016-17 Panini Revolution By the Numbers
*COSMIC/100: 1.2X TO 3X BASIC
1 Stephen Curry 5.00 12.00
2 James Harden 1.25 3.00
3 Kevin Durant 2.50 6.00
4 DeMarcus Cousins .50 1.25
5 LeBron James 5.00 12.00
6 Damian Lillard 1.50 4.00
7 Anthony Davis 2.00 5.00
8 Russell Westbrook 1.00 2.50
9 DeMar DeRozan .75 2.00
10 Paul George 1.00 2.50
11 Rajon Rondo .75 2.00
12 Russell Westbrook 1.00 2.50
13 John Wall .75 2.00
14 Chris Paul 1.00 2.50
15 Ricky Rubio .50 1.25
16 Andre Drummond .60 1.50
17 DeAndre Jordan .50 1.25
18 Dwight Howard .75 2.00
19 Hassan Whiteside .50 1.25
20 DeMarcus Cousins .50 1.25

2016-17 Panini Revolution Revolutionaries
*COSMIC/100: 1X TO 2.5X BASIC
1 Bill Russell 6.00 15.00
2 Oscar Robertson 5.00 12.00
3 Jerry West 5.00 12.00
4 Wilt Chamberlain 6.00 15.00
5 Pete Maravich 3.00 8.00
6 Julius Erving 5.00 12.00
7 Larry Bird 8.00 20.00
8 Magic Johnson 8.00 20.00
9 Hakeem Olajuwon 4.00 10.00
10 David Robinson 4.00 10.00
11 Scottie Pippen 4.00 10.00
12 Karl Malone 3.00 8.00
13 Shaquille O'Neal 6.00 15.00
14 Allen Iverson 3.00 8.00
15 Yao Ming 5.00 12.00
16 Kobe Bryant 15.00 40.00

2016-17 Panini Revolution Rookie Autographs
*FUTURA/25: .6X TO 1.5X BASIC
1 Brandon Ingram 50.00 120.00
2 Dario Saric 6.00 15.00
3 Jaylen Brown 125.00 300.00
4 Buddy Hield 12.00 30.00
5 Kris Dunn 6.00 15.00
6 Jamal Murray 75.00 200.00
7 Marquese Chriss 5.00 12.00
8 Jakob Poeltl 8.00 20.00
9 Thon Maker 5.00 12.00
10 Caris LeVert 10.00 25.00
11 Dragan Bender 4.00 10.00
12 Dejounte Murray 40.00 100.00
13 Denzel Valentine 4.00 10.00
14 Damian Jones 4.00 10.00
15 Juan Hernangomez 8.00 20.00

2016-17 Panini Revolution Rookie Autographs Futura
*FUTURA: .6X TO 1.5X BASIC
STATED PRINT RUN 25 SER.#'d SETS
6 Jamal Murray 125.00 300.00

2016-17 Panini Revolution Rookie Revolution
*COSMIC/100: 1.2X TO 3X BASIC
1 Dario Saric .60 1.50
2 Brandon Ingram 1.50 4.00
3 Jaylen Brown 8.00 20.00
4 Ben Simmons 1.25 3.00
5 Dragan Bender .40 1.00
6 Kris Dunn .60 1.50
7 Buddy Hield 1.25 3.00
8 Jamal Murray 5.00 12.00
9 Marquese Chriss .50 1.25
10 Jakob Poeltl .75 2.00
11 Thon Maker .50 1.25
12 Domantas Sabonis 2.50 6.00
13 Taurean Prince .50 1.25
14 Georgios Papagiannis .40 1.00
15 Denzel Valentine .40 1.00
16 Juan Hernangomez .75 2.00
17 Wade Baldwin IV .40 1.00
18 Henry Ellenson .40 1.00
19 Malik Beasley .75 2.00
20 Caris LeVert 1.00 2.50
21 DeAndre' Bembry .60 1.50
22 Malachi Richardson .40 1.00
23 Timothe Luwawu-Cabarrot .60 1.50
24 Brice Johnson .40 1.00
25 Pascal Siakam 2.50 6.00
26 Skal Labissiere .40 1.00
27 Dejounte Murray 2.00 5.00
28 Damian Jones .40 1.00

2016-17 Panini Revolution Showstoppers
*COSMIC/100: .75X TO 2X BASIC
1 Carmelo Anthony 3.00 8.00
2 Stephen Curry 15.00 40.00
3 Anthony Davis 6.00 15.00
4 Kevin Durant 8.00 20.00
5 James Harden 4.00 10.00
6 Kyrie Irving 4.00 10.00
7 LeBron James 15.00 40.00
8 Dirk Nowitzki 5.00 12.00
9 Chris Paul 3.00 8.00
10 Karl-Anthony Towns 4.00 10.00
11 Dwyane Wade 4.00 10.00
12 Russell Westbrook 3.00 8.00

2016-17 Panini Revolution Star Gazing
*COSMIC/100: 1.2X TO 3X BASIC
1 LaMarcus Aldridge .60 1.50
2 Carmelo Anthony 1.00 2.50
3 Jimmy Butler 1.25 3.00
4 DeMarcus Cousins .50 1.25
5 Stephen Curry 5.00 12.00
6 Anthony Davis 2.00 5.00
7 DeMar DeRozan .75 2.00
8 Kevin Durant 2.50 6.00
9 Paul George 1.00 2.50
10 Blake Griffin .60 1.50
11 James Harden 1.25 3.00
12 Kyrie Irving 1.25 3.00
13 LeBron James 5.00 12.00
14 DeAndre Jordan .50 1.25
15 Kawhi Leonard 1.50 4.00
16 Damian Lillard 1.50 4.00
17 Dirk Nowitzki 1.50 4.00
18 Chris Paul 1.00 2.50
19 Derrick Rose 1.00 2.50
20 Klay Thompson 1.50 4.00
21 Karl-Anthony Towns 1.25 3.00
22 Dwyane Wade 1.25 3.00
23 John Wall .75 2.00
24 Russell Westbrook 1.00 2.50

2017-18 Panini Revolution
1 Steven Adams .30 .75
2 DeMarcus Cousins .30 .75
3 Kemba Walker .30 .75
4 Carmelo Anthony .60 1.50
5 Jrue Holiday .50 1.25
6 Rodney Hood .25 .60
7 Kenneth Faried .30 .75
8 Eric Bledsoe .30 .75
9 Nikola Vucevic .30 .75
10 Kawhi Leonard 1.00 2.50

11 Wesley Matthews .25 .60
12 Devin Booker 1.00 2.50
13 Aaron Gordon .40 1.00
14 Dwight Howard .50 1.25
15 Isaiah Thomas .30 .75
16 Reggie Jackson .30 .75
17 Kyle Lowry .40 1.00
18 Kent Bazemore .25 .60
19 Damian Lillard 1.00 2.50
20 Dennis Schroder .30 .75
21 Paul George .60 1.50
22 Kevin Durant 1.50 4.00
23 Thaddeus Young .25 .60
24 Dario Saric .30 .75
25 Jeff Teague .25 .60
26 LaMarcus Aldridge .40 1.00
27 Myles Turner .40 1.00
28 Khris Middleton .50 1.25
29 Marc Gasol .40 1.00
30 Al Horford .40 1.00
31 Elfrid Payton .25 .60
32 Zach Randolph .40 1.00
33 Tony Parker .60 1.50
34 Ricky Rubio .30 .75
35 LeBron James 3.00 8.00
36 Pau Gasol .60 1.50
37 Dion Waiters .25 .60
38 Serge Ibaka .30 .75
39 Ryan Anderson .25 .60
40 Anthony Davis 1.00 2.50
41 Tyson Chandler .30 .75
42 Brook Lopez .30 .75
43 Gordon Hayward .30 .75
44 Stephen Curry 3.00 8.00
45 DeAndre Jordan .30 .75
46 Andrew Wiggins .50 1.25
47 Nicolas Batum .25 .60
48 Derrick Rose .60 1.50
49 Julius Randle .40 1.00
50 Joakim Noah .25 .60
51 Ben Simmons .40 1.00
52 Robin Lopez .25 .60
53 Draymond Green .50 1.25
54 Jusuf Nurkic .30 .75
55 Kentavious Caldwell-Pope .30 .75
56 Bradley Beal .50 1.25
57 Blake Griffin .40 1.00
58 Mike Conley .30 .75
59 Marcin Gortat .25 .60
60 Dwyane Wade .75 2.00
61 Chris Paul .60 1.50
62 Klay Thompson 1.00 2.50
63 C.J. McCollum .40 1.00
64 Willie Cauley-Stein .25 .60
65 John Wall .50 1.25
66 Vince Carter .75 2.00
67 Jabari Parker .25 .60
68 Malcolm Brogdon .30 .75
69 Avery Bradley .25 .60
70 Chandler Parsons .25 .60
71 Gary Harris .30 .75
72 Dirk Nowitzki 1.00 2.50
73 Kevin Love .40 1.00
74 D'Angelo Russell .30 .75
75 Victor Oladipo .30 .75
76 Giannis Antetokounmpo 2.00 5.00
77 Jeremy Lin .60 1.50
78 Kyrie Irving .75 2.00
79 Russell Westbrook .60 1.50
80 Jimmy Butler .60 1.50
81 JJ Redick .40 1.00
82 Zach LaVine .60 1.50
83 Trevor Ariza .25 .60
84 DeMar DeRozan .50 1.25
85 Otto Porter Jr. .30 .75
86 Ersan Ilyasova .25 .60
87 Hassan Whiteside .30 .75
88 Paul Millsap .30 .75
89 Karl-Anthony Towns .60 1.50
90 Rudy Gobert .50 1.25
91 Danilo Gallinari .30 .75
92 Trevor Booker .25 .60
93 Goran Dragic .30 .75
94 Harrison Barnes .30 .75
95 James Harden .75 2.00
96 Kristaps Porzingis .50 1.25
97 Andre Drummond .30 .75
98 Nikola Jokic 2.50 6.00
99 Tobias Harris .30 .75
100 Brandon Ingram .50 1.25
101 Markelle Fultz RC 1.00 2.50
102 Kyle Kuzma RC 1.50 4.00
103 Jonathan Isaac RC 1.00 2.50
104 Dillon Brooks RC 1.25 3.00
105 Malik Monk RC 1.50 4.00
106 Jordan Bell RC .40 1.00
107 Justin Patton RC .40 1.00
108 Sterling Brown RC .40 1.00
109 Terrance Ferguson RC .40 1.00
110 Bogdan Bogdanovic RC 1.00 2.50
111 Lonzo Ball RC 1.50 4.00
112 Tony Bradley RC .40 1.00
113 Lauri Markkanen RC 2.50 6.00
114 Wesley Iwundu RC .40 1.00
115 Luke Kennard RC .75 2.00
116 Ante Zizic RC .50 1.25
117 D.J. Wilson RC .40 1.00
118 Sindarius Thornwell RC .40 1.00
119 Jarrett Allen RC 1.00 2.50
120 Thomas Bryant RC .60 1.50
121 Jayson Tatum RC 15.00 40.00
122 Derrick White RC 1.50 4.00
123 Frank Ntilikina RC .50 1.25
124 Frank Mason III RC .40 1.00
125 Donovan Mitchell RC 4.00 10.00
126 Jawun Evans RC .40 1.00
127 T.J. Leaf RC .40 1.00
128 Wayne Selden Jr. RC .40 1.00
129 OG Anunoby RC 2.00 5.00
130 Damyean Dotson RC .50 1.25
131 Josh Jackson RC .50 1.25
132 Josh Hart RC 1.00 2.50
133 Dennis Smith Jr. RC .50 1.25
134 Ivan Rabb RC .40 1.00
135 Bam Adebayo RC 2.50 6.00
136 Dwayne Bacon RC .40 1.00
137 John Collins RC 1.00 2.50
138 Zhou Qi RC .75 2.00
139 Tyler Lydon RC .40 1.00
140 Mike James RC .40 1.00
141 De'Aaron Fox RC 3.00 8.00
142 Frank Jackson RC .40 1.00
143 Zach Collins RC .60 1.50
144 Semi Ojeleye RC .50 1.25
145 Justin Jackson RC .40 1.00
146 Tyler Dorsey RC .40 1.00
147 Harry Giles RC .40 1.00
148 Guerschon Yabusele RC .40 1.00
149 Caleb Swanigan RC .40 1.00
150 Milos Teodosic RC .50 1.25

2017-18 Panini Revolution Astro

*ASTRO: .75X TO 2X BASIC
*ASTRO RC: .75X TO 2X BASIC RC

2017-18 Panini Revolution Chinese New Year

*NEW YEAR: 1.5X TO 4X BASIC
*NEW YEAR RC: 1.5X TO 4X BASIC RC

2017-18 Panini Revolution Cosmic

*COSMIC: 2X TO 5X BASIC
*COSMIC RC: 2X TO 5X BASIC RC
STATED PRINT RUN 100 SER.#'d SETS
35 LeBron James 20.00 50.00
111 Lonzo Ball 15.00 40.00
113 Lauri Markkanen 12.00 30.00
121 Jayson Tatum 125.00 300.00
125 Donovan Mitchell 20.00 50.00

2017-18 Panini Revolution Cubic

*CUBIC: 3X TO 8X BASIC
*CUBIC RC: 3X TO 8X BASIC RC
STATED PRINT RUN 50 SER.#'d SETS
35 LeBron James 25.00 60.00
111 Lonzo Ball 25.00 60.00
113 Lauri Markkanen 20.00 50.00
121 Jayson Tatum 200.00 500.00
125 Donovan Mitchell 30.00 80.00

2017-18 Panini Revolution Fractal

*FRACTAL: 1.2X TO 3X BASIC
*FRACTAL RC: 1.2X TO 3X BASIC RC

2017-18 Panini Revolution Groove

*GROOVE: .75X TO 2X BASIC
*GROOVE RC: .75X TO 2X BASIC RC

2017-18 Panini Revolution Impact

*IMPACT: 1.2X TO 3X BASIC
*IMPACT RC: 1.2X TO 3X BASIC RC

2017-18 Panini Revolution Sunburst

*SUNBURST: 2.5X TO 6X BASIC
*SUNBURST RC: 2.5X TO 6X BASIC RC
STATED PRINT RUN 75 SER.#'d SETS
35 LeBron James 20.00 50.00
111 Lonzo Ball 20.00 50.00
113 Lauri Markkanen 15.00 40.00
121 Jayson Tatum 150.00 400.00
125 Donovan Mitchell 25.00 60.00

2017-18 Panini Revolution Vortex

*IMPACT: 1X TO 2.5X BASIC
1 Ben Simmons .50 1.25
2 DeAndre Jordan .40 1.00
3 DeMar DeRozan .60 1.50
4 Hassan Whiteside .40 1.00
5 Anthony Davis 1.25 3.00
6 Kemba Walker .40 1.00
7 Russell Westbrook .75 2.00
8 Stephen Curry 4.00 10.00
9 Eric Bledsoe .40 1.00
10 Draymond Green .60 1.50
11 LaMarcus Aldridge .50 1.25
12 Mike Conley .40 1.00
13 Rudy Gobert .60 1.50
14 Giannis Antetokounmpo 2.50 6.00
15 DeMarcus Cousins .40 1.00
16 Dwyane Wade 1.00 2.50
17 Joel Embiid 1.00 2.50
18 Klay Thompson 1.25 3.00
19 Damian Lillard 1.25 3.00
20 James Harden 1.00 2.50
21 Pau Gasol .75 2.00
22 Marc Gasol .50 1.25
23 John Wall .60 1.50
24 Andrew Wiggins .60 1.50
25 Carmelo Anthony .75 2.00
26 LeBron James 4.00 10.00
27 Devin Booker 1.25 3.00
28 Kevin Durant 2.00 5.00
29 Tony Parker .75 2.00
30 Blake Griffin .50 1.25
31 Kyle Lowry .50 1.25
32 Goran Dragic .40 1.00
33 Bradley Beal .60 1.50
34 Karl-Anthony Towns .75 2.00
35 Kristaps Porzingis .60 1.50
36 Dirk Nowitzki 1.25 3.00

2017-18 Panini Revolution Vortex Cubic

*CUBIC: 2.5X TO 6X BASIC
STATED PRINT RUN 50 SER.#'d SETS

2017-18 Panini Revolution Autographs

EXCHANGE DEADLINE 07/05/2019
1 Damian Lillard 25.00 60.00
2 Kevin Durant 50.00 120.00
3 Dirk Nowitzki 50.00 120.00
4 Karl-Anthony Towns 25.00 60.00
5 Marc Gasol 6.00 15.00
6 Joel Embiid 25.00 60.00
7 Nikola Jokic 150.00 400.00
8 Kareem Abdul-Jabbar 25.00 60.00
9 Kobe Bryant 500.00 1,000.00
10 Kyrie Irving 40.00 100.00
11 Dominique Wilkins 10.00 25.00
12 C.J. McCollum 8.00 20.00
13 Harrison Barnes 6.00 15.00
14 John Wall 15.00 40.00
16 Shaquille O'Neal 40.00 100.00
17 Reggie Miller 60.00 150.00
18 Jason Kidd 15.00 40.00
19 Anfernee Hardaway 25.00 60.00
20 Ben Wallace 10.00 25.00
21 Tim Hardaway 6.00 15.00
A-TM Tracy McGrady 75.00 200.00
23 Latrell Sprewell 10.00 25.00
24 Giannis Antetokounmpo 75.00 200.00
25 Anthony Davis 25.00 60.00
26 Julius Randle 5.00 12.00
27 Gordon Hayward 15.00 40.00
28 Zach LaVine 10.00 25.00
29 Aaron Gordon 8.00 20.00

2017-18 Panini Revolution Autographs Cubic

*CUBIC: .6X TO 1.5X BASIC
STATED PRINT RUN 50 SER.#'d SETS
EXCHANGE DEADLINE 07/05/2019
15 Alonzo Mourning 60.00 150.00

2017-18 Panini Revolution Liftoff!

1 Karl-Anthony Towns 2.00 5.00
2 Aaron Gordon 1.25 3.00
3 DeMar DeRozan 1.50 4.00
4 Andrew Wiggins 1.50 4.00
5 LeBron James 10.00 25.00
6 Giannis Antetokounmpo 6.00 15.00
7 Kevin Durant 5.00 12.00
8 John Wall 1.50 4.00
9 Russell Westbrook 2.00 5.00
10 Blake Griffin 1.25 3.00

2017-18 Panini Revolution Liftoff! Cubic

*CUBIC: 2X TO 5X BASIC
STATED PRINT RUN 50 SER.#'d SETS
5 LeBron James 100.00 250.00

2017-18 Panini Revolution Liftoff! Impact

*IMPACT: 1X TO 2.5X BASIC
5 LeBron James 25.00 60.00

2017-18 Panini Revolution Revolutionaries

*IMPACT: .6X TO 1.5X BASIC
*CUBIC/50: 2X TO 5X BASIC
1 Patrick Ewing 1.25 3.00
2 John Havlicek 1.50 4.00
3 Julius Erving 2.00 5.00
4 Karl Malone 1.50 4.00
5 Grant Hill 1.25 3.00
6 Larry Bird 3.00 8.00
7 John Stockton 1.50 4.00
8 Kareem Abdul-Jabbar 2.50 6.00
9 Allen Iverson 2.00 5.00
10 Shaquille O'Neal 2.50 6.00
11 Gary Payton 1.25 3.00
12 Jerry West 1.50 4.00
13 Scottie Pippen 2.00 5.00
14 Hakeem Olajuwon 1.50 4.00
15 David Robinson 1.50 4.00
16 Tracy McGrady 1.25 3.00
17 Isiah Thomas 1.25 3.00
18 Kobe Bryant 6.00 15.00
19 Jason Kidd 1.25 3.00
20 Oscar Robertson 1.50 4.00
21 Reggie Miller 1.50 4.00
22 Magic Johnson 3.00 8.00

2017-18 Panini Revolution Rookie Autographs

EXCHANGE DEADLINE 07/05/2019
*CUBIC/50: .75X TO 2X BASIC
1 Markelle Fultz 20.00 50.00
2 Lonzo Ball 25.00 60.00
3 Jayson Tatum 200.00 500.00
4 Luke Kennard 6.00 15.00
5 Jordan Bell 3.00 8.00
6 De'Aaron Fox 40.00 100.00
7 OG Anunoby 15.00 40.00
8 Jonathan Isaac 10.00 25.00
9 John Collins 12.00 30.00
10 Zach Collins 5.00 12.00
11 Frank Ntilikina 4.00 10.00
12 Malik Monk 12.00 30.00
13 Bam Adebayo 10.00 25.00
14 Harry Giles 3.00 8.00
15 Jarrett Allen 6.00 15.00
17 Dwayne Bacon 3.00 8.00
18 Donovan Mitchell 75.00 200.00
19 Terrance Ferguson 3.00 8.00
20 Dennis Smith Jr. 4.00 10.00
RAJJK Josh Jackson 4.00 10.00

2017-18 Panini Revolution Rookie Revolution

*IMPACT: .6X TO 1.5X BASIC
*CUBIC/50: 2.5X TO 6X BASIC
1 John Collins 1.25 3.00
2 Dennis Smith Jr. .60 1.50
3 Harry Giles .50 1.25
4 Zach Collins .75 2.00
5 Markelle Fultz 1.25 3.00
6 Malik Monk 2.00 5.00
7 Lonzo Ball 2.00 5.00
8 Luke Kennard 1.00 2.50
9 Jayson Tatum 6.00 15.00
10 Donovan Mitchell 5.00 12.00
11 Josh Jackson .60 1.50
12 Bam Adebayo 3.00 8.00
13 De'Aaron Fox 4.00 10.00
14 Justin Jackson .50 1.25
15 Jonathan Isaac 1.25 3.00
16 D.J. Wilson .50 1.25
17 Frank Ntilikina .60 1.50
18 T.J. Leaf .50 1.25

2017-18 Panini Revolution Showstoppers

*IMPACT: .75X TO 2X BASIC
1 Kevin Durant 5.00 12.00
2 Markelle Fultz 2.00 5.00
3 Stephen Curry 10.00 25.00
4 Lonzo Ball 3.00 8.00
5 LeBron James 10.00 25.00
6 Jayson Tatum 10.00 25.00
7 James Harden 2.50 6.00
8 Josh Jackson 1.00 2.50
9 Russell Westbrook 2.00 5.00
10 Kobe Bryant 10.00 25.00

2017-18 Panini Revolution Showstoppers Cubic

*CUBIC: 1.2X TO 3X BASIC
STATED PRINT RUN 50 SER.#'d SETS
4 Lonzo Ball 20.00 50.00
5 LeBron James 30.00 80.00
6 Jayson Tatum 30.00 80.00
10 Kobe Bryant 20.00 50.00

2018-19 Panini Revolution

*ASTRO: .75X TO 2X BASIC
*CHINESE NY: .75X TO 2X BASIC
*FRACTAL: .75X TO 2X BASIC
*GROOVE: .75X TO 2X BASIC
*IMPACT: .75X TO 2X BASIC
1 Goran Dragic .30 .75
2 Jeremy Lin .60 1.50
3 Anthony Davis 1.00 2.50
4 Kemba Walker .30 .75
5 Aaron Gordon .40 1.00
6 Dennis Smith Jr. .25 .60
7 Jusuf Nurkic .30 .75
8 Klay Thompson 1.00 2.50
9 Kawhi Leonard 1.00 2.50
10 Marcin Gortat .25 .60
11 Hassan Whiteside .30 .75
12 John Collins .40 1.00
13 Nikola Mirotic .25 .60
14 Tony Parker .60 1.50
15 Nikola Vucevic .30 .75
16 Dirk Nowitzki 1.00 2.50
17 De'Aaron Fox .75 2.00
18 Kevin Durant 1.50 4.00
19 Danny Green .30 .75
20 Tobias Harris .30 .75
21 Dion Waiters .25 .60
22 Taurean Prince .25 .60
23 Elfrid Payton .30 .75
24 Nicolas Batum .25 .60
25 Ben Simmons .40 1.00
26 DeAndre Jordan .30 .75
27 Buddy Hield .40 1.00
28 Draymond Green .50 1.25
29 Ricky Rubio .30 .75
30 Lou Williams .30 .75
31 Eric Bledsoe .30 .75
32 Kyrie Irving 1.00 2.50
33 Enes Kanter .30 .75
34 Michael Kidd-Gilchrist .25 .60
35 Joel Embiid 1.00 2.50
36 Nikola Jokic 2.00 5.00
37 Zach Randolph .30 .75
38 Chris Paul .75 2.00
39 Donovan Mitchell 1.25 3.00
40 LeBron James 3.00 8.00
41 Giannis Antetokounmpo 2.00 5.00
42 Jaylen Brown .60 1.50
43 Kristaps Porzingis .50 1.25
44 Lauri Markkanen .60 1.50
45 Markelle Fultz .30 .75
46 Isaiah Thomas .30 .75
47 Willie Cauley-Stein .25 .60
48 James Harden .75 2.00
49 Rudy Gobert .50 1.25
50 Lonzo Ball .40 1.00
51 Khris Middleton .40 1.00
52 Jayson Tatum 1.50 4.00
53 Tim Hardaway Jr. .25 .60
54 Zach LaVine .60 1.50
55 Trevor Ariza .25 .60
56 Paul Millsap .30 .75
57 DeMar DeRozan .50 1.25
58 Eric Gordon .30 .75
59 Joe Ingles .30 .75
60 Kyle Kuzma .40 1.00
61 Jimmy Butler .60 1.50
62 Gordon Hayward .40 1.00
63 Russell Westbrook .60 1.50
64 Jabari Parker .25 .60
65 TJ Warren .25 .60
66 Andre Drummond .30 .75
67 Pau Gasol .60 1.50
68 Clint Capela .30 .75
69 John Wall .50 1.25
70 Brandon Ingram .40 1.00
71 Andrew Wiggins .50 1.25
72 D'Angelo Russell .40 1.00
73 Paul George .60 1.50
74 Kevin Love .40 1.00
75 Devin Booker 1.00 2.50
76 Blake Griffin .40 1.00
77 LaMarcus Aldridge .40 1.00
78 Myles Turner .40 1.00
79 Bradley Beal .50 1.25
80 Mike Conley .30 .75
81 Karl-Anthony Towns .60 1.50
82 DeMarre Carroll .25 .60
83 Dennis Schroder .30 .75
84 Kyle Korver .30 .75
85 Damian Lillard 1.00 2.50
86 Reggie Jackson .30 .75
87 Dejounte Murray .50 1.25
88 Victor Oladipo .30 .75
89 Otto Porter Jr. .30 .75
90 Marc Gasol .40 1.00
91 Derrick Rose .75 2.00
92 Jarrett Allen .40 1.00
93 Evan Fournier .30 .75
94 JR Smith .30 .75
95 CJ McCollum .40 1.00
96 Stephen Curry 3.00 8.00
97 Kyle Lowry .40 1.00
98 Tyreke Evans .25 .60
99 Dwight Howard .50 1.25
100 Dillon Brooks .40 1.00
101 Mo Bamba RC .60 1.50
102 Jarred Vanderbilt RC .75 2.00
103 Shai Gilgeous-Alexander RC 12.00 30.00
104 Melvin Frazier Jr. RC .40 1.00
105 Zhaire Smith RC .40 1.00
106 Isaac Bonga RC .50 1.25
107 Grayson Allen RC .75 2.00
108 Deandre Ayton RC 1.25 3.00
109 Landry Shamet RC .60 1.50
110 Elie Okobo RC .40 1.00
111 Wendell Carter Jr. RC 1.00 2.50
112 Bruce Brown RC .75 2.00
113 Miles Bridges RC 1.00 2.50
114 Mitchell Robinson RC 1.00 2.50
115 Donte DiVincenzo RC 1.00 2.50
116 Kostas Antetokounmpo RC .50 1.25
117 Chandler Hutchison RC .50 1.25
118 Robert Williams III RC .75 2.00
119 Marvin Bagley III RC .60 1.50
120 Jevon Carter RC .60 1.50
121 Collin Sexton RC 1.25 3.00
122 Hamidou Diallo RC .60 1.50
123 Jerome Robinson RC .40 1.00
124 Khyri Thomas RC .40 1.00
125 Lonnie Walker IV RC .75 2.00
126 Vincent Edwards RC .40 1.00
127 Aaron Holiday RC .60 1.50
128 Luka Doncic RC 25.00 60.00
129 Jacob Evans III RC .40 1.00
130 Jalen Brunson RC 3.00 8.00
131 Kevin Knox RC .50 1.25
132 De'Anthony Melton RC .75 2.00
133 Michael Porter Jr. RC 1.50 4.00
134 Justin Jackson RC .40 1.00
135 Kevin Huerter RC .75 2.00
136 Chimezie Metu RC .50 1.25
137 Anfernee Simons RC 2.00 5.00
138 Dzanan Musa RC .40 1.00
139 Jaren Jackson Jr RC 3.00 8.00
140 Devonte' Graham RC .60 1.50
141 Mikal Bridges RC 2.00 5.00
142 Keita Bates-Diop RC .50 1.25
143 Troy Brown Jr. RC .50 1.25
144 Svi Mykhailiuk RC .50 1.25
145 Josh Okogie RC .60 1.50
146 Shake Milton RC .60 1.50
147 Moritz Wagner RC .75 2.00
148 Omari Spellman RC .40 1.00
149 Gary Trent Jr. RC .75 2.00
150 Trae Young RC 3.00 8.00

2018-19 Panini Revolution Sunburst

*SUNBURST: 2.5X TO 6X BASIC
*SUNBURST RC: 2.5X TO 6X BASIC RC
STATED PRINT RUN 75 SER.#'d SETS
146 Shake Milton 50.00 120.00

2018-19 Panini Revolution Autographs

*INFINITE: .75X TO 2X BASIC
EXCHANGE DEADLINE 06/14/2020
1 Charles Barkley 100.00 250.00
2 Kobe Bryant 300.00 600.00
3 Stephen Curry 300.00 600.00
4 Kevin Durant EXCH 50.00 120.00
5 Allen Iverson 40.00 100.00
6 Reggie Miller EXCH 30.00 80.00
7 Dwyane Wade 40.00 100.00
8 Karl Malone 15.00 40.00
9 Damian Lillard 20.00 50.00
10 Kyrie Irving 20.00 50.00
11 Dirk Nowitzki 50.00 120.00
12 Julius Erving EXCH 15.00 40.00
13 John Stockton 15.00 40.00
14 Kawhi Leonard 60.00 150.00
15 Tracy McGrady 15.00 40.00
16 Anfernee Hardaway EXCH 20.00 50.00
17 Jason Kidd 15.00 40.00
18 Joel Embiid EXCH 20.00 50.00
19 Kristaps Porzingis 10.00 25.00
20 Dominique Wilkins 12.00 30.00
21 Steve Kerr 10.00 25.00
22 Karl-Anthony Towns 12.00 30.00
23 Bill Walton 20.00 50.00
24 Zach LaVine 12.00 30.00
25 Donovan Mitchell EXCH 25.00 60.00
26 Jayson Tatum 25.00 60.00
27 Kyle Kuzma 12.00 30.00
28 Lauri Markkanen 12.00 30.00
29 Jason Williams 15.00 40.00
30 Giannis Antetokounmpo 100.00 250.00

2018-19 Panini Revolution Liftoff!

*IMPACT: .6X TO 1.5X BASIC
*CUBIC/50: 2.5X TO 6X BASIC
1 DeMar DeRozan 1.00 2.50
2 Giannis Antetokounmpo 4.00 10.00
3 Anthony Davis 2.00 5.00
4 LeBron James 6.00 15.00
5 Kevin Durant 3.00 8.00
6 Russell Westbrook 1.25 3.00
7 Donovan Mitchell 2.50 6.00
8 Zach LaVine 1.25 3.00
9 Dennis Smith Jr. .50 1.25
10 Blake Griffin .75 2.00

2018-19 Panini Revolution Liftoff! Cubic

*CUBIC/50: 2.5X TO 6X BASIC
3 Anthony Davis 15.00 40.00
4 LeBron James 75.00 200.00

2018-19 Panini Revolution Liftoff! Impact

*IMPACT: .6X TO 1.5X BASIC
4 LeBron James 12.00 30.00

2018-19 Panini Revolution Rookie Autographs

*INFINITE/25: 1X TO 2.5X BASIC
*CNY/20-77: 1X TO 2.5X BASIC
EXCHANGE DEADLINE 06/14/2020
1 Deandre Ayton 15.00 40.00
2 Marvin Bagley III 8.00 20.00
3 Luka Doncic 400.00 800.00
4 Jaren Jackson Jr. 100.00 250.00
5 Trae Young 200.00 500.00
6 Mo Bamba 8.00 20.00
7 Wendell Carter Jr. 12.00 30.00
8 Collin Sexton 15.00 40.00
9 Kevin Knox 6.00 15.00
10 Mikal Bridges 25.00 60.00
11 Shai Gilgeous-Alexander 400.00 800.00
12 Michael Porter Jr. 75.00 200.00
13 Troy Brown Jr. 6.00 15.00
14 Anfernee Simons 25.00 60.00
15 Kevin Huerter EXCH 10.00 25.00
16 Zhaire Smith 5.00 12.00
17 Donte DiVincenzo 10.00 25.00
18 Lonnie Walker IV 10.00 25.00
19 Moritz Wagner 10.00 25.00
20 Jerome Robinson 5.00 12.00

2018-19 Panini Revolution Rookie Autographs Infinite

*INFINITE/25: 1X TO 2.5X BASIC
STATED PRINT RUN 25 SER.#'d SETS
EXCHANGE DEADLINE 07/05/2019
4 Jaren Jackson Jr. 300.00 600.00

2018-19 Panini Revolution Rookie Revolution

*IMPACT: .6X TO 1.5X BASIC
*CUBIC/50: 2.5X TO 6X BASIC
1 Luka Doncic 30.00 80.00
2 Troy Brown Jr. .60 1.50
3 Trae Young 15.00 40.00
4 Donte DiVincenzo 1.25 3.00
5 Wendell Carter Jr. 1.25 3.00
6 Kevin Huerter 1.00 2.50
7 Kevin Knox .60 1.50
8 Shai Gilgeous-Alexander 5.00 12.00
9 Deandre Ayton 1.50 4.00
10 Jerome Robinson .50 1.25
11 Jaren Jackson Jr. 4.00 10.00
12 Zhaire Smith .50 1.25
13 Mo Bamba .75 2.00
14 Lonnie Walker IV 1.00 2.50
15 Collin Sexton 1.50 4.00
16 Grayson Allen 1.00 2.50
17 Mikal Bridges 2.50 6.00
18 Miles Bridges 1.25 3.00
19 Marvin Bagley III .75 2.00
20 Michael Porter Jr. 2.00 5.00

2018-19 Panini Revolution Rookie Revolution Cubic

*CUBIC/50: 2.5X TO 6X BASIC
9 Deandre Ayton 25.00 60.00

2018-19 Panini Revolution Rookie Revolution Impact

*IMPACT: .6X TO 1.5X BASIC
1 Luka Doncic 60.00 150.00

2018-19 Panini Revolution Shock Wave

*IMPACT: .6X TO 1.5X BASIC
*CUBIC/50: 2X TO 5X BASIC
1 Chris Paul 1.50 4.00
2 Anthony Davis 2.00 5.00
3 Stephen Curry 6.00 15.00
4 Kyrie Irving 2.00 5.00
5 Donovan Mitchell 2.50 6.00
6 LeBron James 6.00 15.00
7 Kevin Durant 3.00 8.00
8 Blake Griffin .75 2.00
9 Dwight Howard 1.00 2.50
10 Joel Embiid 2.00 5.00
11 Karl-Anthony Towns 1.25 3.00
12 Dennis Smith Jr. .50 1.25
13 John Wall 1.00 2.50
14 Kristaps Porzingis 1.00 2.50
15 Giannis Antetokounmpo 4.00 10.00
16 Dirk Nowitzki 2.00 5.00
17 Jayson Tatum 3.00 8.00
18 DeMar DeRozan 1.00 2.50
19 Damian Lillard 2.00 5.00
20 Russell Westbrook 1.25 3.00
21 Lonzo Ball .75 2.00
22 Lauri Markkanen 1.25 3.00
23 Ben Simmons .75 2.00
24 James Harden 1.50 4.00
25 Paul George 1.25 3.00

2018-19 Panini Revolution Shock Wave Cubic

*CUBIC/50: 2X TO 5X BASIC
6 LeBron James 50.00 120.00

2018-19 Panini Revolution Supernova

*IMPACT: .6X TO 1.5X BASIC
*CUBIC/50: 2X TO 5X BASIC
1 Anthony Davis 2.00 5.00
2 Stephen Curry 6.00 15.00
3 Kyrie Irving 2.00 5.00
4 Donovan Mitchell 2.50 6.00
5 LeBron James 6.00 15.00
6 Kevin Durant 3.00 8.00
7 Giannis Antetokounmpo 4.00 10.00
8 Russell Westbrook 1.25 3.00
9 Ben Simmons .75 2.00
10 James Harden 1.50 4.00

2018-19 Panini Revolution Supernova Cubic

*CUBIC/50: 2X TO 5X BASIC
5 LeBron James 50.00 120.00

2018-19 Panini Revolution Vortex

*IMPACT: .6X TO 1.5X BASIC
*CUBIC/50: 2X TO 5X BASIC
1 LeBron James 8.00 20.00
2 Dirk Nowitzki 2.00 5.00
3 Blake Griffin .75 2.00
4 Kyle Kuzma .75 2.00
5 DeMar DeRozan 1.00 2.50
6 Bradley Beal 1.00 2.50
7 Joel Embiid 2.00 5.00
8 Kemba Walker .60 1.50
9 Russell Westbrook 1.25 3.00
10 Anthony Davis 2.00 5.00
11 Victor Oladipo .60 1.50
12 Dennis Smith Jr. .50 1.25
13 Lauri Markkanen 1.25 3.00
14 DeAndre Jordan .60 1.50
15 Kyrie Irving 2.00 5.00
16 CJ McCollum .75 2.00
17 Kristaps Porzingis 1.00 2.50
18 James Harden 1.50 4.00
19 Donovan Mitchell 2.50 6.00
20 DeMarcus Cousins .60 1.50
21 Giannis Antetokounmpo 4.00 10.00
22 Paul George 1.25 3.00
23 Kevin Durant 3.00 8.00
24 Goran Dragic .60 1.50
25 Jayson Tatum 3.00 8.00
26 Dwight Howard 1.00 2.50
27 Damian Lillard 2.00 5.00
28 Chris Paul 1.50 4.00
29 Karl-Anthony Towns 1.25 3.00
30 Kawhi Leonard 2.00 5.00
31 Lonzo Ball .75 2.00
32 Jimmy Butler 1.25 3.00
33 Stephen Curry 6.00 15.00
34 John Wall 1.00 2.50
35 Ben Simmons .75 2.00

2018-19 Panini Revolution Vortex Cubic

*CUBIC/50: 2X TO 5X BASIC
1 LeBron James 75.00 200.00

2019-20 Panini Revolution

COMPLETE SET (150)
*ASTRO: .75X TO 2X BASIC
*CHINESE NY: .75X TO 2X BASIC
*FRACTAL: .75X TO 2X BASIC
*GROOVE: .75X TO 2X BASIC
1 Ben Simmons .40 1.00
2 Jae Crowder .25 .60
3 Caris LeVert .30 .75
4 Jimmy Butler .75 2.00
5 Julius Randle .50 1.25
6 Tim Hardaway Jr. .25 .60
7 Kristaps Porzingis .50 1.25
8 Bam Adebayo .60 1.50
9 Joel Embiid .75 2.00
10 Kyrie Irving .75 2.00
11 T.J. Warren .30 .75
12 Myles Turner .40 1.00
13 Trae Young 1.00 2.50
14 LeBron James 3.00 8.00
15 Lonzo Ball .40 1.00
16 DeMar DeRozan .50 1.25
17 John Collins .40 1.00
18 Montrezl Harrell .30 .75
19 Steven Adams .30 .75
20 Dennis Smith Jr. .25 .60
21 Thomas Bryant .30 .75
22 Shai Gilgeous-Alexander 2.00 5.00
23 Nikola Jokic 2.00 5.00
24 Jahlil Okafor .25 .60
25 Derrick Rose .75 2.00
26 Paul George .60 1.50
27 Al Horford .40 1.00
28 Hassan Whiteside .25 .60
29 Clint Capela .30 .75
30 Collin Sexton .50 1.25
31 Buddy Hield .30 .75
32 Zach LaVine .60 1.50
33 Michael Porter Jr. .60 1.50
34 Kevin Love .40 1.00
35 Eric Bledsoe .30 .75
36 Jonathan Isaac .40 1.00
37 LaMarcus Aldridge .40 1.00
38 Mo Bamba .30 .75
39 Victor Oladipo .30 .75
40 Chris Paul .75 2.00
41 Pascal Siakam .60 1.50
42 Stephen Curry 3.00 8.00
43 Kevin Durant 1.25 3.00
44 Kemba Walker .30 .75
45 Lonnie Walker IV .30 .75
46 Jaylen Brown .60 1.50
47 De'Aaron Fox .60 1.50
48 Bradley Beal .50 1.25
49 Paul Millsap .30 .75
50 Goran Dragic .30 .75
51 Malcolm Brogdon .30 .75
52 Jaren Jackson Jr. .60 1.50
53 Aaron Gordon .40 1.00
54 Marvin Bagley III .30 .75
55 Andre Drummond .30 .75
56 Miles Bridges .40 1.00
57 Deandre Ayton .40 1.00
58 Damian Lillard 1.00 2.50
59 Karl-Anthony Towns .60 1.50
60 Ricky Rubio .30 .75
61 Russell Westbrook .60 1.50
62 Jordan Clarkson .40 1.00
63 Draymond Green .50 1.25
64 Donovan Mitchell .75 2.00
65 Devin Booker .10 .25
66 John Wall .50 1.25
67 Blake Griffin .40 1.00
68 Kawhi Leonard 1.00 2.50
69 DeMarcus Cousins .30 .75
70 Gary Harris .30 .75
71 Danilo Gallinari .30 .75
72 Kevin Knox II .25 .60
73 Luka Doncic 2.50 6.00
74 Gordon Hayward .30 .75
75 Jayson Tatum 1.50 4.00
76 Giannis Antetokounmpo 2.00 5.00
77 Andrew Wiggins .50 1.25
78 Klay Thompson 1.00 2.50
79 Brandon Ingram .40 1.00
80 DeAndre Jordan .30 .75
81 Marc Gasol .40 1.00
82 Jamal Murray .60 1.50
83 Wendell Carter Jr. .40 1.00
84 Lauri Markkanen .50 1.25
85 Terry Rozier .30 .75
86 Jrue Holiday .50 1.25
87 Kevin Huerter .40 1.00
88 James Harden .75 2.00
89 CJ McCollum .40 1.00
90 Anthony Davis 1.00 2.50
91 Mike Conley .30 .75
92 Kyle Kuzma .50 1.25
93 Derrick White .40 1.00
94 Jeff Teague .25 .60
95 Jonas Valanciunas .30 .75
96 Kyle Lowry .40 1.00
97 Khris Middleton .40 1.00
98 Brook Lopez .30 .75
99 Rudy Gobert .50 1.25
100 D'Angelo Russell .40 1.00
101 Zion Williamson RC 3.00 8.00
102 Ja Morant RC 4.00 10.00
103 RJ Barrett RC 1.50 4.00
104 De'Andre Hunter RC 1.50 4.00
105 Jarrett Culver RC .40 1.00
106 Coby White RC 1.25 3.00
107 Jaxson Hayes RC .60 1.50
108 Rui Hachimura RC 1.50 4.00
109 Cam Reddish RC .60 1.50
110 Cameron Johnson RC 1.00 2.50
111 PJ Washington Jr. RC 1.25 3.00
112 Tyler Herro RC 2.00 5.00
113 Romeo Langford RC .40 1.00
114 Sekou Doumbouya RC .40 1.00
115 Justin Robinson RC .40 1.00
116 Nickeil Alexander-Walker RC .60 1.50
117 Goga Bitadze RC .60 1.50
118 Luka Samanic RC .50 1.25
119 Matisse Thybulle RC .75 2.00
120 Brandon Clarke RC .75 2.00
121 Grant Williams RC .60 1.50

122 Ty Jerome RC .75 2.00
123 Nassir Little RC .60 1.50
124 Dylan Windler RC .50 1.25
125 Mfiondu Kabengele RC .50 1.25
126 Jordan Poole RC 1.50 4.00
127 Keldon Johnson RC 1.25 3.00
128 Kevin Porter Jr. RC .75 2.00
129 Nicolas Claxton RC .75 2.00
130 KZ Okpala RC .50 1.25
131 Carsen Edwards RC .50 1.25
132 Bruno Fernando RC .50 1.25
133 Cody Martin RC .60 1.50
134 Bol Bol RC 1.00 2.50
135 Isaiah Roby RC .50 1.25
136 Daniel Gafford RC .75 2.00
137 Alen Smailagic RC .40 1.00
138 Eric Paschall RC .50 1.25
139 Admiral Schofield RC .50 1.25
140 Jaylen Nowell RC .50 1.25
141 Ignas Brazdeikis RC .50 1.25
142 Terance Mann RC .75 2.00
143 Quinndary Weatherspoon RC .40 1.00
144 Tacko Fall RC .50 1.25
145 Kyle Guy RC .50 1.25
146 Jordan Bone RC .40 1.00
147 Jalen Lecque RC .40 1.00
148 Talen Horton-Tucker RC .60 1.50
149 Darius Bazley RC .40 1.00
150 Darius Garland RC 1.50 4.00

2019-20 Panini Revolution Chinese New Year Emerald
*CNY EMERALD: 2X TO 5X BASIC
*CNY EMERALD RC: 2X TO 5X BASIC RC
STATED PRINT RUN 88 SER.#'d SETS
101 Zion Williamson 50.00 120.00
102 Ja Morant 50.00 120.00

2019-20 Panini Revolution Cosmic
*COSMIC: 2X TO 5X BASIC
*COSMIC RC: 2X TO 5X BASIC RC
STATED PRINT RUN 100 SER.#'d SETS
101 Zion Williamson 50.00 120.00
102 Ja Morant 50.00 120.00

2019-20 Panini Revolution Cubic
*CUBIC: 3X TO 8X BASIC
*CUBIC RC: 3X TO 8X BASIC RC
STATED PRINT RUN 50 SER.#'d SETS
101 Zion Williamson 75.00 200.00
102 Ja Morant 75.00 200.00

2019-20 Panini Revolution Impact
*IMPACT: 1.5X TO 4X BASIC
*IMPACT RC: 1.5X TO 4X BASIC RC
STATED PRINT RUN 149 SER.#'d SETS
101 Zion Williamson 40.00 100.00
102 Ja Morant 40.00 100.00

2019-20 Panini Revolution Sunburst
*SUNBURST: 2.5X TO 6X BASIC
*SUNBURST RC: 2.5X TO 6X BASIC RC
STATED PRINT RUN 75 SER.#'d SETS
101 Zion Williamson 60.00 150.00
102 Ja Morant 60.00 150.00

2019-20 Panini Revolution Autographs Infinite
*INFINITE: .75X TO 2X BASIC
STATED PRINT RUNT 25 SER.#'d SETS
EXCHANGE DEADLINE 07/17/2021
1 Peja Stojakovic 15.00 40.00
10 Pascal Siakam 20.00 50.00
14 Chris Bosh 20.00 50.00
16 Kobe Bryant 1,500.00 3,000.00
20 Dwyane Wade 75.00 200.00

2019-20 Panini Revolution Liftoff
1 Donovan Mitchell 1.50 4.00
2 LeBron James 12.00 30.00
3 Giannis Antetokounmpo 4.00 10.00
4 Russell Westbrook 1.25 3.00
5 Ben Simmons .75 2.00
6 Zion Williamson 30.00 80.00
7 Ja Morant 15.00 40.00
8 RJ Barrett 2.00 5.00
9 Rui Hachimura 2.00 5.00
10 Brandon Clarke 1.00 2.50

2019-20 Panini Revolution Liftoff Cubic
*CUBIC/50: 2X TO 5X BASIC
STATED PRINT RUN 50 SER.#'d SETS
2 LeBron James 150.00 400.00
3 Giannis Antetokounmpo 20.00 50.00
6 Zion Williamson 200.00 500.00
7 Ja Morant 125.00 300.00
8 RJ Barrett 15.00 40.00
9 Rui Hachimura 25.00 60.00
10 Brandon Clarke 10.00 25.00

2019-20 Panini Revolution Liftoff Fractal
*FRACTAL: .6X TO 1.5X BASIC
2 LeBron James 20.00 50.00
6 Zion Williamson 60.00 150.00
7 Ja Morant 40.00 100.00

2019-20 Panini Revolution Rookie Autographs
EXCHANGE DEADLINE 07/17/2021
*CNY/22-45: 1X TO 2.5X BASIC
1 Carsen Edwards 6.00 15.00
2 Zion Williamson EXCH 500.00 1,000.00
3 Tyler Herro 75.00 200.00
4 RJ Barrett 60.00 150.00
5 Matisse Thybulle 10.00 25.00
6 De'Andre Hunter 20.00 50.00
7 Brandon Clarke 10.00 25.00
8 Cam Reddish 8.00 20.00
9 Nickeil Alexander-Walker 8.00 20.00
10 Jaxson Hayes 8.00 20.00
11 Cameron Johnson 12.00 30.00
RA-JMT Ja Morant 200.00 500.00
13 Nassir Little 8.00 20.00
14 Rui Hachimura 60.00 150.00
15 Romeo Langford 5.00 12.00
16 Jarrett Culver 5.00 12.00
17 Chuma Okeke 20.00 50.00
18 Coby White 25.00 60.00
19 Darius Bazley 5.00 12.00
20 PJ Washington Jr. 15.00 40.00

2019-20 Panini Revolution Rookie Autographs Infinite
*INFINITE: 1X TO 2.5X BASIC
STATED PRINT RUNT 25 SER.#'d SETS
EXCHANGE DEADLINE 07/17/2021
2 Zion Williamson EXCH 1,250.00 2,500.00
3 Tyler Herro 200.00 500.00
RA-JMT Ja Morant 800.00 1,500.00
18 Coby White 125.00 300.00

2019-20 Panini Revolution Rookie Revolution
1 Zion Williamson 40.00 100.00
2 Ja Morant 25.00 60.00
3 RJ Barrett 2.00 5.00
4 De'Andre Hunter 2.00 5.00
5 Darius Garland 2.00 5.00
6 Jarrett Culver .50 1.25
7 Coby White 1.50 4.00
8 Jaxson Hayes .75 2.00
9 Rui Hachimura 2.00 5.00
10 Cam Reddish .75 2.00
11 Cameron Johnson 1.25 3.00
12 PJ Washington Jr. 1.50 4.00
13 Tyler Herro 2.50 6.00
14 Romeo Langford .50 1.25
15 Sekou Doumbouya .50 1.25
16 Nassir Little .75 2.00
17 Nickeil Alexander-Walker .75 2.00
18 Brandon Clarke 1.00 2.50
19 Matisse Thybulle 1.00 2.50
20 Luka Samanic .60 1.50

2019-20 Panini Revolution Rookie Revolution Cubic
*CUBIC/50: 2X TO 5X BASIC
STATED PRINT RUN 50 SER.#'d SETS
1 Zion Williamson 300.00 600.00
2 Ja Morant 125.00 300.00
3 RJ Barrett 20.00 50.00

2019-20 Panini Revolution Rookie Revolution Fractal
*FRACTAL: .6X TO 1.5X BASIC
1 Zion Williamson 60.00 150.00
2 Ja Morant 40.00 100.00

2019-20 Panini Revolution Shock Wave
1 Damian Lillard 2.00 5.00
2 LeBron James 12.00 30.00
3 Russell Westbrook 1.25 3.00
4 James Harden 1.50 4.00
5 Trae Young 2.00 5.00
6 Luka Doncic 5.00 12.00
7 Giannis Antetokounmpo 4.00 10.00
8 Paul George 1.25 3.00
9 Kawhi Leonard 2.00 5.00
10 Kemba Walker .60 1.50
11 Jayson Tatum 3.00 8.00
12 Donovan Mitchell 1.50 4.00
13 D'Angelo Russell .60 1.50
14 De'Aaron Fox 1.25 3.00
15 Joel Embiid 1.50 4.00
16 Ben Simmons .75 2.00
17 Anthony Davis 2.00 5.00
18 Nikola Jokic 4.00 10.00
19 Stephen Curry 6.00 15.00
20 Bradley Beal 1.00 2.50
21 Zion Williamson 12.00 30.00
22 Ja Morant 5.00 12.00
23 RJ Barrett 2.00 5.00
24 De'Andre Hunter 2.00 5.00
25 Coby White 1.50 4.00

2019-20 Panini Revolution Shock Wave Cubic
*CUBIC/50: 2X TO 5X BASIC
STATED PRINT RUN 50 SER.#'d SETS
2 LeBron James 150.00 400.00
21 Zion Williamson 150.00 400.00
22 Ja Morant 40.00 100.00

2019-20 Panini Revolution Shock Wave Fractal
*FRACTAL: .6X TO 1.5X BASIC
21 Zion Williamson 25.00 60.00

2019-20 Panini Revolution Supernova
*FRACTAL: .6X TO 1.5X BASIC
1 Stephen Curry 6.00 15.00
2 LeBron James 12.00 30.00
3 Giannis Antetokounmpo 4.00 10.00
4 James Harden 1.50 4.00
5 Kawhi Leonard 2.00 5.00
6 Paul George 1.25 3.00
7 Russell Westbrook 1.25 3.00
8 Ben Simmons .75 2.00
9 Anthony Davis 2.00 5.00
10 Luka Doncic 12.00 30.00

2019-20 Panini Revolution Supernova Cubic
*CUBIC/50: 2X TO 5X BASIC
STATED PRINT RUN 50 SER.#'d SETS
2 LeBron James 150.00 400.00
3 Giannis Antetokounmpo 25.00 60.00
10 Luka Doncic 150.00 400.00

2019-20 Panini Revolution Vortex
*FRACTAL: .6X TO 1.5X BASIC
1 Anthony Davis 2.00 5.00
2 Ben Simmons .75 2.00
3 Bradley Beal 1.00 2.50
4 Damian Lillard 2.00 5.00
5 D'Angelo Russell .60 1.50
6 De'Aaron Fox 1.25 3.00
7 DeMar DeRozan 1.00 2.50
8 Devin Booker .20 .50
9 Donovan Mitchell 1.50 4.00
10 Giannis Antetokounmpo 4.00 10.00
11 James Harden 1.50 4.00
12 Jayson Tatum 3.00 8.00
13 Joel Embiid 1.50 4.00
14 Kawhi Leonard 2.00 5.00
15 Kemba Walker .60 1.50
16 Kristaps Porzingis 1.00 2.50
17 LeBron James 12.00 30.00
18 Luka Doncic 12.00 30.00
19 Marc Gasol .75 2.00
20 Marvin Bagley III .60 1.50
21 Nikola Jokic 4.00 10.00
22 Paul George 1.25 3.00
23 Russell Westbrook 1.25 3.00
24 Stephen Curry 6.00 15.00
25 Trae Young 2.00 5.00
26 Chris Paul 1.50 4.00
27 Jimmy Butler 1.50 4.00
28 Rudy Gobert 1.00 2.50
29 Victor Oladipo .60 1.50
30 Karl-Anthony Towns 1.25 3.00
31 Blake Griffin .75 2.00
32 Jamal Murray 1.25 3.00
33 Kevin Love .75 2.00
34 Kyle Lowry .75 2.00
35 Clint Capela .60 1.50

2019-20 Panini Revolution Vortex Cubic
*CUBIC/50: 2X TO 5X BASIC
STATED PRINT RUN 50 SER.#'d SETS
17 LeBron James 150.00 400.00
18 Luka Doncic 150.00 400.00

2020-21 Panini Revolution
*ASIA RED: .5X TO 1.2X BASIC
*CNY: .6X TO 1.5X BASIC
*ASIA HOLO SILVER: .75X TO 2X BASIC
*ASTRO: .75X TO 2X BASIC
*FRACTAL: .75X TO 2X BASIC
*GROOVE: .75X TO 2X BASIC
*IMPACT/149: 1.5X TO 4X BASIC
*CNY EMERALD/88: 2X TO 5X BASIC
*SUNBURST/75: 2.5X TO 6X BASIC
1 Ben Simmons .40 1.00
2 LaMarcus Aldridge .40 1.00
3 Kevin Durant 1.50 4.00
4 Steven Adams .40 1.00
5 Davis Bertans .30 .75
6 Brandon Ingram .50 1.25
7 Kyrie Irving .75 2.00
8 CJ McCollum .40 1.00
9 Eric Gordon .30 .75
10 Blake Griffin .40 1.00
11 De'Aaron Fox .60 1.50
12 Andre Drummond .40 1.00
13 Norman Powell .30 .75
14 Buddy Hield .40 1.00
15 Andrew Wiggins .50 1.25
16 Kawhi Leonard 1.00 2.50
17 Mike Conley .30 .75
18 Aron Baynes .25 .60
19 Marvin Bagley III .30 .75
20 Jaylen Brown .60 1.50
21 Tyler Herro .75 2.00
22 Jayson Tatum 1.50 4.00
23 Anthony Davis 1.00 2.50
24 Kristaps Porzingis .50 1.25
25 Deandre Ayton .40 1.00
26 Klay Thompson 1.00 2.50
27 John Wall .50 1.25
28 Bam Adebayo .60 1.50
29 Jamal Murray .60 1.50
30 Kelly Oubre Jr. .40 1.00
31 Lonzo Ball .50 1.25
32 Shai Gilgeous-Alexander 2.00 5.00
33 Devin Booker 1.00 2.50
34 Fred VanVleet .60 1.50
35 Al Horford .40 1.00
36 DeMar DeRozan .50 1.25
37 Luka Doncic 2.50 6.00
38 Kemba Walker .40 1.00
39 Domantas Sabonis .50 1.25
40 Karl-Anthony Towns .60 1.50
41 Draymond Green .50 1.25
42 Tobias Harris .40 1.00
43 James Harden .75 2.00
44 Devonte' Graham .30 .75
45 Kyle Lowry .50 1.25
46 Kevin Love .40 1.00
47 Aaron Gordon .40 1.00
48 Brandon Clarke .40 1.00
49 Coby White .50 1.25
50 Lou Williams .40 1.00
51 Terry Rozier .40 1.00
52 Miles Bridges .40 1.00
53 Rui Hachimura .50 1.25
54 D'Angelo Russell .40 1.00
55 Michael Porter Jr. .50 1.25
56 RJ Barrett .60 1.50
57 Goran Dragic .40 1.00
58 Giannis Antetokounmpo 2.00 5.00
59 Derrick Rose .60 1.50
60 Jaren Jackson Jr. .60 1.50
61 Jusuf Nurkic .40 1.00
62 Caris LeVert .40 1.00
63 Victor Oladipo .30 .75
64 Dejounte Murray .40 1.00
65 Trae Young 1.00 2.50
66 Nikola Jokic 2.00 5.00
67 Jonas Valanciunas .30 .75
68 Lauri Markkanen .50 1.25
69 Kyle Kuzma .50 1.25
70 Russell Westbrook .75 2.00
71 Joel Embiid 1.00 2.50
72 Kevin Huerter .30 .75
73 Tim Hardaway Jr. .25 .60
74 LeBron James 3.00 8.00
75 Zion Williamson 1.25 3.00
76 Mitchell Robinson .40 1.00
77 Chris Paul .75 2.00
78 Jimmy Butler .75 2.00
79 Paul George .60 1.50
80 Nikola Vucevic .40 1.00
81 Zach LaVine .60 1.50
82 Jrue Holiday .40 1.00
83 Ja Morant 1.25 3.00
84 Elfrid Payton .30 .75
85 Pascal Siakam .60 1.50
86 Rudy Gobert .50 1.25
87 Khris Middleton .50 1.25
88 Markelle Fultz .30 .75
89 Collin Sexton .40 1.00
90 Stephen Curry 3.00 8.00
91 Myles Turner .40 1.00
92 Brook Lopez .30 .75
93 Damian Lillard 1.00 2.50
94 Christian Wood .30 .75
95 Gordon Hayward .40 1.00
96 Carmelo Anthony .60 1.50
97 Jarrett Culver .25 .60
98 John Collins .40 1.00
99 Donovan Mitchell .75 2.00
100 Bradley Beal .50 1.25
101 James Wiseman RC .75 2.00
102 Jaden McDaniels RC 2.00 5.00
103 Tyrell Terry RC .50 1.25
104 Desmond Bane RC 2.00 5.00
105 Xavier Tillman RC .75 2.00
106 Cole Anthony RC 1.50 4.00
107 Nico Mannion RC .60 1.50
108 Kira Lewis Jr. RC .60 1.50
109 Kenyon Martin Jr. RC 1.00 2.50
110 Obi Toppin RC 1.25 3.00
111 Cassius Stanley RC .60 1.50
112 Daniel Oturu RC .60 1.50
113 Jahmi'us Ramsey RC .60 1.50
114 Saddiq Bey RC 1.25 3.00
115 Immanuel Quickley RC 1.50 4.00
116 Tyrese Haliburton RC 5.00 12.00
117 Grant Riller RC .60 1.50
118 Devin Vassell RC 2.00 5.00
119 Deni Avdija RC 1.50 4.00
120 Jordan Nwora RC .75 2.00
121 Robert Woodard II RC .60 1.50
122 Elijah Hughes RC .60 1.50
123 Precious Achiuwa RC 1.25 3.00
124 Tyler Bey RC .60 1.50
125 Anthony Edwards RC 20.00 50.00
126 Udoka Azubuike RC .75 2.00
127 Onyeka Okongwu RC 1.25 3.00
128 RJ Hampton RC .60 1.50
129 Cassius Winston RC .60 1.50
130 Malachi Flynn RC .60 1.50
131 Jalen Smith RC 1.25 3.00
132 Aleksej Pokusevski RC .75 2.00
133 Saben Lee RC .60 1.50
134 Killian Hayes RC .60 1.50
135 Josh Green RC 1.25 3.00
136 Payton Pritchard RC 2.00 5.00
137 Tre Jones RC 1.00 2.50
138 CJ Elleby RC .60 1.50
139 Nick Richards RC .75 2.00
140 LaMelo Ball RC 5.00 12.00
141 Skylar Mays RC .60 1.50
142 Isaac Okoro RC 1.00 2.50
143 Patrick Williams RC 1.50 4.00
144 Jae'Sean Tate RC .75 2.00
145 Vernon Carey Jr. RC .60 1.50
146 Zeke Nnaji RC .75 2.00
147 Aaron Nesmith RC 1.25 3.00
148 Tyrese Maxey RC 5.00 12.00
149 Theo Maledon RC .60 1.50
150 Isaiah Stewart RC 1.25 3.00

2020-21 Panini Revolution Cosmic
*COSMIC: 2X TO 5X BASIC
STATED PRINT RUN 100 SER.#'d SETS

2020-21 Panini Revolution Cubic
*CUBIC: 3X TO 8X BASIC
STATED PRINT RUN 50 SER.#'d SETS

2020-21 Panini Revolution Autographs
EXCHANGE DEADLINE 09/03/2022
*FRACTAL: .5X TO 1.2X BASIC
*INFINITE: .75X TO 2X BASIC
1 Ja Morant 200.00 500.00
2 Charles Barkley 75.00 200.00
3 Gary Payton 25.00 60.00
4 Allen Iverson 75.00 200.00
5 John Collins 8.00 20.00
6 Magic Johnson 75.00 200.00
7 Andrew Wiggins 12.00 30.00
8 Karl-Anthony Towns 30.00 80.00
9 Wendell Carter Jr. 6.00 15.00
10 Trae Young 60.00 150.00
11 RJ Barrett 40.00 100.00
12 Stephen Curry 400.00 800.00
13 Steve Kerr 20.00 50.00
14 Karl Malone 40.00 100.00
15 Jrue Holiday 8.00 20.00
16 Julius Erving 60.00 150.00
17 Nikola Vucevic 8.00 20.00
18 Hakeem Olajuwon 40.00 100.00
19 Ricky Rubio 10.00 25.00
20 Ray Allen 25.00 60.00
21 De'Aaron Fox 25.00 60.00
22 Shaquille O'Neal 150.00 400.00
23 Jaren Jackson Jr. 12.00 30.00
24 Larry Bird 75.00 200.00
25 Al Horford 8.00 20.00
26 Oscar Robertson 60.00 150.00
27 Chris Mullin 12.00 30.00
28 David Robinson 30.00 80.00
29 Jason Williams 40.00 100.00
30 Grant Hill 25.00 60.00

2020-21 Panini Revolution Liftoff!
1 Kawhi Leonard 2.00 5.00
2 Jayson Tatum 3.00 8.00
3 Anthony Davis 2.00 5.00
4 Zion Williamson 8.00 20.00
5 LeBron James 12.00 30.00
6 James Harden 1.50 4.00
7 Ja Morant 15.00 40.00
8 Luka Doncic 12.00 30.00
9 Damian Lillard 2.00 5.00
10 Giannis Antetokounmpo 4.00 10.00

2020-21 Panini Revolution Liftoff! Cubic
*CUBIC/50: 2X TO 5X BASIC
STATED PRINT RUN 50 SER.#'d SETS
2 Jayson Tatum 40.00 100.00
4 Zion Williamson 75.00 200.00
5 LeBron James 200.00 500.00
8 Luka Doncic 200.00 500.00
10 Giannis Antetokounmpo 30.00 80.00

2020-21 Panini Revolution Liftoff! Fractal
*FRACTAL: .6X TO 1.5X BASIC
4 Zion Williamson 25.00 60.00
5 LeBron James 25.00 60.00
8 Luka Doncic 25.00 60.00

2020-21 Panini Revolution Rookie Autographs
EXCHANGE DEADLINE 09/03/2022
*FRACTAL: .6X TO 1.5X BASIC
*CNY/20-50: .75X TO 2X BASIC
Deni Avdija 15.00 40.00
2 Tyrese Maxey 75.00 200.00
3 LaMelo Ball 300.00 600.00
4 Obi Toppin 12.00 30.00
5 Isaac Okoro 10.00 25.00
6 Jalen Smith 12.00 30.00
7 Anthony Edwards 125.00 300.00
8 Killian Hayes 6.00 15.00
9 James Wiseman 8.00 20.00
10 Onyeka Okongwu 12.00 30.00
11 Patrick Williams 15.00 40.00
12 Tyrese Haliburton 75.00 200.00
13 Saddiq Bey 12.00 30.00
14 Devin Vassell 20.00 50.00
15 Payton Pritchard 20.00 50.00
16 Josh Green 12.00 30.00
17 Udoka Azubuike 8.00 20.00
18 Kira Lewis Jr. 6.00 15.00
19 Cole Anthony 15.00 40.00
20 RJ Hampton 6.00 15.00

2020-21 Panini Revolution Rookie Autographs Infinite
*INFINITE: .75X TO 2X BASIC
STATED PRINT RUNT 25 SER.#'d SETS
EXCHANGE DEADLINE 09/03/2022
3 LaMelo Ball 1,500.00 3,000.00
7 Anthony Edwards 600.00 1,200.00

2020-21 Panini Revolution Rookie Revolution
*FRACTAL: .6X TO 1.5X BASIC
1 Obi Toppin 1.25 3.00
2 James Wiseman .75 2.00
3 Cole Anthony 1.50 4.00
4 Patrick Williams 1.50 4.00
5 Josh Green 1.25 3.00
6 Anthony Edwards 15.00 40.00
7 Kira Lewis Jr. .60 1.50
8 RJ Hampton .60 1.50
9 Killian Hayes .60 1.50
10 Jalen Smith 1.25 3.00
11 LaMelo Ball 20.00 50.00
12 Devin Vassell 2.00 5.00
13 Tyrese Haliburton 5.00 12.00
14 Isaac Okoro 1.00 2.50
15 Aaron Nesmith 1.25 3.00
16 Onyeka Okongwu 1.25 3.00
17 Deni Avdija 1.50 4.00
18 Aleksej Pokusevski .75 2.00
19 Precious Achiuwa 1.25 3.00
20 Tyrese Maxey 5.00 12.00

2020-21 Panini Revolution Rookie Revolution Cubic
STATED PRINT RUN 50 SER.#'d SETS
6 Anthony Edwards 150.00 400.00
11 LaMelo Ball 200.00 500.00
20 Tyrese Maxey 75.00 200.00

2020-21 Panini Revolution Shock Wave
*FRACTAL: .6X TO 1.5X BASIC
1 Luka Doncic 12.00 30.00
2 Anthony Davis 2.00 5.00
3 Jayson Tatum 3.00 8.00
4 Jimmy Butler 1.50 4.00
5 Damian Lillard 2.00 5.00
6 Pascal Siakam 1.25 3.00
7 Joel Embiid 2.00 5.00
8 Devin Booker 2.00 5.00
9 Bradley Beal 1.00 2.50
10 Kemba Walker .75 2.00
11 RJ Barrett 1.25 3.00
12 Rudy Gobert 1.00 2.50
13 Giannis Antetokounmpo 4.00 10.00
14 Kawhi Leonard 2.00 5.00
15 Ben Simmons .75 2.00
16 Karl-Anthony Towns 1.25 3.00
17 Zion Williamson 8.00 20.00
18 Stephen Curry 6.00 15.00
19 Ja Morant 12.00 30.00
20 Trae Young 2.00 5.00
21 Donovan Mitchell 1.50 4.00
22 Jamal Murray 1.25 3.00
23 LeBron James 12.00 30.00
24 Nikola Jokic 4.00 10.00
25 James Harden 1.50 4.00

2020-21 Panini Revolution Shock Wave Cubic
*CUBIC/50: 2X TO 5X BASIC
STATED PRINT RUN 50 SER.#'d SETS
1 Luka Doncic 100.00 250.00
8 Devin Booker 15.00 40.00
17 Zion Williamson 75.00 200.00
18 Stephen Curry 75.00 200.00
19 Ja Morant 100.00 250.00
21 Donovan Mitchell 15.00 40.00
23 LeBron James 100.00 250.00
24 Nikola Jokic 15.00 40.00

2020-21 Panini Revolution Supernova
*FRACTAL: .6X TO 1.5X BASIC
1 LeBron James 12.00 30.00
2 Jimmy Butler 1.50 4.00
3 Trae Young 2.00 5.00
4 Devin Booker 2.00 5.00
5 Kawhi Leonard 2.00 5.00
6 Donovan Mitchell 1.50 4.00
7 Giannis Antetokounmpo 4.00 10.00
8 Russell Westbrook 1.25 3.00
9 Nikola Jokic 4.00 10.00
10 Luka Doncic 12.00 30.00

2020-21 Panini Revolution Supernova Cubic
*CUBIC/50: 2X TO 5X BASIC
STATED PRINT RUN 50 SER.#'d SETS
1 LeBron James 150.00 400.00
4 Devin Booker 15.00 40.00
6 Donovan Mitchell 15.00 40.00
9 Nikola Jokic 15.00 40.00
10 Luka Doncic 150.00 400.00

2020-21 Panini Revolution Vortex
*FRACTAL: .6X TO 1.5X BASIC
1 Donovan Mitchell 1.50 4.00
2 Paul George 1.25 3.00
3 LeBron James 12.00 30.00
4 Rudy Gobert 1.00 2.50
5 Bradley Beal 1.00 2.50
6 Devin Booker 2.00 5.00
7 Khris Middleton 1.00 2.50
8 RJ Barrett 1.25 3.00
9 Giannis Antetokounmpo 4.00 10.00
10 John Wall 1.00 2.50
11 Klay Thompson 2.00 5.00
12 Luka Doncic 12.00 30.00
13 Jimmy Butler 1.50 4.00
14 Ja Morant 8.00 20.00
15 Trae Young 2.00 5.00
16 Jamal Murray 1.25 3.00
17 Chris Paul 1.50 4.00
18 Kyle Lowry 1.00 2.50
19 Jayson Tatum 3.00 8.00
20 Joel Embiid 2.00 5.00
21 Nikola Jokic 4.00 10.00
22 Anthony Davis 2.00 5.00
23 Kyrie Irving 1.50 4.00
24 Zach LaVine 1.25 3.00
25 James Harden 1.50 4.00
26 Kawhi Leonard 2.00 5.00
27 Damian Lillard 2.00 5.00
28 Pascal Siakam 1.25 3.00
29 Zion Williamson 8.00 20.00
30 Deandre Ayton .75 2.00
31 Bam Adebayo 1.25 3.00
32 D'Angelo Russell .75 2.00
33 Ben Simmons .75 2.00
34 Jaylen Brown 1.25 3.00
35 Domantas Sabonis 1.00 2.50

2020-21 Panini Revolution Vortex Cubic
*CUBIC/50: 2X TO 5X BASIC
STATED PRINT RUN 50 SER.#'d SETS
1 Donovan Mitchell 15.00 40.00
3 LeBron James 150.00 400.00
6 Devin Booker 15.00 40.00
12 Luka Doncic 150.00 400.00
14 Ja Morant 50.00 120.00
21 Nikola Jokic 15.00 40.00
29 Zion Williamson 75.00 200.00

2021-22 Panini Revolution
COMMON CARD (1-100) .25 .60
SEMISTARS .30 .75
UNLISTED STARS .40 1.00
COMMON ROOKIE (101-150) .50 1.25
ROOKIE SEMISTARS .60 1.50
ROOKIE UNLISTED .75 2.00
*ASIA RED: .5X TO 1.2X BASIC
*GROOVE: .6X TO 1.5X BASIC
*ASTRO: .75X TO 2X BASIC
*FRACTAL: .75X TO 2X BASIC
*IMPACT: 1.5X TO 4X BASIC
*COSMIC/99: 3X TO 8X BASIC
*ASIA HOLO SLVR/99: 3X TO 8X BASIC
*CHINESE NY EMRLD/88: 3X TO 8X BASIC
*75TH ANNV/75: 3X TO 8X BASIC
*SUNBURST/60: 4X TO 10X BASIC
*CUBIC/50: 4X TO 10X BASIC
1 LaMelo Ball 1.00 2.50
2 Aaron Gordon .40 1.00
3 Dillon Brooks .40 1.00
4 Giannis Antetokounmpo 2.00 5.00
5 Christian Wood .30 .75
6 Domantas Sabonis .50 1.25
7 Jordan Poole .60 1.50
8 Kevin Durant 1.25 3.00
9 Harrison Barnes .30 .75
10 OG Anunoby .40 1.00
11 Gordon Hayward .30 .75
12 Karl-Anthony Towns .60 1.50
13 Jaren Jackson Jr. .60 1.50
14 Jrue Holiday .50 1.25
15 Kevin Porter Jr. .30 .75
16 Myles Turner .40 1.00
17 Draymond Green .50 1.25
18 James Harden .75 2.00
19 Tyrese Haliburton .75 2.00
20 Pascal Siakam .60 1.50
21 Terry Rozier III .30 .75
22 Anthony Edwards 2.00 5.00
23 Desmond Bane .75 2.00
24 Khris Middleton .40 1.00
25 Zion Williamson 1.00 2.50
26 Jerami Grant .40 1.00
27 Kawhi Leonard 1.00 2.50
28 Kyrie Irving .75 2.00
29 Jimmy Butler .60 1.50
30 Julius Randle .50 1.25
31 Trae Young 1.00 2.50
32 D'Angelo Russell .40 1.00
33 Luka Doncic 2.50 6.00
34 DeMar DeRozan .50 1.25
35 Brandon Ingram .50 1.25
36 Saddiq Bey .30 .75
37 Paul George .60 1.50
38 Ben Simmons .40 1.00
39 Tyler Herro .60 1.50
40 RJ Barrett .60 1.50
41 John Collins .40 1.00
42 Damian Lillard 1.00 2.50
43 Kristaps Porzingis .50 1.25
44 Zach LaVine .60 1.50
45 Jonas Valanciunas .30 .75
46 Killian Hayes .40 1.00
47 Reggie Jackson .30 .75
48 Joel Embiid 1.00 2.50
49 Bam Adebayo .60 1.50
50 Derrick Rose .60 1.50
51 Clint Capela .40 1.00
52 CJ McCollum .30 .75
53 Jalen Brunson .75 2.00
54 Nikola Vucevic .40 1.00
55 Gary Trent Jr. .30 .75
56 Chris Paul .75 2.00
57 LeBron James 3.00 8.00
58 Tyrese Maxey 1.00 2.50
59 Kyle Lowry .40 1.00
60 Donovan Mitchell .75 2.00
61 Cole Anthony .40 1.00
62 Norman Powell .30 .75
63 Dejounte Murray .40 1.00
64 Darius Garland .60 1.50
65 Seth Curry .30 .75
66 Deandre Ayton .40 1.00
67 Anthony Davis 1.00 2.50
68 Jayson Tatum 1.50 4.00
69 Bradley Beal .50 1.25
70 Rudy Gobert .50 1.25
71 Wendell Carter Jr. .40 1.00
72 Shai Gilgeous-Alexander 2.00 5.00
73 Keldon Johnson .50 1.25
74 Jarrett Allen .40 1.00
75 Bobby Portis .30 .75
76 Devin Booker 1.00 2.50
77 Russell Westbrook .60 1.50
78 Jaylen Brown .60 1.50
79 Kyle Kuzma .50 1.25
80 Bojan Bogdanovic .30 .75
81 Mo Bamba .30 .75
82 Luguentz Dort .40 1.00
83 Derrick White .40 1.00
84 Collin Sexton .40 1.00
85 Jusuf Nurkic .30 .75
86 Stephen Curry 2.50 6.00
87 Carmelo Anthony .60 1.50
88 Dennis Schroder .40 1.00
89 Montrezl Harrell .30 .75
90 Nikola Jokic 2.00 5.00
91 Ja Morant 1.25 3.00
92 Darius Bazley .25 .60
93 John Wall .50 1.25
94 Malcolm Brogdon .30 .75
95 Lonzo Ball .40 1.00
96 Andrew Wiggins .50 1.25
97 De'Aaron Fox .60 1.50
98 Fred VanVleet .50 1.25
99 Miles Bridges .30 .75
100 Michael Porter Jr. .50 1.25
101 Sharife Cooper RC .60 1.50
102 Jericho Sims RC 1.00 2.50
103 Jalen Johnson RC 2.50 6.00
104 Moses Moody RC 1.50 4.00
105 Ziaire Williams RC 1.00 2.50
106 Georgios Kalaitzakis RC .75 2.00
107 Isaiah Jackson RC .75 2.00
108 Jonathan Kuminga RC 2.50 6.00
109 Cameron Thomas RC 1.50 4.00
110 Isaiah Todd RC .60 1.50
111 Josh Giddey RC 2.50 6.00
112 Dalano Banton RC 1.00 2.50
113 Aaron Wiggins RC 1.00 2.50
114 Santi Aldama RC 1.00 2.50
115 Jalen Green RC 4.00 10.00
116 Miles McBride RC 1.25 3.00
117 Jared Butler RC .75 2.00
118 Bones Hyland RC 1.00 2.50
119 Ayo Dosunmu RC 1.50 4.00
120 Cade Cunningham RC 5.00 12.00
121 Brandon Boston Jr. RC .75 2.00
122 Day'Ron Sharpe RC .75 2.00
123 Jeremiah Robinson-Earl RC .75 2.00
124 Josh Christopher RC .60 1.50
125 Joe Wieskamp RC .60 1.50
126 Jalen Suggs RC 2.00 5.00
127 Usman Garuba RC .60 1.50
128 Luka Garza RC .75 2.00
129 Jaden Springer RC .75 2.00
130 Greg Brown III RC .60 1.50
131 James Bouknight RC .60 1.50
132 Austin Reaves RC 4.00 10.00
133 JT Thor RC .75 2.00
134 Joshua Primo RC .60 1.50
135 Davion Mitchell RC .75 2.00
136 Corey Kispert RC 1.00 2.50
137 Trey Murphy III RC 2.50 6.00
138 Tre Mann RC 1.25 3.00
139 Chris Duarte RC .60 1.50
140 Quentin Grimes RC 1.50 4.00
141 Kai Jones RC .60 1.50
142 Sandro Mamukelashvili RC 1.00 2.50
143 Evan Mobley RC 3.00 8.00
144 Kessler Edwards RC .75 2.00
145 Scottie Barnes RC 2.50 6.00
146 Franz Wagner RC 2.50 6.00
147 Keon Johnson RC .75 2.00
148 Charles Bassey RC .75 2.00
149 Alperen Sengun RC 2.50 6.00
150 Herbert Jones RC 1.00 2.50

2021-22 Panini Revolution Autographs
COMMON CARD 3.00 8.00
SEMISTARS 4.00 10.00
UNLISTED STARS 5.00 12.00
*FRACTAL/100: .5X TO 1.2X BASIC
*INFINITE/25: .75X TO 2X BASIC
1 PJ Washington Jr. 5.00 12.00
2 Ray Allen 40.00 100.00
3 Vince Carter 75.00 200.00
4 Anthony Edwards 100.00 250.00
5 Charles Barkley 75.00 200.00
6 Karl Malone 40.00 100.00
7 CJ McCollum 15.00 40.00
8 Kevin Johnson 8.00 20.00
9 Anthony Davis 50.00 120.00
10 Nikola Jokic 75.00 200.00
11 T.J. Warren 3.00 8.00
12 Larry Bird 100.00 250.00
13 Julius Randle 6.00 15.00
14 Kristaps Porzingis 15.00 40.00
15 Jamal Crawford 5.00 12.00
16 Mike Conley 4.00 10.00
17 Bill Russell 200.00 500.00
18 Trae Young 100.00 250.00
19 Boban Marjanovic 10.00 25.00
20 James Wiseman 4.00 10.00
21 Ja Morant 200.00 500.00
22 Jason Williams 25.00 60.00
24 Tyrese Haliburton 40.00 100.00
25 Jamal Murray 20.00 50.00
26 Sam Jones 20.00 50.00
27 Shaquille O'Neal 150.00 400.00
28 Luka Doncic 400.00 800.00
29 Myles Turner 5.00 12.00
30 Ben Wallace 25.00 60.00

2021-22 Panini Revolution Liftoff!
COMMON CARD .50 1.25
SEMISTARS .60 1.50
UNLISTED STARS .75 2.00
*FRACTAL: 1X TO 2.5X BASIC
*CUBIC/50:4X TO 10X BASIC
1 Ja Morant 2.50 6.00
2 Jayson Tatum 3.00 8.00
3 Jalen Johnson 2.50 6.00
4 Anthony Edwards 4.00 10.00

5 Zach LaVine 1.25 3.00
6 John Collins .75 2.00
7 Zion Williamson 2.00 5.00
8 Donovan Mitchell 1.50 4.00
9 Jalen Green 4.00 10.00
10 LeBron James 6.00 15.00

2021-22 Panini Revolution Prime Time Performers

COMMON CARD 6.00 15.00
SEMISTARS 8.00 20.00
UNLISTED STARS 10.00 25.00
1 Trae Young 125.00 300.00
2 Stephen Curry 200.00 500.00
3 Giannis Antetokounmpo 150.00 400.00
4 LaMelo Ball 150.00 400.00
5 Ja Morant 200.00 500.00
6 Kevin Durant 100.00 250.00
7 Bradley Beal 40.00 100.00
8 Donovan Mitchell 40.00 100.00
9 Chris Paul 60.00 150.00
10 Russell Westbrook 40.00 100.00
11 Jayson Tatum 125.00 300.00
12 Karl-Anthony Towns 40.00 100.00
13 Cade Cunningham 300.00 600.00
14 Damian Lillard 100.00 250.00
15 Jalen Green 300.00 600.00
16 LeBron James 200.00 500.00
17 Jalen Suggs 60.00 150.00
18 Joel Embiid 60.00 150.00
19 Klay Thompson 125.00 300.00
20 Evan Mobley 200.00 500.00
21 Jimmy Butler 60.00 150.00
22 Julius Randle 25.00 60.00
23 Kawhi Leonard 75.00 200.00
24 Scottie Barnes 200.00 500.00
25 Luka Doncic 200.00 500.00

2021-22 Panini Revolution Rookie Autographs

COMMON CARD 5.00 12.00
SEMISTARS 6.00 15.00
UNLISTED STARS 8.00 20.00
EXCHANGE DEADLINE 10/27/2023
*FRACTAL/100: .6X TO 1.5X BASIC
*INFINITE/25: .75X TO 2X BASIC
1 Jalen Suggs 20.00 50.00
2 Cade Cunningham 150.00 400.00
3 Evan Mobley 125.00 300.00
4 Jonathan Kuminga 100.00 250.00
5 Isaiah Todd 6.00 15.00
6 Alperen Sengun 40.00 100.00
7 Jalen Green 125.00 300.00
8 Scottie Barnes 125.00 300.00
9 Josh Giddey 100.00 250.00
10 Franz Wagner 40.00 100.00
11 Moses Moody 15.00 40.00
12 Jalen Johnson 25.00 60.00
13 Chris Duarte 6.00 15.00
14 Ziaire Williams 10.00 25.00
15 James Bouknight 6.00 15.00
16 Kai Jones 6.00 15.00
17 Corey Kispert 10.00 25.00
18 Tre Mann 12.00 30.00
19 Trey Murphy III 25.00 60.00
20 Davion Mitchell 40.00 100.00

2021-22 Panini Revolution Rookie Revolution

COMMON CARD .50 1.25
SEMISTARS .60 1.50
UNLISTED STARS .75 2.00
*FRACTAL: .6X TO 1.5X BASIC
*CUBIC/50: 4X TO 10X BASIC
1 Evan Mobley 3.00 8.00
2 Alperen Sengun 2.50 6.00
3 Jalen Suggs 2.00 5.00
4 Jeremiah Robinson-Earl .75 2.00
5 Jonathan Kuminga 2.50 6.00
6 Bones Hyland 1.00 2.50
7 Davion Mitchell .75 2.00
8 James Bouknight .60 1.50
9 Cade Cunningham 5.00 12.00
10 Chris Duarte .60 1.50
11 Scottie Barnes 2.50 6.00
12 Herbert Jones 1.00 2.50
13 Josh Giddey 2.50 6.00
14 Ayo Dosunmu 1.50 4.00
15 Franz Wagner 2.50 6.00
16 Tre Mann 1.25 3.00
17 Ziaire Williams 1.00 2.50
18 Joshua Primo .60 1.50
19 Jalen Green 4.00 10.00
20 Moses Moody 1.50 4.00

2021-22 Panini Revolution Shock Wave

COMMON CARD .50 1.25
SEMISTARS .60 1.50
UNLISTED STARS .75 2.00
*FRACTAL: .6X TO 1.5X BASIC
*CUBIC/50: 4X TO 10X BASIC
1 Kyrie Irving 1.50 4.00
2 Josh Giddey 6.00 15.00
3 Trae Young 2.00 5.00
4 Ja Morant 2.50 6.00
5 LeBron James 6.00 15.00
6 Cade Cunningham 8.00 20.00
7 Luka Doncic 5.00 12.00
8 Jalen Suggs 2.00 5.00
9 Devin Booker 2.00 5.00
10 Franz Wagner 2.50 6.00
11 James Harden 1.50 4.00
12 Davion Mitchell .75 2.00
13 Joel Embiid 2.00 5.00
14 Kawhi Leonard 2.00 5.00
15 Giannis Antetokounmpo 4.00 10.00
16 Jalen Green 8.00 20.00
17 Jayson Tatum 3.00 8.00
18 Scottie Barnes 8.00 20.00
19 Stephen Curry 5.00 12.00
20 Chris Duarte .60 1.50
21 Damian Lillard 2.00 5.00
22 Jonathan Kuminga 6.00 15.00
23 Anthony Davis 2.00 5.00
24 Evan Mobley 6.00 15.00
25 Kevin Durant 2.50 6.00

2021-22 Panini Revolution Star Factor

COMMON CARD 6.00 15.00
SEMISTARS 8.00 20.00
UNLISTED STARS 10.00 25.00
1 Zach LaVine 15.00 40.00
2 Ja Morant 125.00 300.00
3 LaMelo Ball 150.00 400.00
4 Luka Doncic 150.00 400.00
5 Anthony Davis 25.00 60.00
6 Donovan Mitchell 20.00 50.00
7 Damian Lillard 25.00 60.00
8 LeBron James 150.00 400.00
9 Stephen Curry 125.00 300.00
10 Paul George 15.00 40.00
11 Nikola Jokic 40.00 100.00
12 Trae Young 40.00 100.00
13 Jayson Tatum 100.00 250.00
14 Devin Booker 50.00 120.00
15 Anthony Edwards 75.00 200.00
16 Giannis Antetokounmpo 75.00 200.00
17 James Harden 20.00 50.00
18 Zion Williamson 25.00 60.00
19 Kevin Durant 30.00 80.00
20 Jalen Suggs 75.00 200.00
21 Cade Cunningham 150.00 400.00
22 Jalen Green 150.00 400.00
23 Evan Mobley 150.00 400.00
24 Scottie Barnes 150.00 400.00
25 Josh Giddey 100.00 250.00

2021-22 Panini Revolution Supernova

COMMON CARD .50 1.25
SEMISTARS .60 1.50
UNLISTED STARS .75 2.00
*FRACTAL: 1X TO 2.5X BASIC
*CUBIC/50: 4X TO 10X BASIC
1 Luka Doncic 5.00 12.00
2 Jalen Green 8.00 20.00
3 Jayson Tatum 3.00 8.00
4 Stephen Curry 5.00 12.00
5 LeBron James 6.00 15.00
6 James Harden 1.50 4.00
7 Giannis Antetokounmpo 4.00 10.00
8 Trae Young 2.00 5.00
9 Kevin Durant 2.50 6.00
10 Cade Cunningham 10.00 25.00

2021-22 Panini Revolution Vortex

COMMON CARD .50 1.25
SEMISTARS .60 1.50
UNLISTED STARS .75 2.00
*FRACTAL: 1X TO 2.5X BASIC
*CUBIC/50: 4X TO 10X BASIC
1 Scottie Barnes 2.50 6.00
2 Kyrie Irving 1.50 4.00
3 Jonathan Kuminga 2.50 6.00
4 LeBron James 6.00 15.00
5 Zach LaVine 1.25 3.00
6 Devin Booker 2.00 5.00
7 Miles Bridges .60 1.50
8 Davion Mitchell .75 2.00
9 Chris Paul 1.50 4.00
10 Giannis Antetokounmpo 4.00 10.00
11 Stephen Curry 5.00 12.00
12 Josh Giddey 2.50 6.00
13 Anthony Davis 2.00 5.00
14 Cade Cunningham 5.00 12.00
15 DeMar DeRozan 1.00 2.50
16 Franz Wagner 2.50 6.00
17 Nikola Jokic 4.00 10.00
18 Joel Embiid 2.00 5.00
19 Rudy Gobert 1.00 2.50
20 Jalen Green 4.00 10.00
21 Chris Duarte .60 1.50
22 Trae Young 3.00 8.00
23 Evan Mobley 3.00 8.00
24 Luka Doncic 5.00 12.00
25 Karl-Anthony Towns 1.25 3.00
26 James Harden 1.50 4.00
27 LaMelo Ball 2.00 5.00
28 Kawhi Leonard 2.00 5.00
29 Domantas Sabonis 1.00 2.50
30 Jayson Tatum 3.00 8.00
31 Damian Lillard 2.00 5.00
32 Ja Morant 2.50 6.00
33 Kevin Durant 2.50 6.00
34 Jalen Suggs 2.00 5.00
35 Donovan Mitchell 1.50 4.00

2023-24 Panini Revolution

*WINTER: .4X TO 1X BASIC
*AVALANCHE: .6X TO 1.5X BASIC
*GROOVE: .6X TO 1.5X BASIC
*ASTRO: .75X TO 2X BASIC
*BLIZZARD: .75X TO 2X BASIC
*CHINESE NEW YEAR: .75X TO 2X BASIC
*FRACTAL: .75X TO 2X BASIC
1 Damian Lillard 1.00 2.50
2 Jimmy Butler .60 1.50
3 Dejounte Murray .50 1.25
4 Andrew Wiggins .50 1.25
5 Jalen Williams .75 2.00
6 Cameron Johnson .40 1.00
7 Bradley Beal .50 1.25
8 Russell Westbrook .60 1.50
9 Jarrett Allen .40 1.00
10 Terry Rozier III .50 1.25
11 Chet Holmgren 1.00 2.50
12 Deandre Ayton .40 1.00
13 Ja Morant 1.25 3.00
14 Kyle Kuzma .50 1.25
15 Marcus Smart .50 1.25
16 Kristaps Porzingis .50 1.25
17 Kawhi Leonard 1.00 2.50
18 Cade Cunningham 1.00 2.50
19 Julius Randle .50 1.25
20 Aaron Gordon .40 1.00
21 James Harden .75 2.00
22 Giannis Antetokounmpo 2.00 5.00
23 Kyrie Irving .75 2.00
24 Desmond Bane .50 1.25
25 Evan Mobley .60 1.50
26 DeMar DeRozan .60 1.50
27 Paul George .60 1.50
28 Rui Hachimura .40 1.00
29 Bam Adebayo .60 1.50
30 Cameron Thomas .50 1.25
31 Jabari Smith Jr. .60 1.50
32 Keegan Murray .50 1.25
33 CJ McCollum .40 1.00
34 Draymond Green .50 1.25
35 Jayson Tatum 1.50 4.00
36 Tobias Harris .40 1.00
37 Brandon Ingram .50 1.25
38 Mikal Bridges .50 1.25
39 Josh Giddey .50 1.25
40 OG Anunoby .50 1.25
41 Fred VanVleet .60 1.50
42 Rudy Gobert .50 1.25
43 Anthony Edwards 2.00 5.00
44 Shaedon Sharpe .75 2.00
45 Tyrese Haliburton .75 2.00
46 PJ Washington Jr. .40 1.00
47 Jaden Ivey .50 1.25
48 Buddy Hield .40 1.00
49 Pascal Siakam .60 1.50
50 John Collins .40 1.00
51 Chris Paul .75 2.00
52 Jamal Murray .75 2.00
53 Nikola Vucevic .40 1.00
54 Malcolm Brogdon .40 1.00
55 Collin Sexton .50 1.25
56 Cole Anthony .40 1.00
57 Nikola Jokic 2.00 5.00
58 Darius Garland .60 1.50
59 Khris Middleton .40 1.00
60 Scottie Barnes .50 1.25
61 Austin Reaves 1.00 2.50
62 Jalen Duren .50 1.25
63 Jaren Jackson Jr. .60 1.50
64 Lauri Markkanen .60 1.50
65 Stephen Curry 3.00 8.00
66 Tyrese Maxey .75 2.00
67 Kevin Durant 1.25 3.00
68 Trae Young .75 2.00
69 Karl-Anthony Towns .60 1.50
70 Tyler Herro .60 1.50
71 Anfernee Simons .50 1.25
72 Jaylen Brown .75 2.00
73 Jalen Brunson .75 2.00
74 Alperen Sengun .60 1.50
75 Anthony Davis 1.00 2.50
76 Shai Gilgeous-Alexander 2.00 5.00
77 Michael Porter Jr. .50 1.25
78 Devin Vassell .50 1.25
79 Bennedict Mathurin .60 1.50
80 D'Angelo Russell .40 1.00
81 Jordan Poole .60 1.50
82 Keldon Johnson .50 1.25
83 Luka Doncic 2.50 6.00
84 Donovan Mitchell .75 2.00
85 LaMelo Ball 1.00 2.50
86 Franz Wagner .60 1.50
87 Domantas Sabonis .60 1.50
88 LeBron James 3.00 8.00
89 Jalen Green .60 1.50
90 Paolo Banchero 1.00 2.50
91 Myles Turner .40 1.00
92 Jalen Johnson .50 1.25
93 Immanuel Quickley .40 1.00
94 Klay Thompson 1.00 2.50
95 Joel Embiid 1.00 2.50
96 Zach LaVine .60 1.50
97 De'Aaron Fox .75 2.00
98 Zion Williamson 1.00 2.50
99 Devin Booker 1.00 2.50
100 Spencer Dinwiddie .30 .75
101 Amen Thompson RC 4.00 10.00
102 Cason Wallace RC 1.50 4.00
103 Kobe Bufkin RC 1.00 2.50
104 Victor Wembanyama RC 12.00 30.00
105 Anthony Black RC 1.50 4.00
106 Brandon Miller RC 3.00 8.00
107 Jalen Hood-Schifino RC .75 2.00
108 Taylor Hendricks RC .75 2.00
109 Scoot Henderson RC 2.50 6.00
110 Gradey Dick RC 1.50 4.00
111 Cam Whitmore RC 2.00 5.00
112 Jarace Walker RC 1.50 4.00
113 Jett Howard RC 1.00 2.50
114 Jaime Jaquez Jr. RC 1.25 3.00
115 Nick Smith Jr. RC 1.00 2.50
116 Jordan Hawkins RC 1.25 3.00
117 Ausar Thompson RC 2.00 5.00
118 Keyonte George RC 2.50 6.00
119 Bilal Coulibaly RC 2.00 5.00
120 Dereck Lively II RC 1.50 4.00
121 Brandin Podziemski RC 2.50 6.00
122 Noah Clowney RC 1.00 2.50
123 Dariq Whitehead RC 1.00 2.50
124 Kris Murray RC .75 2.00
125 Olivier-Maxence Prosper RC .75 2.00
126 Marcus Sasser RC 1.25 3.00
127 Ben Sheppard RC .75 2.00
128 Brice Sensabaugh RC 1.25 3.00
129 Julian Strawther RC 1.00 2.50
130 Kobe Brown RC .75 2.00
131 Trayce Jackson-Davis RC 1.00 2.50
132 Jalen Pickett RC .60 1.50
133 Leonard Miller RC .75 2.00
134 Colby Jones RC .75 2.00
135 Julian Phillips RC .75 2.00
136 Andre Jackson Jr. RC 1.25 3.00
137 Hunter Tyson RC .75 2.00
138 Jordan Walsh RC .75 2.00
139 Maxwell Lewis RC .60 1.50
140 Craig Porter Jr. RC 1.00 2.50
141 Rayan Rupert RC .75 2.00
142 GG Jackson II RC 1.50 4.00
143 Keyontae Johnson RC .75 2.00
144 Jalen Wilson RC .75 2.00
145 Amari Bailey RC .75 2.00
146 Markquis Nowell RC .75 2.00
147 Toumani Camara RC 1.50 4.00
148 Emoni Bates RC 1.00 2.50
149 Sasha Vezenkov RC .60 1.50
150 Vasilije Micic RC .75 2.00

2023-24 Panini Revolution Asia Holo Silver

*ASIA HOLO SILVER: 3X TO 8X BASIC
STATED PRINT RUN 75 SER.#'d SETS
104 Victor Wembanyama 500.00 1,000.00

2023-24 Panini Revolution Chinese New Year Emerald

*CHINESE NY EMERALD: 2.5X TO 6X BASIC
STATED PRINT RUN 88 SER.#'d SETS
104 Victor Wembanyama 400.00 800.00

2023-24 Panini Revolution Cosmic

*COSMIC: 2.5X TO 6X BASIC
STATED PRINT RUN 99 SER.#'d SETS
104 Victor Wembanyama 400.00 800.00

2023-24 Panini Revolution Cubic

*CUBIC: 4X TO 10X BASIC
STATED PRINT RUN 50 SER.#'d SETS
104 Victor Wembanyama 600.00 1,200.00
106 Brandon Miller 100.00 250.00

2023-24 Panini Revolution Future Frame

*FUTURE FRAME: 4X TO 10X BASIC
STATED PRINT RUN 60 SER.#'d SETS
104 Victor Wembanyama 600.00 1,200.00

2023-24 Panini Revolution Impact

*IMPACT: 1.5X TO 4X BASIC
STATED PRINT RUN 149 SER.#'d SETS
104 Victor Wembanyama 300.00 600.00

2023-24 Panini Revolution Neutron

*NEUTRON: 2X TO 5X BASIC
STATED PRINT RUN 125 SER.#'d SETS
104 Victor Wembanyama 350.00 700.00

2023-24 Panini Revolution Red Swirl

*RED SWIRL: 1.5X TO 4X BASIC
STATED PRINT RUN 199 SER.#'d SETS
104 Victor Wembanyama 300.00 600.00

2023-24 Panini Revolution Sunburst

*SUNBURST: 3X TO 8X BASIC
STATED PRINT RUN 75 SER.#'d SETS
104 Victor Wembanyama 500.00 1,000.00

2023-24 Panini Revolution Autographs

*LEVELS: .4X TO 1X BASIC
*ASIA: .5X TO 1.2X BASIC
*FRACTAL/75: .6X TO 1.5X BASIC
*INFINITE/25: .75X TO 2X BASIC
1 Alperen Sengun 10.00 25.00
1 Cole Anthony 6.00 15.00
2 Luka Doncic 400.00 800.00
2 James Wiseman 5.00 12.00
3 Ja Morant 125.00 300.00
3 Obi Toppin 6.00 15.00
4 Stephen Curry 500.00 1,000.00
5 Tyrese Maxey 40.00 100.00
6 Jabari Smith Jr. 10.00 25.00
7 Anthony Edwards 125.00 300.00
8 Jaden Ivey 8.00 20.00
9 Deandre Ayton 6.00 15.00
10 Ochai Agbaji 6.00 15.00
11 Shaedon Sharpe 12.00 30.00
12 Desmond Bane 8.00 20.00
14 Josh Giddey 8.00 20.00
15 Bennedict Mathurin 10.00 25.00
17 Ivica Zubac 6.00 15.00
18 Ayo Dosunmu 6.00 15.00
19 Jalen Williams 12.00 30.00
20 Landry Shamet 4.00 10.00
21 Calvin Murphy 6.00 15.00
25 Herbert Jones 6.00 15.00
28 James Harden 75.00 200.00
29 Nikola Jokic 125.00 300.00
30 Dwyane Wade 60.00 150.00
31 Marcus Smart 8.00 20.00
32 Johnny Davis 5.00 12.00
33 Jalen Duren 8.00 20.00
34 Onyeka Okongwu 5.00 12.00
35 Max Strus 6.00 15.00
36 Magic Johnson 50.00 120.00
37 Tracy McGrady 100.00 250.00
38 B.J. Armstrong 6.00 15.00
39 Shawn Kemp 20.00 50.00
40 Alex English 8.00 20.00
41 Juwan Howard 6.00 15.00
42 Dominique Wilkins 25.00 60.00
43 Peja Stojakovic 6.00 15.00
44 Mike Miller 5.00 12.00
45 Mark Aguirre 5.00 12.00
46 Bill Laimbeer 6.00 15.00
47 Fat Lever 6.00 15.00
48 Clyde Drexler 25.00 60.00
49 Karl Malone 30.00 80.00

2023-24 Panini Revolution Prime Time Performers

1 Stephen Curry 60.00 150.00
2 Luka Doncic 60.00 150.00
3 LeBron James 75.00 200.00
4 Giannis Antetokounmpo 30.00 80.00
5 Jayson Tatum 25.00 60.00
6 Ja Morant 25.00 60.00
7 Damian Lillard 15.00 40.00
8 Trae Young 12.00 30.00
9 Nikola Jokic 30.00 80.00
10 LaMelo Ball 15.00 40.00
11 Kevin Durant 20.00 50.00
12 Zion Williamson 15.00 40.00
13 Donovan Mitchell 12.00 30.00
14 Joel Embiid 15.00 40.00
15 Shai Gilgeous-Alexander 30.00 80.00
16 Victor Wembanyama 800.00 1,500.00
17 Brandon Miller 25.00 60.00
18 Dereck Lively II 12.00 30.00
19 Marcus Sasser 10.00 25.00
20 Scoot Henderson 20.00 50.00
21 Amen Thompson 30.00 80.00
22 Ausar Thompson 15.00 40.00
23 Anthony Black 12.00 30.00
24 Bilal Coulibaly 15.00 40.00
25 Cason Wallace 12.00 30.00

2023-24 Panini Revolution Rookie Autographs

*LEVELS: .4X TO 1X BASIC
*ASIA: .5X TO 1.2X BASIC
*FRACTAL/100: .5X TO 1.2X BASIC
*CHINESE NEW YEAR/28: .75X TO 2X BASIC
*INFINITE/25: .75X TO 2X BASIC
1 Amen Thompson 30.00 80.00
2 Ben Sheppard 6.00 15.00
3 Jalen Wilson 6.00 15.00
4 Dariq Whitehead 8.00 20.00
5 Kobe Bufkin 8.00 20.00
6 Olivier-Maxence Prosper 6.00 15.00
7 Kobe Brown 6.00 15.00
8 Julian Strawther 8.00 20.00
9 Jordan Walsh 6.00 15.00
11 Rayan Rupert 6.00 15.00
12 Ausar Thompson 15.00 40.00
13 Kris Murray 6.00 15.00
14 Marcus Sasser 10.00 25.00
15 Bilal Coulibaly 15.00 40.00
16 Colby Jones 6.00 15.00
17 Maxwell Lewis 5.00 12.00
18 Brice Sensabaugh 10.00 25.00
19 GG Jackson II 40.00 100.00
20 Noah Clowney 8.00 20.00
21 Keyonte George 30.00 80.00
22 Andre Jackson Jr 10.00 25.00
23 Cason Wallace 25.00 60.00
24 Brandin Podziemski 30.00 80.00
25 Dereck Lively II 12.00 30.00

2023-24 Panini Revolution Rookie Revolution

*ASIA: .6X TO 1.5X BASIC
*FRACTAL: .6X TO 1.5X BASIC
*LEVELS: .6X TO 1.5X BASIC
*COSMIC/99: 2.5X TO 6X BASIC
*SUNBURST/75: 3X TO 8X BASIC
*CUBIC/50: 4X TO 10X BASIC
1 Jaime Jaquez Jr. 1.25 3.00
2 Jalen Hood-Schifino .75 2.00
3 Gradey Dick 1.50 4.00
4 Dereck Lively II 1.50 4.00
5 Ausar Thompson 2.00 5.00
6 Anthony Black 1.50 4.00
7 Marcus Sasser 1.25 3.00
8 Keyonte George 2.50 6.00
9 Kobe Bufkin 1.00 2.50
10 Taylor Hendricks .75 2.00
11 Scoot Henderson 2.50 6.00
12 Cason Wallace 1.50 4.00
13 Jett Howard 1.00 2.50
14 Victor Wembanyama 25.00 60.00
15 Amen Thompson 4.00 10.00
16 Jarace Walker 1.50 4.00
17 Jordan Hawkins 1.25 3.00
18 Brandon Miller 3.00 8.00
19 Cam Whitmore 2.00 5.00
20 Bilal Coulibaly 2.00 5.00

2023-24 Panini Revolution Shock Wave

*ASIA: .6X TO 1.5X BASIC
*FRACTAL: .6X TO 1.5X BASIC
*LEVELS: .6X TO 1.5X BASIC
*COSMIC/99: 2.5X TO 6X BASIC
*SUNBURST/75: 3X TO 8X BASIC
*CUBIC/50: 4X TO 10X BASIC
1 Cade Cunningham 2.00 5.00
2 Nikola Jokic 4.00 10.00
3 Ja Morant 2.50 6.00
4 Giannis Antetokounmpo 4.00 10.00
5 Stephen Curry 6.00 15.00
6 LeBron James 6.00 15.00
7 Jaime Jaquez Jr. 1.25 3.00
8 Anthony Edwards 4.00 10.00
9 Brandon Miller 3.00 8.00
10 Jett Howard 1.00 2.50
11 Dereck Lively II 1.50 4.00
12 Gradey Dick 1.50 4.00
13 Jalen Hood-Schifino .75 2.00
14 Scoot Henderson 2.50 6.00
15 Victor Wembanyama 25.00 60.00
16 Jarace Walker 1.50 4.00
17 Cam Whitmore 2.00 5.00
18 Marcus Sasser 1.25 3.00
19 Jordan Hawkins 1.25 3.00
20 Amen Thompson 4.00 10.00
21 Ausar Thompson 2.00 5.00
22 Cason Wallace 1.50 4.00
23 Keyonte George 2.50 6.00
24 Bilal Coulibaly 2.00 5.00
25 Kobe Bufkin 1.00 2.50

2023-24 Panini Revolution Star Factor

1 Stephen Curry 50.00 125.00
2 Luka Doncic 40.00 100.00
3 Jayson Tatum 25.00 60.00
4 Trae Young 12.00 30.00
5 Anthony Edwards 30.00 80.00
6 Amen Thompson 30.00 80.00
7 Ausar Thompson 15.00 40.00
8 Cason Wallace 12.00 30.00
9 Scoot Henderson 20.00 50.00
10 Victor Wembanyama 150.00 400.00
11 Anthony Black 12.00 30.00
12 Brandon Miller 25.00 60.00
13 Cam Whitmore 15.00 40.00
14 Jordan Hawkins 10.00 25.00
15 Dereck Lively II 12.00 30.00
16 Jaime Jaquez Jr. 10.00 25.00
17 Jalen Hood-Schifino 6.00 15.00
18 LeBron James 50.00 125.00
19 Keyonte George 20.00 50.00
20 Marcus Sasser 10.00 25.00

2023-24 Panini Revolution Supernova

*ASIA: .6X TO 1.5X BASIC
*FRACTAL: .6X TO 1.5X BASIC
*LEVELS: .6X TO 1.5X BASIC
*COSMIC/99: 2.5X TO 6X BASIC
*SUNBURST/75: 3X TO 8X BASIC
*CUBIC/50: 4X TO 10X BASIC
1 Luka Doncic 5.00 12.00
2 Jayson Tatum 3.00 8.00
3 Giannis Antetokounmpo 4.00 10.00
4 Stephen Curry 6.00 15.00
5 LeBron James 6.00 15.00
6 Victor Wembanyama 25.00 60.00
7 Amen Thompson 4.00 10.00
8 Ausar Thompson 2.00 5.00
9 Scoot Henderson 2.50 6.00
10 Brandon Miller 3.00 8.00

2023-24 Panini Revolution Vortex

*ASIA: .6X TO 1.5X BASIC
*FRACTAL: .6X TO 1.5X BASIC
*LEVELS: .6X TO 1.5X BASIC
*COSMIC/99: 2.5X TO 6X BASIC
*SUNBURST/75: 3X TO 8X BASIC
*CUBIC/50: 4X TO 10X BASIC
1 Victor Wembanyama 25.00 60.00
2 Anthony Black 1.50 4.00
3 Brandon Miller 3.00 8.00
4 Cam Whitmore 2.00 5.00
5 Gradey Dick 1.50 4.00
6 Jarace Walker 1.50 4.00
7 Jordan Hawkins 1.25 3.00
8 Marcus Sasser 1.25 3.00
9 Scoot Henderson 2.50 6.00
10 Taylor Hendricks .75 2.00
11 Jett Howard 1.00 2.50
12 Jalen Hood-Schifino .75 2.00
13 Jaime Jaquez Jr. 1.25 3.00
14 Amen Thompson 4.00 10.00
15 Ausar Thompson 2.00 5.00
16 Bilal Coulibaly 2.00 5.00
17 Cason Wallace 1.50 4.00
18 Dereck Lively II 1.50 4.00
19 Kobe Bufkin 1.00 2.50
20 Keyonte George 2.50 6.00
21 Brandin Podziemski 2.50 6.00
22 Noah Clowney 1.00 2.50
23 Dariq Whitehead 1.00 2.50
24 Kris Murray .75 2.00
25 LeBron James 6.00 15.00
26 Ja Morant 2.50 6.00
27 Giannis Antetokounmpo 4.00 10.00
28 Stephen Curry 6.00 15.00
29 Jayson Tatum 3.00 8.00
30 Nikola Jokic 4.00 10.00
31 Damian Lillard 2.00 5.00
32 Kyrie Irving 1.50 4.00
33 Kevin Durant 2.50 6.00
34 Anthony Edwards 4.00 10.00
35 Donovan Mitchell 1.50 4.00

2024-25 Panini Revolution

*ASTRO: .5X TO 1.2X BASIC
*BLUE STORM: .5X TO 1.2X BASIC
*FRACTAL: .5X TO 1.2X BASIC
*GROOVE: .5X TO 1.2X BASIC
*CHINESE NY: .6X TO 1.5X BASIC
*RED SWIRL: .6X TO 1.5X BASIC
*RED ASTRO/299: .75X TO 2X BASIC
*BLUE COSMO/285: .75X TO 2X BASIC
*LIGHTNING/175: .75X TO 2X BASIC
*FIREWORKS/149: 1X TO 2.5X BASIC
*GREEN STORM/149: 1X TO 2.5X BASIC
*RED SCOPE/135: 1X TO 2.5X BASIC
*GREEN ASTRO/125: 1X TO 2.5X BASIC
*NEUTRON/125: 1X TO 2.5X BASIC
*BLUE ASTRO/99: 1.25X TO 3X BASIC
*COSMIC/99: 1.25X TO 3X BASIC
*CHINESE NY EMERALD/88: 1.25X TO 3X BASIC
*GREEN COSMO/75: 1.25X TO 3X BASIC
*SUNBURST/75: 1.25X TO 3X BASIC
*FUTURE FRAME/60: 1.25X TO 3X BASIC
*CUBIC/50: 1.5X TO 4X BASIC
*TEAL SWIRL/49: 1.5X TO 4X BASIC
*TEAL SCOPE/35: 2X TO 5X BASIC
*INFINITE/25: 2.5X TO 6X BASIC
*LEVELS/25: 2.5X TO 6X BASIC
*PINK STORM/20: 3X TO 8X BASIC
*PURPLE ASTRO/15: 3X TO 8X BASIC
1 Jalen Brunson .75 2.00
2 CJ McCollum .30 .75
3 Giannis Antetokounmpo 1.50 4.00
4 Scottie Barnes .50 1.25
5 Khris Middleton .40 1.00
6 Stephen Curry 3.00 8.00
7 Keldon Johnson .30 .75
8 Shai Gilgeous-Alexander 2.00 5.00
9 Ausar Thompson .60 1.50
10 Josh Giddey .50 1.25
11 Deandre Ayton .30 .75
12 Russell Westbrook .60 1.50
13 Luka Doncic 2.50 6.00
14 Keyonte George .50 1.25
15 Michael Porter Jr. .40 1.00
16 Cameron Thomas .40 1.00
17 Shaedon Sharpe .50 1.25
18 Derrick White .40 1.00
19 De'Aaron Fox .75 2.00
20 Ja Morant 1.25 3.00
21 Cameron Johnson .30 .75
22 Damian Lillard 1.00 2.50
23 Draymond Green .50 1.25
24 Devin Vassell .50 1.25
25 Mikal Bridges .40 1.00
26 Kristaps Porzingis .50 1.25
27 Trae Young .75 2.00
28 Jordan Poole .40 1.00
29 Paul George .60 1.50
30 Jalen Johnson .60 1.50
31 LeBron James 3.00 8.00
32 Cade Cunningham 1.00 2.50
33 Kyrie Irving 1.00 2.50
34 Jimmy Butler III .60 1.50
35 Tyrese Maxey .75 2.00
36 John Collins .30 .75
37 Klay Thompson 1.00 2.50
38 Joel Embiid .60 1.50
39 Franz Wagner .60 1.50
40 Anthony Edwards 2.00 5.00
41 Jaren Jackson Jr. .60 1.50
42 Donovan Mitchell .75 2.00
43 James Harden .75 2.00
44 Myles Turner .30 .75
45 RJ Barrett .50 1.25
46 Jalen Green .75 2.00
47 Jalen Duren .40 1.00
48 Bogdan Bogdanovic .30 .75
49 Domantas Sabonis .60 1.50
50 Zion Williamson 1.00 2.50
51 Austin Reaves .50 1.25
52 Anfernee Simons .40 1.00
53 Tyler Herro .60 1.50
54 Desmond Bane .40 1.00
55 Jalen Williams .75 2.00
56 Immanuel Quickley .30 .75
57 Miles Bridges .30 .75
58 Bam Adebayo .50 1.25
59 Donte DiVincenzo .40 1.00
60 Darius Garland .50 1.25
61 Ivica Zubac .40 1.00
62 Jaden Ivey .50 1.25
63 Pascal Siakam .50 1.25
64 Anthony Davis 1.00 2.50
65 Alperen Sengun .60 1.50
66 Lauri Markkanen .40 1.00
67 Paolo Banchero 1.00 2.50
68 Jayson Tatum 1.25 3.00
69 Jonathan Kuminga .50 1.25
70 Brandon Miller .60 1.50
71 Kyle Kuzma .30 .75
72 Naz Reid .40 1.00
73 Nicolas Claxton .30 .75
74 Kawhi Leonard .75 2.00
75 Cason Wallace .50 1.25
76 Nikola Jokic 2.00 5.00
77 Scoot Henderson .50 1.25
78 Kevin Durant 1.25 3.00
79 Victor Wembanyama 3.00 8.00
80 Nikola Vucevic .30 .75
81 Zach LaVine .60 1.50
82 Jrue Holiday .50 1.25
83 Devin Booker 1.00 2.50
84 Jamal Murray .60 1.50
85 DeMar DeRozan .50 1.25
86 Chet Holmgren .60 1.50
87 Karl-Anthony Towns .60 1.50
88 Chris Paul .60 1.50
89 LaMelo Ball .75 2.00
90 Julius Randle .40 1.00
91 Tyrese Haliburton .75 2.00
92 Jaylen Brown .60 1.50
93 Dejounte Murray .40 1.00
94 Jarrett Allen .30 .75
95 Coby White .40 1.00
96 Brandon Ingram .40 1.00
97 Fred VanVleet .40 1.00
98 Bradley Beal .50 1.25
99 Jonas Valanciunas .30 .75
100 Jalen Suggs .40 1.00
101 Jamal Shead RC 1.00 2.50
102 Kel'el Ware RC 2.00 5.00
103 Harrison Ingram RC .75 2.00
104 Zaccharie Risacher RC 2.50 6.00
105 Rob Dillingham RC 2.00 5.00
106 Alexandre Sarr RC 2.50 6.00
107 Tristen Newton RC .75 2.00
108 Donovan Clingan RC 2.00 5.00
109 Dalton Knecht RC 2.50 6.00
110 Cody Williams RC 1.00 2.50
111 Jonathan Mogbo RC 1.25 3.00
112 Johnny Furphy RC 1.25 3.00
113 Cam Christie RC 1.00 2.50
114 Ron Holland II RC 1.50 4.00
115 Dillon Jones RC .75 2.00
116 Stephon Castle RC 5.00 12.00
117 KJ Simpson Jr. RC .75 2.00
118 Bronny James Jr. RC 2.50 6.00
119 Kyshawn George RC 1.25 3.00
120 Baylor Scheierman RC 1.00 2.50
121 Bub Carrington RC 1.00 2.50
122 Ajay Mitchell RC 1.25 3.00
123 Tidjane Salaun RC .75 2.00
124 Jared McCain RC 2.50 6.00
125 Devin Carter RC 1.00 2.50
126 Nikola Durisic RC 1.00 2.50
127 Antonio Reeves RC .75 2.00
128 Tyler Smith RC 1.00 2.50
129 Matas Buzelis RC 4.00 10.00
130 Jaylen Wells RC 2.50 6.00
131 Adem Bona RC 1.00 2.50
132 Pelle Larsson RC 1.00 2.50
133 Nikola Topic RC 2.50 6.00
134 Zach Edey RC 2.50 6.00
135 Bobi Klintman RC 1.00 2.50
136 Tyler Kolek RC 1.25 3.00
137 Ryan Dunn RC 1.00 2.50
138 Jaylon Tyson RC .75 2.00
139 Oso Ighodaro RC 1.00 2.50
140 AJ Johnson RC 1.50 4.00
141 DaRon Holmes II RC 1.00 2.50
142 Tristan da Silva RC 2.00 5.00
143 Pacome Dadiet RC 1.00 2.50
144 Isaiah Collier RC 1.50 4.00
145 Reed Sheppard RC 2.50 6.00
146 Kyle Filipowski RC 2.00 5.00
147 Cam Spencer RC .75 2.00
148 Terrence Shannon Jr. RC 1.50 4.00
149 Yves Missi RC 2.00 5.00
150 Ja'Kobe Walter RC 1.00 2.50
151 Kareem Abdul-Jabbar LGD 1.25 3.00
152 Steve Nash LGD .75 2.00
153 Julius Erving LGD 1.00 2.50
154 John Stockton LGD .75 2.00
155 Magic Johnson LGD 1.00 2.50
156 Kevin Garnett LGD 1.00 2.50
157 David Robinson LGD .75 2.00
158 Isiah Thomas LGD .60 1.50
159 Larry Bird LGD 1.25 3.00
160 Dwyane Wade LGD .75 2.00
161 Tim Duncan LGD 1.00 2.50
162 Dominique Wilkins LGD .60 1.50
163 Allen Iverson LGD 1.00 2.50
164 Patrick Ewing LGD .60 1.50
165 Carmelo Anthony LGD .60 1.50
166 Shaquille O'Neal LGD 1.00 2.50
167 Gary Payton LGD .60 1.50
168 Hakeem Olajuwon LGD .75 2.00
169 Karl Malone LGD .75 2.00
170 Yao Ming LGD .75 2.00
171 Charles Barkley LGD 1.00 2.50
172 Dennis Rodman LGD 1.00 2.50
173 Tracy McGrady LGD .75 2.00
174 Dirk Nowitzki LGD 1.00 2.50
175 Clyde Drexler LGD .60 1.50

2024-25 Panini Revolution Around the Rim Autographs

*IMPACT/25-100: .5X TO 1.2X BASIC
*INFINITE/15-25: .6X TO 1.5X BASIC
1 Matas Buzelis 30.00 80.00
2 Karl Malone 30.00 80.00
3 Ja Morant 100.00 250.00
4 Anthony Davis 40.00 100.00
5 Kevin Durant 75.00 200.00
6 Shai Gilgeous-Alexander 200.00 500.00
7 Giannis Antetokounmpo 150.00 400.00
8 Luka Doncic 300.00 600.00
9 Damian Lillard 75.00 200.00
10 Paolo Banchero 50.00 120.00
11 James Harden 75.00 200.00
12 Bub Carrington 15.00 40.00

13 Trae Young 40.00 100.00
14 Stephen Curry 500.00 1,000.00
15 Donovan Clingan 15.00 40.00
17 Zach Edey 20.00 50.00
18 Anthony Edwards 150.00 400.00
19 Jayson Tatum 100.00 250.00
20 Hakeem Olajuwon 30.00 80.00
21 Kareem Abdul-Jabbar 60.00 150.00
22 Reed Sheppard 20.00 50.00
23 Allen Iverson 50.00 120.00
24 Tidjane Salaun 6.00 15.00
25 Patrick Ewing 50.00 120.00

2024-25 Panini Revolution Autographs

*IMPACT/49-100: .5X TO 1.2X BASIC
*CHINESE NY/28: .6X TO 1.5X BASIC
*INFINITE/25: .6X TO 1.5X BASIC
1 Franz Wagner 10.00 25.00
3 Dyson Daniels 8.00 20.00
6 Shaedon Sharpe 8.00 20.00
7 Jaden Ivey 8.00 20.00
8 Amen Thompson 15.00 40.00
9 Ausar Thompson 10.00 25.00
10 Jaden Hardy 6.00 15.00
12 Jalen Duren 6.00 15.00
15 Keegan Murray 5.00 12.00
16 Chet Holmgren 40.00 100.00
17 Jalen Suggs 6.00 15.00
18 Anfernee Simons 6.00 15.00
19 Jalen Green 12.00 30.00
20 Bruce Brown 5.00 12.00
21 Kristaps Porzingis 8.00 20.00
23 Josh Giddey 8.00 20.00
24 Bennedict Mathurin 8.00 20.00
28 Rudy Gobert 6.00 15.00
29 Cason Wallace 8.00 20.00
30 Deandre Ayton 5.00 12.00
31 Keyonte George 8.00 20.00
33 Nikola Vucevic 5.00 12.00
34 Devin Vassell 8.00 20.00
35 Cade Cunningham 40.00 100.00
36 Michael Porter Jr. 6.00 15.00
37 Tyler Herro 10.00 25.00
38 Tayshaun Prince 8.00 20.00
39 Ray Allen 30.00 80.00
40 Jeremy Lin 40.00 100.00
41 Grant Hill 25.00 60.00
42 Paul Pierce 25.00 60.00
43 Larry Bird 60.00 150.00
44 Isiah Thomas 10.00 25.00
45 Rick Barry 8.00 20.00
46 Steve Francis 6.00 15.00
47 Bob Cousy 60.00 150.00
48 Kevin McHale 10.00 25.00
49 Joakim Noah 6.00 15.00
50 John Stockton 30.00 80.00

2024-25 Panini Revolution Hardwood Legacy

*RED ASTRO/299: .75X TO 2X BASIC
*BLUE COSMO/285: .75X TO 2X BASIC
*RED SCOPE/135: 1X TO 2.5X BASIC
*BLUE ASTRO/99: 1.25X TO 3X BASIC
*GREEN STORM/99: 1.25X TO 3X BASIC
*TEAL SWIRL/35: 2X TO 5X BASIC
1 Luka Doncic 3.00 8.00
2 LeBron James 4.00 10.00
3 Stephen Curry 4.00 10.00
4 Jayson Tatum 1.50 4.00
5 Shai Gilgeous-Alexander 2.50 6.00
6 Giannis Antetokounmpo 2.00 5.00
7 Nikola Jokic 2.50 6.00
8 Anthony Edwards 2.50 6.00
9 Kevin Durant 1.50 4.00
10 Victor Wembanyama 4.00 10.00
11 Kareem Abdul-Jabbar 1.50 4.00
12 Dirk Nowitzki 1.25 3.00
13 Dwyane Wade 1.00 2.50
14 Tim Duncan 1.25 3.00
15 Magic Johnson 1.50 4.00
16 Kevin Garnett 1.25 3.00
17 David Robinson 1.00 2.50
18 Larry Bird 1.50 4.00
19 Hakeem Olajuwon 1.00 2.50
20 Shaquille O'Neal 1.25 3.00
21 Zaccharie Risacher 1.50 4.00
22 Alexandre Sarr 1.50 4.00
23 Reed Sheppard 1.50 4.00
24 Stephon Castle 3.00 8.00
25 Matas Buzelis 2.50 6.00

2024-25 Panini Revolution Kaboom Horizontal

1 Anthony Edwards 800.00 1,500.00
2 Zion Williamson 300.00 600.00
3 Kyrie Irving 400.00 800.00
4 Tyrese Maxey 400.00 800.00
5 Tyrese Haliburton 500.00 1,000.00
6 Jaylen Brown 500.00 1,000.00
7 Nikola Jokic 800.00 1,500.00
8 Giannis Antetokounmpo 500.00 1,000.00
9 Luka Doncic 1,000.00 2,000.00
10 Shai Gilgeous-Alexander 1,000.00 2,000.00
11 Ja Morant 400.00 800.00
12 Jayson Tatum 500.00 1,000.00
13 Stephen Curry 1,500.00 3,000.00
14 LeBron James 2,000.00 4,000.00
15 Victor Wembanyama 1,500.00 3,000.00
16 Zaccharie Risacher 400.00 800.00
17 Alexandre Sarr 350.00 700.00
18 Reed Sheppard 400.00 800.00
19 Stephon Castle 800.00 1,500.00
20 Zach Edey 350.00 700.00
21 Jared McCain 800.00 1,500.00
22 Bub Carrington 350.00 700.00
23 Tidjane Salaun 150.00 400.00
24 Cody Williams 200.00 500.00
25 Matas Buzelis 500.00 1,000.00
26 Dalton Knecht 300.00 600.00
27 Ron Holland II 350.00 700.00
28 Rob Dillingham 300.00 600.00
29 Kel'el Ware 300.00 600.00
30 Ja'Kobe Walter 200.00 500.00
31 Julius Erving 350.00 700.00
32 Anthony Davis 400.00 800.00
33 Derrick Rose 500.00 1,000.00
34 Shaquille O'Neal 800.00 1,500.00
35 Larry Bird 800.00 1,500.00

2024-25 Panini Revolution Kaboom Vertical

1 Luka Doncic 1,000.00 2,000.00
2 LeBron James 2,000.00 4,000.00
3 Stephen Curry 1,500.00 3,000.00
4 Jayson Tatum 500.00 1,000.00
5 Ja Morant 400.00 800.00
6 Shai Gilgeous-Alexander 1,000.00 2,000.00
7 Giannis Antetokounmpo 500.00 1,000.00
8 Nikola Jokic 800.00 1,500.00
9 Anthony Edwards 800.00 1,500.00
10 Kevin Durant 350.00 700.00
11 Trae Young 350.00 700.00
12 Paolo Banchero 500.00 1,000.00
13 Jalen Brunson 600.00 1,200.00
14 Damian Lillard 300.00 600.00
15 Victor Wembanyama 1,500.00 3,000.00
16 Zaccharie Risacher 400.00 800.00
17 Alexandre Sarr 350.00 700.00
18 Reed Sheppard 400.00 800.00
19 Stephon Castle 800.00 1,500.00
20 Ron Holland II 350.00 700.00
21 Donovan Clingan 300.00 600.00
22 Rob Dillingham 300.00 600.00
23 Matas Buzelis 500.00 1,000.00
24 Dalton Knecht 300.00 600.00
25 Bronny James Jr. 400.00 800.00
26 Dirk Nowitzki 350.00 700.00
27 Dwyane Wade 350.00 700.00
28 Jared McCain 800.00 1,500.00
29 Pau Gasol 300.00 600.00
30 Tim Duncan 350.00 700.00

2024-25 Panini Revolution Liftoff!

*FRACTAL: .5X TO 1.2X BASIC
*NEUTRON/125: 1X TO 2.5X BASIC
*COSMIC/99: 1.25X TO 3X BASIC
*SUNBURST/75: 1.25X TO 3X BASIC
*CUBIC/50: 1.5X TO 4X BASIC
*INFINITE/25: 2.5X TO 6X BASIC
1 Donovan Clingan 1.25 3.00
2 Victor Wembanyama 4.00 10.00
3 Anthony Davis 1.25 3.00
4 Anthony Edwards 2.50 6.00
5 LeBron James 4.00 10.00
6 Ja Morant 1.50 4.00
7 Jayson Tatum 1.50 4.00
8 Alexandre Sarr 1.50 4.00
9 Zion Williamson 1.25 3.00
10 Matas Buzelis 2.50 6.00
11 Chet Holmgren .75 2.00
12 Zaccharie Risacher 1.50 4.00
13 Zach Edey 1.50 4.00
14 Kevin Durant 1.50 4.00
15 Paolo Banchero 1.25 3.00

2024-25 Panini Revolution New Wave

*RED ASTRO/299: .75X TO 2X BASIC
*BLUE COSMO/285: .75X TO 2X BASIC
*RED SCOPE/135: 1X TO 2.5X BASIC
*BLUE ASTRO/99: 1.25X TO 3X BASIC
*GREEN STORM/99: 1.25X TO 3X BASIC
*TEAL SWIRL/35: 2X TO 5X BASIC
1 Johnny Furphy 1.00 2.50
2 Matas Buzelis 3.00 8.00
3 Tristan da Silva 1.50 4.00
4 Dalton Knecht 2.00 5.00
5 Cody Williams .75 2.00
6 Bronny James Jr. 2.00 5.00
7 Rob Dillingham 1.50 4.00
8 Devin Carter .75 2.00
9 Zaccharie Risacher 2.00 5.00
10 Zach Edey 2.00 5.00
11 Kel'el Ware 1.50 4.00
12 Alexandre Sarr 2.00 5.00
13 Antonio Reeves .60 1.50
14 Jared McCain 2.00 5.00
15 Reed Sheppard 2.00 5.00
16 Ron Holland II 1.25 3.00
17 Tidjane Salaun .60 1.50
18 Stephon Castle 4.00 10.00
19 Donovan Clingan 1.50 4.00
20 Jaylen Wells 2.00 5.00
21 Ja'Kobe Walter .75 2.00
22 Nikola Topic 2.00 5.00
23 Bub Carrington 1.50 4.00
24 Kyle Filipowski 1.50 4.00
25 Tyler Kolek 1.00 2.50

2024-25 Panini Revolution Prime Time Performers

1 Damian Lillard 25.00 60.00
2 Zaccharie Risacher 30.00 80.00
3 Tyrese Haliburton 20.00 50.00
4 Giannis Antetokounmpo 40.00 100.00
5 Shai Gilgeous-Alexander 50.00 125.00
6 Tristan da Silva 25.00 60.00
7 Devin Booker 25.00 60.00
8 Tidjane Salaun 10.00 25.00
9 Ja Morant 30.00 80.00
10 Kevin Durant 30.00 80.00
11 Zach Edey 30.00 80.00
12 Stephen Curry 80.00 200.00
13 De'Aaron Fox 20.00 50.00
14 Luka Doncic 60.00 150.00
15 Nikola Jokic 50.00 125.00
16 LeBron James 80.00 200.00
17 Reed Sheppard 30.00 80.00
18 Matas Buzelis 50.00 125.00
19 Alexandre Sarr 30.00 80.00
20 Victor Wembanyama 80.00 200.00
21 Stephon Castle 60.00 150.00
22 Zion Williamson 25.00 60.00
23 Anthony Edwards 50.00 125.00
24 Ron Holland II 20.00 50.00
25 Kawhi Leonard 20.00 50.00
26 Kyrie Irving 25.00 60.00
27 Bronny James Jr. 30.00 80.00
28 Jayson Tatum 30.00 80.00
29 Paul George 15.00 40.00
30 Jalen Brunson 20.00 50.00

2024-25 Panini Revolution Revolution Signatures

*COSMO/35: .5X TO 1.2X BASIC
*LEVELS/25: .6X TO 1.5X BASIC
*SCOPE/20: .6X TO 1.5X BASIC
1 Cade Cunningham 40.00 100.00
2 Jalen Duren 6.00 15.00
3 Jaden Hardy 6.00 15.00
4 Paolo Banchero 50.00 120.00
6 Cason Wallace 8.00 20.00
7 Johnny Davis 5.00 12.00
8 Adam Flagler 6.00 15.00
9 Bennedict Mathurin 8.00 20.00
11 Keyonte George 8.00 20.00
12 David Duke Jr. 4.00 10.00
13 Jay Huff 5.00 12.00
14 Trey Jemison III 5.00 12.00
15 Amir Coffey 4.00 10.00
16 Mark Williams 5.00 12.00
17 Chris Livingston 5.00 12.00
18 Kenneth Lofton Jr. 5.00 12.00
19 Perry Dozier Jr. 4.00 10.00
20 Dariq Whitehead 5.00 12.00
21 Ricky Council IV 4.00 10.00
22 Josh Minott 4.00 10.00
23 Ausar Thompson 10.00 25.00
24 Amen Thompson 15.00 40.00
25 Blake Wesley 4.00 10.00
26 Johnny Juzang 5.00 12.00
28 Jabari Walker 4.00 10.00
31 Jaden Springer 4.00 10.00
32 Olivier-Maxence Prosper 5.00 12.00
33 Oscar Tshiebwe 6.00 15.00
36 TyTy Washington Jr. 4.00 10.00
37 Jalen Suggs 6.00 15.00
38 Mouhamed Gueye 6.00 15.00
39 DaRon Holmes II 8.00 20.00
40 Trey Alexander 5.00 12.00
41 Reece Beekman 6.00 15.00
42 Trentyn Flowers 5.00 12.00
43 Judah Mintz 5.00 12.00
46 Jalen Bridges 5.00 12.00
47 Keshad Johnson 5.00 12.00
48 Ulrich Chomche 5.00 12.00
49 Ariel Hukporti 5.00 12.00
50 Cam Spencer 6.00 15.00
51 Anton Watson 5.00 12.00
52 Kevin McCullar Jr. 6.00 15.00
53 Tristen Newton 6.00 15.00
54 Enrique Freeman 5.00 12.00
55 Quinten Post 12.00 30.00
56 KJ Simpson Jr. 6.00 15.00
57 Pelle Larsson 8.00 20.00
58 Jamal Shead 8.00 20.00
59 Antonio Reeves 6.00 15.00
60 Harrison Ingram 6.00 15.00
61 Nikola Durisic 8.00 20.00
62 Baylor Scheierman 8.00 20.00
63 Reed Sheppard 20.00 50.00
65 Dillon Jones 6.00 15.00
66 Pacome Dadiet 8.00 20.00
67 Tidjane Salaun 6.00 15.00
68 Donovan Clingan 15.00 40.00
69 Kyshawn George 10.00 25.00
70 Zach Edey 20.00 50.00
71 AJ Johnson 12.00 30.00
72 Matas Buzelis 30.00 80.00
73 Bub Carrington 15.00 40.00
74 Devin Carter 8.00 20.00
75 Yves Missi 15.00 40.00
76 Jared McCain 20.00 50.00
77 Tristan da Silva 15.00 40.00
78 Jaylon Tyson 6.00 15.00
79 Ja'Kobe Walter 8.00 20.00
80 Dalton Knecht 20.00 50.00
81 Jonathan Mogbo 10.00 25.00
82 Bobi Klintman 8.00 20.00
83 Johnny Furphy 10.00 25.00
84 Jaylen Wells 20.00 50.00
85 Oso Ighodaro 8.00 20.00
86 Ajay Mitchell 10.00 25.00
87 Tyler Kolek 10.00 25.00
88 Adem Bona 8.00 20.00
89 Cam Christie 8.00 20.00
90 Craig Hodges 5.00 12.00
91 Vin Baker 5.00 12.00
93 Antoine Carr 5.00 12.00
94 Mark Aguirre 5.00 12.00
95 Gerald Wilkins 4.00 10.00
96 Charlie Scott 8.00 20.00
97 Alton Lister 4.00 10.00
98 James Donaldson 4.00 10.00
99 Cedric Ceballos 5.00 12.00
100 Rik Smits 5.00 12.00

2024-25 Panini Revolution Ring Bearers

*FRACTAL: .5X TO 1.2X BASIC
*NEUTRON/125: 1X TO 2.5X BASIC
*COSMIC/99: 1.25X TO 3X BASIC
*SUNBURST/75: 1.25X TO 3X BASIC
*CUBIC/50: 1.5X TO 4X BASIC
*INFINITE/25: 2.5X TO 6X BASIC
1 Stephen Curry 4.00 10.00
2 LeBron James 4.00 10.00
3 Jayson Tatum 1.50 4.00
4 Nikola Jokic 2.50 6.00
5 Giannis Antetokounmpo 2.00 5.00
6 Kevin Durant 1.50 4.00
7 Jaylen Brown .75 2.00
8 Tim Duncan 1.25 3.00
9 Dirk Nowitzki 1.25 3.00
10 Shaquille O'Neal 1.25 3.00
11 Magic Johnson 1.50 4.00
12 Kevin Garnett 1.25 3.00
13 Hakeem Olajuwon 1.00 2.50
14 Larry Bird 1.50 4.00
15 Dwyane Wade 1.00 2.50

2024-25 Panini Revolution Rookie Autographs

*IMPACT/100: .5X TO 1.2X BASIC
*CHINESE NY/28: .75X TO 2X BASIC
*INFINITE/25: .75X TO 2X BASIC
1 Bub Carrington 15.00 40.00
2 Dalton Knecht 20.00 50.00
3 Zach Edey 20.00 50.00
4 Jaylon Tyson 6.00 15.00
5 Yves Missi 15.00 40.00
6 Matas Buzelis 30.00 80.00
7 DaRon Holmes II 8.00 20.00
8 Jared McCain 20.00 50.00
9 AJ Johnson 12.00 30.00
10 Kyshawn George 10.00 25.00
11 Reed Sheppard 20.00 50.00
12 Pacome Dadiet 8.00 20.00
13 Dillon Jones 6.00 15.00
14 Tristan da Silva 15.00 40.00
16 Jonathan Mogbo 10.00 25.00
17 Baylor Scheierman 8.00 20.00
18 Devin Carter 8.00 20.00
19 Johnny Furphy 10.00 25.00
20 Bobi Klintman 8.00 20.00
21 Ja'Kobe Walter 8.00 20.00
22 Tyler Kolek 10.00 25.00
23 Donovan Clingan 15.00 40.00
24 Ajay Mitchell 10.00 25.00
25 Tidjane Salaun 6.00 15.00

2024-25 Panini Revolution Rookie Revolution

*FRACTAL: .5X TO 1.2X BASIC
*NEUTRON/125: 1X TO 2.5X BASIC
*COSMIC/99: 1.25X TO 3X BASIC
*SUNBURST/75: 1.25X TO 3X BASIC
*CUBIC/50: 1.5X TO 4X BASIC
*INFINITE/25: 2.5X TO 6X BASIC
1 Reed Sheppard 2.50 6.00
2 Stephon Castle 5.00 12.00
3 Cody Williams 1.00 2.50
4 Rob Dillingham 2.00 5.00
5 Jared McCain 2.50 6.00
6 Dalton Knecht 2.50 6.00
7 Ja'Kobe Walter 1.00 2.50
8 Bronny James Jr. 2.50 6.00
9 Kel'el Ware 2.00 5.00
10 Tidjane Salaun .75 2.00
11 Nikola Topic 2.50 6.00
12 Zach Edey 2.50 6.00
13 Bub Carrington 2.00 5.00
14 Matas Buzelis 4.00 10.00
15 Devin Carter 1.00 2.50
16 Alexandre Sarr 2.50 6.00
17 Zaccharie Risacher 2.50 6.00
18 Ron Holland II 1.50 4.00
19 Tristan da Silva 2.00 5.00
20 Donovan Clingan 2.00 5.00

2024-25 Panini Revolution Showstoppers

*FRACTAL: .5X TO 1.2X BASIC
*NEUTRON/125: 1X TO 2.5X BASIC
*COSMIC/99: 1.25X TO 3X BASIC
*SUNBURST/75: 1.25X TO 3X BASIC
*CUBIC/50: 1.5X TO 4X BASIC
*INFINITE/25: 2.5X TO 6X BASIC
1 Zion Williamson 1.25 3.00
2 Nikola Jokic 2.50 6.00
3 Trae Young 1.00 2.50
4 Giannis Antetokounmpo 2.00 5.00
5 Dalton Knecht 1.50 4.00
6 Stephen Curry 4.00 10.00
7 LeBron James 4.00 10.00
8 Anthony Edwards 2.50 6.00
9 Donovan Mitchell 1.00 2.50
10 Damian Lillard 1.25 3.00
11 Luka Doncic 3.00 8.00
12 Zaccharie Risacher 1.50 4.00
13 Jayson Tatum 1.50 4.00
14 Alexandre Sarr 1.50 4.00
15 Jalen Brunson 1.00 2.50
16 Devin Booker 1.25 3.00
17 Bronny James Jr. 1.50 4.00
18 Tyrese Haliburton 1.00 2.50
19 Shai Gilgeous-Alexander 2.50 6.00
20 Kawhi Leonard 1.00 2.50
21 Tyrese Maxey 1.00 2.50
22 Victor Wembanyama 4.00 10.00
23 Rob Dillingham 1.25 3.00
24 Stephon Castle 3.00 8.00
25 Reed Sheppard 1.50 4.00

2024-25 Panini Revolution Star Factor

1 Kevin Durant 25.00 60.00
2 Dalton Knecht 25.00 60.00
3 Jalen Brunson 15.00 40.00
4 Stephon Castle 50.00 125.00
5 Bronny James Jr. 25.00 60.00
6 Donovan Clingan 20.00 50.00
7 Nikola Jokic 40.00 100.00
8 Victor Wembanyama 60.00 150.00
9 Zaccharie Risacher 25.00 60.00
10 Rob Dillingham 20.00 50.00
11 Shai Gilgeous-Alexander 40.00 100.00
12 Trae Young 15.00 40.00
13 Paolo Banchero 20.00 50.00
14 Ron Holland II 15.00 40.00
15 Jayson Tatum 25.00 60.00
16 LeBron James 60.00 150.00
17 Alexandre Sarr 25.00 60.00
18 Damian Lillard 20.00 50.00
19 Luka Doncic 50.00 125.00
20 Giannis Antetokounmpo 30.00 80.00
21 Stephen Curry 60.00 150.00
22 Reed Sheppard 25.00 60.00
23 Anthony Edwards 40.00 100.00
24 Matas Buzelis 40.00 100.00
25 Ja Morant 25.00 60.00

2024-25 Panini Revolution Star Gazing

*RED ASTRO/299: .75X TO 2X BASIC
*BLUE COSMO/285: .75X TO 2X BASIC
*RED SCOPE/135: 1X TO 2.5X BASIC
*BLUE ASTRO/99: 1.25X TO 3X BASIC
*GREEN STORM/99: 1.25X TO 3X BASIC
*TEAL SWIRL/35: 2X TO 5X BASIC
1 Tyrese Maxey 1.00 2.50
2 Ja Morant 1.50 4.00
3 Jayson Tatum 1.50 4.00
4 Stephon Castle 3.00 8.00
5 Shai Gilgeous-Alexander 2.50 6.00
6 Reed Sheppard 1.50 4.00
7 Nikola Jokic 2.50 6.00
8 Trae Young 1.00 2.50
9 Luka Doncic 3.00 8.00
10 Damian Lillard 1.25 3.00
11 Paolo Banchero 1.25 3.00
12 Giannis Antetokounmpo 2.00 5.00
13 Matas Buzelis 2.50 6.00
14 Bronny James Jr. 1.50 4.00
15 Kevin Durant 1.50 4.00
16 Zaccharie Risacher 1.50 4.00
17 Rob Dillingham 1.25 3.00
18 Stephen Curry 4.00 10.00
19 Alexandre Sarr 1.50 4.00
20 Donovan Clingan 1.25 3.00
21 LeBron James 4.00 10.00
22 Anthony Edwards 2.50 6.00
23 Victor Wembanyama 4.00 10.00
24 Jalen Brunson 1.00 2.50
25 Jaylen Brown .75 2.00

2024-25 Panini Revolution Supernova

*FRACTAL: .5X TO 1.2X BASIC
*NEUTRON/125: 1X TO 2.5X BASIC
*COSMIC/99: 1.25X TO 3X BASIC
*SUNBURST/75: 1.25X TO 3X BASIC
*CUBIC/50: 1.5X TO 4X BASIC
*INFINITE/25: 2.5X TO 6X BASIC
1 Jaylen Brown .75 2.00
2 Ron Holland II 1.00 2.50
3 De'Aaron Fox 1.00 2.50
4 Jayson Tatum 1.50 4.00
5 Shai Gilgeous-Alexander 2.50 6.00
6 Anthony Edwards 2.50 6.00
7 James Harden 1.00 2.50
8 Kevin Durant 1.50 4.00
9 Giannis Antetokounmpo 2.00 5.00
10 Cody Williams .60 1.50
11 Bub Carrington 1.25 3.00
12 Kyrie Irving 1.25 3.00
13 Tidjane Salaun .50 1.25
14 LeBron James 4.00 10.00
15 Joel Embiid .75 2.00
16 Stephon Castle 3.00 8.00
17 Zaccharie Risacher 1.50 4.00
18 Reed Sheppard 1.50 4.00
19 Jimmy Butler III .75 2.00
20 Ja Morant 1.50 4.00
21 Stephen Curry 4.00 10.00
22 Luka Doncic 3.00 8.00
23 Victor Wembanyama 4.00 10.00
24 Nikola Jokic 2.50 6.00
25 Paul George .75 2.00

2024-25 Panini Revolution Vortex

*RED ASTRO/299: .75X TO 2X BASIC
*BLUE COSMO/285: .75X TO 2X BASIC
*RED SCOPE/135: 1X TO 2.5X BASIC
*BLUE ASTRO/99: 1.25X TO 3X BASIC
*GREEN STORM/99: 1.25X TO 3X BASIC
*TEAL SWIRL/35: 2X TO 5X BASIC
1 Alexandre Sarr 1.50 4.00
2 Nikola Jokic 2.50 6.00
3 Reed Sheppard 1.50 4.00
4 Jayson Tatum 1.50 4.00
5 Tidjane Salaun .50 1.25
6 Anthony Edwards 2.50 6.00
7 Luka Doncic 3.00 8.00
8 Zaccharie Risacher 1.50 4.00
9 Bub Carrington 1.25 3.00
10 Giannis Antetokounmpo 2.00 5.00
11 Dalton Knecht 1.50 4.00
12 LeBron James 4.00 10.00
13 Joel Embiid .75 2.00
14 Kevin Durant 1.50 4.00
15 Anthony Davis 1.25 3.00
16 Ron Holland II 1.00 2.50
17 Victor Wembanyama 4.00 10.00
18 Zion Williamson 1.25 3.00
19 Stephon Castle 3.00 8.00
20 Shai Gilgeous-Alexander 2.50 6.00
21 Ja Morant 1.50 4.00
22 Tyrese Haliburton 1.00 2.50
23 Trae Young 1.00 2.50
24 Stephen Curry 4.00 10.00
25 Chet Holmgren .75 2.00

2009-10 Panini Season Update

COMPLETE SET (200) 25.00 50.00
1 Kobe Bryant HL 2.50 6.00
2 Brandon Jennings HL .30 .75
3 Allen/Nowitzki/Duncan HL .75 2.00
4 Kevin Durant HL 1.25 3.00
5 Rajon Rondo HL .40 1.00
6 Ben Gordon HL .25 .60
7 Gasol/Odom/Kobe HL 2.50 6.00
8 Jason Kidd HL .50 1.25
9 Vince Carter HL .60 1.50
10 NBA All-Star Game HL .25 .60
11 Dwyane Wade HL .60 1.50
12 Malone/Pippen HL .75 2.00
13 Kobe Bryant HL 2.50 6.00
14 Kevin Durant HL 1.25 3.00
15 Don Nelson HL .30 .75
16 Josh Smith HL .20 .50
17 Tyreke Evans HL .25 .60
18 LeBron James HL 2.50 6.00
19 2010 NBA Lottery HL .25 .60
20 Los Angeles Lakers HL 2.50 6.00
21 Rajon Rondo .40 1.00
22 Paul Pierce .50 1.25
23 Kevin Garnett .60 1.50
24 Rasheed Wallace .40 1.00
25 Glen Davis .20 .50
26 Ray Allen .50 1.25
27 Brook Lopez .30 .75
28 Devin Harris .20 .50
29 Courtney Lee .20 .50
30 Chris Douglas-Roberts .20 .50
31 Al Harrington .25 .60
32 David Lee .20 .50
33 Tracy McGrady .60 1.50
34 Danilo Gallinari .25 .60
35 Amare Stoudemire SP 4.00 10.00
36 Andre Iguodala .30 .75
37 Louis Williams .30 .75
38 Allen Iverson .60 1.50
39 Samuel Dalembert .20 .50
40 Elton Brand .25 .60
41 Thaddeus Young .20 .50
42 Chris Bosh .40 1.00
43 Jarrett Jack .20 .50
44 Andrea Bargnani .20 .50
45 Hedo Turkoglu .25 .60
46 Jose Calderon .20 .50
47 Jason Kidd .50 1.25
48 Dirk Nowitzki .75 2.00
49 Caron Butler .25 .60
50 Jason Terry .25 .60
51 Shawn Marion .30 .75
52 Brendan Haywood .20 .50
53 Aaron Brooks .20 .50
54 Trevor Ariza .20 .50
55 Luis Scola .25 .60
56 Shane Battier .30 .75
57 Kevin Martin .25 .60
58 Zach Randolph .30 .75
59 Rudy Gay .30 .75
60 O.J. Mayo .30 .75
61 Marc Gasol .30 .75
62 Mike Conley Jr. .25 .60
63 Darrell Arthur .20 .50
64 David West .25 .60
65 Emeka Okafor .25 .60
66 Chris Paul .60 1.50
67 Peja Stojakovic .25 .60
68 Morris Peterson .20 .50
69 Tim Duncan .75 2.00
70 Manu Ginobili .60 1.50
71 George Hill .25 .60
72 Tony Parker .50 1.25
73 Richard Jefferson .25 .60
74 Antonio McDyess .25 .60
75 Joakim Noah .25 .60
76 Derrick Rose .50 1.25
77 Kirk Hinrich .25 .60
78 Luol Deng .25 .60
79 Carlos Boozer SP 6.00 15.00
80 Brad Miller .20 .50
81 Antawn Jamison .25 .60
82 LeBron James 2.50 6.00
83 Anderson Varejao .20 .50
84 Shaquille O'Neal 1.00 2.50
85 Mo Williams .25 .60
86 J.J. Hickson .20 .50
87 Ben Gordon .25 .60
88 Tayshaun Prince .30 .75
89 Richard Hamilton .30 .75
90 Ben Wallace .40 1.00
91 Rodney Stuckey .20 .50
92 Jason Maxiell .20 .50
93 Danny Granger .25 .60
94 Roy Hibbert .25 .60
95 Mike Dunleavy .20 .50
96 Troy Murphy .20 .50
97 Dahntay Jones .20 .50
98 Brandon Rush .20 .50
99 Andrew Bogut .25 .60
100 John Salmons .25 .60
101 Luke Ridnour .25 .60
102 Carlos Delfino .25 .60
103 Michael Redd .25 .60
104 Carmelo Anthony .50 1.25
105 Chris Andersen .30 .75
106 J.R. Smith .30 .75
107 Nene .25 .60
108 Chauncey Billups .40 1.00
109 Al Jefferson .20 .50
110 Kevin Love .30 .75
111 Corey Brewer .20 .50
112 Ryan Gomes .20 .50
113 LaMarcus Aldridge .30 .75
114 Brandon Roy .40 1.00
115 Rudy Fernandez .20 .50
116 Andre Miller .30 .75
117 Juwan Howard .25 .60
118 Nicolas Batum .25 .60
119 Kevin Durant 1.25 3.00
120 Russell Westbrook .60 1.50
121 Jeff Green .25 .60
122 Nenad Krstic .20 .50
123 Nick Collison .20 .50
124 Deron Williams .25 .60
125 Carlos Boozer .25 .60
126 Mehmet Okur .20 .50
127 Paul Millsap .25 .60
128 Andrei Kirilenko .25 .60
129 Monta Ellis .25 .60
130 Anthony Morrow .20 .50
131 Corey Maggette .25 .60
132 C.J. Watson .20 .50
133 Kobe Bryant 2.50 6.00
134 Pau Gasol .50 1.25
135 Lamar Odom .25 .60
136 Andrew Bynum .25 .60
137 Ron Artest .30 .75
138 Derek Fisher .30 .75
139 Luke Walton .25 .60
140 Amare Stoudemire .25 .60
141 Steve Nash .60 1.50
142 Jason Richardson .30 .75
143 Robin Lopez .20 .50
144 Grant Hill .50 1.25
145 Channing Frye .20 .50
146 Spencer Hawes .20 .50
147 Beno Udrih .20 .50
148 Jason Thompson .20 .50
149 Carl Landry .20 .50
150 Donte Greene .20 .50
151 Andres Nocioni .20 .50
152 Josh Smith .20 .50
153 Jamal Crawford .30 .75
154 Al Horford .30 .75
155 Joe Johnson .30 .75
156 Mike Bibby .30 .75
157 Marvin Williams .25 .60
158 Gerald Wallace .25 .60
159 Stephen Jackson .25 .60
160 Raymond Felton .20 .50
161 Boris Diaw .25 .60
162 D.J. Augustin .20 .50
163 Michael Beasley .20 .50
164 Dwyane Wade .60 1.50
165 Jermaine O'Neal .30 .75
166 Udonis Haslem .20 .50
167 Chris Bosh SP 6.00 15.00
168 LeBron James 8.00 20.00
169 Dwight Howard .40 1.00
170 Vince Carter .60 1.50
171 Rashard Lewis .25 .60
172 J.J. Redick .30 .75
173 Jameer Nelson .20 .50
174 Matt Barnes .20 .50
175 Al Thornton .20 .50
176 Josh Howard .25 .60
177 Randy Foye .20 .50
178 Mike Miller .25 .60
179 Andray Blatche .20 .50
180 Shaun Livingston .20 .50
181 LeBron James AS 2.50 6.00
182 Dwight Howard AS .40 1.00
183 Dwyane Wade AS .60 1.50
184 Chris Bosh AS .40 1.00
185 Rajon Rondo AS .40 1.00
186 Joe Johnson AS .30 .75
187 Paul Pierce AS .50 1.25
188 Derrick Rose AS .50 1.25
189 Al Horford AS .30 .75
190 David Lee AS .20 .50
191 Carmelo Anthony AS .50 1.25
192 Dirk Nowitzki AS .75 2.00
193 Chauncey Billups AS .40 1.00
194 Deron Williams AS .25 .60
195 Amare Stoudemire AS .25 .60
196 Pau Gasol AS .50 1.25
197 Steve Nash AS .60 1.50
198 Kevin Durant AS 1.25 3.00
199 Chris Kaman AS .25 .60
200 Tim Duncan AS .75 2.00

2009-10 Panini Season Update Gold

*GOLD: 5X TO 12X BASE HI
STATED PRINT RUN 24 SER.#'d SETS
35 Amare Stoudemire 3.00 8.00
79 Carlos Boozer 3.00 8.00
167 Chris Bosh 5.00 12.00
168 LeBron James 20.00 50.00

2009-10 Panini Season Update Silver

*SILVER: 2.5X TO 6X BASE HI
STATED PRINT RUN 99 SER.#'d SETS
35 Amare Stoudemire 1.50 4.00
79 Carlos Boozer 1.50 4.00
167 Chris Bosh 2.50 6.00
168 LeBron James 12.00 30.00

2009-10 Panini Season Update All-Star Patches

COMPLETE SET (5) 25.00 60.00
STATED PRINT RUN 499 SER.#'d SETS
1 Kobe Bryant 75.00 200.00
2 Dirk Nowitzki 15.00 40.00
3 Chris Bosh 8.00 20.00
4 LeBron James 75.00 200.00
5 Dwyane Wade 15.00 40.00

2009-10 Panini Season Update Christmas Cards Materials

PRINT RUN 499 SER.#'d SETS
*PRIME: .75X TO 2X BASE HI
PRIME PRINT RUN 25 SER.#'d SETS
1 Andre Miller 4.00 10.00
2 Amare Stoudemire 3.00 8.00
3 Anthony Carter 2.50 6.00
4 Arron Afflalo 2.50 6.00
5 Brandon Roy 5.00 12.00
6 Carlos Arroyo 3.00 8.00
7 Carmelo Anthony 6.00 15.00
8 Channing Frye 2.50 6.00
9 Chauncey Billups 5.00 12.00
10 Daequan Cook 2.50 6.00
11 Dorell Wright 2.50 6.00
12 Dwight Howard 5.00 12.00
13 Dwyane Wade 8.00 20.00
14 Earl Clark 2.50 6.00
15 Goran Dragic 12.00 30.00
16 J.J. Redick 4.00 10.00
17 J.R. Smith 4.00 10.00
18 Jameer Nelson 2.50 6.00
19 Jared Dudley 2.50 6.00
20 Jason Richardson 4.00 10.00
21 Jason Williams 3.00 8.00
22 Jeff Pendergraph 2.50 6.00
23 Jermaine O'Neal 4.00 10.00
24 Jerryd Bayless 2.50 6.00
25 Joel Anthony 4.00 10.00
26 LaMarcus Aldridge 4.00 10.00
27 Louis Amundson 2.50 6.00
28 Marcin Gortat 3.00 8.00
29 Mario Chalmers 3.00 8.00
30 Martell Webster 2.50 6.00
31 Matt Barnes 2.50 6.00
32 Michael Beasley 2.50 6.00
33 Mickael Pietrus 2.50 6.00
34 Quentin Richardson 2.50 6.00
35 Rashard Lewis 3.00 8.00
36 Robin Lopez 2.50 6.00
37 Ryan Anderson 2.50 6.00
38 Steve Nash 8.00 20.00
39 Ty Lawson 3.00 8.00
40 Udonis Haslem 2.50 6.00

2009-10 Panini Season Update Lakers Legacy

COMPLETE SET (10) 4.00 10.00
1 Kobe Bryant 4.00 10.00
2 Derek Fisher .60 1.50
3 Nick Van Exel .60 1.50
4 Pau Gasol 1.00 2.50
5 Robert Horry .50 1.25
6 Kareem Abdul-Jabbar 2.00 5.00
7 Gary Payton .75 2.00
8 Luke Walton .50 1.25
9 Lamar Odom .50 1.25
10 Andrew Bynum .40 1.00

2009-10 Panini Season Update Lakers Legacy Jerseys

COMPLETE SET (10) 25.00 60.00
1 Kobe Bryant 8.00 20.00
2 Derek Fisher 3.00 8.00
3 Nick Van Exel 3.00 8.00
4 Pau Gasol 3.00 8.00
5 Robert Horry 3.00 8.00
6 Kareem Abdul-Jabbar 10.00 25.00
7 Gary Payton 3.00 8.00
8 Luke Walton 3.00 8.00
9 Lamar Odom 3.00 8.00
10 Andrew Bynum 3.00 8.00

2009-10 Panini Season Update Lakers Legacy Jerseys Prime

*PRIME: 1.25X TO 3X HI COLUMN
STATED PRINT RUN 10 TO 49 SER.#'d SETS
1 Kobe Bryant/49 20.00 50.00
6 Kareem Abdul-Jabbar/49 20.00 50.00
10 Andrew Bynum/15 15.00 40.00

2009-10 Panini Season Update Playoff Debuts

COMPLETE SET (19) 8.00 20.00
*GOLD: 2X TO 5X BASE HI
GOLD PRINT RUN 24 SER.#'d SETS
*SILVER: 1X TO 2.5X BASE HI
SILVER PRINT RUN 99 SER.#'d SETS
1 Kevin Durant 2.50 6.00
2 Brandon Jennings .60 1.50
3 Robin Lopez .40 1.00
4 D.J. Augustin .40 1.00
5 Wesley Matthews .60 1.50
6 Taj Gibson .50 1.25
7 Nate Robinson .50 1.25
8 Russell Westbrook 1.25 3.00
9 Adam Morrison .40 1.00
10 DeJuan Blair .50 1.25
11 Jeff Teague .50 1.25
12 Jeff Pendergraph .40 1.00
13 J.J. Hickson .40 1.00
14 Rodrigue Beaubois .40 1.00
15 Jeff Green .50 1.25
16 Raymond Felton .40 1.00
17 Jamal Crawford .60 1.50
18 Ty Lawson .50 1.25
19 Ryan Anderson .40 1.00

2009-10 Panini Season Update Rookie Challenge

COMPLETE SET (16) 10.00 25.00
1 Stephen Curry 40.00 100.00
2 Tyreke Evans .60 1.50
3 Brandon Jennings .75 2.00
4 Anthony Morrow .50 1.25
5 Brook Lopez .75 2.00
6 Danilo Gallinari .60 1.50
7 DeJuan Blair .60 1.50
8 Eric Gordon .60 1.50
9 Jonas Jerebko .60 1.50
10 Jonny Flynn .50 1.25
11 Kevin Love .75 2.00
12 Marc Gasol .75 2.00
13 Michael Beasley .50 1.25
14 O.J. Mayo .50 1.25
15 Omri Casspi .50 1.25
16 Russell Westbrook 1.50 4.00

2009-10 Panini Season Update Rookie Challenge Jerseys

1 Stephen Curry 100.00 250.00
2 Tyreke Evans 1.50 4.00
3 Brandon Jennings 2.00 5.00
4 Anthony Morrow 2.00 5.00
5 Brook Lopez 3.00 8.00
6 Danilo Gallinari 2.50 6.00
7 DeJuan Blair 1.50 4.00
8 Eric Gordon 2.50 6.00
9 Jonas Jerebko 1.50 4.00
10 Jonny Flynn 1.25 3.00
11 Kevin Love 3.00 8.00
12 Marc Gasol 3.00 8.00
13 Michael Beasley 2.00 5.00
14 O.J. Mayo 2.00 5.00
15 Omri Casspi 1.25 3.00
16 Russell Westbrook 6.00 15.00

2009-10 Panini Season Update Rookie Challenge Jerseys Signatures

STATED PRINT RUN 25 SER.#'d SETS
1 Stephen Curry 1,500.00 3,000.00
2 Tyreke Evans 6.00 15.00
3 Brandon Jennings 8.00 20.00
7 DeJuan Blair 6.00 15.00
9 Jonas Jerebko 6.00 15.00
10 Jonny Flynn 5.00 12.00
11 Kevin Love 8.00 20.00
13 Michael Beasley 5.00 12.00
15 Omri Casspi 5.00 12.00

2009-10 Panini Season Update Rookie Challenge Signatures

PRINT RUN 49 SER.#'d SETS
1 Stephen Curry 1,000.00 2,000.00
2 Tyreke Evans 5.00 12.00
3 Brandon Jennings 6.00 15.00
7 DeJuan Blair 5.00 12.00
9 Jonas Jerebko 5.00 12.00
10 Jonny Flynn 4.00 10.00
11 Kevin Love 6.00 15.00
13 Michael Beasley 4.00 10.00
15 Omri Casspi 4.00 10.00
16 Russell Westbrook 30.00 80.00

2009-10 Panini Season Update Rookie Duals Signatures

STATED PRINT RUN 49 TO 99 SER.#'d SETS
1 B.Griffin/B.Jennings/49 25.00 60.00
2 B.Griffin/S.Curry/49 800.00 1,500.00
3 B.Griffin/T.Evans/49 25.00 60.00
4 T.Evans/B.Jennings/49 6.00 15.00
5 T.Evans/S.Curry/49 800.00 1,500.00
6 B.Jennings/S.Curry/49 800.00 1,500.00
7 S.Curry/D.Collison/49 800.00 1,500.00
8 B.Griffin/T.Griffin/49 25.00 60.00
9 T.Griffin/E.Clark/99 4.00 10.00
10 J.Harden/S.Ibaka/99 75.00 200.00
11 J.Harden/E.Maynor/99 40.00 100.00
12 S.Ibaka/E.Maynor/99 6.00 15.00
13 J.Harden/B.Mullens/99 25.00 60.00
14 S.Ibaka/B.Mullens/99 6.00 15.00
15 W.Ellington/T.Lawson/99 5.00 12.00
16 J.Flynn/W.Ellington/99 5.00 12.00
17 T.Lawson/J.Flynn/99 5.00 12.00
18 T.Gibson/T.Lawson/99 5.00 12.00
19 T.Gibson/J.Johnson/99 5.00 12.00
20 J.Johnson/J.Teague/99 5.00 12.00
21 T.Gibson/J.Teague/99 5.00 12.00
22 H.Thabeet/D.Carroll/99 5.00 12.00
23 H.Thabeet/S.Young/99 4.00 10.00
24 D.Carroll/S.Young/99 5.00 12.00
25 D.Carroll/D.DeRozan/99 30.00 80.00
26 A.Price/T.Hansbrough/99 5.00 12.00
27 DeRozan/Hansbrough/99 30.00 80.00
28 S.Curry/J.Hill/49 400.00 800.00
29 J.Hill/T.Williams/99 4.00 10.00
30 T.Williams/G.Henderson/99 4.00 10.00
31 J.Harden/T.Williams/99 40.00 100.00
32 J.Holiday/T.Williams/99 6.00 15.00
33 T.Williams/A.Daye/99 4.00 10.00
34 J.Flynn/J.Hill/99 4.00 10.00
35 J.Harden/J.Teague/99 40.00 100.00
36 D.Collison/J.Teague/99 6.00 15.00
37 T.Douglas/L.Hudson/99 4.00 10.00
38 T.Douglas/Ellington/99 5.00 12.00
39 T.Hansbrough/B.Mullens/99 5.00 12.00
40 T.Hansbrough/L.Hudson/99 5.00 12.00
41 R.Beaubois/T.Evans/49 5.00 12.00
42 S.Curry/R.Beaubois/49 800.00 1,500.00
43 R.Beaubois/O.Casspi/99 4.00 10.00
44 T.Evans/O.Casspi/49 4.00 10.00
45 O.Casspi/J.Pendergraph/99 4.00 10.00
46 J.Jerebko/A.Daye/99 5.00 12.00
47 J.Jerebko/D.Summers/99 5.00 12.00
48 D.Summers/A.Daye/99 4.00 10.00
49 O.Casspi/J.Jerebko/99 4.00 10.00
50 D.Collison/M.Thornton/99 6.00 15.00
51 M.Thornton/D.Brown/99 5.00 12.00
52 J.Holiday/J.Meeks/99 6.00 15.00
53 J.Pendergraph/P.Mills/99 8.00 20.00
54 O.Casspi/J.Brockman/99 4.00 10.00
55 T.Evans/J.Brockman/49 5.00 12.00
56 J.Brockman/T.Griffin/99 4.00 10.00
57 D.Andersen/J.Hill/99 4.00 10.00
58 J.Hill/C.Budinger/99 4.00 10.00
59 J.Taylor/C.Budinger/99 4.00 10.00
60 J.Taylor/D.Andersen/99 4.00 10.00
61 J.Pendergraph/D.Cunningham/99 4.00 10.00
62 D.Cunningham/P.Mills/99 8.00 20.00
63 W.Matthews/S.Gaines/99 6.00 15.00
64 A.Price/J.Meeks/99 4.00 10.00
65 B.Jennings/J.Meeks/49 6.00 15.00
66 D.Blair/D.Summers/99 5.00 12.00
67 D.Blair/E.Clark/99 5.00 12.00
68 D.Blair/J.Johnson/99 5.00 12.00
69 D.DeRozan/D.Blair/99 30.00 80.00
70 H.Thabeet/S.Ibaka/99 6.00 15.00
71 W.Matthews/T.Douglas/99 6.00 15.00
72 W.Ellington/L.Hudson/99 5.00 12.00
73 L.Hudson/S.Gaines/99 4.00 10.00
74 J.Holiday/C.Budinger/99 6.00 15.00
75 R.Beaubois/DeRozan/99 30.00 80.00

2009-10 Panini Season Update Rookie Triples Signatures

STATED PRINT RUN 25 TO 49 SER.#'d SETS
1 Evans/Curry/Jennings/25 500.00 1,000.00
2 Harden/Maynor/Ibaka/49 50.00 120.00
3 Griffin/Blair/DeRozan/25 75.00 200.00
4 Collison/Beaubois/Flynn/49 8.00 20.00
5 Hill/Budinger/Taylor/49 8.00 20.00
6 Gibson/Lawson/Williams/49 8.00 20.00
7 Hnsbrgh/Price/Hndrsn/49 8.00 20.00
8 Griffin/Griffin/Clark/25 20.00 50.00
9 Daye/Jerebko/Summers/49 8.00 20.00
10 Thabeet/Young/Carroll/49 8.00 20.00
11 Evans/Casspi/Brock/25 8.00 20.00
12 Hnsbrgh/Mullens/Meeks/49 8.00 20.00
13 Collison/Thornton/Brown/49 8.00 20.00
14 Pndrgrph/Cnghm/Mills/49 10.00 25.00
15 Curry/Flynn/Lawson/25 400.00 800.00
16 Clark/Daye/Johnson/49 8.00 20.00
17 Holiday/Teague/Beaubois/49 8.00 20.00
18 Douglas/Hudson/Meeks/49 8.00 20.00
19 Blair/DeRozan/Carroll/49 30.00 80.00
20 Matthews/Douglas/Hudson/49 8.00 20.00
21 Jennings/Collison/Flynn/25 8.00 20.00
22 Williams/Henderson/Teague/49 8.00 20.00
23 Griffin/Thabeet/Harden/25 75.00 200.00
24 Flynn/Clark/Holiday/49 8.00 20.00
25 Hnsbrgh/Elngtn/Lawson/49 8.00 20.00

2009-10 Panini Season Update Signatures

STATED PRINT RUN ONE TO 100 SER.#'d SETS
28 Darryl Dawkins/99 12.00 30.00
33 Mark Price/50 12.00 30.00
34 Mark Price/25 15.00 40.00
35 Robert Horry/50 12.00 30.00
37 Hakeem Olajuwon/50 20.00 50.00
38 Hakeem Olajuwon/25 25.00 60.00
39 Joe Dumars/50 8.00 20.00
40 Joe Dumars/25 10.00 25.00
41 Dominique Wilkins/50 12.00 30.00
42 Dominique Wilkins/25 15.00 40.00
44 Elgin Baylor/25 15.00 40.00
45 Sidney Moncrief/50 6.00 15.00
46 Sidney Moncrief/25 8.00 20.00

2010-11 Panini Season Update

COMPLETE SET (200) 20.00 50.00
EXCH.EXPIRATION 1/20/2013
1 Glen Davis .25 .60
2 Jeff Green .30 .75
3 Kevin Garnett 1.00 2.50
4 Paul Pierce .60 1.50
5 Rajon Rondo .50 1.25
6 Ray Allen .60 1.50
7 Shaquille O'Neal 1.50 4.00
8 Anthony Morrow .25 .60
9 Brook Lopez .30 .75
10 Deron Williams .30 .75
11 Kris Humphries .25 .60
12 Sasha Vujacic .25 .60
13 Travis Outlaw .30 .75
14 Amare Stoudemire .40 1.00
15 Carmelo Anthony .60 1.50
16 Chauncey Billups .50 1.25
17 Ronny Turiaf .25 .60
18 Shawne Williams .25 .60
19 Toney Douglas .25 .60
20 Andre Iguodala .40 1.00
21 Andres Nocioni .25 .60
22 Elton Brand .30 .75
23 Jrue Holiday .50 1.25
24 Louis Williams .25 .60
25 Spencer Hawes .25 .60
26 Thaddeus Young .25 .60
27 Andrea Bargnani .25 .60
28 DeMar DeRozan .60 1.50
29 Jose Calderon .25 .60
30 Leandro Barbosa .30 .75
31 Linas Kleiza .25 .60
32 Sonny Weems .25 .60
33 Carlos Boozer .30 .75
34 Derrick Rose .75 2.00
35 Joakim Noah .40 1.00
36 Kyle Korver .30 .75
37 Luol Deng .30 .75
38 Ronnie Brewer .25 .60
39 Taj Gibson .25 .60
40 Anderson Varejao .25 .60
41 Antawn Jamison .30 .75
42 Daniel Gibson .25 .60
43 J.J. Hickson .25 .60
44 Baron Davis .40 1.00
45 Ramon Sessions .25 .60
46 Austin Daye .25 .60
47 Ben Gordon .30 .75
48 Charlie Villanueva .25 .60
49 Richard Hamilton .50 1.25
50 Rodney Stuckey .25 .60
51 Tayshaun Prince .40 1.00
52 Tracy McGrady .60 1.50
53 Danny Granger .25 .60
54 Darren Collison .25 .60
55 Jeff Foster .25 .60
56 Mike Dunleavy .25 .60
57 Roy Hibbert .30 .75
58 T.J. Ford .25 .60
59 Tyler Hansbrough .25 .60
60 Andrew Bogut .30 .75
61 Brandon Jennings .25 .60
62 Carlos Delfino .25 .60
63 Corey Maggette .30 .75
64 Drew Gooden .25 .60
65 Ersan Ilyasova .30 .75
66 John Salmons .25 .60
67 Luc Mbah a Moute .25 .60
68 Al Horford .40 1.00
69 Jamal Crawford .40 1.00
70 Jeff Teague .25 .60
71 Joe Johnson .40 1.00
72 Josh Smith .25 .60
73 Marvin Williams .25 .60
74 Boris Diaw .30 .75
75 D.J. Augustin .25 .60
76 Gerald Henderson .25 .60
77 Stephen Jackson .30 .75
78 Tyrus Thomas .25 .60
79 Chris Bosh .50 1.25
80 Dwyane Wade .75 2.00
81 Eddie House .25 .60
82 LeBron James 3.00 8.00
83 Mike Miller .30 .75
84 Mike Bibby .40 1.00
85 Udonis Haslem .30 .75
86 Brandon Bass .25 .60
87 Dwight Howard .50 1.25
88 Gilbert Arenas .30 .75
89 Hedo Turkoglu .30 .75
90 J.J. Redick .40 1.00
91 Jameer Nelson .25 .60
92 Jason Richardson .40 1.00
93 Andray Blatche .25 .60
94 JaVale McGee .30 .75
95 Kirk Hinrich .30 .75
96 Nick Young .25 .60
97 Rashard Lewis .30 .75
98 Caron Butler .25 .60
99 Dirk Nowitzki 1.00 2.50
100 Jason Kidd .60 1.50
101 Jason Terry .30 .75
102 Peja Stojakovic .30 .75
103 Corey Brewer .25 .60
104 Shawn Marion .40 1.00
105 Tyson Chandler .30 .75
106 Goran Dragic .50 1.25
107 Kevin Martin .30 .75
108 Kyle Lowry .40 1.00
109 Luis Scola .30 .75
110 Yao Ming .75 2.00
111 Marc Gasol .40 1.00
112 Shane Battier .30 .75
113 Mike Conley Jr. .30 .75
114 O.J. Mayo .25 .60
115 Rudy Gay .40 1.00
116 Zach Randolph .40 1.00
117 Chris Paul .75 2.00
118 David West .40 1.00
119 Emeka Okafor .30 .75
120 Carl Landry .25 .60
121 Trevor Ariza .25 .60
122 DeJuan Blair .25 .60
123 George Hill .30 .75
124 Manu Ginobili .75 2.00
125 Richard Jefferson .30 .75
126 Tim Duncan 1.00 2.50
127 Tony Parker .60 1.50
128 Al Harrington .30 .75
129 Arron Afflalo .25 .60
130 Danilo Gallinari .25 .60
131 Raymond Felton .40 1.00
132 Wilson Chandler .25 .60
133 Chris Andersen .40 1.00
134 J.R. Smith .40 1.00
135 Kenyon Martin .40 1.00
136 Nene .30 .75
137 Anthony Randolph .25 .60
138 Darko Milicic .25 .60
139 Kevin Love .40 1.00
140 Luke Ridnour .25 .60
141 Martell Webster .30 .75
142 Michael Beasley .30 .75
143 Andre Miller .30 .75
144 Gerald Wallace .30 .75
145 Brandon Roy .50 1.25
146 LaMarcus Aldridge .40 1.00
147 Nicolas Batum .30 .75
148 Rudy Fernandez .25 .60
149 Wesley Matthews .25 .60
150 James Harden 1.00 2.50
151 Kendrick Perkins .25 .60
152 Kevin Durant 1.50 4.00
153 Russell Westbrook .60 1.50
154 Serge Ibaka .30 .75
155 Al Jefferson .25 .60
156 Andrei Kirilenko .30 .75
157 C.J. Miles .25 .60
158 Devin Harris .25 .60
159 Paul Millsap .30 .75
160 Raja Bell .30 .75
161 Andris Biedrins .25 .60
162 Al Thornton .25 .60
163 David Lee .25 .60
164 Dorell Wright .25 .60
165 Monta Ellis .30 .75
166 Reggie Williams .30 .75
167 Stephen Curry 3.00 8.00
168 Mo Williams .30 .75
169 Blake Griffin .40 1.00
170 Chris Kaman .25 .60
171 Eric Gordon .30 .75
172 Ryan Gomes .25 .60
173 Andrew Bynum .25 .60
174 Derek Fisher .40 1.00
175 Kobe Bryant 3.00 8.00
176 Lamar Odom .30 .75
177 Pau Gasol .60 1.50
178 Ron Artest .40 1.00
179 Channing Frye .25 .60
180 Aaron Brooks .25 .60
181 Grant Hill .60 1.50
182 Marcin Gortat .30 .75
183 Steve Nash .75 2.00
184 Vince Carter .75 2.00
185 Beno Udrih .25 .60
186 Marcus Thornton .25 .60
187 Francisco Garcia .25 .60
188 Omri Casspi .25 .60
189 Samuel Dalembert .25 .60
190 Tyreke Evans .30 .75
191 Blake Griffin .40 1.00
192 Ray Allen .60 1.50
193 Kobe Bryant 3.00 8.00
194 Kevin Durant 1.50 4.00
195 Kevin Love .40 1.00
196 George Karl .40 1.00
197 Blake Griffin .40 1.00
198 Derrick Rose .75 2.00
199 Lamar Odom .30 .75
200 Kevin Love .40 1.00

2010-11 Panini Season Update Gold

*GOLD: 5X TO 12X BASE HI
STATED PRINT RUN 24 SER.#'d SETS

2010-11 Panini Season Update Silver

*SILVER: 2.5X TO 6X BASE HI
STATED PRINT RUN 99 SER.#'d SETS

2010-11 Panini Season Update All-Stars

COMPLETE SET (25) 8.00 20.00
1 Al Horford .40 1.00
2 Amare Stoudemire .40 1.00
3 Carmelo Anthony .60 1.50
4 Chauncey Billups .50 1.25
5 Chris Bosh .50 1.25
6 Chris Kaman .25 .60
7 David Lee .25 .60
8 Deron Williams .30 .75
9 Derrick Rose .75 2.00
10 Dirk Nowitzki 1.00 2.50
11 Dwight Howard .50 1.25
12 Gerald Wallace .30 .75
13 Jason Kidd .60 1.50
14 Joe Johnson .40 1.00
15 Kevin Durant 1.50 4.00
16 Kevin Garnett 1.00 2.50
17 LeBron James 3.00 8.00
18 Pau Gasol .60 1.50
19 Paul Pierce .60 1.50
20 Rajon Rondo .50 1.25
21 Steve Nash .75 2.00
22 Tim Duncan 1.00 2.50
23 Zach Randolph .40 1.00
24 Kobe Bryant 3.00 8.00
25 Chris Paul .75 2.00

2010-11 Panini Season Update All-Stars Materials

1 Al Horford 2.50 6.00
2 Amare Stoudemire 2.50 6.00
3 Carmelo Anthony 4.00 10.00
4 Chauncey Billups 3.00 8.00
5 Chris Bosh 3.00 8.00
6 Chris Kaman 1.50 4.00
7 David Lee 1.50 4.00
8 Deron Williams 2.00 5.00
9 Derrick Rose 5.00 12.00
10 Dirk Nowitzki 6.00 15.00
11 Dwight Howard 3.00 8.00
12 Gerald Wallace 2.00 5.00
13 Jason Kidd 4.00 10.00
14 Joe Johnson 2.50 6.00
15 Kevin Durant 6.00 15.00
16 Kevin Garnett 6.00 15.00
17 LeBron James 10.00 25.00
18 Pau Gasol 4.00 10.00
19 Paul Pierce 4.00 10.00
20 Rajon Rondo 3.00 8.00
21 Steve Nash 5.00 12.00
22 Tim Duncan 6.00 15.00
23 Zach Randolph 2.50 6.00
24 Kobe Bryant 12.00 30.00
25 Chris Paul 5.00 12.00

2010-11 Panini Season Update Green Week Jerseys

STATED PRINT RUN 10 TO 799 SER.#'d SETS
2 Anthony Carter/799 1.50 4.00
3 Arron Afflalo/799 1.50 4.00
4 Brandon Bass/799 1.50 4.00
5 Brandon Roy/99 3.00 8.00
6 Caron Butler/25 2.00 5.00
7 Chauncey Billups/50 2.00 5.00
8 Chris Andersen/699 2.50 6.00
9 Dante Cunningham/799 1.50 4.00
10 Dirk Nowitzki/399 6.00 15.00
11 Dwight Howard/99 3.00 8.00
12 J.R. Smith/499 2.50 6.00
13 Jameer Nelson/449 1.50 4.00
14 Jason Terry/649 2.00 5.00
15 Juwan Howard/799 2.00 5.00
16 LaMarcus Aldridge/799 2.50 6.00
17 Marcin Gortat/749 2.00 5.00
18 Martell Webster/799 2.00 5.00
19 Mickael Pietrus/349 1.50 4.00
20 Nene/699 2.00 5.00
21 Nicolas Batum/799 2.00 5.00
22 Rashard Lewis/799 2.00 5.00
23 Rudy Fernandez/749 1.50 4.00
24 Ryan Anderson/799 2.00 5.00
25 Shawn Marion/799 2.50 6.00
26 Ty Lawson/799 1.50 4.00
27 Vince Carter/799 5.00 12.00
28 Erick Dampier/799 1.50 4.00
29 Matt Barnes/799 1.50 4.00
30 Jerryd Bayless/799 1.50 4.00

2010-11 Panini Season Update Green Week Jerseys Prime

*PRIME: 1X TO 2.5X BASE HI
STATED PRINT RUN ONE TO 49 SER.#'d SETS
1 Andre Miller/49 5.00 12.00
8 Chris Andersen/29 8.00 20.00
20 Nene/15 6.00 15.00

2010-11 Panini Season Update Rookie Challenge

COMPLETE SET (15) 5.00 12.00
1 DeMarcus Cousins .75 2.00
2 Derrick Favors .40 1.00
3 Eric Bledsoe .50 1.25
4 Gary Neal .30 .75
5 Greg Monroe .30 .75
6 Landry Fields .25 .60
7 Wesley Johnson .25 .60
8 Brandon Jennings .25 .60
9 DeJuan Blair .25 .60
10 DeMar DeRozan .60 1.50
11 James Harden 1.00 2.50
12 Jrue Holiday .50 1.25
13 Serge Ibaka .30 .75
14 Stephen Curry 8.00 20.00
15 Wesley Matthews .25 .60

2010-11 Panini Season Update Rookie Challenge Materials

STATED PRINT RUN 799 SER.#'d SETS
1 DeMarcus Cousins 6.00 15.00
2 Derrick Favors 3.00 8.00
3 Eric Bledsoe 4.00 10.00
4 Gary Neal 2.50 6.00
5 Greg Monroe 2.50 6.00
6 Landry Fields 2.00 5.00
7 Wesley Johnson 2.00 5.00
8 Brandon Jennings 2.00 5.00
9 DeJuan Blair 2.00 5.00
10 DeMar DeRozan 5.00 12.00
11 James Harden 8.00 20.00
12 Jrue Holiday 4.00 10.00
13 Serge Ibaka 2.50 6.00
14 Stephen Curry 25.00 60.00
15 Wesley Matthews 2.00 5.00

2010-11 Panini Season Update Rookie Challenge Materials Signatures

STATED PRINT RUN 25 SER.#'d SETS
1 DeMarcus Cousins 25.00 60.00
2 Derrick Favors 8.00 20.00
3 Eric Bledsoe 10.00 25.00
4 Gary Neal 6.00 15.00
5 Greg Monroe 6.00 15.00
6 Landry Fields 5.00 12.00
7 Wesley Johnson 5.00 12.00
8 Brandon Jennings 5.00 12.00
9 DeJuan Blair 5.00 12.00
10 DeMar DeRozan 50.00 120.00
11 James Harden 60.00 150.00
12 Jrue Holiday 10.00 25.00
13 Serge Ibaka 6.00 15.00
14 Stephen Curry 600.00 1,200.00
15 Wesley Matthews 5.00 12.00

2010-11 Panini Season Update Rookie Challenge Signatures

STATED PRINT RUN 49 SER.#'d SETS
1 DeMarcus Cousins 10.00 25.00
2 Derrick Favors 5.00 12.00
3 Eric Bledsoe 6.00 15.00
4 Gary Neal 4.00 10.00
5 Greg Monroe 4.00 10.00
6 Landry Fields 3.00 8.00
7 Wesley Johnson 3.00 8.00
8 Brandon Jennings 8.00 20.00
9 DeJuan Blair 5.00 12.00
10 DeMar DeRozan 25.00 60.00
11 James Harden 40.00 100.00
12 Jrue Holiday 6.00 15.00
13 Serge Ibaka 6.00 15.00
14 Stephen Curry 500.00 1,000.00
15 Wesley Matthews 6.00 15.00

2010-11 Panini Season Update Rookie Duals Signatures

STATED PRINT RUN 10 TO 99 SER.#'d SETS
4 E.Turner/D.Favors 5.00 12.00
5 E.Turner/D.Cousins 10.00 25.00
6 E.Turner/W.Johnson 4.00 10.00
7 D.Favors/W.Johnson 5.00 12.00
8 D.Favors/D.Cousins 10.00 25.00
9 W.Johnson/D.Cousins 10.00 25.00
10 W.Johnson/E.Udoh 3.00 8.00
11 D.Cousins/E.Udoh 10.00 25.00
12 D.Cousins/G.Monroe 10.00 25.00
13 E.Udoh/E.Monroe 4.00 10.00
14 E.Udoh/A.Aminu 4.00 10.00
15 G.Monroe/A.Aminu 4.00 10.00
16 G.Monroe/G.Hayward 12.00 30.00
17 A.Aminu/G.Hayward 12.00 30.00
18 A.Aminu/P.George 25.00 60.00
19 G.Hayward/P.George 40.00 100.00
20 G.Hayward/C.Aldrich 12.00 30.00
21 P.George/C.Aldrich 25.00 60.00
22 P.George/X.Henry 25.00 60.00
23 C.Aldrich/X.Henry 3.00 8.00
24 C.Aldrich/E.Davis 4.00 10.00
25 X.Henry/E.Davis 4.00 10.00
26 X.Henry/P.Patterson 4.00 10.00
27 P.Patterson/E.Davis 4.00 10.00
28 E.Davis/L.Sanders 4.00 10.00
29 P.Patterson/L.Sanders 4.00 10.00
30 L.Babbitt/E.Williams 3.00 8.00
31 L.Babbitt/A.Johnson 3.00 8.00
32 E.Bledsoe/Warren 6.00 15.00
33 E.Bledsoe/D.Orton 6.00 15.00
34 E.Bledsoe/P.Patterson 6.00 15.00
35 C.Brackins/E.Turner 4.00 10.00
36 T.Booker/J.Crawford 3.00 8.00
37 T.Booker/Seraphin 3.00 8.00
38 D.James/D.Pittman 3.00 8.00
39 D.James/A.Bradley 5.00 12.00
40 A.Bradley/Harangody 5.00 12.00
41 A.Bradley/S.Erden 5.00 12.00
42 D.Jones/Q.Pondexter 3.00 8.00
43 J.Crawford/Seraphin 3.00 8.00
44 G.Vasquez/X.Henry 3.00 8.00
45 G.Vasquez/D.Orton 3.00 8.00
46 D.Orton/L.Hayward 3.00 8.00
47 L.Hayward/W.Johnson 3.00 8.00
48 L.Hayward/N.Pekovic 5.00 12.00
49 Whiteside/D.Cousins 10.00 25.00
50 T.White/G.Monroe 4.00 10.00
51 A.Rautins/L.Fields 3.00 8.00
52 A.Rautins/T.Mozgov 4.00 10.00
53 L.Fields/T.Mozgov 4.00 10.00
54 Stephenson/P.George 25.00 60.00
55 Stephenson/D.Pittman 5.00 12.00
56 D.Ebanks/D.Caracter 3.00 8.00
57 G.Lawal/S.Alabi 3.00 8.00
58 J.Evans/G.Hayward 12.00 30.00
59 G.Neal/G.Forbes 4.00 10.00
60 J.Lin/O.Asik 60.00 150.00
61 J.Lin/E.Udoh 60.00 150.00
62 W.Warren/C.Aldrich 3.00 8.00
63 W.Warren/X.Henry 3.00 8.00
64 J.Anderson/G.Neal 4.00 10.00
65 O.Asik/S.Erden 5.00 12.00
66 D.Jones/J.Crawford 3.00 8.00
67 D.Orton/H.Whiteside 6.00 15.00
68 Whiteside/A.Johnson 6.00 15.00
69 A.Johnson/T.White 3.00 8.00
70 T.White/A.Rautins 3.00 8.00
71 L.Fields/Stephenson 5.00 12.00
72 Stephenson/Ebanks 5.00 12.00
73 D.Ebanks/G.Lawal 3.00 8.00
74 S.Alabi/L.Harangody 3.00 8.00
75 Harangody/Warren 3.00 8.00

2010-11 Panini Season Update Signatures

STATED PRINT RUN 10 TO 299 SER.#'d SETS
2 Jeff Green/199 4.00 10.00
9 Brook Lopez/99 4.00 10.00
11 Kris Humphries/299 3.00 8.00
19 Toney Douglas/299 3.00 8.00
24 Louis Williams/199 4.00 10.00
27 Andrea Bargnani/99 3.00 8.00
28 DeMar DeRozan/25 12.00 30.00
29 Jose Calderon/199 3.00 8.00
32 Sonny Weems/299 3.00 8.00
38 Ronnie Brewer/299 3.00 8.00
41 Antawn Jamison/99 4.00 10.00
42 Daniel Gibson/99 3.00 8.00
46 Austin Daye/299 3.00 8.00
48 Charlie Villanueva/99 3.00 8.00
56 Mike Dunleavy/99 3.00 8.00
57 Roy Hibbert/299 4.00 10.00
58 T.J. Ford/199 3.00 8.00
59 Tyler Hansbrough/99 3.00 8.00
70 Jeff Teague/299 3.00 8.00
72 Josh Smith/99 3.00 8.00
76 Gerald Henderson/299 3.00 8.00
77 Stephen Jackson/199 4.00 10.00
90 J.J. Redick/99 5.00 12.00
91 Jameer Nelson/25 3.00 8.00
94 JaVale McGee/299 4.00 10.00
106 Goran Dragic/99 15.00 40.00
112 Shane Battier/25 4.00 10.00
115 Rudy Gay/299 5.00 12.00
122 DeJuan Blair/299 3.00 8.00
123 George Hill/299 4.00 10.00
131 Raymond Felton/49 3.00 8.00
134 J.R. Smith/299 3.00 8.00
138 Darko Milicic/299 3.00 8.00
140 Luke Ridnour/299 3.00 8.00
143 Andre Miller/299 4.00 10.00
149 Wesley Matthews/299 3.00 8.00
150 James Harden/49 50.00 120.00
152 Kevin Durant/24 75.00 200.00
154 Serge Ibaka/299 4.00 10.00
156 Andrei Kirilenko/99 3.00 8.00
158 Devin Harris/25 3.00 8.00
163 David Lee/25 3.00 8.00
165 Monta Ellis/299 4.00 10.00
167 Stephen Curry/99 500.00 1,000.00
169 Blake Griffin/15 25.00 60.00
171 Eric Gordon/299 4.00 10.00
172 Ryan Gomes/299 3.00 8.00
175 Kobe Bryant/49 1,500.00 3,000.00
180 Aaron Brooks/299 3.00 8.00
185 Beno Udrih/299 3.00 8.00
186 Marcus Thornton/299 3.00 8.00
188 Omri Casspi/299 3.00 8.00
189 Samuel Dalembert/299 3.00 8.00
190 Tyreke Evans/99 4.00 10.00
193 Kobe Bryant/49 1,500.00 3,000.00
194 Kevin Durant/24 125.00 300.00

2010-11 Panini Season Update Throwback Threads

STATED PRINT RUN 199 TO 799 SER.#'d SETS
1 Jermaine O'Neal/799 3.00 8.00
2 Dikembe Mutombo/299 5.00 12.00
3 Tracy McGrady/799 5.00 12.00
4 Larry Johnson/299 4.00 10.00
5 Stephen Jackson/499 2.50 6.00
6 Scottie Pippen/399 8.00 20.00
7 Raja Bell/799 2.50 6.00
8 Toni Kukoc/399 3.00 8.00
9 Marcin Gortat/499 2.50 6.00
10 Kelly Tripucka/299 2.00 5.00
11 Jason Kidd/499 5.00 12.00
12 Ron Harper/399 3.00 8.00
13 Amare Stoudemire/199 3.00 8.00
14 Chuck Person/299 2.50 6.00
15 Tyson Chandler/599 2.50 6.00
16 Xavier McDaniel/299 2.50 6.00
17 Raymond Felton/299 2.00 5.00
18 Moses Malone/299 5.00 12.00
19 Trevor Ariza/499 2.00 5.00
20 Tom Chambers/299 3.00 8.00

2010-11 Panini Season Update Throwback Threads Prime

*PRIME: 1X TO 2.5X BASE HI
STATED PRINT RUN 25 TO 49 SER.#'d SETS

2012-13 Panini Signatures

PRINT RUNS B/WN 10-99 COPIES PER
SOME CARDS ARE NOT SERIAL #'d
NO PRICING ON QTY 15 OR LESS
EXCHANGE DEADLINE 01/24/2014
1A Anthony Davis/49 75.00 200.00
1B Anthony Davis/25 VAR 100.00 250.00
2A Kyrie Irving/49 75.00 200.00
2B Kyrie Irving/25 VAR 100.00 250.00
21 Norris Cole/99 3.00 8.00
23 Tobias Harris/99 10.00 25.00
27 Nando De Colo 3.00 8.00
29 Kent Bazemore 5.00 12.00
31 Orlando Johnson 3.00 8.00
32 Jeff Taylor 3.00 8.00
35 Draymond Green 30.00 80.00
38 Tyler Zeller 3.00 8.00
41 Andrew Nicholson 3.00 8.00
42 Chris Copeland 3.00 8.00
43 Gustavo Ayon 3.00 8.00
45A Jimmy Butler 60.00 150.00
45B Jimmy Butler VAR 60.00 150.00
46 Tornike Shengelia 3.00 8.00
47 Jan Vesely 3.00 8.00
48 Ben Hansbrough 3.00 8.00
50 Mirza Teletovic 6.00 15.00
52 E'Twaun Moore 4.00 10.00
55 Victor Claver 3.00 8.00
57 Marquis Teague 3.00 8.00
59 Bernard James 3.00 8.00
60 Nolan Smith 3.00 8.00
62 Brian Roberts 3.00 8.00
63 Donatas Motiejunas 4.00 10.00
64 Jared Cunningham 3.00 8.00
65 Viacheslav Kravtsov 3.00 8.00
74 Alan Anderson 3.00 8.00
83 Alonzo Gee/99 3.00 8.00
85 Dorell Wright 3.00 8.00
96 Carlos Delfino 3.00 8.00
98 Corey Brewer 3.00 8.00
105 Johan Petro 3.00 8.00
113 Trevor Booker 3.00 8.00
116 Jason Maxiell 3.00 8.00
119A Marvin Williams 3.00 8.00
119B Marvin Williams VAR/99 3.00 8.00
122A Nick Collison/49 3.00 8.00
123 Nikola Pekovic 3.00 8.00
129 Ronnie Brewer 3.00 8.00
131A Kobe Bryant/75 400.00 800.00
131B Kobe Bryant/49 VAR 400.00 800.00
132A Blake Griffin/49 12.00 30.00
132B Blake Griffin/25 VAR 30.00 80.00
133A Kevin Durant/49 60.00 150.00
138 Doug Christie 3.00 8.00
140 Jim Jackson 4.00 10.00
147 Larry Bird/25 30.00 60.00
157 C.J. Watson 3.00 8.00
161 Anthony Morrow 3.00 8.00
173 Zaza Pachulia 3.00 8.00
174 Toney Douglas 3.00 8.00
176 Luc Mbah a Moute 3.00 8.00
182 Sean Elliott 6.00 15.00
184 Tim Hardaway 8.00 20.00
188 Anthony Mason 4.00 10.00
190 Mark Aguirre 4.00 10.00

2012-13 Panini Signatures Die Cut Autographs

PRINT RUNS B/WN 10-99 COPIES PER
SOME CARDS ARE NOT SERIAL #'d
NO PRICING ON QTY 15 OR LESS
EXCHANGE DEADLINE 01/24/2014
1 Anthony Davis/49 150.00 400.00
2 Kyrie Irving/99 40.00 100.00
27 Nando De Colo 3.00 8.00
29 Kent Bazemore 5.00 12.00
31 Orlando Johnson 3.00 8.00
32 Jeff Taylor 3.00 8.00
35 Draymond Green 40.00 100.00
38 Tyler Zeller 3.00 8.00
41 Andrew Nicholson 3.00 8.00
42 Chris Copeland 3.00 8.00
43 Gustavo Ayon 3.00 8.00
45 Jimmy Butler EXCH 30.00 80.00
46 Tornike Shengelia 3.00 8.00
47 Jan Vesely 3.00 8.00
48 Ben Hansbrough 3.00 8.00
49 Kendall Marshall/25 4.00 10.00
50 Mirza Teletovic 4.00 10.00
52 E'Twaun Moore 4.00 10.00
55 Victor Claver 3.00 8.00
59 Bernard James 3.00 8.00
60 Nolan Smith 3.00 8.00
62 Brian Roberts 3.00 8.00
63 Donatas Motiejunas 4.00 10.00
64 Jared Cunningham 3.00 8.00
65 Viacheslav Kravtsov 3.00 8.00
74 Alan Anderson 3.00 8.00
83 Alonzo Gee 3.00 8.00
85 Dorell Wright 3.00 8.00
96 Carlos Delfino 3.00 8.00
98 Corey Brewer 3.00 8.00
105 Johan Petro 3.00 8.00
119 Marvin Williams 3.00 8.00
129 Ronnie Brewer 3.00 8.00
131 Kobe Bryant/49 400.00 800.00
132 Blake Griffin/25 15.00 40.00
133 Kevin Durant/49 75.00 150.00
138 Doug Christie 3.00 8.00
140 Jim Jackson 4.00 10.00
147 Larry Bird/25 EXCH 40.00 100.00

2012-13 Panini Signatures Die Cut Autographs Red

PRINT RUNS B/WN 5-49 COPIES PER
NO PRICING ON QTY 15 OR LESS
EXCHANGE DEADLINE 01/24/2014
1 Anthony Davis/25 200.00 500.00
2 Kyrie Irving/25 60.00 150.00
20 Iman Shumpert/25 EXCH 5.00 12.00
22 Alec Burks/49 5.00 12.00
24 Isaiah Thomas/49 6.00 15.00
27 Nando De Colo/49 3.00 8.00
29 Kent Bazemore/49 5.00 12.00
31 Orlando Johnson/49 3.00 8.00
32 Jeff Taylor/49 3.00 8.00
35 Draymond Green/49 50.00 120.00
41 Andrew Nicholson/49 3.00 8.00
43 Gustavo Ayon/49 3.00 8.00
44 MarShon Brooks/49 EXCH 3.00 8.00
45 Jimmy Butler/49 25.00 60.00
47 Jan Vesely/49 3.00 8.00
48 Ben Hansbrough/49 3.00 8.00
52 E'Twaun Moore/49 4.00 10.00
54 Jon Leuer/49 3.00 8.00
55 Victor Claver/49 3.00 8.00

59 Bernard James/49 3.00 8.00
60 Nolan Smith/49 3.00 8.00
62 Brian Roberts/49 3.00 8.00
64 Jared Cunningham/49 3.00 8.00
65 Viacheslav Kravtsov/49 3.00 8.00
83 Alonzo Gee/25 4.00 10.00
85 Dorell Wright/25 4.00 10.00
98 Corey Brewer/25 4.00 10.00
105 Johan Petro/25 4.00 10.00
131 Kobe Bryant/25 500.00 1,000.00
133 Kevin Durant/25 100.00 200.00
138 Doug Christie/25 4.00 10.00

2012-13 Panini Signatures Red

PRINT RUNS B/WN 5-49 COPIES PER
SOME CARDS ARE NOT SERIAL #'d
NO PRICING ON QTY 15 OR LESS
EXCHANGE DEADLINE 01/24/2014
1A Anthony Davis/25 100.00 250.00
20 Iman Shumpert/49 EXCH 4.00 10.00
22 Alec Burks/49 5.00 12.00
24 Isaiah Thomas/49 6.00 15.00
25 Evan Fournier/49 EXCH 5.00 12.00
27 Nando De Colo/49 3.00 8.00
31 Orlando Johnson/49 3.00 8.00
32 Jeff Taylor/49 3.00 8.00
35 Draymond Green/49 40.00 100.00
38 Tyler Zeller/49 3.00 8.00
41 Andrew Nicholson/49 3.00 8.00
42 Chris Copeland/49 3.00 8.00
43 Gustavo Ayon/49 3.00 8.00
44 MarShon Brooks/49 EXCH 3.00 8.00
45A Jimmy Butler/49 EXCH 30.00 80.00
45B Jimmy Butler/49 VAR EXCH 30.00 80.00
47 Jan Vesely/49 3.00 8.00
48 Ben Hansbrough/49 3.00 8.00
50 Mirza Teletovic/49 6.00 15.00
52 E'Twaun Moore/49 4.00 10.00
54 Jon Leuer/49 3.00 8.00
55 Victor Claver/49 3.00 8.00
57 Marquis Teague/49 3.00 8.00
59 Bernard James/49 3.00 8.00
60 Nolan Smith/49 3.00 8.00
63 Donatas Motiejunas/49 4.00 10.00
64 Jared Cunningham/49 3.00 8.00
65 Viacheslav Kravtsov/49 3.00 8.00
74 Alan Anderson/49 3.00 8.00
83 Alonzo Gee/49 3.00 8.00
85 Dorell Wright/49 3.00 8.00
96 Carlos Delfino/49 3.00 8.00
98 Corey Brewer/49 3.00 8.00
105 Johan Petro/49 3.00 8.00
116 Jason Maxiell/49 3.00 8.00
119A Marvin Williams/49 3.00 8.00
119B Marvin Williams/25 VAR 4.00 10.00
129 Ronnie Brewer/49 3.00 8.00
131A Kobe Bryant/49 400.00 800.00
131B Kobe Bryant/25 VAR 500.00 1,000.00
132A Blake Griffin/25 15.00 40.00
133A Kevin Durant/25 100.00 200.00
138 Doug Christie/49 3.00 8.00
140 Jim Jackson/49 4.00 10.00
157 C.J. Watson/49 3.00 8.00
161 Anthony Morrow/49 3.00 8.00
173 Zaza Pachulia/49 3.00 8.00
174 Toney Douglas/49 3.00 8.00
176 Luc Mbah a Moute/49 3.00 8.00
182 Sean Elliott/49 6.00 15.00
183 Detlef Schrempf/49 5.00 12.00
184 Tim Hardaway/49 8.00 20.00
188 Anthony Mason/49 6.00 15.00
190 Mark Aguirre/49 4.00 10.00

2012-13 Panini Signatures Film Autographs

PRINT RUNS B/WN 10-99 COPIES PER
SOME CARDS ARE NOT SERIAL #'d
NO PRICING ON QTY 20 OR LESS
EXCHANGE DEADLINE 01/24/2014
28 Alonzo Gee/49 3.00 8.00
49 Corey Brewer/49 3.00 8.00
59 Greivis Vasquez/49 3.00 8.00
72 Marvin Williams/49 3.00 8.00
84 Kobe Bryant/75 400.00 800.00
85 Blake Griffin/25 15.00 40.00
86 Kevin Durant/49 60.00 150.00
88 Toney Douglas/49 3.00 8.00
95 Zaza Pachulia/49 3.00 8.00
103 Ian Mahinmi/49 3.00 8.00
108 Jarvis Varnado 4.00 10.00
111 Detlef Schrempf/25 10.00 25.00
114 Antoine Walker/49 15.00 40.00
117 John Starks/49 10.00 25.00
119 Tim Hardaway/49 8.00 20.00
129 Larry Bird/20 75.00 200.00
135 Sean Elliott/49 8.00 20.00
136 Anthony Davis/49 150.00 400.00
137 Kyrie Irving/99 50.00 120.00
155 Iman Shumpert/49 EXCH 4.00 10.00
157 Alec Burks/49 5.00 12.00
162 Nando De Colo 3.00 8.00
164 Kent Bazemore 5.00 12.00
167 Jeff Taylor 3.00 8.00
169 Jae Crowder 6.00 15.00
170 Draymond Green 15.00 40.00
173 Tyler Zeller/49 3.00 8.00
176 Andrew Nicholson/49 3.00 8.00
177 Chris Copeland/49 3.00 8.00
179 MarShon Brooks/49 EXCH 3.00 8.00
183 Ben Hansbrough 3.00 8.00
187 E'Twaun Moore 4.00 10.00
189 Jon Leuer 3.00 8.00
194 Bernard James 3.00 8.00
195 Nolan Smith/49 3.00 8.00
197 Brian Roberts 3.00 8.00
199 Jared Cunningham 3.00 8.00

2012-13 Panini Signatures Film Autographs Red

PRINT RUNS B/WN 4-49 COPIES PER
NO PRICING ON QTY 15 OR LESS
EXCHANGE DEADLINE 01/24/2014
30 Anthony Morrow/25 4.00 10.00
49 Corey Brewer/25 4.00 10.00
59 Greivis Vasquez/25 12.00 30.00
72 Marvin Williams/25 4.00 10.00
84 Kobe Bryant/49 400.00 800.00
86 Kevin Durant/25 EXCH 100.00 200.00
88 Toney Douglas/25 4.00 10.00
95 Zaza Pachulia/25 4.00 10.00
98 Trevor Booker/25 4.00 10.00
111 Detlef Schrempf/25 6.00 15.00
114 Antoine Walker/25 20.00 50.00
117 John Starks/25 12.00 30.00
119 Tim Hardaway/25 10.00 25.00
135 Sean Elliott/25 5.00 12.00
136 Anthony Davis/25 200.00 500.00
137 Kyrie Irving/25 60.00 150.00
157 Alec Burks/25 6.00 15.00
159 Isaiah Thomas/25 8.00 20.00
162 Nando De Colo/49 3.00 8.00
164 Kent Bazemore/49 5.00 12.00
167 Jeff Taylor/25 4.00 10.00
169 Jae Crowder/49 6.00 15.00
170 Draymond Green/25 25.00 60.00
173 Tyler Zeller/25 4.00 10.00
176 Andrew Nicholson/25 4.00 10.00
177 Chris Copeland/49 3.00 8.00
180 Jimmy Butler/49 20.00 50.00
187 E'Twaun Moore/25 5.00 12.00
194 Bernard James/25 4.00 10.00
197 Brian Roberts/49 3.00 8.00
199 Jared Cunningham/49 3.00 8.00

2012-13 Panini Signatures Legends

STATED PRINT RUN 25 SER.#'d SETS
ALL VERSIONS EQUALLY PRICED
1 Scottie Pippen 8.00 20.00
11 Allen Iverson 5.00 12.00
21 Shaquille O'Neal 10.00 25.00
31 Gary Payton 4.00 10.00
41 Larry Bird 10.00 25.00
51 Magic Johnson 10.00 25.00
61 David Robinson 5.00 12.00
71 Dominique Wilkins 4.00 10.00
81 Hakeem Olajuwon 8.00 20.00
91 Clyde Drexler 5.00 12.00
101 John Stockton 6.00 15.00
111 Isiah Thomas 6.00 15.00
121 Karl Malone 5.00 12.00
131 James Worthy 5.00 12.00
141 Anfernee Hardaway 8.00 20.00
151 Oscar Robertson 6.00 15.00
161 Drazen Petrovic 20.00 50.00
171 Patrick Ewing 5.00 12.00
181 Yao Ming 6.00 15.00
191 Shawn Kemp 5.00 12.00
201 Alonzo Mourning 10.00 25.00
211 Dennis Rodman 8.00 20.00
221 Kareem Abdul-Jabbar 10.00 25.00
231 Bill Walton 5.00 12.00
241 Julius Erving 8.00 20.00

2012-13 Panini Signatures Legends Green

*GREEN: 1X TO 2.5X BASIC
STATED PRINT RUN 5 SER.#'d SETS
ALL VERSIONS EQUALLY PRICED
11 Allen Iverson 25.00 60.00
91 Clyde Drexler 25.00 60.00
171 Patrick Ewing 25.00 60.00

2012-13 Panini Signatures Rookies

STATED PRINT RUN 25 SER.#'d SETS
ALL VERSIONS EQUALLY PRICED
1 Anthony Davis 40.00 100.00
11 Kyrie Irving 15.00 40.00
21 Damian Lillard 40.00 100.00
31 Andre Drummond 3.00 8.00
41 Bradley Beal 10.00 25.00
51 Kemba Walker 5.00 12.00
61 Chandler Parsons 1.50 4.00
64 Chandler Parsons 1.50 4.00
71 Harrison Barnes 2.50 6.00
81 Klay Thompson 25.00 60.00
91 Michael Kidd-Gilchrist 1.50 4.00
101 Brandon Knight 1.50 4.00
111 Alexey Shved 1.25 3.00
121 Derrick Williams 1.25 3.00
128 Derrick Williams 1.25 3.00
131 Dion Waiters 1.50 4.00
141 Jared Sullinger 1.25 3.00

2012-13 Panini Signatures Rookies Green

*GREEN: 1.2X TO 3X BASIC
STATED PRINT RUN 5 SER.#'d SETS
ALL VERSIONS EQUALLY PRICED
11 Kyrie Irving 50.00 120.00

2012-13 Panini Signatures Stars

STATED PRINT RUN 25 SER.#'d SETS
ALL VERSIONS EQUALLY PRICED
1 Kevin Durant 12.00 30.00
11 Derrick Rose 5.00 12.00
21 Russell Westbrook 5.00 12.00
31 Blake Griffin 3.00 8.00
38 Blake Griffin 3.00 8.00
41 Kobe Bryant 25.00 60.00
51 Chris Paul 6.00 15.00
61 Dirk Nowitzki 6.00 15.00
71 John Wall 4.00 10.00
81 Dwight Howard 3.00 8.00
91 Kevin Garnett 8.00 20.00
101 Steve Nash 6.00 15.00
111 James Harden 6.00 15.00
121 Rajon Rondo 4.00 10.00
128 Rajon Rondo 4.00 10.00
131 Jeremy Lin 5.00 12.00
141 LeBron James 25.00 60.00
151 Carmelo Anthony 5.00 12.00
161 Chris Bosh 4.00 10.00
171 Amar'e Stoudemire 3.00 8.00
181 Dwyane Wade 5.00 12.00
191 Tim Duncan 8.00 20.00
201 Vince Carter 6.00 15.00
211 Manu Ginobili 6.00 15.00
221 Paul Pierce 5.00 12.00
231 Deron Williams 2.50 6.00
241 Andre Iguodala 3.00 8.00
247 Andre Iguodala 3.00 8.00
251 Paul George 6.00 15.00
261 LaMarcus Aldridge 3.00 8.00
271 Kevin Love 3.00 8.00
281 Tony Parker 5.00 12.00
291 Joakim Noah 2.50 6.00
301 Goran Dragic 3.00 8.00
311 Grant Hill 5.00 12.00
321 Stephen Curry 25.00 60.00
331 Danny Granger 2.00 5.00
341 Ricky Rubio 2.50 6.00
351 David Lee 2.00 5.00
361 Zach Randolph 3.00 8.00
371 Ray Allen 2.50 6.00
381 Pau Gasol 5.00 12.00
391 Rudy Gay 3.00 8.00

2012-13 Panini Signatures Stars Green

*GREEN: 1X TO 2.5X BASIC
STATED PRINT RUN 5 SER.#'d SETS
ALL VERSIONS EQUALLY PRICED
1 Kevin Durant 50.00 120.00
181 Dwyane Wade 30.00 80.00
371 Ray Allen 15.00 40.00

2013-14 Panini Signatures

1-200 PRINT RUN 25 SER.#'d SETS
200-300 PRINT RUN 15 SER.#'d SETS
301-400 PRINT RUN 15 SER.#'d SETS
ALL VERSIONS EQUALLY PRICED
1 Kobe Bryant 20.00 50.00
11 Kevin Durant 8.00 20.00
21 Blake Griffin 2.50 6.00
31 Kyrie Irving 8.00 20.00
41 Anthony Davis 8.00 20.00
51 Russell Westbrook 4.00 10.00
61 Chris Paul 5.00 12.00
71 Kevin Love 2.50 6.00
81 Paul George 4.00 10.00
91 LeBron James 20.00 50.00
101 Damian Lillard 8.00 20.00
111 Dirk Nowitzki 6.00 15.00
121 Carmelo Anthony 4.00 10.00
131 James Harden 5.00 12.00
141 Derrick Rose 4.00 10.00
151 Stephen Curry 20.00 50.00
161 DeMar DeRozan 3.00 8.00
171 Dwight Howard 3.00 8.00
181 Dwyane Wade 5.00 12.00
191 Rajon Rondo 3.00 8.00
201 Shaquille O'Neal 12.00 30.00
211 Magic Johnson 12.00 30.00
221 Larry Bird 12.00 30.00
231 Julius Erving 8.00 20.00
241 Grant Hill 6.00 15.00
251 Jason Kidd 5.00 12.00
261 Tracy McGrady 5.00 12.00
271 Kareem Abdul-Jabbar 10.00 25.00
281 Dennis Rodman 8.00 20.00
291 Moses Malone 5.00 12.00
301 M.Carter-Williams RC 2.50 6.00
311 Victor Oladipo RC 5.00 12.00
321 Anthony Bennett RC 2.00 5.00
331 Ben McLemore RC 2.50 6.00
341 Cody Zeller RC 2.50 6.00
351 G.Antetokounmpo RC 100.00 250.00
361 Kentavious Caldwell-Pope RC 3.00 8.00
371 Nate Wolters RC 2.00 5.00
381 Steven Adams RC 5.00 12.00
391 Tim Hardaway Jr. RC 4.00 10.00

2013-14 Panini Signatures Blue

*BLUE 1-200: .6X TO 1.5X BASIC
*BLUE 201-300: .5X TO 1.2X BASIC
*BLUE 301-400: .5X TO 1.2X BASIC
1-200 PRINT RUN 15 SER.#'d SETS
201-400 PRINT RUN 10 SER.#'d SETS

2013-14 Panini Signatures Green

*GREEN 1-200: 1X TO 2.5X BASIC
*GREEN 201-300: .75X TO 2X BASIC
*GREEN 301-400: .75X TO 2X BASIC
1-200 PRINT RUN 5 SER.#'d SETS
201-400 PRINT RUN 3 SER.#'d SETS

2013-14 Panini Signatures Red

*RED 1-200: .75X TO 2X BASIC
*RED 201-300: .6X TO 1.5X BASIC
*RED 301-400: .6X TO 1.5X BASIC
1-200 PRINT RUN 10 SER.#'d SETS
201-400 PRINT RUN 8 SER.#'d SETS

2013-14 Panini Signatures '14 Draft X-Change

EXCHANGE DEADLINE 12/12/2015
1 Andrew Wiggins Pick 1 8.00 20.00
2 Jabari Parker Pick 2 3.00 8.00
3 Joel Embiid Pick 3 25.00 60.00
4 Aaron Gordon Pick 4 3.00 8.00
5 Dante Exum Pick 5 2.50 6.00
6 Marcus Smart Pick 6 2.50 6.00
7 Julius Randle Pick 7 8.00 20.00
8 Nik Stauskas Pick 8 1.50 4.00
9 Noah Vonleh Pick 9 2.00 5.00
10 Elfrid Payton Pick 10 2.50 6.00
11 Doug McDermott Pick 11 2.50 6.00
12 P.J. Hairston Pick 26 1.50 4.00
13 Zach LaVine Pick 13 20.00 50.00
14 TJ Warren Pick 14 3.00 8.00
15 Adreian Payne Pick 15 1.50 4.00
16 Jusuf Nurkic Pick 16 2.50 6.00
17 James Young Pick 17 1.50 4.00
18 Tyler Ennis Pick 18 1.50 4.00
19 Gary Harris Pick 19 3.00 8.00
20 Bruno Caboclo Pick 20 2.00 5.00
21 Mitch McGary Pick 21 1.50 4.00
22 Jordan Adams Pick 22 1.50 4.00
23 Rodney Hood Pick 23 3.00 8.00
24 Shabazz Napier Pick 24 2.00 5.00
25 Clint Capela Pick 25 3.00 8.00

2013-14 Panini Signatures Dynamic Ink

PRINT RUNS B/WN 25-249 COPIES PER
EXCHANGE DEADLINE 11/28/2015
3 Bill Walton/35 8.00 20.00
4 Julius Erving/25 40.00 100.00
5 Christian Laettner/35 5.00 12.00
6 Jodie Meeks/199 3.00 8.00
8 Harrison Barnes/35 12.00 30.00
9 Kenyon Martin/199 5.00 12.00
10 Jonas Valanciunas/99 4.00 10.00
11 Xavier Henry/49 3.00 8.00
12 Chris Copeland/199 3.00 8.00
13 Eric Maynor/199 3.00 8.00
14 Marvin Williams/199 3.00 8.00
16 Tyler Zeller/49 3.00 8.00
17 Orlando Johnson/199 3.00 8.00
18 Trevor Booker/199 3.00 8.00
20 Kevin Love/25 20.00 50.00
21 Jason Thompson/99 3.00 8.00
23 Gerald Henderson/99 3.00 8.00
24 Ersan Ilyasova/99 3.00 8.00
25 Marcin Gortat/75 3.00 8.00
26 Courtney Lee/99 3.00 8.00
28 B.Grant/199 EXCH 4.00 10.00
29 Dana Barros/199 3.00 8.00
31 Tracy McGrady/35 20.00 50.00
32 Kyrie Irving/35 50.00 120.00
33 Kevin Durant/35 50.00 120.00
34 Kobe Bryant/25 500.00 1,000.00
35 Ryan Anderson/75 3.00 8.00

2013-14 Panini Signatures Endorsements

PRINT RUNS B/WN 25-249 COPIES PER
EXCHANGE DEADLINE 11/28/2015
2 Spencer Haywood/249 5.00 12.00
3 Darrell Griffith/249 4.00 10.00
4 Jon McGlocklin/249 6.00 15.00
5 Ron Harper/249 5.00 12.00
6 Anfernee Hardaway/49 12.00 30.00
7 Grant Hill/49 15.00 40.00
8 Eddie Johnson/249 3.00 8.00
11 Connie Hawkins/149 6.00 15.00
12 Jamal Mashburn/175 4.00 10.00
14 Patrick Beverley/249 3.00 8.00
15 Jason Smith/249 3.00 8.00
18 Ray Allen/20 15.00 40.00
19 James Jones/249 3.00 8.00
21 Harrison Barnes/25 10.00 25.00
22 Ramon Sessions/249 3.00 8.00
24 Nick Collison/249 3.00 8.00
25 Steve Blake/249 3.00 8.00
26 Nick Young/49 10.00 25.00
28 Dwight Howard/20 20.00 50.00
30 Jordan Crawford/249 3.00 8.00
32 David Thompson/99 5.00 12.00
33 Adrian Dantley/99 5.00 12.00
36 Scottie Pippen/20 60.00 120.00
37 Satch Sanders/99 6.00 15.00
38 Jamaal Wilkes/199 4.00 10.00
40 Marques Johnson/249 4.00 10.00
41 A.C. Green/49 6.00 15.00
43 Bruce Bowen/249 4.00 10.00
44 Keith Van Horn/249 4.00 10.00
45 Jerome Williams/249 3.00 8.00
46 Rael LaFrentz/249 5.00 12.00
47 Vlade Divac/249 5.00 12.00
48 Vernon Maxwell/249 4.00 10.00
49 Jason Kidd/20 20.00 50.00
51 Darryl Dawkins/249 4.00 10.00
52 Fred Jones/249 3.00 8.00
53 Bob Dandridge/249 4.00 10.00
54 Jack Sikma/249 5.00 12.00
55 Chris Andersen/25 50.00 100.00

2013-14 Panini Signatures Film

STATED PRINT RUN 35 SER.#'d SETS
1 Dwyane Wade 5.00 12.00
2 J.J. Hickson 1.50 4.00
3 Ray Allen 4.00 10.00
4 Steve Nash 5.00 12.00
5 Al Horford 2.50 6.00
6 Joakim Noah 2.50 6.00
7 Bradley Beal 4.00 10.00
8 Kevin Martin 2.00 5.00
9 Danny Granger 1.50 4.00
10 Mike Conley 2.50 6.00
11 Enes Kanter 2.00 5.00
12 Raymond Felton 1.50 4.00
13 J.J. Redick 2.50 6.00
14 Taj Gibson 1.50 4.00
15 Al Jefferson 1.50 4.00
16 Joe Johnson 2.00 5.00
17 Brandon Bass 1.50 4.00
18 Klay Thompson 8.00 20.00
19 Monta Ellis 2.00 5.00
20 David Lee 1.50 4.00
21 Eric Bledsoe 2.00 5.00
22 Ricky Rubio 2.00 5.00
23 J.R. Smith 2.50 6.00
24 Tayshaun Prince 2.50 6.00
25 Alec Burks 2.00 5.00
26 John Wall 3.00 8.00
27 Brandon Jennings 1.50 4.00
28 Kobe Bryant 20.00 50.00
29 David West 2.00 5.00
30 Nate Robinson 1.50 4.00
31 Eric Gordon 2.00 5.00
32 Roy Hibbert 1.50 4.00
33 Jameer Nelson 1.50 4.00
34 Thabo Sefolosha 1.50 4.00
35 Alexey Shved 1.50 4.00
36 Jonas Valanciunas 2.00 5.00
37 Brandon Knight 2.00 5.00
38 Kyle Korver 2.00 5.00
39 DeAndre Jordan 2.00 5.00
40 Nene 2.00 5.00
41 Evan Turner 1.50 4.00
42 Rudy Gay 2.50 6.00
43 James Harden 8.00 20.00
44 Thaddeus Young 1.50 4.00
45 Amare Stoudemire 2.50 6.00
46 Josh Smith 1.50 4.00
47 Brook Lopez 2.50 6.00
48 Kyrie Irving 8.00 20.00
49 DeMar DeRozan 3.00 8.00
50 Nick Young 1.50 4.00
51 George Hill 2.00 5.00
52 Russell Westbrook 4.00 10.00
53 Jared Sullinger 1.50 4.00
54 Tiago Splitter 1.50 4.00
55 Anderson Varejao 1.50 4.00
56 Jrue Holiday 3.00 8.00
57 Carlos Boozer 2.00 5.00
58 LaMarcus Aldridge 2.50 6.00
59 DeMarcus Cousins 2.50 6.00
60 Nicolas Batum 2.00 5.00
61 Gerald Henderson 1.50 4.00
62 Ryan Anderson 1.50 4.00
63 Jason Terry 2.00 5.00
64 Tim Duncan 6.00 15.00
65 Andre Drummond 2.50 6.00
66 Kawhi Leonard 8.00 20.00
67 Carmelo Anthony 4.00 10.00
68 Lance Stephenson 2.00 5.00
69 Deron Williams 2.00 5.00
70 Nikola Vucevic 3.00 8.00
71 Serge Ibaka 2.00 5.00
72 Glen Davis 1.50 4.00
73 JaVale McGee 2.00 5.00
74 Tony Parker 4.00 10.00
75 Andre Iguodala 2.50 6.00
76 Kemba Walker 2.50 6.00
77 Caron Butler 2.00 5.00
78 LeBron James 20.00 50.00
79 Derrick Favors 1.50 4.00
80 Pau Gasol 4.00 10.00
81 Goran Dragic 2.00 5.00
82 Shane Battier 2.00 5.00
83 Jeff Green 1.50 4.00
84 Tristan Thompson 1.50 4.00
85 Andrei Kirilenko 2.50 6.00
86 Kenneth Faried 2.00 5.00
87 Chandler Parsons 1.50 4.00
88 Luol Deng 2.00 5.00
89 Paul George 4.00 10.00
90 Derrick Rose 10.00 25.00
91 Gordon Hayward 2.00 5.00
92 Shawn Marion 2.00 5.00
93 Jeff Teague 1.50 4.00
94 Ty Lawson 1.50 4.00
95 Anthony Davis 8.00 20.00
96 Kevin Durant 8.00 20.00
97 Chris Bosh 3.00 8.00
98 Manu Ginobili 5.00 12.00
99 Dion Waiters 1.50 4.00
100 Paul Millsap 2.00 5.00
101 Greg Monroe 1.50 4.00
102 Stephen Curry 20.00 50.00
103 Jeremy Lin 4.00 10.00
104 Tyreke Evans 2.00 5.00
105 Arron Afflalo 1.50 4.00
106 Kevin Garnett 6.00 15.00
107 Chris Paul 5.00 12.00
108 Marc Gasol 2.50 6.00
109 Dirk Nowitzki 6.00 15.00
110 Paul Pierce 4.00 10.00
111 Harrison Barnes 2.50 6.00
112 Steve Blake 1.50 4.00
113 Jimmer Fredette 2.50 6.00
114 Tyson Chandler 2.00 5.00
115 Avery Bradley 1.50 4.00
116 Kevin Love 2.50 6.00
117 Damian Lillard 8.00 20.00
118 Marcin Gortat 1.50 4.00
119 Dwight Howard 3.00 8.00
120 Rajon Rondo 3.00 8.00
121 Iman Shumpert 1.50 4.00
122 Zach Randolph 2.00 5.00
123 Jimmy Butler 5.00 12.00
124 Vince Carter 5.00 12.00
125 Blake Griffin 2.50 6.00
126 Mahmoud Abdul-Rauf 1.50 4.00
127 Scottie Pippen 6.00 15.00
128 Arvydas Sabonis 3.00 8.00
129 Clyde Drexler 4.00 10.00
130 Pete Maravich 4.00 10.00
131 Wilt Chamberlain 8.00 20.00
132 Chris Mullin 3.00 8.00
133 Kareem Abdul-Jabbar 8.00 20.00
134 Michael Cooper 2.50 6.00
135 Karl Malone 5.00 12.00
136 Dan Majerle 2.00 5.00
137 Jason Kidd 4.00 10.00
138 Drazen Petrovic 4.00 10.00
139 Dominique Wilkins 4.00 10.00
140 Robert Parish 3.00 8.00
141 Oscar Robertson 4.00 10.00
142 Tracy McGrady 4.00 10.00
143 Jerry West 6.00 15.00
144 Shawn Kemp 4.00 10.00
145 Isiah Thomas 4.00 10.00
146 Vlade Divac 2.50 6.00
147 Patrick Ewing 4.00 10.00
148 Robert Horry 2.50 6.00
149 George Gervin 4.00 10.00
150 Bernard King 3.00 8.00
151 Larry Bird 10.00 25.00
152 Grant Hill 4.00 10.00
153 Elgin Baylor 2.50 6.00
154 Yao Ming 5.00 12.00
155 John Stockton 5.00 12.00
156 Xavier McDaniel 2.00 5.00
157 Gary Payton 4.00 10.00
158 James Worthy 3.00 8.00
159 Dennis Rodman 6.00 15.00
160 Alonzo Mourning 4.00 10.00
161 Magic Johnson 10.00 25.00
162 Dikembe Mutombo 4.00 10.00
163 Hakeem Olajuwon 5.00 12.00
164 Mark Price 2.50 6.00
165 David Robinson 5.00 12.00
166 Michael Finley 2.50 6.00
167 Allen Iverson 5.00 12.00
168 Julius Erving 6.00 15.00
169 Dennis Johnson 2.00 5.00
170 Joe Dumars 3.00 8.00
171 Shaquille O'Neal 10.00 25.00
172 Anfernee Hardaway 6.00 15.00
173 Moses Malone 4.00 10.00
174 Steve Francis 2.00 5.00
175 Kevin McHale 4.00 10.00
176 Pero Antic 1.50 4.00
177 C.J. McCollum 6.00 15.00
178 Kelly Olynyk 2.00 5.00
179 Anthony Bennett 1.50 4.00
180 Shane Larkin 1.50 4.00
181 Cody Zeller 2.00 5.00
182 Tim Hardaway Jr. 3.00 8.00
183 Nerlens Noel 2.00 5.00
184 Dwight Buycks 1.50 4.00
185 Kentavious Caldwell-Pope 2.50 6.00
186 Nate Wolters 1.50 4.00
187 Michael Carter-Williams 2.00 5.00
188 Shabazz Muhammad 1.50 4.00
189 Victor Oladipo 4.00 10.00
190 Tony Snell 2.00 5.00
191 Alex Len 2.00 5.00
192 Ben McLemore 2.00 5.00
193 Archie Goodwin 1.50 4.00
194 Luigi Datome 1.50 4.00
195 Trey Burke 2.00 5.00
196 Matthew Dellavedova 2.50 6.00
197 Steven Adams 4.00 10.00
198 Giannis Antetokounmpo 150.00 400.00
199 Otto Porter 2.50 6.00
200 Mason Plumlee 2.00 5.00

2013-14 Panini Signatures Film Onyx

*ONYX: .5X TO 1.2X BASIC
STATED PRINT RUN 20 SER.#'d SETS

2013-14 Panini Signatures Film Rookie Autographs

PRINT RUNS B/WN 25-249 COPIES PER
EXCHANGE DEADLINE 11/28/2015
1 M.Carter-Williams/99 4.00 10.00
2 Gal Mekel/249 3.00 8.00
3 Nate Wolters/249 3.00 8.00
4 Dwight Buycks/249 3.00 8.00
5 Kelly Olynyk/249 4.00 10.00
6 Shabazz Muhammad/49 3.00 8.00
7 Otto Porter/25 10.00 25.00
8 Victor Oladipo/99 6.00 15.00
9 Solomon Hill/249 4.00 10.00
10 Tony Snell/199 4.00 10.00
11 Carrick Felix/249 3.00 8.00
12 Trey Burke/99 3.00 8.00
13 Shane Larkin/249 3.00 8.00
14 Alex Len/25 4.00 10.00
15 G.Antetokounmpo/199 EXCH 300.00 600.00
16 Mason Plumlee/249 4.00 10.00
17 Archie Goodwin/249 3.00 8.00
18 Tim Hardaway Jr./249 6.00 15.00
19 Gorgui Dieng/249 4.00 10.00
20 Peyton Siva/249 3.00 8.00
21 Nemanja Nedovic/249 3.00 8.00
22 Phil Pressey/249 3.00 8.00
23 Luigi Datome/249 3.00 8.00
24 Ben McLemore/49 3.00 8.00
25 Cody Zeller/25 4.00 10.00

2013-14 Panini Signatures Film Veteran Autographs

PRINT RUNS B/WN 25-149 COPIES PER
EXCHANGE DEADLINE 11/28/2015
1 Bradley Beal/49 15.00 40.00
3 Timofey Mozgov/249 3.00 8.00
4 Thabo Sefolosha/35 8.00 20.00
6 Jared Dudley/75 3.00 8.00
7 K.Irving/35 EXCH 50.00 120.00
8 Kevin Durant/45 75.00 150.00
9 K.Bryant/25 EXCH 600.00 1,200.00
10 Goran Dragic/75 15.00 40.00
11 Andrew Bogut/35 10.00 25.00
12 Kevin Martin/35 4.00 10.00
14 Randy Foye/75 3.00 8.00
16 Harrison Barnes/25 8.00 20.00
18 Kawhi Leonard/35 75.00 200.00
19 Andrea Bargnani/35 3.00 8.00
20 Lance Stephenson/249 4.00 10.00
22 Jimmer Fredette/149 5.00 12.00
23 Earl Clark/249 3.00 8.00
24 C.J. Watson/249 3.00 8.00
25 James Anderson/249 3.00 8.00
26 Andre Drummond/35 12.00 30.00
27 Brandon Rush/249 3.00 8.00
28 Corey Brewer/249 3.00 8.00
29 J.J. Redick/35 10.00 25.00
31 Steve Blake/249 3.00 8.00
34 Landry Fields/199 3.00 8.00
35 Boris Diaw/49 10.00 25.00
36 Udonis Haslem/249 8.00 20.00
37 Draymond Green/249 10.00 25.00
38 Jordan Crawford/249 3.00 8.00
39 Patrick Patterson/249 3.00 8.00
40 Christian Laettner/25 10.00 25.00
42 Ronnie Brewer/249 3.00 8.00
43 Ersan Ilyasova/49 3.00 8.00
44 Kyle Korver/35 4.00 10.00
45 Marcin Gortat/35 20.00 50.00
46 Tobias Harris/149 5.00 12.00
47 Brandon Bass/35 3.00 8.00
49 Anthony Davis/35 40.00 80.00
50 Tracy McGrady/35 30.00 80.00
51 Byron Scott/35 5.00 12.00
52 Jason Kidd/35 15.00 40.00
53 Tom Chambers/49 5.00 12.00
54 Dikembe Mutombo/35 15.00 40.00
55 Toni Kukoc/49 20.00 50.00
57 Steve Smith/249 4.00 10.00
58 D.Coleman/49 EXCH 5.00 12.00
59 Jalen Rose/35 10.00 25.00
60 Avery Johnson/35 4.00 10.00
62 Jamal Mashburn/249 4.00 10.00
64 Clyde Drexler/35 30.00 60.00
66 Luc Longley/249 4.00 10.00
68 Kevin Love/35 20.00 50.00
71 Kareem Abdul-Jabbar/35 40.00 80.00
72 D.Robinson/35 EXCH 25.00 60.00
73 Gary Payton/35 12.00 30.00
74 Anfernee Hardaway/35 40.00 80.00
75 Jarrett Jack/49 4.00 10.00

2013-14 Panini Signatures Franchise Graphs

PRINT RUNS B/WN 25-149 COPIES PER
EXCHANGE DEADLINE 11/28/2015
1 Gordon Hayward/25 20.00 50.00
4 Zach Randolph/25 10.00 25.00
5 Dwight Howard/35 15.00 40.00
6 Jeff Green/35 3.00 8.00
7 Kevin Love/25 12.00 30.00
8 Stephen Curry/25 500.00 1,000.00
9 Kobe Bryant/25 600.00 1,200.00
10 Kevin Durant/25 75.00 200.00
11 Chris Bosh/25 10.00 25.00
12 Kawhi Leonard/49 50.00 120.00
13 Jonas Valanciunas/25 6.00 15.00
14 Andre Drummond/25 20.00 50.00
16 Kyrie Irving/35 50.00 120.00
17 Anthony Davis/35 60.00 120.00
20 LaMarcus Aldridge/25 20.00 50.00
21 Victor Oladipo/35 20.00 50.00
22 M.Carter-Williams/49 4.00 10.00
23 G.Antetokounmpo/149 400.00 800.00
24 Alex Len/35 4.00 10.00
25 Ben McLemore/35 4.00 10.00

2013-14 Panini Signatures Hall Hopefuls Signatures

PRINT RUNS B/WN 20-149 COPIES PER
EXCHANGE DEADLINE 11/28/2015
2 S.Nash/20 EXCH 40.00 100.00
5 Tracy McGrady/20 12.00 30.00
7 Grant Hill/20 30.00 80.00
8 Jason Kidd/20 25.00 60.00
9 Spencer Haywood/50 5.00 12.00
10 Chris Bosh/20 6.00 15.00
12 Kevin Durant/20 60.00 150.00
13 Tim Hardaway/125 10.00 25.00
14 Mark Aguirre/149 4.00 10.00
15 Alonzo Mourning/20 25.00 60.00

2013-14 Panini Signatures History of the Hall Autographs

PRINT RUNS B/WN 20-99 COPIES PER
EXCHANGE DEADLINE 11/28/2015
3 Dan Issel/99 6.00 15.00
6 Bob McAdoo/75 15.00 40.00
7 Jerry Lucas/35 12.00 30.00
8 Walt Frazier/20 12.00 30.00
9 Nate Thurmond/20 12.00 30.00
10 Adrian Dantley/99 5.00 12.00
11 Alex English/99 6.00 15.00
12 Nate Archibald/35 8.00 20.00
13 Dennis Rodman/20 25.00 60.00
14 C.Mullin/20 EXCH 6.00 15.00
15 Bernard King/20 15.00 40.00

2013-14 Panini Signatures Ringing Endorsements

STATED PRINT RUN 20 SER.#'d SETS
EXCHANGE DEADLINE 11/28/2015
1 Scottie Pippen 150.00 250.00
3 Hakeem Olajuwon 30.00 60.00
4 Magic Johnson 50.00 100.00
5 Bill Russell 1,000.00 2,000.00
6 Chris Bosh 30.00 60.00
8 Tony Parker 60.00 120.00
9 Jason Terry 8.00 20.00
10 Tayshaun Prince 10.00 25.00

2013-14 Panini Signatures Rookie Signatures

PRINT RUNS B/WN 99-199 COPIES PER
EXCHANGE DEADLINE 11/28/2015
1 Dwight Buycks/199 3.00 8.00
2 G.Antetokounmpo/199 150.00 400.00
3 M.Carter-Williams/125 4.00 10.00
5 Gorgui Dieng/199 4.00 10.00
6 Andre Roberson/199 4.00 10.00
7 Steven Adams/199 8.00 20.00
8 Archie Goodwin/199 3.00 8.00
10 Lorenzo Brown/199 3.00 8.00
11 Victor Oladipo/99 12.00 30.00
12 Ian Clark/199 3.00 8.00
13 Ray McCallum/199 3.00 8.00
15 Anthony Bennett/125 3.00 8.00
16 Nerlens Noel/99 4.00 10.00
17 Matthew Dellavedova/199 5.00 12.00
18 Carrick Felix/199 3.00 8.00
19 Jamaal Franklin/199 3.00 8.00
20 Toure Murry/199 3.00 8.00
21 Tim Hardaway Jr./199 6.00 15.00
22 Ryan Kelly/199 3.00 8.00
23 Trey Burke/99 4.00 10.00
25 James Southerland/199 3.00 8.00
26 Nate Wolters/199 3.00 8.00
27 Tony Snell/199 4.00 10.00
28 Kelly Olynyk/199 4.00 10.00
29 Phil Pressey/199 3.00 8.00
30 Mason Plumlee/199 4.00 10.00
31 Gal Mekel/199 3.00 8.00
32 Jeff Withey/199 3.00 8.00
33 Peyton Siva/199 3.00 8.00
34 Solomon Hill/199 4.00 10.00
35 Tony Mitchell/199 3.00 8.00
37 Shane Larkin/199 3.00 8.00
38 Dennis Schroder/199 10.00 25.00
39 Erik Murphy/199 3.00 8.00
40 Miroslav Raduljica/199 3.00 8.00

2013-14 Panini Spectra

STATED PRINT RUN 199 SER.#'d SETS
EXCHANGE DEADLINE 1/16/2016
1 Derrick Rose 2.50 6.00
2 Monta Ellis 1.25 3.00
3 Jeff Green 1.00 2.50
4 Chris Paul 3.00 8.00
5 Carmelo Anthony 2.50 6.00
6 Kobe Bryant 40.00 100.00
7 Damian Lillard 5.00 12.00
8 Jeff Teague 1.00 2.50
9 Derrick Favors 1.00 2.50
10 Nikola Vucevic 2.00 5.00
11 Luol Deng 1.25 3.00
12 Dirk Nowitzki 4.00 10.00
13 Avery Bradley 1.00 2.50
14 DeAndre Jordan 1.25 3.00
15 Andrea Bargnani 1.00 2.50
16 Steve Nash 3.00 8.00
17 Nicolas Batum 1.25 3.00
18 Paul Millsap 1.25 3.00
19 Enes Kanter 1.25 3.00

20 Jameer Nelson 1.00 2.50
21 Carlos Boozer 1.25 3.00
22 Jose Calderon 1.00 2.50
23 Jared Sullinger 1.00 2.50
24 Goran Dragic 1.25 3.00
25 J.R. Smith 1.50 4.00
26 DeMarcus Cousins 1.50 4.00
27 Ty Lawson 1.00 2.50
28 Kyle Korver 1.25 3.00
29 Paul George 2.50 6.00
30 Tony Parker 2.50 6.00
31 Kyrie Irving 5.00 12.00
32 Shawn Marion 1.25 3.00
33 DeMar DeRozan 2.00 5.00
34 Eric Bledsoe 1.25 3.00
35 Evan Turner 1.00 2.50
36 Isaiah Thomas 1.25 3.00
37 Kenneth Faried 1.25 3.00
38 Kemba Walker 1.50 4.00
39 David West 1.25 3.00
40 Manu Ginobili 3.00 8.00
41 Dion Waiters 1.00 2.50
42 Ryan Anderson 1.00 2.50
43 Kyle Lowry 1.50 4.00
44 Channing Frye 1.00 2.50
45 Thaddeus Young 1.00 2.50
46 Rudy Gay 1.25 3.00
47 Nate Robinson 1.00 2.50
48 Gerald Henderson 1.00 2.50
49 Lance Stephenson 1.25 3.00
50 Tim Duncan 4.00 10.00
51 Tristan Thompson 1.00 2.50
52 Anthony Davis 5.00 12.00
53 Jonas Valanciunas 1.25 3.00
54 Stephen Curry 12.00 30.00
55 Spencer Hawes 1.00 2.50
56 LeBron James 40.00 100.00
57 Kevin Love 1.50 4.00
58 Al Jefferson 1.00 2.50
59 Roy Hibbert 1.00 2.50
60 Kawhi Leonard 5.00 12.00
61 O.J. Mayo 1.00 2.50
62 Jrue Holiday 2.00 5.00
63 Joe Johnson 1.25 3.00
64 Klay Thompson 5.00 12.00
65 Kevin Durant 5.00 12.00
66 Dwyane Wade 3.00 8.00
67 Kevin Martin 1.25 3.00
68 John Wall 2.00 5.00
69 Brandon Jennings 1.00 2.50
70 James Harden 3.00 8.00
71 Caron Butler 1.25 3.00
72 Mike Conley 1.50 4.00
73 Brook Lopez 1.50 4.00
74 David Lee 1.00 2.50
75 Russell Westbrook 2.50 6.00
76 Chris Bosh 2.00 5.00
77 Nikola Pekovic 1.00 2.50
78 Bradley Beal 2.50 6.00
79 Josh Smith 1.00 2.50
80 Dwight Howard 2.00 5.00
81 Brandon Knight 1.25 3.00
82 Zach Randolph 1.25 3.00
83 Paul Pierce 2.50 6.00
84 Harrison Barnes 1.50 4.00
85 Serge Ibaka 1.25 3.00
86 Ray Allen 2.50 6.00
87 Gordon Hayward 1.25 3.00
88 Marcin Gortat 1.00 2.50
89 Greg Monroe 1.00 2.50
90 Chandler Parsons 1.00 2.50
91 Blake Griffin 1.50 4.00
92 Marc Gasol 1.50 4.00
93 Kevin Garnett 4.00 10.00
94 Pau Gasol 2.50 6.00
95 LaMarcus Aldridge 1.50 4.00
96 Al Horford 1.50 4.00
97 Alec Burks 1.25 3.00
98 Arron Afflalo 1.00 2.50
99 Andre Drummond 1.50 4.00
100 Jeremy Lin 2.50 6.00
101 N.Noel JSY AU RC 4.00 10.00
102 K.Olynyk JSY AU RC 4.00 10.00
103 G.Mekel JSY AU RC 3.00 8.00
104 O.Porter JSY AU RC 5.00 12.00
105 N.Wolters JSY AU RC 3.00 8.00
106 M.Plumlee JSY AU RC 4.00 10.00
107 C.McCollum JSY AU RC 12.00 30.00
108 A.Goodwin JSY AU RC 3.00 8.00
109 S.Larkin JSY AU RC 3.00 8.00
110 T.Snell JSY AU RC 4.00 10.00
111 A.Len JSY AU RC 4.00 10.00
112 T.Burke JSY AU RC 4.00 10.00
113 B.McLemore JSY AU RC 4.00 10.00
114 S.Hill JSY AU RC 4.00 10.00
115 R.Gobert JSY AU RC 15.00 40.00
116 K.Caldwell-Pope JSY AU RC 5.00 12.00
117 T.Hardaway Jr. JSY AU RC 6.00 15.00
118 A.Bennett JSY AU RC 3.00 8.00
119 C.Zeller JSY AU RC 4.00 10.00
120 G.Antetokounmpo JSY AU RC 600.00 1,200.00
121 M.Carter-Williams JSY AU RC 4.00 10.00
122 M.Dellavedova JSY AU RC 5.00 12.00
123 J.Franklin JSY AU RC 3.00 8.00
124 V.Oladipo JSY AU RC 8.00 20.00
125 S.Adams JSY AU RC 8.00 20.00

2013-14 Panini Spectra Blue

*BLUE: .6X TO 1.5X BASIC
STATED PRINT RUN 65 SER.#'d SETS
6 Kobe Bryant 60.00 150.00
56 LeBron James 60.00 150.00
60 Kawhi Leonard 8.00 20.00

2013-14 Panini Spectra Red Die Cut Variations

*RED DC: 2X TO 5X BASIC
STATED PRINT RUN 25 SER.#'d SETS
1 Derrick Rose 60.00 120.00
6 Kobe Bryant 100.00 200.00
50 Tim Duncan 25.00 60.00
56 LeBron James 300.00 600.00
60 Kawhi Leonard 25.00 60.00

2013-14 Panini Spectra Rookie Jerseys Autographs Light Blue

*LT BLUE: .5X TO 1.2X BASIC
PRINT RUNS B/WN 5-99 COPIES PER
NO PRICING ON QTY 5
EXCHANGE DEADLINE 1/16/2016

2013-14 Panini Spectra Rookie Jerseys Autographs Orange

*ORANGE: .6X TO 1.5X BASIC
PRINT RUNS B/WN 5-60 COPIES PER
NO PRICING ON QTY 5
EXCHANGE DEADLINE 1/16/2016
120 Giannis Antetokounmpo/60 1,000.00 2,000.00

2013-14 Panini Spectra All-Stars Jersey Autographs

STATED PRINT RUN 125 SER.#'d SETS
EXCHANGE DEADLINE 1/16/2016
17 Brad Daugherty 5.00 12.00
19 Fat Lever 4.00 10.00

2013-14 Panini Spectra All-Stars Jersey Autographs Light Blue

PRINT RUNS B/WN 25-60 COPIES PER
EXCHANGE DEADLINE 1/16/2016
1 Kobe Bryant/40 500.00 1,000.00
4 Steve Nash/25 40.00 100.00
5 Tony Parker/25 20.00 50.00
6 Kevin Durant/40 75.00 200.00
7 Kevin Love/25 6.00 15.00
8 Tyson Chandler/25 5.00 12.00
9 Larry Bird/25 50.00 120.00
10 James Harden/25 60.00 150.00
11 Andrei Kirilenko/25 6.00 15.00
13 Kyrie Irving/25 50.00 120.00
15 Caron Butler/25 5.00 12.00
17 Brad Daugherty/60 6.00 15.00
19 Fat Lever/49 5.00 12.00
21 Tracy McGrady/25 30.00 80.00
22 Al Horford/25 6.00 15.00
23 David Robinson/25 25.00 60.00
24 Jason Kidd/25 20.00 50.00
25 Grant Hill/25 20.00 50.00

2013-14 Panini Spectra All-Stars Jersey Autographs Orange

*ORANGE: .4X TO 1X LT BLUE
PRINT RUNS B/WN 15-25 COPIES PER
NO PRICING ON QTY 15
EXCHANGE DEADLINE 1/16/2016

2013-14 Panini Spectra Double Team Jerseys

PRINT RUNS B/WN 49-75 COPIES PER
1 K.Garnett/P.Pierce/75 10.00 25.00
2 K.Irving/D.Waiters/75 12.00 30.00
3 D.Nowitzki/M.Ellis/75 10.00 25.00
4 A.Drummond/G.Monroe/75 4.00 10.00
5 S.Curry/H.Barnes/75 6.00 15.00
6 D.Howard/J.Harden/75 10.00 25.00
7 B.Griffin/C.Paul/75 8.00 20.00
8 K.Bryant/P.Gasol/75 12.00 30.00
9 L.James/D.Wade/75 12.00 30.00
10 K.Love/R.Rubio/75 4.00 10.00
11 K.Durant/R.Westbrook/75 12.00 30.00
12 D.Lillard/L.Aldridge/75 10.00 25.00
13 T.Duncan/T.Parker/75 10.00 25.00
14 J.Wall/B.Beal/75 15.00 40.00
15 S.O'Neal /A.Hardaway/49 15.00 40.00
16 L.Bird/K.McHale/49 12.00 30.00
17 P.Ewing/C.Oakley/49 8.00 20.00
18 M.Johnson/K.Abdul-Jabbar/49 15.00 40.00
19 K.Malone/J.Stockton/49 12.00 30.00
20 I.Thomas/J.Dumars/49 6.00 15.00
21 H.Olajuwon/C.Drexler/49 15.00 40.00
22 G.Payton/S.Kemp/49 12.00 30.00
23 A.English/D.Issel/49 5.00 12.00
24 S.Pippen/R.Parish/49 10.00 25.00
25 L.Nance/M.Price/49 4.00 10.00

2013-14 Panini Spectra Hall of Fame Jersey Autographs

STATED PRINT RUN 99 SER.#'d SETS
EXCHANGE DEADLINE 1/16/2016
2 Arvydas Sabonis 12.00 30.00
22 Alex English 6.00 15.00

2013-14 Panini Spectra Hall of Fame Jersey Autographs Light Blue

PRINT RUNS B/WN 25-60 COPIES PER
EXCHANGE DEADLINE 1/16/2016
1 Larry Bird/20 50.00 100.00
2 Arvydas Sabonis/60 12.00 30.00
3 Rick Barry/20 15.00 40.00
4 Clyde Drexler/20 30.00 60.00
5 Dominique Wilkins/20 12.00 30.00
6 Karl Malone/20 60.00 120.00
7 Scottie Pippen/20 75.00 200.00
8 Gary Payton/20 20.00 50.00
9 David Robinson/20 30.00 60.00
10 Bob Lanier/20 12.00 30.00
11 Gail Goodrich/20 10.00 25.00
13 John Havlicek/20 75.00 200.00
14 Julius Erving/20 50.00 100.00
15 Hakeem Olajuwon/20 30.00 60.00
16 Robert Parish/20 12.00 30.00
17 James Worthy/20 30.00 60.00
18 George Gervin/20 15.00 40.00
19 Kareem Abdul-Jabbar/20 20.00 50.00
21 Dennis Rodman/20 40.00 80.00
22 Alex English/60 8.00 20.00

2013-14 Panini Spectra Indelible Ink Jerseys

PRINT RUNS B/WN 75-199 COPIES PER
EXCHANGE DEADLINE 1/16/2016
4 Jack Sikma/199 5.00 12.00
8 Steve Blake/149 3.00 8.00
15 Bill Laimbeer/99 5.00 12.00
17 Ryan Anderson/75 3.00 8.00
18 Nick Collison/199 3.00 8.00
32 George Hill/149 4.00 10.00
40 Sean Elliott/149 6.00 15.00

2013-14 Panini Spectra Indelible Ink Jerseys Light Blue

PRINT RUNS B/WN 25-99 COPIES PER
EXCHANGE DEADLINE 1/16/2016
1 Danny Manning/20 5.00 12.00
2 Kevin Love/25 6.00 15.00
3 Tony Parker/25 12.00 30.00
4 Jack Sikma/99 6.00 15.00
7 Bradley Beal/25 12.00 30.00
8 Steve Blake/99 4.00 10.00
9 James Harden/25 60.00 150.00
10 Steve Nash/25 40.00 100.00
11 Kawhi Leonard/75 60.00 150.00
12 Magic Johnson/25 40.00 100.00
13 Dominique Wilkins/25 20.00 50.00
15 Bill Laimbeer/60 6.00 15.00
17 Ryan Anderson/75 4.00 10.00
18 Nick Collison/75 4.00 10.00
20 Kobe Bryant/40 500.00 1,000.00
21 Larry Bird/25 40.00 100.00
22 Glen Rice/25 10.00 25.00
23 Anfernee Hardaway/25 50.00 120.00
25 Kyrie Irving/25 50.00 120.00
28 Kevin Durant/40 60.00 150.00
31 Julius Erving/25 30.00 80.00
32 George Hill/99 5.00 12.00
36 Joe Dumars/25 8.00 20.00
40 Sean Elliott/99 6.00 15.00

2013-14 Panini Spectra Indelible Ink Jerseys Orange

*ORANGE: .4X TO 1X LT BLUE
PRINT RUNS B/WN 15-60 COPIES PER
NO PRICING ON QTY 15
EXCHANGE DEADLINE 1/16/2016

2013-14 Panini Spectra Jerseys Autographs

PRINT RUNS B/WN 49-149 COPIES PER
EXCHANGE DEADLINE 1/16/2016
20 Kenny Sky Walker/49 8.00 20.00
26 Tom Chambers/49 5.00 12.00
30 Kurt Rambis/49 6.00 15.00
37 Thabo Sefolosha/49 8.00 20.00
50 Mark Price/75 5.00 12.00

2013-14 Panini Spectra Jerseys Autographs Light Blue

PRINT RUNS B/WN 30-75 COPIES PER
EXCHANGE DEADLINE 1/16/2016
8 Jerry West/30 40.00 80.00
10 Kelly Tripucka/30 5.00 12.00
11 Ty Lawson/30 4.00 10.00
14 Shaquille O'Neal 30 75.00 150.00
16 Terry Cummings/75 5.00 12.00
17 Andrei Kirilenko/30 6.00 15.00
18 John Havlicek/30 40.00 80.00
20 Kenny Sky Walker/30 10.00 25.00
22 Kevin Love/30 15.00 40.00
23 Fred Brown/75 5.00 12.00
26 Tom Chambers/30 10.00 25.00
27 Anfernee Hardaway/30 60.00 120.00
29 Buck Williams/49 5.00 12.00
30 Kurt Rambis/30 6.00 15.00
34 Kobe Bryant/30 500.00 1,000.00
35 Ryan Anderson/30 4.00 10.00
37 Thabo Sefolosha/30 10.00 25.00
40 Caron Butler/30 5.00 12.00
45 Jayson Williams/75 4.00 10.00
47 Avery Johnson/30 6.00 15.00
50 Mark Price/49 6.00 15.00

2013-14 Panini Spectra Jerseys Autographs Orange

*ORANGE: .4X TO 1X LT BLUE
PRINT RUNS B/WN 12-25 COPIES PER
NO PRICING ON QTY 12
EXCHANGE DEADLINE 1/16/2016
14 Shaquille O'Neal 20 150.00 400.00
18 John Havlicek/20 60.00 150.00
27 Anfernee Hardaway/20 50.00 120.00
34 Kobe Bryant/20 500.00 1,000.00
50 Mark Price/20 20.00 50.00

2013-14 Panini Spectra Marks Memorabilia

PRINT RUNS B/WN 125-199 COPIES PER
EXCHANGE DEADLINE 1/16/2016
12 Robert Horry/125 5.00 12.00
13 Alex English/199 6.00 15.00

2013-14 Panini Spectra Marks Memorabilia Light Blue

PRINT RUNS B/WN 20-99 COPIES PER
EXCHANGE DEADLINE 1/16/2016
4 Hakeem Olajuwon/20 30.00 60.00
5 Gail Goodrich/20 10.00 25.00
6 Larry Johnson/75 10.00 25.00
7 Tracy McGrady/20 40.00 80.00
8 Grant Hill/20 30.00 60.00
12 Robert Horry/49 6.00 15.00
14 Bob Lanier/20 8.00 20.00
15 Terry Cummings/99 5.00 12.00
16 James Worthy/20 15.00 40.00

2013-14 Panini Spectra Marks Memorabilia Orange

*ORANGE: .4X TO 1X LT BLUE
PRINT RUNS B/WN 15-60 COPIES PER
NO PRICING ON QTY 15
EXCHANGE DEADLINE 1/16/2016

2013-14 Panini Spectra Materials

STATED PRINT RUN 25 SER.#'d SETS
1 Jared Sullinger 2.50 6.00
2 Kevin Durant 15.00 40.00
3 Kenneth Faried 3.00 8.00
4 Tim Duncan 12.00 30.00
6 Kevin Garnett 10.00 25.00
7 Kobe Bryant 20.00 50.00
8 Stephen Curry 30.00 80.00
9 Kevin Love 4.00 10.00
10 Kemba Walker 4.00 10.00
11 Kyrie Irving 10.00 25.00
12 Russell Westbrook 6.00 15.00
13 James Harden 8.00 20.00
15 Blake Griffin 12.00 30.00
16 Paul Pierce 6.00 15.00
17 LeBron James 20.00 50.00
18 O.J. Mayo 2.50 6.00
19 Ricky Rubio 3.00 8.00
20 Anthony Davis 10.00 25.00
21 Dirk Nowitzki 10.00 25.00
22 Damian Lillard 10.00 25.00
23 Dwight Howard 5.00 12.00
24 Al Horford 4.00 10.00
25 Chris Paul 8.00 20.00
26 Monta Ellis 3.00 8.00
27 Dwyane Wade 10.00 25.00
28 Bradley Beal 6.00 15.00
29 Carmelo Anthony 6.00 15.00
30 Kawhi Leonard 10.00 25.00

2013-14 Panini Spectra Rookie Jumbo Jerseys

STATED PRINT RUN 75 SER.#'d SETS
1 Nate Wolters 2.50 6.00
2 Rudy Gobert 10.00 25.00
3 Steven Adams 6.00 15.00
4 C.J. McCollum 10.00 25.00
5 Tim Hardaway Jr. 5.00 12.00
6 Shane Larkin 2.50 6.00
7 Cody Zeller 3.00 8.00
8 Kelly Olynyk 3.00 8.00
9 Trey Burke 3.00 8.00
10 Matthew Dellavedova 4.00 10.00
11 Otto Porter 4.00 10.00
12 Solomon Hill 3.00 8.00
13 Victor Oladipo 6.00 15.00
14 Luigi Datome 2.50 6.00
15 Mason Plumlee 3.00 8.00
16 Kentavious Caldwell-Pope 4.00 10.00
17 Archie Goodwin 2.50 6.00
18 Anthony Bennett 2.50 6.00
19 Tony Snell 3.00 8.00
20 Giannis Antetokounmpo 200.00 500.00
21 Nerlens Noel 3.00 8.00
22 Alex Len 3.00 8.00
23 Michael Carter-Williams 3.00 8.00
24 Gal Mekel 2.50 6.00
25 Ben McLemore 3.00 8.00

2013-14 Panini Spectra Spectacular Swatch Signatures

PRINT RUNS B/WN 75-199 COPIES PER
EXCHANGE DEADLINE 1/16/2016
3 Thaddeus Young/199 3.00 8.00
5 Fat Lever/199 4.00 10.00
15 Fred Brown/199 4.00 10.00
19 Kawhi Leonard/75 75.00 200.00
20 Mark Price/175 8.00 20.00
23 Larry Johnson/75 8.00 20.00
27 Alex English/149 6.00 15.00
43 Marcin Gortat/175 8.00 20.00
65 Ryan Anderson/75 3.00 8.00
68 Thabo Sefolosha/75 4.00 10.00
72 Tom Chambers/149 5.00 12.00
80 Steve Mix/99 3.00 8.00
99 Kevin Willis/99 4.00 10.00

2013-14 Panini Spectra Spectacular Swatch Signatures Light Blue

PRINT RUNS B/WN 20-60 COPIES PER
EXCHANGE DEADLINE 1/16/2016
1 Buck Williams/60 8.00 20.00
5 Fat Lever/60 5.00 12.00
6 Tony Parker/20 50.00 100.00
7 Kyrie Irving/20 75.00 150.00
9 Kareem Abdul-Jabbar/20 30.00 80.00
10 Avery Johnson/20 12.00 30.00
12 Scottie Pippen/20 100.00 250.00
15 Fred Brown/60 5.00 12.00
16 Clyde Drexler/20 40.00 80.00
18 George Hill/60 4.00 10.00
19 Kawhi Leonard/35 100.00 250.00
20 Mark Price/60 12.00 30.00
23 Larry Johnson/35 10.00 25.00
27 Alex English/60 8.00 20.00
28 Steve Blake/60 4.00 10.00
29 Kelly Tripucka/60 5.00 12.00
30 Gary Payton/20 20.00 50.00
32 Stephen Curry/20 500.00 1,000.00
35 Grant Hill/20 20.00 50.00
41 David Robinson/20 40.00 80.00
42 Tyson Chandler/20 5.00 12.00
43 Marcin Gortat/60 10.00 25.00
48 Nick Collison/60 4.00 10.00
49 Kenny Sky Walker/49 8.00 20.00
52 Steve Nash/20 40.00 100.00
56 Hakeem Olajuwon/20 30.00 60.00
57 Anthony Mason/60 8.00 20.00
61 Brad Daugherty/60 6.00 15.00
65 Ryan Anderson/35 4.00 10.00
68 Thabo Sefolosha/35 10.00 25.00
70 Kevin Durant/20 100.00 200.00
72 Tom Chambers/49 6.00 15.00
73 Glen Rice/35 10.00 25.00
75 James Harden/20 30.00 60.00
79 Kevin Love/20 40.00 80.00
80 Steve Mix/60 4.00 10.00
85 Josh Smith/20 4.00 10.00
87 Bob Lanier/20 8.00 20.00
90 Kurt Rambis/49 6.00 15.00
95 Karl Malone/20 50.00 100.00
97 Bradley Beal/20 20.00 50.00
99 Kevin Willis/60 5.00 12.00

2013-14 Panini Spectra Spectacular Swatch Signatures Orange

*ORANGE: .4X TO 1X LT BLUE
PRINT RUNS B/WN 15-35 COPIES PER
NO PRICING ON QTY 15
EXCHANGE DEADLINE 1/16/2016

2013-14 Panini Spectra Swatches

PRINT RUNS B/WN 15-49 COPIES PER
1 Elgin Baylor/15 3.00 8.00
2 Dan Majerle/49 2.50 6.00
3 Dwight Howard/49 4.00 10.00
4 Rajon Rondo/25 4.00 10.00
5 Shaquille O'Neal /49 12.00 30.00
6 Kevin Garnett/49 8.00 20.00
7 Moses Malone/49 5.00 12.00
8 Russell Westbrook/49 5.00 12.00
9 Patrick Ewing/49 8.00 20.00
10 LeBron James/49 15.00 40.00
11 Brad Daugherty/49 3.00 8.00
12 Jason Kidd/49 8.00 20.00
13 Chris Paul/49 6.00 15.00
14 Kevin Durant/49 10.00 25.00
15 Avery Johnson/49 2.50 6.00
16 Kobe Bryant/49 25.00 60.00
17 Dominique Wilkins/49 5.00 12.00
18 James Harden/49 6.00 15.00
19 Kurt Rambis/49 3.00 8.00
20 Ricky Rubio/49 2.50 6.00
21 Reggie Lewis/49 10.00 25.00
22 Anfernee Hardaway/49 12.00 30.00
23 Dwyane Wade/49 6.00 15.00
24 Kenneth Faried/49 2.50 6.00
25 Joe Dumars/49 4.00 10.00
26 Stephen Curry/49 6.00 15.00
27 Scottie Pippen/49 8.00 20.00
28 John Wall/49 4.00 10.00
29 Robert Horry/49 3.00 8.00
30 Anthony Davis/49 6.00 15.00
31 Tracy McGrady/25 6.00 15.00
32 David Robinson/49 6.00 15.00
33 Carmelo Anthony/49 5.00 12.00
34 Tim Duncan/49 6.00 15.00
35 Fat Lever/49 2.50 6.00
36 Kevin Love/49 3.00 8.00
37 Robert Parish/49 3.00 8.00
39 Larry Johnson/49 4.00 10.00
40 Dirk Nowitzki/49 8.00 20.00
41 Xavier McDaniel/49 2.50 6.00
42 Julius Erving/49 8.00 20.00
43 Kemba Walker/49 3.00 8.00
44 Paul George/49 5.00 12.00
45 Alex English/49 4.00 10.00
46 Kyrie Irving/49 8.00 20.00
47 Clyde Drexler/49 15.00 40.00
48 Paul Pierce/49 5.00 12.00
49 Bill Laimbeer/49 6.00 15.00
50 Damian Lillard/49 10.00 25.00

2013-14 Panini Spectra Threads Autographs

PRINT RUNS B/WN 35-149 COPIES PER
EXCHANGE DEADLINE 1/16/2016
*ORANGE: .4X TO 1X LT BLUE
8 Bill Laimbeer/149 8.00 20.00
11 Jeff Malone/149 6.00 15.00
14 Taj Gibson/125 5.00 12.00
16 Kenneth Faried/25 6.00 15.00
17 Andrew Bogut/35 6.00 15.00
20 Greg Monroe/125 5.00 12.00
21 Jodie Meeks/149 5.00 12.00
28 Charles Oakley/149 8.00 20.00
29 Enes Kanter/125 6.00 15.00

2013-14 Panini Spectra Threads Autographs Light Blue

PRINT RUNS B/WN 25-60 COPIES PER
EXCHANGE DEADLINE 1/16/2016
4 Stephen Curry/25 800.00 1,500.00
5 Bradley Beal/25 20.00 50.00
6 Kareem Abdul-Jabbar/25 100.00 250.00
8 Bill Laimbeer/25 12.00 30.00
12 Avery Johnson/25 10.00 25.00
15 David Robinson/25 50.00 120.00
22 Terry Cummings/25 10.00 25.00
23 Robert Horry/60 12.00 30.00
24 Thabo Sefolosha/25 10.00 25.00
25 Gary Payton/25 20.00 50.00
27 Anthony Mason/75 10.00 25.00
31 John Stockton/25 50.00 120.00
35 Grant Hill/25 20.00 50.00

2013-14 Panini Spectra Threads Autographs Orange

*ORANGE: .4X TO 1X LT BLUE
PRINT RUNS B/WN 15-49 COPIES PER
EXCHANGE DEADLINE 1/16/2016

2014-15 Panini Spectra

*BLUE VET/49: .5X TO 1.2X BASE HI
*BLUE RK/99: .5X TO 1.2X BASE HI
*ORANGE RK/25: .75X TO 2X BASE HI
*RED DIE CUT/25: 1.2X TO 3X BASE HI
1 Zach Randolph 2.00 5.00
2 Kenneth Faried 1.25 3.00
3 Kevin Durant 6.00 15.00
4 Goran Dragic 2.00 5.00
5 Michael Kidd-Gilchrist 1.25 3.00
6 Bradley Beal 3.00 8.00
7 Dwight Howard 2.50 6.00
8 Carmelo Anthony 3.00 8.00
9 Pete Maravich 6.00 15.00
10 Al Horford 2.00 5.00
11 Luol Deng 1.50 4.00
12 David Robinson 4.00 10.00
13 Klay Thompson 5.00 12.00
14 Kawhi Leonard 5.00 12.00
15 Derrick Rose 4.00 10.00
16 Shawn Kemp 3.00 8.00
17 DeAndre Jordan 1.50 4.00
18 Moses Malone 3.00 8.00
19 John Stockton 4.00 10.00
20 Rajon Rondo 2.50 6.00
21 Thaddeus Young 1.25 3.00
22 Eric Bledsoe 1.50 4.00
23 Andre Drummond 1.50 4.00
24 John Havlicek 4.00 10.00
25 Dirk Nowitzki 5.00 12.00
26 Giannis Antetokounmpo 12.00 30.00
27 Magic Johnson 8.00 20.00
28 Trevor Ariza 1.25 3.00
29 Tony Parker 3.00 8.00
30 Dennis Schroder 2.00 5.00
31 Russell Westbrook 3.00 8.00
32 Nick Young 1.25 3.00
33 Damian Lillard 5.00 12.00
34 Joakim Noah 2.00 5.00
35 Omer Asik 1.25 3.00
36 Gordon Hayward 1.50 4.00
37 Jared Sullinger 1.25 3.00
38 Marc Gasol 2.00 5.00
39 Marcin Gortat 1.25 3.00
40 Stephen Curry 40.00 100.00
41 Serge Ibaka 1.50 4.00
42 Shaquille O'Neal 8.00 20.00
43 Lance Stephenson 1.50 4.00
44 LaMarcus Aldridge 2.00 5.00
45 Blake Griffin 2.50 6.00
46 Kyle Lowry 2.50 6.00
47 Chandler Parsons 1.25 3.00
48 Brandon Knight 1.25 3.00
49 Kareem Abdul-Jabbar 6.00 15.00
50 Jeff Green 1.50 4.00
51 Ricky Rubio 1.50 4.00
52 Amar'e Stoudemire 2.00 5.00
53 Brandon Jennings 1.25 3.00
54 Nicolas Batum 1.50 4.00
55 Tim Duncan 5.00 12.00
56 Pau Gasol 3.00 8.00
57 Mike Conley 1.50 4.00
58 Victor Oladipo 1.50 4.00
59 JaVale McGee 1.50 4.00
60 Anthony Davis 5.00 12.00
61 Larry Bird 8.00 20.00
62 Deron Williams 1.50 4.00
63 Hakeem Olajuwon 4.00 10.00
64 Paul George 3.00 8.00
65 Andrea Bargnani 1.25 3.00
66 Tyson Chandler 2.00 5.00
67 Chris Bosh 2.50 6.00
68 Trey Burke 1.25 3.00
69 LeBron James 40.00 100.00
70 Grant Hill 3.00 8.00
71 DeMar DeRozan 2.50 6.00
72 Ty Lawson 1.25 3.00
73 Rudy Gay 2.00 5.00
74 Kobe Bryant 40.00 100.00
75 Clyde Drexler 3.00 8.00
76 Kevin Garnett 5.00 12.00
77 Channing Frye 1.25 3.00
78 Scottie Pippen 5.00 12.00
79 David Lee 1.25 3.00
80 Bill Russell 6.00 15.00
81 John Wall 2.50 6.00
82 Kyrie Irving 4.00 10.00
83 Anfernee Hardaway 5.00 12.00
84 Chris Paul 3.00 8.00
85 Nikola Pekovic 1.25 3.00
86 DeMarcus Cousins 1.50 4.00
87 Al Jefferson 1.25 3.00
88 Dwyane Wade 4.00 10.00
89 Michael Carter-Williams 1.25 3.00
90 Roy Hibbert 1.50 4.00
91 Walt Frazier 3.00 8.00
92 Josh Smith 1.25 3.00
93 Wilt Chamberlain 6.00 15.00
94 Karl Malone 4.00 10.00
95 James Harden 4.00 10.00
96 Elgin Baylor 4.00 10.00
97 Kevin Love 2.00 5.00
98 George Gervin 3.00 8.00
99 Nerlens Noel 1.25 3.00
100 Jeremy Lin 4.00 10.00
101 Jabari Parker JSY AU RC 5.00 12.00
102 A.Wiggins JSY AU RC 40.00 100.00
103 Joel Embiid JSY AU RC 100.00 250.00
104 Marcus Smart JSY AU RC 15.00 40.00
105 Julius Randle JSY AU RC 20.00 50.00
106 Aaron Gordon JSY AU RC 20.00 50.00
107 Nik Stauskas JSY AU RC 4.00 10.00
108 Elfrid Payton JSY AU RC 6.00 15.00
109 Doug McDermott JSY AU RC 6.00 15.00
110 Zach LaVine JSY AU RC 40.00 100.00
111 Shabazz Napier JSY AU RC 5.00 12.00
112 Gary Harris JSY AU RC 6.00 15.00
113 Rodney Hood JSY AU RC 5.00 12.00
114 James Ennis JSY AU RC 4.00 10.00
115 Tyler Ennis JSY AU RC 4.00 10.00
116 Noah Vonleh JSY AU RC 4.00 10.00
117 T.J. Warren JSY AU RC 6.00 15.00
118 Johnny O'Bryant JSY AU RC 4.00 10.00
119 C.J. Wilcox JSY AU RC 4.00 10.00
120 Adreian Payne JSY AU RC 4.00 10.00
121 Damien Inglis JSY AU RC 4.00 10.00
122 Jordan Adams JSY AU RC 4.00 10.00
123 Mitch McGary JSY AU RC 4.00 10.00
124 Kyle Anderson JSY AU RC 6.00 15.00
125 Spencer Dinwiddie JSY AU RC 6.00 15.00
126 K.J. McDaniels JSY AU RC 4.00 10.00
127 Joe Harris JSY AU RC 6.00 15.00
128 P.J. Hairston JSY AU RC 4.00 10.00
129 Jarnell Stokes JSY AU RC 4.00 10.00
130 Jerami Grant JSY AU RC 20.00 50.00
131 Cory Jefferson JSY AU RC 4.00 10.00
132 Markel Brown JSY AU RC 4.00 10.00
133 James Young JSY AU RC 4.00 10.00

2014-15 Panini Spectra Double Team Jerseys

STATED PRINT RUN B/WN 35-49 COPIES PER
DTATL A.Horford/J.Teague/49 6.00 15.00
DTBOS A.Bradley/J.Sullinger/49 4.00 10.00
DTBRK J.Johnson/D.Williams/49 5.00 12.00
DTCHI J.Butler/D.Rose/49 15.00 40.00
DTCLE K.Irving/L.James/49 75.00 200.00
DTDAL D.Nowitzki/M.Ellis/49 15.00 40.00
DTDEN K.Faried/T.Lawson/35 4.00 10.00
DTDET A.Drummond/G.Monroe/49 5.00 12.00
DTGSW K.Thompson/S.Curry/49 60.00 150.00
DTHOU D.Howard/J.Harden/49 12.00 30.00
DTLAC B.Griffin/C.Paul/49 10.00 25.00
DTLAL K.Bryant/S.Nash/49 75.00 200.00
DTMEM M.Gasol/M.Conley/35 6.00 15.00
DTMIA C.Bosh/D.Wade/49 12.00 30.00
DTMIN T.Young/G.Dieng/49 4.00 10.00
DTNYK T.Hardaway/C.Anthony/49 10.00 25.00
DTOKC R.Westbrook/K.Durant/49 20.00 50.00
DTORL V.Oladipo/N.Vucevic/49 5.00 12.00
DTPHX E.Bledsoe/G.Dragic/49 6.00 15.00
DTPOR L.Aldridge/N.Batum/35 6.00 15.00
DTSAC D.Collison/D.Cousins/49 5.00 12.00
DTSAS T.Duncan/T.Parker/49 15.00 40.00
DTTOR D.DeRozan/T.Ross/49 8.00 20.00
DTWAS B.Beal/J.Wall/49 10.00 25.00

2014-15 Panini Spectra Franchise Fabrics

STATED PRINT RUN 25 SER.#'d SETS
FRAAD Anthony Davis 20.00 50.00
FRAAH Al Horford 8.00 20.00
FRAAI Allen Iverson 20.00 50.00
FRAAM Alonzo Mourning 12.00 30.00
FRAAS Arvydas Sabonis 10.00 25.00
FRAAW Antoine Walker 6.00 15.00
FRABB Bradley Beal 12.00 30.00
FRABD Brad Daugherty 6.00 15.00
FRABG Blake Griffin 8.00 20.00
FRACA Carmelo Anthony 12.00 30.00
FRACB Chris Bosh 12.00 30.00
FRACD Clyde Drexler 12.00 30.00
FRACM Chris Mullin 10.00 25.00
FRACR Clifford Robinson 8.00 20.00
FRADC DeMarcus Cousins 6.00 15.00
FRADD DeMar DeRozan 10.00 25.00
FRADH Dwight Howard 10.00 25.00
FRADM1 Danny Manning 6.00 15.00
FRADM2 Dikembe Mutombo 12.00 30.00
FRADN Dirk Nowitzki 20.00 50.00
FRADR1 David Robinson 15.00 40.00
FRADR2 Derrick Rose 15.00 40.00
FRADW Dominique Wilkins 12.00 30.00
FRAEI Ersan Ilyasova 5.00 12.00
FRAEM Earl Monroe 12.00 30.00
FRAGD Goran Dragic 8.00 20.00
FRAGM Greg Monroe 5.00 12.00
FRAGP Gary Payton 12.00 30.00
FRAHG Hal Greer 8.00 20.00
FRAHO Hakeem Olajuwon 15.00 40.00
FRAJD Joe Dumars 10.00 25.00
FRAJK Jason Kidd 12.00 30.00
FRAJR Jalen Rose 6.00 15.00
FRAJS1 Jared Sullinger 5.00 12.00
FRAJS2 John Stockton 15.00 40.00
FRAJW1 James Worthy 12.00 30.00
FRAJW2 John Wall 10.00 25.00
FRAKA Kareem Abdul-Jabbar 25.00 60.00
FRAKB Kobe Bryant 75.00 200.00
FRAKD Kevin Durant 25.00 60.00
FRAKF Kenneth Faried 5.00 12.00
FRAKG Kevin Garnett 20.00 50.00
FRAKM Karl Malone 15.00 40.00
FRALB Larry Bird 30.00 80.00
FRALBJ LeBron James 75.00 200.00
FRALJ Larry Johnson 10.00 25.00
FRAMC Michael Carter-Williams 5.00 12.00
FRAMF Michael Finley 8.00 20.00
FRAMK Michael Kidd-Gilchrist 5.00 12.00
FRAPE Patrick Ewing 12.00 30.00
FRARH Roy Hibbert 6.00 15.00
FRARL Reggie Lewis 8.00 20.00
FRARR Ricky Rubio 6.00 15.00
FRASC Stephen Curry 75.00 200.00
FRASK Shawn Kemp 12.00 30.00
FRASO Shaquille O'Neal 30.00 80.00
FRATD Tim Duncan 20.00 50.00
FRATM Tracy McGrady 12.00 30.00
FRAVO Victor Oladipo 6.00 15.00
FRAWD Walter Davis 6.00 15.00
FRAYM Yao Ming 20.00 50.00
FRAZR Zach Randolph 8.00 20.00

2014-15 Panini Spectra Freshman Fabrics

STATED PRINT RUN 49 SER.#'d SETS
FREAG Aaron Gordon 12.00 30.00
FREAP Adreian Payne 2.50 6.00
FREAW Andrew Wiggins 12.00 30.00
FREBC Bruno Caboclo 3.00 8.00
FRECE Cleanthony Early 2.50 6.00
FRECJ Cory Jefferson 2.50 6.00
FRECW C.J. Wilcox 2.50 6.00
FREDE Dante Exum 4.00 10.00
FREDI Damien Inglis 2.50 6.00
FREDM Doug McDermott 4.00 10.00
FREEP Elfrid Payton 4.00 10.00
FREGH Gary Harris 4.00 10.00
FREGR Glenn Robinson III 3.00 8.00
FREJA Jordan Adams 2.50 6.00
FREJE1 James Ennis 2.50 6.00
FREJE2 Joel Embiid 25.00 60.00
FREJG Jerami Grant 12.00 30.00
FREJH Joe Harris 4.00 10.00
FREJO Johnny O'Bryant 2.50 6.00
FREJP Jabari Parker 3.00 8.00
FREJR Julius Randle 12.00 30.00
FREJS Jarnell Stokes 2.50 6.00
FREJY James Young 2.50 6.00
FREKA Kyle Anderson 4.00 10.00
FREKM K.J. McDaniels 2.50 6.00
FREMB Markel Brown 2.50 6.00
FREMM Mitch McGary 2.50 6.00
FREMS Marcus Smart 10.00 25.00
FRENS Nik Stauskas 2.50 6.00
FRENV Noah Vonleh 2.50 6.00
FREPH P.J. Hairston 2.50 6.00
FRERH Rodney Hood 3.00 8.00
FRERS Russ Smith 2.50 6.00
FRESD Spencer Dinwiddie 4.00 10.00
FRESN Shabazz Napier 3.00 8.00
FRETE Tyler Ennis 2.50 6.00
FRETW T.J. Warren 4.00 10.00
FREZL Zach LaVine 15.00 40.00

2014-15 Panini Spectra Global Icons

1 Luis Scola 12.00 30.00
2 Marcin Gortat 10.00 25.00
3 Andrew Wiggins 50.00 125.00
4 Tony Parker 25.00 60.00
5 Dennis Schroder 15.00 40.00
6 Drazen Petrovic 20.00 50.00
7 Ben Gordon 12.00 30.00
8 Nik Stauskas 10.00 25.00
9 Luigi Datome 10.00 25.00
10 Mirza Teletovic 10.00 25.00
11 Nikola Pekovic 10.00 25.00
12 Joel Embiid 100.00 250.00
13 Festus Ezeli 10.00 25.00
14 Ian Mahinmi 10.00 25.00
15 Yao Ming 40.00 100.00
16 Goran Dragic 15.00 40.00
17 Bismack Biyombo 10.00 25.00
18 Pau Gasol 25.00 60.00
19 Anderson Varejao 10.00 25.00
20 Sergey Karasev 10.00 25.00
21 Peja Stojakovic 12.00 30.00
22 Marc Gasol 15.00 40.00
23 Pablo Prigioni 10.00 25.00
24 Luc Longley 12.00 30.00
25 Lucas Nogueira 12.00 30.00
26 Boris Diaw 12.00 30.00
27 Patrick Ewing 25.00 60.00
28 Jusuf Nurkic 30.00 80.00
29 Kevin Seraphin 10.00 25.00
30 Giannis Antetokounmpo 100.00 250.00
31 Tristan Thompson 10.00 25.00
32 Timofey Mozgov 10.00 25.00
33 Manu Ginobili 30.00 80.00
34 Dirk Nowitzki 40.00 100.00
35 Jonas Valanciunas 12.00 30.00
36 Luc Mbah a Moute 10.00 25.00
37 Nikola Mirotic 15.00 40.00
38 Evan Fournier 10.00 25.00
39 Dikembe Mutombo 25.00 60.00
40 Andrea Bargnani 10.00 25.00
41 Andrew Nicholson 10.00 25.00
42 Rik Smits 12.00 30.00
43 Leandro Barbosa 12.00 30.00
44 Kostas Papanikolaou 10.00 25.00
45 Detlef Schrempf 15.00 40.00
46 Zoran Dragic 12.00 30.00
47 Clint Capela 40.00 100.00
48 Matthew Dellavedova 12.00 30.00
49 Thabo Sefolosha 12.00 30.00
50 Tyler Ennis 10.00 25.00
51 Luol Deng 10.00 25.00
52 Nene 12.00 30.00

53 Gheorghe Muresan 10.00 25.00
54 Cory Joseph 10.00 25.00
55 Rudy Gobert 25.00 60.00
56 Patty Mills 15.00 40.00
57 J.J. Barea 12.00 30.00
58 Bojan Bogdanovic 15.00 40.00
59 Ricky Rubio 12.00 30.00
60 Bruno Caboclo 12.00 30.00
61 Marco Belinelli 10.00 25.00
62 Kelly Olynyk 10.00 25.00
63 Zaza Pachulia 10.00 25.00
64 Jonas Jerebko 10.00 25.00
65 Kyrie Irving 30.00 80.00
66 Nikola Vucevic 12.00 30.00
67 Manute Bol 15.00 40.00
68 Steve Nash 30.00 80.00
69 Nicolas Batum 12.00 30.00
70 Gorgui Dieng 10.00 25.00
71 Arvydas Sabonis 20.00 50.00
72 Mychal Thompson 12.00 30.00
73 Vlade Divac 15.00 40.00
74 Rick Fox 12.00 30.00
75 Donatas Motiejunas 10.00 25.00
76 Steven Adams 20.00 50.00
77 Dante Exum 15.00 40.00
78 Jose Calderon 10.00 25.00
79 Robert Sacre 10.00 25.00
80 Pero Antic 10.00 25.00
81 Ersan Ilyasova 10.00 25.00
82 Tiago Splitter 10.00 25.00
83 Alex Len 10.00 25.00
84 Danilo Gallinari 10.00 25.00
85 Enes Kanter 12.00 30.00
86 Andrew Bogut 12.00 30.00
87 Rony Seikaly 12.00 30.00
88 Swen Nater 10.00 25.00
89 Damjan Rudez 10.00 25.00
90 Omer Asik 10.00 25.00
91 Damien Inglis 10.00 25.00
92 Tim Duncan 40.00 100.00
93 Zydrunas Ilgauskas 12.00 30.00
94 Hedo Turkoglu 12.00 30.00
95 Omri Casspi 10.00 25.00
96 Greivis Vasquez 12.00 30.00
97 Anthony Bennett 10.00 25.00
98 Toni Kukoc 20.00 50.00
99 Al Horford 15.00 40.00
100 Joe Ingles 15.00 40.00

2014-15 Panini Spectra Hall of Fame Autograph Materials

STATED PRINT RUN B/WN 35-60 COPIES PER
HOFAD Adrian Dantley 12.00 30.00
HOFAG Artis Gilmore 15.00 40.00
HOFAM Alonzo Mourning 20.00 50.00
HOFCD Clyde Drexler 20.00 50.00
HOFDR1 David Robinson 60.00 150.00
HOFDR2 Dennis Rodman 75.00 200.00
HOFDW Dominique Wilkins 20.00 50.00
HOFGG1 Gail Goodrich 12.00 30.00
HOFGG2 George Gervin 20.00 50.00
HOFGP Gary Payton 20.00 50.00
HOFHO Hakeem Olajuwon 60.00 150.00
HOFIT Isiah Thomas 20.00 50.00
HOFJE Julius Erving 60.00 150.00
HOFJS John Stockton 50.00 120.00
HOFJW1 Jamaal Wilkes 12.00 30.00
HOFJW2 James Worthy 20.00 50.00
HOFKA Kareem Abdul-Jabbar 75.00 200.00
HOFKM Karl Malone 50.00 120.00
HOFLB Larry Bird 75.00 200.00
HOFMJ Magic Johnson 75.00 200.00
HOFMR Mitch Richmond 15.00 40.00
HOFRP Robert Parish 15.00 40.00
HOFRS Ralph Sampson 12.00 30.00

2014-15 Panini Spectra Jersey Autographs

STATED PRINT RUN B/WN 100-125 COPIES PER
*ORANGE/25: .8X TO 2X BASE HI
1 Andrew Nicholson/125 3.00 8.00
2 Antoine Walker/125 4.00 10.00
3 Brandan Wright/125 3.00 8.00
4 C.J. Watson/125 3.00 8.00
5 C.J. Wilcox/125 3.00 8.00
6 Carl Landry/100 3.00 8.00
7 Clifford Robinson/125 5.00 12.00
8 Cory Jefferson/125 3.00 8.00
9 Dan Issel/125 6.00 15.00
10 Dante Exum/100 5.00 12.00
11 Dikembe Mutombo/100 8.00 20.00
12 Eddie Johnson/125 3.00 8.00
13 Michael Cage/125 3.00 8.00
15 Gary Harris/125 5.00 12.00
16 James Ennis/125 3.00 8.00
17 James Jones/125 3.00 8.00
19 Jarnell Stokes/125 3.00 8.00
21 Joe Harris/125 5.00 12.00
22 Jordan Adams/125 3.00 8.00
23 K.J. McDaniels/125 3.00 8.00
25 Danny Green/100 4.00 10.00
26 Lavoy Allen/125 3.00 8.00
28 Luigi Datome/125 3.00 8.00
29 Mark Price/125 5.00 12.00
30 Markel Brown/125 3.00 8.00
31 Maurice Harkless/125 3.00 8.00
32 Nick Collison/125 4.00 10.00
38 Reggie Jackson/125 4.00 10.00
39 Robert Horry/125 5.00 12.00
40 Robert Parish/100 6.00 15.00
41 Rodney Hood/125 4.00 10.00
42 Russ Smith/125 3.00 8.00
43 Shabazz Napier/125 4.00 10.00
44 Spencer Dinwiddie/125 5.00 12.00
45 Spencer Hawes/125 3.00 8.00
46 Steve Blake/125 3.00 8.00
47 Thaddeus Young/125 3.00 8.00
48 Timofey Mozgov/125 3.00 8.00
50 Zach LaVine/125 20.00 50.00

2014-15 Panini Spectra Millenial Memorabilia

STATED PRINT RUN B/WN 25-35 COPIES PER
MMAB Anthony Bennett/25 5.00 12.00
MMAD Andre Drummond/35 6.00 15.00
MMAD Anthony Davis/25 20.00 50.00
MMAL Alex Len/25 5.00 12.00
MMAW Andrew Wiggins/25 25.00 60.00
MMBB Bradley Beal/35 12.00 30.00
MMBG Blake Griffin/35 8.00 20.00
MMBJ Brandon Jennings/25 5.00 12.00
MMBM Ben McLemore/25 5.00 12.00
MMCM C.J. McCollum/25 8.00 20.00
MMCP Chandler Parsons/25 5.00 12.00
MMCZ Cody Zeller/25 5.00 12.00
MMDC DeMarcus Cousins/35 6.00 15.00
MMDD DeMar DeRozan/35 10.00 25.00
MMDG Draymond Green/35 10.00 25.00
MMDG Danilo Gallinari/25 5.00 12.00
MMDG Danny Green/25 6.00 15.00
MMDR Derrick Rose/35 15.00 40.00
MMGM Greg Monroe/25 5.00 12.00
MMIT Isaiah Thomas/25 6.00 15.00
MMJB Jimmy Butler/35 12.00 30.00
MMJE Joel Embiid/25 50.00 125.00
MMJH James Harden/35 15.00 40.00
MMJH Jrue Holiday/35 10.00 25.00
MMJL Jeremy Lin/25 25.00 60.00
MMJP Jabari Parker/25 6.00 15.00
MMJR Julius Randle/25 25.00 60.00
MMJT Jeff Teague/25 5.00 12.00
MMJV Jonas Valanciunas/25 6.00 15.00
MMJW John Wall/25 10.00 25.00
MMKF Kenneth Faried/35 5.00 12.00
MMKI Kyrie Irving/35 15.00 40.00
MMKL Kawhi Leonard/25 20.00 50.00
MMKT Klay Thompson/25 20.00 50.00
MMKW Kemba Walker/25 8.00 20.00
MMMS Marcus Smart/25 20.00 50.00
MMNP Nikola Pekovic/25 5.00 12.00
MMNV Nikola Vucevic/25 6.00 15.00
MMOP Otto Porter/25 5.00 12.00
MMSA Steven Adams/25 10.00 25.00
MMSC Stephen Curry/35 75.00 200.00
MMSI Serge Ibaka/25 6.00 15.00
MMSM Shabazz Muhammad/25 5.00 12.00
MMTE Tyreke Evans/35 6.00 15.00
MMTG Taj Gibson/25 5.00 12.00
MMTL Ty Lawson/35 5.00 12.00
MMTS Tiago Splitter/25 5.00 12.00
MMTT Tristan Thompson/35 5.00 12.00
MMVO Victor Oladipo/25 6.00 15.00
MMWM Wesley Matthews/25 5.00 12.00

2014-15 Panini Spectra Rookie Jumbo Jerseys

STATED PRINT RUN 49 SER.#'d SETS
RJJAG Aaron Gordon 15.00 40.00
RJJAP Adreian Payne 3.00 8.00
RJJAW Andrew Wiggins 15.00 40.00
RJJBC Bruno Caboclo 4.00 10.00
RJJCE Cleanthony Early 3.00 8.00
RJJDE Dante Exum 5.00 12.00
RJJDM Doug McDermott 5.00 12.00
RJJEP Elfrid Payton 5.00 12.00
RJJGH Gary Harris 5.00 12.00
RJJGR Glenn Robinson III 4.00 10.00
RJJJA Jordan Adams 3.00 8.00
RJJJE Joel Embiid 30.00 80.00
RJJJH Joe Harris 3.00 8.00
RJJJP Jabari Parker 4.00 10.00
RJJJR Julius Randle 15.00 40.00
RJJJY James Young 3.00 8.00
RJJKM K.J. McDaniels 3.00 8.00
RJJMS Marcus Smart 12.00 30.00
RJJNS Nik Stauskas 3.00 8.00
RJJNV Noah Vonleh 3.00 8.00
RJJRH Rodney Hood 4.00 10.00
RJJSN Shabazz Napier 4.00 10.00
RJJTE Tyler Ennis 3.00 8.00
RJJTW T.J. Warren 5.00 12.00
RJJZL Zach LaVine 20.00 50.00

2014-15 Panini Spectra Spectacular Swatches Signatures

STATED PRINT RUN B/WN 35-149 COPIES PER
*ORANGE/25: .75X TO 2X pr/75-149
*ORANGE/25: .5X TO 1.2X pr/35-49
SSAD Adrian Dantley/49 12.00 30.00
SSAE Alex English/49 15.00 40.00
SSAM Alonzo Mourning/35 40.00 100.00
SSAP Adreian Payne/149 5.00 12.00
SSAW Andrew Wiggins/35 40.00 100.00
SSBB Bradley Beal/35 20.00 50.00
SSBL Brook Lopez/35 12.00 30.00
SSBM Ben McLemore/35 8.00 20.00
SSCA1 Carmelo Anthony/35 75.00 200.00
SSCA2 Chris Andersen/35 10.00 25.00
SSCE Cleanthony Early/149 5.00 12.00
SSCL Courtney Lee/49 8.00 20.00
SSCZ Cody Zeller/35 8.00 20.00
SSDB Dee Brown/75 10.00 25.00
SSDC DeMarre Carroll/149 5.00 12.00
SSDE Dante Exum/35 12.00 30.00
SSDF Derrick Favors/35 8.00 20.00
SSDG Danny Green/35 10.00 25.00
SSDM1 Danny Manning/35 10.00 25.00
SSDM2 Dikembe Mutombo/35 40.00 100.00
SSDR David Robinson/35 60.00 150.00
SSDW Dominique Wilkins/35 20.00 50.00
SSEP Elfrid Payton/49 12.00 30.00
SSGD1 Goran Dragic/35 10.00 25.00
SSGD2 Gorgui Dieng/149 5.00 12.00
SSGH1 Gary Harris/149 8.00 20.00
SSGH2 Gordon Hayward/35 20.00 50.00
SSGH3 Grant Hill/35 40.00 100.00
SSGP Gary Payton/35 40.00 100.00
SSHO Hakeem Olajuwon/35 60.00 150.00
SSIT1 Isaiah Thomas/149 6.00 15.00
SSIT2 Isiah Thomas/35 40.00 100.00
SSJC Jose Calderon/35 8.00 20.00
SSJH Joe Harris/149 8.00 20.00
SSJK Jason Kidd/35 40.00 100.00
SSJL Jerry Lucas/35 15.00 40.00
SSJP Jabari Parker/35 10.00 25.00
SSJR Julius Randle/35 40.00 100.00
SSJS1 Jared Sullinger/35 8.00 20.00
SSJS2 J.R. Smith/35 15.00 40.00
SSJT Jeff Teague/49 8.00 20.00
SSJW John Wall/35 20.00 50.00
SSKA1 Kareem Abdul-Jabbar/35 100.00 250.00
SSKA2 Kenny Anderson/149 6.00 15.00
SSKB Kobe Bryant/35 1,000.00 2,000.00
SSKC Kentavious Caldwell-Pope/35 10.00 25.00
SSKD Kevin Durant/35 125.00 300.00
SSKF Kenneth Faried/35 8.00 20.00
SSKI Kyrie Irving/35 60.00 150.00
SSKL Kevin Love/35 12.00 30.00
SSLA LaMarcus Aldridge/35 12.00 30.00
SSLS1 Lance Stephenson/49 10.00 25.00
SSLS2 Luis Scola/35 10.00 25.00
SSMA Mark Aguirre/49 10.00 25.00
SSMC Mike Conley/35 10.00 25.00
SSMF Michael Finley/35 12.00 30.00
SSMJ Marques Johnson/149 6.00 15.00
SSMK Michael Kidd-Gilchrist/35 8.00 20.00
SSMS Marcus Smart/35 30.00 80.00
SSMT Mirza Teletovic/149 5.00 12.00
SSNS Nik Stauskas/35 8.00 20.00
SSNV1 Nick Van Exel/35 12.00 30.00
SSNV2 Noah Vonleh/35 8.00 20.00
SSNY Nick Young/49 8.00 20.00
SSOP Otto Porter/35 10.00 25.00
SSQA Quincy Acy/149 5.00 12.00
SSRH Ron Harper/75 12.00 30.00
SSRL Robin Lopez/149 5.00 12.00
SSRS Robert Sacre/149 5.00 12.00
SSSA Steven Adams/149 10.00 25.00
SSSC Stephen Curry/35 1,000.00 2,000.00
SSSE Sean Elliott/49 12.00 30.00
SSSH Spencer Hawes/149 5.00 12.00
SSSM Sidney Moncrief/90 12.00 30.00
SSSN1 Shabazz Napier/149 6.00 15.00
SSSN2 Steve Nash/35 60.00 150.00
SSTC Tyson Chandler/35 12.00 30.00
SSTH Tobias Harris/49 8.00 20.00
SSTL Ty Lawson/35 8.00 20.00
SSTP Tony Parker/35 40.00 100.00
SSTS1 Tiago Splitter/35 8.00 20.00
SSTS2 Tony Snell/149 5.00 12.00
SSTW T.J. Warren/49 12.00 30.00
SSTY Thaddeus Young/149 5.00 12.00
SSWD Walter Davis/149 6.00 15.00
SSZL Zach LaVine/149 40.00 100.00

2014-15 Panini Spectra Spectacular Swatches Signatures Prizms Orange

*ORANGE: 1X TO 2.5X BASE HI
STATED PRINT RUN 25 SER.#'d SETS
SSJR Julius Randle 50.00 125.00
SSKA1 Kareem Abdul-Jabbar 125.00 300.00
SSMJ Marques Johnson 12.00 30.00

2014-15 Panini Spectra Superstar Autograph Materials

STATED PRINT RUN 35 SER.#'d SETS
3 Bradley Beal 20.00 50.00
4 Aaron Gordon 40.00 100.00
5 Julius Randle 40.00 100.00
6 Victor Oladipo 40.00 100.00
7 Marcus Smart 30.00 80.00
9 Grant Hill 60.00 150.00
10 Stephen Curry 1,000.00 2,000.00
11 Tony Parker 50.00 120.00
12 Jason Kidd 50.00 120.00
13 Tracy McGrady 100.00 250.00
15 Chris Bosh 15.00 40.00
16 Andrew Wiggins 40.00 100.00
17 Jabari Parker 10.00 25.00
18 John Wall 20.00 50.00
19 Kyrie Irving 75.00 200.00
20 Larry Bird 100.00 250.00
21 Magic Johnson 100.00 250.00
22 Kevin Durant 125.00 300.00
23 Carmelo Anthony 75.00 200.00
25 Kobe Bryant 1,000.00 2,000.00

2014-15 Panini Spectra Swatches

STATED PRINT RUN B/WN 25-49 COPIES PER
SAB Andrew Bogut/35 4.00 10.00
SAG Aaron Gordon/49 15.00 40.00
SAW Andrew Wiggins/49 15.00 40.00
SBC Bruno Caboclo/49 4.00 10.00
SBG Blake Griffin/25 5.00 12.00
SBL Bill Laimbeer/35 5.00 12.00
SCA Chris Andersen/35 4.00 10.00
SCE Cleanthony Early/49 3.00 8.00
SCR Clifford Robinson/35 5.00 12.00
SDC DeMarcus Cousins/25 4.00 10.00
SDE Dante Exum/49 5.00 12.00
SDM1 Dikembe Mutombo/35 8.00 20.00
SDM2 Doug McDermott/49 5.00 12.00
SDN Dirk Nowitzki/25 12.00 30.00
SDW Deron Williams/35 4.00 10.00
SEK Enes Kanter/25 4.00 10.00
SEP Elfrid Payton/49 5.00 12.00
SGD Goran Dragic/25 5.00 12.00
SGH1 Gary Harris/49 5.00 12.00
SGH2 Gerald Henderson/25 3.00 8.00
SGR Glenn Robinson III/49 4.00 10.00
SJE Joel Embiid/49 30.00 80.00
SJH1 James Harden/25 10.00 25.00
SJH2 Joe Harris/49 5.00 12.00
SJH3 John Henson/35 3.00 8.00
SJN Joakim Noah/35 5.00 12.00
SJP Jabari Parker/49 4.00 10.00
SJR Julius Randle/49 15.00 40.00
SJS Jared Sullinger/35 3.00 8.00
SJV Jonas Valanciunas/35 4.00 10.00
SJW John Wall/25 6.00 15.00
SJY James Young/49 5.00 12.00
SKI Kyrie Irving/25 10.00 25.00
SKK Kyle Korver/25 4.00 10.00
SKM K.J. McDaniels/49 3.00 8.00
SMS Marcus Smart/49 12.00 30.00
SNS Nik Stauskas/49 3.00 8.00
SPE Patrick Ewing/25 8.00 20.00
SPH P.J. Hairston/49 3.00 8.00
SRH1 Rodney Hood/49 4.00 10.00
SRH2 Roy Hibbert/35 4.00 10.00
SRR Ricky Rubio/25 4.00 10.00
SSI Serge Ibaka/35 4.00 10.00
SSN1 Steve Nash/25 10.00 25.00
SSN2 Shabazz Napier/49 4.00 10.00
STE Tyreke Evans/35 4.00 10.00
STH Tobias Harris/35 4.00 10.00
STS Tiago Splitter/35 3.00 8.00
SZL Zach LaVine/49 20.00 50.00
SZR Zach Randolph/35 5.00 12.00

2014-15 Panini Spectra Top Tier Threads

STATED PRINT RUN B/WN 25-35 COPIES PER
TTAD Adrian Dantley/25 8.00 20.00
TTAE Alex English/35 10.00 25.00
TTAH Anfernee Hardaway/25 20.00 50.00
TTAI Allen Iverson/25 20.00 50.00
TTCD Clyde Drexler/35 12.00 30.00
TTDJ Dennis Johnson/25 8.00 20.00
TTDN Dirk Nowitzki/35 20.00 50.00
TTDR1 David Robinson/35 15.00 40.00
TTDR2 Derrick Rose/35 15.00 40.00
TTDW Dwyane Wade/35 15.00 40.00
TTGH Grant Hill/35 12.00 30.00
TTGP Gary Payton/35 12.00 30.00
TTHO Hakeem Olajuwon/25 15.00 40.00
TTJS John Stockton/25 15.00 40.00
TTKA Kareem Abdul-Jabbar/25 25.00 60.00
TTKB Kobe Bryant/35 75.00 200.00
TTKD Kevin Durant/35 25.00 60.00
TTKG Kevin Garnett/35 20.00 50.00
TTKI Kyrie Irving/35 15.00 40.00
TTKL Kevin Love/35 8.00 20.00
TTKM Karl Malone/35 15.00 40.00
TTLB Larry Bird/25 30.00 80.00
TTLJ LeBron James/35 75.00 200.00
TTMM Moses Malone/25 12.00 30.00
TTPE Patrick Ewing/35 12.00 30.00
TTRW Russell Westbrook/35 12.00 30.00
TTSO Shaquille O'Neal/25 30.00 80.00
TTSP Scottie Pippen/25 20.00 50.00
TTTD Tim Duncan/35 20.00 50.00
TTYM Yao Ming/25 20.00 50.00

2014-15 Panini Spectra Triple Double Threads

STATED PRINT RUN B/WN 25-49 COPIES PER
TDAW Antoine Walker/49 6.00 15.00
TDCD Clyde Drexler/25 12.00 30.00
TDCM Chris Mullin/25 10.00 25.00
TDCW Chris Webber/35 10.00 25.00
TDDM Dikembe Mutombo/25 12.00 30.00
TDDR David Robinson/49 15.00 40.00
TDFL Fat Lever/25 8.00 20.00
TDGH Grant Hill/49 12.00 30.00
TDGP Gary Payton/25 12.00 30.00
TDHO Hakeem Olajuwon/25 15.00 40.00
TDJK Jason Kidd/25 12.00 30.00
TDJN Joakim Noah/25 8.00 20.00
TDLB Larry Bird/49 30.00 80.00
TDLBJ LeBron James/25 100.00 250.00
TDLJ Larry Johnson/25 10.00 25.00
TDMF Michael Finley/35 8.00 20.00
TDMJ1 Magic Johnson/25 30.00 80.00
TDMJ2 Mark Jackson/35 6.00 15.00
TDSC Stephen Curry/49 75.00 200.00
TDTD Tim Duncan/25 20.00 50.00

2015-16 Panini Spectra

1-100 PRINT RUN 215 SER.#'d SETS
JSY AU RC NOT SERIAL NUMBERED
EXCHANGE DEADLINE 12/15/2017
*ORANGE/25: .75X TO 2X BASIC
*RED DC/25: 2X TO 5X BASIC
1 Russell Westbrook 2.50 6.00
2 Bradley Beal 2.00 5.00
3 Danilo Gallinari 1.25 3.00
4 Zach Randolph 1.50 4.00
5 Andre Drummond 1.50 4.00
6 John Stockton 3.00 8.00
7 DeAndre Jordan 1.25 3.00
8 Shawn Kemp 2.50 6.00
9 DeMar DeRozan 2.00 5.00
10 Paul Millsap 1.25 3.00
11 Serge Ibaka 1.25 3.00
12 Marcin Gortat 1.00 2.50
13 Kenneth Faried 1.25 3.00
14 Dwight Howard 2.00 5.00
15 Reggie Jackson 1.25 3.00
16 Karl Malone 2.50 6.00
17 Rajon Rondo 2.00 5.00
18 Gary Payton 2.50 6.00
19 Kyle Lowry 1.50 4.00
20 Jeff Teague 1.00 2.50
21 Kevin Durant 6.00 15.00
22 Tim Duncan 4.00 10.00
23 Kevin Love 1.50 4.00
24 James Harden 3.00 8.00
25 Giannis Antetokounmpo 8.00 20.00
26 Rudy Gay 1.50 4.00
27 Oscar Robertson 4.00 10.00
28 Steve Nash 2.50 6.00
29 Isaiah Thomas 1.25 3.00
30 Tobias Harris 1.25 3.00
31 Gordon Hayward 1.50 4.00
32 Tony Parker 2.50 6.00
33 LeBron James 12.00 30.00
34 Anthony Davis 4.00 10.00
35 Jabari Parker 1.00 2.50
36 Allen Iverson 4.00 10.00
37 DeMarcus Cousins 1.50 4.00
38 Yao Ming 4.00 10.00
39 Avery Bradley 1.00 2.50
40 Nikola Vucevic 1.25 3.00
41 Derrick Favors 1.25 3.00
42 Kawhi Leonard 5.00 12.00
43 Kyrie Irving 3.00 8.00
44 Tyreke Evans 1.25 3.00
45 Greg Monroe 1.25 3.00
46 Patrick Ewing 2.50 6.00
47 Eric Bledsoe 1.25 3.00
48 Dennis Rodman 4.00 10.00
49 Carmelo Anthony 2.50 6.00
50 Dwyane Wade 3.00 8.00
51 Damian Lillard 4.00 10.00
52 Dirk Nowitzki 4.00 10.00
53 Derrick Rose 2.50 6.00
54 Wilt Chamberlain 6.00 15.00
55 Stephen Curry 12.00 30.00
56 Jason Kidd 2.50 6.00
57 Brandon Knight 1.00 2.50
58 Alonzo Mourning 2.50 6.00
59 Arron Afflalo 1.00 2.50
60 Hassan Whiteside 1.25 3.00
61 C.J. McCollum 1.50 4.00
62 Deron Williams 1.25 3.00
63 Jimmy Butler 3.00 8.00
64 Pete Maravich 4.00 10.00
65 Klay Thompson 4.00 10.00
66 Scottie Pippen 4.00 10.00
67 Kobe Bryant 12.00 30.00
68 Brook Lopez 1.50 4.00
69 Elgin Baylor 3.00 8.00
70 Chris Bosh 2.00 5.00
71 Andrew Wiggins 2.00 5.00
72 Zaza Pachulia 1.00 2.50
73 Pau Gasol 2.50 6.00
74 Magic Johnson 6.00 15.00
75 Draymond Green 2.00 5.00
76 Kareem Abdul-Jabbar 5.00 12.00
77 Latrell Sprewell 1.25 3.00
78 Jordan Clarkson 1.50 4.00
79 Thaddeus Young 1.00 2.50
80 Kemba Walker 1.50 4.00
81 Ricky Rubio 1.25 3.00
82 Marc Gasol 1.50 4.00
83 Paul George 2.50 6.00
84 Larry Bird 6.00 15.00
85 Blake Griffin 1.50 4.00
86 Tracy McGrady 2.50 6.00
87 Julius Randle 2.00 5.00
88 Nerlens Noel 1.00 2.50
89 Shaquille O'Neal 5.00 12.00
90 Nicolas Batum 1.00 2.50
91 Kevin Garnett 4.00 10.00
92 Mike Conley 1.50 4.00
93 Monta Ellis 1.25 3.00
94 Julius Erving 4.00 10.00
95 Chris Paul 3.00 8.00
96 Al Horford 1.50 4.00
97 Bill Russell 5.00 12.00
98 Dominique Wilkins 2.50 6.00
99 Isaiah Canaan 1.00 2.50
100 John Wall 2.00 5.00
101 K.Towns JSY AU RC 60.00 150.00
102 D.Russell JSY AU RC 12.00 30.00
103 J.Okafor JSY AU RC 4.00 10.00
104 E.Mudiay JSY AU RC 4.00 10.00
105 K.Porzingis JSY AU RC 30.00 80.00
106 M.Hezonja JSY AU RC 4.00 10.00
107 J.Winslow JSY AU RC 5.00 12.00
108 Cauley-Stein JSY AU RC 4.00 10.00
109 Tyus Jones JSY AU RC 4.00 10.00
110 Stanley Johnson JSY AU RC 4.00 10.00
111 Frank Kaminsky JSY AU RC 4.00 10.00
112 Devin Booker JSY AU RC 300.00 600.00
113 Myles Turner JSY AU RC 12.00 30.00
114 Trey Lyles JSY AU RC 4.00 10.00
115 Jerian Grant JSY AU RC 3.00 8.00
116 Nemanja Bjelica JSY AU RC 5.00 12.00
117 Cameron Payne JSY AU RC 5.00 12.00
118 Kelly Oubre Jr. JSY AU RC 10.00 25.00
119 Terry Rozier JSY AU RC 12.00 30.00
120 Rondae Hollis-Jefferson JSY AU RC 4.00 10.00
121 Bobby Portis JSY AU RC 8.00 20.00
122 N.Jokic JSY AU RC 1,000.00 2,000.00
123 Justin Anderson JSY AU RC 3.00 8.00
124 R.J. Hunter JSY AU RC 3.00 8.00
125 Raul Neto JSY AU RC 3.00 8.00
126 Marcelo Huertas JSY AU RC 3.00 8.00
127 Salah Mejri JSY AU RC 3.00 8.00
128 Norman Powell JSY AU RC 6.00 15.00
129 Sasha Kaun JSY AU RC 3.00 8.00
130 Pat Connaughton JSY AU RC 5.00 12.00
131 Richaun Holmes JSY AU RC 5.00 12.00
132 J.Simmons JSY AU RC 4.00 10.00
133 Cristiano Felicio JSY AU RC 4.00 10.00

2015-16 Panini Spectra City Limits

1 Dwight Howard 12.00 30.00
2 Stephen Curry 150.00 400.00
3 Tim Duncan 25.00 60.00
4 Magic Johnson 40.00 100.00
5 Anthony Davis 25.00 60.00
6 Shaquille O'Neal 30.00 80.00
7 Patrick Ewing 15.00 40.00
8 Dwyane Wade 20.00 50.00
9 Russell Westbrook 15.00 40.00
10 Dirk Nowitzki 25.00 60.00
11 Karl Malone 15.00 40.00
12 Scottie Pippen 25.00 60.00
13 James Harden 20.00 50.00
14 Larry Bird 40.00 100.00
15 Allen Iverson 25.00 60.00
16 Chris Paul 20.00 50.00
17 Carmelo Anthony 15.00 40.00
18 Damian Lillard 25.00 60.00
19 John Stockton 20.00 50.00
20 Derrick Rose 15.00 40.00
21 Kevin Durant 40.00 100.00
22 Kobe Bryant 200.00 500.00
23 LeBron James 200.00 500.00
24 Blake Griffin 10.00 25.00
25 Kyrie Irving 20.00 50.00

2015-16 Panini Spectra Franchise Fabrics

STATED PRINT RUN 49 SER.#'d SETS
1 Jimmy Butler 10.00 25.00
2 Monta Ellis 4.00 10.00
3 Al Horford 5.00 12.00
4 Arron Afflalo 3.00 8.00
5 Chris Paul 10.00 25.00
6 Dennis Rodman 12.00 30.00
7 John Wall 6.00 15.00
8 Omri Casspi 3.00 8.00
9 Rajon Rondo 6.00 15.00
10 Ricky Rubio 4.00 10.00
11 Chandler Parsons 3.00 8.00
12 Mike Conley 5.00 12.00
13 Marc Gasol 5.00 12.00
14 Tony Parker 8.00 20.00
15 Kobe Bryant 125.00 300.00
16 Grant Hill 8.00 20.00
17 Blake Griffin 5.00 12.00
18 Reggie Lewis 5.00 12.00
19 Tim Duncan 12.00 30.00
20 Dennis Schroder 5.00 12.00
21 Kenneth Faried 4.00 10.00
22 Zach Randolph 5.00 12.00
23 LeBron James 125.00 300.00
24 Kyle Lowry 5.00 12.00
25 Andrew Wiggins 6.00 15.00
26 Jalen Rose 6.00 15.00
27 Dwyane Wade 10.00 25.00
28 Scottie Pippen 12.00 30.00
29 Bradley Beal 6.00 15.00
30 Jared Sullinger 3.00 8.00
31 Andre Drummond 5.00 12.00
32 Elfrid Payton 4.00 10.00
33 Dirk Nowitzki 12.00 30.00
34 Rudy Gobert 6.00 15.00
35 Anthony Davis 12.00 30.00
36 John Stockton 10.00 25.00
37 Jabari Parker 3.00 8.00
38 Timofey Mozgov 3.00 8.00
39 Marcus Smart 6.00 15.00
40 Nikola Vucevic 4.00 10.00
41 Chris Bosh 6.00 15.00
42 Nerlens Noel 3.00 8.00
43 Stephen Curry 100.00 250.00
44 George Hill 4.00 10.00
45 Kevin Durant 20.00 50.00
46 Kevin Duckworth 3.00 8.00
47 Carmelo Anthony 8.00 20.00
48 Joakim Noah 3.00 8.00
49 Isaiah Thomas 4.00 10.00
50 Hassan Whiteside 4.00 10.00
51 Klay Thompson 12.00 30.00
52 Eric Bledsoe 4.00 10.00
53 James Harden 10.00 25.00
54 Charles Oakley 4.00 10.00
55 Russell Westbrook 8.00 20.00
56 Manu Ginobili 10.00 25.00
57 DeMarcus Cousins 5.00 12.00
58 Jusuf Nurkic 4.00 10.00
59 Kemba Walker 5.00 12.00
60 Donatas Motiejunas 3.00 8.00
61 Dwight Howard 6.00 15.00
62 Brandon Knight 3.00 8.00
63 Paul George 8.00 20.00
64 Danny Manning 4.00 10.00
65 Damian Lillard 12.00 30.00

2015-16 Panini Spectra Freshman Fabrics

STATED PRINT RUN 35 SER.#'d SETS
1 Kelly Oubre Jr. 8.00 20.00
2 Karl-Anthony Towns 15.00 40.00
3 Nikola Jokic 125.00 300.00
4 Kristaps Porzingis 8.00 20.00
5 Richaun Holmes 4.00 10.00
6 Jarell Martin 2.50 6.00
7 Montrezl Harrell 8.00 20.00
8 Devin Booker 6.00 15.00
9 Josh Richardson 4.00 10.00
10 Jerian Grant 2.50 6.00
11 Terry Rozier 10.00 25.00
12 D'Angelo Russell 6.00 15.00
13 Salah Mejri 2.50 6.00
14 Mario Hezonja 3.00 8.00
15 Jonathon Simmons 3.00 8.00
16 Stanley Johnson 3.00 8.00
17 Pat Connaughton 4.00 10.00
18 Myles Turner 10.00 25.00
19 Justin Anderson 2.50 6.00
20 Nemanja Bjelica 4.00 10.00
21 Rondae Hollis-Jefferson 3.00 8.00
22 Jahlil Okafor 5.00 12.00
23 Jordan Mickey 2.50 6.00
24 Justise Winslow 4.00 10.00
25 R.J. Hunter 2.50 6.00
26 Frank Kaminsky 3.00 8.00
27 Anthony Brown 2.50 6.00
28 Trey Lyles 3.00 8.00
29 Tyus Jones 3.00 8.00
30 Cameron Payne 4.00 10.00
31 Bobby Portis 6.00 15.00
32 Emmanuel Mudiay 3.00 8.00
34 Willie Cauley-Stein 3.00 8.00
35 Marcelo Huertas 2.50 6.00

2015-16 Panini Spectra Game Time Materials

STATED PRINT RUN 49 SER.#'d SETS
1 Anthony Davis 12.00 30.00
2 Scottie Pippen 12.00 30.00
3 Al Horford 5.00 12.00
4 Serge Ibaka 4.00 10.00
5 Julius Randle 6.00 15.00
6 Victor Oladipo 4.00 10.00
7 Zach Randolph 5.00 12.00
8 Brad Daugherty 4.00 10.00
9 James Harden 10.00 25.00
10 Isaiah Canaan 3.00 8.00
11 Kevin Durant 20.00 50.00
12 Terrence Ross 4.00 10.00
13 Bojan Bogdanovic 4.00 10.00
14 Andre Iguodala 5.00 12.00
15 Chris Bosh 6.00 15.00
16 LaMarcus Aldridge 5.00 12.00
17 Kyrie Irving 10.00 25.00
18 Clyde Drexler 8.00 20.00
19 Paul George 8.00 20.00
20 Kenny Smith 4.00 10.00
21 Russell Westbrook 8.00 20.00
22 Gary Harris 4.00 10.00
23 Nicolas Batum 3.00 8.00
24 Al Jefferson 3.00 8.00
25 Giannis Antetokounmpo 25.00 60.00
26 DeMarre Carroll 3.00 8.00
27 LeBron James 75.00 200.00
28 Dennis Rodman 12.00 30.00
29 Nerlens Noel 3.00 8.00
30 Larry Bird 20.00 50.00
31 Monta Ellis 4.00 10.00
32 Tobias Harris 4.00 10.00
33 Deron Williams 4.00 10.00
34 DeAndre Jordan 4.00 10.00
35 Tyreke Evans 4.00 10.00
36 Jonas Valanciunas 4.00 10.00
37 Dirk Nowitzki 12.00 30.00
38 Gary Payton 8.00 20.00
39 Kobe Bryant 75.00 200.00
40 Mike Bibby 4.00 10.00
41 John Wall 6.00 15.00
42 Rodney Hood 4.00 10.00
43 Draymond Green 6.00 15.00
44 Kyle Korver 4.00 10.00
45 Jrue Holiday 6.00 15.00
46 DeMarcus Cousins 5.00 12.00
47 Stephen Curry 75.00 200.00
48 Thaddeus Young 3.00 8.00
49 Arvydas Sabonis 5.00 12.00
50 Langston Galloway 3.00 8.00

2015-16 Panini Spectra Indelible Ink Materials

PRINT RUNS B/WN 35-60 COPIES PER
EXCHANGE DEADLINE 12/15/2017
*ORANGE: .6X TO 1.5X BASIC
1 Nikola Mirotic/60 6.00 15.00
2 Elfrid Payton/60 8.00 20.00
3 Matthew Dellavedova/60 8.00 20.00
4 Blake Griffin/35 15.00 40.00
5 Donatas Motiejunas/60 6.00 15.00
6 Kyrie Irving/35 75.00 200.00
7 John Wall/35 12.00 30.00
8 Mo Williams/60 8.00 20.00
9 Jonas Valanciunas/60 8.00 20.00
10 Zach LaVine/60 40.00 100.00
11 T.J. Warren/60 10.00 25.00
12 Alec Burks/60 6.00 15.00
13 Gary Harris/60 8.00 20.00
14 Klay Thompson/35 125.00 300.00
15 Tim Hardaway Jr./60 8.00 20.00
16 Marcin Gortat/60 6.00 15.00
17 Thaddeus Young/60 6.00 15.00
18 Kobe Bryant/35 1,500.00 3,000.00
19 Kevin Durant/35 150.00 400.00
20 Mason Plumlee/60 6.00 15.00

2015-16 Panini Spectra Marks Memorabilia

PRINT RUNS B/WN 35-65 COPIES PER
EXCHANGE DEADLINE 12/15/2017
1 Ray Allen/35 50.00 120.00
2 Jalen Rose/65 10.00 25.00
3 Robert Horry/65 10.00 25.00
4 Isiah Thomas/35 12.00 30.00
5 John Starks/65 12.00 30.00
6 Michael Finley/65 12.00 30.00
7 Gary Payton/35 40.00 100.00
8 Karl Malone/35 60.00 150.00
9 Dennis Rodman/35 125.00 300.00
10 Hakeem Olajuwon/65 75.00 200.00

2015-16 Panini Spectra Materials

PRINT RUNS B/WN 28-49 COPIES PER
1 Jeff Teague/49 3.00 8.00
2 Harrison Barnes/49 4.00 10.00
3 Jordan Clarkson/49 5.00 12.00
4 Aaron Gordon/49 5.00 12.00
5 Derrick Rose/49 8.00 20.00
6 Alonzo Mourning/49 8.00 20.00
7 James Harden/49 10.00 25.00
8 Hakeem Olajuwon/49 10.00 25.00
9 Anthony Davis/49 12.00 30.00
10 Patrick Ewing/49 8.00 20.00
11 Marcin Gortat/49 3.00 8.00
12 Derrick Favors/49 4.00 10.00
13 Vince Carter/49 10.00 25.00
14 C.J. McCollum/49 5.00 12.00
15 Kyrie Irving/49 10.00 25.00
16 Bernard King/49 6.00 15.00
17 Paul George/49 8.00 20.00
18 Jeff Malone/28 3.00 8.00
19 Kevin Durant/49 20.00 50.00
20 Richard Hamilton/49 5.00 12.00
21 Joe Johnson/49 4.00 10.00
22 Danilo Gallinari/49 4.00 10.00
23 Goran Dragic/49 5.00 12.00
24 Kawhi Leonard/49 15.00 40.00
25 LeBron James/49 75.00 200.00
26 Christian Laettner/49 4.00 10.00
27 Chris Paul/49 10.00 25.00
28 Karl Malone/49 8.00 20.00
29 Russell Westbrook/49 8.00 20.00
30 Shaquille O'Neal/49 15.00 40.00
31 Kevin Love/49 5.00 12.00
32 Pau Gasol/49 8.00 20.00
33 Michael Carter-Williams/49 3.00 8.00
34 DeMar DeRozan/49 6.00 15.00
35 Dirk Nowitzki/49 12.00 30.00
36 Dante Exum/49 4.00 10.00
37 Kobe Bryant/49 75.00 200.00
38 Kevin Garnett/49 12.00 30.00
39 Damian Lillard/49 12.00 30.00
40 Trey Burke/49 3.00 8.00
41 Brandon Jennings/49 3.00 8.00
42 Rudy Gay/49 5.00 12.00
43 Eric Gordon/49 4.00 10.00
44 Alec Burks/49 3.00 8.00
45 Stephen Curry/49 75.00 200.00
46 Eddie Johnson/35 3.00 8.00
47 Andrew Wiggins/49 6.00 15.00
48 Mark Jackson/49 4.00 10.00
49 John Wall/49 6.00 15.00
50 Chris Andersen/49 4.00 10.00

2015-16 Panini Spectra Rookie Jumbo Jerseys

STATED PRINT RUN 49 SER.#'d SETS
1 Frank Kaminsky 3.00 8.00
2 Jarell Martin 2.50 6.00
3 Jerian Grant 2.50 6.00
4 Terry Rozier 10.00 25.00
5 Karl-Anthony Towns 15.00 40.00
6 Justin Anderson 2.50 6.00
8 Norman Powell 5.00 12.00
9 Willie Cauley-Stein 3.00 8.00
10 Salah Mejri 2.50 6.00
11 Devin Booker 30.00 80.00
12 Sam Dekker 2.50 6.00
13 Nemanja Bjelica 4.00 10.00
14 Rondae Hollis-Jefferson 3.00 8.00
15 D'Angelo Russell 10.00 25.00
16 R.J. Hunter 2.50 6.00
17 Mario Hezonja 3.00 8.00
18 Joe Young 2.50 6.00
19 Tyus Jones 3.00 8.00
20 Luis Montero 2.50 6.00
21 Myles Turner 10.00 25.00
22 Jordan Mickey 2.50 6.00
23 Cameron Payne 4.00 10.00
24 Bobby Portis 6.00 15.00
25 Jahlil Okafor 3.00 8.00
26 Raul Neto 2.50 6.00
27 Justise Winslow 4.00 10.00
28 Pat Connaughton 4.00 10.00
29 Stanley Johnson 3.00 8.00
30 Delon Wright 3.00 8.00
31 Trey Lyles 3.00 8.00
32 Rakeem Christmas 2.50 6.00
33 Kelly Oubre Jr. 8.00 20.00
35 Emmanuel Mudiay 3.00 8.00

2015-16 Panini Spectra Spectacular Swatch Signatures

PRINT RUNS B/WN 35-149 COPIES PER
EXCHANGE DEADLINE 12/15/2017
1 Kyrie Irving/35 75.00 200.00
2 Isaiah Thomas/149 6.00 15.00

3 John Wall/35 10.00 25.00
4 Andrew Wiggins/35 40.00 100.00
5 Eric Bledsoe/40 6.00 15.00
6 Gary Harris/149 6.00 15.00
7 Norris Cole/99 5.00 12.00
8 T.J. Warren/149 8.00 20.00
9 Jonas Valanciunas/149 6.00 15.00
10 Gordon Hayward/149 8.00 20.00
11 Festus Ezeli/149 5.00 12.00
12 Blake Griffin/35 15.00 40.00
13 Al Horford/40 15.00 40.00
14 Andrew Bogut/99 6.00 15.00
15 Doug McDermott/149 6.00 15.00
16 Elfrid Payton/99 6.00 15.00
17 Dwight Howard/35 40.00 100.00
18 Victor Oladipo/35 6.00 15.00
19 Tristan Thompson/99 5.00 12.00
20 Klay Thompson/35 125.00 300.00
21 Zach LaVine/149 40.00 100.00
22 Nene/149 6.00 15.00
23 Bojan Bogdanovic/149 6.00 15.00
24 Timofey Mozgov/149 5.00 12.00
25 Kobe Bryant/35 1,500.00 3,000.00
26 Alec Burks/99 5.00 12.00
27 Jae Crowder/149 5.00 12.00
28 Marcin Gortat/149 5.00 12.00
29 Dennis Schroder/149 8.00 20.00
30 Dante Exum/35 6.00 15.00
31 David Robinson/35 75.00 200.00
32 Jason Kidd/35 60.00 150.00
33 Dikembe Mutombo/149 40.00 100.00
34 Grant Hill/35 60.00 150.00
35 John Stockton/35 75.00 200.00
36 Karl Malone/35 75.00 200.00
37 Bill Laimbeer/149 15.00 40.00
38 Thaddeus Young/99 5.00 12.00
39 Magic Johnson/35 125.00 300.00
40 Michael Carter-Williams/40 5.00 12.00
42 Jahlil Okafor/35 6.00 15.00
43 Mario Hezonja/99 6.00 15.00
44 Jerian Grant/149 5.00 12.00
45 Nemanja Bjelica/149 8.00 20.00
46 Emmanuel Mudiay/35 6.00 15.00
47 D'Angelo Russell/35 20.00 50.00
48 Karl-Anthony Towns/35 75.00 200.00
49 Willie Cauley-Stein/149 6.00 15.00
50 Myles Turner/149 20.00 50.00

2015-16 Panini Spectra Spectacular Swatch Signatures Prizms Light Blue

*LT.BLUE: .5X TO 1.2X BASIC
STATED PRINT RUN 49 SER.#'d SETS
EXCHANGE DEADLINE 12/15/2017
41 Kristaps Porzingis 75.00 200.00

2015-16 Panini Spectra Spectacular Swatch Signatures Prizms Orange

*ORANGE: .6X TO 1.5X BASIC
STATED PRINT RUN 25 SER.#'d SETS
EXCHANGE DEADLINE 12/15/2017
12 Blake Griffin 20.00 50.00
13 Al Horford 20.00 50.00
17 Dwight Howard 50.00 120.00
20 Klay Thompson 150.00 400.00
25 Kobe Bryant 2,000.00 4,000.00
31 David Robinson 100.00 250.00
34 Grant Hill 75.00 200.00
35 John Stockton 100.00 250.00
36 Karl Malone 100.00 250.00
39 Magic Johnson 150.00 400.00
48 Karl-Anthony Towns 100.00 250.00

2015-16 Panini Spectra Superstar Material Autographs

STATED PRINT RUN 30 SER.#'d SETS
EXCHANGE DEADLINE 12/15/2017
1 Kobe Bryant 800.00 1,500.00
2 Kevin Durant 125.00 300.00
3 Kyrie Irving 60.00 150.00
4 Blake Griffin 10.00 25.00
5 Anthony Davis 75.00 200.00
6 John Wall 12.00 30.00
7 Dwight Howard 20.00 50.00
8 Andrew Wiggins 12.00 30.00
9 Klay Thompson 60.00 150.00
10 Andre Drummond 10.00 25.00
11 Kristaps Porzingis 40.00 100.00
12 Karl-Anthony Towns 40.00 100.00
13 D'Angelo Russell 25.00 60.00
14 Jahlil Okafor 8.00 20.00
15 Emmanuel Mudiay 8.00 20.00
16 John Stockton 50.00 120.00
17 Karl Malone 50.00 120.00
18 Hakeem Olajuwon 50.00 120.00
19 Magic Johnson 100.00 250.00
20 David Robinson 50.00 120.00

2015-16 Panini Spectra Swatches

STATED PRINT RUN 49 SER.#'d SETS
1 Paul George 8.00 20.00
2 Bill Walton 8.00 20.00
3 Damian Lillard 12.00 30.00
4 Kevin McHale 8.00 20.00
5 Rajon Rondo 6.00 15.00
6 Brook Lopez 5.00 12.00
7 Chandler Parsons 3.00 8.00
8 Monta Ellis 4.00 10.00
9 Derrick Rose 8.00 20.00
10 Brandon Knight 3.00 8.00
11 Chris Paul 10.00 25.00
12 Clyde Drexler 8.00 20.00
13 John Wall 6.00 15.00
14 Michael Redd 4.00 10.00
15 Tim Duncan 12.00 30.00
16 O.J. Mayo 3.00 8.00
17 Kenneth Faried 4.00 10.00
18 Marc Gasol 5.00 12.00
19 Kyrie Irving 10.00 25.00
20 T.J. Warren 5.00 12.00
21 Kobe Bryant 75.00 200.00
22 David Robinson 10.00 25.00
23 Blake Griffin 5.00 12.00
24 Rafer Alston 3.00 8.00
25 Bradley Beal 6.00 15.00
26 Ben McLemore 3.00 8.00
27 Andre Drummond 5.00 12.00
28 Zach Randolph 5.00 12.00
29 LeBron James 75.00 200.00
30 Tony Parker 8.00 20.00
31 Andrew Wiggins 6.00 15.00
32 Elton Brand 4.00 10.00
33 Dwyane Wade 10.00 25.00
34 Rory Sparrow 3.00 8.00
35 Marcus Smart 6.00 15.00
36 George Hill 4.00 10.00
37 Reggie Jackson 4.00 10.00
38 Elfrid Payton 4.00 10.00
39 Dirk Nowitzki 12.00 30.00
40 Kyle Lowry 5.00 12.00
41 Anthony Davis 12.00 30.00
42 Herb Williams 3.00 8.00
43 Jabari Parker 3.00 8.00
44 Shaquille O'Neal 15.00 40.00
45 Isaiah Thomas 4.00 10.00
46 Paul Millsap 4.00 10.00
47 Nerlens Noel 3.00 8.00
49 Stephen Curry 75.00 200.00
50 Rudy Gobert 6.00 15.00
51 Kevin Durant 20.00 50.00
52 Joe Smith 4.00 10.00
53 Carmelo Anthony 8.00 20.00
54 Vlade Divac 5.00 12.00
55 Kemba Walker 5.00 12.00
56 Nikola Mirotic 3.00 8.00
57 Dwight Howard 6.00 15.00
58 Eric Bledsoe 4.00 10.00
59 James Harden 10.00 25.00
60 Alvan Adams 3.00 8.00
61 Russell Westbrook 8.00 20.00
62 Keith Van Horn 4.00 10.00
63 DeMarcus Cousins 5.00 12.00
64 Zach LaVine 12.00 30.00
65 Jimmy Butler 10.00 25.00

2016-17 Panini Spectra Neon Blue

*NEON BLUE 1-100: 1X TO 2.5X BASIC
*NEON BLUE 101-141: .5X TO 1.25X BASIC
1-100 PRINT RUN 60 SER.#'d SETS
101-141 PRINT RUN 99 SER.#'d SETS
EXCHANGE DEADLINE 12/28/2018

2016-17 Panini Spectra Neon Green

*NEON GREEN 1-100: 2.5X TO 6X BASIC
*NEON GREEN 101-141: .5X TO 1.2X BASIC
STATED PRINT RUN 25 SER.#'d SETS
EXCHANGE DEADLINE 12/28/2018

2016-17 Panini Spectra Pink

*PINK 1-100: 1.2X TO 3X BASIC
*PINK 101-141: .6X TO 1.5X BASIC
PRINT RUNS B/WN 45-49 COPIES PER
EXCHANGE DEADLINE 12/28/2018

2016-17 Panini Spectra Catalysts Materials

STATED PRINT RUN 149 SER.#'d SETS
1 Dennis Schroder 3.00 8.00
2 Marcus Smart 4.00 10.00
3 Isaiah Thomas 2.50 6.00
4 Kemba Walker 2.50 6.00
5 Michael Kidd-Gilchrist 2.00 5.00
7 Jimmy Butler 6.00 15.00
8 Kyrie Irving 6.00 15.00
9 Deron Williams 2.50 6.00
10 Harrison Barnes 2.50 6.00
11 Kentavious Caldwell-Pope 2.50 6.00
12 Stephen Curry 40.00 100.00
14 James Harden 6.00 15.00
15 Jeff Teague 2.00 5.00
16 Monta Ellis 2.50 6.00
17 Jamal Crawford 3.00 8.00
18 Chris Paul 5.00 12.00
19 D'Angelo Russell 5.00 12.00
20 Jordan Clarkson 3.00 8.00
21 Mike Conley 2.50 6.00
22 Goran Dragic 3.00 8.00
24 Ricky Rubio 2.50 6.00
26 Derrick Rose 5.00 12.00
29 Eric Bledsoe 2.50 6.00
30 Damian Lillard 8.00 20.00
31 C.J. McCollum 3.00 8.00
32 Darren Collison 2.00 5.00
33 Rudy Gay 3.00 8.00
34 Tony Parker 5.00 12.00
35 Kyle Lowry 3.00 8.00
36 DeMar DeRozan 4.00 10.00
39 John Wall 4.00 10.00
40 Bradley Beal 4.00 10.00

2016-17 Panini Spectra Catalysts Materials Neon Blue

*NEON BLUE: .5X TO 1.2X BASIC
PRINT RUNS B/WN 72-99 COPIES PER
13 Patrick Beverley/99 2.50 6.00
37 Alec Burks/99 3.00 8.00

2016-17 Panini Spectra Catalysts Materials Neon Green

*NEON GREEN: 1X TO 2.5X BASIC
PRINT RUNS B/WN 11-25 COPIES PER
NO PRICING ON QTY 17 OR LESS
6 Rajon Rondo/25 10.00 25.00
25 Tyreke Evans/25 6.00 15.00
27 Victor Oladipo/25 6.00 15.00
28 Elfrid Payton/25 6.00 15.00
37 Alec Burks/25 6.00 15.00

2016-17 Panini Spectra Catalysts Materials Pink

*PINK: .6X TO 1.5X BASIC
STATED PRINT RUN 49 SER.#'d SETS
6 Rajon Rondo 6.00 15.00
13 Patrick Beverley 3.00 8.00
23 Matthew Dellavedova 4.00 10.00
25 Tyreke Evans 4.00 10.00
27 Victor Oladipo 4.00 10.00
28 Elfrid Payton 4.00 10.00
37 Alec Burks 4.00 10.00
38 George Hill 4.00 10.00

2016-17 Panini Spectra Global Icons Memorabilia Autographs

STATED PRINT RUN 199 SER.#'d SETS
EXCHANGE DEADLINE 12/28/2018
2 Jakob Poeltl 6.00 15.00
7 J.J. Barea 20.00 50.00
8 Thon Maker 4.00 10.00
15 Jonas Valanciunas 4.00 10.00

2016-17 Panini Spectra Global Icons Memorabilia Autographs Neon Blue

*NEON BLUE: .5X TO 1.2X BASIC
STATED PRINT RUN 99 SER.#'d SETS
EXCHANGE DEADLINE 12/28/2018
1 Karl-Anthony Towns 20.00 50.00
3 Buddy Hield 12.00 30.00
4 Joel Embiid 100.00 250.00
6 Kristaps Porzingis 10.00 25.00
10 Jamal Murray 100.00 250.00
11 Dragan Bender 4.00 10.00
12 Zaza Pachulia 4.00 10.00
13 Luol Deng 5.00 12.00
14 Danilo Gallinari 5.00 12.00

2016-17 Panini Spectra Global Icons Memorabilia Autographs Neon Green

*NEON GREEN: .75X TO 2X BASIC
STATED PRINT RUN 25 SER.#'d SETS
EXCHANGE DEADLINE 12/28/2018
4 Joel Embiid 200.00 500.00

2016-17 Panini Spectra In the Zone Memorabilia Autographs

STATED PRINT RUN 149 SER.#'d SETS
EXCHANGE DEADLINE 12/28/2018
4 Dahntay Jones 3.00 8.00
5 Walter Berry 3.00 8.00
6 Brent Barry 3.00 8.00
7 Shane Battier 4.00 10.00
8 Walter Davis 5.00 12.00
12 Denzel Valentine 3.00 8.00
13 Chinanu Onuaku 3.00 8.00
14 Diamond Stone 3.00 8.00
15 Juan Hernangomez 6.00 15.00
16 Deyonta Davis 3.00 8.00
17 Tobias Harris 5.00 12.00
18 Demetrius Jackson 3.00 8.00
19 Cheick Diallo 3.00 8.00
20 Damian Jones 3.00 8.00
21 Georgios Papagiannis 3.00 8.00
23 Ivica Zubac 8.00 20.00
26 Nemanja Bjelica 3.00 8.00
27 Josh Richardson 4.00 10.00
34 Justin Anderson 3.00 8.00

2016-17 Panini Spectra In the Zone Memorabilia Autographs Neon Blue

*NEON BLUE: .5X TO 1.2X BASIC
STATED PRINT RUN 99 SER.#'d SETS
EXCHANGE DEADLINE 12/28/2018
1 Kobe Bryant 500.00 1,000.00
3 Magic Johnson 60.00 150.00
10 Grant Hill 25.00 60.00
11 Avery Bradley 4.00 10.00
24 Cody Zeller 4.00 10.00
25 C.J. McCollum 6.00 15.00
28 Brandon Knight 5.00 12.00
29 Victor Oladipo 5.00 12.00
31 Marcin Gortat 4.00 10.00
32 Devin Harris 4.00 10.00
33 Andre Drummond 6.00 15.00
35 LaMarcus Aldridge 6.00 15.00

2016-17 Panini Spectra In the Zone Memorabilia Autographs Neon Green

*NEON GREEN: .75X TO 2X BASIC
STATED PRINT RUN 25 SER.#'d SETS
EXCHANGE DEADLINE 12/28/2018
11 Avery Bradley 6.00 15.00
24 Cody Zeller 6.00 15.00
25 C.J. McCollum 10.00 25.00
28 Brandon Knight 8.00 20.00
29 Victor Oladipo 8.00 20.00
31 Marcin Gortat 6.00 15.00
32 Devin Harris 6.00 15.00
33 Andre Drummond 10.00 25.00
35 LaMarcus Aldridge 8.00 20.00

2016-17 Panini Spectra Locked In Memorabilia Autographs

STATED PRINT RUN 199 SER.#'d SETS
EXCHANGE DEADLINE 12/28/2018
4 Tyler Johnson 3.00 8.00
5 Malcolm Brogdon 10.00 25.00
10 Kay Felder 3.00 8.00
11 Demetrius Jackson 3.00 8.00
21 Michael Kidd-Gilchrist 3.00 8.00
24 Skal Labissiere 3.00 8.00
26 Ron Baker 3.00 8.00
32 Sean Kilpatrick 3.00 8.00
35 Juan Hernangomez 6.00 15.00
37 Thaddeus Young 3.00 8.00
40 Cheick Diallo 3.00 8.00
41 Henry Ellenson 3.00 8.00
44 Norman Powell 5.00 12.00
45 Pascal Siakam 20.00 50.00
46 Tony Allen 3.00 8.00
49 Bojan Bogdanovic 4.00 10.00
52 Steven Adams 4.00 10.00
57 Mason Plumlee 3.00 8.00
58 Allen Crabbe 3.00 8.00

2016-17 Panini Spectra Locked In Memorabilia Autographs Neon Blue

*NEON BLUE: .5X TO 1.2X BASIC
STATED PRINT RUN 99 SER.#'d SETS
EXCHANGE DEADLINE 12/28/2018
1 C.J. McCollum 6.00 15.00
3 Kobe Bryant 800.00 1,500.00
6 Denzel Valentine 4.00 10.00
7 Dwyane Wade 60.00 150.00
8 Kyrie Irving 75.00 200.00
9 Kevin Love 10.00 25.00
13 Blake Griffin 6.00 15.00
14 Diamond Stone 4.00 10.00
16 Marc Gasol 6.00 15.00
17 Jrue Holiday 8.00 20.00
19 Goran Dragic 6.00 15.00
20 Justise Winslow 5.00 12.00
22 George Hill 5.00 12.00
25 Kristaps Porzingis 10.00 25.00
27 Carmelo Anthony 75.00 200.00
28 Julius Randle 8.00 20.00
29 Tristan Thompson 5.00 12.00
31 Jeremy Lin 75.00 200.00
33 Danilo Gallinari 5.00 12.00
34 Jamal Murray 75.00 200.00
36 Jordan Clarkson 25.00 60.00
39 Buddy Hield 12.00 30.00
42 Andre Drummond 6.00 15.00
43 DeMar DeRozan 40.00 100.00
47 Eric Gordon 5.00 12.00
49 Devin Booker 125.00 300.00
50 Eric Bledsoe 5.00 12.00
51 Dragan Bender 4.00 10.00
54 Stephen Curry 600.00 1,200.00
55 Elfrid Payton 5.00 12.00
59 Klay Thompson 100.00 250.00
60 John Wall 8.00 20.00

2016-17 Panini Spectra Locked In Memorabilia Autographs Neon Green

*NEON GREEN: .75X TO 2X BASIC
STATED PRINT RUN 25 SER.#'d SETS
EXCHANGE DEADLINE 12/28/2018
14 Diamond Stone 5.00 12.00
23 Malachi Richardson 5.00 12.00

2016-17 Panini Spectra Next Era Materials

STATED PRINT RUN 149 SER.#'d SETS
*NEON BLUE/99: .5X TO 1.2X BASIC
*PINK/49: .6X TO 1.5X BASIC
*NEON GREEN/25: 1X TO 2.5X BASIC
1 Brandon Ingram 8.00 20.00
2 Jaylen Brown 15.00 40.00
3 Dragan Bender 2.00 5.00
4 Jamal Murray 15.00 40.00
5 Marquese Chriss 2.50 6.00
6 Jakob Poeltl 4.00 10.00
7 Thon Maker 2.50 6.00
8 Georgios Papagiannis 2.00 5.00
9 Denzel Valentine 2.00 5.00
10 Juan Hernangomez 4.00 10.00
11 Wade Baldwin IV 2.00 5.00
12 Henry Ellenson 2.00 5.00
13 Malik Beasley 4.00 10.00
14 Caris LeVert 5.00 12.00
15 Malachi Richardson 2.00 5.00
17 Brice Johnson 2.00 5.00
18 Pascal Siakam 12.00 30.00
19 Skal Labissiere 2.00 5.00
20 Dejounte Murray 10.00 25.00
21 Damian Jones 2.00 5.00
22 Deyonta Davis 2.00 5.00
23 Ivica Zubac 5.00 12.00
24 Cheick Diallo 2.00 5.00
25 Tyler Ulis 2.50 6.00
26 Malcolm Brogdon 6.00 15.00
27 Chinanu Onuaku 2.00 5.00
28 Patrick McCaw 2.00 5.00
29 Kay Felder 2.00 5.00
30 Andrew Wiggins 4.00 10.00
32 Jabari Parker 2.00 5.00
33 Jahlil Okafor 2.00 5.00
34 Kristaps Porzingis 5.00 12.00
35 D'Angelo Russell 4.00 10.00
36 Myles Turner 3.00 8.00
37 Emmanuel Mudiay 2.00 5.00
39 Devin Booker 12.00 30.00

2016-17 Panini Spectra Rising Stars Memorabilia Autographs

STATED PRINT RUN 199 SER.#'d SETS
*NEON GREEN/25: .75X TO 2X BASIC
1 Brandon Ingram 15.00 40.00
2 Buddy Hield 12.00 30.00
3 Kris Dunn 6.00 15.00
4 Jaylen Brown 150.00 400.00
5 Malcolm Brogdon 12.00 30.00
6 Tyler Ulis 5.00 12.00
7 Patrick McCaw 4.00 10.00
9 Kay Felder 4.00 10.00
10 Marquese Chriss 5.00 12.00
11 Thon Maker 5.00 12.00
13 Joel Embiid 75.00 200.00
14 Jabari Parker 4.00 10.00
15 Julius Randle 8.00 20.00
16 Kristaps Porzingis 10.00 25.00
18 Devin Booker 75.00 200.00
19 Myles Turner 6.00 15.00
20 Denzel Valentine 4.00 10.00
21 Pascal Siakam 25.00 60.00
22 Zach LaVine 12.00 30.00
24 Malachi Richardson 4.00 10.00
25 Wade Baldwin IV 4.00 10.00

2016-17 Panini Spectra Rising Stars Memorabilia Autographs Neon Blue

*NEON BLUE: .5X TO 1.2X BASIC
STATED PRINT RUN 99 SER.#'d SETS
EXCHANGE DEADLINE 12/28/2018
16 Karl-Anthony Towns 20.00 50.00
23 Dario Saric 8.00 20.00

2016-17 Panini Spectra Rising Stars Memorabilia Autographs Neon Green

*NEON GREEN: .75X TO 2X BASIC
STATED PRINT RUN 25 SER.#'d SETS
EXCHANGE DEADLINE 12/28/2018

2016-17 Panini Spectra Spectacular Swatch Autographs

STATED PRINT RUN 25-149 SER.#'d SETS
EXCHANGE DEADLINE 12/28/2018
*BLUE/75-99: .5X TO 1.2X p/r 149
*BLUE/75-99: .5X TO 1.2X p/r 49-99
*PINK/49: .5X TO 1.2X p/r 149
*PINK/49: .5X TO 1.2X p/r 49-99
*GREEN/25: .6X TO 1.5X p/r 149
*GREEN/25: .6X TO 1.5X p/r 49-99
1 Larry Bird/25 125.00 300.00
2 Denzel Valentine/149 4.00 10.00
3 David Robinson/49 40.00 100.00
4 Junior Bridgeman/149 5.00 12.00
5 Anfernee Hardaway/49 75.00 200.00
6 Damian Jones/149 4.00 10.00
7 Dragan Bender/99 5.00 12.00
9 Kobe Bryant/25 1,000.00 2,000.00
12 Tim Hardaway/149 15.00 40.00
13 Ricky Rubio/49 6.00 15.00
14 Kevin Durant/25 125.00 300.00
15 Jaylen Brown/49 EXCH 150.00 400.00
16 DeAndre' Bembry/149 6.00 15.00
17 C.J. McCollum/99 8.00 20.00
18 Robert Parish/99 10.00 25.00
19 Allen Iverson/25 125.00 300.00
20 Thon Maker/149 5.00 12.00
21 Yao Ming/49 100.00 250.00
22 Taurean Prince/149 5.00 12.00
23 Jimmy Butler/49 40.00 100.00
24 Caris LeVert/149 10.00 25.00
27 Kenny Smith/99 6.00 15.00
29 Carmelo Anthony/25 100.00 250.00
30 Zaza Pachulia/149 4.00 10.00
31 Pau Gasol/49 40.00 100.00
32 Skal Labissiere/149 EXCH 4.00 10.00
33 Marc Gasol/49 8.00 20.00
34 Demetrius Jackson/149 4.00 10.00
35 Buddy Hield/99 15.00 40.00
36 Brice Johnson/149 EXCH 4.00 10.00
37 Jamal Murray/99 100.00 250.00
39 Karl Malone/25 60.00 150.00
40 Al-Farouq Aminu/149 4.00 10.00
41 Karl-Anthony Towns/49 25.00 60.00
42 Dennis Scott/149 4.00 10.00
43 Brandon Ingram/49 20.00 50.00
44 Wade Baldwin IV/149 4.00 10.00
45 Kris Dunn/99 8.00 20.00
46 Dan Issel/49 10.00 25.00
47 Nikola Mirotic/99 5.00 12.00
48 Jakob Poeltl/149 8.00 20.00
49 Magic Johnson/25 125.00 300.00
50 Cedric Maxwell/149 5.00 12.00
51 Andrew Wiggins/49 10.00 25.00
52 Mark Price/149 6.00 15.00
53 Tony Parker/49 30.00 80.00
54 Henry Ellenson/149 4.00 10.00
55 Zach Randolph/99 8.00 20.00
56 Diamond Stone/149 4.00 10.00

2016-17 Panini Spectra Spectacular Swatches

PRINT RUNS B/WN 134-149 COPIES PER
3 Isaiah Thomas/134 3.00 8.00
8 Kemba Walker/149 3.00 8.00
10 Dwyane Wade/149 8.00 20.00
13 Dirk Nowitzki/149 10.00 25.00
14 Deron Williams/149 3.00 8.00
19 Draymond Green/149 5.00 12.00
20 Stephen Curry/149 60.00 150.00
21 Eric Gordon/149 3.00 8.00
22 James Harden/149 8.00 20.00
23 Paul George/149 6.00 15.00
25 Blake Griffin/149 4.00 10.00
29 Mike Conley/149 3.00 8.00
30 Marc Gasol/149 4.00 10.00
31 Hassan Whiteside/149 3.00 8.00
32 Goran Dragic/149 4.00 10.00
33 Giannis Antetokounmpo/149 40.00 100.00
34 Jabari Parker/149 2.50 6.00
35 Andrew Wiggins/149 5.00 12.00
39 Brandon Jennings/149 2.50 6.00
40 Derrick Rose/149 6.00 15.00
42 Russell Westbrook/149 6.00 15.00
43 Evan Fournier/149 3.00 8.00
44 Serge Ibaka/149 3.00 8.00
46 Nerlens Noel/149 2.50 6.00
48 Eric Bledsoe/149 3.00 8.00
51 DeMarcus Cousins/149 3.00 8.00
52 Willie Cauley-Stein/149 3.00 8.00
54 LaMarcus Aldridge/149 4.00 10.00
56 Tony Parker/149 6.00 15.00
57 DeMar DeRozan/149 5.00 12.00
58 Kyle Lowry/149 4.00 10.00
59 Gordon Hayward/149 4.00 10.00
61 Markieff Morris/149 2.50 6.00
62 Bradley Beal/149 5.00 12.00
63 John Wall/149 5.00 12.00
64 Kevin Love/149 4.00 10.00

2016-17 Panini Spectra Spectacular Swatches Neon Blue

*NEON BLUE: .5X TO 1.2X BASIC
PRINT RUNS B/WN 83-99 COPIES PER
1 Dwight Howard/99 6.00 15.00
2 Paul Millsap/99 4.00 10.00
4 Avery Bradley/99 3.00 8.00
5 Rondae Hollis-Jefferson/99 3.00 8.00
6 Brook Lopez/99 4.00 10.00
7 Nicolas Batum/99 4.00 10.00
9 Bobby Portis/99 5.00 12.00
11 LeBron James/99 40.00 100.00
12 Kyrie Irving/99 10.00 25.00
15 Danilo Gallinari/99 4.00 10.00
16 Emmanuel Mudiay/99 3.00 8.00
17 Andre Drummond/99 5.00 12.00
18 Stanley Johnson/99 3.00 8.00
24 Monta Ellis/99 3.00 8.00
26 DeAndre Jordan/99 4.00 10.00
36 Ricky Rubio/99 4.00 10.00
41 Steven Adams/99 4.00 10.00
45 Jahlil Okafor/99 3.00 8.00
55 Kawhi Leonard/99 12.00 30.00
60 Joe Johnson/99 5.00 12.00
65 Jeff Teague/99 3.00 8.00

2016-17 Panini Spectra Spectacular Swatches Neon Green

*NEON GREEN: 1X TO 2.5X BASIC
PRINT RUNS B/WN 8-25 COPIES PER
NO PRICING ON QTY 18 OR LESS
4 Avery Bradley/25 6.00 15.00
5 Rondae Hollis-Jefferson/25 6.00 15.00
6 Brook Lopez/25 8.00 20.00
7 Nicolas Batum/25 8.00 20.00
9 Bobby Portis/25 10.00 25.00
11 LeBron James/25 80.00 200.00
13 Dirk Nowitzki/25 25.00 60.00
15 Danilo Gallinari/25 8.00 20.00
16 Emmanuel Mudiay/25 6.00 15.00
17 Andre Drummond/25 10.00 25.00
18 Stanley Johnson/25 6.00 15.00
24 Monta Ellis/25 8.00 20.00
27 Jordan Clarkson/25 8.00 20.00
36 Ricky Rubio/25 8.00 20.00
37 Langston Galloway/25 6.00 15.00
38 Tyreke Evans/25 8.00 20.00
41 Steven Adams/25 8.00 20.00
45 Jahlil Okafor/25 6.00 15.00
47 Brandon Knight/25 8.00 20.00
50 Al-Farouq Aminu/25 6.00 15.00
53 Darren Collison/25 6.00 15.00
60 Joe Johnson/25 10.00 25.00
65 Jeff Teague/20 6.00 15.00

2016-17 Panini Spectra Spectacular Swatches Pink

*PINK: .6X TO 1.5X BASIC
PRINT RUNS B/WN 41-49 COPIES PER
1 Dwight Howard/49 8.00 20.00
2 Paul Millsap/49 5.00 12.00
4 Avery Bradley/49 4.00 10.00
5 Rondae Hollis-Jefferson/49 4.00 10.00
6 Brook Lopez/49 5.00 12.00
7 Nicolas Batum/49 5.00 12.00
9 Bobby Portis/49 6.00 15.00
11 LeBron James/49 50.00 125.00
12 Kyrie Irving/49 12.00 30.00
15 Danilo Gallinari/49 5.00 12.00
16 Emmanuel Mudiay/49 4.00 10.00
17 Andre Drummond/49 6.00 15.00
18 Stanley Johnson/49 4.00 10.00
24 Monta Ellis/49 5.00 12.00
26 DeAndre Jordan/49 5.00 12.00
27 Jordan Clarkson/49 6.00 15.00
36 Ricky Rubio/49 5.00 12.00
37 Langston Galloway/49 4.00 10.00
38 Tyreke Evans/49 5.00 12.00
41 Steven Adams/49 5.00 12.00
45 Jahlil Okafor/49 4.00 10.00
47 Brandon Knight/49 5.00 12.00
49 Evan Turner/49 4.00 10.00
50 Al-Farouq Aminu/49 4.00 10.00
53 Darren Collison/49 4.00 10.00
55 Kawhi Leonard/49 15.00 40.00
60 Joe Johnson/49 6.00 15.00
65 Jeff Teague/49 4.00 10.00

2016-17 Panini Spectra Triple Threat Materials

STATED PRINT RUN 149 SER.#'d SETS
*NEON BLUE/99: .5X TO 1.2X BASIC
*PINK/49: .6X TO 1.5X BASIC
1 LeBron James 100.00 250.00
5 Al Horford 4.00 10.00
7 Marc Gasol 4.00 10.00
8 Paul Millsap 3.00 8.00
9 Hassan Whiteside 3.00 8.00
11 DeMarcus Cousins 3.00 8.00
12 Carmelo Anthony 6.00 15.00
13 Brandon Ingram 10.00 25.00
15 Malcolm Brogdon 8.00 20.00
16 Paul George 6.00 15.00
17 Anthony Davis 12.00 30.00
18 Dirk Nowitzki 10.00 25.00
19 Devin Booker 20.00 50.00

2016-17 Panini Spectra Triple Threat Materials Neon Green

*NEON GREEN: 1X TO 2.5X BASIC
STATED PRINT RUN 25 SER.#'d SETS
14 Jaylen Brown 50.00 125.00

2017-18 Panini Spectra

JSY AU RC PRINT RUN BTWN 30-299 SER.#'d SETS
EXCHANGE DEADLINE 1/6/2020
1 Paul George 1.50 4.00
2 Dennis Schroder .75 2.00
3 Jayson Tatum RC 60.00 150.00
4 Anthony Davis 2.50 6.00
5 Giannis Antetokounmpo 5.00 12.00
6 Draymond Green 1.25 3.00
7 Kyrie Irving 2.00 5.00
8 Zach Randolph 1.00 2.50
9 Kristaps Porzingis 1.25 3.00
10 Goran Dragic .75 2.00
11 Carmelo Anthony 1.50 4.00
12 Taurean Prince .60 1.50
13 Rudy Gobert 1.25 3.00
14 DeMarcus Cousins .75 2.00
15 Khris Middleton 1.25 3.00
16 Klay Thompson 2.50 6.00
17 Jaylen Brown 2.50 6.00
18 Kyle Kuzma RC 2.50 6.00
19 Lonzo Ball RC 2.50 6.00
20 Donovan Mitchell RC 10.00 25.00
21 Russell Westbrook 1.50 4.00
22 Lauri Markkanen RC 4.00 10.00
23 Ricky Rubio .75 2.00
24 Jrue Holiday 1.25 3.00
25 Eric Bledsoe .75 2.00
26 Kevin Durant 4.00 10.00
27 Al Horford 1.00 2.50
28 Willie Cauley-Stein .60 1.50
29 Markelle Fultz RC 1.50 4.00
30 Hassan Whiteside .75 2.00
31 Jamal Murray 1.50 4.00
32 James Harden 2.00 5.00
33 LeBron James 8.00 20.00
34 Harrison Barnes .75 2.00
35 Victor Oladipo .75 2.00
36 Blake Griffin 1.00 2.50
37 DeMar DeRozan 1.25 3.00
38 Brandon Ingram 1.25 3.00
39 D'Angelo Russell .75 2.00
40 Kemba Walker .75 2.00
41 Nikola Jokic 6.00 15.00
42 Zhou Qi RC 1.25 3.00
43 Kevin Love 1.00 2.50
44 Dirk Nowitzki 2.50 6.00
45 Myles Turner 1.00 2.50
46 Lou Williams .75 2.00
47 Kyle Lowry 1.00 2.50
48 Brook Lopez .75 2.00
49 Rondae Hollis-Jefferson .60 1.50
50 Dwight Howard 1.25 3.00
51 De'Aaron Fox RC 10.00 25.00
52 Chris Paul 1.50 4.00
53 Dwyane Wade 2.00 5.00
54 Dennis Smith Jr. RC .75 2.00
55 Frank Ntilikina RC .75 2.00
56 DeAndre Jordan .75 2.00
57 Bogdan Bogdanovic RC 1.50 4.00
58 Jonathan Isaac RC 1.50 4.00
59 Jordan Bell RC .60 1.50
60 Josh Jackson RC .75 2.00
61 Damian Lillard 2.50 6.00
62 LaMarcus Aldridge 1.00 2.50
63 Tobias Harris .75 2.00
64 Marc Gasol 1.00 2.50
65 Milos Teodosic RC .75 2.00
66 Devin Booker 2.50 6.00
67 Joel Embiid 2.00 5.00
68 Bradley Beal 1.25 3.00
69 Jimmy Butler 1.50 4.00
70 Aaron Gordon 1.00 2.50
71 CJ McCollum 1.00 2.50
72 Kawhi Leonard 2.50 6.00
73 Andre Drummond .75 2.00
74 Mike Conley .75 2.00
75 Zach LaVine 1.50 4.00
76 Bam Adebayo RC 4.00 10.00
77 JJ Redick 1.00 2.50
78 John Wall 1.25 3.00
79 Andrew Wiggins 1.25 3.00
80 Malik Monk RC 2.50 6.00
81 OG Anunoby RC 3.00 8.00
82 Pau Gasol 1.50 4.00
83 Reggie Jackson .75 2.00
84 Frank Mason III RC .60 1.50
85 Stephen Curry 8.00 20.00
86 Isaiah Thomas .75 2.00
87 Ben Simmons 1.00 2.50
88 John Collins RC 1.50 4.00
89 Karl-Anthony Towns 1.50 4.00
90 Nikola Vucevic .75 2.00
91 Kobe Bryant 8.00 20.00
92 Shaquille O'Neal 3.00 8.00
93 Reggie Miller 2.00 5.00
94 Allen Iverson 2.50 6.00
95 Scottie Pippen 2.50 6.00
96 Chris Webber 1.50 4.00
97 Magic Johnson 4.00 10.00
98 Larry Bird 4.00 10.00
99 Julius Erving 2.50 6.00
100 Patrick Ewing 1.50 4.00
101 Donovan Mitchell JSY AU/299 100.00 250.00
102 Markelle Fultz JSY AU/299 12.00 30.00
103 Frank Ntilikina JSY AU/299 6.00 15.00
104 Terrance Ferguson JSY AU/299 RC 5.00 12.00
105 Jayson Tatum JSY AU/99 500.00 1,000.00
106 Josh Hart JSY AU/30 RC 30.00 80.00
107 Ante Zizic JSY AU/299 RC 6.00 15.00
108 Justin Patton JSY AU/299 RC 5.00 12.00
109 De'Aaron Fox JSY AU/299 100.00 250.00
110 Lonzo Ball JSY AU/299 20.00 50.00
111 Dwayne Bacon JSY AU/299 RC 5.00 12.00
112 Semi Ojeleye JSY AU/299 RC 6.00 15.00
113 Harry Giles JSY AU/299 RC 5.00 12.00
114 Tony Bradley JSY AU/299 RC 5.00 12.00
115 John Collins JSY AU/299 12.00 30.00
116 Josh Jackson JSY AU/299 6.00 15.00
117 Bam Adebayo JSY AU/299 30.00 80.00
118 Kyle Kuzma JSY AU/299 20.00 50.00
119 Dennis Smith Jr. JSY AU/299 6.00 15.00
120 Luke Kennard JSY AU/299 RC 10.00 25.00
121 Frank Jackson JSY AU/299 RC 5.00 12.00
122 Sindarius Thornwell JSY AU/299 RC 5.00 12.00
123 Ivan Rabb JSY AU/299 RC 5.00 12.00
124 Wes Iwundu JSY AU/299 RC 5.00 12.00
125 Jonathan Isaac JSY AU/299 12.00 30.00
126 Caleb Swanigan JSY AU/299 RC 5.00 12.00
127 D.J. Wilson JSY AU/299 RC 5.00 12.00
128 Lauri Markkanen JSY AU/299 30.00 80.00
129 Derrick White JSY AU/299 RC 20.00 50.00
130 Malik Monk JSY AU/299 20.00 50.00
131 Frank Mason III JSY AU/299 5.00 12.00
132 TJ Leaf JSY AU/299 5.00 12.00
133 Jarrett Allen JSY AU/299 RC 12.00 30.00
134 Zach Collins JSY AU/299 RC 8.00 20.00
135 Jordan Bell JSY AU/299 5.00 12.00

2017-18 Panini Spectra Neon Blue

*NEON BLUE: .75X TO 2X BASIC
*NEON BLUE RC: .75X TO 2X BASIC RC
*NEON BLUE JSY AU: .5X TO 1.2X BASE
PRINT RUNS B/WN 76-99 COPIES PER
33 LeBron James 40.00 100.00
85 Stephen Curry 40.00 100.00
91 Kobe Bryant 40.00 100.00

2017-18 Panini Spectra Neon Green

*NEON GREEN: 1.2X TO 3X BASIC
*NEON GREEN RC: 1.2X TO 3X BASIC RC
*NEON GREEN JSY AU: .6X TO 1.5X BASE
STATED PRINT RUN 49 SER.#'d SETS
33 LeBron James 60.00 150.00
85 Stephen Curry 60.00 150.00
91 Kobe Bryant 60.00 150.00

2017-18 Panini Spectra Neon Pink

*NEON PINK: 2X TO 5X BASIC
*NEON PINK RC: 2X TO 5X BASIC RC
*NEON PINK JSY AU: .75X TO 2X BASE
STATED PRINT RUN 25 SER.#'d SETS
33 LeBron James 100.00 250.00
85 Stephen Curry 100.00 250.00
91 Kobe Bryant 100.00 250.00

2017-18 Panini Spectra Red

*RED: .75X TO 2X BASIC
*RED RC: .6X TO 1.5X BASIC RC
STATED PRINT RUN 75 SER.#'d SETS
3 Jayson Tatum 150.00 400.00
18 Kyle Kuzma 5.00 12.00
20 Donovan Mitchell 25.00 60.00
22 Lauri Markkanen 15.00 40.00
29 Markelle Fultz 12.00 30.00
33 LeBron James 75.00 200.00
55 Frank Ntilikina 6.00 15.00
58 Jonathan Isaac 5.00 12.00
76 Bam Adebayo 60.00 150.00
80 Malik Monk 5.00 12.00
81 OG Anunoby 4.00 10.00
88 John Collins 8.00 20.00

2017-18 Panini Spectra Silver

*SILVER: 1.25X TO 3X BASIC
*SILVER RC: 1.25X TO 1.3X BASIC RC
33 LeBron James 40.00 100.00
85 Stephen Curry 40.00 100.00
91 Kobe Bryant 40.00 100.00

2017-18 Panini Spectra White Sparkle

*WHITE SPRKLE: 3X TO 8X BASIC
*WHITE SPRKLE RC: 3X TO 8X BASIC RC
33 LeBron James 150.00 400.00
41 Nikola Jokic 75.00 200.00
51 De'Aaron Fox 75.00 200.00
85 Stephen Curry 125.00 300.00
91 Kobe Bryant 125.00 300.00

2017-18 Panini Spectra Catalysts Memorabilia
STATED PRINT RUN 199 SER.#'d SETS
*NEON BLUE/99: .5X TO 1.2X
*NEON GREEN/25: 1X TO 2.5X
1 Willie Cauley-Stein 2.50 6.00
2 Russell Westbrook 6.00 15.00
3 Harrison Barnes 3.00 8.00
4 Devin Booker 10.00 25.00
5 Tobias Harris 3.00 8.00
7 Buddy Hield 4.00 10.00
8 Brook Lopez 3.00 8.00
9 Tyreke Evans 2.50 6.00
10 Bradley Beal 5.00 12.00
11 Yogi Ferrell 2.50 6.00
12 Paul George 6.00 15.00
13 Marcin Gortat 2.50 6.00
14 Rudy Gobert 5.00 12.00
15 Andrew Wiggins 5.00 12.00
16 Otto Porter Jr. 3.00 8.00
17 Ryan Anderson 2.50 6.00
18 Kevin Durant 15.00 40.00
19 Nikola Jokic 25.00 60.00
20 Rodney Hood 2.50 6.00
21 Nikola Mirotic 2.50 6.00
22 Kristaps Porzingis 5.00 12.00
23 Jabari Parker 2.50 6.00
24 Michael Kidd-Gilchrist 2.50 6.00
25 DeAndre Jordan 3.00 8.00
26 Klay Thompson 10.00 25.00
27 DeMarre Carroll 2.50 6.00
28 Blake Griffin 4.00 10.00
29 Kyle Lowry 4.00 10.00
30 Dario Saric 3.00 8.00
31 Kyrie Irving 8.00 20.00
32 Kawhi Leonard 10.00 25.00
33 Dennis Schroder 3.00 8.00
35 Jeff Teague 2.50 6.00
36 Malcolm Brogdon 3.00 8.00
37 Nicolas Batum 2.50 6.00
38 DeMarcus Cousins 3.00 8.00
39 Seth Curry 4.00 10.00
40 Elfrid Payton 2.50 6.00

2017-18 Panini Spectra Epic Legends Memorabilia
STATED PRINT RUN 149 SER.#'d SETS
*NEON BLUE/99: .5X TO 1.2X
*NEON GREEN/25: 1X TO 2.5X
1 Grant Hill 6.00 15.00
2 Danny Manning 3.00 8.00
3 Tree Rollins 2.50 6.00
4 David Robinson 12.00 30.00
5 Artis Gilmore 5.00 12.00
6 Chris Webber 6.00 15.00
7 Mitch Kupchak 3.00 8.00
8 Allen Iverson 20.00 50.00
9 Bernard King 5.00 12.00
10 Kevin Johnson 4.00 10.00
11 Shaquille O'Neal 20.00 50.00
12 John Stockton 8.00 20.00
13 Paul Silas 4.00 10.00
14 Antawn Jamison 3.00 8.00
15 Charles Oakley 3.00 8.00
16 B.J. Armstrong 4.00 10.00
17 Kelly Tripucka 3.00 8.00
18 Christian Laettner 4.00 10.00
19 Danny Granger 2.50 6.00
20 Reggie Lewis 5.00 12.00
21 Darrell Griffith 3.00 8.00
22 Joe Smith 3.00 8.00
23 George Gervin 6.00 15.00
24 Karl Malone 8.00 20.00
25 Kurt Rambis 3.00 8.00
26 Mitch Richmond 5.00 12.00
27 Nick Van Exel 4.00 10.00
28 Jamaal Wilkes 4.00 10.00
29 Paul Pierce 6.00 15.00
30 Tim Duncan 10.00 25.00

2017-18 Panini Spectra Global Icons Autographs
STATED PRINT RUN BTWN 49-149 SER.#'d SETS
EXCHANGE DEADLINE 1/6/2020
*NEON BLUE/49: .5X TO 1.2X p/r 99-149
*NEON BLUE/49: .4X TO 1X p/r 49
*NEON GREEN/25: .6X TO 1.5X p/r 99-149
*NEON GREEN/25: .5X TO 1.2X p/r 49
1 Toni Kukoc/149 6.00 15.00
2 Andrei Kirilenko/149 4.00 10.00
3 Zydrunas Ilgauskas/149 4.00 10.00
4 Arvydas Sabonis/135 6.00 15.00
5 Yao Ming/49 100.00 250.00
6 Dirk Nowitzki/49 100.00 250.00
7 Pau Gasol/49 20.00 50.00
8 Giannis Antetokounmpo/49 200.00 500.00
9 Tony Parker/49 15.00 40.00
10 Kristaps Porzingis/99 15.00 40.00
11 Jonas Jerebko/149 3.00 8.00
12 Nikola Jokic/149 125.00 300.00
13 Dominique Wilkins/99 15.00 40.00
14 Clint Capela/149 4.00 10.00
15 Jonas Valanciunas/149 4.00 10.00
16 Serge Ibaka/149 4.00 10.00
17 Enes Kanter/149 4.00 10.00
18 Nene/149 4.00 10.00
19 Thon Maker/149 3.00 8.00
20 Rudy Gobert/149 6.00 15.00

2017-18 Panini Spectra Illustrious Legends Signatures
STATED PRINT RUN BTWN 10-149 SER.#'d SETS
NO PRICING ON QTY 10
EXCHANGE DEADLINE 1/6/2020
*NEON BLUE/34-49: .5X TO 1.2X
*NEON GREEN/25: .6X TO 1.5X
1 Hersey Hawkins/149 4.00 10.00
2 Jermaine O'Neal/149 6.00 15.00
3 Spud Webb/149 10.00 25.00
4 Allan Houston/149 5.00 12.00
5 John Lucas/149 5.00 12.00
6 Reggie Miller/49 125.00 300.00
7 Spencer Haywood/149 6.00 15.00
8 Magic Johnson/49 60.00 150.00
9 Dick Barnett/149 5.00 12.00
10 Nate Thurmond/99 6.00 15.00
11 Corey Maggette/149 5.00 12.00
12 Bill Walton/149 25.00 60.00
13 Andrei Kirilenko/149 5.00 12.00
14 Shawn Kemp/99 15.00 40.00
15 Clark Kellogg/149 6.00 15.00
16 Allen Iverson/49 75.00 200.00
17 Mike Bibby/149 6.00 15.00
18 Jerry West/49 25.00 60.00
19 Mark Price/149 6.00 15.00
20 Artis Gilmore/99 8.00 20.00
21 Tom Van Arsdale/149 6.00 15.00
22 Danny Manning/149 5.00 12.00
23 Brad Daugherty/149 5.00 12.00
24 Antawn Jamison/149 5.00 12.00
25 A.C. Green/149 6.00 15.00
26 Karl Malone/49 25.00 60.00
27 Bob Dandridge/149 6.00 15.00
28 Alonzo Mourning/49 20.00 50.00
29 Shawn Bradley/149 4.00 10.00
30 Elvin Hayes/99 8.00 20.00
31 Fred Brown/149 5.00 12.00
32 Jo Jo White/149 6.00 15.00
33 Bill Laimbeer/149 6.00 15.00
34 Adrian Dantley/149 6.00 15.00
35 Damon Stoudamire/149 6.00 15.00
37 Bryant Reeves/149 4.00 10.00
38 Ray Allen/49 50.00 120.00
39 Eddie Jones/149 6.00 15.00
40 Lenny Wilkens/149 8.00 20.00

2017-18 Panini Spectra In The Zone Autographs
STATED PRINT RUN BTWN 49-99 SER.#'d SETS
EXCHANGE DEADLINE 1/6/2020
*NEON BLUE/49: .5X TO 1.2X
*NEON GREEN/35: .5X TO 1.2X
*NEON PINK/25: .6X TO 1.5X p/r 75-99
*NEON PINK/25: .5X TO 1.2X p/r 49
1 Magic Johnson/49 100.00 250.00
2 Jason Williams/99 40.00 100.00
3 Giannis Antetokounmpo/75 200.00 500.00
4 Marc Gasol/75 8.00 20.00
5 Kobe Bryant/99 500.00 1,000.00
6 Vince Carter/75 60.00 150.00
7 Shaquille O'Neal/49 100.00 250.00
8 James Worthy/75 10.00 25.00
9 Damian Lillard/49 100.00 250.00
10 Rudy Gobert/99 10.00 25.00
11 Anthony Davis/49 60.00 150.00
12 P.J. Brown/99 5.00 12.00
13 Karl-Anthony Towns/75 12.00 30.00
14 Ricky Rubio/75 6.00 15.00
16 D'Angelo Russell/75 6.00 15.00
17 Reggie Miller/49 125.00 300.00
18 Kemba Walker/75 6.00 15.00
19 Kyrie Irving/49 60.00 150.00
20 Al Attles/99 8.00 20.00
21 Blake Griffin/49 8.00 20.00
22 Chris Herren/99 6.00 15.00
23 Hakeem Olajuwon/75 50.00 120.00
24 Kevin Love/75 8.00 20.00
25 Kevin Durant/99 100.00 250.00
26 Kristaps Porzingis/75 20.00 50.00
27 Chris Paul/49 60.00 150.00
28 Jermaine O'Neal/75 8.00 20.00
29 Larry Bird/49 100.00 250.00
30 Elden Campbell/99 5.00 12.00

2017-18 Panini Spectra Locked In Autographs
STATED PRINT RUN BTWN 49-149 SER.#'d SETS
EXCHANGE DEADLINE 1/6/2020
*NEON BLUE/49: .5X TO 1.2X p/r 99-149
*NEON BLUE/49: .4X TO 1X p/r 49
*NEON GREEN/25: .6X TO 1.5X p/r 99-149
*NEON GREEN/25: .5X TO 1.2X p/r 49
1 Clyde Drexler/49 25.00 60.00
2 Tony Parker/49 20.00 50.00
3 Artis Gilmore/99 6.00 15.00
4 Grant Hill/49 25.00 60.00
5 Kemba Walker/99 4.00 10.00
6 Chris Paul/49 50.00 120.00
7 Paul Millsap/99 4.00 10.00
8 Blake Griffin/49 6.00 15.00
9 Kentavious Caldwell-Pope/99 4.00 10.00
10 Ricky Rubio/49 10.00 25.00
11 Hakeem Olajuwon/49 40.00 100.00
12 Vince Carter/49 50.00 120.00
13 Frank Ramsey/149 15.00 40.00
14 Jeremy Lin/49 40.00 100.00
15 Christian Laettner/99 8.00 20.00
16 Kyrie Irving/49 40.00 100.00
17 Rodney Hood/99 3.00 8.00
18 Giannis Antetokounmpo/49 125.00 300.00
19 Reggie Miller/49 60.00 150.00
20 Marc Gasol/49 6.00 15.00
21 James Worthy/49 10.00 25.00
22 Elvin Hayes/99 6.00 15.00
23 Adrian Dantley/149 5.00 12.00
24 Kristaps Porzingis/49 20.00 50.00
25 Mike Conley/99 4.00 10.00
26 Damian Lillard/49 75.00 200.00
27 Nikola Jokic/99 125.00 300.00
28 Karl-Anthony Towns/49 20.00 50.00
29 Allen Iverson/49 75.00 200.00
30 Brandon Ingram/49 20.00 50.00
31 Bob McAdoo/149 6.00 15.00
32 Isiah Thomas/125 15.00 40.00
33 Larry Brown/99 5.00 12.00
34 D'Angelo Russell/49 8.00 20.00
35 Richard Hamilton/99 6.00 15.00
36 Anthony Davis/49 40.00 100.00
37 Steve Kerr/99 12.00 30.00
38 Andrew Wiggins/49 10.00 25.00
39 Bernard King/99 6.00 15.00
40 Kevin Love/49 10.00 25.00

2017-18 Panini Spectra Next Era Memorabilia
STATED PRINT RUN 199 SER.#'d SETS
*NEON BLUE/99: .5X TO 1.2X
*NEON GREEN/25: .75X TO 2X
1 Caleb Swanigan 1.50 4.00
2 D.J. Wilson 1.50 4.00
3 Lonzo Ball 6.00 15.00
4 TJ Leaf 1.50 4.00
5 Jonathan Isaac 5.00 12.00
7 Dennis Smith Jr. 2.00 5.00
8 Derrick White 6.00 15.00
9 Luke Kennard 3.00 8.00
10 Ante Zizic 2.00 5.00
11 Markelle Fultz 4.00 10.00
12 Harry Giles 1.50 4.00
13 Jayson Tatum 40.00 100.00
14 Terrance Ferguson 1.50 4.00
15 Lauri Markkanen 10.00 25.00
16 Jordan Bell 1.50 4.00
17 Zach Collins 2.50 6.00
18 Dwayne Bacon 1.50 4.00
19 Donovan Mitchell 15.00 40.00
20 Justin Patton 1.50 4.00
21 Josh Jackson 2.00 5.00
22 John Collins 4.00 10.00
23 De'Aaron Fox 12.00 30.00
24 Jarrett Allen 4.00 10.00
25 Frank Ntilikina 2.00 5.00
26 Kyle Kuzma 6.00 15.00
27 Malik Monk 6.00 15.00
28 Semi Ojeleye 2.00 5.00
29 Bam Adebayo 10.00 25.00

2017-18 Panini Spectra Rising Stars Signatures
STATED PRINT RUN BTWN 99-199 SER.#'d SETS
EXCHANGE DEADLINE 1/6/2020
*NEON BLUE/49: .5X TO 1.2X BASE
*NEON GREEN/35: .5X TO 1.2X BASE
*NEON PINK/25: .6X TO 1.5X BASE
1 Jayson Tatum/99 400.00 800.00
2 Josh Jackson/99 6.00 15.00
3 Ante Zizic/199 6.00 15.00
4 Lauri Markkanen/199 30.00 80.00
5 De'Aaron Fox/99 75.00 200.00
6 Malik Monk/199 20.00 50.00
7 Frank Jackson/199 5.00 12.00
8 Sindarius Thornwell/199 5.00 12.00
9 Harry Giles/199 EXCH 5.00 12.00
10 Maxi Kleber/199 8.00 20.00
11 John Collins/199 12.00 30.00
12 Zach Collins/199 8.00 20.00
13 Bam Adebayo/199 30.00 80.00
14 Lonzo Ball/99 20.00 50.00
15 Dennis Smith Jr./199 EXCH 6.00 15.00
16 Markelle Fultz/99 12.00 30.00
17 Frank Mason III/199 5.00 12.00
18 Sterling Brown/199 5.00 12.00
19 Ivan Rabb/199 5.00 12.00
20 Bogdan Bogdanovic/199 12.00 30.00
21 Jonathan Isaac/199 12.00 30.00
22 Justin Jackson/199 5.00 12.00
23 D.J. Wilson/199 5.00 12.00
24 Luke Kennard/199 10.00 25.00
25 Derrick White/199 20.00 50.00
26 Semi Ojeleye/199 6.00 15.00
27 Frank Ntilikina/199 6.00 15.00
28 TJ Leaf/199 5.00 12.00
29 Milos Teodosic/199 6.00 15.00
30 Dillon Brooks/199 15.00 40.00
31 Jordan Bell/199 5.00 12.00
32 Kyle Kuzma/199 20.00 50.00
33 Zhou Qi/199 10.00 25.00
34 Justin Patton/199 5.00 12.00
35 Donovan Mitchell/199 75.00 200.00

2017-18 Panini Spectra Spectacular Swatches
STATED PRINT RUN 99 SER.#'d SETS
*NEON BLUE/49: .5X TO 1.2X
*NEON GREEN/25: .6X TO 1.5X
1 Nerlens Noel 2.00 5.00
2 Kevin Love 3.00 8.00
3 Jamal Crawford 3.00 8.00
5 Mike Conley 2.50 6.00
6 Stephen Curry 40.00 100.00
7 Paul Millsap 2.50 6.00
8 Damian Lillard 8.00 20.00
9 Avery Bradley 2.00 5.00
10 Giannis Antetokounmpo 40.00 100.00
11 Reggie Jackson 2.50 6.00
12 D'Angelo Russell 2.50 6.00
13 Rudy Gay 2.50 6.00
14 Rajon Rondo 4.00 10.00
15 CJ McCollum 3.00 8.00
16 LeBron James 40.00 100.00
17 Danilo Gallinari 2.50 6.00
18 Anthony Davis 8.00 20.00
19 JJ Redick 3.00 8.00
20 John Wall 4.00 10.00
21 Victor Oladipo 2.50 6.00
22 Marcus Smart 3.00 8.00
23 Enes Kanter 2.50 6.00
24 Dion Waiters 2.00 5.00
25 Jamal Murray 5.00 12.00
26 Carmelo Anthony 5.00 12.00
27 Khris Middleton 4.00 10.00
28 Dwight Howard 4.00 10.00
29 Marquese Chriss 2.00 5.00
30 Marc Gasol 3.00 8.00

2017-18 Panini Spectra Triple Threats Memorabilia
STATED PRINT RUN 99 SER.#'d SETS
*NEON BLUE/49: .5X TO 1.2X
*NEON GREEN/25: .6X TO 1.5X
1 Paul George 6.00 15.00
2 Tim Hardaway Jr. 3.00 8.00
3 Karl-Anthony Towns 6.00 15.00
4 Stephen Curry 60.00 150.00
5 Ben Simmons 4.00 10.00
6 Thon Maker 2.50 6.00
7 Dwyane Wade 8.00 20.00
8 Bobby Portis 2.50 6.00
9 Anthony Davis 10.00 25.00
11 Pau Gasol 6.00 15.00
12 Juan Hernangomez 4.00 10.00
13 John Wall 5.00 12.00
14 Kevin Durant 15.00 40.00
15 James Harden 8.00 20.00
16 Patrick Beverley 2.50 6.00
17 Damian Lillard 10.00 25.00
18 Jusuf Nurkic 3.00 8.00
19 Blake Griffin 4.00 10.00
20 Jarell Martin 2.50 6.00
21 Giannis Antetokounmpo 60.00 150.00
22 Pascal Siakam 8.00 20.00
23 Brandon Ingram 5.00 12.00
24 LeBron James 60.00 150.00
25 Carmelo Anthony 6.00 15.00
26 Thaddeus Young 2.50 6.00
27 Kyrie Irving 8.00 20.00
28 Al Jefferson 3.00 8.00
29 Derrick Rose 6.00 15.00
30 Markieff Morris 2.50 6.00
31 Andrew Wiggins 5.00 12.00
32 Willy Hernangomez 2.50 6.00
33 Jimmy Butler 6.00 15.00
34 Russell Westbrook 6.00 15.00
36 Allen Crabbe 2.50 6.00
37 Dirk Nowitzki 10.00 25.00
38 Draymond Green 5.00 12.00
39 Dwight Howard 5.00 12.00
40 Steven Adams 3.00 8.00

2017-18 Panini Spectra Vested Veterans Memorabilia
STATED PRINT RUN BTWN 87-99 SER.#'d SETS
*NEON BLUE/49: .5X TO 1.2X
*NEON GREEN/25: .6X TO 1.5X
1 Evan Turner/99 2.00 5.00
2 Julius Randle/99 3.00 8.00
3 Harrison Barnes/99 2.50 6.00
5 Ben Simmons/99 3.00 8.00
6 Nikola Vucevic/99 2.50 6.00
7 Buddy Hield/99 3.00 8.00
8 Serge Ibaka/99 2.50 6.00
9 Brandon Ingram/99 4.00 10.00
10 DeMar DeRozan/99 4.00 10.00
11 Andre Drummond/99 2.50 6.00
12 Goran Dragic/99 2.50 6.00
13 James Harden/99 6.00 15.00
14 Trevor Ariza/99 2.00 5.00
15 Pau Gasol/99 2.50 6.00
16 Vince Carter/99 6.00 15.00
17 Kemba Walker/99 2.50 6.00
18 Aaron Gordon/99 3.00 8.00
19 Hassan Whiteside/87 2.50 6.00
20 Dwyane Wade/99 6.00 15.00
21 Gary Harris/99 2.50 6.00
22 Karl-Anthony Towns/99 5.00 12.00
23 LaMarcus Aldridge/99 3.00 8.00
24 Al Horford/99 3.00 8.00
25 Eric Gordon/99 2.50 6.00
26 Myles Turner/99 3.00 8.00
27 Dirk Nowitzki/99 8.00 20.00
28 Jrue Holiday/99 4.00 10.00
29 Jimmy Butler/99 5.00 12.00
30 Joel Embiid/99 6.00 15.00

2018-19 Panini Spectra
1-100 STATED PRINT RUN 175 SER.#'d SETS
JSY AU STATED PRINT RUN 299 SER.#'d SETS
EXCHANGE DEADLINE 11/17/2020
1 John Collins 1.25 3.00
2 Gary Harris 1.00 2.50
3 Dennis Smith Jr. .75 2.00
4 Andrew Wiggins 1.50 4.00
5 Andre Drummond 1.00 2.50
6 Luka Doncic RC 75.00 200.00
7 LeBron James 15.00 40.00
8 Kevin Knox 1.00 2.50
9 T.J. Warren 1.00 2.50
10 Kyrie Irving 3.00 8.00
11 Jeremy Lin 2.00 5.00
12 Nikola Jokic 6.00 15.00
13 DeAndre Jordan 1.00 2.50
14 Karl-Anthony Towns 2.00 5.00
15 Reggie Jackson 1.00 2.50
16 Trae Young RC 12.00 30.00
17 Kyle Kuzma 1.25 3.00
18 Wendell Carter Jr. RC 2.00 5.00
19 Kemba Walker 1.00 2.50
20 Jayson Tatum 5.00 12.00
21 James Harden 2.50 6.00
22 Russell Westbrook 2.00 5.00
23 Mike Conley 1.00 2.50
24 Derrick Rose 2.50 6.00
25 Kevin Love 1.00 2.50
26 Collin Sexton RC 2.50 6.00
27 Lonzo Ball 1.25 3.00
28 Miles Bridges RC 2.50 6.00
29 Tony Parker 1.25 3.00
30 Jaylen Brown 1.25 3.00
31 Clint Capela 1.00 2.50
32 Paul George 1.50 4.00
33 Marc Gasol 1.25 3.00
34 Giannis Antetokounmpo 6.00 15.00
35 Jordan Clarkson 1.25 3.00
36 Jaren Jackson Jr. RC 6.00 15.00
37 Brandon Ingram 1.25 3.00
38 Mikal Bridges RC 4.00 10.00
39 Nikola Vucevic 1.00 2.50
40 Caris LeVert 1.25 3.00
41 Chris Paul 2.50 6.00
42 Steven Adams 1.00 2.50
43 Anthony Davis 3.00 8.00
44 Khris Middleton 1.25 3.00
45 Zach LaVine 2.00 5.00
46 Marvin Bagley III RC 5.00 12.00
47 Tobias Harris 1.00 2.50
48 Kawhi Leonard 3.00 8.00
49 Aaron Gordon 1.25 3.00
50 D'Angelo Russell 1.25 3.00
51 DeMar DeRozan 1.50 4.00
52 Damian Lillard 3.00 8.00
53 Jrue Holiday 1.50 4.00
54 Eric Bledsoe 1.00 2.50
55 Lauri Markkanen 2.00 5.00
56 Michael Porter Jr. RC 3.00 8.00
57 Danilo Gallinari 1.00 2.50
58 Kyle Lowry 1.25 3.00
59 Josh Richardson 1.00 2.50
60 Kristaps Porzingis 1.50 4.00
61 LaMarcus Aldridge 1.25 3.00
62 CJ McCollum 1.25 3.00
63 Nikola Mirotic .75 2.00
64 Victor Oladipo 1.25 3.00
65 Stephen Curry 15.00 40.00
66 Mo Bamba RC 1.25 3.00
67 Lou Williams 1.00 2.50
68 Serge Ibaka 1.00 2.50
69 Goran Dragic 1.00 2.50
70 Tim Hardaway Jr. .75 2.00
71 Rudy Gay 1.25 3.00
72 Donovan Mitchell 4.00 10.00
73 Julius Randle 1.25 3.00
74 Bojan Bogdanovic 1.00 2.50
75 Kevin Durant 5.00 12.00
76 Shai Gilgeous-Alexander RC 40.00 100.00
77 Buddy Hield 1.25 3.00
78 Jimmy Butler 2.00 5.00
79 Dwyane Wade 2.50 6.00
80 Enes Kanter 1.00 2.50
81 Harrison Barnes 1.00 2.50
82 Rudy Gobert 1.50 4.00
83 Donte DiVincenzo RC 2.00 5.00
84 Domantas Sabonis 1.50 4.00
85 Klay Thompson 3.00 8.00
86 Deandre Ayton RC 2.50 6.00
87 De'Aaron Fox 2.50 6.00
88 Ben Simmons 1.25 3.00
89 John Wall 1.50 4.00
90 Allonzo Trier .75 2.00
91 Dirk Nowitzki 3.00 8.00
92 Ricky Rubio 1.00 2.50
93 Landry Shamet RC 1.25 3.00
94 Blake Griffin 1.25 3.00
95 Draymond Green 1.50 4.00
96 Grayson Allen RC 1.50 4.00
97 Devin Booker 3.00 8.00
98 Joel Embiid 3.00 8.00
99 Bradley Beal 1.50 4.00
100 Jamal Murray 2.50 6.00
101 Dzanan Musa JSY AU RC 4.00 10.00
102 Omari Spellman JSY AU RC 4.00 10.00
103 Jacob Evans III JSY AU RC 4.00 10.00
104 Trae Young JSY AU 300.00 600.00
105 Jerome Robinson JSY AU RC 4.00 10.00
106 Kevin Knox JSY AU RC 5.00 12.00
107 Aaron Holiday JSY AU RC 6.00 15.00
108 Luka Doncic JSY AU 1,000.00 2,000.00
109 Collin Sexton JSY AU 12.00 30.00
110 Mikal Bridges JSY AU 20.00 50.00
111 Elie Okobo JSY AU RC 4.00 10.00
112 Robert Williams III JSY AU RC 8.00 20.00
113 Jalen Brunson JSY AU RC 75.00 200.00
114 Troy Brown Jr. JSY AU 5.00 12.00
115 Jevon Carter JSY AU RC 6.00 15.00
116 Landry Shamet JSY AU 6.00 15.00
117 Anfernee Simons JSY AU RC 25.00 60.00
118 Marvin Bagley III JSY AU 6.00 15.00
119 Deandre Ayton JSY AU 12.00 30.00
120 Mo Bamba JSY AU 6.00 15.00
121 Grayson Allen JSY AU 8.00 20.00
122 Shai Gilgeous-Alexander JSY AU 500.00 1,000.00
123 Jaren Jackson Jr. JSY AU 150.00 400.00
124 Wendell Carter Jr. JSY AU 10.00 25.00
125 Josh Okogie JSY AU RC 6.00 15.00
126 Lonnie Walker IV JSY AU RC 8.00 20.00
127 Chandler Hutchison JSY AU RC 5.00 12.00
128 Michael Porter Jr. JSY AU 15.00 40.00
129 Donte DiVincenzo JSY AU 10.00 25.00
130 Moritz Wagner JSY AU RC 8.00 20.00
131 Hamidou Diallo JSY AU RC 8.00 20.00
132 Svi Mykhailiuk JSY AU 5.00 12.00
133 Jarred Vanderbilt JSY AU 8.00 20.00
134 Zhaire Smith JSY AU 4.00 10.00
135 Kevin Huerter JSY AU RC 8.00 20.00

2018-19 Panini Spectra Red
*RED: .6X TO 1.5X BASIC
*RED RC: .5X TO 1.2X BASIC RC
STATED PRINT RUN 99 SER.#'d SETS

2018-19 Panini Spectra Silver
*SILVER: .6X TO 1.5X BASIC
*SILVER RC: .6X TO 1.5X BASIC RC

2018-19 Panini Spectra White Sparkle
*WHT SPKL: 2.5X TO 6X BASIC
*WHT SPKL RC: 2.5X TO 6X BASIC RC

2018-19 Panini Spectra Award Winning Autographs
PRINT RUNS B/WN 25-75 COPIES PER
EXCHANGE DEADLINE 11/17/2020
*NEON BLUE/60: .4X TO 1X p/r 75
1 Dwyane Wade/70 20.00 50.00
2 David Thompson/75 6.00 15.00
3 Julius Erving/25 20.00 50.00
4 Tom Heinsohn/75 10.00 25.00
5 Oscar Robertson/25 20.00 50.00
6 Marcus Camby/75 4.00 10.00
7 Jerry Lucas/75 6.00 15.00
8 Dave Cowens/75 6.00 15.00
9 Stephen Curry/25 500.00 1,000.00
10 Chauncey Billups/75 6.00 15.00
11 Larry Bird/65 25.00 60.00
13 Magic Johnson/25 30.00 80.00
14 Darrell Griffith/75 4.00 10.00
15 Jason Kidd/49 8.00 20.00
16 Mark Eaton/75 5.00 12.00
17 Walt Frazier/75 8.00 20.00
18 Ralph Sampson/75 4.00 10.00
19 Allen Iverson/25 25.00 60.00
20 Joe Dumars/75 6.00 15.00
21 Damian Lillard/25 20.00 50.00
22 Alvan Adams/75 4.00 10.00
23 Kareem Abdul-Jabbar/25 25.00 60.00
24 Ernie DiGregorio/75 4.00 10.00
25 Paul Pierce/49 10.00 25.00
26 Sidney Moncrief/75 3.00 8.00
27 Nate Archibald/75 6.00 15.00
28 Mark Jackson/75 4.00 10.00
29 Karl Malone/55 15.00 40.00
30 Dikembe Mutombo/75 8.00 20.00

2018-19 Panini Spectra Award Winning Autographs Neon Green
*NEON GRN: .5X TO 1.2X p/r 75
PRINT RUNS B/WN 35-49 COPIES PER
EXCHANGE DEADLINE 11/17/2020
15 Jason Kidd/35 10.00 25.00

2018-19 Panini Spectra Award Winning Autographs Neon Pink
*NEON PINK: .6X TO 1.5X p/r 75
*NEON PINK: .5X TO 1.2X p/r 49
PRINT RUNS B/WN 15-25 COPIES PER
NO PRICING QTY 15 OR LESS
EXCHANGE DEADLINE 11/17/2020
15 Jason Kidd/25 12.00 30.00

2018-19 Panini Spectra Epic Legends Memorabilia
PRINT RUNS B/WN 77-99 COPIES PER
*NEON BLUE/49: .5X TO 1.2X
1 Allen Iverson/99 20.00 50.00
2 Alvin Robertson/99 3.00 8.00
3 Charles Barkley/99 20.00 50.00
4 Chris Mullin/99 5.00 12.00
5 Chris Webber/99 12.00 30.00
6 David Robinson/99 12.00 30.00
7 Dee Brown/77 3.00 8.00
8 Dominique Wilkins/99 6.00 15.00
9 Ernie DiGregorio/99 3.00 8.00
10 Gary Payton/99 12.00 30.00
11 Glen Rice/99 4.00 10.00
12 Grant Hill/99 6.00 15.00
13 Horace Grant/99 4.00 10.00
14 Isiah Thomas/99 6.00 15.00
15 John Stockton/99 8.00 20.00
16 Karl Malone/99 8.00 20.00
17 Kobe Bryant/99 50.00 120.00
18 Larry Bird/99 25.00 60.00
19 Magic Johnson/99 25.00 60.00
21 Mark Jackson/99 3.00 8.00
22 Patrick Ewing/99 6.00 15.00
23 Shaquille O'Neal/99 20.00 50.00
24 Shawn Kemp/99 12.00 30.00
25 Steve Kerr/99 5.00 12.00
27 Toni Kukoc/99 5.00 12.00
28 Tracy McGrady/99 12.00 30.00
29 Vinnie Johnson/99 4.00 10.00
30 World B. Free/99 3.00 8.00

2018-19 Panini Spectra Epic Legends Memorabilia Neon Green
PRINT RUNS B/WN 19-25 COPIES PER

2018-19 Panini Spectra Headliners
1 Stephen Curry 125.00 300.00
2 LeBron James 125.00 300.00
3 Giannis Antetokounmpo 100.00 250.00
4 Anthony Davis 60.00 150.00
5 James Harden 50.00 120.00
6 Kevin Durant 75.00 200.00
7 Joel Embiid 25.00 60.00
8 Russell Westbrook 30.00 80.00
9 Kawhi Leonard 30.00 80.00
10 Ben Simmons 8.00 20.00
11 Paul George 12.00 30.00
12 Kobe Bryant 125.00 300.00
13 Kyrie Irving 20.00 50.00
14 Dwyane Wade 40.00 100.00
15 Nikola Jokic 40.00 100.00
16 Dirk Nowitzki 75.00 200.00
17 Donovan Mitchell 40.00 100.00
18 Allen Iverson 60.00 150.00
19 Shaquille O'Neal 75.00 200.00
20 Tim Duncan 15.00 40.00
21 Marvin Bagley III 8.00 20.00
22 Jaren Jackson Jr. 25.00 60.00
23 Luka Doncic 400.00 800.00
24 Deandre Ayton 50.00 120.00
25 Trae Young 150.00 400.00

2018-19 Panini Spectra Icons Autographs
PRINT RUNS B/WN 25-75 COPIES PER
EXCHANGE DEADLINE 11/17/2020
*NEON BLUE/60: .4X TO 1X p/r 75
*NEON GRN: .5X TO 1.2X p/r 75
1 John Stockton/25 20.00 50.00
2 Oscar Robertson/25 20.00 50.00
3 Bob Lanier/75 6.00 15.00
4 Sam Jones/75 6.00 15.00
6 Nick Van Exel/75 5.00 12.00
7 Peja Stojakovic/75 4.00 10.00
8 Gail Goodrich/75 5.00 12.00
9 Robert Horry/75 5.00 12.00
10 Jalen Rose/75 5.00 12.00
11 Latrell Sprewell/75 6.00 15.00
12 George McGinnis/75 6.00 15.00
13 B.J. Armstrong/75 5.00 12.00
14 Luke Walton/75 3.00 8.00
15 Stephen Jackson/75 4.00 10.00
16 Mitch Richmond/75 6.00 15.00
17 Tom "Satch" Sanders/75 5.00 12.00
18 Kenny "Sky" Walker/75 3.00 8.00
19 Rik Smits/75 4.00 10.00
20 Dan Issel/75 6.00 15.00
21 Cuttino Mobley/75 3.00 8.00
22 Rafer Alston/75 3.00 8.00
23 Rony Seikaly/75 3.00 8.00
24 Paul Silas/75 5.00 12.00
25 Vlade Divac/75 5.00 12.00
26 Wally Szczerbiak/75 4.00 10.00
27 Jim Jackson/75 4.00 10.00
28 John Salley/75 4.00 10.00
29 Vin Baker/75 3.00 8.00
30 Antonio McDyess/75 4.00 10.00

2018-19 Panini Spectra Icons Autographs Neon Pink
*NEON PINK: .6X TO 1.5X p/r 75
PRINT RUNS B/WN 15-25 COPIES PER
NO PRICING QTY 15 OR LESS
EXCHANGE DEADLINE 11/17/2020
11 Latrell Sprewell/25 8.00 20.00

2018-19 Panini Spectra Illustrious Legends Signatures
PRINT RUNS B/WN 25-75 COPIES PER
EXCHANGE DEADLINE 11/17/2020
*NEON BLUE/60: .4X TO 1X p/r 75
*NEON GRN/35-49: .5X TO 1.2X p/r 75
*NEON GRN/35-49: .4X TO 1X p/r 49
1 Charles Barkley/49 75.00 200.00
2 Mark Aguirre/75 4.00 10.00
3 Larry Bird/25 40.00 100.00
4 Alvan Adams/75 4.00 10.00
5 Kevin McHale/49 8.00 20.00
6 Dee Brown/75 4.00 10.00
7 Nate Archibald/75 6.00 15.00
8 Vlade Divac/75 5.00 12.00
9 World B. Free/75 4.00 10.00
10 Robert Horry/75 5.00 12.00
11 Kobe Bryant/49 400.00 800.00
12 Tom Heinsohn/75 5.00 12.00
13 Magic Johnson/25 30.00 80.00
14 Tim Hardaway/75 6.00 15.00
15 Steve Kerr/75 6.00 15.00
16 Paul Silas/75 5.00 12.00
17 Dave Cowens/75 6.00 15.00
18 Kevin Johnson/75 5.00 12.00
19 Mark Jackson/75 5.00 12.00
20 Avery Johnson/75 4.00 10.00
21 Karl Malone/25 20.00 50.00
22 Toni Kukoc/75 6.00 15.00
23 Oscar Robertson/25 15.00 40.00
24 Jamal Mashburn/75 4.00 10.00
25 Nick Van Exel/75 5.00 12.00
26 Ernie DiGregorio/75 4.00 10.00
27 Louie Dampier/75 5.00 12.00
28 Wally Szczerbiak/75 4.00 10.00
29 Gail Goodrich/75 5.00 12.00
30 Jalen Rose/75 4.00 10.00
31 Allen Iverson/25 40.00 100.00
32 Rony Seikaly/75 3.00 8.00
33 Tracy McGrady/49 15.00 40.00
34 Mark Price/75 5.00 12.00
35 Elvin Hayes/75 6.00 15.00

2018-19 Panini Spectra Illustrious Legends Signatures Neon Pink
*NEON PINK: .6X TO 1.5X p/r 75
*NEON PINK: .5X TO 1.2X p/r 49
PRINT RUNS B/WN 15-25 COPIES PER
NO PRICING QTY 15 OR LESS
EXCHANGE DEADLINE 11/17/2020
33 Tracy McGrady/25 25.00 60.00

2018-19 Panini Spectra In The Zone Autographs
PRINT RUNS B/WN 25-75 COPIES PER
EXCHANGE DEADLINE 11/17/2020
*NEON BLUE/60: .4X TO 1X p/r 75
1 JR Smith/75 5.00 12.00
2 Donovan Mitchell/49 20.00 50.00
3 Bam Adebayo/75 20.00 50.00
4 Lonzo Ball/49 12.00 30.00
5 Allen Crabbe/75 3.00 8.00
6 Gordon Hayward/75 5.00 12.00
7 Kyle Kuzma/75 10.00 25.00
9 Terry Rozier/75 4.00 10.00
10 Kyrie Irving/49 20.00 50.00
11 Cody Zeller/75 3.00 8.00
12 Jayson Tatum/49 20.00 50.00
13 Patrick Beverley/75 3.00 8.00
14 LaMarcus Aldridge/49 6.00 15.00
15 Caris LeVert/75 5.00 12.00
16 Khris Middleton/75 10.00 25.00
17 JJ Redick/75 5.00 12.00
18 Kevin Durant/49 40.00 100.00
19 Myles Turner/75 5.00 12.00
20 Damian Lillard/25 25.00 60.00
21 John Collins/75 5.00 12.00
22 Isaiah Thomas/49 5.00 12.00
23 Jose Calderon/75 3.00 8.00
24 De'Aaron Fox/75 15.00 40.00
25 J.J. Barea/75 5.00 12.00
26 Mike Conley/75 4.00 10.00
27 Nikola Mirotic/75 3.00 8.00
28 Dwyane Wade/25 30.00 80.00
29 Marcin Gortat/75 3.00 8.00
30 Giannis Antetokounmpo/49 60.00 150.00

2018-19 Panini Spectra In The Zone Autographs Neon Green
*NEON GRN: .5X TO 1.2X p/r 75
*NEON GRN: .4X TO 1X p/r 49
PRINT RUNS B/WN 35-49 COPIES PER
EXCHANGE DEADLINE 11/17/2020
2 Donovan Mitchell/35 30.00 80.00
30 Giannis Antetokounmpo/35 75.00 200.00

2018-19 Panini Spectra In The Zone Autographs Neon Pink
*NEON PINK: .6X TO 1.5X p/r 75
*NEON PINK: .5X TO 1.2X p/r 49
PRINT RUNS B/WN 15-25 COPIES PER
NO PRICING QTY 15 OR LESS
EXCHANGE DEADLINE 11/17/2020
2 Donovan Mitchell/25 40.00 100.00
30 Giannis Antetokounmpo/25 100.00 250.00

2018-19 Panini Spectra Making it Rain Autographs
PRINT RUNS B/WN 25-75 COPIES PER
EXCHANGE DEADLINE 11/17/2020
1 John Starks/75 4.00 10.00
2 Damian Lillard/25 15.00 40.00
3 Bryon Russell/75 3.00 8.00
5 Dee Brown/75 3.00 8.00
6 Jalen Rose/75 3.00 8.00
7 Isaiah Rider/75 3.00 8.00
8 Mark Jackson/75 3.00 8.00
9 Jeff Hornacek/75 4.00 10.00
11 Jose Calderon/75 3.00 8.00
12 John Stockton/25 20.00 50.00
13 Charlie Ward/75 4.00 10.00
14 Nick Van Exel/75 5.00 12.00
16 Joe Dumars/75 6.00 15.00
17 Jamal Mashburn/75 5.00 12.00
18 Robert Horry/75 5.00 12.00
19 Nick Anderson/75 5.00 12.00
20 Sam Cassell/75 6.00 15.00
21 Brent Barry/75 3.00 8.00
22 Ray Allen/35 15.00 40.00
23 Clifford Robinson/75 5.00 12.00
24 Peja Stojakovic/75 4.00 10.00
25 Derek Harper/75 4.00 10.00
26 Latrell Sprewell/75 6.00 15.00
27 Jason Williams/75 8.00 20.00
28 Allan Houston/75 5.00 12.00
29 Wally Szczerbiak/75 4.00 10.00
30 J.J. Barea/75 4.00 10.00

2018-19 Panini Spectra Making it Rain Autographs Neon Blue
*NEON GRN: .4X TO 1X p/r 75
STATED PRINT RUN 60 SER.#'d SETS
EXCHANGE DEADLINE 11/17/2020
10 Mitch Richmond 6.00 15.00
27 Jason Williams 15.00 40.00

2018-19 Panini Spectra Making it Rain Autographs Neon Green
*NEON GRN: .5X TO 1.2X p/r 75
*NEON GRN: .4X TO 1X p/r 35
PRINT RUNS B/WN 35-49 COPIES PER
EXCHANGE DEADLINE 11/17/2020
10 Mitch Richmond/49 8.00 20.00
26 Latrell Sprewell/49 6.00 15.00
27 Jason Williams/49 20.00 50.00

2018-19 Panini Spectra Making it Rain Autographs Neon Pink
*NEON PINK: .6X TO 1.5X p/r 75
*NEON PINK: .5X TO 1.2X p/r 35
*NEON PINK: .4X TO 1X p/r 25
PRINT RUNS B/WN 15-25 COPIES PER
NO PRICING QTY 15 OR LESS

EXCHANGE DEADLINE 11/17/2020
1 John Starks/25 8.00 20.00
10 Mitch Richmond/25 10.00 25.00
26 Latrell Sprewell/25 8.00 20.00
27 Jason Williams/25 25.00 60.00

2018-19 Panini Spectra Neon Blue
*NEON BLUE: .6X TO 1.5X BASIC
*NEON BLUE RC: .6X TO 1.5X BASIC RC
*NEON BLUE JSY AU: .5X TO 1.2X BASE
1-100 STATED PRINT RUN 75 SER.#'d SETS
JSY AU STATED PRINT RUN 99 SER.#'d SETS
EXCHANGE DEADLINE 11/17/2020
104 Trae Young JSY AU 400.00 800.00

2018-19 Panini Spectra Neon Green
*NEON GRN: .75X TO 2X BASIC
*NEON GRN RC: .75X TO 2X BASIC RC
*NEON GRN JSY AU: .75X TO 2X BASE
STATED PRINT RUN 49 SER.#'d SETS
EXCHANGE DEADLINE 11/17/2020
104 Trae Young JSY AU 500.00 1,000.00
126 Lonnie Walker IV JSY AU 12.00 30.00

2018-19 Panini Spectra Neon Pink
*NEON PINK: 1.2X TO 3X BASIC
*NEON PINK RC: 1.2X TO 3X BASIC RC
*NEON PINK JSY AU: 1X TO 2.5X BASE
STATED PRINT RUN 25 SER.#'d SETS
EXCHANGE DEADLINE 11/17/2020
104 Trae Young JSY AU 1,000.00 2,000.00
126 Lonnie Walker IV JSY AU 15.00 40.00

2018-19 Panini Spectra Next Era Memorabilia
STATED PRINT RUN 99 SER.#'d SETS
*NEON BLUE/49: .5X TO 1.2X
*NEON GRN/25: .6X TO 1.5X
1 Aaron Holiday 3.00 8.00
2 Anfernee Simons 10.00 25.00
3 Chandler Hutchison 2.50 6.00
4 Collin Sexton 6.00 15.00
5 Deandre Ayton 6.00 15.00
6 Donte DiVincenzo 5.00 12.00
7 Grayson Allen 4.00 10.00
8 Jacob Evans III 2.00 5.00
9 Jaren Jackson Jr. 15.00 40.00
10 Jerome Robinson 2.00 5.00
11 Josh Okogie 3.00 8.00
12 Kevin Huerter 4.00 10.00
13 Kevin Knox 2.50 6.00
14 Landry Shamet 3.00 8.00
15 Lonnie Walker IV 4.00 10.00
16 Luka Doncic 100.00 250.00
17 Marvin Bagley III 3.00 8.00
18 Michael Porter Jr. 8.00 20.00
19 Mikal Bridges 10.00 25.00
20 Mo Bamba 3.00 8.00
21 Robert Williams III 4.00 10.00
22 Shai Gilgeous-Alexander 40.00 100.00
23 Trae Young 15.00 40.00
24 Wendell Carter Jr. 5.00 12.00
25 Zhaire Smith 2.00 5.00
26 Bruce Brown 4.00 10.00
27 De'Anthony Melton 4.00 10.00
28 Devonte' Graham 3.00 8.00
29 Dzanan Musa 2.00 5.00
30 Elie Okobo 2.00 5.00
31 Gary Trent Jr. 4.00 10.00
32 Hamidou Diallo 3.00 8.00
33 Jalen Brunson 15.00 40.00
34 Jarred Vanderbilt 4.00 10.00
35 Jevon Carter 3.00 8.00
36 Keita Bates-Diop 2.50 6.00
37 Moritz Wagner 4.00 10.00
38 Omari Spellman 2.00 5.00
39 Svi Mykhailiuk 2.50 6.00
40 Troy Brown Jr. 2.50 6.00

2018-19 Panini Spectra Radiant Signatures
PRINT RUNS B/WN 25-75 COPIES PER
EXCHANGE DEADLINE 11/17/2020
*NEON BLUE/60: .4X TO 1X p/r 75
*NEON GRN/49: .5X TO 1.2X p/r 75
*NEON PINK/25: .6X TO 1.5X p/r 75
1 Jose Calderon/75 4.00 10.00
2 Damian Lillard/25 50.00 120.00
3 Cuttino Mobley/75 4.00 10.00
4 Rick Fox/75 5.00 12.00
5 Rafer Alston/75 5.00 12.00
6 Avery Johnson/75 5.00 12.00
8 Mark Aguirre/75 5.00 12.00
9 Jonas Jerebko/75 4.00 10.00
10 Sam Cassell/75 5.00 12.00
11 Rik Smits/75 5.00 12.00
12 Walt Frazier/75 10.00 25.00
13 Xavier McDaniel/75 5.00 12.00
14 Gail Goodrich/75 6.00 15.00
15 Terrell Brandon/75 4.00 10.00
16 Bill Walton/75 20.00 50.00
17 Ish Smith/75 4.00 10.00
18 Tom ""Satch"" Sanders/75 6.00 15.00
19 Zydrunas Ilgauskas/75 5.00 12.00
20 Kevin Willis/75 5.00 12.00
21 Dee Brown/75 5.00 12.00
22 George Gervin/75 10.00 25.00
23 Keyon Dooling/75 4.00 10.00
24 Reggie Jackson/75 5.00 12.00
25 James Silas/75 6.00 15.00
26 Horace Grant/75 6.00 15.00
27 Jeff Hornacek/75 5.00 12.00
28 Kenny ""Sky"" Walker/75 4.00 10.00
29 Sam Perkins/75 5.00 12.00
30 Jerian Grant/75 4.00 10.00

2018-19 Panini Spectra Rising Stars Signatures
STATED PRINT RUN 75 SER.#'d SETS
EXCHANGE DEADLINE 11/17/2020
1 Robert Williams III 8.00 20.00
2 Grayson Allen 8.00 20.00
3 Troy Brown Jr. 5.00 12.00
4 Jaren Jackson Jr. 150.00 400.00
5 Gary Trent Jr. 8.00 20.00
6 Josh Okogie 6.00 15.00
7 Lonnie Walker IV 8.00 20.00
8 Aaron Holiday 6.00 15.00
9 Mikal Bridges 20.00 50.00
10 Deandre Ayton 12.00 30.00
11 Shai Gilgeous-Alexander 300.00 600.00
12 Hamidou Diallo 6.00 15.00
13 Wendell Carter Jr. 10.00 25.00
14 Jarred Vanderbilt 8.00 20.00
15 Allonzo Trier 4.00 10.00
16 Kevin Huerter 8.00 20.00
17 Luka Doncic 500.00 1,000.00
18 Anfernee Simons 20.00 50.00
19 Mo Bamba 6.00 15.00
20 Donte DiVincenzo 10.00 25.00
21 Svi Mykhailiuk 5.00 12.00
22 Jacob Evans III 4.00 10.00
23 Zhaire Smith 4.00 10.00
24 Jerome Robinson 4.00 10.00
25 De'Anthony Melton 8.00 20.00
26 Kevin Knox 5.00 12.00
27 Marvin Bagley III 6.00 15.00
28 Chandler Hutchison 5.00 12.00
29 Moritz Wagner 8.00 20.00
30 Dzanan Musa 4.00 10.00
31 Trae Young 200.00 500.00
32 Jalen Brunson 50.00 120.00
33 Devonte' Graham 6.00 15.00
34 Jevon Carter 6.00 15.00
37 Michael Porter Jr. 15.00 40.00
38 Collin Sexton 12.00 30.00
39 Omari Spellman 4.00 10.00
40 Elie Okobo 4.00 10.00

2018-19 Panini Spectra Rising Stars Signatures Neon Blue
*NEON BLUE: .4X TO 1X BASIC
STATED PRINT RUN 60 SER.#'d SETS
EXCHANGE DEADLINE 11/17/2020

2018-19 Panini Spectra Rising Stars Signatures Neon Green
*NEON GRN: .5X TO 1.2X BASIC
STATED PRINT RUN 49 SER.#'d SETS
EXCHANGE DEADLINE 11/17/2020

2018-19 Panini Spectra Rising Stars Signatures Neon Pink
*NEON PINK: .6X TO 1.5X BASIC
STATED PRINT RUN 25 SER.#'d SETS
EXCHANGE DEADLINE 11/17/2020

2018-19 Panini Spectra Signatures
BK
BK
*NEON BLUE/60: .4X TO 1X BASIC
*NEON GRN/49: .5X TO 1.2X BASIC
*NEON PINK/25: .6X TO 1.5X BASIC
1 Joe Dumars/75 8.00 20.00
2 Nick Anderson/75 5.00 12.00
3 Tyus Jones/75 4.00 10.00
4 Jerome Williams/75 4.00 10.00
5 Rick Mahorn/75 4.00 10.00
6 Theo Ratliff/75 4.00 10.00
7 Kelly Olynyk/75 4.00 10.00
8 Vin Baker/75 4.00 10.00
9 Magic Johnson/70 40.00 100.00
10 Clifford Robinson/75 6.00 15.00
11 Zaza Pachulia/75 4.00 10.00
12 Xavier McDaniel/75 5.00 12.00
13 Isaiah Rider/75 5.00 12.00
14 Kenny Anderson/75 5.00 12.00
15 Marcus Camby/75 5.00 12.00
16 Tree Rollins/75 4.00 10.00
17 Sean Elliott/75 5.00 12.00
18 Herb Williams/75 4.00 10.00
19 JJ Redick/75 6.00 15.00
20 Brad Davis/75 5.00 12.00
21 Lauri Markkanen/75 10.00 25.00
22 Jim Jackson/75 5.00 12.00
23 Will Perdue/75 4.00 10.00
24 Rudy Tomjanovich/75 5.00 12.00
25 Bryon Russell/75 4.00 10.00
26 Antonio McDyess/75 5.00 12.00
27 Doug Christie/75 5.00 12.00
28 Yogi Ferrell/75 4.00 10.00
29 Terry Rozier/75 5.00 12.00
30 Muggsy Bogues/75 10.00 25.00
31 Luke Walton/75 4.00 10.00
32 John Salley/75 5.00 12.00
33 Walter Davis/75 6.00 15.00
34 Sarunas Marciulionis/75 6.00 15.00
35 Scott Skiles/75 5.00 12.00
36 Mark Eaton/75 6.00 15.00
37 Darrell Griffith/75 5.00 12.00
38 Charlie Ward/75 5.00 12.00
39 Latrell Sprewell/75 8.00 20.00
40 Larry Nance/75 5.00 12.00

2018-19 Panini Spectra Spectacular Swatches
STATED PRINT RUN 99 SER.#'d SETS
1 LeBron James 40.00 100.00
2 Stephen Curry 40.00 100.00
3 Dirk Nowitzki 10.00 25.00
4 James Harden 8.00 20.00
5 Russell Westbrook 6.00 15.00
6 Kevin Durant 15.00 40.00
7 Giannis Antetokounmpo 20.00 50.00
8 Damian Lillard 10.00 25.00
9 Kawhi Leonard 10.00 25.00
10 Anthony Davis 10.00 25.00
11 Kyrie Irving 10.00 25.00
12 Chris Paul 8.00 20.00
13 Joel Embiid 10.00 25.00
14 Paul George 6.00 15.00
15 Karl-Anthony Towns 6.00 15.00
16 Victor Oladipo 3.00 8.00
17 Donovan Mitchell 12.00 30.00
18 Ben Simmons 4.00 10.00
19 Klay Thompson 10.00 25.00
20 CJ McCollum 4.00 10.00
21 Devin Booker 10.00 25.00
22 LaMarcus Aldridge 4.00 10.00
23 Kristaps Porzingis 5.00 12.00
24 DeMar DeRozan 5.00 12.00
25 John Wall 5.00 12.00
26 Kemba Walker 3.00 8.00
27 Bradley Beal 5.00 12.00
28 Gordon Hayward 4.00 10.00
29 Brandon Ingram 4.00 10.00
30 Jayson Tatum 15.00 40.00

2018-19 Panini Spectra Spectacular Swatches Neon Blue
*NEON BLUE: .5X TO 1.2X BASIC
STATED PRINT RUN 49 SER.#'d SETS

2018-19 Panini Spectra Spectacular Swatches Neon Green
*NEON BLUE: .8X TO 2X BASIC
PRINT RUNS B/WN 12-25 COPIES PER
NO PRICING QTY 15 OR LESS

2019-20 Panini Spectra
JSY AU STATED PRINT RUN 60-149 SER.#'d SETS
EXCHANGE DEADLINE 12/26/2021
1 Klay Thompson 2.50 6.00
2 Fred VanVleet 1.25 3.00
3 Kawhi Leonard 2.50 6.00
4 Goran Dragic .75 2.00
5 Trae Young 2.50 6.00
6 Robert Covington .60 1.50
7 Devonte' Graham .75 2.00
8 Evan Fournier .75 2.00
9 Kristaps Porzingis 1.25 3.00
10 Damian Lillard 2.50 6.00
11 D'Angelo Russell .75 2.00
12 Kyle Lowry 1.00 2.50
13 Lou Williams 1.00 2.50
14 Jimmy Butler 2.00 5.00
15 John Collins 1.00 2.50
16 Lonzo Ball 1.00 2.50
17 Terry Rozier .75 2.00
18 Nikola Vucevic .75 2.00
19 Tim Hardaway Jr. .60 1.50
20 CJ McCollum 1.00 2.50
21 Draymond Green 1.25 3.00
22 Mike Conley .75 2.00
23 Montrezl Harrell .75 2.00
24 Bam Adebayo 1.50 4.00
25 Vince Carter 2.00 5.00
26 Brandon Ingram 1.00 2.50
27 Miles Bridges 1.00 2.50
28 Aaron Gordon 1.00 2.50
29 Jamal Murray 1.50 4.00
30 Carmelo Anthony 1.50 4.00
31 Russell Westbrook 1.50 4.00
32 Donovan Mitchell 2.00 5.00
33 Anthony Davis 2.50 6.00
34 Giannis Antetokounmpo 5.00 12.00
35 Kemba Walker .75 2.00
36 Jrue Holiday 1.25 3.00
37 Zach LaVine 1.50 4.00
38 Ben Simmons 1.00 2.50
39 Nikola Jokic 5.00 12.00
40 Buddy Hield .75 2.00
41 James Harden 2.00 5.00
42 Rudy Gobert 1.25 3.00
43 LeBron James 8.00 20.00
44 Khris Middleton 1.00 2.50
45 Jayson Tatum 4.00 10.00
46 Marcus Morris Sr. .60 1.50
47 Wendell Carter Jr. 1.00 2.50
48 Joel Embiid 2.00 5.00
49 Paul Millsap .75 2.00
50 De'Aaron Fox 1.50 4.00
51 Clint Capela .75 2.00
52 John Wall 1.25 3.00
53 Rajon Rondo 1.25 3.00
54 Brook Lopez .75 2.00
55 Jaylen Brown 1.50 4.00
56 Julius Randle 1.25 3.00
57 Lauri Markkanen 1.25 3.00
58 Tobias Harris .75 2.00
59 Derrick Rose 2.00 5.00
60 Harrison Barnes .75 2.00
61 Malcolm Brogdon .75 2.00
62 Bradley Beal 1.25 3.00
63 Dwight Howard 1.25 3.00
64 Eric Bledsoe .75 2.00
65 Kevin Durant 3.00 8.00
66 Kevin Knox II .60 1.50
67 Collin Sexton 1.25 3.00
68 Josh Richardson .60 1.50
69 Blake Griffin 1.00 2.50
70 DeMar DeRozan 1.25 3.00
71 Myles Turner 1.00 2.50
72 Christian Wood RC .75 2.00
73 Jaren Jackson Jr. 1.50 4.00
74 Karl-Anthony Towns 1.50 4.00
75 Kyrie Irving 2.00 5.00
76 Shai Gilgeous-Alexander 5.00 12.00
77 Kevin Love 1.00 2.50
78 Devin Booker .25 .60
79 Andre Drummond .75 2.00
80 LaMarcus Aldridge 1.00 2.50
81 Domantas Sabonis 1.25 3.00
82 Will Barton .60 1.50
83 Dillon Brooks .75 2.00
84 Andrew Wiggins 1.25 3.00
85 Jarrett Allen 1.00 2.50
86 Chris Paul 2.00 5.00
87 Tristan Thompson .60 1.50
88 Deandre Ayton 1.00 2.50
89 Reggie Jackson .75 2.00
90 Dejounte Murray 1.00 2.50
91 Paul George 1.50 4.00
92 Kyle Kuzma 1.25 3.00
93 Jonas Valanciunas .75 2.00
94 Jeff Teague .60 1.50
95 DeAndre Jordan .75 2.00
96 Steven Adams .75 2.00
97 Luka Doncic 6.00 15.00
98 Ricky Rubio .75 2.00
99 Stephen Curry 8.00 20.00
100 Pascal Siakam 1.50 4.00
101 Darius Garland 2.50 6.00
102 Admiral Schofield RC .75 2.00
103 Cam Reddish RC 1.00 2.50
104 Quinndary Weatherspoon RC .60 1.50
105 Sekou Doumbouya RC .60 1.50
106 Ky Bowman .75 2.00
107 Brandon Clarke RC 1.25 3.00
108 Dylan Windler RC .75 2.00
109 Zion Williamson RC 5.00 12.00
110 KZ Okpala RC .75 2.00
111 Talen Horton-Tucker 1.00 2.50
112 Jaylen Nowell RC .75 2.00
113 Cameron Johnson RC 1.50 4.00
114 Tremont Waters RC .75 2.00
115 Nickeil Alexander-Walker RC 1.00 2.50
116 Nicolo Melli .75 2.00
117 Grant Williams RC 1.00 2.50
118 Mfiondu Kabengele RC .75 2.00
119 Ja Morant RC 10.00 25.00
120 Carsen Edwards RC .75 2.00
121 Coby White RC 2.00 5.00
122 Bol Bol RC 1.50 4.00
123 PJ Washington Jr. RC 2.00 5.00
124 Kyle Guy RC .75 2.00
125 Goga Bitadze RC .75 2.00
126 Daniel Gafford 1.25 3.00
127 Darius Bazley RC .60 1.50
128 Jordan Poole RC 2.50 6.00
129 RJ Barrett RC 2.50 6.00
130 Bruno Fernando RC .75 2.00
131 Jaxson Hayes RC 1.00 2.50
132 Isaiah Roby RC .75 2.00
133 Tyler Herro RC 3.00 8.00
134 Tacko Fall .75 2.00
135 Luka Samanic RC .75 2.00
136 Terance Mann 1.25 3.00
137 Ty Jerome RC 1.25 3.00
138 Keldon Johnson RC 2.00 5.00
139 De'Andre Hunter RC 2.50 6.00
140 Cody Martin RC 1.00 2.50
141 Rui Hachimura RC 2.50 6.00
142 Ignas Brazdeikis RC .75 2.00
143 Romeo Langford RC .60 1.50
144 Kendrick Nunn 1.00 2.50
145 Matisse Thybulle RC 1.25 3.00
146 Nicolas Claxton 1.25 3.00
147 Nassir Little RC 1.00 2.50
148 Kevin Porter Jr. RC 1.25 3.00
149 Jarrett Culver RC .60 1.50
150 Eric Paschall RC .75 2.00
151 Shaquille O'Neal 4.00 10.00
152 James Harden 2.00 5.00
153 Allen Iverson 2.50 6.00
154 Blake Griffin 1.00 2.50
155 Dominique Wilkins 1.50 4.00
156 Kevin Durant 3.00 8.00
157 Charles Barkley 2.00 5.00
158 Kyrie Irving 2.00 5.00
159 Scottie Pippen 2.50 6.00
160 Russell Westbrook 1.50 4.00
161 Tim Duncan 2.50 6.00
162 Giannis Antetokounmpo 5.00 12.00
163 Steve Nash 2.00 5.00
164 Zach LaVine 1.50 4.00
165 Dirk Nowitzki 2.50 6.00
166 Chris Paul 2.00 5.00
167 Magic Johnson 3.00 8.00
168 Kawhi Leonard 2.50 6.00
169 Karl Malone 2.00 5.00
170 Stephen Curry 8.00 20.00
171 Kevin Garnett 2.50 6.00
172 Jason Richardson 1.00 2.50
173 LeBron James 8.00 20.00
174 Donovan Mitchell 2.00 5.00
175 Derrick Rose 2.00 5.00
176 KZ Okpala JSY AU/149 6.00 15.00
177 Tyler Herro JSY AU/149 60.00 150.00
178 Kyle Guy JSY AU/149 6.00 15.00
179 Sekou Doumbouya JSY AU/149 5.00 12.00
180 Goga Bitadze JSY AU/149 8.00 20.00
181 Zion Williamson JSY AU/60 300.00 600.00
182 Grant Williams JSY AU/149 8.00 20.00
183 De'Andre Hunter JSY AU/99 20.00 50.00
184 Dylan Windler JSY AU/149 6.00 15.00
185 Jaxson Hayes JSY AU/149 8.00 20.00
186 Eric Paschall JSY AU/149 6.00 15.00
187 Romeo Langford JSY AU/149 5.00 12.00
188 Jaylen Nowell JSY AU/149 6.00 15.00
189 Nickeil Alexander-Walker JSY AU/149 8.00 20.00
190 Luka Samanic JSY AU/149 6.00 15.00
191 Ja Morant JSY AU/99 300.00 600.00
192 Ty Jerome JSY AU/149 10.00 25.00
193 Jarrett Culver JSY AU/99 5.00 12.00
194 Mfiondu Kabengele JSY AU/149 6.00 15.00
195 Cameron Johnson JSY AU/149 12.00 30.00
196 Cody Martin JSY AU/149 8.00 20.00
197 Matisse Thybulle JSY AU/149 10.00 25.00
198 Quinndary Weatherspoon JSY AU/149 5.00 12.00
199 Brandon Clarke JSY AU/149 10.00 25.00
200 Keldon Johnson JSY AU/149 15.00 40.00
201 RJ Barrett JSY AU/99 20.00 50.00
202 Bruno Fernando JSY AU/149 6.00 15.00
203 Cam Reddish JSY AU/99 8.00 20.00
204 Jordan Poole JSY AU/149 20.00 50.00
205 PJ Washington Jr. JSY AU/149 15.00 40.00
206 Isaiah Roby JSY AU/149 6.00 15.00
207 Nassir Little JSY AU/149 8.00 20.00
208 Tremont Waters JSY AU/149 6.00 15.00
209 Darius Bazley JSY AU/149 5.00 12.00
210 Carsen Edwards JSY AU/149 6.00 15.00
211 Rui Hachimura JSY AU/99 20.00 50.00
212 Admiral Schofield JSY AU/149 6.00 15.00
213 Coby White JSY AU/99 15.00 40.00
214 Kevin Porter Jr. JSY AU/149 10.00 25.00
215 Bol Bol JSY AU/149 12.00 30.00
216 Ignas Brazdeikis JSY AU/149 6.00 15.00
217 Chuma Okeke JSY AU/149 6.00 15.00

2019-20 Panini Spectra Celestial
*CELESTIAL: 1.25X TO 3X BASIC
*CELESTIAL RC: 1.2X TO 3X BASIC RC
*CELESTIAL JSY AU: .5X TO 1.2X BASE
1-175 STATED PRINT RUN 99 SER.#'d SETS
JSY AU STATED PRINT RUN 49-99 SER.#'d SETS
EXCHANGE DEADLINE 12/26/2021

2019-20 Panini Spectra Intersteller
*INTERSTELLER: 1.2X TO 3X BASIC
*INTERSTELLER RC: 1X TO 2.5X BASIC RC
*INTERSTELLER JSY AU: .6X TO 1.5X BASE
1-175 STATED PRINT RUN 49 SER.#'d SETS
JSY AU STATED PRINT RUN 25-49 SER.#'d SETS
EXCHANGE DEADLINE 12/26/2021
1 Klay Thompson 12.00 30.00
2 Fred VanVleet 5.00 12.00
3 Kawhi Leonard 60.00 150.00
5 Trae Young 50.00 120.00
10 Damian Lillard 30.00 80.00
14 Jimmy Butler 12.00 30.00
25 Vince Carter 12.00 30.00
29 Jamal Murray 12.00 30.00
32 Donovan Mitchell 25.00 60.00
33 Anthony Davis 30.00 80.00
34 Giannis Antetokounmpo 75.00 200.00
38 Ben Simmons 12.00 30.00
39 Nikola Jokic 12.00 30.00
41 James Harden 12.00 30.00
43 LeBron James 400.00 800.00
45 Jayson Tatum 30.00 80.00
65 Kevin Durant 50.00 120.00
73 Jaren Jackson Jr. 12.00 30.00
75 Kyrie Irving 10.00 25.00
76 Shai Gilgeous-Alexander 12.00 30.00
78 Devin Booker 30.00 80.00
86 Chris Paul 12.00 30.00
91 Paul George 10.00 25.00
97 Luka Doncic 300.00 600.00
99 Stephen Curry 40.00 100.00
101 Darius Garland 20.00 50.00
105 Sekou Doumbouya 2.00 5.00
107 Brandon Clarke 50.00 120.00
109 Zion Williamson 500.00 1,000.00
111 Talen Horton-Tucker 100.00 250.00
113 Cameron Johnson 25.00 60.00
115 Nickeil Alexander-Walker 12.00 30.00
119 Ja Morant 400.00 800.00
121 Coby White 125.00 300.00
122 Bol Bol 60.00 150.00
123 PJ Washington Jr. 20.00 50.00
128 Jordan Poole 12.00 30.00
129 RJ Barrett 100.00 250.00
131 Jaxson Hayes 20.00 50.00
133 Tyler Herro 100.00 250.00
134 Tacko Fall 15.00 40.00
138 Keldon Johnson 50.00 120.00
139 De'Andre Hunter 20.00 50.00
141 Rui Hachimura 100.00 250.00
145 Matisse Thybulle 30.00 80.00
148 Kevin Porter Jr. 4.00 10.00
149 Jarrett Culver 25.00 60.00
150 Eric Paschall 15.00 40.00
151 Shaquille O'Neal 40.00 100.00
152 James Harden 15.00 40.00
153 Allen Iverson 40.00 100.00
156 Kevin Durant 50.00 120.00
157 Charles Barkley 20.00 50.00
158 Kyrie Irving 15.00 40.00
159 Scottie Pippen 25.00 60.00
161 Tim Duncan 25.00 60.00
162 Giannis Antetokounmpo 75.00 200.00
163 Steve Nash 20.00 50.00
164 Zach LaVine 12.00 30.00
165 Dirk Nowitzki 30.00 80.00
166 Chris Paul 15.00 40.00
167 Magic Johnson 20.00 50.00
168 Kawhi Leonard 100.00 250.00
169 Karl Malone 10.00 25.00
170 Stephen Curry 125.00 300.00
171 Kevin Garnett 30.00 80.00
173 LeBron James 400.00 800.00
174 Donovan Mitchell 25.00 60.00
175 Derrick Rose 25.00 60.00
185 Jaxson Hayes JSY AU/49 25.00 60.00
189 Nickeil Alexander-Walker JSY AU/49 25.00 60.00
191 Ja Morant JSY AU/49 1,000.00 2,000.00

2019-20 Panini Spectra Meta
*INTERSTELLER: 1.5X TO 4X BASIC
*INTERSTELLER RC: 1.2X TO 3X BASIC RC
*INTERSTELLER JSY AU: 1.2X TO 3X BASE
1-175 STATED PRINT RUN 25 SER.#'d SETS
JSY AU STATED PRINT RUN 15-25 SER.#'d SETS
EXCHANGE DEADLINE 12/26/2021
1 Klay Thompson 20.00 50.00
2 Fred VanVleet 15.00 40.00
3 Kawhi Leonard 75.00 200.00
5 Trae Young 75.00 200.00
9 Kristaps Porzingis 20.00 50.00
10 Damian Lillard 40.00 100.00
11 D'Angelo Russell 12.00 30.00
14 Jimmy Butler 20.00 50.00
16 Lonzo Ball 10.00 25.00
18 Nikola Vucevic 8.00 20.00
25 Vince Carter 15.00 40.00
29 Jamal Murray 15.00 40.00
30 Carmelo Anthony 12.00 30.00
32 Donovan Mitchell 30.00 80.00
33 Anthony Davis 75.00 200.00
34 Giannis Antetokounmpo 100.00 250.00
37 Zach LaVine 12.00 30.00
38 Ben Simmons 20.00 50.00
39 Nikola Jokic 20.00 50.00
41 James Harden 20.00 50.00
43 LeBron James 500.00 1,000.00
45 Jayson Tatum 40.00 100.00
65 Kevin Durant 60.00 150.00
73 Jaren Jackson Jr. 20.00 50.00
75 Kyrie Irving 12.00 30.00
76 Shai Gilgeous-Alexander 15.00 40.00
78 Devin Booker 40.00 100.00
86 Chris Paul 15.00 40.00
91 Paul George 12.00 30.00
97 Luka Doncic 400.00 800.00
99 Stephen Curry 50.00 120.00
101 Darius Garland 50.00 120.00
105 Sekou Doumbouya 2.50 6.00
107 Brandon Clarke 75.00 200.00
109 Zion Williamson 800.00 1,500.00
111 Talen Horton-Tucker 125.00 300.00
113 Cameron Johnson 30.00 80.00
115 Nickeil Alexander-Walker 20.00 50.00
119 Ja Morant 600.00 1,200.00
121 Coby White 150.00 400.00
122 Bol Bol 100.00 250.00
128 Jordan Poole 15.00 40.00
129 RJ Barrett 125.00 300.00
131 Jaxson Hayes 30.00 80.00
133 Tyler Herro 125.00 300.00
134 Tacko Fall 25.00 60.00
138 Keldon Johnson 75.00 200.00
139 De'Andre Hunter 40.00 100.00
141 Rui Hachimura 125.00 300.00
145 Matisse Thybulle 40.00 100.00
147 Nassir Little 15.00 40.00
148 Kevin Porter Jr. 5.00 12.00
150 Eric Paschall 30.00 80.00
151 Shaquille O'Neal 60.00 150.00
152 James Harden 25.00 60.00
153 Allen Iverson 60.00 150.00
155 Dominique Wilkins 12.00 30.00
156 Kevin Durant 75.00 200.00
157 Charles Barkley 40.00 100.00
158 Kyrie Irving 40.00 100.00
159 Scottie Pippen 50.00 120.00
160 Russell Westbrook 25.00 60.00
161 Tim Duncan 50.00 120.00
162 Giannis Antetokounmpo 200.00 500.00
163 Steve Nash 50.00 120.00
164 Zach LaVine 25.00 60.00
165 Dirk Nowitzki 60.00 150.00
166 Chris Paul 40.00 100.00
167 Magic Johnson 40.00 100.00
168 Kawhi Leonard 150.00 400.00
169 Karl Malone 25.00 60.00
170 Stephen Curry 300.00 600.00
171 Kevin Garnett 60.00 150.00
172 Jason Richardson 10.00 25.00
173 LeBron James 800.00 1,500.00
174 Donovan Mitchell 40.00 100.00
175 Derrick Rose 40.00 100.00
179 Sekou Doumbouya JSY AU/25 12.00 30.00
183 De'Andre Hunter JSY AU/25 75.00 200.00
185 Jaxson Hayes JSY AU/25 75.00 200.00
189 Nickeil Alexander-Walker JSY AU/25 40.00 100.00
191 Ja Morant JSY AU/25 2,500.00 5,000.00
199 Brandon Clarke JSY AU/25 150.00 400.00
216 Ignas Brazdeikis JSY AU/25 40.00 100.00
217 Chuma Okeke JSY AU/25 75.00 200.00

2019-20 Panini Spectra Silver
*SILVER: .75X TO 2X BASIC
*SILVER RC: .6X TO 1.5X BASIC RC
1 Klay Thompson 6.00 15.00
2 Fred VanVleet 6.00 15.00
3 Kawhi Leonard 20.00 50.00
5 Trae Young 40.00 100.00
9 Kristaps Porzingis 6.00 15.00
10 Damian Lillard 10.00 25.00
31 Russell Westbrook 6.00 15.00
32 Donovan Mitchell 8.00 20.00
33 Anthony Davis 12.00 30.00
34 Giannis Antetokounmpo 50.00 120.00
41 James Harden 6.00 15.00
43 LeBron James 150.00 400.00
45 Jayson Tatum 15.00 40.00
65 Kevin Durant 30.00 80.00
76 Shai Gilgeous-Alexander 8.00 20.00
78 Devin Booker 8.00 20.00
97 Luka Doncic 150.00 400.00
99 Stephen Curry 40.00 100.00
101 Darius Garland 12.00 30.00
105 Sekou Doumbouya 1.25 3.00
107 Brandon Clarke 40.00 100.00
109 Zion Williamson 500.00 1,000.00
111 Talen Horton-Tucker 40.00 100.00
113 Cameron Johnson 20.00 50.00
115 Nickeil Alexander-Walker 8.00 20.00
119 Ja Morant 300.00 600.00
121 Coby White 75.00 200.00
122 Bol Bol 40.00 100.00
129 RJ Barrett 75.00 200.00
131 Jaxson Hayes 20.00 50.00
133 Tyler Herro 50.00 120.00
134 Tacko Fall 15.00 40.00
138 Keldon Johnson 25.00 60.00
139 De'Andre Hunter 20.00 50.00
141 Rui Hachimura 40.00 100.00
145 Matisse Thybulle 20.00 50.00
147 Nassir Little 8.00 20.00
148 Kevin Porter Jr. 2.50 6.00
151 Shaquille O'Neal 12.00 30.00
152 James Harden 12.00 30.00
153 Allen Iverson 12.00 30.00
156 Kevin Durant 40.00 100.00
157 Charles Barkley 20.00 50.00
159 Scottie Pippen 12.00 30.00
160 Russell Westbrook 12.00 30.00
161 Tim Duncan 12.00 30.00
162 Giannis Antetokounmpo 60.00 150.00
165 Dirk Nowitzki 30.00 80.00
166 Chris Paul 8.00 20.00
167 Magic Johnson 12.00 30.00
168 Kawhi Leonard 75.00 200.00
170 Stephen Curry 60.00 150.00
171 Kevin Garnett 12.00 30.00
173 LeBron James 150.00 400.00
174 Donovan Mitchell 15.00 40.00
175 Derrick Rose 15.00 40.00

2019-20 Panini Spectra Variations
3 Kawhi Leonard 5.00 12.00
5 Trae Young 5.00 12.00
10 Damian Lillard 5.00 12.00
31 Russell Westbrook 3.00 8.00
33 Anthony Davis 8.00 20.00
34 Giannis Antetokounmpo 10.00 25.00
38 Ben Simmons 2.00 5.00
39 Nikola Jokic 10.00 25.00
41 James Harden 4.00 10.00
43 LeBron James 30.00 80.00
48 Joel Embiid 4.00 10.00
75 Kyrie Irving 4.00 10.00
97 Luka Doncic 40.00 100.00
101 Darius Garland 5.00 12.00
109 Zion Williamson 150.00 400.00
119 Ja Morant 100.00 250.00
123 PJ Washington Jr. 4.00 10.00
129 RJ Barrett 20.00 50.00
131 Jaxson Hayes 2.00 5.00
133 Tyler Herro 20.00 50.00
139 De'Andre Hunter 5.00 12.00
141 Rui Hachimura 15.00 40.00
149 Jarrett Culver 1.25 3.00
150 Eric Paschall 1.50 4.00

2019-20 Panini Spectra Variations Celestial
*CELESTIAL: .75X TO 2X BASIC
STATED PRINT RUN 99 SER.#'d SETS
3 Kawhi Leonard 25.00 60.00
33 Anthony Davis 25.00 60.00
34 Giannis Antetokounmpo 25.00 60.00
43 LeBron James 200.00 500.00
97 Luka Doncic 150.00 400.00
109 Zion Williamson 400.00 800.00
119 Ja Morant 300.00 600.00
133 Tyler Herro 60.00 150.00
141 Rui Hachimura 40.00 100.00

2019-20 Panini Spectra Variations Intersteller
*INTERSTELLER: 1X TO 2.5X BASIC
3 Kawhi Leonard 30.00 80.00
5 Trae Young 25.00 60.00
33 Anthony Davis 30.00 80.00
34 Giannis Antetokounmpo 30.00 80.00
43 LeBron James 300.00 600.00
97 Luka Doncic 200.00 500.00
109 Zion Williamson 500.00 1,000.00
119 Ja Morant 400.00 800.00
133 Tyler Herro 75.00 200.00
141 Rui Hachimura 50.00 120.00

2019-20 Panini Spectra Variations Meta
*META: 1.2X TO 3X BASIC
3 Kawhi Leonard 75.00 200.00
5 Trae Young 60.00 150.00
10 Damian Lillard 40.00 100.00
33 Anthony Davis 75.00 200.00
34 Giannis Antetokounmpo 75.00 200.00
39 Nikola Jokic 15.00 40.00
41 James Harden 15.00 40.00
43 LeBron James 400.00 800.00
97 Luka Doncic 300.00 600.00
101 Darius Garland 20.00 50.00
109 Zion Williamson 1,000.00 2,000.00
119 Ja Morant 600.00 1,200.00
123 PJ Washington Jr. 20.00 50.00
129 RJ Barrett 75.00 200.00
131 Jaxson Hayes 15.00 40.00
133 Tyler Herro 125.00 300.00
139 De'Andre Hunter 15.00 40.00
141 Rui Hachimura 75.00 200.00
150 Eric Paschall 15.00 40.00

2019-20 Panini Spectra Variations Silver
*SILVER: .75X TO 2X BASIC
3 Kawhi Leonard 25.00 60.00
33 Anthony Davis 25.00 60.00
34 Giannis Antetokounmpo 25.00 60.00
43 LeBron James 200.00 500.00
97 Luka Doncic 150.00 400.00
109 Zion Williamson 400.00 800.00
119 Ja Morant 300.00 600.00
133 Tyler Herro 75.00 200.00
141 Rui Hachimura 40.00 100.00

2019-20 Panini Spectra Aspiring Autographs
STATED PRINT RUN 49 SER.#'d SETS
EXCHANGE DEADLINE 12/26/2021
*META/25: .5X TO 1.2X BASIC
1 PJ Washington Jr. 15.00 40.00
2 Dylan Windler 6.00 15.00
3 Carsen Edwards 6.00 15.00
4 Nickeil Alexander-Walker 8.00 20.00
5 Kevin Porter Jr. 10.00 25.00
6 Jarrett Culver 5.00 12.00
7 Matisse Thybulle 10.00 25.00
8 KZ Okpala 6.00 15.00
9 RJ Barrett 20.00 50.00
10 Goga Bitadze 8.00 20.00
11 Isaiah Roby 6.00 15.00
12 Jaxson Hayes 8.00 20.00
13 Rui Hachimura 20.00 50.00
14 Luka Samanic 6.00 15.00
15 Bol Bol 12.00 30.00
16 Mfiondu Kabengele 6.00 15.00
17 Quinndary Weatherspoon 5.00 12.00
18 Tyler Herro 25.00 60.00
19 Bruno Fernando 6.00 15.00
20 Zion Williamson 150.00 400.00
21 Nassir Little 8.00 20.00
22 Eric Paschall 6.00 15.00
23 Admiral Schofield 6.00 15.00
24 Ja Morant 200.00 500.00
25 Ignas Brazdeikis 6.00 15.00
26 Cameron Johnson 12.00 30.00
27 Brandon Clarke 10.00 25.00
28 Kyle Guy 6.00 15.00
29 Cam Reddish 8.00 20.00
30 Grant Williams 8.00 20.00
31 Tremont Waters 6.00 15.00
32 Romeo Langford 5.00 12.00
33 Coby White 15.00 40.00
34 Ty Jerome 10.00 25.00
35 Jaylen Nowell 6.00 15.00
36 Cody Martin 8.00 20.00
37 Keldon Johnson 15.00 40.00
38 Sekou Doumbouya 5.00 12.00
39 Jordan Poole 20.00 50.00
40 De'Andre Hunter 20.00 50.00
41 Darius Bazley 5.00 12.00
42 Chuma Okeke 8.00 20.00

2019-20 Panini Spectra Catalysts Signatures
PRINT RUNS B/WN 15-49 COPIES PER
EXCHANGE DEADLINE 12/26/2021
*META/25: .5X TO 1.2X p/r 35-49
1 Nemanja Bjelica/49 5.00 12.00
2 Lauri Markkanen/35 10.00 25.00
3 Kevin Knox II/35 5.00 12.00
5 Wendell Carter Jr./49 8.00 20.00
7 Gary Harris/49 6.00 15.00
8 Karl-Anthony Towns/25 20.00 50.00
9 Montrezl Harrell/49 6.00 15.00
10 Vince Carter/25 75.00 200.00
11 Allen Crabbe/49 5.00 12.00
12 Nikola Jokic/35 150.00 400.00
13 Jaren Jackson Jr./35 50.00 120.00
15 Myles Turner/49 8.00 20.00
18 Jrue Holiday/25 10.00 25.00
19 Thaddeus Young/49 5.00 12.00
20 Kristaps Porzingis/35 30.00 80.00
21 Rondae Hollis-Jefferson/49 5.00 12.00
22 Zach LaVine/35 30.00 80.00
23 Julius Randle/49 10.00 25.00
24 Giannis Antetokounmpo/15 400.00 800.00
25 Collin Sexton/49 10.00 25.00
27 Avery Bradley/49 6.00 15.00
28 Lonzo Ball/25 8.00 20.00
29 Ersan Ilyasova/49 5.00 12.00
30 De'Aaron Fox/35 40.00 100.00

2019-20 Panini Spectra Color Blast
1 Damian Lillard 600.00 1,200.00
2 LeBron James 4,000.00 8,000.00
3 Zion Williamson 1,500.00 3,000.00
4 Giannis Antetokounmpo 500.00 1,000.00
5 Tyler Herro 1,000.00 2,000.00
6 Ben Simmons 150.00 400.00
7 Charles Barkley 200.00 500.00
8 Trae Young 400.00 800.00
9 Darius Garland 800.00 1,500.00
10 Kawhi Leonard 300.00 600.00
11 Donovan Mitchell 200.00 500.00
12 Stephen Curry 2,000.00 4,000.00
13 Ja Morant 3,000.00 6,000.00
14 James Harden 1,000.00 2,000.00
15 Rui Hachimura 150.00 400.00
16 Luka Doncic 4,000.00 8,000.00
17 Eric Paschall 75.00 200.00
18 Paul George 400.00 800.00
19 Kendrick Nunn 75.00 200.00
20 Anthony Davis 150.00 400.00
21 Bradley Beal 150.00 400.00
22 Kyrie Irving 800.00 1,500.00
23 RJ Barrett 500.00 1,000.00
24 Russell Westbrook 500.00 1,000.00
25 Coby White 400.00 800.00

2019-20 Panini Spectra Icons Autographs
STATED PRINT RUN 49-149 SER.#'d SETS
EXCHANGE DEADLINE 12/26/2021
*CELESTIAL/75: .4X TO 1X p/r 99-149
*INTERSTELLAR/49: .5X TO 1.2X p/r 99-149
*META/25: .6X TO 1.5X p/r 99-149
1 Dennis Rodman/99 40.00 100.00
2 Antonio Daniels/99 4.00 10.00
3 Rick Fox/49 5.00 12.00
4 Jim Jackson/149 5.00 12.00
5 Jalen Rose/99 5.00 12.00
6 Rick Mahorn/99 5.00 12.00
7 Nate McMillan/149 5.00 12.00
8 Ernie DiGregorio/99 5.00 12.00
9 Magic Johnson/49 60.00 150.00
10 Theo Ratliff/149 4.00 10.00
11 Stephon Marbury/99 8.00 20.00
12 Isaiah Rider/149 5.00 12.00
13 Ralph Sampson/99 5.00 12.00
14 James Silas/99 5.00 12.00
15 Chauncey Billups/99 8.00 20.00
16 Mark Eaton/99 5.00 12.00
17 Aaron McKie/99 4.00 10.00
18 Kenyon Martin/99 5.00 12.00
19 Kevin Garnett/49 60.00 150.00
20 Larry Nance/99 5.00 12.00
21 Richard Hamilton/99 6.00 15.00
22 Walter Davis/149 6.00 15.00
23 Jason Terry/99 5.00 12.00
24 Marcus Camby/99 5.00 12.00
25 B.J. Armstrong/149 6.00 15.00
26 Clifford Robinson/99 6.00 15.00
27 Bryon Russell/99 4.00 10.00
28 Scott Skiles/99 5.00 12.00
29 Jerry West/49 30.00 80.00
30 Otis Birdsong/99 6.00 15.00

2019-20 Panini Spectra Illustrious Legends Signatures
PRINT RUNS B/WN 15-99 COPIES PER
EXCHANGE DEADLINE 12/26/2021
*CELESTIAL/75: .4X TO 1X p/r 99
*INTERSTELLAR/49: .5X TO 1.2X p/r 99
*META/25: .6X TO 1.5X p/r 49-99
1 George Gervin/99 12.00 30.00
3 Dave Cowens/99 8.00 20.00
5 Lenny Wilkens/99 8.00 20.00
6 Elgin Baylor/49 30.00 80.00
7 Bob McAdoo/99 8.00 20.00
8 Walt Frazier/99 10.00 25.00
9 Adrian Dantley/99 6.00 15.00
10 Bernard King/99 8.00 20.00
11 Calvin Murphy/99 6.00 15.00
13 Bill Walton/99 20.00 50.00
15 Rick Fox/99 5.00 12.00
16 James Worthy/49 15.00 40.00
17 Alex English/99 8.00 20.00
18 Artis Gilmore/99 8.00 20.00
19 Arvydas Sabonis/99 10.00 25.00
20 Chris Mullin/99 10.00 25.00
21 Ralph Sampson/99 5.00 12.00
23 Kevin Johnson/99 6.00 15.00
25 George McGinnis/99 6.00 15.00

2019-20 Panini Spectra In The Zone Autographs
PRINT RUNS B/WN 15-99 COPIES PER
EXCHANGE DEADLINE 12/26/2021
*CELESTIAL/60-75: .4X TO 1X p/r 75-99
*INTERSTELLAR/49: .5X TO 1.2X p/r 75-99
*META/25: .6X TO 1.5X p/r 49-99
1 Avery Bradley/99 3.00 8.00
2 JJ Redick/49 12.00 30.00
3 Ersan Ilyasova/99 3.00 8.00
4 Kristaps Porzingis/49 20.00 50.00
5 Zach LaVine/49 30.00 80.00
7 Goran Dragic/99 4.00 10.00
8 Stephen Curry/15 1,000.00 2,000.00
9 Myles Turner/99 5.00 12.00
11 Montrezl Harrell/99 4.00 10.00
12 Lonzo Ball/49 6.00 15.00
13 Rondae Hollis-Jefferson/99 3.00 8.00
14 De'Aaron Fox/49 50.00 120.00
15 Kevin Knox II/49 4.00 10.00
16 Kevin Durant/15 150.00 400.00
17 Wendell Carter Jr./99 5.00 12.00
18 Giannis Antetokounmpo/15 800.00 1,500.00
20 Karl-Anthony Towns/25 20.00 50.00
21 Thaddeus Young/75 3.00 8.00
22 Vince Carter/49 50.00 120.00
23 Josh Richardson/99 3.00 8.00
24 Nikola Jokic/49 200.00 500.00
25 Jaren Jackson Jr./49 50.00 120.00
27 Collin Sexton/99 6.00 15.00

2019-20 Panini Spectra NBA Champions Signatures
PRINT RUNS B/WN 15-49 COPIES PER
EXCHANGE DEADLINE 12/26/2021
*META/25: .5X TO 1.2X p/r 35-49
1 Jason Terry/49 20.00 50.00
4 Clyde Drexler/25 40.00 100.00
5 A.C. Green/49 8.00 20.00
6 Dennis Rodman/35 100.00 250.00
7 Richard Hamilton/49 20.00 50.00
9 Dave Cowens/49 10.00 25.00
11 Robert Parish/49 10.00 25.00
13 Horace Grant/49 8.00 20.00
14 Paul Pierce/25 125.00 300.00
15 Toni Kukoc/49 20.00 50.00
16 Tony Parker/35 60.00 150.00
17 Pascal Siakam/25 75.00 200.00
19 Bill Walton/49 20.00 50.00
21 Rick Fox/49 12.00 30.00
23 B.J. Armstrong/49 10.00 25.00
24 Chris Bosh/25 25.00 60.00
25 Mark Aguirre/49 6.00 15.00
26 James Worthy/35 25.00 60.00
27 Chauncey Billups/49 30.00 80.00
28 Kevin Durant/15 200.00 500.00

2019-20 Panini Spectra Radiant Signatures
PRINT RUNS B/WN 25-149 COPIES PER
EXCHANGE DEADLINE 12/26/2021
*CELESTIAL/60-75: .4X TO 1X p/r 75-99
*INTERSTELLAR/49: .5X TO 1.2X p/r 75-99
*META/25: .6X TO 1.5X p/r 49-99
1 Avery Bradley/99 3.00 8.00
2 Clifford Robinson/99 5.00 12.00
3 Chauncey Billups/99 10.00 25.00
4 DeAndre' Bembry/99 3.00 8.00
5 Nate McMillan/149 4.00 10.00
6 Allen Iverson/49 50.00 120.00
7 Justin Holiday/149 3.00 8.00
8 John Wall/49 8.00 20.00
9 Scott Skiles/99 4.00 10.00
10 CJ McCollum/99 5.00 12.00
11 Larry Nance/99 4.00 10.00
12 Otto Porter Jr./99 3.00 8.00
13 Mason Plumlee/149 3.00 8.00
14 B.J. Armstrong/149 5.00 12.00
15 Dario Saric/99 4.00 10.00
16 Dwyane Wade/49 50.00 120.00
17 Royce O'Neale/149 3.00 8.00
18 Jerry West/49 30.00 80.00
19 Montrezl Harrell/99 4.00 10.00
20 Stephon Marbury/99 10.00 25.00
21 Marcus Camby/99 4.00 10.00
22 Rick Fox/99 4.00 10.00
23 Aaron Holiday/99 4.00 10.00
24 Wesley Matthews/99 3.00 8.00
25 Robert Covington/99 3.00 8.00
26 Magic Johnson/49 50.00 120.00
27 Bryon Russell/99 3.00 8.00
28 Dennis Rodman/99 50.00 120.00
29 Theo Ratliff/149 3.00 8.00
30 Julius Randle/99 6.00 15.00
31 Mark Eaton/99 4.00 10.00
32 Ralph Sampson/99 4.00 10.00
33 Al-Farouq Aminu/99 3.00 8.00
34 Cedi Osman/149 4.00 10.00
35 John Stockton/25 75.00 200.00

2019-20 Panini Spectra Rookie Jersey Autographs Wave
*WAVE: .75X TO 2X BASIC
STATED PRINT RUN 39 SER.#'d SETS
EXCHANGE DEADLINE 12/26/2021
177 Tyler Herro 200.00 500.00
179 Sekou Doumbouya 8.00 20.00
185 Jaxson Hayes 50.00 120.00
189 Nickeil Alexander-Walker 40.00 100.00
191 Ja Morant 2,000.00 4,000.00
197 Matisse Thybulle 100.00 250.00
199 Brandon Clarke 150.00 400.00
200 Keldon Johnson 75.00 200.00
203 Cam Reddish 12.00 30.00
209 Darius Bazley 8.00 20.00
211 Rui Hachimura 200.00 500.00
213 Coby White 200.00 500.00
214 Kevin Porter Jr. 15.00 40.00
217 Chuma Okeke 75.00 200.00

2019-20 Panini Spectra Signatures
PRINT RUNS B/WN 25-149 COPIES PER
EXCHANGE DEADLINE 12/26/2021
*CELESTIAL/60-75: .4X TO 1X p/r 75-99
*INTERSTELLAR/49: .5X TO 1.2X p/r 75-99
*META/25: .6X TO 1.5X p/r 49-99
1 Dwyane Wade/49 50.00 120.00
2 Junior Bridgeman/99 3.00 8.00
3 Jerry West/49 30.00 80.00
4 Micheal Ray Richardson/149 5.00 12.00
5 Kevin McHale/49 10.00 25.00
6 Elden Campbell/99 3.00 8.00
7 Peja Stojakovic/99 4.00 10.00
8 Spencer Haywood/99 4.00 10.00
9 Michael Cooper/99 5.00 12.00
10 Kenny Sky Walker/99 4.00 10.00
11 John Stockton/25 40.00 100.00
12 Jerome Williams/99 3.00 8.00
13 Andrew Wiggins/99 12.00 30.00
14 Cazzie Russell/99 4.00 10.00
15 Chris Bosh/49 10.00 25.00
16 Sean Elliott/99 4.00 10.00
17 Dave Cowens/99 8.00 20.00
18 Charlie Ward/99 4.00 10.00
19 Carlos Boozer/99 4.00 10.00
20 Alvan Adams/99 3.00 8.00
21 John Wall/49 20.00 50.00
22 Brent Barry/99 3.00 8.00
23 Hakeem Olajuwon/49 30.00 80.00
24 Doug Collins/99 5.00 12.00
25 Dennis Rodman/99 40.00 100.00
26 Eddie Jones/99 4.00 10.00
27 Avery Johnson/99 3.00 8.00
28 Anfernee Simons/149 8.00 20.00
29 Thaddeus Young/99 3.00 8.00
30 Ersan Ilyasova/99 3.00 8.00
31 Oscar Robertson/25 75.00 200.00
32 Larry Hughes/99 4.00 10.00
33 Grant Hill/35 20.00 50.00
34 Quentin Richardson/149 3.00 8.00
35 Jaren Jackson Jr./99 30.00 80.00

2020-21 Panini Spectra
JSY AU STATED PRINT RUN 99-149 SER.#'d SETS
EXCHANGE DEADLINE 2/4/2023
*ASIA: .5X TO 1.2X BASIC
*ASIA RED: .5X TO 1.2X BASIC
*SILVER: .75X TO 2X BASIC
1 Aaron Gordon 1.00 2.50
2 Kemba Walker 1.00 2.50
3 Evan Fournier .75 2.00
4 Luka Doncic 6.00 15.00
5 Dillon Brooks 1.00 2.50
6 De'Aaron Fox 1.50 4.00
7 Duncan Robinson 1.00 2.50
8 Lauri Markkanen 1.25 3.00
9 CJ McCollum 1.00 2.50
10 Blake Griffin 1.00 2.50
11 Luguentz Dort 1.50 4.00
12 RJ Barrett 1.50 4.00
13 Chris Paul 2.00 5.00
14 Rudy Gobert 1.25 3.00
15 Marcus Smart 1.00 2.50
16 Khris Middleton 1.25 3.00
17 Trae Young 2.50 6.00
18 Buddy Hield 1.00 2.50
19 Myles Turner 1.00 2.50
20 Nikola Jokic 5.00 12.00
21 Bojan Bogdanovic .75 2.00
22 Jerami Grant 1.00 2.50
23 Kristaps Porzingis 1.25 3.00
24 Gary Trent Jr. 1.00 2.50
25 Giannis Antetokounmpo 5.00 12.00
26 Mike Conley .75 2.00
27 Kelly Oubre Jr. 1.00 2.50
28 Deandre Ayton 1.00 2.50
29 Jrue Holiday 1.00 2.50
30 Terry Rozier 1.00 2.50
31 Devonte' Graham .75 2.00
32 Kevin Durant 4.00 10.00
33 Harrison Barnes .75 2.00
34 Draymond Green 1.25 3.00
35 Zach LaVine 1.50 4.00
36 John Collins 1.00 2.50
37 Devin Booker 2.50 6.00
38 Christian Wood .75 2.00
39 D'Angelo Russell 1.00 2.50
40 Jimmy Butler 2.00 5.00
41 Collin Sexton 1.00 2.50
42 Victor Oladipo .75 2.00
43 John Wall 1.25 3.00
44 Ja Morant 3.00 8.00
45 Andrew Wiggins 1.25 3.00
46 Derrick Rose 1.50 4.00
47 Jamal Murray 1.50 4.00
48 Anthony Davis 2.50 6.00
49 Karl-Anthony Towns 1.50 4.00
50 Brandon Clarke 1.00 2.50
51 Tyler Herro 2.00 5.00
52 Pascal Siakam 1.50 4.00
53 Jaylen Brown 1.50 4.00
54 DeMar DeRozan 1.25 3.00
55 Alec Burks .60 1.50
56 Nikola Vucevic 1.00 2.50
57 Zion Williamson 3.00 8.00
58 Gordon Hayward 1.00 2.50
59 Bam Adebayo 1.50 4.00
60 Shai Gilgeous-Alexander 5.00 12.00
61 Keldon Johnson 1.50 4.00
62 Andre Drummond 1.00 2.50
63 Damian Lillard 2.50 6.00
64 Michael Porter Jr. 1.25 3.00
65 Lonzo Ball 1.25 3.00
66 Donovan Mitchell 2.00 5.00
67 Jayson Tatum 4.00 10.00
68 Kyle Kuzma 1.25 3.00
69 Russell Westbrook 2.00 5.00
70 Kendrick Nunn .75 2.00
71 Fred VanVleet 1.50 4.00
72 Paul George 1.50 4.00
73 Julius Randle 1.00 2.50
74 Malik Beasley .75 2.00
75 Carmelo Anthony 1.50 4.00
76 Tim Hardaway Jr. .60 1.50
77 Coby White 1.25 3.00
78 Kyle Lowry 1.25 3.00
79 Ben Simmons 1.00 2.50
80 Tobias Harris 1.00 2.50
81 LeBron James 8.00 20.00
82 Patrick Beverley .60 1.50
83 Lou Williams 1.00 2.50
84 Steven Adams 1.00 2.50
85 Domantas Sabonis 1.25 3.00
86 De'Andre Hunter 1.00 2.50
87 Bradley Beal 1.25 3.00
88 Rui Hachimura 1.25 3.00
89 Joe Harris .75 2.00
90 LaMarcus Aldridge 1.00 2.50
91 Darius Garland 1.50 4.00
92 Joel Embiid 2.50 6.00
93 James Harden 2.00 5.00
94 Darius Bazley .60 1.50
95 Malcolm Brogdon 1.00 2.50
96 Brandon Ingram 1.25 3.00
97 Kawhi Leonard 2.50 6.00
98 Kyrie Irving 2.00 5.00
99 Stephen Curry 8.00 20.00
100 Cam Reddish 1.25 3.00
101 Anthony Edwards 12.00 30.00
102 LaMelo Ball 10.00 25.00
103 Tyrese Haliburton 10.00 25.00
104 James Wiseman 1.50 4.00
105 Cole Anthony 3.00 8.00
106 Immanuel Quickley 3.00 8.00
107 Desmond Bane 4.00 10.00
108 Patrick Williams 3.00 8.00
109 Tyrese Maxey 10.00 25.00
110 Xavier Tillman 1.50 4.00
111 Isaac Okoro 2.00 5.00
112 Payton Pritchard 4.00 10.00
113 Deni Avdija 3.00 8.00
114 Theo Maledon 1.25 3.00
115 Precious Achiuwa 2.50 6.00
116 Saddiq Bey 2.50 6.00
117 Isaiah Joe 1.50 4.00
118 Devin Vassell 4.00 10.00
119 Jordan Nwora 1.50 4.00
120 Jaden McDaniels 4.00 10.00
121 Isaiah Stewart 2.50 6.00
122 Killian Hayes 1.25 3.00
123 Obi Toppin 2.50 6.00
124 Kira Lewis Jr. 1.25 3.00
125 CJ Elleby 1.25 3.00
126 Aaron Nesmith 2.50 6.00
127 Onyeka Okongwu 2.50 6.00
128 Reggie Perry 1.25 3.00
129 Aleksej Pokusevski 1.50 4.00
130 Josh Green 2.50 6.00
131 Jalen Smith 2.50 6.00
132 Malachi Flynn 1.25 3.00
133 Paul Reed 1.50 4.00
134 Skylar Mays 1.25 3.00
135 Saben Lee 1.25 3.00
136 Caleb Martin 2.50 6.00
137 Robert Woodard II 1.25 3.00
138 Cassius Winston 1.25 3.00
139 Daniel Oturu 1.25 3.00
140 Tre Jones 2.00 5.00
141 Sam Merrill 2.00 5.00
142 Tyler Bey 1.25 3.00
143 Nico Mannion 1.25 3.00
144 Jae'Sean Tate 1.50 4.00
145 Jahmi'us Ramsey 1.25 3.00
146 Facundo Campazzo 1.50 4.00
147 Udoka Azubuike 1.50 4.00
148 Tyrell Terry 1.00 2.50
149 Zeke Nnaji 1.50 4.00
150 RJ Hampton 1.25 3.00
151 LeBron James SD 12.00 30.00
152 Paul George SD 2.50 6.00
153 Kevin Durant SD 6.00 15.00
154 Kawhi Leonard SD 4.00 10.00
155 Luka Doncic SD 10.00 25.00
156 Giannis Antetokounmpo SD 8.00 20.00
157 James Harden SD 3.00 8.00
158 Kyrie Irving SD 3.00 8.00
159 Stephen Curry SD 12.00 30.00
160 Ben Simmons SD 1.50 4.00
161 Anthony Davis SD 4.00 10.00
162 Nikola Jokic SD 8.00 20.00
163 Joel Embiid SD 4.00 10.00
164 Damian Lillard SD 4.00 10.00
165 Zion Williamson SD 5.00 12.00
166 Ja Morant SD 5.00 12.00
167 Russell Westbrook SD 3.00 8.00
168 Carmelo Anthony SD 2.50 6.00
169 Derrick Rose SD 2.50 6.00
170 Bradley Beal SD 2.00 5.00
171 Dirk Nowitzki SD 4.00 10.00
172 Paul Pierce SD 2.50 6.00
173 Shaquille O'Neal SD 6.00 15.00
174 Charles Barkley SD 4.00 10.00
175 Tim Duncan SD 4.00 10.00
176 Isaiah Joe JSY AU/149 RC 10.00 25.00
177 Aaron Nesmith JSY AU/149 RC 15.00 40.00
178 Malachi Flynn JSY AU/149 RC 8.00 20.00
179 Jaden McDaniels JSY AU/149 RC 25.00 60.00
180 Facundo Campazzo JSY AU/149 RC 10.00 25.00
181 Tyrell Terry JSY AU/149 RC 6.00 15.00
182 CJ Elleby JSY AU/149 RC 8.00 20.00
183 Zeke Nnaji JSY AU/149 RC 10.00 25.00
184 Immanuel Quickley JSY AU/149 RC 20.00 50.00
185 Kira Lewis Jr. JSY AU/149 RC 8.00 20.00
186 Obi Toppin JSY AU/149 RC 15.00 40.00
187 Desmond Bane JSY AU/149 RC 50.00 120.00
188 Killian Hayes JSY AU/149 RC 8.00 20.00
189 Onyeka Okongwu JSY AU/149 RC 15.00 40.00
190 Cole Anthony JSY AU/149 RC 20.00 50.00
191 Precious Achiuwa JSY AU/149 RC 15.00 40.00
192 Josh Green JSY AU/149 RC 15.00 40.00
193 Isaiah Stewart JSY AU/149 RC 15.00 40.00
194 Anthony Edwards JSY AU/99 RC 400.00 800.00
195 Tyrese Haliburton JSY AU/149 RC 200.00 500.00
196 Jordan Nwora JSY AU/149 RC 10.00 25.00
197 Daniel Oturu JSY AU/149 RC 8.00 20.00
198 Udoka Azubuike JSY AU/149 RC 10.00 25.00
199 Aleksej Pokusevski JSY AU/149 RC 10.00 25.00
200 Devin Vassell JSY AU/149 RC 25.00 60.00
201 Deni Avdija JSY AU/149 RC 20.00 50.00
202 Jalen Smith JSY AU/149 RC 15.00 40.00
203 Patrick Williams JSY AU/149 RC 20.00 50.00
204 Tyrese Maxey JSY AU/149 RC 150.00 400.00
205 Tre Jones JSY AU/149 RC 12.00 30.00
206 Payton Pritchard JSY AU/149 RC 25.00 60.00
207 RJ Hampton JSY AU/149 RC 8.00 20.00
208 Vernon Carey Jr. JSY AU/149 RC 8.00 20.00
209 James Wiseman JSY AU/99 RC 10.00 25.00
210 Saddiq Bey JSY AU/149 RC 15.00 40.00
211 Jahmi'us Ramsey JSY AU/149 RC 8.00 20.00
212 Theo Maledon JSY AU/149 RC 8.00 20.00
213 Robert Woodard II JSY AU/149 RC 8.00 20.00
214 Xavier Tillman JSY AU/149 RC 10.00 25.00
215 LaMelo Ball JSY AU/99 RC 200.00 500.00
216 Nico Mannion JSY AU/149 RC 8.00 20.00
217 Isaac Okoro JSY AU/149 RC 12.00 30.00

2020-21 Panini Spectra Astral
*ASTRAL: 1.5X TO 4X BASIC
*ASTRAL JSY AU: .75X TO 2X BASE
1-175 STATED PRINT RUN 35 SER.#'d SETS
JSY AU STATED PRINT RUN 35 SER.#'d SETS
EXCHANGE DEADLINE 2/4/2023
101 Anthony Edwards 50.00 120.00

2020-21 Panini Spectra Celestial
*CELESTIAL: 1.2X TO 3X BASIC
*CELESTIAL JSY AU: .5X TO 1.2X BASE
1-175 STATED PRINT RUN 99 SER.#'d SETS
JSY AU STATED PRINT RUN 75-99 SER.#'d SETS
EXCHANGE DEADLINE 2/4/2023
101 Anthony Edwards 40.00 100.00

2020-21 Panini Spectra Interstellar
*INTERSTELLAR: 1.5X TO 4X BASIC
*INTERSTELLAR JSY AU: .6X TO 1.5X BASE
1-175 STATED PRINT RUN 49 SER.#'d SETS
JSY AU STATED PRINT RUN 49 SER.#'d SETS
EXCHANGE DEADLINE 2/4/2023
101 Anthony Edwards 50.00 120.00

2020-21 Panini Spectra Meta
*META: 2.5X TO 6X BASIC
*META JSY AU: 1.2X TO 3X BASE
1-175 STATED PRINT RUN 25 SER.#'d SETS
JSY AU STATED PRINT RUN 25 SER.#'d SETS
EXCHANGE DEADLINE 2/4/2023
101 Anthony Edwards 75.00 200.00

2020-21 Panini Spectra Aspiring Autographs
STATED PRINT RUN 35-49 SER.#'d SETS
EXCHANGE DEADLINE 2/4/2023
*ASTRAL/25-35: .5X TO 1.2X BASIC
*META/25: .6X TO 1.5X BASIC
1 Markus Howard/49 8.00 20.00
2 Anthony Edwards/35 300.00 600.00
3 James Wiseman/35 8.00 20.00
4 Isaac Okoro/49 40.00 100.00
5 Deni Avdija/49 40.00 100.00
6 Tyrese Maxey/49 100.00 250.00
7 Tyler Bey/49 6.00 15.00
8 Aaron Nesmith/49 12.00 30.00
9 Skylar Mays/49 6.00 15.00
10 Caleb Martin/49 12.00 30.00
11 Theo Maledon/49 6.00 15.00
12 Devin Vassell/49 30.00 80.00
13 Isaiah Stewart/49 30.00 80.00
14 Mason Jones/49 5.00 12.00
15 Saddiq Bey/49 40.00 100.00
16 LaMelo Ball/35 800.00 1,500.00
17 Patrick Williams/49 75.00 200.00
18 Daniel Oturu/49 6.00 15.00
19 Onyeka Okongwu/49 12.00 30.00
20 Desmond Bane/49 40.00 100.00
21 Nathan Knight/49 6.00 15.00
22 Nick Richards/49 8.00 20.00
23 Cassius Winston/49 6.00 15.00
24 Sam Merrill/49 10.00 25.00
25 Devon Dotson/49 6.00 15.00
26 Immanuel Quickley/49 40.00 100.00
27 Reggie Perry/49 6.00 15.00
28 RJ Hampton/49 6.00 15.00
29 Cole Anthony/49 40.00 100.00
30 Grant Riller/49 6.00 15.00
31 Kira Lewis Jr./49 6.00 15.00
32 Josh Green/49 12.00 30.00
33 Robert Woodard II/49 6.00 15.00
34 Xavier Tillman/49 8.00 20.00
35 Elijah Hughes/49 6.00 15.00
36 Vernon Carey Jr./49 6.00 15.00
38 Aleksej Pokusevski/49 8.00 20.00
39 Tyrese Haliburton/35 100.00 250.00
40 Tyrell Terry/49 5.00 12.00
41 Jae'Sean Tate/49 40.00 100.00
42 Jalen Harris/49 5.00 12.00

2020-21 Panini Spectra Award Winning Autographs
26 Tim Hardaway 30.00 80.00
49 David Robinson 75.00 200.00

2020-21 Panini Spectra Catalysts Signatures
STATED PRINT RUN 49 SER.#'d SETS
EXCHANGE DEADLINE 2/4/2023
*ASTRAL/35: .5X TO 1.2X BASIC
*META/25: .6X TO 1.5X BASIC
2 Anthony Davis 100.00 250.00
4 JJ Redick 8.00 20.00
6 Luguentz Dort 15.00 40.00
7 Alex Caruso 15.00 40.00
8 Myles Turner 8.00 20.00
9 Anfernee Simons 10.00 25.00
10 Zach Collins 6.00 15.00
11 Carsen Edwards 6.00 15.00
12 Jamal Murray 40.00 100.00
13 Khris Middleton 10.00 25.00
14 Brandon Clarke 8.00 20.00
15 Boban Marjanovic 12.00 30.00
16 Luka Doncic 1,000.00 2,000.00
18 Cedi Osman 6.00 15.00
19 CJ McCollum 15.00 40.00
20 Bryn Forbes 6.00 15.00
21 Daniel Theis 12.00 30.00
22 Joe Harris 6.00 15.00
23 Aron Baynes 5.00 12.00
25 Jarrett Allen 8.00 20.00
26 Duncan Robinson 12.00 30.00
27 Thanasis Antetokounmpo 40.00 100.00
28 Nikola Jokic 125.00 300.00
29 Nerlens Noel 5.00 12.00
30 Robert Williams III 6.00 15.00

2020-21 Panini Spectra Color Blast
1 Giannis Antetokounmpo 1,000.00 2,000.00
2 Stephen Curry 2,500.00 5,000.00
3 Kevin Durant 500.00 1,000.00
4 James Harden 200.00 500.00
5 Nikola Jokic 400.00 800.00
6 Damian Lillard 300.00 600.00
7 Kawhi Leonard 300.00 600.00
8 Anthony Davis 300.00 600.00
9 Luka Doncic 3,000.00 6,000.00
10 LeBron James 3,000.00 6,000.00
11 Bradley Beal 125.00 300.00
12 Zion Williamson 800.00 1,500.00
13 Ja Morant 1,000.00 2,000.00
14 Jayson Tatum 800.00 1,500.00
15 Donovan Mitchell 400.00 800.00
16 Joel Embiid 300.00 600.00
17 Tyrese Maxey 600.00 1,200.00
18 Trae Young 300.00 600.00
19 Deni Avdija 150.00 400.00
20 Immanuel Quickley 150.00 400.00
21 LaMelo Ball 2,000.00 4,000.00
22 James Wiseman 40.00 100.00
23 Anthony Edwards 2,500.00 5,000.00
24 Cole Anthony 200.00 400.00
25 Tyrese Haliburton 1,000.00 2,000.00

2020-21 Panini Spectra Full Spectrum Signatures
STATED PRINT RUN 49 SER.#'d SETS
EXCHANGE DEADLINE 2/4/2023
*ASTRAL/35: .5X TO 1.2X BASIC
*META/25: .6X TO 1.5X BASIC
1 Domantas Sabonis 12.00 30.00
2 Delon Wright 5.00 12.00
3 Justin Holiday 5.00 12.00
4 Kevin Garnett 100.00 250.00
5 Gordon Hayward 12.00 30.00
6 Larry Nance Jr. 6.00 15.00
7 Collin Sexton 15.00 40.00
8 Luke Kennard 6.00 15.00
9 Dorian Finney-Smith 6.00 15.00
10 Daniel Theis 12.00 30.00
11 Tobias Harris 8.00 20.00
12 Troy Brown Jr. 6.00 15.00
13 Brent Barry 6.00 15.00
14 Darius Miles 5.00 12.00
15 Lamar Odom 8.00 20.00
16 Spencer Haywood 8.00 20.00
17 Meyers Leonard 5.00 12.00
18 Danilo Gallinari 6.00 15.00
19 Robert Horry 12.00 30.00
20 Cameron Johnson 10.00 25.00
21 Ivica Zubac 8.00 20.00
22 Nassir Little 6.00 15.00
23 Kelly Oubre Jr. 12.00 30.00
24 Jalen Brunson 12.00 30.00
25 Avery Bradley 5.00 12.00
26 Terry Cummings 8.00 20.00
27 Tomas Satoransky 5.00 12.00
28 Spencer Dinwiddie 6.00 15.00

2020-21 Panini Spectra Hall of Fame Signatures
19 Elvin Hayes 20.00 50.00
50 Walt Frazier 15.00 40.00

2020-21 Panini Spectra Icons Autographs
STATED PRINT RUN 49-99 SER.#'d SETS
EXCHANGE DEADLINE 2/4/2023
*CELESTIAL/35: .5X TO 1.2X BASIC
*INTERSTELLAR/25: .6X TO 1.5X BASIC
*ASTRAL/20: .6X TO 1.5X BASIC
1 Oscar Robertson/49 40.00 100.00
2 Shawn Kemp/49 30.00 80.00
3 Lenny Wilkens/99 8.00 20.00
4 Mitch Richmond/49 10.00 25.00
5 Dennis Rodman/49 50.00 120.00
6 Rasheed Wallace/49 30.00 80.00
7 Richard Hamilton/99 10.00 25.00
8 Artis Gilmore/99 10.00 25.00
9 Tony Parker/49 15.00 40.00
10 Jack Sikma/99 8.00 20.00
11 Danny Manning/99 6.00 15.00
12 Jerry West/49 40.00 100.00
13 David Robinson/49 40.00 100.00
14 Dominique Wilkins/49 15.00 40.00
15 Dikembe Mutombo/49 20.00 50.00
16 Gary Payton/49 15.00 40.00
17 Sarunas Marciulionis/49 8.00 20.00
18 Tim Hardaway/49 12.00 30.00
19 Isiah Thomas/49 20.00 50.00
20 Mark Jackson/99 6.00 15.00
21 Harold Miner/99 6.00 15.00
22 Chris Mullin/49 10.00 25.00
23 Alex English/99 8.00 20.00
24 Sam Perkins/99 6.00 15.00
25 Shaquille O'Neal/49 60.00 150.00
26 Kenny Smith/99 6.00 15.00
27 Mike Bibby/49 8.00 20.00
28 Baron Davis/49 8.00 20.00
29 Maurice Cheeks/99 8.00 20.00
30 Magic Johnson/49 50.00 120.00

2020-21 Panini Spectra Illustrious Legends Signatures
STATED PRINT RUN 49-99 SER.#'d SETS
EXCHANGE DEADLINE 2/4/2023
*CELESTIAL: .5X TO 1.2X BASIC
*INTERSTELLAR: .6X TO 1.5X BASIC
*META: .75X TO 2X BASIC
1 Shawn Kemp/99 30.00 80.00
2 Horace Grant/99 15.00 40.00
3 Calvin Natt/99 6.00 15.00
4 Lenny Wilkens/49 8.00 20.00
5 Spencer Haywood/99 8.00 20.00
6 Greg Ostertag/99 5.00 12.00
7 Derek Fisher/99 12.00 30.00
8 Magic Johnson/49 60.00 150.00
9 Robert Horry/99 12.00 30.00
10 Dominique Wilkins/49 15.00 40.00
11 Rick Barry/99 10.00 25.00
12 Adrian Dantley/99 8.00 20.00
13 John Stockton/49 40.00 100.00
14 Karl Malone/49 40.00 100.00
15 Dino Radja/99 6.00 15.00
16 Jason Williams/49 60.00 150.00
17 Allen Iverson/49 75.00 200.00
18 Baron Davis/99 8.00 20.00
19 Mark Jackson/99 6.00 15.00
20 Richard Jefferson/99 5.00 12.00
21 Nate Archibald/99 10.00 25.00
22 Jerry West/49 40.00 100.00
23 Dwyane Wade/49 60.00 150.00
24 Alex English/99 8.00 20.00
25 Gary Payton/99 15.00 40.00

2020-21 Panini Spectra In The Zone Autographs
STATED PRINT RUN 49-99 SER.#'d SETS
EXCHANGE DEADLINE 2/4/2023
*CELESTIAL: .5X TO 1.2X BASIC
*INTERSTELLAR: .6X TO 1.5X BASIC
*META: .75X TO 2X BASIC
1 Jarrett Culver/99 5.00 12.00
2 Luka Doncic/49 1,000.00 2,000.00
3 Otto Porter Jr./99 5.00 12.00
5 Ricky Rubio/99 8.00 20.00
6 Jalen Brunson/99 12.00 30.00
7 Sekou Doumbouya/99 5.00 12.00
8 Cam Reddish/99 15.00 40.00
9 Boban Marjanovic/99 12.00 30.00
10 Duncan Robinson/49 20.00 50.00
11 Kevin Garnett/49 100.00 250.00
12 Kawhi Leonard/49 75.00 200.00
13 Kelly Oubre Jr./99 10.00 25.00
14 Danilo Gallinari/75 6.00 15.00
15 LaMarcus Aldridge/75 12.00 30.00
16 Anfernee Simons/99 12.00 30.00
17 Jarrett Allen/99 8.00 20.00
18 Luke Kennard/75 6.00 15.00
19 Jrue Holiday/99 12.00 30.00
20 Tony Parker/49 15.00 40.00
21 De'Andre Hunter/49 8.00 20.00
22 Chuma Okeke/99 8.00 20.00
23 Tim Hardaway/99 12.00 30.00
25 Bradley Beal/49 15.00 40.00
26 Dominique Wilkins/49 15.00 40.00
27 Michael Porter Jr./99 10.00 25.00
28 Robin Lopez/99 5.00 12.00

2020-21 Panini Spectra Private Signings Association Version
5 Isaac Okoro 25.00 60.00
45 CJ Elleby 8.00 20.00

2020-21 Panini Spectra Private Signings Icon Version
1 Anthony Edwards 300.00 600.00
2 James Wiseman 8.00 20.00

2020-21 Panini Spectra Radiant Signatures
STATED PRINT RUN 49-99 SER.#'d SETS
EXCHANGE DEADLINE 2/4/2023
*CELESTIAL/35: .5X TO 1.2X BASIC
*INTERSTELLAR/25: .6X TO 1.5X BASIC
*ASTRAL/20: .6X TO 1.5X BASIC
1 Lamar Odom/49 15.00 40.00
2 Kyle Kuzma/49 12.00 30.00
3 Ja Morant/49 150.00 400.00
4 Lauri Markkanen/49 10.00 25.00
5 Jason Terry/99 6.00 15.00
6 Elton Brand/99 12.00 30.00
7 Shake Milton/99 6.00 15.00
9 Buddy Hield/49 8.00 20.00
10 Kevin Durant/49 200.00 500.00
12 CJ McCollum/49 15.00 40.00
14 Detlef Schrempf/99 8.00 20.00
15 Gary Harris/99 6.00 15.00
16 Sarunas Marciulionis/49 8.00 20.00
17 Nickeil Alexander-Walker/99 12.00 30.00
18 Anfernee Hardaway/49 75.00 200.00
20 Dikembe Mutombo/49 20.00 50.00
21 Chris Mullin/49 12.00 30.00
22 De'Andre Hunter/49 8.00 20.00
24 Ben McLemore/99 5.00 12.00
25 Wally Szczerbiak/49 6.00 15.00
26 Dwyane Wade/49 75.00 200.00
27 Mikal Bridges/99 10.00 25.00
28 Robin Lopez/99 5.00 12.00
29 Nassir Little/99 6.00 15.00
30 Bobby Portis/99 8.00 20.00
31 Micheal Ray Richardson/99 5.00 12.00
32 Jarrett Culver/99 5.00 12.00
33 Dwight Powell/99 5.00 12.00
34 Dale Ellis/99 6.00 15.00
35 Solomon Hill/99 5.00 12.00

2020-21 Panini Spectra Rookie Dual Patch Autographs
1 A.Edwards/L.Ball 3,000.00 6,000.00
2 A.Edwards/J.Wiseman 1,000.00 2,000.00
3 J.Wiseman/L.Ball 150.00 400.00
4 O.Toppin/T.Haliburton 300.00 600.00
5 D.Avdija/K.Hayes 125.00 300.00

2020-21 Panini Spectra Signatures
STATED PRINT RUN 49-99 SER.#'d SETS
EXCHANGE DEADLINE 2/4/2023
*CELESTIAL: .5X TO 1.2X BASIC
*INTERSTELLAR: .6X TO 1.5X BASIC
*ASTRAL: .6X TO 1.5X BASIC
1 Ray Allen/49 40.00 100.00
2 Dwyane Wade/49 75.00 200.00
3 Charles Oakley/75 8.00 20.00
4 Quentin Richardson/75 5.00 12.00
5 Tim Legler/75 5.00 12.00
6 Alex Caruso/49 15.00 40.00
7 Aron Baynes/75 5.00 12.00
8 Avery Bradley/75 5.00 12.00
9 Brandon Clarke/75 8.00 20.00
10 Cameron Johnson/75 10.00 25.00
11 Nate Archibald/75 10.00 25.00
12 Luguentz Dort/75 15.00 40.00
13 Robert Parish/75 10.00 25.00
15 Myles Turner/75 8.00 20.00
16 Larry Nance Jr./75 6.00 15.00
17 David Robinson/49 40.00 100.00
18 Dennis Rodman/49 50.00 120.00
19 John Stockton/49 40.00 100.00
20 Kevin Garnett/49 100.00 250.00
22 Troy Brown Jr./75 6.00 15.00
23 Micheal Ray Richardson/99 5.00 12.00
24 Ben McLemore/75 5.00 12.00
25 Danny Manning/75 6.00 15.00
26 Dorian Finney-Smith/99 6.00 15.00
27 Jack Sikma/99 8.00 20.00
28 JJ Redick/75 8.00 20.00
29 Joe Harris/75 6.00 15.00
30 Carsen Edwards/75 6.00 15.00
31 Jarred Vanderbilt/49 8.00 20.00
32 Roy Hibbert/49 5.00 12.00
33 Artis Gilmore/49 10.00 25.00
34 James Johnson/99 5.00 12.00
35 Grant Hill/49 30.00 80.00

2020-21 Panini Spectra Variations
*SILVER: .75X TO 2X BASIC
*CELESTIAL/99: 1.2X TO 3X BASIC
*INTER/49: 1.5X TO 4X BASIC
*META/25: 2.5X TO 6X BASIC
104 James Wiseman 1.50 4.00

2022-23 Panini Spectra
COMPLETE SET (245)
JSY AU STATED PRINT RUN 49-199 SER.#'d SETS
1 Buddy Hield 1.00 2.50
2 Cade Cunningham 3.00 8.00
3 Mikal Bridges 1.25 3.00
4 Cameron Thomas 1.50 4.00
5 Josh Giddey 1.50 4.00
6 Jalen Brunson 2.00 5.00
7 Jayson Tatum 4.00 10.00
8 Collin Sexton 1.25 3.00
9 Jonathan Kuminga 2.50 6.00
10 Anthony Davis 2.50 6.00
11 De'Aaron Fox 2.00 5.00
12 James Harden 2.00 5.00
13 Jaylen Brown 2.00 5.00
14 Joel Embiid 1.50 4.00
15 Keldon Johnson 1.25 3.00
16 Fred VanVleet 1.25 3.00
17 Jarrett Allen 1.00 2.50
18 Gary Trent Jr. 1.00 2.50
19 OG Anunoby 1.25 3.00
20 Marcus Smart 1.25 3.00
21 Cameron Johnson .75 2.00
22 Dorian Finney-Smith .75 2.00
23 Malcolm Brogdon .75 2.00
24 Shaquille O'Neal 4.00 10.00
25 Charles Barkley 2.50 6.00
26 Allen Iverson 2.50 6.00
27 Evan Mobley 2.50 6.00
28 Bojan Bogdanovic 1.00 2.50
29 Tyrese Haliburton 2.00 5.00
30 Spencer Dinwiddie .75 2.00
31 Myles Turner 1.00 2.50
32 Giannis Antetokounmpo 5.00 12.00

33 CJ McCollum 1.00 2.50
34 Jrue Holiday 1.25 3.00
35 Saddiq Bey .75 2.00
36 Brandon Ingram 1.25 3.00
37 Dejounte Murray 1.25 3.00
38 Kevin Porter Jr. .75 2.00
39 John Collins 1.00 2.50
40 LaMelo Ball 2.50 6.00
41 Desmond Bane 1.25 3.00
42 Kelly Oubre Jr. 1.00 2.50
43 PJ Washington Jr. 1.00 2.50
44 Tyler Herro 1.50 4.00
45 Harrison Barnes .75 2.00
46 Jimmy Butler 2.00 5.00
47 Kevin Huerter 1.00 2.50
48 Cole Anthony 1.00 2.50
49 Franz Wagner 2.50 6.00
50 Bradley Beal 1.25 3.00
51 Kristaps Porzingis 1.25 3.00
52 Kevin Durant 3.00 8.00
53 Michael Porter Jr. 1.25 3.00
54 Chris Paul 2.00 5.00
55 Nikola Jokic 5.00 12.00
56 D'Angelo Russell .75 2.00
57 Rui Hachimura 1.00 2.50
58 Rudy Gobert 1.25 3.00
59 Karl-Anthony Towns 1.50 4.00
60 Shai Gilgeous-Alexander 5.00 12.00
61 Julius Randle 1.25 3.00
62 Damian Lillard 2.50 6.00
63 Anfernee Simons 1.25 3.00
64 Kawhi Leonard 2.50 6.00
65 Jordan Poole 1.50 4.00
66 Jordan Clarkson 1.00 2.50
67 Klay Thompson 2.50 6.00
68 RJ Barrett 1.50 4.00
69 Stephen Curry 8.00 20.00
70 Lauri Markkanen 1.50 4.00
71 Jerami Grant 1.25 3.00
72 Andrew Wiggins 1.25 3.00
73 Quentin Grimes .75 2.00
74 Russell Westbrook 1.50 4.00
75 Cam Reddish .75 2.00
76 Paul George 1.50 4.00
77 Bones Hyland .75 2.00
78 Aaron Gordon 1.00 2.50
79 LeBron James 8.00 20.00
80 Tyrese Maxey 2.00 5.00
81 Anthony Edwards 5.00 12.00
82 Cameron Johnson .75 2.00
83 Devin Booker 2.50 6.00
84 Jamal Murray 1.50 4.00
85 Tim Hardaway Jr. .75 2.00
86 Kyle Kuzma 1.25 3.00
87 Jalen McDaniels 1.00 2.50
88 Josh Green 1.00 2.50
89 Bam Adebayo 1.50 4.00
90 Malik Monk 1.00 2.50
91 Jalen Suggs 1.25 3.00
92 Luka Doncic 6.00 15.00
93 Kyrie Irving 2.00 5.00
94 Domantas Sabonis 1.25 3.00
95 Deandre Ayton 1.00 2.50
96 Christian Wood .60 1.50
97 Jalen Green 3.00 8.00
98 De'Andre Hunter 1.00 2.50
99 Alperen Sengun 1.25 3.00
100 Ja Morant 3.00 8.00
101 Terry Rozier III 1.25 3.00
102 Jaren Jackson Jr. 1.50 4.00
103 Zion Williamson 2.50 6.00
104 Trae Young 2.50 6.00
105 Khris Middleton 1.25 3.00
106 Trey Murphy III 1.25 3.00
107 Scottie Barnes 1.50 4.00
108 Devin Vassell 1.25 3.00
109 Tre Jones 1.00 2.50
110 Derrick White 1.00 2.50
111 Josh Hart 1.00 2.50
112 Tobias Harris .75 2.00
113 De'Anthony Melton .75 2.00
114 Nikola Vucevic 1.00 2.50
115 Pascal Siakam 1.50 4.00
116 Bobby Portis 1.00 2.50
117 Wendell Carter Jr. 1.00 2.50
118 Jaden McDaniels 1.00 2.50
119 Luguentz Dort 1.00 2.50
120 Norman Powell 1.00 2.50
121 Malik Beasley .75 2.00
122 Dillon Brooks 1.00 2.50
123 Brandon Clarke .75 2.00
124 Herbert Jones 1.00 2.50
125 Devonte' Graham .75 2.00
126 Jonas Valanciunas .75 2.00
127 Zach LaVine 2.00 5.00
128 Immanuel Quickley 1.00 2.50
129 Max Strus 1.00 2.50
130 Al Horford 1.00 2.50
131 Marvin Bagley III .75 2.00
132 Lonnie Walker IV .75 2.00
133 Robert Williams III .75 2.00
134 DeMar DeRozan 1.25 3.00
135 Draymond Green 1.25 3.00
136 Kevin Love 1.00 2.50
137 Jose Alvarado 1.00 2.50
138 Markelle Fultz .75 2.00
139 Kenyon Martin Jr. 1.00 2.50
140 James Wiseman .75 2.00
141 Ayo Dosunmu 1.25 3.00
142 Darius Garland 1.50 4.00
143 Anfernee Hardaway 2.50 6.00
144 Magic Johnson 4.00 10.00
145 Kevin Garnett 2.50 6.00
146 Donovan Mitchell 2.00 5.00
147 Pau Gasol 1.50 4.00
148 Dirk Nowitzki 2.50 6.00
149 Dwyane Wade 2.00 5.00
150 Vince Carter 2.00 5.00
151 Paolo Banchero RC 10.00 25.00
152 Jabari Smith Jr. RC 5.00 12.00
153 Josh Minott RC 1.50 4.00
154 Kenneth Lofton Jr. RC 2.00 5.00
155 Kevon Harris RC 1.25 3.00
156 Bryce McGowens RC 1.50 4.00
157 Shaedon Sharpe RC 6.00 15.00
158 Dyson Daniels RC 4.00 10.00
159 Jabari Walker RC 1.25 3.00
160 Jalen Williams RC 8.00 20.00
161 Ousmane Dieng RC 2.00 5.00
162 Isaiah Mobley RC 1.50 4.00
163 Jalen Duren RC 5.00 12.00
164 Ochai Agbaji RC 2.00 5.00
165 Jaden Hardy RC 2.50 6.00
166 AJ Griffin RC 1.25 3.00
167 Tari Eason RC 4.00 10.00
168 Christian Koloko RC 1.50 4.00
169 Jake LaRavia RC 1.50 4.00
170 Christian Braun RC 4.00 10.00
171 Peyton Watson RC 2.50 6.00
172 TyTy Washington Jr. RC 1.50 4.00
173 Blake Wesley RC 1.50 4.00
174 Nikola Jovic RC 3.00 8.00
175 David Roddy RC 2.00 5.00
176 Wendell Moore Jr. RC 1.50 4.00
177 MarJon Beauchamp RC 1.50 4.00
178 Patrick Baldwin Jr. RC 1.50 4.00
179 Walker Kessler RC 3.00 8.00
180 Malaki Branham RC 1.50 4.00
181 Andrew Nembhard RC 3.00 8.00
182 Caleb Houstan RC 1.50 4.00
183 Dalen Terry RC 1.50 4.00
184 Max Christie RC 4.00 10.00
185 Moussa Diabate RC 1.50 4.00
186 Kennedy Chandler RC 1.50 4.00
187 Mark Williams RC 3.00 8.00
188 Jordan Goodwin RC 1.25 3.00
189 Trevor Keels RC 1.25 3.00
190 Johnny Davis RC 1.50 4.00
191 Jaylin Williams RC 2.00 5.00
192 Simone Fontecchio RC 1.50 4.00
193 Jeremy Sochan RC 5.00 12.00
194 A.J. Green RC 1.50 4.00
195 Keegan Murray RC 4.00 10.00
196 Bennedict Mathurin RC 5.00 12.00
197 Orlando Robinson RC 1.25 3.00
198 Tyrese Martin RC 1.25 3.00
199 Chet Holmgren RC 8.00 20.00
200 Ryan Rollins RC 1.50 4.00
201 Bennedict Mathurin AU JSY/199 75.00 200.00
202 AJ Griffin AU JSY/199 10.00 25.00
203 Jeremy Sochan AU JSY/49 100.00 250.00
204 Jalen Duren AU JSY/199 40.00 100.00
205 Jalen Williams AU JSY/199 60.00 150.00
206 Shaedon Sharpe AU JSY/199 100.00 250.00
207 Walker Kessler AU JSY/199 25.00 60.00
208 Paolo Banchero AU JSY/199 200.00 500.00
209 MarJon Beauchamp AU JSY/199 12.00 30.00
210 Tari Eason AU JSY/199 30.00 80.00
211 Mark Williams AU JSY/199 25.00 60.00
212 Johnny Davis AU JSY/199 12.00 30.00
213 Ochai Agbaji AU JSY/199 15.00 40.00
214 Jaden Ivey AU JSY/199 40.00 100.00
215 Christian Braun AU JSY/199 30.00 80.00
216 Blake Wesley AU JSY/199 12.00 30.00
217 Jake LaRavia AU JSY/199 12.00 30.00
218 Ousmane Dieng AU JSY/199 15.00 40.00
219 Malaki Branham AU JSY/49 12.00 30.00
220 David Roddy AU JSY/199 15.00 40.00
221 Nikola Jovic AU JSY/199 25.00 60.00
222 Wendell Moore Jr. AU JSY/199 12.00 30.00
223 TyTy Washington Jr. AU JSY/199 12.00 30.00
224 Peyton Watson AU JSY/199 20.00 50.00
225 Andrew Nembhard AU JSY/199 25.00 60.00
226 Jaden Hardy AU JSY/199 25.00 60.00
227 Keegan Murray AU JSY/199 75.00 200.00
228 Max Christie AU JSY/199 30.00 80.00
229 Christian Koloko AU JSY/199 12.00 30.00
230 Patrick Baldwin Jr. AU JSY/199 12.00 30.00
231 Kennedy Chandler AU JSY/199 12.00 30.00
232 Moussa Diabate AU JSY/199 12.00 30.00
233 Trevor Keels AU JSY/199 10.00 25.00
234 Isaiah Mobley AU JSY/199 12.00 30.00
235 Jabari Walker AU JSY/199 10.00 25.00
236 Ryan Rollins AU JSY/199 12.00 30.00
237 Tyrese Martin AU JSY/199 10.00 25.00
238 Dyson Daniels AU JSY/199 30.00 80.00
239 Caleb Houstan AU JSY/199 12.00 30.00
240 Jaylin Williams AU JSY/199 15.00 40.00
241 Bryce McGowens AU JSY/199 12.00 30.00
242 Kenneth Lofton Jr. AU JSY/199 15.00 40.00
243 Vince Williams Jr. AU JSY/199 15.00 40.00
244 Chet Holmgren AU JSY/199 150.00 400.00
245 Jabari Smith Jr. AU JSY/199 40.00 100.00

2022-23 Panini Spectra Aspiring Autographs

COMPLETE SET (46)
STATED PRINT RUN 99 SER.#'d SETS
EXCHANGE DEADLINE 2/16/2025
*ASIA: .4X TO 1X BASIC
*GREEN/50: .5X TO 1.2X BASIC
*PURPLE/35: .6X TO 1.5X BASIC
*PINK/25: .75X TO 2X BASIC
1 Jaden Ivey 50.00 120.00
2 Trevor Keels 5.00 12.00
3 E.J. Liddell 6.00 15.00
4 Moussa Diabate 6.00 15.00
5 Chet Holmgren 125.00 300.00
6 Jaden Hardy 10.00 25.00
7 Walker Kessler 12.00 30.00
9 Isaiah Mobley 6.00 15.00
10 Jake LaRavia 6.00 15.00
12 Jabari Smith Jr. 50.00 120.00
13 Christian Koloko 6.00 15.00
14 Keegan Murray 50.00 120.00
15 AJ Griffin 5.00 12.00
16 Tari Eason 15.00 40.00
17 Jeremy Sochan 40.00 100.00
18 Shaedon Sharpe 60.00 150.00
19 Paolo Banchero 150.00 400.00
20 Jalen Williams 30.00 80.00
21 Dalen Terry 6.00 15.00
22 Bennedict Mathurin 50.00 120.00
23 Dyson Daniels 15.00 40.00
24 Ochai Agbaji 8.00 20.00
25 Ousmane Dieng 8.00 20.00
26 Johnny Davis 6.00 15.00
27 David Roddy 8.00 20.00
28 Christian Braun 15.00 40.00
29 Blake Wesley 6.00 15.00
30 TyTy Washington Jr. 6.00 15.00
32 Jalen Duren 20.00 50.00
33 Mark Williams 12.00 30.00
34 Nikola Jovic 12.00 30.00
35 Wendell Moore Jr. 6.00 15.00
36 Max Christie 25.00 60.00
37 MarJon Beauchamp 6.00 15.00
38 Caleb Houstan 6.00 15.00
39 Malaki Branham 6.00 15.00
40 Jordan Goodwin 5.00 12.00
41 Kennedy Chandler 6.00 15.00
42 Scotty Pippen Jr. 8.00 20.00
43 Jaylin Williams 8.00 20.00
44 Kenneth Lofton Jr. 8.00 20.00
45 Jabari Walker 5.00 12.00
46 Tyrese Martin 5.00 12.00
47 Kevon Harris 5.00 12.00
48 Ryan Rollins 6.00 15.00
49 Josh Minott 6.00 15.00

2022-23 Panini Spectra Catalysts Signatures

COMPLETE SET (34)
STATED PRINT RUN 75-99 SER.#'d SETS
EXCHANGE DEADLINE 2/16/2025
*ASIA: .4X TO 1X BASIC
*ASTRAL/49: .5X TO 1.2X BASIC
*META/25: .6X TO 1.5X BASIC
1 Grayson Allen/99 6.00 15.00
2 Jarred Vanderbilt/99 5.00 12.00
3 Boban Marjanovic/99 6.00 15.00
4 Caleb Martin/99 6.00 15.00
5 Derrick White/99 12.00 30.00
6 Monte Morris/99 4.00 10.00
7 Jonas Valanciunas/99 5.00 12.00
8 Doug McDermott/99 4.00 10.00
9 Kevin Huerter/99 6.00 15.00
10 Danny Green/99 6.00 15.00
11 Isaac Okoro/99 5.00 12.00
12 Isaiah Stewart/99 5.00 12.00
13 Adrian Dantley/99 6.00 15.00
14 Gary Harris/99 5.00 12.00
15 Cameron Payne/99 5.00 12.00
16 Max Strus/99 6.00 15.00
17 Kenyon Martin Jr./99 6.00 15.00
18 Herbert Jones/99 6.00 15.00
19 Gary Trent Jr./99 5.00 12.00
20 Evan Fournier/99 5.00 12.00
21 Nicolas Batum/99 5.00 12.00
22 Cameron Johnson/75 5.00 12.00
23 Georges Niang/99 5.00 12.00
24 De'Anthony Melton/99 5.00 12.00
25 Brent Barry/99 5.00 12.00
26 Robert Parish/99 8.00 20.00
27 Jalen McDaniels/99 6.00 15.00
28 Dale Ellis/99 6.00 15.00
30 Ivica Zubac/99 6.00 15.00
31 Ayo Dosunmu/99 8.00 20.00
32 Malik Monk/99 6.00 15.00
33 Kenny "Sky" Walker/99 5.00 12.00
34 Tim Hardaway/99 8.00 20.00
35 John Starks/99 6.00 15.00

2022-23 Panini Spectra Color Blast

COMPLETE SET (25)
1 Jayson Tatum 800.00 1,500.00
2 Luka Doncic 1,250.00 2,500.00
3 Stephen Curry 1,500.00 3,000.00
4 Kevin Durant 300.00 600.00
5 Kyrie Irving 300.00 600.00
6 James Harden 300.00 600.00
7 Ja Morant 400.00 800.00
8 Nikola Jokic 500.00 1,000.00
9 LeBron James 1,500.00 3,000.00
10 Giannis Antetokounmpo 1,000.00 2,000.00
11 Damian Lillard 300.00 600.00
12 Donovan Mitchell 150.00 400.00
13 Zion Williamson 400.00 800.00
14 LaMelo Ball 300.00 600.00
15 Anthony Edwards 800.00 1,500.00
16 Joel Embiid 300.00 600.00
17 Shai Gilgeous-Alexander 500.00 1,000.00
18 Trae Young 300.00 600.00
19 Jalen Williams 800.00 1,500.00
20 Bennedict Mathurin 1,000.00 2,000.00
21 Jaden Ivey 1,000.00 2,000.00
22 Keegan Murray 1,000.00 2,000.00
23 Jabari Smith Jr. 1,000.00 2,000.00
24 Chet Holmgren 2,000.00 4,000.00
25 Paolo Banchero 2,500.00 5,000.00

2022-23 Panini Spectra Colorgraphs

COMPLETE SET (23)
STATED PRINT RUN 75-99 SER.#'d SETS
EXCHANGE DEADLINE 2/16/2025
*ASIA: .4X TO 1X BASIC
*ASTRAL/49: .5X TO 1.2X BASIC
*META/25: .75X TO 2X BASIC
1 Luka Doncic/75 300.00 600.00
2 Deandre Ayton/99 10.00 25.00
3 Tyrese Haliburton/99 100.00 250.00
4 Jordan Poole/99 40.00 100.00
5 Nikola Jokic/75 125.00 300.00
6 RJ Barrett/99 15.00 40.00
7 Khris Middleton/99 12.00 30.00
8 Jaren Jackson Jr./75 40.00 100.00
9 Anthony Edwards/75 200.00 500.00
10 Stephen Curry/75 500.00 1,000.00
12 Rudy Gobert/99 12.00 30.00
13 Paul George/75 100.00 250.00
14 Saddiq Bey/99 8.00 20.00
15 Brandon Ingram/75 40.00 100.00
16 Ray Allen/75 50.00 120.00
17 Cade Cunningham/99 125.00 300.00
18 Charles Barkley/75 75.00 200.00
19 Seth Curry/99 8.00 20.00
21 Paolo Banchero /75 300.00 600.00
22 Jaden Ivey/75 75.00 200.00
23 Bennedict Mathurin/75 75.00 200.00
24 Jabari Smith Jr./75 75.00 200.00
25 Keegan Murray/75 75.00 200.00

2023-24 Panini Spectra

JSY AU STATED PRINT RUN 99-199 SER.#'d SETS
*INTERNATIONAL: .4X TO 1X BASIC
*MENAGERIE: 1.5X TO 4X BASIC
*CELESTIAL JSY AU/99: .5X TO 1.2X BASIC
*SUPERNOVA JSY AU/75: .6X TO 1.5X BASIC
*INTERSTELLAR JSY AU/49: .75X TO 2X BASIC
*ASTRAL JSY AU/35: 1X TO 2.5X BASIC
*META JSY AU/25: 1.25X TO 3X BASIC
*BLUE WAVE FOTL JSY AU/20: 1.25X TO 3X BASIC
1 Karl-Anthony Towns .75 2.00
2 Jerami Grant .60 1.50
3 Devin Vassell .60 1.50
4 Klay Thompson 1.25 3.00
5 Ivica Zubac .50 1.25
6 Trae Young 1.00 2.50
7 Nikola Vucevic .50 1.25
8 Chris Paul 1.00 2.50
9 Malik Monk .60 1.50
10 Draymond Green .60 1.50
11 Anthony Davis 1.25 3.00
12 Shaedon Sharpe 1.00 2.50
13 Bradley Beal .60 1.50
14 Paul George .75 2.00
15 Michael Porter Jr. .60 1.50
16 OG Anunoby .60 1.50
17 Alperen Sengun .75 2.00
18 Dejounte Murray .60 1.50
19 Anfernee Simons .60 1.50
20 Tobias Harris .50 1.25
21 Jayson Tatum 2.00 5.00
22 Austin Reaves 1.25 3.00
23 Luka Doncic 3.00 8.00
24 Jaden Ivey .60 1.50
25 Lauri Markkanen .75 2.00
26 LeBron James 4.00 10.00
27 Jakob Poeltl .40 1.00
28 Keldon Johnson .60 1.50
29 Josh Giddey .60 1.50
30 Tyler Herro .75 2.00
31 Gary Trent Jr. .50 1.25
32 Ja Morant 1.50 4.00
33 Damian Lillard 1.25 3.00
34 Miles Bridges .50 1.25
35 Trey Murphy III .60 1.50
36 Fred VanVleet .75 2.00
37 Rudy Gobert .60 1.50
38 Jimmy Butler .75 2.00
39 Russell Westbrook .75 2.00
40 Brandon Ingram .60 1.50
41 Nikola Jokic 2.50 6.00
42 Jaren Jackson Jr. .75 2.00
43 Jalen Suggs .60 1.50
44 Derrick Rose .75 2.00
45 D'Angelo Russell .50 1.25
46 DeMar DeRozan .75 2.00
47 Jalen Johnson .60 1.50
48 Cameron Thomas .60 1.50
49 Khris Middleton .50 1.25
50 Domantas Sabonis .75 2.00
51 Deandre Ayton .50 1.25
52 Jonathan Kuminga 1.25 3.00
53 Alex Caruso .50 1.25
54 Mikal Bridges .60 1.50
55 Naz Reid .50 1.25
56 CJ McCollum .50 1.25
57 RJ Barrett .75 2.00
58 Rui Hachimura .50 1.25
59 Jordan Poole .75 2.00
60 Bogdan Bogdanovic .50 1.25
61 Collin Sexton .60 1.50
62 Donovan Mitchell 1.00 2.50
63 Coby White .50 1.25
64 Immanuel Quickley .50 1.25
65 Duncan Robinson .50 1.25
66 Tyrese Maxey 1.00 2.50
67 Scottie Barnes .60 1.50
68 Derrick White .60 1.50
69 Desmond Bane .60 1.50
70 Zion Williamson 1.25 3.00
71 Kevin Durant 1.50 4.00
72 Jaylen Brown 1.00 2.50
73 Marvin Bagley III .40 1.00
74 De'Aaron Fox 1.00 2.50
75 Saddiq Bey .50 1.25
76 Jarrett Allen .50 1.25
77 Jalen Green .75 2.00
78 Joel Embiid 1.25 3.00
79 Evan Mobley .75 2.00
80 Dillon Brooks .50 1.25
81 Stephen Curry 4.00 10.00
82 LaMelo Ball 1.25 3.00
83 Jabari Smith Jr. .75 2.00
84 Kelly Oubre Jr. .50 1.25
85 Jonas Valanciunas .40 1.00
86 Tim Hardaway Jr. .40 1.00
87 Tyrese Haliburton 1.00 2.50
88 Jrue Holiday .60 1.50
89 Kyle Kuzma .60 1.50
90 Cade Cunningham 1.25 3.00
91 Darius Garland .75 2.00
92 Kristaps Porzingis .60 1.50
93 Max Strus .50 1.25
94 Kyrie Irving 1.00 2.50
95 Pascal Siakam .75 2.00
96 Jeremy Sochan .60 1.50
97 Kawhi Leonard 1.25 3.00
98 Malik Beasley .50 1.25
99 Zach LaVine .75 2.00
100 Buddy Hield .50 1.25
101 Jalen Brunson 1.00 2.50
102 Andrew Wiggins .60 1.50
103 Paolo Banchero 1.25 3.00
104 Brook Lopez .40 1.00
105 Chet Holmgren 1.25 3.00
106 Bam Adebayo .75 2.00
107 Jalen Williams 1.00 2.50
108 Donte DiVincenzo .50 1.25
109 Jordan Clarkson .50 1.25
110 Julius Randle .60 1.50
111 Franz Wagner .75 2.00
112 Myles Turner .50 1.25
113 Shai Gilgeous-Alexander 2.50 6.00
114 Devin Booker 1.25 3.00
115 Aaron Gordon .50 1.25
116 John Collins .50 1.25
117 Keegan Murray .60 1.50
118 Jamal Murray 1.00 2.50
119 James Harden 1.00 2.50
120 Grayson Allen .50 1.25
121 Anthony Edwards 2.50 6.00
122 Terry Rozier III .60 1.50
123 Bennedict Mathurin .75 2.00
124 Cameron Johnson .50 1.25
125 Giannis Antetokounmpo 2.50 6.00
126 Kobe Brown RC .75 2.00
127 Hunter Tyson RC .75 2.00
128 Noah Clowney RC 1.00 2.50
129 Ben Sheppard RC .75 2.00
130 Olivier-Maxence Prosper RC .75 2.00
131 Vasilije Micic RC .75 2.00
132 Andre Jackson Jr. RC 1.25 3.00
133 Julian Phillips RC .75 2.00
134 Seth Lundy RC .60 1.50
135 Keyonte George RC 2.50 6.00
136 Leonard Miller RC .75 2.00
137 Victor Wembanyama RC 20.00 50.00
138 Cam Whitmore RC 2.00 5.00
139 Jalen Hood-Schifino RC .75 2.00
140 Rayan Rupert RC .75 2.00
141 Nick Smith Jr. RC 1.00 2.50
142 Scoot Henderson RC 2.50 6.00
143 Jordan Hawkins RC 1.25 3.00
144 Kris Murray RC .75 2.00
145 GG Jackson II RC 1.50 4.00
146 Brandin Podziemski RC 2.50 6.00
147 Anthony Black RC 1.50 4.00
148 Jalen Wilson RC .75 2.00
149 Dereck Lively II RC 1.50 4.00
150 Amen Thompson RC 4.00 10.00
151 Keyontae Johnson RC .75 2.00
152 Jett Howard RC 1.00 2.50
153 Gradey Dick RC 1.50 4.00
154 Lester Quinones RC .60 1.50
155 Marcus Sasser RC 1.25 3.00
156 Ausar Thompson RC 2.00 5.00
157 Emoni Bates RC 1.00 2.50
158 Julian Strawther RC 1.00 2.50
159 Jalen Pickett RC .60 1.50
160 Sasha Vezenkov RC .60 1.50
161 Brandon Miller RC 3.00 8.00
162 Chris Livingston RC .75 2.00
163 Colby Jones RC .75 2.00
164 Cason Wallace RC 1.50 4.00
165 Duop Reath RC .75 2.00
166 Brice Sensabaugh RC 1.25 3.00
167 Amari Bailey RC .75 2.00
168 Jarace Walker RC 1.50 4.00
169 Bilal Coulibaly RC 2.00 5.00
170 Jaime Jaquez Jr. RC 1.25 3.00
171 Kobe Bufkin RC 1.00 2.50
172 Dariq Whitehead RC 1.00 2.50
173 Toumani Camara RC 1.50 4.00
174 Taylor Hendricks RC .75 2.00
175 Trayce Jackson-Davis RC 1.00 2.50
176 Damian Lillard SD 1.25 3.00
177 Magic Johnson SD 2.00 5.00
178 Shaquille O'Neal SD 1.50 4.00
179 LeBron James SD 4.00 10.00
180 Yao Ming SD 1.25 3.00
181 Paolo Banchero SD 1.25 3.00
182 Keyonte George SD 2.50 6.00
183 Trae Young SD 1.00 2.50
184 Larry Bird SD 2.00 5.00
185 Amen Thompson SD 4.00 10.00
186 Jaime Jaquez Jr. SD 1.25 3.00
187 Scoot Henderson SD 2.50 6.00
188 Ja Morant SD 1.50 4.00
189 Stephen Curry SD 4.00 10.00
190 Luka Doncic SD 3.00 8.00
191 Kevin Durant SD 1.50 4.00
192 Jayson Tatum SD 2.00 5.00
193 Brandon Miller SD 3.00 8.00
194 Tim Duncan SD 1.25 3.00
195 Victor Wembanyama SD 20.00 50.00
196 Ausar Thompson SD 2.00 5.00
197 Anthony Edwards SD 2.50 6.00
198 Allen Iverson SD 1.25 3.00
199 Brandin Podziemski SD 2.50 6.00
200 Dirk Nowitzki SD 1.25 3.00
201 Keyonte George JSY AU/199 30.00 80.00
202 Bilal Coulibaly JSY AU/199 25.00 60.00
203 GG Jackson II JSY AU/199 20.00 50.00
205 Kris Murray JSY AU/199 10.00 25.00
206 Marcus Sasser JSY AU/199 15.00 40.00
207 Duop Reath JSY AU/199 10.00 25.00
208 Ricky Council IV JSY AU RC/199 12.00 30.00
209 Oscar Tshiebwe JSY AU RC/199 12.00 30.00
210 Mouhamed Gueye JSY AU RC/199 10.00 25.00
211 Colby Jones JSY AU/199 10.00 25.00
212 Olivier-Maxence Prosper JSY AU/199 10.00 25.00
213 Andre Jackson Jr. JSY AU/199 15.00 40.00
214 Jordan Walsh JSY AU RC/199 10.00 25.00
215 Amari Bailey JSY AU/199 10.00 25.00
217 Kobe Bufkin JSY AU/199 12.00 30.00
218 Noah Clowney JSY AU/199 12.00 30.00
219 Dariq Whitehead JSY AU/199 12.00 30.00
220 Brice Sensabaugh JSY AU/199 15.00 40.00
221 Julian Strawther JSY AU/99 12.00 30.00
222 Sasha Vezenkov JSY AU/199 8.00 20.00
224 Kobe Brown JSY AU/199 10.00 25.00
225 Amen Thompson JSY AU/199 50.00 120.00
226 Ausar Thompson JSY AU/199 25.00 60.00
227 Cason Wallace JSY AU/199 20.00 50.00
228 Maxwell Lewis JSY AU RC/199 8.00 20.00
229 Seth Lundy JSY AU/199 8.00 20.00
230 Leonard Miller JSY AU/199 10.00 25.00
231 Keyontae Johnson JSY AU/199 10.00 25.00
232 Lester Quinones JSY AU/199 8.00 20.00
233 Trayce Jackson-Davis JSY AU/199 12.00 30.00
234 Jalen Pickett JSY AU/199 8.00 20.00
237 Ben Sheppard JSY AU/199 10.00 25.00
238 Chris Livingston JSY AU/199 10.00 25.00
239 Sidy Cissoko JSY AU RC/199 10.00 25.00
240 Isaiah Wong JSY AU RC/199 10.00 25.00
241 Toumani Camara JSY AU/199 20.00 50.00
243 Dereck Lively II JSY AU/199 20.00 50.00
244 Brandin Podziemski JSY AU/199 30.00 80.00
245 Craig Porter Jr. JSY AU RC/199 12.00 30.00

2023-24 Panini Spectra Astral

*ASTRAL: 3X TO 8X BASIC
STATED PRINT RUN 49 SER.#'d SETS
137 Victor Wembanyama/49 300.00 600.00
195 Victor Wembanyama SD/49 300.00 600.00

2023-24 Panini Spectra Celestial

*CELESTIAL: 1.5X TO 4X BASIC
STATED PRINT RUN 125 SER.#'d SETS
137 Victor Wembanyama/125 125.00 300.00
195 Victor Wembanyama SD/125 125.00 300.00

2023-24 Panini Spectra International Blue and Orange

*INT BLUE & ORNG: 4X TO 10X BASIC
STATED PRINT RUN 25 SER.#'d SETS
137 Victor Wembanyama 400.00 800.00
195 Victor Wembanyama SD 400.00 800.00

2023-24 Panini Spectra International Green

*INT GREEN: 2.5X TO 6X BASIC
STATED PRINT RUN 75 SER.#'d SETS
137 Victor Wembanyama 200.00 500.00
195 Victor Wembanyama SD 200.00 500.00

2023-24 Panini Spectra International Red and Yellow

*INT RED & YELLOW: 3X TO 8X BASIC
STATED PRINT RUN 49 SER.#'d SETS
137 Victor Wembanyama 300.00 600.00
195 Victor Wembanyama SD 300.00 600.00

2023-24 Panini Spectra Interstellar

*INTERSTELLAR: 2X TO 5X BASIC
STATED PRINT RUN 99 SER.#'d SETS
137 Victor Wembanyama/99 150.00 400.00
195 Victor Wembanyama SD/99 150.00 400.00

2023-24 Panini Spectra Meta

*META: 4X TO 10X BASIC
STATED PRINT RUN 25 SER.#'d SETS
137 Victor Wembanyama 400.00 800.00
195 Victor Wembanyama SD 400.00 800.00

2023-24 Panini Spectra Psychedelic

*PSYCHEDELIC: 2X TO 5X BASIC
137 Victor Wembanyama 150.00 400.00
195 Victor Wembanyama SD 150.00 400.00

2023-24 Panini Spectra Aspiring Autographs

STATED PRINT RUN BTWN 65-99 SER.#'d SETS
*GREEN/50: .5X TO 1.2X BASIC
*PURPLE/34-35: .6X TO 1.5X BASIC
*PINK/25: .75X TO 2X BASIC
1 Ausar Thompson/65 15.00 40.00
2 Cason Wallace/75 12.00 30.00
3 Kobe Bufkin/75 8.00 20.00
4 Noah Clowney/99 8.00 20.00
5 Kris Murray/99 6.00 15.00
6 Ben Sheppard/99 6.00 15.00
7 Brice Sensabaugh/75 10.00 25.00
8 Dariq Whitehead/75 8.00 20.00
9 Julian Strawther/99 8.00 20.00
10 Amen Thompson/65 30.00 80.00
11 Kobe Brown/99 6.00 15.00
12 Jalen Pickett/99 5.00 12.00
13 Leonard Miller/75 6.00 15.00
14 Bilal Coulibaly/75 15.00 40.00
15 Colby Jones/99 6.00 15.00
17 Andre Jackson Jr./99 10.00 25.00
18 Hunter Tyson/99 6.00 15.00
19 Jordan Walsh/99 6.00 15.00
20 Maxwell Lewis/75 5.00 12.00
21 Seth Lundy/99 5.00 12.00
23 Dereck Lively II/75 12.00 30.00
25 Isaiah Wong/99 6.00 15.00
26 Chris Livingston/99 6.00 15.00
27 Tristan Vukcevic/99 6.00 15.00
28 Brandin Podziemski/65 30.00 80.00

2023-24 Panini Spectra Aspiring Patches

STATED PRINT RUN 149 SER.#'d SETS
*CELESTIAL/99: .5X TO 1.2X BASIC
*INTERSTELLAR/75: .6X TO 1.5X BASIC
*ASTRAL/49: .75X TO 2X BASIC
*META/25: 1X TO 2.5X BASIC
1 Jarace Walker 6.00 15.00
2 Victor Wembanyama 125.00 300.00
3 Toumani Camara 6.00 15.00
4 Marcus Sasser 5.00 12.00
5 Anthony Black 6.00 15.00
6 Dereck Lively II 6.00 15.00
7 Jalen Hood-Schifino 3.00 8.00
8 Cason Wallace 6.00 15.00
9 Ausar Thompson 8.00 20.00
10 Bilal Coulibaly 8.00 20.00
11 GG Jackson II 6.00 15.00
12 Jaime Jaquez Jr. 5.00 12.00
13 Cam Whitmore 8.00 20.00
14 Taylor Hendricks 3.00 8.00
15 Nick Smith Jr. 4.00 10.00
16 Jordan Hawkins 5.00 12.00
17 Jett Howard 4.00 10.00
18 Emoni Bates 4.00 10.00
19 Scoot Henderson 10.00 25.00
20 Brandin Podziemski 10.00 25.00
21 Gradey Dick 6.00 15.00
22 Amen Thompson 15.00 40.00
23 Trayce Jackson-Davis 4.00 10.00
24 Keyonte George 10.00 25.00
25 Brandon Miller 12.00 30.00

2023-24 Panini Spectra Brilliance Jerseys

STATED PRINT RUN 149 SER.#'d SETS
*CELESTIAL/99: .5X TO 1.2X BASIC
*INTERSTELLAR/75: .6X TO 1.5X BASIC
*ASTRAL/49: .75X TO 2X BASIC
*META/15-25: 1X TO 2.5X BASIC
1 Jayson Tatum 12.00 30.00
2 Donovan Mitchell 6.00 15.00
3 Kawhi Leonard 8.00 20.00
5 Jalen Green 5.00 12.00
6 Jamal Murray 6.00 15.00
7 Bam Adebayo 5.00 12.00
8 Zach LaVine 5.00 12.00
9 Damian Lillard 8.00 20.00
11 Stephen Curry 40.00 100.00
13 LeBron James 40.00 100.00
15 Giannis Antetokounmpo 15.00 40.00
16 Trae Young 6.00 15.00
17 De'Aaron Fox 6.00 15.00
18 Devin Booker 8.00 20.00
19 DeMar DeRozan 5.00 12.00
20 Darius Garland 5.00 12.00
21 Julius Randle 4.00 10.00
22 Paul George 5.00 12.00
23 Zion Williamson 8.00 20.00
25 Jalen Brunson 6.00 15.00

2023-24 Panini Spectra Catalysts Signatures

STATED PRINT RUN BTWN 49-99 SER.#'d SETS
*INTERSTELLAR/49: .5X TO 1.2X p/r 99
*INTERSTELLAR/35: .5X TO 1.2X p/r 49
*ASTRAL/49: .6X TO 1.5X p/r 99
*ASTRAL/35: .5X TO 1.2X p/r 49
*META/25: .75X TO 2X p/r 99
*META/25: .6X TO 1.5X p/r 49
1 Jaden Hardy/49 10.00 25.00
2 Franz Wagner/49 12.00 30.00
3 Dyson Daniels/99 8.00 20.00
4 Vince Williams Jr./99 6.00 15.00
5 Josh Giddey/49 10.00 25.00
6 Brook Lopez/99 5.00 12.00
7 Yuta Watanabe/99 6.00 15.00
8 De'Anthony Melton/99 6.00 15.00
9 Khris Middleton/49 8.00 20.00
11 Danilo Gallinari/99 5.00 12.00
12 B.J. Armstrong/99 6.00 15.00
13 Corey Kispert/99 5.00 12.00
14 Adrian Dantley/99 6.00 15.00
15 Charles Oakley/99 6.00 15.00
16 Gary Harris/99 5.00 12.00
17 Boban Marjanovic/99 6.00 15.00
18 Walker Kessler/99 6.00 15.00
19 Tony Parker/49 12.00 30.00
20 Kristaps Porzingis/49 15.00 40.00
21 Gail Goodrich/99 6.00 15.00
22 Bogdan Bogdanovic/99 6.00 15.00
23 Davion Mitchell/99 5.00 12.00
24 Nate Archibald/99 8.00 20.00
25 Lenny Wilkens/99 8.00 20.00
26 Ousmane Dieng/99 6.00 15.00
27 Dale Ellis/99 6.00 15.00
28 Detlef Schrempf/99 5.00 12.00
29 Yuta Tabuse/99 6.00 15.00
30 Michael Cooper/99 6.00 15.00
31 Max Strus/99 6.00 15.00
32 Daniel Gafford/99 6.00 15.00
33 Nicolas Batum/99 4.00 10.00
34 Bill Laimbeer/99 6.00 15.00
35 Gabe Vincent/99 6.00 15.00

2023-24 Panini Spectra Color Blast

1 Keyonte George 800.00 1,500.00
2 Kevin Durant 400.00 800.00
3 Tim Duncan 800.00 1,500.00
4 Dereck Lively II 1,000.00 2,000.00
5 Shai Gilgeous-Alexander 1,250.00 2,500.00
6 Tyrese Haliburton 400.00 800.00
7 Anthony Black 500.00 1,000.00
8 Ausar Thompson 500.00 1,000.00
9 Cason Wallace 500.00 1,000.00
10 Stephen Curry 2,500.00 5,000.00
11 Bilal Coulibaly 500.00 1,000.00
12 Nikola Jokic 800.00 1,500.00
13 Brandin Podziemski 1,000.00 2,000.00
14 Amen Thompson 1,000.00 2,000.00
15 Giannis Antetokounmpo 1,000.00 2,000.00
16 Ja Morant 800.00 1,500.00
17 Brandon Miller 1,500.00 3,000.00
18 Jayson Tatum 800.00 1,500.00
19 LeBron James 2,500.00 5,000.00
20 Victor Wembanyama 8,000.00 12,000.00
21 Scoot Henderson 1,000.00 2,000.00
22 Anthony Edwards 1,500.00 3,000.00
23 Jordan Hawkins 350.00 700.00
24 Jaime Jaquez Jr. 600.00 1,200.00
25 Luka Doncic 1,500.00 3,000.00

2023-24 Panini Spectra Colorgraphs

STATED PRINT RUN BTWN 49-99 SER.#'d SETS
*ASTRAL/35: .6X TO 1.5X p/r 75-99
*ASTRAL/35: .5X TO 1.2X p/r 49
*META/25: .75X TO 2X p/r 99
*META/25: .6X TO 1.5X p/r 49
1 Chet Holmgren/75 50.00 120.00
2 Anthony Davis/49 50.00 120.00
3 Donovan Mitchell/49 40.00 100.00
4 Anthony Edwards/49 150.00 400.00
5 Zach LaVine/75 10.00 25.00
6 De'Aaron Fox/75 25.00 60.00
7 Larry Bird/49 75.00 200.00
8 Julius Randle/49 10.00 25.00
9 Tyrese Maxey/75 30.00 80.00
10 Desmond Bane/99 8.00 20.00
11 Shai Gilgeous-Alexander/49 200.00 500.00
12 Carmelo Anthony/49 60.00 150.00
13 Alperen Sengun/99 10.00 25.00
14 Chris Paul/49 40.00 100.00
15 Stephen Curry/49 300.00 600.00
16 Ja Morant/49 125.00 300.00
17 Julius Erving/49 60.00 150.00
18 Paolo Banchero /49 60.00 150.00
19 David Robinson/49 40.00 100.00
20 Klay Thompson/49 100.00 250.00
21 Trae Young/49 40.00 100.00
22 Fred VanVleet/75 10.00 25.00
23 Russell Westbrook/75 40.00 100.00
24 Damian Lillard/49 40.00 100.00
25 Cade Cunningham/75 40.00 100.00

2023-24 Panini Spectra Deep Space Signatures

STATED PRINT RUN BTWN 35-99 SER.#'d SETS
*INTERSTELLAR/49-75: .5X TO 1.2X p/r 75-99
*ASTRAL/35-49: .6X TO 1.5X p/r 75-99
*ASTRAL/49: .4X TO 1X p/r 49
*META/25: .75X TO 2X p/r 75-99
*META/25: .5X TO 1.2X p/r 35
1 Jalen Green/75 10.00 25.00
2 Jeremy Sochan/99 8.00 20.00
4 Raymond Felton/99 4.00 10.00
5 Caris LeVert/99 6.00 15.00
7 Ben Wallace/99 8.00 20.00
9 Arvydas Sabonis/99 8.00 20.00
11 Dave Bing/99 8.00 20.00
12 Ayo Dosunmu/99 6.00 15.00
13 Glen Rice/99 6.00 15.00
14 Charlie Scott/99 6.00 15.00
15 Luol Deng /49 8.00 20.00
16 Mike Bibby/99 6.00 15.00
17 Dell Curry/99 6.00 15.00
18 Matt Barnes/99 4.00 10.00
19 Bruce Bowen/99 5.00 12.00
20 Dominique Wilkins/75 10.00 25.00
21 Collin Sexton/75 8.00 20.00
22 Isaac Okoro/99 5.00 12.00
23 Bob McAdoo/99 8.00 20.00
25 Evan Mobley/75 10.00 25.00
26 Nikola Jokic/35 125.00 300.00

27 Magic Johnson/35 60.00 150.00
28 John Wall/99 8.00 20.00
29 GG Jackson II/75 12.00 30.00
30 Duop Reath/99 6.00 15.00
31 Toumani Camara/99 12.00 30.00
32 Trayce Jackson-Davis/99 8.00 20.00
33 Wally Szczerbiak/99 5.00 12.00
34 Landry Shamet/99 4.00 10.00

2023-24 Panini Spectra Full Capacity

1 Brandon Miller 100.00 250.00
2 Ja Morant 30.00 80.00
3 Ausar Thompson 25.00 60.00
4 Bilal Coulibaly 25.00 60.00
5 Stephen Curry 80.00 200.00
6 Chet Holmgren 25.00 60.00
7 Victor Wembanyama 350.00 700.00
8 Tyrese Haliburton 20.00 50.00
9 Shai Gilgeous-Alexander 50.00 120.00
10 Giannis Antetokounmpo 50.00 125.00
11 Zion Williamson 25.00 60.00
12 Jordan Hawkins 15.00 40.00
13 Scoot Henderson 30.00 80.00
14 Keyonte George 30.00 80.00
15 Nikola Jokic 50.00 125.00
16 Donovan Mitchell 20.00 50.00
17 Paolo Banchero 25.00 60.00
18 Gradey Dick 20.00 50.00
19 Jayson Tatum 40.00 100.00
20 Kevin Durant 30.00 80.00
21 Luka Doncic 60.00 150.00
22 Jaime Jaquez Jr. 15.00 40.00
23 Anthony Edwards 75.00 200.00
24 Amen Thompson 50.00 120.00
25 LeBron James 125.00 300.00

2023-24 Panini Spectra Icons Autographs

STATED PRINT RUN BTWN 35-99 SER.#'d SETS
*INTERSTELLAR/75: .5X TO 1.2X p/r 99
*ASTRAL/49: .6X TO 1.5X p/r 99
*ASTRAL/35-49: .5X TO 1.2X p/r 75
*META/25: .75X TO 2X p/r 99
*META/25: .6X TO 1.5X p/r 75
*META/25: .5X TO 1.2X p/r 35-49
1 Kareem Abdul-Jabbar/35 75.00 200.00
2 Jack Sikma/99 6.00 15.00
3 Jerry West/49 30.00 80.00
4 James Worthy/75 12.00 30.00
5 Rick Fox/99 6.00 15.00
6 Dave Cowens/75 10.00 25.00
7 Jerry Stackhouse/99 6.00 15.00
8 Ralph Sampson/99 6.00 15.00
9 Rik Smits/99 5.00 12.00
10 Luis Scola/99 5.00 12.00
11 Spud Webb/99 6.00 15.00
12 Antoine Walker/99 6.00 15.00
14 Vlade Divac/99 6.00 15.00
15 Doug Collins/99 6.00 15.00
16 Maurice Cheeks/99 6.00 15.00
17 Metta World Peace/75 8.00 20.00
18 Jason Terry/99 6.00 15.00
19 Steve Francis/99 6.00 15.00
20 Carlos Boozer/99 5.00 12.00
22 Jermaine O'Neal/99 6.00 15.00
23 Patrick Ewing/49 60.00 150.00
24 Jamal Crawford/75 8.00 20.00
25 David Thompson/99 8.00 20.00
26 Elvin Hayes/99 8.00 20.00
27 Sam Cassell/99 5.00 12.00
28 Chauncey Billups/99 8.00 20.00
29 World B. Free/99 5.00 12.00
30 Allan Houston/99 6.00 15.00

2023-24 Panini Spectra Illustrious Legends Signatures

STATED PRINT RUN BTWN 35-99 SER.#'d SETS
*ASTRAL/35-49: .6X TO 1.5X p/r 99
*ASTRAL/35-49: .5X TO 1.2X p/r 75
*META/25: .75X TO 2X p/r 99
*META/25: .6X TO 1.5X p/r 75
*META/25: .5X TO 1.2X p/r 35-49
1 Ray Allen/49 30.00 80.00
2 Tracy McGrady/35 40.00 100.00
3 Alonzo Mourning/49 25.00 60.00
4 Jason Kidd/49 15.00 40.00
5 Dominique Wilkins/75 12.00 30.00
6 Kevin McHale/75 12.00 30.00
8 Chris Mullin/99 8.00 20.00
9 Shawn Kemp/99 10.00 25.00
10 Gilbert Arenas/75 8.00 20.00
11 Gary Payton/75 12.00 30.00
12 Chris Bosh/49 12.00 30.00
13 Bernard King/75 10.00 25.00
14 Anfernee Hardaway/75 40.00 100.00
16 John Stockton/49 30.00 80.00
17 Rick Barry/75 10.00 25.00
18 Paul Pierce/49 15.00 40.00
19 Isiah Thomas/75 12.00 30.00
20 Shaquille O'Neal /35 75.00 200.00
21 Magic Johnson/35 40.00 100.00
22 Grant Hill/75 20.00 50.00
23 Tim Hardaway/99 8.00 20.00
24 Dirk Nowitzki/49 75.00 200.00
25 Steve Nash/35 20.00 50.00

2023-24 Panini Spectra Max Impact Jerseys

STATED PRINT RUN 149 SER.#'d SETS
*CELESTIAL/99: .5X TO 1.2X BASIC
*INTERSTELLAR/75: .6X TO 1.5X BASIC
*ASTRAL/49: .75X TO 2X BASIC
*META/25: 1X TO 2.5X BASIC
1 Anthony Black 6.00 15.00
3 Brandon Miller 12.00 30.00
4 Ausar Thompson 8.00 20.00
6 LeBron James 40.00 100.00
7 Cason Wallace 6.00 15.00
8 Jordan Hawkins 5.00 12.00
9 Victor Wembanyama 125.00 300.00
10 Marcus Sasser 5.00 12.00
11 James Harden 6.00 15.00
12 Joel Embiid 8.00 20.00
13 Russell Westbrook 5.00 12.00
14 Jaylen Brown 6.00 15.00
15 Amen Thompson 15.00 40.00
16 Dereck Lively II 6.00 15.00
17 Jaime Jaquez Jr. 6.00 15.00
19 Tyrese Maxey 6.00 15.00
20 Gradey Dick 6.00 15.00
21 Jimmy Butler 5.00 12.00
22 Scoot Henderson 10.00 25.00
23 Bilal Coulibaly 8.00 20.00
24 Brandin Podziemski 10.00 25.00
25 Keyonte George 10.00 25.00

2023-24 Panini Spectra Next Era Jerseys

STATED PRINT RUN 149 SER.#'d SETS
*CELESTIAL/99: .5X TO 1.2X BASIC
*INTERSTELLAR/75: .6X TO 1.5X BASIC
*ASTRAL/49: .75X TO 2X BASIC
*META/25: 1X TO 2.5X BASIC
1 Nick Smith Jr. 4.00 10.00
2 Julian Strawther 4.00 10.00
3 Taylor Hendricks 3.00 8.00
4 Amen Thompson 15.00 40.00
5 Jordan Hawkins 5.00 12.00
6 Marcus Sasser 5.00 12.00
7 Keyonte George 10.00 25.00
8 Gradey Dick 6.00 15.00
9 Cam Whitmore 8.00 20.00
10 Ausar Thompson 8.00 20.00
11 Anthony Black 6.00 15.00
12 Bilal Coulibaly 8.00 20.00
13 Dereck Lively II 6.00 15.00
14 Jett Howard 4.00 10.00
15 GG Jackson II 6.00 15.00
16 Jalen Hood-Schifino 3.00 8.00
17 Victor Wembanyama 125.00 300.00
18 Scoot Henderson 10.00 25.00
19 Kobe Bufkin 4.00 10.00
20 Trayce Jackson-Davis 4.00 10.00
21 Cason Wallace 6.00 15.00
22 Jarace Walker 6.00 15.00
23 Brandin Podziemski 10.00 25.00
24 Brandon Miller 12.00 30.00
25 Jaime Jaquez Jr. 5.00 12.00

2023-24 Panini Spectra Radiant Signatures

STATED PRINT RUN BTWN 49-99 SER.#'d SETS
*INTERSTELLAR/75: .5X TO 1.2X p/r 99
*ASTRAL/49: .6X TO 1.5X p/r 99
*ASTRAL/35-49: .5X TO 1.2X p/r 49-75
*META/25: .75X TO 2X p/r 99
*META/25: .6X TO 1.5X p/r 75
*META/25: .5X TO 1.2X p/r 49
1 Keegan Murray/75 10.00 25.00
2 Moses Moody/99 8.00 20.00
3 Jalen Duren/75 10.00 25.00
4 Jeremy Lin/75 75.00 200.00
5 Norman Powell/99 6.00 15.00
6 Danny Granger/99 5.00 12.00
8 Mahmoud Abdul-Rauf/99 5.00 12.00
9 Caleb Martin/99 5.00 12.00
10 Manu Ginobili/49 30.00 80.00
11 RJ Barrett/75 12.00 30.00
12 Domantas Sabonis/75 12.00 30.00
14 Ivica Zubac/99 6.00 15.00
15 Luke Kennard/99 5.00 12.00
16 Mark Williams/99 6.00 15.00
17 Andrea Bargnani/99 6.00 15.00
18 Rolando Blackman/99 5.00 12.00
19 Doc Rivers/75 8.00 20.00
20 Derrick Coleman/99 6.00 15.00
22 A.C. Green/99 5.00 12.00
23 Alvan Adams/99 5.00 12.00
24 Malik Beasley/99 6.00 15.00
25 Nikola Jovic/99 6.00 15.00
26 Kirk Hinrich /99 5.00 12.00
27 Malaki Branham/99 5.00 12.00
28 Royce O'Neale/99 5.00 12.00
29 Vin Baker/99 5.00 12.00
30 Pau Gasol/49 15.00 40.00
31 Jerry West/49 30.00 80.00
32 Jaren Jackson Jr./75 12.00 30.00
34 Muggsy Bogues/99 10.00 25.00
35 Scottie Barnes/75 10.00 25.00

2023-24 Panini Spectra RetroSpect Autographs

STATED PRINT RUN BTWN 35-99 SER.#'d SETS
*INTERSTELLAR/49-75: .5X TO 1.2X p/r 75-99
*ASTRAL/49: .6X TO 1.5X p/r 99
*ASTRAL/35-49: .5X TO 1.2X p/r 49-75
*META/25: .75X TO 2X p/r 99
*META/25: .6X TO 1.5X p/r 75
*META/25: .5X TO 1.2X p/r 35-49
1 Charles Barkley/35 75.00 200.00
2 Ben Simmons/49 10.00 25.00
4 Alex Caruso/99 6.00 15.00
5 Jarrett Allen/99 6.00 15.00
6 Kenyon Martin/99 5.00 12.00
7 Donte DiVincenzo/99 6.00 15.00
8 Mark Aguirre/99 5.00 12.00
9 Jeff Hornacek/99 5.00 12.00
10 Lauri Markkanen/75 12.00 30.00
12 Deandre Ayton/75 8.00 20.00
13 Amar'e Stoudemire/75 10.00 25.00
14 Clint Capela/99 5.00 12.00
16 Tony Allen/99 6.00 15.00
17 Dejounte Murray/75 10.00 25.00
18 Andrew Wiggins/75 10.00 25.00
19 Jonas Valanciunas/99 5.00 12.00
21 Latrell Sprewell/99 8.00 20.00
22 Nickeil Alexander-Walker/99 4.00 10.00
23 Elton Brand/99 5.00 12.00
25 CJ McCollum/49 10.00 25.00
26 Rasheed Wallace/49 12.00 30.00
27 Al Horford/99 6.00 15.00
28 Peja Stojakovic/99 6.00 15.00
29 Steven Adams/99 6.00 15.00
30 Victor Oladipo/99 5.00 12.00

2023-24 Panini Spectra Rookie Dual Patch Autographs

STATED PRINT RUN BTWN 25-49 SER.#'d SETS
*ASTRAL/35: .5X TO 1.2X p/r 49
*META/25: .6X TO 1.5X p/r 49
*META/15: .5X TO 1.2X p/r 25
2 Brandin Podziemski
Trayce Jackson-Davis/49 100.00 250.00
3 Bilal Coulibaly
Cason Wallace/49 75.00 200.00
4 Keyonte George
Brice Sensabaugh/49 75.00 200.00
5 Amen Thompson
Ausar Thompson/25 150.00 400.00

2023-24 Panini Spectra Sky High Signatures

STATED PRINT RUN BTWN 49-99 SER.#'d SETS
*INTERSTELLAR/49-75: .5X TO 1.2X p/r 75-99
*ASTRAL/49: .6X TO 1.5X p/r 99
*ASTRAL/49: .5X TO 1.2X p/r 75
*META/25: .75X TO 2X p/r 99
*META/25: .6X TO 1.5X p/r 75
1 John Wall/75 10.00 25.00
2 Shaedon Sharpe/75 15.00 40.00
3 Jalen Johnson/99 8.00 20.00
4 Quentin Grimes/99 6.00 15.00
5 Precious Achiuwa/99 5.00 12.00
6 Cameron Thomas/99 8.00 20.00
7 Austin Reaves/99 15.00 40.00
10 Anfernee Simons/75 10.00 25.00
11 Tari Eason/99 8.00 20.00
12 Devin Harris/99 4.00 10.00
13 Terance Mann/99 5.00 12.00
14 Kenny "Sky" Walker/99 5.00 12.00
15 Oscar Tshiebwe/99 8.00 20.00
16 Ricky Council IV/99 8.00 20.00
17 Olivier-Maxence Prosper/99 6.00 15.00
18 Mouhamed Gueye/99 6.00 15.00
19 Kobe Brown/99 6.00 15.00
21 Marcus Sasser/99 10.00 25.00
22 Marcus Camby/75 6.00 15.00
23 Hakeem Olajuwon/75 15.00 40.00
24 Terquavion Smith/99 6.00 15.00
25 Xavier Tillman/99 6.00 15.00
26 Roy Hibbert/99 5.00 12.00
27 Isaiah Rider/99 6.00 15.00
28 MarJon Beauchamp/99 5.00 12.00
29 Jericho Sims/99 4.00 10.00
30 Dee Brown/99 5.00 12.00
31 Day'Ron Sharpe/99 5.00 12.00
32 Moritz Wagner/99 6.00 15.00
33 Craig Porter Jr. /99 8.00 20.00
35 Dante Exum/99 5.00 12.00

2023-24 Panini Spectra Titan

1 Karl-Anthony Towns 1.25 3.00
2 Taylor Hendricks .75 2.00
3 Jalen Hood-Schifino .75 2.00
4 Bradley Beal 1.00 2.50
5 Scottie Barnes 1.00 2.50
6 Magic Johnson 3.00 8.00
7 Cameron Thomas 1.00 2.50
8 Victor Wembanyama 40.00 100.00
9 Jaylen Brown 1.50 4.00
10 Franz Wagner 1.25 3.00
11 Ausar Thompson 2.00 5.00
12 Trae Young 1.50 4.00
13 Russell Westbrook 1.25 3.00
14 Tracy McGrady 1.50 4.00
15 Darius Garland 1.25 3.00
16 Cade Cunningham 2.00 5.00
17 Allen Iverson 2.00 5.00
18 Trayce Jackson-Davis 1.00 2.50
19 Tyrese Maxey 1.50 4.00
20 Anthony Davis 2.00 5.00
21 Damian Lillard 2.00 5.00
22 Jamal Murray 1.50 4.00
23 Larry Bird 3.00 8.00
24 Bilal Coulibaly 2.00 5.00
25 Dejounte Murray 1.00 2.50
26 Devin Booker 2.00 5.00
27 Anthony Edwards 4.00 10.00
28 Joel Embiid 2.00 5.00
29 RJ Barrett 1.25 3.00
30 Cam Whitmore 2.00 5.00
31 Austin Reaves 2.00 5.00
32 Pascal Siakam 1.25 3.00
33 De'Aaron Fox 1.50 4.00
34 Paul George 1.25 3.00
35 Alperen Sengun 1.25 3.00
36 James Harden 1.50 4.00
37 Jaime Jaquez Jr. 1.50 4.00
38 Carmelo Anthony 1.25 3.00
39 Jalen Williams 1.50 4.00
40 Jordan Hawkins 1.25 3.00
41 Klay Thompson 2.00 5.00
42 GG Jackson II 1.25 3.00
43 Shaedon Sharpe 1.50 4.00
44 Jalen Brunson 1.50 4.00
45 Shaquille O'Neal 2.50 6.00
46 Keyonte George 2.50 6.00
47 Donovan Mitchell 1.50 4.00
48 Brandin Podziemski 2.50 6.00
49 Marcus Sasser 1.25 3.00
50 Jimmy Butler 1.25 3.00
51 Dereck Lively II 1.50 4.00
52 Cason Wallace 1.50 4.00
53 Shai Gilgeous-Alexander 4.00 10.00
54 Kristaps Porzingis 1.50 4.00
55 Paolo Banchero 2.00 5.00
56 Bam Adebayo 1.25 3.00
57 Jaren Jackson Jr. 1.25 3.00
58 Luka Doncic 5.00 12.00
59 Julius Randle 1.00 2.50
60 Dirk Nowitzki 2.00 5.00
61 Jalen Green 1.25 3.00
62 Brandon Ingram 1.00 2.50
63 Zach LaVine 1.25 3.00
64 Kobe Bufkin 1.00 2.50
65 Nikola Jokic 4.00 10.00
66 Tyler Herro 1.25 3.00
67 Chris Paul 1.50 4.00
68 Kareem Abdul-Jabbar 2.50 6.00
69 LeBron James 6.00 15.00
70 Julian Strawther 1.00 2.50
71 Yao Ming 2.00 5.00
72 Nick Smith Jr. 1.00 2.50
73 Kyrie Irving 1.50 4.00
74 LaMelo Ball 2.00 5.00
75 Anfernee Simons 1.00 2.50
76 Lauri Markkanen 1.25 3.00
77 Brandon Miller 3.00 8.00
78 Devin Vassell 1.00 2.50
79 Tyrese Haliburton 1.50 4.00
80 Vasilije Micic 1.00 2.50
81 Chet Holmgren 2.00 5.00
82 Jayson Tatum 3.00 8.00
83 Gradey Dick 1.50 4.00
84 Ja Morant 2.50 6.00
85 Anthony Black 1.50 4.00
86 Tim Duncan 2.00 5.00
87 DeMar DeRozan 1.25 3.00
88 Mikal Bridges 1.00 2.50
89 Zion Williamson 2.00 5.00
90 Stephen Curry 6.00 15.00
91 Kawhi Leonard 2.00 5.00
92 Domantas Sabonis 1.25 3.00
93 Amen Thompson 4.00 10.00
94 Keldon Johnson 1.00 2.50
95 Jarace Walker 1.50 4.00
96 Jett Howard 1.00 2.50
97 Toumani Camara 1.50 4.00
98 Scoot Henderson 2.50 6.00
99 Giannis Antetokounmpo 4.00 10.00
100 Kevin Durant 2.50 6.00

2023-24 Panini Spectra Wavelength Autographs

STATED PRINT RUN BTWN 25-49 SER.#'d SETS
*ASTRAL/15-35: .5X TO 1.2X BASIC
1 Scottie Barnes/49 12.00 30.00
2 Giannis Antetokounmpo/25 300.00 600.00
3 Paolo Banchero /25 75.00 200.00
4 Chet Holmgren/25 60.00 150.00
5 Dwyane Wade/35 40.00 100.00
6 Dennis Rodman/49 40.00 100.00
7 Brandon Ingram/49 12.00 30.00
8 Jalen Brunson/49 75.00 200.00
9 Cade Cunningham/25 50.00 120.00
10 Cason Wallace/49 20.00 50.00
11 Amen Thompson/25 50.00 120.00
12 Ausar Thompson/25 25.00 60.00
13 Brandin Podziemski/35 30.00 80.00
14 Keyonte George/25 30.00 80.00

2017-18 Panini Status

COMPLETE SET (150) 25.00 60.00
1 JJ Redick .40 1.00
2 Jimmy Butler .60 1.50
3 Bojan Bogdanovic .30 .75
4 Dirk Nowitzki 1.00 2.50
5 Avery Bradley .25 .60
6 Dwight Howard .50 1.25
7 Ricky Rubio .30 .75
8 John Wall .50 1.25
9 Marcus Morris .25 .60
10 Kemba Walker .30 .75
11 Dennis Schroder .30 .75
12 Damian Lillard 1.00 2.50
13 T.J. Warren .30 .75
14 Ben Simmons .40 1.00
15 Jusuf Nurkic .30 .75
16 Rodney Hood .25 .60
17 Jeff Teague .25 .60
18 Jrue Holiday .50 1.25
19 DeMar DeRozan .50 1.25
20 Harrison Barnes .30 .75
21 Kevin Love .40 1.00
22 Marcin Gortat .25 .60
23 Marc Gasol .40 1.00
24 Andre Drummond .30 .75
25 C.J. McCollum .40 1.00
26 George Hill .30 .75
27 Eric Bledsoe .30 .75
28 LeBron James 3.00 8.00
29 Karl-Anthony Towns .60 1.50
30 Paul George .60 1.50
31 Zach LaVine .60 1.50
32 Wesley Matthews .25 .60
33 Mike Conley .30 .75
34 Tim Hardaway Jr. .30 .75
35 Isaiah Thomas .30 .75
36 Derrick Rose .60 1.50
37 Al Horford .40 1.00
38 DeAndre Jordan .30 .75
39 Brook Lopez .30 .75
40 Anthony Davis 1.00 2.50
41 DeMarre Carroll .25 .60
42 Devin Booker 1.00 2.50
43 Serge Ibaka .30 .75
44 Vince Carter .75 2.00
45 Gary Harris .30 .75
46 D'Angelo Russell .30 .75
47 Brandon Ingram .50 1.25
48 Aaron Gordon .40 1.00
49 Kevin Durant 1.50 4.00
50 Giannis Antetokounmpo 2.00 5.00
51 Kawhi Leonard 1.00 2.50
52 Klay Thompson 1.00 2.50
53 Chris Paul .60 1.50
54 Rajon Rondo .50 1.25
55 Nikola Vucevic .30 .75
56 Victor Oladipo .30 .75
57 Willie Cauley-Stein .25 .60
58 Jabari Parker .25 .60
59 Steven Adams .30 .75
60 Gordon Hayward .30 .75
61 Dion Waiters .25 .60
62 Kyle Lowry .40 1.00
63 Tony Parker .60 1.50
64 Jordan Clarkson .40 1.00
65 Blake Griffin .40 1.00
66 Andrew Wiggins .50 1.25
67 Chandler Parsons .25 .60
68 Taurean Prince .25 .60
69 Nikola Jokic 2.50 6.00
70 Myles Turner .40 1.00
71 Elfrid Payton .25 .60
72 Draymond Green .50 1.25
73 Ryan Anderson .25 .60
74 Bradley Beal .50 1.25
75 Goran Dragic .30 .75
76 Kris Dunn .25 .60
77 Kristaps Porzingis .50 1.25
78 Hassan Whiteside .30 .75
79 Joel Embiid .75 2.00
80 James Harden .75 2.00
81 Seth Curry .40 1.00
82 Rudy Gobert .50 1.25
83 Stephen Curry 3.00 8.00
84 Danilo Gallinari .30 .75
85 Zach Randolph .40 1.00
86 Jeremy Lin .60 1.50
87 Russell Westbrook .60 1.50
88 Carmelo Anthony .60 1.50
89 Dario Saric .30 .75
90 Nicolas Batum .25 .60
91 LaMarcus Aldridge .40 1.00
92 Julius Randle .40 1.00
93 Dwyane Wade .75 2.00
94 Reggie Jackson .30 .75
95 Paul Millsap .30 .75
96 DeMarcus Cousins .30 .75
97 Malcolm Brogdon .30 .75
98 Kent Bazemore .25 .60
99 Kyrie Irving .75 2.00
100 Pau Gasol .60 1.50
101 Semi Ojeleye RC .50 1.25
102 Malik Monk RC 1.50 4.00
103 Tyler Dorsey RC .40 1.00
104 Justin Patton RC .40 1.00
105 Thomas Bryant RC .60 1.50
106 Terrance Ferguson RC .40 1.00
107 Kyle Kuzma RC 1.50 4.00
108 Markelle Fultz RC 1.00 2.50
109 Davon Reed RC .40 1.00
110 Jonathan Isaac RC 1.00 2.50
111 Ante Zizic RC .50 1.25
112 Luke Kennard RC .75 2.00
113 Damyean Dotson RC .50 1.25
114 D.J. Wilson RC .40 1.00
115 Bogdan Bogdanovic RC 1.00 2.50
116 Jarrett Allen RC 1.00 2.50
117 Tony Bradley RC .40 1.00
118 Lonzo Ball RC 1.50 4.00
119 Wesley Iwundu RC .40 1.00
120 Lauri Markkanen RC 2.50 6.00
121 Jordan Bell RC .40 1.00
122 Donovan Mitchell RC 4.00 10.00
123 Sterling Brown RC .40 1.00
124 T.J. Leaf RC .40 1.00
125 Guerschon Yabusele RC .40 1.00
126 OG Anunoby RC 2.00 5.00
127 Derrick White RC 1.50 4.00
128 Jayson Tatum RC 10.00 25.00
129 Frank Mason III RC .40 1.00
130 Frank Ntilikina RC .50 1.25
131 Jawun Evans RC .40 1.00
132 Bam Adebayo RC 2.50 6.00
133 Ike Anigbogu RC .40 1.00
134 John Collins RC 1.00 2.50
135 Wayne Selden Jr. RC .40 1.00
136 Tyler Lydon RC .40 1.00
137 Josh Hart RC 1.00 2.50
138 Josh Jackson RC .50 1.25
139 Ivan Rabb RC .40 1.00
140 Dennis Smith Jr. RC .50 1.25
141 Dwayne Bacon RC .40 1.00
142 Justin Jackson RC .40 1.00
143 Sindarius Thornwell RC .40 1.00
144 Harry Giles RC .40 1.00
145 Milos Teodosic RC .50 1.25
146 Caleb Swanigan RC .40 1.00
147 Frank Jackson RC .40 1.00
148 De'Aaron Fox RC 3.00 8.00
149 Mike James RC .40 1.00
150 Zach Collins RC .60 1.50

2017-18 Panini Status Aqua

*AQUA: .75X TO 2X BASIC
*AQUA RC: .5X TO 1.2X BASIC RC

2017-18 Panini Status Aspirations

COMPLETE SET (150)
*ASP: 2.5X TO 6X BASIC
PRINT RUNS B/WN 45-99 COPIES PER
28 LeBron James/77 40.00 100.00
83 Stephen Curry/70 40.00 100.00
122 Donovan Mitchell/55 30.00 80.00
128 Jayson Tatum/99 75.00 200.00

2017-18 Panini Status Blue

*BLUE: 1.5X TO 4X BASIC
*BLUE RC: .75X TO 2X BASIC RC
STATED PRINT RUN 199 SER.#'d SETS

2017-18 Panini Status Green

*GREEN: 2X TO 5X BASIC
*GREEN RC: 1X TO 2.5X BASIC RC
STATED PRINT RUN 75 SER.#'d SETS
122 Donovan Mitchell 20.00 50.00
128 Jayson Tatum 12.00 30.00

2017-18 Panini Status Orange

*ORANGE: 1X TO 2.5X BASIC
*ORANGE RC: .5X TO 1.2X BASIC RC

2017-18 Panini Status Purple

*PURPLE: 1.5X TO 4X BASIC
*PURPLE RC: .75X TO 2X BASIC RC
STATED PRINT RUN 149 SER.#'d SETS

2017-18 Panini Status Red

*RED: 1.2X TO 3X BASIC
*RED RC: .6X TO 1.5X BASIC RC
STATED PRINT RUN 299 SER.#'d SETS

2017-18 Panini Status Status

*STAT p/r 55: 1X TO 2.5X BASIC RC
*STAT p/r 30-50: 2.5X TO 6X BASIC
*STAT p/r 30-50: 1.2X TO 3X BASIC RC
*STAT p/r 20-27: 3X TO 8X BASIC
*STAT p/r 20-27: 1.5X TO 4X BASIC RC
PRINT RUNS B/WN 1-55 COPIES PER
NO PRICING ON QTY 17 OR LESS
28 LeBron James/23 30.00 80.00
122 Donovan Mitchell/45 40.00 100.00

2017-18 Panini Status Draft Night Autographs

PRINT RUNS B/WN 23-32 COPIES PER
EXCHANGE DEADLINE 7/31/2019
1 Damyean Dotson/32 6.00 15.00
2 De'Aaron Fox/24 60.00 150.00
3 Dwayne Bacon/32 5.00 12.00
4 Edmond Sumner/24 8.00 20.00
5 Frank Jackson/32 5.00 12.00
6 Frank Ntilikina/32 6.00 15.00
7 Ike Anigbogu/32 5.00 12.00
8 Jarrett Allen/24 12.00 30.00
9 Jawun Evans/32 5.00 12.00
10 Jayson Tatum/31 125.00 300.00
11 John Collins/24 12.00 30.00
12 Jonathan Isaac/24 12.00 30.00
13 Justin Jackson/24 5.00 12.00
14 Justin Patton/24 5.00 12.00
15 Lauri Markkanen/24 50.00 120.00
16 Lonzo Ball/31 20.00 50.00
17 Luke Kennard/24 10.00 25.00
18 Markelle Fultz/31 12.00 30.00
19 OG Anunoby/24 25.00 60.00
20 T.J. Leaf/24 5.00 12.00
21 Thomas Bryant/32 8.00 20.00
22 Wesley Iwundu/29 5.00 12.00
23 Zach Collins/27 8.00 20.00
24 Malik Monk/23 15.00 40.00
25 Dennis Smith Jr./23 6.00 15.00
26 Bam Adebayo/24 20.00 50.00

2017-18 Panini Status Draft Night Hats

PRINT RUNS B/WN 28-99 COPIES PER
1 Jayson Tatum/99 125.00 300.00
2 De'Aaron Fox/56 10.00 25.00
3 Bam Adebayo/99 20.00 50.00
4 Zach Collins/56 5.00 12.00
5 Frank Ntilikina/99 4.00 10.00
6 Dennis Smith Jr./99 4.00 10.00
7 Luke Kennard/99 6.00 15.00
8 Jonathan Isaac/99 8.00 20.00
9 OG Anunoby/28 15.00 40.00
10 John Collins/28 8.00 20.00
11 Lauri Markkanen/28 12.00 30.00
12 Malik Monk/99 12.00 30.00
13 Lonzo Ball/99 10.00 25.00
14 Justin Patton/99 3.00 8.00
15 Jarrett Allen/28 8.00 20.00
16 Markelle Fultz/99 8.00 20.00
17 Justin Jackson/56 3.00 8.00

2017-18 Panini Status Draft Night Hats Prime

*PRIME/25: .75X TO 2X BASIC
PRINT RUNS B/WN 14-25 COPIES PER
NO PRICING ON QTY 17 OR LESS
1 Jayson Tatum/25 300.00 600.00
2 De'Aaron Fox/25 60.00 150.00
3 Bam Adebayo/25 20.00 50.00
8 Jonathan Isaac/25 20.00 50.00
13 Lonzo Ball/25 30.00 80.00

2017-18 Panini Status Elite Signatures

EXCHANGE DEADLINE 7/31/2019
1 Kobe Bryant EXCH 300.00 600.00
2 Magic Johnson 20.00 50.00
3 Damian Lillard 20.00 50.00
4 Seth Curry 4.00 10.00
5 Steven Adams 6.00 15.00
6 Jerry Stackhouse 5.00 12.00
7 Mark Aguirre 3.00 8.00
8 Frank Ramsey 6.00 15.00
9 Henry Ellenson 2.50 6.00
10 Aaron Gordon 4.00 10.00
11 LaMarcus Aldridge 4.00 10.00
12 Kelly Oubre Jr. 4.00 10.00
13 Cedric Maxwell 3.00 8.00
14 Kyrie Irving 15.00 40.00
15 Chris Paul 15.00 40.00
16 Cliff Hagan 5.00 12.00
17 Robert Horry 4.00 10.00
18 Jamal Mashburn 3.00 8.00
19 Myles Turner 4.00 10.00
20 Tim Hardaway 5.00 12.00
21 Michael Cooper 3.00 8.00
22 Grant Hill 8.00 20.00
23 Alex English 5.00 12.00
24 Steve Kerr 5.00 12.00
25 John Starks 3.00 8.00
26 Andre Drummond 3.00 8.00
28 Latrell Sprewell 8.00 20.00
29 Marquese Chriss 2.50 6.00
30 Kevin Durant EXCH 30.00 80.00

2017-18 Panini Status Elite Signatures Pink

*PINK/99: .5X TO 1.2X BASIC
*PINK/25: .6X TO 1.5X BASIC
PRINT RUNS B/WN 25-99 COPIES PER
EXCHANGE DEADLINE 7/31/2019
27 Richard Jefferson/99 4.00 10.00
30 Kevin Durant/25 EXCH 60.00 150.00

2017-18 Panini Status Factions

*RED/299: .6X TO 1.5X BASIC
*BLUE/199: .75X TO 2X BASIC
*PURPLE/149: .75X TO 2X BASIC
1 McCollum/Lillard/Nurkic 1.25 3.00
2 Blake Griffin
Danilo Gallinari
DeAndre Jordan .50 1.25
3 Kyle Lowry
DeMar DeRozan
Jonas Valanciunas .60 1.50
4 Dion Waiters
Hassan Whiteside
Goran Dragic .40 1.00
5 Wiggins/Butler/Towns .75 2.00
6 Horford/Hayward/Irving 1.00 2.50
7 Noah/Hardaway/Porzingis .60 1.50
8 Rose/Love/James 4.00 10.00
9 Nikola Vucevic
Aaron Gordon
Elfrid Payton .50 1.25
10 Curry/Durant/Thompson 4.00 10.00
11 Leonard/Parker/Gasol 1.25 3.00
12 Lopez/Randle/Ball 1.25 3.00
13 Beal/Gortat/Wall .60 1.50
14 Giannis/Brogdon/Middleton 2.50 6.00
15 Davis/Cousins/Holiday 1.25 3.00
16 Dwight Howard
Jeremy Lamb
Kemba Walker .60 1.50
17 Anthony/George/Westbrook .75 2.00
18 Andre Drummond
Avery Bradley
Reggie Jackson .40 1.00
19 Simmons/Embiid/Fultz 1.00 2.50
20 Harden/Paul/Anderson 1.00 2.50
21 Olajuwon/Drexler/Horry 1.00 2.50
22 Kidd/Terry/Nowitzki 1.25 3.00
23 Isiah Thomas
Joe Dumars
Bill Laimbeer .75 2.00
24 Manu/Duncan/Parker 1.25 3.00
25 Kareem/Worthy/Magic 2.00 5.00
26 Shaq/Mourning/Howard 1.50 4.00
27 McHale/Bird/Parish 2.00 5.00
28 Ben Wallace
Chauncey Billups
Richard Hamilton .60 1.50
29 Wilt/Goodrich/West 1.50 4.00
30 Shaq/Rice/Kobe 4.00 10.00

2017-18 Panini Status Foundations

*FOUND: 1.2X TO 3X BASIC
*FOUND RC: .6X TO 1.5X BASIC RC

2017-18 Panini Status Freshman Signatures

EXCHANGE DEADLINE 7/31/2019
1 Markelle Fultz 6.00 15.00
2 Lonzo Ball 15.00 40.00
3 Jayson Tatum 125.00 300.00
5 De'Aaron Fox 15.00 40.00
6 Jonathan Isaac 6.00 15.00
7 Frank Ntilikina 3.00 8.00
8 Dennis Smith Jr. EXCH 3.00 8.00
9 Zach Collins 4.00 10.00
10 Luke Kennard 5.00 12.00
11 Bam Adebayo 12.00 30.00
13 T.J. Leaf 2.50 6.00
14 Harry Giles 2.50 6.00
15 Jarrett Allen 6.00 15.00
16 Tyler Lydon 2.50 6.00
17 Kyle Kuzma 10.00 25.00
18 Derrick White 10.00 25.00
19 Frank Jackson 2.50 6.00
21 Ivan Rabb 2.50 6.00
22 Semi Ojeleye 3.00 8.00
23 Jordan Bell 2.50 6.00
24 Dwayne Bacon 2.50 6.00
25 Damyean Dotson 3.00 8.00
26 Ike Anigbogu 2.50 6.00
27 Guerschon Yabusele 2.50 6.00
28 Zhou Qi 5.00 12.00
29 Kadeem Allen 2.50 6.00
30 Alec Peters 2.50 6.00

2017-18 Panini Status Freshman Signatures Pink

*PINK: .5X TO 1.2X BASIC
STATED PRINT RUN 149 SER.#'d SETS
EXCHANGE DEADLINE 7/31/2019
20 Wesley Iwundu 3.00 8.00

2017-18 Panini Status Legendary Signatures

PRINT RUN B/WN 49-199 COPIES PER
EXCHANGE DEADLINE 7/31/2019
*PINK/99: 4X TO 1X BASIC
*PINK/25: .6X TO 1.5X BASIC
1 Magic Johnson/49 25.00 60.00
2 Anfernee Hardaway/199 12.00 30.00
3 Kobe Bryant/49 EXCH 400.00 800.00
4 Grant Hill/199 12.00 30.00
5 Larry Bird/49 30.00 80.00
6 Richard Hamilton/199 6.00 15.00
7 Willis Reed/199 20.00 50.00
8 Nate Archibald/199 6.00 15.00
9 Walt Frazier/199 8.00 20.00
10 Dave Cowens/199 8.00 20.00

2017-18 Panini Status Materials

*PINK/25: .75X TO 2X BASIC
1 Carmelo Anthony 4.00 10.00
2 Brook Lopez 2.00 5.00
3 Damian Lillard 4.00 10.00
4 Rondae Hollis-Jefferson 1.50 4.00
5 Shaquille O'Neal 8.00 20.00
6 Tim Duncan 6.00 15.00
7 Rudy Gobert 3.00 8.00
8 LeBron James 20.00 50.00
9 Gordon Hayward 2.00 5.00
10 Kevin Love 2.50 6.00
11 Trevor Booker 1.50 4.00
12 Joe Johnson 2.00 5.00
13 Danny Granger 1.50 4.00
14 Ricky Rubio 2.00 5.00
15 Kemba Walker 2.00 5.00
16 Grant Hill 4.00 10.00
17 Tony Parker 4.00 10.00
18 Bradley Beal 3.00 8.00
19 David Robinson 5.00 12.00
20 C.J. McCollum 2.50 6.00
21 Willy Hernangomez 1.50 4.00
22 Iman Shumpert 1.50 4.00
23 Gorgui Dieng 1.50 4.00
24 Kyrie Irving 3.00 8.00
25 Aaron Gordon 2.50 6.00
26 Myles Turner 2.50 6.00
27 Jimmy Butler 4.00 10.00
28 Joe Smith 2.00 5.00
29 John Wall 3.00 8.00
30 Kristaps Porzingis 3.00 8.00
31 Terrance Ferguson 1.50 4.00
32 Bam Adebayo 10.00 25.00
33 Wesley Iwundu 1.50 4.00
34 Davon Reed 1.50 4.00
35 Frank Mason III 1.50 4.00
36 Ante Zizic 2.00 5.00
37 Semi Ojeleye 2.00 5.00
38 Jonathan Isaac 4.00 10.00
39 Ivan Rabb 1.50 4.00
40 Derrick White 6.00 15.00
41 Frank Ntilikina 2.00 5.00
42 Jayson Tatum 6.00 15.00
43 Josh Jackson 2.00 5.00
44 Lonzo Ball 6.00 15.00
45 Harry Giles 1.50 4.00
46 Tyler Dorsey 1.50 4.00
47 OG Anunoby 8.00 20.00
48 Markelle Fultz 4.00 10.00
49 De'Aaron Fox 3.00 8.00
50 Caleb Swanigan 1.50 4.00
51 John Collins 4.00 10.00
52 Tyler Lydon 1.50 4.00
53 Dwayne Bacon 1.50 4.00
54 Zach Collins 2.50 6.00
55 Frank Jackson 1.50 4.00
56 Sterling Brown 1.50 4.00
57 Jawun Evans 1.50 4.00
58 Justin Patton 1.50 4.00
59 Luke Kennard 3.00 8.00
60 Donovan Mitchell 6.00 15.00

2017-18 Panini Status New Breed Autographs

EXCHANGE DEADLINE 7/31/2019
*PINK/149: .5X TO 1.2X BASIC
1 Markelle Fultz 10.00 25.00
2 Lonzo Ball 12.00 30.00
3 Jayson Tatum 125.00 300.00
4 Josh Jackson 3.00 8.00

5 De'Aaron Fox 15.00 40.00
6 Jonathan Isaac 8.00 20.00
7 Frank Ntilikina 3.00 8.00
8 Dennis Smith Jr. EXCH 3.00 8.00
9 Lauri Markkanen 12.00 30.00
10 Malik Monk 6.00 15.00
11 Donovan Mitchell 30.00 80.00
12 Justin Jackson 2.50 6.00
13 D.J. Wilson 2.50 6.00
14 John Collins 6.00 15.00
16 OG Anunoby 12.00 30.00
17 Caleb Swanigan 2.50 6.00
18 Tony Bradley 2.50 6.00
19 Josh Hart 6.00 15.00
20 Davon Reed 2.50 6.00
21 Frank Mason III 2.50 6.00
22 Daniel Theis 8.00 20.00
23 Ante Zizic 3.00 8.00
24 Jawun Evans 2.50 6.00
25 Tyler Dorsey 2.50 6.00
26 Sterling Brown 2.50 6.00
27 Sindarius Thornwell 2.50 6.00
28 Wayne Selden Jr. 2.50 6.00
29 Kadeem Allen 2.50 6.00
30 Treveon Graham 3.00 8.00

2017-18 Panini Status Rookie Credentials

*RED/299: .6X TO 1.5X BASIC
*BLUE/199: .75X TO 2X BASIC
*PURPLE/149: .75X TO 2X BASIC
1 Terrance Ferguson .30 .75
2 Josh Hart .75 2.00
3 Luke Kennard .60 1.50
4 Dwayne Bacon .30 .75
5 Lonzo Ball 1.25 3.00
6 Frank Jackson .30 .75
7 Donovan Mitchell 3.00 8.00
8 Derrick White 1.25 3.00
9 Semi Ojeleye .40 1.00
10 Jawun Evans .30 .75
11 Kyle Kuzma 1.25 3.00
12 Josh Jackson .40 1.00
13 D.J. Wilson .30 .75
14 Justin Jackson .30 .75
15 Wesley Iwundu .30 .75
16 De'Aaron Fox 2.50 6.00
17 Sterling Brown .30 .75
18 Jayson Tatum 4.00 10.00
19 Malik Monk 1.25 3.00
20 Bam Adebayo 2.00 5.00
21 Markelle Fultz .75 2.00
22 Ivan Rabb .30 .75
23 Jarrett Allen .75 2.00
24 Harry Giles .30 .75
25 Lauri Markkanen 2.00 5.00
26 Zach Collins .50 1.25
27 T.J. Leaf .30 .75
28 Frank Mason III .30 .75
29 Tyler Dorsey .30 .75
30 John Collins .75 2.00
31 Jonathan Isaac .75 2.00
32 Dennis Smith Jr. .40 1.00
33 Tony Bradley .30 .75
34 Caleb Swanigan .30 .75
35 Jordan Bell .30 .75
36 Milos Teodosic .40 1.00
37 OG Anunoby 1.50 4.00
38 Frank Ntilikina .40 1.00
39 Justin Patton .30 .75
40 Tyler Lydon .30 .75

2017-18 Panini Status Rookie Essentials Relics

1 Tony Bradley 1.25 3.00
2 Malik Monk 5.00 12.00
3 Wesley Iwundu 1.25 3.00
4 Bam Adebayo 8.00 20.00
5 D.J. Wilson 1.25 3.00
6 Markelle Fultz 3.00 8.00
7 Harry Giles 1.25 3.00
8 Josh Jackson 1.50 4.00
9 OG Anunoby 6.00 15.00
10 Frank Ntilikina 1.50 4.00
11 Derrick White 5.00 12.00
12 Luke Kennard 2.50 6.00
13 Ivan Rabb 1.25 3.00
15 T.J. Leaf 1.25 3.00
16 Lonzo Ball 5.00 12.00
17 Terrance Ferguson 1.25 3.00
18 De'Aaron Fox 10.00 25.00
19 Tyler Lydon 1.25 3.00
20 Dennis Smith Jr. 1.50 4.00
21 Frank Jackson 1.25 3.00
22 Donovan Mitchell 12.00 30.00
23 Zach Collins 2.00 5.00
24 Justin Patton 1.25 3.00
25 John Collins 3.00 8.00
26 Jayson Tatum 15.00 40.00
27 Jarrett Allen 3.00 8.00
28 Jonathan Isaac 3.00 8.00
29 Caleb Swanigan 1.25 3.00
30 Frank Mason III 1.25 3.00

2017-18 Panini Status Signatures

EXCHANGE DEADLINE 7/31/2019
*PINK/25: .6X TO 1.5X BASIC
1 Markelle Fultz 12.00 30.00
2 Lonzo Ball 20.00 50.00
3 Jayson Tatum 125.00 300.00
4 Lauri Markkanen 20.00 50.00
5 Frank Ntilikina 3.00 8.00
6 Jonathan Isaac 8.00 20.00
7 Dennis Smith Jr. EXCH 3.00 8.00
8 Treveon Graham 3.00 8.00
9 Ante Zizic 3.00 8.00
10 Bogdan Bogdanovic 8.00 20.00
11 Thomas Bryant 4.00 10.00
12 Alex Caruso 40.00 100.00
13 Alfonzo McKinnie 4.00 10.00
14 Milos Teodosic 3.00 8.00
15 Daniel Theis 8.00 20.00
16 David Nwaba 2.50 6.00
17 Royce O'Neale 3.00 8.00
18 Cedi Osman 5.00 12.00
19 Mike James 2.50 6.00
20 Ryan Arcidiacono 4.00 10.00
21 Matt Costello 3.00 8.00
22 Brandon Paul 2.50 6.00
23 Abdel Nader 3.00 8.00
24 Dillon Brooks 8.00 20.00
25 Damyean Dotson 3.00 8.00
26 Ike Anigbogu 2.50 6.00
27 Guerschon Yabusele 2.50 6.00
28 Zhou Qi 8.00 20.00
29 Kadeem Allen 2.50 6.00
30 Alec Peters 2.50 6.00
31 Allen Iverson 30.00 80.00
32 Karl Malone 12.00 30.00
33 Magic Johnson 20.00 50.00
34 Hakeem Olajuwon 12.00 30.00
35 Clyde Drexler 15.00 40.00
36 Manu Ginobili 20.00 50.00
37 Isaiah Thomas 3.00 8.00
38 Kobe Bryant 400.00 800.00
39 Kevin Durant EXCH 40.00 100.00
40 Shaquille O'Neal EXCH 40.00 100.00

2017-18 Panini Status Status Quo

*RED/299: .6X TO 1.5X BASIC
*BLUE/199: .75X TO 2X BASIC
*PURPLE/149: .6X TO 1.5X BASIC
1 Reggie Miller 1.00 2.50
2 John Stockton 1.00 2.50
3 Kobe Bryant 4.00 10.00
4 Manu Ginobili 1.00 2.50
5 Dirk Nowitzki 1.25 3.00
6 Tim Duncan 1.25 3.00
7 John Havlicek 1.00 2.50
8 Tony Parker .75 2.00
9 Larry Bird 2.00 5.00
10 Magic Johnson 2.00 5.00

2017-18 Panini Status Swatches

STATED PRINT RUN 99 SER.#'d SETS
1 Dirk Nowitzki 8.00 20.00
2 Rudy Gobert 4.00 10.00
3 Trevor Ariza 2.00 5.00
4 Kevin Garnett 8.00 20.00
5 JJ Redick 3.00 8.00
6 Andrew Wiggins 4.00 10.00
7 Larry Bird 12.00 30.00
8 Carmelo Anthony 5.00 12.00
9 Kyrie Irving 4.00 10.00
10 C.J. McCollum 3.00 8.00
11 Kenneth Faried 2.50 6.00
12 John Wall 4.00 10.00
13 Hakeem Olajuwon 6.00 15.00
14 Gordon Hayward 2.50 6.00
15 Kobe Bryant 8.00 20.00
16 Karl-Anthony Towns 5.00 12.00
17 Brook Lopez 2.50 6.00
18 Nikola Vucevic 2.50 6.00
19 Kevin Love 3.00 8.00
20 Derrick Favors 2.00 5.00
21 Grant Hill 5.00 12.00
22 Zach LaVine 5.00 12.00
23 DeAndre Jordan 2.50 6.00
24 Chris Paul 5.00 12.00
25 Udonis Haslem 2.00 5.00
26 Ricky Rubio 2.50 6.00
27 Nicolas Batum 2.00 5.00

2017-18 Panini Status Symbols

*RED/299: .6X TO 1.5X BASIC
*BLUE/199: .75X TO 2X BASIC
*PURPLE/149: .75X TO 2X BASIC
1 Giannis Antetokounmpo 2.50 6.00
2 James Harden 1.00 2.50
3 Larry Bird 2.00 5.00
4 Draymond Green .60 1.50
5 Allen Iverson 1.25 3.00
6 Kobe Bryant 4.00 10.00
7 Dirk Nowitzki 1.25 3.00
8 Stephen Curry 4.00 10.00
9 Tim Duncan 1.25 3.00
10 Russell Westbrook .75 2.00
11 Magic Johnson 2.00 5.00
12 Jeff Hornacek .40 1.00
13 Julius Erving 1.25 3.00
14 Klay Thompson 1.25 3.00
15 Hakeem Olajuwon 1.00 2.50
16 Damian Lillard 1.25 3.00
17 Kevin Garnett 1.25 3.00
18 LeBron James 4.00 10.00
19 Kristaps Porzingis .60 1.50
20 Kawhi Leonard 1.25 3.00

2018-19 Panini Status

1 Aaron Gordon .30 .75
2 Paul George .50 1.25
3 Jeremy Lin .50 1.25
4 Derrick Rose .60 1.50
5 Chris Paul .50 1.25
6 Reggie Jackson .25 .60
7 Draymond Green .40 1.00
8 Kyle Lowry .30 .75
9 De'Aaron Fox .60 1.50
10 Caris LeVert .30 .75
11 Evan Fournier .25 .60
12 Dennis Schroder .25 .60
13 Vince Carter .60 1.50
14 Andrew Wiggins .40 1.00
15 Clint Capela .25 .60
16 Lauri Markkanen .50 1.25
17 DeMarcus Cousins .25 .60
18 Kawhi Leonard .75 2.00
19 Willie Cauley-Stein .20 .50
20 D'Angelo Russell .30 .75
21 Josh Richardson .25 .60
22 Steven Adams .25 .60
23 Mike Conley .25 .60
24 Giannis Antetokounmpo 1.50 4.00
25 Eric Gordon .25 .60
26 Zach LaVine .50 1.25
27 Tobias Harris .25 .60
28 Serge Ibaka .25 .60
29 Devin Booker .75 2.00
30 Jarrett Allen .30 .75
31 Goran Dragic .25 .60
32 Nikola Jokic 1.50 4.00
33 Marc Gasol .30 .75
34 Khris Middleton .30 .75
35 DeMar DeRozan .30 .75
36 Jabari Parker .20 .50
37 Lou Williams .25 .60
38 Joel Embiid .75 2.00
39 T.J. Warren .25 .60
40 Kristaps Porzingis .40 1.00
41 Hassan Whiteside .25 .60
42 Gary Harris .25 .60
43 Garrett Temple .20 .50
44 Eric Bledsoe .25 .60
45 LaMarcus Aldridge .30 .75
46 Kevin Love .25 .60
47 Danilo Gallinari .25 .60
48 Ben Simmons .30 .75
49 Trevor Ariza .20 .50
50 Tim Hardaway Jr. .20 .50
51 Dwyane Wade .60 1.50
52 Jamal Murray .60 1.50
53 Anthony Davis .75 2.00
54 Victor Oladipo .25 .60
55 Pau Gasol .50 1.25
56 George Hill .25 .60
57 LeBron James 2.50 6.00
58 Jimmy Butler .50 1.25
59 Kemba Walker .25 .60
60 Enes Kanter .25 .60
61 Bradley Beal .40 1.00
62 Donovan Mitchell 1.00 2.50
63 Jrue Holiday .40 1.00
64 Bojan Bogdanovic .25 .60
65 Harrison Barnes .25 .60
66 Rodney Hood .25 .60
67 Kyle Kuzma .30 .75
68 JJ Redick .30 .75
69 Jeremy Lamb .20 .50
70 Damian Lillard .75 2.00
71 John Wall .40 1.00
72 Rudy Gobert .40 1.00
73 Nikola Mirotic .20 .50
74 Myles Turner .30 .75
75 Dennis Smith Jr. .20 .50
76 Stephen Curry 2.50 6.00
77 Brandon Ingram .30 .75
78 Kyrie Irving .75 2.00
79 Malik Monk .30 .75
80 CJ McCollum .30 .75
81 Dwight Howard .40 1.00
82 Joe Ingles .25 .60
83 Julius Randle .30 .75
84 Blake Griffin .30 .75
85 DeAndre Jordan .25 .60
86 Kevin Durant 1.25 3.00
87 Lonzo Ball .30 .75
88 Jayson Tatum 1.25 3.00
89 Tony Parker .50 1.25
90 Jusuf Nurkic .25 .60
91 Taurean Prince .20 .50
92 Karl-Anthony Towns .50 1.25
93 James Harden .60 1.50
94 Andre Drummond .25 .60
95 Dirk Nowitzki .75 2.00
96 Klay Thompson .75 2.00
97 Buddy Hield .30 .75
98 Jaylen Brown .50 1.25
99 Nikola Vucevic .25 .60
100 Russell Westbrook .60 1.50
101 Landry Shamet RC .60 1.50
102 Deandre Ayton RC 1.25 3.00
103 Elie Okobo RC .40 1.00
104 Mo Bamba RC .60 1.50
105 Jarred Vanderbilt RC .75 2.00
106 Shai Gilgeous-Alexander RC 10.00 25.00
107 Keita Bates-Diop RC .50 1.25
108 Zhaire Smith RC .40 1.00
109 Chimezie Metu RC .50 1.25
110 Grayson Allen RC .75 2.00
111 Robert Williams III RC .75 2.00
112 Marvin Bagley III RC .60 1.50
113 Jevon Carter RC .60 1.50
114 Wendell Carter Jr. RC 1.00 2.50
115 Bruce Brown RC .75 2.00
116 Miles Bridges RC 1.00 2.50
117 Allonzo Trier RC .40 1.00
118 Donte DiVincenzo RC 1.00 2.50
119 Ryan Broekhoff RC .60 1.50
120 Chandler Hutchison RC .50 1.25
121 Jacob Evans III RC .40 1.00
122 Luka Doncic RC 20.00 50.00
123 Jalen Brunson RC 3.00 8.00
124 Collin Sexton RC 1.25 3.00
125 Hamidou Diallo RC .60 1.50
126 Jerome Robinson RC .40 1.00
127 Gary Clark RC .40 1.00
128 Lonnie Walker IV RC .75 2.00
129 Mitchell Robinson RC 1.00 2.50
130 Aaron Holiday RC .60 1.50
131 Dzanan Musa RC .40 1.00
132 Jaren Jackson Jr. RC 3.00 8.00
133 Devonte' Graham RC .60 1.50
134 Kevin Knox RC .50 1.25
135 De'Anthony Melton RC .75 2.00
136 Michael Porter Jr. RC 1.50 4.00
137 Johnathan Williams RC .60 1.50
138 Kevin Huerter RC .75 2.00
139 Kostas Antetokounmpo RC .50 1.25
140 Anfernee Simons RC 2.00 5.00
141 Omari Spellman RC .40 1.00
142 Trae Young RC 3.00 8.00
143 Gary Trent Jr. RC .75 2.00
144 Mikal Bridges RC 2.00 5.00
145 Svi Mykhailiuk RC .50 1.25
146 Troy Brown Jr. RC .50 1.25
147 Rodions Kurucs RC .50 1.25
148 Josh Okogie RC .60 1.50
149 Yuta Watanabe RC .60 1.50
150 Moritz Wagner RC .75 2.00
151 Landry Shamet .30 .75
152 Deandre Ayton .60 1.50
153 Elie Okobo .20 .50
154 Mo Bamba .30 .75
155 Jarred Vanderbilt .30 .75
156 Shai Gilgeous-Alexander 10.00 25.00
157 Keita Bates-Diop .25 .60
158 Zhaire Smith .20 .50
159 Chimezie Metu .25 .60
160 Grayson Allen .40 1.00
161 Robert Williams III .40 1.00
162 Marvin Bagley III .30 .75
163 Jevon Carter .30 .75
164 Wendell Carter Jr. .50 1.25
165 Bruce Brown .40 1.00
166 Miles Bridges .50 1.25
167 Allonzo Trier .20 .50
168 Donte DiVincenzo .50 1.25
169 Ryan Broekhoff .30 .75
170 Chandler Hutchison .25 .60
171 Jacob Evans III .20 .50
172 Luka Doncic 20.00 50.00
173 Jalen Brunson 1.50 4.00
174 Collin Sexton .60 1.50
175 Hamidou Diallo .30 .75
176 Jerome Robinson .20 .50
177 Gary Clark .20 .50
178 Lonnie Walker IV .40 1.00
179 Mitchell Robinson .50 1.25
180 Aaron Holiday .30 .75
181 Dzanan Musa .20 .50
182 Jaren Jackson Jr. 1.50 4.00
183 Devonte' Graham .30 .75
184 Kevin Knox .25 .60
185 De'Anthony Melton .40 1.00
186 Michael Porter Jr. .75 2.00
187 Johnathan Williams .30 .75
188 Kevin Huerter .40 1.00
189 Kostas Antetokounmpo .25 .60
190 Anfernee Simons 1.00 2.50
191 Omari Spellman .20 .50
192 Trae Young 1.50 4.00
193 Gary Trent Jr. .40 1.00
194 Mikal Bridges 1.00 2.50
195 Svi Mykhailiuk .25 .60
196 Troy Brown Jr. .25 .60
197 Rodions Kurucs .25 .60
198 Josh Okogie .30 .75
199 Yuta Watanabe .30 .75
200 Moritz Wagner .40 1.00

2018-19 Panini Status Aqua

*AQUA: 1X TO 2.5X BASIC
*AQUA RC: .5X TO 1.2X BASIC RC

2018-19 Panini Status Aspirations

*ASP p/r 55-99: 2X TO 5X BASIC
*ASP p/r 55-99: 1X TO 2.5X BASIC RC
*ASP p/r 23: 1.5X TO 4X BASIC RC
PRINT RUNS B/WN 23-99 COPIES PER

2018-19 Panini Status Blue

*BLUE: 1.5X TO 4X BASIC
*BLUE RC: 1.5X TO 4X BASIC RC

2018-19 Panini Status Green

*GREEN: 1X TO 2.5X BASIC
*GREEN RC: .5X TO 1.2X BASIC RC

2018-19 Panini Status Orange

*ORANGE: 1X TO 2.5X BASIC
*ORANGE RC: .5X TO 1.2X BASIC RC

2018-19 Panini Status Purple

*PURPLE: 1X TO 2.5X BASIC
*PURPLE RC: 1X TO 2.5X BASIC RC
172 Luka Doncic 50.00 120.00

2018-19 Panini Status Red

*RED: 1X TO 2.5X BASIC
*RED RC: 1X TO 2.5X BASIC RC
172 Luka Doncic 50.00 120.00

2018-19 Panini Status Status

*STAT p/r 77: 1X TO 2.5X BASIC RC
*STAT p/r 26-45: 2.5X TO 6X BASIC
*STAT p/r 26-45: 1.2X TO 3X BASIC RC
*STAT p/r 20-25: 3X TO 8X BASIC
*STAT p/r 20-25: 1.5X TO 4X BASIC RC
PRINT RUNS B/WN 1-77 COPIES PER
NO PRICING ON QTY 19 OR LESS
122 Luka Doncic/77 400.00 800.00

2018-19 Panini Status Court Vision

*AQUA: .6X TO 1.5X BASIC
*GREEN: .6X TO 1.5X BASIC
*ORANGE: .6X TO 1.5X BASIC
1 DeMar DeRozan .60 1.50
2 John Wall .60 1.50
3 Jrue Holiday .60 1.50
4 De'Aaron Fox 1.00 2.50
5 LeBron James 4.00 10.00
6 Kyle Lowry .50 1.25
7 Chris Paul 1.00 2.50
8 Trae Young 8.00 20.00
9 Damian Lillard 1.25 3.00
10 Ben Simmons .50 1.25

2018-19 Panini Status Draft Night Autographs

STATED PRINT RUN 32 SER.#'d SETS
EXCHANGE DEADLINE 9/20/2020
1 Aaron Holiday 20.00 50.00
2 Bruce Brown 10.00 25.00
3 Chandler Hutchison 6.00 15.00
4 Collin Sexton 30.00 80.00
5 Deandre Ayton 60.00 150.00
6 Donte DiVincenzo 12.00 30.00
7 Dzanan Musa 5.00 12.00
8 Grayson Allen 20.00 50.00
9 Hamidou Diallo 10.00 25.00
10 Jaren Jackson Jr. 125.00 300.00
11 Kevin Knox 15.00 40.00
12 Khyri Thomas 5.00 12.00
13 Landry Shamet 20.00 50.00
14 Lonnie Walker IV 50.00 120.00
15 Luka Doncic 2,000.00 4,000.00
16 Marvin Bagley III 8.00 20.00
17 Michael Porter Jr. 125.00 300.00
18 Mikal Bridges 25.00 60.00
19 Mo Bamba 8.00 20.00
20 Moritz Wagner 10.00 25.00
21 Rodions Kurucs 6.00 15.00
22 Shai Gilgeous-Alexander 500.00 1,000.00
23 Svi Mykhailiuk 6.00 15.00
24 Trae Young 500.00 1,000.00
25 Zhaire Smith 5.00 12.00

2018-19 Panini Status Elite Series

*AQUA: .6X TO 1.5X BASIC
*GREEN: .6X TO 1.5X BASIC
*ORANGE: .6X TO 1.5X BASIC
1 Dirk Nowitzki 1.50 4.00
2 Anthony Davis 1.50 4.00
3 Zach LaVine 1.00 2.50
4 Jimmy Butler 1.00 2.50
5 Damian Lillard 1.50 4.00
6 Chris Paul 1.25 3.00
7 Kyrie Irving 1.50 4.00
8 Devin Booker 1.50 4.00
9 Karl-Anthony Towns 1.00 2.50
10 Khris Middleton .60 1.50
11 Klay Thompson 1.50 4.00
12 Victor Oladipo .50 1.25
13 LaMarcus Aldridge .60 1.50
14 Kemba Walker .50 1.25
15 John Wall .75 2.00
16 Kawhi Leonard 1.50 4.00
17 Kevin Durant 2.50 6.00
18 DeMar DeRozan .75 2.00
19 James Harden 1.25 3.00
20 Ben Simmons .60 1.50
21 Russell Westbrook 1.00 2.50
22 LeBron James 5.00 12.00
23 Paul George 1.00 2.50
24 Donovan Mitchell 2.00 5.00
25 Stephen Curry 5.00 12.00
26 Giannis Antetokounmpo 3.00 8.00
27 Jayson Tatum 2.50 6.00
28 Joel Embiid 1.50 4.00
29 Andre Drummond .50 1.25
30 Dwyane Wade 1.25 3.00

2018-19 Panini Status Elite Signatures

EXCHANGE DEADLINE 9/20/2020
*PINK/25: .6X TO 1.5X BASIC
1 Stephen Curry 150.00 400.00
2 Marcus Camby 3.00 8.00
3 Andrew Wiggins 6.00 15.00
4 Kelly Olynyk 2.50 6.00
6 Mahmoud Abdul-Rauf 2.50 6.00
7 Gary Harris 3.00 8.00
8 Vin Baker 2.50 6.00
9 Joe Dumars 5.00 12.00
10 Udonis Haslem 2.50 6.00
12 Bryon Russell 2.50 6.00
13 Kevin Love 6.00 15.00
14 Sean Elliott 3.00 8.00
15 JJ Redick 4.00 10.00
16 Doug Christie 3.00 8.00
17 Serge Ibaka 3.00 8.00
18 Herb Williams 2.50 6.00
19 George McGinnis 5.00 12.00
20 Jose Calderon 2.50 6.00
21 Kyrie Irving 15.00 40.00
22 Scott Skiles 3.00 8.00
23 Nikola Jokic 100.00 250.00
24 Mychal Thompson 2.50 6.00
26 Darrell Griffith 3.00 8.00
27 Terry Rozier 3.00 8.00
28 Yogi Ferrell 2.50 6.00
29 Lauri Markkanen 8.00 20.00
30 Rick Mahorn 2.50 6.00

2018-19 Panini Status Factions

*BLUE: .6X TO 1.5X BASIC
*PURPLE: .6X TO 1.5X BASIC
*RED: .6X TO 1.5X BASIC
1 Smmns/Btlr/Embd 1.25 3.00
2 Bldse/Mddltn/Anttknmpo 2.50 6.00
3 LVne/Prts/Crtr .75 2.00
4 Sxtn/Clrksn/Love 1.00 2.50
5 Brwn/Ttm/Irvng 2.00 5.00
6 Gllnri/Glgs-Alxndr/Hrrs 3.00 8.00
7 Jcksn/Gsl/Cnly 2.50 6.00
8 Hrtr/Prnce/Yng 6.00 15.00
9 Dragic/McGruder/Richardson .40 1.00
10 Wlkr/Btm/Brdgs .75 2.00
11 Mtchll/Alln/Rbc 1.50 4.00
12 Bgly/Fox/Cly-Sin 1.00 2.50
13 Trr/Sith/Knox .40 1.00
14 Ingrm/Kzma/Jms 4.00 10.00
15 Grdn/Isc/Bmba .50 1.25
16 Nwtzki/Dncc/Brns 2.00 5.00
17 Russell/Allen/LeVert .50 1.25
18 Hrrs/Mrry/Jkc 2.50 6.00
19 Oladipo/Sabonis/Turner .60 1.50
20 Dvs/Hldy/Mrtc 1.25 3.00
21 Drummond/Griffin/Jackson .50 1.25
22 Lwry/Skm/Lnrd 1.25 3.00
23 Paul/Cpla/Hrdn 1.00 2.50
24 DRzn/Aldrdge/Wlkr .60 1.50
25 Wrrn/Atn/Bkr 1.25 3.00
26 Grge/Wstbok/Adms .75 2.00
27 Wggns/Twns/Rose 1.00 2.50
28 McCllm/Llrd/Nrkc 1.25 3.00
29 Grn/Drnt/Crry 4.00 10.00
30 Hwrd/Beal/Wall .60 1.50

2018-19 Panini Status Freshman Signatures

EXCHANGE DEADLINE 9/20/2020
*PINK/25: .6X TO 1.5X BASIC
1 De'Anthony Melton 5.00 12.00
2 Marvin Bagley III 4.00 10.00
3 Isaac Bonga 3.00 8.00
4 Collin Sexton 12.00 30.00
5 Bruce Brown 5.00 12.00
6 Troy Brown Jr. 3.00 8.00
7 Jarred Vanderbilt 5.00 12.00
8 Lonnie Walker IV 6.00 15.00
9 Shake Milton 40.00 100.00
11 Dzanan Musa 2.50 6.00
12 Jaren Jackson Jr. 40.00 100.00
13 Alize Johnson 4.00 10.00
15 Duncan Robinson 60.00 150.00
16 Devonte' Graham 4.00 10.00
17 Ryan Broekhoff 4.00 10.00
18 Anfernee Simons 12.00 30.00
19 Daryl Macon 2.50 6.00
20 Moritz Wagner 5.00 12.00
22 Mo Bamba 6.00 15.00
23 Mitchell Robinson 15.00 40.00
24 Jerome Robinson 2.50 6.00
25 J.P. Macura 5.00 12.00
26 Josh Okogie 4.00 10.00
27 Kenrich Williams 6.00 15.00
28 Chandler Hutchison 3.00 8.00
29 Gary Clark 2.50 6.00
30 Robert Williams III 4.00 10.00

2018-19 Panini Status Legendary Signatures

EXCHANGE DEADLINE 9/20/2020
*PINK/25: .6X TO 1.5X BASIC
1 Richard Hamilton 6.00 15.00
2 Charles Barkley EXCH 75.00 200.00
3 Nick Van Exel 8.00 20.00
4 Kobe Bryant EXCH 60.00 150.00
5 Bill Walton 20.00 50.00
6 Magic Johnson 20.00 50.00
7 Latrell Sprewell 8.00 20.00
8 Dennis Rodman 15.00 40.00
9 Glen Rice 4.00 10.00
10 Walt Frazier 6.00 15.00

2018-19 Panini Status Legendary Status Materials

1 Clifford Robinson 2.50 6.00
2 Clyde Drexler 4.00 10.00
3 David Robinson 3.00 8.00
4 Hakeem Olajuwon 3.00 8.00
5 Gerald Wallace 2.00 5.00
6 Glen Rice 2.50 6.00
7 James Worthy 4.00 10.00
8 Jason Kidd 4.00 10.00
9 Jermaine O'Neal 2.00 5.00
10 Jerry Stackhouse 3.00 8.00
11 Joe Dumars 3.00 8.00
12 John Starks 2.00 5.00
13 Karl Malone 5.00 12.00
14 Kenny Anderson 2.00 5.00
15 Kevin Garnett 3.00 8.00
16 Kobe Bryant 20.00 50.00
17 Larry Johnson 3.00 8.00

2018-19 Panini Status New Breed Autographs

EXCHANGE DEADLINE 9/20/2020
*PINK/25: .6X TO 1.5X BASIC
2 Grayson Allen 6.00 15.00
3 Vincent Edwards 2.50 6.00
4 Aaron Holiday 4.00 10.00
6 Trae Young 125.00 300.00
8 Wendell Carter Jr. 6.00 15.00
9 Chimezie Metu 5.00 12.00
11 Ray Spalding 2.50 6.00
13 Jared Terrell 2.50 6.00
15 Omari Spellman 2.50 6.00
16 Deandre Ayton EXCH 12.00 30.00
17 Allonzo Trier 2.50 6.00
18 Michael Porter Jr. 10.00 25.00
19 Hamidou Diallo 4.00 10.00
20 Donte DiVincenzo 6.00 15.00
21 Svi Mykhailiuk 3.00 8.00
23 Yante Maten 2.50 6.00
25 Torrey Craig 10.00 25.00
26 Luka Doncic 500.00 1,000.00
27 Angel Delgado 2.50 6.00
28 Kevin Knox 3.00 8.00
29 Keenan Evans 2.50 6.00
30 Zhaire Smith 2.50 6.00
NBSGA Shai Gilgeous-Alexander 400.00 800.00

2018-19 Panini Status Quo

*BLUE: .6X TO 1.5X BASIC
*PURPLE: .6X TO 1.5X BASIC
*RED: .6X TO 1.5X BASIC
1 Dirk Nowitzki 1.25 3.00
2 Kobe Bryant 4.00 10.00
3 John Stockton 1.00 2.50
4 Tim Duncan 1.25 3.00
5 Reggie Miller 1.00 2.50
6 Jerry West 1.00 2.50
7 Bill Russell 1.50 4.00
8 Russell Westbrook .75 2.00
9 Stephen Curry 4.00 10.00
10 Mike Conley .40 1.00

2018-19 Panini Status Rookie Credentials

*AQUA: .6X TO 1.5X BASIC
*GREEN: .6X TO 1.5X BASIC
*ORANGE: .6X TO 1.5X BASIC
1 Gary Trent Jr. .75 2.00
2 Michael Porter Jr. 1.50 4.00
3 Svi Mykhailiuk .50 1.25
4 Kevin Huerter .75 2.00
5 Aaron Holiday .60 1.50
6 Deandre Ayton 1.25 3.00
7 Robert Williams III .75 2.00
8 Trae Young 12.00 30.00
9 Elie Okobo .40 1.00
10 Kevin Knox .50 1.25
11 Bruce Brown .75 2.00
12 Troy Brown Jr. .50 1.25
13 Keita Bates-Diop .50 1.25
14 Josh Okogie .60 1.50
15 Anfernee Simons 2.00 5.00
16 Marvin Bagley III .60 1.50
17 Jacob Evans III .40 1.00
18 Mo Bamba .60 1.50
19 Jevon Carter .60 1.50
20 Mikal Bridges 2.00 5.00
21 Hamidou Diallo .60 1.50
22 Donte DiVincenzo 1.00 2.50
23 Allonzo Trier .40 1.00
24 Grayson Allen .75 2.00
25 Moritz Wagner .75 2.00
26 Luka Doncic 12.00 30.00
27 Dzanan Musa .40 1.00
28 Wendell Carter Jr. 1.00 2.50
29 Jalen Brunson 3.00 8.00
30 Shai Gilgeous-Alexander 4.00 10.00
31 De'Anthony Melton .75 2.00
32 Lonnie Walker IV .75 2.00
33 Mitchell Robinson 1.00 2.50
34 Chandler Hutchison .50 1.25
35 Landry Shamet .60 1.50
36 Jaren Jackson Jr. 3.00 8.00
37 Omari Spellman .40 1.00
38 Collin Sexton 1.25 3.00
39 Devonte' Graham .60 1.50
40 Jerome Robinson .40 1.00

2018-19 Panini Status Rookie Essentials Relics

1 Zhaire Smith 1.50 4.00
2 Kevin Huerter 3.00 8.00
3 Aaron Holiday 2.50 6.00
4 Deandre Ayton 6.00 15.00
5 Jacob Evans III 1.50 4.00
6 Trae Young 20.00 50.00
7 Jalen Brunson 12.00 30.00
8 Kevin Knox 3.00 8.00
9 Hamidou Diallo 2.50 6.00
10 Michael Porter Jr. 6.00 15.00
11 Moritz Wagner 3.00 8.00
12 Josh Okogie 2.50 6.00
13 Anfernee Simons 8.00 20.00
14 Marvin Bagley III 4.00 10.00
15 Dzanan Musa 1.50 4.00
16 Mo Bamba 2.50 6.00
17 Devonte' Graham 2.50 6.00
18 Mikal Bridges 8.00 20.00
19 De'Anthony Melton 3.00 8.00
20 Troy Brown Jr. 2.00 5.00
21 Jevon Carter 2.50 6.00
22 Grayson Allen 3.00 8.00
23 Landry Shamet 2.50 6.00
24 Luka Doncic 12.00 30.00
25 Omari Spellman 1.50 4.00
26 Wendell Carter Jr. 4.00 10.00
27 Gary Trent Jr. 3.00 8.00
28 Shai Gilgeous-Alexander 3.00 8.00
29 Svi Mykhailiuk 2.00 5.00
30 Donte DiVincenzo 4.00 10.00
31 Jarred Vanderbilt 3.00 8.00
32 Chandler Hutchison 2.00 5.00
33 Robert Williams III 3.00 8.00
34 Jaren Jackson Jr. 4.00 10.00
35 Elie Okobo 1.50 4.00
36 Collin Sexton 3.00 8.00
37 Bruce Brown 3.00 8.00
38 Jerome Robinson 1.50 4.00
39 Keita Bates-Diop 2.00 5.00
40 Lonnie Walker IV 3.00 8.00

2018-19 Panini Status Rookie Prominence

*BLUE: .6X TO 1.5X BASIC
*PURPLE: .6X TO 1.5X BASIC
*RED: .6X TO 1.5X BASIC
1 Deandre Ayton 1.25 3.00
2 Marvin Bagley III .60 1.50
3 Luka Doncic 30.00 80.00
4 Jaren Jackson Jr. 3.00 8.00
5 Trae Young 8.00 20.00
6 Mo Bamba .60 1.50
7 Wendell Carter Jr. 1.00 2.50
8 Collin Sexton 1.25 3.00
9 Kevin Knox .50 1.25
10 Mikal Bridges 2.00 5.00
11 Shai Gilgeous-Alexander 4.00 10.00
12 Jerome Robinson .40 1.00
13 Michael Porter Jr. 1.50 4.00
14 Troy Brown Jr. .50 1.25
15 Miles Bridges 1.00 2.50
16 Donte DiVincenzo 1.00 2.50
17 Lonnie Walker IV .75 2.00
18 Kevin Huerter .75 2.00
19 Josh Okogie .60 1.50
20 Grayson Allen .75 2.00
21 Chandler Hutchison .50 1.25
22 Aaron Holiday .60 1.50
23 Anfernee Simons 2.00 5.00
24 Moritz Wagner .75 2.00
25 Landry Shamet .60 1.50
26 Robert Williams III .75 2.00
27 Jacob Evans III .40 1.00
28 Dzanan Musa .40 1.00
29 Omari Spellman .40 1.00
30 Elie Okobo .40 1.00
31 Jevon Carter .60 1.50
32 Jalen Brunson 3.00 8.00
33 Devonte' Graham .60 1.50
34 Mitchell Robinson 1.00 2.50
35 Hamidou Diallo .60 1.50
36 Yuta Watanabe .60 1.50
37 Allonzo Trier .40 1.00
38 Kostas Antetokounmpo .50 1.25
39 Rodions Kurucs .50 1.25
40 Svi Mykhailiuk .50 1.25

2018-19 Panini Status Swatches

1 Wilson Chandler 1.50 4.00
2 Wesley Matthews 1.50 4.00
3 Tyus Jones 1.50 4.00
4 Trey Lyles 1.50 4.00
5 Thaddeus Young 1.50 4.00
6 Terrence Ross 2.00 5.00
7 Taj Gibson 1.50 4.00
8 Steven Adams 2.00 5.00
9 Serge Ibaka 2.00 5.00
10 Rudy Gobert 3.00 8.00
11 Rondae Hollis-Jefferson 1.50 4.00
12 Otto Porter Jr. 2.00 5.00
13 Nikola Jokic 12.00 30.00
14 Nicolas Batum 1.50 4.00
15 Mario Hezonja 1.50 4.00
16 Lance Stephenson 2.00 5.00
17 Klay Thompson 6.00 15.00
18 Kevin Love 2.00 5.00

2018-19 Panini Status Symbols

*BLUE: .6X TO 1.5X BASIC
*PURPLE: .6X TO 1.5X BASIC
*RED: .6X TO 1.5X BASIC
1 Stephen Curry 4.00 10.00
2 Kobe Bryant 4.00 10.00
3 LeBron James 4.00 10.00
4 James Harden 1.00 2.50
5 Russell Westbrook .75 2.00
6 Tim Duncan 1.25 3.00
7 Charles Barkley 1.00 2.50
8 Anthony Davis 1.25 3.00
9 Shaquille O'Neal 1.50 4.00
10 Dwyane Wade 1.00 2.50
11 Paul Pierce .75 2.00
12 Kevin Garnett 1.25 3.00
13 Scottie Pippen 1.25 3.00
14 Dennis Rodman 1.25 3.00
15 Larry Bird 2.00 5.00
16 Magic Johnson 2.00 5.00
17 Julius Erving 1.25 3.00
18 Giannis Antetokounmpo 2.50 6.00
19 Kyrie Irving 1.25 3.00
20 Kevin Durant 2.00 5.00

2018-19 Panini Status Top Status

*AQUA: .6X TO 1.5X BASIC
*GREEN: .6X TO 1.5X BASIC
*ORANGE: .6X TO 1.5X BASIC
1 David Robinson 1.00 2.50
2 Anthony Davis 1.25 3.00
3 Hakeem Olajuwon .60 1.50
4 John Wall .60 1.50
5 Kareem Abdul-Jabbar 1.50 4.00
6 Dwight Howard .60 1.50
7 Yao Ming 1.25 3.00
8 Deandre Ayton 1.00 2.50

9 Allen Iverson 1.25 3.00
10 Ben Simmons .50 1.25
11 Patrick Ewing .75 2.00
12 Kyrie Irving 1.25 3.00
13 Magic Johnson 2.00 5.00
14 Derrick Rose 1.00 2.50
15 Bill Walton .75 2.00
16 LeBron James 4.00 10.00
17 Tim Duncan 1.25 3.00
18 Markelle Fultz .40 1.00
19 Shaquille O'Neal 1.50 4.00
20 Karl-Anthony Towns .75 2.00

2019-20 Panini Status

*BLUE: .75X TO 2X BASIC
*RED: .75X TO 2X BASIC
*WHITE DIAMONDS/125: 2X TO 5X BASIC
*GRN ESCHER SQUARES/49: 4X TO 10X BASIC
1 Jordan Poole 2.00 5.00
2 Mike Conley .30 .75
3 DeMar DeRozan .50 1.25
4 Jimmy Butler .75 2.00
5 Sekou Doumbouya .50 1.25
6 D'Angelo Russell .30 .75
7 Danny Green .30 .75
8 Nickeil Alexander-Walker .75 2.00
9 Gordon Hayward .30 .75
10 Josh Okogie .30 .75
11 RJ Barrett 2.00 5.00
12 Eric Paschall .60 1.50
13 Miles Bridges .40 1.00
14 Brook Lopez .30 .75
15 Buddy Hield .30 .75
16 Ky Bowman .60 1.50
17 Landry Shamet .30 .75
18 Seth Curry .30 .75
19 Kyrie Irving .75 2.00
20 Kevin Love .40 1.00
21 Derrick Jones Jr. .25 .60
22 Jonathan Isaac .40 1.00
23 Admiral Schofield .60 1.50
24 LaMarcus Aldridge .40 1.00
25 Goga Bitadze .75 2.00
26 Zach LaVine .60 1.50
27 Norman Powell .30 .75
28 Ja Morant 5.00 12.00
29 Goran Dragic .30 .75
30 Juancho Hernangomez .40 1.00
31 Hassan Whiteside .30 .75
32 Bobby Portis .25 .60
33 Bojan Bogdanovic .30 .75
34 De'Anthony Melton .25 .60
35 Russell Westbrook .60 1.50
36 Luka Samanic .60 1.50
37 JJ Redick .40 1.00
38 Joe Ingles .30 .75
39 Darius Garland 2.00 5.00
40 Eric Gordon .30 .75
41 Bogdan Bogdanovic .40 1.00
42 Bradley Beal .50 1.25
43 Jrue Holiday .50 1.25
44 Bol Bol 1.25 3.00
45 Trae Young 1.00 2.50
46 Davis Bertans .25 .60
47 Frank Ntilikina .25 .60
48 Devin Booker .10 .25
49 Jaylen Nowell .60 1.50
50 Lauri Markkanen .50 1.25
51 Draymond Green .50 1.25
52 Matisse Thybulle 1.00 2.50
53 T.J. Warren .30 .75
54 Spencer Dinwiddie .30 .75
55 Terry Rozier .30 .75
56 Rui Hachimura 2.00 5.00
57 Maxi Kleber .25 .60
58 CJ McCollum .40 1.00
59 Mitchell Robinson .40 1.00
61 Dylan Windler .60 1.50
62 Cam Reddish .75 2.00
63 Al Horford .40 1.00
64 Jayson Tatum 1.50 4.00
65 Daniel Gafford 1.00 2.50
66 Michael Porter Jr. .60 1.50
67 Zion Williamson 4.00 10.00
68 Montrezl Harrell .30 .75
69 Caris LeVert .30 .75
70 Jarrett Culver .50 1.25
71 Cody Martin .75 2.00
72 Jae Crowder .25 .60
73 Patty Mills .40 1.00
74 Devonte' Graham .30 .75
75 Dwight Powell .25 .60
76 Khris Middleton .40 1.00
77 Andre Drummond .30 .75
78 Jonas Valanciunas .30 .75
79 KZ Okpala .60 1.50
80 Ignas Brazdeikis .60 1.50
81 Josh Jackson .25 .60
82 Larry Nance Jr. .30 .75
83 Marcus Smart .30 .75
84 Kyle Kuzma .50 1.25
85 Pascal Siakam .60 1.50
86 Isaiah Roby .60 1.50
87 Kris Dunn .25 .60
88 Danuel House Jr. .25 .60
89 Nicolo Melli .60 1.50
90 Joel Embiid .75 2.00
91 Mfiondu Kabengele .60 1.50
92 Kyle Guy .60 1.50
93 John Wall .50 1.25
94 Nikola Jokic 2.00 5.00
95 Kevin Porter Jr. 1.00 2.50
96 Jaxson Hayes .75 2.00
97 Blake Griffin .40 1.00
98 Kristaps Porzingis .50 1.25
99 Aaron Gordon .40 1.00
100 Lonnie Walker IV .30 .75
101 Shai Gilgeous-Alexander 2.00 5.00
102 Jaylen Brown .60 1.50
103 Dennis Schroder .50 1.25
104 Aron Baynes .25 .60
105 PJ Washington Jr. 1.50 4.00
106 Cameron Johnson 1.25 3.00
107 De'Andre Hunter 2.00 5.00
108 Carsen Edwards .60 1.50
109 Collin Sexton .50 1.25
110 Mo Bamba .30 .75
111 Tremont Waters .60 1.50
112 Kevin Huerter .40 1.00
113 Ben Simmons .40 1.00
114 Otto Porter Jr. .25 .60
115 Luguentz Dort 2.00 5.00
116 Paul George .60 1.50
117 Stephen Curry 3.00 8.00
118 Torrey Craig .25 .60
119 Marvin Bagley III .30 .75
120 Karl-Anthony Towns .60 1.50
121 Markelle Fultz .30 .75
122 Lou Williams .40 1.00
123 Jamal Murray .60 1.50
124 De'Aaron Fox .60 1.50
125 Brandon Clarke 1.00 2.50
126 Damian Lillard 1.00 2.50
127 Ty Jerome 1.00 2.50
128 Tobias Harris .30 .75
129 Brandon Ingram .40 1.00
130 Robert Covington .25 .60
131 Keldon Johnson 1.50 4.00
132 Ricky Rubio .30 .75
133 Tristan Thompson .25 .60
134 Thomas Bryant .30 .75
135 Rudy Gobert .50 1.25
136 Julius Randle .50 1.25
137 Klay Thompson 1.00 2.50
138 Tyler Herro 2.50 6.00
139 Romeo Langford .50 1.25
140 Darius Bazley .50 1.25
141 Luka Doncic 2.50 6.00
142 Harrison Barnes .30 .75
143 John Collins .40 1.00
144 Evan Fournier .30 .75
145 Dwight Howard .50 1.25
146 Deandre Ayton .40 1.00
147 Kendrick Nunn .75 2.00
148 Will Barton .25 .60
149 Chris Paul .75 2.00
150 Dejounte Murray .40 1.00
151 Elfrid Payton .25 .60
152 Grant Williams .75 2.00
153 Jeff Teague .25 .60
154 Domantas Sabonis .50 1.25
155 Wendell Carter Jr. .40 1.00
156 Donovan Mitchell .75 2.00
157 Malik Beasley .30 .75
158 Eric Bledsoe .30 .75
159 Kyle Lowry .40 1.00
160 Danilo Gallinari .30 .75
161 Joe Harris .30 .75
162 Victor Oladipo .30 .75
163 Tim Hardaway Jr. .25 .60
164 Kawhi Leonard 1.00 2.50
165 Kevin Durant 1.25 3.00
166 Quinndary Weatherspoon .50 1.25
167 Lonzo Ball .40 1.00
168 Dillon Brooks .30 .75
169 Langston Galloway .25 .60
170 James Harden .75 2.00
171 Derrick Favors .25 .60
172 Troy Brown Jr. .25 .60
173 Giannis Antetokounmpo 2.00 5.00
174 Fred VanVleet .50 1.25
175 LeBron James 3.00 8.00
176 Steven Adams .30 .75
177 Malcolm Brogdon .30 .75
178 Tacko Fall .60 1.50
179 Bam Adebayo .60 1.50
180 Anfernee Simons .60 1.50
181 Luke Kennard .30 .75
182 Kevon Looney .25 .60
183 Marc Gasol .40 1.00
184 Cody Zeller .25 .60
185 Kemba Walker .30 .75
186 Malik Monk .40 1.00
187 Bruno Fernando .60 1.50
188 Jaren Jackson Jr. .60 1.50
189 Terance Mann 1.00 2.50
190 Donte DiVincenzo .30 .75
191 Christian Wood .30 .75
192 Andrew Wiggins .50 1.25
193 Kelly Oubre Jr. .30 .75
194 Myles Turner .40 1.00
195 Anthony Davis 1.00 2.50
196 Derrick Rose .75 2.00
197 Nassir Little .75 2.00
198 Carmelo Anthony .60 1.50
199 Josh Richardson .25 .60
200 Coby White 1.50 4.00

2019-20 Panini Status New Beginnings

*BLUE: .75X TO 2X BASIC
*RED: .75X TO 2X BASIC
*WHT DIAMONDS/125: 2X TO 5X BASIC
*GRN ESCHER SQUARES/49: 4X TO 10X BASIC
1 Ja Morant 4.00 10.00
2 Darius Garland 1.50 4.00
3 Keldon Johnson 1.25 3.00
4 Nickeil Alexander-Walker .60 1.50
5 Carsen Edwards .50 1.25
6 Darius Bazley .40 1.00
7 Goga Bitadze .60 1.50
8 De'Andre Hunter 1.50 4.00
9 Brandon Clarke .75 2.00
10 Luguentz Dort 1.50 4.00
11 Grant Williams .60 1.50
12 Kevin Porter Jr. .60 1.50
13 Kendrick Nunn .60 1.50
14 Matisse Thybulle .75 2.00
15 RJ Barrett 1.50 4.00
16 Ky Bowman .50 1.25
17 Jarrett Culver .40 1.00
18 Jordan Poole 1.50 4.00
19 Luka Samanic .50 1.25
20 Terence Davis II .60 1.50
21 PJ Washington Jr. 1.25 3.00
22 Coby White 1.25 3.00
23 Rui Hachimura 1.50 4.00
24 Cameron Johnson 1.00 2.50
25 Jaxson Hayes .60 1.50
26 Sekou Doumbouya .40 1.00
27 Eric Paschall .50 1.25
28 Tyler Herro 2.00 5.00
29 Cam Reddish .60 1.50
30 Zion Williamson 3.00 8.00

2019-20 Panini Status New Kids on the Court Autographs

STATED PRINT RUN 10-30 SER.#'d SETS
NO PRICING ON QTY 15 AND BELOW
1 Tacko Fall/30 6.00 15.00
2 Naz Reid/25 20.00 50.00
3 Kendrick Nunn/30 8.00 20.00
4 De'Andre Hunter/30 20.00 50.00
5 Tremont Waters/25 6.00 15.00
6 Isaiah Roby/25 6.00 15.00
7 Coby White/30 15.00 40.00
8 Talen Horton-Tucker/25 8.00 20.00
9 Grant Williams/25 8.00 20.00
10 Sekou Doumbouya/30 5.00 12.00
11 Jaylen Nowell/25 6.00 15.00
14 Brandon Clarke/25 10.00 25.00
15 Dylan Windler/25 6.00 15.00
19 Nickeil Alexander-Walker/25 8.00 20.00
20 Chuma Okeke/30 8.00 20.00
21 Bruno Fernando/25 6.00 15.00
25 Darius Bazley/30 5.00 12.00
26 Jarrett Culver/30 5.00 12.00
27 RJ Barrett/30 20.00 50.00
29 Daniel Gafford/25 10.00 25.00
30 Nicolas Claxton/30 10.00 25.00

2019-20 Panini Status Newbie Status Signatures

STATED PRINT RUN 10-30 SER.#'d SETS
NO PRICING ON QTY 15 AND BELOW
1 Allen Smailagic/25 5.00 12.00
2 Chris Clemons/25 5.00 12.00
3 Ky Bowman/25 6.00 15.00
4 Terance Mann/25 10.00 25.00
5 RJ Barrett/30 20.00 50.00
6 Jarrett Culver/30 5.00 12.00
7 Brandon Clarke/30 10.00 25.00
8 Darius Bazley/30 5.00 12.00
9 Nickeil Alexander-Walker/30 8.00 20.00
10 Coby White/30 15.00 40.00
11 Nicolas Claxton/30 10.00 25.00
12 Garrison Mathews/25 8.00 20.00
13 Tacko Fall/25 6.00 15.00
14 Jaylen Nowell/25 6.00 15.00
20 Grant Williams/25 8.00 20.00
21 Cody Martin/25 8.00 20.00
22 Isaiah Roby/25 6.00 15.00
23 Quinndary Weatherspoon/25 5.00 12.00
25 Tremont Waters/25 6.00 15.00
26 Sekou Doumbouya/30 5.00 12.00
27 De'Andre Hunter/30 20.00 50.00
29 Terence Davis II/30 8.00 20.00
30 Jalen Lecque/25 5.00 12.00

2019-20 Panini Status Prominence Signatures

1 Dennis Rodman 60.00 150.00
2 Kevin Garnett 40.00 100.00
5 Jerry West 40.00 100.00
6 Allen Iverson 60.00 150.00
7 John Stockton 30.00 80.00
9 Hakeem Olajuwon 30.00 80.00
10 Magic Johnson 60.00 150.00
PSDWD Dwyane Wade 40.00 100.00

2019-20 Panini Status Renowned Autographs

STATED PRINT RUN 25-30 SER.#'d SETS
1 Torrey Craig/25 6.00 15.00
2 Markelle Fultz/25 8.00 20.00
3 Kelly Oubre Jr./25 8.00 20.00
4 Devonte' Graham/25 8.00 20.00
5 Spencer Dinwiddie/25 8.00 20.00
6 Donovan Mitchell/30 20.00 50.00
7 Shawn Kemp/30 30.00 80.00
8 Alex Caruso/25 20.00 50.00
9 Ray Allen/30 40.00 100.00
10 Stephon Marbury/30 12.00 30.00
11 Deron Williams/25 8.00 20.00
12 Karl-Anthony Towns/30 15.00 40.00
13 Jason Kidd/30 25.00 60.00
14 Paul Pierce/30 40.00 100.00
15 Lou Williams/25 10.00 25.00
16 Pascal Siakam/25 15.00 40.00
17 Toni Kukoc/25 12.00 30.00
18 Luke Kennard/25 8.00 20.00
20 Zach LaVine/25 15.00 40.00
21 DeAndre Jordan/25 8.00 20.00
22 Richard Jefferson/25 6.00 15.00
23 Shai Gilgeous-Alexander/25 400.00 800.00
24 Trae Young/30 75.00 200.00
25 George Gervin/30 15.00 40.00
26 Tim Hardaway/30 12.00 30.00
27 JJ Redick/30 10.00 25.00
28 Jason Williams/25 20.00 50.00
29 Baron Davis/30 8.00 20.00
30 Dave Bing/30 12.00 30.00

2019-20 Panini Status Status Symbols

*BLUE: .75X TO 2X BASIC
*RED: .75X TO 2X BASIC
*WHITE DIAMONDS/125: 2.5X TO 6X BASIC
*GRN ESCHER SQUARES/49: 4X TO 10X BASIC
1 Paul Pierce 1.00 2.50
2 Tim Duncan 1.50 4.00
3 John Wall .75 2.00
4 Giannis Antetokounmpo 3.00 8.00
5 Kyle Lowry .60 1.50
6 James Harden 1.25 3.00
7 Donovan Mitchell 1.25 3.00
8 Joel Embiid 1.25 3.00
9 Devin Booker .15 .40
10 Kevin Garnett 1.50 4.00
11 Karl Malone 1.25 3.00
12 John Stockton 1.25 3.00
13 Allen Iverson 1.50 4.00
14 Magic Johnson 2.00 5.00
15 Dwyane Wade 1.25 3.00
16 Julius Erving 1.25 3.00
17 LeBron James 5.00 12.00
18 Chris Webber .75 2.00
19 Anfernee Hardaway 1.50 4.00
20 Kawhi Leonard 1.50 4.00
21 Trae Young 1.50 4.00
22 Luka Doncic 4.00 10.00
23 Shaquille O'Neal 2.50 6.00
24 Larry Bird 2.50 6.00
25 Scottie Pippen 1.50 4.00
26 Jayson Tatum 2.50 6.00
27 Pascal Siakam 1.00 2.50
28 Damian Lillard 1.50 4.00
29 Stephen Curry 5.00 12.00
30 Dirk Nowitzki 1.50 4.00

2019-20 Panini Status Trophy Club

*BLUE: .75X TO 2X BASIC
*RED: .75X TO 2X BASIC
*WHITE DIAMONDS/125: 2.5X TO 6X BASIC
*GRN ESCHER SQUARES/49: 4X TO 10X BASIC
1 Dwyane Wade 1.25 3.00
2 Kevin Durant 2.00 5.00
3 Kyrie Irving 1.25 3.00
4 Kyle Lowry .60 1.50
5 LeBron James 5.00 12.00
6 Andre Iguodala .50 1.25
7 Tim Duncan 1.50 4.00
8 Paul Pierce 1.00 2.50
9 Jason Kidd 1.00 2.50
10 Pascal Siakam 1.00 2.50
11 Ray Allen 1.00 2.50
12 David Robinson 1.25 3.00
13 Gary Payton 1.00 2.50
14 Derek Fisher .60 1.50
15 Patty Mills .60 1.50
16 Draymond Green .75 2.00
17 Hakeem Olajuwon 1.25 3.00
18 Glen Rice .50 1.25
19 Kevin Garnett 1.50 4.00
20 Tony Parker .75 2.00
21 Klay Thompson 1.50 4.00
22 Kawhi Leonard 1.50 4.00
23 LeBron James 5.00 12.00
24 Toni Kukoc .75 2.00
25 Jason Terry .50 1.25
26 Dirk Nowitzki 1.50 4.00
27 Kawhi Leonard 1.50 4.00
28 Fred VanVleet .75 2.00
29 Stephen Curry 5.00 12.00
30 Shaquille O'Neal 2.50 6.00

2019-20 Panini Status Upper Echelon

*BLUE: .75X TO 2X BASIC
*RED: .75X TO 2X BASIC
*WHITE DIAMONDS/125: 2.5X TO 6X BASIC
*GRN ESCHER SQUARES/49: 4X TO 10X BASIC
1 James Harden 1.25 3.00
2 Kawhi Leonard 1.50 4.00
3 Zion Williamson 3.00 8.00
4 Anthony Davis 1.50 4.00
5 Luka Doncic 4.00 10.00
6 LeBron James 5.00 12.00
7 Nikola Jokic 3.00 8.00
8 Trae Young 1.50 4.00
9 Stephen Curry 5.00 12.00
10 Giannis Antetokounmpo 3.00 8.00

1987 Panini Stickers

141 Michael Jordan 150.00 400.00

1990-91 Panini Stickers

COMPLETE SET (180) 8.00 20.00
1 Magic Johnson .40 1.00
2 Mychal Thompson .08 .25
3 Vlade Divac .15 .40
4 Byron Scott .08 .25
5 James Worthy .20 .50
6 A.C. Green .08 .25
7 Jerome Kersey .08 .25
8 Clyde Drexler .40 1.00
9 Buck Williams .08 .25
10 Kevin Duckworth .08 .25
11 Terry Porter .08 .25
12 Cliff Robinson .15 .40
13 Tom Chambers .08 .25
14 Dan Majerle .15 .40
15 Mark West .08 .25
16 Kevin Johnson .15 .40
17 Jeff Hornacek .15 .40
18 Kurt Rambis .08 .25
19 Nate McMillan .08 .25
20 Shawn Kemp .50 1.25
21 Dale Ellis .08 .25
22 Michael Cage .08 .25
23 Xavier McDaniel .08 .25
24 Derrick McKey .08 .25
25 Manute Bol .08 .25
26 Chris Mullin .20 .50
27 Terry Teagle .08 .25
28 Tim Hardaway .75 2.00
29 Sarunas Marciulionis .08 .25
30 Mitch Richmond .40 1.00
31 Gary Grant .08 .25
32 Danny Manning .15 .40
33 Benoit Benjamin .08 .25
34 Ron Harper .15 .40
35 Ken Norman .08 .25
36 Charles Smith .08 .25
37 Harold Pressley .08 .25
38 Antoine Carr .08 .25
39 Danny Ainge .15 .40
40 Wayman Tisdale .08 .25
41 Ralph Sampson .08 .25
42 Vinny Del Negro .08 .25
43 David Robinson .50 1.25
44 Sean Elliott .20 .50
45 Terry Cummings .15 .40
46 Willie Anderson .08 .25
47 Rod Strickland .15 .40
48 Frank Brickowski .08 .25
49 Karl Malone .60 1.50
50 Darrell Griffith .08 .25
51 John Stockton .60 1.50
52 Blue Edwards .08 .25
53 Mark Eaton .08 .25
54 Thurl Bailey .08 .25
55 Rolando Blackman .08 .25
56 Sam Perkins .08 .25
57 James Donaldson .08 .25
58 Herb Williams .08 .25
59 Roy Tarpley .08 .25
60 Derek Harper .08 .25
61 Michael Adams .08 .25
62 Blair Rasmussen .08 .25
63 Jerome Lane .08 .25
64 Walter Davis .08 .25
65 Todd Lichti .08 .25
66 Joe Barry Carroll .08 .25
67 Vernon Maxwell .08 .25
68 Otis Thorpe .08 .25
69 Hakeem Olajuwon .40 1.00
70 Buck Johnson .08 .25
71 Eric (Sleepy) Floyd .08 .25
72 Mitchell Wiggins .08 .25
73 Tony Campbell .08 .25
74 Tod Murphy .08 .25
75 Tyrone Corbin .08 .25
76 Sam Mitchell .08 .25
77 Randy Breuer .08 .25
78 Pooh Richardson .08 .25
79 Rex Chapman .15 .40
80 Dell Curry .08 .25
81 Muggsy Bogues .15 .40
82 J.R. Reid .08 .25
83 Armon Gilliam .08 .25
84 Kelly Tripucka .08 .25
85 Dennis Rodman .50 1.25
86 Joe Dumars .20 .50
87 Isiah Thomas .20 .50
88 Bill Laimbeer .15 .40
89 Vinnie Johnson .08 .25
90 James Edwards .08 .25
91 Michael Jordan 1.50 4.00
92 Stacey King .08 .25
93 Scottie Pippen .60 1.50
94 John Paxson .08 .25
95 Horace Grant .08 .25
96 Craig Hodges .08 .25
97 Brad Lohaus .08 .25
98 Jack Sikma .08 .25
99 Ricky Pierce .08 .25
100 Greg Anderson .08 .25
101 Alvin Robertson .08 .25
102 Jay Humphries .08 .25
103 Mark Price .15 .40
104 Winston Bennett .08 .25
105 Brad Daugherty .08 .25
106 Craig Ehlo .08 .25
107 Larry Nance .08 .25
108 Hot Rod Williams .08 .25
109 Rik Smits .15 .40
110 Chuck Person .08 .25
111 Reggie Miller .40 1.00
112 LaSalle Thompson .08 .25
113 Detlef Schrempf .15 .40
114 Vern Fleming .08 .25
115 Moses Malone .15 .40
116 Doc Rivers .15 .40
117 Dominique Wilkins .25 .60
118 Spud Webb .15 .40
119 Kevin Willis .08 .25
120 Kenny Smith .08 .25
121 Otis Smith .08 .25
122 Sidney Green .08 .25
123 Nick Anderson .08 .25
124 Scott Skiles .08 .25
125 Jerry Reynolds .08 .25
126 Terry Catledge .08 .25
127 Charles Barkley .40 1.00
128 Ron Anderson .08 .25
129 Hersey Hawkins .08 .25
130 Mike Gminski .08 .25
131 Johnny Dawkins .08 .25
132 Rick Mahorn .08 .25
133 Michael Smith .08 .25
134 Reggie Lewis .08 .25
135 Larry Bird 1.00 2.50
136 Kevin McHale .20 .50
137 Joe Kleine .08 .25
138 Robert Parish .15 .40
139 Maurice Cheeks .08 .25
140 Patrick Ewing .40 1.00
141 Charles Oakley .15 .40
142 Gerald Wilkins .08 .25
143 Kenny Walker .15 .40
144 Mark Jackson .08 .25
145 Mark Alarie .08 .25
146 John Williams .08 .25
147 Darrell Walker .08 .25
148 Bernard King .08 .25
149 Harvey Grant .08 .25
150 Ledell Eackles .08 .25
151 Glen Rice .50 1.25
152 Kevin Edwards .08 .25
153 Tellis Frank .08 .25
154 Rony Seikaly .08 .25
155 Billy Thompson .08 .25
156 Sherman Douglas .08 .25
157 Roy Hinson .08 .25
158 Chris Morris .08 .25
159 Lester Conner .08 .25
160 Sam Bowie .08 .25
161 Purvis Short .08 .25
162 Mookie Blaylock .15 .40
A John Stockton AS .25 .60
B Magic Johnson AS .25 .60
C A.C. Green AS .08 .25
D Hakeem Olajuwon AS .25 .60
E James Worthy AS .15 .40
F Isiah Thomas AS .15 .40
G Michael Jordan AS .75 2.00
H Larry Bird AS .40 1.00
I Patrick Ewing AS .25 .60
J Charles Barkley AS .25 .60
K Michael Jordan .75 2.00
L Larry Bird .40 1.00
M Hakeem Olajuwon .25 .60
N NBA Finals .08 .25
O NBA Finals .08 .25
P NBA Finals .08 .25
Q NBA Finals .08 .25
R NBA Finals .08 .25
XX Panini Album .40 1.00

1991-92 Panini Stickers

COMPLETE SET (192) 50.00 120.00
1 NBA Official Licensed Product Logo .08 .25
2 1991 NBA Finals Logo .08 .25
3 Chris Mullin .30 .75
4 Mitch Richmond .30 .75
5 Alton Lister .08 .25
6 Tim Hardaway .30 .75
7 Tom Tolbert .08 .25
8 Rod Higgins .08 .25
9 Charles Smith .08 .25
10 Ron Harper .20 .50
11 Olden Polynice .08 .25
12 Ken Norman .08 .25
13 Gary Grant .08 .25
14 Danny Manning .15 .40
15 Sam Perkins .10 .30
16 Vlade Divac .10 .30
17 James Worthy .30 .75
18 Magic Johnson .75 2.00
19 A.C. Green .20 .50
20 Byron Scott .20 .50
21 Kevin Johnson .15 .40
22 Mark West .08 .25
23 Dan Majerle .15 .40
24 Jeff Hornacek .30 .75
25 Xavier McDaniel .08 .25
26 Tom Chambers .20 .50
27 Terry Porter .08 .25
28 Kevin Duckworth .08 .25
29 Clyde Drexler .40 1.00
30 Jerome Kersey .08 .25
31 Buck Williams .15 .40
32 Danny Ainge .20 .50
33 Wayman Tisdale .08 .25
34 Antoine Carr .08 .25
35 Lionel Simmons .08 .25
36 Travis Mays .08 .25
37 Rory Sparrow .08 .25
38 Duane Causwell .08 .25
39 Benoit Benjamin .08 .25
40 Michael Cage .08 .25
41 Derrick McKey .08 .25
42 Shawn Kemp .30 .75
43 Gary Payton .60 1.50
44 Ricky Pierce .08 .25
45 Derek Harper .15 .40
46 James Donaldson .08 .25
47 Randy White .08 .25
48 Rodney McCray .08 .25
49 Alex English .20 .50
50 Rolando Blackman .15 .40
51 Orlando Woolridge .08 .25
52 Todd Lichti .08 .25
53 Chris Jackson .08 .25
54 Blair Rasmussen .08 .25
55 Reggie Williams .08 .25
56 Marcus Liberty .08 .25
57 Hakeem Olajuwon .50 1.25
58 Kenny Smith .08 .25
59 Vernon Maxwell .08 .25
60 Otis Thorpe .10 .30
61 Buck Johnson .08 .25
62 Larry Smith .08 .25
63 Pooh Richardson .08 .25
64 Felton Spencer .08 .25
65 Tod Murphy .08 .25
66 Tyrone Corbin .08 .25
67 Tony Campbell .08 .25
68 Sam Mitchell .15 .40
69 Dennis Scott .10 .30
70 Nick Anderson .10 .30
71 Terry Catledge .08 .25
72 Scott Skiles .20 .50
73 Otis Smith .08 .25
74 Greg Kite .08 .25
75 Terry Cummings .15 .40
76 Rod Strickland .10 .30
77 David Robinson .60 1.50
78 Willie Anderson .08 .25
79 Sean Elliott .20 .50
80 Paul Pressey .08 .25
81 John Stockton .75 2.00
82 Jeff Malone .08 .25
83 Mark Eaton .08 .25
84 Thurl Bailey .08 .25
85 Karl Malone .75 2.00
86 Blue Edwards .08 .25
87 Kevin Johnson .15 .40
88 '91 Western Division .10 .30
89 NBA All-Star Weekend .08 .25
90 Magic Johnson AS .40 1.00
91 Karl Malone AS .40 1.00
92 David Robinson AS .30 .75
93 Chris Mullin AS .20 .50
94 Charles Barkley AS .30 .75
95 '91 Eastern Division .10 .30
96 Michael Jordan AS 12.00 30.00
97 Isiah Thomas AS .30 .75
98 Charles Barkley AS .40 1.00
99 Patrick Ewing AS .30 .75
100 Larry Bird AS .50 1.25
101 Dominique Wilkins .40 1.00
102 Kevin Willis .10 .30
103 John Battle .08 .25
104 Doc Rivers .20 .50
105 Spud Webb .10 .30
106 Moses Malone .15 .40
107 J.R. Reid .08 .25
108 Johnny Newman .08 .25
109 Rex Chapman .15 .40
110 Muggsy Bogues .20 .50
111 Mike Gminski .08 .25
112 Kendall Gill .15 .40
113 Scottie Pippen .60 1.50
114 Bill Cartwright .10 .30
115 John Paxson .10 .30
116 Michael Jordan 12.00 30.00
117 Horace Grant .15 .40
118 B.J. Armstrong .08 .25
119 Brad Daugherty .08 .25
120 Larry Nance .10 .30
121 Hot Rod Williams .08 .25
122 Craig Ehlo .08 .25
123 Darnell Valentine .08 .25
124 Danny Ferry .08 .25
125 Isiah Thomas .40 1.00
126 James Edwards .08 .25
127 Bill Laimbeer .20 .50
128 Vinnie Johnson .08 .25
129 Joe Dumars .30 .75
130 Dennis Rodman .40 1.00
131 Reggie Miller .40 1.00
132 Detlef Schrempf .10 .30
133 Chuck Person .08 .25
134 LaSalle Thompson .08 .25
135 Vern Fleming .08 .25
136 Rik Smits .08 .25
137 Dale Ellis .10 .30
138 Frank Brickowski .08 .25
139 Jay Humphries .08 .25
140 Jack Sikma .08 .25
141 Fred Roberts .08 .25
142 Alvin Robertson .08 .25
143 Robert Parish .20 .50
144 Kevin McHale .30 .75
145 Kevin Gamble .08 .25
146 Larry Bird .75 2.00
147 Reggie Lewis .15 .40
148 Brian Shaw .15 .40
149 Sherman Douglas .08 .25
150 Rony Seikaly .08 .25
151 Glen Rice .30 .75
152 Grant Long .08 .25
153 Billy Thompson .08 .25
154 Willie Burton .08 .25
155 Reggie Theus .10 .30
156 Sam Bowie .10 .30
157 Derrick Coleman .10 .30
158 Drazen Petrovic .60 1.50
159 Mookie Blaylock .10 .30
160 Chris Morris .08 .25
161 Gerald Wilkins .08 .25
162 Charles Oakley .10 .30
163 Patrick Ewing .40 1.00
164 Kiki Vandeweghe .08 .25
165 Maurice Cheeks .15 .40
166 John Starks .20 .50
167 Hersey Hawkins .10 .30
168 Rick Mahorn .08 .25
169 Charles Barkley .50 1.25
170 Rickey Green .08 .25
171 Ron Anderson .08 .25
172 Armon Gilliam .08 .25
173 Bernard King .15 .40
174 Ledell Eackles .08 .25
175 John Williams .08 .25
176 Darrell Walker .08 .25
177 Haywoode Workman .08 .25
178 Harvey Grant .08 .25
179 Derrick Coleman ART .08 .25
180 Dee Brown ART .08 .25
181 Lionel Simmons ART .08 .25
182 Felton Spencer ART .08 .25
183 Dennis Scott ART .08 .25
184 Gary Payton ART .40 1.00
185 Travis Mays ART .08 .25
186 Kendall Gill ART .10 .30
187 All-NBA 1st Team .10 .30
188 Charles Barkley AS .40 1.00
189 Patrick Ewing AS .30 .75
190 Michael Jordan AS 40.00 100.00
191 Karl Malone AS .50 1.25
192 Magic Johnson AS .50 1.25
XX Panini Album 1.25 3.00

1992-93 Panini Stickers

COMPLETE SET (192) 15.00 40.00
1 Shaquille O'Neal 2.50 6.00
2 Tracy Murray .08 .25
3 Robert Horry .50 1.25
4 Bryant Stith .08 .25
5 Randy Woods .08 .25
6 Adam Keefe .08 .25
7 Byron Houston .08 .25
8 Duane Cooper .08 .25
9 Western Playoffs (Action scene left) .08 .25
10 Western Playoffs (Action scene right) .08 .25
11 Clyde Drexler .50 1.25
12 Michael Jordan 5.00 12.00
13 Eastern Playoffs (Action scene left) .08 .25
14 Eastern Playoffs (Action scene right) .08 .25
15 Chicago Bulls Logo .08 .25
16 1992 NBA Finals (Action scene upper left; Michael Jordan pictured) 2.00 5.00
17 1992 NBA Finals (Action scene upper right; Michael Jordan pictured) 2.00 5.00
18 1992 NBA Finals (Action scene lower left; Michael Jordan pictured) 2.00 5.00
19 1992 NBA Finals (Action scene lower right; Michael Jordan pictured) 2.00 5.00
20 Michael Jordan MVP 10.00 25.00
21 Tim Hardaway .40 1.00
22 Chris Mullin .40 1.00
23 Billy Owens .20 .50
24 Sarunas Marciulionis .20 .50
25 Jeff Grayer .08 .25
26 Tyrone Hill .08 .25
27 Danny Manning .20 .50
28 Ron Harper .20 .50
29 Ken Norman .08 .25
30 Charles Smith .08 .25
31 Gary Grant .08 .25
32 Doc Rivers .20 .50
33 James Worthy .40 1.00
34 Sam Perkins .20 .50
35 Byron Scott .20 .50
36 Sedale Threatt .08 .25
37 Elden Campbell .08 .25
38 A.C. Green .20 .50
39 Charles Barkley .50 1.25
40 Kevin Johnson .20 .50
41 Tom Chambers .20 .50
42 Dan Majerle .20 .50
43 Mark West .08 .25
44 Danny Ainge .20 .50
45 Buck Williams .20 .50
46 Clyde Drexler .50 1.25
47 Jerome Kersey .08 .25
48 Terry Porter .08 .25
49 Clifford Robinson .08 .25
50 Kevin Duckworth .08 .25
51 Mitch Richmond .30 .75
52 Lionel Simmons .08 .25
53 Wayman Tisdale .08 .25
54 Spud Webb .08 .25
55 Duane Causwell .08 .25
56 Jim Les .08 .25

57 Eddie Johnson .08 .25
58 Ricky Pierce .08 .25
59 Shawn Kemp .30 .75
60 Benoit Benjamin .08 .25
61 Gary Payton .50 1.25
62 Dana Barros .08 .25
63 Herb Williams .08 .25
64 Doug Smith .08 .25
65 Terry Davis .08 .25
66 Derek Harper .20 .50
67 Mike Iuzzolino .08 .25
68 Rodney McCray .08 .25
69 Greg Anderson .08 .25
70 Reggie Williams .08 .25
71 Dikembe Mutombo .40 1.00
72 Mark Macon .08 .25
73 Winston Garland .08 .25
74 Chris Jackson .08 .25
75 Otis Thorpe .08 .25
76 Hakeem Olajuwon .50 1.25
77 Vernon Maxwell .08 .25
78 Kenny Smith .08 .25
79 Avery Johnson .20 .50
80 Sleepy Floyd .08 .25
81 Pooh Richardson .08 .25
82 Tony Campbell .08 .25
83 Thurl Bailey .08 .25
84 Doug West .08 .25
85 Gerald Glass .08 .25
86 Felton Spencer .08 .25
87 David Robinson .50 1.25
88 Terry Cummings .08 .25
89 Sidney Green .08 .25
90 Sean Elliott .20 .50
91 Willie Anderson .08 .25
92 Antoine Carr .08 .25
93 Clyde Drexler FF .30 .75
94 Patrick Ewing FF .25 .60
95 Magic Johnson FF .40 1.00
96 Scottie Pippen FF .30 .75
97 John Stockton FF .40 1.00
98 Tim Hardaway FF .10 .30
99 David Robinson FF .30 .75
100 Karl Malone FF .30 .75
101 Chris Mullin FF .20 .50
102 Michael Jordan FF 30.00 80.00
103 Mark Eaton .08 .25
104 Karl Malone .50 1.25
105 Jeff Malone .08 .25
106 John Stockton .60 1.50
107 David Benoit .08 .25
108 Jay Humphries .08 .25
109 Alvin Robertson .08 .25
110 Moses Malone .20 .50
111 Sam Vincent .08 .25
112 Frank Brickowski .08 .25
113 Fred Roberts .08 .25
114 Blue Edwards .08 .25
115 Stacey Augmon .08 .25
116 Rumeal Robinson .08 .25
117 Paul Graham .08 .25
118 Dominique Wilkins .50 1.25
119 Kevin Willis .08 .25
120 Duane Ferrell .08 .25
121 Tyrone Bogues .15 .40
122 Kendall Gill .08 .25
123 Dell Curry .08 .25
124 Larry Johnson .25 .60
125 Johnny Newman .08 .25
126 J.R. Reid .08 .25
127 Scottie Pippen .75 2.00
128 Michael Jordan 10.00 25.00
129 Bill Cartwright .10 .30
130 Horace Grant .20 .50
131 John Paxson .20 .50
132 B.J. Armstrong .08 .25
133 Mark Price .20 .50
134 Brad Daugherty .08 .25
135 Larry Nance .20 .50
136 Craig Ehlo .15 .40
137 Hot Rod Williams .08 .25
138 Terrell Brandon .10 .30
139 Joe Dumars .40 1.00
140 Isiah Thomas .50 1.25
141 Dennis Rodman .50 1.25
142 Orlando Woolridge .08 .25
143 John Salley .20 .50
144 Bill Laimbeer .20 .50
145 Reggie Miller .50 1.25
146 Detlef Schrempf .20 .50
147 Chuck Person .08 .25
148 Micheal Williams .08 .25
149 Rik Smits .08 .25
150 Vern Fleming .08 .25
151 Lester Conner .08 .25
152 Nick Anderson .08 .25
153 Scott Skiles .15 .40
154 Terry Catledge .08 .25
155 Jerry Reynolds .08 .25
156 Dennis Scott .08 .25
157 Rick Fox .08 .25
158 Reggie Lewis .08 .25
159 Robert Parish .20 .50
160 Kevin Gamble .08 .25
161 Kevin McHale .25 .60
162 John Bagley .08 .25
163 Steve Smith .25 .60
164 Glen Rice .25 .60
165 Grant Long .08 .25
166 Rony Seikaly .08 .25
167 Bimbo Coles .08 .25
168 Willie Burton .08 .25
169 Derrick Coleman .08 .25
170 Drazen Petrovic .40 1.00
171 Sam Bowie .08 .25
172 Chris Morris .08 .25
173 Mookie Blaylock .08 .25
174 Chris Dudley .08 .25
175 Patrick Ewing .40 1.00
176 Mark Jackson .20 .50
177 Xavier McDaniel .08 .25
178 John Starks .15 .40
179 Charles Oakley .08 .25
180 Rolando Blackman .08 .25
181 Hersey Hawkins .08 .25
182 Johnny Dawkins .08 .25
183 Armon Gilliam .08 .25
184 Jeff Hornacek .20 .50
185 Tim Perry .08 .25
186 Andrew Lang .08 .25
187 Pervis Ellison .08 .25
188 Michael Adams .08 .25
189 Harvey Grant .08 .25
190 Ledell Eackles .08 .25
191 A.J. English .08 .25
192 David Wingate .08 .25
XX Panini Album 1.00 2.50

1993-94 Panini Stickers

COMPLETE SET (253) 10.00 25.00
1 John Paxson (top part of photo) .30 .75
2 John Paxson (bottom part of photo) .30 .75
3 Charles Barkley (top part of photo) .75 2.00
4 Charles Barkley (bottom part of photo) .75 2.00
5 Victor Alexander .20 .50
6 Chris Gatling .20 .50
7 Tim Hardaway .40 1.00
8 Warriors Team Logo .20 .50
9 Tyrone Hill .20 .50
10 Sarunas Marciulionis .30 .75
11 Chris Mullin .40 1.00
12 Billy Owens .25 .60
13 Latrell Sprewell .50 1.25
14 Gary Grant .20 .50
15 Ron Harper .30 .75
16 Mark Jackson .25 .60
17 Clippers Team Logo .20 .50
18 Danny Manning .25 .60
19 Ken Norman .20 .50
20 Stanley Roberts .20 .50
21 Loy Vaught .20 .50
22 John Williams .20 .50
23 Sam Bowie .25 .60
24 Elden Campbell .25 .60
25 Vlade Divac .30 .75
26 Lakers Team Logo .20 .50
27 A.C. Green .25 .60
28 Anthony Peeler .25 .60
29 Doug Christie .25 .60
30 Sedale Threatt .20 .50
31 James Worthy .40 1.00
32 Danny Ainge .30 .75
33 Charles Barkley .75 2.00
34 Cedric Ceballos .25 .60
35 Suns Team Logo .20 .50
36 Tom Chambers .30 .75
37 Richard Dumas .20 .50
38 Kevin Johnson .30 .75
39 Dan Majerle .30 .75
40 Oliver Miller .20 .50
41 Clyde Drexler .50 1.25
42 Mario Elie .25 .60
43 Harvey Grant .25 .60
44 Trail Blazers Team Logo .20 .50
45 Jerome Kersey .25 .60
46 Terry Porter .25 .60
47 Clifford Robinson .30 .75
48 Rod Strickland .25 .60
49 Buck Williams .25 .60
50 Anthony Bonner .20 .50
51 Duane Causwell .20 .50
52 Kurt Rambis .25 .60
53 Kings Team Logo .20 .50
54 Mitch Richmond .40 1.00
55 Lionel Simmons .20 .50
56 Wayman Tisdale .25 .60
57 Spud Webb .25 .60
58 Walt Williams .30 .75
59 Dana Barros .20 .50
60 Eddie Johnson .20 .50
61 Shawn Kemp .50 1.25
62 Supersonics Team Logo .20 .50
63 Derrick McKey .25 .60
64 Nate McMillan .25 .60
65 Gary Payton .40 1.00
66 Sam Perkins .25 .60
67 Ricky Pierce .20 .50
68 Terry Davis .20 .50
69 Derek Harper .25 .60
70 Donald Hodge .20 .50
71 Mavericks Team Logo .20 .50
72 Mike Iuzzolino .20 .50
73 Jim Jackson .25 .60
74 Sean Rooks .20 .50
75 Doug Smith .20 .50
76 Randy White .20 .50
77 LaPhonso Ellis .25 .60
78 Scott Hastings .25 .60
79 Mahmoud Abdul-Rauf .25 .60
80 Nuggets Team Logo .20 .50
81 Marcus Liberty .20 .50
82 Mark Macon .20 .50
83 Dikembe Mutombo .50 1.25
84 Robert Pack .20 .50
85 Reggie Williams .20 .50
86 Scott Brooks .20 .50
87 Sleepy Floyd .25 .60
88 Carl Herrera .25 .60
89 Rockets Team Logo .20 .50
90 Robert Horry .30 .75
91 Vernon Maxwell .25 .60
92 Hakeem Olajuwon .60 1.50
93 Kenny Smith .25 .60
94 Otis Thorpe .30 .75
95 Thurl Bailey .20 .50
96 Chris Smith .20 .50
97 Mike Brown .20 .50
98 Timberwolves Team Logo .20 .50
99 Christian Laettner .30 .75
100 Luc Longley .25 .60
101 Chuck Person .25 .60
102 Doug West .25 .60
103 Micheal Williams .20 .50
104 Willie Anderson .20 .50
105 Antoine Carr .20 .50
106 Terry Cummings .25 .60
107 Spurs Team Logo .20 .50
108 Sean Elliott .30 .75
109 Dale Ellis .20 .50
110 Avery Johnson .25 .60
111 J.R. Reid .25 .60
112 David Robinson .60 1.50
113 David Benoit .20 .50
114 Tyrone Corbin .20 .50
115 Mark Eaton .30 .75
116 Jazz Team Logo .20 .50
117 Jay Humphries .25 .60
118 Jeff Malone .25 .60
119 Karl Malone .60 1.50
120 Felton Spencer .20 .50
121 John Stockton .60 1.50
122 Anthony Avent .20 .50
123 Frank Brickowski .20 .50
124 Todd Day .20 .50
125 Bucks Team Logo .20 .50
126 Blue Edwards .20 .50
127 Brad Lohaus .20 .50
128 Moses Malone .50 1.25
129 Lee Mayberry .20 .50
130 Eric Murdock .20 .50
131 Stacey Augmon .25 .60
132 Mookie Blaylock .30 .75
133 Duane Ferrell .20 .50
134 Hawks Team Logo .20 .50
135 Steve Henson .20 .50
136 Adam Keefe .20 .50
137 Jon Koncak .20 .50
138 Dominique Wilkins .50 1.25
139 Kevin Willis .25 .60
140 Muggsy Bogues .30 .75
141 Dell Curry .30 .75
142 Kenny Gattison .20 .50
143 Hornets Team Logo .20 .50
144 Kendall Gill .20 .50
145 Larry Johnson .40 1.00
146 Alonzo Mourning .50 1.25
147 Johnny Newman .20 .50
148 David Wingate .20 .50
149 B.J. Armstrong .30 .75
150 Bill Cartwright .25 .60
151 Horace Grant .30 .75
152 Bulls Team Logo .20 .50
153 Stacey King .20 .50
154 John Paxson .30 .75
155 Will Perdue .20 .50
156 Scottie Pippen .75 2.00
157 Scott Williams .20 .50
158 Terrell Brandon .25 .60
159 Brad Daugherty .25 .60
160 Craig Ehlo .20 .50
161 Cavaliers Team Logo .20 .50
162 Danny Ferry .20 .50
163 Larry Nance .30 .75
164 Mark Price .30 .75
165 Gerald Wilkins .25 .60
166 Hot Rod Williams .25 .60
167 Mark Aguirre .25 .60
168 Joe Dumars .40 1.00
169 Bill Laimbeer .30 .75
170 Pistons Team Logo .20 .50
171 Terry Mills .20 .50
172 Olden Polynice .20 .50
173 Alvin Robertson .25 .60
174 Dennis Rodman .75 2.00
175 Isiah Thomas .50 1.25
176 Dale Davis .25 .60
177 Vern Fleming .25 .60
178 Reggie Miller .60 1.50
179 Pacers Team Logo .20 .50
180 Pooh Richardson .20 .50
181 Detlef Schrempf .30 .75
182 Malik Sealy .25 .60
183 Rik Smits .25 .60
184 LaSalle Thompson .20 .50
185 Nick Anderson .25 .60
186 Anthony Bowie .20 .50
187 Shaquille O'Neal 1.50 4.00
188 Magic Team Logo .20 .50
189 Donald Royal .20 .50
190 Dennis Scott .20 .50
191 Scott Skiles .25 .60
192 Tom Tolbert .20 .50
193 Jeff Turner .20 .50
194 Alaa Abdelnaby .20 .50
195 Dee Brown .25 .60
196 Sherman Douglas .20 .50
197 Celtics Team Logo .20 .50
198 Rick Fox .25 .60
199 Kevin Gamble .20 .50
200 Xavier McDaniel .30 .75
201 Robert Parish .40 1.00
202 Lorenzo Williams .20 .50
203 Bimbo Coles .20 .50
204 Matt Geiger .20 .50
205 Harold Miner .25 .60
206 Heat Team Logo .20 .50
207 Glen Rice .30 .75
208 John Salley .25 .60
209 Rony Seikaly .25 .60
210 Brian Shaw .20 .50
211 Steve Smith .25 .60
212 Rafael Addison .20 .50
213 Kenny Anderson .25 .60
214 Benoit Benjamin .25 .60
215 Nets Team Logo .20 .50
216 Derrick Coleman .30 .75
217 Chris Dudley .20 .50
218 Rick Mahorn .25 .60
219 Chris Morris .20 .50
220 Rumeal Robinson .20 .50
221 Greg Anthony .20 .50
222 Rolando Blackman .20 .50
223 Patrick Ewing .50 1.25
224 Knicks Team Logo .20 .50
225 Anthony Mason .25 .60
226 Charles Oakley .30 .75
227 Doc Rivers .25 .60
228 Charles Smith .25 .60
229 John Starks .30 .75
230 Ron Anderson .20 .50
231 Johnny Dawkins .25 .60
232 Armon Gilliam .20 .50
233 76ers Team Logo .20 .50
234 Hersey Hawkins .20 .50
235 Jeff Hornacek .25 .60
236 Andrew Lang .20 .50
237 Tim Perry .20 .50
238 Clarence Weatherspoon .20 .50
239 Michael Adams .25 .60
240 Rex Chapman .20 .50
241 Kevin Duckworth .25 .60
242 Bullets Team Logo .20 .50
243 Pervis Ellison .20 .50
244 Tom Gugliotta .25 .60
245 Don MacLean .20 .50
246 Brent Price .20 .50
247 LaBradford Smith .20 .50
A Charles Barkley MVP .75 2.00
B Mahmoud Abdul-Rauf MIP .25 .60
C Shaquille O'Neal ROY 1.50 4.00
D Hakeem Olajuwon Def POY .60 1.50
E John Stockton CV .60 1.50
F Clifford Robinson SM .30 .75
XX Panini Album .75 2.00

1994-95 Panini Stickers

COMPLETE SET (230) 30.00 80.00
1 Toronto Raptors .40 1.00
2 Toronto Raptors .40 1.00
3 Vancouver Grizzlies .40 1.00
4 Vancouver Grizzlies .40 1.00
5 Stacey Augmon .50 1.25
6 Mookie Blaylock .60 1.50
7 Craig Ehlo .40 1.00
8 Duane Ferrell .40 1.00
9 Adam Keefe .40 1.00
10 Andrew Lang .40 1.00
11 Danny Manning .50 1.25
12 Kevin Willis .50 1.25
13 Dee Brown .50 1.25
14 Sherman Douglas .40 1.00
15 Pervis Ellison .40 1.00
16 Rick Fox .40 1.00
17 Kevin Gamble .40 1.00
18 Xavier McDaniel .40 1.00
19 Dino Radja .40 1.00
20 Dominique Wilkins 1.00 2.50
21 Michael Adams .40 1.00
22 Muggsy Bogues .50 1.25
23 Dell Curry .40 1.00
24 Kenny Gattison .40 1.00
25 Hersey Hawkins .40 1.00
26 Larry Johnson .75 2.00
27 Alonzo Mourning 1.00 2.50
28 Robert Parish .60 1.50
29 B.J. Armstrong .60 1.50
30 Steve Kerr .60 1.50
31 Toni Kukoc .75 2.00
32 Luc Longley .50 1.25
33 Pete Myers .40 1.00
34 Will Perdue .40 1.00
35 Scottie Pippen 1.50 4.00
36 Bill Wennington .40 1.00
37 Terrell Brandon .40 1.00
38 Michael Cage .40 1.00
39 Brad Daugherty .50 1.25
40 Tyrone Hill .40 1.00
41 Chris Mills .50 1.25
42 Mark Price .60 1.50
43 Gerald Wilkins .50 1.25
44 John Williams .40 1.00
45 Greg Anderson .40 1.00
46 Joe Dumars .60 1.50
47 Allan Houston .60 1.50
48 Lindsey Hunter .40 1.00
49 Eric Leckner .40 1.00
50 Mark Macon .40 1.00
51 Terry Mills .40 1.00
52 Mark West .40 1.00
53 Antonio Davis .50 1.25
54 Dale Davis .40 1.00
55 Mark Jackson .50 1.25
56 Derrick McKey .40 1.00
57 Reggie Miller 1.25 3.00
58 Byron Scott .50 1.25
59 Rik Smits .50 1.25
60 Haywoode Workman .40 1.00
61 Vernell Bimbo Coles .40 1.00
62 Matt Geiger .40 1.00
63 Grant Long .40 1.00
64 Harold Miner .40 1.00
65 Glen Rice .60 1.50
66 John Salley .40 1.00
67 Rony Seikaly .40 1.00
68 Steve Smith .50 1.25
69 Vin Baker .60 1.50
70 Jon Barry .40 1.00
71 Anthony Cook .40 1.00
72 Todd Day .40 1.00
73 Brad Lohaus .40 1.00
74 Lee Mayberry .40 1.00
75 Eric Murdock .40 1.00
76 Ed Pinckney .40 1.00
77 Kenny Anderson .50 1.25
78 Benoit Benjamin .40 1.00
79 P.J. Brown .40 1.00
80 Derrick Coleman .60 1.50
81 Kevin Edwards .40 1.00
82 Armon Gilliam .40 1.00
83 Chris Morris .40 1.00
84 Rex Walters .40 1.00
85 Greg Anthony .40 1.00
86 Hubert Davis .40 1.00
87 Patrick Ewing 1.00 2.50
88 Derek Harper .50 1.25
89 Anthony Mason .50 1.25
90 Charles Oakley .60 1.50
91 Charles Smith .40 1.00
92 John Starks .60 1.50
93 Nick Anderson .60 1.50
94 Anthony Avent .40 1.00
95 Horace Grant .60 1.50
96 Anfernee Hardaway 1.25 3.00
97 Shaquille O'Neal 2.50 6.00
98 Donald Royal .40 1.00
99 Dennis Scott .50 1.25
100 Jeff Turner .40 1.00
101 Dana Barros .40 1.00
102 Shawn Bradley .40 1.00
103 Johnny Dawkins .40 1.00
104 Jeff Malone .40 1.00
105 Tim Perry .40 1.00
106 Clarence Weatherspoon .40 1.00
107 Scott Williams .40 1.00
108 Orlando Woolridge .40 1.00
109 Rex Chapman .40 1.00
110 Calbert Cheaney .50 1.25
111 Kevin Duckworth .40 1.00
112 Tom Gugliotta .40 1.00
113 Don MacLean .40 1.00
114 Gheorghe Muresan .40 1.00
115 Brent Price .40 1.00
116 Scott Skiles .40 1.00
117 Tony Campbell .40 1.00
118 Lucious Harris .40 1.00
119 Donald Hodge .40 1.00
120 Jim Jackson .50 1.25
121 Popeye Jones .40 1.00
122 Jamal Mashburn .60 1.50
123 Sean Rooks .40 1.00
124 Doug Smith .40 1.00
125 Mahmoud Abdul-Rauf .40 1.00
126 LaPhonso Ellis .40 1.00
127 Dikembe Mutombo 1.00 2.50
128 Robert Pack .50 1.25
129 Rodney Rogers .40 1.00
130 Bryant Stith .40 1.00
131 Brian Williams .40 1.00
132 Reggie Williams .40 1.00
133 Victor Alexander .40 1.00
134 Chris Gatling .40 1.00
135 Tim Hardaway .75 2.00
136 Keith Jennings .40 1.00
137 Chris Mullin .75 2.00
138 Billy Owens .40 1.00
139 Latrell Sprewell .75 2.00
140 Chris Webber 1.25 3.00
141 Sam Cassell .60 1.50
142 Mario Elie .40 1.00
143 Carl Herrera .40 1.00
144 Robert Horry .60 1.50
145 Vernon Maxwell .40 1.00
146 Hakeem Olajuwon 1.25 3.00
147 Kenny Smith .50 1.25
148 Otis Thorpe .40 1.00
149 Terry Dehere .40 1.00
150 Harold Ellis .40 1.00
151 Gary Grant .40 1.00
152 Ron Harper .50 1.25
153 Pooh Richardson .40 1.00
154 Malik Sealy .40 1.00
155 Elmore Spencer .40 1.00
156 Loy Vaught .40 1.00
157 Elden Campbell .40 1.00
158 Doug Christie .50 1.25
159 Vlade Divac .60 1.50
160 Anthony Peeler .40 1.00
161 Tony Smith .40 1.00
162 Sedale Threatt .40 1.00
163 Nick Van Exel .60 1.50
164 James Worthy .75 2.00
165 Thurl Bailey .40 1.00
166 Mike Brown .40 1.00
167 Stacey King .40 1.00
168 Christian Laettner .50 1.25
169 Isaiah Rider .60 1.50
170 Chris Smith .40 1.00
171 Doug West .40 1.00
172 Micheal Williams .40 1.00
173 Danny Ainge .60 1.50
174 Charles Barkley 1.50 4.00
175 Cedric Ceballos .50 1.25
176 A.C. Green .50 1.25
177 Frank Johnson .40 1.00
178 Kevin Johnson .60 1.50
179 Dan Majerle .60 1.50
180 Oliver Miller .50 1.25
181 Mark Bryant .40 1.00
182 Clyde Drexler 1.00 2.50
183 Harvey Grant .40 1.00
184 Jerome Kersey .40 1.00
185 Terry Porter .50 1.25
186 Clifford Robinson .50 1.25
187 Rod Strickland .40 1.00
188 Buck Williams .40 1.00
189 Randy Brown .40 1.00
190 Olden Polynice .40 1.00
191 Mitch Richmond .75 2.00
192 Lionel Simmons .40 1.00
193 Andre Spencer .40 1.00
194 Wayman Tisdale .40 1.00
195 Spud Webb .50 1.25
196 Walt Williams .40 1.00
197 Willie Anderson .40 1.00
198 Vinny Del Negro .40 1.00
199 Sean Elliott .50 1.25
200 Dale Ellis .40 1.00
201 Avery Johnson .50 1.25
202 Chuck Person .50 1.25
203 David Robinson 1.25 3.00
204 Dennis Rodman 1.50 4.00
205 Kendall Gill .40 1.00
206 Ervin Johnson .40 1.00
207 Shawn Kemp 1.00 2.50
208 Sarunas Marciulionis .40 1.00
209 Nate McMillan .50 1.25
210 Gary Payton 1.00 2.50
211 Sam Perkins .40 1.00
212 Detlef Schrempf .60 1.50
213 David Benoit .40 1.00
214 Tyrone Corbin .40 1.00
215 Jeff Hornacek .50 1.25
216 Jay Humphries .50 1.25
217 Karl Malone 1.25 3.00
218 Felton Spencer .40 1.00
219 John Stockton 1.25 3.00
220 Luther Wright .40 1.00
A Chris Webber ART 1.25 3.00
B Anfernee Hardaway ART 1.25 3.00
C Vin Baker ART .60 1.50
D Jamal Mashburn ART .60 1.50
E Isaiah Rider ART .60 1.50
F Dino Radja ART .50 1.25
G Nick Van Exel ART .60 1.50
H Toni Kukoc ART .75 2.00
I Lindsey Hunter ART .40 1.00
J Shawn Bradley ART .40 1.00
XX Panini Album .40 1.00

1995-96 Panini Stickers

COMPLETE SET (288) 15.00 40.00
1 Dee Brown .20 .50
2 Sherman Douglas .15 .40
3 Pervis Ellison .15 .40
4 Rick Fox .15 .40
5 Greg Minor .15 .40
6 Celtics Team Logo .15 .40
7 Eric Montross .15 .40
8 Dino Radja .15 .40
9 David Wesley .15 .40
10 Rex Chapman .15 .40
11 Bimbo Coles .15 .40
12 Kevin Gamble .15 .40
13 Matt Geiger .15 .40
14 Billy Owens .15 .40
15 Heat Team Logo .15 .40
16 Khalid Reeves .15 .40
17 Glen Rice .25 .60
18 Kevin Willis .15 .40
19 Kenny Anderson .20 .50
20 P.J. Brown .15 .40
21 Chris Childs .15 .40
22 Derrick Coleman .20 .50
23 Kevin Edwards .15 .40
24 Nets Team Logo .15 .40
25 Armon Gilliam .15 .40
26 Chris Morris .15 .40
27 Jayson Williams .15 .40
28 Anthony Bonner .15 .40
29 Hubert Davis .15 .40
30 Patrick Ewing .40 1.00
31 Derek Harper .20 .50
32 Anthony Mason .15 .40
33 Knicks Team Logo .15 .40
34 Charles Oakley .20 .50
35 Charles Smith .15 .40
36 John Starks .25 .60
37 Nick Anderson .15 .40
38 Horace Grant .20 .50
39 Anfernee Hardaway .60 1.50
40 Shaquille O'Neal 1.00 2.50
41 Donald Royal .15 .40
42 Magic Team Logo .15 .40
43 Dennis Scott .15 .40
44 Brian Shaw .15 .40
45 Jeff Turner .15 .40
46 Derrick Alston .15 .40
47 Dana Barros .20 .50
48 Shawn Bradley .15 .40
49 Willie Burton .20 .50
50 Jeff Malone .15 .40
51 76ers Team Logo .15 .40
52 Clarence Weatherspoon .15 .40
53 Scott Williams .15 .40
54 Sharone Wright .15 .40
55 Mitchell Butler .15 .40
56 Calbert Cheaney .15 .40
57 Juwan Howard .25 .60
58 Don MacLean .15 .40
59 Gheorghe Muresan .15 .40
60 Bullets Team Logo .15 .40
61 Doug Overton .15 .40
62 Scott Skiles .15 .40
63 Chris Webber .30 .75
64 Stacey Augmon .20 .50
65 Mookie Blaylock .25 .60
66 Craig Ehlo .15 .40
67 Andrew Lang .15 .40
68 Grant Long .15 .40
69 Hawks Team Logo .15 .40
70 Ken Norman .15 .40
71 Steve Smith .20 .50
72 Spud Webb .25 .60
73 Tony Bennett .15 .40
74 Muggsy Bogues .20 .50
75 Scott Burrell .15 .40
76 Dell Curry .25 .60
77 Kendall Gill .15 .40
78 Hornets Team Logo .15 .40
79 Larry Johnson .30 .75
80 Alonzo Mourning .40 1.00
81 Robert Parish .30 .75
82 Ron Harper .20 .50
83 Michael Jordan 8.00 20.00
84 Steve Kerr .25 .60
85 Toni Kukoc .30 .75
86 Luc Longley .20 .50
87 Bulls Team Logo .15 .40
88 Will Perdue .20 .50
89 Scottie Pippen .60 1.50
90 Bill Wennington .15 .40
91 Terrell Brandon .20 .50
92 Michael Cage .15 .40
93 Danny Ferry .15 .40
94 Tyrone Hill .15 .40
95 Chris Mills .15 .40
96 Cavaliers Team Logo .15 .40
97 Bobby Phills .20 .50
98 Mark Price .25 .60
99 John Williams .15 .40
100 Bill Curley .15 .40
101 Joe Dumars .25 .60
102 Grant Hill .40 1.00
103 Allan Houston .20 .50
104 Lindsey Hunter .15 .40
105 Pistons Team Logo .15 .40
106 Mark Macon .15 .40
107 Terry Mills .15 .40
108 Mark West .15 .40
109 Antonio Davis .15 .40
110 Dale Davis .15 .40
111 Duane Ferrell .15 .40
112 Mark Jackson .20 .50
113 Derrick McKey .15 .40
114 Pacers Team Logo .15 .40
115 Reggie Miller .50 1.25
116 Rik Smits .20 .50
117 Haywoode Workman .15 .40
118 Vin Baker .20 .50
119 Jon Barry .15 .40
120 Marty Conlon .15 .40
121 Todd Day .15 .40
122 Lee Mayberry .15 .40
123 Bucks Team Logo .15 .40
124 Eric Mobley .15 .40
125 Eric Murdock .15 .40
126 Glenn Robinson .25 .60
127 Willie Anderson .15 .40
128 B.J. Armstrong .25 .60
129 Acie Earl .15 .40
130 Jerome Kersey .15 .40
131 Tony Massenburg .15 .40
132 Raptors Team Logo .15 .40
133 Oliver Miller .15 .40
134 John Salley .15 .40
135 B.J. Tyler .15 .40
136 Larry Johnson POW .30 .75
137 Shawn Kemp POW .40 1.00
138 Karl Malone POW .50 1.25
139 Jamal Mashburn POW .25 .60
140 Alonzo Mourning POW .40 1.00
141 Hakeem Olajuwon POW .50 1.25
142 Shaquille O'Neal POW 1.00 2.50
143 David Robinson POW .50 1.25
144 Chris Webber POW .30 .75
145 Lucious Harris .15 .40
146 Jim Jackson .20 .50
147 Popeye Jones .15 .40
148 Jason Kidd .40 1.00
149 Jamal Mashburn .25 .60
150 Mavericks Team Logo .15 .40
151 George McCloud .15 .40
152 Roy Tarpley .20 .50
153 Lorenzo Williams .15 .40
154 Mahmoud Abdul-Rauf .20 .50
155 LaPhonso Ellis .20 .50
156 Dikembe Mutombo .40 1.00
157 Robert Pack .15 .40
158 Jalen Rose .30 .75
159 Nuggets Team Logo .15 .40
160 Bryant Stith .15 .40
161 Brian Williams .15 .40
162 Reggie Williams .15 .40
163 Chucky Brown .15 .40
164 Sam Cassell .25 .60
165 Clyde Drexler .40 1.00
166 Mario Elie .15 .40
167 Carl Herrera .15 .40
168 Rockets Team Logo .15 .40
169 Robert Horry .25 .60
170 Hakeem Olajuwon .50 1.25
171 Kenny Smith .20 .50
172 Tom Gugliotta .15 .40
173 Christian Laettner .20 .50
174 Darrick Martin .15 .40
175 Isaiah Rider .25 .60
176 Sean Rooks .15 .40
177 Timberwolves Team Logo .15 .40
178 Chris Smith .15 .40
179 Doug West .15 .40
180 Micheal Williams .15 .40
181 Vinny Del Negro .15 .40
182 Sean Elliott .20 .50
183 Avery Johnson .20 .50
184 Chuck Person .20 .50
185 J.R. Reid .15 .40
186 Spurs Team Logo .15 .40
187 Doc Rivers .20 .50
188 David Robinson .50 1.25
189 Dennis Rodman .50 1.25
190 David Benoit .15 .40
191 Jeff Hornacek .20 .50
192 Adam Keefe .15 .40
193 Karl Malone .50 1.25
194 Bryon Russell .15 .40
195 Jazz Team Logo .15 .40
196 Felton Spencer .15 .40
197 John Stockton .50 1.25
198 Jamie Watson .15 .40
199 Greg Anthony .15 .40
200 Benoit Benjamin .15 .40
201 Blue Edwards .15 .40
202 Doug Edwards .15 .40
203 Kenny Gattison .15 .40
204 Grizzlies Team Logo .15 .40
205 Antonio Harvey .15 .40
206 Byron Scott .25 .60
207 Larry Stewart .15 .40
208 Chris Gatling .15 .40
209 Tim Hardaway .30 .75
210 Donyell Marshall .15 .40
211 Chris Mullin .25 .60
212 Carlos Rogers .15 .40
213 Warriors Team Logo .15 .40
214 Clifford Rozier .15 .40
215 Rony Seikaly .15 .40
216 Latrell Sprewell .25 .60
217 Terry Dehere .15 .40
218 Harold Ellis .15 .40
219 Lamond Murray .15 .40
220 Bo Outlaw .15 .40
221 Pooh Richardson .15 .40
222 Clippers Team Logo .15 .40
223 Rodney Rogers .20 .50
224 Malik Sealy .15 .40
225 Loy Vaught .15 .40
226 Sam Bowie .15 .40
227 Elden Campbell .15 .40
228 Cedric Ceballos .20 .50
229 Vlade Divac .25 .60
230 Eddie Jones .25 .60
231 Lakers Team Logo .15 .40
232 Anthony Peeler .15 .40
233 Sedale Threatt .15 .40
234 Nick Van Exel .25 .60
235 Charles Barkley .60 1.50
236 A.C. Green .20 .50
237 Kevin Johnson .25 .60
238 Dan Majerle .25 .60
239 Danny Manning .20 .50
240 Suns Team Logo .15 .40
241 Elliot Perry .15 .40
242 Wesley Person .15 .40
243 Wayman Tisdale .15 .40
244 Chris Dudley .15 .40
245 Harvey Grant .15 .40
246 Aaron McKie .15 .40
247 Terry Porter .15 .40
248 Clifford Robinson .25 .60
249 Trail Blazers Team Logo .15 .40
250 Rod Strickland .15 .40
251 Otis Thorpe .20 .50
252 Buck Williams .15 .40
253 Randy Brown .25 .60
254 Brian Grant .20 .50
255 Bobby Hurley .15 .40
256 Olden Polynice .15 .40
257 Mitch Richmond .30 .75

258 Kings Team Logo .15 .40
259 Lionel Simmons .15 .40
260 Michael Smith .15 .40
261 Walt Williams .15 .40
262 Vincent Askew .15 .40
263 Hersey Hawkins .20 .50
264 Shawn Kemp .40 1.00
265 Sarunas Marciulionis .25 .60
266 Nate McMillan .15 .40
267 Supersonics Team Logo .15 .40
268 Gary Payton .40 1.00
269 Sam Perkins .15 .40
270 Detlef Schrempf .25 .60
271 Chris Gatling LL .15 .40
272 Popeye Jones LL .15 .40
273 Steve Kerr LL .25 .60
274 Karl Malone LL .50 1.25
275 Dikembe Mutombo LL .40 1.00
276 Shaquille O'Neal LL 1.00 2.50
277 Scottie Pippen LL .60 1.50
278 Dennis Rodman LL .50 1.25
279 John Stockton LL .50 1.25
280 Spud Webb LL .25 .60
281 Brian Grant ROO .25 .60
282 Grant Hill ROO .40 1.00
283 Juwan Howard ROO .25 .60
284 Eddie Jones ROO .25 .60
285 Jason Kidd ROO .40 1.00
286 Eric Montross ROO .15 .40
287 Wesley Person ROO .15 .40
288 Glenn Robinson ROO .25 .60
XX Panini Album .75 2.00

1996-97 Panini Stickers

COMPLETE SET (288) 15.00 40.00
1 NBA Logo .15 .40
2 Eastern Conference Logo .15 .40
3 Western Conference Logo .15 .40
4 Dana Barros .15 .40
5 Dee Brown .15 .40
6 Todd Day .15 .40
7 Rick Fox .15 .40
8 Eric Montross .15 .40
9 Dino Radja .15 .40
10 Boston Celtics Logo .15 .40
11 David Wesley .15 .40
12 Eric Williams .15 .40
13 Keith Askins .15 .40
14 Rex Chapman .15 .40
15 Sasha Danilovic .15 .40
16 Chris Gatling .15 .40
17 Tim Hardaway .30 .75
18 Alonzo Mourning .40 1.00
19 Miami Heat Logo .15 .40
20 Kurt Thomas .15 .40
21 Walt Williams .15 .40
22 Shawn Bradley .15 .40
23 P.J. Brown .15 .40
24 Vern Fleming .15 .40
25 Kendall Gill .25 .60
26 Armon Gilliam .15 .40
27 New Jersey Nets Logo .15 .40
28 Ed O'Bannon .15 .40
29 Khalid Reeves .15 .40
30 Jayson Williams .15 .40
31 Willie Anderson .15 .40
32 Chris Childs .15 .40
33 Hubert Davis .15 .40
34 Patrick Ewing .40 1.00
35 Derek Harper .20 .50
36 New York Knicks Logo .15 .40
37 Anthony Mason .20 .50
38 Charles Oakley .25 .60
39 John Starks .25 .60
40 Nick Anderson .15 .40
41 Horace Grant .25 .60
42 Anfernee Hardaway .60 1.50
43 Jon Koncak .15 .40
44 Shaquille O'Neal 1.00 2.50
45 Orlando Magic Logo .15 .40
46 Donald Royal .15 .40
47 Dennis Scott .20 .50
48 Brian Shaw .15 .40
49 Derrick Coleman .20 .50
50 Richard Dumas .15 .40
51 Tony Massenburg .15 .40
52 Vernon Maxwell .15 .40
53 Ed Pinckney .15 .40
54 Trevor Ruffin .15 .40
55 Philadelphia 76ers Logo .15 .40
56 Jerry Stackhouse .30 .75
57 Clarence Weatherspoon .15 .40
58 Calbert Cheaney .15 .40
59 Juwan Howard .25 .60
60 Tim Legler .15 .40
61 Gheorghe Muresan .15 .40
62 Robert Pack .15 .40
63 Washington Bullets Logo .15 .40
64 Brent Price .15 .40
65 Rasheed Wallace .30 .75
66 Chris Webber .30 .75
67 Stacey Augmon .20 .50
68 Mookie Blaylock .25 .60
69 Craig Ehlo .15 .40
70 Alan Henderson .15 .40
71 Christian Laettner .25 .60
72 Atlanta Hawks Logo .15 .40
73 Grant Long .15 .40
74 Sean Rooks .15 .40
75 Steve Smith .20 .50
76 Kenny Anderson .20 .50
77 Scott Burrell .15 .40
78 Dell Curry .25 .60
79 Matt Geiger .15 .40
80 Darrin Hancock .15 .40
81 Larry Johnson .30 .75
82 Glen Rice .25 .60
83 Charlotte Hornets Logo .15 .40
84 George Zidek .15 .40
85 Jud Buechler .15 .40
86 Ron Harper .20 .50
87 Steve Kerr .20 .50
88 Toni Kukoc .25 .60
89 Luc Longley .20 .50
90 Chicago Bulls Logo .15 .40
91 Scottie Pippen .60 1.50
92 Dennis Rodman .60 1.50
93 Bill Wennington .15 .40
94 Terrell Brandon .20 .50
95 Michael Cage .15 .40
96 Danny Ferry .15 .40
97 Tyrone Hill .15 .40
98 Dan Majerle .25 .60
99 Chris Mills .15 .40
100 Bobby Phills .15 .40
101 Cleveland Cavaliers Logo .15 .40
102 Bob Sura .15 .40
103 Joe Dumars .30 .75
104 Grant Hill .40 1.00
105 Allan Houston .25 .60
106 Lindsey Hunter .15 .40
107 Terry Mills .15 .40
108 Detroit Pistons Logo .15 .40
109 Theo Ratliff .15 .40
110 Don Reid .15 .40
111 Otis Thorpe .20 .50
112 Antonio Davis .15 .40
113 Dale Davis .15 .40
114 Mark Jackson .20 .50
115 Derrick McKey .15 .40
116 Reggie Miller .50 1.25
117 Ricky Pierce .20 .50
118 Indiana Pacers Logo .15 .40
119 Rik Smits .20 .50
120 Haywoode Workman .15 .40
121 Vin Baker .20 .50
122 Benoit Benjamin .15 .40
123 Terry Cummings .20 .50
124 Sherman Douglas .15 .40
125 Milwaukee Bucks Logo .15 .40
126 Lee Mayberry .15 .40
127 Johnny Newman .15 .40
128 Shawn Respert .15 .40
129 Glenn Robinson .25 .60
130 Doug Christie .15 .40
131 Jimmy King .15 .40
132 Oliver Miller .15 .40
133 Tracy Murray .15 .40
134 Alvin Robertson .15 .40
135 Toronto Raptors Logo .15 .40
136 Carlos Rogers .15 .40
137 Damon Stoudamire .25 .60
138 Sharone Wright .15 .40
139 Mookie Blaylock FG .25 .60
140 Terrell Brandon FG .20 .50
141 Anfernee Hardaway FG .60 1.50
142 Tim Hardaway FG .30 .75
143 Jason Kidd FG .40 1.00
144 Gary Payton FG .40 1.00
145 John Stockton FG .50 1.25
146 Nick Van Exel FG .25 .60
147 Tony Dumas .15 .40
148 Lucious Harris .15 .40
149 Jim Jackson .15 .40
150 Popeye Jones .15 .40
151 Jason Kidd .40 1.00
152 Dallas Mavericks Logo .15 .40
153 Jamal Mashburn .25 .60
154 George McCloud .15 .40
155 Cherokee Parks .15 .40
156 Mahmoud Abdul-Rauf .20 .50
157 Dale Ellis .20 .50
158 LaPhonso Ellis .15 .40
159 Don MacLean .15 .40
160 Antonio McDyess .25 .60
161 Dikembe Mutombo .40 1.00
162 Denver Nuggets Logo .15 .40
163 Jalen Rose .20 .50
164 Bryant Stith .15 .40
165 Chucky Brown .15 .40
166 Mark Bryant .15 .40
167 Sam Cassell .20 .50
168 Pete Chilcutt .15 .40
169 Houston Rockets Logo .15 .40
170 Clyde Drexler .40 1.00
171 Mario Elie .15 .40
172 Robert Horry .25 .60
173 Hakeem Olajuwon .50 1.25
174 Kevin Garnett .75 2.00
175 Tom Gugliotta .15 .40
176 Andrew Lang .15 .40
177 Darrick Martin .15 .40
178 Sam Mitchell .15 .40
179 Minnesota Timberwolves Logo .15 .40
180 Terry Porter .15 .40
181 Isaiah Rider .20 .50
182 Doug West .15 .40
183 Cory Alexander .15 .40
184 Vinny Del Negro .15 .40
185 Sean Elliott .25 .60
186 Avery Johnson .25 .60
187 Will Perdue .15 .40
188 San Antonio Spurs Logo .15 .40
189 Chuck Person .20 .50
190 David Robinson .50 1.25
191 Charles Smith .15 .40
192 David Benoit .15 .40
193 Antoine Carr .15 .40
194 Jeff Hornacek .20 .50
195 Adam Keefe .15 .40
196 Karl Malone .50 1.25
197 Chris Morris .15 .40
198 Utah Jazz Logo .15 .40
199 Felton Spencer .15 .40
200 John Stockton .50 1.25
201 Greg Anthony .15 .40
202 Anthony Avent .15 .40
203 Blue Edwards .15 .40
204 Chris King .15 .40
205 Lawrence Moten .15 .40
206 Vancouver Grizzlies Logo .15 .40
207 Eric Murdock .15 .40
208 Bryant Reeves .20 .50
209 Gerald Wilkins .15 .40
210 B.J. Armstrong .20 .50
211 Jerome Kersey .15 .40
212 Donyell Marshall .15 .40
213 Chris Mullin .30 .75
214 Golden State Warriors Logo .15 .40
215 Rony Seikaly .20 .50
216 Joe Smith .20 .50
217 Latrell Sprewell .25 .60
218 Kevin Willis .20 .50
219 Brent Barry .20 .50
220 Terry Dehere .15 .40
221 Lamond Murray .15 .40
222 Eric Piatkowski .15 .40
223 Pooh Richardson .15 .40
224 Los Angeles Clippers Logo .15 .40
225 Rodney Rogers .15 .40
226 Malik Sealy .15 .40
227 Loy Vaught .15 .40
228 Elden Campbell .15 .40
229 Cedric Ceballos .20 .50
230 Vlade Divac .25 .60
231 Eddie Jones .25 .60
232 George Lynch .15 .40
233 Los Angeles Lakers Logo .15 .40
234 Anthony Peeler .15 .40
235 Sedale Threatt .15 .40
236 Nick Van Exel .25 .60
237 Charles Barkley .60 1.50
238 Michael Finley .25 .60
239 A.C. Green .20 .50
240 Kevin Johnson .25 .60
241 Danny Manning .20 .50
242 Elliot Perry .15 .40
243 Phoenix Suns Logo .15 .40
244 Wayman Tisdale .20 .50
245 Wesley Person .15 .40
246 Chris Dudley .15 .40
247 Harvey Grant .15 .40
248 Aaron McKie .20 .50
249 Clifford Robinson .25 .60
250 Portland Trail Blazers Logo .15 .40
251 James Robinson .15 .40
252 Arvydas Sabonis .25 .60
253 Rod Strickland .25 .60
254 Buck Williams .25 .60
255 Tyus Edney .15 .40
256 Kevin Gamble .15 .40
257 Brian Grant .20 .50
258 Sarunas Marciulionis .15 .40
259 Sacramento Kings Logo .15 .40
260 Billy Owens .15 .40
261 Olden Polynice .15 .40
262 Mitch Richmond .30 .75
263 Michael Smith .15 .40
264 Vincent Askew .15 .40
265 Hersey Hawkins .15 .40
266 Ervin Johnson .15 .40
267 Shawn Kemp .40 1.00
268 Nate McMillan .15 .40
269 Seattle Supersonics Logo .15 .40
270 Gary Payton .40 1.00
271 Sam Perkins .20 .50
272 Detlef Schrempf .20 .50
273 Mahmoud Abdul-Rauf LL .20 .50
274 Tim Legler LL .15 .40
275 Anthony Mason LL .20 .50
276 Gheorghe Muresan LL .15 .40
277 Dikembe Mutombo LL .40 1.00
278 Gary Payton LL .40 1.00
279 Dennis Rodman LL .60 1.50
280 John Stockton LL .50 1.25
281 Michael Finley .25 .60
282 Kevin Garnett .75 2.00
283 Antonio McDyess .25 .60
284 Bryant Reeves .15 .40
285 Arvydas Sabonis .25 .60
286 Joe Smith .20 .50
287 Jerry Stackhouse .30 .75
288 Damon Stoudamire .25 .60

1998-99 Panini Stickers

COMPLETE SET (156) 250.00 500.00
1 NBA Logo 1.25 3.00
2 Dana Barros 1.25 3.00
3 Ron Mercer 1.50 4.00
4 Kenny Anderson 1.50 4.00
5 Antoine Walker 2.00 5.00
6 Walter McCarty 1.25 3.00
7 Tim Hardaway 2.50 6.00
8 Alonzo Mourning 4.00 10.00
9 Jamal Mashburn 2.00 5.00
10 Dan Majerle 2.00 5.00
11 P.J. Brown 1.25 3.00
12 Jayson Williams 1.25 3.00
13 Sam Cassell 1.50 4.00
14 Kendall Gill 1.50 4.00
15 Keith Van Horn 2.00 5.00
16 Kerry Kittles 1.50 4.00
17 Patrick Ewing 4.00 10.00
18 Latrell Sprewell 2.50 6.00
19 Larry Johnson 3.00 8.00
20 Marcus Camby 1.50 4.00
21 Allan Houston 2.00 5.00
22 Anfernee Hardaway 4.00 10.00
23 Nick Anderson 1.25 3.00
24 Derek Strong 1.25 3.00
25 Bo Outlaw 1.25 3.00
26 Horace Grant 2.00 5.00
27 Theo Ratliff 1.50 4.00
28 Allen Iverson 5.00 12.00
29 Tim Thomas 1.50 4.00
31 Scott Williams 1.25 3.00
32 Juwan Howard 1.50 4.00
33 Mitch Richmond 2.50 6.00
34 Tracy Murray 1.25 3.00
35 Rod Strickland 1.50 4.00
36 Calbert Cheaney 1.25 3.00
37 Dikembe Mutombo 3.00 8.00
38 Mookie Blaylock 1.50 4.00
39 Tyrone Corbin 1.25 3.00
40 Steve Smith 1.50 4.00
41 Alan Henderson 1.25 3.00
42 Anthony Mason 1.50 4.00
43 Derrick Coleman 1.50 4.00
44 David Wesley 1.25 3.00
45 Glen Rice 2.00 5.00
46 Bobby Phills 1.25 3.00
47 Ron Harper 2.00 5.00
48 Toni Kukoc 2.00 5.00
49 Mark Bryant 1.25 3.00
50 Brent Barry 1.50 4.00
51 Andrew Lang 1.25 3.00
52 Shawn Kemp 4.00 10.00
53 Wesley Person 1.25 3.00
54 Derek Anderson 1.50 4.00
55 Brevin Knight 1.25 3.00
56 Zydrunas Ilgauskas 2.00 5.00
57 Grant Hill 4.00 10.00
58 Jerry Stackhouse 2.00 5.00
59 Joe Dumars 2.00 5.00
60 Christian Laettner 1.50 4.00
61 Bison Dele 1.25 3.00
62 Rik Smits 1.50 4.00
63 Jalen Rose 1.50 4.00
64 Mark Jackson 1.50 4.00
65 Reggie Miller 4.00 10.00
66 Chris Mullin 2.50 6.00
67 Tyrone Hill 1.25 3.00
68 Glenn Robinson 2.00 5.00
69 Armon Gilliam 1.25 3.00
70 Terrell Brandon 1.50 4.00
71 Ray Allen 4.00 10.00
72 Reggie Slater 1.25 3.00
73 John Wallace 1.25 3.00
74 Doug Christie 1.50 4.00
75 Charles Oakley 1.50 4.00
76 Tracy McGrady 4.00 10.00
77 Shawn Bradley 1.25 3.00
78 Michael Finley 2.00 5.00
79 A.C. Green 1.50 4.00
80 Chris Anstey 1.25 3.00
81 Hot Rod Williams 1.25 3.00
82 Nick Van Exel 2.00 5.00
83 Bryant Stith 1.25 3.00
84 Eric Williams 1.25 3.00
85 Chauncey Billups 2.50 6.00
86 Antonio McDyess 1.50 4.00
87 Charles Barkley 4.00 10.00
88 Scottie Pippen 4.00 10.00
89 Hakeem Olajuwon 4.00 10.00
90 Matt Maloney 1.25 3.00
91 Rodrick Rhodes 1.25 3.00
92 Kevin Garnett 5.00 12.00
93 Sam Mitchell 1.25 3.00
94 Malik Sealy 1.25 3.00
95 Stephon Marbury 2.50 6.00
96 Anthony Peeler 1.25 3.00
97 David Robinson 4.00 10.00
98 Sean Elliott 2.00 5.00
99 Tim Duncan 5.00 12.00
100 Avery Johnson 1.50 4.00
101 Steve Kerr 1.50 4.00
102 Karl Malone 4.00 10.00
103 John Stockton 4.00 10.00
104 Howard Eisley 1.25 3.00
105 Bryon Russell 1.25 3.00
106 Jeff Hornacek 1.50 4.00
107 Bryant Reeves 1.25 3.00
108 Shareef Abdur-Rahim 2.00 5.00
109 Sam Mack 1.25 3.00
110 Tony Massenburg 1.25 3.00
111 Michael Smith 1.25 3.00
112 John Starks 2.00 5.00
113 Terry Cummings 1.50 4.00
114 Erick Dampier 1.25 3.00
115 Chris Mills 1.25 3.00
116 Donyell Marshall 1.25 3.00
117 Rodney Rogers 1.25 3.00
118 Darrick Martin 1.25 3.00
119 Lorenzen Wright 1.25 3.00
120 Lamond Murray 1.25 3.00
121 Pooh Richardson 1.25 3.00
122 Shaquille O'Neal 8.00 20.00
123 Robert Horry 1.50 4.00
124 Eddie Jones 2.00 5.00
125 Kobe Bryant 15.00 40.00
126 Rick Fox 1.25 3.00
127 Jason Kidd 4.00 10.00
128 Rex Chapman 1.50 4.00
129 Clifford Robinson 1.25 3.00
130 Tom Gugliotta 1.25 3.00
131 Danny Manning 1.50 4.00
132 Isaiah Rider 1.50 4.00
133 Damon Stoudamire 2.00 5.00
134 Stacey Augmon 1.50 4.00
135 Rasheed Wallace 2.50 6.00
136 Arvydas Sabonis 2.00 5.00
137 Chris Webber 4.00 10.00
138 Terry Dehere 1.25 3.00
139 Tariq Abdul-Wahad 1.25 3.00
140 Vlade Divac 2.00 5.00
141 Corliss Williamson 1.25 3.00
142 Vin Baker 1.50 4.00
143 Hersey Hawkins 1.25 3.00
144 Dale Ellis 1.25 3.00
145 Detlef Schrempf 2.00 5.00
146 Gary Payton 3.00 8.00
147 Tim Duncan 5.00 12.00
148 Rod Strickland 1.50 4.00
149 Dikembe Mutombo 3.00 8.00
150 Avery Johnson 1.50 4.00
151 Shaquille O'Neal 8.00 20.00
152 Michael Olowokandi 2.50 6.00
153 Mike Bibby 4.00 10.00
154 Raef LaFrentz 2.50 6.00
155 Robert Traylor 2.00 5.00
156 Vince Carter 10.00 25.00

1999-00 Panini Stickers

COMPLETE SET (210) 400.00 800.00
1 NBA Logo 1.50 4.00
2 Boston Celtics Logo 1.50 4.00
3 Kenny Anderson 2.00 5.00
4 Dana Barros 1.50 4.00
5 Calbert Cheaney 1.50 4.00
6 Paul Pierce 5.00 12.00
7 Vitaly Potapenko 1.50 4.00
8 Antoine Walker 2.50 6.00
9 P.J. Brown 1.50 4.00
10 Tim Hardaway 3.00 8.00
11 Miami Heat Logo 1.50 4.00
12 Voshon Lenard 1.50 4.00
13 Dan Majerle 2.50 6.00
14 Jamal Mashburn 2.00 5.00
15 Alonzo Mourning 5.00 12.00
16 New Jersey Nets Logo 1.50 4.00
17 Scott Burrell 1.50 4.00
18 Kendall Gill 2.50 6.00
19 Kerry Kittles 2.00 5.00
20 Stephon Marbury 3.00 8.00
21 Keith Van Horn 2.00 5.00
22 Jayson Williams 1.50 4.00
23 Marcus Camby 2.00 5.00
24 Patrick Ewing 5.00 12.00
25 New York Knicks Logo 1.50 4.00
26 Allan Houston 2.00 5.00
27 Larry Johnson 2.50 6.00
28 Latrell Sprewell 3.00 8.00
29 Charlie Ward 1.50 4.00
30 Orlando Magic Logo 1.50 4.00
31 Tariq Abdul-Wahad 1.50 4.00
32 Darrell Armstrong 1.50 4.00
33 Michael Doleac 1.50 4.00
34 Chris Gatling 1.50 4.00
35 Matt Harpring 1.50 4.00
36 Charles Outlaw 1.50 4.00
37 Matt Geiger 1.50 4.00
38 Larry Hughes 2.00 5.00
39 Philadelphia 76ers Logo 1.50 4.00
40 Allen Iverson 6.00 15.00
41 George Lynch 1.50 4.00
42 Billy Owens 1.50 4.00
43 Theo Ratliff 2.00 5.00
44 Washington Wizards Logo 1.50 4.00
45 Isaac Austin 1.50 4.00
46 Juwan Howard 2.00 5.00
47 Mitch Richmond 3.00 8.00
48 Rod Strickland 2.00 5.00
49 Chris Whitney 1.50 4.00
50 Lorenzo Williams 1.50 4.00
51 Bimbo Coles 1.50 4.00
52 LaPhonso Ellis 1.50 4.00
53 Atlanta Hawks Logo 1.50 4.00
54 Alan Henderson 1.50 4.00
55 Jim Jackson 1.50 4.00
56 Dikembe Mutombo 4.00 10.00
57 Isaiah Rider 2.00 5.00
58 Charlotte Hornets Logo 1.50 4.00
59 Elden Campbell 1.50 4.00
60 Derrick Coleman 2.00 5.00
61 Eddie Jones 2.50 6.00
62 Anthony Mason 2.50 6.00
63 Brad Miller 2.00 5.00
64 David Wesley 1.50 4.00
65 B.J. Armstrong 1.50 4.00
66 Randy Brown 1.50 4.00
67 Chicago Bulls Logo 1.50 4.00
68 Kornell David 1.50 4.00
69 Hersey Hawkins 1.50 4.00
70 Toni Kukoc 3.00 8.00
71 Dickey Simpkins 1.50 4.00
72 Cleveland Cavaliers Logo 1.50 4.00
73 Danny Ferry 1.50 4.00
74 Cedric Henderson 1.50 4.00
75 Zydrunas Ilgauskas 2.00 5.00
76 Shawn Kemp 5.00 12.00
77 Brevin Knight 1.50 4.00
78 Wesley Person 1.50 4.00
79 Jud Buechler 1.50 4.00
80 Grant Hill 5.00 12.00
81 Detroit Pistons Logo 1.50 4.00
82 Lindsey Hunter 1.50 4.00
83 Christian Laettner 2.00 5.00
84 Jerry Stackhouse 2.50 6.00
85 Jerome Williams 1.50 4.00
86 Indiana Pacers Logo 1.50 4.00
87 Dale Davis 1.50 4.00
88 Mark Jackson 2.00 5.00
89 Reggie Miller 5.00 12.00
90 Sam Perkins 1.50 4.00
91 Jalen Rose 2.00 5.00
92 Rik Smits 2.00 5.00
93 Ray Allen 5.00 12.00
94 Sam Cassell 2.00 5.00
95 Milwaukee Bucks Logo 1.50 4.00
96 Dale Ellis 1.50 4.00
97 Danny Manning 2.00 5.00
98 Glenn Robinson 2.00 5.00
99 Tim Thomas 2.00 5.00
100 Toronto Raptors Logo 1.50 4.00
101 Vince Carter 6.00 15.00
102 Doug Christie 2.00 5.00
103 Dell Curry 1.50 4.00
104 Antonio Davis 1.50 4.00
105 Tracy McGrady 5.00 12.00
106 Kevin Willis 1.50 4.00
107 Shawn Bradley 1.50 4.00
108 Cedric Ceballos 1.50 4.00
109 Dallas Mavericks Logo 1.50 4.00
110 Michael Finley 2.50 6.00
111 Dirk Nowitzki 8.00 20.00
112 Robert Pack 1.50 4.00
113 Hubert Davis 1.50 4.00
114 Denver Nuggets Logo 1.50 4.00
115 Cory Alexander 1.50 4.00
116 Chauncey Billups 2.50 6.00
117 Raef LaFrentz 2.00 5.00
118 Antonio McDyess 2.00 5.00
119 Ron Mercer 2.00 5.00
120 Nick Van Exel 2.00 5.00
121 Cuttino Mobley 2.00 5.00
122 Hakeem Olajuwon 5.00 12.00
123 Houston Rockets Logo 1.50 4.00
124 Charles Barkley 5.00 12.00
125 Shandon Anderson 1.50 4.00
126 Walt Williams 1.50 4.00
127 Matt Bullard 1.50 4.00
128 Minnesota Timberwolves Logo 1.50 4.00
129 Terrell Brandon 1.50 4.00
130 Kevin Garnett 6.00 15.00
131 Radoslav Nesterovic 2.50 6.00
132 Anthony Peeler 1.50 4.00
133 Malik Sealy 1.50 4.00
134 Joe Smith 2.00 5.00
135 Tim Duncan 6.00 15.00
136 Mario Elie 1.50 4.00
137 San Antonio Spurs Logo 1.50 4.00
138 Terry Porter 1.50 4.00
139 Avery Johnson 2.00 5.00
140 David Robinson 5.00 12.00
141 Malik Rose 1.50 4.00
142 Utah Jazz logo 1.50 4.00
143 Howard Eisley 1.50 4.00
144 Karl Malone 5.00 12.00
145 Greg Ostertag 1.50 4.00
146 Bryon Russell 1.50 4.00
147 Jeff Hornacek 3.00 8.00
148 John Stockton 5.00 12.00
149 Shareef Abdur-Rahim 2.50 6.00
150 Mike Bibby 2.50 6.00
151 Vancouver Grizzlies Logo 1.50 4.00
152 Othella Harrington 1.50 4.00
153 Felipe Lopez 1.50 4.00
154 Bryant Reeves 1.50 4.00
155 Dennis Scott 1.50 4.00
156 Golden State Warriors Logo 1.50 4.00
157 Mookie Blaylock 1.50 4.00
158 Antawn Jamison 2.50 6.00
159 Donyell Marshall 2.00 5.00
160 Chris Mills 1.50 4.00
161 John Starks 2.50 6.00
162 Terry Cummings 2.00 5.00
163 Derek Anderson 1.50 4.00
164 Tyrone Nesby 1.50 4.00
165 Los Angeles Clippers Logo 1.50 4.00
166 Michael Olowokandi 1.50 4.00
167 Eric Piatkowski 1.50 4.00
168 Brian Skinner 1.50 4.00
169 Maurice Taylor 1.50 4.00
170 Los Angeles Lakers Logo 1.50 4.00
171 Kobe Bryant 20.00 50.00
172 Derek Fisher 2.00 5.00
173 Rick Fox 1.50 4.00
174 Robert Horry 2.00 5.00
175 A.C. Green 2.00 5.00
176 Glen Rice 2.50 6.00
177 Tom Gugliotta 2.00 5.00
178 Anfernee Hardaway 5.00 12.00
179 Phoenix Suns Logo 1.50 4.00
180 Jason Kidd 5.00 12.00
181 Luc Longley 2.00 5.00
182 Clifford Robinson 2.00 5.00
183 Rodney Rogers 1.50 4.00
184 Portland Trail Blazers Logo 1.50 4.00
185 Scottie Pippen 5.00 12.00
186 Arvydas Sabonis 2.00 5.00
187 Detlef Schrempf 2.00 5.00
188 Steve Smith 2.00 5.00
189 Damon Stoudamire 2.50 6.00
190 Rasheed Wallace 3.00 8.00
191 Nick Anderson 1.50 4.00
192 Vlade Divac 2.50 6.00
193 Sacramento Kings Logo 1.50 4.00
194 Peja Stojakovic 2.50 6.00
195 Chris Webber 5.00 12.00
196 Jason Williams 4.00 10.00
197 Corliss Williamson 1.50 4.00
198 Seattle Supersonics Logo 1.50 4.00
199 Vin Baker 2.00 5.00
200 Brent Barry 2.00 5.00
201 Greg Foster 1.50 4.00
202 Horace Grant 2.00 5.00
203 Vernon Maxwell 1.50 4.00
204 Gary Payton 4.00 10.00
205 Elton Brand 5.00 12.00
206 Steve Francis 5.00 12.00
207 Baron Davis 6.00 15.00
208 Lamar Odom 5.00 12.00
209 Jonathan Bender 2.50 6.00
210 Wally Szczerbiak 4.00 10.00

2009-10 Panini Stickers

COMPLETE SET (384) 300.00 600.00
1 Boston Celtics Logo .10 .25
2 Kevin Garnett 1.00 2.50
3 Paul Pierce .60 1.50
4 Rajon Rondo .50 1.25
5 Lester Hudson .25 .60
6 Ray Allen .60 1.50
7 Kendrick Perkins .25 .60
8 Eddie House .25 .60
9 Glen Davis .25 .60
10 Rasheed Wallace .50 1.25
11 Robert Parish .50 1.25
12 New Jersey Nets Logo .10 .25
13 Devin Harris .25 .60
14 Brook Lopez .40 1.00
15 Yi Jianlian .50 1.25
16 Terrence Williams .25 .60
17 Bobby Simmons .25 .60
18 New Jersey Nets Records .10 .25
19 Jarvis Hayes .25 .60
20 Tony Battie .25 .60
21 Rafer Alston .25 .60
22 Courtney Lee .25 .60
23 New York Knicks Logo .10 .25
24 Al Harrington .30 .75
25 Danilo Gallinari .30 .75
26 Chris Duhon .25 .60
27 Jordan Hill .25 .60
28 Wilson Chandler .30 .75
29 Willis Reed .60 1.50
30 Nate Robinson .30 .75
31 David Lee .25 .60
32 Jared Jeffries .25 .60
33 Darko Milicic .25 .60
34 Philadelphia 76ers Logo .10 .25
35 Andre Iguodala .40 1.00
36 Thaddeus Young .25 .60
37 Samuel Dalembert .25 .60
38 Jrue Holiday 1.25 3.00
39 Elton Brand .30 .75
40 Billy Cunningham .40 1.00
41 Louis Williams .40 1.00
42 Willie Green .25 .60
43 Jason Kapono .25 .60
44 Primoz Brezec .25 .60
45 Toronto Raptors Logo .10 .25
46 Chris Bosh .50 1.25
47 Andrea Bargnani .25 .60
48 Jose Calderon .25 .60
49 DeMar DeRozan 15.00 40.00
50 Rasho Nesterovic .25 .60
51 Toronto Raptors Records .10 .25
52 Marco Belinelli .25 .60
53 Jarrett Jack .30 .75
54 Antoine Wright .25 .60
55 Hedo Turkoglu .30 .75
56 Chicago Bulls Logo .10 .25
57 Derrick Rose .60 1.50
58 Luol Deng .30 .75
59 John Salmons .30 .75
60 James Johnson .30 .75
61 Brad Miller .30 .75
62 Chicago Bulls Records .10 .25
63 Joakim Noah .25 .60
64 Tyrus Thomas .25 .60
65 Jannero Pargo .25 .60
66 Kirk Hinrich .30 .75
67 Cleveland Cavaliers Logo .10 .25
68 LeBron James 20.00 50.00
69 Mo Williams .25 .60
70 Delonte West .25 .60
71 Danny Green .40 1.00
72 Daniel Gibson .25 .60
73 Cleveland Cavaliers Records .10 .25
74 Anthony Parker .25 .60
75 Shaquille O'Neal 1.25 3.00
76 Anderson Varejao .25 .60
77 Zydrunas Ilgauskas .30 .75
78 Detroit Pistons Logo .10 .25
79 Tayshaun Prince .40 1.00
80 Richard Hamilton .40 1.00
81 Rodney Stuckey .25 .60
82 Austin Daye .25 .60
83 Ben Gordon .30 .75
84 Isiah Thomas .40 1.00
85 Will Bynum .25 .60
86 Kwame Brown .25 .60
87 Charlie Villanueva .25 .60
88 Ben Wallace .50 1.25
89 Indiana Pacers Logo .10 .25
90 Danny Granger .25 .60
91 Mike Dunleavy .25 .60
92 T.J. Ford .25 .60
93 Tyler Hansbrough .30 .75
94 Jeff Foster .25 .60
95 Indiana Pacers Records .10 .25
96 Earl Watson .25 .60
97 Dahntay Jones .25 .60
98 Troy Murphy .25 .60
99 Brandon Rush .25 .60
100 Milwaukee Bucks Logo .10 .25
101 Andrew Bogut .30 .75
102 Michael Redd .30 .75
103 Francisco Elson .25 .60
104 Brandon Jennings .40 1.00
105 Charlie Bell .25 .60
106 Luke Ridnour .30 .75
107 Luc Mbah A Moute .25 .60
108 Hakim Warrick .25 .60
109 Ersan Ilyasova .25 .60
110 Oscar Robertson .50 1.25
111 Atlanta Hawks Logo .10 .25
112 Joe Johnson .40 1.00
113 Josh Smith .25 .60
114 Mike Bibby .40 1.00
115 Jeff Teague .30 .75
116 Al Horford .40 1.00
117 Bob Pettit .50 1.25
118 Maurice Evans .25 .60
119 Zaza Pachulia .25 .60
120 Marvin Williams .25 .60
121 Jamal Crawford .40 1.00
122 Charlotte Bobcats Logo .10 .25
123 Boris Diaw .30 .75
124 Gerald Wallace .30 .75
125 Raja Bell .30 .75
126 Gerald Henderson .25 .60
127 DeSagana Diop .25 .60
128 Charlotte Bobcats Records .10 .25
129 D.J. Augustin .25 .60
130 Vladimir Radmanovic .25 .60
131 Tyson Chandler .30 .75
132 Raymond Felton .25 .60
133 Miami Heat Logo .10 .25
134 Dwyane Wade .75 2.00
135 Mario Chalmers .30 .75
136 Michael Beasley .25 .60
137 Chris Quinn .25 .60
138 Udonis Haslem .25 .60
139 Miami Heat Records .10 .25
140 Daequan Cook .25 .60
141 Joel Anthony .40 1.00
142 Quentin Richardson .25 .60
143 Jermaine O'Neal .40 1.00
144 Orlando Magic Logo .10 .25
145 Dwight Howard .50 1.25
146 Rashard Lewis .30 .75
147 Jameer Nelson .25 .60
148 Mickael Pietrus .25 .60
149 J.J. Redick .40 1.00
150 Orlando Magic Records .10 .25
151 Anthony Johnson .25 .60
152 Vince Carter .75 2.00
153 Ryan Anderson .25 .60
154 Matt Barnes .25 .60
155 Washington Wizards Logo .10 .25
156 Antawn Jamison .30 .75
157 Gilbert Arenas .30 .75
158 Caron Butler .30 .75
159 Nick Young .25 .60
160 Andray Blatche .25 .60
161 Elvin Hayes .60 1.50
162 Mike James .25 .60
163 Mike Miller .30 .75
164 Randy Foye .25 .60
165 Fabricio Oberto .25 .60
166 Andre Iguodala MIN .40 1.00
167 Joe Johnson MIN .40 1.00
168 O.J. Mayo MIN .25 .60
169 Anthony Morrow 3PT .25 .60
170 Jameer Nelson 3PT .25 .60
171 Troy Murphy 3PT .25 .60
172 Chris Paul STEAL .75 2.00
173 Dwyane Wade STEAL .75 2.00
174 Jason Kidd STEAL .60 1.50
175 David Lee DD .25 .60
176 Dwight Howard DD .50 1.25
177 Chris Paul DD .75 2.00
178 Terry Cummings PTT .30 .75
179 Blake Griffin PTT 1.50 4.00
180 Walt Frazier PTT .60 1.50
181 Jordan Hill PTT .25 .60
182 Pau Gasol PTT .60 1.50
183 Marc Gasol PTT .40 1.00
184 Kevin Durant PTT 1.50 4.00
185 James Harden PTT 40.00 100.00
186 Mitch Richmond PTT .40 1.00
187 Omri Casspi PTT .25 .60
188 Chris Mullin PTT .50 1.25
189 Stephen Curry PTT 150.00 400.00
190 Alvan Adams PTT .25 .60
191 Taylor Griffin PTT .25 .60
192 Jose Calderon FT .25 .60
193 Ray Allen FT .60 1.50
194 Steve Nash FT .75 2.00
195 Dwight Howard BL .50 1.25
196 Chris Andersen BL .40 1.00

197 Marcus Camby BL .30 .75
198 Chris Paul AST .75 2.00
199 Deron Williams AST .30 .75
200 Steve Nash AST .75 2.00
201 Dwight Howard REB .50 1.25
202 David Lee REB .25 .60
203 Troy Murphy REB .25 .60
204 Denver Nuggets Logo .10 .25
205 Carmelo Anthony .60 1.50
206 Chauncey Billups .50 1.25
207 J.R. Smith .40 1.00
208 Ty Lawson .30 .75
209 Nene .30 .75
210 Denver Nuggets Records .10 .25
211 Kenyon Martin .30 .75
212 Arron Afflalo .25 .60
213 Chris Andersen .40 1.00
214 Joey Graham .25 .60
215 Minnesota Timberwolves Logo .10 .25
216 Al Jefferson .25 .60
217 Ryan Gomes .25 .60
218 Kevin Love .40 1.00
219 Jonny Flynn UER .25 .60
220 Ryan Hollins .25 .60
221 Minnesota Timberwolves Records .10 .25
222 Damien Wilkins .25 .60
223 Corey Brewer .25 .60
224 Ramon Sessions .25 .60
225 Sasha Pavlovic .25 .60
226 Oklahoma City Thunder Logo .10 .25
227 Kevin Durant 1.50 4.00
228 Jeff Green .30 .75
229 Russell Westbrook .75 2.00
230 James Harden 40.00 100.00
231 Nenad Krstic .25 .60
232 Oklahoma City Thunder Records .10 .25
233 Thabo Sefolosha .25 .60
234 Shaun Livingston .25 .60
235 Kevin Ollie .25 .60
236 Kyle Weaver .25 .60
237 Portland Trail Blazers Logo .10 .25
238 Brandon Roy .50 1.25
239 LaMarcus Aldridge .40 1.00
240 Travis Outlaw .25 .60
241 Jeff Pendergraph .25 .60
242 Steve Blake .25 .60
243 Bill Walton .60 1.50
244 Rudy Fernandez .25 .60
245 Greg Oden .25 .60
246 Joel Przybilla .25 .60
247 Andre Miller .40 1.00
248 Utah Jazz Logo .10 .25
249 Deron Williams .30 .75
250 Carlos Boozer .30 .75
251 Mehmet Okur .25 .60
252 Eric Maynor .25 .60
253 Ronnie Brewer .25 .60
254 Karl Malone .50 1.25
255 Andrei Kirilenko .30 .75
256 C.J. Miles .25 .60
257 Kyle Korver .30 .75
258 Paul Millsap .30 .75
259 Golden State Warriors Logo .10 .25
260 Stephen Jackson .30 .75
261 Monta Ellis .30 .75
262 Corey Maggette .30 .75
263 Stephen Curry 150.00 400.00
264 Kelenna Azubuike .25 .60
265 Rick Barry .30 .75
266 Andris Biedrins .25 .60
267 Anthony Morrow .25 .60
268 Ronny Turiaf .25 .60
269 C.J. Watson .25 .60
270 Los Angeles Clippers Logo .10 .25
271 Eric Gordon .30 .75
272 Al Thornton .25 .60
273 Chris Kaman .30 .75
274 Blake Griffin 1.50 4.00
275 Marcus Camby .30 .75
276 Los Angeles Clippers Records .10 .25
277 Rasual Butler .25 .60
278 Baron Davis .30 .75
279 Sebastian Telfair .25 .60
280 Craig Smith .25 .60
281 Los Angeles Lakers Logo .10 .25
282 Kobe Bryant 8.00 20.00
283 Pau Gasol .60 1.50
284 Andrew Bynum .25 .60
285 Adam Morrison .25 .60
286 Lamar Odom .30 .75
287 Kareem Abdul-Jabbar 1.25 3.00
288 Derek Fisher .40 1.00
289 Sasha Vujacic .25 .60
290 Jordan Farmar .25 .60
291 Ron Artest .40 1.00
292 Phoenix Suns Logo .10 .25
293 Steve Nash .75 2.00
294 Jason Richardson .40 1.00
295 Amare Stoudemire .30 .75
296 Earl Clark .25 .60
297 Leandro Barbosa .30 .75
298 Phoenix Suns Records .10 .25
299 Channing Frye .25 .60
300 Grant Hill .60 1.50
301 Jared Dudley .25 .60
302 Goran Dragic 2.00 5.00
303 Sacramento Kings Logo .10 .25
304 Kevin Martin .30 .75
305 Andres Nocioni .25 .60
306 Francisco Garcia .25 .60
307 Tyreke Evans .30 .75
308 Spencer Hawes .25 .60
309 Sacramento Kings Records .10 .25
310 Jason Thompson .25 .60
311 Beno Udrih .25 .60
312 Sean May .25 .60
313 Sergio Rodriguez .25 .60
314 Dallas Mavericks Logo .10 .25
315 Dirk Nowitzki 1.00 2.50
316 Jason Kidd .60 1.50
317 Josh Howard .30 .75
318 Rodrigue Beaubois .25 .60
319 Jason Terry .30 .75
320 Dallas Mavericks Records .10 .25
321 Jose Barea .40 1.00
322 Erick Dampier .25 .60
323 Shawn Marion .40 1.00
324 Tim Thomas .25 .60
325 Houston Rockets Logo .10 .25
326 Yao Ming 1.00 2.50
327 Tracy McGrady .75 2.00
328 Luis Scola .30 .75
329 Jermaine Taylor .25 .60
330 Aaron Brooks .25 .60
331 Clyde Drexler .60 1.50
332 Shane Battier .40 1.00
333 Carl Landry .25 .60
334 Kyle Lowry .40 1.00
335 Trevor Ariza .25 .60
336 Memphis Grizzlies Logo .10 .25
337 O.J. Mayo .25 .60
338 Rudy Gay .40 1.00
339 Marc Gasol .40 1.00
340 Hasheem Thabeet .25 .60
341 Mike Conley Jr. .30 .75
342 Memphis Grizzlies Records .10 .25
343 Darrell Arthur .25 .60
344 Marko Jaric .25 .60
345 Zach Randolph .40 1.00
346 Steven Hunter .25 .60
347 New Orleans Hornets Logo .10 .25
348 Chris Paul .75 2.00
349 David West .30 .75
350 Peja Stojakovic .30 .75
351 Darren Collison .40 1.00
352 Ike Diogu .25 .60
353 New Orleans Hornets Records .10 .25
354 James Posey .25 .60
355 Emeka Okafor .30 .75
356 Hilton Armstrong .25 .60
357 Devin Brown .25 .60
358 San Antonio Spurs Logo .10 .25
359 Tony Parker .60 1.50
360 Tim Duncan 1.00 2.50
361 Manu Ginobili .75 2.00
362 DeJuan Blair .30 .75
363 Roger Mason .25 .60
364 George Gervin .50 1.25
365 Matt Bonner .25 .60
366 Michael Finley .40 1.00
367 Richard Jefferson .30 .75
368 Antonio McDyess .30 .75
369 Kobe Bryant PTS 8.00 20.00
370 Dwyane Wade PTS .75 2.00
371 LeBron James PTS 20.00 50.00
372 Shaquille O'Neal FG 1.25 3.00
373 Nene FG .30 .75
374 Andris Biedrins FG .25 .60
375 Dwyane Wade SCO .75 2.00
376 LeBron James SCO 20.00 50.00
377 Kobe Bryant SCO 8.00 20.00
378 LeBron James PRA 20.00 50.00
379 Dwyane Wade PRA .75 2.00
380 Chris Paul PRA .75 2.00
381 LeBron James MVP 20.00 50.00
382 Kobe Bryant FIN MVP 8.00 20.00
383 Jason Terry 6th Man .30 .75
384 Derrick Rose ROY .60 1.50

2010-11 Panini Stickers

COMPLETE SET (378) 60.00 150.00
1 NBA Logo .40 1.00
2 2011 All-Star Game Logo .40 1.00
3 2011 Playoffs Logo .40 1.00
4 2011 Finals Logo .40 1.00
5 Western Conference Logo .40 1.00
6 Eastern Conference Logo .40 1.00
7 Boston Celtics Logo .40 1.00
8 Paul Pierce .60 1.50
9 Ray Allen .60 1.50
10 Shaquille O'Neal 1.50 4.00
11 Rajon Rondo .50 1.25
12 Rasheed Wallace .40 1.00
13 Jermaine O'Neal .40 1.00
14 Nate Robinson .30 .75
15 Boston Celtics Leaders .40 1.00
16 Glen Davis .25 .60
17 Kevin Garnett 1.00 2.50
18 New Jersey Nets Logo .40 1.00
19 Brook Lopez .30 .75
20 Travis Outlaw .30 .75
21 Jordan Farmar .25 .60
22 Devin Harris .25 .60
23 Anthony Morrow .25 .60
24 Kris Humphries .25 .60
25 Troy Murphy .25 .60
26 Terrence Williams .25 .60
27 Johan Petro .25 .60
28 New York Knicks Logo .40 1.00
29 Amare Stoudemire .40 1.00
30 Danilo Gallinari .30 .75
31 Kelenna Azubuike .25 .60
32 Wilson Chandler .30 .75
33 Bill Walker .25 .60
34 Ronny Turiaf .25 .60
35 Toney Douglas .25 .60
36 Raymond Felton .25 .60
37 Anthony Randolph .25 .60
38 Philadelphia 76ers Logo .40 1.00
39 Andre Iguodala .40 1.00
40 Louis Williams .30 .75
41 Thaddeus Young .25 .60
42 Elton Brand .30 .75
43 Jodie Meeks .25 .60
44 Marreese Speights .25 .60
45 Jrue Holiday .50 1.25
46 Spencer Hawes .25 .60
47 Andres Nocioni .25 .60
48 Toronto Raptors Logo .40 1.00
49 Andrea Bargnani .25 .60
50 Leandro Barbosa .30 .75
51 Amir Johnson .25 .60
52 Jarrett Jack .30 .75
53 Jose Calderon .25 .60
54 DeMar DeRozan .60 1.50
55 Sonny Weems .25 .60
56 Julian Wright .25 .60
57 Marcus Banks .25 .60
58 Chicago Bulls Logo .40 1.00
59 Derrick Rose .75 2.00
60 Carlos Boozer .30 .75
61 Luol Deng .30 .75
62 Chicago Bulls Leaders .40 1.00
63 Joakim Noah .40 1.00
64 Ronnie Brewer .25 .60
65 Flip Murray .25 .60
66 Kyle Korver .30 .75
67 Jannero Pargo .25 .60
68 Taj Gibson .75 2.00
69 Cleveland Cavaliers Logo .40 1.00
70 Antawn Jamison .30 .75
71 J.J. Hickson .25 .60
72 Mo Williams .30 .75
73 Jamario Moon .25 .60
74 Anthony Parker .25 .60
75 Ryan Hollins .25 .60
76 Ramon Sessions .25 .60
77 Cleveland Cavaliers Leaders .40 1.00
78 Daniel Gibson .25 .60
79 Anderson Varejao .25 .60
80 Detroit Pistons Logo .40 1.00
81 Richard Hamilton .50 1.25
82 Rodney Stuckey .25 .60
83 Tayshaun Prince .40 1.00
84 Jonas Jerebko .25 .60
85 Ben Gordon .30 .75
86 Chris Wilcox .25 .60
87 DaJuan Summers .25 .60
88 Ben Wallace .50 1.25
89 Austin Daye .25 .60
90 Indiana Pacers Logo .40 1.00
91 Danny Granger .30 .75
92 Roy Hibbert .30 .75
93 T.J. Ford .25 .60
94 Darren Collison .25 .60
95 Dahntay Jones .25 .60
96 Brandon Rush .25 .60
97 A.J. Price .25 .60
98 Mike Dunleavy .25 .60
99 Tyler Hansbrough .25 .60
100 Milwaukee Bucks Logo .40 1.00
101 Brandon Jennings .30 .75
102 Corey Maggette .30 .75
103 Andrew Bogut .30 .75
104 Carlos Delfino .25 .60
105 John Salmons .25 .60
106 Drew Gooden .30 .75
107 Chris Douglas-Roberts .25 .60
108 Milwaukee Bucks Leaders .40 1.00
109 Luc Mbah a Moute .25 .60
110 Ersan Ilyasova .30 .75
111 Atlanta Hawks Logo .40 1.00
112 Joe Johnson .40 1.00
113 Josh Smith .25 .60
114 Mike Bibby .40 1.00
115 Jamal Crawford .40 1.00
116 Al Horford .40 1.00
117 Maurice Evans .25 .60
118 Jeff Teague .25 .60
119 Marvin Williams .25 .60
120 Zaza Pachulia .25 .60
121 Charlotte Bobcats Logo .40 1.00
122 Stephen Jackson .30 .75
123 Gerald Wallace .30 .75
124 Boris Diaw .30 .75
125 Charlotte Bobcats Leaders .40 1.00
126 Nazr Mohammed .25 .60
127 D.J. Augustin .25 .60
128 Shaun Livingston .25 .60
129 Erick Dampier .25 .60
130 Tyrus Thomas .25 .60
131 Gerald Henderson .25 .60
132 Miami Heat Logo .40 1.00
133 Dwyane Wade .75 2.00
134 LeBron James 15.00 40.00
135 Chris Bosh .50 1.25
136 Udonis Haslem .25 .60
137 Zydrunas Ilgauskas .30 .75
138 Mike Miller .30 .75
139 Carlos Arroyo .25 .60
140 Mario Chalmers .30 .75
141 Joel Anthony .25 .60
142 Orlando Magic Logo .40 1.00
143 Dwight Howard .50 1.25
144 Quentin Richardson .25 .60
145 Vince Carter .75 2.00
146 Rashard Lewis .30 .75
147 Jameer Nelson .30 .75
148 Ryan Anderson .30 .75
149 J.J. Redick .40 1.00
150 Orlando Magic Leaders .40 1.00
151 Marcin Gortat .25 .60
152 Mickael Pietrus .25 .60
153 Washington Wizards Logo .40 1.00
154 Gilbert Arenas .30 .75
155 Yi Jianlian .40 1.00
156 Andray Blatche .25 .60
157 Josh Howard .30 .75
158 Al Thornton .25 .60
159 Kirk Hinrich .30 .75
160 Nick Young .25 .60
161 Fabricio Oberto .25 .60
162 JaVale McGee .30 .75
163 Dallas Mavericks Logo .40 1.00
164 Dirk Nowitzki 1.00 2.50
165 Jason Kidd .60 1.50
166 Caron Butler .25 .60
167 Jason Terry .30 .75
168 DeShawn Stevenson .25 .60
169 Shawn Marion .40 1.00
170 Brendan Haywood .25 .60
171 Dallas Mavericks Leaders .40 1.00
172 Rodrigue Beaubois .25 .60
173 Tyson Chandler .30 .75
174 Houston Rockets Logo .40 1.00
175 Aaron Brooks .25 .60
176 Kevin Martin .30 .75
177 Yao Ming .75 2.00
178 Houston Rockets Leaders .40 1.00
179 Shane Battier .30 .75
180 Kyle Lowry .40 1.00
181 Chase Budinger .25 .60
182 Chuck Hayes .25 .60
183 Brad Miller .30 .75
184 Luis Scola .30 .75
185 Memphis Grizzlies Logo .40 1.00
186 O.J. Mayo .75 2.00
187 Mike Conley Jr. .30 .75
188 Rudy Gay .40 1.00
189 Memphis Grizzlies Leaders .40 1.00
190 Zach Randolph .40 1.00
191 Sam Young .25 .60
192 Hasheem Thabeet .25 .60
193 Marc Gasol .40 1.00
194 Darrell Arthur .25 .60
195 Hamed Haddadi .25 .60
196 New Orleans Hornets Logo .40 1.00
197 Chris Paul .75 2.00
198 Peja Stojakovic .30 .75
199 Trevor Ariza .25 .60
200 Emeka Okafor .30 .75
201 David West .30 .75
202 Marcus Thornton .25 .60
203 Aaron Gray .25 .60
204 Darius Songaila .25 .60
205 Marco Belinelli .25 .60
206 San Antonio Spurs Logo .40 1.00
207 Tim Duncan 1.00 2.50
208 Manu Ginobili .75 2.00
209 Tony Parker .60 1.50
210 San Antonio Spurs Leaders .40 1.00
211 Richard Jefferson .30 .75
212 DeJuan Blair .25 .60
213 Matt Bonner .25 .60
214 Tiago Splitter .30 .75
215 Antonio McDyess .30 .75
216 George Hill .30 .75
217 Denver Nuggets Logo .40 1.00
218 Carmelo Anthony .60 1.50
219 Chauncey Billups .50 1.25
220 Chris Andersen .40 1.00
221 Arron Afflalo .25 .60
222 Ty Lawson .25 .60
223 Kenyon Martin .40 1.00
224 Al Harrington .30 .75
225 Denver Nuggets Leaders .40 1.00
226 J.R. Smith .40 1.00
227 Nene .30 .75
228 Minnesota Timberwolves Logo .40 1.00
229 Kevin Love .40 1.00
230 Sebastian Telfair .25 .60
231 Corey Brewer .25 .60
232 Jonny Flynn .25 .60
233 Michael Beasley .25 .60
234 Kosta Koufos .25 .60
235 Luke Ridnour .25 .60
236 Martell Webster .30 .75
237 Darko Milicic .25 .60
238 Oklahoma City Thunder Logo .40 1.00
239 Kevin Durant 1.50 4.00
240 Russell Westbrook .60 1.50
241 Jeff Green .30 .75
242 James Harden 1.00 2.50
243 Serge Ibaka .30 .75
244 Nenad Krstic .25 .60
245 Nick Collison .25 .60
246 Oklahoma City Thunder Leaders .40 1.00
247 Eric Maynor .25 .60
248 Thabo Sefolosha .25 .60
249 Portland Trail Blazers Logo .40 1.00
250 LaMarcus Aldridge .40 1.00
251 Andre Miller .30 .75
252 Jerryd Bayless .25 .60
253 Dante Cunningham .30 .75
254 Nicolas Batum .30 .75
255 Marcus Camby .30 .75
256 Brandon Roy .50 1.25
257 Greg Oden .25 .60
258 Rudy Fernandez .25 .60
259 Utah Jazz Logo .40 1.00
260 Deron Williams .30 .75
261 Al Jefferson .25 .60
262 Mehmet Okur .25 .60
263 Utah Jazz Leaders .40 1.00
264 C.J. Miles .25 .60
265 Andrei Kirilenko .30 .75
266 Raja Bell .30 .75
267 Sundiata Gaines .25 .60
268 Paul Millsap .30 .75
269 Ronnie Price .25 .60
270 Golden State Warriors Logo .40 1.00
271 Monta Ellis .30 .75
272 Stephen Curry 20.00 50.00
273 Andris Biedrins .25 .60
274 Golden State Warriors Leaders .40 1.00
275 Dorell Wright .25 .60
276 Reggie Williams .30 .75
277 David Lee .25 .60
278 Charlie Bell .25 .60
279 Dan Gadzuric .25 .60
280 Vladimir Radmanovic .25 .60
281 Los Angeles Clippers Logo .40 1.00
282 Chris Kaman .25 .60
283 Eric Gordon .30 .75
284 Baron Davis .40 1.00
285 Rasual Butler .25 .60
286 Craig Smith .25 .60
287 Randy Foye .25 .60
288 Ryan Gomes .25 .60
289 Brian Cook .25 .60
290 Blake Griffin .40 1.00
291 Los Angeles Lakers Logo .40 1.00
292 Kobe Bryant 6.00 15.00
293 Ron Artest .40 1.00
294 Pau Gasol .60 1.50
295 Los Angeles Lakers Leaders .40 1.00
296 Derek Fisher .40 1.00
297 Lamar Odom .30 .75
298 Andrew Bynum .25 .60
299 Steve Blake .25 .60
300 Luke Walton .25 .60
301 Sasha Vujacic .25 .60
302 Phoenix Suns Logo .40 1.00
303 Steve Nash .75 2.00
304 Goran Dragic .50 1.25
305 Hedo Turkoglu .30 .75
306 Phoenix Suns Leaders .40 1.00
307 Jared Dudley .25 .60
308 Channing Frye .25 .60
309 Grant Hill .60 1.50
310 Jason Richardson .40 1.00
311 Robin Lopez .25 .60
312 Hakim Warrick .25 .60
313 Sacramento Kings Logo .40 1.00
314 Tyreke Evans .30 .75
315 Carl Landry .25 .60
316 Beno Udrih .25 .60
317 Jason Thompson .25 .60
318 Omri Casspi .25 .60
319 Donte Greene .25 .60
320 Francisco Garcia .25 .60
321 Antoine Wright .25 .60
322 Samuel Dalembert .25 .60
323 Kobe Bryant 2000 3.00 8.00
324 Kobe Bryant 2000 3.00 8.00
325 Kobe Bryant 2001 3.00 8.00
326 Kobe Bryant 2001 3.00 8.00
327 Kobe Bryant 2002 3.00 8.00
328 Kobe Bryant 2002 3.00 8.00
329 Kobe Bryant 2004 3.00 8.00
330 Kobe Bryant 2008 3.00 8.00
331 Kobe Bryant 2009 3.00 8.00
332 Kobe Bryant 2009 3.00 8.00
333 Kobe Bryant 2010 3.00 8.00
334 Kobe Bryant 2010 3.00 8.00
335 Kobe Bryant 2010 3.00 8.00
336 NBA Europe 2010 .40 1.00
337 NBA Europe 2010 .40 1.00
338 NBA Europe 2010 .40 1.00
339 NBA Europe 2010 .40 1.00
340 NBA London 2011 .40 1.00
341 Noche Latina 2010 .40 1.00
342 Noche Latina 2010 .40 1.00
343 NBA Mexico 2010 .40 1.00
344 NBA China 2010 .40 1.00
345 NBA China 2010 .40 1.00
346 NBA China 2010 .40 1.00
347 NBA without borders .40 1.00
348 NBA without borders .40 1.00
349 John Wall 1.25 3.00
350 Evan Turner .30 .75
351 Derrick Favors .40 1.00
352 Wesley Johnson .25 .60
353 DeMarcus Cousins .75 2.00
354 Ekpe Udoh .25 .60
355 Greg Monroe .30 .75
356 Al-Farouq Aminu .30 .75
357 Gordon Hayward 1.00 2.50
358 Paul George 12.00 30.00
359 Cole Aldrich .25 .60
360 Xavier Henry .25 .60
361 Ed Davis .30 .75
362 Patrick Patterson .30 .75
363 Larry Sanders .25 .60
364 Luke Babbitt .25 .60
365 Eric Bledsoe .50 1.25
366 Avery Bradley .40 1.00
367 James Anderson .25 .60
368 Craig Brackins .25 .60
369 Elliot Williams .25 .60
370 Trevor Booker .25 .60
371 Damion James .25 .60
372 Dominique Jones .25 .60
373 LeBron James MVP 25.00 60.00
374 Tyreke Evans ROY .30 .75
375 Jamal Crawford 6th Man .40 1.00
376 Kobe Bryant FIN MVP 8.00 20.00
377 Dwyane Wade AS MVP .75 2.00
378 Dwight Howard DEF POY .50 1.25

2012-13 Panini Stickers

COMPLETE SET (360) 60.00 150.00
1 Paul Pierce .60 1.50
2 Rajon Rondo .50 1.25
3 Kevin Garnett 1.00 2.50
4 Avery Bradley .25 .60
5 Brandon Bass .25 .60
6 Jason Terry .30 .75
7 Jeff Green .25 .60
8 Chris Wilcox .25 .60
9 Deron Williams .30 .75
10 Brook Lopez .30 .75
11 Gerald Wallace .30 .75
12 MarShon Brooks .25 .60
13 Kris Humphries .25 .60
14 C.J. Watson .25 .60
15 Joe Johnson .30 .75
16 Reggie Evans .25 .60
17 Carmelo Anthony .60 1.50
18 Amare Stoudemire .40 1.00
19 Tyson Chandler .30 .75
20 J.R. Smith .40 1.00
21 Jason Kidd .60 1.50
22 Marcus Camby .40 1.00
23 Raymond Felton .25 .60
24 Iman Shumpert .30 .75
25 Jrue Holiday .50 1.25
26 Evan Turner .25 .60
27 Andrew Bynum .25 .60
28 Thaddeus Young .25 .60
29 Lavoy Allen .25 .60
30 Spencer Hawes .25 .60
31 Dorell Wright .25 .60
32 Nick Young .25 .60
33 Andrea Bargnani .25 .60
34 DeMar DeRozan .50 1.25
35 Jose Calderon .25 .60
36 Ed Davis .25 .60
37 Amir Johnson .25 .60
38 Linas Kleiza .25 .60
39 Landry Fields .25 .60
40 Kyle Lowry .40 1.00
41 Derrick Rose .60 1.50
42 Luol Deng .30 .75
43 Joakim Noah .30 .75
44 Carlos Boozer .30 .75
45 Marco Belinelli .25 .60
46 Kirk Hinrich .30 .75
47 Richard Hamilton .40 1.00
48 Taj Gibson .25 .60
49 Kyrie Irving 2.50 6.00
50 Tristan Thompson .40 1.00
51 Alonzo Gee .25 .60
52 Daniel Gibson .25 .60
53 Anderson Varejao .25 .60
54 Samardo Samuels .25 .60
55 C.J. Miles .25 .60
56 Omri Casspi .25 .60
57 Greg Monroe .25 .60
58 Brandon Knight .30 .75
59 Tayshaun Prince .40 1.00
60 Jason Maxiell .25 .60
61 Corey Maggette .30 .75
62 Rodney Stuckey .25 .60
63 Jonas Jerebko .25 .60
64 Austin Daye .25 .60
65 Roy Hibbert .30 .75
66 Danny Granger .25 .60
67 David West .30 .75
68 Paul George .60 1.50
69 Tyler Hansbrough .25 .60
70 George Hill .30 .75
71 D.J. Augustin .25 .60
72 Gerald Green .30 .75
73 Brandon Jennings .25 .60
74 Monta Ellis .30 .75
75 Ersan Ilyasova .25 .60
76 Luc Mbah A Moute .25 .60
77 Drew Gooden .30 .75
78 Samuel Dalembert .25 .60
79 Ekpe Udoh .25 .60
80 Mike Dunleavy .25 .60
81 Al Horford .40 1.00
82 Josh Smith .25 .60
83 Jeff Teague .25 .60
84 Zaza Pachulia .25 .60
85 Kyle Korver .30 .75
86 Louis Williams .30 .75
87 Anthony Morrow .25 .60
88 Devin Harris .25 .60
89 Kemba Walker 1.00 2.50
90 Gerald Henderson .25 .60
91 Bismack Biyombo .30 .75
92 Ramon Sessions .25 .60
93 B.J. Mullens .25 .60
94 Ben Gordon .30 .75
95 Reggie Williams .30 .75
96 Tyrus Thomas .25 .60
97 LeBron James 6.00 15.00
98 Dwyane Wade .75 2.00
99 Chris Bosh .50 1.25
100 Udonis Haslem .30 .75
101 Mario Chalmers .30 .75
102 Shane Battier .30 .75
103 Norris Cole .25 .60
104 Ray Allen .60 1.50
105 Jameer Nelson .25 .60
106 Glen Davis .25 .60
107 Hedo Turkoglu .30 .75
108 J.J. Redick .40 1.00
109 Nikola Vucevic 1.00 2.50
110 Gustavo Ayon .25 .60
111 Arron Afflalo .25 .60
112 Al Harrington .30 .75
113 John Wall .50 1.25
114 Nene .30 .75
115 Jordan Crawford .25 .60
116 Trevor Ariza .25 .60
117 Trevor Booker .25 .60
118 Kevin Seraphin .25 .60
119 Emeka Okafor .30 .75
120 Chris Singleton .25 .60
121 Dirk Nowitzki 1.00 2.50
122 Shawn Marion .40 1.00
123 Vince Carter .75 2.00
124 Rodrigue Beaubois .25 .60
125 Darren Collison .25 .60
126 Chris Kaman .30 .75
127 Elton Brand .30 .75
128 O.J. Mayo .25 .60
129 Kevin Martin .30 .75
130 Chandler Parsons .30 .75
131 Patrick Patterson .25 .60
132 Jeremy Lin .60 1.50
133 Shaun Livingston .25 .60
134 Omer Asik .25 .60
135 Gary Forbes .25 .60
136 Carlos Delfino .25 .60
137 Rudy Gay .40 1.00
138 Marc Gasol .40 1.00
139 Mike Conley .30 .75
140 Zach Randolph .40 1.00
141 Marreese Speights .25 .60
142 Tony Allen .25 .60
143 Darrell Arthur .25 .60
144 Jerryd Bayless .25 .60
145 Eric Gordon .30 .75
146 Jason Smith .25 .60
147 Ryan Anderson .25 .60
148 Al-Farouq Aminu .25 .60
149 Greivis Vasquez .25 .60
150 Xavier Henry .25 .60
151 Lance Thomas .25 .60
152 Robin Lopez .25 .60
153 Tim Duncan 1.00 2.50
154 Tony Parker .60 1.50
155 Manu Ginobili .75 2.00
156 Gary Neal .25 .60
157 Kawhi Leonard 40.00 100.00
158 Tiago Splitter .25 .60
159 Matt Bonner .25 .60
160 Stephen Jackson .30 .75
161 Ty Lawson .25 .60
162 Danilo Gallinari .25 .60
163 Wilson Chandler .30 .75
164 Kenneth Faried .30 .75
165 Andre Miller .30 .75
166 Andre Iguodala .40 1.00
167 Timofey Mozgov .25 .60
168 JaVale McGee .30 .75
169 Kevin Love .40 1.00
170 Ricky Rubio .30 .75
171 Nikola Pekovic .25 .60
172 Derrick Williams .25 .60
173 Andrei Kirilenko .30 .75
174 J.J. Barea .30 .75
175 Luke Ridnour .30 .75
176 Brandon Roy .30 .75
177 Kevin Durant 1.50 4.00
178 Russell Westbrook .60 1.50
179 James Harden .75 2.00
180 Serge Ibaka .30 .75
181 Thabo Sefolosha .25 .60
182 Nick Collison .25 .60
183 Kendrick Perkins .25 .60
184 Daequan Cook .25 .60
185 LaMarcus Aldridge .40 1.00
186 Nicolas Batum .30 .75
187 J.J. Hickson .25 .60
188 Nolan Smith .25 .60
189 Luke Babbitt .25 .60
190 Wesley Matthews .25 .60
191 Ronnie Price .25 .60
192 Elliot Williams .25 .60
193 Paul Millsap .30 .75
194 Al Jefferson .25 .60
195 Gordon Hayward .40 1.00
196 Derrick Favors .30 .75
197 Alec Burks .40 1.00
198 Enes Kanter .40 1.00
199 Mo Williams .30 .75
200 Marvin Williams .25 .60
201 David Lee .25 .60
202 Stephen Curry 3.00 8.00
203 Klay Thompson 6.00 15.00
204 Carl Landry .25 .60
205 Charles Jenkins .25 .60
206 Jarrett Jack .30 .75
207 Brandon Rush .25 .60
208 Andrew Bogut .30 .75
209 Chris Paul .75 2.00
210 Blake Griffin .40 1.00
211 DeAndre Jordan .30 .75
212 Caron Butler .30 .75
213 Grant Hill .60 1.50
214 Eric Bledsoe .30 .75
215 Chauncey Billups .50 1.25
216 Lamar Odom .30 .75
217 Kobe Bryant 3.00 8.00
218 Pau Gasol .60 1.50
219 Steve Nash .75 2.00
220 Dwight Howard .50 1.25
221 Metta World Peace .30 .75
222 Steve Blake .25 .60
223 Jordan Hill .25 .60
224 Antawn Jamison .30 .75
225 Marcin Gortat .25 .60
226 Jared Dudley .25 .60
227 Channing Frye .25 .60
228 Luis Scola .30 .75
229 Markieff Morris .40 1.00
230 Wesley Johnson .25 .60
231 Goran Dragic .40 1.00
232 Michael Beasley .25 .60
233 Tyreke Evans .30 .75
234 DeMarcus Cousins .40 1.00
235 Isaiah Thomas .50 1.25
236 Marcus Thornton .25 .60
237 Jimmer Fredette .40 1.00
238 Jason Thompson .25 .60
239 Aaron Brooks .25 .60
240 Chuck Hayes .25 .60
241 Anthony Davis 6.00 15.00
242 Michael Kidd-Gilchrist .30 .75
243 Bradley Beal 2.00 5.00
244 Dion Waiters .30 .75
245 Thomas Robinson .25 .60
246 Damian Lillard 6.00 15.00
247 Harrison Barnes .50 1.25
248 Terrence Ross .60 1.50
249 Andre Drummond .60 1.50
250 Austin Rivers .40 1.00
251 Miami Heat NBA Champs
Dwyane Wade
LeBron James 3.00 8.00
252 LeBron James MVP 8.00 20.00
253 LeBron James
Kevin Durant Finals 3.00 8.00
254 Oklahoma City
Thunder West Champs .40 1.00
255 Miami Heat East Champs
Chris Bosh .50 1.25
256 Kobe Bryant
LeBron James ASG 12.00 30.00
257 Kevin Durant ASG 1.50 4.00
258 Blake Griffin ASG .40 1.00
259 2012 All-Star Game .20 .50
260 Deron Williams ASG .30 .75
261 Kevin Love ASG .40 1.00
262 LeBron James MVP 8.00 20.00
263 Kyrie Irving ROY 2.50 6.00
264 James Harden 6th Man .75 2.00
265 Tyson Chandler D-POY .30 .75
266 Ryan Anderson MIP .25 .60
A1 NBA Logo FOIL .15 .40
A2 NBA Trophy Logo FOIL .15 .40
A3 Eastern Conference Logo FOIL .15 .40
A4 Western Conference Logo FOIL .15 .40
A5 Boston Celtics Logo FOIL .15 .40
A6 Brooklyn Nets Logo FOIL .15 .40
A7 New York Knicks Logo FOIL .15 .40
A8 Philadelphia 76ers Logo FOIL .15 .40
A9 Toronto Raptors Logo FOIL .15 .40
A10 Chicago Bulls Logo FOIL .15 .40
A11 Cleveland Cavaliers Logo FOIL .15 .40
A12 Detroit Pistons Logo FOIL .15 .40
A13 Indiana Pacers Logo FOIL .15 .40
A14 Milwaukee Bucks Logo FOIL .15 .40
A15 Atlanta Hawks Logo FOIL .15 .40
A16 Charlotte Bobcats Logo FOIL .15 .40
A17 Miami Heat Logo FOIL .15 .40
A18 Orlando Magic Logo FOIL .15 .40
A19 Washington Wizards Logo FOIL .15 .40
A20 Dallas Mavericks Logo FOIL .15 .40
A21 Houston Rockets Logo FOIL .15 .40
A22 Memphis Grizzlies Logo FOIL .15 .40
A23 New Orleans Hornets Logo FOIL .15 .40
A24 San Antonio Spurs Logo FOIL .15 .40
A25 Denver Nuggets Logo FOIL .15 .40
A26 Minnesota Timberwolves Logo FOIL.15 .40
A27 Oklahoma City Thunder Logo FOIL.15 .40
A28 Portland Trail Blazers Logo FOIL .15 .40
A29 Utah Jazz Logo FOIL .15 .40
A30 Golden State Warriors Logo FOIL .15 .40
A31 Los Angeles Clippers Logo FOIL .15 .40
A32 Los Angeles Lakers Logo FOIL .15 .40
A33 Phoenix Suns Logo FOIL .15 .40
A34 Sacramento Kings Logo FOIL .15 .40
A35 Paul Pierce FOIL .50 1.25
A36 Rajon Rondo FOIL .40 1.00
A37 Deron Williams FOIL .25 .60
A38 Brook Lopez FOIL .25 .60
A39 Carmelo Anthony FOIL .50 1.25
A40 Amare Stoudemire FOIL .30 .75
A41 Jrue Holiday FOIL .40 1.00
A42 Evan Turner FOIL .20 .50
A43 Andrea Bargnani FOIL .20 .50
A44 DeMar DeRozan FOIL .40 1.00
A45 Derrick Rose FOIL .50 1.25
A46 Luol Deng FOIL .25 .60
A47 Kyrie Irving FOIL 10.00 25.00

A48 Tristan Thompson FOIL	.30	.75
A49 Greg Monroe FOIL	.20	.50
A50 Brandon Knight FOIL	.25	.60
A51 Roy Hibbert FOIL	.25	.60
A52 Danny Granger FOIL	.20	.50
A53 Brandon Jennings FOIL	.20	.50
A54 Monta Ellis FOIL	.25	.60
A55 Al Horford FOIL	.30	.75
A56 Josh Smith FOIL	.20	.50
A57 Kemba Walker FOIL	.75	2.00
A58 Gerald Henderson FOIL	.20	.50
A59 LeBron James FOIL	15.00	40.00
A60 Dwyane Wade FOIL	.60	1.50
A61 Jameer Nelson FOIL	.20	.50
A62 Glen Davis FOIL	.20	.50
A63 John Wall FOIL	.40	1.00
A64 Nene FOIL	.25	.60
A65 Dirk Nowitzki FOIL	.75	2.00
A66 Shawn Marion FOIL	.30	.75
A67 Kevin Martin FOIL	.25	.60
A68 Jeremy Lin FOIL	.50	1.25
A69 Rudy Gay FOIL	.30	.75
A70 Marc Gasol FOIL	.30	.75
A71 Eric Gordon FOIL	.25	.60
A72 Anthony Davis FOIL	15.00	40.00
A73 Tim Duncan FOIL	.75	2.00
A74 Tony Parker FOIL	.50	1.25
A75 Ty Lawson FOIL	.20	.50
A76 Danilo Gallinari FOIL	.20	.50
A77 Kevin Love FOIL	.30	.75
A78 Ricky Rubio FOIL	.25	.60
A79 Kevin Durant FOIL	6.00	15.00
A80 Russell Westbrook FOIL	.50	1.25
A81 LaMarcus Aldridge FOIL	.30	.75
A82 Nicolas Batum FOIL	.25	.60
A83 Paul Millsap FOIL	.25	.60
A84 Al Jefferson FOIL	.20	.50
A85 David Lee FOIL	.20	.50
A86 Stephen Curry FOIL	2.50	6.00
A87 Chris Paul FOIL	.60	1.50
A88 Blake Griffin FOIL	.30	.75
A89 Kobe Bryant FOIL	2.50	6.00
A90 Steve Nash FOIL	.60	1.50
A91 Marcin Gortat FOIL	.20	.50
A92 Goran Dragic FOIL	.30	.75
A93 Tyreke Evans FOIL	.25	.60
A94 DeMarcus Cousins FOIL	.30	.75

2013-14 Panini Stickers

COMPLETE SET (363)	25.00	60.00
1 NBA Logo	.20	.50
2 NBA Logo	.20	.50
3 NBA Champions	.20	.50
4 NBA Champions	.20	.50
5 Brandon Bass	.15	.40
6 Jeff Green	.15	.40
7 Rajon Rondo	.30	.75
8 Jared Sullinger	.15	.40
9 Gerald Wallace	.20	.50
10 Keith Bogans	.15	.40
11 Avery Bradley	.15	.40
12 MarShon Brooks	.15	.40
13 Rajon Rondo	.30	.75
14 Jeff Green	.15	.40
15 Brook Lopez	.25	.60
16 Andray Blatche	.15	.40
17 Brook Lopez	.25	.60
18 Kevin Garnett	.60	1.50
19 Reggie Evans	.15	.40
20 Andrei Kirilenko	.25	.60
21 Paul Pierce	.40	1.00
22 Joe Johnson	.20	.50
23 Deron Williams	.20	.50
24 Deron Williams	.20	.50
25 Tyson Chandler	.20	.50
26 Andrea Bargnani	.15	.40
27 Carmelo Anthony	.40	1.00
28 Amar'e Stoudemire	.25	.60
29 Carmelo Anthony	.40	1.00
30 Metta World Peace	.20	.50
31 Iman Shumpert	.15	.40
32 Raymond Felton	.15	.40
33 J.R. Smith	.25	.60
34 Tyson Chandler	.20	.50
35 Kwame Brown	.15	.40
36 LaVoy Allen	.15	.40
37 Evan Turner	.15	.40
38 Spencer Hawes	.15	.40
39 Arnett Moultrie	.15	.40
40 Thaddeus Young	.15	.40
41 Evan Turner	.15	.40
42 Michael Carter-Williams	.20	.50
43 Jason Richardson	.25	.60
44 Thaddeus Young	.15	.40
45 Jonas Valanciunas	.20	.50
46 Tyler Hansbrough	.15	.40
47 Rudy Gay	.20	.50
48 Amir Johnson	.15	.40
49 Landry Fields	.15	.40
50 Rudy Gay	.20	.50
51 DeMar DeRozan	.30	.75
52 Kyle Lowry	.25	.60
53 Terrence Ross	.20	.50
54 DeMar DeRozan	.30	.75
55 Joakim Noah	.25	.60
56 Carlos Boozer	.20	.50
57 Derrick Rose	.40	1.00
58 Luol Deng	.20	.50
59 Mike Dunleavy	.15	.40
60 Taj Gibson	.15	.40
61 Jimmy Butler	.50	1.25
62 Kirk Hinrich	.20	.50
63 Derrick Rose	.40	1.00
64 Joakim Noah	.25	.60
65 Andrew Bynum	.15	.40
66 Anderson Varejao	.15	.40
67 Kyrie Irving	.75	2.00
68 Tyler Zeller	.15	.40
69 Tristan Thompson	.15	.40
70 Kyrie Irving	.75	2.00
71 Jarrett Jack	.20	.50
72 C.J. Miles	.15	.40
73 Dion Waiters	.15	.40
74 Dion Waiters	.15	.40
75 Andre Drummond	.25	.60
76 Greg Monroe	.15	.40
77 Greg Monroe	.15	.40
78 Jonas Jerebko	.15	.40
79 Josh Smith	.15	.40
80 Chauncey Billups	.30	.75
81 Brandon Jennings	.15	.40
82 Kyle Singler	.15	.40
83 Rodney Stuckey	.15	.40
84 Andre Drummond	.25	.60
85 Roy Hibbert	.15	.40
86 Chris Copeland	.15	.40
87 Paul George	.40	1.00
88 Danny Granger	.15	.40
89 Luis Scola	.20	.50
90 David West	.20	.50
91 Paul George	.40	1.00
92 George Hill	.20	.50
93 Lance Stephenson	.20	.50
94 Roy Hibbert	.15	.40
95 Larry Sanders	.15	.40
96 Ekpe Udoh	.15	.40
97 Larry Sanders	.15	.40
98 Zaza Pachulia	.15	.40
99 John Henson	.15	.40
100 Ersan Ilyasova	.15	.40
101 Brandon Knight	.20	.50
102 O.J. Mayo	.15	.40
103 Luke Ridnour	.15	.40
104 Ersan Ilyasova	.15	.40
105 Al Horford	.25	.60
106 Elton Brand	.20	.50
107 Al Horford	.25	.60
108 DeMarre Carroll	.15	.40
109 Paul Millsap	.20	.50
110 Kyle Korver	.20	.50
111 John Jenkins	.15	.40
112 Jeff Teague	.15	.40
113 Louis Williams	.20	.50
114 Louis Williams	.20	.50
115 Bismack Biyombo	.15	.40
116 Al Jefferson	.15	.40
117 Kemba Walker	.25	.60
118 Jeff Adrien	.15	.40
119 Michael Kidd-Gilchrist	.15	.40
120 Jeff Taylor	.15	.40
121 Gerald Henderson	.15	.40
122 Ramon Sessions	.15	.40
123 Kemba Walker	.25	.60
124 Michael Kidd-Gilchrist	.15	.40
125 Chris Bosh	.30	.75
126 Chris Andersen	.20	.50
127 LeBron James	2.00	5.00
128 Udonis Haslem	.20	.50
129 LeBron James	2.00	5.00
130 Ray Allen	.40	1.00
131 Mario Chalmers	.20	.50
132 Norris Cole	.15	.40
133 Dwyane Wade	.50	1.25
134 Dwyane Wade	.50	1.25
135 Nikola Vucevic	.30	.75
136 Glen Davis	.15	.40
137 Nikola Vucevic	.30	.75
138 Maurice Harkless	.15	.40
139 Tobias Harris	.25	.60
140 Andrew Nicholson	.15	.40
141 Hedo Turkoglu	.20	.50
142 Arron Afflalo	.15	.40
143 Jameer Nelson	.15	.40
144 Tobias Harris	.25	.60
145 Emeka Okafor	.15	.40
146 Kevin Seraphin	.15	.40
147 John Wall	.30	.75
148 Trevor Ariza	.15	.40
149 Trevor Booker	.15	.40
150 Nene	.20	.50
151 Martell Webster	.15	.40
152 Bradley Beal	.40	1.00
153 John Wall	.30	.75
154 Bradley Beal	.40	1.00
155 Brandan Wright	.15	.40
156 Jae Crowder	.15	.40
157 Dirk Nowitzki	.60	1.50
158 Shawn Marion	.15	.40
159 Dirk Nowitzki	.60	1.50
160 Vince Carter	.50	1.25
161 Jose Calderon	.15	.40
162 Wayne Ellington	.15	.40
163 Monta Ellis	.20	.50
164 Shawn Marion	.20	.50
165 Omer Asik	.15	.40
166 Dwight Howard	.30	.75
167 James Harden	.50	1.25
168 Donatas Motiejunas	.20	.50
169 Chandler Parsons	.20	.50
170 Francisco Garcia	.15	.40
171 Patrick Beverley	.15	.40
172 James Harden	.50	1.25
173 Jeremy Lin	.40	1.00
174 Jeremy Lin	.40	1.00
175 Marc Gasol	.25	.60
176 Kosta Koufos	.15	.40
177 Marc Gasol	.25	.60
178 Ed Davis	.15	.40
179 Quincy Pondexter	.15	.40
180 Tayshaun Prince	.25	.60
181 Zach Randolph	.30	.75
182 Tony Allen	.15	.40
183 Mike Conley	.25	.60
184 Zach Randolph	.30	.75
185 Anthony Davis	.75	2.00
186 Jason Smith	.15	.40
187 Anthony Davis	.75	2.00
188 Al-Farouq Aminu	.15	.40
189 Ryan Anderson	.15	.40
190 Tyreke Evans	.20	.50
191 Eric Gordon	.20	.50
192 Jrue Holiday	.30	.75
193 Brian Roberts	.15	.40
194 Ryan Anderson	.15	.40
195 Tiago Splitter	.15	.40
196 Tim Duncan	.60	1.50
197 Tim Duncan	.60	1.50
198 Kawhi Leonard	.75	2.00
199 Danny Green	.20	.50
200 Marco Belinelli	.15	.40
201 Manu Ginobili	.50	1.25
202 Cory Joseph	.15	.40
203 Tony Parker	.40	1.00
204 Tony Parker	.40	1.00
205 JaVale McGee	.20	.50
206 J.J. Hickson	.15	.40
207 Ty Lawson	.15	.40
208 Wilson Chandler	.20	.50
209 Kenneth Faried	.20	.50
210 Danilo Gallinari	.20	.50
211 Randy Foye	.15	.40
212 Ty Lawson	.15	.40
213 Andre Miller	.20	.50
214 Danilo Gallinari	.20	.50
215 Nikola Pekovic	.15	.40
216 Kevin Love	.25	.60
217 Kevin Love	.25	.60
218 Chase Budinger	.15	.40
219 Derrick Williams	.15	.40
220 Jose Barea	.20	.50
221 Kevin Martin	.20	.50
222 Ricky Rubio	.20	.50
223 Alexy Shved	.15	.40
224 Ricky Rubio	.20	.50
225 Kendrick Perkins	.15	.40
226 Nick Collison	.15	.40
227 Kevin Durant	.75	2.00
228 Serge Ibaka	.20	.50
229 Kevin Durant	.75	2.00
230 Jeremy Lamb	.15	.40
231 Reggie Jackson	.20	.50
232 Thabo Sefolosha	.20	.50
233 Russell Westbrook	.40	1.00
234 Russell Westbrook	.40	1.00
235 Meyers Leonard	.15	.40
236 Robin Lopez	.15	.40
237 LaMarcus Aldridge	.25	.60
238 LaMarcus Aldridge	.25	.60
239 Victor Claver	.15	.40
240 Thomas Robinson	.15	.40
241 Nicolas Batum	.20	.50
242 Damian Lillard	.75	2.00
243 Wesley Matthews	.15	.40
244 Damian Lillard	.75	2.00
245 Enes Kanter	.20	.50
246 Derrick Favors	.20	.50
247 Gordon Hayward	.20	.50
248 Jeremy Evans	.15	.40
249 Marvin Williams	.15	.40
250 Gordon Hayward	.20	.50
251 Brandon Rush	.15	.40
252 Alec Burks	.15	.40
253 John Lucas III	.15	.40
254 Derrick Favors	.15	.40
255 Andrew Bogut	.20	.50
256 Festus Ezeli	.15	.40
257 Stephen Curry	2.00	5.00
258 David Lee	.15	.40
259 Harrison Barnes	.25	.60
260 Draymond Green	.40	1.00
261 Andre Iguodala	.25	.60
262 Stephen Curry	2.00	5.00
263 Klay Thompson	.75	2.00
264 David Lee	.15	.40
265 Ryan Hollins	.15	.40
266 DeAndre Jordan	.25	.60
267 Chris Paul	.50	1.25
268 Matt Barnes	.15	.40
269 Blake Griffin	.25	.60
270 Darren Collison	.15	.40
271 Jamal Crawford	.25	.60
272 Chris Paul	.50	1.25
273 J.J. Redick	.25	.60
274 Blake Griffin	.25	.60
275 Jordan Hill	.15	.40
276 Chris Kaman	.15	.40
277 Kobe Bryant	2.00	5.00
278 Pau Gasol	.40	1.00
279 Wesley Johnson	.15	.40
280 Nick Young	.15	.40
281 Steve Blake	.15	.40
282 Kobe Bryant	2.00	5.00
283 Steve Nash	.50	1.25
284 Pau Gasol	.40	1.00
285 Marcin Gortat	.15	.40
286 Michael Beasley	.15	.40
287 Marcin Gortat	.15	.40
288 Goran Dragic	.20	.50
289 Markieff Morris	.15	.40
290 Marcus Morris	.20	.50
291 Eric Bledsoe	.20	.50
292 Goran Dragic	.20	.50
293 Kendall Marshall	.20	.50
294 Goran Dragic	.20	.50
295 DeMarcus Cousins	.25	.60
296 Patrick Patterson	.15	.40
297 DeMarcus Cousins	.25	.60
298 Jason Thompson	.15	.40
299 John Salmons	.15	.40
300 Jimmer Fredette	.25	.60
301 Isaiah Thomas	.25	.60
302 Marcus Thornton	.15	.40
303 Greivis Vasquez	.15	.40
304 Isaiah Thomas	.20	.50
305 Carmelo Anthony	.40	1.00
306 Dwight Howard	.30	.75
307 DeAndre Jordan	.25	.60
308 Kevin Durant	.75	2.00
309 Rajon Rondo	.30	.75
310 Jose Calderon	.15	.40
311 Chris Paul	.50	1.25
312 Serge Ibaka	.20	.50
313 Zach Randolph	.20	.50
314 David Lee	.15	.40
315 Kobe Bryant	2.00	5.00
316 Marc Gasol	.25	.60
317 Tim Duncan	.60	1.50
318 Danilo Gallinari	.20	.50
319 Dirk Nowitzki	.60	1.50
320 Andrew Bogut	.20	.50
321 Tony Parker	.40	1.00
322 Steve Nash	.50	1.25
323 Kevin Durant	.75	2.00
324 Anderson Varejao	.15	.40
325 All-Star Game	.20	.50
326 All-Star Game	.20	.50
327 All-Star Game	.20	.50
328 All-Star Game	.20	.50
329 All-Star Game	.20	.50
330 Rising Star Challenge	.20	.50
331 Rising Star Challenge	.20	.50
332 Terrence Ross	.20	.50
333 Kyrie Irving	.75	2.00
334 Chris Paul	.50	1.25
335 All-Star Game	.20	.50
336 Anthony Bennett	.15	.40
337 Victor Oladipo	.40	1.00
338 Otto Porter	.25	.60
339 Cody Zeller	.20	.50
340 Alex Len	.20	.50
341 Nerlens Noel	.20	.50
342 Ben McLemore	.20	.50
343 Kentavious Caldwell-Pope	.25	.60
344 Trey Burke	.20	.50
345 C.J. McCollum	.60	1.50
346 Damian Lillard	.75	2.00
347 Anthony Davis	.75	2.00
348 Bradley Beal	.40	1.00
349 Harrison Barnes	.25	.60
350 Michael Kidd-Gilchrist	.15	.40
351 Dion Waiters	.15	.40
352 Terrence Ross	.15	.40
353 Andre Drummond	.20	.50
354 Tyler Zeller	.15	.40
355 John Henson	.15	.40
356 Festus Ezeli	.15	.40
357 Jared Sullinger	.15	.40
358 LeBron James	2.00	5.00
359 Marc Gasol	.25	.60
360 Damian Lillard	.75	2.00
361 J.R. Smith	.25	.60
362 Paul George	.40	1.00
363 LeBron James	2.00	5.00

2014-15 Panini Stickers

COMPLETE SET (470)	50.00	120.00
1 Panini Knight Logo	.10	.25
2 NBA Logo	.10	.25
3 Rajon Rondo FOIL	.40	1.00
4 Jeff Green FOIL	.25	.60
5 Celtics Home Jersey	.10	.25
6 Celtics Road Jersey	.10	.25
7 Rajon Rondo	.30	.75
8 Jeff Green	.20	.50
9 Avery Bradley	.15	.40
10 Brandon Bass	.15	.40
11 Celtics Logo	.10	.25
12 Jared Sullinger	.15	.40
13 Kelly Olynyk	.15	.40
14 Tyler Zeller	.15	.40
15 Marcus Smart	.60	1.50
16 Joe Johnson FOIL	.25	.60
17 Deron Williams FOIL	.25	.60
18 Nets Home Jersey	.10	.25
19 Nets Road Jersey	.10	.25
20 Joe Johnson	.20	.50
21 Deron Williams	.20	.50
22 Kevin Garnett	.60	1.50
23 Mason Plumlee	.15	.40
24 Nets Logo	.10	.25
25 Alan Anderson	.15	.40
26 Brook Lopez	.25	.60
27 Andrei Kirilenko	.20	.50
28 Mirza Teletovic	.15	.40
29 Carmelo Anthony FOIL	.50	1.25
30 Tim Hardaway Jr. FOIL	.25	.60
31 Knicks Home Jersey	.10	.25
32 Knicks Road Jersey	.10	.25
33 Carmelo Anthony	.40	1.00
34 Tim Hardaway Jr.	.20	.50
35 Amar'e Stoudemire	.25	.60
36 J.R. Smith	.25	.60
37 Knicks Logo	.10	.25
38 Andrea Bargnani	.15	.40
39 Pablo Prigioni	.15	.40
40 Jose Calderon	.15	.40
41 Iman Shumpert	.15	.40
42 M.Carter-Williams FOIL	.15	.40
43 Tony Wroten FOIL	.15	.40
44 76ers Home Jersey	.10	.25
45 76ers Road Jersey	.10	.25
46 Michael Carter-Williams	.15	.40
47 Alexey Shved	.15	.40
48 Nerlens Noel	.15	.40
49 Henry Sims	.15	.40
50 76ers Logo	.10	.25
51 Tony Wroten	.15	.40
52 Joel Embiid	12.00	30.00
53 Jason Richardson	.25	.60
54 Hollis Thompson	.15	.40
55 DeMar DeRozan FOIL	.40	1.00
56 Kyle Lowry FOIL	.40	1.00
57 Raptors Home Jersey	.10	.25
58 Raptors Road Jersey	.10	.25
59 DeMar DeRozan	.30	.75
60 Kyle Lowry	.30	.75
61 Greivis Vasquez	.20	.50
62 Jonas Valanciunas	.20	.50
63 Raptors Logo	.10	.25
64 Terrence Ross	.15	.40
65 Amir Johnson	.15	.40
66 Patrick Patterson	.15	.40
67 Louis Williams	.20	.50
68 Derrick Rose FOIL	.60	1.50
69 Joakim Noah FOIL	.30	.75
70 Bulls Home Jersey	.10	.25
71 Bulls Road Jersey	.10	.25
72 Derrick Rose	.50	1.25
73 Joakim Noah	.25	.60
74 Pau Gasol	.40	1.00
75 Tony Snell	.15	.40
76 Bulls Logo	.10	.25
77 Kirk Hinrich	.20	.50
78 Jimmy Butler	.40	1.00
79 Taj Gibson	.15	.40
80 Mike Dunleavy	.15	.40
81 Kyrie Irving FOIL	.60	1.50
82 LeBron James FOIL	2.50	6.00
83 Cavaliers Home Jersey	.10	.25
84 Cavaliers Road Jersey	.10	.25
85 Kyrie Irving	.50	1.25
86 LeBron James	2.00	5.00
87 Dion Waiters	.15	.40
88 Tristan Thompson	.15	.40
89 Cavaliers Logo	.10	.25
90 Shawn Marion	.15	.40
91 Kevin Love	.25	.60
92 Anderson Varejao	.15	.40
93 Matt Dellavedova	.20	.50
94 Andre Drummond FOIL	.25	.60
95 Greg Monroe FOIL	.20	.50
96 Pistons Home Jersey	.10	.25
97 Pistons Road Jersey	.10	.25
98 Greg Monroe	.15	.40
99 Andre Drummond	.20	.50
100 Brandon Jennings	.15	.40
101 Josh Smith	.15	.40
102 Pistons Logo	.10	.25
103 Kyle Singler	.15	.40
104 Kentavious Caldwell-Pope	.20	.50
105 Jonas Jerebko	.15	.40
106 Luigi Datome	.15	.40
107 Roy Hibbert FOIL	.25	.60
108 David West FOIL	.25	.60
109 Pacers Home Jersey	.10	.25
110 Pacers Road Jersey	.10	.25
111 Paul George	.40	1.00
112 David West	.20	.50
113 Roy Hibbert	.20	.50
114 Luis Scola	.20	.50
115 Pacers Logo	.10	.25
116 Rodney Stuckey	.15	.40
117 C.J. Watson	.15	.40
118 George Hill	.20	.50
119 Ian Mahinmi	.15	.40
120 Jabari Parker FOIL	.25	.60
121 G.Antetokounmpo FOIL	25.00	60.00
122 Bucks Home Jersey	.10	.25
123 Bucks Road Jersey	.10	.25
124 Jabari Parker	.20	.50
125 Giannis Antetokounmpo	25.00	60.00
126 Brandon Knight	.15	.40
127 Larry Sanders	.15	.40
128 Bucks Logo	.10	.25
129 Ersan Ilyasova	.15	.40
130 John Henson	.15	.40
131 Nate Wolters	.20	.50
132 Zaza Pachulia	.15	.40
133 Jeff Teague FOIL	.20	.50
134 Paul Millsap FOIL	.25	.60
135 Hawks Home Jersey	.10	.25
136 Hawks Road Jersey	.10	.25
137 Jeff Teague	.15	.40
138 Paul Millsap	.20	.50
139 Al Horford	.25	.60
140 Dennis Schroder	.25	.60
141 Hawks Logo	.10	.25
142 Elton Brand	.25	.60
143 Kyle Korver	.20	.50
144 Pero Antic	.15	.40
145 DeMarre Carroll	.15	.40
146 Al Jefferson FOIL	.20	.50
147 Kemba Walker FOIL	.30	.75
148 Hornets Home Jersey	.10	.25
149 Hornets Road Jersey	.10	.25
150 Al Jefferson	.15	.40
151 Kemba Walker	.25	.60
152 Michael Kidd-Gilchrist	.15	.40
153 Gerald Henderson	.15	.40
154 Hornets Logo	.10	.25
155 Bismack Biyombo	.15	.40
156 Cody Zeller	.15	.40
157 Lance Stephenson	.20	.50
158 Noah Vonleh	.15	.40
159 Chris Bosh FOIL	.40	1.00
160 Dwyane Wade FOIL	.60	1.50
161 Heat Home Jersey	.10	.25
162 Heat Road Jersey	.10	.25
163 Chris Bosh	.30	.75
164 Dwyane Wade	.50	1.25
165 Mario Chalmers	.20	.50
166 Udonis Haslem	.20	.50
167 Heat Logo	.10	.25
168 Josh McRoberts	.15	.40
169 Chris Andersen	.20	.50
170 Luol Deng	.20	.50
171 Norris Cole	.15	.40
172 Nikola Vucevic FOIL	.25	.60
173 Victor Oladipo FOIL	.25	.60
174 Magic Home Jersey	.10	.25
175 Magic Road Jersey	.10	.25
176 Nikola Vucevic	.20	.50
177 Victor Oladipo	.20	.50
178 Tobias Harris	.20	.50
179 Aaron Gordon	.75	2.00
180 Magic Logo	.10	.25
181 Maurice Harkless	.15	.40
182 Channing Frye	.15	.40
183 Elfrid Payton	.25	.60
184 Evan Fournier	.15	.40
185 John Wall FOIL	.40	1.00
186 Bradley Beal FOIL	.50	1.25
187 Wizards Home Jersey	.10	.25
188 Wizards Road Jersey	.10	.25
189 John Wall	.30	.75
190 Bradley Beal	.40	1.00
191 Nene	.20	.50
192 Paul Pierce	.40	1.00
193 Wizards Logo	.10	.25
194 Otto Porter	.20	.50
195 Marcin Gortat	.15	.40
196 Martell Webster	.15	.40
197 Andre Miller	.20	.50
198 Dirk Nowitzki FOIL	.75	2.00
199 Monta Ellis FOIL	.25	.60
200 Mavericks Home Jersey	.10	.25
201 Mavericks Road Jersey	.10	.25
202 Dirk Nowitzki	.60	1.50
203 Monta Ellis	.20	.50
204 Tyson Chandler	.25	.60
205 Devin Harris	.15	.40
206 Mavericks Logo	.10	.25
207 Raymond Felton	.15	.40
208 Jae Crowder	.15	.40
209 Jameer Nelson	.15	.40
210 Chandler Parsons	.15	.40
211 Dwight Howard FOIL	.40	1.00
212 James Harden FOIL	.60	1.50
213 Rockets Home Jersey	.10	.25
214 Rockets Road Jersey	.10	.25
215 Dwight Howard	.30	.75
216 James Harden	.50	1.25
217 Trevor Ariza	.15	.40
218 Donatas Motiejunas	.15	.40
219 Rockets Logo	.10	.25
220 Patrick Beverley	.15	.40
221 Terrence Jones	.15	.40
222 Troy Daniels	.15	.40
223 Robert Covington	.20	.50
224 Marc Gasol FOIL	.30	.75
225 Zach Randolph FOIL	.30	.75
226 Grizzlies Home Jersey	.10	.25
227 Grizzlies Road Jersey	.10	.25
228 Marc Gasol	.25	.60
229 Zach Randolph	.25	.60
230 Tayshaun Prince	.25	.60
231 Mike Conley	.20	.50
232 Grizzlies Logo	.10	.25
233 Vince Carter	.50	1.25
234 Tony Allen	.15	.40
235 Courtney Lee	.15	.40
236 Kosta Koufos	.15	.40
237 Anthony Davis FOIL	.75	2.00
238 Jrue Holiday FOIL	.40	1.00
239 Pelicans Home Jersey	.10	.25
240 Pelicans Road Jersey	.10	.25
241 Jrue Holiday	.30	.75
242 Anthony Davis	.60	1.50
243 Eric Gordon	.20	.50
244 Jeff Withey	.15	.40
245 Pelicans Logo	.10	.25
246 Ryan Anderson	.15	.40
247 Omer Asik	.15	.40
248 Austin Rivers	.15	.40
249 Tyreke Evans	.20	.50
250 Tim Duncan FOIL	.75	2.00
251 Kawhi Leonard FOIL	.75	2.00
252 Spurs Home Jersey	.10	.25
253 Spurs Road Jersey	.10	.25
254 Tim Duncan	.60	1.50
255 Kawhi Leonard	.60	1.50
256 Tony Parker	.40	1.00
257 Manu Ginobili	.50	1.25
258 Spurs Logo	.10	.25
259 Patty Mills	.25	.60
260 Tiago Splitter	.15	.40
261 Boris Diaw	.20	.50
262 Marco Belinelli	.15	.40
263 Ty Lawson FOIL	.20	.50
264 Danilo Gallinari FOIL	.20	.50
265 Nuggets Home Jersey	.10	.25
266 Nuggets Road Jersey	.10	.25
267 Ty Lawson	.15	.40
268 Danilo Gallinari	.15	.40
269 Wilson Chandler	.15	.40
270 Kenneth Faried	.15	.40
271 Nuggets Logo	.10	.25
272 Arron Afflalo	.15	.40
273 JaVale McGee	.20	.50
274 J.J. Hickson	.15	.40
275 Timofey Mozgov	.15	.40
276 Ricky Rubio FOIL	.25	.60
277 Kevin Martin FOIL	.25	.60
278 Timberwolves Home Jersey	.10	.25
279 Timberwolves Road Jersey	.10	.25
280 Andrew Wiggins	.75	2.00
281 Ricky Rubio	.20	.50
282 Nikola Pekovic	.15	.40
283 Corey Brewer	.15	.40
284 Timberwolves Logo	.10	.25
285 Gorgui Dieng	.15	.40
286 Jose Barea	.20	.50
287 Thaddeus Young	.15	.40
288 Kevin Martin	.20	.50
289 Kevin Durant FOIL	1.00	2.50
290 Russell Westbrook FOIL	.50	1.25
291 Thunder Home Jersey	.10	.25
292 Thunder Road Jersey	.10	.25
293 Kevin Durant	.75	2.00
294 Russell Westbrook	.40	1.00
295 Reggie Jackson	.20	.50
296 Serge Ibaka	.20	.50
297 Thunder Logo	.10	.25
298 Jeremy Lamb	.15	.40
299 Nick Collison	.20	.50
300 Kendrick Perkins	.15	.40
301 Steven Adams	.30	.75
302 Damian Lillard FOIL	.75	2.00
303 LaMarcus Aldridge FOIL	.30	.75
304 Trail Blazers Home Jersey	.10	.25
305 Trail Blazers Road Jersey	.10	.25
306 Damian Lillard	.60	1.50
307 LaMarcus Aldridge	.25	.60
308 Dorell Wright	.15	.40
309 Robin Lopez	.15	.40
310 Trail Blazers Logo	.10	.25
311 Nicolas Batum	.20	.50
312 Thomas Robinson	.15	.40
313 Wesley Matthews	.15	.40
314 C.J. McCollum	.25	.60
315 Gordon Hayward FOIL	.25	.60
316 Trey Burke FOIL	.20	.50
317 Jazz Home Jersey	.10	.25
318 Jazz Road Jersey	.10	.25
319 Gordon Hayward	.20	.50
320 Trey Burke	.15	.40
321 Derrick Favors	.15	.40
322 Alec Burks	.20	.50
323 Jazz Logo	.10	.25
324 Enes Kanter	.20	.50
325 Rudy Gobert	.40	1.00
326 Jeremy Evans	.15	.40
327 Dante Exum	.25	.60
328 Stephen Curry FOIL	2.50	6.00
329 Klay Thompson FOIL	.75	2.00
330 Warriors Home Jersey	.10	.25
331 Warriors Road Jersey	.10	.25
332 Stephen Curry	2.00	5.00
333 Klay Thompson	.60	1.50
334 David Lee	.15	.40
335 Andre Iguodala	.25	.60
336 Warriors Logo	.10	.25
337 Draymond Green	.30	.75
338 Harrison Barnes	.20	.50
339 Shaun Livingston	.20	.50
340 Andrew Bogut	.20	.50
341 Chris Paul FOIL	.50	1.25
342 Blake Griffin FOIL	.30	.75
343 Clippers Home Jersey	.10	.25
344 Clippers Road Jersey	.10	.25
345 Chris Paul	.40	1.00
346 Blake Griffin	.25	.60
347 J.J. Redick	.25	.60
348 Spencer Hawes	.15	.40
349 Clippers Logo	.10	.25
350 DeAndre Jordan	.20	.50
351 Matt Barnes	.20	.50
352 Glen Davis	.15	.40
353 Jamal Crawford	.25	.60
354 Kobe Bryant FOIL	6.00	15.00
355 Nick Young FOIL	.20	.50
356 Lakers Home Jersey	.10	.25
357 Lakers Road Jersey	.10	.25
358 Kobe Bryant	2.00	5.00
359 Nick Young	.15	.40
360 Steve Nash	.50	1.25
361 Jeremy Lin	.50	1.25
362 Lakers Logo	.10	.25
363 Carlos Boozer	.20	.50
364 Jordan Hill	.15	.40
365 Ryan Kelly	.15	.40
366 Julius Randle	.75	2.00
367 Isaiah Thomas FOIL	.25	.60
368 Goran Dragic FOIL	.30	.75
369 Suns Home Jersey	.10	.25
370 Suns Road Jersey	.10	.25
371 Eric Bledsoe	.20	.50
372 Goran Dragic	.25	.60
373 Isaiah Thomas	.20	.50
374 Gerald Green	.20	.50
375 Suns Logo	.10	.25
376 Marcus Morris	.15	.40
377 Markieff Morris	.15	.40
378 Miles Plumlee	.15	.40
379 T.J. Warren	.25	.60
380 Rudy Gay FOIL	.30	.75
381 DeMarcus Cousins FOIL	.25	.60
382 Kings Home Jersey	.10	.25
383 Kings Road Jersey	.10	.25
384 Rudy Gay	.25	.60
385 DeMarcus Cousins	.20	.50
386 Ben McLemore	.15	.40
387 Ray McCallum	.15	.40
388 Kings Logo	.10	.25
389 Darren Collison	.15	.40
390 Derrick Williams	.15	.40
391 Jason Thompson	.15	.40
392 Nik Stauskas	.15	.40
393 Manu Ginobili	.50	1.25
394 Matt Dellavedova	.20	.50
395 Mirza Teletovic	.15	.40
396 Nene	.20	.50
397 Serge Ibaka	.20	.50
398 Tony Parker	.40	1.00
399 Dennis Schroder	.25	.60
400 Andrea Bargnani	.15	.40
401 Jose Barea	.20	.50
402 Goran Dragic	.25	.60
403 Victor Claver	.15	.40
404 Enes Kanter	.20	.50
405 Global Games - Manchester	.10	.25
406 Global Games - Manila	.10	.25
407 Global Games - Rio de Janeiro	.10	.25
408 Global Games - Taipei	.10	.25
409 Global Games - Shanghai	.10	.25
410 Global Games - Beijing	.10	.25
411 Global Games - Istanbul	.10	.25
412 Global Games - London	.10	.25
413 Christmas Day Games Logo	.10	.25
414 Bulls		
Nets	.10	.25
415 Thunder		
Knicks	.10	.25
416 Heat		
Lakers	.10	.25
417 Rockets		
Spurs	.10	.25
418 Clippers		
Warriors	.10	.25
419 Kyrie Irving		
All-Star Game MVP	.50	1.25
420 John Wall		
Dunk Contest	.30	.75
421 Rising Stars Challenge	.10	.25
422 Andre Drummond		
Rising Stars Challenge MVP	.20	.50
423 Trey Burke		
Skills Challenge Team	.15	.40
424 Damian Lillard		
Skills Challenge Team	.60	1.50
425 Marco Belinelli		
{3-Point Shooting Contest	.15	.40
426 All-Star Game Logo	.10	.25
427 Paul George AS	.40	1.00
428 Carmelo Anthony AS	.40	1.00
429 LeBron James AS	2.00	5.00
430 Stephen Curry AS	2.00	5.00
431 Kevin Durant AS	.75	2.00
432 James Harden AS	.50	1.25
433 Chris Paul AS	.40	1.00
434 Western Conference First Round	.10	.25
435 Western Conference First Round	.10	.25
436 Western Conference Second Round	.10	.25
437 Western Conference Finals	.10	.25
438 Eastern Conference First Round	.10	.25
439 Eastern Conference First Round	.10	.25
440 Eastern Conference First Round	.10	.25
441 Eastern Conference Finals	.10	.25
442 NBA Finals Game 1	.10	.25
443 NBA Finals Game 2	.10	.25
444 NBA Finals Game 3	.10	.25
445 NBA Finals Game 4	.10	.25
446 NBA Finals Game 5	.10	.25
447 NBA Champions	.10	.25
448 NBA Champions	.10	.25
449 Kawhi Leonard		
NBA Finals MVP	.60	1.50
450 Alonzo Mourning HOF	.40	1.00
451 Nolan Richardson HOF	.25	.60
452 Mitch Richmond HOF	.30	.75
453 Gary Williams HOF	.25	.60
454 Hall of Fame Logo	.10	.25
455 David Stern HOF	.25	.60
456 Doug McDermott	.25	.60
457 Zach LaVine	1.00	2.50
458 Rodney Hood	.20	.50
459 Shabazz Napier	.20	.50
460 P.J. Hairston	.15	.40
461 James Young	.15	.40
462 Gary Harris	.25	.60
463 Kevin Durant		

MVP .75 2.00
464 Michael Carter-Williams
Rookie of the Year .15 .40
465 Joakim Noah
Defensive Player of the Year .25 .60
466 Jamal Crawford
Sixth Man of the Year .25 .60
467 Goran Dragic
Most Improved Player of the Year .25 .60
468 Luol Deng
Kennedy Citizenship Award .20 .50
469 Mike Conley
NBA Sportsmanship Award .20 .50
470 Shane Battier
Twyman-Stokes Teammate of the Year .20 .50

2015-16 Panini Stickers

COMPLETE SET (483) 20.00 50.00
1 Dirk Nowitzki
Highest-scoring international player .75 2.00
2 Panini Knight Logo .10 .25
3 NBA Logo .10 .25
4 Kobe Bryant
#3 on All-Time scoring list 2.50 6.00
5 Klay Thompson
Record for points in a quarter .75 2.00
6 Kyrie Irving
NBA-best 57 points in one game .60 1.50
7 Russell Westbrook
Registers 11 triple-doubles .50 1.25
8 Anthony Davis
Historic Statline .75 2.00
9 Avery Bradley FOIL .20 .50
10 Boston Celtics
Home Jersey .10 .25
11 Boston Celtics
Away Jersey .10 .25
12 Marcus Smart FOIL .40 1.00
13 Marcus Smart .40 1.00
14 Boston Celtics Logo .10 .25
15 Avery Bradley .20 .50
16 Jared Sullinger .20 .50
17 Evan Turner .20 .50
18 Tyler Zeller .20 .50
19 Kelly Olynyk .20 .50
20 Isaiah Thomas .25 .60
21 Terry Rozier .75 2.00
22 Brook Lopez FOIL .30 .75
23 Brooklyn Nets
Home Jersey .10 .25
24 Brooklyn Nets
Away Jersey .10 .25
25 Joe Johnson FOIL .25 .60
26 Joe Johnson .25 .60
27 Brooklyn Nets Logo .10 .25
28 Brook Lopez .30 .75
29 Bojan Bogdanovic .25 .60
30 Shane Larkin .20 .50
31 Thaddeus Young .20 .50
32 Jarrett Jack .25 .60
33 Thomas Robinson .20 .50
34 Markel Brown .20 .50
35 Carmelo Anthony FOIL .50 1.25
36 New York Knicks
Home Jersey .10 .25
37 New York Knicks
Away Jersey .10 .25
38 Kristaps Porzingis FOIL 8.00 20.00
39 Carmelo Anthony .50 1.25
40 New York Knicks Logo .10 .25
41 Kristaps Porzingis 8.00 20.00
42 Cleanthony Early .20 .50
43 Langston Galloway .20 .50
44 Robin Lopez .20 .50
45 Jose Calderon .20 .50
46 Arron Afflalo .20 .50
47 Derrick Williams .20 .50
48 Tony Wroten FOIL .20 .50
49 Philadelphia 76ers
Home Jersey .10 .25
50 Philadelphia 76ers
Away Jersey .10 .25
51 Nerlens Noel FOIL .20 .50
52 Nerlens Noel .20 .50
53 Philadelphia 76ers Logo .10 .25
54 Tony Wroten .20 .50
55 Robert Covington .25 .60
56 Isaiah Canaan .20 .50
57 Jahlil Okafor .25 .60
58 Jerami Grant .30 .75
59 Joel Embiid .75 2.00
60 JaKarr Sampson .20 .50
61 DeMar DeRozan FOIL .40 1.00
62 Toronto Raptors
Home Jersey .10 .25
63 Toronto Raptors
Away Jersey .10 .25
64 Kyle Lowry FOIL .30 .75
65 DeMar DeRozan .40 1.00
66 Toronto Raptors Logo .10 .25
67 Kyle Lowry .30 .75
68 Jonas Valanciunas .25 .60
69 Terrence Ross .25 .60
70 DeMarre Carroll .20 .50
71 Patrick Patterson .20 .50
72 Bruno Caboclo .20 .50
73 James Johnson .20 .50
74 Derrick Rose FOIL .50 1.25
75 Chicago Bulls
Home Jersey .10 .25
76 Chicago Bulls
Away Jersey .10 .25
77 Jimmy Butler FOIL .60 1.50
78 Derrick Rose .50 1.25
79 Chicago Bulls Logo .10 .25
80 Pau Gasol .50 1.25
81 Jimmy Butler .60 1.50
82 Joakim Noah .20 .50
83 Taj Gibson .20 .50
84 Nikola Mirotic .20 .50
85 Doug McDermott .25 .60
86 Tony Snell .20 .50
87 LeBron James FOIL 2.50 6.00
88 Cleveland Cavaliers
Home Jersey .10 .25
89 Cleveland Cavaliers
Away Jersey .10 .25
90 Kyrie Irving FOIL .60 1.50
91 LeBron James 2.50 6.00
92 Cleveland Cavaliers Logo .10 .25
93 Kyrie Irving .60 1.50
94 Iman Shumpert .20 .50
95 Timofey Mozgov .20 .50
96 Tristan Thompson .20 .50
97 Kevin Love .30 .75
98 Matthew Dellavedova .25 .60
99 J.R. Smith .30 .75
100 Andre Drummond FOIL .30 .75
101 Detroit Pistons
Home Jersey .10 .25
102 Detroit Pistons
Away Jersey .10 .25
103 Brandon Jennings FOIL .20 .50
104 Andre Drummond .30 .75
105 Detroit Pistons Logo .10 .25
106 Brandon Jennings .20 .50
107 Kentavious Caldwell-Pope .20 .50
108 Reggie Jackson .25 .60
109 Stanley Johnson .25 .60
110 Spencer Dinwiddie .25 .60
111 Jodie Meeks .20 .50
112 Marcus Morris .20 .50
113 Paul George FOIL .50 1.25
114 Indiana Pacers
Home Jersey .10 .25
115 Indiana Pacers
Away Jersey .10 .25
116 George Hill FOIL .25 .60
117 Paul George .50 1.25
118 Indiana Pacers Logo .10 .25
119 George Hill .25 .60
120 C.J. Miles .20 .50
121 Rodney Stuckey .20 .50
122 Solomon Hill .20 .50
123 Myles Turner .75 2.00
124 Monta Ellis .20 .50
125 Joe Young .20 .50
126 Giannis Antetokounmpo FOIL 1.50 4.00
127 Milwaukee Bucks
Home Jersey .10 .25
128 Milwaukee Bucks
Away Jersey .10 .25
129 Jabari Parker FOIL .20 .50
130 Giannis Antetokounmpo 1.50 4.00
131 Milwaukee Bucks Logo .10 .25
132 Jabari Parker .20 .50
133 Michael Carter-Williams .20 .50
134 Khris Middleton .40 1.00
135 Greg Monroe .25 .60
136 O.J. Mayo .20 .50
137 Tyler Ennis .20 .50
138 John Henson .20 .50
139 Al Horford .30 .75
140 Atlanta Hawks
Home Jersey .10 .25
141 Atlanta Hawks
Away Jersey .10 .25
142 Jeff Teague .20 .50
143 Al Horford .30 .75
144 Atlanta Hawks Logo .10 .25
145 Jeff Teague .20 .50
146 Kyle Korver .25 .60
147 Paul Millsap .25 .60
148 Dennis Schroder .30 .75
149 Thabo Sefolosha .20 .50
150 Tiago Splitter .20 .50
151 Tim Hardaway Jr. .25 .60
152 Kemba Walker .30 .75
153 Charlotte Hornets
Home Jersey .10 .25
154 Charlotte Hornets
Away Jersey .10 .25
155 Al Jefferson .20 .50
156 Kemba Walker .30 .75
157 Charlotte Hornets Logo .10 .25
158 Al Jefferson .20 .50
159 Michael Kidd-Gilchrist .20 .50
160 Nicolas Batum .20 .50
161 Marvin Williams .20 .50
162 Frank Kaminsky .20 .50
163 Jeremy Lin .60 1.50
164 Cody Zeller .20 .50
165 Chris Bosh .40 1.00
166 Miami Heat
Home Jersey .10 .25
167 Miami Heat
Away Jersey .10 .25
168 Dwyane Wade .60 1.50
169 Dwyane Wade .60 1.50
170 Miami Heat Logo .10 .25
171 Chris Bosh .40 1.00
172 Luol Deng .25 .60
173 Goran Dragic .30 .75
174 Hassan Whiteside .25 .60
175 Justise Winslow .30 .75
176 Chris Andersen .25 .60
177 Mario Chalmers .25 .60
178 Victor Oladipo .25 .60
179 Orlando Magic
Home Jersey .10 .25
180 Orlando Magic
Away Jersey .10 .25
181 Nikola Vucevic .25 .60
182 Victor Oladipo .25 .60
183 Orlando Magic Logo .10 .25
184 Nikola Vucevic .25 .60
185 Elfrid Payton .25 .60
186 Tobias Harris .25 .60
187 Mario Hezonja .25 .60
188 Aaron Gordon .30 .75
189 Channing Frye .20 .50
190 Evan Fournier .25 .60
191 John Wall .40 1.00
192 Washington Wizards
Home Jersey .10 .25
193 Washington Wizards
Away Jersey .10 .25
194 Bradley Beal .40 1.00
195 John Wall .40 1.00
196 Washington Wizards Logo .10 .25
197 Bradley Beal .40 1.00
198 Marcin Gortat .20 .50
199 Martell Webster .20 .50
200 Nene .25 .60
201 Otto Porter Jr. .25 .60
202 Kris Humphries .20 .50
203 Ramon Sessions .20 .50
204 Chandler Parsons .20 .50
205 Dallas Mavericks
Home Jersey .10 .25
206 Dallas Mavericks
Away Jersey .10 .25
207 Dirk Nowitzki .75 2.00
208 Dirk Nowitzki .75 2.00
209 Dallas Mavericks Logo .10 .25
210 Chandler Parsons .20 .50
211 Wesley Matthews .20 .50
212 J.J. Barea .25 .60
213 Devin Harris .20 .50
214 Deron Williams .25 .60
215 Justin Anderson .20 .50
216 Charlie Villanueva .20 .50
217 James Harden .60 1.50
218 Houston Rockets
Home Jersey .10 .25
219 Houston Rockets
Away Jersey .10 .25
220 Dwight Howard .40 1.00
221 James Harden .60 1.50
222 Houston Rockets Logo .10 .25
223 Dwight Howard .40 1.00
224 Trevor Ariza .20 .50
225 Sam Dekker .20 .50
226 Patrick Beverley .20 .50
227 Donatas Motiejunas .20 .50
228 Corey Brewer .20 .50
229 Terrence Jones .20 .50
230 Mike Conley .30 .75
231 Memphis Grizzlies
Home Jersey .10 .25
232 Memphis Grizzlies
Away Jersey .10 .25
233 Zach Randolph .30 .75
234 Zach Randolph .30 .75
235 Memphis Grizzlies Logo .10 .25
236 Mike Conley .30 .75
237 Marc Gasol .30 .75
238 Tony Allen .20 .50
239 Courtney Lee .20 .50
240 Jeff Green .20 .50
241 Jordan Adams .20 .50
242 Vince Carter .60 1.50
243 Anthony Davis .75 2.00
244 New Orleans Pelicans
Home Jersey .10 .25
245 New Orleans Pelicans
Away Jersey .10 .25
246 Tyreke Evans .25 .60
247 Anthony Davis .75 2.00
248 New Orleans Pelicans Logo .10 .25
249 Tyreke Evans .25 .60
250 Jrue Holiday .40 1.00
251 Eric Gordon .25 .60
252 Alexis Ajinca .20 .50
253 Omer Asik .20 .50
254 Ryan Anderson .20 .50
255 Quincy Pondexter .20 .50
256 Tony Parker .50 1.25
257 San Antonio Spurs
Home Jersey .10 .25
258 San Antonio Spurs
Away Jersey .10 .25
259 Kwahi Leonard 1.25 3.00
260 Kwahi Leonard 1.25 3.00
261 San Antonio Spurs Logo .10 .25
262 Tim Duncan .75 2.00
263 Tony Parker .50 1.25
264 Manu Ginobili .60 1.50
265 Lamarcus Aldridge .30 .75
266 Danny Green .25 .60
267 Kyle Anderson .20 .50
268 Boris Diaw .25 .60
269 Kenneth Faried .25 .60
270 Denver Nuggets
Home Jersey .10 .25
271 Denver Nuggets
Away Jersey .10 .25
272 Emmanuel Mudiay .25 .60
273 Kenneth Faried .25 .60
274 Denver Nuggets Logo .10 .25
275 Danilo Gallinari .25 .60
276 Randy Foye .20 .50
277 Emmanuel Mudiay .25 .60
278 Jusuf Nurkic .25 .60
279 Wilson Chandler .25 .60
280 Gary Harris .25 .60
281 J.J. Hickson .20 .50
282 Andrew Wiggins .40 1.00
283 Minnesota Timberwolves
Home Jersey .10 .25
284 Minnesota Timberwolves
Away Jersey .10 .25
285 Ricky Rubio .25 .60
286 Andrew Wiggins .40 1.00
287 Minnesota Timberwolves Logo .10 .25
288 Ricky Rubio .25 .60
289 Kevin Garnett .75 2.00
290 Zach LaVine .75 2.00
291 Kevin Martin .25 .60
292 Karl-Anthony Towns 8.00 20.00
293 Shabazz Muhammad .20 .50
294 Anthony Bennett .20 .50
295 Kevin Durant 1.25 3.00
296 Oklahoma City Thunder
Home Jersey .10 .25
297 Oklahoma City Thunder
Away Jersey .10 .25
298 Russell Westbrook .50 1.25
299 Kevin Durant 1.25 3.00
300 Oklahoma City Thunder Logo .10 .25
301 Russell Westbrook .50 1.25
302 Serge Ibaka .25 .60
303 Enes Kanter .20 .50
304 Dion Waiters .20 .50
305 Anthony Morrow .20 .50
306 Steven Adams .25 .60
307 Mitch McGary .20 .50
308 Damian Lillard .75 2.00
309 Portland Trail Blazers
Home Jersey .10 .25
310 Portland Trail Blazers
Away Jersey .10 .25
311 C.J. McCollum .30 .75
312 Damian Lillard .75 2.00
313 Portland Trail Blazers Logo .10 .25
314 Gerald Henderson .20 .50
315 C.J. McCollum .30 .75
316 Meyers Leonard .20 .50
317 Noah Vonleh .20 .50
318 Ed Davis .20 .50
319 Al-Farouq Aminu .20 .50
320 Allen Crabbe .20 .50
321 Derrick Favors .25 .60
322 Utah Jazz
Home Jersey .10 .25
323 Utah Jazz
Away Jersey .10 .25
324 Gordon Hayward .30 .75
325 Gordon Hayward .30 .75
326 Utah Jazz Logo .10 .25
327 Derrick Favors .25 .60
328 Rudy Gobert .40 1.00
329 Trey Burke .20 .50
330 Dante Exum .25 .60
331 Alec Burks .20 .50
332 Rodney Hood .25 .60
333 Joe Ingles .25 .60
334 Stephen Curry 2.50 6.00
335 Golden State Warriors
Home Jersey .10 .25
336 Golden State Warriors
Away Jersey .10 .25
337 Klay Thompson .75 2.00
338 Stephen Curry 2.50 6.00
339 Golden State Warriors Logo .10 .25
340 Klay Thompson .75 2.00
341 Harrison Barnes .25 .60
342 Andre Iguodala .30 .75
343 Draymond Green .40 1.00
344 Andrew Bogut .25 .60
345 Shaun Livingston .20 .50
346 Leandro Barbosa .20 .50
347 Chris Paul .60 1.50
348 Los Angeles Clippers
Home Jersey .10 .25
349 Los Angeles Clippers
Away Jersey .10 .25
350 Blake Griffin .30 .75
351 Chris Paul .60 1.50
352 Los Angeles Clippers Logo .10 .25
353 Blake Griffin .30 .75
354 DeAndre Jordan .25 .60
355 J.J. Redick .30 .75
356 Jamal Crawford .30 .75
357 Lance Stephenson .25 .60
358 Paul Pierce .50 1.25
359 Josh Smith .30 .75
360 Kobe Bryant 2.50 6.00
361 Los Angeles Lakers
Home Jersey .10 .25
362 Los Angeles Lakers
Away Jersey .10 .25
363 Julius Randle .40 1.00
364 Kobe Bryant 2.50 6.00
365 Los Angeles Lakers Logo .10 .25
366 Julius Randle .40 1.00
367 Jordan Clarkson .30 .75
368 D'Angelo Russell .75 2.00
369 Lou Williams .25 .60
370 Roy Hibbert .25 .60
371 Nick Young .20 .50
372 Ryan Kelly .20 .50
373 Eric Bledsoe .25 .60
374 Phoenix Suns
Home Jersey .10 .25
375 Phoenix Suns
Away Jersey .10 .25
376 Brandon Knight .20 .50
377 Eric Bledsoe .25 .60
378 Phoenix Suns Logo .10 .25
379 Brandon Knight .20 .50
380 Alex Len .20 .50
381 Tyson Chandler .25 .60
382 T.J. Warren .30 .75
383 Archie Goodwin .20 .50
384 Markieff Morris .20 .50
385 P.J. Tucker .20 .50
386 DeMarcus Cousins .30 .75
387 Sacramento Kings
Home Jersey .10 .25
388 Sacramento Kings
Away Jersey .10 .25
389 Rudy Gay .30 .75
390 DeMarcus Cousins .30 .75
391 Sacramento Kings Logo .10 .25
392 Rudy Gay .30 .75
393 Rajon Rondo .40 1.00
394 Darren Collison .20 .50
395 Willie Cauley-Stein .25 .60
396 Ben McLemore .20 .50
397 Marco Belinelli .20 .50
398 Omri Casspi .20 .50
399 Trey Lyles .25 .60
400 Devin Booker 10.00 25.00
401 Cameron Payne .30 .75
402 Kelly Oubre Jr. .60 1.50
403 Rashad Vaughn .20 .50
404 Jerian Grant .20 .50
405 Bobby Portis .50 1.25
406 Rondae Hollis-Jefferson .25 .60
407 Tyus Jones .25 .60
408 All-Star Game FOIL .10 .25
409 Zach LaVine .75 2.00
410 Zach LaVine .75 2.00
411 Russell Westbrook .50 1.25
412 Stephen Curry 2.50 6.00
413 Stephen Curry 2.50 6.00
414 2016 All-Star Toronto FOIL .10 .25
415 Patrick Beverley .20 .50
416 Patrick Beverley .20 .50
417 LaMarcus Aldridge .30 .75
418 Stephen Curry 2.50 6.00
419 Tim Duncan .75 2.00
420 Kevin Durant 1.25 3.00
421 James Harden .60 1.50
422 Damian Lillard .75 2.00
423 Dirk Nowitzki .75 2.00
424 Chris Paul .60 1.50
425 Klay Thompson .75 2.00
426 Carmelo Anthony .50 1.25
427 Jimmy Butler .60 1.50
428 Pau Gasol .50 1.25
429 Al Horford .30 .75
430 Kyrie Irving .60 1.50
431 LeBron James 2.50 6.00
432 Kyle Lowry .30 .75
433 Jeff Teague .20 .50
434 John Wall .40 1.00
435 Warriors v Pelicans .20 .50
436 Trail Blazers v Grizzles .20 .50
437 Clippers v Spurs .20 .50
438 Rockets v Mavericks .20 .50
439 Warriors v Grizzlies .20 .50
440 Clippers v Rockets .20 .50
441 Warriors v Rockets .20 .50
442 Hawks v Nets .20 .50
443 Raptors v Wizards .20 .50
444 Bulls v Bucks .20 .50
445 Cavaliers v Celtics .20 .50
446 Hawks v Wizards .20 .50
447 Bulls v Cavaliers .20 .50
448 Hawks v Cavaliers .20 .50
449 The Finals
Game 1 .20 .50
450 The Finals
Game 2 .20 .50
451 The Finals
Game 3 .20 .50
452 The Finals
Game 4 .20 .50
453 The Finals
Game 5 .20 .50
454 The Finals
Game 6 .20 .50
455 Warriors Team .20 .50
456 Warriors Team .20 .50
457 Andre Iguodala MVP .30 .75
458 Warriors Championship Logo .10 .25
459 Warriors Championship Logo .10 .25
460 Larry O'Brien Trophy .40 1.00
461 Stephen Curry MVP 2.50 6.00
462 Andrew Wiggins ROY .40 1.00
463 Kawhi Leonard DPOY 1.00 2.50
464 Lou Williams
6th Man .25 .60
465 Jimmy Butler
Most Improved .60 1.50
466 Joakim Noah
Citizenship Award .20 .50
467 Kyle Korver
Sportsmanship Award .25 .60
468 Basketball HOF .20 .50
469 John Calipari .30 .75
470 Louie Dampier .30 .75
471 Spencer Haywood .30 .75
472 Tommy Heinsohn .30 .75
473 Dikembe Mutombo .50 1.25
474 Jo Jo White .30 .75
475 Kobe Bryant Championship 1 2.50 6.00
476 Kobe Bryant Championship 2 2.50 6.00
477 Kobe Bryant Championship 3 2.50 6.00
478 Kobe Bryant Championship 4 2.50 6.00
479 Kobe Bryant Championship 5 2.50 6.00
480 Kobe Bryant Photo 1 2.50 6.00
481 Kobe Bryant Photo 2 2.50 6.00
482 Kobe Bryant Photo 3 2.50 6.00
483 Kobe Bryant Photo 4 2.50 6.00

2016-17 Panini Stickers

COMPLETE SET (449) 25.00 60.00
1 2015-16 NBA Season Highlights .60 1.50
2 2015-16 NBA Season Highlights 2.00 5.00
3 2015-16 NBA Season Highlights .10 .25
4 2015-16 NBA Season Highlights .40 1.00
5 2015-16 NBA Season Highlights 2.00 5.00
6 2015-16 NBA Season Highlights .10 .25
7 2015-16 NBA Season Highlights .10 .25
8 2015-16 NBA Season Highlights .10 .25
9 Avery Bradley FOIL .20 .50
10 Isaiah Thomas FOIL .25 .60
11 Jae Crowder FOIL .20 .50
12 Boston Celtics Logo .10 .25
13 Isaiah Thomas .20 .50
14 Avery Bradley .15 .40
15 Jae Crowder .15 .40
16 Marcus Smart .30 .75
17 Al Horford .25 .60
18 Demetrius Jackson .15 .40
19 Jaylen Brown 1.25 3.00
20 Boston Celtics Home-Away Jerseys .10 .25
21 Brook Lopez FOIL .25 .60
22 Bojan Bogdanovic FOIL .25 .60
23 Rondae Hollis-Jefferson FOIL .20 .50
24 Brooklyn Nets Logo .10 .25
25 Brook Lopez .20 .50
26 Rondae Hollis-Jefferson .15 .40
27 Bojan Bogdanovic .20 .50
28 Jeremy Lin .50 1.25
29 Chris McCullough .15 .40
30 Luis Scola .20 .50
31 Isaiah Whitehead .15 .40
32 Brooklyn Nets Home-Away Jerseys .10 .25
33 Carmelo Anthony FOIL .50 1.25
34 Kristaps Porzingis
Illustrated .40 1.00
35 Derrick Rose FOIL .50 1.25
36 New York Knicks Logo .10 .25
37 Carmelo Anthony .40 1.00
38 Kristaps Porzingis .40 1.00
39 Derrick Rose .40 1.00
40 Courtney Lee .15 .40
41 Joakim Noah .15 .40
42 Lance Thomas .15 .40
43 Brandon Jennings .15 .40
44 New York Knicks Home-Away Jerseys .10 .25
45 Jahlil Okafor
Illustrated .15 .40
46 Nerlens Noel FOIL .20 .50
47 Robert Covington FOIL .25 .60
48 Philadelphia 76ers Logo .10 .25
49 Jahlil Okafor .15 .40
50 Nerlens Noel .15 .40
51 Robert Covington .20 .50
52 Joel Embiid .60 1.50
53 Gerald Henderson .15 .40
54 Ben Simmons .50 1.25
55 Jerami Grant .25 .60
56 Philadelphia 76ers
Home-Away Jerseys .10 .25
57 Kyle Lowry FOIL .30 .75
58 Jonas Valanciunas FOIL .25 .60
59 DeMar DeRozan
Illustrated .30 .75
60 Toronto Raptors Logo .10 .25
61 Kyle Lowry .25 .60
62 DeMar DeRozan .30 .75
63 Jonas Valanciunas .20 .50
64 DeMarre Carroll .15 .40
65 Norman Powell .25 .60
66 Cory Joseph .15 .40
67 Patrick Patterson .15 .40
68 Toronto Raptors Home-Away Jerseys .10 .25
69 Jimmy Butler
Illustrated .50 1.25
70 Nikola Mirotic FOIL .20 .50
71 Dwyane Wade FOIL .60 1.50
72 Chicago Bulls Logo .10 .25
73 Jimmy Butler .50 1.25
74 Bobby Portis .25 .60
75 Nikola Mirotic .15 .40
76 Rajon Rondo .30 .75
77 Dwyane Wade .50 1.25
78 Robin Lopez .15 .40
79 Tony Snell .15 .40
80 Chicago Bulls Home-Away Jerseys .10 .25
81 LeBron James FOIL 2.50 6.00
82 Kyrie Irving
Illustrated .50 1.25
83 Kevin Love FOIL .30 .75
84 Cleveland Cavaliers Logo .10 .25
85 LeBron James 2.00 5.00
86 Kyrie Irving .50 1.25
87 Kevin Love .25 .60
88 J.R. Smith .25 .60
89 Channing Frye .15 .40
90 Tristan Thompson .20 .50
91 Iman Shumpert .15 .40
92 Cleveland Cavaliers
Home-Away Jerseys .10 .25
93 Kentavious Caldwell-Pope FOIL .25 .60
94 Reggie Jackson FOIL .25 .60
95 Andre Drummond FOIL .30 .75
96 Detroit Pistons Logo .10 .25
97 Andre Drummond .25 .60
98 Reggie Jackson .20 .50
99 Stanley Johnson .15 .40
100 Tobias Harris .25 .60
101 Kentavious Caldwell-Pope .20 .50
102 Aron Baynes .15 .40
103 Marcus Morris .15 .40
104 Detroit Pistons Home-Away Jerseys .10 .25
105 Paul George
Illustrated .40 1.00
106 Monta Ellis FOIL .25 .60
107 Myles Turner FOIL .30 .75
108 Indiana Pacers Logo .10 .25
109 Paul George .40 1.00
110 Myles Turner .25 .60
111 Monta Ellis .20 .50
112 Jeff Teague .15 .40
113 Al Jefferson .15 .40
114 Thaddeus Young .15 .40
115 C.J. Miles .15 .40
116 Indiana Pacers Home-Away Jerseys .10 .25
117 Jabari Parker FOIL .20 .50
118 Giannis Antetokounmpo FOIL 1.50 4.00
119 Khris Middleton FOIL .30 .75
120 Milwaukee Bucks Logo .10 .25
121 Giannis Antetokounmpo 1.25 3.00
122 Jabari Parker .15 .40
123 Khris Middleton .25 .60
124 Greg Monroe .15 .40
125 Matthew Dellavedova .20 .50
126 John Henson .15 .40
127 Michael Carter-Williams .15 .40
128 Milwaukee Bucks
Home-Away Jerseys .10 .25
129 Paul Millsap FOIL .25 .60
130 Kyle Korver FOIL .25 .60
131 Dwight Howard FOIL .40 1.00
132 Atlanta Hawks Logo .10 .25
133 Paul Millsap .20 .50
134 Dennis Schroder .25 .60
135 Kent Bazemore .15 .40
136 Dwight Howard .30 .75
137 Kyle Korver .20 .50
138 Thabo Sefolosha .15 .40
139 Tiago Splitter .15 .40
140 Atlanta Hawks Home-Away Jerseys .10 .25
141 Frank Kaminsky FOIL .20 .50
142 Kemba Walker FOIL .25 .60
143 Nicolas Batum FOIL .25 .60
144 Charlotte Hornets Logo .10 .25
145 Kemba Walker .20 .50
146 Frank Kaminsky .15 .40
147 Nicolas Batum .20 .50
148 Michael Kidd-Gilchrist .15 .40
149 Marco Belinelli .15 .40
150 Marvin Williams .15 .40
151 Roy Hibbert .20 .50
152 Charlotte Hornets
Home-Away Jerseys .10 .25
153 Goran Dragic FOIL .30 .75
154 Justise Winslow FOIL .25 .60
155 Hassan Whiteside FOIL .25 .60
156 Miami Heat Logo .10 .25
157 Goran Dragic .25 .60
158 Hassan Whiteside .20 .50
159 Chris Bosh .30 .75
160 Justise Winslow .20 .50
161 Udonis Haslem .20 .50
162 Josh Richardson .20 .50
163 Tyler Johnson .15 .40
164 Miami Heat Home-Away Jerseys .10 .25
165 Elfrid Payton FOIL .25 .60
166 Nikola Vucevic FOIL .30 .75
167 Evan Fournier FOIL .25 .60
168 Orlando Magic Logo .10 .25
169 Mario Hezonja .15 .40
170 Aaron Gordon .25 .60
171 Nikola Vucevic .25 .60
172 Elfrid Payton .20 .50
173 Evan Fournier .20 .50
174 Bismack Biyombo .15 .40
175 Serge Ibaka .20 .50
176 Orlando Magic Home-Away Jerseys .10 .25
177 John Wall
Illustrated .30 .75
178 Marcin Gortat FOIL .20 .50
179 Bradley Beal FOIL .40 1.00
180 Washington Wizards Logo .10 .25
181 John Wall .30 .75
182 Markieff Morris .15 .40
183 Bradley Beal .30 .75
184 Marcin Gortat .15 .40
185 Kelly Oubre Jr. .30 .75
186 Otto Porter .10 .25
187 Ian Mahinmi .15 .40
188 Washington Wizards
Home-Away Jerseys .10 .25
189 Dallas Mavericks Logo .10 .25
190 Dirk Nowitzki .60 1.50
191 Justin Anderson .15 .40
192 Deron Williams .20 .50
193 Harrison Barnes .20 .50
194 Andrew Bogut .25 .60
195 J.J. Barea .20 .50
196 Wesley Matthews .15 .40
197 Dallas Mavericks
Home-Away Jerseys .10 .25
198 Wesley Matthews FOIL .20 .50
199 Dirk Nowitzki
Illustrated .60 1.50
200 J.J. Barea FOIL .25 .60
201 Houston Rockets Logo .10 .25
202 James Harden .50 1.25
203 Trevor Ariza .15 .40
204 Clint Capela .20 .50
205 Michael Beasley .15 .40
206 Patrick Beverley .15 .40
207 Corey Brewer .15 .40
208 Ryan Anderson .15 .40
209 Houston Rockets
Home-Away Jerseys .10 .25
210 Trevor Ariza FOIL .20 .50
211 James Harden
Illustrated .50 1.25
212 Patrick Beverley FOIL .20 .50
213 Memphis Grizzlies Logo .10 .25
214 Mike Conley .20 .50
215 Marc Gasol .25 .60
216 Zach Randolph .25 .60
217 JaMychal Green .20 .50
218 Chandler Parsons .15 .40
219 Vince Carter .50 1.25
220 Tony Allen .15 .40
221 Memphis Grizzlies
Home-Away Jerseys .10 .25
222 Mike Conley FOIL .25 .60
223 Zach Randolph FOIL .30 .75
224 Marc Gasol FOIL .30 .75
225 New Orleans Pelicans Logo .10 .25
226 Anthony Davis .75 2.00
227 Jrue Holiday .30 .75
228 Tyreke Evans .20 .50
229 E'Twaun Moore .15 .40
230 Omer Asik .15 .40
231 Dante Cunningham .15 .40
232 Buddy Hield .50 1.25
233 New Orleans Pelicans
Home-Away Jerseys .10 .25
234 Anthony Davis
Illustrated .75 2.00
235 Jrue Holiday FOIL .40 1.00
236 Tyreke Evans FOIL .25 .60
237 San Antonio Spurs Logo .10 .25
238 Kawhi Leonard .60 1.50
239 LaMarcus Aldridge .25 .60
240 Tony Parker .40 1.00
241 Patty Mills .25 .60
242 Manu Ginobili .50 1.25
243 Danny Green .20 .50
244 Pau Gasol .40 1.00
245 San Antonio Spurs
Home-Away Jerseys .10 .25
246 Kawhi Leonard FOIL .75 2.00
247 LaMarcus Aldridge FOIL .30 .75
248 Tony Parker
Illustrated .40 1.00
249 Denver Nuggets Logo .10 .25
250 Emmanuel Mudiay .15 .40
251 Danilo Gallinari .20 .50
252 Kenneth Faried .20 .50
253 Nikola Jokic 1.25 3.00
254 Will Barton .15 .40
255 Jusuf Nurkic .20 .50
256 Joffrey Lauvergne .15 .40
257 Denver Nuggets Home-Away Jerseys .10 .25
258 Emmanuel Mudiay FOIL .20 .50
259 Kenneth Faried FOIL .25 .60
260 Danilo Gallinari FOIL .25 .60
261 Minnesota Timberwolves Logo .10 .25
262 Karl-Anthony Towns .50 1.25
263 Andrew Wiggins .30 .75
264 Zach LaVine .50 1.25
265 Ricky Rubio .20 .50
266 Shabazz Muhammad .15 .40
267 Nemanja Bjelica .15 .40
268 Kris Dunn .25 .60
269 Minnesota Timberwolves
Home-Away Jerseys .10 .25
270 Zach LaVine FOIL .60 1.50
271 Andrew Wiggins
Illustrated .30 .75
272 Karl-Anthony Towns FOIL .60 1.50
273 Oklahoma City Thunder Logo .10 .25
274 Russell Westbrook .40 1.00
275 Steven Adams .20 .50
276 Enes Kanter .15 .40
277 Victor Oladipo .20 .50
278 Nick Collison .15 .40
279 Cameron Payne .25 .60
280 Domantas Sabonis 1.00 2.50
281 Oklahoma City Thunder
Home-Away Jerseys .10 .25
282 Victor Oladipo FOIL .25 .60
283 Russell Westbrook
Illustrated .40 1.00
284 Steven Adams FOIL .25 .60
285 Portland Trail Blazers Logo .10 .25
286 Damian Lillard .60 1.50

287 C.J. McCollum .25 .60
288 Al-Farouq Aminu .15 .40
289 Mason Plumlee .15 .40
290 Ed Davis .15 .40
291 Meyers Leonard .15 .40
292 Evan Turner .15 .40
293 Portland Trail Blazers
Home-Away Jerseys .10 .25
294 Damian Lillard
Illustrated .60 1.50
295 C.J. McCollum FOIL .30 .75
296 Al-Farouq Aminu FOIL .20 .50
297 Utah Jazz Logo .10 .25
298 Gordon Hayward .25 .60
299 Rudy Gobert .30 .75
300 Rodney Hood .20 .50
301 Derrick Favors .15 .40
302 Alec Burks .20 .50
303 Trey Lyles .20 .50
304 George Hill .20 .50
305 Utah Jazz Home-Away Jerseys .10 .25
306 Gordon Hayward FOIL .30 .75
307 Derrick Favors FOIL .20 .50
308 Rudy Gobert FOIL .40 1.00
309 Golden State Warriors Logo .10 .25
310 Stephen Curry 2.00 5.00
311 Klay Thompson .60 1.50
312 Draymond Green .30 .75
313 Kevin Durant 1.00 2.50
314 David West .20 .50
315 Shaun Livingston .15 .40
316 Zaza Pachulia .12 .30
317 Golden State Warriors
Home-Away Jerseys .10 .25
318 Stephen Curry FOIL 2.50 6.00
319 Draymond Green FOIL .40 1.00
320 Klay Thompson
Illustrated .60 1.50
321 Los Angeles Clippers Logo .10 .25
322 Chris Paul .40 1.00
323 Blake Griffin .25 .60
324 DeAndre Jordan .20 .50
325 J.J. Redick .25 .60
326 Jamal Crawford .25 .60
327 Austin Rivers .20 .50
328 Paul Pierce .40 1.00
329 Los Angeles Clippers
Home-Away Jerseys .10 .25
330 Chris Paul FOIL .50 1.25
331 Blake Griffin
Illustrated .25 .60
332 DeAndre Jordan FOIL .25 .60
333 Los Angeles Lakers Logo .10 .25
334 D'Angelo Russell .30 .75
335 Jordan Clarkson .25 .60
336 Julius Randle .30 .75
337 Larry Nance Jr. .15 .40
338 Luol Deng .20 .50
339 Lou Williams .25 .60
340 Brandon Ingram .60 1.50
341 Los Angeles Lakers
Home-Away Jerseys .10 .25
342 Jordan Clarkson FOIL .30 .75
343 Julius Randle FOIL .40 1.00
344 D'Angelo Russell
Illustrated .30 .75
345 Phoenix Suns Logo .10 .25
346 Devin Booker 1.00 2.50
347 Eric Bledsoe .20 .50
348 Brandon Knight .20 .50
349 Alex Len .15 .40
350 T.J. Warren .20 .50
351 Dragan Bender .15 .40
352 Marquese Chriss .20 .50
353 Phoenix Suns Home-Away Jerseys .10 .25
354 Eric Bledsoe FOIL .25 .60
355 Devin Booker FOIL 1.25 3.00
356 Brandon Knight FOIL .25 .60
357 Sacramento Kings Logo .10 .25
358 DeMarcus Cousins .20 .50
359 Rudy Gay .25 .60
360 Willie Cauley-Stein .20 .50
361 Darren Collison .15 .40
362 Ben McLemore .15 .40
363 Omri Casspi .15 .40
364 Kosta Koufos .15 .40
365 Sacramento Kings
Home-Away Jerseys .10 .25
366 DeMarcus Cousins FOIL .25 .60
367 Rudy Gay FOIL .30 .75
368 Willie Cauley-Stein FOIL .25 .60
369 Pelicans vs. Heat
2015 Christmas Day Matchups .10 .25
370 Bulls vs. Thunder
2015 Christmas Day Matchups .10 .25
371 Cavaliers vs. Warriors
2015 Christmas Day Matchups .10 .25
372 Spurs vs. Rockets
2015 Christmas Day Matchups .10 .25
373 Clippers vs. Lakers
2015 Christmas Day Matchups .10 .25
374 2016 NBA All-Star Game Logo .10 .25
375 Slam Dunk Contest Winner
Left .10 .25
376 Slam Dunk Contest Winner
Right .10 .25
377 2016 All-Star Game MVP .10 .25
378 3-Point Contest Winner
Left .10 .25
379 3-Point Contest Winner
Right .10 .25
380 2016 Rising Stars Challenge MVP .10 .25
381 Skills Challenge Winner
Left .10 .25
382 Skills Challenge Winner
Right .10 .25
383 Kobe Bryant
Western Conference All-Stars 2.00 5.00
384 Stephen Curry
Western Conference All-Stars 2.00 5.00
385 Anthony Davis
Western Conference All-Stars .75 2.00
386 Kevin Durant
Western Conference All-Stars 1.00 2.50
387 James Harden
Western Conference All-Stars .50 1.25
388 Kawhi Leonard
Western Conference All-Stars .60 1.50
389 Chris Paul
Western Conference All-Stars .40 1.00
390 Klay Thompson
Western Conference All-Stars .60 1.50
391 Russell Westbrook
Western Conference All-Stars .40 1.00
392 Carmelo Anthony
Eastern Conference All-Stars .40 1.00
393 DeMar DeRozan
Eastern Conference All-Stars .30 .75
394 Andre Drummond
Eastern Conference All-Stars .25 .60
395 Pau Gasol
Eastern Conference All-Stars .40 1.00
396 Paul George
Eastern Conference All-Stars .40 1.00
397 LeBron James
Eastern Conference All-Stars 2.00 5.00
398 Kyle Lowry
Eastern Conference All-Stars .25 .60
399 Dwyane Wade
Eastern Conference All-Stars .50 1.25
400 John Wall
Eastern Conference All-Stars .30 .75
401 Warriors vs. Rockets
2016 Playoffs .10 .25
402 Clippers vs. Trail Blazers
2016 Playoffs .10 .25
403 Thunder vs. Mavericks
2016 Playoffs .10 .25
404 Spurs vs. Grizzlies
2016 Playoffs .10 .25
405 Warriors vs. Trail Blazers
2016 Playoffs .10 .25
406 Spurs vs. Thunder
2016 Playoffs .10 .25
407 Warriors vs. Thunder
2016 Playoffs .10 .25
408 Cavaliers vs. Raptors
2016 Playoffs .10 .25
409 Cavaliers vs. Hawks
2016 Playoffs .10 .25
410 Raptors vs. Heat
2016 Playoffs .10 .25
411 Cavaliers vs. Pistons
2016 Playoffs .10 .25
412 Hawks vs. Celtics
2016 Playoffs .10 .25
413 Heat vs. Hornets
2016 Playoffs .10 .25
414 Raptors vs. Pacers
2016 Playoffs .10 .25
415 Game 1
2016 Finals .10 .25
416 Game 2
2016 Finals .10 .25
417 Game 3
2016 Finals .10 .25
418 Game 4
2016 Finals .10 .25
419 Game 5
2016 Finals .10 .25
420 Game 6
2016 Finals .10 .25
421 Game 7
2016 Finals .10 .25
422 Cavaliers Team
Left .10 .25
423 Cavaliers Team
Right .10 .25
424 Larry O'Brien Trophy .10 .25
425 Cavaliers Champions Logo
Left .10 .25
426 Cavaliers Champions Logo
Right .10 .25
427 LeBron James
2016 NBA Finals MVP 2.00 5.00
428 Stephen Curry
MVP 2.00 5.00
429 Karl-Anthony Towns
ROY .50 1.25
430 Kawhi Leonard
DPOY .60 1.50
431 Jamal Crawford
6th Man Award .25 .60
432 C.J. McCollum
Most Improved Player .25 .60
433 Wayne Ellington
Kennedy Citizenship Award .15 .40
434 Mike Conley Jr.
NBA Sportsmanship Award .20 .50
435 Jamal Murray
7th Overall Draft Pick 1.25 3.00
436 Jakob Poeltl
9th Overall Draft Pick .30 .75
437 Thon Maker
10th Overall Draft Pick .20 .50
438 Denzel Valentine
14th Overall Draft Pick .15 .40
439 Wade Baldwin IV
17th Overall Draft Pick .15 .40
440 Henry Ellenson
18th Overall Draft Pick .15 .40
441 Malik Beasley
19th Overall Draft Pick .30 .75
442 Brice Johnson
25th Overall Draft Pick .15 .40
443 Dejounte Murray
29th Overall Draft Pick .75 2.00
444 Western Conference
Northwest Division .10 .25
445 Western Conference
Pacific Division .10 .25
446 Western Conference
Southwest Division .10 .25
447 Eastern Conference
Atlantic Division .10 .25
448 Eastern Conference
Central Division .10 .25
449 Eastern Conference
Southeast Division .10 .25

2017-18 Panini Stickers

COMPLETE SET (449) 25.00 60.00
1 Panini Logo FOIL .20 .50
2 NBA Season Highlights
Nov. 7, 2016
Stephen Curry 1.50 4.00
3 NBA Season Highlights
Dec. 1, 2016
HOU @ GSW .10 .25
4 NBA Season Highlights
Feb. 3, 2017
Boston Celtics .10 .25
5 NBA Season Highlights
Mar. 3, 2017
Cleveland Cavaliers .10 .25
6 NBA Season Highlights
Mar. 7, 2017
Dirk Nowitzki .50 1.25
7 NBA Season Highlights
Mar. 24, 2017
Devin Booker .50 1.25
8 NBA Season Highlights
Apr. 9, 2017
Russell Westbrook .30 .75
9 NBA Season Highlights
Apr. 12, 2017
Giannis Antetokounmpo 1.00 2.50
10 Kent Bazemore FOIL .20 .50
11 Ersan Ilyasova FOIL .20 .50
12 Dennis Schroeder FOIL .25 .60
13 Mike Budenholzer CO .20 .50
14 Dennis Schroder .20 .50
15 Kent Bazemore .15 .40
16 Malcolm Delaney .15 .40
17 Taurean Prince .15 .40
18 Marco Belinelli .15 .40
19 Ersan Ilyasova .15 .40
20 John Collins .40 1.00
21 Atlanta Hawks Team Logo .10 .25
22 Al Horford FOIL .30 .75
23 Marcus Smart FOIL .30 .75
24 Isaiah Thomas FOIL .25 .60
25 Brad Stevens CO .20 .50
26 Isaiah Thomas .20 .50
27 Al Horford .25 .60
28 Gordon Hayward .25 .60
29 Marcus Smart .25 .60
30 Jae Crowder .15 .40
31 Jaylen Brown .60 1.50
32 Jayson Tatum 12.00 30.00
33 Boston Celtics Team Logo .10 .25
34 D'Angelo Russell FOIL .25 .60
35 Trevor Booker FOIL .20 .50
36 Sean Kilpatrick FOIL .20 .50
37 Kenny Atkinson CO .15 .40
38 Trevor Booker .15 .40
39 Sean Kilpatrick .15 .40
40 Jeremy Lin .40 1.00
41 D'Angelo Russell .20 .50
42 DeMarre Carroll .15 .40
43 Allen Crabbe .15 .40
44 Rondae Hollis-Jefferson .15 .40
45 Brooklyn Nets Team Logo .10 .25
46 Nicolas Batum FOIL .20 .50
47 Michael Kidd-Gilchrist FOIL .20 .50
48 Kemba Walker FOIL .25 .60
49 Steve Clifford CO .15 .40
50 Kemba Walker .20 .50
51 Dwight Howard .30 .75
52 Nicolas Batum .15 .40
53 Marvin Williams .15 .40
54 Michael Kidd-Gilchrist .15 .40
55 Cody Zeller .15 .40
56 Frank Kaminsky .15 .40
57 Charlotte Hornets Team Logo .10 .25
58 Dwyane Wade FOIL .60 1.50
59 Zach LaVine FOIL .50 1.25
60 Robin Lopez FOIL .20 .50
61 Fred Hoiberg CO .15 .40
62 Dwyane Wade .50 1.25
63 Robin Lopez .15 .40
64 Bobby Portis .15 .40
65 Zach LaVine .40 1.00
66 Kris Dunn .15 .40
67 Jerian Grant .15 .40
68 Denzel Valentine .15 .40
69 Chicago Bulls Team Logo .10 .25
70 Kyrie Irving FOIL .60 1.50
71 Kevin Love FOIL .30 .75
72 LeBron James FOIL 2.50 6.00
73 Tyronn Lue CO .25 .60
74 LeBron James 2.00 5.00
75 Kyrie Irving .50 1.25
76 Kevin Love .25 .60
77 J.R. Smith .20 .50
78 Tristan Thompson .15 .40
79 Iman Shumpert .15 .40
80 Richard Jefferson .15 .40
81 Cleveland Cavaliers Team Logo .10 .25
82 Andre Drummond FOIL .25 .60
83 Tobias Harris FOIL .25 .60
84 Reggie Jackson FOIL .25 .60
85 Stan Van Gundy CO .25 .60
86 Tobias Harris .20 .50
87 Reggie Jackson .20 .50
88 Andre Drummond .20 .50
89 Jon Leuer .15 .40
90 Ish Smith .15 .40
91 Avery Bradley .15 .40
92 Luke Kennard .30 .75
93 Detroit Pistons Team Logo .10 .25
94 Myles Turner FOIL .30 .75
95 Victor Oladipo FOIL .25 .60
96 Thaddeus Young FOIL .20 .50
97 Nate McMillan CO .15 .40
98 Myles Turner .25 .60
99 Thaddeus Young .15 .40
100 Victor Oladipo .20 .50
101 Glenn Robinson III .15 .40
102 Al Jefferson .20 .50
103 Cory Joseph .15 .40
104 Darren Collison .15 .40
105 Indiana Pacers Team Logo .10 .25
106 Dion Waiters FOIL .20 .50
107 Goran Dragic FOIL .25 .60
108 Hassan Whiteside FOIL .25 .60
109 Erik Spoelstra CO .25 .60
110 Goran Dragic .20 .50
111 Hassan Whiteside .20 .50
112 Dion Waiters .15 .40
113 Tyler Johnson .15 .40
114 Justise Winslow .15 .40
115 Josh Richardson .20 .50
116 Kelly Olynyk .15 .40
117 Miami Heat Team Logo .10 .25
118 Jabari Parker FOIL .20 .50
119 Malcolm Brogdon FOIL .25 .60
120 Giannis Antetokounmpo FOIL 1.50 4.00
121 Jason Kidd CO .40 1.00
122 Giannis Antetokounmpo 1.25 3.00
123 Jabari Parker .15 .40
124 Khris Middleton .30 .75
125 Greg Monroe .15 .40
126 Malcolm Brogdon .20 .50
127 Tony Snell .15 .40
128 Matthew Dellavedova .20 .50
129 Milwaukee Bucks Team Logo .10 .25
130 Joakim Noah FOIL .20 .50
131 Courtney Lee FOIL .20 .50
132 Kristaps Porzingis FOIL .40 1.00
133 Jeff Hornacek CO .20 .50
134 Carmelo Anthony .40 1.00
135 Kristaps Porzingis .30 .75
136 Courtney Lee .15 .40
137 Joakim Noah .15 .40
138 Lance Thomas .15 .40
139 Tim Hardaway Jr. .20 .50
140 Willy Hernangomez .15 .40
141 New York Knicks Team Logo .10 .25
142 Aaron Gordon FOIL .30 .75
143 Evan Fournier FOIL .25 .60
144 Elfrid Payton FOIL .20 .50
145 Frank Vogel CO .15 .40
146 Evan Fournier .20 .50
147 Terrence Ross .20 .50
148 Elfrid Payton .15 .40
149 Nikola Vucevic .20 .50
150 Aaron Gordon .25 .60
151 Bismack Biyombo .15 .40
152 Jonathan Isaac .40 1.00
153 Orlando Magic Team Logo .10 .25
154 Joel Embiid FOIL .60 1.50
155 Dario Saric FOIL .20 .50
156 Robert Covington FOIL .20 .50
157 Brett Brown CO .15 .40
158 Joel Embiid .50 1.25
159 Robert Covington .15 .40
160 Jahlil Okafor .15 .40
161 Dario Saric .20 .50
162 Ben Simmons .25 .60
163 J.J. Redick .25 .60
164 Markelle Fultz .40 1.00
165 Philadelphia 76ers Team Logo .10 .25
166 DeMar DeRozan FOIL .40 1.00
167 Kyle Lowry FOIL .30 .75
168 Jonas Valanciunas FOIL .25 .60
169 Dwane Casey CO .15 .40
170 DeMar DeRozan .30 .75
171 Kyle Lowry .25 .60
172 Serge Ibaka .25 .60
173 Jonas Valanciunas .20 .50
174 Norman Powell .25 .60
175 C.J. Miles .15 .40
176 OG Anunoby .75 2.00
177 Toronto Raptors Team Logo .10 .25
178 John Wall FOIL .40 1.00
179 Markieff Morris FOIL .20 .50
180 Bradley Beal FOIL .40 1.00
181 Scott Brooks CO .15 .40
182 John Wall .30 .75
183 Bradley Beal .30 .75
184 Markieff Morris .15 .40
185 Otto Porter Jr. .20 .50
186 Marcin Gortat .15 .40
187 Kelly Oubre Jr. .25 .60
188 Ian Mahinmi .15 .40
189 Washington Wizards Team Logo .10 .25
190 Dirk Nowitzki FOIL .75 2.00
191 Yogi Ferrell FOIL .20 .50
192 Harrison Barnes FOIL .25 .60
193 Rick Carlisle CO .20 .50
194 Harrison Barnes .20 .50
195 Dirk Nowitzki .60 1.50
196 Wesley Matthews .25 .60
197 Seth Curry .25 .60
198 Yogi Ferrell .15 .40
199 J.J. Barea .20 .50
200 Dennis Smith Jr. .25 .60
201 Dallas Mavericks Team Logo .10 .25
202 Paul Millsap FOIL .25 .60
203 Nikola Jokic FOIL 2.00 5.00
204 Kenneth Faried FOIL .25 .60
205 Mike Malone CO .15 .40
206 Paul Millsap .20 .50
207 Nikola Jokic 1.50 4.00
208 Kenneth Faried .20 .50
209 Gary Harris .20 .50
210 Wilson Chandler .20 .50
211 Emmanuel Mudiay .15 .40
212 Jamal Murray .40 1.00
213 Denver Nuggets Team Logo .10 .25
214 Stephen Curry FOIL 2.50 6.00
215 Draymond Green FOIL .40 1.00
216 Kevin Durant FOIL 1.25 3.00
217 Steve Kerr CO .15 .40
218 Stephen Curry 2.00 5.00
219 Kevin Durant 1.00 2.50
220 Klay Thompson .60 1.50
221 Draymond Green .30 .75
222 Andre Iguodala .25 .60
223 Shaun Livingston .20 .50
224 Zaza Pachulia .15 .40
225 Golden State Warriors Team Logo .10 .25
226 James Harden FOIL .60 1.50
227 Chris Paul FOIL .50 1.25
228 Eric Gordon FOIL .25 .60
229 Mike D'Antoni CO .20 .50
230 James Harden .50 1.25
231 Eric Gordon .20 .50
232 Chris Paul .40 1.00
233 Ryan Anderson .15 .40
234 Clint Capela .20 .50
235 Trevor Ariza .15 .40
236 P.J. Tucker .15 .40
237 Houston Rockets Team Logo .10 .25
238 Blake Griffin FOIL .30 .75
239 Danilo Gallinari FOIL .25 .60
240 DeAndre Jordan FOIL .25 .60
241 Doc Rivers CO .25 .60
242 Blake Griffin .25 .60
243 DeAndre Jordan .20 .50
244 Danilo Gallinari .20 .50
245 Austin Rivers .20 .50
246 Patrick Beverley .15 .40
247 Lou Williams .20 .50
248 Wesley Johnson .15 .40
249 Los Angeles Clippers Team Logo .10 .25
250 Brandon Ingram FOIL .40 1.00
251 Julius Randle FOIL .30 .75
252 Jordan Clarkson FOIL .30 .75
253 Luke Walton CO .15 .40
254 Jordan Clarkson .25 .60
255 Julius Randle .25 .60
256 Brandon Ingram .30 .75
257 Lonzo Ball .60 1.50
258 Brook Lopez .20 .50
259 Luol Deng .20 .50
260 Corey Brewer .15 .40
261 Los Angeles Lakers Team Logo .10 .25
262 Marc Gasol FOIL .30 .75
263 Mike Conley FOIL .25 .60
264 Chandler Parsons FOIL .20 .50
265 David Fizdale CO .15 .40
266 Marc Gasol .25 .60
267 Mike Conley .20 .50
268 Brandan Wright .15 .40
269 Troy Daniels .15 .40
270 Ben McLemore .15 .40
271 Chandler Parsons .15 .40
272 Tyreke Evans .15 .40
273 Memphis Grizzlies Team Logo .10 .25
274 Jimmy Butler FOIL .50 1.25
275 Karl-Anthony Towns FOIL .50 1.25
276 Andrew Wiggins FOIL .40 1.00
277 Tom Thibodeau CO .20 .50
278 Karl-Anthony Towns .40 1.00
279 Andrew Wiggins .30 .75
280 Jimmy Butler .40 1.00
281 Jeff Teague .15 .40
282 Gorgui Dieng .15 .40
283 Jamal Crawford .25 .60
284 Taj Gibson .15 .40
285 Minnesota Timberwolves Team Logo .10 .25
286 Anthony Davis FOIL .75 2.00
287 Jrue Holiday FOIL .40 1.00
288 DeMarcus Cousins FOIL .25 .60
289 Alvin Gentry CO .15 .40
290 Anthony Davis .60 1.50
291 DeMarcus Cousins .20 .50
292 Jrue Holiday .30 .75
293 Jordan Crawford .15 .40
294 E'Twaun Moore .15 .40
295 Solomon Hill .15 .40
296 Rajon Rondo .30 .75
297 New Orleans Pelicans Team Logo .10 .25
298 Russell Westbrook FOIL .50 1.25
299 Paul George FOIL .50 1.25
300 Steven Adams FOIL .25 .60
301 Billy Donovan CO .30 .75
302 Russell Westbrook .40 1.00
303 Paul George .40 1.00
304 Steven Adams .20 .50
305 Enes Kanter .20 .50
306 Andre Roberson .15 .40
307 Jerami Grant .40 1.00
308 Doug McDermott .15 .40
309 Oklahoma City Thunder Team Logo .10 .25
310 Devin Booker FOIL .75 2.00
311 Eric Bledsoe FOIL .25 .60
312 Marquese Chriss FOIL .25 .60
313 Earl Watson CO .15 .40
314 Devin Booker .60 1.50
315 Eric Bledsoe .20 .50
316 T.J. Warren .20 .50
317 Marquese Chriss .15 .40
318 Tyson Chandler .20 .50
319 Alan Williams .15 .40
320 Josh Jackson .20 .50
321 Phoenix Suns Team Logo .10 .25
322 Damian Lillard FOIL .75 2.00
323 Jusuf Nurkic FOIL .25 .60
324 C.J. McCollum FOIL .30 .75
325 Terry Stotts CO .15 .40
326 Damian Lillard .60 1.50
327 C.J. McCollum .20 .50
328 Jusuf Nurkic .20 .50
329 Maurice Harkless .15 .40
330 Evan Turner .15 .40
331 Noah Vonleh .15 .40
332 Zach Collins .25 .60
333 Portland Trail Blazers Team Logo .10 .25
334 George Hill FOIL .25 .60
335 Buddy Hield FOIL .30 .75
336 Willie Cauley-Stein FOIL .20 .50
337 Dave Joerger CO .15 .40
338 George Hill .20 .50
339 Buddy Hield .25 .60
340 Zach Randolph .20 .50
341 Willie Cauley-Stein .15 .40
342 Kosta Koufos .15 .40
343 De'Aaron Fox 2.00 5.00
344 Justin Jackson .15 .40
345 Sacramento Kings Team Logo .10 .25
346 Tony Parker FOIL .50 1.25
347 LaMarcus Aldridge FOIL .30 .75
348 Kawhi Leonard FOIL .75 2.00
349 Gregg Popovich CO .60 1.50
350 Kawhi Leonard .60 1.50
351 Tony Parker .40 1.00
352 Rudy Gay .25 .60
353 LaMarcus Aldridge .25 .60
354 Pau Gasol .40 1.00
355 Danny Green .25 .60
356 Dejounte Murray .25 .60
357 San Antonio Spurs Team Logo .10 .25
358 Rudy Gobert FOIL .40 1.00
359 Ricky Rubio FOIL .25 .60
360 Derrick Favors FOIL .20 .50
361 Quin Snyder CO .20 .50
362 Rudy Gobert .30 .75
363 Ricky Rubio .20 .50
364 Rodney Hood .15 .40
365 Joe Ingles .20 .50
366 Joe Johnson .20 .50
367 Derrick Favors .15 .40
368 Donovan Mitchell 4.00 10.00
369 Utah Jazz Team Logo .10 .25
370 Celtics v Knicks
'16 Christmas Day Match-ups .10 .25
371 Warriors v Cavaliers
'16 Christmas Day Match-ups .10 .25
372 Bulls v Spurs
'16 Christmas Day Match-ups .10 .25
373 Timberwolves v Thunder
'16 Christmas Day Match-ups .10 .25
374 Clippers v Lakers
'16 Christmas Day Match-ups .10 .25
375 2017 NBA All-Star Game Logo FOIL .20 .50
376 Glenn Robinson III
'17 NBA All Star Game Slam Dunk Contest Winner
puzzle 1 .15 .40
377 Glenn Robinson III
'17 NBA All Star Game Slam Dunk Contest Winner
puzzle 2 .15 .40
378 2017 NBA All-Star Game MVP .15 .40
379 Eric Gordon
'17 NBA All Star Game 3-Point Contest Winner
puzzle 1 .20 .50
380 Eric Gordon
'17 NBA All Star Game 3-Point Contest Winner
puzzle 2 .20 .50
381 2018 NBA All-Star Game Logo .10 .25
382 Kristaps Porzingis
'17 NBA All Star Game Skills Challenge Winner
puzzle 1 .30 .75
383 Kristaps Porzingis
'17 NBA All Star Game Skills Challenge Winner
puzzle 2 .30 .75
384 Stephen Curry
Western Conference All-Stars 2.00 5.00
385 James Harden
Western Conference All-Stars .50 1.25
386 Kevin Durant
Western Conference All-Stars 1.00 2.50
387 Kawhi Leonard
Western Conference All-Stars .60 1.50
388 Anthony Davis
Western Conference All-Stars .60 1.50
389 Russell Westbrook
Western Conference All-Stars .40 1.00
390 Klay Thompson
Western Conference All-Stars .60 1.50
391 Marc Gasol
Western Conference All-Stars .25 .60
392 DeAndre Jordan
Western Conference All-Stars .20 .50
393 Kyrie Irving
Eastern Conference All-Stars .50 1.25
394 DeMar DeRozan
Eastern Conference All-Stars .30 .75
395 LeBron James
Eastern Conference All-Stars 2.00 5.00
396 Jimmy Butler
Eastern Conference All-Stars .40 1.00
397 Giannis Antetokounmpo
Eastern Conference All-Stars 1.25 3.00
398 Isaiah Thomas
Eastern Conference All-Stars .20 .50
399 John Wall
Eastern Conference All-Stars .30 .75
400 Kyle Lowry
Eastern Conference All-Stars .25 .60
401 Kemba Walker
Eastern Conference All-Stars .20 .50
402 Warriors vs. Trail Blazers .10 .25
403 Clippers vs. Jazz .10 .25
404 Rockets vs. Thunder .10 .25
405 Spurs vs. Grizzlies .10 .25
406 Warriors vs. Jazz .10 .25
407 Spurs vs. Rockets .10 .25
408 Warriors vs. Spurs .10 .25
409 Celtics vs. Cavaliers .10 .25
410 Celtics vs. Wizards .10 .25
411 Cavaliers vs. Raptors .10 .25
412 Celtics vs. Bulls .10 .25
413 Wizards vs. Hawks .10 .25
414 Raptors vs. Bucks .10 .25
415 Cavaliers vs. Pacers .10 .25
416 Game 1
'17 NBA Finals .10 .25
417 Game 2
'17 NBA Finals .10 .25
418 Game 3
'17 NBA Finals .10 .25
419 Game 4
'17 NBA Finals .10 .25
420 Game 5
'17 NBA Finals .10 .25
421 2017 NBA Champions Logo
puzzle 1 .10 .25
422 2017 NBA Champions Logo
puzzle 2 .10 .25
423 Larry O'Brien Trophy FOIL .15 .40
424 Golden State Warriors Team Photo
puzzle 1 .10 .25
425 Golden State Warriors Team Photo
puzzle 2 .10 .25
426 Kevin Durant
2017 NBA Finals MVP 1.00 2.50
427 Russell Westbrook
Most Valuable Player
16-17 NBA Awards .40 1.00
428 Malcolm Brogdon
Rookie of the Year
16-17 NBA Awards .20 .50
429 Draymond Green
Defensive Player of the Year
16-17 NBA Awards .30 .75
430 Eric Gordon
Sixth Man of the Year
16-17 NBA Awards .20 .50
431 Giannis Antetokounmpo
Most Improved Player
16-17 NBA Awards 1.25 3.00
432 Kemba Walker
NBA Sportsmanship Award
16-17 NBA Awards .20 .50
433 Dirk Nowitzki
Teammate of the Year Award
16-17 NBA Awards .60 1.50
434 Markelle Fultz
NBA Draft .40 1.00
435 Lonzo Ball
NBA Draft .60 1.50
436 Jayson Tatum
NBA Draft 12.00 30.00
437 Josh Jackson
NBA Draft .20 .50
438 De'Aaron Fox
NBA Draft 2.00 5.00
439 Lauri Markkanen
NBA Draft 1.00 2.50
440 Malik Monk
NBA Draft .60 1.50
441 Bam Adebayo
NBA Draft 1.00 2.50
442 T.J. Leaf
NBA Draft .15 .40
443 NBA Logo
puzzle 1 .10 .25
444 NBA Logo
puzzle 2 .10 .25
445 NBA Logo
puzzle 3 .10 .25
446 NBA Logo
puzzle 4 .10 .25
447 NBA Logo
puzzle 5 .10 .25
448 NBA Logo
puzzle 6 .10 .25

2018-19 Panini Stickers

1 Panini Knight Logo .10 .25
2 Russell Westbrook
Oct. 28, 2017 .40 1.00
3 Kobe Bryant
Dec. 18, 2017 2.00 5.00
4 Lauri Markkanen
Jan. 15, 2018 .40 1.00
5 James Harden
Jan. 30, 2018 .50 1.25
6 Nikola Jokic
Feb. 15, 2018 1.25 3.00
7 Dirk Nowitzki
Feb. 28, 2018 .60 1.50
8 LeBron James
Apr. 6, 2018 2.00 5.00
9 Markelle Fultz
Apr. 11, 2018 .20 .50
10 Atlanta Hawks Team Logo .10 .25
11 John Collins FOIL .30 .75
12 Taurean Prince FOIL .20 .50
13 Kent Bazemore FOIL .20 .50
14 Lloyd Pierce .15 .40
15 Kent Bazemore .15 .40
16 Jeremy Lin .40 1.00
17 Dewayne Dedmon .15 .40
18 Taurean Prince .15 .40
19 Trae Young 12.00 30.00
20 John Collins .25 .60
21 Miles Plumlee .15 .40
22 Tyler Dorsey .15 .40
23 Boston Celtics Team Logo .10 .25
24 Jayson Tatum FOIL 1.25 3.00
25 Gordon Hayward FOIL .30 .75
26 Kyrie Irving FOIL .75 2.00
27 Brad Stevens .15 .40
28 Kyrie Irving .60 1.50
29 Jaylen Brown .40 1.00
30 Al Horford .25 .60
31 Jayson Tatum 1.00 2.50
32 Gordon Hayward .25 .60
33 Marcus Morris .15 .40
34 Terry Rozier .20 .50
35 Marcus Smart .25 .60
36 Brooklyn Nets Team Logo .10 .25
37 D'Angelo Russell FOIL .30 .75
38 Spencer Dinwiddie FOIL .25 .60
39 Rondae Hollis-Jefferson FOIL .20 .50
40 Kenny Atkinson .15 .40
41 Shabazz Napier .15 .40
42 Allen Crabbe .15 .40
43 Jarrett Allen .25 .60
44 DeMarre Carroll .15 .40
45 D'Angelo Russell .25 .60
46 Rondae Hollis-Jefferson .15 .40
47 Spencer Dinwiddie .20 .50
48 Caris LeVert .25 .60
49 Charlotte Hornets Team Logo .10 .25
50 Kemba Walker FOIL .25 .60
51 Jeremy Lamb FOIL .20 .50
52 Nicolas Batum FOIL .20 .50
53 James Borrego .15 .40
54 Nicolas Batum .15 .40
55 Tony Parker .40 1.00
56 Miles Bridges .40 1.00
57 Marvin Williams .15 .40
58 Michael Kidd-Gilchrist .15 .40
59 Kemba Walker .20 .50
60 Jeremy Lamb .15 .40
61 Frank Kaminsky .15 .40
62 Chicago Bulls Team Logo .10 .25
63 Lauri Markkanen FOIL .50 1.25
64 Kris Dunn FOIL .20 .50
65 Zach LaVine FOIL .50 1.25
66 Fred Hoiberg .15 .40
67 Robin Lopez .15 .40
68 Bobby Portis .25 .60
69 Justin Holiday .15 .40
70 Lauri Markkanen .40 1.00
71 Kris Dunn .15 .40
72 Denzel Valentine .15 .40
73 Zach LaVine .40 1.00
74 Wendell Carter Jr. .40 1.00
75 Cleveland Cavaliers Team Logo .10 .25
76 Larry Nance Jr. FOIL .20 .50
77 Kyle Korver FOIL .25 .60
78 Kevin Love FOIL .25 .60
79 Tyronn Lue .20 .50
80 Kevin Love .20 .50
81 George Hill .20 .50
82 JR Smith .25 .60
83 Kyle Korver .20 .50
84 Tristan Thompson .15 .40
85 Jordan Clarkson .25 .60
86 Larry Nance Jr. .15 .40
87 Collin Sexton .50 1.25
88 Detroit Pistons Team Logo .10 .25
89 Reggie Jackson FOIL .25 .60
90 Andre Drummond FOIL .25 .60
91 Blake Griffin FOIL .30 .75

92 Dwane Casey	.15	.40
93 Blake Griffin	.25	.60
94 Andre Drummond	.20	.50
95 Reggie Jackson	.20	.50
96 Stanley Johnson	.15	.40
97 Ish Smith	.15	.40
98 Luke Kennard	.20	.50
99 Jon Leuer	.15	.40
100 Reggie Bullock	.15	.40
101 Indiana Pacers Team Logo	.10	.25
102 Victor Oladipo FOIL	.25	.60
103 Myles Turner FOIL	.30	.75
104 Darren Collison FOIL	.20	.50
105 Nate McMillan	.20	.50
106 Bojan Bogdanovic	.20	.50
107 Darren Collison	.15	.40
108 Thaddeus Young	.15	.40
109 Victor Oladipo	.20	.50
110 Cory Joseph	.15	.40
111 Myles Turner	.25	.60
112 Tyreke Evans	.15	.40
113 Domantas Sabonis	.30	.75
114 Miami Heat Team Logo	.10	.25
115 Tyler Johnson FOIL	.20	.50
116 Goran Dragic FOIL	.25	.60
117 Kelly Olynyk FOIL	.20	.50
118 Erik Spoelstra	.15	.40
119 Goran Dragic	.20	.50
120 Hassan Whiteside	.20	.50
121 Josh Richardson	.20	.50
122 Kelly Olynyk	.15	.40
123 Justise Winslow	.20	.50
124 Tyler Johnson	.15	.40
125 Dwyane Wade	.50	1.25
126 Dion Waiters	.15	.40
127 Milwaukee Bucks Team Logo	.10	.25
128 Eric Bledsoe FOIL	.25	.60
129 Khris Middleton FOIL	.30	.75
130 Giannis Antetokounmpo FOIL	1.50	4.00
131 Mike Budenholzer	.15	.40
132 Giannis Antetokounmpo	1.25	3.00
133 Eric Bledsoe	.20	.50
134 Khris Middleton	.25	.60
135 John Henson	.15	.40
136 Tony Snell	.15	.40
137 Malcolm Brogdon	.25	.60
138 Thon Maker	.15	.40
139 Brook Lopez	.20	.50
140 New York Knicks Team Logo	.10	.25
141 Kristaps Porzingis FOIL	.40	1.00
142 Enes Kanter FOIL	.25	.60
143 Tim Hardaway Jr. FOIL	.20	.50
144 David Fizdale	.15	.40
145 Tim Hardaway Jr.	.15	.40
146 Kristaps Porzingis	.30	.75
147 Courtney Lee	.15	.40
148 Enes Kanter	.20	.50
149 Mario Hezonja	.15	.40
150 Emmanuel Mudiay	.15	.40
151 Frank Ntilikina	.15	.40
152 Kevin Knox	.20	.50
153 Orlando Magic Team Logo	.10	.25
154 Nikola Vucevic FOIL	.25	.60
155 Evan Fournier FOIL	.25	.60
156 Aaron Gordon FOIL	.30	.75
157 Steve Clifford	.15	.40
158 D.J. Augustin	.15	.40
159 Aaron Gordon	.25	.60
160 Evan Fournier	.20	.50
161 Nikola Vucevic	.20	.50
162 Jonathon Simmons	.15	.40
163 Mo Bamba	.25	.60
164 Terrence Ross	.20	.50
165 Jonathan Isaac	.25	.60
166 Philadelphia 76ers Team Logo	.10	.25
167 Dario Saric FOIL	.25	.60
168 Ben Simmons FOIL	.30	.75
169 Joel Embiid FOIL	.75	2.00
170 Brett Brown	.15	.40
171 Robert Covington	.20	.50
172 Joel Embiid	.60	1.50
173 Ben Simmons	.25	.60
174 JJ Redick	.25	.60
175 Dario Saric	.20	.50
176 Markelle Fultz	.20	.50
177 T.J. McConnell	.15	.40
178 Wilson Chandler	.15	.40
179 Toronto Raptors Team Logo	.10	.25
180 Kyle Lowry FOIL	.30	.75
181 Serge Ibaka FOIL	.25	.60
182 Jonas Valanciunas FOIL	.30	.75
183 Nick Nurse	.25	.60
184 Kawhi Leonard	.60	1.50
185 Kyle Lowry	.25	.60
186 Serge Ibaka	.20	.50
187 Jonas Valanciunas	.25	.60
188 Pascal Siakam	.40	1.00
189 OG Anunoby	.25	.60
190 Fred VanVleet	.30	.75
191 Danny Green	.20	.50
192 Washington Wizards Team Logo	.10	.25
193 John Wall FOIL	.40	1.00
194 Otto Porter Jr. FOIL	.25	.60
195 Bradley Beal FOIL	.40	1.00
196 Scott Brooks	.15	.40
197 Bradley Beal	.30	.75
198 John Wall	.30	.75
199 Otto Porter Jr.	.20	.50
200 Kelly Oubre Jr.	.25	.60
201 Markieff Morris	.15	.40
202 Dwight Howard	.30	.75
203 Tomas Satoransky	.15	.40
204 Austin Rivers	.20	.50
205 Dallas Mavericks Team Logo	.10	.25
206 Dennis Smith Jr. FOIL	.20	.50
207 Dirk Nowitzki FOIL	.75	2.00
208 Harrison Barnes FOIL	.25	.60
209 Rick Carlisle	.20	.50
210 Harrison Barnes	.20	.50
211 Wesley Matthews	.15	.40
212 Dennis Smith Jr.	.15	.40
213 Dwight Powell	.15	.40
214 Dirk Nowitzki	.60	1.50
215 J.J. Barea	.25	.60
216 DeAndre Jordan	.20	.50
217 Luka Doncic	15.00	40.00
218 Denver Nuggets Team Logo	.10	.25
219 Gary Harris FOIL	.25	.60
220 Jamal Murray FOIL	.60	1.50
221 Nikola Jokic FOIL	1.50	4.00
222 Michael Malone	.25	.60
223 Gary Harris	.20	.50
224 Will Barton	.15	.40
225 Nikola Jokic	1.25	3.00
226 Michael Porter Jr.	.60	1.50
227 Jamal Murray	.50	1.25
228 Paul Millsap	.20	.50
229 Trey Lyles	.15	.40
230 Isaiah Thomas	.20	.50
231 Golden State Warriors Team Logo	.10	.25
232 Kevin Durant FOIL	1.25	3.00
233 Stephen Curry FOIL	2.50	6.00
234 Draymond Green FOIL	.40	1.00
235 Steve Kerr	.30	.75
236 Stephen Curry	2.00	5.00
237 Kevin Durant	1.00	2.50
238 Klay Thompson	.60	1.50
239 Draymond Green	.30	.75
240 Andre Iguodala	.20	.50
241 Shaun Livingston	.20	.50
242 Quinn Cook	.20	.50
243 DeMarcus Cousins	.20	.50
244 Houston Rockets Team Logo	.10	.25
245 James Harden FOIL	.60	1.50
246 Clint Capela FOIL	.25	.60
247 Chris Paul FOIL	.60	1.50
248 Mike D'Antoni	.15	.40
249 James Harden	.50	1.25
250 Chris Paul	.50	1.25
251 Clint Capela	.20	.50
252 Eric Gordon	.20	.50
253 P.J. Tucker	.15	.40
254 Gerald Green	.20	.50
255 Ryan Anderson	.15	.40
256 Zhou Qi	.15	.40
257 Los Angeles Clippers Team Logo	.10	.25
258 Tobias Harris FOIL	.25	.60
259 Lou Williams FOIL	.25	.60
260 Danilo Gallinari FOIL	.25	.60
261 Doc Rivers	.25	.60
262 Tobias Harris	.20	.50
263 Avery Bradley	.15	.40
264 Lou Williams	.20	.50
265 Danilo Gallinari	.20	.50
266 Shai Gilgeous-Alexander	1.50	4.00
267 Patrick Beverley	.15	.40
268 Wesley Johnson	.15	.40
269 Milos Teodosic	.15	.40
270 Los Angeles Lakers Team Logo	.10	.25
271 Kyle Kuzma FOIL	.30	.75
272 Brandon Ingram FOIL	.30	.75
273 Lonzo Ball FOIL	.30	.75
274 Luke Walton	.15	.40
275 LeBron James	2.00	5.00
276 Lonzo Ball	.25	.60
277 Brandon Ingram	.25	.60
278 Kentavious Caldwell-Pope	.15	.40
279 Kyle Kuzma	.25	.60
280 Lance Stephenson	.20	.50
281 Josh Hart	.20	.50
282 Michael Beasley	.15	.40
283 Memphis Grizzlies Team Logo	.10	.25
284 Marc Gasol FOIL	.30	.75
285 Mike Conley FOIL	.25	.60
286 JaMychal Green FOIL	.20	.50
287 J.B. Bickerstaff	.15	.40
288 Marc Gasol	.25	.60
289 Mike Conley	.20	.50
290 Wayne Selden	.20	.50
291 Dillon Brooks	.25	.60
292 JaMychal Green	.15	.40
293 Andrew Harrison	.15	.40
294 Jaren Jackson Jr.	1.25	3.00
295 Chandler Parsons	.15	.40
296 Minnesota Timberwolves Team Logo	.10	.25
297 Jeff Teague FOIL	.20	.50
298 Karl-Anthony Towns FOIL	.50	1.25
299 Jimmy Butler FOIL	.50	1.25
300 Tom Thibodeau	.15	.40
301 Jimmy Butler	.40	1.00
302 Karl-Anthony Towns	.40	1.00
303 Andrew Wiggins	.30	.75
304 Taj Gibson	.15	.40
305 Jeff Teague	.15	.40
306 Gorgui Dieng	.15	.40
307 Tyus Jones	.15	.40
308 Derrick Rose	.50	1.25
309 New Orleans Pelicans Team Logo	.10	.25
310 Anthony Davis FOIL	.75	2.00
311 Jrue Holiday FOIL	.40	1.00
312 Nikola Mirotic FOIL	.20	.50
313 Alvin Gentry	.15	.40
314 Anthony Davis	.60	1.50
315 Jrue Holiday	.30	.75
316 Julius Randle	.25	.60
317 E'Twaun Moore	.15	.40
318 Elfrid Payton	.20	.50
319 Nikola Mirotic	.15	.40
320 Cheick Diallo	.15	.40
321 Darius Miller	.15	.40
322 Oklahoma City Thunder Team Logo	.10	.25
323 Steven Adams FOIL	.25	.60
324 Russell Westbrook FOIL	.50	1.25
325 Paul George FOIL	.50	1.25
326 Billy Donovan	.15	.40
327 Russell Westbrook	.40	1.00
328 Paul George	.40	1.00
329 Steven Adams	.20	.50
330 Dennis Schroder	.20	.50
331 Andre Roberson	.15	.40
332 Terrance Ferguson	.15	.40
333 Alex Abrines	.15	.40
334 Patrick Patterson	.15	.40
335 Phoenix Suns Team Logo	.10	.25
336 Josh Jackson FOIL	.20	.50
337 TJ Warren FOIL	.20	.50
338 Devin Booker FOIL	.75	2.00
339 Igor Kokoskov	.15	.40
340 Devin Booker	.60	1.50
341 Brandon Knight	.15	.40
342 TJ Warren	.15	.40
343 Trevor Ariza	.15	.40
344 Josh Jackson	.15	.40
345 Marquese Chriss	.15	.40
346 Dragan Bender	.15	.40
347 Deandre Ayton	.50	1.25
348 Portland Trail Blazers Team Logo	.10	.25
349 Jusuf Nurkic FOIL	.25	.60
350 Damian Lillard FOIL	.75	2.00
351 CJ McCollum FOIL	.30	.75
352 Terry Stotts	.15	.40
353 Damian Lillard	.60	1.50
354 CJ McCollum	.25	.60
355 Al-Farouq Aminu	.15	.40
356 Jusuf Nurkic	.20	.50
357 Evan Turner	.15	.40
358 Maurice Harkless	.15	.40
359 Zach Collins	.20	.50
360 Meyers Leonard	.15	.40
361 Sacramento Kings Team Logo	.10	.25
362 Zach Randolph FOIL	.25	.60
363 De'Aaron Fox FOIL	.60	1.50
364 Willie Cauley-Stein FOIL	.20	.50
365 Dave Joerger	.15	.40
366 Willie Cauley-Stein	.15	.40
367 Bogdan Bogdanovic	.25	.60
368 De'Aaron Fox	.50	1.25
369 Zach Randolph	.20	.50
370 Buddy Hield	.25	.60
371 Marvin Bagley III	.25	.60
372 Justin Jackson	.15	.40
373 Skal Labissiere	.15	.40
374 San Antonio Spurs Team Logo	.10	.25
375 Dejounte Murray FOIL	.40	1.00
376 Pau Gasol FOIL	.50	1.25
377 LaMarcus Aldridge FOIL	.30	.75
378 Gregg Popovich	.60	1.50
379 LaMarcus Aldridge	.25	.60
380 Manu Ginobili	.50	1.25
381 DeMar DeRozan	.30	.75
382 Patty Mills	.25	.60
383 Marco Belinelli	.15	.40
384 Pau Gasol	.40	1.00
385 Dejounte Murray	.30	.75
386 Rudy Gay	.25	.60
387 Utah Jazz Team Logo	.10	.25
388 Donovan Mitchell FOIL	1.00	2.50
389 Ricky Rubio FOIL	.25	.60
390 Rudy Gobert FOIL	.40	1.00
391 Quin Snyder	.15	.40
392 Donovan Mitchell	.75	2.00
393 Rudy Gobert	.30	.75
394 Joe Ingles	.20	.50
395 Ricky Rubio	.20	.50
396 Thabo Sefolosha	.15	.40
397 Jae Crowder	.15	.40
398 Alec Burks	.15	.40
399 Royce O'Neale	.15	.40
400 76ers at Knicks	.10	.25
401 Cavaliers at Warriors	.10	.25
402 Wizards at Celtics	.10	.25
403 Rockets at Thunder	.10	.25
404 Timberwolves at Lakers	.10	.25
405 18 NBA All-Star Game Logo	.10	.25
406 Donovan Mitchell Slam Dunk Contest Winner Left	.75	2.00
407 Donovan Mitchell Slam Dunk Contest Winner Right	.75	2.00
408 LeBron James '18 NBA All-Star Game MVP	2.00	5.00
409 Devin Booker 3-Point Contest Winner Left	.60	1.50
410 Devin Booker 3-Point Contest Winner Right	.60	1.50
411 19 NBA All-Star Game Logo	.10	.25
412 Spencer Dinwiddie Skills Challenge Winner Left	.20	.50
413 Spencer Dinwiddie Skills Challenge Winner Right	.20	.50
414 LeBron James Team LeBron All-Stars	2.00	5.00
415 Bradley Beal Team LeBron All-Stars	.30	.75
416 Anthony Davis Team LeBron All-Stars	.60	1.50
417 Andre Drummond Team LeBron All-Stars	.20	.50
418 Kevin Durant Team LeBron All-Stars	1.00	2.50
419 Paul George Team LeBron All-Stars	.40	1.00
420 Kyrie Irving Team LeBron All-Stars	.60	1.50
421 Kemba Walker Team LeBron All-Stars	.20	.50
422 Russell Westbrook Team LeBron All-Stars	.40	1.00
423 Stephen Curry Team Stephen All-Stars	2.00	5.00
424 Giannis Antetokounmpo Team Stephen All-Stars	1.25	3.00
425 DeMar DeRozan Team Stephen All-Stars	.30	.75
426 Joel Embiid Team Stephen All-Stars	.60	1.50
427 James Harden Team Stephen All-Stars	.50	1.25
428 Damian Lillard Team Stephen All-Stars	.60	1.50
429 Kyle Lowry Team Stephen All-Stars	.25	.60
430 Klay Thompson Team Stephen All-Stars	.60	1.50
431 Karl-Anthony Towns Team Stephen All-Stars	.40	1.00
432 Rockets vs. Timberwolves	.10	.25
433 Thunder vs. Jazz	.10	.25
434 Trail Blazers vs. Pelicans	.10	.25
435 Warriors vs. Spurs	.10	.25
436 Rockets vs. Jazz	.10	.25
437 Warriors vs. Pelicans	.10	.25
438 Rockets vs. Warriors	.10	.25
439 Celtics vs. Cavaliers	.10	.25
440 Raptors vs. Cavaliers	.10	.25
441 Celtics vs. 76ers	.10	.25
442 Raptors vs. Wizards	.10	.25
443 Cavaliers vs. Pacers	.10	.25
444 76ers vs. Heat	.10	.25
445 Celtics vs. Bucks	.10	.25
446 Game 1 '18 NBA Finals Left	.10	.25
447 Game 1 '18 NBA Finals Right	.10	.25
448 Game 2 '18 NBA Finals Left	.10	.25
449 Game 2 '18 NBA Finals Right	.10	.25
450 Game 3 '18 NBA Finals Left	.10	.25
451 Game 3 '18 NBA Finals Right	.10	.25
452 Game 4 '18 NBA Finals Left	.10	.25
453 Game 4 '18 NBA Finals Right	.10	.25
454 2018 NBA Champions Logo Left	.10	.25
455 2018 NBA Champions Logo Right	.10	.25
456 Larry O'Brien Trophy	.10	.25
457 Golden State Warriors Team Photo Left	.10	.25
458 Golden State Warriors Team Photo Right	.10	.25
459 Kevin Durant '18 NBA Finals MVP	1.00	2.50
460 James Harden Most Valuable Player	.50	1.25
461 Ben Simmons Rookie of the Year	.25	.60
462 Rudy Gobert Defensive Player of the Year	.30	.75
463 Lou Williams Sixth Man of the Year	.20	.50
464 Victor Oladipo Most Improved Player	.20	.50
465 Kemba Walker NBA Sportsmanship Award	.20	.50
466 Jamal Crawford Teammate of the Year Award	.25	.60
467 Mikal Bridges 10th Overall Pick	.75	2.00
468 Jerome Robinson 13th Overall Pick	.15	.40
469 Troy Brown Jr. 15th Overall Pick	.20	.50
470 Donte DiVincenzo 17th Overall Pick	.40	1.00
471 Lonnie Walker IV 18th Overall Pick	.30	.75
472 Josh Okogie 20th Overall Pick	.25	.60
473 Grayson Allen 21st Overall Pick	.30	.75
474 Aaron Holiday 23rd Overall Pick	.25	.60
475 Moritz Wagner 25th Overall Pick	.30	.75
476 Jacob Evans III 28th Overall Pick	.15	.40
477 NBA Logo Top Left FOIL	.15	.40
478 NBA Logo Top Right FOIL	.15	.40
479 NBA Logo Middle Left FOIL	.15	.40
480 NBA Logo Middle Right FOIL	.15	.40
481 NBA Logo Bottom Left FOIL	.15	.40
482 NBA Logo Bottom Right FOIL	.15	.40

1987-88 Panini Spanish Stickers

COMPLETE SET (161)	200.00	400.00
1 Larry Bird	40.00	100.00
2 Kareem Abdul-Jabbar	40.00	100.00
3 Earvin Magic Johnson	40.00	100.00
4 Michael Jordan	500.00	1,000.00
5 Isiah Thomas	20.00	50.00
6 Stephen Baeck	.20	.50
7 Tony Balogun	.20	.50
8 Alexandr Belostenni	.20	.50
9 Karl Brown	.20	.50
10 Fanis Christodoulou	.20	.50
11 Danko Cvjeticanin	.20	.50
12 Sandro Dell'Agnello	.20	.50
13 Vlade Divac	3.00	8.00
14 Nikos Filippou	.20	.50
15 Nikos Gallis	1.25	3.00
16 Valeri Goborov	.20	.50
17 Andrea Gracis	.20	.50
18 Henning Harnisch	.20	.50
19 Colin Irish	.20	.50
20 Pertram Koch	.20	.50
21 Jens Kujawa	.20	.50
22 Rimas Kurtinaitis	.75	2.00
23 Bob McAdoo	4.00	10.00
24 Walter Magnifico	8.00	20.00
25 Sharunas Marchulenis	2.00	5.00
26 Sven Meyer	.20	.50
27 Igor Miglinieks	.20	.50
28 Jacques Monclar	.20	.50
29 Frederic Monetti	.20	.50
30 Stephane Ostrowski	.75	2.00
31 Drazen Petrovic	10.00	25.00
32 Dino Radja	1.50	4.00
33 Zoran Radovic	.40	1.00
34 Antonello Riva	1.50	4.00
35 Oscar Schmidt	6.00	15.00
36 Christian Soule	.20	.50
37 Titt Sokk	.20	.50
38 Francesco Vescovi	.20	.50
39 Georges Vestris	.20	.50
40 Alexander Volkov	1.50	4.00
41 Stojan Vrankovic	1.25	3.00
42 Panagiotis Yiannakis	.20	.50

1990-91 Panini Stickers Greek

COMPLETE SET (180)	600.00	1,200.00
1 Magic Johnson	4.00	10.00
2 Mychal Thompson	1.00	2.50
3 Vlade Divac	1.50	4.00
4 Byron Scott	1.00	2.50
5 James Worthy	2.00	5.00
6 A.C. Green	1.00	2.50
7 Jerome Kersey	1.00	2.50
8 Clyde Drexler	4.00	10.00
9 Buck Williams	1.00	2.50
10 Kevin Duckworth	1.00	2.50
11 Terry Porter	1.00	2.50
12 Cliff Robinson	1.50	4.00
13 Tom Chambers	1.00	2.50
14 Dan Majerle	1.50	4.00
15 Mark West	1.00	2.50
16 Kevin Johnson	1.50	4.00
17 Jeff Hornacek	1.50	4.00
18 Kurt Rambis	1.00	2.50
19 Nate McMillan	1.00	2.50
20 Shawn Kemp	5.00	12.00
21 Dale Ellis	1.00	2.50
22 Michael Cage	1.00	2.50
23 Xavier McDaniel	1.00	2.50
24 Derrick McKey	1.00	2.50
25 Manute Bol	1.00	2.50
26 Chris Mullin	2.00	5.00
27 Terry Teagle	1.00	2.50
28 Tim Hardaway	2.00	5.00
29 Sarunas Marciulionis	1.00	2.50
30 Mitch Richmond	4.00	10.00
31 Gary Grant	1.00	2.50
32 Danny Manning	1.50	4.00
33 Benoit Benjamin	1.00	2.50
34 Ron Harper	1.50	4.00
35 Ken Norman	1.00	2.50
36 Charles Smith	1.00	2.50
37 Harold Pressley	1.00	2.50
38 Antoine Carr	1.00	2.50
39 Danny Ainge	1.50	4.00
40 Wayman Tisdale	1.00	2.50
41 Ralph Sampson	1.00	2.50
42 Vinny Del Negro	1.00	2.50
43 David Robinson	5.00	12.00
44 Sean Elliott	2.00	5.00
45 Terry Cummings	1.50	4.00
46 Willie Anderson	1.00	2.50
47 Rod Strickland	1.50	4.00
48 Frank Brickowski	1.00	2.50
49 Karl Malone	6.00	15.00
50 Darrell Griffith	1.00	2.50
51 John Stockton	6.00	15.00
52 Blue Edwards	1.00	2.50
53 Mark Eaton	1.00	2.50
54 Thurl Bailey	1.00	2.50
55 Rolando Blackman	1.00	2.50
56 Sam Perkins	1.00	2.50
57 James Donaldson	1.00	2.50
58 Herb Williams	1.00	2.50
59 Roy Tarpley	1.00	2.50
60 Derek Harper	1.00	2.50
61 Michael Adams	1.00	2.50
62 Blair Rasmussen	1.00	2.50
63 Jerome Lane	1.00	2.50
64 Walter Davis	1.00	2.50
65 Todd Lichti	1.00	2.50
66 Joe Barry Carroll	1.00	2.50
67 Vernon Maxwell	1.00	2.50
68 Otis Thorpe	1.00	2.50
69 Hakeem Olajuwon	4.00	10.00
70 Buck Johnson	1.00	2.50
71 Eric (Sleepy) Floyd	1.00	2.50
72 Mitchell Wiggins	1.00	2.50
73 Tony Campbell	1.00	2.50
74 Tod Murphy	1.00	2.50
75 Tyrone Corbin	1.00	2.50
76 Sam Mitchell	1.00	2.50
77 Randy Breuer	1.00	2.50
78 Pooh Richardson	1.00	2.50
79 Rex Chapman	1.50	4.00
80 Dell Curry	1.00	2.50
81 Muggsy Bogues	1.50	4.00
82 J.R. Reid	1.00	2.50
83 Armon Gilliam	1.00	2.50
84 Kelly Tripucka	1.00	2.50
85 Dennis Rodman	5.00	12.00
86 Joe Dumars	2.00	5.00
87 Isiah Thomas	2.00	5.00
88 Bill Laimbeer	1.50	4.00
89 Vinnie Johnson	1.00	2.50
90 James Edwards	1.00	2.50
91 Michael Jordan	150.00	300.00
92 Stacey King	1.00	2.50
93 Scottie Pippen	6.00	15.00
94 John Paxson	1.00	2.50
95 Horace Grant	1.00	2.50
96 Craig Hodges	1.00	2.50
97 Brad Lohaus	1.00	2.50
98 Jack Sikma	1.00	2.50
99 Ricky Pierce	1.00	2.50
100 Greg Anderson	1.00	2.50
101 Alvin Robertson	1.00	2.50
102 Jay Humphries	1.00	2.50
103 Mark Price	1.50	4.00
104 Winston Bennett	1.00	2.50
105 Brad Daugherty	1.00	2.50
106 Craig Ehlo	1.00	2.50
107 Larry Nance	1.00	2.50
108 Hot Rod Williams	1.00	2.50
109 Rik Smits	1.50	4.00
110 Chuck Person	1.00	2.50
111 Reggie Miller	4.00	10.00
112 LaSalle Thompson	1.00	2.50
113 Detlef Schrempf	1.50	4.00
114 Vern Fleming	1.00	2.50
115 Moses Malone	1.50	4.00
116 Doc Rivers	1.50	4.00
117 Dominique Wilkins	2.50	6.00
118 Spud Webb	1.50	4.00
119 Kevin Willis	1.00	2.50
120 Kenny Smith	1.00	2.50
121 Otis Smith	1.00	2.50
122 Sidney Green	1.00	2.50
123 Nick Anderson	1.00	2.50
124 Scott Skiles	1.00	2.50
125 Jerry Reynolds	1.00	2.50
126 Terry Catledge	1.00	2.50
127 Charles Barkley	4.00	10.00
128 Ron Anderson	1.00	2.50
129 Hersey Hawkins	1.00	2.50
130 Mike Gminski	1.00	2.50
131 Johnny Dawkins	1.00	2.50
132 Rick Mahorn	1.00	2.50
133 Michael Smith	1.00	2.50
134 Reggie Lewis	1.00	2.50
135 Larry Bird	10.00	25.00
136 Kevin McHale	2.00	5.00
137 Joe Kleine	1.00	2.50
138 Robert Parish	1.50	4.00
139 Maurice Cheeks	1.00	2.50
140 Patrick Ewing	4.00	10.00
141 Charles Oakley	1.50	4.00
142 Gerald Wilkins	1.00	2.50
143 Kenny Walker	1.50	4.00
144 Mark Jackson	1.00	2.50
145 Mark Alarie	1.00	2.50
146 John Williams	1.00	2.50
147 Darrell Walker	1.00	2.50
148 Bernard King	1.00	2.50
149 Harvey Grant	1.00	2.50
150 Ledell Eackles	1.00	2.50
151 Glen Rice	5.00	12.00
152 Kevin Edwards	1.00	2.50
153 Tellis Frank	1.00	2.50
154 Rony Seikaly	1.00	2.50
155 Billy Thompson	1.00	2.50
156 Sherman Douglas	1.00	2.50
157 Roy Hinson	1.00	2.50
158 Chris Morris	1.00	2.50
159 Lester Conner	1.00	2.50
160 Sam Bowie	1.00	2.50
161 Purvis Short	1.00	2.50
162 Mookie Blaylock	1.50	4.00
A John Stockton AS	2.50	6.00
B Magic Johnson AS	2.50	6.00
C A.C. Green AS	1.00	2.50
D Hakeem Olajuwon AS	2.50	6.00
E James Worthy AS	1.50	4.00
F Isiah Thomas AS	1.25	3.00
G Michael Jordan AS	150.00	300.00
H Larry Bird AS	4.00	10.00
I Patrick Ewing AS	2.50	6.00
J Charles Barkley AS	2.50	6.00
K Michael Jordan	150.00	300.00
L Larry Bird	4.00	10.00
M Hakeem Olajuwon	2.50	6.00
N NBA Finals	1.00	2.50
O NBA Finals	1.00	2.50
P NBA Finals	1.00	2.50
Q NBA Finals	1.00	2.50
R NBA Finals	1.00	2.50

1988-89 Panini Stickers Spanish

COMPLETE SET (292)	250.00	450.00
1 NBA Official	.40	1.00
2 NBA Official	.40	1.00
3 Boston Celtics Logo	.40	1.00
4 Jimmy Rodgers CO	.40	1.00
5 Dennis Johnson	1.50	4.00
6 Brian Shaw	.75	2.00
7 Danny Ainge	1.25	3.00
8 Larry Bird	15.00	40.00
9 Kevin McHale	3.00	8.00
10 Robert Parish	1.50	4.00
11 Robert Parish IA	.75	2.00
12 Celtics Jersey	.40	1.00
13 Charlotte Hornets	.40	1.00
14 Dick Harter CO	.40	1.00
15 Rex Chapman	2.00	5.00
16 Muggsy Bogues	2.00	5.00
17 Kelly Tripucka	.40	1.00
18 Robert Reid	.40	1.00
19 Kurt Rambis	.75	2.00
20 Dave Hoppen	.40	1.00
21 Muggsy Bogues IA	.75	2.00
22 Hornets Jersey	.40	1.00
23 New Jersey Nets Logo	.40	1.00
24 Willis Reed CO	.75	2.00
25 John Bagley	.40	1.00
26 Dennis Hopson	.40	1.00
27 Mike McGee	.40	1.00
28 Roy Hinson	.40	1.00
29 Buck Williams	.75	2.00
30 Joe Barry Carroll	.40	1.00
31 Roy Hinson IA	.40	1.00
32 Nets Jersey	.40	1.00
33 New York Knicks Logo	.40	1.00
34 Rick Pitino CO	1.25	3.00
35 Mark Jackson	3.00	8.00
36 Trent Tucker	.40	1.00
37 Johnny Newman	.40	1.00
38 Gerald Wilkins	.40	1.00
39 Charles Oakley	.40	1.00
40 Patrick Ewing	6.00	15.00
41 Gerald Wilkins IA	.40	1.00
42 Knicks Jersey	.40	1.00
43 Philadelphia 76ers	.40	1.00
44 Jim Lynam CO	.40	1.00
45 Maurice Cheeks	1.25	3.00
46 Hersey Hawkins	1.50	4.00
47 Ron Anderson	.40	1.00
48 Charles Barkley	8.00	20.00
49 Cliff Robinson	.40	1.00
50 Mike Gminski	.75	2.00
51 Hersey Hawkins IA	.75	2.00
52 76ers Jersey	.40	1.00
53 Washington Bullets	.40	1.00
54 Wes Unseld CO	.75	2.00
55 Jeff Malone	.75	2.00
56 Darrell Walker	.40	1.00
57 Bernard King	.75	2.00
58 Terry Catledge	.40	1.00
59 John Williams	.40	1.00
60 Dave Feitl	.40	1.00
61 Jeff Malone IA	.40	1.00
62 Bullets Jersey	.40	1.00
63 Atlanta Hawks Logo	.40	1.00
64 Mike Fratello CO	.40	1.00
65 Doc Rivers	1.25	3.00
66 Spud Webb	1.00	2.50
67 Reggie Theus	.75	2.00
68 Dominique Wilkins	5.00	12.00
69 Kevin Willis	.75	2.00
70 Moses Malone	2.00	5.00
71 Reggie Theus IA	.40	1.00
72 Hawks Jersey	.40	1.00
73 Chicago Bulls Logo	.40	1.00
74 Doug Collins CO	1.00	2.50
75 Craig Hodges	.40	1.00
76 Michael Jordan	30.00	80.00
77 Scottie Pippen	15.00	40.00
78 Horace Grant	3.00	8.00
79 Brad Sellers	.40	1.00
80 Bill Cartwright	.75	2.00
81 Brad Sellers IA	.40	1.00
82 Bulls Jersey	.40	1.00
83 Cleveland Cavaliers	.40	1.00
84 Lenny Wilkens CO	.75	2.00
85 Mark Price	1.50	4.00
86 Ron Harper	1.50	4.00
87 Hot Rod Williams	.40	1.00
88 Mike Sanders	.40	1.00
89 Larry Nance	.75	2.00
90 Brad Daugherty	.75	2.00
91 Mike Sanders IA	.40	1.00
92 Cavaliers Jersey	.40	1.00
93 Detroit Pistons Logo	.40	1.00
94 Chuck Daly CO	1.50	4.00
95 Isiah Thomas	4.00	10.00
96 Joe Dumars	3.00	8.00
97 Dennis Rodman	8.00	20.00
98 Adrian Dantley	1.25	3.00
99 John Salley	.75	2.00
100 Bill Laimbeer	1.25	3.00
101 Dennis Rodman IA	5.00	12.00
102 Pistons Jersey	.40	1.00
103 Indiana Pacers Logo	.40	1.00
104 Dick Versace CO	.60	1.50
105 Vern Fleming	.40	1.00
106 Reggie Miller	15.00	40.00
107 Chuck Person	.75	2.00
108 Herb Williams	.40	1.00
109 Steve Stipanovich	.40	1.00
110 Rik Smits	2.00	5.00
111 Chuck Person IA	.40	1.00
112 Pacers Jersey	.40	1.00
113 Milwaukee Bucks Logo	.40	1.00
114 Del Harris CO	.40	1.00
115 Sidney Moncrief	1.25	3.00
116 Jay Humphries	.40	1.00
117 Paul Pressey	.40	1.00
118 Ricky Pierce	.75	2.00
119 Terry Cummings	.75	2.00
120 Jack Sikma	.75	2.00
121 Jay Humphries IA	.40	1.00
122 Bucks Jersey	.40	1.00
123 Mavericks Logo	.40	1.00
124 John MacLeod CO	.40	1.00
125 Derek Harper	.75	2.00
126 Rolando Blackman	1.00	2.50
127 Detlef Schrempf	1.50	4.00
128 Mark Aguirre	.75	2.00
129 Sam Perkins	.75	2.00
130 James Donaldson	.40	1.00
131 Sam Perkins IA	.60	1.50
132 Mavericks Jersey	.40	1.00
133 Denver Nuggets Logo	.40	1.00
134 Doug Moe CO	.40	1.00
135 Walter Davis	.75	2.00
136 Michael Adams	.40	1.00
137 Fat Lever	.75	2.00
138 Alex English	1.25	3.00
139 Wayne Cooper	.40	1.00
140 Danny Schayes	.40	1.00
141 Fat Lever IA	.40	1.00
142 Nuggets Jersey	.40	1.00
143 Houston Rockets Logo	.40	1.00
144 Don Chaney CO	.40	1.00
145 Sleepy Floyd	.40	1.00
146 Mike Woodson	.40	1.00
147 Purvis Short	.40	1.00
148 Buck Johnson	.40	1.00
149 Otis Thorpe	.75	2.00
150 Hakeem Olajuwon	5.00	12.00
151 Otis Thorpe IA	.40	1.00
152 Rockets Jersey	.40	1.00
153 Miami Heat Logo	.40	1.00
154 Ron Rothstein CO	.75	2.00
155 Jon Sundvold	.40	1.00
156 Kevin Edwards	.40	1.00
157 Grant Long	.75	2.00
158 Billy Thompson	.75	2.00
159 Dwayne Washington	.40	1.00
160 Rony Seikaly	1.25	3.00
161 Rony Seikaly IA	.40	1.00
162 Heat Jersey	.40	1.00
163 San Antonio Spurs	.40	1.00
164 Larry Brown CO	2.00	5.00
165 Johnny Dawkins	.75	2.00
166 Alvin Robertson	.40	1.00
167 Willie Anderson	.40	1.00
168 Albert King	.40	1.00
169 Greg Anderson	.40	1.00
170 Frank Brickowski	.40	1.00
171 Willie Anderson IA	.40	1.00
172 Spurs Jersey	.40	1.00
173 Utah Jazz Logo	.40	1.00
174 Jerry Sloan CO	3.00	8.00
175 John Stockton	8.00	20.00
176 Darrell Griffith	.75	2.00
177 Marc Iavaroni	.40	1.00
178 Thurl Bailey	.40	1.00
179 Karl Malone	8.00	20.00
180 Mark Eaton	.75	2.00
181 Thurl Bailey IA	.40	1.00
182 Jazz Jersey	.40	1.00
183 Golden State Warriors	.40	1.00
184 Don Nelson CO	.75	2.00
185 Mitch Richmond	6.00	15.00
186 Winston Garland	.40	1.00
187 Larry Smith	.40	1.00
188 Chris Mullin	2.50	6.00
189 Ralph Sampson	.75	2.00
190 Manute Bol	.75	2.00
191 Ralph Sampson IA	.40	1.00
192 Warriors Jersey	.40	1.00
193 Los Angeles Clippers	.40	1.00
194 Don Casey CO	.40	1.00
195 Gary Grant	.40	1.00

196 Quintin Dailey .40 1.00
197 Norm Nixon .75 2.00
198 Ken Norman .40 1.00
199 Danny Manning 1.50 4.00
200 Benoit Benjamin .40 1.00
201 Ken Norman IA .40 1.00
202 Clippers Jersey .40 1.00
203 Los Angeles Lakers .40 1.00
204 Pat Riley CO 1.50 4.00
205 Magic Johnson 10.00 25.00
206 Byron Scott 1.25 3.00
207 James Worthy 2.50 6.00
208 A.C. Green 1.50 4.00
209 Mychal Thompson .75 2.00
210 Kareem Abdul-Jabbar 6.00 15.00
211 Byron Scott IA .75 2.00
212 Lakers Jersey .40 1.00
213 Phoenix Suns Logo .40 1.00
214 Cotton Fitzsimmons CO .75 2.00
215 Kevin Johnson 2.00 5.00
216 Dan Majerle 2.00 5.00
217 Eddie Johnson .40 1.00
218 Armon Gilliam .40 1.00
219 Tom Chambers 1.25 3.00
220 Mark West .40 1.00
221 Kevin Johnson IA .75 2.00
222 Suns Jersey .40 1.00
223 Portland Trail .40 1.00
224 Mike Schuler CO .40 1.00
225 Terry Porter .75 2.00
226 Clyde Drexler 6.00 15.00
227 Jerome Kersey .40 1.00
228 Kiki Vandeweghe 1.25 3.00
229 Steve Johnson .40 1.00
230 Kevin Duckworth .40 1.00
231 Jerome Kersey IA .40 1.00
232 Trail Blazers Jersey .40 1.00
233 Sacramento Kings Logo .40 1.00
234 Jerry Reynolds CO .40 1.00
235 Kenny Smith .75 2.00
236 Rodney McCray .40 1.00
237 Derek Smith .75 2.00
238 Ed Pinckney .40 1.00
239 Jim Petersen .40 1.00
240 LaSalle Thompson .40 1.00
241 Kenny Smith IA .40 1.00
242 Kings Jersey .40 1.00
243 Seattle Supersonics .40 1.00
244 Bernie Bickerstaff CO .40 1.00
245 Nate McMillan .75 2.00
246 Dale Ellis .75 2.00
247 Xavier McDaniel .40 1.00
248 Derrick McKey .40 1.00
249 Michael Cage .40 1.00
250 Alton Lister .40 1.00
251 Xavier McDaniel IA .40 1.00
252 Supersonics Jersey .40 1.00
253 AS Puzzle
Patrick Ewing
Hakeem Olajuwon 1.25 3.00
254 AS Puzzle
Karl Malone 1.25 3.00
255 AS Puzzle .40 1.00
256 AS Puzzle .40 1.00
257 AS Puzzle
Fat Lever .40 1.00
258 AS Puzzle .40 1.00
259 Lenny Wilkens CO AS .75 2.00
260 Isiah Thomas AS 1.50 4.00
261 Michael Jordan AS 10.00 25.00
262 Dominique Wilkins AS 2.50 6.00
263 Charles Barkley AS 4.00 10.00
264 Moses Malone AS 1.25 3.00
265 Mark Jackson AS 1.25 3.00
266 Mark Price AS .75 2.00
267 Larry Nance AS .75 2.00
268 Terry Cummings AS .75 2.00
269 Kevin McHale AS 1.25 3.00
270 Brad Daugherty AS .40 1.00
271 Patrick Ewing AS 2.00 5.00
272 Pat Riley CO AS 1.25 3.00
273 John Stockton AS 5.00 12.00
274 Dale Ellis AS .40 1.00
275 Alex English AS .75 2.00
276 Karl Malone AS 4.00 10.00
277 Hakeem Olajuwon AS 3.00 8.00
278 Kareem Abdul-Jabbar AS 3.00 8.00
279 Clyde Drexler AS 3.00 8.00
280 Chris Mullin AS 1.25 3.00
281 James Worthy AS 1.50 4.00
282 Tom Chambers AS .75 2.00
283 Kevin Duckworth AS .40 1.00
284 Mark Eaton AS .40 1.00
285 Michael Jordan AW 15.00 40.00
286 Mark Jackson AW 1.25 3.00
287 Charles Barkley AW 3.00 8.00
288 Jack Sikma AW .40 1.00
289 Michael Cage AW .40 1.00
290 Mark Eaton AW .40 1.00
291 John Stockton AW 4.00 10.00
292 Doug Moe CO AW .40 1.00
XX Album
Dominique Wilkins
Larry Bird 6.00 15.00

1989-90 Panini Stickers Spanish

COMPLETE SET (272) 125.00 275.00
1 Boston Celtics Logo .40 1.00
2 Dennis Johnson .75 2.00
3 Reggie Lewis .75 2.00
4 Kelvin Upshaw .40 1.00
5 Kevin Gamble .40 1.00
6 Larry Bird 8.00 20.00
7 Ed Pinckney .40 1.00
8 Kevin McHale 2.00 5.00
9 Robert Parish .75 2.00
10 Miami Heat Logo .40 1.00
11 Jon Sundvold .40 1.00
12 Rory Sparrow .40 1.00
13 Dwayne Washington .40 1.00
14 Billy Thompson .40 1.00
15 Grant Long .40 1.00
16 Kevin Edwards .40 1.00
17 Pat Cummings .40 1.00
18 Rony Seikaly .40 1.00
19 New Jersey Nets Logo .40 1.00
20 Dennis Hopson .40 1.00
21 Lester Conner .40 1.00
22 Chris Morris .40 1.00
23 Charles Shackleford .40 1.00
24 Purvis Short .40 1.00
25 Roy Hinson .40 1.00
26 Sam Bowie .60 1.50
27 Joe Barry Carroll .40 1.00
28 New York Knicks Logo .40 1.00
29 Mark Jackson 1.00 2.50
30 Rod Strickland .75 2.00
31 Gerald Wilkins .40 1.00
32 Trent Tucker .40 1.00
33 Johnny Newman .40 1.00
34 Kenny Walker .40 1.00
35 Charles Oakley .60 1.50
36 Patrick Ewing 3.00 8.00
37 Philadelphia 76ers Logo .40 1.00
38 Scott Brooks .40 1.00
39 Johnny Dawkins .40 1.00
40 Hersey Hawkins .75 2.00
41 Derek Smith .75 2.00
42 Ron Anderson .40 1.00
43 Charles Barkley 5.00 12.00
44 Rick Mahorn .40 1.00
45 Mike Gminski .40 1.00
46 Washington Bullets Logo .40 1.00
47 Steve Colter .40 1.00
48 Jeff Malone .40 1.00
49 Ledell Eackles .40 1.00
50 Darrell Walker .40 1.00
51 Bernard King .75 2.00
52 Charles Jones .40 1.00
53 Mark Alarie .40 1.00
54 Harvey Grant .40 1.00
55 Atlanta Hawks Logo .40 1.00
56 Anthony Webb .75 2.00
57 Glenn Rivers .75 2.00
58 John Battle .40 1.00
59 Dominique Wilkins 3.00 8.00
60 Cliff Levingston .40 1.00
61 Jon Koncak .40 1.00
62 Antoine Carr .40 1.00
63 Moses Malone 1.25 3.00
64 Chicago Bulls Logo .75 2.00
65 Craig Hodges .40 1.00
66 John Paxson .75 2.00
67 Michael Jordan 20.00 50.00
68 Scottie Pippen 6.00 15.00
69 Charles Davis .40 1.00
70 Horace Grant 1.00 2.50
71 Will Perdue .40 1.00
72 Bill Cartwright .75 2.00
73 Cleveland Cavaliers Logo .40 1.00
74 Mark Price .75 2.00
75 Craig Ehlo .60 1.50
76 Chris Dudley .40 1.00
77 Randolph Keys .40 1.00
78 Larry Nance .75 2.00
79 John Williams .40 1.00
80 Paul Mokeski .40 1.00
81 Wayne Rollins .40 1.00
82 Pistons .40 1.00
83 Isiah Thomas 2.50 6.00
84 Vinnie Johnson .60 1.50
85 Joe Dumars 1.25 3.00
86 Mark Aguirre .60 1.50
87 Dennis Rodman 4.00 10.00
88 John Salley .75 2.00
89 James Edwards .40 1.00
90 Bill Laimbeer .75 2.00
91 Indiana Pacers Logo .40 1.00
92 Reggie Miller 4.00 10.00
93 Vern Fleming .40 1.00
94 Randy Wittman .40 1.00
95 Chuck Person .40 1.00
96 Mike Sanders .40 1.00
97 Rickey Green .40 1.00
98 Lasalle Thompson .40 1.00
99 Rik Smits .75 2.00
100 Milwaukee Bucks Logo .40 1.00
101 Jay Humphries .40 1.00
102 Ricky Pierce .40 1.00
103 Paul Pressey .40 1.00
104 Alvin Robertson .40 1.00
105 Tony Brown .40 1.00
106 Fred Roberts .40 1.00
107 Randy Breuer .40 1.00
108 Jack Sikma .60 1.50
109 Orlando Magic Logo .40 1.00
110 Sam Vincent .40 1.00
111 Reggie Theus .75 2.00
112 Scott Skiles .75 2.00
113 Otis Smith .40 1.00
114 Sidney Green .40 1.00
115 Nick Anderson 1.25 3.00
116 Terry Catledge .40 1.00
117 Mark Acres .40 1.00
118 Hornets .40 1.00
119 Muggsy Bogues 1.00 2.50
120 Dell Curry .40 1.00
121 Rex Chapman .75 2.00
122 Kelly Tripucka .40 1.00
123 Jerry Sichting .40 1.00
124 Brian Rowsom .40 1.00
125 J.R. Reid .40 1.00
126 Stuart Gray .40 1.00
127 Dallas Mavericks Logo .40 1.00
128 Brad Davis .40 1.00
129 Derek Harper .75 2.00
130 Rolando Blackman .75 2.00
131 Adrian Dantley .75 2.00
132 Herb Williams .40 1.00
133 Bill Wennington .40 1.00
134 Sam Perkins .75 2.00
135 James Donaldson .40 1.00
136 Denver Nuggets Logo .40 1.00
137 Walter Davis .75 2.00
138 Michael Adams .40 1.00
139 Lafayette Lever .40 1.00
140 Alex English .75 2.00
141 Todd Lichti .40 1.00
142 Jerome Lane .40 1.00
143 Tim Kempton .40 1.00
144 Blair Rasmussen .40 1.00
145 Houston Rockets Logo .40 1.00
146 Eric Floyd .40 1.00
147 Mike Woodson .40 1.00
148 Derrick Chievous .40 1.00
149 John Lucas .50 1.25
150 Buck Johnson .40 1.00
151 Otis Thorpe .40 1.00
152 Larry Smith .40 1.00
153 Akeem Olajuwon 5.00 12.00
154 Minnesota Twolves Logo .40 1.00
155 Pooh Richardson .40 1.00
156 Sidney Lowe .40 1.00
157 Doug West .40 1.00
158 Adrian Branch .75 2.00
159 Tony Campbell .40 1.00
160 David Rivers .40 1.00
161 Steve Johnson .40 1.00
162 Brad Lohaus .40 1.00
163 San Antonio Spurs Logo .40 1.00
164 Maurice Cheeks .75 2.00
165 Vernon Maxwell .40 1.00
166 Zarko Paspalj .40 1.00
167 Sean Elliott 2.00 5.00
168 Terry Cummings .75 2.00
169 Frank Brickowski .40 1.00
170 Willie Anderson .40 1.00
171 David Robinson 10.00 25.00
172 Utah Jazz Logo .40 1.00
173 John Stockton 6.00 15.00
174 Darrell Griffith .60 1.50
175 Bobby Hansen .40 1.00
176 Karl Malone 6.00 15.00
177 Mike Brown .40 1.00
178 Thurl Bailey .40 1.00
179 Eric Leckner .40 1.00
180 Mark Eaton .40 1.00
181 Golden State Warrior Logo .40 1.00
182 Winston Garland .40 1.00
183 Mitch Richmond 2.00 5.00
184 Sarunas Marciulionis .75 2.00
185 Terry Teagle .40 1.00
186 Chris Mullin 1.50 4.00
187 Rod Higgins .40 1.00
188 Uwe Blab .40 1.00
189 Manute Bol .40 1.00
190 Los Angeles Clippers Logo .40 1.00
191 Gary Grant .40 1.00
192 Ron Harper .75 2.00
193 Ken Norman .40 1.00
194 Charles Smith .40 1.00
195 Danny Manning .75 2.00
196 Joe Wolf .40 1.00
197 Benoit Benjamin .40 1.00
198 Ken Bannister .40 1.00
199 Los Angeles Lakers Logo .40 1.00
200 Earvin Johnson 8.00 20.00
201 Byron Scott .75 2.00
202 Michael Cooper .75 2.00
203 Orlando Woolridge .40 1.00
204 James Worthy 1.50 4.00
205 A.C. Green .75 2.00
206 Vlade Divac 2.50 6.00
207 Mychal Thompson .40 1.00
208 Phoenix Suns Logo .40 1.00
209 Kevin Johnson .75 2.00
210 Jeff Hornacek 1.50 4.00
211 Greg Grant .40 1.00
212 Dan Majerle .75 2.00
213 Tim Perry .40 1.00
214 Eddie Johnson .40 1.00
215 Tom Chambers .75 2.00
216 Andrew Lang .40 1.00
217 Portland Trail Blazers Logo .40 1.00
218 Clyde Drexler 5.00 12.00
219 Terry Porter .75 2.00
220 Drazen Petrovic 3.00 8.00
221 Jerome Kersey .40 1.00
222 Mark Bryant .40 1.00
223 Danny Young .40 1.00
224 Wayne Cooper .40 1.00
225 Kevin Duckworth .40 1.00
226 Sacramento Kings Logo .40 1.00
227 Danny Ainge 1.25 3.00
228 Michael Jackson .40 1.00
229 Vinny Del Negro .40 1.00
230 Kenny Smith .75 2.00
231 Harold Pressley .40 1.00
232 Rodney McCray .40 1.00
233 Wayman Tisdale .40 1.00
234 Greg Kite .40 1.00
235 Seattle Supersonics Logo .40 1.00
236 Sedale Threatt .40 1.00
237 Avery Johnson 1.25 3.00
238 Nate McMillan .60 1.50
239 Dale Ellis .40 1.00
240 Xavier McDaniel .40 1.00
241 Derrick McKey .40 1.00
242 Michael Cage .40 1.00
243 Olden Polynice .40 1.00
244 Charles Barkley 3.00 8.00
245 Larry Bird 4.00 10.00
246 Tom Chambers .75 2.00
247 Adrian Dantley .75 2.00
248 Clyde Drexler 3.00 8.00
249 Joe Dumars .75 2.00
250 Dale Ellis .40 1.00
251 Patrick Ewing 1.50 4.00
252 A.C. Green .75 2.00
253 Earvin Johnson 4.00 10.00
254 Michael Jordan 12.50 30.00
255 Bill Laimbeer .75 2.00
256 Jeff Malone .40 1.00
257 Karl Malone 3.00 8.00
258 Moses Malone .75 2.00
259 Xavier McDaniel .40 1.00
260 Akeem Olajuwon 2.50 6.00
261 Robert Parish .75 2.00
262 Mark Price .75 2.00
263 Jack Sikma .40 1.00
264 John Stockton 4.00 10.00
265 Isiah Thomas 2.00 5.00
266 Dominique Wilkins 2.50 6.00
267 James Worthy 1.25 3.00
268 NBA Logo .40 1.00
269 Puzzle Card .40 1.00
270 Puzzle Card .40 1.00
271 Puzzle Card .40 1.00
272 Puzzle Card .40 1.00

1990-91 Panini Stickers Spanish

COMPLETE SET (217) 150.00 300.00
1 NBA Logo .40 1.00
2 Boston Celtics Logo .40 1.00
3 Reggie Lewis .60 1.50
4 Larry Bird 6.00 15.00
5 Michael Smith .40 1.00
6 Kevin McHale 2.00 5.00
7 Joe Kleine .40 1.00
8 Robert Parish 1.25 3.00
9 Miami Heat Logo .40 1.00
10 Sherman Douglas .40 1.00
11 Kevin Edwards .40 1.00
12 Glen Rice 2.00 5.00
13 Billy Thompson 1.25 3.00
14 Tellis Frank .60 1.50
15 Rony Seikaly .40 1.00
16 New Jersey Nets Logo .40 1.00
17 Mookie Blaylock .75 2.00
18 Lester Conner .40 1.00
19 Purvis Short .40 1.00
20 Chris Morris .40 1.00
21 Roy Hinson .40 1.00
22 Sam Bowie .60 1.50
23 New York Knicks Logo .40 1.00
24 Maurice Cheeks .75 2.00
25 Mark Jackson 1.25 3.00
26 Gerald Wilkins .40 1.00
27 Kenny Walker .40 1.00
28 Charles Oakley .40 1.00
29 Patrick Ewing 4.00 10.00
30 Philadelphia 76ers Logo .40 1.00
31 Johnny Dawkins .40 1.00
32 Hersey Hawkins .60 1.50
33 Ron Anderson .40 1.00
34 Charles Barkley 5.00 12.00
35 Rick Mahorn .40 1.00
36 Mike Gminski .40 1.00
37 Washington Bullets Logo .40 1.00
38 Ledell Eackles .40 1.00
39 Darrell Walker .40 1.00
40 Bernard King .75 2.00
41 John Williams .40 1.00
42 Mark Alarie .60 1.50
43 Harvey Grant .40 1.00
44 Atlanta Hawks Logo .40 1.00
45 Anthony Webb .75 2.00
46 Doc Rivers .75 2.00
47 Kenny Smith .75 2.00
48 Dominique Wilkins 4.00 10.00
49 Kevin Willis .75 2.00
50 Moses Malone 1.25 3.00
51 Charlotte Hornets Logo .40 1.00
52 Muggsy Bogues .75 2.00
53 Rex Chapman .75 2.00
54 Dell Curry .75 2.00
55 Kelly Tripucka .40 1.00
56 Armon Gilliam .40 1.00
57 J.R. Reid .40 1.00
58 Chicago Bulls Logo .40 1.00
59 Craig Hodges .40 1.00
60 John Paxson .75 2.00
61 Michael Jordan 20.00 50.00
62 Scottie Pippen 6.00 15.00
63 Horace Grant 1.00 2.50
64 Stacey King .40 1.00
65 Cleveland Cavaliers Logo .40 1.00
66 Mark Price .75 2.00
67 Craig Ehlo .60 1.50
68 Winston Bennett .40 1.00
69 John Williams .40 1.00
70 Larry Nance .75 2.00
71 Brad Daugherty .40 1.00
72 Detroit Pistons Logo .40 1.00
73 Isiah Thomas 4.00 10.00
74 Joe Dumars 2.50 6.00
75 Vinnie Johnson .75 2.00
76 Dennis Rodman 4.00 10.00
77 Bill Laimbeer .75 2.00
78 James Edwards .40 1.00
79 Indiana Pacers Logo .40 1.00
80 Vern Fleming .40 1.00
81 Reggie Miller 5.00 12.00
82 Chuck Person .40 1.00
83 LaSalle Thompson .40 1.00
84 Detlef Schrempf .75 2.00
85 Rik Smits .75 2.00
86 Milwaukee Bucks Logo .40 1.00
87 Alvin Robertson .40 1.00
88 Jay Humphries .40 1.00
89 Ricky Pierce .40 1.00
90 Brad Lohaus .40 1.00
91 Jack Sikma .60 1.50
92 Greg Anderson .40 1.00
93 Dallas Mavericks Logo .40 1.00
94 Derek Harper .75 2.00
95 Rolando Blackman .75 2.00
96 Brad Davis .60 1.50
97 Roy Tarpley .40 1.00
98 Herb Williams .40 1.00
99 James Donaldson .40 1.00
100 Denver Nuggets Logo .40 1.00
101 Michael Adams .40 1.00
102 Walter Davis .75 2.00
103 Todd Lichti .40 1.00
104 Jerome Lane .40 1.00
105 Blair Rasmussen .40 1.00
106 Joe Barry Carroll .40 1.00
107 Houston Rockets Logo .40 1.00
108 Eric Floyd .40 1.00
109 Mitchell Wiggins .40 1.00
110 Vernon Maxwell .40 1.00
111 Otis Thorpe .60 1.50
112 Buck Johnson .40 1.00
113 Hakeem Olajuwon 5.00 12.00
114 Minnesota T-wolves Logo .40 1.00
115 Pooh Richardson .40 1.00
116 Tony Campbell .40 1.00
117 Tyrone Corbin .40 1.00
118 Sam Mitchell .60 1.50
119 Tod Murphy .40 1.00
120 Randy Breuer .40 1.00
121 Orlando Magic Logo .40 1.00
122 Scott Skiles .75 2.00
123 Otis Smith .40 1.00
124 Terry Catledge .40 1.00
125 Jerry Reynolds .40 1.00
126 Nick Anderson .75 2.00
127 Sidney Green .40 1.00
128 San Antonio Spurs Logo .40 1.00
129 Rod Strickland .60 1.50
130 Willie Anderson .40 1.00
131 Sean Elliott 1.25 3.00
132 Terry Cummings .75 2.00
133 Frank Brickowski .40 1.00
134 David Robinson 6.00 15.00
135 Utah Jazz Logo .40 1.00
136 John Stockton 6.00 15.00
137 Darrell Griffith .40 1.00
138 Theodore Edwards .40 1.00
139 Karl Malone 6.00 15.00
140 Thurl Bailey .40 1.00
141 Mark Eaton .40 1.00
142 Golden St. Warriors Logo .40 1.00
143 Tim Hardaway 2.00 5.00
144 Mitch Richmond 2.00 5.00
145 Chris Mullin 2.00 5.00
146 Sarunas Marciulionis .75 2.00
147 Terry Teagle .40 1.00
148 Manute Bol .40 1.00
149 L.A. Clippers Logo .40 1.00
150 Gary Grant .40 1.00
151 Ron Harper .75 2.00
152 Ken Norman .40 1.00
153 Charles Smith .40 1.00
154 Danny Manning .75 2.00
155 Benoit Benjamin .40 1.00
156 L.A. Lakers Logo .40 1.00
157 Magic Johnson 6.00 15.00
158 Byron Scott 1.00 2.50
159 James Worthy 2.00 5.00
160 A.C. Green 1.00 2.50
161 Vlade Divac .75 2.00
162 Mychal Thompson .60 1.50
163 Phoenix Suns Logo .40 1.00
164 Kevin Johnson .75 2.00
165 Jeff Hornacek .75 2.00
166 Dan Majerle .75 2.00
167 Tom Chambers .75 2.00
168 Kurt Rambis .75 2.00
169 Mark West .40 1.00
170 Portland Trailblazers Logo .40 1.00
171 Terry Porter .75 2.00
172 Clyde Drexler 5.00 12.00
173 Jerome Kersey .40 1.00
174 Cliff Robinson 1.25 3.00
175 Buck Williams .75 2.00
176 Kevin Duckworth .40 1.00
177 Sacramento Kings Logo .40 1.00
178 Vinny Del Negro .60 1.50
179 Danny Ainge 1.25 3.00
180 Wayman Tisdale .60 1.50
181 Antoine Carr .40 1.00
182 Greg Kite .40 1.00
183 Ralph Sampson .75 2.00
184 Seattle Sonics Logo .40 1.00
185 Nate McMillan .60 1.50
186 Dale Ellis .60 1.50
187 Xavier McDaniel .60 1.50
188 Shawn Kemp 2.00 5.00
189 Derrick McKey .40 1.00
190 Michael Cage .40 1.00
191 Dennis Rodman AW 1.00 2.50
192 Dennis Rodman AW 1.00 2.50
193 Darrell Walker AW .40 1.00
194 Darrell Walker AW .40 1.00
195 Ricky Pierce AW .40 1.00
196 Ricky Pierce AW .40 1.00
197 Isiah Thomas AW 1.00 2.50
198 Isiah Thomas AW 1.00 2.50
199 David Robinson AW 1.50 4.00
200 David Robinson AW 1.50 4.00
201 Magic Johnson AW 1.50 4.00
202 Magic Johnson AW 1.50 4.00
203 Larry Bird AW 2.00 5.00
204 Larry Bird AW 2.00 5.00
205 Michael Jordan AW 4.00 10.00
206 Michael Jordan AW 4.00 10.00
207 Hakeem Olajuwon AW 1.25 3.00
208 Hakeem Olajuwon AW 1.25 3.00
209 Puzzle Card #1 .40 1.00
210 Puzzle Card #2 .40 1.00
211 Puzzle Card #3 .40 1.00
212 Puzzle Card #4 .40 1.00
213 Puzzle Card #5 .40 1.00
214 Puzzle Card #6 .40 1.00
215 Puzzle Card #7 .40 1.00
216 Puzzle Card #8 .40 1.00
217 Puzzle Card #9 .40 1.00

2009-10 Panini Threads

COMP.SET w/o RCs (100) 15.00 30.00
RC STATED PRINT RUN 126 TO 700 SETS
ASTERISK CARDS FROM PANINI UPDATE
1 LeBron James 3.00 8.00
2 Dwyane Wade .75 2.00
3 Chris Paul .75 2.00
4 Kobe Bryant 3.00 8.00
5 Dirk Nowitzki 1.00 2.50
6 Dwight Howard .50 1.25
7 Al Jefferson .25 .60
8 Chris Bosh .50 1.25
9 Kevin Durant 1.50 4.00
10 Danny Granger .25 .60
11 Tim Duncan 1.00 2.50
12 Antawn Jamison .30 .75
13 Deron Williams .30 .75
14 Carmelo Anthony .60 1.50
15 Zach Randolph .30 .75
16 Brandon Roy .50 1.25
17 Stephen Jackson .30 .75
18 Pau Gasol .60 1.50
19 Tony Parker .60 1.50
20 David West .30 .75
21 Devin Harris .25 .60
22 Joe Johnson .30 .75
23 Amare Stoudemire .30 .75
24 Yao Ming 1.00 2.50
25 Caron Butler .30 .75
26 Kevin Martin .30 .75
27 Vince Carter .75 2.00
28 David Lee .25 .60
29 Andre Iguodala .30 .75
30 Paul Pierce .60 1.50
31 Carlos Boozer .30 .75
32 Troy Murphy .25 .60
33 Steve Nash .75 2.00
34 Shaquille O'Neal 1.25 3.00
35 Al Harrington .30 .75
36 Ben Gordon .30 .75
37 LaMarcus Aldridge .40 1.00
38 Gilbert Arenas .30 .75
39 Andre Miller .40 1.00
40 Chauncey Billups .50 1.25
41 Gerald Wallace .30 .75
42 Jamal Crawford .40 1.00
43 Michael Redd .30 .75
44 Derrick Rose .60 1.50
45 Monta Ellis .30 .75
46 Hedo Turkoglu .30 .75
47 Kevin Garnett 1.00 2.50
48 Richard Jefferson .30 .75
49 Mehmet Okur .25 .60
50 Baron Davis .30 .75
51 Rudy Gay .40 1.00
52 Rashard Lewis .30 .75
53 Corey Maggette .30 .75
54 Richard Hamilton .40 1.00
55 John Salmons .30 .75
56 Ron Artest .40 1.00
57 Jameer Nelson .25 .60
58 Russell Westbrook .75 2.00
59 Allen Iverson .75 2.00
60 O.J. Mayo .25 .60
61 Rajon Rondo .50 1.25
62 Jason Terry .30 .75
63 Mo Williams .30 .75
64 Josh Smith .25 .60
65 Jeff Green .30 .75
66 Nate Robinson .30 .75
67 Andris Biedrins .25 .60
68 Tracy McGrady .75 2.00
69 Raymond Felton .25 .60
70 Josh Howard .30 .75
71 Charlie Villanueva .25 .60
72 Jose Calderon .25 .60
73 Ray Allen .60 1.50
74 Andrew Bogut .30 .75
75 Emeka Okafor .30 .75
76 Paul Millsap .30 .75
77 Jason Kidd .60 1.50
78 Elton Brand .30 .75
79 Nene .30 .75
80 T.J. Ford .25 .60
81 Andrew Bynum .25 .60
82 Randy Foye .25 .60
83 Manu Ginobili .75 2.00
84 Marcus Camby .30 .75
85 Shawn Marion .30 .75
86 Al Thornton .25 .60
87 Mike Bibby .40 1.00
88 Jason Richardson .40 1.00
89 Al Horford .40 1.00
90 Tayshaun Prince .40 1.00
91 Luis Scola .30 .75
92 Brad Miller .30 .75
93 Boris Diaw .30 .75
94 Brook Lopez .40 1.00
95 Lamar Odom .30 .75
96 Luol Deng .30 .75
97 Andrea Bargnani .25 .60
98 Jermaine O'Neal .40 1.00
99 Rasheed Wallace .50 1.25
100 Michael Beasley .25 .60
101 Blake Griffin/640 AU RC 40.00 100.00
102 Hasheem Thabeet/315 AU RC 4.00 10.00
103 James Harden/660 AU RC 150.00 400.00
104 Tyreke Evans/150 AU RC 5.00 12.00
105 R.Beaubois/640 AU RC 4.00 10.00
106 Jonny Flynn/625 AU RC 4.00 10.00
107 Stephen Curry/625 AU RC 1,500.00 3,000.00
108 Jordan Hill/700 AU RC 4.00 10.00
109 Derrick Brown/150 AU RC 4.00 10.00
110 B.Jennings/640 AU RC 6.00 15.00
111 T.Williams/160 AU RC 4.00 10.00
112 G.Henderson/630 AU RC 4.00 10.00
113 T.Hansbrough/650 AU RC 5.00 12.00
114 Earl Clark/625 AU RC 4.00 10.00
115 Austin Daye/700 AU RC 4.00 10.00
116 James Johnson/630 AU RC 5.00 12.00
117 Jrue Holiday/630 AU RC 20.00 50.00
118 Ty Lawson/330 AU RC 5.00 12.00
119 Jeff Teague/660 AU RC 5.00 12.00
120 Eric Maynor/126 AU RC 4.00 10.00
121 Darren Collison/160 AU RC 6.00 15.00
122 Dante Cunningham/650 AU RC 4.00 10.00
123 Omri Casspi/660 AU RC 4.00 10.00
124 B.J. Mullens/630 AU RC 4.00 10.00
125 Taj Gibson/330 AU RC 5.00 12.00
126 DeMarre Carroll/630 AU RC 5.00 12.00
127 Wayne Ellington/630 AU RC 5.00 12.00
128 Toney Douglas/630 AU RC 4.00 10.00
129 Jeff Pendergraph/660 AU RC 4.00 10.00
130 DaJuan Summers/630 AU RC 4.00 10.00
131 Sam Young/365 AU RC 5.00 12.00
132 DeJuan Blair/625 AU RC 5.00 12.00
133 Jodie Meeks/625 AU RC 4.00 10.00
134 Chase Budinger/640 AU RC 4.00 10.00
135 Taylor Griffin/640 AU RC 4.00 10.00
136 DeMar DeRozan/700 RC* 125.00 300.00
137 Jonas Jerebko/700 RC* 5.00 12.00
138 Wesley Matthews/683 RC* 6.00 15.00
139 Marcus Thornton/696 RC* 5.00 12.00
140 Jermaine Taylor/696 RC* 4.00 10.00

2009-10 Panini Threads Century Proof Gold

*GOLD: 1.5X TO 4X BASE HI
STATED PRINT RUN 99 SER.#'d SETS

2009-10 Panini Threads Century Proof Orange

*ORANGE: .5X TO 1.25X BASE HI

2009-10 Panini Threads Century Proof Platinum

*PLATINUM: 3X TO 8X BASE HI
STATED PRINT RUN 25 SER.#'d SETS

2009-10 Panini Threads Century Proof Silver

*SILVER: .75X TO 2X BASE HI
STATED PRINT RUN 249 SER.#'d SETS

2009-10 Panini Threads ABA Legends

COMPLETE SET (10) 6.00 15.00
*PROOF: .75X TO 2X BASE HI
PRINT RUN 100 SER.#'d SETS
1 Dan Issel 1.25 3.00
2 Rick Barry 1.25 3.00
3 Artis Gilmore 2.00 5.00
4 George Gervin 2.00 5.00
5 David Thompson 1.25 3.00
6 Louie Dampier 1.00 2.50
7 Moses Malone 2.50 6.00
8 Connie Hawkins 2.00 5.00
9 George McGinnis 1.50 4.00
10 Billy Cunningham 1.50 4.00

2009-10 Panini Threads ABA Legends Autographs

STATED PRINT RUN 25 SER.#'d SETS
1 Dan Issel 10.00 25.00
2 Rick Barry 20.00 40.00
3 Artis Gilmore 20.00 40.00
4 George Gervin 25.00 50.00
5 David Thompson 15.00 30.00
8 Connie Hawkins 25.00 50.00
9 George McGinnis 8.00 20.00

2009-10 Panini Threads Century Collection Materials

STATED PRINT RUN 100 TO 250 SER.#'d SETS
1 Dwight Howard/250 4.00 10.00
2 Tim Duncan/100 8.00 20.00
3 Kobe Bryant/250 8.00 20.00
4 Tracy McGrady/250 6.00 15.00
6 Mike Bibby/250 3.00 8.00
9 Jason Kidd/250 5.00 12.00
10 LaMarcus Aldridge/250 3.00 8.00
11 Michael Beasley/250 2.00 5.00
12 Andre Iguodala/250 3.00 8.00
13 Elton Brand/250 2.50 6.00
14 LeBron James/100 10.00 25.00
17 Chris Paul/250 6.00 15.00
19 Dwyane Wade/250 6.00 15.00

2009-10 Panini Threads Century Collection Materials Prime

*PRIME: .75X TO 2X BASE HI
STATED PRINT RUN 5 TO 25 SER.#'d SETS
8 Dirk Nowitzki/20 15.00 40.00
15 Amare Stoudemire/25 5.00 12.00
18 Gilbert Arenas/25 5.00 12.00
20 Tony Parker/20 10.00 25.00

2009-10 Panini Threads Century Stars

COMPLETE SET (25) 15.00 30.00
*PROOF: .6X TO 1.5X BASE HI
PROOF PRINT RUN 100 SER.#'d SETS
1 Joe Johnson .75 2.00
2 Kevin Garnett 2.00 5.00
3 LeBron James 6.00 15.00
4 Jason Kidd 1.25 3.00
5 Carmelo Anthony 1.25 3.00
6 Yao Ming 2.00 5.00
7 Baron Davis .60 1.50
8 Kobe Bryant 6.00 15.00
9 Chris Paul 1.50 4.00
10 Kevin Durant 3.00 8.00
11 Vince Carter 1.50 4.00
12 Grant Hill 1.25 3.00
13 Tony Parker 1.25 3.00
14 Carlos Boozer .60 1.50
15 Antawn Jamison .60 1.50
16 Derrick Rose 1.25 3.00
17 Richard Hamilton .75 2.00
18 Danny Granger .50 1.25
19 Dwyane Wade 1.50 4.00
20 Andrew Bogut .60 1.50
21 Devin Harris .50 1.25
22 Nate Robinson .60 1.50
23 Elton Brand .60 1.50
24 Brandon Roy 1.00 2.50
25 Chris Bosh 1.00 2.50

2009-10 Panini Threads Century Stars Autographs

STATED PRINT RUN 10 TO 50 SER.#'d SETS
4 Jason Kidd/25 15.00 40.00
8 Kobe Bryant/50 500.00 1,000.00
13 Tony Parker/25 15.00 40.00
18 Danny Granger/25 8.00 20.00

2009-10 Panini Threads Century Stars Materials

STATED PRINT RUN 100 TO 250 SER.#'d SETS
2 Kevin Garnett/250 8.00 20.00
3 LeBron James/100 10.00 25.00
4 Jason Kidd/250 5.00 12.00
6 Yao Ming/250 8.00 20.00
8 Kobe Bryant/250 8.00 20.00
9 Chris Paul/250 6.00 15.00
10 Kevin Durant/250 6.00 15.00
14 Carlos Boozer/250 2.50 6.00
19 Dwyane Wade/250 6.00 15.00
20 Andrew Bogut/250 2.50 6.00
22 Nate Robinson/250 2.50 6.00
23 Elton Brand/250 2.50 6.00
25 Chris Bosh/250 4.00 10.00

2009-10 Panini Threads Century Stars Materials Prime

*PRIME: .75X TO 2X BASE HI
STATED PRINT RUN 3 TO 25 SER.#'d SETS
10 Kevin Durant/25 15.00 40.00
21 Devin Harris/25 4.00 10.00

2009-10 Panini Threads Generations

COMPLETE SET (15) 10.00 25.00
*PROOF: 1X TO 2.5X BASE HI
PROOF PRINT RUN 100 SER.#'d SETS
1 J.West/K.Bryant 6.00 15.00
2 M.Redd/O.Robertson 1.00 2.50
3 C.Mullin/S.Jackson 1.00 2.50
4 C.Anthony/D.Thompson 1.25 3.00
5 B.Gordon/I.Thomas .75 2.00
6 K.Johnson/S.Nash 1.50 4.00
7 J.Hill/W.Reed 1.25 3.00
8 S.Curry/T.Hardaway 30.00 80.00
9 A.Dantley/D.Williams .60 1.50
10 D.Granger/J.Rose .60 1.50
11 P.Gasol/V.Divac 1.25 3.00
12 K.Durant/X.McDaniel 3.00 8.00
13 J.Havlicek/L.Bird 3.00 8.00
14 A.English/C.Billups 1.00 2.50
15 C.Hawkins/R.Artest 1.00 2.50

2009-10 Panini Threads Generations Autographs
STATED PRINT RUN 25 TO 50 SER.#'d SETS
1 J.West/K.Bryant/25 2,000.00 4,000.00
7 J.Hill/W.Reed/50 25.00 60.00
8 S.Curry/T.Hardaway/50 800.00 1,500.00

2009-10 Panini Threads Generations Materials
STATED PRINT RUN 100 SER.#'d SETS
1 J.West/K.Bryant 20.00 50.00
3 C.Mullin/S.Jackson 4.00 10.00

2009-10 Panini Threads Jerseys
STATED PRINT RUN 25 TO 100 SER.#'d SETS
1 LeBron James/100 8.00 20.00
2 Dwyane Wade/100 4.00 10.00
3 Chris Paul/100 6.00 15.00
4 Kobe Bryant/100 8.00 20.00
5 Dirk Nowitzki/100 8.00 20.00
6 Dwight Howard/100 4.00 10.00
8 Chris Bosh/100 4.00 10.00
9 Kevin Durant/100 8.00 20.00
11 Tim Duncan/100 8.00 20.00
13 Deron Williams/100 2.50 6.00
16 Brandon Roy/100 4.00 10.00
17 Stephen Jackson/100 2.50 6.00
18 Pau Gasol/100 5.00 12.00
19 Tony Parker/100 5.00 12.00
20 David West/100 2.50 6.00
24 Yao Ming/100 8.00 20.00
28 David Lee/100 2.00 5.00
29 Andre Iguodala/100 3.00 8.00
30 Paul Pierce/100 5.00 12.00
31 Carlos Boozer/100 2.50 6.00
37 LaMarcus Aldridge/100 3.00 8.00
38 Gilbert Arenas/100 2.50 6.00
41 Gerald Wallace/100 2.50 6.00
44 Derrick Rose/100 5.00 12.00
47 Kevin Garnett/100 8.00 20.00
60 O.J. Mayo/100 2.00 5.00
61 Rajon Rondo/100 4.00 10.00
62 Jason Terry/100 2.50 6.00
66 Nate Robinson/100 2.50 6.00
68 Tracy McGrady/100 6.00 15.00
70 Josh Howard/100 2.50 6.00
72 Jose Calderon/100 2.00 5.00
73 Ray Allen/100 5.00 12.00
74 Andrew Bogut/100 2.50 6.00
76 Paul Millsap/100 2.50 6.00
77 Jason Kidd/100 5.00 12.00
78 Elton Brand/100 2.50 6.00
79 Nene/100 2.50 6.00
81 Andrew Bynum/100 2.00 5.00
83 Manu Ginobili/25 6.00 15.00
87 Mike Bibby/100 3.00 8.00
90 Tayshaun Prince/100 3.00 8.00
97 Andrea Bargnani/100 2.00 5.00
98 Jermaine O'Neal/100 3.00 8.00
100 Michael Beasley/100 2.00 5.00

2009-10 Panini Threads Jerseys Prime
*PRIME: .75X TO 2X BASE HI
STATED PRINT RUNS 5 TO 25 SER.#'d SETS
1 LeBron James/25 25.00 60.00
2 Dwyane Wade/25 10.00 25.00
12 Antawn Jamison/25 5.00 12.00
22 Joe Johnson/25 6.00 15.00
23 Amare Stoudemire/25 5.00 12.00
26 Kevin Martin/20 5.00 12.00
35 Al Harrington/25 5.00 12.00
43 Michael Redd/25 5.00 12.00
49 Mehmet Okur/25 4.00 10.00
52 Rashard Lewis/25 5.00 12.00
64 Josh Smith/25 4.00 10.00

2009-10 Panini Threads Kobe Bryant Letters
STATED PRINT RUN 240 SER.#'d SETS
1 Kobe Bryant 400.00 800.00

2009-10 Panini Threads Legends
COMPLETE SET (15) 8.00 20.00
*PROOF: .6X TO 1.5X BASE HI
PROOF PRINT RUN 100 SER.#'d SETS
1 Magic Johnson 5.00 12.00
2 Willis Reed 2.00 5.00
3 Kareem Abdul-Jabbar 4.00 10.00
4 John Havlicek 3.00 8.00
5 Isiah Thomas 1.25 3.00
6 Slick Watts .75 2.00
7 David Thompson 1.00 2.50
8 Jerry West 2.00 5.00
9 Danny Ainge 1.25 3.00
10 Alex English 1.50 4.00
11 Hal Greer 1.50 4.00
12 Artis Gilmore 1.50 4.00
13 Walt Frazier 2.00 5.00
14 Chris Mullin 1.50 4.00
15 Tom Heinsohn 1.25 3.00

2009-10 Panini Threads Legends Autographs
STATED PRINT RUN 25 SER.#'d SETS
2 Willis Reed 40.00 100.00
4 John Havlicek 20.00 40.00
7 David Thompson 20.00 40.00
8 Jerry West 25.00 50.00
10 Alex English 10.00 25.00
12 Artis Gilmore 10.00 25.00
13 Walt Frazier 10.00 25.00
14 Chris Mullin 15.00 30.00

2009-10 Panini Threads Legends Materials
STATED PRINT RUN 50 TO 100 SER.#'d SETS
*PRIME: .6X TO 1.5X BASE HI
PRIME PRINT RUN 10 TO 25 SETS
1 Magic Johnson/100 6.00 15.00
3 Kareem Abdul-Jabbar/100 6.00 15.00
5 Isiah Thomas/100 5.00 12.00
8 Jerry West/50 8.00 20.00
9 Danny Ainge/100 5.00 12.00
10 Alex English/100 6.00 15.00
12 Artis Gilmore/100 6.00 15.00
13 Walt Frazier/50 6.00 15.00
14 Chris Mullin/100 6.00 15.00
15 Tom Heinsohn/100 5.00 12.00

2009-10 Panini Threads Rookie Collection Materials
STATED PRINT RUN 250 SER.#'d SETS
*PRIME: .75X TO 2X BASE HI
PRIME PRINT RUN 25 SER.#'d SETS
1 Blake Griffin 10.00 25.00
2 Hasheem Thabeet 1.50 4.00
3 James Harden 25.00 60.00
4 Tyreke Evans 2.00 5.00
5 Jonny Flynn 1.50 4.00
6 Stephen Curry 125.00 300.00
7 Jordan Hill 1.50 4.00
8 DeMar DeRozan 20.00 50.00
9 Brandon Jennings 2.50 6.00
10 Terrence Williams 1.50 4.00
11 Gerald Henderson 1.50 4.00
12 Tyler Hansbrough 2.00 5.00
13 Earl Clark 1.50 4.00
14 Austin Daye 1.50 4.00
15 James Johnson 2.00 5.00
16 Jrue Holiday 8.00 20.00
17 Ty Lawson 2.00 5.00
18 Jeff Teague 2.00 5.00
19 Eric Maynor 1.50 4.00
20 Darren Collison 2.50 6.00
21 Omri Casspi 1.50 4.00
22 B.J. Mullens 1.50 4.00
23 Rodrigue Beaubois 1.50 4.00
24 Taj Gibson 2.00 5.00
25 DeMarre Carroll 1.50 4.00
26 Wayne Ellington 2.00 5.00
27 Toney Douglas 1.50 4.00
28 Jeff Pendergraph 1.50 4.00
29 DaJuan Summers 1.50 4.00
30 Sam Young 1.50 4.00
31 DeJuan Blair 2.00 5.00
32 Jodie Meeks 1.50 4.00
33 Chase Budinger 1.50 4.00
34 Taylor Griffin 1.50 4.00
35 Jermaine Taylor 1.50 4.00

2009-10 Panini Threads Rookie Collection Materials Signatures
STATED PRINT RUN 50 SER.#'d SETS
1 Blake Griffin 100.00 200.00
2 Hasheem Thabeet 5.00 12.00
4 Tyreke Evans 6.00 15.00
5 Jonny Flynn 5.00 12.00
6 Stephen Curry 1,000.00 2,000.00
7 Jordan Hill 5.00 12.00
9 Brandon Jennings 8.00 20.00
10 Terrence Williams 5.00 12.00
11 Gerald Henderson 5.00 12.00
12 Tyler Hansbrough 6.00 15.00
13 Earl Clark 5.00 12.00
14 Austin Daye 5.00 12.00
15 James Johnson 6.00 15.00
16 Jrue Holiday 25.00 60.00
17 Ty Lawson 6.00 15.00
18 Jeff Teague 6.00 15.00
21 Omri Casspi 5.00 12.00
22 B.J. Mullens 5.00 12.00
23 Rodrigue Beaubois 5.00 12.00
25 DeMarre Carroll 6.00 15.00
27 Toney Douglas 5.00 12.00
28 Jeff Pendergraph 5.00 12.00
29 DaJuan Summers 5.00 12.00
30 Sam Young 5.00 12.00
31 DeJuan Blair 6.00 15.00
32 Jodie Meeks 6.00 15.00
33 Chase Budinger 5.00 12.00
34 Taylor Griffin 5.00 12.00
35 Jermaine Taylor 5.00 12.00

2009-10 Panini Threads Rookie Collection Materials Prime Signatures
*PRIME: .5X TO 1.25X HI COLUMN
STATED PRINT RUN 25 SER.#'d SETS
1 Blake Griffin 125.00 300.00
6 Stephen Curry 1,500.00 3,000.00

2009-10 Panini Threads Rookie Preview Jerseys
STATED PRINT RUN 100 SER.#'d SETS
INSERTED INTO RETAIL PACKS
1 Blake Griffin 10.00 25.00
2 Hasheem Thabeet 1.50 4.00
3 James Harden 25.00 60.00
4 Tyreke Evans 2.00 5.00
5 Jonny Flynn 1.50 4.00
6 Stephen Curry 150.00 400.00
7 Jordan Hill 1.50 4.00
8 DeMar DeRozan 20.00 50.00
9 Brandon Jennings 2.50 6.00
10 Terrence Williams 1.50 4.00
11 Gerald Henderson 1.50 4.00
12 Tyler Hansbrough 2.00 5.00
13 Earl Clark 1.50 4.00
14 Austin Daye 1.50 4.00
15 James Johnson 2.00 5.00
16 Jrue Holiday 8.00 20.00
17 Ty Lawson 2.00 5.00
18 Jeff Teague 2.00 5.00
19 Eric Maynor 1.50 4.00
20 Darren Collison 2.50 6.00
21 Omri Casspi 1.50 4.00
22 B.J. Mullens 1.50 4.00
23 Rodrigue Beaubois 1.50 4.00
24 Taj Gibson 2.00 5.00
25 DeMarre Carroll 2.00 5.00
26 Wayne Ellington 2.00 5.00
27 Toney Douglas 1.50 4.00
28 Jeff Pendergraph 1.50 4.00
29 DaJuan Summers 1.50 4.00
30 Sam Young 1.50 4.00
31 DeJuan Blair 2.00 5.00
32 Chase Budinger 1.50 4.00
33 Jermaine Taylor 1.50 4.00

2009-10 Panini Threads Rookie Preview Jerseys Autographs
STATED PRINT RUN 50 SER.#'d SETS
INSERTED INTO RETAIL PACKS
1 Blake Griffin 40.00 100.00
2 Hasheem Thabeet 4.00 10.00
4 Tyreke Evans 5.00 12.00
5 Jonny Flynn 4.00 10.00
6 Stephen Curry 1,000.00 2,000.00
7 Jordan Hill 4.00 10.00
9 Brandon Jennings 6.00 15.00
10 Terrence Williams 5.00 12.00
11 Gerald Henderson 4.00 10.00
12 Tyler Hansbrough 5.00 12.00
13 Earl Clark 4.00 10.00
14 Austin Daye 4.00 10.00
15 James Johnson 5.00 12.00
16 Jrue Holiday 20.00 50.00
17 Ty Lawson 5.00 12.00
18 Jeff Teague 5.00 12.00
21 Omri Casspi 4.00 10.00
22 B.J. Mullens 4.00 10.00
23 Rodrigue Beaubois 4.00 10.00
25 DeMarre Carroll 5.00 12.00
27 Toney Douglas 4.00 10.00
28 Jeff Pendergraph 4.00 10.00
29 DaJuan Summers 4.00 10.00
30 Sam Young 4.00 10.00
31 DeJuan Blair 5.00 12.00
32 Chase Budinger 4.00 10.00
33 Jermaine Taylor 4.00 10.00

2009-10 Panini Threads Silver Signatures
STATED PRINT RUN 10 TO 99 SER.#'d SETS
4 Kobe Bryant/99 1,000.00 2,000.00
5 Dirk Nowitzki/25 125.00 300.00
10 Danny Granger/99 5.00 12.00
19 Tony Parker/50 15.00 40.00
21 Devin Harris/50 5.00 12.00
28 David Lee/50 5.00 12.00
29 Andre Iguodala/50 10.00 25.00
71 Charlie Villanueva/50 5.00 12.00
77 Jason Kidd/25 20.00 50.00
87 Mike Bibby/50 8.00 20.00

2009-10 Panini Threads Team Threads Away
COMPLETE SET (50) 25.00 50.00
HOME VERSION: .4X TO 1X AWAY
1 Joe Johnson 1.00 2.50
2 Mike Bibby 1.00 2.50
3 Paul Pierce 1.50 4.00
4 Rajon Rondo 1.25 3.00
5 Gerald Wallace .75 2.00
6 Joakim Noah .60 1.50
7 LeBron James 12.00 30.00
8 Shaquille O'Neal 3.00 8.00
9 Dirk Nowitzki 2.50 6.00
10 Shawn Marion 1.00 2.50
11 Carmelo Anthony 1.50 4.00
12 Ben Gordon .75 2.00
13 Richard Hamilton 1.00 2.50
14 Stephen Jackson .75 2.00
15 Tracy McGrady 2.00 5.00
16 Danny Granger .60 1.50
17 Baron Davis .75 2.00
18 Marcus Camby .75 2.00
19 Kobe Bryant 8.00 20.00
20 Ron Artest 1.00 2.50
21 O.J. Mayo .60 1.50
22 Dwyane Wade 2.00 5.00
23 Jermaine O'Neal 1.00 2.50
24 Andrew Bogut .75 2.00
25 Michael Redd .75 2.00
26 Kevin Love 1.00 2.50
27 Devin Harris .60 1.50
28 Rafer Alston .60 1.50
29 Chris Paul 2.00 5.00
30 Peja Stojakovic .75 2.00
31 David Lee .60 1.50
32 Nate Robinson .75 2.00
33 Kevin Durant 4.00 10.00
34 Dwight Howard 1.25 3.00
35 Vince Carter 2.00 5.00
36 Andre Iguodala 1.00 2.50
37 Elton Brand .75 2.00
38 Amare Stoudemire .75 2.00
39 Steve Nash 2.00 5.00
40 Brandon Roy 1.25 3.00
41 LaMarcus Aldridge 1.00 2.50
42 Kevin Martin .75 2.00
43 Tim Duncan 2.50 6.00
44 Tony Parker 1.50 4.00
45 Chris Bosh 1.50 4.00
46 Hedo Turkoglu .75 2.00
47 Deron Williams .75 2.00
48 Carlos Boozer .75 2.00
49 Antawn Jamison .75 2.00
50 Gilbert Arenas .75 2.00

2009-10 Panini Threads Team Threads Away Autographs
STATED PRINT RUN 5 TO 25 SER.#'d SETS
*HOME VERSION: .4X TO 1X AWAY
ASTERISK CARDS FROM PANINI UPDATE
2 Mike Bibby/25 30.00 60.00
4 Rajon Rondo/25 30.00 80.00
16 Danny Granger/25* 8.00 20.00
19 Kobe Bryant/25 800.00 1,500.00
23 Jermaine O'Neal/25 8.00 20.00
26 Kevin Love/25 25.00 50.00
27 Devin Harris/25 8.00 20.00
36 Andre Iguodala/25 8.00 20.00
37 Elton Brand/25 8.00 20.00
44 Tony Parker/25 30.00 80.00
45 Chris Bosh/25* 8.00 20.00
47 Deron Williams/25* 25.00 60.00
48 Carlos Boozer/25 15.00 40.00

2009-10 Panini Threads Triple Threat
COMPLETE SET 6.00 15.00
*PROOF: .6X TO 1.5X BASE HI
PROOF PRINT RUN 100 SER.#'d SETS
1 LeBron James 6.00 15.00
2 Chris Paul 1.50 4.00
3 Jason Kidd 1.25 3.00
4 Kobe Bryant 6.00 15.00
5 Andre Miller .75 2.00
6 Rajon Rondo 1.00 2.50
7 Pau Gasol 1.25 3.00
8 Tracy McGrady 1.50 4.00
9 Dwight Howard 1.00 2.50
10 Russell Westbrook 1.50 4.00

2009-10 Panini Threads Triple Threat Autographs
STATED PRINT RUN 50 SER.#'d SETS
3 Jason Kidd 12.00 30.00
4 Kobe Bryant 500.00 1,000.00

2009-10 Panini Threads Triple Threat Materials
STATED PRINT RUN 90 TO 100 SER.#'d SETS
1 LeBron James/90 10.00 25.00
2 Chris Paul/100 6.00 15.00
3 Jason Kidd/100 5.00 12.00
4 Kobe Bryant/100 8.00 20.00
6 Rajon Rondo/100 4.00 10.00
7 Pau Gasol/95 5.00 12.00
8 Tracy McGrady/100 6.00 15.00
9 Dwight Howard/100 4.00 10.00

2009-10 Panini Threads Triple Threat Materials Prime
*PRIME: .75X TO 2X BASE HI
STATED PRINT RUN 5 TO 25 SER.#'d SETS
4 Kobe Bryant/25 20.00 50.00

2010-11 Panini Threads
COMP.SET w/o RCs (100) 15.00 30.00
ROOKIE PRINT RUN 399 SER.#'d SETS
*ORANGE/199: 1.25X TO 3X BASE HI
*SILVER/199: 1.25X TO 3X BASE HI
*GOLD/99: 1.5X TO 4X BASE HI
EXCH.EXPIRATION 5/24/2012
1 Al-Farouq Aminu AU RC 4.00 10.00
2 Andy Rautins AU RC 3.00 8.00
3 Willie Warren AU RC 3.00 8.00
4 Cole Aldrich AU RC 3.00 8.00
5 Craig Brackins AU RC 3.00 8.00
6 Da'Sean Butler AU RC 4.00 10.00
7 Damion James AU RC 3.00 8.00
8 Daniel Orton AU RC 3.00 8.00
9 DeMarcus Cousins AU RC 10.00 25.00
10 Derrick Favors AU RC 5.00 12.00
11 Devin Ebanks AU RC 3.00 8.00
12 Dexter Pittman AU RC 3.00 8.00
13 Dominique Jones AU RC 3.00 8.00
14 Ed Davis AU RC 4.00 10.00
15 Ekpe Udoh AU RC 3.00 8.00
16 Elliot Williams AU RC 3.00 8.00
17 Eric Bledsoe AU RC 6.00 15.00
18 Evan Turner AU RC 4.00 10.00
19 Gani Lawal AU RC 3.00 8.00
20 Gordon Hayward AU RC 12.00 30.00
21 Greg Monroe AU RC 4.00 10.00
22 Greivis Vasquez AU RC 3.00 8.00
23 Hassan Whiteside AU RC 6.00 15.00
24 James Anderson AU RC 3.00 8.00
25 John Wall AU RC 15.00 40.00
26 Xavier Henry AU RC 3.00 8.00
27 Lance Stephenson AU RC 5.00 12.00
28 Larry Sanders AU RC 3.00 8.00
29 Lazar Hayward AU RC 3.00 8.00
30 Luke Babbitt AU RC 3.00 8.00
31 Luke Harangody AU RC 3.00 8.00
32 Patrick Patterson AU RC 4.00 10.00
33 Paul George AU RC 75.00 200.00
34 Quincy Pondexter AU RC 3.00 8.00
35 Stanley Robinson AU RC 3.00 8.00
36 Keith Gallon AU RC 3.00 8.00
37 Trevor Booker AU RC 3.00 8.00
38 Wesley Johnson AU RC 3.00 8.00
39 Andrew Bogut .30 .75
40 John Salmons .25 .60
41 Brandon Jennings .25 .60
42 Michael Beasley .25 .60
43 Martell Webster .30 .75
44 Kevin Love .40 1.00
45 Brook Lopez .30 .75
46 Troy Murphy .25 .60
47 Devin Harris .25 .60
48 Chris Paul .75 2.00
49 David West .30 .75
50 Marcus Thornton .25 .60
51 Amare Stoudemire .40 1.00
52 Anthony Randolph .25 .60
53 Danilo Gallinari .30 .75
54 Raymond Felton .25 .60
55 Kevin Durant 1.50 4.00
56 Russell Westbrook .60 1.50
57 Jeff Green .30 .75
58 Dwight Howard .50 1.25
59 Vince Carter .75 2.00
60 Rashard Lewis .30 .75
61 J.J. Redick .40 1.00
62 Andre Iguodala .40 1.00
63 Allen Iverson .75 2.00
64 Elton Brand .30 .75
65 Steve Nash .75 2.00
66 Robin Lopez .25 .60
67 Channing Frye .25 .60
68 LaMarcus Aldridge .40 1.00
69 Brandon Roy .50 1.25
70 Andre Miller .30 .75
71 Greg Oden .25 .60
72 Tyreke Evans .25 .60
73 Samuel Dalembert .25 .60
74 Carl Landry .25 .60
75 Tim Duncan 1.00 2.50
76 Tony Parker .60 1.50
77 Manu Ginobili .75 2.00
78 Richard Jefferson .30 .75
79 Andrea Bargnani .25 .60
80 Jose Calderon .25 .60
81 Leandro Barbosa .30 .75
82 Deron Williams .30 .75
83 Al Jefferson .25 .60
84 Paul Millsap .30 .75
85 Al Thornton .25 .60
86 Kirk Hinrich .25 .60
87 Josh Howard .30 .75
88 Joe Johnson .30 .75
89 Josh Smith .25 .60
90 Al Horford .30 .75
91 Jamal Crawford .40 1.00
92 Paul Pierce .60 1.50
93 Rajon Rondo .50 1.25
94 Kevin Garnett 1.00 2.50
95 Shaquille O'Neal 1.50 4.00
96 Stephen Jackson .30 .75
97 Gerald Wallace .30 .75
98 Gerald Henderson .25 .60
99 Carlos Boozer .30 .75
100 Derrick Rose .75 2.00
101 Luol Deng .30 .75
102 Joakim Noah .40 1.00
103 Antawn Jamison .30 .75
104 Daniel Gibson .25 .60
105 Mo Williams .30 .75
106 Dirk Nowitzki 1.00 2.50
107 Jason Kidd .60 1.50
108 Jason Terry .30 .75
109 Carmelo Anthony .60 1.50
110 Chauncey Billups .50 1.25
111 Al Harrington .30 .75
112 Nene .30 .75
113 Ben Gordon .30 .75
114 Richard Hamilton .50 1.25
115 Tracy McGrady .60 1.50
116 Monta Ellis .30 .75
117 Stephen Curry 6.00 15.00
118 David Lee .25 .60
119 Shane Battier .30 .75
120 Kevin Martin .30 .75
121 Luis Scola .30 .75
122 Yao Ming .75 2.00
123 Danny Granger .25 .60
124 Mike Dunleavy .25 .60
125 Tyler Hansbrough .25 .60
126 Baron Davis .40 1.00
127 Eric Gordon .30 .75
128 Chris Kaman .25 .60
129 Kobe Bryant 3.00 8.00
130 Derek Fisher .40 1.00
131 Pau Gasol .60 1.50
132 Lamar Odom .30 .75
133 Rudy Gay .40 1.00
134 Marc Gasol .40 1.00
135 Zach Randolph .40 1.00
136 Chris Bosh .50 1.25
137 Dwyane Wade .75 2.00
138 LeBron James 3.00 8.00

2010-11 Panini Threads Century Proof Platinum
*PLATINUM: 3X TO 8X BASE HI
STATED PRINT RUN 25 SER.#'d SETS
117 Stephen Curry 75.00 200.00
129 Kobe Bryant 50.00 120.00
138 LeBron James 50.00 120.00

2010-11 Panini Threads All-Time Big Men
COMPLETE SET (25) 12.50 25.00
*PROOF: .75X TO 2X BASE HI
PROOF: STATED PRINT RUN 99 SER.#'d SETS
1 Bill Russell 3.00 8.00
2 Kareem Abdul-Jabbar 3.00 8.00
3 Bill Walton 1.50 4.00
4 Artis Gilmore 1.25 3.00
5 Hakeem Olajuwon 2.00 5.00
6 Patrick Ewing 1.50 4.00
7 Walt Bellamy 1.25 3.00
8 Wes Unseld 1.25 3.00
9 Dolph Schayes 1.25 3.00
10 Elvin Hayes 1.25 3.00
11 Karl Malone 2.00 5.00
12 Wayne Embry .75 2.00
13 Alonzo Mourning 1.50 4.00
14 Arnie Risen .75 2.00
15 Bill Cartwright .75 2.00
16 Bob Lanier 1.50 4.00
17 Clyde Lovellette 1.25 3.00
18 Wilt Chamberlain 3.00 8.00
19 Dave Cowens 1.50 4.00
20 David Robinson 2.00 5.00
21 Moses Malone 1.50 4.00
22 Nate Thurmond 1.25 3.00
23 Mark Eaton 1.00 2.50
24 George Mikan 3.00 8.00
25 Robert Parish 1.50 4.00

2010-11 Panini Threads All-Time Big Men Autographs
STATED PRINT RUN 10 TO 49 SER.#'d SETS
1 Bill Russell/25 400.00 800.00
2 Kareem Abdul-Jabbar/25 75.00 200.00
3 Bill Walton/25 20.00 50.00
4 Artis Gilmore/49 10.00 25.00
5 Hakeem Olajuwon/25 40.00 100.00
7 Walt Bellamy/49 10.00 25.00
8 Wes Unseld/49 10.00 25.00
9 Dolph Schayes/49 40.00 100.00
13 Alonzo Mourning/25 25.00 60.00
14 Arnie Risen/49 10.00 25.00
15 Bill Cartwright/49 6.00 15.00
16 Bob Lanier/25 12.00 30.00
17 Clyde Lovellette/25 10.00 25.00
19 Dave Cowens/10 20.00 50.00
22 Nate Thurmond/25 10.00 25.00
25 Robert Parish/49 12.00 30.00

2010-11 Panini Threads All-Time Big Men Materials
STATED PRINT RUN 399 SER.#'d SETS
*PRIME/50: 1.25X TO 3X BASE HI
5 Hakeem Olajuwon 6.00 15.00
6 Patrick Ewing 6.00 15.00
11 Karl Malone 6.00 15.00
13 Alonzo Mourning 5.00 12.00
23 Mark Eaton 3.00 8.00

2010-11 Panini Threads Century Collection Materials
STATED PRINT RUN 399 SER.#'d SETS
*PRIME: .75X TO 2X BASE HI
PRIME STATED PRINT RUN 50 SER.#'d SETS
1 Ben Gordon 3.00 8.00
2 Yi Jianlian 4.00 10.00
3 Wayne Ellington 2.50 6.00
4 Tyler Hansbrough 2.50 6.00
5 Trevor Ariza 2.50 6.00
6 Thaddeus Young 2.50 6.00
7 Terrence Williams 2.50 6.00
8 Samuel Dalembert 2.50 6.00
9 Ron Artest 4.00 10.00
10 Rodrigue Beaubois 2.50 6.00
11 Luis Scola 3.00 8.00
12 Josh Howard 3.00 8.00
13 Jonny Flynn 2.50 6.00
14 Joakim Noah 4.00 10.00
15 James Harden 10.00 25.00
16 J.J. Barea 3.00 8.00
17 Elton Brand 3.00 8.00
18 Earl Clark 2.50 6.00
19 DeMarre Carroll 2.50 6.00
20 David West 2.50 6.00
21 Brandon Jennings 2.50 6.00
22 Andre Iguodala 2.50 6.00
23 Stephen Curry 30.00 80.00
24 Michael Redd 3.00 8.00
25 James Johnson 2.50 6.00

2010-11 Panini Threads Century Legends
COMPLETE SET (15) 7.50 15.00
*PROOF: .6X TO 1.5X BASE HI
PROOF: STATED PRINT RUN 99 SER.#'d SETS
1 Adrian Dantley 1.25 3.00
2 Bob Dandridge .75 2.00
3 Calvin Murphy 1.00 2.50
4 Frank Ramsey 1.25 3.00
5 Gary Payton 2.00 5.00
6 Jerry Lucas 1.25 3.00
7 Jerry Sloan 1.25 3.00
8 Jo Jo White 1.00 2.50
9 Kelly Tripucka .75 2.00
10 Robert Horry 1.25 3.00
11 Sam Perkins .75 2.00
12 Scottie Pippen 3.00 8.00
13 Spencer Haywood 1.25 3.00
14 Toni Kukoc 1.25 3.00
15 World B. Free 1.00 2.50

2010-11 Panini Threads Century Legends Autographs
STATED PRINT RUN 10 TO 50 SER.#'d SETS
1 Adrian Dantley/25 5.00 12.00
2 Bob Dandridge/50 8.00 20.00
4 Frank Ramsey/50 8.00 20.00
9 Kelly Tripucka/25 8.00 20.00
10 Robert Horry/50 20.00 50.00
14 Toni Kukoc/50 20.00 50.00

2010-11 Panini Threads Century Legends Materials
STATED PRINT RUN 399 SER.#'d SETS
5 Gary Payton 5.00 12.00
11 Sam Perkins 2.00 5.00
12 Scottie Pippen 8.00 20.00
14 Toni Kukoc 3.00 8.00

2010-11 Panini Threads Century Legends Materials Prime
*PRIME: .75X TO 2X BASE HI
STATED PRINT RUN 50 SER.#'d SETS
12 Scottie Pippen 25.00 60.00

2010-11 Panini Threads Century Stars
COMPLETE SET (25) 10.00 20.00
*PROOF: .6X TO 1.5X BASE HI
PROOF STATED PRINT RUN 99 SER.#'d SETS
1 Al Jefferson .50 1.25
2 Allen Iverson 1.50 4.00
3 Amare Stoudemire .75 2.00
4 Andrea Bargnani .50 1.25
5 Anthony Randolph .50 1.25
6 Carlos Boozer .60 1.50
7 Caron Butler .60 1.50
8 Chauncey Billups 1.00 2.50
9 Chris Bosh 1.00 2.50
10 Chris Kaman .50 1.25
11 Chris Paul 1.50 4.00
12 Derrick Rose 1.50 4.00
13 Dirk Nowitzki 2.00 5.00
14 Dwight Howard 1.00 2.50
15 Dwyane Wade 1.50 4.00
16 Joe Johnson .75 2.00
17 Kevin Durant 3.00 8.00
18 Kevin Garnett 2.00 5.00
19 LeBron James 6.00 15.00
20 Paul Pierce 1.25 3.00
21 Rudy Gay .75 2.00
22 Russell Westbrook 1.25 3.00
23 Shaquille O'Neal 3.00 8.00
24 Steve Nash 1.50 4.00
25 Tim Duncan 2.00 5.00

2010-11 Panini Threads Century Stars Autographs
STATED PRINT RUN 5 TO 25 SER.#'d SETS
4 Andrea Bargnani/25 5.00 12.00
5 Anthony Randolph/25 5.00 12.00
8 Chauncey Billups/25 10.00 25.00
9 Chris Bosh/25 15.00 40.00
22 Russell Westbrook/25 60.00 150.00

2010-11 Panini Threads Century Stars Materials
STATED PRINT RUN 99 TO 399 SER.#'d SETS
1 Al Jefferson/399 2.50 6.00
2 Allen Iverson/99 8.00 20.00
4 Andrea Bargnani/399 2.50 6.00
6 Carlos Boozer/399 3.00 8.00
7 Caron Butler/399 3.00 8.00
8 Chauncey Billups/399 5.00 12.00
13 Dirk Nowitzki/399 10.00 25.00
14 Dwight Howard/399 5.00 12.00
15 Dwyane Wade/399 8.00 20.00
20 Paul Pierce/399 6.00 15.00
23 Shaquille O'Neal/399 20.00 50.00
25 Tim Duncan/399 10.00 25.00

2010-11 Panini Threads Century Stars Materials Prime
*PRIME: 1X TO 2.5X BASE HI
STATED PRINT RUN 50 SER.#'d SETS
12 Derrick Rose 20.00 50.00
24 Steve Nash 20.00 50.00

2010-11 Panini Threads Jerseys
STATED PRINT RUN 99 TO 399 SER.#'d SETS
39 Andrew Bogut/299 2.50 6.00
41 Brandon Jennings/399 2.50 6.00
42 Michael Beasley/399 2.00 5.00
44 Kevin Love/399 3.00 8.00
47 Devin Harris/299 2.00 5.00
48 Chris Paul/399 6.00 15.00
49 David West/399 2.00 5.00
52 Anthony Randolph/399 2.00 5.00
54 Raymond Felton/399 2.00 5.00
58 Dwight Howard/399 4.00 10.00
59 Vince Carter/399 6.00 15.00
60 Rashard Lewis/399 2.50 6.00
61 J.J. Redick/399 3.00 8.00
62 Andre Iguodala/399 3.00 8.00
63 Allen Iverson/99 6.00 15.00
64 Elton Brand/399 3.00 8.00
65 Steve Nash/399 6.00 15.00
66 Robin Lopez/399 2.00 5.00
67 Channing Frye/399 2.00 5.00
68 LaMarcus Aldridge/399 3.00 8.00
69 Brandon Roy/399 4.00 10.00
70 Andre Miller/399 2.50 6.00
71 Greg Oden/399 2.00 5.00
73 Samuel Dalembert/399 2.00 5.00
75 Tim Duncan/399 8.00 20.00
76 Tony Parker/399 5.00 12.00
77 Manu Ginobili/399 6.00 15.00
78 Richard Jefferson/399 2.50 6.00
79 Andrea Bargnani/399 2.00 5.00
80 Jose Calderon/399 2.00 5.00
81 Leandro Barbosa/399 2.50 6.00
82 Deron Williams/399 2.50 6.00
83 Al Jefferson/399 2.00 5.00
86 Kirk Hinrich/299 2.50 6.00
90 Al Horford/399 3.00 8.00
92 Paul Pierce/399 5.00 12.00
95 Shaquille O'Neal/399 12.00 30.00
96 Stephen Jackson/399 2.50 6.00
98 Gerald Henderson/349 2.00 5.00
99 Carlos Boozer/399 2.50 6.00
102 Joakim Noah/399 3.00 8.00
103 Antawn Jamison/399 2.50 6.00
106 Dirk Nowitzki/399 8.00 20.00
108 Jason Terry/399 2.50 6.00
110 Chauncey Billups/399 4.00 10.00
112 Nene/399 2.50 6.00
113 Ben Gordon/399 2.50 6.00
115 Tracy McGrady/399 5.00 12.00
117 Stephen Curry/199 25.00 60.00
119 Shane Battier/399 2.50 6.00
120 Kevin Martin/399 2.50 6.00
121 Luis Scola/399 2.50 6.00
124 Mike Dunleavy/99 2.00 5.00
125 Tyler Hansbrough/399 2.00 5.00
129 Kobe Bryant/399 25.00 60.00
130 Derek Fisher/399 3.00 8.00
131 Pau Gasol/399 5.00 12.00
132 Lamar Odom/399 2.50 6.00
137 Dwyane Wade/399 6.00 15.00

2010-11 Panini Threads Jerseys Prime
*PRIME: .75X TO 2X BASE HI
STATED PRINT RUN 25 TO 50 SER.#'d SETS
100 Derrick Rose/50 12.00 30.00

2010-11 Panini Threads Rookie Collection Materials
STATED PRINT RUN 399 SER.#'d SETS
*PRIME: .75X TO 2X BASE HI
PRIME STATED PRINT RUN 50 SER.#'d SETS
1 John Wall 6.00 15.00
2 Evan Turner 1.50 4.00
3 Derrick Favors 2.00 5.00
4 Wesley Johnson 1.25 3.00
5 DeMarcus Cousins 4.00 10.00
6 Ekpe Udoh 1.25 3.00
7 Greg Monroe 1.50 4.00
8 Al-Farouq Aminu 1.50 4.00
9 Gordon Hayward 5.00 12.00
10 Paul George 10.00 25.00
11 Cole Aldrich 1.25 3.00
12 Xavier Henry 1.25 3.00
13 Patrick Patterson 1.50 4.00
14 Larry Sanders 1.25 3.00
15 Luke Babbitt 1.25 3.00
16 Eric Bledsoe 2.50 6.00
17 Avery Bradley 2.00 5.00
18 James Anderson 1.25 3.00
19 Craig Brackins 1.25 3.00
20 Elliot Williams 1.25 3.00
21 Trevor Booker 1.25 3.00
22 Damion James 1.25 3.00
23 Dominique Jones 1.25 3.00
24 Quincy Pondexter 1.25 3.00
25 Jordan Crawford 1.25 3.00
26 Greivis Vasquez 1.25 3.00
27 Daniel Orton 1.25 3.00
28 Lazar Hayward 1.25 3.00
29 Dexter Pittman 1.25 3.00
30 Hassan Whiteside 2.50 6.00
31 Andy Rautins 1.25 3.00
32 Lance Stephenson 2.00 5.00
33 Da'Sean Butler 1.50 4.00
34 Devin Ebanks 1.25 3.00
35 Gani Lawal 1.25 3.00

2010-11 Panini Threads Rookie Collection Materials Signatures
STATED PRINT RUN 50 SER.#'d SETS
*SIG.PRIME: .75X TO 2X HI
SIG.PRIME PRINT RUN 25 SER.#'d SETS
1 John Wall 40.00 100.00
2 Evan Turner 5.00 12.00
3 Derrick Favors 6.00 15.00
4 Wesley Johnson 4.00 10.00
5 DeMarcus Cousins 12.00 30.00
6 Ekpe Udoh 4.00 10.00
7 Greg Monroe 5.00 12.00
8 Al-Farouq Aminu 5.00 12.00
9 Gordon Hayward 15.00 40.00
10 Paul George 75.00 200.00
11 Cole Aldrich 4.00 10.00
12 Xavier Henry 4.00 10.00
13 Patrick Patterson 5.00 12.00
14 Larry Sanders 4.00 10.00
15 Luke Babbitt 4.00 10.00
16 Eric Bledsoe 8.00 20.00
17 Avery Bradley 6.00 15.00
18 James Anderson 4.00 10.00
19 Craig Brackins 4.00 10.00
20 Elliot Williams 4.00 10.00
21 Trevor Booker 4.00 10.00
22 Damion James 4.00 10.00
23 Dominique Jones 4.00 10.00
24 Quincy Pondexter 4.00 10.00
25 Jordan Crawford 4.00 10.00
26 Greivis Vasquez 4.00 10.00
27 Daniel Orton 4.00 10.00
28 Lazar Hayward 4.00 10.00
29 Dexter Pittman 4.00 10.00
30 Hassan Whiteside 8.00 20.00
31 Andy Rautins 4.00 10.00
32 Lance Stephenson 6.00 15.00
33 Da'Sean Butler 5.00 12.00
34 Devin Ebanks 4.00 10.00
35 Gani Lawal 4.00 10.00

2010-11 Panini Threads Rookie Team Threads Away
COMPLETE SET (40) 20.00 40.00
*HOME VERSION: .4X TO 1X BASE HI
1 Al-Farouq Aminu .60 1.50

2009-10 Panini Threads Generations Autographs

2 Andy Rautins .50 1.25
3 Avery Bradley .75 2.00
4 Cole Aldrich .50 1.25
5 Craig Brackins .50 1.25
6 Darington Hobson .50 1.25
7 Damion James .50 1.25
8 Daniel Orton .50 1.25
9 DeMarcus Cousins 1.50 4.00
10 Derrick Favors .75 2.00
11 Brian Zoubek .50 1.25
12 Jeremy Lin 3.00 8.00
13 Dominique Jones .50 1.25
14 Ed Davis .60 1.50
15 Ekpe Udoh .50 1.25
16 Elliot Williams .50 1.25
17 Eric Bledsoe 1.00 2.50
18 Evan Turner .60 1.50
19 Gani Lawal .50 1.25
20 Gordon Hayward 2.00 5.00
21 Greg Monroe .60 1.50
22 Greivis Vasquez .50 1.25
23 Hassan Whiteside 1.00 2.50
24 James Anderson .50 1.25
25 John Wall 2.50 6.00
26 Jordan Crawford .50 1.25
27 Lance Stephenson .75 2.00
28 Larry Sanders .50 1.25
29 Lazar Hayward .50 1.25
30 Luke Babbitt .50 1.25
31 Luke Harangody .50 1.25
32 Patrick Patterson .60 1.50
33 Paul George 4.00 10.00
34 Quincy Pondexter .50 1.25
35 Stanley Robinson .50 1.25
36 Keith Gallon .50 1.25
37 Trevor Booker .50 1.25
38 Wesley Johnson .50 1.25
39 Willie Warren .50 1.25
40 Xavier Henry .50 1.25

2010-11 Panini Threads Rookie Team Threads Home Autographs

STATED PRINT RUN 77 TO 99 SER.#'d SETS
1 Al-Farouq Aminu/97 5.00 12.00
2 Andy Rautins/99 4.00 10.00
3 Avery Bradley/97 6.00 15.00
4 Cole Aldrich/99 4.00 10.00
5 Craig Brackins/99 4.00 10.00
6 Darington Hobson/99 4.00 10.00
7 Damion James/99 4.00 10.00
8 Daniel Orton/99 4.00 10.00
9 DeMarcus Cousins/99 25.00 60.00
10 Derrick Favors/99 6.00 15.00
11 Brian Zoubek/99 EXCH 4.00 10.00
12 Jeremy Lin/99 75.00 200.00
13 Dominique Jones/99 4.00 10.00
14 Ed Davis/99 5.00 12.00
15 Ekpe Udoh/99 4.00 10.00
16 Elliot Williams/99 4.00 10.00
17 Eric Bledsoe/99 8.00 20.00
18 Evan Turner/99 5.00 12.00
19 Gani Lawal/99 4.00 10.00
20 Gordon Hayward/99 15.00 40.00
21 Greg Monroe/99 5.00 12.00
22 Greivis Vasquez/99 4.00 10.00
23 Hassan Whiteside/99 8.00 20.00
24 James Anderson/99 4.00 10.00
25 John Wall/99 30.00 80.00
26 Jordan Crawford/99 4.00 10.00
27 Lance Stephenson/99 6.00 15.00
28 Larry Sanders/99 4.00 10.00
29 Lazar Hayward/99 4.00 10.00
30 Luke Babbitt/99 4.00 10.00
31 Luke Harangody/77 4.00 10.00
32 Patrick Patterson/99 5.00 12.00
33 Paul George/99 75.00 200.00
34 Quincy Pondexter/99 4.00 10.00
35 Stanley Robinson/99 EXCH 4.00 10.00
36 Keith Gallon/99 4.00 10.00
37 Trevor Booker/99 4.00 10.00
38 Wesley Johnson/99 4.00 10.00
39 Willie Warren/99 4.00 10.00
40 Xavier Henry/99 4.00 10.00

2010-11 Panini Threads Silver Signatures

STATED PRINT RUN 9 TO 49 SER.#'d SETS
39 Andrew Bogut/24 5.00 12.00
41 Brandon Jennings/24 4.00 10.00
42 Michael Beasley/24 4.00 10.00
44 Kevin Love/24 12.00 30.00
45 Brook Lopez/24 5.00 12.00
46 Troy Murphy/24 EXCH 4.00 10.00
47 Devin Harris/24 4.00 10.00
50 Marcus Thornton/49 4.00 10.00
51 Amare Stoudemire/24 6.00 15.00
52 Anthony Randolph/24 4.00 10.00
56 Russell Westbrook/49 50.00 120.00
59 Vince Carter/24 40.00 100.00
61 J.J. Redick/24 10.00 25.00
65 Steve Nash/24 60.00 150.00
66 Robin Lopez/49 4.00 10.00
67 Channing Frye/49 4.00 10.00
68 LaMarcus Aldridge/24 12.00 30.00
69 Brandon Roy/24 8.00 20.00
72 Tyreke Evans/49 5.00 12.00
73 Samuel Dalembert/49 4.00 10.00
74 Carl Landry/49 4.00 10.00
76 Tony Parker/24 15.00 40.00
79 Andrea Bargnani/24 4.00 10.00
82 Deron Williams/24 5.00 12.00
87 Josh Howard/24 5.00 12.00
93 Rajon Rondo/24 12.00 30.00
95 Shaquille O'Neal/24 75.00 200.00
97 Gerald Wallace/24 5.00 12.00
98 Gerald Henderson/49 4.00 10.00
100 Derrick Rose/24 50.00 120.00
101 Luol Deng/24 5.00 12.00
105 Mo Williams/24 5.00 12.00
107 Jason Kidd/24 20.00 50.00
110 Chauncey Billups/24 10.00 25.00
114 Richard Hamilton/24 10.00 25.00
117 Stephen Curry/24 1,000.00 2,000.00
125 Tyler Hansbrough/49 4.00 10.00
128 Chris Kaman/24 4.00 10.00
129 Kobe Bryant/24 1,500.00 3,000.00
130 Derek Fisher/24 6.00 15.00
131 Pau Gasol/24 12.00 30.00
132 Lamar Odom/24 10.00 25.00
134 Marc Gasol/24 10.00 25.00
135 Zach Randolph/24 6.00 15.00
136 Chris Bosh/24 15.00 40.00

2010-11 Panini Threads Team Threads Away

COMPLETE SET (50) 30.00 60.00
*HOME VERSION: .4X TO 1X BASE HI
1 Josh Smith .60 1.50
2 Al Horford 1.00 2.50
3 Shaquille O'Neal 4.00 10.00
4 Kevin Garnett 2.50 6.00
5 Stephen Jackson .75 2.00
6 Derrick Rose 2.00 5.00
7 Carlos Boozer .75 2.00
8 Antawn Jamison .75 2.00
9 Dirk Nowitzki 2.50 6.00
10 Jason Kidd 1.50 4.00
11 Chauncey Billups 1.25 3.00
12 Chris Andersen 1.00 2.50
13 Tracy McGrady 1.50 4.00
14 Tayshaun Prince 1.00 2.50
15 Monta Ellis .75 2.00
16 David Lee .60 1.50
17 Yao Ming 2.00 5.00
18 Kevin Martin .75 2.00
19 Darren Collison .60 1.50
20 Randy Foye .60 1.50
21 Eric Gordon .75 2.00
22 Kobe Bryant 8.00 20.00
23 Pau Gasol 1.50 4.00
24 Marc Gasol 1.00 2.50
25 Zach Randolph 1.00 2.50
26 LeBron James 8.00 20.00
27 Chris Bosh 1.25 3.00
28 Brandon Jennings .60 1.50
29 John Salmons .60 1.50
30 Michael Beasley .60 1.50
31 Brook Lopez .75 2.00
32 Troy Murphy .60 1.50
33 Chris Paul 2.00 5.00
34 David West .75 2.00
35 Amare Stoudemire 1.00 2.50
36 Anthony Randolph .60 1.50
37 Kevin Durant 4.00 10.00
38 Russell Westbrook 1.50 4.00
39 Dwight Howard 1.25 3.00
40 Andre Iguodala 1.00 2.50
41 Steve Nash 2.00 5.00
42 Andre Miller .75 2.00
43 Tyreke Evans .75 2.00
44 Richard Jefferson .75 2.00
45 Andrea Bargnani .60 1.50
46 Leandro Barbosa .75 2.00
47 Deron Williams .75 2.00
48 Al Jefferson .60 1.50
49 Al Thornton .60 1.50
50 Kirk Hinrich .75 2.00

2010-11 Panini Threads Team Threads Away Autographs

STATED PRINT RUN 10 TO 99 SER.#'d SETS
*HOME VERSION: .4X TO 1X BASE HI
HOME PRINT RUN 10 TO 99 SER.#'d SETS
2 Al Horford/49 8.00 20.00
3 Shaquille O'Neal/15 100.00 250.00
10 Jason Kidd/25 25.00 60.00
12 Chris Andersen/25 20.00 50.00
19 Darren Collison/49 5.00 12.00
20 Randy Foye/49 5.00 12.00
22 Kobe Bryant/99 1,500.00 3,000.00
24 Marc Gasol/25 12.00 30.00
25 Zach Randolph/49 12.00 30.00
28 Brandon Jennings/49 8.00 20.00
38 Russell Westbrook/49 60.00 150.00
40 Andre Iguodala/25 8.00 20.00
43 Tyreke Evans/49 5.00 12.00
47 Deron Williams/25 8.00 20.00
49 Al Thornton/49 5.00 12.00

2010-11 Panini Threads Triple Threat

COMPLETE SET (10) 7.50 15.00
*PROOF: .6X TO 1.5X BASE HI
PROOF STATED PRINT RUN 99 SER.#'d SETS
1 Jason Kidd 1.25 3.00
2 Deron Williams .60 1.50
3 Andre Iguodala .75 2.00
4 Russell Westbrook 1.25 3.00
5 LeBron James 6.00 15.00
6 Carlos Boozer .60 1.50
7 Rajon Rondo 1.00 2.50
8 Kobe Bryant 6.00 15.00
9 Brandon Roy 1.00 2.50
10 Steve Nash 1.50 4.00

2010-11 Panini Threads Triple Threat Autographs

STATED PRINT RUN 5 TO 50 SER.#'d SETS
1 Jason Kidd/15 40.00 100.00
4 Russell Westbrook/50 60.00 150.00
7 Rajon Rondo/15 20.00 50.00
8 Kobe Bryant/50 1,500.00 3,000.00
9 Brandon Roy/50 12.00 30.00

2010-11 Panini Threads Triple Threat Materials

STATED PRINT RUN 399 SER.#'d SETS
2 Deron Williams 2.50 6.00
3 Andre Iguodala 3.00 8.00
6 Carlos Boozer 2.50 6.00
8 Kobe Bryant 40.00 100.00
9 Brandon Roy 4.00 10.00

2010-11 Panini Threads Triple Threat Materials Prime

*PRIME: .75X TO 2X BASE HI
STATED PRINT RUN 50 SER.#'d SETS
10 Steve Nash 25.00 60.00

2012-13 Panini Threads

COMP.SET w/o RCs (150) 12.00 30.00
*RED: .75X TO 2X BASE HI
*SILVER/99: 2X TO 5X BASE HI
*GOLD/25: 4X TO 10X BASE HI
1 Al Horford .40 1.00
2 Jeff Teague .25 .60
3 Josh Smith .25 .60
4 Joe Johnson .30 .75
5 Kirk Hinrich .30 .75
6 Paul Pierce .60 1.50
7 Ray Allen .60 1.50
8 Rajon Rondo .50 1.25
9 Kevin Garnett 1.00 2.50
10 Avery Bradley .25 .60
11 Brandon Bass .25 .60
12 D.J. Augustin .25 .60
13 Gerald Henderson .25 .60
14 Corey Maggette .30 .75
15 Derrick Rose .60 1.50
16 Carlos Boozer .30 .75
17 Luol Deng .30 .75
18 Joakim Noah .30 .75
19 Richard Hamilton .40 1.00
20 John Lucas III .25 .60
21 Anderson Varejao .25 .60
22 Antawn Jamison .30 .75
23 Omri Casspi .25 .60
24 Dirk Nowitzki 1.00 2.50
25 Jason Terry .30 .75
26 Shawn Marion .40 1.00
27 Jason Kidd .60 1.50
28 Vince Carter .75 2.00
29 Delonte West .25 .60
30 Ty Lawson .25 .60
31 Danilo Gallinari .25 .60
32 Andre Miller .30 .75
33 JaVale McGee .30 .75
34 Arron Afflalo .25 .60
35 Al Harrington .30 .75
36 Greg Monroe .25 .60
37 Rodney Stuckey .25 .60
38 Tayshaun Prince .40 1.00
39 Ben Gordon .30 .75
40 Jason Maxiell .25 .60
41 Stephen Curry 3.00 8.00
42 Andrew Bogut .30 .75
43 David Lee .25 .60
44 Nate Robinson .25 .60
45 Dorell Wright .25 .60
46 Brandon Rush .25 .60
47 Kevin Martin .30 .75
48 Luis Scola .30 .75
49 Kyle Lowry .40 1.00
50 Goran Dragic .40 1.00
51 Courtney Lee .25 .60
52 Danny Granger .25 .60
53 David West .30 .75
54 George Hill .30 .75
55 Roy Hibbert .30 .75
56 Paul George .60 1.50
57 Darren Collison .25 .60
58 Chris Paul .75 2.00
59 Blake Griffin .40 1.00
60 Nick Young .25 .60
61 Caron Butler .30 .75
62 Mo Williams .30 .75
63 DeAndre Jordan .30 .75
64 Kobe Bryant 3.00 8.00
65 Andrew Bynum .25 .60
66 Pau Gasol .60 1.50
67 Ramon Sessions .25 .60
68 Devin Ebanks .25 .60
69 Metta World Peace .30 .75
70 Rudy Gay .40 1.00
71 Zach Randolph .40 1.00
72 O.J. Mayo .25 .60
73 Marc Gasol .40 1.00
74 Marreese Speights .25 .60
75 Mike Conley .30 .75
76 LeBron James 3.00 8.00
77 Chris Bosh .50 1.25
78 Dwyane Wade .75 2.00
79 Mario Chalmers .30 .75
80 Shane Battier .30 .75
81 Mike Miller .30 .75
82 Monta Ellis .30 .75
83 Brandon Jennings .25 .60
84 Ersan Ilyasova .25 .60
85 Drew Gooden .30 .75
86 Luc Mbah a Moute .25 .60
87 Kevin Love .40 1.00
88 Ricky Rubio .30 .75
89 Nikola Pekovic .25 .60
90 Luke Ridnour .25 .60
91 Michael Beasley .25 .60
92 Wesley Johnson .25 .60
93 Eric Gordon .30 .75
94 Jarrett Jack .30 .75
95 Chris Kaman .30 .75
96 Marco Belinelli .25 .60
97 Greivis Vasquez .25 .60
98 Kevin Durant 1.50 4.00
99 Russell Westbrook .60 1.50
100 James Harden .75 2.00
101 Serge Ibaka .30 .75
102 Kendrick Perkins .25 .60
103 Derek Fisher .30 .75
104 Dwight Howard .50 1.25
105 Jameer Nelson .25 .60
106 J.J. Redick .40 1.00
107 Glen Davis .25 .60
108 Jason Richardson .40 1.00
109 Ryan Anderson .25 .60
110 Andre Iguodala .40 1.00
111 Evan Turner .25 .60
112 Louis Williams .30 .75
113 Jrue Holiday .50 1.25
114 Elton Brand .30 .75
115 Thaddeus Young .25 .60
116 Steve Nash .75 2.00
117 Grant Hill .60 1.50
118 Jared Dudley .25 .60
119 Marcin Gortat .25 .60
120 Channing Frye .25 .60
121 Shannon Brown .25 .60
122 Tyreke Evans .30 .75
123 DeMarcus Cousins .40 1.00
124 Marcus Thornton .25 .60
125 Terrence Williams .25 .60
126 Jason Thompson .25 .60
127 Tim Duncan 1.00 2.50
128 Tony Parker .60 1.50
129 Manu Ginobili .75 2.00
130 Stephen Jackson .30 .75
131 Danny Green .30 .75
132 Gary Neal .25 .60
133 Andrea Bargnani .25 .60
134 DeMar DeRozan .50 1.25
135 Jose Calderon .25 .60
136 Jerryd Bayless .25 .60
137 Linas Kleiza .25 .60
138 Ed Davis .25 .60
139 Al Jefferson .25 .60
140 Devin Harris .25 .60
141 Paul Millsap .30 .75
142 Derrick Favors .30 .75
143 Gordon Hayward .40 1.00
144 DeMarre Carroll .25 .60
145 Josh Howard .30 .75
146 John Wall .50 1.25
147 Jordan Crawford .25 .60
148 Nene .30 .75
149 Cartier Martin RC .40 1.00
150 Trevor Booker .25 .60
151 Kyrie Irving AU RC 100.00 250.00
152 Derrick Williams AU RC 5.00 12.00
153 Enes Kanter AU RC 8.00 20.00
154 Tristan Thompson AU RC 8.00 20.00
155 Jan Vesely AU RC 5.00 12.00
156 Bismack Biyombo AU RC 6.00 15.00
157 Brandon Knight AU RC 6.00 15.00
158 Kemba Walker AU RC 20.00 50.00
159 Klay Thompson AU RC 100.00 250.00
160 Alec Burks AU RC 8.00 20.00
161 Markieff Morris AU RC 8.00 20.00
162 Marcus Morris AU RC 8.00 20.00
163 Kawhi Leonard AU RC 125.00 300.00
164 Nikola Vucevic AU RC 20.00 50.00
165 Iman Shumpert AU RC 6.00 15.00
166 Chris Singleton AU RC 5.00 12.00
167 Tobias Harris AU RC 15.00 40.00
168 Nolan Smith AU RC 5.00 12.00
169 Kenneth Faried AU RC 6.00 15.00
170 Reggie Jackson AU RC 8.00 20.00
171 MarShon Brooks AU RC 5.00 12.00
172 Jordan Hamilton AU RC 5.00 12.00
173 JaJuan Johnson AU RC 5.00 12.00
174 Norris Cole AU RC 5.00 12.00
175 Cory Joseph AU RC 6.00 15.00
176 Jimmy Butler AU RC 50.00 120.00
177 Justin Harper AU RC 5.00 12.00
178 Shelvin Mack AU RC 6.00 15.00
179 Tyler Honeycutt AU RC 5.00 12.00
180 Jordan Williams AU RC 6.00 15.00
181 Trey Thompkins AU RC 5.00 12.00
182 Chandler Parsons AU RC 6.00 15.00
183 Jeremy Tyler AU RC 5.00 12.00
184 Jon Leuer AU RC 5.00 12.00
185 Darius Morris AU RC 6.00 15.00
186 Malcolm Lee AU RC 5.00 12.00
187 Charles Jenkins AU RC 5.00 12.00
189 Andrew Goudelock AU RC 5.00 12.00
190 Travis Leslie AU RC 5.00 12.00
192 Josh Selby AU RC 5.00 12.00
193 Lavoy Allen AU RC 5.00 12.00
195 DeAndre Liggins AU RC 5.00 12.00
196 E'Twaun Moore AU RC 6.00 15.00
197 Isaiah Thomas AU RC 10.00 25.00
198 Ivan Johnson AU RC 5.00 12.00
199 Greg Stiemsma AU RC 5.00 12.00
200 Lance Thomas AU RC 5.00 12.00
201 Anthony Davis AU RC 100.00 250.00
202 M.Kidd-Gilchrist AU RC 6.00 15.00
203 Bradley Beal AU RC 40.00 100.00
204 Dion Waiters AU RC 6.00 15.00
205 Thomas Robinson AU RC 5.00 12.00
206 Robbie Hummel AU RC 5.00 12.00
207 Harrison Barnes AU RC 10.00 25.00
208 Terrence Ross AU RC 12.00 30.00
209 Andre Drummond AU RC 12.00 30.00
210 Austin Rivers AU RC 8.00 20.00
211 Meyers Leonard AU RC 6.00 15.00
212 Jeremy Lamb AU RC 8.00 20.00
213 Kendall Marshall AU RC 5.00 12.00
214 John Henson AU RC 6.00 15.00
215 Moe Harkless AU RC 6.00 15.00
216 Royce White AU RC 5.00 12.00
217 Tyler Zeller AU RC 5.00 12.00
218 Terrence Jones AU RC 5.00 12.00
219 Andrew Nicholson AU RC 5.00 12.00
220 Evan Fournier AU RC 8.00 20.00
221 Jared Sullinger AU RC 5.00 12.00
222 Fab Melo AU RC 5.00 12.00
223 John Jenkins AU RC 5.00 12.00
224 Jared Cunningham AU RC 5.00 12.00
225 Tony Wroten AU RC 5.00 12.00
226 Miles Plumlee AU RC 5.00 12.00
227 Arnett Moultrie AU RC 5.00 12.00
228 Perry Jones AU RC 5.00 12.00
229 Marquis Teague AU RC 5.00 12.00
230 Festus Ezeli AU RC 5.00 12.00
231 Jeff Taylor AU RC 5.00 12.00
232 Robert Sacre AU RC 5.00 12.00
233 Bernard James AU RC 5.00 12.00
234 Jae Crowder AU RC 10.00 25.00
235 Draymond Green AU RC 30.00 80.00
236 Orlando Johnson AU RC 5.00 12.00
237 Quincy Acy AU RC 5.00 12.00
238 Quincy Miller AU RC 5.00 12.00
240 Will Barton AU RC 10.00 25.00
241 Tyshawn Taylor AU RC 5.00 12.00
242 Doron Lamb AU RC 5.00 12.00
243 Mike Scott AU RC 6.00 15.00
244 Kim English AU RC 5.00 12.00
246 Darius Miller AU RC 6.00 15.00
247 Kevin Murphy AU RC 5.00 12.00
248 Kyle O'Quinn AU RC 6.00 15.00
249 Kris Joseph AU RC 5.00 12.00
250 T.Shengelia AU RC EXCH 5.00 12.00

2012-13 Panini Threads Authentic Threads

1 Ray Allen 5.00 12.00
2 Tim Duncan 8.00 20.00
3 LeBron James 40.00 100.00
4 Jason Kidd 5.00 12.00
5 Anderson Varejao 2.00 5.00
6 Antawn Jamison 2.50 6.00
7 Andre Iguodala 3.00 8.00
8 Jameer Nelson 2.00 5.00
9 Marc Gasol 3.00 8.00
10 Kevin Martin 2.50 6.00
11 Nick Collison 2.00 5.00
12 Jamal Crawford 3.00 8.00
13 Joe Johnson 2.50 6.00
14 Tyrus Thomas 2.00 5.00
15 Jordan Crawford 2.00 5.00
16 George Hill 2.50 6.00
17 Tayshaun Prince 3.00 8.00
18 Taj Gibson 2.00 5.00
19 Luol Deng 2.50 6.00
20 Manu Ginobili 6.00 15.00
21 O.J. Mayo 2.00 5.00
22 Dirk Nowitzki 8.00 20.00
23 John Salmons 2.50 6.00
24 Channing Frye 2.00 5.00
25 Devin Harris 2.00 5.00
26 Pau Gasol 5.00 12.00
27 Randy Foye 2.00 5.00
28 Caron Butler 2.50 6.00
29 Josh Smith 2.00 5.00
30 David Lee 2.00 5.00
31 DeMar DeRozan 4.00 10.00
32 Jose Calderon 2.00 5.00
33 Evan Turner 2.00 5.00
34 Thaddeus Young 2.00 5.00
35 Landry Fields 2.00 5.00
36 Amare Stoudemire 3.00 8.00
37 Brook Lopez 2.50 6.00
38 Kris Humphries 2.00 5.00
39 Deron Williams 2.50 6.00
40 J.J. Redick 3.00 8.00
41 Glen Davis 2.00 5.00
42 LaMarcus Aldridge 3.00 8.00
43 James Harden 8.00 20.00
44 Anthony Mason 2.50 6.00
45 Luke Ridnour 2.50 6.00
46 Wayne Ellington 2.00 5.00
47 Tony Parker 5.00 12.00
48 Derrick Rose 5.00 12.00
49 D.J. Augustin 2.00 5.00
50 Kevin Durant 12.00 30.00
51 Al Jefferson 2.00 5.00
52 Josh Howard 2.50 6.00
53 Drew Gooden 2.50 6.00
54 Udonis Haslem 2.50 6.00
55 Chris Kaman 2.50 6.00
56 Emeka Okafor 2.50 6.00
57 Rajon Rondo 4.00 10.00
58 Kevin Garnett 8.00 20.00
59 Kenny Anderson 2.50 6.00
60 John Wall 4.00 10.00
61 Joakim Noah 2.50 6.00
62 Jrue Holiday 4.00 10.00
63 Mike Conley 2.50 6.00
64 David West 2.50 6.00
65 Elton Brand 2.50 6.00
66 Chase Budinger 2.00 5.00
67 Andrew Bynum 2.00 5.00
68 Dwight Howard 4.00 10.00
69 Rudy Fernandez 2.00 5.00
70 Al Horford 3.00 8.00
71 Brandon Knight 2.50 6.00
72 Kyrie Irving 20.00 50.00
73 Derrick Williams 2.00 5.00
74 MarShon Brooks 2.00 5.00
75 Markieff Morris 3.00 8.00

2012-13 Panini Threads Authentic Threads Prime

*PRIME: 1X TO 2.5X BASE HI
STATED PRINT RUN ONE TO 25 SER.#'d SETS
20 Manu Ginobili/25 10.00 25.00
48 Derrick Rose/25 30.00 80.00

2012-13 Panini Threads Century Greats

COMPLETE SET (25) 12.00 30.00
1 Larry Bird 2.50 6.00
2 Moses Malone 1.25 3.00
3 Shaquille O'Neal 2.50 6.00
4 Patrick Ewing 1.25 3.00
5 Bill Sharman 1.00 2.50
6 Bill Russell 2.50 6.00
7 John Havlicek 1.50 4.00
8 Hakeem Olajuwon 1.50 4.00
9 Kareem Abdul-Jabbar 2.50 6.00
10 Wilt Chamberlain 2.50 6.00
11 Julius Erving 2.00 5.00
12 Scottie Pippen 2.00 5.00
13 Magic Johnson 2.50 6.00
14 Jerry West 1.50 4.00
15 David Robinson 1.25 3.00
16 Isiah Thomas 1.50 4.00
17 James Worthy 1.25 3.00
18 Nate Archibald 1.00 2.50
19 Elvin Hayes 1.00 2.50
20 Clyde Drexler 1.25 3.00
21 Elgin Baylor 2.00 5.00
22 Oscar Robertson 1.50 4.00
23 Walt Frazier 1.25 3.00
24 Bill Walton 1.25 3.00
25 K.C. Jones .75 2.00

2012-13 Panini Threads Century Stars

1 Chris Paul 8.00 20.00
2 Tim Duncan 10.00 25.00
3 Kevin Garnett 10.00 25.00
4 Kobe Bryant 30.00 80.00
5 Dirk Nowitzki 10.00 25.00
6 Blake Griffin 4.00 10.00
7 Kevin Durant 15.00 40.00
8 Dwight Howard 5.00 12.00
9 Steve Nash 8.00 20.00
10 LeBron James 30.00 80.00
11 Paul Pierce 6.00 15.00
12 Tony Parker 6.00 15.00
13 Dwyane Wade 8.00 20.00
14 Derrick Rose 6.00 15.00
15 Carmelo Anthony 6.00 15.00
16 Josh Smith 2.50 6.00
17 Amare Stoudemire 4.00 10.00
18 Kevin Martin 3.00 8.00
19 Carlos Boozer 3.00 8.00
20 Zach Randolph 4.00 10.00
21 Tyreke Evans 3.00 8.00
22 Kevin Love 4.00 10.00
23 Russell Westbrook 6.00 15.00
24 LaMarcus Aldridge 4.00 10.00
25 Deron Williams 3.00 8.00

2012-13 Panini Threads Floor Generals

COMPLETE SET (20) 8.00 20.00
1 Rajon Rondo 1.00 2.50
2 Derrick Rose 1.25 3.00
3 John Wall 1.00 2.50
4 Deron Williams .60 1.50
5 Steve Nash 1.50 4.00
6 Russell Westbrook 1.25 3.00
7 Chris Paul 1.50 4.00
8 Stephen Curry 6.00 15.00
9 Ty Lawson .50 1.25
10 Raymond Felton .50 1.25
11 Tony Parker 1.25 3.00
12 Dwyane Wade 1.50 4.00
13 Brandon Jennings .50 1.25
14 Jrue Holiday 1.00 2.50
15 Jason Kidd 1.50 4.00
16 Ramon Sessions .50 1.25
17 Ricky Rubio .60 1.50
18 Kyrie Irving 3.00 8.00
19 Devin Harris .50 1.25
20 Jeremy Lin 1.25 3.00

2012-13 Panini Threads High Flyers

COMPLETE SET (30) 10.00 25.00
1 Blake Griffin .75 2.00
2 LeBron James 6.00 15.00
3 Rudy Gay .75 2.00
4 Derrick Rose 1.25 3.00
5 Russell Westbrook 1.25 3.00
6 JaVale McGee .60 1.50
7 Josh Smith .50 1.25
8 Dwyane Wade 1.50 4.00
9 Dwight Howard 1.00 2.50
10 DeMar DeRozan 1.00 2.50
11 Kevin Durant 3.00 8.00
12 Jeremy Evans .50 1.25
13 DeAndre Jordan .60 1.50
14 J.R. Smith .75 2.00
15 Alonzo Gee .50 1.25
16 Kenneth Faried .60 1.50
17 Paul George 1.25 3.00
18 John Wall 1.00 2.50
19 Andre Iguodala .75 2.00
20 Gerald Green .60 1.50
21 Vince Carter 1.50 4.00
22 Tracy McGrady 1.25 3.00
23 Nate Robinson .50 1.25
24 Jason Richardson .75 2.00
25 Kobe Bryant 6.00 15.00
26 Gerald Wallace .60 1.50
27 Shannon Brown .50 1.25
28 Terrence Williams .50 1.25
29 Serge Ibaka .60 1.50
30 Amare Stoudemire .75 2.00

2012-13 Panini Threads Inside Presence

COMPLETE SET (25) 8.00 20.00
1 Tim Duncan 2.00 5.00
2 Andrew Bynum .50 1.25
3 Kevin Love .75 2.00
4 Dwight Howard 1.00 2.50
5 Pau Gasol 1.25 3.00
6 Blake Griffin .75 2.00
7 Brook Lopez .60 1.50
8 Al Jefferson .50 1.25
9 DeMarcus Cousins .75 2.00
10 Kevin Garnett 2.00 5.00
11 Greg Monroe .50 1.25
12 Marc Gasol .75 2.00
13 Nikola Pekovic .50 1.25
14 Chris Kaman .60 1.50
15 Roy Hibbert .60 1.50
16 Al Horford .75 2.00
17 Andrew Bogut .60 1.50
18 Tyson Chandler .60 1.50
19 LaMarcus Aldridge .75 2.00
20 JaVale McGee .60 1.50
21 DeAndre Jordan .60 1.50
22 Joakim Noah .60 1.50
23 Nene .60 1.50
24 Marcin Gortat .50 1.25
25 Tristan Thompson .75 2.00

2012-13 Panini Threads Private Signings

1 Deron Williams 10.00 25.00
2 Antawn Jamison 10.00 25.00
3 Tyson Chandler 10.00 25.00
4 Monta Ellis 10.00 25.00

2012-13 Panini Threads Rookie Team Threads

COMPLETE SET (22) 15.00 40.00
1 Kemba Walker 2.50 6.00
2 Kenneth Faried .75 2.00
3 Kawhi Leonard 8.00 20.00
5 Ivan Johnson .60 1.50
6 Bismack Biyombo .75 2.00
7 Chris Singleton .60 1.50
8 Marcus Morris 1.00 2.50
9 Reggie Jackson 1.00 2.50
10 Enes Kanter 1.00 2.50
11 Lavoy Allen .60 1.50
12 Damian Lillard 6.00 15.00
13 Terrence Ross 1.50 4.00
14 Meyers Leonard .75 2.00
15 John Henson .75 2.00
16 Royce White .60 1.50
17 Tyler Zeller .60 1.50
18 Terrence Jones .60 1.50
19 Andrew Nicholson .60 1.50
20 Fab Melo .60 1.50
21 Evan Fournier 1.00 2.50
22 John Jenkins .60 1.50
23 Marquis Teague .60 1.50

2012-13 Panini Threads Rookie Team Threads Autographs

1 Kyrie Irving 100.00 250.00
2 Brandon Knight 6.00 15.00
3 Isaiah Thomas 10.00 25.00
5 Klay Thompson 125.00 300.00
6 Iman Shumpert 6.00 15.00
7 Chandler Parsons 6.00 15.00
8 Derrick Williams 5.00 12.00
9 Tristan Thompson 8.00 20.00
10 Kawhi Leonard 125.00 300.00
11 Jimmer Fredette 8.00 20.00
12 Markieff Morris 8.00 20.00
13 Norris Cole 5.00 12.00
14 Thomas Robinson 5.00 12.00
15 Harrison Barnes 15.00 40.00
16 Austin Rivers 8.00 20.00
17 Anthony Davis 125.00 300.00
18 Bradley Beal 20.00 50.00
19 Michael Kidd-Gilchrist 6.00 15.00
20 Jeremy Lamb 8.00 20.00
21 Kendall Marshall 5.00 12.00
22 Jared Sullinger 5.00 12.00
23 Andre Drummond 12.00 30.00
24 Perry Jones 5.00 12.00
25 Dion Waiters 6.00 15.00

2012-13 Panini Threads Signage

1 Willis Reed 12.00 30.00
2 DeMarcus Cousins 8.00 20.00
3 Artis Gilmore 10.00 25.00
4 Stephen Curry 800.00 1,500.00
5 Kobe Bryant 1,000.00 2,000.00
6 Andrew Bynum 5.00 12.00
7 Bill Walton 20.00 50.00
8 Blake Griffin 8.00 20.00
9 Steve Nash 50.00 120.00
10 Grant Hill 30.00 80.00
11 Larry Bird 100.00 250.00
12 Michael Finley 8.00 20.00
13 Kevin Durant 100.00 250.00
14 Dave Cowens 12.00 30.00
15 Tom Chambers 8.00 20.00
16 Wesley Matthews 5.00 12.00
17 Kevin Love 12.00 30.00
18 Magic Johnson 75.00 200.00
19 Chris Mullin 10.00 25.00
20 World B. Free 6.00 15.00
21 James Worthy 12.00 30.00
22 Trevor Booker EXCH 5.00 12.00
23 Joe Dumars 10.00 25.00
24 David Robinson 30.00 80.00
25 Jrue Holiday 20.00 50.00
26 Elvin Hayes 10.00 25.00
27 Cedric Ceballos 6.00 15.00
28 Lenny Wilkens 10.00 25.00
29 Josh Smith 5.00 12.00
30 Monta Ellis 6.00 15.00
31 Rolando Blackman 6.00 15.00
32 Roy Hibbert 6.00 15.00
33 Clyde Lovellette 10.00 25.00
34 Ben Gordon 6.00 15.00
35 Tayshaun Prince 15.00 40.00
36 Sean Elliott 6.00 15.00
37 Robert Parish 12.00 30.00
38 Carlos Boozer 6.00 15.00
39 Jamal Mashburn 6.00 15.00
40 Allan Houston EXCH 6.00 15.00
41 Brook Lopez 6.00 15.00
42 Tim Hardaway 10.00 25.00
43 Andre Iguodala 8.00 20.00
44 Zach Randolph 8.00 20.00
45 Mike Conley 6.00 15.00
46 Kyle Lowry 8.00 20.00
47 Kurt Rambis 8.00 20.00
48 Jason Kidd 25.00 60.00
49 Tyson Chandler EXCH 6.00 15.00
50 Dolph Schayes 10.00 25.00

2012-13 Panini Threads Talented Twosomes

COMPLETE SET (14) 10.00 25.00
1 K.Durant/R.Westbrook 3.00 8.00
2 L.Deng/C.Boozer .60 1.50
3 L.James/D.Wade 6.00 15.00
4 P.Pierce/R.Rondo 1.25 3.00
5 K.Bryant/P.Gasol 6.00 15.00
6 T.Evans/D.Cousins .75 2.00
7 T.Lawson/A.Miller .60 1.50
8 Z.Randolph/M.Gasol .75 2.00
9 T.Parker/T.Duncan 2.00 5.00
10 C.Anthony/A.Stoudemire 1.25 3.00
11 S.Curry/D.Lee 6.00 15.00
12 R.Gay/M.Conley .60 1.50
13 A.Jefferson/P.Millsap .60 1.50
14 B.Knight/G.Monroe .60 1.50

2012-13 Panini Threads Team Threads

COMPLETE SET (25) 20.00 50.00
1 Metta World Peace 1.25 3.00
2 Kevin Garnett 4.00 10.00
3 Dwight Howard 2.00 5.00
4 LeBron James 12.00 30.00
5 Louis Williams 1.25 3.00
6 Manu Ginobili 3.00 8.00
7 Jason Terry 1.25 3.00
8 Carmelo Anthony 2.50 6.00
9 Kevin Love 1.50 4.00
10 George Hill 1.25 3.00
11 Jeff Teague 1.00 2.50
12 Serge Ibaka 1.25 3.00
13 Paul Pierce 2.50 6.00
14 Ricky Rubio 1.25 3.00
15 Marcin Gortat 1.00 2.50
16 Jeremy Lin 2.50 6.00
17 Marc Gasol 1.50 4.00
18 Ersan Ilyasova 1.00 2.50
19 Nicolas Batum 1.25 3.00
20 Nick Young 1.00 2.50
21 Gordon Hayward 1.50 4.00
22 Brandon Rush 1.00 2.50
23 David West 1.25 3.00
24 Luis Scola 1.25 3.00
25 Luol Deng 1.25 3.00

2012-13 Panini Threads Team Threads Autographs

1 James Harden 75.00 200.00
2 Kobe Bryant 1,000.00 2,000.00
3 Kevin Durant 100.00 250.00
4 Kevin Love 20.00 50.00
6 Stephen Curry 800.00 1,500.00
7 Chris Paul EXCH 75.00 200.00
8 Tony Parker 40.00 100.00
10 Marcus Thornton 5.00 12.00
11 Vince Carter 75.00 200.00
12 JaVale McGee 6.00 15.00
13 Derrick Favors 6.00 15.00
15 Darren Collison 5.00 12.00
16 Andrew Bogut 15.00 40.00
17 Evan Turner 5.00 12.00
18 Landry Fields 5.00 12.00
19 Ray Allen 75.00 200.00
21 Danilo Gallinari 5.00 12.00
23 Greg Monroe 5.00 12.00

24 Eric Gordon 6.00 15.00
25 Kevin Martin 6.00 15.00

2012-13 Panini Threads Triple Threat Materials

*PRIME/25: 1.25X TO 3X BASE HI
1 Lopez/Big Al/Dwight 4.00 10.00
2 Martin/Dehzn/Granger 4.00 10.00
3 Gasol/Horford/Barg 3.00 8.00
4 Dragic/Barea/Gordon 3.00 8.00
5 Duncan/Gasol/Scola 8.00 20.00
6 Lawson/Rondo/DWill 4.00 10.00
7 Harden/Wstbrk/Durant 12.00 30.00
8 Gasol/Kobe/Bynum 25.00 60.00
9 Lee/Griffin/Cousins 3.00 8.00
10 Zach/Boozer/Amare 3.00 8.00
11 Pierce/Gay/Granger 5.00 12.00
12 Butler/Iguodala/Deng 3.00 8.00
13 Harden/Mayo/Conley 6.00 15.00
14 Carter/Dirk/Pierce 8.00 20.00
15 Rip/Manu/Gordon 6.00 15.00
16 Turner/Fields/Hywrd 3.00 8.00
17 Augustin/Hedo/Zach 3.00 8.00
18 Rose/Williams/Paul 6.00 15.00
19 Bosh/Wade/LeBron 25.00 60.00
20 Brooks/Redick/Wright 3.00 8.00
21 Dwight/O'Neal/Gasol 4.00 10.00
22 Brand/Kaman/Hawes 2.50 6.00
23 Okafor/Davis/Haywd 2.50 6.00
24 Felton/Conley/Miller 2.50 6.00
25 Nelson/Harris/Davis 2.50 6.00

2013 Panini Threads 2011 Draft All-Star Game

COMPLETE SET (6) 10.00 25.00
1 Kyrie Irving 8.00 20.00
2 Derrick Williams 1.50 4.00
3 Brandon Knight 2.00 5.00
4 Kenneth Faried 2.00 5.00
5 Kemba Walker 2.00 5.00
6 Klay Thompson 2.50 6.00

2013 Panini Threads 2012 Draft All-Star Game

COMPLETE SET (6) 8.00 20.00
1 Anthony Davis 5.00 12.00
2 Michael Kidd-Gilchrist 2.50 6.00
3 Thomas Robinson .75 2.00
4 Harrison Barnes 2.50 6.00
5 Austin Rivers 2.00 5.00
6 Jared Sullinger 2.00 5.00

2014-15 Panini Threads

1 Al Horford .60 1.50
2 Al Jefferson .40 1.00
3 Alec Burks .50 1.25
4 Alonzo Mourning 1.00 2.50
5 Amar'e Stoudemire .60 1.50
6 Amir Johnson .40 1.00
7 Anderson Varejao .40 1.00
8 Andre Drummond .50 1.25
9 Andrew Bogut .50 1.25
10 Anthony Davis 1.50 4.00
11 Anthony Morrow .40 1.00
12 Arron Afflalo .40 1.00
13 Artis Gilmore .75 2.00
14 Austin Rivers .40 1.00
15 Avery Bradley .40 1.00
16 Ben McLemore .40 1.00
17 Bernard King .75 2.00
18 Blake Griffin .60 1.50
19 Bradley Beal 1.00 2.50
20 Brandon Jennings .40 1.00
21 Brandon Knight .40 1.00
22 Brook Lopez .60 1.50
23 Carlos Boozer .50 1.25
24 Carmelo Anthony 1.00 2.50
25 Caron Butler .50 1.25
26 Chandler Parsons .40 1.00
27 Channing Frye .40 1.00
28 Chris Andersen .50 1.25
29 Chris Bosh .75 2.00
30 Chris Mullin .75 2.00
31 Chris Paul 1.00 2.50
32 Cody Zeller .40 1.00
33 Corey Brewer .40 1.00
34 Courtney Lee .40 1.00
35 Damian Lillard 1.50 4.00
36 Danilo Gallinari .40 1.00
37 Danny Green .50 1.25
38 Darren Collison .40 1.00
39 David Lee .40 1.00
40 David Robinson 1.25 3.00
41 David West .50 1.25
42 DeAndre Jordan .50 1.25
43 DeMar DeRozan .75 2.00
44 DeMarcus Cousins .50 1.25
45 DeMarre Carroll .40 1.00
46 Dennis Schroder .60 1.50
47 Deron Williams .50 1.25
48 Derrick Favors .40 1.00
49 Derrick Rose 1.25 3.00
50 Devin Harris .40 1.00
51 Dirk Nowitzki 1.50 4.00
52 Dominique Wilkins 1.00 2.50
53 Donatas Motiejunas .40 1.00
54 Draymond Green .75 2.00
55 Dwight Howard .75 2.00
56 Dwyane Wade 1.25 3.00
57 Enes Kanter .50 1.25
58 Eric Bledsoe .50 1.25
59 Eric Gordon .50 1.25
60 Ersan Ilyasova .40 1.00
61 Evan Fournier .40 1.00
62 Evan Turner .40 1.00
63 Gary Payton 1.00 2.50
64 Giannis Antetokounmpo 4.00 10.00
65 Glen Rice .60 1.50
66 Goran Dragic .60 1.50
67 Gordon Hayward .50 1.25
68 Gorgui Dieng .40 1.00
69 Greg Monroe .40 1.00
70 Hakeem Olajuwon 1.25 3.00
71 Harrison Barnes .50 1.25
72 Henry Sims RC .40 1.00
73 Hollis Thompson .40 1.00
74 Iman Shumpert .40 1.00
75 Isaiah Thomas .50 1.25
76 Jamal Crawford .60 1.50
77 Jameer Nelson .40 1.00
78 James Harden 1.25 3.00
79 Jared Sullinger .40 1.00
80 Jarrett Jack .50 1.25
81 Jason Thompson .40 1.00
82 Jeff Green .50 1.25
83 Jeff Teague .40 1.00
84 Jeremy Lin 1.25 3.00
85 Jimmy Butler 1.00 2.50
86 J.J. Redick .60 1.50
87 Joakim Noah .60 1.50
88 Joe Dumars .75 2.00
89 Joe Johnson .50 1.25
90 John Stockton 1.25 3.00
91 John Wall .75 2.00
92 Jonas Valanciunas .50 1.25
93 Jordan Hill .40 1.00
94 Jose Calderon .40 1.00
95 Josh Smith .40 1.00
96 Jrue Holiday .75 2.00
97 Julius Erving 1.50 4.00
98 Kareem Abdul-Jabbar 2.00 5.00
99 Karl Malone 1.25 3.00
100 Kawhi Leonard 1.50 4.00
101 Kelly Olynyk .40 1.00
102 Kemba Walker .60 1.50
103 Kenneth Faried .40 1.00
104 Kentavious Caldwell-Pope .50 1.25
105 Kevin Durant 2.00 5.00
106 Kevin Garnett 1.50 4.00
107 Kevin Love .60 1.50
108 Kevin McHale 1.00 2.50
109 Kirk Hinrich .50 1.25
110 Klay Thompson 1.50 4.00
111 Kobe Bryant 5.00 12.00
112 Kyle Korver .50 1.25
113 Kyle Lowry .75 2.00
114 Kyrie Irving 1.25 3.00
115 LaMarcus Aldridge .60 1.50
116 Lance Stephenson .50 1.25
117 Larry Bird 2.50 6.00
118 Larry Sanders .40 1.00
119 LeBron James 5.00 12.00
120 Luc Mbah a Moute .40 1.00
121 Luis Scola .50 1.25
122 Luol Deng .50 1.25
123 Magic Johnson 2.50 6.00
124 Manu Ginobili 1.25 3.00
125 Marc Gasol .60 1.50
126 Marcin Gortat .40 1.00
127 Marcus Morris .40 1.00
128 Mario Chalmers .50 1.25
129 Markieff Morris .40 1.00
130 Marvin Williams .40 1.00
131 Matt Barnes .50 1.25
132 Maurice Harkless .40 1.00
133 Michael Carter-Williams .40 1.00
134 Michael Kidd-Gilchrist .40 1.00
135 Mike Conley .50 1.25
136 Mike Dunleavy .40 1.00
137 Miles Plumlee .40 1.00
138 Mirza Teletovic .40 1.00
139 Mo Williams .50 1.25
140 Monta Ellis .50 1.25
141 Nene .50 1.25
142 Nerlens Noel .40 1.00
143 Nick Young .40 1.00
144 Nicolas Batum .50 1.25
145 Nikola Pekovic .40 1.00
146 Nikola Vucevic .50 1.25
147 Norris Cole .40 1.00
148 O.J. Mayo .40 1.00
149 Omer Asik .40 1.00
150 Omri Casspi .40 1.00
151 Otto Porter .50 1.25
152 Patrick Beverley .40 1.00
153 Patrick Patterson .40 1.00
154 Pau Gasol 1.00 2.50
155 Paul George 1.00 2.50
156 Paul Millsap .50 1.25
157 Paul Pierce 1.00 2.50
158 Rajon Rondo .75 2.00
159 Reggie Jackson .50 1.25
160 Ricky Rubio .50 1.25
161 Robin Lopez .40 1.00
162 Rodney Stuckey .40 1.00
163 Roy Hibbert .50 1.25
164 Rudy Gay .60 1.50
165 Rudy Gobert 1.00 2.50
166 Russell Westbrook 1.00 2.50
167 Shane Larkin .40 1.00
168 Scottie Pippen 1.50 4.00
169 Serge Ibaka .50 1.25
170 Shaquille O'Neal 2.50 6.00
171 Shawn Marion .50 1.25
172 Solomon Hill .40 1.00
173 Stephen Curry 5.00 12.00
174 Steve Blake .40 1.00
175 Steven Adams .75 2.00
176 Terrence Jones .40 1.00
177 Terrence Ross .50 1.25
178 Thaddeus Young .40 1.00
179 Tiago Splitter .40 1.00
180 Tim Duncan 1.50 4.00
181 Tim Hardaway Jr. .50 1.25
182 Timofey Mozgov .40 1.00
183 Tobias Harris .50 1.25
184 Tony Allen .40 1.00
185 Tony Parker 1.00 2.50
186 Trevor Ariza .40 1.00
187 Tony Wroten .40 1.00
188 Trey Burke .40 1.00
189 Tristan Thompson .40 1.00
190 Ty Lawson .40 1.00
191 Tyreke Evans .50 1.25
192 Tyson Chandler .60 1.50
193 Victor Oladipo .50 1.25
194 Vince Carter 1.25 3.00
195 Walt Frazier 1.00 2.50
196 Wesley Johnson .40 1.00
197 Wesley Matthews .40 1.00
198 Wilson Chandler .40 1.00
199 Zach Randolph .60 1.50
200 Zaza Pachulia .40 1.00
201 Andrew Wiggins TT RC 6.00 15.00
202 Jabari Parker TT RC 1.50 4.00
203 Damjan Rudez TT RC 1.25 3.00
204 Bojan Bogdanovic TT RC 2.00 5.00
205 Elfrid Payton TT RC 2.00 5.00
206 P.J. Hairston TT RC 1.25 3.00
207 Jordan Adams TT RC 1.25 3.00
208 Julius Randle TT RC 6.00 15.00
209 Dante Exum TT RC 2.00 5.00
210 Doug McDermott TT RC 2.00 5.00
211 Zach LaVine TT RC 8.00 20.00
212 Nikola Mirotic TT RC 2.00 5.00
213 Cleanthony Early TT RC 1.25 3.00
214 Glenn Robinson III TT RC 1.50 4.00
215 K.J. McDaniels TT RC 1.50 4.00
216 Marcus Smart TT RC 5.00 12.00
217 Rodney Hood TT RC 1.50 4.00
218 Jordan Clarkson TT RC 5.00 12.00
219 James Young TT RC 1.25 3.00
220 Aaron Gordon TT RC 6.00 15.00
221 Gary Harris TT RC 2.00 5.00
222 Adreian Payne TT RC 1.25 3.00
223 Jusuf Nurkic TT RC 4.00 10.00
224 Kostas Papanikolaou TT RC 1.25 3.00
225 Noah Vonleh TT RC 1.25 3.00
226 Cory Jefferson TT RC 1.25 3.00
227 Shabazz Napier TT RC 1.50 4.00
228 Nik Stauskas TT RC 1.25 3.00
229 James Ennis TT RC 1.25 3.00
230 Kyle Anderson TT RC 2.00 5.00
231 Joel Embiid TT RC 12.00 30.00
232 Tyler Ennis TT RC 2.00 5.00
233 Nick Johnson TT RC 1.25 3.00
234 T.J. Warren TT RC 2.00 5.00
235 Joe Ingles TT RC 2.00 5.00
236 Jerami Grant TT RC 6.00 15.00
237 Joe Harris TT RC 2.00 5.00
238 Erick Green TT RC 1.25 3.00
239 Markel Brown TT RC 1.25 3.00
240 Tarik Black TT RC 1.25 3.00
241 Joel Embiid LTHR RC 15.00 40.00
242 Aaron Gordon LTHR RC 8.00 20.00
243 Bojan Bogdanovic LTHR RC 2.50 6.00
244 Jordan Adams LTHR RC 1.50 4.00
245 Zach LaVine LTHR RC 10.00 25.00
246 Dante Exum LTHR RC 2.50 6.00
247 Glenn Robinson III LTHR RC 2.00 5.00
248 Jabari Parker LTHR RC 2.00 5.00
249 Rodney Hood LTHR RC 2.00 5.00
250 Damjan Rudez LTHR RC 1.50 4.00
251 Joe Ingles LTHR RC 2.50 6.00
252 Elfrid Payton LTHR RC 2.50 6.00
253 Andrew Wiggins LTHR RC 8.00 20.00
254 Damien Inglis LTHR RC 1.50 4.00
255 Tarik Black LTHR RC 1.50 4.00
256 Joe Harris LTHR RC 2.50 6.00
257 P.J. Hairston LTHR RC 1.50 4.00
258 K.J. McDaniels LTHR RC 1.50 4.00
259 Kostas Papanikolaou LTHR RC 1.50 4.00
260 T.J. Warren LTHR RC 2.50 6.00
261 Marcus Smart LTHR RC 6.00 15.00
262 Jarnell Stokes LTHR RC 1.50 4.00
263 Russ Smith LTHR RC 1.50 4.00
264 Cleanthony Early LTHR RC 1.50 4.00
265 Clint Capela LTHR RC 6.00 15.00
266 C.J. Wilcox LTHR RC 1.50 4.00
267 Doug McDermott LTHR RC 2.50 6.00
268 Tyler Ennis LTHR RC 2.50 6.00
269 Nikola Mirotic LTHR RC 2.50 6.00
270 James Ennis LTHR RC 1.50 4.00
271 Cory Jefferson LTHR RC 1.50 4.00
272 James Young LTHR RC 1.50 4.00
273 Shabazz Napier LTHR RC 2.00 5.00
274 Jusuf Nurkic LTHR RC 5.00 12.00
275 Adreian Payne LTHR RC 1.50 4.00
276 Jordan Clarkson LTHR RC 6.00 15.00
277 Nik Stauskas LTHR RC 1.50 4.00
278 Gary Harris LTHR RC 2.50 6.00
279 Nick Johnson LTHR RC 1.50 4.00
280 Devyn Marble LTHR RC 1.50 4.00
281 Kyle Anderson LTHR RC 2.50 6.00
282 Noah Vonleh LTHR RC 1.50 4.00
283 Cameron Bairstow LTHR RC 1.50 4.00
284 Julius Randle LTHR RC 8.00 20.00
285 Erick Green LTHR RC 1.50 4.00
286 Joel Embiid ETCH RC 10.00 25.00
287 Aaron Gordon ETCH RC 5.00 12.00
288 Bojan Bogdanovic ETCH RC 1.50 4.00
289 Jordan Adams ETCH RC 1.00 2.50
290 Zach LaVine ETCH RC 6.00 15.00
291 Dante Exum ETCH RC 1.50 4.00
292 Glenn Robinson III ETCH RC 1.25 3.00
293 Jabari Parker ETCH RC 1.25 3.00
294 Rodney Hood ETCH RC 1.50 4.00
295 Damjan Rudez ETCH RC 1.00 2.50
296 Joe Ingles ETCH RC 1.50 4.00
297 Elfrid Payton ETCH RC 1.50 4.00
298 Andrew Wiggins ETCH RC 5.00 12.00
299 Damien Inglis ETCH RC 1.00 2.50
300 Tarik Black ETCH RC 1.00 2.50
301 Joe Harris ETCH RC 1.50 4.00
302 P.J. Hairston ETCH RC 1.00 2.50
303 K.J. McDaniels ETCH RC 1.00 2.50
304 Kostas Papanikolaou ETCH RC 1.00 2.50
305 T.J. Warren ETCH RC 1.50 4.00
306 Marcus Smart ETCH RC 4.00 10.00
307 Jarnell Stokes ETCH RC 1.00 2.50
308 Russ Smith ETCH RC 1.00 2.50
309 Cleanthony Early ETCH RC 1.00 2.50
310 Clint Capela ETCH RC 4.00 10.00
311 C.J. Wilcox ETCH RC 1.00 2.50
312 Doug McDermott ETCH RC 1.50 4.00
313 Tyler Ennis ETCH RC 1.50 4.00
314 Nikola Mirotic ETCH RC 1.50 4.00
315 James Ennis ETCH RC 1.00 2.50
316 Cory Jefferson ETCH RC 1.00 2.50
317 James Young ETCH RC 1.00 2.50
318 Shabazz Napier ETCH RC 1.25 3.00
319 Jusuf Nurkic ETCH RC 3.00 8.00
320 Adreian Payne ETCH RC 1.00 2.50
321 Jordan Clarkson ETCH RC 4.00 10.00
322 Nik Stauskas ETCH RC 1.00 2.50
323 Gary Harris ETCH RC 1.50 4.00
324 Nick Johnson ETCH RC 1.00 2.50
325 Devyn Marble ETCH RC 1.00 2.50
326 Kyle Anderson ETCH RC 1.50 4.00
327 Noah Vonleh ETCH RC 1.00 2.50
328 Cameron Bairstow ETCH RC 1.00 2.50
329 Julius Randle ETCH RC 5.00 12.00
330 Erick Green ETCH RC 1.00 2.50
331 Joel Embiid WOOD RC 12.00 30.00
332 Aaron Gordon WOOD RC 6.00 15.00
333 Bojan Bogdanovic WOOD RC 2.00 5.00
334 Jordan Adams WOOD RC 1.25 3.00
335 Zach LaVine WOOD RC 8.00 20.00
336 Dante Exum WOOD RC 2.00 5.00
337 Glenn Robinson III WOOD RC 1.50 4.00
338 Jabari Parker WOOD RC 1.50 4.00
339 Rodney Hood WOOD RC 1.50 4.00
340 Damjan Rudez WOOD RC 1.25 3.00
341 Joe Ingles WOOD RC 2.00 5.00
342 Elfrid Payton WOOD RC 2.00 5.00
343 Andrew Wiggins WOOD RC 6.00 15.00
344 Damien Inglis WOOD RC 1.25 3.00
345 Tarik Black WOOD RC 1.25 3.00
346 Joe Harris WOOD RC 2.00 5.00
347 P.J. Hairston WOOD RC 1.25 3.00
348 K.J. McDaniels WOOD RC 1.25 3.00
349 Kostas Papanikolaou WOOD RC 1.25 3.00
350 T.J. Warren WOOD RC 2.00 5.00
351 Marcus Smart WOOD RC 5.00 12.00
352 Jarnell Stokes WOOD RC 1.25 3.00
353 Russ Smith WOOD RC 1.25 3.00
354 Cleanthony Early WOOD RC 1.25 3.00
355 Clint Capela WOOD RC 5.00 12.00
356 C.J. Wilcox WOOD RC 1.25 3.00
357 Doug McDermott WOOD RC 2.00 5.00
358 Tyler Ennis WOOD RC 2.00 5.00
359 Nikola Mirotic WOOD RC 2.00 5.00
360 James Ennis WOOD RC 1.25 3.00
361 Cory Jefferson WOOD RC 1.25 3.00
362 James Young WOOD RC 1.25 3.00
363 Shabazz Napier WOOD RC 1.50 4.00
364 Jusuf Nurkic WOOD RC 4.00 10.00
365 Adreian Payne WOOD RC 1.25 3.00
366 Jordan Clarkson WOOD RC 5.00 12.00
367 Nik Stauskas WOOD RC 1.25 3.00
368 Gary Harris WOOD RC 2.00 5.00
369 Nick Johnson WOOD RC 1.25 3.00
370 Devyn Marble WOOD RC 1.25 3.00
371 Kyle Anderson WOOD RC 2.00 5.00
372 Noah Vonleh WOOD RC 1.25 3.00
373 Cameron Bairstow WOOD RC 1.25 3.00
374 Julius Randle WOOD RC 6.00 15.00
375 Erick Green WOOD RC 1.25 3.00

2014-15 Panini Threads Century Proof Gold

*VETS: .6X TO 1.5X BASE HI
STATED PRINT RUN 25 SER.#'d SETS

2014-15 Panini Threads Century Proof Red

*VETS: .5X TO 1.2X BASE HI
STATED PRINT RUN 199 SER.#'d SETS

2014-15 Panini Threads ABA Legends

1 Louie Dampier 2.00 5.00
2 Artis Gilmore 2.50 6.00
3 Billy Paultz 1.50 4.00
4 Julius Erving 5.00 12.00
5 Charlie Scott 2.00 5.00
6 Freddie Lewis 1.25 3.00
7 Jimmy Jones 1.25 3.00
8 Ron Boone 1.25 3.00
9 George Gervin 3.00 8.00
10 Dan Issel 2.50 6.00

2014-15 Panini Threads Authentic Threads

STATED PRINT RUN B/WN 78-199 COPIES PER
*PRIME: 1.5X TO 4X BASE HI
1 Al Horford/199 2.50 6.00
2 Jae Crowder/199 1.50 4.00
3 Derrick Favors/199 1.50 4.00
4 Carmelo Anthony/199 4.00 10.00
5 Harrison Barnes/199 2.00 5.00
6 Jimmy Butler/199 4.00 10.00
7 Andre Drummond/199 2.00 5.00
8 Jared Sullinger/199 1.50 4.00
9 Danny Green/199 2.00 5.00
10 Kevin Durant/199 8.00 20.00
11 Chris Paul/199 4.00 10.00
12 John Wall/199 3.00 8.00
13 DeAndre Jordan/199 2.00 5.00
14 Klay Thompson/78 6.00 15.00
15 Chris Andersen/199 2.00 5.00
16 Goran Dragic/199 2.50 6.00
17 Kirk Hinrich/199 2.00 5.00
18 Draymond Green/199 3.00 8.00
19 Jrue Holiday/199 3.00 8.00
20 Bradley Beal/199 4.00 10.00
21 Dwight Howard/199 3.00 8.00
22 Stephen Curry/199 40.00 100.00
23 Dirk Nowitzki/199 6.00 15.00
24 Kawhi Leonard/199 6.00 15.00
25 Marc Gasol/199 2.50 6.00
26 Joakim Noah/199 2.50 6.00
27 Iman Shumpert/199 1.50 4.00
28 DeMarcus Cousins/199 2.50 6.00
29 Ersan Ilyasova/199 1.50 4.00
30 Anderson Varejao/199 1.50 4.00
31 Dwyane Wade/199 5.00 12.00
32 Jeff Teague/199 1.50 4.00
33 David Lee/199 1.50 4.00
34 Kenneth Faried/199 1.50 4.00
35 James Harden/199 5.00 12.00
36 Norris Cole/199 1.50 4.00
37 Kobe Bryant/199 40.00 100.00
38 Greg Monroe/199 1.50 4.00
39 Deron Williams/199 2.00 5.00
40 Chris Bosh/199 3.00 8.00

2014-15 Panini Threads Century Greats

*RED: .5X TO 1.2X BASE HI
1 Larry Bird 5.00 12.00
2 Magic Johnson 5.00 12.00
3 Julius Erving 3.00 8.00
4 Scottie Pippen 3.00 8.00
5 John Stockton 2.50 6.00
6 Moses Malone 2.00 5.00
7 Dominique Wilkins 2.00 5.00
8 David Robinson 2.50 6.00
9 Bill Russell 4.00 10.00
10 Kareem Abdul-Jabbar 4.00 10.00
11 Oscar Robertson 2.50 6.00
12 Karl Malone 2.50 6.00
13 Wilt Chamberlain 4.00 10.00
14 Hakeem Olajuwon 2.50 6.00
15 Jerry West 3.00 8.00
16 Gary Payton 2.00 5.00
17 Clyde Drexler 2.00 5.00
18 John Havlicek 2.50 6.00
19 Chet Walker 1.00 2.50
20 George Mikan 4.00 10.00

2014-15 Panini Threads Century Greats Century Proof Gold

*GOLD: .6X TO 1.5X BASE HI
STATED PRINT RUN 25 SER.#'d SETS
13 Wilt Chamberlain 10.00 25.00

2014-15 Panini Threads Century Greats Threads

STATED PRINT RUN 199 SER.#'d SETS
*PRIME: 1.2X TO 3X BASE HI
1 Yao Ming 8.00 20.00
2 Larry Johnson 4.00 10.00
3 Kareem Abdul-Jabbar 10.00 25.00
4 Scottie Pippen 8.00 20.00
5 Kevin McHale 5.00 12.00
6 Magic Johnson 6.00 15.00
7 Jason Kidd 5.00 12.00
8 John Stockton 6.00 15.00
9 Shaquille O'Neal 12.00 30.00
10 Hakeem Olajuwon 6.00 15.00
11 Karl Malone 6.00 15.00
12 Robert Parish 4.00 10.00
13 Grant Hill 5.00 12.00
14 Julius Erving 8.00 20.00
15 Patrick Ewing 5.00 12.00
16 David Robinson 6.00 15.00
17 Joe Dumars 4.00 10.00
18 Moses Malone 5.00 12.00
19 Larry Bird 12.00 30.00
20 Tracy McGrady 5.00 12.00
21 Alex English 4.00 10.00
22 Gary Payton 5.00 12.00
23 Dikembe Mutombo 5.00 12.00
24 Alonzo Mourning 5.00 12.00
25 Tim Hardaway 4.00 10.00
26 Clyde Drexler 5.00 12.00
27 Chris Mullin 4.00 10.00
28 Allen Iverson 8.00 20.00
29 Mitch Richmond 4.00 10.00
30 Artis Gilmore 4.00 10.00

2014-15 Panini Threads Debut Threads

STATED PRINT RUN 199 SER.#'d SETS
1 Julius Randle 6.00 15.00
2 Cory Jefferson 1.25 3.00
3 Jarnell Stokes 1.25 3.00
4 Andrew Wiggins 15.00 40.00
5 Noah Vonleh 1.25 3.00
6 James Ennis 1.25 3.00
7 Marcus Smart 5.00 12.00
8 Elfrid Payton 2.00 5.00
9 Kyle Anderson 2.00 5.00
10 Markel Brown 1.25 3.00
11 T.J. Warren 2.00 5.00
12 Rodney Hood 1.50 4.00
13 Joel Embiid 12.00 30.00
14 Tyler Ennis 1.25 3.00
15 K.J. McDaniels 1.25 3.00
16 Jabari Parker 1.50 4.00
17 Nik Stauskas 1.25 3.00
18 Doug McDermott 2.00 5.00
19 P.J. Hairston 1.25 3.00
20 Glenn Robinson III 1.50 4.00
21 Adreian Payne 1.25 3.00
22 C.J. Wilcox 1.25 3.00
23 Joe Harris 3.00 8.00
24 Dante Exum 2.00 5.00
25 Shabazz Napier 1.50 4.00
26 Cleanthony Early 1.25 3.00
27 Damien Inglis 1.25 3.00
28 Zach LaVine 8.00 20.00
29 James Young 3.00 8.00
30 Russ Smith 1.25 3.00
31 Aaron Gordon 6.00 15.00
32 Gary Harris 2.00 5.00
33 Jordan Adams 1.25 3.00
34 Johnny O'Bryant 1.25 3.00
35 Jerami Grant 6.00 15.00
36 Mitch McGary 1.25 3.00
37 Bruno Caboclo 1.50 4.00

2014-15 Panini Threads Floor Generals

*RED: .6X TO 1.5X BASE HI
*GOLD: .8X TO 2X BASE HI
1 Elfrid Payton 1.25 3.00
2 Rajon Rondo 1.50 4.00
3 Patrick Beverley .75 2.00
4 Tony Parker 2.00 5.00
5 Mike Conley 1.00 2.50
6 Ricky Rubio 1.00 2.50
7 Russell Westbrook 2.00 5.00
8 Brandon Knight .75 2.00
9 Mario Chalmers 1.00 2.50
10 George Hill 1.00 2.50
11 Michael Carter-Williams .75 2.00
12 Goran Dragic 1.25 3.00
13 Damian Lillard 3.00 8.00
14 Trey Burke .75 2.00
15 Stephen Curry 3.00 8.00
16 John Wall 1.50 4.00
17 Kyrie Irving 2.50 6.00
18 Derrick Rose 2.50 6.00
19 Chris Paul 2.00 5.00
20 Jeff Teague .75 2.00

2014-15 Panini Threads Freshman Pairs Jerseys

STATED PRINT RUN 199 SER.#'d SETS
1 A.Wiggins/J.Parker 8.00 20.00
2 D.Exum/J.Embiid 15.00 40.00
3 A.Wiggins/J.Embiid 15.00 40.00
4 D.Exum/A.Wiggins 8.00 20.00
5 J.Parker/D.Exum 2.50 6.00
6 A.Gordon/E.Payton 8.00 20.00
7 M.McGary/N.Stauskas 1.50 4.00
8 A.Wiggins/Z.LaVine 10.00 25.00
9 A.Gordon/J.Parker 8.00 20.00
10 B.Caboclo/D.Exum 2.50 6.00
11 R.Smith/S.Napier 2.00 5.00
12 Z.LaVine/A.Gordon 10.00 25.00
13 D.Inglis/D.Exum 2.50 6.00
14 R.Hood/J.Parker 2.00 5.00
15 T.Ennis/P.Hairston 1.50 4.00
16 M.Smart/M.Brown 6.00 15.00
17 J.Young/J.Stokes 1.50 4.00
18 R.Hood/R.Smith 2.00 5.00
19 D.McDermott/N.Stauskas 2.50 6.00
20 J.Young/J.Randle 8.00 20.00
21 K.Anderson/Z.LaVine 10.00 25.00
22 A.Payne/G.Harris 2.50 6.00

2014-15 Panini Threads Freshman Pairs Jerseys Prime

*PRIME: .6X TO 1.5X BASE HI
STATED PRINT RUN 25 SER.#'d SETS

2014-15 Panini Threads High Flyers

*RED: .5X TO 1.2X BASE HI
1 Blake Griffin 1.25 3.00
2 Terrence Ross .75 2.00
3 Kenneth Faried .60 1.50
4 LeBron James 8.00 20.00
5 Gerald Green .75 2.00
6 Russell Westbrook 1.50 4.00
7 DeAndre Jordan .75 2.00
8 Aaron Gordon 3.00 8.00
9 DeMar DeRozan 1.25 3.00
10 Zach LaVine 4.00 10.00
11 Anthony Davis 2.50 6.00
12 Kobe Bryant 8.00 20.00
13 Kevin Durant 3.00 8.00
14 Josh Smith .60 1.50
15 Paul George 1.50 4.00
16 Andrew Wiggins 3.00 8.00
17 James Harden 2.00 5.00
18 John Wall 1.25 3.00
19 Rudy Gay 1.00 2.50
20 Serge Ibaka .75 2.00

2014-15 Panini Threads Rookie Jumbo Materials

STATED PRINT RUN 199 SER.#'d SETS
1 Andrew Wiggins 12.00 30.00
2 Jabari Parker 3.00 8.00
3 Joel Embiid 25.00 60.00
4 Aaron Gordon 12.00 30.00
5 Dante Exum 4.00 10.00
6 Marcus Smart 10.00 25.00
7 Julius Randle 12.00 30.00
8 Nik Stauskas 2.50 6.00
9 Noah Vonleh 2.50 6.00
10 Elfrid Payton 4.00 10.00
11 Doug McDermott 4.00 10.00
12 Zach LaVine 15.00 40.00
13 T.J. Warren 4.00 10.00
14 Adreian Payne 2.50 6.00
15 James Young 2.50 6.00
16 Tyler Ennis 2.50 6.00
17 Gary Harris 4.00 10.00
18 Bruno Caboclo 3.00 8.00
19 Mitch McGary 2.50 6.00
20 Jordan Adams 2.50 6.00
21 Rodney Hood 3.00 8.00
22 Shabazz Napier 3.00 8.00
23 P.J. Hairston 2.50 6.00
24 C.J. Wilcox 2.50 6.00
25 Kyle Anderson 4.00 10.00
26 Jarnell Stokes 2.50 6.00
27 Spencer Dinwiddie 4.00 10.00
28 Glenn Robinson III 3.00 8.00
29 Russ Smith 2.50 6.00
30 Cory Jefferson 2.50 6.00

2014-15 Panini Threads Rookie Jumbo Materials Prime

*PRIME: .6X TO 1.5X BASE HI
STATED PRINT RUN 25 SER.#'d SETS
1 Andrew Wiggins 30.00 80.00

2014-15 Panini Threads Rookie Signage

1 Damjan Rudez 3.00 8.00
2 Joe Harris 5.00 12.00
3 Andrew Wiggins 30.00 80.00
4 Lucas Nogueira 3.00 8.00
5 Aaron Gordon 15.00 40.00
6 T.J. Warren 8.00 20.00
7 Jabari Parker 4.00 10.00
8 Joel Embiid 75.00 200.00
9 Tyler Ennis 3.00 8.00
10 Damien Inglis 3.00 8.00
11 Rodney Hood 4.00 10.00
12 Zach LaVine 40.00 100.00
13 Elfrid Payton 5.00 12.00
14 Johnny O'Bryant 3.00 8.00
15 K.J. McDaniels 3.00 8.00
16 Jerami Grant 15.00 40.00
17 James Ennis 3.00 8.00
18 Erick Green 3.00 8.00
19 Shabazz Napier 4.00 10.00
20 P.J. Hairston 3.00 8.00
21 Nik Stauskas 3.00 8.00
22 C.J. Wilcox 3.00 8.00
23 Adreian Payne 3.00 8.00
24 Mitch McGary 3.00 8.00
25 Noah Vonleh 3.00 8.00
26 Marcus Smart 12.00 30.00
27 Jusuf Nurkic 10.00 25.00
28 Doug McDermott 5.00 12.00
29 Julius Randle 15.00 40.00
30 Gary Harris 5.00 12.00

2014-15 Panini Threads Rookie Threads

1 Julius Randle 10.00 25.00
2 Cory Jefferson 2.00 5.00
3 Jarnell Stokes 2.00 5.00
4 Andrew Wiggins 10.00 25.00
5 Noah Vonleh 2.00 5.00
6 James Ennis 2.00 5.00
7 Marcus Smart 8.00 20.00
8 Elfrid Payton 3.00 8.00
9 Kyle Anderson 3.00 8.00
10 Markel Brown 2.00 5.00
11 T.J. Warren 3.00 8.00
12 Rodney Hood 2.50 6.00
13 Joel Embiid 20.00 50.00
14 Tyler Ennis 2.00 5.00
15 K.J. McDaniels 2.00 5.00
16 Jabari Parker 4.00 10.00
17 Nik Stauskas 2.00 5.00
18 Doug McDermott 3.00 8.00
19 P.J. Hairston 2.00 5.00
20 Glenn Robinson III 2.50 6.00
21 Adreian Payne 2.00 5.00
22 Mitch McGary 2.00 5.00
23 Joe Harris 3.00 8.00
24 Dante Exum 3.00 8.00
25 Shabazz Napier 2.50 6.00
26 Cleanthony Early 2.00 5.00
27 Bruno Caboclo 2.50 6.00
28 Zach LaVine 12.00 30.00
29 James Young 2.00 5.00
30 Russ Smith 2.00 5.00
31 Aaron Gordon 10.00 25.00
32 Gary Harris 3.00 8.00
33 Jordan Adams 2.00 5.00
34 Julius Randle 10.00 25.00
35 Cory Jefferson 2.00 5.00
36 Jarnell Stokes 2.00 5.00
37 Andrew Wiggins 4.00 10.00
38 Noah Vonleh 2.00 5.00
39 James Ennis 2.00 5.00
40 Marcus Smart 8.00 20.00
41 Elfrid Payton 3.00 8.00
42 Kyle Anderson 3.00 8.00
43 Markel Brown 2.00 5.00
44 T.J. Warren 3.00 8.00
45 Rodney Hood 2.50 6.00
46 Joel Embiid 20.00 50.00
47 Tyler Ennis 2.00 5.00
48 K.J. McDaniels 2.00 5.00
49 Jabari Parker 2.50 6.00
50 Nik Stauskas 2.00 5.00
51 Doug McDermott 3.00 8.00
52 P.J. Hairston 2.00 5.00
53 Glenn Robinson III 2.50 6.00
54 Adreian Payne 2.00 5.00
55 Mitch McGary 2.00 5.00
56 Joe Harris 3.00 8.00
57 Dante Exum 3.00 8.00
58 Shabazz Napier 2.50 6.00
59 Cleanthony Early 2.00 5.00
60 Bruno Caboclo 2.50 6.00
61 Zach LaVine 12.00 30.00
62 James Young 2.00 5.00
63 Russ Smith 2.00 5.00
64 Aaron Gordon 10.00 25.00
65 Gary Harris 3.00 8.00
66 Jordan Adams 2.00 5.00
67 Julius Randle 10.00 25.00
68 Cory Jefferson 2.00 5.00
69 Jarnell Stokes 2.00 5.00
70 Andrew Wiggins 5.00 12.00
71 Noah Vonleh 2.00 5.00
72 James Ennis 2.00 5.00
73 Marcus Smart 8.00 20.00
74 Elfrid Payton 3.00 8.00
75 Kyle Anderson 3.00 8.00
76 Markel Brown 2.00 5.00
77 T.J. Warren 3.00 8.00
78 Rodney Hood 2.50 6.00
79 Joel Embiid 20.00 50.00
80 Tyler Ennis 2.00 5.00
81 K.J. McDaniels 2.00 5.00
82 Jabari Parker 2.50 6.00
83 Nik Stauskas 2.00 5.00
84 Doug McDermott 3.00 8.00
85 P.J. Hairston 2.00 5.00
86 Glenn Robinson III 2.50 6.00
87 Adreian Payne 2.00 5.00
88 Mitch McGary 2.00 5.00
89 Joe Harris 3.00 8.00
90 Dante Exum 3.00 8.00
91 Shabazz Napier 2.50 6.00
92 Cleanthony Early 2.00 5.00
93 Bruno Caboclo 2.50 6.00
94 Zach LaVine 12.00 30.00
95 James Young 2.00 5.00
96 Russ Smith 2.00 5.00
97 Aaron Gordon 10.00 25.00
98 Gary Harris 3.00 8.00
99 Jordan Adams 2.00 5.00
100 Andrew Wiggins 10.00 25.00

2014-15 Panini Threads Rookie Threads Signatures

STATED PRINT RUN B/WN 149-249 COPIES PER
1 Andrew Wiggins/149 15.00 40.00
2 Jabari Parker/149 4.00 10.00
3 Joel Embiid/149 125.00 300.00
4 Dante Exum/149 5.00 12.00
5 Rodney Hood/249 4.00 10.00
6 Glenn Robinson III/249 4.00 10.00
7 T.J. Warren/249 5.00 12.00
8 Marcus Smart/149 12.00 30.00
9 Nik Stauskas/249 3.00 8.00
10 Zach LaVine/249 40.00 100.00
11 Spencer Dinwiddie/249 5.00 12.00
12 Kyle Anderson/249 5.00 12.00
13 Damien Inglis/249 3.00 8.00
14 Johnny O'Bryant/249 3.00 8.00
15 Tyler Ennis/149 3.00 8.00
16 Aaron Gordon/149 15.00 40.00
17 Doug McDermott/249 5.00 12.00
18 Adreian Payne/249 3.00 8.00
19 Gary Harris/249 5.00 12.00
20 Jordan Adams/249 3.00 8.00
21 Cory Jefferson/249 3.00 8.00
22 Jarnell Stokes/249 3.00 8.00
23 Joe Harris/249 5.00 12.00
24 Markel Brown/249 3.00 8.00
25 Mitch McGary/249 3.00 8.00
26 C.J. Wilcox/249 3.00 8.00
27 Elfrid Payton/249 5.00 12.00
28 James Ennis/249 3.00 8.00
29 Shabazz Napier/249 4.00 10.00
30 James Young/249 3.00 8.00
31 Jerami Grant/249 15.00 40.00
32 Julius Randle/149 15.00 40.00
33 K.J. McDaniels/249 3.00 8.00
34 P.J. Hairston/249 3.00 8.00
35 Noah Vonleh/149 3.00 8.00

2014-15 Panini Threads Rookie Threads Signatures Prime

*PRIME: .8X TO 2X BASE HI
STATED PRINT RUN 25 SER.#'d SETS

2014-15 Panini Threads Rookie View Autographs

1 Russ Smith 3.00 8.00
2 Markel Brown 3.00 8.00

3 Cory Jefferson 3.00 8.00
4 K.J. McDaniels 3.00 8.00
5 Johnny O'Bryant 3.00 8.00
6 Jarnell Stokes 3.00 8.00
7 Joe Harris 5.00 12.00
8 Cleanthony Early 3.00 8.00
9 P.J. Hairston 3.00 8.00
10 Jerami Grant 15.00 40.00
11 Rodney Hood 4.00 10.00
12 Kyle Anderson 5.00 12.00
13 Aaron Gordon 15.00 40.00
14 Noah Vonleh 3.00 8.00
15 Tyler Ennis 3.00 8.00
16 Nik Stauskas 3.00 8.00
17 Elfrid Payton 5.00 12.00
18 Jabari Parker 4.00 10.00
19 Julius Randle 15.00 40.00
20 Andrew Wiggins 15.00 40.00
21 Joel Embiid 125.00 300.00
22 Bruno Caboclo 4.00 10.00
23 Spencer Dinwiddie 5.00 12.00
24 Glenn Robinson III 4.00 10.00
25 T.J. Warren 5.00 12.00
26 James Young 3.00 8.00
27 Doug McDermott 5.00 12.00
28 Gary Harris 5.00 12.00
29 Shabazz Napier 4.00 10.00
30 Jordan Adams 3.00 8.00
31 Damien Inglis 3.00 8.00
32 Mitch McGary 3.00 8.00
33 Marcus Smart 12.00 30.00
34 Zach LaVine 40.00 100.00
35 Adreian Payne 3.00 8.00
36 C.J. Wilcox 3.00 8.00

2014-15 Panini Threads Signage

STATED PRINT RUN B/WN 49-199 COPIES PER
1 Roy Hibbert/99 4.00 10.00
2 Kyle Korver/99 4.00 10.00
3 Lance Stephenson/199 4.00 10.00
4 Tristan Thompson/49 3.00 8.00
5 Steve Blake/199 3.00 8.00
6 Henry Sims/199 3.00 8.00
7 Josh Smith/49 3.00 8.00
8 Lavoy Allen/199 3.00 8.00
9 Brook Lopez/49 5.00 12.00
10 James Jones/199 3.00 8.00
11 Andrew Nicholson/199 3.00 8.00
12 Otto Porter/49 4.00 10.00
13 Trey Burke/49 3.00 8.00
14 Mike Muscala/199 3.00 8.00
15 Victor Oladipo/49 4.00 10.00
16 Ben McLemore/49 3.00 8.00
17 Nerlens Noel/49 3.00 8.00
18 Carl Landry/99 3.00 8.00
19 Troy Daniels/199 3.00 8.00
20 Jason Terry/49 4.00 10.00
21 Dennis Schroder/199 5.00 12.00
22 Maurice Harkless/199 3.00 8.00
23 Kobe Bryant/49 500.00 1,000.00
24 Kevin Durant/49 100.00 250.00
25 Solomon Hill/199 3.00 8.00
26 Kevin Love/49 5.00 12.00
27 C.J. McCollum/49 5.00 12.00
28 Manu Ginobili/49 20.00 50.00
29 Paul George/49 30.00 80.00
30 Dwyane Wade/49 60.00 150.00
31 Carmelo Anthony/49 30.00 80.00
32 Anthony Bennett/49 3.00 8.00
33 Luis Scola/99 4.00 10.00
34 Jrue Holiday/99 6.00 15.00
35 Kevin Martin/49 4.00 10.00
36 Adrian Dantley/199 5.00 12.00
37 Hal Greer/49 5.00 12.00
38 Kareem Abdul-Jabbar/49 100.00 250.00
39 Rick Barry/49 6.00 15.00
40 Dominique Wilkins/49 12.00 30.00
42 Gary Payton/49 12.00 30.00
43 Clyde Drexler/49 20.00 50.00
44 James Worthy/49 12.00 30.00
45 Dan Issel/199 6.00 15.00
46 George Gervin/49 12.00 30.00
47 Jerry West/49 30.00 80.00
48 Julius Erving/49 60.00 150.00
49 David Robinson/49 60.00 150.00
50 Chris Mullin/49 12.00 30.00

2014-15 Panini Threads Talented Twosomes

1 E.Bledsoe/G.Dragic 1.00 2.50
2 L.Aldridge/D.Lillard 2.50 6.00
3 K.Durant/R.Westbrook 3.00 8.00
4 K.Thompson/S.Curry 8.00 20.00
5 B.Griffin/C.Paul 1.50 4.00
6 B.Beal/J.Wall 1.50 4.00
7 M.Ellis/D.Nowitzki 2.50 6.00
8 K.Lowry/D.DeRozan 1.25 3.00
9 M.Ginobili/T.Parker 2.00 5.00
10 C.Bosh/D.Wade 2.00 5.00
11 K.Irving/L.James 8.00 20.00
12 R.Rubio/A.Wiggins 3.00 8.00
13 C.Anthony/T.Hardaway Jr. 1.50 4.00
14 Z.Randolph/M.Conley 1.00 2.50
15 D.Howard/J.Harden 2.00 5.00

2014-15 Panini Threads Team Threads

1 Jeff Teague 1.25 3.00
2 Al Jefferson 1.25 3.00
3 Kyrie Irving 4.00 10.00
4 Brandon Jennings 1.25 3.00
5 Paul George 3.00 8.00
6 Kobe Bryant 15.00 40.00
7 Luol Deng 1.50 4.00
8 Jrue Holiday 2.50 6.00
9 Victor Oladipo 1.50 4.00
10 LaMarcus Aldridge 2.00 5.00
11 DeMar DeRozan 2.50 6.00
12 Paul Millsap 1.50 4.00
13 Lance Stephenson 1.50 4.00
14 LeBron James 15.00 40.00
15 Andre Drummond 1.50 4.00
16 Roy Hibbert 1.50 4.00
17 Marc Gasol 2.00 5.00
18 Giannis Antetokounmpo 12.00 30.00
19 Carmelo Anthony 3.00 8.00
20 Nerlens Noel 1.25 3.00
21 DeMarcus Cousins 1.50 4.00
22 Kyle Lowry 2.50 6.00
23 Rajon Rondo 2.50 6.00
24 Derrick Rose 8.00 20.00
25 Dirk Nowitzki 5.00 12.00
26 Klay Thompson 5.00 12.00
27 Blake Griffin 2.00 5.00
28 Zach Randolph 2.00 5.00
29 Brandon Knight 1.25 3.00
30 Tim Hardaway Jr. 1.50 4.00
31 Goran Dragic 2.00 5.00
32 Kawhi Leonard 5.00 12.00
33 Gordon Hayward 1.50 4.00
34 Avery Bradley 1.25 3.00
35 Joakim Noah 2.00 5.00
36 Chandler Parsons 1.25 3.00
37 Stephen Curry 15.00 40.00
38 Chris Paul 3.00 8.00
39 Chris Bosh 2.50 6.00
40 Ricky Rubio 1.50 4.00
41 Kevin Durant 6.00 15.00
42 Eric Bledsoe 1.50 4.00
43 Tim Duncan 5.00 12.00
44 John Wall 6.00 15.00
45 Deron Williams 1.50 4.00
46 Pau Gasol 3.00 8.00
47 Ty Lawson 1.25 3.00
48 Dwight Howard 2.50 6.00
49 DeAndre Jordan 1.50 4.00
50 Dwyane Wade 4.00 10.00
51 Anthony Davis 5.00 12.00
52 Russell Westbrook 3.00 8.00
53 Damian Lillard 5.00 12.00
54 Tony Parker 3.00 8.00
55 Bradley Beal 3.00 8.00
56 Kevin Garnett 5.00 12.00
57 Kevin Love 2.00 5.00
58 Kenneth Faried 1.25 3.00
59 James Harden 4.00 10.00
60 Jeremy Lin 4.00 10.00

2014-15 Panini Threads Threads Signatures

STATED PRINT RUN B/WN 15-99 COPIES PER
NO PRICING ON QTY 15 OR LESS
1 Kobe Bryant/35 600.00 1,200.00
2 Kevin Durant/35 125.00 300.00
3 Kyrie Irving/35 40.00 100.00
4 Deron Williams/35 4.00 10.00
5 Otto Porter/35 4.00 10.00
6 Cody Zeller/35 3.00 8.00
7 Michael Carter-Williams/99 3.00 8.00
8 Victor Oladipo/35 4.00 10.00
9 Tobias Harris/99 4.00 10.00
10 Al Horford/35 5.00 12.00
11 Bradley Beal/99 8.00 20.00
12 Ryan Kelly/99 3.00 8.00
13 Taj Gibson/99 3.00 8.00
14 Carmelo Anthony/35 20.00 50.00
17 Tiago Splitter/75 3.00 8.00
18 Jared Dudley/99 3.00 8.00
19 Andre Iguodala/99 5.00 12.00
20 Steve Nash/35 40.00 100.00
21 J.R. Smith/99 5.00 12.00
22 Chris Bosh/35 6.00 15.00
23 Brandon Knight/99 3.00 8.00
24 Andre Drummond/99 4.00 10.00
25 Josh Smith/35 3.00 8.00
26 Kevin Martin/99 4.00 10.00
27 Caron Butler/99 4.00 10.00
28 Anthony Bennett/35 3.00 8.00
29 Tristan Thompson/99 4.00 10.00
30 Udonis Haslem/99 3.00 8.00
31 Jodie Meeks/99 3.00 8.00
32 Kyle Korver/99 4.00 10.00
33 Derrick Favors/99 3.00 8.00
34 Gordon Hayward/75 4.00 10.00
35 Luis Scola/99 4.00 10.00
36 Jordan Hill/99 3.00 8.00
37 James Jones/99 3.00 8.00
38 Brook Lopez/99 5.00 12.00
39 Ryan Anderson/99 3.00 8.00
40 Alan Anderson/99 3.00 8.00
41 Maurice Harkless/99 3.00 8.00
42 Gerald Wallace/99 3.00 8.00
43 Austin Rivers/99 3.00 8.00
44 Draymond Green/99 15.00 40.00
45 Enes Kanter/99 4.00 10.00
46 Corey Brewer/99 3.00 8.00
47 Greg Monroe/65 3.00 8.00
48 Nick Young/99 3.00 8.00
49 Tony Snell/75 3.00 8.00
50 Nick Collison/99 4.00 10.00
52 Tony Allen/65 3.00 8.00
53 J.J. Redick/65 5.00 12.00
54 Nikola Pekovic/75 3.00 8.00
55 Danny Green/99 4.00 10.00
56 Michael Kidd-Gilchrist/35 3.00 8.00
57 Mason Plumlee/99 3.00 8.00
58 Gorgui Dieng/99 3.00 8.00
59 Timofey Mozgov/99 3.00 8.00
60 Kentavious Caldwell-Pope/99 3.00 8.00
61 Alex Len/35 3.00 8.00
62 Trey Burke/99 3.00 8.00
63 Andrea Bargnani/99 3.00 8.00
64 Brandon Bass/99 3.00 8.00
65 George Hill/99 4.00 10.00

2014-15 Panini Threads Threads Signatures Prime

*PRIME: .6X TO 1.5X BASE HI
STATED PRINT RUN 25 SER.#'d SETS
LACK OF PRICING DUE TO MARKET INFO
44 Draymond Green/25 30.00 80.00

2014-15 Panini Threads View Autographs

1 Amar'e Stoudemire 5.00 12.00
2 Brandon Jennings 5.00 12.00
3 Caron Butler 4.00 10.00
4 Chris Bosh 10.00 25.00
5 Derrick Favors 3.00 8.00
6 Evan Turner 3.00 8.00
7 John Wall 6.00 15.00
8 Larry Sanders 3.00 8.00
9 Pau Gasol 40.00 100.00
10 Samuel Dalembert 3.00 8.00
11 Steve Nash 50.00 120.00
12 Xavier Henry 3.00 8.00
13 DeMarcus Cousins 4.00 10.00
14 Boris Diaw 4.00 10.00

2014-15 Panini Threads Voices of the Game Autographs

STATED PRINT RUN B/WN 49-499 COPIES PER
1 Craig Sager/499 75.00 200.00
2 Rick Kamla/499 2.50 6.00
3 Ernie Johnson/499 75.00 200.00
4 Kenny Smith/99 4.00 10.00
5 Bob Knight/49 100.00 250.00
6 Steve Smith/299 4.00 10.00
7 Clark Kellogg/499 3.00 8.00
8 Walt Frazier/99 8.00 20.00
9 Chris Webber/49 60.00 150.00
10 Dick Vitale/99 75.00 200.00
11 Phil Chenier/349 3.00 8.00
12 Ron Boone/299 3.00 8.00
13 Mychal Thompson/349 3.00 8.00
14 Shaquille O'Neal/49 100.00 250.00
15 Michael Cage/349 3.00 8.00
16 Jon McGlocklin/199 4.00 10.00
17 Doug Collins/199 10.00 25.00
18 Grant Hill/49 15.00 40.00
19 Sidney Moncrief/349 2.50 6.00
20 Brent Barry/99 4.00 10.00

2015-16 Panini Threads

COMP.SET w/o RCs (150) 20.00 50.00
1 Ricky Rubio .30 .75
2 Goran Dragic .40 1.00
3 Joe Johnson .30 .75
4 Evan Fournier .30 .75
5 Pau Gasol .60 1.50
6 Zaza Pachulia .25 .60
7 DeMar DeRozan .50 1.25
8 Andre Iguodala .40 1.00
9 Brook Lopez .40 1.00
10 Julius Randle .50 1.25
11 Kevin Garnett 1.00 2.50
12 Dwyane Wade .75 2.00
13 Gary Harris .30 .75
14 Tobias Harris .30 .75
15 Jimmy Butler .75 2.00
16 Deron Williams .30 .75
17 Kyle Lowry .40 1.00
18 Klay Thompson 1.00 2.50
19 Thaddeus Young .25 .60
20 Kobe Bryant 3.00 8.00
21 Kevin Martin .30 .75
22 Hassan Whiteside .30 .75
23 Will Barton .25 .60
24 Elfrid Payton .30 .75
25 Nikola Mirotic .25 .60
26 Wesley Matthews .25 .60
27 Jonas Valanciunas .30 .75
28 Draymond Green .50 1.25
29 Bojan Bogdanovic .30 .75
30 Roy Hibbert .30 .75
31 Zach LaVine 1.00 2.50
32 Luol Deng .30 .75
33 Jameer Nelson .25 .60
34 Nikola Vucevic .30 .75
35 Doug McDermott .30 .75
36 Chandler Parsons .25 .60
37 DeMarre Carroll .25 .60
38 Festus Ezeli .25 .60
39 Jarrett Jack .30 .75
40 Lou Williams .30 .75
41 Gordon Hayward .40 1.00
42 Nicolas Batum .25 .60
43 LeBron James 3.00 8.00
44 Tim Duncan 1.00 2.50
45 George Hill .30 .75
46 Mike Conley .40 1.00
47 Luis Scola .30 .75
48 Blake Griffin .40 1.00
49 Nerlens Noel .25 .60
50 Ben McLemore .25 .60
51 Rudy Gobert .50 1.25
52 Marvin Williams .25 .60
53 Kevin Love .40 1.00
54 Tony Parker .60 1.50
55 Paul George .60 1.50
56 Zach Randolph .40 1.00
57 Jae Crowder .25 .60
58 DeAndre Jordan .30 .75
59 Tony Wroten .25 .60
60 DeMarcus Cousins .40 1.00
61 Derrick Favors .30 .75
62 Kemba Walker .40 1.00
63 Kyrie Irving .75 2.00
64 Manu Ginobili .75 2.00
65 Monta Ellis .30 .75
66 Marc Gasol .40 1.00
67 Isaiah Thomas .30 .75
68 J.J. Redick .40 1.00
69 Nik Stauskas .25 .60
70 Rajon Rondo .50 1.25
71 Rodney Hood .30 .75
72 Al Jefferson .25 .60
73 Mo Williams .30 .75
74 Kawhi Leonard 1.25 3.00
75 Rodney Stuckey .25 .60
76 Courtney Lee .25 .60
77 Avery Bradley .25 .60
78 Chris Paul .75 2.00
79 Jerami Grant .40 1.00
80 Rudy Gay .40 1.00
81 Alec Burks .25 .60
82 Jeremy Lin .75 2.00
83 Timofey Mozgov .25 .60
84 LaMarcus Aldridge .40 1.00
85 Jordan Hill .25 .60
86 Jeff Green .25 .60
87 Jared Sullinger .25 .60
88 Paul Pierce .60 1.50
89 Isaiah Canaan .25 .60
90 Darren Collison .25 .60
91 Damian Lillard 1.00 2.50
92 John Wall .50 1.25
93 Marcus Morris .25 .60
94 Dwight Howard .50 1.25
95 Khris Middleton .50 1.25
96 Eric Gordon .30 .75
97 Marcus Smart .50 1.25
98 Brandon Knight .25 .60
99 Russell Westbrook .60 1.50
100 Paul Millsap .30 .75
101 C.J. McCollum .40 1.00
102 Otto Porter .30 .75
103 Kentavious Caldwell-Pope .30 .75
104 James Harden .75 2.00
105 Greg Monroe .30 .75
106 Anthony Davis 1.00 2.50
107 Carmelo Anthony .60 1.50
108 Eric Bledsoe .30 .75
109 Kevin Durant 1.50 4.00
110 Al Horford .40 1.00
111 Mason Plumlee .25 .60
112 Bradley Beal .50 1.25
113 Andre Drummond .40 1.00
114 Ty Lawson .25 .60
115 Giannis Antetokounmpo 2.00 5.00
116 Ryan Anderson .25 .60
117 Langston Galloway .25 .60
118 Markieff Morris .25 .60
119 Serge Ibaka .30 .75
120 Jeff Teague .25 .60
121 Meyers Leonard .25 .60
122 Marcin Gortat .25 .60
123 Reggie Jackson .30 .75
124 Trevor Ariza .25 .60
125 Michael Carter-Williams .25 .60
126 Jrue Holiday .50 1.25
127 Robin Lopez .25 .60
128 Tyson Chandler .30 .75
129 Enes Kanter .25 .60
130 Kent Bazemore .25 .60
131 Al-Farouq Aminu .25 .60
132 Nene .30 .75
133 Brandon Jennings .25 .60
134 Corey Brewer .25 .60
135 Jabari Parker .25 .60
136 Tyreke Evans .30 .75
137 Jose Calderon .25 .60
138 T.J. Warren .40 1.00
139 Dion Waiters .25 .60
140 Kyle Korver .30 .75
141 Danilo Gallinari .30 .75
142 Victor Oladipo .30 .75
143 Derrick Rose .60 1.50
144 Dirk Nowitzki 1.00 2.50
145 Stephen Curry 3.00 8.00
146 Kenneth Faried .30 .75
147 Sasha Vujacic .25 .60
148 Jordan Clarkson .40 1.00
149 Andrew Wiggins .50 1.25
150 Chris Bosh .50 1.25
151 R.J. Hunter RC .50 1.25
152 Frank Kaminsky RC .60 1.50
153 Salah Mejri RC .40 1.00
154 Josh Richardson RC .75 2.00
155 Terry Rozier RC 2.00 5.00
156 Kristaps Porzingis RC 3.00 8.00
157 Cliff Alexander RC .50 1.25
158 Anthony Brown RC .50 1.25
159 Myles Turner RC 2.00 5.00
160 Luis Montero RC .50 1.25
161 Rashad Vaughn RC .50 1.25
162 Jahlil Okafor RC .60 1.50
163 Sam Dekker RC .50 1.25
164 Justin Anderson RC .50 1.25
165 Trey Lyles RC .60 1.50
166 Larry Nance Jr. RC 1.00 2.50
167 Cristiano Felicio RC .60 1.50
168 Boban Marjanovic RC 1.50 4.00
169 Nemanja Bjelica RC .75 2.00
170 D'Angelo Russell RC 2.00 5.00
171 Raul Neto RC .50 1.25
172 Jerian Grant RC .50 1.25
173 Sasha Kaun RC .50 1.25
174 Justise Winslow RC .75 2.00
175 Tyus Jones RC .60 1.50
176 Marcelo Huertas RC .50 1.25
177 Rakeem Christmas RC .50 1.25
178 Bobby Portis RC 1.25 3.00
179 Nikola Jokic RC 60.00 150.00
180 Delon Wright RC .60 1.50
181 Richaun Holmes RC .75 2.00
182 Jordan Mickey RC .50 1.25
183 Stanley Johnson RC .60 1.50
184 Karl-Anthony Towns RC 3.00 8.00
185 Willie Cauley-Stein RC .60 1.50
186 Mario Hezonja RC .60 1.50
187 Aaron Harrison RC .60 1.50
188 Cameron Payne RC .75 2.00
189 Norman Powell RC 1.00 2.50
190 Devin Booker RC 8.00 20.00
191 Rondae Hollis-Jefferson RC .60 1.50
192 Joe Young RC .50 1.25
193 T.J. McConnell RC 2.00 5.00
194 Kelly Oubre Jr. RC 1.50 4.00
195 Jonathon Simmons RC .60 1.50
196 Montrezl Harrell RC 1.50 4.00
197 Darrun Hilliard RC .50 1.25
198 Walter Tavares RC .50 1.25
199 Pat Connaughton RC .60 1.50
200 Emmanuel Mudiay RC .60 1.50
201 Boban Marjanovic LTHR 2.00 5.00
202 Myles Turner LTHR 2.50 6.00
203 Jarell Martin LTHR RC .60 1.50
204 Pat Connaughton LTHR 1.00 2.50
205 Montrezl Harrell LTHR 2.00 5.00
206 Cameron Payne LTHR 1.00 2.50
207 Willie Cauley-Stein LTHR .75 2.00
208 Emmanuel Mudiay LTHR .75 2.00
209 Jonathon Simmons LTHR .75 2.00
210 Jahlil Okafor LTHR .75 2.00
211 Kevon Looney LTHR RC 2.00 5.00
212 Mario Hezonja LTHR .75 2.00
213 Karl-Anthony Towns LTHR 4.00 10.00
214 Rakeem Christmas LTHR .60 1.50
215 Tyus Jones LTHR .75 2.00
216 Larry Nance Jr. LTHR 1.25 3.00
217 Justin Anderson LTHR .60 1.50
218 Bobby Portis LTHR 1.50 4.00
219 Marcelo Huertas LTHR .60 1.50
220 Norman Powell LTHR 1.25 3.00
221 Justise Winslow LTHR 1.00 2.50
222 Trey Lyles LTHR .75 2.00
223 Sam Dekker LTHR .60 1.50
224 Terry Rozier LTHR 2.50 6.00
225 Frank Kaminsky LTHR .75 2.00
226 T.J. McConnell LTHR 2.50 6.00
227 Rondae Hollis-Jefferson LTHR .75 2.00
228 Kristaps Porzingis LTHR 4.00 10.00
229 Josh Richardson LTHR 1.00 2.50
230 Chris McCullough LTHR RC .60 1.50
231 R.J. Hunter LTHR .60 1.50
232 Jordan Mickey LTHR .60 1.50
233 Devin Booker LTHR 12.00 30.00
234 Jordan Mickey LTHR .60 1.50
235 Delon Wright LTHR .75 2.00
236 Jerian Grant LTHR .60 1.50
237 D'Angelo Russell LTHR 2.50 6.00
238 Stanley Johnson LTHR .75 2.00
239 Richaun Holmes LTHR 1.00 2.50
240 Kelly Oubre Jr. LTHR 2.00 5.00
241 Nikola Jokic LTHR 60.00 150.00
242 Raul Neto LTHR .60 1.50
243 Nemanja Bjelica LTHR 1.00 2.50
244 Rashad Vaughn LTHR .60 1.50
245 Anthony Brown LTHR .60 1.50
246 Boban Marjanovic WOOD 3.00 8.00
247 Myles Turner WOOD 4.00 10.00
248 Jarell Martin WOOD 1.00 2.50
249 Pat Connaughton WOOD 1.50 4.00
250 Montrezl Harrell WOOD 3.00 8.00
251 Cameron Payne WOOD 1.50 4.00
252 Willie Cauley-Stein WOOD 1.25 3.00
253 Emmanuel Mudiay WOOD 1.25 3.00
254 Jonathon Simmons WOOD 1.25 3.00
255 Jahlil Okafor WOOD 1.25 3.00
256 Kevon Looney WOOD RC 3.00 8.00
257 Mario Hezonja WOOD 1.25 3.00
258 Karl-Anthony Towns WOOD 6.00 15.00
259 Rakeem Christmas WOOD 1.00 2.50
260 Tyus Jones WOOD 1.25 3.00
261 Larry Nance Jr. WOOD 2.00 5.00
262 Justin Anderson WOOD 1.00 2.50
263 Bobby Portis WOOD 2.50 6.00
264 Marcelo Huertas WOOD 1.00 2.50
265 Norman Powell WOOD 2.00 5.00
266 Justise Winslow WOOD 1.50 4.00
267 Trey Lyles WOOD 1.25 3.00
268 Sam Dekker WOOD 1.00 2.50
269 Terry Rozier WOOD 4.00 10.00
270 Frank Kaminsky WOOD 1.25 3.00
271 T.J. McConnell WOOD 4.00 10.00
272 Rondae Hollis-Jefferson WOOD 1.00 2.50
273 Kristaps Porzingis WOOD 6.00 15.00
274 Josh Richardson WOOD 1.50 4.00
275 Chris McCullough WOOD 1.00 2.50
276 R.J. Hunter WOOD 1.00 2.50
277 Joe Young WOOD 1.00 2.50
278 Devin Booker WOOD 20.00 50.00
279 Jordan Mickey WOOD 1.00 2.50
280 Delon Wright WOOD 1.25 3.00
281 Jerian Grant WOOD 1.00 2.50
282 D'Angelo Russell WOOD 4.00 10.00
283 Stanley Johnson WOOD 1.25 3.00
284 Richaun Holmes WOOD 1.50 4.00
285 Kelly Oubre Jr. WOOD 3.00 8.00
286 Nikola Jokic WOOD 100.00 250.00
287 Raul Neto WOOD 1.00 2.50
288 Nemanja Bjelica WOOD 1.50 4.00
289 Rashad Vaughn WOOD 1.00 2.50
290 Anthony Brown WOOD 1.00 2.50
291 Boban Marjanovic ETCH 2.00 5.00
292 Myles Turner ETCH 2.50 6.00
293 Jarell Martin ETCH .60 1.50
294 Pat Connaughton ETCH 1.00 2.50
295 Montrezl Harrell ETCH 2.00 5.00
296 Cameron Payne ETCH 1.00 2.50
297 Willie Cauley-Stein ETCH .75 2.00
298 Emmanuel Mudiay ETCH .75 2.00
299 Jonathon Simmons ETCH .75 2.00
300 Jahlil Okafor ETCH .75 2.00
301 Kevon Looney ETCH RC 2.00 5.00
302 Mario Hezonja ETCH .75 2.00
303 Karl-Anthony Towns ETCH 4.00 10.00
304 Rakeem Christmas ETCH .60 1.50
305 Tyus Jones ETCH .75 2.00
306 Larry Nance Jr. ETCH 1.25 3.00
307 Justin Anderson ETCH .60 1.50
308 Bobby Portis ETCH 1.50 4.00
309 Marcelo Huertas ETCH .60 1.50
310 Norman Powell ETCH 1.25 3.00
311 Justise Winslow ETCH 1.00 2.50
312 Trey Lyles ETCH .75 2.00
313 Sam Dekker ETCH .60 1.50
314 Terry Rozier ETCH 2.50 6.00
315 Frank Kaminsky ETCH .75 2.00
316 T.J. McConnell ETCH 2.50 6.00
317 Rondae Hollis-Jefferson ETCH .75 2.00
318 Kristaps Porzingis ETCH 4.00 10.00
319 Josh Richardson ETCH 1.00 2.50
320 Chris McCullough ETCH .60 1.50
321 R.J. Hunter ETCH .60 1.50
322 Joe Young ETCH .60 1.50
323 Devin Booker ETCH 12.00 30.00
324 Jordan Mickey ETCH .60 1.50
325 Delon Wright ETCH .75 2.00
326 Jerian Grant ETCH .60 1.50
327 D'Angelo Russell ETCH 2.50 6.00
328 Stanley Johnson ETCH .75 2.00
329 Richaun Holmes ETCH 1.00 2.50
330 Kelly Oubre Jr. ETCH 2.00 5.00
331 Nikola Jokic ETCH 60.00 150.00
332 Raul Neto ETCH .60 1.50
333 Nemanja Bjelica ETCH 1.00 2.50
334 Rashad Vaughn ETCH .60 1.50
335 Anthony Brown ETCH .60 1.50

2015-16 Panini Threads Century Proof Gold

*RED 1-150: 2.5X TO 6X BASIC
1-150 PRINT RUN 25 SER.#'d SETS
151-200 PRINT RUN 10 SER.#'d SETS

2015-16 Panini Threads Century Proof Red

*RED 1-150: .6X TO 1.5X BASIC
*RED 151-200: .6X TO 1.5X BASIC
STATED PRINT RUN 99 SER.#'d SETS
179 Nikola Jokic 40.00 100.00

2015-16 Panini Threads Authentic Threads

STATED PRINT RUN 99-199 SER.#'d SETS
2 Kevin Garnett/199 6.00 15.00
3 Mike Bibby/199 2.00 5.00
4 Tony Parker/199 4.00 10.00
5 Kyrie Irving/99 5.00 12.00
6 Jared Sullinger/199 1.50 4.00
7 Dwight Howard/99 3.00 8.00
8 Markieff Morris/199 1.50 4.00
9 Bobby Jackson/199 1.50 4.00
10 Carmelo Anthony/99 4.00 10.00
11 Joe Smith/199 2.00 5.00
12 LaMarcus Aldridge/199 2.50 6.00
13 Rick Fox/199 2.00 5.00
14 Anthony Davis/199 6.00 15.00
15 Avery Bradley/99 1.50 4.00
16 Joakim Noah/99 1.50 4.00
18 Mo Williams/199 2.00 5.00
20 Brad Daugherty/199 2.00 5.00
21 Keith Van Horn/199 2.00 5.00
22 Russell Westbrook/199 4.00 10.00
23 Kobe Bryant/199 20.00 50.00
24 Doug McDermott/99 2.00 5.00
25 Stephen Curry/99 20.00 50.00
26 Kelly Olynyk/99 1.50 4.00
27 John Wall/99 3.00 8.00
28 Serge Ibaka/99 2.00 5.00
29 Brent Barry/199 1.50 4.00
30 DeMarcus Cousins/199 2.50 6.00
32 Tim Duncan/199 6.00 15.00
33 Kevin Durant/199 10.00 25.00
34 Eric Gordon/199 2.00 5.00
35 James Harden/99 5.00 12.00
36 Kentavious Caldwell-Pope/199 2.00 5.00
37 LeBron James/199 20.00 50.00
38 T.J. Warren/199 2.50 6.00
40 Kawhi Leonard/199 8.00 20.00

2015-16 Panini Threads Century Collection Materials

STATED PRINT RUN 57-75 SER.#'d SETS
1 Cazzie Russell/75 2.50 6.00
2 Larry Johnson/75 4.00 10.00
3 David Robinson/75 6.00 15.00
4 Michael Redd/75 2.50 6.00
6 Ray Allen/75 4.00 10.00
7 Isiah Thomas/75 3.00 8.00
8 Shaquille O'Neal/75 10.00 25.00
10 Karl Malone/75 5.00 12.00
11 Charles Oakley/75 2.50 6.00
13 Dennis Rodman/75 8.00 20.00
14 Patrick Ewing/75 5.00 12.00
15 Gary Payton/75 5.00 12.00
16 Richard Hamilton/75 3.00 8.00
17 Jamal Mashburn/75 2.50 6.00
18 Steve Kerr/57 2.50 6.00
19 Alonzo Mourning/75 5.00 12.00
20 Kenny Smith/75 2.50 6.00
21 Clifford Robinson/75 3.00 8.00
22 Manute Bol/75 3.00 8.00
23 Doc Rivers/75 3.00 8.00
24 Grant Hill/75 3.00 8.00
25 Mike Bibby/75 2.50 6.00
26 Scottie Pippen/75 8.00 20.00
27 John Starks/75 3.00 8.00
28 Toni Kukoc/75 3.00 8.00
29 Alvan Adams/75 2.00 5.00
30 Kevin Duckworth/75 2.00 5.00
31 Danny Manning/75 2.50 6.00
32 Mark Aguirre/75 2.50 6.00
33 Dominique Wilkins/75 5.00 12.00
34 Ralph Sampson/75 2.50 6.00
35 Hakeem Olajuwon/75 6.00 15.00
36 Shane Battier/75 2.50 6.00
37 John Stockton/75 6.00 15.00
38 World B. Free/75 2.50 6.00
39 Ben Wallace/75 2.50 6.00
40 Larry Bird/75 12.00 30.00

2015-16 Panini Threads Century Greats

*RED/99: .75X TO 2X BASIC
*GOLD/25: 1.2X TO 3X BASIC
1 Karl Malone 1.00 2.50
2 Bill Russell 2.00 5.00
3 Wilt Chamberlain 2.50 6.00
4 Elgin Baylor 1.25 3.00
5 John Havlicek .75 2.00
6 Patrick Ewing 1.00 2.50
7 Elvin Hayes 1.00 2.50
8 David Robinson 1.25 3.00
9 Shaquille O'Neal 2.00 5.00
10 Hakeem Olajuwon 1.25 3.00
11 Jerry West 1.25 3.00
12 Isiah Thomas .60 1.50
13 Bob Cousy 1.00 2.50
14 Julius Erving 1.50 4.00
15 Larry Bird 2.50 6.00
16 Clyde Drexler 1.00 2.50
17 Magic Johnson 2.50 6.00
18 John Stockton 1.25 3.00
19 Kareem Abdul-Jabbar 2.00 5.00
20 Oscar Robertson 1.50 4.00

2015-16 Panini Threads Century Greats Threads

STATED PRINT RUN 170-199 SER.#'d SETS
1 Scottie Pippen/199 6.00 15.00
2 Adrian Dantley/199 2.50 6.00
3 Clifford Robinson/199 2.50 6.00
4 Mark Aguirre/199 2.00 5.00
5 Ralph Sampson/199 2.50 6.00
6 Alonzo Mourning/199 4.00 10.00
7 Kenny Smith/199 2.00 5.00
8 Gary Payton/199 4.00 10.00
9 Toni Kukoc/199 2.50 6.00
10 Isiah Thomas/199 2.50 6.00
11 Larry Bird/199 10.00 25.00
12 Ben Wallace/199 2.00 5.00
13 Michael Redd/199 2.00 5.00
14 Danny Manning/199 2.00 5.00
15 Ray Allen/199 3.00 8.00
16 Dennis Rodman/199 6.00 15.00
17 Shaquille O'Neal/199 8.00 20.00
18 Grant Hill/199 4.00 10.00
19 Clyde Drexler/199 4.00 10.00
20 John Stockton/199 5.00 12.00
21 Larry Johnson/199 3.00 8.00
22 Charles Oakley/199 2.00 5.00
23 David Robinson/199 5.00 12.00
24 Patrick Ewing/199 4.00 10.00
25 Richard Hamilton/199 2.50 6.00
26 Doc Rivers/199 2.50 6.00
27 Steve Kerr/170 2.50 6.00
28 Hakeem Olajuwon/199 5.00 12.00
29 Karl Malone/199 4.00 10.00
30 World B. Free/199 2.00 5.00

2015-16 Panini Threads Century Signatures

PRINT RUNS B/WN 25-199 COPIES PER
1 Sam Bowie/199 2.50 6.00
2 Oscar Robertson/25 25.00 60.00
3 Cuttino Mobley/199 2.50 6.00
4 Wes Unseld/199 5.00 12.00
5 Larry Nance/199 3.00 8.00
6 Calvin Murphy/170 3.00 8.00
7 Terry Cummings/199 3.00 8.00
9 Wayne Embry/199 2.50 6.00
10 Julius Erving/25 30.00 80.00
11 Ron Harper/199 4.00 10.00
12 Anfernee Hardaway/111 10.00 25.00
13 Theo Ratliff/199 2.50 6.00
14 Bernard King/149 5.00 12.00
15 Raef LaFrentz/199 2.50 6.00
16 Dikembe Mutombo/199 6.00 15.00
17 Billy Paultz/199 4.00 10.00
18 Magic Johnson/25 25.00 60.00
19 Tony Delk/199 2.50 6.00
20 John Stockton/25 15.00 40.00
21 Antoine Carr/199 2.50 6.00
22 Larry Brown/199 8.00 20.00
23 Will Perdue/199 2.50 6.00
24 Frank Ramsey/199 10.00 25.00
25 Eddie Jones/199 4.00 10.00
26 Scott Brooks/199 2.50 6.00
27 Paul Westphal/199 4.00 10.00
28 Larry Bird/25 40.00 100.00
29 Kenny Anderson/199 3.00 8.00
30 Karl Malone/25 25.00 60.00

2015-16 Panini Threads Century Stars

1 Kobe Bryant 20.00 50.00
2 Tim Duncan 12.00 30.00
3 Andrew Wiggins 6.00 15.00
4 LeBron James 25.00 60.00
5 Carmelo Anthony 8.00 20.00
6 Anthony Davis 12.00 30.00
7 Kyrie Irving 10.00 25.00
8 James Harden 10.00 25.00
9 Dirk Nowitzki 12.00 30.00
10 Russell Westbrook 8.00 20.00
11 Derrick Rose 8.00 20.00
12 John Wall 6.00 15.00
13 Kevin Garnett 8.00 20.00
14 Kevin Durant 20.00 50.00
15 Dwight Howard 6.00 15.00
16 Stephen Curry 25.00 60.00
17 Damian Lillard 12.00 30.00
18 Chris Paul 10.00 25.00
19 Dwyane Wade 10.00 25.00
20 Blake Griffin 5.00 12.00

2015-16 Panini Threads Debut Threads

STATED PRINT RUN 199 SER.#'d SETS
1 Justin Anderson 1.25 3.00
2 Rondae Hollis-Jefferson 1.50 4.00
3 Jordan Mickey 1.25 3.00
4 Myles Turner 5.00 12.00
5 D'Angelo Russell 5.00 12.00
6 Delon Wright 1.50 4.00
7 R.J. Hunter 1.25 3.00
8 Stanley Johnson 1.50 4.00
9 Devin Booker 4.00 10.00
10 Kelly Oubre Jr. 4.00 10.00
11 Mario Hezonja 1.50 4.00
12 Emmanuel Mudiay 1.50 4.00
13 Cameron Payne 2.00 5.00
14 Terry Rozier 5.00 12.00
15 Bobby Portis 3.00 8.00
16 Kristaps Porzingis 5.00 12.00
17 Justise Winslow 2.00 5.00
18 Montrezl Harrell 4.00 10.00
20 Jerian Grant 1.25 3.00
21 Frank Kaminsky 1.50 4.00
22 Chris McCullough 1.50 4.00
23 Sam Dekker 1.25 3.00
24 Richaun Holmes 2.00 5.00
25 Willie Cauley-Stein 1.50 4.00
26 Tyus Jones 1.50 4.00
27 Anthony Brown 1.25 3.00
28 Trey Lyles 1.50 4.00
29 Karl-Anthony Towns 6.00 15.00
30 Jahlil Okafor 1.50 4.00

2015-16 Panini Threads Floor Generals

*RED/99: .75X TO 2X BASIC
*GOLD/25: 1.2X TO 3X BASIC
1 Jason Kidd 1.00 2.50
2 LeBron James 5.00 12.00
3 Allen Iverson 1.50 4.00
4 Kyrie Irving 1.25 3.00
5 Russell Westbrook 1.00 2.50
6 Kyle Lowry .60 1.50
7 Tony Parker 1.00 2.50
8 Jeff Teague .40 1.00
9 John Stockton 1.25 3.00
10 Pete Maravich 1.50 4.00
11 Chris Paul 1.25 3.00
12 James Harden 1.25 3.00
13 Steve Nash 1.00 2.50
14 Damian Lillard 1.50 4.00
15 Isiah Thomas .60 1.50
16 Michael Carter-Williams .40 1.00
17 Stephen Curry 5.00 12.00
18 Ty Lawson .40 1.00
19 Gary Payton 1.00 2.50
20 John Wall .75 2.00

2015-16 Panini Threads Hardwood Pioneers

*RED/49: .75X TO 2X BASIC
*GOLD/25: 1.2X TO 3X BASIC
1 Bob Pettit .60 1.50
2 Bob Cousy 1.00 2.50
3 Elgin Baylor 1.25 3.00
4 Wilt Chamberlain 2.50 6.00
5 Lenny Wilkens .60 1.50
6 Clyde Lovellette .60 1.50
7 Bill Russell 2.00 5.00
8 George Mikan 1.25 3.00
9 Oscar Robertson 1.50 4.00
10 Sam Jones .60 1.50

2015-16 Panini Threads High Flyers

*RED/99: .75X TO 2X BASIC
*GOLD/25: 1.2X TO 3X BASIC
1 DeAndre Jordan .50 1.25
2 Kobe Bryant 5.00 12.00
3 Russell Westbrook 1.00 2.50
4 Dwight Howard .75 2.00
5 Kenny Walker .40 1.00
6 Julius Erving 1.50 4.00
7 Clyde Drexler 1.00 2.50
8 Blake Griffin .60 1.50
9 Scottie Pippen 1.50 4.00
10 Zach LaVine 1.50 4.00
11 Dee Brown .40 1.00
12 Spud Webb .50 1.25
13 Darrell Griffith .50 1.25
14 Larry Nance .50 1.25
15 Shaquille O'Neal 2.00 5.00
16 Dominique Wilkins 1.00 2.50
17 Tracy McGrady 1.00 2.50
18 LeBron James 5.00 12.00
19 Victor Oladipo .50 1.25
20 Shawn Kemp 1.00 2.50

2015-16 Panini Threads Precision Players

*RED/99: .75X TO 2X BASIC
*GOLD/25: 1.2X TO 3X BASIC
1 Kyrie Irving 1.25 3.00
2 Klay Thompson 1.50 4.00
3 Damian Lillard 1.50 4.00
4 Anthony Davis 1.50 4.00
5 Kevin Love .60 1.50
6 LaMarcus Aldridge .60 1.50
7 DeMar DeRozan .75 2.00
8 Al Horford .60 1.50
9 Bradley Beal .75 2.00
10 Kawhi Leonard 2.00 5.00
11 Tobias Harris .50 1.25
12 Tim Duncan 1.50 4.00
13 Chris Paul 1.25 3.00
14 Dirk Nowitzki 1.50 4.00
15 Jimmy Butler 1.25 3.00
16 Blake Griffin .60 1.50
17 Pau Gasol 1.00 2.50
18 Wesley Matthews .40 1.00
19 Andrew Wiggins .75 2.00
20 Chandler Parsons .40 1.00

2015-16 Panini Threads Rookie Signage

1 Kelly Oubre Jr. 8.00 20.00
2 Justise Winslow 4.00 10.00
3 Rondae Hollis-Jefferson 3.00 8.00
4 Stanley Johnson 3.00 8.00
5 Kevon Looney 8.00 20.00
6 Myles Turner 8.00 20.00
7 Larry Nance Jr. 5.00 12.00
8 Karl-Anthony Towns 30.00 80.00
9 Rashad Vaughn 2.50 6.00
10 Emmanuel Mudiay 3.00 8.00
11 Terry Rozier 10.00 25.00
12 Willie Cauley-Stein 8.00 20.00
13 Justin Anderson 2.50 6.00
14 Frank Kaminsky 3.00 8.00
15 Nemanja Bjelica 4.00 10.00
16 Trey Lyles 3.00 8.00
17 Raul Neto 2.50 6.00
18 D'Angelo Russell 8.00 20.00
19 Delon Wright 3.00 8.00
20 Kristaps Porzingis 20.00 50.00
21 Sam Dekker 2.50 6.00
22 Tyus Jones 3.00 8.00
23 Bobby Portis 6.00 15.00
24 Devin Booker 200.00 500.00
25 Nikola Jokic 800.00 1,500.00
26 Jerian Grant 2.50 6.00
27 Darrun Hilliard 2.50 6.00
28 Jahlil Okafor 3.00 8.00
29 Cameron Payne 4.00 10.00

2015-16 Panini Threads Rookie Team Threads

1 Devin Booker 12.00 30.00
2 Raul Neto 1.00 2.50
3 Rashad Vaughn 1.00 2.50
4 Norman Powell 2.00 5.00
5 Karl-Anthony Towns 20.00 50.00
6 Justin Anderson 1.00 2.50
7 Mario Hezonja 1.25 3.00
8 Larry Nance Jr. 2.00 5.00
9 Frank Kaminsky 1.25 3.00
10 Jordan Mickey 1.00 2.50
11 Cameron Payne 1.50 4.00
12 Nikola Jokic 75.00 200.00
13 Sam Dekker 1.00 2.50
14 Boban Marjanovic 3.00 8.00
15 D'Angelo Russell 4.00 10.00
16 Bobby Portis 2.50 6.00
17 Willie Cauley-Stein 1.25 3.00
18 R.J. Hunter 1.00 2.50
19 Justise Winslow 1.50 4.00
20 Anthony Brown 1.00 2.50
21 Kelly Oubre Jr. 3.00 8.00
22 Marcelo Huertas 1.00 2.50
23 Jonathon Simmons 1.25 3.00
24 Jerian Grant 1.00 2.50
25 Jahlil Okafor 1.25 3.00
26 Rondae Hollis-Jefferson 1.25 3.00
27 Emmanuel Mudiay 1.25 3.00
28 Chris McCullough 1.00 2.50
29 Myles Turner 4.00 10.00
30 Nemanja Bjelica 1.50 4.00
31 Terry Rozier 4.00 10.00
32 Richaun Holmes 1.50 4.00
33 Delon Wright 1.25 3.00
34 Pat Connaughton 1.50 4.00
35 Kristaps Porzingis 6.00 15.00
36 Tyus Jones 1.25 3.00
37 Stanley Johnson 1.25 3.00
38 Montrezl Harrell 3.00 8.00
39 Trey Lyles 1.25 3.00
40 T.J. McConnell 4.00 10.00

2015-16 Panini Threads Rookie Threads

*PRIME/25: 2X TO 5X BASIC
1 Karl-Anthony Towns 6.00 15.00
2 Karl-Anthony Towns 6.00 15.00
3 Karl-Anthony Towns 6.00 15.00
4 Karl-Anthony Towns 6.00 15.00
5 Karl-Anthony Towns 6.00 15.00
6 D'Angelo Russell 4.00 10.00
7 D'Angelo Russell 4.00 10.00
8 D'Angelo Russell 4.00 10.00
9 D'Angelo Russell 4.00 10.00
10 D'Angelo Russell 4.00 10.00
11 Jahlil Okafor 2.50 6.00
12 Jahlil Okafor 2.50 6.00
13 Jahlil Okafor 1.50 4.00
14 Jahlil Okafor 1.50 4.00
15 Jahlil Okafor 1.50 4.00
16 Kristaps Porzingis 5.00 12.00
17 Kristaps Porzingis 5.00 12.00
18 Kristaps Porzingis 5.00 12.00
19 Kristaps Porzingis 5.00 12.00
20 Kristaps Porzingis 5.00 12.00
21 Mario Hezonja 1.50 4.00
22 Mario Hezonja 1.50 4.00
23 Mario Hezonja 1.50 4.00
24 Mario Hezonja 1.50 4.00
25 Mario Hezonja 1.50 4.00
26 Willie Cauley-Stein 1.50 4.00
27 Willie Cauley-Stein 1.50 4.00
28 Willie Cauley-Stein 1.50 4.00
29 Willie Cauley-Stein 1.50 4.00
30 Willie Cauley-Stein 1.50 4.00
31 Emmanuel Mudiay 1.50 4.00
32 Emmanuel Mudiay 1.50 4.00
33 Emmanuel Mudiay 1.50 4.00
34 Emmanuel Mudiay 1.50 4.00
35 Emmanuel Mudiay 1.50 4.00
36 Stanley Johnson 1.50 4.00
37 Stanley Johnson 1.50 4.00
38 Stanley Johnson 1.50 4.00
39 Stanley Johnson 1.50 4.00
40 Stanley Johnson 1.50 4.00
41 Frank Kaminsky 1.50 4.00
42 Frank Kaminsky 1.50 4.00
43 Frank Kaminsky 1.50 4.00
44 Frank Kaminsky 1.50 4.00
45 Frank Kaminsky 1.50 4.00
46 Justise Winslow 2.00 5.00
47 Justise Winslow 2.00 5.00
48 Justise Winslow 2.00 5.00
49 Justise Winslow 2.00 5.00
50 Justise Winslow 2.00 5.00
51 Myles Turner 5.00 12.00
52 Myles Turner 5.00 12.00
53 Myles Turner 5.00 12.00
54 Myles Turner 5.00 12.00
55 Myles Turner 5.00 12.00
56 Trey Lyles 1.50 4.00
57 Trey Lyles 1.50 4.00
58 Trey Lyles 1.50 4.00
59 Trey Lyles 1.50 4.00
60 Trey Lyles 1.50 4.00
61 Devin Booker 4.00 10.00
62 Devin Booker 4.00 10.00
63 Devin Booker 4.00 10.00
64 Devin Booker 4.00 10.00
65 Devin Booker 4.00 10.00
66 Cameron Payne 2.00 5.00
67 Cameron Payne 2.00 5.00
68 Cameron Payne 2.00 5.00
69 Cameron Payne 2.00 5.00
70 Cameron Payne 2.00 5.00
71 Kelly Oubre Jr. 4.00 10.00
72 Kelly Oubre Jr. 4.00 10.00
73 Kelly Oubre Jr. 4.00 10.00
74 Kelly Oubre Jr. 4.00 10.00
75 Kelly Oubre Jr. 4.00 10.00
76 Terry Rozier 5.00 12.00
77 Terry Rozier 5.00 12.00
78 Terry Rozier 5.00 12.00
79 Terry Rozier 5.00 12.00
80 Terry Rozier 5.00 12.00
86 Sam Dekker 1.25 3.00
87 Sam Dekker 1.25 3.00
88 Sam Dekker 1.25 3.00
89 Sam Dekker 1.25 3.00
90 Sam Dekker 1.25 3.00
91 Jerian Grant 1.25 3.00
92 Jerian Grant 1.25 3.00
93 Jerian Grant 1.25 3.00
94 Jerian Grant 1.25 3.00
95 Jerian Grant 1.25 3.00
96 Delon Wright 1.50 4.00
97 Delon Wright 1.50 4.00
98 Delon Wright 1.50 4.00
99 Delon Wright 1.50 4.00
100 Delon Wright 1.50 4.00

2015-16 Panini Threads Rookie Threads Signatures

PRINT RUNS B/WN 99-199 COPIES PER
1 Karl-Anthony Towns/199 30.00 80.00
2 D'Angelo Russell/199 20.00 50.00
3 Jahlil Okafor/199 4.00 10.00
4 Emmanuel Mudiay/199 4.00 10.00
5 Kristaps Porzingis/99 30.00 80.00
7 Justise Winslow/199 5.00 12.00
8 Willie Cauley-Stein/199 4.00 10.00
9 Tyus Jones/199 4.00 10.00
10 Stanley Johnson/199 4.00 10.00
11 Frank Kaminsky/199 4.00 10.00
12 Devin Booker/199 200.00 500.00
13 Myles Turner/199 12.00 30.00
14 Trey Lyles/199 4.00 10.00
15 Jerian Grant/199 3.00 8.00
17 Delon Wright/199 4.00 10.00
18 Cameron Payne/199 5.00 12.00
19 Kelly Oubre Jr./199 10.00 25.00
20 Terry Rozier/199 12.00 30.00
21 Sam Dekker/199 3.00 8.00
22 Rondae Hollis-Jefferson/199 4.00 10.00
23 Justin Anderson/199 3.00 8.00
24 Bobby Portis/199 8.00 20.00
25 Kevon Looney/199 10.00 25.00
26 R.J. Hunter/199 3.00 8.00
27 Jarell Martin/199 3.00 8.00
28 Anthony Brown/199 3.00 8.00
29 Chris McCullough/199 3.00 8.00
30 Montrezl Harrell/199 12.00 30.00
31 Jordan Mickey/199 3.00 8.00
32 Walter Tavares/199 3.00 8.00
34 Pat Connaughton/199 5.00 12.00

2015-16 Panini Threads Rookie Threads Signatures Prime

*PRIME/25: .6X TO 1.5X BASIC
PRINT RUNS B/WN 15-25 COPIES PER
NO PRIICNG ON QTY 15
35 Joe Young/25 15.00 40.00

2015-16 Panini Threads Signage

PRINT RUNS B/WN 15-199 COPIES PER
NO PRICING ON QTY 15
1 Trey Burke/199 2.50 6.00
3 Rodney Stuckey/199 2.50 6.00
4 Cody Zeller/199 2.50 6.00
5 Tom Gugliotta/199 2.50 6.00
6 Derrick Williams/99 2.50 6.00
7 Jeff Malone/199 2.50 6.00
9 Artis Gilmore/99 5.00 12.00
11 Kevin Willis/199 2.50 6.00
12 Anfernee Hardaway/49 10.00 25.00
13 Bob McAdoo/199 5.00 12.00
15 Cedric Maxwell/199 3.00 8.00
16 Julius Randle/99 10.00 25.00
17 Sam Bowie/199 2.50 6.00
19 Chris Mullin/99 6.00 15.00
21 Chase Budinger/199 2.50 6.00
22 Anthony Bennett/199 2.50 6.00
23 Steve Novak/199 2.50 6.00
24 Otto Porter/99 3.00 8.00
25 Jason Smith/199 2.50 6.00
27 Tony Delk/199 2.50 6.00
29 Kentavious Caldwell-Pope/99 3.00 8.00
31 Courtney Lee/199 2.50 6.00
32 Gary Payton/49 8.00 20.00
33 Jusuf Nurkic/199 3.00 8.00
34 Alex Len/99 2.50 6.00
35 Ron Harper/199 4.00 10.00
36 Nerlens Noel/99 2.50 6.00
37 Glenn Robinson III/199 2.50 6.00
39 Tayshaun Prince/99 3.00 8.00
41 Wayne Embry/199 2.50 6.00
44 Bob Lanier/83 8.00 20.00
45 Cuttino Mobley/199 2.50 6.00
46 Andre Drummond/99 4.00 10.00
47 Antoine Carr/199 2.50 6.00
49 C.J. McCollum/199 6.00 15.00

2015-16 Panini Threads Team Threads

1 DeMar DeRozan 2.00 5.00
2 Dwyane Wade 3.00 8.00
3 James Harden 3.00 8.00
4 Brook Lopez 1.50 4.00
5 Tim Duncan 4.00 10.00
6 Andre Iguodala 1.50 4.00
7 Kevin Love 1.50 4.00
8 Rudy Gay 1.50 4.00
9 Andrew Wiggins 2.00 5.00
10 Kyrie Irving 3.00 8.00
11 Derrick Rose 2.50 6.00
12 Gordon Hayward 1.50 4.00
13 Chris Paul 3.00 8.00
14 Rudy Gobert 2.00 5.00
15 LaMarcus Aldridge 1.50 4.00
16 Kyle Korver 1.25 3.00
17 Jimmy Butler 3.00 8.00
18 Tony Parker 2.50 6.00
19 Ricky Rubio 1.25 3.00
20 Damian Lillard 4.00 10.00
21 LeBron James 15.00 40.00
22 Eric Bledsoe 1.25 3.00
23 Russell Westbrook 2.50 6.00
24 Pau Gasol 2.50 6.00
25 John Wall 2.00 5.00
26 Al Jefferson 1.00 2.50
27 Dwight Howard 2.00 5.00
28 Kobe Bryant 15.00 40.00
29 Kenneth Faried 1.25 3.00
30 Klay Thompson 4.00 10.00
31 Kevin Durant 6.00 15.00
32 Kyle Lowry 1.50 4.00
33 Blake Griffin 1.50 4.00
34 Jeff Teague 1.00 2.50
35 DeMarcus Cousins 1.50 4.00
36 Greg Monroe 1.25 3.00
37 Paul George 2.50 6.00
38 Paul Pierce 2.50 6.00
39 Monta Ellis 1.25 3.00
40 Mike Conley 1.50 4.00
41 Anthony Davis 4.00 10.00
42 Andre Drummond 1.50 4.00
43 Marc Gasol 1.50 4.00
44 Goran Dragic 1.50 4.00
45 Carmelo Anthony 2.50 6.00
46 Zach Randolph 1.50 4.00
47 Al Horford 1.50 4.00
48 Tyreke Evans 1.25 3.00
49 Chandler Parsons 1.00 2.50
50 Stephen Curry 15.00 40.00
51 Dirk Nowitzki 4.00 10.00
52 Tyson Chandler 1.25 3.00
53 Kawhi Leonard 5.00 12.00
54 Joakim Noah 1.00 2.50
55 Draymond Green 2.00 5.00
56 Danny Green 1.25 3.00
57 Chris Bosh 2.00 5.00
58 Jabari Parker 1.00 2.50
59 Bradley Beal 2.00 5.00
60 DeAndre Jordan 1.25 3.00

2015-16 Panini Threads Threads Signatures

PRINT RUNS B/WN 17-49 COPIES PER
*PRIME/25: .6X TO 1.5X BASIC
1 Trey Burke/35 3.00 8.00
2 John Wall/25 15.00 40.00
4 Marcus Smart/39 6.00 15.00
6 Zach Randolph/35 5.00 12.00
7 Rafer Alston/49 3.00 8.00
8 Kobe Bryant/25 500.00 1,000.00
9 Tyson Chandler/35 4.00 10.00
10 Anthony Davis/25 30.00 80.00
11 Goran Dragic/35 5.00 12.00
12 Chris Webber/25 40.00 100.00
13 Mike Conley/35 5.00 12.00
14 Harrison Barnes/35 4.00 10.00
16 Jrue Holiday/35 6.00 15.00
17 Brad Daugherty/49 4.00 10.00
18 Chris Paul/25 40.00 100.00
19 Josh Smith/35 3.00 8.00
20 Blake Griffin/25 15.00 40.00
24 Richard Hamilton/35 5.00 12.00
25 Jusuf Nurkic/49 4.00 10.00
26 Tyreke Evans/35 4.00 10.00
27 Reggie Jackson/49 4.00 10.00
28 Dwyane Wade/25 30.00 80.00
29 Al Horford/35 15.00 40.00
31 Andrea Bargnani/35 3.00 8.00
33 Wesley Matthews/49 3.00 8.00
34 Otto Porter/35 4.00 10.00
35 Timofey Mozgov/49 3.00 8.00
36 Ben McLemore/35 3.00 8.00
37 Donatas Motiejunas/49 3.00 8.00
38 Carmelo Anthony/20 15.00 40.00
39 Steve Kerr/35 10.00 25.00
40 Kyrie Irving/25 12.00 30.00
41 Brandon Knight/35 3.00 8.00
42 Andrew Wiggins/25 15.00 40.00
43 Nik Stauskas/49 3.00 8.00
44 Chris Andersen/35 4.00 10.00
45 Cody Zeller/35 3.00 8.00
47 Isaiah Canaan/49 3.00 8.00
48 Kevin Durant/25 50.00 120.00
49 C.J. McCollum/35 8.00 20.00
51 Danilo Gallinari/35 4.00 10.00
52 Kevin Love/35 10.00 25.00
53 DeMarre Carroll/49 3.00 8.00
54 Joe Johnson/35 4.00 10.00
55 Matthew Dellavedova/49 12.00 30.00
56 Andre Drummond/35 6.00 15.00
57 Jordan Clarkson/49 5.00 12.00
58 Allen Iverson/25 50.00 120.00
59 Michael Carter-Williams/35 3.00 8.00
60 Pau Gasol/25 10.00 25.00
61 Danny Manning/35 4.00 10.00
62 Victor Oladipo/35 4.00 10.00
63 T.J. Warren/49 5.00 12.00
64 Julius Randle/35 8.00 20.00
65 Tim Hardaway Jr./49 4.00 10.00

2015-16 Panini Threads Triple Threat Materials

STATED PRINT RUN 199 SER.#'d SETS
1 Nicolas Batum 1.50 4.00
2 Carmelo Anthony 4.00 10.00
3 Tim Duncan 6.00 15.00
4 Aaron Gordon 2.50 6.00
5 Kawhi Leonard 8.00 20.00
6 Andrew Wiggins 3.00 8.00
7 Dante Exum 2.00 5.00
8 Brook Lopez 2.50 6.00
9 Iman Shumpert 1.50 4.00
10 Kevin Durant 10.00 25.00
11 Rajon Rondo 3.00 8.00
12 Clyde Drexler 4.00 10.00
13 Tony Parker 4.00 10.00
14 LeBron James 20.00 50.00
15 Bradley Beal 3.00 8.00
16 Kobe Bryant 20.00 50.00
17 David West 2.00 5.00
18 Chris Andersen 2.00 5.00
19 John Henson 1.50 4.00
20 LaMarcus Aldridge 2.50 6.00
21 Terrence Ross 2.00 5.00
22 Damian Lillard 6.00 15.00
23 Trey Burke 1.50 4.00
24 Russell Westbrook 4.00 10.00
25 C.J. McCollum 2.50 6.00
26 Brandon Jennings 1.50 4.00
27 George Hill 2.00 5.00
28 Eric Bledsoe 2.00 5.00
29 Marcus Smart 3.00 8.00
30 Manu Ginobili 5.00 12.00

2015-16 Panini Threads Voices of the Game Autographs

PRINT RUNS B/WN 10-199 COPIES PER
NO PRICING ON QTY 10
1 Bob Knight/49 100.00 250.00
3 Chris Webber/49 25.00 60.00
4 Kenny Smith/115 3.00 8.00
5 Steve Kerr/99 10.00 25.00
6 Doug Collins/199 4.00 10.00
7 Jalen Rose/199 4.00 10.00
8 Avery Johnson/199 3.00 8.00
9 Rick Fox/199 3.00 8.00
10 Grant Hill/49 25.00 60.00

2016-17 Panini Threads

COMP.SET w/o RCs (150) 20.00 50.00
1 Paul George .50 1.25
2 Marcus Smart .40 1.00
3 Andrew Wiggins .40 1.00
4 Jimmy Butler .60 1.50
5 DeAndre Jordan .25 .60
6 Jeremy Lin .60 1.50
7 Rudy Gay .30 .75
8 Harrison Barnes .25 .60
9 Ersan Ilyasova .20 .50
10 Tony Snell .20 .50
11 Al Horford .30 .75
12 James Harden .60 1.50
13 Andre Drummond .30 .75
14 Evan Fournier .25 .60
15 Gordon Hayward .30 .75
16 Dion Waiters .20 .50
17 Will Barton .20 .50
18 Marc Gasol .30 .75
19 Robin Lopez .20 .50
20 Ricky Rubio .25 .60
21 Rudy Gobert .40 1.00
22 Cody Zeller .20 .50
23 Trevor Booker .20 .50
24 Andre Roberson .20 .50
25 Dirk Nowitzki .75 2.00
26 JaMychal Green .25 .60
27 Nicolas Batum .25 .60
28 Justise Winslow .25 .60
29 Trey Lyles .25 .60
30 Mike Conley .25 .60
31 D'Angelo Russell .40 1.00
32 Bojan Bogdanovic .25 .60
33 Enes Kanter .20 .50
34 Marcin Gortat .20 .50
35 Greg Monroe .20 .50
36 J.R. Smith .30 .75
37 Joakim Noah .20 .50
38 Solomon Hill .20 .50
39 Tim Hardaway Jr. .25 .60
40 Hassan Whiteside .25 .60
41 Jae Crowder .20 .50
42 Avery Bradley .20 .50
43 Dennis Schroder .30 .75
44 Thaddeus Young .20 .50
45 Kentavious Caldwell-Pope .25 .60
46 Maurice Harkless .20 .50
47 Klay Thompson .75 2.00
48 Serge Ibaka .25 .60
49 C.J. McCollum .30 .75
50 Kevin Durant 1.25 3.00
51 Paul Millsap .25 .60
52 Bradley Beal .40 1.00
53 Danny Green .25 .60
54 Emmanuel Mudiay .20 .50
55 Tyler Johnson .20 .50
56 Ty Lawson .20 .50
57 Jusuf Nurkic .25 .60
58 Victor Oladipo .25 .60
59 Joel Embiid .75 2.00
60 Anthony Davis 1.00 2.50
61 Tony Parker .50 1.25
62 Blake Griffin .30 .75
63 DeMarcus Cousins .30 .75
64 LeBron James 2.50 6.00
65 Elfrid Payton .25 .60
66 Luol Deng .25 .60
67 Terrence Ross .25 .60
68 Marvin Williams .20 .50
69 Steven Adams .25 .60
70 Stephen Curry 2.50 6.00
71 Robert Covington .25 .60
72 Taj Gibson .20 .50
73 Kristaps Porzingis .50 1.25
74 Derrick Rose .50 1.25
75 Wilson Chandler .25 .60
76 Zach LaVine .60 1.50
77 Reggie Jackson .25 .60
78 Kevin Love .30 .75
79 Jrue Holiday .40 1.00
80 E'Twaun Moore .20 .50
81 Pau Gasol .50 1.25
82 Derrick Favors .20 .50
83 Rodney Hood .25 .60
84 Karl-Anthony Towns .60 1.50
85 Chris Paul .50 1.25
86 Kyle Lowry .30 .75
87 Nikola Vucevic .30 .75
88 Nick Young .20 .50
89 Gorgui Dieng .20 .50
90 Marcus Morris .20 .50
91 Clint Capela .25 .60
92 Tristan Thompson .25 .60
93 Arron Afflalo .20 .50
94 DeMar DeRozan .40 1.00
95 Carmelo Anthony .50 1.25
96 Allen Crabbe .20 .50
97 Luc Mbah a Moute .20 .50
98 Dwyane Wade .60 1.50
99 Darren Collison .20 .50
100 Myles Turner .30 .75
101 Mason Plumlee .20 .50
102 Tim Frazier .20 .50
103 Brandon Knight .25 .60
104 John Wall .40 1.00
105 Kemba Walker .25 .60
106 Markieff Morris .20 .50
107 Eric Bledsoe .25 .60
108 Michael Kidd-Gilchrist .20 .50
109 Jabari Parker .20 .50
110 Ryan Anderson .20 .50
111 Vince Carter .60 1.50
112 Jonas Valanciunas .25 .60
113 Matthew Dellavedova .25 .60
114 Lou Williams .30 .75
115 Devin Booker 1.25 3.00
116 Damian Lillard .75 2.00
117 Monta Ellis .25 .60
118 Tobias Harris .30 .75
119 Jeff Teague .20 .50
120 LaMarcus Aldridge .30 .75
121 Giannis Antetokounmpo 1.50 4.00
122 Draymond Green .40 1.00
123 Jahlil Okafor .20 .50
124 Danilo Gallinari .25 .60
125 Brook Lopez .25 .60
126 Kyrie Irving .60 1.50
127 Dwight Howard .40 1.00
128 Russell Westbrook .50 1.25
129 Sean Kilpatrick .20 .50
130 Wesley Matthews .20 .50
131 T.J. Warren .25 .60
132 Patrick Beverley .20 .50
133 Tyson Chandler .20 .50
134 Brandon Jennings .20 .50
135 Trevor Ariza .20 .50
136 J.J. Barea .20 .50
137 Kawhi Leonard .75 2.00
138 Otto Porter .25 .60
139 Deron Williams .25 .60
140 Jordan Clarkson .30 .75
141 Tony Allen .25 .60
142 Isaiah Thomas .25 .60
143 Sergio Rodriguez .20 .50
144 Kyle Korver .20 .50
145 Andre Iguodala .30 .75
146 Goran Dragic .25 .60
147 Aaron Gordon .30 .75
148 Cory Joseph .20 .50
149 Rajon Rondo .40 1.00
150 J.J. Redick .30 .75
151 Domantas Sabonis RC 2.50 6.00
152 Henry Ellenson RC .40 1.00
153 Willy Hernangomez RC .60 1.50
154 DeAndre' Bembry RC .60 1.50
155 Damian Jones RC .40 1.00
156 Ben Simmons RC 1.25 3.00
157 Malcolm Brogdon RC 1.25 3.00
158 Buddy Hield RC 1.25 3.00
159 A.J. Hammons RC .40 1.00
160 Taurean Prince RC .50 1.25
161 Malcolm Delaney RC .40 1.00
162 Malik Beasley RC .75 2.00
163 Mindaugas Kuzminskas RC .40 1.00
164 Brice Johnson RC .40 1.00
165 Deyonta Davis RC .40 1.00
166 Brandon Ingram RC 1.50 4.00
167 Diamond Stone RC .40 1.00
168 Jamal Murray RC 3.00 8.00
169 Kay Felder RC .40 1.00
170 Georgios Papagiannis RC .40 1.00
171 Yogi Ferrell RC .50 1.25
172 Caris LeVert RC 1.00 2.50
173 Davis Bertans RC .60 1.50
174 Pascal Siakam RC 2.50 6.00
175 Ivica Zubac RC 1.00 2.50
176 Jaylen Brown RC 3.00 8.00
177 Stephen Zimmerman RC .40 1.00
178 Marquese Chriss RC .50 1.25
179 Dario Saric RC .60 1.50
180 Denzel Valentine RC .40 1.00
181 Tomas Satoransky RC .60 1.50
182 Malachi Richardson RC .40 1.00
183 Ron Baker RC .40 1.00
184 Skal Labissiere RC .40 1.00
185 Cheick Diallo RC .40 1.00
186 Dragan Bender RC .40 1.00
187 Isaiah Whitehead RC .40 1.00
188 Jakob Poeltl RC .75 2.00
189 Rodney McGruder RC .50 1.25
190 Juan Hernangomez RC .75 2.00
191 Patrick McCaw RC .50 1.25
192 T. Luwawu-Cabarrot RC .60 1.50
193 Chinanu Onuaku RC .40 1.00
194 Dejounte Murray RC 2.00 5.00
195 Tyler Ulis RC .50 1.25
196 Kris Dunn RC .60 1.50
197 Demetrius Jackson RC .40 1.00
198 Thon Maker RC .50 1.25
199 Dorian Finney-Smith RC .50 1.25
200 Wade Baldwin IV RC .40 1.00
201 Deyonta Davis LTHR .50 1.25
202 Patrick McCaw LTHR .50 1.25
203 Georgios Papagiannis LTHR .50 1.25
204 Kris Dunn LTHR .75 2.00
205 Jaylen Brown LTHR 4.00 10.00
206 Denzel Valentine LTHR .50 1.25
207 Domantas Sabonis LTHR 3.00 8.00
208 Skal Labissiere LTHR .50 1.25
209 Ben Simmons LTHR 1.50 4.00
210 Isaiah Whitehead LTHR .50 1.25
211 Brandon Ingram LTHR 2.00 5.00
212 Dejounte Murray LTHR 2.50 6.00
213 Caris LeVert LTHR 1.25 3.00
214 Demetrius Jackson LTHR .50 1.25
215 Marquese Chriss LTHR .60 1.50
216 Tomas Satoransky LTHR .75 2.00
217 Henry Ellenson LTHR .50 1.25
218 Cheick Diallo LTHR .50 1.25
219 Malcolm Brogdon LTHR 1.50 4.00
220 Jakob Poeltl LTHR 1.00 2.50
221 Jamal Murray LTHR 4.00 10.00
222 Tyler Ulis LTHR .60 1.50
223 Ivica Zubac LTHR 1.25 3.00
224 Thon Maker LTHR .60 1.50
225 Dario Saric LTHR .75 2.00
226 Malachi Richardson LTHR .50 1.25
227 Damian Jones LTHR .50 1.25
228 Dragan Bender LTHR .50 1.25
229 Buddy Hield LTHR 1.50 4.00
230 Juan Hernangomez LTHR 1.00 2.50
231 Damian Jones WOOD .75 2.00
232 Domantas Sabonis WOOD 5.00 12.00
233 Isaiah Whitehead WOOD .75 2.00
234 Marquese Chriss WOOD 1.00 2.50
235 Jamal Murray WOOD 6.00 15.00
236 Deyonta Davis WOOD .75 2.00
237 Thon Maker WOOD 1.00 2.50
238 Kris Dunn WOOD 1.25 3.00
239 Dragan Bender WOOD .75 2.00
240 Skal Labissiere WOOD .75 2.00
241 Brandon Ingram WOOD 3.00 8.00
242 Malcolm Brogdon WOOD 2.50 6.00
243 Tyler Ulis WOOD 1.00 2.50
244 Patrick McCaw WOOD .75 2.00
245 Dario Saric WOOD 1.25 3.00
246 Jaylen Brown WOOD 6.00 15.00
247 Buddy Hield WOOD 2.50 6.00
248 Ben Simmons WOOD 2.50 6.00
249 Dejounte Murray WOOD 4.00 10.00
250 Jakob Poeltl WOOD 1.50 4.00
251 Ivica Zubac WOOD 2.00 5.00
252 Georgios Papagiannis WOOD .75 2.00
253 Malachi Richardson WOOD .75 2.00
254 Denzel Valentine WOOD .75 2.00
255 Domantas Sabonis ETCH 3.00 8.00
256 Henry Ellenson ETCH .50 1.25
257 Damian Jones ETCH .50 1.25
258 Ben Simmons ETCH 1.50 4.00
259 Malcolm Brogdon ETCH 1.50 4.00
260 Buddy Hield ETCH 1.50 4.00
261 A.J. Hammons ETCH .50 1.25
262 Brice Johnson ETCH .50 1.25
263 Deyonta Davis ETCH .50 1.25
264 Brandon Ingram ETCH 2.00 5.00
265 Diamond Stone ETCH .50 1.25
266 Jamal Murray ETCH 4.00 10.00
267 Georgios Papagiannis ETCH .50 1.25
268 Caris LeVert ETCH 1.25 3.00
269 Ivica Zubac ETCH 1.25 3.00
270 Jaylen Brown ETCH 4.00 10.00
271 Marquese Chriss ETCH .60 1.50
272 Dario Saric ETCH .75 2.00
273 Denzel Valentine ETCH .50 1.25
274 Tomas Satoransky ETCH .75 2.00
275 Malachi Richardson ETCH .50 1.25
276 Skal Labissiere ETCH .50 1.25
277 Cheick Diallo ETCH .50 1.25
278 Dragan Bender ETCH .50 1.25
279 Isaiah Whitehead ETCH .50 1.25
280 Jakob Poeltl ETCH 1.00 2.50
281 Juan Hernangomez ETCH 1.00 2.50
282 Patrick McCaw ETCH .50 1.25
283 Dejounte Murray ETCH 2.50 6.00
284 Tyler Ulis ETCH .60 1.50
285 Kris Dunn ETCH .75 2.00
286 Demetrius Jackson ETCH .50 1.25
287 Thon Maker ETCH .60 1.50

2016-17 Panini Threads Century Proof Dazzle

*DAZZLE: 1.2X TO 3X BASIC
*DAZZLE RC: .6X TO 1.5X BASIC RC

2016-17 Panini Threads Century Proof Dazzle Orange

*ORANGE: 4X TO 10X BASIC
*ORANGE RC: 4X TO 10X BASIC RC
STATED PRINT RUN 25 SER.#'d SETS

2016-17 Panini Threads Century Proof Holo

*HOLO: 1.5X TO 4X BASIC
*HOLO RC: 1X TO 2.5X BASIC RC

2016-17 Panini Threads Century Proof Red

*RED: 1.5X TO 4X BASIC
*RED: 1.5X TO 4X BASIC RC
STATED PRINT RUN 199 SER.#'d SETS

2016-17 Panini Threads Authentic Threads

1 Karl-Anthony Towns 6.00 15.00
2 Jeff Teague 2.00 5.00
3 LeBron James 40.00 100.00
4 DeMar DeRozan 4.00 10.00
5 Marc Gasol 3.00 8.00
6 Blake Griffin 3.00 8.00
7 Dwyane Wade 6.00 15.00
8 Draymond Green 4.00 10.00
9 Eric Gordon 2.50 6.00
10 Kawhi Leonard 8.00 20.00
11 James Harden 6.00 15.00
12 Damian Lillard 8.00 20.00
13 DeMarcus Cousins 2.50 6.00
14 Anthony Davis 10.00 25.00
15 Dennis Schroder 3.00 8.00
16 D'Angelo Russell 4.00 10.00
17 Kyle Lowry 3.00 8.00
18 Kyrie Irving 6.00 15.00
19 Andre Drummond 3.00 8.00
20 Devin Booker 12.00 30.00
21 Kevin Love 3.00 8.00
22 Andrew Wiggins 4.00 10.00
23 DeAndre Jordan 2.50 6.00
24 Emmanuel Mudiay 2.00 5.00
25 Ricky Rubio 2.50 6.00
26 John Wall 4.00 10.00
27 Goran Dragic 3.00 8.00
28 Dirk Nowitzki 8.00 20.00
29 Serge Ibaka 2.50 6.00
30 Brook Lopez 2.50 6.00
31 Kemba Walker 2.50 6.00
32 Derrick Rose 5.00 12.00
33 Elfrid Payton 2.50 6.00
34 Dwight Howard 4.00 10.00
35 Bradley Beal 4.00 10.00
36 Eric Bledsoe 2.50 6.00
37 Harrison Barnes 2.50 6.00
38 Danilo Gallinari 2.50 6.00
39 Chris Paul 5.00 12.00
40 Carmelo Anthony 5.00 12.00

2016-17 Panini Threads Autographs

1 Trey Lyles 3.00 8.00
2 Mike Muscala 2.50 6.00
3 James Ennis 2.50 6.00
4 Cody Zeller 2.50 6.00
5 C.J. McCollum 8.00 20.00
6 Justin Hamilton 2.50 6.00
7 Ian Clark 2.50 6.00
8 Josh Huestis 2.50 6.00
9 Larry Nance Jr. 2.50 6.00
10 Sean Kilpatrick 2.50 6.00
11 Mario Hezonja 2.50 6.00
12 Richaun Holmes 3.00 8.00
13 Dwight Powell 2.50 6.00
14 E'Twaun Moore 2.50 6.00
15 Maurice Harkless 2.50 6.00
16 Victor Oladipo 3.00 8.00
17 Kyle O'Quinn 2.50 6.00
18 Justin Anderson 2.50 6.00
19 Kobe Bryant 1,000.00 2,000.00
20 Michael Carter-Williams 2.50 6.00
21 Langston Galloway 2.50 6.00
22 Jordan McRae 2.50 6.00
23 Kevin Love 6.00 15.00
24 Kevin Durant 100.00 250.00
25 Jeremy Lin 30.00 80.00
26 Zach LaVine 40.00 100.00
27 Karl-Anthony Towns 15.00 40.00
28 Carmelo Anthony 40.00 100.00
29 Kyrie Irving 75.00 200.00
30 Anthony Davis 60.00 150.00

2016-17 Panini Threads Automatic

1 Steve Nash 5.00 12.00
2 Giannis Antetokounmpo 15.00 40.00
3 Carmelo Anthony 5.00 12.00
4 Russell Westbrook 5.00 12.00
5 Kyle Lowry 3.00 8.00
6 Damian Lillard 8.00 20.00
7 Dirk Nowitzki 8.00 20.00
8 DeMar DeRozan 4.00 10.00
9 Kobe Bryant 25.00 60.00
10 Jimmy Butler 6.00 15.00
11 Kyrie Irving 6.00 15.00
12 Steve Kerr 3.00 8.00
13 John Wall 4.00 10.00
14 James Harden 6.00 15.00
15 C.J. McCollum 3.00 8.00
16 Kevin Durant 12.00 30.00
17 Ray Allen 5.00 12.00
18 Stephen Curry 25.00 60.00
19 Larry Bird 12.00 30.00
20 Klay Thompson 8.00 20.00

2016-17 Panini Threads Board of Directors

*DAZZLE: .75X TO 2X BASIC
*RED: .6X TO 1.5X BASIC
*HOLO: 1X TO 2.5X BASIC
*ORANGE/25: 2X TO 5X BASIC
1 Marcin Gortat .30 .75
2 Hassan Whiteside .40 1.00
3 Hakeem Olajuwon 1.00 2.50
4 DeAndre Jordan .40 1.00
5 Dennis Rodman 1.00 2.50
6 Anthony Davis 1.50 4.00
7 Wilt Chamberlain 1.50 4.00
8 Dwight Howard .60 1.50
9 Bill Russell 1.50 4.00
10 Karl-Anthony Towns 1.00 2.50

11 Karl Malone .75 2.00
12 Andre Drummond .50 1.25
13 Shaquille O'Neal 1.50 4.00
14 Rudy Gobert .60 1.50
15 Patrick Ewing .60 1.50

2016-17 Panini Threads Bringing Down the House

1 John Wall 3.00 8.00
2 Julius Erving 6.00 15.00
3 Damian Lillard 6.00 15.00
4 Shaquille O'Neal 8.00 20.00
5 Russell Westbrook 4.00 10.00
6 Zach LaVine 5.00 12.00
7 Giannis Antetokounmpo 12.00 30.00
8 Anthony Davis 8.00 20.00
9 DeMar DeRozan 3.00 8.00
10 Dwight Howard 3.00 8.00
11 Shawn Kemp 4.00 10.00
12 Dominique Wilkins 3.00 8.00
13 Kevin Durant 10.00 25.00
14 Kobe Bryant 20.00 50.00
15 Derrick Rose 4.00 10.00

2016-17 Panini Threads Century Collection Materials

STATED PRINT RUN 99 SER.#'d SETS
1 Jamal Mashburn 2.50 6.00
2 Tracy McGrady 5.00 12.00
3 Kevin McHale 5.00 12.00
4 Scottie Pippen 6.00 15.00
5 Joe Dumars 3.00 8.00
6 Robert Parish 4.00 10.00
7 Kiki Vandeweghe 2.50 6.00
8 Kareem Abdul-Jabbar 10.00 25.00
9 Gary Payton 5.00 12.00
10 Chris Mullin 3.00 8.00
11 Grant Hill 4.00 10.00
12 Clyde Drexler 5.00 12.00
13 Shaquille O'Neal 4.00 10.00
14 Brent Barry 2.00 5.00
15 Alonzo Mourning 10.00 25.00
16 Alex English 2.50 6.00
17 Karl Malone 5.00 12.00
18 Anfernee Hardaway 5.00 12.00
19 Jason Kidd 5.00 12.00
20 John Stockton 5.00 12.00
21 Nick Van Exel 3.00 8.00
22 Michael Finley 3.00 8.00
23 Patrick Ewing 4.00 10.00
24 Kobe Bryant 25.00 60.00
25 Hakeem Olajuwon 6.00 15.00
26 Larry Johnson 4.00 10.00
27 David Robinson 4.00 10.00
28 Allen Iverson 5.00 12.00
29 Larry Bird 10.00 25.00
30 Tim Duncan 4.00 10.00

2016-17 Panini Threads Century Stars

1 Stephen Curry 40.00 100.00
2 LeBron James 40.00 100.00
3 Russell Westbrook 8.00 20.00
4 Kyrie Irving 10.00 25.00
5 Kevin Durant 20.00 50.00
6 Ben Simmons 10.00 25.00
7 Brandon Ingram 12.00 30.00
8 Jaylen Brown 25.00 60.00
9 Kris Dunn 5.00 12.00
10 Buddy Hield 10.00 25.00

2016-17 Panini Threads Debut Threads

*PRIME/25: .75X TO 2X BASIC
1 Isaiah Whitehead 2.00 5.00
2 Pascal Siakam 12.00 30.00
3 Henry Ellenson 2.00 5.00
4 Kris Dunn 3.00 8.00
5 Marquese Chriss 2.50 6.00
6 Ivica Zubac 5.00 12.00
7 Jakob Poeltl 4.00 10.00
8 Jamal Murray 15.00 40.00
9 Kay Felder 2.00 5.00
10 Caris LeVert 5.00 12.00
11 Damian Jones 2.00 5.00
12 Tyler Ulis 2.50 6.00
13 Diamond Stone 2.00 5.00
14 Brandon Ingram 8.00 20.00
15 Thon Maker 2.50 6.00
16 Skal Labissiere 2.00 5.00
17 Denzel Valentine 2.00 5.00
18 Malachi Richardson 2.00 5.00
19 A.J. Hammons 2.00 5.00
20 Dragan Bender 2.00 5.00
21 Deyonta Davis 2.00 5.00
22 Jaylen Brown 15.00 40.00
23 Demetrius Jackson 2.00 5.00
24 Cheick Diallo 2.00 5.00
25 Brice Johnson 2.00 5.00
26 Buddy Hield 6.00 15.00
27 Juan Hernangomez 4.00 10.00
28 Patrick McCaw 2.00 5.00
29 Malcolm Brogdon 6.00 15.00
30 Stephen Zimmerman 2.00 5.00

2016-17 Panini Threads Floor Generals

*DAZZLE: .75X TO 2X BASIC
*RED: .6X TO 1.5X BASIC
*HOLO: 1X TO 2.5X BASIC
*ORANGE/25: 2X TO 5X BASIC
1 James Harden 1.00 2.50
2 Ricky Rubio .40 1.00
3 Chris Paul .75 2.00
4 Kyrie Irving 1.00 2.50
5 Damian Lillard 1.25 3.00
6 Stephen Curry 4.00 10.00
7 Mark Jackson .40 1.00
8 Anfernee Hardaway 1.25 3.00
9 John Stockton .75 2.00
10 Jason Kidd .75 2.00
11 Russell Westbrook .75 2.00
12 Steve Francis .40 1.00
13 John Wall .60 1.50
14 Gary Payton .75 2.00
15 Rajon Rondo .60 1.50

2016-17 Panini Threads Front-Row Seat

*DAZZLE: .75X TO 2X BASIC
*RED: .6X TO 1.5X BASIC
*HOLO: 1X TO 2.5X BASIC
*ORANGE/25: 2X TO 5X BASIC
1 Dwyane Wade 1.00 2.50
2 Paul George .75 2.00
3 Carmelo Anthony .75 2.00
4 Kawhi Leonard 1.25 3.00
5 Damian Lillard 1.25 3.00
6 Stephen Curry 4.00 10.00
7 Al Horford .50 1.25
8 Paul Millsap .40 1.00
9 Kevin Love .50 1.25
10 DeMarcus Cousins .40 1.00
11 Mike Conley .40 1.00
12 Anthony Davis 1.50 4.00
13 Karl-Anthony Towns 1.00 2.50
14 Russell Westbrook .75 2.00
15 DeAndre Jordan .40 1.00
16 Kevin Durant 2.00 5.00
17 John Wall .60 1.50
18 Kyle Lowry .50 1.25
19 Andre Drummond .50 1.25
20 LaMarcus Aldridge .50 1.25
21 Kyrie Irving 1.00 2.50
22 James Harden 1.00 2.50
23 Marc Gasol .50 1.25
24 Chris Paul .75 2.00
25 Klay Thompson 1.25 3.00
26 LeBron James 4.00 10.00
27 Jimmy Butler 1.00 2.50
28 Draymond Green .60 1.50
29 Gordon Hayward .50 1.25
30 Blake Griffin .50 1.25

2016-17 Panini Threads Hardwood Pioneers

*DAZZLE: .75X TO 2X BASIC
*RED: .6X TO 1.5X BASIC
*HOLO: 1X TO 2.5X BASIC
*ORANGE/25: 2X TO 5X BASIC
1 Dave DeBusschere .50 1.25
2 Wilt Chamberlain 1.50 4.00
3 Elgin Baylor 1.00 2.50
4 Oscar Robertson 1.25 3.00
5 Larry Bird 2.00 5.00
6 Elvin Hayes .60 1.50
7 Jerry West 1.25 3.00
8 Lenny Wilkens .50 1.25
9 Earl Monroe .75 2.00
10 Bill Russell 1.50 4.00
11 Kareem Abdul-Jabbar 1.50 4.00
12 Magic Johnson 2.00 5.00
13 John Havlicek 1.25 3.00
14 Gail Goodrich .50 1.25
15 Julius Erving 1.25 3.00

2016-17 Panini Threads High Octane

*DAZZLE: .75X TO 2X BASIC
*RED: .6X TO 1.5X BASIC
*HOLO: 1X TO 2.5X BASIC
*ORANGE/25: 2X TO 5X BASIC
1 Allen Iverson .75 2.00
2 Derrick Rose .75 2.00
3 Spud Webb .50 1.25
4 Russell Westbrook .75 2.00
5 Manu Ginobili 1.00 2.50
6 Avery Bradley .30 .75
7 Clyde Drexler .75 2.00
8 Elfrid Payton .40 1.00
9 Isiah Thomas .75 2.00
10 Dennis Schroder .50 1.25
11 Muggsy Bogues .40 1.00
12 Eric Bledsoe .40 1.00
13 Isaiah Thomas .40 1.00
14 Dwyane Wade 1.00 2.50
15 Chris Paul .75 2.00
16 Jeff Teague .30 .75
17 Kenny Smith .40 1.00
18 Victor Oladipo .40 1.00
19 Nate Archibald .50 1.25
20 Kyrie Irving 1.00 2.50
21 James Harden 1.00 2.50
22 John Wall .60 1.50
23 Damon Stoudamire .50 1.25
24 Tony Parker .75 2.00
25 Rajon Rondo .60 1.50

2016-17 Panini Threads Materials

1 Joakim Noah 2.00 5.00
2 Adreian Payne 2.00 5.00
3 Karl-Anthony Towns 6.00 15.00
4 Al-Farouq Aminu 2.00 5.00
5 Jusuf Nurkic 2.50 6.00
6 Dante Exum 2.50 6.00
7 Rajon Rondo 4.00 10.00
8 Jeff Teague 2.00 5.00
9 LeBron James 25.00 60.00
10 Andrew Bogut 3.00 8.00
11 DeMar DeRozan 4.00 10.00
12 Marc Gasol 3.00 8.00
13 Blake Griffin 3.00 8.00
14 Dwyane Wade 6.00 15.00
15 Draymond Green 4.00 10.00
16 Eric Gordon 2.50 6.00
17 Andre Iguodala 3.00 8.00
18 Kawhi Leonard 8.00 20.00
19 James Harden 6.00 15.00
20 Deron Williams 2.50 6.00
21 Brandon Knight 2.50 6.00
22 Damian Lillard 8.00 20.00
23 DeMarcus Cousins 2.50 6.00
24 Bojan Bogdanovic 2.50 6.00
25 Anthony Davis 10.00 25.00
26 Dennis Schroder 3.00 8.00
27 D'Angelo Russell 4.00 10.00
28 Kyle Lowry 3.00 8.00
29 Derrick Favors 2.00 5.00
30 Aaron Gordon 3.00 8.00
31 Kyrie Irving 6.00 15.00
32 Andre Drummond 3.00 8.00
33 Devin Booker 12.00 30.00
34 Greg Monroe 2.00 5.00
35 Kevin Love 2.00 5.00
36 Jrue Holiday 4.00 10.00
37 Brandon Jennings 2.00 5.00
38 Ben McLemore 2.00 5.00
39 Jonas Valanciunas 2.50 6.00
40 Al Horford 3.00 8.00
41 Andrew Wiggins 4.00 10.00
42 Dwight Powell 2.00 5.00
43 DeAndre Jordan 2.50 6.00
44 Emmanuel Mudiay 2.00 5.00
45 Marcin Gortat 2.00 5.00
46 Ricky Rubio 2.50 6.00
47 John Wall 4.00 10.00
48 DeMarre Carroll 2.00 5.00
49 Goran Dragic 3.00 8.00
50 Al Jefferson 2.00 5.00
51 Dirk Nowitzki 8.00 20.00
52 Serge Ibaka 2.50 6.00
53 J.J. Barea 2.50 6.00
54 Brook Lopez 2.50 6.00
55 Kemba Walker 2.50 6.00
56 Derrick Rose 5.00 12.00
57 Elfrid Payton 2.50 6.00
58 Dwight Howard 4.00 10.00
59 Bradley Beal 4.00 10.00
60 Eric Bledsoe 2.50 6.00
61 Jeremy Lamb 2.00 5.00
62 Harrison Barnes 2.50 6.00
63 Justin Anderson 2.00 5.00
64 C.J. McCollum 3.00 8.00
65 Danilo Gallinari 2.50 6.00
66 Chris Paul 5.00 2.00
67 Darren Collison 2.00 5.00
68 Devin Harris 2.00 5.00
69 Michael Kidd-Gilchrist 2.00 5.00
70 Carmelo Anthony 5.00 2.00

2016-17 Panini Threads NBA Legends Ink

PRINT RUNS B/WN 10-99 COPIES PER
NO PRICING ON QTY 10
1 Kobe Bryant/99 800.00 1,500.00
2 Vin Baker/99 5.00 12.00
3 Bill Willoughby/99 5.00 12.00
4 Magic Johnson/99 40.00 100.00
5 Spud Webb/99 6.00 15.00
6 Walter Berry/99 4.00 10.00
7 Dan Issel/99 8.00 20.00
8 Tom Gugliotta/99 4.00 10.00
9 World B. Free/99 5.00 12.00
10 Elvin Hayes/59 8.00 20.00
11 Bob Dandridge/99 6.00 15.00
12 Sidney Moncrief/99 5.00 12.00
13 Zydrunas Ilgauskas/99 5.00 12.00
14 Kenny Anderson/49 5.00 12.00
15 Dennis Scott/49 4.00 10.00
16 Shane Battier/69 5.00 12.00
17 Vinny Del Negro/99 5.00 12.00
18 Dennis Rodman/99 40.00 100.00
19 Vernon Maxwell/49 4.00 10.00
20 Rashard Lewis/99 5.00 12.00
21 Kurt Rambis/49 6.00 15.00
22 Juwan Howard/99 5.00 12.00
23 Kevin Willis/99 4.00 10.00
24 Ron Harper/99 6.00 15.00
25 Raef LaFrentz/99 4.00 10.00
26 Larry Nance/99 5.00 12.00
27 Scottie Pippen/49 75.00 200.00
29 Avery Johnson/99 5.00 12.00
30 Kendall Gill/99 6.00 15.00

2016-17 Panini Threads Rookie Signage

PRINT RUNS B/WN 199-299 COPIES PER
1 Brandon Ingram/199 12.00 30.00
2 Jaylen Brown/199 75.00 200.00
3 Kris Dunn/199 5.00 12.00
4 Buddy Hield/299 10.00 25.00
6 Jamal Murray/199 25.00 60.00
8 Kay Felder/199 3.00 8.00
9 Marquese Chriss/199 4.00 10.00
10 Dragan Bender/199 3.00 8.00
11 Malcolm Brogdon/199 10.00 25.00
12 Denzel Valentine/299 3.00 8.00
13 Taurean Prince/299 4.00 10.00
14 DeAndre' Bembry/299 5.00 12.00
15 Brice Johnson/199 3.00 8.00
16 Wade Baldwin IV/199 3.00 8.00
17 Malachi Richardson/199 3.00 8.00
18 Juan Hernangomez/199 6.00 15.00
19 Ivica Zubac/299 8.00 20.00
20 Cheick Diallo/299 3.00 8.00
22 Henry Ellenson/199 3.00 8.00
23 Georges Niang/199 5.00 12.00
24 Jakob Poeltl/199 6.00 15.00
25 Pascal Siakam/199 20.00 50.00
26 Domantas Sabonis/199 20.00 50.00
27 Dario Saric/199 5.00 12.00
28 Damian Jones/199 3.00 8.00
29 Skal Labissiere/199 3.00 8.00
30 Diamond Stone/299 3.00 8.00
31 Paul Zipser/199 3.00 8.00
32 Demetrius Jackson/299 3.00 8.00
33 Deyonta Davis/299 3.00 8.00
34 Malik Beasley/199 6.00 15.00
35 Georgios Papagiannis/299 3.00 8.00
36 Mindaugas Kuzminskas/299 3.00 8.00
37 Thon Maker/299 4.00 10.00
38 Jake Layman/299 4.00 10.00
39 Michael Gbinije/299 3.00 8.00
40 T. Luwawu-Cabarrot/299 5.00 12.00

2016-17 Panini Threads Signage

PRINT RUNS B/WN 49-99 COPIES PER
1 C.J. McCollum/99 6.00 15.00
2 Victor Oladipo/99 5.00 12.00
3 Trey Lyles/99 5.00 12.00
4 Jason Terry/99 5.00 12.00
5 Norman Powell/99 6.00 15.00
6 Jeremy Lin/49 40.00 100.00
7 Zach LaVine/99 12.00 30.00
8 Justise Winslow/49 5.00 12.00
9 Tristan Thompson/49 5.00 12.00
10 Rondae Hollis-Jefferson/99 4.00 10.00
11 Kevin Durant/99 100.00 250.00
12 Kyrie Irving/99 25.00 60.00
13 Blake Griffin/49 10.00 25.00
14 Jabari Parker/75 4.00 10.00
15 Andrew Wiggins/99 15.00 40.00
16 Isaiah Thomas/49 5.00 12.00
17 Karl-Anthony Towns/99 25.00 60.00
18 Carmelo Anthony/49 40.00 100.00
19 Kristaps Porzingis/99 12.00 30.00
20 Kobe Bryant/99 1,000.00 2,000.00
21 Marc Gasol/49 6.00 15.00
22 Myles Turner/75 6.00 15.00
23 Devin Booker/49 150.00 400.00
24 John Wall/49 12.00 30.00
25 Andre Drummond/99 6.00 15.00
26 Anthony Davis/49 60.00 150.00
27 J.J. Barea/99 5.00 12.00
28 Sean Kilpatrick/99 4.00 10.00
29 Al Horford/49 6.00 15.00
30 E'Twaun Moore/99 4.00 10.00

2016-17 Panini Threads Swingmen

1 LeBron James 40.00 100.00
2 Gordon Hayward 5.00 12.00
3 Nicolas Batum 4.00 10.00
4 Larry Bird 20.00 50.00
5 Klay Thompson 12.00 30.00
6 Julius Erving 12.00 30.00
7 Andre Iguodala 5.00 12.00
8 Andrew Wiggins 6.00 15.00
9 Kevin Durant 20.00 50.00
10 Otto Porter 4.00 10.00
11 Paul George 8.00 20.00
12 Kobe Bryant 40.00 100.00
13 Carmelo Anthony 8.00 20.00
14 Jerry West 12.00 30.00
15 Giannis Antetokounmpo 25.00 60.00
16 Scottie Pippen 10.00 25.00
17 DeMar DeRozan 6.00 15.00
18 Tobias Harris 5.00 12.00
19 Kawhi Leonard 12.00 30.00
20 Harrison Barnes 4.00 10.00

2016-17 Panini Threads Team Threads Die Cuts

1 Dwyane Wade 4.00 10.00
2 Kyrie Irving 4.00 10.00
3 Isaiah Thomas 1.50 4.00
4 Avery Bradley 1.25 3.00
5 Blake Griffin 2.00 5.00
6 Justise Winslow 1.50 4.00
7 Carmelo Anthony 3.00 8.00
8 Kristaps Porzingis 3.00 8.00
9 Jordan Clarkson 2.00 5.00
10 Jeremy Lin 4.00 10.00
11 Anthony Davis 6.00 15.00
12 Jrue Holiday 2.50 6.00
13 DeMar DeRozan 2.50 6.00
14 Ryan Anderson 1.25 3.00
15 Devin Booker 8.00 20.00
16 Andrew Wiggins 2.50 6.00
17 Karl-Anthony Towns 4.00 10.00
18 Stephen Curry 15.00 40.00
19 Kevin Durant 8.00 20.00
20 John Wall 2.50 6.00
21 Joel Embiid 5.00 12.00
22 Robert Covington 1.50 4.00
23 Giannis Antetokounmpo 10.00 25.00
24 Jabari Parker 1.25 3.00
25 Jimmy Butler 4.00 10.00
26 LeBron James 15.00 40.00
27 Chris Paul 3.00 8.00
28 Marc Gasol 2.00 5.00
29 Mike Conley 1.50 4.00
30 Dwight Howard 2.50 6.00
31 Dennis Schroder 2.00 5.00
32 Goran Dragic 2.00 5.00
33 Frank Kaminsky 1.25 3.00
34 Kemba Walker 1.50 4.00
35 Gordon Hayward 2.00 5.00
36 Rodney Hood 1.50 4.00
37 DeMarcus Cousins 1.50 4.00
38 Rudy Gay 2.00 5.00
39 Aaron Gordon 2.00 5.00
40 Serge Ibaka 1.50 4.00
41 Deron Williams 1.50 4.00
42 Dirk Nowitzki 5.00 12.00
43 Brook Lopez 1.50 4.00
44 Danilo Gallinari 1.50 4.00
45 Nikola Jokic 30.00 80.00
46 Paul George 3.00 8.00
47 Jeff Teague 1.25 3.00
48 Reggie Jackson 1.50 4.00
49 Andre Drummond 2.00 5.00
50 Kyle Lowry 2.00 5.00
51 James Harden 4.00 10.00
52 Kawhi Leonard 5.00 12.00
53 LaMarcus Aldridge 2.00 5.00
54 Eric Bledsoe 1.50 4.00
55 Russell Westbrook 3.00 8.00
56 Steven Adams 1.50 4.00
57 Damian Lillard 5.00 12.00
58 C.J. McCollum 2.00 5.00
59 Markieff Morris 1.25 3.00
60 D'Angelo Russell 2.50 6.00

2016-17 Panini Threads Team Threads Die Cuts Autographs

STATED PRINT RUN 99 SER.#'d SETS
1 Dwyane Wade 75.00 200.00
2 Kyrie Irving 75.00 200.00
3 Isaiah Thomas 10.00 25.00
4 Avery Bradley 3.00 8.00
5 Blake Griffin 10.00 25.00
6 Justise Winslow 4.00 10.00
7 Carmelo Anthony 60.00 150.00
8 Kristaps Porzingis 20.00 50.00
9 Jordan Clarkson 20.00 50.00
10 Jeremy Lin 60.00 150.00
11 Anthony Davis 60.00 150.00
12 Jrue Holiday 25.00 60.00
13 DeMar DeRozan 20.00 50.00
14 Ryan Anderson 3.00 8.00
15 Devin Booker 100.00 250.00
16 Andrew Wiggins 25.00 60.00
17 Karl-Anthony Towns 40.00 100.00
18 Stephen Curry 800.00 1,500.00
19 Kevin Durant 150.00 400.00
20 John Wall 15.00 40.00

2016-17 Panini Threads Team Threads Rookie Die Cuts

1 Brandon Ingram 5.00 12.00
2 Jaylen Brown 15.00 40.00
3 Kris Dunn 2.00 5.00
4 Buddy Hield 4.00 10.00
5 Patrick McCaw 1.25 3.00
6 Jamal Murray 10.00 25.00
7 Tyler Ulis 1.50 4.00
8 Kay Felder 1.25 3.00
9 Marquese Chriss 1.50 4.00
10 Dragan Bender 1.25 3.00
11 Malcolm Brogdon 4.00 10.00
12 Denzel Valentine 1.25 3.00
13 Taurean Prince 1.50 4.00
14 DeAndre' Bembry 2.00 5.00
15 Brice Johnson 1.25 3.00
16 Wade Baldwin IV 1.25 3.00
17 Malachi Richardson 1.25 3.00
18 Juan Hernangomez 2.50 6.00
19 Ivica Zubac 3.00 8.00
20 Cheick Diallo 1.25 3.00
21 Jakob Poeltl 2.50 6.00
22 Pascal Siakam 8.00 20.00
23 Domantas Sabonis 8.00 20.00
24 Dario Saric 2.00 5.00
25 Damian Jones 1.25 3.00
26 Skal Labissiere 1.25 3.00
27 Demetrius Jackson 1.25 3.00
28 Deyonta Davis 1.25 3.00
29 Malik Beasley 2.50 6.00
30 Tomas Satoransky 2.00 5.00
31 Thon Maker 1.50 4.00
32 Chinanu Onuaku 1.25 3.00
33 Dorian Finney-Smith 1.50 4.00
34 Caris LeVert 3.00 8.00
35 Henry Ellenson 1.25 3.00
36 Georges Niang 2.00 5.00
37 Diamond Stone 1.25 3.00
38 Paul Zipser 1.25 3.00
39 Georgios Papagiannis 1.25 3.00
40 Ben Simmons 4.00 10.00

2016-17 Panini Threads Team Threads Rookie Die Cuts Autographs

STATED PRINT RUN 199 SER.#'d SETS
1 Brandon Ingram 12.00 30.00
2 Jaylen Brown 75.00 200.00
3 Kris Dunn 5.00 12.00
4 Buddy Hield 10.00 25.00
5 Patrick McCaw 3.00 8.00
6 Jamal Murray 25.00 60.00
7 Tyler Ulis 4.00 10.00
8 Kay Felder 3.00 8.00
9 Marquese Chriss 4.00 10.00
10 Dragan Bender 3.00 8.00
11 Malcolm Brogdon 10.00 25.00
12 Denzel Valentine 3.00 8.00
13 Taurean Prince 4.00 10.00
14 DeAndre' Bembry 5.00 12.00
15 Brice Johnson 3.00 8.00
16 Wade Baldwin IV 3.00 8.00
17 Malachi Richardson 3.00 8.00
18 Juan Hernangomez 6.00 15.00
19 Ivica Zubac 8.00 20.00
20 Cheick Diallo 3.00 8.00
21 Jakob Poeltl 6.00 15.00
22 Pascal Siakam 20.00 50.00
23 Domantas Sabonis 20.00 50.00
24 Dario Saric 5.00 12.00
25 Damian Jones 3.00 8.00
26 Skal Labissiere 3.00 8.00
27 Demetrius Jackson 3.00 8.00
28 Deyonta Davis 3.00 8.00
29 Malik Beasley 6.00 15.00
30 Tomas Satoransky 5.00 12.00
31 Thon Maker 4.00 10.00
32 Chinanu Onuaku 3.00 8.00
33 Dorian Finney-Smith 4.00 10.00

2016-17 Panini Threads The Rooks

1 Skal Labissiere 3.00 8.00
2 Taurean Prince 4.00 10.00
3 Jakob Poeltl 6.00 15.00
4 Deyonta Davis 3.00 8.00
5 Dejounte Murray 15.00 40.00
6 Jamal Murray 25.00 60.00
7 Pascal Siakam 20.00 50.00
8 Domantas Sabonis 20.00 50.00
9 Dario Saric 5.00 12.00
10 Ben Simmons 10.00 25.00
11 Cheick Diallo 3.00 8.00
12 Malik Beasley 6.00 15.00
13 Juan Hernangomez 6.00 15.00
14 Brandon Ingram 12.00 30.00
15 Tyler Ulis 4.00 10.00
16 Georgios Papagiannis 3.00 8.00
17 Ivica Zubac 8.00 20.00
18 Henry Ellenson 3.00 8.00
19 Denzel Valentine 3.00 8.00
20 Malcolm Brogdon 10.00 25.00
21 Dragan Bender 3.00 8.00
22 Brice Johnson 3.00 8.00
23 Patrick McCaw 3.00 8.00
24 Diamond Stone 3.00 8.00
25 Kris Dunn 5.00 12.00
26 Caris LeVert 8.00 20.00
27 Jaylen Brown 25.00 60.00
28 Damian Jones 3.00 8.00
29 Malachi Richardson 3.00 8.00
30 Buddy Hield 10.00 25.00
31 Isaiah Whitehead 3.00 8.00
32 Stephen Zimmerman 3.00 8.00
33 Timothe Luwawu-Cabarrot 5.00 12.00
34 Marquese Chriss 4.00 10.00
35 Thon Maker 4.00 10.00

2017-18 Panini Threads

COMPLETE SET (100) 25.00 60.00
1 Damian Lillard 1.00 2.50
2 Draymond Green .50 1.25
3 Kyle Lowry .40 1.00
4 DeAndre Jordan .30 .75
5 Hassan Whiteside .30 .75
6 Dennis Schroder .30 .75
7 Anthony Davis 1.00 2.50
8 Zach LaVine .60 1.50
9 Russell Westbrook .60 1.50
10 Jamal Murray .60 1.50
11 CJ McCollum .40 1.00
12 Kevin Durant 1.50 4.00
13 DeMar DeRozan .50 1.25
14 Brandon Ingram .50 1.25
15 Giannis Antetokounmpo 2.00 5.00
16 Kyrie Irving .75 2.00
17 DeMarcus Cousins .30 .75
18 LeBron James 3.00 8.00
19 Aaron Gordon .40 1.00
20 Nikola Jokic 2.50 6.00
21 Zach Randolph .40 1.00
22 James Harden .75 2.00
23 Rodney Hood .25 .60
24 Kentavious Caldwell-Pope .30 .75
25 Eric Bledsoe .30 .75
26 Jaylen Brown 1.00 2.50
27 Tim Hardaway Jr. .30 .75
28 Kevin Love .40 1.00
29 Ben Simmons .40 1.00
30 Tobias Harris .30 .75
31 Pau Gasol .60 1.50
32 Chris Paul .60 1.50
33 John Wall .50 1.25
34 Mike Conley .30 .75
35 Jimmy Butler .60 1.50
36 D'Angelo Russell .30 .75
37 Kristaps Porzingis .50 1.25
38 Dwyane Wade .75 2.00
39 Joel Embiid .75 2.00
40 Andre Drummond .30 .75
41 LaMarcus Aldridge .40 1.00
42 Victor Oladipo .30 .75
43 Bradley Beal .50 1.25
44 Marc Gasol .40 1.00
45 Andrew Wiggins .50 1.25
46 Kemba Walker .30 .75
47 Carmelo Anthony .60 1.50
48 Harrison Barnes .30 .75
49 Devin Booker 1.00 2.50
50 Stephen Curry 3.00 8.00
51 Manu Ginobili .75 2.00
52 Blake Griffin .40 1.00
53 Marcin Gortat .25 .60
54 Goran Dragic .30 .75
55 Karl-Anthony Towns .60 1.50
56 Dwight Howard .50 1.25
57 Paul George .60 1.50
58 Dirk Nowitzki 1.00 2.50
59 TJ Warren .30 .75
60 Klay Thompson 1.00 2.50
61 Bam Adebayo RC 3.00 8.00
62 Cedi Osman RC 1.00 2.50
63 Guerschon Yabusele RC .50 1.25
64 Bogdan Bogdanovic RC 1.25 3.00
65 Frank Jackson RC .50 1.25
66 Frank Ntilikina RC .60 1.50
67 Brandon Paul RC .50 1.25
68 Lonzo Ball RC 2.00 5.00
69 Josh Hart RC 1.25 3.00
70 Dillon Brooks RC 1.50 4.00
71 Jordan Bell RC .50 1.25
72 Josh Jackson RC .60 1.50
73 Ivan Rabb RC .50 1.25
74 Justin Jackson RC .50 1.25
75 Zach Collins RC .75 2.00
76 Sindarius Thornwell RC .50 1.25
77 Daniel Theis RC 1.00 2.50
78 Jayson Tatum RC 12.00 30.00
79 Maxi Kleber RC .75 2.00
80 Dennis Smith Jr. RC .60 1.50
81 Markelle Fultz RC 1.25 3.00
82 John Collins RC 1.25 3.00
83 Justin Patton RC .50 1.25
84 OG Anunoby RC 2.50 6.00
85 Terrance Ferguson RC .50 1.25
86 Jonathan Isaac RC 1.25 3.00
87 TJ Leaf RC .50 1.25
88 Kyle Kuzma RC 2.00 5.00
89 Frank Mason III RC .50 1.25
90 De'Aaron Fox RC 4.00 10.00
91 Zhou Qi RC 1.00 2.50
92 Dwayne Bacon RC .50 1.25
93 Harry Giles RC .50 1.25
94 Malik Monk RC 2.00 5.00
95 Jarrett Allen RC 1.25 3.00
96 Semi Ojeleye RC .60 1.50
97 Luke Kennard RC 1.00 2.50
98 Donovan Mitchell RC 5.00 12.00
99 Caleb Swanigan RC .50 1.25
100 Lauri Markkanen RC 3.00 8.00

2017-18 Panini Threads Dazzle

*DAZZLE: 1X TO 2.5X BASIC
*DAZZLE RC: .6X TO 1.5X BASIC
STATED PRINT RUN 199 SER.#'d SETS
78 Jayson Tatum 6.00 15.00
98 Donovan Mitchell 10.00 25.00

2017-18 Panini Threads Dazzle Blue

*DAZ BLUE: 2X TO 5X BASIC
*DAZ BLUE RC: 1X TO 2.5X BASIC
STATED PRINT RUN 25 SER.#'d SETS
18 LeBron James 75.00 200.00
78 Jayson Tatum 12.00 30.00
98 Donovan Mitchell 20.00 50.00

2017-18 Panini Threads Dazzle Red

*DAZ RED: 1.2X TO 3X BASIC
*DAZ RED RC: .75X TO 2X BASIC
STATED PRINT RUN 99 SER.#'d SETS
18 LeBron James 20.00 50.00
78 Jayson Tatum 8.00 20.00
98 Donovan Mitchell 12.00 30.00

2017-18 Panini Titanium Draft Pick

PRINT RUNS B/WN 1-60 COPIES PER
NO PRICING ON QTY 16 OR LESS
202 Ike Anigbogu/47 3.00 8.00
206 Sterling Brown/46 3.00 8.00
208 Wayne Selden Jr./60 3.00 8.00
209 Cedi Osman/31 6.00 15.00
210 Dwayne Bacon/40 3.00 8.00
212 Jawun Evans/39 3.00 8.00
216 Tony Bradley/28 3.00 8.00
218 Zhou Qi/43 25.00 60.00
219 Davon Reed/32 3.00 8.00
220 Frank Mason III/34 3.00 8.00
222 Jordan Bell/38 3.00 8.00
224 Dillon Brooks/45 10.00 25.00

2017-18 Panini Titanium Jersey Number

PRINT RUNS B/WN 1-99 COPIES PER
NO PRICING ON QTY 16 OR LESS
203 Jayson Tatum/99 30.00 80.00
204 Justin Patton/24 3.00 8.00
205 Lauri Markkanen/24 75.00 200.00
206 Sterling Brown/23 3.00 8.00
219 Davon Reed/32 3.00 8.00
223 Josh Jackson/20 4.00 10.00
224 Dillon Brooks/24 10.00 25.00

2017-18 Panini Threads Box Topper Memorabilia

*JUMBO: .6X TO 1.5X BASIC
1 Grant Hill 5.00 12.00
2 Ricky Rubio 2.50 6.00
3 Jameer Nelson 2.00 5.00
4 Gordon Hayward 2.50 6.00
5 Larry Bird 12.00 30.00
6 Rudy Gobert 4.00 10.00
7 Nikola Vucevic 2.50 6.00
8 Andrew Wiggins 4.00 10.00
9 Rodney Hood 2.00 5.00
10 Zach LaVine 5.00 12.00
11 Brook Lopez 2.50 6.00
12 Dirk Nowitzki 10.00 25.00
13 Noah Vonleh 2.00 5.00
14 Derrick Favors 2.00 5.00
15 John Wall 4.00 10.00
16 Carmelo Anthony 5.00 12.00
17 Kris Dunn 2.00 5.00
18 Karl-Anthony Towns 5.00 12.00
19 Shaquille O'Neal 10.00 25.00
20 Gorgui Dieng 2.00 5.00
21 Kenneth Faried 2.50 6.00
22 Kevin Garnett 6.00 15.00
23 Kyrie Irving 10.00 25.00
24 Kobe Bryant 10.00 25.00
25 Damian Lillard 8.00 20.00

2017-18 Panini Threads Box Topper Rookie Memorabilia

*JUMBO: .6X TO 1.5X BASIC
1 Caleb Swanigan 2.00 5.00
2 De'Aaron Fox 15.00 40.00
3 Dennis Smith Jr. 2.50 6.00
4 Derrick White 8.00 20.00
5 Donovan Mitchell 12.00 30.00
6 Frank Jackson 2.00 5.00
7 Frank Ntilikina 2.50 6.00
8 Jarrett Allen 5.00 12.00
9 Jawun Evans 2.00 5.00
10 Jayson Tatum 15.00 40.00
11 John Collins 5.00 12.00
12 Jordan Bell 2.00 5.00
13 Josh Jackson 2.50 6.00
14 Justin Patton 2.00 5.00
15 Lonzo Ball 8.00 20.00
16 Luke Kennard 4.00 10.00
17 Malik Monk 4.00 10.00
18 Markelle Fultz 6.00 15.00
19 OG Anunoby 10.00 25.00
20 Sterling Brown 2.00 5.00
21 TJ Leaf 2.00 5.00
22 Tony Bradley 2.00 5.00
23 Tyler Dorsey 2.00 5.00
24 Tyler Lydon 2.00 5.00
25 Zach Collins 3.00 8.00

2018-19 Panini Threads

1 Joel Embiid 1.00 2.50
2 Ben Simmons .40 1.00
3 Jimmy Butler .60 1.50
4 JJ Redick .40 1.00
5 Giannis Antetokounmpo 2.00 5.00
6 Khris Middleton .40 1.00
7 Eric Bledsoe .30 .75
8 Brook Lopez .30 .75
9 Zach LaVine .60 1.50
10 Lauri Markkanen .60 1.50
11 Jabari Parker .25 .60
12 Kris Dunn .25 .60
13 Kevin Love .30 .75
14 Tristan Thompson .25 .60
15 Cedi Osman .30 .75
16 Kyrie Irving 1.00 2.50
17 Jayson Tatum 1.50 4.00
18 Jaylen Brown .60 1.50
19 Gordon Hayward .40 1.00
20 Montrezl Harrell .40 1.00
21 Tobias Harris .30 .75
22 Danilo Gallinari .30 .75
23 Lou Williams .30 .75
24 Mike Conley .30 .75
25 Marc Gasol .40 1.00
26 Jeremy Lin .60 1.50
27 Vince Carter .75 2.00
28 Taurean Prince .25 .60
29 Dwyane Wade .75 2.00
30 Josh Richardson .30 .75
31 Goran Dragic .30 .75
32 Rodney McGruder .25 .60
33 Kemba Walker .30 .75
34 Joakim Noah .25 .60
35 Marvin Williams .25 .60
36 Jeremy Lamb .25 .60
37 Donovan Mitchell 1.25 3.00
38 Ricky Rubio .30 .75
39 Rudy Gobert .50 1.25
40 Joe Ingles .30 .75
41 De'Aaron Fox .75 2.00
42 Willie Cauley-Stein .25 .60
43 Buddy Hield .40 1.00
44 Kristaps Porzingis .50 1.25
45 DeAndre Jordan .30 .75
46 Tim Hardaway Jr. .25 .60
47 LeBron James 3.00 8.00
48 Brandon Ingram .40 1.00
49 Kyle Kuzma .40 1.00
50 Lonzo Ball .40 1.00
51 Jonathan Isaac .40 1.00
52 Nikola Vucevic .30 .75
53 Aaron Gordon .40 1.00
54 Dirk Nowitzki 1.00 2.50
55 Harrison Barnes .30 .75
56 Dennis Smith Jr. .25 .60
57 D'Angelo Russell .40 1.00
58 Caris LeVert .40 1.00
59 Jarrett Allen .40 1.00
60 Nikola Jokic 2.00 5.00
61 Jamal Murray .75 2.00
62 Gary Harris .30 .75
63 Domantas Sabonis .50 1.25
64 Victor Oladipo .30 .75
65 Myles Turner .40 1.00
66 Anthony Davis 1.00 2.50

67 Jrue Holiday .50 1.25
68 Julius Randle .40 1.00
69 Nikola Mirotic .25 .60
70 Blake Griffin .40 1.00
71 Andre Drummond .30 .75
72 Reggie Jackson .30 .75
73 Kawhi Leonard 1.00 2.50
74 Kyle Lowry .40 1.00
75 Pascal Siakam .60 1.50
76 James Harden .75 2.00
77 Chris Paul .75 2.00
78 Clint Capela .30 .75
79 LaMarcus Aldridge .40 1.00
80 DeMar DeRozan .50 1.25
81 Pau Gasol .60 1.50
82 Bryn Forbes .30 .75
83 Devin Booker 1.00 2.50
84 Josh Jackson .25 .60
85 T.J. Warren .30 .75
86 Russell Westbrook .60 1.50
87 Paul George .60 1.50
88 Steven Adams .30 .75
89 Andrew Wiggins .50 1.25
90 Karl-Anthony Towns .60 1.50
91 Robert Covington .30 .75
92 Damian Lillard 1.00 2.50
93 CJ McCollum .40 1.00
94 Jusuf Nurkic .30 .75
95 Stephen Curry 3.00 8.00
96 Kevin Durant 1.50 4.00
97 Klay Thompson 1.00 2.50
98 John Wall .50 1.25
99 Bradley Beal .50 1.25
100 Trevor Ariza .25 .60
101 Luka Doncic ASOC RC 20.00 50.00
102 Deandre Ayton ASOC RC 1.50 4.00
103 Trae Young ASOC RC 4.00 10.00
104 Marvin Bagley III ASOC RC .75 2.00
105 Kevin Knox ASOC RC .60 1.50
106 Jaren Jackson Jr. ASOC RC 4.00 10.00
107 Wendell Carter Jr. ASOC RC 1.25 3.00
108 Allonzo Trier ASOC RC .50 1.25
109 Mo Bamba ASOC RC .75 2.00
110 Collin Sexton ASOC RC 1.50 4.00
111 Shai Gilgeous-Alexander ASOC RC 12.00 30.00
112 Michael Porter Jr. ASOC RC 2.00 5.00
113 Miles Bridges ASOC RC 1.25 3.00
114 Mikal Bridges ASOC RC 2.50 6.00
115 Donte DiVincenzo ASOC RC 1.25 3.00
116 Kevin Huerter ASOC RC 1.00 2.50
117 Grayson Allen ASOC RC 1.00 2.50
118 Josh Okogie ASOC RC .75 2.00
119 Mitchell Robinson ASOC RC 1.25 3.00
120 Landry Shamet ASOC RC .75 2.00
121 Troy Brown Jr. ASOC RC .60 1.50
122 Jerome Robinson ASOC RC .50 1.25
123 Omari Spellman ASOC RC .50 1.25
124 Jalen Brunson ASOC RC 4.00 10.00
125 Hamidou Diallo ASOC RC .75 2.00
126 Aaron Holiday ASOC RC .75 2.00
127 Jacob Evans III ASOC RC .50 1.25
128 Chandler Hutchison ASOC RC .60 1.50
129 Lonnie Walker IV ASOC RC 1.00 2.50
130 Zhaire Smith ASOC RC .50 1.25
131 Kobe Bryant ASOC SP 6.00 15.00
132 Kevin Durant ASOC SP 3.00 8.00
133 Kyrie Irving ASOC SP 2.00 5.00
134 Stephen Curry ASOC SP 6.00 15.00
135 LeBron James ASOC SP 6.00 15.00
136 Ben Simmons ASOC SP .75 2.00
137 James Harden ASOC SP 1.50 4.00
138 Russell Westbrook ASOC SP 1.25 3.00
139 Anthony Davis ASOC SP 2.00 5.00
140 Giannis Antetokounmpo ASOC SP 4.00 10.00
141 Luka Doncic ICON 8.00 20.00
142 Deandre Ayton ICON 1.50 4.00
143 Trae Young ICON 4.00 10.00
144 Marvin Bagley III ICON .75 2.00
145 Kevin Knox ICON .60 1.50
146 Jaren Jackson Jr. ICON 4.00 10.00
147 Wendell Carter Jr. ICON 1.25 3.00
148 Allonzo Trier ICON .50 1.25
149 Mo Bamba ICON .75 2.00
150 Collin Sexton ICON 1.50 4.00
151 Shai Gilgeous-Alexander ICON 5.00 12.00
152 Michael Porter Jr. ICON 2.00 5.00
153 Miles Bridges ICON 1.25 3.00
154 Mikal Bridges ICON 2.50 6.00
155 Donte DiVincenzo ICON 1.25 3.00
156 Kevin Huerter ICON 1.00 2.50
157 Grayson Allen ICON 1.00 2.50
158 Josh Okogie ICON .75 2.00
159 Mitchell Robinson ICON 1.25 3.00
160 Landry Shamet ICON .75 2.00
161 Troy Brown Jr. ICON .60 1.50
162 Jerome Robinson ICON .50 1.25
163 Omari Spellman ICON .50 1.25
164 Jalen Brunson ICON 4.00 10.00
165 Hamidou Diallo ICON .75 2.00
166 Aaron Holiday ICON .75 2.00
167 Jacob Evans III ICON .50 1.25
168 Chandler Hutchison ICON .60 1.50
169 Lonnie Walker IV ICON 1.00 2.50
170 Zhaire Smith ICON .50 1.25
171 Kobe Bryant ICON SP 6.00 15.00
172 Kevin Durant ICON SP 3.00 8.00
173 Kyrie Irving ICON SP 2.00 5.00
174 Stephen Curry ICON SP 6.00 15.00
175 LeBron James ICON SP 6.00 15.00
176 Ben Simmons ICON SP .75 2.00
177 James Harden ICON SP 1.50 4.00
178 Russell Westbrook ICON SP 1.25 3.00
179 Anthony Davis ICON SP 2.00 5.00
180 Giannis Antetokounmpo ICON SP 4.00 10.00
181 Luka Doncic STAT 8.00 20.00
182 Deandre Ayton STAT 1.50 4.00
183 Trae Young STAT 4.00 10.00
184 Marvin Bagley III STAT .75 2.00
185 Kevin Knox STAT .60 1.50
186 Jaren Jackson Jr. STAT 4.00 10.00
187 Wendell Carter Jr. STAT 1.25 3.00
188 Allonzo Trier STAT .50 1.25
189 Mo Bamba STAT .75 2.00
190 Collin Sexton STAT 1.50 4.00
191 Shai Gilgeous-Alexander STAT 5.00 12.00
192 Michael Porter Jr. STAT 2.00 5.00
193 Miles Bridges STAT 1.25 3.00
194 Mikal Bridges STAT 2.50 6.00
195 Donte DiVincenzo STAT 1.25 3.00
196 Kevin Huerter STAT 1.00 2.50
197 Grayson Allen STAT 1.00 2.50
198 Josh Okogie STAT .75 2.00
199 Mitchell Robinson STAT 1.25 3.00
200 Landry Shamet STAT .75 2.00
201 Troy Brown Jr. STAT .60 1.50
202 Jerome Robinson STAT .50 1.25
203 Omari Spellman STAT .50 1.25
204 Jalen Brunson STAT 4.00 10.00
205 Hamidou Diallo STAT .75 2.00
206 Aaron Holiday STAT .75 2.00
207 Jacob Evans III STAT .50 1.25
208 Chandler Hutchison STAT .60 1.50
209 Lonnie Walker IV STAT 1.00 2.50
210 Zhaire Smith STAT .50 1.25
211 Kobe Bryant STAT SP 6.00 15.00
212 Kevin Durant STAT SP 3.00 8.00
213 Kyrie Irving STAT SP 2.00 5.00
214 Stephen Curry STAT SP 6.00 15.00
215 LeBron James STAT SP 6.00 15.00
216 Ben Simmons STAT SP .75 2.00
217 James Harden STAT SP 1.50 4.00
218 Russell Westbrook STAT SP 1.25 3.00
219 Anthony Davis STAT SP 2.00 5.00
220 Giannis Antetokounmpo STAT SP 4.00 10.00

2018-19 Panini Threads Dazzle
*DAZZLE: .5X TO 1.2X BASIC
*DAZZLE RC: .5X TO 1.2X BASIC
101 Luka Doncic ASOC 15.00 40.00
141 Luka Doncic ICON 20.00 50.00
181 Luka Doncic STAT 20.00 50.00

2018-19 Panini Threads Premium
*PREM: 1.2X TO 3X BASIC
*PREM RC: .6X TO 1.5X BASIC
*PREM SP: .6X TO 1.5X BASIC
STATED PRINT RUN 199 SER.#'d SETS
101 Luka Doncic ASOC 20.00 50.00

2018-19 Panini Threads Premium Blue
*PREM BLU: 1.5X TO 4X BASIC
*PREM RC: .75X TO 2X BASIC
*PREM SP: .75X TO 2X BASIC
STATED PRINT RUN 75 SER.#'d SETS
101 Luka Doncic ASOC 75.00 200.00
103 Trae Young ASOC 30.00 80.00

2018-19 Panini Threads Authentic Threads
1 Aaron Gordon 3.00 8.00
2 Andre Drummond 2.50 6.00
3 Andrew Wiggins 4.00 10.00
4 Anthony Davis 8.00 20.00
5 Ben Simmons 3.00 8.00
6 Bradley Beal 4.00 10.00
7 Brandon Ingram 3.00 8.00
8 Buddy Hield 3.00 8.00
9 Chris Paul 6.00 15.00
10 CJ McCollum 3.00 8.00
11 Damian Lillard 8.00 20.00
12 D'Angelo Russell 3.00 8.00
13 De'Aaron Fox 6.00 15.00
14 DeMar DeRozan 4.00 10.00
15 Dennis Smith Jr. 2.00 5.00
16 Devin Booker 8.00 20.00
17 Dirk Nowitzki 8.00 20.00
18 Donovan Mitchell 10.00 25.00
19 Draymond Green 4.00 10.00
20 Dwyane Wade 6.00 15.00
21 Fred VanVleet 4.00 10.00
22 Giannis Antetokounmpo 15.00 40.00
23 Gordon Hayward 3.00 8.00
24 Jamal Murray 6.00 15.00
25 James Harden 6.00 15.00
26 Jarrett Allen 3.00 8.00
27 Jaylen Brown 5.00 12.00
28 Jayson Tatum 12.00 30.00
29 Joe Ingles 2.50 6.00
30 Joel Embiid 8.00 20.00
31 John Wall 4.00 10.00
32 Josh Jackson 2.00 5.00
33 Karl-Anthony Towns 5.00 12.00
34 Kawhi Leonard 8.00 20.00
35 Kemba Walker 2.50 6.00
36 Kevin Durant 12.00 30.00
37 Kevin Love 2.50 6.00
38 Klay Thompson 8.00 20.00
39 Kristaps Porzingis 4.00 10.00
40 Kyle Kuzma 3.00 8.00
41 Kyrie Irving 8.00 20.00
42 LaMarcus Aldridge 3.00 8.00
43 Lauri Markkanen 5.00 12.00
44 LeBron James 25.00 60.00
46 Marc Gasol 3.00 8.00
47 Mike Conley 2.50 6.00
48 Nikola Jokic 15.00 40.00
49 Otto Porter Jr. 2.50 6.00
50 Pau Gasol 5.00 12.00
51 Paul George 5.00 12.00
52 Ricky Rubio 2.50 6.00
53 Rudy Gobert 4.00 10.00
54 Russell Westbrook 5.00 12.00
55 Stephen Curry 25.00 60.00
56 Tim Hardaway Jr. 2.00 5.00
57 Tony Parker 5.00 12.00
58 Victor Oladipo 2.50 6.00
59 Vince Carter 6.00 15.00
60 Zach LaVine 5.00 12.00

2018-19 Panini Threads Automatic
*DAZZLE: .5X TO 1.2X BASIC
1 Stephen Curry 6.00 15.00
2 Kyrie Irving 2.00 5.00
3 Russell Westbrook 1.25 3.00
4 James Harden 1.50 4.00
5 Anthony Davis 2.00 5.00
6 Kevin Durant 3.00 8.00
7 LeBron James 6.00 15.00
8 Dirk Nowitzki 2.00 5.00
9 Giannis Antetokounmpo 4.00 10.00
10 Kawhi Leonard 2.00 5.00

2018-19 Panini Threads Board of Directors
*DAZZLE: .5X TO 1.2X BASIC
*PREM: .6X TO 1.5X BASIC
*PREM BLU: .8X TO 2X BASIC
1 Andre Drummond .60 1.50
2 DeAndre Jordan .60 1.50
3 Joel Embiid 2.00 5.00
4 Giannis Antetokounmpo 4.00 10.00
5 Rudy Gobert 1.00 2.50
6 Anthony Davis 2.00 5.00
7 Karl-Anthony Towns 1.25 3.00
8 Steven Adams .60 1.50
9 Jusuf Nurkic .60 1.50
10 LaMarcus Aldridge .75 2.00
11 Blake Griffin .75 2.00
12 Marc Gasol .75 2.00
13 Julius Randle .75 2.00
14 Bam Adebayo 1.25 3.00
15 Aaron Gordon .75 2.00

2018-19 Panini Threads Bringing Down the House
*DAZZLE: .5X TO 1.2X BASIC
1 Joel Embiid 2.00 5.00
2 LeBron James 6.00 15.00
3 Russell Westbrook 1.25 3.00
4 Giannis Antetokounmpo 4.00 10.00
5 Rudy Gobert 1.00 2.50
6 Zach LaVine 1.25 3.00
7 Victor Oladipo .60 1.50
8 Donovan Mitchell 2.50 6.00
9 Kevin Durant 3.00 8.00
10 Ben Simmons .75 2.00

2018-19 Panini Threads Century Collection
*DAZZLE: .5X TO 1.2X BASIC
1 Kobe Bryant 6.00 15.00
2 Larry Bird 3.00 8.00
3 Magic Johnson 3.00 8.00
4 Julius Erving 2.00 5.00
5 Bill Russell 2.50 6.00
6 Kareem Abdul-Jabbar 2.50 6.00
7 Scottie Pippen 2.00 5.00
8 Karl Malone 1.50 4.00
9 Shaquille O'Neal 2.50 6.00
10 Allen Iverson 2.00 5.00
11 Wilt Chamberlain 2.50 6.00
12 David Robinson 1.50 4.00
13 John Stockton 1.50 4.00
14 Charles Barkley 1.50 4.00
15 Hakeem Olajuwon 1.00 2.50
16 Oscar Robertson 1.50 4.00
17 Kevin Durant 3.00 8.00
18 LeBron James 6.00 15.00
19 Stephen Curry 6.00 15.00
20 Russell Westbrook 1.25 3.00

2018-19 Panini Threads Century Collection Dazzle
*DAZZLE: .5X TO 1.2X BASIC
14 Charles Barkley 10.00 25.00

2018-19 Panini Threads Floor Generals
*DAZZLE: .5X TO 1.2X BASIC
*PREM: .6X TO 1.5X BASIC
*PREM BLU: .8X TO 2X BASIC
1 Damian Lillard 2.00 5.00
2 Luka Doncic 20.00 50.00
3 Devin Booker 2.00 5.00
4 Trae Young 8.00 20.00
5 Lonzo Ball .75 2.00
6 Ricky Rubio .60 1.50
7 Eric Bledsoe .60 1.50
8 Kyle Lowry .75 2.00
9 Jamal Murray 1.50 4.00
10 Mike Conley .60 1.50
11 Goran Dragic .60 1.50
12 Jrue Holiday 1.00 2.50
13 Kemba Walker .60 1.50
14 Ben Simmons .75 2.00
15 John Wall 1.00 2.50
16 Chris Paul 1.50 4.00
17 Kyrie Irving 2.00 5.00
18 Russell Westbrook 1.25 3.00
19 Stephen Curry 6.00 15.00
20 James Harden 1.50 4.00

2018-19 Panini Threads Floor Generals Premium
*PREM: .6X TO 1.5X BASIC
STATED PRINT RUN 199 SER.#'d SETS
2 Luka Doncic 100.00 250.00

2018-19 Panini Threads Floor Generals Premium Blue
*PREM BLU: .8X TO 2X BASIC
STATED PRINT RUN 85 SER.#'d SETS
2 Luka Doncic 200.00 500.00

2018-19 Panini Threads High Octane
*DAZZLE: .5X TO 1.2X BASIC
*PREM: .6X TO 1.5X BASIC
*PREM BLU: .8X TO 2X BASIC
1 Anthony Davis 2.00 5.00
2 Russell Westbrook 1.25 3.00
3 James Harden 1.50 4.00
4 Kevin Durant 3.00 8.00
5 LeBron James 6.00 15.00
6 Stephen Curry 6.00 15.00
7 Giannis Antetokounmpo 4.00 10.00
8 Donovan Mitchell 2.50 6.00
9 Jayson Tatum 3.00 8.00
10 Karl-Anthony Towns 1.25 3.00

2018-19 Panini Threads High Octane Premium Blue
*PREM BLU: .8X TO 2X BASIC
STATED PRINT RUN 85 SER.#'d SETS
5 LeBron James 10.00 25.00
6 Stephen Curry 8.00 20.00

2018-19 Panini Threads In Motion
*DAZZLE: .5X TO 1.2X BASIC
1 Kawhi Leonard 2.00 5.00
2 Russell Westbrook 1.25 3.00
3 Anthony Davis 2.00 5.00
4 Giannis Antetokounmpo 4.00 10.00
5 James Harden 1.50 4.00
6 Rudy Gobert 1.00 2.50
7 Donovan Mitchell 2.50 6.00
8 Nikola Jokic 4.00 10.00
9 Joel Embiid 2.00 5.00
10 Jimmy Butler 1.25 3.00
11 Ben Simmons .75 2.00
12 LeBron James 6.00 15.00
13 Lonzo Ball .75 2.00
14 Kevin Durant 3.00 8.00
15 Luka Doncic 8.00 20.00

2018-19 Panini Threads In Motion Dazzle
*DAZZLE: .5X TO 1.2X BASIC
15 Luka Doncic 12.00 30.00

2018-19 Panini Threads Next Wave
*DAZZLE: .5X TO 1.2X BASIC
1 Deandre Ayton 1.50 4.00
2 Trae Young 8.00 20.00
3 Luka Doncic 8.00 20.00
4 Marvin Bagley III .75 2.00
5 Jaren Jackson Jr. 4.00 10.00
6 Mo Bamba .75 2.00
7 Wendell Carter Jr. 1.25 3.00
8 Shai Gilgeous-Alexander 5.00 12.00
9 Michael Porter Jr. 2.00 5.00
10 Miles Bridges 1.25 3.00
11 Grayson Allen 1.00 2.50
12 Aaron Holiday .75 2.00
13 Collin Sexton 1.50 4.00
14 Kevin Knox .60 1.50
15 Allonzo Trier .50 1.25

2018-19 Panini Threads Our Time
*DAZZLE: .5X TO 1.2X BASIC
1 Donovan Mitchell 2.50 6.00
2 Jayson Tatum 3.00 8.00
3 Devin Booker 2.00 5.00
4 Fred VanVleet 1.00 2.50
5 Aaron Gordon .75 2.00
6 Brandon Ingram .75 2.00
7 Myles Turner .75 2.00
8 Jamal Murray 1.50 4.00
9 Jaylen Brown 1.25 3.00
10 Ben Simmons .75 2.00
11 Karl-Anthony Towns 1.25 3.00
12 Nikola Jokic 4.00 10.00
13 Joel Embiid 2.00 5.00
14 Giannis Antetokounmpo 4.00 10.00
15 Luka Doncic 8.00 20.00

2018-19 Panini Threads Our Time Dazzle
*DAZZLE: .5X TO 1.2X BASIC
15 Luka Doncic 10.00 25.00

2018-19 Panini Threads Rookie Signatures
EXCHANGE DEADLINE 10/15/2020
*PREM: .4X TO 1X BASIC
*GOLD: .75X TO 2X BASIC
1 Deandre Ayton 25.00 60.00
2 Marvin Bagley III 4.00 10.00
3 Luka Doncic 300.00 600.00
4 Jaren Jackson Jr. 40.00 100.00
5 Trae Young 125.00 300.00
6 Mo Bamba 4.00 10.00
7 Wendell Carter Jr. 6.00 15.00
8 Collin Sexton 8.00 20.00
9 Kevin Knox 3.00 8.00
10 Mikal Bridges 12.00 30.00
11 Shai Gilgeous-Alexander 200.00 500.00
12 Michael Porter Jr. 10.00 25.00
13 Troy Brown Jr. 3.00 8.00
14 Anfernee Simons 12.00 30.00
15 Kevin Huerter 5.00 12.00
16 Zhaire Smith 2.50 6.00
17 Donte DiVincenzo 6.00 15.00
18 Lonnie Walker IV 5.00 12.00
19 Moritz Wagner 5.00 12.00
20 Jerome Robinson 2.50 6.00
21 Allonzo Trier 2.50 6.00
22 Gary Trent Jr. 5.00 12.00
23 Grayson Allen 5.00 12.00
24 Omari Spellman 2.50 6.00
25 Jalen Brunson 20.00 50.00
26 Josh Okogie 4.00 10.00
27 Yuta Watanabe 20.00 50.00
28 Jarred Vanderbilt 5.00 12.00
29 Hamidou Diallo 4.00 10.00
30 Chimezie Metu 3.00 8.00
31 Dzanan Musa 2.50 6.00
32 Svi Mykhailiuk 3.00 8.00
33 Aaron Holiday 4.00 10.00
34 De'Anthony Melton 5.00 12.00
35 Chandler Hutchison 3.00 8.00
36 Keita Bates-Diop 3.00 8.00
37 Kostas Antetokounmpo 3.00 8.00
38 Jevon Carter 4.00 10.00
39 Elie Okobo 2.50 6.00
40 Landry Shamet 4.00 10.00

2018-19 Panini Threads Rookie Threads
*PRIME: .6X TO 1.5X BASIC
1 Aaron Holiday 3.00 8.00
2 Allonzo Trier 2.00 5.00
3 Anfernee Simons 10.00 25.00
4 Bruce Brown 4.00 10.00
5 Chandler Hutchison 2.50 6.00
6 Collin Sexton 6.00 15.00
7 De'Anthony Melton 4.00 10.00
8 Deandre Ayton 6.00 15.00
9 Devonte' Graham 3.00 8.00
10 Donte DiVincenzo 5.00 12.00
11 Elie Okobo 2.00 5.00
12 Gary Trent Jr. 4.00 10.00
13 Grayson Allen 4.00 10.00
14 Jacob Evans III 2.00 5.00
15 Jalen Brunson 15.00 40.00
16 Jaren Jackson Jr. 15.00 40.00
17 Jerome Robinson 2.00 5.00
18 Josh Okogie 3.00 8.00
19 Kevin Huerter 4.00 10.00
20 Kevin Knox 2.50 6.00
21 Khyri Thomas 2.00 5.00
22 Kostas Antetokounmpo 2.50 6.00
23 Landry Shamet 3.00 8.00
24 Lonnie Walker IV 4.00 10.00
25 Luka Doncic 30.00 80.00
26 Marvin Bagley III 3.00 8.00
27 Melvin Frazier Jr. 2.00 5.00
28 Michael Porter Jr. 8.00 20.00
29 Mikal Bridges 10.00 25.00
30 Mitchell Robinson 5.00 12.00
31 Mo Bamba 3.00 8.00
32 Moritz Wagner 4.00 10.00
33 Robert Williams III 4.00 10.00
34 Rodions Kurucs 2.50 6.00
35 Shai Gilgeous-Alexander 20.00 50.00
36 Svi Mykhailiuk 2.50 6.00
37 Trae Young 15.00 40.00
38 Wendell Carter Jr. 5.00 12.00
39 Yuta Watanabe 3.00 8.00
40 Zhaire Smith 2.00 5.00

2018-19 Panini Threads Rookie Threads Prime
*PRIME: .6X TO 1.5X BASIC
STATED PRINT RUN 25 SER.#'d SETS
25 Luka Doncic 50.00 120.00

2018-19 Panini Threads Shoot to Thrill
*DAZZLE: .5X TO 1.2X BASIC
1 Buddy Hield .75 2.00
2 Reggie Miller 1.50 4.00
3 Stephen Curry 6.00 15.00
4 Trae Young 8.00 20.00
5 Larry Bird 3.00 8.00
6 Steve Nash 1.50 4.00
7 Dirk Nowitzki 2.00 5.00
8 Khris Middleton .75 2.00
9 Otto Porter Jr. .60 1.50
10 Klay Thompson 2.00 5.00
11 Kyrie Irving 2.00 5.00
12 LeBron James 6.00 15.00
13 Kevin Durant 3.00 8.00
14 Damian Lillard 2.00 5.00
15 Jayson Tatum 3.00 8.00
16 Paul George 1.25 3.00
17 Kawhi Leonard 2.00 5.00
18 James Harden 1.50 4.00
19 Kyle Korver .60 1.50
20 Seth Curry .60 1.50

2018-19 Panini Threads Signage Signatures
EXCHANGE DEADLINE 10/15/2020
*PREM/195-200: .4X TO 1X BASIC
*PREM/100: .5X TO 1.2X BASIC
*PREM/40-55: .6X TO 1.5X BASIC
*PREM/20-30: .8X TO 2X BASIC
*GOLD/25: .8X TO 2X BASIC
2 Montrezl Harrell 4.00 10.00
3 Terry Rozier 3.00 8.00
5 Patrick Beverley 2.50 6.00
6 Kelly Olynyk 2.50 6.00
7 Harry Giles 2.50 6.00
8 Yogi Ferrell 2.50 6.00
9 Jarrett Allen 4.00 10.00
11 Nick Anderson 3.00 8.00
12 Aron Baynes 2.50 6.00
13 Xavier McDaniel 3.00 8.00
14 Lauri Markkanen 6.00 15.00
15 Dee Brown 3.00 8.00
16 Zydrunas Ilgauskas 3.00 8.00
17 Elfrid Payton 3.00 8.00
18 Wally Szczerbiak 3.00 8.00
19 Vin Baker 2.50 6.00
21 Raef LaFrentz 2.50 6.00
22 Brad Davis 3.00 8.00
23 Seth Curry 3.00 8.00
24 Damian Jones 2.50 6.00
25 Justin Jackson 2.50 6.00
27 Taurean Prince 2.50 6.00
28 John Starks 3.00 8.00
29 Caris LeVert 4.00 10.00
31 Maxi Kleber 3.00 8.00
32 Dell Curry 4.00 10.00
33 Khris Middleton 4.00 10.00
35 Jordan Bell 2.50 6.00
38 Jerry Stackhouse 5.00 12.00
39 Bruce Bowen 3.00 8.00
40 Jason Williams 3.00 8.00
41 Muggsy Bogues 4.00 10.00
42 Meyers Leonard 2.50 6.00
43 Fred Hoiberg 2.50 6.00
44 Furkan Korkmaz 3.00 8.00
45 Kurt Rambis 3.00 8.00
46 Jerome Williams 3.00 8.00
47 Zach LaVine 6.00 15.00
48 John Salley 3.00 8.00
49 Cuttino Mobley 2.50 6.00
50 Rudy Tomjanovich 3.00 8.00
51 Mark Eaton 4.00 10.00
52 Frank Jackson 3.00 8.00
53 Jerami Grant 4.00 10.00
54 Allonzo McKinnie 2.50 6.00
57 Ish Smith 2.50 6.00
58 Tyrone Wallace 2.50 6.00
59 John Collins 4.00 10.00
60 Josh Hart 3.00 8.00

2018-19 Panini Threads Signage Signatures Premium
*PREM/195-200: .4X TO 1X BASIC
*PREM/100: .5X TO 1.2X BASIC
*PREM/40-55: .6X TO 1.5X BASIC
*PREM/20-30: .8X TO 2X BASIC
PRINT RUN B/WN 20-200 SER.#'d SETS
EXCHANGE DEADLINE 10/15/2020
4 Kevin Durant/20 EXCH 50.00 120.00
10 Kyrie Irving/20 20.00 50.00
14 Lauri Markkanen/100 15.00 40.00
26 Stephen Curry/20 400.00 800.00
36 Giannis Antetokounmpo/30 75.00 200.00
37 Allen Iverson/20 25.00 60.00
55 Damian Lillard/20 30.00 80.00

2018-19 Panini Threads Swingmen
*DAZZLE: .5X TO 1.2X BASIC
*PREM: .6X TO 1.5X BASIC
*PREM BLU: .8X TO 2X BASIC
1 Giannis Antetokounmpo 4.00 10.00
2 LeBron James 6.00 15.00
3 Kevin Durant 3.00 8.00
4 James Harden 1.50 4.00
5 Paul George 1.25 3.00
6 Klay Thompson 2.00 5.00
7 DeMar DeRozan 1.00 2.50
8 Jimmy Butler 1.25 3.00
9 Gordon Hayward .75 2.00
10 Dwyane Wade 1.50 4.00
11 Andre Iguodala .60 1.50
12 Bradley Beal 1.00 2.50
13 CJ McCollum .75 2.00
14 Harrison Barnes .60 1.50
15 Rudy Gay .75 2.00

2018-19 Panini Threads Threedom!
*DAZZLE: .5X TO 1.2X BASIC
1 Damian Lillard 2.00 5.00
2 Stephen Curry 6.00 15.00
3 Kyrie Irving 2.00 5.00
4 Jimmy Butler 1.25 3.00
5 Kevin Durant 3.00 8.00
6 James Harden 1.50 4.00
7 Karl-Anthony Towns 1.25 3.00
8 Malcolm Brogdon .75 2.00
9 Rudy Gay .75 2.00
10 Dirk Nowitzki 2.00 5.00
11 Buddy Hield .75 2.00
12 Jayson Tatum 3.00 8.00
13 Khris Middleton .75 2.00
14 Kawhi Leonard 2.00 5.00
15 LeBron James 6.00 15.00

2013-14 Panini Titanium
1 Jrue Holiday .60 1.50
2 Gerald Wallace .40 1.00
3 Nikola Vucevic .60 1.50
4 Deron Williams .40 1.00
5 Luol Deng .40 1.00
6 Channing Frye .30 .75
7 Damian Lillard 1.50 4.00
8 Manu Ginobili 1.00 2.50
9 Dirk Nowitzki 1.25 3.00
10 Tim Duncan 1.25 3.00
11 Greivis Vasquez .30 .75
12 Dion Waiters .30 .75
13 Dwight Howard .60 1.50
14 Evan Turner .30 .75
15 Kyrie Irving 1.50 4.00
16 Gerald Henderson .30 .75
17 Chris Bosh .60 1.50
18 Paul George .75 2.00
19 Arron Afflalo .30 .75
20 James Harden 1.00 2.50
21 Chris Paul 1.00 2.50
22 Zach Randolph .40 1.00
23 Carmelo Anthony .75 2.00
24 Derrick Favors .30 .75
25 Brandon Knight .40 1.00
26 Josh Smith .30 .75
27 Kemba Walker .50 1.25
28 Amar'e Stoudemire .50 1.25
29 Jameer Nelson .30 .75
30 Al Horford .50 1.25
31 Kobe Bryant 4.00 10.00
32 Rudy Gay .40 1.00
33 John Wall .60 1.50
34 Danny Granger .30 .75
35 Jeff Green .30 .75
36 Ricky Rubio .40 1.00
37 Rajon Rondo .60 1.50
38 Roy Hibbert .30 .75
39 Kevin Martin .40 1.00
40 Eric Bledsoe .40 1.00
41 Jeremy Lin .75 2.00
42 Kevin Garnett 1.25 3.00
43 Carl Landry .30 .75
44 Blake Griffin .50 1.25
45 Enes Kanter .40 1.00
46 Al Jefferson .30 .75
47 Paul Millsap .40 1.00
49 Dwyane Wade 1.00 2.50
50 Anthony Davis 1.50 4.00
51 Andre Drummond .50 1.25
52 Joakim Noah .50 1.25
53 Serge Ibaka .40 1.00
54 Jason Richardson .50 1.25
55 DeMarcus Cousins .50 1.25
56 Nicolas Batum .40 1.00
57 Paul Pierce .75 2.00
58 LeBron James 4.00 10.00
59 DeMar DeRozan .60 1.50
60 LaMarcus Aldridge .50 1.25
61 J.J. Redick .50 1.25
62 Gordon Hayward .50 1.25
63 Bradley Beal .75 2.00
64 Tyson Chandler .40 1.00
65 Mike Conley .50 1.25
66 Harrison Barnes .50 1.25
67 Thaddeus Young .30 .75
68 Shawn Marion .40 1.00
69 Jeff Teague .30 .75
70 Kevin Love .50 1.25
71 Carlos Boozer .40 1.00
72 O.J. Mayo .40 1.00
73 DeAndre Jordan .40 1.00
74 Andre Miller .40 1.00
75 Steve Nash 1.00 2.50
76 Klay Thompson 1.50 4.00
77 Anderson Varejao .30 .75
78 Pau Gasol .75 2.00
79 Kenneth Faried .40 1.00
80 Brandon Jennings .30 .75
81 Russell Westbrook .75 2.00
82 Tyreke Evans .40 1.00
83 Vince Carter 1.00 2.50
84 Marcin Gortat .30 .75
85 Jimmer Fredette .50 1.25
86 Monta Ellis .40 1.00
87 Nikola Pekovic .30 .75
88 George Hill .40 1.00
89 Derrick Rose .75 2.00
90 Goran Dragic .40 1.00
91 Andrew Bogut .40 1.00
92 Mario Chalmers .40 1.00
93 Larry Sanders .30 .75
94 Joe Johnson .40 1.00
95 Stephen Curry 4.00 10.00
96 J.R. Smith .50 1.25
97 Tony Parker .75 2.00
98 Marc Gasol .50 1.25
99 Kevin Durant 2.00 5.00
100 Ty Lawson .30 .75

2013-14 Panini Titanium Draft Position
*JSY NUM p/r 15-19: .75X TO 2X RET RC
*JSY NUM p/r 15-19: 1.5X TO 4X RET VET
*JSY NUM p/r 20-25: .6X TO 1.5X RET RC
*JSY NUM p/r 20-25: 1.2X TO 3X RET VET
*JSY NUM p/r 26-36: .5X TO 1.2X RET RC
*JSY NUM p/r 26-36: 1X TO 2.5X RET VET
*JSY NUM p/r 37-49: .4X TO 1X RET RC
*JSY NUM p/r 56-60: .5X TO 1.2X RET VET
PRINT RUNS B/WN 1-60 COPIES PER
NO PRICING ON QTY 14 OR LESS
115 Giannis Antetokounmpo/15 1,000.00 2,000.00
126 Rudy Gobert/27 40.00 100.00
179 Manu Ginobili/57 12.00 30.00

2013-14 Panini Titanium Draft Year
*DRAFT YR: .5X TO 1.2X BASIC RETAIL
PRINT RUNS B/WN 1-99 COPIES PER
NO PRICING ON QTY 13 OR LESS
143 Kobe Bryant/96 60.00 150.00

2013-14 Panini Titanium Electric Endorsements
PRINT RUNS B/WN 25-299 COPIES PER
EXCHANGE DEADLINE 8/26/2015
1 Kobe Bryant/75 1,000.00 2,000.00
2 Harrison Barnes/99 5.00 12.00
3 Carlos Delfino/299 3.00 8.00
4 Blake Griffin/25 25.00 60.00
5 Mark Jackson/99 4.00 10.00
6 Isaiah Thomas/299 4.00 10.00
7 Luc Mbah a Moute/299 3.00 8.00
8 Kevin Durant/75 125.00 300.00
9 Sean Elliott/299 5.00 12.00
10 Anfernee Hardaway/49 100.00 250.00
11 Eddie Jones/149 4.00 10.00
12 Kyrie Irving/49 60.00 150.00
13 Kawhi Leonard/249 75.00 200.00
14 Jarrett Jack/99 4.00 10.00
15 MarShon Brooks/199 3.00 8.00
16 Tony Parker/49 30.00 80.00
17 Grant Hill/49 40.00 100.00
18 Stephen Curry/49 500.00 1,000.00
19 Michael Finley/49 8.00 20.00
20 Kenny Walker/249 3.00 8.00

2013-14 Panini Titanium Jersey Number
*JSY NUM p/r 15-19: .75X TO 2X RET RC
*JSY NUM p/r 15-19: 1.5X TO 4X RET VET
*JSY NUM p/r 20-25: .6X TO 1.5X RET RC
*JSY NUM p/r 20-25: 1.2X TO 3X RET VET
*JSY NUM p/r 26-36: .5X TO 1.2X RET RC
*JSY NUM p/r 26-36: 1X TO 2.5X RET VET
*JSY NUM p/r 37-49: .4X TO 1X RET RC
*JSY NUM p/r 37-49: .75X TO 2X RET VET
*JSY NUM p/r 50-100: .5X TO 1.2X RET VET
PRINT RUNS B/WN 1-100 COPIES PER
NO PRICING ON QTY 14 OR LESS
115 G.Antetokounmpo/34 2,000.00 4,000.00
172 Kevin Durant/35 30.00 80.00

2013-14 Panini Titanium Titanum 22
*TITAN 22 1-100: 8X TO 20X BASIC RET.
*TITAN 22 101-1142: .6X TO 1.5X BASIC RET.
*TITAN 22 143-200: 1.2X TO 3X BASIC RET.
STATED PRINT RUN 22 SER.#'d SETS

2013-14 Panini Titanium Atomic Numbers
STATED PRINT RUN 99 SER.#'d SETS
1 Bernard King 3.00 8.00
2 Clyde Drexler 4.00 10.00
3 Danny Ainge 2.50 6.00
4 Dave DeBusschere 2.50 6.00
5 Elgin Baylor 2.50 6.00
6 George Karl 2.50 6.00
7 Jamaal Franklin 1.50 4.00
8 Jay Williams 1.50 4.00
9 Otto Porter 2.50 6.00
10 Rolando Blackman 2.00 5.00
11 Isaiah Thomas 2.00 5.00
12 Taj Gibson 1.50 4.00
13 Tiago Splitter 1.50 4.00
14 Moses Malone 4.00 10.00
15 Tom Chambers 2.50 6.00
16 Miles Plumlee 1.50 4.00
17 Jim Jackson 1.50 4.00
18 Matt Barnes 1.50 4.00
19 Larry Nance 2.00 5.00
20 John Salley 2.00 5.00
21 John Drew 2.50 6.00
22 Rod Higgins 2.50 6.00

2013-14 Panini Titanium Conductors
STATED PRINT RUN 49 SER.#'d SETS
1 Jrue Holiday 5.00 12.00
2 Steve Nash 8.00 20.00
3 Raymond Felton 2.50 6.00
4 Deron Williams 3.00 8.00
5 Chris Paul 8.00 20.00
6 Stephen Curry 30.00 80.00
7 Tony Parker 6.00 15.00
8 Jeremy Lin 6.00 15.00
9 Jose Calderon 2.50 6.00
10 Russell Westbrook 6.00 15.00
11 Mario Chalmers 3.00 8.00
12 Damian Lillard 12.00 30.00
13 Rajon Rondo 5.00 12.00
14 John Wall 5.00 12.00
15 Kyrie Irving 12.00 30.00
16 Mike Conley 4.00 10.00
17 Ty Lawson 2.50 6.00
18 Ricky Rubio 5.00 12.00
19 Pete Maravich 6.00 15.00
20 John Stockton 8.00 20.00
21 Jason Kidd 6.00 15.00
22 Mark Jackson 3.00 8.00
23 Magic Johnson 15.00 40.00
24 Isiah Thomas 6.00 15.00
25 Gary Payton 6.00 15.00
26 Tim Hardaway 5.00 12.00
27 Oscar Robertson 6.00 15.00
28 Bob Cousy 10.00 25.00

2013-14 Panini Titanium Double Jerseys
PRINT RUNS B/WN 149-279 COPIES PER
1 Amar'e Stoudemire/279 4.00 10.00
2 Taj Gibson/279 2.50 6.00
3 JaVale McGee/279 3.00 8.00
4 Deron Williams/279 3.00 8.00
5 Jeremy Lin/279 6.00 15.00
6 LeBron James/279 75.00 200.00
7 Samuel Dalembert/279 2.50 6.00

8 Tyson Chandler/279 3.00 8.00
9 Andre Iguodala/279 4.00 10.00
10 Caron Butler/279 3.00 8.00
11 Kobe Bryant/279 75.00 200.00
12 Joakim Noah/279 4.00 10.00
13 Damian Lillard/279 12.00 30.00
14 Andrew Bynum/279 2.50 6.00
15 Chris Kaman/279 3.00 8.00
16 Brandon Jennings/279 2.50 6.00
17 Goran Dragic/279 3.00 8.00
18 Kenneth Faried/249 3.00 8.00
19 Michael Beasley/279 2.50 6.00
20 Tim Duncan/279 10.00 25.00
21 Paul Pierce/279 6.00 15.00
22 Elton Brand/279 3.00 8.00
23 Carmelo Anthony/279 6.00 15.00
24 Kevin Garnett/279 10.00 25.00
25 Jimmer Fredette/279 2.50 6.00
26 Klay Thompson/279 12.00 30.00
27 Blake Griffin/279 4.00 10.00
28 Dwight Howard/279 5.00 12.00
29 O.J. Mayo/279 2.50 6.00
30 Russell Westbrook/279 6.00 15.00
31 Omer Asik/279 2.50 6.00
32 Zach Randolph/279 3.00 8.00
33 Arron Afflalo/279 2.50 6.00
34 John Wall/279 5.00 12.00
35 Derrick Rose/279 6.00 15.00
36 Udonis Haslem/279 3.00 8.00
37 Greg Monroe/279 2.50 6.00
38 Kevin Love/279 4.00 10.00
39 Rajon Rondo/249 5.00 12.00
40 Ty Lawson/279 2.50 6.00
41 Nick Young/279 2.50 6.00
42 Rodney Stuckey/229 2.50 6.00
43 Evan Turner/279 2.50 6.00
44 Anthony Davis/279 12.00 30.00
45 Dwyane Wade/279 8.00 20.00
46 DeMar DeRozan/279 5.00 12.00
47 Chris Paul/249 8.00 20.00
48 Kevin Durant/279 12.00 30.00
49 Xavier Henry/149 2.50 6.00
50 Tony Parker/249 6.00 15.00

2013-14 Panini Titanium Double Double Jerseys Prime

*PRIME: .75X TO 2X BASIC
PRINT RUNS B/WN 3-25 COPIES PER
NO PRICING ON QTY 10 OR LESS

2013-14 Panini Titanium Draft Day Autographs

EXCHANGE DEADLINE 8/26/2015
1 Ben McLemore 4.00 10.00
2 Otto Porter 5.00 12.00
3 Michael Carter-Williams 4.00 10.00
4 Victor Oladipo 12.00 30.00
5 C.J. McCollum 12.00 30.00
6 Shabazz Muhammad 3.00 8.00
7 Rudy Gobert 12.00 30.00
8 Shane Larkin 3.00 8.00
9 Tony Mitchell 3.00 8.00
10 Mason Plumlee 4.00 10.00
11 Trey Burke 4.00 10.00
12 Alex Len 4.00 10.00
13 Anthony Bennett 3.00 8.00
14 Sergey Karasev EXCH 3.00 8.00
15 Andre Roberson 4.00 10.00
16 Ricky Ledo 3.00 8.00
17 Giannis Antetokounmpo 600.00 1,200.00
18 Gorgui Dieng 4.00 10.00
19 Allen Crabbe 3.00 8.00
20 Steven Adams 12.00 30.00

2013-14 Panini Titanium Elements Jerseys

*PRIME/15-25: 1X TO 2.5X BASIC
1 Carmelo Anthony 5.00 12.00
2 Grant Hill 5.00 12.00
3 Marcin Gortat 2.00 5.00
4 Ryan Anderson 2.00 5.00
5 Tristan Thompson 2.00 5.00
6 Magic Johnson 12.00 30.00
7 Paul Pierce 5.00 12.00
8 Rasheed Wallace 3.00 8.00
9 Kobe Bryant 25.00 60.00
10 Brandon Jennings 2.00 5.00
11 Joe Johnson 2.50 6.00
12 Blake Griffin 3.00 8.00
13 Alex English 4.00 10.00
14 Danny Green 2.50 6.00
15 J.J. Barea 2.50 6.00
16 Thabo Sefolosha 2.50 6.00
17 LaMarcus Aldridge 3.00 8.00
18 Nene 2.50 6.00
19 Thaddeus Young 2.00 5.00
20 Kevin Martin 2.50 6.00
21 Serge Ibaka 2.50 6.00
22 Metta World Peace 2.50 6.00
23 Kevin Durant 10.00 25.00
24 Jared Sullinger 2.00 5.00
25 Dirk Nowitzki 8.00 20.00
26 Jrue Holiday 4.00 10.00
27 Al Horford 3.00 8.00
28 Bradley Beal 5.00 12.00
29 Kyle Lowry 3.00 8.00
30 Chandler Parsons 2.00 5.00
31 Kenneth Faried 2.50 6.00
32 LeBron James 25.00 60.00
33 Michael Kidd-Gilchrist 2.00 5.00
34 Shaquille O'Neal 12.00 30.00
35 Tracy McGrady 5.00 12.00
36 Raymond Felton 2.00 5.00
37 Luol Deng 2.50 6.00
38 Kawhi Leonard 10.00 25.00
39 Carlos Boozer 2.50 6.00
40 David Lee 2.00 5.00
41 Spencer Hawes 2.00 5.00
42 Amar'e Stoudemire 3.00 8.00
43 Chris Paul 6.00 15.00
44 Deron Williams 2.50 6.00
45 Jason Richardson 3.00 8.00
46 Kemba Walker 3.00 8.00
47 Norris Cole 2.00 5.00
48 Robert Parish 4.00 10.00
49 Will Bynum 2.00 5.00
50 Klay Thompson 10.00 25.00
51 Rajon Rondo 4.00 10.00
52 Nate Robinson 2.00 5.00
53 John Wall 4.00 10.00
54 Iman Shumpert 2.00 5.00
55 Darren Collison 2.00 5.00
56 Bismack Biyombo 2.00 5.00
57 Clyde Drexler 5.00 12.00
58 Kenyon Martin 3.00 8.00
59 Dwyane Wade 6.00 15.00
60 Joakim Noah 3.00 8.00
61 Kevin McHale 5.00 12.00
62 Michael Beasley 2.00 5.00
63 Damian Lillard 10.00 25.00
64 Ty Lawson 2.00 5.00
65 Mike Miller 2.50 6.00
66 Kevin Love 3.00 8.00
67 James Harden 6.00 15.00
68 Andre Miller 2.50 6.00
69 Brook Lopez 3.00 8.00
70 DeAndre Jordan 2.50 6.00
71 Bill Laimbeer 3.00 8.00
72 Greivis Vasquez 2.00 5.00
73 Jameer Nelson 2.00 5.00
74 Pau Gasol 5.00 12.00
75 Tim Duncan 8.00 20.00

2013-14 Panini Titanium Enshrinement Ink

PRINT RUNS B/WN 25-199 COPIES PER
EXCHANGE DEADLINE 8/26/2015
1 Joe Dumars/25 8.00 20.00
2 Nate Archibald/25 8.00 20.00
3 Earl Monroe/25 15.00 40.00
4 John Stockton/25 50.00 120.00
5 Chris Mullin/149 12.00 30.00
6 Alex English/199 8.00 20.00
7 Bailey Howell/199 6.00 15.00
8 Gail Goodrich/25 6.00 15.00
9 Nate Thurmond/25 12.00 30.00
10 Bob Lanier/25 12.00 30.00
11 Kareem Abdul-Jabbar/49 100.00 250.00
12 Robert Parish/25 20.00 50.00
14 Jamaal Wilkes/199 5.00 12.00
15 Wes Unseld/25 20.00 50.00
16 Larry Bird/49 100.00 250.00
17 Gary Payton/49 20.00 50.00
18 Ralph Sampson/25 15.00 40.00
19 Artis Gilmore/25 12.00 30.00
20 Jerry West/25 30.00 80.00
21 Bob McAdoo/199 10.00 25.00
22 Isiah Thomas/25 30.00 80.00
23 Jerry Lucas/25 20.00 50.00
24 Adrian Dantley/199 6.00 15.00
25 Elgin Baylor/25 30.00 80.00
26 Scottie Pippen/49 75.00 200.00
27 David Thompson/199 6.00 15.00
28 Magic Johnson/49 100.00 250.00
29 Karl Malone/49 50.00 120.00
30 Connie Hawkins/199 8.00 20.00

2013-14 Panini Titanium Fundamentals

STATED PRINT RUN 199 SER.#'d SETS
1 Tim Duncan 4.00 10.00
2 Carmelo Anthony 2.50 6.00
3 Deron Williams 1.25 3.00
4 Kyle Lowry 1.50 4.00
5 Greivis Vasquez 1.00 2.50
6 Steve Nash 3.00 8.00
7 Klay Thompson 5.00 12.00
8 Tony Parker 2.50 6.00
9 Dennis Rodman 4.00 10.00
10 Magic Johnson 6.00 15.00
11 Tayshaun Prince 1.50 4.00
12 James Harden 3.00 8.00
13 Kemba Walker 1.50 4.00
14 Goran Dragic 1.25 3.00
15 J.J. Hickson 1.00 2.50
16 Dirk Nowitzki 4.00 10.00
17 Andre Miller 1.25 3.00
18 Chris Paul 3.00 8.00
19 John Stockton 3.00 8.00
20 Hakeem Olajuwon 3.00 8.00
21 Shane Battier 1.25 3.00
22 Kyrie Irving 5.00 12.00
23 Tyreke Evans 1.25 3.00
24 Ricky Rubio 1.25 3.00
25 Kevin Garnett 4.00 10.00
26 Steve Novak 1.00 2.50
27 Ray Allen 2.50 6.00
28 Andre Iguodala 1.50 4.00
29 Karl Malone 3.00 8.00
30 David Robinson 3.00 8.00
31 LeBron James 12.00 30.00
32 Stephen Curry 12.00 30.00
33 Ryan Anderson 1.00 2.50
34 Gordon Hayward 1.25 3.00
35 DeMarcus Cousins 1.50 4.00
36 Kevin Martin 1.25 3.00
37 Chauncey Billups 2.00 5.00
38 Antawn Jamison 1.25 3.00
39 Kareem Abdul-Jabbar 5.00 12.00
40 George Mikan 5.00 12.00
41 Kobe Bryant 12.00 30.00
42 LaMarcus Aldridge 1.50 4.00
43 Ty Lawson 1.00 2.50
44 Damian Lillard 5.00 12.00
45 Jose Calderon 1.00 2.50
46 Jimmer Fredette 1.50 4.00
47 Pau Gasol 2.50 6.00
48 Kyle Korver 1.25 3.00
49 Larry Bird 6.00 15.00
50 Oscar Robertson 2.50 6.00

2013-14 Panini Titanium Game Gear Duals

PRINT RUNS B/WN 49-155 COPIES PER
1 A.Bradley/R.Rondo/125 6.00 15.00
2 K.Walker/M.Gilchrist/155 5.00 12.00
3 D.Nowitzki/J.Kidd/155 15.00 40.00
4 B.Griffin/C.Paul/125 10.00 25.00
5 D.Wade/L.James/155 40.00 100.00
6 E.Udoh/E.Ilyasova/155 3.00 8.00
7 K.Garnett/P.Pierce/155 12.00 30.00
8 K.Durant/R.Westbrook/155 15.00 40.00
9 E.Turner/T.Young/155 3.00 8.00
10 D.Lillard/K.Irving/155 15.00 40.00
11 D.Howard/J.Harden/155 10.00 25.00
12 G.Hill/P.George/155 8.00 20.00
13 A.Horford/J.Teague/125 5.00 12.00
14 K.Bryant/P.Gasol/155 40.00 100.00
15 C.Bosh/U.Haslem/155 6.00 15.00
16 K.Love/K.Martin/155 5.00 12.00
17 D.Waiters/K.Irving/155 15.00 40.00
18 N.Vucevic/V.Oladipo/155 8.00 20.00
19 E.Bledsoe/G.Dragic/155 4.00 10.00
20 I.Thomas/J.Fredette/155 5.00 12.00
21 A.Davis/A.Rivers/155 15.00 40.00
22 C.Anthony/T.Chandler/155 8.00 20.00
23 D.Rose/J.Noah/155 8.00 20.00
24 M.Gasol/Z.Randolph/155 5.00 12.00
25 N.Cole/R.Allen/155 8.00 20.00
26 H.Barnes/S.Curry/155 40.00 100.00
27 K.Faried/T.Lawson/125 4.00 10.00
28 C.Anthony/M.Williams/155 8.00 20.00
29 D.Howard/H.Olajuwon/79 10.00 25.00
30 C.Paul/D.Williams/125 10.00 25.00
31 M.Morris/M.Morris/155 4.00 10.00
32 D.Nowitzki/K.Love/155 12.00 30.00
33 A.Bennett/L.Johnson/155 6.00 15.00
34 M.Johnson/S.Nash/49 20.00 50.00
35 K.Jabbar/T.Duncan/49 15.00 40.00
36 T.Splitter/T.Duncan/155 12.00 30.00
37 A.Johnson/D.DeRozan/155 6.00 15.00
38 B.Beal/J.Wall/155 8.00 20.00
39 J.Butler/T.Gibson/155 10.00 25.00
40 P.Ewing/T.Chandler/79 8.00 20.00
41 J.Noah/S.Pippen/125 12.00 30.00
42 G.Payton/R.Westbrook/49 8.00 20.00
43 I.Thomas/I.Thomas/79 8.00 20.00
44 J.Lin/Y.Ming/79 20.00 50.00
45 D.Brown/D.Wilkins/49 8.00 20.00
46 M.Ginobili/T.Parker/125 10.00 25.00
47 D.Favors/G.Hayward/155 4.00 10.00
48 D.Williams/J.Terry/155 4.00 10.00
49 F.Lever/T.Lawson/155 3.00 8.00
50 J.Worthy/K.Bryant/49 40.00 100.00

2013-14 Panini Titanium Game Gear Duals Prime

*PRIME: .75X TO 2X BASIC
PRINT RUNS B/WN 2-25 COPIES PER
NO PRICING ON QTY 10 OR LESS

2013-14 Panini Titanium Gamers

1 Tracy McGrady 6.00 15.00
2 Grant Hill 6.00 15.00
3 LeBron James 30.00 80.00
4 Steve Nash 8.00 20.00
5 Jason Kidd 6.00 15.00
6 Paul Pierce 6.00 15.00
7 Rasheed Wallace 4.00 10.00
8 Deron Williams 3.00 8.00
9 Blake Griffin 4.00 10.00
10 Clyde Drexler 6.00 15.00
11 Dwight Howard 5.00 12.00
12 Allen Iverson 8.00 20.00
13 Ray Allen 6.00 15.00
14 Tim Duncan 10.00 25.00
15 Shaquille O'Neal 15.00 40.00
16 Eric Gordon 3.00 8.00
17 Kevin Durant 12.00 30.00
18 Pau Gasol 6.00 15.00
19 Dwyane Wade 8.00 20.00
20 Dirk Nowitzki 10.00 25.00
21 Joakim Noah 4.00 10.00
22 Al Horford 4.00 10.00
23 Kobe Bryant 30.00 80.00
24 Carmelo Anthony 6.00 15.00
25 Kyrie Irving 12.00 30.00

2013-14 Panini Titanium Gamers Prime

*PRIME: .75X TO 2X BASIC
PRINT RUNS B/WN 2-25 COPIES PER
NO PRICING ON QTY 10 OR LESS
MANY NOT PRICED DUE TO LACK OF INFC
1 Tracy McGrady/25 20.00 50.00
2 Grant Hill/25 20.00 50.00
3 LeBron James/25 75.00 200.00
7 Rasheed Wallace/25 20.00 50.00
10 Clyde Drexler/25 15.00 40.00
13 Ray Allen/25 15.00 40.00
14 Tim Duncan/25 20.00 50.00
23 Kobe Bryant/25 75.00 200.00

2013-14 Panini Titanium Luster

STATED PRINT RUN 99 SER.#'d SETS
1 Kobe Bryant 25.00 60.00
2 James Harden 6.00 15.00
3 Steve Nash 6.00 15.00
4 Jeremy Lin 5.00 12.00
5 LeBron James 25.00 60.00
6 Deron Williams 2.50 6.00
7 Derrick Rose 5.00 12.00
8 Carmelo Anthony 5.00 12.00
9 Kyrie Irving 10.00 25.00
10 Chandler Parsons 2.00 5.00
11 Blake Griffin 3.00 8.00
12 Damian Lillard 10.00 25.00
13 Ricky Rubio 2.50 6.00
14 Stephen Curry 25.00 60.00
15 Kevin Durant 10.00 25.00
16 Vince Carter 6.00 15.00
17 Jeff Teague 2.00 5.00
18 Rajon Rondo 4.00 10.00
19 John Wall 4.00 10.00
20 Chris Paul 6.00 15.00
21 Brandon Jennings 2.00 5.00
22 Paul George 5.00 12.00
23 Tyreke Evans 2.00 5.00
24 Shawn Marion 2.50 6.00
25 Chris Bosh 4.00 10.00

2013-14 Panini Titanium Metallic Marks

PRINT RUNS B/WN 25-299 COPIES PER
EXCHANGE DEADLINE 8/26/2015
1 Kevin Durant/99 EXCH 125.00 300.00
2 Danilo Gallinari/25 5.00 12.00
3 Detlef Schrempf/299 6.00 15.00
4 Stephen Curry/25 600.00 1,200.00
5 David Thompson/299 6.00 15.00
6 Kyrie Irving/49 60.00 150.00
7 Kurt Rambis/299 6.00 15.00
8 Raymond Felton/25 4.00 10.00
9 Muggsy Bogues/299 12.00 30.00
10 Blake Griffin/49 12.00 30.00
11 Marcin Gortat/99 4.00 10.00
12 Reggie Theus/299 5.00 12.00
13 Tony Parker/25 20.00 50.00
14 Kobe Bryant/49 1,000.00 2,000.00
15 Klay Thompson/25 125.00 300.00
18 Scottie Pippen/49 75.00 200.00
19 Monta Ellis/25 EXCH 5.00 12.00
20 Byron Mullens/299 4.00 10.00
21 Greivis Vasquez/249 4.00 10.00
22 John Starks/299 6.00 15.00
23 Cedric Ceballos/299 4.00 10.00
24 Kent Bazemore/299 4.00 10.00
25 Michael Cage/299 4.00 10.00

2013-14 Panini Titanium New Wave Signatures

1 Anthony Davis 60.00 150.00
2 Jared Sullinger 3.00 8.00
3 Derrick Williams 3.00 8.00
4 Alec Burks 4.00 10.00
5 MarShon Brooks 3.00 8.00
6 Kyle Lowry 5.00 12.00
7 Danilo Gallinari 4.00 10.00
8 Jeff Ayres 3.00 8.00
9 Greg Monroe 3.00 8.00
10 Daniel Orton 3.00 8.00
11 Bradley Beal 20.00 50.00
12 Jared Cunningham 3.00 8.00
13 Enes Kanter 4.00 10.00
14 Kawhi Leonard 100.00 250.00
15 Norris Cole 3.00 8.00
16 Stephen Jackson 4.00 10.00
17 Jrue Holiday 6.00 15.00
18 Tyshawn Taylor 3.00 8.00
19 Al-Farouq Aminu 3.00 8.00
20 Landry Fields 3.00 8.00
21 Eric Gordon 4.00 10.00
22 Patrick Beverley 3.00 8.00
23 Tristan Thompson 3.00 8.00
24 Nikola Vucevic 6.00 15.00
25 Dorell Wright 3.00 8.00
26 Terrence Ross 4.00 10.00
27 Gerald Henderson 3.00 8.00
28 Hollis Thompson 3.00 8.00
29 Gordon Hayward 4.00 10.00
30 Lance Stephenson 4.00 10.00
31 Harrison Barnes 5.00 12.00
32 Festus Ezeli 3.00 8.00
33 Jan Vesely 3.00 8.00
34 Iman Shumpert 3.00 8.00
35 Henry Sims 5.00 12.00
36 Austin Rivers 4.00 10.00
37 Tyreke Evans 4.00 10.00
38 Ersan Ilyasova 3.00 8.00
39 Patrick Patterson 3.00 8.00
40 Ish Smith 3.00 8.00
41 Andre Drummond 5.00 12.00
42 Draymond Green 20.00 50.00
43 Robbie Hummel 3.00 8.00
44 Tobias Harris 5.00 12.00
45 Andre Iguodala 6.00 15.00
46 Blake Griffin EXCH 5.00 12.00
47 Nick Young 3.00 8.00
48 E'Twaun Moore 3.00 8.00
49 James Anderson 3.00 8.00
50 Derrick Favors 3.00 8.00
51 Meyers Leonard 3.00 8.00
52 Quincy Miller 3.00 8.00
53 Kemba Walker 5.00 12.00
54 Kenneth Faried 4.00 10.00
55 Chandler Parsons EXCH 3.00 8.00
56 James Harden 30.00 80.00
57 Ty Lawson 3.00 8.00
58 D.J. Augustin 3.00 8.00
59 Andrea Bargnani 3.00 8.00
60 Robert Sacre 3.00 8.00
61 DeMarre Carroll 3.00 8.00
62 Khris Middleton 10.00 25.00
63 Jimmer Fredette 5.00 12.00
64 Greg Smith 3.00 8.00
65 Jon Leuer 3.00 8.00
66 Stephen Curry 300.00 600.00
67 Alexey Shved 3.00 8.00
68 Diante Garrett 3.00 8.00
69 Greivis Vasquez 3.00 8.00
70 Michael Kidd-Gilchrist 3.00 8.00
71 Maurice Harkless 3.00 8.00
72 Kyrie Irving 100.00 250.00
73 Klay Thompson 100.00 250.00
74 Reggie Jackson 4.00 10.00
75 Jason Smith 3.00 8.00
76 Nikola Pekovic 3.00 8.00
77 Perry Jones 3.00 8.00
78 Kent Bazemore 3.00 8.00
79 Courtney Lee 3.00 8.00
80 Alan Anderson 3.00 8.00

2013-14 Panini Titanium Reserve Signatures

PRINT RUNS B/WN 25-299 COPIES PER
EXCHANGE DEADLINE 8/26/2015
1 Kobe Bryant/49 EXCH 1,000.00 2,000.00
3 Mario Chalmers/99 4.00 10.00
4 Eddie Jones/199 4.00 10.00
5 Nikola Vucevic/225 EXCH 6.00 15.00
6 Norm Nixon/299 4.00 10.00
7 Larry Johnson/199 12.00 30.00
8 Kyrie Irving/49 60.00 150.00
9 Anthony Davis/49 60.00 150.00
10 DeAndre Jordan/25 4.00 10.00
11 MarShon Brooks/249 3.00 8.00
12 Isiah Thomas/25 20.00 50.00
13 Karl Malone/49 50.00 120.00
14 Xavier Henry/299 3.00 8.00
15 Mitch Richmond/249 12.00 30.00
16 Jerryd Bayless/299 3.00 8.00
17 Kevin Durant/49 125.00 300.00
18 Bismack Biyombo/299 3.00 8.00
19 Jerry Lucas/49 12.00 30.00
20 Grant Hill/49 30.00 60.00
21 Kendall Gill/299 10.00 25.00
22 Dee Brown/299 4.00 10.00
23 Horace Grant/49 12.00 30.00
24 Dorell Wright/299 3.00 8.00
25 Keith Van Horn/249 4.00 10.00

2013-14 Panini Titanium Retail

101-200 PRINT RUN 149 COPIES PER
1 Jrue Holiday .40 1.00
2 Gerald Wallace .25 .60
3 Nikola Vucevic .40 1.00
4 Deron Williams .25 .60
5 Luol Deng .25 .60
6 Channing Frye .20 .50
7 Damian Lillard 1.00 2.50
8 Manu Ginobili .60 1.50
9 Dirk Nowitzki .75 2.00
10 Tim Duncan .75 2.00
11 Greivis Vasquez .20 .50
12 Dion Waiters .20 .50
13 Dwight Howard .40 1.00
14 Evan Turner .20 .50
15 Kyrie Irving 1.00 2.50
16 Gerald Henderson .20 .50
17 Chris Bosh .40 1.00
18 Paul George .50 1.25
19 Arron Afflalo .20 .50
20 James Harden .60 1.50
21 Chris Paul .60 1.50
22 Zach Randolph .25 .60
23 Carmelo Anthony .50 1.25
24 Derrick Favors .25 .60
25 Brandon Knight .25 .60
26 Josh Smith .30 .75
27 Kemba Walker .30 .75
28 Amar'e Stoudemire .30 .75
29 Jameer Nelson .20 .50
30 Al Horford .20 .50
31 Kobe Bryant 2.50 6.00
32 Rudy Gay .25 .60
33 John Wall .40 1.00
34 Danny Granger .20 .50
35 Jeff Green .20 .50
36 Ricky Rubio .25 .60
37 Rajon Rondo .40 1.00
38 Roy Hibbert .20 .50
39 Kevin Martin .25 .60
40 Eric Bledsoe .25 .60
41 Jeremy Lin .50 1.25
42 Kevin Garnett .75 2.00
44 Blake Griffin .30 .75
45 Enes Kanter .25 .60
46 Al Jefferson .20 .50
47 Paul Millsap .25 .60
48 Steve Novak .20 .50
49 Dwyane Wade .60 1.50
50 Anthony Davis 1.00 2.50
51 Andre Drummond .30 .75
52 Joakim Noah .30 .75
53 Serge Ibaka .30 .75
54 Jason Richardson .20 .50
55 DeMarcus Cousins .30 .75
56 Nicolas Batum .25 .60
57 Paul Pierce .50 1.25
58 LeBron James 2.50 6.00
59 DeMar DeRozan .40 1.00
60 LaMarcus Aldridge .30 .75
61 J.J. Redick .30 .75
62 Gordon Hayward .25 .60
63 Bradley Beal .50 1.25
64 Tyson Chandler .25 .60
65 Mike Conley .25 .60
66 Harrison Barnes .30 .75
67 Thaddeus Young .20 .50
68 Shawn Marion .25 .60
69 Jeff Teague .20 .50
70 Kevin Love .30 .75
71 Carlos Boozer .25 .60
72 O.J. Mayo .20 .50
73 DeAndre Jordan .25 .60
74 Andre Miller .25 .60
75 Steve Nash .60 1.50
76 Klay Thompson 1.00 2.50
77 Anderson Varejao .20 .50
78 Pau Gasol .50 1.25
79 Kenneth Faried .25 .60
80 Brandon Jennings .20 .50
81 Russell Westbrook .50 1.25
82 Tyreke Evans .25 .60
83 Vince Carter .60 1.50
84 Marcin Gortat .20 .50
85 Jimmer Fredette .30 .75
86 Monta Ellis .25 .60
87 Nikola Pekovic .20 .50
88 George Hill .25 .60
89 Derrick Rose .50 1.25
90 Goran Dragic .25 .60
91 Andrew Bogut .25 .60
92 Mario Chalmers .25 .60
93 Larry Sanders .20 .50
94 Joe Johnson .25 .60
95 Stephen Curry 2.50 6.00
96 J.R. Smith .30 .75
97 Tony Parker .50 1.25
98 Marc Gasol .30 .75
99 Kevin Durant 1.00 2.50
100 Ty Lawson .20 .50
101 Anthony Bennett RC 2.50 6.00
102 Victor Oladipo RC 6.00 15.00
103 Otto Porter RC 4.00 10.00
104 Cody Zeller RC 3.00 8.00
105 Alex Len RC 3.00 8.00
106 Nerlens Noel RC 3.00 8.00
107 Ben McLemore RC 3.00 8.00
108 Kentavious Caldwell-Pope RC 4.00 10.00
109 Trey Burke RC 3.00 8.00
110 C.J. McCollum RC 10.00 25.00
111 M.Carter-Williams RC 3.00 8.00
112 Steven Adams RC 6.00 15.00
113 Kelly Olynyk RC 3.00 8.00
114 Shabazz Muhammad RC 2.50 6.00
115 G.Antetokounmpo RC 300.00 600.00
116 Dennis Schroder RC 8.00 20.00
117 Shane Larkin RC 2.50 6.00
118 Sergey Karasev RC 2.50 6.00
119 Tony Snell RC 3.00 8.00
120 Gorgui Dieng RC 3.00 8.00
121 Mason Plumlee RC 3.00 8.00
122 Solomon Hill RC 3.00 8.00
123 Tim Hardaway Jr. RC 5.00 12.00
124 Reggie Bullock RC 3.00 8.00
125 Andre Roberson RC 3.00 8.00
126 Rudy Gobert RC 10.00 25.00
127 Archie Goodwin RC 2.50 6.00
128 Nemanja Nedovic RC 2.50 6.00
129 Allen Crabbe RC 2.50 6.00
130 Carrick Felix RC 2.50 6.00
131 Isaiah Canaan RC 2.50 6.00
132 Glen Rice Jr. RC 2.50 6.00
133 Ray McCallum RC 2.50 6.00
134 Tony Mitchell RC 2.50 6.00
135 Nate Wolters RC 2.50 6.00
136 Jeff Withey RC 2.50 6.00
137 Jamaal Franklin RC 2.50 6.00
138 Ricky Ledo RC 2.50 6.00
139 Erik Murphy RC 2.50 6.00
140 Ryan Kelly RC 2.50 6.00
141 Peyton Siva RC 2.50 6.00
142 Vitor Faverani RC 2.50 6.00
143 Kobe Bryant 15.00 40.00
144 James Harden 4.00 10.00
145 Steve Nash 4.00 10.00
146 Dwight Howard 2.50 6.00
147 LeBron James 15.00 40.00
148 Deron Williams 1.50 4.00
149 Derrick Rose 3.00 8.00
150 Anthony Davis 6.00 15.00
151 Kyrie Irving 6.00 15.00
152 Dwyane Wade 4.00 10.00
153 Kevin Garnett 5.00 12.00
154 Carmelo Anthony 3.00 8.00
155 Kenneth Faried 1.50 4.00
156 Tim Duncan 5.00 12.00
157 Blake Griffin 2.00 5.00
158 Paul Pierce 3.00 8.00
159 Damian Lillard 6.00 15.00
160 Rajon Rondo 2.50 6.00
161 Tony Parker 3.00 8.00
162 Chris Paul 4.00 10.00
163 DeMarcus Cousins 2.00 5.00
164 Tyson Chandler 1.50 4.00
165 Brandon Jennings 1.25 3.00
166 Kawhi Leonard 6.00 15.00
167 Paul George 3.00 8.00
168 Russell Westbrook 3.00 8.00
169 John Wall 2.50 6.00
170 Dirk Nowitzki 5.00 12.00
171 Larry Sanders 1.25 3.00
172 Kevin Durant 6.00 15.00
173 Joakim Noah 1.50 4.00
174 Zach Randolph 2.00 5.00
175 Vince Carter 4.00 10.00
176 Kevin Love 2.00 5.00
177 Stephen Curry 15.00 40.00
178 Marcin Gortat 1.25 3.00
179 Manu Ginobili 4.00 10.00
180 Ricky Rubio 1.50 4.00
181 Isiah Thomas 3.00 8.00
182 Dominique Wilkins 3.00 8.00
183 Kevin McHale 3.00 8.00
184 Hakeem Olajuwon 4.00 10.00
185 David Robinson 4.00 10.00
186 Julius Erving 5.00 12.00
187 Bill Russell 6.00 15.00
188 Magic Johnson 8.00 20.00
189 Larry Bird 8.00 20.00
190 Wilt Chamberlain 6.00 15.00
191 Karl Malone 4.00 10.00
192 Anfernee Hardaway 3.00 8.00
193 Oscar Robertson 3.00 8.00
194 Jason Kidd 3.00 8.00
195 Grant Hill 3.00 8.00
196 Kareem Abdul-Jabbar 6.00 15.00
197 Pete Maravich 3.00 8.00
198 Shaquille O'Neal 8.00 20.00
199 Scottie Pippen 5.00 12.00
200 Gary Payton 3.00 8.00

2013-14 Panini Titanium Rookie Jerseys

PRINT RUNS B/WN 85-325 COPIES PER
ALL VERSIONS EQUALLY PRICED
1 Anthony Bennett/325 2.00 5.00
2 Victor Oladipo/325 5.00 12.00
3 Otto Porter/325 3.00 8.00
4 Cody Zeller/325 2.50 6.00
5 Alex Len/325 2.50 6.00
6 Nerlens Noel/325 2.50 6.00
7 Ben McLemore/325 2.50 6.00
8 Kentavious Caldwell-Pope/325 3.00 8.00
9 Trey Burke/325 2.50 6.00
10 C.J. McCollum/325 8.00 20.00
11 M.Carter-Williams/325 2.50 6.00
12 Steven Adams/325 5.00 12.00
13 Kelly Olynyk/325 2.50 6.00
14 Shabazz Muhammad/325 2.00 5.00
15 G.Antetokounmpo/325 125.00 300.00
16 Shane Larkin/325 2.00 5.00
17 Tony Snell/325 2.50 6.00
18 Mason Plumlee/325 2.50 6.00
19 Tim Hardaway Jr./325 4.00 10.00
20 Glen Rice Jr./325 2.00 5.00
21 Anthony Bennett/325 2.00 5.00
22 Victor Oladipo/325 5.00 12.00
23 Otto Porter/325 3.00 8.00
24 Cody Zeller/325 2.50 6.00
25 Alex Len/325 2.50 6.00
26 Nerlens Noel/325 2.50 6.00
27 Ben McLemore/325 2.50 6.00
28 Kentavious Caldwell-Pope/325 3.00 8.00
29 Trey Burke/325 2.50 6.00
30 C.J. McCollum/325 8.00 20.00
31 Michael Carter-Williams/325 2.50 6.00
32 Steven Adams/325 5.00 12.00
33 Kelly Olynyk/325 2.50 6.00
34 Shabazz Muhammad/325 2.00 5.00
35 G.Antetokounmpo/325 125.00 300.00
36 Shane Larkin/325 2.00 5.00
37 Tony Snell/325 2.50 6.00
38 Mason Plumlee/325 2.50 6.00
39 Tim Hardaway Jr./325 4.00 10.00
40 Glen Rice Jr./325 2.00 5.00
41 Anthony Bennett/325 2.00 5.00
42 Victor Oladipo/325 5.00 12.00
43 Otto Porter/325 3.00 8.00
44 Cody Zeller/325 2.50 6.00
45 Alex Len/325 2.50 6.00
46 Nerlens Noel/325 2.50 6.00
47 Ben McLemore/325 2.50 6.00
48 Kentavious Caldwell-Pope/325 3.00 8.00
49 Trey Burke/325 2.50 6.00
50 C.J. McCollum/325 8.00 20.00
51 Michael Carter-Williams/325 2.50 6.00
52 Steven Adams/325 5.00 12.00
53 Kelly Olynyk/325 2.50 6.00
54 Shabazz Muhammad/325 2.00 5.00
55 G.Antetokounmpo/325 125.00 300.00
56 Shane Larkin/325 2.00 5.00
57 Tony Snell/325 2.50 6.00
58 Mason Plumlee/325 2.50 6.00
59 Tim Hardaway Jr./325 4.00 10.00
60 Glen Rice Jr./325 2.00 5.00
61 Anthony Bennett/325 2.00 5.00
62 Victor Oladipo/325 5.00 12.00
63 Otto Porter/325 3.00 8.00
64 Cody Zeller/325 2.50 6.00
65 Alex Len/325 2.50 6.00
66 Nerlens Noel/325 2.50 6.00
67 Ben McLemore/325 2.50 6.00
68 Kentavious Caldwell-Pope/325 3.00 8.00
69 Trey Burke/325 2.50 6.00
70 C.J. McCollum/325 8.00 20.00
71 Michael Carter-Williams/325 2.50 6.00
72 Steven Adams/325 5.00 12.00
73 Kelly Olynyk/325 2.50 6.00
74 Shabazz Muhammad/325 2.00 5.00
75 G.Antetokounmpo/325 125.00 300.00
76 Shane Larkin/325 2.00 5.00
77 Tony Snell/325 2.50 6.00
78 Mason Plumlee/325 2.50 6.00
79 Tim Hardaway Jr./325 4.00 10.00
80 Glen Rice Jr./325 2.00 5.00
81 Anthony Bennett/85 3.00 8.00
82 Victor Oladipo/85 6.00 15.00
83 Otto Porter/85 4.00 10.00
84 Cody Zeller/85 3.00 8.00
85 Alex Len/85 3.00 8.00
86 Nerlens Noel/85 3.00 8.00
87 Ben McLemore/85 3.00 8.00
88 Kentavious Caldwell-Pope/85 4.00 10.00
89 Trey Burke/85 3.00 8.00
90 C.J. McCollum/85 10.00 25.00
91 M.Carter-Williams/85 3.00 8.00
92 Steven Adams/85 6.00 15.00
93 Kelly Olynyk/85 3.00 8.00
94 Shabazz Muhammad/85 2.50 6.00
95 G.Antetokounmpo/85 125.00 300.00
96 Shane Larkin/85 2.50 6.00
97 Tony Snell/85 3.00 8.00
98 Mason Plumlee/85 3.00 8.00
99 Tim Hardaway Jr./85 5.00 12.00
100 Glen Rice Jr./85 2.50 6.00

2013-14 Panini Titanium Strength

STATED PRINT RUN 99 SER.#'d SETS
1 Anthony Davis 8.00 20.00
2 Josh Smith 1.50 4.00
3 Kobe Bryant 20.00 50.00
4 Paul Pierce 4.00 10.00
5 Tim Duncan 6.00 15.00
6 Pau Gasol 4.00 10.00
7 Dwight Howard 3.00 8.00
8 Kevin Durant 8.00 20.00
9 Zach Randolph 2.00 5.00
10 Serge Ibaka 2.00 5.00
11 Chris Bosh 3.00 8.00
12 Anderson Varejao 1.50 4.00
13 Marc Gasol 2.50 6.00
14 Tyson Chandler 2.00 5.00
15 LeBron James 20.00 50.00
16 DeMarcus Cousins 2.50 6.00
17 Blake Griffin 2.50 6.00
18 Kenneth Faried 2.00 5.00
19 Dwyane Wade 5.00 12.00
20 Kevin Garnett 6.00 15.00
21 Carmelo Anthony 4.00 10.00
22 Dirk Nowitzki 6.00 15.00
23 Joakim Noah 2.50 6.00
24 Metta World Peace 2.00 5.00
25 Nate Robinson 1.50 4.00

2013-14 Panini Titanium Team Titans

STATED PRINT RUN 149 SER.#'d SETS
1 A.Drummond/G.Monroe 2.50 6.00
2 D.Waiters/K.Irving 8.00 20.00
3 E.Bledsoe/G.Dragic 2.00 5.00
4 D.Wade/L.James 20.00 50.00
5 K.Bryant/P.Gasol 20.00 50.00
6 B.Griffin/C.Paul 5.00 12.00
7 K.Thompson/S.Curry 40.00 100.00
8 B.Beal/J.Wall 4.00 10.00
9 D.Lillard/L.Aldridge 8.00 20.00
10 B.Lopez/D.Williams 2.50 6.00
11 K.Love/R.Rubio 2.50 6.00
12 K.Durant/R.Westbrook 8.00 20.00
13 C.Anthony/T.Chandler 4.00 10.00
14 D.Howard/J.Harden 5.00 12.00
15 P.George/R.Hibbert 4.00 10.00
16 D.Nowitzki/S.Marion 6.00 15.00
17 T.Duncan/T.Parker 6.00 15.00
18 K.Faried/T.Lawson 2.00 5.00
19 E.Turner/T.Young 1.50 4.00
20 D.Rose/J.Noah 4.00 10.00
21 D.DeRozan/K.Lowry 3.00 8.00
22 D.Favors/G.Hayward 2.00 5.00
23 M.Conley/Z.Randolph 2.50 6.00
24 A.Bradley/R.Rondo 3.00 8.00
25 A.Davis/J.Holiday 8.00 20.00

2013-14 Panini Titanium Titanic Threads Jumbo

PRINT RUNS B/WN 99-299 COPIES PER
1 Al Horford/299 4.00 10.00
2 Andrew Bynum/299 2.50 6.00
3 Chauncey Billups/299 5.00 12.00
4 Deron Williams/299 3.00 8.00
5 Jamal Crawford/299 4.00 10.00
6 Kareem Abdul-Jabbar/99 8.00 20.00
7 Larry Johnson/299 5.00 12.00
8 Robert Parish/99 5.00 12.00
9 Tracy McGrady/99 6.00 15.00
10 Zach Randolph/99 3.00 8.00
11 Alex English/99 5.00 12.00
12 Anfernee Hardaway/99 12.00 30.00
13 Chris Bosh/299 5.00 12.00
14 Kevin Martin/299 3.00 8.00
15 James Harden/299 8.00 20.00
16 Karl Malone/299 8.00 20.00
17 LeBron James/299 15.00 40.00
18 Russell Westbrook/299 6.00 15.00
19 James Worthy/99 6.00 15.00
20 Isiah Thomas/99 6.00 15.00
21 Al-Farouq Aminu/198 2.50 6.00
22 Antawn Jamison/299 3.00 8.00
23 Dirk Nowitzki/299 10.00 25.00
24 Chris Paul/299 8.00 20.00

25 Jason Kidd/299 6.00 15.00
26 Brandon Bass/299 2.50 6.00
27 Magic Johnson/99 15.00 40.00
28 Scottie Pippen/99 10.00 25.00
29 Jeff Green/299 2.50 6.00
30 Shane Battier/299 3.00 8.00
31 Alonzo Mourning/99 6.00 15.00
32 Anthony Davis/99 12.00 30.00
33 Clyde Drexler/99 6.00 15.00
34 Dominique Wilkins/99 6.00 15.00
35 Vinnie Johnson/99 4.00 10.00
36 Kenneth Faried/299 3.00 8.00
37 Metta World Peace/299 3.00 8.00
38 Shaquille O'Neal/99 15.00 40.00
39 Tyson Chandler/299 3.00 8.00
40 Nate Robinson/299 2.50 6.00
41 Andray Blatche/299 2.50 6.00
42 Bill Laimbeer/99 4.00 10.00
43 Damian Lillard/99 12.00 30.00
44 Dwight Howard/299 5.00 12.00
45 Mike Miller/299 3.00 8.00
46 Jeremy Lin/299 6.00 15.00
47 Patrick Ewing/99 6.00 15.00
48 Stephen Curry/299 40.00 100.00
49 Jayson Williams/299 2.50 6.00
50 Tayshaun Prince/99 4.00 10.00
51 Andre Iguodala/299 4.00 10.00
52 Nate Wolters/299 2.50 6.00
53 Danilo Gallinari/299 3.00 8.00
54 Dwyane Wade/99 8.00 20.00
55 Jermaine O'Neal/299 3.00 8.00
56 Kevin Garnett/299 6.00 15.00
57 Pau Gasol/299 6.00 15.00
58 Moses Malone/99 6.00 15.00
59 Luol Deng/299 3.00 8.00
60 Kevin Durant/299 12.00 30.00
61 Andre Miller/299 3.00 8.00
62 Jodie Meeks/299 2.50 6.00
63 David Robinson/99 8.00 20.00
64 Fat Lever/299 3.00 8.00
65 Joakim Noah/299 4.00 10.00
66 Kevin McHale/99 6.00 15.00
67 Paul Pierce/299 6.00 15.00
68 Steve Nash/299 8.00 20.00
69 Raymond Felton/299 2.50 6.00
70 Jason Terry/299 3.00 8.00
71 Carlos Boozer/299 3.00 8.00
72 Andrei Kirilenko/99 4.00 10.00
73 DeMar DeRozan/299 5.00 12.00
74 Gary Payton/99 6.00 15.00
75 Joe Dumars/299 5.00 12.00
76 Kevin Love/299 4.00 10.00
77 Rajon Rondo/299 5.00 12.00
78 Taj Gibson/299 2.50 6.00
79 Victor Oladipo/299 5.00 12.00
80 G.Antetokounmpo/299 125.00 300.00
81 Amar'e Stoudemire/99 4.00 10.00
82 DeMarcus Cousins/299 4.00 10.00
83 Carmelo Anthony/299 6.00 15.00
84 Gerald Wallace/99 3.00 8.00
85 John Wall/99 5.00 12.00
86 Kobe Bryant/299 75.00 200.00
87 Ray Allen/299 6.00 15.00
88 Tim Duncan/299 10.00 25.00
89 Mario Chalmers/299 3.00 8.00
90 Larry Bird/99 15.00 40.00
91 Ben McLemore/299 3.00 8.00
92 Caron Butler/299 3.00 8.00
93 Channing Frye/99 2.50 6.00
94 Grant Hill/299 6.00 15.00
95 John Stockton/99 8.00 20.00
96 Kyrie Irving/99 12.00 30.00
97 Kendrick Perkins/299 2.50 6.00
98 Tony Parker/99 6.00 15.00
99 Anthony Bennett/299 2.50 6.00
100 M.Carter-Williams/299 3.00 8.00

2013-14 Panini Titanium Titans

STATED PRINT RUN 199 SER.#'d SETS
1 Kevin Garnett 4.00 10.00
2 Tim Duncan 4.00 10.00
3 Dirk Nowitzki 4.00 10.00
4 Kobe Bryant 12.00 30.00
5 LeBron James 10.00 25.00
6 Paul Pierce 2.50 6.00
7 Steve Nash 3.00 8.00
8 Dwyane Wade 3.00 8.00
9 Vince Carter 3.00 8.00
10 Dwight Howard 2.00 5.00
11 Chris Paul 3.00 8.00
12 Blake Griffin 1.50 4.00
13 Kyrie Irving 5.00 12.00
14 Anthony Davis 5.00 12.00
15 Tony Parker 2.50 6.00
16 Carmelo Anthony 2.50 6.00
17 Kevin Durant 5.00 12.00
18 James Harden 3.00 8.00
19 Russell Westbrook 2.50 6.00
20 Stephen Curry 12.00 30.00
21 Marc Gasol 1.50 4.00
22 Kenneth Faried 1.25 3.00
23 Joakim Noah 1.50 4.00
24 Ray Allen 2.50 6.00
25 Damian Lillard 5.00 12.00

2017-18 Panini Vanguard

1-100 STATED PRINT RUN 49 SER.#'d SETS
AU RC STATED PRINT RUN 99 SER.#'d SETS
JSY AU STATED PRINT RUN 99 SER.#'d SETS
EXCHANGE DEADLINE 02/29/2020
1 Joel Embiid 3.00 8.00
2 Klay Thompson 4.00 10.00
3 Kyle Lowry 1.50 4.00
4 Brandon Ingram 2.00 5.00
5 Donovan Mitchell RC 40.00 100.00
6 Anthony Davis 4.00 10.00
7 John Collins RC 4.00 10.00
8 Dennis Schroder 1.25 3.00
9 Kobe Bryant 12.00 30.00
10 LeBron James 20.00 50.00
11 Elfrid Payton 1.00 2.50
12 Draymond Green 2.00 5.00
13 DeMar DeRozan 2.00 5.00
14 Marc Gasol 1.50 4.00
15 Markelle Fultz RC 4.00 10.00
16 DeMarcus Cousins 1.25 3.00
17 Josh Hart RC 4.00 10.00
18 Taurean Prince 1.00 2.50
19 Shaquille O'Neal 5.00 12.00
20 Kevin Love 1.50 4.00
21 Devin Booker 4.00 10.00
22 Kevin Durant 6.00 15.00
23 Ricky Rubio 1.25 3.00
24 Mike Conley 1.25 3.00
25 Jayson Tatum RC 60.00 150.00
26 Kristaps Porzingis 2.00 5.00
27 Bam Adebayo RC 15.00 40.00
28 Kyrie Irving 3.00 8.00
29 Larry Bird 6.00 15.00
30 George Hill 1.25 3.00
31 Damian Lillard 4.00 10.00
32 Chris Paul 2.50 6.00
33 Rudy Gobert 2.00 5.00
34 Dwyane Wade 3.00 8.00
35 Lauri Markkanen RC 10.00 25.00
36 Enes Kanter 1.25 3.00
37 Frank Ntilikina RC 2.00 5.00
38 Jaylen Brown 4.00 10.00
39 Magic Johnson 6.00 15.00
40 Dirk Nowitzki 4.00 10.00
41 CJ McCollum 1.50 4.00
42 James Harden 3.00 8.00
43 John Wall 2.00 5.00
44 Goran Dragic 1.25 3.00
45 Kyle Kuzma RC 6.00 15.00
46 Russell Westbrook 2.50 6.00
47 Jonathan Isaac RC 4.00 10.00
48 D'Angelo Russell 1.25 3.00
49 Pete Maravich 4.00 10.00
50 Harrison Barnes 1.25 3.00
51 Zach Randolph 1.50 4.00
52 Victor Oladipo 1.25 3.00
53 Bradley Beal 2.00 5.00
54 Eric Bledsoe 1.25 3.00
55 Dennis Smith Jr. 2.00 5.00
56 Paul George 2.50 6.00
57 Jordan Bell RC 1.50 4.00
58 Spencer Dinwiddie 1.25 3.00
59 Tim Duncan 4.00 10.00
60 Jamal Murray 2.50 6.00
61 Vince Carter 3.00 8.00
62 Myles Turner 1.50 4.00
63 Marcin Gortat 1.00 2.50
64 Giannis Antetokounmpo 8.00 20.00
65 Dillon Brooks RC 5.00 12.00
66 Carmelo Anthony 2.50 6.00
67 OG Anunoby RC 8.00 20.00
68 Kemba Walker 1.25 3.00
69 Kevin Garnett 4.00 10.00
70 Nikola Jokic 10.00 25.00
71 Tony Parker 2.50 6.00
72 Lonzo Ball RC 6.00 15.00
73 Lou Williams 1.25 3.00
74 Jimmy Butler 2.50 6.00
75 Bogdan Bogdanovic RC 4.00 10.00
76 Aaron Gordon 1.50 4.00
77 Maxi Kleber RC 2.50 6.00
78 Dwight Howard 2.00 5.00
79 Allen Iverson 4.00 10.00
80 Blake Griffin 1.50 4.00
81 Kawhi Leonard 4.00 10.00
82 DeAndre Jordan 1.25 3.00
83 Khris Middleton 2.00 5.00
84 Andrew Wiggins 2.00 5.00
85 De'Aaron Fox RC 12.00 30.00
86 Nikola Vucevic 1.25 3.00
87 Zhou Qi RC 3.00 8.00
88 Zach LaVine 2.50 6.00
89 Stephon Marbury 1.25 3.00
90 Andre Drummond 1.25 3.00
91 LaMarcus Aldridge 1.50 4.00
92 Isaiah Thomas 1.25 3.00
93 Tyreke Evans 1.00 2.50
94 Karl-Anthony Towns 2.50 6.00
95 Josh Jackson RC 2.00 5.00
96 Ben Simmons 1.50 4.00
97 Malik Monk RC 6.00 15.00
98 Kris Dunn 1.00 2.50
99 Drazen Petrovic 1.50 4.00
100 Stephen Curry 12.00 30.00
101 Kyle Kuzma AU 12.00 30.00
102 Bogdan Bogdanovic AU 6.00 15.00
103 Dennis Smith Jr. AU 4.00 10.00
104 Brandon Paul AU RC 3.00 8.00
105 John Collins AU 10.00 25.00
106 Tyler Cavanaugh AU RC 3.00 8.00
107 Malik Monk AU EXCH 12.00 30.00
108 Harry Giles AU RC 3.00 8.00
109 Lonzo Ball AU 25.00 60.00
110 TJ Leaf AU RC 3.00 8.00
111 Lauri Markkanen AU 15.00 40.00
112 Daniel Theis AU RC 10.00 25.00
113 Jordan Bell AU 3.00 8.00
114 Cedi Osman AU RC 6.00 15.00
115 Luke Kennard AU RC 6.00 15.00
116 Markelle Fultz AU 12.00 30.00
117 Jonathan Isaac AU 8.00 20.00
118 Zach Collins AU RC 5.00 12.00
119 Jayson Tatum AU 60.00 150.00
120 Milos Teodosic AU RC 4.00 10.00
121 Frank Ntilikina AU 4.00 10.00
122 Maxi Kleber AU 5.00 12.00
123 De'Aaron Fox AU 25.00 60.00
124 Zhou Qi AU 15.00 40.00
125 Frank Mason III AU RC 3.00 8.00
126 Dillon Brooks AU 10.00 25.00
127 Bam Adebayo AU 20.00 50.00
128 OG Anunoby AU 15.00 40.00
129 Donovan Mitchell AU 125.00 300.00
130 Dwayne Bacon AU RC 3.00 8.00
131 Lonzo Ball JSY AU 100.00 250.00
132 Donovan Mitchell JSY AU 150.00 400.00
133 Jayson Tatum JSY AU 200.00 500.00
134 Kyle Kuzma JSY AU 15.00 40.00
135 Markelle Fultz JSY AU 15.00 40.00
136 Lauri Markkanen JSY AU 20.00 50.00
137 Frank Ntilikina JSY AU 5.00 12.00
138 Dennis Smith Jr. JSY AU 5.00 12.00
140 De'Aaron Fox JSY AU 100.00 250.00
141 Josh Jackson JSY AU 5.00 12.00
143 Frank Mason III JSY AU 4.00 10.00
144 Malik Monk JSY AU 15.00 40.00
145 Jonathan Isaac JSY AU 20.00 50.00
146 Bam Adebayo JSY AU 100.00 250.00
147 Harry Giles JSY AU 4.00 10.00
148 Zach Collins JSY AU 6.00 15.00
149 OG Anunoby JSY AU 20.00 50.00
152 John Collins JSY AU 40.00 100.00
154 Tony Bradley JSY AU RC 4.00 10.00
155 Justin Jackson JSY AU RC 4.00 10.00
156 Caleb Swanigan JSY AU RC 4.00 10.00
157 Derrick White JSY AU RC 20.00 50.00
158 Terrance Ferguson JSY AU RC 4.00 10.00
159 Semi Ojeleye JSY AU 5.00 12.00
160 Dwayne Bacon JSY AU 4.00 10.00

2017-18 Panini Vanguard Purple

*PRPL 1-100: .6X TO 1.5X BASIC
*PRPL 1-100 RC: .6X TO 1.5X BASIC
*PRPL 101-130: .5X TO 1.2X BASIC
*PRPL 131-160: .6X TO 1.5X BASIC
1-100 STATED PRINT RUN 25 SER.#'d SETS
AU STATED PRINT RUN 49 SER.#'d SETS
JSY AU STATED PRINT RUN 25 SER.#'d SETS
EXCHANGE DEADLINE 11/2/2019
112 Daniel Theis AU 12.00 30.00
133 Jayson Tatum JSY AU 500.00 1,000.00
139 Jordan Bell JSY AU 6.00 15.00
142 Luke Kennard JSY AU 12.00 30.00
151 Josh Hart JSY AU 30.00 80.00
153 Justin Patton JSY AU 6.00 15.00

2017-18 Panini Vanguard Beyond the Arc Scripts

PRINT RUNS B/WN 25-99 COPIES PER
EXCHANGE DEADLINE 02/29/2020
*PURPLE/25: .6X TO 1.5X p/r 99
*PURPLE/25: .5X TO 1.2X p/r 49
*PURPLE/25: .4X TO 1X p/r 25
1 Glen Rice/99 3.00 8.00
2 Kobe Bryant/25 EXCH 1,500.00 3,000.00
3 Dan Majerle/99 3.00 8.00
5 Lou Williams/99 3.00 8.00
6 Ray Allen/49 40.00 100.00
7 Wayne Ellington/99 2.50 6.00
8 Eric Gordon/49 4.00 10.00
9 Mike Bibby/99 4.00 10.00
10 Chauncey Billups/99 12.00 30.00
11 Allan Houston/99 4.00 10.00
12 Stephen Curry/25 800.00 1,500.00
13 Mitch Richmond/99 10.00 25.00
14 Larry Bird/25 75.00 200.00
15 Damon Stoudamire/99 10.00 25.00
16 Jason Kidd/49 20.00 50.00
17 Antoine Walker/99 3.00 8.00
18 Trevor Ariza/99 2.50 6.00
19 Dell Curry/99 6.00 15.00
20 Latrell Sprewell/99 15.00 40.00
21 Antawn Jamison/99 3.00 8.00
22 Reggie Miller/25 75.00 200.00
23 Stephen Jackson/99 3.00 8.00
24 Kevin Love/49 10.00 25.00
25 John Starks/99 10.00 25.00
26 Gary Payton/49 20.00 50.00
27 Eddie Jones/99 4.00 10.00
28 Joe Ingles/99 EXCH 6.00 15.00
29 Jason Williams/99 30.00 80.00
30 Kyle Korver/99 3.00 8.00

2017-18 Panini Vanguard Cosmic Force Signatures

PRINT RUNS B/WN 25-99 COPIES PER
EXCHANGE DEADLINE 02/29/2020
*PURPLE/25: .6X TO 1.5X p/r 99
*PURPLE/25: .5X TO 1.2X p/r 49
*PURPLE/25: .4X TO 1X p/r 25
1 Dikembe Mutombo/99 8.00 20.00
2 Kevin Love/49 EXCH 10.00 25.00
3 Rudy Gobert/99 12.00 30.00
4 LaMarcus Aldridge/49 8.00 20.00
5 Al Horford/49 5.00 12.00
6 Nikola Mirotic/49 3.00 8.00
7 Bill Walton/99 10.00 25.00
8 Kareem Abdul-Jabbar/25 100.00 250.00
9 Robert Parish/99 10.00 25.00
10 David Robinson/49 40.00 100.00
11 Enes Kanter/99 3.00 8.00
12 Dennis Rodman/49 40.00 100.00
13 Willie Cauley-Stein/99 2.50 6.00
14 Joel Embiid/49 50.00 120.00
15 Nikola Jokic/49 EXCH 150.00 400.00
16 Shaquille O'Neal/25 100.00 250.00
17 Dave Cowens/99 6.00 15.00
18 Alonzo Mourning/49 20.00 50.00
19 Ben Wallace/99 EXCH 12.00 30.00
20 Hakeem Olajuwon/49 40.00 100.00
21 Zaza Pachulia/99 2.50 6.00
22 Kristaps Porzingis/49 20.00 50.00
23 Arvydas Sabonis/99 8.00 20.00
24 Artis Gilmore/49 10.00 25.00
25 Myles Turner/99 4.00 10.00
26 Karl Malone/25 40.00 100.00
27 Ralph Sampson/99 6.00 15.00
28 Karl-Anthony Towns/49 15.00 40.00
29 Jermaine O'Neal/99 4.00 10.00
30 Marc Gasol/49 EXCH 5.00 12.00
31 Charles Barkley/25 150.00 400.00

2017-18 Panini Vanguard High Voltage Signatures

PRINT RUNS B/WN 25-99 COPIES PER
EXCHANGE DEADLINE 02/29/2020
*PURPLE/25: .6X TO 1.5X p/r 99
*PURPLE/25: .5X TO 1.2X p/r 49
*PURPLE/25: .4X TO 1X p/r 25
1 David Thompson/99 8.00 20.00
2 John Stockton/25 60.00 150.00
3 Jrue Holiday/99 8.00 20.00
4 Dwyane Wade/25 75.00 200.00
5 Calvin Murphy/49 5.00 12.00
6 Kobe Bryant/25 EXCH 1,500.00 3,000.00
7 Mike Conley/49 4.00 10.00
8 Isaiah Thomas/49 4.00 10.00
9 Mark Price/99 8.00 20.00
10 Jason Kidd/49 25.00 60.00
11 Jerry Stackhouse/99 10.00 25.00
13 Danny Green/99 3.00 8.00
14 Damian Lillard/25 75.00 200.00
15 Nate Archibald/49 6.00 15.00
16 Stephen Curry/25 600.00 1,200.00
17 Zach Randolph/49 5.00 12.00
18 Gary Payton/49 20.00 50.00
19 Terrell Brandon/99 2.50 6.00
20 Vince Carter/49 25.00 60.00
21 Mike Bibby/99 4.00 10.00
22 Clyde Drexler/49 20.00 50.00
23 Rudy Gay/99 3.00 8.00
25 Chauncey Billups/99 12.00 30.00
26 Kevin Durant/25 125.00 300.00
27 Kenny Smith/49 4.00 10.00
28 Grant Hill/49 15.00 40.00
29 Isaiah Rider/99 3.00 8.00
30 Anfernee Hardaway/49 25.00 60.00
31 Derek Harper/99 3.00 8.00
32 Tracy McGrady/49 20.00 50.00
33 Michael Cooper/99 3.00 8.00
34 Magic Johnson/25 60.00 150.00
35 Lenny Wilkens/99 8.00 20.00
36 Allen Iverson/25 75.00 200.00
37 Walt Frazier/49 12.00 30.00
38 Kemba Walker/49 12.00 30.00
39 Cedric Ceballos/99 12.00 30.00
40 Tony Parker/49 20.00 50.00

2017-18 Panini Vanguard Hot off the Press Autographs

STATED PRINT RUN 99 SER.#'d SETS
EXCHANGE DEADLINE 02/29/2020
*PURPLE/49: .5X TO 1.2X BASIC
1 Frank Mason III 4.00 10.00
2 Bam Adebayo 40.00 100.00
3 Lonzo Ball 40.00 100.00
4 OG Anunoby 20.00 50.00
5 Kyle Kuzma 15.00 40.00
6 Josh Hart 10.00 25.00
7 Frank Ntilikina 5.00 12.00
8 Maxi Kleber 6.00 15.00
9 De'Aaron Fox 40.00 100.00
10 Zhou Qi 15.00 40.00
11 Malik Monk EXCH 15.00 40.00
12 Terrance Ferguson 4.00 10.00
13 Donovan Mitchell 125.00 300.00
14 TJ Leaf 4.00 10.00
15 Markelle Fultz 15.00 40.00
16 Bogdan Bogdanovic 20.00 50.00
17 Dennis Smith Jr. 5.00 12.00
18 Brandon Paul 4.00 10.00
19 John Collins 10.00 25.00
20 Tyler Cavanaugh 4.00 10.00
21 Jonathan Isaac 10.00 25.00
22 Zach Collins 6.00 15.00
23 Jayson Tatum 200.00 500.00
24 Milos Teodosic 5.00 12.00
25 Lauri Markkanen 25.00 60.00
26 Daniel Theis 10.00 25.00
27 Jordan Bell 4.00 10.00
28 Cedi Osman 8.00 20.00
29 Luke Kennard 8.00 20.00
30 Dillon Brooks 12.00 30.00

2017-18 Panini Vanguard In Focus Autographs

PRINT RUNS B/WN 25-99 COPIES PER
EXCHANGE DEADLINE 02/29/2020
*PURPLE/25: .6X TO 1.5X p/r 99
*PURPLE/25: .5X TO 1.2X p/r 49
*PURPLE/25: .4X TO 1X p/r 25
1 Magic Johnson/25 60.00 150.00
2 Shaun Livingston/99 3.00 8.00
3 Giannis Antetokounmpo/49 300.00 600.00
4 Iman Shumpert/99 2.50 6.00
5 D'Angelo Russell/49 12.00 30.00
6 Patrick Patterson/99 2.50 6.00
7 Andre Drummond/49 4.00 10.00
8 Avery Bradley/49 3.00 8.00
9 Kevin Durant/25 125.00 300.00
10 Joe Johnson/99 EXCH 3.00 8.00
12 Channing Frye/99 2.50 6.00
13 Andrew Wiggins/49 12.00 30.00
14 Darren Collison/99 2.50 6.00
15 Gordon Hayward/49 4.00 10.00
16 Thon Maker/99 2.50 6.00
17 Kentavious Caldwell-Pope/49 4.00 10.00
18 Aaron Gordon/49 5.00 12.00
19 JJ Redick/99 10.00 25.00
20 Allen Iverson/25 75.00 200.00
21 Justise Winslow/99 2.50 6.00
23 Jonas Valanciunas/99 3.00 8.00
24 Brandon Ingram/49 EXCH 20.00 50.00
25 Evan Turner/99 2.50 6.00
26 Buddy Hield/49 5.00 12.00
27 D.J. Augustin/99 2.50 6.00
28 Devin Harris/99 2.50 6.00
29 Dwyane Wade/25 75.00 200.00
30 Rony Seikaly/99 2.50 6.00
31 Jerry West/25 40.00 100.00
32 Ryan Anderson/99 2.50 6.00
33 Jeremy Lin/49 12.00 30.00
34 Malcolm Brogdon/99 3.00 8.00
35 Glen Rice/99 3.00 8.00
36 Doug McDermott/99 2.50 6.00
37 Tyson Chandler/49 4.00 10.00
38 Emmanuel Mudiay/99 2.50 6.00
39 Damian Lillard/25 75.00 200.00
40 Nerlens Noel/99 2.50 6.00

2017-18 Panini Vanguard Postseason Heroes Autographed Materials

STATED PRINT RUN 25 SER.#'d SETS
EXCHANGE DEADLINE 02/29/2020
1 Bill Walton 20.00 50.00
2 Hakeem Olajuwon 75.00 200.00
3 Cedric Maxwell 6.00 15.00
4 Kevin Love 8.00 20.00
5 Jason Kidd 40.00 100.00
6 Kobe Bryant EXCH 1,500.00 3,000.00
7 Dennis Rodman 60.00 150.00
8 Kevin Durant 150.00 400.00
9 Joe Dumars 12.00 30.00
10 Dirk Nowitzki 150.00 400.00
11 B.J. Armstrong 8.00 20.00
12 Clyde Drexler 40.00 100.00
13 Bill Laimbeer 12.00 30.00
14 Ray Allen 75.00 200.00
15 Tony Parker 30.00 80.00
16 Stephen Curry 600.00 1,200.00
17 Richard Hamilton 12.00 30.00
18 Shaquille O'Neal 150.00 400.00
19 Robert Parish 15.00 40.00
20 David Robinson 75.00 200.00

2017-18 Panini Vanguard V-Team Signatures Swatches

PRINT RUNS B/WN 25-99 COPIES PER
EXCHANGE DEADLINE 02/29/2020
*PURPLE/25: .6X TO 1.5X p/r 99
*PURPLE/25: .5X TO 1.2X p/r 49
*PURPLE/25: .4X TO 1X p/r 25
1 DeMarre Carroll/99 4.00 10.00
2 Joel Embiid/49 40.00 100.00
3 Seth Curry/99 6.00 15.00
4 Al Horford/99 6.00 15.00
5 Harrison Barnes/49 6.00 15.00
6 Kevin Durant/25 100.00 250.00
7 Trevor Ariza/99 4.00 10.00
8 Anthony Davis/25 60.00 150.00
9 Rudy Gay/99 5.00 12.00
10 Brandon Ingram/49 EXCH 10.00 25.00
11 Evan Turner/99 4.00 10.00
12 Clint Capela/99 5.00 12.00
13 Rudy Gobert/99 12.00 30.00
14 Khris Middleton/99 8.00 20.00
15 Joe Ingles/99 5.00 12.00
16 Dwyane Wade/25 125.00 300.00
17 Elfrid Payton/99 4.00 10.00
19 Gary Harris/99 5.00 12.00
20 Vince Carter/49 40.00 100.00
21 Malcolm Brogdon/99 5.00 12.00
22 Marcus Smart/99 6.00 15.00
23 Willie Cauley-Stein/99 4.00 10.00
24 Zach LaVine/99 15.00 40.00
25 Reggie Jackson/95 5.00 12.00
26 Chris Paul/25 75.00 200.00
27 Myles Turner/99 6.00 15.00
28 Blake Griffin/25 20.00 50.00
29 Andrew Wiggins/25 12.00 30.00
30 D'Angelo Russell/49 6.00 15.00
31 Thaddeus Young/99 4.00 10.00
32 Buddy Hield/49 8.00 20.00
33 James Johnson/99 4.00 10.00
34 Nikola Jokic/99 150.00 400.00
35 Michael Kidd-Gilchrist/99 4.00 10.00
36 Damian Lillard/25 75.00 200.00
37 Jrue Holiday/99 12.00 30.00
38 Giannis Antetokounmpo/25 150.00 400.00
39 Enes Kanter/99 5.00 12.00
40 LaMarcus Aldridge/49 8.00 20.00
41 Patrick Beverley/99 4.00 10.00
42 Andre Drummond/99 5.00 12.00
43 Tim Hardaway Jr./99 5.00 12.00
44 Avery Bradley/99 4.00 10.00
45 Nerlens Noel/99 4.00 10.00
46 Kyrie Irving/25 40.00 100.00
47 Ryan Anderson/99 4.00 10.00
48 Karl-Anthony Towns/49 15.00 40.00
49 Thon Maker/99 4.00 10.00
50 Kristaps Porzingis/49 20.00 50.00

2014-15 Paramount

COMPLETE SET (100)
1 Tony Parker 1.25 3.00
2 Kobe Bryant 6.00 15.00
3 Damian Lillard 2.00 5.00
4 Kevin Durant 2.50 6.00
5 Paul George 1.25 3.00
6 Dirk Nowitzki 2.00 5.00
7 Anthony Davis 2.00 5.00
8 Russell Westbrook 1.25 3.00
9 James Harden 1.50 4.00
10 Blake Griffin .75 2.00
11 Stephen Curry 2.00 5.00
12 LeBron James 4.00 10.00
13 Derrick Rose 1.50 4.00
14 Kyrie Irving 1.50 4.00
15 Rajon Rondo 1.00 2.50
16 Dwyane Wade 1.50 4.00
17 Carmelo Anthony 1.25 3.00
18 Tim Duncan 2.00 5.00
19 Kevin Love .75 2.00
20 Chris Paul 1.25 3.00
21 Magic Johnson 3.00 8.00
22 Larry Bird 3.00 8.00
23 Scottie Pippen 2.00 5.00
24 Allen Iverson 2.00 5.00
25 Chris Webber 1.00 2.50
26 Andrew Wiggins RC 8.00 20.00
27 Jabari Parker RC 1.25 3.00
28 Joel Embiid RC 10.00 25.00
29 Aaron Gordon RC 5.00 12.00
30 Dante Exum RC 1.50 4.00
31 Marcus Smart RC 4.00 10.00
32 Julius Randle RC 5.00 12.00
33 Nik Stauskas RC 1.00 2.50
34 Noah Vonleh RC 1.00 2.50
35 Elfrid Payton RC 1.50 4.00
36 Doug McDermott RC 1.50 4.00
37 Zach LaVine RC 6.00 15.00
38 T.J. Warren RC 1.50 4.00
39 Adreian Payne RC 1.00 2.50
40 Cleanthony Early RC 1.00 2.50
41 James Young RC 1.00 2.50
42 Tyler Ennis RC 1.00 2.50
43 Gary Harris RC 1.50 4.00
44 Bruno Caboclo RC 1.25 3.00
45 Mitch McGary RC 1.00 2.50
46 Jordan Adams RC 1.00 2.50
47 Shabazz Napier RC 1.25 3.00
48 Rodney Hood RC 1.25 3.00
49 Glenn Robinson III RC 1.25 3.00
50 P.J. Hairston RC 1.00 2.50
51 Tony Parker SP 8.00 20.00
52 Kobe Bryant SP 40.00 100.00
53 Damian Lillard SP 12.00 30.00
54 Kevin Durant SP 15.00 40.00
55 Paul George SP 8.00 20.00
56 Dirk Nowitzki SP 12.00 30.00
57 Anthony Davis SP 12.00 30.00
58 Russell Westbrook SP 8.00 20.00
59 James Harden SP 10.00 25.00
60 Blake Griffin SP 5.00 12.00
61 Stephen Curry SP 40.00 100.00
62 LeBron James SP 40.00 100.00
63 Derrick Rose SP 10.00 25.00
64 Kyrie Irving SP 10.00 25.00
65 Rajon Rondo SP 6.00 15.00
66 Dwyane Wade SP 10.00 25.00
67 Carmelo Anthony SP 8.00 20.00
68 Tim Duncan SP 12.00 30.00
69 Kevin Love SP 5.00 12.00
70 Chris Paul SP 8.00 20.00
71 Magic Johnson SP 20.00 50.00
72 Larry Bird SP 20.00 50.00
73 Scottie Pippen SP 12.00 30.00
74 Allen Iverson SP 12.00 30.00
75 Chris Webber SP 6.00 15.00
76 Andrew Wiggins SP 125.00 250.00
77 Jabari Parker SP 4.00 10.00
78 Joel Embiid SP 30.00 80.00
79 Aaron Gordon SP 15.00 40.00
80 Dante Exum SP 5.00 12.00
81 Marcus Smart SP 12.00 30.00
82 Julius Randle SP 15.00 40.00
83 Nik Stauskas SP 3.00 8.00
84 Noah Vonleh SP 3.00 8.00
85 Elfrid Payton SP 5.00 12.00
86 Doug McDermott SP 5.00 12.00
87 Zach LaVine SP 20.00 50.00
88 T.J. Warren SP 5.00 12.00
89 Adreian Payne SP 3.00 8.00
90 Cleanthony Early SP 3.00 8.00
91 James Young SP 3.00 8.00
92 Tyler Ennis SP 3.00 8.00
93 Gary Harris SP 5.00 12.00
94 Bruno Caboclo SP 4.00 10.00
95 Mitch McGary SP 3.00 8.00
96 Jordan Adams SP 3.00 8.00
97 Shabazz Napier SP 4.00 10.00
98 Rodney Hood SP 4.00 10.00
99 Glenn Robinson III SP 4.00 10.00
100 P.J. Hairston SP 3.00 8.00

2014-15 Paramount Blue

*BLUE VETS: 4X TO 10X BASE HI
*BLUE RK: 2X TO 5X BASE HI
STATED PRINT RUN 25 SER.#'d SETS
18 Tim Duncan 10.00 25.00
26 Andrew Wiggins 75.00 150.00
27 Jabari Parker 6.00 15.00

2014-15 Paramount Bronze

*GOLD VETS: 2X TO 5X BASE HI
*GOLD RK: 1X TO 2.5X BASE HI
STATED PRINT RUN 50 SER.#'d SETS

2014-15 Paramount Next Day Autographs

STATED PRINT RUN B/WN 49-110 COPIES PER
EXCHANGE DEADLINE 7/7/2016
NDAG Aaron Gordon/100 40.00 100.00
NDAP Adreian Payne/100 4.00 10.00
NDAW Andrew Wiggins/100 125.00 300.00
NDBC Bruno Caboclo/100 5.00 12.00
NDCE Cleanthony Early/100 4.00 10.00
NDCJ Cory Jefferson/100 4.00 10.00
NDCW C.J. Wilcox/100 4.00 10.00
NDDI Damien Inglis/100 4.00 10.00
NDDM Doug McDermott/100 6.00 15.00
NDEP Elfrid Payton/100 12.00 30.00
NDGH Gary Harris/105 40.00 100.00
NDGR Glenn Robinson III/100 5.00 12.00
NDJA Jordan Adams/100 4.00 10.00
NDJE Joel Embiid/49 400.00 800.00
NDJG Jerami Grant/100 20.00 50.00
NDJH Joe Harris/100 6.00 15.00
NDJO Johnny O'Bryant/85 4.00 10.00
NDJP Jabari Parker/110 5.00 12.00
NDJR Julius Randle/100 125.00 300.00
NDJS Jarnell Stokes/101 4.00 10.00
NDJY James Young/100 4.00 10.00
NDKA Kyle Anderson/100 6.00 15.00
NDKM K.J. McDaniels/100 4.00 10.00
NDMB Markel Brown/100 4.00 10.00
NDMM Mitch McGary/101 4.00 10.00
NDMS Marcus Smart/100 20.00 50.00
NDNS Nik Stauskas/100 4.00 10.00
NDNV Noah Vonleh/100 4.00 10.00
NDPH P.J. Hairston/100 4.00 10.00
NDRH Rodney Hood/100 5.00 12.00
NDRS Russ Smith/98 4.00 10.00
NDSD Spencer Dinwiddie/100 20.00 50.00
NDSN Shabazz Napier/100 5.00 12.00
NDTA Thanasis Antetokounmpo/97 8.00 20.00
NDTE Tyler Ennis/97 4.00 10.00
NDTW T.J. Warren/94 15.00 40.00
NDZL Zach LaVine/100 300.00 600.00

2014-15 Paramount Past and Present Jerseys

STATED PRINT RUN B/WN 20-40 COPIES PER
1 Paul Millsap/20 3.00 8.00
2 LeBron James/40 25.00 60.00
3 Monta Ellis/40 3.00 8.00
4 Kevin Garnett/40 10.00 25.00
5 James Harden/40 10.00 25.00
6 Chris Andersen/25 3.00 8.00
7 Dwight Howard/40 5.00 12.00
8 Brandon Knight/20 2.50 6.00
9 Al Jefferson/20 2.50 6.00
10 Brandon Jennings/20 2.50 6.00
11 Joe Johnson/40 3.00 8.00
12 David Lee/20 2.50 6.00
13 O.J. Mayo/25 2.50 6.00
14 Steve Nash/40 8.00 20.00
15 Carmelo Anthony/40 6.00 15.00
16 Chris Paul/40 6.00 15.00
17 Goran Dragic/40 4.00 10.00
18 Chris Bosh/40 3.00 8.00
19 Eric Bledsoe/40 3.00 8.00
20 Andre Iguodala/40 4.00 10.00

2014-15 Paramount Past and Present Jerseys Prime

*PRIME: 1X TO 2.5X BASE HI
STATED PRINT RUN B/WN 15-25 COPIES PER
1 Paul Millsap/15 25.00 60.00
2 LeBron James/20 100.00 200.00
4 Kevin Garnett/25 20.00 50.00
6 Chris Andersen/15 15.00 40.00
7 Dwight Howard/20 25.00 60.00
15 Carmelo Anthony/25 15.00 40.00

2014-15 Paramount Penmanship Autographs

STATED PRINT RUN B/WN 35-99 COPIES PER
EXCHANGE DEADLINE 7/7/2016
1 Kobe Bryant/35 1,500.00 3,000.00
2 Karl Malone/35 40.00 100.00
3 Magic Johnson/35 125.00 300.00
4 Larry Bird/35 125.00 300.00
5 John Stockton/35 40.00 100.00
6 Kevin Durant/35 125.00 300.00
7 Kareem Abdul-Jabbar/35 150.00 400.00
8 Anthony Davis/35 60.00 150.00
9 Kyrie Irving/35 40.00 100.00
10 Steve Nash/49 50.00 120.00
11 Jason Kidd/49 20.00 50.00
12 Kevin Love/49 6.00 15.00
13 Tony Parker/49 20.00 50.00
14 Stephen Curry/49 1,000.00 2,000.00
15 Grant Hill/49 30.00 80.00
16 Anthony Bennett/49 4.00 10.00
18 DeMarcus Cousins/49 5.00 12.00
19 Ben McLemore/49 4.00 10.00
21 Tyson Chandler/49 6.00 15.00
22 C.J. McCollum/49 6.00 15.00
23 Harrison Barnes/49 5.00 12.00
24 Andre Drummond/49 5.00 12.00
25 LaMarcus Aldridge/49 6.00 15.00
26 Artis Gilmore/49 12.00 30.00
27 M.Carter-Williams/49 4.00 10.00
29 Jason Terry/49 5.00 12.00
30 Dolph Schayes/49 6.00 15.00
31 Danny Manning/49 5.00 12.00
32 Kenny Smith/49 5.00 12.00
33 Kyle Korver/49 5.00 12.00
34 Luis Scola/49 5.00 12.00
36 Danny Green/99 5.00 12.00
37 Tiago Splitter/99 4.00 10.00
38 Allan Houston/99 6.00 15.00
39 Thabo Sefolosha/99 4.00 10.00
40 Jeff Green/99 5.00 12.00
41 Nick Young/99 5.00 12.00
43 Iman Shumpert/99 4.00 10.00
44 Jason Thompson/99 4.00 10.00
45 Kyle Lowry/99 20.00 50.00
46 Alex English/99 8.00 20.00
47 Kevin Willis/99 5.00 12.00
48 Kurt Rambis/99 5.00 12.00
49 Robert Horry/99 15.00 40.00
50 Sam Perkins/99 5.00 12.00
51 D.J. Augustin/99 5.00 12.00
52 Enes Kanter/99 5.00 12.00
53 John Starks/99 6.00 15.00
54 Isaiah Thomas/99 5.00 12.00
55 Mark Price/99 6.00 15.00
56 Dee Brown/99 5.00 12.00
57 Cazzie Russell/99 6.00 15.00
58 Eddie Jones/99 6.00 15.00
59 Jo Jo White/99 6.00 15.00
60 Steve Blake/99 4.00 10.00

2014-15 Paramount Penmanship Autographs Blue

*BLUE: .5X TO 1.2X BASE HI
STATED PRINT RUN 25 SER.#'d SETS
EXCHANGE DEADLINE 7/7/2016
14 Stephen Curry 1,500.00 3,000.00

2014-15 Paramount Penmanship Rookie Autographs

*BLUE: .6X TO 1.5X BASE HI
STATED PRINT RUN 99 SER.#'d SETS
EXCHANGE DEADLINE 7/7/2016
1 Andrew Wiggins 20.00 50.00
2 Jabari Parker 5.00 12.00
3 Joel Embiid 75.00 200.00
4 Aaron Gordon 20.00 50.00
5 Dante Exum 6.00 15.00
6 Marcus Smart 15.00 40.00
7 Julius Randle 20.00 50.00
8 Nik Stauskas 4.00 10.00
9 Noah Vonleh 4.00 10.00
10 Elfrid Payton 6.00 15.00
11 Doug McDermott 6.00 15.00
12 Zach LaVine 150.00 400.00
13 T.J. Warren 6.00 15.00
14 Adreian Payne 4.00 10.00
15 James Young 4.00 10.00
16 Tyler Ennis 4.00 10.00
17 Gary Harris 6.00 15.00
18 Bruno Caboclo 5.00 12.00
19 Mitch McGary 4.00 10.00
20 Jordan Adams 4.00 10.00
22 Shabazz Napier 5.00 12.00
24 C.J. Wilcox 4.00 10.00
25 Kyle Anderson 6.00 15.00
26 Jusuf Nurkic 12.00 30.00
28 Joe Harris 6.00 15.00
29 Jarnell Stokes 4.00 10.00
30 Spencer Dinwiddie 6.00 15.00
31 Glenn Robinson III 6.00 15.00
33 Russ Smith 4.00 10.00
34 Dwight Powell 5.00 12.00
36 Cory Jefferson 4.00 10.00
37 Johnny O'Bryant 4.00 10.00
38 Damjan Rudez 4.00 10.00
39 Damien Inglis 4.00 10.00
40 Jordan Clarkson 15.00 40.00

2014-15 Paramount Rookie Impressions Autographs

STATED PRINT RUN 49 SER.#'d SETS
EXCHANGE DEADLINE 7/7/2016
1 Aaron Gordon 25.00 60.00
2 Adreian Payne 5.00 12.00
3 Andrew Wiggins 75.00 200.00
4 Bruno Caboclo 6.00 15.00
5 C.J. Wilcox 5.00 12.00
6 Cleanthony Early 5.00 12.00
7 Cory Jefferson 5.00 12.00
8 Damien Inglis 5.00 12.00
9 Doug McDermott 8.00 20.00
10 Elfrid Payton 8.00 20.00
11 Gary Harris 8.00 20.00
12 Glenn Robinson III 6.00 15.00
13 Jabari Parker 6.00 15.00
14 James Young 5.00 12.00
15 Jarnell Stokes 5.00 12.00
16 Jerami Grant 25.00 60.00
17 Joe Harris 8.00 20.00
18 Joel Embiid 300.00 600.00
19 Johnny O'Bryant 5.00 12.00
20 Jordan Adams 5.00 12.00
21 Julius Randle 75.00 200.00
22 K.J. McDaniels 5.00 12.00
23 Kyle Anderson 8.00 20.00
24 Marcus Smart 20.00 50.00
25 Markel Brown 5.00 12.00
26 Mitch McGary 5.00 12.00
27 Nik Stauskas 5.00 12.00
28 Noah Vonleh 5.00 12.00
29 Rodney Hood 6.00 15.00
30 Russ Smith 5.00 12.00
31 Shabazz Napier 6.00 15.00

32 Spencer Dinwiddie 8.00 20.00
33 T.J. Warren 8.00 20.00
34 Tyler Ennis 5.00 12.00
35 Zach LaVine 300.00 600.00

2014-15 Paramount Rookie Jumbo Jerseys

STATED PRINT RUN 49 SER.#'d SETS
*PRIME: 1X TO 2.5X BASE HI
1 Damien Inglis 2.50 6.00
2 Markel Brown 2.50 6.00
3 Gary Harris 4.00 10.00
4 P.J. Hairston 2.50 6.00
5 James Young 2.50 6.00
6 Spencer Dinwiddie 4.00 10.00
7 Aaron Gordon 12.00 30.00
8 Joel Embiid 25.00 60.00
9 C.J. Wilcox 2.50 6.00
10 K.J. McDaniels 2.50 6.00
11 Dante Exum 4.00 10.00
12 Mitch McGary 2.50 6.00
13 Glenn Robinson III 3.00 8.00
14 Rodney Hood 3.00 8.00
15 Jarnell Stokes 2.50 6.00
16 T.J. Warren 4.00 10.00
17 Adreian Payne 2.50 6.00
18 Johnny O'Bryant 2.50 6.00
19 Cleanthony Early 2.50 6.00
20 Kyle Anderson 4.00 10.00
21 Doug McDermott 4.00 10.00
22 Nik Stauskas 2.50 6.00
23 Jabari Parker 3.00 8.00
24 Russ Smith 2.50 6.00
25 Jerami Grant 12.00 30.00
26 Tyler Ennis 2.50 6.00
27 Andrew Wiggins 12.00 30.00
28 Jordan Adams 2.50 6.00
29 Cory Jefferson 2.50 6.00
30 Marcus Smart 10.00 25.00
31 Elfrid Payton 4.00 10.00
32 Noah Vonleh 2.50 6.00
33 James Ennis 2.50 6.00
34 Joe Harris 4.00 10.00
35 Shabazz Napier 3.00 8.00
36 Zach LaVine 15.00 40.00
37 Bruno Caboclo 3.00 8.00
38 Julius Randle 12.00 30.00

2014-15 Paramount Rookies Home and Away Jerseys

STATED PRINT RUN 40 SER.#'d SETS
1 Andrew Wiggins 12.00 30.00
2 Glenn Robinson III 3.00 8.00
3 Elfrid Payton 4.00 10.00
5 Aaron Gordon 12.00 30.00
6 Damien Inglis 2.50 6.00
8 James Young 2.50 6.00
9 Russ Smith 2.50 6.00
10 K.J. McDaniels 2.50 6.00
12 Rodney Hood 3.00 8.00
13 Noah Vonleh 2.50 6.00
14 Adreian Payne 2.50 6.00
15 Zach LaVine 15.00 40.00
16 Markel Brown 2.50 6.00
17 Doug McDermott 4.00 10.00
18 Spencer Dinwiddie 4.00 10.00
19 Jerami Grant 12.00 30.00
20 Dante Exum 4.00 10.00
21 Cory Jefferson 2.50 6.00
22 Jarnell Stokes 2.50 6.00
23 James Ennis 2.50 6.00
25 Bruno Caboclo 3.00 8.00
26 Gary Harris 4.00 10.00
28 Joel Embiid 25.00 60.00
30 Mitch McGary 2.50 6.00
31 Marcus Smart 10.00 25.00
32 T.J. Warren 4.00 10.00
33 Joe Harris 4.00 10.00
34 Cleanthony Early 2.50 6.00
35 Julius Randle 12.00 30.00
36 P.J. Hairston 2.50 6.00
37 Jabari Parker 3.00 8.00
38 C.J. Wilcox 2.50 6.00

2014-15 Paramount Rookies Home and Away Jerseys Prime

*PRIME: .8X TO 2X BASE HI
STATED PRINT RUN 25 SER.#'d SETS

1977-78 Pepsi All-Stars

COMPLETE SET (8) 350.00 550.00
1 Rick Barry 15.00 40.00
2 Dave Cowens 15.00 40.00
3 Julius Erving 40.00 75.00
4 Kareem Abdul-Jabbar 40.00 75.00
5 Pete Maravich 150.00 300.00
6 Bob McAdoo 20.00 50.00
7 David Thompson 15.00 40.00
8 Bill Walton 40.00 75.00

1974-75 Picture Buttons

COMPLETE SET (11) 300.00 600.00
1 Kareem Abdul-Jabbar 50.00 100.00
2 Bill Bradley 40.00 80.00
3 Dave DeBusschere 25.00 50.00
4 Walt Frazier 40.00 80.00
5 John Havlicek 50.00 100.00
6 Bob Lanier 25.00 50.00
7 Jerry Lucas 12.50 25.00
8 Pete Maravich 75.00 125.00
9 Willis Reed 40.00 100.00
10 Jerry West 50.00 100.00
11 JoJo White 12.50 25.00

1997 Pinnacle Inside WNBA

COMPLETE SET (81) 15.00 40.00
1 Lisa Leslie RC 4.00 10.00
2 Cynthia Cooper RC 6.00 15.00
3 Rebecca Lobo RC 2.00 5.00
4 Michele Timms RC 2.00 5.00
5 Ruthie Bolton-Holifield RC 1.50 4.00
6 Michelle Edwards RC .60 1.50
7 Vicky Bullett RC .50 1.25
8 Tammi Reiss RC .50 1.25
9 Penny Toler RC .50 1.25
10 Tia Jackson RC .30 .75
11 Rhonda Mapp RC .40 1.00
12 Elena Baranova RC 1.00 2.50
13 Tina Thompson RC 4.00 10.00
14 Merlakia Jones RC .50 1.25
15 Tora Suber RC .50 1.25
16 Sophia Witherspoon RC .50 1.25
17 Tajama Abraham RC .30 .75
18 Jessie Hicks RC .30 .75
19 Tina Nicholson RC .30 .75
20 Tiffany Woosley RC .40 1.00
21 Chantel Tremitiere RC .30 .75
22 Daedra Charles RC .30 .75
23 Nancy Lieberman-Cline RC 1.25 3.00
24 Denique Graves RC .30 .75
25 Toni Foster RC .50 1.25
26 Sheryl Swoopes RC 4.00 10.00
27 Kym Hampton RC .50 1.25
28 Sharon Manning RC .30 .75
29 Janice Lawrence Braxton RC .30 .75
30 Sue Wicks RC .50 1.25
31 Lady Hardmon RC .30 .75
32 Jamila Wideman RC .50 1.25
33 Bridgette Gordon RC .30 .75
34 Lynette Woodard RC .75 2.00
35 Kim Perrot RC 1.25 3.00
36 Teresa Weatherspoon RC 2.50 6.00
37 Andrea Stinson RC .75 2.00
38 Janeth Arcain RC .30 .75
39 Pamela McGee RC .50 1.25
40 Tamecka Dixon RC .50 1.25
41 Wendy Palmer RC 1.00 2.50
42 Umeki Webb RC .30 .75
43 Isabelle Fijalkowski RC .30 .75
44 Jennifer Gillom RC 1.00 2.50
45 Latasha Byears RC .50 1.25
46 Haixia Zheng RC .30 .75
47 Kisha Ford RC .30 .75
48 Eva Nemcova RC .60 1.50
49 Penny Moore RC .50 1.25
50 Mwadi Mabika RC .30 .75
51 Kim Williams RC .30 .75
52 Wanda Guyton RC .30 .75
53 Vickie Johnson RC .50 1.25
54 Deborah Carter RC .30 .75
55 Bridget Pettis RC .30 .75
56 Andrea Congreaves RC .30 .75
57 Haixia Zheng HS .30 .75
58 Tammi Reiss HS .50 1.25
59 Jennifer Gillom HS 1.00 2.50
60 Bridgette Gordon HS .30 .75
61 Janice Lawrence Braxton HS .30 .75
62 Cynthia Cooper HS 6.00 15.00
63 Teresa Weatherspoon HS 2.50 6.00
64 Elena Baranova HS 1.00 2.50
65 N. Lieberman-Cline HS 1.25 3.00
66 Andrea Congreaves HS .30 .75
67 Sophia Witherspoon HS .30 .75
68 Vicky Bullett HS .50 1.25
69 R.Bolton-Holifield HS 1.50 4.00
70 Tina Thompson HS 4.00 10.00
71 Lynette Woodard HS .75 2.00
72 Jamila Wideman HS .50 1.25
73 Lisa Leslie SG 4.00 10.00
74 Wendy Palmer SG 1.00 2.50
75 Michele Timms SG 2.00 5.00
76 R.Bolton-Holifield SG 1.50 4.00
77 Andrea Stinson SG .75 2.00
78 Lynette Woodard SG .75 2.00
79 Cynthia Cooper SG 6.00 15.00
80 Rebecca Lobo SG 2.00 5.00
81 Checklist .20 .50

1997 Pinnacle Inside WNBA Court Collection

COMPLETE SET (81) 40.00 100.00
*COURT: 1.25X TO 3X HI COLUMN
STATED ODDS 1:7

1997 Pinnacle Inside WNBA Executive Collection

*EXEC: 4X TO 10X BASE CARD HI
STATED ODDS 1:47

1997 Pinnacle Inside WNBA Cans

COMPLETE SET (17) 10.00 25.00
1 Andrea Stinson .50 1.25
2 Vicky Bullett .30 .75
3 Lynette Woodard .50 1.25
4 Michelle Edwards .40 1.00
5 Cynthia Cooper 4.00 10.00
6 Tina Thompson 2.50 6.00
7 Lisa Leslie 2.50 6.00
8 Jamila Wideman .30 .75
9 Teresa Weatherspoon 1.50 4.00
10 Rebecca Lobo 1.25 3.00
11 Michele Timms 1.25 3.00
12 Bridget Pettis .20 .50
13 Bridgette Gordon .20 .50
14 Ruthie Bolton-Holifield 1.00 2.50
15 Wendy Palmer .60 1.50
16 Elena Baranova .60 1.50
17 WNBA League .40 1.00

1997 Pinnacle Inside WNBA My Town

COMPLETE SET (8) 12.00 30.00
1 Lisa Leslie 5.00 12.00
2 Lady Hardmon .40 1.00
3 Michele Timms 2.50 6.00
4 Ruthie Bolton-Holifield 2.00 5.00
5 Andrea Stinson 1.00 2.50
6 Michelle Edwards .75 2.00
7 Cynthia Cooper 8.00 20.00
8 Rebecca Lobo 2.50 6.00

1997 Pinnacle Inside WNBA Team Development

COMPLETE SET (8) 10.00 25.00
1 Tina Thompson 8.00 20.00
2 Pamela McGee 1.00 2.50
3 Jamila Wideman 1.00 2.50
4 Eva Nemcova 1.25 3.00
5 Tammi Reiss 1.00 2.50
6 Sue Wicks 1.00 2.50
7 Tora Suber 1.00 2.50
8 Toni Foster 1.00 2.50

1998 Pinnacle WNBA

COMPLETE SET (85) 10.00 25.00
1 Rhonda Blades RC .30 .75
2 Lisa Leslie 1.25 3.00
3 Jennifer Gillom .50 1.25
4 Ruthie Bolton-Holifield .75 2.00
5 Wendy Palmer .50 1.25
6 Sophia Witherspoon .30 .75
7 Eva Nemcova .30 .75
8 Andrea Stinson .50 1.25
9 Heidi Burge RC .30 .75
10 Cynthia Cooper 1.50 4.00
11 Christy Smith RC .30 .75
12 Penny Moore .30 .75
13 Penny Toler .30 .75
14 Bridget Pettis .20 .50
15 Tora Suber .30 .75
16 Elena Baranova .50 1.25
17 Rebecca Lobo .75 2.00
18 Isabelle Fijalkowski .20 .50
19 Vicky Bullett .30 .75
20 Tina Thompson .75 2.00
21 Andrea Kuklova RC .30 .75
22 Rita Williams RC .40 1.00
23 Tamecka Dixon .30 .75
24 Michele Timms .75 2.00
25 Bridgette Gordon .20 .50
26 Tammi Reiss .30 .75
27 Kym Hampton .30 .75
28 Janice Braxton .30 .75
29 Rhonda Mapp .25 .60
30 Janeth Arcain .20 .50
31 Lynette Woodard .50 1.25
32 Tammy Jackson RC .30 .75
33 Haixia Zheng .20 .50
34 Toni Foster .30 .75
35 Chantel Tremitiere .30 .75
36 Vickie Johnson .30 .75
37 Michelle Edwards .40 1.00
38 Wanda Guyton .20 .50
39 Kim Perrot .60 1.50
40 Sheryl Swoopes 1.25 3.00
41 Merlakia Jones .30 .75
42 Teresa Weatherspoon .75 2.00
43 Kim Williams .20 .50
44 Lady Hardmon .20 .50
45 Latasha Byears .30 .75
46 Umeki Webb .20 .50
47 Pamela McGee .30 .75
48 Nikki McCray RC 1.25 3.00
49 Cindy Brown RC .75 2.00
50 Tiffany Woosley .20 .50
51 Andrea Congreaves .20 .50
52 Jamila Wideman .30 .75
53 Mwadi Mabika .30 .75
54 Murriel Page RC .50 1.25
55 Mikiko Hagiwara RC .30 .75
56 Linda Burgess RC .30 .75
57 Olympia Scott RC .30 .75
58 Dena Head RC .30 .75
59 Quacy Barnes RC .30 .75
60 Suzie McConnell-Serio RC 1.00 2.50
61 Trena Trice RC .30 .75
62 Rushia Brown RC .30 .75
63 Kisha Ford .20 .50
64 Sharon Manning .20 .50
65 Tangela Smith RC .30 .75
66 Jim Lewis CO .20 .50
67 Nancy Lieberman-Cline CO .75 2.00
68 Van Chancellor CO .30 .75
69 Denise Taylor CO .30 .75
70 Heidi VanDerveer CO .30 .75
71 Marynell Meadors CO .30 .75
72 Linda Hill-MacDonald CO .20 .50
73 Nancy Darsch CO .30 .75
74 Cheryl Miller CO 1.25 3.00
75 Julie Rousseau CO .30 .75
76 Rebecca Lobo P .40 1.00
77 Jennifer Gillom P .25 .60
78 Janeth Arcain P .10 .25
79 Rhonda Mapp P .12 .30
80 Cynthia Cooper P .75 2.00
81 Tina Thompson P .40 1.00
82 Kym Hampton P .15 .40
83 Cynthia Cooper P .75 2.00
84 Checklist .20 .50
85 Checklist .20 .50
S66 Sheryl Swoopes PROMO .75 2.00

1998 Pinnacle WNBA Court Collection

*COURT: 1.25X TO 3X BASE CARD HI
STATED ODDS 1:3

1998 Pinnacle WNBA Arena Collection

*ARENA: 4X TO 10X BASE CARD HI
STATED ODDS 1:19

1998 Pinnacle WNBA Coast to Coast

COMPLETE SET (10) 10.00 25.00
1 Lynette Woodard 1.00 2.50
2 Nikki McCray 2.50 6.00
3 Lisa Leslie 2.50 6.00
4 Andrea Stinson 1.00 2.50
5 Eva Nemcova .60 1.50
6 Cynthia Cooper 3.00 8.00
7 Teresa Weatherspoon 1.50 4.00
8 Wendy Palmer 1.00 2.50
9 Ruthie Bolton-Holifield 1.50 4.00
10 Michele Timms 1.50 4.00

1998 Pinnacle WNBA Number Ones

COMPLETE SET (9) 8.00 20.00
1 Malgorzata Dydek 2.50 6.00
2 Ticha Penicheiro 3.00 8.00
3 Murriel Page 1.50 4.00
4 Korie Hlede 2.00 5.00
5 Allison Feaster 1.50 4.00
6 Cindy Blodgett 2.00 5.00
7 Tracy Reid 1.25 3.00
8 Alicia Thompson 1.00 2.50
9 Nyree Roberts 1.00 2.50

1998 Pinnacle WNBA Planet Pinnacle

COMPLETE SET (10) 12.00 30.00
1 Korie Hlede 2.50 6.00
2 Eva Nemcova 1.25 3.00
3 Haixia Zheng .75 2.00
4 Michele Timms 3.00 8.00
5 Ticha Penicheiro 4.00 10.00
6 Elena Baranova 2.00 5.00
7 Rebecca Lobo 3.00 8.00
8 Isabelle Fijalkowski .75 2.00
9 Andrea Congreaves .75 2.00
10 Sheryl Swoopes 5.00 12.00

2013-14 Pinnacle

COMPLETE SET (300) 60.00 150.00
1 C.J. McCollum RC 1.00 2.50
2 Allen Crabbe RC .25 .60
3 Victor Oladipo RC .60 1.50
4 Ian Clark RC .30 .75
5 G.Antetokounmpo RC 25.00 60.00
6 Reggie Bullock RC .30 .75
7 Luigi Datome RC .25 .60
8 Ricky Ledo RC .25 .60
9 Erik Murphy RC .25 .60
10 Kelly Olynyk RC .30 .75
11 Jeff Withey RC .25 .60
12 Archie Goodwin RC .25 .60
13 Steven Adams RC .60 1.50
14 Dwight Buycks RC .25 .60
15 Elias Harris RC .25 .60
16 Isaiah Canaan RC .25 .60
17 Robert Covington RC .40 1.00
18 Sergey Karasev RC .25 .60
19 Cody Zeller RC .30 .75
20 Pero Antic RC .25 .60
21 Ben McLemore RC .30 .75
22 Alex Len RC .30 .75
23 Ognjen Kuzmic RC .25 .60
24 Gorgui Dieng RC .30 .75
25 Jamaal Franklin RC .25 .60
26 Nemanja Nedovic RC .25 .60
27 Kentavious Caldwell-Pope RC .40 1.00
28 Carrick Felix RC .25 .60
29 Mason Plumlee RC .30 .75
30 Miroslav Raduljica RC .25 .60
31 Glen Rice Jr. RC .25 .60
32 Nerlens Noel RC .30 .75
33 Andre Roberson RC .30 .75
34 Shabazz Muhammad RC .25 .60
35 Ryan Kelly RC .25 .60
36 Tony Mitchell RC .25 .60
37 Gal Mekel RC .25 .60
38 Anthony Bennett RC .25 .60
39 Vitor Faverani RC .25 .60
40 Dennis Schroder RC .75 2.00
41 Trey Burke RC .30 .75
42 M.Carter-Williams RC .30 .75
43 Tim Hardaway Jr. RC .50 1.25
44 Nate Wolters RC .25 .60
45 Solomon Hill RC .30 .75
46 Otto Porter RC .40 1.00
47 Shane Larkin RC .25 .60
48 Tony Snell RC .30 .75
49 Phil Pressey RC .25 .60
50 Ray McCallum RC .25 .60
51 Josh Smith .20 .50
52 Andrei Kirilenko .30 .75
53 Chauncey Billups .40 1.00
54 Mike Conley .30 .75
55 Kawhi Leonard 1.00 2.50
56 Marcus Morris .25 .60
57 Serge Ibaka .25 .60
58 Tayshaun Prince .30 .75
59 Will Bynum .20 .50
60 Bradley Beal .50 1.25
61 Jared Sullinger .20 .50
62 Taj Gibson .20 .50
63 Draymond Green .50 1.25
64 Ray Allen .50 1.25
65 Carl Landry .20 .50
66 Evan Turner .20 .50
67 Anthony Davis 1.00 2.50
68 Tony Allen .20 .50
69 Ty Lawson .20 .50
70 Emeka Okafor .25 .60
71 Marquis Teague .20 .50
72 Paul Pierce .50 1.25
73 Jonas Jerebko .20 .50
74 Marc Gasol .30 .75
75 Damian Lillard 1.00 2.50
76 Andrew Nicholson .20 .50
77 J.R. Smith .30 .75
78 Zach Randolph .30 .75
79 Rodney Stuckey .20 .50
80 Eric Maynor .20 .50
81 Jamal Crawford .30 .75
82 Mike Dunleavy .20 .50
83 David Lee .25 .60
84 Udonis Haslem .20 .50
85 Robin Lopez .20 .50
86 Jeremy Lamb .25 .60
87 Tyreke Evans .25 .60
88 Tony Wroten .20 .50
89 Dirk Nowitzki .75 2.00
90 John Wall .40 1.00
91 Louis Williams .25 .60
92 Ramon Sessions .20 .50
93 Brandon Knight .25 .60
94 Kosta Koufos .20 .50
95 Manu Ginobili .60 1.50
96 Luis Scola .25 .60
97 Thabo Sefolosha .20 .50
98 Nick Young .25 .60
99 Evan Fournier .25 .60
100 Alec Burks .25 .60
101 Kyle Korver .25 .60
102 Kirk Hinrich .20 .50
103 Andrew Bogut .25 .60
104 Norris Cole .20 .50
105 DeMarcus Cousins .30 .75
106 Jason Richardson .30 .75
107 Pablo Prigioni .20 .50
108 Kobe Bryant 2.50 6.00
109 Jae Crowder .20 .50
110 Derrick Favors .20 .50
111 John Jenkins .20 .50
112 Michael Kidd-Gilchrist .20 .50
113 Andre Drummond .30 .75
114 Blake Griffin .30 .75
115 Joel Freeland .20 .50
116 E'Twaun Moore .20 .50
117 Austin Rivers .20 .50
118 Pau Gasol .30 .75
119 J.J. Hickson .20 .50
120 Enes Kanter .25 .60
121 Jeff Teague .20 .50
122 Joakim Noah .30 .75
123 Andre Iguodala .30 .75
124 LeBron James 2.50 6.00
125 Victor Claver .20 .50
126 Kendrick Perkins .20 .50
127 Alexey Shved .20 .50
128 Steve Blake .20 .50
129 Monta Ellis .25 .60
130 Gordon Hayward .25 .60
131 Elton Brand .25 .60
132 Kemba Walker .30 .75
133 Stephen Curry 2.50 6.00
134 Larry Sanders .20 .50
135 Tiago Splitter .20 .50
136 Marcin Gortat .20 .50
137 Amar'e Stoudemire .30 .75
138 Robert Sacre .20 .50
139 JaVale McGee .25 .60
140 John Lucas III .20 .50
141 Al Horford .30 .75
142 Jimmy Butler .60 1.50
143 Jeremy Lin .50 1.25
144 Mario Chalmers .25 .60
145 Greivis Vasquez .20 .50
146 Spencer Hawes .20 .50
147 Carmelo Anthony .50 1.25
148 Steve Nash .60 1.50
149 Samuel Dalembert .20 .50
150 Amir Johnson .20 .50
151 Rajon Rondo .40 1.00
152 Bismack Biyombo .20 .50
153 Klay Thompson 1.00 2.50
154 O.J. Mayo .20 .50
155 LaMarcus Aldridge .30 .75
156 Jameer Nelson .20 .50
157 Eric Gordon .25 .60
158 Chris Paul .60 1.50
159 Jordan Hamilton .20 .50
160 D.J. Augustin .20 .50
161 MarShon Brooks .20 .50
162 Derrick Rose .50 1.25
163 James Harden .60 1.50
164 Dwyane Wade .60 1.50
165 Will Barton .20 .50
166 Kevin Durant 1.00 2.50
167 Corey Brewer .20 .50
168 David West .25 .60
169 Shawn Marion .25 .60
170 DeMar DeRozan .40 1.00
171 Kris Humphries .20 .50
172 Al Jefferson .20 .50
173 Kent Bazemore .20 .50
174 John Henson .20 .50
175 Tim Duncan .75 2.00
176 P.J. Tucker .30 .75
177 Andrea Bargnani .20 .50
178 DeAndre Jordan .25 .60
179 Kenneth Faried .25 .60
180 Jonas Valanciunas .25 .60
181 Jeff Green .20 .50
182 Tyler Zeller .20 .50
183 Dwight Howard .40 1.00
184 Ersan Ilyasova .20 .50
185 Isaiah Thomas .25 .60
186 Thaddeus Young .20 .50
187 Raymond Felton .20 .50
188 George Hill .25 .60
189 Vince Carter .60 1.50
190 Kyle Lowry .30 .75
191 Brandon Bass .20 .50
192 Luol Deng .25 .60
193 Harrison Barnes .30 .75
194 Ricky Rubio .25 .60
195 Meyers Leonard .20 .50
196 Nikola Vucevic .40 1.00
197 Jrue Holiday .40 1.00
198 J.J. Redick .30 .75
199 Nate Robinson .20 .50
200 Landry Fields .20 .50
201 Avery Bradley .20 .50
202 Tristan Thompson .20 .50
203 Chandler Parsons .20 .50
204 Chris Andersen .25 .60
205 Eric Bledsoe .25 .60
206 Ronnie Brewer .20 .50
207 Derrick Williams .20 .50
208 Danny Granger .20 .50
209 Chris Kaman .25 .60
210 Rudy Gay .25 .60
211 Kevin Garnett .75 2.00
212 Jarrett Jack .25 .60
213 Aaron Brooks .20 .50
214 Kevin Martin .25 .60
215 Tony Parker .50 1.25
216 Markieff Morris .20 .50
217 Iman Shumpert .20 .50
218 Jared Dudley .20 .50
219 Randy Foye .20 .50
220 Terrence Ross .25 .60
221 Joe Johnson .25 .60
222 Kyrie Irving 1.00 2.50
223 Roy Hibbert .20 .50
224 Nikola Pekovic .20 .50
225 Jimmer Fredette .30 .75
226 Lavoy Allen .20 .50
227 Al-Farouq Aminu .20 .50
228 Chris Copeland .20 .50
229 Anderson Varejao .20 .50
230 Boris Diaw .25 .60
231 Jason Terry .25 .60
232 Earl Clark .20 .50
233 Paul George .50 1.25
234 Brandon Jennings .20 .50
235 Nicolas Batum .25 .60
236 Tobias Harris .30 .75
237 Ryan Anderson .20 .50
238 Matt Barnes .20 .50
239 Timofey Mozgov .20 .50
240 Danny Green .25 .60
241 Deron Williams .25 .60
242 C.J. Miles .20 .50
243 Lance Stephenson .25 .60
244 Chris Bosh .40 1.00
245 Goran Dragic .25 .60
246 Russell Westbrook .50 1.25
247 Kevin Love .30 .75
248 Ryan Hollins .20 .50
249 Andrew Bynum .20 .50
250 Brook Lopez .30 .75
251 Dikembe Mutombo .50 1.25
252 Dan Issel .40 1.00
253 Magic Johnson 1.25 3.00
254 Oscar Robertson .50 1.25
255 Wilt Chamberlain 1.00 2.50
256 Shawn Kemp .50 1.25
257 Gheorghe Muresan .20 .50
258 David Robinson .60 1.50
259 Patrick Ewing .50 1.25
260 Jason Williams .25 .60
261 Yao Ming .60 1.50
262 Michael Finley .30 .75
263 Dominique Wilkins .50 1.25
264 Mark Price .30 .75
265 George McGinnis .30 .75
266 Christian Laettner .30 .75
267 Julius Erving .75 2.00
268 Nate Thurmond .30 .75
269 Manute Bol .30 .75
270 Clyde Drexler .50 1.25
271 George Mikan 1.00 2.50
272 Bob Lanier .40 1.00
273 Larry Bird 1.25 3.00
274 Isiah Thomas .50 1.25
275 Elgin Baylor .30 .75
276 Anfernee Hardaway .75 2.00
277 World B. Free .25 .60
278 Karl Malone .60 1.50
279 Walt Frazier .50 1.25
280 Bill Walton .50 1.25
281 David Thompson .30 .75
282 Bill Russell 1.00 2.50
283 Rolando Blackman .25 .60
284 Alonzo Mourning .50 1.25
285 George Gervin .50 1.25
286 John Stockton .60 1.50
287 Tom Chambers .30 .75
288 Eddie Jones .25 .60
289 Larry Nance .25 .60
290 Scottie Pippen .75 2.00
291 Nate Archibald .40 1.00
292 Jason Kidd .50 1.25
293 Spud Webb .30 .75
294 Gary Payton .50 1.25
295 Shaquille O'Neal 1.25 3.00
296 Drazen Petrovic .40 1.00
297 Kareem Abdul-Jabbar 1.00 2.50
298 Dennis Rodman .75 2.00
299 Rick Barry .40 1.00
300 Hakeem Olajuwon .60 1.50

2013-14 Pinnacle Artist's Proofs

*AP 1-50: 1X TO 2.5X BASIC
*AP 51-300: 1.2X TO 3X BASIC
5 Giannis Antetokounmpo 200.00 500.00

2013-14 Pinnacle Artist's Proofs Blue

*AP BLUE 1-50: .6X TO 1.5X BASIC
*AP BLUE 51-300: .6X TO 1.5X BASIC
5 Giannis Antetokounmpo 125.00 300.00

2013-14 Pinnacle Artist's Proofs Green

*AP GREEN 1-50: X TO X BASIC
*AP GREEN 51-300: X TO X BASIC
STATED PRINT RUN 25 SER.#'d SETS
5 Giannis Antetokounmpo 1,000.00 2,000.00

2013-14 Pinnacle Artist's Proofs Red

*AP RED 1-50: .6X TO 1.5X BASIC
*AP RED 51-300: .6X TO 1.5X BASIC
5 Giannis Antetokounmpo 125.00 300.00

2013-14 Pinnacle Autographs

EXCHANGE DEADLINE 7/15/2015
1 Kyrie Irving 75.00 200.00
2 Al Horford 4.00 10.00
3 Alan Anderson 2.50 6.00
4 Alex Len 3.00 8.00
5 Al-Farouq Aminu 2.50 6.00
6 Allan Houston 4.00 10.00
7 Allen Crabbe 2.50 6.00
8 Andre Drummond 4.00 10.00
9 Andre Miller 3.00 8.00
10 Andre Roberson 3.00 8.00
11 Andrei Kirilenko 4.00 10.00
12 Andrew Bogut 3.00 8.00
13 Anfernee Hardaway 50.00 120.00
14 Antawn Jamison 3.00 8.00
15 Anthony Bennett 2.50 6.00
16 Anthony Davis 40.00 100.00
17 Anthony Mason 3.00 8.00
18 Archie Goodwin 2.50 6.00
19 Artis Gilmore 5.00 12.00
20 Bailey Howell 4.00 10.00
21 Ben Gordon 3.00 8.00
22 Ben McLemore 3.00 8.00
23 Bill Cartwright 3.00 8.00
24 Bill Sharman 4.00 10.00
25 Blake Griffin 4.00 10.00
26 Bob Dandridge 3.00 8.00
27 Bobby Jackson 2.50 6.00
28 Brent Barry 2.50 6.00
29 Brook Lopez 4.00 10.00
30 Bruce Bowen 3.00 8.00
31 Bryon Russell 2.50 6.00
32 Ian Clark 3.00 8.00
33 C.J. McCollum 25.00 60.00
34 C.J. Miles 2.50 6.00
35 Calvin Murphy 3.00 8.00
36 Campy Russell 3.00 8.00
37 Carl Landry 2.50 6.00
38 Caron Butler 3.00 8.00
39 Cazzie Russell 3.00 8.00
40 Cedric Maxwell 3.00 8.00
41 Chase Budinger 2.50 6.00
42 Chris Kaman 3.00 8.00
43 Chris Mullin 10.00 25.00
44 Chris Whitney 2.50 6.00
45 Clyde Drexler 20.00 50.00
46 Cody Zeller 3.00 8.00
47 Connie Hawkins 10.00 25.00
48 Corey Brewer 2.50 6.00
49 Courtney Lee 2.50 6.00
50 D.J. Augustin 2.50 6.00
51 Dale Davis 3.00 8.00
52 Damon Jones 2.50 6.00
53 Dan Majerle 3.00 8.00
54 Danny Manning 3.00 8.00
55 Darrell Walker 3.00 8.00
56 David Robinson 30.00 80.00
57 David Thompson 4.00 10.00
58 Dennis Schroder 8.00 20.00
59 Derek Anderson 2.50 6.00
60 Deron Williams 3.00 8.00
61 Derrick Coleman 4.00 10.00
62 Derrick Favors 2.50 6.00
63 Doc Rivers 3.00 8.00
64 Dominique Wilkins 10.00 25.00
65 Draymond Green 20.00 50.00
66 Dwight Howard 8.00 20.00
67 Dwyane Wade 20.00 50.00
68 Earl Clark 2.50 6.00
69 Earl Monroe 6.00 15.00
70 Eric Maynor 2.50 6.00
71 Erik Murphy 2.50 6.00
72 Ersan Ilyasova 2.50 6.00
73 Fat Lever 3.00 8.00
74 Gary Payton 12.00 30.00
75 George Hill 3.00 8.00
76 Giannis Antetokounmpo 500.00 1,000.00
77 Glen Rice Jr. 2.50 6.00
78 Gorgui Dieng 3.00 8.00
79 Grant Hill 20.00 50.00
80 Carrick Felix 2.50 6.00
81 Greg Anthony 2.50 6.00
82 Greg Ostertag 2.50 6.00
83 Hakeem Olajuwon 40.00 100.00
84 Harrison Barnes 4.00 10.00
85 Harvey Grant 2.50 6.00
86 Horace Grant 4.00 10.00
87 Isaiah Canaan 2.50 6.00
88 Isiah Thomas 15.00 40.00
89 Jamaal Franklin 2.50 6.00
90 Jalen Rose 3.00 8.00
91 Ish Smith 2.50 6.00
92 Jan Vesely 2.50 6.00
93 Jared Dudley 2.50 6.00
94 Jared Jeffries 2.50 6.00
95 Jarrett Jack 3.00 8.00
96 Jason Kidd 15.00 40.00
97 Jeff Malone 3.00 8.00
98 Jeff Ayres 2.50 6.00
99 Jeff Taylor 2.50 6.00
100 Jeff Withey 2.50 6.00
101 Jimmer Fredette 4.00 10.00
102 Jo Jo White 3.00 8.00
103 John Henson 2.50 6.00
104 John Lucas 3.00 8.00
105 John Salley 3.00 8.00
106 Jon Leuer 2.50 6.00
107 Jonas Jerebko 2.50 6.00
108 Josh Harrellson 2.50 6.00
109 Josh Smith 2.50 6.00
110 K.C. Jones 4.00 10.00
111 Kareem Abdul-Jabbar 75.00 200.00
112 Kawhi Leonard 60.00 150.00
113 Kelly Olynyk 3.00 8.00
114 Kenny Walker 2.50 6.00
115 Kentavious Caldwell-Pope 4.00 10.00
116 Kevin Durant 125.00 300.00
117 Kevin Willis 3.00 8.00
118 Khris Middleton 12.00 30.00
119 Kobe Bryant 800.00 1,500.00
120 Kurt Rambis 4.00 10.00
121 Jayson Williams 2.50 6.00
122 Kyle Lowry 4.00 10.00
123 Dennis Rodman 40.00 100.00
124 Lamond Murray 2.50 6.00
125 Lance Stephenson 3.00 8.00
126 Larry Bird 100.00 250.00
127 Lavoy Allen 2.50 6.00
128 Leonard Robinson 2.50 6.00
129 Lindsey Hunter 2.50 6.00
130 Luc Longley 3.00 8.00
131 Magic Johnson 100.00 250.00
132 Nick Collison 2.50 6.00
133 Marcus Thornton 2.50 6.00
134 Mark Jackson 3.00 8.00
135 MarShon Brooks 2.50 6.00
136 Marvin Williams 2.50 6.00
137 Mason Plumlee 3.00 8.00
138 Maurice Harkless 2.50 6.00
139 Michael Cage 2.50 6.00
140 Michael Carter-Williams 3.00 8.00
141 Michael Finley 4.00 10.00
142 Micheal Ray Richardson 3.00 8.00
143 Mike Conley 4.00 10.00
144 Mitch Richmond 10.00 25.00
145 Muggsy Bogues 12.00 30.00
146 Nate Archibald 5.00 12.00
147 Nate Wolters 2.50 6.00
148 Nemanja Nedovic 2.50 6.00
149 Nerlens Noel 3.00 8.00
150 Nick Anderson 3.00 8.00
151 Nick Young 2.50 6.00
152 Nikola Pekovic 2.50 6.00
153 Nikola Vucevic 5.00 12.00
154 Hollis Thompson 2.50 6.00
155 Otto Porter 4.00 10.00
156 Peja Stojakovic 3.00 8.00
157 Peyton Siva 2.50 6.00
158 Ray McCallum 2.50 6.00
159 Phil Pressey 2.50 6.00
160 Reggie Jackson 3.00 8.00
161 Richard Jefferson 3.00 8.00
162 Rick Fox 3.00 8.00
163 Ricky Ledo 2.50 6.00
164 Robbie Hummel 2.50 6.00
165 Rod Strickland 3.00 8.00
166 Roy Hibbert 2.50 6.00
167 Rudy Gobert 10.00 25.00
168 Ryan Kelly 2.50 6.00
169 Sam Jones 8.00 20.00
170 Scott Skiles 3.00 8.00
171 Scottie Pippen 75.00 200.00
172 Shelvin Mack 2.50 6.00
173 Shabazz Muhammad 2.50 6.00
174 Shane Larkin 2.50 6.00
175 Sidney Moncrief 4.00 10.00
176 Sleepy Floyd 3.00 8.00
177 Solomon Hill 3.00 8.00
178 Steve Kerr 4.00 10.00
179 Tayshaun Prince 4.00 10.00
180 Terry Porter 4.00 10.00
181 Tim Hardaway Jr. 5.00 12.00
182 Satch Sanders 5.00 12.00
183 Tom Gugliotta 3.00 8.00
184 Toni Kukoc 5.00 12.00
185 Tracy McGrady 30.00 80.00
186 Gal Mekel 2.50 6.00

187 Tony Snell 3.00 8.00
188 Travis Best 2.50 6.00
189 Trey Burke 3.00 8.00
190 Victor Oladipo 6.00 15.00
191 Vin Baker 2.50 6.00
192 Vince Carter 30.00 80.00
193 Vinny Del Negro 2.50 6.00
194 Vlade Divac 4.00 10.00
195 Walt Bellamy 4.00 10.00
196 Wes Unseld 5.00 12.00
197 World B. Free 3.00 8.00
198 Xavier Henry 2.50 6.00
199 Zach Randolph 3.00 8.00
200 Zydrunas Ilgauskas 3.00 8.00

2013-14 Pinnacle Awaiting the Call

COMPLETE SET (15) 8.00 20.00
1 Jason Kidd 1.00 2.50
2 Grant Hill 1.00 2.50
3 Kobe Bryant 5.00 12.00
4 Tim Duncan 1.50 4.00
5 Shaquille O'Neal 2.50 6.00
6 Dwyane Wade 1.25 3.00
7 Kevin Garnett 1.50 4.00
8 LeBron James 5.00 12.00
9 Paul Pierce 1.00 2.50
10 Ray Allen 1.00 2.50
11 Tony Parker 1.00 2.50
12 Steve Nash 1.25 3.00
13 Chris Bosh .75 2.00
14 Chris Paul 1.25 3.00
15 Vince Carter 1.25 3.00

2013-14 Pinnacle Awaiting the Call Artist's Proofs

*AP: .6X TO 1.5X BASIC

2013-14 Pinnacle Awaiting the Call Artist's Proofs Green

*AP GREEN: 1.5X TO 4X BASIC
STATED PRINT RUN 25 SER.#'d SETS
8 LeBron James 15.00 40.00

2013-14 Pinnacle Awaiting the Call Die Cuts

*DIE CUT: 1X TO 2.5X BASIC
STATED PRINT RUN 99 SER.#'d SETS
8 LeBron James 10.00 25.00

2013-14 Pinnacle Behind the Numbers

COMPLETE SET (20) 8.00 20.00
1 Tim Duncan 1.50 4.00
2 Kyrie Irving 2.00 5.00
3 Kobe Bryant 5.00 12.00
4 Kevin Durant 2.00 5.00
5 Blake Griffin .60 1.50
6 Damian Lillard 2.00 5.00
7 LeBron James 5.00 12.00
8 Chris Paul 1.25 3.00
9 Ricky Rubio .50 1.25
10 Stephen Curry 5.00 12.00
11 Rajon Rondo .75 2.00
12 Dwight Howard .75 2.00
13 Carmelo Anthony 1.00 2.50
14 Derrick Rose 1.00 2.50
15 Dirk Nowitzki 1.50 4.00
16 Patrick Ewing 1.00 2.50
17 Dennis Rodman 1.50 4.00
18 Larry Bird 2.50 6.00
19 Magic Johnson 2.50 6.00
20 Shaquille O'Neal 2.50 6.00

2013-14 Pinnacle Behind the Numbers Artist's Proofs

*AP: .6X TO 1.5X BASIC

2013-14 Pinnacle Behind the Numbers Artist's Proofs Green

*AP GREEN: 1.5X TO 4X BASIC
STATED PRINT RUN 25 SER.#'d SETS

2013-14 Pinnacle Behind the Numbers Die Cuts

*DIE CUT: 1X TO 2.5X BASIC
STATED PRINT RUN 99 SER.#'d SETS

2013-14 Pinnacle Big Bang

COMPLETE SET (20) 6.00 15.00
1 Andre Drummond .60 1.50
2 Anderson Varejao .40 1.00
3 Tyson Chandler .50 1.25
4 Joakim Noah .60 1.50
5 Al Horford .60 1.50
6 DeAndre Jordan .50 1.25
7 Marcin Gortat .40 1.00
8 Nikola Vucevic .75 2.00
9 Kevin Love .60 1.50
10 Enes Kanter .50 1.25
11 Dwight Howard .75 2.00
12 Al Jefferson .40 1.00
13 Marc Gasol .60 1.50
14 Udonis Haslem .50 1.25
15 Tim Duncan 1.50 4.00
16 David Lee .40 1.00
17 Pau Gasol 1.00 2.50
18 Roy Hibbert .40 1.00
19 Jonas Valanciunas .50 1.25
20 Serge Ibaka .50 1.25

2013-14 Pinnacle Big Bang Artist's Proofs

*AP: .6X TO 1.5X BASIC

2013-14 Pinnacle Big Bang Artist's Proofs Green

*AP GREEN: 1.5X TO 4X BASIC
STATED PRINT RUN 25 SER.#'d SETS

2013-14 Pinnacle Big Bang Die Cuts

*DIE CUT: 1X TO 2.5X BASIC
STATED PRINT RUN 99 SER.#'d SETS

2013-14 Pinnacle Clear Vision 1st Quarter

1 Kobe Bryant 10.00 25.00
2 Serge Ibaka 1.00 2.50
3 Paul George 2.00 5.00
4 Brandon Knight 1.00 2.50
5 Joakim Noah 1.25 3.00
6 Avery Bradley .75 2.00
7 Tony Parker 2.00 5.00
8 Marcin Gortat .75 2.00
9 Carmelo Anthony 2.00 5.00
10 Dwyane Wade 2.50 6.00
11 Manu Ginobili 2.50 6.00
12 George Hill 1.00 2.50
13 Andre Drummond 1.25 3.00
14 Jimmy Butler 2.50 6.00
15 Jeff Teague .75 2.00
16 Tim Duncan 3.00 8.00
17 Eric Bledsoe 1.00 2.50
18 Eric Gordon 1.00 2.50
19 Chris Bosh 1.50 4.00
20 Larry Sanders .75 2.00
21 Jeremy Lin 2.00 5.00
22 Ty Lawson .75 2.00
23 Derrick Rose 2.00 5.00
24 Al Horford 1.25 3.00
25 Kawhi Leonard 4.00 10.00
26 Thaddeus Young .75 2.00
27 Anthony Davis 4.00 10.00
28 Zach Randolph 1.00 2.50
29 J.J. Redick 1.25 3.00
30 James Harden 2.50 6.00
31 Kenneth Faried 1.00 2.50
32 Michael Kidd-Gilchrist .75 2.00
33 John Wall 1.50 4.00
34 Jimmer Fredette 1.25 3.00
35 Evan Turner .75 2.00
36 Ricky Rubio 1.00 2.50
37 Mike Conley 1.25 3.00
38 Amar'e Stoudemire 1.25 3.00
39 Dwight Howard 1.50 4.00
40 Vince Carter 2.50 6.00
41 Kemba Walker 1.25 3.00
42 Bradley Beal 2.00 5.00
43 Isaiah Thomas 1.00 2.50
44 Tobias Harris 1.25 3.00
45 Kevin Love 1.25 3.00
46 Pau Gasol 2.00 5.00
47 Nicolas Batum 1.00 2.50
48 Stephen Curry 10.00 25.00
49 Shawn Marion 1.00 2.50
50 Paul Pierce 2.00 5.00
51 Gordon Hayward 1.00 2.50
52 DeMarcus Cousins 1.25 3.00
53 Nikola Vucevic 1.50 4.00
54 John Henson .75 2.00
55 Steve Nash 2.50 6.00
56 Jared Sullinger .75 2.00
57 Harrison Barnes 1.25 3.00
58 Dirk Nowitzki 3.00 8.00
59 Kris Humphries .75 2.00
60 Derrick Favors .75 2.00
61 LaMarcus Aldridge 1.25 3.00
62 Russell Westbrook 2.00 5.00
63 Ersan Ilyasova .75 2.00
64 Chris Paul 2.50 6.00
65 JaVale McGee 1.00 2.50
66 David Lee .75 2.00
67 Anderson Varejao .75 2.00
68 Deron Williams 1.00 2.50
69 Jonas Valanciunas 1.00 2.50
70 Damian Lillard 4.00 10.00
71 Kevin Durant 4.00 10.00
72 LeBron James 10.00 25.00
73 Blake Griffin 1.25 3.00
74 Chandler Parsons .75 2.00
75 Greg Monroe .75 2.00
76 Kyrie Irving 4.00 10.00
77 Rajon Rondo 1.50 4.00
78 DeMar DeRozan 1.50 4.00
79 Goran Dragic 1.00 2.50
80 Tyson Chandler 1.00 2.50
81 Magic Johnson 5.00 12.00
82 Larry Bird 5.00 12.00
83 David Robinson 2.50 6.00
84 Hakeem Olajuwon 2.50 6.00
85 Pete Maravich 2.00 5.00
86 Wilt Chamberlain 4.00 10.00
87 Shaquille O'Neal 5.00 12.00
88 George Gervin 2.00 5.00
89 Anfernee Hardaway 3.00 8.00
90 Karl Malone 2.50 6.00
91 Scottie Pippen 3.00 8.00
92 Gary Payton 2.00 5.00
93 Earl Monroe 2.00 5.00
94 Kareem Abdul-Jabbar 4.00 10.00
95 Shawn Kemp 2.00 5.00
96 Isiah Thomas 1.50 4.00
97 Dennis Rodman 3.00 8.00
98 Grant Hill 2.00 5.00
99 Jason Kidd 2.00 5.00
100 John Stockton 2.50 6.00

2013-14 Pinnacle Clear Vision 2nd Quarter

*2ND QTR: 1X TO 2.5X BASIC
STATED PRINT RUN 36 SER.#'d SETS
79 Goran Dragic 12.00 30.00

2013-14 Pinnacle Clear Vision 3rd Quarter

*3RD QTR: 1.5X TO 4X BASIC
STATED PRINT RUN 24 SER.#'d SETS
79 Goran Dragic 15.00 40.00

2013-14 Pinnacle Essence of the Game Autographs

PRINT RUNS B/WN 25-199 COPIES PER
EXCHANGE DEADLINE 7/15/2015
1 D.J. Augustin/199 4.00 10.00
2 Andre Miller/99 5.00 12.00
3 Ersan Ilyasova/199 4.00 10.00
4 Andray Blatche/199 4.00 10.00
5 Jordan Crawford/199 4.00 10.00
6 Ronnie Brewer/179 4.00 10.00
7 Tyreke Evans/49 5.00 12.00
8 John Lucas/199 4.00 10.00
9 Darrell Griffith/199 5.00 12.00
10 Steve Smith/199 5.00 12.00
11 Nicolas Batum/199 EXCH 5.00 12.00
12 Allan Houston/99 6.00 15.00
13 Kenneth Faried/99 5.00 12.00
14 Kyrie Irving/99 75.00 200.00
15 Goran Dragic/99 5.00 12.00
16 Marcin Gortat/99 4.00 10.00
17 B.J. Armstrong/99 6.00 15.00
18 Greivis Vasquez/199 4.00 10.00
19 Blake Griffin/99 6.00 15.00
20 Maurice Harkless/199 4.00 10.00
21 Tiago Splitter/149 4.00 10.00
22 Norm Nixon/199 5.00 12.00
23 Reggie Theus/199 5.00 12.00
24 Kevin Martin/49 5.00 12.00
25 Andrew Bogut/99 5.00 12.00
26 Derrick Favors/49 4.00 10.00
27 J.J. Redick/99 6.00 15.00
28 Jared Dudley/25 4.00 10.00
29 Zydrunas Ilgauskas/199 5.00 12.00
30 Mike Conley/99 6.00 15.00
31 Ty Lawson/49 4.00 10.00
32 Nick Van Exel/49 25.00 60.00
33 Spud Webb/199 8.00 20.00
34 Andre Drummond/49 6.00 15.00
35 Kawhi Leonard/99 75.00 200.00
36 Iman Shumpert/199 4.00 10.00
37 Nikola Pekovic/199 4.00 10.00
38 Steve Blake/199 4.00 10.00
39 Jimmer Fredette/149 6.00 15.00
40 Steve Francis/49 12.00 30.00
41 Charles Oakley/199 6.00 15.00
42 Zach Randolph/49 5.00 12.00
43 Chuck Person/99 5.00 12.00
44 Kobe Bryant/99 800.00 1,500.00
45 Kevin Durant/99 125.00 300.00
46 Chase Budinger/149 4.00 10.00
47 Monta Ellis/49 5.00 12.00
48 Ramon Sessions/199 4.00 10.00
49 Shannon Brown/199 4.00 10.00
50 DeMarcus Cousins/25 6.00 15.00

2013-14 Pinnacle Jamfest

COMPLETE SET (20) 8.00 20.00
1 Terrence Ross .50 1.25
2 Paul George 1.00 2.50
3 Harrison Barnes .60 1.50
4 Kenneth Faried .50 1.25
5 Blake Griffin .60 1.50
6 DeMar DeRozan .75 2.00
7 DeAndre Jordan .50 1.25
8 J.R. Smith .60 1.50
9 LeBron James 5.00 12.00
10 Kevin Durant 2.00 5.00
11 Kobe Bryant 5.00 12.00
12 Amar'e Stoudemire .60 1.50
13 Vince Carter 1.25 3.00
14 James Harden 1.25 3.00
15 Dwyane Wade 1.25 3.00
16 Dominique Wilkins 1.00 2.50
17 Clyde Drexler 1.00 2.50
18 Julius Erving 1.50 4.00
19 Larry Nance .50 1.25
20 Darryl Dawkins .50 1.25

2013-14 Pinnacle Jamfest Artist's Proofs

*AP: .6X TO 1.5X BASIC

2013-14 Pinnacle Jamfest Artist's Proofs Green

*AP GREEN: 2X TO 5X BASIC
STATED PRINT RUN 25 SER.#'d SETS

2013-14 Pinnacle Jamfest Die Cuts

*DIE CUT: 1X TO 2.5X BASIC
STATED PRINT RUN 99 SER.#'d SETS

2013-14 Pinnacle Museum Collection

*MUSEUM 1-50: 1.5X TO 4X BASIC
*MUSEUM 51-300: 2X TO 5X BASIC

2013-14 Pinnacle Performers Jerseys

1 Tim Duncan 6.00 15.00
2 Monta Ellis 2.00 5.00
3 Michael Kidd-Gilchrist 1.50 4.00
4 Mo Williams 2.00 5.00
5 J.R. Smith 2.50 6.00
6 Nick Young 1.50 4.00
7 Matt Barnes 1.50 4.00
8 Pablo Prigioni 1.50 4.00
9 Dirk Nowitzki 6.00 15.00
10 Kobe Bryant 20.00 50.00
11 Kevin Durant 8.00 20.00
12 Dwight Howard 3.00 8.00
13 Tony Parker 4.00 10.00
14 Kevin Love 2.50 6.00
15 Russell Westbrook 4.00 10.00
16 Rajon Rondo 3.00 8.00
17 Raymond Felton 1.50 4.00
18 Amar'e Stoudemire 2.50 6.00
19 Ryan Anderson 1.50 4.00
20 Stephen Curry 20.00 50.00
21 Steve Nash 5.00 12.00
22 Ty Lawson 1.50 4.00
23 Ben Gordon 2.00 5.00
24 Kyrie Irving 8.00 20.00
25 Chris Bosh 3.00 8.00
26 Kawhi Leonard 8.00 20.00
27 Zach Randolph 2.00 5.00
28 LeBron James 20.00 50.00
29 Andre Drummond 2.50 6.00
30 Kenneth Faried 2.00 5.00
31 Brandan Wright 1.50 4.00
32 Carl Landry 1.50 4.00
33 Carlos Delfino 1.50 4.00
34 Carmelo Anthony 4.00 10.00
35 Anthony Davis 8.00 20.00
36 Al Jefferson 1.50 4.00
37 Dwyane Wade 5.00 12.00
38 Danny Green 2.00 5.00
39 DeAndre Jordan 2.00 5.00
40 DeMar DeRozan 3.00 8.00
41 Deron Williams 2.00 5.00
42 Derrick Favors 1.50 4.00
43 Derrick Rose 4.00 10.00
44 Dion Waiters 1.50 4.00
45 Ersan Ilyasova 1.50 4.00
46 Jason Terry 2.00 5.00
47 Gerald Henderson 1.50 4.00
48 Glen Davis 1.50 4.00
49 Gordon Hayward 2.00 5.00
50 Jason Richardson 2.50 6.00
51 Paul Pierce 4.00 10.00
52 Andrew Bynum 1.50 4.00
53 MarShon Brooks 1.50 4.00
54 LaMarcus Aldridge 2.50 6.00
55 Kevin Garnett 6.00 15.00
56 Evan Fournier 2.00 5.00
57 Roy Hibbert 1.50 4.00
58 Blake Griffin 2.50 6.00
59 Channing Frye 1.50 4.00
60 Omer Asik 1.50 4.00
61 David Lee 1.50 4.00
62 Rodney Stuckey 1.50 4.00
63 Kirk Hinrich 2.00 5.00
64 Joakim Noah 2.50 6.00
65 Avery Bradley 1.50 4.00

2013-14 Pinnacle Performers Jerseys Prime

*PRIME: 1.2X TO 3X BASIC
PRINT RUN B/WN 1-25 COPIES PER
NO PRICING ON QTY 10 OR LESS

2013-14 Pinnacle Pinnacle of Success Autographs

PRINT RUNS B/WN 25-199 COPIES PER
EXCHANGE DEADLINE 7/15/2015
1 Stephen Curry/99 500.00 1,000.00
2 Jason Terry/99 5.00 12.00
3 Joakim Noah/99 6.00 15.00
4 John Havlicek/25 75.00 200.00
5 Ralph Sampson/99 5.00 12.00
6 Toni Kukoc/199 12.00 30.00
7 Scottie Pippen/49 75.00 200.00
8 Steve Kerr/99 12.00 30.00
9 Sean Elliott/199 6.00 15.00
10 Elvin Hayes/99 8.00 20.00
11 Michael Finley/99 6.00 15.00
12 Rick Mahorn/199 4.00 10.00
13 Mark Jackson/99 5.00 12.00
14 Kobe Bryant/99 800.00 1,500.00
15 Kevin Durant/49 125.00 300.00
16 Chris Bosh/49 8.00 20.00
17 Tony Parker/49 40.00 100.00
18 Hakeem Olajuwon/49 40.00 100.00
19 Steve Nash/25 75.00 200.00
20 Gail Goodrich/99 6.00 15.00
21 Jerry West/49 30.00 80.00
22 Walt Bellamy/99 6.00 15.00
23 Mario Chalmers/99 EXCH 5.00 12.00
24 Chris Andersen/49 10.00 25.00
25 Tom Heinsohn/199 40.00 100.00
26 Sidney Moncrief/199 6.00 15.00
27 Spencer Haywood/199 6.00 15.00
28 Horace Grant/99 12.00 30.00
29 Kyrie Irving/99 75.00 200.00
30 Norris Cole/199 4.00 10.00
31 Byron Scott/99 6.00 15.00
32 Julius Erving/49 50.00 120.00
33 Larry Bird/49 100.00 250.00
34 Magic Johnson/49 EXCH 100.00 250.00
35 Tyson Chandler/99 5.00 12.00
36 Glen Rice/99 5.00 12.00
37 Grant Hill/99 25.00 60.00
38 Bill Laimbeer/199 6.00 15.00
39 Bill Walton/99 10.00 25.00
40 Jack Sikma/199 6.00 15.00
41 A.C. Green/199 6.00 15.00
42 Robert Horry/199 6.00 15.00
43 Anderson Varejao/99 4.00 10.00
44 Kyle Lowry/199 6.00 15.00
45 Jonas Valanciunas/199 5.00 12.00
46 Kenny Smith/99 5.00 12.00
47 Jrue Holiday/99 12.00 30.00
48 Vlade Divac/199 6.00 15.00
49 Bob Dandridge/199 5.00 12.00
50 Bill Cartwright/199 5.00 12.00

2013-14 Pinnacle Position Powers

1 Pete Maravich 1.00 2.50
2 Magic Johnson 2.50 6.00
3 John Stockton 1.25 3.00
4 Mark Jackson .50 1.25
5 Kobe Bryant 5.00 12.00
6 Clyde Drexler 1.00 2.50
7 George Gervin 1.00 2.50
8 Allen Iverson 1.25 3.00
9 LeBron James 5.00 12.00
10 Larry Bird 2.50 6.00
11 Julius Erving 1.50 4.00
12 Scottie Pippen 1.50 4.00
13 Karl Malone 1.25 3.00
14 Tim Duncan 1.50 4.00
15 Dirk Nowitzki 1.50 4.00
16 Dennis Rodman 1.50 4.00
17 Shaquille O'Neal 2.50 6.00
18 Bill Russell 2.00 5.00
19 Kareem Abdul-Jabbar 2.00 5.00
20 Wilt Chamberlain 2.00 5.00

2013-14 Pinnacle Position Powers Artist's Proofs

*AP: .6X TO 1.5X BASIC

2013-14 Pinnacle Position Powers Artist's Proofs Green

*AP GREEN: 1.5X TO 4X BASIC
STATED PRINT RUN 25 SER.#'d SETS

2013-14 Pinnacle Position Powers Die Cuts

*DIE CUT: 1X TO 2.5X BASIC
STATED PRINT RUN 99 SER.#'d SETS

2013-14 Pinnacle Scoring Kings

COMPLETE SET (15) 8.00 20.00
1 Kareem Abdul-Jabbar 2.00 5.00
2 Karl Malone 1.25 3.00
3 Kobe Bryant 5.00 12.00
4 Wilt Chamberlain 2.00 5.00
5 Julius Erving 1.50 4.00
6 Moses Malone 1.00 2.50
7 Shaquille O'Neal 2.50 6.00
8 Dan Issel .75 2.00
9 Elvin Hayes .75 2.00
10 Hakeem Olajuwon 1.25 3.00
11 Oscar Robertson 1.00 2.50
12 Dominique Wilkins 1.00 2.50
13 George Gervin 1.00 2.50
14 John Havlicek 1.50 4.00
15 Alex English .75 2.00

2013-14 Pinnacle Scoring Kings Artist's Proofs

*AP: .6X TO 1.5X BASIC

2013-14 Pinnacle Scoring Kings Artist's Proofs Green

*AP GREEN: 1.5X TO 4X BASIC
STATED PRINT RUN 25 SER.#'d SETS

2013-14 Pinnacle Scoring Kings Die Cuts

*DIE CUT: 1X TO 2.5X BASIC
STATED PRINT RUN 99 SER.#'d SETS

2013-14 Pinnacle Team 2020

1 Anthony Bennett .40 1.00
2 Kyrie Irving 2.00 5.00
3 Brandon Knight .50 1.25
4 Bradley Beal 1.00 2.50
5 Harrison Barnes .60 1.50
6 Draymond Green 1.00 2.50
7 John Wall .75 2.00
8 Kawhi Leonard 2.00 5.00
9 Anthony Davis 2.00 5.00
10 Otto Porter .60 1.50
11 Dennis Schroder 1.25 3.00
12 Nerlens Noel .50 1.25
13 Trey Burke .50 1.25
14 Jimmy Butler 1.25 3.00
15 Chandler Parsons .40 1.00
16 Dion Waiters .40 1.00
17 Nikola Vucevic .75 2.00
18 Blake Griffin .60 1.50
19 Shane Larkin .40 1.00
20 Norris Cole .40 1.00
21 Tobias Harris .60 1.50
22 Shabazz Muhammad .40 1.00
23 Michael Carter-Williams .50 1.25
24 Andre Drummond .60 1.50
25 Damian Lillard 2.00 5.00
26 Victor Oladipo 1.00 2.50
27 Klay Thompson 2.00 5.00
28 Ben McLemore .50 1.25
29 Cody Zeller .50 1.25
30 C.J. McCollum 1.50 4.00

2013-14 Pinnacle Team 2020 Artist's Proofs

*AP: .6X TO 1.5X BASIC

2013-14 Pinnacle Team 2020 Artist's Proofs Green

*AP GREEN: 1.5X TO 4X BASIC
STATED PRINT RUN 25 SER.#'d SETS

2013-14 Pinnacle Team 2020 Die Cuts

*DIE CUT: 1X TO 2.5X BASIC
STATED PRINT RUN 99 SER.#'d SETS

2013-14 Pinnacle Team Pinnacle

COMPLETE SET (20) 8.00 20.00
1 K.Durant/D.Wade 2.00 5.00
2 R.Westbrook/T.Parker 1.00 2.50
3 L.James/K.Bryant 20.00 50.00
4 B.Griffin/A.Davis 2.00 5.00
5 C.Paul/D.Rose 1.25 3.00
6 C.Anthony/K.Durant 2.00 5.00
7 D.Lillard/K.Irving 2.00 5.00
8 H.Barnes/V.Carter 1.25 3.00
9 B.Beal/C.Parsons 1.00 2.50
10 P.Gasol/M.Gasol 1.00 2.50
11 O.Mayo/D.DeRozan .75 2.00
12 R.Rondo/J.Wall .75 2.00
13 R.Rubio/D.Williams .50 1.25
14 D.Nowitzki/K.Love 1.50 4.00
15 D.Howard/R.Hibbert .75 2.00
16 P.George/P.Pierce 1.00 2.50
17 K.Garnett/T.Duncan 1.50 4.00
18 K.Bryant/K.Durant 10.00 25.00
19 L.James/K.Durant 5.00 12.00
20 K.Irving/K.Bryant 8.00 20.00

2013-14 Pinnacle Team Pinnacle Artist's Proofs

*AP: .6X TO 1.5X BASIC

2013-14 Pinnacle Team Pinnacle Artist's Proofs Green

*AP GREEN: 1.5X TO 4X BASIC
STATED PRINT RUN 25 SER.#'d SETS

2013-14 Pinnacle Team Pinnacle Die Cuts

*DIE CUT: 1X TO 2.5X BASIC
STATED PRINT RUN 99 SER.#'d SETS

2013-14 Pinnacle The Naturals

COMPLETE SET (20) 8.00 20.00
1 LeBron James 5.00 12.00
2 Kobe Bryant 5.00 12.00
3 Blake Griffin .60 1.50
4 Kyrie Irving 2.00 5.00
5 Anthony Davis 2.00 5.00
6 Harrison Barnes .60 1.50
7 Tim Duncan 1.50 4.00
8 Yao Ming 1.25 3.00
9 Shaquille O'Neal 2.50 6.00
10 Patrick Ewing 1.00 2.50
11 David Robinson 1.25 3.00
12 Allen Iverson 1.25 3.00
13 Derrick Rose 1.00 2.50
14 Kevin Durant 2.00 5.00
15 Paul Pierce 1.00 2.50
16 Kevin Garnett 1.50 4.00
17 Grant Hill 1.00 2.50
18 Jason Kidd 1.00 2.50
19 Ray Allen 1.00 2.50
20 Carmelo Anthony 1.00 2.50

2013-14 Pinnacle The Naturals Artist's Proofs

*AP: .6X TO 1.5X BASIC

2013-14 Pinnacle The Naturals Artist's Proofs Green

*AP GREEN: 2X TO 5X BASIC
STATED PRINT RUN 25 SER.#'d SETS

2013-14 Pinnacle The Naturals Die Cuts

*DIE CUT: 1.25X TO 3X BASIC
STATED PRINT RUN 99 SER.#'d SETS

2013-14 Pinnacle Upstarts Jerseys

1 Anthony Bennett 1.50 4.00
2 Victor Oladipo 4.00 10.00
3 Otto Porter 2.50 6.00
4 Nerlens Noel 2.00 5.00
5 Ben McLemore 2.00 5.00
6 Kentavious Caldwell-Pope 2.50 6.00
7 Trey Burke 2.00 5.00
8 Michael Carter-Williams 2.00 5.00
9 Steven Adams 4.00 10.00
10 Kelly Olynyk 2.00 5.00
11 Shabazz Muhammad 1.50 4.00
12 Giannis Antetokounmpo 125.00 300.00
13 Tony Snell 2.00 5.00
14 Shane Larkin 1.50 4.00
15 Mason Plumlee 2.00 5.00
16 Tim Hardaway Jr. 3.00 8.00
17 Andre Roberson 2.00 5.00
18 Archie Goodwin 1.50 4.00
19 Glen Rice Jr. 1.50 4.00
20 Nate Wolters 1.50 4.00
21 Jeff Withey 1.50 4.00
22 Dennis Schroder 5.00 12.00
23 Jamaal Franklin 1.50 4.00
24 Erik Murphy 1.50 4.00
25 Peyton Siva 1.50 4.00
26 Ryan Kelly 1.50 4.00
27 Isaiah Canaan 1.50 4.00
28 Alex Len 2.00 5.00
29 C.J. McCollum 6.00 15.00
30 Cody Zeller 2.00 5.00
31 Solomon Hill 2.00 5.00
32 Reggie Bullock 2.00 5.00
33 Allen Crabbe 1.50 4.00
34 Tony Mitchell 1.50 4.00
35 Ricky Ledo 1.50 4.00

2013-14 Pinnacle Upstarts Jerseys Prime

*BLUE PRIME: 1.2X TO 3X BASIC
STATED PRINT RUN 25 SER.#'d SETS

2013-14 Pinnacle Z-Team

COMPLETE SET (20) 8.00 20.00
1 Kobe Bryant 5.00 12.00
2 LeBron James 5.00 12.00
3 Anthony Davis 2.00 5.00
4 Kyrie Irving 2.00 5.00
5 Kevin Durant 2.00 5.00
6 Carmelo Anthony 1.00 2.50
7 Derrick Rose 1.00 2.50
8 John Wall .75 2.00
9 James Harden 1.25 3.00
10 Chris Paul 1.25 3.00
11 Paul George 1.00 2.50
12 Rajon Rondo .75 2.00
13 Kawhi Leonard 2.00 5.00
14 Kenneth Faried .50 1.25
15 Damian Lillard 2.00 5.00
16 Ricky Rubio .50 1.25
17 Brandon Knight .50 1.25
18 Blake Griffin .60 1.50
19 Dirk Nowitzki 1.50 4.00
20 Stephen Curry 5.00 12.00

2013-14 Pinnacle Z-Team Artist's Proofs

*AP: .6X TO 1.5X BASIC

2013-14 Pinnacle Z-Team Artist's Proofs Green

*AP GREEN: 2.5X TO 6X BASIC
STATED PRINT RUN 25 SER.#'d SETS
1 Kobe Bryant 60.00 150.00
2 LeBron James 60.00 150.00
4 Kyrie Irving 20.00 50.00
5 Kevin Durant 30.00 80.00
20 Stephen Curry 60.00 150.00

2013-14 Pinnacle Z-Team Die Cuts

*DIE CUT: 1.25X TO 3X BASIC
STATED PRINT RUN 99 SER.#'d SETS

2017-18 Pinnacle

251 Justin Patton .50 1.25
252 Jonathan Isaac 1.25 3.00
253 Terrance Ferguson .50 1.25
254 Lonzo Ball 2.00 5.00
255 Ike Anigbogu .50 1.25
256 Bam Adebayo 3.00 8.00
257 Donovan Mitchell 5.00 12.00
258 De'Aaron Fox 4.00 10.00
259 Jarrett Allen 1.25 3.00
260 Frank Ntilikina .60 1.50
261 Milos Teodosic .60 1.50
262 Josh Jackson .60 1.50
263 Tyler Lydon .50 1.25
264 Malik Monk 2.00 5.00
265 Cedi Osman 1.00 2.50
266 D.J. Wilson .50 1.25
267 Frank Mason III .50 1.25
268 Dennis Smith Jr. .60 1.50
269 Jordan Bell .30 .75
270 Jayson Tatum 6.00 15.00
271 Sindarius Thornwell .50 1.25
272 Lauri Markkanen 3.00 8.00
273 Abdel Nader .60 1.50
274 Markelle Fultz 1.25 3.00
275 Dillon Brooks 1.50 4.00

2017-18 Pinnacle Artist Proof Blue

*AP BLUE: .5X TO 1.2X BASIC
STATED PRINT RUN 199 SER.#'d SETS

2017-18 Pinnacle Artist Proof Red

*AP RED: .5X TO 1.2X BASIC
STATED PRINT RUN 249 SER.#'d SETS

2017-18 Pinnacle Artist Proof Silver

*AP SILVER: .6X TO 1.5X BASIC
STATED PRINT RUN 99 SER.#'d SETS

1968-69 Pipers Minnesota Team Issue

COMPLETE SET (10) 35.00 75.00
1 Frank Card 2.00 5.00
2 Connie Hawkins 15.00 40.00
3 Art Heyman 3.00 8.00
4 Arvesta Kelly 2.50 6.00
5 Mike Lewis 2.50 6.00
6 George Sutor 2.00 5.00
7 Steve Vacendak 2.00 5.00
8 Chico Vaughn 2.00 5.00
9 Tom Washington 3.00 8.00
10 Charlie Williams 3.00 8.00

1990-91 Pistons Star

COMPLETE SET (14) 1.50 4.00
1 Mark Aguirre .20 .50
2 William Bedford .08 .25
3 Joe Dumars .40 1.00
4 James Edwards .08 .25
5 David Greenwood .08 .25
6 Scott Hastings .08 .25
7 Gerald Henderson .08 .25
8 Vinnie Johnson .20 .50
9 Bill Laimbeer .40 1.00
10 Dennis Rodman .60 1.50
11 John Salley .08 .25
12 Isiah Thomas .40 1.00
13 Chuck Daly CO .20 .50
14 Maia A. Porche PRES .08 .25

1977-78 Pistons Team Issue

COMPLETE SET (11) 20.00 35.00
1 Roger Brown 1.25 3.00
2 M.L. Carr 3.00 8.00
3 Leon Douglas 1.25 3.00
4 Al Eberhard 1.25 3.00
5 Chris Ford 2.50 6.00
6 Larry Jones 1.25 3.00
7 Al Menendez 1.25 3.00
8 Eric Money 1.25 3.00
9 Willie Norwood 1.25 3.00
10 Howard Porter 1.50 4.00
11 Ralph Simpson 1.50 4.00

1978-79 Pistons Team Issue

COMPLETE SET (13) 20.00 35.00
1 M.L. Carr 1.00 2.50
2 Leon Douglas .75 2.00
3 Chris Ford 1.50 4.00
4 Gus Gerard .75 2.00
5 Bubbles Hawkins .75 2.00
6 Bob Lanier 3.00 8.00
7 John Long .75 2.00
8 Ben Poquette .75 2.00
9 Kevin Porter 1.00 2.50
10 Terry Tyler .75 2.00
11 Dick Vitale CO 5.00 10.00
12 Al Menendez ACO
Mike Abdenor TR .75 2.00
13 Mike Brunker ACO
Richie Adubato ACO .75 2.00

1990-91 Pistons Unocal

COMPLETE SET (16) 3.00 8.00
1 Mark Aguirre .30 .75
2 Chuck Daly CO .60 1.50
3 Joe Dumars .60 1.50
4 James Edwards .20 .50
5 Vinnie Johnson .30 .75
6 Vinnie Johnson
(The Shot) .30 .75
7 Bill Laimbeer .30 .75
8 Lawrence O'Brien
Trophy .20 .50
9 Dennis Rodman .75 2.00
10 John Salley .20 .50
11 Isiah Thomas .75 2.00
12 Isiah Thomas MVP .75 2.00
13 Celebration Card .20 .50
14 Team Photo .50 1.25
15 Two Championship Rings .20 .50
16 1990 World Champions .20 .50

1991-92 Pistons Unocal

COMPLETE SET (16) 3.00 8.00
1 Mark Aguirre .30 .75
2 Dave Bing .40 1.00
3 Chuck Daly CO .30 .75
4 Joe Dumars .60 1.50
5 Joe Dumars
1991 Pistons MVP .60 1.50
6 Bill Laimbeer .30 .75
7 Bill Laimbeer
All-Time Leading Rebounder .30 .75
8 Dennis Rodman .60 1.50
9 John Salley .20 .50
10 Isiah Thomas .75 2.00
11 Isiah Thomas
All-Time Leading Scorer .75 2.00
12 Darrell Walker .20 .50
13 Orlando Woolridge .20 .50
14 Team Photo
1989 World Champs .50 1.25
15 Mark Aguirre
Joe Dumars
Bill Laimbeer
Dennis Rodman
Isiah Thomas
Chuck Daly CO .30 .75
16 Brad Sellers
Bob McCann
Charles Thomas
William Bedford
Lance Blanks .20 .50

2007-08 Pistons Upper Deck

COMPLETE SET (5) 1.25 3.00
1 Richard Hamilton .50 1.25
2 Chauncey Billups .50 1.25
3 Tayshaun Prince .40 1.00
4 Rasheed Wallace .50 1.25
5 Chris Webber .50 1.25

2008 Playoff Contenders

COMP.SET w/o AU's (50) 8.00 20.00
COMMON CARD (1-50) .25 .60
COMMON AU (51-130) 3.00 8.00
OVERALL AUTO ODDS 5 PER BOX
EXCHANGE DEADLINE 8/4/2010
78 D.Rose AU/88 * 150.00 300.00
103 M.Beasley AU/88 * 30.00 60.00
112 O.Mayo AU/88 * 40.00 80.00

2008 Playoff Contenders Playoff Ticket

COMMON CARD (51-130) 1.00 2.50
OVERALL INSERT ODDS 1:3

2009-10 Playoff Contenders

COMP.SET w/o SPs (100) 25.00 50.00
AU RC APPROX.ODDS FOUR PER BOX
1 Kevin Garnett 1.25 3.00
2 Paul Pierce .75 2.00
3 Rajon Rondo .60 1.50
4 Dirk Nowitzki 1.25 3.00
5 Jason Terry .40 1.00
6 Josh Howard .40 1.00
7 Shawn Marion .50 1.25
8 Brook Lopez .50 1.25
9 Devin Harris .30 .75
10 Yi Jianlian .60 1.50
11 Luis Scola .40 1.00
12 Tracy McGrady 1.00 2.50
13 Trevor Ariza .30 .75
14 Danilo Gallinari .40 1.00
15 Darko Milicic .30 .75
16 David Lee .30 .75
17 Nate Robinson .40 1.00

18 Allen Iverson 1.00 2.50
19 Marc Gasol .50 1.25
20 O.J. Mayo .30 .75
21 Zach Randolph .50 1.25
22 Andre Iguodala .50 1.25
23 Elton Brand .40 1.00
24 Thaddeus Young .30 .75
25 Chris Paul 1.00 2.50
26 David West .40 1.00
27 Peja Stojakovic .40 1.00
28 Andrea Bargnani .30 .75
29 Chris Bosh .60 1.50
30 Jarrett Jack .40 1.00
31 Jose Calderon .30 .75
32 Michael Finley .50 1.25
33 Richard Jefferson .40 1.00
34 Tim Duncan 1.25 3.00
35 Tony Parker .75 2.00
36 Derrick Rose .75 2.00
37 Joakim Noah .30 .75
38 Tyrus Thomas .30 .75
39 Carmelo Anthony .75 2.00
40 Chauncey Billups .60 1.50
41 J.R. Smith .50 1.25
42 Nene .40 1.00
43 LeBron James 4.00 10.00
44 Shaquille O'Neal 1.50 4.00
45 Zydrunas Ilgauskas .40 1.00
46 Al Jefferson .30 .75
47 Kevin Love .50 1.25
48 Ryan Gomes .30 .75
49 Ben Gordon .40 1.00
50 Richard Hamilton .50 1.25
51 Tayshaun Prince .50 1.25
52 Andre Miller .50 1.25
53 Brandon Roy .60 1.50
54 LaMarcus Aldridge .50 1.25
55 Rudy Fernandez .30 .75
56 Danny Granger .30 .75
57 T.J. Ford .30 .75
58 Troy Murphy .30 .75
59 Jeff Green .40 1.00
60 Kevin Durant 2.00 5.00
61 Russell Westbrook 1.00 2.50
62 Andrew Bogut .40 1.00
63 Kurt Thomas .30 .75
64 Michael Redd .40 1.00
65 Andrei Kirilenko .40 1.00
66 Deron Williams .40 1.00
67 Mehmet Okur .30 .75
68 Joe Johnson .40 1.00
69 Josh Smith .30 .75
70 Mike Bibby .50 1.25
71 Anthony Randolph .40 1.00
72 Corey Maggette .40 1.00
73 Stephen Jackson .40 1.00
74 Boris Diaw .40 1.00
75 D.J. Augustin .30 .75
76 Gerald Wallace .40 1.00
77 Raja Bell .40 1.00
78 Al Thornton .30 .75
79 Baron Davis .40 1.00
80 Chris Kaman .40 1.00
81 Eric Gordon .40 1.00
82 Daequan Cook .30 .75
83 Dwyane Wade 1.00 2.50
84 Jermaine O'Neal .50 1.25
85 Andrew Bynum .30 .75
86 Kobe Bryant 4.00 10.00
87 Pau Gasol .75 2.00
88 Ron Artest .50 1.25
89 Dwight Howard .60 1.50
90 Jameer Nelson .30 .75
91 Vince Carter 1.00 2.50
92 Amare Stoudemire .40 1.00
93 Grant Hill .75 2.00
94 Steve Nash 1.00 2.50
95 Antawn Jamison .40 1.00
96 Caron Butler .40 1.00
97 Gilbert Arenas .40 1.00
98 Andres Nocioni .30 .75
99 Kevin Martin .40 1.00
100 Sean May .30 .75
101 Blake Griffin SP AU RC 20.00 50.00
102 Hasheem Thabeet SP AU RC 4.00 10.00
103 James Harden SP AU RC 300.00 600.00
104 Tyreke Evans SP AU RC 5.00 12.00
105 Jonny Flynn SP AU RC 4.00 10.00
106 Stephen Curry SP AU RC 3,000.00 6,000.00
107 Jordan Hill SP AU RC 4.00 10.00
108 Brandon Jennings SP AU RC 6.00 15.00
109 T.Williams SP AU RC 4.00 10.00
110 G.Henderson AU RC 4.00 10.00
111 Tyler Hansbrough SP AU RC 5.00 12.00
112 Earl Clark SP AU RC 4.00 10.00
113 Austin Daye AU RC 4.00 10.00
114 James Johnson AU RC 5.00 12.00
115 Jrue Holiday AU RC 20.00 50.00
116 Ty Lawson AU RC 5.00 12.00
117 Jeff Teague AU RC 5.00 12.00
118 Eric Maynor AU RC 4.00 10.00
119 Darren Collison AU RC 6.00 15.00
120 Omri Casspi AU RC 4.00 10.00
121 B.J. Mullens AU RC 4.00 10.00
122 Rodrigue Beaubois AU RC 4.00 10.00
123 Taj Gibson AU RC 5.00 12.00
124 DeMarre Carroll AU RC 5.00 12.00
125 Wayne Ellington AU RC 5.00 12.00
126 Toney Douglas AU RC 4.00 10.00
127 J.Pendergraph AU RC 4.00 10.00
128 Jermaine Taylor AU RC 4.00 10.00
129 D.Cunningham SP AU RC 4.00 10.00
130 DaJuan Summers AU RC 4.00 10.00
131 Sam Young AU RC 4.00 10.00
132 DeJuan Blair AU RC 5.00 12.00
133 Jodie Meeks AU RC 4.00 10.00
134 Chase Budinger AU RC 4.00 10.00
135 Taylor Griffin AU RC 4.00 10.00
136 Kareem Abdul-Jabbar 4.00 10.00
137 Isiah Thomas 1.25 3.00
138 Bernard King 1.50 4.00
139 Danny Manning 1.00 2.50
140 Larry Bird 5.00 12.00
141 Artis Gilmore 1.50 4.00
142 Jalen Rose 1.00 2.50
143 John Havlicek 3.00 8.00
144 A.C. Green 1.25 3.00
145 Spencer Haywood .75 2.00
146 Hal Greer 1.50 4.00
147 Oscar Robertson 1.50 4.00
148 World B. Free 1.00 2.50
149 Sidney Moncrief 1.00 2.50
150 Maurice Cheeks 1.00 2.50

2009-10 Playoff Contenders Classic Tickets Signatures

STATED PRINT RUN 25 SER.#'d SETS
136 Kareem Abdul-Jabbar 125.00 300.00
137 Isiah Thomas 40.00 100.00
138 Bernard King 20.00 50.00
139 Danny Manning 12.00 30.00
140 Larry Bird 150.00 400.00
141 Artis Gilmore 15.00 40.00
142 Jalen Rose 15.00 40.00
143 John Havlicek 100.00 250.00
144 A.C. Green 12.00 30.00
145 Spencer Haywood 20.00 50.00
146 Hal Greer 40.00 100.00
147 Oscar Robertson 75.00 200.00
149 Sidney Moncrief 12.00 30.00
150 Maurice Cheeks 12.00 30.00

2009-10 Playoff Contenders Playoff Tickets

STATED PRINT RUN 5 TO 50 SER.#'d SETS
86 Kobe Bryant/50 1,500.00 3,000.00

2009-10 Playoff Contenders Award Contenders

COMPLETE SET (20) 8.00 20.00
*BLACK: 1X TO 2.5X BASE HI
BLACK PRINT RUN 50 SER.#'d SETS
*GOLD: .75X TO 2X BASE HI
GOLD PRINT RUN 100 SER.#'d SETS
1 Kobe Bryant 6.00 15.00
2 Danny Granger .50 1.25
3 Al Harrington .60 1.50
4 Ben Gordon .60 1.50
5 Carmelo Anthony 1.25 3.00
6 Chris Bosh 1.00 2.50
7 Dirk Nowitzki 2.00 5.00
8 Dwyane Wade 1.50 4.00
9 Kevin Love .75 2.00
10 LeBron James 6.00 15.00
11 Tony Parker 1.25 3.00
12 Michael Redd .60 1.50
13 Ray Allen 1.25 3.00
14 Tim Duncan 2.00 5.00
15 Tracy McGrady 1.50 4.00
16 Deron Williams .60 1.50
17 Dwight Howard 1.00 2.50
18 Paul Pierce 1.25 3.00
19 Chris Paul 1.50 4.00
20 Chauncey Billups 1.00 2.50

2009-10 Playoff Contenders Award Contenders Autographs

STATED PRINT RUN 5 TO 50 SER.#'d SETS
1 Kobe Bryant/50 1,500.00 3,000.00

2009-10 Playoff Contenders Draft Class

COMPLETE SET (20) 10.00 25.00
*BLACK: .75X TO 2X BASE HI
BLACK PRINT RUN 50 SER.#'d SETS
*GOLD: .6X TO 1.5X BASE HI
GOLD PRINT RUN 100 SER.#'d SETS
1 Andrea Bargnani .75 2.00
2 Adam Morrison .75 2.00
3 J.J. Redick 1.25 3.00
4 Jordan Farmar .75 2.00
5 Daniel Gibson .75 2.00
6 Greg Oden .75 2.00
7 Kevin Durant 5.00 12.00
8 Al Horford 1.25 3.00
9 Mike Conley Jr. 1.00 2.50
10 Yi Jianlian 1.50 4.00
11 Joakim Noah .75 2.00
12 Acie Law .75 2.00
13 Thaddeus Young .75 2.00
14 Al Thornton .75 2.00
15 Aaron Brooks .75 2.00
16 Ramon Sessions .75 2.00
17 Derrick Rose 2.00 5.00
18 Michael Beasley .75 2.00
19 Russell Westbrook 2.50 6.00
20 Danilo Gallinari 1.00 2.50
21 Eric Gordon 1.00 2.50
22 D.J. Augustin .75 2.00
23 Brook Lopez .75 2.00
24 Anthony Randolph .75 2.00
25 Paul Millsap 1.00 2.50

2009-10 Playoff Contenders Draft Tandems

COMPLETE SET (20) 15.00 30.00
*BLACK: .6X TO 1.5X BASE HI
BLACK PRINT RUN 50 SER.#'d SETS
*GOLD: .5X TO 1.25X BASE HI
GOLD PRINT RUN 100 SER.#'d SETS
1 H.Thabeet/M.Beasley .75 2.00
2 A.Bargnani/T.Duncan 3.00 8.00
3 C.Bosh/C.Paul 2.50 6.00
4 K.Love/R.Felton 1.25 3.00
5 E.Gordon/R.Foye 1.00 2.50
6 C.Kaman/Y.Jianlian 1.50 4.00
7 A.Stoudemire/J.Noah 1.00 2.50
8 J.Worthy/L.Johnson 1.50 4.00
9 A.Mourning/S.Bradley 2.00 5.00
10 D.Mutombo/G.Rice 2.00 5.00
11 M.Richmond/S.Moncrief 1.25 3.00
12 C.Brewer/K.Hinrich 1.00 2.50
13 A.Bynum/P.Pierce 2.00 5.00
14 D.Harper/R.Horry 1.00 2.50
15 J.Rose/K.Malone 1.50 4.00
16 D.Majerle/T.Hardaway 1.25 3.00
17 B.Griffin/M.Johnson 5.00 12.00
18 D.Williams/J.Harden 8.00 20.00
19 C.Mullin/S.Curry 25.00 60.00
20 D.Schrempf/J.Hill 1.25 3.00

2009-10 Playoff Contenders Legendary Contenders

COMPLETE SET (20) 10.00 25.00
*BLACK: .75X TO 2X BASE HI
BLACK PRINT RUN 50 SER.#'d SETS
*GOLD: .6X TO 1.5X BASE HI
GOLD PRINT RUN 100 SER.#'d SETS
1 Willis Reed 2.50 6.00
2 Shawn Bradley 1.00 2.50
3 Jeff Hornacek 1.25 3.00
4 Dolph Schayes 1.50 4.00
6 Bill Laimbeer 1.50 4.00
7 Kenny Walker 1.00 2.50
8 Connie Hawkins 2.00 5.00
9 Clyde Drexler 2.50 6.00
10 Rony Seikaly 1.00 2.50
11 Larry Johnson 1.50 4.00
12 Cedric Ceballos 1.00 2.50
14 Kurt Rambis 1.00 2.50
15 Joe Dumars 2.00 5.00
16 Bobby Wanzer 1.00 2.50
17 Dan Majerle 1.25 3.00
18 George McGinnis 1.50 4.00
19 Gheorghe Muresan 1.00 2.50

2009-10 Playoff Contenders Lottery Winners

COMPLETE SET (30) 15.00 30.00
*BLACK: 1X TO 2.5X BASE HI
BLACK PRINT RUN 50 SER.#'d SETS
*GOLD: .75X TO 2X BASE HI
GOLD PRINT RUN 100 SER.#'d SETS
1 LeBron James 6.00 15.00
2 Allen Iverson 1.50 4.00
3 Tim Duncan 2.00 5.00
4 Yao Ming 2.00 5.00
5 Derrick Rose 2.00 5.00
6 Kevin Garnett 2.00 5.00
7 Blake Griffin 3.00 8.00
8 Jason Kidd 1.25 3.00
9 Carmelo Anthony 1.25 3.00
10 Deron Williams .60 1.50
11 Chris Paul 1.50 4.00
12 Rudy Gay .75 2.00
13 Brandon Roy 1.00 2.50
14 LaMarcus Aldridge .75 2.00
15 Andrea Bargnani .50 1.25
16 Andre Iguodala .75 2.00
17 Chris Bosh 1.00 2.50
18 Jeff Green .60 1.50
19 Dwyane Wade 1.50 4.00
20 Chris Kaman .60 1.50
21 Paul Pierce 1.25 3.00
22 Andrew Bynum .50 1.25
23 Kevin Durant 3.00 8.00
24 Joakim Noah .50 1.25
25 Al Thornton .50 1.25
26 Charlie Villanueva .50 1.25
27 Emeka Okafor .60 1.50
28 Michael Beasley .50 1.25
29 Mike Bibby .75 2.00
30 Shane Battier .75 2.00

2009-10 Playoff Contenders One-Two Punch

COMPLETE SET (25) 15.00 0.00
*BLACK: .6X TO 1.5X BASE HI
BLACK PRINT RUN 50 SER.#'d SETS
*GOLD: .5X TO 1.25X BASE HI
GOLD PRINT RUN 100 SER.#'d SETS
1 B.Roy/G.Oden 2.00 5.00
2 J.Green/K.Durant 6.00 5.00
3 C.Bosh/H.Turkoglu 2.00 5.00
4 E.Brand/T.Young 1.25 3.00
5 A.Randolph/R.Bell 1.25 3.00
6 S.Jackson/R.Felton 1.25 3.00
7 D.Nowitzki/J.Howard 4.00 0.00
8 B.Gordon/C.Villanueva 1.25 3.00
9 S.Battier/T.Ariza 1.50 4.00
10 C.Kaman/M.Camby 1.25 3.00
11 L.Odom/P.Gasol 2.50 6.00
12 D.Harris/R.Alston 1.00 2.50
13 D.West/P.Stojakovic 1.25 3.00
14 C.Billups/J.Smith 2.00 5.00
15 A.Jefferson/K.Love 1.50 4.00
16 C.Boozer/D.Williams 1.25 3.00
17 O.Mayo/R.Gay 1.50 4.00
18 R.Rondo/R.Allen 2.50 6.00
19 L.Barbosa/S.Nash 3.00 8.00
20 A.Horford/M.Bibby 1.50 4.00
21 D.Rose/J.Noah 2.50 6.00
22 A.Varejao/S.O'Neal 5.00 12.00
23 R.Hamilton/T.Prince 1.50 4.00
24 D.Granger/T.Murphy 1.00 2.50
25 M.Beasley/U.Haslem 1.00 2.50

2009-10 Playoff Contenders Perennial Contenders

COMPLETE SET (20) 10.00 25.00
*BLACK: .75X TO 2X BASE HI
BLACK PRINT RUN 50 SER.#'d SETS
*GOLD: .6X TO 1.5X BASE HI
GOLD PRINT RUN 100 SER.#'d SETS
1 Rasheed Wallace 1.25 3.00
2 Joakim Noah .60 1.50
3 Shaquille O'Neal 3.00 8.00
4 Jason Terry .75 2.00
5 Chauncey Billups 1.25 3.00
6 Tayshaun Prince 1.00 2.50
7 Tracy McGrady 2.00 5.00
8 Kobe Bryant 8.00 20.00
9 Nate Robinson .75 2.00
10 Vince Carter 2.00 5.00
11 Grant Hill 1.25 3.00
12 Greg Oden .60 1.50
13 Tony Parker 1.50 4.00
14 Carlos Boozer .75 2.00
15 Ron Artest 1.00 2.50
16 Paul Pierce 1.50 4.00
17 Deron Williams .75 2.00
18 Ben Wallace 1.25 3.00
19 LeBron James 8.00 20.00
20 Andre Iguodala 1.25 3.00

2009-10 Playoff Contenders Perennial Contenders Autographs

STATED PRINT RUN 5 TO 50 SER.#'d SETS
8 Kobe Bryant/50 500.00 1,000.00

2009-10 Playoff Contenders Rookie of the Year Contenders

COMPLETE SET (15) 10.00 25.00
*BLACK: 1.25X TO 3X BASE HI
BLACK PRINT RUN 50 SER.#'d SETS
*GOLD: .75X TO 2X BASE HI
GOLD PRINT RUN 100 SER.#'d SETS
1 Blake Griffin 4.00 10.00
2 DeJuan Blair .75 2.00
3 Omri Casspi .60 1.50
4 Chase Budinger .60 1.50
5 Hasheem Thabeet .60 1.50
6 James Harden 12.00 30.00
7 Brandon Jennings 1.00 2.50
8 Jonny Flynn .60 1.50
9 Jordan Hill .60 1.50
10 Stephen Curry 125.00 300.00
11 Terrence Williams .60 1.50
12 Ty Lawson .75 2.00
13 Tyler Hansbrough .75 2.00
14 Tyreke Evans .75 2.00
15 Taj Gibson .75 2.00

2009-10 Playoff Contenders Rookie of the Year Contenders Autographs

STATED PRINT RUN 25 SER.#'d SETS
1 Blake Griffin 50.00 100.00
2 DeJuan Blair 6.00 15.00
3 Omri Casspi 5.00 12.00
4 Chase Budinger 5.00 12.00
5 Hasheem Thabeet 5.00 12.00
6 James Harden 200.00 500.00
7 Brandon Jennings 8.00 20.00
8 Jonny Flynn 5.00 12.00
9 Jordan Hill 5.00 12.00
10 Stephen Curry 2,500.00 5,000.00
11 Terrence Williams 5.00 12.00
12 Ty Lawson 6.00 15.00
13 Tyler Hansbrough 6.00 15.00
14 Tyreke Evans 6.00 15.00
15 Taj Gibson 6.00 15.00

2009-10 Playoff Contenders Round Numbers

COMPLETE SET (25) 20.00 40.00
*BLACK: .6X TO 1.5X BASE HI
BLACK PRINT RUN 50 SER.#'d SETS
*GOLD: .5X TO 1.25X BASE HI
GOLD PRINT RUN 100 SER.#'d SETS
1 M.Redd/R.Sessions 1.00 2.50
2 L.Aldridge/T.Duncan 3.00 8.00
3 C.Bosh/P.Gasol 2.00 5.00
4 B.Gordon/V.Carter 2.50 6.00
5 R.Lewis/T.Ariza 1.00 2.50
6 C.Anthony/P.Pierce 2.00 5.00
7 D.Howard/G.Oden 1.50 4.00
8 K.Garnett/T.Hansbrough 3.00 8.00
9 B.Griffin/K.Bryant 10.00 25.00
10 C.Boozer/P.Millsap 1.00 2.50
11 O.Mayo/T.Williams .75 2.00
12 B.Jennings/C.Paul 2.50 6.00
13 S.Nash/T.Lawson 2.50 6.00
14 D.Wade/S.Curry 25.00 60.00
15 M.Ellis/S.Jackson 1.00 2.50
16 B.Roy/J.Flynn 1.50 4.00
17 J.Kidd/T.Evans 2.00 5.00
18 D.Rose/J.Harden 8.00 20.00
19 A.Bogut/H.Thabeet .60 1.50
20 M.Ginobili/M.Williams 2.50 6.00
21 D.Williams/G.Henderson .75 2.00
22 J.Hill/K.Durant 5.00 12.00
23 A.Bargnani/D.Nowitzki 3.00 8.00
24 A.Stoudemire/E.Brand 1.00 2.50
25 G.Arenas/M.Chalmers 1.00 2.50

2009-10 Playoff Contenders Round Numbers Autographs

STATED PRINT RUN 10 TO 25 SER.#'d SETS
9 B.Griffin/K.Bryant/25 1,500.00 3,000.00

2010-11 Playoff Contenders Patches

COMP.SET w/o RCs (100) 15.00 40.00
EXCH.EXPIRATION 8/16/2010
1 Kobe Bryant 4.00 10.00
2 Pau Gasol .75 2.00
3 Sasha Vujacic .30 .75
4 Lamar Odom .40 1.00
5 Blake Griffin .50 1.25
6 Baron Davis .50 1.25
7 Eric Gordon .40 1.00
8 Stephen Curry 4.00 10.00
9 Monta Ellis .50 1.25
10 David Lee .30 .75
11 Channing Frye .30 .75
12 Steve Nash 1.00 2.50
13 Robin Lopez .30 .75
14 Samuel Dalembert .30 .75
15 Tyreke Evans .40 1.00
16 Carl Landry .30 .75
17 Carmelo Anthony .75 2.00
18 Chauncey Billups .60 1.50
19 Al Harrington .40 1.00
20 Chris Andersen .30 .75
21 LaMarcus Aldridge .50 1.25
22 Marcus Camby .40 1.00
23 Brandon Roy .60 1.50
24 Al Jefferson .30 .75
25 Deron Williams .40 1.00
26 Andrei Kirilenko .40 1.00
27 Kevin Durant 2.00 5.00
28 Jeff Green .30 .75
29 Russell Westbrook .75 2.00
30 James Harden 1.25 3.00
31 Jonny Flynn .30 .75
32 Anthony Tolliver .30 .75
33 Kevin Love .50 1.25
34 Caron Butler .40 1.00
35 Brendan Haywood .30 .75
36 Dirk Nowitzki 1.25 3.00
37 Jason Kidd .75 2.00
38 Aaron Brooks .30 .75
39 Kevin Martin .40 1.00
40 Yao Ming 1.00 2.50
41 DeJuan Blair .30 .75
42 Richard Jefferson .40 1.00
43 Tony Parker .75 2.00
44 Tim Duncan 1.25 3.00
45 Trevor Ariza .30 .75
46 Chris Paul 1.00 2.50
47 David West .40 1.00
48 Mike Conley Jr. .40 1.00
49 Marc Gasol .50 1.25
50 Zach Randolph .50 1.25
51 O.J. Mayo .40 1.00
52 Rajon Rondo .60 1.50
53 Shaquille O'Neal 2.00 5.00
54 Paul Pierce .75 2.00
55 Kevin Garnett 1.25 3.00
56 Brook Lopez .40 1.00
57 Terrence Williams .30 .75
58 Devin Harris .30 .75
59 Toney Douglas .30 .75
60 Amare Stoudemire .75 2.00
61 Danilo Gallinari .40 1.00
62 Jrue Holiday .60 1.50
63 Elton Brand .40 1.00
64 Andre Iguodala .50 1.25
65 DeMar DeRozan .75 2.00
66 Andrea Bargnani .30 .75
67 Leandro Barbosa .40 1.00
68 Joakim Noah .50 1.25
69 Derrick Rose 1.00 2.50
70 Carlos Boozer .40 1.00
71 Taj Gibson .30 .75
72 Tayshaun Prince .50 1.25
73 Ben Gordon .40 1.00
74 Tracy McGrady .75 2.00
75 Daniel Gibson .30 .75
76 Antawn Jamison .40 1.00
77 Ramon Sessions .30 .75
78 Darren Collison .30 .75
79 Tyler Hansbrough .30 .75
80 Danny Granger .30 .75
81 Andrew Bogut .40 1.00
82 Brandon Jennings .30 .75
83 John Salmons .30 .75
84 Jamal Crawford .50 1.25
85 Joe Johnson .50 1.25
86 Josh Smith .30 .75
87 Al Horford .50 1.25
88 Stephen Jackson .40 1.00
89 Gerald Henderson .30 .75
90 Gerald Wallace .40 1.00
91 Dwyane Wade 1.00 2.50
92 Chris Bosh .60 1.50
93 LeBron James 4.00 10.00
94 Mike Miller .40 1.00
95 Dwight Howard .60 1.50
96 Vince Carter 1.00 2.50
97 Jameer Nelson .30 .75
98 Al Thornton .30 .75
99 JaVale McGee .40 1.00
100 Andray Blatche .30 .75
101 John Wall AU RC 40.00 100.00
102 Evan Turner AU RC 3.00 8.00
103 Derrick Favors AU RC 4.00 10.00
104 Wesley Johnson AU RC 2.50 6.00
105 DeMarcus Cousins AU RC 12.00 30.00
106 Ekpe Udoh AU RC 2.50 6.00
107 Greg Monroe AU RC 3.00 8.00
108 Al-Farouq Aminu AU RC 3.00 8.00
109 Gordon Hayward AU RC 25.00 60.00
110 Paul George AU RC 125.00 300.00
111 Cole Aldrich AU RC 2.50 6.00
112 Xavier Henry AU RC 2.50 6.00
113 Ed Davis AU RC 3.00 8.00
114 Patrick Patterson AU RC 3.00 8.00
115 Larry Sanders AU RC 2.50 6.00
116 Luke Babbitt AU RC 2.50 6.00
117 Eric Bledsoe AU RC 6.00 15.00
118 Avery Bradley AU RC 4.00 10.00
119 James Anderson AU RC 2.50 6.00
120 Gary Neal AU RC 3.00 8.00
121 Elliot Williams AU RC 2.50 6.00
122 Trevor Booker AU RC 2.50 6.00
123 Damion James AU RC 2.50 6.00
124 Dominique Jones AU RC 2.50 6.00
125 Quincy Pondexter AU RC 2.50 6.00
126 Jordan Crawford AU RC 2.50 6.00
127 Greivis Vasquez AU RC 2.50 6.00
128 Daniel Orton AU RC 2.50 6.00
129 Lazar Hayward AU RC 2.50 6.00
130 Dexter Pittman AU RC 2.50 6.00
131 Hassan Whiteside AU RC 8.00 20.00
132 Lance Stephenson AU RC 4.00 10.00
133 Gary Forbes AU RC 2.50 6.00
134 Devin Ebanks AU RC 2.50 6.00
135 Gani Lawal AU RC 2.50 6.00
136 Luke Harangody AU RC 2.50 6.00
137 Willie Warren AU RC 2.50 6.00
138 Terrico White AU RC 2.50 6.00
139 Jeremy Evans AU RC 2.50 6.00
140 Timofey Mozgov AU RC 2.50 6.00
141 Jeremy Lin AU RC 100.00 250.00
142 Sherron Collins AU RC 2.50 6.00
143 Armon Johnson AU RC 2.50 6.00
144 Tiago Splitter AU RC 3.00 8.00
145 Landry Fields AU RC 2.50 6.00
146 Andy Rautins AU RC 2.50 6.00
147 Kevin Seraphin AU RC 2.50 6.00
148 Solomon Alabi AU RC 2.50 6.00
149 Derrick Caracter AU RC 2.50 6.00
150 Omer Asik AU RC 4.00 10.00
151 John Wall AU SP 40.00 100.00
152 Evan Turner AU SP 4.00 10.00
153 Derrick Favors AU SP 5.00 12.00
154 Wesley Johnson AU SP 3.00 8.00
155 DeMarcus Cousins AU SP 12.00 30.00
156 Ekpe Udoh AU SP 3.00 8.00
157 Greg Monroe AU SP 4.00 10.00
158 Al-Farouq Aminu AU SP 4.00 10.00
159 Gordon Hayward AU SP 12.00 30.00
160 Paul George AU SP 100.00 250.00
161 Cole Aldrich AU SP 3.00 8.00
162 Xavier Henry AU SP 3.00 8.00
163 Ed Davis AU SP 4.00 10.00
164 Patrick Patterson AU SP 4.00 10.00
165 Larry Sanders AU SP 3.00 8.00
166 Luke Babbitt AU SP 3.00 8.00
167 Eric Bledsoe AU SP 6.00 15.00
168 Avery Bradley AU SP 5.00 12.00
169 James Anderson AU SP 3.00 8.00
170 Gary Neal AU SP 4.00 10.00
171 Elliot Williams AU SP 3.00 8.00
172 Trevor Booker AU SP 3.00 8.00
173 Damion James AU SP 3.00 8.00
174 Dominique Jones AU SP 3.00 8.00
175 Quincy Pondexter AU SP 3.00 8.00
176 Jordan Crawford AU SP 3.00 8.00
177 Greivis Vasquez AU SP 3.00 8.00
178 Daniel Orton AU SP 3.00 8.00
179 Lazar Hayward AU SP 3.00 8.00
180 Dexter Pittman AU SP 3.00 8.00
181 Hassan Whiteside AU SP 10.00 25.00
182 Lance Stephenson AU SP 5.00 12.00
183 Gary Forbes AU SP 3.00 8.00
184 Devin Ebanks AU SP 3.00 8.00
185 Gani Lawal AU SP 3.00 8.00
186 Luke Harangody AU SP 3.00 8.00
187 Willie Warren AU SP 3.00 8.00
188 Terrico White AU SP 3.00 8.00
189 Jeremy Evans AU SP 3.00 8.00
190 Timofey Mozgov AU SP 4.00 10.00
191 Jeremy Lin AU SP 200.00 500.00
192 Sherron Collins AU SP 3.00 8.00
193 Armon Johnson AU SP 3.00 8.00
194 Tiago Splitter AU SP 4.00 10.00
195 Landry Fields AU SP 3.00 8.00
196 Andy Rautins AU SP 3.00 8.00
197 Kevin Seraphin AU SP 3.00 8.00
198 Solomon Alabi AU SP 3.00 8.00
199 Derrick Caracter AU SP 3.00 8.00
200 Omer Asik AU SP 5.00 12.00

2010-11 Playoff Contenders Patches Die Cuts Black

*DC BLACK: 2X TO 5X BASE HI
STATED PRINT RUN 49 SER.#'d SETS

2010-11 Playoff Contenders Patches Die Cuts Gold

*DC GOLD: 1.5X TO 4X BASE HI
STATED PRINT RUN 99 SER.#'d SETS
1 Kobe Bryant 25.00 60.00
8 Stephen Curry 25.00 60.00
93 LeBron James 25.00 60.00

2010-11 Playoff Contenders Patches Die Cuts Silver

*DC SILVER: 1X TO 2.5X BASE HI
STATED PRINT RUN 299 SER.#'d SETS
1 Kobe Bryant 15.00 40.00
8 Stephen Curry 15.00 40.00
93 LeBron James 15.00 40.00

2010-11 Playoff Contenders Patches One-Two Punch

COMPLETE SET (25) 20.00 40.00
*DC BLACK: 1.25X TO 3X BASE HI
DC BLACK PRINT RUN 49 SER.#'d SETS
*DC GOLD: 1X TO 2.5X BASE HI
DC GOLD PRINT RUN 99 SER.#'d SETS
*DC SILVER: .6X TO 1.5X BASE HI
DC SILVER PRINT RUN 299 SER.#'d SETS
1 R.Rondo/S.O'Neal 3.00 8.00
2 R.Allen/P.Pierce 1.25 3.00
3 R.Rondo/K.Garnett 2.00 5.00
4 D.Rose/J.Noah 1.50 4.00
5 B.Jennings/A.Bogut .60 1.50
6 S.Curry/M.Ellis 6.00 15.00
7 K.Durant/R.Westbrook 3.00 8.00
8 J.Kidd/D.Nowitzki 2.00 5.00
9 T.Douglas/A.Stoudemire .75 2.00
10 L.James/D.Wade 6.00 15.00
11 C.Bosh/L.James 6.00 15.00
12 B.Griffin/B.Davis .75 2.00
13 B.Gordon/B.Wallace 1.00 2.50
14 C.Anthony/Nene 1.25 3.00
15 D.Harris/B.Lopez .60 1.50
16 J.Johnson/A.Horford .75 2.00
17 J.Nelson/D.Howard 1.00 2.50
18 T.Evans/C.Landry .60 1.50
19 J.Flynn/M.Beasley .50 1.25
20 J.Holiday/E.Brand 1.00 2.50
21 C.Paul/E.Okafor 1.50 4.00
22 O.J. Mayo/M.Gasol .75 2.00
23 K.Bryant/P.Gasol 6.00 15.00
24 K.Bryant/D.Fisher 6.00 15.00
25 S.Nash/C.Frye 1.50 4.00

2010-11 Playoff Contenders Patches Place in History

COMPLETE SET (25) 12.50 30.00
*DC BLACK: 1.25X TO 3X BASE HI
DC BLACK PRINT RUN 49 SER.#'d SETS
*DC GOLD: 1X TO 2.5X BASE HI
DC GOLD PRINT RUN 99 SER.#'d SETS
*DC SILVER: .6X TO 1.5X BASE HI
DC SILVER PRINT RUN 299 SER.#'d SETS
1 James Harden 2.00 5.00
2 Brook Lopez .60 1.50
3 Joakim Noah .75 2.00
4 J.J. Redick .75 2.00
5 Andrew Bogut .60 1.50
6 Andre Iguodala .75 2.00
7 Carmelo Anthony 1.25 3.00
8 Amare Stoudemire .75 2.00
9 Pau Gasol 1.25 3.00
10 Hedo Turkoglu .60 1.50
11 Shawn Marion .75 2.00
12 Dirk Nowitzki 2.00 5.00
13 Chauncey Billups 1.00 2.50
14 Kobe Bryant 6.00 15.00
15 Kevin Garnett 2.00 5.00
16 Jason Kidd 1.25 3.00
17 Shawn Bradley .50 1.25
18 Shaquille O'Neal 3.00 8.00
19 Larry Johnson 1.00 2.50
20 Gary Payton 1.25 3.00
21 Sean Elliott .60 1.50
22 Hersey Hawkins .50 1.25
23 Scottie Pippen 2.00 5.00
24 Walter Berry .50 1.25
25 Chris Mullin 1.00 2.50

2010-11 Playoff Contenders Patches Place in History Autographs Gold

STATED PRINT RUN 10 TO 49 SER.#'d SETS
1 James Harden/49 40.00 100.00
2 Brook Lopez/49 6.00 15.00
3 Joakim Noah/49 8.00 20.00
4 J.J. Redick/49 6.00 15.00
5 Andrew Bogut/49 8.00 20.00
6 Andre Iguodala/49 6.00 15.00
8 Amare Stoudemire/49 10.00 25.00
9 Pau Gasol/49 20.00 50.00
12 Dirk Nowitzki/49 50.00 125.00
13 Chauncey Billups/49 8.00 20.00
14 Kobe Bryant/49 1,500.00 3,000.00
16 Jason Kidd/49 12.00 30.00
19 Larry Johnson/15 50.00 120.00
20 Gary Payton/49 10.00 25.00
21 Sean Elliott/15 12.00 30.00
22 Hersey Hawkins/49 6.00 15.00
23 Scottie Pippen/49 50.00 120.00
24 Walter Berry/49 6.00 15.00
25 Chris Mullin/49 12.50 30.00

2010-11 Playoff Contenders Patches Rookie of the Year Contenders

COMPLETE SET (15) 10.00 25.00
*DC BLACK: 1.25X TO 3X BASE HI
DC BLACK PRINT RUN 49 SER.#'d SETS
*DC GOLD: 1X TO 2.5X BASE HI
DC GOLD PRINT RUN 99 SER.#'d SETS
*DC SILVER: .6X TO 1.5X BASE HI
DC SILVER PRINT RUN 299 SER.#'d SETS
1 John Wall 2.50 6.00
2 Blake Griffin .75 2.00
3 Evan Turner .60 1.50
4 Wesley Johnson .50 1.25
5 Derrick Favors .75 2.00
6 DeMarcus Cousins 1.50 4.00
7 Gordon Hayward 2.00 5.00
8 Cole Aldrich .50 1.25
9 Ekpe Udoh .50 1.25
10 Ed Davis .60 1.50
11 Xavier Henry .50 1.25
12 Greg Monroe .60 1.50
13 James Anderson .50 1.25
14 Patrick Patterson .60 1.50
15 Al-Farouq Aminu .60 1.50

2010-11 Playoff Contenders Patches Rookie of the Year Contenders Autographs Gold

STATED PRINT RUN 49 SER.#'d SETS
1 John Wall 50.00 120.00
2 Blake Griffin 20.00 50.00
3 Evan Turner 6.00 15.00
4 Wesley Johnson 5.00 12.00
5 Derrick Favors 8.00 20.00
6 DeMarcus Cousins 15.00 40.00
7 Gordon Hayward 20.00 50.00
8 Cole Aldrich 5.00 12.00
9 Ekpe Udoh 5.00 12.00
10 Ed Davis 6.00 15.00
11 Xavier Henry 5.00 12.00
12 Greg Monroe 6.00 15.00
13 James Anderson 5.00 12.00
14 Patrick Patterson 6.00 15.00
15 Al-Farouq Aminu 6.00 15.00

2010-11 Playoff Contenders Patches Starting Blocks

COMPLETE SET (30) 20.00 40.00
*DC BLACK: 1.25X TO 3X BASE HI
DC BLACK PRINT RUN 49 SER.#'d SETS
*DC GOLD: 1X TO 2.5X BASE HI
DC GOLD PRINT RUN 99 SER.#'d SETS
*DC SILVER: .6X TO 1.5X BASE HI
DC SILVER PRINT RUN 299 SER.#'d SETS
1 T.Evans/D.Cousins 1.50 4.00
2 S.Curry/E.Udoh 6.00 15.00
3 M.Speights/E.Turner .60 1.50
4 B.Lopez/D.Favors .75 2.00
5 A.Daye/G.Monroe .60 1.50
6 B.Jennings/L.Sanders .50 1.25
7 D.Carroll/X.Henry .50 1.25
8 D.Rose/T.Gibson 1.50 4.00
9 J.McGee/J.Wall 2.50 6.00
10 J.Flynn/W.Johnson .50 1.25
11 D.DeRozan/E.Davis 1.25 3.00
12 D.Gallinari/T.Douglas .60 1.50
13 J.Evans/G.Hayward 2.00 5.00
14 B.Lopez/D.James .60 1.50
15 E.Gordon/B.Griffin .75 2.00
16 D.J. Augustin/G.Henderson .50 1.25
17 T.Young/J.Holiday 1.00 2.50
18 J.Noah/J.Johnson .75 2.00
19 T.Hansbrough/P.George 4.00 10.00
20 T.Evans/O.Casspi .60 1.50
21 T.Gibson/J.Johnson .50 1.25
22 B.Griffin/A.Aminu .75 2.00
23 A.Brooks/P.Patterson .60 1.50
24 R.Stuckey/G.Monroe .60 1.50
25 J.Noah/D.Rose 1.50 4.00
26 H.Whiteside/T.Evans 1.00 2.50
27 A.Horford/J.Crawford .75 2.00
28 A.Bargnani/D.DeRozan 1.25 3.00
29 R.Rondo/A.Bradley 1.00 2.50
30 R.Gay/G.Vasquez .75 2.00

2010-11 Playoff Contenders Patches Starting Blocks Autographs Gold

STATED PRINT RUN 25 TO 49 SER.#'d SETS
1 T.Evans/D.Cousins/49 10.00 25.00
2 S.Curry/E.Udoh/49 500.00 1,000.00
4 B.Lopez/D.Favors/49 6.00 15.00
5 A.Daye/G.Monroe/49 6.00 15.00
6 B.Jennings/L.Sanders/49 6.00 15.00
7 D.Carroll/X.Henry/49 6.00 15.00
8 D.Rose/T.Gibson/49 40.00 100.00
9 J.McGee/J.Wall/49 50.00 120.00
10 J.Flynn/W.Johnson/49 6.00 15.00
11 D.DeRozan/E.Davis/49 12.00 30.00
12 D.Gallinari/T.Douglas/25 6.00 15.00
13 J.Evans/G.Hayward/49 12.00 30.00
14 B.Lopez/D.James/49 6.00 15.00
15 E.Gordon/B.Griffin/49 10.00 25.00
16 D.J. Augustin/G.Henderson/49 6.00 15.00
18 J.Noah/J.Johnson/49 6.00 15.00
19 T.Hansbrough/P.George/49 60.00 150.00
20 T.Evans/O.Casspi/49 6.00 15.00
21 T.Gibson/J.Johnson/49 6.00 15.00
22 B.Griffin/A.Aminu/49 12.00 30.00
23 A.Brooks/P.Patterson/49 6.00 15.00
25 J.Noah/D.Rose/49 50.00 120.00
26 H.Whiteside/T.Evans/49 6.00 15.00
27 A.Horford/J.Crawford/49 6.00 15.00
28 A.Bargnani/D.DeRozan/49 12.00 30.00
29 R.Rondo/A.Bradley/49 12.00 30.00

2009-10 Playoff National Treasures

COMP.SET w/o RCs (185) 800.00 1,500.00
1-185 PRINT RUN 99 SER.#'d SETS
186-200 RC PRINT RUN 99 SER.#'d SETS
1 Kobe Bryant 400.00 800.00
2 LeBron James 600.00 1,200.00
3 Dwight Howard 4.00 10.00
4 Derrick Rose 5.00 12.00
5 Dwyane Wade 6.00 15.00
6 Kevin Garnett 8.00 20.00
7 Chris Paul 6.00 15.00
8 Paul Pierce 5.00 12.00

9 Shaquille O'Neal 10.00 25.00
10 Pau Gasol 5.00 12.00
11 Carmelo Anthony 5.00 12.00
12 Steve Nash 6.00 15.00
13 David Lee 2.00 5.00
14 Allen Iverson 6.00 15.00
15 Kevin Durant 12.00 30.00
16 Monta Ellis 2.50 6.00
17 Dirk Nowitzki 8.00 20.00
18 Chris Bosh 4.00 10.00
19 Brandon Roy 4.00 10.00
20 Amare Stoudemire 2.50 6.00
21 Joe Johnson 3.00 8.00
22 Zach Randolph 3.00 8.00
23 Carlos Boozer 2.50 6.00
24 Rudy Gay 3.00 8.00
25 Stephen Jackson 2.50 6.00
26 Corey Maggette 2.50 6.00
27 Brook Lopez 3.00 8.00
28 Aaron Brooks 2.00 5.00
29 Rodney Stuckey 2.00 5.00
30 Chris Kaman 2.50 6.00
31 O.J. Mayo 2.00 5.00
32 Tim Duncan 8.00 20.00
33 Al Jefferson 2.00 5.00
34 Andre Iguodala 3.00 8.00
35 Deron Williams 2.50 6.00
36 David West 2.50 6.00
37 Mo Williams 2.50 6.00
38 Gerald Wallace 2.50 6.00
39 Andrea Bargnani 2.00 5.00
40 Antawn Jamison 2.50 6.00
41 Luol Deng 2.50 6.00
42 Al Harrington 2.50 6.00
43 Jamal Crawford 3.00 8.00
44 Jason Terry 2.50 6.00
45 Baron Davis 2.50 6.00
46 Russell Westbrook 6.00 15.00
47 Michael Beasley 2.00 5.00
48 Caron Butler 2.50 6.00
49 Carl Landry 2.00 5.00
50 LaMarcus Aldridge 3.00 8.00
51 Ray Allen 5.00 12.00
52 Trevor Ariza 2.00 5.00
53 Tony Parker 5.00 12.00
54 Chauncey Billups 4.00 10.00
55 Luis Scola 2.50 6.00
56 Josh Smith 2.50 6.00
57 Andrew Bynum 2.00 5.00
58 Marc Gasol 3.00 8.00
59 Jason Richardson 3.00 8.00
60 Jeff Green 2.50 6.00
61 Danny Granger 2.00 5.00
62 Nene 2.50 6.00
63 Vince Carter 6.00 15.00
64 Charlie Villanueva 2.50 6.00
65 Rajon Rondo 4.00 10.00
66 Eric Gordon 2.50 6.00
67 Elton Brand 2.50 6.00
68 D.J. Augustin 2.00 5.00
69 Derek Fisher 3.00 8.00
70 Devin Harris 2.00 5.00
71 Emeka Okafor 2.00 5.00
72 Jason Kidd 5.00 12.00
73 Jermaine O'Neal 3.00 8.00
74 Josh Howard 2.50 6.00
75 Kevin Love 3.00 8.00
76 Lamar Odom 2.50 6.00
77 Mike Bibby 2.50 6.00
78 Randy Foye 2.00 5.00
79 Richard Hamilton 3.00 8.00
80 Ron Artest 3.00 8.00
81 Ronnie Brewer 2.00 5.00
82 Rudy Fernandez 2.00 5.00
83 Ryan Gomes 2.00 5.00
84 Shane Battier 3.00 8.00
85 T.J. Ford 2.00 5.00
86 Ben Gordon 2.50 6.00
87 Rashard Lewis 2.50 6.00
88 Shawn Marion 3.00 8.00
89 Troy Murphy 2.00 5.00
90 Chris Duhon 2.00 5.00
91 Raymond Felton 2.00 5.00
92 Andre Miller 3.00 8.00
93 Jarrett Jack 2.50 6.00
94 Mike Conley Jr. 2.50 6.00
95 Kendrick Perkins 2.00 5.00
96 Chris Andersen 3.00 8.00
97 Greg Oden 3.00 8.00
98 Danilo Gallinari 2.50 6.00
99 Yi Jianlian 4.00 10.00
100 Wilson Chandler 2.50 6.00
101 Ed Macauley LEG 3.00 8.00
102 Bob Cousy LEG 8.00 20.00
103 Bob Pettit LEG 4.00 10.00
104 Dolph Schayes LEG 3.00 8.00
105 Bill Russell LEG 10.00 25.00
106 Bill Sharman LEG 3.00 8.00
107 Elgin Baylor LEG 8.00 20.00
108 Cliff Hagan LEG 3.00 8.00
109 Jerry Lucas LEG 3.00 8.00
110 Oscar Robertson LEG 4.00 10.00
111 Jerry West LEG 5.00 12.00
112 Hal Greer LEG 4.00 10.00
113 Slater Martin LEG 3.00 8.00
114 Frank Ramsey LEG 3.00 8.00
115 Willis Reed LEG 5.00 12.00
116 Jack Twyman LEG 3.00 8.00
117 John Havlicek LEG 8.00 20.00
118 Sam Jones LEG 4.00 10.00
119 Nate Thurmond LEG 2.50 6.00
120 Billy Cunningham LEG 3.00 8.00
121 Tom Heinsohn LEG 3.00 8.00
122 Rick Barry LEG 2.50 6.00
123 Walt Frazier LEG 5.00 12.00
124 Bobby Wanzer LEG 2.00 5.00
125 Clyde Lovellette LEG 3.00 8.00
126 Wes Unseld LEG 3.00 8.00
127 K.C. Jones LEG 3.00 8.00
128 Lenny Wilkens LEG 3.00 8.00
129 Elvin Hayes LEG 5.00 12.00
130 Earl Monroe LEG 4.00 10.00
131 Nate Archibald LEG 4.00 10.00
132 Dave Cowens LEG 4.00 10.00
133 Harry Gallatin LEG 3.00 8.00
134 Connie Hawkins LEG 4.00 10.00
135 Bob Lanier LEG 4.00 10.00
136 Walt Bellamy LEG 2.50 6.00
137 Dan Issel LEG 2.50 6.00
138 Bill Walton LEG 5.00 12.00
139 Kareem Abdul-Jabbar LEG 10.00 25.00
140 Vern Mikkelsen LEG 3.00 8.00
141 George Gervin LEG 4.00 10.00
142 Gail Goodrich LEG 3.00 8.00
143 David Thompson LEG 2.50 6.00
144 Alex English LEG 4.00 10.00
145 Bailey Howell LEG 3.00 8.00
146 Larry Bird LEG 12.00 30.00
147 Marques Haynes LEG 3.00 8.00
148 Arnie Risen LEG 3.00 8.00
149 Kevin McHale LEG 5.00 12.00
150 Bob McAdoo LEG 4.00 10.00
151 Isiah Thomas LEG 3.00 8.00
152 Magic Johnson LEG 12.00 30.00
153 Robert Parish LEG 4.00 10.00
154 James Worthy LEG 4.00 10.00
155 Clyde Drexler LEG 5.00 12.00
156 Lynette Woodard LEG 3.00 8.00
157 Jalen Rose LEG 2.50 6.00
158 Joe Dumars LEG 4.00 10.00
159 Dominique Wilkins LEG 5.00 12.00
160 Adrian Dantley LEG 2.50 6.00
161 Patrick Ewing LEG 5.00 12.00
162 Hakeem Olajuwon LEG 4.00 10.00
163 David Robinson LEG 6.00 15.00
164 John Stockton LEG 5.00 12.00
165 John Kundla LEG 3.00 8.00
166 Earl Lloyd LEG 3.00 8.00
167 Alonzo Mourning LEG 5.00 12.00
168 Bernard King LEG 4.00 10.00
169 Bill Laimbeer LEG 3.00 8.00
170 Scottie Pippen LEG 8.00 20.00
171 Chris Mullin LEG 4.00 10.00
172 Danny Manning LEG 2.50 6.00
173 Dennis Rodman LEG 6.00 15.00
174 Detlef Schrempf LEG 3.00 8.00
175 Dikembe Mutombo LEG 5.00 12.00
176 George McGinnis LEG 3.00 8.00
177 Jeff Hornacek LEG 2.50 6.00
178 Sidney Moncrief LEG 2.50 6.00
179 Pat Riley LEG 3.00 8.00
180 Tom Gola LEG 3.00 8.00
181 Calvin Murphy LEG 2.50 6.00
182 Nancy Lieberman LEG 4.00 10.00
183 Meadowlark Lemon LEG 3.00 8.00
184 Geese Ausbie LEG 3.00 8.00
185 Curly Neal LEG 3.00 8.00
186 Jonas Jerebko RC 6.00 15.00
187 Marcus Thornton RC 6.00 15.00
188 Wesley Matthews RC 8.00 20.00
189 Serge Ibaka RC 8.00 20.00
190 A.J. Price RC 5.00 12.00
191 Jon Brockman RC 5.00 12.00
192 Dante Cunningham RC 5.00 12.00
193 Derrick Brown RC 5.00 12.00
194 Sundiata Gaines RC 5.00 12.00
195 Marcus Landry RC 5.00 12.00
196 Lester Hudson RC 5.00 12.00
197 Danny Green RC 15.00 40.00
198 David Andersen RC 5.00 12.00
199 DeMar DeRozan 60.00 150.00
200 Ricky Rubio RC 15.00 40.00
201 Blake Griffin JSY AU RC 400.00 800.00
202 Hasheem Thabeet JSY AU RC 12.00 30.00
203 Jms Harden JSY AU RC 10,000.00 20,000.00
204 Tyreke Evans JSY AU RC 60.00 150.00
205 Jonny Flynn JSY AU RC 12.00 30.00
206 Stph Curry JSY AU RC 60,000.00 100,000.00
207 Jordan Hill JSY AU RC 12.00 30.00
208 D. DeRozan JSY AU RC 1,000.00 2,000.00
209 B.Jennings JSY AU RC 20.00 50.00
210 T.Williams JSY AU RC 12.00 30.00
211 G.Henderson JSY AU RC 12.00 30.00
212 T.Hansbrough JSY AU RC 15.00 40.00
213 Earl Clark JSY AU RC 12.00 30.00
214 Austin Daye JSY AU RC 12.00 30.00
215 James Johnson JSY AU RC 15.00 40.00
216 Jrue Holiday JSY AU RC 200.00 500.00
217 Ty Lawson JSY AU RC 15.00 40.00
218 Jeff Teague JSY AU RC 15.00 40.00
219 Eric Maynor JSY AU RC 12.00 30.00
220 D.Collison JSY AU RC 15.00 40.00
221 Omri Casspi JSY AU RC 12.00 30.00
222 B.J. Mullens JSY AU RC 12.00 30.00
223 R.Beaubois JSY AU RC 12.00 30.00
224 Taj Gibson JSY AU RC 12.00 30.00
225 DeMarre Carroll JSY AU RC 15.00 40.00
226 Wayne Ellington JSY AU RC 12.00 30.00
227 Toney Douglas JSY AU RC 12.00 30.00
228 Jeff Pendergraph JSY AU RC 12.00 30.00
229 Jermaine Taylor JSY AU RC 12.00 30.00
230 DaJuan Summers JSY AU RC 12.00 30.00
231 Sam Young JSY AU RC 12.00 30.00
232 DeJuan Blair JSY AU RC 12.00 30.00
233 Jodie Meeks JSY AU RC 12.00 30.00
234 Chase Budinger JSY AU RC 12.00 30.00
235 Taylor Griffin JSY AU RC 12.00 30.00
236 Tyreke Evans JSY AU/97 15.00 40.00
237 Darren Collison JSY AU 20.00 50.00
238 Hasheem Thabeet JSY AU 12.00 30.00

2009-10 Playoff National Treasures Century Gold

201-238 PRINT RUN 25 SER.#'d SETS
201 Blake Griffin JSY AU 600.00 1,200.00
202 Hasheem Thabeet JSY AU 15.00 40.00
203 James Harden JSY AU 4,000.00 6,000.00
204 Tyreke Evans JSY AU 75.00 200.00
205 Jonny Flynn JSY AU 15.00 40.00
206 S.Curry JSY AU 40,000.00 80,000.00
207 Jordan Hill JSY AU 15.00 40.00
208 DeMar DeRozan JSY AU 1,500.00 3,000.00
209 Brandon Jennings JSY AU 25.00 60.00
210 Terrence Williams JSY AU 15.00 40.00
211 Gerald Henderson JSY AU 15.00 40.00
212 Tyler Hansbrough JSY AU 20.00 50.00
213 Earl Clark JSY AU 15.00 40.00
214 Austin Daye JSY AU 15.00 40.00
215 James Johnson JSY AU 20.00 50.00
216 Jrue Holiday JSY AU 100.00 250.00
217 Ty Lawson JSY AU 20.00 50.00
218 Jeff Teague JSY AU 20.00 50.00
219 Eric Maynor JSY AU 15.00 40.00
220 Darren Collison JSY AU 25.00 60.00
221 Omri Casspi JSY AU 15.00 40.00
222 B.J. Mullens JSY AU 15.00 40.00
223 Rodrigue Beaubois JSY AU 15.00 40.00
224 Taj Gibson JSY AU 20.00 50.00
225 DeMarre Carroll JSY AU 20.00 50.00
226 Wayne Ellington JSY AU 15.00 40.00
227 Toney Douglas JSY AU 15.00 40.00
228 Jeff Pendergraph JSY AU 15.00 40.00
229 Jermaine Taylor JSY AU 15.00 40.00
230 DaJuan Summers JSY AU 15.00 40.00
231 Sam Young JSY AU 15.00 40.00
232 DeJuan Blair JSY AU 15.00 40.00
233 Jodie Meeks JSY AU 15.00 40.00
234 Chase Budinger JSY AU 15.00 40.00
235 Taylor Griffin JSY AU 15.00 40.00
236 Tyreke Evans JSY AU 20.00 50.00
237 Darren Collison JSY AU 25.00 60.00
238 Hasheem Thabeet JSY AU 15.00 40.00

2009-10 Playoff National Treasures 25th Anniversary Team

COMPLETE SET (10) 25.00 50.00
STATED PRINT RUN 25 SER.#'d SETS
1 Dolph Schayes 3.00 8.00
2 Bob Pettit 4.00 10.00
3 Bill Russell 10.00 25.00
4 George Mikan 10.00 25.00
5 Bob Cousy 8.00 20.00
6 Bill Sharman 4.00 10.00
7 Sam Jones 4.00 10.00
8 Paul Arizin 3.00 8.00
9 Bob Davies 3.00 8.00
10 Red Auerbach 4.00 10.00

2009-10 Playoff National Treasures 25th Anniversary Team Signatures

STATED PRINT RUN 5 TO 25 SER.#'d SETS
1 Dolph Schayes/25 15.00 40.00
2 Bob Pettit/25 40.00 100.00
6 Bill Sharman/25 40.00 100.00

2009-10 Playoff National Treasures 35th Anniversary Team

COMPLETE SET (10) 30.00 80.00
STATED PRINT RUN 35 SER.#'d SETS
1 Kareem Abdul-Jabbar 12.00 30.00
2 Elgin Baylor 10.00 25.00
3 Bob Cousy 10.00 25.00
4 John Havlicek 10.00 25.00
5 George Mikan 12.00 30.00
6 Bob Pettit 5.00 12.00
7 Oscar Robertson 5.00 12.00
8 Bill Russell 12.00 30.00
9 Jerry West 6.00 15.00
10 Wilt Chamberlain 15.00 40.00

2009-10 Playoff National Treasures 35th Anniversary Team Signatures

STATED PRINT RUN 5 TO 25 SER.#'d SETS
1 Kareem Abdul-Jabbar/25 150.00 400.00
4 John Havlicek/25 100.00 250.00
6 Bob Pettit/25 40.00 100.00
9 Jerry West/25 125.00 300.00

2009-10 Playoff National Treasures All Decade

STATED PRINT RUN 25 SER.#'d SETS
1 George Mikan 12.00 30.00
2 Bob Cousy 10.00 25.00
3 Bill Russell 12.00 30.00
4 Oscar Robertson 5.00 12.00
5 Dolph Schayes 4.00 10.00
6 John Havlicek 10.00 25.00
7 Jerry West 6.00 15.00
8 Kareem Abdul-Jabbar 12.00 30.00
9 Larry Bird 15.00 40.00
10 Magic Johnson 15.00 40.00
11 Dominique Wilkins 6.00 15.00
12 Scottie Pippen 10.00 25.00
13 Shaquille O'Neal 10.00 25.00
14 Kobe Bryant 30.00 80.00
15 Jason Kidd 6.00 15.00
16 Dirk Nowitzki 10.00 25.00
17 Tim Duncan 10.00 25.00
18 Kevin Garnett 10.00 25.00
19 Tracy McGrady 8.00 20.00
20 Steve Nash 8.00 20.00

2009-10 Playoff National Treasures All Decade Materials

STATED PRINT RUN 10 TO 99 SER.#'d SETS
1 George Mikan/99 15.00 40.00
8 Kareem Abdul-Jabbar/25 15.00 40.00
12 Scottie Pippen/49 12.00 30.00
13 Shaquille O'Neal/49 15.00 40.00
14 Kobe Bryant/99 100.00 250.00
16 Dirk Nowitzki/99 12.00 30.00
17 Tim Duncan/99 12.00 30.00
18 Kevin Garnett/99 10.00 25.00
19 Tracy McGrady/99 10.00 25.00
20 Steve Nash/49 10.00 25.00

2009-10 Playoff National Treasures All Decade Materials Prime

*PRIME: .6X TO 1.5X HI COLUMN
STATED PRINT RUN 5 TO 25 SER.#'d SETS
10 Magic Johnson/25 30.00 80.00
11 Dominique Wilkins/25 12.00 30.00
14 Kobe Bryant/25 150.00 400.00

2009-10 Playoff National Treasures All Decade Materials Signatures

STATED PRINT RUN ONE TO 25 SER.#'d SETS
14 Kobe Bryant/25 2,000.00 4,000.00

2009-10 Playoff National Treasures All Decade Signatures

STATED PRINT RUN 3 TO 25 SER.#'d SETS
14 Kobe Bryant/25 2,000.00 4,000.00

2009-10 Playoff National Treasures All NBA

STATED PRINT RUN 25 SER.#'d SETS
1 Karl Malone 6.00 15.00
2 Elgin Baylor 12.00 30.00
3 Jerry West 8.00 20.00
4 Kareem Abdul-Jabbar 15.00 40.00
5 Bob Cousy 12.00 30.00
6 Bob Pettit 6.00 15.00
7 Magic Johnson 20.00 50.00
8 Larry Bird 20.00 50.00
9 Oscar Robertson 6.00 15.00
10 Dolph Schayes 5.00 12.00
11 Hakeem Olajuwon 6.00 15.00
12 Kobe Bryant 40.00 100.00
13 George Gervin 6.00 15.00
14 Rick Barry 4.00 10.00
15 Bill Sharman 6.00 15.00
16 David Robinson 10.00 25.00
17 John Havlicek 12.00 30.00
18 Walt Frazier 8.00 20.00
19 Ed Macauley 6.00 15.00
20 Elvin Hayes 8.00 20.00
21 Isiah Thomas 5.00 12.00
22 Jerry Lucas 5.00 12.00
23 Nate Archibald 6.00 15.00
24 Scottie Pippen 12.00 30.00
25 Bill Russell 15.00 40.00

2009-10 Playoff National Treasures All NBA Materials

STATED PRINT RUN 10 TO 99 SER.#'d SETS
1 Karl Malone/99 10.00 25.00
4 Kareem Abdul-Jabbar/25 20.00 50.00
11 Hakeem Olajuwon/99 15.00 40.00
12 Kobe Bryant/99 100.00 250.00
24 Scottie Pippen/49 15.00 40.00

2009-10 Playoff National Treasures All NBA Materials Prime

STATED PRINT RUN 5 TO 25 SER.#'d SETS
1 Karl Malone/25 20.00 50.00
7 Magic Johnson/25 40.00 100.00
11 Hakeem Olajuwon/25 30.00 80.00
12 Kobe Bryant/25 200.00 500.00

2009-10 Playoff National Treasures All NBA Materials Signatures

STATED PRINT RUN ONE TO 25 SER.#'d SETS
12 Kobe Bryant/25 2,500.00 5,000.00

2009-10 Playoff National Treasures All NBA Signatures

STATED PRINT RUN 4 TO 49 SER.#'d SETS
10 Dolph Schayes/25 20.00 50.00
11 Hakeem Olajuwon/25 75.00 200.00
12 Kobe Bryant/25 1,500.00 3,000.00
15 Bill Sharman/25 60.00 150.00
18 Walt Frazier/25 40.00 100.00
23 Nate Archibald/49 12.00 30.00

2009-10 Playoff National Treasures Biography Materials

STATED PRINT RUN 49 TO 99 SER.#'d SETS
1 Kobe Bryant/99 100.00 250.00
2 LeBron James/49 100.00 250.00
3 Kevin Durant/49 20.00 50.00
4 Dirk Nowitzki/99 12.00 30.00
5 Dwyane Wade/99 10.00 25.00
6 Carmelo Anthony/99 8.00 20.00
7 Chris Bosh/49 6.00 15.00
8 Dwight Howard/99 6.00 15.00
9 Tim Duncan/99 12.00 30.00
10 Shaquille O'Neal/49 15.00 40.00

2009-10 Playoff National Treasures Biography Materials Prime

*PRIME: .6X TO 1.5X HI COLUMN
STATED PRINT RUN ONE TO 25 SER.#'d SETS
1 Kobe Bryant/25 150.00 400.00

2009-10 Playoff National Treasures Biography Materials Autographs

STATED PRINT RUN 3 TO 25 SER.#'d SETS
1 Kobe Bryant/25 2,000.00 4,000.00

2009-10 Playoff National Treasures Century Materials

STATED PRINT RUN ONE TO 99 SER.#'d SETS
1 Kobe Bryant/99 100.00 250.00
2 LeBron James/49 100.00 250.00
3 Dwight Howard/99 6.00 15.00
4 Derrick Rose/99 8.00 20.00
5 Dwyane Wade/99 10.00 25.00
6 Kevin Garnett/99 12.00 30.00
7 Chris Paul/99 10.00 25.00
8 Paul Pierce/99 8.00 20.00
9 Shaquille O'Neal/49 15.00 40.00
10 Pau Gasol/99 8.00 20.00
11 Carmelo Anthony/99 8.00 20.00
12 Steve Nash/49 10.00 25.00
13 David Lee/49 3.00 8.00
14 Allen Iverson/99 10.00 25.00
15 Kevin Durant/49 10.00 25.00
16 Monta Ellis/49 4.00 10.00
17 Dirk Nowitzki/99 12.00 30.00
18 Chris Bosh/49 6.00 15.00
19 Brandon Roy/49 6.00 15.00
20 Amare Stoudemire/99 4.00 10.00
21 Joe Johnson/99 5.00 12.00
23 Carlos Boozer/99 4.00 10.00
24 Rudy Gay/99 5.00 12.00
26 Corey Maggette/99 4.00 10.00
27 Brook Lopez/99 5.00 12.00
29 Rodney Stuckey/99 3.00 8.00
30 Chris Kaman/49 4.00 10.00
31 O.J. Mayo/99 3.00 8.00
32 Tim Duncan/99 12.00 30.00
33 Al Jefferson/99 3.00 8.00
34 Andre Iguodala/99 5.00 12.00
35 Deron Williams/25 8.00 20.00
36 David West/99 4.00 10.00
38 Gerald Wallace/99 4.00 10.00
39 Andrea Bargnani/99 3.00 8.00
40 Antawn Jamison/49 4.00 10.00
41 Luol Deng/99 4.00 10.00
44 Jason Terry/99 4.00 10.00
45 Baron Davis/99 4.00 10.00
46 Russell Westbrook/99 10.00 25.00
47 Michael Beasley/99 3.00 8.00
48 Caron Butler/49 4.00 10.00
49 Carl Landry/99 3.00 8.00
50 LaMarcus Aldridge/99 5.00 12.00
51 Ray Allen/99 8.00 20.00
52 Trevor Ariza/99 3.00 8.00
53 Tony Parker/99 8.00 20.00
54 Chauncey Billups/25 6.00 15.00
55 Luis Scola/99 4.00 10.00
56 Josh Smith/99 3.00 8.00
58 Marc Gasol/99 5.00 12.00
59 Jason Richardson/99 5.00 12.00
60 Jeff Green/99 4.00 10.00
61 Danny Granger/99 3.00 8.00
62 Nene/99 4.00 10.00
63 Vince Carter/99 10.00 25.00
65 Rajon Rondo/99 6.00 15.00
66 Eric Gordon/99 4.00 10.00
67 Elton Brand/99 4.00 10.00
68 D.J. Augustin/99 3.00 8.00
69 Derek Fisher/49 5.00 12.00
70 Devin Harris/99 3.00 8.00
71 Emeka Okafor/49 4.00 10.00
73 Jermaine O'Neal/99 5.00 12.00
75 Kevin Love/99 5.00 12.00
76 Lamar Odom/99 4.00 10.00
77 Mike Bibby/99 5.00 12.00
78 Randy Foye/99 3.00 8.00
79 Richard Hamilton/99 5.00 12.00
80 Ron Artest/99 5.00 12.00
82 Rudy Fernandez/99 3.00 8.00
84 Shane Battier/99 5.00 12.00
85 T.J. Ford/99 3.00 8.00
86 Ben Gordon/99 4.00 10.00
87 Rashard Lewis/99 4.00 10.00
88 Shawn Marion/99 5.00 12.00
89 Troy Murphy/99 3.00 8.00
90 Chris Duhon/99 3.00 8.00
91 Raymond Felton/99 3.00 8.00
92 Andre Miller/99 5.00 12.00
94 Mike Conley Jr./99 4.00 10.00
96 Chris Andersen/99 5.00 12.00
97 Greg Oden/99 5.00 12.00
99 Yi Jianlian/99 6.00 15.00
100 Wilson Chandler/99 4.00 10.00
121 Tom Heinsohn/25 5.00 12.00
130 Earl Monroe/25 6.00 15.00
132 Dave Cowens/49 6.00 15.00
135 Bob Lanier/99 6.00 15.00
139 Kareem Abdul-Jabbar/25 15.00 40.00
144 Alex English/25 6.00 15.00
149 Kevin McHale/99 8.00 20.00
153 Robert Parish/49 6.00 15.00
155 Clyde Drexler/25 8.00 20.00
158 Joe Dumars/25 6.00 15.00
161 Patrick Ewing/99 8.00 20.00
162 Hakeem Olajuwon/99 6.00 15.00
167 Alonzo Mourning/99 8.00 20.00
168 Bernard King/99 6.00 15.00
170 Scottie Pippen/49 12.00 30.00
171 Chris Mullin/99 6.00 15.00
172 Danny Manning/99 4.00 10.00
174 Detlef Schrempf/99 5.00 12.00
175 Dikembe Mutombo/99 8.00 20.00
177 Jeff Hornacek/99 4.00 10.00
193 Derrick Brown/25 3.00 8.00

2009-10 Playoff National Treasures Century Materials Prime

*PRIME: .75X TO 2X BASE HI
STATED PRINT RUN ONE TO 25 SER.#'d SETS
14 Allen Iverson/25 20.00 50.00
121 Tom Heinsohn/15 10.00 25.00
137 Dan Issel/25 6.00 15.00
144 Alex English/25 8.00 20.00
152 Magic Johnson/25 25.00 60.00
158 Joe Dumars/25 8.00 20.00
159 Dominique Wilkins/25 12.00 30.00
160 Adrian Dantley/25 6.00 15.00
161 Patrick Ewing/25 15.00 40.00
164 John Stockton/25 10.00 25.00
168 Bernard King/25 8.00 20.00
171 Chris Mullin/25 12.50 30.00

2009-10 Playoff National Treasures Century Materials Signatures

STATED PRINT RUN ONE TO 99 SER.#'d SETS
1 Kobe Bryant/25 800.00 1,500.00
14 Allen Iverson/25 100.00 250.00
19 Brandon Roy/25 12.00 30.00
20 Amare Stoudemire/25 8.00 20.00
30 Chris Kaman/49 8.00 20.00
34 Andre Iguodala/49 8.00 20.00
35 Deron Williams/25 8.00 20.00
39 Andrea Bargnani/49 8.00 20.00
45 Baron Davis/99 8.00 20.00
49 Carl Landry/99 8.00 20.00
53 Tony Parker/25 15.00 40.00
54 Chauncey Billups/25 8.00 20.00
57 Andrew Bynum/25 8.00 20.00
68 D.J. Augustin/99 8.00 20.00
71 Emeka Okafor/49 8.00 20.00
85 T.J. Ford/25 8.00 20.00
96 Chris Andersen/99 12.00 30.00
132 Dave Cowens/99 10.00 25.00
144 Alex English/28 8.00 20.00
168 Bernard King/99 8.00 20.00
171 Chris Mullin/49 20.00 40.00
172 Danny Manning/49 12.50 30.00
174 Detlef Schrempf/99 8.00 20.00

2009-10 Playoff National Treasures Century Materials Prime Signatures

STATED PRINT RUN ONE TO 25 SER.#'d SETS
30 Chris Kaman/25 10.00 25.00
34 Andre Iguodala/25 10.00 25.00
49 Carl Landry/25 10.00 25.00
96 Chris Andersen/25 30.00 60.00
132 Dave Cowens/25 15.00 30.00
168 Bernard King/25 10.00 25.00
171 Chris Mullin/25 30.00 80.00
172 Danny Manning/25 15.00 40.00
193 Derrick Brown/25 10.00 25.00

2009-10 Playoff National Treasures Century Signatures

STATED PRINT RUN 5 TO 99 SER.#'d SETS
ASTERISK CARDS FROM PANINI UPDATE
1 Kobe Bryant/25* 800.00 1,500.00
28 Aaron Brooks/25 6.00 15.00
30 Chris Kaman/25 6.00 15.00
34 Andre Iguodala/25 6.00 15.00
39 Andrea Bargnani/25 6.00 15.00
45 Baron Davis/25 6.00 15.00
46 Russell Westbrook/25 75.00 200.00
47 Michael Beasley/25 6.00 15.00
52 Trevor Ariza/25 6.00 15.00
54 Chauncey Billups/25 8.00 20.00
64 Charlie Villanueva/25 6.00 15.00
68 D.J. Augustin/25 6.00 15.00
70 Devin Harris/25 6.00 15.00
71 Emeka Okafor/25 6.00 15.00
73 Jermaine O'Neal/25 6.00 15.00
74 Josh Howard/25 6.00 15.00
75 Kevin Love/25 20.00 50.00
77 Mike Bibby/25 6.00 15.00
78 Randy Foye/25 5.00 12.00
79 Richard Hamilton/25 6.00 15.00
80 Ron Artest/25 12.00 30.00
81 Ronnie Brewer/25 6.00 15.00
84 Shane Battier/25 8.00 20.00
85 T.J. Ford/25 6.00 15.00
96 Chris Andersen/25 6.00 15.00
104 Dolph Schayes/25 12.00 30.00
108 Cliff Hagan/25 6.00 15.00
112 Hal Greer/25 6.00 15.00
114 Frank Ramsey/25 12.00 30.00
115 Willis Reed/25 60.00 150.00
119 Nate Thurmond/25 10.00 25.00
123 Walt Frazier/25 12.00 30.00
124 Bobby Wanzer/25 10.00 25.00
126 Wes Unseld/25 15.00 40.00
128 Lenny Wilkens/25 10.00 25.00
129 Elvin Hayes/25 15.00 30.00
131 Nate Archibald/25 10.00 25.00
132 Dave Cowens/25 10.00 25.00
133 Harry Gallatin/25 10.00 25.00
137 Dan Issel/17 8.00 20.00
141 George Gervin/25 10.00 25.00
142 Gail Goodrich/25 10.00 25.00
143 David Thompson/25 10.00 25.00
145 Bailey Howell/25 10.00 25.00
147 Marques Haynes/25 12.00 30.00
148 Arnie Risen/25 10.00 25.00
150 Bob McAdoo/25 12.00 30.00
153 Robert Parish/25 15.00 40.00
154 James Worthy/25 30.00 80.00
155 Clyde Drexler/25 20.00 50.00
162 Hakeem Olajuwon/25 25.00 60.00
168 Bernard King/25 10.00 25.00
169 Bill Laimbeer/15 12.00 30.00
171 Chris Mullin/25 15.00 40.00
172 Danny Manning/25 10.00 25.00
174 Detlef Schrempf/25 20.00 50.00
175 Dikembe Mutombo/25 12.00 30.00
176 George McGinnis/25 10.00 25.00
177 Jeff Hornacek/25 10.00 25.00
178 Sidney Moncrief/25 8.00 20.00
179 Pat Riley/25 15.00 40.00
181 Calvin Murphy/25 8.00 20.00
182 Nancy Lieberman/25 8.00 20.00
183 Meadowlark Lemon/25 15.00 40.00
186 Jonas Jerebko/99 5.00 12.00
187 Marcus Thornton/99 5.00 12.00
188 Wesley Matthews/99 6.00 15.00
189 Serge Ibaka/99 6.00 15.00
190 A.J. Price/99 4.00 10.00
191 Jon Brockman/99 4.00 10.00
192 Dante Cunningham/99 4.00 10.00
193 Derrick Brown/99 4.00 10.00
194 Sundiata Gaines/99 4.00 10.00
195 Marcus Landry/99 4.00 10.00
196 Lester Hudson/99 4.00 10.00
197 Danny Green/99 6.00 15.00
198 David Andersen/99 4.00 10.00
199 DeMar DeRozan/99 125.00 300.00
200 Ricky Rubio/99 60.00 150.00

2009-10 Playoff National Treasures Champions

COMPLETE SET (10) 40.00 80.00
STATED PRINT RUN 25 SER.#'d SETS
1 John Kundla 5.00 12.00
2 Vern Mikkelsen 5.00 12.00
3 Earl Lloyd 5.00 12.00
4 Dolph Schayes 5.00 12.00
5 Arnie Risen 5.00 12.00
6 Bobby Wanzer 3.00 8.00
7 Clyde Drexler 8.00 20.00
8 Chauncey Billups 6.00 15.00
9 Shaquille O'Neal 15.00 40.00
10 Tony Parker 8.00 20.00

2009-10 Playoff National Treasures Champions Signature Combos

STATED PRINT RUN 5 TO 25 SER.#'d SETS
3 D.Cowens/J.Havlicek/25 30.00 80.00
4 E.Hayes/W.Unseld/25 25.00 50.00

2009-10 Playoff National Treasures Champions Signatures

STATED PRINT RUN 5 TO 99 SER.#'d SETS
4 Dolph Schayes/25 10.00 25.00
6 Bobby Wanzer/99 6.00 15.00
7 Clyde Drexler/25 20.00 50.00
10 Tony Parker/15 12.00 30.00

2009-10 Playoff National Treasures Colossal Materials

STATED PRINT RUN 5 TO 99 SER.#'d SETS
1 Kobe Bryant/99 60.00 150.00
2 Blake Griffin/25 12.00 30.00
3 Kevin Durant/49 15.00 40.00
4 James Harden/25 100.00 250.00
5 Dirk Nowitzki/99 10.00 25.00
6 Tyreke Evans/25 2.50 6.00
7 Carmelo Anthony/49 6.00 15.00
8 Jonny Flynn/25 2.00 5.00
9 Chris Bosh/25 5.00 12.00
10 Stephen Curry/25 1,000.00 2,000.00
11 David Lee/25 2.50 6.00
12 DeMar DeRozan/25 40.00 100.00
14 Brandon Jennings/25 3.00 8.00
15 Steve Nash/49 12.00 30.00
16 Terrence Williams/25 2.00 5.00
18 Omri Casspi/25 2.00 5.00
19 Andre Iguodala/99 4.00 10.00
20 Darren Collison/25 3.00 8.00
22 Taj Gibson/25 2.50 6.00
23 Russell Westbrook/99 8.00 20.00
24 Ty Lawson/25 2.50 6.00
25 Danny Granger/99 2.50 6.00
26 DeJuan Blair/25 2.50 6.00
27 Ray Allen/99 6.00 15.00
28 Chase Budinger/25 2.00 5.00
29 Rajon Rondo/99 5.00 12.00
30 Sam Young/25 2.00 5.00
32 Jrue Holiday/25 10.00 25.00
33 LeBron James/49 75.00 200.00
34 Tyler Hansbrough/25 2.50 6.00
35 Dwyane Wade/99 8.00 20.00
36 Amare Stoudemire/99 3.00 8.00
37 Derrick Rose/99 6.00 15.00
38 Dwight Howard/99 5.00 12.00
40 Tim Duncan/99 10.00 25.00
41 Brandon Roy/49 5.00 12.00
42 Chris Paul/49 8.00 20.00
43 Pau Gasol/99 6.00 15.00
44 Shaquille O'Neal/49 12.00 30.00
45 Josh Smith/99 2.50 6.00
47 Paul Pierce/99 6.00 15.00
48 Eric Gordon/99 3.00 8.00
49 Tony Parker/99 6.00 15.00
50 Kevin Garnett/25 10.00 25.00

2009-10 Playoff National Treasures Colossal Materials Prime

STATED PRINT RUN ONE TO 25 SER.#'d SETS
1 Kobe Bryant/25 150.00 400.00

2009-10 Playoff National Treasures Colossal Materials Jersey Numbers

*JSY NUMB: SAME VALUE AS BASE
STATED PRINT RUN 10 TO 99 SER.#'d SETS
23 Russell Westbrook/25 8.00 20.00
27 Ray Allen/25 8.00 20.00
43 Pau Gasol/25 10.00 25.00
47 Paul Pierce/99 6.00 15.00

2009-10 Playoff National Treasures Colossal Materials Signatures

STATED PRINT RUN 3 TO 49 SER.#'d SETS
*JSY NUMBER: .4X TO 1X HI COLUMN
JSY NUMBER PRINT RUN 4 TO 49 SETS
1 Kobe Bryant/25 1,000.00 2,000.00
4 James Harden/49 200.00 500.00
6 Tyreke Evans/49 20.00 50.00
8 Jonny Flynn/49 4.00 10.00
9 Chris Bosh/25 15.00 40.00
10 Stephen Curry/49 2,000.00 4,000.00
12 DeMar DeRozan/49 75.00 200.00
14 Brandon Jennings/49 6.00 15.00
16 Terrence Williams/49 4.00 10.00
18 Omri Casspi/49 4.00 10.00
19 Andre Iguodala/49 6.00 15.00
20 Darren Collison/49 6.00 15.00
24 Ty Lawson/49 12.00 30.00
26 DeJuan Blair/49 5.00 12.00
28 Chase Budinger/49 4.00 10.00
30 Sam Young/49 4.00 10.00
32 Jrue Holiday/49 15.00 40.00
34 Tyler Hansbrough/49 5.00 12.00
41 Brandon Roy/25 12.00 30.00
49 Tony Parker/15 15.00 40.00

2009-10 Playoff National Treasures Colossal Materials Prime Signatures

STATED PRINT RUN ONE TO 25 SER.#'d SETS
*JSY NUMBER: .4X TO 1X HI COLUMN
JSY NUMBER PRINT RUN ONE TO 25 SETS
12 DeMar DeRozan/25 200.00 500.00
14 Brandon Jennings/25 15.00 40.00
26 DeJuan Blair/25 12.00 30.00
32 Jrue Holiday/25 50.00 120.00

2009-10 Playoff National Treasures NBA Gear Dual

STATED PRINT RUN 10 TO 49 SER.#'d SETS
1 Kobe Bryant/49 60.00 150.00
2 LeBron James/49 75.00 200.00
3 Blake Griffin/25 12.00 30.00
5 James Harden/25 100.00 250.00
6 Dwyane Wade/99 6.00 15.00
7 Tyreke Evans/25 2.50 6.00
8 Carmelo Anthony/49 5.00 12.00
9 Jonny Flynn/25 2.00 5.00
10 Chris Paul/99 6.00 15.00
11 Stephen Curry/25 1,000.00 2,000.00
12 Dwight Howard/99 4.00 10.00
13 DeMar DeRozan/25 40.00 100.00
14 Earl Clark/25 2.00 5.00
15 Brandon Jennings/25 3.00 8.00
16 Gerald Henderson/25 2.00 5.00
17 Terrence Williams/25 2.00 5.00
18 Toney Douglas/25 2.00 5.00
19 Omri Casspi/25 2.00 5.00
20 Wayne Ellington/25 2.50 6.00
21 Darren Collison/25 3.00 8.00
22 Austin Daye/25 2.00 5.00
23 Taj Gibson/25 2.50 6.00
24 Jeff Teague/25 2.50 6.00
25 Ty Lawson/25 2.50 6.00
26 Eric Maynor/25 2.00 5.00
27 DeJuan Blair/25 2.50 6.00
28 James Johnson/25 2.50 6.00
29 Chase Budinger/25 2.00 5.00
30 Jordan Hill/25 2.00 5.00
31 Sam Young/25 2.00 5.00
32 Hasheem Thabeet/25 2.00 5.00
33 Jrue Holiday/25 10.00 25.00
34 Rodrigue Beaubois/25 2.00 5.00
35 Tyler Hansbrough/25 2.50 6.00

2009-10 Playoff National Treasures NBA Gear Dual Prime

*PRIME: .5X TO 1.25X BASE HI
STATED PRINT RUN 5 TO 49 SER.#'d SETS
1 Kobe Bryant/49 40.00 80.00
8 Carmelo Anthony/25 10.00 25.00
10 Chris Paul/20 10.00 25.00
29 Chase Budinger/25 8.00 20.00

2009-10 Playoff National Treasures NBA Gear Dual Signatures

STATED PRINT RUN 3 TO 30 SER.#'d SETS
*PRIME: .5X TO 1.25X HI COLUMN
PRIME PRINT RUN 3 TO 49 SETS
1 Kobe Bryant/25 800.00 1,500.00
3 Blake Griffin/25 60.00 150.00
5 James Harden/30 200.00 500.00
7 Tyreke Evans/30 10.00 25.00
9 Jonny Flynn/30 4.00 10.00
11 Stephen Curry/30 5,000.00 10,000.00
13 DeMar DeRozan/30 75.00 200.00
14 Earl Clark/30 4.00 10.00
15 Brandon Jennings/30 6.00 15.00
16 Gerald Henderson/30 4.00 10.00

17 Terrence Williams/30 4.00 10.00
18 Toney Douglas/30 4.00 10.00
19 Omri Casspi/30 4.00 10.00
20 Wayne Ellington/30 5.00 12.00
21 Darren Collison/30 6.00 15.00
22 Austin Daye/30 4.00 10.00
23 Taj Gibson/30 5.00 12.00
24 Jeff Teague/30 5.00 12.00
25 Ty Lawson/30 5.00 12.00
26 Eric Maynor/25 4.00 10.00
27 DeJuan Blair/30 5.00 12.00
28 James Johnson/30 5.00 12.00
29 Chase Budinger/30 4.00 10.00
30 Jordan Hill/30 4.00 10.00
31 Sam Young/30 4.00 10.00
32 Hasheem Thabeet/30 4.00 10.00
33 Jrue Holiday/30 20.00 50.00
34 Rodrigue Beaubois/30 4.00 10.00
35 Tyler Hansbrough/30 5.00 12.00

2009-10 Playoff National Treasures NBA Gear Trios

STATED PRINT RUN 10 TO 99 SER.#'d SETS
1 Kobe Bryant/99 15.00 30.00
2 LeBron James/49 12.00 30.00
3 Blake Griffin/25 30.00 80.00
5 James Harden/25 125.00 300.00
6 Dwyane Wade/99 8.00 20.00
7 Tyreke Evans/25 3.00 8.00
8 Carmelo Anthony/49 6.00 15.00
9 Jonny Flynn/25 2.50 6.00
10 Chris Paul/99 8.00 20.00
11 Stephen Curry/25 1,250.00 2,500.00
12 Dwight Howard/99 5.00 12.00
13 DeMar DeRozan/25 60.00 150.00
14 Earl Clark/25 2.50 6.00
15 Brandon Jennings/25 4.00 10.00
16 Gerald Henderson/25 2.50 6.00
17 Terrence Williams/25 2.50 6.00
18 Toney Douglas/25 2.50 6.00
19 Omri Casspi/25 2.50 6.00
20 Wayne Ellington/25 3.00 8.00
21 Darren Collison/25 4.00 10.00
22 Austin Daye/25 2.50 6.00
23 Taj Gibson/25 3.00 8.00
24 Jeff Teague/25 3.00 8.00
25 Ty Lawson/25 3.00 8.00
26 Eric Maynor/25 2.50 6.00
27 DeJuan Blair/25 3.00 8.00
28 James Johnson/25 3.00 8.00
29 Chase Budinger/25 2.50 6.00
30 Jordan Hill/25 2.50 6.00
31 Sam Young/25 2.50 6.00
32 Hasheem Thabeet/25 2.50 6.00
33 Jrue Holiday/25 12.00 30.00
34 Rodrigue Beaubois/25 2.50 6.00
35 Tyler Hansbrough/25 3.00 8.00

2009-10 Playoff National Treasures NBA Gear Trios Prime

*PRIME: .5X TO 1.25X BASE HI
STATED PRINT RUN 5 TO 49 SER.#'d SETS
1 Kobe Bryant/49 40.00 75.00
8 Carmelo Anthony/49 12.00 30.00
10 Chris Paul/49 12.00 30.00

2009-10 Playoff National Treasures NBA Gear Trios Signatures

STATED PRINT RUN 3 TO 30 SER.#'d SETS
*PRIME: .6X TO 1.5X HI COLUMN
PRIME PRINT RUN 3 TO 49 SETS
1 Kobe Bryant/25 800.00 1,500.00
5 James Harden/30 200.00 500.00
7 Tyreke Evans/30 10.00 25.00
9 Jonny Flynn/30 4.00 10.00
11 Stephen Curry/30 5,000.00 10,000.00
13 DeMar DeRozan/30 125.00 300.00
14 Earl Clark/30 4.00 10.00
15 Brandon Jennings/30 6.00 15.00
16 Gerald Henderson/30 4.00 10.00
17 Terrence Williams/30 4.00 10.00
18 Toney Douglas/30 4.00 10.00
19 Omri Casspi/30 4.00 10.00
20 Wayne Ellington/30 5.00 12.00
21 Darren Collison/30 6.00 15.00
22 Austin Daye/30 4.00 10.00
23 Taj Gibson/30 10.00 25.00
24 Jeff Teague/30 5.00 12.00
25 Ty Lawson/30 5.00 12.00
26 Eric Maynor/25 4.00 10.00
27 DeJuan Blair/30 5.00 12.00
28 James Johnson/30 5.00 12.00
29 Chase Budinger/30 4.00 10.00
30 Jordan Hill/30 4.00 10.00
31 Sam Young/30 4.00 10.00
32 Hasheem Thabeet/30 4.00 10.00
33 Jrue Holiday/30 15.00 40.00
34 Rodrigue Beaubois/30 4.00 10.00
35 Tyler Hansbrough/30 5.00 12.00

2009-10 Playoff National Treasures NBA Greatest

COMPLETE SET (30) 125.00 250.00
PRINT RUN 25 SER.#'d SETS
1 Kareem Abdul-Jabbar 15.00 40.00
2 Nate Archibald 6.00 15.00
3 Rick Barry 4.00 10.00
4 Larry Bird 20.00 50.00
5 Bob Cousy 12.00 30.00
6 Dave Cowens 6.00 15.00
7 Clyde Drexler 8.00 20.00
8 Walt Frazier 8.00 20.00
9 George Gervin 6.00 15.00
10 Hal Greer 6.00 15.00
11 John Havlicek 12.00 30.00
12 Elvin Hayes 8.00 20.00
13 Magic Johnson 20.00 50.00
14 Kevin McHale 8.00 20.00
15 George Mikan 15.00 40.00
16 Earl Monroe 6.00 15.00
17 Shaquille O'Neal 15.00 40.00
18 Robert Parish 6.00 15.00
19 Scottie Pippen 12.00 30.00
20 Willis Reed 8.00 20.00
21 Oscar Robertson 6.00 15.00
22 Bill Russell 15.00 40.00
23 Dolph Schayes 5.00 12.00
24 Isiah Thomas 5.00 12.00
25 Nate Thurmond 4.00 10.00
26 Wes Unseld 5.00 12.00
27 Bill Walton 8.00 20.00
28 Jerry West 8.00 20.00
29 Lenny Wilkens 5.00 12.00
30 James Worthy 6.00 15.00

2009-10 Playoff National Treasures NBA Greatest Materials

STATED PRINT RUN 10 TO 99 SER.#'d SETS
1 Kareem Abdul-Jabbar/25 20.00 50.00
6 Dave Cowens/99 8.00 20.00
7 Clyde Drexler/25 12.00 30.00
14 Kevin McHale/99 10.00 25.00
15 George Mikan/99 20.00 50.00
16 Earl Monroe/25 8.00 20.00
17 Shaquille O'Neal/49 20.00 50.00
18 Robert Parish/49 8.00 20.00
19 Scottie Pippen/49 15.00 40.00

2009-10 Playoff National Treasures NBA Greatest Materials Prime

*PRIME: .6X TO 1.5X HI COLUMN
STATED PRINT RUN 5 TO 25 SER.#'d SETS
13 Magic Johnson/25 15.00 40.00

2009-10 Playoff National Treasures NBA Greatest Materials Signatures

STATED PRINT RUN ONE TO 49 SER.#'d SETS
6 Dave Cowens/49 10.00 25.00
7 Clyde Drexler/25 25.00 60.00

2009-10 Playoff National Treasures NBA Greatest Materials Prime Signatures

STATED PRINT RUN ONE TO 25 SER.#'d SETS
6 Dave Cowens/25 20.00 50.00

2009-10 Playoff National Treasures NBA Greatest Signature Combos

STATED PRINT RUN 5 TO 99 SER.#'d SETS
1 B.Pettit/L.Wilkens/25 25.00 50.00
4 E.Hayes/W.Unseld/25 25.00 60.00

2009-10 Playoff National Treasures NBA Greatest Signature Quads

STATED PRINT RUN 3 TO 15 SER.#'d SETS
2 McH/Parish/Wltn/Bird/15 150.00 300.00

2009-10 Playoff National Treasures NBA Greatest Signatures

STATED PRINT RUN 3 TO 25 SER.#'d SETS
2 Nate Archibald/25 12.00 30.00
6 Dave Cowens/25 12.00 30.00
7 Clyde Drexler/25 25.00 60.00
8 Walt Frazier/25 12.00 30.00
10 Hal Greer/25 12.00 30.00
18 Robert Parish/25 12.00 30.00
20 Willis Reed/25 40.00 100.00
23 Dolph Schayes/25 12.00 30.00
25 Nate Thurmond/25 15.00 40.00
26 Wes Unseld/25 20.00 50.00
27 Bill Walton/25 12.00 30.00
30 James Worthy/25 30.00 60.00

2009-10 Playoff National Treasures Notable Nicknames

STATED PRINT RUN 10 TO 99 SER.#'d SETS
BC Billy Cunningham/55 125.00 300.00
BW Bill Walton/99 100.00 250.00
CD Clyde Drexler/25 400.00 800.00
DC Dave Cowens/99 100.00 250.00
DW Dominique Wilkins/25 500.00 1,000.00
EH Elvin Hayes/25 150.00 400.00
EM Earl Monroe/99 125.00 300.00
FR Frank Ramsey/49 150.00 400.00
GG George Gervin/99 125.00 300.00
HG Harry Gallatin/49 300.00 600.00
JH John Havlicek/49 500.00 1,000.00
LB Larry Bird/25 1,000.00 2,000.00
NT Nate Thurmond/25 125.00 300.00
OR Oscar Robertson/25 400.00 800.00
WR Willis Reed/99 125.00 300.00
JWE Jerry West/25 400.00 800.00
KB1 Kobe Bryant Mamba/99 5,000.00 10,000.00
KB2 Kobe Bryant MVP/35 3,000.00 6,000.00

2009-10 Playoff National Treasures Pen Pals

STATED PRINT RUN 50 SER.#'d SETS
1 Blake Griffin 75.00 200.00
2 Hasheem Thabeet 4.00 10.00
3 James Harden 500.00 1,000.00
4 Jordan Hill 4.00 10.00
5 Stephen Curry 5,000.00 10,000.00
6 Tyler Hansbrough 5.00 12.00
7 Tyreke Evans 12.00 30.00
8 B.Griffin/H.Thabeet 20.00 50.00
9 B.Griffin/T.Hansbrough 20.00 50.00
10 D.Collison/J.Holiday 15.00 40.00
11 D.Blair/S.Young 5.00 12.00
12 E.Clark/T.Williams 4.00 10.00
13 J.Harden/J.Hill 200.00 500.00
14 J.Johnson/J.Teague 5.00 12.00
15 C.Budinger/J.Hill 4.00 10.00
16 T.Lawson/T.Hansbrough 5.00 12.00
17 Blair/Thabeet/Flynn 5.00 12.00

2009-10 Playoff National Treasures Signature Patches College

STATED PRINT RUN 25 TO 77 SER.#'d SETS
2 Carmelo Anthony/27 30.00 80.00
3 Bill Walton/77 15.00 40.00
4 Dominique Wilkins/25 15.00 40.00
7 Dave Cowens/27 15.00 40.00
8 Oscar Robertson/27 40.00 100.00
9 David Thompson/27 12.50 30.00
10 Rick Barry/26 12.50 30.00
13 Isiah Thomas/27 15.00 40.00
15 Jerry West/26 40.00 80.00
17 John Havlicek/28 30.00 60.00
19 Kareem Abdul-Jabbar/27 40.00 80.00
25 Magic Johnson/27 40.00 100.00

2009-10 Playoff National Treasures Signature Patches NBA Team

STATED PRINT RUN 49 TO 100 SER.#'d SETS
1 Bill Russell/49 500.00 1,000.00
2 Carmelo Anthony/53 20.00 50.00
3 Bill Walton/50 10.00 25.00
5 Bob Cousy/54 40.00 100.00
6 Nate Thurmond/53 12.00 30.00
7 Dave Cowens/52 12.00 30.00
8 Oscar Robertson/53 40.00 100.00
9 David Thompson/51 10.00 25.00
10 Rick Barry/51 10.00 25.00
11 Dennis Rodman/53 25.00 60.00
12 Robert Parish/49 12.00 30.00
13 Isiah Thomas/53 15.00 40.00
14 Scottie Pippen/53 100.00 250.00
15 Jerry West/54 30.00 80.00
17 John Havlicek/52 25.00 60.00
18 Steve Nash/25 50.00 120.00
19 Kareem Abdul-Jabbar/54 40.00 100.00
23 Larry Bird/49 60.00 150.00
24 Kobe Bryant/100 500.00 1,000.00
25 Magic Johnson/51 50.00 120.00

2009-10 Playoff National Treasures Souvenir Cuts

STATED PRINT RUN ONE TO 25 SER.#'d SETS
1 George Mikan/15 125.00 250.00
6 Andy Phillip/25 75.00 200.00
7 Paul Arizin/25 25.00 60.00

2009-10 Playoff National Treasures Timeline Materials Custom Names

STATED PRINT RUN 10 TO 99 SER.#'d SETS
*NICKNAMES: .4X TO 1X BASE HI
1 Kobe Bryant/99 200.00 500.00
2 LeBron James/99 300.00 600.00
3 Tyreke Evans/49 2.50 6.00
4 Brandon Jennings/49 3.00 8.00
5 Stephen Curry/49 1,500.00 3,000.00
6 Jonny Flynn/49 2.00 5.00
7 Taj Gibson/49 2.50 6.00
9 Ty Lawson/49 2.50 6.00
10 Shaquille O'Neal/49 12.00 30.00
11 DeJuan Blair/49 2.50 6.00
12 Dirk Nowitzki/99 10.00 25.00
14 Dwyane Wade/99 8.00 20.00
15 Derrick Rose/99 6.00 15.00
16 Carmelo Anthony/49 6.00 15.00
17 David Lee/25 2.50 6.00
18 Chris Bosh/25 5.00 12.00
19 Brook Lopez/99 4.00 10.00
20 Dwight Howard/99 5.00 12.00
21 Joe Johnson/99 4.00 10.00
22 Tim Duncan/99 10.00 25.00
23 James Harden/49 100.00 250.00
24 Steve Nash/25 20.00 50.00
25 Darren Collison/49 3.00 8.00
27 Omri Casspi/49 2.00 5.00
28 Chris Paul/99 8.00 20.00
29 Blake Griffin/49 12.00 30.00
30 Pau Gasol/99 6.00 15.00

2009-10 Playoff National Treasures Timeline Materials Custom Names Prime

*PRIME: .6X TO 1.5X HI COLUMN
STATED PRINT RUN 3 TO 30 SER.#'d SETS
*NICKNAMES: .4X TO 1X BASE HI

2009-10 Playoff National Treasures Timeline Materials Custom Names Signatures

STATED PRINT RUN 3 TO 30 SER.#'d SETS
*NICKNAMES: .4X TO 1X BASE HI
1 Kobe Bryant/25 1,000.00 2,000.00
3 Tyreke Evans/30 6.00 15.00
4 Brandon Jennings/30 8.00 20.00
5 Stephen Curry/30 5,000.00 10,000.00
6 Jonny Flynn/30 5.00 12.00
7 Taj Gibson/30 6.00 15.00
9 Ty Lawson/30 6.00 15.00
11 DeJuan Blair/30 6.00 15.00
17 David Lee/25 5.00 12.00
18 Chris Bosh/25 20.00 50.00
23 James Harden/30 500.00 1,000.00
25 Darren Collison/30 8.00 20.00
27 Omri Casspi/30 5.00 12.00
29 Blake Griffin/30 75.00 200.00

2009-10 Playoff National Treasures Timeline Materials Custom Names Prime Signatures

STATED PRINT RUN ONE TO 25 SER.#'d SETS
*NICKNAMES: .4X TO 1X BASE HI
4 Brandon Jennings/25 25.00 60.00
5 Stephen Curry/25 6,000.00 12,000.00
6 Jonny Flynn/25 6.00 15.00
7 Taj Gibson/25 8.00 20.00

2010-11 Playoff National Treasures

1-185 PRINT RUN 99 SER.#'d SETS
JSY AU RC PRINT RUN 71 TO 99 SETS
1 Josh Smith 2.50 6.00
2 Al Horford 4.00 10.00
3 Jamal Crawford 4.00 10.00
4 Joe Johnson 4.00 10.00
5 Kevin Garnett 10.00 25.00
6 Shaquille O'Neal 15.00 40.00
7 Rajon Rondo 5.00 12.00
8 Ray Allen 6.00 15.00
9 Paul Pierce 6.00 15.00
10 D.J. Augustin 2.50 6.00
11 Stephen Jackson 3.00 8.00
12 Joakim Noah 4.00 10.00
13 Derrick Rose 8.00 20.00
14 Luol Deng 3.00 8.00
15 Carlos Boozer 3.00 8.00
16 Antawn Jamison 3.00 8.00
17 Baron Davis 4.00 10.00
18 Dirk Nowitzki 10.00 25.00
19 Tyson Chandler 3.00 8.00
20 Jason Kidd 6.00 15.00
21 Shawn Marion 4.00 10.00
22 Raymond Felton 2.50 6.00
23 Nene 3.00 8.00
24 Danilo Gallinari 3.00 8.00
25 Ty Lawson 2.50 6.00
26 Tayshaun Prince 4.00 10.00
27 Rodney Stuckey 2.50 6.00
28 Ben Gordon 3.00 8.00
29 Richard Hamilton 5.00 12.00
30 Monta Ellis 3.00 8.00
31 David Lee 2.50 6.00
32 Stephen Curry 200.00 500.00
33 Kevin Martin 3.00 8.00
34 Luis Scola 3.00 8.00
35 Kyle Lowry 4.00 10.00
36 Danny Granger 2.50 6.00
37 Roy Hibbert 3.00 8.00
38 Darren Collison 2.50 6.00
39 Eric Gordon 3.00 8.00
40 Blake Griffin 4.00 10.00
41 Mo Williams 3.00 8.00
42 Kobe Bryant 100.00 250.00
43 Derek Fisher 4.00 10.00
44 Andrew Bynum 2.50 6.00
45 Lamar Odom 3.00 8.00
46 Pau Gasol 6.00 15.00
47 O.J. Mayo 2.50 6.00
48 Rudy Gay 4.00 10.00
49 Mike Conley Jr. 3.00 8.00
50 Zach Randolph 4.00 10.00
51 Dwyane Wade 8.00 20.00
52 Chris Bosh 5.00 12.00
53 Mike Bibby 4.00 10.00
54 LeBron James 125.00 300.00
55 Andrew Bogut 3.00 8.00
56 Brandon Jennings 2.50 6.00
57 John Salmons 2.50 6.00
58 Kevin Love 4.00 10.00
59 Michael Beasley 2.50 6.00
60 Anthony Morrow 2.50 6.00
61 Brook Lopez 3.00 8.00
62 Deron Williams 3.00 8.00
63 Chris Paul 8.00 20.00
64 David West 3.00 8.00
65 Emeka Okafor 3.00 8.00
66 Trevor Ariza 2.50 6.00
67 Amare Stoudemire 4.00 10.00
68 Carmelo Anthony 6.00 15.00
69 Chauncey Billups 5.00 12.00
70 James Harden 10.00 25.00
71 Kevin Durant 15.00 40.00
72 Russell Westbrook 6.00 15.00
73 Dwight Howard 5.00 12.00
74 Jameer Nelson 2.50 6.00
75 Jason Richardson 4.00 10.00
76 Andre Iguodala 4.00 10.00
77 Elton Brand 3.00 8.00
78 Jrue Holiday 5.00 12.00
79 Grant Hill 6.00 15.00
80 Steve Nash 8.00 20.00
81 Vince Carter 8.00 20.00
82 Brandon Roy 5.00 12.00
83 Gerald Wallace 3.00 8.00
84 LaMarcus Aldridge 4.00 10.00
85 Wesley Matthews 2.50 6.00
86 Marcus Thornton 2.50 6.00
87 Tyreke Evans 3.00 8.00
88 Manu Ginobili 8.00 20.00
89 Richard Jefferson 3.00 8.00
90 Tim Duncan 10.00 25.00
91 Tony Parker 6.00 15.00
92 Andrea Bargnani 2.50 6.00
93 DeMar DeRozan 6.00 15.00
94 Leandro Barbosa 3.00 8.00
95 Al Jefferson 2.50 6.00
96 Devin Harris 2.50 6.00
97 Paul Millsap 3.00 8.00
98 Andray Blatche 2.50 6.00
99 Nick Young 2.50 6.00
100 Rashard Lewis 3.00 8.00
101 Julius Erving 8.00 20.00
102 Bill Russell 12.00 30.00
103 Oscar Robertson 10.00 25.00
104 Dave Bing 5.00 12.00
105 Elvin Hayes 5.00 12.00
106 Wilt Chamberlain 12.00 30.00
107 Larry Bird 15.00 40.00
108 Karl Malone 8.00 20.00
109 Jerry Sloan 4.00 10.00
110 Pete Maravich 10.00 25.00
111 Bill Walton 6.00 15.00
112 Scottie Pippen 10.00 25.00
113 Henry Bibby 2.50 6.00
114 Dominique Wilkins 6.00 15.00
115 Kareem Abdul-Jabbar 12.00 30.00
116 Kiki Vandeweghe 3.00 8.00
117 Norm Nixon 2.50 6.00
118 Anfernee Hardaway 10.00 25.00
119 David Robinson 8.00 20.00
120 Kevin McHale 6.00 15.00
121 Dolph Schayes 5.00 12.00
122 Danny Schayes 3.00 8.00
123 Walt Frazier 6.00 15.00
124 Tim Hardaway 5.00 12.00
125 Magic Johnson 15.00 40.00
126 Clyde Drexler 6.00 15.00
127 Dale Ellis 3.00 8.00
128 Bailey Howell 4.00 10.00
129 Mark Price 4.00 10.00
130 Alonzo Mourning 6.00 15.00
131 Byron Scott 4.00 10.00
132 Chris Mullin 5.00 12.00
133 John Salley 3.00 8.00
134 Jerry West 8.00 20.00
135 Dennis Scott 2.50 6.00
136 Walter Berry 2.50 6.00
137 Wes Unseld 5.00 12.00
138 John Stockton 6.00 15.00
139 K.C. Jones 4.00 10.00
140 Rex Chapman 4.00 10.00
141 Patrick Ewing 6.00 15.00
142 Tom Chambers 4.00 10.00
143 Dell Curry 4.00 10.00
144 Hakeem Olajuwon 8.00 20.00
145 Danny Ainge 4.00 10.00
146 Rickey Green 4.00 10.00
147 Dave DeBusschere 4.00 10.00
148 Vlade Divac 4.00 10.00
149 Mark Eaton 4.00 10.00
150 Shawn Kemp 6.00 15.00
151 Jamal Mashburn 3.00 8.00
152 Sam Jones 5.00 12.00
153 Xavier McDaniel 3.00 8.00
154 Elgin Baylor 8.00 20.00
155 David Thompson 4.00 10.00
156 George Gervin 6.00 15.00
157 Albert King 3.00 8.00
158 Isiah Thomas 6.00 15.00
159 Willis Reed 6.00 15.00
160 Walt Bellamy 5.00 12.00
161 Bob Cousy 10.00 25.00
162 Gary Payton 6.00 15.00
163 Jalen Rose 3.00 8.00
164 Chris Webber 5.00 12.00
165 Sean Elliott 3.00 8.00
166 Steve Kerr 5.00 12.00
167 Christian Laettner 4.00 10.00
168 Dan Issel 5.00 12.00
169 Sidney Wicks 4.00 10.00
170 Dan Majerle 3.00 8.00
171 Rick Barry 5.00 12.00
172 George Mikan 12.00 30.00
173 Dikembe Mutombo 6.00 15.00
174 Gail Goodrich 4.00 10.00
175 Darryl Dawkins 4.00 10.00
176 Doc Rivers 4.00 10.00
177 Mitch Richmond 5.00 12.00
178 John Paxson 3.00 8.00
179 John Havlicek 8.00 20.00
180 Moses Malone 6.00 15.00
181 Glen Rice 4.00 10.00
182 Buck Williams 3.00 8.00
183 Ron Harper 4.00 10.00
184 Bob Love 4.00 10.00
185 Dave Cowens 6.00 15.00
186 Devin Ebanks RC 3.00 8.00
187 Craig Brackins RC 3.00 8.00
188 Kevin Seraphin RC 3.00 8.00
189 Omer Asik RC 5.00 12.00
190 Gary Forbes RC 3.00 8.00
191 Semih Erden RC 3.00 8.00
192 Nikola Pekovic RC 5.00 12.00
193 Manny Harris RC 5.00 12.00
194 Jeremy Lin RC 100.00 250.00
195 Jeremy Evans RC 3.00 8.00
196 Eugene Jeter RC 5.00 12.00
197 Samardo Samuels RC 3.00 8.00
198 Ishmael Smith RC 5.00 12.00
199 Armon Johnson RC 3.00 8.00
200 Derrick Caracter RC 3.00 8.00
201 John Wall JSY AU/99 RC 500.00 1,000.00
202 Evan Turner JSY AU/99 RC 20.00 50.00
203 D.Favors JSY AU/99 RC 25.00 60.00
204 W.Johnson JSY AU/99 RC 15.00 40.00
205 D.Cousins JSY AU/99 RC 300.00 600.00
206 Ekpe Udoh JSY AU/99 RC 15.00 40.00
207 G.Monroe JSY AU/99 RC 20.00 50.00
208 A.Aminu JSY AU/99 RC 20.00 50.00
209 G.Hayward JSY AU/99 RC 125.00 300.00
210 P.George JSY AU/99 RC 1,000.00 2,000.00
211 Cole Aldrich JSY AU/99 RC 15.00 40.00
212 Xavier Henry JSY AU/99 RC 15.00 40.00
213 Ed Davis JSY AU/75 RC 20.00 50.00
214 P.Patterson JSY AU/99 RC 20.00 50.00
215 Larry Sanders JSY AU/71 RC 15.00 40.00
216 Luke Babbitt JSY AU/99 RC 15.00 40.00
217 E.Bledsoe JSY AU/86 RC 75.00 200.00
218 A.Bradley JSY AU/99 RC 25.00 60.00
219 J.Anderson JSY AU/99 RC 15.00 40.00
220 Elliot Williams JSY AU/99 RC 15.00 40.00
221 Trevor Booker JSY AU/99 RC 15.00 40.00
222 Damion James JSY AU/99 RC 15.00 40.00
223 D.Jones JSY AU/99 RC 15.00 40.00
224 Q.Pondexter JSY AU/99 RC 15.00 40.00
225 J.Crawford JSY AU/99 RC 15.00 40.00
226 G.Vasquez JSY AU/99 RC 15.00 40.00
227 Daniel Orton JSY AU/99 RC 15.00 40.00
228 L.Hayward JSY AU/99 RC 15.00 40.00
229 H.Whiteside JSY AU/99 RC 30.00 80.00
230 Terrico White JSY AU/99 RC 15.00 40.00
231 Andy Rautins JSY AU/99 RC 15.00 40.00
232 L.Stphnsn JSY AU/99 RC 60.00 150.00
233 L.Harangody JSY AU/99 RC 15.00 40.00
234 Willie Warren JSY AU/99 RC 15.00 40.00
235 Gani Lawal JSY AU/99 RC 15.00 40.00
236 Dexter Pittman JSY AU/99 RC 15.00 40.00
237 T.Mozgov JSY AU/99 RC 20.00 50.00
238 Landry Fields JSY AU/99 RC 15.00 40.00
239 Gary Neal JSY AU/99 RC 20.00 50.00

2010-11 Playoff National Treasures Century Gold

JSY AU STATED PRINT RUN 25 SETS
201 John Wall JSY AU 1,500.00 2,500.00
202 Evan Turner JSY AU 40.00 100.00
203 Derrick Favors JSY AU 125.00 300.00
204 Wesley Johnson JSY AU 30.00 80.00
205 D. Cousins JSY AU 600.00 1,200.00
206 Ekpe Udoh JSY AU 30.00 80.00
207 Greg Monroe JSY AU 100.00 250.00
208 Al-Farouq Aminu JSY AU 40.00 100.00
209 Gordon Hayward JSY AU 500.00 1,000.00
210 Paul George JSY AU 2,000.00 6,000.00
211 Cole Aldrich JSY AU 30.00 80.00
212 Xavier Henry JSY AU 30.00 80.00
213 Ed Davis JSY AU 40.00 100.00
214 Patrick Patterson JSY AU 40.00 100.00
215 Larry Sanders JSY AU 30.00 80.00
216 Luke Babbitt JSY AU 30.00 80.00
217 Eric Bledsoe JSY AU 200.00 500.00
218 Avery Bradley JSY AU 100.00 250.00
219 James Anderson JSY AU 30.00 80.00
220 Elliot Williams JSY AU 30.00 80.00
221 Trevor Booker JSY AU 30.00 80.00
222 Damion James JSY AU 30.00 80.00
223 Dominique Jones JSY AU 30.00 80.00
224 Quincy Pondexter JSY AU 30.00 80.00
225 Jordan Crawford JSY AU 30.00 80.00
226 Greivis Vasquez JSY AU 30.00 80.00
227 Daniel Orton JSY AU 30.00 80.00
228 Lazar Hayward JSY AU 30.00 80.00
229 Hassan Whiteside JSY AU 150.00 400.00
230 Terrico White JSY AU 30.00 80.00
231 Andy Rautins JSY AU 30.00 80.00
232 Lance Stephenson JSY AU 125.00 300.00
233 Luke Harangody JSY AU 30.00 80.00
234 Willie Warren JSY AU 30.00 80.00
235 Gani Lawal JSY AU 30.00 80.00
236 Dexter Pittman JSY AU 30.00 80.00
237 Timofey Mozgov JSY AU 40.00 100.00
238 Landry Fields JSY AU 30.00 80.00
239 Gary Neal JSY AU 40.00 100.00

2010-11 Playoff National Treasures ABA Legends

STATED PRINT RUN 25 SER.#'d SETS
1 Julius Erving 12.00 30.00
2 Rick Barry 8.00 20.00
3 Moses Malone 10.00 25.00
4 Billy Cunningham 8.00 20.00
5 George Gervin 10.00 25.00
6 Dan Issel 8.00 20.00
7 Connie Hawkins 8.00 20.00
8 Artis Gilmore 8.00 20.00
9 George McGinnis 6.00 15.00
10 Wilt Chamberlain 20.00 50.00

2010-11 Playoff National Treasures ABA Legends Signatures

STATED PRINT RUN 10 TO 99 SER.#'d SETS
2 Rick Barry/99 25.00 60.00
4 Billy Cunningham/99 60.00 150.00
5 George Gervin/25 25.00 60.00
6 Dan Issel/25 20.00 50.00
7 Connie Hawkins/99 30.00 80.00
8 Artis Gilmore/99 15.00 40.00
9 George McGinnis/99 30.00 80.00

2010-11 Playoff National Treasures All Decade

STATED PRINT RUN 25 SER.#'d SETS
1 George Mikan 12.00 30.00
2 Bill Russell 12.00 30.00
3 Elgin Baylor 8.00 20.00
4 Jerry West 6.00 15.00
5 Sam Jones 5.00 12.00
6 Kareem Abdul-Jabbar 12.00 30.00
7 George Gervin 6.00 15.00
8 John Havlicek 8.00 20.00
9 Magic Johnson 15.00 40.00
10 Larry Bird 15.00 40.00
11 Julius Erving 8.00 20.00
12 Kevin McHale 6.00 15.00
13 Dominique Wilkins 6.00 15.00
14 David Robinson 8.00 20.00
15 Clyde Drexler 8.00 20.00
16 Gary Payton 6.00 15.00
17 LeBron James 30.00 80.00
18 Kobe Bryant 30.00 80.00
19 Paul Pierce 6.00 15.00
20 Dirk Nowitzki 10.00 25.00

2010-11 Playoff National Treasures All Decade Materials

STATED PRINT RUN ONE TO 99 SER.#'d SETS
1 George Mikan/25 40.00 100.00
3 Elgin Baylor/49 10.00 25.00
5 Sam Jones/49 6.00 15.00
6 Kareem Abdul-Jabbar/99 40.00 100.00
7 George Gervin/49 8.00 20.00
10 Larry Bird/49 40.00 100.00
11 Julius Erving/49 15.00 40.00
12 Kevin McHale/99 8.00 20.00
13 Dominique Wilkins/25 10.00 25.00
14 David Robinson/99 10.00 25.00
15 Clyde Drexler/99 8.00 20.00
16 Gary Payton/99 8.00 20.00
17 LeBron James/99 60.00 150.00
18 Kobe Bryant/99 60.00 150.00
19 Paul Pierce/99 8.00 20.00
20 Dirk Nowitzki/99 12.00 30.00

2010-11 Playoff National Treasures All Decade Materials Prime

*PRIME: .6X TO 1.5X BASE HI
STATED PRINT RUN ONE TO 25 SER.#'d SETS

2010-11 Playoff National Treasures All Decade Materials Signatures

STATED PRINT RUN 5 TO 25 SER.#'d SETS
3 Elgin Baylor/25 30.00 80.00
5 Sam Jones/25 15.00 40.00
7 George Gervin/25 20.00 50.00
13 Dominique Wilkins/25 20.00 50.00
14 David Robinson/25 50.00 120.00
15 Clyde Drexler/25 25.00 60.00
16 Gary Payton/25 25.00 60.00
18 Kobe Bryant/25 2,000.00 4,000.00
19 Paul Pierce/25 40.00 100.00

2010-11 Playoff National Treasures All Decade Signatures

STATED PRINT RUN 10 TO 25 SER.#'d SETS
3 Elgin Baylor/25 40.00 100.00
5 Sam Jones/25 15.00 40.00
7 George Gervin/25 25.00 60.00
8 John Havlicek/25 75.00 200.00
12 Kevin McHale/25 25.00 60.00
13 Dominique Wilkins/25 20.00 50.00
14 David Robinson/25 40.00 100.00
15 Clyde Drexler/25 30.00 80.00
16 Gary Payton/25 30.00 80.00
18 Kobe Bryant/25 1,500.00 3,000.00
19 Paul Pierce/25 40.00 100.00

2010-11 Playoff National Treasures All NBA

STATED PRINT RUN 25 SER.#'d SETS
1 George Mikan 12.00 30.00
2 Bill Walton 6.00 15.00
3 Chris Mullin 5.00 12.00
4 Clyde Drexler 6.00 15.00
5 Connie Hawkins 5.00 12.00
6 Dominique Wilkins 6.00 15.00
7 Earl Monroe 4.00 10.00
8 Gail Goodrich 4.00 10.00
9 Harry Gallatin 4.00 10.00
10 John Stockton 6.00 15.00
11 Moses Malone 6.00 15.00
12 Patrick Ewing 6.00 15.00
13 Sidney Moncrief 2.50 6.00
14 Spencer Haywood 4.00 10.00
15 Tim Hardaway 5.00 12.00
16 Wes Unseld 5.00 12.00
17 Willis Reed 6.00 15.00
18 Alonzo Mourning 6.00 15.00
19 Bernard King 5.00 12.00
20 Julius Erving 8.00 20.00
21 Kevin McHale 6.00 15.00
22 Kevin Durant 15.00 40.00
23 Kobe Bryant 30.00 80.00
24 Kevin Garnett 10.00 25.00
25 Steve Nash 8.00 20.00

2010-11 Playoff National Treasures All NBA Materials

STATED PRINT RUN 25 TO 99 SER.#'d SETS
1 George Mikan/25 15.00 40.00
3 Chris Mullin/49 6.00 15.00
4 Clyde Drexler/99 8.00 20.00
6 Dominique Wilkins/25 8.00 20.00
7 Earl Monroe/99 5.00 12.00
10 John Stockton/99 8.00 20.00
12 Patrick Ewing/99 8.00 20.00
15 Tim Hardaway/49 6.00 15.00
18 Alonzo Mourning/49 8.00 20.00
19 Bernard King/49 6.00 15.00
20 Julius Erving/49 10.00 25.00
21 Kevin McHale/99 8.00 20.00
22 Kevin Durant/49 20.00 50.00
23 Kobe Bryant/99 40.00 100.00
24 Kevin Garnett/99 12.00 30.00
25 Steve Nash/99 10.00 25.00

2010-11 Playoff National Treasures All NBA Materials Prime

*PRIME: .6X TO 1.5X BASE HI
STATED PRINT RUN ONE TO 25 SER.#'d SETS
7 Earl Monroe/25 8.00 20.00
12 Patrick Ewing/25 12.00 30.00
18 Alonzo Mourning/25 12.00 30.00
20 Julius Erving/25 15.00 40.00
22 Kevin Durant/25 30.00 80.00
23 Kobe Bryant/25 60.00 150.00
24 Kevin Garnett/25 20.00 50.00
25 Steve Nash/25 15.00 40.00

2010-11 Playoff National Treasures All NBA Materials Signatures

STATED PRINT RUN 5 TO 25 SER.#'d SETS
3 Chris Mullin/25 15.00 40.00
4 Clyde Drexler/25 25.00 60.00
6 Dominique Wilkins/25 20.00 50.00
7 Earl Monroe/25 12.00 30.00
15 Tim Hardaway/25 15.00 40.00
19 Bernard King/25 15.00 40.00
23 Kobe Bryant/25 1,500.00 3,000.00

2010-11 Playoff National Treasures All NBA Signatures

STATED PRINT RUN 10 TO 99 SER.#'d SETS
3 Chris Mullin/49 12.00 30.00
5 Connie Hawkins/99 20.00 50.00
6 Dominique Wilkins/49 15.00 40.00
7 Earl Monroe/25 15.00 40.00
8 Gail Goodrich/99 6.00 15.00
9 Harry Gallatin/99 6.00 15.00
13 Sidney Moncrief/99 10.00 25.00
14 Spencer Haywood/99 10.00 25.00
15 Tim Hardaway/99 12.00 30.00
16 Wes Unseld/99 10.00 25.00
17 Willis Reed/49 40.00 100.00
19 Bernard King/99 12.00 30.00
21 Kevin McHale/25 25.00 60.00
23 Kobe Bryant/99 1,000.00 2,000.00
25 Steve Nash/25 75.00 200.00

2010-11 Playoff National Treasures Biography Materials

STATED PRINT RUN 25 TO 99 SER.#'d SETS
1 Kevin Durant/49 15.00 40.00
2 Kobe Bryant/99 30.00 80.00
3 Blake Griffin/25 4.00 10.00
4 LeBron James/99 30.00 80.00
5 Dirk Nowitzki/99 10.00 25.00
6 Derrick Rose/99 8.00 20.00
7 Chris Paul/99 8.00 20.00
8 Zach Randolph/99 4.00 10.00
9 Steve Nash/99 8.00 20.00
10 Tyreke Evans/99 3.00 8.00
11 Al Jefferson/99 2.50 6.00
12 Tony Parker/49 6.00 15.00
13 Stephen Curry/25 150.00 400.00
14 Joakim Noah/99 4.00 10.00
15 Dwight Howard/49 5.00 12.00
16 Kevin Martin/99 3.00 8.00
17 Monta Ellis/99 3.00 8.00
18 Kevin Garnett/99 10.00 25.00
19 Kevin Love/99 4.00 10.00
20 Russell Westbrook/99 6.00 15.00

2010-11 Playoff National Treasures Biography Materials Prime

*PRIME: .75X TO 2X BASE HI
STATED PRINT RUN 5 TO 25 SER.#'d SETS
9 Steve Nash/25 15.00 40.00

2010-11 Playoff National Treasures Biography Materials Autographs

STATED PRINT RUN 10 TO 25 SER.#'d SETS
2 Kobe Bryant/25 2,000.00 4,000.00
8 Zach Randolph/25 12.00 30.00
10 Tyreke Evans/20 8.00 20.00
11 Al Jefferson/25 8.00 20.00
12 Tony Parker/25 50.00 120.00
13 Stephen Curry/25 800.00 1,500.00
14 Joakim Noah/25 8.00 20.00
16 Kevin Martin/25 8.00 20.00
17 Monta Ellis/25 10.00 25.00
19 Kevin Love/25 20.00 50.00
20 Russell Westbrook/25 125.00 300.00

2010-11 Playoff National Treasures Century Materials

STATED PRINT RUN ONE TO 99 SER.#'d SETS
1 Josh Smith/25 4.00 10.00
2 Al Horford/25 6.00 15.00
4 Joe Johnson/25 6.00 15.00
5 Kevin Garnett/25 15.00 40.00
6 Shaquille O'Neal/25 25.00 60.00
7 Rajon Rondo/25 8.00 20.00
8 Ray Allen/49 10.00 25.00
9 Paul Pierce/25 10.00 25.00
10 D.J. Augustin/25 4.00 10.00
11 Stephen Jackson/25 5.00 12.00
12 Joakim Noah/25 6.00 15.00
13 Derrick Rose/25 12.00 30.00
14 Luol Deng/25 5.00 12.00
15 Carlos Boozer/25 5.00 12.00
16 Antawn Jamison/25 5.00 12.00
18 Dirk Nowitzki/25 15.00 40.00
19 Tyson Chandler/25 5.00 12.00
20 Jason Kidd/25 10.00 25.00
21 Shawn Marion/25 6.00 15.00
23 Nene/25 5.00 12.00
24 Danilo Gallinari/49 5.00 12.00
25 Ty Lawson/49 4.00 10.00
26 Tayshaun Prince/25 6.00 15.00
27 Rodney Stuckey/15 4.00 10.00

28 Ben Gordon/25 5.00 12.00
29 Richard Hamilton/49 8.00 20.00
30 Monta Ellis/49 5.00 12.00
31 David Lee/25 4.00 10.00
32 Stephen Curry/25 150.00 400.00
33 Kevin Martin/49 5.00 12.00
34 Luis Scola/49 5.00 12.00
35 Kyle Lowry/49 6.00 15.00
36 Danny Granger/49 4.00 10.00
37 Roy Hibbert/49 5.00 12.00
38 Darren Collison/49 4.00 10.00
39 Eric Gordon/25 5.00 12.00
40 Blake Griffin/49 6.00 15.00
41 Mo Williams/25 5.00 12.00
42 Kobe Bryant/25 100.00 250.00
43 Derek Fisher/25 6.00 15.00
44 Andrew Bynum/99 4.00 10.00
45 Lamar Odom/99 5.00 12.00
46 Pau Gasol/99 10.00 25.00
47 O.J. Mayo/25 4.00 10.00
48 Rudy Gay/25 6.00 15.00
49 Mike Conley Jr./25 5.00 12.00
50 Zach Randolph/25 6.00 15.00
51 Dwyane Wade/25 12.00 30.00
52 Chris Bosh/49 8.00 20.00
54 LeBron James/99 75.00 200.00
55 Andrew Bogut/49 5.00 12.00
56 Brandon Jennings/49 4.00 10.00
57 John Salmons/25 4.00 10.00
58 Kevin Love/25 6.00 15.00
59 Michael Beasley/25 4.00 10.00
60 Anthony Morrow/25 4.00 10.00
61 Brook Lopez/25 5.00 12.00
63 Chris Paul/25 12.00 30.00
64 David West/25 5.00 12.00
65 Emeka Okafor/25 5.00 12.00
66 Trevor Ariza/49 4.00 10.00
67 Amare Stoudemire/25 6.00 15.00
68 Carmelo Anthony/25 10.00 25.00
69 Chauncey Billups/49 8.00 20.00
70 James Harden/25 15.00 40.00
71 Kevin Durant/49 25.00 60.00
72 Russell Westbrook/49 10.00 25.00
73 Dwight Howard/25 8.00 20.00
74 Jameer Nelson/25 4.00 10.00
75 Jason Richardson/25 6.00 15.00
76 Andre Iguodala/49 6.00 15.00
77 Elton Brand/99 5.00 12.00
78 Jrue Holiday/49 8.00 20.00
79 Grant Hill/99 10.00 25.00
80 Steve Nash/99 12.00 30.00
81 Vince Carter/99 12.00 30.00
82 Brandon Roy/99 8.00 20.00
84 LaMarcus Aldridge/99 6.00 15.00
85 Wesley Matthews/99 4.00 10.00
87 Tyreke Evans/99 5.00 12.00
88 Manu Ginobili/99 12.00 30.00
89 Richard Jefferson/99 5.00 12.00
90 Tim Duncan/99 15.00 40.00
91 Tony Parker/49 10.00 25.00
92 Andrea Bargnani/99 4.00 10.00
93 DeMar DeRozan/99 8.00 20.00
94 Leandro Barbosa/99 5.00 12.00
95 Al Jefferson/99 4.00 10.00
96 Devin Harris/99 4.00 10.00
97 Paul Millsap/99 5.00 12.00
99 Nick Young/99 4.00 10.00
101 Julius Erving/49 12.00 30.00
106 Wilt Chamberlain/25 75.00 200.00
107 Larry Bird/49 25.00 60.00
108 Karl Malone/99 10.00 25.00
112 Scottie Pippen/99 15.00 40.00
114 Dominique Wilkins/25 10.00 25.00
115 Kareem Abdul-Jabbar/25 20.00 50.00
116 Kiki Vandeweghe/99 5.00 12.00
118 Anfernee Hardaway/99 15.00 40.00
119 David Robinson/49 12.00 30.00
120 Kevin McHale/49 10.00 25.00
126 Clyde Drexler/49 10.00 25.00
128 Bailey Howell/99 6.00 15.00
129 Mark Price/99 6.00 15.00
130 Alonzo Mourning/49 8.00 20.00
132 Chris Mullin/49 8.00 20.00
135 Dennis Scott/99 4.00 10.00
138 John Stockton/99 10.00 25.00
141 Patrick Ewing/99 10.00 25.00
142 Tom Chambers/25 6.00 15.00
144 Hakeem Olajuwon/99 12.00 30.00
149 Mark Eaton/49 6.00 15.00
152 Sam Jones/49 8.00 20.00
154 Elgin Baylor/99 12.00 30.00
156 George Gervin/49 10.00 25.00
163 Jalen Rose/99 5.00 12.00
164 Chris Webber/99 8.00 20.00
170 Dan Majerle/99 5.00 12.00
172 George Mikan/25 12.00 30.00
173 Dikembe Mutombo/25 10.00 25.00
181 Glen Rice/99 6.00 15.00
183 Ron Harper/99 6.00 15.00
186 Devin Ebanks/99 4.00 10.00
187 Craig Brackins/99 4.00 10.00
188 Kevin Seraphin/99 4.00 10.00
194 Jeremy Lin/99 125.00 300.00

2010-11 Playoff National Treasures Century Materials Prime

*PRIME: 1.25X TO 3X BASE HI
STATED PRINT RUN ONE TO 25 SER.#'d SETS
42 Kobe Bryant/25 125.00 300.00
112 Scottie Pippen/25 40.00 100.00
130 Alonzo Mourning/25 20.00 50.00
164 Chris Webber/25 15.00 40.00

2010-11 Playoff National Treasures Century Materials Prime Signatures

STATED PRINT RUN ONE TO 25 SER.#'d SETS
2 Al Horford/25 12.00 30.00
4 Joe Johnson/25 15.00 40.00
10 D.J. Augustin/25 12.00 30.00
11 Stephen Jackson/25 12.00 30.00
12 Joakim Noah/25 25.00 60.00
16 Antawn Jamison/25 12.00 30.00
20 Jason Kidd/25 40.00 100.00
25 Ty Lawson/25 15.00 40.00
30 Monta Ellis/25 15.00 40.00
31 David Lee/25 12.00 30.00
33 Kevin Martin/25 12.00 30.00
36 Danny Granger/25 12.00 30.00
37 Roy Hibbert/25 15.00 40.00
38 Darren Collison/25 15.00 40.00
42 Kobe Bryant/25 3,000.00 6,000.00
44 Andrew Bynum/25 15.00 40.00
48 Rudy Gay/25 15.00 40.00
49 Mike Conley Jr./25 15.00 40.00
50 Zach Randolph/25 15.00 40.00
61 Brook Lopez/25 15.00 40.00
150 James Harden/25 200.00 500.00
72 Russell Westbrook/20 125.00 300.00
74 Jameer Nelson/25 15.00 40.00
78 Jrue Holiday/25 20.00 50.00
79 Grant Hill/25 50.00 120.00
81 Vince Carter/25 50.00 125.00
82 Brandon Roy/25 15.00 40.00
84 LaMarcus Aldridge/25 15.00 40.00
87 Tyreke Evans/15 15.00 40.00
91 Tony Parker/25 30.00 80.00
92 Andrea Bargnani/25 12.00 30.00
93 DeMar DeRozan/25 60.00 150.00
96 Devin Harris/25 12.00 30.00
116 Kiki Vandeweghe/25 12.00 30.00
129 Mark Price/25 20.00 50.00
142 Tom Chambers/15 15.00 40.00
144 Hakeem Olajuwon/25 30.00 80.00
168 Dan Issel/25 12.00 30.00
170 Dan Majerle/25 12.00 30.00
173 Dikembe Mutombo/25 30.00 80.00
181 Glen Rice/25 15.00 40.00
183 Ron Harper/25 15.00 40.00
186 Devin Ebanks/25 12.00 30.00
194 Jeremy Lin/25 400.00 800.00

2010-11 Playoff National Treasures Century Materials Signatures

STATED PRINT RUN ONE TO 99 SER.#'d SETS
1 Josh Smith/25 8.00 20.00
2 Al Horford/99 8.00 20.00
4 Joe Johnson/25 8.00 20.00
7 Rajon Rondo/49 25.00 60.00
8 Ray Allen/25 40.00 100.00
9 Paul Pierce/25 40.00 100.00
10 D.J. Augustin/99 8.00 20.00
11 Stephen Jackson/99 8.00 20.00
12 Joakim Noah/25 8.00 20.00
16 Antawn Jamison/99 8.00 20.00
19 Tyson Chandler/35 8.00 20.00
20 Jason Kidd/25 25.00 60.00
24 Danilo Gallinari/25 10.00 25.00
25 Ty Lawson/99 8.00 20.00
28 Ben Gordon/25 8.00 20.00
30 Monta Ellis/99 8.00 20.00
31 David Lee/49 8.00 20.00
32 Stephen Curry/25 800.00 1,500.00
33 Kevin Martin/99 8.00 20.00
36 Danny Granger/99 8.00 20.00
37 Roy Hibbert/99 8.00 20.00
38 Darren Collison/49 8.00 20.00
41 Mo Williams/99 8.00 20.00
42 Kobe Bryant/49 1,500.00 3,000.00
43 Derek Fisher/49 8.00 20.00
44 Andrew Bynum/49 8.00 20.00
48 Rudy Gay/99 8.00 20.00
49 Mike Conley Jr./99 8.00 20.00
50 Zach Randolph/99 8.00 20.00
55 Andrew Bogut/99 8.00 20.00
56 Brandon Jennings/99 8.00 20.00
58 Kevin Love/25 10.00 25.00
61 Brook Lopez/25 8.00 20.00
65 Emeka Okafor/25 8.00 20.00
66 Trevor Ariza/49 8.00 20.00
69 Chauncey Billups/25 15.00 40.00
70 James Harden/49 125.00 300.00
72 Russell Westbrook/49 75.00 200.00
74 Jameer Nelson/99 8.00 20.00
76 Andre Iguodala/49 8.00 20.00
78 Jrue Holiday/49 12.00 30.00
79 Grant Hill/25 40.00 100.00
81 Vince Carter/25 40.00 100.00
82 Brandon Roy/25 8.00 20.00
84 LaMarcus Aldridge/49 8.00 20.00
85 Wesley Matthews/99 8.00 20.00
87 Tyreke Evans/49 8.00 20.00
91 Tony Parker/25 25.00 60.00
92 Andrea Bargnani/49 8.00 20.00
93 DeMar DeRozan/49 40.00 100.00
95 Al Jefferson/25 8.00 20.00
96 Devin Harris/25 8.00 20.00
114 Dominique Wilkins/25 20.00 50.00
116 Kiki Vandeweghe/99 8.00 20.00
119 David Robinson/25 40.00 100.00
126 Clyde Drexler/25 25.00 60.00
128 Bailey Howell/99 8.00 20.00
129 Mark Price/49 12.00 30.00
132 Chris Mullin/49 12.00 30.00
142 Tom Chambers/49 8.00 20.00
144 Hakeem Olajuwon/25 40.00 100.00
152 Sam Jones/49 15.00 40.00
154 Elgin Baylor/25 40.00 100.00
163 Jalen Rose/99 10.00 25.00
170 Dan Majerle/99 6.00 15.00
173 Dikembe Mutombo/25 15.00 40.00
181 Glen Rice/49 10.00 25.00
183 Ron Harper/99 8.00 20.00
186 Devin Ebanks/99 8.00 20.00
187 Craig Brackins/99 8.00 20.00
194 Jeremy Lin/99 300.00 600.00

2010-11 Playoff National Treasures Century Signatures

STATED PRINT RUN ONE TO 99 SER.#'d SETS
1 Josh Smith/25 6.00 15.00
2 Al Horford/25 6.00 15.00
4 Joe Johnson/25 6.00 15.00
7 Rajon Rondo/49 12.00 30.00
8 Ray Allen/25 30.00 80.00
9 Paul Pierce/25 40.00 100.00
10 D.J. Augustin/99 6.00 15.00
11 Stephen Jackson/99 6.00 15.00
12 Joakim Noah/99 6.00 15.00
16 Antawn Jamison/99 6.00 15.00
17 Baron Davis/25 8.00 20.00
19 Tyson Chandler/20 6.00 15.00
20 Jason Kidd/25 20.00 50.00
22 Raymond Felton/99 6.00 15.00
24 Danilo Gallinari/25 10.00 25.00
25 Ty Lawson/99 6.00 15.00
28 Ben Gordon/25 6.00 15.00
30 Monta Ellis/49 8.00 20.00
31 David Lee/25 6.00 15.00
32 Stephen Curry/49 600.00 1,200.00
33 Kevin Martin/99 6.00 15.00
36 Danny Granger/25 6.00 15.00
37 Roy Hibbert/99 6.00 15.00
38 Darren Collison/25 6.00 15.00
41 Mo Williams/99 6.00 15.00
42 Kobe Bryant/99 1,500.00 3,000.00
43 Derek Fisher/49 8.00 20.00
44 Andrew Bynum/25 12.00 30.00
48 Rudy Gay/99 6.00 15.00
49 Mike Conley Jr./99 6.00 15.00
50 Zach Randolph/49 8.00 20.00
52 Chris Bosh/25 15.00 40.00
53 Mike Bibby/99 8.00 20.00
55 Andrew Bogut/25 10.00 25.00
56 Brandon Jennings/25 8.00 20.00
58 Kevin Love/25 15.00 40.00
61 Brook Lopez/49 6.00 15.00
62 Deron Williams/25 8.00 20.00
65 Emeka Okafor/25 6.00 15.00
66 Trevor Ariza/49 6.00 15.00
69 Chauncey Billups/25 12.00 30.00
70 James Harden/49 75.00 200.00
72 Russell Westbrook/49 75.00 200.00
74 Jameer Nelson/49 6.00 15.00
76 Andre Iguodala/49 8.00 20.00
78 Jrue Holiday/49 12.00 30.00
79 Grant Hill/25 75.00 200.00
80 Steve Nash/25 75.00 200.00
81 Vince Carter/25 75.00 200.00
82 Brandon Roy/25 10.00 25.00
84 LaMarcus Aldridge/25 8.00 20.00
85 Wesley Matthews/99 6.00 15.00
87 Tyreke Evans/49 6.00 15.00
91 Tony Parker/49 15.00 40.00
92 Andrea Bargnani/49 6.00 15.00
93 DeMar DeRozan/25 75.00 200.00
95 Al Jefferson/25 6.00 15.00
96 Devin Harris/99 6.00 15.00
103 Oscar Robertson/25 75.00 200.00
105 Elvin Hayes/49 12.00 30.00
111 Bill Walton/25 25.00 60.00
114 Dominique Wilkins/25 15.00 40.00
116 Kiki Vandeweghe/99 6.00 15.00
120 Kevin McHale/25 15.00 40.00
121 Dolph Schayes/49 6.00 15.00
123 Walt Frazier/49 15.00 40.00
124 Tim Hardaway/75 12.00 30.00
127 Dale Ellis/99 6.00 15.00
128 Bailey Howell/99 6.00 15.00
129 Mark Price/99 6.00 15.00
131 Byron Scott/99 8.00 20.00
132 Chris Mullin/49 10.00 25.00
136 Walter Berry/99 6.00 15.00
137 Wes Unseld/99 6.00 15.00
139 K.C. Jones/20 8.00 20.00
142 Tom Chambers/99 6.00 15.00
143 Dell Curry/99 10.00 25.00
144 Hakeem Olajuwon/25 75.00 200.00
148 Vlade Divac/99 6.00 15.00
149 Mark Eaton/99 6.00 15.00
151 Jamal Mashburn/99 6.00 15.00
152 Sam Jones/25 8.00 20.00
153 Xavier McDaniel/99 6.00 15.00
154 Elgin Baylor/25 40.00 100.00
155 David Thompson/99 10.00 25.00
156 George Gervin/25 15.00 40.00
158 Isiah Thomas/49 30.00 80.00
159 Willis Reed/49 40.00 100.00
160 Walt Bellamy/50 6.00 15.00
162 Gary Payton/25 30.00 80.00
163 Jalen Rose/49 10.00 25.00
165 Sean Elliott/25 12.00 30.00
167 Christian Laettner/49 10.00 25.00
168 Dan Issel/25 8.00 20.00
170 Dan Majerle/99 10.00 25.00
171 Rick Barry/99 20.00 50.00
173 Dikembe Mutombo/49 20.00 50.00
174 Gail Goodrich/99 8.00 20.00
175 Darryl Dawkins/99 12.00 30.00
176 Doc Rivers/49 10.00 25.00
179 John Havlicek/15 75.00 200.00
181 Glen Rice/49 12.00 30.00
183 Ron Harper/99 15.00 40.00
184 Bob Love/99 6.00 15.00
185 Dave Cowens/25 15.00 40.00
186 Devin Ebanks/15 6.00 15.00
187 Craig Brackins/99 6.00 15.00
189 Omer Asik/99 5.00 12.00
190 Gary Forbes/99 5.00 12.00
191 Semih Erden/99 5.00 12.00
192 Nikola Pekovic/99 8.00 20.00
194 Jeremy Lin/99 125.00 300.00
195 Jeremy Evans/99 5.00 12.00
196 Eugene Jeter/25 8.00 20.00
198 Ishmael Smith/49 8.00 20.00
200 Derrick Caracter/99 5.00 12.00

2010-11 Playoff National Treasures Champions

STATED PRINT RUN 25 SER.#'d SETS
1 Bill Russell 12.00 30.00
2 Kareem Abdul-Jabbar 12.00 30.00
3 Oscar Robertson 6.00 15.00
4 David Robinson 8.00 20.00
5 John Havlicek 8.00 20.00
6 Rick Barry 5.00 12.00
7 Hakeem Olajuwon 8.00 20.00
8 Dennis Rodman 8.00 20.00
9 Isiah Thomas 6.00 15.00
10 Robert Horry 4.00 10.00

2010-11 Playoff National Treasures Champions Signatures

STATED PRINT RUN 10 TO 25 SER.#'d SETS
3 Oscar Robertson/25 75.00 200.00
5 John Havlicek/25 75.00 200.00
6 Rick Barry/25 20.00 50.00
7 Hakeem Olajuwon/25 60.00 150.00
8 Dennis Rodman/25 60.00 150.00
9 Isiah Thomas/25 40.00 100.00
10 Robert Horry/25 40.00 100.00

2010-11 Playoff National Treasures Champions Signatures Combos

STATED PRINT RUN 2 TO 20 SER.#'d SETS
2 D.Rodman/B.Laimbeer/20 40.00 100.00
7 Pierce/Rondo/15 100.00 250.00
9 E.Hayes/W.Unseld/20 30.00 80.00
10 T.Parker/R.Horry/20 40.00 100.00

2010-11 Playoff National Treasures Colossal Materials

STATED PRINT RUN 5 TO 99 SER.#'d SETS
1 Kevin Durant/49 8.00 20.00
2 Al Horford/99 4.00 10.00
3 Al Jefferson/99 2.50 6.00
4 Alex English/99 3.00 8.00
5 Pau Gasol/99 6.00 15.00
6 Larry Bird/25 15.00 40.00
7 Brook Lopez/49 3.00 8.00
8 John Wall/99 6.00 15.00
9 James Harden/99 10.00 25.00
10 Gary Payton/49 6.00 15.00
11 Patrick Ewing/99 8.00 20.00
12 Ray Allen/49 6.00 15.00
13 DeMarcus Cousins/99 4.00 10.00
14 Derrick Rose/99 8.00 20.00
15 Landry Fields/99 1.25 3.00
16 Kevin Love/99 4.00 10.00
17 Dikembe Mutombo/99 6.00 15.00
18 Kobe Bryant/99 12.00 30.00
19 Evan Turner/99 1.50 4.00
20 Stephen Curry/25 30.00 80.00
21 Tyreke Evans/99 3.00 8.00
22 Wesley Johnson/99 1.25 3.00
23 Rajon Rondo/99 6.00 15.00
24 Blake Griffin/25 4.00 10.00
25 Hakeem Olajuwon/49 6.00 15.00
26 Dwight Howard/99 5.00 12.00
28 Gordon Hayward/99 5.00 12.00
29 Jalen Rose/49 3.00 8.00
30 Jonny Flynn/99 2.50 6.00
31 Bill Laimbeer/99 3.00 8.00
32 Andrew Bogut/49 3.00 8.00
33 Brandon Jennings/49 2.50 6.00
34 Caron Butler/49 3.00 8.00
35 Clyde Drexler/49 8.00 20.00
36 Cole Aldrich/99 1.25 3.00
37 Detlef Schrempf/99 8.00 20.00
38 Eric Bledsoe/99 2.50 6.00
39 Robert Horry/25 6.00 15.00
40 Tim Duncan/99 10.00 25.00
41 Toni Kukoc/45 6.00 15.00
42 Xavier McDaniel/49 3.00 8.00
43 Kelly Tripucka/49 2.50 6.00
44 Luke Babbitt/99 1.25 3.00
46 Robert Parish/20 5.00 12.00
48 Chris Bosh/25 5.00 12.00
49 Xavier Henry/99 1.25 3.00
50 Paul George/99 10.00 25.00

2010-11 Playoff National Treasures Colossal Materials Prime Signatures

STATED PRINT RUN ONE TO 25 SER.#'d SETS
2 Al Horford/25 10.00 25.00
4 Alex English/25 15.00 40.00
8 John Wall/25 75.00 200.00
18 Kobe Bryant/25 2,500.00 5,000.00
19 Evan Turner/25 30.00 80.00
25 Hakeem Olajuwon/25 75.00 200.00
28 Gordon Hayward/25 25.00 60.00
45 Mark Price/25 75.00 200.00
46 Robert Parish/25 12.00 30.00
50 Paul George/25 200.00 500.00

2010-11 Playoff National Treasures Colossal Materials Signatures

STATED PRINT RUN ONE TO 49 SER.#'d SETS
2 Al Horford/25 6.00 15.00
3 Al Jefferson/25 6.00 15.00
4 Alex English/49 6.00 15.00
9 James Harden/20 40.00 100.00
13 DeMarcus Cousins/25 12.00 30.00
15 Landry Fields/49 4.00 10.00
16 Kevin Love/15 15.00 40.00
17 Dikembe Mutombo/25 20.00 50.00
18 Kobe Bryant/20 2,000.00 4,000.00
19 Evan Turner/49 5.00 12.00
21 Tyreke Evans/25 10.00 25.00
22 Wesley Johnson/49 6.00 15.00
28 Gordon Hayward/49 15.00 40.00
30 Jonny Flynn/25 6.00 15.00
31 Bill Laimbeer/49 5.00 12.00
32 Andrew Bogut/25 12.00 30.00
33 Brandon Jennings/25 4.00 10.00
34 Caron Butler/23 6.00 15.00
36 Cole Aldrich/49 4.00 10.00
37 Detlef Schrempf/49 10.00 25.00
38 Eric Bledsoe/49 8.00 20.00
41 Toni Kukoc/20 25.00 60.00
42 Xavier McDaniel/20 10.00 25.00
44 Luke Babbitt/49 4.00 10.00
46 Robert Parish/25 10.00 25.00
49 Xavier Henry/49 4.00 10.00
50 Paul George/49 75.00 200.00

2010-11 Playoff National Treasures Colossal Materials Jersey Numbers

STATED PRINT RUN 5 TO 99 SER.#'d SETS
1 Kevin Durant/99 15.00 40.00
2 Al Horford/99 4.00 10.00
3 Al Jefferson/99 2.50 6.00
4 Alex English/99 3.00 8.00
5 Pau Gasol/99 6.00 15.00
6 Larry Bird/25 15.00 40.00
7 Brook Lopez/49 3.00 8.00
8 John Wall/99 6.00 15.00
9 James Harden/40 10.00 25.00
10 Gary Payton/99 6.00 15.00
11 Patrick Ewing/99 8.00 20.00
12 Ray Allen/49 6.00 15.00
13 DeMarcus Cousins/99 4.00 10.00
14 Derrick Rose/99 8.00 20.00
15 Landry Fields/99 1.25 3.00
16 Kevin Love/20 6.00 15.00
17 Dikembe Mutombo/99 6.00 15.00
18 Kobe Bryant/49 75.00 200.00
19 Evan Turner/99 1.50 4.00
20 Stephen Curry/25 30.00 80.00
21 Tyreke Evans/99 3.00 8.00
22 Wesley Johnson/99 1.25 3.00
23 Rajon Rondo/99 6.00 15.00
24 Blake Griffin/25 12.00 30.00
25 Hakeem Olajuwon/49 6.00 15.00
26 Dwight Howard/49 5.00 12.00
28 Gordon Hayward/99 5.00 12.00
29 Jalen Rose/49 3.00 8.00
30 Jonny Flynn/99 2.50 6.00
31 Bill Laimbeer/99 3.00 8.00
32 Andrew Bogut/99 3.00 8.00
33 Brandon Jennings/49 2.50 6.00
34 Caron Butler/49 3.00 8.00
35 Clyde Drexler/49 8.00 20.00
36 Cole Aldrich/99 1.25 3.00
37 Detlef Schrempf/99 8.00 20.00
38 Eric Bledsoe/99 2.50 6.00
39 Robert Horry/25 6.00 15.00
40 Tim Duncan/99 10.00 25.00
41 Toni Kukoc/99 6.00 15.00
42 Xavier McDaniel/49 3.00 8.00
43 Kelly Tripucka/99 2.50 6.00
44 Luke Babbitt/99 1.25 3.00
46 Robert Parish/35 6.00 15.00
48 Chris Bosh/25 5.00 12.00
49 Xavier Henry/99 1.25 3.00
50 Paul George/99 10.00 25.00

2010-11 Playoff National Treasures Colossal Materials Jersey Numbers Prime Signatures

STATED PRINT RUN ONE TO 25 SER.#'d SETS
2 Al Horford/25 10.00 25.00
4 Alex English/25 12.00 30.00
9 James Harden/25 100.00 250.00
19 Evan Turner/25 12.00 30.00
21 Tyreke Evans/15 20.00 50.00
25 Hakeem Olajuwon/15 50.00 100.00
28 Gordon Hayward/25 25.00 60.00
31 Bill Laimbeer/25 15.00 40.00
42 Xavier McDaniel/25 10.00 25.00
43 Kelly Tripucka/20 10.00 25.00
44 Luke Babbitt/25 4.00 10.00
45 Mark Price/15 40.00 100.00
49 Xavier Henry/25 6.00 15.00
50 Paul George/25 150.00 400.00

2010-11 Playoff National Treasures Colossal Materials Jersey Numbers Signatures

STATED PRINT RUN 2 TO 49 SER.#'d SETS
2 Al Horford/25 6.00 15.00
3 Al Jefferson/25 6.00 15.00
4 Alex English/49 6.00 15.00
7 Brook Lopez/25 6.00 15.00
8 John Wall/15 75.00 200.00
9 James Harden/15 100.00 250.00
12 Ray Allen/20 30.00 80.00
13 DeMarcus Cousins/25 12.00 30.00
15 Landry Fields/49 4.00 10.00
17 Dikembe Mutombo/25 25.00 60.00
19 Evan Turner/49 12.00 30.00
22 Wesley Johnson/49 4.00 10.00
28 Gordon Hayward/49 15.00 40.00
29 Jalen Rose/15 30.00 80.00
31 Bill Laimbeer/15 12.00 30.00
32 Andrew Bogut/25 12.00 30.00
33 Brandon Jennings/25 4.00 10.00
34 Caron Butler/25 6.00 15.00
36 Cole Aldrich/49 4.00 10.00
37 Detlef Schrempf/49 10.00 25.00
38 Eric Bledsoe/49 8.00 20.00
41 Toni Kukoc/15 25.00 60.00
42 Xavier McDaniel/49 6.00 15.00
43 Kelly Tripucka/18 6.00 15.00
44 Luke Babbitt/49 4.00 10.00
45 Mark Price/20 40.00 100.00
46 Robert Parish/15 10.00 25.00
49 Xavier Henry/49 4.00 10.00
50 Paul George/49 125.00 300.00

2010-11 Playoff National Treasures Hall of Fame

STATED PRINT RUN 25 SER.#'d SETS
1 Clyde Drexler 8.00 20.00
2 Jerry West 10.00 25.00
3 Larry Bird 20.00 50.00
4 Wes Unseld 6.00 15.00
5 Chris Mullin 6.00 15.00
6 Julius Erving 10.00 25.00
7 Rick Barry 6.00 15.00
8 Oscar Robertson 12.00 30.00
9 Artis Gilmore 6.00 15.00
10 Isiah Thomas 8.00 20.00
11 James Worthy 6.00 15.00
12 Moses Malone 8.00 20.00
13 Dominique Wilkins 8.00 20.00
14 Kareem Abdul-Jabbar 15.00 40.00
15 Dan Issel 6.00 15.00
16 Elgin Baylor 10.00 25.00
17 Robert Parish 8.00 20.00
18 John Stockton 10.00 25.00
19 David Robinson 10.00 25.00
20 Kevin McHale 8.00 20.00
21 Earl Monroe 5.00 12.00
22 Scottie Pippen 12.00 30.00
23 Joe Dumars 5.00 12.00
24 George Mikan 15.00 40.00
25 Bill Russell 15.00 40.00
26 George Gervin 8.00 20.00
27 Dennis Rodman 10.00 25.00
28 Karl Malone 10.00 25.00
29 John Havlicek 10.00 25.00
30 Magic Johnson 20.00 50.00

2010-11 Playoff National Treasures Hall of Fame Materials

STATED PRINT RUN ONE TO 99 SER.#'d SETS
1 Clyde Drexler/25 8.00 20.00
3 Larry Bird/49 15.00 40.00
5 Chris Mullin/49 5.00 12.00
6 Julius Erving/99 8.00 20.00
11 James Worthy/99 6.00 15.00
12 Moses Malone/99 6.00 15.00
13 Dominique Wilkins/25 8.00 20.00
14 Kareem Abdul-Jabbar/25 12.00 30.00
16 Elgin Baylor/49 6.00 15.00
17 Robert Parish/99 6.00 15.00
18 John Stockton/99 6.00 15.00
19 David Robinson/49 8.00 20.00
20 Kevin McHale/99 6.00 15.00
21 Earl Monroe/99 4.00 10.00
22 Scottie Pippen/49 8.00 20.00
23 Joe Dumars/99 4.00 10.00
24 George Mikan/25 12.00 30.00
26 George Gervin/49 6.00 15.00
28 Karl Malone/99 8.00 20.00

2010-11 Playoff National Treasures Hall of Fame Materials Prime

*PRIME: 1X TO 2.5X BASE HI
STATED PRINT RUN ONE TO 25 SER.#'d SETS
15 Dan Issel/25 12.00 30.00
22 Scottie Pippen/25 40.00 100.00
23 Joe Dumars/25 10.00 25.00
28 Karl Malone/25 15.00 40.00

2010-11 Playoff National Treasures Hall of Fame Materials Prime Signatures

STATED PRINT RUN ONE TO 25 SER.#'d SETS
5 Chris Mullin/25 30.00 80.00
9 Artis Gilmore/25 20.00 50.00
10 Isiah Thomas/25 25.00 60.00
11 James Worthy/25 25.00 60.00
15 Dan Issel/25 50.00 120.00
17 Robert Parish/25 15.00 40.00
21 Earl Monroe/25 20.00 50.00
23 Joe Dumars/25 25.00 60.00

2010-11 Playoff National Treasures Hall of Fame Materials Signatures

STATED PRINT RUN ONE TO 49 SER.#'d SETS
1 Clyde Drexler/25 25.00 60.00
5 Chris Mullin/49 12.00 30.00
11 James Worthy/25 25.00 60.00
13 Dominique Wilkins/25 20.00 50.00
16 Elgin Baylor/25 60.00 150.00
17 Robert Parish/25 12.00 30.00
19 David Robinson/25 25.00 60.00
21 Earl Monroe/25 12.00 30.00
23 Joe Dumars/49 12.00 30.00

2010-11 Playoff National Treasures Hall of Fame Signatures

STATED PRINT RUN 10 TO 25 SER.#'d SETS
3 Larry Bird/25 75.00 150.00
4 Wes Unseld/25 25.00 60.00
5 Chris Mullin/25 20.00 50.00
7 Rick Barry/25 10.00 25.00
8 Oscar Robertson/25 100.00 200.00
9 Artis Gilmore/25 10.00 25.00
10 Isiah Thomas/25 15.00 40.00
11 James Worthy/25 15.00 40.00
13 Dominique Wilkins/25 25.00 60.00
15 Dan Issel/25 10.00 25.00
16 Elgin Baylor/25 20.00 50.00
17 Robert Parish/25 10.00 25.00
20 Kevin McHale/25 30.00 80.00
21 Earl Monroe/25 10.00 25.00
23 Joe Dumars/25 10.00 25.00
26 George Gervin/25 12.00 30.00
27 Dennis Rodman/25 25.00 60.00
29 John Havlicek/25 40.00 100.00

2010-11 Playoff National Treasures Hall of Fame Signatures Combos

STATED PRINT RUN 10 TO 50 SER.#'d SETS
3 J.Havlicek/J.West/25 40.00 100.00
4 Lovellette/Schayes/50 10.00 25.00
5 R.Parish/Olajuwon/25 35.00 70.00

2010-11 Playoff National Treasures NBA Gear Dual

STATED PRINT RUN 25 TO 99 SER.#'d SETS
1 John Wall/99 8.00 20.00
2 Joakim Noah/99 5.00 12.00
3 Blake Griffin/25 10.00 25.00
4 Tyreke Evans/50 4.00 10.00
5 LeBron James/99 40.00 100.00
6 Evan Turner/99 2.00 5.00
7 Kobe Bryant/99 25.00 60.00
8 DeMarcus Cousins/99 5.00 12.00
9 Kevin Durant/49 10.00 25.00
10 Landry Fields/99 1.50 4.00
11 Stephen Curry/25 40.00 100.00
12 Greg Monroe/99 2.00 5.00
13 Andrew Bogut/49 4.00 10.00
14 Gordon Hayward/99 6.00 15.00
15 Brandon Jennings/99 3.00 8.00
16 Wesley Johnson/99 1.50 4.00
17 LaMarcus Aldridge/99 5.00 12.00
18 Al-Farouq Aminu/99 2.00 5.00
19 Dirk Nowitzki/99 12.00 30.00
20 Paul George/99 12.00 30.00
21 Josh Smith/99 3.00 8.00
22 Xavier Henry/99 1.50 4.00
23 Avery Bradley/99 2.50 6.00
24 Larry Sanders/99 1.50 4.00
25 Cole Aldrich/99 1.50 4.00
26 Luke Babbitt/99 1.50 4.00
27 Greivis Vasquez/99 1.50 4.00
28 Eric Bledsoe/99 3.00 8.00
29 James Anderson/99 1.50 4.00
30 Patrick Patterson/99 2.00 5.00
31 Elliot Williams/99 1.50 4.00
32 Ed Davis/99 2.00 5.00
33 Damion James/99 1.50 4.00
34 Daniel Orton/99 1.50 4.00
35 Lazar Hayward/99 1.50 4.00

2010-11 Playoff National Treasures NBA Gear Dual Prime

*PRIME STARS: .6X TO 1.5X BASE HI
*PRIME ROOKIES: .75X TO 2X BASE HI
STATED PRINT RUN ONE TO 49 SER.#'d SETS

2010-11 Playoff National Treasures NBA Gear Dual Prime Signatures

STATED PRINT RUN ONE TO 49 SER.#'d SETS
6 Evan Turner/49 6.00 15.00
7 Kobe Bryant/49 1,500.00 3,000.00
10 Landry Fields/49 5.00 12.00
12 Greg Monroe/49 6.00 15.00
14 Gordon Hayward/49 20.00 50.00
20 Paul George/25 125.00 300.00
23 Avery Bradley/25 8.00 20.00
24 Larry Sanders/25 5.00 12.00
25 Cole Aldrich/49 5.00 12.00
29 James Anderson/49 5.00 12.00
30 Patrick Patterson/49 6.00 15.00
31 Elliot Williams/25 5.00 12.00
33 Damion James/49 5.00 12.00
34 Daniel Orton/49 5.00 12.00
35 Lazar Hayward/49 5.00 12.00

2010-11 Playoff National Treasures NBA Gear Dual Signatures

STATED PRINT RUN 5 TO 30 SER.#'d SETS
4 Tyreke Evans/30 5.00 12.00
6 Evan Turner/30 5.00 12.00
7 Kobe Bryant/30 1,500.00 3,000.00
8 DeMarcus Cousins/30 30.00 80.00
10 Landry Fields/30 4.00 10.00
11 Stephen Curry/25 800.00 1,500.00
12 Greg Monroe/30 5.00 12.00
14 Gordon Hayward/30 12.00 30.00
15 Brandon Jennings/30 4.00 10.00
16 Wesley Johnson/30 4.00 10.00
18 Al-Farouq Aminu/30 5.00 12.00
20 Paul George/30 125.00 300.00
22 Xavier Henry/30 4.00 10.00
23 Avery Bradley/30 6.00 15.00
24 Larry Sanders/30 4.00 10.00
25 Cole Aldrich/30 4.00 10.00
26 Luke Babbitt/30 4.00 10.00
27 Greivis Vasquez/30 4.00 10.00
28 Eric Bledsoe/30 8.00 20.00
29 James Anderson/30 4.00 10.00
30 Patrick Patterson/30 5.00 12.00
31 Elliot Williams/30 4.00 10.00
32 Ed Davis/30 5.00 12.00
33 Damion James/30 4.00 10.00
34 Daniel Orton/30 4.00 10.00
35 Lazar Hayward/30 4.00 10.00

2010-11 Playoff National Treasures NBA Gear Trios

STATED PRINT RUN 25 TO 99 SER.#'d SETS
1 John Wall/99 10.00 25.00
2 Joakim Noah/99 6.00 15.00
3 Blake Griffin/25 6.00 15.00
4 Tyreke Evans/99 5.00 12.00
5 LeBron James/99 15.00 40.00
6 Evan Turner/99 2.50 6.00
7 Kobe Bryant/99 15.00 40.00
8 DeMarcus Cousins/99 6.00 15.00
9 Kevin Durant/49 10.00 25.00
10 Landry Fields/99 2.00 5.00
11 Stephen Curry/25 50.00 125.00
12 Greg Monroe/99 2.50 6.00
13 Andrew Bogut/49 5.00 12.00
14 Gordon Hayward/99 8.00 20.00
15 Brandon Jennings/49 4.00 10.00
16 Wesley Johnson/99 2.00 5.00
17 LaMarcus Aldridge/99 6.00 15.00
18 Al-Farouq Aminu/99 2.50 6.00
19 Dirk Nowitzki/99 15.00 40.00
20 Paul George/99 12.00 30.00
21 Josh Smith/99 4.00 10.00
22 Xavier Henry/99 2.00 5.00
23 Avery Bradley/99 3.00 8.00
24 Larry Sanders/99 2.00 5.00
25 Cole Aldrich/99 2.00 5.00
26 Luke Babbitt/99 2.00 5.00
27 Greivis Vasquez/99 2.00 5.00
28 Eric Bledsoe/99 4.00 10.00
29 James Anderson/99 2.00 5.00
30 Patrick Patterson/99 2.50 6.00
31 Elliot Williams/99 2.00 5.00
32 Ed Davis/99 2.50 6.00
33 Damion James/99 2.00 5.00
34 Daniel Orton/99 2.00 5.00
35 Lazar Hayward/99 2.00 5.00

2010-11 Playoff National Treasures NBA Gear Trios Prime

*PRIME: .6X TO 1.5X BASE HI
STATED PRINT RUN ONE TO 49 SER.#'d SETS
1 John Wall/49 20.00 50.00
7 Kobe Bryant/49 40.00 100.00

2010-11 Playoff National Treasures NBA Gear Trios Prime Signatures

STATED PRINT RUN ONE TO 49 SER.#'d SETS
4 Tyreke Evans/25 25.00 60.00
6 Evan Turner/49 20.00 50.00
10 Landry Fields/49 5.00 12.00
12 Greg Monroe/49 6.00 15.00
14 Gordon Hayward/49 20.00 50.00
20 Paul George/25 30.00 80.00
24 Larry Sanders/25 15.00 40.00
25 Cole Aldrich/49 10.00 25.00
27 Greivis Vasquez/25 25.00 60.00
29 James Anderson/49 5.00 12.00
30 Patrick Patterson/49 6.00 15.00
33 Damion James/49 5.00 12.00
34 Daniel Orton/49 5.00 12.00
35 Lazar Hayward/49 5.00 12.00

2010-11 Playoff National Treasures NBA Gear Trios Signatures

STATED PRINT RUN 5 TO 30 SER.#'d SETS
4 Tyreke Evans/30 5.00 12.00
6 Evan Turner/30 5.00 12.00
7 Kobe Bryant/30 1,500.00 3,000.00
8 DeMarcus Cousins/30 12.00 30.00
10 Landry Fields/30 4.00 10.00
11 Stephen Curry/25 1,000.00 2,000.00
12 Greg Monroe/30 5.00 12.00
14 Gordon Hayward/30 15.00 40.00
15 Brandon Jennings/30 4.00 10.00
16 Wesley Johnson/30 4.00 10.00
18 Al-Farouq Aminu/30 5.00 12.00
20 Paul George/30 75.00 200.00
22 Xavier Henry/30 4.00 10.00
23 Avery Bradley/30 6.00 15.00
24 Larry Sanders/30 4.00 10.00
25 Cole Aldrich/30 4.00 10.00
26 Luke Babbitt/30 4.00 10.00
27 Greivis Vasquez/30 4.00 10.00
28 Eric Bledsoe/30 20.00 50.00
29 James Anderson/30 4.00 10.00
30 Patrick Patterson/30 5.00 12.00
31 Elliot Williams/30 4.00 10.00
32 Ed Davis/30 5.00 12.00

33 Damion James/30 4.00 10.00
34 Daniel Orton/30 4.00 10.00
35 Lazar Hayward/30 4.00 10.00

2010-11 Playoff National Treasures Notable Nicknames
STATED PRINT RUN 10 TO 99 SER.#'d SETS
1 David Robinson/25 125.00 300.00
2 Isiah Thomas/49 100.00 250.00
3 Gary Payton/49 100.00 250.00
4 Dennis Rodman/25 125.00 300.00
6 Jason Terry/49 EXCH 30.00 80.00
7 Hakeem Olajuwon/25 125.00 300.00
9 Earl Monroe/25 30.00 80.00
10 Robert Parish/99 20.00 50.00
12 Darryl Dawkins/99 60.00 150.00
13 Larry Johnson/99 100.00 250.00
14 Dan Majerle/99 100.00 250.00
15 James Worthy/25 50.00 120.00
16 David Thompson/99 100.00 250.00
17 Vince Carter/35 1,000.00 2,000.00
18 Chris Andersen/99 150.00 300.00
19 Kevin Johnson/49 60.00 150.00
20 LaMarcus Aldridge/25 40.00 100.00
21 Dan Issel/49 15.00 40.00

2010-11 Playoff National Treasures Pen Pals
STATED PRINT RUN 5 TO 25 SER.#'d SETS
1 C.Brackins/Pondexter/25 8.00 20.00
2 J.Wall/E.Turner/25 25.00 60.00
3 W.Johnson/G.Hayward/25 10.00 25.00
4 C.Aldrich/X.Henry/25 8.00 20.00
5 E.Bledsoe/A.Aminu/25 10.00 25.00
6 P.George/L.Babbitt/25 40.00 100.00
7 E.Turner/X.Henry/25 8.00 20.00
8 D.Favors/D.James/25 8.00 20.00
9 Wall/Turner/Favors/15 40.00 100.00
10 Johnson/Cousins/Udoh/15 12.00 30.00
11 Monroe/Aminu/Hayward/15 12.00 30.00
12 Johnson/Monroe/Jones/15 8.00 20.00
13 Cousins/Aldrich/Orton/15 12.00 30.00
14 Brackins/James/Udoh/15 8.00 20.00

2010-11 Playoff National Treasures Private Signings
STATED PRINT RUN 25 TO 99 SER.#'d SETS
1 Dennis Rodman/25 75.00 200.00
2 Elvin Hayes/99 15.00 40.00
3 Dominique Wilkins/49 25.00 60.00
4 Nate Archibald/99 10.00 25.00
5 Rick Barry/99 15.00 40.00

2010-11 Playoff National Treasures Signature Patches NBA Team
STATED PRINT RUN 10 TO 99 SER.#'d SETS
1 Stephen Curry/99 2,000.00 4,000.00
2 John Wall/25 100.00 250.00
3 Chris Bosh/25 40.00 100.00
5 Kobe Bryant/49 2,000.00 4,000.00
7 Blake Griffin/25 50.00 120.00
9 Jason Terry/49 EXCH 12.00 30.00
10 Jalen Rose/99 8.00 20.00
12 Russell Westbrook/25 75.00 200.00
15 Bill Walton/49 20.00 50.00
16 Elvin Hayes/49 12.00 30.00
17 Kevin Durant/25 150.00 400.00
18 Kevin Love/25 20.00 50.00
21 Adrian Dantley/99 8.00 20.00
22 Earl Monroe/99 15.00 40.00
23 John Havlicek/49 60.00 150.00
25 Joe Dumars/49 10.00 25.00

2010-11 Playoff National Treasures Souvenir Cuts
STATED PRINT RUN ONE TO 30 SER.#'d SETS
7 Paul Arizin/15 75.00 200.00
8 Paul Endacott/30 75.00 200.00
9 Al Cervi/25 60.00 150.00

2010-11 Playoff National Treasures Springfield Bound
STATED PRINT RUN 25 SER.#'d SETS
1 Kobe Bryant 60.00 150.00
2 Shaquille O'Neal 30.00 80.00
3 Jason Kidd 12.00 30.00
4 Steve Nash 15.00 40.00
5 Paul Pierce 12.00 30.00
6 Tim Duncan 20.00 50.00
7 LeBron James 60.00 150.00
8 Ray Allen 12.00 30.00
9 Dirk Nowitzki 20.00 50.00
10 Kevin Garnett 20.00 50.00

2010-11 Playoff National Treasures Springfield Bound Signatures
STATED PRINT RUN 25 SER.#'d SETS
1 Kobe Bryant 1,500.00 3,000.00
3 Jason Kidd 100.00 250.00
4 Steve Nash 100.00 250.00
5 Paul Pierce 100.00 250.00
8 Ray Allen 100.00 250.00

2010-11 Playoff National Treasures Timeline Materials Custom Names
STATED PRINT RUN 25 TO 99 SER.#'d SETS
1 Kobe Bryant/99 75.00 200.00
2 Kevin Garnett/49 12.00 30.00
3 Stephen Jackson/99 4.00 10.00
4 Alonzo Mourning/49 8.00 20.00
5 Amare Stoudemire/99 5.00 12.00
6 Andrew Bogut/49 4.00 10.00
7 DeMar DeRozan/99 8.00 20.00
8 Jodie Meeks/99 3.00 8.00
9 Kevin Durant/49 20.00 50.00
10 Paul Pierce/99 8.00 20.00
11 Toney Douglas/99 3.00 8.00
12 Jonny Flynn/99 3.00 8.00
13 Mark Price/99 5.00 12.00
14 Brandon Jennings/49 3.00 8.00
15 Carlos Boozer/99 4.00 10.00
16 DeJuan Blair/99 3.00 8.00
17 Derek Fisher/99 5.00 12.00
18 James Harden/99 12.00 30.00
19 James Jones/99 3.00 8.00
20 Jrue Holiday/99 6.00 15.00
21 LeBron James/99 75.00 200.00
22 Chris Paul/99 10.00 25.00
23 Kevin Love/99 5.00 12.00
24 Lamar Odom/99 4.00 10.00
25 LaMarcus Aldridge/99 5.00 12.00
26 Rajon Rondo/99 6.00 15.00
27 Russell Westbrook/99 8.00 20.00
28 Stephen Curry/25 125.00 300.00
29 Wesley Matthews/99 3.00 8.00
30 Dwight Howard/99 6.00 15.00

2010-11 Playoff National Treasures Timeline Materials Custom Names Prime
*PRIME: .75X TO 2X BASE HI
STATED PRINT RUN 5 TO 25 SER.#'d SETS
1 Kobe Bryant/25 150.00 400.00

2010-11 Playoff National Treasures Timeline Materials Custom Names Prime Signatures
STATED PRINT RUN 5 TO 25 SER.#'d SETS
1 Kobe Bryant/25 2,000.00 4,000.00
3 Stephen Jackson/20 15.00 40.00
7 DeMar DeRozan/25 75.00 200.00
9 Kevin Durant/25 200.00 500.00
10 Paul Pierce/25 50.00 120.00
11 Toney Douglas/25 10.00 25.00
12 Jonny Flynn/25 10.00 25.00
18 James Harden/23 125.00 300.00
20 Jrue Holiday/23 40.00 100.00
25 LaMarcus Aldridge/16 20.00 50.00

2010-11 Playoff National Treasures Timeline Materials Custom Names Signatures
STATED PRINT RUN 10 TO 30 SER.#'d SETS
1 Kobe Bryant/30 1,500.00 3,000.00
3 Stephen Jackson/30 12.00 30.00
7 DeMar DeRozan/30 60.00 150.00
8 Jodie Meeks/30 6.00 15.00
10 Paul Pierce/30 30.00 80.00
11 Toney Douglas/30 6.00 15.00
12 Jonny Flynn/30 6.00 15.00
13 Mark Price/30 15.00 40.00
14 Brandon Jennings/30 10.00 25.00
16 DeJuan Blair/30 6.00 15.00
17 Derek Fisher/30 15.00 40.00
18 James Harden/30 75.00 200.00
20 Jrue Holiday/30 20.00 50.00
23 Kevin Love/30 15.00 40.00
25 LaMarcus Aldridge/30 15.00 40.00
26 Rajon Rondo/30 20.00 50.00
27 Russell Westbrook/30 75.00 200.00
28 Stephen Curry/25 1,000.00 2,000.00
29 Wesley Matthews/30 6.00 15.00

2010-11 Playoff National Treasures Timeline Materials Custom Team Nicknames
STATED PRINT RUN 10 TO 99 SER.#'d SETS
1 Kobe Bryant/99 75.00 200.00
2 Kevin Garnett/49 12.00 30.00
3 Stephen Jackson/99 4.00 10.00
4 Alonzo Mourning/99 4.00 10.00
5 Amare Stoudemire/99 5.00 12.00
6 Andrew Bogut/49 4.00 10.00
7 DeMar DeRozan/99 8.00 20.00
9 Kevin Durant/49 20.00 50.00
10 Paul Pierce/99 8.00 20.00
11 Toney Douglas/49 3.00 8.00
12 Jonny Flynn/99 3.00 8.00
14 Brandon Jennings/49 3.00 8.00
15 Carlos Boozer/99 4.00 10.00
16 DeJuan Blair/99 3.00 8.00
17 Derek Fisher/25 5.00 12.00
18 James Harden/99 12.00 30.00
19 James Jones/99 3.00 8.00
20 Jrue Holiday/99 6.00 15.00
21 LeBron James/99 75.00 200.00
22 Chris Paul/99 10.00 25.00
23 Kevin Love/99 5.00 12.00
24 Lamar Odom/99 4.00 10.00
25 LaMarcus Aldridge/99 5.00 12.00
26 Rajon Rondo/99 6.00 15.00
27 Russell Westbrook/99 8.00 20.00
28 Stephen Curry/25 40.00 100.00
29 Wesley Matthews/99 3.00 8.00
30 Dwight Howard/99 6.00 15.00
31 Jodie Meeks/99 3.00 8.00

2010-11 Playoff National Treasures Timeline Materials Custom Team Nicknames Prime
*PRIME: .75X TO 2X BASE HI
STATED PRINT RUN 2 TO 25 SER.#'d SETS

2010-11 Playoff National Treasures Timeline Materials Custom Team Nicknames Prime Signatures
STATED PRINT RUN 5 TO 25 SER.#'d SETS
1 Kobe Bryant/23 2,000.00 4,000.00
7 DeMar DeRozan/25 75.00 200.00
11 Toney Douglas/17 10.00 25.00
18 James Harden/15 100.00 250.00
25 LaMarcus Aldridge/15 20.00 50.00

2010-11 Playoff National Treasures Timeline Materials Custom Team Nicknames Signatures
STATED PRINT RUN 5 TO 30 SER.#'d SETS
1 Kobe Bryant/30 1,500.00 3,000.00
3 Stephen Jackson/30 12.00 30.00
7 DeMar DeRozan/30 60.00 150.00
8 Jodie Meeks/30 6.00 15.00
11 Toney Douglas/30 6.00 15.00
12 Jonny Flynn/30 6.00 15.00
14 Brandon Jennings/30 10.00 25.00
16 DeJuan Blair/30 6.00 15.00
17 Derek Fisher/30 15.00 40.00
18 James Harden/30 75.00 200.00
20 Jrue Holiday/30 20.00 50.00
23 Kevin Love/30 15.00 40.00
25 LaMarcus Aldridge/30 15.00 40.00
27 Russell Westbrook/30 75.00 200.00
28 Stephen Curry/25 1,000.00 2,000.00
29 Wesley Matthews/30 6.00 15.00

1977-78 Post Auerbach Tips
COMPLETE SET (12) 60.00 120.00
COMMON TIP (1-12) 6.00 12.00

1995 Post Honeycomb Posters
COMPLETE SET (3) 2.00 5.00
1 Patrick Ewing .75 2.00
2 Shawn Kemp .75 2.00
3 Alonzo Mourning .75 2.00

2006-07 Press Pass Legends
COMPLETE SET (70) 20.00 50.00
1 Ronnie Brewer .60 1.50
2 J.J. Redick 1.25 3.00
3 Shelden Williams .40 1.00
4 Adam Morrison .50 1.25
5 Rajon Rondo 2.00 5.00
6 Tyrus Thomas .50 1.25
7 Rodney Carney .40 1.00
8 Shawne Williams .40 1.00
9 Maurice Ager .40 1.00
10 Shannon Brown .40 1.00
11 Cedric Simmons .40 1.00
12 Mardy Collins .40 1.00
13 LaMarcus Aldridge 1.50 4.00
14 Hilton Armstrong .40 1.00
15 Rudy Gay .75 2.00
16 Marcus Williams .40 1.00
17 Randy Foye .50 1.25
18 Brandon Roy 1.25 3.00
19 Sidney Moncrief .40 1.00
20 Nate Thurmond .60 1.50
21 Larry Nance .50 1.25
22 Sue Bird 2.00 5.00
23 Diana Taurasi 2.00 5.00
24 Jay Bilas .60 1.50
25 Sleepy Floyd .40 1.00
26 Dominique Wilkins 1.00 2.50
27 Clyde Drexler .75 2.00
27B Clyde Drexler Color 1.00 2.50
28 Elvin Hayes .60 1.50
28B Elvin Hayes Color .75 2.00
29 Hakeem Olajuwon 1.25 3.00
30 Steve Alford .60 1.50
31 Calbert Cheaney .60 1.50
32 Scott May .60 1.50
33 Isiah Thomas 1.00 2.50
34 Larry Bird 2.00 5.00
34B Larry Bird 2.50 6.00
35 Connie Hawkins .60 1.50
36 Danny Manning .50 1.25
36B Danny Manning Color .60 1.50
37 Jo Jo White .50 1.25
38 Rex Chapman .60 1.50
39 Dan Issel .50 1.25
40 Pat Riley .75 2.00
41 Pete Maravich 1.00 2.50
42 Wes Unseld .60 1.50
43 Rick Barry .50 1.25
44 Lou Hudson .40 1.00
45 David Robinson 1.00 2.50
46 Spud Webb .50 1.25
47 David Thompson .50 1.25
48 Brad Daugherty .50 1.25
49 Bob McAdoo .50 1.25
50 Sam Perkins .40 1.00
51 Kenny Smith .50 1.25
52 Bill Laimbeer .50 1.25
53 Adrian Dantley .50 1.25
54 John Havlicek .60 1.50
55 A.C. Green .60 1.50
56 Bill Russell 2.00 5.00
57 Walt Frazier .75 2.00
58 Mark Jackson .50 1.25
59 Bernard King .50 1.25
60 Henry Bibby .40 1.00
61 Bill Walton .75 2.00
61B Bill Walton Color 1.00 2.50
62 Stacey Augmon .40 1.00
63 Reggie Theus .50 1.25
64 Ralph Sampson .50 1.25
65 Jerry West 1.00 2.50
66 Dean Smith .60 1.50
67 Digger Phelps .60 1.50
68 John Wooden .60 1.50
69 Jerry Tarkanian .60 1.50
70 Larry Bird CL 1.25 3.00
NNO Rip Hamilton Ball 12.50 30.00
NNO Lamar Odom Ball 15.00 40.00
NNO Elton Brand Ball 15.00 40.00

2006-07 Press Pass Legends Bronze
*BRONZE: .5X TO 1.25X BASE HI
PRINT RUN 899 SER.#'d SETS

2006-07 Press Pass Legends Emerald
*EMERALD: 2X TO 5X BASE HI
PRINT RUN 25 SER.#'d SETS

2006-07 Press Pass Legends Gold
*GOLD: 1X TO 2.5X BASE HI
PRINT RUN 99 SER.#'d SETS

2006-07 Press Pass Legends Silver
*SILVER: .6X TO 1.5X BASE HI
PRINT RUN 499 SER.#'d SETS

2006-07 Press Pass Legends Alumni Association
COMPLETE SET (10) 10.00 25.00
STATED ODDS 1:9
1 S.Moncrief/R.Brewer 1.50 4.00
2 J.Bilas/J.J.Redick 2.50 6.00
3 C.Drexler/E.Hayes 2.00 5.00
4 I.Thomas/S.Alford 2.50 6.00
5 J.White/D.Manning 1.50 4.00
6 P.Riley/D.Issel 1.50 4.00
7 P.Maravich/Ty.Thomas 6.00 15.00
8 B.McAdoo/S.Perkins 1.50 4.00
9 A.Dantley/B.Laimbeer 1.50 4.00
10 D.Turasi/S.Bird 3.00 8.00

2006-07 Press Pass Legends Alumni Association Autographs
PRINT RUN 50 SER.#'d SETS
1 S.Moncrief/R.Brewer 15.00 40.00
2 J.Bilas/J.J.Redick 20.00 40.00
3 C.Drexler/E.Hayes 20.00 50.00
4 I.Thomas/S.Alford 25.00 60.00
5 J.White/D.Manning 25.00 60.00
6 P.Riley/D.Issel 25.00 60.00
9 A.Dantley/B.Laimbeer 25.00 60.00
9A Dantley Red Teach/Laimbeer/26 30.00 80.00

2006-07 Press Pass Legends Center Court Cuts
2 Bill Russell/75 600.00 1,200.00
2B Bill Russell Red 600.00 1,200.00

2006-07 Press Pass Legends Legendary Legacy
COMPLETE SET (10) 8.00 20.00
STATED ODDS 1:9
1 Clyde Drexler 1.00 2.50
2 Steve Alford .75 2.00
3 Isiah Thomas 1.25 3.00
4 Larry Bird 2.50 6.00
5 Danny Manning .60 1.50
6 Pat Riley 1.00 2.50
7 Sam Perkins .50 1.25
8 Bill Walton 1.00 2.50
9 Jerry West 1.25 3.00
10 Pete Maravich 1.25 3.00

2006-07 Press Pass Legends Legendary Legacy Autographs
PRINT RUN LISTED IN CL BELOW
2 Steve Alford/155 6.00 15.00
3 Isiah Thomas/75 15.00 40.00
4 Larry Bird/50 90.00 180.00
5 Danny Manning/50 15.00 40.00
6 Pat Riley/125 20.00 50.00
7 Sam Perkins/400 6.00 15.00
8 Bill Walton/50 10.00 25.00
9 Jerry West/175 25.00 60.00

2006-07 Press Pass Legends Legendary Legacy Autographs Platinum
PRINT RUNS LISTED IN CL BELOW
2 Steve Alford/25 20.00 50.00
3 Isiah Thomas/25 20.00 50.00
4 Larry Bird/18 100.00 200.00
5 Danny Manning/25 30.00 60.00
6 Pat Riley/25 30.00 80.00
7 Sam Perkins/25 15.00 40.00
9 Jerry West/25 50.00 120.00

2006-07 Press Pass Legends Naismith Award Winners
COMPLETE SET (10) 8.00 20.00
STATED ODDS 1:9
1 Pete Maravich 1.25 3.00
2 Bill Walton 1.00 2.50
3 David Thompson .60 1.50
4 Scott May .75 2.00
5 Larry Bird 2.50 6.00
6 Ralph Sampson .60 1.50
7 David Robinson 1.25 3.00
8 Danny Manning .60 1.50
9 Calbert Cheaney .75 2.00
10 J.J. Redick 1.50 4.00

2006-07 Press Pass Legends Naismith Award Winners Autographs
PRINT RUNS LISTED IN CL BELOW
2 Bill Walton/75 10.00 25.00
3 David Thompson/275 10.00 25.00
3F D.Thompson Red/20 12.00 30.00
4 Scott May/400 5.00 12.00
4A Scott May Red/34 6.00 15.00
6 Ralph Sampson/400 6.00 15.00
6B Ralph Sampson Red 8.00 20.00
7 David Robinson/50 30.00 80.00
8 Danny Manning/100 12.50 30.00
8B D.Manning Red/49 15.00 40.00
9 Calbert Cheaney/400 5.00 12.00
10 J.J. Redick/275 10.00 25.00
10A J.J. Redick Go Duke/24 12.00 30.00

2006-07 Press Pass Legends Naismith Award Winners Autographs Platinum
PRINT RUNS LISTED IN CL BELOW
2 Bill Walton 15.00 40.00
3 David Thompson 15.00 40.00
5 Larry Bird 100.00 200.00
7 David Robinson 60.00 150.00
8 Danny Manning 20.00 50.00
9 Calbert Cheaney 8.00 20.00

2006-07 Press Pass Legends Saturday Swatches
APPROXIMATE ODDS ONE PER BOX
*PRIME: .6X TO 1.25X BASE HI
PRIME PRINT RUN 50 SER.#'d SETS
1 Ronnie Brewer 3.00 8.00
2 David Lee 2.00 5.00
3 Rodney Carney 2.00 5.00
4 Shannon Brown 2.00 5.00
5 Danny Granger 2.00 5.00
6 Sean May 2.00 5.00
7 LaMarcus Aldridge 6.00 15.00
8 Rudy Gay 4.00 10.00
9 Kyle Lowry 10.00 25.00
10 Chris Paul 6.00 15.00
11 Brandon Roy 6.00 15.00

2006-07 Press Pass Legends Signatures
APPROXIMATELY TWO TO THREE PER BOX
1 LaMarcus Aldridge 8.00 20.00
2 L.Aldridge Red/25 8.00 20.00
3 Steve Alford 6.00 15.00
5 Alford Red 1987 Champs/25 15.00 40.00
6 Hilton Armstrong 2.50 6.00
9 Stacey Augmon 4.00 10.00
11 Rick Barry 10.00 25.00
12 R.Barry Go Canes/24 20.00 50.00
13 Rick Barry Red/30 12.50 30.00
14 Henry Bibby 4.00 10.00
19 Henry Bibby Red/22 6.00 15.00
20 Jay Bilas 4.00 10.00
21 Bilas 21 1986 37-3/51 10.00 25.00
23 Bilas '86 37-3/21 15.00 40.00
51 Larry Bird 40.00 100.00
53 Ronnie Brewer 4.00 10.00
55 Calbert Cheaney 4.00 10.00
59 Adrian Dantley 6.00 15.00
60 Brad Daugherty 4.00 10.00
61 Daugherty Go Heels/35 8.00 20.00
62 Daugherty Red Go Heels/24 20.00 50.00
63 Clyde Drexler 12.50 30.00
64 Eric Sleepy Floyd 4.00 10.00
66 Eric Sleepy Floyd/16 10.00 25.00
67 Eric Sleepy Floyd Red/54 8.00 20.00
68 Randy Foye 3.00 8.00
69 R.Foye Foyeboy/25 10.00 25.00
70 Randy Foye Red/24 10.00 25.00
71 Walt Frazier 8.00 20.00
75 Rudy Gay 5.00 12.00
78 A.C. Green 4.00 10.00
79 A.C. Green 45/80 6.00 15.00
80 A.C. Green Red/25 8.00 20.00
83 John Havlicek 12.50 30.00
86 Connie Hawkins 8.00 20.00
87 C.Hawkins Go Hawkeyes/24 20.00 50.00
89 Elvin Hayes 4.00 10.00
90 Elvin Hayes Red/25 8.00 20.00
91 Hayes Red The Big E/25 15.00 40.00
92 Lou Hudson 4.00 10.00
93 Lou Hudson Red/28 10.00 25.00
94 Dan Issel 4.00 10.00
97 Bernard King 6.00 15.00
98 Bill Laimbeer 6.00 15.00
99 B.Laimbeer 1978 Final 4/25 20.00 50.00
100 B.Laimbeer Red/25 20.00 50.00
101 Danny Manning 12.00 30.00
104 Scott May Red 4.00 10.00
105 Sidney Moncrief 4.00 10.00
107 Moncrief Go Hogs/22 12.50 30.00
108 Moncrief Red/30 6.00 15.00
109 Adam Morrison 8.00 20.00
110 A.Morrison Go Zags/37 15.00 30.00
112 Larry Nance 4.00 10.00
114 Larry Nance Red/32 6.00 15.00
116 Hakeem Olajuwon 15.00 40.00
117 Sam Perkins 8.00 20.00
118 Digger Phelps 8.00 20.00
119 D.Phelps Go Irish/25 10.00 25.00
121 J.J. Redick 12.50 30.00
122 Pat Riley 12.50 30.00
123 David Robinson 30.00 75.00
124 D.Robinson Red/24 75.00 150.00
125 Rajon Rondo 12.00 30.00
126 Brandon Roy 8.00 20.00
128 Brandon Roy Red/25 15.00 40.00
129 Ralph Sampson 6.00 15.00
130 R.Sampson Red/86 8.00 20.00
131 Kenny Smith 8.00 20.00
132 Kenny Smith Jet/20 12.50 30.00
133 Kenny Smith Red/69 8.00 20.00
135 K.Smith Red Jet/26 8.00 20.00
136 Dean Smith 75.00 150.00
138 Jerry Tarkanian 10.00 25.00
142 Tarkanian Red/23 15.00 40.00
143 Diana Taurasi 8.00 20.00
145 Reggie Theus 4.00 10.00
148 Isiah Thomas 10.00 25.00
150 Tyrus Thomas 3.00 8.00
151 Thomas T-Time Gx Trgs/25 10.00 25.00
153 David Thompson 10.00 25.00
162 Nate Thurmond 4.00 10.00
163 Thurmond Red/25 10.00 25.00
165 Wes Unseld 4.00 10.00
168 Bill Walton 15.00 40.00
169 Bill Walton Red/17 15.00 40.00
170 Spud Webb 5.00 12.00
171 Jerry West 20.00 50.00
175 Jo Jo White 6.00 15.00
176 Jo Jo White Red/24 12.50 30.00
178 Dominique Wilkins 15.00 40.00
179 D.Wilkins Rd/24 25.00 60.00
181 Shelden Williams 2.50 6.00
185 John Wooden 75.00 150.00
186 John Wooden UCLA/25 75.00 150.00

2007-08 Press Pass Legends
COMPLETE SET (70) 20.00 40.00
1 Jared Dudley .60 1.50
2 Jason Smith .50 1.25
3 Josh McRoberts .50 1.25
4 Taurean Green .50 1.25
5 Javaris Crittenton .50 1.25
6 Glen Davis .60 1.50
7 Nick Fazekas .50 1.25
8 Aaron Gray .50 1.25
9 Morris Almond .50 1.25
10 Acie Law .50 1.25
11 Aaron Afflalo .60 1.50
12 Brandan Wright .60 1.50
13 Nick Young .75 2.00
14 Gabe Pruitt .50 1.25
15 Spencer Hawes .50 1.25
16 Sean Elliott .60 1.50
17 Lafette Lever .60 1.50
18 Byron Scott .60 1.50
19 Robert Parish .75 2.00
20 Scottie Pippen 1.25 3.00
21 Dan Majerle .60 1.50
22 Tree Rollins .50 1.25
23 Sue Bird 2.50 6.00
24 Jay Bilas .75 2.00
25 Bobby Hurley .75 2.00
26 George Gervin 1.00 2.50
27 Dominique Wilkins 1.25 3.00
28 Kenny Anderson .60 1.50
29 Willis Reed 1.25 3.00
30 Larry Bird 3.00 8.00
31 Artis Gilmore .60 1.50
32 JoJo White .60 1.50
33 Rolando Blackman .60 1.50
34 Dan Issel .60 1.50
35 Pete Maravich 2.00 5.00
36 Joe Dumars .75 2.00
37 Hal Greer 1.00 2.50
38 Rick Barry .60 1.50
39 Glen Rice .75 2.00
40 David Robinson 1.50 4.00
41 Michael Cooper .75 2.00
42 Calvin Murphy .60 1.50
43 John Paxson .75 2.00
44 John Havlicek 1.50 4.00
45 Jerry Lucas .75 2.00
46 A.C. Green .60 1.50
47 Lenny Wilkens .75 2.00
48 Bill Russell 2.50 6.00
49 Elgin Baylor .75 2.00
50 Alex English .60 1.50
51 Dick McGuire .75 2.00
52 Sherman Douglas .75 2.00
53 Henry Bibby .50 1.25
54 Bill Walton 1.00 2.50
55 Kiki Vandeweghe .60 1.50
56 Phil Ford .75 2.00
57 George Karl .75 2.00
58 Sam Perkins .60 1.50
59 Kenny Smith .60 1.50
60 James Worthy 1.25 3.00
61 Stacey Augmon .50 1.25
62 Larry Johnson 1.00 2.50
63 Jerry Tarkanian .75 2.00
64 Gus Williams .50 1.25
65 Nate Archibald .60 1.50
66 Muggsy Bogues .60 1.50
67 Detlef Schrempf .75 2.00
68 Earl Monroe .75 2.00
69 Jerry West 2.00 5.00
70 Tarkanian/L.Johnson/S.Augmon 1.00 2.50

2007-08 Press Pass Legends Bronze
*BRONZE: .5X TO 1.25X BASE HI
BRONZE PRINT RUN 899 SER.#'d SETS

2007-08 Press Pass Legends Emerald
*EMERALD: 2.5X TO 6X BASE HI
PRINT RUN 25 SER.#'d SETS

2007-08 Press Pass Legends Gold
*GOLD: 1.25X TO 3X BASE HI
GOLD PRINT RUN 99 SER.#'d SETS

2007-08 Press Pass Legends Silver
*SILVER: .6X TO 1.5X BASE HI
PRINT RUN 499 SER.#'d SETS

2007-08 Press Pass Legends All-American
COMPLETE SET (11) 8.00 20.00
STATED ODDS 1:9
1 Sean Elliott .60 1.50
2 Larry Bird 3.00 8.00
3 Glen Davis .60 1.50
4 Pete Maravich 2.00 5.00
5 David Robinson 1.50 4.00
6 John Paxson .75 2.00
7 Acie Law .50 1.25
8 Aaron Afflalo .60 1.50
9 James Worthy 1.25 3.00
10 Larry Johnson 1.00 2.50
11 Nick Fazekas .50 1.25

2007-08 Press Pass Legends All-American Autographs
PRINT RUNS LISTED IN CHECKLIST
EXCH EXPIRATION DATE 10/1/08
1 Sean Elliott/258 10.00 25.00
2 Larry Bird/50 125.00 300.00
3 Glen Davis/255 5.00 12.00
6 John Paxson/236 12.00 30.00
6A John Paxson Red/23 25.00 60.00
7 Acie Law/245 6.00 15.00
8 Aaron Afflalo/232 5.00 12.00
9 James Worthy/25 40.00 100.00
10 Larry Johnson 25.00 60.00
11 Nick Fazekas 4.00 10.00
11A Nick Fazekas Red/31 5.00 12.00

2007-08 Press Pass Legends Alumni Association
COMPLETE SET (10) 10.00 25.00
STATED ODDS 1:9
1 L.Lever/B.Scott .60 1.50
2 B.Hurley/J.McRoberts .75 2.00
3 K.Anderson/J.Crittenton .60 1.50
4 P.Maravich/G.Davis 2.00 5.00
5 J.Lucas/J.Havlicek 1.50 4.00
6 H.Bibby/K.Vandeweghe .60 1.50
7 J.Worthy/B.Wright 1.25 3.00
8 L.Johnson/S.Augmon 1.00 2.50
9 N.Young/G.Williams .75 2.00
10 D.Schrempf/S.Hawes .75 2.00

2007-08 Press Pass Legends Alumni Association Autographs
PRINT RUNS LISTED IN CHECKLIST
1 L.Lever/B.Scott/50 15.00 30.00
2 B.Hurley/J.McRoberts/48 15.00 30.00
3 K.Anderson/J.Crittenton/45 10.00 25.00
6 H.Bibby/K.Vandeweghe 10.00 25.00
7 J.Worthy/B.Wright 12.00 30.00
8 L.Johnson/S.Augmon 25.00 50.00
9 N.Young/G.Williams/46 10.00 25.00
SBDT S.Bird/D.Taurasi/25 150.00 400.00

2007-08 Press Pass Legends Center Court Cuts
PRINT RUNS LISTED IN CHECKLIST
2 Bill Russell/53 600.00 1,200.00
2A Bill Russell Red/13 1,000.00 2,000.00
2B Bill Russell Red #6/19 1,000.00 2,000.00

2007-08 Press Pass Legends Legendary Legacy
COMPLETE SET (10) 8.00 20.00
STATED ODDS 1:9
1 Robert Parish 1.00 2.50
2 Scottie Pippen 1.50 4.00
3 Willis Reed 1.50 4.00
4 Larry Bird 4.00 10.00
5 Joe Dumars 1.00 2.50
6 David Robinson 2.00 5.00
7 Elgin Baylor 1.00 2.50
8 James Worthy 1.50 4.00
9 Nate Archibald .75 2.00
10 Earl Monroe 1.00 2.50

2007-08 Press Pass Legends Legendary Legacy Marks
PRINT RUNS LISTED IN CHECKLIST
1 Robert Parish Red/265 8.00 20.00
2 Scottie Pippen/35 60.00 150.00
2A Scottie Pippen Red/50 60.00 150.00
3 Willis Reed/100 40.00 100.00
4 Larry Bird/50 40.00 80.00
5 Joe Dumars/25 8.00 20.00
7 Elgin Baylor/129 15.00 30.00
8 James Worthy/50 20.00 40.00
9 Nate Archibald/24 8.00 20.00
10 Earl Monroe/42 10.00 25.00
10B Earl Monroe Red/50 10.00 25.00

2007-08 Press Pass Legends Select Swatches
APPROXIMATELY 1:18 PACKS
*PREMIUM: .5X TO 1.25X BASE HI
PREMIUM PRINT RUN 50 SER.#'d SETS
PATCH PRINT RUN 10 SER.#'d SETS
1 Rudy Gay 2.50 6.00
2 Nick Fazekas 2.00 5.00
3 LaMarcus Aldridge 3.00 8.00
4 Acie Law 2.00 5.00
5 Brandan Wright 2.50 6.00
6 Nick Young 3.00 8.00
7 Brandon Roy 4.00 10.00

2007-08 Press Pass Legends Signatures
APPROXIMATELY FOUR PER BOX
EXCHANGE EXPIRATION 10/1/08
1 Arron Afflalo 5.00 12.00
4 Morris Almond 4.00 10.00
5 Morris Almond Go Rice/25 6.00 15.00
6 Kenny Anderson 5.00 12.00
7 Kenny Anderson Red/48 6.00 15.00
9 Nate Archibald 5.00 12.00
10 Nate Archibald Red/25 15.00 30.00
11 Stacey Augmon 4.00 10.00
13 Stacey Augmon Red/68 6.00 15.00
14 Rick Barry 6.00 15.00
15 Rick Barry Go Canes/35 15.00 30.00
16 Rick Barry Red/40 15.00 30.00
17 Elgin Baylor 40.00 100.00
18 Henry Bibby 4.00 10.00
22 Jay Bilas 10.00 25.00
23 J.Bilas ESPN Duke 21/39 15.00 40.00
34 Jay Bilas Red/62 20.00 50.00
35 Larry Bird 125.00 300.00
36 Sue Bird 50.00 120.00
38 Sue Bird Red 60.00 150.00
39 Rolando Blackman 6.00 15.00
40 R.Blackman Ro Silk/38 20.00 40.00
41 Rolando Blackman Red/25 25.00 50.00
42 Muggsy Bogues 6.00 15.00
43 M.Bogues Go Deacs/26 25.00 50.00
44 Muggsy Bogues Red/52 10.00 25.00
46 Michael Cooper 4.00 10.00
49 Michael Cooper Red 6.00 15.00
51 Javaris Crittenton 4.00 10.00
52 Javaris Crittenton Red/158 5.00 12.00
53 Glen Davis 6.00 15.00
54 Sherman Douglas 4.00 10.00
56 Sherman Douglas Red/82 5.00 12.00
57 Jared Dudley 4.00 10.00
58 Joe Dumars 6.00 15.00
59 Sean Elliott 5.00 12.00
62 Alex English 4.00 10.00
64 Alex English Red 6.00 15.00
69 Phil Ford 10.00 25.00
72 George Gervin 12.00 30.00
74 George Gervin Red/45 20.00 50.00
75 Artis Gilmore 5.00 12.00
76 Artis Gilmore A-Train/199 12.00 30.00
78 Artis Gilmore Red/186 10.00 25.00
79 A.Gilmore Red A-Train/74 15.00 40.00
81 Aaron Gray 4.00 10.00
84 Hal Greer 20.00 50.00
85 Hal Greer Go Herd/25 50.00 120.00
86 Hal Greer Red/50 30.00 80.00
87 Spencer Hawes 4.00 10.00
91 Spencer Hawes Red/50 5.00 12.00
92 Bobby Hurley 12.00 30.00
94 Bobby Hurley Red/46 20.00 50.00
95 Dan Issel 6.00 15.00
96 Dan Issel The Horse/25 30.00 60.00
98 Larry Johnson 8.00 20.00
99 George Karl 12.00 30.00
103 George Karl Red/57 20.00 50.00
104 Lafayette Lever 6.00 15.00
105 Lafayette Lever Fat/25 25.00 50.00
106 L.Lever Red Fat/50 15.00 30.00
107 Jerry Lucas 10.00 25.00
108 Jerry Lucas Go Bucks/25 30.00 60.00
109 Jerry Lucas Red/50 15.00 30.00
110 Dan Majerle 8.00 20.00
111 Dan Majerle Thunder/25 30.00 80.00
112 Dan Majerle Red/50 15.00 40.00
113 Dick McGuire 6.00 15.00
114 Dick McGuire Red/50 10.00 25.00
115 D.McGuire Red Tricky/25 15.00 40.00
116 Earl Monroe 12.00 30.00
117 Calvin Murphy 4.00 10.00
118 Calvin Murphy Red/50 6.00 15.00
120 Robert Parish 8.00 20.00
121 John Paxson 6.00 15.00
123 John Paxson Go Irish/14 20.00 40.00
125 Sam Perkins Smooth 6.00 15.00
127 Scottie Pippen 75.00 150.00
129 Willis Reed Go Tigers/25 75.00 200.00
130 Willis Reed Red/25 75.00 200.00
131 Glen Rice 41 5.00 12.00
133 David Robinson 25.00 50.00
137 Tree Rollins 4.00 10.00
140 Tree Rollins Red/46 5.00 12.00
141 Detlef Schrempf 8.00 20.00
142 D.Schrempf Go Huskies/25 25.00 50.00
144 Byron Scott 4.00 10.00
146 Byron Scott Red/100 15.00 30.00
147 Jason Smith 4.00 10.00
150 Jerry Tarkanian 12.00 30.00
154 Jerry Tarkanian Red/50 10.00 25.00
155 Lenny Wilkens 4.00 10.00
156 Lenny Wilkens Lefty/25 15.00 30.00
157 Lenny Wilkens Red/50 15.00 30.00
158 Dominique Wilkins 15.00 40.00
160 Dominique Wilkins Red/77 30.00 80.00
162 D.Wilk Red Hum.Hi.Film/23 40.00 100.00
163 Gus Williams 4.00 10.00
165 Gus Williams Red/50 5.00 12.00
166 James Worthy 25.00 60.00
167 Brandan Wright 6.00 15.00
168 Nick Young 6.00 15.00
169 Josh McRoberts 6.00 15.00

2007-08 Press Pass Legends Student and Teacher Signatures
SAJT S.Augmon/J.Tarkanian 25.00 60.00
SAJT L.Johnson/J.Tarkanian 30.00 80.00

2008-09 Press Pass Legends
COMPLETE SET (70) 12.00 30.00
1 Jerryd Bayless .50 1.25
2 Sonny Weems .40 1.00
3 Trent Plaisted .40 1.00
4 DeVon Hardin .40 1.00
5 Marreese Speights .50 1.25
6 Patrick Ewing Jr. .40 1.00
7 Roy Hibbert .50 1.25
8 Eric Gordon 1.00 2.50
9 D.J. White .40 1.00
10 Danilo Gallinari 1.00 2.50
11 Mario Chalmers .60 1.50

12 Darnell Jackson .40 1.00
13 Brandon Rush .40 1.00
14 Michael Beasley .60 1.50
15 Anthony Randolph .40 1.00
16 Joey Dorsey .40 1.00
17 Chris Douglas-Roberts .40 1.00
18 Derrick Rose 2.50 6.00
19 J.J. Hickson .40 1.00
20 J.R. Giddens .40 1.00
21 Kosta Koufos .40 1.00
22 Malik Hairston .40 1.00
23 Bryce Taylor .60 1.50
24 Brook Lopez .75 2.00
25 Robin Lopez .50 1.25
26 Chris Lofton .60 1.50
27 Candace Parker 1.50 4.00
28 D.J. Augustin .60 1.50
29 DeAndre Jordan .75 2.00
30 Kevin Love 1.25 3.00
31 Russell Westbrook 3.00 8.00
32 O.J. Mayo .50 1.25
33 Shan Foster .40 1.00
34 Courtney Lee .50 1.25
35 Sean Elliott .50 1.25
36 Sidney Moncrief .50 1.25
37 Corliss Williamson .40 1.00
38 Larry Nance .50 1.25
39 Bobby Hurley .60 1.50
40 Sleepy Floyd .40 1.00
41 Clyde Drexler .75 2.00
42 Calbert Cheaney .40 1.00
43 Larry Bird 2.00 5.00
44 Danny Manning .50 1.25
45 Rolando Blackman .50 1.25
46 Cliff Hagan .50 1.25
47 Darrell Griffith .40 1.00
48 Bailey Howell .60 1.50
49 David Robinson 1.25 3.00
50 Sidney Lowe .60 1.50
51 Michael Cooper .50 1.25
52 Calvin Murphy .50 1.25
53 Willis Reed 1.00 2.50
54 Brad Daugherty .50 1.25
55 Nate Archibald .50 1.25
56 James Worthy .60 1.50
57 Jerry Lucas .60 1.50
58 Elgin Baylor 1.00 2.50
59 Mark Jackson .50 1.25
60 Ernie Grunfeld .60 1.50
61 Bernard King .50 1.25
62 Henry Bibby .40 1.00
63 Gail Goodrich .50 1.25
64 Bill Walton 1.00 2.50
65 John Wooden .75 2.00
66 Stacey Augmon .40 1.00
67 Jerry Tarkanian .60 1.50
68 Gus Williams .40 1.00
69 Jerry West 1.25 3.00
70 UCLA CL .75 2.00

2008-09 Press Pass Legends Bronze
*BRONZE: .5X TO 1.25X BASE HI
BRONZE PRINT RUN 750 SER.#'d SETS

2008-09 Press Pass Legends Emerald
*EMERALD: 2X TO 5X BASE HI
EMERALD PRINT RUN 25 SETS

2008-09 Press Pass Legends Gold
*GOLD: .75X TO 2X BASE HI
GOLD PRINT RUN 99 SETS

2008-09 Press Pass Legends Silver
*SILVER: .6X TO 1.5X BASE HI
SILVER PRINT RUN 199 SETS

2008-09 Press Pass Legends All-American
COMPLETE SET (10) 10.00 25.00
STATED ODDS 1:9
1 Sidney Moncrief .75 2.00
2 Bobby Hurley 1.00 2.50
3 Larry Bird 3.00 8.00
4 Brandon Rush .60 1.50
5 Michael Beasley 1.00 2.50
6 Brad Daugherty .75 2.00
7 Derrick Rose 4.00 10.00
8 Candace Parker 2.50 6.00
9 D.J. Augustin 1.00 2.50
10 Kevin Love 2.00 5.00

2008-09 Press Pass Legends All-American Autographs
STATED PRINT RUN 30 TO 271 SER.#'d SETS
1 Sidney Moncrief/271 6.00 15.00
2 Bobby Hurley/195 10.00 25.00
3 Larry Bird/50 75.00 200.00
4 Brandon Rush/159 4.00 10.00
5 Michael Beasley/160 5.00 12.00
6 Brad Daugherty/210 5.00 12.00
7 Derrick Rose/165 40.00 100.00
8 Candace Parker/46 50.00 120.00
9 D.J. Augustin/105 6.00 15.00
10 Kevin Love/78 12.00 30.00
AACC Calbert Cheaney/266 4.00 10.00
AACW Corliss Williamson/165 4.00 10.00
AADG Darrell Griffith/270 8.00 20.00
AADM Danny Manning/169 8.00 20.00
AADR David Robinson/30 50.00 120.00

2008-09 Press Pass Legends All-American Autographs Platinum
STATED PRINT RUN ONE TO 25 SETS
7 Derrick Rose/25 75.00 200.00
8 Candace Parker/25 60.00 150.00
9 D.J. Augustin/25 12.00 30.00
10 Kevin Love/25 25.00 60.00
AADM Danny Manning/25 15.00 40.00
AADR David Robinson/25 60.00 150.00

2008-09 Press Pass Legends Alumni Association
COMPLETE SET (10) 6.00 15.00
STATED ODDS 1:9
1 S.Elliott/J.Bayless 1.50 4.00
2 S.Moncrief/C.Williamson 1.25 3.00
3 C.Cheaney/E.Gordon 1.50 4.00
4 D.Manning/B.Rush 1.50 4.00
5 J.Lucas/K.Koufos 1.25 3.00
7 G.Goodrich/R.Westbrook 2.00 5.00
6 B.Walton/K.Love 2.00 5.00
8 E.Grunfeld/B.King 1.50 4.00
9 R.Blackman/M.Beasley 2.00 5.00
10 G.Williams/O.Mayo 1.50 4.00

2008-09 Press Pass Legends Alumni Association Autographs
STATED PRINT RUN 38 TO 50 SER.#'d SETS
1 S.Elliott/J.Bayless/50 20.00 40.00
2 Moncrief/Williamson/49 10.00 25.00
3 Cheaney/E.Gordon/50 10.00 25.00
4 Manning/B.Rush/50 15.00 40.00
5 J.Lucas/Koufos/50 10.00 25.00
7 Goodrich/Westbrook/50 60.00 150.00
6 B.Walton/K.Love/50 25.00 60.00
9 Blackman/Beasley/49 20.00 50.00
10 G.Williams/Mayo/50 15.00 40.00
AABLRL B.Lopez/R.Lopez/38 20.00 40.00
AAJWBD Worthy/Daugherty/50 20.00 50.00
AAMCJG M.Cooper/Giddens/50 10.00 25.00
AASFRH S.Floyd/Hibbert/50 20.00 40.00

2008-09 Press Pass Legends Legendary Legacy
COMPLETE SET (10) 5.00 12.00
STATED ODDS 1:9
1 Clyde Drexler 1.25 3.00
2 Bobby Hurley 1.00 2.50
3 Larry Bird 3.00 8.00
4 Danny Manning .75 2.00
5 Bailey Howell 1.00 2.50
6 David Robinson 2.00 5.00
7 Calvin Murphy .75 2.00
8 Jerry Lucas 1.00 2.50
9 Gail Goodrich .75 2.00
10 Bill Walton 1.50 4.00

2008-09 Press Pass Legends Legendary Legacy Autographs
STATED PRINT RUN ONE TO 259 SETS
1 Clyde Drexler/98 20.00 50.00
2 Bobby Hurley/200 10.00 25.00
3 Larry Bird/50 40.00 100.00
4 Danny Manning/146 8.00 20.00
5 Bailey Howell/213 5.00 12.00
6 David Robinson/30 40.00 100.00
7 Calvin Murphy/255 5.00 12.00
8 Jerry Lucas/100 6.00 15.00
9 Gail Goodrich/160 5.00 12.00
10 Bill Walton/50 6.00 15.00
10B Bill Walton Red/25* 15.00 40.00
LLBD Brad Daugherty/210 5.00 12.00
LLCW Corliss Williamson/165 5.00 12.00
LLDG Darrell Griffith/259 5.00 12.00
LLJW Jerry West/102 20.00 50.00
LLJW2 Jerry West Red/26* 50.00 100.00
LLJWO James Worthy/50 20.00 50.00

2008-09 Press Pass Legends Legendary Legacy Autographs Platinum
STATED PRINT RUN 4 TO 25 SETS
1 Clyde Drexler 30.00 80.00
2 Bobby Hurley 12.50 30.00
3 Larry Bird 50.00 120.00
4 Danny Manning 10.00 25.00
5 Bailey Howell 10.00 25.00
6 David Robinson 50.00 100.00
7 Calvin Murphy 10.00 25.00
8 Jerry Lucas 10.00 25.00
9 Gail Goodrich/25 10.00 25.00
10 Bill Walton 15.00 40.00
LLBD Brad Daugherty 10.00 25.00
LLJW Jerry West 20.00 50.00
LLJWO James Worthy 25.00 60.00
LLJWO1 J.Worthy Big Game/25* 40.00 80.00

2008-09 Press Pass Legends Select Signatures
APPROX.THREE AU's PER MINI BOX
AR Anthony Randolph 4.00 10.00
AR1 A.Randolph Red/46* 5.00 12.00
BD Brad Daugherty 4.00 10.00
BH Bailey Howell 6.00 15.00
BH1 B.Howell Go Dawgs/25* 10.00 25.00
BH2 B.Howell Red/46* 8.00 20.00
BHU Bobby Hurley 10.00 25.00
BHU1 B.Hurley Go Duke/25* 75.00 150.00
BHU2 B.Hurley Red/46* 12.00 30.00
BK Bernard King 6.00 15.00
BK1 B.King Go Vols/18* 25.00 60.00
BK2 B.King Red/50* 8.00 20.00
BL Brook Lopez 8.00 20.00
BL2 B.Lopez Red/25* 8.00 20.00
BR Brandon Rush 4.00 10.00
BW Bill Walton 8.00 20.00
CC Calbert Cheaney 4.00 10.00
CC1 C.Cheaney Go Big Red/25* 6.00 15.00
CC2 C.Cheaney Red/50* 5.00 12.00
CD Clyde Drexler 15.00 40.00
CD1 C.Drexler The Glide/25* 60.00 120.00
CD2 C.Drexler Red/50* 10.00 25.00
CDR Chris Douglas-Roberts 4.00 10.00
CDR2 C.Douglas-Roberts Red/50* 5.00 12.00
CH Cliff Hagan 4.00 10.00
CH2 Cliff Hagen Red/51* 5.00 12.00
CL Courtney Lee 6.00 15.00
CM Calvin Murphy 4.00 10.00
CM1 Calvin Murphy Murph/25* 5.00 12.00
CM2 C.Murphy Red/49* 5.00 12.00
CP Candace Parker Red 30.00 80.00
CP1 C.Parker Blue Go Vols/2* 30.00 80.00
CW Corliss Williamson 4.00 10.00
CW1 C.Williamson Big Nasty/15* 8.00 20.00
DA D.J. Augustin 6.00 15.00
DG Darrell Griffith 4.00 10.00
DG2 D.Griffith Red/48* 6.00 15.00
DGA Danilo Gallinari 6.00 15.00
DGA2 D.Gallinari Red/13* 10.00 25.00
DJ DeAndre Jordan 8.00 20.00
DM Danny Manning 8.00 20.00
DM1 D.Manning Red/58* 10.00 25.00
DR David Robinson 20.00 40.00
DRO Derrick Rose 20.00 50.00
DRO1 D.Rose D.Pooh Rose/25* 40.00 100.00
DRO2 Derrick Rose Red/50* 50.00 100.00
DW D.J. White 4.00 10.00
DW1 D.White Red Go IU/25* 10.00 25.00
EB Elgin Baylor 10.00 25.00
EB1 E.Baylor Go Chieftains/25* 25.00 60.00
EB2 E.Baylor Red/50* 15.00 40.00
EG Eric Gordon 8.00 20.00
EG2 E.Gordon Red/46* 10.00 25.00
EGR Ernie Grunfeld 8.00 20.00
EGR1 E.Grunfeld Red/50* 10.00 25.00
GG Gail Goodrich 5.00 12.00
GW Gus Williams 4.00 10.00
GW2 G.Williams Red/125* 6.00 15.00
HB Henry Bibby 4.00 10.00
JB Jerryd Bayless 5.00 12.00
JB2 J.Bayless Red/50* 8.00 20.00
JD Joey Dorsey 4.00 10.00
JD1 J.Dorsey Red Hulk/47* 6.00 15.00
JG J.R. Giddens 4.00 10.00
JG1 J.Giddens Red/54* 5.00 12.00
JL Jerry Lucas 6.00 15.00
JT Jerry Tarkanian 6.00 15.00
JT1 Jerry Tarkanian Red/50* 8.00 20.00
JW Jerry West 25.00 50.00
JWD John Wooden 40.00 80.00
JWO James Worthy 15.00 30.00
JWO1 J.Worthy Red/59* 15.00 40.00
KK Kosta Koufos 4.00 10.00
KK2 Kosta Koufos Red/54* 6.00 15.00
KL Kevin Love Red 20.00 50.00
LB Larry Bird 30.00 60.00
LN Larry Nance 4.00 10.00
MB Michael Beasley 5.00 12.00
MB2 M.Beasley 27/30* 25.00 50.00
MB3 M. Beasley Red/25* 15.00 40.00
MC Michael Cooper 6.00 15.00
MJ Mark Jackson 5.00 12.00
MS Marreese Speights 4.00 10.00
OM O.J. Mayo 8.00 20.00
OM1 O.J. Mayo Red/39* 10.00 25.00
OM2 O.Mayo Red Juice/50* 20.00 40.00
RB Rolando Blackman 4.00 10.00
RB1 R.Blackman Go K-State/25* 10.00 25.00
RB2 Rolando Blackman Red/49* 6.00 15.00
RH Roy Hibbert 5.00 12.00
RL Robin Lopez 5.00 12.00
RL2 R.Lopez Red/48* 6.00 15.00
RW Russell Westbrook 75.00 200.00
RW2 R.Westbrook Red/25 125.00 300.00
SA Stacey Augmon 4.00 10.00
SA1 S.Augmon Plasticman/25* 15.00 30.00
SA2 S.Augmon Red/50* 6.00 15.00
SE Sean Elliott 4.00 10.00
SE1 S.Elliott Red/50* 8.00 20.00
SF Sleepy Floyd 4.00 10.00
SL Sidney Lowe 4.00 10.00
SM Sidney Moncrief 4.00 10.00
SM1 S.Moncrief Super Sid/25* 30.00 60.00

2008-09 Press Pass Legends Select Swatches
*PLATINUM: .6X TO 1.5X BASE
PLATINUM PRINT RUN 50 SER. #'d SETS
SSWAR Anthony Randolph 2.50 6.00
SSWBL Brook Lopez 2.50 6.00
SSWBR Brandon Rush 2.50 6.00
SSWDA D.J. Augustin 2.50 6.00
SSWDR Derrick Rose 4.00 10.00
SSWJD Joey Dorsey 2.50 6.00
SSWRH Roy Hibbert 1.50 4.00
SSWRL Robin Lopez 2.50 6.00
SSWRW Russell Westbrook 8.00 20.00

2008-09 Press Pass Legends Student and Teacher Signatures
PRINT RUN 25 SER.#'d SETS
STBWJW Walton/Wooden 125.00 300.00
STGGJW Goodrich/Wooden 60.00 150.00
STHBJW Bibby/Wooden 75.00 150.00

2009-10 Prestige
COMP.SET w/o RCs (150) 10.00 25.00
1 Joe Johnson .40 1.00
2 Josh Smith .25 .60
3 Mike Bibby .40 1.00
4 Jamal Crawford .40 1.00
5 Kevin Garnett 1.00 2.50
6 Paul Pierce .60 1.50
7 Ray Allen .60 1.50
8 Rajon Rondo .50 1.25
9 Gerald Wallace .30 .75
10 Boris Diaw .30 .75
11 Emeka Okafor .30 .75
12 Ben Gordon .30 .75
13 John Salmons .30 .75
14 Derrick Rose .60 1.50
15 Luol Deng .30 .75
16 LeBron James 3.00 8.00
17 Mo Williams .30 .75
18 Zydrunas Ilgauskas .30 .75
19 Delonte West .25 .60
20 Shaquille O'Neal 1.25 3.00
21 Dirk Nowitzki 1.00 2.50
22 Jason Terry .30 .75
23 Josh Howard .30 .75
24 Jason Kidd .60 1.50
25 Carmelo Anthony .60 1.50
26 Chauncey Billups .50 1.25
27 Nene .30 .75
28 Richard Hamilton .40 1.00
29 Allen Iverson .75 2.00
30 Tayshaun Prince .40 1.00
31 Rasheed Wallace .50 1.25
32 Stephen Jackson .30 .75
33 Corey Maggette .30 .75
34 Yao Ming 1.00 2.50
35 Tracy McGrady .75 2.00
36 Ron Artest .40 1.00
37 Luis Scola .30 .75
38 Danny Granger .25 .60
39 T.J. Ford .25 .60
40 Mike Dunleavy .25 .60
41 Marquis Daniels .25 .60
42 Zach Randolph .40 1.00
43 Al Thornton .25 .60
44 Eric Gordon .30 .75
45 Baron Davis .30 .75
46 Kobe Bryant 3.00 8.00
47 Pau Gasol .60 1.50
48 Lamar Odom .30 .75
49 Derek Fisher .40 1.00
50 O.J. Mayo .30 .75
51 Rudy Gay .40 1.00
52 Marc Gasol .40 1.00
53 Dwyane Wade .75 2.00
54 Jermaine O'Neal .40 1.00
55 Michael Beasley .25 .60
56 Udonis Haslem .25 .60
57 Michael Redd .30 .75
58 Charlie Villanueva .25 .60
59 Al Jefferson .25 .60
60 Ryan Gomes .25 .60
61 Kevin Love .40 1.00
62 Devin Harris .25 .60
63 Brook Lopez .40 1.00
64 Yi Jianlian .50 1.25
65 Chris Paul .75 2.00
66 David West .30 .75
67 Peja Stojakovic .30 .75
68 Rasual Butler .25 .60
69 Al Harrington .30 .75
70 Nate Robinson .30 .75
71 David Lee .25 .60
72 Larry Hughes .30 .75
73 Kevin Durant 1.50 4.00
74 Jeff Green .30 .75
75 Russell Westbrook .75 2.00
76 Dwight Howard .50 1.25
77 Rashard Lewis .30 .75
78 Hedo Turkoglu .30 .75
79 Jameer Nelson .25 .60
80 Vince Carter .75 2.00
81 Andre Iguodala .40 1.00
82 Andre Miller .40 1.00
83 Thaddeus Young .25 .60
84 Elton Brand .30 .75
85 Amare Stoudemire .40 1.00
86 Steve Nash .75 2.00
87 Jason Richardson .40 1.00
88 Brandon Roy .50 1.25
89 LaMarcus Aldridge .40 1.00
90 Greg Oden .25 .60
91 Kevin Martin .30 .75
92 Andres Nocioni .25 .60
93 Jason Thompson .25 .60
94 Tony Parker .60 1.50
95 Tim Duncan 1.00 2.50
96 Manu Ginobili .75 2.00
97 Michael Finley .40 1.00
98 Richard Jefferson .30 .75
99 Chris Bosh .50 1.25
100 Andrea Bargnani .25 .60
101 Shawn Marion .40 1.00
102 Deron Williams .50 1.25
103 Mehmet Okur .25 .60
104 Carlos Boozer .30 .75
105 Ronnie Brewer .25 .60
106 Antawn Jamison .30 .75
107 Caron Butler .30 .75
108 Nick Young .25 .60
109 Andray Blatche .25 .60
110 Randy Foye .25 .60
111 Kareem Abdul-Jabbar 2.00 5.00
112 Bob Dandridge .40 1.00
113 Alvan Adams .40 1.00
114 A.C. Green .60 1.50
115 Dave Bing .75 2.00
116 Larry Bird 2.50 6.00
117 Nate Thurmond .50 1.25
118 Michael Cooper .60 1.50
119 Bob Cousy 1.50 4.00
120 Adrian Dantley .50 1.25
121 Darryl Dawkins .60 1.50
122 Clyde Drexler 1.00 2.50
123 Elvin Hayes 1.00 2.50
124 Walt Frazier 1.00 2.50
125 World B. Free .50 1.25
126 George Gervin .75 2.00
127 Gail Goodrich .60 1.50
128 Tim Hardaway .60 1.50
129 Connie Hawkins .75 2.00
130 K.C. Jones .60 1.50
131 Bernard King .75 2.00
132 Bob Lanier .75 2.00
133 Dan Majerle .50 1.25
134 Karl Malone .75 2.00
135 Sam Perkins .40 1.00
136 Slick Watts .40 1.00
137 Bob McAdoo .75 2.00
138 Xavier McDaniel .40 1.00
139 Sidney Moncrief .50 1.25
140 Robert Parish .75 2.00
141 Oscar Robertson .75 2.00
142 Paul Silas .60 1.50
143 Moses Malone 1.00 2.50
144 Dennis Rodman 1.25 3.00
145 Bill Russell 2.00 5.00
146 Bill Bradley .75 2.00
147 Bill Walton 1.00 2.50
148 Spud Webb .50 1.25
149 Cedric Ceballos .40 1.00
150 Jerry West 1.00 2.50
151 Blake Griffin RC 4.00 10.00
152 Hasheem Thabeet RC .60 1.50
153 James Harden RC 6.00 15.00
154 Tyreke Evans RC .75 2.00
155 Blake Griffin College RC 4.00 10.00
156 Jonny Flynn RC .60 1.50
157 Stephen Curry RC 75.00 200.00
158 Jordan Hill RC .60 1.50
159 DeMar DeRozan RC 6.00 15.00
160 Brandon Jennings SP 10.00 25.00
161 Terrence Williams RC .60 1.50
162 Gerald Henderson RC .60 1.50
163 Tyler Hansbrough SP 10.00 25.00
164 Earl Clark RC .60 1.50
165 Austin Daye RC .60 1.50
166 James Johnson RC .75 2.00
167 Jrue Holiday RC 3.00 8.00
168 Ty Lawson RC .75 2.00
169 Jeff Teague RC .75 2.00
170 Eric Maynor RC .75 2.00
171 Darren Collison RC 1.00 2.50
172 Hasheem Thabeet UConn RC .60 1.50
173 Omri Casspi RC .60 1.50
174 B.J. Mullens RC .60 1.50
175 Rodrigue Beaubois RC .60 1.50
176 Taj Gibson SP 8.00 20.00
177 DeMarre Carroll SP 6.00 15.00
178 Wayne Ellington RC .75 2.00
179 Toney Douglas RC .60 1.50
180 Tyreke Evans Memphis RC .75 2.00
181 Jeff Pendergraph RC .60 1.50
182 Jermaine Taylor RC .60 1.50
183 Dante Cunningham RC .60 1.50
184 DaJuan Summers RC .60 1.50
185 Sam Young RC .60 1.50
186 DeJuan Blair RC .75 2.00
187 Jon Brockman RC .60 1.50
188 Derrick Brown RC .60 1.50
189 Jodie Meeks RC .60 1.50
190 Jonas Jerebko SP 5.00 12.00
191 Marcus Thornton RC .75 2.00
192 Chase Budinger RC .60 1.50
193 Goran Suton RC .60 1.50
194 Danny Green RC 1.00 2.50
195 Taylor Griffin RC .60 1.50
196 A.J. Price RC .60 1.50
197 Jrue Holiday UCLA RC 3.00 8.00
198 Lester Hudson RC .60 1.50
199 Jack McClinton RC .60 1.50
200 Patrick Beverley RC 1.00 2.50
201 Blake Griffin RC 4.00 10.00
202 Hasheem Thabeet RC .60 1.50
203 James Harden RC 6.00 15.00
204 Tyreke Evans RC .75 2.00
205 Jordan Hill Arizona SP 8.00 20.00
206 Jonny Flynn RC .60 1.50
207 Stephen Curry RC 75.00 200.00
208 Jordan Hill RC .60 1.50
209 DeMar DeRozan RC 6.00 15.00
210 Brandon Jennings RC 1.00 2.50
211 Terrence Williams RC .60 1.50
212 Gerald Henderson RC .60 1.50
213 Tyler Hansbrough RC .75 2.00
214 Earl Clark RC .60 1.50
215 Austin Daye RC .60 1.50
216 James Johnson RC .75 2.00
217 Jrue Holiday RC 3.00 8.00
218 Ty Lawson SP 8.00 20.00
219 Jeff Teague RC .75 2.00
220 Eric Maynor SP 6.00 15.00
221 Darren Collison RC 1.00 2.50
222 Tyler Hansbrough RC .75 2.00
223 Omri Casspi RC .60 1.50
224 B.J. Mullens RC .60 1.50
225 Rodrigue Beaubois RC .60 1.50
226 Taj Gibson RC .75 2.00
227 DeMarre Carroll RC .75 2.00
228 Wayne Ellington RC .75 2.00
229 Toney Douglas RC .60 1.50
230 Stephen Curry Davidson RC 75.00 200.00
231 Jeff Pendergraph RC .60 1.50
232 Jermaine Taylor RC .60 1.50
233 Dante Cunningham SP 5.00 12.00
234 DaJuan Summers RC .60 1.50
235 Sam Young RC .60 1.50
236 DeJuan Blair RC .75 2.00
237 Jon Brockman RC .60 1.50
238 Derrick Brown RC .60 1.50
239 Jodie Meeks RC .60 1.50
240 Jonas Jerebko RC .75 2.00
241 Marcus Thornton RC .75 2.00
242 Chase Budinger RC .75 2.00
243 Goran Suton RC .60 1.50
244 Danny Green RC 1.00 2.50
245 Taylor Griffin RC .60 1.50
246 A.J. Price RC .60 1.50
247 James Johnson Wake SP 6.00 15.00
248 Lester Hudson RC .60 1.50
249 Jack McClinton RC .60 1.50
250 Patrick Beverley RC 1.00 2.50
251 Wesley Matthews RC* 1.00 2.50
252 Patrick Mills RC* 1.50 4.00
253 Serge Ibaka RC* 1.00 2.50
254 Marcus Landry RC* .60 1.50
255 Sundiata Gaines RC* .60 1.50
251A Wesley Matthews AU* 5.00 12.00
252A Patrick Mills AU* 12.00 30.00
253A Serge Ibaka AU* 5.00 12.00
254A Marcus Landry AU* 3.00 8.00
255A Sundiata Gaines AU* 3.00 8.00

2009-10 Prestige Bonus Shots Black Signatures
STATED PRINT RUN 25 TO 250 SER.#'d SETS
ASTERISK CARDS FROM PANINI UPDATE
46 Kobe Bryant/25 1,000.00 2,000.00
120 Adrian Dantley/100 5.00 12.00
124 Walt Frazier/100 10.00 25.00
129 Connie Hawkins/100 8.00 20.00
137 Bob McAdoo/50 15.00 30.00
139 Sidney Moncrief/100 5.00 12.00
141 Oscar Robertson/50 20.00 50.00
145 Bill Russell/50 300.00 6,000.00
147 Bill Walton/50 10.00 25.00
151 Blake Griffin/25 75.00 200.00
153 James Harden/25 150.00 400.00
154 Tyreke Evans/25 5.00 12.00
155 Blake Griffin/25 75.00 200.00
157 Stephen Curry/25 1,500.00 3,000.00
158 Jordan Hill/25 4.00 10.00
160 Brandon Jennings/25 6.00 15.00
161 Terrence Williams/25 4.00 10.00
162 Gerald Henderson/25 4.00 10.00
163 Tyler Hansbrough/25 5.00 12.00
164 Earl Clark/25 4.00 10.00
165 Austin Daye/25 4.00 10.00
166 James Johnson/25 5.00 12.00
167 Jrue Holiday/25 15.00 40.00
169 Jeff Teague/25 5.00 12.00
171 Darren Collison/50 6.00 15.00
173 Omri Casspi/50 5.00 12.00
174 B.J. Mullens/50 4.00 10.00
175 Rodrigue Beaubois/50 4.00 10.00
176 Taj Gibson/50 5.00 12.00
177 DeMarre Carroll/50 5.00 12.00
179 Toney Douglas/50 4.00 10.00
180 Tyreke Evans/50 5.00 12.00
182 Jermaine Taylor/100 4.00 10.00
183 Dante Cunningham/100 4.00 10.00
186 DeJuan Blair/100 5.00 12.00
188 Derrick Brown/100 4.00 10.00
189 Jodie Meeks/100 4.00 10.00
191 Marcus Thornton/100 5.00 12.00
192 Chase Budinger/100 4.00 10.00
193 Goran Suton/100 4.00 10.00
194 Danny Green/100 20.00 50.00
197 Jrue Holiday/25 15.00 40.00
199 Jack McClinton/100 4.00 10.00
201 Blake Griffin/25 75.00 200.00
202 Hasheem Thabeet/25 4.00 10.00
203 James Harden/25 150.00 400.00
204 Tyreke Evans/25 12.00 30.00
205 Jordan Hill/25 4.00 10.00
207 Stephen Curry/25 1,500.00 3,000.00
208 Jordan Hill/25 4.00 10.00
210 Brandon Jennings/25 6.00 15.00
211 Terrence Williams/25 4.00 10.00
212 Gerald Henderson/25 4.00 10.00
213 Tyler Hansbrough/25 5.00 12.00
214 Earl Clark/25 4.00 10.00
216 James Johnson/25 5.00 12.00
217 Jrue Holiday/25 15.00 40.00
219 Jeff Teague/25 5.00 12.00
221 Darren Collison/50 6.00 15.00
222 Tyler Hansbrough/25 5.00 12.00
223 Omri Casspi/50 4.00 10.00
224 B.J. Mullens/50 4.00 10.00
225 Rodrigue Beaubois/50 4.00 10.00
226 Taj Gibson/50 5.00 12.00
227 DeMarre Carroll/50 5.00 12.00
229 Toney Douglas/50 4.00 10.00
230 Stephen Curry/25 1,500.00 3,000.00
231 Jeff Pendergraph/100 4.00 10.00
232 Jermaine Taylor/100 4.00 10.00
233 Dante Cunningham/100 4.00 10.00
236 DeJuan Blair/100 5.00 12.00
238 Derrick Brown/100 4.00 10.00
239 Jodie Meeks/100 4.00 10.00
241 Marcus Thornton/100 5.00 12.00
242 Chase Budinger/100 4.00 10.00
243 Goran Suton/100 4.00 10.00
244 Danny Green/100 20.00 50.00
246 A.J. Price/100 4.00 10.00
247 James Johnson/50 5.00 12.00
249 Jack McClinton/100 4.00 10.00
251 Wesley Matthews/250* 6.00 15.00
252 Patrick Mills/250* 12.00 30.00
253 Serge Ibaka/250* 6.00 15.00
254 Marcus Landry/250* 4.00 10.00
255 Sundiata Gaines/250* 4.00 10.00

2009-10 Prestige Bonus Shots Green
*GREEN 1-150: 3X TO 8X BASE HI
*GREEN 151-250: 1.5X TO 4X BASE HI
STATED PRINT RUN 25 SER.#'d SETS
SP CARDS SAME VALUE AS NON SP
29 Allen Iverson 6.00 15.00
157 Stephen Curry 400.00 800.00
159 DeMar DeRozan 60.00 150.00
207 Stephen Curry 400.00 800.00
209 DeMar DeRozan 60.00 150.00
230 Stephen Curry 400.00 800.00

2009-10 Prestige Bonus Shots Orange
*ORANGE 1-150: .75X TO 2X BASE HI
*ORANGE 151-250: .6X TO 1.5X BASE HI
STATED PRINT RUN 300 SER.#'d SETS
SP CARDS SAME VALUE AS NON SP
157 Stephen Curry 150.00 400.00
159 DeMar DeRozan 15.00 40.00
207 Stephen Curry 150.00 400.00
209 DeMar DeRozan 15.00 40.00
230 Stephen Curry 150.00 400.00

2009-10 Prestige Draft Picks Light Blue
*BLUE: .4X TO 1X BASE HI
PRINT RUN 999 SER.#'d SETS
SP CARDS SAME VALUE AS NON SP
153 James Harden 8.00 20.00
157 Stephen Curry 100.00 250.00
159 DeMar DeRozan 10.00 25.00
207 Stephen Curry 100.00 250.00
209 DeMar DeRozan 10.00 25.00
230 Stephen Curry 100.00 250.00

2009-10 Prestige Draft Picks Light Blue Autographs
STATED PRINT RUN 50 TO 699 SER.#'d SETS
151 Blake Griffin/50 60.00 150.00
153 James Harden/100 150.00 400.00
154 Tyreke Evans/50 3.00 8.00
155 Blake Griffin/50 60.00 150.00
157 Stephen Curry/100 800.00 1,500.00
158 Jordan Hill/50 2.50 6.00
160 Brandon Jennings/100 4.00 10.00
161 Terrence Williams/100 2.50 6.00
162 Gerald Henderson/50 2.50 6.00
163 Tyler Hansbrough/100 3.00 8.00
164 Earl Clark/100 2.50 6.00
165 Austin Daye/100 2.50 6.00
166 James Johnson/50 3.00 8.00
167 Jrue Holiday/100 12.00 30.00
169 Jeff Teague/100 3.00 8.00
171 Darren Collison/399 4.00 10.00
173 Omri Casspi/499 2.50 6.00
174 B.J. Mullens/499 2.50 6.00
175 Rodrigue Beaubois/499 2.50 6.00
176 Taj Gibson/499 3.00 8.00
177 DeMarre Carroll/499 2.50 6.00
179 Toney Douglas/399 2.50 6.00
180 Tyreke Evans/50 3.00 8.00
181 Jeff Pendergraph/399 2.50 6.00
182 Jermaine Taylor/699 2.50 6.00
183 Dante Cunningham/699 2.50 6.00
186 DeJuan Blair/699 3.00 8.00
188 Derrick Brown/699 2.50 6.00
189 Jodie Meeks/699 2.50 6.00
191 Marcus Thornton/699 3.00 8.00
192 Chase Budinger/699 2.50 6.00
193 Goran Suton/699 2.50 6.00
194 Danny Green/499 4.00 10.00
196 A.J. Price/699 2.50 6.00
197 Jrue Holiday/100 12.00 30.00
199 Jack McClinton/699 2.50 6.00
201 Blake Griffin/50 40.00 100.00
203 James Harden/100 150.00 400.00
204 Tyreke Evans/50 3.00 8.00
205 Jordan Hill/50 2.50 6.00
207 Stephen Curry/100 800.00 1,500.00
208 Jordan Hill/25 2.50 6.00
210 Brandon Jennings/100 4.00 10.00
211 Terrence Williams/100 2.50 6.00
212 Gerald Henderson/50 2.50 6.00
213 Tyler Hansbrough/100 3.00 8.00
214 Earl Clark/100 2.50 6.00
215 Austin Daye/100 2.50 6.00
216 James Johnson/50 3.00 8.00
217 Jrue Holiday/100 12.00 30.00
219 Jeff Teague/100 3.00 8.00
221 Darren Collison/399 4.00 10.00
222 Tyler Hansbrough/100 3.00 8.00
223 Omri Casspi/499 2.50 6.00
224 B.J. Mullens/499 2.50 6.00
225 Rodrigue Beaubois/499 2.50 6.00
226 Taj Gibson/499 3.00 8.00
227 DeMarre Carroll/499 3.00 8.00
229 Toney Douglas/399 2.50 6.00
230 Stephen Curry/100 800.00 1,500.00
231 Jeff Pendergraph/100 2.50 6.00
232 Jermaine Taylor/699 2.50 6.00
233 Dante Cunningham/699 2.50 6.00
236 DeJuan Blair/699 3.00 8.00
238 Derrick Brown/699 2.50 6.00
239 Jodie Meeks/699 2.50 6.00
241 Marcus Thornton/699 3.00 8.00
242 Chase Budinger/699 2.50 6.00
243 Goran Suton/499 2.50 6.00
244 Danny Green/499 4.00 10.00
246 A.J. Price/699 2.50 6.00
247 James Johnson/50 3.00 8.00
249 Jack McClinton/699 2.50 6.00

2009-10 Prestige Connections
COMPLETE SET (10) 10.00 25.00
1 L.Walton/J.Hill .75 2.00
2 Y.Ming/S.Yue 2.50 6.00
3 Y.Ming/Y.Jianlian 2.50 6.00
4 M.Gasol/P.Gasol 1.50 4.00
5 J.Posey/D.West .75 2.00
6 J.Johnson/J.Teague .75 2.00
7 J.Holiday/D.Collison 3.00 8.00
8 B.Griffin/T.Hansbrough 5.00 12.00
9 D.Curry/S.Curry 30.00 80.00
10 S.Jackson/J.Smith .75 2.00

2009-10 Prestige Connections Materials
PRINT RUN 250 SER.#'d SETS
6 J.Johnson/J.Teague 4.00 10.00
7 J.Holiday/D.Collison 5.00 12.00
8 B.Griffin/T.Hansbrough 15.00 40.00

2009-10 Prestige Franchise Favorites
COMPLETE SET (19) 8.00 20.00
1 Amare Stoudemire .60 1.50
2 Carmelo Anthony 1.25 3.00
3 Chris Bosh 1.00 2.50
4 Chris Paul 1.50 4.00
5 Deron Williams .60 1.50
6 Dirk Nowitzki 2.00 5.00
7 Dwight Howard 1.00 2.50
8 Dwyane Wade 1.50 4.00
9 Kobe Bryant 6.00 15.00
10 LeBron James 6.00 15.00
11 Paul Pierce 1.25 3.00
12 Tim Duncan 2.00 5.00
13 Yao Ming 2.00 5.00
14 Danny Granger .50 1.25
15 Michael Redd .60 1.50
16 Ben Gordon .60 1.50
17 Gilbert Arenas .60 1.50
18 Kevin Durant 3.00 8.00
19 Brandon Roy 1.00 2.50

2009-10 Prestige Hardcourt Heroes
COMPLETE SET (20) 6.00 15.00
1 Joe Johnson .60 1.50
2 Rajon Rondo .75 2.00
3 Ben Gordon .50 1.25
4 LeBron James 5.00 12.00
5 Josh Howard .50 1.25
6 Carmelo Anthony 1.00 2.50
7 Yao Ming 1.50 4.00
8 Danny Granger .40 1.00
9 Baron Davis .50 1.25
10 Pau Gasol 1.00 2.50
11 Jermaine O'Neal .60 1.50
12 Michael Redd .50 1.25
13 Devin Harris .40 1.00
14 David Lee .40 1.00
15 Kevin Durant 2.50 6.00
16 Amare Stoudemire .50 1.25
17 Brandon Roy .75 2.00
18 Tony Parker 1.00 2.50
19 Chris Bosh .75 2.00
20 Carlos Boozer .50 1.25
BG Blake Griffin PROMO 5.00 12.00
JH Jordan Hill PROMO .75 2.00

2009-10 Prestige Hardcourt Heroes Materials
STATED PRINT RUN 250 SER.#'d SETS
1 Joe Johnson 3.00 8.00
5 Josh Howard 2.50 6.00
7 Yao Ming 8.00 20.00
11 Jermaine O'Neal 3.00 8.00
14 David Lee 2.00 5.00
17 Brandon Roy 4.00 10.00
19 Chris Bosh 4.00 10.00
20 Carlos Boozer 2.50 6.00

2009-10 Prestige Inside the Numbers
COMPLETE SET (10) 4.00 10.00
1 Derrick Rose 1.25 3.00
2 Tim Duncan 2.00 5.00
3 Kobe Bryant 6.00 15.00
4 Richard Hamilton .75 2.00
5 T.J. Ford .50 1.25
6 Gilbert Arenas .60 1.50
7 Deron Williams .60 1.50
8 Marcus Camby .60 1.50
9 Chauncey Billups 1.00 2.50
10 O.J. Mayo .50 1.25

2009-10 Prestige Inside the Numbers Materials
STATED PRINT RUN 100 TO 250 SER.#'d SETS
2 Tim Duncan/150 8.00 20.00
3 Kobe Bryant/100 10.00 25.00
7 Deron Williams/250 2.50 6.00
10 O.J. Mayo/100 2.00 5.00

2009-10 Prestige Inside the Numbers Signatures
STATED PRINT RUN 25 SER.#'d SETS
3 Kobe Bryant 800.00 1,500.00

2009-10 Prestige NBA Draft Class
COMPLETE SET (34) 25.00 50.00
1 Blake Griffin 5.00 12.00
2 Hasheem Thabeet .75 2.00
3 James Harden 8.00 20.00
4 Tyreke Evans 1.00 2.50
5 Rodrigue Beaubois .75 2.00
6 Jonny Flynn .75 2.00
7 Stephen Curry 150.00 400.00
8 Jordan Hill .75 2.00
9 DeMar DeRozan 5.00 12.00
10 Brandon Jennings 1.25 3.00
11 Terrence Williams .75 2.00
12 Gerald Henderson .75 2.00
13 Tyler Hansbrough 1.00 2.50
14 Earl Clark .75 2.00
15 Austin Daye .75 2.00
16 James Johnson 1.00 2.50
17 Jrue Holiday 4.00 10.00
18 Ty Lawson 1.00 2.50
19 Jeff Teague 1.00 2.50
20 Eric Maynor .75 2.00
21 Darren Collison 1.25 3.00
23 Omri Casspi .75 2.00
24 B.J. Mullens .75 2.00
25 Taj Gibson 1.00 2.50
26 DeMarre Carroll 1.00 2.50
27 Wayne Ellington 1.00 2.50
28 Toney Douglas .75 2.00
29 Jeff Pendergraph .75 2.00
30 DaJuan Summers .75 2.00
31 Sam Young .75 2.00
32 DeJuan Blair 1.00 2.50
33 Jodie Meeks .75 2.00
34 Chase Budinger .75 2.00
35 Taylor Griffin .75 2.00
36 Patrick Mills 2.00 5.00

2009-10 Prestige NBA Draft Class Autographs
1 Blake Griffin 30.00 80.00
2 Hasheem Thabeet 3.00 8.00
3 James Harden 200.00 500.00
4 Tyreke Evans 4.00 10.00
5 Rodrigue Beaubois 3.00 8.00
6 Jonny Flynn 3.00 8.00
7 Stephen Curry 1,000.00 2,000.00
8 Jordan Hill 3.00 8.00
10 Brandon Jennings 5.00 12.00
11 Terrence Williams 3.00 8.00
12 Gerald Henderson 3.00 8.00
13 Tyler Hansbrough 4.00 10.00
14 Earl Clark 3.00 8.00
15 Austin Daye 3.00 8.00
16 James Johnson 4.00 10.00
17 Jrue Holiday 15.00 40.00
18 Ty Lawson 4.00 10.00
19 Jeff Teague 4.00 10.00
20 Eric Maynor 4.00 10.00
21 Darren Collison 5.00 12.00
23 Omri Casspi 3.00 8.00
24 B.J. Mullens 3.00 8.00
25 Taj Gibson 4.00 10.00
26 DeMarre Carroll 4.00 10.00
27 Wayne Ellington 4.00 10.00
28 Toney Douglas 3.00 8.00
29 Jeff Pendergraph 3.00 8.00
30 DaJuan Summers/249 3.00 8.00
31 Sam Young 3.00 8.00
32 DeJuan Blair 4.00 10.00
33 Jodie Meeks 3.00 8.00
34 Chase Budinger 3.00 8.00
35 Taylor Griffin 3.00 8.00

2009-10 Prestige NBA Draft Class Autographs Logos
STATED PRINT RUN 124 TO 125 SER.#'d SETS
1 Blake Griffin 75.00 200.00
2 Hasheem Thabeet/124 4.00 10.00
3 James Harden 300.00 600.00
4 Tyreke Evans 5.00 12.00
5 Rodrigue Beaubois 4.00 10.00
6 Jonny Flynn 4.00 10.00
7 Stephen Curry 1,500.00 3,000.00
8 Jordan Hill 4.00 10.00
10 Brandon Jennings 6.00 15.00
11 Terrence Williams/124 4.00 10.00
12 Gerald Henderson 4.00 10.00
13 Tyler Hansbrough 5.00 12.00
14 Earl Clark/124 4.00 10.00
15 Austin Daye 4.00 10.00
16 James Johnson 5.00 12.00
17 Jrue Holiday/124 20.00 50.00
18 Ty Lawson 5.00 12.00
19 Jeff Teague 5.00 12.00
20 Eric Maynor 4.00 10.00
21 Darren Collison 6.00 15.00
23 Omri Casspi 4.00 10.00
24 B.J. Mullens 4.00 10.00
25 Taj Gibson 5.00 12.00
26 DeMarre Carroll 5.00 12.00
27 Wayne Ellington 5.00 12.00
28 Toney Douglas 4.00 10.00
29 Jeff Pendergraph 4.00 10.00
30 DaJuan Summers 4.00 10.00
31 Sam Young 4.00 10.00
32 DeJuan Blair 5.00 12.00
33 Jodie Meeks 4.00 10.00
34 Chase Budinger 4.00 10.00
35 Taylor Griffin 4.00 10.00

2009-10 Prestige NBA Draft Class Autographs Logos College
STATED PRINT RUN 93 TO 100 SER.#'d SETS
1 Blake Griffin/99 75.00 150.00
2 Hasheem Thabeet/100 5.00 12.00
3 James Harden/100 400.00 800.00
4 Tyreke Evans/100 6.00 15.00
5 Rodrigue Beaubois/100 5.00 12.00
6 Jonny Flynn/100 5.00 12.00
7 Stephen Curry/100 2,000.00 4,000.00
8 Jordan Hill/100 5.00 12.00
10 Brandon Jennings/100 8.00 20.00
11 Terrence Williams/100 5.00 12.00
12 Gerald Henderson/100 5.00 12.00
13 Tyler Hansbrough/100 20.00 50.00
14 Earl Clark/100 5.00 12.00
15 Austin Daye/100 5.00 12.00
16 James Johnson/100 6.00 15.00
17 Jrue Holiday/100 25.00 60.00
18 Ty Lawson/98 6.00 15.00
19 Jeff Teague/100 6.00 15.00
21 Darren Collison/100 8.00 20.00
23 Omri Casspi/100 6.00 15.00
24 B.J. Mullens/100 5.00 12.00
25 Taj Gibson/100 6.00 15.00
26 DeMarre Carroll/100 6.00 15.00
27 Wayne Ellington/100 6.00 15.00
28 Toney Douglas/93 5.00 12.00
29 Jeff Pendergraph/100 5.00 12.00
30 DaJuan Summers/100 5.00 12.00
31 Sam Young/98 5.00 12.00
32 DeJuan Blair/100 6.00 15.00
33 Jodie Meeks/99 15.00 40.00
34 Chase Budinger/99 5.00 12.00
35 Taylor Griffin/100 5.00 12.00

2009-10 Prestige Old School
COMPLETE SET (18) 10.00 25.00
1 Connie Hawkins 2.00 5.00
2 Bob McAdoo 2.00 5.00
3 Dan Issel 1.25 3.00
4 Kevin McHale 2.50 6.00
5 David Thompson 1.25 3.00
6 Bill Bradley 2.00 5.00
7 Ralph Sampson 1.25 3.00
8 Kenny Walker 1.00 2.50
9 Bryant Reeves 1.00 2.50
10 Dave Cowens 2.00 5.00
11 Joe Dumars 2.00 5.00
12 Oscar Robertson 2.00 5.00
13 Mark Aguirre 1.25 3.00
14 Chris Mullin 2.00 5.00
15 Al Attles 1.25 3.00
16 Walt Frazier 2.50 6.00
17 Dell Curry 1.50 4.00
18 Bill Walton 2.50 6.00

2009-10 Prestige Old School Materials
COMPLETE SET (2) 6.00 15.00
STATED PRINT RUN 250 SER.#'d SETS
4 Kevin McHale 6.00 15.00
14 Chris Mullin 5.00 12.00

2009-10 Prestige Old School Signatures
STATED PRINT RUN 50 TO 100 SER.#'d SETS
ASTERISK CARDS FROM PANINI UPDATE
1 Connie Hawkins*/100 12.00 30.00
2 Bob McAdoo/100 20.00 40.00
3 Dan Issel/100 10.00 25.00
4 Kevin McHale*/100 25.00 60.00
5 David Thompson/100 8.00 20.00
8 Kenny Walker*/100 8.00 20.00
10 Dave Cowens/99 8.00 20.00
12 Oscar Robertson/50 50.00 100.00
14 Chris Mullin*/100 15.00 40.00
15 Al Attles/100 10.00 25.00
16 Walt Frazier*/100 8.00 20.00
17 Dell Curry/96 8.00 20.00
18 Bill Walton/82 15.00 40.00

2009-10 Prestige Playmakers
COMPLETE SET (18) 6.00 15.00
1 Rajon Rondo 1.00 2.50
2 Mike Bibby .75 2.00
3 D.J. Augustin .50 1.25
4 Chauncey Billups 1.00 2.50
5 Danny Granger .50 1.25
6 Shane Battier .75 2.00
7 Derek Fisher .75 2.00
8 Kevin Love .75 2.00
9 David West .60 1.50
10 Nate Robinson .60 1.50
11 Russell Westbrook 1.50 4.00
12 Jameer Nelson .50 1.25
13 Brandon Roy .60 1.50
14 Deron Williams .60 1.50
15 Jason Terry .60 1.50
16 Tayshaun Prince .75 2.00
17 Michael Redd .60 1.50
18 Devin Harris .50 1.25

2009-10 Prestige Playmakers Materials
STATED PRINT RUN 250 SER.#'d SETS
2 Mike Bibby 3.00 8.00
6 Shane Battier 3.00 8.00
10 Nate Robinson 2.50 6.00
13 Brandon Roy 4.00 10.00
14 Deron Williams 2.50 6.00
15 Jason Terry 2.50 6.00

2009-10 Prestige Playmakers Signatures
STATED PRINT RUN 50 TO 100 SER.#'d SETS
ASTERISK CARDS FROM PANINI UPDATE
2 Mike Bibby/100 5.00 12.00
8 Kevin Love/50 15.00 40.00
11 Russell Westbrook/100 50.00 120.00
13 Brandon Roy*/57 10.00 25.00
14 Deron Williams*/100 8.00 20.00
18 Devin Harris*/100 5.00 12.00

2009-10 Prestige Preferred Materials
STATED PRINT RUN 150 TO 250 SETS
1 Brandon Roy/250 4.00 10.00
2 Jermaine O'Neal/250 3.00 8.00
4 LaMarcus Aldridge/250 3.00 8.00
5 David Lee/250 2.00 5.00
6 Joe Johnson/250 3.00 8.00
7 Elton Brand/250 2.50 6.00
8 Dirk Nowitzki/250 8.00 20.00
9 Tracy McGrady/250 6.00 15.00
10 Tim Duncan/150 8.00 20.00

2009-10 Prestige Prestigious Picks Green
STATED PRINT RUN 500 SER.#'d SETS
*BLACK: 1X TO 2.5X BASE HI
BLACK PRINT RUN 25 SER.#'d SETS
*GOLD: .5X TO 1.25X BASE HI
GOLD PRINT RUN 100 SER.#'d SETS
1 Blake Griffin 6.00 15.00
2 Hasheem Thabeet 1.00 2.50
3 James Harden 20.00 50.00
4 Tyreke Evans 1.25 3.00
5 Jonny Flynn 1.00 2.50
6 Stephen Curry 125.00 300.00
7 Jordan Hill 1.00 2.50
8 DeMar DeRozan 10.00 25.00
9 Brandon Jennings 1.50 4.00
10 Terrence Williams 1.00 2.50
11 Gerald Henderson 1.00 2.50
12 Tyler Hansbrough 1.25 3.00
13 Earl Clark 1.00 2.50
14 Austin Daye 1.00 2.50
15 James Johnson 1.25 3.00
16 Jrue Holiday 5.00 12.00
17 Ty Lawson 1.25 3.00
18 Jeff Teague 1.25 3.00
19 Eric Maynor 1.00 2.50
20 Darren Collison 1.50 4.00
21 Omri Casspi 1.00 2.50
22 B.J. Mullens 1.00 2.50
23 Rodrigue Beaubois 1.00 2.50
24 Taj Gibson 1.25 3.00
25 DeMarre Carroll 1.25 3.00
26 Wayne Ellington 1.25 3.00
27 Toney Douglas 1.00 2.50
28 Jeff Pendergraph 1.00 2.50
29 Jeff Pendergraph 1.00 2.50
30 DaJuan Summers 1.00 2.50
31 Sam Young 1.00 2.50
32 DeJuan Blair 1.25 3.00
33 Jodie Meeks 1.00 2.50
34 Chase Budinger 1.00 2.50
35 Taylor Griffin 1.00 2.50
36 Blake Griffin 6.00 15.00
37 Hasheem Thabeet 1.00 2.50
38 Jordan Hill 1.00 2.50
39 Tyler Hansbrough 1.25 3.00
40 Jonny Flynn 1.00 2.50
41 James Harden 10.00 25.00
42 DeMar DeRozan 6.00 15.00
43 Gerald Henderson 1.00 2.50
44 Jrue Holiday 5.00 12.00
45 B.J. Mullens 1.00 2.50
46 Darren Collison 1.50 4.00
47 Chase Budinger 1.00 2.50
48 Wayne Ellington 1.25 3.00
49 Jodie Meeks 1.00 2.50
50 Tyreke Evans 1.25 3.00

2009-10 Prestige Prestigious Picks Signatures Black
STATED PRINT RUN 50 TO 100 SER.#'d SETS
1 Blake Griffin/100 30.00 80.00
3 James Harden/50 200.00 500.00
4 Tyreke Evans/50 5.00 12.00
6 Stephen Curry/50 1,000.00 2,000.00
7 Jordan Hill/50 4.00 10.00
9 Brandon Jennings/50 6.00 15.00
10 Terrence Williams/50 4.00 10.00
11 Gerald Henderson/50 4.00 10.00
12 Tyler Hansbrough/50 5.00 12.00
13 Earl Clark/50 4.00 10.00
14 Austin Daye/50 4.00 10.00
15 James Johnson/50 4.00 10.00
16 Jrue Holiday/50 20.00 50.00
18 Jeff Teague/50 5.00 12.00
20 Darren Collison/50 6.00 15.00
21 Omri Casspi/50 4.00 10.00
22 B.J. Mullens/50 4.00 10.00
23 Rodrigue Beaubois/50 4.00 10.00
24 Taj Gibson/50 5.00 12.00
25 DeMarre Carroll/50 4.00 10.00
27 Toney Douglas/50 4.00 10.00
28 Jeff Pendergraph/50 4.00 10.00
29 Jeff Pendergraph/50 4.00 10.00
32 DeJuan Blair/50 5.00 12.00
33 Jodie Meeks/50 4.00 10.00
34 Chase Budinger/50 4.00 10.00
36 Blake Griffin/50 40.00 80.00
38 Jordan Hill/50 4.00 10.00
39 Tyler Hansbrough/50 5.00 12.00
41 James Harden/50 50.00 120.00
43 Gerald Henderson/50 4.00 10.00
44 Jrue Holiday/50 20.00 50.00
45 B.J. Mullens/50 4.00 10.00
46 Darren Collison/50 6.00 15.00
47 Chase Budinger/50 4.00 10.00
49 Jodie Meeks/50 4.00 10.00
50 Tyreke Evans/50 5.00 12.00

2009-10 Prestige Prestigious Picks Materials Blue
*BLACK: 1.25X TO 3X BASE HI
BLACK PRINT RUN 25 SER.#'d SETS
*GOLD: .6X TO 1.5X BASE HI
GOLD PRINT RUN 50 SER.#'d SETS
*GREEN: .5X TO 1.25X BASE HI
GREEN PRINT RUN 100 SER.#'d SETS
*PLATINUM PATCH: 1.5X TO 4X BASE HI
PLATINUM PRINT RUN 25 SER.#'d SETS
1 Blake Griffin 10.00 25.00
2 Hasheem Thabeet 1.00 2.50
3 James Harden 20.00 50.00
4 Tyreke Evans 1.25 3.00
5 Jonny Flynn 1.00 2.50
6 Stephen Curry 125.00 300.00
7 Jordan Hill 1.00 2.50
8 DeMar DeRozan 6.00 15.00
9 Brandon Jennings 1.50 4.00
10 Terrence Williams 1.00 2.50
11 Gerald Henderson 1.00 2.50
12 Tyler Hansbrough 1.25 3.00
13 Earl Clark 1.00 2.50
14 Austin Daye 1.00 2.50
15 James Johnson 1.25 3.00
16 Jrue Holiday 5.00 12.00
17 Ty Lawson 1.25 3.00
18 Jeff Teague 1.25 3.00
19 Eric Maynor 1.00 2.50
20 Darren Collison 1.50 4.00
21 Omri Casspi 1.00 2.50
22 B.J. Mullens 1.00 2.50
23 Rodrigue Beaubois 1.00 2.50
24 Taj Gibson 1.25 3.00
25 DeMarre Carroll 1.25 3.00
26 Wayne Ellington 1.25 3.00
27 Toney Douglas 1.00 2.50
29 Jeff Pendergraph 1.00 2.50
30 DaJuan Summers 1.00 2.50
31 Sam Young 1.00 2.50
32 DeJuan Blair 1.25 3.00
33 Jodie Meeks 1.00 2.50
34 Chase Budinger 1.00 2.50
35 Taylor Griffin 1.00 2.50
38 Jordan Hill 1.00 2.50
46 Darren Collison 1.50 4.00
47 Chase Budinger 1.00 2.50
49 Jodie Meeks 1.00 2.50
50 Tyreke Evans 1.25 3.00

2009-10 Prestige Prestigious Pros Black Signatures
STATED PRINT RUN 25 SER.#'d SETS
1 Kobe Bryant 1,000.00 2,000.00

2009-10 Prestige Prestigious Pros Green
STATED PRINT RUN 500 SER.#'d SETS
*BLACK: 1.25X TO 3X BASE HI
BLACK PRINT RUN 25 SER.#'d SETS
*GOLD: 1X TO 2.5X BASE HI
GOLD PRINT RUN 100 SER.#'d SETS
1 Kobe Bryant 6.00 15.00
2 LeBron James 6.00 15.00
3 Dwyane Wade 1.50 4.00
4 Chris Paul 1.50 4.00
5 Kevin Garnett 2.00 5.00
6 Josh Howard .60 1.50
7 Gilbert Arenas .60 1.50
8 Steve Nash 1.50 4.00
9 Dirk Nowitzki 2.00 5.00
10 Danny Granger .50 1.25
11 Yao Ming 2.00 5.00
12 Joe Johnson .75 2.00
13 Carmelo Anthony 1.25 3.00
14 Richard Hamilton .75 2.00
15 Stephen Jackson .60 1.50
16 Zach Randolph .75 2.00
17 Rudy Gay .75 2.00
18 Michael Redd .60 1.50
19 Al Jefferson .60 1.50
20 Emeka Okafor .60 1.50
21 Devin Harris .50 1.25
22 Tracy McGrady 1.50 4.00
23 Ben Gordon .60 1.50
24 Al Harrington .60 1.50
25 Kevin Durant 3.00 8.00
26 Dwight Howard 1.00 2.50
27 Andre Iguodala .75 2.00
28 Brandon Roy 1.00 2.50
29 Paul Pierce 1.25 3.00
30 Jamal Crawford .75 2.00
31 Kevin Martin .60 1.50
32 Tim Duncan 2.00 5.00
33 Allen Iverson 1.50 4.00
34 Chris Bosh 1.00 2.50
35 Deron Williams .60 1.50
36 Mo Williams .60 1.50
37 Antawn Jamison .60 1.50
38 Vince Carter 1.50 4.00
39 Ron Artest .75 2.00
40 Amare Stoudemire .60 1.50
41 O.J. Mayo .50 1.25
42 Shawn Marion .75 2.00
43 Chauncey Billups 1.00 2.50
44 Tony Parker 1.25 3.00
45 LaMarcus Aldridge .75 2.00
46 Ray Allen 1.25 3.00
47 Pau Gasol 1.25 3.00
48 Derrick Rose 1.25 3.00
49 Russell Westbrook 1.50 4.00
50 Richard Jefferson .60 1.50

2009-10 Prestige Prestigious Pros Materials Black
*BLACK: 1.25X TO 3X BASE HI
BLACK PRINT RUN 25 SER.#'d SETS
1A Kobe Bryant AU/25 800.00 1,500.00

2009-10 Prestige Prestigious Pros Materials Blue
STATED PRINT RUN 150 TO 250 SER.#'d SETS
1 Kobe Bryant/200 10.00 25.00
4 Chris Paul/250 6.00 15.00
5 Kevin Garnett/250 8.00 20.00
6 Josh Howard/250 2.50 6.00
9 Dirk Nowitzki/250 8.00 20.00
11 Yao Ming/250 8.00 20.00
12 Joe Johnson/250 3.00 8.00
19 Al Jefferson/250 2.00 5.00
22 Tracy McGrady/250 6.00 15.00
24 Al Harrington/250 2.50 6.00
26 Dwight Howard/250 4.00 10.00
27 Andre Iguodala/250 3.00 8.00
28 Brandon Roy/250 4.00 10.00
31 Kevin Martin/250 2.50 6.00
32 Tim Duncan/150 8.00 20.00
34 Chris Bosh/250 4.00 10.00
35 Deron Williams/250 2.50 6.00
41 O.J. Mayo/150 2.00 5.00
45 LaMarcus Aldridge/250 3.00 8.00

2009-10 Prestige Prestigious Pros Materials Gold
*GOLD: .6X TO 1.5X BASE HI
GOLD PRINT RUN 50 SER.#'d SETS
1A Kobe Bryant AU/50 600.00 1,200.00

2009-10 Prestige Prestigious Pros Materials Green
*GREEN: .5X TO 1.25X BASE HI
GREEN PRINT RUN 100 SER.#'d SETS
1A Kobe Bryant AU/100 500.00 1,000.00

2009-10 Prestige Stars of the NBA
COMPLETE SET (20) 15.00 30.00
1 LeBron James 6.00 15.00
2 Kobe Bryant 6.00 15.00
3 Dwyane Wade 1.50 4.00
4 Dirk Nowitzki 2.00 5.00
5 Dwight Howard 1.00 2.50
6 Chris Paul 1.50 4.00
7 Shaquille O'Neal 2.50 6.00
8 Kevin Durant 3.00 8.00
9 Danny Granger .50 1.25
10 Kevin Garnett 2.00 5.00
11 Allen Iverson 1.50 4.00
12 Carmelo Anthony 1.25 3.00
13 Yao Ming 2.00 5.00
14 O.J. Mayo .50 1.25
15 Vince Carter 1.50 4.00
16 Tim Duncan 2.00 5.00
17 Chris Bosh 1.00 2.50
18 Deron Williams .60 1.50
19 Gilbert Arenas .60 1.50
20 Ben Gordon .60 1.50

2009-10 Prestige Stars of the NBA Materials
STATED PRINT RUN 100 TO 250 SER.#'d SETS
2 Kobe Bryant/100 15.00 40.00
4 Dirk Nowitzki/250 8.00 20.00
5 Dwight Howard/250 4.00 10.00
6 Chris Paul/250 6.00 15.00
10 Kevin Garnett/250 8.00 20.00
13 Yao Ming/250 8.00 20.00
14 O.J. Mayo/250 2.00 5.00
16 Tim Duncan/150 8.00 20.00
17 Chris Bosh/250 4.00 10.00
18 Deron Williams/250 2.50 6.00

2009-10 Prestige Stat Stars
COMPLETE SET (20) 10.00 25.00
1 O.J. Mayo .50 1.25
2 Kevin Love .75 2.00
3 Derrick Rose 1.25 3.00
4 Kevin Durant 3.00 8.00
5 Luis Scola .60 1.50
6 Ramon Sessions .50 1.25
7 Dwyane Wade 1.50 4.00
8 LeBron James 6.00 15.00
9 Kobe Bryant 6.00 15.00
10 Dirk Nowitzki 2.00 5.00
11 Dwight Howard 1.00 2.50
12 Troy Murphy .50 1.25
13 Tim Duncan 2.00 5.00
14 Yao Ming 2.00 5.00
15 Chris Paul 1.50 4.00
16 Deron Williams .60 1.50
17 Jose Calderon .50 1.25
18 Ray Allen 1.25 3.00
19 Shaquille O'Neal 2.50 6.00
20 Rashard Lewis .60 1.50

2009-10 Prestige Stat Stars Materials
STATED PRINT RUN 150 TO 250 SER.#'d SETS
1 O.J. Mayo/200 2.00 5.00
5 Luis Scola/250 2.50 6.00
9 Kobe Bryant/150 15.00 40.00
10 Dirk Nowitzki/250 8.00 20.00
11 Dwight Howard/250 4.00 10.00
13 Tim Duncan/150 8.00 20.00
14 Yao Ming/250 8.00 20.00
15 Chris Paul/250 6.00 15.00
16 Deron Williams/250 2.50 6.00
17 Jose Calderon/250 2.00 5.00

2009-10 Prestige Super Sophs
COMPLETE SET (9) 6.00 15.00
1 Derrick Rose 2.00 5.00
2 Marc Gasol 1.25 3.00
3 Russell Westbrook 2.50 6.00
4 Rudy Fernandez .75 2.00
5 O.J. Mayo .75 2.00
6 Danilo Gallinari 1.00 2.50
7 Michael Beasley .75 2.00
8 Eric Gordon 1.00 2.50
9 Brook Lopez 1.25 3.00

2009-10 Prestige Super Sophs Signatures
STATED PRINT RUN 57 TO 100 SETS
3 Russell Westbrook/57* 60.00 150.00
8 Eric Gordon/100* 8.00 20.00

2009-10 Prestige True Colors
COMPLETE SET (10) 4.00 10.00
1 Kobe Bryant 6.00 15.00
2 Tim Duncan 2.00 5.00
3 Paul Pierce 1.25 3.00
4 Zydrunas Ilgauskas .60 1.50
5 Dirk Nowitzki 2.00 5.00
6 Jeff Foster .50 1.25
7 Michael Redd .60 1.50
8 Samuel Dalembert .50 1.25
9 Andrei Kirilenko .60 1.50
10 Brendan Haywood .50 1.25

2009-10 Prestige True Colors Materials
STATED PRINT RUN 50 TO 250 SER.#'d SETS
1 Kobe Bryant/50 15.00 40.00
2 Tim Duncan/150 8.00 20.00
4 Zydrunas Ilgauskas/250 2.50 6.00
5 Dirk Nowitzki/250 8.00 20.00
6 Jeff Foster/250 2.00 5.00
8 Samuel Dalembert/250 2.00 5.00
9 Andrei Kirilenko/250 2.50 6.00

2009-10 Prestige True Colors Signatures
STATED PRINT RUN 25 SER.#'d SETS
1 Kobe Bryant 1,000.00 2,000.00

2010-11 Prestige
COMPLETE SET (250) 60.00 150.00
ASTERISK CARDS INSERTED IN SEASON UPDATE
1 Al Horford .40 1.00
2 Jamal Crawford .40 1.00
3 Josh Smith .25 .60
4 Mike Bibby .40 1.00
5 Glen Davis .25 .60
6 Kendrick Perkins .25 .60
7 Kevin Garnett 1.00 2.50
8 Rajon Rondo .50 1.25
9 Boris Diaw .30 .75
10 D.J. Augustin .25 .60
11 Gerald Wallace .30 .75
12 Stephen Jackson .30 .75
13 Derrick Rose .75 2.00
14 Joakim Noah .40 1.00
15 Luol Deng .30 .75
16 Taj Gibson .25 .60
17 Anderson Varejao .25 .60
18 Antawn Jamison .30 .75
19 Anthony Parker .25 .60
20 LeBron James 3.00 8.00
21 Caron Butler .30 .75
22 Dirk Nowitzki 1.00 2.50
23 Jason Kidd .60 1.50
24 Shawn Marion .40 1.00
25 Carmelo Anthony .60 1.50
26 Chauncey Billups .50 1.25
27 J.R. Smith .40 1.00
28 Nene .30 .75
29 Ben Gordon .30 .75
30 Richard Hamilton .50 1.25
31 Rodney Stuckey .25 .60
32 Tayshaun Prince .40 1.00
33 Andris Biedrins .25 .60
34 Anthony Randolph .25 .60
35 Monta Ellis .30 .75
36 Stephen Curry 3.00 8.00
37 Aaron Brooks .25 .60
38 Kevin Martin .30 .75
39 Shane Battier .30 .75
40 Trevor Ariza .25 .60
41 Dahntay Jones .25 .60
42 Danny Granger .25 .60
43 T.J. Ford .25 .60
44 Troy Murphy .25 .60
45 Baron Davis .40 1.00
46 Blake Griffin .40 1.00
47 Chris Kaman .25 .60
48 Eric Gordon .30 .75
49 Kobe Bryant 3.00 8.00
50 Lamar Odom .30 .75
51 Pau Gasol .60 1.50
52 Ron Artest .40 1.00
53 Marc Gasol .40 1.00
54 Mike Conley Jr. .30 .75
55 O.J. Mayo .25 .60
56 Zach Randolph .40 1.00
57 Dwyane Wade .75 2.00
58 James Jones .25 .60
59 Jermaine O'Neal .40 1.00
60 Michael Beasley .25 .60
61 Andrew Bogut .30 .75
62 Brandon Jennings .25 .60
63 Ersan Ilyasova .30 .75
64 Luc Mbah a Moute .25 .60
65 Al Jefferson .25 .60
66 Corey Brewer .25 .60
67 Kevin Love .40 1.00
68 Ramon Sessions .25 .60
69 Brook Lopez .30 .75
70 Courtney Lee .25 .60
71 Devin Harris .25 .60
72 Yi Jianlian .40 1.00
73 Chris Paul .75 2.00
74 David West .30 .75
75 Emeka Okafor .30 .75
76 Marcus Thornton .25 .60
77 Danilo Gallinari .30 .75
78 David Lee .25 .60
79 Toney Douglas .25 .60
80 Wilson Chandler .30 .75
81 James Harden 1.00 2.50
82 Jeff Green .30 .75
83 Kevin Durant 1.50 4.00
84 Russell Westbrook .60 1.50
85 Dwight Howard .50 1.25
86 Jameer Nelson .25 .60
87 Rashard Lewis .30 .75
88 Vince Carter .75 2.00
89 Andre Iguodala .40 1.00
90 Elton Brand .30 .75
91 Louis Williams .30 .75
92 Thaddeus Young .25 .60
93 Amare Stoudemire .40 1.00
94 Jason Richardson .40 1.00
95 Leandro Barbosa .30 .75
96 Steve Nash .75 2.00
97 Andre Miller .30 .75
98 Brandon Roy .50 1.25
99 Greg Oden .25 .60
100 LaMarcus Aldridge .40 1.00
101 Beno Udrih .25 .60
102 Carl Landry .25 .60
103 Jason Thompson .25 .60
104 Tyreke Evans .30 .75
105 George Hill .30 .75
106 Manu Ginobili .75 2.00
107 Tim Duncan 1.00 2.50
108 Tony Parker .60 1.50
109 Andrea Bargnani .25 .60
110 Chris Bosh .50 1.25
111 Hedo Turkoglu .30 .75
112 Jarrett Jack .30 .75
113 Andrei Kirilenko .30 .75
114 Deron Williams .30 .75
115 Mehmet Okur .25 .60
116 Paul Millsap .30 .75
117 Al Thornton .25 .60
118 Andray Blatche .25 .60
119 JaVale McGee .30 .75
120 Nick Young .25 .60
121 Alvan Adams .25 .60
122 Charles Oakley .40 1.00
123 Chris Webber .50 1.25
124 Connie Hawkins .50 1.25
125 Dell Curry .40 1.00
126 Gary Payton .60 1.50
127 Gheorghe Muresan .25 .60
128 Hal Greer .30 .75
129 Jalen Rose .30 .75
130 Jamal Mashburn .30 .75
131 James Worthy .50 1.25
132 Joe Dumars .40 1.00
133 John Stockton .60 1.50
134 K.C. Jones .40 1.00
135 Kelly Tripucka .25 .60
136 Kurt Rambis .25 .60
137 Larry Bird 1.50 4.00
138 Larry Johnson .50 1.25
139 Magic Johnson 1.50 4.00
140 Maurice Cheeks .30 .75
141 Michael Cooper .40 1.00
142 Mike Dunleavy, Sr. .40 1.00
143 Moses Malone .60 1.50
144 Muggsy Bogues .30 .75
145 Nate Thurmond .50 1.25
146 Pete Maravich 1.00 2.50
147 Quinn Buckner .25 .60
148 Rolando Blackman .30 .75
149 Sidney Moncrief .25 .60
150 Toni Kukoc .40 1.00
151 John Wall RC 2.50 6.00
152 Evan Turner RC .60 1.50
153 Derrick Favors RC .75 2.00
154 Wesley Johnson RC .50 1.25
155 DeMarcus Cousins RC 1.50 4.00
156 Ekpe Udoh RC .50 1.25
157 Greg Monroe RC .60 1.50
158 Al-Farouq Aminu RC .60 1.50
159 Gordon Hayward RC 2.00 5.00
160 Paul George RC 6.00 15.00
161 Cole Aldrich RC .50 1.25
162 Xavier Henry RC .50 1.25
163 Ed Davis RC .60 1.50
164 Patrick Patterson RC .60 1.50
165 Larry Sanders RC .50 1.25
166 Luke Babbitt RC .50 1.25
167 Kevin Seraphin RC .50 1.25
168 Eric Bledsoe RC 1.00 2.50
169 Avery Bradley RC .75 2.00
170 James Anderson RC .50 1.25
171 Craig Brackins RC .50 1.25
172 Elliot Williams RC .50 1.25
173 Trevor Booker RC .50 1.25
174 Damion James RC .50 1.25
175 Dominique Jones RC .50 1.25
176 Quincy Pondexter RC .50 1.25
177 Jordan Crawford RC .50 1.25
178 Greivis Vasquez RC .50 1.25
179 Daniel Orton RC .50 1.25
180 Lazar Hayward RC .50 1.25
181 Tibor Pleiss RC .75 2.00
182 Dexter Pittman RC .50 1.25
183 Hassan Whiteside RC 1.00 2.50
184 Armon Johnson RC .50 1.25
185 Brian Zoubek RC .50 1.25
186 Terrico White RC .50 1.25
187 Jeremy Lin RC 3.00 8.00
188 Andy Rautins RC .50 1.25
189 Landry Fields RC .50 1.25
190 Lance Stephenson RC .75 2.00
191 Jarvis Varnado RC .50 1.25
192 Da'Sean Butler RC .60 1.50
193 Devin Ebanks RC .50 1.25
194 Wesley Johnson RC .50 1.25
195 Terrico White RC .50 1.25
196 Gani Lawal RC .50 1.25
197 Keith Gallon RC .50 1.25
198 Lance Stephenson RC .75 2.00
199 John Wall RC 2.50 6.00
200 Solomon Alabi RC .50 1.25
201 Devin Ebanks RC .50 1.25
202 Luke Harangody RC .50 1.25
203 Hassan Whiteside RC 1.00 2.50
204 Willie Warren RC .50 1.25
205 Andy Rautins RC .50 1.25
206 Evan Turner RC .60 1.50
207 Keith Gallon RC .50 1.25
208 Derrick Caracter RC .50 1.25
209 Stanley Robinson RC .50 1.25
210 Jeremy Lin RC 3.00 8.00
211 John Wall RC 2.50 6.00
212 Evan Turner RC .60 1.50
213 Derrick Favors RC .75 2.00
214 Wesley Johnson RC .50 1.25
215 DeMarcus Cousins RC 1.50 4.00
216 Ekpe Udoh RC .50 1.25
217 Greg Monroe RC .60 1.50
218 Al-Farouq Aminu RC .60 1.50
219 Gordon Hayward RC 2.00 5.00
220 Paul George RC 6.00 15.00
221 Cole Aldrich RC .50 1.25
222 Xavier Henry RC .50 1.25
223 Ed Davis RC .60 1.50
224 Patrick Patterson RC .60 1.50
225 Larry Sanders RC .50 1.25
226 Luke Babbitt RC .50 1.25
227 Eric Bledsoe RC 1.00 2.50
228 Avery Bradley RC .75 2.00
229 James Anderson RC .50 1.25
230 Craig Brackins RC .50 1.25
231 Elliot Williams RC .50 1.25
232 Trevor Booker RC .50 1.25
233 Damion James RC .50 1.25
234 Dominique Jones RC .50 1.25
235 Quincy Pondexter RC .50 1.25
236 Jordan Crawford RC .50 1.25
237 Greivis Vasquez RC .50 1.25
238 Daniel Orton RC .50 1.25
239 Lazar Hayward RC .50 1.25
240 Dexter Pittman RC .50 1.25
241 Da'Sean Butler RC .60 1.50
242 Luke Harangody RC .50 1.25
243 Willie Warren RC .50 1.25
244 Gani Lawal RC .50 1.25
245 Stanley Robinson RC .50 1.25
246 Gary Neal RC* .60 1.50
247 Gary Forbes RC* .50 1.25
248 Omer Asik RC* .75 2.00
249 Semih Erden RC* .50 1.25
250 Timofey Mozgov RC* .60 1.50

2010-11 Prestige Bonus Shots Gold
*GOLD 1-150: 1.5X TO 4X BASE HI
*GOLD 151-245: 1.5X TO 4X BASE HI
GOLD PRINT RUN 249 SER.#'d SETS

2010-11 Prestige Bonus Shots Green
*GREEN 1-150: 4X TO 10X BASE HI
*GREEN 151-245: 1.5X TO 4X BASE HI
GREEN PRINT RUN 25 SER.#'d SETS

2010-11 Prestige Bonus Shots Orange
*ORANGE 1-150: .1.25X TO 3X BASE HI
*ORANGE 151-245: 1.25X TO 3X BASE HI
STATED PRINT RUN 499 SER.#'d SETS

2010-11 Prestige Bonus Shots Purple
*PURPLE 1-150: 3X TO 8X BASE HI
*PURPLE 151-245: 3X TO 8X BASE HI
PURPLE PRINT RUN 49 SER.#'d SETS

2010-11 Prestige Bonus Shots Black Signatures
STATED PRINT RUN 25 TO 99 SER.#'d SETS
ASTERISK CARDS INSERTED IN SEASON UPDATE
16 Taj Gibson/25 5.00 12.00
30 Richard Hamilton/50 6.00 15.00
37 Aaron Brooks/99 5.00 12.00
43 T.J. Ford/25 5.00 12.00
46 Blake Griffin/99 20.00 50.00
49 Kobe Bryant/49 1,500.00 3,000.00
52 Ron Artest/50 15.00 40.00
59 Jermaine O'Neal/50 5.00 12.00
60 Michael Beasley/25 10.00 25.00
67 Kevin Love/25 12.00 30.00
71 Devin Harris/25 5.00 12.00

75 Emeka Okafor/50 5.00 12.00
76 Marcus Thornton/99 5.00 12.00
79 Toney Douglas/99 5.00 12.00
81 James Harden/99 20.00 50.00
89 Andre Iguodala/50 5.00 12.00
93 Amare Stoudemire/25 15.00 40.00
98 Brandon Roy/50 8.00 20.00
102 Carl Landry/50 5.00 12.00
104 Tyreke Evans/99 5.00 12.00
121 Alvan Adams/50 5.00 12.00
126 Gary Payton/25 20.00 40.00
128 Hal Greer/50 5.00 12.00
145 Nate Thurmond/25 8.00 20.00
149 Sidney Moncrief/50 5.00 12.00
151 John Wall/99 30.00 80.00
152 Evan Turner/25 5.00 12.00
153 Derrick Favors/99 6.00 15.00
154 Wesley Johnson/99 4.00 10.00
155 DeMarcus Cousins/99 25.00 60.00
156 Ekpe Udoh/99 4.00 10.00
158 Al-Farouq Aminu/99 5.00 12.00
161 Cole Aldrich/99 4.00 10.00
162 Xavier Henry/99 4.00 10.00
163 Ed Davis/99 5.00 12.00
164 Patrick Patterson/99 5.00 12.00
166 Luke Babbitt/99 4.00 10.00
167 Kevin Seraphin/25 4.00 10.00
168 Eric Bledsoe/99 8.00 20.00
169 Avery Bradley/99 6.00 15.00
170 James Anderson/99 4.00 10.00
171 Craig Brackins/25 4.00 10.00
175 Dominique Jones/25 4.00 10.00
176 Quincy Pondexter/99 4.00 10.00
177 Jordan Crawford/99 4.00 10.00
179 Daniel Orton/99 4.00 10.00
180 Lazar Hayward/99 4.00 10.00
184 Armon Johnson/99 4.00 10.00
186 Terrico White/99 4.00 10.00
187 Jeremy Lin/99 60.00 150.00
188 Andy Rautins/99 4.00 10.00
189 Landry Fields/99 4.00 10.00
190 Lance Stephenson/99 6.00 15.00
192 Da'Sean Butler/99 5.00 12.00
194 Wesley Johnson/99 4.00 10.00
195 Terrico White/99 4.00 10.00
196 Gani Lawal/99 4.00 10.00
197 Keith Gallon/99 4.00 10.00
198 Lance Stephenson/99 6.00 15.00
199 John Wall/99 30.00 80.00
200 Solomon Alabi/99 4.00 10.00
202 Luke Harangody/99 4.00 10.00
205 Andy Rautins/99 4.00 10.00
206 Evan Turner/25 5.00 12.00
207 Keith Gallon/99 4.00 10.00
210 Jeremy Lin/99 75.00 200.00
211 John Wall/99 30.00 80.00
212 Evan Turner/25 5.00 12.00
213 Derrick Favors/99 6.00 15.00
214 Wesley Johnson/99 4.00 10.00
215 DeMarcus Cousins/99 25.00 60.00
216 Ekpe Udoh/99 4.00 10.00
218 Al-Farouq Aminu/99 5.00 12.00
221 Cole Aldrich/99 4.00 10.00
222 Xavier Henry/99 4.00 10.00
223 Ed Davis/99 5.00 12.00
224 Patrick Patterson/99 5.00 12.00
226 Luke Babbitt/99 4.00 10.00
227 Eric Bledsoe/99 8.00 20.00
228 Avery Bradley/99 6.00 15.00
229 James Anderson/99 4.00 10.00
230 Craig Brackins/25 4.00 10.00
234 Dominique Jones/25 4.00 10.00
235 Quincy Pondexter/99 4.00 10.00
236 Jordan Crawford/99 4.00 10.00
238 Daniel Orton/99 4.00 10.00
239 Lazar Hayward/99 4.00 10.00
241 Da'Sean Butler/99 5.00 12.00
242 Luke Harangody/99 4.00 10.00
244 Gani Lawal/99 4.00 10.00
246 Gary Neal/99* 5.00 12.00
247 Gary Forbes/99* 4.00 10.00
248 Omer Asik/99* 6.00 15.00
249 Semih Erden/99* 4.00 10.00
250 Timofey Mozgov/99* 5.00 12.00

2010-11 Prestige Draft Picks Light Blue

*LIGHT BLUE: .75X TO 2X BASE HI
STATED PRINT RUN 999 SER.#'d SETS

2010-11 Prestige Draft Picks Rights Autographs

STATED PRINT RUN 25 TO 199 SER.#'d SETS
ASTERISK CARDS INSERTED IN SEASON UPDATE
151 John Wall/99 30.00 80.00
152 Evan Turner/25 5.00 12.00
153 Derrick Favors/199 5.00 12.00
154 Wesley Johnson/99 3.00 8.00
155 DeMarcus Cousins/199 10.00 25.00
156 Ekpe Udoh/199 3.00 8.00
158 Al-Farouq Aminu/199 4.00 10.00
161 Cole Aldrich/199 3.00 8.00
162 Xavier Henry/199 3.00 8.00
163 Ed Davis/199 4.00 10.00
164 Patrick Patterson/99 4.00 10.00
166 Luke Babbitt/199 3.00 8.00
167 Kevin Seraphin/25 3.00 8.00
168 Eric Bledsoe/199 6.00 15.00
169 Avery Bradley/199 5.00 12.00
170 James Anderson/199 3.00 8.00
171 Craig Brackins/25 3.00 8.00
175 Dominique Jones/25 10.00 25.00
176 Quincy Pondexter/199 3.00 8.00
177 Jordan Crawford/199 3.00 8.00
179 Daniel Orton/199 3.00 8.00
180 Lazar Hayward/199 3.00 8.00
182 Dexter Pittman/49 3.00 8.00
184 Armon Johnson/199 3.00 8.00
186 Terrico White/199 3.00 8.00
187 Jeremy Lin/199 50.00 125.00
188 Andy Rautins/199 3.00 8.00
189 Landry Fields/199 3.00 8.00
190 Lance Stephenson/199 5.00 12.00
192 Da'Sean Butler/199 4.00 10.00
194 Wesley Johnson/99 3.00 8.00
195 Terrico White/199 3.00 8.00
196 Gani Lawal/199 3.00 8.00
197 Keith Gallon/99 3.00 8.00
198 Lance Stephenson/199 5.00 12.00
199 John Wall/99 40.00 100.00
200 Solomon Alabi/199 3.00 8.00
202 Luke Harangody/199 3.00 8.00
205 Andy Rautins/199 3.00 8.00
206 Evan Turner/25 4.00 10.00
207 Keith Gallon/99 3.00 8.00
210 Jeremy Lin/199 60.00 150.00
211 John Wall/99 30.00 60.00
212 Evan Turner/25 15.00 40.00
213 Derrick Favors/199 5.00 12.00
214 Wesley Johnson/99 3.00 8.00
215 DeMarcus Cousins/199 10.00 25.00
216 Ekpe Udoh/199 3.00 8.00
218 Al-Farouq Aminu/199 4.00 10.00
221 Cole Aldrich/199 3.00 8.00
222 Xavier Henry/199 3.00 8.00
223 Ed Davis/199 4.00 10.00
224 Patrick Patterson/99 4.00 10.00
226 Luke Babbitt/199 3.00 8.00
227 Eric Bledsoe/199 6.00 15.00
228 Avery Bradley/199 5.00 12.00
229 James Anderson/199 3.00 8.00
230 Craig Brackins/25 3.00 8.00
234 Dominique Jones/25 10.00 25.00
235 Quincy Pondexter/199 3.00 8.00
236 Jordan Crawford/199 3.00 8.00
238 Daniel Orton/199 3.00 8.00
239 Lazar Hayward/199 3.00 8.00
240 Dexter Pittman/49 3.00 8.00
244 Gani Lawal/199 3.00 8.00
246 Gary Neal/199* 4.00 10.00
247 Gary Forbes/199* 3.00 8.00
248 Omer Asik/199* 5.00 12.00
249 Semih Erden/199* 3.00 8.00
250 Timofey Mozgov/199* 4.00 10.00

2010-11 Prestige Franchise Favorites

COMPLETE SET (30) 15.00 30.00
1 Ray Allen 1.00 2.50
2 Brook Lopez .50 1.25
3 Al Harrington .50 1.25
4 Allen Iverson 1.25 3.00
5 Andrea Bargnani .40 1.00
6 Luol Deng .50 1.25
7 Antawn Jamison .50 1.25
8 Tayshaun Prince .60 1.50
9 Danny Granger .40 1.00
10 Brandon Jennings .40 1.00
11 Joe Johnson .60 1.50
12 Stephen Jackson .50 1.25
13 Dwyane Wade 1.25 3.00
14 Dwight Howard .75 2.00
15 Al Thornton .40 1.00
16 Dirk Nowitzki 1.50 4.00
17 Kevin Martin .50 1.25
18 Zach Randolph .60 1.50
19 Chris Paul 1.25 3.00
20 Tim Duncan 1.50 4.00
21 Carmelo Anthony 1.00 2.50
22 Kevin Love .60 1.50
23 LaMarcus Aldridge .60 1.50
24 Kevin Durant 2.50 6.00
25 Deron Williams .50 1.25
26 Monta Ellis .50 1.25
27 Baron Davis .60 1.50
28 Kobe Bryant 5.00 12.00
29 Steve Nash 1.25 3.00
30 Tyreke Evans .50 1.25

2010-11 Prestige Franchise Favorites Materials

STATED PRINT RUN 50 TO 249 SER.#'d SETS
*PRIME: .75X TO 2X BASE HI
PRIME PRINT RUN 5 TO 49 SER.#'d SETS
1 Ray Allen/149 5.00 12.00
2 Brook Lopez/249 2.50 6.00
4 Allen Iverson/199 6.00 15.00
5 Andrea Bargnani/249 2.00 5.00
6 Luol Deng/249 2.50 6.00
8 Tayshaun Prince/249 3.00 8.00
9 Danny Granger/249 2.00 5.00
10 Brandon Jennings/249 2.00 5.00
11 Joe Johnson/249 3.00 8.00
13 Dwyane Wade/249 6.00 15.00
14 Dwight Howard/249 4.00 10.00
16 Dirk Nowitzki/249 8.00 20.00
17 Kevin Martin/249 2.50 6.00
19 Chris Paul/249 6.00 15.00
20 Tim Duncan/249 8.00 20.00
21 Carmelo Anthony/249 5.00 12.00
22 Kevin Love/249 3.00 8.00
23 LaMarcus Aldridge/249 3.00 8.00
24 Kevin Durant/50 8.00 20.00
25 Deron Williams/249 2.50 6.00
27 Baron Davis/249 3.00 8.00
28 Kobe Bryant/249 12.00 30.00
29 Steve Nash/249 6.00 15.00
30 Tyreke Evans/249 2.50 6.00

2010-11 Prestige Franchise Favorites Signatures

STATED PRINT RUN 10 TO 49 SER.#'d SETS
10 Brandon Jennings/25 15.00 40.00
22 Kevin Love/25 12.00 30.00
25 Deron Williams/25 10.00 25.00
27 Baron Davis/49 6.00 15.00
28 Kobe Bryant/49 1,500.00 3,000.00
30 Tyreke Evans/25 10.00 25.00

2010-11 Prestige Hardcourt Heroes

COMPLETE SET (20) 10.00 25.00
1 LeBron James 5.00 12.00
2 Kevin Durant 2.50 6.00
3 David Lee .40 1.00
4 Chris Bosh .75 2.00
5 Pau Gasol 1.00 2.50
6 Dwight Howard .75 2.00
7 Chris Paul 1.25 3.00
8 Carlos Boozer .50 1.25
9 Dirk Nowitzki 1.50 4.00
10 Dwyane Wade 1.25 3.00
11 Marc Gasol .60 1.50
12 Amare Stoudemire .60 1.50
13 Tim Duncan 1.50 4.00
14 Carmelo Anthony 1.00 2.50
15 Kobe Bryant 5.00 12.00
16 Deron Williams .50 1.25
17 Gerald Wallace .50 1.25
18 Josh Smith .40 1.00
19 Steve Nash 1.25 3.00
20 Brook Lopez .50 1.25

2010-11 Prestige Hardcourt Heroes Materials

STATED PRINT RUN 50 TO 249 SER.#'d SETS
*PRIME: .75X TO 2X BASE HI
PRIME PRINT RUN 10 TO 49 SER.#'d SETS
1 LeBron James/50 10.00 25.00
2 Kevin Durant/50 8.00 20.00
4 Chris Bosh/249 4.00 10.00
5 Pau Gasol/249 5.00 12.00
6 Dwight Howard/249 4.00 10.00
7 Chris Paul/249 6.00 15.00
8 Carlos Boozer/249 2.50 6.00
9 Dirk Nowitzki/249 8.00 20.00
10 Dwyane Wade/249 6.00 15.00
11 Marc Gasol/249 3.00 8.00
12 Amare Stoudemire/249 3.00 8.00
13 Tim Duncan/249 8.00 20.00
14 Carmelo Anthony/249 5.00 12.00
15 Kobe Bryant/249 12.00 30.00
16 Deron Williams/249 2.50 6.00
17 Gerald Wallace/249 2.50 6.00
18 Josh Smith/249 2.00 5.00
19 Steve Nash/249 6.00 15.00
20 Brook Lopez/249 2.50 6.00

2010-11 Prestige Hardcourt Heroes Signatures

STATED PRINT RUN 10 TO 25 SER.#'d SETS
12 Amare Stoudemire/25 15.00 40.00
15 Kobe Bryant/25 1,500.00 3,000.00
16 Deron Williams/25 5.00 12.00

2010-11 Prestige Inside the Numbers

COMPLETE SET (10) 4.00 10.00
1 Danny Granger .40 1.00
2 Dwyane Wade 1.25 3.00
3 Dwight Howard .75 2.00
4 Chris Bosh .75 2.00
5 Carmelo Anthony 1.00 2.50
6 Aaron Brooks .40 1.00
7 Dirk Nowitzki 1.50 4.00
8 Stephen Jackson .50 1.25
9 David West .50 1.25
10 Zach Randolph .60 1.50

2010-11 Prestige Inside the Numbers Materials

STATED PRINT RUN 149 TO 249 SER.#'d SETS
*PRIME: .75X TO 2X BASE HI
PRIME PRINT RUN 25 TO 49 SER.#'d SETS
1 Danny Granger/149 2.00 5.00
2 Dwyane Wade/249 6.00 15.00
3 Dwight Howard/249 4.00 10.00
4 Chris Bosh/249 4.00 10.00
5 Carmelo Anthony/249 5.00 12.00
7 Dirk Nowitzki/249 8.00 20.00
9 David West/249 2.50 6.00

2010-11 Prestige Inside the Numbers Signatures

STATED PRINT RUN 25 SER.#'d SETS
INSERTED IN PACKS OF SEASON UPDATE
1 Danny Granger* 6.00 15.00

2010-11 Prestige NBA Draft Class

COMPLETE SET (40) 40.00 80.00
STATED PRINT RUN 499 SER.#'d SETS
1 John Wall 4.00 10.00
2 Evan Turner 1.00 2.50
3 Derrick Favors 1.25 3.00
4 Wesley Johnson .75 2.00
5 DeMarcus Cousins 2.50 6.00
6 Ekpe Udoh .75 2.00
7 Greg Monroe 1.00 2.50
8 Al-Farouq Aminu 1.00 2.50
9 Gordon Hayward 3.00 8.00
10 Paul George 6.00 15.00
11 Cole Aldrich .75 2.00
12 Xavier Henry .75 2.00
13 Ed Davis 1.00 2.50
14 Patrick Patterson 1.00 2.50
15 Larry Sanders .75 2.00
16 Luke Babbitt .75 2.00
17 Kevin Seraphin .75 2.00
18 Eric Bledsoe 1.50 4.00
19 Avery Bradley 1.25 3.00
20 James Anderson .75 2.00
21 Craig Brackins .75 2.00
22 Elliot Williams .75 2.00
23 Trevor Booker .75 2.00
24 Damion James .75 2.00
25 Dominique Jones .75 2.00
26 Quincy Pondexter .75 2.00
27 Jordan Crawford .75 2.00
28 Greivis Vasquez .75 2.00
29 Daniel Orton .75 2.00
30 Lazar Hayward .75 2.00
31 Dexter Pittman .75 2.00
32 Da'Sean Butler 1.00 2.50
33 Luke Harangody .75 2.00
34 Willie Warren .75 2.00
35 Gani Lawal .75 2.00
36 Hassan Whiteside 1.50 4.00
37 Andy Rautins .75 2.00
38 Lance Stephenson 1.25 3.00
39 Devin Ebanks .75 2.00
40 Keith Gallon .75 2.00

2010-11 Prestige NBA Draft Class Draft Logo Signatures

STATED PRINT RUN 199 TO 499 SER.#'d SETS
LOGOMAN PRINT RUN 10 SER.#'d SETS
1 John Wall/199 30.00 80.00
2 Evan Turner/199 3.00 8.00
3 Derrick Favors/199 4.00 10.00
4 Wesley Johnson/299 2.50 6.00
5 DeMarcus Cousins/299 20.00 50.00
6 Ekpe Udoh/299 2.50 6.00
7 Greg Monroe/299 3.00 8.00
8 Al-Farouq Aminu/299 3.00 8.00
9 Gordon Hayward/299 10.00 25.00
10 Paul George/299 30.00 80.00
11 Cole Aldrich/299 2.50 6.00
12 Xavier Henry/299 2.50 6.00
13 Ed Davis/299 3.00 8.00
14 Patrick Patterson/299 3.00 8.00
15 Larry Sanders/399 2.50 6.00
16 Luke Babbitt/399 2.50 6.00
17 Kevin Seraphin/399 2.50 6.00
18 Eric Bledsoe/399 5.00 12.00
19 Avery Bradley/396 4.00 10.00
20 James Anderson/399 2.50 6.00
21 Craig Brackins/399 2.50 6.00
22 Elliot Williams/399 2.50 6.00
23 Trevor Booker/399 2.50 6.00
24 Damion James/499 2.50 6.00
25 Dominique Jones/499 2.50 6.00
26 Quincy Pondexter/399 2.50 6.00
27 Jordan Crawford/499 2.50 6.00
28 Greivis Vasquez/499 2.50 6.00
29 Daniel Orton/499 2.50 6.00
30 Lazar Hayward/499 2.50 6.00
31 Dexter Pittman/499 2.50 6.00
32 Da'Sean Butler/499 3.00 8.00
33 Luke Harangody/499 2.50 6.00
34 Willie Warren/399 2.50 6.00
35 Gani Lawal/399 2.50 6.00
36 Hassan Whiteside/399 5.00 12.00
37 Andy Rautins/499 2.50 6.00
38 Lance Stephenson/499 8.00 20.00
39 Devin Ebanks/499 2.50 6.00
40 Keith Gallon/499 2.50 6.00

2010-11 Prestige NBA Draft Class Signatures

STATED PRINT RUN 263 TO 299 SER.#'d SETS
1 John Wall/283 25.00 60.00
2 Evan Turner/299 4.00 10.00
3 Derrick Favors/295 5.00 12.00
4 Wesley Johnson/299 3.00 8.00
5 DeMarcus Cousins/299 15.00 40.00
6 Ekpe Udoh/299 3.00 8.00
7 Greg Monroe/299 4.00 10.00
8 Al-Farouq Aminu/296 4.00 10.00
9 Gordon Hayward/299 12.00 30.00
10 Paul George/299 30.00 80.00
11 Cole Aldrich/299 3.00 8.00
12 Xavier Henry/292 3.00 8.00
13 Ed Davis/299 4.00 10.00
14 Patrick Patterson/299 4.00 10.00
15 Larry Sanders/299 3.00 8.00
16 Luke Babbitt/299 3.00 8.00
17 Kevin Seraphin/299 3.00 8.00
18 Eric Bledsoe/297 6.00 15.00
19 Avery Bradley/298 5.00 12.00
20 James Anderson/299 3.00 8.00
21 Craig Brackins/299 3.00 8.00
22 Elliot Williams/299 3.00 8.00
23 Trevor Booker/294 3.00 8.00
24 Damion James/299 3.00 8.00
25 Dominique Jones/299 3.00 8.00
26 Quincy Pondexter/299 3.00 8.00
27 Jordan Crawford/299 3.00 8.00
28 Greivis Vasquez/299 3.00 8.00
29 Daniel Orton/299 3.00 8.00
30 Lazar Hayward/299 3.00 8.00
31 Dexter Pittman/299 3.00 8.00
32 Da'Sean Butler/299 4.00 10.00
33 Luke Harangody/284 3.00 8.00
34 Willie Warren/292 3.00 8.00
35 Gani Lawal/299 3.00 8.00
36 Hassan Whiteside/263 6.00 15.00
37 Andy Rautins/299 3.00 8.00
38 Lance Stephenson/299 4.00 10.00
39 Devin Ebanks/299 3.00 8.00
40 Keith Gallon/299 3.00 8.00

2010-11 Prestige Old School

COMPLETE SET (20) 15.00 30.00
1 Earl Monroe 1.25 3.00
2 George Gervin 2.00 5.00
3 Paul Westphal 1.25 3.00
4 Elgin Baylor 2.50 6.00
5 Doc Rivers 1.25 3.00
6 Gail Goodrich 1.25 3.00
7 Gary Payton 2.00 5.00
8 Isiah Thomas 2.00 5.00
9 Jeff Hornacek 1.00 2.50
10 Kelly Tripucka .75 2.00
11 Maurice Cheeks 1.00 2.50
12 Nate Archibald 1.25 3.00
13 Rick Barry 1.50 4.00
14 Sidney Moncrief .75 2.00
15 Campy Russell .75 2.00
16 Vlade Divac 1.25 3.00
17 Alonzo Mourning 2.00 5.00
18 Sean Elliott 1.00 2.50
19 Cedric Maxwell 1.25 3.00
20 Rolando Blackman 1.00 2.50

2010-11 Prestige Old School Materials

STATED PRINT RUN 25 TO 249 SER.#'d SETS
*PRIME: .75X TO 2X BASE HI
PRIME PRINT RUN 25 TO 49 SER.#'d SETS
1 Earl Monroe/25 6.00 15.00
7 Gary Payton/249 6.00 15.00
9 Jeff Hornacek/149 3.00 8.00
10 Kelly Tripucka/249 2.50 6.00
11 Maurice Cheeks/249 3.00 8.00
17 Alonzo Mourning/249 6.00 15.00
20 Rolando Blackman/249 3.00 8.00

2010-11 Prestige Old School Signatures

STATED PRINT RUN 49 SER.#'d SETS
ASTERISK CARDS INSERTED IN SEASON UPDATE
1 Earl Monroe* 8.00 20.00
2 George Gervin 8.00 20.00
3 Paul Westphal* 8.00 20.00
4 Elgin Baylor* 10.00 25.00
5 Doc Rivers* 10.00 25.00
6 Gail Goodrich 8.00 20.00
7 Gary Payton* 10.00 25.00
8 Isiah Thomas* 12.00 30.00
9 Jeff Hornacek 8.00 20.00
12 Nate Archibald 8.00 20.00
13 Rick Barry 8.00 20.00
14 Sidney Moncrief* 8.00 20.00
15 Campy Russell* 8.00 20.00
16 Vlade Divac* 15.00 40.00
18 Sean Elliott* 15.00 40.00
19 Cedric Maxwell* 8.00 20.00

2010-11 Prestige Playmakers

COMPLETE SET (20) 15.00 30.00
1 Steve Nash 1.50 4.00
2 Chris Paul 1.50 4.00
3 Devin Harris .50 1.25
4 Jose Calderon .50 1.25
5 Stephen Curry 6.00 15.00
6 Tony Parker 1.25 3.00
7 Baron Davis .75 2.00
8 Andre Iguodala .75 2.00
9 Chris Duhon .50 1.25
10 Mike Conley Jr. .60 1.50
11 Raymond Felton .50 1.25
12 Jason Kidd 1.25 3.00
13 Brandon Jennings .50 1.25
14 Derrick Rose 1.50 4.00
15 Jameer Nelson .50 1.25
16 LeBron James 6.00 15.00
17 Andre Miller .60 1.50
18 Tyreke Evans .60 1.50
19 Darren Collison .50 1.25
20 Jonny Flynn .50 1.25

2010-11 Prestige Playmakers Materials

STATED PRINT RUN 50 TO 249 SER.#'d SETS
*PRIME: .75X TO 2X HI
PRIME PRINT RUN 5 TO 49 SER.#'d SETS
1 Steve Nash/249 6.00 15.00
2 Chris Paul/249 6.00 15.00
3 Devin Harris/249 2.00 5.00
4 Jose Calderon/249 2.00 5.00
5 Stephen Curry/249 25.00 60.00
6 Tony Parker/249 5.00 12.00
7 Baron Davis/249 3.00 8.00
8 Andre Iguodala/249 3.00 8.00
9 Chris Duhon/249 2.00 5.00
10 Mike Conley Jr./100 2.50 6.00
11 Raymond Felton/249 2.00 5.00
12 Jason Kidd/249 5.00 12.00
13 Brandon Jennings/249 2.00 5.00
14 Derrick Rose/149 6.00 15.00
15 Jameer Nelson/249 2.00 5.00
16 LeBron James/50 10.00 25.00
17 Andre Miller/249 2.50 6.00
18 Tyreke Evans/249 2.50 6.00
19 Darren Collison/249 2.00 5.00
20 Jonny Flynn/249 2.00 5.00

2010-11 Prestige Playmakers Signatures

STATED PRINT RUN 10 TO 49 SETS
INSERTED IN PACKS OF SEASON UPDATE
1 Steve Nash/25 40.00 100.00
3 Devin Harris/25 6.00 15.00
5 Stephen Curry/49 1,000.00 2,000.00
6 Tony Parker/42 15.00 40.00
13 Brandon Jennings/25 10.00 25.00

2010-11 Prestige Preferred Materials

COMPLETE SET (9) 20.00 40.00
STATED PRINT RUN 199 TO 249 SER.#'d SETS
MAT.SIG.PRINT RUN 10 TO 15 SETS
2 Allen Iverson/199 5.00 12.00
3 Jason Kidd/249 5.00 12.00
4 Devin Harris/249 2.00 5.00
5 Chris Bosh/249 4.00 10.00
6 Richard Hamilton/249 4.00 10.00
7 Amare Stoudemire/249 3.00 8.00
8 Russell Westbrook/99 5.00 12.00
9 Al Jefferson/249 2.00 5.00
10 Andrea Bargnani/249 2.00 5.00

2010-11 Prestige Preferred Materials Patches

*PATCH: .75X TO 2X BASE HI
STATED PRINT RUN 25 SER.#'d SETS
PATCH SIG.PRINT RUN 5 TO 10 SER.#'d SETS
1 Rajon Rondo/25 10.00 25.00

2010-11 Prestige Preferred Materials Signatures

STATED PRINT RUN 10 TO 15 SER.#'d SETS
4 Devin Harris/15 8.00 20.00
5 Chris Bosh/15 12.00 30.00
6 Richard Hamilton/15 8.00 20.00
7 Amare Stoudemire/15 15.00 40.00
10 Andrea Bargnani/15 8.00 20.00

2010-11 Prestige Preferred Signatures

STATED PRINT RUN 10 TO 40 SER.#'d SETS
4 Devin Harris/25 6.00 15.00
7 Amare Stoudemire/40 8.00 20.00
10 Andrea Bargnani/25 6.00 15.00

2010-11 Prestige Prestigious Picks Green

COMPLETE SET (35) 40.00 80.00
STATED PRINT RUN 499 SER.#'d SETS
*BLACK: 1.25X TO 3X BASE HI
BLACK PRINT RUN 25 SER.#'d SETS
*GOLD: .6X TO 1.5X BASE HI
GOLD PRINT RUN 99 SER.#'d SETS
*ORANGE: .6X TO 1.5X BASE HI
ORANGE PRINT RUN 299 SER.#'d SETS
1 John Wall 4.00 10.00
2 Evan Turner 1.00 2.50
3 Derrick Favors 1.25 3.00
4 Wesley Johnson .75 2.00
5 DeMarcus Cousins 2.50 6.00
6 Ekpe Udoh .75 2.00
7 Greg Monroe 1.00 2.50
8 Al-Farouq Aminu 1.00 2.50
9 Gordon Hayward 3.00 8.00
10 Paul George 6.00 15.00
11 Cole Aldrich .75 2.00
12 Xavier Henry .75 2.00
13 Ed Davis 1.00 2.50
14 Patrick Patterson 1.00 2.50
15 Larry Sanders .75 2.00
16 Luke Babbitt .75 2.00
17 Eric Bledsoe 1.50 4.00
18 Avery Bradley 1.25 3.00
19 James Anderson .75 2.00
20 Craig Brackins .75 2.00
21 Elliot Williams .75 2.00
22 Trevor Booker .75 2.00
23 Damion James .75 2.00
24 Dominique Jones .75 2.00
25 Quincy Pondexter .75 2.00
26 Jordan Crawford .75 2.00
27 Greivis Vasquez .75 2.00
28 Daniel Orton .75 2.00
29 Lazar Hayward .75 2.00
30 Dexter Pittman .75 2.00
31 Da'Sean Butler 1.00 2.50
32 Luke Harangody .75 2.00
33 Willie Warren .75 2.00
34 Gani Lawal .75 2.00
35 Stanley Robinson .75 2.00

2010-11 Prestige Prestigious Picks Materials Green

STATED PRINT RUN 499 SER.#'d SETS
*BLACK: .6X TO 1.5X BASE HI
BLACK PRINT RUN 25 SER.#'d SETS
*GOLD: .5X TO 1.25X BASE HI
GOLD PRINT RUN 99 SER.#'d SETS
1 John Wall 6.00 15.00
2 Evan Turner 1.50 4.00
3 Derrick Favors 2.00 5.00
4 Wesley Johnson 1.25 3.00
5 DeMarcus Cousins 4.00 10.00
6 Ekpe Udoh 1.25 3.00
7 Greg Monroe 1.50 4.00
8 Al-Farouq Aminu 1.50 4.00
9 Gordon Hayward 5.00 12.00
10 Paul George 10.00 25.00
11 Cole Aldrich 1.25 3.00
12 Xavier Henry 1.25 3.00
13 Ed Davis 1.50 4.00
14 Patrick Patterson 1.50 4.00
15 Larry Sanders 1.25 3.00
16 Luke Babbitt 1.25 3.00
17 Eric Bledsoe 2.50 6.00
18 Avery Bradley 2.00 5.00
19 James Anderson 1.25 3.00
20 Craig Brackins 1.25 3.00
21 Elliot Williams 1.25 3.00
22 Trevor Booker 1.25 3.00
23 Damion James 1.25 3.00
24 Dominique Jones 1.25 3.00
25 Quincy Pondexter 1.25 3.00
26 Jordan Crawford 1.25 3.00
27 Greivis Vasquez 1.25 3.00
28 Daniel Orton 1.25 3.00
29 Lazar Hayward 1.25 3.00
30 Dexter Pittman 1.25 3.00
31 Da'Sean Butler 1.50 4.00
32 Luke Harangody 1.25 3.00
33 Willie Warren 1.25 3.00
34 Gani Lawal 1.25 3.00

2010-11 Prestige Prestigious Picks Signatures Black

STATED PRINT RUN 25 TO 249 SER.#'d SETS
1 John Wall/49 40.00 100.00
2 Evan Turner/25 12.00 30.00
3 Derrick Favors/249 4.00 10.00
4 Wesley Johnson/249 2.50 6.00
5 DeMarcus Cousins/249 12.00 30.00
6 Ekpe Udoh/249 2.50 6.00
8 Al-Farouq Aminu/249 3.00 8.00
11 Cole Aldrich/249 2.50 6.00
12 Xavier Henry/249 2.50 6.00
13 Ed Davis/249 3.00 8.00
14 Patrick Patterson/149 3.00 8.00
16 Luke Babbitt/249 2.50 6.00
17 Eric Bledsoe/249 5.00 12.00
18 Avery Bradley/249 4.00 10.00
19 James Anderson/249 2.50 6.00
24 Dominique Jones/25 8.00 20.00
25 Quincy Pondexter/249 2.50 6.00
26 Jordan Crawford/249 2.50 6.00
28 Daniel Orton/249 2.50 6.00
29 Lazar Hayward/249 2.50 6.00
30 Dexter Pittman/49 2.50 6.00
31 Da'Sean Butler/49 5.00 12.00
32 Luke Harangody/99 2.50 6.00
34 Gani Lawal/249 2.50 6.00

2010-11 Prestige Prestigious Pros Green

COMPLETE SET (65) 40.00 80.00
STATED PRINT RUN 499 SER.#'d SETS
*BLACK: 1.25X TO 3X BASE HI
BLACK PRINT RUN 25 SER.#'d SETS
*GOLD: .5X TO 1.25X BASE HI
GOLD PRINT RUN 99 SER.#'d SETS
*ORANGE: .6X TO 1.5X BASE HI
ORANGE PRINT RUN 299 SER.#'d SETS
1 Ray Allen 1.50 4.00
2 Glen Davis .60 1.50
3 Kevin Garnett 2.50 6.00
4 Yi Jianlian 1.00 2.50
5 Terrence Williams .60 1.50
6 Bill Walker .60 1.50
7 Chris Duhon .60 1.50
8 Elton Brand .75 2.00
9 Thaddeus Young .60 1.50
10 Hedo Turkoglu .75 2.00
11 Jose Calderon .60 1.50
12 Joakim Noah 1.00 2.50
13 Kirk Hinrich .75 2.00
14 Shaquille O'Neal 4.00 10.00
15 Zydrunas Ilgauskas .75 2.00
16 LeBron James 8.00 20.00
17 Richard Hamilton 1.25 3.00
18 Rodney Stuckey .60 1.50
19 Mike Dunleavy .60 1.50
20 Troy Murphy .60 1.50
21 Andrew Bogut .75 2.00
22 Michael Redd .75 2.00
23 Al Horford 1.00 2.50
24 Mike Bibby 1.00 2.50
25 D.J. Augustin .60 1.50
26 Tyson Chandler .75 2.00
27 Carlos Arroyo .60 1.50
28 Mario Chalmers .75 2.00
29 Dwyane Wade 2.00 5.00
30 Marcin Gortat .75 2.00
31 Mickael Pietrus .60 1.50
32 Randy Foye .60 1.50
33 Nick Young .60 1.50
34 Shawn Marion 1.00 2.50
35 Caron Butler .75 2.00
36 Shane Battier .75 2.00
37 Luis Scola .75 2.00
38 Marc Gasol 1.00 2.50
39 O.J. Mayo .60 1.50
40 David West .75 2.00
41 Peja Stojakovic .75 2.00
42 Richard Jefferson .75 2.00
43 Tim Duncan 2.50 6.00
44 Arron Afflalo .60 1.50
45 J.R. Smith 1.00 2.50
46 Kevin Love 1.00 2.50
47 Al Jefferson .60 1.50
48 Greg Oden .60 1.50
49 Rudy Fernandez .60 1.50
50 Russell Westbrook 1.50 4.00
51 Jeff Green .75 2.00
52 Andrei Kirilenko .75 2.00
53 Carlos Boozer .75 2.00
54 Andris Biedrins .60 1.50
55 Anthony Randolph .60 1.50
56 Baron Davis 1.00 2.50
57 Chris Kaman .60 1.50
58 Derek Fisher 1.00 2.50
59 Ron Artest 1.00 2.50
60 Kobe Bryant 8.00 20.00
61 Leandro Barbosa .75 2.00
62 Grant Hill 1.50 4.00
63 Channing Frye .60 1.50
64 Omri Casspi .60 1.50
65 Tyreke Evans .75 2.00

2010-11 Prestige Prestigious Pros Materials Black

*BLACK: .6X TO 1.5X BASE HI
STATED PRINT RUN 10 TO 25 SER.#'d SETS

2010-11 Prestige Prestigious Pros Materials Gold

*GOLD: .5X TO 1.25X BASE HI
STATED PRINT RUN 25 TO 99 SER.#'d SETS

2010-11 Prestige Prestigious Pros Materials Green

STATED PRINT RUN 50 TO 499 SER.#'d SETS
BLACK PRINT RUN 10 TO 25 SER.#'d SETS
GOLD PRINT RUN 25 TO 99 SER.#'d SETS
PLATINUM PRINT RUN 5 TO 25 SETS
1 Ray Allen/199 5.00 12.00
2 Glen Davis 2.00 5.00
3 Kevin Garnett 8.00 20.00
5 Terrence Williams 2.00 5.00
6 Bill Walker 2.00 5.00
7 Chris Duhon 2.00 5.00
8 Elton Brand 2.50 6.00
9 Thaddeus Young 2.00 5.00
10 Hedo Turkoglu 2.50 6.00
11 Jose Calderon 2.00 5.00
12 Joakim Noah 3.00 8.00
13 Kirk Hinrich 2.50 6.00
14 Shaquille O'Neal 12.00 30.00
15 Zydrunas Ilgauskas 2.50 6.00
16 LeBron James/50 10.00 25.00
17 Richard Hamilton 4.00 10.00
18 Rodney Stuckey 2.00 5.00
19 Mike Dunleavy 2.00 5.00
20 Troy Murphy 2.00 5.00
21 Andrew Bogut 2.50 6.00
22 Michael Redd 2.50 6.00
23 Al Horford 3.00 8.00
24 Mike Bibby 3.00 8.00
25 D.J. Augustin 2.00 5.00
27 Carlos Arroyo 2.00 5.00
28 Mario Chalmers 2.50 6.00
29 Dwyane Wade 6.00 15.00
30 Marcin Gortat 2.50 6.00
31 Mickael Pietrus 2.00 5.00
32 Randy Foye 2.00 5.00
33 Nick Young 2.00 5.00
34 Shawn Marion 3.00 8.00
35 Caron Butler 2.50 6.00
36 Shane Battier 2.50 6.00
37 Luis Scola 2.50 6.00
38 Marc Gasol 3.00 8.00
39 O.J. Mayo 2.00 5.00
40 David West 2.50 6.00
41 Peja Stojakovic 2.50 6.00
42 Richard Jefferson 2.50 6.00
43 Tim Duncan 8.00 20.00
44 Arron Afflalo 2.00 5.00
45 J.R. Smith 3.00 8.00
46 Kevin Love 3.00 8.00
47 Al Jefferson 2.00 5.00
48 Greg Oden 2.00 5.00
49 Rudy Fernandez 2.00 5.00
50 Russell Westbrook/99 5.00 12.00
51 Jeff Green 2.50 6.00
52 Andrei Kirilenko 2.50 6.00
53 Carlos Boozer 2.50 6.00
54 Andris Biedrins 2.00 5.00
55 Anthony Randolph 2.00 5.00
56 Baron Davis 3.00 8.00
57 Chris Kaman 2.00 5.00
58 Derek Fisher 3.00 8.00
59 Ron Artest 3.00 8.00
60 Kobe Bryant 12.00 30.00
61 Leandro Barbosa 2.50 6.00
62 Grant Hill 6.00 15.00
63 Channing Frye 2.00 5.00
64 Omri Casspi 2.00 5.00
65 Tyreke Evans 2.50 6.00

2010-11 Prestige Prestigious Pros Materials Patches Platinum

*PATCH: .75X TO 2X BASE HI
STATED PRINT RUN 5 TO 25 SER.#'d SETS

2010-11 Prestige Prestigious Pros Signatures Black

STATED PRINT RUN 24 TO 49 SER.#'d SETS
5 Terrence Williams/49 5.00 12.00
25 D.J. Augustin/49 5.00 12.00
32 Randy Foye/49 5.00 12.00
36 Shane Battier/49 5.00 12.00
46 Kevin Love/25 8.00 20.00
56 Baron Davis/49 6.00 15.00
57 Chris Kaman/24 5.00 12.00
59 Ron Artest/25 12.50 30.00
60 Kobe Bryant/49 1,500.00 3,000.00
64 Omri Casspi/49 5.00 12.00
65 Tyreke Evans/49 10.00 25.00

2010-11 Prestige Stars of the NBA

COMPLETE SET (14) 15.00 30.00
1 Rajon Rondo 1.25 3.00
2 Joe Johnson 1.00 2.50
3 Amare Stoudemire 1.00 2.50
4 Tyreke Evans .75 2.00
5 Paul Pierce 1.50 4.00
6 Russell Westbrook 1.50 4.00
7 Kobe Bryant 8.00 20.00
8 Derrick Rose 2.00 5.00

9 Monta Ellis .75 2.00
10 David Lee .60 1.50
11 Caron Butler .75 2.00
12 LeBron James 8.00 20.00
13 Pau Gasol 1.50 4.00
14 Chauncey Billups 1.25 3.00
15 Kevin Martin .75 2.00

2010-11 Prestige Stars of the NBA Materials

STATED PRINT RUN 50 TO 249 SER.#'d SETS
2 Joe Johnson/249 3.00 8.00
3 Amare Stoudemire/249 3.00 8.00
4 Tyreke Evans/249 2.50 6.00
5 Paul Pierce/249 5.00 12.00
6 Russell Westbrook/99 5.00 12.00
7 Kobe Bryant/249 12.00 30.00
8 Derrick Rose/149 6.00 15.00
11 Caron Butler/249 2.50 6.00
12 LeBron James/50 8.00 20.00
13 Pau Gasol/249 5.00 12.00
14 Chauncey Billups/249 4.00 10.00
15 Kevin Martin/249 2.50 6.00

2010-11 Prestige Stars of the NBA Materials Prime

*PRIME: .75X TO 2X HI
STATED PRINT RUN 5 TO 49 SER.#'d SETS

2010-11 Prestige Stars of the NBA Signatures

STATED PRINT RUN 10 TO 25 SER.#'d SETS
3 Amare Stoudemire/25 15.00 40.00
4 Tyreke Evans/25 12.00 30.00
7 Kobe Bryant/25 1,500.00 3,000.00

2010-11 Prestige Stat Stars

COMPLETE SET (25) 20.00 40.00
1 Kevin Durant 3.00 8.00
2 LeBron James 6.00 15.00
3 Carmelo Anthony 1.25 3.00
4 Kobe Bryant 6.00 15.00
5 Dwyane Wade 1.50 4.00
6 Monta Ellis .60 1.50
7 Dirk Nowitzki 2.00 5.00
8 Dwight Howard 1.00 2.50
9 Marcus Camby .60 1.50
10 Zach Randolph .75 2.00
11 David Lee .50 1.25
12 Pau Gasol 1.25 3.00
13 Carlos Boozer .60 1.50
14 Steve Nash 1.50 4.00
15 Chris Paul 1.50 4.00
16 Deron Williams .60 1.50
17 Rajon Rondo 1.00 2.50
18 Jason Kidd 1.25 3.00
19 Baron Davis .75 2.00
20 Andrew Bogut .60 1.50
21 Josh Smith .50 1.25
22 Brendan Haywood .50 1.25
23 Chris Andersen .75 2.00
24 Samuel Dalembert .50 1.25
25 Brook Lopez .60 1.50

2010-11 Prestige Stat Stars Materials

STATED PRINT RUN 50 TO 249 SER.#'d SETS
*PRIME: .75X TO 2X HI
PRIME PRINT RUN 10 TO 49 SER.#'d SETS
1 Kevin Durant/50 8.00 20.00
2 LeBron James/50 10.00 25.00
3 Carmelo Anthony/249 5.00 12.00
4 Kobe Bryant/249 8.00 20.00
5 Dwyane Wade/249 6.00 15.00
7 Dirk Nowitzki/249 8.00 20.00
8 Dwight Howard/249 4.00 10.00
9 Marcus Camby/249 2.50 6.00
12 Pau Gasol/249 5.00 12.00
13 Carlos Boozer/249 2.50 6.00
14 Steve Nash/249 6.00 15.00
15 Chris Paul/249 6.00 15.00
16 Deron Williams/249 2.50 6.00
18 Jason Kidd/249 5.00 12.00
19 Baron Davis/249 3.00 8.00
20 Andrew Bogut/249 2.50 6.00
21 Josh Smith/249 2.00 5.00
22 Brendan Haywood/249 2.00 5.00
23 Chris Andersen/249 3.00 8.00
24 Samuel Dalembert/249 2.00 5.00
25 Brook Lopez/249 2.50 6.00

2010-11 Prestige Stat Stars Signatures

STATED PRINT RUN 10 TO 25 SER.#'d SETS
4 Kobe Bryant/25 1,500.00 3,000.00
16 Deron Williams/25 12.00 30.00
19 Baron Davis/25 10.00 25.00

2010-11 Prestige Super Sophs

COMPLETE SET (5) 4.00 10.00
1 Tyreke Evans .75 2.00
2 Brandon Jennings .60 1.50
3 Stephen Curry 8.00 20.00
4 Darren Collison .60 1.50
5 DeJuan Blair .60 1.50

2010-11 Prestige Super Sophs Materials

STATED PRINT RUN 249 SER.#'d SETS
*PRIME: .75X TO 2X HI
PRIME PRINT RUN 5 TO 49 SER.#'d SETS
1 Tyreke Evans/249 2.50 6.00
2 Brandon Jennings/249 2.00 5.00
3 Stephen Curry/249 25.00 60.00
4 Darren Collison/249 2.00 5.00
5 DeJuan Blair/249 2.00 5.00

2010-11 Prestige Super Sophs Signatures

STATED PRINT RUN 25 SER.#'d SETS
INSERTED IN PACKS OF SEASON UPDATE
2 Brandon Jennings/25 10.00 25.00
3 Stephen Curry/25 1,500.00 3,000.00

2010-11 Prestige True Colors

1 Kobe Bryant 6.00 15.00
2 Tim Duncan 2.00 5.00
3 Paul Pierce 1.25 3.00
4 Dirk Nowitzki 2.00 5.00
5 Tony Parker 1.25 3.00

2010-11 Prestige True Colors Materials

STATED PRINT RUN 249 SER.#'d SETS
*PRIME: .75X TO 2X HI
PRIME PRINT RUN 10 TO 49 SER.#'d SETS
1 Kobe Bryant/249 8.00 20.00
2 Tim Duncan/249 8.00 20.00
3 Paul Pierce/249 5.00 12.00
4 Dirk Nowitzki/249 8.00 20.00
5 Tony Parker/249 5.00 12.00

2010-11 Prestige True Colors Signatures

STATED PRINT RUN 25 SER.#'d SETS
ASTERISK CARDS INSERTED IN SEASON UPDATE
1 Kobe Bryant/25 1,500.00 3,000.00
5 Tony Parker/25* 15.00 40.00

2012-13 Prestige

ROOKIES INSERTED ONE PER PACK
1 LaMarcus Aldridge .40 1.00
2 Ray Allen .60 1.50
3 Al-Farouq Aminu .25 .60
4 JaVale McGee .30 .75
5 Ryan Anderson .25 .60
6 Carmelo Anthony .60 1.50
7 Trevor Ariza .25 .60
8 D.J. Augustin .25 .60
9 J.J. Barea .30 .75
10 Andrea Bargnani .25 .60
11 Nicolas Batum .30 .75
12 Michael Beasley .25 .60
13 Rodrigue Beaubois .25 .60
14 DeJuan Blair .25 .60
15 Andrew Bogut .30 .75
16 Trevor Booker .25 .60
17 Carlos Boozer .30 .75
18 Chris Bosh .50 1.25
19 Avery Bradley .25 .60
20 Elton Brand .30 .75
21 Kobe Bryant 3.00 8.00
22 Andrew Bynum .25 .60
23 Jose Calderon .25 .60
24 Vince Carter .75 2.00
25 Mario Chalmers .30 .75
26 Tyson Chandler .30 .75
27 Darren Collison .25 .60
28 Mike Conley .30 .75
29 DeMarcus Cousins .40 1.00
30 Jamal Crawford .40 1.00
31 Jordan Crawford .25 .60
32 Stephen Curry 3.00 8.00
33 Ed Davis .25 .60
34 Glen Davis .25 .60
35 Boris Diaw .30 .75
36 Luol Deng .30 .75
37 DeMar DeRozan .50 1.25
38 Goran Dragic .40 1.00
39 Jared Dudley .25 .60
40 Tim Duncan 1.00 2.50
41 Kevin Durant 1.50 4.00
42 Devin Ebanks .25 .60
43 Monta Ellis .30 .75
44 Tyreke Evans .25 .60
45 Raymond Felton .25 .60
46 Landry Fields .25 .60
47 Channing Frye .25 .60
48 Danilo Gallinari .25 .60
49 Kevin Garnett 1.00 2.50
50 Marc Gasol .40 1.00
51 Pau Gasol .60 1.50
52 Rudy Gay .40 1.00
53 Paul George .60 1.50
54 Taj Gibson .25 .60
55 Manu Ginobili .75 2.00
56 Drew Gooden .25 .60
57 Ben Gordon .30 .75
58 Eric Gordon .30 .75
59 Marcin Gortat .25 .60
60 Danny Granger .25 .60
61 Blake Griffin .40 1.00
62 Tyler Hansbrough .25 .60
63 James Harden .75 2.00
64 Al Harrington .30 .75
65 Gordon Hayward .40 1.00
66 Gerald Henderson .25 .60
67 Roy Hibbert .30 .75
68 George Hill .30 .75
69 Grant Hill .60 1.50
70 Jrue Holiday .50 1.25
71 Al Horford .40 1.00
72 Dwight Howard .50 1.25
73 Kris Humphries .25 .60
74 Serge Ibaka .30 .75
75 Andre Iguodala .40 1.00
76 Ersan Ilyasova .25 .60
77 Jarrett Jack .30 .75
78 Stephen Jackson .30 .75
79 LeBron James 3.00 8.00
80 Antawn Jamison .30 .75
81 Al Jefferson .25 .60
82 Brandon Jennings .30 .75
83 Joe Johnson .30 .75
84 DeAndre Jordan .30 .75
85 Chris Kaman .30 .75
86 Jason Kidd .60 1.50
87 Carl Landry .25 .60
88 Ty Lawson .25 .60
89 Courtney Lee .25 .60
90 David Lee .25 .60
91 Jeremy Lin .60 1.50
92 Brook Lopez .30 .75
93 Kevin Love .40 1.00
94 Kyle Lowry .40 1.00
95 Corey Maggette .25 .60
96 Shawn Marion .40 1.00
97 Kevin Martin .30 .75
98 Wesley Matthews .25 .60
99 O.J. Mayo .25 .60
100 Andre Miller .30 .75
101 Paul Millsap .30 .75
102 Greg Monroe .25 .60
103 Steve Nash .75 2.00
104 Jameer Nelson .25 .60
105 Nene .30 .75
106 Steve Novak .25 .60
107 Joakim Noah .30 .75
108 Dirk Nowitzki 1.00 2.50
109 Emeka Okafor .30 .75
110 Tony Parker .60 1.50
111 Chris Paul .75 2.00
112 Tayshaun Prince .40 1.00
113 Zach Randolph .40 1.00
114 Jason Richardson .40 1.00
115 Luke Ridnour .30 .75
116 Nate Robinson .25 .60
117 Rajon Rondo .50 1.25
118 Derrick Rose .60 1.50
119 Ricky Rubio .30 .75
120 Luis Scola .30 .75
121 Ramon Sessions .25 .60
122 J.R. Smith .40 1.00
123 Josh Smith .25 .60
124 Marreese Speights .25 .60
125 Amare Stoudemire .40 1.00
126 Rodney Stuckey .25 .60
127 Jeff Teague .25 .60
128 Jason Terry .30 .75
129 Jason Thompson .25 .60
130 Marcus Thornton .25 .60
131 Hedo Turkoglu .30 .75
132 Evan Turner .25 .60
133 Ekpe Udoh .25 .60
134 Anderson Varejao .25 .60
135 Dwyane Wade .75 2.00
136 John Wall .50 1.25
137 Gerald Wallace .30 .75
138 David West .30 .75
139 Delonte West .25 .60
140 Russell Westbrook .60 1.50
141 Deron Williams .30 .75
142 Louis Williams .30 .75
143 Mo Williams .30 .75
144 Metta World Peace .30 .75
145 Dorell Wright .25 .60
146 Nick Young .25 .60
147 Richard Hamilton .40 1.00
148 Thaddeus Young .25 .60
149 Kirk Hinrich .30 .75
150 Paul Pierce .60 1.50
151 Kyrie Irving RC 5.00 12.00
152 Derrick Williams RC .50 1.25
153 Brandon Knight RC .60 1.50
154 MarShon Brooks RC .50 1.25
155 Klay Thompson RC 5.00 12.00
156 Kemba Walker RC 2.00 5.00
157 Isaiah Thomas RC 1.00 2.50
158 Kenneth Faried RC .60 1.50
159 Iman Shumpert RC .60 1.50
160 Chandler Parsons RC .60 1.50
161 Tristan Thompson RC .75 2.00
162 Kawhi Leonard RC 6.00 15.00
163 Jimmer Fredette RC .75 2.00
164 Vernon Macklin RC .50 1.25
165 Markieff Morris RC .75 2.00
166 Alec Burks RC .75 2.00
167 Norris Cole RC .50 1.25
168 Ivan Johnson RC .50 1.25
169 Jeremy Pargo RC .50 1.25
170 Gustavo Ayon RC .50 1.25
171 Charles Jenkins RC .50 1.25
172 Nikola Vucevic RC 2.00 5.00
173 Donald Sloan RC .50 1.25
174 Bismack Biyombo RC .60 1.50
175 Tobias Harris RC 1.50 4.00
176 Jeremy Tyler RC .50 1.25
177 Jon Leuer RC .50 1.25
178 Jan Vesely RC .50 1.25
179 Chris Singleton RC .50 1.25
180 Enes Kanter RC .60 1.50
181 Jordan Williams RC .50 1.25
182 Jordan Hamilton RC .50 1.25
183 Josh Harrellson RC .50 1.25
184 Andrew Goudelock RC .50 1.25
185 Lavoy Allen RC .50 1.25
186 Lance Thomas RC .50 1.25
187 Cory Higgins RC .50 1.25
188 Nolan Smith RC .50 1.25
189 Marcus Morris RC .75 2.00
190 Trey Thompkins RC .50 1.25
191 Elliot Williams .25 .60
192 Terrel Harris RC .50 1.25
193 Shelvin Mack RC .50 1.25
194 JaJuan Johnson RC .50 1.25
195 Reggie Jackson RC .75 2.00
196 Greg Stiemsma RC .60 1.50
197 E'Twaun Moore RC .60 1.50
198 Josh Selby RC .50 1.25
199 Jimmy Butler RC 5.00 12.00
200 Cory Joseph RC .60 1.50
201 Anthony Davis RC 6.00 15.00
202 Austin Rivers RC .75 2.00
203 Jeremy Lamb RC .75 2.00
204 Michael Kidd-Gilchrist RC .60 1.50
205 Terrence Ross RC 1.25 3.00
206 Andre Drummond RC 1.25 3.00
207 Thomas Robinson RC .50 1.25
208 Kendall Marshall RC .50 1.25
209 Terrence Jones RC .50 1.25
210 Meyers Leonard RC .50 1.25
211 Harrison Barnes RC 1.00 2.50
212 Bradley Beal RC 4.00 10.00
213 Dion Waiters RC .60 1.50
214 Damian Lillard RC 5.00 12.00
215 John Henson RC .60 1.50
216 Moe Harkless RC .60 1.50
217 Royce White RC .50 1.25
218 Tyler Zeller RC .50 1.25
219 Andrew Nicholson RC .50 1.25
220 Evan Fournier RC .75 2.00
221 Jared Sullinger RC .60 1.50
222 Fab Melo RC .50 1.25
223 Tony Wroten RC .60 1.50
224 Perry Jones RC .50 1.25
225 Miles Plumlee RC .50 1.25
226 Jared Cunningham RC .50 1.25
227 John Jenkins RC .50 1.25
228 Marquis Teague RC .50 1.25
229 Festus Ezeli RC .50 1.25
230 Arnett Moultrie RC .50 1.25
231 Bernard James RC .50 1.25
232 Orlando Johnson RC .50 1.25
233 Jeff Taylor RC .50 1.25
234 Quincy Acy RC .50 1.25
235 Justin Harper RC .50 1.25
236 Jae Crowder RC 1.00 2.50
237 Draymond Green RC 3.00 8.00
238 Quincy Miller RC .50 1.25
239 Khris Middleton RC 2.50 6.00
240 Will Barton RC 1.00 2.50
241 Kim English RC .50 1.25
242 Darius Miller RC .60 1.50
243 Doron Lamb RC .50 1.25
244 Mike Scott RC .60 1.50
245 Justin Hamilton RC .50 1.25
246 Tornike Shengelia RC .50 1.25
247 Kyle O'Quinn RC .60 1.50
248 Robert Sacre RC .50 1.25
249 Tyshawn Taylor RC .50 1.25
250 Kris Joseph RC .50 1.25

2012-13 Prestige Bonus Shots Gold

*GOLD: 1X TO 2.5X BASE HI
STATED PRINT RUN 249 SER.#'d SETS

2012-13 Prestige All-Stars East

COMPLETE SET (14) 20.00 50.00
1 Dwyane Wade 3.00 8.00
2 Derrick Rose 2.50 6.00
3 Dwight Howard 2.00 5.00
4 LeBron James 12.00 30.00
5 Carmelo Anthony 2.50 6.00
6 Chris Bosh 2.00 5.00
7 Luol Deng 1.25 3.00
8 Roy Hibbert 1.25 3.00
9 Andre Iguodala 1.50 4.00
10 Rajon Rondo 2.00 5.00
11 Paul Pierce 2.50 6.00
12 Deron Williams 1.25 3.00
13 Tom Thibodeau 1.50 4.00
14 Team Photo 4.00 10.00

2012-13 Prestige All-Stars West

COMPLETE SET (14) 20.00 50.00
1 Kobe Bryant 12.00 30.00
2 Chris Paul 3.00 8.00
3 Andrew Bynum 1.00 2.50
4 Blake Griffin 1.50 4.00
5 Kevin Durant 6.00 15.00
6 LaMarcus Aldridge 1.50 4.00
7 Marc Gasol 1.50 4.00
8 Kevin Love 1.50 4.00
9 Steve Nash 3.00 8.00
10 Dirk Nowitzki 4.00 10.00
11 Tony Parker 2.50 6.00
12 Russell Westbrook 2.50 6.00
13 Scott Brooks 1.00 2.50
14 Team Photo 4.00 10.00

2012-13 Prestige Connections

COMPLETE SET (25) 12.00 30.00
1 A.Davis/M.Kidd-Gilchrist 5.00 12.00
2 Marc.Morris/Mark.Morris .60 1.50
3 R.Westbrook/K.Love 1.00 2.50
4 J.Holiday/D.Collison .75 2.00
5 V.Carter/A.Jamison 1.25 3.00
6 J.Terry/M.Ginobili 1.25 3.00
7 L.Aldridge/K.Durant 2.50 6.00
8 J.Wall/R.Rondo .75 2.00
9 C.Paul/B.Griffin 1.25 3.00
10 D.DeRozan/T.Gibson .75 2.00
11 O.J. Mayo/N.Young .40 1.00
12 T.Parker/N.Batum 1.00 2.50
13 M.Gasol/P.Gasol 1.00 2.50
14 E.Turner/M.Conley .50 1.25
15 D.Rose/T.Evans 1.00 2.50
16 T.Chandler/D.Howard .75 2.00
17 S.Nash/D.Nowitzki 1.50 4.00
18 D.Fisher/K.Bryant 5.00 12.00
19 J.Noah/A.Horford .60 1.50
20 D.Wade/L.James 5.00 12.00
21 R.Gay/R.Allen 1.00 2.50
22 R.Hamilton/B.Gordon .60 1.50
23 S.Marion/A.Stoudemire .60 1.50
24 K.Malone/J.Stockton 1.25 3.00
25 M.Johnson/L.Bird 2.50 6.00

2012-13 Prestige Distinctive Ink

1 Kevin Durant 75.00 200.00
2 Kobe Bryant 500.00 1,000.00
3 Gordon Hayward 6.00 15.00
4 O.J. Mayo EXCH 6.00 15.00
5 Danilo Gallinari 6.00 15.00
6 Marcin Gortat 6.00 15.00
7 Monta Ellis 6.00 15.00
8 Stephen Jackson 6.00 15.00
9 Andrew Bogut 6.00 15.00
10 Danny Granger EXCH 6.00 15.00

2012-13 Prestige Franchise Favorites

COMPLETE SET (25) 10.00 25.00
1 Kevin Durant 2.50 6.00
2 Kevin Martin .50 1.25
3 Al Horford .60 1.50
4 Stephen Curry 5.00 12.00
5 Dirk Nowitzki 1.50 4.00
6 LeBron James 5.00 12.00
7 Paul Pierce 1.00 2.50
8 Deron Williams .50 1.25
9 Dwight Howard .75 2.00
10 Kobe Bryant 5.00 12.00
11 Blake Griffin .60 1.50
12 Ricky Rubio .60 1.50
13 Joakim Noah .50 1.25
14 Danny Granger .40 1.00
15 Manu Ginobili 1.25 3.00
16 Tayshaun Prince .60 1.50
17 Marc Gasol .60 1.50
18 Carmelo Anthony 1.00 2.50
19 Kyrie Irving 3.00 8.00
20 John Wall .75 2.00
21 DeMar DeRozan .75 2.00
22 Andre Iguodala .60 1.50
23 Tony Parker 1.00 2.50
24 Kevin Love .60 1.50
25 Ty Lawson .40 1.00

2012-13 Prestige Hardcourt Heroes

COMPLETE SET (25) 10.00 25.00
1 Rajon Rondo .75 2.00
2 Carmelo Anthony 1.00 2.50
3 Kevin Durant 2.50 6.00
4 Kobe Bryant 5.00 12.00
5 LeBron James 5.00 12.00
6 Dirk Nowitzki 1.50 4.00
7 Kevin Love .60 1.50
8 Dwyane Wade 1.25 3.00
9 Derrick Rose 1.00 2.50
10 Dwight Howard .75 2.00
11 Tim Duncan 1.50 4.00
12 LaMarcus Aldridge .60 1.50
13 Blake Griffin .60 1.50
14 Steve Nash 1.25 3.00
15 Josh Smith .40 1.00
16 Andrew Bynum .40 1.00
17 Tyreke Evans .50 1.25
18 Russell Westbrook 1.00 2.50
19 Chris Paul 1.25 3.00
20 Brandon Jennings .40 1.00
21 John Wall .75 2.00
22 Kevin Garnett 1.50 4.00
23 Al Jefferson .40 1.00
24 Rudy Gay .60 1.50
25 Monta Ellis .50 1.25

2012-13 Prestige Inside the Numbers Materials

1 Kevin Durant 10.00 25.00
2 Kobe Bryant 20.00 50.00
3 Tyson Chandler 2.00 5.00
4 Rajon Rondo 4.00 10.00
5 Ricky Rubio 8.00 20.00
6 Joe Johnson 2.00 5.00
7 Chris Paul 5.00 12.00
8 Steve Nash 5.00 12.00
9 Serge Ibaka 2.00 5.00
10 Dwight Howard 3.00 8.00
11 Mike Conley 2.00 5.00
12 Kevin Love 2.50 6.00
13 Andrew Bynum 1.50 4.00
14 DeAndre Jordan 2.00 5.00
15 Josh Smith 1.50 4.00
16 DeMarcus Cousins 2.50 6.00
17 Blake Griffin 2.50 6.00
18 LeBron James 20.00 50.00
19 Russell Westbrook 4.00 10.00
20 Carmelo Anthony 4.00 10.00
21 Derrick Rose 10.00 25.00
22 Dwyane Wade 5.00 12.00
23 Jose Calderon 1.50 4.00
24 Deron Williams 2.00 5.00
25 John Wall 3.00 8.00
26 Jason Kidd 4.00 10.00
27 Paul Pierce 4.00 10.00
28 LaMarcus Aldridge 2.50 6.00
29 Marcus Camby 2.00 5.00
30 Metta World Peace 2.00 5.00
31 David Lee 1.50 4.00
32 Kyrie Irving 15.00 40.00
33 Stephen Curry 20.00 50.00
34 Tony Parker 4.00 10.00
35 Luol Deng 2.00 5.00
36 Marc Gasol 2.50 6.00
37 Manu Ginobili 5.00 12.00
38 Ryan Anderson 1.50 4.00
39 Kevin Garnett 6.00 15.00
40 Andre Miller 2.00 5.00
41 James Harden 5.00 12.00
42 Antawn Jamison 2.00 5.00
43 Tim Duncan 6.00 15.00
44 Dirk Nowitzki 6.00 15.00
45 Jordan Crawford 1.50 4.00
46 Greg Monroe 1.50 4.00
47 Kenneth Faried 2.00 5.00
48 Baron Davis 2.00 5.00
49 Ty Lawson 1.50 4.00
50 Amare Stoudemire 2.50 6.00

2012-13 Prestige Inside the Numbers Materials Prime

*PRIME: 1.25X TO 3X BASE HI
STATED PRINT RUN 25 SER.#'d SETS
5 Ricky Rubio 40.00 100.00
21 Derrick Rose 12.00 30.00
23 Jose Calderon 10.00 25.00
26 Jason Kidd 12.00 30.00
27 Paul Pierce 12.00 30.00
37 Manu Ginobili 12.00 30.00
47 Kenneth Faried 40.00 100.00

2012-13 Prestige Old School Signatures

STATED PRINT RUN 25 TO 99 SETS
1 Rick Barry/49 12.00 30.00
2 Walt Bellamy/99 6.00 15.00
3 Tom Chambers/99 6.00 15.00
4 Bob Lanier/49 10.00 25.00
5 Spud Webb/99 EXCH 8.00 20.00
6 Kenny Anderson/99 6.00 15.00
7 Rod Strickland/99 6.00 15.00
8 Steve Smith/99 6.00 15.00
9 Vlade Divac/99 EXCH 6.00 15.00
10 Adrian Dantley/99 6.00 15.00
11 Buck Williams/99 6.00 15.00
12 Sidney Moncrief/99 6.00 15.00
13 Reggie Theus/99 6.00 15.00
14 Eddie Johnson/99 6.00 15.00
15 Kevin Willis/99 6.00 15.00
16 Larry Johnson/99 EXCH 6.00 15.00
17 Detlef Schrempf/99 6.00 15.00
18 Fat Lever/99 6.00 15.00
19 Kenny Walker/99 6.00 15.00
21 Dikembe Mutombo/49 10.00 25.00
22 Sam Perkins/99 EXCH 6.00 15.00
23 Cedric Ceballos/99 EXCH 6.00 15.00
24 Dan Majerle/99 6.00 15.00
25 Terry Porter/99 6.00 15.00
26 Jamal Mashburn/99 6.00 15.00
27 Danny Manning/49 6.00 15.00
28 Mitch Richmond/99 6.00 15.00
29 Glen Rice/49 8.00 20.00
30 Chris Mullin/99 8.00 20.00
31 Steve Kerr/49 10.00 25.00
32 Joe Dumars/49 8.00 20.00
33 John Stockton/25 75.00 200.00
34 Rex Chapman/99 6.00 15.00
35 Kurt Rambis/99 6.00 15.00
36 Robert Parish/49 8.00 20.00
37 Maurice Cheeks/99 6.00 15.00

2012-13 Prestige Playmakers

1 Kobe Bryant 80.00 200.00
2 LeBron James 80.00 200.00
3 Kevin Durant 40.00 100.00
4 Blake Griffin 10.00 25.00
5 Derrick Rose 15.00 40.00
6 Kevin Love 10.00 25.00
7 Dwight Howard 12.00 30.00
8 Deron Williams 8.00 20.00
9 Dirk Nowitzki 25.00 60.00
10 Dwyane Wade 20.00 50.00
11 LaMarcus Aldridge 10.00 25.00
12 Tony Parker 15.00 40.00
13 David Lee 6.00 15.00
14 Russell Westbrook 15.00 40.00
15 Josh Smith 6.00 15.00
16 Rudy Gay 10.00 25.00
17 Brandon Jennings 6.00 15.00
18 Carmelo Anthony 15.00 40.00
19 Al Jefferson 6.00 15.00
20 Chris Paul 20.00 50.00
21 Rajon Rondo 12.00 30.00
22 John Wall 12.00 30.00
23 Joe Johnson 8.00 20.00
24 Paul Pierce 15.00 40.00
25 Danny Granger 6.00 15.00

2012-13 Prestige Prestigious Picks Signatures

1 Kyrie Irving 30.00 80.00
2 Derrick Williams 2.50 6.00
3 Enes Kanter 4.00 10.00
4 Tristan Thompson 4.00 10.00
5 Jan Vesely 2.50 6.00
6 Bismack Biyombo 3.00 8.00
7 Brandon Knight 3.00 8.00
8 Kemba Walker 20.00 50.00
9 Jimmer Fredette 4.00 10.00
10 Klay Thompson 75.00 200.00
11 Alec Burks 4.00 10.00
12 Markieff Morris 4.00 10.00
13 Marcus Morris 4.00 10.00
14 Kawhi Leonard 150.00 400.00
15 Nikola Vucevic 10.00 25.00
16 Iman Shumpert 3.00 8.00
17 Chris Singleton 2.50 6.00
18 Tobias Harris 8.00 20.00
19 Nolan Smith 2.50 6.00
20 Kenneth Faried 3.00 8.00
21 Reggie Jackson 4.00 10.00
22 MarShon Brooks 2.50 6.00
23 Jordan Hamilton 2.50 6.00
24 JaJuan Johnson 2.50 6.00
25 Norris Cole 2.50 6.00
26 Cory Joseph 3.00 8.00
27 Jimmy Butler 50.00 120.00
28 Shelvin Mack 3.00 8.00
29 Tyler Honeycutt 2.50 6.00
30 Jordan Williams 3.00 8.00
31 Trey Thompkins 2.50 6.00
32 Chandler Parsons 3.00 8.00
33 Jeremy Tyler 2.50 6.00
34 Jon Leuer 2.50 6.00
35 Darius Morris 3.00 8.00
36 Malcolm Lee 2.50 6.00
37 Charles Jenkins 2.50 6.00
38 Josh Harrellson 2.50 6.00
39 Andrew Goudelock 2.50 6.00
40 Josh Selby 2.50 6.00
41 Isaiah Thomas 15.00 40.00
42 Lavoy Allen 2.50 6.00
43 E'Twaun Moore 3.00 8.00
44 Courtney Fortson 2.50 6.00
45 Anthony Davis 125.00 300.00
46 Michael Kidd-Gilchrist 3.00 8.00
47 Bradley Beal 25.00 60.00
48 Dion Waiters 3.00 8.00
49 Thomas Robinson 2.50 6.00
51 Harrison Barnes 5.00 12.00
52 Terrence Ross 6.00 15.00
53 Andre Drummond 6.00 15.00
54 Austin Rivers 4.00 10.00
55 Meyers Leonard 3.00 8.00
56 Jeremy Lamb 4.00 10.00
57 Kendall Marshall 2.50 6.00
58 John Henson 3.00 8.00
59 Moe Harkless 3.00 8.00
60 Royce White 2.50 6.00
61 Tyler Zeller 2.50 6.00
62 Terrence Jones 2.50 6.00
63 Andrew Nicholson 2.50 6.00
64 Evan Fournier 4.00 10.00
65 Jared Sullinger 2.50 6.00
66 Fab Melo 2.50 6.00
67 John Jenkins 2.50 6.00
68 Jared Cunningham 2.50 6.00
69 Tony Wroten 2.50 6.00
70 Miles Plumlee 2.50 6.00
71 Arnett Moultrie 2.50 6.00
72 Perry Jones 2.50 6.00
73 Marquis Teague 2.50 6.00
74 Festus Ezeli 2.50 6.00
75 Bernard James 2.50 6.00

2012-13 Prestige Prestigious Pros Signatures

3 Kobe Bryant 400.00 800.00
4 Blake Griffin 30.00 80.00
5 Andrea Bargnani 4.00 10.00
6 Stephen Curry 300.00 600.00
7 Tyreke Evans EXCH 4.00 10.00
8 Raymond Felton EXCH 4.00 10.00
9 Jeff Teague 4.00 10.00
10 Devin Ebanks 4.00 10.00
11 George Hill 4.00 10.00
12 Mike Conley 4.00 10.00
13 Al Horford 4.00 10.00
14 Paul Millsap EXCH 6.00 15.00
15 Stephen Jackson 6.00 15.00
17 Marcus Thornton 6.00 15.00
18 Marcin Gortat EXCH 8.00 20.00
19 Brook Lopez 4.00 10.00
20 Jordan Crawford 4.00 10.00
21 Zach Randolph 6.00 15.00
23 Luol Deng 4.00 10.00
24 Kevin Love 15.00 40.00
25 Derek Fisher 5.00 12.00

2012-13 Prestige Stars of the NBA

COMPLETE SET (25) 8.00 20.00
1 Russell Westbrook 1.00 2.50
2 Pau Gasol 1.00 2.50
3 Greg Monroe .40 1.00
4 DeMarcus Cousins .60 1.50
5 Chris Bosh .75 2.00
6 Joe Johnson .50 1.25
7 Elton Brand .50 1.25
8 Shawn Marion .60 1.50
9 LeBron James 5.00 12.00
10 Louis Williams .50 1.25
11 Tyson Chandler .50 1.25
12 David Lee .40 1.00
13 Rudy Gay .60 1.50
14 Dirk Nowitzki 1.50 4.00
15 James Harden 1.25 3.00
16 Kevin Martin .50 1.25
17 Marcus Thornton .40 1.00
18 Chris Paul 1.25 3.00
19 Brook Lopez .50 1.25
20 Andrew Bogut .50 1.25
21 Ty Lawson .40 1.00
22 Raymond Felton .40 1.00
23 Carlos Boozer .50 1.25
24 Ray Allen 1.00 2.50
25 Amare Stoudemire .60 1.50

2012-13 Prestige True Colors Materials

1 Deron Williams 2.00 5.00
2 Jason Kidd 4.00 10.00
3 Andre Iguodala 2.50 6.00
4 Ricky Rubio 5.00 12.00
5 Danny Granger 1.50 4.00
6 Ryan Anderson 1.50 4.00
7 Paul Millsap 2.00 5.00
8 LeBron James 20.00 50.00
9 Kevin Garnett 6.00 15.00
10 Dwight Howard 3.00 8.00
11 Ty Lawson 1.50 4.00
12 Al Horford 2.50 6.00
13 Steve Nash 5.00 12.00
14 DeMarcus Cousins 2.50 6.00
15 Carmelo Anthony 4.00 10.00
16 Ray Allen 4.00 10.00
17 Tim Duncan 6.00 15.00
18 Eric Gordon 2.00 5.00
19 Kyrie Irving 12.00 30.00
20 Andrea Bargnani 1.50 4.00
21 Russell Westbrook 4.00 10.00
22 Brandon Jennings 1.50 4.00
23 Baron Davis 2.00 5.00
24 Luol Deng 2.00 5.00
25 Stephen Curry 6.00 15.00
26 Kevin Durant 10.00 25.00
27 Jrue Holiday 3.00 8.00
28 Andrew Bynum 1.50 4.00
29 Luis Scola 2.00 5.00
30 Brandon Knight 1.50 4.00
31 Klay Thompson 12.00 30.00
32 Tristan Thompson 2.00 5.00
33 Jordan Crawford 1.50 4.00
34 Drew Gooden 2.00 5.00
35 Danilo Gallinari 2.00 5.00
36 Michael Beasley 1.50 4.00
37 David West 2.00 5.00
38 Raymond Felton 1.50 4.00
39 Kemba Walker 5.00 12.00
40 Kawhi Leonard 5.00 12.00
41 Josh Smith 1.50 4.00
42 Anderson Varejao 1.50 4.00
43 O.J. Mayo 1.50 4.00
44 Mario Chalmers 2.00 5.00
45 Glen Davis 1.50 4.00
46 Mo Williams 2.00 5.00
47 Joakim Noah 2.00 5.00
48 Jared Dudley 2.00 5.00
49 Brook Lopez 2.00 5.00
50 Chris Kaman 2.00 5.00

2012-13 Prestige True Colors Materials Prime

*PRIME: 1.25X TO 3X BASE HI
STATED PRINT RUN 25 SER.#'d SETS
8 LeBron James 40.00 100.00
15 Carmelo Anthony 12.00 30.00
16 Ray Allen 10.00 25.00

2013-14 Prestige

COMPLETE SET (200) 20.00 50.00
1 Kendrick Perkins .25 .60
2 Austin Rivers .30 .75
3 Andre Iguodala .40 1.00
4 Dwight Howard .50 1.25
5 Paul George .60 1.50
6 Omer Asik .25 .60
7 Kyle Singler .25 .60
8 Anderson Varejao .25 .60
9 Kemba Walker .40 1.00
10 Nene .30 .75
11 Evan Turner .25 .60
12 Nicolas Batum .30 .75
13 Kevin Durant 1.25 3.00
14 Greivis Vasquez .25 .60
15 Chris Bosh .50 1.25
16 Tony Wroten .25 .60
17 Jeff Green .25 .60
18 David Lee .25 .60
19 JaVale McGee .30 .75
20 Derrick Favors .25 .60
21 Michael Kidd-Gilchrist .25 .60
22 Jeff Teague .25 .60
23 Jason Richardson .40 1.00
24 Wesley Matthews .25 .60
25 Andre Miller .30 .75
26 Ryan Anderson .25 .60
27 Dwyane Wade .75 2.00
28 Andrew Bogut .30 .75
29 Eric Bledsoe .30 .75
30 Al Jefferson .25 .60
31 Kenneth Faried .25 .60
32 Tristan Thompson .25 .60
33 Ramon Sessions .25 .60
34 Josh Smith .25 .60
35 Jrue Holiday .50 1.25
36 DeMarcus Cousins .40 1.00
37 Reggie Jackson .30 .75
38 Terrence Ross .30 .75
39 LeBron James 3.00 8.00
40 Bradley Beal .60 1.50
41 Danny Granger .25 .60
42 Harrison Barnes .40 1.00
43 Andrew Bynum .25 .60
44 Tyler Zeller .25 .60
45 Brook Lopez .40 1.00
46 Louis Williams .30 .75
47 Thaddeus Young .25 .60
48 Isaiah Thomas .30 .75
49 Russell Westbrook .60 1.50
50 Jonas Valanciunas .30 .75

51 Chauncey Billups .50 1.25
52 Metta World Peace .30 .75
53 David West .30 .75
54 Kent Bazemore .25 .60
55 Ty Lawson .25 .60
56 Derrick Rose .60 1.50
57 Deron Williams .30 .75
58 Andrew Nicholson .25 .60
59 Goran Dragic .30 .75
60 Emeka Okafor .30 .75
61 Serge Ibaka .30 .75
62 Andrei Kirilenko .40 1.00
63 Ray Allen .60 1.50
64 Pau Gasol .60 1.50
65 George Hill .30 .75
66 Klay Thompson 1.25 3.00
67 Wilson Chandler .30 .75
68 Jimmy Butler .75 2.00
69 Gerald Wallace .30 .75
70 Gordon Hayward .30 .75
71 Danilo Gallinari .30 .75
72 Tyreke Evans .30 .75
73 Amar'e Stoudemire .40 1.00
74 Kevin Love .40 1.00
75 Shane Battier .30 .75
76 Steve Blake .25 .60
77 DeAndre Jordan .30 .75
78 Richard Jefferson .30 .75
79 Chris Kaman .30 .75
80 John Wall .50 1.25
81 Joe Johnson .30 .75
82 Derek Fisher .30 .75
83 Marcin Gortat .25 .60
84 Kawhi Leonard 1.25 3.00
85 Carmelo Anthony .60 1.50
86 Ricky Rubio .30 .75
87 Udonis Haslem .30 .75
88 Steve Nash .75 2.00
89 Roy Hibbert .25 .60
90 Paul Millsap .30 .75
91 Enes Kanter .30 .75
92 Kirk Hinrich .30 .75
93 Avery Bradley .25 .60
94 Jameer Nelson .25 .60
95 Marcus Morris .30 .75
96 Manu Ginobili .75 2.00
97 Ersan Ilyasova .25 .60
98 Nikola Pekovic .25 .60
99 Marc Gasol .40 1.00
100 DeMar DeRozan .50 1.25
101 Greg Oden .25 .60
102 Brandon Rush .25 .60
103 Dirk Nowitzki 1.00 2.50
104 Luol Deng .30 .75
105 Jared Sullinger .25 .60
106 Maurice Harkless .25 .60
107 Markieff Morris .25 .60
108 Tiago Splitter .25 .60
109 J.R. Smith .40 1.00
110 Brandon Jennings .25 .60
111 Mike Conley .40 1.00
112 Chris Paul .75 2.00
113 Chandler Parsons .25 .60
114 Andre Drummond .40 1.00
115 O.J. Mayo .25 .60
116 Nate Robinson .25 .60
117 Kevin Garnett 1.00 2.50
118 Nikola Vucevic .50 1.25
119 Kendall Marshall .25 .60
120 Tim Duncan 1.00 2.50
121 Tyson Chandler .30 .75
122 J.J. Redick .40 1.00
123 Tayshaun Prince .40 1.00
124 Larry Sanders .25 .60
125 James Harden .75 2.00
126 Brandon Knight .30 .75
127 Shawn Marion .30 .75
128 Taj Gibson .25 .60
129 Paul Pierce .60 1.50
130 Tobias Harris .40 1.00
131 Damian Lillard 1.25 3.00
132 Tony Parker .60 1.50
133 Al-Farouq Aminu .25 .60
134 John Henson .25 .60
135 Tony Allen .25 .60
136 Jamal Crawford .40 1.00
137 Jeremy Lin .60 1.50
138 Rudy Gay .30 .75
139 Vince Carter .75 2.00
140 Byron Mullens .25 .60
141 Rajon Rondo .50 1.25
142 Steve Novak .25 .60
143 LaMarcus Aldridge .40 1.00
144 Amir Johnson .25 .60
145 Anthony Davis 1.25 3.00
146 Monta Ellis .30 .75
147 J.J. Hickson .25 .60
148 Greg Monroe .25 .60
149 Thomas Robinson .30 .75
150 Zach Randolph .30 .75
151 Al Horford .40 1.00
152 Kyrie Irving 1.25 3.00
153 Draymond Green .60 1.50
154 Kobe Bryant 3.00 8.00
155 Alexey Shved .25 .60
156 Jimmer Fredette .40 1.00
157 Arron Afflalo .25 .60
158 Joakim Noah .40 1.00
159 Stephen Curry 3.00 8.00
160 Blake Griffin .40 1.00
161 Anthony Bennett RC .50 1.25
162 Victor Oladipo RC 1.25 3.00
163 Otto Porter RC .75 2.00
164 Cody Zeller RC .60 1.50
165 Alex Len RC .60 1.50
166 Nerlens Noel RC .60 1.50
167 Ben McLemore RC .60 1.50
168 Kentavious Caldwell-Pope RC .75 2.00
169 Trey Burke RC .60 1.50
170 C.J. McCollum RC 2.00 5.00
171 M.Carter-Williams RC .60 1.50
172 Steven Adams RC 1.25 3.00
173 Kelly Olynyk RC .60 1.50
174 Shabazz Muhammad RC .50 1.25
175 G.Antetokounmpo RC 25.00 60.00
176 Carrick Felix RC .50 1.25
177 Dennis Schroeder RC 1.50 4.00
178 Shane Larkin RC .50 1.25
179 Sergey Karasev RC .50 1.25
180 Tony Snell RC .60 1.50
181 Gorgui Dieng RC .60 1.50
182 Mason Plumlee RC .60 1.50
183 Solomon Hill RC .60 1.50
184 Tim Hardaway Jr. RC 1.00 2.50
185 Reggie Bullock RC .60 1.50
186 Andre Roberson RC .60 1.50
187 Archie Goodwin RC .50 1.25
188 Ricky Ledo RC .50 1.25
189 Phil Pressey RC .50 1.25
190 Jamaal Franklin RC .50 1.25
191 Peyton Siva RC .50 1.25
192 Glen Rice Jr. RC .50 1.25
193 Ray McCallum RC .50 1.25
194 Elias Harris RC .50 1.25
195 C.J. Leslie RC .50 1.25
196 Tony Mitchell RC .50 1.25
197 Ryan Kelly RC .50 1.25
198 Ian Clark RC .60 1.50
199 Allen Crabbe RC .50 1.25
200 Erik Murphy RC .50 1.25

2013-14 Prestige Bonus Shots Blue

*BLUE 1-160: 1X TO 2.5X BASIC
*BLUE 161-200: 1X TO 2.5X BASIC
175 Giannis Antetokounmpo 125.00 300.00

2013-14 Prestige Bonus Shots Red

*RED 1-160: 1X TO 2.5X BASIC
*RED 161-200: 1X TO 2.5X BASIC
175 Giannis Antetokounmpo 125.00 300.00

2013-14 Prestige Bonus Shots Silver

*SILVER 1-160: 1X TO 2.5X BASIC
*SILVER 161-200: 1X TO 2.5X BASIC
175 Giannis Antetokounmpo 125.00 300.00

2013-14 Prestige Bonus Shots Autographs

EXCHANGE DEADLINE 5/6/2015
1 Kenyon Martin 5.00 12.00
2 DeSagana Diop 3.00 8.00
3 Ricky Davis 4.00 10.00
4 Greg Stiemsma 3.00 8.00
5 P.J. Tucker 5.00 12.00
6 John Lucas III 3.00 8.00
7 Nicolas Batum 4.00 10.00
8 Marcus Thornton 3.00 8.00
9 Ish Smith 3.00 8.00
10 Kyle O'Quinn 3.00 8.00
11 DeAndre Liggins 3.00 8.00
12 Luc Longley 4.00 10.00
13 Marquis Daniels 3.00 8.00
14 C.J. Miles 3.00 8.00
15 Jon Leuer 3.00 8.00
16 Jeff Taylor 3.00 8.00
17 Keith Bogans 3.00 8.00
18 Khris Middleton 10.00 25.00
19 Earl Clark 3.00 8.00
20 Anthony Mason 4.00 10.00
21 Antoine Walker 4.00 10.00
22 Antonio Davis 4.00 10.00
23 Bonzi Wells 3.00 8.00
24 Brandon Rush 3.00 8.00
25 Bruce Bowen 4.00 10.00
26 Byron Scott 5.00 12.00
27 Cedric Maxwell 4.00 10.00
28 Dahntay Jones 3.00 8.00
29 Darrell Griffith 4.00 10.00
30 John Paxson 4.00 10.00
31 Kenny Anderson 4.00 10.00
32 Luc Mbah a Moute 3.00 8.00
33 Mark Price 5.00 12.00
34 Maurice Cheeks 5.00 12.00
35 Terry Porter 5.00 12.00
36 Walt Williams 3.00 8.00
37 Xavier McDaniel 4.00 10.00
38 Corey Brewer 3.00 8.00
39 Zydrunas Ilgauskas 4.00 10.00
40 Ekpe Udoh 3.00 8.00
41 Goran Dragic 4.00 10.00
42 James Johnson 3.00 8.00
43 Jan Vesely 3.00 8.00
44 Jerryd Bayless 3.00 8.00
45 Nikola Pekovic 3.00 8.00
46 Rolando Blackman 4.00 10.00
47 Danny Green 4.00 10.00
48 Gerald Henderson 3.00 8.00
49 Alvan Adams 3.00 8.00
50 Chris Mullin 6.00 15.00
51 Dan Majerle 4.00 10.00
52 Derrick Coleman 5.00 12.00
53 Chris Bosh 6.00 15.00
54 James Worthy 6.00 15.00
55 Shane Battier 4.00 10.00
56 Tyreke Evans 4.00 10.00
57 Joe Johnson 4.00 10.00
58 Walt Frazier 8.00 20.00
59 Artis Gilmore 6.00 15.00
60 Brent Barry 3.00 8.00
61 Nick Van Exel 5.00 12.00
62 Michael Finley 5.00 12.00
63 Harrison Barnes 5.00 12.00
64 Jordan Hill 3.00 8.00
65 Steve Francis 4.00 10.00
66 Robert Parish 6.00 15.00
67 Peja Stojakovic 4.00 10.00
68 Kelly Tripucka 4.00 10.00
69 Jason Terry 4.00 10.00
70 Danilo Gallinari 4.00 10.00
71 Charlie Villanueva 3.00 8.00
72 Brandon Knight 4.00 10.00
73 Bill Walton 8.00 20.00
74 Andrei Kirilenko 6.00 15.00
75 Devin Harris 3.00 8.00
76 Richard Jefferson 4.00 10.00
77 Steve Novak 3.00 8.00
78 Kris Humphries 3.00 8.00
79 John Henson 3.00 8.00
80 Anderson Varejao 3.00 8.00
81 Dikembe Mutombo 8.00 20.00
82 Eric Gordon 4.00 10.00
83 Carl Landry 3.00 8.00
84 Kyle Korver 4.00 10.00
85 Kendrick Perkins 3.00 8.00
86 B.J. Armstrong 5.00 12.00
87 Andrew Bogut 4.00 10.00
88 Marcin Gortat 3.00 8.00
89 Robert Horry 5.00 12.00
90 Kyrie Irving EXCH 30.00 80.00
91 Boris Diaw 4.00 10.00
92 Xavier Henry 3.00 8.00
93 Dave Cowens 5.00 12.00
94 Will Perdue 3.00 8.00
95 Kevin Durant 50.00 120.00
96 Spencer Haywood 5.00 12.00
97 Sleepy Floyd 4.00 10.00
98 Rodney Stuckey 3.00 8.00
99 Kobe Bryant 400.00 800.00
100 Michael Cage 3.00 8.00

2013-14 Prestige Bonus Shots Autographs Blue

*BLUE: .4X TO 1X BASE HI
PRINT RUNS B/WN 5-99 COPIES PER
EXCHANGE DEADLINE 5/6/2015

2013-14 Prestige Bonus Shots Autographs Red

*RED: .6X TO 1.5X BASE HI
PRINT RUNS B/WN 5-99 COPIES PER
EXCHANGE DEADLINE 5/6/2015

2013-14 Prestige Bonus Shots Materials

1 Jared Sullinger 2.00 5.00
2 Paul Pierce 5.00 12.00
3 Brandon Bass 2.00 5.00
4 Larry Bird 10.00 25.00
5 Rajon Rondo 4.00 10.00
6 Reggie Lewis 8.00 20.00
7 Avery Bradley 2.00 5.00
8 Dee Brown 2.50 6.00
9 Zaza Pachulia 2.00 5.00
10 Jeff Teague 2.00 5.00
11 John Jenkins 2.00 5.00
12 Gerald Wallace 2.50 6.00
13 Nene 2.50 6.00
14 Brook Lopez 3.00 8.00
15 Michael Kidd-Gilchrist 2.50 6.00
16 Kemba Walker 3.00 8.00
17 Gerald Henderson 2.00 5.00
18 Tyrus Thomas 2.00 5.00
19 Richard Hamilton 2.50 6.00
20 Luol Deng 2.50 6.00
21 Joakim Noah 3.00 8.00
22 Tristan Thompson 2.00 5.00
23 Tyler Zeller 2.00 5.00
24 Dirk Nowitzki 8.00 20.00
25 Tim Duncan 8.00 20.00
26 Manu Ginobili 6.00 15.00
27 Tony Parker 3.00 8.00
28 Kenneth Faried 2.50 6.00
29 Jordan Hamilton 2.00 5.00
30 Alex English 4.00 10.00
31 Jalen Rose 2.50 6.00
32 Kyle Singler 2.00 5.00
33 Andre Drummond 3.00 8.00
34 Rick Mahorn 2.00 5.00
35 Isiah Thomas 5.00 12.00
36 Klay Thompson 10.00 25.00
37 Harrison Barnes 3.00 8.00
38 Carl Landry 2.00 5.00
39 Jeremy Lin 5.00 12.00
40 Carlos Delfino 2.00 5.00
41 Orlando Johnson 2.00 5.00
42 Danny Granger 2.00 5.00
43 David West 2.50 6.00
44 Danny Manning 2.50 6.00
45 Caron Butler 2.50 6.00
46 Lamar Odom 2.50 6.00
47 Eric Bledsoe 2.50 6.00
48 Chris Paul 6.00 15.00
49 Blake Griffin 5.00 12.00
50 Kobe Bryant 10.00 25.00
51 Pau Gasol 5.00 12.00
52 Metta World Peace 2.50 6.00
53 Zach Randolph 2.50 6.00
54 Marc Gasol 3.00 8.00
55 LeBron James 10.00 25.00
56 Joel Anthony 2.00 5.00
57 John Henson 2.00 5.00
58 Luc Mbah a Moute 2.00 5.00
59 Monta Ellis 2.50 6.00
60 Drew Gooden 2.50 6.00
61 Kevin Love 3.00 8.00
62 Austin Rivers 2.50 6.00
63 Anthony Davis 10.00 25.00
64 Darius Miller 2.00 5.00
65 Amar'e Stoudemire 3.00 8.00
66 Carmelo Anthony 5.00 12.00
67 Tyson Chandler 2.50 6.00
68 Pablo Prigioni 2.00 5.00
69 Andrew Nicholson 2.00 5.00
70 Hedo Turkoglu 2.50 6.00
71 Glen Davis 2.00 5.00
72 Jameer Nelson 2.00 5.00
73 Evan Turner 2.00 5.00
74 Jrue Holiday 4.00 10.00
75 Jason Richardson 3.00 8.00
76 Nick Young 2.00 5.00
77 Kendall Marshall 2.00 5.00
78 Channing Frye 2.00 5.00
79 Damian Lillard 10.00 25.00
80 LaMarcus Aldridge 3.00 8.00
81 Isaiah Thomas 2.50 6.00
82 Jonas Valanciunas 2.50 6.00
83 DeMar DeRozan 4.00 10.00
84 Al Jefferson 2.00 5.00
85 John Wall 4.00 10.00
86 Anthony Bennett 2.00 5.00
87 Victor Oladipo 5.00 12.00
88 Otto Porter 3.00 8.00
89 Nerlens Noel 2.50 6.00
90 Ben McLemore 2.50 6.00
91 Kentavious Caldwell-Pope 3.00 8.00
92 Trey Burke 2.50 6.00
93 Michael Carter-Williams 2.50 6.00
94 Steven Adams 5.00 12.00
95 Kelly Olynyk 2.50 6.00
96 Shabazz Muhammad 2.00 5.00
97 Tony Snell 2.50 6.00
98 Mason Plumlee 2.50 6.00
99 Tim Hardaway Jr. 4.00 10.00
100 Glen Rice Jr. 2.00 5.00

2013-14 Prestige Bonus Shots Materials Prime

*PRIME: .75X TO 2X BASE HI
PRINT RUNS B/WN 10-25 COPIES PER

2013-14 Prestige Connections

1 C.Bosh/A.Mourning 1.00 2.50
2 D.Lee/R.Barry .75 2.00
3 H.Olajuwon/D.Howard 1.25 3.00
4 B.King/C.Anthony 1.00 2.50
5 D.Robinson/T.Duncan 1.50 4.00
6 D.Williams/P.Pierce 1.00 2.50
7 B.Walton/B.Griffin 1.00 2.50
8 B.Lanier/G.Monroe .75 2.00
9 R.Westbrook/G.Payton 1.00 2.50
10 K.Johnson/G.Dragic .60 1.50
11 J.Harden/C.Drexler 1.25 3.00
12 D.Rose/S.Pippen 1.50 4.00
13 B.Lopez/D.Dawkins .60 1.50
14 D.Nowitzki/M.Aguirre 1.50 4.00
15 K.Faried/A.English .75 2.00
16 K.Bryant/M.Johnson 5.00 12.00
17 R.Rondo/N.Archibald .75 2.00
18 A.Horford/D.Wilkins 1.00 2.50
19 R.Parish/J.Sullinger .75 2.00
20 M.Ginobili/S.Elliott 1.25 3.00

2013-14 Prestige Distinctive Ink

PRINT RUNS B/WN 15-99 COPIES PER
2013-14 Prestige Bonus Shots Autographs
1 Derrick Williams/50 4.00 10.00
2 Kendall Marshall/99 4.00 10.00
3 Karl Malone/25 30.00 80.00
4 Chris Bosh/15 12.00 30.00
5 Tiago Splitter/99 4.00 10.00
6 Larry Bird/50 50.00 100.00
7 Magic Johnson/50 30.00 60.00
8 Dwight Howard/15 20.00 50.00
9 Dwight Howard/99 8.00 20.00
11 Kobe Bryant/99 400.00 800.00
12 David West/99 5.00 12.00
13 Antawn Jamison/99 5.00 12.00
15 Kevin Durant/75 40.00 100.00
16 Rajon Rondo/25 15.00 40.00
19 Kyrie Irving/50 EXCH 30.00 80.00
20 Norris Cole/99 4.00 10.00
21 Tyson Chandler/50 5.00 12.00
22 Jeff Teague/99 4.00 10.00
23 Nicolas Batum/99 5.00 12.00
24 Jarrett Jack/99 5.00 12.00
25 J.J. Redick/99 6.00 15.00
26 Jeff Green/99 4.00 10.00
27 Scottie Pippen/50 50.00 120.00
29 Gary Payton/50 15.00 40.00
30 Tyreke Evans/25 6.00 15.00
32 Steve Francis/50 5.00 12.00
33 Isiah Thomas/50 10.00 25.00
34 Rick Fox/50 12.00 30.00
35 Grant Hill/15 25.00 60.00
36 Nate Archibald/25 8.00 20.00
37 J.R. Smith/99 6.00 15.00
38 Horace Grant/99 10.00 25.00
39 David Thompson/99 6.00 15.00
40 Tom Chambers/99 4.00 10.00

2013-14 Prestige Franchise Favorites

1 Al Horford .60 1.50
2 Rajon Rondo .75 2.00
3 Brook Lopez .60 1.50
4 Kemba Walker .60 1.50
5 Derrick Rose 1.00 2.50
6 Kyrie Irving 2.00 5.00
7 Dirk Nowitzki 1.50 4.00
8 Kenneth Faried .50 1.25
9 Greg Monroe .40 1.00
10 Stephen Curry 5.00 12.00
11 James Harden 1.25 3.00
12 Roy Hibbert .40 1.00
13 Chris Paul 1.25 3.00
14 Kobe Bryant 5.00 12.00
15 Marc Gasol .60 1.50
16 LeBron James 5.00 12.00
17 Larry Sanders .40 1.00
18 Kevin Love .60 1.50
19 Anthony Davis 2.00 5.00
20 Carmelo Anthony 1.00 2.50
21 Kevin Durant 2.00 5.00
22 Jameer Nelson .40 1.00
23 Evan Turner .40 1.00
24 Marcin Gortat .40 1.00
25 LaMarcus Aldridge .60 1.50
26 Isaiah Thomas .75 2.00
27 Tim Duncan 1.50 4.00
28 DeMar DeRozan .75 2.00
29 Gordon Hayward .50 1.25
30 John Wall .75 2.00

2013-14 Prestige Hardcourt Heroes

1 Carmelo Anthony 1.00 2.50
2 Kobe Bryant 5.00 12.00
3 Kevin Durant 2.00 5.00
4 Monta Ellis .50 1.25
5 Rudy Gay .50 1.25
6 Blake Griffin .60 1.50
7 James Harden 1.25 3.00
8 LeBron James 5.00 12.00
9 Al Jefferson .40 1.00
10 David Lee .40 1.00
11 Damian Lillard 2.00 5.00
12 Dirk Nowitzki 1.50 4.00
13 Tony Parker 1.00 2.50
14 Chris Paul 1.25 3.00
15 Paul Pierce 1.00 2.50
16 Zach Randolph .50 1.25
17 Rajon Rondo .75 2.00
18 Dwyane Wade 1.25 3.00
19 Russell Westbrook 1.00 2.50
20 Deron Williams .60 1.50

2013-14 Prestige NBA Materials

1 Jrue Holiday 4.00 10.00
2 LeBron James 10.00 25.00
3 Deron Williams 2.50 6.00
4 Russell Westbrook 5.00 12.00
5 Al Horford 3.00 8.00
6 Kyrie Irving 10.00 25.00
7 Paul Pierce 5.00 12.00
8 Dirk Nowitzki 8.00 20.00
9 Ben Gordon 2.50 6.00
10 Devin Harris 2.00 5.00
11 Tim Duncan 8.00 20.00
12 Shane Battier 2.50 6.00
13 Monta Ellis 2.50 6.00
14 Terrence Ross 2.50 6.00
15 Anthony Davis 6.00 15.00
16 Austin Rivers 2.50 6.00
17 Thabo Sefolosha 2.50 6.00
18 Thaddeus Young 2.00 5.00
19 DeMar DeRozan 4.00 10.00
20 Thomas Robinson 2.00 5.00
21 Manu Ginobili 6.00 15.00
22 Drew Gooden 2.50 6.00
23 Kendall Marshall 2.00 5.00
24 Blake Griffin 3.00 8.00
25 Al Jefferson 2.00 5.00

2013-14 Prestige NBA Materials Prime

*PRIME: .75X TO 2X BASE HI
PRINT RUNS B/WN 12-25 COPIES PER
NO PRICING ON QTY 12

2013-14 Prestige Old School Signatures

PRINT RUNS B/WN 10-99 COPIES PER
NO PRICING ON QTY 10
EXCHANGE DEADLINE 5/6/2015
1 Allan Houston/49 6.00 15.00
2 World B. Free/50 5.00 12.00
3 Spencer Haywood/99 6.00 15.00
5 Wes Unseld/25 8.00 20.00
6 Scottie Pippen/50 60.00 150.00
7 Connie Hawkins/99 8.00 20.00
8 Michael Cooper/99 6.00 15.00
9 A.C. Green/99 6.00 15.00
10 Larry Nance/99 5.00 12.00
11 Dominique Wilkins/75 10.00 25.00
12 Bob Dandridge/99 5.00 12.00
13 George Gervin/50 10.00 25.00
14 Jo Jo White/99 5.00 12.00
15 Bailey Howell/99 6.00 15.00
16 Slick Watts/99 4.00 10.00
17 George McGinnis/99 6.00 15.00
18 Lenny Wilkens/50 6.00 15.00
19 Hal Greer/50 5.00 12.00
20 Darryl Dawkins/99 5.00 12.00
21 Len Elmore/99 5.00 12.00
22 Nate Thurmond/25 6.00 15.00
23 Rory Sparrow/99 4.00 10.00
24 Herb Williams/99 4.00 10.00
25 Otis Birdsong/99 5.00 12.00
26 Gail Goodrich/50 6.00 15.00
29 Campy Russell/99 5.00 12.00
30 Gus Williams/99 4.00 10.00
31 Satch Sanders/99 8.00 20.00
32 Bill Laimbeer/99 6.00 15.00
33 John Lucas/99 5.00 12.00
34 Dan Meminger/99 5.00 12.00
35 Reggie Theus/99 5.00 12.00
36 Sidney Moncrief/99 6.00 15.00
38 James Worthy/25 10.00 25.00
40 Hot Rod Williams/99 4.00 10.00
41 Bill Walton/99 10.00 25.00
44 Dave Stallworth/99 6.00 15.00
46 Buck Williams/99 6.00 15.00
47 Henry Bibby/99 4.00 10.00
48 Paul Westphal/99 6.00 15.00
49 Mel Daniels/99 6.00 15.00
50 Bobby Jones/99 8.00 20.00
51 Mark Aguirre/99 5.00 12.00
54 Sam Jones/25 10.00 25.00
55 Dennis Rodman/25 15.00 40.00
56 Harry Gallatin/99 6.00 15.00
59 Hakeem Olajuwon/75 15.00 40.00
60 Bernard King/99 8.00 20.00

2013-14 Prestige Playmakers

1 James Harden 8.00 20.00
2 Stephen Curry 30.00 80.00
3 Kobe Bryant 20.00 50.00
4 Carmelo Anthony 6.00 15.00
5 Tim Duncan 10.00 25.00
6 Kevin Durant 12.00 30.00
7 Blake Griffin 4.00 10.00
8 Dwight Howard 5.00 12.00
9 LaMarcus Aldridge 4.00 10.00
10 Kyrie Irving 12.00 30.00
11 LeBron James 20.00 50.00
12 Damian Lillard 12.00 30.00
13 Kevin Love 4.00 10.00
14 Steve Nash 8.00 20.00
15 Tony Parker 6.00 15.00
16 Chris Paul 8.00 20.00
17 Rajon Rondo 5.00 12.00
18 Derrick Rose 6.00 15.00
19 Dwyane Wade 8.00 20.00
20 Russell Westbrook 6.00 15.00
21 Ricky Rubio 3.00 8.00
22 John Wall 5.00 12.00
23 Blake Griffin 4.00 10.00
24 Dirk Nowitzki 10.00 25.00
25 Paul George 6.00 15.00

2013-14 Prestige Prestigious Picks

1 Anthony Bennett 1.50 4.00
2 Victor Oladipo 4.00 10.00
3 Otto Porter 2.50 6.00
4 Cody Zeller 2.00 5.00
5 Alex Len 2.00 5.00
6 Nerlens Noel 2.00 5.00
7 Ben McLemore 2.00 5.00
8 Kentavious Caldwell-Pope 2.50 6.00
9 Trey Burke 2.00 5.00
10 C.J. McCollum 6.00 15.00
11 Michael Carter-Williams 2.00 5.00
12 Steven Adams 4.00 10.00
13 Kelly Olynyk 2.00 5.00
14 Shabazz Muhammad 1.50 4.00
15 Shane Larkin 1.50 4.00
16 Tim Hardaway Jr. 3.00 8.00
17 Glen Rice Jr. 1.50 4.00
18 Mason Plumlee 2.00 5.00
19 Dennis Schroeder 5.00 12.00
20 Sergey Karasev 1.50 4.00
21 Reggie Bullock 2.00 5.00
22 Tony Mitchell 1.50 4.00
23 Archie Goodwin 1.50 4.00
24 Rudy Gobert 6.00 15.00
25 Tony Snell 2.00 5.00

2013-14 Prestige Prestigious Pioneers

1 Kareem Abdul-Jabbar 2.00 5.00
2 Al Attles .50 1.25
3 Elgin Baylor .60 1.50
4 Wilt Chamberlain 2.00 5.00
5 Bob Cousy 1.50 4.00
6 Walt Frazier 1.00 2.50
7 Artis Gilmore .75 2.00
8 John Havlicek 1.50 4.00
9 Clyde Lovellette .60 1.50
10 Pete Maravich 2.00 5.00
11 George Mikan 2.00 5.00
12 Vern Mikkelsen .60 1.50
13 Bob Pettit .60 1.50
14 Willis Reed 1.00 2.50
15 Oscar Robertson 1.00 2.50
16 Bill Russell 2.00 5.00
17 Dolph Schayes .60 1.50
19 Jerry West 1.50 4.00
20 Lenny Wilkens .60 1.50

2013-14 Prestige Prestigious Posts

COMPLETE SET (10) 6.00 15.00
1 Andrew Bogut 1.00 2.50
2 Chris Bosh 1.50 4.00
3 Tyson Chandler 1.00 2.50
4 DeMarcus Cousins 1.25 3.00
5 Tim Duncan 3.00 8.00
6 Marc Gasol 1.25 3.00
7 Roy Hibbert .75 2.00
8 Dwight Howard 1.50 4.00
9 Brook Lopez 1.25 3.00
10 Joakim Noah 1.25 3.00

2013-14 Prestige Prestigious Premieres Signatures

EXCHANGE DEADLINE 5/6/2015
1 Nate Wolters 3.00 8.00
2 Erik Murphy 3.00 8.00
3 C.J. Leslie 3.00 8.00
4 Kelly Olynyk 4.00 10.00
5 Anthony Bennett 3.00 8.00
6 Trey Burke 4.00 10.00
7 Jeff Withey 3.00 8.00
8 Phil Pressey 3.00 8.00
9 Peyton Siva 3.00 8.00
10 Shabazz Muhammad 3.00 8.00
11 Victor Oladipo 15.00 40.00
12 C.J. McCollum 15.00 40.00
13 Grant Jerrett 3.00 8.00
14 Archie Goodwin 3.00 8.00
15 Mason Plumlee 4.00 10.00
16 Giannis Antetokounmpo 200.00 500.00
17 Otto Porter 5.00 12.00
18 Michael Carter-Williams 4.00 10.00
19 Jamaal Franklin 3.00 8.00
20 Elias Harris 3.00 8.00
21 Solomon Hill 4.00 10.00
22 Carrick Felix 3.00 8.00
23 Cody Zeller 4.00 10.00
24 Steven Adams 8.00 20.00
25 Ian Clark 4.00 10.00
26 Allen Crabbe 3.00 8.00
27 Tim Hardaway Jr. 6.00 15.00
28 Dennis Schroeder 10.00 25.00
29 Alex Len 4.00 10.00
30 Ben McLemore 4.00 10.00
31 Tony Snell 4.00 10.00
32 Glen Rice Jr. 3.00 8.00
33 Reggie Bullock 4.00 10.00
34 Shane Larkin 3.00 8.00
35 Nerlens Noel 4.00 10.00
36 Kentavious Caldwell-Pope 5.00 12.00
37 Ryan Kelly 3.00 8.00
38 Tony Mitchell 3.00 8.00
39 Andre Roberson 4.00 10.00
40 Isaiah Canaan 3.00 8.00

2013-14 Prestige Prestigious Pros

1 LaMarcus Aldridge 2.00 5.00
2 Carmelo Anthony 3.00 8.00
3 Bradley Beal 3.00 8.00
4 Carlos Boozer 1.50 4.00
5 Chris Bosh 2.50 6.00
6 Kobe Bryant 10.00 25.00
7 Mike Conley 2.00 5.00
8 DeMarcus Cousins 2.00 5.00
9 Jamal Crawford 2.00 5.00
10 Anthony Davis 6.00 15.00
11 Luol Deng 1.50 4.00
12 DeMar DeRozan 2.50 6.00
13 Goran Dragic 1.50 4.00
14 Kevin Durant 6.00 15.00
15 Monta Ellis 1.50 4.00
16 Tyreke Evans 1.50 4.00
17 Marc Gasol 2.00 5.00
18 Rudy Gay 1.50 4.00
19 Paul George 3.00 8.00
20 Manu Ginobili 4.00 10.00
21 Ben Gordon 1.50 4.00
22 Blake Griffin 2.00 5.00
23 Jameer Nelson 1.25 3.00
24 Gordon Hayward 2.00 5.00
25 Jrue Holiday 2.50 6.00
26 Dwight Howard 2.50 6.00
27 Serge Ibaka 1.50 4.00
28 Kyrie Irving 6.00 15.00
29 LeBron James 10.00 25.00
30 Al Jefferson 1.25 3.00
31 Brandon Jennings 1.25 3.00
32 Joe Johnson 1.50 4.00
33 Ty Lawson 1.25 3.00
34 David Lee 1.25 3.00
35 Damian Lillard 6.00 15.00
36 Brook Lopez 2.00 5.00
37 Joakim Noah 2.00 5.00
38 Chandler Parsons 1.25 3.00
39 Chris Paul 4.00 10.00
40 Paul Pierce 3.00 8.00
41 Zach Randolph 1.50 4.00
42 J.R. Smith 2.00 5.00
43 Josh Smith 1.25 3.00
44 Klay Thompson 6.00 15.00
45 Dwyane Wade 4.00 10.00
46 Kemba Walker 2.00 5.00
47 John Wall 2.50 6.00
48 David West 1.50 4.00
49 Russell Westbrook 3.00 8.00
50 Deron Williams 1.50 4.00

2013-14 Prestige Stars of the NBA Signatures

PRINT RUNS B/WN 10-99 COPIES PER
NO PRICING ON QTY 10
EXCHANGE DEADLINE 5/6/2015
1 Dwight Howard/25 30.00 60.00
2 J.R. Smith/25 6.00 15.00
3 Tyson Chandler/25 5.00 12.00
4 Kevin Love/25 20.00 50.00
7 Deron Williams/25 5.00 12.00
8 Dwyane Wade/25 90.00 150.00
9 Tyreke Evans/25 5.00 12.00
10 Rajon Rondo/25 15.00 40.00
11 Connie Hawkins/99 8.00 20.00
15 Norris Cole/99 6.00 15.00
16 Harrison Barnes/50 6.00 15.00
17 Dan Issel/99 8.00 20.00
18 Rolando Blackman/99 5.00 12.00
20 Ryan Anderson/99 4.00 10.00
21 J.J. Redick/25 30.00 60.00
22 Goran Dragic/25 15.00 40.00
23 Kobe Bryant/50 500.00 1,000.00
24 Kevin Durant/50 40.00 100.00
25 Kyrie Irving/50 50.00 120.00
26 David West/99 5.00 12.00
27 Danny Green/99 5.00 12.00
29 Antawn Jamison/99 5.00 12.00
30 Nick Young/99 4.00 10.00
31 Marcin Gortat/25 12.00 30.00
35 Ty Lawson/25 4.00 10.00
36 John Lucas/99 5.00 12.00
37 MarShon Brooks/49 6.00 15.00
38 Andre Drummond/25 20.00 50.00
39 Isaiah Thomas/99 12.00 30.00
40 Bradley Beal/25 12.00 30.00
41 Kawhi Leonard/25 30.00 80.00
42 Reggie Theus/99 5.00 12.00
43 Blake Griffin/50 40.00 80.00
44 Nikola Vucevic/99 8.00 20.00
45 Jeff Green/25 4.00 10.00
46 Danilo Gallinari/25 5.00 12.00
48 Bill Laimbeer/99 6.00 15.00
49 Andre Miller/25 5.00 12.00
53 Mark Aguirre/99 5.00 12.00
55 Taj Gibson/99 4.00 10.00
57 Steve Nash/25 40.00 100.00
58 James Harden/25 EXCH 30.00 80.00
59 Monta Ellis/25 EXCH 5.00 12.00

2013-14 Prestige True Colors Materials

1 Joe Johnson 2.50 6.00
2 Tristan Thompson 2.00 5.00
3 Kyle Singler 2.00 5.00
4 David West 2.50 6.00
5 Buck Williams 2.00 5.00
6 Russell Westbrook 5.00 12.00
7 Jeff Teague 2.00 5.00
8 Gerald Wallace 2.50 6.00
9 Kyrie Irving 6.00 15.00
10 Grant Hill 5.00 12.00
11 Danny Granger 2.00 5.00
12 Steve Novak 2.00 5.00
13 Kevin Durant 6.00 15.00
14 Kendall Marshall 2.00 5.00
15 DeShawn Stevenson 2.00 5.00
16 Dirk Nowitzki 8.00 20.00
17 Andre Drummond 3.00 8.00
18 Ronny Turiaf 2.00 5.00
19 Karl Malone 6.00 15.00
20 Nick Anderson 2.50 6.00
21 Monta Ellis 2.50 6.00
22 Fat Lever 2.50 6.00
23 Jae Crowder 2.00 5.00
24 Klay Thompson 10.00 25.00
25 Ron Harper 3.00 8.00
26 Patrick Ewing 5.00 12.00
27 Glen Davis 2.00 5.00
28 Jason Richardson 2.00 5.00
29 Danny Ainge 3.00 8.00
30 Kenneth Faried 2.50 6.00
31 Harrison Barnes 3.00 8.00
32 Eric Bledsoe 2.50 6.00
33 Raymond Felton 2.00 5.00
34 Arron Afflalo 2.00 5.00
35 Ersan Ilyasova 2.00 5.00
36 Larry Bird 12.00 30.00
37 Andre Miller 2.50 6.00
38 Draymond Green 5.00 12.00
39 DeAndre Jordan 2.50 6.00
40 J.R. Smith 3.00 8.00
41 Marcin Gortat 2.00 5.00
42 Luc Mbah a Moute 2.00 5.00
43 Michael Kidd-Gilchrist 2.00 5.00
44 Alex English 4.00 10.00
45 Carl Landry 2.00 5.00
46 Danny Manning 2.50 6.00
47 Carmelo Anthony 5.00 12.00
48 Goran Dragic 2.50 6.00
49 D.J. Augustin 2.00 5.00
50 Taj Gibson 2.00 5.00
51 Andre Iguodala 3.00 8.00
52 John Lucas 2.00 5.00
53 Chris Paul 6.00 15.00
54 Amar'e Stoudemire 3.00 8.00
55 Michael Beasley 2.00 5.00
56 Thaddeus Young 2.00 5.00
57 Carlos Boozer 2.50 6.00
58 Rodney Stuckey 2.00 5.00
59 Carlos Delfino 2.00 5.00
60 Blake Griffin 3.00 8.00
61 Lance Thomas 2.00 5.00
62 Omer Asik 2.00 5.00
63 Evan Turner 2.00 5.00
64 Zydrunas Ilgauskas 2.00 5.00
65 Bob Lanier 4.00 10.00
66 Brent Barry 2.00 5.00
67 Shaquille O'Neal 12.00 30.00
68 Austin Rivers 2.50 6.00
69 Zaza Pachulia 2.00 5.00
70 Lavoy Allen 2.00 5.00
71 Tyler Zeller 2.00 5.00
72 Rick Mahorn 2.00 5.00

73 Roy Hibbert 2.00 5.00
74 Cazzie Russell 2.50 6.00
75 Anthony Davis 10.00 25.00

2013-14 Prestige True Colors Materials Prime

*PRIME: .75X TO 2X BASE HI
PRINT RUNS B/WN 5-25 COPIES PER
NO PRICING ON QTY 10 OR LESS

2014-15 Prestige

COMPLETE SET (200) 40.00 80.00
1 Ricky Rubio .30 .75
2 Jamal Crawford .40 1.00
3 Tiago Splitter .25 .60
4 Al Horford .40 1.00
5 Jordan Hill .25 .60
6 Ben McLemore .25 .60
7 Kyle Lowry .50 1.25
8 Corey Brewer .25 .60
9 Nerlens Noel .30 .75
10 Enes Kanter .30 .75
11 Robin Lopez .25 .60
12 Jameer Nelson .25 .60
13 Tim Duncan 1.00 2.50
14 Al Jefferson .25 .60
15 Jose Calderon .25 .60
16 Blake Griffin .40 1.00
17 Kyrie Irving .75 2.00
18 Damian Lillard 1.00 2.50
19 Nick Collison .30 .75
20 Eric Bledsoe .30 .75
21 Roy Hibbert .30 .75
22 James Harden .75 2.00
23 Tim Hardaway Jr. .30 .75
24 Alex Len .25 .60
25 Josh Smith .25 .60
26 Bradley Beal .60 1.50
27 LaMarcus Aldridge .40 1.00
28 Danilo Gallinari .25 .60
29 Nick Young .25 .60
30 Eric Gordon .30 .75
31 Rudy Gay .40 1.00
32 Jared Sullinger .25 .60
33 Al-Farouq Aminu .25 .60
34 Tobias Harris .30 .75
35 Jrue Holiday .50 1.25
36 Brandon Bass .25 .60
37 Lance Stephenson .30 .75
38 David Lee .25 .60
39 Nicolas Batum .30 .75
40 Ersan Ilyasova .25 .60
41 Russell Westbrook .60 1.50
42 Jason Thompson .25 .60
43 Tony Parker .60 1.50
44 Amar'e Stoudemire .40 1.00
45 Kawhi Leonard 1.00 2.50
46 Brandon Jennings .25 .60
47 LeBron James 3.00 8.00
48 David West .30 .75
49 Nikola Pekovic .25 .60
50 George Hill .30 .75
51 Ryan Anderson .25 .60
52 Jason Terry .30 .75
53 Tony Snell .25 .60
54 Amir Johnson .25 .60
55 Kelly Olynyk .25 .60
56 Brandon Knight .25 .60
57 Luol Deng .30 .75
58 DeAndre Jordan .30 .75
59 Nikola Vucevic .30 .75
60 Gerald Green .30 .75
61 Serge Ibaka .30 .75
62 JaVale McGee .25 .60
63 Tony Wroten .25 .60
64 Anderson Varejao .25 .60
65 Kemba Walker .40 1.00
66 Brook Lopez .40 1.00
67 Manu Ginobili .75 2.00
68 DeMar DeRozan .50 1.25
69 Norris Cole .25 .60
70 Gerald Henderson .25 .60
71 Shawn Marion .30 .75
72 Jeff Green .30 .75
73 Trey Burke .25 .60
74 Andre Drummond .30 .75
75 Kenneth Faried .25 .60
76 C.J. McCollum .40 1.00
77 Marc Gasol .40 1.00
78 O.J. Mayo .25 .60
79 Dennis Schroder .40 1.00
80 Giannis Antetokounmpo 2.50 6.00
81 Stephen Curry 3.00 8.00
82 Jeff Teague .25 .60
83 Tristan Thompson .25 .60
84 Andre Iguodala .40 1.00
85 Kentavious Caldwell-Pope .30 .75
86 Carlos Boozer .30 .75
87 Marcin Gortat .25 .60
88 Deron Williams .30 .75
89 Otto Porter .30 .75
90 Goran Dragic .40 1.00
91 Steve Nash .75 2.00
92 Jeremy Lin .75 2.00
93 Ty Lawson .25 .60
94 Andrew Bogut .30 .75
95 Kevin Durant 1.25 3.00
96 Carmelo Anthony .60 1.50
97 Marco Belinelli .25 .60
98 Derrick Favors .30 .75
99 Pau Gasol .60 1.50
100 Gordon Hayward .30 .75
101 Steven Adams .50 1.25
102 Jimmy Butler .60 1.50
103 Tyreke Evans .30 .75
104 Anthony Bennett .25 .60
105 Kevin Garnett 1.00 2.50
106 Caron Butler .30 .75
107 Mason Plumlee .25 .60
108 Derrick Rose .75 2.00
109 Paul George .60 1.50
110 Taj Gibson .25 .60
111 Gorgui Dieng .25 .60
112 Joakim Noah .40 1.00
113 Tyson Chandler .40 1.00
114 Anthony Davis 1.00 2.50
115 Kevin Love .40 1.00
116 Chandler Parsons .25 .60
117 Matt Barnes .30 .75
118 Dion Waiters .25 .60
119 Paul Millsap .30 .75
120 Greg Monroe .25 .60
121 Tayshaun Prince .40 1.00
122 Jodie Meeks .25 .60
123 Victor Oladipo .30 .75
124 Archie Goodwin .25 .60
125 Klay Thompson 1.00 2.50
126 Channing Frye .25 .60
127 Michael Carter-Williams .25 .60
128 Dirk Nowitzki 1.00 2.50
129 Paul Pierce .60 1.50
130 Harrison Barnes .30 .75
131 Terrence Jones .25 .60
132 Joe Johnson .30 .75
133 Vince Carter .75 2.00
134 Arron Afflalo .25 .60
135 Kevin Martin .30 .75
136 Chris Bosh .50 1.25
137 Mike Conley .30 .75
138 Dwight Howard .50 1.25
139 Rajon Rondo .50 1.25
140 Isaiah Thomas .30 .75
141 Terrence Ross .30 .75
142 John Wall .50 1.25
143 Wesley Matthews .50 1.25
144 Avery Bradley .25 .60
145 Kobe Bryant 3.00 8.00
146 Chris Paul .60 1.50
147 Monta Ellis .30 .75
148 DeMarcus Cousins .30 .75
149 Randy Foye .25 .60
150 J.J. Redick .40 1.00
151 Thaddeus Young .25 .60
152 Jonas Valanciunas .30 .75
153 Zach Randolph .40 1.00
154 Michael Kidd-Gilchrist .25 .60
155 Kyle Korver .30 .75
156 Cody Zeller .25 .60
157 Nene .30 .75
158 Dwyane Wade .75 2.00
159 J.R. Smith .40 1.00
160 Michael Beasley .25 .60
161 Andrew Wiggins RC 2.50 6.00
162 Jabari Parker RC .60 1.50
163 Joel Embiid RC 5.00 12.00
164 Aaron Gordon RC 2.50 6.00
165 Dante Exum RC .75 2.00
166 Marcus Smart RC 2.00 5.00
167 Julius Randle RC 2.50 6.00
168 Nik Stauskas RC .50 1.25
169 Noah Vonleh RC .50 1.25
170 Elfrid Payton RC .75 2.00
171 Doug McDermott RC .75 2.00
172 Zach LaVine RC 3.00 8.00
173 T.J. Warren RC .75 2.00
174 Adreian Payne RC .50 1.25
175 James Young RC .50 1.25
176 Tyler Ennis RC .50 1.25
177 Gary Harris RC .75 2.00
178 Mitch McGary RC .50 1.25
179 Jordan Adams RC .50 1.25
180 Rodney Hood RC .60 1.50
181 Shabazz Napier RC .60 1.50
182 P.J. Hairston RC .50 1.25
183 C.J. Wilcox RC .50 1.25
184 Josh Huestis RC .50 1.25
185 Kyle Anderson RC .75 2.00
186 Damien Inglis RC .50 1.25
187 K.J. McDaniels RC .50 1.25
188 Joe Harris RC .75 2.00
189 Cleanthony Early RC .50 1.25
190 Jarnell Stokes RC .50 1.25
191 Johnny O'Bryant RC .50 1.25
192 Erick Green RC .50 1.25
193 Spencer Dinwiddie RC .75 2.00
194 Jerami Grant RC 2.50 6.00
195 Jordan Clarkson RC 2.00 5.00
196 Russ Smith RC .50 1.25
197 Thanasis Antetokounmpo RC 1.00 2.50
198 Jordan McRae RC .50 1.25
199 Xavier Thames RC .50 1.25
200 Cory Jefferson RC .50 1.25

2014-15 Prestige Bonus Shots Blue

*VETS: 1.2X TO 3X BASE HI
*ROOKIES: 1.5X TO 4X BASE HI
STATED PRINT RUN 99 SER.#'d SETS

2014-15 Prestige Bonus Shots Orange Die Cuts

*VETS: 2.5X TO 6X BASE HI
*ROOKIES: 3X TO 8X BASE HI
STATED PRINT RUN 25 SER.#'d SETS
47 LeBron James 12.00 30.00
80 Giannis Antetokounmpo 25.00 60.00

2014-15 Prestige Bonus Shots Purple

*VETS: 1.5X TO 4X BASE HI
*ROOKIES: 2X TO 5X BASE HI
STATED PRINT RUN 49 SER.#'d SETS

2014-15 Prestige Bonus Shots Red

*VETS: 1X TO 2.5X BASE HI
*ROOKIES: 1.2X TO 3X BASE HI
STATED PRINT RUN 199 SER.#'d SETS

2014-15 Prestige Bonus Shots Autographs

PRINT RUNS B/WN 10-99 COPIES PER
NO PRICING ON QTY 10
*BLUE/25: .5X TO 1.2X BASE HI
*RED/49: .4X TO 1X BASE HI
*RED/25: .5X TO 1.2X BASE HI
3 Gorgui Dieng/49 4.00 10.00
9 Terry Porter/49 4.00 10.00
13 Tim Hardaway Jr./49 5.00 12.00
21 Khris Middleton/49 8.00 20.00
23 Rudy Gobert/99 10.00 25.00
29 Horace Grant/49 6.00 15.00
31 Tony Snell/49 4.00 10.00
33 Luigi Datome/99 4.00 10.00
39 Isaiah Thomas/49 12.00 30.00
49 Rick Mahorn/49 5.00 12.00
53 Solomon Hill/99 4.00 10.00
61 Gal Mekel/49 4.00 10.00
63 Isaiah Canaan/99 4.00 10.00
67 Marvin Williams/49 4.00 10.00
71 P.J. Tucker/99 5.00 12.00
77 Brandan Wright/49 4.00 10.00
79 Sean Elliott/49 6.00 15.00
83 Ryan Kelly/49 4.00 10.00
89 Mark Aguirre/49 5.00 12.00
91 Dennis Schroder/49 6.00 15.00
93 Phil Pressey/49 4.00 10.00
97 Steven Adams/49 8.00 20.00

2014-15 Prestige Connections

1 D.Williams/J.Kidd 1.00 2.50
2 D.Robinson/T.Duncan 1.50 4.00
3 B.Cousy/R.Rondo 1.25 3.00
4 A.Iverson/M.Carter-Williams 1.50 4.00
5 B.Walton/L.Aldridge 1.00 2.50
6 T.Lawson/F.Lever .40 1.00
7 A.Gilmore/J.Noah .75 2.00
8 M.Price/K.Irving 1.25 3.00
9 A.Drummond/B.Laimbeer .60 1.50
10 B.Griffin/B.McAdoo .60 1.50
11 R.Barry/K.Thompson 1.50 4.00
12 E.Baylor/K.Bryant 5.00 12.00
13 A.Mourning/A.Davis 1.50 4.00
14 M.Malone/D.Howard 1.00 2.50
15 T.Porter/D.Lillard 1.50 4.00
16 L.James/O.Robertson 5.00 12.00
17 D.Wade/J.Dumars 1.25 3.00
18 C.Andersen/D.Rodman 1.50 4.00
19 K.Durant/G.Gervin 2.00 5.00
20 L.Bird/C.Anthony 2.50 6.00

2014-15 Prestige Franchise Favorites

1 Al Horford .60 1.50
2 Rajon Rondo .75 2.00
3 Deron Williams .50 1.25
4 Gerald Henderson .40 1.00
5 Derrick Rose 1.25 3.00
6 LeBron James 5.00 12.00
7 Dirk Nowitzki 1.50 4.00
8 Ty Lawson .40 1.00
9 Greg Monroe .40 1.00
10 Stephen Curry 5.00 12.00
11 James Harden 1.25 3.00
12 Paul George 1.00 2.50
13 Blake Griffin .60 1.50
14 Kobe Bryant 5.00 12.00
15 Mike Conley .50 1.25
16 Dwyane Wade 1.25 3.00
17 Ersan Ilyasova .40 1.00
18 Ricky Rubio .50 1.25
19 Anthony Davis 1.50 4.00
20 Carmelo Anthony 1.00 2.50
21 Kevin Durant 2.00 5.00
22 Nikola Vucevic .50 1.25
23 Michael Carter-Williams .40 1.00
24 Goran Dragic .60 1.50
25 LaMarcus Aldridge .60 1.50
26 DeMarcus Cousins .50 1.25
27 Tim Duncan 1.50 4.00
28 DeMar DeRozan .75 2.00
29 Gordon Hayward .50 1.25
30 John Wall .75 2.00

2014-15 Prestige Hardcourt Heroes

1 Joe Johnson .50 1.25
2 Chris Bosh .75 2.00
3 Dirk Nowitzki 1.50 4.00
4 Damian Lillard 1.50 4.00
5 Vince Carter 1.25 3.00
6 LeBron James 5.00 12.00
7 Russell Westbrook 1.00 2.50
8 Stephen Curry 5.00 12.00
9 Kevin Durant 2.00 5.00
10 Jeff Green .50 1.25
11 Kobe Bryant 5.00 12.00
12 Carmelo Anthony 1.00 2.50
13 Anthony Davis 1.50 4.00
14 Chris Paul 1.00 2.50
15 Dwyane Wade 1.25 3.00
16 Kevin Love .60 1.50
17 Manu Ginobili 1.50 4.00
18 Klay Thompson 1.50 4.00
19 Tim Duncan 1.50 4.00
20 Kyrie Irving 1.25 3.00

2014-15 Prestige Mystery Rookies

1 Andrew Wiggins 6.00 15.00
2 Dante Exum 2.00 5.00
3 Marcus Smart 5.00 12.00
4 T.J. Warren 2.00 5.00
5 James Young 1.25 3.00
6 Jabari Parker 1.50 4.00
7 Jerami Grant 6.00 15.00
8 Nick Johnson 1.25 3.00
9 Glenn Robinson III 1.50 4.00
10 Joe Harris 2.00 5.00
11 Jordan Adams 1.25 3.00
12 Aaron Gordon 6.00 15.00
13 Julius Randle 6.00 15.00
14 Zach LaVine 8.00 20.00
15 Gary Harris 2.00 5.00
16 Kyle Anderson 2.00 5.00
17 Markel Brown 1.25 3.00
18 Bruno Caboclo 1.50 4.00
19 Semaj Christon 1.25 3.00
20 Damien Inglis 1.25 3.00
21 Russ Smith 1.25 3.00
22 Joel Embiid 12.00 30.00
23 Nik Stauskas 1.25 3.00
24 Doug McDermott 2.00 5.00
25 Rodney Hood 1.50 4.00
26 Cleanthony Early 1.25 3.00
27 Jordan Clarkson 5.00 12.00
28 Mitch McGary 1.25 3.00
29 Thanasis Antetokounmpo 2.50 6.00
30 Jarnell Stokes 1.25 3.00
31 Adreian Payne 1.25 3.00
32 Tyler Ennis 1.25 3.00
33 Noah Vonleh 1.25 3.00
34 Elfrid Payton 2.00 5.00
35 Shabazz Napier 1.50 4.00
36 P.J. Hairston 1.25 3.00
37 Cory Jefferson 1.25 3.00
38 Xavier Thames 1.25 3.00
39 Lamar Patterson 1.25 3.00
40 Jordan McRae 1.25 3.00

2014-15 Prestige NBA Materials

STATED PRINT RUN 99 SER.#'d SETS
*PURPLE/199: .4X TO 1X BASIC
1 Andray Blatche 2.00 5.00
2 Andre Iguodala 3.00 8.00
3 Brandon Bass 2.00 5.00
4 Carlos Boozer 2.50 6.00
5 Chris Bosh 4.00 10.00
6 David Lee 2.00 5.00
7 DeAndre Jordan 2.50 6.00
8 Harrison Barnes 2.50 6.00
9 J.R. Smith 3.00 8.00
10 Jamal Crawford 3.00 8.00
11 Jimmy Butler 5.00 12.00
12 Joe Johnson 2.50 6.00
13 Jordan Hill 2.00 5.00
14 Kevin Garnett 8.00 20.00
15 Kevin Love 3.00 8.00
16 Mario Chalmers 2.50 6.00
17 Nick Collison 2.50 6.00
18 Pau Gasol 5.00 12.00
19 Paul Pierce 3.00 8.00
20 Raymond Felton 2.00 5.00
21 Serge Ibaka 2.50 6.00
22 Taj Gibson 2.00 5.00
23 Steven Adams 4.00 10.00
24 Tony Snell 2.00 5.00
25 Tyson Chandler 3.00 8.00

2014-15 Prestige Prestigious Pioneers

1 George Mikan 2.00 5.00
2 Bob Pettit .60 1.50
3 Bob Cousy 1.25 3.00
4 Dolph Schayes .60 1.50
5 Bill Russell 2.00 5.00
6 Elgin Baylor 1.25 3.00
7 Bill Sharman .75 2.00
8 Wilt Chamberlain 2.00 5.00
9 Oscar Robertson 1.25 3.00
10 Jerry West 1.50 4.00
11 Willis Reed 1.00 2.50
12 Hal Greer .60 1.50
13 John Havlicek 1.25 3.00
14 Pete Maravich 2.00 5.00
15 Rick Barry .75 2.00
16 Julius Erving 1.50 4.00
17 Kareem Abdul-Jabbar 2.00 5.00
18 Larry Bird 2.50 6.00
19 Magic Johnson 2.50 6.00
20 Dominique Wilkins 1.00 2.50

2014-15 Prestige Prestigious Posts

1 DeAndre Jordan .75 2.00
2 Andre Drummond .75 2.00
3 Kevin Love 1.00 2.50
4 Joakim Noah 1.00 2.50
5 Dwight Howard 1.25 3.00
6 Tim Duncan 2.50 6.00
7 Anthony Davis 2.50 6.00
8 Blake Griffin 1.00 2.50
9 Marcin Gortat .60 1.50
10 LaMarcus Aldridge 1.00 2.50

2014-15 Prestige Prestigious Premieres Signatures

PPAG Aaron Gordon 10.00 25.00
PPAP Adreian Payne 4.00 10.00
PPAW Andrew Wiggins 20.00 50.00
PPBC Bruno Caboclo 5.00 12.00
PPCE Cleanthony Early 4.00 10.00
PPCJ Cory Jefferson 4.00 10.00
PPCW C.J. Wilcox 4.00 10.00
PPDD Doug McDermott 4.00 10.00
PPDE Dante Exum 6.00 15.00
PPEP Elfrid Payton 6.00 15.00
PPGH Gary Harris 6.00 15.00
PPGR Glenn Robinson III 5.00 12.00
PPJA Jordan Adams 4.00 10.00
PPJE Joel Embiid 50.00 120.00
PPJP Jabari Parker 5.00 12.00
PPJR Julius Randle 10.00 25.00
PPJS Jarnell Stokes 4.00 10.00
PPJY James Young 4.00 10.00
PPKA Kyle Anderson 4.00 10.00
PPMM Mitch McGary 4.00 10.00
PPMS Marcus Smart 15.00 40.00
PPNS Nik Stauskas 4.00 10.00
PPNV Noah Vonleh 4.00 10.00
PPRH Rodney Hood 5.00 12.00
PPRS Russ Smith 4.00 10.00
PPSN Shabazz Napier 5.00 12.00
PPSP Spencer Dinwiddie 6.00 15.00
PPTA Thanasis Antetokounmpo 8.00 20.00
PPTE Tyler Ennis 4.00 10.00
PPTJ T.J. Warren 6.00 15.00
PPZL Zach LaVine 12.00 30.00

2014-15 Prestige True Colors Materials

*PURPLE/49-199: .5X TO 1.2X BASIC
*PRIME/25: .75X TO 2X BASIC
1 Jimmy Butler/75 5.00 12.00
2 Ty Lawson/75 2.00 5.00
3 Kevin Love/75 3.00 8.00
4 Kenneth Faried/75 2.00 5.00
5 Al Horford/75 3.00 8.00
6 Pau Gasol/75 5.00 12.00
7 DeMarcus Cousins/75 2.50 6.00
8 Russell Westbrook/75 5.00 12.00
9 James Harden/75 6.00 15.00
10 Tim Duncan/75 8.00 20.00
11 Jrue Holiday/75 4.00 10.00
12 Tyson Chandler/75 3.00 8.00
13 Kevin Durant/75 10.00 25.00
14 Kobe Bryant/75 25.00 60.00
15 Blake Griffin/75 3.00 8.00
16 Ricky Rubio/75 2.50 6.00
17 Dirk Nowitzki/75 8.00 20.00
18 Steve Nash/75 6.00 15.00
19 Jeff Teague/75 2.00 5.00
20 Tony Parker/75 5.00 12.00
21 M.Carter-Williams/75 2.00 5.00
22 Zach Randolph/75 3.00 8.00
23 LeBron James/75 25.00 60.00
24 Kyrie Irving/75 6.00 15.00
25 Carmelo Anthony/75 5.00 12.00
26 David Robinson/49 6.00 15.00
27 Patrick Ewing/49 5.00 12.00
28 Dikembe Mutombo/49 5.00 12.00
29 Gary Payton/49 5.00 12.00
30 Julius Erving/49 8.00 20.00
31 Hakeem Olajuwon/49 6.00 15.00
32 Scottie Pippen/49 8.00 20.00
33 Shaquille O'Neal/49 12.00 30.00
34 Clyde Drexler/49 5.00 12.00
35 Zydrunas Ilgauskas/49 2.50 6.00
36 Joe Dumars/49 4.00 10.00
37 Aaron Gordon/99 10.00 25.00
38 Gary Harris/99 3.00 8.00
39 James Ennis/99 2.00 5.00
40 Elfrid Payton/99 3.00 8.00
41 Julius Randle/99 10.00 25.00
42 Mitch McGary/99 2.00 5.00
43 Noah Vonleh/99 2.00 5.00
44 Shabazz Napier/99 2.50 6.00
45 Tyler Ennis/99 2.00 5.00
46 P.J. Hairston/99 2.00 5.00
47 Joe Harris/99 3.00 8.00
48 Adreian Payne/99 2.00 5.00
49 Glenn Robinson III/99 2.50 6.00
51 Doug McDermott/99 3.00 8.00
52 Kyle Anderson/99 3.00 8.00
53 Johnny O'Bryant/99 2.00 5.00
54 Rodney Hood/99 2.50 6.00
55 Spencer Dinwiddie/99 3.00 8.00
56 Thanasis Antetokounmpo/99 4.00 10.00
57 Cleanthony Early/99 2.00 5.00
58 Markel Brown/99 2.00 5.00
59 Cory Jefferson/99 2.00 5.00
60 Andrew Wiggins/99 6.00 15.00
61 Jabari Parker/99 2.50 6.00
62 Jordan Adams/99 2.00 5.00
63 Damien Inglis/99 2.00 5.00
64 Marcus Smart/99 8.00 20.00
65 Nik Stauskas/99 2.00 5.00
66 Russ Smith/99 2.00 5.00
67 T.J. Warren/99 3.00 8.00
68 Zach LaVine/99 12.00 30.00
69 Jarnell Stokes/99 2.00 5.00
70 Jerami Grant/99 10.00 25.00
71 K.J. McDaniels/99 2.00 5.00
72 C.J. Wilcox/99 2.00 5.00
73 James Young/99 2.00 5.00
74 Joel Embiid/99 20.00 50.00
75 Bruno Caboclo/99 2.50 6.00

2014-15 Prestige Plus

1 Ricky Rubio .40 1.00
2 Jamal Crawford .50 1.25
3 Tiago Splitter .30 .75
4 Al Horford .50 1.25
5 Jordan Hill .30 .75
6 Ben McLemore .30 .75
7 Kyle Lowry .60 1.50
8 Corey Brewer .30 .75
9 Nerlens Noel .30 .75
10 Enes Kanter .40 1.00
11 Robin Lopez .30 .75
12 Jameer Nelson .30 .75
13 Tim Duncan 1.25 3.00
14 Al Jefferson .30 .75
15 Jose Calderon .30 .75
16 Blake Griffin .50 1.25
17 Kyrie Irving 1.00 2.50
18 Damian Lillard 1.25 3.00
19 Nick Collison .40 1.00
20 Eric Bledsoe .40 1.00
21 Roy Hibbert .40 1.00
22 James Harden 1.00 2.50
23 Tim Hardaway Jr. .40 1.00
24 Alex Len .30 .75
25 Josh Smith .30 .75
26 Bradley Beal .75 2.00
27 LaMarcus Aldridge .50 1.25
28 Danilo Gallinari .30 .75
29 Nick Young .30 .75
30 Eric Gordon .40 1.00
31 Rudy Gay .50 1.25
32 Jared Sullinger .30 .75
33 Al-Farouq Aminu .30 .75
34 Tobias Harris .40 1.00
35 Jrue Holiday .60 1.50
36 Brandon Bass .30 .75
37 Lance Stephenson .40 1.00
38 David Lee .30 .75
39 Nicolas Batum .40 1.00
40 Ersan Ilyasova .30 .75
41 Russell Westbrook .75 2.00
42 Jason Thompson .30 .75
43 Tony Parker .75 2.00
44 Amar'e Stoudemire .50 1.25
45 Kawhi Leonard 1.25 3.00
46 Brandon Jennings .30 .75
47 LeBron James 4.00 10.00
48 David West .40 1.00
49 Nikola Pekovic .30 .75
50 George Hill .40 1.00
51 Ryan Anderson .30 .75
52 Jason Terry .40 1.00
53 Tony Snell .30 .75
54 Amir Johnson .30 .75
55 Kelly Olynyk .30 .75
56 Brandon Knight .30 .75
57 Luol Deng .40 1.00
58 DeAndre Jordan .40 1.00
59 Nikola Vucevic .40 1.00
60 Gerald Green .40 1.00
61 Serge Ibaka .40 1.00
62 JaVale McGee .40 1.00
63 Tony Wroten .30 .75
64 Anderson Varejao .30 .75
65 Kemba Walker .50 1.25
66 Brook Lopez .50 1.25
67 Manu Ginobili 1.00 2.50
68 DeMar DeRozan .60 1.50
69 Norris Cole .30 .75
70 Gerald Henderson .30 .75
71 Shawn Marion .40 1.00
72 Jeff Green .40 1.00
73 Trey Burke .30 .75
74 Andre Drummond .40 1.00
75 Kenneth Faried .30 .75
76 C.J. McCollum .50 1.25
77 Marc Gasol .50 1.25
78 O.J. Mayo .30 .75
79 Dennis Schroder .50 1.25
80 Giannis Antetokounmpo 3.00 8.00
81 Stephen Curry 4.00 10.00
82 Jeff Teague .30 .75
83 Tristan Thompson .30 .75
84 Andre Iguodala .50 1.25
85 Kentavious Caldwell-Pope .40 1.00
86 Carlos Boozer .40 1.00
87 Marcin Gortat .30 .75
88 Deron Williams .40 1.00
89 Otto Porter .40 1.00
90 Goran Dragic .50 1.25
91 Steve Nash 1.00 2.50
92 Jeremy Lin 1.00 2.50
93 Ty Lawson .30 .75
94 Andrew Bogut .40 1.00
95 Kevin Durant 1.50 4.00
96 Carmelo Anthony .75 2.00
97 Marco Belinelli .30 .75
98 Derrick Favors .30 .75
99 Pau Gasol .75 2.00
100 Gordon Hayward .40 1.00
101 Steven Adams .60 1.50
102 Jimmy Butler .75 2.00
103 Tyreke Evans .40 1.00
104 Anthony Bennett .30 .75
105 Kevin Garnett 1.25 3.00
106 Caron Butler .40 1.00
107 Mason Plumlee .30 .75
108 Derrick Rose 1.00 2.50
109 Paul George .75 2.00
110 Taj Gibson .30 .75
111 Gorgui Dieng .30 .75
112 Joakim Noah .50 1.25
113 Tyson Chandler .50 1.25
114 Anthony Davis 1.25 3.00
115 Kevin Love .50 1.25
116 Chandler Parsons .30 .75
117 Matt Barnes .40 1.00
118 Dion Waiters .30 .75
119 Paul Millsap .40 1.00
120 Greg Monroe .30 .75
121 Tayshaun Prince .50 1.25
122 Jodie Meeks .30 .75
123 Victor Oladipo .40 1.00
124 Archie Goodwin .30 .75
125 Klay Thompson 1.25 3.00
126 Channing Frye .30 .75
127 Michael Carter-Williams .30 .75
128 Dirk Nowitzki 1.25 3.00
129 Paul Pierce .75 2.00
130 Harrison Barnes .40 1.00
131 Terrence Jones .30 .75
132 Joe Johnson .40 1.00
133 Vince Carter 1.00 2.50
134 Arron Afflalo .30 .75
135 Kevin Martin .40 1.00
136 Chris Bosh .60 1.50
137 Mike Conley .40 1.00
138 Dwight Howard .60 1.50
139 Rajon Rondo .60 1.50
140 Isaiah Thomas .40 1.00
141 Terrence Ross .40 1.00
142 John Wall .60 1.50
143 Wesley Matthews .30 .75
144 Avery Bradley .30 .75
145 Kobe Bryant 4.00 10.00
146 Chris Paul .75 2.00
147 Monta Ellis .40 1.00
148 DeMarcus Cousins .40 1.00
149 Randy Foye .30 .75
150 J.J. Redick .50 1.25
151 Thaddeus Young .30 .75
152 Jonas Valanciunas .40 1.00
153 Zach Randolph .50 1.25
154 Michael Kidd-Gilchrist .30 .75
155 Kyle Korver .40 1.00
156 Cody Zeller .30 .75
157 Nene .40 1.00
158 Dwyane Wade 1.00 2.50
159 J.R. Smith .50 1.25
160 Michael Beasley .30 .75
161 Andrew Wiggins RC 3.00 8.00
162 Jabari Parker RC .75 2.00
163 Joel Embiid RC 6.00 15.00
164 Aaron Gordon RC 3.00 8.00
165 Dante Exum RC 1.00 2.50
166 Marcus Smart RC 2.50 6.00
167 Julius Randle RC 3.00 8.00
168 Nik Stauskas RC .60 1.50
169 Noah Vonleh RC .60 1.50
170 Elfrid Payton RC 1.00 2.50
171 Doug McDermott RC 1.00 2.50
172 Zach LaVine RC 4.00 10.00
173 T.J. Warren RC 1.00 2.50
174 Adreian Payne RC .60 1.50
175 James Young RC .60 1.50
176 Tyler Ennis RC .60 1.50
177 Gary Harris RC 1.00 2.50
178 Mitch McGary RC .60 1.50
179 Jordan Adams RC .60 1.50
180 Rodney Hood RC .75 2.00
181 Shabazz Napier RC .75 2.00
182 P.J. Hairston RC .60 1.50
183 C.J. Wilcox RC .60 1.50
184 Josh Huestis RC .60 1.50
185 Kyle Anderson RC 1.00 2.50
186 Damien Inglis RC .60 1.50
187 K.J. McDaniels RC .60 1.50
188 Joe Harris RC 1.00 2.50
189 Cleanthony Early RC .60 1.50
190 Jarnell Stokes RC .60 1.50
191 Johnny O'Bryant RC .60 1.50
192 Erick Green RC .60 1.50
193 Spencer Dinwiddie RC 1.00 2.50
194 Jerami Grant RC 3.00 8.00
195 Jordan Clarkson RC 2.50 6.00
196 Russ Smith RC .60 1.50
197 Thanasis Antetokounmpo RC 1.25 3.00
198 Jordan McRae RC .60 1.50
199 Xavier Thames RC .60 1.50
200 Cory Jefferson RC .60 1.50

2014-15 Prestige Plus Bonus Shots Blue

*VETS: 1X TO 2.5X BASE HI
*ROOKIES: 1.2X TO 3X BASE HI
STATED PRINT RUN 99 SER.#'d SETS

2014-15 Prestige Plus Bonus Shots Orange Die Cuts

*VETS: 2X TO 5X BASE HI
*ROOKIES: 2.5X TO 6X BASE HI
STATED PRINT RUN 25 SER.#'d SETS

2014-15 Prestige Plus Bonus Shots Purple

*VETS: 1.2X TO 3X BASE HI
*ROOKIES: 1.5X TO 4X BASE HI
STATED PRINT RUN 49 SER.#'d SETS

2014-15 Prestige Plus Bonus Shots Red

*VETS: .75X TO 2X BASE HI
*ROOKIES: 1X TO 2.5X BASE HI
STATED PRINT RUN 199 SER.#'d SETS

2014-15 Prestige Plus Bonus Shots Autographs

*RED/49: .4X TO 1X BASE HI
*BLUE/25: .5X TO 1.2X BASE HI
STATED PRINT RUN 10-99
NO PRICING ON QTY 10 OR LESS
1 Glen Rice Jr./99 4.00 10.00
3 Gorgui Dieng/99 4.00 10.00
11 Arnett Moultrie/99 4.00 10.00
13 Tim Hardaway Jr./99 5.00 12.00
17 Glen Rice/25 6.00 15.00
23 Rudy Gobert/99 10.00 25.00
27 Enes Kanter/25 5.00 12.00
29 Horace Grant/99 6.00 15.00
37 Harry Gallatin/25 6.00 15.00
39 Isaiah Thomas/99 12.00 30.00
45 Greg Anthony/25 4.00 10.00
47 Cedric Maxwell/25 5.00 12.00
57 Marcin Gortat/25 20.00 50.00
59 Amir Johnson/99 4.00 10.00
75 Dan Majerle/25 5.00 12.00
79 Sean Elliott/99 6.00 15.00
81 Hollis Thompson/99 4.00 10.00
87 Bismack Biyombo/99 4.00 10.00
91 Dennis Schroder/99 6.00 15.00
94 Ryan Anderson/25 4.00 10.00
97 Steven Adams/99 8.00 20.00
99 Greg Buckner/99 4.00 10.00

2014-15 Prestige Plus Connections

1 D.Williams/J.Kidd 1.25 3.00
2 D.Robinson/T.Duncan 2.00 5.00
3 B.Cousy/R.Rondo 1.50 4.00
4 A.Iverson/M.Carter-Williams 2.00 5.00
5 B.Walton/L.Aldridge 1.25 3.00
6 T.Lawson/F.Lever .50 1.25
7 A.Gilmore/J.Noah 1.00 2.50
8 M.Price/K.Irving 1.50 4.00
9 A.Drummond/B.Laimbeer .75 2.00
10 B.Griffin/B.McAdoo .75 2.00
11 R.Barry/K.Thompson 2.00 5.00
12 E.Baylor/K.Bryant 6.00 15.00
13 A.Mourning/A.Davis 2.00 5.00
14 M.Malone/D.Howard 1.25 3.00
15 T.Porter/D.Lillard 2.00 5.00
16 L.James/O.Robertson 6.00 15.00
17 D.Wade/J.Dumars 1.50 4.00
18 C.Andersen/D.Rodman 2.00 5.00
19 K.Durant/G.Gervin 2.50 6.00
20 L.Bird/C.Anthony 3.00 8.00

2014-15 Prestige Plus Franchise Favorites

1 Al Horford .75 2.00
2 Rajon Rondo 1.00 2.50
3 Deron Williams .60 1.50
4 Gerald Henderson .50 1.25
5 Derrick Rose 1.50 4.00
6 LeBron James 6.00 15.00
7 Dirk Nowitzki 2.00 5.00
8 Ty Lawson .50 1.25
9 Greg Monroe .50 1.25
10 Stephen Curry 6.00 15.00
11 James Harden 1.50 4.00
12 Paul George 1.25 3.00
13 Blake Griffin .75 2.00
14 Kobe Bryant 6.00 15.00
15 Mike Conley .60 1.50
16 Dwyane Wade 1.50 4.00
17 Ersan Ilyasova .50 1.25
18 Ricky Rubio .60 1.50
19 Anthony Davis 2.00 5.00
20 Carmelo Anthony 1.25 3.00
21 Kevin Durant 2.50 6.00
22 Nikola Vucevic .60 1.50
23 Michael Carter-Williams .50 1.25
24 Goran Dragic .75 2.00
25 LaMarcus Aldridge .75 2.00
26 DeMarcus Cousins .60 1.50
27 Tim Duncan 2.00 5.00
28 DeMar DeRozan 1.00 2.50
29 Gordon Hayward .60 1.50
30 John Wall 1.00 2.50

2014-15 Prestige Plus Hardcourt Heroes

1 Joe Johnson .60 1.50
2 Chris Bosh 1.00 2.50
3 Dirk Nowitzki 2.00 5.00
4 Damian Lillard 2.00 5.00
5 Vince Carter 1.50 4.00
6 LeBron James 6.00 15.00
7 Russell Westbrook 1.25 3.00
8 Stephen Curry 6.00 15.00
9 Kevin Durant 2.50 6.00
10 Jeff Green .60 1.50
11 Kobe Bryant 6.00 15.00
12 Carmelo Anthony 1.25 3.00
13 Anthony Davis 2.00 5.00
14 Chris Paul 1.25 3.00
15 Dwyane Wade 1.50 4.00
16 Kevin Love .75 2.00
17 Manu Ginobili 1.50 4.00
18 Klay Thompson 2.00 5.00
19 Tim Duncan 2.00 5.00
20 Kyrie Irving 1.50 4.00

2014-15 Prestige Plus NBA Materials

PRINT RUN B/WN 99-199 COPIES PER
1 Andray Blatche/99 2.00 5.00
2 Andre Iguodala/99 3.00 8.00
3 Brandon Bass/99 2.00 5.00
4 Carlos Boozer/99 2.50 6.00

5 Chris Bosh/99 4.00 10.00
6 David Lee/99 2.00 5.00
7 DeAndre Jordan/99 2.50 6.00
8 Harrison Barnes/99 2.50 6.00
9 J.R. Smith/99 3.00 8.00
10 Jamal Crawford/99 3.00 8.00
11 Jimmy Butler/99 5.00 12.00
12 Joe Johnson/99 2.50 6.00
13 Jordan Hill/99 2.00 5.00
14 Kevin Garnett/99 8.00 20.00
15 Kevin Love/99 3.00 8.00
16 Mario Chalmers/99 2.50 6.00
17 Nick Collison/99 2.50 6.00
18 Pau Gasol/199 5.00 12.00
19 Paul Pierce/99 5.00 12.00
20 Raymond Felton/199 2.00 5.00
21 Serge Ibaka/99 2.50 6.00
22 Taj Gibson/99 2.00 5.00
23 Steven Adams/99 4.00 10.00
24 Tony Snell/99 2.00 5.00
25 Tyson Chandler/199 3.00 8.00

2014-15 Prestige Plus Playmakers

1 Kevin Durant 15.00 40.00
2 LeBron James 75.00 150.00
3 Kevin Love 5.00 12.00
4 Anthony Davis 12.00 30.00
5 DeMarcus Cousins 4.00 10.00
6 Chris Paul 8.00 20.00
7 Carmelo Anthony 8.00 20.00
8 Stephen Curry 40.00 100.00
9 Blake Griffin 5.00 12.00
10 Dirk Nowitzki 12.00 30.00
11 James Harden 10.00 25.00
12 Andre Drummond 4.00 10.00
13 Al Jefferson 3.00 8.00
14 LaMarcus Aldridge 5.00 12.00
15 Goran Dragic 5.00 12.00
16 Tim Duncan 12.00 30.00
17 Dwight Howard 8.00 20.00
18 Isaiah Thomas 4.00 10.00
19 Paul George 8.00 20.00
20 Kyrie Irving 15.00 40.00
21 Kyle Lowry 6.00 15.00
22 Mike Conley 4.00 10.00
23 Joakim Noah 5.00 12.00
24 Kenneth Faried 3.00 8.00
25 Paul Millsap 4.00 10.00

2014-15 Prestige Plus Prestigious Pioneers

1 George Mikan 2.50 6.00
2 Bob Pettit .75 2.00
3 Bob Cousy 1.50 4.00
4 Dolph Schayes .75 2.00
5 Bill Russell 2.50 6.00
6 Elgin Baylor 1.50 4.00
7 Bill Sharman 1.00 2.50
8 Wilt Chamberlain 2.50 6.00
9 Oscar Robertson 1.50 4.00
10 Jerry West 2.00 5.00
11 Willis Reed 1.25 3.00
12 Hal Greer .75 2.00
13 John Havlicek 1.50 4.00
14 Pete Maravich 2.50 6.00
15 Rick Barry 1.00 2.50
16 Julius Erving 2.00 5.00
17 Kareem Abdul-Jabbar 2.50 6.00
18 Larry Bird 3.00 8.00
19 Magic Johnson 3.00 8.00
20 Dominique Wilkins 1.25 3.00

2014-15 Prestige Plus Prestigious Posts

1 DeAndre Jordan 1.00 2.50
2 Andre Drummond 1.00 2.50
3 Kevin Love 1.25 3.00
4 Joakim Noah 1.25 3.00
5 Dwight Howard 1.50 4.00
6 Tim Duncan 3.00 8.00
7 Anthony Davis 3.00 8.00
8 Blake Griffin 1.25 3.00
9 Marcin Gortat .75 2.00
10 LaMarcus Aldridge 1.25 3.00

2014-15 Prestige Plus Prestigious Premieres Signatures

PPAG Aaron Gordon 10.00 25.00
PPAP Adreian Payne 8.00 20.00
PPAW Andrew Wiggins 100.00 200.00
PPBC Bruno Caboclo 4.00 10.00
PPCE Cleanthony Early 3.00 8.00
PPCJ Cory Jefferson 3.00 8.00
PPCW C.J. Wilcox 3.00 8.00
PPDD Doug McDermott 5.00 12.00
PPDE Dante Exum 5.00 12.00
PPEP Elfrid Payton 15.00 40.00
PPGH Gary Harris 5.00 12.00
PPGR Glenn Robinson III 4.00 10.00
PPJA Jordan Adams 3.00 8.00
PPJE Joel Embiid 20.00 50.00
PPJP Jabari Parker 4.00 10.00
PPJR Julius Randle 20.00 50.00
PPJS Jarnell Stokes 3.00 8.00
PPJY James Young 3.00 8.00
PPKA Kyle Anderson 8.00 20.00
PPMM Mitch McGary 3.00 8.00
PPMS Marcus Smart 25.00 60.00
PPNS Nik Stauskas 3.00 8.00
PPNV Noah Vonleh 8.00 20.00
PPRH Rodney Hood 4.00 10.00
PPRS Russ Smith 3.00 8.00
PPSN Shabazz Napier 4.00 10.00
PPSP Spencer Dinwiddie 5.00 12.00
PPTA Thanasis Antetokounmpo 6.00 15.00
PPTE Tyler Ennis 5.00 12.00
PPTJ T.J. Warren 5.00 12.00
PPZL Zach LaVine 10.00 25.00

2014-15 Prestige Plus Prestigious Pros

1 Kobe Bryant 15.00 40.00
2 Anthony Davis 5.00 12.00
3 DeMarcus Cousins 1.50 4.00
4 Monta Ellis 1.50 4.00
5 Tim Duncan 5.00 12.00
6 Chris Paul 3.00 8.00
7 Victor Oladipo 1.50 4.00
8 Josh Smith 1.25 3.00
9 Manu Ginobili 4.00 10.00
10 Rajon Rondo 2.50 6.00
11 Paul Pierce 3.00 8.00
12 Mike Conley 1.50 4.00
13 Ricky Rubio 1.50 4.00
14 Tristan Thompson 1.25 3.00
15 DeAndre Jordan 1.50 4.00
16 Paul George 3.00 8.00
17 Stephen Curry 15.00 40.00
18 Kevin Durant 6.00 15.00
19 Isaiah Thomas 1.50 4.00
20 Jonas Valanciunas 1.50 4.00
21 Ty Lawson 1.25 3.00
22 Michael Carter-Williams 1.25 3.00
23 Chris Bosh 2.50 6.00
24 Derrick Rose 4.00 10.00
25 Al Horford 1.25 3.00
26 Gerald Green 1.50 4.00
27 LaMarcus Aldridge 2.00 5.00
28 John Wall 2.50 6.00
29 Jameer Nelson 1.25 3.00
30 Marcin Gortat 1.25 3.00
31 Kevin Garnett 5.00 12.00
32 Trevor Ariza 1.25 3.00
33 Klay Thompson 5.00 12.00
34 Taj Gibson 1.25 3.00
35 Kemba Walker 2.00 5.00
36 Kenneth Faried 1.25 3.00
37 Joakim Noah 2.00 5.00
38 Al Jefferson 1.25 3.00
39 Carmelo Anthony 3.00 8.00
40 Damian Lillard 5.00 12.00
41 Serge Ibaka 1.50 4.00
42 Kyle Lowry 2.50 6.00
43 Jimmy Butler 3.00 8.00
44 Andrew Bogut 1.50 4.00
45 Steve Nash 4.00 10.00
46 Nicolas Batum 1.50 4.00
47 Marc Gasol 1.50 4.00
48 Blake Griffin 2.00 5.00
49 Kevin Love 2.00 5.00
50 Rudy Gay 2.00 5.00
51 Andre Drummond 1.50 4.00
52 Paul Millsap 1.50 4.00
53 Trey Burke 1.25 3.00
54 Roy Hibbert 1.50 4.00
55 Tony Parker 3.00 8.00
56 Lance Stephenson 1.25 3.00
57 Jeff Green 1.50 4.00
58 Vince Carter 4.00 10.00
59 Pau Gasol 3.00 8.00
60 Kyle Korver 1.50 4.00
61 Mario Chalmers 1.50 4.00
62 Thaddeus Young 1.25 3.00
63 Jeff Teague 1.25 3.00
64 Brandon Jennings 1.25 3.00
65 Robin Lopez 1.25 3.00
66 Derrick Favors 1.25 3.00
67 Greg Monroe 1.25 3.00
68 Zach Randolph 2.00 5.00
69 Dwight Howard 2.50 6.00
70 Goran Dragic 2.00 5.00
71 Dirk Nowitzki 5.00 12.00
72 DeMar DeRozan 2.50 6.00
73 James Harden 4.00 10.00
74 LeBron James 15.00 40.00
75 Kyrie Irving 4.00 10.00

2014-15 Prestige Plus True Colors Materials

STATED PRINT RUN 99-199
*PRIME/25: .75X TO 2X BASE HI
1 Jimmy Butler/199 5.00 12.00
2 Ty Lawson/199 2.00 5.00
3 Kevin Love/199 3.00 8.00
4 Kenneth Faried/199 2.00 5.00
5 Al Horford/199 3.00 8.00
6 Pau Gasol/199 5.00 12.00
7 DeMarcus Cousins/199 2.50 6.00
8 Russell Westbrook/199 5.00 12.00
9 James Harden/199 6.00 15.00
10 Tim Duncan/199 8.00 20.00
11 Jrue Holiday/199 4.00 10.00
12 Tyson Chandler/199 3.00 8.00
13 Kevin Durant/199 10.00 25.00
14 Kobe Bryant/199 10.00 25.00
15 Blake Griffin/199 3.00 8.00
16 Ricky Rubio/199 2.50 6.00
17 Dirk Nowitzki/199 8.00 20.00
18 Steve Nash/199 6.00 15.00
19 Jeff Teague/199 2.00 5.00
20 Tony Parker/199 5.00 12.00
21 M.Carter-Williams/199 2.00 5.00
22 Zach Randolph/199 3.00 8.00
23 LeBron James/199 25.00 60.00
24 Kyrie Irving/199 6.00 15.00
25 Carmelo Anthony/199 5.00 12.00
26 David Robinson/99 6.00 15.00
27 Patrick Ewing/199 5.00 12.00
28 Dikembe Mutombo/199 5.00 12.00
29 Gary Payton/199 5.00 12.00
30 Julius Erving/199 8.00 20.00
31 Hakeem Olajuwon/99 6.00 15.00
32 Scottie Pippen/199 8.00 20.00
33 Shaquille O'Neal/99 12.00 30.00
34 Clyde Drexler/199 5.00 12.00
35 Zydrunas Ilgauskas/99 2.50 6.00
36 Joe Dumars/99 4.00 10.00
37 Aaron Gordon/199 10.00 25.00
38 Gary Harris/199 3.00 8.00
39 James Ennis/199 8.00 20.00
40 Elfrid Payton/199 3.00 8.00
41 Julius Randle/199 10.00 25.00
42 Mitch McGary/199 2.00 5.00
43 Noah Vonleh/199 2.00 5.00
44 Shabazz Napier/199 2.50 6.00
45 Tyler Ennis/199 2.00 5.00
46 P.J. Hairston/199 2.00 5.00
47 Joe Harris/199 3.00 8.00
48 Adreian Payne/199 2.00 5.00
49 Glenn Robinson III/199 2.50 6.00
51 Doug McDermott/199 3.00 8.00
52 Kyle Anderson/199 3.00 8.00
53 Johnny O'Bryant/199 2.00 5.00
54 Rodney Hood/199 2.50 6.00
55 Spencer Dinwiddie/199 3.00 8.00
56 Thanasis Antetokounmpo/199 4.00 10.00
57 Cleanthony Early/199 2.00 5.00
58 Markel Brown/199 2.00 5.00
59 Cory Jefferson/199 2.00 5.00
60 Andrew Wiggins/199 10.00 25.00
61 Jabari Parker/199 2.50 6.00
62 Jordan Adams/199 2.00 5.00
63 Damien Inglis/199 2.00 5.00
64 Marcus Smart/199 8.00 20.00
65 Nik Stauskas/199 2.00 5.00
66 Russ Smith/199 2.00 5.00
67 T.J. Warren/199 3.00 8.00
68 Zach LaVine/199 12.00 30.00
69 Jarnell Stokes/199 2.00 5.00
70 Jerami Grant/199 10.00 25.00
71 K.J. McDaniels/199 2.00 5.00
72 C.J. Wilcox/199 2.00 5.00
73 James Young/199 2.00 5.00
74 Joel Embiid/199 20.00 50.00
75 Bruno Caboclo/199 2.50 6.00

2014-15 Prestige Premium

COMPLETE SET (200) 50.00 120.00
1 Ricky Rubio .60 1.50
2 Jamal Crawford .75 2.00
3 Tiago Splitter .50 1.25
4 Al Horford .75 2.00
5 Jordan Hill .50 1.25
6 Ben McLemore .50 1.25
7 Kyle Lowry 1.00 2.50
8 Corey Brewer .50 1.25
9 Nerlens Noel .50 1.25
10 Enes Kanter .60 1.50
11 Robin Lopez .50 1.25
12 Jameer Nelson .50 1.25
13 Tim Duncan 2.00 5.00
14 Al Jefferson .50 1.25
15 Jose Calderon .50 1.25
16 Blake Griffin .75 2.00
17 Kyrie Irving 1.50 4.00
18 Damian Lillard 2.00 5.00
19 Nick Collison .60 1.50
20 Eric Bledsoe .60 1.50
21 Roy Hibbert .60 1.50
22 James Harden 1.50 4.00
23 Tim Hardaway Jr. .60 1.50
24 Alex Len .50 1.25
25 Josh Smith .50 1.25
26 Bradley Beal 1.25 3.00
27 LaMarcus Aldridge .75 2.00
28 Danilo Gallinari .50 1.25
29 Nick Young .50 1.25
30 Eric Gordon .60 1.50
31 Rudy Gay .75 2.00
32 Jared Sullinger .50 1.25
33 Al-Farouq Aminu .50 1.25
34 Tobias Harris .50 1.25
35 Jrue Holiday 1.00 2.50
36 Brandon Bass .50 1.25
37 Lance Stephenson .50 1.25
38 David Lee .50 1.25
39 Nicolas Batum .60 1.50
40 Ersan Ilyasova .50 1.25
41 Russell Westbrook 1.25 3.00
42 Jason Thompson .50 1.25
43 Tony Parker 1.25 3.00
44 Amar'e Stoudemire .75 2.00
45 Kawhi Leonard 2.00 5.00
46 Brandon Jennings .50 1.25
47 LeBron James 6.00 15.00
48 David West .60 1.50
49 Nikola Pekovic .50 1.25
50 George Hill .60 1.50
51 Ryan Anderson .50 1.25
52 Jason Terry .60 1.50
53 Tony Snell .50 1.25
54 Amir Johnson .50 1.25
55 Kelly Olynyk .50 1.25
56 Brandon Knight .50 1.25
57 Luol Deng .60 1.50
58 DeAndre Jordan .60 1.50
59 Nikola Vucevic .60 1.50
60 Gerald Green .60 1.50
61 Serge Ibaka .60 1.50
62 JaVale McGee .60 1.50
63 Tony Wroten .50 1.25
64 Anderson Varejao .50 1.25
65 Kemba Walker .75 2.00
66 Brook Lopez .75 2.00
67 Manu Ginobili 1.50 4.00
68 DeMar DeRozan 1.00 2.50
69 Norris Cole .50 1.25
70 Gerald Henderson .50 1.25
71 Shawn Marion .60 1.50
72 Jeff Green .60 1.50
73 Trey Burke .50 1.25
74 Andre Drummond .60 1.50
75 Kenneth Faried .50 1.25
76 C.J. McCollum .75 2.00
77 Marc Gasol .75 2.00
78 O.J. Mayo .50 1.25
79 Dennis Schroder .75 2.00
80 Giannis Antetokounmpo 5.00 12.00
81 Stephen Curry 6.00 15.00
82 Jeff Teague .50 1.25
83 Tristan Thompson .50 1.25
84 Andre Iguodala .75 2.00
85 Kentavious Caldwell-Pope .60 1.50
86 Carlos Boozer .60 1.50
87 Marcin Gortat .50 1.25
88 Deron Williams .60 1.50
89 Otto Porter .60 1.50
90 Goran Dragic .75 2.00
91 Steve Nash 1.50 4.00
92 Jeremy Lin 1.50 4.00
93 Ty Lawson .50 1.25
94 Andrew Bogut .60 1.50
95 Kevin Durant 2.50 6.00
96 Carmelo Anthony 1.25 3.00
97 Marco Belinelli .50 1.25
98 Derrick Favors .50 1.25
99 Pau Gasol 1.25 3.00
100 Gordon Hayward .60 1.50
101 Steven Adams 1.00 2.50
102 Jimmy Butler 1.25 3.00
103 Tyreke Evans .60 1.50
104 Anthony Bennett .50 1.25
105 Kevin Garnett 2.00 5.00
106 Caron Butler .60 1.50
107 Mason Plumlee .50 1.25
108 Derrick Rose 1.50 4.00
109 Paul George 1.25 3.00
110 Taj Gibson .50 1.25
111 Gorgui Dieng .50 1.25
112 Joakim Noah .75 2.00
113 Tyson Chandler .75 2.00
114 Anthony Davis 2.00 5.00
115 Kevin Love .75 2.00
116 Chandler Parsons .50 1.25
117 Matt Barnes .60 1.50
118 Dion Waiters .50 1.25
119 Paul Millsap .60 1.50
120 Greg Monroe .50 1.25
121 Tayshaun Prince .75 2.00
122 Jodie Meeks .50 1.25
123 Victor Oladipo .60 1.50
124 Archie Goodwin .50 1.25
125 Klay Thompson 2.00 5.00
126 Channing Frye .50 1.25
127 Michael Carter-Williams .50 1.25
128 Dirk Nowitzki 2.00 5.00
129 Paul Pierce 1.25 3.00
130 Harrison Barnes .60 1.50
131 Terrence Jones .50 1.25
132 Joe Johnson .60 1.50
133 Vince Carter 1.50 4.00
134 Arron Afflalo .50 1.25
135 Kevin Martin .60 1.50
136 Chris Bosh 1.00 2.50
137 Mike Conley .60 1.50
138 Dwight Howard 1.00 2.50
139 Rajon Rondo 1.00 2.50
140 Isaiah Thomas .60 1.50
141 Terrence Ross .60 1.50
142 John Wall 1.00 2.50
143 Wesley Matthews .50 1.25
144 Avery Bradley .50 1.25
145 Kobe Bryant 6.00 15.00
146 Chris Paul 1.25 3.00
147 Monta Ellis .60 1.50
148 DeMarcus Cousins .60 1.50
149 Randy Foye .50 1.25
150 J.J. Redick .75 2.00
151 Thaddeus Young .50 1.25
152 Jonas Valanciunas .60 1.50
153 Zach Randolph .75 2.00
154 Michael Kidd-Gilchrist .50 1.25
155 Kyle Korver .60 1.50
156 Cody Zeller .50 1.25
157 Nene .60 1.50
158 Dwyane Wade 1.50 4.00
159 J.R. Smith .75 2.00
160 Michael Beasley .50 1.25
161 Andrew Wiggins RC 5.00 12.00
162 Jabari Parker RC 1.25 3.00
163 Joel Embiid RC 10.00 25.00
164 Aaron Gordon RC 5.00 12.00
165 Dante Exum RC 1.50 4.00
166 Marcus Smart RC 4.00 10.00
167 Julius Randle RC 5.00 12.00
168 Nik Stauskas RC 1.00 2.50
169 Noah Vonleh RC 1.00 2.50
170 Elfrid Payton RC 1.50 4.00
171 Doug McDermott RC 1.50 4.00
172 Zach LaVine RC 6.00 15.00
173 T.J. Warren RC 1.50 4.00
174 Adreian Payne RC 1.00 2.50
175 James Young RC 1.00 2.50
176 Tyler Ennis RC 1.00 2.50
177 Gary Harris RC 1.50 4.00
178 Mitch McGary RC 1.00 2.50
179 Jordan Adams RC 1.00 2.50
180 Rodney Hood RC 1.25 3.00
181 Shabazz Napier RC 1.25 3.00
182 P.J. Hairston RC 1.00 2.50
183 C.J. Wilcox RC 1.00 2.50
184 Bruno Caboclo RC 1.25 3.00
185 Kyle Anderson RC 1.50 4.00
186 Damien Inglis RC 1.00 2.50
187 K.J. McDaniels RC 1.00 2.50
188 Joe Harris RC 1.50 4.00
189 Cleanthony Early RC 1.00 2.50
190 Jarnell Stokes RC 1.00 2.50
191 Johnny O'Bryant RC 1.00 2.50
192 Erick Green RC 1.00 2.50
193 Spencer Dinwiddie RC 1.50 4.00
194 Jerami Grant RC 5.00 12.00
195 Jordan Clarkson RC 4.00 10.00
196 Russ Smith RC 1.00 2.50
197 Thanasis Antetokounmpo RC 2.00 5.00
198 Jordan McRae RC 1.00 2.50
199 Xavier Thames RC 1.00 2.50
200 Cory Jefferson RC 1.00 2.50

2014-15 Prestige Premium Bonus Shots Blue

*VETS: .6X TO 1.5X BASE HI
*ROOKIES: .75X TO 2X BASE HI
STATED PRINT RUN 99 SER.#'d SETS

2014-15 Prestige Premium Bonus Shots Orange Die Cuts

*VETS: 1.2X TO 3X BASE HI
*ROOKIES: 1.5X TO 4X BASE HI
STATED PRINT RUN 25 SER.#'d SETS

2014-15 Prestige Premium Bonus Shots Purple

*VETS: .8X TO 2X BASE HI
*ROOKIES: 1X TO 2.5X BASE HI
STATED PRINT RUN 49 SER.#'d SETS

2014-15 Prestige Premium Bonus Shots Red

*VETS: .5X TO 1.2X BASE HI
*ROOKIES: .6X TO 1.5X BASE HI
STATED PRINT RUN 199 SER.#'d SETS

2014-15 Prestige Premium Bonus Shots Autographs

PRINT RUNS B/WN 15-199 COPIES PER
NO PRICING ON QTY 15 OR LESS
*BLUE/75: .4X TO 1X BASIC
*BLUE/25: .5X TO 1.2 BASIC
*ORANGE/49: .4X TO 1X BASIC
*RED/49-99: .4X TO 1X BASIC
*RED/25: .5X TO 1.2X BASIC
7 David Thompson/49 6.00 15.00
8 Hakeem Olajuwon/15 12.00 30.00
10 Anfernee Hardaway/25 15.00 40.00
11 Arnett Moultrie/199 4.00 10.00
12 Bill Sharman/25 12.00 30.00
13 Tim Hardaway Jr./199 5.00 12.00
15 Danny Green/49 5.00 12.00
17 Glen Rice/49 6.00 15.00
20 Nerlens Noel/99 4.00 10.00
23 Rudy Gobert/199 10.00 25.00
29 Horace Grant/149 6.00 15.00
30 Kentavious Caldwell-Pope/99 5.00 12.00
31 Tony Snell/199 4.00 10.00
32 Elvin Hayes/49 10.00 25.00
33 Luigi Datome/199 4.00 10.00
42 Gail Goodrich/49 8.00 20.00
44 Steve Kerr/25 8.00 20.00
50 Nick Van Exel/25 6.00 15.00
53 Solomon Hill/199 4.00 10.00
57 Marcin Gortat/49 15.00 40.00
58 Clyde Drexler/49 12.00 30.00
60 C.J. McCollum/99 6.00 15.00
61 Gal Mekel/199 4.00 10.00
63 Isaiah Canaan/199 4.00 10.00
66 Anthony Davis/49 40.00 100.00
68 Victor Oladipo/99 5.00 12.00
70 M.Carter-Williams/99 4.00 10.00
71 P.J. Tucker/199 5.00 12.00
73 Ray McCallum/199 4.00 10.00
75 Dan Majerle/49 5.00 12.00
78 Cody Zeller/99 4.00 10.00
79 Sean Elliott/149 6.00 15.00
80 Trey Burke/99 4.00 10.00
81 Hollis Thompson/199 4.00 10.00
82 Robert Parish/25 8.00 20.00
83 Ryan Kelly/199 4.00 10.00
85 Kurt Rambis/49 5.00 12.00
88 Otto Porter/99 5.00 12.00
91 Dennis Schroder/199 6.00 15.00
92 Bradley Beal/25 10.00 25.00
93 Phil Pressey/199 4.00 10.00
96 Jason Kidd/49 15.00 40.00
97 Steven Adams/149 8.00 20.00
99 Greg Buckner/149 4.00 10.00

2014-15 Prestige Premium Bonus Shots Materials

PRINT RUNS B/WN 49-99 COPIES PER
*ORANGE/25: .6 TO 1.5X BASIC
1 J.J. Redick/75 3.00 8.00
2 Stephen Curry/99 25.00 60.00
3 Joe Johnson/75 2.50 6.00
4 Trey Burke/75 2.00 5.00
5 Kevin Durant/99 5.00 12.00
6 Al Horford/75 3.00 8.00
7 Manu Ginobili/75 6.00 15.00
8 Chris Andersen/75 2.50 6.00
9 Pau Gasol/99 5.00 12.00
10 Dikembe Mutombo/99 5.00 12.00
11 Isaiah Thomas/75 2.50 6.00
12 Steve Nash/99 6.00 15.00
13 Tristan Thompson/75 2.00 5.00
14 John Wall/99 4.00 10.00
15 Kyrie Irving/99 6.00 15.00
16 Alex English/75 4.00 10.00
17 Marc Gasol/99 3.00 8.00
18 Chris Paul/99 5.00 12.00
19 Paul George/75 5.00 12.00
20 Dirk Nowitzki/99 8.00 20.00
21 James Harden/99 6.00 15.00
22 Steven Adams/75 4.00 10.00
23 Jose Calderon/75 2.00 5.00
24 Ty Lawson/75 2.00 5.00
25 Kobe Bryant/99 25.00 60.00
26 Allen Iverson/99 8.00 20.00
27 Damian Lillard/99 8.00 20.00
28 M.Carter-Williams/75 4.00 10.00
29 Paul Pierce/75 5.00 12.00
30 Dominique Wilkins/75 5.00 12.00
31 Jason Kidd/75 5.00 12.00
32 Taj Gibson/75 2.00 5.00
33 Josh Smith/75 2.00 5.00
34 Tyreke Evans/75 2.50 6.00
35 Kevin Garnett/99 8.00 20.00
36 Larry Johnson/75 4.00 10.00
37 David Lee/75 2.00 5.00
38 Michael Kidd-Gilchrist/75 2.00 5.00
39 Ray Allen/75 5.00 12.00
40 Dwight Howard/99 4.00 10.00
41 Jeff Green/75 2.50 6.00
42 Tayshaun Prince/75 3.00 8.00
43 Jrue Holiday/75 4.00 10.00
44 Tyson Chandler/75 3.00 8.00
45 Kevin Love/99 3.00 8.00
46 Anthony Davis/99 8.00 20.00
47 Mike Conley/75 2.50 6.00
48 DeAndre Jordan/75 2.50 6.00
49 Ricky Rubio/75 2.50 6.00
50 Goran Dragic/75 3.00 8.00
51 Jeff Teague/75 2.00 5.00
52 Terrence Ross/75 2.50 6.00
53 Kareem Abdul-Jabbar/49 10.00 25.00
54 Victor Oladipo/75 2.50 6.00
55 Kevin McHale/75 5.00 12.00
56 Monta Ellis/75 2.50 6.00
57 Avery Bradley/75 2.00 5.00
58 DeMar DeRozan/99 4.00 10.00
59 Russell Westbrook/99 5.00 12.00
60 Grant Hill/75 5.00 12.00
61 Jeremy Lin/75 6.00 15.00
62 Thaddeus Young/75 2.00 5.00
63 Karl Malone/49 6.00 15.00
64 Zach Randolph/75 3.00 8.00
65 Klay Thompson/75 8.00 20.00
66 Ben McLemore/75 2.00 5.00
67 Nikola Vucevic/75 2.50 6.00
68 DeMarcus Cousins/75 2.50 6.00
69 Ryan Anderson/75 2.00 5.00
70 Greg Monroe/75 2.00 5.00
71 Jimmy Butler/75 5.00 12.00
72 Tim Duncan/99 8.00 20.00
73 Dion Waiters/75 2.00 5.00
74 Kawhi Leonard/75 8.00 20.00
75 LaMarcus Aldridge/75 3.00 8.00
76 Blake Griffin/99 3.00 8.00
77 Norris Cole/75 2.00 5.00
78 Dennis Schroder/99 3.00 8.00
79 Serge Ibaka/75 2.50 6.00
80 Harrison Barnes/75 2.50 6.00
81 Joakim Noah/99 3.00 8.00
82 Tony Parker/99 5.00 12.00
83 Kemba Walker/75 3.00 8.00
84 Shawn Kemp/75 5.00 12.00
85 Lance Stephenson/75 2.50 6.00
86 Brandon Jennings/75 2.00 5.00
87 Otto Porter/75 2.50 6.00
88 Deron Williams/75 2.50 6.00
89 Shaquille O'Neal/49 12.00 30.00
90 Iman Shumpert/75 2.00 5.00
91 Joe Dumars/75 4.00 10.00
92 Tim Hardaway Jr./75 2.50 6.00
93 Kenneth Faried/75 2.00 5.00
94 Hakeem Olajuwon/75 6.00 15.00
95 LeBron James/99 25.00 60.00
96 Carmelo Anthony/99 5.00 12.00
97 Derrick Rose/75 6.00 15.00
98 Patrick Ewing/49 5.00 12.00
99 Shawn Marion/75 2.50 6.00
100 Michael Finley/75 3.00 8.00

2014-15 Prestige Premium Connections

1 D.Williams/J.Kidd 1.25 3.00
2 D.Robinson/T.Duncan 2.00 5.00
3 B.Cousy/R.Rondo 1.50 4.00
4 A.Iverson/M.Carter-Williams 2.00 5.00
5 B.Walton/L.Aldridge 1.25 3.00
6 T.Lawson/F.Lever .50 1.25
7 A.Gilmore/J.Noah 1.00 2.50
8 M.Price/K.Irving 1.50 4.00
9 A.Drummond/B.Laimbeer .75 2.00
10 B.Griffin/B.McAdoo .75 2.00
11 R.Barry/K.Thompson 2.00 5.00
12 E.Baylor/K.Bryant 6.00 15.00
13 A.Mourning/A.Davis 2.00 5.00
14 M.Malone/D.Howard 1.25 3.00
15 T.Porter/D.Lillard 2.00 5.00
16 L.James/O.Robertson 6.00 15.00
17 D.Wade/J.Dumars 1.50 4.00
18 C.Andersen/D.Rodman 2.00 5.00
19 K.Durant/G.Gervin 2.50 6.00
20 L.Bird/C.Anthony 3.00 8.00

2014-15 Prestige Premium Distinctive Ink

PRINT RUNS B/WN 10-175 COPIES PER
NO PRICING ON QTY 10
2 Khris Middleton/175 8.00 20.00
3 Kobe Bryant/25 1,000.00 2,000.00
4 Robert Parish/25 15.00 40.00
8 Tyler Zeller/175 4.00 10.00
10 Spencer Hawes/175 4.00 10.00
11 Bill Walton/25 40.00 100.00
12 Tony Snell/175 4.00 10.00
13 Kevin Durant/25 150.00 400.00
14 Marcin Gortat/49 4.00 10.00
16 Jason Thompson/149 4.00 10.00
20 Rick Mahorn/175 5.00 12.00
22 Dennis Schroder/175 6.00 15.00
24 Chase Budinger/49 4.00 10.00
26 Mark Aguirre/149 5.00 12.00
28 Brandan Wright/175 4.00 10.00
30 Tim Hardaway Jr./175 5.00 12.00
32 Nate Wolters/175 5.00 12.00
33 Anthony Davis/25 75.00 200.00
38 Jordan Crawford/175 4.00 10.00
40 Alan Anderson/175 4.00 10.00

2014-15 Prestige Premium Franchise Favorites

1 Al Horford 1.25 3.00
2 Rajon Rondo 1.50 4.00
3 Deron Williams 1.00 2.50
4 Gerald Henderson .75 2.00
5 Derrick Rose 2.50 6.00
6 LeBron James 10.00 25.00
7 Dirk Nowitzki 3.00 8.00
8 Ty Lawson .75 2.00
9 Greg Monroe .75 2.00
10 Stephen Curry 10.00 25.00
11 James Harden 2.50 6.00
12 Paul George 2.00 5.00
13 Blake Griffin 1.25 3.00
14 Kobe Bryant 10.00 25.00
15 Mike Conley 1.00 2.50
16 Dwyane Wade 2.50 6.00
17 Ersan Ilyasova .75 2.00
18 Ricky Rubio 1.00 2.50
19 Anthony Davis 3.00 8.00
20 Carmelo Anthony 2.00 5.00
21 Kevin Durant 4.00 10.00
22 Nikola Vucevic 1.00 2.50
23 Michael Carter-Williams .75 2.00
24 Goran Dragic 1.25 3.00
25 LaMarcus Aldridge 1.25 3.00
26 DeMarcus Cousins 1.00 2.50
27 Tim Duncan 3.00 8.00
28 DeMar DeRozan 1.50 4.00
29 Gordon Hayward 1.00 2.50
30 John Wall 1.50 4.00

2014-15 Prestige Premium Hardcourt Heroes

1 Joe Johnson .60 1.50
2 Chris Bosh 1.00 2.50
3 Dirk Nowitzki 2.00 5.00
4 Damian Lillard 2.00 5.00
5 Vince Carter 1.50 4.00
6 LeBron James 6.00 15.00
7 Russell Westbrook 1.25 3.00
8 Stephen Curry 6.00 15.00
9 Kevin Durant 2.50 6.00
10 Jeff Green .60 1.50
11 Kobe Bryant 6.00 15.00
12 Carmelo Anthony 1.25 3.00
13 Anthony Davis 2.00 5.00
14 Chris Paul 1.25 3.00
15 Dwyane Wade 1.50 4.00
16 Kevin Love .75 2.00
17 Manu Ginobili 1.50 4.00
18 Klay Thompson 2.00 5.00
19 Tim Duncan 2.00 5.00
20 Kyrie Irving 1.50 4.00

2014-15 Prestige Premium Old School Signatures

PRINT RUNS B/WN 15-175 COPIES PER
NO PRICING ON QTY 15 OR LESS
2 Dick Van Arsdale/175 6.00 15.00
6 Cedric Ceballos/175 5.00 12.00
8 Horace Grant/149 8.00 20.00
10 Dan Issel/175 8.00 20.00
18 David Thompson/149 6.00 15.00
20 Tim Hardaway/175 8.00 20.00
23 George Karl/25 6.00 15.00
24 Micheal Ray Richardson/175 5.00 12.00
26 Bob Dandridge/175 6.00 15.00
30 Rick Mahorn/175 5.00 12.00
32 John Salley/175 5.00 12.00
34 Maurice Cheeks/175 5.00 12.00
35 George Gervin/25 12.00 30.00
36 Gary Trent/175 4.00 10.00
37 Wayne Embry/149 10.00 25.00
38 Mark Aguirre/149 5.00 12.00
40 Jack Sikma/175 6.00 15.00
41 Michael Curry/175 4.00 10.00
44 Jim Jackson/175 5.00 12.00
46 Eddie Johnson/175 4.00 10.00
47 John Lucas/144 5.00 12.00
52 Terry Porter/175 4.00 10.00
54 Tom Van Arsdale/175 5.00 12.00
55 Joe Dumars/25 8.00 20.00
56 Harvey Grant/175 4.00 10.00
57 George McGinnis/149 4.00 10.00
58 Adrian Smith/175 5.00 12.00
60 Doug Collins/175 6.00 15.00

2014-15 Prestige Premium Playmakers

1 Kevin Durant 20.00 50.00
2 LeBron James 75.00 150.00
3 Kevin Love 6.00 15.00
4 Anthony Davis 15.00 40.00
5 DeMarcus Cousins 15.00 40.00
6 Chris Paul 10.00 25.00
7 Carmelo Anthony 10.00 25.00
8 Stephen Curry 50.00 120.00
9 Blake Griffin 6.00 15.00
10 Dirk Nowitzki 15.00 40.00
11 James Harden 12.00 30.00
12 Andre Drummond 5.00 12.00
13 Al Jefferson 4.00 10.00
14 LaMarcus Aldridge 6.00 15.00
15 Goran Dragic 6.00 15.00
16 Tim Duncan 15.00 40.00
17 Dwight Howard 8.00 20.00
18 Isaiah Thomas 5.00 12.00
19 Paul George 10.00 25.00
20 Kyrie Irving 20.00 50.00
21 Kyle Lowry 8.00 20.00
22 Mike Conley 5.00 12.00
23 Joakim Noah 6.00 15.00
24 Kenneth Faried 4.00 10.00
25 Paul Millsap 5.00 12.00

2014-15 Prestige Premium Preeminent Ink

PRINT RUNS B/WN 10-175 COPIES PER
5 Dee Brown/175 5.00 12.00
10 Kyrie Irving/25 25.00 60.00
13 Reggie Jackson/149 5.00 12.00
14 Thaddeus Young/175 4.00 10.00
18 Kevin Durant/25 30.00 80.00
21 JaVale McGee/49 5.00 12.00
23 Wesley Matthews/175 4.00 10.00
24 Tim Hardaway Jr./175 5.00 12.00
28 Blake Griffin/25 20.00 50.00
37 Anthony Davis/25 75.00 150.00
38 Marcin Gortat/49 15.00 40.00

2014-15 Prestige Premium Prestigious Pioneers

1 George Mikan 2.50 6.00
2 Bob Pettit .75 2.00
3 Bob Cousy 1.50 4.00
4 Dolph Schayes .75 2.00
5 Bill Russell 2.50 6.00
6 Elgin Baylor 1.50 4.00
7 Bill Sharman 1.00 2.50
8 Wilt Chamberlain 2.50 6.00
9 Oscar Robertson 1.50 4.00
10 Jerry West 2.00 5.00
11 Willis Reed 1.25 3.00
12 Hal Greer .75 2.00
13 John Havlicek 1.50 4.00
14 Pete Maravich 2.50 6.00
15 Rick Barry 1.00 2.50
16 Julius Erving 2.00 5.00
17 Kareem Abdul-Jabbar 2.50 6.00
18 Larry Bird 3.00 8.00
19 Magic Johnson 3.00 8.00
20 Dominique Wilkins 1.25 3.00

2014-15 Prestige Premium Prestigious Posts

1 DeAndre Jordan 1.00 2.50
2 Andre Drummond 1.00 2.50
3 Kevin Love 1.25 3.00
4 Joakim Noah 1.25 3.00
5 Dwight Howard 1.50 4.00
6 Tim Duncan 3.00 8.00
7 Anthony Davis 3.00 8.00
8 Blake Griffin 1.25 3.00
9 Marcin Gortat .75 2.00
10 LaMarcus Aldridge 1.25 3.00

2014-15 Prestige Premium Prestigious Premieres Signatures

PPAG Aaron Gordon 6.00 15.00
PPAP Adreian Payne 3.00 8.00
PPAW Andrew Wiggins 100.00 200.00
PPBC Bruno Caboclo 4.00 10.00
PPCE Cleanthony Early 3.00 8.00
PPCJ Cory Jefferson 3.00 8.00
PPCW C.J. Wilcox 3.00 8.00
PPDD Doug McDermott 5.00 12.00
PPDE Dante Exum 5.00 12.00
PPEP Elfrid Payton 5.00 12.00
PPGH Gary Harris 5.00 12.00
PPGR Glenn Robinson III 4.00 10.00
PPJA Jordan Adams 3.00 8.00
PPJE Joel Embiid 20.00 50.00
PPJP Jabari Parker 4.00 10.00
PPJR Julius Randle 15.00 40.00
PPJS Jarnell Stokes 3.00 8.00
PPJY James Young 3.00 8.00
PPKA Kyle Anderson 8.00 20.00
PPMM Mitch McGary 3.00 8.00
PPMS Marcus Smart 12.00 30.00
PPNS Nik Stauskas 3.00 8.00
PPNV Noah Vonleh 8.00 20.00
PPRH Rodney Hood 4.00 10.00
PPRS Russ Smith 3.00 8.00
PPSN Shabazz Napier 5.00 12.00
PPSP Spencer Dinwiddie 5.00 12.00

PPTA Thanasis Antetokounmpo 6.00 15.00
PPTE Tyler Ennis 3.00 8.00
PPTJ T.J. Warren 5.00 12.00
PPZL Zach LaVine 12.00 30.00

2014-15 Prestige Premium Prestigious Pros

1 Kobe Bryant 15.00 40.00
2 Anthony Davis 5.00 12.00
3 DeMarcus Cousins 1.50 4.00
4 Monta Ellis 1.50 4.00
5 Tim Duncan 5.00 12.00
6 Chris Paul 3.00 8.00
7 Victor Oladipo 1.50 4.00
8 Josh Smith 1.25 3.00
9 Manu Ginobili 4.00 10.00
10 Rajon Rondo 2.50 6.00
11 Paul Pierce 3.00 8.00
12 Mike Conley 1.50 4.00
13 Ricky Rubio 1.50 4.00
14 Tristan Thompson 1.25 3.00
15 DeAndre Jordan 1.50 4.00
16 Paul George 3.00 8.00
17 Stephen Curry 15.00 40.00
18 Kevin Durant 6.00 15.00
19 Isaiah Thomas 1.50 4.00
20 Jonas Valanciunas 1.50 4.00
21 Ty Lawson 1.25 3.00
22 Michael Carter-Williams 1.25 3.00
23 Chris Bosh 2.50 6.00
24 Derrick Rose 4.00 10.00
25 Al Horford 2.00 5.00
26 Gerald Green 1.50 4.00
27 LaMarcus Aldridge 2.00 5.00
28 John Wall 2.50 6.00
29 Jameer Nelson 1.25 3.00
30 Marcin Gortat 1.25 3.00
31 Kevin Garnett 5.00 12.00
32 Trevor Ariza 1.25 3.00
33 Klay Thompson 5.00 12.00
34 Taj Gibson 1.25 3.00
35 Kemba Walker 2.00 5.00
36 Kenneth Faried 1.25 3.00
37 Joakim Noah 2.00 5.00
38 Al Jefferson 1.25 3.00
39 Carmelo Anthony 3.00 8.00
40 Damian Lillard 5.00 12.00
41 Serge Ibaka 1.50 4.00
42 Kyle Lowry 2.50 6.00
43 Jimmy Butler 3.00 8.00
44 Andrew Bogut 1.50 4.00
45 Steve Nash 4.00 10.00
46 Nicolas Batum 1.50 4.00
47 Marc Gasol 2.00 5.00
48 Blake Griffin 2.00 5.00
49 Kevin Love 2.00 5.00
50 Rudy Gay 2.00 5.00
51 Andre Drummond 1.50 4.00
52 Paul Millsap 1.50 4.00
53 Tony Parker 1.25 3.00
54 Roy Hibbert 1.50 4.00
55 Tony Parker 3.00 8.00
56 Lance Stephenson 1.50 4.00
57 Jeff Green 1.50 4.00
58 Vince Carter 4.00 10.00
59 Pau Gasol 3.00 8.00
60 Kyle Korver 1.50 4.00
61 Mario Chalmers 1.50 4.00
62 Thaddeus Young 1.25 3.00
63 Jeff Teague 1.25 3.00
64 Brandon Jennings 1.25 3.00
65 Robin Lopez 1.25 3.00
66 Derrick Favors 1.25 3.00
67 Greg Monroe 1.25 3.00
68 Zach Randolph 2.00 5.00
69 Dwight Howard 2.50 6.00
70 Goran Dragic 2.00 5.00
71 Dirk Nowitzki 5.00 12.00
72 DeMar DeRozan 2.50 6.00
73 James Harden 4.00 10.00
74 LeBron James 15.00 40.00
75 Kyrie Irving 4.00 10.00

2014-15 Prestige Premium Stars of the NBA Signatures

PRINT RUNS B/WN 10-175 COPIES PER
NO PRICING ON QTY 10
10 John Salley/175 5.00 12.00
11 Tristan Thompson/25 4.00 10.00
12 Kevin Durant/25 75.00 150.00
14 Marcin Gortat/49 4.00 10.00
18 Kevin Willis/149 5.00 12.00
21 Blake Griffin/25 30.00 80.00
22 Andrea Bargnani/25 4.00 10.00
24 Allan Houston/49 10.00 25.00
27 Nikola Vucevic/149 5.00 12.00
28 Isaiah Thomas/175 5.00 12.00
30 Eddie Jones/175 6.00 15.00
32 Nate Thurmond/25 15.00 40.00
34 Terrence Ross/149 5.00 12.00
45 David Thompson/149 6.00 15.00
47 Mahmoud Abdul-Rauf/175 12.00 30.00
49 Antoine Walker/175 5.00 12.00
55 Adrian Dantley/149 6.00 15.00
57 Dan Issel/175 8.00 20.00
59 Bob Dandridge/175 6.00 15.00

2015-16 Prestige

1 J.R. Smith .40 1.00
2 Luol Deng .30 .75
3 Tristan Thompson .25 .60
4 Chris Paul .75 2.00
5 Jeremy Lin .75 2.00
6 Josh Smith .25 .60
7 Thaddeus Young .25 .60
8 Kevin Garnett 1.00 2.50
9 Henry Sims .25 .60
10 Kevin Love .40 1.00
11 Khris Middleton .50 1.25
12 Matthew Dellavedova .30 .75
13 Al Jefferson .25 .60
14 Matt Barnes .25 .60
15 Jordan Hill .25 .60
16 Corey Brewer .25 .60
17 Tony Wroten .25 .60
18 Jameer Nelson .25 .60
19 Kosta Koufos .25 .60
20 Brandon Bass .25 .60
21 Michael Carter-Williams .25 .60
22 Avery Bradley .25 .60
23 Gerald Henderson .25 .60
24 Spencer Hawes .25 .60
25 Carlos Boozer .30 .75
26 Tim Duncan 1.00 2.50
27 David West .30 .75
28 Nerlens Noel .25 .60
29 LaMarcus Aldridge .40 1.00
30 Giannis Antetokounmpo 2.00 5.00
31 DeAndre Jordan .30 .75
32 Marcus Smart .50 1.25
33 Joe Ingles .30 .75
34 Tobias Harris .30 .75
35 Tony Allen .25 .60
36 Kawhi Leonard 1.25 3.00
37 C.J. Watson .25 .60
38 Hollis Thompson .25 .60
39 Wesley Matthews .25 .60
40 Zaza Pachulia .25 .60
41 Marc Gasol .40 1.00
42 Tyler Zeller .25 .60
43 Derrick Williams .25 .60
44 Courtney Lee .25 .60
45 Monta Ellis .30 .75
46 Manu Ginobili .75 2.00
47 Luis Scola .30 .75
48 Robert Covington .30 .75
49 Arron Afflalo .25 .60
50 Derrick Rose .60 1.50
51 Jeff Green .25 .60
52 Jared Sullinger .25 .60
53 Andre Miller .30 .75
54 Vince Carter .75 2.00
55 Al-Farouq Aminu .25 .60
56 Danny Green .30 .75
57 Roy Hibbert .30 .75
58 Nicolas Batum .25 .60
59 Nikola Mirotic .25 .60
60 Robin Lopez .25 .60
61 DeMarre Carroll .25 .60
62 Evan Turner .25 .60
63 Shane Larkin .25 .60
64 Zach Randolph .40 1.00
65 Rajon Rondo .50 1.25
66 Brandon Knight .25 .60
67 Omer Asik .25 .60
68 Chris Kaman .25 .60
69 Mike Dunleavy .25 .60
70 Paul Millsap .30 .75
71 Pau Gasol .60 1.50
72 Blake Griffin .40 1.00
73 Andrea Bargnani .25 .60
74 Mike Conley .40 1.00
75 Tyson Chandler .30 .75
76 Gerald Green .30 .75
77 Eric Gordon .30 .75
78 Damian Lillard 1.00 2.50
79 Aaron Brooks .25 .60
80 Goran Dragic .40 1.00
81 Jimmy Butler .75 2.00
82 J.J. Redick .40 1.00
83 Jason Smith .25 .60
84 Al Horford .40 1.00
85 Alan Anderson .25 .60
86 Dion Waiters .25 .60
87 Greg Monroe .30 .75
88 Jabari Parker .25 .60
89 LeBron James 3.00 8.00
90 Joakim Noah .25 .60
91 Dwyane Wade .75 2.00
92 Jamal Crawford .40 1.00
93 Wesley Johnson .25 .60
94 Kyle Korver .30 .75
95 Brook Lopez .40 1.00
96 Kevin Durant 1.50 4.00
97 Amir Johnson .25 .60
98 Ersan Ilyasova .25 .60
99 Timofey Mozgov .25 .60
100 Kyrie Irving .75 2.00
101 Nikola Vucevic .30 .75
102 Enes Kanter .25 .60
103 Jusuf Nurkic .30 .75
104 Harrison Barnes .30 .75
105 Thabo Sefolosha .25 .60
106 Jrue Holiday .50 1.25
107 Michael Kidd-Gilchrist .25 .60
108 Greivis Vasquez .25 .60
109 Jason Thompson .25 .60
110 Boris Diaw .30 .75
111 Elfrid Payton .30 .75
112 Steven Adams .30 .75
113 Ty Lawson .30 .75
114 Draymond Green .50 1.25
115 Jeff Teague .25 .60
116 Norris Cole .25 .60
117 Alec Burks .25 .60
118 Kyle Lowry .40 1.00
119 Darren Collison .25 .60
120 Tiago Splitter .25 .60
121 Victor Oladipo .30 .75
122 Andrew Wiggins .50 1.25
123 Kenneth Faried .30 .75
124 Stephen Curry 3.00 8.00
125 Hassan Whiteside .30 .75
126 Ryan Anderson .25 .60
127 Derrick Favors .30 .75
128 Jonas Valanciunas .30 .75
129 Tim Hardaway Jr. .30 .75
130 Tony Parker .60 1.50
131 Devin Harris .25 .60
132 Gorgui Dieng .25 .60
133 Danilo Gallinari .30 .75
134 Klay Thompson 1.00 2.50
135 Chris Andersen .25 .60
136 Tyreke Evans .30 .75
137 Rudy Gobert .50 1.25
138 Patrick Patterson .25 .60
139 Carmelo Anthony .60 1.50
140 Marcus Morris .25 .60
141 Chandler Parsons .25 .60
142 Ricky Rubio .30 .75
143 Wilson Chandler .30 .75
144 Bradley Beal .50 1.25
145 Mario Chalmers .25 .60
146 Andre Drummond .50 1.25
147 Trey Burke .25 .60
148 DeMar DeRozan .50 1.25
149 Langston Galloway .25 .60
150 Markieff Morris .25 .60
151 Dirk Nowitzki 1.00 2.50
152 Nikola Pekovic .25 .60
153 Gary Harris .30 .75
154 Nene .30 .75
155 Chris Bosh .50 1.25
156 Jodie Meeks .25 .60
157 Dante Exum .30 .75
158 Trevor Ariza .25 .60
159 Nick Young .25 .60
160 P.J. Tucker .25 .60
161 Bojan Bogdanovic .30 .75
162 Kevin Martin .30 .75
163 Solomon Hill .25 .60
164 John Wall .50 1.25
165 Lance Stephenson .30 .75
166 Brandon Jennings .25 .60
167 Gordon Hayward .40 1.00
168 Donatas Motiejunas .25 .60
169 Jordan Clarkson .40 1.00
170 Eric Bledsoe .30 .75
171 Joe Johnson .30 .75
172 Zach LaVine 1.00 2.50
173 Paul George .60 1.50
174 Marcin Gortat .25 .60
175 Kemba Walker .40 1.00
176 Caron Butler .30 .75
177 Ben McLemore .25 .60
178 Dwight Howard .50 1.25
179 Kobe Bryant 3.00 8.00
180 Reggie Jackson .30 .75
181 Deron Williams .30 .75
182 Andrew Bogut .30 .75
183 George Hill .30 .75
184 Otto Porter .30 .75
185 Marvin Williams .25 .60
186 Kentavious Caldwell-Pope .30 .75
187 DeMarcus Cousins .40 1.00
188 James Harden .75 2.00
189 Aaron Gordon .40 1.00
190 Russell Westbrook .60 1.50
191 Jarrett Jack .30 .75
192 Andre Iguodala .40 1.00
193 Anthony Davis 1.00 2.50
194 Paul Pierce .60 1.50
195 Cody Zeller .25 .60
196 Terrence Ross .30 .75
197 Rudy Gay .40 1.00
198 Patrick Beverley .25 .60
199 Channing Frye .25 .60
200 Serge Ibaka .30 .75
201 Stanley Johnson RC .60 1.50
202 Jordan Mickey RC .50 1.25
203 Jerian Grant RC .50 1.25
204 Darrun Hilliard RC .50 1.25
205 Rashad Vaughn RC .50 1.25
206 Andrew Harrison RC .60 1.50
207 Karl-Anthony Towns RC 3.00 8.00
208 Rondae Hollis-Jefferson RC .60 1.50
209 Kristaps Porzingis RC 3.00 8.00
210 R.J. Hunter RC .50 1.25
211 Frank Kaminsky RC .60 1.50
212 Larry Nance Jr. RC 1.00 2.50
213 Trey Lyles RC .60 1.50
214 Pat Connaughton RC .75 2.00
215 Kelly Oubre Jr. RC 1.50 4.00
216 Tyus Jones RC .60 1.50
217 D'Angelo Russell RC 2.00 5.00
218 Bobby Portis RC 1.25 3.00
219 Mario Hezonja RC .60 1.50
220 Anthony Brown RC .50 1.25
221 Devin Booker RC 12.00 30.00
222 Montrezl Harrell RC 1.50 4.00
223 Cameron Payne RC .75 2.00
224 Rakeem Christmas RC .50 1.25
225 Sam Dekker RC .50 1.25
226 Kevon Looney RC 1.50 4.00
227 Jahlil Okafor RC .60 1.50
228 Justin Anderson RC .50 1.25
229 Justise Winslow RC .75 2.00
230 Pierre Jackson RC .50 1.25
231 Myles Turner RC 2.00 5.00
232 Walter Tavares RC .50 1.25
233 Delon Wright RC .60 1.50
234 Joe Young RC .50 1.25
235 Terry Rozier RC 2.00 5.00
236 Norman Powell RC 1.00 2.50
237 Emmanuel Mudiay RC .60 1.50
238 Jarell Martin RC .50 1.25
239 Willie Cauley-Stein RC .60 1.50
240 Chris McCullough RC .60 1.50

2015-16 Prestige Bonus Shots Blue

*BLUE: 1.2X TO 3X BASIC
*BLUE RC: 1.2X TO 3X BASIC
STATED PRINT RUN 99 SER.#'d SETS
207 Karl-Anthony Towns 20.00 50.00

2015-16 Prestige Bonus Shots Light Blue

*LT.BLUE VET: .5X TO 1.2X BASIC
*LT.BLUE RC: .5X TO 1.2X BASIC

2015-16 Prestige Bonus Shots Orange Die Cuts

*ORANGE: 1X TO 2.5X BASIC
*ORANGE RC: 1X TO 2.5X BASIC
STATED PRINT RUN 149 SER.#'d SETS

2015-16 Prestige Bonus Shots Purple

*PURPLE: 1.5X TO 4X BASIC
*PURPLE RC: 1.5X TO 4X BASIC
STATED PRINT RUN 49 SER.#'d SETS
207 Karl-Anthony Towns 25.00 60.00
221 Devin Booker 25.00 60.00

2015-16 Prestige Bonus Shots Red

*RED: .75X TO 2X BASIC
*RED RC: .75X TO 2X BASIC
STATED PRINT RUN 25 SER.#'d SETS

2015-16 Prestige Acetate Rookies

1 Pierre Jackson .75 2.00
2 Stanley Johnson 1.00 2.50
3 Rakeem Christmas .75 2.00
4 Emmanuel Mudiay 1.00 2.50
5 Kevon Looney 2.50 6.00
6 Darrun Hilliard .75 2.00
7 Bobby Portis 2.00 5.00
8 Sam Dekker .75 2.00
9 Branden Dawson .75 2.00
10 Trey Lyles 1.00 2.50
11 Joe Young .75 2.00
12 Willie Cauley-Stein 1.00 2.50
13 Walter Tavares .75 2.00
14 Jahlil Okafor 1.00 2.50
15 Larry Nance Jr. 1.50 4.00
16 Nikola Jokic 75.00 200.00
17 Justin Anderson .75 2.00
18 Tyus Jones 1.00 2.50
19 Jonathon Simmons 1.00 2.50
20 Jerian Grant .75 2.00
21 Norman Powell 1.50 4.00
22 Justise Winslow 1.25 3.00
23 Montrezl Harrell 2.50 6.00
24 D'Angelo Russell 3.00 8.00
25 Anthony Brown .75 2.00
26 Cliff Alexander .75 2.00
27 Rondae Hollis-Jefferson 1.00 2.50
28 Cameron Payne 1.25 3.00
29 Tyler Harvey .75 2.00
30 Myles Turner 3.00 8.00
31 Richaun Holmes 1.25 3.00
32 Mario Hezonja 1.00 2.50
33 Jordan Mickey .75 2.00
34 Karl-Anthony Towns 5.00 12.00
35 R.J. Hunter .75 2.00
36 Josh Huestis .75 2.00
37 Kelly Oubre Jr. 2.50 6.00
38 Rashad Vaughn .75 2.00
39 Aaron Harrison 1.00 2.50
40 Devin Booker 12.00 30.00
41 Dakari Johnson .75 2.00
42 Kristaps Porzingis 5.00 12.00
43 Chris McCullough .75 2.00
44 Josh Richardson 1.25 3.00
45 Jarell Martin .75 2.00
46 Ryan Boatright .75 2.00
47 Terry Rozier 3.00 8.00
48 Delon Wright 1.00 2.50
49 Andrew Harrison 1.00 2.50
50 Frank Kaminsky 1.00 2.50

2015-16 Prestige Bonus Shots Autographs

PRINT RUNS B/WN 10-49 COPIES PER
NO PRICING ON QTY 10
EXCHANGE DEADLINE 4/19/2017
1 Robert Covington/49 5.00 12.00
2 Lorenzo Brown/49 4.00 10.00
4 Ian Clark/49 4.00 10.00
7 Dwight Powell/49 4.00 10.00
9 James Ennis/49 4.00 10.00
10 Cameron Bairstow/49 4.00 10.00
11 Reggie Bullock/49 4.00 10.00
13 Mike Muscala/49 4.00 10.00
18 Antonio McDyess/49 5.00 12.00
35 James Michael McAdoo/49 4.00 10.00
36 Jabari Brown/49 4.00 10.00
37 Eddie Jones/49 6.00 15.00
43 Isaiah Canaan/49 4.00 10.00
50 Hollis Thompson/49 4.00 10.00
54 Chuck Person/25 6.00 15.00
55 John Salley/49 4.00 10.00
56 Kurt Rambis/25 6.00 15.00
58 Jeff Malone/49 4.00 10.00
61 Kenny Walker/25 5.00 12.00
65 Mason Plumlee/49 4.00 10.00
68 Bojan Bogdanovic/49 5.00 12.00
69 Charles Oakley/49 6.00 15.00
70 Glenn Robinson III/49 4.00 10.00
73 Satch Sanders/25 10.00 25.00
79 Larry Nance/25 6.00 15.00
81 Scott Brooks/25 6.00 15.00
82 Mark Price/49 6.00 15.00
83 Keith Van Horn/25 6.00 15.00
85 Maurice Cheeks/25 6.00 15.00
90 Nikola Mirotic/25 5.00 12.00
100 Will Perdue/25 5.00 12.00

2015-16 Prestige Brilliant Beginnings

*STARBURST: .6X TO 1.5X BASIC
1 Rajon Rondo .75 2.00
2 Tyreke Evans .50 1.25
3 Larry Bird 2.50 6.00
4 Tim Duncan 1.50 4.00
5 Alonzo Mourning 1.00 2.50
6 David Robinson 1.25 3.00
7 Steve Nash 1.00 2.50
8 Kobe Bryant 5.00 12.00
9 Tracy McGrady 1.00 2.50
10 Chris Paul 1.25 3.00
11 Chris Andersen .50 1.25
12 Dwight Howard .75 2.00
13 Magic Johnson 2.50 6.00
14 Ray Allen .75 2.00
15 Kevin Garnett 1.50 4.00
16 Allen Iverson 1.50 4.00
17 Dikembe Mutombo 1.00 2.50
18 Kevin Durant 2.50 6.00
19 James Harden 1.50 4.00
20 Shawn Kemp 1.00 2.50
21 J.R. Smith .60 1.50
22 Carmelo Anthony 1.00 2.50
23 Karl Malone 1.00 2.50
24 Chris Webber .75 2.00
25 Hakeem Olajuwon 1.25 3.00
26 Dwyane Wade 1.25 3.00
27 Tony Parker 1.25 3.00
28 Kyrie Irving 1.25 3.00
29 Deron Williams .50 1.25
30 LeBron James 5.00 12.00
31 Pau Gasol 1.00 2.50
32 Baron Davis .50 1.25
33 John Stockton 1.25 3.00
34 Latrell Sprewell .50 1.25
35 Paul Pierce 1.00 2.50
36 Chris Bosh .75 2.00
37 Grant Hill 1.00 2.50
38 Anthony Davis 1.50 4.00
39 Joakim Noah .50 1.25
40 Kevin Love .60 1.50
41 Joe Johnson .50 1.25
42 Vince Carter 1.25 3.00
43 Dirk Nowitzki 1.50 4.00
44 Shaquille O'Neal 2.00 5.00
45 Jason Kidd 1.00 2.50
46 Anfernee Hardaway 1.50 4.00
47 Manu Ginobili 1.25 3.00
48 John Wall .75 2.00
49 Blake Griffin .60 1.50
50 Stephen Curry 5.00 12.00

2015-16 Prestige Distinctive Ink

PRINT RUNS B/WN 21-199 COPIES PER
EXCHANGE DEADLINE 4/19/2017
1 James Worthy/49 10.00 25.00
2 Michael Carter-Williams/49 4.00 10.00
3 Kobe Bryant/25 500.00 1,000.00
4 Steve Novak/149 3.00 8.00
5 Chris Webber/25 40.00 100.00
6 Julius Randle/49 8.00 20.00
7 Mike Muscala/199 3.00 8.00
8 Robert Covington/199 4.00 10.00
9 Jo Jo White/149 5.00 12.00
10 Victor Oladipo/49 5.00 12.00
11 Vlade Divac/149 5.00 12.00
12 Kentavious Caldwell-Pope/49 5.00 12.00
13 Kevin Durant/25 25.00 60.00
14 Andre Roberson/199 3.00 8.00
15 Andrew Wiggins/49 12.00 30.00
16 Kevin Willis/149 3.00 8.00
17 Walter Davis/149 3.00 8.00
18 C.J. McCollum/49 6.00 15.00
19 Walt Frazier/49 10.00 25.00
20 Ben McLemore/49 4.00 10.00
21 Danny Manning/149 4.00 10.00
22 Nerlens Noel/49 4.00 10.00
23 Kyrie Irving/25 20.00 50.00
24 Donatas Motiejunas/199 3.00 8.00
26 Michael Kidd-Gilchrist/49 4.00 10.00
27 Nikola Mirotic/99 4.00 10.00
28 Otto Porter/49 5.00 12.00
29 Paul Westphal/149 5.00 12.00
30 Alex Len/49 4.00 10.00
31 Jamaal Wilkes/149 5.00 12.00
32 Jordan Clarkson/199 5.00 12.00
33 Carmelo Anthony/21 12.00 30.00
34 Jerami Grant/199 5.00 12.00
35 Ricky Rubio/49 5.00 12.00
36 Noah Vonleh/49 4.00 10.00
37 Norm Nixon/149 3.00 8.00
38 Trey Burke/49 4.00 10.00
39 Christian Laettner/49 5.00 12.00
40 Anthony Bennett/49 4.00 10.00
41 Dolph Schayes/149 5.00 12.00
42 Ricky Pierce/199 3.00 8.00
43 Allen Iverson/25 50.00 120.00
44 Terry Cummings/149 4.00 10.00
45 Enes Kanter/149 3.00 8.00
46 Mason Plumlee/199 3.00 8.00
47 Gary Payton/49 10.00 25.00
48 Shabazz Muhammad/149 3.00 8.00
49 Clyde Drexler/49 10.00 25.00
50 Cody Zeller/49 4.00 10.00

2015-16 Prestige Franchise Favorites

*CRYSTAL/99: 1.2X TO 3X
*CHECK/125: 1.2X TO 3X
1 Hakeem Olajuwon 1.25 3.00
2 John Stockton 1.25 3.00
3 Blake Griffin .60 1.50
4 Joe Dumars .75 2.00
5 Kyrie Irving 1.25 3.00
6 Jerry West 1.00 2.50
7 Kevin Durant 2.50 6.00
8 Tim Duncan 1.50 4.00
9 Isiah Thomas .60 1.50
10 Dirk Nowitzki 1.50 4.00
11 Patrick Ewing 1.00 2.50
12 Bill Russell 2.00 5.00
13 Anthony Davis 1.50 4.00
14 David Robinson 1.25 3.00
15 LeBron James 5.00 12.00
16 Larry Bird 2.50 6.00
17 Russell Westbrook 1.00 2.50
18 Kobe Bryant 5.00 12.00
19 Julius Erving 1.50 4.00
20 Dwyane Wade 1.25 3.00

2015-16 Prestige Freshman Fabrics

*PRIME/25: .75X TO 2X BASIC
1 Karl-Anthony Towns 8.00 20.00
2 D'Angelo Russell 4.00 10.00
3 Jahlil Okafor 4.00 10.00
4 Kristaps Porzingis 8.00 20.00
5 Myles Turner 6.00 15.00
6 Willie Cauley-Stein 2.00 5.00
7 Emmanuel Mudiay 2.00 5.00
8 Stanley Johnson 2.00 5.00
9 Frank Kaminsky 2.00 5.00
10 Justise Winslow 2.50 6.00

2015-16 Prestige Freshman Fabrics Jumbo

*PRIME/25: .75X TO 2X BASIC
1 Karl-Anthony Towns 8.00 20.00
2 D'Angelo Russell 6.00 15.00
3 Jahlil Okafor 2.00 5.00
4 Kristaps Porzingis 6.00 15.00
5 Montrezl Harrell 2.00 5.00
6 Willie Cauley-Stein 2.00 5.00
7 Emmanuel Mudiay 2.00 5.00
8 Stanley Johnson 2.00 5.00
9 Frank Kaminsky 2.00 5.00
10 Justise Winslow 2.00 5.00
11 Myles Turner 6.00 15.00
12 Trey Lyles 2.00 5.00
13 Devin Booker 20.00 50.00
14 Cameron Payne 2.50 6.00
15 Kelly Oubre Jr. 2.50 6.00
16 Terry Rozier 6.00 15.00
17 R.J. Hunter 1.50 4.00
18 Sam Dekker 1.50 4.00
19 Jerian Grant 1.50 4.00
20 Delon Wright 1.50 4.00
21 Justin Anderson 1.50 4.00
22 Bobby Portis 4.00 10.00
23 Rondae Hollis-Jefferson 2.00 5.00
24 Tyus Jones 2.00 5.00
25 Kevon Looney 5.00 12.00

2015-16 Prestige Freshman Flashback Jumbo Materials

*PRIME/25: 1X TO 2.5X BASIC
1 Andre Drummond 2.50 6.00
2 Anthony Davis 6.00 15.00
3 Bradley Beal 3.00 8.00
4 Tristan Thompson 1.50 4.00
5 Enes Kanter 1.50 4.00
6 Harrison Barnes 2.00 5.00
7 Iman Shumpert 1.50 4.00
8 Jimmy Butler 5.00 12.00
9 Kawhi Leonard 8.00 20.00
10 Kemba Walker 2.50 6.00
11 Kenneth Faried 2.00 5.00
12 Klay Thompson 6.00 15.00
13 Kyrie Irving 5.00 12.00
14 Nikola Vucevic 2.00 5.00
15 Tobias Harris 2.00 5.00

2015-16 Prestige Freshman Flashback Jumbo Materials Prime

2 Anthony Davis 30.00 80.00
9 Kawhi Leonard 30.00 80.00
12 Klay Thompson 12.00 30.00

2015-16 Prestige NBA Materials

*PRIME/25: .75X TO 2X BASIC
1 Carmelo Anthony 4.00 10.00
2 Chris Bosh 3.00 8.00
3 Clyde Drexler 4.00 10.00
4 David Robinson 5.00 12.00
5 Dikembe Mutombo 4.00 10.00
6 Grant Hill 4.00 10.00
7 Jared Sullinger 1.50 4.00
8 Joakim Noah 1.50 4.00
9 Kevin Love 2.50 6.00
10 Larry Bird 8.00 20.00
11 Patrick Ewing 4.00 10.00
12 Shaquille O'Neal 8.00 20.00
13 Victor Oladipo 2.00 5.00
14 Kyrie Irving 5.00 12.00
15 John Wall 3.00 8.00
16 Derrick Rose 4.00 10.00
17 Marcus Smart 3.00 8.00
18 Andre Drummond 2.50 6.00
19 Stephen Curry 20.00 50.00
20 Blake Griffin 2.50 6.00
21 Damian Lillard 6.00 15.00
22 Kyle Lowry 2.50 6.00
23 Trey Burke 1.50 4.00
24 DeMar DeRozan 3.00 8.00
25 Dwyane Wade 5.00 12.00

2015-16 Prestige NBA Passport Signatures

STATED PRINT RUN 99 SER.#'d SETS
EXCHANGE DEADLINE 4/19/2017
1 Karl-Anthony Towns 100.00 250.00
2 D'Angelo Russell 60.00 150.00
3 Jahlil Okafor 5.00 12.00
4 Emmanuel Mudiay 5.00 12.00
5 Kristaps Porzingis 100.00 250.00
6 Mario Hezonja 5.00 12.00
7 Justise Winslow 6.00 15.00
8 Willie Cauley-Stein 15.00 40.00
9 Stanley Johnson 5.00 12.00
10 Frank Kaminsky 5.00 12.00
11 Devin Booker 125.00 300.00
12 Myles Turner 15.00 40.00
13 Jerian Grant 4.00 10.00
14 Trey Lyles 5.00 12.00
15 Cameron Payne 6.00 15.00
16 Delon Wright 5.00 12.00
17 Rashad Vaughn 4.00 10.00
18 Kelly Oubre Jr. 12.00 30.00
19 Sam Dekker 4.00 10.00
20 Terry Rozier 15.00 40.00
21 Rondae Hollis-Jefferson 5.00 12.00
22 Bobby Portis 10.00 25.00
23 Justin Anderson 4.00 10.00
24 Jarell Martin 4.00 10.00
25 R.J. Hunter 4.00 10.00
26 Anthony Brown 4.00 10.00
28 Chris McCullough 4.00 10.00
29 Jordan Mickey 4.00 10.00
30 Larry Nance Jr. 8.00 20.00
31 Montrezl Harrell 12.00 30.00
32 Dakari Johnson 4.00 10.00
33 Darrun Hilliard 4.00 10.00
34 Pat Connaughton 6.00 15.00
35 Rakeem Christmas 4.00 10.00
36 Richaun Holmes 6.00 15.00
38 Andrew Harrison 5.00 12.00
40 Joe Young 4.00 10.00
42 Tyler Harvey 4.00 10.00
43 Branden Dawson 4.00 10.00
44 Tyus Jones 5.00 12.00
46 Aaron Harrison 5.00 12.00
48 Josh Richardson 6.00 15.00
49 Walter Tavares 4.00 10.00

2015-16 Prestige Old School Signatures

PRINT RUNS B/WN 20-199 COPIES PER
EXCHANGE DEADLINE 4/19/2017
1 Jeff Malone/199 3.00 8.00
2 Theo Ratliff/199 3.00 8.00
4 Gary Payton/49 15.00 40.00
5 Larry Brown/49 6.00 15.00
7 Keith Van Horn/199 4.00 10.00
8 Hakeem Olajuwon/49 12.00 30.00
9 Ricky Pierce/199 3.00 8.00
10 Cazzie Russell/199 4.00 10.00
11 John Lucas/199 4.00 10.00
12 Will Perdue/199 3.00 8.00
13 Charles Oakley/199 4.00 10.00
14 Fat Lever/199 4.00 10.00
16 Magic Johnson/25 30.00 80.00
17 Maurice Cheeks/199 4.00 10.00
18 Kevin McHale/49 10.00 25.00
19 Terry Cummings/199 4.00 10.00
20 Vin Baker/199 3.00 8.00
21 Kenny Walker/199 3.00 8.00
22 Billy Paultz/199 5.00 12.00
23 Scott Skiles/199 4.00 10.00
24 Avery Johnson/49 5.00 12.00
25 Mario Elie/199 3.00 8.00
26 Julius Erving/25 40.00 100.00
27 Walter Davis/199 3.00 8.00
28 Tracy McGrady/49 15.00 40.00
29 Kevin Willis/199 3.00 8.00
30 Kendall Gill/199 3.00 8.00
31 Bobby Jones/199 4.00 10.00
32 Brad Daugherty/199 4.00 10.00
33 Satch Sanders/199 8.00 20.00
34 Bob Dandridge/199 3.00 8.00
35 Larry Nance/199 4.00 10.00
36 John Stockton/25 20.00 50.00
37 Norm Nixon/199 3.00 8.00
38 Clyde Drexler/49 10.00 25.00
39 Chuck Person/199 4.00 10.00
40 Bill Cartwright/199 4.00 10.00
41 Kenny Anderson/199 4.00 10.00
42 Tom Gugliotta/199 3.00 8.00
43 Robert Parish/49 8.00 20.00
44 Cedric Maxwell/199 4.00 10.00
45 Rik Smits/199 4.00 10.00
46 David Robinson/49 20.00 50.00
48 Grant Hill/49 10.00 25.00
49 Kurt Rambis/199 4.00 10.00
50 Tom Chambers/199 4.00 10.00

2015-16 Prestige Playmakers

*LT.BLUE/99: .75X TO 2X BASIC
*BRONZE/49: 1X TO 2.5X BASIC
1 Klay Thompson 1.50 4.00
2 Andrew Wiggins .75 2.00
3 LeBron James 5.00 12.00
4 Carmelo Anthony 1.00 2.50
5 Russell Westbrook 1.00 2.50
6 Stephen Curry 5.00 12.00
7 Damian Lillard 1.50 4.00
8 James Harden 1.25 3.00
9 Derrick Rose 1.00 2.50
10 Kawhi Leonard 2.00 5.00
11 Dwight Howard .75 2.00
12 Kobe Bryant 5.00 12.00
13 Anthony Davis 1.50 4.00
14 Manu Ginobili 1.25 3.00
15 Chris Bosh .75 2.00
16 Tony Parker 1.00 2.50
17 DeMar DeRozan .75 2.00
18 John Wall .75 2.00
19 Dirk Nowitzki 1.50 4.00
20 Kevin Durant 2.50 6.00
21 Dwyane Wade 1.25 3.00
22 Kyrie Irving 1.25 3.00
23 Blake Griffin .60 1.50
24 Bradley Beal .75 2.00
25 Chris Paul 1.25 3.00

2015-16 Prestige Preeminent Ink

PRINT RUNS B/WN 20-149 COPIES PER
EXCHANGE DEADLINE 4/19/2017
1 Michael Carter-Williams/49 4.00 10.00
3 Alex Len/49 4.00 10.00
4 Satch Sanders/149 5.00 12.00
5 Michael Kidd-Gilchrist/49 4.00 10.00
6 Karl Malone/25 20.00 50.00
7 Chris Webber/49 50.00 120.00
8 Allen Iverson/25 40.00 100.00
9 Carl Landry/149 3.00 8.00
10 Bill Russell/20 200.00 500.00
11 Kentavious Caldwell-Pope/49 5.00 12.00
12 Cedric Maxwell/149 4.00 10.00
13 Otto Porter/49 5.00 12.00
14 Chase Budinger/149 3.00 8.00
15 Kevin Love/49 6.00 15.00
16 John Stockton/25 20.00 50.00
19 Shabazz Muhammad/49 4.00 10.00
20 Kobe Bryant/25 500.00 1,000.00
21 Ben McLemore/49 4.00 10.00
22 Kurt Rambis/49 4.00 10.00
23 Cody Zeller/49 4.00 10.00
24 Chuck Person/149 4.00 10.00
25 Clyde Drexler/49 15.00 40.00
26 Julius Erving/25 25.00 60.00
27 Anthony Davis/49 30.00 80.00
28 Chris Paul/30 40.00 100.00
29 Trey Burke/49 4.00 10.00
30 Alan Anderson/149 3.00 8.00
31 Nerlens Noel/49 4.00 10.00
32 John Lucas/149 4.00 10.00
33 Victor Oladipo/49 5.00 12.00
34 Rik Smits/149 4.00 10.00
35 Dennis Rodman/49 15.00 40.00
36 Magic Johnson/25 30.00 80.00
37 Oscar Robertson/25 30.00 80.00
38 Kevin Durant/25 50.00 120.00
39 Noah Vonleh/49 4.00 10.00
40 Dorell Wright/149 3.00 8.00
41 Julius Randle/49 10.00 25.00
42 Kenny Walker/149 3.00 8.00
44 Nikola Mirotic/99 4.00 10.00
45 Tracy McGrady/49 12.00 30.00
46 Larry Bird/25 30.00 80.00
49 C.J. McCollum/49 6.00 15.00
50 Maurice Harkless/149 3.00 8.00

2015-16 Prestige Prestigious Passers

*CRYSTAL/99: 1.2X TO 3X
*CHECK/125: 1.2X TO 3X
1 Chris Paul 1.25 3.00
2 John Wall .75 2.00
3 Damian Lillard 1.50 4.00
4 Russell Westbrook 1.00 2.50
5 LeBron James 5.00 12.00
6 Stephen Curry 5.00 12.00
7 Tony Parker 1.00 2.50
8 Kyrie Irving 1.25 3.00
9 Magic Johnson 2.50 6.00
10 John Stockton 1.25 3.00
11 Isiah Thomas .60 1.50
12 Jason Kidd 1.00 2.50
13 Steve Nash 1.00 2.50
14 Ty Lawson .40 1.00
15 Tim Hardaway .75 2.00

2015-16 Prestige Prestigious Picks

*LT.BLUE/99: 1X TO 2.5X BASIC
*BRONZE/49: 1.2X TO 3X BASIC
1 Chris McCullough .40 1.00
2 Kelly Oubre Jr. 1.25 3.00
3 Delon Wright .50 1.25
4 Mario Hezonja .50 1.25
5 Jahlil Okafor .50 1.25
6 Rakeem Christmas .40 1.00
7 Stanley Johnson .40 1.00

8 Sam Dekker .40 1.00
9 Anthony Brown .40 1.00
10 Trey Lyles .50 1.25
11 Dakari Johnson .40 1.00
12 Kevon Looney 1.25 3.00
13 Devin Booker 5.00 12.00
14 Montrezl Harrell 1.25 3.00
15 Jarell Martin .40 1.00
16 Rashad Vaughn .40 1.00
17 Justise Winslow .60 1.50
18 Stanley Johnson .50 1.25
19 Bobby Portis 1.00 2.50
20 Willie Cauley-Stein .50 1.25
21 D'Angelo Russell 1.50 4.00
22 Kristaps Porzingis 2.50 6.00
23 Emmanuel Mudiay .50 1.25
24 Myles Turner 1.50 4.00
25 Jerian Grant .40 1.00
26 Rondae Hollis-Jefferson .50 1.25
27 Karl-Anthony Towns 2.50 6.00
28 Terry Rozier 1.50 4.00
29 Cameron Payne .60 1.50
30 Tyus Jones .50 1.25
31 Darrun Hilliard .40 1.00
32 Larry Nance Jr. .75 2.00
33 R.J. Hunter .40 1.00
34 Frank Kaminsky .50 1.25
35 Jordan Mickey .40 1.00

2015-16 Prestige Prestigious Premieres Signatures

STATED PRINT RUN 299 SER.#'d SETS
*CHECK/25: .6X TO 1.5X BASIC
EXCHANGE DEADLINE 4/19/2017
1 Karl-Anthony Towns 75.00 200.00
2 D'Angelo Russell 15.00 40.00
3 Jahlil Okafor 4.00 10.00
4 Emmanuel Mudiay 4.00 10.00
5 Kristaps Porzingis 50.00 120.00
6 Mario Hezonja 4.00 10.00
7 Justise Winslow 5.00 12.00
8 Willie Cauley-Stein 8.00 20.00
9 Stanley Johnson 4.00 10.00
10 Frank Kaminsky 4.00 10.00
11 Devin Booker 100.00 250.00
12 Myles Turner 10.00 25.00
13 Jerian Grant 3.00 8.00
14 Trey Lyles 4.00 10.00
15 Cameron Payne 5.00 12.00
16 Delon Wright 4.00 10.00
17 Rashad Vaughn 3.00 8.00
18 Kelly Oubre Jr. 10.00 25.00
19 Sam Dekker 3.00 8.00
20 Terry Rozier 12.00 30.00
21 Rondae Hollis-Jefferson 4.00 10.00
22 Bobby Portis 8.00 20.00
23 Justin Anderson 3.00 8.00
24 Jarell Martin 3.00 8.00
25 R.J. Hunter 3.00 8.00
26 Anthony Brown 3.00 8.00
28 Chris McCullough 3.00 8.00
29 Jordan Mickey 3.00 8.00
30 Larry Nance Jr. 6.00 15.00
31 Montrezl Harrell 10.00 25.00
32 Dakari Johnson 3.00 8.00
33 Darrun Hilliard 3.00 8.00
34 Pat Connaughton 5.00 12.00
35 Rakeem Christmas 3.00 8.00
36 Richaun Holmes 5.00 12.00
38 Andrew Harrison 4.00 10.00
40 Joe Young 3.00 8.00
42 Tyler Harvey 3.00 8.00
43 Branden Dawson 3.00 8.00
44 Tyus Jones 8.00 20.00
46 Aaron Harrison 4.00 10.00
48 Josh Richardson 5.00 12.00
49 Walter Tavares 3.00 8.00

2015-16 Prestige Prestigious Pros

*LT.BLUE/99: .75X TO 2X BASIC
*BRONZE/49: 1X TO 2.5X BASIC
1 Kenneth Faried .50 1.25
2 Russell Westbrook 1.00 2.50
3 Marc Gasol .60 1.50
4 Kobe Bryant 5.00 12.00
5 Paul Millsap .50 1.25
6 John Wall .75 2.00
7 Manu Ginobili 1.25 3.00
8 LeBron James 5.00 12.00
9 Dwight Howard .75 2.00
10 Carmelo Anthony 1.00 2.50
11 Chris Bosh .75 2.00
12 Tony Parker 1.00 2.50
13 Al Horford .60 1.50
14 Dirk Nowitzki 1.50 4.00
15 Kyle Lowry .60 1.50
16 Kyrie Irving 1.25 3.00
17 Bradley Beal .75 2.00
18 Kevin Durant 2.50 6.00
19 Goran Dragic .60 1.50
20 Stephen Curry 5.00 12.00
21 Kawhi Leonard 2.00 5.00
22 Kevin Love .60 1.50
23 Klay Thompson 1.50 4.00
24 Joakim Noah .40 1.00
25 Eric Bledsoe .50 1.25
26 Tim Duncan 1.50 4.00
27 Mike Conley .60 1.50
28 Chris Paul 1.25 3.00
29 DeMarcus Cousins .60 1.50
30 Blake Griffin .60 1.50
31 Andre Drummond .60 1.50
32 James Harden 1.25 3.00
33 Rudy Gay .60 1.50
34 Damian Lillard 1.50 4.00
35 Zach Randolph .60 1.50
36 Dwyane Wade 1.25 3.00
37 Andrew Wiggins .75 2.00
38 Anthony Davis 1.50 4.00
39 DeMar DeRozan .75 2.00
40 Derrick Rose 1.00 2.50

2015-16 Prestige Stars of the NBA Signatures

PRINT RUNS B/WN 25-149 COPIES PER
EXCHANGE DEADLINE 4/19/2017
1 Shaquille O'Neal/25 50.00 120.00
3 Allen Iverson/25 60.00 150.00
5 Chris Webber/25 60.00 150.00
6 Hakeem Olajuwon/25 20.00 50.00
7 Paul George/25 25.00 60.00
8 Nerlens Noel/49 6.00 15.00
9 Alonzo Mourning/25 20.00 50.00
10 Artis Gilmore/49 8.00 20.00
11 Blake Griffin/25 15.00 40.00
12 Walt Frazier/49 10.00 25.00
13 Dennis Rodman/25 20.00 50.00
14 Roy Hibbert/149 4.00 10.00
15 Jerry West/25 20.00 50.00
16 John Stockton/25 20.00 50.00
18 Nick Van Exel/49 40.00 100.00
19 Kareem Abdul-Jabbar/25 30.00 80.00
20 Nikola Mirotic/99 4.00 10.00
21 Julius Erving/25 40.00 100.00
22 Clyde Drexler/25 15.00 40.00
23 Oscar Robertson/25 25.00 60.00
24 Peja Stojakovic/49 10.00 25.00
27 Chris Paul/28 40.00 100.00
28 Charles Oakley/149 4.00 10.00
30 Bernard King/49 8.00 20.00
31 Jabari Parker/25 5.00 12.00
32 James Worthy/49 10.00 25.00
33 Anfernee Hardaway/49 20.00 50.00
34 Harrison Barnes/49 10.00 25.00
35 Ricky Rubio/25 6.00 15.00
36 Victor Oladipo/49 5.00 12.00
37 Yao Ming/25 15.00 40.00
38 Damon Stoudamire/149 5.00 12.00
39 Andrew Wiggins/49 30.00 80.00
40 Vin Baker/149 3.00 8.00
41 David Robinson/25 15.00 40.00
42 Vlade Divac/149 5.00 12.00
43 Wes Unseld/49 8.00 20.00
47 Magic Johnson/25 25.00 60.00
48 Robert Parish/149 6.00 15.00
49 Carmelo Anthony/25 20.00 50.00
50 Brandon Knight/149 3.00 8.00

2015-16 Prestige Stat Stars

*CRYSTAL/99: 1.2X TO 3X
*CHECK/125: 1.2X TO 3X
1 Dwight Howard .75 2.00
2 Wilt Chamberlain 2.50 6.00
3 Tim Duncan 1.50 4.00
4 Magic Johnson 2.50 6.00
5 Bill Russell 2.00 5.00
6 Stephen Curry 5.00 12.00
7 Russell Westbrook 1.00 2.50
8 Larry Brown .60 1.50
9 Kevin Durant 2.50 6.00
10 Kawhi Leonard 2.00 5.00
11 Steve Nash 1.00 2.50
12 John Stockton 1.25 3.00
13 Allen Iverson 1.50 4.00
14 Steve Kerr .60 1.50
15 Julius Erving 1.50 4.00
16 DeAndre Jordan .50 1.25
17 Dikembe Mutombo 1.00 2.50
18 Chris Paul 1.25 3.00
19 Kobe Bryant 5.00 12.00
20 Anthony Davis 1.50 4.00
21 John Wall .75 2.00
22 Dennis Rodman 1.50 4.00
23 Jerry West 1.00 2.50
24 LeBron James 5.00 12.00
25 Artis Gilmore .75 2.00

2015-16 Prestige True Colors Materials

*PRIME/25: 1X TO 2.5X BASIC
1 Allen Iverson 4.00 10.00
2 Chris Andersen 1.50 4.00
3 Clifford Robinson 2.00 5.00
4 Danny Manning 1.50 4.00
5 DeMarcus Cousins 2.00 5.00
6 Dirk Nowitzki 5.00 12.00
7 Hakeem Olajuwon 4.00 10.00
8 Jimmy Butler 4.00 10.00
9 Kenny Anderson 1.50 4.00
10 Kobe Bryant 15.00 40.00
11 Nikola Vucevic 1.50 4.00
12 Ray Allen 2.50 6.00
13 Tim Duncan 5.00 12.00
14 Kevin Durant 8.00 20.00
15 Anthony Davis 5.00 12.00
16 Andrew Wiggins 2.50 6.00
17 LeBron James 15.00 40.00
18 Chandler Parsons 1.25 3.00
19 Brandon Jennings 1.25 3.00
20 James Harden 4.00 10.00
21 Chris Paul 4.00 10.00
22 Tony Parker 3.00 8.00
23 Bradley Beal 2.50 6.00
24 Aaron Gordon 2.00 5.00
25 Elfrid Payton 1.50 4.00

2016-17 Prestige

COMPLETE SET (200) 20.00 50.00
1 Kenneth Faried .30 .75
2 Jose Calderon .25 .60
3 Isaiah Thomas .30 .75
4 Anthony Davis 1.25 3.00
5 Paul George .60 1.50
6 Nick Collison .25 .60
7 Stephen Curry 3.00 8.00
8 Andrew Wiggins .50 1.25
9 Kent Bazemore .25 .60
10 Aaron Gordon .40 1.00
11 Chandler Parsons .25 .60
12 Eric Bledsoe .30 .75
13 Andre Drummond .40 1.00
14 Evan Turner .25 .60
15 Giannis Antetokounmpo 2.00 5.00
16 Jeremy Lin .75 2.00
17 Dante Exum .30 .75
18 Nene .30 .75
19 DeMarcus Cousins .30 .75
20 J.J. Redick .40 1.00
21 David Lee .25 .60
22 Dwight Howard .50 1.25
23 DeMar DeRozan .50 1.25
24 Matthew Dellavedova .30 .75
25 Julius Randle .50 1.25
26 Trevor Ariza .25 .60
27 Kevin Durant 1.50 4.00
28 Elfrid Payton .30 .75
29 Eric Gordon .30 .75
30 Jeremy Lamb .25 .60
31 Enes Kanter .25 .60
32 Wesley Matthews .25 .60
33 Willie Cauley-Stein .30 .75
34 Dwyane Wade .75 2.00
35 Nik Stauskas .25 .60
36 Josh McRoberts .25 .60
37 J.R. Smith .40 1.00
38 Zach Randolph .40 1.00
39 Mason Plumlee .25 .60
40 Emmanuel Mudiay .25 .60
41 Paul Pierce .60 1.50
42 Kyle Lowry .60 1.50
43 Kelly Olynyk .25 .60
44 Devin Booker 1.50 4.00
45 Kentavious Caldwell-Pope .30 .75
46 Jared Sullinger .25 .60
47 Dennis Schroder .40 1.00
48 Tyreke Evans .30 .75
49 Monta Ellis .30 .75
50 Kawhi Leonard 1.00 2.50
51 Jameer Nelson .25 .60
52 Cory Joseph .25 .60
53 Danilo Gallinari .30 .75
54 Dion Waiters .25 .60
55 Jahlil Okafor .25 .60
56 Brook Lopez .30 .75
57 Serge Ibaka .30 .75
58 Jordan Clarkson .40 1.00
59 Klay Thompson 1.00 2.50
60 Karl-Anthony Towns .75 2.00
61 Roy Hibbert .25 .60
62 Russell Westbrook .60 1.50
63 Ryan Anderson .25 .60
64 Derrick Favors .25 .60
65 Greg Monroe .25 .60
66 Jimmy Butler .75 2.00
67 Marc Gasol .40 1.00
68 Ty Lawson .25 .60
69 Deron Williams .30 .75
70 Tony Parker .60 1.50
71 Jordan Hill .25 .60
72 Paul Millsap .30 .75
73 C.J. McCollum .40 1.00
74 Al Jefferson .25 .60
75 Jonas Valanciunas .30 .75
76 Iman Shumpert .25 .60
77 Jabari Parker .25 .60
78 Gordon Hayward .40 1.00
79 Reggie Jackson .30 .75
80 Matt Barnes .25 .60
81 Marcus Smart .25 .60
82 Jrue Holiday .50 1.25
83 Chris Paul .60 1.50
84 Andrew Bogut .40 1.00
85 Omri Casspi .25 .60
86 Patrick Beverley .25 .60
87 Rajon Rondo .50 1.25
88 Justise Winslow .30 .75
89 Joakim Noah .25 .60
90 Luis Scola .30 .75
91 Damian Lillard 1.00 2.50
92 Jusuf Nurkic .30 .75
93 Mike Conley .30 .75
94 Tyson Chandler .30 .75
95 Kemba Walker .30 .75
96 Victor Oladipo .30 .75
97 Andre Iguodala .40 1.00
98 Nerlens Noel .25 .60
99 Kevin Love .40 1.00
100 Nikola Vucevic .40 1.00
101 Harrison Barnes .30 .75
102 Kristaps Porzingis .60 1.50
103 Zach LaVine .75 2.00
104 Kyle Korver .30 .75
105 Justin Anderson .25 .60
106 Tony Snell .25 .60
107 Stanley Johnson .25 .60
108 Pau Gasol .60 1.50
109 Al Horford .40 1.00
110 Joe Johnson .40 1.00
111 Myles Turner .40 1.00
112 Kyrie Irving .75 2.00
113 Omer Asik .25 .60
114 Marvin Williams .25 .60
115 Langston Galloway .25 .60
116 Hassan Whiteside .30 .75
117 Jerryd Bayless .25 .60
118 Anthony Bennett .25 .60
119 Derrick Rose .60 1.50
120 JaVale McGee .30 .75
121 DeAndre Jordan .30 .75
122 LaMarcus Aldridge .40 1.00
123 Nikola Mirotic .30 .75
124 Rudy Gay .40 1.00
125 Carmelo Anthony .60 1.50
126 Luol Deng .30 .75
127 Arron Afflalo .25 .60
128 Avery Bradley .25 .60
129 Brandon Knight .30 .75
130 Jeff Teague .25 .60
131 Trey Lyles .30 .75
132 Tobias Harris .40 1.00
133 Draymond Green .50 1.25
134 Al-Farouq Aminu .25 .60
135 Dirk Nowitzki 1.00 2.50
136 Goran Dragic .40 1.00
137 Joel Embiid 1.00 2.50
138 D'Angelo Russell .50 1.25
139 Jodie Meeks .25 .60
140 Robin Lopez .25 .60
141 Steven Adams .30 .75
142 Vince Carter .75 2.00
143 Brandon Jennings .25 .60
144 Rondae Hollis-Jefferson .25 .60
145 E'Twaun Moore .25 .60
146 James Harden .75 2.00
147 Ricky Rubio .25 .60
148 LeBron James 3.00 8.00
149 Blake Griffin .40 1.00
150 Cody Zeller .25 .60
151 Ben Simmons RC 1.50 4.00
152 Brandon Ingram RC 2.00 5.00
153 Jaylen Brown RC 4.00 10.00
154 Dragan Bender RC .50 1.25
155 Kris Dunn RC .75 2.00
156 Buddy Hield RC 1.50 4.00
157 Jamal Murray RC 8.00 20.00
158 Marquese Chriss RC .60 1.50
159 Jakob Poeltl RC 1.00 2.50
160 Thon Maker RC .60 1.50
161 Domantas Sabonis RC 3.00 8.00
162 Taurean Prince RC .60 1.50
163 Georgios Papagiannis RC .50 1.25
164 Denzel Valentine RC .50 1.25
165 Juan Hernangomez RC 1.00 2.50
166 Wade Baldwin IV RC .50 1.25
167 Henry Ellenson RC .50 1.25
168 Malik Beasley RC 1.00 2.50
169 Caris LeVert RC 1.25 3.00
170 DeAndre' Bembry RC .75 2.00
171 Malachi Richardson RC .50 1.25
172 Timothe Luwawu-Cabarrot RC .75 2.00
173 Brice Johnson RC .50 1.25
174 Pascal Siakam RC 3.00 8.00
175 Skal Labissiere RC .50 1.25
176 Dejounte Murray RC 2.50 6.00
177 Damian Jones RC .50 1.25
178 Deyonta Davis RC .50 1.25
179 Ivica Zubac RC 1.25 3.00
180 Cheick Diallo RC .50 1.25
181 Tyler Ulis RC .60 1.50
182 Malcolm Brogdon RC 1.50 4.00
183 Chinanu Onuaku RC .50 1.25
184 Patrick McCaw RC .50 1.25
185 Diamond Stone RC .50 1.25
186 Stephen Zimmerman RC .50 1.25
187 Isaiah Whitehead RC .50 1.25
188 Demetrius Jackson RC .50 1.25
189 A.J. Hammons RC .50 1.25
190 Kay Felder RC .50 1.25
191 Jake Layman RC .60 1.50
192 Georges Niang RC .75 2.00
193 Joel Bolomboy RC .50 1.25
194 Sheldon McClellan RC .50 1.25
195 Tim Quarterman RC .50 1.25
196 Tomas Satoransky RC .75 2.00
197 Mindaugas Kuzminskas RC .50 1.25
198 Ron Baker RC .50 1.25
199 Marshall Plumlee RC .50 1.25
200 Dario Saric RC .75 2.00

2016-17 Prestige Bonus Shots Red

*RED: 1.5X TO 4X BASIC
*RED RC: .75X TO 2X BASIC
STATED PRINT RUN 75 SER.#'d SETS
157 Jamal Murray 20.00 50.00

2016-17 Prestige Crystal

*CRYSTAL: 2X TO 5X BASIC
*CRYSTAL RC: 1X TO 2.5X BASIC

2016-17 Prestige Horizon

*HORIZON: 1.2X TO 3X BASIC
*HORIZON RC: .6X TO 1.5X BASIC

2016-17 Prestige Metallized

*METALIZED: 2.5X TO 6X BASIC
*METALIZED RC: 1.2X TO 3X BASIC
RANDON INSERTS IN PACKS

2016-17 Prestige Rain

*RAIN: 1X TO 2.5X BASIC
*RAIN RC: .5X TO 1.2X BASIC

2016-17 Prestige Acetate Rookies

1 Brandon Ingram 2.50 6.00
2 Ben Simmons 2.00 5.00
3 Dario Saric 1.00 2.50
4 Marquese Chriss .75 2.00
5 Dragan Bender .60 1.50
6 Patrick McCaw .60 1.50
7 Kris Dunn 1.00 2.50
8 Jaylen Brown 5.00 12.00
9 Thon Maker .75 2.00
10 Wade Baldwin IV .60 1.50
11 Denzel Valentine .60 1.50
12 Tyler Ulis .75 2.00
13 Kay Felder .60 1.50
14 Taurean Prince .75 2.00
15 Brice Johnson .60 1.50
16 Buddy Hield 2.00 5.00
17 Jamal Murray 8.00 20.00
18 Domantas Sabonis 4.00 10.00
19 Henry Ellenson .60 1.50
20 Malcolm Brogdon 2.00 5.00
21 Pascal Siakam 4.00 10.00
22 Jakob Poeltl 1.00 2.50
23 Diamond Stone .60 1.50
24 Ivica Zubac 1.50 4.00
25 Jake Layman .75 2.00

2016-17 Prestige Acetate Veterans

1 LeBron James 8.00 20.00
2 Giannis Antetokounmpo 5.00 12.00
3 Stephen Curry 8.00 20.00
4 Kevin Durant 4.00 10.00
5 Kyrie Irving 2.00 5.00
6 John Wall 1.25 3.00
7 Damian Lillard 2.50 6.00
8 Russell Westbrook 1.50 4.00
9 James Harden 2.00 5.00
10 Paul George 1.50 4.00
11 Karl-Anthony Towns 2.00 5.00
12 Jimmy Butler 2.00 5.00
13 Dwyane Wade 2.00 5.00
14 Blake Griffin 1.00 2.50
15 D'Angelo Russell 1.25 3.00
16 Carmelo Anthony 1.50 4.00
17 Kristaps Porzingis 1.50 4.00
18 DeMarcus Cousins .75 2.00
19 DeMar DeRozan 1.25 3.00
20 Anthony Davis 3.00 8.00
21 Kawhi Leonard 2.50 6.00
22 Devin Booker 4.00 10.00
23 Andrew Wiggins 1.25 3.00
24 Joel Embiid 2.50 6.00
25 Chris Paul 1.50 4.00

2016-17 Prestige All-Time Greats

COMPLETE SET (20) 15.00 40.00
*RAIN: .6X TO 1.5X BASIC
*HORIZON: .75X TO 2X BASIC
*CRYSTAL: 1.2X TO 3X BASIC
1 Patrick Ewing .75 2.00
2 Dominique Wilkins .75 2.00
3 Mitch Richmond .60 1.50
4 Ray Allen 1.00 2.50
5 Robert Parish .75 2.00
6 Joe Dumars .60 1.50
7 Magic Johnson 2.50 6.00
8 Ralph Sampson .50 1.25
9 Julius Erving 1.50 4.00
10 Bill Walton 1.00 2.50
11 Shaquille O'Neal 2.00 5.00
12 Tracy McGrady 1.00 2.50
13 Allen Iverson 1.00 2.50
14 Scottie Pippen 1.25 3.00
15 Alonzo Mourning 1.00 2.50
16 Isiah Thomas 1.00 2.50
17 Bill Russell 2.00 5.00
18 Steve Nash 1.00 2.50
19 Walt Frazier .60 1.50
20 Jason Kidd 1.00 2.50

2016-17 Prestige Bonus Shots Signatures

1 Mike Muscala 3.00 8.00
2 Cody Zeller 3.00 8.00
3 C.J. McCollum 5.00 12.00
4 E'Twaun Moore 3.00 8.00
5 Justin Hamilton 3.00 8.00
6 Ian Clark 3.00 8.00
7 James Ennis 3.00 8.00
8 Josh Huestis 3.00 8.00
9 Dwight Powell 3.00 8.00
10 Victor Oladipo 4.00 10.00
11 Maurice Harkless 3.00 8.00
12 Steve Novak 3.00 8.00
13 Walter Tavares 3.00 8.00
14 Michael Carter-Williams 3.00 8.00
15 Reggie Bullock 3.00 8.00
16 Langston Galloway 3.00 8.00
17 Noah Vonleh 3.00 8.00
18 Troy Daniels 3.00 8.00
19 Jason Smith 3.00 8.00
20 Allen Crabbe 3.00 8.00
21 Kevon Looney 5.00 12.00
22 Alan Anderson 3.00 8.00
23 Aaron Harrison 3.00 8.00
24 Jordan Clarkson 5.00 12.00
25 Jeff Withey 3.00 8.00
26 Jordan McRae 3.00 8.00
27 C.J. Miles 3.00 8.00
28 T.J. McConnell 4.00 10.00
29 Jason Terry 6.00 15.00
30 Alex Len 3.00 8.00
31 James Johnson 3.00 8.00
32 Hollis Thompson 3.00 8.00
33 Isaiah Canaan 3.00 8.00
34 Jason Terry 6.00 15.00
35 Deron Williams 4.00 10.00
36 Glenn Robinson III 3.00 8.00
37 Norman Powell 5.00 12.00
38 Brian Roberts 3.00 8.00
39 Michael Kidd-Gilchrist 3.00 8.00
40 P.J. Tucker 3.00 8.00
41 Tyler Ennis 3.00 8.00
42 Tristan Thompson 4.00 10.00
43 Rondae Hollis-Jefferson 3.00 8.00
44 Rashad Vaughn 3.00 8.00
45 Terrence Jones 3.00 8.00
46 Dante Exum 4.00 10.00
47 Ed Davis 3.00 8.00
48 Alec Burks 4.00 10.00
50 Bill Willoughby 4.00 10.00
51 Vin Baker 3.00 8.00
52 Chris Herren 3.00 8.00
53 Zydrunas Ilgauskas 4.00 10.00
55 Bob Dandridge 5.00 12.00
56 Charlie Bell 3.00 8.00
57 Tony Campbell 3.00 8.00
58 Jim Chones 3.00 8.00
60 Chucky Brown 3.00 8.00
61 Mark Price 5.00 12.00
62 Harvey Grant 3.00 8.00
63 Rick Fox 4.00 10.00
64 Jim Jackson 4.00 10.00
65 Jeff Malone 3.00 8.00
67 Sean Elliott 4.00 10.00
68 Jonathan Bender 3.00 8.00
69 Jared Jeffries 3.00 8.00
70 Gary Trent 3.00 8.00
71 Cedric Ceballos 5.00 12.00
72 Dale Ellis 3.00 8.00
73 Chris Whitney 3.00 8.00
74 Kevin Willis 3.00 8.00
75 Vinny Del Negro 4.00 10.00
76 Kenny Walker 3.00 8.00
77 Jamal Mashburn 4.00 10.00
78 Bo Kimble 3.00 8.00
79 Ron Boone 4.00 10.00
80 Dell Curry 5.00 12.00
81 Tree Rollins 3.00 8.00
82 Damon Jones 3.00 8.00
83 Lamond Murray 3.00 8.00
85 Dan Majerle 4.00 10.00
86 Mark Landsberger 3.00 8.00
87 Dan Issel 6.00 15.00
88 Mario Elie 6.00 15.00
89 Junior Bridgeman 4.00 10.00
90 Denzel Valentine 3.00 8.00
91 Taurean Prince 4.00 10.00
92 Juan Hernangomez 12.00 30.00
93 Chinanu Onuaku 3.00 8.00
94 Jake Layman 4.00 10.00
95 Damian Jones 3.00 8.00
96 Georgios Papagiannis 3.00 8.00
97 Domantas Sabonis 20.00 50.00
98 Wade Baldwin IV 3.00 8.00
99 Michael Gbinije 3.00 8.00
100 Demetrius Jackson 3.00 8.00

2016-17 Prestige Distinctive Ink

PRINT RUNS B/WN 75-499 COPIES PER
1 C.J. McCollum/149 8.00 20.00
2 Victor Oladipo/75 4.00 10.00
3 Dwight Powell/199 2.50 6.00
4 Michael Carter-Williams/199 2.50 6.00
5 Jordan Clarkson/199 8.00 20.00
6 Jeremy Lin/75 30.00 80.00
7 Jabari Parker/75 3.00 8.00
8 Allen Crabbe/199 2.50 6.00
9 Kevin Love/75 5.00 12.00
10 Dwyane Wade/75 50.00 120.00
11 Kyrie Irving/75 40.00 100.00
12 Dirk Nowitzki/75 100.00 250.00
13 D'Angelo Russell/75 15.00 40.00
14 Bobby Portis/199 8.00 20.00
15 Marc Gasol/75 8.00 20.00
16 Blake Griffin/75 10.00 25.00
17 Carmelo Anthony/75 40.00 100.00
18 Shawn Kemp/199 25.00 60.00
19 Scottie Pippen/75 60.00 150.00
20 Rick Fox/199 3.00 8.00
21 Dan Majerle/199 3.00 8.00
22 Adrian Dantley/199 4.00 10.00
23 Karl Malone/75 20.00 50.00
24 Yao Ming/75 100.00 250.00
25 Artis Gilmore/75 6.00 15.00

2016-17 Prestige Franchise Favorites

COMPLETE SET (15) 10.00 25.00
*RAIN: .6X TO 1.5X BASIC
*HORIZON: .75X TO 2X BASIC
*CRYSTAL: 1.2X TO 3X BASIC
1 Dirk Nowitzki 1.50 4.00
2 Jimmy Butler 1.25 3.00
3 Kyrie Irving 1.25 3.00
4 Blake Griffin .60 1.50
5 Mike Conley .50 1.25
6 Paul Millsap .50 1.25
7 Kemba Walker .50 1.25
8 DeMarcus Cousins .50 1.25
9 Carmelo Anthony 1.00 2.50
10 Tony Parker 1.00 2.50
11 Klay Thompson 1.50 4.00
12 Kyle Lowry .60 1.50
13 Anthony Davis 2.00 5.00
14 Gordon Hayward .60 1.50
15 Andre Drummond .60 1.50

2016-17 Prestige Freshman Fabrics Jumbo

STATED PRINT RUN 99 SER. #'d SETS
1 A.J. Hammons 1.50 4.00
2 Brandon Ingram 6.00 15.00
3 Brice Johnson 1.50 4.00
4 Buddy Hield 5.00 12.00
5 Caris LeVert 4.00 10.00
6 Cheick Diallo 1.50 4.00
7 Chinanu Onuaku 1.50 4.00
8 Damian Jones 1.50 4.00
9 Dario Saric 10.00 25.00
10 Demetrius Jackson 1.50 4.00
11 Denzel Valentine 1.50 4.00
12 Deyonta Davis 1.50 4.00
13 Diamond Stone 1.50 4.00
14 Domantas Sabonis 10.00 25.00
15 Dragan Bender 1.50 4.00
16 Georges Niang 2.50 6.00
17 Georgios Papagiannis 1.50 4.00
18 Henry Ellenson 1.50 4.00
19 Isaiah Whitehead 1.50 4.00
20 Ivica Zubac 4.00 10.00
21 Jakob Poeltl 3.00 8.00
22 Jamal Murray 12.00 30.00
23 Jaylen Brown 5.00 12.00
24 Juan Hernangomez 3.00 8.00
25 Kay Felder 1.50 4.00
26 Kris Dunn 2.50 6.00
27 Malachi Richardson 1.50 4.00
28 Malcolm Brogdon 5.00 12.00
29 Malik Beasley 3.00 8.00
30 Marquese Chriss 2.00 5.00
31 Pascal Siakam 10.00 25.00
32 Patrick McCaw 1.50 4.00
33 Skal Labissiere 1.50 4.00
34 Stephen Zimmerman 1.50 4.00
35 Thon Maker 2.00 5.00
36 Timothe Luwawu-Cabarrot 2.50 6.00
37 Tyler Ulis 2.00 5.00
38 Wade Baldwin IV 1.50 4.00
39 Taurean Prince 2.00 5.00

2016-17 Prestige Hardcourt Heroes

COMPLETE SET (15) 6.00 15.00
*RAINBOW/25: 1X TO 2.5X BASIC
1 Kyrie Irving 1.25 3.00
2 Dwyane Wade 1.25 3.00
3 Kevin Durant 2.50 6.00
4 Blake Griffin .60 1.50
5 Andrew Wiggins .75 2.00
6 Eric Bledsoe .50 1.25
7 Bradley Beal .75 2.00
8 Paul Millsap .50 1.25
9 Al Horford .60 1.50
10 Kawhi Leonard 1.50 4.00
11 Kyle Lowry .60 1.50
12 Rudy Gay .60 1.50
13 Derrick Rose 1.00 2.50
14 Jordan Clarkson .60 1.50
15 Goran Dragic .60 1.50

2016-17 Prestige Highlight Reel

COMPLETE SET (10) 10.00 25.00
*RAIN: .6X TO 1.5X BASIC
*HORIZON: .75X TO 2X BASIC
*CRYSTAL: 1.2X TO 3X BASIC
1 Anthony Davis 2.00 5.00
2 Aaron Gordon .60 1.50
3 Kevin Durant 2.50 6.00
4 Russell Westbrook 1.00 2.50
5 Damian Lillard 1.50 4.00
6 James Harden 1.25 3.00
7 Dwyane Wade 1.25 3.00
8 Myles Turner .60 1.50
9 Brandon Ingram 1.50 4.00
10 Joel Embiid 1.50 4.00

2016-17 Prestige Inside the Numbers

*RAIN: .6X TO 1.5X BASIC
*HORIZON: .75X TO 2X BASIC
*CRYSTAL: 1.2X TO 3X BASIC
1 Stephen Curry 5.00 12.00
2 James Harden 1.25 3.00
3 Kevin Durant 2.50 6.00
4 DeMarcus Cousins .50 1.25
5 LeBron James 5.00 12.00
6 Damian Lillard 1.50 4.00
7 Anthony Davis 2.00 5.00
8 Russell Westbrook 1.00 2.50
9 DeMar DeRozan .75 2.00
10 Paul George 1.00 2.50
11 Andre Drummond .60 1.50
12 DeAndre Jordan .50 1.25
13 Hassan Whiteside .50 1.25
14 Dwight Howard .75 2.00
15 Pau Gasol 1.00 2.50
16 Rajon Rondo .75 2.00
17 John Wall .75 2.00
18 Chris Paul 1.00 2.50
19 Ricky Rubio .50 1.25
20 Kyle Lowry .60 1.50

2016-17 Prestige Jerseys

STATED PRINT RUN 199 SER. #'d SETS
*PRIME/25: 1X TO 2.5X BASIC
1 Andrew Wiggins 3.00 8.00
2 Bradley Beal 3.00 8.00
3 Carmelo Anthony 4.00 10.00
4 David Robinson 5.00 12.00
5 DeMarre Carroll 1.50 4.00
6 Jimmy Butler 5.00 12.00
7 Deron Williams 2.00 5.00
8 Dirk Nowitzki 6.00 15.00
9 Doug McDermott 2.00 5.00
10 Draymond Green 3.00 8.00
11 Dwyane Wade 5.00 12.00
12 Elfrid Payton 2.00 5.00
13 Elton Brand 2.00 5.00
14 Emmanuel Mudiay 1.50 4.00
15 Enes Kanter 1.50 4.00
16 Frank Kaminsky 1.50 4.00
17 George Hill 2.00 5.00
18 Goran Dragic 2.50 6.00
19 Hassan Whiteside 2.00 5.00
20 J.J. Redick 2.50 6.00
21 Jahlil Okafor 1.50 4.00
22 John Stockton 4.00 10.00
23 Kemba Walker 2.00 5.00
24 Kevin Durant 10.00 25.00
25 Kevin Love 2.50 6.00
26 LeBron James 20.00 50.00
27 Manu Ginobili 5.00 12.00
28 Mason Plumlee 1.50 4.00
29 Myles Turner 2.50 6.00
30 Paul George 4.00 10.00

2016-17 Prestige NBA Passport Signatures

PRINT RUNS B/WN 99-199 COPIES PER
1 Brandon Ingram/99 50.00 120.00
2 Denzel Valentine/99 3.00 8.00
3 Taurean Prince/99 4.00 10.00
4 Juan Hernangomez/149 6.00 15.00
5 Wade Baldwin IV/99 3.00 8.00
6 Malcolm Brogdon/149 12.00 30.00
7 Brice Johnson/149 3.00 8.00
8 DeAndre' Bembry/99 5.00 12.00
9 Kay Felder/149 3.00 8.00
10 Jaylen Brown/99 125.00 300.00
11 Kris Dunn/99 5.00 12.00
12 Thon Maker/99 4.00 10.00
13 Jamal Murray/99 60.00 150.00
14 Buddy Hield/99 12.00 30.00
15 Jakob Poeltl/99 6.00 15.00
16 Marquese Chriss/99 4.00 10.00
17 Henry Ellenson/99 3.00 8.00
18 Dragan Bender/99 3.00 8.00
19 Patrick McCaw/149 3.00 8.00
20 Tyler Ulis/99 4.00 10.00
21 Chinanu Onuaku/149 3.00 8.00
22 Domantas Sabonis/99 15.00 40.00
23 Cheick Diallo/149 3.00 8.00
24 Timothe Luwawu-Cabarrot/99 5.00 12.00
25 Malik Beasley/125 6.00 15.00

2016-17 Prestige Old School Signatures

PRINT RUNS B/WN 49-199 COPIES PER
1 Karl Malone/49 25.00 60.00
2 Jo Jo White/199 8.00 20.00
3 A.C. Green/199 5.00 12.00
4 Adrian Dantley/199 4.00 10.00
5 Alex English/199 4.00 10.00
6 Spud Webb/199 10.00 25.00
7 Shawn Kemp/49 40.00 100.00
8 Kenny Walker/49 4.00 10.00
9 Dan Issel/49 8.00 20.00
10 Scottie Pippen/49 40.00 100.00
11 Kurt Rambis/199 5.00 12.00
12 John Stockton/199 30.00 80.00
13 Kobe Bryant/49 1,000.00 2,000.00
14 Tom Heinsohn/99 40.00 100.00
15 Kiki Vandeweghe/49 5.00 12.00
16 Dan Majerle/99 4.00 10.00
17 Rick Barry/199 8.00 20.00
18 Rudy Tomjanovich/49 5.00 12.00
19 Vlade Divac/49 6.00 15.00
20 Christian Laettner/49 8.00 20.00

2016-17 Prestige Playmakers

1 Kyrie Irving 10.00 25.00
2 Chris Paul 8.00 20.00
3 John Wall 6.00 15.00
4 DeMar DeRozan 6.00 15.00
5 LeBron James 30.00 80.00
6 Russell Westbrook 8.00 20.00
7 James Harden 10.00 25.00
8 Goran Dragic 5.00 12.00
9 Ty Lawson 3.00 8.00
10 Jeff Teague 3.00 8.00
11 Stephen Curry 40.00 100.00
12 Deron Williams 4.00 10.00
13 Kristaps Porzingis 8.00 20.00
14 Karl-Anthony Towns 10.00 25.00
15 Tony Parker 8.00 20.00
16 Kevin Durant 20.00 50.00
17 Jimmy Butler 10.00 25.00
18 Kawhi Leonard 12.00 30.00
19 Anthony Davis 15.00 40.00
20 Paul George 8.00 20.00
21 DeMarcus Cousins 4.00 10.00
22 Damian Lillard 12.00 30.00
23 Mike Conley 4.00 10.00
24 DeAndre Jordan 4.00 10.00
25 Giannis Antetokounmpo 20.00 50.00
26 Dirk Nowitzki 12.00 30.00
27 Blake Griffin 5.00 12.00
28 C.J. McCollum 5.00 12.00
29 Isaiah Thomas 4.00 10.00
30 Andre Drummond 5.00 12.00

2016-17 Prestige Preeminent Ink
PRINT RUNS B/WN 49-199 COPIES PER
1 Bill Willoughby/199 4.00 10.00
2 Vin Baker/199 4.00 10.00
3 Zydrunas Ilgauskas/199 4.00 10.00
4 Brian Grant/199 4.00 10.00
5 Bob Dandridge/199 5.00 12.00
6 Jim Chones/199 3.00 8.00
7 Chucky Brown/199 3.00 8.00
8 Mark Price/199 5.00 12.00
9 Rick Fox/99 3.00 8.00
10 Jim Jackson/199 4.00 10.00
11 Jeff Malone/99 2.50 6.00
12 Kevin Willis/99 2.50 6.00
13 Luol Deng/99 3.00 8.00
14 Zach Randolph/99 4.00 10.00
15 Paul Millsap/99 3.00 8.00
16 Nikola Vucevic/99 4.00 10.00
17 Danilo Gallinari/99 3.00 8.00
18 Avery Bradley/99 2.50 6.00
19 Zaza Pachulia/99 2.50 6.00
20 Jae Crowder/99 2.50 6.00
21 Tony Allen/99 2.50 6.00
22 Nicolas Batum/99 3.00 8.00
23 Kent Bazemore/99 2.50 6.00
24 Dwight Powell/199 3.00 8.00
25 Hassan Whiteside/99 3.00 8.00
26 Al Horford/99 4.00 10.00
27 Andrew Wiggins/49 25.00 60.00
28 Kevin Love/49 8.00 20.00
29 Nikola Jokic/199 125.00 300.00
30 Kristaps Porzingis/99 12.00 30.00
31 Karl-Anthony Towns/49 20.00 50.00
32 Devin Booker/99 75.00 200.00
33 Justise Winslow/99 3.00 8.00
34 C.J. McCollum/99 4.00 10.00
35 Myles Turner/99 4.00 10.00
36 Draymond Green/99 20.00 50.00
37 Zach LaVine/99 20.00 50.00
38 Kenneth Faried/99 3.00 8.00
39 DeMar DeRozan/49 12.00 30.00
40 Dirk Nowitzki/49 100.00 250.00

2016-17 Prestige Prestigious Passers
COMPLETE SET (10) 10.00 25.00
*RAIN: .6X TO 1.5X BASIC
*HORIZON: .75X TO 2X BASIC
*CRYSTAL: 1.2X TO 3X BASIC
1 Rajon Rondo .75 2.00
2 Russell Westbrook 1.00 2.50
3 John Wall .75 2.00
4 Chris Paul 1.00 2.50
5 Ricky Rubio .50 1.25
6 James Harden 1.25 3.00
7 Draymond Green .75 2.00
8 Damian Lillard 1.50 4.00
9 LeBron James 5.00 12.00
10 Stephen Curry 5.00 12.00

2016-17 Prestige Prestigious Picks
1 Ben Simmons 12.00 30.00
2 Brandon Ingram 15.00 40.00
3 Jaylen Brown 30.00 80.00
4 Dragan Bender 4.00 10.00
5 Kris Dunn 6.00 15.00
6 Buddy Hield 12.00 30.00
7 Jamal Murray 30.00 80.00
8 Marquese Chriss 5.00 12.00
9 Jakob Poeltl 8.00 20.00
10 Thon Maker 5.00 12.00
11 Domantas Sabonis 25.00 60.00
12 Taurean Prince 5.00 12.00
13 Georgios Papagiannis 4.00 10.00
14 Denzel Valentine 4.00 10.00
15 Juan Hernangomez 8.00 20.00
16 Wade Baldwin IV 4.00 10.00
17 Henry Ellenson 4.00 10.00
18 Malik Beasley 8.00 20.00
19 Caris LeVert 10.00 25.00
20 DeAndre' Bembry 6.00 15.00
21 Malachi Richardson 4.00 10.00
22 Timothe Luwawu-Cabarrot 6.00 15.00
23 Brice Johnson 4.00 10.00
24 Pascal Siakam 25.00 60.00
25 Skal Labissiere 4.00 10.00
26 Dejounte Murray 20.00 50.00
27 Damian Jones 4.00 10.00
28 Deyonta Davis 4.00 10.00
29 Ivica Zubac 10.00 25.00
30 Cheick Diallo 4.00 10.00
31 Tyler Ulis 5.00 12.00
32 Malcolm Brogdon 12.00 30.00
33 Chinanu Onuaku 4.00 10.00
34 Patrick McCaw 4.00 10.00
35 Diamond Stone 4.00 10.00
36 Stephen Zimmerman 4.00 10.00
37 Isaiah Whitehead 4.00 10.00
38 Demetrius Jackson 4.00 10.00
39 A.J. Hammons 4.00 10.00
40 Kay Felder 4.00 10.00

2016-17 Prestige Prestigious Pioneers
COMPLETE SET (20) 10.00 25.00
*RAINBOW: 1X TO 2.5X BASIC
1 Julius Erving 1.50 4.00
2 Shaquille O'Neal 2.00 5.00
3 Allen Iverson 1.00 2.50
4 Oscar Robertson 1.50 4.00
5 Hakeem Olajuwon 1.25 3.00
6 Jerry West 1.50 4.00
7 Latrell Sprewell .50 1.25
8 Dennis Rodman 1.25 3.00
9 Bill Russell 2.00 5.00
10 James Worthy .75 2.00
11 Larry Bird 2.50 6.00
12 David Robinson 1.25 3.00
13 Yao Ming 1.50 4.00
14 George Gervin 1.00 2.50
15 Karl Malone 1.00 2.50
16 John Stockton 1.00 2.50
17 Isiah Thomas 1.00 2.50
18 Chris Webber .60 1.50
19 Grant Hill .75 2.00
20 Shawn Kemp 1.00 2.50

2016-17 Prestige Prestigious Premieres Signatures
1 Denzel Valentine 3.00 8.00
2 Taurean Prince 4.00 10.00
3 Juan Hernangomez 6.00 15.00
4 Chinanu Onuaku 3.00 8.00
5 Jake Layman 4.00 10.00
6 Damian Jones 3.00 8.00
7 Georgios Papagiannis 3.00 8.00
8 Domantas Sabonis 20.00 50.00
9 Wade Baldwin IV 3.00 8.00
10 Michael Gbinije 3.00 8.00
11 Demetrius Jackson 3.00 8.00
12 Malcolm Brogdon 10.00 25.00
13 Ivica Zubac 8.00 20.00
14 Deyonta Davis 3.00 8.00
15 Brice Johnson 3.00 8.00
16 DeAndre' Bembry 5.00 12.00
17 Pascal Siakam 20.00 50.00
18 Cheick Diallo 3.00 8.00
19 Timothe Luwawu-Cabarrot 5.00 12.00
20 Kay Felder 3.00 8.00
21 Jaylen Brown 75.00 200.00
22 Thon Maker 4.00 10.00
23 Mindaugas Kuzminskas 3.00 8.00
24 Malik Beasley 6.00 15.00
25 Jamal Murray 50.00 120.00
26 Buddy Hield 10.00 25.00
27 Kris Dunn 5.00 12.00
28 Jakob Poeltl 6.00 15.00
29 Marquese Chriss 4.00 10.00
30 Henry Ellenson 3.00 8.00
31 Dragan Bender 3.00 8.00
32 Georges Niang 5.00 12.00
33 A.J. Hammons 3.00 8.00
34 Patrick McCaw 3.00 8.00
35 Diamond Stone 3.00 8.00
36 Tyler Ulis 4.00 10.00
37 Ron Baker 3.00 8.00
38 Caris LeVert 8.00 20.00
39 Brandon Ingram 25.00 60.00
40 Malachi Richardson 3.00 8.00
41 Dejounte Murray 50.00 120.00
42 Dario Saric 5.00 12.00
43 Joel Bolomboy 3.00 8.00
44 Kyle Wiltjer 3.00 8.00
45 Willy Hernangomez 4.00 10.00
46 Sheldon McClellan 3.00 8.00
47 Paul Zipser 3.00 8.00
48 Marshall Plumlee 3.00 8.00
49 Tim Quarterman 3.00 8.00
50 Fred VanVleet 60.00 150.00

2016-17 Prestige Prestigious Pros
1 Paul Millsap 2.50 6.00
2 Al Horford 3.00 8.00
3 Brook Lopez 2.50 6.00
4 Kemba Walker 2.50 6.00
5 Jimmy Butler 6.00 15.00
6 LeBron James 20.00 50.00
7 Dirk Nowitzki 8.00 20.00
8 Kenneth Faried 2.50 6.00
9 Andre Drummond 3.00 8.00
10 Stephen Curry 25.00 60.00
11 James Harden 6.00 15.00
12 Paul George 5.00 12.00
13 Chris Paul 5.00 12.00
14 D'Angelo Russell 4.00 10.00
15 Marc Gasol 3.00 8.00
16 Justise Winslow 2.50 6.00
17 Giannis Antetokounmpo 15.00 40.00
18 Karl-Anthony Towns 6.00 15.00
19 Anthony Davis 10.00 25.00
20 Carmelo Anthony 5.00 12.00
21 Russell Westbrook 5.00 12.00
22 Nikola Vucevic 3.00 8.00
23 Jahlil Okafor 2.00 5.00
24 Eric Bledsoe 2.50 6.00
25 Damian Lillard 8.00 20.00
26 DeMarcus Cousins 2.50 6.00
27 Kawhi Leonard 8.00 20.00
28 DeMar DeRozan 4.00 10.00
29 Gordon Hayward 3.00 8.00
30 John Wall 4.00 10.00

2016-17 Prestige Reminiscent
COMPLETE SET (15) 10.00 25.00
*RAINBOW: 1X TO 2.5X BASIC
1 Durant/Ingram 2.50 6.00
2 Brown/Butler 3.00 8.00
3 Nikola Mirotic
Dragan Bender .40 1.00
4 Dunn/Wall .75 2.00
5 Beal/Hield 1.25 3.00
6 Thompson/Murray 3.00 8.00
7 Chriss/Williams .50 1.25
8 Andrew Bogut
Jakob Poeltl .75 2.00
9 Porzingis/Maker 1.00 2.50
10 Domantas Sabonis
Greg Monroe 2.50 6.00
11 Evan Turner
Denzel Valentine .40 1.00
12 Murray/Barton 2.00 5.00
13 DeMarre Carroll
Taurean Prince .50 1.25
14 Simmons/Griffin 1.25 3.00
15 Henry Ellenson
Kevin Love .60 1.50

2016-17 Prestige Rookie Class
COMPLETE SET (25) 20.00 50.00
*RAIN: .6X TO 1.5X BASIC
*HORIZON: .75X TO 2X BASIC
*CRYSTAL: 1.2X TO 3X BASIC
1 Brandon Ingram 1.50 4.00
2 Jaylen Brown 3.00 8.00
3 Kris Dunn .60 1.50
4 Dragan Bender .40 1.00
5 Marquese Chriss .50 1.25
6 Buddy Hield 1.25 3.00
7 Jamal Murray 8.00 20.00
8 Jakob Poeltl .75 2.00
9 Thon Maker .50 1.25
10 Denzel Valentine .40 1.00
11 Domantas Sabonis 2.50 6.00
12 Dejounte Murray 2.00 5.00
13 Juan Hernangomez .75 2.00
14 Taurean Prince .50 1.25
15 Henry Ellenson .40 1.00
16 Caris LeVert 1.00 2.50
17 Timothe Luwawu-Cabarrot .60 1.50
18 Brice Johnson .40 1.00
19 Wade Baldwin IV .40 1.00
20 Georgios Papagiannis .40 1.00
21 Dario Saric .60 1.50
22 Malik Beasley .75 2.00
23 DeAndre' Bembry .60 1.50
24 Malachi Richardson .40 1.00
25 Pascal Siakam 2.50 6.00

2016-17 Prestige Stars of the NBA Signatures
PRINT RUNS B/WN 49-199 COPIES PER
1 Stephen Curry/49 300.00 600.00
2 Dennis Schroder/199 4.00 10.00
3 Kristaps Porzingis/199 12.00 30.00
4 John Wall/49 12.00 30.00
5 DeMar DeRozan/199 8.00 20.00
6 Paul George/49 25.00 60.00
7 Jonas Valanciunas/199 3.00 8.00
8 Isaiah Thomas/199 3.00 8.00
9 E'Twaun Moore/199 2.50 6.00
10 Will Barton/199 2.50 6.00
11 Anthony Davis/49 50.00 120.00
12 Myles Turner/199 4.00 10.00
13 Jabari Parker/49 3.00 8.00
14 Tobias Harris/199 4.00 10.00
15 D'Angelo Russell/49 10.00 25.00
16 Tony Parker/99 12.00 30.00
17 Kyrie Irving/49 40.00 100.00
18 Devin Booker/199 125.00 300.00
19 Pau Gasol/49 10.00 25.00
20 Gordon Hayward/199 4.00 10.00
21 Michael Carter-Williams/199 2.50 6.00
22 Jae Crowder/199 2.50 6.00
23 Matthew Dellavedova/199 3.00 8.00
24 Kyle Lowry/49 10.00 25.00
25 Thaddeus Young/99 3.00 8.00
26 Victor Oladipo/49 4.00 10.00
27 Karl-Anthony Towns/49 25.00 60.00
28 Seth Curry/199 8.00 20.00
29 Jordan Clarkson/99 8.00 20.00
30 Dirk Nowitzki/49 100.00 250.00
31 Elfrid Payton/49 4.00 10.00
32 LaMarcus Aldridge/49 10.00 25.00
33 Mike Muscala/199 2.50 6.00
34 Blake Griffin/49 5.00 12.00
35 Eric Bledsoe/49 4.00 10.00
36 C.J. McCollum/199 10.00 25.00
37 Draymond Green/49 12.00 30.00
38 Goran Dragic/199 4.00 10.00
39 Carmelo Anthony/49 40.00 100.00
40 Kevin Durant/49 100.00 250.00

2016-17 Prestige Stat Stars
COMPLETE SET (20) 6.00 15.00
*RAINBOW: 1X TO 2.5X BASIC
1 DeMarcus Cousins .50 1.25
2 Giannis Antetokounmpo 3.00 8.00
3 Jimmy Butler 1.25 3.00
4 Karl-Anthony Towns 1.25 3.00
5 LeBron James 5.00 12.00
6 Isaiah Thomas .50 1.25
7 Chris Paul 1.00 2.50
8 Marc Gasol .60 1.50
9 Stephen Curry 5.00 12.00
10 Hassan Whiteside .50 1.25
11 Kemba Walker .50 1.25
12 Carmelo Anthony 1.00 2.50
13 Damian Lillard 1.50 4.00
14 Jeremy Lin 1.25 3.00
15 John Wall .75 2.00
16 Paul George 1.00 2.50
17 Anthony Davis 2.00 5.00
18 DeMar DeRozan .75 2.00
19 James Harden 1.25 3.00
20 Russell Westbrook 1.00 2.50

2016-17 Prestige Teamwork
COMPLETE SET (30) 10.00 25.00
*RAINBOW/25: 1X TO 2.5X BASIC
1 Okafor/Embiid 1.50 4.00
2 Parker/Antetokounmpo 3.00 8.00
3 Wade/Butler 1.25 3.00
4 Irving/James 5.00 12.00
5 Isaiah Thomas
Al Horford .60 1.50
6 Griffin/Paul 1.00 2.50
7 Marc Gasol
Mike Conley .60 1.50
8 Dennis Schroder
Paul Millsap .60 1.50
9 Hassan Whiteside
Justise Winslow .50 1.25
10 Kemba Walker
Nicolas Batum .50 1.25
11 Gordon Hayward
Rodney Hood .60 1.50
12 Rudy Gay
DeMarcus Cousins .60 1.50
13 Rose/Anthony 1.00 2.50
14 Russell/Clarkson .75 2.00
15 Aaron Gordon
Elfrid Payton .60 1.50
16 Williams/Nowitzki 1.50 4.00
17 Jeremy Lin
Brook Lopez 1.25 3.00
18 Danilo Gallinari
Emmanuel Mudiay .50 1.25
19 Teague/George 1.00 2.50
20 Davis/Evans 2.00 5.00
21 Andre Drummond
Reggie Jackson .60 1.50
22 DeMar DeRozan
Kyle Lowry .75 2.00
23 Harden/Anderson 1.25 3.00
24 Leonard/Aldridge 1.50 4.00
25 Bledsoe/Booker 2.50 6.00
26 Westbrook/Adams 1.00 2.50
27 Towns/Wiggins 1.25 3.00
28 McCollum/Lillard 1.50 4.00
29 Curry/Durant 5.00 12.00
30 Beal/Wall .75 2.00

2016-17 Prestige True Colors Materials
STATED PRINT RUN 199 SER.#'d SETS
*PRIME/25: 1X TO 2.5X BASIC
1 Aaron Gordon 3.00 8.00
2 Al Horford 3.00 8.00
3 Allen Iverson 6.00 15.00
4 Manu Ginobili 6.00 15.00
5 Andrew Wiggins 4.00 10.00
6 Kevin Love 3.00 8.00
7 Bojan Bogdanovic 2.50 6.00
8 Bradley Beal 4.00 10.00
9 Brook Lopez 2.50 6.00
10 C.J. McCollum 3.00 8.00
11 Carmelo Anthony 5.00 12.00
12 Dan Issel 4.00 10.00
13 Danny Manning 2.50 6.00
14 DeAndre Jordan 2.50 6.00
15 Deron Williams 2.50 6.00
17 Gorgui Dieng 2.00 5.00
18 Grant Hill 4.00 10.00
19 Jamal Crawford 3.00 8.00
20 Jeff Teague 2.00 5.00
21 Jimmy Butler 6.00 15.00
22 Justise Winslow 2.50 6.00
23 Jusuf Nurkic 2.50 6.00
24 Karl Malone 5.00 12.00
25 Karl-Anthony Towns 6.00 15.00
26 Kawhi Leonard 8.00 20.00
27 Kyrie Irving 6.00 15.00
28 Stephen Curry 25.00 60.00
29 Klay Thompson 8.00 20.00
30 Kyle Lowry 3.00 8.00
31 Michael Kidd-Gilchrist 2.00 5.00

2017-18 Prestige
COMPLETE SET (200) 20.00 50.00
1 Ben Simmons .30 .75
2 Joel Embiid .60 1.50
3 JJ Redick .30 .75
4 Dario Saric .25 .60
5 Robert Covington .20 .50
6 Giannis Antetokounmpo 1.50 4.00
7 Malcolm Brogdon .25 .60
8 Khris Middleton .40 1.00
9 Thon Maker .20 .50
10 Matthew Dellavedova .25 .60
11 Kris Dunn .20 .50
12 Nikola Mirotic .20 .50
13 Justin Holiday .20 .50
14 Cameron Payne .20 .50
15 Robin Lopez .20 .50
16 LeBron James 2.50 6.00
17 Derrick Rose .50 1.25
18 Dwyane Wade .60 1.50
19 Jae Crowder .20 .50
20 Kevin Love .30 .75
21 Kyrie Irving .60 1.50
22 Gordon Hayward .25 .60
23 Al Horford .25 .60
24 Jaylen Brown .75 2.00
25 Marcus Smart .30 .75
26 Blake Griffin .30 .75
27 DeAndre Jordan .25 .60
28 Danilo Gallinari .25 .60
29 Patrick Beverley .20 .50
30 Lou Williams .20 .50
31 Marc Gasol .30 .75
32 Mike Conley .25 .60
33 Chandler Parsons .20 .50
34 Mario Chalmers .25 .60
35 JaMychal Green .20 .50
36 Dennis Schroder .25 .60
37 Kent Bazemore .20 .50
38 Taurean Prince .25 .60
39 DeAndre' Bembry .25 .60
40 Mike Muscala .20 .50
41 Hassan Whiteside .25 .60
42 Goran Dragic .25 .60
43 Dion Waiters .20 .50
44 James Johnson .20 .50
45 Justise Winslow .20 .50
46 Kemba Walker .30 .75
47 Dwight Howard .40 1.00
48 Michael Kidd-Gilchrist .20 .50
49 Marvin Williams .20 .50
50 Jeremy Lamb .20 .50
51 Rudy Gobert .40 1.00
52 Ricky Rubio .25 .60
53 Derrick Favors .20 .50
54 Rodney Hood .20 .50
55 Alec Burks .20 .50
56 Willie Cauley-Stein .20 .50
57 Skal Labissiere .20 .50
58 Vince Carter .60 1.50
59 Buddy Hield .30 .75
60 George Hill .25 .60
61 Kristaps Porzingis .40 1.00
62 Tim Hardaway Jr. .25 .60
63 Courtney Lee .20 .50
64 Michael Beasley .20 .50
65 Willy Hernangomez .25 .60
66 Brandon Ingram .40 1.00
67 Jordan Clarkson .30 .75
68 Kentavious Caldwell-Pope .25 .60
69 Julius Randle .30 .75
70 Brook Lopez .25 .60
71 Elfrid Payton .25 .60
72 Aaron Gordon .30 .75
73 Nikola Vucevic .20 .50
74 Evan Fournier .25 .60
75 Bismack Biyombo .20 .50
76 Dirk Nowitzki .75 2.00
77 Harrison Barnes .25 .60
78 Nerlens Noel .20 .50
79 Wesley Matthews .20 .50
80 J.J. Barea .25 .60
81 Jeremy Lin .50 1.25
82 D'Angelo Russell .25 .60
83 Sean Kilpatrick .20 .50
84 Caris LeVert .25 .60
85 Allen Crabbe .20 .50
86 Nikola Jokic 2.00 5.00
87 Jamal Murray .50 1.25
88 Paul Millsap .25 .60
89 Gary Harris .20 .50
90 Juan Hernangomez .30 .75
91 Lance Stephenson .25 .60
92 Myles Turner .30 .75
93 Victor Oladipo .25 .60
94 Thaddeus Young .20 .50
95 Darren Collison .20 .50
96 Anthony Davis .75 2.00
97 Jrue Holiday .40 1.00
98 DeMarcus Cousins .25 .60
99 Rajon Rondo .40 1.00
100 Solomon Hill .20 .50
101 Andre Drummond .25 .60
102 Reggie Jackson .25 .60
103 Avery Bradley .20 .50
104 Stanley Johnson .20 .50
105 Tobias Harris .25 .60
106 DeMar DeRozan .40 1.00
107 Kyle Lowry .30 .75
108 Jonas Valanciunas .25 .60
109 Serge Ibaka .25 .60
110 C.J. Miles 20.00 50.00
111 James Harden .60 1.50
112 Chris Paul .50 1.25
113 Ryan Anderson .20 .50
114 Eric Gordon .25 .60
115 Trevor Ariza .20 .50
116 Kawhi Leonard .75 2.00
117 Manu Ginobili .60 1.50
118 LaMarcus Aldridge .30 .75
119 Pau Gasol .50 1.25
120 Rudy Gay .25 .60
121 Devin Booker .75 2.00
122 Eric Bledsoe .25 .60
123 Marquese Chriss .20 .50
124 Tyler Ulis .20 .50
125 Alex Len .20 .50
126 Russell Westbrook .50 1.25
127 Paul George .50 1.25
128 Steven Adams .25 .60
129 Carmelo Anthony .50 1.25
130 Andre Roberson .20 .50
131 Karl-Anthony Towns .50 1.25
132 Andrew Wiggins .40 1.00
133 Jimmy Butler .50 1.25
134 Jamal Crawford .30 .75
135 Jeff Teague .20 .50
136 Damian Lillard .75 2.00
137 CJ McCollum .30 .75
138 Evan Turner .20 .50
139 Jusuf Nurkic .25 .60
140 Al-Farouq Aminu .20 .50
141 Stephen Curry 2.50 6.00
142 Kevin Durant 1.25 3.00
143 Klay Thompson .75 2.00
144 Andre Iguodala .30 .75
145 Draymond Green .40 1.00
146 John Wall .40 1.00
147 Bradley Beal .40 1.00
148 Marcin Gortat .20 .50
149 Otto Porter Jr. .25 .60
150 Markieff Morris .20 .50
151 Markelle Fultz RC 1.00 2.50
152 Lonzo Ball RC 1.50 4.00
153 Jayson Tatum RC 5.00 12.00
154 Josh Jackson RC 1.00 2.50
155 De'Aaron Fox RC 3.00 8.00
156 Jonathan Isaac RC 1.00 2.50
157 Lauri Markkanen RC 2.50 6.00
158 Frank Ntilikina RC .50 1.25
159 Dennis Smith Jr. RC .50 1.25
160 Zach Collins RC .60 1.50
161 Malik Monk RC 1.50 4.00
162 Luke Kennard RC .75 2.00
163 Donovan Mitchell RC 4.00 10.00
164 Bam Adebayo RC 2.50 6.00
165 Justin Jackson RC .40 1.00
166 Justin Patton RC .40 1.00
167 D.J. Wilson RC .40 1.00
168 TJ Leaf RC .40 1.00
169 John Collins RC 1.00 2.50
170 Harry Giles RC .40 1.00
171 Terrance Ferguson RC .40 1.00
172 Jarrett Allen RC 1.00 2.50
173 OG Anunoby RC 2.00 5.00
174 Tyler Lydon RC .40 1.00
175 Caleb Swanigan RC .40 1.00
176 Kyle Kuzma RC 1.50 4.00
177 Tony Bradley RC .40 1.00
178 Derrick White RC 1.50 4.00
179 Josh Hart RC 1.00 2.50
180 Frank Jackson RC .40 1.00
181 Davon Reed RC .40 1.00
182 Wes Iwundu RC .40 1.00
183 Frank Mason III RC .40 1.00
184 Ivan Rabb RC .40 1.00
185 Semi Ojeleye RC .50 1.25
186 Jawun Evans RC .40 1.00
187 Dwayne Bacon RC .40 1.00
188 Tyler Dorsey RC .40 1.00
189 Thomas Bryant RC .60 1.50
190 Jordan Bell RC .60 1.50
191 Damyean Dotson RC .50 1.25
192 Dillon Brooks RC 1.25 3.00
193 Sterling Brown RC .40 1.00
194 Ike Anigbogu RC .40 1.00
195 Milos Teodosic RC .50 1.25
196 Furkan Korkmaz RC .60 1.50
197 Guerschon Yabusele RC .40 1.00
198 Sindarius Thornwell RC .40 1.00
199 Wayne Selden RC .40 1.00
200 Zhou Qi RC .75 2.00

2017-18 Prestige Crystal
*CRYSTAL: 1.5X TO 4X BASIC
*CRYSTAL RC: 1.5X TO 4X BASIC RC
STATED PRINT RUN 199 SER.#'d SETS

2017-18 Prestige Horizon
*HORIZON: 1X TO 2.5X BASIC
*HORIZON RC: 1X TO 2.5X BASIC RC

2017-18 Prestige Mist
*MIST: 1X TO 2.5X BASIC
*MIST RC: 1X TO 2.5X BASIC RC

2017-18 Prestige Rain
*RAIN: 1X TO 2.5X BASIC
*RAIN RC: 1X TO 2.5X BASIC RC

2017-18 Prestige All Time Greats
*CRYSTAL: 1X TO 2.5X BASIC
*HORIZON: .6X TO 1.5X BASIC
*MIST: .6X TO 1.5X BASIC
*RAIN: .6X TO 1.5X BASIC
1 Kobe Bryant 4.00 10.00
2 Magic Johnson 2.00 5.00
3 Larry Bird 2.00 5.00
4 Julius Erving 1.25 3.00
5 Pete Maravich 1.25 3.00
6 Shaquille O'Neal 1.50 4.00
7 Scottie Pippen 1.25 3.00
8 Anfernee Hardaway 1.25 3.00
9 Grant Hill .75 2.00
10 Wilt Chamberlain 1.50 4.00
11 Kareem Abdul-Jabbar 1.50 4.00
12 Hakeem Olajuwon 1.00 2.50
13 David Robinson 1.00 2.50
14 Oscar Robertson 1.00 2.50
15 Karl Malone 1.00 2.50
16 John Stockton 1.00 2.50
17 Allen Iverson 1.25 3.00
18 Clyde Drexler .75 2.00
19 Reggie Miller 1.00 2.50
20 Bob Pettit .50 1.25

2017-18 Prestige Bonus Shots Signatures
EXCHANGE DEADLINE 8/21/2019
1 Ante Zizic 3.00 8.00
2 Guerschon Yabusele 2.50 6.00
3 Zhou Qi 10.00 25.00
4 Thomas Bryant 4.00 10.00
5 Ike Anigbogu 2.50 6.00
7 D.J. Augustin 2.50 6.00
8 Dwight Powell 2.50 6.00
9 De'Aaron Fox 25.00 60.00
10 Lonzo Ball 30.00 80.00
11 Zach Collins 4.00 10.00
12 Caleb Swanigan 2.50 6.00
13 Jayson Tatum 150.00 400.00
14 Devin Booker 125.00 300.00
15 Jonathan Isaac 6.00 15.00
16 Giannis Antetokounmpo 100.00 250.00
17 JJ Redick 4.00 10.00
18 Khris Middleton 5.00 12.00
19 Sterling Brown 2.50 6.00
20 Davon Reed 2.50 6.00
21 Mason Plumlee 2.50 6.00
22 Lauri Markkanen 15.00 40.00
24 Seth Curry 4.00 10.00
27 Manu Ginobili 20.00 50.00
28 Amir Johnson 2.50 6.00
29 Cameron Payne 2.50 6.00
30 Kelly Oubre Jr. 4.00 10.00
31 Mike Muscala 2.50 6.00
32 Wayne Selden 2.50 6.00
33 Treveon Graham 3.00 8.00
34 Ivica Zubac 3.00 8.00
35 Danny Green 3.00 8.00
37 Cody Zeller 2.50 6.00
38 Tomas Satoransky 3.00 8.00
39 Paul Zipser 2.50 6.00
40 Dennis Smith Jr. EXCH 3.00 8.00
41 Josh Jackson 3.00 8.00
42 Frank Ntilikina 3.00 8.00
43 Malik Monk 10.00 25.00
44 Luke Kennard 5.00 12.00
45 Donovan Mitchell 75.00 200.00
46 Bam Adebayo 15.00 40.00
47 Justin Jackson 2.50 6.00
49 D.J. Wilson 2.50 6.00
50 TJ Leaf 2.50 6.00
51 John Collins 6.00 15.00
52 Harry Giles 2.50 6.00
53 Jarrett Allen 12.00 30.00
55 Tyler Lydon 2.50 6.00
56 Kyle Kuzma 10.00 25.00
57 Tony Bradley 2.50 6.00
58 Derrick White 10.00 25.00
60 Frank Jackson 2.50 6.00
61 Wes Iwundu 2.50 6.00
62 Frank Mason III 2.50 6.00
63 Ivan Rabb 2.50 6.00
64 Semi Ojeleye 3.00 8.00
65 Jordan Bell 2.50 6.00
66 Jawun Evans 2.50 6.00
67 Dwayne Bacon 2.50 6.00
68 Tyler Dorsey 2.50 6.00
69 Johnathan Motley 2.50 6.00
70 Kobe Bryant 500.00 1,000.00
71 Kevin Durant EXCH 75.00 200.00
72 Kyrie Irving 40.00 100.00
74 Nikola Jokic 125.00 300.00
75 Yogi Ferrell 2.50 6.00
76 Mike Conley 3.00 8.00
77 Lou Williams 3.00 8.00
78 Chris McCullough 2.50 6.00
79 Dakari Johnson 2.50 6.00

2017-18 Prestige Bonus Shots Signatures Crystal
*CRYSTAL: .5X TO 1.2X BASIC
EXCHANGE DEADLINE 8/21/2019
6 Damyean Dotson 4.00 10.00
25 Robert Covington 3.00 8.00
26 Josh Richardson 4.00 10.00
36 Steven Adams 4.00 10.00
73 Jakob Poeltl 4.00 10.00

2017-18 Prestige Hardcourt Heroes
*CRYSTAL: 1X TO 2.5X BASIC
*HORIZON: .6X TO 1.5X BASIC
*MIST: .6X TO 1.5X BASIC
*RAIN: .6X TO 1.5X BASIC
1 Ben Simmons .50 1.25
2 Joel Embiid 1.00 2.50
3 Khris Middleton .60 1.50
4 Lauri Markkanen 2.00 5.00
5 Derrick Rose .75 2.00
6 Blake Griffin .50 1.25
7 Mike Conley .40 1.00
8 Dennis Schroder .40 1.00
9 Hassan Whiteside .40 1.00
10 Malik Monk 1.25 3.00
11 Donovan Mitchell 3.00 8.00
12 Buddy Hield .50 1.25
13 Kristaps Porzingis .60 1.50
14 Lonzo Ball 1.25 3.00
15 Harrison Barnes .40 1.00
16 D'Angelo Russell .40 1.00
17 Myles Turner .50 1.25
18 DeMarcus Cousins .40 1.00
19 Kyle Lowry .50 1.25
20 Chris Paul .75 2.00

2017-18 Prestige Highlight Reel
*CRYSTAL: 1X TO 2.5X BASIC
*HORIZON: .6X TO 1.5X BASIC
*MIST: .6X TO 1.5X BASIC
*RAIN: .6X TO 1.5X BASIC
1 Ben Simmons .50 1.25
2 DeMarcus Cousins .40 1.00
3 Lonzo Ball 1.25 3.00
4 LeBron James 4.00 10.00
5 Blake Griffin .50 1.25
6 Markelle Fultz .75 2.00
7 Jayson Tatum 4.00 10.00
8 Giannis Antetokounmpo 2.50 6.00
9 Dennis Smith Jr. .40 1.00
10 Donovan Mitchell 3.00 8.00

2017-18 Prestige Micro Etch Rookies
*RED: .4X TO 1X BASIC
*ORANGE: .5X TO 1.2X BASIC
*GREEN: .6X TO 1.5X BASIC
1 Markelle Fultz 1.25 3.00
2 Lonzo Ball 2.00 5.00
3 Jayson Tatum 6.00 15.00
4 Josh Jackson .60 1.50
5 De'Aaron Fox 4.00 10.00
6 Jonathan Isaac 1.25 3.00
7 Lauri Markkanen 3.00 8.00
8 Frank Ntilikina .60 1.50
9 Dennis Smith Jr. .60 1.50
10 Zach Collins .75 2.00
11 Malik Monk 2.00 5.00
12 Luke Kennard 1.00 2.50
13 Donovan Mitchell 5.00 12.00
14 Bam Adebayo 3.00 8.00
15 Justin Jackson .50 1.25
16 Justin Patton .50 1.25
17 D.J. Wilson .60 1.50
18 TJ Leaf .50 1.25
19 John Collins 1.25 3.00
20 Harry Giles .50 1.25
21 Terrance Ferguson .50 1.25
22 Jarrett Allen 1.25 3.00
23 OG Anunoby 2.50 6.00
24 Tyler Lydon .50 1.25
25 Caleb Swanigan .50 1.25
26 Kyle Kuzma 2.00 5.00
27 Tony Bradley .50 1.25
28 Derrick White 2.00 5.00
29 Josh Hart 1.25 3.00
30 Frank Jackson .50 1.25
31 Davon Reed .50 1.25
32 Wes Iwundu .50 1.25
33 Frank Mason III .50 1.25
34 Ivan Rabb .50 1.25
35 Semi Ojeleye .60 1.50
36 Jordan Bell .60 1.50
37 Jawun Evans .50 1.25
38 Dwayne Bacon .50 1.25
39 Tyler Dorsey .50 1.25
40 Thomas Bryant .75 2.00
41 Sindarius Thornwell .50 1.25
42 Damyean Dotson .60 1.50
43 Dillon Brooks 1.50 4.00
44 Sterling Brown .50 1.25
45 Bogdan Bogdanovic 1.25 3.00
46 Milos Teodosic .60 1.50
47 Wayne Selden .50 1.25
48 Guerschon Yabusele .50 1.25
49 Zhou Qi 1.00 2.50
50 Mike James .50 1.25

2017-18 Prestige Old School Signatures
EXCHANGE DEADLINE 8/21/2019
1 Magic Johnson 15.00 40.00
2 Mark Price 4.00 10.00
3 Tracy McGrady 10.00 25.00
4 Rod Strickland 3.00 8.00
5 David Thompson 5.00 12.00
6 Jerry Stackhouse 5.00 12.00
7 Gary Payton 6.00 15.00
9 Mark Aguirre 3.00 8.00
10 Glen Rice 3.00 8.00
11 Alex English 5.00 12.00
12 Detlef Schrempf 4.00 10.00
13 Jamal Mashburn 3.00 8.00
14 Chauncey Billups 6.00 15.00
16 Charles Oakley 3.00 8.00
17 Gail Goodrich 4.00 10.00
18 Tony Delk 2.50 6.00
19 Cedric Maxwell 3.00 8.00

2017-18 Prestige Old School Signatures Crystal
*CRYSTAL: .5X TO 1.2X BASIC
EXCHANGE DEADLINE 8/21/2019
8 Kenny Smith 4.00 10.00
15 Tim Hardaway 6.00 15.00

2017-18 Prestige Playmakers
1 Lonzo Ball 20.00 50.00
2 Ben Simmons 4.00 10.00
3 Markelle Fultz 6.00 15.00
4 Giannis Antetokounmpo 20.00 50.00
5 Kyrie Irving 8.00 20.00
6 Jayson Tatum 25.00 60.00
7 Kevin Durant 15.00 40.00
8 LeBron James 20.00 50.00
9 Kristaps Porzingis 5.00 12.00
10 Anthony Davis 10.00 25.00
11 Kawhi Leonard 10.00 25.00
12 De'Aaron Fox 20.00 50.00
13 Joel Embiid 8.00 20.00
14 Kobe Bryant 20.00 50.00
15 Dennis Smith Jr. 3.00 8.00
16 Shaquille O'Neal 12.00 30.00
17 Julius Erving 10.00 25.00
18 Magic Johnson 15.00 40.00
19 Larry Bird 15.00 40.00
20 James Harden 8.00 20.00
21 Russell Westbrook 6.00 15.00
22 Allen Iverson 12.00 30.00
23 Damian Lillard 10.00 25.00
24 Stephen Curry 20.00 50.00
25 Karl-Anthony Towns 6.00 15.00

2017-18 Prestige Prestigious Picks
1 Markelle Fultz 6.00 15.00
2 Lonzo Ball 25.00 60.00

3 Jayson Tatum 40.00 100.00
4 Josh Jackson 3.00 8.00
5 De'Aaron Fox 20.00 50.00
6 Jonathan Isaac 6.00 15.00
7 Lauri Markkanen 15.00 40.00
8 Frank Ntilikina 3.00 8.00
9 Dennis Smith Jr. 3.00 8.00
10 Zach Collins 4.00 10.00
11 Malik Monk 10.00 25.00
12 Luke Kennard 5.00 12.00
13 Donovan Mitchell 50.00 120.00
14 Bam Adebayo 15.00 40.00
15 Justin Jackson 2.50 6.00
16 Justin Patton 2.50 6.00
17 D.J. Wilson 2.50 6.00
18 TJ Leaf 2.50 6.00
19 John Collins 6.00 15.00
20 Harry Giles 2.50 6.00
21 Terrance Ferguson 2.50 6.00
22 Jarrett Allen 6.00 15.00
23 OG Anunoby 12.00 30.00
24 Tyler Lydon 2.50 6.00
25 Kyle Kuzma 10.00 25.00

2017-18 Prestige Rookie Class
*CRYSTAL: 1X TO 2.5X BASIC
*HORIZON: .6X TO 1.5X BASIC
*MIST: .6X TO 1.5X BASIC
*RAIN: .6X TO 1.5X BASIC
1 Markelle Fultz .75 2.00
2 Lonzo Ball 1.25 3.00
3 Jayson Tatum 4.00 10.00
4 Josh Jackson .40 1.00
5 De'Aaron Fox 2.50 6.00
6 Jonathan Isaac .75 2.00
7 Lauri Markkanen 2.00 5.00
8 Frank Ntilikina .40 1.00
9 Dennis Smith Jr. .40 1.00
10 Zach Collins .50 1.25
11 Malik Monk 1.25 3.00
12 Luke Kennard .60 1.50
13 Donovan Mitchell 3.00 8.00
14 Bam Adebayo 2.00 5.00
15 Justin Jackson .30 .75
16 Justin Patton .30 .75
17 D.J. Wilson .30 .75
18 TJ Leaf .30 .75
19 John Collins .75 2.00
20 Jarrett Allen .75 2.00
21 Milos Teodosic .40 1.00
22 Kyle Kuzma 1.25 3.00
23 OG Anunoby 1.50 4.00
24 Jordan Bell .30 .75
25 Guerschon Yabusele .30 .75

2017-18 Prestige Stars of the NBA
*CRYSTAL: 1X TO 2.5X BASIC
*HORIZON: .6X TO 1.5X BASIC
*MIST: .6X TO 1.5X BASIC
*RAIN: .6X TO 1.5X BASIC
1 Kyrie Irving 1.00 2.50
2 LeBron James 4.00 10.00
3 Russell Westbrook .75 2.00
4 James Harden 1.00 2.50
5 Kevin Durant 2.00 5.00
6 Stephen Curry 4.00 10.00
7 Karl-Anthony Towns .75 2.00
8 Jimmy Butler .75 2.00
9 Kawhi Leonard 1.25 3.00
10 Dirk Nowitzki 1.25 3.00
11 Dwyane Wade 1.00 2.50
12 Kemba Walker .40 1.00
13 John Wall .60 1.50
14 Damian Lillard 1.25 3.00
15 Gordon Hayward .40 1.00

2017-18 Prestige Stat Stars
*CRYSTAL: 1X TO 2.5X BASIC
*HORIZON: .6X TO 1.5X BASIC
*MIST: .6X TO 1.5X BASIC
*RAIN: .6X TO 1.5X BASIC
1 LeBron James 4.00 10.00
2 Giannis Antetokounmpo 2.50 6.00
3 Anthony Davis 1.25 3.00
4 DeMar DeRozan .60 1.50
5 James Harden 1.00 2.50
6 Russell Westbrook .75 2.00
7 Damian Lillard 1.25 3.00
8 John Wall .60 1.50
9 Stephen Curry 4.00 10.00
10 Kawhi Leonard 1.25 3.00

1980-81 Pride New Orleans WBL
COMPLETE SET (11) 50.00 100.00
1 Kathy Andrykowski 4.00 10.00
2 Sybil Blalock 4.00 10.00
3 Cindy Brogden 7.50 15.00
4 Vicky Chapman 4.00 10.00
5 Beverly Crusoe 4.00 10.00
6 Sharon Farrah 4.00 10.00
7 Eileen Feeney 4.00 10.00
8 Augusta Forest 4.00 10.00
9 Bertha Hardy 4.00 10.00
10 Sue Peters 4.00 10.00
11 Heidi Wayment 4.00 10.00

2008 Prime Cuts Playoff Contenders Autographs
OVERALL AU/MEM ODDS 4 PER BOX
EXCHANGE DEADLINE 6/26/2010
23 O.J. Mayo 30.00 60.00
24 Michael Beasley 15.00 40.00
25 Derrick Rose 150.00 300.00

1985 Prism/Jewel Stickers
COMPLETE SET (14) 6,000.00 12,000.00
1 Kareem Abdul-Jabbar 100.00 250.00
2 Larry Bird 200.00 500.00
3 Bird vs. Worthy 150.00 400.00
4 Julius Erving 100.00 250.00
5 Patrick Ewing 100.00 250.00
6 Magic Johnson 150.00 400.00
7 Michael Jordan 5,000.00 10,000.00
8 Moses Malone 75.00 200.00
9 Malone vs. Jabbar 75.00 200.00
10 Sidney Moncrief 75.00 200.00
11 Ralph Sampson 60.00 150.00
12 Isiah Thomas 75.00 200.00
13 Kelly Tripucka 40.00 100.00
14 Buck Williams 40.00 100.00

2024-25 Prizm Deca
1 Desmond Bane .40 1.00
2 Julius Randle .40 1.00
3 Tidjane Salaun RC .75 2.00
4 Dereck Lively II .40 1.00
5 Russell Westbrook .60 1.50
6 Jordan Clarkson .40 1.00
7 Anfernee Simons .40 1.00
8 Tari Eason .40 1.00
9 Isaiah Hartenstein .30 .75
10 Jamal Murray .60 1.50
11 Johnny Furphy RC 1.25 3.00
12 Tyler Herro .60 1.50
13 Shai Gilgeous-Alexander 2.00 5.00
14 GG Jackson II .40 1.00
15 Scoot Henderson .50 1.25
16 Cam Whitmore .40 1.00
17 Baylor Scheierman RC 1.00 2.50
18 Tyrese Haliburton .75 2.00
19 Paolo Banchero 1.00 2.50
20 Kyrie Irving 1.00 2.50
21 Jaylen Wells RC 2.50 6.00
22 Kevin Durant 1.25 3.00
23 Keldon Johnson .30 .75
24 Jared McCain RC 3.00 8.00
25 Nicolas Claxton .30 .75
26 Trae Young .75 2.00
27 Jalen Green .75 2.00
28 Reed Sheppard RC 2.50 6.00
29 P.J. Washington Jr. .30 .75
30 Darius Garland .50 1.25
31 Tyler Kolek RC 1.25 3.00
32 Jaime Jaquez Jr. .40 1.00
33 Rui Hachimura .40 1.00
34 Terrence Shannon Jr. RC 1.50 4.00
35 Tristan da Silva RC 2.00 5.00
36 Bilal Coulibaly .50 1.25
37 Andrew Wiggins .50 1.25
38 Victor Wembanyama 3.00 8.00
39 Anthony Davis 1.00 2.50
40 Devin Vassell .50 1.25
41 Devin Booker 1.00 2.50
42 Coby White .40 1.00
43 Mikal Bridges .40 1.00
44 Cam Spencer RC .75 2.00
45 Jalen Williams .75 2.00
46 Brook Lopez .30 .75
47 Terry Rozier III .30 .75
48 Bronny James Jr. RC 2.50 6.00
49 Gradey Dick .50 1.25
50 Malik Beasley .30 .75
51 Fred VanVleet .40 1.00
52 Devin Carter RC 1.00 2.50
53 Jonathan Mogbo RC 1.25 3.00
54 Ron Holland II RC 1.50 4.00
55 Ausar Thompson .60 1.50
56 Brandon Ingram .40 1.00
57 Michael Porter Jr. .40 1.00
58 Pacome Dadiet RC 1.00 2.50
59 Jaylen Brown .60 1.50
60 Donovan Clingan RC 2.00 5.00
61 Ben Simmons .40 1.00
62 Jaden Ivey .50 1.25
63 Zach Edey RC 2.50 6.00
64 Alexandre Sarr RC 2.50 6.00
65 Jordan Hawkins .30 .75
66 Luka Doncic 2.50 6.00
67 Nikola Jokic 2.00 5.00
68 Derrick White .40 1.00
69 Brandon Miller .60 1.50
70 Pelle Larsson RC 1.00 2.50
71 Matas Buzelis RC 4.00 10.00
72 Cody Williams RC 1.00 2.50
73 T.J. McConnell .30 .75
74 Ajay Mitchell RC 1.25 3.00
75 Dillon Jones RC .75 2.00
76 Zaccharie Risacher RC 2.50 6.00
77 Collin Sexton .40 1.00
78 Cam Christie RC 1.00 2.50
79 Kel'el Ware RC 2.00 5.00
80 Kyle Kuzma .30 .75
81 Kyshawn George RC 1.25 3.00
82 Kyle Filipowski RC 1.50 4.00
83 Jarrett Allen .30 .75
84 Bobi Klintman RC 1.00 2.50
85 RJ Barrett .50 1.25
86 Naz Reid .40 1.00
87 Dejounte Murray .40 1.00
88 Harrison Barnes .30 .75
89 Stephen Curry 3.00 8.00
90 Donte DiVincenzo .40 1.00
91 Cason Wallace .50 1.25
92 Bobby Portis .30 .75
93 Ivica Zubac .40 1.00
94 Lauri Markkanen .40 1.00
95 Zion Williamson 1.00 2.50
96 Jalen Johnson .50 1.25
97 De'Andre Hunter .40 1.00
98 Nikola Djurisic RC 1.00 2.50
99 Jusuf Nurkic .30 .75
100 Shaedon Sharpe .50 1.25
101 Jonathan Kuminga .50 1.25
102 Scottie Barnes .50 1.25
103 Myles Turner .30 .75
104 Jordan Poole .40 1.00
105 Yuki Kawamura RC 1.00 2.50
106 Zach LaVine .60 1.50
107 James Harden .75 2.00
108 Keegan Murray .30 .75
109 LaMelo Ball .75 2.00
110 Paul George .60 1.50
111 Keyonte George .50 1.25
112 Yongxi "Jacky" Cui RC 1.50 4.00
113 Josh Hart .30 .75
114 Alperen Sengun .60 1.50
115 Daniel Gafford .30 .75
116 Ja'Kobe Walter .50 1.25
117 Bennedict Mathurin .50 1.25
118 Jamal Shead RC 1.00 2.50
119 Jalen Brunson .75 2.00
120 Marcus Smart .40 1.00
121 Dennis Schroder .40 1.00
122 Dalton Knecht RC 2.50 6.00
123 Josh Giddey .50 1.25
124 Giannis Antetokounmpo 1.50 4.00
125 Jeremy Sochan .40 1.00
126 Kawhi Leonard .75 2.00
127 Franz Wagner .60 1.50
128 Rudy Gobert .40 1.00
129 Nikola Topic RC 2.50 6.00
130 Jaren Jackson Jr. .60 1.50
131 Kristaps Porzingis .50 1.25
132 Chet Holmgren .60 1.50
133 Jayson Tatum 1.25 3.00
134 Bradley Beal .50 1.25
135 Austin Reaves .50 1.25
136 Miles Bridges .30 .75
137 CJ McCollum .30 .75
138 Ja Morant 1.25 3.00
139 KJ Simpson Jr. RC .75 2.00
140 Jalen Duren .40 1.00
141 Nikola Vucevic .40 1.00
142 Aaron Gordon .40 1.00
143 De'Aaron Fox .75 2.00
144 Yves Missi RC 2.00 5.00
145 Bub Carrington RC 2.00 5.00
146 Cole Anthony .40 1.00
147 Khris Middleton .40 1.00
148 Evan Mobley .60 1.50
149 Immanuel Quickley .30 .75
150 D'Angelo Russell .30 .75
151 Jaylon Tyson RC .75 2.00
152 Harrison Ingram RC .75 2.00
153 Alex Caruso .40 1.00
154 AJ Johnson RC 1.50 4.00
155 Tristen Newton RC .75 2.00
156 Jalen Suggs .40 1.00
157 Kyle Lowry .40 1.00
158 Donovan Mitchell .75 2.00
159 Trey Murphy III .50 1.25
160 Tre Mann .30 .75
161 Draymond Green .50 1.25
162 John Collins .30 .75
163 Brandin Podziemski .50 1.25
164 Bam Adebayo .50 1.25
165 Antonio Reeves RC .75 2.00
166 Karl-Anthony Towns .60 1.50
167 Derrick Jones Jr. .25 .60
168 Jabari Smith Jr. .40 1.00
169 Mark Williams .30 .75
170 Adem Bona RC 1.00 2.50
171 DeMar DeRozan .50 1.25
172 Gary Trent Jr. .30 .75
173 Cameron Johnson .30 .75
174 Stephon Castle RC 5.00 12.00
175 Domantas Sabonis .60 1.50
176 Jrue Holiday .50 1.25
177 Jimmy Butler III .60 1.50
178 Damian Lillard 1.00 2.50
179 Cameron Thomas .40 1.00
180 Amen Thompson 1.00 2.50
181 OG Anunoby .30 .75
182 Malaki Branham .30 .75
183 Guerschon Yabusele .30 .75
184 Robert Williams III .30 .75
185 Bogdan Bogdanovic .30 .75
186 Isaiah Collier RC 1.50 4.00
187 Pascal Siakam .50 1.25
188 Klay Thompson 1.00 2.50
189 Ryan Dunn RC 1.00 2.50
190 Kevin McCullar Jr. RC .75 2.00
191 Tyler Smith RC 1.00 2.50
192 Deandre Ayton .30 .75
193 Tyrese Maxey .75 2.00
194 Anthony Edwards 2.00 5.00
195 Rob Dillingham RC 2.00 5.00
196 Joel Embiid .60 1.50
197 Cade Cunningham 1.00 2.50
198 LeBron James 3.00 8.00
199 Chris Paul .60 1.50
200 Oso Ighodaro RC 1.00 2.50
201 Julius Erving LEG 1.00 2.50
202 Tim Duncan LEG 1.00 2.50
203 Larry Bird LEG 1.25 3.00
204 Magic Johnson LEG 1.25 3.00
205 Steve Nash LEG .75 2.00
206 Yao Ming LEG .75 2.00
207 Karl Malone LEG .75 2.00
208 Hakeem Olajuwon LEG .75 2.00
209 Patrick Ewing LEG .60 1.50
210 Ray Allen LEG .60 1.50
211 Dirk Nowitzki LEG 1.00 2.50
212 Tony Parker LEG .60 1.50
213 Steve Kerr LEG .50 1.25
214 David Robinson LEG .75 2.00
215 John Stockton LEG .75 2.00
216 Pau Gasol LEG .60 1.50
217 Dwyane Wade LEG .75 2.00
218 Isiah Thomas LEG .60 1.50
219 Dominique Wilkins LEG .60 1.50
220 Dennis Rodman LEG 1.00 2.50
221 Kareem Abdul-Jabbar LEG 1.25 3.00
222 Shaquille O'Neal LEG 1.00 2.50
223 Vince Carter LEG .75 2.00
224 Clyde Drexler LEG .60 1.50
225 Carmelo Anthony LEG .60 1.50
226 Pete Maravich LEG 1.00 2.50
227 Allen Iverson LEG 1.00 2.50
228 Charles Barkley LEG 1.00 2.50
229 Kevin Garnett LEG 1.00 2.50
230 Tracy McGrady LEG .75 2.00
231 Derrick Rose LEG .75 2.00
232 Gary Payton LEG .60 1.50
233 Brandon Roy LEG .60 1.50
234 Gilbert Arenas LEG .40 1.00
235 Paul Pierce LEG .60 1.50
236 Manu Ginobili LEG .60 1.50
237 Alonzo Mourning LEG .60 1.50
238 Jason Kidd LEG .60 1.50
239 Chris Bosh LEG .50 1.25
240 Anfernee Hardaway LEG .60 1.50
241 Bam Adebayo AS .50 1.25
242 Luka Doncic AS 2.50 6.00
243 Giannis Antetokounmpo AS 1.50 4.00
244 Kevin Durant AS 1.25 3.00
245 Tyrese Haliburton AS .75 2.00
246 Shai Gilgeous-Alexander AS 2.00 5.00
247 Damian Lillard AS 1.00 2.50
248 LeBron James AS 3.00 8.00
249 Jayson Tatum AS 1.25 3.00
250 Nikola Jokic AS 2.00 5.00
251 Paolo Banchero AS 1.00 2.50
252 Devin Booker AS 1.00 2.50
253 Scottie Barnes AS .50 1.25
254 Stephen Curry AS 3.00 8.00
255 Jaylen Brown AS .60 1.50
256 Anthony Davis AS 1.00 2.50
257 Jalen Brunson AS .75 2.00
258 Anthony Edwards AS 2.00 5.00
259 Tyrese Maxey AS .75 2.00
260 Paul George AS .60 1.50
261 Donovan Mitchell AS .75 2.00
262 Kawhi Leonard AS .75 2.00
263 Karl-Anthony Towns AS .60 1.50
264 Trae Young AS .75 2.00
265 Joel Embiid AS .60 1.50
266 Julius Randle AS .40 1.00
267 Domantas Sabonis AS .60 1.50
268 Ja Morant AS 1.25 3.00
269 Kyrie Irving AS 1.00 2.50
270 De'Aaron Fox AS .75 2.00
271 Giannis Antetokounmpo ANBA 1.50 4.00
272 Luka Doncic ANBA 2.50 6.00
273 Shai Gilgeous-Alexander ANBA 2.00 5.00
274 Nikola Jokic ANBA 2.00 5.00
275 Jayson Tatum ANBA 1.25 3.00
276 Chet Holmgren ANBA .60 1.50
277 Victor Wembanyama ANBA 3.00 8.00
278 Brandon Miller ANBA .60 1.50
279 Jaime Jaquez Jr. ANBA .40 1.00
280 Brandin Podziemski ANBA .50 1.25
281 Bam Adebayo ANBA .50 1.25
282 Anthony Davis ANBA 1.00 2.50
283 Rudy Gobert ANBA .40 1.00
284 Herbert Jones ANBA .30 .75
285 Victor Wembanyama ANBA 3.00 8.00
286 LeBron James MVP 5.00 12.00
287 Stephen Curry MVP 5.00 12.00
288 Kevin Durant MVP 2.00 5.00
289 LeBron James MVP 5.00 12.00
290 Giannis Antetokounmpo MVP 2.50 6.00
291 Jaylen Brown MVP 1.00 2.50
292 Kawhi Leonard MVP 1.25 3.00
293 Nikola Jokic MVP 3.00 8.00
294 LeBron James MVP 5.00 12.00
295 Shaquille O'Neal MVP 1.50 4.00
296 Larry Bird MVP 2.00 5.00
297 Hakeem Olajuwon MVP 1.25 3.00
298 Dirk Nowitzki MVP 1.50 4.00
299 Dwyane Wade MVP 1.25 3.00
300 Tim Duncan MVP 1.50 4.00

2024-25 Prizm Deca Prizms Blue
*BLUE: 3X TO 8X BASIC
STATED PRINT RUN 149 SER. #'D SETS
174 Stephon Castle 60.00 150.00

2024-25 Prizm Deca Prizms Mojo
*MOJO: 10X TO 25X BASIC
STATED PRINT RUN 25 SER. #'D SETS
174 Stephon Castle 200.00 500.00

2024-25 Prizm Deca Prizms Orange
*ORANGE: 5X TO 12X BASIC
STATED PRINT RUN 49 SER. #'D SETS
174 Stephon Castle 100.00 250.00

2024-25 Prizm Deca Prizms Purple
*PURPLE: 3X TO 8X BASIC
STATED PRINT RUN 99 SER. #'D SETS
174 Stephon Castle 60.00 150.00

2024-25 Prizm Deca Prizms Red
*RED: 3X TO 8X BASIC
STATED PRINT RUN 199 SER. #'D SETS
174 Stephon Castle 60.00 150.00

2024-25 Prizm Deca Prizms Silver
*SILVER: 1.5X TO 4X BASIC
174 Stephon Castle 30.00 80.00

2024-25 Prizm Deca Brilliance
*SILVER: 1X TO 2.5X BASIC
*MOJO/25: 10X TO 25X BASIC
1 Kevin Durant 1.25 3.00
2 Luka Doncic 2.50 6.00
3 Trae Young .75 2.00
4 Stephen Curry 3.00 8.00
5 Damian Lillard 1.00 2.50
6 Giannis Antetokounmpo 1.50 4.00
7 Nikola Jokic 2.00 5.00
8 Shai Gilgeous-Alexander 2.00 5.00
9 Jayson Tatum 1.25 3.00
10 Ja Morant 1.25 3.00
11 Reed Sheppard 1.25 3.00
12 Bronny James Jr. 1.25 3.00
13 Zaccharie Risacher 1.25 3.00
14 Donovan Clingan 1.00 2.50
15 Anthony Edwards 2.00 5.00
16 LeBron James 3.00 8.00
17 Victor Wembanyama 3.00 8.00
18 Matas Buzelis 4.00 10.00
19 De'Aaron Fox .75 2.00
20 Ron Holland II .75 2.00

2024-25 Prizm Deca Downtown Bound
*SILVER: 1X TO 2.5X BASIC
*MOJO/25: 10X TO 25X BASIC
1 Shai Gilgeous-Alexander 2.00 5.00
2 Anthony Edwards 2.00 5.00
3 Kevin Durant 1.25 3.00
4 Stephen Curry 3.00 8.00
5 Luka Doncic 2.50 6.00
6 Paul George .60 1.50
7 James Harden .75 2.00
8 Jayson Tatum 1.25 3.00
9 Ja Morant 1.25 3.00
10 LeBron James 3.00 8.00
11 Trae Young .75 2.00
12 Devin Booker 1.00 2.50
13 Kyrie Irving 1.00 2.50
14 Damian Lillard 1.00 2.50
15 Reed Sheppard 1.00 2.50
16 Stephon Castle 4.00 10.00
17 Dalton Knecht 1.25 3.00
18 Zaccharie Risacher 1.25 3.00
19 Rob Dillingham 1.00 2.50
20 Larry Bird 1.25 3.00
21 Dirk Nowitzki 1.00 2.50
22 Ray Allen .60 1.50
23 Vince Carter .75 2.00
24 Jared McCain 1.50 4.00
25 Carmelo Anthony .60 1.50

2024-25 Prizm Deca Explosion
*SILVER: 1X TO 2.5X BASIC
*MOJO/25: 10X TO 25X BASIC
1 Dalton Knecht 1.25 3.00
2 Donovan Mitchell .75 2.00
3 Rob Dillingham 1.00 2.50
4 Trae Young .75 2.00
5 Ja Morant 1.25 3.00
6 Shai Gilgeous-Alexander 2.00 5.00
7 Victor Wembanyama 3.00 8.00
8 Zion Williamson 1.00 2.50
9 Luka Doncic 2.50 6.00
10 LeBron James 3.00 8.00
11 Stephen Curry 3.00 8.00
12 Paolo Banchero 1.00 2.50
13 Giannis Antetokounmpo 1.50 4.00
14 Damian Lillard 1.00 2.50
15 Tidjane Salaun .40 1.00
16 Jayson Tatum 1.25 3.00
17 Cody Williams .50 1.25
18 Nikola Jokic 2.00 5.00
19 Alexandre Sarr 1.25 3.00
20 Zaccharie Risacher 1.25 3.00
21 Kevin Durant 1.25 3.00
22 Anthony Edwards 2.00 5.00
23 Reed Sheppard 1.25 3.00
24 Jalen Brunson .75 2.00
25 Stephon Castle 4.00 10.00

2024-25 Prizm Deca Finalists
*SILVER: 1X TO 2.5X BASIC
*MOJO/25: 10X TO 25X BASIC
1 Stephen Curry 3.00 8.00
2 LeBron James 3.00 8.00
3 Giannis Antetokounmpo 1.50 4.00
4 Nikola Jokic 2.00 5.00
5 Kawhi Leonard .75 2.00
6 Anthony Davis 1.00 2.50
7 Kevin Durant 1.25 3.00
8 Kyrie Irving 1.00 2.50
9 Jayson Tatum 1.25 3.00
10 Jaylen Brown .60 1.50
11 Kevin Garnett 1.00 2.50
12 David Robinson .75 2.00
13 Hakeem Olajuwon .75 2.00
14 Dennis Rodman 1.00 2.50
15 Julius Erving 1.00 2.50
16 Tim Duncan 1.00 2.50
17 Dirk Nowitzki 1.00 2.50
18 Magic Johnson 1.25 3.00
19 Shaquille O'Neal 1.00 2.50
20 Larry Bird 1.25 3.00

2024-25 Prizm Deca Signatures
*SILVER: .5X TO 1.2X BASIC
*RED/75-99: .5X TO 1.2X BASIC
*RED/30-49: .6X TO 1.5X BASIC
*RED/15: .75X TO 2X BASIC
*PURPLE/75: .5X TO 1.2X BASIC
*PURPLE/35-49: .6X TO 1.5X BASIC
*BLUE/35-49: .6X TO 1.5X BASIC
*BLUE/15: .75X TO 2X BASIC
*MOJO/25: .75X TO 2X BASIC
*GREEN SHMR FOTL/15-25: .75X TO 2X BASIC
1 Stephen Curry 400.00 800.00
2 Zion Williamson 30.00 80.00
3 Luka Doncic 400.00 800.00
4 Kevin Durant 60.00 150.00
5 Chet Holmgren 25.00 60.00
6 Cade Cunningham 40.00 100.00
7 Paolo Banchero 50.00 120.00
8 Amen Thompson 40.00 100.00
10 Ausar Thompson 10.00 25.00
11 Giannis Antetokounmpo 100.00 250.00
13 Ja Morant 75.00 200.00
14 Trae Young 40.00 100.00
15 Damian Lillard 40.00 100.00
16 Jayson Tatum 100.00 250.00
17 Jabari Smith Jr. 6.00 15.00
20 Jaden Ivey 6.00 15.00
21 Jaden Hardy 6.00 15.00
22 Jalen Duren 6.00 15.00
24 Lauri Markkanen 6.00 15.00
25 Cason Wallace 8.00 20.00
26 Jonathan Kuminga 8.00 20.00
27 Deandre Ayton 5.00 12.00
28 Andrew Wiggins 8.00 20.00
29 Shaedon Sharpe 8.00 20.00
30 Tyler Herro 10.00 25.00
31 Jeremy Sochan 6.00 15.00
32 Mark Williams 5.00 12.00
33 Trey Murphy III 8.00 20.00
34 Jake LaRavia 5.00 12.00
35 Andrew Nembhard 5.00 12.00
36 Matas Buzelis 40.00 100.00
37 Reed Sheppard 40.00 100.00
38 Donovan Clingan 15.00 40.00
39 Ja'Kobe Walter 8.00 20.00
40 Jared McCain 25.00 60.00
41 Tidjane Salaun 6.00 15.00
42 Bub Carrington 15.00 40.00
43 Dalton Knecht 20.00 50.00
44 Bobi Klintman 8.00 20.00
45 Devin Carter 8.00 20.00
46 Yves Missi 15.00 40.00
47 Kyshawn George 10.00 25.00
48 Tristan da Silva 15.00 40.00
49 Johnny Furphy 8.00 20.00
50 Jaylon Tyson 6.00 15.00
51 AJ Johnson 12.00 30.00
52 Adem Bona 8.00 20.00
53 Pacome Dadiet 8.00 20.00
54 Tyler Kolek 10.00 25.00
55 DaRon Holmes II 8.00 20.00
56 Terrence Shannon Jr. 20.00 50.00
57 Oso Ighodaro 8.00 20.00
58 Dillon Jones 6.00 15.00
59 Baylor Scheierman 8.00 20.00
60 Ajay Mitchell 10.00 25.00
61 Zach Edey 20.00 50.00
62 Jaylen Wells 20.00 50.00
63 Nikola Djurisic 8.00 20.00
64 Harrison Ingram 6.00 15.00
66 Anton Watson 5.00 12.00
67 Antonio Reeves 6.00 15.00
69 Kevin McCullar Jr. 6.00 15.00
70 Cam Christie 8.00 20.00
71 Quinten Post 12.00 30.00
72 Tristen Newton 6.00 15.00
73 Cam Spencer 6.00 15.00
74 Pelle Larsson 8.00 20.00
75 Jamal Shead 8.00 20.00
76 Derrick Rose 100.00 250.00
77 Dwyane Wade 20.00 50.00
78 Dirk Nowitzki 60.00 150.00
79 Allen Iverson 40.00 100.00
80 Kevin Garnett 40.00 100.00
81 Carmelo Anthony 40.00 100.00
82 Kareem Abdul-Jabbar 40.00 100.00
83 Yao Ming 40.00 100.00
84 Larry Bird 40.00 100.00
85 Tracy McGrady 20.00 50.00
86 Ray Allen 20.00 50.00
87 Manu Ginobili 20.00 50.00
88 Magic Johnson 40.00 100.00
89 Grant Hill 12.00 30.00
90 Hakeem Olajuwon 20.00 50.00
91 Clyde Drexler 12.00 30.00
92 Tony Parker 12.00 30.00
93 Brandon Roy 12.00 30.00
94 Anfernee Hardaway 20.00 50.00
95 Gilbert Arenas 6.00 15.00
96 Doc Rivers 6.00 15.00
97 DeMarcus Cousins 5.00 12.00
98 Jermaine O'Neal 5.00 12.00
99 Dominique Wilkins 10.00 25.00
100 Shawn Kemp 10.00 25.00

2024-25 Prizm Deca Superstars
*SILVER: 1X TO 2.5X BASIC
*MOJO/25: 10X TO 25X BASIC
1 Anthony Edwards 2.00 5.00
2 Ja Morant 1.25 3.00
3 Luka Doncic 2.50 6.00
4 Stephen Curry 3.00 8.00
5 Victor Wembanyama 3.00 8.00
6 LeBron James 3.00 8.00
7 Nikola Jokic 2.00 5.00
8 Shai Gilgeous-Alexander 2.00 5.00
9 Jayson Tatum 1.25 3.00
10 Giannis Antetokounmpo 1.50 4.00

1989-90 ProCards CBA
COMPLETE SET (207) 50.00 120.00
1 Sioux Falls Checklist .30 .75
2 Ben Wilson .30 .75
3 Leonard Harris .40 1.00
4 Laurent Crawford .30 .75
5 Steve Grayer .50 1.25
6 Jim Lampley .30 .75
7 Eric Brown .30 .75
8 Dennis Nutt .50 1.25
9 Ralph Lewis .30 .75
10 Lashun McDaniel .30 .75
11 Leo Parent .30 .75
12 Ron Ekker .30 .75
13 Terry Gould .30 .75
14 Wichita Falls CL .30 .75
15 Mark Peterson .30 .75
16 Greg Van Soelen .30 .75
17 Maurice Selvin .30 .75
18 Michael Tait .40 1.00
19 Deon Hunter .40 1.00
20 Randy Henry .30 .75
21 Kenny McClary .40 1.00
22 Earl Walker .30 .75
23 Jeff Hodge .30 .75
24 Martin Nessley .50 1.25
25 On Court Staff .30 .75
26 Rapid City Checklist .30 .75
27 Daren Queenan .40 1.00
28 Carey Scurry .30 .75
29 Keith Smart 1.25 3.00
30 Jim Thomas .50 1.25
31 Pearl Washington .75 2.00
32 Chris Childs 2.00 5.00
33 Jarvis Basnight .50 1.25
34 Dwight Boyd .30 .75
35 Raymond Brown .40 1.00
36 Sylvester Gray .40 1.00
37 Eric Musselman CO 1.25 3.00
38 Quad City Checklist .30 .75
39 Kenny Gattison 1.25 3.00
40 Lafester Rhodes .30 .75
41 Perry Young .40 1.00
42 Wiley Brown .40 1.00
43 Jose Slaughter .75 2.00
44 Gerald Greene .40 1.00
45 Lloyd Daniels 1.50 4.00
46 Bill Jones .30 .75
47 Sean Couch .30 .75
48 Marty Eggleston .40 1.00
49 Mauro Panaggio CO .40 1.00
50 Dan Panaggio CO .30 .75
51 Pensacola Checklist .30 .75
52 Joe Mullaney CO 1.00 2.50
53 Mark Wade .30 .75
54 Larry Houzer .30 .75
55 Clifford Lett .30 .75
56 Tony Dawson .40 1.00
57 Johnathan Edwards .30 .75
58 Jim Farmer .60 1.50
59 Dwayne Taylor .30 .75
60 Bob McCann .40 1.00
61 Omaha Checklist .30 .75
62 Silks Rodie .30 .75
63 Racers Front Office .30 .75
64 Rodie-Team Mascot .30 .75
65 Tim Price .30 .75
66 Barry Glanzer .30 .75
67 Greg Wiltjer .40 1.00
68 Ron Kellogg .30 .75
69 Tat Hunter .30 .75
70 Reginald Turner .30 .75
71 Jerry Adams .30 .75
72 Roland Gray .30 .75
73 Tim Legler 1.25 3.00
74 Corey Gaines .60 1.50
75 Columbus Checklist .30 .75
76 Gary Youmans .30 .75
77 Kelvin Ramsey .75 2.00
78 Chip Engelland 1.50 4.00
79 Brian Martin .30 .75
80 Ray Hall .30 .75
81 Jay Burson .40 1.00
82 Bill Martin .60 1.50
83 Eric Mudd .30 .75
84 Tom Schafer .30 .75
85 Steve Harris .40 1.00
86 Eric Newsome .30 .75
87 Rockford Checklist .30 .75
88 Charley Rosen 1.50 4.00
89 Tom Hart .30 .75
90 Team Picture .30 .75
91 Brent Carmichael .30 .75
92 Fred Cofield .40 1.00
93 Darren Guest .30 .75
94 Bobby Parks .30 .75
95 Elston Turner .60 1.50
96 Adrian McKinnon .30 .75
97 Gary Massey .30 .75
98 Tim Dillon .40 1.00
99 Herb Blunt .30 .75
100 Greg Grissom .30 .75
101 Albany Checklist .30 .75
102 Leroy Witherspoon .30 .75
103 Vincent Askew 2.00 5.00
104 Clinton Smith .30 .75
105 Andre Patterson .40 1.00
106 Jim Ferrer .30 .75
107 Willie Glass .60 1.50
108 Darryl Joe .30 .75
109 Mario Elie 2.50 6.00
110 Dave Popson .75 2.00
111 Danny Pearson .30 .75
112 Doc Nunnally .30 .75
113 Gene Espeland .30 .75
114 Gerald Oliver CO .30 .75
115 Santa Barbara CL .30 .75
116 Luther Burks .40 1.00
117 Brian Christensen .30 .75
118 Kevin Francewar .30 .75
119 Leon Wood 1.25 3.00
120 Derrick Gervin .75 2.00
121 Larry Spriggs .75 2.00
122 Michael Phelps .40 1.00
123 Mike Ratliff .30 .75
124 Steffond Johnson .40 1.00
125 Mitch McMullen .30 .75
126 Sonny Allen .30 .75
127 Don Ford .60 1.50
128 Grand Rapids CL .30 .75
129 Lorenzo Sutton .30 .75
130 Willie Simmons .40 1.00
131 Kenny Fields .40 1.00
132 Winston Crite .30 .75
133 Eric McLaughlin .30 .75
134 Tony Brown .40 1.00
135 Ricky Wilson .40 1.00
136 Milt Newton .40 1.00
137 Albert Springs .30 .75
138 Herbert Crook .40 1.00
139 Mike Mashak ACO .30 .75
140 Jim Sleeper .30 .75
141 Tulsa Checklist .30 .75
142 Terry Faggins .30 .75
143 Ozell Jones .40 1.00
144 Brian Rahilly .30 .75
145 Duane Washington .60 1.50
146 Ron Spivey .30 .75
147 Henry Bibby CO .60 1.50
148 Al Gipson .40 1.00
149 Greg Jones .30 .75
150 Andre Moore .60 1.50
151 Tracy Moore .60 1.50
152 Steve Bontrager .30 .75
153 Bubby Breaker Mascot .30 .75
154 LaCrosse Checklist .30 .75
155 Mike Williams .30 .75
156 Vince Hamilton .40 1.00
157 John Harris .30 .75
158 Tony White .30 .75
159 Todd Alexander .30 .75
160 Richard Johnson .30 .75
161 Leo Rautins 1.00 2.50
162 Dwayne McClain 1.00 2.50
163 Carlos Clark 1.00 2.50
164 Vada Martin .30 .75
165 Flip Saunders 1.50 4.00
166 Topeka Checklist .30 .75
167 Cedric Hunter .30 .75
168 Elfrem Jackson .30 .75
169 Glen Clem .30 .75
170 Mike Richmond .30 .75
171 Jim Rowinski .30 .75
172 Craig Jackson .30 .75
173 Tony Mack .30 .75
174 Hubert Henderson .30 .75
175 Kevin Nixon .30 .75
176 Haywoode Workman 1.25 3.00
177 Porter Cutrell .30 .75
178 Mike Riley .30 .75
179 Cedar Rapids CL .30 .75
180 Bullet Bear .30 .75
181 George Whittaker .30 .75
182 Tom Domako .30 .75
183 Al Lorenzen .30 .75
184 Darryl Johnson .40 1.00
185 Mel Braxton .30 .75
186 Orlando Graham .30 .75
187 Reggie Owens .30 .75
188 John Starks 6.00 15.00
189 Kenny Drummond .30 .75
190 Mark Plansky .30 .75
191 Anthony Blakley .40 1.00
192 Everette Stephens .75 2.00
193 San Jose Checklist .30 .75
194 Cory Russell .30 .75
195 Jim Ellis .30 .75
196 Butch Hays .60 1.50
197 Mike Doktorczyk .30 .75
198 Scooter Barry 1.50 4.00
199 Monroe Douglass .30 .75
200 Scott Fisher .40 1.00
201 David Boone .30 .75
202 Jervis Cole .30 .75
203 Freddie Banks .30 .75
204 Richard Morton .30 .75
205 Dan Williams .30 .75
206 Mike Thibault CO .30 .75
207 Omaha Coaches
Omaha Racers .30 .75

1990-91 ProCards CBA
COMPLETE SET (203) 40.00 100.00
1 Jim Les .75 2.00
2 Ron Moore .25 .60
3 Rod Mason .25 .60
4 Paul Weakly .25 .60

5 Brian Howard .40 1.00
6 Pat Bolden .25 .60
7 Mike Thibault CO .30 .75
8 Tim Legler 1.00 2.50
9 Cedric Hunter .30 .75
10 Mark Peterson .25 .60
11 Greg Wiltjer .40 1.00
12 The Idelman's .25 .60
13 The Silks and Rodie .25 .60
14 Basketball Staff .25 .60
15 Front Office Staff .25 .60
16 Omaha Checklist .25 .60
17 Calvin Duncan .25 .60
18 Pat Durham .40 1.00
19 Steve Grayer .40 1.00
20 Roy Marble .60 1.50
21 Tony Martin .30 .75
22 Shawn McDaniel .25 .60
23 Peter Thibeaux .25 .60
24 Clarence Thompson .25 .60
25 Demone Webster .25 .60
26 A.J. Wynder .40 1.00
27 Steve Kahl .25 .60
28 Steve Bontranger .25 .60
29 Cedar Rapids CL .25 .60
30 Skeeter Henry .40 1.00
31 Eugene McDowell .25 .60
32 Bruce Wheatley .25 .60
33 Mark Wade .30 .75
34 Cheyenne Gibson .25 .60
35 Clifford Lett .30 .75
36 Larry Houzer .25 .60
37 Tony Dawson .25 .60
38 Richard Hollis .30 .75
39 Ed Leonard and
Joe Corona .25 .60
40 Front Office Staff .25 .60
41 Torry the Tornado .25 .60
42 Fred Bryan .25 .60
43 Jim Goodman .25 .60
44 Pensacola Checklist .25 .60
45 Joe Fredrick .25 .60
46 Everette Stephens .60 1.50
47 Mario Donaldson .25 .60
48 Dan Godfread .25 .60
49 Haakon Austefjord .25 .60
50 Gary Massey .25 .60
51 Chris Childs 1.25 3.00
52 Gerry Wright .25 .60
53 Marty Conlon 1.00 2.50
54 Tony Costner .25 .60
55 Steve Hayes CO .50 1.25
56 Tom Hart .25 .60
57 Paul Kulick .25 .60
58 Rockford Team Photo .25 .60
59 Rockford Checklist .25 .60
60 Mike Williams .25 .60
61 Brian Rahilly .25 .60
62 Bill Martin .40 1.00
63 Vince Hamilton .30 .75
64 Dwayne McClain .75 2.00
65 Bart Kofoed .40 1.00
66 Dominic Pressley .30 .75
67 Herb Dixon .25 .60
68 Todd Mitchell .30 .75
69 Ben Mitchell .25 .60
70 Flip Saunders 1.25 3.00
71 LaCrosse Checklist .25 .60
72 Keith Smart 1.00 2.50
73 Stevie Thompson .75 2.00
74 Brian Rowsom .40 1.00
75 Tony Martin .30 .75
76 Joe Ward .25 .60
77 Fennis Dembo .40 1.00
78 Glenn Puddy .25 .60
79 Lanard Copeland .60 1.50
80 Carl Brown .25 .60
81 Rapid City Checklist .25 .60
82 Dennis Nutt .40 1.00
83 Leonard Harris .30 .75
84 Tharon Mayes .30 .75
85 Melvin McCants .40 1.00
86 Tracy Mitchell .30 .75
87 Ken Redfield .30 .75
88 Frank Ross .25 .60
89 Michael Phelps .30 .75
90 Brian Christensen .25 .60
91 Kevin McKenna .60 1.50
92 Steve Raab .25 .60
93 Clay Moser .25 .60
94 Tony Khing .25 .60
95 Little Dude .25 .60
96 Sioux Falls Checklist .25 .60
97 Perry Young .40 1.00
98 Ozell Jones .40 1.00
99 Willie Simmons .25 .60
100 Alvin Heggs .25 .60
101 Kelsey Weems .30 .75
102 Anthony Frederick .30 .75
103 Royce Jeffries .25 .60
104 Darryl McDonald .60 1.50
105 Sgt. Slammer .25 .60
106 Charley Rosen 1.25 3.00
107 Oklahoma City CL .25 .60
108 Keith Wilson .25 .60
109 James Carter .25 .60
110 Tracy Moore .40 1.00
111 Mark Plansky .30 .75
112 Charles Bradley .25 .60
113 Leroy Combs .25 .60
114 Anthony Mason 4.00 10.00
115 Gary Voce .40 1.00
116 Jim Lampley .30 .75
117 Henry Bibby CO .60 1.50
118 Tulsa Checklist .25 .60
119 Texans Logo .25 .60
120 Ennis Whatley .75 2.00
121 Mike Mitchell .40 1.00
122 Derrick Taylor .30 .75
123 Kenny Atkinson .25 .60
124 Jaren Jackson .50 1.25
125 Cedric Ball .25 .60
126 Chris Munk .25 .60
127 Mark Becker .25 .60
128 Rodney Blake .25 .60
129 Kurt Portmann .25 .60
130 Henry James .40 1.00
131 John Treloar ACO .25 .60
132 Dave Whitney ACO .25 .60
133 Mike Davis ACO .50 1.25
134 Wichita Falls CL .25 .60
135 Milt Wagner 1.00 2.50
136 Phil Henderson .60 1.50
137 Tony Harris .25 .60
138 Steve Bardo .40 1.00
139 A.J. Wynder .40 1.00
140 Joel DeBortoli .40 1.00
141 Tim Anderson .25 .60
142 Ron Draper .25 .60
143 Barry Sumpter .30 .75
144 Demone Webster .25 .60
145 Thunderbird Dance Team .25 .60
146 Mauro Panaggio CO .40 1.00
147 Dan Panaggio CO .25 .60
148 Quad City Checklist .25 .60
149 Albert King .40 1.00
150 Keith Smith .25 .60
151 Mario Elie 2.00 5.00
152 Albert Springs .25 .60
153 Jeff Fryer .25 .60
154 Clinton Smith .25 .60
155 Vincent Askew 1.50 4.00
156 Paul Graham .75 2.00
157 Ben McDonald .60 1.50
158 Willie McDuffie .25 .60
159 George Karl CO 2.50 6.00
160 Terry Stotts 1.00 2.50
161 Doc Nunnally .25 .60
162 Albany Checklist .25 .60
163 Reggie Fox .25 .60
164 Sedric Toney .30 .75
165 Ron Draper .25 .60
166 Alex Austin .25 .60
167 Robert Brickey .40 1.00
168 Ricky Blanton .40 1.00
169 Stan Kimbrough .25 .60
170 Ron Cavenall .25 .60
171 Grand Rapids CL .25 .60
172 Darren Henrie .25 .60
173 Duane Washington .50 1.25
174 Barry Stevens .25 .60
175 Craig Neal .25 .60
176 Ron Spivey .25 .60
177 Kenny Hammonds .25 .60
178 Brian Martin .25 .60
179 Jerome Henderson .25 .60
180 John McIntyre .25 .60
181 Chris Childs 1.25 3.00
182 The Jacobson's .25 .60
183 Columbus Checklist .25 .60
184 Luther Burks .25 .60
185 Lee Campbell .25 .60
186 Corey Gaines .40 1.00
187 Mike Higgins .25 .60
188 Ron Kellogg .25 .60
189 Bart Kofoed .40 1.00
190 Jim Rowinski .25 .60
191 Riley Smith .25 .60
192 Yakima Checklist .25 .60
193 Mike Yoest .25 .60
194 Freddie Banks .30 .75
195 Scooter Barry 1.25 3.00
196 Richard Morton .25 .60
197 Kelby Stuckey .25 .60
198 Jervis Cole .25 .60
199 Kenny McClary .30 .75
200 Joe Wallace .25 .60
201 Mark Tillmon .30 .75
202 Greg Butler .30 .75
203 San Jose Checklist .25 .60

1991-92 ProCards CBA

COMPLETE SET (206) 30.00 80.00
1 Chris Childs 1.25 3.00
2 Mark Tillmon .30 .75
3 Greg Butler .30 .75
4 Keith Hill .20 .50
5 Jean Derouillere .20 .50
6 Levy Middlebrooks .20 .50
7 Tank Collins .20 .50
8 Sam Williams .20 .50
9 Herman Kull CO .20 .50
10 Don Ford ACO .40 1.00
11 Charles Charlesworth TR .20 .50
12 Calvin Oldham .20 .50
13 Larry Smith .20 .50
14 Trent Jackson .20 .50
15 Rob Rose .40 1.00
16 Walter Bond .40 1.00
17 Jeff Majerle .40 1.00
18 Brad Baldridge .20 .50
19 Kurt Portman .20 .50
20 Cedric Jenkins .30 .75
21 John Treloar CO .20 .50
22 Mike Davis ACO .60 1.50
23 Dave Whitney ACO .20 .50
24 Wichita Falls CL .20 .50
25 Tim Dillon .20 .50
26 Kenny Miller .20 .50
27 Stevie Wise .20 .50
28 Dan Godfread .20 .50
29 Mario Donaldson .20 .50
30 Steve Berger .20 .50
31 Corey Beasley .20 .50
32 Danny Jones .20 .50
33 Lanny Van Eman CO .20 .50
34 Tony Morocco ACO .20 .50
35 Rockford CL .20 .50
36 Bobby Martin .40 1.00
37 Dwight Moody .30 .75
38 Tim Anderson .30 .75
39 A.J. Wynder .40 1.00
40 Keith Robinson .30 .75
41 Steve Scheffler .60 1.50
42 Anthony Bowie 1.00 2.50
43 Tony Harris .40 1.00
44 Barry Mitchell .30 .75
45 Tom Sheehey .20 .50
46 Dan Panaggio CO .20 .50
47 Mike Mashak ACO .20 .50
48 Quad City CL .20 .50
49 Bernard Thompson .40 1.00
50 Daryll Walker .20 .50
51 Darryl Kennedy .30 .75
52 Stevie Thompson .40 1.00
53 Kelsey Weems .30 .75
54 Steve Burtt .40 1.00
55 Junie Lewis .20 .50
56 Chris Harris .20 .50
57 Jeff Hodge .20 .50
58 Demone Webster .20 .50
59 Henry Bibby CO .50 1.25
60 Oklahoma City CL .20 .50
61 Jarvis Basnight .30 .75
62 Ed Horton .30 .75
63 Stanley Brundy .20 .50
64 Irving Thomas .30 .75
65 Nate Johnston .20 .50
66 Keith Smart .75 2.00
67 Larry Robinson .20 .50
68 Michael Anderson .20 .50
69 Eric Musselman CO .60 1.50
70 Duane Ticknor ACO .20 .50
71 Rapid City CL .20 .50
72 Bakersfield CL .20 .50
73 Lyndon Jones .30 .75
74 Warren Bradley .20 .50
75 Anthony Corbitt .20 .50
76 Tony Karasek .20 .50
77 Mark Peterson .20 .50
78 Dan Palombizio .40 1.00
79 Ricky Hall .20 .50
80 John Cooper .40 1.00
81 Carl Thomas .30 .75
82 Travis Williams .20 .50
83 Gerald Oliver CO .20 .50
84 Kevin Kacer TR
Terry Stotts ACO
Dave Carrington ACO
Walter Jordan ACO .50 1.25
85 Fort Wayne CL .20 .50
86 Ronn McMahon .20 .50
87 Sean Tyson .20 .50
88 McKinley Singleton .20 .50
89 Teo Alibegovic .20 .50
90 Joey Johnson .20 .50
91 Riley Smith .20 .50
92 Alex Austin .20 .50
93 Dennis Williams .20 .50
94 Luther Burks .20 .50
95 Bill Klucas CO .20 .50
96 Jack Miller ACO .20 .50
97 Yakima CL .20 .50
98 Roy Fisher .40 1.00
99 Reggie Isaac .20 .50
100 Reggie Jordan .40 1.00
101 Cedric Lewis .20 .50
102 Jeff Martin .40 1.00
103 Dyron Nix .50 1.25
104 Walter Watts .20 .50
105 Gary Waites .20 .50
106 Gerald Paddio .40 1.00
107 Bruce Stewart CO .20 .50
108 Jeff Burkhamer ACO .20 .50
109 Grand Rapids CL .20 .50
110 Petur Gudmundsson .75 2.00
111 Ralph Lewis .20 .50
112 John Smith .20 .50
113 Tony Farmer .30 .75
114 Matt Roe .40 1.00
115 Darryl McDonald .60 1.50
116 Corey Gaines .40 1.00
117 Richard Rellford .30 .75
118 Ken Redfield .30 .75
119 Chuckie White .20 .50
120 Kevin McKenna CO .50 1.25
121 Clay Moser ACO .20 .50
122 Donald Royal 1.50 4.00
123 Wayne Tinkle .20 .50
124 Jim Usevitch .20 .50
125 Eric Dunn .20 .50
126 Jeffty Connelly .20 .50
127 Alan Pollard .20 .50
128 Clifford Scales .30 .75
129 Harold Wright .20 .50
130 Willie Simms .20 .50
131 Michael Holton .40 1.00
132 Terrill Hall .20 .50
133 Calvin Duncan
Guard
Assistant CO .20 .50
134 Steve Hayes CO .50 1.25
135 Yakima CL .20 .50
136 Duane Washington .50 1.25
137 Kermit Holmes .20 .50
138 Mike Goodson .20 .50
139 Byron Dinkins .40 1.00
140 Leonard Harris .30 .75
141 Louis Banks .20 .50
142 James Bradley .30 .75
143 Jeff King .20 .50
144 Ron Spivey .60 1.50
145 Orlando Graham .20 .50
146 Vincent Chickerella CO .20 .50
147 Columbus CL .20 .50
148 Daron Hoges .20 .50
149 Von McDade .20 .50
150 Byron Irvin .40 1.00
151 Patrick Tompkins .20 .50
152 Brian Rahilly .20 .50
153 Kenny Battle .40 1.00
154 Jaren Jackson .40 1.00
155 Troy Truvillion .20 .50
156 Mark Davis .40 1.00
157 Vince Hamilton .25 .60
158 Don Zierden ACO
and Mike McCollow ACO .20 .50
159 LaCrosse CL .20 .50
160 Derrick Chievous .40 1.00
161 Jeff Sanders .40 1.00
162 Marc Brown .20 .50
163 Johnnie Hilliad .30 .75
164 Jerry Johnson .20 .50
165 Dave Popson .30 .75
166 Derrick Rowland .20 .50
167 Jose Slaughter .50 1.25
168 Steve Wright .20 .50
169 Charley Rosen CO 1.00 2.50
170 Lowes Moore ACO .30 .75
171 Albany CL .30 .75
172 Jasper Hooks .20 .50
173 Tracy Moore .30 .75
174 Keith Wilson .20 .50
175 Shawn McDaniel .20 .50
176 Sam Johnson .20 .50
177 Jeff Fryer .20 .50
178 A.C. Carver .20 .50
179 Jawann Oldham .60 1.50
180 Lefty Moore .20 .50
181 Anthony Blakley .40 1.00
182 Steve Bontranger CO .20 .50
183 Tulsa CL .20 .50
184 Cedric Hunter .30 .75
185 Ronnie Grandison .30 .75
186 Ricky Jones .40 1.00
187 Tim Legler .75 2.00
188 Chip Engelland 1.25 3.00
189 Brian Howard .40 1.00
190 Greg Wiltjer .20 .50
191 Rod Mason .20 .50
192 Roland Gray .20 .50
193 Tat Hunter .20 .50
194 Mike Thibault CO .30 .75
195 Omaha CL .20 .50
196 Chris Collier .20 .50
197 Skeeter Henry .30 .75
198 Emmett Smith .20 .50
199 Anthony Houston .40 1.00
200 Michael Cutright .30 .75
201 Michael Ansley .60 1.50
202 Eugene McDowell .40 1.00
203 Eric Johnson .20 .50
204 Mo McHone CO .30 .75
205 Birmingham CL .20 .50
206 Sioux Falls CL .20 .50

1987 Pro Basketball Reading Kit

COMPLETE SET (40) 75.00 135.00
1 Ralph Sampson
Hakeem Olajuwon 1.50 4.00
2 Cheryl Miller 1.50 4.00
3 Paul Arizin 1.00 2.50
4 Walt Frazier 1.25 3.00
5 Joe Fulks 1.00 2.50
6 Manute Bol .75 2.00
7 Referees .75 2.00
8 Bob Pettit 1.25 3.00
9 Patrick Ewing 2.00 5.00
10 Bob Pettit 1.25 3.00
11 Charles Barkley 2.50 6.00
12 Maurice Stokes 1.00 2.50
13 Madison Square Garden .75 2.00
14 Artis Gilmore 1.00 2.50
15 Dr. James Naismith .75 2.00
16 George Mikan 1.25 3.00
17 ABA .75 2.00
18 Spud Webb .75 2.00
19 John Havlicek 1.25 3.00
20 Bob Cousy 2.00 5.00
21 Moses Malone 1.50 4.00
22 Eddie Gottlieb .75 2.00
23 Jerry West 2.50 6.00
24 Dave DeBusschere 1.25 3.00
25 Magic Johnson 3.00 8.00
26 Hall of Fame .75 2.00
27 Minneapolis Lakers .75 2.00
28 Kareem Abdul-Jabbar 3.00 8.00
29 Dolph Schayes 1.00 2.50
30 Elgin Baylor 1.25 3.00
31 Julius Erving 4.00 10.00
32 Jerry Krause .75 2.00
33 Wilt Chamberlain 4.00 10.00
35 Bill Sharman 1.00 2.50
36 Larry Bird 4.00 10.00
37 Bill Russell 3.00 8.00
38 Philadelphia 76ers .75 2.00
39 Oscar Robertson 2.50 6.00
40 Bill Walton 2.00 5.00

1994 Pro Mags Promos

COMPLETE SET (3) 4.00 10.00
1 Shaquille O'Neal UER
name spelled O'Neil 2.00 5.00
2 Grant Hill 2.00 5.00
3 Jason Kidd 2.00 5.00

1994 Pro Mags

COMPLETE SET (135) 40.00 100.00
1 Stacey Augmon .50 1.25
2 Mookie Blaylock .40 1.00
3 Doug Edwards .40 1.00
4 Adam Keefe .40 1.00
5 Danny Manning .50 1.25
6 Dee Brown .40 1.00
7 Sherman Douglas .40 1.00
8 Rick Fox .40 1.00
9 Xavier McDaniel .40 1.00
10 Robert Parish .60 1.50
11 Muggsy Bogues .50 1.25
12 Dell Curry .40 1.00
13 Hersey Hawkins .40 1.00
14 Larry Johnson .75 2.00
15 Alonzo Mourning 1.25 3.00
16 B.J. Armstrong .40 1.00
17 Horace Grant .50 1.25
18 Toni Kukoc .75 2.00
19 John Paxson .50 1.25
20 Scottie Pippen 2.00 5.00
21 Brad Daugherty .50 1.25
22 John Williams .40 1.00
23 Chris Mills .40 1.00
24 Larry Nance .50 1.25
25 Gerald Wilkins .40 1.00
26 Doug Smith .40 1.00
27 Jim Jackson .40 1.00
28 Popeye Jones .40 1.00
29 Jamal Mashburn .60 1.50
30 Randy White .40 1.00
31 Mahmoud Abdul-Rauf .40 1.00
32 LaPhonso Ellis .40 1.00
33 Dikembe Mutombo .60 1.50
34 Reggie Williams .40 1.00
35 Rodney Rogers .40 1.00
36 Joe Dumars .75 2.00
37 Sean Elliott .60 1.50
38 Allan Houston .60 1.50
39 Lindsey Hunter .40 1.00
40 Terry Mills .40 1.00
41 Tim Hardaway .75 2.00
42 Chris Mullin .75 2.00
43 Billy Owens .40 1.00
44 Latrell Sprewell .75 2.00
45 Chris Webber 2.50 6.00
46 Robert Horry .60 1.50
47 Vernon Maxwell .40 1.00
48 Hakeem Olajuwon .75 2.00
49 Kenny Smith .50 1.25
50 Otis Thorpe .40 1.00
51 Dale Davis .40 1.00
52 Reggie Miller 1.25 3.00
53 Pooh Richardson .40 1.00
54 Rik Smits .50 1.25
55 LaSalle Thompson .40 1.00
56 Dominique Wilkins 1.00 2.50
57 Ron Harper .50 1.25
58 Mark Jackson .50 1.25
59 Stanley Roberts .40 1.00
60 Loy Vaught .40 1.00
61 Sam Bowie .40 1.00
62 Vlade Divac .60 1.50
63 George Lynch .40 1.00
64 Anthony Peeler .40 1.00
65 James Worthy .75 2.00
66 Harold Miner .40 1.00
67 Glen Rice .60 1.50
68 Rony Seikaly .50 1.25
69 Brian Shaw .40 1.00
70 Steve Smith .50 1.25
71 Vin Baker .60 1.50
72 Theodore Edwards .40 1.00
73 Todd Day .40 1.00
74 Eric Murdock .40 1.00
75 Jon Barry .40 1.00
76 Thurl Bailey .40 1.00
77 Christian Laettner .50 1.25
78 Chuck Person .50 1.25
79 Doug West .40 1.00
80 Micheal Williams .40 1.00
81 Derrick Coleman .60 1.50
82 Rick Mahorn .40 1.00
83 Johnny Newman .40 1.00
84 Kenny Anderson .50 1.25
85 Rex Walters .40 1.00
86 Greg Anthony .40 1.00
87 Rolando Blackman .50 1.25
88 Patrick Ewing .75 2.00
89 Charles Oakley .50 1.25
90 John Starks .50 1.25
91 Nick Anderson .40 1.00
92 Anfernee Hardaway 1.00 2.50
93 Donald Royal .40 1.00
94 Dennis Scott .40 1.00
95 Scott Skiles .40 1.00
96 Dana Barros .40 1.00
97 Shawn Bradley .40 1.00
98 Johnny Dawkins .40 1.00
99 Tim Perry .40 1.00
100 Clarence Weatherspoon .40 1.00
101 Charles Barkley 1.50 4.00
102 Cedric Ceballos .40 1.00
103 Malcolm Mackey .40 1.00
104 Dan Majerle .60 1.50
105 Danny Ainge .60 1.50
106 Clyde Drexler .75 2.00
107 Jerome Kersey .40 1.00
108 Rod Strickland .40 1.00
109 Buck Williams .40 1.00
110 Clifford Robinson .40 1.00
111 Mitch Richmond .60 1.50
112 Lionel Simmons .40 1.00
113 Wayman Tisdale .40 1.00
114 Walt Williams .40 1.00
115 Spud Webb .60 1.50
116 Dale Ellis .40 1.00
117 J.R. Reid .40 1.00
118 David Robinson 1.00 2.50
119 Dennis Rodman 1.50 4.00
120 Vinny Del Negro .40 1.00
121 Kendall Gill .40 1.00
122 Ervin Johnson .40 1.00
123 Shawn Kemp .75 2.00
124 Gary Payton .60 1.50
125 Sam Perkins .50 1.25
126 Karl Malone 1.50 4.00
127 Tyrone Corbin .40 1.00
128 Jeff Hornacek .50 1.25
129 Felton Spencer .40 1.00
130 John Stockton 2.00 5.00
131 Michael Adams .40 1.00
132 Calbert Cheaney .40 1.00
133 Tom Gugliotta .40 1.00
134 Don MacLean .40 1.00
135 Pervis Ellison .40 1.00

1994-95 Pro Mags Rookie Showcase

COMPLETE SET (12) 10.00 25.00
1 Tony Dumas .50 1.25
2 Brian Grant 1.00 2.50
3 Juwan Howard 1.00 2.50
4 Donyell Marshall .60 1.50
5 Eric Mobley .40 1.00
6 Eric Montross .40 1.00
7 Carlos Rogers .50 1.25
8 Jalen Rose 1.50 4.00
9 Charlie Ward .60 1.50
10 Grant Hill 3.00 8.00
11 Glenn Robinson 1.25 3.00
12 Jason Kidd 3.00 8.00

1995 Pro Mags

COMPLETE SET (145) 60.00 150.00
1 Stacey Augmon .60 1.50
2 Mookie Blaylock .50 1.25
3 Ken Norman .50 1.25
4 Steve Smith .60 1.50
5 Grant Long .50 1.25
6 Eric Williams .75 2.00
7 Eric Montross .50 1.25
8 Sherman Douglas .50 1.25
9 Dee Brown .50 1.25
10 Dino Radja .50 1.25
11 Larry Johnson .75 2.00
12 Alonzo Mourning 1.00 2.50
13 Muggsy Bogues .60 1.50
14 Scott Burrell .50 1.25
15 Kendall Gill .50 1.25
16 Dennis Rodman 1.50 4.00
17 Scottie Pippen 1.25 3.00
18 Ron Harper .60 1.50
19 Toni Kukoc .75 2.00
20 Dickey Simpkins .50 1.25
21 Danny Ferry .50 1.25
22 Tyrone Hill .50 1.25
23 Michael Cage .50 1.25
24 Chris Mills .50 1.25
25 Terrell Brandon .50 1.25
26 Jason Kidd 1.25 3.00
27 Jamal Mashburn .75 2.00
28 Tony Dumas .50 1.25
29 Roy Tarpley .50 1.25
30 Jim Jackson .50 1.25
31 Dikembe Mutombo .75 2.00
32 Jalen Rose 1.00 2.50
33 Robert Pack .50 1.25
34 Antonio McDyess 1.00 2.50
35 Reggie Williams .50 1.25
36 Grant Hill 1.25 3.00
37 Joe Dumars .75 2.00
38 Lindsey Hunter .50 1.25
39 Allan Houston .60 1.50
40 Terry Mills .50 1.25
41 Tim Hardaway .75 2.00
42 Chris Mullin .75 2.00
43 Joe Smith 1.00 2.50
44 Latrell Sprewell .75 2.00
45 Donyell Marshall .50 1.25
46 Hakeem Olajuwon 1.00 2.50
47 Robert Horry .60 1.50
48 Sam Cassell .75 2.00
49 Kenny Smith .60 1.50
50 Clyde Drexler 1.00 2.50
51 Reggie Miller 1.00 2.50
52 Mark Jackson .75 2.00
53 Rik Smits .60 1.50
54 Dale Davis .50 1.25
55 Derrick McKey .50 1.25
56 Loy Vaught .50 1.25
57 Terry Dehere .50 1.25
58 Lamond Murray .50 1.25
59 Eric Piatkowski .50 1.25
60 Pooh Richardson .50 1.25
61 Vlade Divac .75 2.00
62 Anthony Peeler .50 1.25
63 Nick Van Exel .75 2.00
64 Cedric Ceballos .50 1.25
65 Eddie Jones 1.00 2.50
66 Sasha Danilovic .75 2.00
67 Glen Rice .75 2.00
68 Khalid Reeves .50 1.25
69 Billy Owens .50 1.25
70 Kevin Willis .50 1.25
71 Glenn Robinson .60 1.50
72 Vin Baker .60 1.50
73 Todd Day .50 1.25
74 Eric Mobley .50 1.25
75 Jon Barry .50 1.25
76 Isaiah Rider .75 2.00
77 Christian Laettner .60 1.50
78 Kevin Garnett 6.00 15.00
79 Doug West .50 1.25
80 Sean Rooks .50 1.25
81 Derrick Coleman .60 1.50
82 Rick Mahorn .60 1.50
83 Rex Walters .50 1.25
84 Kenny Anderson .60 1.50
85 Ed O'Bannon .75 2.00
86 Patrick Ewing 1.00 2.50
87 John Starks .60 1.50
88 Charles Oakley .60 1.50
89 Anthony Mason .50 1.25
90 Derek Harper .60 1.50
91 Anfernee Hardaway 1.25 3.00
92 Brian Shaw .50 1.25
93 Shaquille O'Neal 2.00 5.00
94 Brooks Thompson .50 1.25
95 Horace Grant .60 1.50
96 Tim Perry .50 1.25
97 Sharone Wright .50 1.25
98 Jerry Stackhouse 2.50 6.00
99 Clarence Weatherspoon .50 1.25
100 Vernon Maxwell .50 1.25
101 Charles Barkley 1.25 3.00
102 Danny Manning .60 1.50
103 Michael Finley 2.50 6.00
104 Kevin Johnson .75 2.00
105 Wayman Tisdale .50 1.25
106 Randolph Childress .75 2.00
107 Gary Trent .75 2.00
108 James Robinson .50 1.25
109 Buck Williams .50 1.25
110 Clifford Robinson .50 1.25
111 Corliss Williamson .75 2.00
112 Bobby Hurley .50 1.25
113 Brian Grant .60 1.50
114 Mitch Richmond .75 2.00
115 Walt Williams .50 1.25
116 David Robinson 1.25 3.00
117 Will Perdue .50 1.25
118 Chuck Person .50 1.25
119 Sean Elliott .50 1.25
120 Vinny Del Negro .50 1.25
121 Ervin Johnson .50 1.25
122 Shawn Kemp .75 2.00
123 Sam Perkins .50 1.25
124 Detlef Schrempf .75 2.00
125 Gary Payton .75 2.00
126 Karl Malone 1.00 2.50
127 John Stockton 1.00 2.50
128 Felton Spencer .50 1.25
129 Jeff Hornacek .60 1.50
130 Adam Keefe .50 1.25
131 Chris Webber 1.00 2.50
132 Juwan Howard .75 2.00
133 Calbert Cheaney .50 1.25
134 Rasheed Wallace 2.50 6.00
135 Gheorghe Muresan .50 1.25
136 Ed Pinckney .50 1.25
137 Tony Massenburg .50 1.25
138 Damon Stoudamire 2.00 5.00
139 Acie Earl .50 1.25
140 Alvin Robertson .50 1.25
141 Greg Anthony .50 1.25
142 Benoit Benjamin .50 1.25
143 Antonio Harvey .50 1.25
144 Byron Scott .75 2.00
145 Bryant Reeves .75 2.00

1995-96 Pro Mags Die Cuts

COMPLETE SET (27) 12.00 30.00
1 Charles Barkley 2.00 5.00
2 Patrick Ewing 1.50 4.00
3 Anfernee Hardaway 1.50 4.00
4 Tim Hardaway 1.25 3.00
5 Grant Hill 1.50 4.00
6 Larry Johnson 1.25 3.00
7 Magic Johnson 3.00 8.00
8 Shawn Kemp 1.25 3.00
9 Jason Kidd 1.50 4.00
10 Karl Malone 1.50 4.00
11 Jamal Mashburn 1.25 3.00
12 Reggie Miller 1.50 4.00
13 Shaquille O'Neal 2.00 5.00
14 Hakeem Olajuwon 1.25 3.00
15 Scottie Pippen 2.00 5.00
16 Mitch Richmond 1.25 3.00
17 Isaiah Rider .75 2.00
18 David Robinson 1.50 4.00
19 Glenn Robinson 1.25 3.00
20 Dennis Rodman 2.50 6.00
21 Jerry Stackhouse 1.50 4.00
22 John Stockton 2.00 5.00
23 Damon Stoudamire 1.25 3.00
24 Nick Van Exel 1.25 3.00
25 Chris Webber 1.25 3.00

1995 Pro Mags Lost In Space

COMPLETE SET (6) 8.00 20.00
LIS1 Anfernee Hardaway 3.00 8.00
LIS2 Antonio McDyess 1.25 3.00
LIS3 Isaiah Rider 2.00 5.00
LIS4 Ed O'Bannon 1.00 2.50
LIS5 Latrell Sprewell 2.00 5.00
LIS6 Robert Pack 1.25 3.00

1995 Pro Mags USA Basketball

COMPLETE SET (10) 8.00 20.00
1 Hakeem Olajuwon 1.25 3.00
2 Glenn Robinson .75 2.00
3 Karl Malone 1.25 3.00
4 Shaquille O'Neal 2.50 6.00
5 Reggie Miller 1.25 3.00
6 David Robinson 1.50 4.00
7 John Stockton 1.25 3.00
8 Anfernee Hardaway 1.50 4.00
9 Scottie Pippen 1.50 4.00
10 Grant Hill 1.50 4.00

1997-98 Pro Mags Heroes of the Locker Room

COMPLETE SET 15.00 30.00
1 Kobe Bryant 10.00 25.00
2 Tim Duncan 3.00 8.00
3 Grant Hill 1.50 4.00
4 Kevin Garnett 2.50 6.00
5 Karl Malone 2.00 5.00
6 Keith Van Horn 1.50 4.00

1992 Pro Set Club

COMPLETE SET (9) 2.00 5.00
COMMON CARD (1-9) .15 .40
9 Basketball
Pro Player
(David Robinson) 1.00 2.50

1991-92 Pro Set Prototypes

1 Tom Chambers 40.00 80.00
2 Patrick Ewing 75.00 200.00
3 Magic Johnson 100.00 250.00
4 Michael Jordan 300.00 600.00
5 Karl Malone 80.00 200.00

1995 Pro Stamps

COMPLETE SET (12) 15.00 40.00
NNO Collector's Album 1.25 3.00
SHEET1 Brooks Thompson
Larry Johnson
Robert Pack
Mitch Richmond
Stacey Augmon
Terry Dehere
Charles Barkley
Bryant Reeves
Derek Harper
Corliss Williamson
Rex Walters
Tyrone Hill 2.00 5.00
SHEET2 Horace Grant
Derrick McKey
Antonio McDyess
Brian Grant
Mookie Blaylock
Loy Vaught
Gary Payton
Benoit Benjamin
Anthony Mason
Joe Smith
Rick Mahorn
Randolph Childress 1.50 4.00
SHEET3 Ervin Johnson
Dale Davis
Reggie Williams
Bobby Hurley
Ken Norman
Clifford Robinson
Detlef Schrempf
Antonio Harvey
Charles Oakley
Latrell Sprewell
Derrick Coleman
Gary Trent 1.50 4.00
SHEET4 Shawn Kemp
Rik Smits
Patrick Ewing
Corliss Williamson
Steve Smith
Buck Williams
Sam Perkins
Greg Anthony
John Starks
Rony Seikaly
Grant Long
James Robinson 1.50 4.00
SHEET5 Hakeem Olajuwon
Cedric Ceballos
Jason Kidd
Glen Rice
Glenn Robinson
Alvin Robertson
Toni Kukoc

David Robinson
Calbert Cheaney
Grant Hill
Isaiah Rider
Danny Ferry 2.50 6.00
SHEET6 Robert Horry
Nick Van Exel
Jamal Mashburn
Sasha Danilovic
Vin Baker
Ed Pinckney
Ron Harper
Will Perdue
Juwan Howard
Joe Dumars
Dino Radja
Sean Rooks 1.50 4.00
SHEET7 Sam Cassell
Anthony Peeler
Tony Dumas
Charles Barkley
Khalid Reeves
Damon Stoudamire
Scottie Pippen
Chuck Person
Chris Webber
Lindsey Hunter
Dee Brown
Doug West 2.00 5.00
SHEET8 Kenny Smith
Vlade Divac
Roy Tarpley
Anfernee Hardaway
Billy Owens
Tony Massenburg
Dennis Rodman
Sean Elliott
Adam Keefe
Rasheed Wallace
Sherman Douglas
Kevin Garnett 2.00 5.00
SHEET9 Clyde Drexler
Kendall Gill
Eddie Jones
Jerry Stackhouse
Kevin Willis
Acie Earl
Wayman Tisdale
Dickey Simpkins
Jeff Hornacek
Gheorghe Muresan
Eric Montross
Christian Laettner 2.00 5.00
SHEET10 Anfernee Hardaway
Scott Burrell
Jim Jackson
Sharone Wright
Todd Day
Pooh Richardson
Kevin Johnson
Vinny Del Negro
Felton Spencer
Allan Houston
Eric Williams
Tyrone Hill 2.00 5.00
SHEET11 Brian Shaw
Muggsy Bogues
Dikembe Mutombo
Tim Perry
Hakeem Olajuwon
Eric Piatkowski
Michael Finley
Reggie Miller
John Stockton
Terry Mills
Ed O'Bannon
Michael Cage 2.00 5.00
SHEET12 Dennis Scott
Alonzo Mourning
Jalen Rose
Walt Williams
Eric Murdock
Lamond Murray
Danny Manning
Mark Jackson
Karl Malone
Tim Hardaway
Kenny Anderson
Chris Mills 2.00 5.00

1991 Pro Stars Posters
COMPLETE SET (3) 4.00 10.00
2 Michael Jordan 2.00 5.00

1993-94 Quad City Thunder CBA
COMPLETE SET (13) 1.25 3.00
1 Mike Bell .15 .40
2 Gary Collier .15 .40
3 Tate George .20 .50
4 Bill Jones .15 .40
5 Randolph Keys .20 .50
6 Richard Manning .15 .40
7 Kevin Pritchard .20 .50
8 LaBradford Smith .15 .40
9 Maurice Stokes .30 .75
10 Barry Sumpter .15 .40
11 Shon Tarver .15 .40
12 Thunder Coaches .15 .40
13 Team Picture .15 .40

1979-80 Quaker Iron-Ons
COMPLETE SET (9) 125.00 250.00
1 Kareem Abdul-Jabbar 20.00 40.00
2 Rick Barry 10.00 25.00
3 Julius Erving 25.00 50.00
4 George Gervin 15.00 40.00
5 Elvin Hayes 10.00 20.00
6 Maurice Lucas 5.00 12.00
7 Pete Maravich 45.00 90.00
8 David Thompson 10.00 20.00
9 Paul Westphal 6.00 12.00

1987 Quaker Sports Illustrated Mini Posters
COMPLETE SET (7) 60.00 150.00
1 Larry Bird 12.50 30.00
2 Julius Erving 6.00 15.00
3 Magic Johnson 10.00 25.00
5 Hakeem Olajuwon 8.00 20.00
6 Spud Webb 4.00 10.00
7 Dominique Wilkins 5.00 12.00

1961-64 Rawlings
COMPLETE SET (7) 125.00 250.00
1 Richie Guerin 10.00 25.00
2 Cliff Hagan 17.50 35.00
3 John Havlicek 40.00 70.00
4 Gus Johnson 10.00 25.00
5 Bob Pettit 40.00 70.00
6 Frank Ramsey 10.00 25.00
7 Len Wilkens 25.00 60.00

1992-93 Reebok Shawn Kemp
COMPLETE SET (7) 15.00 30.00
COMMON CARD (1-3) 3.00 8.00
COMMON CARD (4-7) 1.25 3.00

1998 Reebok Rebecca Lobo Postcard
1 Rebecca Lobo 1.25 3.00

2005-06 Reflections
COMP.SET w/o RC's (100) 20.00 50.00
RC PRINT RUN 1499 SER.#'d SETS
1 Al Harrington .50 1.25
2 Josh Smith .50 1.25
3 Josh Childress .40 1.00
4 Joe Johnson .50 1.25
5 Paul Pierce 1.00 2.50
6 Antoine Walker .50 1.25
7 Gary Payton 1.00 2.50
8 Al Jefferson .40 1.00
9 Emeka Okafor .50 1.25
10 Primoz Brezec .40 1.00
11 Gerald Wallace .50 1.25
12 Michael Jordan 6.00 15.00
13 Ben Gordon .50 1.25
14 Luol Deng .50 1.25
15 Kirk Hinrich .50 1.25
16 LeBron James 5.00 12.00
17 Dajuan Wagner .40 1.00
18 Drew Gooden .50 1.25
19 Larry Hughes .50 1.25
20 Dirk Nowitzki 1.50 4.00
21 Jason Terry .50 1.25
22 Michael Finley .60 1.50
23 Jerry Stackhouse .50 1.25
24 Andre Miller .50 1.25
25 Carmelo Anthony 1.00 2.50
26 Kenyon Martin .50 1.25
27 Earl Boykins .40 1.00
28 Rasheed Wallace .60 1.50
29 Ben Wallace .75 2.00
30 Richard Hamilton .75 2.00
31 Chauncey Billups .75 2.00
32 Baron Davis .60 1.50
33 Derek Fisher .60 1.50
34 Jason Richardson .60 1.50
35 Tracy McGrady 1.00 2.50
36 Yao Ming 1.25 3.00
37 Juwan Howard .50 1.25
38 Jermaine O'Neal .50 1.25
39 Ron Artest .50 1.25
40 Jamaal Tinsley .40 1.00
41 Corey Maggette .50 1.25
42 Elton Brand .50 1.25
43 Shaun Livingston .50 1.25
44 Kobe Bryant 5.00 12.00
45 Brian Cook .40 1.00
46 Lamar Odom .50 1.25
47 Mike Miller .50 1.25
48 Pau Gasol 1.00 2.50
49 Shane Battier .50 1.25
50 Shaquille O'Neal 2.00 5.00
51 Dwyane Wade 1.25 3.00
52 Udonis Haslem .40 1.00
53 Joe Smith .50 1.25
54 Michael Redd .50 1.25
55 Desmond Mason .40 1.00
56 Kevin Garnett 1.50 4.00
57 Wally Szczerbiak .50 1.25
58 Sam Cassell .50 1.25
59 Vince Carter 1.25 3.00
60 Jason Kidd 1.00 2.50
61 Richard Jefferson .50 1.25
62 Jamaal Magloire .40 1.00
63 J.R. Smith .60 1.50
64 Bostjan Nachbar .40 1.00
65 Allan Houston .50 1.25
66 Stephon Marbury .75 2.00
67 Jamal Crawford .60 1.50
68 Dwight Howard .75 2.00
69 Grant Hill 1.00 2.50
70 Jameer Nelson .40 1.00
71 Steve Francis .60 1.50
72 Allen Iverson 1.25 3.00
73 Andre Iguodala .60 1.50
74 Chris Webber .75 2.00
75 Samuel Dalembert .40 1.00
76 Amare Stoudemire .60 1.50
77 Steve Nash 1.25 3.00
78 Quentin Richardson .40 1.00
79 Shawn Marion .50 1.25
80 Damon Stoudamire .60 1.50
81 Zach Randolph .60 1.50
82 Sebastian Telfair .50 1.25
83 Peja Stojakovic .50 1.25
84 Mike Bibby .60 1.50
85 Cuttino Mobley .40 1.00
86 Manu Ginobili 1.25 3.00
87 Tim Duncan 1.50 4.00
88 Tony Parker 1.00 2.50
89 Ray Allen 1.00 2.50
90 Rashard Lewis .50 1.25
91 Luke Ridnour .50 1.25
92 Ronald Murray .40 1.00
93 Chris Bosh .75 2.00
94 Morris Peterson .40 1.00
95 Rafael Araujo .40 1.00
96 Andrei Kirilenko .50 1.25
97 Raul Lopez .40 1.00
98 Carlos Boozer .50 1.25
99 Antawn Jamison .50 1.25
100 Gilbert Arenas .60 1.50
101 Travis Diener RC 1.00 2.50
102 Julius Hodge RC 1.00 2.50
103 David Lee RC 1.50 4.00
104 Sarunas Jasikevicius RC 1.50 4.00
105 Jason Maxiell RC 1.25 3.00
106 Luther Head RC 1.00 2.50
107 Amir Johnson RC 1.50 4.00
108 Linas Kleiza RC 1.25 3.00
109 Uros Slokar RC 1.50 4.00
110 Andray Blatche RC 1.50 4.00
111 Sean May RC 1.00 2.50
112 Alex Acker RC 1.00 2.50
113 Nate Robinson RC 1.50 4.00
114 Brandon Bass RC 1.25 3.00
115 Ike Diogu RC 1.00 2.50
116 Daniel Ewing RC 1.25 3.00
117 Salim Stoudamire RC 1.25 3.00
118 Dijon Thompson RC 1.00 2.50
119 Danny Granger RC 1.50 4.00
120 Chris Taft RC 1.00 2.50
121 Louis Williams RC 4.00 10.00
122 Channing Frye RC 1.25 3.00
123 Francisco Garcia RC 1.00 2.50
124 Ryan Gomes RC 1.25 3.00
125 Von Wafer RC 1.00 2.50
126 Jarrett Jack RC 1.50 4.00
127 Lawrence Roberts RC 1.00 2.50
128 Ricky Sanchez RC 1.50 4.00
129 C.J. Miles RC 1.25 3.00
130 Ersan Ilyasova RC 1.25 3.00
131 Robert Whaley RC 1.00 2.50
132 Monta Ellis RC 2.00 5.00
133 Bracey Wright RC 1.00 2.50
134 Johan Petro RC 1.00 2.50
135 Will Bynum RC 1.25 3.00
136 Andrew Bynum RC 1.25 3.00
137 Martynas Andriuskevicius RC 1.00 2.50
138 Charlie Villanueva RC 1.25 3.00
139 Antoine Wright RC 1.25 3.00
140 Joey Graham RC 1.25 3.00
141 Wayne Simien RC 1.00 2.50
142 Hakim Warrick RC 1.25 3.00
143 Gerald Green RC 1.50 4.00
144 Marvin Williams RC 1.50 4.00
145 Deron Williams RC 2.50 6.00
146 Rashad McCants RC 1.00 2.50
147 Martell Webster RC 1.25 3.00
148 Raymond Felton RC 1.25 3.00
149 Chris Paul RC 8.00 20.00
150 Andrew Bogut RC 2.00 5.00

2005-06 Reflections Blue
*BLUE VETS: 2X TO 5X BASE HI
*BLUE RCs: 1.5X TO 4X BASE HI
PRINT RUN 50 SER.#'d SETS
RC PLAYERS HAVE AUTOGRAPHS
NOT ALL RCs WERE PRODUCED
12 Michael Jordan 300.00 600.00
149 Chris Paul AU 40.00 100.00

2005-06 Reflections Green
*GREEN VETS: 3X TO 8X BASE HI
*GREEN RCs: 1.25X TO 3X BASE HI
PRINT RUN 25 SER.#'d SETS
RC PLAYERS HAVE PATCH SWATCH
NOT ALL RCs WERE PRODUCED
12 Michael Jordan 400.00 800.00

2005-06 Reflections Purple
*PURPLE VETS: .6X TO 1.5X BASE HI
1-100 PURPLE STATED ODDS 1:3
*PURPLE RCs: .6X TO 1.5X BASE HI
PURPLE RC PRINT RUN 250 SER.#'d SETS
12 Michael Jordan 20.00 50.00

2005-06 Reflections Red
*RED VETS: 1X TO 2.5X BASE HI
PRINT RUN 100 SER.#'d SETS
RC PLAYERS HAVE JSY SWATCH
NOT ALL RC's WERE PRODUCED
12 Michael Jordan 100.00 250.00
44 Kobe Bryant 10.00 25.00

2005-06 Reflections Compare and Contrast Autographs
PRINT RUN 30 SER.#'d SETS
AB Andriuskevicius/Bogut 15.00 40.00
AK A.Miller/K.Hinrich 10.00 25.00
AT T.Ariza/D.Thompson 8.00 20.00
BH C.Billups/R.Hamilton 20.00 50.00
BT A.Bogut/C.Taft 15.00 40.00
CO J.Childress/L.Odom 10.00 25.00
DF B.Davis/D.Fisher 12.00 30.00
EF D.Ewing/R.Felton 10.00 25.00
FL C.Frye/D.Lee 12.00 30.00
FP R.Felton/C.Paul 40.00 100.00
GG D.Granger/J.Graham 12.00 30.00
GS B.Gordon/J.R.Smith 12.00 30.00
GW G.Green/M.Webster 12.00 30.00
IC I.Diogu/C.Frye 10.00 25.00
IJ A.Iguodala/R.Jefferson 12.00 30.00
JA A.Jamison/G.Arenas 12.00 30.00
JJ R.Jefferson/A.Jamison 10.00 25.00
JM L.James/T.McGrady 1,000.00 2,000.00
KG A.Kirilenko/P.Gasol 20.00 50.00
LJ M.Jordan/L.James 3,000.00 6,000.00
LT S.Livingston/S.Telfair 10.00 25.00
MF R.McCants/R.Felton 10.00 25.00
MH Y.Ming/D.Howard 40.00 100.00
MK S.Marbury/J.Kidd 20.00 50.00
MM B.Miller/J.Magloire 10.00 25.00
NB S.Nash/M.Bibby 50.00 100.00
NT J.Nelson/S.Telfair 10.00 25.00
PW C.Paul/D.Williams 75.00 200.00
RC M.Redd/J.Crawford 15.00 40.00
SF S.Stoudamire/C.Frye 10.00 25.00
SP P.Stojakovic/P.Pierce 20.00 50.00
SS D.Stoudamire/S.Stoud 15.00 40.00
SW W.Simien/H.Warrick 10.00 25.00
TP C.Taft/J.Petro 8.00 20.00
VW C.Villanueva/H.Warrick 10.00 25.00
WB G.Wallace/P.Brezec 10.00 25.00
WH D.Williams/L.Head 20.00 50.00
WM Mv.Williams/S.May 12.00 30.00
WV Mv.Williams/C.Villanueva 10.00 25.00
WW A.Wright/M.Webster 10.00 25.00

2005-06 Reflections Compare and Contrast Jerseys
PRINT RUN 100 SER.#'d SETS
AB A.Houston/J.Crawford 4.00 10.00
AL R.Allen/R.Lewis 5.00 12.00
AR S.Abdur-Rahim/Z.Randolph 4.00 10.00
BC C.Butler/B.Cook 4.00 10.00
BJ K.Bryant/M.Jordan 200.00 500.00
BM C.Bosh/D.Marshall 4.00 10.00
BN E.Boykins/Nene 4.00 10.00
BT A.Bogut/C.Taft 5.00 12.00
BW P.Brezec/G.Wallace 4.00 10.00
FM R.Felton/R.McCants 8.00 20.00
FR D.Fisher/J.Richardson 4.00 10.00
GP M.Ginobili/T.Parker 10.00 25.00
GS F.Garcia/S.Stoudamire 4.00 10.00
GW G.Green/M.Webster 4.00 10.00
HC A.Harrington/J.Childress 4.00 10.00
HT D.Harris/S.Telfair 4.00 10.00
JJ M.Jordan/L.James 40.00 80.00
LB R.Lopez/C.Boozer 4.00 10.00
MC B.Miller/E.Curry 4.00 10.00
MR D.Miles/Z.Randolph 4.00 10.00
MS M.Miller/S.Swift 4.00 10.00
OA J.O'Neal/R.Artest 4.00 10.00
OH S.O'Neal/U.Haslem 10.00 25.00
PF C.Paul/R.Felton 12.50 30.00
PR M.Peterson/J.Rose 4.00 10.00
RA J.Rose/R.Araujo 4.00 10.00
SC W.Szczerbiak/S.Cassell 4.00 10.00
SF S.Stoudamire/C.Frye 4.00 10.00
SH J.Stackhouse/D.Harris 4.00 10.00
SK Joe Smith/T.Kukoc 5.00 12.00
SM W.Simien/S.May 4.00 10.00
TJ J.Tinsley/S.Jackson 4.00 10.00
WG D.Williams/F.Garcia 6.00 15.00
WI D.Wagner/Z.Ilgauskas 4.00 10.00
WK C.Webber/K.Korver 8.00 20.00
WM Mv.Williams/S.May 4.00 10.00
WV H.Warrick/C.Villanueva 4.00 10.00
WW Mv.Williams/H.Warrick 4.00 10.00

2005-06 Reflections Compare and Contrast Quad Jerseys
PRINT RUN 50 SER.#'d SETS
ADHC Arenas/Dixon/Houstn/Crwfrd 8.00 20.00
ALRM Allen/Lewis/Redd/Mason 8.00 20.00
BBPW Kobe/Butler/Payton/Walker 40.00 100.00
BMIG Brand/Magg/Ilgaus/Gooden 6.00 15.00
BNLB Boykins/Nene/Lopez/Boozer 6.00 15.00
FHMH Francis/Hill/Marb/Hou 8.00 20.00
FSFH Fizer/JoSmith/Francis/Hill 12.50 30.00
GPBH Manu/Parker/Billups/Rip 12.50 30.00
GSWH Garnett/Szcz/Sheed/Rip 12.50 30.00
HCVA Hinrich/Curry/Vexel/A-Rahim 6.00 15.00
HCWJ Hrngtn/Chldrss/Walker/BigAl 6.00 15.00
JASF SJcksn/Artest/Stack/Finley 6.00 15.00
JGKJ LeBron/Gooden/Kidd/R-Jeff 15.00 40.00
JJBA MJ/LeBron/Kobe/Melo 500.00 1,000.00
JMSM JoJhnsn/Marion/Bassy/Miles 6.00 15.00
KDPA Korver/Dalmb/MPete/Araujo 8.00 20.00
LBBC Lvngstn/Brand/Butler/Cook 6.00 15.00
MFMW May/Felton/McCants/Williams 10.00 25.00
MJMM Marion/Jhnsn/Miller/Cuttino 8.00 20.00
MNBW K-Mart/Nene/Brezec/G.Wallace 6.00 15.00
PFHW Pietrus/Fish/Ju.Howard/Wesley 8.00 20.00
RPWC J-Rich/Mo-Pete/Webb/Crwfrd 12.00 30.00
TFMM Jet/Finley/A.Miller/K-Mart 10.00 25.00

2005-06 Reflections Compare and Contrast Octa Jerseys
PRINT RUN 25 SER.#'d SETS
2 AI/AJ/DS/BU/DH/SL/JN/DW 15.00 40.00
3 DH/BG/LD/JS/AB/MW/CP/DW 20.00 50.00
4 KB/LO/CB/VD/MB/PS/BM/CM 75.00 200.00
5 LJ/DG/ZI/DW/KH/LD/TC/EC 60.00 120.00
6 TD/TP/MG/BU/DN/MF/JT/JS 20.00 50.00
7 RA/RL/LR/RM/AM/KM/N/EB 25.00 60.00
9 GA/JH/AJ/JD/JO/RA/JT/SJ 10.00 25.00
10 PP/AW/GP/AJ/SD/AI/KK/CW 15.00 40.00
11 CB/JR/RA/DM/MR/DM/TK/MF 25.00 60.00
12 TM/YM/DW/JH/PG/SB/SS/MM 40.00 80.00

2005-06 Reflections Fabrics
STATED ODDS 1:6
*FABRIC BLUE/50: .6X TO 1.5X BASE HI
*FABRIC GREEN/25: .75X TO 2X BASE HI
*FABRIC RED/100: .5X TO 1.25X BASE HI
AH Al Harrington 2.00 5.00
AJ Antawn Jamison 2.00 5.00
AK Andrei Kirilenko 2.00 5.00
AM Andre Miller 2.00 5.00
AR Carlos Arroyo 1.50 4.00
AS Amare Stoudemire 2.50 6.00
BD Baron Davis 2.50 6.00
BG Ben Gordon 2.00 5.00
BW Ben Wallace 3.00 8.00
CA Carmelo Anthony 4.00 10.00
CB Chauncey Billups SP 3.00 8.00
CM Corey Maggette 2.00 5.00
DH Dwight Howard 3.00 8.00
DM Desmond Mason SP 2.00 5.00
DN Dirk Nowitzki 6.00 15.00
GA Gilbert Arenas 2.50 6.00
GP Gary Payton 4.00 10.00
JC Jamal Crawford 2.50 6.00
JK Jason Kidd 4.00 10.00
JN Jameer Nelson SP 1.50 4.00
JR J.R. Smith 2.50 6.00
JS Josh Smith 2.00 5.00
KB Kobe Bryant 40.00 100.00
KG Kevin Garnett 6.00 15.00
KK Kyle Korver 2.00 5.00
LD Luol Deng 2.00 5.00
LJ LeBron James 15.00 40.00
LO Lamar Odom 2.00 5.00
MB Mike Bibby 2.50 6.00
MJ Michael Jordan SP 40.00 100.00
MR Michael Redd SP 2.00 5.00
PG Pau Gasol 4.00 10.00
PP Paul Pierce 4.00 10.00
PS Peja Stojakovic 2.00 5.00
RJ Richard Jefferson 2.00 5.00
SB Shane Battier 2.00 5.00
SM Stephon Marbury 3.00 8.00
SN Steve Nash 5.00 12.00
SO Shaquille O'Neal 8.00 20.00
TD Tim Duncan 6.00 15.00
TM Tracy McGrady 4.00 10.00
YM Yao Ming 5.00 12.00

2005-06 Reflections Fabrics Dual Swatch
*DUAL SWATCH: .6X TO 1.5X BASE FAB HI
PRINT RUN 50 SER.#'d SETS
*BLUE: .75X TO 2X BASE FAB HI
BLUE PRINT RUN 25 SER.#'d SETS

2005-06 Reflections Fabrics Triple Swatch
*TRIPLE SWATCH: 1.25X TO 3X BASE FAB HI
PRINT RUN 25 SER.#'d SETS
*BLUE: 1.5X TO 4X BASE FAB HI
BLUE PRINT RUN 20 SER.#'d SETS

2005-06 Reflections Signatures
STATED ODDS 1:34
SP's/PRINT RUNS LISTED IN CHECKLIST
AA Alex Acker 2.00 5.00
AH Al Harrington 3.00 8.00
AI Andre Iguodala/35 10.00 25.00
AJ Antawn Jamison SP 4.00 10.00
AM Andre Miller SP 4.00 10.00
AN Martynas Andriuskevicius 2.00 5.00
AR Carlos Arroyo 8.00 20.00
BG Ben Gordon/35 8.00 20.00
BU Beno Udrih 3.00 8.00
BW Ben Wallace/35 10.00 25.00
CA Carmelo Anthony/35 15.00 40.00
CD Chris Duhon 3.00 8.00
CK Chris Kaman SP 3.00 8.00
CM Corey Maggette SP 3.00 8.00
CW Chris Wilcox SP 3.00 8.00
DA David Harrison 3.00 8.00
DF Derek Fisher 3.00 8.00
DH Dwight Howard/35 15.00 40.00
DM Desmond Mason 3.00 8.00
DS Damon Stoudamire SP 4.00 10.00
DW Dorell Wright 3.00 8.00
FG Francisco Garcia 2.00 5.00
GP Gary Payton/35 10.00 25.00
GR Danny Granger 3.00 8.00
HW Hakim Warrick 2.50 6.00
JA Jalen Rose 4.00 10.00
JG Joey Graham 2.50 6.00
JH Josh Howard SP 3.00 8.00
JJ Jarrett Jack 3.00 8.00
JK Jason Kidd/35 12.50 30.00
JM Jamaal Magloire 3.00 8.00
JN Jameer Nelson SP 3.00 8.00
JO Amir Johnson 3.00 8.00
JP Johan Petro 2.00 5.00
JS Jerry Stackhouse SP 6.00 15.00
JU Julius Hodge 2.00 5.00
JV Jackson Vroman 3.00 8.00
KA Kareem Rush 3.00 8.00
KH Kirk Hinrich/35 10.00 25.00
KM Kevin Martin 3.00 8.00
LH Luther Head 2.00 5.00
LJ LeBron James/35 1,000.00 2,000.00
LK Linas Kleiza 2.50 6.00
LU Luke Jackson 3.00 8.00
MD Marquis Daniels SP 3.00 8.00
MJ Michael Jordan/35 1,500.00 3,000.00
MP Morris Peterson 3.00 8.00
MW Maurice Williams 3.00 8.00
NR Nate Robinson SP 8.00 20.00
PA Pavel Podkolzin 3.00 8.00
PB Primoz Brezec 3.00 8.00
PP Paul Pierce/35 10.00 25.00
PS Pape Sow 3.00 8.00
RA Rafael Araujo 3.00 8.00
RM Ronald Murray 3.00 8.00
SB Shane Battier 3.00 8.00
SM Stephon Marbury/35 10.00 25.00
SN Steve Nash/35 25.00 60.00
SS Salim Stoudamire 2.50 6.00
SV Sasha Vujacic 3.00 8.00
TA Tony Allen 3.00 8.00
TK Toni Kukoc 3.00 8.00
TM Tracy McGrady/35 15.00 40.00
TR Trevor Ariza 3.00 8.00
UH Udonis Haslem 3.00 8.00
VK Viktor Khryapa 3.00 8.00
WS Wayne Simien SP 2.00 5.00
YM Yao Ming/35 25.00 60.00

2005-06 Reflections Signatures Blue
*BLUE: .6X TO 1.5X BASE HI
PRINT RUN 15 TO 50 SER.#'d SETS
AB Andrew Bogut/50 20.00 50.00
BY Andrew Bynum/50 6.00 15.00
CF Channing Frye/50 10.00 25.00
CP Chris Paul/50 20.00 50.00
CV Charlie Villanueva/50 6.00 15.00
GA Gilbert Arenas/50 8.00 20.00
GG Gerald Green/50 8.00 20.00
JC Josh Childress/50 5.00 12.00
JR J.R. Smith/50 6.00 15.00
JW Jason Williams/50 20.00 50.00
LO Lamar Odom/50 8.00 20.00
MA Marvin Williams/50 8.00 20.00
MB Mike Bibby/50 6.00 15.00
MC Rashad McCants/50 3.00 8.00
PG Pau Gasol/50 10.00 25.00
QR Quentin Richardson/50 5.00 12.00
RF Raymond Felton/50 12.00 30.00
RH Richard Hamilton/50 10.00 25.00
RJ Richard Jefferson/50 5.00 12.00
SL Shaun Livingston/50 5.00 12.00
WE Martell Webster/50 5.00 12.00
WI Deron Williams/50 25.00 60.00

2005-06 Reflections Signatures Green
*GREEN: .75X TO 2X BASE HI
PRINT RUN 10 TO 25 SER.#'d SETS
AB Andrew Bogut/25 25.00 60.00
BY Andrew Bynum/25 8.00 20.00
CF Channing Frye/25 12.00 30.00
CP Chris Paul/25 50.00 120.00
CV Charlie Villanueva/25 8.00 20.00
GA Gilbert Arenas/25 10.00 25.00
GG Gerald Green/25 10.00 25.00
JC Josh Childress/25 6.00 15.00
JR J.R. Smith/25 8.00 20.00
JW Jason Williams/25 40.00 100.00
LO Lamar Odom/25 10.00 25.00
MA Marvin Williams/25 10.00 25.00
MB Mike Bibby/25 8.00 20.00
MC Rashad McCants/25 4.00 10.00
PG Pau Gasol/25 12.50 30.00
QR Quentin Richardson/25 6.00 15.00
RF Raymond Felton/25 15.00 40.00
RH Richard Hamilton/25 12.50 30.00
RJ Richard Jefferson/25 6.00 15.00
SE Sean May/25 6.00 15.00
SL Shaun Livingston/25 6.00 15.00
WE Martell Webster/25 6.00 15.00
WI Deron Williams/25 30.00 80.00

2005-06 Reflections Signatures Red
*RED: .5X TO 1.25X BASE HI
PRINT RUN 25 TO 100 SER.#'d SETS
BY Andrew Bynum/100 5.00 12.00
CV Charlie Villanueva/100 5.00 12.00
GG Gerald Green/100 6.00 15.00
JC Josh Childress/100 4.00 10.00
JR J.R. Smith/100 5.00 12.00
JW Jason Williams/100 25.00 60.00
LJ LeBron James/25 1,250.00 2,500.00
MB Mike Bibby/100 5.00 12.00
MC Rashad McCants/100 2.50 6.00
QR Quentin Richardson/100 4.00 10.00
RH Richard Hamilton/100 8.00 20.00
RJ Richard Jefferson/100 4.00 10.00
SE Sean May/100 4.00 10.00

2006-07 Reflections
COMP.SET w/o SP's 25.00 60.00
111-125 RC PRINT RUN 799 SER.#'d SETS
126-149 RC PRINT RUN 399 SER.#'d SETS
1 Josh Childress .40 1.00
2 Joe Johnson .60 1.50
3 Marvin Williams .40 1.00
4 Dan Dickau .40 1.00
5 Paul Pierce 1.00 2.50
6 Wally Szczerbiak .50 1.25
7 Raymond Felton .40 1.00
8 Emeka Okafor .50 1.25
9 Kareem Rush .40 1.00
10 Gerald Wallace .50 1.25
11 Tyson Chandler .50 1.25
12 Luol Deng .50 1.25
13 Ben Gordon .50 1.25
14 Michael Jordan 5.00 12.00
15 Larry Hughes .50 1.25
16 Zydrunas Ilgauskas .50 1.25
17 LeBron James 5.00 12.00
18 Donyell Marshall .40 1.00
19 Marquis Daniels .40 1.00
20 Josh Howard .50 1.25
21 Dirk Nowitzki 1.50 4.00
22 Jason Terry .50 1.25
23 Carmelo Anthony 1.00 2.50
24 Earl Boykins .40 1.00
25 Marcus Camby .50 1.25
26 Kenyon Martin .50 1.25
27 Chauncey Billups .75 2.00
28 Richard Hamilton .60 1.50
29 Rasheed Wallace .75 2.00
30 Baron Davis .60 1.50
31 Ike Diogu .40 1.00
32 Mike Dunleavy .40 1.00
33 Troy Murphy .40 1.00
34 Luther Head .40 1.00
35 Tracy McGrady 1.00 2.50
36 Yao Ming 1.50 4.00
37 Jermaine O'Neal .60 1.50
38 Peja Stojakovic .50 1.25
39 Jamaal Tinsley .40 1.00
40 Chris Kaman .40 1.00
41 Sam Cassell .50 1.25
42 Shaun Livingston .50 1.25
43 Cuttino Mobley .50 1.25
44 Kobe Bryant 5.00 12.00
45 Devean George .40 1.00
46 Lamar Odom .50 1.25
47 Pau Gasol 1.00 2.50
48 Bobby Jackson .40 1.00
49 Mike Miller .50 1.25
50 Shaquille O'Neal 2.50 6.00
51 Dwyane Wade 1.25 3.00
52 Jason Williams .75 2.00
53 Andrew Bogut .50 1.25
54 T.J. Ford .40 1.00
55 Michael Redd .50 1.25
56 Ricky Davis .50 1.25
57 Kevin Garnett 1.50 4.00
58 Troy Hudson .40 1.00
59 Vince Carter 1.25 3.00
60 Jason Collins .40 1.00
61 Richard Jefferson .50 1.25
62 Jason Kidd 1.00 2.50
63 Desmond Mason .40 1.00
64 Chris Paul 1.25 3.00
65 J.R. Smith .60 1.50
66 Steve Francis .60 1.50
67 Channing Frye .40 1.00
68 Stephon Marbury .75 2.00
69 Dwight Howard .75 2.00
70 Darko Milicic .40 1.00
71 Jameer Nelson .40 1.00
72 Andre Iguodala .60 1.50
73 Allen Iverson 1.50 4.00
74 Chris Webber .75 2.00
75 Boris Diaw .50 1.25
76 Shawn Marion .60 1.50
77 Steve Nash 1.25 3.00
78 Amare Stoudemire .60 1.50
79 Juan Dixon .40 1.00
80 Darius Miles .40 1.00
81 Sebastian Telfair .40 1.00
82 Ron Artest .60 1.50
83 Mike Bibby .60 1.50
84 Brad Miller .50 1.25
85 Tim Duncan 1.50 4.00
86 Manu Ginobili 1.25 3.00
87 Robert Horry .60 1.50
88 Tony Parker 1.00 2.50
89 Ray Allen 1.00 2.50
90 Rashard Lewis .50 1.25
91 Luke Ridnour .50 1.25
92 Chris Bosh .75 2.00
93 Joey Graham .40 1.00
94 Charlie Villanueva .40 1.00
95 Carlos Boozer .50 1.25
96 Andrei Kirilenko .50 1.25
97 Deron Williams .50 1.25
98 Gilbert Arenas .60 1.50
99 Caron Butler .50 1.25
100 Antawn Jamison .50 1.25
101 Adam Morrison RC 2.00 5.00
102 Tyrus Thomas RC 2.00 5.00
103 Rudy Gay RC 3.00 8.00
104 Andrea Bargnani RC 2.00 5.00
105 LaMarcus Aldridge RC 6.00 15.00
106 Brandon Roy RC 5.00 12.00
107 Randy Foye RC 2.00 5.00
108 Marcus Williams RC 1.50 4.00
109 Rodney Carney RC 1.50 4.00
110 Shelden Williams RC 1.50 4.00
111 Patrick O'Bryant RC 1.00 2.50
112 Cedric Simmons RC 1.00 2.50
113 Jordan Farmar RC 1.25 3.00
114 J.J. Redick RC 3.00 8.00
115 Tarence Kinsey RC 1.00 2.50
116 Kevin Pittsnogle RC 1.25 3.00
117 Ronnie Brewer RC 1.50 4.00
118 Shawne Williams RC 1.00 2.50
119 Allan Ray RC 1.00 2.50
120 Shannon Brown RC 1.00 2.50
121 Kyle Lowry RC 5.00 12.00
122 Mardy Collins RC 1.00 2.50
123 Hilton Armstrong RC 1.00 2.50
124 Maurice Ager RC 1.00 2.50
125 Quincy Douby RC 1.00 2.50
126 Rajon Rondo RC 6.00 15.00
127 Mike Gansey RC 1.25 3.00
128 Joel Freeland RC 1.25 3.00
129 Josh Boone RC 1.25 3.00
130 Saer Sene RC 1.25 3.00
131 Denham Brown RC 1.25 3.00
132 Renaldo Balkman RC 1.50 4.00
133 Will Blalock RC 1.25 3.00
134 David Noel RC 1.25 3.00
135 Steve Novak RC 1.50 4.00
136 Solomon Jones RC 1.25 3.00
137 Dee Brown RC 1.25 3.00
138 Hassan Adams RC 1.25 3.00
139 Bobby Jones RC 1.25 3.00
140 Thabo Sefolosha RC 1.50 4.00
141 James White RC 1.25 3.00
142 Paul Davis RC 1.25 3.00
143 P.J. Tucker RC 2.00 5.00
144 Ryan Hollins RC 1.25 3.00
145 Damir Markota RC 1.25 3.00
146 Leon Powe RC 1.25 3.00
147 James Augustine RC 1.25 3.00
148 Alexander Johnson RC 1.25 3.00
149 Daniel Gibson RC 1.50 4.00

2006-07 Reflections Blue
*1-100 BLUE: 2X TO 5X BASE HI
*101-110 BLUE RC: .75X TO 2X BASE HI
*111-125 BLUE RC: 1.25X TO 3X BASE HI
*126-149 BLUE RC: 1X TO 2.5X BASE HI
BLUE PRINT RUN 49 SER.#'d SETS
17 LeBron James 60.00 150.00

2006-07 Reflections Copper
*1-100 COPPER: 1.5X TO 4X BASE HI
*101-110 COPPER RC: .5X TO 1.25X BASE HI
*111-125 COPPER RC: .75X TO 2X BASE HI
*126-149 COPPER RC: .6X TO 1.5X BASE HI
COPPER PRINT RUN 99 SER.#'d SETS
17 LeBron James 50.00 120.00

2006-07 Reflections Dual Fabric
APPROXIMATE ODDS 1:12
*GOLD FABRIC: .6X TO 1.5X BASE HI
GOLD PRINT RUN 100 SER.#'d SETS
*COPPER FABRIC: .75X TO 2X BASE HI
COPPER PRINT RUN 50 SER.#'d SETS
*PATCH BLUE: 1.5X TO 4X BASE HI
PAT.BLUE PRINT RUN 15 SER.#'d SETS
AH R.Allen/R.Hamilton 4.00 10.00
AI G.Arenas/A.Iguodala 4.00 10.00
AN R.Araujo/N.Hilario 3.00 8.00
AW C.Anthony/H.Warrick 6.00 15.00
BC C.Butler/B.Gordon 3.00 8.00
BD C.Boozer/L.Deng 3.00 8.00
BG B.Bowen/M.Ginobili 8.00 20.00
BH E.Brand/D.Howard 5.00 12.00
BM K.Bryant/T.McGrady 60.00 150.00
CB T.Chandler/K.Brown 3.00 8.00
CR E.Curry/Z.Randolph 4.00 10.00
DM R.Davis/R.McCants 3.00 8.00
DP T.Duncan/T.Parker 10.00 25.00
DR B.Davis/J.Richardson 4.00 10.00
DS M.Dunleavy/P.Stojakovic 3.00 8.00
FR S.Francis/N.Robinson 4.00 10.00
FV C.Frye/C.Villanueva 2.50 6.00
FW R.Felton/D.Williams 3.00 8.00
GC D.George/B.Cook 2.50 6.00
GJ K.Garnett/R.Jefferson 10.00 25.00
HB M.Bibby/K.Hinrich 4.00 10.00
HH J.Howard/D.Harris 3.00 8.00
HR J.Howard/J.Rose 3.00 8.00
JH E.Jones/L.Hughes 4.00 10.00
JJ M.Jordan/L.James 300.00 600.00
JW J.Johnson/M.Williams 4.00 10.00
KH J.Kidd/G.Hill 6.00 15.00
KW C.Webber/K.Korver 5.00 12.00
LF F.Jones/L.Jackson 2.50 6.00
LO R.Lewis/E.Okafor 3.00 8.00
MG D.Mason/J.Graham 2.50 6.00
MI D.Mutombo/Z.Ilgauskas 4.00 10.00
MK J.McInnis/N.Krstic 2.50 6.00
MM C.Maggette/C.Mobley 3.00 8.00
MN S.Nash/S.Marion 8.00 20.00
NS S.Nash/A.Stoudemire 8.00 20.00
NT J.Nelson/S.Telfair 2.50 6.00
NU B.Nachbar/B.Udrih 2.50 6.00
OW J.Williams/S.O'Neal 15.00 40.00
PJ P.Pierce/A.Jamison 6.00 15.00
RB M.Redd/A.Bogut 3.00 8.00
SJ W.Szczerbiak/A.Jefferson 3.00 8.00
SM S.Swift/D.Milicic 2.50 6.00
TO J.Tinsley/J.O'Neal 4.00 10.00
WB B.Wallace/C.Bosh 5.00 12.00
WC J.Williams/S.Cassell 5.00 12.00
WK C.Webber/A.Kirilenko 5.00 12.00
WN R.Wallace/D.Nowitzki 10.00 25.00
WP A.Walker/T.Prince 4.00 10.00

2006-07 Reflections Mirror Image Dual Auto Jersey
PRINT RUN 25 SER.#'d SETS
AB R.Artest/B.Bowen 20.00 50.00
BD B.Davis/C.Billups 40.00 100.00
BH D.Howard/A.Bogut 40.00 100.00
BO E.Brand/E.Okafor 15.00 40.00
BP M.Bibby/C.Paul 75.00 200.00
CI V.Carter/A.Iguodala 75.00 200.00
GB K.Garnett/C.Bosh 125.00 300.00
JJ M.Jordan/L.James 4,000.00 8,000.00
NK S.Nash/J.Kidd 75.00 200.00
TR S.Telfair/N.Robinson 15.00 40.00

1991 Pro Stars Posters

2006-07 Reflections Mirror Image Dual Jersey
PRINT RUN 100 SER.#'d SETS
*PATCHES: .75X TO 2X BASE HI
PATCH PRINT RUN 50 SER.#'d SETS
AB R.Artest/B.Bowen 6.00 15.00
BD B.Davis/C.Billups 8.00 20.00
BH D.Howard/A.Bogut 8.00 20.00
BO E.Brand/E.Okafor 5.00 12.00
BP M.Bibby/C.Paul 12.00 30.00
BS K.Brown/S.Swift 12.00 30.00
CI V.Carter/A.Iguodala 12.00 30.00
CS J.Childress/J.Smith 4.00 10.00
DB T.Duncan/E.Brand 15.00 40.00
DH L.Hughes/M.Daniels 5.00 12.00
FM S.Francis/S.Marbury 8.00 20.00
FV C.Frye/C.Villanueva 4.00 10.00
GB K.Garnett/C.Bosh 15.00 40.00
HB K.Bryant/R.Hamilton 125.00 300.00
HD R.Hamilton/R.Davis 6.00 15.00
HM G.Hill/T.McGrady 10.00 25.00
JA L.James/C.Anthony 150.00 400.00
JH K.Hinrich/S.Jasikevicius 5.00 12.00
JJ M.Jordan/L.James 400.00 800.00
JR A.Jamison/J.Richardson 6.00 15.00
KM A.Kirilenko/D.Milicic 5.00 12.00
MH S.Marion/D.Howard 8.00 20.00
MO J.Magloire/J.O'Neal 6.00 15.00
MP A.Miller/T.Parker 10.00 25.00
NG D.Nowitzki/P.Gasol 15.00 40.00
NK S.Nash/J.Kidd 12.00 30.00
OM Y.Ming/S.O'Neal 25.00 60.00
PR P.Pierce/J.Richardson 10.00 25.00
RG M.Redd/B.Gordon 5.00 12.00
RJ Q.Richardson/J.Johnson 6.00 15.00
SG W.Szczerbiak/M.Ginobili 12.00 30.00
SO A.Stoudemire/J.O'Neal 6.00 15.00
TM J.Tinsley/J.McInnis 4.00 10.00
TR S.Telfair/N.Robinson 5.00 12.00
WO C.Webber/L.Odom 8.00 20.00

2006-07 Reflections Signature Copper
*COPPER: .75X TO 2X SILVER HI
STATED PRINT RUN 10-20 SER.#'d SETS

2006-07 Reflections Signature Gold
*GOLD: .6X TO 1.5X SILVER HI
STATED PRINT RUN 25 TO 50 SER.#'d SETS
MJ Michael Jordan/25 3,000.00 6,000.00

2006-07 Reflections Signature Silver
APPROXIMATE ODDS 1:12
AB Andrea Bargnani 4.00 10.00
AD Hassan Adams 3.00 8.00
AI Andre Iguodala 5.00 12.00
AJ Al Jefferson 3.00 8.00
BA Brent Barry 3.00 8.00
BB Bruce Bowen 4.00 10.00
BD Baron Davis 5.00 12.00
BJ Bobby Jackson 3.00 8.00
BM Brad Miller 4.00 10.00
BN Denham Brown 3.00 8.00
BO Andrew Bogut 4.00 10.00
BR Brandon Roy 10.00 25.00
BS Bobby Simmons 3.00 8.00
CA Carmelo Anthony 40.00 100.00
CB Chauncey Billups 12.00 30.00
CD Chris Duhon 3.00 8.00
CH Chris Bosh 12.00 30.00
CM Cuttino Mobley 4.00 10.00
CP Chris Paul 50.00 120.00
CS Cedric Simmons 3.00 8.00
DA Marquis Daniels 3.00 8.00
DB Dee Brown 3.00 8.00
DE Daniel Ewing 3.00 8.00
DG Daniel Gibson 4.00 10.00
DH Dwight Howard 25.00 60.00
DN David Noel 3.00 8.00
DR David Robinson 50.00 120.00
EB Elton Brand 4.00 10.00
EO Emeka Okafor 4.00 10.00
FR Raymond Felton 3.00 8.00
HA Hilton Armstrong 3.00 8.00
HO Hakeem Olajuwon 50.00 120.00
ID Ike Diogu 3.00 8.00
JB Josh Boone 3.00 8.00
JJ Joe Johnson 5.00 12.00
JK Jason Kidd 12.00 30.00
JS Bobby Jones 3.00 8.00
JT Jarrett Jack 4.00 10.00
JW James White 3.00 8.00
KG Kevin Garnett 100.00 250.00
KL Kyle Lowry 15.00 40.00
LA LaMarcus Aldridge 12.00 30.00
LJ LeBron James 1,000.00 2,000.00
LO Lamar Odom 4.00 10.00
LR Luke Ridnour 4.00 10.00
MA Maurice Ager 3.00 8.00
MB Mike Bibby 8.00 20.00
MC Mardy Collins 3.00 8.00
MD Desmond Mason 3.00 8.00
MR Michael Redd 4.00 10.00
MW Marcus Williams 3.00 8.00
NO Steve Novak 4.00 10.00
NR Nate Robinson 4.00 10.00
PD Paul Davis 3.00 8.00
PO Patrick O'Bryant 3.00 8.00
PP Paul Pierce 30.00 80.00
PS Peja Stojakovic 4.00 10.00
PT P.J. Tucker 5.00 12.00
QD Quincy Douby 3.00 8.00
RA Ron Artest 5.00 12.00
RB Ronnie Brewer 5.00 12.00
RC Rodney Carney 3.00 8.00
RF Randy Foye 4.00 10.00
RG Rudy Gay 6.00 15.00
RJ Richard Jefferson 4.00 10.00
RM Rashad McCants 3.00 8.00
RR Rajon Rondo 15.00 40.00
RT Ronny Turiaf 4.00 10.00
RY Ryan Hollins 3.00 8.00
SJ Solomon Jones 3.00 8.00
SN Steve Nash 60.00 150.00
SW Shelden Williams 3.00 8.00
TT Tyrus Thomas 4.00 10.00
VC Vince Carter 60.00 150.00
WI Shawne Williams 3.00 8.00
WM Marvin Williams 3.00 8.00
WS Wayne Simien 3.00 8.00
YM Yao Ming 150.00 400.00

1987-88 Rockford Lightning CBA
COMPLETE SET (10) 1.50 4.00
COMMON CARD (1-10) .15 .40
1 Fred Cofield .30 .75
2 Bruce Douglas .15 .40
3 John Fox .15 .40
4 Carl Henry .30 .75
5 Jim Lampley .15 .40
6 Pete Myers .30 .75
7 Richard Rellford .15 .40
8 Charley Rosen CO .40 1.00
9 John Schweitz .30 .75
10 David Wood .50 1.25

2001 Rockers Fleer WNBA
COMPLETE SET (9) 4.00 10.00
1 Eva Nemcova 1.25 3.00
2 Ann Wauters 1.25 3.00
3 Merlakia Jones .40 1.00
4 Mery Andrade .40 1.00
5 Cleveland Rockers .40 1.00
6 Rushia Brown .40 1.00
7 Helen Darling .40 1.00
8 Vicky Hall .40 1.00
9 Chasity Melvin .40 1.00

1971-72 Rockets Carnation Milk
COMPLETE SET 300.00 600.00
1 Dick Cunningham 30.00 60.00
2 Dick Gibbs 30.00 60.00
3 Elvin Hayes 75.00 150.00
4 Stu Lantz 50.00 100.00
5 Cliff Meely 30.00 60.00
6 Calvin Murphy 50.00 100.00
7 Mike Newlin 40.00 75.00
8 Rudy Tomjanovich 60.00 120.00

1969-70 Rockets Coca-Cola
COMPLETE SET (9) 75.00 150.00
1 Rick Adelman 8.00 20.00
2 Jim Barnett 5.00 10.00
3 John Block 5.00 10.00
4 Elvin Hayes 12.50 25.00
5 Toby Kimball 5.00 10.00
6 Stu Lantz 8.00 20.00
7 Pat Riley 15.00 40.00
8 John Trapp 5.00 10.00
9 Art Williams 5.00 10.00

1971-72 Rockets Denver Team Issue
COMPLETE SET (2) 15.00 30.00
1 Byron Beck
Art Becker
Julian Hammond
Marv Roberts
Ralph Simpson
Dwight Waller
Chuck Williams
Steve Wilson 7.50 15.00
2 Stan Albeck ACO
Larry Brown
Alex Hannum CO
Julius Keye
Del Klone GM
Dave Robisch
Al Smith
Lloyd Williams TR 10.00 20.00

1968-69 Rockets Jack in the Box
COMPLETE SET (14) 50.00 90.00
1 Rick Adelman 2.50 6.00
2 Harry Barnes SP 20.00 50.00
3 Jim Barnett .75 2.00
4 John Block .60 1.50
5 Henry Finkel SP 20.00 50.00
6 Elvin Hayes 3.00 8.00
7 Toby Kimball .60 1.50
8 Don Kojis .60 1.50
9 Stu Lantz 1.25 3.00
10 Pat Riley 4.00 10.00
11 Bobby Smith 1.50 4.00
12 John Trapp .60 1.50
13 Art Williams .60 1.50
14 Bernie Williams 1.00 2.50

1978-79 Rockets Photos
COMPLETE SET 15.00 30.00
1 Rick Barry 3.00 8.00
2 Alonzo Bradley 1.00 2.50
3 Jacky Dorsey 1.00 2.50
4 Mike Dunleavy 1.50 4.00
5 Moses Malone 2.50 6.00
6 Calvin Murphy 2.00 5.00
7 Mike Newlin 1.25 3.00
8 Jackie Robinson 1.00 2.50
9 Rudy Tomjanovich 2.00 5.00
10 Slick Watts 1.25 3.00

1975-76 Rockets Team Issue
COMPLETE SET (8) 12.50 25.00
1 John Johnson 1.50 4.00
2 Kevin Kunnert 1.25 3.00
3 Mike Newlin 1.50 4.00
4 Ed Ratleff 1.25 3.00
5 Ron Riley 1.25 3.00
6 Rudy White 1.25 3.00
7 Dave Wohl 1.25 3.00
8 Tom Nissalke CO 1.25 3.00

1977-78 Rockets Team Issue
COMPLETE SET 10.00 20.00
1 John Johnson 1.50 4.00
2 Kevin Kunnert 1.25 3.00
3 Mike Newlin 1.50 4.00
4 Tom Nissalke CO 1.25 3.00
5 Ed Ratleff 1.25 3.00
6 Ron Riley 1.25 3.00
7 Rudy White 1.25 3.00
8 Dave Wohl 1.50 4.00

1990-91 Rockets Team Issue
COMPLETE SET (5) 4.00 10.00
1 Dave Jamerson .30 .75
2 Buck Johnson .30 .75
3 Hakeem Olajuwon 3.00 8.00
4 Otis Thorpe .60 1.50
5 David Wood .30 .75

1971-72 Rockets Team Photo
1 Team Photo
Curtis Perry
Elvin Hayes
Dick Cunningham
John Egan
Dick Gibbs
Rudy Tomjanovich
Mike Newlin
Jim Davis
Cliff Meely
Calvin Murphy
Stu Lantz
John Vallely 6.00 12.00

2008-09 Rockets Upper Deck
COMPLETE SET (14) 2.50 6.00
1 Yao Ming .75 2.00
2 Tracy McGrady .50 1.25
3 Shane Battier .25 .60
4 Rafer Alston .20 .50
5 Luis Scola .25 .60
6 Chuck Hayes .20 .50
7 Steve Francis .30 .75
8 Luther Head .20 .50
9 Carl Landry .20 .50
10 Dikembe Mutombo .30 .75
11 Ron Artest .30 .75
12 Joey Dorsey .20 .50
13 Rick Adelman CO .20 .50
14 Hakeem Olajuwon .60 1.50

2009-10 Rookies and Stars
COMP.SET w/o SPs (115) 12.50 30.00
AU RC PRINT RUNS LISTED IN CHECKLIST
ASTERISK CARDS FROM PANINI UPDATE
1 Josh Smith .25 .60
2 Joe Johnson .40 1.00
3 Mike Bibby .40 1.00
4 Paul Pierce .60 1.50
5 Ray Allen .60 1.50
6 Rajon Rondo .50 1.25
7 Kevin Garnett 1.00 2.50
8 Gerald Wallace .30 .75
9 Boris Diaw .30 .75
10 Raja Bell .30 .75
11 Derrick Rose .60 1.50
12 John Salmons .30 .75
13 Kirk Hinrich .30 .75
14 LeBron James 3.00 8.00
15 Shaquille O'Neal 1.25 3.00
16 Mo Williams .30 .75
17 Dirk Nowitzki 1.00 2.50
18 Josh Howard .30 .75
19 Jason Kidd .60 1.50
20 Jason Terry .30 .75
21 Shawn Marion .40 1.00
22 Carmelo Anthony .60 1.50
23 Chauncey Billups .50 1.25
24 J.R. Smith .30 .75
25 Richard Hamilton .40 1.00
26 Tayshaun Prince .40 1.00
27 Allen Iverson .75 2.00
28 Stephen Jackson .30 .75
29 Corey Maggette .30 .75
30 Monta Ellis .30 .75
31 Yao Ming 1.00 2.50
32 Tracy McGrady .75 2.00
33 Trevor Ariza .25 .60
34 Danny Granger .25 .60
35 Mike Dunleavy .25 .60
36 T.J. Ford .25 .60
37 Al Thornton .25 .60
38 Eric Gordon .30 .75
39 Kobe Bryant 3.00 8.00
40 Pau Gasol .60 1.50
41 Ron Artest .30 .75
42 Andrew Bynum .40 1.00
43 Rudy Gay .40 1.00
44 O.J. Mayo .25 .60
45 Mike Conley Jr. .30 .75
46 Zach Randolph .40 1.00
47 Dwyane Wade .75 2.00
48 Michael Beasley .25 .60
49 Jermaine O'Neal .40 1.00
50 Udonis Haslem .25 .60
51 Michael Redd .30 .75
52 Ramon Sessions .25 .60
53 Andrew Bogut .30 .75
54 Al Jefferson .25 .60
55 Ryan Gomes .25 .60
56 Kevin Love .40 1.00
57 Devin Harris .25 .60
58 Brook Lopez .40 1.00
59 Rafer Alston .25 .60
60 Chris Paul .75 2.00
61 David West .30 .75
62 Peja Stojakovic .30 .75
63 Al Harrington .30 .75
64 Nate Robinson .30 .75
65 Wilson Chandler .30 .75
66 Kevin Durant 1.50 4.00
67 Jeff Green .30 .75
68 Russell Westbrook .75 2.00
69 Dwight Howard .50 1.25
70 Rashard Lewis .30 .75
71 Jameer Nelson .25 .60
72 Vince Carter .75 2.00
73 Andre Iguodala .40 1.00
74 Elton Brand .30 .75
75 Thaddeus Young .25 .60
76 Amare Stoudemire .30 .75
77 Steve Nash .75 2.00
78 Leandro Barbosa .30 .75
79 Channing Frye .25 .60
80 Brandon Roy .50 1.25
81 LaMarcus Aldridge .40 1.00
82 Greg Oden .25 .60
83 Kevin Martin .30 .75
84 Andres Nocioni .25 .60
85 Spencer Hawes .25 .60
86 Tony Parker .60 1.50
87 Tim Duncan 1.00 2.50
88 Manu Ginobili .75 2.00
89 Richard Jefferson .30 .75
90 Chris Bosh .50 1.25
91 Hedo Turkoglu .25 .60
92 Andrea Bargnani .25 .60
93 Deron Williams .30 .75
94 Mehmet Okur .30 .75
95 Andrei Kirilenko .30 .75
96 Ronnie Brewer .25 .60
97 Antawn Jamison .30 .75
98 Gilbert Arenas .30 .75
99 Caron Butler .30 .75
100 Randy Foye .25 .60
101 Kareem Abdul-Jabbar 1.25 3.00
102 Elvin Hayes .60 1.50
103 Karl Malone .50 1.25
104 Arnie Risen .40 1.00
105 Jalen Rose .30 .75
106 Dave DeBusschere .40 1.00
107 Artis Gilmore .50 1.25
108 Nate Archibald .50 1.25
109 Mark Eaton .25 .60
110 Darryl Dawkins .40 1.00
111 Spencer Haywood .25 .60
112 Bill Cartwright .30 .75
113 Moses Malone .60 1.50
114 Magic Johnson 1.50 4.00
115 Sleepy Floyd .30 .75
116 Dante Cunningham RC .50 1.25
117 Jon Brockman RC .60 1.50
118 Jonas Jerebko RC .60 1.50
119 Derrick Brown RC .50 1.25
120 DJonte Christmas RC .50 1.25
121 Marcus Thornton RC .60 1.50
122 Danny Green RC .75 2.00
123 Goran Suton RC .50 1.25
124 Jack McClinton RC .50 1.25
125 A.J. Price RC .50 1.25
126 Serge Ibaka RC .75 2.00
127 DeMar DeRozan RC 6.00 15.00
128 Chris Hunter RC .50 1.25
129 Lester Hudson RC .50 1.25
130 David Andersen RC .50 1.25
131 Blake Griffin AU/449 RC 20.00 50.00
132 H.Thabeet AU/449 RC 4.00 10.00
133 James Harden AU/449 RC 200.00 500.00
134 Tyreke Evans AU/379 RC 5.00 12.00
135 Jonny Flynn AU/449 RC 4.00 10.00
136 Stephen Curry AU/449 RC 2,000.00 4,000.00
137 Jordan Hill AU/449 RC 4.00 10.00
138 Dante Cunningham AU/437 RC 4.00 10.00
139 B.Jennings AU/379 RC 6.00 15.00
140 T.Williams AU/356 RC 4.00 10.00
141 Gerald Henderson AU/449 RC 4.00 10.00
142 T.Hansbrough AU/449 RC 5.00 12.00
143 Earl Clark AU/449 RC 4.00 10.00
144 Austin Daye AU/369 RC 4.00 10.00
145 James Johnson AU/449 RC 5.00 12.00
146 Jrue Holiday AU/449 RC 20.00 50.00
147 Ty Lawson AU/369 RC 5.00 12.00
148 Jeff Teague AU/449 RC 5.00 12.00
149 Eric Maynor AU/369 RC 4.00 10.00
150 Darren Collison AU/347 RC 6.00 15.00
151 Omri Casspi AU/449 RC 4.00 10.00
152 B.J. Mullens AU/379 RC 4.00 10.00
153 R.Beaubois AU/390 RC 4.00 10.00
154 Taj Gibson AU/369 RC 5.00 12.00
155 DeMarre Carroll AU/449 RC 5.00 12.00
156 Wayne Ellington AU/416 RC 5.00 12.00
157 Toney Douglas AU/379 RC 4.00 10.00
158 Jermaine Taylor AU/449 RC 4.00 10.00
159 Jeff Pendergraph AU/449 RC 4.00 10.00
160 DaJuan Summers AU/378 RC 4.00 10.00
161 Sam Young AU/369 RC 4.00 10.00
162 DeJuan Blair AU/449 RC 5.00 12.00
163 Chase Budinger AU/369 RC 4.00 10.00
164 Jodie Meeks AU/449 RC 4.00 10.00
165 Taylor Griffin AU/380 RC 4.00 10.00
166 D.Derozan AU/499 RC* 150.00 400.00
167 W.Matthews AU/499 RC* 6.00 15.00
168 Serge Ibaka AU/499 RC* 6.00 15.00
169 M.Thornton AU/499 RC* 5.00 12.00
170 J.Jerebko AU/499 RC* 5.00 12.00

2009-10 Rookies and Stars Gold
*GOLD 1-115: 1X TO 2.5X BASE HI
*GOLD 116-130: .75X TO 2X BASE HI
*GOLD 131-165: .6X TO 1.5X BASE HI
GOLD 1-130 PRINT RUN 500 SER.#'d SETS
GOLD 131-165 PRINT RUN 25 SER.#'d SETS
136 Stephen Curry AU 4,000.00 8,000.00

2009-10 Rookies and Stars Gold Holofoil
*GOLD STARS: 2X TO 5X BASE HI
*GOLD RCs: 1.25X TO 3X BASE HI
STATED PRINT RUN 250 SER.#'d SETS

2009-10 Rookies and Stars Current NBA Team Patches Signatures
STATED PRINT RUN 199 SER.#'d SETS
1 Kobe Bryant 500.00 1,000.00

2009-10 Rookies and Stars Dress for Success Materials
STATED PRINT RUN 299 SER.#'d SETS
*PRIME: 1X TO 2.5X BASE HI
PRIME PRINT RUN 50 SER.#'d SETS
1 Blake Griffin 8.00 20.00
2 Hasheem Thabeet 1.25 3.00
3 James Harden 20.00 50.00
4 Tyreke Evans 1.50 4.00
5 Jonny Flynn 1.25 3.00
6 Stephen Curry 125.00 300.00
7 Jordan Hill 1.25 3.00
8 DeMar DeRozan 15.00 40.00
9 Brandon Jennings 2.00 5.00
10 Terrence Williams 1.25 3.00
11 Gerald Henderson 1.25 3.00
12 Tyler Hansbrough 1.50 4.00
13 Earl Clark 1.25 3.00
14 Austin Daye 1.25 3.00
15 James Johnson 1.50 4.00
16 Jrue Holiday 6.00 15.00
17 Ty Lawson 1.50 4.00
18 Jeff Teague 1.50 4.00
19 Eric Maynor 1.25 3.00
20 Darren Collison 2.00 5.00
21 Omri Casspi 1.25 3.00
22 B.J. Mullens 1.25 3.00
23 Rodrigue Beaubois 1.50 4.00
24 Taj Gibson 1.50 4.00
25 DeMarre Carroll 1.50 4.00
26 Wayne Ellington 1.50 4.00
27 Toney Douglas 1.25 3.00
28 Jermaine Taylor 1.25 3.00
29 Jeff Pendergraph 1.25 3.00
30 DaJuan Summers 1.25 3.00
31 Sam Young 1.25 3.00
32 DeJuan Blair 1.50 4.00
33 Chase Budinger 1.25 3.00
34 Jodie Meeks 1.25 3.00
35 Taylor Griffin 1.25 3.00

2009-10 Rookies and Stars Dress for Success Materials Signatures
STATED PRINT RUN 25 SER.#'d SETS
1 Blake Griffin 25.00 60.00
2 Hasheem Thabeet 4.00 10.00
3 James Harden 300.00 600.00
4 Tyreke Evans 5.00 12.00
5 Jonny Flynn 4.00 10.00
6 Stephen Curry 1,500.00 3,000.00
7 Jordan Hill 4.00 10.00
9 Brandon Jennings 6.00 15.00
10 Terrence Williams 4.00 10.00
11 Gerald Henderson 4.00 10.00
12 Tyler Hansbrough 5.00 12.00
13 Earl Clark 4.00 10.00
14 Austin Daye 4.00 10.00
15 James Johnson 5.00 12.00
16 Jrue Holiday 20.00 50.00
18 Jeff Teague 5.00 12.00
21 Omri Casspi 4.00 10.00
22 B.J. Mullens 4.00 10.00
23 Rodrigue Beaubois 4.00 10.00
25 DeMarre Carroll 5.00 12.00
26 Wayne Ellington 5.00 12.00
27 Toney Douglas 4.00 10.00
28 Jermaine Taylor 4.00 10.00
29 Jeff Pendergraph 4.00 10.00
30 DaJuan Summers 4.00 10.00
32 DeJuan Blair 5.00 12.00
33 Chase Budinger 4.00 10.00
34 Jodie Meeks 4.00 10.00
35 Taylor Griffin 4.00 10.00

2009-10 Rookies and Stars Freshman Orientation Materials
STATED PRINT RUN 299 SER.#'d SETS
*PRIME: 1X TO 2.5X BASE HI
PRIME PRINT RUN 50 SER.#'d SETS
1 Blake Griffin 8.00 20.00
2 Hasheem Thabeet 1.25 3.00
3 James Harden 20.00 50.00
4 Tyreke Evans 1.50 4.00
5 Jonny Flynn 1.25 3.00
6 Stephen Curry 125.00 300.00
7 Jordan Hill 1.25 3.00
8 DeMar DeRozan 15.00 40.00
9 Brandon Jennings 2.00 5.00
10 Terrence Williams 1.25 3.00
11 Gerald Henderson 1.25 3.00
12 Tyler Hansbrough 1.50 4.00
13 Earl Clark 1.25 3.00
14 Austin Daye 1.25 3.00
15 James Johnson 1.50 4.00
16 Jrue Holiday 6.00 15.00
17 Ty Lawson 1.50 4.00
18 Jeff Teague 1.50 4.00
19 Eric Maynor 1.25 3.00
20 Darren Collison 2.00 5.00
21 Omri Casspi 1.25 3.00
22 B.J. Mullens 1.25 3.00
23 Rodrigue Beaubois 1.25 3.00
24 Taj Gibson 1.50 4.00
25 DeMarre Carroll 1.50 4.00
26 Wayne Ellington 1.50 4.00
27 Toney Douglas 1.25 3.00
28 Jermaine Taylor 1.25 3.00
29 Jeff Pendergraph 1.25 3.00
30 DaJuan Summers 1.25 3.00
31 Sam Young 1.25 3.00
32 DeJuan Blair 1.50 4.00
33 Chase Budinger 1.25 3.00
34 Jodie Meeks 1.25 3.00
35 Taylor Griffin 1.25 3.00

2009-10 Rookies and Stars Freshman Orientation Materials Signatures
STATED PRINT RUN 25 SER.#'d SETS
1 Blake Griffin 60.00 150.00
2 Hasheem Thabeet 4.00 10.00
3 James Harden 300.00 600.00
4 Tyreke Evans 5.00 12.00
5 Jonny Flynn 4.00 10.00
6 Stephen Curry 1,500.00 3,000.00
7 Jordan Hill 4.00 10.00
9 Brandon Jennings 6.00 15.00
10 Terrence Williams 4.00 10.00
11 Gerald Henderson 4.00 10.00
12 Tyler Hansbrough 5.00 12.00
13 Earl Clark 4.00 10.00
14 Austin Daye 4.00 10.00
15 James Johnson 5.00 12.00
16 Jrue Holiday 20.00 50.00
18 Jeff Teague 5.00 12.00
21 Omri Casspi 4.00 10.00
22 B.J. Mullens 4.00 10.00
23 Rodrigue Beaubois 5.00 12.00
24 Taj Gibson 5.00 12.00
25 DeMarre Carroll 5.00 12.00
26 Wayne Ellington 5.00 12.00
27 Toney Douglas 4.00 10.00
28 Jermaine Taylor 4.00 10.00
29 Jeff Pendergraph 4.00 10.00
30 DaJuan Summers 4.00 10.00
32 DeJuan Blair 5.00 12.00
33 Chase Budinger 4.00 10.00
34 Jodie Meeks 4.00 10.00
35 Taylor Griffin 4.00 10.00

2009-10 Rookies and Stars Gold Materials
STATED PRINT RUN 99 TO 250 SER.#'d SETS
1 Josh Smith/250 2.00 5.00
3 Mike Bibby/250 3.00 8.00
13 Kirk Hinrich/250 2.50 6.00
14 LeBron James/250 8.00 20.00
17 Dirk Nowitzki/99 8.00 20.00
18 Josh Howard/250 2.50 6.00
19 Jason Kidd/250 5.00 12.00
20 Jason Terry/250 2.50 6.00
22 Carmelo Anthony/250 5.00 12.00
26 Tayshaun Prince/250 3.00 8.00
28 Stephen Jackson/250 2.50 6.00
31 Yao Ming/250 8.00 20.00
32 Tracy McGrady/250 6.00 15.00
39 Kobe Bryant/99 12.00 30.00
42 Andrew Bynum/250 2.00 5.00
45 Mike Conley Jr./250 2.50 6.00
47 Dwyane Wade/250 6.00 15.00
48 Michael Beasley/250 2.00 5.00
49 Jermaine O'Neal/100 3.00 8.00
50 Udonis Haslem/250 2.00 5.00
51 Michael Redd/250 2.50 6.00
53 Andrew Bogut/250 2.50 6.00
54 Al Jefferson/250 2.00 5.00
56 Kevin Love/250 3.00 8.00
57 Devin Harris/199 2.00 5.00
62 Peja Stojakovic/250 2.50 6.00
63 Al Harrington/250 2.50 6.00
66 Kevin Durant/250 6.00 15.00
69 Dwight Howard/250 4.00 10.00
70 Rashard Lewis/250 2.50 6.00
73 Andre Iguodala/250 3.00 8.00
74 Elton Brand/250 2.50 6.00
75 Thaddeus Young/250 2.00 5.00
76 Amare Stoudemire/250 2.50 6.00
77 Steve Nash/250 6.00 15.00
80 Brandon Roy/250 4.00 10.00
81 LaMarcus Aldridge/250 3.00 8.00
82 Greg Oden/250 2.00 5.00
84 Andres Nocioni/250 2.00 5.00
86 Tony Parker/250 5.00 12.00
87 Tim Duncan/250 8.00 20.00
88 Manu Ginobili/250 6.00 15.00
92 Andrea Bargnani/250 2.00 5.00
93 Deron Williams/250 2.50 6.00
94 Carlos Boozer/250 2.50 6.00
95 Andrei Kirilenko/250 2.50 6.00
127 DeMar DeRozan/250 25.00 60.00

2009-10 Rookies and Stars Gold Stars
COMPLETE SET (15) 8.00 20.00
*BLACK: .75X TO 2X BASE HI
BLACK PRINT RUN 100 SER.#'d SETS
*GOLD: .5X TO 1.25X BASE HI
GOLD PRINT RUN 500 SER.#'d SETS
*HOLOFOIL: .6X TO 1.5X BASE HI
HOLO PRINT RUN 250 SER.#'d SETS
1 Dwyane Wade 1.50 4.00
2 Kobe Bryant 6.00 15.00
3 LeBron James 6.00 15.00
4 Dirk Nowitzki 2.00 5.00
5 Danny Granger .50 1.25
6 Kevin Durant 3.00 8.00
7 Chris Paul 1.50 4.00
8 Carmelo Anthony 1.25 3.00
9 Chris Bosh 1.00 2.50
10 Brandon Roy 1.00 2.50
11 Joe Johnson .75 2.00
12 Devin Harris .50 1.25
13 Deron Williams .60 1.50
14 Dwight Howard 1.00 2.50
15 Paul Pierce 1.25 3.00

2009-10 Rookies and Stars Gold Stars Materials
*PRIME: 1X TO 2.5X BASE HI
PRIME PRINT RUN 10 TO 50 SER.#'d SETS
1 Dwyane Wade 5.00 12.00
2 Kobe Bryant 12.00 30.00
3 LeBron James 8.00 20.00
4 Dirk Nowitzki 6.00 15.00
6 Kevin Durant 6.00 15.00
7 Chris Paul 5.00 12.00
8 Carmelo Anthony 4.00 10.00
9 Chris Bosh 3.00 8.00
10 Brandon Roy 3.00 8.00
11 Joe Johnson 2.50 6.00
12 Devin Harris 1.50 4.00
13 Deron Williams 2.00 5.00
14 Dwight Howard 3.00 8.00

2009-10 Rookies and Stars Gold Stars Signatures
STATED PRINT RUN 10 TO 25 SER.#'d SETS
2 Kobe Bryant/25 800.00 1,500.00

2009-10 Rookies and Stars Moments in Time
COMPLETE SET (15) 15.00 30.00
*BLACK: .75X TO 2X BASE HI
BLACK PRINT RUN 100 SER.#'d SETS
*GOLD: .5X TO 1.25X BASE HI
GOLD PRINT RUN 500 SER.#'d SETS
*HOLOFOIL: .6X TO 1.5X BASE HI
HOLO PRINT RUN 250 SER.#'d SETS
1 Bob Pettit 1.25 3.00
2 Wilt Chamberlain 4.00 10.00
3 John Havlicek 2.50 6.00
4 Bill Russell 3.00 8.00
5 Willis Reed 1.50 4.00
6 Jerry West 1.50 4.00
7 Bill Walton 1.50 4.00
8 Darryl Dawkins 1.00 2.50
9 Magic Johnson 4.00 10.00
10 Spud Webb .75 2.00
11 Larry Bird 4.00 10.00
12 Kareem Abdul-Jabbar 3.00 8.00
13 Shaquille O'Neal 3.00 8.00
14 LeBron James 8.00 20.00
15 Kobe Bryant 8.00 20.00

2009-10 Rookies and Stars Prime Cuts
STATED PRINT RUN 25 TO 50 SER.#'d SETS
1 Mike Bibby/50 6.00 15.00
2 Dirk Nowitzki/50 15.00 40.00
3 Tracy McGrady/25 12.00 30.00
4 Elton Brand/50 4.00 10.00
5 Brandon Roy/50 8.00 20.00
6 Michael Beasley/50 4.00 10.00
7 Andre Iguodala/50 6.00 15.00
8 Amare Stoudemire/50 5.00 12.00
9 Andrea Bargnani/50 4.00 10.00
10 Manu Ginobili/50 12.00 30.00
11 Nate Robinson/50 5.00 12.00
12 Al Jefferson/50 4.00 10.00
13 O.J. Mayo/50 4.00 10.00
14 Tony Parker/50 10.00 25.00
15 Carlos Boozer/50 5.00 12.00

2009-10 Rookies and Stars Prime Cuts Signatures
STATED PRINT RUN 25 SER.#'d SETS
1 Mike Bibby 12.00 30.00
2 Dirk Nowitzki 150.00 400.00
6 Michael Beasley 10.00 25.00
7 Andre Iguodala 20.00 50.00
15 Carlos Boozer 10.00 25.00

2009-10 Rookies and Stars Retired NBA Team Patches Signatures
STATED PRINT RUN 99 TO 394 SER.#'d SETS
1 Willis Reed/99 40.00 100.00
2 Elvin Hayes/99 8.00 20.00
3 Sidney Moncrief/199 6.00 15.00
4 Danny Manning/199 6.00 15.00
5 Bill Laimbeer/199 6.00 15.00
6 Dan Majerle/99 6.00 15.00
7 Bob Cousy/199 15.00 40.00
8 Earl Monroe/99 12.50 30.00
9 Darryl Dawkins/99 10.00 25.00
10 Adrian Dantley/99 6.00 15.00
11 Byron Scott/199 10.00 25.00
12 Nate Thurmond/199 8.00 20.00
13 Cazzie Russell/199 6.00 15.00
14 Tim Hardaway/199 6.00 15.00
15 Kurt Rambis/99 12.50 30.00
16 Rick Barry/199 8.00 20.00
17 Manute Bol/199 30.00 60.00
18 Artis Gilmore/199 8.00 20.00
19 Spencer Haywood/394 6.00 15.00

2009-10 Rookies and Stars Sharp Shooters
COMPLETE SET (15) 6.00 15.00
*BLACK: .75X TO 2X BASE HI
BLACK PRINT RUN 100 SER.#'d SETS
*GOLD: .5X TO 1.25X BASE HI
GOLD PRINT RUN 500 SER.#'d SETS
*HOLOFOIL: .6X TO 1.5X BASE HI
HOLO PRINT RUN 250 SER.#'d SETS
1 Anthony Morrow .75 2.00
2 D.J. Augustin .75 2.00
3 Jameer Nelson .75 2.00
4 Jason Kapono .75 2.00
5 Kelenna Azubuike .75 2.00
6 Kevin Durant 5.00 12.00
7 Mehmet Okur .75 2.00
8 Mo Williams 1.00 2.50
9 Steve Nash 2.50 6.00
10 Troy Murphy .75 2.00
11 Chauncey Billups 1.50 4.00
12 David West 1.00 2.50
13 Dirk Nowitzki 4.00 10.00
14 Manu Ginobili 2.50 6.00
15 Ray Allen 2.00 5.00

2009-10 Rookies and Stars Sharp Shooters Materials
*PRIME: .75X TO 2X BASE HI
PRIME PRINT RUN 50 SER.#'d SETS
6 Kevin Durant 8.00 20.00
9 Steve Nash 6.00 15.00
13 Dirk Nowitzki 8.00 20.00
14 Manu Ginobili 6.00 15.00

2009-10 Rookies and Stars Signatures
STATED PRINT RUN 25 TO 250 SER.#'d SETS
3 Mike Bibby/25 6.00 15.00
17 Dirk Nowitzki/25 75.00 200.00
19 Jason Kidd/25 15.00 40.00
39 Kobe Bryant/25 800.00 1,500.00
42 Andrew Bynum/25 5.00 12.00
48 Michael Beasley/25 6.00 15.00
56 Kevin Love/25 12.00 30.00
73 Andre Iguodala/25 12.00 30.00
94 Carlos Boozer/25 6.00 15.00
102 Elvin Hayes/25 8.00 20.00
104 Arnie Risen/25 6.00 15.00
107 Artis Gilmore/50 6.00 15.00
108 Nate Archibald/25 12.00 30.00
111 Spencer Haywood/25 10.00 25.00
115 Sleepy Floyd/25 8.00 20.00
117 Jon Brockman/250 3.00 8.00
121 Marcus Thornton/250 4.00 10.00
122 Danny Green/250 8.00 20.00
123 Goran Suton/250 3.00 8.00
124 Jack McClinton/250 3.00 8.00
125 A.J. Price/250 3.00 8.00
129 Lester Hudson/250 3.00 8.00

2009-10 Rookies and Stars Stardom
COMPLETE SET (15) 8.00 20.00
*BLACK: .75X TO 2X BASE HI
BLACK PRINT RUN 100 SER.#'d SETS
*GOLD: .5X TO 1.25X BASE HI
GOLD PRINT RUN 500 SER.#'d SETS
*HOLOFOIL: .6X TO 1.5X BASE HI
HOLO PRINT RUN 250 SER.#'d SETS
1 Mike Bibby 1.00 2.50
2 Rajon Rondo 1.25 3.00
3 Raja Bell .75 2.00
4 Kirk Hinrich .75 2.00
5 Shaquille O'Neal 3.00 8.00
6 Jason Terry .75 2.00
7 Chauncey Billups 1.25 3.00
8 Baron Davis .75 2.00
9 Kobe Bryant 8.00 20.00
10 O.J. Mayo .60 1.50
11 Jermaine O'Neal 1.00 2.50
12 Elton Brand .75 2.00
13 Greg Oden .60 1.50
14 Tim Duncan 2.50 6.00
15 Hedo Turkoglu .75 2.00

2009-10 Rookies and Stars Stardom Materials
1 Mike Bibby 2.50 6.00
4 Kirk Hinrich 2.00 5.00
6 Jason Terry 2.00 5.00
9 Kobe Bryant 8.00 20.00
11 Jermaine O'Neal 2.50 6.00
12 Elton Brand 2.00 5.00
13 Greg Oden 1.50 4.00
14 Tim Duncan 6.00 15.00

2009-10 Rookies and Stars Stardom Signatures
STATED PRINT RUN 50 SER.#'d SETS
1 Mike Bibby 8.00 20.00
9 Kobe Bryant 500.00 1,000.00

2009-10 Rookies and Stars Statistical Standouts Materials

STATED PRINT RUN 99 TO 299 SER.#'d SETS
*PRIME: .75X TO 2X BASE HI
PRIME PRINT RUN 10 TO 50 SER.#'d SETS
1 Chris Paul/299 6.00 15.00
2 Dirk Nowitzki/299 8.00 20.00
3 Dwyane Wade/299 6.00 15.00
4 Kobe Bryant/99 10.00 25.00
5 LeBron James/299 8.00 20.00
6 Al Jefferson/299 2.00 5.00
8 Dwight Howard/299 4.00 10.00
9 Stephen Jackson/299 2.50 6.00
11 Devin Harris/299 2.00 5.00
12 Joe Johnson/299 3.00 8.00
13 Pau Gasol/299 5.00 12.00
14 Tony Parker/299 5.00 12.00
15 Kevin Martin/299 2.50 6.00

2009-10 Rookies and Stars Statistical Standouts Materials Signatures

STATED PRINT RUN 25 SER.#'d SETS
2 Dirk Nowitzki 100.00 250.00
4 Kobe Bryant 800.00 1,500.00

2009-10 Rookies and Stars Studio Combo Rookies

COMPLETE SET (10) 10.00 25.00
*BLACK: .75X TO 2X BASE HI
BLACK PRINT RUN 100 SER.#'d SETS
*GOLD: .5X TO 1.25X BASE HI
GOLD PRINT RUN 500 SER.#'d SETS
*HOLOFOIL: .6X TO 1.5X BASE HI
HOLO PRINT RUN 250 SER.#'d SETS
1 B.Griffin/T.Griffin 3.00 8.00
2 C.Budinger/J.Hill .50 1.25
3 D.DeRozan/T.Gibson 3.00 8.00
4 T.Lawson/T.Hansbrough .60 1.50
5 J.Johnson/J.Teague .60 1.50
6 D.Collison/J.Holiday 2.50 6.00
7 J.Harden/J.Pendergraph 5.00 12.00
8 D.Blair/H.Thabeet .60 1.50
9 S.Curry/T.Evans 20.00 50.00
10 B.Griffin/T.Hansbrough 3.00 8.00

2009-10 Rookies and Stars Studio Combo Rookies Materials

STATED PRINT RUN 299 SER.#'d SETS
*PRIME: 1X TO 2.5X BASE HI
PRIME PRINT RUN 50 SER.#'d SETS
1 B.Griffin/T.Griffin 6.00 15.00
2 C.Budinger/J.Hill 2.00 5.00
3 D.DeRozan/T.Gibson 6.00 15.00
4 T.Lawson/T.Hansbrough 1.25 3.00
5 J.Johnson/J.Teague 1.25 3.00
6 D.Collison/J.Holiday 5.00 12.00
7 J.Harden/J.Pendergraph 10.00 25.00
8 D.Blair/H.Thabeet 1.25 3.00
9 S.Curry/T.Evans 125.00 300.00
10 B.Griffin/T.Hansbrough 6.00 15.00

2009-10 Rookies and Stars Studio Combo Rookies Signatures

STATED PRINT RUN 50 SER.#'d SETS
1 B.Griffin/T.Griffin 25.00 60.00
2 C.Budinger/J.Hill 10.00 25.00
4 T.Lawson/T.Hansbrough 20.00 50.00
5 J.Johnson/J.Teague 10.00 25.00
6 D.Collison/J.Holiday 15.00 40.00
7 J.Harden/J.Pendergraph 40.00 100.00
8 D.Blair/H.Thabeet 12.50 30.00
9 S.Curry/T.Evans 800.00 1,500.00
10 B.Griffin/T.Hansbrough 50.00 120.00

2009-10 Rookies and Stars Team Leaders

COMPLETE SET (30) 20.00 50.00
*BLACK: .75X TO 2X BASE HI
BLACK PRINT RUN 100 SER.#'d SETS
*GOLD: .5X TO 1.25X BASE HI
GOLD PRINT RUN 500 SER.#'d SETS
*HOLOFOIL: .6X TO 1.5X BASE HI
HOLO PRINT RUN 250 SER.#'d SETS
1 Atlanta Hawks 1.00 2.50
2 Boston Celtics 2.50 6.00
3 Charlotte Bobcats .75 2.00
4 Chicago Bulls 1.50 4.00
5 Cleveland Cavaliers 8.00 20.00
6 Dallas Mavericks 2.50 6.00
7 Denver Nuggets 1.50 4.00
8 Detroit Pistons 1.00 2.50
9 Golden State Warriors .75 2.00
10 Houston Rockets 2.50 6.00
11 Indiana Pacers .60 1.50
12 Los Angeles Clippers .75 2.00
13 Los Angeles Lakers 8.00 20.00
14 Memphis Grizzlies 1.00 2.50
15 Miami Heat 2.00 5.00
16 Milwaukee Bucks .75 2.00
17 Minnesota Timberwolves .60 1.50
18 New Jersey Nets 1.00 2.50
19 New Orleans Hornets 2.00 5.00
20 New York Knicks .75 2.00
21 Oklahoma City Thunder 4.00 10.00
22 Orlando Magic 1.25 3.00
23 Philadelphia 76ers 1.00 2.50
24 Phoenix Suns 3.00 8.00
25 Portland Trail Blazers 1.25 3.00
26 Sacramento Kings .75 2.00
27 San Antonio Spurs 2.50 6.00
28 Toronto Raptors 1.25 3.00
29 Utah Jazz .75 2.00
30 Washington Wizards .75 2.00

2010-11 Rookies and Stars

COMP.SET w/o RCs (115) 12.50 30.00
AU RC PRINT RUNS LISTED IN CHECKLIST
ASTERISK CARDS INSERTED IN SEASON UPDATE
EXCH EXPIRATION 5/10/12
1 Ray Allen .60 1.50
2 Paul Pierce .60 1.50
3 Rajon Rondo .50 1.25
4 Kevin Garnett 1.00 2.50
5 Brook Lopez .30 .75
6 Devin Harris .25 .60
7 Troy Murphy .25 .60
8 Amare Stoudemire .40 1.00
9 Anthony Randolph .25 .60
10 Danilo Gallinari .30 .75
11 Andre Iguodala .40 1.00
12 Elton Brand .30 .75
13 Thaddeus Young .25 .60
14 Andrea Bargnani .25 .60
15 Leandro Barbosa .30 .75
16 Jose Calderon .25 .60
17 Carlos Boozer .30 .75
18 Derrick Rose .75 2.00
19 Joakim Noah .40 1.00
20 Luol Deng .30 .75
21 Antawn Jamison .30 .75
22 Mo Williams .30 .75
23 Daniel Gibson .25 .60
24 Ben Gordon .30 .75
25 Richard Hamilton .50 1.25
26 Tayshaun Prince .40 1.00
27 Danny Granger .25 .60
28 Tyler Hansbrough .25 .60
29 Mike Dunleavy .25 .60
30 Andrew Bogut .30 .75
31 Brandon Jennings .25 .60
32 John Salmons .25 .60
33 Joe Johnson .40 1.00
34 Josh Smith .25 .60
35 Al Horford .40 1.00
36 Jamal Crawford .40 1.00
37 Gerald Henderson .25 .60
38 Stephen Jackson .30 .75
39 Gerald Wallace .30 .75
40 LeBron James 3.00 8.00
41 Dwyane Wade .75 2.00
42 Chris Bosh .50 1.25
43 Dwight Howard .50 1.25
44 Vince Carter .75 2.00
45 J.J. Redick .40 1.00
46 Josh Howard .25 .60
47 Al Thornton .25 .60
48 Gilbert Arenas .30 .75
49 Kirk Hinrich .30 .75
50 Dirk Nowitzki 1.00 2.50
51 Jason Kidd .60 1.50
52 Shawn Marion .40 1.00
53 Caron Butler .30 .75
54 Kevin Martin .30 .75
55 Shane Battier .30 .75
56 Luis Scola .30 .75
57 Yao Ming .75 2.00
58 Marc Gasol .40 1.00
59 Rudy Gay .40 1.00
60 Zach Randolph .40 1.00
61 Chris Paul .75 2.00
62 Emeka Okafor .30 .75
63 David West .30 .75
64 Tim Duncan 1.00 2.50
65 Tony Parker .60 1.50
66 Richard Jefferson .30 .75
67 Carmelo Anthony .60 1.50
68 Chauncey Billups .50 1.25
69 Chris Andersen .40 1.00
70 Nene .30 .75
71 Kevin Love .40 1.00
72 Michael Beasley .25 .60
73 Jonny Flynn .25 .60
74 Brandon Roy .50 1.25
75 Rudy Fernandez .25 .60
76 Greg Oden .25 .60
77 Kevin Durant 1.50 4.00
78 Russell Westbrook .60 1.50
79 Jeff Green .30 .75
80 Deron Williams .30 .75
81 Al Jefferson .30 .75
82 Andrei Kirilenko .30 .75
83 Paul Millsap .30 .75
84 David Lee .25 .60
85 Monta Ellis .30 .75
86 Stephen Curry 20.00 50.00
87 Eric Gordon .30 .75
88 Chris Kaman .25 .60
89 Baron Davis .40 1.00
90 Kobe Bryant 3.00 8.00
91 Pau Gasol .60 1.50
92 Lamar Odom .30 .75
93 Ron Artest .40 1.00
94 Steve Nash .75 2.00
95 Hedo Turkoglu .30 .75
96 Channing Frye .25 .60
97 Grant Hill .60 1.50
98 Tyreke Evans .30 .75
99 Samuel Dalembert .25 .60
100 Carl Landry .25 .60
101 Rolando Blackman .30 .75
102 Joe Dumars .40 1.00
103 Wayne Embry .40 1.00
104 Walt Frazier .60 1.50
105 Gail Goodrich .40 1.00
106 John Havlicek .75 2.00
107 Rod Hundley .40 1.00
108 Phil Jackson .50 1.25
109 K.C. Jones .40 1.00
110 Clyde Lovellette .50 1.25
111 Jerry Lucas .40 1.00
112 Nate McMillan .25 .60
113 Willis Reed .60 1.50
114 Paul Silas .40 1.00
115 Jerry West .75 2.00
116 Armon Johnson RC .50 1.25
117 Sherron Collins RC .50 1.25
118 Terrico White RC .50 1.25
119 Darington Hobson RC .50 1.25
120 Landry Fields RC .50 1.25
121 Tony Gaffney RC .50 1.25
122 Ben Uzoh RC .50 1.25
123 Ishmael Smith RC .75 2.00
124 Tweety Carter RC .50 1.25
125 Tiago Splitter RC .60 1.50
126 Solomon Alabi RC .50 1.25
127 Magnum Rolle RC .50 1.25
128 Pape Sy RC .50 1.25
129 Jeremy Lin RC 3.00 8.00
130 Derrick Caracter RC .50 1.25
131 J.Crawford AU/443 RC 2.50 6.00
132 Luke Harangody AU/460 RC 2.50 6.00
133 Avery Bradley AU/449 RC 4.00 10.00
134 Kevin Seraphin AU/499 RC 2.50 6.00
135 Dominique Jones AU/453 RC 2.50 6.00
136 Greg Monroe AU/454 RC 3.00 8.00
137 Ekpe Udoh AU/457 RC 2.50 6.00
138 P.Patterson AU/455 RC 3.00 8.00
139 L.Stephenson AU/457 RC 4.00 10.00
140 Paul George AU/455 RC 60.00 150.00
141 Eric Bledsoe AU/499 RC 5.00 12.00
142 Willie Warren AU/455 RC 2.50 6.00
143 Al-Farouq Aminu AU/499 RC 3.00 8.00
144 Devin Ebanks AU/455 RC 2.50 6.00
145 Xavier Henry AU/455 RC 2.50 6.00
146 Greivis Vasquez AU/455 RC 2.50 6.00
147 Dexter Pittman AU/455 RC 2.50 6.00
148 Da'Sean Butler AU/455 RC 3.00 8.00
149 Keith Gallon AU/455 RC 2.50 6.00
150 Larry Sanders AU/455 RC 2.50 6.00
151 Lazar Hayward AU/455 RC 2.50 6.00
152 Wes.Johnson AU/452 RC 2.50 6.00
153 Derrick Favors AU/458 RC 4.00 10.00
154 Damion James AU/454 RC 2.50 6.00
155 Craig Brackins AU/455 RC 2.50 6.00
156 Q.Pondexter AU/461 RC 2.50 6.00
157 Andy Rautins AU/499 RC 2.50 6.00
158 Cole Aldrich AU/450 RC 2.50 6.00
159 Daniel Orton AU/449 RC 2.50 6.00
160 Evan Turner AU/455 RC 3.00 8.00
161 Gani Lawal AU/457 RC 2.50 6.00
162 Elliot Williams AU/461 RC 2.50 6.00
163 Luke Babbitt AU/454 RC 2.50 6.00
164 D.Cousins AU/454 RC 20.00 50.00
165 H. Whiteside AU/458 RC 5.00 12.00
166 J.Anderson AU/459 RC 2.50 6.00
167 Ed Davis AU/455 RC 3.00 8.00
168 G.Hayward AU/455 RC 10.00 25.00
169 Trevor Booker AU/456 RC 2.50 6.00
170 John Wall AU/454 RC 30.00 80.00
171 Landry Fields AU/499* 2.50 6.00
172 Gary Neal AU/499 RC* 3.00 8.00
173 Omer Asik AU/499 RC* 4.00 10.00
174 Semih Erden AU/411 RC* 2.50 6.00
175 Gary Forbes AU/499 RC* 2.50 6.00

2010-11 Rookies and Stars Gold

*GOLD STARS: 1X TO 2.5X BASE HI
*GOLD 116-130: .6X TO 1.5X BASE HI
*GOLD 131-175: .75X TO 2X BASE HI
GOLD 1-130 PRINT RUN 499 SER.#'d SETS
GOLD 131-175 PRINT RUN 25 SER.#'d SETS
ASTERISK CARDS INSERTED IN SEASON UPDATE

2010-11 Rookies and Stars Gold Holofoil

*HOLO STARS: 2X TO 5X BASE HI
*HOLO RCs: 1.25X TO 3X BASE HI
STATED PRINT RUN 199 SER.#'d SETS

2010-11 Rookies and Stars Gold Materials

STATED PRINT RUN 25 TO 299 SER.#'d SETS
1 Ray Allen/50 5.00 12.00
2 Paul Pierce/299 5.00 12.00
3 Rajon Rondo/299 4.00 10.00
4 Kevin Garnett/50 8.00 20.00
6 Devin Harris/299 2.00 5.00
11 Andre Iguodala/299 3.00 8.00
12 Elton Brand/299 2.50 6.00
13 Thaddeus Young/299 2.50 6.00
14 Andrea Bargnani/299 2.00 5.00
15 Leandro Barbosa/299 2.50 6.00
18 Derrick Rose/50 6.00 15.00
19 Joakim Noah/299 3.00 8.00
20 Luol Deng/50 2.50 6.00
21 Antawn Jamison/299 2.50 6.00
24 Ben Gordon/299 2.50 6.00
26 Tayshaun Prince/299 3.00 8.00
28 Tyler Hansbrough/299 2.00 5.00
29 Mike Dunleavy/99 2.00 5.00
30 Andrew Bogut/100 2.50 6.00
31 Brandon Jennings/299 2.00 5.00
33 Joe Johnson/54 3.00 8.00
37 Gerald Henderson/299 2.00 5.00
38 Stephen Jackson/299 2.50 6.00
39 Gerald Wallace/99 2.50 6.00
41 Dwyane Wade/199 6.00 15.00
43 Dwight Howard/299 4.00 10.00
44 Vince Carter/299 6.00 15.00
45 J.J. Redick/299 3.00 8.00
46 Josh Howard/299 2.50 6.00
48 Gilbert Arenas/299 2.50 6.00
49 Kirk Hinrich/299 2.50 6.00
51 Jason Kidd/50 5.00 12.00
52 Shawn Marion/299 3.00 8.00
53 Caron Butler/299 2.50 6.00
54 Kevin Martin/299 2.50 6.00
55 Shane Battier/299 2.50 6.00
56 Luis Scola/199 2.50 6.00
58 Marc Gasol/99 3.00 8.00
59 Rudy Gay/99 3.00 8.00
61 Chris Paul/299 6.00 15.00
62 Emeka Okafor/299 2.50 6.00
63 David West/299 2.50 6.00
64 Tim Duncan/299 8.00 20.00
65 Tony Parker/299 5.00 12.00
66 Richard Jefferson/299 2.50 6.00
67 Carmelo Anthony/25 5.00 12.00
68 Chauncey Billups/299 4.00 10.00
70 Nene/299 2.50 6.00
71 Kevin Love/299 3.00 8.00
72 Michael Beasley/299 2.00 5.00
73 Jonny Flynn/299 2.00 5.00
74 Brandon Roy/299 4.00 10.00
75 Rudy Fernandez/299 2.00 5.00
76 Greg Oden/299 2.00 5.00
78 Russell Westbrook/299 5.00 12.00
80 Deron Williams/299 2.50 6.00
81 Al Jefferson/299 2.00 5.00
82 Andrei Kirilenko/299 2.50 6.00
86 Stephen Curry/299 40.00 100.00
87 Eric Gordon/99 2.50 6.00
88 Chris Kaman/150 2.00 5.00
89 Baron Davis/100 3.00 8.00
91 Pau Gasol/299 5.00 12.00
92 Lamar Odom/299 2.50 6.00
93 Ron Artest/299 3.00 8.00
94 Steve Nash/299 6.00 15.00
95 Hedo Turkoglu/299 2.50 6.00
96 Channing Frye/299 2.00 5.00
99 Samuel Dalembert/299 2.00 5.00
101 Rolando Blackman/50 2.50 6.00
102 Joe Dumars/99 3.00 8.00
118 Terrico White/299 2.00 5.00
129 Jeremy Lin/299 12.00 30.00

2010-11 Rookies and Stars Dress for Success Materials

STATED PRINT RUN 15 TO 299 SER.#'d SETS
*PRIME: .75X TO 2X BASE HI
PRIME PRINT RUN 10 TO 49 SER.#'d SETS
1 John Wall/299 5.00 12.00
2 Andre Miller/299 2.50 6.00
3 Evan Turner/299 1.50 4.00
4 Wesley Johnson/299 1.25 3.00
5 Andris Biedrins/299 2.00 5.00
6 Derrick Favors/299 2.00 5.00
7 Ekpe Udoh/299 1.25 3.00
8 Emeka Okafor/299 2.50 6.00
9 Eric Gordon/99 2.50 6.00
10 Caron Butler/299 2.50 6.00
11 Gani Lawal/299 1.25 3.00
12 Gerald Henderson/299 2.00 5.00
13 Goran Dragic/199 4.00 10.00
14 Gordon Hayward/299 5.00 12.00
15 Greg Monroe/299 1.50 4.00
16 Greg Oden/299 2.00 5.00
17 Greivis Vasquez/299 1.25 3.00
18 Hassan Whiteside/299 2.50 6.00
19 J.J. Barea/299 2.50 6.00
20 J.J. Redick/299 3.00 8.00
21 J.R. Smith/299 3.00 8.00
22 James Anderson/299 1.25 3.00
23 Jeff Green/15 2.50 6.00
24 Dwight Howard/299 4.00 10.00
25 Jose Calderon/299 2.00 5.00
26 Lance Stephenson/299 2.00 5.00
27 Marcus Camby/299 2.50 6.00
28 Mike Dunleavy/99 2.00 5.00
29 DeMarcus Cousins/299 4.00 10.00
30 Joakim Noah/299 3.00 8.00
31 Xavier Henry/299 1.25 3.00
32 Nene/299 2.50 6.00
33 Al-Farouq Aminu/299 1.50 4.00
34 Larry Sanders/299 1.25 3.00
35 Paul George/299 10.00 25.00

2010-11 Rookies and Stars Dress for Success Materials Signatures

STATED PRINT RUN 5 TO 25 SER.#'d SETS
PRIME SIG.PRINT RUN 10 SER.#'d SETS
1 John Wall/25 50.00 100.00
2 Andre Miller/25 6.00 15.00
3 Evan Turner/25 15.00 40.00
4 Wesley Johnson/25 4.00 10.00
6 Derrick Favors/25 20.00 50.00
7 Ekpe Udoh/25 4.00 10.00
9 Eric Gordon/25 8.00 20.00
11 Gani Lawal/25 4.00 10.00
12 Gerald Henderson/25 6.00 15.00
13 Goran Dragic/25 40.00 100.00
14 Gordon Hayward/25 15.00 40.00
15 Greg Monroe/25 15.00 40.00
17 Greivis Vasquez/25 4.00 10.00
18 Hassan Whiteside/25 8.00 20.00
19 J.J. Barea/25 20.00 50.00
21 J.R. Smith/25 6.00 15.00
22 James Anderson/25 4.00 10.00
26 Lance Stephenson/25 6.00 15.00
27 Marcus Camby/25 6.00 15.00
28 Mike Dunleavy/25 6.00 15.00
29 DeMarcus Cousins/25 25.00 60.00
31 Xavier Henry/25 4.00 10.00
33 Al-Farouq Aminu/25 5.00 12.00
34 Larry Sanders/25 4.00 10.00
35 Paul George/25 75.00 150.00

2010-11 Rookies and Stars Freshman Orientation Double Materials

STATED PRINT RUN 399 SER.#'d SETS
*PRIME: 1X TO 2.5X BASE HI
PRIME: PRINT RUN 25 TO 49 SER.#'d SETS
1 John Wall 6.00 15.00
2 Evan Turner 1.50 4.00
3 Derrick Favors 2.00 5.00
4 Wesley Johnson 1.25 3.00
5 DeMarcus Cousins 4.00 10.00
6 Ekpe Udoh 1.25 3.00
7 Greg Monroe 1.50 4.00
8 Al-Farouq Aminu 1.50 4.00
9 Gordon Hayward 5.00 12.00
10 Paul George 10.00 25.00
11 Cole Aldrich 1.25 3.00
12 Xavier Henry 1.25 3.00
13 Patrick Patterson 1.50 4.00
14 Larry Sanders 1.25 3.00
15 Luke Babbitt 1.25 3.00
16 Eric Bledsoe 2.50 6.00
17 Avery Bradley 2.00 5.00
18 James Anderson 1.25 3.00
19 Craig Brackins 1.25 3.00
20 Elliot Williams 1.25 3.00
21 Trevor Booker 1.25 3.00
22 Damion James 1.25 3.00
23 Dominique Jones 1.25 3.00
24 Quincy Pondexter 1.25 3.00
25 Jordan Crawford 1.25 3.00
26 Greivis Vasquez 1.25 3.00
27 Daniel Orton 1.25 3.00
28 Lazar Hayward 1.25 3.00
29 Dexter Pittman 1.25 3.00
30 Hassan Whiteside 2.50 6.00
31 Lance Stephenson 2.00 5.00
32 Da'Sean Butler 1.50 4.00
33 Devin Ebanks 1.25 3.00
34 Gani Lawal 1.25 3.00
35 Luke Harangody 1.25 3.00

2010-11 Rookies and Stars Freshman Orientation Double Materials Signatures

STATED PRINT RUN 49 SER.#'d SETS
PRIME SIG.PRINT RUN 10 SER.#'d SETS
1 John Wall 30.00 80.00
2 Evan Turner 4.00 10.00
3 Derrick Favors 5.00 12.00
4 Wesley Johnson 3.00 8.00
5 DeMarcus Cousins 10.00 25.00
6 Ekpe Udoh 3.00 8.00
7 Greg Monroe 4.00 10.00
8 Al-Farouq Aminu 4.00 10.00
9 Gordon Hayward 12.00 30.00
10 Paul George 50.00 120.00
11 Cole Aldrich 3.00 8.00
12 Xavier Henry 3.00 8.00
13 Patrick Patterson 4.00 10.00
14 Larry Sanders 3.00 8.00
15 Luke Babbitt 3.00 8.00
16 Eric Bledsoe 6.00 15.00
17 Avery Bradley 5.00 12.00
18 James Anderson 3.00 8.00
19 Craig Brackins 3.00 8.00
20 Elliot Williams 3.00 8.00
21 Trevor Booker 3.00 8.00
22 Damion James 3.00 8.00
23 Dominique Jones 3.00 8.00
24 Quincy Pondexter 3.00 8.00
25 Jordan Crawford 3.00 8.00
26 Greivis Vasquez 3.00 8.00
27 Daniel Orton 3.00 8.00
28 Lazar Hayward EXCH 3.00 8.00
29 Dexter Pittman 3.00 8.00
30 Hassan Whiteside 6.00 15.00
31 Lance Stephenson 5.00 12.00
32 Da'Sean Butler 4.00 10.00
33 Devin Ebanks 3.00 8.00
34 Gani Lawal 3.00 8.00
35 Luke Harangody 3.00 8.00

2010-11 Rookies and Stars Game Garb Materials

STATED PRINT RUN 10 TO 49 SER.#'d SETS
1 Al Horford/49 6.00 15.00
2 Ben Gordon/49 5.00 12.00
3 Brook Lopez/49 5.00 12.00
4 Caron Butler/25 5.00 12.00
5 Chris Kaman/25 4.00 10.00
6 Danny Granger/15 4.00 10.00
7 Eric Gordon/25 5.00 12.00
8 Grant Hill/49 10.00 25.00
9 Luol Deng/15 5.00 12.00
11 Nene/49 5.00 12.00
12 Paul Pierce/49 10.00 25.00
13 Steve Nash/25 12.00 30.00
14 Tim Duncan/49 15.00 40.00
15 Vince Carter/49 12.00 30.00

2010-11 Rookies and Stars Game Garb Materials Signatures

STATED PRINT RUN 5 TO 49 SER.#'d SETS
1 Al Horford/25 8.00 20.00
2 Ben Gordon/25 8.00 20.00
5 Chris Kaman/49 8.00 20.00
7 Eric Gordon/25 10.00 25.00

2010-11 Rookies and Stars Moments in Time

COMPLETE SET (15) 7.50 15.00
*BLACK: .75X TO 2X BASE HI
BLACK PRINT RUN 99 SER.#'d SETS
*GOLD: .5X TO 1.25X BASE HI
GOLD PRINT RUN 499 SER.#'d SETS
*HOLO: .6X TO 1.5X BASE HI
HOLO PRINT RUN 199 SER.#'d SETS
1 Bob Cousy 2.00 5.00
2 Elgin Baylor 1.50 4.00
3 Jerry West 1.50 4.00
4 John Havlicek 1.50 4.00
5 George Gervin 1.25 3.00
6 Kareem Abdul-Jabbar 2.50 6.00
7 Larry Bird 3.00 8.00
8 Magic Johnson 3.00 8.00
9 92 USA Men's Olympic 2.50 6.00
10 A.C. Green .75 2.00
11 John Stockton 1.25 3.00
12 Karl Malone 1.50 4.00
13 LeBron James 6.00 15.00
14 Kobe Bryant 6.00 15.00
15 Tyreke Evans .60 1.50

2010-11 Rookies and Stars Prime Cuts

STATED PRINT RUN 25 TO 50 SER.#'d SETS
1 Allen Iverson/50 20.00 50.00
2 Alonzo Mourning/50 15.00 40.00
3 Andre Iguodala/50 10.00 25.00
4 Carmelo Anthony/50 15.00 40.00
5 Chris Paul/50 20.00 50.00
6 Clyde Drexler/50 15.00 40.00
7 Dirk Nowitzki/50 25.00 60.00
8 Dwight Howard/50 12.00 30.00
9 Dwyane Wade/25 20.00 50.00
10 Gary Payton/50 12.00 30.00
11 John Stockton/50 15.00 40.00
12 Kareem Abdul-Jabbar/50 30.00 80.00
13 Karl Malone/50 20.00 50.00
14 Magic Johnson/50 40.00 100.00
15 Vince Carter/50 20.00 50.00

2010-11 Rookies and Stars Retired NBA Team Patches Signatures

STATED PRINT RUN 54 TO 99 SER.#'d SETS
1 Bill Cartwright/99 15.00 40.00
2 Bob Dandridge/99 8.00 20.00
3 Chris Ford/99 10.00 25.00
4 Dennis Rodman/99 40.00 100.00
5 G.Muresan/99 EXCH 8.00 20.00
6 Kelly Tripucka/99 6.00 15.00
7 Kevin Johnson/99 EXCH 20.00 50.00
8 Maurice Cheeks/99 6.00 15.00
9 Dominique Wilkins/54 15.00 40.00
10 Xavier McDaniel/99 6.00 15.00

2010-11 Rookies and Stars Sharp Shooters

COMPLETE SET (15) 5.00 12.00
*BLACK: .75X TO 2X BASE HI
BLACK: STATED PRINT RUN 99 SER.#'d SETS
*GOLD: .5X TO 1.25X BASE HI
GOLD: STATED PRINT RUN 499 SER.#'d SETS
*HOLO: .6X TO 1.5X BASE HI
HOLO STATED PRINT RUN 199 SER.#'d SETS
1 Dwight Howard 1.25 3.00
2 Kendrick Perkins .60 1.50
3 Nene .75 2.00
4 Marc Gasol 1.00 2.50
5 Andrew Bynum .60 1.50
6 Carlos Boozer .75 2.00
7 Amare Stoudemire 1.00 2.50
8 Al Horford 1.00 2.50
9 David Lee .60 1.50
10 Paul Millsap .75 2.00
11 Pau Gasol 1.50 4.00
12 Kevin Garnett 2.50 6.00
13 Chris Bosh 1.25 3.00
14 Tim Duncan 2.50 6.00
15 Rajon Rondo 1.25 3.00

2010-11 Rookies and Stars Sharp Shooters Materials

STATED PRINT RUN 99 SER.#'d SETS
*PRIME: .75X TO 2X BASE HI
PRIME PRINT RUN ONE TO 49 SER.#'d SETS
1 Dwight Howard 4.00 10.00
3 Nene 2.50 6.00
4 Marc Gasol 3.00 8.00
5 Andrew Bynum 2.00 5.00
8 Al Horford 3.00 8.00
11 Pau Gasol 5.00 12.00
12 Kevin Garnett 8.00 20.00
14 Tim Duncan 8.00 20.00
15 Rajon Rondo 4.00 10.00

2010-11 Rookies and Stars Sharp Shooters Signatures

STATED PRINT RUN 10 TO 49 SER.#'d SETS
4 Marc Gasol/25 12.00 30.00
5 Andrew Bynum/49 8.00 20.00
6 Carlos Boozer/49 6.00 15.00
7 Amare Stoudemire/15 25.00 60.00
8 Al Horford/49 6.00 15.00
9 David Lee/49 6.00 15.00
11 Pau Gasol/15 15.00 40.00
15 Rajon Rondo/15 25.00 60.00

2010-11 Rookies and Stars Signatures

STATED PRINT RUN 5 TO 49 SER.#'d SETS
8 Amare Stoudemire/15 30.00 80.00
11 Andre Iguodala/25 4.00 10.00
14 Andrea Bargnani/49 6.00 15.00
28 Tyler Hansbrough/99 4.00 10.00
37 Gerald Henderson/149 4.00 10.00
46 Josh Howard/99 4.00 10.00
51 Jason Kidd/25 20.00 50.00
55 Shane Battier/49 4.00 10.00
62 Emeka Okafor/25 4.00 10.00
73 Jonny Flynn/199 4.00 10.00
86 Stephen Curry/49 1,000.00 2,000.00
89 Baron Davis/25 10.00 25.00
90 Kobe Bryant/99 1,500.00 3,000.00
93 Ron Artest/25 10.00 25.00
98 Tyreke Evans/99 4.00 10.00
100 Carl Landry/99 4.00 10.00
105 Gail Goodrich/49 8.00 20.00
106 John Havlicek/25 40.00 100.00
116 Armon Johnson/99 2.50 6.00
118 Terrico White/299 2.50 6.00
120 Landry Fields/349 2.50 6.00
126 Solomon Alabi/350 2.50 6.00
129 Jeremy Lin/499 75.00 200.00

2010-11 Rookies and Stars Stardom

COMPLETE SET (15) 10.00 20.00
*BLACK: .75X TO 2X BASE HI
BLACK STATED PRINT RUN 99 SER.#'d SETS
*GOLD: .5X TO 1.25X BASE HI
GOLD STATED PRINT RUN 499 SER.#'d SETS
*HOLO: .6X TO 1.5X BASE HI
HOLO STATED PRINT RUN 199 SER.#'d SETS
1 Kobe Bryant 6.00 15.00
2 LeBron James 6.00 15.00
3 Dirk Nowitzki 2.00 5.00
4 Dwight Howard 1.00 2.50
5 Paul Pierce 1.25 3.00
6 Chris Paul 1.50 4.00
7 Chris Bosh 1.00 2.50
8 Kevin Durant 3.00 8.00
9 Tyreke Evans .60 1.50
10 Steve Nash 1.50 4.00
11 Deron Williams .60 1.50
12 Derrick Rose 1.50 4.00
13 Dwyane Wade 1.50 4.00
14 Brandon Jennings .50 1.25
15 Carlos Boozer .60 1.50

2010-11 Rookies and Stars Stardom Materials

STATED PRINT RUN 50 TO 99 SER.#'d SETS
1 Kobe Bryant/99 8.00 20.00
3 Dirk Nowitzki/99 8.00 20.00
4 Dwight Howard/99 4.00 10.00
5 Paul Pierce/99 5.00 12.00
6 Chris Paul/99 6.00 15.00
10 Steve Nash/99 6.00 15.00
11 Deron Williams/99 2.50 6.00
12 Derrick Rose/50 6.00 15.00
13 Dwyane Wade/99 6.00 15.00
14 Brandon Jennings/99 2.00 5.00

2010-11 Rookies and Stars Stardom Signatures

STATED PRINT RUN 49 SER.#'d SETS
1 Kobe Bryant 1,500.00 3,000.00
9 Tyreke Evans 6.00 15.00
14 Brandon Jennings 10.00 25.00

2010-11 Rookies and Stars Statistical Standouts Materials

STATED PRINT RUN 25 TO 199 SER.#'d SETS
*PRIME: .75X TO 2X BASE HI
PRIME PRINT RUN 5 TO 49 SER.#'d SETS
2 Carmelo Anthony/25 5.00 12.00
3 Kobe Bryant/199 8.00 20.00
4 Dirk Nowitzki/199 8.00 20.00
6 Joe Johnson/199 3.00 8.00
7 Steve Nash/199 6.00 15.00
8 Deron Williams/199 2.50 6.00
9 Rajon Rondo/199 4.00 10.00
10 Jason Kidd/149 5.00 12.00
11 Dwight Howard/199 4.00 10.00
12 Marcus Camby/199 2.50 6.00
13 Andrew Bogut/100 2.50 6.00
14 Josh Smith/25 2.00 5.00
15 Chris Andersen/199 3.00 8.00

2010-11 Rookies and Stars Statistical Standouts Materials Signatures

STATED PRINT RUN 10 TO 25 SER.#'d SETS
3 Kobe Bryant/25 1,500.00 3,000.00
6 Joe Johnson/25 10.00 25.00
8 Deron Williams/25 12.00 30.00
9 Rajon Rondo/25 20.00 50.00
10 Jason Kidd/25 20.00 50.00
12 Marcus Camby/25 10.00 25.00
15 Chris Andersen/25 20.00 50.00

2010-11 Rookies and Stars Studio Combo Rookies

COMPLETE SET (10) 7.50 15.00
*BLACK: .75X TO 2X BASE HI
BLACK PRINT RUN 99 SER.#'d SETS
*GOLD: .5X TO 1.25X BASE HI
GOLD PRINT RUN 499 SER.#'d SETS
*HOLO: .6X TO 1.5X BASE HI
HOLO PRINT RUN 199 SER.#'d SETS
1 E.Turner/J.Wall 3.00 8.00
2 W.Johnson/D.Favors 1.50 4.00
3 E.Udoh/D.Cousins 1.50 4.00
4 G.Monroe/A.Aminu 1.00 2.50
5 G.Hayward/P.George 1.50 4.00
6 J.Wall/D.Cousins 4.00 10.00
7 C.Aldrich/X.Henry 1.00 2.50
8 E.Bledsoe/P.Patterson 1.50 4.00
9 D.Ebanks/D.Butler 1.00 2.50
10 J.Wall/D.Orton 2.50 6.00

2010-11 Rookies and Stars Studio Combo Rookies Materials

STATED PRINT RUN 399 SER.#'d SETS
*PRIME: .75X TO 2X BASE HI
PRIME PRINT RUN 49 SER.#'d SETS
1 E.Turner/J.Wall 8.00 20.00
2 W.Johnson/D.Favors 6.00 15.00
3 E.Udoh/D.Cousins 4.00 10.00
4 G.Monroe/A.Aminu 3.00 8.00
5 G.Hayward/P.George 4.00 10.00
6 J.Wall/D.Cousins 10.00 25.00
7 C.Aldrich/X.Henry 3.00 8.00
8 E.Bledsoe/P.Patterson 5.00 12.00
9 D.Ebanks/D.Butler 3.00 8.00
10 J.Wall/D.Orton 8.00 20.00

2010-11 Rookies and Stars Studio Combo Rookies Signatures

STATED PRINT RUN 49 SER.#'d SETS
1 E.Turner/J.Wall 30.00 60.00
2 W.Johnson/D.Favors 15.00 40.00
3 E.Udoh/D.Cousins 10.00 25.00
4 G.Monroe/A.Aminu 10.00 25.00
5 G.Hayward/P.George 20.00 50.00
6 J.Wall/D.Cousins 40.00 100.00
7 C.Aldrich/X.Henry 10.00 25.00
8 E.Bledsoe/P.Patterson 10.00 25.00
9 D.Ebanks/D.Butler 10.00 25.00
10 J.Wall/D.Orton 30.00 60.00

2010-11 Rookies and Stars Superstars

COMPLETE SET (15) 7.50 15.00
*BLACK: .75X TO 2X BASE HI
BLACK STATED PRINT RUN 99 SER.#'d SETS
*GOLD: .5X TO 1.25X BASE HI
GOLD STATED PRINT RUN 499 SER.#'d SETS
*HOLO: .6X TO 1.5X BASE HI
HOLO STATED PRINT RUN 199 SER.#'d SETS
1 Kobe Bryant 6.00 15.00
2 LeBron James 6.00 15.00
3 Dwight Howard 1.00 2.50
4 Dwyane Wade 1.50 4.00
5 Kevin Durant 3.00 8.00
6 Steve Nash 1.50 4.00
7 Dirk Nowitzki 2.00 5.00
8 Andrew Bogut .60 1.50
9 Deron Williams .60 1.50
10 Carmelo Anthony 1.25 3.00
11 Rajon Rondo 1.00 2.50
12 Brandon Roy 1.00 2.50
13 Tim Duncan 2.00 5.00
14 Josh Smith .50 1.25
15 Chris Bosh 1.00 2.50

2010-11 Rookies and Stars Superstars Materials

STATED PRINT RUN 25 TO 299 SER.#'d SETS
*PRIME: .75X TO 2X BASE HI
PRIME STATED PRINT RUN 5 TO 49 SETS
1 Kobe Bryant/299 8.00 20.00
3 Dwight Howard/299 4.00 10.00
4 Dwyane Wade/299 6.00 15.00
6 Steve Nash/299 6.00 15.00
7 Dirk Nowitzki/299 8.00 20.00
8 Andrew Bogut/100 2.50 6.00
9 Deron Williams/299 2.50 6.00
10 Carmelo Anthony/25 5.00 12.00
11 Rajon Rondo/299 4.00 10.00
12 Brandon Roy/299 4.00 10.00
13 Tim Duncan/299 8.00 20.00
14 Josh Smith/25 2.00 5.00

2010-11 Rookies and Stars Superstars Signatures

STATED PRINT RUN 5 TO 49 SER.#'d SETS
1 Kobe Bryant/49 1,500.00 3,000.00
9 Deron Williams/25 12.50 30.00
11 Rajon Rondo/15 25.00 60.00
12 Brandon Roy/49 8.00 20.00

2010-11 Rookies and Stars Team Leaders

COMPLETE SET (30) 12.50 25.00
*BLACK: .75X TO 2X BASE HI
BLACK STATED PRINT RUN 99 SER.#'d SETS
*GOLD: .5X TO 1.25X BASE HI
GOLD STATED PRINT RUN 499 SER.#'d SETS
*HOLO: .6X TO 1.5X BASE HI
HOLO STATED PRINT RUN 199 SER.#'d SETS
1 Horford/Johnson/Smith .75 2.00
2 Garnett/Pierce/Rondo 2.00 5.00
3 Wallace/Jackson/Diaw .60 1.50
4 Boozer/Deng/Rose 1.50 4.00
5 Varejao/Williams/Jamison .60 1.50
6 Butler/Kidd/Nowitzki 2.00 5.00
7 Anthony/Billups/Nene 1.25 3.00
8 Hamilton/Prince/Gordon 1.00 2.50
9 Ellis/Lee/Curry 6.00 15.00
10 Martin/Brooks/Scola .60 1.50
11 Dunleavy/Ford/Granger .50 1.25
12 Davis/Gordon/Kaman .75 2.00
13 Gasol/Odom/Bryant 6.00 15.00
14 Gasol/Mayo/Randolph .75 2.00
15 Wade/James/Bosh 6.00 15.00
16 Jennings/Salmons/Bogut .60 1.50
17 Love/Beasley/Webster .75 2.00
18 Murphy/Harris/Lopez .60 1.50
19 Paul/West/Ariza 1.50 4.00
20 Gallinari/Stoud/Randolph .75 2.00
21 Durant/Green/Westbrook 3.00 8.00
22 Howard/Lewis/Carter 1.50 4.00

23 Iguodala/Young/Brand .75 2.00
24 Nash/Richardson/Frye 1.50 4.00
25 Roy/Aldridge/Miller 1.00 2.50
26 Dalembert/Landry/Evans .60 1.50
27 Duncan/Ginobili/Parker 2.00 5.00
28 Bargnani/Calderon/Barbosa .60 1.50
29 Jefferson/Kirilenko/Williams .60 1.50
30 Howard/Thornton/Arenas .60 1.50

2010-11 Rookies and Stars Kids Foot Locker

COMPLETE SET (6) 6.00 15.00
1 Kobe Bryant 5.00 12.00
2 Wesley Johnson .40 1.00
3 Rajon Rondo .75 2.00
4 Derrick Rose 1.25 3.00
5 Evan Turner .50 1.25
6 John Wall 2.00 5.00

2009-10 Rookies and Stars Longevity

COMP.SET w/o SPs (115) 15.00 30.00
1 Josh Smith .25 .60
2 Joe Johnson .40 1.00
3 Mike Bibby .40 1.00
4 Paul Pierce .60 1.50
5 Ray Allen .60 1.50
6 Rajon Rondo .50 1.25
7 Kevin Garnett 1.00 2.50
8 Gerald Wallace .30 .75
9 Boris Diaw .30 .75
10 Raja Bell .30 .75
11 Derrick Rose .60 1.50
12 John Salmons .30 .75
13 Kirk Hinrich .30 .75
14 LeBron James 3.00 8.00
15 Shaquille O'Neal 1.25 3.00
16 Mo Williams .30 .75
17 Dirk Nowitzki 1.00 2.50
18 Josh Howard .30 .75
19 Jason Kidd .60 1.50
20 Jason Terry .30 .75
21 Shawn Marion .40 1.00
22 Carmelo Anthony .60 1.50
23 Chauncey Billups .50 1.25
24 J.R. Smith .40 1.00
25 Richard Hamilton .40 1.00
26 Tayshaun Prince .40 1.00
27 Allen Iverson .75 2.00
28 Stephen Jackson .30 .75
29 Corey Maggette .30 .75
30 Monta Ellis .30 .75
31 Yao Ming 1.00 2.50
32 Tracy McGrady .75 2.00
33 Trevor Ariza .25 .60
34 Danny Granger .25 .60
35 Mike Dunleavy .25 .60
36 T.J. Ford .25 .60
37 Al Thornton .25 .60
38 Eric Gordon .30 .75
39 Kobe Bryant 3.00 8.00
40 Pau Gasol .60 1.50
41 Ron Artest .40 1.00
42 Andrew Bynum .25 .60
43 Rudy Gay .40 1.00
44 O.J. Mayo .25 .60
45 Mike Conley Jr. .30 .75
46 Zach Randolph .40 1.00
47 Dwyane Wade .75 2.00
48 Michael Beasley .25 .60
49 Jermaine O'Neal .40 1.00
50 Udonis Haslem .25 .60
51 Michael Redd .30 .75
52 Ramon Sessions .25 .60
53 Andrew Bogut .30 .75
54 Al Jefferson .25 .60
55 Ryan Gomes .25 .60
56 Kevin Love .40 1.00
57 Devin Harris .25 .60
58 Brook Lopez .40 1.00
59 Rafer Alston .25 .60
60 Chris Paul .75 2.00
61 David West .30 .75
62 Peja Stojakovic .30 .75
63 Al Harrington .30 .75
64 Nate Robinson .30 .75
65 Wilson Chandler .30 .75
66 Kevin Durant 1.50 4.00
67 Jeff Green .30 .75
68 Russell Westbrook .75 2.00
69 Dwight Howard .50 1.25
70 Rashard Lewis .30 .75
71 Jameer Nelson .25 .60
72 Vince Carter .75 2.00
73 Andre Iguodala .40 1.00
74 Elton Brand .30 .75
75 Thaddeus Young .25 .60
76 Amare Stoudemire .30 .75
77 Steve Nash .75 2.00
78 Leandro Barbosa .30 .75
79 Channing Frye .25 .60
80 Brandon Roy .50 1.25
81 LaMarcus Aldridge .40 1.00
82 Greg Oden .25 .60
83 Kevin Martin .30 .75
84 Andres Nocioni .25 .60
85 Spencer Hawes .25 .60
86 Tony Parker .60 1.50
87 Tim Duncan 1.00 2.50
88 Manu Ginobili .75 2.00
89 Richard Jefferson .30 .75
90 Chris Bosh .50 1.25
91 Hedo Turkoglu .30 .75
92 Andrea Bargnani .25 .60
93 Deron Williams .30 .75
94 Carlos Boozer .30 .75
95 Andrei Kirilenko .30 .75
96 Ronnie Brewer .25 .60
97 Antawn Jamison .30 .75
98 Gilbert Arenas .30 .75
99 Caron Butler .30 .75
100 Randy Foye .25 .60
101 Kareem Abdul-Jabbar 1.25 3.00
102 Elvin Hayes .60 1.50
103 Karl Malone .50 1.25
104 Arnie Risen .40 1.00
105 Jalen Rose .30 .75
106 Dave DeBusschere .40 1.00
107 Artis Gilmore .50 1.25
108 Nate Archibald .50 1.25
109 Mark Eaton .25 .60
110 Darryl Dawkins .40 1.00
111 Spencer Haywood .25 .60
112 Bill Cartwright .30 .75
113 Moses Malone .60 1.50
114 Magic Johnson 1.50 4.00
115 Sleepy Floyd .30 .75
116 Dante Cunningham RC .40 1.00
117 Jon Brockman RC .40 1.00
118 Jonas Jerebko RC .50 1.25
119 Derrick Brown RC .40 1.00
120 Dionte Christmas RC .40 1.00
121 Marcus Thornton RC .50 1.25
122 Danny Green RC .60 1.50
123 Goran Suton RC .40 1.00
124 Jack McClinton RC .40 1.00
125 A.J. Price RC .40 1.00
126 Serge Ibaka RC .60 1.50
127 DeMar DeRozan RC 5.00 12.00
128 Chris Hunter RC .40 1.00
129 Lester Hudson RC .40 1.00
130 David Andersen RC .40 1.00

2009-10 Rookies and Stars Longevity Ruby

*1-130 RUBY: 2X TO 5X BASE HI
1-130 RUBY PRINT RUN 250 SER.#'d SETS
131-164 PRINT RUN 43 TO 49 SER.#'d SETS
131 Blake Griffin AU 100.00 250.00
132 Hasheem Thabeet AU 5.00 12.00
133 James Harden AU 125.00 300.00
134 Tyreke Evans AU 6.00 15.00
135 Jonny Flynn AU 5.00 12.00
136 Stephen Curry AU 1,500.00 3,000.00
137 Jordan Hill AU 5.00 12.00
139 Brandon Jennings AU 8.00 20.00
140 Terrence Williams AU 5.00 12.00
141 Gerald Henderson AU 5.00 12.00
142 Tyler Hansbrough AU 6.00 15.00
143 Earl Clark AU 5.00 12.00
144 Austin Daye AU 5.00 12.00
145 James Johnson AU/43 6.00 15.00
146 Jrue Holiday AU 25.00 60.00
147 Ty Lawson AU 5.00 12.00
148 Jeff Teague AU 6.00 15.00
149 Eric Maynor AU 5.00 12.00
150 Darren Collison AU 8.00 20.00
151 Omri Casspi AU 5.00 12.00
152 B.J. Mullens AU 5.00 12.00
153 Rodrigue Beaubois AU 5.00 12.00
154 Taj Gibson AU 6.00 15.00
155 DeMarre Carroll AU 6.00 15.00
156 Wayne Ellington AU 6.00 15.00
157 Toney Douglas AU 5.00 12.00
158 Jermaine Taylor AU 5.00 12.00
159 Jeff Pendergraph AU 5.00 12.00
160 DaJuan Summers AU 5.00 12.00
161 Sam Young AU 5.00 12.00
162 DeJuan Blair AU/48 6.00 15.00
163 Chase Budinger AU 5.00 12.00
164 Jodie Meeks AU 5.00 12.00
165 Taylor Griffin AU 5.00 12.00

2009-10 Rookies and Stars Longevity Dress for Success Materials Jerseys

STATED PRINT RUN 299 SER.#'d SETS
1 Blake Griffin 8.00 20.00
2 Hasheem Thabeet 1.25 3.00
3 James Harden 20.00 50.00
4 Tyreke Evans 1.50 4.00
5 Jonny Flynn 1.25 3.00
6 Stephen Curry 125.00 300.00
7 Jordan Hill 1.25 3.00
8 DeMar DeRozan 15.00 40.00
9 Brandon Jennings 2.00 5.00
10 Terrence Williams 1.25 3.00
11 Gerald Henderson 1.25 3.00
12 Tyler Hansbrough 1.50 4.00
13 Earl Clark 1.25 3.00
14 Austin Daye 1.25 3.00
15 James Johnson 1.50 4.00
16 Jrue Holiday 6.00 15.00
17 Ty Lawson 1.50 4.00
18 Jeff Teague 1.50 4.00
19 Eric Maynor 1.25 3.00
20 Darren Collison 2.00 5.00
21 Omri Casspi 1.25 3.00
22 B.J. Mullens 1.25 3.00
23 Rodrigue Beaubois 1.25 3.00
24 Taj Gibson 1.50 4.00
25 DeMarre Carroll 1.50 4.00
26 Wayne Ellington 1.50 4.00
27 Toney Douglas 1.25 3.00
28 Jermaine Taylor 1.25 3.00
29 Jeff Pendergraph 1.25 3.00
30 DaJuan Summers 1.25 3.00
31 Sam Young 1.25 3.00
32 DeJuan Blair 1.50 4.00
33 Chase Budinger 1.25 3.00
34 Jodie Meeks 1.25 3.00
35 Taylor Griffin 1.25 3.00

2009-10 Rookies and Stars Longevity Freshman Orientation Materials Jerseys

STATED PRINT RUN 299 SER.#'d SETS
1 Blake Griffin 8.00 20.00
2 Hasheem Thabeet 1.25 3.00
3 James Harden 20.00 50.00
4 Tyreke Evans 1.50 4.00
5 Jonny Flynn 1.25 3.00
6 Stephen Curry 125.00 300.00
7 Jordan Hill 1.25 3.00
8 DeMar DeRozan 15.00 40.00
9 Brandon Jennings 2.00 5.00
10 Terrence Williams 1.25 3.00
11 Gerald Henderson 1.25 3.00
12 Tyler Hansbrough 1.50 4.00
13 Earl Clark 1.25 3.00
14 Austin Daye 1.25 3.00
15 James Johnson 1.50 4.00
16 Jrue Holiday 6.00 15.00
17 Ty Lawson 1.50 4.00
18 Jeff Teague 1.50 4.00
19 Eric Maynor 1.25 3.00
20 Darren Collison 2.00 5.00
21 Omri Casspi 1.25 3.00
22 B.J. Mullens 1.25 3.00
23 Rodrigue Beaubois 1.25 3.00
24 Taj Gibson 1.50 4.00
25 DeMarre Carroll 1.50 4.00
26 Wayne Ellington 1.50 4.00
27 Toney Douglas 1.25 3.00
28 Jermaine Taylor 1.25 3.00
29 Jeff Pendergraph 1.25 3.00
30 DaJuan Summers 1.25 3.00
31 Sam Young 1.25 3.00
32 DeJuan Blair 1.50 4.00
33 Chase Budinger 1.25 3.00
34 Jodie Meeks 1.25 3.00
35 Taylor Griffin 1.25 3.00

2009-10 Rookies and Stars Longevity Materials Ruby

STATED PRINT RUN 99 TO 250 SER.#'d SETS
*SAPPHIRE: .6X TO 1.5X BASE HI
SAPPHIRE PRINT RUN 25 SER.#'d SETS
1 Josh Smith/250 2.00 5.00
3 Mike Bibby/250 3.00 8.00
13 Kirk Hinrich/250 2.50 6.00
14 LeBron James/250 8.00 20.00
17 Dirk Nowitzki/250 8.00 20.00
18 Josh Howard/250 2.50 6.00
19 Jason Kidd/250 5.00 12.00
20 Jason Terry/250 2.50 6.00
22 Carmelo Anthony/250 5.00 12.00
26 Tayshaun Prince/250 3.00 8.00
31 Yao Ming/250 8.00 20.00
32 Tracy McGrady/250 6.00 15.00
39 Kobe Bryant/99 12.00 30.00
40 Pau Gasol/250 5.00 12.00
42 Andrew Bynum/250 2.00 5.00
44 O.J. Mayo/250 2.00 5.00
45 Mike Conley Jr./250 2.50 6.00
47 Dwyane Wade/250 6.00 15.00
49 Jermaine O'Neal/150 3.00 8.00
50 Udonis Haslem/250 2.00 5.00
51 Michael Redd/250 2.50 6.00
53 Andrew Bogut/250 2.50 6.00
54 Al Jefferson/250 2.00 5.00
56 Kevin Love/250 3.00 8.00
57 Devin Harris/150 2.00 5.00
60 Chris Paul/250 6.00 15.00
62 Peja Stojakovic/250 2.50 6.00
63 Al Harrington/250 2.50 6.00
64 Nate Robinson/250 2.50 6.00
66 Kevin Durant/150 8.00 20.00
69 Dwight Howard/250 4.00 10.00
70 Rashard Lewis/250 2.50 6.00
73 Andre Iguodala/250 3.00 8.00
74 Elton Brand/250 2.50 6.00
75 Thaddeus Young/250 2.00 5.00
76 Amare Stoudemire/250 2.50 6.00
77 Steve Nash/150 6.00 15.00
80 Brandon Roy/250 4.00 10.00
81 LaMarcus Aldridge/250 3.00 8.00
82 Greg Oden/250 2.00 5.00
83 Kevin Martin/250 2.50 6.00
84 Andres Nocioni/250 2.00 5.00
86 Tony Parker/250 5.00 12.00
87 Tim Duncan/250 8.00 20.00
88 Manu Ginobili/250 6.00 15.00
90 Chris Bosh/250 4.00 10.00
92 Andrea Bargnani/250 2.00 5.00
93 Deron Williams/250 2.50 6.00
94 Carlos Boozer/250 2.50 6.00
95 Andrei Kirilenko/250 2.50 6.00
101 Kareem Abdul-Jabbar/250 10.00 25.00
102 Elvin Hayes/250 5.00 12.00
103 Karl Malone/250 4.00 10.00
113 Moses Malone/150 5.00 12.00
115 Sleepy Floyd/250 2.50 6.00
127 DeMar DeRozan/250 25.00 60.00

2009-10 Rookies and Stars Longevity Signatures

STATED PRINT RUN 10 TO 999 SER.#'d SETS
3 Mike Bibby/25 6.00 15.00
19 Jason Kidd/25 15.00 40.00
39 Kobe Bryant/25 800.00 1,500.00
42 Andrew Bynum/100 8.00 20.00
56 Kevin Love/25 12.00 30.00
102 Elvin Hayes/25 10.00 25.00
104 Arnie Risen/25 6.00 15.00
107 Artis Gilmore/50 6.00 15.00
108 Nate Archibald/25 15.00 40.00
111 Spencer Haywood/25 10.00 25.00
117 Jon Brockman/874 2.00 5.00
121 Marcus Thornton/374 2.50 6.00
122 Danny Green/874 3.00 8.00
123 Goran Suton/773 2.00 5.00
124 Jack McClinton/474 2.00 5.00
125 A.J. Price/674 2.00 5.00
129 Lester Hudson/999 2.00 5.00

2010-11 Rookies and Stars Longevity

COMP.SET w/o RCs (115) 20.00 50.00
EXCH EXPIRATION 5/10/12
1 Ray Allen 1.00 2.50
2 Paul Pierce 1.00 2.50
3 Rajon Rondo .75 2.00
4 Kevin Garnett 1.50 4.00
5 Brook Lopez .50 1.25
6 Devin Harris .40 1.00
7 Troy Murphy .40 1.00
8 Amare Stoudemire .60 1.50
9 Anthony Randolph .40 1.00
10 Danilo Gallinari .50 1.25
11 Andre Iguodala .60 1.50
12 Elton Brand .50 1.25
13 Thaddeus Young .50 1.25
14 Andrea Bargnani .40 1.00
15 Leandro Barbosa .50 1.25
16 Jose Calderon .40 1.00
17 Carlos Boozer .50 1.25
18 Derrick Rose 1.25 3.00
19 Joakim Noah .60 1.50
20 Luol Deng .50 1.25
21 Antawn Jamison .50 1.25
22 Mo Williams .50 1.25
23 Daniel Gibson .40 1.00
24 Ben Gordon .50 1.25
25 Richard Hamilton .75 2.00
26 Tayshaun Prince .60 1.50
27 Danny Granger .40 1.00
28 Tyler Hansbrough .40 1.00
29 Mike Dunleavy .40 1.00
30 Andrew Bogut .50 1.25
31 Brandon Jennings .50 1.25
32 John Salmons .40 1.00
33 Joe Johnson .60 1.50
34 Josh Smith .60 1.50
35 Al Horford .60 1.50
36 Jamal Crawford .60 1.50
37 Gerald Henderson .40 1.00
38 Stephen Jackson .50 1.25
39 Gerald Wallace .50 1.25
40 LeBron James 5.00 12.00
41 Dwyane Wade 1.25 3.00
42 Chris Bosh .75 2.00
43 Dwight Howard .75 2.00
44 Vince Carter 1.25 3.00
45 J.J. Redick .60 1.50
46 Josh Howard .50 1.25
47 Al Thornton .40 1.00
48 Gilbert Arenas .50 1.25
49 Kirk Hinrich .50 1.25
50 Dirk Nowitzki 1.50 4.00
51 Jason Kidd 1.00 2.50
52 Shawn Marion .60 1.50
53 Caron Butler .50 1.25
54 Kevin Martin .50 1.25
55 Shane Battier .50 1.25
56 Luis Scola .50 1.25
57 Yao Ming 1.25 3.00
58 Marc Gasol .60 1.50
59 Rudy Gay .60 1.50
60 Zach Randolph .60 1.50
61 Chris Paul 1.25 3.00
62 Emeka Okafor .50 1.25
63 David West .50 1.25
64 Tim Duncan 1.50 4.00
65 Tony Parker 1.00 2.50
66 Richard Jefferson .50 1.25
67 Carmelo Anthony 1.00 2.50
68 Chauncey Billups 1.00 2.50
69 Chris Andersen .60 1.50
70 Nene .50 1.25
71 Kevin Love .60 1.50
72 Michael Beasley .60 1.50
73 Jonny Flynn .40 1.00
74 Brandon Roy .40 1.00
75 Rudy Fernandez .40 1.00
76 Greg Oden .40 1.00
77 Kevin Durant 2.50 6.00
78 Russell Westbrook 1.00 2.50
79 Jeff Green .50 1.25
80 Deron Williams .50 1.25
81 Al Jefferson .40 1.00
82 Andrei Kirilenko .50 1.25
83 Paul Millsap .50 1.25
84 David Lee .40 1.00
85 Monta Ellis .50 1.25
86 Stephen Curry 40.00 100.00
87 Eric Gordon .50 1.25
88 Chris Kaman .40 1.00
89 Baron Davis .60 1.50
90 Kobe Bryant 5.00 12.00
91 Pau Gasol 1.00 2.50
92 Lamar Odom .50 1.25
93 Ron Artest .60 1.50
94 Steve Nash 1.25 3.00
95 Hedo Turkoglu .50 1.25
96 Channing Frye .40 1.00
97 Grant Hill 1.00 2.50
98 Tyreke Evans .50 1.25
99 Samuel Dalembert .40 1.00
100 Carl Landry .40 1.00
101 Rolando Blackman .50 1.25
102 Joe Dumars .60 1.50
103 Wayne Embry .50 1.25
104 Walt Frazier 1.00 2.50
105 Gail Goodrich .60 1.50
106 John Havlicek 1.25 3.00
107 Rod Hundley .60 1.50
108 Phil Jackson .75 2.00
109 K.C. Jones .60 1.50
110 Clyde Lovellette .75 2.00
111 Jerry Lucas .60 1.50
112 Nate McMillan .40 1.00
113 Willis Reed 1.00 2.50
114 Paul Silas .60 1.50
115 Jerry West 1.25 3.00
116 Armon Johnson RC .60 1.50
117 Sherron Collins RC .60 1.50
118 Terrico White RC .60 1.50
119 Darington Hobson RC .60 1.50
120 Landry Fields RC .60 1.50
121 Tony Gaffney RC .60 1.50
122 Ben Uzoh RC .60 1.50
123 Ishmael Smith RC 1.00 2.50
124 Tweety Carter RC .60 1.50
125 Tiago Splitter RC .75 2.00
126 Solomon Alabi RC .60 1.50
127 Magnum Rolle RC .60 1.50
128 Pape Sy RC .60 1.50
129 Jeremy Lin RC 4.00 10.00
130 Derrick Caracter RC .60 1.50

2010-11 Rookies and Stars Longevity Ruby

*RUBY 1-130: 2X TO 5X BASE HI
1-130 RUBY PRINT RUN 250 SER.#'d SETS
131-170 PRINT RUN 5 TO 49 SER.#'d SETS
86 Stephen Curry 150.00 400.00
131 Jordan Crawford AU/49 4.00 10.00
132 Luke Harangody AU/49 4.00 10.00
133 Avery Bradley AU/49 6.00 15.00
134 Kevin Seraphin AU/49 4.00 10.00
135 Dominique Jones AU/49 4.00 10.00
136 Greg Monroe AU/49 5.00 12.00
137 Ekpe Udoh AU/49 4.00 10.00
138 Patrick Patterson AU/49 5.00 12.00
139 Lance Stephenson AU/49 6.00 15.00
140 Paul George AU/49 100.00 250.00
141 Eric Bledsoe AU/49 8.00 20.00
142 Willie Warren AU/49 4.00 10.00
144 Devin Ebanks AU/49 4.00 10.00
145 Xavier Henry AU/49 4.00 10.00
146 Greivis Vasquez AU/49 4.00 10.00
147 Dexter Pittman AU/49 4.00 10.00
148 Da'Sean Butler AU/49 5.00 12.00
149 Keith Gallion AU/49 4.00 10.00
150 Larry Sanders AU/49 4.00 10.00
151 Lazar Hayward AU/49 4.00 10.00
152 Wesley Johnson AU/49 4.00 10.00
153 Derrick Favors AU/49 6.00 15.00
154 Damion James AU/49 4.00 10.00
155 Craig Brackins AU/49 4.00 10.00
156 Quincy Pondexter AU/49 4.00 10.00
157 Andy Rautins AU/49 4.00 10.00
158 Cole Aldrich AU/49 4.00 10.00
159 Daniel Orton AU/49 4.00 10.00
160 Evan Turner AU/49 5.00 12.00
161 Gani Lawal AU/49 4.00 10.00
162 Elliot Williams AU/49 4.00 10.00
163 Luke Babbitt AU/49 4.00 10.00
166 James Anderson AU/49 4.00 10.00
167 Ed Davis AU/49 5.00 12.00
168 Gordon Hayward AU/49 15.00 40.00
169 Trevor Booker AU/49 4.00 10.00
170 John Wall AU/49 40.00 100.00

2010-11 Rookies and Stars Longevity Sapphire

*SAPPHIRE 1-130: 3X TO 8X BASE HI
1-130 PRINT RUN 25 SER.#'d SETS

2010-11 Rookies and Stars Longevity Dress for Success Materials

STATED PRINT RUN 99 TO 299 SER.#'d SETS
1 John Wall/299 6.00 15.00
2 Andre Miller/299 2.50 6.00
3 Evan Turner/299 1.50 4.00
4 Wesley Johnson/299 1.25 3.00
5 Andris Biedrins/299 2.00 5.00
6 Derrick Favors/299 2.00 5.00
7 Ekpe Udoh/299 1.25 3.00
8 Emeka Okafor/299 2.50 6.00
9 Eric Gordon/99 2.50 6.00
10 Evan Turner/299 1.50 4.00
11 Gani Lawal/299 1.25 3.00
12 Gerald Henderson/299 2.00 5.00
13 Goran Dragic/199 4.00 10.00
14 Gordon Hayward/299 5.00 12.00
15 Greg Monroe/299 1.50 4.00
16 Greg Oden/299 2.00 5.00
17 Greivis Vasquez/299 1.25 3.00
18 Hassan Whiteside/299 2.50 6.00
19 J.J. Barea/299 2.50 6.00
20 J.J. Redick/299 3.00 8.00
21 J.R. Smith/299 3.00 8.00
22 James Anderson/299 1.25 3.00
24 Dwight Howard/299 4.00 10.00
25 Jose Calderon/299 2.00 5.00
26 Lance Stephenson/299 2.00 5.00
27 Marcus Camby/299 2.50 6.00
28 Mike Dunleavy/199 2.00 5.00
29 DeMarcus Cousins/299 4.00 10.00
30 Wesley Johnson/299 1.25 3.00
31 Xavier Henry/299 1.25 3.00
32 Derrick Favors/299 2.00 5.00
33 Al-Farouq Aminu/299 1.50 4.00
34 Larry Sanders/299 1.25 3.00
35 Paul George/299 10.00 25.00

2010-11 Rookies and Stars Longevity Freshman Orientation Materials

STATED PRINT RUN 299 SER.#'d SETS
1 John Wall 6.00 15.00
2 Evan Turner 1.50 4.00
3 Derrick Favors 2.00 5.00
4 Wesley Johnson 1.25 3.00
5 DeMarcus Cousins 4.00 10.00
6 Ekpe Udoh 1.25 3.00
7 Greg Monroe 1.50 4.00
8 Al-Farouq Aminu 1.50 4.00
9 Gordon Hayward 5.00 12.00
10 Paul George 8.00 20.00
11 Cole Aldrich 1.25 3.00
12 Xavier Henry 1.25 3.00
13 Patrick Patterson 1.50 4.00
14 Larry Sanders 1.25 3.00
15 Luke Babbitt 1.25 3.00
16 Eric Bledsoe 2.50 6.00
17 Avery Bradley 2.00 5.00
18 James Anderson 1.25 3.00
19 Craig Brackins 1.25 3.00
20 Elliot Williams 1.25 3.00
21 Trevor Booker 1.25 3.00
22 Damion James 1.25 3.00
23 Dominique Jones 1.25 3.00
24 Quincy Pondexter 1.25 3.00
25 Jordan Crawford 1.25 3.00
26 Greivis Vasquez 1.25 3.00
27 Daniel Orton 1.25 3.00
28 Lazar Hayward 1.25 3.00
29 Dexter Pittman 1.25 3.00
30 Hassan Whiteside 2.50 6.00
31 Lance Stephenson 2.00 5.00
32 Da'Sean Butler 1.50 4.00
33 Devin Ebanks 1.25 3.00
34 Gani Lawal 1.25 3.00
35 Luke Harangody 1.25 3.00

2010-11 Rookies and Stars Longevity Materials Sapphire

STATED PRINT RUN 25 SER.#'d SETS
1 Ray Allen 8.00 20.00
2 Paul Pierce 8.00 20.00
3 Rajon Rondo 6.00 15.00
4 Kevin Garnett 12.00 30.00
6 Devin Harris 3.00 8.00
11 Andre Iguodala 5.00 12.00
12 Elton Brand 4.00 10.00
13 Thaddeus Young 3.00 8.00
15 Leandro Barbosa 4.00 10.00
16 Jose Calderon 3.00 8.00
18 Derrick Rose 10.00 25.00
19 Joakim Noah 5.00 12.00
20 Luol Deng 4.00 10.00
21 Antawn Jamison 4.00 10.00
24 Ben Gordon 4.00 10.00
26 Tayshaun Prince 5.00 12.00
28 Tyler Hansbrough 3.00 8.00
29 Mike Dunleavy 3.00 8.00
30 Andrew Bogut 4.00 10.00
31 Brandon Jennings 3.00 8.00
33 Joe Johnson 5.00 12.00
34 Josh Smith 3.00 8.00
35 Al Horford 5.00 12.00
37 Gerald Henderson 3.00 8.00
38 Stephen Jackson 4.00 10.00
39 Gerald Wallace 4.00 10.00
41 Dwyane Wade 10.00 25.00
43 Dwight Howard 6.00 15.00
44 Vince Carter 10.00 25.00
45 J.J. Redick 5.00 12.00
46 Josh Howard 4.00 10.00
48 Gilbert Arenas 4.00 10.00
49 Kirk Hinrich 4.00 10.00
50 Dirk Nowitzki 12.00 30.00
51 Jason Kidd 8.00 20.00
52 Shawn Marion 5.00 12.00
53 Caron Butler 4.00 10.00
54 Kevin Martin 4.00 10.00
55 Shane Battier 4.00 10.00
56 Luis Scola 4.00 10.00
58 Marc Gasol 5.00 12.00
59 Rudy Gay 5.00 12.00
61 Chris Paul 10.00 25.00
62 Emeka Okafor 4.00 10.00
63 David West 4.00 10.00
64 Tim Duncan 12.00 30.00
65 Tony Parker 8.00 20.00
66 Richard Jefferson 4.00 10.00
67 Carmelo Anthony 8.00 20.00
68 Chauncey Billups 6.00 15.00
69 Chris Andersen 5.00 12.00
70 Nene 4.00 10.00
71 Kevin Love 5.00 12.00
72 Michael Beasley 3.00 8.00
73 Jonny Flynn 3.00 8.00
74 Brandon Roy 6.00 15.00
75 Rudy Fernandez 3.00 8.00
76 Greg Oden 3.00 8.00
78 Russell Westbrook 8.00 20.00
80 Deron Williams 4.00 10.00
82 Andrei Kirilenko 4.00 10.00
86 Stephen Curry 25.00 60.00
88 Chris Kaman 3.00 8.00
89 Baron Davis 5.00 12.00
90 Kobe Bryant 20.00 50.00
91 Pau Gasol 8.00 20.00
92 Lamar Odom 4.00 10.00
93 Ron Artest 5.00 12.00
94 Steve Nash 10.00 25.00
95 Hedo Turkoglu 4.00 10.00
96 Channing Frye 3.00 8.00
97 Grant Hill 10.00 25.00
99 Samuel Dalembert 3.00 8.00
101 Rolando Blackman 4.00 10.00
102 Joe Dumars 5.00 12.00
118 Terrico White 3.00 8.00
129 Jeremy Lin 100.00 200.00

2010-11 Rookies and Stars Longevity Signatures

STATED PRINT RUN 5 TO 799 SER.#'d SETS
8 Amare Stoudemire/15 25.00 60.00
11 Andre Iguodala/25 4.00 10.00
14 Andrea Bargnani/49 5.00 12.00
28 Tyler Hansbrough/99 4.00 10.00
37 Gerald Henderson/149 4.00 10.00
46 Josh Howard/99 4.00 10.00
51 Jason Kidd/25 20.00 50.00
62 Emeka Okafor/25 4.00 10.00
73 Jonny Flynn/199 4.00 10.00
86 Stephen Curry/49 1,000.00 2,000.00
89 Baron Davis/20 10.00 25.00
90 Kobe Bryant/49 1,500.00 3,000.00
93 Ron Artest/25 12.00 30.00
98 Tyreke Evans/99 4.00 10.00
100 Carl Landry/99 4.00 10.00
105 Gail Goodrich/49 8.00 20.00
106 John Havlicek/25 40.00 100.00
116 Armon Johnson/149 2.50 6.00
117 Sherron Collins/799 2.50 6.00
118 Terrico White/299 2.50 6.00
119 Darington Hobson/799 2.50 6.00
120 Landry Fields/349 2.50 6.00
121 Tony Gaffney/799 2.50 6.00
123 Ishmael Smith/799 4.00 10.00
124 Tweety Carter/499 2.50 6.00
125 Tiago Splitter/799 3.00 8.00
126 Solomon Alabi/350 2.50 6.00
127 Magnum Rolle/799 2.50 6.00
128 Pape Sy/799 2.50 6.00
129 Jeremy Lin/599 75.00 200.00
130 Derrick Caracter/799 2.50 6.00

1978-79 Royal Crown Cola

COMPLETE SET 1,500.00 3,000.00
1 Kareem Abdul-Jabbar 150.00 300.00
2 Nate Archibald 50.00 100.00
3 Rick Barry 50.00 100.00
4 Jim Chones 25.00 50.00
5 Doug Collins 40.00 80.00
6 Dave Cowens 50.00 100.00
7 Adrian Dantley 45.00 90.00
8 Walter Davis 45.00 85.00
9 John Drew 20.00 45.00
10 Julius Erving 175.00 350.00
11 Walt Frazier 50.00 100.00
12 George Gervin 60.00 120.00
13 Artis Gilmore 45.00 90.00
14 Elvin Hayes 45.00 90.00
15 Dan Issel 45.00 90.00
16 Marques Johnson 35.00 70.00
17 Mickey Johnson 20.00 45.00
18 Bernard King 50.00 100.00
19 Bob Lanier 50.00 100.00
20 Maurice Lucas 35.00 65.00
21 Pete Maravich 300.00 475.00
22 Bob McAdoo 45.00 90.00
23 George McGinnis 30.00 60.00
24 Eric Money 25.00 45.00
25 Earl Monroe 45.00 90.00
26 Calvin Murphy 35.00 75.00
27 Robert Parish 60.00 120.00
28 Billy Paultz 25.00 45.00
29 Jack Sikma 35.00 65.00
30 Ricky Sobers 25.00 45.00
31 David Thompson 60.00 120.00
32 Rudy Tomjanovich 45.00 90.00
33 Wes Unseld 45.00 90.00
34 Norm Van Lier 30.00 60.00
35 Bill Walton 75.00 150.00
36 Marvin Webster 25.00 45.00
37 Scott Wedman 25.00 45.00
38 Paul Westphal 40.00 75.00
39 Jo Jo White 35.00 70.00
40 John Williamson 25.00 45.00
41 Brian Winters 40.00 80.00

1979-80 Royal Crown Cola Cans

COMPLETE SET (35) 225.00 450.00
1 Dave Cowens 7.50 15.00
2 Nate Archibald 5.00 10.00
3 Artis Gilmore 7.50 15.00
4 David Thompson 7.50 15.00
5 Bob Lanier 5.00 10.00
6 Rick Barry 10.00 20.00
7 Rudy Tomjanovich 5.00 10.00
8 Kareem Abdul-Jabbar 20.00 40.00
9 Brian Winters 2.00 5.00
10 Bernard King 3.00 8.00
11 Pete Maravich 25.00 50.00
12 Bob McAdoo 5.00 10.00
13 Doug Collins 5.00 10.00
14 George McGinnis 5.00 10.00
15 Walter Davis 2.00 5.00
16 Paul Westphal 5.00 10.00
17 Robert Parish 7.50 15.00
18 Bill Walton 12.50 25.00
19 George Gervin 12.50 25.00
20 Elvin Hayes 7.50 15.00
21 Norm Van Lier 2.00 5.00
22 Dan Issel 7.50 15.00
23 Julius Erving 20.00 40.00
24 Jim Chones 2.00 5.00
25 Jo Jo White 3.00 8.00
26 Calvin Murphy 6.00 12.00
27 Earl Monroe 7.50 15.00
28 Billy Paultz 2.00 5.00
29 John Drew 2.00 5.00
30 John Williamson 2.00 5.00
31 Jack Sikma 3.00 8.00
32 Scott Wedman 2.00 5.00
33 Ricky Sobers 2.00 5.00
34 Maurice Lucas 3.00 8.00
35 Marvin Webster 2.00 5.00

1952 Royal Desserts

COMPLETE SET (8) 7,000.00 9,500.00
1 Fred Schaus 350.00 700.00
2 Dick McGuire 400.00 850.00
3 Jack Nichols 250.00 500.00
4 Frank Brian 250.00 500.00
5 Joe Fulks 700.00 1,200.00
6 George Mikan 3,000.00 4,000.00
7 Jim Pollard 700.00 1,200.00
8 Buddy Jeanette 400.00 800.00

1970-71 Royals Cincinnati Team Issue

COMPLETE SET (12) 50.00 100.00
1 Nate Archibald 8.00 20.00
2 Bob Arnzen 2.00 5.00
3 Moe Barr 2.00 5.00
4 Bob Cousy 12.50 25.00
5 Johnny Green 3.00 8.00
6 Greg Hyder 2.00 5.00
7 Darrall Imhoff 3.00 8.00
8 Sam Lacey 3.00 8.00
9 Charlie Paulk 2.00 5.00
10 Flynn Robinson 3.00 8.00
11 Tom Van Arsdale 3.00 8.00
12 Norm Van Lier 5.00 10.00

1972 7-11 Cups

COMPLETE SET 300.00 600.00
1 Kareem Abdul-Jabbar 20.00 40.00
2 Mahdi Abdul-Rahman 5.00 10.00
3 Nate Archibald 8.00 20.00
4 Rick Barry 8.00 20.00
5 Dave Bing 6.00 15.00
6 Austin Carr 5.00 10.00
7 Wilt Chamberlain 25.00 50.00
8 Dave DeBusschere 8.00 20.00
9 Walt Frazier 10.00 20.00
10 Gail Goodrich 6.00 15.00
11 Hal Greer 6.00 15.00
12 Happy Hairston 5.00 10.00
13 John Havlicek 10.00 25.00
14 Connie Hawkins 8.00 20.00
15 Elvin Hayes 10.00 20.00
16 Spencer Haywood 5.00 10.00
17 Lou Hudson 5.00 10.00
18 John Johnson 5.00 10.00
19 Don Kojis 5.00 10.00
20 Bob Lanier 7.50 15.00
21 Kevin Loughery 5.00 10.00
22 Jerry Lucas 6.00 15.00
23 Pete Maravich 50.00 100.00
24 Jack Marin 5.00 10.00
25 Jim McMillian 5.00 10.00
26 Jeff Mullins 5.00 10.00
27 Geoff Petrie 5.00 10.00
28 Willis Reed 8.00 20.00
29 Oscar Robertson 15.00 30.00
30 Paul Silas 6.00 15.00
31 Jerry Sloan 8.00 20.00
32 Elmore Smith 5.00 10.00
33 Nate Thurmond 6.00 15.00
34 Wes Unseld 6.00 15.00
35 Dick Van Arsdale 6.00 12.00
36 Tom Van Arsdale 6.00 12.00
37 Chet Walker 6.00 12.00
38 John Warren 5.00 10.00
39 Jerry West 25.00 50.00
40 Jo Jo White 6.00 15.00

1981 7-Up Jumbos

COMPLETE SET (7) 30.00 75.00
3 Magic Johnson BK 15.00 40.00
5 Ann Meyers BK 6.00 15.00

1976-77 76ers Canada Dry Cans

COMPLETE SET (14) 37.50 75.00
1 Henry Bibby 2.50 6.00
2 Joe Bryant 2.50 6.00
3 Harvey Catchings 1.50 4.00
4 Darryl Dawkins 5.00 10.00
5 Al Domenico TR 1.50 4.00
6 Mike Dunleavy 3.00 8.00
7 Julius Erving 15.00 30.00
8 Lloyd Free 2.50 6.00
9 Terry Furlow 1.50 4.00
10 Caldwell Jones 2.50 6.00
11 George McGinnis 5.00 10.00
12 Jack McMahon ACO 1.50 4.00

13 Steve Mix 1.50 4.00
14 Gene Shue CO 3.00 8.00

2001-02 76ers Fleer
COMPLETE SET (6) 2.00 5.00
NNO Larry Brown CO .40 1.00
NNO Eric Snow .30 .75
NNO Aaron McKie .30 .75
NNO Allen Iverson 1.25 3.00
NNO Team Photo .40 1.00
NNO Dikembe Mutombo .75 2.00

2001-02 76ers Fleer NBA All-Star Jam Session
COMPLETE SET (6) 3.00 8.00
1 Speedy Claxton .50 1.25
2 Derrick Coleman .60 1.50
3 Allen Iverson 2.00 5.00
4 Aaron McKie .50 1.25
5 Dikembe Mutombo 1.25 3.00
6 Eric Snow .50 1.25

1989-90 76ers Kodak
COMPLETE SET (16) 6.00 15.00
1 Ron Anderson .20 .50
2 Charles Barkley 3.00 8.00
3 Scott Brooks .40 1.00
4 Lanard Copeland .20 .50
5 Johnny Dawkins .40 1.00
6 Mike Gminski .40 1.00
7 Hersey Hawkins .75 2.00
8 Rick Mahorn .30 .75
9 Kurt Nimphius .20 .50
10 Kenny Payne .20 .50
11 Derek Smith .40 1.00
12 Bob Thornton .20 .50
13 Big Shot (Team Mascot) .20 .50
14 Jim Lynam CO .20 .50
15 Fred Carter ACO .20 .50
16 Buzz Braman ACO .75 2.00

1975-76 76ers McDonald's Standups
COMPLETE SET (6) 6.00 15.00
1 Fred Carter 1.25 3.00
2 Harvey Catchings 1.25 3.00
3 Doug Collins 3.00 8.00
4 Billy Cunningham 3.00 8.00
5 George McGinnis 2.00 5.00
6 Steve Mix 1.25 3.00

1979-80 76ers Stand-ups
COMPLETE SET (12) 60.00 120.00
1 Henry Bibby 3.00 8.00
2 Joe Bryant 3.00 8.00
3 Harvey Catchings 2.50 6.00
4 Doug Collins 7.50 15.00
5 Darryl Dawkins 6.00 12.00
6 Mike Dunleavy 5.00 12.00
7 Julius Erving 30.00 55.00
8 Lloyd Free 5.00 10.00
9 Terry Furlow 2.50 6.00
10 Caldwell Jones 2.50 6.00
11 George McGinnis 5.00 10.00
12 Steve Mix 2.50 6.00

1969-70 76ers Team Issue
COMPLETE SET (11) 25.00 60.00
1 Archie Clark 2.50 6.00
2 Bill Cunningham 8.00 20.00
3 Hal Greer 5.00 12.00
4 Matt Guokas 3.00 8.00
5 Fred Hetzel 1.50 4.00
6 Darrall Imhoff 1.50 4.00
7 Luke Jackson 2.50 6.00
8 Wally Jones 2.50 6.00
9 Bud Ogden 1.50 4.00
10 Jack Ramsay CO 3.00 8.00
11 George Wilson 1.50 4.00

1970-71 76ers Team Issue
COMPLETE SET (13) 20.00 40.00
1 Dennis Awtrey 1.00 2.50
2 Archie Clark 1.50 4.00
3 Billy Cunningham 3.00 8.00
4 Connie Dierking 1.25 3.00
5 Fred Foster 1.00 2.50
6 Hal Greer 2.00 5.00
7 Al Henry 1.00 2.50
8 Bailey Howell 1.25 3.00
9 Luke Jackson 1.25 3.00
10 Wally Jones 1.50 4.00
11 Bud Ogden 1.00 2.50
12 Jack Ramsay CO 2.00 5.00
13 Jim Washington 1.25 3.00

1976-77 76ers Team Issue Black and White
COMPLETE SET (12) 15.00 30.00
1 Henry Bibby 1.50 4.00
2 Joe Bryant 1.50 4.00
3 Fred Carter 1.25 3.00
4 Harvey Catchings 1.25 3.00
5 Lloyd Free 2.00 5.00
6 Steve Mix 1.25 3.00
7 Coniel Norman 1.25 3.00
8 F. Eugene Dixon Jr. PRES 1.25 3.00
9 Al Domenico TR 1.25 3.00
10 Jack McMahon CO 1.25 3.00
11 Gene Shue CO 1.50 4.00
12 Pat Williams VP 1.25 3.00

1976-77 76ers Team Issue Color
COMPLETE SET (12) 20.00 50.00
1 Henry Bibby 1.25 3.00
2 Joe Bryant 1.50 4.00
3 Harvey Catchings .75 2.00
4 Doug Collins 3.00 8.00
5 Darryl Dawkins 2.50 6.00
6 Mike Dunleavy 2.00 5.00
7 Julius Erving 12.00 30.00
8 Lloyd Free 2.00 5.00
9 Terry Furlow .75 2.00
10 Caldwell Jones 1.25 3.00
11 George McGinnis 1.50 4.00
12 Steve Mix .75 2.00

1997 Scholastic Ultimate NBA Postcards
COMPLETE SET (30) 6.00 15.00
1 Greg Anthony .20 .50
2 Vin Baker .20 .50
3 Shawn Bradley .20 .50
4 Terrell Brandon .20 .50
5 Elden Campbell .20 .50
6 Sam Cassell .30 .75
7 Joe Dumars .40 1.00
8 Patrick Ewing .40 1.00
9 Kevin Garnett 1.50 4.00
10 Kevin Johnson .30 .75
11 Shawn Kemp .25 .60
12 Toni Kukoc .30 .75
13 Karl Malone .60 1.50
14 Jamal Mashburn .30 .75
15 Antonio McDyess .30 .75
16 Alonzo Mourning .40 1.00
17 Dino Radja .20 .50
18 Glen Rice .30 .75
19 Mitch Richmond .30 .75
20 David Robinson .40 1.00
21 Arvydas Sabonis .30 .75
22 Dennis Scott .20 .50
23 Joe Smith .25 .60
24 Steve Smith .30 .75
25 Rik Smits .20 .50
26 John Starks .20 .50
27 Damon Stoudamire .30 .75
28 Loy Vaught .20 .50
29 Clarence Weatherspoon .20 .50
30 Chris Webber .75 2.00

1995 Score Board Phone Card Promo
NNO Shaquille O'Neal
Hakeem Olajuwon 4.00 10.00

2012-13 Select
COMP.SET w/o AUs (150) 75.00 200.00
AU SER.#'d B/WN 149-449 COPIES PER
JSY AU SER.#'d 149-399 COPIES PER
EXCHANGE DEADLINE 10/03/2014
1 Al Horford .50 1.25
2 Anthony Morrow .30 .75
3 Jeff Teague .30 .75
4 Josh Smith .30 .75
5 Brook Lopez .40 1.00
6 Deron Williams .40 1.00
7 Gerald Wallace .40 1.00
8 Joe Johnson .40 1.00
9 Kris Humphries .30 .75
10 Brandon Bass .30 .75
11 Courtney Lee .30 .75
12 Jason Terry .40 1.00
13 Jeff Green .30 .75
14 Kevin Garnett 1.25 3.00
15 Paul Pierce .75 2.00
16 Rajon Rondo .60 1.50
17 Ben Gordon .40 1.00
18 Gerald Henderson .30 .75
19 Carlos Boozer .40 1.00
20 Derrick Rose .75 2.00
21 Joakim Noah .40 1.00
22 Luol Deng .40 1.00
23 Nate Robinson .30 .75
24 Taj Gibson .30 .75
25 Anderson Varejao .30 .75
26 Darren Collison .30 .75
27 Dirk Nowitzki 1.25 3.00
28 O.J. Mayo .30 .75
29 Vince Carter 1.00 2.50
30 Andre Iguodala .50 1.25
31 Danilo Gallinari .30 .75
32 JaVale McGee .40 1.00
33 Ty Lawson .30 .75
34 Wilson Chandler .40 1.00
35 Greg Monroe .30 .75
36 Rodney Stuckey .30 .75
37 Andrew Bogut .40 1.00
38 David Lee .30 .75
39 Stephen Curry 10.00 25.00
40 James Harden 1.00 2.50
41 Jeremy Lin .75 2.00
42 Danny Granger .30 .75
43 David West .40 1.00
44 Paul George .75 2.00
45 Roy Hibbert .40 1.00
46 Blake Griffin .50 1.25
47 Chauncey Billups .60 1.50
48 Chris Paul 1.00 2.50
49 DeAndre Jordan .40 1.00
50 Eric Bledsoe .40 1.00
51 Grant Hill .75 2.00
52 Antawn Jamison .40 1.00
53 Dwight Howard .60 1.50
54 Kobe Bryant 10.00 25.00
55 Metta World Peace .40 1.00
56 Pau Gasol .75 2.00
57 Steve Blake .30 .75
58 Steve Nash 1.00 2.50
59 Marc Gasol .50 1.25
60 Marreese Speights .30 .75
61 Mike Conley .40 1.00
62 Rudy Gay .50 1.25
63 Zach Randolph .50 1.25
64 Chris Bosh .60 1.50
65 Dwyane Wade 1.00 2.50
66 LeBron James 10.00 25.00
67 Mario Chalmers .40 1.00
68 Ray Allen .75 2.00
69 Shane Battier .40 1.00
70 Brandon Jennings .30 .75
71 Ersan Ilyasova .30 .75
72 Monta Ellis .40 1.00
73 Andrei Kirilenko .40 1.00
74 Brandon Roy .40 1.00
75 Kevin Love .50 1.25
76 Ricky Rubio .40 1.00
77 Eric Gordon .40 1.00
78 Ryan Anderson .30 .75
79 Amar'e Stoudemire .50 1.25
80 Carmelo Anthony .75 2.00
81 Jason Kidd .75 2.00
82 J.R. Smith .50 1.25
83 Marcus Camby .50 1.25
84 Raymond Felton .30 .75
85 Tyson Chandler .40 1.00
86 Kendrick Perkins .30 .75
87 Kevin Martin .40 1.00
88 Kevin Durant 2.00 5.00
89 Russell Westbrook .75 2.00
90 Serge Ibaka .40 1.00
91 Arron Afflalo .30 .75
92 Glen Davis .30 .75
93 Jameer Nelson .30 .75
94 Andrew Bynum .30 .75
95 Evan Turner .30 .75
96 Jason Richardson .50 1.25
97 Jrue Holiday .60 1.50
98 Nick Young .30 .75
99 Goran Dragic .50 1.25
100 Marcin Gortat .30 .75
101 Michael Beasley .30 .75
102 LaMarcus Aldridge .50 1.25
103 Nicolas Batum .40 1.00
104 Wesley Matthews .30 .75
105 DeMarcus Cousins .50 1.25
106 Marcus Thornton .30 .75
107 Tyreke Evans .40 1.00
108 DeJuan Blair .30 .75
109 Manu Ginobili 1.00 2.50
110 Tim Duncan 1.25 3.00
111 Tony Parker .75 2.00
112 Andrea Bargnani .30 .75
113 DeMar DeRozan .60 1.50
114 Kyle Lowry .50 1.25
115 Al Jefferson .30 .75
116 Derrick Favors .40 1.00
117 Gordon Hayward .50 1.25
118 Mo Williams .40 1.00
119 John Wall .60 1.50
120 Nene .40 1.00
121 Danny Ainge .50 1.25
122 Nate Archibald .60 1.50
123 Elgin Baylor 1.25 3.00
124 Walt Bellamy .40 1.00
125 Wilt Chamberlain 1.50 4.00
126 Darryl Dawkins .30 .75
127 Vlade Divac .50 1.25
128 Julius Erving 1.25 3.00
129 Patrick Ewing .75 2.00
130 Walt Frazier .75 2.00
131 Horace Grant .50 1.25
132 Anfernee Hardaway 1.25 3.00
133 John Havlicek 1.00 2.50
134 Dennis Johnson .40 1.00
135 Magic Johnson 1.50 4.00
136 Bernard King .60 1.50
137 Toni Kukoc .50 1.25
138 Jerry Lucas .50 1.25
139 Moses Malone .75 2.00
140 Kevin McHale .60 1.50
141 Earl Monroe .60 1.50
142 Shaquille O'Neal 1.50 4.00
143 Willis Reed .75 2.00
144 Bill Russell 1.50 4.00
145 Rik Smits .40 1.00
146 John Starks .40 1.00
147 Isiah Thomas 1.00 2.50
148 David Thompson .50 1.25
149 Spud Webb .40 1.00
150 Damian Lillard RC 25.00 60.00
151 Kyrie Irving AU/149 RC 150.00 400.00
152 Anthony Davis AU/149 RC 150.00 400.00
153 Derrick Williams AU/149 RC 3.00 8.00
154 M.Kidd-Gilchrist AU/149 RC 4.00 10.00
155 Enes Kanter AU/149 RC 5.00 12.00
156 Bradley Beal AU/149 RC 15.00 40.00
157 Tristan Thompson AU/149 5.00 12.00
158 Dion Waiters AU/149 4.00 10.00
159 Jonas Valanciunas AU/149 6.00 15.00
160 Thomas Robinson AU/149 RC 3.00 8.00
161 Jan Vesely AU/199 3.00 8.00
162 Bismack Biyombo AU/399 RC 4.00 10.00
163 Harrison Barnes AU/149 RC 6.00 15.00
164 Brandon Knight AU/149 RC 4.00 10.00
165 Terrence Ross AU/149 8.00 20.00
166 Kemba Walker AU/149 RC 25.00 60.00
167 A. Drummond AU/149 RC 8.00 20.00
168 Jimmer Fredette AU/149 5.00 12.00
169 Austin Rivers AU/149 RC 5.00 12.00
170 Klay Thompson AU/149 125.00 300.00
171 Meyers Leonard AU/149 4.00 10.00
172 Alec Burks AU/299 RC 5.00 12.00
173 Jeremy Lamb AU/149 5.00 12.00
174 Markieff Morris AU/299 RC 5.00 12.00
175 Kendall Marshall AU/199 3.00 8.00
176 Marcus Morris AU/299 RC 5.00 12.00
177 John Henson AU/149 4.00 10.00
178 Kawhi Leonard AU/199 150.00 400.00
179 Maurice Harkless AU/299 RC 4.00 10.00
180 Nikola Vucevic AU/399 RC 60.00 150.00
181 Royce White AU/299 RC 3.00 8.00
182 Iman Shumpert AU/199 RC 3.00 8.00
183 Tyler Zeller AU/199 3.00 8.00
184 Chris Singleton AU/399 RC 3.00 8.00
185 Terrence Jones AU/199 3.00 8.00
186 Tobias Harris AU/299 RC 10.00 25.00
187 A.Nicholson AU/299 RC 3.00 8.00
188 Donatas Motiejunas AU/299 RC 4.00 10.00
189 Evan Fournier AU/299 RC 5.00 12.00
190 Nolan Smith AU/399 RC 3.00 8.00
191 Jared Sullinger AU/149 RC 3.00 8.00
192 Kenneth Faried AU/199 4.00 10.00
193 Fab Melo AU/199 RC 3.00 8.00
194 Reggie Jackson AU/399 RC 5.00 12.00
195 John Jenkins AU/399 RC 3.00 8.00
196 MarShon Brooks AU/399 RC 3.00 8.00
197 Jared Cunningham AU/399 RC 3.00 8.00
198 Jordan Hamilton AU/449 RC 3.00 8.00
199 Tony Wroten AU/199 3.00 8.00
200 Miles Plumlee AU/399 RC 3.00 8.00
201 Norris Cole AU/199 3.00 8.00
202 Arnett Moultrie AU/399 RC 3.00 8.00
203 Perry Jones AU/399 RC 3.00 8.00
204 Cory Joseph AU/449 RC 4.00 10.00
205 Marquis Teague AU/399 RC 3.00 8.00
206 Jimmy Butler AU/399 RC 125.00 300.00
207 Festus Ezeli AU/399 RC 3.00 8.00
208 E'Twaun Moore AU/399 RC 4.00 10.00
209 DeAndre Liggins AU/449 RC 3.00 8.00
210 Kyle Singler AU/449 RC 3.00 8.00
211 Chandler Parsons AU/299 RC 4.00 10.00
212 Quincy Acy AU/449 RC 3.00 8.00
213 Tyler Honeycutt AU/449 RC 3.00 8.00
214 Bernard James AU/449 RC 3.00 8.00
215 Charles Jenkins AU/349 3.00 8.00
216 Jae Crowder AU/449 RC 6.00 15.00
217 Darius Morris AU/449 RC 4.00 10.00
218 D. Green AU/449 RC 20.00 50.00
219 Malcolm Lee AU/449 RC 3.00 8.00
220 Orlando Johnson AU/449 RC 3.00 8.00
221 Jon Leuer AU/349 RC 3.00 8.00
222 Will Barton AU/449 RC 6.00 15.00
223 Tyshawn Taylor AU/449 RC 3.00 8.00
224 Julyan Stone AU/449 RC 3.00 8.00
225 Doron Lamb AU/449 RC 3.00 8.00
226 Kim English AU/449 RC 3.00 8.00
227 Mike Scott AU/449 RC 4.00 10.00
228 Kevin Murphy AU/449 RC 3.00 8.00
229 Kyle O'Quinn AU/449 RC 4.00 10.00
230 Lavoy Allen AU/399 RC 3.00 8.00
231 Tornike Shengelia AU/449 RC 3.00 8.00
232 Darius Miller AU/449 RC 4.00 10.00
233 Isaiah Thomas AU/449 RC 6.00 15.00
234 Trey Thompkins AU/449 RC 3.00 8.00
235 Robert Sacre AU/449 RC 3.00 8.00
236 Kyrie Irving JSY AU/149 RC 60.00 150.00
237 D.Williams JSY AU/149 RC 3.00 8.00
238 Enes Kanter JSY AU/199 RC 5.00 12.00
239 T.Thompson JSY AU/149 RC 5.00 12.00
240 J.Valanciunas JSY AU/199 RC 6.00 15.00
241 Jan Vesely JSY AU/249 RC 3.00 8.00
242 Bismack Biyombo JSY AU/299 4.00 10.00
243 Brandon Knight JSY AU/149 RC 4.00 10.00
244 K. Walker JSY AU/149 RC 12.00 30.00
245 J.Fredette JSY AU/199 RC 5.00 12.00
246 K. Thompson JSY AU/199 RC 125.00 300.00
247 Alec Burks JSY AU/299 RC 5.00 12.00
248 Markieff Morris JSY AU/299 RC 5.00 12.00
249 Marcus Morris JSY AU/299 RC 5.00 12.00
250 K. Leonard JSY AU/249 RC 200.00 500.00
251 N.Vucevic JSY AU/399 RC 12.00 30.00
252 Iman Shumpert JSY AU/199 RC 4.00 10.00
253 Chris Singleton JSY AU/399 RC 3.00 8.00
254 Tobias Harris JSY AU/299 RC 10.00 25.00
255 Nolan Smith JSY AU/299 RC 3.00 8.00
256 Kenneth Faried JSY AU/249 RC 4.00 10.00
257 Reggie Jackson JSY AU/399 RC 5.00 12.00
258 M.Brooks JSY AU/399 RC 3.00 8.00
259 Jordan Hamilton JSY AU/399 3.00 8.00
260 Norris Cole JSY AU/249 RC 3.00 8.00
261 Cory Joseph JSY AU/399 4.00 10.00
262 J. Butler JSY AU/399 RC 150.00 400.00
263 Kyle Singler JSY AU/399 3.00 8.00
264 Trey Thompkins JSY AU/399 3.00 8.00
265 C.Parsons JSY AU/299 RC 4.00 10.00
266 Lavoy Allen JSY AU/399 RC 3.00 8.00
267 Isaiah Thomas JSY AU/399 6.00 15.00
268 Tyler Honeycutt JSY AU/399 3.00 8.00
269 Malcolm Lee JSY AU/399 3.00 8.00
270 A. Davis JSY AU/149 RC 200.00 500.00
271 Kidd-Gilchrist JSY AU/149 RC 4.00 10.00
272 B. Beal JSY AU/149 RC 25.00 60.00
273 T.Robinson JSY AU/149 RC 3.00 8.00
274 Dion Waiters JSY AU/199 RC 4.00 10.00
275 H.Barnes JSY AU/149 RC 6.00 15.00
276 Terrence Ross JSY AU/199 RC 8.00 20.00
277 A.Drummond JSY AU/149 RC 8.00 20.00
278 Austin Rivers JSY AU/149 RC 5.00 12.00
279 M.Leonard JSY AU/199 RC 4.00 10.00
280 Jeremy Lamb JSY AU/199 RC 5.00 12.00
281 Kendall Marshall JSY AU/249 RC 3.00 8.00
282 John Henson JSY AU/199 RC 4.00 10.00
283 Royce White JSY AU/299 RC 3.00 8.00
284 Tyler Zeller JSY AU/249 RC 3.00 8.00
285 Terrence Jones JSY AU/399 RC 3.00 8.00
286 A.Nicholson JSY AU/299 RC 3.00 8.00
287 Evan Fournier JSY AU/299 RC 5.00 12.00
288 Jared Sullinger JSY AU/149 RC 3.00 8.00
289 Tony Wroten JSY AU/249 RC 3.00 8.00
290 Miles Plumlee JSY AU/399 RC 3.00 8.00
291 Arnett Moultrie JSY AU/399 RC 3.00 8.00
292 Perry Jones JSY AU/399 RC 3.00 8.00
293 M.Teague JSY AU/399 RC 3.00 8.00
294 Festus Ezeli JSY AU/399 RC 3.00 8.00
295 Bernard James JSY AU/399 3.00 8.00
297 Jae Crowder JSY AU/399 6.00 15.00
298 D. Green JSY AU/399 20.00 50.00
299 Orlando Johnson JSY AU/399 3.00 8.00
300 Quincy Miller JSY AU/399 RC 3.00 8.00
301 Quincy Acy JSY AU/399 3.00 8.00
302 Khris Middleton JSY AU/399 RC 15.00 40.00
303 Kyle O'Quinn JSY AU/399 4.00 10.00
304 Tyshawn Taylor JSY AU/399 3.00 8.00
305 Doron Lamb JSY AU/399 3.00 8.00
306 Kris Joseph JSY AU/399 RC 3.00 8.00
307 Kim English JSY AU/399 3.00 8.00
308 Robert Sacre JSY AU/399 3.00 8.00
309 Kevin Murphy JSY AU/399 3.00 8.00
310 Fab Melo JSY AU/249 RC 3.00 8.00
311 D. Lillard JSY AU/49 RC 150.00 400.00

2012-13 Select Prizms
*PRIZM: 3X TO 8X BASIC
*PRIZM AU: .5X TO 1.2X BASIC
*PRIZM JSY AU: .5X TO 1.2X BASIC
AU SER.#'d B/WN 99-199 COPIES PER
JSY AU SER.#'d 99-199 COPIES PER
EXCHANGE DEADLINE 10/03/2014
15 Paul Pierce 8.00 20.00
27 Dirk Nowitzki 20.00 50.00
39 Stephen Curry 200.00 500.00
40 James Harden 40.00 100.00
44 Paul George 40.00 100.00
48 Chris Paul 15.00 40.00
53 Dwight Howard 12.00 30.00
54 Kobe Bryant 300.00 600.00
58 Steve Nash 12.00 30.00
65 Dwyane Wade 60.00 150.00
66 LeBron James 800.00 1,500.00
68 Ray Allen 12.00 30.00
80 Carmelo Anthony 8.00 20.00
88 Kevin Durant 125.00 300.00
89 Russell Westbrook 20.00 50.00
99 Goran Dragic 8.00 20.00
109 Manu Ginobili 12.00 30.00
110 Tim Duncan 15.00 40.00
111 Tony Parker 6.00 15.00
114 Kyle Lowry 6.00 15.00
119 John Wall 6.00 15.00
125 Wilt Chamberlain 12.00 30.00
132 Anfernee Hardaway 12.00 30.00
142 Shaquille O'Neal 15.00 40.00
144 Bill Russell 8.00 20.00
150 Damian Lillard 200.00 500.00
151 Kyrie Irving AU/99 125.00 300.00
152 Anthony Davis AU/99 300.00 600.00
156 Bradley Beal AU/99 60.00 150.00
170 Klay Thompson AU/149 125.00 300.00
178 Kawhi Leonard AU/199 300.00 600.00
206 Jimmy Butler AU/199 300.00 600.00
244 Kemba Walker JSY AU/99 40.00 100.00
246 Klay Thompson JSY AU/199 150.00 400.00
250 Kawhi Leonard JSY AU/199 500.00 1,000.00
262 Jimmy Butler JSY AU/199 300.00 600.00
270 Anthony Davis JSY AU/99 400.00 800.00
272 Bradley Beal JSY AU/199 60.00 150.00
298 Draymond Green JSY AU/199 40.00 100.00
302 Khris Middleton JSY AU/199 60.00 150.00

2012-13 Select All-Star Selections
1 Kevin Durant 4.00 10.00
2 LeBron James 8.00 20.00
3 Dwight Howard 1.25 3.00
4 Kobe Bryant 8.00 20.00
5 James Harden 2.00 5.00
6 Dirk Nowitzki 2.50 6.00
7 Dwyane Wade 2.00 5.00
8 Chris Paul 2.00 5.00
9 Kevin Garnett 2.50 6.00
10 Tim Duncan 2.50 6.00
11 Grant Hill 1.50 4.00
12 Shaquille O'Neal 3.00 8.00
13 George Gervin 1.50 4.00
14 David Thompson 1.00 2.50
15 Chris Webber 1.00 2.50
16 Allen Iverson 1.50 4.00
17 Gary Payton 1.25 3.00
18 Karl Malone 1.50 4.00
19 Dominique Wilkins 1.25 3.00
20 Hakeem Olajuwon 2.00 5.00
21 David Robinson 1.50 4.00
22 Larry Bird 3.00 8.00
23 Julius Erving 2.50 6.00
24 Magic Johnson 3.00 8.00
25 Clyde Drexler 1.50 4.00

2012-13 Select Hall Selections
1 Larry Bird 3.00 8.00
2 Kareem Abdul-Jabbar 3.00 8.00
3 Elgin Baylor 2.50 6.00
4 Wilt Chamberlain 3.00 8.00
5 Patrick Ewing 1.50 4.00
6 John Stockton 2.00 5.00
7 David Robinson 1.50 4.00
8 Hakeem Olajuwon 2.00 5.00
9 Scottie Pippen 2.50 6.00
10 Bill Russell 3.00 8.00
11 Dennis Rodman 2.50 6.00
12 Pete Maravich 2.00 5.00
13 Julius Erving 2.50 6.00
14 Karl Malone 1.50 4.00
15 Jerry West 2.00 5.00
16 Oscar Robertson 2.00 5.00
17 George Mikan 3.00 8.00
18 Clyde Drexler 1.50 4.00
19 Bill Walton 1.50 4.00
20 James Worthy 1.50 4.00
21 Moses Malone 1.50 4.00
22 Don Nelson 1.00 2.50
23 Wes Unseld 1.25 3.00
24 Drazen Petrovic 1.00 2.50
25 Dave Cowens 1.50 4.00

2012-13 Select Hot Rookies
1 Anthony Davis 60.00 150.00
2 Dion Waiters 1.00 2.50
3 Damian Lillard 50.00 120.00
4 Michael Kidd-Gilchrist 1.00 2.50
5 Thomas Robinson .75 2.00
6 Austin Rivers 1.25 3.00
7 Bradley Beal 6.00 15.00
8 Jonas Valanciunas 1.50 4.00
9 Harrison Barnes 1.50 4.00
10 Jae Crowder 1.50 4.00
11 Tyler Zeller .75 2.00
12 Andre Drummond 2.00 5.00
13 Kyle Singler .75 2.00
14 Meyers Leonard 1.00 2.50
15 Maurice Harkless 1.00 2.50
16 Jared Sullinger .75 2.00
17 John Henson 1.00 2.50
18 Festus Ezeli .75 2.00
20 Perry Jones .75 2.00
21 Mirza Teletovic 1.00 2.50
22 Kendall Marshall .75 2.00
23 Miles Plumlee .75 2.00
24 Draymond Green 5.00 12.00
25 Bernard James .75 2.00
26 Pablo Prigioni .75 2.00
27 Darius Miller 1.00 2.50
28 Terrence Jones .75 2.00
29 Fab Melo .75 2.00
30 Alexey Shved .75 2.00
31 Kyrie Irving 8.00 20.00
32 Kemba Walker 3.00 8.00
33 Kenneth Faried 1.00 2.50
34 Kawhi Leonard 60.00 150.00
35 Klay Thompson 25.00 60.00
36 E'Twaun Moore 1.00 2.50
37 Chandler Parsons 1.00 2.50
38 Isaiah Thomas 1.50 4.00
39 Brandon Knight 1.00 2.50
40 Nikola Vucevic 3.00 8.00
41 MarShon Brooks .75 2.00
42 Derrick Williams .75 2.00
43 Jimmer Fredette 1.25 3.00
44 Norris Cole .75 2.00
45 Enes Kanter 1.25 3.00
46 Marcus Morris 1.25 3.00
47 Tristan Thompson 1.25 3.00
48 Tobias Harris 2.50 6.00
49 Markieff Morris 1.25 3.00
50 Lavoy Allen .75 2.00

2012-13 Select Hot Rookies Prizms
*PRIZM: 1.2X TO 3X BASIC
STATED PRINT RUN 25 SER.#'d SETS
1 Anthony Davis 500.00 1,000.00
3 Damian Lillard 400.00 800.00
34 Kawhi Leonard 800.00 1,500.00
35 Klay Thompson 125.00 300.00

2012-13 Select Hot Stars
1 Kobe Bryant 40.00 100.00
2 Kevin Durant 10.00 25.00
3 Dwyane Wade 3.00 8.00
4 Dwight Howard 2.00 5.00
5 LeBron James 40.00 100.00
6 Paul Pierce 2.50 6.00
7 Kyrie Irving 25.00 60.00
8 Blake Griffin 1.50 4.00
9 Kevin Love 1.50 4.00
10 Carmelo Anthony 2.50 6.00
11 Deron Williams 1.25 3.00
12 James Harden 3.00 8.00
13 Russell Westbrook 2.50 6.00
14 Tim Duncan 4.00 10.00
15 Chris Paul 3.00 8.00
16 Rajon Rondo 2.00 5.00
17 Kevin Garnett 4.00 10.00
18 Kemba Walker 4.00 10.00
19 Chris Bosh 2.00 5.00
20 Derrick Rose 2.50 6.00
21 Dirk Nowitzki 4.00 10.00
22 Stephen Curry 30.00 80.00
23 Jeremy Lin 2.50 6.00
24 Steve Nash 3.00 8.00
25 Marc Gasol 1.50 4.00

2012-13 Select In-Flight Selections
1 Blake Griffin 1.00 2.50
2 Anthony Davis 8.00 20.00
3 LeBron James 8.00 20.00
4 Rajon Rondo 1.25 3.00
5 Derrick Rose 1.50 4.00
6 Kobe Bryant 8.00 20.00
7 Chris Paul 2.00 5.00
8 O.J. Mayo .60 1.50
9 Dwyane Wade 2.00 5.00
10 Serge Ibaka .75 2.00
11 Andre Iguodala 1.00 2.50
12 Harrison Barnes 1.25 3.00
13 Paul George 1.50 4.00
14 Thomas Robinson .60 1.50
15 Tyson Chandler .75 2.00
16 Vince Carter 2.00 5.00
17 Dion Waiters .75 2.00
18 Jason Terry .75 2.00
19 Tyreke Evans .75 2.00
20 Kevin Durant 4.00 10.00
21 Kevin Love 1.00 2.50
22 Michael Kidd-Gilchrist .75 2.00
23 Jeremy Lin 1.50 4.00
24 Kawhi Leonard 8.00 20.00
25 Ricky Rubio .75 2.00

2012-13 Select In-Flight Selections Prizms
*PRIZM: 1.25X TO 3X BASIC
24 Kawhi Leonard 60.00 150.00

2012-13 Select Select Stars Jersey Autographs
PRINT RUNS B/WN 20-199 COPIES PER
EXCHANGE DEADLINE 10/03/2014
*PRIZMS/49-99: .5X TO 1.2X BASIC
1 Kevin Durant/199 125.00 300.00
2 Kobe Bryant/199 1,500.00 3,000.00
3 Blake Griffin/199 8.00 20.00
4 Zach Randolph/299 8.00 20.00
5 Joakim Noah/299 6.00 15.00
6 David Lee/299 EXCH 5.00 12.00
7 DeMarcus Cousins/299 8.00 20.00
9 J.J. Redick/299 8.00 20.00
10 Marcus Thornton/299 6.00 15.00
11 Andre Iguodala/299 8.00 20.00
12 Carlos Boozer/299 EXCH 5.00 12.00
13 Derrick Favors/299 6.00 15.00
14 Kevin Love/199 8.00 20.00
15 Kirk Hinrich/299 EXCH 6.00 15.00
16 LaMarcus Aldridge/199 8.00 20.00
17 Brook Lopez/199 6.00 15.00
18 Rashard Lewis/299 8.00 20.00
19 Stephen Curry/125 800.00 1,500.00
20 Stephen Jackson/199 6.00 15.00
21 Taj Gibson/199 5.00 12.00
22 Tayshaun Prince/199 EXCH 8.00 20.00
24 Tony Allen/199 5.00 12.00
25 Ty Lawson/299 5.00 12.00

2012-13 Select White Hot Rookies
1 Anthony Davis 75.00 200.00
2 Dion Waiters 1.25 3.00
3 Damian Lillard 60.00 150.00
4 Michael Kidd-Gilchrist 1.25 3.00
5 Thomas Robinson 1.00 2.50
6 Austin Rivers 1.50 4.00
7 Bradley Beal 8.00 20.00
8 Jonas Valanciunas 2.00 5.00
9 Harrison Barnes 2.00 5.00
10 Jae Crowder 2.00 5.00
11 Tyler Zeller 1.00 2.50
12 Andre Drummond 2.50 6.00
13 Kyle Singler 1.00 2.50
14 Meyers Leonard 1.25 3.00
15 Maurice Harkless 1.25 3.00
16 Jared Sullinger 1.00 2.50
17 John Henson 1.25 3.00
18 Festus Ezeli 1.00 2.50
19 Tornike Shengelia 1.00 2.50
20 Perry Jones 1.00 2.50
21 Mirza Teletovic 1.25 3.00
22 Kendall Marshall 1.00 2.50
23 Miles Plumlee 1.00 2.50
24 Draymond Green 6.00 15.00
25 Bernard James 1.00 2.50
26 Pablo Prigioni 1.00 2.50
27 Darius Miller 1.25 3.00
28 Terrence Jones 1.00 2.50
29 Fab Melo 1.00 2.50
30 Alexey Shved 1.00 2.50
31 Kyrie Irving 10.00 25.00
32 Kemba Walker 4.00 10.00
33 Kenneth Faried 1.25 3.00
34 Kawhi Leonard 75.00 200.00
35 Klay Thompson 30.00 80.00
36 E'Twaun Moore 1.25 3.00
37 Chandler Parsons 1.25 3.00
38 Isaiah Thomas 2.00 5.00
39 Brandon Knight 1.25 3.00
40 Nikola Vucevic 4.00 10.00
41 MarShon Brooks 1.00 2.50
42 Derrick Williams 1.00 2.50
43 Jimmer Fredette 1.50 4.00
44 Norris Cole 1.00 2.50
45 Enes Kanter 1.50 4.00
46 Marcus Morris 1.50 4.00
47 Tristan Thompson 1.50 4.00
48 Tobias Harris 3.00 8.00
49 Markieff Morris 1.50 4.00
50 Lavoy Allen 1.00 2.50

2012-13 Select White Hot Rookies Prizms
*PRIZM: 1.2X TO 3X BASIC
STATED PRINT RUN 25 SER.#'d SETS
1 Anthony Davis 500.00 1,000.00
3 Damian Lillard 400.00 800.00
34 Kawhi Leonard 800.00 1,500.00
35 Klay Thompson 150.00 400.00

2012-13 Select White Hot Stars
1 Kobe Bryant 40.00 100.00
2 Kevin Durant 10.00 25.00
3 Dwyane Wade 3.00 8.00
4 Dwight Howard 2.00 5.00
5 LeBron James 40.00 100.00
6 Paul Pierce 2.50 6.00
7 Kyrie Irving 25.00 60.00
8 Blake Griffin 1.50 4.00
9 Kevin Love 1.50 4.00
10 Carmelo Anthony 2.50 6.00
11 Deron Williams 1.25 3.00
12 James Harden 3.00 8.00
13 Russell Westbrook 2.50 6.00
14 Tim Duncan 4.00 10.00
15 Chris Paul 3.00 8.00
16 Rajon Rondo 2.00 5.00
17 Kevin Garnett 4.00 10.00
18 Kemba Walker 4.00 10.00
19 Chris Bosh 2.00 5.00
20 Derrick Rose 2.50 6.00
21 Dirk Nowitzki 4.00 10.00
22 Stephen Curry 30.00 80.00
23 Jeremy Lin 2.50 6.00
24 Steve Nash 3.00 8.00
25 Marc Gasol 1.50 4.00

2012-13 Select White Hot Stars Prizms
STATED PRINT RUN 25 SER.#'d SETS
1 Kobe Bryant 300.00 600.00
2 Kevin Durant 60.00 150.00
3 Dwyane Wade 40.00 100.00
5 LeBron James 500.00 1,000.00
7 Kyrie Irving 500.00 1,000.00
22 Stephen Curry 75.00 200.00

2013-14 Select
COMPLETE SET (200) 75.00 200.00
1 Ersan Ilyasova .30 .75
2 James Harden 1.00 2.50
3 Danny Granger .30 .75
4 Goran Dragic .40 1.00
5 Manu Ginobili 1.00 2.50
6 Taj Gibson .30 .75
7 Gerald Wallace .40 1.00
8 DeMarcus Cousins .50 1.25
9 Klay Thompson 1.50 4.00
10 Joakim Noah .50 1.25
11 Kendrick Perkins .30 .75
12 J.J. Redick .50 1.25
13 Jordan Hill .30 .75
14 Al-Farouq Aminu .30 .75
15 Rajon Rondo .60 1.50
16 Tyler Hansbrough .30 .75
17 Brook Lopez .50 1.25
18 Eric Bledsoe .40 1.00
19 Jeremy Lin .75 2.00
20 Shawn Marion .40 1.00
21 Jimmy Butler 1.00 2.50
22 Zach Randolph .40 1.00
23 Shane Battier .40 1.00
24 LeBron James 4.00 10.00
25 Terrence Jones .30 .75
26 Tristan Thompson .30 .75
27 Carlos Boozer .40 1.00
28 Thabo Sefolosha .40 1.00
29 Chris Paul 1.00 2.50
30 Josh Smith .30 .75
31 Tiago Splitter .30 .75
32 Larry Sanders .30 .75
33 Kobe Bryant 4.00 10.00
34 Paul George .75 2.00
35 David Lee .30 .75
36 Kawhi Leonard 1.50 4.00
37 Jose Calderon .30 .75
38 Eric Gordon .40 1.00
39 Mike Conley .50 1.25
40 Harrison Barnes .50 1.25
41 Jan Vesely .30 .75
42 Jrue Holiday .60 1.50
43 Nick Young .30 .75
44 Vince Carter 1.00 2.50
45 Marc Gasol .50 1.25
46 Gerald Green .40 1.00
47 Rodney Stuckey .30 .75
48 Michael Beasley .30 .75
49 Mario Chalmers .30 .75
50 George Hill .40 1.00
51 Marcus Thornton .30 .75
52 Arron Afflalo .30 .75
53 Evan Turner .30 .75
54 Gerald Henderson .30 .75
55 Nicolas Batum .40 1.00
56 Greivis Vasquez .30 .75
57 Dwight Howard .60 1.50
58 Chris Kaman .40 1.00
59 Ricky Rubio .40 1.00
60 Blake Griffin .50 1.25
61 Nikola Vucevic .60 1.50
62 Damian Lillard 1.50 4.00
63 Thomas Robinson .30 .75
64 Kyle Lowry .50 1.25
65 John Wall .60 1.50
66 Greg Monroe .30 .75
67 Jamal Crawford .50 1.25
68 Lance Stephenson .40 1.00
69 Tyson Chandler .40 1.00
70 John Henson .30 .75
71 Anthony Davis 1.50 4.00
72 Tony Parker .75 2.00
73 DeMar DeRozan .60 1.50
74 Jason Richardson .50 1.25
75 Kevin Garnett 1.25 3.00

76 Spencer Hawes .30 .75
77 Tony Allen .30 .75
78 Andrew Bogut .40 1.00
79 Glen Davis .30 .75
80 Tyreke Evans .40 1.00
81 Dwyane Wade 1.00 2.50
82 Derrick Favors .30 .75
83 Marcin Gortat .30 .75
84 Iman Shumpert .30 .75
85 Ty Lawson .30 .75
86 Stephen Curry 4.00 10.00
87 Chris Bosh .60 1.50
88 J.J. Hickson .30 .75
89 Marcus Morris .40 1.00
90 Thaddeus Young .30 .75
91 Roy Hibbert .30 .75
92 Paul Millsap .40 1.00
93 Jimmer Fredette .50 1.25
94 O.J. Mayo .30 .75
95 Luis Scola .40 1.00
96 Jameer Nelson .30 .75
97 Kevin Martin .40 1.00
98 Kyrie Irving 1.50 4.00
99 Isaiah Thomas .40 1.00
100 Wesley Matthews .30 .75
101 Brandon Jennings .30 .75
102 Al Jefferson .30 .75
103 Danilo Gallinari .40 1.00
104 Tayshaun Prince .50 1.25
105 Raymond Felton .30 .75
106 Khris Middleton 1.00 2.50
107 Amare Stoudemire .50 1.25
108 Miles Plumlee .30 .75
109 Tim Duncan 1.25 3.00
110 Jonas Valanciunas .40 1.00
111 Anderson Varejao .30 .75
112 Andrei Kirilenko .50 1.25
113 Steve Nash 1.00 2.50
114 David West .40 1.00
115 Rudy Gay .40 1.00
116 J.R. Smith .50 1.25
117 Serge Ibaka .40 1.00
118 Deron Williams .40 1.00
119 Marvin Williams .30 .75
120 Trevor Ariza .30 .75
121 Andray Blatche .30 .75
122 Carmelo Anthony .75 2.00
123 J.J. Barea .40 1.00
124 Andre Drummond .50 1.25
125 Avery Bradley .30 .75
126 Pau Gasol .75 2.00
127 Markieff Morris .30 .75
128 Al Horford .50 1.25
129 Martell Webster .30 .75
130 Joe Johnson .40 1.00
131 Jeff Green .30 .75
132 Derrick Rose .75 2.00
133 Russell Westbrook .75 2.00
134 Kirk Hinrich .40 1.00
135 Bradley Beal .75 2.00
136 Kevin Durant 1.50 4.00
137 LaMarcus Aldridge .50 1.25
138 Kemba Walker .50 1.25
139 Jeff Teague .30 .75
140 Monta Ellis .40 1.00
141 Kenneth Faried .40 1.00
142 Dirk Nowitzki 1.25 3.00
143 Nikola Pekovic .30 .75
144 Brandon Bass .30 .75
145 Michael Kidd-Gilchrist .30 .75
146 Kevin Love .50 1.25
147 Danny Green .40 1.00
148 Dion Waiters .30 .75
149 Kris Humphries .30 .75
150 Chandler Parsons .30 .75
151 Luol Deng .40 1.00
152 Andre Iguodala .50 1.25
153 Enes Kanter .40 1.00
154 Kyle Korver .40 1.00
155 Richard Jefferson .30 .75
156 Ray Allen .75 2.00
157 Gordon Hayward .40 1.00
158 JaVale McGee .40 1.00
159 Paul Pierce .75 2.00
160 DeAndre Jordan .40 1.00
161 Gorgui Dieng RC .60 1.50
162 Dwight Buycks RC .50 1.25
163 Shane Larkin RC .50 1.25
164 Dennis Schroder RC 1.50 4.00
165 Vitor Faverani RC .50 1.25
166 Kentavious Caldwell-Pope RC .75 2.00
167 Phil Pressey RC .50 1.25
168 Nate Wolters RC .50 1.25
169 Tony Snell RC .60 1.50
170 Solomon Hill RC .60 1.50
171 Lorenzo Brown RC .50 1.25
172 Sergey Karasev RC .50 1.25
173 Tony Mitchell RC .50 1.25
174 Nerlens Noel RC .60 1.50
175 Victor Oladipo RC 1.25 3.00
176 Brandon Davies RC .50 1.25
177 Archie Goodwin RC .50 1.25
178 G.Antetokounmpo RC 60.00 150.00
179 Reggie Bullock RC .60 1.50
180 Trey Burke RC .60 1.50
181 Luigi Datome RC .50 1.25
182 C.J. McCollum RC 2.00 5.00
183 Shabazz Muhammad RC .50 1.25
184 Kelly Olynyk RC .60 1.50
185 Cody Zeller RC .60 1.50
186 Tim Hardaway Jr. RC 1.00 2.50
187 Anthony Bennett RC .50 1.25
188 Gal Mekel RC .50 1.25
189 Matthew Dellavedova RC .75 2.00
190 M.Carter-Williams RC .60 1.50
191 Peyton Siva RC .60 1.50
192 Otto Porter RC .75 2.00
193 Alex Len RC .60 1.50
194 Glen Rice Jr. RC .50 1.25
195 Steven Adams RC 1.25 3.00
196 Ben McLemore RC .60 1.50
197 Mason Plumlee RC .60 1.50
198 Nemanja Nedovic RC .50 1.25
199 Rudy Gobert RC 2.00 5.00
200 Pero Antic RC .50 1.25

2013-14 Select Prizms

*PRIZMS: 2X TO 5X BASIC
*PRIZMS RC: 1.2X TO 3X BASIC
24 LeBron James 50.00 120.00
33 Kobe Bryant 50.00 120.00
86 Stephen Curry 50.00 120.00
178 Giannis Antetokounmpo 400.00 800.00

2013-14 Select Prizms Blue

*PRIZMS BLUE: 4X TO 10X BASIC
*PRIZMS BLUE RC: 2.5X TO 6X BASIC
STATED PRINT RUN 49 SER.#'d SETS
24 LeBron James 100.00 250.00
33 Kobe Bryant 100.00 250.00
86 Stephen Curry 100.00 250.00
178 Giannis Antetokounmpo 800.00 1,500.00

2013-14 Select Prizms Purple

*PRIZMS PURPLE: 3X TO 8X BASIC
*PRIZMS PURPLE RC: 2X TO 5X BASIC
STATED PRINT RUN 99 SER.#'d SETS
24 LeBron James 75.00 200.00
33 Kobe Bryant 75.00 200.00
86 Stephen Curry 75.00 200.00
178 Giannis Antetokounmpo 600.00 1,200.00

2013-14 Select Clutch

*PRIZMS: 2X TO 5X BASIC
*PURPLE/99: 2.5X TO 6X BASIC
*BLUE/49: 3X TO 8X BASIC
1 Dirk Nowitzki 2.00 5.00
2 Ray Allen 1.25 3.00
3 Kobe Bryant 20.00 50.00
4 Robert Horry .75 2.00
5 Chauncey Billups 1.00 2.50
6 LeBron James 15.00 40.00
7 Kevin Durant 2.50 6.00
8 Larry Bird 3.00 8.00
9 Dwyane Wade 1.50 4.00
10 Paul Pierce 1.25 3.00
11 Damian Lillard 2.50 6.00
12 Vinnie Johnson .75 2.00
13 Jerry West 2.00 5.00
14 Steve Kerr .75 2.00
15 Magic Johnson 3.00 8.00

2013-14 Select Draft Selections

*PRIZMS: 1.25X TO 3X BASIC
*PRIZMS PURPLE/99: 1.5X TO 4X BASIC
*PRIZMS BLUE/49: 2X TO 5X BASIC
1 Anthony Bennett .60 1.50
2 Victor Oladipo 1.50 4.00
3 Otto Porter 1.00 2.50
4 Cody Zeller .75 2.00
5 Alex Len .75 2.00
6 Nerlens Noel .75 2.00
7 Ben McLemore .75 2.00
8 Kentavious Caldwell-Pope 1.00 2.50
9 Trey Burke .75 2.00
10 C.J. McCollum 2.50 6.00
11 Michael Carter-Williams .75 2.00
12 Steven Adams 1.50 4.00
13 Kelly Olynyk .75 2.00
14 Shabazz Muhammad .60 1.50
15 Giannis Antetokounmpo 100.00 250.00
16 Shane Larkin .60 1.50
17 Sergey Karasev .60 1.50
18 Tony Snell .75 2.00
19 Gorgui Dieng .75 2.00
20 Mason Plumlee .75 2.00
21 Solomon Hill .75 2.00
22 Tim Hardaway Jr. 1.25 3.00
23 Rudy Gobert 2.50 6.00
24 Archie Goodwin .60 1.50
25 Nate Wolters .60 1.50

2013-14 Select Franchise Signatures

EXCHANGE DEADLINE 12/25/2015
4 Udonis Haslem 4.00 10.00
5 Bob Dandridge 4.00 10.00
6 Jack Sikma 5.00 12.00
10 Kyrie Irving EXCH 60.00 150.00
11 Anthony Davis 75.00 200.00
14 Gerald Henderson 3.00 8.00
15 Bruce Bowen 4.00 10.00
16 Zydrunas Ilgauskas 4.00 10.00
25 Michael Cooper 5.00 12.00

2013-14 Select Franchise Signatures Blue

*BLUE: .5X TO 1.2X PURPLE
PRINT RUNS B/WN 20-49 COPIES PER
EXCHANGE DEADLINE 12/25/2015
18 Elgin Baylor/20 75.00 200.00

2013-14 Select Franchise Signatures Purple

*PURPLE: .5X TO 1.2X BASIC
PRINT RUNS B/WN 30-60 COPIES PER
EXCHANGE DEADLINE 12/25/2015
1 Kyle Lowry/60 20.00 50.00
2 Kevin Love/30 6.00 15.00
3 Serge Ibaka/30 5.00 12.00
7 Allan Houston/49 6.00 15.00
8 Isiah Thomas/30 30.00 80.00
12 Bradley Beal/30 30.00 60.00
13 Roy Hibbert/30 4.00 10.00
17 Michael Finley/30 6.00 15.00
19 Kevin Durant/30 100.00 250.00
20 Kobe Bryant/30 1,250.00 2,500.00
21 Tony Parker/30 25.00 60.00
22 Jared Sullinger/30 4.00 10.00
23 Shaquille O'Neal/30 100.00 250.00
24 Goran Dragic/30 5.00 12.00
25 Michael Cooper/60 6.00 15.00

2013-14 Select Hall Selections Signatures

EXCHANGE DEADLINE 12/25/2015
9 Bob McAdoo 6.00 15.00
21 Dan Issel 6.00 15.00

2013-14 Select Hall Selections Signatures Prizms Blue

*BLUE: .5X TO 1.2X PURPLE
STATED PRINT RUN 20 SER.#'d SETS
EXCHANGE DEADLINE 12/25/2015
23 Nate Thurmond 10.00 25.00

2013-14 Select Hall Selections Signatures Prizms Purple

*PURPLE: .6X TO 1.5X BASIC
STATED PRINT RUN 30 SER.#'d SETS
EXCHANGE DEADLINE 12/25/2015
1 Chris Mullin 10.00 25.00
2 Dolph Schayes 8.00 20.00
3 Robert Parish 10.00 25.00
4 Gail Goodrich 10.00 25.00
5 Hakeem Olajuwon 75.00 200.00
6 Magic Johnson 150.00 400.00
7 Karl Malone 50.00 120.00
8 Scottie Pippen 200.00 500.00
10 Adrian Dantley 8.00 20.00
11 Clyde Drexler 40.00 100.00
12 Joe Dumars 12.00 30.00
13 Ralph Sampson 6.00 15.00
14 James Worthy 25.00 60.00
15 Kevin McHale 20.00 50.00
16 Kareem Abdul-Jabbar 150.00 400.00
17 Larry Bird 150.00 400.00
18 David Robinson 75.00 200.00
19 Jerry Lucas 12.00 30.00
20 Bernard King 10.00 25.00
22 Nate Archibald 10.00 25.00
24 Dennis Rodman 50.00 120.00
25 Julius Erving 60.00 150.00

2013-14 Select Jersey Autographs

EXCHANGE DEADLINE 12/25/2015
2 Eddie Johnson 5.00 12.00
12 Buck Williams 6.00 15.00
16 Kobe Bryant 1,500.00 3,000.00
21 Dee Brown 6.00 15.00
22 Rory Sparrow 5.00 12.00
30 Steve Mix 5.00 12.00
33 John Wall 20.00 50.00
34 Steve Smith 6.00 15.00
36 Nick Collison 5.00 12.00
37 Anthony Mason 6.00 15.00
38 Scottie Pippen 125.00 300.00
39 Charles Oakley 8.00 20.00

2013-14 Select Jersey Autographs Blue

*BLUE: .5X TO 1.2X PURPLE
PRINT RUNS B/WN 20-49 COPIES PER
EXCHANGE DEADLINE 12/25/2015

2013-14 Select Jersey Autographs Purple

*PURPLE: .5X TO 1.2X BASIC
PRINT RUNS B/WN 30-99 COPIES PER
EXCHANGE DEADLINE 12/25/2015
1 Derrick Favors/30 6.00 15.00
2 Eddie Johnson/99 6.00 15.00
3 Kenny Sky Walker/49 6.00 15.00
4 Kyrie Irving/30 125.00 300.00
5 Tracy McGrady/30 150.00 400.00
6 Kenneth Faried/30 8.00 20.00
7 Al Horford/30 10.00 25.00
8 Deron Williams/30 8.00 20.00
9 Harrison Barnes/30 10.00 25.00
10 Steve Nash/30 75.00 200.00
11 Enes Kanter/30 8.00 20.00
13 Kevin Willis/49 8.00 20.00
14 Shaquille O'Neal/30 125.00 300.00
15 James Harden/30 75.00 200.00
17 Stephen Curry/30 1,000.00 2,000.00
18 Andre Drummond/30 10.00 25.00
19 Andre Iguodala/30 10.00 25.00
20 Goran Dragic/30 8.00 20.00
21 Dee Brown/99 8.00 20.00
23 Jalen Rose/30 8.00 20.00
24 Ralph Sampson/30 8.00 20.00
25 Kevin Durant/30 125.00 300.00
26 Kevin Love/30 10.00 25.00
27 Bradley Beal/30 20.00 50.00
28 Josh Smith/30 6.00 15.00
29 Mike Conley/30 10.00 25.00
31 Karl Malone/30 50.00 120.00
32 Alex English/49 12.00 30.00
33 John Wall/30 25.00 60.00
35 Tom Chambers/49 10.00 25.00
38 Scottie Pippen/30 150.00 400.00
40 James Worthy/30 25.00 60.00

2013-14 Select Red Hot

1 J.R. Smith 1.00 2.50
2 DeMarcus Cousins 1.00 2.50
3 Kobe Bryant 25.00 60.00
4 Victor Oladipo 1.50 4.00
5 Jeff Teague .60 1.50
6 Russell Westbrook 1.50 4.00
7 Shawn Marion .75 2.00
8 Harrison Barnes 1.00 2.50
9 Chris Paul 2.00 5.00
10 Ricky Rubio .75 2.00
11 Jameer Nelson .60 1.50
12 Tony Parker 1.50 4.00
13 Kevin Durant 3.00 8.00
14 Nate Wolters .60 1.50
15 Paul Millsap .75 2.00
16 Joakim Noah 1.00 2.50
17 Monta Ellis .75 2.00
18 Klay Thompson 3.00 8.00
19 Zach Randolph .75 2.00
20 Kevin Love 1.00 2.50
21 Thaddeus Young .60 1.50
22 Tim Duncan 2.50 6.00
23 Kyrie Irving 3.00 8.00
24 Ben McLemore .75 2.00
25 Rajon Rondo 1.25 3.00
26 Derrick Rose 1.50 4.00
27 Kenneth Faried .75 2.00
28 James Harden 2.00 5.00
29 Dwyane Wade 2.00 5.00
30 Tyreke Evans .75 2.00
31 Eric Bledsoe .75 2.00
32 Derrick Favors .60 1.50
33 Damian Lillard 3.00 8.00
34 Giannis Antetokounmpo 75.00 200.00
35 Paul Pierce 1.50 4.00
36 Anderson Varejao .60 1.50
37 Dirk Nowitzki 2.50 6.00
38 Roy Hibbert .60 1.50
39 LeBron James 20.00 50.00
40 Anthony Davis 3.00 8.00
41 Nicolas Batum .75 2.00
42 Marcin Gortat .60 1.50
43 Michael Carter-Williams .75 2.00
44 Trey Burke .75 2.00
45 Brook Lopez 1.00 2.50
46 Dion Waiters .60 1.50
47 Brandon Jennings .60 1.50
48 Paul George 1.50 4.00
49 O.J. Mayo .60 1.50
50 Amare Stoudemire 1.00 2.50

2013-14 Select Rookie Jersey Autographs

EXCHANGE DEADLINE 12/25/2015
*PURPLE/60-99: .5X TO 1.2X BASIC
*BLUE/35-49: .6X TO 1.5X BASIC
1 Giannis Antetokounmpo 600.00 1,200.00
2 Mason Plumlee 5.00 12.00
3 Glen Rice Jr. 4.00 10.00
4 Erik Murphy 4.00 10.00
5 Victor Oladipo 10.00 25.00
6 Luigi Datome 4.00 10.00
7 Otto Porter 6.00 15.00
8 Nerlens Noel 5.00 12.00
9 Trey Burke 5.00 12.00
10 Steven Adams 10.00 25.00
11 Shane Larkin 4.00 10.00
12 Tim Hardaway Jr. 8.00 20.00
13 Nate Wolters 4.00 10.00
14 Ricky Ledo 4.00 10.00
15 Matthew Dellavedova 6.00 15.00
16 Rudy Gobert 15.00 40.00
17 Cody Zeller 5.00 12.00
18 Ben McLemore 5.00 12.00
19 C.J. McCollum 15.00 40.00
20 Kelly Olynyk 5.00 12.00
21 Tony Snell 5.00 12.00
22 Archie Goodwin 4.00 10.00
23 Tony Mitchell 4.00 10.00
24 Gal Mekel 4.00 10.00
25 Peyton Siva 4.00 10.00
26 Anthony Bennett 4.00 10.00
27 Alex Len 5.00 12.00
28 Kentavious Caldwell-Pope 6.00 15.00
29 Michael Carter-Williams 5.00 12.00
30 Shabazz Muhammad 4.00 10.00

2013-14 Select Signatures

EXCHANGE DEADLINE 12/25/2015
1 Marcin Gortat 4.00 10.00
3 John Lucas 5.00 12.00
4 Cazzie Russell 5.00 12.00
8 P.J. Tucker 6.00 15.00
9 Kobe Bryant 1,000.00 2,000.00
10 Nick Collison 4.00 10.00
11 Brandon Bass 4.00 10.00
13 George McGinnis 6.00 15.00
14 Fat Lever 6.00 15.00
17 Derrick Coleman 6.00 15.00
18 Kevin Durant 125.00 300.00
19 Patrick Beverley 4.00 10.00
20 Jan Vesely 4.00 10.00
21 Roy Hibbert 4.00 10.00
23 Jay Williams 4.00 10.00
24 Theo Ratliff 4.00 10.00
27 Vin Baker 4.00 10.00
29 Jon Leuer 4.00 10.00
30 Tobias Harris 6.00 15.00
33 Clifford Robinson 6.00 15.00
34 B.J. Armstrong 6.00 15.00
38 Ramon Sessions 4.00 10.00
39 Nando De Colo 4.00 10.00
40 Taj Gibson 4.00 10.00
43 Gus Williams 4.00 10.00
48 Brian Roberts 4.00 10.00
49 Greg Oden 4.00 10.00
50 Enes Kanter 5.00 12.00

2013-14 Select Signatures Blue

*BLUE: .5X TO 1.2X PURPLE
PRINT RUNS B/WN 15-49 COPIES PER
NO PRICING ON QTY 15 OR LESS
EXCHANGE DEADLINE 12/25/2015
9 Kobe Bryant/20 2,000.00 4,000.00
18 Kevin Durant/20 200.00 500.00

2013-14 Select Signatures Purple

*PURPLE/99: .5X TO 1.2X BASIC
PRINT RUNS B/WN 25-99 COPIES PER
EXCHANGE DEADLINE 12/25/2015
2 Steve Nash/25 75.00 200.00
5 Jason Kidd/25 40.00 100.00
6 Gail Goodrich/25 12.00 30.00
7 Byron Scott/25 12.00 30.00
12 Kevin Love/25 12.00 30.00
13 George McGinnis/25 12.00 30.00
15 Julius Erving/25 100.00 250.00
16 George Gervin/25 20.00 50.00
22 Al Horford/25 12.00 30.00
25 Earl Monroe/25 20.00 50.00
26 Peja Stojakovic/25 10.00 25.00
28 Kyrie Irving/25 100.00 250.00
32 Andre Iguodala/25 12.00 30.00
35 Kevin McHale/25 20.00 50.00
36 Steve Francis/25 10.00 25.00
37 Magic Johnson/25 125.00 300.00
41 Bradley Beal/25 20.00 50.00
42 Andre Drummond/25 12.00 30.00
44 Danny Manning/25 10.00 25.00
45 Hakeem Olajuwon/25 75.00 200.00
46 Kenny Smith/25 10.00 25.00
47 John Stockton/25 100.00 250.00

2013-14 Select Skills

*PRIZMS: 1.5X TO 4X BASIC
*PURPLE/99: 2.5X TO 6X BASIC
*BLUE/49: 3X TO 8X BASIC
1 Kemba Walker .75 2.00
2 John Wall 1.00 2.50
3 Dwight Howard 1.00 2.50
4 Tim Duncan 2.00 5.00
5 Damian Lillard 2.50 6.00
6 Stephen Curry 12.00 30.00
7 Blake Griffin .75 2.00
8 Rajon Rondo 1.00 2.50
9 DeMar DeRozan 1.00 2.50
10 Greg Monroe .50 1.25
11 LeBron James 12.00 30.00
12 Dirk Nowitzki 2.00 5.00
13 Marc Gasol .75 2.00
14 Kenneth Faried .60 1.50
15 Kevin Durant 2.50 6.00
16 Chris Paul 1.50 4.00
17 DeMarcus Cousins .75 2.00
18 Paul Pierce 1.25 3.00
19 Derrick Rose 1.25 3.00
20 Paul George 1.25 3.00
21 Dwyane Wade 1.50 4.00
22 James Harden 1.50 4.00
23 Anthony Davis 2.50 6.00
24 Kevin Love .75 2.00
25 Russell Westbrook 1.25 3.00
26 Kobe Bryant 12.00 30.00
27 LaMarcus Aldridge .75 2.00
28 Carmelo Anthony 1.25 3.00
29 Kyrie Irving 2.50 6.00
30 Kyle Korver .60 1.50

2013-14 Select Skills Prizms Blue

*BLUE: 3X TO 8X BASIC
STATED PRINT RUN 49 SER.#'d SETS

2013-14 Select Sky High

1 Blake Griffin .60 1.50
2 Nate Robinson .40 1.00
3 Vince Carter 1.25 3.00
4 Jason Richardson .60 1.50
5 Dwight Howard .75 2.00
6 Kevin Durant 2.00 5.00
7 Kobe Bryant 20.00 50.00
8 LeBron James 20.00 50.00
9 Terrence Ross .50 1.25
10 Gerald Green .50 1.25

2013-14 Select Sky High Prizms

*PRIZMS: 1.5X TO 4X BASIC
7 Kobe Bryant 150.00 400.00
8 LeBron James 150.00 400.00

2013-14 Select Sky High Prizms Blue

*BLUE: 3X TO 8X BASIC
STATED PRINT RUN 49 SER.#'d SETS
7 Kobe Bryant 200.00 500.00
8 LeBron James 200.00 500.00

2013-14 Select Sky High Prizms Purple

*PURPLE: 2.5X TO 6X BASIC
STATED PRINT RUN 99 SER.#'d SETS
7 Kobe Bryant 150.00 400.00
8 LeBron James 150.00 400.00

2013-14 Select Stars

1 Kyrie Irving 2.00 5.00
2 Anthony Davis 2.00 5.00
3 Kobe Bryant 5.00 12.00
4 Kevin Love .60 1.50
5 Dirk Nowitzki 1.50 4.00
6 Damian Lillard 2.00 5.00
7 Carmelo Anthony 1.00 2.50
8 Tim Duncan 1.50 4.00
9 Paul George 1.00 2.50
10 Kevin Durant 2.00 5.00

2013-14 Select Stars Prizms

*PRIZMS: 1.5X TO 4X BASIC
3 Kobe Bryant 50.00 120.00

2013-14 Select Stars Prizms Blue

*BLUE: 3X TO 8X BASIC
STATED PRINT RUN 49 SER.#'d SETS
3 Kobe Bryant 150.00 400.00

2013-14 Select Stars Prizms Purple

*PURPLE: 2.5X TO 6X BASIC
STATED PRINT RUN 99 SER.#'d SETS
3 Kobe Bryant 125.00 300.00

2013-14 Select Swatches

2 James Jones 2.00 5.00
3 Amare Stoudemire 3.00 8.00
4 Robert Parish 4.00 10.00
5 Michael Beasley 2.00 5.00
6 Raymond Felton 2.00 5.00
7 LeBron James 40.00 100.00
8 Al Horford 3.00 8.00
9 Kemba Walker 3.00 8.00
10 Klay Thompson 10.00 25.00
11 Dikembe Mutombo 5.00 12.00
12 Patrick Ewing 5.00 12.00
14 Alex English 4.00 10.00
15 DeJuan Blair 2.00 5.00
16 Kyrie Irving 10.00 25.00
17 Dwyane Wade 6.00 15.00
18 Kevin Garnett 8.00 20.00
19 Jimmy Butler 6.00 15.00
20 Anthony Davis 10.00 25.00
21 Bill Laimbeer 3.00 8.00
22 Norris Cole 2.00 5.00
23 DeMarcus Cousins 3.00 8.00
24 Clyde Drexler 5.00 12.00
25 MarShon Brooks 2.00 5.00
26 Dirk Nowitzki 8.00 20.00
27 Kevin Love 3.00 8.00
28 Paul Pierce 5.00 12.00
29 Andre Drummond 3.00 8.00
30 Jrue Holiday 4.00 10.00
31 Jayson Williams 2.00 5.00
32 Jermaine O'Neal 2.50 6.00
33 Joe Dumars 4.00 10.00
34 Shaquille O'Neal 12.00 30.00
35 Tayshaun Prince 3.00 8.00
36 Kenneth Faried 2.50 6.00
37 Ricky Rubio 2.50 6.00
38 Monta Ellis 2.50 6.00
39 Brandon Jennings 2.00 5.00
40 Joakim Noah 3.00 8.00
41 Bob Lanier 4.00 10.00
42 Chris Mullin 4.00 10.00
43 Scottie Pippen 8.00 20.00
44 Walter Berry 2.00 5.00
45 Boris Diaw 2.50 6.00
46 James Harden 6.00 15.00
47 Carmelo Anthony 5.00 12.00
48 Stephen Curry 40.00 100.00
49 Josh Smith 2.00 5.00
50 Anderson Varejao 2.00 5.00
51 Bernard King 4.00 10.00
52 Grant Hill 5.00 12.00
53 Karl Malone 6.00 15.00
54 Ray Allen 5.00 12.00
55 Tobias Harris 3.00 8.00
56 Dwight Howard 4.00 10.00
57 Kevin Durant 10.00 25.00
58 O.J. Mayo 2.00 5.00
59 Harrison Barnes 3.00 8.00
60 Jeremy Lin 5.00 12.00
61 Anfernee Hardaway 8.00 20.00
62 Larry Johnson 4.00 10.00
65 Tyson Chandler 2.50 6.00
66 Paul George 5.00 12.00
67 Russell Westbrook 5.00 12.00
68 Bradley Beal 5.00 12.00
69 Andre Iguodala 3.00 8.00
70 Tony Parker 5.00 12.00
74 Nate Robinson 2.00 5.00
75 Derrick Favors 2.00 5.00
76 Blake Griffin 3.00 8.00
78 Deron Williams 2.50 6.00
79 David Lee 2.00 5.00
81 Jose Calderon 2.00 5.00
84 Udonis Haslem 2.50 6.00
85 Caron Butler 2.50 6.00
87 Tim Duncan 8.00 20.00
88 Al Jefferson 2.00 5.00
90 Xavier McDaniel 2.50 6.00
92 Tracy McGrady 5.00 12.00
94 Danilo Gallinari 2.50 6.00
95 Steve Novak 2.00 5.00
96 Kobe Bryant 40.00 100.00
97 John Wall 4.00 10.00
98 Michael Kidd-Gilchrist 2.00 5.00
99 Pau Gasol 5.00 12.00
100 DeMar DeRozan 4.00 10.00

2013-14 Select Swatches Prizms

*PRIZMS: 1.25X TO 3X BASIC
STATED PRINT RUN 25 SER.#'d SETS
7 LeBron James 125.00 300.00
48 Stephen Curry 125.00 300.00
96 Kobe Bryant 125.00 300.00

2013-14 Select Swatches Prizms Blue

*PRIZMS BLUE: 1.25X TO 3X BASIC
PRINT RUNS B/WN 35-49 COPIES PER

2013-14 Select Swatches Prizms Purple

*PRIZMS PURPLE: .75X TO 2X BASIC
PRINT RUNS B/WN 60-99 COPIES PER
1 Kelly Tripucka 5.00 12.00
13 Hakeem Olajuwon 12.00 30.00
15 DeJuan Blair 4.00 10.00
63 John Stockton 12.00 30.00
71 Reggie Lewis 6.00 15.00
72 David Robinson 12.00 30.00
77 Damian Lillard 20.00 50.00
80 Marc Gasol 6.00 15.00
83 Kevin McHale 10.00 25.00
86 Chris Paul 12.00 30.00
89 Steve Nash 12.00 30.00
91 Paul Westphal 6.00 15.00

2013-14 Select Top Selections Jersey Autographs

EXCHANGE DEADLINE 12/25/2015
1 Charles Oakley 6.00 15.00
2 Cedric Maxwell 5.00 12.00
3 Bill Cartwright 5.00 12.00
15 Kevin Durant 125.00 300.00
18 Kobe Bryant 1,250.00 2,500.00
24 Kenyon Martin 6.00 15.00
29 Larry Johnson 25.00 60.00

2013-14 Select Top Selections Jersey Autographs Prizms Blue

*PRIZMS BLUE: .5X TO 1.2X PURPLE
PRINT RUNS B/WN 15-49 COPIES PER
NO PRICING ON QTY 15
EXCHANGE DEADLINE 12/25/2015

2013-14 Select Top Selections Jersey Autographs Prizms Purple

*PRIZMS PURPLE: .5X TO 1.2X BASIC
PRINT RUNS B/WN 20-99 COPIES PER
EXCHANGE DEADLINE 12/25/2015
4 Dikembe Mutombo/30 20.00 50.00
5 Chris Bosh/30 12.00 30.00
6 Kevin Love/30 8.00 20.00
7 Harrison Barnes/30 8.00 20.00
8 James Harden/30 75.00 200.00
9 Kareem Abdul-Jabbar/30 150.00 400.00
10 Fred Brown/99 6.00 15.00
11 Larry Bird/30 150.00 400.00
12 Sidney Moncrief/79 8.00 20.00
13 David Robinson/30 75.00 200.00
14 Grant Hill/30 20.00 50.00
16 Kawhi Leonard/75 75.00 200.00
17 LaMarcus Aldridge/30 8.00 20.00
19 Bob Lanier/20 10.00 25.00
20 Robert Parish/30 10.00 25.00
21 Magic Johnson/30 150.00 400.00
22 John Wall/30 10.00 25.00
23 Dan Majerle/99 6.00 15.00
24 Kenyon Martin/99 8.00 20.00
25 Kyrie Irving/30 75.00 200.00
26 Bradley Beal/30 12.00 30.00
27 Kelly Tripucka/30 6.00 15.00
28 Cazzie Russell/99 6.00 15.00
30 Bernard King/30 10.00 25.00

2013-14 Select White Hot

*PURPLE/99: 2.5X TO 6X BASIC
*BLUE/49: 3X TO 8X BASIC
*PRIZMS/25: 5X TO 12X BASIC
1 LeBron James 15.00 40.00
2 Kemba Walker .75 2.00
3 Ty Lawson .50 1.25
4 Jeremy Lin 1.25 3.00
5 Chris Bosh 1.00 2.50
6 Jrue Holiday 1.00 2.50
7 Nikola Vucevic 1.00 2.50
8 Rudy Gay .60 1.50
9 Kyrie Irving 2.50 6.00
10 Victor Oladipo 1.25 3.00
11 Al Horford .75 2.00
12 Luol Deng .60 1.50
13 Andre Drummond .75 2.00
14 Blake Griffin .75 2.00
15 Larry Sanders .50 1.25
16 Tyson Chandler .60 1.50
17 Evan Turner .50 1.25
18 Manu Ginobili 1.50 4.00
19 Kobe Bryant 15.00 40.00
20 Anthony Bennett .50 1.25
21 Kevin Garnett 2.00 5.00
22 Carlos Boozer .60 1.50
23 Andre Iguodala .75 2.00
24 DeAndre Jordan .60 1.50
25 Ersan Ilyasova .50 1.25
26 Carmelo Anthony 1.25 3.00
27 Goran Dragic .60 1.50
28 DeMar DeRozan 1.00 2.50
29 Kevin Durant 2.50 6.00
30 C.J. McCollum 2.00 5.00
31 Deron Williams .60 1.50
32 Vince Carter 1.50 4.00
33 Stephen Curry 12.00 30.00
34 Marc Gasol .75 2.00
35 Nikola Pekovic .50 1.25
36 Serge Ibaka .75 2.00
37 LaMarcus Aldridge .75 2.00
38 Bradley Beal 1.25 3.00
39 Damian Lillard 2.50 6.00
40 Nerlens Noel .60 1.50
41 Al Jefferson .50 1.25
42 Dirk Nowitzki 2.00 5.00
43 Dwight Howard 1.00 2.50
44 Mike Conley .75 2.00
45 Kevin Martin .60 1.50
46 Russell Westbrook 1.25 3.00
47 Isaiah Thomas .60 1.50
48 John Wall 1.00 2.50
49 Michael Carter-Williams .60 1.50
50 Steven Adams 1.25 3.00

2013-14 Select Young Bloods

*PRIZMS: 1.5X TO 4X BASIC
*PURPLE/99: 2.5X TO 6X BASIC
*BLUE/49: 3X TO 8X BASIC
1 James Harden 1.50 4.00
2 Kemba Walker .75 2.00
3 Michael Carter-Williams .60 1.50
4 Anthony Davis 2.50 6.00
5 Victor Oladipo 1.25 3.00
6 Damian Lillard 2.50 6.00
7 Kenneth Faried .60 1.50
8 Kyrie Irving 2.50 6.00
9 Jimmy Butler 1.50 4.00
10 Cody Zeller .60 1.50

2014-15 Select

1 Stephen Curry CON 5.00 12.00
2 Dwyane Wade CON 1.25 3.00
3 Victor Oladipo CON .50 1.25
4 Larry Sanders CON .40 1.00
5 Marcin Gortat CON .40 1.00
6 LaMarcus Aldridge CON .60 1.50
7 Serge Ibaka CON .50 1.25
8 Roy Hibbert CON .50 1.25
9 Klay Thompson CON 1.50 4.00
10 Chris Bosh CON .75 2.00
11 Nikola Vucevic CON .50 1.25
12 Ersan Ilyasova CON .40 1.00
13 Tim Duncan CON 1.50 4.00
14 Damian Lillard CON 1.50 4.00
15 Anthony Davis CON 1.50 4.00
16 Deron Williams CON .50 1.25
17 Andre Iguodala CON .60 1.50
18 Luol Deng CON .50 1.25
19 Goran Dragic CON .60 1.50
20 Kobe Bryant CON 5.00 12.00
21 Tony Parker CON 1.00 2.50
22 Al Jefferson CON .40 1.00
23 Jrue Holiday CON .75 2.00
24 Kevin Garnett CON 1.50 4.00
25 Derrick Rose CON 1.25 3.00
26 James Harden CON 1.25 3.00
27 Miles Plumlee CON .40 1.00
28 Nick Young CON .40 1.00
29 Patty Mills CON .60 1.50
30 Michael Kidd-Gilchrist CON .40 1.00
31 Tyreke Evans CON .50 1.25
32 Ricky Rubio CON .50 1.25
33 Joakim Noah CON .60 1.50
34 Dwight Howard CON .75 2.00
35 Isaiah Thomas CON .50 1.25
36 Jeremy Lin CON 1.25 3.00
37 Rudy Gay CON .60 1.50
38 Chris Paul CON 1.00 2.50
39 Brandon Jennings CON .40 1.00
40 Al Horford CON .60 1.50
41 Pau Gasol CON 1.00 2.50
42 Terrence Jones CON .40 1.00
43 Markieff Morris CON .40 1.00
44 DeMar DeRozan CON .75 2.00
45 Ben McLemore CON .40 1.00
46 Blake Griffin CON .60 1.50
47 Andre Drummond CON .50 1.25
48 Michael Carter-Williams CON .40 1.00
49 Jimmy Butler CON 1.00 2.50
50 Trevor Ariza CON .40 1.00
51 Gordon Hayward CON .50 1.25
52 Kyle Lowry CON .75 2.00
53 Darren Collison CON .40 1.00
54 Ty Lawson CON .40 1.00
55 Josh Smith CON .40 1.00
56 Nerlens Noel CON .40 1.00
57 LeBron James CON 5.00 12.00
58 Dirk Nowitzki CON 1.50 4.00
59 Trey Burke CON .40 1.00
60 Terrence Ross CON .50 1.25
61 Vince Carter CON 1.25 3.00
62 Kenneth Faried CON .40 1.00
63 Carmelo Anthony CON 1.00 2.50
64 Rajon Rondo CON .75 2.00
65 Kyrie Irving CON 1.25 3.00
66 Chandler Parsons CON .40 1.00
67 Derrick Favors CON .40 1.00
68 Bradley Beal CON 1.00 2.50
69 Zach Randolph CON .60 1.50
70 Kevin Durant CON 2.00 5.00
71 Jose Calderon CON .40 1.00
72 Jeff Teague CON .40 1.00
73 Kevin Love CON .60 1.50
74 Monta Ellis CON .50 1.25
75 Giannis Antetokounmpo CON 4.00 10.00
76 John Wall CON .75 2.00
77 Mike Conley CON .50 1.25
78 Russell Westbrook CON 1.00 2.50
79 Paul George CON 1.00 2.50
80 Wesley Matthews CON .40 1.00
81 Bruno Caboclo CON RC .50 1.25
82 P.J. Hairston CON RC .40 1.00
83 Marcus Smart CON RC 1.50 4.00
84 Zach LaVine CON RC 2.50 6.00
85 Nik Stauskas CON RC .40 1.00
86 Elfrid Payton CON RC .60 1.50
87 Dante Exum CON RC .60 1.50
88 James Young CON RC .40 1.00
89 Julius Randle CON RC 2.00 5.00

90 Joel Embiid CON RC 4.00 10.00
91 Aaron Gordon CON RC 2.00 5.00
92 Adreian Payne CON RC .40 1.00
93 Gary Harris CON RC .60 1.50
94 Doug McDermott CON RC .60 1.50
95 Shabazz Napier CON RC .50 1.25
96 Cleanthony Early CON RC .40 1.00
97 T.J. Warren CON RC .60 1.50
98 Mitch McGary CON RC .40 1.00
99 Jabari Parker CON RC .50 1.25
100 Andrew Wiggins CON RC 2.00 5.00
101 Kobe Bryant PRE 5.00 12.00
102 Russell Westbrook PRE 1.00 2.50
103 Mirza Teletovic PRE .40 1.00
104 Reggie Jackson PRE .50 1.25
105 Danilo Gallinari PRE .40 1.00
106 Hollis Thompson PRE .40 1.00
107 Derrick Rose PRE 1.25 3.00
108 Kevin Durant PRE 2.00 5.00
109 Paul Pierce PRE 1.00 2.50
110 Tim Hardaway Jr. PRE .50 1.25
111 Tony Snell PRE .40 1.00
112 Tayshaun Prince PRE .60 1.50
113 Stephen Curry PRE 5.00 12.00
114 Carmelo Anthony PRE 1.00 2.50
115 DeMarcus Cousins PRE .50 1.25
116 Eric Gordon PRE .50 1.25
117 Paul Millsap PRE .50 1.25
118 Shareef Abdur-Rahim PRE .50 1.25
119 LeBron James PRE 5.00 12.00
120 Andrew Wiggins PRE 2.00 5.00
121 Avery Bradley PRE .40 1.00
122 J.J. Redick PRE .60 1.50
123 Kyle Korver PRE .60 1.50
124 Danny Granger PRE .40 1.00
125 Kyrie Irving PRE 1.25 3.00
126 Marcus Smart PRE 1.50 4.00
127 Robin Lopez PRE .40 1.00
128 Kelly Olynyk PRE .40 1.00
129 Otto Porter PRE .50 1.25
130 David West PRE .50 1.25
131 James Harden PRE 1.25 3.00
132 Dante Exum PRE .60 1.50
133 Amar'e Stoudemire PRE .60 1.50
134 Tony Wroten PRE .50 1.25
135 Jonas Valanciunas PRE .50 1.25
136 Chris Copeland PRE .40 1.00
137 Tony Parker PRE 1.00 2.50
138 James Young PRE .40 1.00
139 Andrea Bargnani PRE .40 1.00
140 Jodie Meeks PRE .40 1.00
141 Jae Crowder PRE .40 1.00
142 Mason Plumlee PRE .40 1.00
143 Damian Lillard PRE 1.50 4.00
144 Jabari Parker PRE .50 1.25
145 Marco Belinelli PRE .40 1.00
146 Tobias Harris PRE .50 1.25
147 Shawn Marion PRE .50 1.25
148 Jarrett Jack PRE .50 1.25
149 Chris Paul PRE 1.00 2.50
150 Julius Randle PRE 2.00 5.00
151 Gerald Green PRE .50 1.25
152 Norris Cole PRE .40 1.00
153 C.J. McCollum PRE .60 1.50
154 Tyson Chandler PRE .60 1.50
155 Blake Griffin PRE .60 1.50
156 Zach LaVine PRE 2.50 6.00
157 Tiago Splitter PRE .40 1.00
158 JaVale McGee PRE .50 1.25
159 Draymond Green PRE .75 2.00
160 Gerald Henderson PRE .40 1.00
161 Wes Unseld PRE .75 2.00
162 Chris Webber PRE .75 2.00
163 Nate Thurmond PRE .60 1.50
164 Larry Johnson PRE .75 2.00
165 Allen Iverson PRE 1.50 4.00
166 Julius Erving PRE 1.50 4.00
167 Baron Davis PRE .60 1.50
168 Magic Johnson PRE 2.50 6.00
169 Karl Malone PRE 1.25 3.00
170 Hakeem Olajuwon PRE 1.25 3.00
171 Sam Perkins PRE .50 1.25
172 Bill Bradley PRE .75 2.00
173 Tim Hardaway PRE .75 2.00
174 Shaquille O'Neal PRE 2.50 6.00
175 Pete Maravich PRE 2.00 5.00
176 Alonzo Mourning PRE 1.00 2.50
177 Scottie Pippen PRE 1.50 4.00
178 Isiah Thomas PRE 1.00 2.50
179 Bob Lanier PRE .75 2.00
180 Jalen Rose PRE .50 1.25
181 Jerome Williams PRE .40 1.00
182 Doug Collins PRE .60 1.50
183 George Gervin PRE 1.00 2.50
184 Wilt Chamberlain PRE 2.00 5.00
185 Bojan Bogdanovic PRE .60 1.50
186 Jusuf Nurkic PRE 1.25 3.00
187 Clint Capela PRE 1.50 4.00
188 Markel Brown PRE .40 1.00
189 Johnny O'Bryant PRE .40 1.00
190 Damien Inglis PRE .40 1.00
191 Lucas Nogueira PRE .40 1.00
192 Rodney Hood PRE .50 1.25
193 Noah Vonleh PRE .40 1.00
194 Cameron Bairstow PRE .40 1.00
195 Russ Smith PRE .40 1.00
196 Jarnell Stokes PRE .40 1.00
197 Spencer Dinwiddie PRE .60 1.50
198 Tyler Ennis PRE .40 1.00
199 Kyle Anderson PRE .60 1.50
200 Glenn Robinson III PRE .50 1.25
201 Larry Bird COU 6.00 15.00
202 David Robinson COU 3.00 8.00
203 Clyde Drexler COU 2.50 6.00
204 John Stockton COU 3.00 8.00
205 Chris Mullin COU 2.00 5.00
206 Scottie Pippen COU 4.00 10.00
207 Magic Johnson COU 6.00 15.00
208 Christian Laettner COU 1.50 4.00
209 Kobe Bryant COU 12.00 30.00
210 Derrick Rose COU 3.00 8.00
211 Stephen Curry COU 12.00 30.00
212 LeBron James COU 30.00 80.00
213 Kyrie Irving COU 3.00 8.00
214 James Harden COU 3.00 8.00
215 Kevin Durant COU 5.00 12.00
216 Klay Thompson COU 4.00 10.00
217 Anthony Davis COU 4.00 10.00
218 Rudy Gay COU 1.50 4.00
219 Kenneth Faried COU 1.00 2.50
220 Mason Plumlee COU 1.00 2.50
221 Tyson Chandler COU 1.50 4.00
222 Chris Paul COU 2.50 6.00
223 Kevin Love COU 1.50 4.00
224 Carmelo Anthony COU 2.50 6.00
225 Russell Westbrook COU 2.50 6.00
226 Karl Malone COU 3.00 8.00
227 Anfernee Hardaway COU 4.00 10.00
228 Grant Hill COU 2.50 6.00
229 Gary Payton COU 2.50 6.00
230 Jason Kidd COU 2.50 6.00
231 Shaquille O'Neal COU 6.00 15.00
232 Dwight Howard COU 2.00 5.00
233 Chris Bosh COU 2.00 5.00
234 Deron Williams COU 1.25 3.00
235 Ray Allen COU 2.50 6.00
236 Andre Drummond COU 1.25 3.00
237 Allen Iverson COU 4.00 10.00
238 Vince Carter COU 3.00 8.00
239 Tim Hardaway COU 2.00 5.00
240 Hakeem Olajuwon COU 3.00 8.00
241 Shawn Kemp COU 2.50 6.00
242 Dikembe Mutombo COU 2.50 6.00
243 Manute Bol COU 1.50 4.00
244 Nate Archibald COU 2.00 5.00
245 Dennis Rodman COU 4.00 10.00
246 Kareem Abdul-Jabbar COU 5.00 12.00
247 Mark Jackson COU 1.25 3.00
248 Bill Russell COU 5.00 12.00
249 Oscar Robertson COU 3.00 8.00
250 Bob Cousy COU 3.00 8.00
251 Moses Malone COU 2.50 6.00
252 Latrell Sprewell COU 2.00 5.00
253 Dave DeBusschere COU 1.50 4.00
254 Jerry West COU 4.00 10.00
255 Vlade Divac COU 1.50 4.00
256 Dion Waiters COU 1.00 2.50
257 Greg Monroe COU 1.00 2.50
258 Bradley Beal COU 2.50 6.00
259 Chris Andersen COU 1.25 3.00
260 Steven Adams COU 2.00 5.00
261 J.R. Smith COU 1.50 4.00
262 Kevin Martin COU 1.25 3.00
263 John Henson COU 1.00 2.50
264 Marc Gasol COU 1.50 4.00
265 Manu Ginobili COU 3.00 8.00
266 Steve Nash COU 3.00 8.00
267 Kemba Walker COU 1.50 4.00
268 Jamal Crawford COU 1.50 4.00
269 Brook Lopez COU 1.50 4.00
270 Tony Parker COU 2.50 6.00
271 Damian Lillard COU 4.00 10.00
272 John Wall COU 2.00 5.00
273 DeMarcus Cousins COU 1.25 3.00
274 Lance Stephenson COU 1.25 3.00
275 Dennis Schroder COU 1.50 4.00
276 Taj Gibson COU 1.00 2.50
277 Joe Johnson COU 1.00 2.50
278 Nicolas Batum COU 1.25 3.00
279 Eric Bledsoe COU 1.25 3.00
280 Omer Asik COU 1.00 2.50
281 Cory Jefferson COU 1.00 2.50
282 Zach LaVine COU 6.00 15.00
283 Adreian Payne COU 1.00 2.50
285 Gary Harris COU 1.50 4.00
286 Rodney Hood COU 1.25 3.00
287 Nik Stauskas COU 1.25 3.00
288 Bruno Caboclo COU 1.25 3.00
289 Elfrid Payton COU 1.50 4.00
290 Jordan Adams COU 1.00 2.50
291 James Ennis COU 1.25 3.00
293 Jabari Parker COU 1.25 3.00
294 Andrew Wiggins COU 5.00 12.00
295 Doug McDermott COU 1.50 4.00
296 Julius Randle COU 5.00 12.00
297 Dante Exum COU 1.50 4.00
298 Marcus Smart COU 4.00 10.00
299 C.J. Wilcox COU 1.00 2.50
300 Damjan Rudez COU 1.00 2.50

2014-15 Select Concourse Prizms Blue

*CON BLUE: 1.5X TO 4X BASE HI
STATED PRINT RUN 249 SER.#'d SETS
1 Stephen Curry 40.00 100.00
20 Kobe Bryant 40.00 100.00
57 LeBron James 40.00 100.00

2014-15 Select Concourse Prizms Orange

*CON. RED: 3X TO 8X BASE HI
STATED PRINT RUN 60 SER.#'d SETS
1 Stephen Curry 75.00 200.00
20 Kobe Bryant 75.00 200.00
57 LeBron James 75.00 200.00
90 Joel Embiid 75.00 200.00

2014-15 Select Concourse Prizms Red

*CON. RED: 2.5X TO 6X BASE HI
STATED PRINT RUN 149 SER.#'d SETS
1 Stephen Curry 60.00 150.00
20 Kobe Bryant 60.00 150.00
57 LeBron James 60.00 150.00

2014-15 Select Courtside Prizms Copper

*COUR.COPPER: 2.5X TO 6X BASE HI
STATED PRINT RUN 49 SER.#'d SETS
209 Kobe Bryant 300.00 600.00
211 Stephen Curry 150.00 400.00
212 LeBron James 300.00 600.00
215 Kevin Durant 60.00 150.00
224 Carmelo Anthony 40.00 100.00

2014-15 Select Premier Prizms Light Blue Die Cut

*PRE.LIGHT BLUE: 2X TO 5X BASE HI
STATED PRINT RUN 199 SER.#'d SETS
101 Kobe Bryant 50.00 120.00
113 Stephen Curry 50.00 120.00
119 LeBron James 50.00 120.00

2014-15 Select Premier Prizms Light Purple Die Cut

*PRE.LIGHT PURP: 1.5X TO 4X BASE HI
STATED PRINT RUN 99 SER.#'d SETS
101 Kobe Bryant 40.00 100.00
113 Stephen Curry 40.00 100.00
119 LeBron James 50.00 120.00

2014-15 Select Premier Prizms Tie Dye Die Cut

*PRE.TIE DYE: 8X TO 20X BASE HI
STATED PRINT RUN 25 SER.#'d SETS
101 Kobe Bryant 200.00 500.00
113 Stephen Curry 200.00 500.00
119 LeBron James 300.00 600.00

2014-15 Select Prizms Blue and Silver

*CON.BLUE SILV: 1.5X TO 4X BASE HI
*PRE.BLUE SILV: 1.5X TO 4X BASE HI
*COUR.BLUE SILV: 1.5X TO 4X BASE HI
1 Stephen Curry CON 40.00 100.00
20 Kobe Bryant CON 40.00 100.00
57 LeBron James CON 40.00 100.00
101 Kobe Bryant PRE 40.00 100.00
113 Stephen Curry PRE 40.00 100.00
119 LeBron James PRE 40.00 100.00
209 Kobe Bryant COU 150.00 400.00
211 Stephen Curry COU 125.00 300.00
212 LeBron James COU 125.00 300.00

2014-15 Select Prizms Purple and White

*CON.PURP WHITE: 1.5X TO 4X BASE HI
*PRE.PURP WHITE: 1.5X TO 4X BASE HI
*COUR.PURP WHITE: 1.5X TO 4X BASE HI
1 Stephen Curry CON 40.00 100.00
20 Kobe Bryant CON 40.00 100.00
57 LeBron James CON 40.00 100.00
101 Kobe Bryant PRE 40.00 100.00
113 Stephen Curry PRE 40.00 100.00
119 LeBron James PRE 40.00 100.00
209 Kobe Bryant COU 150.00 400.00
211 Stephen Curry COU 125.00 300.00
212 LeBron James COU 125.00 300.00

2014-15 Select Prizms Silver

*CON.SILVER: 1.25X TO 3X BASE HI
*PRE.SILVER: 1.25X TO 3X BASE HI
*COUR.SILVER: 1.25X TO 3X BASE HI
1 Stephen Curry CON 30.00 80.00
20 Kobe Bryant CON 30.00 80.00
57 LeBron James CON 30.00 80.00
101 Kobe Bryant PRE 30.00 80.00
113 Stephen Curry PRE 30.00 80.00
119 LeBron James PRE 30.00 80.00
209 Kobe Bryant COU 150.00 400.00
211 Stephen Curry COU 125.00 300.00
212 LeBron James COU 125.00 300.00

2014-15 Select Prizms Tie Dye

*CON.TIE DYE: 8X TO 20X BASE HI
*PRE.TIE DYE: 8X TO 20X BASE HI
*COUR.TIE DYE: 8X TO 20X BASE HI
STATED PRINT RUN 25 SER.#'d SETS
1 Stephen Curry CON 200.00 500.00
20 Kobe Bryant CON 300.00 600.00
57 LeBron James CON 300.00 600.00
75 Giannis Antetokounmpo CON 300.00 600.00
101 Kobe Bryant PRE 200.00 500.00
113 Stephen Curry PRE 200.00 500.00
119 LeBron James PRE 300.00 600.00
209 Kobe Bryant COU 1,000.00 2,000.00
211 Stephen Curry COU 1,000.00 2,000.00
212 LeBron James COU 1,250.00 2,500.00
231 Shaquille O'Neal COU 300.00 600.00

2014-15 Select City to City Jerseys

STATED PRINT RUN 199 SER.#'d SETS
*COPPER/49: .6X TO 1.5X BASE HI
*TIE DYE/25: 1.5X TO 4X BASE HI
1 Shaquille O'Neal 25.00 60.00
2 LeBron James 100.00 250.00
3 Tracy McGrady 12.00 30.00
4 Vince Carter 12.00 30.00
5 Dwight Howard 6.00 15.00
6 Steve Nash 12.00 30.00
7 Carmelo Anthony 12.00 30.00
8 Monta Ellis 4.00 10.00
9 Chris Bosh 6.00 15.00
10 Ray Allen 12.00 30.00
11 Chris Andersen 4.00 10.00
12 Chris Paul 8.00 20.00
13 Grant Hill 8.00 20.00
14 Paul Pierce 8.00 20.00
15 Kevin Garnett 12.00 30.00
16 Jason Kidd 12.00 30.00
17 Clyde Drexler 8.00 20.00
18 Scottie Pippen 25.00 60.00
19 Amar'e Stoudemire 5.00 12.00
20 Deron Williams 4.00 10.00
21 Larry Johnson 8.00 20.00
22 Marcin Gortat 3.00 8.00
23 Alonzo Mourning 8.00 20.00
24 Dikembe Mutombo 8.00 20.00
25 Joe Johnson 4.00 10.00

2014-15 Select Die Cut Autographs

1 Jeff Green/40 8.00 20.00
2 Otto Porter/25 8.00 20.00
3 Nerlens Noel/25 6.00 15.00
4 Kevin Martin/25 8.00 20.00
5 John Stockton/25 40.00 100.00
6 Walt Frazier/25 15.00 40.00
7 Joe Dumars/25 12.00 30.00
8 Alex English/40 8.00 20.00
9 George Gervin/25 12.00 30.00
10 Karl Malone/25 40.00 100.00
11 Tracy McGrady/25 60.00 150.00
12 Allen Iverson/25 75.00 200.00
13 Clyde Drexler/25 20.00 50.00
14 Grant Hill/25 25.00 60.00
16 Chris Mullin/25 12.00 30.00
17 Toni Kukoc/40 12.00 30.00
18 Muggsy Bogues/99 8.00 20.00
19 Carmelo Anthony/25 50.00 120.00
20 M.Carter-Williams/25 6.00 15.00
21 Jason Terry/25 8.00 20.00
22 Tristan Thompson/25 6.00 15.00
23 Ryan Anderson/40 6.00 15.00
24 Stephen Curry/25 1,000.00 2,000.00
25 Troy Daniels/99 4.00 10.00
26 Al Horford/25 10.00 25.00
27 Chris Bosh/25 12.00 30.00
28 Jordan Hill/25 6.00 15.00
29 Shane Battier/25 8.00 20.00
30 Ty Lawson/25 6.00 15.00
31 Gorgui Dieng/99 4.00 10.00
32 Eric Gordon/25 8.00 20.00
33 Jrue Holiday/40 12.00 30.00
34 P.J. Tucker/99 5.00 12.00
35 Marvin Williams/99 4.00 10.00
36 Marcin Gortat/40 6.00 15.00
37 Bradley Beal/25 15.00 40.00
38 Lance Stephenson/40 8.00 20.00
39 Hakeem Olajuwon/25 40.00 100.00
40 Robert Parish/25 12.00 30.00
41 Adrian Dantley/40 10.00 25.00
42 Kurt Rambis/40 8.00 20.00
43 Vlade Divac/99 6.00 15.00
44 Spud Webb/99 10.00 25.00
45 Dikembe Mutombo/40 20.00 50.00
46 John Starks/99 20.00 50.00
47 Jason Kidd/25 20.00 50.00
48 Eddie Jones/99 6.00 15.00
49 Luc Longley/99 5.00 12.00
50 Bruce Bowen/99 6.00 15.00
51 Robert Horry/40 10.00 25.00
52 Michael Cooper/40 10.00 25.00
53 Andrea Bargnani/25 6.00 15.00
54 Udonis Haslem/99 5.00 12.00
55 Matthew Dellavedova/99 5.00 12.00
56 John Wall/25 12.00 30.00
57 Danilo Gallinari/25 6.00 15.00
58 Austin Rivers/25 6.00 15.00
59 Mike Conley/40 8.00 20.00
60 Zach Randolph/25 10.00 25.00
61 Marcus Smart/99 15.00 40.00
62 Andrew Wiggins/99 40.00 100.00
63 Kyle Anderson/99 6.00 15.00
64 Zach LaVine/99 60.00 150.00
65 Nik Stauskas/99 4.00 10.00
66 Elfrid Payton/99 6.00 15.00
67 T.J. Warren/99 6.00 15.00
68 Rodney Hood/99 5.00 12.00
69 Dante Exum/99 6.00 15.00
70 Mitch McGary/99 4.00 10.00
71 Lucas Nogueira/99 4.00 10.00
72 James Young/99 4.00 10.00
73 P.J. Hairston/99 4.00 10.00
74 Julius Randle/99 20.00 50.00
75 Jabari Parker/99 5.00 12.00
76 Gary Harris/99 6.00 15.00
77 Joe Harris/99 6.00 15.00
78 Shabazz Napier/99 5.00 12.00
79 Noah Vonleh/99 4.00 10.00
80 Tyler Ennis/99 4.00 10.00
81 Jordan Clarkson/99 15.00 40.00
82 Joel Embiid/99 100.00 250.00
83 Aaron Gordon/99 20.00 50.00
84 Jusuf Nurkic/99 12.00 30.00
85 Doug McDermott/99 6.00 15.00
86 Russ Smith/99 4.00 10.00
87 Cameron Bairstow/99 4.00 10.00
88 Jarnell Stokes/99 4.00 10.00
89 James Ennis/99 4.00 10.00
90 Adreian Payne/99 4.00 10.00
91 Glenn Robinson III/99 5.00 12.00
92 C.J. Wilcox/99 4.00 10.00
93 Cleanthony Early/99 4.00 10.00
94 Devyn Marble/99 4.00 10.00
95 Spencer Dinwiddie/99 6.00 15.00
96 Damien Inglis/99 4.00 10.00
97 Jerami Grant/99 20.00 50.00
98 Nikola Mirotic/99 6.00 15.00
99 Jordan Adams/99 4.00 10.00
100 Cory Jefferson/99 4.00 10.00

2014-15 Select Double Team Jerseys

STATED PRINT RUN 149 SER.#'d SETS
*COPPER/49: .6X TO 1.5X BASE HI
*TIE DYE/25: 1.5X TO 4X BASE HI
1 K.Durant/R.Westbrook 15.00 40.00
3 K.Love/L.James 50.00 120.00
4 K.Irving/L.James 75.00 200.00
5 D.Williams/J.Johnson 4.00 10.00
6 A.Stoudemire/C.Anthony 8.00 20.00
7 J.Butler/J.Noah 8.00 20.00
8 A.Drummond/G.Monroe 4.00 10.00
9 P.George/R.Hibbert 8.00 20.00
10 A.Horford/K.Korver 5.00 12.00
11 K.Walker/M.Kidd-Gilchrist 5.00 12.00
12 C.Andersen/C.Bosh 6.00 15.00
13 D.Wade/L.Deng 10.00 25.00
14 B.Beal/J.Wall 8.00 20.00
15 M.Gortat/Nene 3.00 8.00
16 D.Nowitzki/T.Chandler 12.00 30.00
17 M.Ellis/R.Rondo 6.00 15.00
18 D.Howard/J.Harden 10.00 25.00
19 M.Gasol/Z.Randolph 5.00 12.00
20 A.Davis/T.Evans 12.00 30.00
21 T.Duncan/T.Parker 12.00 30.00
22 D.Green/K.Leonard 12.00 30.00
23 A.Afflalo/K.Faried 3.00 8.00
24 D.Lillard/L.Aldridge 12.00 30.00
25 K.Thompson/S.Curry 100.00 250.00
26 A.Bogut/D.Lee 4.00 10.00
27 B.Griffin/C.Paul 8.00 20.00
28 J.Lin/K.Bryant 125.00 300.00
29 E.Bledsoe/G.Dragic 5.00 12.00
30 B.McLemore/D.Cousins 4.00 10.00

2014-15 Select Fame Game Autographs

1 Larry Bird/60 60.00 150.00
2 John Stockton/60 40.00 100.00
3 Magic Johnson/60 60.00 150.00
4 Jerry West/60 30.00 80.00
5 Elgin Baylor/60 40.00 100.00
7 Dominique Wilkins/60 12.00 30.00
8 James Worthy/60 12.00 30.00
9 Rick Barry/60 10.00 25.00
10 Walt Frazier/60 12.00 30.00
11 Robert Parish/149 8.00 20.00
12 George Gervin/149 8.00 20.00
13 Dolph Schayes/99 6.00 15.00
14 Joe Dumars/149 8.00 20.00
15 Nate Thurmond/149 6.00 15.00
16 Nate Archibald/149 8.00 20.00
17 Isiah Thomas/149 25.00 60.00
18 Alex English/149 8.00 20.00
19 Dan Issel/149 6.00 15.00
20 Sarunas Marciulionis/199 6.00 15.00

2014-15 Select Fame Game Autographs Prizms Copper

*COPPER: .6X TO 1.5X BASE HI
STATED PRINT RUN 49 SER.#'d SETS
9 Rick Barry 12.00 30.00
12 George Gervin 15.00 40.00

2014-15 Select Jersey Autographs

STATED PRINT RUN B/WN 35-199 COPIES PER
1 Al Horford/35 6.00 15.00
2 Otto Porter/35 5.00 12.00
3 Trey Burke/35 4.00 10.00
4 Robert Sacre/199 4.00 10.00
5 Bradley Beal/35 10.00 25.00
6 Andre Iguodala/35 10.00 25.00
7 Tristan Thompson/35 4.00 10.00
8 Andrea Bargnani/35 4.00 10.00
9 Brook Lopez/35 6.00 15.00
10 Rodney Stuckey/40 4.00 10.00
11 Zach Randolph/35 6.00 15.00
12 Danny Green/35 5.00 12.00
13 Patty Mills/199 20.00 50.00
14 Andre Drummond/35 5.00 12.00
15 J.R. Smith/35 6.00 15.00
16 Ty Lawson/35 4.00 10.00
17 Luigi Datome/199 4.00 10.00
18 Stephen Curry/35 600.00 1,200.00
19 Ben Gordon/35 5.00 12.00
20 Shane Battier/35 5.00 12.00
21 Gordon Hayward/99 5.00 12.00
22 Hal Greer/35 6.00 15.00
23 Michael Carter-Williams/35 4.00 10.00
24 John Stockton/35 40.00 100.00
25 Cedric Maxwell/199 6.00 15.00
26 Artis Gilmore/35 8.00 20.00
27 Fred Brown/199 4.00 10.00
28 Ryan Anderson/35 4.00 10.00
29 Victor Oladipo/35 12.00 30.00
30 Doug Collins/199 6.00 15.00
31 Steve Smith/199 5.00 12.00
32 Larry Johnson/35 8.00 20.00
33 Michael Kidd-Gilchrist/35 4.00 10.00
34 Clyde Drexler/35 20.00 50.00
35 Kiki Vandeweghe/199 5.00 12.00
36 Dan Majerle/99 5.00 12.00
37 Tiago Splitter/35 4.00 10.00
38 Jonas Valanciunas/99 5.00 12.00
39 Gerald Henderson/99 4.00 10.00
40 Chris Bosh/35 8.00 20.00
41 Andre Miller/35 5.00 12.00
42 Kelly Olynyk/99 4.00 10.00
43 Kyle Singler/199 4.00 10.00
44 Thaddeus Young/199 4.00 10.00
45 Carmelo Anthony/35 15.00 40.00
46 Jose Calderon/35 4.00 10.00
47 Jason Terry/35 5.00 12.00
48 Brandon Knight/35 4.00 10.00
49 Luol Deng/125 5.00 12.00
50 Dennis Schroder/199 6.00 15.00
51 Kyle Korver/35 5.00 12.00
52 C.J. McCollum/35 25.00 60.00
53 DeMarre Carroll/199 4.00 10.00
54 Jeff Green/35 5.00 12.00
55 George Hill/35 5.00 12.00
57 Perry Jones/199 4.00 10.00
58 Eric Gordon/35 5.00 12.00
59 Jrue Holiday/35 8.00 20.00
60 Anthony Davis/35 60.00 150.00
61 Chris Kaman/35 5.00 12.00
62 Tayshaun Prince/35 12.00 30.00
63 Kevin Love/35 6.00 15.00
64 J.J. Redick/35 6.00 15.00
65 Raymond Felton/35 4.00 10.00
66 Walter Berry/199 4.00 10.00
67 Alex Len/35 4.00 10.00
68 Ben McLemore/35 4.00 10.00
69 Carl Landry/35 4.00 10.00
70 Alan Anderson/199 4.00 10.00

2014-15 Select Jersey Autographs Prizms Tie Dye

*TIE DYE: 1X TO 2.5X BASE HI
STATED PRINT RUN 25 SER.#'d SETS
13 Patty Mills/25 60.00 150.00
18 Stephen Curry/25 1,000.00 2,000.00

2014-15 Select On Hallowed Ground Jerseys

STATED PRINT RUN 149 SER.#'d SETS
*COPPER/49: .75X TO 2X BASE HI
*TIE DYE/25: 2X TO 5X BASE HI
1 Kareem Abdul-Jabbar 12.00 30.00
2 Dennis Rodman 10.00 25.00
3 Patrick Ewing 6.00 15.00
4 Gary Payton 6.00 15.00
5 Magic Johnson 15.00 40.00
6 Alex English 5.00 12.00
7 Kevin McHale 6.00 15.00
8 Clyde Drexler 6.00 15.00
9 Robert Parish 5.00 12.00
10 Larry Bird 15.00 40.00
11 Hakeem Olajuwon 8.00 20.00
12 Karl Malone 8.00 20.00
13 David Robinson 8.00 20.00
14 John Stockton 8.00 20.00
15 Alonzo Mourning 6.00 15.00

2014-15 Select On Hallowed Ground Jerseys Prizms Tie Dye

*TIE DYE: 2X TO 5X BASE HI
STATED PRINT RUN 25 SER.#'d SETS

2014-15 Select Rookie Jersey Autographs

STATED PRINT RUN 199 SER.#'d SETS
*ORANGE/60: .5X TO 1.2X BASE HI
*TIE DYE/25: .75X TO 2X BASE HI
1 Andrew Wiggins 25.00 60.00
2 Jabari Parker 6.00 15.00
3 Joel Embiid 100.00 250.00
4 Markel Brown 5.00 12.00
5 T.J. Warren 8.00 20.00
6 James Ennis 5.00 12.00
7 Gary Harris 8.00 20.00
8 Adreian Payne 5.00 12.00
9 Marcus Smart 20.00 50.00
10 Kyle Anderson 8.00 20.00
11 Russ Smith 5.00 12.00
12 Noah Vonleh 5.00 12.00
13 Zach LaVine 30.00 80.00
14 C.J. Wilcox 5.00 12.00
15 Tyler Ennis 5.00 12.00
16 Doug McDermott 8.00 20.00
17 Spencer Dinwiddie 8.00 20.00
18 Damien Inglis 5.00 12.00
19 P.J. Hairston 5.00 12.00
20 K.J. McDaniels 5.00 12.00
21 James Young 5.00 12.00
22 Bruno Caboclo 6.00 15.00
23 Mitch McGary 5.00 12.00
24 Nik Stauskas 5.00 12.00
25 Aaron Gordon 25.00 60.00
26 Elfrid Payton 8.00 20.00
27 Shabazz Napier 6.00 15.00
28 Dante Exum 8.00 20.00
29 Rodney Hood 6.00 15.00
30 Johnny O'Bryant 5.00 12.00

2014-15 Select Rookie Signatures

STATED PRINT RUN 275 SER.#'d SETS
RSAG Aaron Gordon 12.00 30.00
RSAP Adreian Payne 3.00 8.00
RSAW Andrew Wiggins 40.00 100.00
RSBB Bojan Bogdanovic 5.00 12.00
RSCB Cameron Bairstow 3.00 8.00
RSCE Cleanthony Early 3.00 8.00
RSCJ Cory Jefferson 3.00 8.00
RSDE Dante Exum 5.00 12.00
RSDM Doug McDermott 5.00 12.00
RSDR Damjan Rudez 3.00 8.00
RSEP Elfrid Payton 5.00 12.00
RSGH Gary Harris 5.00 12.00
RSGR Glenn Robinson III 4.00 10.00
RSJC Jordan Clarkson 12.00 30.00
RSJE Joel Embiid 200.00 500.00
RSJP Jabari Parker 4.00 10.00
RSJR Julius Randle 15.00 40.00
RSJY James Young 3.00 8.00
RSMB Markel Brown 3.00 8.00
RSMM Mitch McGary 3.00 8.00
RSMS Marcus Smart 15.00 40.00
RSNS Nik Stauskas 3.00 8.00
RSNV Noah Vonleh 3.00 8.00
RSRH Rodney Hood 4.00 10.00
RSSN Shabazz Napier 4.00 10.00
RSTE Tyler Ennis 3.00 8.00
RSTW T.J. Warren 5.00 12.00
RSZD Zoran Dragic 4.00 10.00
RSZL Zach LaVine 125.00 300.00

2014-15 Select Rookie Signatures Prizms Copper

*COPPER: .75X TO 2X BASE HI
STATED PRINT RUN 49 SER.#'d SETS

2014-15 Select Rookie Swatches

STATED PRINT RUN 199 SER.#'d SETS
*PURPLE: .5X TO 1.2X BASE HI
1 Jabari Parker 2.50 6.00
2 Aaron Gordon 10.00 25.00
3 Russ Smith 2.00 5.00
4 Bruno Caboclo 2.50 6.00
5 Joel Embiid 60.00 150.00
6 Andrew Wiggins 10.00 25.00
7 K.J. McDaniels 2.00 5.00
8 Cleanthony Early 2.00 5.00
9 Nik Stauskas 2.00 5.00
10 Dante Exum 3.00 8.00
11 P.J. Hairston 2.00 5.00
12 Doug McDermott 3.00 8.00
13 C.J. Wilcox 2.00 5.00
14 Rodney Hood 2.50 6.00
15 Marcus Smart 8.00 20.00
16 Shabazz Napier 2.50 6.00
17 Cory Jefferson 2.00 5.00
18 T.J. Warren 3.00 8.00
19 Julius Randle 10.00 25.00
20 Tyler Ennis 2.00 5.00
21 Zach LaVine 12.00 30.00
22 Noah Vonleh 2.00 5.00
23 Damien Inglis 2.00 5.00
24 Elfrid Payton 3.00 8.00
25 Spencer Dinwiddie 3.00 8.00
26 Mitch McGary 2.00 5.00
27 Adreian Payne 2.00 5.00
28 Kyle Anderson 3.00 8.00
29 James Ennis 2.00 5.00
30 Gary Harris 3.00 8.00

2014-15 Select Rookie Swatches Prizms Orange

*ORANGE: .6X TO 1.5X BASE HI
STATED PRINT RUN 60 SER.#'d SETS

2014-15 Select Rookie Swatches Prizms Tie Dye

*TIE DYE: 1X TO 2.5X BASE HI
STATED PRINT RUN 25 SER.#'d SETS
5 Joel Embiid 100.00 250.00

2014-15 Select Signatures

STATED PRINT RUN B/WN 60-99 COPIES PER
STATED PRINT RUN B/WN 149-199 COPIES PER
1 Kobe Bryant/60 75.00 200.00
2 Shaquille O'Neal/60 60.00 150.00
3 Kevin Durant/60 60.00 120.00
4 Julius Erving/60 40.00 100.00
5 Karl Malone/60 25.00 60.00
6 John Wall/60 20.00 50.00
7 Anthony Davis/60 30.00 80.00
8 Kyrie Irving/60 40.00 100.00
9 Reggie Jackson/199 4.00 10.00
10 Jason Kidd/60 10.00 25.00
11 Ray Allen/60 20.00 50.00
12 Tracy McGrady/60 15.00 40.00
13 Kevin Love/60 15.00 40.00
14 Vince Carter/60 15.00 40.00
15 Anthony Bennett/60 5.00 12.00
16 Grant Hill/60 12.00 30.00
17 Tony Parker/60 12.00 30.00
18 Victor Oladipo/60 6.00 15.00
19 Rick Fox/99 5.00 12.00
20 Ben McLemore/75 5.00 12.00
23 Artis Gilmore/75 10.00 25.00
24 Andre Drummond/75 6.00 15.00
25 Bradley Beal/75 12.00 30.00
26 Harrison Barnes/75 6.00 15.00
27 Patty Mills/199 8.00 20.00
28 C.J. McCollum/149 4.00 10.00
29 Michael Carter-Williams/149 2.50 6.00
30 Trey Burke/149 2.50 6.00
31 Allan Houston/149 4.00 10.00
32 Dick Van Arsdale/199 4.00 10.00
33 Jared Sullinger/149 2.50 6.00
34 Kevin Martin/149 3.00 8.00
35 Scott Brooks/149 2.50 6.00
36 Tiago Splitter/199 2.50 6.00
37 Kurt Rambis/199 3.00 8.00
38 Tom Chambers/199 3.00 8.00
39 Toni Kukoc/199 6.00 15.00
41 Kendall Gill/199 4.00 10.00
42 Mahmoud Abdul-Rauf/199 3.00 8.00
43 Muggsy Bogues/199 4.00 10.00
44 Mark Price/199 4.00 10.00
45 Scott Skiles/199 3.00 8.00
46 Spud Webb/199 5.00 12.00
47 Tim Hardaway/199 5.00 12.00
48 Rudy Tomjanovich/199 4.00 10.00
49 Kelly Olynyk/199 2.50 6.00

2014-15 Select Signatures Prizms Copper

*COPPER: 1X TO 2.5X BASE p/r 149-199
*COPPER: .5X TO 1.2X BASE p/r60-99
STATED PRINT RUN 49 SER.#'d SETS
34 Kevin Martin 5.00 12.00
44 Mark Price 10.00 25.00
46 Spud Webb 8.00 20.00

2014-15 Select Sparks Jerseys

STATED PRINT RUN B/WN 40-149 COPIES PER
*COPPER/49: .5X TO 1.2X BASE HI
*TIE DYE/25: .75X TO 2X BASE HI
1 Manu Ginobili/149 10.00 25.00
2 Chris Paul/149 8.00 20.00
3 Klay Thompson/149 15.00 40.00
4 James Harden/149 10.00 25.00
5 Mike Conley/149 4.00 10.00
6 Eric Gordon/149 4.00 10.00
7 Monta Ellis/149 4.00 10.00
8 LeBron James/149 50.00 120.00
9 Kemba Walker/149 5.00 12.00
10 Kyrie Irving/149 10.00 25.00
11 Patty Mills/149 5.00 12.00
12 Ty Lawson/149 3.00 8.00
13 Russell Westbrook/149 8.00 20.00
14 John Wall/149 6.00 15.00
15 Avery Bradley/149 4.00 10.00
16 Damian Lillard/149 12.00 30.00
17 Jeff Teague/149 3.00 8.00
18 Kawhi Leonard/149 12.00 30.00
19 Stephen Curry/149 50.00 120.00
20 Jose Calderon/149 3.00 8.00
21 Michael Carter-Williams/149 3.00 8.00
22 Deron Williams/149 4.00 10.00
23 Rajon Rondo/149 6.00 15.00
24 Goran Dragic/149 5.00 12.00
25 Reggie Jackson/149 4.00 10.00
26 Gordon Hayward/149 4.00 10.00
27 Mario Chalmers/149 4.00 10.00
28 Tim Hardaway Jr./149 4.00 10.00
29 Jeff Green/149 4.00 10.00
30 Tony Parker/149 8.00 20.00

2014-15 Select Sparks Jerseys Prizms Copper

*COPPER: .5X TO 1.2X BASE HI
STATED PRINT RUN B/WN 10-49 COPIES PER
NO PRICING ON QTY 10 OR LESS

2014-15 Select Sparks Jerseys Prizms Tie Dye

*TIE DYE: .75X TO 2X BASE HI
STATED PRINT RUN 25 SER.#'d SETS
3 Klay Thompson/25 30.00 80.00
8 LeBron James/25 100.00 250.00
18 Kawhi Leonard/25 25.00 60.00
19 Stephen Curry/25 100.00 250.00

2014-15 Select Swatches

STATED PRINT RUN 75 SER.#'d SETS
*PURPLE/99: .5X TO 1.2X BASE HI
1 Alex Len 3.00 8.00
2 Dan Majerle 4.00 10.00
3 Deron Williams 4.00 10.00
4 Bill Laimbeer 5.00 12.00
5 Greg Monroe 3.00 8.00
6 Bradley Beal 8.00 20.00
7 DeMar DeRozan 6.00 15.00
8 Hakeem Olajuwon 10.00 25.00
9 Allen Iverson 12.00 30.00
10 Kyrie Irving 10.00 25.00
11 Danny Manning 4.00 10.00
12 Bismack Biyombo 3.00 8.00
13 Jason Kidd 8.00 20.00
14 DeMarcus Cousins 4.00 10.00
15 Amar'e Stoudemire 5.00 12.00
16 Magic Johnson 20.00 50.00
17 David Lee 3.00 8.00
18 Chris Andersen 3.00 8.00
19 Dwight Howard 6.00 15.00
20 Julius Erving 12.00 30.00
21 Blake Griffin 5.00 12.00
22 Clifford Robinson 3.00 8.00
23 Harrison Barnes 4.00 10.00
24 Kobe Bryant 40.00 100.00
25 Enes Kanter 4.00 10.00
26 Chris Paul 8.00 20.00
27 Eric Bledsoe 4.00 10.00
28 Al Horford 5.00 12.00
29 Dwyane Wade 10.00 25.00
30 Danny Green 4.00 10.00
31 Bobby Jackson 3.00 8.00
32 Gary Payton 8.00 20.00
33 Dennis Rodman 12.00 30.00
34 Andrew Bogut 4.00 10.00
35 Kevin Durant 15.00 40.00
36 Dikembe Mutombo 8.00 20.00
37 Anfernee Hardaway 5.00 12.00
38 Jeff Green 4.00 10.00
39 Carmelo Anthony 8.00 20.00
40 Ersan Ilyasova 3.00 8.00
41 Adrian Dantley 5.00 12.00
42 Dirk Nowitzki 12.00 30.00
43 Joakim Noah 5.00 12.00
44 Brandon Knight 3.00 8.00
45 DeAndre Jordan 4.00 10.00
46 John Stockton 10.00 25.00
47 Andre Drummond 4.00 10.00
48 David West 4.00 10.00
49 Larry Bird 20.00 50.00
50 Ben Wallace 5.00 12.00
51 LeBron James 40.00 100.00

52 Damian Lillard 12.00 30.00
53 J.J. Redick 5.00 12.00
54 Aaron Brooks 3.00 8.00
55 J.R. Smith 5.00 12.00
56 Chris Mullin 6.00 15.00
57 James Harden 10.00 25.00
58 Anthony Davis 12.00 30.00
59 Iman Shumpert 3.00 8.00
60 Clyde Drexler 8.00 20.00
61 Gerald Green 4.00 10.00
62 Alex English 6.00 15.00
63 Grant Hill 8.00 20.00
64 David Robinson 10.00 25.00
65 Gordon Hayward 4.00 10.00
66 Kawhi Leonard 12.00 30.00
67 Draymond Green 6.00 15.00
68 Chris Bosh 6.00 15.00
69 Dion Waiters 3.00 8.00
70 Al Jefferson 3.00 8.00

2014-15 Select Swatches Prizms Tie Dye
*TIE DYE: .75X TO 2X BASE HI
STATED PRINT RUN B/WN 10-25 COPIES PER
NO PRICING ON QTY 10 OR LESS
8 Hakeem Olajuwon/25 20.00 50.00
9 Allen Iverson/25 40.00 100.00
24 Kobe Bryant/25 125.00 300.00
33 Dennis Rodman/25 40.00 100.00
35 Kevin Durant/25 60.00 150.00
37 Anfernee Hardaway/25 30.00 80.00
42 Dirk Nowitzki/25 20.00 50.00
51 LeBron James/25 125.00 300.00

2015-16 Select
1 Andrew Wiggins CON .75 2.00
2 Bojan Bogdanovic CON .50 1.25
3 Dennis Schroder CON .60 1.50
4 Frank Kaminsky CON RC .50 1.25
5 James Young CON .40 1.00
6 Jusuf Nurkic CON .50 1.25
7 Kobe Bryant CON 5.00 12.00
8 Myles Turner CON RC 1.50 4.00
9 Reggie Jackson CON .50 1.25
10 Terrence Ross CON .50 1.25
11 Aaron Harrison CON RC .50 1.25
12 Brook Lopez CON .60 1.50
13 Deron Williams CON .50 1.25
14 Gary Harris CON .50 1.25
15 Jarell Martin CON RC .40 1.00
16 Karl-Anthony Towns CON RC 2.50 6.00
17 Kristaps Porzingis CON RC 2.50 6.00
18 Nemanja Bjelica CON RC .60 1.50
19 Robin Lopez CON .40 1.00
20 Terry Rozier CON RC 1.50 4.00
21 Alec Burks CON .40 1.00
22 Carmelo Anthony CON 1.00 2.50
23 Derrick Rose CON 1.00 2.50
24 Goran Dragic CON .60 1.50
25 Jeff Teague CON .40 1.00
26 Kawhi Leonard CON 2.00 5.00
27 Kyle Lowry CON .60 1.50
28 Nicolas Batum CON .40 1.00
29 Rodney Stuckey CON .40 1.00
30 Tim Duncan CON 1.50 4.00
31 Alex Len CON .40 1.00
32 Chris Paul CON 1.25 3.00
33 Dirk Nowitzki CON 1.50 4.00
34 Gordon Hayward CON .60 1.50
35 Jerian Grant CON RC .40 1.00
36 Oscar Robertson CON 1.50 4.00
37 Kyrie Irving CON 1.25 3.00
38 Nik Stauskas CON .40 1.00
39 Rondae Hollis-Jefferson CON RC .50 1.25
40 Trey Burke CON .50 1.25
41 Al-Farouq Aminu CON .40 1.00
42 Corey Brewer CON .40 1.00
43 Dwyane Wade CON 1.25 3.00
44 Ian Mahinmi CON .40 1.00
45 Jimmy Butler CON 1.25 3.00
46 Kemba Walker CON .60 1.50
47 LeBron James CON 5.00 12.00
48 Nikola Mirotic CON .40 1.00
49 Rudy Gay CON .60 1.50
50 Tyreke Evans CON .50 1.25
51 Amare Stoudemire CON .60 1.50
52 Damian Lillard CON 1.50 4.00
53 Elfrid Payton CON .50 1.25
54 J.J. Barea CON .50 1.25
55 John Wall CON .75 2.00
56 Kenneth Faried CON .50 1.25
57 Manu Ginobili CON 1.25 3.00
58 Nikola Vucevic CON .50 1.25
59 Russell Westbrook CON 1.00 2.50
60 Victor Oladipo CON .50 1.25
61 Andre Iguodala CON .60 1.50
62 D'Angelo Russell CON RC 1.50 4.00
63 Emmanuel Mudiay CON RC .50 1.25
64 Jabari Parker CON .40 1.00
65 Jordan Clarkson CON .60 1.50
66 Kevin Durant CON 2.50 6.00
67 Marc Gasol CON .60 1.50
68 Noah Vonleh CON .40 1.00
69 Kelly Oubre Jr. CON RC 1.25 3.00
70 Walter Tavares CON RC .40 1.00
71 Anthony Davis CON 1.50 4.00
72 Darrun Hilliard CON RC .40 1.00
73 Eric Bledsoe CON .50 1.25
74 Jahlil Okafor CON RC .50 1.25
75 Josh Smith CON .50 1.25
76 Kevin Love CON .60 1.50
77 Marcus Smart CON .75 2.00
78 Omer Asik CON .40 1.00
79 Serge Ibaka CON .50 1.25
80 Willie Cauley-Stein CON RC .50 1.25
81 Arron Afflalo CON .40 1.00
82 Delon Wright CON RC .50 1.25
83 Ersan Ilyasova CON .40 1.00
84 JaKarr Sampson CON .40 1.00
85 Justin Anderson CON RC .40 1.00
86 Kevon Looney CON RC 1.25 3.00
87 Mario Hezonja CON RC .50 1.25
88 Otto Porter CON .50 1.25
89 Stanley Johnson CON RC .50 1.25
90 Zach LaVine CON 1.50 4.00
91 Blake Griffin CON .60 1.50
92 DeMarcus Cousins CON .60 1.50
93 Evan Turner CON .40 1.00
94 James Harden CON 1.25 3.00
95 Justise Winslow CON RC .60 1.50
96 Klay Thompson CON 1.50 4.00
97 Montrezl Harrell CON RC 1.25 3.00
98 Paul George CON 1.00 2.50
99 Stephen Curry CON 5.00 12.00
100 Zach Randolph CON .60 1.50
101 Anthony Davis PRE 1.50 4.00
102 Cameron Payne PRE RC 1.00 2.50
103 Derrick Rose PRE 1.00 2.50
104 Greg Monroe PRE .50 1.25
105 Jerian Grant PRE .40 1.00
106 Jrue Holiday PRE .75 2.00
107 Kyrie Irving PRE 1.25 3.00
108 Montrezl Harrell PRE 1.25 3.00
109 Raul Neto PRE RC .40 1.00
110 Tim Duncan PRE 1.50 4.00
111 Aaron Gordon PRE .60 1.50
112 Carmelo Anthony PRE 1.00 2.50
113 Duje Dukan PRE RC .40 1.00
114 Harrison Barnes PRE .50 1.25
115 Joakim Noah PRE .40 1.00
116 Julius Randle PRE .75 2.00
117 LaMarcus Aldridge PRE .60 1.50
118 Nerlens Noel PRE .40 1.00
119 Reggie Jackson PRE .50 1.25
120 Tim Hardaway Jr. PRE .50 1.25
121 Al Jefferson PRE .40 1.00
122 Chris Andersen PRE .50 1.25
123 Dwight Howard PRE .75 2.00
124 Hassan Whiteside PRE .50 1.25
125 Joe Ingles PRE .50 1.25
126 Justise Winslow PRE .60 1.50
127 Lance Thomas PRE .40 1.00
128 Nikola Jokic PRE RC 100.00 250.00
129 R.J. Hunter PRE RC .40 1.00
130 Tony Parker PRE 1.00 2.50
131 Andre Drummond PRE .60 1.50
132 Chris McCullough PRE RC .40 1.00
133 Dwyane Wade PRE 1.25 3.00
134 Isaiah Thomas PRE .50 1.25
135 Joe Johnson PRE .50 1.25
136 Karl-Anthony Towns PRE 2.50 6.00
137 Larry Nance Jr. PRE RC .75 2.00
138 Norman Powell PRE RC .75 2.00
139 Robert Covington PRE .50 1.25
140 Trey Lyles PRE .50 1.25
141 Andrew Wiggins PRE .75 2.00
142 Chris Paul PRE 1.25 3.00
143 Elfrid Payton PRE .50 1.25
144 J.J. Hickson PRE .40 1.00
145 Joe Young PRE RC .40 1.00
146 Kelly Oubre Jr. PRE 1.25 3.00
147 LeBron James PRE 5.00 12.00
148 Pat Connaughton PRE RC .60 1.50
149 Rudy Gobert PRE .75 2.00
150 Ty Lawson PRE .40 1.00
151 Blake Griffin PRE .60 1.50
152 Damian Lillard PRE 1.50 4.00
153 Emmanuel Mudiay PRE .50 1.25
154 Jabari Parker PRE .50 1.25
155 John Wall PRE .75 2.00
156 Kevin Durant PRE 2.50 6.00
157 Marco Belinelli PRE .40 1.00
158 Pau Gasol PRE 1.00 2.50
159 Russell Westbrook PRE 1.00 2.50
160 Tyson Chandler PRE .50 1.25
161 Bobby Portis PRE RC 1.00 2.50
162 D'Angelo Russell PRE 1.50 4.00
163 Eric Bledsoe PRE .50 1.25
164 Jahlil Okafor PRE .50 1.25
165 Jonathon Simmons PRE RC .50 1.25
166 Kevin Garnett PRE 1.50 4.00
167 Matthew Dellavedova PRE .50 1.25
168 Paul Pierce PRE 1.00 2.50
169 Sam Dekker PRE RC .40 1.00
170 Tyus Jones PRE RC .50 1.25
171 Bradley Beal PRE .75 2.00
172 DeMar DeRozan PRE .75 2.00
173 Evan Fournier PRE .50 1.25
174 James Harden PRE 1.25 3.00
175 Jordan Hill PRE .40 1.00
176 Klay Thompson PRE 1.50 4.00
177 Maurice Harkless PRE .40 1.00
178 Avery Bradley PRE .40 1.00
179 Stephen Curry PRE 5.00 12.00
180 Walter Tavares PRE .40 1.00
181 Branden Dawson PRE RC .40 1.00
182 DeMarre Carroll PRE .40 1.00
183 Frank Kaminsky PRE .50 1.25
184 Jeff Green PRE .40 1.00
185 Jordan Mickey PRE RC .40 1.00
186 Kobe Bryant PRE 5.00 12.00
187 Mike Conley PRE .60 1.50
188 Rajon Rondo PRE .75 2.00
189 T.J. Warren PRE .60 1.50
190 Wesley Matthews PRE .40 1.00
191 Brandon Knight PRE .40 1.00
192 Deron Williams PRE .50 1.25
193 Giannis Antetokounmpo PRE 3.00 8.00
194 Jeremy Lin PRE 1.25 3.00
195 Josh Richardson PRE RC .60 1.50
196 Kristaps Porzingis PRE 2.50 6.00
197 Monta Ellis PRE .50 1.25
198 Rashad Vaughn PRE RC .40 1.00
199 Tiago Splitter PRE .40 1.00
200 Willie Cauley-Stein PRE .50 1.25
201 Bradley Beal COU 2.00 5.00
202 Cameron Payne COU 1.50 4.00
203 Devin Booker COU RC 40.00 100.00
204 Jerian Grant COU 1.00 2.50
205 Kemba Walker COU 1.50 4.00
206 Marc Gasol COU 1.50 4.00
207 Paul George COU 2.50 6.00
208 Stanley Johnson COU 1.25 3.00
209 Allen Crabbe COU 1.00 2.50
210 Chandler Parsons COU 1.00 2.50
211 Draymond Green COU 2.00 5.00
212 Jimmy Butler COU 3.00 8.00
213 Kenneth Faried COU 1.25 3.00
214 Marcin Gortat COU 1.00 2.50
215 Raul Neto COU 1.00 2.50
216 T.J. Warren COU 1.50 4.00
217 Andrew Wiggins COU 2.00 5.00
218 Damian Lillard COU 4.00 10.00
219 Elfrid Payton COU 1.25 3.00
220 Joe Young COU 1.00 2.50
221 Kentavious Caldwell-Pope COU 1.25 3.00
222 Marcus Smart COU 2.00 5.00
223 Rakeem Christmas COU RC 1.00 2.50
224 Thabo Sefolosha COU 1.00 2.50
225 Anthony Brown COU RC 1.00 2.50
226 D'Angelo Russell COU 4.00 10.00
227 Emmanuel Mudiay COU 1.25 3.00
228 Jonas Valanciunas COU 1.25 3.00
229 Khris Middleton COU 2.00 5.00
230 Mario Hezonja COU 1.25 3.00
231 Rashad Vaughn COU 1.00 2.50
232 Tobias Harris COU 1.25 3.00
233 Austin Rivers COU 1.25 3.00
234 Danilo Gallinari COU 1.25 3.00
235 Enes Kanter COU 1.00 2.50
236 Jordan Clarkson COU 1.50 4.00
237 Klay Thompson COU 4.00 10.00
238 Michael Carter-Williams COU 1.00 2.50
239 Reggie Jackson COU 1.25 3.00
240 Trey Lyles COU 1.25 3.00
241 Ben McLemore COU 1.00 2.50
242 Darren Collison COU 1.00 2.50
243 Eric Gordon COU 1.25 3.00
244 Jrue Holiday COU 2.00 5.00
245 Kristaps Porzingis COU 6.00 15.00
246 Myles Turner COU 4.00 10.00
247 R.J. Hunter COU 1.00 2.50
248 Tristan Thompson COU 1.00 2.50
249 Bojan Bogdanovic COU 1.00 2.50
250 DeAndre Jordan COU 1.25 3.00
251 George Hill COU 1.25 3.00
252 Justin Anderson COU 1.00 2.50
253 Kyle Korver COU 1.25 3.00
254 Nemanja Bjelica COU 1.50 4.00
255 Rondae Hollis-Jefferson COU 1.25 3.00
256 Tyus Jones COU 1.00 2.50
257 Brandon Jennings COU 1.00 2.50
258 Delon Wright COU 1.25 3.00
259 Giannis Antetokounmpo COU 8.00 20.00
260 Justise Winslow COU 1.50 4.00
261 Kyle Lowry COU 1.50 4.00
262 Nene COU 1.25 3.00
263 Rudy Gobert COU 2.00 5.00
264 Victor Oladipo COU 1.25 3.00
265 Brandon Knight COU 1.00 2.50
266 DeMarcus Cousins COU 1.50 4.00
267 Jahlil Okafor COU 1.25 3.00
268 Karl-Anthony Towns COU 6.00 15.00
269 Kyrie Irving COU 3.00 8.00
270 Nikola Mirotic COU 1.00 2.50
271 Sam Dekker COU 1.00 2.50
272 Zach LaVine COU 4.00 10.00
273 C.J. McCollum COU 1.50 4.00
274 Derrick Rose COU 2.50 6.00
275 Jeremy Lamb COU 1.00 2.50
276 Kawhi Leonard COU 5.00 12.00
277 Langston Galloway COU 1.00 2.50
278 Norman Powell COU 2.00 5.00
279 Shane Larkin COU 1.00 2.50
280 Zach Randolph COU 1.50 4.00
281 Anthony Davis COU 4.00 10.00
282 Chris Andersen COU 1.25 3.00
283 Dirk Nowitzki COU 4.00 10.00
284 James Harden COU 3.00 8.00
285 Kevin Love COU 1.50 4.00
286 Russell Westbrook COU 2.50 6.00
287 Tony Parker COU 2.50 6.00
288 Blake Griffin COU 1.50 4.00
289 Chris Bosh COU 2.00 5.00
290 Dwight Howard COU 2.00 5.00
291 Jeremy Lin COU 3.00 8.00
292 Kobe Bryant COU 12.00 30.00
293 Stephen Curry COU 12.00 30.00
294 Vince Carter COU 3.00 8.00
295 Carmelo Anthony COU 2.50 6.00
296 Chris Paul COU 3.00 8.00
297 Dwyane Wade COU 3.00 8.00
298 Kevin Durant COU 6.00 15.00
299 Tim Duncan COU 4.00 10.00
300 LeBron James COU 12.00 30.00

2015-16 Select Concourse Prizms Blue
*BLUE: 1.5X TO 4X BASIC
STATED PRINT RUN 249 SER.#'d SETS
7 Kobe Bryant 50.00 120.00
47 LeBron James 60.00 150.00
99 Stephen Curry 50.00 120.00

2015-16 Select Concourse Prizms Orange
*ORANGE: 3X TO 8X BASIC
*ORANGE RC: 2X TO 5X BASIC RC
STATED PRINT RUN 60 SER.#'d SETS
7 Kobe Bryant 125.00 300.00
16 Karl-Anthony Towns 75.00 200.00
17 Kristaps Porzingis 25.00 60.00
22 Carmelo Anthony 15.00 40.00
23 Derrick Rose 15.00 40.00
26 Kawhi Leonard 20.00 50.00
30 Tim Duncan 15.00 40.00
33 Dirk Nowitzki 15.00 40.00
37 Kyrie Irving 12.00 30.00
43 Dwyane Wade 15.00 40.00
45 Jimmy Butler 15.00 40.00
47 LeBron James 125.00 300.00
52 Damian Lillard 20.00 50.00
57 Manu Ginobili 12.00 30.00
66 Kevin Durant 25.00 60.00
71 Anthony Davis 15.00 40.00
90 Zach LaVine 20.00 50.00
94 James Harden 15.00 40.00
96 Klay Thompson 20.00 50.00
99 Stephen Curry 75.00 200.00

2015-16 Select Concourse Prizms Pink
*PINK: 8X TO 20X BASIC
*PINK RC: 5X TO 12X BASIC RC
STATED PRINT RUN 20 SER.#'d SETS
7 Kobe Bryant 400.00 800.00
16 Karl-Anthony Towns 125.00 300.00
17 Kristaps Porzingis 75.00 200.00
22 Carmelo Anthony 40.00 100.00
23 Derrick Rose 40.00 100.00
26 Kawhi Leonard 50.00 120.00
30 Tim Duncan 40.00 100.00
33 Dirk Nowitzki 40.00 100.00
37 Kyrie Irving 30.00 80.00
43 Dwyane Wade 40.00 100.00
45 Jimmy Butler 40.00 100.00
47 LeBron James 400.00 800.00
52 Damian Lillard 40.00 100.00
57 Manu Ginobili 25.00 60.00
62 D'Angelo Russell 30.00 80.00
66 Kevin Durant 50.00 120.00
71 Anthony Davis 40.00 100.00
90 Zach LaVine 50.00 120.00
94 James Harden 40.00 100.00
96 Klay Thompson 50.00 120.00
99 Stephen Curry 200.00 500.00

2015-16 Select Concourse Prizms Red
*RED: 2X TO 5X BASIC
STATED PRINT RUN 149 SER.#'d SETS
7 Kobe Bryant 60.00 150.00
47 LeBron James 75.00 200.00
99 Stephen Curry 60.00 150.00

2015-16 Select Courtside Prizms Copper
*COPPER: 2X TO 6X BASIC
*COPPER RC: 1.5X TO 4X BASIC RC
STATED PRINT RUN 49 SER.#'d SETS
203 Devin Booker 800.00 1,500.00
245 Kristaps Porzingis 40.00 100.00
259 Giannis Antetokounmpo 100.00 250.00
268 Karl-Anthony Towns 200.00 500.00
278 Norman Powell 25.00 60.00
283 Dirk Nowitzki 30.00 80.00
292 Kobe Bryant 400.00 800.00
293 Stephen Curry 300.00 600.00
294 Vince Carter 25.00 60.00
295 Carmelo Anthony 20.00 50.00
296 Chris Paul 20.00 50.00
297 Dwyane Wade 25.00 60.00
298 Kevin Durant 100.00 250.00
299 Tim Duncan 25.00 60.00
300 LeBron James 400.00 800.00

2015-16 Select Premier Prizms Light Blue Die Cut
*LT.BLUE: .75X TO 2X BASIC
*LT.BLUE RC: .5X TO 1.2X BASIC RC
STATED PRINT RUN 199 SER.#'d SETS
136 Karl-Anthony Towns 10.00 25.00
146 Kelly Oubre Jr. 30.00 80.00
179 Stephen Curry 10.00 25.00
186 Kobe Bryant 125.00 300.00
196 Kristaps Porzingis 15.00 40.00

2015-16 Select Premier Prizms Purple Die Cut
*PURPLE: 1X TO 2.5X BASIC
*PURPLE RC: .6X TO 1.5X BASIC RC
STATED PRINT RUN 99 SER.#'d SETS
136 Karl-Anthony Towns 12.00 30.00
146 Kelly Oubre Jr. 40.00 100.00
147 LeBron James 15.00 40.00
179 Stephen Curry 12.00 30.00
186 Kobe Bryant 150.00 400.00
196 Kristaps Porzingis 20.00 50.00

2015-16 Select Prizms Silver
*SILVER: 1.25X TO 3X BASIC
7 Kobe Bryant CON 30.00 80.00
47 LeBron James CON 40.00 100.00
99 Stephen Curry CON 30.00 80.00
179 Stephen Curry PRE 30.00 80.00
186 Kobe Bryant PRE 30.00 80.00
259 Giannis Antetokounmpo COU 25.00 60.00
268 Karl-Anthony Towns COU 20.00 50.00
278 Norman Powell COU 6.00 15.00
283 Dirk Nowitzki COU 12.00 30.00
292 Kobe Bryant COU 100.00 250.00
293 Stephen Curry COU 100.00 250.00
294 Vince Carter COU 10.00 25.00
295 Carmelo Anthony COU 8.00 20.00
296 Chris Paul COU 10.00 25.00
297 Dwyane Wade COU 10.00 25.00
298 Kevin Durant COU 20.00 50.00
299 Tim Duncan COU 12.00 30.00
300 LeBron James COU 125.00 300.00

2015-16 Select Prizms Tie Dye
*TIE DYE 1-100: 8X TO 20X BASIC
*TIE DYE 1-100: 5X TO 12X BASIC RC
*TIE DYE 101-200: 3X TO 8X BASIC
*TIE DYE 101-200: 2X TO 5X BASIC RC
*TIE DYE 201-300: 2.5X TO 6X BASIC
*TIE DYE 201-300: 1.5X TO 4X BASIC RC
STATED PRINT RUN 25 SER.#'d SETS
1 Andrew Wiggins CON 30.00 80.00
7 Kobe Bryant CON 400.00 800.00
8 Myles Turner CON 25.00 60.00
16 Karl-Anthony Towns CON 125.00 300.00
17 Kristaps Porzingis CON 75.00 200.00
20 Terry Rozier CON 25.00 60.00
26 Kawhi Leonard CON 20.00 50.00
30 Tim Duncan CON 20.00 50.00
45 Jimmy Butler CON 20.00 50.00
47 LeBron James CON 60.00 150.00
69 Kelly Oubre Jr. CON 200.00 500.00
71 Jahlil Okafor CON 25.00 60.00
90 Zach LaVine CON 25.00 60.00
95 Justise Winslow CON 30.00 80.00
98 Paul George CON 15.00 40.00
99 Stephen Curry CON 60.00 150.00
110 Tim Duncan PRE 20.00 50.00
112 Carmelo Anthony PRE 25.00 60.00
126 Justise Winslow PRE 20.00 50.00
128 Nikola Jokic PRE 2,000.00 4,000.00
136 Karl-Anthony Towns PRE 125.00 300.00
141 Andrew Wiggins PRE 30.00 80.00
146 Kelly Oubre Jr. PRE 200.00 500.00
147 LeBron James PRE 60.00 150.00
164 Jahlil Okafor PRE 25.00 60.00
179 Stephen Curry PRE 60.00 150.00
186 Kobe Bryant PRE 400.00 800.00
193 G. Antetokounmpo PRE 15.00 40.00
196 Kristaps Porzingis PRE 75.00 200.00
203 Devin Booker COU 125.00 300.00
207 Paul George COU 15.00 40.00
212 Jimmy Butler COU 20.00 50.00
217 Andrew Wiggins COU 30.00 80.00
245 Kristaps Porzingis COU 125.00 300.00
246 Myles Turner COU 25.00 60.00
259 G. Antetokounmpo COU 20.00 50.00
260 Justise Winslow COU 30.00 80.00
267 Jahlil Okafor COU 25.00 60.00
268 Karl-Anthony Towns COU 125.00 300.00
272 Zach LaVine COU 20.00 50.00
276 Kawhi Leonard COU 20.00 50.00
292 Kobe Bryant COU 800.00 1,500.00
295 Carmelo Anthony COU 25.00 60.00
299 Tim Duncan COU 20.00 50.00
300 LeBron James COU 800.00 1,500.00

2015-16 Select Prizms Tri Color
*TRI CLR: 1.25X TO 3X BASIC
7 Kobe Bryant CON 30.00 80.00
47 LeBron James CON 40.00 100.00
99 Stephen Curry CON 30.00 80.00
179 Stephen Curry PRE 30.00 80.00
186 Kobe Bryant PRE 30.00 80.00

2015-16 Select City to City Jerseys
PRINT RUNS B/WN 35-149 COPIES PER
*TIE DYE/25: .75X TO 2X BASIC
1 Clyde Drexler/49 10.00 25.00
2 LeBron James/149 60.00 150.00
3 Dan Majerle/49 4.00 10.00
4 Nick Young/149 2.50 6.00
5 Jalen Rose/149 3.00 8.00
6 Shaquille O'Neal/49 25.00 60.00
7 Karl Malone/49 10.00 25.00
8 Toni Kukoc/149 8.00 20.00
9 Adrian Dantley/99 4.00 10.00
10 Kevin Garnett/149 10.00 25.00
11 Boris Diaw/149 3.00 8.00
12 Luol Deng/149 3.00 8.00
13 Danilo Gallinari/149 3.00 8.00
14 Ray Allen/99 10.00 25.00
15 Jason Kidd/99 10.00 25.00
16 Tobias Harris/149 3.00 8.00
17 Kelly Tripucka/35 2.50 6.00
18 Wilson Chandler/49 3.00 8.00
19 Al Jefferson/49 2.50 6.00
20 Larry Johnson/149 5.00 12.00
21 Nikola Vucevic/149 3.00 8.00
22 Mark Jackson/99 3.00 8.00
23 Eric Gordon/149 3.00 8.00
24 Raymond Felton/149 2.50 6.00
25 Jrue Holiday/149 5.00 12.00

2015-16 Select Die Cut Autographs
PRINT RUNS B/WN 25-60 COPIES PER
EXCHANGE DEADLINE 9/9/2017
1 Chris Andersen/25 10.00 25.00
2 Reggie Jackson/60 6.00 15.00
3 Jrue Holiday/25 8.00 20.00
4 Jordan Clarkson/60 5.00 12.00
5 Ben McLemore/25 4.00 10.00
6 Ray McCallum/60 3.00 8.00
7 Tyler Ennis/60 3.00 8.00
8 Victor Oladipo/25 5.00 12.00
9 Mike Conley/60 5.00 12.00
10 Harrison Barnes/25 5.00 12.00
11 Thabo Sefolosha/60 3.00 8.00
12 Ryan Anderson/60 3.00 8.00
13 Jason Terry/60 4.00 10.00
14 Shabazz Muhammad/60 3.00 8.00
15 Donatas Motiejunas/60 3.00 8.00
16 Julius Randle/25 10.00 25.00
17 Ed Davis/60 3.00 8.00
18 Josh Smith/25 4.00 10.00
19 Goran Dragic/60 5.00 12.00
20 T.J. Warren/60 5.00 12.00
21 Steven Adams/60 10.00 25.00
22 Brandon Knight/60 3.00 8.00
23 Andre Drummond/25 6.00 15.00
24 Trey Burke/60 3.00 8.00
25 Andrew Bogut/60 3.00 8.00
26 Langston Galloway/60 3.00 8.00
27 Zach Randolph/25 6.00 15.00
28 C.J. McCollum/60 5.00 12.00
29 Michael Carter-Williams/60 8.00 20.00
30 Kevin Martin/25 5.00 12.00
31 Khris Middleton/60 6.00 15.00
32 Alec Burks/60 3.00 8.00
33 Chris Paul/25 75.00 200.00
34 DeMarre Carroll/60 3.00 8.00
35 Brandon Bass/60 3.00 8.00
36 Kentavious Caldwell-Pope/25 3.00 8.00
37 Jusuf Nurkic/60 4.00 10.00
38 Kevin Love/25 12.00 30.00
39 Chris Bosh/25 10.00 25.00
40 Dwyane Wade/25 40.00 100.00
41 Otto Porter/25 5.00 12.00
42 Tony Allen/60 3.00 8.00
43 Oscar Robertson/25 30.00 80.00
44 Chris Mullin/60 10.00 25.00
45 Kareem Abdul-Jabbar/25 25.00 60.00
46 John Stockton/25 20.00 50.00
47 Connie Hawkins/60 8.00 20.00
48 Dennis Rodman/25 15.00 40.00
49 Tracy McGrady/25 15.00 40.00
50 Antonio McDyess/60 4.00 10.00
51 Steve Francis/60 8.00 20.00
52 Yao Ming/25 20.00 50.00
53 Anfernee Hardaway/25 20.00 50.00
54 Rick Barry/25 8.00 20.00
55 Jerry Lucas/60 6.00 15.00
56 Bill Walton/60 30.00 80.00
57 Alex English/60 5.00 12.00
58 Artis Gilmore/25 8.00 20.00
59 Ralph Sampson/60 4.00 10.00
60 Wes Unseld/25 8.00 20.00

2015-16 Select Die Cut Rookie Autographs
STATED PRINT RUN 60 SER.#'d SETS
EXCHANGE DEADLINE 9/9/2017
1 Karl-Anthony Towns 75.00 200.00
2 D'Angelo Russell 40.00 100.00
3 Jahlil Okafor 5.00 12.00
4 Emmanuel Mudiay 5.00 12.00
5 Kristaps Porzingis 100.00 250.00
6 Mario Hezonja 5.00 12.00
7 Justise Winslow 6.00 15.00
8 Willie Cauley-Stein 5.00 12.00
9 Stanley Johnson 5.00 12.00
10 Tyus Jones 5.00 12.00
11 Frank Kaminsky 5.00 12.00
12 Devin Booker 200.00 500.00
13 Myles Turner 15.00 40.00
14 Jerian Grant 4.00 10.00
15 Trey Lyles 5.00 12.00
16 Cameron Payne 6.00 15.00
17 Delon Wright 5.00 12.00
18 Rashad Vaughn 4.00 10.00
19 Kelly Oubre Jr. 6.00 15.00
20 Sam Dekker 4.00 10.00
21 Terry Rozier 6.00 15.00
22 Rondae Hollis-Jefferson 5.00 12.00
23 Bobby Portis 10.00 25.00
24 Justin Anderson 4.00 10.00
25 Kevon Looney 12.00 30.00
26 Jarell Martin 4.00 10.00
27 R.J. Hunter 4.00 10.00
28 Josh Huestis 4.00 10.00
29 Norman Powell 8.00 20.00
30 Jordan Mickey 4.00 10.00
31 Branden Dawson 4.00 10.00
32 Duje Dukan 4.00 10.00
33 Walter Tavares 4.00 10.00
34 Larry Nance Jr. 8.00 20.00
35 Jonathon Simmons 5.00 12.00
36 Aaron Harrison 5.00 12.00
37 Montrezl Harrell 15.00 40.00
38 Nikola Jokic 800.00 1,500.00
39 Raul Neto 4.00 10.00
40 Pat Connaughton 6.00 15.00

2015-16 Select Rookie Jersey Autographs
STATED PRINT RUN 125 SER.#'d SETS
EXCHANGE DEADLINE 9/9/2017
*COPPER/49: .5X TO 1.2X BASIC
1 Karl-Anthony Towns 20.00 50.00
2 D'Angelo Russell 12.00 30.00
3 Jahlil Okafor 4.00 10.00
4 Emmanuel Mudiay 4.00 10.00
5 Kristaps Porzingis 25.00 60.00
6 Mario Hezonja 4.00 10.00
7 Justise Winslow 5.00 12.00
8 Willie Cauley-Stein 6.00 15.00
9 Stanley Johnson 4.00 10.00
10 Tyus Jones 4.00 10.00
11 Frank Kaminsky 4.00 10.00
12 Devin Booker 400.00 800.00
13 Myles Turner 8.00 20.00
14 Jerian Grant 3.00 8.00
15 Trey Lyles 4.00 10.00
16 Cameron Payne 5.00 12.00
17 Delon Wright 4.00 10.00
19 Kelly Oubre Jr. 75.00 200.00
20 Sam Dekker 3.00 8.00
21 Terry Rozier 12.00 30.00
22 Rondae Hollis-Jefferson 3.00 8.00
23 Bobby Portis 8.00 20.00
24 Justin Anderson 3.00 8.00
25 Kevon Looney 10.00 25.00
26 Jarell Martin 3.00 8.00
27 R.J. Hunter 3.00 8.00
28 Anthony Brown 3.00 8.00
29 Chris McCullough 3.00 8.00
30 Jordan Mickey 3.00 8.00
31 Josh Huestis 3.00 8.00
32 Montrezl Harrell 10.00 25.00
33 Richaun Holmes 5.00 12.00

2015-16 Select Rookie Jersey Autographs Prizms Tie Dye
*TIE DYE: 2X TO 5X BASIC
STATED PRINT RUN 25 SER.#'d SETS
EXCHANGE DEADLINE 9/9/2017

2015-16 Select Rookie Signatures
STATED PRINT RUN 199 SER.#'d SETS
EXCHANGE DEADLINE 9/9/2017
*COPPER/49: .5X TO 1.2X BASIC
RSSD Sam Dekker 3.00 8.00
RSFK Frank Kaminsky 4.00 10.00
RSKO Kelly Oubre Jr. 40.00 100.00
RSRH Rondae Hollis-Jefferson 3.00 8.00
RSBP Bobby Portis 8.00 20.00
RSJO Jahlil Okafor 4.00 10.00
RSKL Kevon Looney 10.00 25.00
RSAB Anthony Brown 3.00 8.00
RSRN Raul Neto 3.00 8.00
RSCP Cameron Payne 5.00 12.00
RSJM Jarell Martin 3.00 8.00
RSKP Kristaps Porzingis 60.00 150.00
RSJS Jonathon Simmons 4.00 10.00
RSJR Josh Richardson 5.00 12.00
RSJG Jerian Grant 3.00 8.00
RSMH Mario Hezonja 3.00 8.00
RSTR Terry Rozier 12.00 30.00
RSTM T.J. McConnell 20.00 50.00
RSDR D'Angelo Russell 20.00 50.00
RSJK Jordan Mickey 3.00 8.00
RSLN Larry Nance Jr. 6.00 15.00
RSDL Delon Wright 4.00 10.00
RSJA Justin Anderson 3.00 8.00
RSMT Myles Turner 15.00 40.00
RSWT Walter Tavares 3.00 8.00
RSNP Norman Powell 6.00 15.00
RSDB Devin Booker 300.00 600.00
RSJW Justise Winslow 8.00 20.00
RSWC Willie Cauley-Stein 10.00 25.00
RSEM Emmanuel Mudiay 4.00 10.00
RSKT Karl-Anthony Towns 50.00 120.00
RSRV Rashad Vaughn 3.00 8.00
RSNB Nemanja Bjelica 5.00 12.00
RSDD Duje Dukan 3.00 8.00
RSDH Darrun Hilliard 3.00 8.00
RSNJ Nikola Jokic 1,000.00 2,000.00

2015-16 Select Rookie Swatches
STATED PRINT RUN 149 COPIES PER
*PURPLE/99: .5X TO 1.25X BASIC
*ORANGE/60: .6X TO 1.5X BASIC
*TIE DYE/25: 1.25X TO 3X BASIC
1 Jahlil Okafor 3.00 8.00
2 Mario Hezonja 3.00 8.00
3 Justise Winslow 4.00 10.00
4 Frank Kaminsky 3.00 8.00
5 Karl-Anthony Towns 15.00 40.00
6 Jerian Grant 2.50 6.00
7 Delon Wright 3.00 8.00
8 Willie Cauley-Stein 3.00 8.00
10 D'Angelo Russell 10.00 25.00
11 Kelly Oubre Jr. 8.00 20.00
12 Terry Rozier 10.00 25.00
13 Stanley Johnson 3.00 8.00
14 Sam Dekker 2.50 6.00
15 Jordan Mickey 2.50 6.00
16 Emmanuel Mudiay 3.00 8.00
17 Chris McCullough 2.50 6.00
18 Kevon Looney 8.00 20.00
19 Tyus Jones 3.00 8.00
20 Devin Booker 30.00 80.00
21 Rondae Hollis-Jefferson 3.00 8.00
22 Kristaps Porzingis 15.00 40.00
23 Myles Turner 10.00 25.00
24 Trey Lyles 3.00 8.00
25 Bobby Portis 6.00 15.00
26 Justin Anderson 2.50 6.00
27 Cameron Payne 4.00 10.00
28 Jarell Martin 2.50 6.00
29 R.J. Hunter 2.50 6.00
30 Anthony Brown 2.50 6.00

2015-16 Select Signatures
PRINT RUNS B/WN 99-149 COPIES PER
EXCHANGE DEADLINE 9/9/2017
*COPPER/49: .5X TO 1.2X BASIC
1 Kobe Bryant/99 600.00 1,200.00
2 Clyde Drexler/99 20.00 50.00
3 Bill Walton/149 25.00 60.00
4 Zach LaVine/149 25.00 60.00
5 Gary Harris/149 5.00 12.00
6 Mo Williams/149 5.00 12.00
7 Kevin Durant/99 75.00 200.00
8 Jason Kidd/99 20.00 50.00
9 Robert Parish/149 8.00 20.00
10 Doug McDermott/149 5.00 12.00
11 Elfrid Payton/149 5.00 12.00
12 Blake Griffin/99 6.00 15.00
13 Chris Paul/99 40.00 100.00
14 Kevin Love/99 6.00 15.00
15 Mark Jackson/149 5.00 12.00
16 Carmelo Anthony/99 40.00 100.00
17 Kenny Anderson/149 5.00 12.00
18 T.J. Warren/149 6.00 15.00
19 Julius Erving/99 75.00 200.00
20 Tracy McGrady/99 40.00 100.00
21 Dikembe Mutombo/149 15.00 40.00
22 Victor Oladipo/25 5.00 12.00
24 Mike Conley/149 6.00 15.00
25 Karl Malone/99 25.00 60.00
26 Anfernee Hardaway/99 50.00 120.00
27 Marcin Gortat/149 4.00 10.00
28 Tony Allen/149 4.00 10.00
29 Bojan Bogdanovic/149 5.00 12.00
30 Gary Neal/149 4.00 10.00
31 Anthony Davis/99 40.00 100.00
32 Gary Payton/99 20.00 50.00
33 Allan Houston/149 5.00 12.00
34 Cuttino Mobley/149 5.00 12.00
35 Langston Galloway/149 4.00 10.00
36 Dwyane Wade/99 40.00 100.00
37 Alonzo Mourning/99 20.00 50.00
38 Kenneth Faried/149 5.00 12.00
39 Danny Green/149 4.00 10.00
40 Antoine Carr/149 4.00 10.00
41 Chris Bosh/99 12.00 30.00
42 Nene/149 5.00 12.00
43 Timofey Mozgov/149 4.00 10.00
44 Andre Drummond/149 6.00 15.00
46 Thaddeus Young/149 4.00 10.00
47 Jonas Valanciunas/149 5.00 12.00
48 Joe Ingles/149 4.00 10.00
49 John Wall/99 8.00 20.00
50 J.R. Smith/149 12.00 30.00
51 Sonny Weems/149 4.00 10.00
52 Marcus Smart/99 12.00 30.00
53 Mason Plumlee/149 4.00 10.00
54 Tony Parker/99 20.00 50.00
56 Andrew Wiggins/99 15.00 40.00
57 Julius Randle/99 8.00 20.00
58 Tim Hardaway Jr./149 5.00 12.00
59 Tarik Black/149 5.00 12.00
60 Gordon Hayward/149 6.00 15.00

2015-16 Select Sparks Jerseys
PRINT RUNS B/WN 49-99 COPIES PER
1 John Stockton/49 4.00 10.00
2 Stephen Curry/99 25.00 60.00
3 Gary Payton/99 5.00 12.00
4 Derrick Rose/99 5.00 12.00
5 DeMar DeRozan/99 4.00 10.00
6 Paul George/49 5.00 12.00
7 Carmelo Anthony/99 5.00 12.00
8 Kobe Bryant/99 8.00 20.00
9 Tony Parker/99 5.00 12.00
10 Kyrie Irving/99 6.00 15.00
11 Jimmy Butler/99 6.00 15.00
12 LeBron James/99 10.00 25.00
13 Elfrid Payton/99 2.50 6.00
14 Russell Westbrook/99 4.00 10.00
15 Damian Lillard/99 5.00 12.00
16 Manu Ginobili/99 5.00 12.00
17 Allen Iverson/49 8.00 20.00
18 Kevin Durant/99 6.00 15.00
19 John Wall/99 4.00 10.00
20 Anthony Davis/99 6.00 15.00
21 Jason Kidd/99 5.00 12.00
22 James Harden/99 6.00 15.00
23 Dwyane Wade/99 6.00 15.00
24 Ricky Rubio/99 2.50 6.00
25 Chris Paul/99 4.00 10.00

2015-16 Select Sparks Jerseys Prizms Tie Dye
*TIE DYE: 1X TO 2.5X BASIC
PRINT RUNS B/WN 15-25 COPIES PER
1 John Stockton/25 20.00 50.00
2 Stephen Curry/15 60.00 150.00
3 Gary Payton/25 15.00 40.00
4 Derrick Rose/25 25.00 60.00
7 Carmelo Anthony/15 15.00 40.00
8 Kobe Bryant/25 50.00 120.00
12 LeBron James/25 60.00 150.00
14 Russell Westbrook/25 20.00 50.00
17 Allen Iverson/25 20.00 50.00
18 Kevin Durant/25 20.00 50.00
22 James Harden/25 15.00 40.00

2015-16 Select Swatches
PRINT RUNS B/WN 60-149 COPIES PER
*PURPLE/49-99: .5X TO 1.25X BASIC
*ORANGE/35-60: .6X TO 1.5X BASIC
*TIE DYE/15-25: 1.25X TO 3X BASIC
1 John Wall/99 4.00 10.00
2 Manu Ginobili/60 6.00 15.00
3 Kevin Durant/60 12.00 30.00
4 Zach LaVine/60 8.00 20.00

5 Chris Bosh/149 4.00 10.00
6 Paul George/60 5.00 12.00
7 Rodney Hood/99 2.50 6.00
8 Kevin Love/60 3.00 8.00
9 Marcin Gortat/99 2.00 5.00
10 Dirk Nowitzki/149 8.00 20.00
11 Bradley Beal/99 4.00 10.00
12 Kawhi Leonard/149 10.00 25.00
13 Tobias Harris/149 2.50 6.00
14 Ricky Rubio/99 2.50 6.00
15 Vince Carter/99 6.00 15.00
16 James Harden/60 6.00 15.00
17 Brandon Jennings/99 2.00 5.00
18 Joakim Noah/149 2.00 5.00
19 Nene/149 2.50 6.00
20 Tim Hardaway Jr./60 2.50 6.00
21 Gordon Hayward/99 3.00 8.00
22 DeMarcus Cousins/149 3.00 8.00
23 Russell Westbrook/149 5.00 12.00
24 Eric Gordon/99 2.50 6.00
25 Mike Conley/60 3.00 8.00
26 Dwight Howard/60 4.00 10.00
27 Metta World Peace/149 2.00 5.00
28 Jimmy Butler/99 6.00 15.00
29 Terrence Ross/60 2.50 6.00
30 Kenneth Faried/99 2.50 6.00
31 Kyle Lowry/99 3.00 8.00
32 Damian Lillard/149 8.00 20.00
33 Langston Galloway/149 2.00 5.00
34 Andrew Wiggins/99 4.00 10.00
35 Marc Gasol/149 3.00 8.00
36 Stephen Curry/99 75.00 200.00
37 Kevin Garnett/149 8.00 20.00
38 Derrick Rose/99 5.00 12.00
39 Jose Calderon/149 2.00 5.00
40 Chandler Parsons/99 2.00 5.00
41 DeMar DeRozan/60 4.00 10.00
42 Eric Bledsoe/149 2.50 6.00
43 Carmelo Anthony/60 5.00 12.00
44 Giannis Antetokounmpo/60 40.00 100.00
45 DeAndre Jordan/149 2.50 6.00
46 Klay Thompson/60 8.00 20.00
47 Marcus Smart/99 4.00 10.00
48 Kemba Walker/99 3.00 8.00
49 T.J. Warren/99 3.00 8.00
50 LeBron James/60 75.00 200.00
51 Tony Parker/99 5.00 12.00
52 Nerlens Noel/99 2.00 5.00
53 Ryan Anderson/60 2.00 5.00
54 Mario Chalmers/149 2.50 6.00
55 Chris Paul/99 6.00 15.00
56 Harrison Barnes/99 2.50 6.00
57 Avery Bradley/99 2.00 5.00
58 Dennis Schroder/99 3.00 8.00
59 Alex Len/149 2.00 5.00
60 Kobe Bryant/149 60.00 150.00
61 Tim Duncan/99 8.00 20.00
62 Victor Oladipo/149 2.50 6.00
63 Tyreke Evans/99 2.50 6.00
64 Dwyane Wade/60 6.00 15.00
65 Blake Griffin/99 3.00 8.00
66 Draymond Green/99 4.00 10.00
67 Kyrie Irving/99 6.00 15.00
68 Al Horford/149 3.00 8.00
69 Ian Mahinmi/149 2.00 5.00
70 Jared Sullinger/149 2.00 5.00

2015-16 Select Throwback Memorabilia

PRINT RUNS B/WN 35-149 COPIES PER
1 Kevin Garnett/149 8.00 20.00
2 J.J. Barea/149 2.50 6.00
3 Danilo Gallinari/149 2.50 6.00
4 Richard Jefferson/49 2.50 6.00
5 Devin Harris/49 2.00 5.00
6 Timofey Mozgov/149 2.00 5.00
7 Iman Shumpert/149 2.00 5.00
8 Jeff Green/49 2.00 5.00
9 Al Jefferson/49 2.00 5.00
10 Kevin Martin/149 2.50 6.00
11 Brandon Knight/149 2.00 5.00
12 Pau Gasol/149 5.00 12.00
13 Zaza Pachulia/149 2.00 5.00
14 Robert Covington/149 2.50 6.00
15 Dion Waiters/149 2.00 5.00
16 Tobias Harris/149 2.50 6.00
17 Isaiah Thomas/149 2.50 6.00
18 Jeremy Lin/149 6.00 15.00
19 Amare Stoudemire/149 3.00 8.00
20 LeBron James/149 10.00 25.00
21 Chandler Parsons/149 2.00 5.00
22 Paul Millsap/149 2.50 6.00
23 Darren Collison/149 2.00 5.00
24 Rudy Gay/149 3.00 8.00
25 Evan Turner/149 2.00 5.00
26 Trevor Ariza/149 2.00 5.00
27 J.R. Smith/149 3.00 8.00
28 Jodie Meeks/149 2.00 5.00
29 Andre Miller/149 2.50 6.00
30 Lou Williams/149 2.50 6.00
31 Channing Frye/149 2.00 5.00
32 Paul Pierce/149 5.00 12.00
33 DeJuan Blair/149 2.00 5.00
34 Thabo Sefolosha/149 2.00 5.00
35 Gerald Green/149 2.50 6.00
36 Tyson Chandler/149 2.50 6.00
37 Jamal Crawford/49 3.00 8.00
38 Boris Diaw/149 2.50 6.00
39 Anthony Bennett/149 2.00 5.00
40 Matt Barnes/149 2.00 5.00
41 Corey Brewer/149 2.00 5.00
42 Raymond Felton/149 2.00 5.00
43 DeMarre Carroll/122 2.00 5.00
44 Thaddeus Young/149 2.00 5.00
45 Mike Dunleavy/149 2.00 5.00
46 Vince Carter/149 6.00 15.00
47 Jarrett Jack/149 2.50 6.00
48 Kevin Love/149 3.00 8.00
49 Arron Afflalo/149 2.00 5.00
50 Mo Williams/149 2.50 6.00

2015-16 Select Throwback Memorabilia Prizms Tie Dye

*TIE DYE: 1X TO 2.5X BASIC
PRINT RUNS B/WN 14-25 COPIES PER
20 LeBron James/25 60.00 150.00
46 Vince Carter/25 20.00 50.00

2016-17 Select Prizms Blue

*PRIZMS BLUE: 2X TO 5X BASIC
*PRIZMS BLUE RC: 1.25X TO 3X BASIC RC
STATED PRINT RUN 299 SER.#'d SETS
33 Jaylen Brown 50.00 120.00

2016-17 Select Prizms Copper

*PRIZMS COPPER: 1X TO 2.5X BASIC
*PRIZMS COPPER RC: .6X TO 1.5X BASIC RC
STATED PRINT RUN 49 SER.#'d SETS
232 Dario Saric 30.00 80.00
258 Nikola Jokic 75.00 200.00
270 Buddy Hield 6.00 15.00
275 Jamal Murray 400.00 800.00
279 Skal Labissiere 12.00 30.00
280 Brandon Ingram 300.00 600.00
286 LeBron James 1,000.00 2,000.00
287 Andre Iguodala 10.00 25.00
288 Kawhi Leonard 12.00 30.00
289 LeBron James 1,000.00 2,000.00
290 LeBron James 1,000.00 2,000.00
291 Dirk Nowitzki 20.00 50.00
292 Kobe Bryant 20.00 50.00
293 Kobe Bryant 20.00 50.00
294 Paul Pierce 12.00 30.00
295 Tony Parker 15.00 40.00
296 Dwyane Wade 20.00 50.00
297 Chauncey Billups 6.00 15.00
298 Shaquille O'Neal 10.00 25.00
299 Shaquille O'Neal 10.00 25.00
300 Shaquille O'Neal 10.00 25.00

2016-17 Select Prizms Light Blue Die-Cut

*PRIZMS LT.BLUE: 1.2X TO 3X BASIC
*PRIZMS LT.BLUE RC: .75X TO 2X BASIC RC
STATED PRINT RUN 199 SER.#'d SETS
161 Stephen Curry 15.00 40.00
174 Jaylen Brown 50.00 120.00

2016-17 Select Prizms Maroon

*PRIZMS MARN: 2.5X TO 6X BASIC
*PRIZMS MARN RC: 1.5X TO 4X BASIC RC
STATED PRINT RUN 175 SER.#'d SETS
33 Jaylen Brown 60.00 150.00

2016-17 Select Prizms Neon Yellow Die-Cut

*PRIZMS YLLW: 2X TO 5X BASIC
*PRIZMS YLLW RC: 1.2X TO 3X BASIC RC
STATED PRINT RUN 75 SER.#'d SETS
122 Buddy Hield 10.00 25.00
126 Kris Dunn 3.00 8.00
161 Stephen Curry 50.00 120.00
174 Jaylen Brown 100.00 250.00

2016-17 Select Prizms Orange

*PRIZMS ORNGE: 4X TO 10X BASIC
*PRIZMS ORNGE RC: 2.5X TO 6X BASIC RC
STATED PRINT RUN 60 SER.#'d SETS
33 Jaylen Brown 100.00 250.00

2016-17 Select Prizms Purple Die-Cut

*PRIZMS PURPLE: 1X TO 2.5X BASIC
*PRIZMS PURPLE RC: .6X TO 1.5X BASIC RC
STATED PRINT RUN 99 SER.#'d SETS
101 Brandon Ingram 50.00 120.00
118 Pascal Siakam 40.00 100.00
122 Buddy Hield 12.00 30.00
161 Stephen Curry 25.00 60.00
174 Jaylen Brown 75.00 200.00

2016-17 Select Prizms Silver

*SILVER 1-100: 1X TO 3X BASIC
*SILVER 1-100 RC: .75X TO 2X BASIC RC
*SILVER 101-200: .6X TO 1.5X BASIC
*SILVER 101-200 RC: .4X TO 1X BASIC RC
*SILVER 201-300: .6X TO 1.5X BASIC
*SILVER 201-300 RC: .4X TO 1X BASIC RC
4 Jamal Murray 20.00 50.00
33 Jaylen Brown 25.00 60.00
88 Stephen Curry 20.00 50.00
91 Brandon Ingram 40.00 100.00
101 Brandon Ingram 50.00 120.00
161 Stephen Curry 15.00 40.00
174 Jaylen Brown 25.00 60.00
194 Domantas Sabonis 20.00 50.00
205 Giannis Antetokounmpo 15.00 40.00
251 Ben Simmons 2.50 6.00
253 Devin Booker 25.00 60.00
258 Nikola Jokic 40.00 100.00
273 Domantas Sabonis 40.00 100.00
275 Jamal Murray 75.00 200.00
280 Brandon Ingram 75.00 200.00
286 LeBron James 500.00 1,000.00
289 LeBron James 500.00 1,000.00
290 LeBron James 500.00 1,000.00
292 Kobe Bryant 75.00 200.00
293 Kobe Bryant 75.00 200.00

2016-17 Select Prizms Tie-Dye

*PRIZM TD 1-100: 6X TO 15X BASIC
*PRIZM TD 1-100 RC: 4X TO 10X BASIC RC
*PRIZM TD 101-200: 6X TO 15X BASIC
*PRIZM TD 101-200 RC: 4X TO 10X BASIC RC
*PRIZM TD 201-300: 6X TO 15X BASIC
*PRIZM TD 201-300 RC: 4X TO 10X BASIC RC
STATED PRINT RUN 25 SER.#'d SETS
33 Jaylen Brown 125.00 300.00
174 Jaylen Brown 125.00 300.00
258 Nikola Jokic 150.00 400.00
286 LeBron James 500.00 1,000.00
287 Andre Iguodala 40.00 100.00
288 Kawhi Leonard 150.00 400.00
289 LeBron James 500.00 1,000.00
290 LeBron James 500.00 1,000.00
291 Dirk Nowitzki 150.00 400.00
292 Kobe Bryant 800.00 1,500.00
293 Kobe Bryant 800.00 1,500.00
294 Paul Pierce 75.00 200.00
295 Tony Parker 75.00 200.00
296 Dwyane Wade 75.00 200.00
297 Chauncey Billups 40.00 100.00
298 Shaquille O'Neal 60.00 150.00
299 Shaquille O'Neal 60.00 150.00
300 Shaquille O'Neal 60.00 150.00

2016-17 Select Prizms Tri-Color

*TRICLR 1-100: 1.2X TO 3X BASIC
*TRICLR 1-100 RC: .75X TO 2X BASIC RC
*TRICLR 101-200: .6X TO 1.5X BASIC
*TRICLR 101-200 RC: .4X TO 1X BASIC RC
4 Jamal Murray 75.00 200.00
88 Stephen Curry 15.00 40.00
91 Brandon Ingram 30.00 80.00
101 Brandon Ingram 30.00 80.00
161 Stephen Curry 12.00 30.00

2016-17 Select Prizms White

*PRIZMS WHITE: 2.5X TO 6X BASIC
*PRIZMS WHITE RC: 1.5X TO 4X BASIC RC
STATED PRINT RUN 149 SER.#'d SETS
33 Jaylen Brown 60.00 150.00

2016-17 Select Die-Cut Autographs

PRINT RUNS B/WN 49-99 COPIES PER
*PLSR p/r 49-60: .4X TO 1X p/r 49-60
*PLSR p/r 49-60: .5X TO 1.2X p/r 75-99
*PLSR p/r 35: .5X TO 1.2X p/r 49-60
*PLSR p/r 35: .6X TO 1.5X p/r 75-99
*SCPE p/r 49: .4X TO 1X p/r 49-60
*SCPE p/r 49: .5X TO 1.2X p/r 75-99
*SCPE p/r 25: .6X TO 1.5X p/r 49-60
*SCPE p/r 25: .75X TO 2X p/r 75-99
1 Michael Carter-Williams/60 3.00 8.00
2 Shawn Kemp/99 20.00 50.00
3 Scottie Pippen/49 40.00 100.00
4 Jim Jackson/99 3.00 8.00
5 Yao Ming/49 25.00 60.00
6 Glen Rice/99 4.00 10.00
7 Jeff Hornacek/99 3.00 8.00
8 Kevon Looney/99 4.00 10.00
9 Sean Elliott/99 6.00 15.00
10 Dirk Nowitzki/49 60.00 150.00
11 Artis Gilmore/60 6.00 15.00
12 Rick Barry/49 6.00 15.00
13 D'Angelo Russell/49 6.00 15.00
14 Dennis Rodman/49 20.00 50.00
15 Toni Kukoc/99 10.00 25.00
16 Bernard King/60 6.00 15.00
17 Chauncey Billups/75 5.00 12.00
18 Louie Dampier/75 6.00 15.00
19 Vince Carter/49 12.00 30.00
20 Carmelo Anthony/49 12.00 30.00
21 Adrian Dantley/99 4.00 10.00
22 Dwyane Wade/49 25.00 60.00
23 Jordan Clarkson/99 4.00 10.00
24 Rick Fox/99 3.00 8.00
25 Cedric Ceballos/99 3.00 8.00
26 Kobe Bryant/60 500.00 1,000.00
27 Tristan Thompson/99 3.00 8.00
28 Tyler Ennis/99 2.50 6.00
29 Michael Kidd-Gilchrist/49 3.00 8.00
30 Dante Exum/49 4.00 10.00
31 Latrell Sprewell/99 5.00 12.00
32 David Robinson/49 15.00 40.00
33 Spud Webb/99 5.00 12.00
34 Jalen Rose/99 3.00 8.00
35 Victor Oladipo/99 3.00 8.00
36 Gary Harris/75 3.00 8.00
37 Chris Paul/49 40.00 100.00
38 Shaquille O'Neal/49 30.00 80.00
39 Kevin Durant/49 75.00 200.00
40 Anthony Davis/49 60.00 150.00
41 Anthony Bennett/49 3.00 8.00
42 Cody Zeller/49 3.00 8.00
43 Alex Len/49 3.00 8.00
44 Dan Majerle/99 5.00 12.00
45 Jamal Mashburn/99 5.00 12.00
46 Deron Williams/49 4.00 10.00
47 Reggie Jackson/99 3.00 8.00
48 Horace Grant/99 4.00 10.00
49 Michael Finley/99 4.00 10.00
50 Bob Lanier/49 6.00 15.00
51 Jamaal Wilkes/99 4.00 10.00
52 Brian Grant/99 3.00 8.00
53 David Thompson/75 5.00 12.00
54 Michael Cooper/99 4.00 10.00
55 Kyrie Irving/49 40.00 100.00
56 Kevin Love/49 10.00 25.00
57 Karl Malone/49 20.00 50.00
58 Calvin Murphy/99 4.00 10.00
59 Jeremy Lin/49 50.00 120.00

2016-17 Select Die-Cut Rookie Autographs

STATED PRINTED RUN 199 SER.#'d SETS
*PULSAR/99: .5X TO 1.2X BASIC
*SCOPE/49: .6X TO 1.5X BASIC
1 Domantas Sabonis 40.00 100.00
2 Pascal Siakam 25.00 60.00
3 Malcolm Brogdon 8.00 20.00
4 Jakob Poeltl 5.00 12.00
5 Henry Ellenson 2.50 6.00
6 Wade Baldwin IV 2.50 6.00
7 Ivica Zubac 6.00 15.00
8 Timothe Luwawu-Cabarrot 4.00 10.00
9 Thon Maker 3.00 8.00
10 Jamal Murray 50.00 120.00
11 Buddy Hield 8.00 20.00
12 Cheick Diallo 2.50 6.00
13 Kris Dunn 4.00 10.00
14 Marquese Chriss 3.00 8.00
15 Malik Beasley 5.00 12.00
16 Dragan Bender 2.50 6.00
17 Georges Niang 4.00 10.00
19 Deyonta Davis 2.50 6.00
20 DeAndre' Bembry 4.00 10.00
21 Denzel Valentine 2.50 6.00
22 Damian Jones 2.50 6.00
23 Brice Johnson 2.50 6.00
25 Marshall Plumlee 2.50 6.00
26 Ron Baker 2.50 6.00
27 Brandon Ingram 25.00 60.00
28 Jake Layman 3.00 8.00
29 Jaylen Brown 150.00 400.00
30 Willy Hernangomez 3.00 8.00
31 Paul Zipser 2.50 6.00
32 A.J. Hammons 2.50 6.00
33 Michael Gbinije 2.50 6.00
34 Mindaugas Kuzminskas 2.50 6.00
35 Sean Kilpatrick 2.50 6.00
36 Georgios Papagiannis 2.50 6.00
37 Kay Felder 2.50 6.00
38 Juan Hernangomez 5.00 12.00
39 Demetrius Jackson 2.50 6.00
40 Dorian Finney-Smith 3.00 8.00

2016-17 Select Duets Memorabilia

STATED PRINT RUN 149 SER.#'d SETS
1 James/Irving 40.00 100.00
2 Thompson/Curry 15.00 40.00
3 DeMar DeRozan
Kyle Lowry 4.00 10.00
4 Paul/Griffin 5.00 12.00
5 Wiggins/LaVine 6.00 15.00
6 Anthony/Porzingis 5.00 12.00
7 Beal/Wall 4.00 10.00
9 DeMarcus Cousins
Rudy Gay 3.00 8.00
10 Leonard/Aldridge 8.00 20.00
11 Kemba Walker
Michael Kidd-Gilchrist 2.50 6.00
13 Williams/Nowitzki 8.00 20.00
14 Andre Drummond
Kentavious Caldwell-Pope 3.00 8.00
15 Russell/Clarkson 4.00 10.00
16 Marc Gasol
Mike Conley 3.00 8.00
17 Hassan Whiteside
Justise Winslow 2.50 6.00
18 Monroe/Giannis 12.00 30.00
20 Aaron Gordon
Nikola Vucevic 3.00 8.00
21 McCollum/Lillard 8.00 20.00
23 Bledsoe/Booker 12.00 30.00
24 Thomas/Smart 4.00 10.00

2016-17 Select Duets Memorabilia Prizms Copper

*COPPER: .5X TO 1.2X BASIC
STATED PRINT RUN 49 SER.#'d SETS
19 Westbrook/Adams 6.00 15.00
25 Harden/Beverley 8.00 20.00

2016-17 Select Duets Memorabilia Prizms Purple

*PURPLE: .4X TO 1X BASIC
PRINT RUNS B/WN 78-99 COPIES PER
19 Westbrook/Adams 5.00 12.00
25 Harden/Beverley/78 6.00 15.00

2016-17 Select Duets Memorabilia Prizms Tie-Dye

*TIEDYE: .75X TO 2X BASIC
PRINT RUNS B/WN 10-25 COPIES PER
NO PRICING ON QTY 10
19 Westbrook/Adams 10.00 25.00
24 Thomas/Smart 8.00 20.00

2016-17 Select In Flight Signatures

STATED PRINT RUN 99 SER.#'d SETS
*ORANGE/60: .5X TO 1.2X BASIC
*TIEDYE/25: .75X TO 2X BASIC
1 Julius Erving 75.00 200.00
2 Kobe Bryant 1,250.00 2,500.00
4 Clyde Drexler 30.00 80.00
5 Ray Allen 50.00 120.00
6 Norman Powell 8.00 20.00
7 Shawn Kemp 30.00 80.00
8 Spud Webb 12.00 30.00
10 Kyrie Irving 75.00 200.00
12 Carmelo Anthony 75.00 200.00
13 Jordan Clarkson 12.00 30.00
14 Justise Winslow 6.00 15.00
15 Zach LaVine 40.00 100.00
16 Grant Hill 25.00 60.00
17 Latrell Sprewell 20.00 50.00
18 Eric Bledsoe 6.00 15.00
19 Reggie Jackson 6.00 15.00
20 Evan Fournier 6.00 15.00

2016-17 Select Rookie Signatures

STATED PRINT RUN 299 SER.#'d SETS
1 Brandon Ingram 25.00 60.00
2 Jaylen Brown 150.00 400.00
3 Buddy Hield 8.00 20.00
4 Kris Dunn 4.00 10.00
5 Jamal Murray 60.00 150.00
6 Marquese Chriss 3.00 8.00
7 Jakob Poeltl 5.00 12.00
8 Thon Maker 3.00 8.00
9 Domantas Sabonis 15.00 40.00
10 Dario Saric 4.00 10.00
11 Dragan Bender 2.50 6.00
12 Denzel Valentine 2.50 6.00
13 Taurean Prince 3.00 8.00
14 Skal Labissiere 2.50 6.00
15 Caris LeVert 6.00 15.00
16 Damian Jones 2.50 6.00
17 Demetrius Jackson 2.50 6.00
18 Henry Ellenson 2.50 6.00
19 Wade Baldwin IV 2.50 6.00
20 Juan Hernangomez 12.00 30.00
21 Timothe Luwawu-Cabarrot 4.00 10.00
22 Tyler Ulis 3.00 8.00
24 Malik Beasley 5.00 12.00
25 Mindaugas Kuzminskas 2.50 6.00
27 DeAndre' Bembry 4.00 10.00
29 Malachi Richardson 2.50 6.00
30 Pascal Siakam 25.00 60.00
31 Tomas Satoransky 4.00 10.00
32 Ivica Zubac 6.00 15.00
33 Malcolm Brogdon 8.00 20.00
35 Georges Niang 4.00 10.00
36 Jake Layman 3.00 8.00
37 Kay Felder 2.50 6.00
38 Paul Zipser 2.50 6.00
39 Stephen Zimmerman 2.50 6.00
40 Marshall Plumlee 2.50 6.00

2016-17 Select Rookie Signatures Prizms Orange

*ORANGE: .5X TO 1.2X BASIC

2016-17 Select Rookie Swatches

*PURPLE/99: .5X TO 1.2X BASIC
*ORANGE/60: .6X TO 1.5X BASIC
*TIEDYE/25: 1.25X TO 3X BASIC
1 A.J. Hammons 1.50 4.00
2 Brandon Ingram 6.00 15.00
3 Brice Johnson 1.50 4.00
4 Buddy Hield 5.00 12.00
5 Caris LeVert 4.00 10.00
6 Cheick Diallo 1.50 4.00
7 Chinanu Onuaku 1.50 4.00
8 Damian Jones 1.50 4.00
9 Dejounte Murray 8.00 20.00
10 Demetrius Jackson 1.50 4.00
11 Denzel Valentine 1.50 4.00
12 Deyonta Davis 1.50 4.00
13 Dragan Bender 1.50 4.00
15 Georgios Papagiannis 1.50 4.00
16 Henry Ellenson 1.50 4.00
17 Isaiah Whitehead 1.50 4.00
18 Ivica Zubac 4.00 10.00
19 Jakob Poeltl 3.00 8.00
20 Jamal Murray 12.00 30.00
21 Jaylen Brown 15.00 40.00
22 Juan Hernangomez 3.00 8.00
23 Kay Felder 1.50 4.00
24 Kris Dunn 2.50 6.00
25 Malachi Richardson 1.50 4.00
26 Malcolm Brogdon 5.00 12.00
27 Malik Beasley 3.00 8.00
28 Marquese Chriss 2.00 5.00
29 Pascal Siakam 10.00 25.00
30 Patrick McCaw 1.50 4.00
31 Skal Labissiere 1.50 4.00
32 Stephen Zimmerman 1.50 4.00
33 Thon Maker 2.00 5.00
34 Timothe Luwawu-Cabarrot 2.50 6.00
35 Tyler Ulis 2.00 5.00
36 Wade Baldwin IV 1.50 4.00

2016-17 Select Signatures

PRINT RUNS B/WN 99-149 COPIES PER
*ORANGE/60: .5X TO 1.2X BASIC
*TIEDYE/25: .75X TO 2X BASIC
1 Jeremy Lin/99 50.00 120.00
2 Reggie Jackson/149 6.00 15.00
3 Andrew Wiggins/99 15.00 40.00
4 John Starks/149 12.00 30.00
5 Kevin Durant/99 125.00 300.00
6 Ricky Rubio/99 12.00 30.00
7 Karl-Anthony Towns/99 30.00 80.00
8 Kyrie Irving/99 40.00 100.00
9 Kent Bazemore/149 5.00 12.00
10 Dennis Rodman/99 60.00 150.00
11 Anthony Davis/99 30.00 80.00
13 Jamal Mashburn/149 6.00 15.00
14 Dwyane Wade/99 40.00 100.00
15 Luol Deng/149 6.00 15.00
16 Evan Fournier/149 6.00 15.00
17 Marcelo Huertas/149 5.00 12.00
18 Sean Elliott/149 6.00 15.00
19 Allen Iverson/99 75.00 200.00
20 Marc Gasol/99 12.00 30.00
21 Festus Ezeli/149 5.00 12.00
22 Kobe Bryant/99 1,250.00 2,500.00
23 Shawn Kemp/149 20.00 50.00
26 Kevin Love/99 10.00 25.00
27 Langston Galloway/149 5.00 12.00
28 Jae Crowder/149 5.00 12.00
29 Clint Capela/149 6.00 15.00
31 Goran Dragic/99 8.00 20.00
32 Nicolas Batum/149 6.00 15.00
33 Kenneth Faried/99 6.00 15.00
34 Kristaps Porzingis/99 20.00 50.00
35 Justise Winslow/99 6.00 15.00
36 Jordan Clarkson/99 12.00 30.00
37 Tobias Harris/99 8.00 20.00
38 Boban Marjanovic/149 6.00 15.00
39 Nikola Jokic/149 125.00 300.00
40 Tony Parker/99 30.00 80.00

2016-17 Select Sparks Memorabilia

STATED PRINT RUN 199 SER.#'d SETS
*PURPLE/99: .4X TO 1X BASIC
1 Nikola Mirotic 2.00 5.00
2 J.R. Smith 3.00 8.00
3 Patrick Beverley 2.00 5.00
6 Devin Harris 2.00 5.00
7 Jamal Crawford 3.00 8.00
8 Jeff Green 2.00 5.00
9 Iman Shumpert 2.00 5.00
10 Shabazz Muhammad 2.00 5.00
12 Dante Exum 2.50 6.00
13 Otto Porter 2.50 6.00
18 Justin Anderson 2.00 5.00
19 Doug McDermott 2.50 6.00
20 Eric Gordon 2.50 6.00
22 Matthew Dellavedova 2.00 5.00
23 Chris McCullough 2.00 5.00
24 Brandon Knight 2.50 6.00
25 Marcus Smart 4.00 10.00

2016-17 Select Sparks Memorabilia Prizms Copper

*COPPER: .5X TO 1.2X BASIC
STATED PRINT RUN 49 SER.#'d SETS
17 Leandro Barbosa 2.50 6.00

2016-17 Select Sparks Memorabilia Prizms Tie-Dye

*TIEDYE: .75X TO 2X BASIC
PRINT RUNS B/WN 5-25 COPIES PER
NO PRICING ON QTY 5
4 T.J. Warren/25 5.00 12.00
7 Jamal Crawford/25 100.00 250.00
17 Leandro Barbosa/25 4.00 10.00
21 Rondae Hollis-Jefferson/25 4.00 10.00

2016-17 Select Swatches

1 Cody Zeller 1.50 4.00
2 Jimmy Butler 5.00 12.00
3 Tyler Zeller 1.50 4.00
4 Bojan Bogdanovic 2.00 5.00
5 Marcus Morris 1.50 4.00
6 Doug McDermott 2.00 5.00
7 Kyle Korver 2.00 5.00
8 Frank Kaminsky 1.50 4.00
9 Nikola Mirotic 1.50 4.00
10 Derrick Rose 4.00 10.00
11 LeBron James 25.00 60.00
12 Thabo Sefolosha 1.50 4.00
13 Michael Kidd-Gilchrist 1.50 4.00
14 Terry Rozier 2.50 6.00
15 Brook Lopez 2.00 5.00
16 Tony Parker 4.00 10.00
17 Kyrie Irving 5.00 12.00
18 Kentavious Caldwell-Pope 2.00 5.00
19 Kevin Love 2.50 6.00
20 Trevor Ariza 1.50 4.00
21 James Harden 5.00 12.00
23 Deron Williams 2.00 5.00
24 Nicolas Batum 2.00 5.00
25 DeMarre Carroll 1.50 4.00
26 Danny Green 2.00 5.00
27 Carmelo Anthony 4.00 10.00
28 George Hill 2.00 5.00
29 Monta Ellis 2.00 5.00
30 Dirk Nowitzki 4.00 10.00
31 Bradley Beal 3.00 8.00
32 Jamal Crawford 2.50 6.00
33 J.J. Redick 2.50 6.00
34 Jahlil Okafor 1.50 4.00
36 Russell Westbrook 4.00 10.00
37 Udonis Haslem 2.00 5.00
39 Rudy Gay 2.50 6.00
40 Rudy Gobert 3.00 8.00
41 Marc Gasol 2.50 6.00
42 Adreian Payne 1.50 4.00
43 Derrick Favors 1.50 4.00
44 Mike Conley 2.00 5.00
45 John Henson 1.50 4.00
46 Stephen Curry 12.00 30.00
47 Karl-Anthony Towns 5.00 12.00
48 Joakim Noah 1.50 4.00
49 Damian Lillard 4.00 10.00
50 Kyle Lowry 2.50 6.00
51 Ricky Rubio 2.00 5.00
52 Zach LaVine 5.00 12.00
53 Omer Asik 1.50 4.00
54 Myles Turner 2.50 6.00
55 Joe Johnson 2.50 6.00
57 Kevin Durant 10.00 25.00
58 Serge Ibaka 2.00 5.00
59 Rodney Hood 2.00 5.00
60 Manu Ginobili 5.00 12.00
61 Khris Middleton 2.50 6.00
62 Kawhi Leonard 6.00 15.00
63 Jonas Valanciunas 2.00 5.00
64 Kristaps Porzingis 4.00 10.00

2016-17 Select Swatches Prizms Orange

*ORANGE: .5X TO 1.2X BASIC
STATED PRINT RUN 60 SER.#'d SETS
11 LeBron James 40.00 100.00
35 Roy Hibbert 2.50 6.00
38 Zach Randolph 3.00 8.00

2016-17 Select Swatches Prizms Purple

*PURPLE: .5X TO 1.2X BASIC
STATED PRINT RUN 99 SER.#'d SETS
11 LeBron James 40.00 100.00
38 Zach Randolph 3.00 8.00

2016-17 Select Swatches Prizms Tie-Dye

*TIEDYE: 1X TO 2.5X BASIC
STATED PRINT RUN 25 SER.#'d SETS
2 Jimmy Butler 15.00 40.00
11 LeBron James 125.00 300.00
22 Terrence Ross 5.00 12.00
32 Jamal Crawford 100.00 250.00
35 Roy Hibbert 5.00 12.00
36 Russell Westbrook 25.00 60.00
38 Zach Randolph 6.00 15.00
46 Stephen Curry 60.00 150.00
64 Kristaps Porzingis 20.00 50.00

2016-17 Select Throwback Memorabilia

PRINT RUNS B/WN 50-199 COPIES PER
2 Luol Deng/199 2.50 6.00
3 Michael Beasley/199 2.00 5.00
4 David West/199 2.50 6.00
7 D.J. Augustin/199 2.00 5.00
8 Chandler Parsons/199 2.00 5.00
9 Paul Pierce/199 5.00 12.00
12 Monta Ellis/199 2.50 6.00
13 Iman Shumpert/199 2.00 5.00
14 Jrue Holiday/199 4.00 10.00
15 Jose Calderon/199 2.00 5.00
17 Leandro Barbosa/199 2.00 5.00
18 Michael Carter-Williams/199 2.00 5.00
19 LeBron James/85 40.00 100.00
20 Arron Afflalo/199 2.00 5.00
21 Derrick Williams/199 2.00 5.00
22 Michael Beasley/50 2.00 5.00
23 Eric Gordon/122 2.50 6.00
24 Isaiah Canaan/199 2.00 5.00
25 Jerryd Bayless/199 2.00 5.00
28 Nene/199 2.50 6.00
30 Vince Carter/199 6.00 15.00
31 David West/199 2.50 6.00
32 Vince Carter/199 6.00 15.00
33 Evan Fournier/199 2.50 6.00
34 Channing Frye/199 2.00 5.00
36 Jameer Nelson/199 2.00 5.00
38 Anthony Bennett/199 2.00 5.00
39 Evan Turner/199 2.00 5.00
41 Nicolas Batum/199 2.50 6.00
42 Miles Plumlee/199 2.00 5.00
43 Derrick Rose/199 5.00 12.00
45 Gerald Green/199 2.00 5.00
46 Vince Carter/199 6.00 15.00
47 Isaiah Thomas/199 2.50 6.00
48 Marcus Morris/199 2.00 5.00
49 Deron Williams/199 2.50 6.00

2016-17 Select Throwback Memorabilia Prizms Copper

*COPPER: .5X TO 1.2X BASIC
PRINT RUNS B/WN 48-49 COPIES PER
6 Isaiah Thomas/49 3.00 8.00

2016-17 Select Throwback Memorabilia Prizms Purple

*PURPLE: .4X TO 1X BASIC
STATED PRINT RUN 99 SER.#'d SETS
6 Isaiah Thomas 2.50 6.00
26 Tyson Chandler 2.50 6.00

2016-17 Select Throwback Memorabilia Prizms Tie-Dye

*TIEDYE: .75X TO 2X BASIC
PRINT RUNS B/WN 21-25 COPIES PER
6 Isaiah Thomas/25 5.00 12.00
19 LeBron James/25 125.00 300.00

2017-18 Select

1 Dirk Nowitzki 1.00 2.50
2 Ricky Rubio .30 .75
3 Giannis Antetokounmpo 2.00 5.00
4 Tyler Dorsey RC .50 1.25
5 Jerian Grant .25 .60
6 Josh Jackson RC .60 1.50
7 Al-Farouq Aminu .25 .60
8 Lauri Markkanen RC 3.00 8.00
9 Damian Lillard 1.00 2.50
10 Myles Turner .40 1.00
11 Donovan Mitchell RC 5.00 12.00
12 Rondae Hollis-Jefferson .25 .60
13 Gorgui Dieng .25 .60
14 Tyler Johnson .25 .60
15 Jerryd Bayless .25 .60
16 Jrue Holiday .50 1.25
17 Andre Iguodala .40 1.00
18 LeBron James 3.00 8.00
19 Daniel Theis RC 1.00 2.50
20 Nicolas Batum .25 .60
21 Doug McDermott .25 .60
22 Russell Westbrook .60 1.50
23 Ivan Rabb RC .50 1.25
24 Tyler Ulis .25 .60
25 Joe Johnson .30 .75
26 Justin Patton RC .50 1.25
27 Andrew Wiggins .50 1.25
28 Lonzo Ball RC 2.00 5.00
29 Dante Exum .25 .60
30 Nikola Jokic 2.50 6.00
31 Dwight Howard .50 1.25
32 Stephen Curry 3.00 8.00
33 Jae Crowder .25 .60
34 Victor Oladipo .30 .75
35 Joel Embiid .75 2.00
36 Kawhi Leonard 1.00 2.50
37 Aron Baynes .25 .60
38 Lou Williams .30 .75
39 Davon Reed RC .50 1.25
40 Nikola Mirotic .25 .60
41 Enes Kanter .25 .60
42 Sterling Brown RC .50 1.25
43 Jalen Jones RC .50 1.25
44 Vince Carter .75 2.00
45 John Collins RC 1.25 3.00
46 Kevin Durant 1.50 4.00
47 Ben McLemore .25 .60
48 Malcolm Brogdon .30 .75
49 De'Aaron Fox RC 4.00 10.00
50 Otto Porter Jr. .30 .75
51 Eric Bledsoe .30 .75
52 Terrence Ross .30 .75
53 James Ennis .25 .60
54 Wayne Selden RC .50 1.25
55 John Henson .25 .60
56 Kevin Love .40 1.00
57 Bogdan Bogdanovic RC 1.25 3.00
58 Markieff Morris .25 .60
59 DeAndre Jordan .30 .75
60 Patrick Beverley .25 .60
61 Eric Gordon .30 .75
62 Tobias Harris .30 .75
63 James Harden .75 2.00
64 Josh Richardson .30 .75
65 Jon Leuer .25 .60
66 Klay Thompson 1.00 2.50
67 Brandon Ingram .50 1.25
68 Markelle Fultz RC 1.25 3.00
69 DeMar DeRozan .50 1.25
70 Ramon Sessions .25 .60
71 Ersan Ilyasova .25 .60
72 Tony Parker .60 1.50
73 James Johnson .25 .60
74 Marcus Smart .40 1.00
75 Jonas Valanciunas .30 .75
76 Kris Dunn .25 .60
77 Brook Lopez .30 .75
78 Marquese Chriss .30 .75
79 DeMarcus Cousins .30 .75
80 Raymond Felton .25 .60
81 Garrett Temple .25 .60
82 Trevor Ariza .25 .60
83 Jarrett Allen RC 1.25 3.00
84 Yogi Ferrell .25 .60
85 Jonathon Simmons .25 .60
86 Kyrie Irving .75 2.00
87 Caleb Swanigan RC .50 1.25
88 Meyers Leonard .25 .60
89 Dennis Schroder .30 .75
90 Reggie Jackson .30 .75
91 Gary Harris .30 .75
92 Trevor Booker .25 .60
93 Jayson Tatum RC 15.00 40.00
94 Zach Collins RC .75 2.00
95 Jordan Bell RC .50 1.25
96 LaMarcus Aldridge .40 1.00
97 Carmelo Anthony .60 1.50
98 Mike Muscala .25 .60
99 Derrick White RC 2.00 5.00
100 Ryan Arcidiacono RC .75 2.00
101 Aaron Gordon .60 1.50
102 Lance Stephenson .50 1.25
103 C.J. Miles .40 1.00
104 Nik Stauskas .40 1.00
105 Derrick Rose 1.00 2.50
106 Semi Ojeleye RC .75 2.00
107 Furkan Korkmaz RC 1.00 2.50
108 Tomas Satoransky .50 1.25
109 Kyrie Irving 1.25 3.00
110 John Wall .75 2.00
111 Alex Len .40 1.00
112 Larry Nance Jr. .50 1.25
113 Cedi Osman RC 1.25 3.00
114 Noah Vonleh .40 1.00
115 Devin Booker 1.50 4.00
116 Shabazz Muhammad .40 1.00
117 Bojan Bogdanovic .50 1.25
118 Tony Snell .40 1.00
119 Isaiah Thomas .50 1.25
120 Jordan Clarkson .60 1.50
121 Andre Drummond .50 1.25
122 LeBron James 5.00 12.00
123 Chandler Parsons .40 1.00
124 Norman Powell .60 1.50
125 Dewayne Dedmon .40 1.00
126 Shaun Livingston .50 1.25
127 George Hill .50 1.25
129 Josh Jackson .50 1.25
130 Josh Hart RC 1.50 4.00
131 Andre Roberson .40 1.00
132 Damian Lillard 1.50 4.00
133 Cody Zeller .40 1.00
134 OG Anunoby RC 3.00 8.00
135 Draymond Green .75 2.00
136 Skal Labissiere .40 1.00
137 Maxi Kleber RC 1.00 2.50
138 Wesley Matthews .40 1.00
139 JaMychal Green .40 1.00

140 Justise Winslow .40 1.00
141 Austin Rivers .50 1.25
142 Malik Monk RC 2.50 6.00
143 Stephen Curry 5.00 12.00
144 Pau Gasol 1.00 2.50
145 Kevin Durant 2.50 6.00
146 Steven Adams .50 1.25
147 Giannis Antetokounmpo 3.00 8.00
148 Wes Iwundu RC .60 1.50
149 Jawun Evans RC .60 1.50
150 Kawhi Leonard 1.50 4.00
151 Avery Bradley .40 1.00
152 Manu Ginobili 1.25 3.00
153 D.J. Wilson RC .60 1.50
154 Jimmy Butler 1.00 2.50
155 Elfrid Payton .40 1.00
156 Taj Gibson .40 1.00
157 Goran Dragic .50 1.25
158 Russell Westbrook 1.00 2.50
159 Jaylen Brown 1.50 4.00
160 Kelly Oubre Jr. .60 1.50
161 Lonzo Ball 2.50 6.00
162 Mario Hezonja .40 1.00
163 Danilo Gallinari .50 1.25
164 Robin Lopez .40 1.00
165 E'Twaun Moore .40 1.00
166 Jayson Tatum 20.00 50.00
167 Gordon Hayward .50 1.25
168 Will Barton .40 1.00
169 Jeff Teague .40 1.00
170 Kent Bazemore .40 1.00
171 Bam Adebayo RC 4.00 10.00
172 Michael Kidd-Gilchrist .40 1.00
174 Rodney Hood .40 1.00
175 De'Aaron Fox 5.00 12.00
176 Thomas Bryant RC 1.00 2.50
177 James Harden 1.25 3.00
178 Wilson Chandler .50 1.25
179 Jeremy Lin 1.00 2.50
180 Klay Thompson 1.50 4.00
181 Bobby Portis .40 1.00
182 Nene .50 1.25
183 DeMarre Carroll .40 1.00
184 Ryan Anderson .40 1.00
185 Frank Ntilikina RC .75 2.00
186 Thon Maker .40 1.00
187 Harry Giles RC .60 1.50
188 Zach Randolph .60 1.50
189 J.J. Barea .50 1.25
190 Kristaps Porzingis .75 2.00
191 CJ McCollum .60 1.50
192 Nerlens Noel .40 1.00
193 Derrick Favors .40 1.00
194 Sean Kilpatrick .40 1.00
195 Markelle Fultz 1.50 4.00
196 Tim Hardaway Jr. .50 1.25
197 Ike Anigbogu RC .60 1.50
198 Zhou Qi RC 1.25 3.00
199 JJ Redick .60 1.50
200 Kyle Kuzma RC 2.50 6.00
201 Buddy Hield 1.50 4.00
202 Luke Kennard RC 4.00 10.00
203 Karl-Anthony Towns 2.50 6.00
204 Zaza Pachulia 1.00 2.50
205 Jabari Parker 1.00 2.50
206 Tony Bradley RC 2.00 5.00
207 Frank Jackson RC 2.00 5.00
208 Sindarius Thornwell RC 2.00 5.00
209 Dennis Smith Jr. RC 2.50 6.00
210 Nikola Vucevic 1.25 3.00
211 Bradley Beal 2.00 5.00
212 Damian Lillard 4.00 10.00
213 Justin Jackson RC 2.00 5.00
214 Zach LaVine 2.50 6.00
215 Kyrie Irving 3.00 8.00
216 Kyle Kuzma 8.00 20.00
217 De'Aaron Fox 15.00 40.00
218 Seth Curry 1.50 4.00
219 Dejounte Murray 1.50 4.00
220 Milos Teodosic RC 2.50 6.00
221 Blake Griffin 1.50 4.00
222 LeBron James 12.00 30.00
223 Julius Randle 1.50 4.00
224 Willy Hernangomez 1.00 2.50
225 Harrison Barnes 1.25 3.00
226 Thaddeus Young 1.00 2.50
227 Evan Turner 1.00 2.50
228 Serge Ibaka 1.25 3.00
229 Darren Collison 1.00 2.50
230 Mike Conley 1.25 3.00
231 Ben Simmons 1.50 4.00
232 Kyle Lowry 1.50 4.00
233 Lauri Markkanen 12.00 30.00
234 Willie Cauley-Stein 1.00 2.50
235 James Harden 3.00 8.00
236 Terrance Ferguson RC 2.00 5.00
237 Evan Fournier 1.25 3.00
238 Rudy Gobert 2.00 5.00
239 Dario Saric 1.25 3.00
240 Maurice Harkless 1.00 2.50
241 Lonzo Ball 8.00 20.00
242 Klay Thompson 4.00 10.00
243 Jonathan Isaac RC 5.00 12.00
244 Russell Westbrook 2.50 6.00
245 Hassan Whiteside 1.25 3.00
246 Taurean Prince 1.00 2.50
247 Dwyane Wade 3.00 8.00
248 Rudy Gay 1.25 3.00
249 D'Angelo Russell 1.25 3.00
250 Marvin Williams 1.00 2.50
251 Anthony Davis 4.00 10.00
252 Khris Middleton 2.00 5.00
253 Joe Ingles 1.25 3.00
254 Wesley Johnson 1.00 2.50
255 Guerschon Yabusele RC 1.00 2.50
256 Jayson Tatum 75.00 200.00
257 Dwayne Bacon RC 2.00 5.00
258 Robert Covington 1.00 2.50
259 Stephen Curry 12.00 30.00
260 Marcus Morris 1.00 2.50
261 Ante Zizic RC 2.50 6.00
262 Kentavious Caldwell-Pope 1.25 3.00
263 Jimmy Butler 2.50 6.00
264 Tyson Chandler 1.25 3.00
265 Giannis Antetokounmpo 8.00 20.00
266 TJ Warren 1.25 3.00
267 Kevin Durant 6.00 15.00
268 Rajon Rondo 2.00 5.00
269 Courtney Lee 1.00 2.50
270 Marcin Gortat 1.00 2.50
271 Al Jefferson 1.25 3.00
272 Kemba Walker 1.25 3.00
273 Jamal Murray 2.50 6.00
274 Tyler Lydon RC 2.00 5.00
275 Markelle Fultz 2.50 6.00
276 TJ Leaf RC 2.00 5.00
277 Dion Waiters 1.00 2.50
278 Paul Millsap 1.25 3.00
279 Clint Capela 1.25 3.00
280 Marc Gasol 1.50 4.00
281 Al Horford 1.50 4.00
282 Kawhi Leonard 4.00 10.00
283 Josh Jackson 1.25 3.00
284 Tristan Thompson 1.00 2.50
285 Frank Mason RC 2.00 5.00
286 Stanley Johnson 1.00 2.50
287 Denzel Valentine 1.00 2.50
288 Paul George 2.50 6.00
289 Chris Paul 2.50 6.00
290 Dillon Brooks RC 6.00 15.00
291 Kobe Bryant 12.00 30.00
292 Shaquille O'Neal 5.00 12.00
293 Reggie Miller 3.00 8.00
294 Allen Iverson 4.00 10.00
295 Wilt Chamberlain 5.00 12.00
296 Scottie Pippen 4.00 10.00
297 Magic Johnson 6.00 15.00
298 Larry Bird 6.00 15.00
299 Patrick Ewing 2.50 6.00
300 Pete Maravich 4.00 10.00

2017-18 Select Prizms Blue

*BLUE: 1.2X TO 3X BASIC
*BLUE RC: .6X TO 1.5X BASIC RC
STATED PRINT RUN 299 SER.#'d SETS
8 Lauri Markkanen 12.00 30.00
11 Donovan Mitchell 125.00 300.00
18 LeBron James 50.00 120.00
19 Daniel Theis 5.00 12.00
28 Lonzo Ball 20.00 50.00
49 De'Aaron Fox 50.00 120.00
93 Jayson Tatum 200.00 500.00

2017-18 Select Prizms Copper

*COPPER: 1.2X TO 3X BASIC
*COPPER RC: .6X TO 1.5X BASIC RC
STATED PRINT RUN 49 SER.#'d SETS
216 Kyle Kuzma 6.00 15.00
222 LeBron James 200.00 500.00
231 Ben Simmons 2.50 6.00
241 Lonzo Ball 100.00 250.00
243 Jonathan Isaac 10.00 25.00
256 Jayson Tatum 500.00 1,000.00
291 Kobe Bryant 75.00 200.00

2017-18 Select Prizms Die Cut Light Blue

*DC LT BLUE: 1X TO 2.5X BASIC
*DC LT BLUE RC: .5X TO 1.2X BASIC RC
STATED PRINT RUN 185 SER.#'d SETS
122 LeBron James 60.00 150.00
143 Stephen Curry 8.00 20.00
161 Lonzo Ball 30.00 80.00
166 Jayson Tatum 200.00 500.00
171 Bam Adebayo 40.00 100.00
175 De'Aaron Fox 75.00 200.00
200 Kyle Kuzma 4.00 10.00

2017-18 Select Prizms Die Cut Neon Green

*DC NEON GRN: 2.5X TO 6X BASIC
*DC NEON GRN RC: 1.2X TO 3X BASIC RC
STATED PRINT RUN 65 SER.#'d SETS
122 LeBron James 100.00 250.00
161 Lonzo Ball 75.00 200.00
166 Jayson Tatum 200.00 500.00
171 Bam Adebayo 60.00 150.00
175 De'Aaron Fox 125.00 300.00
200 Kyle Kuzma 10.00 25.00

2017-18 Select Prizms Die Cut Purple

*DC PURPLE: 1.2X TO 3X BASIC
*DC PURPLE RC: .6X TO 1.5X BASIC RC
STATED PRINT RUN 99 SER.#'d SETS
122 LeBron James 75.00 200.00
161 Lonzo Ball 40.00 100.00
166 Jayson Tatum 150.00 400.00
171 Bam Adebayo 60.00 150.00
175 De'Aaron Fox 100.00 250.00
200 Kyle Kuzma 5.00 12.00

2017-18 Select Prizms Die Cut Red

*DC RED: 1X TO 2.5X BASIC
*DC RED RC: .5X TO 1.2X BASIC RC
STATED PRINT RUN 135 SER.#'d SETS
122 LeBron James 75.00 200.00
143 Stephen Curry 20.00 50.00
147 Giannis Antetokounmpo 30.00 80.00
150 Kawhi Leonard 20.00 50.00
161 Lonzo Ball 40.00 100.00
166 Jayson Tatum 150.00 400.00
171 Bam Adebayo 60.00 150.00
175 De'Aaron Fox 75.00 200.00
195 Markelle Fultz 15.00 40.00
200 Kyle Kuzma 4.00 10.00

2017-18 Select Prizms Die Cut Tie Dye

*DC TIE DYE: 5X TO 12X BASIC
*DC TIE DYE: 2.5X TO 6X BASIC RC
STATED PRINT RUN 25 SER.#'d SETS
122 LeBron James 500.00 1,000.00
129 Josh Jackson 6.00 15.00
143 Stephen Curry 50.00 120.00
150 Kawhi Leonard 40.00 100.00
161 Lonzo Ball 125.00 300.00
166 Jayson Tatum 500.00 1,000.00
171 Bam Adebayo 125.00 300.00
175 De'Aaron Fox 400.00 800.00
195 Markelle Fultz 60.00 150.00
198 Zhou Qi 30.00 80.00
200 Kyle Kuzma 15.00 40.00

2017-18 Select Prizms Maroon

*MAROON: 1.2X TO 3X BASIC
*MAROON RC: .6X TO 1.5X BASIC RC
STATED PRINT RUN 199 SER.#'d SETS
11 Donovan Mitchell 75.00 200.00
18 LeBron James 60.00 150.00
49 De'Aaron Fox 40.00 100.00
93 Jayson Tatum 150.00 400.00

2017-18 Select Prizms Orange

*ORANGE: 2.5X TO 6X BASIC
*ORANGE RC: 1.2X TO 3X BASIC RC
STATED PRINT RUN 75 SER.#'d SETS
8 Lauri Markkanen 25.00 60.00
11 Donovan Mitchell 300.00 600.00
18 LeBron James 100.00 250.00
19 Daniel Theis 12.00 30.00
28 Lonzo Ball 40.00 100.00
49 De'Aaron Fox 100.00 250.00
57 Bogdan Bogdanovic 50.00 120.00
93 Jayson Tatum 400.00 800.00

2017-18 Select Prizms Scope

*SCOPE 1-100: 1.5X TO 4X BASIC
*SCOPE 1-100 RC: 1.25X TO 3X BASIC RC
*SCOPE 101-200: 1.5X TO 4X BASIC
*SCOPE 101-200 RC: 1.25X TO 3X BASIC
18 LeBron James 20.00 50.00
93 Jayson Tatum 75.00 200.00
166 Jayson Tatum 75.00 200.00

2017-18 Select Prizms Silver

*SILVER 1-100: 1.5X TO 4X BASIC
*SILVER 1-100 RC: 1.25X TO 3X BASIC RC
*SILVER 101-200: 1.5X TO 4X BASIC
*SILVER 101-200 RC: 1.25X TO 3X BASIC
*SILVER 201-300: 1.5X TO 4X BASIC
*SILVER 201-300 RC: 1.25X TO 3X BASIC
18 LeBron James 20.00 50.00
93 Jayson Tatum 75.00 200.00
166 Jayson Tatum 75.00 200.00
216 Kyle Kuzma 25.00 60.00
222 LeBron James 50.00 120.00
241 Lonzo Ball 25.00 60.00
256 Jayson Tatum 500.00 1,000.00

2017-18 Select Prizms Tie Dye

*TIE DYE1-100: 8X TO 20X BASIC
*TIE DYE 1-100 RC: 4X TO 10X BASIC RC
*TIE DYE 201-300: 4X TO 10X BASIC
*TIE DYE 201-300 RC: 2X TO 5X BASIC
STATED PRINT RUN 25 SER.#'d SETS
11 Donovan Mitchell 600.00 1,200.00
18 LeBron James 500.00 1,000.00
49 De'Aaron Fox 400.00 800.00
93 Jayson Tatum 1,000.00 2,000.00
217 De'Aaron Fox 600.00 1,200.00
222 LeBron James 1,000.00 2,000.00
256 Jayson Tatum 1,500.00 3,000.00
291 Kobe Bryant 500.00 1,000.00

2017-18 Select Prizms Tri Color

*TRI CLR 1-100: 1.2X TO 3X BASIC
*TRI CLR 1-100 RC: .6X TO 1.5X BASIC RC
*TRI CLR 101-200: .75X TO 2X BASIC
*TRI CLR 101-200 RC: .4X TO 1X BASIC RC
8 Lauri Markkanen 10.00 25.00
11 Donovan Mitchell 100.00 250.00
19 Daniel Theis 5.00 12.00
28 Lonzo Ball 15.00 40.00
49 De'Aaron Fox 50.00 120.00
93 Jayson Tatum 100.00 250.00
161 Lonzo Ball 25.00 60.00
166 Jayson Tatum 150.00 400.00
171 Bam Adebayo 30.00 80.00
175 De'Aaron Fox 60.00 150.00
200 Kyle Kuzma 3.00 8.00

2017-18 Select Prizms White

*WHITE: 1.5X TO 4X BASIC
*WHITE RC: .75X TO 2X BASIC RC
STATED PRINT RUN 149 SER.#'d SETS
8 Lauri Markkanen 15.00 40.00
11 Donovan Mitchell 200.00 500.00
18 LeBron James 100.00 250.00
19 Daniel Theis 8.00 20.00
28 Lonzo Ball 25.00 60.00
49 De'Aaron Fox 60.00 150.00
57 Bogdan Bogdanovic 30.00 80.00

2017-18 Select Prizms Zebra

*ZEBRA 1-100: 20X TO 50X BASIC
*ZEBRA 1-100 RC: 10X TO 25X BASIC RC
*ZEBRA 101-200: 12X TO 30X BASIC
*ZEBRA 101-200 RC: 6X TO 15X BASIC
*ZEBRA 201-300: 8X TO 20X BASIC
*ZEBRA 201-300 RC: 4X TO 10X BASIC
8 Lauri Markkanen 125.00 300.00
11 Donovan Mitchell 2,000.00 4,000.00
18 LeBron James 300.00 600.00
19 Daniel Theis 40.00 100.00
28 Lonzo Ball 250.00 600.00
49 De'Aaron Fox 125.00 300.00
57 Bogdan Bogdanovic 30.00 80.00
68 Markelle Fultz 150.00 400.00
93 Jayson Tatum 400.00 800.00
122 LeBron James 300.00 600.00
142 Malik Monk 60.00 150.00
161 Lonzo Ball 150.00 400.00
166 Jayson Tatum 400.00 800.00
171 Bam Adebayo 80.00 200.00
175 De'Aaron Fox 150.00 400.00
195 Markelle Fultz 150.00 400.00
198 Zhou Qi 100.00 250.00
200 Kyle Kuzma 50.00 120.00
216 Kyle Kuzma 50.00 120.00
217 De'Aaron Fox 1,000.00 2,000.00
222 LeBron James 500.00 1,000.00
231 Ben Simmons 20.00 50.00
241 Lonzo Ball 400.00 800.00
243 Jonathan Isaac 60.00 150.00
256 Jayson Tatum 600.00 1,200.00
265 Giannis Antetokounmpo 60.00 150.00
275 Markelle Fultz 150.00 400.00
283 Josh Jackson 75.00 200.00
291 Kobe Bryant 100.00 250.00

2017-18 Select All World

*SILVER: 1X TO 2.5X BASIC
1 Arvydas Sabonis .75 2.00
2 Patrick Ewing 1.00 2.50
3 Kyrie Irving 1.25 3.00
4 Manu Ginobili 1.25 3.00
5 Giannis Antetokounmpo 3.00 8.00
6 Andrei Kirilenko .50 1.25
7 Goran Dragic .50 1.25
8 Dirk Nowitzki 1.50 4.00
9 Yao Ming 1.25 3.00
10 Steve Nash 1.00 2.50
11 Nikola Vucevic .50 1.25
12 Tony Parker 1.00 2.50
13 Drazen Petrovic .60 1.50
14 Dominique Wilkins 1.00 2.50
15 Andrew Wiggins .75 2.00
16 Manute Bol .60 1.50
17 Zhou Qi .75 2.00
18 Tim Duncan 1.50 4.00
19 Sarunas Marciulionis .40 1.00
20 Dikembe Mutombo .75 2.00
21 Kristaps Porzingis .75 2.00
22 Joel Embiid 1.25 3.00
23 Rudy Gobert .75 2.00
24 Toni Kukoc .75 2.00
25 Nikola Jokic 4.00 10.00

2017-18 Select Autographed Memorabilia

PRINT RUNS B/WN 50-149 COPIES PER
EXCHANGE DEADLINE 9/07/2019
*PURPLE/65: .5X TO 1.2X p/r 149
*PURPLE/65: .4X TO 1X p/r 50-99
*PURPLE/35-43: .6X TO 1.5X p/r 149
*PURPLE/35-43: .5X TO 1.2X p/r 50-99
1 Marcus Smart/99 6.00 15.00
3 Seth Curry/149 5.00 12.00
4 Devin Harris/149 3.00 8.00
5 Reggie Jackson/99 5.00 12.00
6 Zaza Pachulia/149 3.00 8.00
7 Detlef Schrempf/149 6.00 15.00
8 Frank Kaminsky/149 3.00 8.00
9 Andre Drummond/99 5.00 12.00
10 Elfrid Payton/149 3.00 8.00
11 World B. Free/149 5.00 12.00
12 Joe Dumars/149 6.00 15.00
13 Andrew Wiggins/50 12.00 30.00
14 Dennis Rodman/50 15.00 40.00
15 Dikembe Mutombo/149 8.00 20.00
16 Damian Lillard/50 20.00 50.00
17 Kyrie Irving/50 25.00 60.00
18 CJ McCollum/99 10.00 25.00
19 Harrison Barnes/99 5.00 12.00
20 Gordon Hayward/99 12.00 30.00
21 Khris Middleton/99 8.00 20.00
22 Nikola Jokic/99 125.00 300.00
23 Ivica Zubac/149 4.00 10.00
24 Mark Price/149 6.00 15.00
25 George Hill/149 4.00 10.00
26 Justise Winslow/149 3.00 8.00
27 Chris McCullough/149 3.00 8.00
28 Kelly Oubre Jr./149 5.00 12.00
29 Mario Hezonja/149 3.00 8.00
30 Ron Baker/149 3.00 8.00
31 Keith Van Horn/149 4.00 10.00
32 Dwight Powell/149 3.00 8.00

2017-18 Select Autographed Memorabilia Prizms Tie Dye

*TIE DIE/21-25: 1.2X TO 3X p/r 149
*TIE DIE/21-25: 1X TO 2.5X p/r 50-99
PRINT RUNS B/WN 4-25 COPIES PER
NO PRICING ON QTY 11 OR LESS
EXCHANGE DEADLINE 9/07/2019
2 LaMarcus Aldridge/25 15.00 40.00

2017-18 Select Draft Selections Memorabilia

*PURPLE/99: .5X TO 1.2X BASIC
*TIE DYE/25: 1.2X TO 3X BASIC
1 Tyler Lydon 1.50 4.00
2 Tony Bradley 1.50 4.00
3 Luke Kennard 3.00 8.00
4 TJ Leaf 1.50 4.00
5 Semi Ojeleye 2.00 5.00
6 Markelle Fultz 4.00 10.00
7 Dwayne Bacon 1.50 4.00
8 Josh Jackson 2.00 5.00
9 Davon Reed 1.50 4.00
10 Justin Patton 1.50 4.00
11 Malik Monk 6.00 15.00
12 D.J. Wilson 1.50 4.00
13 Terrance Ferguson 1.50 4.00
14 Sterling Brown 1.50 4.00
15 Harry Giles 1.50 4.00
16 Lonzo Ball 8.00 20.00
17 Jarrett Allen 4.00 10.00
18 De'Aaron Fox 12.00 30.00
19 OG Anunoby 8.00 20.00
20 Donovan Mitchell 15.00 40.00
21 Tyler Dorsey 1.50 4.00
22 Jordan Bell 3.00 8.00
23 Caleb Swanigan 1.50 4.00
24 John Collins 4.00 10.00
25 Frank Ntilikina 2.00 5.00
DS-JAY Jayson Tatum 40.00 100.00
27 Dennis Smith Jr. 2.00 5.00
28 Jonathan Isaac 2.50 6.00
29 Zach Collins 2.50 6.00
30 Frank Jackson 1.50 4.00
31 Jawun Evans 1.50 4.00
32 Frank Mason 1.50 4.00

2017-18 Select Draft Selections Memorabilia Prizms Purple

20 Donovan Mitchell 25.00 60.00

2017-18 Select Draft Selections Memorabilia Prizms Tie Dye

20 Donovan Mitchell 60.00 150.00

2017-18 Select In Flight Signatures

PRINT RUNS B/WN 60-199 COPIES PER
EXCHANGE DEADLINE 9/07/2019
*GREEN/65: .5X TO 1.2X p/r 149-199
*GREEN/65: .4X TO 1X p/r 60-99
*GREEN/35: .6X TO 1.5X p/r 149-199
*GREEN/35: .5X TO 1.2X p/r 60-99
*TIE DIE/25: .75X TO 2X p/r 149-199
*TIE DIE/25: .6X TO 1.5X p/r 60-99
IFAD Anthony Davis/60 25.00 60.00
IFAG Aaron Gordon/149 6.00 15.00
IFAH Anfernee Hardaway/60 25.00 60.00
IFAI Allen Iverson/60 40.00 100.00
IFCL Caris LeVert/199 5.00 12.00
IFDW Dominique Wilkins/60 12.00 30.00
IFER Eric Gordon/149 4.00 10.00
IFGG George Gervin/149 6.00 15.00
IFGH Grant Hill/60 15.00 40.00
IFGI Giannis Antetokounmpo/60 60.00 150.00
IFHB Harrison Barnes/99 5.00 12.00
IFIR Isaiah Rider/149 4.00 10.00
IFJA Justin Anderson/199 3.00 8.00
IFJS Jerry Stackhouse/199 6.00 15.00
IFJW Justise Winslow/149 3.00 8.00
IFKB Kobe Bryant/60 600.00 1,200.00
IFKD Kevin Durant/60 60.00 150.00
IFKH Khris Middleton/149 12.00 30.00
IFKM Karl Malone/60 25.00 60.00
IFKW Kenny "Sky" Walker/199 3.00 8.00
IFLN Larry Nance Jr./199 4.00 10.00
IFRA Ray Allen/60 15.00 40.00
IFRH Rondae Hollis-Jefferson/199 3.00 8.00
IFRJ Reggie Jackson/149 4.00 10.00
IFSP Spud Webb/199 5.00 12.00

2017-18 Select Phenomenon

*SILVER: 1X TO 2.5X BASIC
P1 Josh Jackson 1.25 3.00
P2 Jamal Murray 8.00 20.00
P3 Frank Ntilikina 1.25 3.00
P4 Brandon Ingram 2.00 5.00
P5 Zach Collins 1.50 4.00
P6 Kristaps Porzingis 2.00 5.00
P7 Donovan Mitchell 125.00 300.00
P8 Kyle Kuzma 4.00 10.00
P9 Markelle Fultz 2.50 6.00
P10 Derrick White 4.00 10.00
P11 De'Aaron Fox 15.00 40.00
P12 Malcolm Brogdon 1.25 3.00
P13 Lauri Markkanen 6.00 15.00
P14 Karl-Anthony Towns 2.50 6.00
P15 Malik Monk 4.00 10.00
P16 Myles Turner 1.50 4.00
P17 Bam Adebayo 30.00 80.00
P18 Josh Hart 2.50 6.00
P19 Lonzo Ball 8.00 20.00
P20 Frank Mason 1.00 2.50
P21 Jonathan Isaac 2.50 6.00
P22 Dario Saric 1.25 3.00
P23 Dennis Smith Jr. 1.25 3.00
P24 Devin Booker 8.00 20.00
P25 Luke Kennard 2.00 5.00
P26 Willy Hernangomez 1.00 2.50
P27 Justin Jackson 1.00 2.50
P28 Milos Teodosic 1.25 3.00
P29 Jayson Tatum 125.00 300.00
P30 Buddy Hield 1.50 4.00

2017-18 Select Phenomenon Prizms Silver

*SILVER: 1X TO 2.5X BASIC
P9 Markelle Fultz 15.00 40.00
P11 De'Aaron Fox 100.00 250.00
P13 Lauri Markkanen 15.00 40.00

2017-18 Select Rookie Jersey Autographs

STATED PRINT RUN 199 SER.#'d SETS
EXCHANGE DEADLINE 9/07/2019
1 Markelle Fultz 20.00 50.00
RJAJJK Josh Jackson 4.00 10.00
3 Lonzo Ball 100.00 250.00
4 Jayson Tatum 75.00 200.00
5 De'Aaron Fox 30.00 80.00
6 Jonathan Isaac 6.00 15.00
7 Derrick White 12.00 30.00
8 Frank Ntilikina 4.00 10.00
9 Dennis Smith Jr. 4.00 10.00
10 Zach Collins 5.00 12.00
11 Malik Monk 12.00 30.00
12 Luke Kennard 6.00 15.00
13 Justin Patton 3.00 8.00
14 D.J. Wilson 4.00 10.00
15 Ante Zizic 4.00 10.00
16 Semi Ojeleye 4.00 10.00
18 John Collins 8.00 20.00
20 Jarrett Allen 8.00 20.00
21 OG Anunoby 6.00 15.00
23 Terrance Ferguson 3.00 8.00
24 Tyler Dorsey 3.00 8.00
26 Caleb Swanigan 3.00 8.00
27 Jordan Bell 3.00 8.00
28 Wes Iwundu 3.00 8.00
29 Frank Jackson 3.00 8.00
30 Frank Mason 3.00 8.00
31 Dwayne Bacon 3.00 8.00
32 Davon Reed 3.00 8.00
33 Jawun Evans 3.00 8.00
34 Bam Adebayo 12.00 30.00
35 Donovan Mitchell 75.00 200.00
36 Ivan Rabb 3.00 8.00

2017-18 Select Rookie Jersey Autographs Prizms Purple

*PURPLE: .5X TO 1.2X BASIC
STATED PRINT RUN 99 SER.#'d SETS
EXCHANGE DEADLINE 9/07/2019
17 TJ Leaf 4.00 10.00

2017-18 Select Rookie Jersey Autographs Prizms Tie Dye

*TIE DIE: 1.2X TO 3X BASIC
STATED PRINT RUN 25 SER.#'d SETS
EXCHANGE DEADLINE 9/07/2019
19 Harry Giles 10.00 25.00

2017-18 Select Rookie Signatures

STATED PRINT RUN 199 SER.#'d SETS
EXCHANGE DEADLINE 9/07/2019
*GREEN/65: .5X TO 1.2X BASIC
*TIE DYE/25: 1X TO 2.5X BASIC
1 Markelle Fultz 15.00 40.00
2 Lonzo Ball 75.00 200.00
3 Jayson Tatum 300.00 600.00
RSJOS Josh Jackson 4.00 10.00
5 De'Aaron Fox 100.00 250.00
6 Jonathan Isaac 10.00 25.00
7 Wes Iwundu 3.00 8.00
8 Sindarius Thornwell 3.00 8.00
9 Josh Hart 8.00 20.00
10 Justin Patton 3.00 8.00
11 Donovan Mitchell 200.00 500.00
12 Kyle Kuzma 12.00 30.00
13 Frank Jackson 3.00 8.00
14 Tony Bradley 3.00 8.00
15 D.J. Wilson 3.00 8.00
16 Caleb Swanigan 3.00 8.00
17 Frank Mason 3.00 8.00
18 TJ Leaf 3.00 8.00
19 Sterling Brown 3.00 8.00
20 John Collins 12.00 30.00
21 Lauri Markkanen 30.00 80.00
22 Semi Ojeleye 4.00 10.00
23 Harry Giles 3.00 8.00
24 Frank Ntilikina 4.00 10.00
25 Dwayne Bacon 3.00 8.00
26 Jarrett Allen 8.00 20.00
27 Dennis Smith Jr. 4.00 10.00
28 Davon Reed 3.00 8.00
29 OG Anunoby 15.00 40.00
30 Zach Collins 5.00 12.00
31 Tyler Lydon 3.00 8.00
32 Malik Monk 12.00 30.00
33 Tyler Dorsey 3.00 8.00
34 Jawun Evans 3.00 8.00
35 Ante Zizic 4.00 10.00
36 Luke Kennard 6.00 15.00
37 Justin Jackson 3.00 8.00
38 Terrance Ferguson 3.00 8.00
RSJOD Jordan Bell 3.00 8.00

2017-18 Select Select Swatches

*PURPLE/99: .5X TO 1.2X BASIC
*COPPER/49: .5X TO 1.2X BASIC
*TIE DYE/25: 1.2X TO 3X BASIC
1 Chris Paul 3.00 8.00
2 Rodney Hood 1.50 4.00
3 Derrick Rose 4.00 10.00
4 Steven Adams 2.00 5.00
5 Gary Harris 2.00 5.00
6 Dirk Nowitzki 6.00 15.00
7 Jamal Murray 4.00 10.00
8 Kevin Love 2.50 6.00
9 Bojan Bogdanovic 2.00 5.00
10 Mario Hezonja 1.50 4.00
11 Danny Green 2.00 5.00
12 Rudy Gobert 3.00 8.00
13 Elfrid Payton 1.50 4.00
14 Willy Hernangomez 1.50 4.00
15 Gordon Hayward 2.00 5.00
16 Zach Randolph 2.50 6.00
17 Juan Hernangomez 2.50 6.00
18 Lance Stephenson 2.00 5.00
19 Brandon Ingram 4.00 10.00
20 Nikola Vucevic 2.00 5.00

2017-18 Select Signatures

PRINT RUNS B/WN 49-149 COPIES PER
EXCHANGE DEADLINE 9/07/2019
*GREEN/65: .5X TO 1.2X p/r 149
*GREEN/65: .4X TO 1X p/r 49-99
*GREEN/35: .6X TO 1.5X p/r 149
*GREEN/35: .5X TO 1.2X p/r 49-99
*TIE DIE/25: .75X TO 2X p/r 149
*TIE DIE/25: .6X TO 1.5X p/r 49
1 Kyrie Irving/49 40.00 100.00
2 Damian Lillard/49 30.00 80.00
3 CJ McCollum/99 10.00 25.00
4 Willy Hernangomez/149 3.00 8.00
5 Malcolm Delaney/149 3.00 8.00
6 Alan Williams/149 3.00 8.00
7 Brice Johnson/149 4.00 10.00
8 Gorgui Dieng/149 3.00 8.00
9 Doug McDermott/149 3.00 8.00
11 Denzel Valentine/149 3.00 8.00
12 J.J. Barea/149 6.00 15.00
13 Jonas Valanciunas/99 5.00 12.00
16 Kyle Korver/99 8.00 20.00
17 Jrue Holiday/99 8.00 20.00
19 Walt Frazier/99 10.00 25.00
20 George Gervin/99 8.00 20.00
21 Nate Archibald/99 6.00 15.00
22 Joe Dumars/99 8.00 20.00
23 Louie Dampier/99 6.00 15.00
24 Rick Barry/99 6.00 15.00
25 Shaquille O'Neal /49 50.00 120.00
26 Allen Iverson/49 40.00 100.00
27 Karl Malone/49 25.00 60.00
SIGJS John Stockton/49 20.00 50.00
29 Larry Bird/49 50.00 120.00
30 Willis Reed/99 40.00 100.00
31 Alex English/99 8.00 20.00
32 Kobe Bryant/49 1,000.00 2,000.00

2017-18 Select Slash and Dash

*SILVER: 1X TO 2.5X BASIC
1 Grant Hill 1.00 2.50
2 Julius Erving 1.50 4.00
3 LeBron James 5.00 12.00
4 Tracy McGrady 1.00 2.50
5 Kobe Bryant 5.00 12.00
6 Derrick Rose 1.00 2.50
7 Goran Dragic .50 1.25
8 John Wall .75 2.00
9 Rajon Rondo .75 2.00
10 Chris Paul 1.00 2.50
11 Kyrie Irving 1.25 3.00
12 Elgin Baylor 1.00 2.50
13 Jeremy Lin 1.00 2.50
14 Magic Johnson 2.50 6.00
15 Jimmy Butler 1.00 2.50
16 Scottie Pippen 1.50 4.00
17 Kevin Durant 2.50 6.00
18 Russell Westbrook 1.00 2.50
19 Manu Ginobili 1.25 3.00
20 Tony Parker 1.00 2.50
21 Allen Iverson 1.50 4.00
22 George Gervin 1.00 2.50
23 Vince Carter 1.25 3.00
24 Walt Frazier 1.00 2.50
25 DeMar DeRozan .75 2.00
26 Dwyane Wade 1.25 3.00
27 Paul George 1.00 2.50
28 Carmelo Anthony 1.00 2.50
29 James Harden 1.25 3.00
30 Bradley Beal .75 2.00

2017-18 Select Sparks Memorabilia

*PURPLE/99: .5X TO 1.2X BASIC
*COPPER/49: .5X TO 1.2X BASIC
1 Allen Iverson 4.00 10.00
2 Andrew Wiggins 3.00 8.00
3 Blake Griffin 2.50 6.00
4 Dirk Nowitzki 6.00 15.00
5 Kevin Garnett 6.00 15.00
6 Kobe Bryant 8.00 20.00
7 Kristaps Porzingis 3.00 8.00
8 Kyrie Irving 4.00 10.00
9 Shaquille O'Neal 8.00 20.00
10 Tim Duncan 6.00 15.00

2017-18 Select Sparks Memorabilia Prizms Tie Dye

*TIE DYE: 1.2X TO 3X BASIC
STATED PRINT RUN 25 SER.#'d SETS
6 Kobe Bryant 50.00 120.00

2017-18 Select Throwback Memorabilia

*PURPLE/99: .5X TO 1.2X BASIC
*COPPER/49: .5X TO 1.2X BASIC
*TIE DYE/25: 1.2X TO 3X BASIC
1 Arron Afflalo 1.50 4.00
2 Carmelo Anthony 4.00 10.00
3 Chris Paul 4.00 10.00
4 Courtney Lee 1.50 4.00
5 David West 2.00 5.00
6 DeMarre Carroll 1.50 4.00
7 Dwyane Wade 5.00 12.00
TMDRS Derrick Rose 4.00 10.00
9 Domantas Sabonis 5.00 12.00
10 Kentavious Caldwell-Pope 2.00 5.00
11 Jeff Teague 1.50 4.00
12 Enes Kanter 2.00 5.00
13 Ersan Ilyasova 1.50 4.00
14 Evan Turner 1.50 4.00
15 Gordon Hayward 2.00 5.00
TMJJN James Johnson 1.50 4.00
17 Jimmy Butler 4.00 10.00
18 JJ Redick 2.50 6.00
19 Joe Johnson 2.00 5.00
20 Joffrey Lauvergne 1.50 4.00
21 Jose Calderon 1.50 4.00
22 Jusuf Nurkic 2.00 5.00
23 Kris Dunn 1.50 4.00
24 Lance Stephenson 2.00 5.00
25 LeBron James 40.00 100.00
26 Marco Belinelli 1.50 4.00
27 Mirza Teletovic 1.50 4.00
28 Omri Casspi 1.50 4.00
29 Raymond Felton 1.50 4.00
30 Richard Jefferson 2.00 5.00
31 Robin Lopez 1.50 4.00
32 Seth Curry 2.50 6.00
TMTRS Terrence Ross 2.00 5.00
34 Timofey Mozgov 1.50 4.00
35 Trevor Ariza 1.50 4.00
36 Trevor Booker 1.50 4.00
37 Trey Lyles 1.50 4.00
38 Vince Carter 5.00 12.00
39 Wesley Matthews 1.50 4.00
40 Zach Randolph 2.50 6.00

2017-18 Select With Authority

*SILVER: 1.25X TO 3X BASIC
WA1 Blake Griffin .60 1.50
WA2 Vince Carter 1.25 3.00
WA3 Kobe Bryant 5.00 12.00
WA4 Isaiah Rider .50 1.25
WA5 John Wall .75 2.00
WA6 Dominique Wilkins 1.00 2.50
WA7 Clyde Drexler 1.00 2.50
WA8 Shawn Kemp 1.00 2.50
WA9 Tracy McGrady 1.00 2.50
WA10 Shaquille O'Neal 2.00 5.00
WA11 LeBron James 5.00 12.00
WA12 Julius Erving 1.50 4.00
WA13 Kevin Durant 2.50 6.00
WA14 Russell Westbrook 1.00 2.50
WA15 DeAndre Jordan .50 1.25

2017-18 Select X Factor Memorabilia

*PURPLE/99: .5X TO 1.2X BASIC
*COPPER/49: .6X TO 1.5X BASIC
*TIE DYE/25: 1.2X TO 3X BASIC
1 Josh Jackson 2.00 5.00
2 LaMarcus Aldridge 2.50 6.00
3 Dennis Smith Jr. 2.00 5.00
4 Paul George 4.00 10.00
5 De'Aaron Fox 12.00 30.00
6 Trey Lyles 1.50 4.00
7 Brook Lopez 2.00 5.00
8 Devin Harris 1.50 4.00
9 Markelle Fultz 4.00 10.00
10 Harrison Barnes 2.00 5.00
11 Jonathan Isaac 4.00 10.00
12 LeBron James 40.00 100.00
XFZCL Zach Collins 2.50 6.00
14 Rondae Hollis-Jefferson 1.50 4.00
15 Aaron Gordon 2.50 6.00
16 Wilson Chandler 1.50 4.00
17 Danilo Gallinari 2.00 5.00
18 Evan Fournier 2.00 5.00
19 Lonzo Ball 6.00 15.00
20 Jameer Nelson 1.50 4.00
21 Frank Ntilikina 2.00 5.00
22 Nikola Jokic 15.00 40.00
23 Malik Monk 6.00 15.00
24 Shawn Marion 2.00 5.00
25 Bradley Beal 3.00 8.00
26 Yogi Ferrell 1.50 4.00
27 Dejounte Murray 2.50 6.00
28 Georgios Papagiannis 1.50 4.00
29 Jayson Tatum 40.00 100.00
30 Kenneth Faried 2.00 5.00

2018-19 Select

1 Stephen Curry 3.00 8.00
2 Deandre Ayton RC 1.50 4.00
3 Dennis Smith Jr. .25 .60
4 Elie Okobo RC .50 1.25
5 Robin Lopez .25 .60
6 Devin Booker 1.00 2.50
7 Shai Gilgeous-Alexander RC 12.00 30.00
8 Jalen Brunson RC 4.00 10.00
9 Grayson Allen RC 1.00 2.50
10 Kris Dunn .25 .60
11 LeBron James 3.00 8.00
12 Rudy Gay .40 1.00
13 Giannis Antetokounmpo 2.00 5.00
14 Al-Farouq Aminu .25 .60
15 Marvin Bagley III RC 3.00 8.00
16 Josh Richardson .30 .75
17 Miles Bridges RC 1.25 3.00
18 Jarrett Allen .40 1.00
19 Chandler Hutchison RC .60 1.50
20 LaMarcus Aldridge .40 1.00
21 Kyrie Irving 1.00 2.50
22 Serge Ibaka .30 .75
23 DeMar DeRozan .50 1.25

2018-19 Select

24 Andre Iguodala .30 .75
25 Luka Doncic RC 15.00 40.00
26 Domantas Sabonis .50 1.25
27 Jerome Robinson RC .50 1.25
28 Jeremy Lin .60 1.50
29 Aaron Holiday RC .75 2.00
30 Malik Monk .40 1.00
31 Kevin Durant 1.50 4.00
32 Taj Gibson .25 .60
33 Anthony Davis 1.00 2.50
34 Monte Morris RC 1.25 3.00
35 Jaren Jackson Jr. RC 4.00 10.00
36 Dwyane Wade .75 2.00
37 Michael Porter Jr. RC 2.00 5.00
38 J.J. Barea .40 1.00
39 Anfernee Simons RC 2.50 6.00
40 Marcus Smart .40 1.00
41 Ben Simmons .40 1.00
42 Terry Rozier .30 .75
43 Damian Lillard 1.00 2.50
44 Brandon Ingram .40 1.00
45 Trae Young RC 4.00 10.00
46 Eric Bledsoe .30 .75
47 Troy Brown Jr. RC .60 1.50
48 John Collins .40 1.00
49 Moritz Wagner RC 1.00 2.50
50 Michael Kidd-Gilchrist .25 .60
51 James Harden .75 2.00
52 Tim Hardaway Jr. .25 .60
53 Paul George .60 1.50
54 Buddy Hield .40 1.00
55 Mo Bamba RC .75 2.00
56 Zhaire Smith RC .50 1.25
57 Evan Fournier .30 .75
58 Jordan Bell .25 .60
59 Landry Shamet RC .75 2.00
60 Nerlens Noel .25 .60
61 Jayson Tatum 1.50 4.00
62 Tony Parker .60 1.50
63 Karl-Anthony Towns .60 1.50
64 Chris Paul .75 2.00
65 Wendell Carter Jr. RC 1.25 3.00
66 Fred VanVleet .50 1.25
67 Donte DiVincenzo RC 1.25 3.00
68 JR Smith .40 1.00
69 Robert Williams III RC 1.00 2.50
70 Nikola Mirotic .25 .60
71 Donovan Mitchell 1.25 3.00
72 Tristan Thompson .25 .60
73 Lonzo Ball .40 1.00
74 D'Angelo Russell .40 1.00
75 Collin Sexton RC 1.50 4.00
76 Gerald Green .30 .75
77 Lonnie Walker IV RC 1.00 2.50
78 Jusuf Nurkic .30 .75
79 Jacob Evans III RC .50 1.25
80 Patrick Beverley .25 .60
81 Joel Embiid 1.00 2.50
82 Vince Carter .75 2.00
83 Kyle Kuzma .40 1.00
84 DeAndre Jordan .30 .75
85 Kevin Knox RC .60 1.50
86 Hamidou Diallo RC .75 2.00
87 Kevin Huerter RC 1.00 2.50
88 Kemba Walker .30 .75
89 Dzanan Musa RC .50 1.25
90 Paul Millsap .30 .75
91 Russell Westbrook .60 1.50
92 Zach Collins .30 .75
93 Kawhi Leonard 1.00 2.50
94 Dennis Schroder .30 .75
95 Mikal Bridges RC 2.50 6.00
96 Hassan Whiteside .30 .75
97 Josh Okogie RC .75 2.00
98 Kevin Love .30 .75
99 Omari Spellman RC .50 1.25
100 Reggie Jackson .30 .75
101 Aaron Gordon .40 1.00
102 Deandre Ayton 1.50 4.00
103 Devonte' Graham RC .75 2.00
104 Shai Gilgeous-Alexander 12.00 30.00
105 Jamal Murray .75 2.00
106 Grayson Allen .50 1.25
107 Kristaps Porzingis .50 1.25
108 Stephen Curry 3.00 8.00
109 Rodney Hood .30 .75
110 Dennis Smith Jr. .25 .60
111 Allen Crabbe .25 .60
112 Marvin Bagley III .75 2.00
113 Dirk Nowitzki 1.00 2.50
114 Miles Bridges 1.25 3.00
115 Jaylen Brown .60 1.50
116 Chandler Hutchison .30 .75
117 Lou Williams .30 .75
118 LeBron James 3.00 8.00
119 Rudy Gobert .50 1.25
120 Giannis Antetokounmpo 2.00 5.00
121 Andrew Wiggins .50 1.25
122 Luka Doncic 15.00 40.00
123 Draymond Green .50 1.25
124 Jerome Robinson .50 1.25
125 Jevon Carter RC .75 2.00
126 Aaron Holiday .75 2.00
127 Marc Gasol .40 1.00
128 Kyrie Irving 1.00 2.50
129 Steven Adams .30 .75
130 DeMar DeRozan .50 1.25
131 Blake Griffin .40 1.00
132 Jaren Jackson Jr. 4.00 10.00
133 Elfrid Payton .30 .75
134 Michael Porter Jr. 2.00 5.00
135 JJ Redick .40 1.00
136 Anfernee Simons 2.50 6.00
137 Markelle Fultz .30 .75
138 Kevin Durant 1.50 4.00
139 Taurean Prince .25 .60
140 Anthony Davis 1.00 2.50
141 Brook Lopez .30 .75
142 Trae Young 4.00 10.00
143 Eric Gordon .30 .75
144 Troy Brown Jr. .60 1.50
145 John Wall .50 1.25
146 Moritz Wagner 1.00 2.50
147 Mike Conley .30 .75
148 Ben Simmons .40 1.00
149 Thaddeus Young .25 .60
150 Damian Lillard 1.00 2.50
151 Caris LeVert .40 1.00
152 Mo Bamba .75 2.00
153 Evan Turner .25 .60
154 Zhaire Smith .50 1.25
155 Josh Hart .30 .75
156 Landry Shamet .75 2.00
157 Nicolas Batum .25 .60
158 James Harden .75 2.00
159 T.J. Warren .30 .75
160 Paul George .60 1.50
161 CJ McCollum .40 1.00
162 Wendell Carter Jr. 1.25 3.00
163 Gary Trent Jr. RC 1.00 2.50
164 Donte DiVincenzo 1.25 3.00
165 Jrue Holiday .50 1.25
166 Robert Williams III 1.00 2.50
167 Nikola Vucevic .30 .75
168 Jayson Tatum 1.50 4.00
169 Trevor Ariza .25 .60
170 Karl-Anthony Towns .60 1.50
171 Dario Saric .30 .75
172 Collin Sexton 1.50 4.00
173 Goran Dragic .30 .75
174 Lonnie Walker IV 1.00 2.50
175 Kawhi Leonard 1.00 2.50
176 Jacob Evans III .50 1.25
177 Patty Mills .30 .75
178 Donovan Mitchell 1.25 3.00
179 Tyreke Evans .25 .60
180 Lonzo Ball .40 1.00
181 De'Anthony Melton RC 1.00 2.50
182 Kevin Knox .60 1.50
183 Harrison Barnes .30 .75
184 Kevin Huerter 1.00 2.50
185 Kent Bazemore .25 .60
186 Dzanan Musa .50 1.25
187 Rajon Rondo .50 1.25
188 Joel Embiid 1.00 2.50
189 Wesley Matthews .25 .60
190 Kyle Kuzma .40 1.00
191 Derrick Favors .25 .60
192 Mikal Bridges 2.50 6.00
193 Isaiah Thomas .30 .75
194 Josh Okogie .75 2.00
195 Khris Middleton .40 1.00
196 Omari Spellman .50 1.25
197 Ricky Rubio .30 .75
198 Russell Westbrook .60 1.50
199 Zach LaVine .60 1.50
200 Kyle Lowry .40 1.00
201 Shai Gilgeous-Alexander 40.00 100.00
202 Jeff Teague .50 1.25
203 Grayson Allen .50 1.25
204 Malcolm Brogdon .75 2.00
205 Stephen Curry 6.00 15.00
206 Ryan Anderson .50 1.25
207 Giannis Antetokounmpo 4.00 10.00
208 Andre Drummond .60 1.50
209 Deandre Ayton 3.00 8.00
210 D.J. Augustin .50 1.25
211 Miles Bridges 2.50 6.00
212 Jimmy Butler 1.25 3.00
213 Chandler Hutchison 1.25 3.00
214 Marcin Gortat .50 1.25
215 LeBron James 6.00 15.00
216 Svi Mykhailiuk RC 1.25 3.00
217 DeMar DeRozan 1.00 2.50
218 Avery Bradley .50 1.25
219 Marvin Bagley III 1.50 4.00
220 Dwight Howard 1.00 2.50
221 Jerome Robinson 1.00 2.50
222 Joe Ingles .60 1.50
223 Aaron Holiday 1.50 4.00
224 MarShon Brooks .50 1.25
225 Kyrie Irving 2.00 5.00
226 Terrance Ferguson .50 1.25
227 Anthony Davis 2.00 5.00
228 Bradley Beal 1.00 2.50
229 Luka Doncic 150.00 400.00
230 Enes Kanter .60 1.50
231 Michael Porter Jr. 4.00 10.00
232 Jonathan Isaac .75 2.00
233 Anfernee Simons 5.00 12.00
234 Myles Turner .75 2.00
235 Ben Simmons .75 2.00
236 Thon Maker .50 1.25
237 Damian Lillard 2.00 5.00
238 Bruce Brown RC 2.00 5.00
239 Jaren Jackson Jr. 8.00 20.00
240 E'Twaun Moore .50 1.25
241 Troy Brown Jr. 1.25 3.00
242 Josh Jackson .50 1.25
243 Moritz Wagner 2.00 5.00
244 Nikola Jokic 4.00 10.00
245 James Harden 1.50 4.00
246 Tobias Harris .60 1.50
247 Paul George 1.25 3.00
248 Chris Paul 1.50 4.00
249 Trae Young 8.00 20.00
250 Frank Ntilikina .50 1.25
251 Zhaire Smith 1.00 2.50
252 Julius Randle .75 2.00
253 Landry Shamet 1.50 4.00
254 Otto Porter Jr. .60 1.50
255 Jayson Tatum 3.00 8.00
256 Trey Burke .50 1.25
257 Karl-Anthony Towns 1.25 3.00
258 Clint Capela .60 1.50
259 Mo Bamba 1.50 4.00
260 George Hill .60 1.50
261 Donte DiVincenzo 2.50 6.00
262 Keita Bates-Diop RC 1.25 3.00
263 Robert Williams III 2.00 5.00
264 Pau Gasol 1.25 3.00
265 Donovan Mitchell 2.50 6.00
266 Victor Oladipo .60 1.50
267 Lonzo Ball .75 2.00
268 De'Aaron Fox 1.50 4.00
269 Wendell Carter Jr. 2.50 6.00
270 Gordon Hayward .75 2.00
271 Lonnie Walker IV 2.00 5.00
272 Kentavious Caldwell-Pope .50 1.25
273 Jacob Evans III 1.00 2.50
274 Reggie Bullock .50 1.25
275 Joel Embiid 2.00 5.00
276 Willie Cauley-Stein .50 1.25
277 Kyle Kuzma .75 2.00
278 DeMarcus Cousins .60 1.50
279 Collin Sexton 3.00 8.00
280 Harry Giles .50 1.25
281 Kevin Huerter 2.00 5.00
282 Klay Thompson 2.00 5.00
283 Dzanan Musa 1.00 2.50
284 Robert Covington .60 1.50
285 Russell Westbrook 1.25 3.00
286 Zach Randolph .60 1.50
287 Kawhi Leonard 2.00 5.00
288 Derrick Rose 1.50 4.00
289 Kevin Knox 1.25 3.00
290 Jabari Parker .50 1.25
291 Josh Okogie 1.50 4.00
292 Kyle Lowry .75 2.00
293 Omari Spellman 1.00 2.50
294 Royce O'Neale .50 1.25
295 Dennis Smith Jr. .50 1.25
296 Kevin Durant 3.00 8.00
297 Al Horford .75 2.00
298 Dillon Brooks .30 .75
299 Mikal Bridges 5.00 12.00
300 Jarred Vanderbilt RC .30 .75

2018-19 Select Prizms Blue Die Cut

*BLUE DC: 2X TO 5X BASIC
*BLUE DC RC: 1X TO 2.5X BASIC RC
STATED PRINT RUN 249 SER.#'d SETS
104 Shai Gilgeous-Alexander 75.00 200.00
122 Luka Doncic 125.00 300.00

2018-19 Select Prizms Copper

*COPPER: 5X TO 12X BASIC
*COPPER RC: 2.5X TO 6X BASIC RC
STATED PRINT RUN 65 SER.#'d SETS
201 Shai Gilgeous-Alexander 500.00 1,000.00
229 Luka Doncic 1,500.00 3,000.00
249 Trae Young 125.00 300.00

2018-19 Select Prizms Light Blue

*LIGHT BLUE: 2X TO 5X BASIC
*LIGHT BLUE RC: 1X TO 2.5X BASIC RC
STATED PRINT RUN 299 SER.#'d SETS
7 Shai Gilgeous-Alexander 75.00 200.00
8 Jalen Brunson 25.00 60.00
25 Luka Doncic 150.00 400.00
45 Trae Young 25.00 60.00

2018-19 Select Prizms Maroon Die Cut

*MAROON DC: 2.5X TO 6X BASIC
*MAROON DC RC: 1.25X TO 3X BASIC RC
STATED PRINT RUN 175 SER.#'d SETS
104 Shai Gilgeous-Alexander 100.00 250.00
122 Luka Doncic 200.00 500.00
142 Trae Young 30.00 80.00

2018-19 Select Prizms Neon Green

*NEON GRN: 5X TO 12X BASIC
*NEON GRN RC: 2.5X TO 6X BASIC RC
STATED PRINT RUN 75 SER.#'d SETS
7 Shai Gilgeous-Alexander 200.00 500.00
8 Jalen Brunson 60.00 150.00
25 Luka Doncic 500.00 1,000.00
45 Trae Young 60.00 150.00

2018-19 Select Prizms Orange Die Cut

104 Shai Gilgeous-Alexander 200.00 500.00
122 Luka Doncic 500.00 1,000.00
142 Trae Young 60.00 150.00

2018-19 Select Prizms Purple Die Cut

*PURPLE DC: 3X TO 8X BASIC
*PURPLE DC RC: 1.5X TO 4X BASIC RC
STATED PRINT RUN 99 SER.#'d SETS
104 Shai Gilgeous-Alexander 125.00 300.00
122 Luka Doncic 300.00 600.00
142 Trae Young 40.00 100.00

2018-19 Select Prizms Red

*RED: 2.5X TO 6X BASIC
*RED RC: 1.25X TO 3X BASIC RC
STATED PRINT RUN 199 SER.#'d SETS
7 Shai Gilgeous-Alexander 100.00 250.00
8 Jalen Brunson 30.00 80.00
25 Luka Doncic 200.00 500.00
45 Trae Young 30.00 80.00

2018-19 Select Prizms Scope

*SCOPE 1-100: 2X TO 5X BASIC
*SCOPE 1-100 RC: 1X TO 2.5X BASIC RC
*SCOPE 101-200: 2X TO 5X BASIC
*SCOPE 101-200 RC: 1X TO 2.5X BASIC
7 Shai Gilgeous-Alexander 50.00 120.00
8 Jalen Brunson 20.00 50.00
25 Luka Doncic 125.00 300.00
45 Trae Young 20.00 50.00
104 Shai Gilgeous-Alexander 50.00 120.00
122 Luka Doncic 125.00 300.00
142 Trae Young 20.00 50.00

2018-19 Select Prizms Silver

*SILVER 1-100: 2X TO 5X BASIC
*SILVER 1-100 RC: 1X TO 2.5X BASIC RC
*SILVER 101-200: 2X TO 5X BASIC
*SILVER 101-200 RC: 1X TO 2.5X BASIC
*SILVER 201-300: 2X TO 5X BASIC
*SILVER 201-300 RC: 1X TO 2.5X BASIC
7 Shai Gilgeous-Alexander 50.00 120.00
8 Jalen Brunson 20.00 50.00
25 Luka Doncic 125.00 300.00
45 Trae Young 20.00 50.00
104 Shai Gilgeous-Alexander 50.00 120.00
122 Luka Doncic 125.00 300.00
142 Trae Young 20.00 50.00
201 Shai Gilgeous-Alexander 150.00 400.00
229 Luka Doncic 1,000.00 2,000.00
249 Trae Young 40.00 100.00

2018-19 Select Prizms Tie Dye

*TIE DYE 1-100: 10X TO 25X BASIC
*TIE DYE 1-100 RC: 5X TO 12X BASIC RC
*TIE DYE 201-300: 10X TO 25X BASIC
*TIE DYE 201-300 RC: 5X TO 12X BASIC
STATED PRINT RUN 25 SER.#'d SETS
7 Shai Gilgeous-Alexander 500.00 1,000.00
8 Jalen Brunson 125.00 300.00
25 Luka Doncic 1,000.00 2,000.00
45 Trae Young 125.00 300.00
201 Shai Gilgeous-Alexander 1,000.00 2,000.00
229 Luka Doncic 3,000.00 6,000.00
249 Trae Young 300.00 600.00

2018-19 Select Prizms Tie Dye Die Cut

*TIE DYE DC: 10X TO 25X BASIC
*TIE DYE DC RC: 5X TO 12X BASIC RC
STATED PRINT RUN 25 SER.#'d SETS
104 Shai Gilgeous-Alexander 500.00 1,000.00
122 Luka Doncic 1,000.00 2,000.00
142 Trae Young 125.00 300.00

2018-19 Select Prizms Tri Color

*TRI CLR 1-100: 2X TO 5X BASIC
*TRI CLR 1-100 RC: 1X TO 2.5X BASIC RC
*TRI CLR 101-200: 2X TO 5X BASIC
*TRI CLR 101-200 RC: 1X TO 2.5X BASIC
7 Shai Gilgeous-Alexander 50.00 120.00
8 Jalen Brunson 20.00 50.00
25 Luka Doncic 125.00 300.00
45 Trae Young 20.00 50.00
104 Shai Gilgeous-Alexander 50.00 120.00
122 Luka Doncic 125.00 300.00
142 Trae Young 20.00 50.00

2018-19 Select Prizms White

*WHITE: 3X TO 8X BASIC
*WHITE RC: 1.5X TO4X BASIC RC
STATED PRINT RUN 149 SER.#'d SETS
7 Shai Gilgeous-Alexander 125.00 300.00
8 Jalen Brunson 40.00 100.00
25 Luka Doncic 300.00 600.00
45 Trae Young 40.00 100.00

2018-19 Select Prizms Zebra

*ZEBRA 1-100: 10X TO 25X BASIC
*ZEBRA 1-100 RC: 5X TO 12X BASIC RC
*ZEBRA 101-200: 10X TO 25X BASIC
*ZEBRA 101-200 RC: 5X TO 12X BASIC
*ZEBRA 201-300: 10X TO 25X BASIC
*ZEBRA 201-300 RC: 5X TO 12X BASIC
7 Shai Gilgeous-Alexander 500.00 1,000.00
8 Jalen Brunson 125.00 300.00
25 Luka Doncic 1,000.00 2,000.00
45 Trae Young 125.00 300.00
104 Shai Gilgeous-Alexander 500.00 1,000.00
122 Luka Doncic 1,000.00 2,000.00
142 Trae Young 125.00 300.00
201 Shai Gilgeous-Alexander 1,000.00 2,000.00
229 Luka Doncic 3,000.00 6,000.00
249 Trae Young 300.00 600.00

2018-19 Select Autographed Memorabilia

STATED PRINT RUN B/WN 69-199 COPIES PER
EXCHANGE DEADLINE 9/06/2020
*PURPLE/40-99: .5X TO 1.2X
*TIE DYE/25: .75X TO 2X
1 Jamal Mashburn/199 5.00 12.00
2 Shawn Bradley/199 4.00 10.00
3 Stephen Jackson/199 5.00 12.00
4 Peja Stojakovic/69 5.00 12.00
5 Clint Capela/199 5.00 12.00
6 Magic Johnson/99 75.00 200.00
7 Rik Smits/149 5.00 12.00
8 Andrew Wiggins/199 8.00 20.00
9 Enes Kanter/199 5.00 12.00
10 Christian Laettner/149 6.00 15.00
12 Derrick Favors/199 4.00 10.00
13 Dan Majerle/160 5.00 12.00
14 Terry Rozier/199 5.00 12.00
15 Tristan Thompson/184 4.00 10.00
16 Kareem Abdul-Jabbar/99 75.00 200.00
18 Karl-Anthony Towns/199 20.00 50.00
19 Luke Walton/149 4.00 10.00
20 JJ Redick/199 6.00 15.00
22 Calvin Murphy/149 5.00 12.00
23 J.J. Barea/199 6.00 15.00
24 Myles Turner/149 6.00 15.00
25 Joe Dumars/199 8.00 20.00
26 Kawhi Leonard/99 EXCH 60.00 150.00
27 Lauri Markkanen/199 10.00 25.00
28 Kevin McHale/99 10.00 25.00
29 Thaddeus Young/167 4.00 10.00

2018-19 Select Autographed Memorabilia Prizms Purple

*PURPLE: .5X TO 1.2X
STATED PRINT RUN B/WN 35-99 COPIES PER
EXCHANGE DEADLINE 9/06/2020
16 Kareem Abdul-Jabbar/65 100.00 250.00

2018-19 Select Draft Selections Memorabilia

*PURPLE/99: .5X TO 1.2X BASIC
*TIE DYE/25: 1.2X TO 3X BASIC
1 Donte DiVincenzo 4.00 10.00
2 Deandre Ayton 5.00 12.00
3 Josh Okogie 2.50 6.00
4 Jaren Jackson Jr. 8.00 20.00
5 Aaron Holiday 2.50 6.00
6 Wendell Carter Jr. 4.00 10.00
7 Landry Shamet 2.50 6.00
8 Mikal Bridges 8.00 20.00
9 Dzanan Musa 1.50 4.00
10 Michael Porter Jr. 6.00 15.00
11 Lonnie Walker IV 3.00 8.00
12 Marvin Bagley III 2.50 6.00
13 Grayson Allen 3.00 8.00
14 Trae Young 12.00 30.00
15 Anfernee Simons 8.00 20.00
16 Collin Sexton 5.00 12.00
17 Robert Williams III 3.00 8.00
18 Shai Gilgeous-Alexander 25.00 60.00
19 Omari Spellman 1.50 4.00
20 Troy Brown Jr. 2.00 5.00
21 Kevin Huerter 3.00 8.00
22 Luka Doncic 75.00 200.00
23 Chandler Hutchison 2.00 5.00
24 Mo Bamba 2.50 6.00
25 Moritz Wagner 3.00 8.00
26 Kevin Knox 2.00 5.00
27 Jacob Evans III 1.50 4.00
28 Jerome Robinson 1.50 4.00
29 Elie Okobo 1.50 4.00
30 Zhaire Smith 1.50 4.00

2018-19 Select Global Icons

*SILVER/99: 2.5X TO 6X BASIC
1 Patrick Ewing 1.25 3.00
2 Kristaps Porzingis 1.00 2.50
3 Drazen Petrovic 1.00 2.50
4 Ricky Rubio .60 1.50
5 Ben Simmons .75 2.00
6 Giannis Antetokounmpo 4.00 10.00
7 Marc Gasol .75 2.00
8 Rudy Gobert 1.00 2.50
9 Hakeem Olajuwon 1.00 2.50
10 Nikola Jokic 4.00 10.00
11 Yao Ming 2.00 5.00
12 Joel Embiid 2.00 5.00
13 Steve Nash 1.50 4.00
14 Pau Gasol 1.25 3.00
15 Dirk Nowitzki 2.00 5.00

2018-19 Select In Flight Signatures

STATED PRINT RUN B/WN 49-199 COPIES PER
EXCHANGE DEADLINE 9/06/2020
*GREEN/99: .5X TO 1.2X p/r 199
*GREEN/35: .6X TO 1.5X p/r 199
*GREEN/35: .5X TO 1.2X p/r 99
*GREEN/35: .4X TO 1X p/r 49
*TIE DYE/25: .75X TO 2X p/r 199
*TIE DYE/25: .6X TO 1.5X p/r 99
*TIE DYE/25: .5X TO 1.2X p/r 49
1 Kobe Bryant/49 1,250.00 2,500.00
2 Dwyane Wade/49 75.00 200.00
3 Damian Lillard/49 75.00 200.00
4 Kyrie Irving/49 75.00 200.00
5 Julius Erving/49 100.00 250.00
6 Kawhi Leonard/49 75.00 200.00
7 Alonzo Mourning/49 40.00 100.00
8 Giannis Antetokounmpo/49 150.00 400.00
9 Andrew Wiggins/99 8.00 20.00
10 Clyde Drexler/99 25.00 60.00
11 Brandon Ingram/99 EXCH 6.00 15.00
12 Antonio McDyess/199 4.00 10.00
13 Cedric Ceballos/99 3.00 8.00
14 Isaiah Rider/199 4.00 10.00
15 Chauncey Billups/199 12.00 30.00
16 Clifford Robinson/199 5.00 12.00
17 Darrell Griffith/199 4.00 10.00
18 Dee Brown/199 4.00 10.00
19 Detlef Schrempf/99 5.00 12.00
20 Jalen Rose/199 4.00 10.00
21 Donovan Mitchell/99 75.00 200.00
22 Kyle Kuzma/199 5.00 12.00
23 Jayson Tatum/99 150.00 400.00
24 Robert Horry/199 5.00 12.00
25 Larry Nance/199 4.00 10.00
26 Latrell Sprewell/99 6.00 15.00
27 Mitch Richmond/199 6.00 15.00
28 Myles Turner/199 5.00 12.00
29 Shareef Abdur-Rahim/199 4.00 10.00
30 Terry Rozier/199 4.00 10.00

2018-19 Select In Flight Signatures Prizms Neon Green

*GREEN/99: .5X TO 1.2X p/r 199
*GREEN/35: .6X TO 1.5X p/r 199
*GREEN/35: .5X TO 1.2X p/r 99
*GREEN/35: .4X TO 1X p/r 49
STATED PRINT RUN B/WN 35-99 COPIES PER
EXCHANGE DEADLINE 9/06/2020

2018-19 Select In Flight Signatures Prizms Tie Dye

*TIE DYE/25: .75X TO 2X p/r 199
*TIE DYE/25: .6X TO 1.5X p/r 99
*TIE DYE/25: .5X TO 1.2X p/r 49
STATED PRINT RUN 25 SER.#'d SETS
EXCHANGE DEADLINE 9/06/2020

2018-19 Select Phenomenon

*SILVER/99: 2.5X TO 6X BASIC
1 Collin Sexton 3.00 8.00
2 Michael Porter Jr. 4.00 10.00
3 Donte DiVincenzo 2.50 6.00
4 Omari Spellman 1.00 2.50
5 Grayson Allen 2.00 5.00
6 Trae Young 8.00 20.00
7 Jaren Jackson Jr. 8.00 20.00
8 Josh Okogie 1.50 4.00
9 Aaron Holiday 1.50 4.00
10 Landry Shamet 1.50 4.00
11 Deandre Ayton 3.00 8.00
12 Mikal Bridges 5.00 12.00
13 Dzanan Musa 1.00 2.50
14 Robert Williams III 2.00 5.00
15 Hamidou Diallo 1.50 4.00
16 Troy Brown Jr. 1.25 3.00
17 Jarred Vanderbilt 2.00 5.00
18 Keita Bates-Diop 1.25 3.00
19 Anfernee Simons 5.00 12.00
20 Lonnie Walker IV 2.00 5.00
21 De'Anthony Melton 2.00 5.00
22 Mo Bamba 1.50 4.00
23 Elie Okobo 1.00 2.50
24 Shai Gilgeous-Alexander 12.00 30.00
25 Jacob Evans III 1.00 2.50
26 Wendell Carter Jr. 2.50 6.00
27 Jerome Robinson 1.00 2.50
28 Kevin Huerter 2.00 5.00
29 Bruce Brown 2.00 5.00
30 Luka Doncic 40.00 100.00
31 Devonte' Graham 1.50 4.00
32 Moritz Wagner 2.00 5.00
33 Gary Trent Jr. 2.00 5.00
34 Svi Mykhailiuk 1.25 3.00
35 Jalen Brunson 8.00 20.00
36 Zhaire Smith 1.00 2.50
37 Jevon Carter 1.50 4.00
38 Kevin Knox 1.25 3.00
39 Chandler Hutchison 1.25 3.00
40 Marvin Bagley III 1.50 4.00

2018-19 Select Rookie Jersey Autographs

STATED PRINT RUN B/WN 99-199 COPIES PER
EXCHANGE DEADLINE 9/06/2020
*PURPLE/99: .5X TO 1.2X p/r 199
*PURPLE/49: .6X TO 1.5X p/r 199
*PURPLE/49: .5X TO 1.2X p/r 99
*TIE DYE/25: 1.2X TO 3X p/r 199
*TIE DYE/25: 1X TO 2.5X p/r 99
1 De'Anthony Melton/199 6.00 15.00
2 Gary Trent Jr./199 6.00 15.00
3 Robert Williams III/199 6.00 15.00
4 Grayson Allen/99 8.00 20.00
5 Bruce Brown/99 8.00 20.00
6 Devonte' Graham/99 6.00 15.00
7 Jalen Brunson/99 75.00 200.00
8 Jaren Jackson Jr./99 60.00 150.00
9 Keita Bates-Diop/99 5.00 12.00
10 Collin Sexton/99 12.00 30.00
11 Landry Shamet/199 EXCH 5.00 12.00
12 Jevon Carter/199 5.00 12.00
13 Kevin Huerter/199 6.00 15.00
14 Chandler Hutchison/199 4.00 10.00
15 Marvin Bagley III/199 5.00 12.00
16 Mikal Bridges/199 15.00 40.00
17 Dzanan Musa/199 3.00 8.00
18 Deandre Ayton/199 10.00 25.00
19 Aaron Holiday/199 5.00 12.00
20 Hamidou Diallo/199 5.00 12.00
21 Lonnie Walker IV/199 6.00 15.00
22 Jacob Evans III/199 3.00 8.00
23 Zhaire Smith/199 3.00 8.00
24 Donte DiVincenzo/199 8.00 20.00
25 Moritz Wagner/199 6.00 15.00
26 Kevin Knox/199 4.00 10.00
27 Shai Gilgeous-Alexander/199 300.00 600.00
28 Trae Young/199 150.00 400.00
29 Mo Bamba/199 5.00 12.00
30 Luka Doncic/199 800.00 1,500.00
31 Anfernee Simons/199 15.00 40.00
32 Troy Brown Jr./199 4.00 10.00
33 Michael Porter Jr./199 12.00 30.00
34 Wendell Carter Jr./199 8.00 20.00
35 Jerome Robinson/199 4.00 10.00
36 Josh Okogie/199 5.00 12.00
37 Svi Mykhailiuk/199 4.00 10.00
38 Omari Spellman/199 3.00 8.00
39 Elie Okobo/199 3.00 8.00
40 Jarred Vanderbilt/199 6.00 15.00

2018-19 Select Rookie Signatures

STATED PRINT RUN 199 SER.#'d SETS
EXCHANGE DEADLINE 9/06/2020
*NEON GREEN/99: .5X TO 1.2X BASIC
*TIE DYE/25: 1X TO 2.5X BASIC
1 De'Anthony Melton 6.00 15.00
2 Gary Trent Jr. 6.00 15.00
3 Robert Williams III 6.00 15.00
4 Grayson Allen 6.00 15.00
5 Bruce Brown 6.00 15.00
6 Devonte' Graham 5.00 12.00
7 Jalen Brunson 75.00 200.00
8 Jaren Jackson Jr. 60.00 150.00
9 Keita Bates-Diop 4.00 10.00
10 Collin Sexton 10.00 25.00
11 Landry Shamet 5.00 12.00
12 Jevon Carter 5.00 12.00
13 Kevin Huerter EXCH 6.00 15.00
14 Chandler Hutchison 4.00 10.00
15 Marvin Bagley III 5.00 12.00
16 Mikal Bridges 15.00 40.00
17 Dzanan Musa 3.00 8.00
18 Deandre Ayton 10.00 25.00
19 Aaron Holiday 5.00 12.00
20 Hamidou Diallo 5.00 12.00
21 Lonnie Walker IV 6.00 15.00
22 Jacob Evans III 3.00 8.00
23 Zhaire Smith 3.00 8.00
24 Donte DiVincenzo 8.00 20.00
25 Moritz Wagner 6.00 15.00
26 Kevin Knox 4.00 10.00
27 Shai Gilgeous-Alexander 300.00 600.00
28 Trae Young 150.00 400.00
29 Mo Bamba 5.00 12.00
30 Luka Doncic 600.00 1,200.00
31 Anfernee Simons 15.00 40.00
32 Troy Brown Jr. 4.00 10.00
33 Michael Porter Jr. 12.00 30.00
34 Wendell Carter Jr. 8.00 20.00
35 Jerome Robinson 3.00 8.00
36 Josh Okogie 5.00 12.00
37 Svi Mykhailiuk 4.00 10.00
38 Omari Spellman 3.00 8.00
39 Elie Okobo 3.00 8.00
40 Jarred Vanderbilt 6.00 15.00

2018-19 Select Signatures

STATED PRINT RUN B/WN 49-199 COPIES PER
EXCHANGE DEADLINE 9/06/2020
*GREEN/99: .5X TO 1.2X p/r 199
*GREEN/35: .6X TO 1.5X p/r 199
*GREEN/35: .5X TO 1.2X p/r 99
*GREEN/35: .4X TO 1X p/r 49
*TIE DYE/25: .75X TO 2X p/r 199
*TIE DYE/25: .6X TO 1.5X p/r 99
*TIE DYE/25: .5X TO 1.2X p/r 49
1 Larry Bird/49 50.00 120.00
2 Gary Harris/199 4.00 10.00
3 Kareem Abdul-Jabbar/49 25.00 60.00
4 John Collins/199 5.00 12.00
5 Paul Pierce/99 EXCH 15.00 40.00
6 Tyus Jones/199 3.00 8.00
7 Bryant Reeves/199 3.00 8.00
8 Dikembe Mutombo/199 8.00 20.00
SG-CBK Charles Barkley/49 75.00 200.00
10 J.J. Barea/199 5.00 12.00
11 Magic Johnson/49 30.00 80.00
12 Elfrid Payton/199 4.00 10.00
13 Oscar Robertson/49 20.00 50.00
14 Gerald Green/199 4.00 10.00
15 Arvydas Sabonis/199 5.00 12.00
16 Wally Szczerbiak/199 4.00 10.00
17 Clint Capela/199 4.00 10.00
18 Elden Campbell/199 3.00 8.00
19 Stephen Curry/49 EXCH 500.00 1,000.00
20 Jack Sikma/199 4.00 10.00
21 John Stockton/49 20.00 50.00
22 Enes Kanter/199 4.00 10.00
23 Ray Allen/99 15.00 40.00
24 Maurice Harkless/199 3.00 8.00
25 Bruce Bowen/199 4.00 10.00
26 Zydrunas Ilgauskas/199 4.00 10.00
27 Dave Cowens/199 6.00 15.00
28 Gail Goodrich/199 5.00 12.00
29 Kevin Durant/49 50.00 120.00
30 Joe Ingles/199 4.00 10.00

2018-19 Select Signatures Prizms Neon Green

*GREEN/99: .5X TO 1.2X p/r 199
*GREEN/35: .6X TO 1.5X p/r 199
*GREEN/35: .5X TO 1.2X p/r 99
*GREEN/35: .4X TO 1X p/r 49
STATED PRINT RUN B/WN 35-99 COPIES PER
EXCHANGE DEADLINE 9/06/2020
1 Larry Bird/35 60.00 150.00
3 Kareem Abdul-Jabbar/35 30.00 80.00
SG-CBK Charles Barkley/35 100.00 250.00
19 Stephen Curry/35 EXCH 500.00 1,000.00

2018-19 Select Signatures Prizms Tie Dye

*TIE DYE/25: .75X TO 2X p/r 199
*TIE DYE/25: .6X TO 1.5X p/r 99
*TIE DYE/25: .5X TO 1.2X p/r 49
STATED PRINT RUN 25 SER.#'d SETS
EXCHANGE DEADLINE 9/06/2020
1 Larry Bird 75.00 200.00
3 Kareem Abdul-Jabbar 40.00 100.00
SG-CBK Charles Barkley 125.00 300.00
11 Magic Johnson 50.00 120.00
13 Oscar Robertson 30.00 80.00
19 Stephen Curry EXCH 600.00 1,200.00

2018-19 Select Slash and Dash

*SILVER/99: 1.5X TO 4X BASIC
1 Tim Hardaway 1.00 2.50
2 Allen Iverson 2.00 5.00
3 Devin Booker 2.00 5.00
4 Vince Carter 1.50 4.00
5 Victor Oladipo .60 1.50
6 Kobe Bryant 6.00 15.00
7 Rajon Rondo 1.00 2.50
8 Goran Dragic .60 1.50
9 Dominique Wilkins 1.25 3.00
10 Kawhi Leonard 2.00 5.00
11 Latrell Sprewell 1.00 2.50
12 LeBron James 6.00 15.00
13 Jerry West 1.50 4.00
14 Tracy McGrady 1.25 3.00
15 Tony Parker 1.25 3.00
16 Jimmy Butler 1.25 3.00
17 Derrick Rose 1.50 4.00
18 Kevin Durant 3.00 8.00
19 Giannis Antetokounmpo 4.00 10.00
20 James Harden 1.50 4.00
21 Donovan Mitchell 2.50 6.00
22 Jeremy Lin 1.25 3.00
23 Oscar Robertson 1.50 4.00
24 John Wall 1.00 2.50
25 Scottie Pippen 2.00 5.00
26 DeMar DeRozan 1.00 2.50
27 Russell Westbrook 1.25 3.00
28 Paul George 1.25 3.00
29 Clyde Drexler 1.25 3.00
30 Kyrie Irving 2.00 5.00

2018-19 Select Sparks Memorabilia

*PURPLE/99: .5X TO 1.2X BASIC
*COPPER/49: .6X TO 1.5X BASIC
*TIE DYE/25: 1.2X TO 3X BASIC
1 Deandre Ayton 5.00 12.00
2 Marvin Bagley III 2.50 6.00
3 Luka Doncic 75.00 200.00
4 Jaren Jackson Jr. 12.00 30.00
5 Trae Young 12.00 30.00
6 Mo Bamba 2.50 6.00
7 Wendell Carter Jr. 4.00 10.00
8 Collin Sexton 5.00 12.00
9 Kevin Knox 2.50 6.00
10 Mikal Bridges 8.00 20.00

2018-19 Select Swatches

*PURPLE/99: .5X TO 1.2X BASIC
*COPPER/49: .6X TO 1.5X BASIC
*TIE DYE/25: 1.25X TO 3X BASIC
1 Jimmy Butler 4.00 10.00
2 Joe Harris 2.00 5.00
3 Joel Embiid 6.00 15.00
4 John Collins 2.50 6.00
5 John Starks 2.00 5.00
6 Jonas Valanciunas 2.50 6.00
7 Jonathan Isaac 2.50 6.00
8 JR Smith 2.50 6.00
9 Jrue Holiday 3.00 8.00
10 Jusuf Nurkic 2.50 6.00
11 Karl Malone 5.00 12.00
12 Karl-Anthony Towns 4.00 10.00
13 Kevin Garnett 6.00 15.00
14 Kevin Love 2.00 5.00
15 Khris Middleton 2.50 6.00
16 Kobe Bryant 20.00 50.00
17 Kristaps Porzingis 3.00 8.00
18 Kyle Lowry 2.50 6.00
19 Kyrie Irving 6.00 15.00
20 Markieff Morris 1.50 4.00

2018-19 Select Throwback Memorabilia

*PURPLE: .5X TO 1.2X BASIC
*COPPER: .6X TO 1.5X BASIC
*TIE DYE: 1.2X TO 3X BASIC
1 Enes Kanter 2.00 5.00
2 Vince Carter 5.00 12.00
4 Raymond Felton 1.50 4.00
5 Derrick Rose 5.00 12.00
6 Carmelo Anthony 4.00 10.00
8 Iman Shumpert 1.50 4.00
9 Jamal Crawford 2.50 6.00
10 Kris Dunn 1.50 4.00
11 Evan Turner 1.50 4.00
12 Paul Millsap 2.00 5.00
13 Omri Casspi 1.50 4.00
14 Taj Gibson 1.50 4.00
15 George Hill 2.00 5.00
16 Trey Burke 1.50 4.00
17 Jose Calderon 1.50 4.00
18 DeMarre Carroll 1.50 4.00
19 Lance Stephenson 2.00 5.00
20 Kyle O'Quinn 1.50 4.00
21 Paul George 4.00 10.00
22 Nicolas Batum 1.50 4.00
23 LeBron James 40.00 100.00
24 Marcin Gortat 1.50 4.00
25 Robin Lopez 1.50 4.00
26 Isaiah Thomas 2.00 5.00
27 Doug McDermott 1.50 4.00
28 Tobias Harris 2.00 5.00
29 Rodney Hood 2.00 5.00
30 Terrence Ross 2.00 5.00
31 Allen Crabbe 1.50 4.00
32 Evan Fournier 2.00 5.00
33 Wesley Matthews 1.50 4.00
34 Julius Randle 2.50 6.00
35 DeAndre Jordan 2.00 5.00
36 Wilson Chandler 1.50 4.00
37 Danilo Gallinari 2.00 5.00
38 Rajon Rondo 3.00 8.00
39 Matthew Dellavedova 2.00 5.00
40 Chandler Parsons 1.50 4.00

2018-19 Select Top Selections
*SILVER/99: 1.5X TO 4X BASIC
1 Patrick Ewing 1.25 3.00
2 Anthony Davis 2.00 5.00
3 Andrew Wiggins 1.00 2.50
4 LeBron James 6.00 15.00
5 Tim Duncan 2.00 5.00
6 Deandre Ayton 1.50 4.00
7 Chris Webber 1.00 2.50
8 Ben Simmons .75 2.00
9 David Robinson 1.50 4.00
10 Karl-Anthony Towns 1.25 3.00
11 Hakeem Olajuwon 1.00 2.50
12 John Wall 1.00 2.50
13 Markelle Fultz .60 1.50
14 Yao Ming 2.00 5.00
15 Allen Iverson 2.00 5.00

2018-19 Select X Factor Memorabilia
*PURPLE/99: .5X TO 1.2X BASIC
*COPPER/49: .6X TO 1.5X BASIC
*TIE DYE/21-25: 1.2X TO 3X BASIC
1 Aaron Gordon 2.50 6.00
2 Al Horford 2.50 6.00
3 Allen Iverson 6.00 15.00
4 Andre Drummond 2.00 5.00
5 Andrew Wiggins 3.00 8.00
6 Bradley Beal 3.00 8.00
7 Brook Lopez 2.00 5.00
8 Allen Crabbe 1.50 4.00
9 Chris Webber 3.00 8.00
10 CJ McCollum 2.50 6.00
11 Clint Capela 2.00 5.00
12 Courtney Lee 1.50 4.00
13 Danilo Gallinari 2.00 5.00
14 DeAndre Jordan 2.00 5.00
15 DeMar DeRozan 3.00 8.00
16 DeMarcus Cousins 2.00 5.00
17 Dennis Smith Jr. 1.50 4.00
18 Derrick Rose 5.00 12.00
19 Draymond Green 3.00 8.00
20 Enes Kanter 2.00 5.00
21 Jamal Crawford 2.50 6.00
22 Jarrett Allen 2.50 6.00
23 Jayson Tatum 10.00 25.00
24 Jaylen Brown 4.00 10.00
25 Jeremy Lamb 1.50 4.00
26 John Wall 3.00 8.00
27 Josh Jackson 1.50 4.00
28 Kawhi Leonard 6.00 15.00
29 Kelly Oubre Jr. 2.50 6.00
30 Kevin Durant 10.00 25.00

2019-20 Select
*SCOPE: 1.5X TO 4X BASIC
*TRI CLR: 1.5X TO 4X BASIC
*BLUE DC/249: 2X TO 5X BASIC
*MAROON DC/175: 2X TO 5X BASIC
*PURPLE DC/99: 2.5X TO 6X BASIC
*ORANGE DC/65: 3X TO 8X BASIC
*DISCO RED/49: 4X TO 10X BASIC
1 Zion Williamson RC 4.00 10.00
2 Dylan Windler RC .60 1.50
3 Tacko Fall RC .60 1.50
4 James Harden .75 2.00
5 Julius Randle .50 1.25
6 Admiral Schofield RC .60 1.50
7 Kyle Guy RC .60 1.50
8 Cameron Johnson RC 1.25 3.00
9 Zach Norvell Jr. RC .60 1.50
10 Darius Garland 1.00 2.50
11 Quinndary Weatherspoon RC .50 1.25
12 Eric Paschall RC .30 .75
13 Talen Horton-Tucker RC .75 2.00
14 Jaren Jackson Jr. .60 1.50
15 Justin Robinson RC .60 1.50
16 Andre Drummond .30 .75
17 Kyle Lowry .40 1.00
18 Carsen Edwards RC .60 1.50
19 Mfiondu Kabengele RC .60 1.50
20 De'Aaron Fox .60 1.50
21 RJ Barrett RC 2.00 5.00
22 Giannis Antetokounmpo 2.00 5.00
23 Terry Rozier .30 .75
24 Jarrett Culver RC .50 1.25
25 Karl-Anthony Towns .60 1.50
26 Anthony Davis 1.00 2.50
27 Kyrie Irving .75 2.00
28 Chris Paul .75 2.00
29 Nassir Little RC .75 2.00
30 Deandre Ayton .40 1.00
31 Romeo Langford RC .50 1.25
32 Goga Bitadze RC .75 2.00
33 Trae Young 1.00 2.50
34 Jaxson Hayes RC .75 2.00
35 Kawhi Leonard 1.00 2.50
36 Ben Simmons .40 1.00
37 KZ Okpala RC .60 1.50
38 CJ McCollum .40 1.00
39 Naz Reid RC 2.00 5.00
40 De'Andre Hunter RC 2.00 5.00
41 Rudy Gobert .50 1.25
42 Grant Williams RC .75 2.00
43 Tremont Waters RC .60 1.50
44 Jaylen Nowell RC .60 1.50
45 Keldon Johnson RC 1.50 4.00
46 Blake Griffin .40 1.00
47 LeBron James 3.00 8.00
48 Coby White RC 1.50 4.00
49 Nickeil Alexander-Walker RC .75 2.00
50 DeMar DeRozan .50 1.25
51 Rui Hachimura RC 2.00 5.00
52 Ignas Brazdeikis RC .60 1.50
53 Ty Jerome RC 1.00 2.50
54 Jayson Tatum 1.50 4.00
55 Kemba Walker .30 .75
56 Bol Bol RC 1.25 3.00
57 Lonzo Ball .40 1.00
58 Cody Martin RC .75 2.00
59 Nicolas Claxton RC 1.00 2.50
60 Derrick Rose .75 2.00
61 Russell Westbrook .60 1.50
62 Isaiah Roby RC .60 1.50
63 Tyler Herro RC 2.50 6.00
64 Jimmy Butler .75 2.00
65 Kevin Durant 1.25 3.00
66 Bradley Beal .50 1.25
67 Luka Doncic 2.50 6.00
68 Collin Sexton .50 1.25
69 Nikola Jokic 2.00 5.00
70 Devin Booker .10 .25
71 Sekou Doumbouya RC .50 1.25
72 Ja Morant RC 5.00 12.00
73 Victor Oladipo .30 .75
74 Joel Embiid .75 2.00
75 Kevin Knox II .25 .60
76 Brandon Clarke RC 1.00 2.50
77 Luka Samanic RC .60 1.50
78 Damian Lillard 1.00 2.50
79 Nikola Vucevic .30 .75
80 Darius Bazley .25 .60
81 Shai Gilgeous-Alexander 2.00 5.00
82 Jalen Lecque RC .50 1.25
83 Zach LaVine .60 1.50
84 John Wall .50 1.25
85 Kevin Porter Jr. RC 1.00 2.50
86 Bruno Fernando RC .60 1.50
87 Marvin Bagley III .30 .75
88 D'Angelo Russell .30 .75
89 Pascal Siakam .60 1.50
90 Donovan Mitchell .75 2.00
91 Stephen Curry 3.00 8.00
92 Jamal Murray .60 1.50
93 PJ Washington Jr. RC 1.50 4.00
94 Jordan Poole RC 2.00 5.00
95 Khris Middleton .40 1.00
96 Cam Reddish RC .75 2.00
97 Matisse Thybulle RC 1.00 2.50
98 Daniel Gafford .50 1.25
99 Paul George .60 1.50
100 Draymond Green .50 1.25
101 JJ Redick .40 1.00
102 Aaron Gordon .40 1.00
103 Kevin Knox II .25 .60
104 Brandon Clarke 1.00 2.50
105 Luka Samanic .60 1.50
106 Damian Lillard 1.00 2.50
107 Nikola Jokic 2.00 5.00
108 Dwight Howard .50 1.25
109 Sekou Doumbouya .50 1.25
110 Isaiah Thomas .30 .75
111 Joel Embiid .75 2.00
112 Al Horford .40 1.00
113 Kevin Love .40 1.00
114 Brandon Ingram .40 1.00
115 Malcolm Brogdon .30 .75
116 Darius Bazley .50 1.25
117 Paul George .60 1.50
118 Eric Bledsoe .30 .75
119 Stephen Curry 3.00 8.00
120 Ja Morant 5.00 12.00
121 John Collins .40 1.00
122 Allonzo Trier .25 .60
123 Kristaps Porzingis .50 1.25
124 Brook Lopez .30 .75
125 Malik Monk .40 1.00
126 Darius Garland 2.00 5.00
127 PJ Washington Jr. 1.50 4.00
128 Fred VanVleet .50 1.25
129 Steven Adams .30 .75
130 Jabari Parker .25 .60
131 Jonas Valanciunas .30 .75
132 Andrew Wiggins .50 1.25
133 Kyle Kuzma .50 1.25
134 Buddy Hield .30 .75
135 Marc Gasol .75 2.00
136 De'Andre Hunter 1.00 2.50
137 Reggie Jackson .30 .75
138 Gary Harris .30 .75
139 Tobias Harris .30 .75
140 James Harden .75 2.00
141 Josh Richardson .25 .60
142 Anthony Davis 1.00 2.50
143 Kyrie Irving .75 2.00
144 Cam Reddish .75 2.00
145 Matisse Thybulle 1.00 2.50
146 DeAndre Jordan .30 .75
147 Ricky Rubio .30 .75
148 Giannis Antetokounmpo 2.00 5.00
149 Trae Young 1.00 2.50
150 Jarrett Allen .40 1.00
151 Jrue Holiday .40 1.00
152 Bam Adebayo .60 1.50
153 LaMarcus Aldridge .40 1.00
154 Cameron Johnson 1.25 3.00
155 Mike Conley .30 .75
156 Delon Wright .25 .60
157 RJ Barrett 2.00 5.00
158 Goga Bitadze .75 2.00
159 Tristan Thompson .25 .60
160 Jarrett Culver .50 1.25
161 Karl-Anthony Towns .60 1.50
162 Ben Simmons .40 1.00
163 Lauri Markkanen .50 1.25
164 Chris Paul .75 2.00
165 Miles Bridges .40 1.00
166 Dennis Smith Jr. .25 .60
167 Romeo Langford .50 1.25
168 Goran Dragic .30 .75
169 Tyler Herro 2.50 6.00
170 Jaxson Hayes .75 2.00
171 Kawhi Leonard 1.00 2.50
172 Blake Griffin .40 1.00
173 LeBron James 3.00 8.00
174 CJ McCollum .40 1.00
175 Mo Bamba .30 .75
176 Devin Booker .10 .25
177 Rudy Gay .30 .75
178 Grant Williams .75 2.00
179 Victor Oladipo .30 .75
180 Jaylen Brown .60 1.50
181 Kemba Walker .30 .75
182 Bojan Bogdanovic .30 .75
183 Lou Williams .40 1.00
184 Clint Capela .30 .75
185 Myles Turner .40 1.00
186 Domantas Sabonis .50 1.25
187 Rui Hachimura 2.00 5.00
188 Harrison Barnes .30 .75
189 Wendell Carter Jr. .40 1.00
190 Jayson Tatum 1.50 4.00
191 Kevin Durant 1.25 3.00
192 Bradley Beal .50 1.25
193 Luka Doncic 2.50 6.00
194 Coby White 1.50 4.00
195 Nickeil Alexander-Walker .75 2.00
196 Donovan Mitchell .75 2.00
197 Russell Westbrook .60 1.50
198 Hassan Whiteside .25 .60
199 Zion Williamson 4.00 10.00
200 Jimmy Butler .75 2.00
201 Kevin Knox II .50 1.25
202 Cameron Johnson 2.50 6.00
203 Malcolm Brogdon .60 1.50
204 Darius Garland 4.00 10.00
205 Paul George 1.25 3.00
206 Draymond Green 1.00 2.50
207 Stephen Curry 6.00 15.00
208 Ja Morant 10.00 25.00
209 Joel Embiid 1.50 4.00
210 Admiral Schofield 1.25 3.00
211 Kevin Porter Jr. 2.00 5.00
212 Carsen Edwards 1.25 3.00
213 Marvin Bagley III .60 1.50
214 De'Aaron Fox 1.25 3.00
215 PJ Washington Jr. 3.00 8.00
216 Dwight Howard 1.00 2.50
217 Tacko Fall 1.25 3.00
218 Jamal Murray 1.25 3.00
219 John Wall 1.00 2.50
220 Andre Drummond .60 1.50
221 Khris Middleton .75 2.00
222 Chris Paul 1.50 4.00
223 Matisse Thybulle 2.00 5.00
224 Deandre Ayton .75 2.00
225 Quinndary Weatherspoon 1.00 2.50
226 Dylan Windler 1.25 3.00
227 Terry Rozier .60 1.50
228 James Harden 1.50 4.00
229 Jordan Poole 4.00 10.00
230 Anthony Davis 2.00 5.00
231 Kyle Lowry .75 2.00
232 CJ McCollum .75 2.00
233 Mfiondu Kabengele 1.25 3.00
234 De'Andre Hunter 4.00 10.00
235 RJ Barrett 4.00 10.00
236 Eric Paschall 1.25 3.00
237 Trae Young 2.00 5.00
238 Jaren Jackson Jr. 1.25 3.00
239 Josh Richardson .50 1.25
240 Ben Simmons .75 2.00
241 Kyrie Irving 1.50 4.00
242 Coby White 3.00 8.00
243 Mike Conley .60 1.50
244 DeAndre Jordan .60 1.50
245 Romeo Langford 1.00 2.50
246 Giannis Antetokounmpo 4.00 10.00
247 Tremont Waters 1.25 3.00
248 Jarrett Culver 1.00 2.50
249 Julius Randle 1.00 2.50
250 Blake Griffin .75 2.00
251 KZ Okpala 1.25 3.00
252 Cody Martin 1.50 4.00
253 Nassir Little 1.50 4.00
254 Delon Wright .50 1.25
255 Rudy Gobert 1.00 2.50
256 Goga Bitadze 1.50 4.00
257 Ty Jerome 2.00 5.00
258 Jaxson Hayes 1.50 4.00
259 Karl-Anthony Towns 1.25 3.00
260 Bol Bol 2.50 6.00
262 Collin Sexton 1.00 2.50
263 Nickeil Alexander-Walker 1.50 4.00
264 DeMar DeRozan 1.00 2.50
265 Rui Hachimura 4.00 10.00
266 Grant Williams 1.50 4.00
267 Tyler Herro 5.00 12.00
268 Jaylen Nowell 1.25 3.00
269 Kawhi Leonard 2.00 5.00
270 Bradley Beal 1.00 2.50
271 Lonzo Ball .75 2.00
272 Damian Lillard 2.00 5.00
273 Nikola Jokic 4.00 10.00
274 Derrick Rose 1.50 4.00
275 Russell Westbrook 1.25 3.00
276 Hassan Whiteside .50 1.25
277 Victor Oladipo .60 1.50
278 Jayson Tatum 3.00 8.00
279 Keldon Johnson 3.00 8.00
280 Brandon Clarke 2.00 5.00
281 Luka Doncic 5.00 12.00
282 D'Angelo Russell .60 1.50
283 Nikola Vucevic .60 1.50
284 Devin Booker .20 .50
285 Sekou Doumbouya 1.00 2.50
286 Ignas Brazdeikis 1.25 3.00
287 Zach LaVine 1.25 3.00
288 Jimmy Butler 1.50 4.00
289 Kemba Walker .60 1.50
290 Bruno Fernando 1.25 3.00
291 Luka Samanic 1.25 3.00
292 Darius Bazley 1.00 2.50
293 Pascal Siakam 1.25 3.00
294 Donovan Mitchell 1.50 4.00
295 Shai Gilgeous-Alexander 4.00 10.00
296 Isaiah Roby 1.25 3.00
297 Zion Williamson 8.00 20.00
298 JJ Redick .75 2.00
299 Kevin Durant 2.50 6.00
300 Cam Reddish 1.50 4.00

2019-20 Select Prizms Disco
*DISCO: 1.5X TO 4X BASIC
207 Stephen Curry 40.00 100.00
261 LeBron James 40.00 100.00

2019-20 Select Prizms Disco Blue
*DISCO BLUE 1-100: 8X TO 20X BASIC
*DISCO BLUE 1-100 RC: 4X TO 10X BASIC RC
*DISCO BLUE 101-200: 5X TO 12X BASIC
*DISCO BLUE 101-200 RC: 2.5X TO 6X BASIC
*DISCO BLUE 201-300: 4X TO 10X BASIC
*DISCO BLUE 201-300 RC: 2X TO 5X BASIC
STATED PRINT RUN 25 SER.#'d SETS
1 Zion Williamson 1,000.00 2,000.00
8 Cameron Johnson 20.00 50.00
10 Darius Garland 40.00 100.00
12 Eric Paschall 40.00 100.00
21 RJ Barrett 125.00 300.00
22 Giannis Antetokounmpo 150.00 400.00
24 Jarrett Culver 5.00 12.00
29 Nassir Little 15.00 40.00
33 Trae Young 150.00 400.00
34 Jaxson Hayes 20.00 50.00
35 Kawhi Leonard 60.00 150.00
39 Naz Reid 75.00 200.00
40 De'Andre Hunter 50.00 120.00
45 Keldon Johnson 20.00 50.00
47 LeBron James 300.00 6,000.00
48 Coby White 150.00 400.00
51 Rui Hachimura 100.00 250.00
56 Bol Bol 40.00 100.00
63 Tyler Herro 500.00 1,000.00
67 Luka Doncic 300.00 600.00
71 Sekou Doumbouya 5.00 12.00
72 Ja Morant 800.00 1,500.00
76 Brandon Clarke 60.00 150.00
81 Shai Gilgeous-Alexander 20.00 50.00
82 Jalen Lecque 30.00 80.00
85 Kevin Porter Jr. 10.00 25.00
86 Bruno Fernando 12.00 30.00
91 Stephen Curry 75.00 200.00
93 PJ Washington Jr. 50.00 120.00
94 Jordan Poole 400.00 800.00
97 Matisse Thybulle 40.00 100.00
104 Brandon Clarke 60.00 150.00
119 Stephen Curry 75.00 200.00
120 Ja Morant 800.00 1,500.00
126 Darius Garland 40.00 100.00
127 PJ Washington Jr. 50.00 120.00
145 Matisse Thybulle 40.00 100.00
148 Giannis Antetokounmpo 150.00 400.00
149 Trae Young 150.00 400.00
154 Cameron Johnson 20.00 50.00
157 RJ Barrett 125.00 300.00
169 Tyler Herro 500.00 1,000.00
170 Jaxson Hayes 20.00 50.00
171 Kawhi Leonard 60.00 150.00
173 LeBron James 300.00 600.00
193 Luka Doncic 300.00 600.00
194 Coby White 150.00 400.00
199 Zion Williamson 1,000.00 2,000.00
202 Cameron Johnson 60.00 150.00
204 Darius Garland 60.00 150.00
207 Stephen Curry 100.00 250.00
208 Ja Morant 1,500.00 3,000.00
211 Kevin Porter Jr. 10.00 25.00
215 PJ Washington Jr. 75.00 200.00
217 Tacko Fall 25.00 60.00
223 Matisse Thybulle 60.00 150.00
229 Jordan Poole 400.00 800.00
234 De'Andre Hunter 75.00 200.00
235 RJ Barrett 200.00 500.00
236 Eric Paschall 60.00 150.00
237 Trae Young 200.00 500.00
242 Coby White 300.00 600.00
246 Giannis Antetokounmpo 300.00 600.00
252 Cody Martin 15.00 40.00
258 Jaxson Hayes 60.00 150.00
260 Bol Bol 60.00 150.00
261 LeBron James 400.00 800.00
263 Nickeil Alexander-Walker 20.00 50.00
267 Tyler Herro 1,000.00 2,000.00
269 Kawhi Leonard 75.00 200.00
278 Jayson Tatum 60.00 150.00
279 Keldon Johnson 60.00 150.00
280 Brandon Clarke 125.00 300.00
281 Luka Doncic 400.00 800.00
290 Bruno Fernando 20.00 50.00
295 Shai Gilgeous-Alexander 25.00 60.00
297 Zion Williamson 2,000.00 4,000.00

2019-20 Select Prizms Light Blue
*LIGHT BLUE: 1.5X TO 4X BASIC
STATED PRINT RUN 299 SER.#'d SETS
1 Zion Williamson 40.00 100.00
72 Ja Morant 75.00 200.00

2019-20 Select Prizms Neon Green
*NEON GRN: 2.5X TO 6X BASIC
*NEON GRN RC: 1.2X TO 3X BASIC RC
STATED PRINT RUN 75 SER.#'d SETS
1 Zion Williamson 500.00 1,000.00
3 Tacko Fall 12.00 30.00
10 Darius Garland 12.00 30.00
12 Eric Paschall 8.00 20.00
21 RJ Barrett 50.00 120.00
22 Giannis Antetokounmpo 40.00 100.00
29 Nassir Little 6.00 15.00
33 Trae Young 20.00 50.00
34 Jaxson Hayes 8.00 20.00
35 Kawhi Leonard 15.00 40.00
39 Naz Reid 25.00 60.00
40 De'Andre Hunter 15.00 40.00
45 Keldon Johnson 8.00 20.00
47 LeBron James 125.00 300.00
48 Coby White 100.00 250.00
49 Nickeil Alexander-Walker 8.00 20.00
51 Rui Hachimura 15.00 40.00
56 Bol Bol 12.00 30.00
63 Tyler Herro 200.00 500.00
67 Luka Doncic 75.00 200.00
71 Sekou Doumbouya 1.50 4.00
72 Ja Morant 300.00 600.00
76 Brandon Clarke 15.00 40.00
81 Shai Gilgeous-Alexander 12.00 30.00
82 Jalen Lecque 10.00 25.00
85 Kevin Porter Jr. 3.00 8.00
91 Stephen Curry 20.00 50.00
93 PJ Washington Jr. 15.00 40.00
94 Jordan Poole 150.00 400.00
97 Matisse Thybulle 6.00 15.00

2019-20 Select Prizms Red
*RED: 1.5X TO 4X BASIC
STATED PRINT RUN 199 SER.#'d SETS
1 Zion Williamson 40.00 100.00
72 Ja Morant 75.00 200.00

2019-20 Select Prizms Silver
*SILVER 1-100: 1.5X TO 4X BASIC
*SILVER 1-100 RC: 1.5X TO 4X BASIC RC
*SILVER 101-200: 1.5X TO 4X BASIC
*SILVER 101-200 RC: 1.5X TO 4X BASIC
*SILVER 201-300: 1.5X TO 4X BASIC
207 Stephen Curry 40.00 100.00
208 Ja Morant 100.00 250.00
261 LeBron James 40.00 100.00
297 Zion Williamson 60.00 150.00

2019-20 Select Prizms Tie Dye
*TIE DYE 1-100: 8X TO 20X BASIC
*TIE DYE 1-100 RC: 4X TO 10X BASIC RC
*TIE DYE 201-300: 4X TO 10X BASIC
*TIE DYE 201-300 RC: 2X TO 5X BASIC
STATED PRINT RUN 25 SER.#'d SETS
1 Zion Williamson 1,000.00 2,000.00
8 Cameron Johnson 20.00 50.00
10 Darius Garland 40.00 100.00
12 Eric Paschall 40.00 100.00
21 RJ Barrett 125.00 300.00
22 Giannis Antetokounmpo 150.00 400.00
29 Nassir Little 15.00 40.00
33 Trae Young 150.00 400.00
34 Jaxson Hayes 20.00 50.00
35 Kawhi Leonard 60.00 150.00
39 Naz Reid 75.00 200.00
40 De'Andre Hunter 50.00 120.00
45 Keldon Johnson 20.00 50.00
47 LeBron James 300.00 600.00
48 Coby White 150.00 400.00
51 Rui Hachimura 100.00 250.00
56 Bol Bol 40.00 100.00
63 Tyler Herro 500.00 1,000.00
67 Luka Doncic 300.00 600.00
71 Sekou Doumbouya 5.00 12.00
72 Ja Morant 800.00 1,500.00
76 Brandon Clarke 60.00 150.00
81 Shai Gilgeous-Alexander 20.00 50.00
82 Jalen Lecque 30.00 80.00
85 Kevin Porter Jr. 10.00 25.00
86 Bruno Fernando 12.00 30.00
91 Stephen Curry 75.00 200.00
93 PJ Washington Jr. 50.00 120.00
94 Jordan Poole 400.00 800.00
97 Matisse Thybulle 40.00 100.00
202 Cameron Johnson 60.00 150.00
204 Darius Garland 60.00 150.00
207 Stephen Curry 100.00 250.00
208 Ja Morant 1,500.00 3,000.00
211 Kevin Porter Jr. 10.00 25.00
215 PJ Washington Jr. 75.00 200.00
217 Tacko Fall 25.00 60.00
221 Khris Middleton 12.00 30.00
223 Matisse Thybulle 60.00 150.00
229 Jordan Poole 400.00 800.00
234 De'Andre Hunter 75.00 200.00
235 RJ Barrett 200.00 500.00
236 Eric Paschall 60.00 150.00
237 Trae Young 200.00 500.00
242 Coby White 300.00 600.00
246 Giannis Antetokounmpo 200.00 500.00
252 Cody Martin 15.00 40.00
258 Jaxson Hayes 60.00 150.00
260 Bol Bol 60.00 150.00
261 LeBron James 500.00 1,000.00
263 Nickeil Alexander-Walker 20.00 50.00
265 Rui Hachimura 125.00 300.00
267 Tyler Herro 1,000.00 2,000.00
269 Kawhi Leonard 75.00 200.00
278 Jayson Tatum 60.00 150.00
279 Keldon Johnson 60.00 150.00
280 Brandon Clarke 125.00 300.00
281 Luka Doncic 400.00 800.00
290 Bruno Fernando 20.00 50.00
295 Shai Gilgeous-Alexander 25.00 60.00
297 Zion Williamson 2,000.00 4,000.00

2019-20 Select Prizms Tie Dye Die Cut
*TIE DYE DC: 5X TO 12X BASIC
*TIE DYE DC RC: 2.5X TO 6X BASIC RC
STATED PRINT RUN 25 SER.#'d SETS
104 Brandon Clarke 60.00 150.00
119 Stephen Curry 75.00 200.00
120 Ja Morant 800.00 1,500.00
126 Darius Garland 40.00 100.00
127 PJ Washington Jr. 50.00 120.00
145 Matisse Thybulle 40.00 100.00
148 Giannis Antetokounmpo 150.00 400.00
149 Trae Young 150.00 400.00
154 Cameron Johnson 20.00 50.00
157 RJ Barrett 125.00 300.00
169 Tyler Herro 500.00 1,000.00
170 Jaxson Hayes 20.00 50.00
171 Kawhi Leonard 60.00 150.00
173 LeBron James 300.00 600.00
187 Rui Hachimura 100.00 250.00
193 Luka Doncic 300.00 600.00
194 Coby White 150.00 400.00
199 Zion Williamson 1,000.00 2,000.00

2019-20 Select Prizms White
*WHITE: 1.5X TO 4X BASIC
*WHITE RC: .8X TO 2X BASIC RC
STATED PRINT RUN 149 SER.#'d SETS
1 Zion Williamson 50.00 120.00
39 Naz Reid 15.00 40.00
47 LeBron James 125.00 300.00
72 Ja Morant 100.00 250.00

2019-20 Select Prizms Zebra
*ZEBRA 1-100: 20X TO 50X BASIC
*ZEBRA 1-100 RC: 10X TO 25X BASIC RC
*ZEBRA 101-200: 12X TO 30X BASIC
*ZEBRA 101-200 RC: 6X TO 15X BASIC
*ZEBRA 201-300: 8X TO 20X BASIC
*ZEBRA 201-300 RC: 4X TO 10X BASIC
1 Zion Williamson 2,500.00 5,000.00
10 Darius Garland 60.00 150.00
12 Eric Paschall 60.00 150.00
21 RJ Barrett 200.00 500.00
22 Giannis Antetokounmpo 150.00 400.00
24 Jarrett Culver 100.00 250.00
33 Trae Young 100.00 250.00
35 Kawhi Leonard 125.00 300.00
39 Naz Reid 40.00 100.00
40 De'Andre Hunter 75.00 200.00
44 Jaylen Nowell 40.00 100.00
47 LeBron James 400.00 800.00
48 Coby White 200.00 500.00
51 Rui Hachimura 150.00 400.00
56 Bol Bol 40.00 100.00
63 Tyler Herro 500.00 1,000.00
67 Luka Doncic 400.00 800.00
71 Sekou Doumbouya 12.00 30.00
72 Ja Morant 1,000.00 2,000.00
76 Brandon Clarke 100.00 250.00
82 Jalen Lecque 50.00 120.00
85 Kevin Porter Jr. 25.00 60.00
91 Stephen Curry 150.00 400.00
94 Jordan Poole 1,000.00 2,000.00
97 Matisse Thybulle 60.00 150.00
104 Brandon Clarke 75.00 200.00
109 Sekou Doumbouya 12.00 30.00
120 Ja Morant 1,000.00 3,000.00
126 Darius Garland 60.00 150.00
127 PJ Washington Jr. 60.00 150.00
136 De'Andre Hunter 60.00 150.00
145 Matisse Thybulle 60.00 150.00
148 Giannis Antetokounmpo 150.00 400.00
149 Trae Young 100.00 250.00
157 RJ Barrett 200.00 500.00
160 Jarrett Culver 75.00 200.00
170 Jaxson Hayes 40.00 100.00
171 Kawhi Leonard 125.00 300.00
173 LeBron James 800.00 1,500.00
187 Rui Hachimura 300.00 600.00
191 Kevin Durant 75.00 200.00
193 Luka Doncic 400.00 800.00
194 Coby White 200.00 500.00
199 Zion Williamson 2,500.00 5,000.00
202 Cameron Johnson 100.00 250.00
204 Darius Garland 150.00 400.00
207 Stephen Curry 200.00 500.00
208 Ja Morant 3,000.00 6,000.00
211 Kevin Porter Jr. 25.00 60.00
212 Carsen Edwards 30.00 80.00
215 PJ Washington Jr. 150.00 400.00
217 Tacko Fall 125.00 300.00
223 Matisse Thybulle 125.00 300.00
225 Quinndary Weatherspoon 25.00 60.00
229 Jordan Poole 1,000.00 2,000.00
230 Anthony Davis 125.00 300.00
233 Mfiondu Kabengele 25.00 60.00
234 De'Andre Hunter 150.00 400.00
235 RJ Barrett 400.00 800.00
236 Eric Paschall 125.00 300.00
237 Trae Young 200.00 500.00
242 Coby White 400.00 800.00
246 Giannis Antetokounmpo 300.00 600.00
248 Jarrett Culver 75.00 200.00
253 Nassir Little 75.00 200.00
258 Jaxson Hayes 125.00 300.00
260 Bol Bol 100.00 250.00
261 LeBron James 800.00 1,500.00
263 Nickeil Alexander-Walker 20.00 50.00
265 Rui Hachimura 200.00 500.00
266 Grant Williams 30.00 80.00
267 Tyler Herro 500.00 1,000.00
268 Jaylen Nowell 15.00 40.00
269 Kawhi Leonard 200.00 500.00
278 Jayson Tatum 200.00 500.00
279 Keldon Johnson 100.00 250.00
280 Brandon Clarke 75.00 200.00
281 Luka Doncic 1,000.00 2,000.00
295 Shai Gilgeous-Alexander 100.00 250.00
297 Zion Williamson 100.00 250.00
299 Kevin Durant 125.00 300.00

2019-20 Select Company
*SILVER: 1X TO 2.5X BASIC
1 Paul George 1.25 3.00
2 Kyrie Irving 1.50 4.00
3 Anthony Davis 2.00 5.00
4 Joel Embiid 1.50 4.00
5 Ben Simmons .75 2.00
6 Russell Westbrook 1.25 3.00
7 Jimmy Butler 1.50 4.00
8 LeBron James 6.00 15.00
9 Luka Doncic 5.00 12.00
10 Stephen Curry 6.00 15.00
11 Kawhi Leonard 2.00 5.00
12 Giannis Antetokounmpo 4.00 10.00
13 Karl-Anthony Towns 1.25 3.00
14 James Harden 1.50 4.00
15 Trae Young 2.00 5.00

2019-20 Select Draft Selections Memorabilia
1 Darius Bazley 1.50 4.00
2 Jaxson Hayes 2.50 6.00
3 Dylan Windler 2.00 5.00
4 Cameron Johnson 4.00 10.00
5 Keldon Johnson 5.00 12.00
6 Romeo Langford 1.50 4.00
7 Nickeil Alexander-Walker 2.50 6.00
8 Zion Williamson 40.00 100.00
9 Matisse Thybulle 3.00 8.00
10 De'Andre Hunter 6.00 15.00
11 Ty Jerome 3.00 8.00
12 Rui Hachimura 6.00 15.00
13 Mfiondu Kabengele 2.00 5.00
14 PJ Washington Jr. 5.00 12.00
15 Kevin Porter Jr. 3.00 8.00
16 Sekou Doumbouya 1.50 4.00
17 Goga Bitadze 2.50 6.00
18 Ja Morant 20.00 50.00
19 Brandon Clarke 3.00 8.00
20 Jarrett Culver 1.50 4.00
21 Nassir Little 2.50 6.00
22 Cam Reddish 2.50 6.00
23 Jordan Poole 6.00 15.00
24 Tyler Herro 8.00 20.00
25 Carsen Edwards 2.00 5.00
26 Coby White 5.00 12.00
27 Luka Samanic 2.00 5.00
28 RJ Barrett 6.00 15.00
29 Grant Williams 2.50 6.00
30 Chuma Okeke 2.50 6.00

2019-20 Select Draft Selections Memorabilia Prizms Copper
*COPPER: .6X TO 1.5X BASIC
STATED PRINT RUN 49 SER.#'d SETS
8 Zion Williamson 100.00 250.00
18 Ja Morant 40.00 100.00

2019-20 Select Draft Selections Memorabilia Prizms Purple
STATED PRINT RUN 99 SER.#'d SETS
8 Zion Williamson 75.00 200.00
18 Ja Morant 30.00 80.00

2019-20 Select Draft Selections Memorabilia Prizms Tie Dye
*TIE DYE: 1.2X TO 3X BASIC
STATED PRINT RUN 25 SER.#'d SETS
8 Zion Williamson 400.00 800.00
18 Ja Morant 150.00 400.00

2019-20 Select Future
1 Darius Bazley 1.00 2.50
2 Brandon Clarke 2.00 5.00
3 Cameron Johnson 2.50 6.00
4 Cam Reddish 1.50 4.00
5 Nickeil Alexander-Walker 1.50 4.00
6 Carsen Edwards 1.25 3.00
7 De'Andre Hunter 4.00 10.00
8 RJ Barrett 4.00 10.00
9 Mfiondu Kabengele 1.25 3.00
10 Sekou Doumbouya 1.00 2.50
11 Jaxson Hayes 1.50 4.00
12 Jarrett Culver 1.00 2.50
13 Keldon Johnson 3.00 8.00
14 Jordan Poole 4.00 10.00
15 Zion Williamson 30.00 80.00
16 Coby White 3.00 8.00
17 Ty Jerome 2.00 5.00
18 Grant Williams 1.50 4.00
19 PJ Washington Jr. 3.00 8.00
20 Goga Bitadze 1.50 4.00
21 Dylan Windler 1.25 3.00
22 Nassir Little 1.50 4.00
23 Romeo Langford 1.00 2.50
24 Tyler Herro 5.00 12.00
25 Matisse Thybulle 2.00 5.00
26 Luka Samanic 1.25 3.00
27 Rui Hachimura 4.00 10.00
28 Tacko Fall 1.25 3.00
29 Kevin Porter Jr. 2.00 5.00
30 Ja Morant 20.00 50.00

2019-20 Select Future Prizms Silver
*SILVER: 1X TO 2.5X BASIC
8 RJ Barrett 15.00 40.00
15 Zion Williamson 125.00 300.00
30 Ja Morant 60.00 150.00

2019-20 Select In Flight Signatures
STATED PRINT RUN B/WN 40-179 COPIES PER
EXCHANGE DEADLINE 9/04/2021
1 Zion Williamson 1,000.00 3,000.00
3 Kevin Garnett 75.00 200.00
4 Kyrie Irving 20.00 50.00
5 Shaquille O'Neal 75.00 200.00
6 RJ Barrett 75.00 200.00
7 Rui Hachimura 75.00 200.00
8 Ja Morant 400.00 800.00
9 Karl-Anthony Towns 12.00 30.00
10 Zach LaVine 12.00 30.00
11 Donovan Mitchell 20.00 50.00
12 Anthony Davis 40.00 100.00
13 JaVale McGee 4.00 10.00
14 Myles Turner 5.00 12.00
15 Allan Houston 4.00 10.00
16 Charles Barkley 40.00 100.00
17 Damian Lillard 25.00 60.00
18 Montrezl Harrell 4.00 10.00
19 Allen Iverson 60.00 150.00
20 Julius Randle 6.00 15.00
21 Derrick Jones Jr. 8.00 20.00
22 Lauri Markkanen 6.00 15.00
23 Dominique Wilkins 8.00 20.00
24 Vince Carter 30.00 80.00
25 Fred VanVleet 6.00 15.00
26 Dwyane Wade 40.00 100.00
27 Steve Francis 5.00 12.00
28 Jaren Jackson Jr. 8.00 20.00
29 Wendell Carter Jr. 5.00 12.00
30 Kevin Porter Jr. 8.00 20.00

2019-20 Select In Flight Signatures Prizms Neon Orange Pulsar
STATED PRINT RUN 35 COPIES PER
EXCHANGE DEADLINE 9/04/2021
1 Zion Williamson 1,000.00 3,000.00
6 RJ Barrett 125.00 300.00
7 Rui Hachimura 125.00 300.00
8 Ja Morant 800.00 1,500.00
11 Donovan Mitchell 30.00 80.00
12 Anthony Davis 125.00 300.00
16 Charles Barkley 75.00 200.00
24 Vince Carter 60.00 150.00
26 Dwyane Wade 60.00 150.00
30 Kevin Porter Jr. 10.00 25.00

2019-20 Select In Flight Signatures Prizms Tie Dye
STATED PRINT RUN 15-25 SER. #'d SETS
EXCHANGE DEADLINE 9/04/2021
8 Ja Morant 800.00 1,500.00
10 Zach LaVine 40.00 100.00
11 Donovan Mitchell 60.00 150.00
13 JaVale McGee 12.00 30.00
16 Charles Barkley 75.00 200.00
18 Montrezl Harrell 20.00 50.00
24 Vince Carter 75.00 200.00
25 Fred VanVleet 20.00 50.00
27 Steve Francis 12.00 30.00
28 Jaren Jackson Jr. 20.00 50.00
29 Wendell Carter Jr. 15.00 40.00
30 Kevin Porter Jr. 12.00 30.00

2019-20 Select Phenomenon
1 Collin Sexton 2.00 5.00
2 Mfiondu Kabengele 1.25 3.00
3 Kevin Knox II 1.00 2.50
4 Goga Bitadze 1.50 4.00
5 Nassir Little 1.50 4.00
6 Darius Bazley 1.00 2.50
7 Carsen Edwards 1.25 3.00
8 Keldon Johnson 3.00 8.00
9 Grant Williams 1.50 4.00
10 Matisse Thybulle 2.00 5.00
11 Deandre Ayton 1.50 4.00
12 PJ Washington Jr. 3.00 8.00
13 Shai Gilgeous-Alexander 8.00 20.00
14 Ja Morant 30.00 80.00
15 Cam Reddish 1.50 4.00
16 Jaxson Hayes 1.50 4.00
17 Coby White 3.00 8.00
18 Romeo Langford 1.00 2.50
19 Tacko Fall 1.25 3.00
20 De'Andre Hunter 4.00 10.00
21 Marvin Bagley III 1.25 3.00
22 Kevin Porter Jr. 2.00 5.00
23 Wendell Carter Jr. 1.50 4.00
24 Brandon Clarke 2.00 5.00
25 Jordan Poole 4.00 10.00
26 Dylan Windler 1.25 3.00
27 Luka Samanic 1.25 3.00
28 Nickeil Alexander-Walker 1.50 4.00

29 Luka Doncic 10.00 25.00
30 Ty Jerome 2.00 5.00
31 Jaren Jackson Jr. 2.50 6.00
32 Sekou Doumbouya 1.00 2.50
33 Mitchell Robinson 1.50 4.00
34 Jarrett Culver 1.00 2.50
35 Tyler Herro 5.00 12.00
36 Cameron Johnson 2.50 6.00
37 RJ Barrett 4.00 10.00
38 Zion Williamson 60.00 150.00
39 Trae Young 4.00 10.00
40 Rui Hachimura 4.00 10.00

2019-20 Select Phenomenon Prizms Silver

*SILVER: 1X TO 2.5X BASIC
14 Ja Morant 60.00 150.00
17 Coby White 15.00 40.00
29 Luka Doncic 60.00 150.00
32 Sekou Doumbouya 2.50 6.00
37 RJ Barrett 25.00 60.00
38 Zion Williamson 200.00 500.00

2019-20 Select Rookie Jersey Autographs

COMMON CARD 3.00 8.00
SEMISTARS 4.00 10.00
UNLISTED STARS 5.00 12.00
STATED PRINT RUN 199 COPIES PER
EXCHANGE DEADLINE 9/04/2021
RJA-ZWL Zion Williamson 800.00 1,500.00
2 Ja Morant 200.00 500.00
3 RJ Barrett 60.00 150.00
4 Rui Hachimura 40.00 100.00
5 De'Andre Hunter 12.00 30.00
6 Jarrett Culver 3.00 8.00
7 Cam Reddish 5.00 12.00
8 Quinndary Weatherspoon 3.00 8.00
9 Coby White 60.00 150.00
10 Jaxson Hayes 5.00 12.00
11 PJ Washington Jr. 10.00 25.00
12 Bol Bol 12.00 30.00
13 Cameron Johnson 8.00 20.00
14 Tyler Herro 40.00 100.00
15 Nassir Little 5.00 12.00
16 Matisse Thybulle 6.00 15.00
17 Romeo Langford 3.00 8.00
18 Brandon Clarke 6.00 15.00
19 Chuma Okeke 5.00 12.00
20 Nickeil Alexander-Walker 5.00 12.00
21 Sekou Doumbouya 3.00 8.00
22 Jaylen Nowell 4.00 10.00
23 Carsen Edwards 4.00 10.00
24 Goga Bitadze 5.00 12.00
25 Ignas Brazdeikis 4.00 10.00
26 Keldon Johnson 10.00 25.00
27 Luka Samanic 4.00 10.00
28 Grant Williams 5.00 12.00
29 Admiral Schofield 4.00 10.00
30 Ty Jerome 6.00 15.00
31 Bruno Fernando 4.00 10.00
32 Kyle Guy 4.00 10.00
33 Dylan Windler 4.00 10.00
34 Kevin Porter Jr. 6.00 15.00
35 KZ Okpala 4.00 10.00
36 Tremont Waters 4.00 10.00
37 Mfiondu Kabengele 4.00 10.00
38 Cody Martin 4.00 10.00
39 Isaiah Roby 4.00 10.00
40 Jordan Poole 12.00 30.00

2019-20 Select Rookie Jersey Autographs Prizms Purple

*PURPLE/99: .5X TO 1.2X BASIC
STATED PRINT RUN 99 COPIES PER
EXCHANGE DEADLINE 9/04/2021
RJA-ZWL Zion Williamson 1,500.00 3,000.00

2019-20 Select Rookie Jersey Autographs Prizms Tie Dye

*TIE DYE/25: 1.2X TO 3X BASIC
STATED PRINT RUN 25 SER. #'d SETS
EXCHANGE DEADLINE 9/04/2021
RJA-ZWL Zion Williamson 3,000.00 6,000.00
9 Coby White 300.00 600.00
15 Nassir Little 30.00 80.00
18 Brandon Clarke 40.00 100.00
20 Nickeil Alexander-Walker 20.00 50.00
26 Keldon Johnson 20.00 50.00
34 Kevin Porter Jr. 20.00 50.00

2019-20 Select Rookie Signatures

STATED PRINT RUN 79-149 SER. #'d SETS
EXCHANGE DEADLINE 9/04/2021
1 Naz Reid 25.00 60.00
2 Jalen Lecque 10.00 25.00
3 Louis King 4.00 10.00
4 Justin Robinson 3.00 8.00
5 Jaylen Hoard 3.00 8.00
6 Luguentz Dort 12.00 30.00
7 Zach Norvell Jr. 4.00 10.00
8 Ja Morant 300.00 600.00
9 RJ Barrett 60.00 150.00
10 Jarrett Culver 3.00 8.00
11 Jaxson Hayes 5.00 12.00
12 Cam Reddish 5.00 12.00
13 Cameron Johnson 8.00 20.00
14 PJ Washington Jr. 12.00 30.00
15 Tyler Herro 150.00 400.00
16 Nickeil Alexander-Walker 5.00 12.00
17 Goga Bitadze 5.00 12.00
18 Luka Samanic 4.00 10.00
19 Brandon Clarke 25.00 60.00
20 Grant Williams 5.00 12.00
RS-TJR Ty Jerome 6.00 15.00
22 Nassir Little 5.00 12.00
23 Dylan Windler 4.00 10.00
24 Mfiondu Kabengele 4.00 10.00
25 Keldon Johnson 10.00 25.00
26 Kevin Porter Jr. 8.00 20.00
27 Nicolas Claxton 6.00 15.00
28 Tacko Fall 25.00 60.00
29 Bruno Fernando 4.00 10.00
30 Cody Martin 5.00 12.00
31 Daniel Gafford 6.00 15.00
33 Admiral Schofield 4.00 10.00
34 Jaylen Nowell 4.00 10.00
35 Isaiah Roby 4.00 10.00
36 Talen Horton-Tucker 5.00 12.00
38 Kyle Guy 4.00 10.00
39 Brian Bowen II 3.00 8.00
40 Jordan Bone 3.00 8.00

2019-20 Select Rookie Signatures Prizms Tie Dye

*TIE DYE: 1X TO 2.5X BASIC
STATED PRINT RUN 25 SER. #'d SETS
EXCHANGE DEADLINE 9/04/2021
6 Luguentz Dort 25.00 60.00
8 Ja Morant 800.00 1,500.00
15 Tyler Herro 500.00 1,000.00
22 Nassir Little 20.00 50.00
25 Keldon Johnson 40.00 100.00
26 Kevin Porter Jr. 20.00 50.00

2019-20 Select Signatures

STATED PRINT RUN B/WN 99-199 COPIES PER
EXCHANGE DEADLINE 9/04/2021
1 Gary Harris 4.00 10.00
2 Horace Grant 5.00 12.00
3 Bob McAdoo 6.00 15.00
4 Lonzo Ball 20.00 50.00
6 Josh Hart 4.00 10.00
7 Christian Laettner 5.00 12.00
8 Harrison Barnes 4.00 10.00
9 Josh Richardson 3.00 8.00
10 Kevin McHale 8.00 20.00
11 Ralph Sampson 4.00 10.00
12 Jamal Mashburn 5.00 12.00
13 Walt Frazier 8.00 20.00
14 Stephen Jackson 3.00 8.00
15 Tyson Chandler 4.00 10.00
16 A.C. Green 5.00 12.00
17 Elfrid Payton 3.00 8.00
18 Quinn Cook 4.00 10.00
19 Peja Stojakovic 4.00 10.00
20 Shawn Bradley 3.00 8.00
21 Toni Kukoc 6.00 15.00
22 Dave Cowens 6.00 15.00
23 Michael Cooper 5.00 12.00
24 Adrian Dantley 5.00 12.00
25 Mark Jackson 4.00 10.00
26 Juwan Howard 4.00 10.00
27 Wally Szczerbiak 4.00 10.00
28 Rik Smits 4.00 10.00
29 Dan Majerle 4.00 10.00
30 John Stockton 15.00 40.00

2019-20 Select Signatures Prizms Tie Dye

*TIE DYE: .75X TO 2X BASIC
STATED PRINT RUN 25 SER. #'d SETS
EXCHANGE DEADLINE 9/04/2021
4 Lonzo Ball 60.00 150.00
30 John Stockton 60.00 150.00

2019-20 Select Sparks Memorabilia

1 Zion Williamson 12.00 30.00
2 Ja Morant 15.00 40.00
3 RJ Barrett 6.00 15.00
4 De'Andre Hunter 6.00 15.00
5 Jarrett Culver 1.50 4.00
6 Jaxson Hayes 2.50 6.00
7 Rui Hachimura 6.00 15.00
8 Coby White 5.00 12.00
9 Cam Reddish 2.50 6.00
10 PJ Washington Jr. 5.00 12.00

2019-20 Select Sparks Memorabilia Prizms Copper

*COPPER: .6X TO 1.5X BASIC
2 Ja Morant 60.00 150.00

2019-20 Select Sparks Memorabilia Prizms Purple

*PURPLE: .5X TO 1.2X BASIC
STATED PRINT RUN 99 SER.#'d SETS
2 Ja Morant 30.00 80.00

2019-20 Select Sparks Memorabilia Prizms Tie Dye

*TIE DYE: 1.2X TO 3X BASIC
STATED PRINT RUN 25 SER.#'d SETS
2 Ja Morant 150.00 400.00

2019-20 Select Swatches

*PURPLE: .5X TO 1.2X BASIC
*COPPER: .6X TO 1.5X BASIC
*TIE DYE: 1.2X TO 3X BASIC
1 Myles Turner 2.50 6.00
2 Karl-Anthony Towns 4.00 10.00
3 Bradley Beal 3.00 8.00
4 Dirk Nowitzki 6.00 15.00
5 Joe Harris 2.00 5.00
6 Thaddeus Young 1.50 4.00
7 J.J. Barea 2.00 5.00
8 John Wall 3.00 8.00
9 Allonzo Trier 1.50 4.00
10 Enes Kanter 1.50 4.00
11 Victor Oladipo 2.00 5.00
12 Andrew Wiggins 3.00 8.00
13 Rondae Hollis-Jefferson 1.50 4.00
14 Derrick Rose 5.00 12.00
15 CJ McCollum 2.50 6.00
16 Jarrett Allen 2.50 6.00
17 Larry Bird 10.00 25.00
18 Shaquille O'Neal 10.00 25.00
19 D'Angelo Russell 2.00 5.00
20 Rudy Gobert 3.00 8.00

2019-20 Select Throwback Memorabilia

1 Vince Carter 5.00 12.00
2 Derrick Rose 5.00 12.00
3 Thaddeus Young 1.50 4.00
4 Kevin Love 2.50 6.00
5 Zach LaVine 4.00 10.00
6 DeAndre Jordan 2.00 5.00
7 Joe Johnson 2.00 5.00
8 Ricky Rubio 2.00 5.00
9 Wesley Matthews 1.50 4.00
10 Enes Kanter 1.50 4.00
11 Domantas Sabonis 3.00 8.00
12 Brook Lopez 2.00 5.00
13 Victor Oladipo 2.00 5.00
14 Jimmy Butler 5.00 12.00
15 Pau Gasol 4.00 10.00
16 Blake Griffin 2.50 6.00
17 Dwight Howard 3.00 8.00
18 Serge Ibaka 2.00 5.00
19 Nerlens Noel 1.50 4.00
20 Kyrie Irving 5.00 12.00
21 Dario Saric 2.00 5.00
22 Eric Gordon 2.00 5.00
23 Harrison Barnes 2.00 5.00
24 Joe Harris 2.00 5.00
25 Terrence Ross 2.50 6.00
26 George Hill 2.00 5.00
27 Rudy Gay 2.00 5.00
28 Al Horford 2.50 6.00
29 DeMarcus Cousins 2.00 5.00
30 D'Angelo Russell 2.00 5.00
31 Dennis Schroder 2.00 5.00
32 Paul Millsap 2.00 5.00
33 Tobias Harris 2.00 5.00
34 Patrick Beverley 2.00 5.00
35 DeMarre Carroll 1.50 4.00
36 LeBron James 20.00 50.00
37 Eric Bledsoe 2.00 5.00
38 Jusuf Nurkic 2.00 5.00
39 Goran Dragic 2.00 5.00
40 JJ Redick 2.50 6.00

2019-20 Select Throwback Memorabilia Prizms Copper

*COPPER: .6X TO 1.5X BASIC
STATED PRINT RUN 49 SER.#'d SETS
36 LeBron James 75.00 200.00

2019-20 Select Throwback Memorabilia Prizms Purple

*PURPLE: .5X TO 1.2X BASIC
STATED PRINT RUN 99 SER.#'d SETS
36 LeBron James 60.00 150.00

2019-20 Select Throwback Memorabilia Prizms Tie Dye

*TIE DYE: 1.2X TO 3X BASIC
1 Vince Carter 12.00 30.00
36 LeBron James 150.00 400.00

2019-20 Select Top Selections

1 Deandre Ayton .75 2.00
2 Tim Duncan 2.00 5.00
3 Karl-Anthony Towns 1.25 3.00
4 Shaquille O'Neal 3.00 8.00
5 Kyrie Irving 1.50 4.00
6 Patrick Ewing 1.25 3.00
7 Blake Griffin .75 2.00
8 Derrick Rose 1.50 4.00
9 Zion Williamson 40.00 100.00
10 LeBron James 12.00 30.00
11 Ben Simmons .75 2.00
12 Allen Iverson 2.00 5.00
13 Anthony Davis 2.00 5.00
14 David Robinson 1.50 4.00
15 John Wall 1.00 2.50

2019-20 Select Top Selections Prizms Silver

*SILVER: 1.2X TO 3X BASIC
9 Zion Williamson 150.00 400.00
10 LeBron James 150.00 400.00

2019-20 Select X Factor Memorabilia Signatures

STATED PRINT RUN 199 COPIES PER
EXCHANGE DEADLINE 9/04/2021
1 P.J. Tucker 4.00 10.00
2 Wesley Matthews 3.00 8.00
3 Otto Porter Jr. 3.00 8.00
4 Chandler Hutchison 3.00 8.00
5 Montrezl Harrell 4.00 10.00
6 Robert Covington 3.00 8.00
8 Thaddeus Young 3.00 8.00
9 Ersan Ilyasova 3.00 8.00
10 Al-Farouq Aminu 3.00 8.00
11 Malcolm Brogdon 4.00 10.00
12 Meyers Leonard 3.00 8.00
13 Danny Green 4.00 10.00
14 Terrence Ross 5.00 12.00
15 Troy Brown Jr. 3.00 8.00
16 Lauri Markkanen 15.00 40.00
17 Pascal Siakam 15.00 40.00
18 Thon Maker 3.00 8.00
19 Dario Saric 4.00 10.00
20 Willie Cauley-Stein 3.00 8.00
21 Chris Bosh 8.00 20.00
22 Doug McDermott 3.00 8.00
24 Larry Nance Jr. 4.00 10.00
25 Jalen Brunson 12.00 30.00

2020-21 Select

COMMON CARD (1-100) .25 .60
SEMISTARS .30 .75
UNLISTED STARS .40 1.00
COMMON RC (1-100) .50 1.25
RC SEMIS .60 1.50
RC UNLISTED .75 2.00
COMMON CARD (101-200) .40 1.00
SEMISTARS .50 1.25
UNLISTED STARS .60 1.50
COMMON RC (101-200) .75 2.00
RC SEMIS 1.00 2.50
RC UNLISTED 1.25 3.00
COMMON CARD (201-300) .50 1.25
SEMISTARS .60 1.50
UNLISTED STARS .75 2.00
COMMON RC (201-300) 1.00 2.50
RC SEMIS 1.25 3.00
RC UNLISTED 1.50 4.00
*BLUE RETAIL: .4X TO 1X BASIC HOBBY
*RD/WHT/ORG FLASH: .75X TO 2X BASIC
*RD/WHT/ORG SHIMMER: .75X TO 2X BASIC
*TRI-COLOR: .75X TO 2X BASIC
*RED WAVE: 1.2X TO 3X BASIC
*SCOPE: 1.2X TO 3X BASIC
1 Zion Williamson 1.25 3.00
2 Trae Young 1.00 2.50
3 Lou Williams .40 1.00
4 Terry Rozier .40 1.00
5 Andre Drummond .40 1.00
6 Andrew Wiggins .50 1.25
7 Victor Oladipo .30 .75
8 Bam Adebayo .60 1.50
9 Mitchell Robinson .40 1.00
10 Chris Paul .75 2.00
11 Tobias Harris .40 1.00
12 James Harden .75 2.00
13 Rui Hachimura .75 2.00
14 Zach LaVine .60 1.50
15 Luka Doncic 2.50 6.00
16 Derrick Rose .60 1.50
17 Eric Bledsoe .30 .75
18 D'Angelo Russell .40 1.00
19 Steven Adams .40 1.00
20 Nikola Vucevic .40 1.00
21 Cameron Johnson .50 1.25
22 Goran Dragic .40 1.00
23 LeBron James 3.00 8.00
24 Damian Lillard 1.00 2.50
25 Marvin Bagley III .30 .75
26 Kyle Lowry .50 1.25
27 Donovan Mitchell .75 2.00
28 Davis Bertans .30 .75
29 Fred VanVleet .60 1.50
30 Duncan Robinson .40 1.00
31 John Wall .50 1.25
32 De'Aaron Fox .60 1.50
33 Deandre Ayton .40 1.00
34 Ben Simmons .40 1.00
35 Danilo Gallinari .30 .75
36 Karl-Anthony Towns .60 1.50
37 Kawhi Leonard 1.00 2.50
38 Kemba Walker .40 1.00
39 Russell Westbrook .75 2.00
40 RJ Barrett .60 1.50
41 Jayson Tatum 1.50 4.00
42 Kyrie Irving .75 2.00
43 Kristaps Porzingis .50 1.25
44 Draymond Green .50 1.25
45 Anthony Davis 1.00 2.50
46 Pascal Siakam .60 1.50
47 Bojan Bogdanovic .30 .75
48 Patty Mills .40 1.00
49 LaMarcus Aldridge .40 1.00
50 Bogdan Bogdanovic .40 1.00
51 Jusuf Nurkic .40 1.00
52 Markelle Fultz .30 .75
53 Brandon Ingram .50 1.25
54 Giannis Antetokounmpo 2.00 5.00
55 Brandon Clarke .40 1.00
56 Domantas Sabonis .50 1.25
57 Stephen Curry 3.00 8.00
58 Nikola Jokic 2.00 5.00
59 Collin Sexton .40 1.00
60 Ja Morant 1.25 3.00
61 Anthony Edwards RC 6.00 15.00
62 James Wiseman RC .75 2.00
63 LaMelo Ball RC 5.00 12.00
64 Patrick Williams RC 1.50 4.00
65 Isaac Okoro RC 1.00 2.50
66 Onyeka Okongwu RC 1.25 3.00
67 Killian Hayes RC .60 1.50
68 Obi Toppin RC 1.25 3.00
69 Deni Avdija RC 1.50 4.00
70 Jalen Smith RC 1.25 3.00
71 Devin Vassell RC 2.00 5.00
72 Tyrese Haliburton RC 5.00 12.00
73 Kira Lewis Jr. RC .60 1.50
74 Aaron Nesmith RC 1.25 3.00
75 Cole Anthony RC 1.50 4.00
76 Isaiah Stewart RC 1.25 3.00
77 Aleksej Pokusevski RC .75 2.00
78 Josh Green RC 1.25 3.00
79 Saddiq Bey RC 1.25 3.00
80 Precious Achiuwa RC 1.25 3.00
81 Tyrese Maxey RC 5.00 12.00
82 Zeke Nnaji RC .75 2.00
83 Facundo Campazzo RC .75 2.00
84 RJ Hampton RC .60 1.50
85 Immanuel Quickley RC 1.50 4.00
86 Payton Pritchard RC 2.00 5.00
87 Udoka Azubuike RC .75 2.00
88 Jaden McDaniels RC 2.00 5.00
89 Malachi Flynn RC .60 1.50
90 Desmond Bane RC 2.00 5.00
91 Tyrell Terry RC .50 1.25
92 Vernon Carey Jr. RC .60 1.50
93 Daniel Oturu RC .60 1.50
94 Theo Maledon RC .60 1.50
95 Xavier Tillman RC .75 2.00
96 Cassius Winston RC .60 1.50
97 Saben Lee RC .60 1.50
98 Kenyon Martin Jr. RC 1.00 2.50
99 Isaiah Joe RC .75 2.00
100 CJ Elleby RC .60 1.50
101 Kevin Durant 2.50 6.00
102 Devonte' Graham .50 1.25
103 Coby White .75 2.00
104 Kevin Love .60 1.50
105 Kristaps Porzingis .75 2.00
106 Michael Porter Jr. .75 2.00
107 Sekou Doumbouya .40 1.00
108 Klay Thompson 1.50 4.00
109 Eric Gordon .50 1.25
110 Malcolm Brogdon .60 1.50
111 Marcus Smart .60 1.50
112 Ivica Zubac .60 1.50
113 LeBron James 5.00 12.00
114 Jaren Jackson Jr. 1.00 2.50
115 Jimmy Butler 1.25 3.00
116 Donte DiVincenzo .60 1.50
117 Giannis Antetokounmpo 3.00 8.00
118 Jrue Holiday .60 1.50
119 Shai Gilgeous-Alexander 3.00 8.00
120 Joel Embiid 1.50 4.00
121 Devin Booker 1.50 4.00
122 CJ McCollum .60 1.50
123 Harrison Barnes .50 1.25
124 Dejounte Murray .60 1.50
125 Terence Davis II .60 1.50
126 Zion Williamson 2.00 5.00
127 Bradley Beal .75 2.00
128 Tim Hardaway Jr. .40 1.00
129 Blake Griffin .60 1.50
130 Rui Hachimura .75 2.00
131 Joe Ingles .50 1.25
132 Carmelo Anthony 1.00 2.50
133 Ricky Rubio .60 1.50
134 Aaron Gordon .60 1.50
135 Julius Randle .60 1.50
136 Jarrett Culver .40 1.00
137 Lonzo Ball .75 2.00
138 Darius Bazley .40 1.00
139 Matisse Thybulle .50 1.25
140 Aron Baynes .40 1.00
141 Derrick White .60 1.50
142 Jamal Murray 1.00 2.50
143 Cam Reddish .75 2.00
144 Josh Okogie .50 1.25
145 Alex Caruso .60 1.50
146 Rudy Gobert .75 2.00
147 Norman Powell .50 1.25
148 Keldon Johnson 1.00 2.50
149 John Collins .60 1.50
150 Luka Doncic 4.00 10.00
151 Jonathan Isaac .60 1.50
152 Brook Lopez .50 1.25
153 Kendrick Nunn .50 1.25
154 Duncan Robinson .60 1.50
155 Anthony Davis 1.50 4.00
156 Paul George 1.00 2.50
157 Myles Turner .60 1.50
158 Eric Paschall .50 1.25
159 Luke Kennard .50 1.25
160 Gary Harris .50 1.25
161 Darius Garland 1.00 2.50
162 Lauri Markkanen .75 2.00
163 Caris LeVert .60 1.50
164 Jaylen Brown 1.00 2.50
165 PJ Washington Jr. .60 1.50
166 Grant Riller 1.00 2.50
167 Nick Richards 1.25 3.00
168 Elijah Hughes 1.00 2.50
169 Anthony Edwards 10.00 25.00
170 Malachi Flynn 1.00 2.50
171 Udoka Azubuike 1.25 3.00
172 Immanuel Quickley 2.50 6.00
173 Caleb Martin 2.00 5.00
174 Tyrese Maxey 8.00 20.00
175 Saddiq Bey 2.00 5.00
176 Aleksej Pokusevski 1.25 3.00
177 Cole Anthony 2.50 6.00
178 Kira Lewis Jr. 1.00 2.50
179 Devin Vassell 3.00 8.00
180 Deni Avdija 2.50 6.00
181 Killian Hayes 1.00 2.50
182 Isaac Okoro 1.50 4.00
183 LaMelo Ball 8.00 20.00
184 James Wiseman 1.25 3.00
185 Patrick Williams 2.50 6.00
186 Onyeka Okongwu 2.00 5.00
187 Obi Toppin 2.00 5.00
188 Jalen Smith 2.00 5.00
189 Tyrese Haliburton 8.00 20.00
190 Aaron Nesmith 2.00 5.00
191 Isaiah Stewart 2.00 5.00
192 Josh Green 2.00 5.00
193 Precious Achiuwa 2.00 5.00
194 Zeke Nnaji 1.25 3.00
195 RJ Hampton 1.00 2.50
196 Payton Pritchard 3.00 8.00
197 Jaden McDaniels 3.00 8.00
198 CJ Elleby 1.00 2.50
199 Cassius Stanley 1.00 2.50
200 Jahmi'us Ramsey 1.00 2.50
201 Luka Doncic 5.00 12.00
202 Nikola Jokic 4.00 10.00
203 Derrick Rose 1.25 3.00
204 Stephen Curry 6.00 15.00
205 Victor Oladipo .60 1.50
206 Montrezl Harrell .75 2.00
207 Aaron Gordon .75 2.00
208 Kawhi Leonard 2.00 5.00
209 Chris Paul 1.50 4.00
210 De'Aaron Fox 1.25 3.00
211 Bam Adebayo 1.25 3.00
212 James Harden 1.50 4.00
213 Zion Williamson 2.50 6.00
214 Jayson Tatum 3.00 8.00
215 Brandon Ingram 1.00 2.50
216 Joel Embiid 2.00 5.00
217 Kyle Lowry 1.00 2.50
218 Donovan Mitchell 1.50 4.00
219 Bradley Beal 1.00 2.50
220 DeMar DeRozan 1.00 2.50
221 Kelly Oubre Jr. .75 2.00
222 Karl-Anthony Towns 1.25 3.00
223 LeBron James 6.00 15.00
224 Giannis Antetokounmpo 4.00 10.00
225 Tyler Herro 1.50 4.00
226 Russell Westbrook 1.50 4.00
227 Trae Young 2.00 5.00
228 Anthony Davis 2.00 5.00
229 Devin Booker 2.00 5.00
230 Carmelo Anthony 1.25 3.00
231 Fred VanVleet 1.25 3.00
232 Rui Hachimura 1.00 2.50
233 Coby White 1.00 2.50
234 Darius Garland 1.25 3.00
235 John Wall 1.00 2.50
236 Jaylen Brown 1.25 3.00
237 Deandre Ayton .75 2.00
238 CJ McCollum .75 2.00
239 Zach LaVine 1.25 3.00
240 Christian Wood .60 1.50
241 Devonte' Graham .60 1.50
242 De'Andre Hunter .75 2.00
243 Klay Thompson 2.00 5.00
244 Kristaps Porzingis .75 2.00
245 Pascal Siakam .75 2.00
246 Bryn Forbes .60 1.50
247 Buddy Hield .75 2.00
248 Damian Lillard 2.00 5.00
249 Ben Simmons .75 2.00
250 Evan Fournier .60 1.50
251 Shai Gilgeous-Alexander 4.00 10.00
252 Kemba Walker .75 2.00
253 D'Angelo Russell .75 2.00
254 Paul George 1.25 3.00
255 Ja Morant 2.50 6.00
256 Khris Middleton 1.00 2.50
257 Jimmy Butler 1.50 4.00
258 RJ Barrett 1.25 3.00
259 Kevin Durant 3.00 8.00
260 Jamal Murray 1.25 3.00
261 Nico Mannion 1.25 3.00
262 Jordan Nwora 1.50 4.00
263 Tre Jones 2.00 5.00
264 Robert Woodard II 1.25 3.00
265 Tyler Bey 1.25 3.00
266 Xavier Tillman 1.50 4.00
267 Theo Maledon 1.25 3.00
268 Daniel Oturu 1.25 3.00
269 Vernon Carey Jr 1.25 3.00
270 Tyrell Terry 1.00 2.50
271 Desmond Bane 4.00 10.00
272 Malachi Flynn 1.25 3.00
273 Jaden McDaniels 4.00 10.00
274 Udoka Azubuike 1.50 4.00
275 Payton Pritchard 4.00 10.00
276 Immanuel Quickley 3.00 8.00
277 RJ Hampton 1.25 3.00
278 Jae'Sean Tate 1.50 4.00
279 Zeke Nnaji 1.50 4.00
280 Tyrese Maxey 10.00 25.00
281 Precious Achiuwa 2.50 6.00
282 Saddiq Bey 2.50 6.00
283 Josh Green 2.50 6.00
284 Aleksej Pokusevski 1.50 4.00
285 Isaiah Stewart 2.50 6.00
286 Cole Anthony 3.00 8.00
287 Aaron Nesmith 2.50 6.00
288 Kira Lewis Jr. 1.25 3.00
289 Tyrese Haliburton 10.00 25.00
290 Devin Vassell 4.00 10.00
291 Jalen Smith 2.50 6.00
292 Deni Avdija 3.00 8.00
293 Obi Toppin 2.50 6.00
294 Killian Hayes 1.25 3.00
295 Onyeka Okongwu 2.50 6.00
296 Isaac Okoro 2.00 5.00
297 Patrick Williams 3.00 8.00
298 LaMelo Ball 10.00 25.00
299 James Wiseman 1.50 4.00
300 Anthony Edwards 12.00 30.00

2020-21 Select Prizms Blue

*BLUE: .6X TO 1.5X BASIC
300 Anthony Edwards 75.00 200.00

2020-21 Select Prizms Blue Die Cut

*BLUE DIE CUT: 1.5X TO 4X BASIC
STATED PRINT RUN 249 SER.#'d SETS
169 Anthony Edwards 125.00 300.00

2020-21 Select Prizms Blue Disco

*BLUE DISCO: 4X TO 10X BASIC
STATED PRINT RUN 25 SER.#'d SETS
61 Anthony Edwards 200.00 500.00
169 Anthony Edwards 250.00 600.00
300 Anthony Edwards 400.00 800.00

2020-21 Select Prizms Blue White Green Flash

*BLUE WHT GRN FLASH/49 1-100: 3X TO 8X BASIC
*BLUE WHT GRN FLASH/25 101-200: 4X TO 10X BASIC
STATED PRINT RUN 10-49 SER.#'d SETS
61 Anthony Edwards 150.00 400.00
169 Anthony Edwards 300.00 600.00

2020-21 Select Prizms Blue White Green Shimmer

*BLUE WHT GRN SHMR/49 1-100: 3X TO 8X BASIC
*BLUE WHT GRN SHMR/25 101-200: 4X TO 10X BASIC
STATED PRINT RUN 10-49 SER.#'d SETS
61 Anthony Edwards 150.00 400.00
169 Anthony Edwards 300.00 600.00

2020-21 Select Prizms Blue White Purple Ice

*BL WHITE PRPLE ICE: .6X TO 1.5X BASIC
300 Anthony Edwards 75.00 200.00

2020-21 Select Prizms Disco

*DISCO: 1.2X TO 3X BASIC
289 Tyrese Haliburton 60.00 150.00
298 LaMelo Ball 60.00 150.00
300 Anthony Edwards 300.00 600.00

2020-21 Select Prizms Green White Purple

*GRN WHT PRPL: .5X TO 1.2X BASIC
300 Anthony Edwards 40.00 100.00

2020-21 Select Prizms Light Blue

*LIGHT BLUE: 1.5X TO 4X BASIC
STATED PRINT RUN 299 SER.#'d SETS
61 Anthony Edwards 75.00 200.00

2020-21 Select Prizms Maroon Die Cut

*MAROON DIE CUT: 1.5X TO 4X BASIC
STATED PRINT RUN 175 SER.#'d SETS
169 Anthony Edwards 125.00 300.00

2020-21 Select Prizms Neon Green

*NEON GREEN: 2.5X TO 6X BASIC
STATED PRINT RUN 75 SER.#'d SETS
61 Anthony Edwards 125.00 300.00

2020-21 Select Prizms Orange Die Cut

*ORANGE DIE CUT: 2X TO 5X BASIC
STATED PRINT RUN 65 SER.#'d SETS
169 Anthony Edwards 150.00 400.00

2020-21 Select Prizms Purple Die Cut

*PURPLE DIE CUT: 2X TO 5X BASIC
STATED PRINT RUN 99 SER.#'d SETS
169 Anthony Edwards 150.00 400.00

2020-21 Select Prizms Red

*RED: 2X TO 5X BASIC
STATED PRINT RUN 199 SER.#'d SETS
61 Anthony Edwards 100.00 250.00

2020-21 Select Prizms Red Disco

*RED DISCO: 3X TO 8X BASIC
STATED PRINT RUN 49 SER.#'d SETS
61 Anthony Edwards 150.00 400.00
169 Anthony Edwards 200.00 500.00
300 Anthony Edwards 300.00 600.00

2020-21 Select Prizms Red White Green Ice

*RD/WHT/GRN ICE: .6X TO 1.5X BASIC
300 Anthony Edwards 75.00 200.00

2020-21 Select Prizms Silver

*SILVER: 1.2X TO 3X BASIC
289 Tyrese Haliburton 60.00 150.00
298 LaMelo Ball 60.00 150.00
300 Anthony Edwards 300.00 600.00

2020-21 Select Prizms Teal White Pink

*TEAL WHT PNK/49 1-100: 3X TO 8X BASIC
*TEAL WHT PNK/25 101-200: 4X TO 10X BASIC
STATED PRINT RUN 10-49 SER.#'d SETS
61 Anthony Edwards 150.00 400.00
169 Anthony Edwards 300.00 600.00

2020-21 Select Prizms Tie Dye

*TIE DYE: 4X TO 10X BASIC
STATED PRINT RUN 25 SER.#'d SETS
61 Anthony Edwards 200.00 500.00
300 Anthony Edwards 400.00 800.00

2020-21 Select Prizms Tie Dye Die Cut

*TIE DYE DIE CUT: 4X TO 10X BASIC
STATED PRINT RUN 25 SER.#'d SETS
169 Anthony Edwards 300.00 600.00

2020-21 Select Prizms White

*WHITE: 2X TO 5X BASIC
STATED PRINT RUN 149 SER.#'d SETS
61 Anthony Edwards 100.00 250.00

2020-21 Select Artistic Selections

COMMON CARD 8.00 20.00
SEMISTARS 10.00 25.00
UNLISTED STARS 12.00 30.00
1 Zion Williamson 60.00 150.00
2 Ja Morant 75.00 200.00
3 LeBron James 100.00 250.00
4 Giannis Antetokounmpo 75.00 200.00
5 Stephen Curry 100.00 250.00
6 Jayson Tatum 60.00 150.00
7 Trae Young 30.00 80.00
8 Luka Doncic 100.00 250.00
9 Kawhi Leonard 30.00 80.00
10 James Harden 25.00 60.00

2020-21 Select Autographed Memorabilia

COMMON CARD p/r 149-249 3.00 8.00
SEMISTARS p/r 149-249 4.00 10.00
UNLISTED STARS p/r 149-249 5.00 12.00
COMMON CARD p/r 49-99 5.00 12.00
SEMISTARS p/r 49-99 6.00 15.00
UNLISTED STARS p/r 49-99 8.00 20.00
STATED PRINT RUN B/WN 49-249 COPIES PER
EXCHANGE DEADLINE 1/28/2023
*PURPLE: .5X TO 1.2X BASIC
1 Nikola Jokic/149 125.00 300.00
2 Domantas Sabonis/249 15.00 40.00
3 Kyle Kuzma/149 15.00 40.00
4 Robert Covington/249 4.00 10.00
5 Tobias Harris/249 5.00 12.00
6 Deron Williams/249 4.00 10.00
7 Karl Malone/49 50.00 120.00
8 Mo Bamba/249 5.00 12.00
9 Grant Hill/99 30.00 80.00
10 Kevin Martin/149 4.00 10.00
11 Nerlens Noel/149 3.00 8.00
12 Dwight Powell/249 3.00 8.00
13 Eric Gordon/249 4.00 10.00
14 Richard Jefferson/249 3.00 8.00
15 Spencer Dinwiddie/249 4.00 10.00
16 Allonzo Trier/249 3.00 8.00
17 Larry Bird/49 125.00 300.00
18 Michael Kidd-Gilchrist/249 3.00 8.00
19 Jamal Murray/99 25.00 60.00
20 J.J. Barea/249 10.00 25.00
21 Dennis Smith Jr./149 3.00 8.00
22 Chris Kaman/249 3.00 8.00
23 Eric Bledsoe/249 4.00 10.00
24 Keita Bates-Diop/249 3.00 8.00
25 Otto Porter Jr./249 3.00 8.00

2020-21 Select Autographed Memorabilia Prizms Tie Dye

*TIE DYE/25: 1.2X TO 3X BASIC
STATED PRINT RUN 25 SER.#'d SETS
EXCHANGE DEADLINE 1/28/2023
7 Karl Malone 125.00 300.00
9 Grant Hill 75.00 200.00
17 Larry Bird 200.00 500.00

2020-21 Select Company

COMMON CARD .40 1.00
SEMISTARS .50 1.25
UNLISTED STARS .60 1.50
*BLUE: 1.2X TO 3X BASIC
*GREEN: 1.2X TO 3X BASIC
*SILVER: 1.2X TO 3X BASIC
*RED: 1.2X TO 3X BASIC
1 Damian Lillard 1.50 4.00
2 Anthony Davis 1.50 4.00
3 Donovan Mitchell 1.25 3.00
4 Luka Doncic 4.00 10.00
5 Trae Young 1.50 4.00
6 Zion Williamson 2.00 5.00
7 Ja Morant 2.00 5.00
8 James Harden 1.25 3.00
9 LeBron James 5.00 12.00
10 Kawhi Leonard 1.50 4.00
11 Jimmy Butler 1.25 3.00
12 Jayson Tatum 2.50 6.00
13 Kevin Durant 2.50 6.00
14 Stephen Curry 5.00 12.00
15 Devin Booker 1.50 4.00
16 Nikola Jokic 3.00 8.00
17 Ben Simmons .60 1.50
18 Karl-Anthony Towns 1.00 2.50
19 Russell Westbrook 1.25 3.00
20 Giannis Antetokounmpo 3.00 8.00
21 Pascal Siakam 1.00 2.50
22 Kyrie Irving 1.25 3.00
23 Paul George 1.00 2.50
24 Joel Embiid 1.50 4.00

2020-21 Select Draft Selections Memorabilia

*PURPLE/99: .6X TO 1.5X BASIC
*COPPER/49: .75X TO 2X BASIC
1 Anthony Edwards 25.00 60.00
2 James Wiseman 2.50 6.00
3 LaMelo Ball 25.00 60.00
4 Patrick Williams 5.00 12.00
5 Isaac Okoro 3.00 8.00
6 Onyeka Okongwu 4.00 10.00
7 Killian Hayes 2.00 5.00
8 Obi Toppin 4.00 10.00
9 Deni Avdija 5.00 12.00
10 Jalen Smith 4.00 10.00
11 Devin Vassell 6.00 15.00
12 Tyrese Haliburton 15.00 40.00
13 Kira Lewis Jr. 2.00 5.00
14 Aaron Nesmith 4.00 10.00
15 Cole Anthony 5.00 12.00
16 Isaiah Stewart 4.00 10.00
17 Aleksej Pokusevski 2.50 6.00

18 Josh Green 4.00 10.00
19 Saddiq Bey 4.00 10.00
20 Precious Achiuwa 4.00 10.00
21 Tyrese Maxey 15.00 40.00
22 Zeke Nnaji 2.50 6.00
23 Tyrell Terry 1.50 4.00
24 RJ Hampton 2.00 5.00
25 Immanuel Quickley 5.00 12.00
26 Payton Pritchard 6.00 15.00
27 Udoka Azubuike 2.50 6.00
28 Jaden McDaniels 6.00 15.00
29 Malachi Flynn 2.00 5.00
30 Desmond Bane 6.00 15.00

2020-21 Select Draft Selections Memorabilia Prizms Tie Dye

STATED PRINT RUN 25 SER.#'d SETS
1 Anthony Edwards 125.00 300.00
3 LaMelo Ball 125.00 300.00

2020-21 Select Duet Selections Memorabilia

1 LeBron James 75.00 200.00
2 Kevin Garnett 10.00 25.00
3 Jusuf Nurkic 3.00 8.00
4 Kawhi Leonard 8.00 20.00
5 Steve Nash 8.00 20.00
6 Bojan Bogdanovic 2.50 6.00
7 DeAndre Jordan 2.50 6.00
8 Vince Carter 8.00 20.00
9 Al Horford 3.00 8.00
10 Charles Barkley 25.00 60.00
11 Domantas Sabonis 4.00 10.00
12 Shawn Kemp 12.00 30.00
13 Chris Webber 12.00 30.00
14 Kevin Love 3.00 8.00
15 Seth Curry 3.00 8.00
16 Danny Green 2.50 6.00
17 DeMar DeRozan 4.00 10.00
18 Shaquille O'Neal 30.00 80.00
19 Zach LaVine 5.00 12.00
20 Paul George 5.00 12.00

2020-21 Select Duet Selections Memorabilia Prizms Tie Dye

STATED PRINT RUN 15-25 SER.#'d SETS
NO PRICING ON QTY 15
1 LeBron James/25 500.00 1,000.00
2 Kevin Garnett/25 100.00 250.00
4 Kawhi Leonard/25 100.00 250.00
5 Steve Nash/25 60.00 150.00
8 Vince Carter/25 60.00 150.00
12 Shawn Kemp/25 60.00 150.00
13 Chris Webber/25 75.00 200.00
14 Kevin Love/25 25.00 60.00
19 Zach LaVine/25 75.00 200.00
20 Paul George/25 40.00 100.00

2020-21 Select En Fuego

COMMON CARD 2.50 6.00
SEMISTARS 3.00 8.00
UNLISTED STARS 4.00 10.00
*SILVER: 1X TO 2.5X BASIC
1 Giannis Antetokounmpo 20.00 50.00
2 Trae Young 10.00 25.00
3 Kawhi Leonard 10.00 25.00
4 James Harden 8.00 20.00
5 Ja Morant 12.00 30.00
6 Donovan Mitchell 8.00 20.00
7 Damian Lillard 10.00 25.00
8 Stephen Curry 30.00 80.00
9 Kyrie Irving 8.00 20.00
10 Ben Simmons 4.00 10.00
11 Jamal Murray 6.00 15.00
12 Jayson Tatum 15.00 40.00
13 LeBron James 30.00 80.00
14 Zion Williamson 12.00 30.00
15 Luka Doncic 25.00 60.00

2020-21 Select Future

COMMON CARD 1.00 2.50
SEMISTARS 1.25 3.00
UNLISTED STARS 1.50 4.00
1 Desmond Bane 4.00 10.00
2 Malachi Flynn 1.25 3.00
3 Jaden McDaniels 4.00 10.00
4 Udoka Azubuike 1.50 4.00
5 Payton Pritchard 4.00 10.00
6 Immanuel Quickley 3.00 8.00
7 RJ Hampton 1.25 3.00
8 Facundo Campazzo 1.50 4.00
9 Zeke Nnaji 1.50 4.00
10 Tyrese Maxey 10.00 25.00
11 Precious Achiuwa 2.50 6.00
12 Saddiq Bey 2.50 6.00
13 Josh Green 2.50 6.00
14 Aleksej Pokusevski 1.50 4.00
15 Isaiah Stewart 2.50 6.00
16 Cole Anthony 3.00 8.00
17 Aaron Nesmith 2.50 6.00
18 Kira Lewis Jr. 1.25 3.00
19 Tyrese Haliburton 10.00 25.00
20 Devin Vassell 4.00 10.00
21 Jalen Smith 2.50 6.00
22 Deni Avdija 3.00 8.00
23 Obi Toppin 2.50 6.00
24 Killian Hayes 1.25 3.00
25 Onyeka Okongwu 2.50 6.00
26 Isaac Okoro 2.00 5.00
27 Patrick Williams 3.00 8.00
28 LaMelo Ball 30.00 80.00
29 James Wiseman 1.50 4.00
30 Anthony Edwards 20.00 50.00

2020-21 Select Future Prizms Silver

10 Tyrese Maxey 20.00 50.00
28 LaMelo Ball 125.00 300.00
30 Anthony Edwards 75.00 200.00

2020-21 Select In Flight Signatures

COMMON CARD p/r 149-249 3.00 8.00
SEMISTARS p/r 149-249 4.00 10.00
UNLISTED STARS p/r 149-249 5.00 12.00
COMMON CARD p/r 49 5.00 12.00
SEMISTARS p/r 49 6.00 15.00
UNLISTED STARS p/r 49 8.00 20.00
STATED PRINT RUN B/WN 49-249 COPIES PER
EXCHANGE DEADLINE 1/28/2023
*NEON GREEN: .5X TO 1.2X BASIC
*NEON ORNG PULSAR: 1.2X TO 3X BASIC
2 Ron Harper/249 8.00 20.00
3 Clyde Drexler/149 40.00 100.00
4 Nick Anderson/249 4.00 10.00
5 Dominique Wilkins/149 15.00 40.00
6 Desmond Mason/249 4.00 10.00
7 Dwight Howard/149 25.00 60.00
8 Spud Webb/249 8.00 20.00
9 Steve Francis/249 10.00 25.00
10 Michael Cooper/249 4.00 10.00
11 Anfernee Hardaway/49 75.00 200.00
12 Kenny Sky Walker/249 4.00 10.00
13 Cam Reddish/149 30.00 80.00
14 Cedric Ceballos/199 4.00 10.00
15 Zach LaVine/149 40.00 100.00
16 Doug Christie/249 4.00 10.00
17 Kenny Smith/149 4.00 10.00
18 Larry Nance/249 4.00 10.00
19 Shawn Kemp/149 30.00 80.00
20 Tom Chambers/249 4.00 10.00
21 Julius Erving/49 100.00 250.00
22 Harold Miner/249 8.00 20.00
23 Vince Carter/149 75.00 200.00
24 Ricky Davis/249 4.00 10.00
25 Jarrett Culver/149 3.00 8.00
26 Isaiah Rider/249 4.00 10.00
27 Baron Davis/249 8.00 20.00
29 Jason Richardson/249 8.00 20.00
30 Gerald Green/249 3.00 8.00

2020-21 Select In Flight Signatures Prizms Tie Dye

STATED PRINT RUN 25 SER.#'d SETS
EXCHANGE DEADLINE 1/28/2023
21 Julius Erving 125.00 300.00

2020-21 Select Numbers

COMMON CARD .40 1.00
SEMISTARS .50 1.25
UNLISTED STARS .60 1.50
*BLUE: 1.25X TO 3X BASIC
*GREEN: 1.25X TO 3X BASIC
*RED: 1.25X TO 3X BASIC
*SILVER: 1.25X TO 3X BASIC
1 LaMelo Ball 4.00 10.00
2 LeBron James 5.00 12.00
3 Jamal Murray 1.00 2.50
4 Damian Lillard 1.50 4.00
5 Jaylen Brown 1.00 2.50
6 Luka Doncic 4.00 10.00
7 Obi Toppin 1.00 2.50
8 James Wiseman .60 1.50
9 Donovan Mitchell 1.25 3.00
10 Kevin Durant 2.50 6.00
11 James Harden 1.25 3.00
12 Bradley Beal .75 2.00
13 Zion Williamson 2.00 5.00
14 Trae Young 1.50 4.00
15 Anthony Edwards 5.00 12.00
16 Patrick Williams 1.25 3.00
17 Jayson Tatum 2.50 6.00
18 Ja Morant 2.00 5.00
19 Kawhi Leonard 1.50 4.00
20 Chris Paul 1.25 3.00
21 Joel Embiid 1.50 4.00
22 Deni Avdija 1.25 3.00
23 Killian Hayes .50 1.25
24 Onyeka Okongwu 1.00 2.50
25 Isaac Okoro .75 2.00
26 Jalen Smith 1.00 2.50
27 Anthony Davis 1.50 4.00
28 Kyrie Irving 1.25 3.00
29 Ben Simmons .60 1.50
30 Stephen Curry 5.00 12.00
31 Giannis Antetokounmpo 3.00 8.00
32 Pascal Siakam 1.00 2.50
33 D'Angelo Russell .60 1.50
34 Zach LaVine 1.00 2.50
35 Jimmy Butler 1.25 3.00
36 Nikola Jokic 3.00 8.00
37 Paul George 1.00 2.50
38 Brandon Ingram .75 2.00
39 De'Aaron Fox 1.00 2.50
40 RJ Barrett 1.00 2.50

2020-21 Select Phenomenon

COMMON CARD .60 1.50
SEMISTARS .75 2.00
UNLISTED STARS 1.00 2.50
*SILVER: 1.5X TO 4X BASIC
1 Anthony Edwards 8.00 20.00
2 Zion Williamson 3.00 8.00
3 James Wiseman 1.00 2.50
4 Tyler Herro 2.00 5.00
5 LaMelo Ball 6.00 15.00
6 Rui Hachimura 1.25 3.00
7 Coby White 1.25 3.00
8 Patrick Williams 2.00 5.00
9 Jarrett Culver .60 1.50
10 Isaac Okoro 1.25 3.00
11 Onyeka Okongwu 1.50 4.00
12 RJ Barrett 1.50 4.00
13 De'Andre Hunter 1.00 2.50
14 Killian Hayes .75 2.00
15 Obi Toppin 1.50 4.00
16 Brandon Clarke 1.00 2.50
17 Deni Avdija 2.00 5.00
18 Kendrick Nunn .75 2.00
19 Jalen Smith 1.50 4.00
20 Ja Morant 3.00 8.00
21 Devin Vassell 2.50 6.00
22 Tyrese Haliburton 6.00 15.00
23 Kira Lewis Jr. .75 2.00
24 Aaron Nesmith 1.50 4.00
25 Cole Anthony 2.00 5.00
26 Isaiah Stewart 1.50 4.00
27 Aleksej Pokusevski 1.00 2.50
28 Josh Green 1.50 4.00
29 Saddiq Bey 1.50 4.00
30 Precious Achiuwa 1.50 4.00
31 Tyrese Maxey 6.00 15.00
32 Zeke Nnaji 1.00 2.50
33 Jae'Sean Tate 1.00 2.50
34 RJ Hampton .75 2.00
35 Immanuel Quickley 2.00 5.00
36 Payton Pritchard 2.50 6.00
37 Udoka Azubuike 1.00 2.50
38 Jaden McDaniels 2.50 6.00
39 Malachi Flynn .75 2.00
40 Desmond Bane 2.50 6.00

2020-21 Select Rookie Jersey Autographs

COMMON CARD 5.00 12.00
SEMISTARS 6.00 15.00
UNLISTED STARS 8.00 20.00
STATED PRINT RUN 199 COPIES PER
EXCHANGE DEADLINE 1/28/2023
*RED WAVE: .5X TO 1.2X BASIC
*PURPLE/99: .5X TO 1.2X BASIC
*NEON ORNG PLSR/30: .75X TO 2X BASIC
*TIE DYE/25: 1X TO 2.5X BASIC
1 Anthony Edwards 400.00 800.00
2 LaMelo Ball 100.00 250.00
3 Isaac Okoro 10.00 25.00
4 Killian Hayes 6.00 15.00
5 Deni Avdija 15.00 40.00
6 Devin Vassell 20.00 50.00
7 Kira Lewis Jr. 6.00 15.00
8 Cole Anthony 15.00 40.00
9 Aleksej Pokusevski 8.00 20.00
10 Saddiq Bey 12.00 30.00
11 Tyrese Maxey 75.00 200.00
12 Jahmi'us Ramsey 6.00 15.00
13 Immanuel Quickley 15.00 40.00
14 Udoka Azubuike 8.00 20.00
15 Malachi Flynn 6.00 15.00
16 Tyrell Terry 5.00 12.00
17 Daniel Oturu 6.00 15.00
18 Xavier Tillman 8.00 20.00
19 Robert Woodard II 6.00 15.00
20 Jordan Nwora 8.00 20.00
21 Nico Mannion 6.00 15.00
22 Tre Jones 10.00 25.00
23 Skylar Mays 6.00 15.00
24 Theo Maledon 6.00 15.00
25 Vernon Carey Jr. 6.00 15.00
26 Desmond Bane 20.00 50.00
27 Jaden McDaniels 20.00 50.00
28 Payton Pritchard 20.00 50.00
29 RJ Hampton 6.00 15.00
30 Zeke Nnaji 8.00 20.00
31 Precious Achiuwa 12.00 30.00
32 Josh Green 12.00 30.00
33 Isaiah Stewart 12.00 30.00
34 Aaron Nesmith 12.00 30.00
35 Tyrese Haliburton 75.00 200.00
36 Jalen Smith 12.00 30.00
37 Obi Toppin 12.00 30.00
38 Onyeka Okongwu 12.00 30.00
39 Patrick Williams 15.00 40.00
40 James Wiseman 8.00 20.00

2020-21 Select Rookie Jersey Autographs Prizms Disco

*DISCO: .6X TO 1.5X BASIC
EXCHANGE DEADLINE 1/28/2023
2 LaMelo Ball 100.00 250.00

2020-21 Select Rookie Jersey Autographs Prizms Neon Orange Pulsar

*ORANGE PULSAR: .75X TO 2X BASIC
STATED PRINT RUN 30 COPIES PER
EXCHANGE DEADLINE 1/28/2023

2020-21 Select Rookie Jersey Autographs Prizms Purple

*PURPLE: .6X TO 1.5X BASIC
STATED PRINT RUN 99 COPIES PER
EXCHANGE DEADLINE 1/28/2023

2020-21 Select Rookie Jersey Autographs Prizms Tie Dye

*TIE DYE: 1X TO 2.5X BASIC
STATED PRINT RUN 25 COPIES PER
1 Anthony Edwards 1,000.00 2,000.00
2 LaMelo Ball 300.00 600.00

2020-21 Select Rookie Selections

COMMON CARD .60 1.50
SEMISTARS .75 2.00
UNLISTED STARS 1.00 2.50
1 LaMelo Ball 6.00 15.00
2 Obi Toppin 1.50 4.00
3 Tyrese Haliburton 6.00 15.00
4 James Wiseman 1.00 2.50
5 Anthony Edwards 8.00 20.00
6 Deni Avdija 2.00 5.00
7 Tyrese Maxey 6.00 15.00
8 Killian Hayes .75 2.00
9 Jalen Smith 1.50 4.00
10 RJ Hampton .75 2.00
11 Aaron Nesmith 1.50 4.00
12 Patrick Williams 2.00 5.00
13 Cole Anthony 2.00 5.00
14 Josh Green 1.50 4.00
15 Precious Achiuwa 1.50 4.00
16 Payton Pritchard 2.50 6.00
17 Devin Vassell 2.50 6.00
18 Onyeka Okongwu 1.50 4.00
19 Isaac Okoro 1.25 3.00
20 Kira Lewis Jr. .75 2.00
21 Aleksej Pokusevski 1.00 2.50
22 Immanuel Quickley 2.00 5.00
23 Jaden McDaniels 2.50 6.00
24 Malachi Flynn .75 2.00
25 Zeke Nnaji 1.00 2.50
26 Udoka Azubuike 1.00 2.50
27 Isaiah Stewart 1.50 4.00
28 Desmond Bane 2.50 6.00
29 Jordan Nwora 1.00 2.50
30 Saddiq Bey 1.50 4.00

2020-21 Select Rookie Selections Prizms Blue

*BLUE: .75X TO 2X BASIC
1 LaMelo Ball 40.00 100.00
5 Anthony Edwards 20.00 50.00

2020-21 Select Rookie Selections Prizms Green

*GREEN: .75X TO 2X BASIC
1 LaMelo Ball 40.00 100.00
5 Anthony Edwards 20.00 50.00

2020-21 Select Rookie Selections Prizms Red

*RED: .75X TO 2X BASIC
1 LaMelo Ball 40.00 100.00
5 Anthony Edwards 20.00 50.00

2020-21 Select Rookie Selections Prizms Silver

*SILVER: 1X TO 2.5X BASIC
1 LaMelo Ball 50.00 120.00
5 Anthony Edwards 25.00 60.00

2020-21 Select Rookie Signatures

COMMON CARD 4.00 10.00
SEMISTARS 5.00 12.00
UNLISTED STARS 6.00 15.00
STATED PRINT RUN 249 COPIES PER
EXCHANGE DEADLINE 1/28/2023
1 Anthony Edwards 400.00 800.00
2 James Wiseman 6.00 15.00
3 LaMelo Ball 75.00 200.00
4 Patrick Williams 12.00 30.00
5 Isaac Okoro 8.00 20.00
6 Onyeka Okongwu 10.00 25.00
7 Killian Hayes 5.00 12.00
8 Obi Toppin 10.00 25.00
9 Deni Avdija 12.00 30.00
10 Jalen Smith 10.00 25.00
11 Devin Vassell 15.00 40.00
12 Tyrese Haliburton 100.00 250.00
13 Kira Lewis Jr. 5.00 12.00
14 Aaron Nesmith 10.00 25.00
15 Cole Anthony 12.00 30.00
16 Isaiah Stewart 10.00 25.00
17 Aleksej Pokusevski 6.00 15.00
18 Josh Green 10.00 25.00
19 Saddiq Bey 10.00 25.00
20 Precious Achiuwa 10.00 25.00
21 Tyrese Maxey 75.00 200.00
22 Zeke Nnaji 6.00 15.00
23 Mason Jones 4.00 10.00
24 RJ Hampton 5.00 12.00
25 Immanuel Quickley 12.00 30.00
26 Payton Pritchard 15.00 40.00
27 Udoka Azubuike 6.00 15.00
28 Jaden McDaniels 15.00 40.00
29 Malachi Flynn 5.00 12.00
30 Desmond Bane 15.00 40.00
31 Tyrell Terry 4.00 10.00
32 Vernon Carey Jr. 5.00 12.00
33 Daniel Oturu 5.00 12.00
34 Theo Maledon 5.00 12.00
35 Xavier Tillman 6.00 15.00
36 Tyler Bey 5.00 12.00
37 Robert Woodard II 5.00 12.00
38 Tre Jones 8.00 20.00
39 Jordan Nwora 6.00 15.00
40 Nico Mannion 6.00 15.00

2020-21 Select Rookie Signatures Prizms Neon Green

STATED PRINT RUN 99 SER.#'d SETS
EXCHANGE DEADLINE 1/28/2023

2020-21 Select Rookie Signatures Prizms Neon Orange Pulsar

STATED PRINT RUN 30 SER.#'d SETS
EXCHANGE DEADLINE 1/28/2023

2020-21 Select Rookie Signatures Prizms Tie Dye

STATED PRINT RUN 25 SER.#'d SETS
EXCHANGE DEADLINE 1/28/2023

2020-21 Select Selection Committee Signatures

EXCHANGE DEADLINE 1/28/2023
1 Kevin Garnett 100.00 250.00
2 Magic Johnson 125.00 300.00
3 Larry Bird 125.00 300.00
4 Karl Malone 50.00 120.00
5 Allen Iverson 100.00 250.00
6 John Stockton 50.00 120.00
7 Clyde Drexler 40.00 100.00
8 Jerry West 40.00 100.00
9 Dennis Rodman 50.00 120.00
10 Isiah Thomas 40.00 100.00

2020-21 Select Selective Swatches

COMMON CARD 1.50 4.00
SEMISTARS 2.00 5.00
UNLISTED STARS 2.50 6.00
1 Karl-Anthony Towns 4.00 10.00
2 LeBron James 25.00 60.00
3 Myles Turner 2.50 6.00
4 Nikola Vucevic 2.50 6.00
6 Markelle Fultz 2.00 5.00
7 Brandon Clarke 2.50 6.00
8 Trae Young 6.00 15.00
9 Chris Paul 5.00 12.00
10 Jamal Murray 4.00 10.00
11 Joel Embiid 6.00 15.00
12 Cam Reddish 3.00 8.00
13 Anfernee Hardaway 6.00 15.00
14 Andrew Wiggins 3.00 8.00
15 Danny Green 2.00 5.00
16 Jarrett Culver 1.50 4.00
17 Shai Gilgeous-Alexander 12.00 30.00
18 Brook Lopez 2.00 5.00
19 PJ Washington Jr. 2.50 6.00
20 Joe Ingles 2.00 5.00
21 Kevin Love 2.50 6.00
22 Miles Bridges 2.50 6.00
23 Wendell Carter Jr. 2.00 5.00
24 Dennis Schroder 2.50 6.00
25 Al Horford 2.50 6.00
26 Montrezl Harrell 2.50 6.00
27 Josh Okogie 2.00 5.00
28 Steve Nash 5.00 12.00
29 Andre Drummond 2.50 6.00
30 Darius Garland 4.00 10.00
31 Jaylen Brown 4.00 10.00
32 Bradley Beal 3.00 8.00
33 RJ Barrett 4.00 10.00
34 Luka Doncic 25.00 60.00
35 Kyle Kuzma 3.00 8.00
36 Aaron Gordon 2.50 6.00
37 Dirk Nowitzki 6.00 15.00
38 Nikola Jokic 12.00 30.00
39 Ben Simmons 2.50 6.00
40 Rudy Gobert 3.00 8.00

2020-21 Select Selective Swatches Prizms Copper

*COPPER: .75X TO 2X BASIC
STATED PRINT RUN 49 SER.#'d SETS
2 LeBron James/49 75.00 200.00
8 Trae Young/49 20.00 50.00
28 Steve Nash/49 12.00 30.00
34 Luka Doncic/49 75.00 200.00

2020-21 Select Selective Swatches Prizms Purple

*PURPLE: .6X TO 1.5X BASIC
STATED PRINT RUN 99 SER.#'d SETS
2 LeBron James/99 60.00 150.00
8 Trae Young/99 15.00 40.00
28 Steve Nash/99 10.00 25.00
34 Luka Doncic/99 60.00 150.00

2020-21 Select Selective Swatches Prizms Tie Dye

*TIE DYE: 1.5X TO 4X BASIC
STATED PRINT RUN 10-25 SER.#'d SETS
NO PRICING ON QTY 15 & BELOW
2 LeBron James/25 200.00 500.00
28 Steve Nash/25 25.00 60.00
37 Dirk Nowitzki/25 25.00 60.00

2020-21 Select Signature Selections

COMMON CARD 4.00 10.00
SEMISTARS 5.00 12.00
UNLISTED STARS 6.00 15.00
EXCHANGE DEADLINE 1/28/2023
1 De'Andre Hunter 6.00 15.00
2 Thomas Bryant 5.00 12.00
3 Fat Lever 6.00 15.00
4 Ricky Rubio 6.00 15.00
5 David Nwaba 4.00 10.00
6 Moritz Wagner 4.00 10.00
7 Robert Horry 12.00 30.00
8 T.J. McConnell 12.00 30.00
9 Chandler Hutchison 5.00 12.00
10 Bobby Portis 6.00 15.00
11 Robert Covington 5.00 12.00
12 Gary Clark 5.00 12.00
13 Thaddeus Young 4.00 10.00
14 Isaac Bonga 4.00 10.00
15 Otto Porter Jr. 4.00 10.00
16 Alvin Robertson 5.00 12.00
17 Jeff Mullins 5.00 12.00
18 Dominique Wilkins 12.00 30.00
19 Kevin Huerter 5.00 12.00
20 Josh Hart 5.00 12.00
21 Mitch Richmond 10.00 25.00
22 Mark Jackson 5.00 12.00
23 Mike Miller 5.00 12.00
24 Chuma Okeke 6.00 15.00
25 Gary Trent Jr. 6.00 15.00
26 Quinn Cook 4.00 10.00
27 Torrey Craig 5.00 12.00
28 Wayne Ellington 4.00 10.00
29 Kenny Anderson 5.00 12.00
30 Quinndary Weatherspoon 4.00 10.00
31 Wes Iwundu 4.00 10.00
32 Anfernee Simons 8.00 20.00
33 Jack Sikma 6.00 15.00
34 Langston Galloway 4.00 10.00
35 JaVale McGee 5.00 12.00
36 Ivica Zubac 6.00 15.00
37 KZ Okpala 5.00 12.00
38 Cam Reddish 8.00 20.00
39 Aron Baynes 4.00 10.00
40 Bruno Fernando 4.00 10.00
41 Arron Afflalo 4.00 10.00
42 Sam Perkins 5.00 12.00
43 Tony Delk 5.00 12.00
44 Anderson Varejao 4.00 10.00
45 Nickeil Alexander-Walker 6.00 15.00
46 Tony Bradley 4.00 10.00
47 Michael Porter Jr. 8.00 20.00
48 E'Twaun Moore 4.00 10.00
49 Ricky Pierce 4.00 10.00
50 Shawn Kemp 30.00 80.00

2020-21 Select Signatures

COMMON CARD p/r 249 3.00 8.00
SEMISTARS p/r 249 4.00 10.00
UNLISTED STARS p/r 249 5.00 12.00
COMMON CARD p/r 49-99 5.00 12.00
SEMISTARS p/r 49-99 6.00 15.00
UNLISTED STARS p/r 49-99 8.00 20.00
STATED PRINT RUN 49-249 SER. #'d SETS
EXCHANGE DEADLINE 1/28/2023
2 Luka Doncic/49 500.00 1,000.00
3 Kelly Oubre Jr./249 10.00 25.00
4 John Stockton/49 30.00 80.00
5 Thomas Bryant/249 4.00 10.00
6 Bradley Beal/49 20.00 50.00
7 RJ Barrett/49 30.00 80.00
8 Charles Barkley/49 75.00 200.00
9 Mike Conley/99 6.00 15.00
10 Allen Iverson/49 100.00 250.00
12 Larry Bird/49 125.00 300.00
13 Derrick Coleman/249 5.00 12.00
14 Anthony Davis/49 40.00 100.00
15 Alex Caruso/249 15.00 40.00
16 Ja Morant/49 300.00 600.00
17 De'Aaron Fox/99 20.00 50.00
18 Shaquille O'Neal /49 125.00 300.00
19 Eric Bledsoe/249 4.00 10.00
20 Karl Malone/49 30.00 80.00
21 Devonte' Graham/249 4.00 10.00
22 Magic Johnson/49 125.00 300.00
23 Boban Marjanovic/249 10.00 25.00
24 Kareem Abdul-Jabbar/49 125.00 300.00
25 Dale Ellis/249 4.00 10.00
26 Trae Young/49 125.00 300.00
27 Lamar Odom/99 8.00 20.00
28 Kevin Durant/49 125.00 300.00
29 Maurice Cheeks/249 5.00 12.00
30 Dwyane Wade/49 75.00 200.00

2020-21 Select Signatures Prizms Neon Green

*NEON GREEN: .5X TO 1.2X BASIC
STATED PRINT RUN 35-99 SER.#'d SETS
EXCHANGE DEADLINE 1/28/2023
1 Spencer Dinwiddie/99 5.00 12.00

2020-21 Select Signatures Prizms Tie Dye

*TIE DYE: .75X TO 2X BASIC
STATED PRINT RUN 25 SER.#'d SETS
EXCHANGE DEADLINE 1/28/2023
15 Alex Caruso 40.00 100.00

2020-21 Select Sparks Memorabilia

COMMON CARD 1.50 4.00
SEMISTARS 2.00 5.00
UNLISTED STARS 2.50 6.00
*PURPLE/99: .6X TO 1.5X BASIC
*COPPER/49: .75X TO 2X BASIC
1 Obi Toppin 4.00 10.00
2 Deni Avdija 5.00 12.00
3 LaMelo Ball 60.00 150.00
4 James Wiseman 2.50 6.00
5 Anthony Edwards 25.00 60.00
6 Patrick Williams 5.00 12.00
7 Killian Hayes 2.00 5.00
8 Isaac Okoro 3.00 8.00
9 Onyeka Okongwu 4.00 10.00
10 Jalen Smith 4.00 10.00

2020-21 Select Sparks Memorabilia Prizms Tie Dye

*TIE DYE: 1.5X TO 4X BASIC
STATED PRINT RUN 25 SER.#'d SETS
3 LaMelo Ball 300.00 600.00
5 Anthony Edwards 150.00 400.00
6 Patrick Williams 60.00 150.00

2020-21 Select Turbo Charged

COMMON CARD .60 1.50
SEMISTARS .75 2.00
UNLISTED STARS 1.00 2.50
1 Luka Doncic 6.00 15.00
2 LeBron James 8.00 20.00
3 Zion Williamson 3.00 8.00
4 Giannis Antetokounmpo 5.00 12.00
5 Anthony Davis 2.50 6.00
6 Kawhi Leonard 2.50 6.00

2020-21 Select Turbo Charged Prizms Blue

*BLUE: .75X TO 2X BASIC
1 Luka Doncic 25.00 60.00
2 LeBron James 25.00 60.00

2020-21 Select Turbo Charged Prizms Green

*GREEN: .75X TO 2X BASIC
1 Luka Doncic 20.00 50.00
2 LeBron James 20.00 50.00

2020-21 Select Turbo Charged Prizms Red

*RED: .75X TO 2X BASIC
1 Luka Doncic 25.00 60.00
2 LeBron James 25.00 60.00

2020-21 Select Turbo Charged Prizms Silver

*SILVER: .75X TO 2X BASIC
1 Luka Doncic 20.00 50.00
2 LeBron James 20.00 50.00

2020-21 Select Unstoppable

COMMON CARD 1.00 2.50
SEMISTARS 1.25 3.00
UNLISTED STARS 1.50 4.00
1 Jamal Murray 2.50 6.00
2 LeBron James 25.00 60.00
3 Paul George 2.50 6.00
4 Trae Young 4.00 10.00
5 Jayson Tatum 6.00 15.00
6 Joel Embiid 4.00 10.00
7 Zion Williamson 5.00 12.00
8 Devin Booker 4.00 10.00
9 Chris Paul 3.00 8.00
10 Damian Lillard 4.00 10.00
11 Anthony Davis 4.00 10.00
12 Kawhi Leonard 4.00 10.00
13 Bradley Beal 2.00 5.00
14 Giannis Antetokounmpo 8.00 20.00
15 Luka Doncic 25.00 60.00

2020-21 Select Unstoppable Prizms Silver

*SILVER: 1X TO 2.5X BASIC
2 LeBron James 150.00 400.00
4 Trae Young 30.00 80.00
5 Jayson Tatum 30.00 80.00
7 Zion Williamson 100.00 250.00
14 Giannis Antetokounmpo 30.00 80.00
15 Luka Doncic 150.00 400.00

2020-21 Select X Factor Memorabilia Signatures

COMMON CARD 3.00 8.00
SEMISTARS 4.00 10.00
UNLISTED STARS 5.00 12.00
STATED PRINT RUN 49-249 COPIES PER
EXCHANGE DEADLINE 1/28/2023
1 Jarrett Allen/249 5.00 12.00
3 Jonas Valanciunas/249 4.00 10.00
4 David Robinson/99 25.00 60.00
5 Nemanja Bjelica/125 3.00 8.00
6 Myles Turner/249 5.00 12.00
8 Nikola Vucevic/149 5.00 12.00
9 Rodney Hood/249 3.00 8.00
10 Ricky Rubio/249 5.00 12.00
11 Andrea Bargnani/249 3.00 8.00
12 Karl-Anthony Towns/49 20.00 50.00
13 Sam Cassell/99 4.00 10.00
14 Hakeem Olajuwon/99 25.00 60.00
15 Doug McDermott/249 4.00 10.00
16 Al Horford/149 5.00 12.00
17 Roy Hibbert/249 3.00 8.00
18 Justin Holiday/249 3.00 8.00
19 Taj Gibson/249 3.00 8.00
20 Terry Cummings/249 5.00 12.00
21 Wesley Matthews/249 3.00 8.00
22 Bradley Beal/99 6.00 15.00
23 Toni Kukoc/149 12.00 30.00
25 TJ Leaf/249 3.00 8.00

2020-21 Select X Factor Memorabilia Signatures Prizms Purple

STATED PRINT RUN 35-99 SER.#'d SETS
EXCHANGE DEADLINE 1/28/2023

2020-21 Select X Factor Memorabilia Signatures Prizms Tie Dye

STATED PRINT RUN 25 SER.#'d SETS
EXCHANGE DEADLINE 1/28/2023

2020-21 Select Youth Explosion Signatures

COMMON CARD 4.00 10.00
SEMISTARS 5.00 12.00
UNLISTED STARS 6.00 15.00
EXCHANGE DEADLINE 1/28/2023
1 Anthony Edwards 200.00 500.00
2 James Wiseman 6.00 15.00
3 LaMelo Ball 75.00 200.00
4 Patrick Williams 12.00 30.00
5 Isaac Okoro 8.00 20.00
6 Onyeka Okongwu 10.00 25.00
7 Killian Hayes 5.00 12.00
8 Obi Toppin 10.00 25.00
9 Deni Avdija 12.00 30.00
10 Ashton Hagans 6.00 15.00
11 Devin Vassell 15.00 40.00
12 Tyrese Haliburton 100.00 250.00
13 Kira Lewis Jr. 5.00 12.00
14 Aaron Nesmith 10.00 25.00
15 Cole Anthony 12.00 30.00
16 Isaiah Stewart 10.00 25.00
17 Aleksej Pokusevski 6.00 15.00
18 Josh Green 10.00 25.00
19 Saddiq Bey 10.00 25.00
20 Precious Achiuwa 10.00 25.00
21 Mason Jones 4.00 10.00
22 Zeke Nnaji 6.00 15.00
23 Caleb Martin 10.00 25.00
24 RJ Hampton 5.00 12.00
25 Immanuel Quickley 12.00 30.00
26 Payton Pritchard 15.00 40.00
27 Udoka Azubuike 6.00 15.00
29 Devon Dotson 5.00 12.00
30 Isaiah Joe 6.00 15.00
32 Vernon Carey Jr. 5.00 12.00
33 Daniel Oturu 5.00 12.00
34 Theo Maledon 5.00 12.00
35 Xavier Tillman 6.00 15.00
36 Tyler Bey 5.00 12.00
37 Robert Woodard II 5.00 12.00
38 Tre Jones 8.00 20.00
39 Jordan Nwora 6.00 15.00

2021-22 Select

*BLUE: .4X TO 1X BASIC
*BLUE SHIMMER: .75X TO 2X BASIC
GRN/WHT/PRPL: .75X TO 2X BASIC
*ORANGE FLASH: .75X TO 2X BASIC
*PRIZMS BLUE: .75X TO 2X BASIC
*RED WAVE: .75X TO 2X BASIC
TRI-COLOR: .75X TO 2X BASIC
*GRN CRCKD ICE: 1.2X TO 3X BASIC
*SCOPE: 1.2X TO 3X BASIC
*SILVER: 1.2X TO 3X BASIC
*LIGHT BLUE/299: 1.5X TO 4X BASIC
*BLUE DIE CUT/249: 1.5X TO 4X BASIC
*RED/199: 2X TO 5X BASIC
*MAROON DIE CUT/175: 2X TO 5X BASIC
*WHITE/149: 2.5X TO 6X BASIC
*NEON GREEN/75: 3X TO 8X BASIC
*RED DISCO/49: 4X TO 10X BASIC
*TEAL/WHT/PNK/49: 4X TO 10X BASIC
1 Buddy Hield .30 .75
2 Luguentz Dort .40 1.00
3 Damian Lillard 1.00 2.50
4 Patrick Williams .40 1.00
5 Evan Mobley RC 3.00 8.00
6 T.J. Warren .25 .60
7 Jalen Green RC 4.00 10.00
8 Joe Harris .30 .75
9 Alex Caruso .40 1.00
10 Karl-Anthony Towns .60 1.50
11 Cade Cunningham RC 5.00 12.00
12 Luka Doncic 2.50 6.00
13 Darius Garland .60 1.50
14 Paul George .60 1.50
15 Franz Wagner RC 2.50 6.00
16 Tobias Harris .30 .75
17 Jalen Johnson RC 2.50 6.00
18 Joe Wieskamp RC .60 1.50
19 Alperen Sengun RC 2.50 6.00
20 Kawhi Leonard 1.00 2.50
21 Cameron Thomas RC 1.50 4.00
22 Luka Garza RC .75 2.00
23 Davion Mitchell RC .75 2.00
24 Quentin Grimes RC 1.50 4.00
25 Gary Trent Jr. .30 .75
26 Trae Young 1.00 2.50
27 Jalen Suggs RC 2.00 5.00
28 Jonathan Kuminga RC 2.50 6.00
29 Anfernee Simons .60 1.50
30 Kelly Oubre Jr. .40 1.00
31 Carmelo Anthony .60 1.50
32 Marcus Smart .40 1.00
33 Day'Ron Sharpe RC .75 2.00
34 Rajon Rondo .50 1.25
35 Giannis Antetokounmpo 2.00 5.00
36 Tre Mann RC 1.25 3.00
37 James Bouknight RC .60 1.50
38 Jordan Clarkson .40 1.00
39 Anthony Davis 1.00 2.50
40 Keon Johnson RC .75 2.00
41 Chris Duarte RC .60 1.50
42 Miles Bridges .30 .75
43 Dejounte Murray .40 1.00
44 Robert Williams III .40 1.00
45 Herbert Jones RC 1.00 2.50
46 Trey Murphy III RC 2.50 6.00
47 James Harden .75 2.00
48 Josh Christopher RC .60 1.50
49 Anthony Edwards 2.00 5.00
50 Kevin Durant 1.25 3.00
51 Chris Paul .75 2.00
52 Montrezl Harrell .30 .75
53 Derrick Rose .60 1.50
54 Russell Westbrook .60 1.50
55 Isaiah Jackson RC .75 2.00
56 Usman Garuba RC .60 1.50
57 Jaren Jackson Jr. .60 1.50
58 Josh Giddey RC 2.50 6.00
59 Bam Adebayo .60 1.50
60 Kevin Love .40 1.00
61 Christian Wood .30 .75
62 Moses Moody RC 1.50 4.00
63 Desmond Bane .75 2.00
64 Santi Aldama RC 1.00 2.50
65 Isaiah Todd RC .60 1.50
66 Victor Oladipo .30 .75
67 Jaylen Brown .60 1.50
68 Joshua Primo RC .60 1.50
69 Bojan Bogdanovic .30 .75
70 Kyle Kuzma .50 1.25
71 Collin Sexton .40 1.00
72 Neemias Queta RC .75 2.00
73 Domantas Sabonis .50 1.25
74 Scottie Barnes RC 2.50 6.00

75 Ja Morant 1.25 3.00
76 Zach LaVine .60 1.50
77 Jayson Tatum 1.50 4.00
78 JT Thor RC .75 2.00
79 Bones Hyland RC 1.00 2.50
80 Kyrie Irving .75 2.00
81 Corey Kispert RC 1.00 2.50
82 Nikola Jokic 2.00 5.00
83 Donovan Mitchell .75 2.00
84 Seth Curry .30 .75
85 Jaden Springer RC .75 2.00
86 Ziaire Williams RC 1.00 2.50
87 Jericho Sims RC 1.00 2.50
88 Julius Randle .50 1.25
89 Bradley Beal .50 1.25
90 Lauri Markkanen .50 1.25
91 Dalano Banton RC 1.00 2.50
92 Nikola Vucevic .40 1.00
93 Elfrid Payton .25 .60
94 Stephen Curry 2.50 6.00
95 Jae'Sean Tate .40 1.00
96 Zion Williamson 1.00 2.50
97 Jimmy Butler .60 1.50
98 Kai Jones RC .60 1.50
99 Brandon Ingram .50 1.25
100 LeBron James 3.00 8.00
101 Santi Aldama 1.00 2.50
102 Jalen Suggs 2.00 5.00
103 John Collins .40 1.00
104 Al Horford .40 1.00
105 Kemba Walker .40 1.00
106 Brook Lopez .30 .75
107 Lonzo Ball .40 1.00
108 Darius Bazley .25 .60
109 Nikola Jokic 2.00 5.00
110 Evan Mobley 3.00 8.00
111 Scottie Barnes 2.50 6.00
112 Jamal Murray .60 1.50
113 Jonas Valanciunas .30 .75
114 Alperen Sengun 2.50 6.00
115 Keon Johnson .75 2.00
116 Cade Cunningham 5.00 12.00
117 Luka Doncic 2.50 6.00
118 Davion Mitchell .75 2.00
119 Onyeka Okongwu .40 1.00
120 Franz Wagner 2.50 6.00
121 Jalen Green 2.50 6.00
122 James Bouknight .60 1.50
123 Jonathan Kuminga 2.50 6.00
124 Andre Drummond .30 .75
125 Ja Morant 1.25 3.00
126 Cameron Thomas 1.50 4.00
127 Luke Kennard .30 .75
128 Day'Ron Sharpe .75 2.00
129 Paul George .60 1.50
130 Fred VanVleet .50 1.25
131 Trae Young 1.00 2.50
132 James Harden .75 2.00
133 Josh Christopher .60 1.50
134 Andrew Wiggins .50 1.25
135 Kevin Durant 1.25 3.00
136 Caris LeVert .30 .75
137 Malik Beasley .30 .75
138 Deandre Ayton .40 1.00
139 Payton Pritchard .40 1.00
140 Giannis Antetokounmpo 2.00 5.00
141 Tre Mann 1.25 3.00
142 Jared Butler RC .75 2.00
143 Josh Giddey 2.50 6.00
144 Anthony Davis 1.00 2.50
145 Kevin Huerter .30 .75
146 Chris Duarte .60 1.50
147 Mikal Bridges .50 1.25
148 DeMar DeRozan .50 1.25
149 Precious Achiuwa .40 1.00
150 Isaiah Jackson .75 2.00
151 Trey Murphy III 2.50 6.00
152 Jarrett Allen .40 1.00
153 Joshua Primo .60 1.50
154 Ayo Dosunmu RC 1.50 4.00
155 Khris Middleton .40 1.00
156 Chris Paul .75 2.00
157 Miles McBride RC 1.25 3.00
158 Devin Booker 1.00 2.50
159 Quentin Grimes 1.50 4.00
160 Isaiah Livers RC .75 2.00
161 Usman Garuba .60 1.50
162 Jaylen Brown .60 1.50
163 Jrue Holiday .50 1.25
164 Blake Griffin .40 1.00
165 Kyle Lowry .40 1.00
166 Clint Capela .40 1.00
167 Mitchell Robinson .40 1.00
168 Devonte' Graham .30 .75
169 Ricky Rubio .40 1.00
170 Isaiah Stewart .40 1.00
171 Zach LaVine .60 1.50
172 Jayson Tatum 1.50 4.00
173 Jusuf Nurkic .30 .75
174 Bones Hyland 1.00 2.50
175 Kyrie Irving .75 2.00
176 Corey Kispert 1.00 2.50
177 Moses Brown .25 .60
178 Donovan Mitchell .75 2.00
179 Rudy Gobert .50 1.25
180 Jaden Springer .75 2.00
181 Ziaire Williams 1.00 2.50
182 Jeremiah Robinson-Earl RC .75 2.00
183 Kai Jones .60 1.50
184 Bradley Beal .50 1.25
185 LaMelo Ball 1.00 2.50
186 Damian Lillard 1.00 2.50
187 Moses Moody 1.50 4.00
188 Duncan Robinson .30 .75
189 Russell Westbrook .60 1.50
190 Jalen Green 4.00 10.00
191 Zion Williamson 1.00 2.50
192 Jimmy Butler .60 1.50
193 Kawhi Leonard 1.00 2.50
194 Brandon Boston Jr. RC .75 2.00
195 LeBron James 3.00 8.00
196 D'Angelo Russell .40 1.00
197 Nickeil Alexander-Walker .30 .75
198 Eric Bledsoe .30 .75
199 Sandro Mamukelashvili RC 1.00 2.50
200 Jalen Johnson 2.50 6.00
201 Myles Turner .75 2.00
202 Dennis Schroder .75 2.00
203 Russell Westbrook 1.25 3.00
204 Gordon Hayward .60 1.50
205 Tim Hardaway Jr. .50 1.25
206 Jayson Tatum 3.00 8.00
207 Karl-Anthony Towns 1.25 3.00
208 Aaron Gordon .75 2.00
209 LaMarcus Aldridge .75 2.00
210 Carmelo Anthony 1.25 3.00
211 Nikola Jokic 4.00 10.00
212 Derrick Rose 1.25 3.00
213 Saddiq Bey .60 1.50
214 Ja Morant 2.50 6.00
215 Trae Young 2.00 5.00
216 Jerami Grant .75 2.00
217 Kawhi Leonard 2.00 5.00
218 Aleksej Pokusevski .60 1.50
219 LeBron James 6.00 15.00
220 Chris Duarte 1.25 3.00
221 Nikola Vucevic .75 2.00
222 Devin Vassell 1.25 3.00
223 Scottie Barnes 5.00 12.00
224 Jalen Brunson 1.50 4.00
225 Tyler Herro 1.25 3.00
226 Jimmy Butler 1.25 3.00
227 Keldon Johnson 1.00 2.50
228 Andre Iguodala .75 2.00
229 Lonnie Walker IV .60 1.50
230 Chris Paul 1.50 4.00
231 OG Anunoby .75 2.00
232 Donovan Mitchell 1.50 4.00
233 Seth Curry .60 1.50
234 Jalen Green 8.00 20.00
235 Tyrese Haliburton 1.50 4.00
236 John Wall 1.00 2.50
237 Kendrick Nunn .60 1.50
238 Anthony Davis 2.00 5.00
239 Lou Williams .75 2.00
240 CJ McCollum .60 1.50
241 Pascal Siakam 1.25 3.00
242 Draymond Green 1.00 2.50
243 Shai Gilgeous-Alexander 4.00 10.00
244 Jalen Suggs 4.00 10.00
245 Tyrese Maxey 2.00 5.00
246 Jonathan Kuminga 5.00 12.00
247 Kevin Durant 2.50 6.00
248 Austin Reaves RC 8.00 20.00
249 Luka Doncic 5.00 12.00
250 Cole Anthony 1.00 2.50
251 Paul George 1.25 3.00
252 Dwight Howard 1.00 2.50
253 Spencer Dinwiddie .60 1.50
254 James Bouknight 1.25 3.00
255 Wendell Carter Jr. .75 2.00
256 Josh Giddey 5.00 12.00
257 Kevin Love .75 2.00
258 Ben Simmons .75 2.00
259 Malcolm Brogdon .60 1.50
260 Damian Lillard 2.00 5.00
261 PJ Washington Jr. .75 2.00
262 Evan Fournier .60 1.50
263 Stephen Curry 5.00 12.00
264 James Harden 1.50 4.00
265 Will Barton .50 1.25
266 Josh Richardson .60 1.50
267 Kevin Porter Jr. .60 1.50
268 Bogdan Bogdanovic .75 2.00
269 Michael Porter Jr. 1.00 2.50
270 Danilo Gallinari .60 1.50
271 Rajon Rondo 1.00 2.50
272 Evan Mobley 6.00 15.00
273 Steven Adams .60 1.50
274 James Wiseman .60 1.50
275 Zach LaVine 1.25 3.00
276 Joshua Primo 1.25 3.00
277 Kristaps Porzingis 1.00 2.50
278 Bradley Beal 1.00 2.50
279 Mike Conley .60 1.50
280 Davion Mitchell 1.50 4.00
281 Richaun Holmes .50 1.25
282 Franz Wagner 5.00 12.00
283 Terrence Ross .60 1.50
284 Jaren Jackson Jr. 1.25 3.00
285 Ziaire Williams 2.00 5.00
286 Juan Toscano-Anderson RC 1.50 4.00
287 Kyle Kuzma 1.00 2.50
288 Cade Cunningham 10.00 25.00
289 Mo Bamba .60 1.50
290 De'Aaron Fox 1.25 3.00
291 RJ Barrett 1.25 3.00
292 Giannis Antetokounmpo 4.00 10.00
293 Terry Rozier III .60 1.50
294 Jaylen Brown 1.25 3.00
295 Zion Williamson 2.00 5.00
296 Julius Randle 1.00 2.50
297 Kyrie Irving 1.50 4.00
298 Cam Reddish .75 2.00
299 Moses Moody 3.00 8.00
300 De'Andre Hunter .75 2.00

2021-22 Select Prizms Orange Die Cut

*ORANGE DIE CUT: 3X TO 8X BASIC
STATED PRINT RUN 65 SER.#'d SETS
116 Cade Cunningham 75.00 200.00
117 Luka Doncic 40.00 100.00
121 Stephen Curry 40.00 100.00
190 Jalen Green 75.00 200.00
195 LeBron James 40.00 100.00

2021-22 Select Prizms Purple Die Cut

*PURPLE DIE CUT: 2.5X TO 6X BASIC
STATED PRINT RUN 99 SER.#'d SETS
116 Cade Cunningham 50.00 120.00
117 Luka Doncic 30.00 80.00
121 Stephen Curry 30.00 80.00
190 Jalen Green 50.00 120.00
195 LeBron James 30.00 80.00

2021-22 Select Prizms Tie Dye Die Cut

*TIE DYE DIE CUT: 6X TO 15X BASIC
STATED PRINT RUN 25 SER.#'d SETS

2021-22 Select Artistic Selections

1 Luka Doncic 100.00 250.00
2 Cade Cunningham 125.00 300.00
3 Stephen Curry 100.00 250.00
4 Kevin Durant 40.00 100.00
5 Zion Williamson 60.00 150.00
6 Zach LaVine 30.00 80.00
7 LeBron James 125.00 300.00
8 Nikola Jokic 30.00 80.00
9 Giannis Antetokounmpo 75.00 200.00
10 Jalen Green 125.00 300.00

2021-22 Select Autographed Memorabilia

COMMON CARD 5.00 12.00
SEMISTARS 6.00 15.00
UNLISTED STARS 8.00 20.00
STATED PRINT RUN B/WN 99-199 COPIES PER
*PURPLE/49-99: .5X TO 1.2X BASIC
*TIE DYE/5-25: .75X TO 2X BASIC
1 Ja Morant/99 300.00 600.00
2 Tobias Harris/149 6.00 15.00
3 Jeff Teague/199 5.00 12.00
4 Larry Bird/99 100.00 250.00
6 Paul Pierce/99 30.00 80.00
7 Collin Sexton/149 8.00 20.00
8 Roy Hibbert/199 6.00 15.00
9 Dillon Brooks/199 8.00 20.00
10 Stephen Jackson/199 6.00 15.00
11 Jamal Murray/99 25.00 60.00
12 Tyus Jones/199 6.00 15.00
13 Julius Randle/149 10.00 25.00
14 Luke Kennard/199 6.00 15.00
15 Caris LeVert/199 6.00 15.00
16 Ricky Rubio/149 8.00 20.00
17 Devin Harris/199 5.00 12.00
18 Stephen Curry/99 500.00 1,000.00
19 Enes Freedom/199 6.00 15.00
20 T.J. Warren/149 5.00 12.00
21 Jason Kidd/99 20.00 50.00
22 Vince Carter/99 50.00 120.00
23 Kyrie Irving/99 40.00 100.00
24 Nikola Jokic/99 75.00 200.00
25 Chris Kaman/163 5.00 12.00

2021-22 Select Company

COMMON CARD .50 1.25
SEMISTARS .60 1.50
UNLISTED STARS .75 2.00
*BLUE: 1.2X TO 3X BASIC
*GREEN: 1.2X TO 3X BASIC
*SILVER: 1.2X TO 3X BASIC
*RED: 1.2X TO 3X BASIC
1 Dominique Wilkins 1.25 3.00
2 Tim Duncan 2.00 5.00
3 Allen Iverson 2.00 5.00
4 Shaquille O'Neal 2.50 6.00
5 Ben Wallace 1.00 2.50
6 Hakeem Olajuwon 1.50 4.00
7 Magic Johnson 2.50 6.00
8 Wilt Chamberlain 2.50 6.00
9 Steve Nash 1.50 4.00
10 Charles Barkley 2.00 5.00
11 Dirk Nowitzki 2.00 5.00
12 Kevin Garnett 2.00 5.00
13 Tracy McGrady 1.25 3.00
14 David Robinson 1.50 4.00
15 Jason Kidd 1.25 3.00
16 Bill Russell 2.50 6.00
17 Larry Bird 2.50 6.00
18 Kareem Abdul-Jabbar 2.50 6.00
19 Patrick Ewing 1.25 3.00
20 Karl Malone 1.50 4.00

2021-22 Select Draft Selections Memorabilia

COMMON CARD 1.25 3.00
SEMISTARS 1.50 4.00
UNLISTED STARS 2.00 5.00
*PURPLE/99: .75X TO 2X BASIC
*COPPER/49: 1X TO 2.5X BASIC
*TIE DYE/25: 2X TO 5X BASIC
1 Alperen Sengun 6.00 15.00
2 Cade Cunningham 12.00 30.00
3 Kai Jones 1.50 4.00
4 Scottie Barnes 6.00 15.00
5 Isaiah Jackson 2.00 5.00
6 Franz Wagner 6.00 15.00
7 Quentin Grimes 4.00 10.00
8 Ziaire Williams 2.50 6.00
9 Jaden Springer 2.00 5.00
10 Chris Duarte 1.50 4.00
11 Trey Murphy III 6.00 15.00
12 Jalen Green 10.00 25.00
13 Jalen Johnson 6.00 15.00
14 Jalen Suggs 5.00 12.00
16 Josh Giddey 6.00 15.00
17 Bones Hyland 2.50 6.00
18 James Bouknight 1.50 4.00
19 Day'Ron Sharpe 2.00 5.00
20 Moses Moody 4.00 10.00
21 Tre Mann 3.00 8.00
22 Evan Mobley 8.00 20.00
23 Keon Johnson 2.00 5.00
24 Jonathan Kuminga 6.00 15.00
26 Davion Mitchell 2.00 5.00
27 Cameron Thomas 4.00 10.00
28 Joshua Primo 1.50 4.00
29 Santi Aldama 2.50 6.00
30 Corey Kispert 2.50 6.00

2021-22 Select En Fuego

COMMON CARD 2.00 5.00
SEMISTARS 2.50 6.00
UNLISTED STARS 3.00 8.00
*SILVER: 1X TO 2.5X BASIC
1 Ja Morant 10.00 25.00
2 Giannis Antetokounmpo 15.00 40.00
3 Kawhi Leonard 8.00 20.00
4 Kyrie Irving 6.00 15.00
5 Joel Embiid 8.00 20.00
6 Anthony Davis 8.00 20.00
7 Jayson Tatum 12.00 30.00
8 LeBron James 25.00 60.00
9 James Harden 6.00 15.00
10 Kevin Durant 10.00 25.00
11 Zion Williamson 8.00 20.00
12 Luka Doncic 20.00 50.00
13 Zach LaVine 5.00 12.00
14 Stephen Curry 20.00 50.00
15 Trae Young 8.00 20.00

2021-22 Select Future

COMMON CARD .50 1.25
SEMISTARS .60 1.50
UNLISTED STARS .75 2.00
*SILVER: 1.25X TO 3X BASIC
1 Quentin Grimes 1.50 4.00
2 Jalen Suggs 2.00 5.00
3 Jaden Springer .75 2.00
4 Corey Kispert 1.00 2.50
5 Alperen Sengun 2.50 6.00
6 Jonathan Kuminga 2.50 6.00
7 Kai Jones .60 1.50
8 Cade Cunningham 5.00 12.00
9 Isaiah Jackson .75 2.00
10 James Bouknight .60 1.50
11 Bones Hyland 1.00 2.50
12 Davion Mitchell .75 2.00
13 Isaiah Todd .60 1.50
14 Evan Mobley 3.00 8.00
15 Trey Murphy III 2.50 6.00
16 Ziaire Williams 1.00 2.50
17 Jalen Johnson 2.50 6.00
18 Scottie Barnes 2.50 6.00
19 Usman Garuba .60 1.50
20 Moses Moody 1.50 4.00
21 Cameron Thomas 1.50 4.00
22 Joshua Primo .60 1.50
23 Ayo Dosunmu 1.50 4.00
24 Josh Giddey 2.50 6.00
25 Tre Mann 1.25 3.00
26 Chris Duarte .60 1.50
27 Keon Johnson .75 2.00
28 Franz Wagner 2.50 6.00
29 Josh Christopher .60 1.50
30 Jalen Green 4.00 10.00

2021-22 Select In Flight Signatures

COMMON CARD 4.00 10.00
SEMISTARS 5.00 12.00
UNLISTED STARS 6.00 15.00
STATED PRINT RUN 149-299 COPIES PER
*NEON GREEN/99: .5X TO 1.2X BASIC
*NEON ORNG PLSR/15-30: .6X TO 1.5X BASIC
*TIE DYE/25: .75X TO 2X BASIC
1 Shaquille O'Neal /149 75.00 200.00
2 Clint Capela/299 6.00 15.00
3 Tyrese Haliburton/249 50.00 120.00
4 Dominique Wilkins/299 12.00 30.00
5 James Wiseman/299 5.00 12.00
6 Allen Iverson/149 60.00 150.00
7 Julius Randle/249 8.00 20.00
8 Anthony Edwards/299 125.00 300.00
9 Ralph Sampson/224 6.00 15.00
10 Ben Wallace/199 20.00 50.00
11 Steve Francis/299 6.00 15.00
12 Clyde Drexler/299 20.00 50.00
13 Vince Carter/249 40.00 100.00
14 George Gervin/249 10.00 25.00
15 Jason Richardson/299 6.00 15.00
16 Andre Drummond/249 5.00 12.00
17 Kendall Gill/299 5.00 12.00
18 Artis Gilmore/299 8.00 20.00
19 Rex Chapman/299 5.00 12.00
20 Brent Barry/299 5.00 12.00
21 Steven Adams/249 5.00 12.00
22 David Thompson/299 8.00 20.00
23 Jamal Crawford/299 6.00 15.00
24 Jason Williams/299 20.00 50.00
25 Anfernee Hardaway/149 40.00 100.00
26 Montrezl Harrell/199 5.00 12.00
27 Ben McLemore/299 4.00 10.00
28 Ron Harper/299 6.00 15.00
29 Cassius Stanley/299 4.00 10.00
30 Gerald Wilkins/299 5.00 12.00

2021-22 Select Numbers

COMMON CARD .40 1.00
SEMISTARS .50 1.25
UNLISTED STARS .60 1.50
*BLUE: 1.25X TO 3X BASIC
*GREEN: 1.25X TO 3X BASIC
*RED: 1.25X TO 3X BASIC
*SILVER: 1.25X TO 3X BASIC
1 De'Aaron Fox 1.00 2.50
2 Jonathan Kuminga 2.00 5.00
3 Kawhi Leonard 1.50 4.00
4 Bam Adebayo 1.00 2.50
5 Stephen Curry 4.00 10.00
6 LeBron James 5.00 12.00
7 Luka Doncic 4.00 10.00
8 Jamal Murray 1.00 2.50
9 Jayson Tatum 2.50 6.00
10 Carmelo Anthony 1.00 2.50
11 Joel Embiid 1.50 4.00
12 Jalen Suggs 1.50 4.00
13 RJ Barrett 1.00 2.50
14 Pascal Siakam 1.00 2.50
15 Damian Lillard 1.50 4.00
16 Jimmy Butler 1.00 2.50
17 Giannis Antetokounmpo 3.00 8.00
18 Kevin Durant 2.00 5.00
19 Zion Williamson 1.50 4.00
20 Russell Westbrook 1.00 2.50
21 Kyrie Irving 1.25 3.00
22 Jalen Green 3.00 8.00
23 Paul George 1.00 2.50
24 Michael Porter Jr. .75 2.00
25 Nikola Jokic 3.00 8.00
26 CJ McCollum .50 1.25
27 Julius Randle .75 2.00
28 Ben Simmons .60 1.50
29 Trae Young 1.50 4.00
30 Anthony Davis 1.50 4.00
31 Donovan Mitchell 1.25 3.00
32 Evan Mobley 2.50 6.00
33 Karl-Anthony Towns 1.00 2.50
34 Chris Paul 1.25 3.00
35 Bradley Beal .75 2.00
36 James Harden 1.25 3.00
37 Devin Booker 1.50 4.00
38 Derrick Rose 1.00 2.50
39 Zach LaVine 1.00 2.50
40 Cade Cunningham 5.00 12.00

2021-22 Select Phenomenon

COMMON CARD .60 1.50
SEMISTARS .75 2.00
UNLISTED STARS 1.00 2.50
*SILVER: 1.5X TO 4X BASIC
1 Trae Young 2.50 6.00
2 James Wiseman .75 2.00
3 Ja Morant 3.00 8.00
4 Luka Doncic 6.00 15.00
5 Zion Williamson 2.50 6.00
6 Jae'Sean Tate 1.00 2.50
7 Shai Gilgeous-Alexander 5.00 12.00
8 Darius Garland 1.50 4.00
9 Tyrese Haliburton 2.00 5.00
10 RJ Barrett 1.50 4.00
11 Jonathan Kuminga 3.00 8.00
12 Corey Kispert 1.25 3.00
13 Chris Duarte .75 2.00
14 Josh Giddey 3.00 8.00
15 Scottie Barnes 3.00 8.00
16 Theo Maledon .75 2.00
17 James Bouknight .75 2.00
18 Gary Trent Jr. .75 2.00
19 Jalen Green 5.00 12.00
20 Davion Mitchell 1.00 2.50
21 Duncan Robinson .75 2.00
22 Immanuel Quickley 1.00 2.50
23 LaMelo Ball 2.50 6.00
24 Saddiq Bey .75 2.00
25 Michael Porter Jr. 1.25 3.00
26 Patrick Williams 1.00 2.50
27 Anthony Edwards 5.00 12.00
28 PJ Washington Jr. 1.00 2.50
29 Deandre Ayton 1.00 2.50
30 Collin Sexton 1.00 2.50
31 Ziaire Williams 1.25 3.00
32 Evan Mobley 4.00 10.00
33 Cade Cunningham 6.00 15.00
34 Isaiah Stewart 1.00 2.50
35 Franz Wagner 3.00 8.00
36 Coby White 1.00 2.50
37 Moses Moody 2.00 5.00
38 Rui Hachimura 1.00 2.50
39 Jalen Suggs 2.50 6.00
40 Joshua Primo .75 2.00

2021-22 Select Rookie Jersey Autographs

COMMON CARD 5.00 12.00
SEMISTARS 6.00 15.00
UNLISTED STARS 8.00 20.00
STATED PRINT RUN 199 COPIES PER
*RED WAVE: .5X TO 1.25X BASIC
*PURPLE/99: .5X TO 1.25X BASIC
*NEON ORNG PLSR/15-30: .75X TO 2X BASIC
1 Isaiah Jackson 8.00 20.00
2 Cameron Thomas 15.00 40.00
3 Cade Cunningham 200.00 500.00
4 Chris Duarte 6.00 15.00
5 Jonathan Kuminga 60.00 150.00
6 Day'Ron Sharpe 8.00 20.00
7 Keon Johnson 8.00 20.00
8 Isaiah Todd 6.00 15.00
9 James Bouknight 6.00 15.00
10 Jeremiah Robinson-Earl 8.00 20.00
11 Alperen Sengun 25.00 60.00
12 Ayo Dosunmu 15.00 40.00
13 Jalen Suggs 40.00 100.00
14 Brandon Boston Jr. 8.00 20.00
15 Scottie Barnes 100.00 250.00
16 Herbert Jones 10.00 25.00
17 Moses Moody 15.00 40.00
18 Jason Preston 6.00 15.00
19 Josh Giddey 75.00 200.00
20 Joshua Primo 6.00 15.00
21 Trey Murphy III 25.00 60.00
23 Evan Mobley 75.00 200.00
24 Jaden Springer 8.00 20.00
25 Davion Mitchell 8.00 20.00
26 Miles McBride 12.00 30.00
27 Kai Jones 6.00 15.00
28 Greg Brown III 6.00 15.00
29 Corey Kispert 10.00 25.00
32 Jared Butler 8.00 20.00
33 Jalen Green 200.00 500.00
34 Tre Mann 12.00 30.00
35 Franz Wagner 60.00 150.00
36 Bones Hyland 10.00 25.00
37 Jalen Johnson 25.00 60.00
38 Luka Garza 8.00 20.00
39 Ziaire Williams 8.00 20.00
40 Kessler Edwards 8.00 20.00

2021-22 Select Rookie Jersey Autographs Prizms Tie Dye

*TIE DYE: 1X TO 2.5X BASIC
STATED PRINT RUN 25 SER.#'d SETS
3 Cade Cunningham 800.00 1,500.00
33 Jalen Green 800.00 1,500.00

2021-22 Select Rookie Revolution

COMMON CARD .60 1.50
SEMISTARS .75 2.00
UNLISTED STARS 1.00 2.50
*BLUE: 1.2X TO 3X BASIC
*GREEN: 1.2X TO 3X BASIC
*SILVER: 1.2X TO 3X BASIC
*RED: 1.2X TO 3X BASIC
1 Tre Mann 1.50 4.00
2 Alperen Sengun 3.00 8.00
3 Josh Christopher .75 2.00
4 Isaiah Jackson 1.00 2.50
5 Isaiah Todd .75 2.00
6 Jalen Johnson 3.00 8.00
7 Cameron Thomas 2.00 5.00
8 Quentin Grimes 2.00 5.00
9 Chris Duarte .75 2.00
10 Jonathan Kuminga 3.00 8.00
11 James Bouknight .75 2.00
12 Evan Mobley 4.00 10.00
13 Scottie Barnes 3.00 8.00
14 Joshua Primo .75 2.00
15 Jalen Suggs 2.50 6.00
16 Keon Johnson 1.00 2.50
17 Kai Jones .75 2.00
18 Jalen Green 8.00 20.00
19 Bones Hyland 1.25 3.00
20 Trey Murphy III 3.00 8.00
21 Usman Garuba .75 2.00
22 Ayo Dosunmu 2.00 5.00
23 Jaden Springer 1.00 2.50
24 Franz Wagner 3.00 8.00
25 Cade Cunningham 8.00 20.00
26 Davion Mitchell 1.00 2.50
27 Ziaire Williams 1.25 3.00
28 Moses Moody 2.00 5.00
29 Josh Giddey 3.00 8.00
30 Corey Kispert 1.25 3.00

2021-22 Select Rookie Signatures

COMMON CARD 4.00 10.00
SEMISTARS 5.00 12.00
UNLISTED STARS 6.00 15.00
STATED PRINT RUN 199 COPIES PER
*NEON GREEN/99: .5X TO 1.25X BASIC
1 Keon Johnson 6.00 15.00
2 Jason Preston 5.00 12.00
3 James Bouknight 5.00 12.00
4 Neemias Queta 6.00 15.00
5 Isaiah Jackson 6.00 15.00
6 Cameron Thomas 12.00 30.00
7 Cade Cunningham 200.00 500.00
8 Chris Duarte 5.00 12.00
9 Jonathan Kuminga 20.00 50.00
10 Herbert Jones 8.00 20.00
11 Moses Moody 12.00 30.00
12 Greg Brown III 5.00 12.00
13 Josh Giddey 75.00 200.00
14 Joe Wieskamp 5.00 12.00
15 Alperen Sengun 25.00 60.00
16 Ayo Dosunmu 12.00 30.00
17 Jalen Suggs 40.00 100.00
18 Jaden Springer 6.00 15.00
19 Scottie Barnes 100.00 250.00
20 Miles McBride 10.00 25.00
21 Kai Jones 5.00 12.00
22 Luka Garza 6.00 15.00
23 Corey Kispert 8.00 20.00
24 Isaiah Livers 6.00 15.00
25 Trey Murphy III 20.00 50.00
26 Josh Christopher 5.00 12.00
27 Evan Mobley 75.00 200.00
28 Tre Mann 10.00 25.00
29 Davion Mitchell 6.00 15.00
30 Bones Hyland 8.00 20.00
31 Jalen Johnson 20.00 50.00
32 Jeremiah Robinson-Earl 6.00 15.00
33 Ziaire Williams 8.00 20.00
34 Kessler Edwards 6.00 15.00
35 Usman Garuba 5.00 12.00
36 Jared Butler 6.00 15.00
37 Jalen Green 200.00 500.00
38 Day'Ron Sharpe 6.00 15.00
39 Franz Wagner 40.00 100.00
40 Isaiah Todd 5.00 12.00

2021-22 Select Signature Selections

COMMON CARD 3.00 8.00
SEMISTARS 4.00 10.00
UNLISTED STARS 5.00 12.00
1 Ty Jerome 4.00 10.00
2 Jae'Sean Tate 5.00 12.00
3 John Drew 3.00 8.00
4 Nate McMillan 4.00 10.00
5 Trey Burke 4.00 10.00
6 Metta World Peace 5.00 12.00
7 Tyus Jones 4.00 10.00
8 Dominique Wilkins 12.00 30.00
9 Devin Harris 3.00 8.00
10 Jalen Rose 4.00 10.00
11 Torrey Craig 4.00 10.00
12 Tony Allen 3.00 8.00
13 Jeff Ruland 4.00 10.00
14 Thomas Bryant 3.00 8.00
15 Ben McLemore 3.00 8.00
16 Larry Bird 75.00 200.00
17 Jim Paxson 4.00 10.00
18 Mike Conley 4.00 10.00
19 Enes Freedom 4.00 10.00
20 Jeff Teague 3.00 8.00
21 Robert Williams III 5.00 12.00
22 Matt Barnes 4.00 10.00
23 Tony Delk 4.00 10.00
24 Grant Williams 5.00 12.00
25 Jalen Brunson 10.00 25.00
28 Sam Jones 6.00 15.00
29 Wayne Ellington 3.00 8.00
30 Shawn Kemp 25.00 60.00
31 Micheal Ray Richardson 4.00 10.00
32 Marques Johnson 4.00 10.00
33 Calvin Natt 4.00 10.00
34 Sterling Brown 3.00 8.00
35 Nassir Little 5.00 12.00
36 Magic Johnson 75.00 200.00
37 Walter McCarty 4.00 10.00
38 Spencer Dinwiddie 4.00 10.00
39 Chuma Okeke 5.00 12.00
40 Kendrick Perkins 4.00 10.00
42 Dale Ellis 4.00 10.00
43 Bonzi Wells 4.00 10.00
44 Danuel House Jr. 4.00 10.00
45 Jaylen Nowell 3.00 8.00
46 Dennis Rodman 30.00 80.00
47 Benoit Benjamin 3.00 8.00
48 Kendrick Nunn 4.00 10.00
49 Frank Jackson 3.00 8.00
50 Horace Grant 5.00 12.00

2021-22 Select Signatures

COMMON CARD 4.00 10.00
SEMISTARS 5.00 12.00
UNLISTED STARS 6.00 15.00
STATED PRINT RUN 149-299 COPIES PER
*NEON GREEN/99: .5X TO 1.2X BASIC
1 Alex English/299 8.00 20.00
2 David Robinson/249 20.00 50.00
3 Tim Hardaway Jr./299 4.00 10.00
4 Paul Pierce/149 20.00 50.00
5 Kristaps Porzingis/214 8.00 20.00
6 Luka Doncic/249 350.00 700.00
7 Mike Conley/199 5.00 12.00
8 Rui Hachimura/149 12.00 30.00
9 Ricky Rubio/249 6.00 15.00
10 Ray Allen/249 30.00 80.00
11 Chauncey Billups/249 8.00 20.00
12 Pat Riley/149 8.00 20.00
13 Charles Barkley/149 75.00 200.00
14 Grant Hill/199 20.00 50.00
15 Gary Payton/299 20.00 50.00
16 Oscar Robertson/169 40.00 100.00
17 Sam Jones/199 8.00 20.00
18 Magic Johnson/199 75.00 200.00
19 Richard Hamilton/299 8.00 20.00
20 Hakeem Olajuwon/149 30.00 80.00
21 Jalen Rose/299 5.00 12.00
22 Nikola Jokic/149 100.00 250.00
23 Mitch Kupchak/299 5.00 12.00
25 Steve Kerr/199 8.00 20.00
26 Kareem Abdul-Jabbar/249 75.00 200.00
27 Jerry Lucas/249 8.00 20.00
28 Jason Kidd/249 20.00 50.00
29 Kevin Johnson/199 6.00 15.00

2021-22 Select Sparks Memorabilia

COMMON CARD 1.50 4.00
SEMISTARS 2.00 5.00
UNLISTED STARS 2.50 6.00
*PURPLE/99: .5X TO 1.25X BASIC
*COPPER/49: .5X TO 1.5X BASIC
1 Davion Mitchell 2.50 6.00
2 Scottie Barnes 8.00 20.00
3 Ziaire Williams 3.00 8.00
4 Jalen Suggs 6.00 15.00
5 Josh Giddey 8.00 20.00
6 Cade Cunningham 15.00 40.00
7 Jonathan Kuminga 8.00 20.00
8 Jalen Green 12.00 30.00
9 Franz Wagner 8.00 20.00
10 Evan Mobley 10.00 25.00

2021-22 Select Sparks Memorabilia Prizms Tie Dye

*TIE DYE: 1.5X TO 4X BASIC
STATED PRINT RUN 25 SER.#'d SETS
2 Scottie Barnes 75.00 200.00
5 Josh Giddey 75.00 200.00
6 Cade Cunningham 100.00 250.00
8 Jalen Green 100.00 250.00

2021-22 Select Throwback Memorabilia

COMMON CARD 1.50 4.00
SEMISTARS 2.00 5.00
UNLISTED STARS 2.50 6.00
*PURPLE/99: .5X TO 1.25X BASIC
*COPPER/49: .5X TO 1.5X BASIC
1 LeBron James 40.00 100.00
2 Chris Paul 5.00 12.00
3 Paul George 4.00 10.00
4 Andrew Wiggins 3.00 8.00
5 Taj Gibson 1.50 4.00
6 T.J. Warren 1.50 4.00
7 Serge Ibaka 2.00 5.00
8 Shai Gilgeous-Alexander 12.00 30.00
9 Enes Freedom 2.00 5.00
10 Gordon Hayward 2.00 5.00
11 Derrick Rose 4.00 10.00
12 Terrence Ross 2.00 5.00
13 Carmelo Anthony 4.00 10.00
14 Dennis Smith Jr. 1.50 4.00
15 Jeff Teague 1.50 4.00
16 Danilo Gallinari 2.00 5.00
17 Dennis Schroder 2.50 6.00
18 Nicolas Batum 2.00 5.00
19 Bojan Bogdanovic 2.00 5.00
20 Markelle Fultz 1.50 4.00

2021-22 Select Throwback Memorabilia Prizms Tie Dye

*TIE DYE: 1.5X TO 4X BASIC
STATED PRINT RUN 25 SER.#'d SETS
1 LeBron James 200.00 500.00
2 Chris Paul 40.00 100.00
3 Paul George 40.00 100.00
11 Derrick Rose 40.00 100.00
13 Carmelo Anthony 40.00 100.00

2021-22 Select Turbo Charged

COMMON CARD .75 2.00
SEMISTARS 1.00 2.50
UNLISTED STARS 1.25 3.00
*BLUE: 1.25X TO 3X BASIC
*GREEN: 1.25X TO 3X BASIC
*RED: 1.25X TO 3X BASIC
*SILVER: 1.25X TO 3X BASIC
1 Zion Williamson 2.50 6.00
2 Jalen Suggs 2.50 6.00
3 Stephen Curry 6.00 15.00
4 Scottie Barnes 3.00 8.00
5 LeBron James 8.00 20.00
6 Cade Cunningham 6.00 15.00
7 Giannis Antetokounmpo 5.00 12.00
8 Jalen Green 5.00 12.00
9 Luka Doncic 6.00 15.00
10 Evan Mobley 4.00 10.00

2021-22 Select Unstoppable

COMMON CARD 1.25 3.00
SEMISTARS 1.50 4.00
UNLISTED STARS 2.00 5.00
*SILVER: 1.25X TO 3X BASIC
1 Luka Doncic 12.00 30.00
2 Kyrie Irving 4.00 10.00
3 Stephen Curry 12.00 30.00
4 Anthony Davis 5.00 12.00
5 LeBron James 15.00 40.00
6 Ja Morant 6.00 15.00
7 Kevin Durant 6.00 15.00
8 Giannis Antetokounmpo 10.00 25.00
9 Zion Williamson 5.00 12.00
10 Kawhi Leonard 5.00 12.00
11 Zach LaVine 3.00 8.00
12 Joel Embiid 5.00 12.00
13 Trae Young 5.00 12.00
14 Jayson Tatum 8.00 20.00
15 James Harden 4.00 10.00

2021-22 Select X-Factor Memorabilia Signatures

COMMON CARD 5.00 12.00
SEMISTARS 6.00 15.00
UNLISTED STARS 8.00 20.00
STATED PRINT RUN B/WN 99-199 COPIES PER
*PURPLE/49-99: .5X TO 1.2X BASIC
*TIE DYE/25: .75X TO 2X BASIC
1 Jonas Valanciunas/149 6.00 15.00
2 James Wiseman/99 6.00 15.00
3 Taj Gibson/199 5.00 12.00
4 Khris Middleton/99 8.00 20.00
5 Jarrett Culver/149 5.00 12.00
6 Zion Williamson/99 150.00 400.00
8 Anthony Davis/99 40.00 100.00
9 PJ Washington Jr./149 8.00 20.00
10 Kevin Garnett/99 75.00 200.00
11 Thaddeus Young/199 5.00 12.00
12 CJ McCollum/99 6.00 15.00

13 Raymond Felton/199 5.00 12.00
14 Mike Conley/99 6.00 15.00
15 Isaac Okoro/149 6.00 15.00
16 Luka Doncic/99 350.00 700.00
17 Myles Turner/149 8.00 20.00
18 Dirk Nowitzki/99 75.00 200.00
19 David Lee/149 6.00 15.00
20 Rui Hachimura/99 8.00 20.00
21 Jarrett Allen/199 8.00 20.00
22 Kristaps Porzingis/99 10.00 25.00
23 Al Harrington/199 6.00 15.00
24 De'Andre Hunter/99 8.00 20.00
25 Steven Adams/149 6.00 15.00

2021-22 Select Youth Explosion Signatures

COMMON CARD 4.00 10.00
SEMISTARS 5.00 12.00
UNLISTED STARS 6.00 15.00
1 Evan Mobley 75.00 200.00
2 Jose Alvarado 15.00 40.00
3 Dalano Banton 8.00 20.00
4 Cade Cunningham 200.00 500.00
5 Sam Hauser 20.00 50.00
6 Ziaire Williams 8.00 20.00
7 Franz Wagner 40.00 100.00
8 JaQuori McLaughlin 4.00 10.00
9 Scottie Lewis 5.00 12.00
10 Jalen Suggs 15.00 40.00
11 Bones Hyland 8.00 20.00
12 Jaden Springer 6.00 15.00
13 Joel Ayayi 5.00 12.00
14 Aaron Henry 4.00 10.00
15 Joe Wieskamp 5.00 12.00
16 Malik Fitts 5.00 12.00
17 Jay Huff 5.00 12.00
18 Austin Reaves 75.00 200.00
19 Charles Bassey 6.00 15.00
20 RJ Nembhard 4.00 10.00
21 Jonathan Kuminga 20.00 50.00
22 Isaiah Livers 6.00 15.00
23 Yves Pons 5.00 12.00
24 Josh Giddey 75.00 200.00
25 Scottie Barnes 75.00 200.00
26 Sandro Mamukelashvili 8.00 20.00
27 Georgios Kalaitzakis 6.00 15.00
28 Jalen Green 200.00 500.00
29 Aaron Wiggins 8.00 20.00
30 Davion Mitchell 6.00 15.00
31 Jericho Sims 8.00 20.00
32 Herbert Jones 8.00 20.00
33 David Duke Jr. 6.00 15.00
34 Kevin Pangos 4.00 10.00
35 Duane Washington Jr. 6.00 15.00
36 Greg Brown III 5.00 12.00
37 Trendon Watford 8.00 20.00
38 Day'Ron Sharpe 6.00 15.00
39 Arnoldas Kulboka 6.00 15.00
40 Justin Champagnie 5.00 12.00

2022-23 Select

COMPLETE SET (300)
*BLUE: .4X TO 1X BASIC
1 Nikola Jokic 2.00 5.00
2 Dejounte Murray .50 1.25
3 Jalen Suggs .50 1.25
4 Kristaps Porzingis .50 1.25
5 DeMar DeRozan .50 1.25
6 Darius Garland .60 1.50
7 Damian Lillard 1.00 2.50
8 Jimmy Butler .75 2.00
9 Tyrese Maxey .75 2.00
10 Andrew Wiggins .50 1.25
11 Malcolm Brogdon .30 .75
12 Karl-Anthony Towns .60 1.50
13 De'Aaron Fox .75 2.00
14 Michael Porter Jr. .50 1.25
15 Jrue Holiday .50 1.25
16 Paul George .60 1.50
17 Anthony Davis 1.00 2.50
18 Cade Cunningham 1.25 3.00
19 Klay Thompson 1.00 2.50
20 Tyrese Haliburton .75 2.00
21 Ayo Dosunmu .50 1.25
22 Jalen Brunson .75 2.00
23 Collin Sexton .50 1.25
24 Zion Williamson 1.00 2.50
25 James Harden .75 2.00
26 LeBron James 3.00 8.00
27 Stephen Curry 3.00 8.00
28 Khris Middleton .50 1.25
29 Christian Wood .25 .60
30 Kyrie Irving .75 2.00
31 Donovan Mitchell .75 2.00
32 Jaylen Brown .75 2.00
33 RJ Barrett .60 1.50
34 Zach LaVine .75 2.00
35 Marcus Smart .50 1.25
36 Fred VanVleet .50 1.25
37 Kevin Durant 1.25 3.00
38 Devin Booker 1.00 2.50
39 Jamal Murray .60 1.50
40 Julius Randle .50 1.25
41 LaMelo Ball 1.00 2.50
42 Anfernee Simons .50 1.25
43 Tyler Herro .60 1.50
44 Evan Mobley 1.00 2.50
45 Lauri Markkanen .60 1.50
46 Anthony Edwards 2.00 5.00
47 Joel Embiid .60 1.50
48 Pascal Siakam .60 1.50
49 Kevin Porter Jr. .30 .75
50 Chris Paul .75 2.00
51 Luka Doncic 2.50 6.00
52 Jalen Green 1.25 3.00
53 Scottie Barnes .60 1.50
54 Keldon Johnson .50 1.25
55 Jayson Tatum 1.50 4.00
56 Shai Gilgeous-Alexander 2.00 5.00
57 Bam Adebayo .60 1.50
58 Ja Morant 1.25 3.00
59 Brandon Ingram .50 1.25
60 Josh Giddey .60 1.50
61 Giannis Antetokounmpo 2.00 5.00
62 Bradley Beal .50 1.25
63 Desmond Bane .50 1.25
64 Devin Vassell .50 1.25
65 Kawhi Leonard 1.00 2.50
66 Trae Young 1.00 2.50
67 Dyson Daniels RC 2.00 5.00
68 Caleb Houstan RC .75 2.00
69 Jabari Smith Jr. RC 2.50 6.00
70 TyTy Washington Jr. RC .75 2.00
71 Shaedon Sharpe RC 3.00 8.00
72 Paolo Banchero RC 5.00 12.00
73 Wendell Moore Jr. RC .75 2.00
74 Peyton Watson RC 1.25 3.00
75 MarJon Beauchamp RC .75 2.00
76 Ousmane Dieng RC 1.00 2.50
77 Andrew Nembhard RC 1.50 4.00
78 David Roddy RC 1.00 2.50
79 Bennedict Mathurin RC 2.50 6.00
80 Jaden Hardy RC 1.25 3.00
81 Keegan Murray RC 2.00 5.00
82 Tari Eason RC 2.00 5.00
83 Chet Holmgren RC 4.00 10.00
84 Trevor Keels RC .60 1.50
85 Christian Braun RC 2.00 5.00
86 Jeremy Sochan RC 2.50 6.00
87 Jaden Ivey RC 2.50 6.00
88 AJ Griffin RC .60 1.50
89 Dalen Terry RC .75 2.00
90 Jalen Williams RC 4.00 10.00
91 Nikola Jovic RC 1.50 4.00
92 Moussa Diabate RC .75 2.00
93 Mark Williams RC 1.50 4.00
94 Jake LaRavia RC .75 2.00
95 Malaki Branham RC .75 2.00
96 Ochai Agbaji RC 1.00 2.50
97 Blake Wesley RC .75 2.00
98 Jalen Duren RC 2.50 6.00
99 Jaylin Williams RC 1.00 2.50
100 Johnny Davis RC .75 2.00
101 Nikola Jokic 2.00 5.00
102 Dejounte Murray .50 1.25
103 Jalen Suggs .50 1.25
104 Kristaps Porzingis .50 1.25
105 DeMar DeRozan .50 1.25
106 Darius Garland .60 1.50
107 Damian Lillard 1.00 2.50
108 Jimmy Butler .75 2.00
109 Tyrese Maxey .75 2.00
110 Andrew Wiggins .50 1.25
111 Malcolm Brogdon .30 .75
112 Karl-Anthony Towns .60 1.50
113 De'Aaron Fox .75 2.00
114 Michael Porter Jr. .50 1.25
115 Jrue Holiday .50 1.25
116 Paul George .60 1.50
117 Anthony Davis 1.00 2.50
118 Cade Cunningham 1.25 3.00
119 Klay Thompson 1.00 2.50
120 Tyrese Haliburton .75 2.00
121 Ayo Dosunmu .50 1.25
122 Jalen Brunson .75 2.00
123 Collin Sexton .50 1.25
124 Zion Williamson 1.00 2.50
125 James Harden .75 2.00
126 LeBron James 3.00 8.00
127 Stephen Curry 3.00 8.00
128 Khris Middleton .50 1.25
129 Christian Wood .25 .60
130 Kyrie Irving .75 2.00
131 Donovan Mitchell .75 2.00
132 Jaylen Brown .75 2.00
133 RJ Barrett .60 1.50
134 Zach LaVine .75 2.00
135 Marcus Smart .50 1.25
136 Fred VanVleet .50 1.25
137 Kevin Durant 1.25 3.00
138 Devin Booker 1.00 2.50
139 Jamal Murray .60 1.50
140 Julius Randle .50 1.25
141 LaMelo Ball 1.00 2.50
142 Anfernee Simons .50 1.25
143 Tyler Herro .60 1.50
144 Evan Mobley 1.00 2.50
145 Lauri Markkanen .60 1.50
146 Anthony Edwards 2.00 5.00
147 Joel Embiid .60 1.50
148 Pascal Siakam .60 1.50
149 Kevin Porter Jr. .30 .75
150 Chris Paul .75 2.00
151 Luka Doncic 2.50 6.00
152 Jalen Green 1.25 3.00
153 Scottie Barnes .60 1.50
154 Keldon Johnson .50 1.25
155 Jayson Tatum 1.50 4.00
156 Shai Gilgeous-Alexander 2.00 5.00
157 Bam Adebayo .60 1.50
158 Ja Morant 1.25 3.00
159 Brandon Ingram .50 1.25
160 Josh Giddey .60 1.50
161 Giannis Antetokounmpo 2.00 5.00
162 Bradley Beal .50 1.25
163 Desmond Bane .50 1.25
164 Devin Vassell .50 1.25
165 Kawhi Leonard 1.00 2.50
166 Trae Young 1.00 2.50
167 Jalen Williams 4.00 10.00
168 TyTy Washington Jr. .75 2.00
169 Paolo Banchero 5.00 12.00
170 Nikola Jovic 1.50 4.00
171 Malaki Branham .75 2.00
172 Dyson Daniels 2.00 5.00
173 Kennedy Chandler .75 2.00
174 Jaden Hardy 1.25 3.00
175 Jake LaRavia .75 2.00
176 Jalen Duren 2.50 6.00
177 Caleb Houstan .75 2.00
178 Jaden Ivey 2.50 6.00
179 MarJon Beauchamp .75 2.00
180 Blake Wesley .75 2.00
181 Max Christie 2.00 5.00
182 Bennedict Mathurin 2.50 6.00
183 Tari Eason 2.00 5.00
184 Jabari Smith Jr. 2.50 6.00
185 Christian Koloko .75 2.00
186 Andrew Nembhard 1.50 4.00
187 Walker Kessler 1.50 4.00
188 Dalen Terry .75 2.00
189 Shaedon Sharpe 3.00 8.00
190 Ousmane Dieng 1.00 2.50
191 Johnny Davis .75 2.00
192 Jeremy Sochan 2.50 6.00
193 Patrick Baldwin Jr. .75 2.00
194 Moussa Diabate .75 2.00
195 Christian Braun 2.00 5.00
196 Chet Holmgren 4.00 10.00
197 Keegan Murray 2.00 5.00
198 AJ Griffin .60 1.50
199 Ochai Agbaji 1.00 2.50
200 Wendell Moore Jr. .75 2.00
201 Nikola Jokic 4.00 10.00
202 Dejounte Murray 1.00 2.50
203 Jalen Suggs 1.00 2.50
204 Kristaps Porzingis 1.00 2.50
205 DeMar DeRozan 1.00 2.50
206 Darius Garland 1.25 3.00
207 Damian Lillard 2.00 5.00
208 Jimmy Butler 1.50 4.00
209 Tyrese Maxey 1.50 4.00
210 Andrew Wiggins 1.00 2.50
211 Malcolm Brogdon .60 1.50
212 Karl-Anthony Towns 1.25 3.00
213 De'Aaron Fox 1.50 4.00
214 Michael Porter Jr. 1.00 2.50
215 Jrue Holiday 1.00 2.50
216 Paul George 1.25 3.00
217 Anthony Davis 2.00 5.00
218 Cade Cunningham 2.50 6.00
219 Klay Thompson 2.00 5.00
220 Tyrese Haliburton 1.50 4.00
221 Ayo Dosunmu 1.00 2.50
222 Jalen Brunson 1.50 4.00
223 Collin Sexton 1.00 2.50
224 Zion Williamson 2.00 5.00
225 James Harden 1.50 4.00
226 LeBron James 6.00 15.00
227 Stephen Curry 6.00 15.00
228 Khris Middleton 1.00 2.50
229 Christian Wood .50 1.25
230 Kyrie Irving 1.50 4.00
231 Donovan Mitchell 1.50 4.00
232 Jaylen Brown 1.50 4.00
233 RJ Barrett 1.25 3.00
234 Zach LaVine 1.50 4.00
235 Marcus Smart 1.00 2.50
236 Fred VanVleet 1.00 2.50
237 Kevin Durant 2.50 6.00
238 Devin Booker 2.00 5.00
239 Jamal Murray 1.25 3.00
240 Julius Randle 1.00 2.50
241 LaMelo Ball 2.00 5.00
242 Anfernee Simons 1.00 2.50
243 Tyler Herro 1.25 3.00
244 Evan Mobley 2.00 5.00
245 Lauri Markkanen 1.25 3.00
246 Anthony Edwards 4.00 10.00
247 Joel Embiid 1.25 3.00
248 Pascal Siakam 1.25 3.00
249 Kevin Porter Jr. .60 1.50
250 Chris Paul 1.50 4.00
251 Luka Doncic 5.00 12.00
252 Jalen Green 2.50 6.00
253 Scottie Barnes 1.25 3.00
254 Keldon Johnson 1.00 2.50
255 Jayson Tatum 3.00 8.00
256 Shai Gilgeous-Alexander 4.00 10.00
257 Bam Adebayo 1.25 3.00
258 Ja Morant 2.50 6.00
259 Brandon Ingram 1.00 2.50
260 Josh Giddey 1.25 3.00
261 Giannis Antetokounmpo 4.00 10.00
262 Bradley Beal 1.00 2.50
263 Desmond Bane 1.00 2.50
264 Devin Vassell 1.00 2.50
265 Kawhi Leonard 2.00 5.00
266 Trae Young 2.00 5.00
267 Ousmane Dieng 2.00 5.00
268 Blake Wesley 1.50 4.00
269 TyTy Washington Jr. 1.50 4.00
270 Nikola Jovic 3.00 8.00
271 Dyson Daniels 4.00 10.00
272 Christian Braun 4.00 10.00
273 David Roddy 2.00 5.00
274 AJ Griffin 1.25 3.00
275 Dalen Terry 1.50 4.00
276 Walker Kessler 3.00 8.00
277 Patrick Baldwin Jr. 1.50 4.00
278 Tari Eason 4.00 10.00
279 Bennedict Mathurin 5.00 12.00
280 Andrew Nembhard 3.00 8.00
281 Jaden Hardy 2.50 6.00
282 Jalen Williams 8.00 20.00
283 MarJon Beauchamp 1.50 4.00
284 Caleb Houstan 1.50 4.00
285 Malaki Branham 1.50 4.00
286 Jalen Duren 5.00 12.00
287 Jake LaRavia 1.50 4.00
288 Kennedy Chandler 1.50 4.00
289 Ochai Agbaji 2.00 5.00
290 Jeremy Sochan 5.00 12.00
291 Jabari Smith Jr. 5.00 12.00
292 Shaedon Sharpe 6.00 15.00
293 Max Christie 4.00 10.00
294 Keegan Murray 4.00 10.00
295 Paolo Banchero 10.00 25.00
296 Chet Holmgren 8.00 20.00
297 Christian Koloko 1.50 4.00
298 Jaden Ivey 5.00 12.00
299 Wendell Moore Jr. 1.50 4.00
300 Johnny Davis 1.50 4.00

2022-23 Select Prizms Blue Cracked Ice

COMPLETE SET (300)
*BLUE CRKD ICE: 1X TO 2.5X BASIC
295 Paolo Banchero 60.00 150.00
296 Chet Holmgren 50.00 120.00

2022-23 Select Prizms Copper Plaid

COMPLETE SET (100)
*COPPER PLAID: 6X TO 15X BASIC
STATED PRINT RUN 49 SER.#'d SETS
72 Paolo Banchero 150.00 400.00
83 Chet Holmgren 125.00 300.00

2022-23 Select Prizms Disco

COMPLETE SET (300)
*DISCO: 1.25X TO 3X BASIC
226 LeBron James 25.00 60.00
227 Stephen Curry 25.00 60.00
295 Paolo Banchero 75.00 200.00
296 Chet Holmgren 60.00 150.00

2022-23 Select Prizms Green Ice

COMPLETE SET (300)
*GREEN ICE: 1.25X TO 3X BASIC
226 LeBron James 25.00 60.00
227 Stephen Curry 25.00 60.00
295 Paolo Banchero 75.00 200.00
296 Chet Holmgren 60.00 150.00

2022-23 Select Prizms Green Shock

COMPLETE SET (300)
*GREEN SHOCK: 1.25X TO 3X BASIC
226 LeBron James 25.00 60.00
227 Stephen Curry 25.00 60.00
295 Paolo Banchero 75.00 200.00
296 Chet Holmgren 60.00 150.00

2022-23 Select Prizms Green Wave

COMPLETE SET (300)
*GREEN WAVE: 6X TO 15X BASIC
STATED PRINT RUN 50 SER.#'d SETS
72 Paolo Banchero 150.00 400.00
83 Chet Holmgren 125.00 300.00
169 Paolo Banchero 150.00 400.00
196 Chet Holmgren 125.00 300.00
295 Paolo Banchero 400.00 800.00
296 Chet Holmgren 300.00 600.00

2022-23 Select Prizms Green White Purple

COMPLETE SET (300)
*BLUE CRKD ICE: 1X TO 2.5X BASIC
295 Paolo Banchero 60.00 150.00
296 Chet Holmgren 50.00 120.00

2022-23 Select Prizms Light Blue Disco

COMPLETE SET (300)
*LIGHT BLUE DISCO: 4X TO 10X BASIC
STATED PRINT RUN 99 SER.#'d SETS
72 Paolo Banchero 100.00 250.00
83 Chet Holmgren 75.00 200.00
169 Paolo Banchero 100.00 250.00
196 Chet Holmgren 75.00 200.00
295 Paolo Banchero 200.00 500.00
296 Chet Holmgren 150.00 400.00

2022-23 Select Prizms Light Green Die Cut

COMPLETE SET (100)
*LIGHT GREEN DIE CUT: 6X TO 15X BASIC
STATED PRINT RUN 49 SER.#'d SETS
169 Paolo Banchero 150.00 400.00
196 Chet Holmgren 125.00 300.00

2022-23 Select Prizms Neon Green

COMPLETE SET (100)
*NEON GREEN: 5X TO 12X BASIC
STATED PRINT RUN 75 SER.#'d SETS
72 Paolo Banchero 125.00 300.00
83 Chet Holmgren 100.00 250.00

2022-23 Select Prizms Orange Die Cut

COMPLETE SET (100)
*ORNG DIE CUT: 5X TO 12X BASIC
STATED PRINT RUN 65 SER.#'d SETS
169 Paolo Banchero 125.00 300.00
196 Chet Holmgren 100.00 250.00

2022-23 Select Prizms Orange Flash

COMPLETE SET (300)
*ORANGE FLASH: 1.25X TO 3X BASIC
295 Paolo Banchero 75.00 200.00
296 Chet Holmgren 60.00 150.00

2022-23 Select Prizms Purple Die Cut

COMPLETE SET (100)
*PRPL DIE CUT: 4X TO 10X BASIC
STATED PRINT RUN 99 SER.#'d SETS
169 Paolo Banchero 100.00 250.00
196 Chet Holmgren 75.00 200.00

2022-23 Select Prizms Red Cracked Ice

COMPLETE SET (300)
*RED CRKD ICE: 1X TO 2.5X BASIC
226 LeBron James 20.00 50.00
227 Stephen Curry 20.00 50.00
295 Paolo Banchero 60.00 150.00
296 Chet Holmgren 50.00 120.00

2022-23 Select Prizms Red Disco

COMPLETE SET (300)
*RED DISCO: 6X TO 15X BASIC
STATED PRINT RUN 49 SER.#'d SETS
72 Paolo Banchero 150.00 400.00
83 Chet Holmgren 125.00 300.00
169 Paolo Banchero 150.00 400.00
196 Chet Holmgren 125.00 300.00
295 Paolo Banchero 400.00 800.00
296 Chet Holmgren 300.00 600.00

2022-23 Select Prizms Red Wave

COMPLETE SET (300)
*RED WAVE: 1.25X TO 3X BASIC
295 Paolo Banchero 75.00 200.00
296 Chet Holmgren 60.00 150.00

2022-23 Select Prizms Silver

COMPLETE SET (300)
*SILVER: 1.25X TO 3X BASIC
295 Paolo Banchero 75.00 200.00
296 Chet Holmgren 60.00 150.00

2022-23 Select Prizms Teal White Pink

COMPLETE SET (300)
*TEAL WHITE PINK: 6X TO 15X BASIC
STATED PRINT RUN 49 SER.#'d SETS
72 Paolo Banchero 150.00 400.00
83 Chet Holmgren 125.00 300.00
169 Paolo Banchero 150.00 400.00
196 Chet Holmgren 125.00 300.00
295 Paolo Banchero 400.00 800.00
296 Chet Holmgren 300.00 600.00

2022-23 Select Prizms Tie-Dye

COMPLETE SET (200)
*TIE-DYE: 10X TO 25X BASIC
STATED PRINT RUN 25 SER.#'d SETS
72 Paolo Banchero 300.00 600.00
83 Chet Holmgren 200.00 500.00
295 Paolo Banchero 600.00 1,200.00
296 Chet Holmgren 500.00 1,000.00

2022-23 Select Prizms Tie-Dye Die-Cut

COMPLETE SET (100)
*TIE-DYE DIE-CUT: 10X TO 25X BASIC
STATED PRINT RUN 25 SER.#'d SETS
169 Paolo Banchero 300.00 600.00
196 Chet Holmgren 200.00 500.00

2022-23 Select Prizms White

COMPLETE SET (100)
*WHITE: 3X TO 8X BASIC
STATED PRINT RUN 149 SER.#'d SETS
72 Paolo Banchero 75.00 200.00
83 Chet Holmgren 60.00 150.00

2022-23 Select Prizms White Disco

COMPLETE SET (300)
*WHITE DISCO: 5X TO 12X BASIC
STATED PRINT RUN 75 SER.#'d SETS
72 Paolo Banchero 125.00 300.00
83 Chet Holmgren 100.00 250.00
169 Paolo Banchero 125.00 300.00
196 Chet Holmgren 100.00 250.00
295 Paolo Banchero 300.00 600.00
296 Chet Holmgren 200.00 500.00

2022-23 Select Artistic Selections

COMPLETE SET (10)
1 Jayson Tatum 40.00 100.00
2 Bennedict Mathurin 75.00 200.00
3 Ja Morant 75.00 200.00
4 LeBron James 100.00 250.00
5 Giannis Antetokounmpo 75.00 200.00
6 Stephen Curry 100.00 250.00
7 Jabari Smith Jr. 75.00 200.00
8 Paolo Banchero 200.00 500.00
9 Jaden Ivey 75.00 200.00
10 Luka Doncic 100.00 250.00

2022-23 Select Autograph Memorabilia

COMPLETE SET (28)
STATED PRINT RUN B/WN 75-199 COPIES PER
*PURPLE/75-99: .5X TO 1.2X BASIC
*BLUE/49: .6X TO 1.5X BASIC
*TIE DYE/15-25: .75X TO 2X BASIC
1 Evan Mobley/199 30.00 80.00
2 Cole Anthony/125 8.00 20.00
3 Karl-Anthony Towns/99 20.00 50.00
4 Myles Turner/199 8.00 20.00
5 Isaac Okoro/199 6.00 15.00
6 Derrick White/199 8.00 20.00
7 Isaiah Stewart/199 6.00 15.00
9 Luke Kennard/199 6.00 15.00
10 Nassir Little/199 8.00 20.00
11 Luguentz Dort/199 8.00 20.00
12 Jonas Valanciunas/199 6.00 15.00
13 Brandon Clarke/199 6.00 15.00
14 Khris Middleton/99 10.00 25.00
15 Chris Paul/75 40.00 100.00
16 Jamal Murray/149 40.00 100.00
17 Rudy Gobert/125 10.00 25.00
18 James Wiseman/199 6.00 15.00
19 Deni Avdija/199 8.00 20.00
20 Al Horford/199 8.00 20.00
21 Duncan Robinson/146 8.00 20.00
23 Jrue Holiday/75 10.00 25.00
24 RJ Barrett/149 12.00 30.00
25 Jalen Suggs/199 10.00 25.00
26 Christian Laettner/199 8.00 20.00
27 Metta World Peace/199 8.00 20.00
28 Bill Laimbeer/199 8.00 20.00
29 Clyde Drexler/99 20.00 50.00
30 Gary Payton/99 20.00 50.00

2022-23 Select Certified

COMPLETE SET (20)
*GREEN: .6X TO 1.5X BASIC
*RED: .75X TO 2X BASIC
*SILVER: .75X TO 2X BASIC
1 Shaedon Sharpe 2.50 6.00
2 Jabari Smith Jr. 2.00 5.00
3 Anthony Edwards 3.00 8.00
4 Jaden Ivey 2.00 5.00
5 Jayson Tatum 2.50 6.00
6 Bennedict Mathurin 2.00 5.00
7 Stephen Curry 5.00 12.00
8 Ja Morant 2.00 5.00
9 Chet Holmgren 3.00 8.00
10 Nikola Jokic 3.00 8.00
11 Paolo Banchero 4.00 10.00
12 Giannis Antetokounmpo 3.00 8.00
13 LaMelo Ball 1.50 4.00
14 Cade Cunningham 2.00 5.00
15 Keegan Murray 1.50 4.00
16 Zion Williamson 1.50 4.00
17 Kevin Durant 2.00 5.00
18 LeBron James 5.00 12.00
19 Trae Young 1.50 4.00
20 Luka Doncic 4.00 10.00

2022-23 Select Color Wheel

COMPLETE SET (23)
1 Kevin Durant 125.00 300.00
2 LaMelo Ball 150.00 400.00
3 Luka Doncic 300.00 600.00
4 Zion Williamson 125.00 300.00
5 Nikola Jokic 350.00 700.00
6 Anthony Edwards 200.00 500.00
7 LeBron James 600.00 1,200.00
8 Ja Morant 200.00 500.00
9 Giannis Antetokounmpo 300.00 600.00
10 Jayson Tatum 150.00 400.00
11 Cade Cunningham 150.00 400.00
12 Trae Young 150.00 400.00
13 Stephen Curry 600.00 1,200.00
14 Shaquille O'Neal 200.00 500.00
15 Anfernee Hardaway 200.00 500.00
16 Magic Johnson 125.00 300.00
17 Allen Iverson 150.00 400.00
18 Keegan Murray 300.00 600.00
19 Chet Holmgren 600.00 1,200.00
20 Jaden Ivey 200.00 500.00
21 Paolo Banchero 1,000.00 2,000.00
22 Jabari Smith Jr. 300.00 600.00
23 Bennedict Mathurin 300.00 600.00

2022-23 Select Draft Selections Memorabilia

COMPLETE SET (30)
*PURPLE/99: .75X TO 2X BASIC
*BLUE/75: 1X TO 2.5X BASIC
*TIE DYE/25: 2.5X TO 6X BASIC
1 Paolo Banchero 12.00 30.00
2 Tari Eason 5.00 12.00
3 Peyton Watson 3.00 8.00
4 Jalen Williams 10.00 25.00
5 MarJon Beauchamp 2.00 5.00
6 Jabari Smith Jr. 6.00 15.00
7 Christian Braun 5.00 12.00
8 Ochai Agbaji 2.50 6.00
9 Dyson Daniels 5.00 12.00
10 Dalen Terry 2.00 5.00
11 Patrick Baldwin Jr. 2.00 5.00
12 Ousmane Dieng 2.50 6.00
13 Jaden Ivey 6.00 15.00
14 David Roddy 2.50 6.00
15 Malaki Branham 2.00 5.00
16 Jalen Duren 6.00 15.00
17 Keegan Murray 5.00 12.00
18 Bennedict Mathurin 6.00 15.00
19 AJ Griffin 1.50 4.00
20 Chet Holmgren 10.00 25.00
21 Mark Williams 4.00 10.00
22 TyTy Washington Jr. 2.00 5.00
23 Johnny Davis 2.00 5.00
24 Jake LaRavia 2.00 5.00
25 Nikola Jovic 4.00 10.00
26 Wendell Moore Jr. 2.00 5.00
27 Blake Wesley 2.00 5.00
28 Jeremy Sochan 6.00 15.00
29 Shaedon Sharpe 8.00 20.00
30 Walker Kessler 4.00 10.00

2022-23 Select En Fuego

COMPLETE SET (10)
*SILVER: 2X TO 5X BASIC
1 Giannis Antetokounmpo 5.00 12.00
2 Luka Doncic 6.00 15.00
3 Stephen Curry 8.00 20.00
4 Zion Williamson 2.50 6.00
5 Trae Young 2.50 6.00
6 Jayson Tatum 4.00 10.00
7 LeBron James 8.00 20.00
8 Kevin Durant 3.00 8.00
9 Ja Morant 3.00 8.00
10 Cade Cunningham 3.00 8.00

2022-23 Select Future

COMPLETE SET (25)
*SILVER: .75X TO 2X BASIC
1 Ousmane Dieng 1.00 2.50
2 Jeremy Sochan 2.50 6.00
3 Ochai Agbaji 1.00 2.50
4 Paolo Banchero 5.00 12.00
5 AJ Griffin .60 1.50
6 Walker Kessler 1.50 4.00
7 Malaki Branham .75 2.00
8 Bennedict Mathurin 2.50 6.00
9 Johnny Davis .75 2.00
10 Christian Braun 2.00 5.00
11 Chet Holmgren 4.00 10.00
12 Jake LaRavia .75 2.00
13 Tari Eason 2.00 5.00
14 Dalen Terry .75 2.00
15 Jabari Smith Jr. 2.50 6.00
16 Caleb Houstan .75 2.00
17 Dyson Daniels 2.00 5.00
18 Andrew Nembhard 1.50 4.00
19 Christian Koloko .75 2.00
20 Jalen Williams 4.00 10.00
21 Shaedon Sharpe 3.00 8.00
22 David Roddy 1.00 2.50
23 Jaden Ivey 2.50 6.00
24 Keegan Murray 2.00 5.00
25 Jalen Duren 2.50 6.00

2022-23 Select In Flight Signatures

COMPLETE SET (28)
STATED PRINT RUN B/WN 75-249 COPIES PER
*RED/75-99: .5X TO 1.2X BASIC
*BLUE/49: .6X TO 1.5X BASIC
*ORNG PULSAR/30: .75X TO 2X BASIC
*TIE DYE/25: .75X TO 2X BASIC
1 Jalen Green/99 40.00 100.00
2 Anfernee Hardaway/149 40.00 100.00
3 Shawn Kemp/149 15.00 40.00
4 RJ Barrett/149 8.00 20.00
5 Obi Toppin/249 5.00 12.00
6 Jamal Crawford/249 5.00 12.00
7 Jordan Poole/125 20.00 50.00
8 Wendell Carter Jr./249 5.00 12.00
9 Dennis Rodman/99 40.00 100.00
10 Anthony Edwards/75 125.00 300.00
12 Brandon Ingram/149 15.00 40.00
13 Myles Turner/249 5.00 12.00
14 Amar'e Stoudemire/125 5.00 12.00
15 Cade Cunningham/99 40.00 100.00
16 Steve Francis/249 5.00 12.00
17 Ray Allen/99 40.00 100.00
18 Jonathan Kuminga/249 20.00 50.00
19 Victor Oladipo/249 4.00 10.00
20 Latrell Sprewell/249 12.00 30.00
21 Josh Hart/249 5.00 12.00
22 Manu Ginobili/99 40.00 100.00
23 Shai Gilgeous-Alexander/99 300.00 600.00
24 Dejounte Murray/99 6.00 15.00
25 Grant Hill/249 12.00 30.00
26 Ja Morant/99 100.00 250.00
27 Jonas Valanciunas/249 4.00 10.00
28 Alperen Sengun/149 6.00 15.00
30 Lonnie Walker IV/149 4.00 10.00

2022-23 Select Numbers

COMPLETE SET (25)
*GREEN: .6X TO 1.5X BASIC
*RED: .75X TO 2X BASIC
*SILVER: .75X TO 2X BASIC
1 Ja Morant 2.00 5.00
2 Zion Williamson 1.50 4.00
3 Cade Cunningham 2.00 5.00
4 LeBron James 5.00 12.00
5 Stephen Curry 5.00 12.00
6 Anthony Edwards 3.00 8.00
7 LaMelo Ball 1.50 4.00
8 Jayson Tatum 2.50 6.00
9 Giannis Antetokounmpo 3.00 8.00
10 Luka Doncic 4.00 10.00
11 Nikola Jokic 3.00 8.00
12 Trae Young 1.50 4.00
13 Kevin Durant 2.00 5.00
14 Pascal Siakam 1.00 2.50
15 James Harden 1.25 3.00
16 Paolo Banchero 4.00 10.00
17 Damian Lillard 1.50 4.00
18 Keegan Murray 1.50 4.00
19 Bennedict Mathurin 2.00 5.00
20 Jabari Smith Jr. 2.00 5.00
21 Donovan Mitchell 1.25 3.00
22 Jaden Ivey 2.00 5.00
23 Jimmy Butler 1.25 3.00
24 Jalen Green 2.00 5.00
25 Paul George 1.00 2.50

2022-23 Select Rookie Jersey Autographs

COMPLETE SET (40)
STATED PRINT RUN B/WN 99-199 COPIES PER
*DISCO: .5X TO 1.2X BASIC
*RED WAVE: .5X TO 1.2X BASIC
*PURPLE/99: .5X TO 1.2X BASIC
*BLUE/49: .6X TO 1.5X BASIC
*NEON ORNG PLSR/30: 1.5X TO 4X BASIC
*GREEN WAVE/25: 1.5X TO 4X BASIC
*TIE DYE/25: 1.5X TO 4X BASIC
1 Jaden Ivey/199 30.00 80.00
2 Jabari Smith Jr./199 30.00 80.00
3 Bennedict Mathurin/199 30.00 80.00
4 AJ Griffin/199 8.00 20.00
5 Jaden Hardy/199 15.00 40.00
6 Jalen Duren/199 30.00 80.00
7 Dalen Terry/199 10.00 25.00
8 Jalen Williams/199 50.00 125.00
9 Jake LaRavia/199 10.00 25.00
10 Malaki Branham/199 10.00 25.00
11 Tari Eason/199 25.00 60.00
12 Christian Braun/199 25.00 60.00
13 Ochai Agbaji/199 12.00 30.00
14 David Roddy/199 12.00 30.00
15 Walker Kessler/199 20.00 50.00
16 MarJon Beauchamp/199 10.00 25.00
17 Mark Williams/199 20.00 50.00
18 Paolo Banchero /199 150.00 400.00
19 Blake Wesley/199 10.00 25.00
20 Wendell Moore Jr./199 10.00 25.00
21 Shaedon Sharpe/199 40.00 100.00
22 Nikola Jovic/199 20.00 50.00
23 Johnny Davis/199 10.00 25.00
24 Dyson Daniels/199 25.00 60.00
25 Patrick Baldwin Jr./199 10.00 25.00
26 Jabari Walker/199 8.00 20.00
27 Peyton Watson/199 15.00 40.00
28 Jeremy Sochan/199 30.00 80.00
29 Keegan Murray/199 25.00 60.00
30 Isaiah Mobley/199 10.00 25.00
31 Ousmane Dieng/199 12.00 30.00
32 Max Christie/199 25.00 60.00
33 Christian Koloko/199 10.00 25.00
34 Caleb Houstan/199 10.00 25.00
35 Chet Holmgren/99 150.00 400.00
36 TyTy Washington Jr./199 10.00 25.00
37 Andrew Nembhard/199 20.00 50.00
38 Trevor Keels/199 8.00 20.00
39 Tyrese Martin/199 8.00 20.00
40 Kendall Brown/199 8.00 20.00

2022-23 Select Rookie Revolution

COMPLETE SET (30)
*GREEN: .6X TO 1.5X BASIC
*RED: .75X TO 2X BASIC
*SILVER: .75X TO 2X BASIC
1 Andrew Nembhard 1.25 3.00
2 Nikola Jovic 1.25 3.00
3 Max Christie 1.50 4.00
4 Walker Kessler 1.25 3.00
5 Keegan Murray 1.50 4.00
6 Malaki Branham .60 1.50
7 Jake LaRavia .60 1.50
8 Jaden Hardy 1.00 2.50
9 Bennedict Mathurin 2.00 5.00
10 Jaden Ivey 2.00 5.00
11 Caleb Houstan .60 1.50
12 Dyson Daniels 1.50 4.00
13 Christian Braun 1.50 4.00
14 Christian Koloko .60 1.50
15 AJ Griffin .50 1.25
16 David Roddy .75 2.00
17 Tari Eason 1.50 4.00
18 Chet Holmgren 3.00 8.00
19 Paolo Banchero 4.00 10.00
20 Ochai Agbaji .75 2.00
21 Jabari Smith Jr. 2.00 5.00
22 Jeremy Sochan 2.00 5.00
23 Ousmane Dieng .75 2.00
24 Johnny Davis .60 1.50
25 Mark Williams 1.25 3.00
26 Dalen Terry .60 1.50
27 Jalen Duren 2.00 5.00
28 Shaedon Sharpe 2.50 6.00
29 Jalen Williams 3.00 8.00
30 MarJon Beauchamp .60 1.50

2022-23 Select Rookie Signatures

COMPLETE SET (40)
STATED PRINT RUN B/WN 99-249 COPIES PER
*DISCO: .5X TO 1.2X BASIC
*RED/99: .6X TO 1.5X BASIC
*BLUE/49: .75X TO 2X BASIC
*NEON ORNG PLSR/30: 2X TO 5X BASIC
*TIE DYE/25: 2X TO 5X BASIC
1 Jabari Smith Jr./249 40.00 100.00
2 Johnny Davis/249 5.00 12.00
3 Dalen Terry/249 5.00 12.00
4 Jake LaRavia/249 5.00 12.00
5 Malaki Branham/249 5.00 12.00
6 Ousmane Dieng/249 6.00 15.00
7 Wendell Moore Jr./249 5.00 12.00
8 Nikola Jovic/249 10.00 25.00
9 Christian Braun/249 12.00 30.00
10 Paolo Banchero /249 125.00 300.00
11 Patrick Baldwin Jr./249 5.00 12.00
12 Walker Kessler/249 10.00 25.00
13 Jeremy Sochan/249 15.00 40.00
14 David Roddy/249 6.00 15.00
15 Jalen Williams/249 40.00 100.00

16 MarJon Beauchamp/249 5.00 12.00
17 Dyson Daniels/249 12.00 30.00
18 Blake Wesley/249 5.00 12.00
19 Tari Eason/249 12.00 30.00
20 TyTy Washington Jr./249 5.00 12.00
21 Chet Holmgren/99 150.00 400.00
22 Peyton Watson/249 8.00 20.00
23 Jaden Hardy/249 8.00 20.00
24 Shaedon Sharpe/249 40.00 100.00
25 Christian Koloko/249 5.00 12.00
26 AJ Griffin/249 4.00 10.00
27 Caleb Houstan/249 5.00 12.00
28 Keegan Murray/249 40.00 100.00
29 Jabari Walker/249 4.00 10.00
30 Mark Williams/249 10.00 25.00
31 Max Christie/249 12.00 30.00
32 Jalen Duren/249 15.00 40.00
33 Andrew Nembhard/249 10.00 25.00
34 Moussa Diabate/249 5.00 12.00
35 Bennedict Mathurin/249 40.00 100.00
36 Bryce McGowens/249 5.00 12.00
37 Ryan Rollins/249 5.00 12.00
38 Kennedy Chandler/249 5.00 12.00
39 Ochai Agbaji/249 6.00 15.00
40 Jaden Ivey/249 40.00 100.00

2022-23 Select Selection Committee Signatures

COMPLETE SET (10)
*GREEN ICE: .5X TO 1.2X BASIC
1 Larry Bird 60.00 150.00
2 Anfernee Hardaway 50.00 120.00
3 Magic Johnson 60.00 150.00
4 Kevin Garnett 60.00 150.00
5 Clyde Drexler 40.00 100.00
6 Grant Hill 25.00 60.00
7 Oscar Robertson 40.00 100.00
8 Paul Pierce 40.00 100.00
9 Pau Gasol 40.00 100.00
10 Gary Payton 25.00 60.00

2022-23 Select Selective Swatches

COMPLETE SET (40)
*PURPLE/99: .75X TO 2X BASIC
*BLUE/75: 1X TO 2.5X BASIC
*COPPER/49: 1.25X TO 3X BASIC
*TIE DYE/25: 2.5X TO 6X BASIC
1 Nikola Jokic 12.00 30.00
2 Kyrie Irving 5.00 12.00
3 Karl-Anthony Towns 4.00 10.00
4 Jamal Murray 4.00 10.00
5 Myles Turner 2.50 6.00
6 Tobias Harris 2.00 5.00
7 Anthony Davis 6.00 15.00
8 Jaren Jackson Jr. 4.00 10.00
9 Trae Young 6.00 15.00
10 LaMelo Ball 6.00 15.00
11 Fred VanVleet 3.00 8.00
12 Pascal Siakam 4.00 10.00
13 Devin Booker 6.00 15.00
14 Chris Paul 5.00 12.00
15 Tyrese Maxey 5.00 12.00
16 Joel Embiid 4.00 10.00
17 Brandon Ingram 3.00 8.00
18 RJ Barrett 4.00 10.00
19 Anfernee Simons 3.00 8.00
20 Luka Doncic 15.00 40.00
21 Russell Westbrook 4.00 10.00
22 Julius Randle 3.00 8.00
23 Bam Adebayo 4.00 10.00
24 Stephen Curry 20.00 50.00
25 Deandre Ayton 2.50 6.00
26 De'Aaron Fox 5.00 12.00
27 Damian Lillard 6.00 15.00
28 Grant Williams 2.00 5.00
29 Jrue Holiday 3.00 8.00
30 Khris Middleton 3.00 8.00
31 Anthony Edwards 12.00 30.00
32 Jayson Tatum 10.00 25.00
33 Giannis Antetokounmpo 12.00 30.00
34 Marcus Smart 3.00 8.00
35 Jaylen Brown 5.00 12.00
36 Zion Williamson 6.00 15.00
37 Bradley Beal 3.00 8.00
38 LeBron James 20.00 50.00
39 Ja Morant 8.00 20.00
40 Klay Thompson 6.00 15.00

2022-23 Select Sensations

COMPLETE SET (25)
*SILVER: .75X TO 2X BASIC
1 Tyrese Haliburton 1.50 4.00
2 Andrew Wiggins 1.00 2.50
3 Bradley Beal 1.00 2.50
4 Devin Booker 2.00 5.00
5 Damian Lillard 2.00 5.00
6 DeMar DeRozan 1.00 2.50
7 Fred VanVleet 1.00 2.50
8 James Harden 1.50 4.00
9 Shai Gilgeous-Alexander 4.00 10.00
10 Tyrese Maxey 1.50 4.00
11 Jaylen Brown 1.50 4.00
12 Darius Garland 1.25 3.00
13 Paul George 1.25 3.00
14 Dejounte Murray 1.00 2.50
15 Jaden Ivey 2.50 6.00
16 Tari Eason 2.00 5.00
17 Paolo Banchero 5.00 12.00
18 AJ Griffin .60 1.50
19 Shaedon Sharpe 3.00 8.00
20 Jabari Smith Jr. 2.50 6.00
21 Keegan Murray 2.00 5.00
22 Bennedict Mathurin 2.50 6.00
23 Jalen Duren 2.50 6.00
24 Dyson Daniels 2.00 5.00
25 Jeremy Sochan 2.50 6.00

2022-23 Select Signature Selections Autographs

COMPLETE SET (50)
*GREEN ICE: .5X TO 1.2X BASIC
1 Anthony Edwards 125.00 300.00
2 Juan Toscano-Anderson 3.00 8.00
3 George McGinnis 5.00 12.00
4 Tim Hardaway Jr. 4.00 10.00
5 Kelly Oubre Jr. 5.00 12.00
6 Caron Butler 4.00 10.00
7 Max Strus 5.00 12.00
8 Bill Laimbeer 5.00 12.00
9 Bobby Portis 5.00 12.00
10 Herbert Jones 5.00 12.00
11 Derrick White 12.00 30.00
12 Pat Connaughton 4.00 10.00
13 Lonnie Walker IV 4.00 10.00
14 Gary Harris 4.00 10.00
15 Kenny "Sky" Walker 4.00 10.00
16 Tony Allen 3.00 8.00
17 Kenyon Martin Jr. 5.00 12.00
18 Luke Kennard 4.00 10.00
19 Alperen Sengun 12.00 30.00
20 Hedo Turkoglu 5.00 12.00
21 Grant Williams 4.00 10.00
22 Derek Harper 4.00 10.00
23 Jose Alvarado 5.00 12.00
24 Duane Washington Jr. 3.00 8.00
25 Franz Wagner 20.00 50.00
26 Dale Ellis 5.00 12.00
27 Austin Reaves 40.00 100.00
28 Mike Miller 4.00 10.00
29 Muggsy Bogues 12.00 30.00
30 Brian Scalabrine 3.00 8.00
31 De'Anthony Melton 4.00 10.00
32 Devin Vassell 10.00 25.00
33 Grayson Allen 5.00 12.00
34 Udonis Haslem 4.00 10.00
35 Isaac Okoro 4.00 10.00
36 Ricky Davis 4.00 10.00
37 Mo Bamba 4.00 10.00
38 Landry Shamet 3.00 8.00
39 Georges Niang 4.00 10.00
40 Kevon Looney 5.00 12.00
41 Thomas Bryant 4.00 10.00
42 Jordan Clarkson 12.00 30.00
43 Swen Nater 5.00 12.00
44 Antawn Jamison 5.00 12.00
45 Andrew Bogut 5.00 12.00
46 Frank Selvy 5.00 12.00
47 Deni Avdija 5.00 12.00
48 Bojan Bogdanovic 5.00 12.00
49 Moses Moody 6.00 15.00
50 Christian Laettner 5.00 12.00

2022-23 Select Signatures

COMPLETE SET (30)
STATED PRINT RUN B/WN 99-249 COPIES PER
*RED/75-99: .5X TO 1.2X BASIC
*BLUE/49: .6X TO 1.5X BASIC
*NEON ORNG PLSR/30: .75X TO 2X BASIC
*TIE DYE/25: .75X TO 2X BASIC
1 Tyrese Haliburton/99 50.00 120.00
2 Khris Middleton/99 8.00 20.00
3 Magic Johnson/99 60.00 150.00
4 Zach Randolph/249 6.00 15.00
5 Scottie Barnes/149 25.00 60.00
6 Richard Hamilton/249 8.00 20.00
7 Luka Doncic/99 300.00 600.00
8 Metta World Peace/149 6.00 15.00
9 Jalen Brunson/249 20.00 50.00
10 Rudy Gobert/149 8.00 20.00
11 Stephen Curry/99 500.00 1,000.00
12 Jayson Tatum/99 125.00 300.00
13 Nikola Jokic/99 125.00 300.00
14 Ayo Dosunmu/249 8.00 20.00
15 Robert Horry/249 6.00 15.00
16 Jalen Rose/249 6.00 15.00
17 Bones Hyland/249 5.00 12.00
18 Dave Cowens/249 8.00 20.00
19 Adrian Dantley/249 6.00 15.00
20 Joe Harris/249 5.00 12.00
21 Trey Murphy III/249 8.00 20.00
22 Buddy Hield/149 6.00 15.00
23 Andre Drummond/125 6.00 15.00
24 Marcus Smart/125 12.00 30.00
25 Steve Kerr/149 12.00 30.00
26 Walt Frazier/149 10.00 25.00
27 Carlos Boozer/249 5.00 12.00
28 Keldon Johnson/249 8.00 20.00
29 Sam Cassell/125 6.00 15.00
30 Hakeem Olajuwon/99 30.00 80.00

2022-23 Select Snapshots

COMPLETE SET (21)
*SILVER: .75X TO 2X BASIC
1 Giannis Antetokounmpo 3.00 8.00
2 Jayson Tatum 2.50 6.00
3 LeBron James 5.00 12.00
4 Ja Morant 2.00 5.00
5 Luka Doncic 4.00 10.00
6 Zion Williamson 1.50 4.00
7 Stephen Curry 5.00 12.00
8 Kevin Durant 2.00 5.00
9 Donovan Mitchell 1.25 3.00
10 Nikola Jokic 3.00 8.00
11 LaMelo Ball 1.50 4.00
12 Anthony Edwards 3.00 8.00
13 Paolo Banchero 4.00 10.00
14 Jaden Ivey 2.00 5.00
15 Jabari Smith Jr. 2.00 5.00
16 Bennedict Mathurin 2.00 5.00
17 Keegan Murray 1.50 4.00
18 Dirk Nowitzki 1.50 4.00
19 Allen Iverson 1.50 4.00
20 Shaquille O'Neal 2.50 6.00

2022-23 Select Sparks Memorabilia

COMPLETE SET (10)
*PURPLE/99: .75X TO 2X BASIC
*BLUE/75: 1X TO 2.5X BASIC
*COPPER/49: 1.25X TO 3X BASIC
*TIE DYE/25: 2.5X TO 6X BASIC
1 Jabari Smith Jr. 6.00 15.00
2 Bennedict Mathurin 6.00 15.00
3 Chet Holmgren 10.00 25.00
4 Paolo Banchero 12.00 30.00
5 Jaden Ivey 6.00 15.00
6 Jeremy Sochan 6.00 15.00
7 Dyson Daniels 5.00 12.00
8 Shaedon Sharpe 8.00 20.00
9 Keegan Murray 5.00 12.00
10 Johnny Davis 2.00 5.00

2022-23 Select Throwback Memorabilia

COMPLETE SET (20)
*PURPLE/99: .75X TO 2X BASIC
*BLUE/75: 1X TO 2.5X BASIC
*COPPER/49: 1.25X TO 3X BASIC
*TIE DYE/11-25: 2.5X TO 6X BASIC
1 Dejounte Murray 2.50 6.00
2 D'Angelo Russell 1.50 4.00
3 Kawhi Leonard 5.00 12.00
4 Zach LaVine 4.00 10.00
5 Al Horford 2.00 5.00
6 Anthony Davis 5.00 12.00
7 Chris Paul 4.00 10.00
8 Malcolm Brogdon 1.50 4.00
9 Shai Gilgeous-Alexander 10.00 25.00
10 Tyrese Haliburton 4.00 10.00
11 CJ McCollum 2.00 5.00
12 Derrick Rose 4.00 10.00
13 Kyrie Irving 4.00 10.00
14 Kristaps Porzingis 2.50 6.00
15 Paul George 3.00 8.00
16 Andrew Wiggins 2.50 6.00
17 Rudy Gobert 2.50 6.00
18 Jimmy Butler 4.00 10.00
19 Collin Sexton 2.50 6.00
20 LeBron James 40.00 100.00

2022-23 Select Thunder Lane

COMPLETE SET (15)
*GREEN: .6X TO 1.5X BASIC
*RED: .75X TO 2X BASIC
*SILVER: .75X TO 2X BASIC
1 Ja Morant 2.50 6.00
2 LeBron James 6.00 15.00
3 Paul George 1.25 3.00
4 John Collins .75 2.00
5 Zach LaVine 1.50 4.00
6 Joel Embiid 1.25 3.00
7 Anthony Davis 2.00 5.00
8 Donovan Mitchell 1.50 4.00
9 Tyrese Maxey 1.50 4.00
10 Zion Williamson 2.00 5.00
11 Bam Adebayo 1.25 3.00
12 Anthony Edwards 4.00 10.00
13 Giannis Antetokounmpo 4.00 10.00
14 Jaylen Brown 1.50 4.00
15 Shai Gilgeous-Alexander 4.00 10.00

2022-23 Select Top Shelf Signatures

COMPLETE SET (17)
*TIE-DIE/25: .75X TO 2X BASIC
1 Jayson Tatum 125.00 300.00
2 Stephen Curry 500.00 1,000.00
3 Paolo Banchero 150.00 400.00
4 Jabari Smith Jr. 100.00 250.00
5 Luka Doncic 350.00 700.00
6 Paul Pierce 30.00 80.00
7 Allen Iverson 75.00 200.00
8 Nikola Jokic 125.00 300.00
9 Anthony Edwards 125.00 300.00
10 Bennedict Mathurin 100.00 250.00
11 Keegan Murray 100.00 250.00
12 Chris Paul 40.00 100.00
13 Jaden Ivey 100.00 250.00
14 Kevin Garnett 75.00 200.00
15 Ja Morant 125.00 300.00
16 Magic Johnson 75.00 200.00
17 Chet Holmgren 150.00 400.00

2022-23 Select Turbo Charged

COMPLETE SET (10)
*GREEN: .6X TO 1.5X BASIC
*RED: .75X TO 2X BASIC
*SILVER: .75X TO 2X BASIC
1 Bennedict Mathurin 2.00 5.00
2 Jaden Ivey 2.00 5.00
3 LeBron James 5.00 12.00
4 Keegan Murray 1.50 4.00
5 Paolo Banchero 4.00 10.00
6 Luka Doncic 4.00 10.00
7 Stephen Curry 5.00 12.00
8 Jabari Smith Jr. 2.00 5.00
9 Ja Morant 2.00 5.00
10 Giannis Antetokounmpo 3.00 8.00

2022-23 Select Unstoppable

COMPLETE SET (20)
*SILVER: 1.25X TO 3X BASIC
1 Trae Young 2.00 5.00
2 Kevin Durant 2.50 6.00
3 Stephen Curry 6.00 15.00
4 Jalen Green 2.50 6.00
5 Joel Embiid 1.25 3.00
6 Giannis Antetokounmpo 4.00 10.00
7 LeBron James 6.00 15.00
8 Zion Williamson 2.00 5.00
9 Jayson Tatum 3.00 8.00
10 Cade Cunningham 2.50 6.00
11 Luka Doncic 5.00 12.00
12 Ja Morant 2.50 6.00
13 Shai Gilgeous-Alexander 4.00 10.00
14 James Harden 1.50 4.00
15 LaMelo Ball 2.00 5.00
16 Nikola Jokic 4.00 10.00
17 Devin Booker 2.00 5.00
18 Anthony Edwards 4.00 10.00
19 Donovan Mitchell 1.50 4.00
20 Paolo Banchero 5.00 12.00

2022-23 Select X-Factor Memorabilia Signatures

COMPLETE SET (27)
STATED PRINT RUN B/WN 75-199 COPIES PER
*PURPLE/75-99: .5X TO 1.2X BASIC
*BLUE/49: .6X TO 1.5X BASIC
*TIE DYE/25: 1X TO 2.5X BASIC
1 Santi Aldama/199 6.00 15.00
2 Shai Gilgeous-Alexander/99 300.00 600.00
3 Jason Kidd/99 15.00 40.00
4 De'Aaron Fox/99 20.00 50.00
5 Keldon Johnson/199 8.00 20.00
7 Obi Toppin/149 6.00 15.00
8 Marcus Smart/199 12.00 30.00
9 Spencer Dinwiddie/149 5.00 12.00
10 Jalen Brunson/199 20.00 50.00
11 Anfernee Simons/199 8.00 20.00
12 Robert Williams III/199 5.00 12.00
13 Josh Giddey/199 30.00 80.00
15 Grant Williams/199 5.00 12.00
16 Herbert Jones/199 6.00 15.00
17 Jalen Green/149 40.00 100.00
18 Jonathan Kuminga/149 15.00 40.00
19 Julius Randle/149 8.00 20.00
20 Pau Gasol/99 40.00 100.00
21 Jaren Jackson Jr./149 40.00 100.00
22 Onyeka Okongwu/199 6.00 15.00
23 Michael Porter Jr./149 8.00 20.00
25 Cade Cunningham/125 40.00 100.00
26 Ray Allen/75 40.00 100.00
27 Manu Ginobili/75 40.00 100.00
28 Jason Terry/199 5.00 12.00
29 Robert Horry/199 6.00 15.00
30 Toni Kukoc/199 8.00 20.00

2022-23 Select Youth Explosion Signatures

COMPLETE SET (39)
*GREEN ICE: .5X TO 1.2X BASIC
1 Jabari Smith Jr. 40.00 100.00
2 Andrew Nembhard 12.00 30.00
3 Scotty Pippen Jr. 8.00 20.00
4 Kenneth Lofton Jr. 8.00 20.00
5 Jaden Ivey 40.00 100.00
6 Kevon Harris 5.00 12.00
7 Isaiah Mobley 6.00 15.00
8 Tari Eason 15.00 40.00
9 Bennedict Mathurin 40.00 100.00
10 Christian Braun 15.00 40.00
11 Ryan Rollins 6.00 15.00
13 Jaylin Williams 8.00 20.00
14 Jamal Cain 6.00 15.00
15 TyTy Washington Jr. 6.00 15.00
16 Chet Holmgren 150.00 400.00
17 Jalen Duren 20.00 50.00
18 Moussa Diabate 6.00 15.00
19 Nikola Jovic 12.00 30.00
20 Jabari Walker 5.00 12.00
21 Jaden Hardy 10.00 25.00
22 Ron Harper Jr. 8.00 20.00
23 AJ Griffin 5.00 12.00
24 Christian Koloko 6.00 15.00
25 Dalen Terry 6.00 15.00
26 David Roddy 8.00 20.00
27 A.J. Green 20.00 50.00
28 Dereon Seabron 5.00 12.00
29 Keegan Murray 40.00 100.00
30 Trevor Keels 5.00 12.00
31 Tyrese Martin 5.00 12.00
32 Bryce McGowens 6.00 15.00
33 Kennedy Chandler 6.00 15.00
34 Caleb Houstan 6.00 15.00
35 Wendell Moore Jr. 6.00 15.00
36 Josh Minott 6.00 15.00
37 Ochai Agbaji 8.00 20.00
38 Julian Champagnie 12.00 30.00
39 Dyson Daniels 15.00 40.00
40 Paolo Banchero 150.00 400.00

2023-24 Select

*BLUE: .4X TO 1X BASIC
1 RJ Barrett .60 1.50
2 Kevin Durant 1.25 3.00
3 Klay Thompson 1.00 2.50
4 Joel Embiid 1.00 2.50
5 Karl-Anthony Towns .60 1.50
6 Cameron Thomas .50 1.25
7 Jalen Brunson .75 2.00
8 Pascal Siakam .60 1.50
9 Jalen Williams .75 2.00
10 DeMar DeRozan .60 1.50
11 Deandre Ayton .40 1.00
12 Cameron Johnson .40 1.00
13 Alperen Sengun .60 1.50
14 Paul George .60 1.50
15 Shaedon Sharpe .75 2.00
16 Zach LaVine .60 1.50
17 Franz Wagner .60 1.50
18 Jordan Poole .60 1.50
19 Lauri Markkanen .60 1.50
20 Anthony Davis 1.00 2.50
21 Kyrie Irving .75 2.00
22 Jaylen Brown .75 2.00
23 Michael Porter Jr. .50 1.25
24 Kawhi Leonard 1.00 2.50
25 Domantas Sabonis .60 1.50
26 Cade Cunningham 1.00 2.50
27 Dejounte Murray .50 1.25
28 Brandon Ingram .50 1.25
29 Tyrese Haliburton .75 2.00
30 Jaren Jackson Jr. .60 1.50
31 Paolo Banchero 1.00 2.50
32 Nikola Jokic 2.00 5.00
33 Jordan Clarkson .40 1.00
34 Mikal Bridges .50 1.25
35 Jamal Murray .75 2.00
36 Zion Williamson 1.00 2.50
37 Anthony Edwards 2.00 5.00
38 Donovan Mitchell .75 2.00
39 Desmond Bane .50 1.25
40 Jimmy Butler .60 1.50
41 Chet Holmgren 1.00 2.50
42 Jalen Green .60 1.50
43 Trae Young .75 2.00
44 Tyrese Maxey .75 2.00
45 Jayson Tatum 1.50 4.00
46 Julius Randle .50 1.25
47 Bradley Beal .50 1.25
48 Devin Vassell .50 1.25
49 De'Aaron Fox .75 2.00
50 Darius Garland .60 1.50
51 Luka Doncic 2.50 6.00
52 Austin Reaves 1.00 2.50
53 LaMelo Ball 1.00 2.50
54 Scottie Barnes .50 1.25
55 Russell Westbrook .60 1.50
56 Stephen Curry 3.00 8.00
57 Shai Gilgeous-Alexander 2.00 5.00
58 Devin Booker 1.00 2.50
59 Bam Adebayo .60 1.50
60 Giannis Antetokounmpo 2.00 5.00
61 Keldon Johnson .50 1.25
62 Kristaps Porzingis .50 1.25
63 Damian Lillard 1.00 2.50
64 James Harden .75 2.00
65 Ja Morant 1.25 3.00
66 LeBron James 3.00 8.00
67 Emoni Bates RC 1.00 2.50
68 Jalen Pickett RC .60 1.50
69 Cam Whitmore RC 2.00 5.00
70 Marcus Sasser RC 1.25 3.00
71 Anthony Black RC 1.50 4.00
72 Jordan Hawkins RC 1.25 3.00
73 Noah Clowney RC 1.00 2.50
74 Sasha Vezenkov RC .60 1.50
75 Keyonte George RC 2.50 6.00
76 Dereck Lively II RC 1.50 4.00
77 Scoot Henderson RC 2.50 6.00
78 Julian Strawther RC 1.00 2.50
79 Kobe Brown RC .75 2.00
80 Brandon Miller RC 3.00 8.00
81 Toumani Camara RC 1.50 4.00
82 Julian Phillips RC .75 2.00
83 Colby Jones RC .75 2.00
84 Trayce Jackson-Davis RC 1.00 2.50
85 Olivier-Maxence Prosper RC .75 2.00
86 Jarace Walker RC 1.50 4.00
87 Victor Wembanyama RC 6.00 15.00
88 Cason Wallace RC 1.50 4.00
89 Nick Smith Jr. RC 1.00 2.50
90 Gradey Dick RC 1.50 4.00
91 Kris Murray RC .75 2.00
92 Vasilije Micic RC .75 2.00
93 Brandin Podziemski RC 2.50 6.00
94 Ben Sheppard RC .75 2.00
95 Ausar Thompson RC 2.00 5.00
96 Amen Thompson RC 4.00 10.00
97 Bilal Coulibaly RC 2.00 5.00
98 Andre Jackson Jr. RC 1.25 3.00
99 Jalen Hood-Schifino RC .75 2.00
100 Jaime Jaquez Jr. RC 1.25 3.00
101 Julian Strawther 1.00 2.50
102 Jaime Jaquez Jr. 1.25 3.00
103 Cason Wallace 1.50 4.00
104 Brandin Podziemski 2.50 6.00
105 Ben Sheppard .75 2.00
106 Vasilije Micic .75 2.00
107 Chris Livingston RC .75 2.00
108 Jalen Pickett .60 1.50
109 Keyonte George 2.50 6.00
110 Kobe Brown .75 2.00
111 Dereck Lively II 1.50 4.00
112 Olivier-Maxence Prosper .75 2.00
113 Anthony Black 1.50 4.00
114 Marcus Sasser 1.25 3.00
115 Toumani Camara 1.50 4.00
116 Jordan Miller 1.00 2.50
117 Trayce Jackson-Davis 1.00 2.50
118 Cam Whitmore 2.00 5.00
119 Nick Smith Jr. 1.00 2.50
120 Kris Murray .75 2.00
121 Victor Wembanyama 6.00 15.00
122 Amen Thompson 4.00 10.00
123 Jalen Hood-Schifino .75 2.00
124 Jordan Hawkins 1.25 3.00
125 Dariq Whitehead RC 1.00 2.50
126 Gradey Dick 1.50 4.00
127 Sasha Vezenkov .60 1.50
128 Ausar Thompson 2.00 5.00
129 Scoot Henderson 2.50 6.00
130 Brandon Miller 3.00 8.00
131 Bilal Coulibaly 2.00 5.00
132 Colby Jones .75 2.00
133 Jarace Walker 1.50 4.00
134 Andre Jackson Jr. 1.25 3.00
135 LeBron James 3.00 8.00
136 Ja Morant 1.25 3.00
137 James Harden .75 2.00
138 Damian Lillard 1.00 2.50
139 Kristaps Porzingis .50 1.25
140 Keldon Johnson .50 1.25
141 Giannis Antetokounmpo 2.00 5.00
142 Bam Adebayo .60 1.50
143 Devin Booker 1.00 2.50
144 Shai Gilgeous-Alexander 2.00 5.00
145 Stephen Curry 3.00 8.00
146 Russell Westbrook .60 1.50
147 Scottie Barnes .50 1.25
148 LaMelo Ball 1.00 2.50
149 Austin Reaves 1.00 2.50
150 Luka Doncic 2.50 6.00
151 Darius Garland .60 1.50
152 De'Aaron Fox .75 2.00
153 Devin Vassell .50 1.25
154 Bradley Beal .50 1.25
155 Julius Randle .50 1.25
156 Jayson Tatum 1.50 4.00
157 Tyrese Maxey .75 2.00
158 Trae Young .75 2.00
159 Jalen Green .60 1.50
160 Chet Holmgren 1.00 2.50
161 Jimmy Butler .60 1.50
162 Desmond Bane .50 1.25
163 Donovan Mitchell .75 2.00
164 Anthony Edwards 2.00 5.00
165 Zion Williamson 1.00 2.50
166 Jamal Murray .75 2.00
167 Mikal Bridges .50 1.25
168 Jordan Clarkson .40 1.00
169 Nikola Jokic 2.00 5.00
170 Paolo Banchero 1.00 2.50
171 Jaren Jackson Jr. .60 1.50
172 Tyrese Haliburton .75 2.00
173 Brandon Ingram .50 1.25
174 Dejounte Murray .50 1.25
175 Cade Cunningham 1.00 2.50
176 Domantas Sabonis .60 1.50
177 Kawhi Leonard 1.00 2.50
178 Michael Porter Jr. .50 1.25
179 Jaylen Brown .75 2.00
180 Kyrie Irving .75 2.00
181 Anthony Davis 1.00 2.50
182 Lauri Markkanen .60 1.50
183 Jordan Poole .60 1.50
184 Franz Wagner .60 1.50
185 Zach LaVine .60 1.50
186 Shaedon Sharpe .75 2.00
187 Paul George .60 1.50
188 Alperen Sengun .60 1.50
189 Cameron Johnson .40 1.00
190 Deandre Ayton .40 1.00
191 DeMar DeRozan .60 1.50
192 Jalen Williams .75 2.00
193 Pascal Siakam .60 1.50
194 Jalen Brunson .75 2.00
195 Cameron Thomas .50 1.25
196 Karl-Anthony Towns .60 1.50
197 Joel Embiid 1.00 2.50
198 Klay Thompson 1.00 2.50
199 Kevin Durant 1.25 3.00
200 RJ Barrett .60 1.50
201 RJ Barrett 1.25 3.00
202 Kevin Durant 2.50 6.00
203 Klay Thompson 2.00 5.00
204 Joel Embiid 2.00 5.00
205 Karl-Anthony Towns 1.25 3.00
206 Cameron Thomas 1.00 2.50
207 Jalen Brunson 1.50 4.00
208 Pascal Siakam 1.25 3.00
209 Jalen Williams 1.50 4.00
210 DeMar DeRozan 1.25 3.00
211 Deandre Ayton .75 2.00
212 Cameron Johnson .75 2.00
213 Alperen Sengun 1.25 3.00
214 Paul George 1.25 3.00
215 Shaedon Sharpe 1.50 4.00
216 Zach LaVine 1.25 3.00
217 Franz Wagner 1.25 3.00
218 Jordan Poole 1.25 3.00
219 Lauri Markkanen 1.25 3.00
220 Anthony Davis 2.00 5.00
221 Kyrie Irving 1.50 4.00
222 Jaylen Brown 1.50 4.00
223 Michael Porter Jr. 1.00 2.50
224 Kawhi Leonard 2.00 5.00
225 Domantas Sabonis 1.25 3.00
226 Cade Cunningham 2.00 5.00
227 Dejounte Murray 1.00 2.50
228 Brandon Ingram 1.00 2.50
229 Tyrese Haliburton 1.50 4.00
230 Jaren Jackson Jr. 1.25 3.00
231 Paolo Banchero 2.00 5.00
232 Nikola Jokic 4.00 10.00
233 Jordan Clarkson .75 2.00
234 Mikal Bridges 1.00 2.50
235 Jamal Murray 1.50 4.00
236 Zion Williamson 2.00 5.00
237 Anthony Edwards 4.00 10.00
238 Donovan Mitchell 1.50 4.00
239 Desmond Bane 1.00 2.50
240 Jimmy Butler 1.25 3.00
241 Chet Holmgren 2.00 5.00
242 Jalen Green 1.25 3.00
243 Trae Young 1.50 4.00
244 Tyrese Maxey 1.50 4.00
245 Jayson Tatum 3.00 8.00
246 Julius Randle 1.00 2.50
247 Bradley Beal 1.00 2.50
248 Devin Vassell 1.00 2.50
249 De'Aaron Fox 1.50 4.00
250 Darius Garland 1.25 3.00
251 Luka Doncic 5.00 12.00
252 Austin Reaves 2.00 5.00
253 LaMelo Ball 2.00 5.00
254 Scottie Barnes 1.00 2.50
255 Russell Westbrook 1.25 3.00
256 Stephen Curry 6.00 15.00
257 Shai Gilgeous-Alexander 4.00 10.00
258 Devin Booker 2.00 5.00
259 Bam Adebayo 1.25 3.00
260 Giannis Antetokounmpo 4.00 10.00
261 Keldon Johnson 1.00 2.50
262 Kristaps Porzingis 1.00 2.50
263 Damian Lillard 2.00 5.00
264 James Harden 1.50 4.00
265 Ja Morant 2.50 6.00
266 LeBron James 6.00 15.00
267 Olivier-Maxence Prosper 1.50 4.00
268 Bilal Coulibaly 4.00 10.00
269 Scoot Henderson 5.00 12.00
270 Jett Howard RC 2.00 5.00
271 Sasha Vezenkov 1.25 3.00
272 Toumani Camara 3.00 8.00
273 Jarace Walker 3.00 8.00
274 Amen Thompson 8.00 20.00
275 Kobe Brown 1.50 4.00
276 Ben Sheppard 1.50 4.00
277 Kris Murray 1.50 4.00
278 Trayce Jackson-Davis 2.00 5.00
279 Colby Jones 1.50 4.00
280 Jordan Hawkins 2.50 6.00
281 Jalen Pickett 1.25 3.00
282 Cam Whitmore 4.00 10.00
283 Julian Strawther 2.00 5.00
284 Ausar Thompson 4.00 10.00
285 Dereck Lively II 3.00 8.00
286 Brandon Miller 6.00 15.00
287 Gradey Dick 3.00 8.00
288 Victor Wembanyama 12.00 30.00
289 Julian Phillips 1.50 4.00
290 Vasilije Micic 1.50 4.00
291 Andre Jackson Jr. 2.50 6.00
292 Marcus Sasser 2.50 6.00
293 Nick Smith Jr. 2.00 5.00
294 Emoni Bates 2.00 5.00
295 Keyonte George 5.00 12.00
296 Anthony Black 3.00 8.00
297 Jalen Hood-Schifino 1.50 4.00
298 Cason Wallace 3.00 8.00
299 Brandin Podziemski 5.00 12.00
300 Jaime Jaquez Jr. 2.50 6.00
301 Toumani Camara 1.50 4.00
302 Jaime Jaquez Jr. 1.25 3.00
303 Marcus Sasser 1.25 3.00
304 Bilal Coulibaly 2.00 5.00
305 Keyonte George 2.50 6.00
306 Kris Murray .75 2.00
307 Cam Whitmore 2.00 5.00
308 Dariq Whitehead 1.00 2.50
309 Jarace Walker 1.50 4.00
310 Nick Smith Jr. 1.00 2.50
311 Victor Wembanyama 12.00 30.00
312 Gradey Dick 1.50 4.00
313 Dereck Lively II 1.50 4.00
314 Chris Livingston .75 2.00
315 Vasilije Micic .75 2.00
316 Ausar Thompson 2.00 5.00
317 Andre Jackson Jr. 1.25 3.00
318 Julian Strawther 1.00 2.50
319 Brandin Podziemski 2.50 6.00
320 Kobe Brown .75 2.00
321 Cason Wallace 1.50 4.00
322 Amen Thompson 4.00 10.00
323 Sasha Vezenkov .60 1.50
324 Scoot Henderson 2.50 6.00
325 Noah Clowney 1.00 2.50
326 Jalen Hood-Schifino .75 2.00
327 Jalen Pickett .60 1.50
328 Anthony Black 1.50 4.00
329 Trayce Jackson-Davis 1.00 2.50
330 Olivier-Maxence Prosper .75 2.00
331 Julian Phillips .75 2.00
332 Brandon Miller 3.00 8.00
333 Ben Sheppard .75 2.00
334 Jordan Hawkins 1.25 3.00
335 LeBron James 3.00 8.00
336 Ja Morant 1.25 3.00
337 James Harden .75 2.00
338 Damian Lillard 1.00 2.50
339 Kristaps Porzingis .50 1.25
340 Keldon Johnson .50 1.25
341 Giannis Antetokounmpo 2.00 5.00
342 Bam Adebayo .60 1.50
343 Devin Booker 1.00 2.50
344 Shai Gilgeous-Alexander 2.00 5.00
345 Stephen Curry 3.00 8.00
346 Russell Westbrook .60 1.50
347 Scottie Barnes .50 1.25
348 LaMelo Ball 1.00 2.50
349 Austin Reaves 1.00 2.50
350 Luka Doncic 2.50 6.00
351 Darius Garland .60 1.50
352 De'Aaron Fox .75 2.00
353 Devin Vassell .50 1.25
354 Bradley Beal .50 1.25
355 Julius Randle .50 1.25
356 Jayson Tatum 1.50 4.00
357 Tyrese Maxey .75 2.00
358 Trae Young .75 2.00
359 Jalen Green .60 1.50
360 Chet Holmgren 1.00 2.50
361 Jimmy Butler .60 1.50
362 Desmond Bane .50 1.25
363 Donovan Mitchell .75 2.00
364 Anthony Edwards 2.00 5.00
365 Zion Williamson 1.00 2.50
366 Jamal Murray .75 2.00
367 Mikal Bridges .50 1.25
368 Jordan Clarkson .40 1.00
369 Nikola Jokic 2.00 5.00
370 Paolo Banchero 1.00 2.50
371 Jaren Jackson Jr. .60 1.50
372 Tyrese Haliburton .75 2.00
373 Brandon Ingram .50 1.25
374 Dejounte Murray .50 1.25
375 Cade Cunningham 1.00 2.50
376 Domantas Sabonis .60 1.50
377 Kawhi Leonard 1.00 2.50
378 Michael Porter Jr. .50 1.25
379 Jaylen Brown .75 2.00
380 Kyrie Irving .75 2.00
381 Anthony Davis 1.00 2.50
382 Lauri Markkanen .60 1.50
383 Jordan Poole .60 1.50
384 Franz Wagner .60 1.50
385 Zach LaVine .60 1.50
386 Shaedon Sharpe .75 2.00
387 Paul George .60 1.50
388 Alperen Sengun .60 1.50
389 Cameron Johnson .40 1.00
390 Deandre Ayton .40 1.00
391 DeMar DeRozan .60 1.50
392 Jalen Williams .75 2.00
393 Pascal Siakam .60 1.50
394 Jalen Brunson .75 2.00
395 Cameron Thomas .50 1.25
396 Karl-Anthony Towns .60 1.50
397 Joel Embiid 1.00 2.50
398 Klay Thompson 1.00 2.50
399 Kevin Durant 1.25 3.00
400 RJ Barrett .60 1.50

2023-24 Select Prizms Blue

*PRIZMS BLUE: .6X TO 1.5X BASIC
87 Victor Wembanyama 25.00 60.00
121 Victor Wembanyama 25.00 60.00
288 Victor Wembanyama 100.00 250.00
311 Victor Wembanyama 40.00 100.00

2023-24 Select Prizms Blue Cracked Ice

*BLUE CRKD ICE: .6X TO 1.5X BASIC
87 Victor Wembanyama 25.00 60.00
121 Victor Wembanyama 25.00 60.00
288 Victor Wembanyama 100.00 250.00
311 Victor Wembanyama 40.00 100.00

2023-24 Select Prizms Blue Die-Cut

*BLUE DIE CUT: 2X TO 5X BASIC
STATED PRINT RUN 249 SER.#'d SETS
121 Victor Wembanyama 150.00 400.00

2023-24 Select Prizms Blue Disco

*BLUE DISCO: 8X TO 20X BASIC
STATED PRINT RUN 25 SER. #'D SETS
87 Victor Wembanyama 1,000.00 2,000.00
121 Victor Wembanyama 1,000.00 2,000.00
288 Victor Wembanyama 1,500.00 3,000.00

2023-24 Select Prizms Blue Flash

*BLUE FLASH: 4X TO 10X BASIC
STATED PRINT RUN 99 SER.#'d SETS
87 Victor Wembanyama 400.00 800.00
121 Victor Wembanyama 400.00 800.00
288 Victor Wembanyama 800.00 1,500.00
311 Victor Wembanyama 400.00 800.00

2023-24 Select Prizms Blue Scope

*BLUE SCOPE: 1.5X TO 4X BASIC
STATED PRINT RUN 249 SER.#'d SETS
87 Victor Wembanyama 150.00 400.00

2023-24 Select Prizms Blue Tectonic
*BLUE TECTONIC: 4X TO 10X BASIC
STATED PRINT RUN 99 SER.#'d SETS
87 Victor Wembanyama 400.00 800.00
121 Victor Wembanyama 400.00 800.00
288 Victor Wembanyama 800.00 1,500.00
311 Victor Wembanyama 400.00 800.00

2023-24 Select Prizms Blue Wave
*BLUE WAVE: 5X TO 12X BASIC
STATED PRINT RUN 75 SER.#'d SETS
87 Victor Wembanyama 500.00 1,000.00
121 Victor Wembanyama 500.00 1,000.00
288 Victor Wembanyama 1,000.00 2,000.00

2023-24 Select Prizms Bronze Checker
*BRONZE CHECKER: 6X TO 15X BASIC
STATED PRINT RUN 49 SER. #'D SETS
87 Victor Wembanyama 600.00 1,200.00

2023-24 Select Prizms Bronze Checker Die-Cut
*BRONZE CHECKER DC: 6X TO 15X BASIC
STATED PRINT RUN 49 SER. #'D SETS
121 Victor Wembanyama 600.00 1,200.00

2023-24 Select Prizms Disco
*DISCO: 1.25X TO 3X BASIC
87 Victor Wembanyama 100.00 250.00
121 Victor Wembanyama 100.00 250.00
288 Victor Wembanyama 500.00 1,000.00

2023-24 Select Prizms Green Ice
*GREEN ICE: 1.25X TO 3X BASIC
87 Victor Wembanyama 75.00 200.00
121 Victor Wembanyama 75.00 200.00
288 Victor Wembanyama 400.00 800.00
311 Victor Wembanyama 100.00 250.00

2023-24 Select Prizms Green Shock
*GREEN SHOCK: 1.25X TO 3X BASIC
87 Victor Wembanyama 75.00 200.00
121 Victor Wembanyama 75.00 200.00
288 Victor Wembanyama 400.00 800.00
311 Victor Wembanyama 100.00 250.00

2023-24 Select Prizms Green Wave
*GREEN WAVE: 6X TO 15X BASIC
STATED PRINT RUN 50 SER. #'D SETS
87 Victor Wembanyama 600.00 1,200.00
121 Victor Wembanyama 600.00 1,200.00
288 Victor Wembanyama 1,250.00 2,500.00

2023-24 Select Prizms Green White Purple
*GRN WHITE PRPL: .6X TO 1.5X BASIC
87 Victor Wembanyama 30.00 80.00
121 Victor Wembanyama 30.00 80.00
288 Victor Wembanyama 125.00 300.00

2023-24 Select Prizms Light Blue
*LIGHT BLUE: 1.5X TO 4X BASIC
STATED PRINT RUN 299 SER.#'d SETS
87 Victor Wembanyama 150.00 400.00

2023-24 Select Prizms Light Blue Disco
*LIGHT BLUE DISCO: 4X TO 10X BASIC
STATED PRINT RUN 99 SER.#'d SETS
87 Victor Wembanyama 400.00 800.00
121 Victor Wembanyama 400.00 800.00
288 Victor Wembanyama 800.00 1,500.00

2023-24 Select Prizms Maroon
*MAROON: 2.5X TO 6X BASIC
STATED PRINT RUN 175 SER.#'d SETS
87 Victor Wembanyama 200.00 500.00
311 Victor Wembanyama 200.00 500.00

2023-24 Select Prizms Maroon Die-Cut
*MAROON DIE CUT: 2.5X TO 6X BASIC
STATED PRINT RUN 175 SER.#'d SETS
121 Victor Wembanyama 200.00 500.00

2023-24 Select Prizms Neon Green
*NEON GREEN: 5X TO 12X BASIC
STATED PRINT RUN 75 SER.#'d SETS
87 Victor Wembanyama 500.00 1,000.00

2023-24 Select Prizms Neon Green Die-Cut
*NEON GREEN DIE CUT: 5X TO 12X BASIC
STATED PRINT RUN 75 SER.#'d SETS
121 Victor Wembanyama 500.00 1,000.00

2023-24 Select Prizms Orange Die-Cut
*ORANGE DIE CUT: 5X TO 12X BASIC
STATED PRINT RUN 65 SER.#'d SETS
121 Victor Wembanyama 500.00 1,000.00

2023-24 Select Prizms Orange Flash
*ORANGE FLASH: 1.25X TO 3X BASIC
87 Victor Wembanyama 60.00 150.00
121 Victor Wembanyama 60.00 150.00
288 Victor Wembanyama 200.00 500.00
311 Victor Wembanyama 75.00 200.00

2023-24 Select Prizms Orange Tectonic
*ORANGE TECTONIC: 1.25X TO 3X BASIC
87 Victor Wembanyama 60.00 150.00
121 Victor Wembanyama 60.00 150.00
288 Victor Wembanyama 300.00 600.00
311 Victor Wembanyama 75.00 200.00

2023-24 Select Prizms Pink Cracked Ice
*PINK CRACKED ICE: 4X TO 10X BASIC
STATED PRINT RUN 99 SER.#'d SETS
87 Victor Wembanyama 400.00 800.00
121 Victor Wembanyama 400.00 800.00
288 Victor Wembanyama 800.00 1,500.00
311 Victor Wembanyama 400.00 800.00

2023-24 Select Prizms Purple Cracked Ice
*PRPL CRACKED ICE: 4X TO 10X BASIC
STATED PRINT RUN 99 SER.#'d SETS
87 Victor Wembanyama 400.00 800.00
121 Victor Wembanyama 400.00 800.00
288 Victor Wembanyama 800.00 1,500.00
311 Victor Wembanyama 400.00 800.00

2023-24 Select Prizms Purple Die-Cut
*PRPL DIE CUT: 4X TO 10X BASIC
STATED PRINT RUN 99 SER.#'d SETS
121 Victor Wembanyama 400.00 800.00

2023-24 Select Prizms Purple Flash
*PURPLE FLASH: 2.5X TO 6X BASIC
STATED PRINT RUN 175 SER.#'d SETS
87 Victor Wembanyama 200.00 500.00
121 Victor Wembanyama 200.00 500.00
311 Victor Wembanyama 300.00 600.00

2023-24 Select Prizms Red
*RED: 2X TO 5X BASIC
STATED PRINT RUN 199 SER.#'d SETS
87 Victor Wembanyama 200.00 500.00

2023-24 Select Prizms Red Cracked Ice
*RED CRKD ICE: .75X TO 2X BASIC
87 Victor Wembanyama 40.00 100.00
121 Victor Wembanyama 40.00 100.00
288 Victor Wembanyama 150.00 400.00
311 Victor Wembanyama 60.00 150.00

2023-24 Select Prizms Red Disco
*RED DISCO: 6X TO 15X BASIC
STATED PRINT RUN 49 SER. #'D SETS
87 Victor Wembanyama 600.00 1,200.00
121 Victor Wembanyama 600.00 1,200.00
288 Victor Wembanyama 1,250.00 2,500.00

2023-24 Select Prizms Scope
*SCOPE: 1.25X TO 3X BASIC
87 Victor Wembanyama 75.00 200.00
121 Victor Wembanyama 75.00 200.00

2023-24 Select Prizms Silver
*SILVER: 1.25X TO 3X BASIC
87 Victor Wembanyama 60.00 150.00
121 Victor Wembanyama 60.00 150.00
288 Victor Wembanyama 400.00 800.00
311 Victor Wembanyama 75.00 200.00

2023-24 Select Prizms Teal White Pink
*TEAL WHITE PINK: 6X TO 15X BASIC
STATED PRINT RUN 49 SER. #'D SETS
87 Victor Wembanyama 600.00 1,200.00
121 Victor Wembanyama 600.00 1,200.00
288 Victor Wembanyama 1,250.00 2,500.00

2023-24 Select Prizms Tectonic
*TECTONIC: 1.25X TO 3X BASIC
87 Victor Wembanyama 60.00 150.00
121 Victor Wembanyama 60.00 150.00
288 Victor Wembanyama 300.00 600.00
311 Victor Wembanyama 75.00 200.00

2023-24 Select Prizms Tie-Dye
*TIE DYE: 8X TO 20X BASIC
STATED PRINT RUN 25 SER. #'D SETS
87 Victor Wembanyama 1,250.00 2,500.00
288 Victor Wembanyama 2,000.00 4,000.00
311 Victor Wembanyama 1,250.00 2,500.00

2023-24 Select Prizms Tie-Dye Die-Cut
*TIE DYE DIE CUT: 8X TO 20X BASIC
STATED PRINT RUN 25 SER. #'D SETS
121 Victor Wembanyama 1,250.00 2,500.00

2023-24 Select Prizms Tri-Color
*TRI COLOR: .6X TO 1.5X BASIC
87 Victor Wembanyama 40.00 100.00
121 Victor Wembanyama 40.00 100.00

2023-24 Select Prizms White
*WHITE: 4X TO 10X BASIC
STATED PRINT RUN 149 SER.#'d SETS
87 Victor Wembanyama 400.00 800.00
311 Victor Wembanyama 400.00 800.00

2023-24 Select Prizms White Die-Cut
*WHITE DIE-CUT: 4X TO 10X BASIC
STATED PRINT RUN 149 SER.#'d SETS
121 Victor Wembanyama 400.00 800.00

2023-24 Select Prizms White Disco
*PINK: 5X TO 12X BASIC
STATED PRINT RUN 75 SER.#'d SETS
87 Victor Wembanyama 500.00 1,000.00
121 Victor Wembanyama 500.00 1,000.00
288 Victor Wembanyama 1,000.00 2,000.00

2023-24 Select Artistic Selections
1 LeBron James 50.00 120.00
2 Amen Thompson 25.00 60.00
3 Victor Wembanyama 200.00 500.00
4 Luka Doncic 40.00 100.00
5 Brandon Miller 25.00 60.00
6 Ja Morant 25.00 60.00
7 Jayson Tatum 25.00 60.00
8 Stephen Curry 50.00 120.00
9 Scoot Henderson 25.00 60.00
10 Ausar Thompson 20.00 50.00

2023-24 Select Autographed Memorabilia
*PURPLE/99: .5X TO 1.2X BASIC
*BLUE/49: .6X TO 1.5X BASIC
*TIE DYE/15-25: .75X TO 2X BASIC
1 Kristaps Porzingis/125 25.00 60.00
2 Jarred Vanderbilt/199 5.00 12.00
3 Fred VanVleet/99 12.00 30.00
4 Jamal Murray/99 12.00 30.00
5 Keldon Johnson/125 8.00 20.00
6 Onyeka Okongwu/199 5.00 12.00
7 Toni Kukoc/199 12.00 30.00
8 Myles Turner/125 6.00 15.00
9 Clint Capela/199 5.00 12.00
10 Day'Ron Sharpe/199 5.00 12.00
11 Herbert Jones/199 6.00 15.00
12 Dyson Daniels/199 8.00 20.00
13 Tyler Herro/125 20.00 50.00
14 Trey Murphy III/199 8.00 20.00
15 Donte DiVincenzo/199 20.00 50.00
18 Russell Westbrook/125 60.00 150.00
19 Nicolas Batum/199 4.00 10.00
20 Ayo Dosunmu/199 6.00 15.00
21 Jonathan Kuminga/199 15.00 40.00
22 Bruce Brown/199 6.00 15.00
23 Obi Toppin/199 6.00 15.00
24 Gilbert Arenas/99 6.00 15.00
25 Johnny Davis/199 5.00 12.00
26 Kevin McHale/125 20.00 50.00
28 Isaac Okoro/199 5.00 12.00
29 Blake Wesley/199 4.00 10.00

2023-24 Select Color Wheel
1 Jayson Tatum 125.00 300.00
2 Kevin Durant 75.00 200.00
3 Amen Thompson 125.00 300.00
4 Anthony Edwards 200.00 500.00
5 Scoot Henderson 125.00 300.00
6 LaMelo Ball 100.00 250.00
7 Yao Ming 100.00 250.00
8 Tim Duncan 100.00 250.00
9 Trae Young 50.00 120.00
10 Victor Wembanyama 2,000.00 4,000.00
11 Nikola Jokic 100.00 250.00
12 Tyrese Haliburton 100.00 250.00
13 Zion Williamson 60.00 150.00
14 Julius Erving 75.00 200.00
15 Giannis Antetokounmpo 125.00 300.00
16 Shai Gilgeous-Alexander 150.00 400.00
17 Ja Morant 100.00 250.00
18 Brandon Miller 400.00 800.00
19 Larry Bird 100.00 250.00
20 Paolo Banchero 150.00 400.00
21 Luka Doncic 200.00 500.00
22 Ausar Thompson 75.00 200.00
23 Stephen Curry 200.00 500.00
24 Damian Lillard 75.00 200.00
25 LeBron James 200.00 500.00

2023-24 Select Draft Selections Memorabilia
*PURPLE/99: .75X TO 2X BASIC
*BLUE/75: 1X TO 2.5X BASIC
*COPPER/49: 1.25X TO 3X BASIC
*TIE DYE/25: 2X TO 5X BASIC
1 Amen Thompson 10.00 25.00
2 Jalen Pickett 1.50 4.00
3 Kobe Brown 2.00 5.00
4 Cam Whitmore 5.00 12.00
5 Jett Howard 2.50 6.00
6 Taylor Hendricks 2.00 5.00
7 Anthony Black 4.00 10.00
8 Jaime Jaquez Jr. 3.00 8.00
9 Jordan Hawkins 3.00 8.00
10 Kobe Bufkin 2.50 6.00
11 Ausar Thompson 5.00 12.00
12 Kris Murray 2.00 5.00
13 Nick Smith Jr. 2.50 6.00
14 Brandon Miller 8.00 20.00
15 Julian Strawther 2.50 6.00
16 Keyonte George 6.00 15.00
17 Andre Jackson Jr. 3.00 8.00
18 Olivier-Maxence Prosper 2.00 5.00
19 Jarace Walker 4.00 10.00
20 Brandin Podziemski 6.00 15.00
21 Toumani Camara 4.00 10.00
22 Dereck Lively II 4.00 10.00
23 Marcus Sasser 3.00 8.00
24 Gradey Dick 4.00 10.00
25 Scoot Henderson 6.00 15.00
26 Cason Wallace 4.00 10.00
27 Trayce Jackson-Davis 2.50 6.00
28 Colby Jones 2.00 5.00
29 Victor Wembanyama 60.00 150.00
30 Bilal Coulibaly 5.00 12.00

2023-24 Select En Fuego
*SILVER: 1.5X TO 4X BASIC
*TIE-DYE/25: 10X TO 25X BASIC
1 Luka Doncic 6.00 15.00
2 Brandon Miller 4.00 10.00
3 Ja Morant 3.00 8.00
4 Victor Wembanyama 30.00 80.00
5 Nikola Jokic 5.00 12.00
6 Jayson Tatum 4.00 10.00
7 Giannis Antetokounmpo 5.00 12.00
8 Stephen Curry 8.00 20.00
9 Scoot Henderson 3.00 8.00
10 LeBron James 8.00 20.00

2023-24 Select Hall Selections Signatures
1 Dirk Nowitzki
Pau Gasol
Tony Parker 150.00 400.00
2 Grant Hill
Jason Kidd
Steve Nash 150.00 400.00
3 Allen Iverson
Shaquille O'Neal
Yao Ming 600.00 1,200.00
4 Charles Barkley
Dominique Wilkins
Joe Dumars 150.00 400.00
5 Adrian Dantley
Hakeem Olajuwon
Patrick Ewing 125.00 300.00

2023-24 Select In Flight Signatures
*RED/99: .5X TO 1.2X BASIC
*BLUE/15-49: .6X TO 1.5X BASIC
*ORNG PULSAR/30: .75X TO 2X BASIC
*TIE DYE/25: .75X TO 2X BASIC
1 Zion Williamson/75 60.00 150.00
2 Tyrese Maxey/125 40.00 100.00
3 James Wiseman/249 5.00 12.00
4 Tracy McGrady/30 75.00 200.00
5 Khris Middleton/99 6.00 15.00
6 Lonnie Walker IV/149 6.00 15.00
7 Jabari Smith Jr./125 15.00 40.00
8 Isiah Thomas/125 15.00 40.00
9 Mac McClung/125 20.00 50.00
11 Jalen Williams/125 20.00 50.00
12 Andre Drummond/149 5.00 12.00
13 Julius Erving/30 60.00 150.00
14 Jaden Ivey/125 8.00 20.00
15 Steve Francis/125 6.00 15.00
16 Dennis Rodman/125 50.00 120.00
17 Christian Braun/149 6.00 15.00
18 Saddiq Bey/149 6.00 15.00
19 Bennedict Mathurin/125 15.00 40.00
20 Josh Giddey/125 15.00 40.00
22 Peja Stojakovic/125 6.00 15.00
23 Gary Trent Jr./149 6.00 15.00
24 Cazzie Russell/125 6.00 15.00
25 Dominique Wilkins/125 20.00 50.00
26 Scottie Barnes/149 20.00 50.00
27 Jason Terry/125 6.00 15.00
28 Zach LaVine/125 20.00 50.00
30 Hakeem Olajuwon/125 40.00 100.00

2023-24 Select Jumbo Rookie Signature Swatches
*WHITE/49: .6X TO 1.5X BASIC
*ORNG PULSAR/30: .6X TO 1.5X BASIC
*TIE DYE/25: .6X TO 1.5X BASIC
*PRPL PULSAR/15: .6X TO 1.5X BASIC
1 Maxwell Lewis 10.00 25.00
2 Noah Clowney 15.00 40.00
3 Bilal Coulibaly 30.00 80.00
4 Rayan Rupert 12.00 30.00
5 Dereck Lively II 25.00 60.00
6 Julian Phillips 12.00 30.00
7 Keyonte George 50.00 120.00
8 Brandin Podziemski 40.00 100.00
9 Ausar Thompson 30.00 80.00
10 Brice Sensabaugh 20.00 50.00
11 Jordan Walsh 12.00 30.00
12 Colby Jones 12.00 30.00
13 Marcus Sasser 20.00 50.00
14 Kris Murray 12.00 30.00
15 Dariq Whitehead 15.00 40.00
16 GG Jackson II 50.00 120.00
17 Sasha Vezenkov 10.00 25.00
18 Andre Jackson Jr. 20.00 50.00
19 Jalen Pickett 10.00 25.00
20 Leonard Miller 12.00 30.00
21 Olivier-Maxence Prosper 12.00 30.00
22 Kobe Bufkin 15.00 40.00
23 Sidy Cissoko 12.00 30.00
24 Hunter Tyson 12.00 30.00
25 Amen Thompson 60.00 150.00
27 Markquis Nowell 12.00 30.00
28 Cason Wallace 25.00 60.00
29 Julian Strawther 15.00 40.00
30 Kobe Brown 12.00 30.00

2023-24 Select Jumbo Rookie Swatches
*PURPLE/99: .75X TO 2X BASIC
*BLUE/75: 1X TO 2.5X BASIC
*COPPER/49: 1.25X TO 3X BASIC
*TIE DYE/25: 2X TO 5X BASIC
1 Emoni Bates 2.50 6.00
2 Bilal Coulibaly 5.00 12.00
3 Kobe Brown 2.00 5.00
4 Jalen Slawson 2.00 5.00
5 Jaime Jaquez Jr. 3.00 8.00
6 Olivier-Maxence Prosper 2.00 5.00
7 Toumani Camara 4.00 10.00
8 Amen Thompson 10.00 25.00
9 Cason Wallace 4.00 10.00
10 Victor Wembanyama 60.00 150.00
11 Hunter Tyson 2.00 5.00
12 Dariq Whitehead 2.50 6.00
13 Jalen Hood-Schifino 2.00 5.00
14 Brandin Podziemski 6.00 15.00
15 Noah Clowney 2.50 6.00
16 Taylor Hendricks 2.00 5.00
17 Ben Sheppard 2.00 5.00
18 Anthony Black 4.00 10.00
19 Jett Howard 2.50 6.00
20 Andre Jackson Jr. 3.00 8.00
21 Rayan Rupert 2.00 5.00
22 Cam Whitmore 5.00 12.00
23 Gradey Dick 4.00 10.00
24 Amari Bailey 2.00 5.00
25 Nick Smith Jr. 2.50 6.00
26 Brandon Miller 8.00 20.00
27 Ausar Thompson 5.00 12.00
28 Trayce Jackson-Davis 2.50 6.00
29 Dereck Lively II 4.00 10.00
30 Scoot Henderson 6.00 15.00
31 Keyonte George 6.00 15.00
32 Kris Murray 2.00 5.00
33 Julian Phillips 2.00 5.00
34 Jalen Pickett 1.50 4.00
35 Kobe Bufkin 2.50 6.00
36 Jordan Hawkins 3.00 8.00
37 Marcus Sasser 3.00 8.00
38 Julian Strawther 2.50 6.00
39 Colby Jones 2.00 5.00
40 Jarace Walker 4.00 10.00

2023-24 Select Lodestars
*GREEN: .75X TO 2X BASIC
*RED: .75X TO 2X BASIC
*SILVER: .75X TO 2X BASIC
1 Scoot Henderson 2.00 5.00
2 Giannis Antetokounmpo 3.00 8.00
3 Brandon Miller 2.50 6.00
4 LeBron James 5.00 12.00
5 Jayson Tatum 2.50 6.00
6 Stephen Curry 5.00 12.00
7 Luka Doncic 4.00 10.00
8 Nikola Jokic 3.00 8.00
9 Victor Wembanyama 12.00 30.00
10 Ja Morant 2.00 5.00

2023-24 Select Lodestars Pink Cracked Ice Prizms
*PINK CRKD ICE: 2X TO 5X BASIC
STATED PRINT RUN 99 SER. #'D SETS
9 Victor Wembanyama 150.00 400.00

2023-24 Select Lodestars Purple Cracked Ice Prizms
*PURPLE CRKD ICE: 2.5X TO 6X BASIC
STATED PRINT RUN 75 SER. #'D SETS
9 Victor Wembanyama 200.00 500.00

2023-24 Select Lodestars Red Flash Prizms
*RED FLASH: 2X TO 5X BASIC
STATED PRINT RUN 99 SER. #'D SETS
9 Victor Wembanyama 150.00 400.00

2023-24 Select Lodestars Tectonic Prizms
*TECTONIC: .75X TO 2X BASIC
9 Victor Wembanyama 60.00 150.00

2023-24 Select Neon Icon
*GREEN: .75X TO 2X BASIC
*RED: .75X TO 2X BASIC
*SILVER: .75X TO 2X BASIC
1 Giannis Antetokounmpo 3.00 8.00
2 Ausar Thompson 1.50 4.00
3 Jaime Jaquez Jr. 1.00 2.50
4 Stephen Curry 5.00 12.00
5 Anthony Edwards 3.00 8.00
6 Kevin Durant 2.00 5.00
7 Scoot Henderson 2.00 5.00
8 Kawhi Leonard 1.50 4.00
9 Bilal Coulibaly 1.50 4.00
10 Zion Williamson 1.50 4.00
11 Brandon Miller 2.50 6.00
12 LeBron James 5.00 12.00
13 Victor Wembanyama 12.00 30.00
14 Tyrese Haliburton 1.25 3.00
15 Jayson Tatum 2.50 6.00
16 Dereck Lively II 1.25 3.00
17 Damian Lillard 1.50 4.00
18 Trae Young 1.25 3.00
19 Donovan Mitchell 1.25 3.00
20 Amen Thompson 3.00 8.00
21 Luka Doncic 4.00 10.00
22 Anthony Black 1.25 3.00
23 Nikola Jokic 3.00 8.00
24 Ja Morant 2.00 5.00
25 Jordan Hawkins 1.00 2.50

2023-24 Select Neon Icon Pink Cracked Ice Prizms
*PINK CRKD ICE: 2X TO 5X BASIC
STATED PRINT RUN 99 SER. #'D SETS
13 Victor Wembanyama 150.00 400.00

2023-24 Select Neon Icon Purple Cracked Ice Prizms
*PURPLE CRKD ICE: 2.5X TO 6X BASIC
STATED PRINT RUN 75 SER. #'D SETS
13 Victor Wembanyama 200.00 500.00

2023-24 Select Neon Icon Red Flash Prizms
*RED FLASH: 2X TO 5X BASIC
STATED PRINT RUN 99 SER. #'D SETS
13 Victor Wembanyama 150.00 400.00

2023-24 Select Neon Icon Tectonic Prizms
*TECTONIC: .75X TO 2X BASIC
13 Victor Wembanyama 60.00 150.00

2023-24 Select Prime Selections Signatures
*WHITE/49: .6X TO 1.5X BASIC
*ORNG PULSAR/30: .6X TO 1.5X BASIC
*TIE DYE/25: .6X TO 1.5X BASIC
*PRPL PULSAR/15: .6X TO 1.5X BASIC
1 Keyonte George 50.00 120.00
2 Amen Thompson 40.00 100.00
3 Kobe Bufkin 10.00 25.00
4 Dereck Lively II 15.00 40.00
5 Ausar Thompson 20.00 50.00
6 Bilal Coulibaly 20.00 50.00
7 Cason Wallace 15.00 40.00
8 Brandin Podziemski 25.00 60.00
9 Marcus Sasser 12.00 30.00
10 Dariq Whitehead 10.00 25.00
11 Amari Bailey 8.00 20.00
13 Julian Phillips 8.00 20.00
14 Rayan Rupert 8.00 20.00
15 GG Jackson II 50.00 120.00
16 Brice Sensabaugh 12.00 30.00
17 Julian Strawther 10.00 25.00
18 Hunter Tyson 8.00 20.00
19 Olivier-Maxence Prosper 8.00 20.00
20 Kris Murray 8.00 20.00
21 Colby Jones 8.00 20.00
22 Ben Sheppard 8.00 20.00
23 Jordan Walsh 8.00 20.00
24 Maxwell Lewis 6.00 15.00
25 Sasha Vezenkov 6.00 15.00
26 Toumani Camara 15.00 40.00
27 Isaiah Wong 8.00 20.00
28 Jordan Miller 10.00 25.00
29 Vasilije Micic 8.00 20.00
30 Sidy Cissoko 8.00 20.00

2023-24 Select Rookie Jersey Autographs
STATED PRINT RUN 199 COPIES PER
*DISCO: .4X TO 1X BASIC
*RED WAVE: .4X TO 1X BASIC
*PURPLE/99: .5X TO 1.2X BASIC
*BLUE/49: .6X TO 1.5X BASIC
*ORNG PULSAR/30: .75X TO 2X BASIC
*TIE DYE/25: .75X TO 2X BASIC
*PRPL PULSAR/15: .75X TO 2X BASIC
1 Julian Phillips 10.00 25.00
2 D'Moi Hodge 8.00 20.00
3 Bilal Coulibaly 25.00 60.00
4 Jordan Walsh 10.00 25.00
5 Dereck Lively II 20.00 50.00
6 Amari Bailey 10.00 25.00
7 Markquis Nowell 10.00 25.00
8 Brandin Podziemski 30.00 80.00
9 Noah Clowney 12.00 30.00
10 Dariq Whitehead 12.00 30.00
11 Kris Murray 10.00 25.00
12 GG Jackson II 20.00 50.00
13 Kobe Brown 10.00 25.00
15 Colin Castleton 8.00 20.00
16 Jalen Wilson 10.00 25.00
17 Marcus Sasser 15.00 40.00
18 Rayan Rupert 10.00 25.00
19 Jalen Pickett 8.00 20.00
20 Leonard Miller 10.00 25.00
21 Colby Jones 10.00 25.00
22 Amen Thompson 50.00 120.00
23 Filip Petrusev 10.00 25.00
24 Hunter Tyson 10.00 25.00
25 Cason Wallace 20.00 50.00
26 Maxwell Lewis 8.00 20.00
27 Toumani Camara 20.00 50.00
28 Sidy Cissoko 10.00 25.00
29 Olivier-Maxence Prosper 10.00 25.00
30 Keyontae Johnson 10.00 25.00
31 Julian Strawther 12.00 30.00
32 Kobe Bufkin 12.00 30.00
33 Sasha Vezenkov 8.00 20.00
34 Vasilije Micic 10.00 25.00
35 Keyonte George 30.00 80.00
36 Chris Livingston 10.00 25.00
38 Ausar Thompson 25.00 60.00
39 Lester Quinones 8.00 20.00
40 Brice Sensabaugh 15.00 40.00

2023-24 Select Rookie Revolution
*GREEN: .75X TO 2X BASIC
*RED: .75X TO 2X BASIC
*SILVER: .75X TO 2X BASIC
1 Toumani Camara 1.50 4.00
2 Keyonte George 2.50 6.00
3 Jordan Hawkins 1.25 3.00
4 Scoot Henderson 2.50 6.00
5 Brandon Miller 3.00 8.00
6 Nick Smith Jr. 1.00 2.50
7 Dereck Lively II 1.50 4.00
8 Colby Jones .75 2.00
9 Victor Wembanyama 12.00 30.00
10 Jarace Walker 1.50 4.00
11 Taylor Hendricks .75 2.00
12 Ausar Thompson 2.00 5.00
13 Ben Sheppard .75 2.00
14 Amen Thompson 4.00 10.00
15 Olivier-Maxence Prosper .75 2.00
16 Kobe Brown .75 2.00
17 Julian Strawther 1.00 2.50
18 Jett Howard 1.00 2.50
19 Brandin Podziemski 2.50 6.00
20 Kris Murray .75 2.00
21 Kobe Bufkin 1.00 2.50
22 Gradey Dick 1.50 4.00
23 Jaime Jaquez Jr. 1.25 3.00
24 Cam Whitmore 2.00 5.00
25 Jalen Hood-Schifino .75 2.00
26 Bilal Coulibaly 2.00 5.00
27 Marcus Sasser 1.25 3.00
28 Anthony Black 1.50 4.00
29 Cason Wallace 1.50 4.00
30 Dariq Whitehead 1.00 2.50

2023-24 Select Rookie Revolution Pink Cracked Ice Prizms
*PINK CRKD ICE: 2X TO 5X BASIC
STATED PRINT RUN 99 SER. #'D SETS
9 Victor Wembanyama 150.00 400.00

2023-24 Select Rookie Revolution Purple Cracked Ice Prizms
*PURPLE CRKD ICE: 2.5X TO 6X BASIC
STATED PRINT RUN 75 SER. #'D SETS
9 Victor Wembanyama 200.00 500.00

2023-24 Select Rookie Revolution Red Flash Prizms
*RED FLASH: 2X TO 5X BASIC
STATED PRINT RUN 99 SER. #'D SETS
9 Victor Wembanyama 150.00 400.00

2023-24 Select Rookie Revolution Tectonic Prizms
*TECTONIC: .75X TO 2X BASIC
9 Victor Wembanyama 60.00 150.00

2023-24 Select Rookie Signatures
STATED PRINT RUN 125-249 COPIES PER
*DISCO: .5X TO 1.2X BASIC
*RED/99: .5X TO 1.2X BASIC
*BLUE/49: .6X TO 1.5X BASIC
*ORNG PULSAR/30: .75X TO 2X BASIC
*TIE DYE/25: .75X TO 2X BASIC
*PRPL PULSAR/15: 1X TO 2.5X BASIC
1 Markquis Nowell/249 5.00 12.00
2 Ausar Thompson/125 12.00 30.00
3 Colin Castleton/249 4.00 10.00
4 Maxwell Lewis/249 4.00 10.00
5 Julian Strawther/125 6.00 15.00
6 Colby Jones/249 5.00 12.00
7 Keyonte George/125 40.00 100.00
8 GG Jackson II/125 10.00 25.00
9 Noah Clowney/249 6.00 15.00
10 Dariq Whitehead/125 6.00 15.00
11 Amari Bailey/249 5.00 12.00
12 Olivier-Maxence Prosper/125 5.00 12.00
13 Andre Jackson Jr./249 8.00 20.00
14 D'Moi Hodge/249 4.00 10.00
15 Brice Sensabaugh/249 8.00 20.00
16 Dereck Lively II/125 10.00 25.00
17 Kobe Brown/249 5.00 12.00
18 Sidy Cissoko/249 5.00 12.00
19 Vasilije Micic/125 5.00 12.00
20 Leonard Miller/249 5.00 12.00
21 Kobe Bufkin/125 6.00 15.00
23 Marcus Sasser/125 8.00 20.00
24 Hunter Tyson/249 5.00 12.00
25 Jordan Walsh/249 5.00 12.00
26 Cason Wallace/125 10.00 25.00
27 Keyontae Johnson/249 5.00 12.00
28 Rayan Rupert/249 5.00 12.00
29 Brandin Podziemski/125 15.00 40.00
30 Toumani Camara/249 10.00 25.00
31 Jalen Wilson/249 5.00 12.00
32 Kris Murray/125 5.00 12.00
33 Sasha Vezenkov/125 4.00 10.00
34 Jalen Pickett/249 4.00 10.00
35 Amen Thompson/125 25.00 60.00
36 Chris Livingston/249 5.00 12.00
37 Filip Petrusev/249 5.00 12.00
39 Lester Quinones/249 4.00 10.00
40 Bilal Coulibaly/125 12.00 30.00

2023-24 Select Select Certified
*GREEN: .75X TO 2X BASIC
*RED: .75X TO 2X BASIC
*SILVER: .75X TO 2X BASIC
1 Joel Embiid 1.50 4.00
2 Nikola Jokic 3.00 8.00
3 Victor Wembanyama 12.00 30.00
4 Stephen Curry 5.00 12.00
5 Amen Thompson 3.00 8.00
6 Jayson Tatum 2.50 6.00
7 LeBron James 5.00 12.00
8 Anthony Black 1.25 3.00
9 Luka Doncic 4.00 10.00
10 Brandon Miller 2.50 6.00
11 Ausar Thompson 1.50 4.00
12 Zion Williamson 1.50 4.00
13 Giannis Antetokounmpo 3.00 8.00
14 Donovan Mitchell 1.25 3.00
15 LaMelo Ball 1.50 4.00
16 Damian Lillard 1.50 4.00
17 Jordan Hawkins 1.00 2.50
18 Ja Morant 2.00 5.00
19 Scoot Henderson 2.00 5.00
20 Shai Gilgeous-Alexander 3.00 8.00

2023-24 Select Select Certified Pink Cracked Ice Prizms
*PINK CRKD ICE: 2X TO 5X BASIC
STATED PRINT RUN 99 SER. #'D SETS
3 Victor Wembanyama 150.00 400.00

2023-24 Select Select Certified Purple Cracked Ice Prizms
*PURPLE CRKD ICE: 2.5X TO 6X BASIC
STATED PRINT RUN 75 SER. #'D SETS
3 Victor Wembanyama 200.00 500.00

2023-24 Select Select Certified Red Flash Prizms
*RED FLASH: 2X TO 5X BASIC
STATED PRINT RUN 99 SER. #'D SETS
3 Victor Wembanyama 150.00 400.00

2023-24 Select Select Certified Tectonic Prizms
*TECTONIC: .75X TO 2X BASIC
3 Victor Wembanyama 60.00 150.00

2023-24 Select Select Few Signatures
*TIE DYE/25: .75X TO 2X BASIC
1 Kareem Abdul-Jabbar 60.00 150.00
2 Karl Malone 50.00 120.00
3 Kevin Garnett 60.00 150.00
4 John Stockton 40.00 100.00
5 Anfernee Hardaway 50.00 120.00
6 Allen Iverson 60.00 150.00
7 Giannis Antetokounmpo 150.00 400.00
8 Luka Doncic 400.00 800.00
9 Nikola Jokic 125.00 300.00
10 Anthony Edwards 125.00 300.00
11 Damian Lillard 60.00 150.00
12 Paolo Banchero 60.00 150.00
13 Anthony Davis 60.00 150.00

2023-24 Select Select Future
*SILVER: 1.5X TO 4X BASIC
1 Scoot Henderson 2.00 5.00
2 Cason Wallace 1.25 3.00
3 Taylor Hendricks .60 1.50
4 Anthony Black 1.25 3.00
5 Duop Reath .60 1.50
6 GG Jackson II 1.25 3.00
7 Amen Thompson 3.00 8.00
8 Ben Sheppard .60 1.50
9 Marcus Sasser 1.00 2.50
10 Jordan Hawkins 1.00 2.50
11 Brandin Podziemski 2.00 5.00
12 Cam Whitmore 1.50 4.00
13 Victor Wembanyama 15.00 40.00
14 Keyonte George 2.00 5.00
15 Trayce Jackson-Davis .75 2.00
16 Toumani Camara 1.25 3.00
17 Gradey Dick 1.25 3.00
18 Jaime Jaquez Jr. 1.00 2.50
19 Brandon Miller 2.50 6.00
20 Ausar Thompson 1.50 4.00
21 Jarace Walker 1.25 3.00
22 Bilal Coulibaly 1.50 4.00
23 Kobe Bufkin .75 2.00
24 Dereck Lively II 1.25 3.00
25 Julian Strawther .75 2.00

2023-24 Select Select Future Tie-Dye Prizms
*TIE DYE: 12X TO 30X BASIC
STATED PRINT RUN 25 SER. #'D SETS
13 Victor Wembanyama 1,000.00 2,000.00

2023-24 Select Select Pairings Signatures
STATED PRINT RUN 25-49 SER. #'D SETS
*TIE DYE/15-25: .5X TO 1.2X BASIC
1 Stephen Curry
Klay Thompson/25 1,000.00 2,000.00
2 Manu Ginobili
Tony Parker/49 100.00 250.00
3 Dirk Nowitzki
Luka Doncic/49 800.00 1,500.00
4 Russell Westbrook
James Harden/49 200.00 500.00
5 De'Aaron Fox
Domantas Sabonis/49 75.00 200.00
6 Brandon Ingram
CJ McCollum/49 40.00 100.00
7 Rasheed Wallace
Chauncey Billups/49 60.00 150.00
8 John Wall
Gilbert Arenas/49 40.00 100.00
9 Moritz Wagner
Franz Wagner/49 40.00 100.00
10 Yuta Watanabe
Rui Hachimura/49 125.00 300.00
11 Desmond Bane
Jaren Jackson Jr./49 50.00 120.00
12 Robin Lopez
Brook Lopez/49 30.00 80.00
13 Mike Bibby
Peja Stojakovic/49 30.00 80.00
14 Ray Allen
Paul Pierce/49 150.00 400.00
15 Steve Nash
Amar'e Stoudemire/49 75.00 200.00
16 Jabari Smith Jr.
Alperen Sengun/49 50.00 120.00
17 Jordan Clarkson
Lauri Markkanen/49 40.00 100.00
18 Trae Young
Dejounte Murray/49 60.00 150.00
19 Evan Mobley
Isaiah Mobley/49 30.00 80.00
20 Tim Hardaway
Tim Hardaway Jr./49 40.00 100.00

2023-24 Select Selection Committee Signatures
1 Shaquille O'Neal 100.00 250.00
2 Dirk Nowitzki 100.00 250.00
3 Dwyane Wade 50.00 120.00
4 Bob Pettit 20.00 50.00
5 Alonzo Mourning 20.00 50.00
6 Karl Malone 30.00 80.00
7 Anfernee Hardaway 50.00 120.00
8 Derek Fisher 12.00 30.00
9 Isiah Thomas 20.00 50.00
10 Gary Payton 20.00 50.00

2023-24 Select Sensations

*SILVER: 1.25X TO 3X BASIC
1 Tyrese Maxey 1.50 4.00
2 Jalen Brunson 1.50 4.00
3 Dereck Lively II 1.50 4.00
4 Ausar Thompson 2.00 5.00
5 Trae Young 1.50 4.00
6 Amen Thompson 4.00 10.00
7 Victor Wembanyama 20.00 50.00
8 Devin Booker 2.00 5.00
9 Franz Wagner 1.25 3.00
10 Tyler Herro 1.25 3.00
11 Lauri Markkanen 1.25 3.00
12 Jaime Jaquez Jr. 1.25 3.00
13 Bilal Coulibaly 2.00 5.00
14 Cade Cunningham 2.00 5.00
15 Anthony Edwards 4.00 10.00
16 LaMelo Ball 2.00 5.00
17 Brandon Miller 3.00 8.00
18 Scoot Henderson 2.50 6.00
19 Keyonte George 2.50 6.00
20 Scottie Barnes 1.00 2.50
21 De'Aaron Fox 1.50 4.00
22 Cameron Thomas 1.00 2.50
23 Tyrese Haliburton 1.50 4.00
24 Jordan Hawkins 1.25 3.00
25 Shai Gilgeous-Alexander 4.00 10.00

2023-24 Select Sensations Tie-Dye Prizms

*TIE-DYE: 10X TO 25X BASIC
STATED PRINT RUN 25 SER. #'D SETS
7 Victor Wembanyama 1,000.00 2,000.00

2023-24 Select Signature Selections

*RED FLASH/49: .6X TO 1.5X BASIC
*WHITE CRKD ICE/25: .75X TO 2X BASIC
*TECTONIC/15: .75X TO 2X BASIC
1 Ousmane Dieng 5.00 12.00
2 Jalen McDaniels 4.00 10.00
3 Larry Nance Jr. 3.00 8.00
4 JT Thor 4.00 10.00
5 Jose Alvarado 5.00 12.00
6 Seth Curry 5.00 12.00
7 Dave Bing 6.00 15.00
8 Orlando Robinson 3.00 8.00
9 Drew Eubanks 3.00 8.00
10 Udonis Haslem 5.00 12.00
11 Ty Jerome 3.00 8.00
12 Xavier Tillman 5.00 12.00
13 Ish Smith 4.00 10.00
14 Sam Merrill 5.00 12.00
15 Patty Mills 5.00 12.00
16 Sam Hauser 10.00 25.00
17 Nate Archibald 6.00 15.00
18 Oshae Brissett 4.00 10.00
19 Day'Ron Sharpe 4.00 10.00
21 Isaac Okoro 4.00 10.00
22 Georges Niang 3.00 8.00
23 Chuma Okeke 4.00 10.00
24 Gary Harris 4.00 10.00
25 Thanasis Antetokounmpo 5.00 12.00
26 Keita Bates-Diop 4.00 10.00
27 Justin Holiday 4.00 10.00
28 Amir Coffey 3.00 8.00
29 Mark Williams 5.00 12.00
30 E.J. Liddell 4.00 10.00
31 Wendell Moore Jr. 4.00 10.00
32 Scotty Pippen Jr. 5.00 12.00
33 Usman Garuba 4.00 10.00
34 Christian Koloko 4.00 10.00
35 Ryan Rollins 5.00 12.00
36 John Konchar 4.00 10.00
37 Torrey Craig 4.00 10.00
40 Johnny Juzang 3.00 8.00
41 Sandro Mamukelashvili 5.00 12.00
42 Moses Brown 3.00 8.00
44 Matt Ryan 4.00 10.00
45 Damian Jones 4.00 10.00
46 Brian Scalabrine 4.00 10.00
47 Outtino Mobley 4.00 10.00
48 Tom Van Arsdale 5.00 12.00
49 Aaron Wiggins 4.00 10.00
50 Dan Majerle 5.00 12.00

2023-24 Select Signatures

STATED PRINT RUN B/WN 75-249 COPIES PER
*RED/99: .5X TO 1.2X BASIC
1 Rick Barry/149 6.00 15.00
2 Chris Paul/149 25.00 60.00
3 Ben Simmons/249 5.00 12.00
4 Gabe Vincent/249 5.00 12.00
6 Kerry Kittles/249 4.00 10.00
7 Jusuf Nurkic/249 5.00 12.00
8 Jaden Hardy/249 6.00 15.00
9 Josh Green/249 4.00 10.00
10 Carlos Boozer/149 4.00 10.00
11 Ben Wallace/149 6.00 15.00
12 Jalen Duren/249 6.00 15.00
13 Ochai Agbaji/249 5.00 12.00
14 Jason Williams/149 20.00 50.00
15 Bojan Bogdanovic/249 5.00 12.00
16 Ja Morant/75 75.00 200.00
17 Jordan Poole/149 8.00 20.00
18 Al Horford/249 5.00 12.00
19 Dorian Finney-Smith/249 4.00 10.00
20 Keegan Murray/149 6.00 15.00
21 Cade Cunningham/149 40.00 100.00
22 Quentin Grimes/249 5.00 12.00
23 RJ Barrett/125 8.00 20.00
24 Andrew Wiggins/125 6.00 15.00
25 Metta World Peace/125 5.00 12.00
27 Steven Adams/249 5.00 12.00
28 Jalen Suggs/249 6.00 15.00
29 Talen Horton-Tucker/249 4.00 10.00
30 Donovan Mitchell/75 25.00 60.00

2023-24 Select Signatures Blue Prizms

*BLUE: .6X TO 1.5X BASIC
STATED PRINT RUN 15-49 SER. #'D SETS
16 Ja Morant 100.00 250.00
30 Donovan Mitchell 30.00 80.00

2023-24 Select Signatures Neon Orange Pulsar Prizms FOTL

*ORNG PULSAR FOTL: .75X TO 2X BASIC
STATED PRINT RUN 30 SER. #'D SETS
16 Ja Morant 125.00 300.00

2023-24 Select Signatures Tie-Dye Prizms

*TIE DYE: .75X TO 2X BASIC
STATED PRINT RUN 25 SER. #'D SETS
16 Ja Morant 125.00 300.00

2023-24 Select Snapshots

1 Kevin Durant 2.00 5.00
2 Shai Gilgeous-Alexander 3.00 8.00
3 Jayson Tatum 2.50 6.00
4 Brandon Miller 2.50 6.00
5 Damian Lillard 1.50 4.00
6 Luka Doncic 4.00 10.00
7 Nikola Jokic 3.00 8.00
8 Amen Thompson 3.00 8.00
9 Tyrese Maxey 1.25 3.00
10 Scoot Henderson 2.00 5.00
11 Vince Carter 1.25 3.00
12 LeBron James 5.00 12.00
13 Stephen Curry 5.00 12.00
14 Giannis Antetokounmpo 3.00 8.00
15 Tim Duncan 1.50 4.00
16 Ja Morant 2.00 5.00
17 Victor Wembanyama 15.00 40.00
18 Tyrese Haliburton 1.25 3.00
19 Ausar Thompson 1.50 4.00
20 Yao Ming 1.50 4.00

2023-24 Select Snapshots Silver Prizms

*SILVER: 1.25X TO 3X BASIC
17 Victor Wembanyama 125.00 300.00

2023-24 Select Snapshots Tie-Dye Prizms

*TIE DYE: 10X TO 25X BASIC
STATED PRINT RUN 25 SER. #'D SETS
4 Brandon Miller 125.00 300.00
17 Victor Wembanyama 1,000.00 2,000.00

2023-24 Select Sparks Memorabilia

*PURPLE/99: .75X TO 2X BASIC
*BLUE/75: 1X TO 2.5X BASIC
*COPPER/49: 1.25X TO 3X BASIC
1 Scoot Henderson 6.00 15.00
2 Ausar Thompson 5.00 12.00
3 Jordan Hawkins 3.00 8.00
4 Cason Wallace 4.00 10.00
5 Brandon Miller 8.00 20.00
6 Bilal Coulibaly 5.00 12.00
7 Victor Wembanyama 75.00 200.00
8 Keyonte George 6.00 15.00
9 Anthony Black 4.00 10.00
10 Amen Thompson 10.00 25.00

2023-24 Select Sparks Tie-Dye Prizms

*TIE DYE/25: 2X TO 5X BASIC
STATED PRINT RUN 25 SER. #'D SETS
5 Brandon Miller 75.00 200.00
7 Victor Wembanyama 800.00 1,500.00

2023-24 Select Starcade

1 Jordan Hawkins 8.00 20.00
2 Amen Thompson 25.00 60.00
3 Damian Lillard 12.00 30.00
4 Anthony Edwards 40.00 100.00
5 Victor Wembanyama 300.00 600.00
6 Cason Wallace 10.00 25.00
7 Ja Morant 15.00 40.00
8 Donovan Mitchell 10.00 25.00
9 Brandon Miller 75.00 200.00
10 De'Aaron Fox 10.00 25.00
11 Tyrese Maxey 10.00 25.00
12 Kevin Durant 15.00 40.00
13 Gradey Dick 10.00 25.00
14 LeBron James 40.00 100.00
15 Zion Williamson 12.00 30.00
16 Zach LaVine 8.00 20.00
17 Luka Doncic 30.00 80.00
18 Ausar Thompson 12.00 30.00
19 Giannis Antetokounmpo 25.00 60.00
20 Bilal Coulibaly 12.00 30.00
21 Trae Young 10.00 25.00
22 Jayson Tatum 20.00 50.00
23 Scoot Henderson 15.00 40.00
24 Kyrie Irving 10.00 25.00
25 Anthony Black 10.00 25.00
26 Stephen Curry 40.00 100.00
27 Tyrese Haliburton 10.00 25.00
28 Joel Embiid 12.00 30.00
29 Nikola Jokic 25.00 60.00
30 Shai Gilgeous-Alexander 25.00 60.00

2023-24 Select Throwback Memorabilia

*PURPLE/99: .75X TO 2X BASIC
*BLUE/75: 1X TO 2.5X BASIC
*COPPER/49: 1.25X TO 3X BASIC
*TIE DYE/25: 2X TO 5X BASIC
1 LeBron James 40.00 100.00
2 Jimmy Butler 4.00 10.00
3 Shai Gilgeous-Alexander 12.00 30.00
4 Derrick Rose 4.00 10.00
5 Kyrie Irving 5.00 12.00
6 Kawhi Leonard 6.00 15.00
8 Buddy Hield 2.50 6.00
9 Gordon Hayward 2.50 6.00
10 DeAndre Jordan 2.00 5.00
11 Aaron Gordon 2.50 6.00
12 Julius Randle 3.00 8.00
13 Mikal Bridges 3.00 8.00
14 DeMar DeRozan 4.00 10.00
15 Cameron Johnson 2.50 6.00
16 Jerami Grant 3.00 8.00
17 Kevin Durant 8.00 20.00
18 Mike Conley 2.00 5.00
19 Rudy Gobert 3.00 8.00
20 Cam Reddish 2.00 5.00

2023-24 Select Thunder Lane

*GREEN: .75X TO 2X BASIC
1 Zion Williamson 2.00 5.00
2 Zach LaVine 1.25 3.00
3 Luka Doncic 5.00 12.00
4 Giannis Antetokounmpo 4.00 10.00
5 Victor Wembanyama 12.00 30.00
6 Nikola Jokic 4.00 10.00
7 Ja Morant 2.50 6.00
8 LeBron James 6.00 15.00
9 Ausar Thompson 2.00 5.00
10 Stephen Curry 6.00 15.00
11 Shai Gilgeous-Alexander 4.00 10.00
12 Brandon Miller 3.00 8.00
13 Amen Thompson 4.00 10.00
14 Jayson Tatum 3.00 8.00
15 Scoot Henderson 2.50 6.00

2023-24 Select Thunder Lane Pink Cracked Ice Prizms

*PINK CRKD ICE: 2X TO 5X BASIC
STATED PRINT RUN 99 SER. #'D SETS
5 Victor Wembanyama 400.00 800.00

2023-24 Select Thunder Lane Purple Cracked Ice Prizms

*PURPLE CRKD ICE: 2.5X TO 6X BASIC
STATED PRINT RUN 75 SER. #'D SETS
5 Victor Wembanyama 500.00 1,000.00

2023-24 Select Thunder Lane Red Flash Prizms

*RED FLASH: 2X TO 5X BASIC
STATED PRINT RUN 99 SER. #'D SETS
5 Victor Wembanyama 400.00 800.00

2023-24 Select Thunder Lane Red Prizms

*RED: .75X TO 2X BASIC
5 Victor Wembanyama 40.00 100.00

2023-24 Select Thunder Lane Silver Prizms

*SILVER: .75X TO 2X BASIC
5 Victor Wembanyama 40.00 100.00

2023-24 Select Thunder Lane Tectonic Prizms

*TECTONIC: .75X TO 2X BASIC
5 Victor Wembanyama 60.00 150.00

2023-24 Select Top Shelf Signatures

*TIE DYE/25: .75X TO 2X BASIC
1 Amen Thompson 30.00 80.00
2 Ausar Thompson 30.00 80.00
3 Cason Wallace 12.00 30.00
4 Keyonte George 40.00 100.00
5 Dereck Lively II 12.00 30.00
6 Brandin Podziemski 30.00 80.00
7 Anthony Davis 60.00 150.00
8 Luka Doncic 300.00 600.00
9 Anthony Edwards 125.00 300.00
10 Giannis Antetokounmpo 200.00 500.00
11 Nikola Jokic 125.00 300.00
12 Ja Morant 75.00 200.00
13 Stephen Curry 300.00 600.00
14 Magic Johnson 60.00 150.00
15 Shaquille O'Neal 75.00 200.00
16 Larry Bird 60.00 150.00
17 Carmelo Anthony 60.00 150.00

2023-24 Select Unstoppable

*SILVER: 1.25X TO 3X BASIC
*TIE-DYE/25: 10X TO 25X BASIC
1 James Harden 1.25 3.00
2 Stephen Curry 5.00 12.00
3 Kevin Durant 2.00 5.00
4 Jimmy Butler 1.00 2.50
5 Donovan Mitchell 1.25 3.00
6 Damian Lillard 1.50 4.00
7 Trae Young 1.25 3.00
8 Giannis Antetokounmpo 3.00 8.00
9 Anthony Davis 1.50 4.00
10 Joel Embiid 1.50 4.00
11 De'Aaron Fox 1.25 3.00
12 Jayson Tatum 2.50 6.00
13 Ja Morant 2.00 5.00
14 LeBron James 5.00 12.00
15 Zion Williamson 1.50 4.00
16 Nikola Jokic 3.00 8.00
17 Anthony Edwards 3.00 8.00
18 Luka Doncic 4.00 10.00
19 Kyrie Irving 1.25 3.00
20 Tyrese Haliburton 1.25 3.00

2023-24 Select X-Factor Memorabilia Signatures

*PURPLE/99: .5X TO 1.2X BASIC
*BLUE/49: .5X TO 1.2X BASIC
*TIE DYE/25: .6X TO 1.5X BASIC
1 Shaedon Sharpe 15.00 40.00
3 Michael Porter Jr. 10.00 25.00
4 Karl-Anthony Towns 12.00 30.00
5 Cameron Thomas 10.00 25.00
6 Immanuel Quickley 8.00 20.00
7 Franz Wagner 12.00 30.00
8 John Wall 10.00 25.00
9 Lauri Markkanen 12.00 30.00
10 Jalen Green 12.00 30.00
12 JJ Redick 8.00 20.00
13 Jrue Holiday 25.00 60.00
14 Deandre Ayton 8.00 20.00
15 Maurice Cheeks 8.00 20.00
16 Josh Hart 8.00 20.00
17 D'Angelo Russell 8.00 20.00
18 Bradley Beal 10.00 25.00
20 Jordan Clarkson 8.00 20.00
21 Tony Parker 25.00 60.00
23 Alperen Sengun 12.00 30.00
24 Dennis Schroder 8.00 20.00
25 Jalen Brunson 60.00 150.00
26 Nikola Vucevic 8.00 20.00
27 Evan Mobley 12.00 30.00
28 Davion Mitchell 6.00 15.00
30 Jeff Hornacek 6.00 15.00

2023-24 Select Youth Explosion Signatures

*RED FLASH/49: .6X TO 1.5X BASIC
*WHITE CRKD ICE/25: .75X TO 2X BASIC
*TECTONIC/15: .75X TO 2X BASIC
1 Terquavion Smith 5.00 12.00
2 Adama Sanogo 5.00 12.00
3 Bilal Coulibaly 12.00 30.00
4 Ausar Thompson 12.00 30.00
5 Dereck Lively II 10.00 25.00
6 Kobe Bufkin 6.00 15.00
7 Ricky Council IV 6.00 15.00
8 Brandin Podziemski 15.00 40.00
9 Noah Clowney 6.00 15.00
10 Amen Thompson 25.00 60.00
11 Kris Murray 5.00 12.00
12 Olivier-Maxence Prosper 5.00 12.00
13 Marcus Sasser 8.00 20.00
15 Brice Sensabaugh 8.00 20.00
16 Julian Strawther 6.00 15.00
19 Jalen Pickett 4.00 10.00
21 Colby Jones 5.00 12.00
24 Hunter Tyson 5.00 12.00
25 Jordan Walsh 5.00 12.00
26 Maxwell Lewis 4.00 10.00
28 Rayan Rupert 5.00 12.00
29 GG Jackson II 10.00 25.00
30 Keyontae Johnson 5.00 12.00
32 Amari Bailey 5.00 12.00
33 Sasha Vezenkov 4.00 10.00
34 Vasilije Micic 5.00 12.00
35 Markquis Nowell 5.00 12.00
36 Chris Livingston 5.00 12.00
37 Filip Petrusev 5.00 12.00
38 D'Moi Hodge 4.00 10.00
39 Lester Quinones 4.00 10.00
40 Colin Castleton 4.00 10.00

2024 Select WNBA

1 Elena Delle Donne .75 2.00
2 Alyssa Thomas .60 1.50
3 Brittney Sykes .40 1.00
4 Jaelyn Brown RC .60 1.50
5 Angel Reese RC 2.00 5.00
6 Jewell Loyd .60 1.50
7 Stephanie Soares .30 .75
8 Napheesa Collier 1.25 3.00
9 Stefanie Dolson .40 1.00
10 Kalani Brown .30 .75
11 Betnijah Laney-Hamilton .40 1.00
12 Skylar Diggins-Smith .60 1.50
13 Breanna Stewart 1.50 4.00
14 Jonquel Jones .75 2.00
15 Maya Moore .75 2.00
16 Celeste Taylor RC .75 2.00
17 Shakira Austin .40 1.00
18 DiJonai Carrington .50 1.25
19 Erica Wheeler .50 1.25
20 Dawn Staley .75 2.00
21 Kahleah Copper .60 1.50
22 Kate Martin RC 2.00 5.00
23 Marine Johannes .60 1.50
24 Isabelle Harrison .40 1.00
25 Diamond Miller .40 1.00
26 Tamika Catchings .60 1.50
27 Nika Muhl RC 1.50 4.00
28 Ivana Dojkic .50 1.25
29 Chennedy Carter .30 .75
30 Sue Bird 1.25 3.00
31 Tyasha Harris .40 1.00
32 Natasha Howard .50 1.25
33 Kamilla Cardoso RC 1.25 3.00
34 Alissa Pili RC .75 2.00
35 Crystal Dangerfield .30 .75
36 Aaliyah Edwards RC .75 2.00
37 Natasha Cloud .50 1.25
38 Jackie Young .75 2.00
39 Satou Sabally .60 1.50
40 Sydney Colson .40 1.00
41 Marquesha Davis RC .60 1.50
42 Ezi Magbegor .50 1.25
43 Alysha Clark .40 1.00
44 Tiffany Mitchell .30 .75
45 Arike Ogunbowale .75 2.00
46 Diana Taurasi 1.25 3.00
47 Zia Cooke .30 .75
48 DeWanna Bonner .60 1.50
49 NaLyssa Smith .30 .75
50 Grace Berger .40 1.00
51 Allisha Gray .50 1.25
52 Aliyah Boston 1.25 3.00
53 Lou Lopez Senechal .30 .75
54 Courtney Williams .50 1.25
55 Haley Jones .30 .75
56 Cameron Brink RC 3.00 8.00
57 Julie Vanloo RC .75 2.00
58 Rickea Jackson RC 1.50 4.00
59 DiDi Richards .30 .75
60 Jacy Sheldon RC 1.25 3.00
61 Maddy Siegrist .40 1.00
62 Cheyenne Parker-Tyus .30 .75
63 Sabrina Ionescu 1.25 3.00
64 Ariel Atkins .50 1.25
65 Rhyne Howard .60 1.50
66 Nyara Sabally .40 1.00
67 Lexie Brown .50 1.25
68 Brittney Griner 1.00 2.50
69 Dorka Juhasz .60 1.50
70 Aerial Powers .30 .75
71 Sophie Cunningham 1.00 2.50
72 Caitlin Clark RC 10.00 25.00
73 Dana Evans .40 1.00
74 Li Yueru .50 1.25
75 Kelsey Plum 1.25 3.00
76 Sheryl Swoopes .60 1.50
77 Dearica Hamby .50 1.25
78 Courtney Vandersloot .50 1.25
79 Lexie Hull .75 2.00
80 Cynthia Cooper-Dyke .60 1.50
81 Katie Lou Samuelson .60 1.50
82 Jordan Horston .40 1.00
83 Tina Charles .50 1.25
84 Kayla McBride .50 1.25
85 Cheryl Miller .75 2.00
86 A'ja Wilson 1.50 4.00
87 Kelsey Mitchell 1.00 2.50
88 Brionna Jones .50 1.25
89 Lauren Jackson .75 2.00
90 Nneka Ogwumike .50 1.25
91 Aari McDonald .40 1.00
92 Moriah Jefferson .30 .75
93 Jordin Canada .40 1.00
94 Chelsea Gray .40 1.00
95 Marina Mabrey .50 1.25
96 Nancy Lieberman .60 1.50
97 Lisa Leslie .75 2.00
98 Kristi Toliver .50 1.25
99 Karlie Samuelson .40 1.00
100 Diamond DeShields .40 1.00
101 Katie Douglas .50 1.25
102 Alysha Clark .40 1.00
103 Ivana Dojkic .50 1.25
104 Jordan Horston .40 1.00
105 Kelsey Plum 1.25 3.00
106 Brittney Sykes .40 1.00
107 Tina Charles .50 1.25
108 Maya Moore .75 2.00
109 Natasha Howard .50 1.25
110 Kalani Brown .30 .75
111 Nyara Sabally .40 1.00
112 Diamond DeShields .40 1.00
113 DiDi Richards .30 .75
114 Allisha Gray .50 1.25
115 Natasha Cloud .50 1.25
116 Li Yueru .50 1.25
117 Dorka Juhasz .60 1.50
118 Kelsey Mitchell 1.00 2.50
119 NaLyssa Smith .30 .75
120 Lou Lopez Senechal .30 .75
121 Moriah Jefferson .30 .75
122 Aari McDonald .40 1.00
123 Elena Delle Donne .75 2.00
124 Napheesa Collier 1.25 3.00
125 Katie Lou Samuelson .60 1.50
126 Aliyah Boston 1.25 3.00
127 Rickea Jackson 1.50 4.00
128 Celeste Taylor .75 2.00
129 DeWanna Bonner .60 1.50
130 Aaliyah Edwards .75 2.00
131 Crystal Dangerfield .30 .75
132 Karlie Samuelson .40 1.00
133 Lauren Jackson .75 2.00
134 Jacy Sheldon 1.25 3.00
135 Ruthie Bolton .40 1.00
136 Betnijah Laney-Hamilton .40 1.00
137 Brittney Griner 1.00 2.50
138 Chelsea Gray .40 1.00
139 Shakira Austin .40 1.00
140 Rhyne Howard .60 1.50
141 Lisa Leslie .75 2.00
142 Jewell Loyd .60 1.50
143 Lexie Hull .75 2.00
144 Kate Martin 2.00 5.00
145 Aerial Powers .30 .75
146 Dana Evans .40 1.00
147 Angel Reese 2.00 5.00
148 Sydney Colson .40 1.00
149 Nneka Ogwumike .50 1.25
150 Sue Bird 1.25 3.00
151 Caitlin Clark 15.00 40.00
152 Erica Wheeler .50 1.25
153 Ariel Atkins .50 1.25
154 Maddy Siegrist .40 1.00
155 Arike Ogunbowale .75 2.00
156 Dawn Staley .75 2.00
157 Grace Berger .40 1.00
158 A'ja Wilson 1.50 4.00
159 Marquesha Davis .40 1.00
160 Julie Vanloo .75 2.00
161 Marine Johannes .60 1.50
162 Nika Muhl 1.50 4.00
163 Courtney Williams .50 1.25
164 Cynthia Cooper-Dyke .60 1.50
165 Haley Jones .30 .75
166 Jonquel Jones .75 2.00
167 Ezi Magbegor .50 1.25
168 Temi Fagbenle .40 1.00
169 Diamond Miller .40 1.00
170 Alissa Pili .75 2.00
171 Kristi Toliver .50 1.25
172 Alyssa Thomas .60 1.50
173 Emily Engstler .40 1.00
174 Sabrina Ionescu 1.25 3.00
175 Cheyenne Parker-Tyus .30 .75
176 Kayla McBride .50 1.25
177 Sevgi Uzun RC .60 1.50
178 Kahleah Copper .60 1.50
179 Kiah Stokes .40 1.00
180 Jackie Young .75 2.00
181 Jaelyn Brown .60 1.50
182 Isabelle Harrison .40 1.00
183 Sheryl Swoopes .60 1.50
184 Tamika Catchings .60 1.50
185 Breanna Stewart 1.50 4.00
186 Courtney Vandersloot .50 1.25
187 Zia Cooke .30 .75
188 Diana Taurasi 1.25 3.00
189 Tiffany Mitchell .30 .75
190 Marina Mabrey .50 1.25
191 Cameron Brink 3.00 8.00
192 Brionna Jones .50 1.25
193 Skylar Diggins-Smith .60 1.50
194 DiJonai Carrington .50 1.25
195 Kamilla Cardoso 1.25 3.00
196 Sophie Cunningham 1.00 2.50
197 Satou Sabally .60 1.50
198 Jordin Canada .40 1.00
199 Chennedy Carter .30 .75
200 Lexie Brown .50 1.25
201 DeWanna Bonner 1.25 3.00
202 Angel Reese 5.00 12.00
203 Rhyne Howard 1.25 3.00
204 Megan Gustafson .75 2.00
205 Kelsey Plum 2.50 6.00
206 Arike Ogunbowale 1.50 4.00
207 Kamilla Cardoso 3.00 8.00
208 Jackie Young 1.50 4.00
209 Kate Martin 5.00 12.00
210 Aaliyah Edwards 2.00 5.00
211 Marquesha Davis .75 2.00
212 Jewell Loyd 1.25 3.00
213 Sophie Cunningham 2.00 5.00
214 Angel McCoughtry .75 2.00
215 Kahleah Copper 1.25 3.00
216 Dawn Staley 1.50 4.00
217 Alissa Pili 2.00 5.00
218 Caitlin Clark 60.00 150.00
219 Marine Johannes 1.25 3.00
220 Ticha Penicheiro 1.00 2.50
221 Nika Muhl 4.00 10.00
222 Alanna Smith 1.25 3.00
223 Ruth Riley 1.00 2.50
224 Rebecca Allen 1.25 3.00
225 Brittney Griner 2.00 5.00
226 Satou Sabally 1.25 3.00
227 Napheesa Collier 2.50 6.00
228 Cameron Brink 8.00 20.00
229 Marina Mabrey 1.00 2.50
230 Teresa Edwards 1.00 2.50
231 Cynthia Cooper-Dyke 1.25 3.00
232 Lexie Hull 1.50 4.00
233 DiJonai Carrington 1.00 2.50
234 Aliyah Boston 2.50 6.00
235 Rickea Jackson 4.00 10.00
236 Lauren Jackson 1.50 4.00
237 Kierstan Bell .60 1.50
238 Natasha Cloud 1.00 2.50
239 Jonquel Jones 1.50 4.00
240 Jacy Sheldon 3.00 8.00
241 Sheryl Swoopes 1.25 3.00
242 Chelsea Gray .75 2.00
243 A'ja Wilson 3.00 8.00
244 Sue Bird 2.50 6.00
245 Maya Moore 1.50 4.00
246 Elena Delle Donne 1.50 4.00
247 Breanna Stewart 3.00 8.00
248 Sabrina Ionescu 2.50 6.00
249 Lisa Leslie 1.50 4.00
250 Diana Taurasi 2.50 6.00

2024 Select WNBA Bronze Checker Prizms

*BRONZE CHECKER/49: 5X TO 12X BASIC
72 Caitlin Clark 500.00 1,000.00
151 Caitlin Clark 500.00 1,000.00

2024 Select WNBA Green Ice Prizms

*GREEN ICE: 2X TO 5X BASIC
72 Caitlin Clark 150.00 400.00
151 Caitlin Clark 150.00 400.00
218 Caitlin Clark 400.00 800.00
228 Cameron Brink 60.00 150.00

2024 Select WNBA Light Blue Disco Prizms

*LIGHT BLUE DISCO/125: 3X TO 8X BASIC
72 Caitlin Clark 300.00 600.00

2024 Select WNBA Neon Green Prizms

*NEON GREEN/75: 4X TO 10X BASIC
72 Caitlin Clark 400.00 800.00
151 Caitlin Clark 400.00 800.00

2024 Select WNBA Orange Prizms

*ORANGE/125: 2.5X TO 6X BASIC
151 Caitlin Clark 200.00 500.00

2024 Select WNBA Pink and Purple Prizms

*PINK & PURPLE/99: 4X TO 10X BASIC
72 Caitlin Clark 400.00 800.00
151 Caitlin Clark 400.00 800.00

2024 Select WNBA Pink Ice Prizms

*PINK ICE: 1X TO 2.5X BASIC
72 Caitlin Clark 75.00 200.00
151 Caitlin Clark 75.00 200.00
218 Caitlin Clark 150.00 400.00

2024 Select WNBA Purple Ice Prizms

*PURPLE ICE/149: 2.5X TO 6X BASIC
72 Caitlin Clark 200.00 500.00
151 Caitlin Clark 200.00 500.00
218 Caitlin Clark 400.00 800.00
228 Cameron Brink 75.00 200.00

2024 Select WNBA Purple Prizms

*PURPLE/149: 2.5X TO 6X BASIC
151 Caitlin Clark 200.00 500.00

2024 Select WNBA Red and Blue Prizms

*RED & BLUE/399: 2X TO 5X BASIC
72 Caitlin Clark 150.00 400.00
151 Caitlin Clark 150.00 400.00

2024 Select WNBA Red Ice Prizms

*RED ICE: 1.25X TO 3X BASIC
72 Caitlin Clark 75.00 200.00
151 Caitlin Clark 75.00 200.00
218 Caitlin Clark 200.00 500.00
228 Cameron Brink 40.00 100.00

2024 Select WNBA Red Prizms

*RED/149: 2.5X TO 6X BASIC
72 Caitlin Clark 200.00 500.00

2024 Select WNBA Silver Flash Prizms

*SILVER FLASH: 1.25X TO 3X BASIC
72 Caitlin Clark 75.00 200.00
151 Caitlin Clark 75.00 200.00
218 Caitlin Clark 400.00 800.00
228 Cameron Brink 75.00 200.00

2024 Select WNBA Silver Prizms

*SILVER: 1.25X TO 3X BASIC
72 Caitlin Clark 40.00 100.00
151 Caitlin Clark 75.00 200.00
218 Caitlin Clark 400.00 800.00
228 Cameron Brink 60.00 150.00

2024 Select WNBA Tie-Dye Prizms

*TIE-DYE/25: 8X TO 20X BASIC
72 Caitlin Clark 800.00 1,500.00
151 Caitlin Clark 800.00 1,500.00
218 Caitlin Clark 1,250.00 2,500.00
228 Cameron Brink 300.00 600.00

2024 Select WNBA White Prizms

*WHITE/99: 4X TO 10X BASIC
72 Caitlin Clark 400.00 800.00
151 Caitlin Clark 400.00 800.00

2024 Select WNBA All-Stars

*FLASH: .75X TO 2X BASIC
*SILVER: .75X TO 2X BASIC
1 Satou Sabally .75 2.00
2 Chelsea Gray .50 1.25
3 Rhyne Howard .75 2.00
4 Elena Delle Donne 1.00 2.50
5 Napheesa Collier 1.50 4.00
6 Arike Ogunbowale 1.00 2.50
7 Brittney Griner 1.25 3.00
8 Aliyah Boston 1.50 4.00
9 Skylar Diggins-Smith .75 2.00
10 Diana Taurasi 1.50 4.00
11 Angel Reese 1.50 4.00
12 Nneka Ogwumike .60 1.50
13 Lisa Leslie 1.00 2.50
14 Courtney Vandersloot .60 1.50
15 Caitlin Clark 20.00 50.00

2024 Select WNBA All-Stars Blue Flash Prizms

*BLUE FLASH/99: 1.5X TO 4X BASIC
15 Caitlin Clark 125.00 300.00

2024 Select WNBA All-Stars Blue Prizms

*BLUE/49: 2.5X TO 6X BASIC
15 Caitlin Clark 200.00 500.00

2024 Select WNBA All-Stars Tie Dye Prizms

*TIE-DYE/25: 5X TO 12X BASIC
15 Caitlin Clark 500.00 1,000.00

2024 Select WNBA All-Stars White Disco Prizms

*WHITE DISCO/75: 2X TO 5X BASIC
15 Caitlin Clark 150.00 400.00

2024 Select WNBA Autographed Memorabilia

*PURPLE/99: .5X TO 1.2X BASIC
*BLUE/49: .6X TO 1.5X BASIC
*TIE-DYE/25: .75X TO 2X BASIC
1 Cameron Brink 75.00 200.00
2 Jackie Young 20.00 50.00
3 Jewell Loyd 15.00 40.00
4 Brittney Griner 25.00 60.00
5 Jacy Sheldon 20.00 50.00
6 Nika Muhl 25.00 60.00
7 Sue Bird 30.00 80.00
8 Maya Moore 20.00 50.00
9 Kamilla Cardoso 20.00 50.00
10 Diana Taurasi 30.00 80.00
11 Arike Ogunbowale 20.00 50.00
12 Chelsea Gray 10.00 25.00
13 A'ja Wilson 40.00 100.00
14 Marine Johannes 15.00 40.00
15 Aliyah Boston 30.00 80.00
16 Betnijah Laney-Hamilton 10.00 25.00
17 Caitlin Clark 1,000.00 2,000.00
18 Angel Reese 75.00 200.00
19 Breanna Stewart 40.00 100.00
20 Rickea Jackson 25.00 60.00

2024 Select WNBA Black Color Blast

1 Rickea Jackson 200.00 500.00
2 Sabrina Ionescu 200.00 500.00
3 Caitlin Clark 3,000.00 6,000.00
4 Angel Reese 300.00 600.00
5 Nika Muhl 150.00 400.00
6 Cameron Brink 600.00 1,200.00
7 A'ja Wilson 200.00 500.00
8 Diana Taurasi 125.00 300.00
9 Kamilla Cardoso 200.00 500.00
10 Kelsey Plum 200.00 500.00

2024 Select WNBA Color Wheel

1 A'ja Wilson 200.00 500.00
2 Cameron Brink 600.00 1,200.00
3 Sabrina Ionescu 200.00 500.00
4 Angel Reese 300.00 600.00
5 Caitlin Clark 3,000.00 6,000.00

2024 Select WNBA Courtside Action Signatures

*ICE: .5X TO 1.2X BASIC
*RED/99: .5X TO 1.2X BASIC
*BLUE/49: .6X TO 1.5X BASIC
*TIE-DYE/25: .75X TO 2X BASIC
1 Allisha Gray 6.00 15.00
2 DeWanna Bonner 8.00 20.00
3 Jackie Young 10.00 25.00
4 Jordin Canada 5.00 12.00
5 Alissa Pili 6.00 15.00
6 Arike Ogunbowale 10.00 25.00
7 Chelsea Gray 5.00 12.00
8 Breanna Stewart 20.00 50.00
9 Tina Charles 6.00 15.00
10 Zia Cooke 4.00 10.00
11 Caitlin Clark 1,000.00 2,000.00
12 Sophie Cunningham 100.00 250.00
13 Skylar Diggins-Smith 8.00 20.00
14 Dana Evans 5.00 12.00
15 Napheesa Collier 30.00 80.00
16 Kelsey Mitchell 12.00 30.00
17 Katie Lou Samuelson 20.00 50.00
18 Shey Peddy 5.00 12.00
19 Kalani Brown 4.00 10.00
20 Brionna Jones 6.00 15.00
21 Natasha Howard 6.00 15.00
22 Nyara Sabally 5.00 12.00
23 Nika Muhl 40.00 100.00
24 Betnijah Laney-Hamilton 5.00 12.00
25 Diamond Miller 5.00 12.00

2024 Select WNBA Draft Selections Signatures

*ICE: .5X TO 1.2X BASIC
*RED/99: .5X TO 1.2X BASIC
*BLUE/49: .6X TO 1.5X BASIC
*TIE-DYE/25: .75X TO 2X BASIC
*WHITE ICE/25: .75X TO 2X BASIC
1 Nika Muhl 40.00 100.00
2 Jewell Loyd 8.00 20.00
3 Kristi Toliver 6.00 15.00
4 Maya Moore 10.00 25.00
5 Jackie Young 10.00 25.00
6 Kalani Brown 4.00 10.00
7 Diana Taurasi 15.00 40.00
8 Brittney Griner 12.00 30.00
9 Rickea Jackson 12.00 30.00
10 Tamika Catchings 8.00 20.00
11 Aaliyah Edwards 6.00 15.00
12 Sue Bird 15.00 40.00
13 Napheesa Collier 30.00 80.00
14 Courtney Vandersloot 6.00 15.00
15 Jacy Sheldon 10.00 25.00
16 Caitlin Clark 1,000.00 2,000.00
17 Aliyah Boston 15.00 40.00
18 Cameron Brink 75.00 200.00
19 Kate Martin 40.00 100.00
20 Alissa Pili 6.00 15.00
21 A'ja Wilson 40.00 100.00
22 Kamilla Cardoso 20.00 50.00
23 Arike Ogunbowale 10.00 25.00
24 Angel Reese 75.00 200.00
25 Maddy Siegrist 5.00 12.00

2024 Select WNBA En Fuego

*FLASH: 1X TO 2.5X BASIC
*SILVER: 1X TO 2.5X BASIC
*BLUE FLASH/99: 2X TO 5X BASIC
*WHITE DISCO/75: 2.5X TO 6X BASIC
*BLUE/49: 3X TO 8X BASIC

*TIE-DYE/25: 5X TO 12X BASIC
1 Aaliyah Edwards 1.00 2.50
2 Sabrina Ionescu 2.50 6.00
3 Lexie Brown 1.00 2.50
4 Rhyne Howard 1.25 3.00
5 Cameron Brink 4.00 10.00
6 Kelsey Plum 2.50 6.00
7 Kahleah Copper 1.25 3.00
8 Angel Reese 2.50 6.00
9 Marina Mabrey 1.00 2.50
10 Napheesa Collier 2.50 6.00
11 Brittney Sykes .75 2.00
12 Skylar Diggins-Smith 1.25 3.00
13 Satou Sabally 1.25 3.00
14 Caitlin Clark 30.00 80.00
15 Alyssa Thomas 1.25 3.00

2024 Select WNBA Select Future
*FLASH: 1X TO 2.5X BASIC
*SILVER: 1X TO 2.5X BASIC
1 Kamilla Cardoso 1.25 3.00
2 Zia Cooke .50 1.25
3 Nika Muhl 1.50 4.00
4 Caitlin Clark 20.00 50.00
5 Kate Martin 2.00 5.00
6 Jordan Horston .60 1.50
7 Cameron Brink 3.00 8.00
8 Jaelyn Brown .60 1.50
9 Angel Reese 2.00 5.00
10 Maddy Siegrist .60 1.50
11 Rhyne Howard 1.00 2.50
12 Shakira Austin .60 1.50
13 Grace Berger .60 1.50
14 Nyara Sabally .60 1.50
15 Rickea Jackson 1.50 4.00
16 Aliyah Boston 2.00 5.00
17 Dana Evans .60 1.50
18 Diamond Miller .60 1.50
19 NaLyssa Smith .50 1.25
20 Haley Jones .50 1.25
21 Alissa Pili .75 2.00
22 Dorka Juhasz 1.00 2.50
23 Jacy Sheldon 1.25 3.00
24 Celeste Taylor .75 2.00
25 Aaliyah Edwards .75 2.00

2024 Select WNBA Select Future Blue Flash Prizms
*BLUE FLASH/99: 2X TO 5X BASIC
4 Caitlin Clark 150.00 400.00

2024 Select WNBA Select Future Blue Prizms
*BLUE/49: 3X TO 8X BASIC
4 Caitlin Clark 300.00 600.00

2024 Select WNBA Select Future Tie Dye Prizms
*TIE-DYE/25: 5X TO 12X BASIC
4 Caitlin Clark 500.00 1,000.00

2024 Select WNBA Select Future White Disco Prizms
*WHITE DISCO/75: 2.5X TO 6X BASIC
4 Caitlin Clark 200.00 500.00

2024 Select WNBA Select Pairings Signatures
1 Arike Ogunbowale
Jewell Loyd 50.00 120.00
2 Sophie Cunningham
Diana Taurasi 150.00 400.00
3 Chelsea Gray
Jackie Young 60.00 150.00
4 Angel Reese
Sheryl Swoopes 75.00 200.00
SPSIOW Caitlin Clark
Kate Martin 1,000.00 2,000.00
6 Diana Taurasi
Sue Bird 150.00 400.00
7 Courtney Vandersloot
Elena Delle Donne 40.00 100.00
8 Aliyah Boston
Dawn Staley 100.00 250.00
9 Lisa Leslie
Cameron Brink 125.00 300.00
10 A'ja Wilson
Aliyah Boston 100.00 250.00

2024 Select WNBA Selective Swatches
*PURPLE/49: .5X TO 1.2X BASIC
*TIE-DYE/25: 1X TO 2.5X BASIC
1 Alissa Pili 3.00 8.00
2 A'ja Wilson 10.00 25.00
3 Kamilla Cardoso 5.00 12.00
4 DeWanna Bonner 4.00 10.00
5 Grace Berger 2.50 6.00
6 Maya Moore 5.00 12.00
7 Diana Taurasi 8.00 20.00
8 Kelsey Plum 8.00 20.00
9 Jewell Loyd 4.00 10.00
10 Brittney Griner 6.00 15.00
11 Caitlin Clark 125.00 300.00
12 Crystal Dangerfield 2.00 5.00
13 Nika Muhl 6.00 15.00
14 Karlie Samuelson 2.50 6.00
15 Marine Johannes 4.00 10.00
16 Kalani Brown 2.00 5.00
17 Dana Evans 2.50 6.00
18 Satou Sabally 4.00 10.00
19 Dearica Hamby 3.00 8.00
20 Diamond Miller 2.50 6.00
21 Rickea Jackson 6.00 15.00
22 Natasha Howard 3.00 8.00
23 Nyara Sabally 2.50 6.00
24 Sabrina Ionescu 8.00 20.00
25 Aaliyah Edwards 3.00 8.00
26 Brionna Jones 3.00 8.00
27 Cameron Brink 20.00 50.00
28 Erica Wheeler 3.00 8.00
29 Angel Reese 15.00 40.00
30 Maddy Siegrist 2.50 6.00
31 Arike Ogunbowale 5.00 12.00
32 Julie Vanloo 3.00 8.00
33 Sue Bird 8.00 20.00
34 Jacy Sheldon 5.00 12.00
35 Nneka Ogwumike 3.00 8.00
36 Dorka Juhasz 4.00 10.00
37 Angel McCoughtry 2.50 6.00
38 Aliyah Boston 8.00 20.00
39 Tina Charles 3.00 8.00
40 Haley Jones 2.00 5.00

2024 Select WNBA Signatures
*ICE: .5X TO 1.2X BASIC
*RED/99: .5X TO 1.2X BASIC
*BLUE/49: .6X TO 1.5X BASIC
*TIE-DYE/25: .75X TO 2X BASIC
*WHITE ICE/25: .75X TO 2X BASIC
1 Lisa Leslie 10.00 25.00
2 Nika Muhl 40.00 100.00
3 Angel Reese 75.00 200.00
4 Cameron Brink 75.00 200.00
5 Angel McCoughtry 5.00 12.00
6 Erica Wheeler 6.00 15.00
7 Rickea Jackson 12.00 30.00
8 Natasha Cloud 6.00 15.00
9 Natasha Howard 6.00 15.00
10 Shey Peddy 5.00 12.00
11 Sophie Cunningham 100.00 250.00
12 Alysha Clark 5.00 12.00
13 Tina Charles 6.00 15.00
14 Jacy Sheldon 10.00 25.00
15 A'ja Wilson 40.00 100.00
16 Marine Johannes 8.00 20.00
17 Skylar Diggins-Smith 8.00 20.00
18 DiJonai Carrington 6.00 15.00
19 Nyara Sabally 5.00 12.00
20 Lauren Jackson 10.00 25.00
21 Alissa Pili 6.00 15.00
22 Kristi Toliver 6.00 15.00
23 Breanna Stewart 20.00 50.00
24 Aaliyah Edwards 6.00 15.00
25 Caitlin Clark 1,000.00 2,000.00

2024 Select WNBA Snapshots
*FLASH: .75X TO 2X BASIC
*SILVER: .75X TO 2X BASIC
1 Arike Ogunbowale 1.25 3.00
2 Aliyah Boston 2.00 5.00
3 Marquesha Davis .60 1.50
4 Jewell Loyd 1.00 2.50
5 Diana Taurasi 2.00 5.00
6 Skylar Diggins-Smith 1.00 2.50
7 Aaliyah Edwards .75 2.00
8 Sabrina Ionescu 2.00 5.00
9 A'ja Wilson 2.50 6.00
10 Jackie Young 1.25 3.00
11 Alyssa Thomas 1.00 2.50
12 Caitlin Clark 20.00 50.00
13 Rhyne Howard 1.00 2.50
14 Breanna Stewart 2.50 6.00
15 Angel Reese 2.00 5.00
16 Rickea Jackson 1.50 4.00
17 Nika Muhl 1.50 4.00
18 Chelsea Gray .60 1.50
19 Kelsey Plum 2.00 5.00
20 Kamilla Cardoso 1.25 3.00
21 Kahleah Copper 1.00 2.50
22 Natasha Cloud .75 2.00
23 Courtney Vandersloot .75 2.00
24 Cameron Brink 3.00 8.00
25 Jacy Sheldon 1.25 3.00

2024 Select WNBA Snapshots Blue Flash Prizms
*BLUE FLASH/99: 2X TO 5X BASIC
12 Caitlin Clark 150.00 400.00

2024 Select WNBA Snapshots Blue Prizms
*BLUE/49: 3X TO 8X BASIC
12 Caitlin Clark 300.00 600.00

2024 Select WNBA Snapshots Tie Dye Prizms
*TIE-DYE/25: 5X TO 12X BASIC
12 Caitlin Clark 500.00 1,000.00

2024 Select WNBA Snapshots White Disco Prizms
*WHITE DISCO/75: 2.5X TO 6X BASIC
12 Caitlin Clark 200.00 500.00

2024 Select WNBA Sparks
*PURPLE/49: .5X TO 1.2X BASIC
*TIE-DYE/25: 1.25X TO 3X BASIC
1 Angel Reese 8.00 20.00
2 Natasha Cloud 3.00 8.00
3 Skylar Diggins-Smith 4.00 10.00
4 Celeste Taylor 3.00 8.00
5 Kelsey Mitchell 6.00 15.00
6 Aaliyah Edwards 3.00 8.00
7 Jewell Loyd 4.00 10.00
8 Chelsea Gray 2.50 6.00
9 Allisha Gray 3.00 8.00
10 Rickea Jackson 6.00 15.00
11 Sophie Cunningham 6.00 15.00
12 Kamilla Cardoso 5.00 12.00
13 Katie Lou Samuelson 4.00 10.00
14 Courtney Vandersloot 3.00 8.00
15 A'ja Wilson 10.00 25.00
16 Satou Sabally 4.00 10.00
17 Alissa Pili 3.00 8.00
18 Alyssa Thomas 4.00 10.00
19 Kelsey Plum 8.00 20.00
20 Lexie Hull 20.00 50.00
21 Sue Bird 8.00 20.00
22 Jackie Young 5.00 12.00
23 DiJonai Carrington 3.00 8.00
24 Nika Muhl 6.00 15.00
25 Kate Martin 20.00 50.00
26 Arike Ogunbowale 5.00 12.00
27 Betnijah Laney-Hamilton 2.50 6.00
28 Julie Vanloo 3.00 8.00
29 Jonquel Jones 5.00 12.00
30 Aliyah Boston 8.00 20.00
31 Lexie Brown 3.00 8.00
32 Maya Moore 5.00 12.00
33 Jordin Canada 2.50 6.00
34 Elena Delle Donne 5.00 12.00
35 Cameron Brink 25.00 60.00
36 Sabrina Ionescu 8.00 20.00
37 Jacy Sheldon 5.00 12.00
38 Caitlin Clark 150.00 400.00
39 Marquesha Davis 2.50 6.00
40 Diana Taurasi 8.00 20.00

2024 Select WNBA Unstoppable
*FLASH: .6X TO 1.5X BASIC
*SILVER: 1X TO 2.5X BASIC
*BLUE FLASH/99: 1.25X TO 3X BASIC
*WHITE DISCO/75: 1.5X TO 4X BASIC
*BLUE/49: 2X TO 5X BASIC
*TIE-DYE/25: 4X TO 10X BASIC
1 Natasha Cloud .75 2.00
2 Jackie Young 1.25 3.00
3 Kahleah Copper 1.00 2.50
4 Kalani Brown .50 1.25
5 Jewell Loyd 1.00 2.50
6 Courtney Williams .75 2.00
7 Breanna Stewart 2.50 6.00
8 Skylar Diggins-Smith 1.00 2.50
9 Lexie Brown .75 2.00
10 Jonquel Jones 1.25 3.00
11 Tina Charles .75 2.00
12 Alyssa Thomas 1.00 2.50
13 A'ja Wilson 2.50 6.00
14 Ticha Penicheiro .75 2.00
15 Arike Ogunbowale 1.25 3.00
16 Kelsey Mitchell 1.50 4.00
17 DeWanna Bonner 1.00 2.50
18 Aerial Powers .50 1.25
19 Aliyah Boston 2.00 5.00
20 Napheesa Collier 2.00 5.00

1990-91 SkyBox Prototypes
COMPLETE SET (10) 30.00 80.00
41 Michael Jordan 40.00 100.00
91 Dennis Rodman 8.00 20.00
138 Magic Johnson 8.00 20.00
151 Rony Seikaly 4.00 10.00
162 Ricky Pierce 4.00 10.00
173 Pooh Richardson 4.00 10.00
224 Kevin Johnson 5.00 12.00
233 Clyde Drexler 6.00 15.00
260 David Robinson 8.00 20.00
282 Karl Malone 8.00 20.00
NNO SkyBox Logo
Distributed at 1990
National Convention 2.00 5.00

1990-91 SkyBox
COMPLETE SET (423) 10.00 20.00
COMPLETE SERIES 1 (300) 6.00 12.00
COMPLETE SERIES 2 (123) 4.00 8.00
1 John Battle .02 .10
2 Duane Ferrell SP RC .08 .25
3 Jon Koncak .02 .10
4 Cliff Levingston SP .08 .25
5 John Long SP .08 .25
6 Moses Malone .08 .25
7 Doc Rivers .02 .10
8 Kenny Smith SP .08 .25
9 Alexander Volkov RC .02 .10
10 Spud Webb .02 .10
11 Dominique Wilkins .08 .25
12 Kevin Willis .02 .10
13 John Bagley .02 .10
14 Larry Bird .40 1.00
15 Kevin Gamble .02 .10
16 Dennis Johnson SP .08 .25
17 Joe Kleine .02 .10
18 Reggie Lewis .02 .10
19 Kevin McHale .02 .10
20 Robert Parish .02 .10
21 Jim Paxson SP .08 .25
22 Ed Pinckney .02 .10
23 Brian Shaw .08 .25
24 Michael Smith .02 .10
25 Richard Anderson SP .08 .25
26 Muggsy Bogues .02 .10
27 Rex Chapman .08 .25
28 Dell Curry .02 .10
29 Armon Gilliam .02 .10
30 Michael Holton SP .08 .25
31 Dave Hoppen .02 .10
32 J.R. Reid RC .02 .10
33 Robert Reid SP .08 .25
34 Brian Rowsom SP .08 .25
35 Kelly Tripucka .02 .10
36 Micheal Williams SP UER .08 .25
37 B.J. Armstrong RC .02 .10
38 Bill Cartwright .02 .10
39 Horace Grant .02 .10
40 Craig Hodges .02 .10
41 Michael Jordan 1.25 3.00
42 Stacey King RC .02 .10
43 Ed Nealy SP .02 .10
44 John Paxson .02 .10
45 Will Perdue .02 .10
46 Scottie Pippen .40 1.00
47 Jeff Sanders SP RC .08 .25
48 Winston Bennett .02 .10
49 Chucky Brown RC .02 .10
50 Brad Daugherty .02 .10
51 Craig Ehlo .02 .10
52 Steve Kerr .08 .25
53 Paul Mokeski SP .08 .25
54 John Morton .02 .10
55 Larry Nance .02 .10
56 Mark Price .02 .10
57 Tree Rollins SP .08 .25
58 Hot Rod Williams .02 .10
59 Steve Alford .02 .10
60 Rolando Blackman .02 .10
61 Adrian Dantley SP .08 .25
62 Brad Davis .02 .10
63 James Donaldson .02 .10
64 Derek Harper .02 .10
65 Anthony Jones SP .08 .25
66 Sam Perkins SP .08 .25
67 Roy Tarpley .02 .10
68 Bill Wennington SP .08 .25
69 Randy White RC .02 .10
70 Herb Williams .02 .10
71 Michael Adams .02 .10
72 Joe Barry Carroll SP .08 .25
73 Walter Davis .02 .10
74 Alex English SP .08 .25
75 Bill Hanzlik .02 .10
76 Tim Kempton SP .08 .25
77 Jerome Lane .02 .10
78 Lafayette Lever SP .08 .25
79 Todd Lichti RC .02 .10
80 Blair Rasmussen .02 .10
81 Danny Schayes SP .08 .25
82 Mark Aguirre .02 .10
83 William Bedford RC .02 .10
84 Joe Dumars .08 .25
85 James Edwards .02 .10
86 David Greenwood SP .08 .25
87 Scott Hastings .02 .10
88 Gerald Henderson SP .08 .25
89 Vinnie Johnson .02 .10
90 Bill Laimbeer .02 .10
91 Dennis Rodman .25 .60
91B Dennis Rodman Left .40 1.00
92 John Salley .02 .10
93 Isiah Thomas .08 .25
94 Manute Bol SP .08 .25
95 Tim Hardaway RC 1.25 3.00
96 Rod Higgins .02 .10
97 Sarunas Marciulionis RC .02 .10
98 Chris Mullin .08 .25
99 Jim Petersen .02 .10
100 Mitch Richmond .10 .30
101 Mike Smrek .02 .10
102 Terry Teagle SP .08 .25
103 Tom Tolbert RC .02 .10
104 Kelvin Upshaw SP .08 .25
105 Anthony Bowie SP RC .08 .25
106 Adrian Caldwell .02 .10
107 Eric(Sleepy) Floyd .02 .10
108 Buck Johnson .02 .10
109 Vernon Maxwell .02 .10
110 Hakeem Olajuwon .15 .40
111 Larry Smith .02 .10
112A Otis Thorpe ERR .60 1.50
112B Otis Thorpe COR .02 .10
113A M. Wiggins SP ERR .60 1.50
113B M. Wiggins SP COR .08 .25
114 Vern Fleming .02 .10
115 Rickey Green SP .08 .25
116 George McCloud RC .08 .25
117 Reggie Miller .10 .30
118A Dyron Nix SP ERR .60 1.50
118B Dyron Nix SP COR .08 .25
119 Chuck Person .02 .10
120 Mike Sanders .02 .10
121 Detlef Schrempf .02 .10
122 Rik Smits .08 .25
123 LaSalle Thompson .02 .10
124 Benoit Benjamin .02 .10
125 Winston Garland .02 .10
126 Tom Garrick .02 .10
127 Gary Grant .02 .10
128 Ron Harper .02 .10
129 Danny Manning .02 .10
130 Jeff Martin .02 .10
131 Ken Norman .02 .10
132 Charles Smith .02 .10
133 Joe Wolf SP .08 .25
134 Michael Cooper SP .08 .25
135 Vlade Divac RC .25 .60
136 Larry Drew .02 .10
137 A.C. Green .02 .10
138 Magic Johnson .30 .75
139 Mark McNamara SP .08 .25
140 Byron Scott .02 .10
141 Mychal Thompson .02 .10
142 Orlando Woolridge SP .08 .25
143 James Worthy .08 .25
144 Terry Davis RC .02 .10
145 Sherman Douglas RC .02 .10
146 Kevin Edwards .02 .10
147 Tellis Frank SP .08 .25
148 Scott Haffner SP .08 .25
149 Grant Long .02 .10
150 Glen Rice RC .40 1.00
151 Rony Seikaly .02 .10
152 Rory Sparrow SP .08 .25
153 Jon Sundvold .02 .10
154 Billy Thompson .02 .10
155 Greg Anderson .02 .10
156 Ben Coleman SP .08 .25
157 Jeff Grayer RC .02 .10
158 Jay Humphries .02 .10
159 Frank Kornet .02 .10
160 Larry Krystkowiak .02 .10
161 Brad Lohaus .02 .10
162 Ricky Pierce .02 .10
163 Paul Pressey SP .08 .25
164 Fred Roberts .02 .10
165 Alvin Robertson .02 .10
166 Jack Sikma .02 .10
167 Randy Breuer .02 .10
168 Tony Campbell .02 .10
169 Tyrone Corbin .02 .10
170 Sidney Lowe SP .08 .25
171 Sam Mitchell RC .02 .10
172 Tod Murphy .02 .10
173 Pooh Richardson RC .02 .10
174 Donald Royal SP RC .08 .25
175 Brad Sellers SP .08 .25
176 Mookie Blaylock RC .15 .40
177 Sam Bowie .02 .10
178 Lester Conner .02 .10
179 Derrick Gervin .02 .10
180 Jack Haley RC .02 .10
181 Roy Hinson .02 .10
182 Dennis Hopson SP .08 .25
183 Chris Morris .02 .10
184 Pete Myers SP RC .08 .25
185 Purvis Short SP .08 .25
186 Maurice Cheeks .02 .10
187 Patrick Ewing .08 .25
188 Stuart Gray .02 .10
189 Mark Jackson .02 .10
190 Johnny Newman SP .08 .25
191 Charles Oakley .02 .10
192 Brian Quinnett .02 .10
193 Trent Tucker .02 .10
194 Kiki Vandeweghe .02 .10
195 Kenny Walker .02 .10
196 Eddie Lee Wilkins .02 .10
197 Gerald Wilkins .02 .10
198 Mark Acres .02 .10
199 Nick Anderson RC .15 .40
200 Michael Ansley .02 .10
201 Terry Catledge .02 .10
202 Dave Corzine SP .08 .25
203 Sidney Green SP .08 .25
204 Jerry Reynolds .02 .10
205 Scott Skiles .02 .10
206 Otis Smith .02 .10
207 Reggie Theus SP .08 .25
208 Jeff Turner .02 .10
209 Sam Vincent .02 .10
210 Ron Anderson .02 .10
211 Charles Barkley .15 .40
212 Scott Brooks SP .08 .25
213 Lanard Copeland SP .08 .25
214 Johnny Dawkins .02 .10
215 Mike Gminski .02 .10
216 Hersey Hawkins .02 .10
217 Rick Mahorn .02 .10
218 Derek Smith SP .08 .25
219 Bob Thornton .02 .10
220 Tom Chambers .02 .10
221 Greg Grant SP RC .08 .25
222 Jeff Hornacek .02 .10
223 Eddie Johnson .02 .10
224A Kevin Johnson Lower .08 .25
224B Kevin Johnson Upper .08 .25
225 Andrew Lang RC .08 .25
226 Dan Majerle .08 .25
227 Mike McGee SP .08 .25
228 Tim Perry .02 .10
229 Kurt Rambis .02 .10
230 Mark West .02 .10
231 Mark Bryant .02 .10
232 Wayne Cooper .02 .10
233 Clyde Drexler .08 .25
234 Kevin Duckworth .02 .10
235 Byron Irvin SP .08 .25
236 Jerome Kersey .02 .10
237 Drazen Petrovic RC .10 .30
238 Terry Porter .02 .10
239 Clifford Robinson RC .15 .40
240 Buck Williams .02 .10
241 Danny Young .02 .10
242 Danny Ainge SP .08 .25
243 Randy Allen SP .08 .25
244A Antoine Carr SP .08 .25
244B Antoine Carr .02 .10
245 Vinny Del Negro SP .08 .25
246 Pervis Ellison SP RC .08 .25
247 Greg Kite SP .08 .25
248 Rodney McCray SP .08 .25
249 Harold Pressley SP .08 .25
250 Ralph Sampson .02 .10
251 Wayman Tisdale .02 .10
252 Willie Anderson .02 .10
253 Uwe Blab SP .08 .25
254 Frank Brickowski SP .08 .25
255 Terry Cummings .02 .10
256 Sean Elliott RC .20 .50
257 Caldwell Jones SP .08 .25
258 Johnny Moore SP .08 .25
259 Zarko Paspalj SP .08 .25
260 David Robinson .30 .75
261 Rod Strickland .08 .25
262 David Wingate SP .08 .25
263 Dana Barros RC .08 .25
264 Michael Cage .02 .10
265 Quintin Dailey .02 .10
266 Dale Ellis .02 .10
267 Steve Johnson SP .08 .25
268 Shawn Kemp RC 1.00 2.50
269 Xavier McDaniel .02 .10
270 Derrick McKey .02 .10
271A Nate McMillan SP ERR .08 .25
271B Nate McMillan COR .02 .10
272 Olden Polynice .02 .10
273 Sedale Threatt .02 .10
274 Thurl Bailey .02 .10
275 Mike Brown .02 .10
276 Mark Eaton .02 .10
277 Blue Edwards RC .02 .10
278 Darrell Griffith .02 .10
279 Bobby Hansen SP .08 .25
280 Eric Johnson .02 .10
281 Eric Leckner SP .08 .25
282 Karl Malone .15 .40
283 Delaney Rudd .02 .10
284 John Stockton .10 .30
285 Mark Alarie .02 .10
286 Steve Colter SP .08 .25
287 Ledell Eackles SP .08 .25
288 Harvey Grant .02 .10
289 Tom Hammonds RC .02 .10
290 Charles Jones RC .02 .10
291 Bernard King .02 .10
292 Jeff Malone SP .08 .25
293 Darrell Walker .02 .10
294 John Williams .02 .10
295 Checklist 1 SP .08 .25
296 Checklist 2 SP .08 .25
297 Checklist 3 SP .08 .25
298 Checklist 4 SP .08 .25
299 Checklist 5 SP .08 .25
300 Danny Ferry SP RC .20 .50
301 Bob Weiss CO .02 .10
302 Chris Ford CO .02 .10
303 Gene Littles CO .02 .10
304 Phil Jackson CO .10 .30
305 Lenny Wilkens CO .10 .30
306 Richie Adubato CO .02 .10
307 Paul Westhead CO .02 .10
308 Chuck Daly CO .10 .30
309 Don Nelson CO .10 .30
310 Don Chaney CO .02 .10
311 Dick Versace CO .02 .10
312 Mike Schuler CO .02 .10
313 Mike Dunleavy CO .02 .10
314 Ron Rothstein CO .02 .10
315 Del Harris CO .02 .10
316 Bill Musselman CO .02 .10
317 Bill Fitch CO .02 .10
318 Stu Jackson CO .02 .10
319 Matt Guokas CO .02 .10
320 Jim Lynam CO .02 .10
321 Cotton Fitzsimmons CO .02 .10
322 Rick Adelman CO .02 .10
323 Dick Motta CO .02 .10
324 Larry Brown CO .02 .10
325 K.C. Jones CO .10 .30
326 Jerry Sloan CO .10 .30
327 Wes Unseld CO .02 .10
328 Atlanta Hawks TC .02 .10
329 Boston Celtics TC .02 .10
330 Charlotte Hornets TC .02 .10
331 Chicago Bulls TC .10 .30
332 Cleveland Cavaliers TC .02 .10
333 Dallas Mavericks TC .02 .10
334 Denver Nuggets TC .02 .10
335 Detroit Pistons TC .02 .10
336 Golden State Warriors TC .02 .10
337 Houston Rockets TC .02 .10
338 Indiana Pacers TC .02 .10
339 Los Angeles Clippers TC .02 .10
340 Los Angeles Lakers TC .02 .10
341 Miami Heat TC .02 .10
342 Milwaukee Bucks TC .02 .10
343 Minnesota Timberwolves TC .02 .10
344 New Jersey Nets TC .02 .10
345 New York Knicks TC .02 .10
346 Orlando Magic TC .02 .10
347 Philadelphia 76ers TC .02 .10
348 Phoenix Suns TC .02 .10
349 Portland Trail Blazers TC .02 .10
350 Sacramento Kings TC .02 .10
351 San Antonio Spurs TC .02 .10
352 Seattle SuperSonics TC .02 .10
353 Utah Jazz TC .02 .10
354 Washington Bullets TC .02 .10
355 Rumeal Robinson RC .02 .10
356 Kendall Gill RC .50 1.25
357 Chris Jackson RC .25 .60
358 Tyrone Hill RC .20 .50
359 Bo Kimble RC .02 .10
360 Willie Burton RC .02 .10
361 Felton Spencer RC .10 .30
362 Derrick Coleman RC .50 1.25
363 Dennis Scott RC .30 .75
364 Lionel Simmons RC .10 .30
365 Gary Payton RC 2.00 5.00
366 Tim McCormick .02 .10
367 Sidney Moncrief .02 .10
368 Kenny Gattison RC .02 .10
369 Randolph Keys .02 .10
370 Johnny Newman .02 .10
371 Dennis Hopson .02 .10
372 Cliff Levingston .02 .10
373 Derrick Chievous .02 .10
374 Danny Ferry .10 .30
375 Alex English .02 .10
376 Lafayette Lever .02 .10
377 Rodney McCray .02 .10
378 T.R. Dunn .02 .10
379 Corey Gaines .02 .10
380 Avery Johnson RC .30 .75
381 Joe Wolf .02 .10
382 Orlando Woolridge .02 .10
383 Tree Rollins .02 .10
384 Steve Johnson .02 .10
385 Kenny Smith .02 .10
386 Mike Woodson .02 .10
387 Greg Dreiling RC .02 .10
388 Micheal Williams .10 .30
389 Randy Wittman .02 .10
390 Ken Bannister .02 .10
391 Sam Perkins .10 .30
392 Terry Teagle .02 .10
393 Milt Wagner .02 .10
394 Frank Brickowski .02 .10
395 Danny Schayes .02 .10
396 Scott Brooks .02 .10
397 Doug West RC .10 .30
398 Chris Dudley RC .02 .10
399 Reggie Theus .10 .30
400 Greg Grant .02 .10
401 Greg Kite .02 .10
402 Mark McNamara .02 .10
403 Manute Bol .02 .10
404 Rickey Green .02 .10
405 Kenny Battle RC .02 .10
406 Ed Nealy .02 .10
407 Danny Ainge .10 .30
408 Steve Colter .02 .10
409 Bobby Hansen .02 .10
410 Eric Leckner .02 .10
411 Rory Sparrow .02 .10
412 Bill Wennington .02 .10
413 Sidney Green .02 .10
414 David Greenwood .02 .10
415 Paul Pressey .02 .10
416 Reggie Williams .02 .10
417 Dave Corzine .02 .10
418 Jeff Malone .02 .10
419 Pervis Ellison .02 .10
420 Byron Irvin .02 .10
421 Checklist 1 .02 .10
422 Checklist 2 .02 .10
423 Checklist 3 .02 .10
NNO SkyBox Salutes the NBA 2.50 6.00

1991-92 SkyBox Prototypes
COMPLETE SET (20) 25.00 60.00
24 Rex Chapman 1.00 2.50
86 Dennis Rodman SP 6.00 15.00
95 Chris Mullin SP 3.00 8.00
97 Mitch Richmond 2.50 6.00
114 Reggie Miller 3.00 8.00
130 Charles Smith 1.00 2.50
137 Magic Johnson 5.00 12.00
143 James Worthy 1.50 4.00
173 Pooh Richardson 1.00 2.50
189 Patrick Ewing 2.50 6.00
205 Dennis Scott 1.00 2.50
211 Charles Barkley 4.00 10.00
216 Hersey Hawkins 1.00 2.50
223 Tom Chambers 1.00 2.50
237 Clyde Drexler 2.50 6.00
238 Kevin Duckworth 1.00 2.50
240 Terry Porter 1.00 2.50
242 Buck Williams 1.00 2.50
268 Ricky Pierce 1.00 2.50
294 Bernard King 1.00 2.50

1991-92 SkyBox
COMPLETE SET (659) 30.00 60.00
COMPLETE SERIES 1 (350) 10.00 20.00
COMPLETE SERIES 2 (309) 20.00 40.00
1 John Battle .20 .50
2 Duane Ferrell .20 .50
3 Jon Koncak .20 .50
4 Moses Malone .50 1.25
5 Tim McCormick .20 .50
6 Sidney Moncrief .30 .75
7 Doc Rivers .30 .75
8 Rumeal Robinson UER .20 .50
9 Spud Webb .30 .75
10 Dominique Wilkins .50 1.25
11 Kevin Willis .25 .60
12 Larry Bird 1.00 2.50
13 Dee Brown .25 .60
14 Kevin Gamble .20 .50
15 Joe Kleine .20 .50
16 Reggie Lewis .30 .75
17 Kevin McHale .50 1.25
18 Robert Parish .40 1.00
19 Ed Pinckney .25 .60
20 Brian Shaw .25 .60
21 Michael Smith .20 .50
22 Stojko Vrankovic .20 .50
23 Muggsy Bogues .30 .75
24 Rex Chapman .25 .60
25 Dell Curry .25 .60
26 Kenny Gattison .20 .50
27 Kendall Gill .30 .75
28 Mike Gminski .20 .50
29 Randolph Keys .20 .50
30 Eric Leckner .20 .50
31 Johnny Newman .20 .50
32 J.R. Reid .20 .50
33 Kelly Tripucka .25 .60
34 B.J. Armstrong .30 .75
35 Bill Cartwright .25 .60
36 Horace Grant .30 .75
37 Craig Hodges .25 .60
38 Dennis Hopson .20 .50
39 Michael Jordan 2.50 6.00
40 Stacey King .25 .60
41 Cliff Levingston .25 .60
42 John Paxson .25 .60
43 Will Perdue .25 .60
44 Scottie Pippen .75 2.00
45 Winston Bennett .20 .50
46 Chucky Brown .20 .50
47 Brad Daugherty .30 .75
48 Craig Ehlo .25 .60
49 Danny Ferry .20 .50
50 Steve Kerr .40 1.00
51 John Morton .20 .50
52 Larry Nance .30 .75
53 Mark Price .30 .75
54 Darnell Valentine .20 .50
55 John Williams .20 .50
56 Steve Alford .25 .60
57 Rolando Blackman .25 .60
58 Brad Davis .20 .50
59 James Donaldson .25 .60
60 Derek Harper .25 .60
61 Fat Lever .25 .60
62 Rodney McCray .25 .60
63 Roy Tarpley .25 .60
64 Kelvin Upshaw .20 .50
65 Randy White .20 .50
66 Herb Williams .25 .60
67 Michael Adams .25 .60
68 Greg Anderson .20 .50
69 Anthony Cook .20 .50
70 Chris Jackson .25 .60
71 Jerome Lane .20 .50
72 Marcus Liberty .20 .50
73 Todd Lichti .20 .50
74 Blair Rasmussen .20 .50
75 Reggie Williams .25 .60
76 Joe Wolf .20 .50
77 Orlando Woolridge .25 .60
78 Mark Aguirre .25 .60
79 William Bedford .20 .50
80 Lance Blanks .20 .50
81 Joe Dumars .40 1.00
82 James Edwards .25 .60
83 Scott Hastings .20 .50
84 Vinnie Johnson .30 .75
85 Bill Laimbeer .30 .75
86 Dennis Rodman .60 1.50
87 John Salley .25 .60
88 Isiah Thomas .50 1.25
89 Mario Elie RC .20 .50
90 Tim Hardaway .40 1.00
91 Rod Higgins .20 .50
92 Tyrone Hill .25 .60
93 Les Jepsen .20 .50
94 Alton Lister .20 .50
95 Sarunas Marciulionis .30 .75
96 Chris Mullin .40 1.00
97 Jim Petersen .20 .50
98 Mitch Richmond .40 1.00
99 Tom Tolbert .20 .50
100 Adrian Caldwell .20 .50
101 Eric(Sleepy) Floyd .25 .60
102 Dave Jamerson .20 .50
103 Buck Johnson .20 .50
104 Vernon Maxwell .25 .60
105 Hakeem Olajuwon .60 1.50
106 Kenny Smith .25 .60
107 Larry Smith .20 .50
108 Otis Thorpe .25 .60
109 Kennard Winchester RC .20 .50
110 David Wood RC .20 .50
111 Greg Dreiling .20 .50
112 Vern Fleming .25 .60
113 George McCloud .20 .50
114 Reggie Miller .50 1.25
115 Chuck Person .25 .60
116 Mike Sanders .20 .50
117 Detlef Schrempf .25 .60
118 Rik Smits .25 .60
119 LaSalle Thompson .20 .50
120 Kenny Williams .20 .50
121 Micheal Williams .20 .50
123 Winston Garland .20 .50
124 Gary Grant .20 .50
125 Ron Harper .30 .75
126 Bo Kimble .25 .60
127 Danny Manning .25 .60
128 Jeff Martin .20 .50
129 Ken Norman .25 .60
130 Olden Polynice .20 .50
131 Charles Smith .25 .60
132 Loy Vaught .25 .60
133 Elden Campbell .25 .60
134 Vlade Divac .25 .60
135 Larry Drew .20 .50

136 A.C. Green .25 .60
137 Magic Johnson 1.00 2.50
138 Sam Perkins .25 .60
139 Byron Scott .30 .75
140 Tony Smith .20 .50
141 Terry Teagle .25 .60
142 Mychal Thompson .25 .60
143 James Worthy .40 1.00
144 Willie Burton .20 .50
145 Bimbo Coles .25 .60
146 Terry Davis .20 .50
147 Sherman Douglas .25 .60
148 Kevin Edwards .20 .50
149 Alec Kessler .20 .50
150 Grant Long .20 .50
151 Glen Rice .30 .75
152 Rony Seikaly .25 .60
153 Jon Sundvold .20 .50
154 Billy Thompson .20 .50
155 Frank Brickowski .20 .50
156 Lester Conner .20 .50
157 Jeff Grayer .20 .50
158 Jay Humphries .25 .60
159 Larry Krystkowiak .20 .50
160 Brad Lohaus .20 .50
161 Dale Ellis .25 .60
162 Fred Roberts .20 .50
163 Alvin Robertson .25 .60
164 Danny Schayes .20 .50
165 Jack Sikma .30 .75
166 Randy Breuer .20 .50
167 Scott Brooks .20 .50
168 Tony Campbell .20 .50
169 Tyrone Corbin .20 .50
170 Gerald Glass .20 .50
171 Sam Mitchell .20 .50
172 Tod Murphy .20 .50
173 Pooh Richardson .25 .60
174 Felton Spencer .20 .50
176 Doug West .20 .50
177 Mookie Blaylock .30 .75
178 Sam Bowie .25 .60
179 Jud Buechler .25 .60
180 Derrick Coleman .30 .75
181 Chris Dudley .20 .50
182 Tate George .20 .50
183 Jack Haley .20 .50
184 Terry Mills RC .20 .50
185 Chris Morris .20 .50
186 Drazen Petrovic .40 1.00
187 Reggie Theus .25 .60
188 Maurice Cheeks .25 .60
189 Patrick Ewing .50 1.25
190 Mark Jackson .25 .60
191 Jerrod Mustaf .20 .50
192 Charles Oakley .25 .60
193 Brian Quinnett .20 .50
194 John Starks RC 1.00 2.50
195 Trent Tucker .25 .60
196 Kiki Vandeweghe .25 .60
197 Kenny Walker .20 .50
198 Gerald Wilkins .25 .60
199 Mark Acres .20 .50
200 Nick Anderson .25 .60
201 Michael Ansley .20 .50
202 Terry Catledge .20 .50
203 Greg Kite .20 .50
204 Jerry Reynolds .20 .50
205 Dennis Scott .25 .60
206 Scott Skiles .25 .60
207 Otis Smith .20 .50
208 Jeff Turner .20 .50
209 Sam Vincent .20 .50
210 Ron Anderson .20 .50
211 Charles Barkley .60 1.50
212 Manute Bol .30 .75
213 Johnny Dawkins .25 .60
214 Armon Gilliam .25 .60
215 Rickey Green .25 .60
216 Hersey Hawkins .25 .60
217 Rick Mahorn .25 .60
218 Brian Oliver .20 .50
219 Andre Turner .20 .50
220 Jayson Williams .25 .60
221 Joe Barry Carroll .20 .50
222 Cedric Ceballos .25 .60
223 Tom Chambers .30 .75
224 Jeff Hornacek .25 .60
225 Kevin Johnson .30 .75
226 Negele Knight .20 .50
227 Andrew Lang .20 .50
228 Dan Majerle .30 .75
229 Xavier McDaniel .25 .60
230 Kurt Rambis .25 .60
231 Mark West .25 .60
232 Alaa Abdelnaby .20 .50
233 Danny Ainge .25 .60
234 Mark Bryant .20 .50
235 Wayne Cooper .20 .50
236 Walter Davis .25 .60
237 Clyde Drexler .50 1.25
238 Kevin Duckworth .25 .60
239 Jerome Kersey .25 .60
240 Terry Porter .25 .60
241 Clifford Robinson .25 .60
242 Buck Williams .25 .60
243 Anthony Bonner .20 .50
244 Antoine Carr .25 .60
245 Duane Causwell .20 .50
246 Bobby Hansen .20 .50
247 Jim Les RC .20 .50
248 Travis Mays .20 .50
249 Ralph Sampson .25 .60
250 Lionel Simmons .20 .50
251 Rory Sparrow .20 .50
252 Wayman Tisdale .25 .60
253 Bill Wennington .25 .60
254 Willie Anderson .25 .60
255 Terry Cummings .30 .75
256 Sean Elliott .25 .60
257 Sidney Green .20 .50
258 David Greenwood .20 .50
259 Avery Johnson .25 .60
260 Paul Pressey .25 .60
261 David Robinson .60 1.50
262 Dwayne Schintzius .20 .50
263 Rod Strickland .25 .60
264 David Wingate .25 .60
265 Dana Barros .25 .60
266 Benoit Benjamin .20 .50
267 Michael Cage .25 .60
268 Quintin Dailey .20 .50
269 Ricky Pierce .25 .60
270 Eddie Johnson .20 .50
271 Shawn Kemp .50 1.25
272 Derrick McKey .20 .50
273 Nate McMillan .25 .60
274 Gary Payton .50 1.25
275 Sedale Threatt .20 .50
276 Thurl Bailey .25 .60
277 Mike Brown .25 .60
278 Tony Brown .20 .50
279 Mark Eaton .30 .75
280 Blue Edwards .20 .50
281 Darrell Griffith .30 .75
282 Jeff Malone .25 .60
283 Karl Malone .60 1.50
284 Delaney Rudd .20 .50
285 John Stockton .60 1.50
286 Andy Toolson .20 .50
287 Mark Alarie .20 .50
288 Ledell Eackles .20 .50
289 Pervis Ellison .20 .50
290 A.J. English .20 .50
291 Harvey Grant .25 .60
292 Tom Hammonds .20 .50
293 Charles Jones .20 .50
294 Bernard King .40 1.00
295 Darrell Walker .20 .50
296 John Williams .20 .50
297 Haywoode Workman RC .20 .50
298 Muggsy Bogues .30 .75
299 Lester Conner .20 .50
300 Michael Adams .25 .60
301 Chris Mullin Minutes .40 1.00
302 Otis Thorpe .25 .60
303 Rich/Hard/Mullin TRIO .40 1.00
304 Darrell Walker .20 .50
305 Jerome Lane .20 .50
306 John Stockton Assists .60 1.50
307 Michael Jordan Points 2.50 6.00
308 Michael Adams .25 .60
309 L.Smith/J.Lane .20 .50
310 Scott Skiles .25 .60
311 H.Olajuwon/D.Robinson .60 1.50
312 Alvin Robertson .25 .60
313 Stay In School Jam .75 2.00
314 Craig Hodges 3P .25 .60
315 Dee Brown SD .25 .60
316 Charles Barkley AS-MVP .60 1.50
317 Behind the Scenes .60 1.50
318 Derrick Coleman ART .30 .75
319 Lionel Simmons ART .20 .50
320 Dennis Scott ART .25 .60
321 Kendall Gill ART .30 .75
322 Dee Brown ART .25 .60
323 Magic Johnson GQ 1.00 2.50
324 Hakeem Olajuwon GQ .60 1.50
325 K.Willis/D.Wilkins GQ .50 1.25
326 K.Willis/D.Wilkins GQ .50 1.25
327 Gerald Wilkins GQ .25 .60
328 Centennial Logo Card .40 1.00
329 Old-Fashioned Ball .40 1.00
330 Women Take the Court .40 1.00
331 The Peach Basket .40 1.00
332 Dr. James Naismith .40 1.00
333 M.Johnson/M.Jordan FIN 2.50 6.00
334 Michael Jordan FIN 2.50 6.00
335 Vlade Divac FIN .25 .60
336 John Paxson FIN .25 .60
337 Bulls Team/M.Jordan 2.50 6.00
338 Language Arts .40 1.00
339 Mathematics .30 .75
340 Vocational Education .40 1.00
341 Social Studies .40 1.00
342 Physical Education .40 1.00
343 Art .40 1.00
344 Science .40 1.00
345 Checklist 1 (1-60) .40 1.00
346 Checklist 2 (61-120) .40 1.00
347 Checklist 3 (121-180) .40 1.00
348 Checklist 4 (181-244) .40 1.00
349 Checklist 5 (245-305) .40 1.00
350 Checklist 6 (306-350) .40 1.00
351 Atlanta Hawks TL .40 1.00
352 Boston Celtics TL .40 1.00
353 Charlotte Hornets TL .40 1.00
354 Chicago Bulls TL .40 1.00
355 Cleveland Cavaliers TL .40 1.00
356 Dallas Mavericks TL .40 1.00
357 Denver Nuggets TL .40 1.00
358 Detroit Pistons TL .40 1.00
359 Golden State Warriors TL .40 1.00
360 Houston Rockets TL .40 1.00
361 Indiana Pacers TL .40 1.00
362 Los Angeles Clippers TL .40 1.00
363 Los Angeles Lakers TL .40 1.00
364 Miami Heat TL .40 1.00
365 Milwaukee Bucks TL .40 1.00
366 Minnesota Timberwolves TL .40 1.00
367 New Jersey Nets TL .40 1.00
368 New York Knicks TL .40 1.00
369 Orlando Magic TL .40 1.00
370 Philadelphia 76ers TL .40 1.00
371 Phoenix Suns TL .40 1.00
372 Portland Trail Blazers TL .40 1.00
373 Sacramento Kings TL .40 1.00
374 San Antonio Spurs TL .40 1.00
375 Seattle Supersonics TL .40 1.00
376 Utah Jazz TL .40 1.00
377 Washington Bullets TL .40 1.00
378 Bob Weiss CO .40 1.00
379 Chris Ford CO .40 1.00
380 Allan Bristow CO .40 1.00
381 Phil Jackson CO .40 1.00
382 Lenny Wilkens CO .40 1.00
383 Richie Adubato CO .40 1.00
384 Paul Westhead CO .40 1.00
385 Chuck Daly CO .40 1.00
386 Don Nelson CO .40 1.00
387 Don Chaney CO .40 1.00
388 Bob Hill CO RC .40 1.00
389 Mike Schuler CO .40 1.00
390 Mike Dunleavy CO .40 1.00
391 Kevin Loughery CO .40 1.00
392 Del Harris CO .40 1.00
393 Jimmy Rodgers CO .40 1.00
394 Bill Fitch CO .40 1.00
395 Pat Riley CO .40 1.00
396 Matt Guokas CO .40 1.00
397 Jim Lynam CO .40 1.00
398 Cotton Fitzsimmons CO .40 1.00
399 Rick Adelman CO .40 1.00
400 Dick Motta CO .40 1.00
401 Larry Brown CO .40 1.00
402 K.C. Jones CO .40 1.00
403 Jerry Sloan CO .40 1.00
404 Wes Unseld CO .40 1.00
405 Mo Cheeks GF .25 .60
406 Dee Brown GF .25 .60
407 Rex Chapman GF .25 .60
408 Michael Jordan GF 2.50 6.00
409 John Williams GF .20 .50
410 James Donaldson GF .25 .60
411 Dikembe Mutombo GF 1.25 3.00
412 Isiah Thomas GF .50 1.25
413 Tim Hardaway GF .40 1.00
414 Hakeem Olajuwon GF .60 1.50
415 Detlef Schrempf GF .25 .60
416 Danny Manning GF .25 .60
417 Magic Johnson GF 1.00 2.50
418 Bimbo Coles GF .25 .60
419 Alvin Robertson GF .25 .60
420 Sam Mitchell GF .20 .50
421 Sam Bowie GF .20 .50
422 Mark Jackson GF .20 .50
423 Orlando Magic GF .20 .50
424 Charles Barkley GF .60 1.50
425 Dan Majerle GF .30 .75
426 Robert Pack GF .20 .50
427 Wayman Tisdale GF .25 .60
428 David Robinson GF .60 1.50
429 Nate McMillan GF .25 .60
430 Karl Malone GF .60 1.50
431 Michael Adams GF .25 .60
432 Duane Ferrell SM .20 .50
433 Kevin McHale SM .50 1.25
434 Dell Curry SM .25 .60
435 B.J. Armstrong SM .30 .75
436 John Williams SM .20 .50
437 Brad Davis SM .20 .50
438 Marcus Liberty SM .20 .50
439 Mark Aguirre SM .25 .60
440 Rod Higgins SM .20 .50
441 Eric (Sleepy) Floyd SM .25 .60
442 Detlef Schrempf SM .25 .60
443 Loy Vaught SM .25 .60
444 Terry Teagle SM .20 .50
445 Kevin Edwards SM .20 .50
446 Dale Ellis SM .20 .50
447 Tod Murphy SM .20 .50
448 Chris Dudley SM .20 .50
449 Mark Jackson SM .20 .50
450 Jerry Reynolds SM .20 .50
451 Ron Anderson SM .20 .50
452 Dan Majerle SM .30 .75
453 Danny Ainge SM .25 .60
454 Jim Les SM .20 .50
455 Paul Pressey SM .25 .60
456 Ricky Pierce SM .25 .60
457 Mike Brown SM .25 .60
458 Ledell Eackles SM .20 .50
459 D.Wilkins/Willis TW .50 1.25
460 L.Bird/R.Parish TW 1.00 2.50
461 R.Chapman/Gill TW .30 .75
462 M.Jordan/S.Pippen TW 2.50 6.00
463 C.Ehlo/M.Price TW .30 .75
464 D.Harper/R.Blackman TW .25 .60
465 R.Williams/C.Jackson TW .25 .60
466 I.Thomas/B.Laimbeer TW .50 1.25
467 T.Hard/C.Mullin TW .40 1.00
468 V.Maxwell/K.Smith TW .40 1.00
469 D.Schrempf/R.Miller TW .50 1.25
470 C.Smith/D.Manning TW .25 .60
471 M.Johnson/J.Worthy TW 1.00 2.50
472 G.Rice/R.Seikaly TW .30 .75
473 J.Hump/A.Robertson TW .20 .50
474 T.Campbell/P.Rich TW .20 .50
475 D.Coleman/S.Bowie TW .30 .75
476 P.Ewing/C.Oakley TW .50 1.25
477 D.Scott/S.Skiles TW .25 .60
478 C.Barkley/H.Hawkins TW .60 1.50
479 K.Johnson/T.Chambers TW .30 .75
480 C.Drexler/T.Porter TW .50 1.25
481 L.Simmons/W.Tisdale TW .25 .60
482 T.Cummings/S.Elliott TW .30 .75
483 E.Johnson/R.Pierce TW .25 .60
484 K.Malone/J.Stockton TW .60 1.50
485 H.Grant/B.King TW .40 1.00
486 Rumeal Robinson RS .20 .50
487 Dee Brown RS .25 .60
488 Kendall Gill RS .30 .75
489 B.J. Armstrong RS .30 .75
490 Danny Ferry RS .20 .50
491 Randy White RS .20 .50
492 Chris Jackson RS .25 .60
493 Lance Blanks RS .20 .50
494 Tim Hardaway RS .40 1.00
495 Vernon Maxwell RS .25 .60
496 Micheal Williams RS .20 .50
497 Charles Smith RS .25 .60
498 Vlade Divac RS .25 .60
499 Willie Burton RS .20 .50
500 Jeff Grayer RS .20 .50
501 Pooh Richardson RS .25 .60
502 Derrick Coleman RS .30 .75
503 John Starks RS 1.00 2.50
504 Dennis Scott RS .25 .60
505 Hersey Hawkins RS .25 .60
506 Negele Knight RS .20 .50
507 Clifford Robinson RS .25 .60
508 Lionel Simmons RS .20 .50
509 David Robinson RS .60 1.50
510 Gary Payton RS .50 1.25
511 Blue Edwards RS .20 .50
512 Harvey Grant RS .25 .60
513 Larry Johnson RC 1.00 2.50
514 Kenny Anderson RC .30 .75
515 Billy Owens RC .30 .75
516 Dikembe Mutombo RC 1.25 3.00
517 Steve Smith RC .50 1.25
518 Doug Smith RC .20 .50
519 Luc Longley RC .50 1.25
520 Mark Macon RC .30 .75
521 Stacey Augmon RC .30 .75
522 Brian Williams RC .30 .75
523 Terrell Brandon RC .25 .60
524 The Ball .40 1.00
525 The Basket .40 1.00
526 The 24-second Shot .40 1.00
527 The Game Program .40 1.00
528 The Championship Gift .40 1.00
529 Championship Trophy .40 1.00
530 Charles Barkley USA .60 1.50
531 Larry Bird USA 1.00 2.50
532 Patrick Ewing USA .50 1.25
533 Magic Johnson USA 1.00 2.50
534 Michael Jordan USA 2.50 6.00
535 Karl Malone USA .60 1.50
536 Chris Mullin USA .40 1.00
537 Scottie Pippen USA .75 2.00
538 David Robinson USA .60 1.50
539 John Stockton USA .60 1.50
540 Chuck Daly CO USA .30 .75
541 P.J.Carlesimo CO USA RC .20 .50
542 M.Krzyzewski CO USA RC 3.00 8.00
543 Lenny Wilkens CO USA .30 .75
544 Team USA 1 6.00 15.00
545 Team USA 2 6.00 15.00
546 Team USA 3 6.00 15.00
547 Willie Anderson USA .25 .60
548 Stacey Augmon USA .30 .75
549 Bimbo Coles USA .25 .60
550 Jeff Grayer USA .20 .50
551 Hersey Hawkins USA .25 .60
552 Dan Majerle USA .30 .75
553 Danny Manning USA .25 .60
554 J.R. Reid USA .20 .50
555 Mitch Richmond USA .40 1.00
556 Charles Smith USA .25 .60
557 Vern Fleming USA .25 .60
558 Joe Kleine USA .20 .50
559 Jon Koncak USA .20 .50
560 Sam Perkins USA .25 .60
561 Alvin Robertson USA .25 .60
562 Wayman Tisdale USA .25 .60
563 Jeff Turner USA .20 .50
564 Tony Campbell MAG .20 .50
565 Joe Dumars MAG .40 1.00
566 Horace Grant MAG .30 .75
567 Reggie Lewis MAG .30 .75
568 Hakeem Olajuwon MAG .60 1.50
569 Sam Perkins MAG .25 .60
570 Chuck Person MAG .25 .60
571 Buck Williams MAG .25 .60
572 Michael Jordan SAL 2.50 6.00
573 Bernard King SAL .40 1.00
574 Moses Malone SAL .50 1.25
575 Robert Parish SAL .40 1.00
576 Pat Riley CO SAL .40 1.00
577 Dee Brown SM .25 .60
578 Rex Chapman SM .25 .60
579 Clyde Drexler SM .50 1.25
580 Blue Edwards SM .20 .50
581 Ron Harper SM .30 .75
582 Kevin Johnson SM .30 .75
583 Michael Jordan SM 2.50 6.00
584 Shawn Kemp SM .50 1.25
585 Xavier McDaniel SM .25 .60
586 Scottie Pippen SM .75 2.00
587 Kenny Smith SM .25 .60
588 Dominique Wilkins SM .50 1.25
589 Michael Adams SS .25 .60
590 Danny Ainge SS .25 .60
591 Larry Bird SS 1.00 2.50
592 Dale Ellis SS .25 .60
593 Hersey Hawkins SS .25 .60
594 Jeff Hornacek SS .25 .60
595 Jeff Malone SS .25 .60
596 Reggie Miller SS .50 1.25
597 Chris Mullin SS .40 1.00
598 John Paxson SS .40 1.00
599 Drazen Petrovic SS .40 1.00
600 Ricky Pierce SS .25 .60
601 Mark Price SS .30 .75
602 Dennis Scott SS .30 .75
603 Manute Bol SMALL .30 .75
604 Jerome Kersey SMALL .25 .60
605 Charles Oakley SMALL .25 .60
606 Scottie Pippen SMALL .75 2.00
607 Terry Porter SMALL .25 .60
608 Dennis Rodman SMALL .60 1.50
609 Sedale Threatt SMALL .20 .50
610 Business .40 1.00
611 Engineering .40 1.00
612 Law .40 1.00
613 Liberal Arts .40 1.00
614 Medicine .40 1.00
615 Maurice Cheeks .25 .60
616 Travis Mays .20 .50
617 Blair Rasmussen .20 .50
618 Alexander Volkov .20 .50
619 Rickey Green .25 .60
620 Bobby Hansen .20 .50
621 John Battle .20 .50
622 Terry Davis .20 .50
623 Walter Davis .25 .60
624 Winston Garland .20 .50
625 Scott Hastings .20 .50
626 Brad Sellers .20 .50
627 Darrell Walker .20 .50
628 Orlando Woolridge .25 .60
629 Tony Brown .20 .50
630 James Edwards .25 .60
631 Doc Rivers .30 .75
632 Jack Haley .20 .50
633 Sedale Threatt .20 .50
634 Moses Malone .50 1.25
635 Thurl Bailey .20 .50
636 Rafael Addison RC .25 .60
637 Tim McCormick .20 .50
638 Xavier McDaniel .25 .60
639 Charles Shackleford .20 .50
640 Mitchell Wiggins .20 .50
641 Jerrod Mustaf .20 .50
642 Dennis Hopson .20 .50
643 Les Jepsen .20 .50
644 Mitch Richmond .40 1.00
645 Dwayne Schintzius .20 .50
646 Spud Webb .30 .75
647 Jud Buechler .25 .60
648 Antoine Carr .25 .60
649 Tyrone Corbin .20 .50
650 Michael Adams .25 .60
651 Ralph Sampson .25 .60
652 Andre Turner .20 .50
653 David Wingate .20 .50
654 Checklist S .60 1.50
655 Checklist K .60 1.50
656 Checklist Y .60 1.50
657 Checklist B .60 1.50
658 Checklist O .60 1.50
659 Checklist X .60 1.50
NNO Clyde Drexler USA 100.00 250.00
NNO Team USA Card 20.00 50.00

1991-92 SkyBox Blister Inserts

COMPLETE SET (6) 1.00 2.50
ONE CARD PER BLISTER PACK
1 USA Basketball .08 .25
2 Stay in School .08 .25
3 Orlando All-Star .08 .25
4 Inside Stuff .08 .25
5 M.Johnson/J.Worthy .40 1.00
6 J.Dumars/I.Thomas .20 .50

1992-93 SkyBox

COMPLETE SET (413) 20.00 50.00
COMPLETE SERIES 1 (327) 12.00 30.00
COMPLETE SERIES 2 (86) 8.00 20.00
1 Stacey Augmon .40 1.00
2 Maurice Cheeks .30 .75
3 Duane Ferrell .25 .60
4 Paul Graham .25 .60
5 Jon Koncak .25 .60
6 Blair Rasmussen .25 .60
7 Rumeal Robinson .25 .60
8 Dominique Wilkins .60 1.50
9 Kevin Willis .30 .75
10 Larry Bird 1.50 4.00
11 Dee Brown .30 .75
12 Sherman Douglas .30 .75
13 Rick Fox .40 1.00
14 Kevin Gamble .25 .60
15 Reggie Lewis .40 1.00
16 Kevin McHale .60 1.50
17 Robert Parish .50 1.25
18 Ed Pinckney .30 .75
19 Muggsy Bogues .40 1.00
20 Dell Curry .30 .75
21 Kenny Gattison .25 .60
22 Kendall Gill .30 .75
23 Mike Gminski .25 .60
24 Tom Hammonds .25 .60
25 Larry Johnson .50 1.25
26 Johnny Newman .25 .60
27 J.R. Reid .30 .75
28 B.J. Armstrong .40 1.00
29 Bill Cartwright .30 .75
30 Horace Grant .40 1.00
31 Michael Jordan 3.00 8.00
32 Stacey King .25 .60
33 John Paxson .30 .75
34 Will Perdue .25 .60
35 Scottie Pippen 1.00 2.50
36 Scott Williams .25 .60
37 John Battle .30 .75
38 Terrell Brandon .30 .75
39 Brad Daugherty .30 .75
40 Craig Ehlo .30 .75
41 Danny Ferry .25 .60
42 Henry James .25 .60
43 Larry Nance .30 .75
44 Mark Price .40 1.00
45 Mike Sanders .30 .75
46 Hot Rod Williams .30 .75
47 Rolando Blackman .30 .75
48 Terry Davis .25 .60
49 Derek Harper .30 .75
50 Donald Hodge .25 .60
51 Mike Iuzzolino .25 .60
52 Fat Lever .30 .75
53 Rodney McCray .25 .60
54 Doug Smith .25 .60
55 Randy White .25 .60
56 Herb Williams .30 .75
57 Greg Anderson .25 .60
58 Walter Davis .30 .75
59 Winston Garland .25 .60
60 Chris Jackson .25 .60
61 Marcus Liberty .25 .60
62 Todd Lichti .25 .60
63 Mark Macon .25 .60
64 Dikembe Mutombo .60 1.50
65 Reggie Williams .25 .60
66 Mark Aguirre .30 .75
67 William Bedford .25 .60
68 Lance Blanks .25 .60
69 Joe Dumars .50 1.25
70 Bill Laimbeer .40 1.00
71 Dennis Rodman 1.00 2.50
72 John Salley .25 .60
73 Isiah Thomas .60 1.50
74 Darrell Walker .25 .60
75 Orlando Woolridge .40 1.00
76 Victor Alexander .25 .60
77 Mario Elie .30 .75
78 Chris Gatling .25 .60
79 Tim Hardaway .50 1.25
80 Tyrone Hill .25 .60
81 Alton Lister .25 .60
82 Sarunas Marciulionis .40 1.00
83 Chris Mullin .50 1.25
84 Billy Owens .30 .75
85 Matt Bullard .25 .60
86 Sleepy Floyd .30 .75
87 Avery Johnson .25 .60
88 Buck Johnson .25 .60
89 Vernon Maxwell .25 .60
90 Hakeem Olajuwon .75 2.00
91 Kenny Smith .30 .75
92 Larry Smith .25 .60
93 Otis Thorpe .30 .75
94 Dale Davis .25 .60
95 Vern Fleming .30 .75
96 George McCloud .25 .60
97 Reggie Miller .75 2.00
98 Chuck Person .30 .75
99 Detlef Schrempf .40 1.00
100 Rik Smits .30 .75
101 LaSalle Thompson .25 .60
102 Micheal Williams .25 .60
103 James Edwards .25 .60
104 Gary Grant .25 .60
105 Ron Harper .40 1.00
106 Bo Kimble .30 .75
107 Danny Manning .30 .75
108 Ken Norman .25 .60
109 Olden Polynice .25 .60
110 Doc Rivers .40 1.00
111 Charles Smith .30 .75
112 Loy Vaught .25 .60
113 Elden Campbell .25 .60
114 Vlade Divac .40 1.00
115 A.C. Green .30 .75
116 Jack Haley .25 .60
117 Sam Perkins .30 .75
118 Byron Scott .40 1.00
119 Tony Smith .25 .60
120 Sedale Threatt .25 .60
121 James Worthy .60 1.50
122 Keith Askins .25 .60
123 Willie Burton .25 .60
124 Bimbo Coles .25 .60
125 Kevin Edwards .25 .60
126 Alec Kessler .25 .60
127 Grant Long .25 .60
128 Glen Rice .40 1.00
129 Rony Seikaly .30 .75
130 Brian Shaw .25 .60
131 Steve Smith .40 1.00
132 Frank Brickowski .25 .60
133 Dale Ellis .30 .75
134 Jeff Grayer .25 .60
135 Jay Humphries .30 .75
136 Larry Krystkowiak .30 .75
137 Moses Malone .40 1.00
138 Fred Roberts .25 .60
139 Alvin Robertson .30 .75
140 Danny Schayes .25 .60
141 Thurl Bailey .30 .75
142 Scott Brooks .30 .75
143 Tony Campbell .25 .60
144 Gerald Glass .25 .60
145 Luc Longley .40 1.00
146 Sam Mitchell .25 .60
147 Pooh Richardson .25 .60
148 Felton Spencer .25 .60
149 Doug West .30 .75
150 Rafael Addison .25 .60
151 Kenny Anderson .30 .75
152 Mookie Blaylock .40 1.00
153 Sam Bowie .25 .60
154 Derrick Coleman .40 1.00
155 Chris Dudley .25 .60
156 Tate George .25 .60
157 Terry Mills .25 .60
158 Chris Morris .30 .75
159 Drazen Petrovic .50 1.25
160 Greg Anthony .25 .60
161 Patrick Ewing .60 1.50
162 Mark Jackson .40 1.00
163 Anthony Mason .40 1.00
164 Tim McCormick .25 .60
165 Xavier McDaniel .30 .75
166 Charles Oakley .40 1.00
167 John Starks .40 1.00
168 Gerald Wilkins .30 .75
169 Nick Anderson .30 .75
170 Terry Catledge .25 .60
171 Jerry Reynolds .25 .60
172 Stanley Roberts .25 .60
173 Dennis Scott .30 .75
174 Scott Skiles .30 .75
175 Jeff Turner .25 .60
176 Sam Vincent .25 .60
177 Brian Williams .30 .75
178 Ron Anderson .25 .60
179 Charles Barkley 1.00 2.50
180 Manute Bol .40 1.00
181 Johnny Dawkins .25 .60
182 Armon Gilliam .25 .60
183 Greg Grant .25 .60
184 Hersey Hawkins .30 .75
185 Brian Oliver .25 .60
186 Charles Shackleford .25 .60
187 Jayson Williams .30 .75
188 Cedric Ceballos .30 .75
189 Tom Chambers .40 1.00
190 Jeff Hornacek .30 .75
191 Kevin Johnson .40 1.00
192 Negele Knight .25 .60
193 Andrew Lang .25 .60
194 Dan Majerle .40 1.00
195 Jerrod Mustaf .25 .60
196 Tim Perry .25 .60
197 Mark West .30 .75
198 Alaa Abdelnaby .25 .60
199 Danny Ainge .40 1.00
200 Mark Bryant .25 .60
201 Clyde Drexler .60 1.50
202 Kevin Duckworth .40 1.00
203 Jerome Kersey .30 .75
204 Robert Pack .25 .60
205 Terry Porter .25 .60
206 Clifford Robinson .30 .75
207 Buck Williams .30 .75
208 Anthony Bonner .25 .60
209 Randy Brown .30 .75
210 Duane Causwell .25 .60
211 Pete Chilcutt .25 .60
212 Dennis Hopson .25 .60
213 Jim Les .25 .60
214 Mitch Richmond .50 1.25
215 Lionel Simmons .25 .60
216 Wayman Tisdale .40 1.00
217 Spud Webb .40 1.00
218 Willie Anderson .30 .75
219 Antoine Carr .30 .75
220 Terry Cummings .30 .75
221 Sean Elliott .40 1.00
222 Sidney Green .25 .60
223 Vinnie Johnson .30 .75
224 David Robinson .75 2.00
225 Rod Strickland .30 .75
226 Greg Sutton .25 .60
227 Dana Barros .25 .60
228 Benoit Benjamin .25 .60
229 Michael Cage .30 .75
230 Eddie Johnson .30 .75
231 Shawn Kemp .60 1.50
232 Derrick McKey .30 .75
233 Nate McMillan .30 .75
234 Gary Payton .60 1.50
235 Ricky Pierce .30 .75
236 David Benoit .25 .60
237 Mike Brown .25 .60
238 Tyrone Corbin .30 .75
239 Mark Eaton .40 1.00
240 Blue Edwards .25 .60
241 Jeff Malone .30 .75
242 Karl Malone .75 2.00
243 Eric Murdock .25 .60
244 John Stockton .75 2.00
245 Michael Adams .30 .75
246 Rex Chapman .30 .75
247 Ledell Eackles .25 .60
248 Pervis Ellison .25 .60
249 A.J. English .25 .60
250 Harvey Grant .30 .75
251 Charles Jones .25 .60
252 Bernard King .50 1.25
253 LaBradford Smith .25 .60
254 Larry Stewart .25 .60
255 Bob Weiss CO .25 .60
256 Chris Ford CO .25 .60
257 Allan Bristow CO .25 .60
258 Phil Jackson CO .60 1.50
259 Lenny Wilkens CO .40 1.00
260 Richie Adubato CO .25 .60
261 Dan Issel CO .50 1.25
262 Ron Rothstein CO .25 .60
263 Don Nelson CO .50 1.25
264 Rudy Tomjanovich CO .50 1.25
265 Bob Hill CO .25 .60
266 Larry Brown CO .40 1.00
267 Randy Pfund CO RC .25 .60
268 Kevin Loughery CO .25 .60
269 Mike Dunleavy CO .25 .60
270 Jimmy Rodgers CO .25 .60
271 Chuck Daly CO .50 1.25
272 Pat Riley CO .50 1.25
273 Matt Guokas CO .25 .60
274 Doug Moe CO .30 .75
275 Paul Westphal CO .40 1.00
276 Rick Adelman CO .25 .60
277 Garry St. Jean CO RC .25 .60
278 Jerry Tarkanian CO RC .40 1.00
279 George Karl CO .30 .75
280 Jerry Sloan CO .40 1.00
281 Wes Unseld CO .50 1.25
282 Dominique Wilkins TT .60 1.50
283 Reggie Lewis TT .40 1.00
284 Kendall Gill TT .30 .75
285 Horace Grant TT .40 1.00
286 Brad Daugherty TT .30 .75
287 Derek Harper TT .30 .75
288 Chris Jackson TT .30 .75
289 Isiah Thomas TT .60 1.50
290 Chris Mullin TT .50 1.25
291 Kenny Smith TT .30 .75
292 Reggie Miller TT .75 2.00
293 Ron Harper TT .40 1.00
294 Vlade Divac TT .40 1.00
295 Glen Rice TT .40 1.00
296 Moses Malone TT .40 1.00
297 Doug West TT .30 .75
298 Derrick Coleman TT .40 1.00
299 Patrick Ewing TT .60 1.50
300 Scott Skiles TT .30 .75
301 Hersey Hawkins TT .30 .75
302 Kevin Johnson TT .40 1.00
303 Clifford Robinson TT .30 .75
304 Spud Webb TT .40 1.00
305 David Robinson TT COR .75 2.00
305A Dav.Robinson TT ERR 299 .75 2.00
306 Shawn Kemp TT .60 1.50
307 John Stockton TT .75 2.00
308 Pervis Ellison TT .25 .60
309 Craig Hodges AS .30 .75
310 Magic Johnson AS MVP 1.50 4.00
311 Cedric Ceballos AS SD .30 .75
312 D.Rodman/Group AS 1.00 2.50
313 K.Malone/Group AS .75 2.00
314 Michael Jordan MVP 3.00 8.00
315 Clyde Drexler FIN .60 1.50
316 Danny Ainge PO .40 1.00
317 Scottie Pippen FIN 1.00 2.50
318 M.Jordan CHAMP 3.00 8.00
319 L.Johnson/D.Mut. ART .50 1.25
320 NBA Stay in School .75 2.00
321 Boys and Girls .25 .60
322 Checklist 1 .20 .50
323 Checklist 2 .20 .50
324 Checklist 3 .20 .50
325 Checklist 4 .20 .50
326 Checklist 5 .20 .50
327 Checklist 6 .20 .50
328 Adam Keefe SP RC .25 .60
329 Sean Rooks SP RC .25 .60
330 Xavier McDaniel .30 .75
331 Kiki Vandeweghe .30 .75
332 Alonzo Mourning SP RC 2.00 5.00
333 Rodney McCray .25 .60
334 Gerald Wilkins .30 .75
335 Tony Bennett SP RC .25 .60
336 LaPhonso Ellis SP RC .40 1.00
337 Bryant Stith SP RC .30 .75
338 Isaiah Morris SP RC .30 .75
339 Olden Polynice .25 .60
340 Jeff Grayer .25 .60
341 Byron Houston SP RC .25 .60
342 Latrell Sprewell SP RC 1.25 3.00
343 Scott Brooks .30 .75
344 Frank Johnson .30 .75
345 Robert Horry SP RC 1.00 2.50
346 David Wood .25 .60
347 Sam Mitchell .25 .60
348 Pooh Richardson .25 .60
349 Malik Sealy SP RC .30 .75

350 Morlon Wiley .25 .60
351 Mark Jackson .40 1.00
352 Stanley Roberts .25 .60
353 Elmore Spencer SP RC .25 .60
354 John Williams .25 .60
355 Randy Woods SP RC .25 .60
356 James Edwards .25 .60
357 Jeff Sanders .25 .60
358 Magic Johnson 1.50 4.00
359 Anthony Peeler SP RC .30 .75
360 Harold Miner SP RC .50 1.25
361 John Salley .30 .75
362 Alaa Abdelnaby .25 .60
363 Todd Day SP RC .30 .75
364 Blue Edwards .25 .60
365 Lee Mayberry SP RC .25 .60
366 Eric Murdock .25 .60
367 Mookie Blaylock .40 1.00
368 Anthony Avent RC .25 .60
369 Christian Laettner SP RC 1.25 3.00
370 Chuck Person .30 .75
371 Chris Smith SP RC .25 .60
372 Micheal Williams .25 .60
373 Rolando Blackman .30 .75
374 Tony Campbell UER .25 .60
375 Hubert Davis SP RC .30 .75
376 Travis Mays .25 .60
377 Doc Rivers .40 1.00
378 Charles Smith .30 .75
379 Rumeal Robinson .25 .60
380 Vinny Del Negro .30 .75
381 Steve Kerr .30 .75
382 Shaquille O'Neal SP RC 3.00 8.00
383 Donald Royal .25 .60
384 Jeff Hornacek .30 .75
385 Andrew Lang .25 .60
386 Tim Perry .25 .60
387 C.Weatherspoon SP RC .40 1.00
388 Danny Ainge .40 1.00
389 Charles Barkley 1.00 2.50
390 Tim Kempton .25 .60
391 Oliver Miller SP RC .30 .75
392 Dave Johnson SP RC .25 .60
393 Tracy Murray SP RC .30 .75
394 Rod Strickland .30 .75
395 Marty Conlon .25 .60
396 Walt Williams SP RC .40 1.00
397 Lloyd Daniels RC .30 .75
398 Dale Ellis .30 .75
399 Dave Hoppen .25 .60
400 Larry Smith .25 .60
401 Doug Overton .30 .75
402 Isaac Austin RC .30 .75
403 Jay Humphries .30 .75
404 Larry Krystkowiak .30 .75
405 Tom Gugliotta SP RC .40 1.00
406 Buck Johnson .25 .60
407 Don MacLean SP RC .30 .75
408 Marlon Maxey SP RC .25 .60
409 Corey Williams SP RC .25 .60
410 D.Majerle OLY .40 1.00
411 Checklist 1 .20 .50
412 Checklist 2 .20 .50
413 Checklist 3 .20 .50
NNO Magic Never Ends Silver 5.00 12.00
NNO Admiral Comes Prep Silver 2.00 5.00
NNO Magic Johnson AU 125.00 300.00
NNO Admiral Comes Prep Gold 2.50 6.00
NNO David Robinson AU 60.00 150.00
NNO Head of the Class 10.00 25.00
NNO Magic Never Ends Gold 6.00 15.00

1992-93 SkyBox Draft Picks

COMPLETE SET (25) 12.00 30.00
COMPLETE SERIES 1 (6) 4.00 10.00
COMPLETE SERIES 2 (19) 8.00 20.00
SER.1/2 STATED ODDS 1:8
DP1 Shaquille O'Neal 10.00 25.00
DP2 Alonzo Mourning 1.50 4.00
DP3 Christian Laettner 1.25 3.00
DP5 LaPhonso Ellis .40 1.00
DP6 Tom Gugliotta .40 1.00
DP7 Walt Williams .40 1.00
DP8 Todd Day .30 .75
DP9 Clarence Weatherspoon .40 1.00
DP10 Adam Keefe .25 .60
DP11 Robert Horry 1.00 2.50
DP12 Harold Miner .50 1.25
DP13 Bryant Stith .30 .75
DP14 Malik Sealy .30 .75
DP15 Anthony Peeler .30 .75
DP16 Randy Woods .25 .60
DP18 Tracy Murray .30 .75
DP19 Don MacLean .30 .75
DP20 Hubert Davis .30 .75
DP21 Jon Barry .25 .60
DP22 Oliver Miller .30 .75
DP23 Lee Mayberry .25 .60
DP24 Latrell Sprewell 1.25 3.00
DP25 Elmore Spencer .25 .60
DP26 Dave Johnson .25 .60
DP27 Byron Houston .25 .60

1992-93 SkyBox Olympic Team

COMPLETE SET (12) 12.00 30.00
SER.1 STATED ODDS 1:6
USA1 Clyde Drexler .75 2.00
USA2 Chris Mullin .60 1.50
USA3 John Stockton .75 2.00
USA4 Karl Malone 1.00 2.50
USA5 Scottie Pippen 2.00 5.00
USA6 Larry Bird 2.50 6.00
USA7 Charles Barkley 1.00 2.50
USA8 Patrick Ewing .75 2.00
USA9 Christian Laettner 1.25 3.00
USA10 David Robinson 1.00 2.50
USA11 Michael Jordan 8.00 20.00
USA12 Magic Johnson 2.00 5.00

1992-93 SkyBox David Robinson

COMPLETE SET (10) 3.00 8.00
COMPLETE SERIES 1 (5) 1.50 4.00
COMPLETE SERIES 2 (5) 1.50 4.00
COMMON D.ROB. (R1-R10) .75 2.00
SER.1/2 STATED ODDS 1:8

1992-93 SkyBox School Ties

COMPLETE SET (18) 8.00 20.00
SER.2 STATED ODDS 1:4
ST1 P.Ewing/A.Mourning 2.00 5.00
ST2 D.Mutombo/S.Floyd .60 1.50
ST3 R.Williams/D.Wingate .25 .60
ST4 K.Anderson/D.Ferrell .30 .75
ST5 Hammonds/J.Barry/M.Price .40 1.00
ST6 J.Salley/D.Scott .30 .75
ST7 R.Addison/D.Johnson .25 .60
ST8 Owens/Coleman/Seikaly .40 1.00
ST9 S.Douglas/D.Schayes .30 .75
ST10 N.Anderson/K.Gill .30 .75
ST11 D.Harper/E.Johnson .30 .75
ST12 M.Liberty/K.Norman .25 .60
ST13 G.Anthony/S.Augmon .40 1.00
ST14 Gilliam/L.Johnson/Green .50 1.25
ST15 E.Spencer/G.Paddio .25 .60
ST16 Worthy/Jordan/Perkins 3.00 8.00
ST17 Reid/Chilcu/Daugherty/Fox .40 1.00
ST18 Davis/Smith/Williams .30 .75

1992-93 SkyBox Thunder and Lightning

COMPLETE SET (9) 15.00 40.00
SER.2 STATED ODDS 1:40
TL1 D.Mutombo/M.Macon 1.50 4.00
TL2 B.Williams/C.Drexler 1.50 4.00
TL3 C.Barkley/K.Johnson 3.00 8.00
TL4 P.Ellison/M.Adams .60 1.50
TL5 L.Johnson/M.Bogues 1.50 4.00
TL6 B.Daugherty/M.Price .60 1.50
TL7 S.Kemp/G.Payton 4.00 10.00
TL8 K.Malone/J.Stockton 4.00 10.00
TL9 B.Owens/T.Hardaway 2.00 5.00

2008-09 SkyBox

COMPLETE SET (230) 40.00 80.00
APPROXIMATE CLOSE ODDS 1:1.25
1 Mike Bibby .30 .75
2 Acie Law .25 .60
3 Al Horford .25 .60
4 Joe Johnson .30 .75
5 Josh Smith .20 .50
6 Marvin Williams .20 .50
7 Ray Allen .50 1.25
8 Glen Davis .20 .50
9 Kevin Garnett .75 2.00
10 Paul Pierce .50 1.25
11 Leon Powe .20 .50
12 Rajon Rondo .40 1.00
13 Raymond Felton .20 .50
14 Adam Morrison .20 .50
15 Emeka Okafor .25 .60
16 Boris Diaw .25 .60
17 Gerald Wallace .25 .60
18 Luol Deng .25 .60
19 Ben Gordon .25 .60
20 Kirk Hinrich .25 .60
21 Joakim Noah .20 .50
22 Andres Nocioni .20 .50
23 Tyrus Thomas .20 .50
24 Daniel Gibson .20 .50
25 Zydrunas Ilgauskas .25 .60
26 LeBron James 2.50 6.00
27 Anderson Varejao .20 .50
28 Ben Wallace .40 1.00
29 Jose Barea .40 1.00
30 Josh Howard .25 .60
31 Jason Kidd .50 1.25
32 Dirk Nowitzki .75 2.00
33 Jason Terry .25 .60
34 Carmelo Anthony .40 1.00
35 Shaun Livingston .20 .50
36 Chauncey Billups .40 1.00
37 Kenyon Martin .25 .60
38 J.R. Smith .30 .75
39 Allen Iverson .60 1.50
40 Richard Hamilton .30 .75
41 Jason Maxiell .20 .50
42 Tayshaun Prince .30 .75
43 Rodney Stuckey .20 .50
44 Rasheed Wallace .40 1.00
45 Kelenna Azubuike .20 .50
46 Matt Barnes .20 .50
47 Corey Maggette .25 .60
48 Monta Ellis .25 .60
49 Jamal Crawford .30 .75
50 Stephen Jackson .25 .60
51 Shane Battier .25 .60
52 Luther Head .20 .50
53 Carl Landry .20 .50
54 Tracy McGrady .50 1.25
55 Yao Ming .75 2.00
56 Luis Scola .25 .60
57 Mike Dunleavy .20 .50
58 Danny Granger .25 .60
59 Troy Murphy .20 .50
60 T.J. Ford .20 .50
61 Jamaal Tinsley .20 .50
62 Elton Brand .25 .60
63 Chris Kaman .20 .50
64 Ricky Davis .25 .60
65 Baron Davis .30 .75
66 Zach Randolph .30 .75
67 Al Thornton .20 .50
68 Kobe Bryant 2.50 6.00
69 Andrew Bynum .20 .50
70 Jordan Farmar .20 .50
71 Pau Gasol .40 1.00
72 Lamar Odom .25 .60
73 Sasha Vujacic .20 .50
74 Mike Conley Jr. .25 .60
75 Rudy Gay .30 .75
76 Kyle Lowry .30 .75
77 Mike Miller .25 .60
78 Hakim Warrick .20 .50
79 Daequan Cook .20 .50
80 Marcus Camby .25 .60
81 Udonis Haslem .20 .50
82 Shawn Marion .30 .75
83 Alonzo Mourning .40 1.00
84 Dwyane Wade .60 1.50
85 Andrew Bogut .25 .60
86 Richard Jefferson .25 .60
87 Desmond Mason .20 .50
88 Michael Redd .25 .60
89 Ramon Sessions .20 .50
90 Mo Williams .25 .60
91 Corey Brewer .25 .60
92 Randy Foye .30 .75
93 Al Jefferson .20 .50
94 Rashad McCants .20 .50
95 Sebastian Telfair .20 .50
96 Josh Boone .20 .50
97 Vince Carter .60 1.50
98 Devin Harris .20 .50
99 Yi Jianlian .40 1.00
100 Keyon Dooling .20 .50
101 Sean Williams .20 .50
102 Tyson Chandler .25 .60
103 Chris Paul .60 1.50
104 Morris Peterson .25 .60
105 Peja Stojakovic .25 .60
106 David West .25 .60
107 Julian Wright .20 .50
108 Al Harrington .25 .60
109 Eddy Curry .20 .50
110 David Lee .20 .50
111 Stephon Marbury .30 .75
112 Cuttino Mobley .20 .50
113 Quentin Richardson .20 .50
114 Keith Bogans .20 .50
115 Maurice Evans .20 .50
116 Dwight Howard .40 1.00
117 Rashard Lewis .25 .60
118 Jameer Nelson .20 .50
119 Hedo Turkoglu .25 .60
120 Samuel Dalembert .20 .50
121 Reggie Evans .20 .50
122 Willie Green .20 .50
123 Andre Iguodala .25 .60
124 Andre Miller .25 .60
125 Thaddeus Young .25 .60
126 Leandro Barbosa .25 .60
127 Jason Richardson .30 .75
128 Grant Hill .50 1.25
129 Steve Nash .60 1.50
130 Shaquille O'Neal 1.00 2.50
131 Amare Stoudemire .30 .75
132 LaMarcus Aldridge .30 .75
133 Steve Blake .20 .50
134 Greg Oden .25 .60
135 Brandon Roy .25 .60
136 Martell Webster .25 .60
137 Beno Udrih .20 .50
138 Ron Artest .30 .75
139 Francisco Garcia .20 .50
140 Kevin Martin .25 .60
141 Brad Miller .20 .50
142 Brent Barry .20 .50
143 Bruce Bowen .25 .60
144 Tim Duncan .75 2.00
145 Michael Finley .30 .75
146 Manu Ginobili .60 1.50
147 Tony Parker .40 1.00
148 Nick Collison .20 .50
149 Kevin Durant 1.25 3.00
150 Jeff Green .25 .60
151 Earl Watson .20 .50
152 Chris Wilcox .20 .50
153 Damien Wilkins .20 .50
154 Andrea Bargnani .25 .60
155 Chris Bosh .40 1.00
156 Jose Calderon .20 .50
157 Jermaine O'Neal .30 .75
158 Jamario Moon .20 .50
159 Anthony Parker .20 .50
160 Carlos Boozer .25 .60
161 Ronnie Brewer .20 .50
162 Andrei Kirilenko .25 .60
163 Kyle Korver .25 .60
164 Mehmet Okur .20 .50
165 Deron Williams .25 .60
166 Gilbert Arenas .30 .75
167 Caron Butler .25 .60
168 Antawn Jamison .25 .60
169 DeShawn Stevenson .25 .60
170 Nick Young .20 .50
171 Al Horford CU .40 1.00
172 Joe Johnson CU .40 1.00
173 Kevin Garnett CU 1.00 2.50
174 Paul Pierce CU .60 1.50
175 Larry Johnson CU .60 1.50
176 Michael Jordan CU 3.00 8.00
177 LeBron James CU 3.00 8.00
178 Ben Wallace CU .50 1.25
179 Dirk Nowitzki CU 1.00 2.50
180 Carmelo Anthony CU .50 1.25
181 Allen Iverson CU .75 2.00
182 Isiah Thomas CU .60 1.50
183 Monta Ellis CU .30 .75
184 Magic Johnson CU 1.25 3.00
185 Kobe Bryant CU 3.00 8.00
186 Dwyane Wade CU .75 2.00
187 Oscar Robertson CU .60 1.50
188 Vince Carter CU .75 2.00
189 Chris Paul CU .75 2.00
190 Patrick Ewing CU .60 1.50
191 Dwight Howard CU .50 1.25
192 Julius Erving CU 1.00 2.50
193 Steve Nash CU .75 2.00
194 Shaquille O'Neal CU 1.25 3.00
195 Brandon Roy CU .30 .75
196 Tim Duncan CU 1.00 2.50
197 Kevin Durant CU 1.50 4.00
198 Chris Bosh CU .50 1.25
199 Deron Williams CU .30 .75
200 Gilbert Arenas CU .40 1.00
201 Derrick Rose RC 6.00 15.00
202 Michael Beasley RC 2.00 5.00
203 O.J. Mayo RC .75 2.00
204 Russell Westbrook RC 12.00 30.00
205 Kevin Love RC 2.00 5.00
206 Danilo Gallinari RC 1.50 4.00
207 Eric Gordon RC 1.50 4.00
208 Joe Alexander RC .60 1.50
209 D.J. Augustin RC 1.00 2.50
210 Brook Lopez RC 1.00 2.50
211 Jerryd Bayless RC .75 2.00
212 Jason Thompson RC .60 1.50
213 Brandon Rush RC .60 1.50
214 Robin Lopez RC .75 2.00
215 Roy Hibbert RC .75 2.00
216 Alexis Ajinca RC .60 1.50
217 George Hill RC 1.00 2.50
218 Donte Greene RC .60 1.50
219 J.J. Hickson RC .75 2.00
220 D.J. White RC .60 1.50
221 Mario Chalmers RC 1.00 2.50
222 Mike Taylor RC .60 1.50
223 Kosta Koufos RC .60 1.50
224 Kyle Weaver RC .60 1.50
225 Rudy Fernandez RC .75 2.00
226 Nicolas Batum RC 1.25 3.00
227 Luc Richard Mbah A Moute RC .75 2.00
228 Marc Gasol RC 2.00 5.00
229 Darrell Jackson RC .60 1.50
230 Richard Hendrix RC .60 1.50

2008-09 SkyBox Ruby

*VETS 1-170: 12X TO 30X BASE HI
*SUBSET 171-200: 10X TO 25X BASE HI
*ROOKIES 201-230: 4X TO 10X BASE HI
STATED PRINT RUN 50 SER.#'d SETS
26 LeBron James 200.00 500.00
29 Jose Barea 15.00 40.00
39 Allen Iverson 20.00 50.00
68 Kobe Bryant 125.00 300.00
84 Dwyane Wade 25.00 60.00
128 Grant Hill 25.00 60.00
149 Kevin Durant 75.00 200.00
176 Michael Jordan CU 200.00 500.00
177 LeBron James CU 150.00 400.00
181 Allen Iverson CU 20.00 50.00
185 Kobe Bryant CU 100.00 250.00
186 Dwyane Wade CU 25.00 60.00
197 Kevin Durant CU 50.00 125.00
204 Russell Westbrook 300.00 600.00

2008-09 SkyBox Emerald Rookie Autographs

COMBINED AUTO ODDS 1:12
202 Michael Beasley 40.00 100.00
203 O.J. Mayo 40.00 100.00
204 Russell Westbrook 300.00 600.00
205 Kevin Love 150.00 300.00
207 Eric Gordon 30.00 80.00
208 Joe Alexander 5.00 12.00
210 Brook Lopez 15.00 40.00
212 Jason Thompson 5.00 12.00
213 Brandon Rush 5.00 12.00
214 Robin Lopez 6.00 15.00
215 Roy Hibbert 6.00 15.00
216 Alexis Ajinca 5.00 12.00
217 George Hill 8.00 20.00
218 Donte Greene 5.00 12.00
219 J.J. Hickson 20.00 50.00
220 D.J. White 5.00 12.00
221 Mario Chalmers 8.00 20.00
222 Mike Taylor 5.00 12.00
224 Kyle Weaver 5.00 12.00
226 Nicolas Batum 30.00 80.00
227 Luc Richard Mbah A Moute 6.00 15.00
229 Darnell Jackson 5.00 12.00
230 Richard Hendrix 5.00 12.00

2008-09 SkyBox Fresh Ink

COMBINED AUTO ODDS 1:12
FICD Chris Duhon 4.00 10.00
FICM Chris Mihm 4.00 10.00
FICW C.J. Watson 4.00 10.00
FIGP Gabe Pruitt 4.00 10.00
FIJF Jordan Farmar 4.00 10.00
FIKD Kevin Durant 50.00 120.00
FIKG Kevin Garnett 50.00 120.00
FIMA Morris Almond 4.00 10.00
FIMW Mario West 4.00 10.00
FIRR Rajon Rondo 10.00 25.00
FISV Sasha Vujacic 4.00 10.00
FIWM Mo Williams 5.00 12.00

2008-09 SkyBox Larger Than Life

COMBINED MEM.ODDS 1:4
*RETAIL GREEN: .4X TO 1X HI COLUMN
*PATCHES: 1.25X TO 3X HI COLUMN
PATCH PRINT RUN 25 SER.#'d SETS
LLAS Amare Stoudemire 2.00 5.00
LLCA Carmelo Anthony 2.50 6.00
LLDN Dirk Nowitzki 5.00 12.00
LLDW Deron Williams 1.50 4.00
LLEB Elton Brand 1.50 4.00
LLGA Gilbert Arenas 2.00 5.00
LLJJ Joe Johnson 2.00 5.00
LLKB Kobe Bryant 40.00 100.00
LLKG Kevin Garnett 5.00 12.00
LLLJ LeBron James 8.00 20.00
LLME Monta Ellis 1.50 4.00
LLMG Manu Ginobili 4.00 10.00
LLPP Paul Pierce 3.00 8.00
LLRA Ray Allen 3.00 8.00
LLRH Richard Hamilton 2.00 5.00
LLSM Shawn Marion 2.00 5.00
LLSN Steve Nash 4.00 10.00
LLSO Shaquille O'Neal 6.00 15.00
LLTD Tim Duncan 5.00 12.00
LLVC Vince Carter 4.00 10.00

2008-09 SkyBox Metal Universe

COMPLETE SET (100) 125.00 300.00
APPROXIMATE ODDS 1:2
1 Kevin Garnett 4.00 10.00
2 LeBron James 75.00 200.00
3 Dwight Howard 2.00 5.00
4 Kobe Bryant 75.00 200.00
5 Carmelo Anthony 2.00 5.00
6 Tim Duncan 4.00 10.00
7 Yao Ming 4.00 10.00
8 Dwyane Wade 3.00 8.00
9 Dirk Nowitzki 4.00 10.00
10 Jason Kidd 2.50 6.00
11 Allen Iverson 3.00 8.00
12 Tracy McGrady 2.50 6.00
13 Steve Nash 3.00 8.00
14 Ray Allen 2.50 6.00
15 Amare Stoudemire 1.50 4.00
16 Vince Carter 3.00 8.00
17 Shaquille O'Neal 5.00 12.00
18 Chris Bosh 2.00 5.00
19 Gilbert Arenas 1.50 4.00
20 Chauncey Billups 2.00 5.00
21 Paul Pierce 2.50 6.00
22 Chris Paul 3.00 8.00
23 Michael Jordan 125.00 300.00
24 Carlos Boozer 1.25 3.00
25 Manu Ginobili 3.00 8.00
26 Shawn Marion 1.50 4.00
27 Tony Parker 2.00 5.00
28 Baron Davis 1.50 4.00
29 Shane Battier 1.25 3.00
30 Kevin Durant 6.00 15.00
31 Yi Jianlian 2.00 5.00
32 Luis Scola 1.25 3.00
33 Josh Howard 1.25 3.00
34 Marcus Camby 1.25 3.00
35 Grant Hill 2.50 6.00
36 Michael Redd 1.25 3.00
37 Caron Butler 1.25 3.00
38 Richard Hamilton 1.50 4.00
39 Rasheed Wallace 2.00 5.00
40 Hedo Turkoglu 1.25 3.00
41 Jason Terry 1.25 3.00
42 Tyson Chandler 1.25 3.00
43 Andrew Bogut 1.25 3.00
44 Tayshaun Prince 1.50 4.00
45 Ben Wallace 2.00 5.00
46 Joe Johnson 1.50 4.00
47 T.J. Ford 1.00 2.50
48 Rashard Lewis 1.25 3.00
49 Jermaine O'Neal 1.50 4.00
50 LaMarcus Aldridge 1.50 4.00
51 Pau Gasol 2.00 5.00
52 Chris Kaman 1.00 2.50
53 Emeka Okafor 1.00 2.50
54 Eddy Curry 1.00 2.50
55 Al Horford 1.50 4.00
56 Josh Smith 1.00 2.50
57 Gerald Wallace 1.25 3.00
58 Ben Gordon 1.25 3.00
59 Monta Ellis 1.25 3.00
60 Elton Brand 1.25 3.00
61 Rudy Gay 1.50 4.00
62 Al Jefferson 1.00 2.50
63 David West 1.25 3.00
64 Jamal Crawford 1.50 4.00
65 Andre Iguodala 1.25 3.00
66 Brandon Roy 1.25 3.00
67 Greg Oden 1.00 2.50
68 Kevin Martin 1.25 3.00
69 Jamario Moon 1.00 2.50
70 Deron Williams 1.25 3.00
71 Derrick Rose 20.00 50.00
72 Michael Beasley 1.50 4.00
73 O.J. Mayo 1.25 3.00
74 Russell Westbrook 50.00 120.00
75 Kevin Love 3.00 8.00
76 Danilo Gallinari 2.50 6.00
77 Eric Gordon 2.50 6.00
78 Joe Alexander 1.00 2.50
79 D.J. Augustin 1.50 4.00
80 Brook Lopez 2.00 5.00
81 Jerryd Bayless 1.25 3.00
82 Jason Thompson 1.00 2.50
83 Brandon Rush 1.00 2.50
84 Anthony Randolph 1.00 2.50
85 Robin Lopez 1.25 3.00
86 Marreese Speights 1.25 3.00
87 Roy Hibbert 1.25 3.00
88 Javale McGee 1.50 4.00
89 J.J. Hickson 1.00 2.50
90 Alexis Ajinca 1.00 2.50
91 Ryan Anderson 1.25 3.00
92 Courtney Lee 1.25 3.00
93 Kosta Koufos 1.00 2.50
94 Nicolas Batum 2.00 5.00
95 George Hill 1.50 4.00
96 D.J. White 1.00 2.50
97 J.R. Giddens 1.00 2.50
98 Luc Richard Mbah A Moute 1.25 3.00
99 Marc Gasol 3.00 8.00
100 Rudy Fernandez 1.25 3.00

2008-09 SkyBox Metal Universe Precious Metal Gems Red

*STARS: 5X TO 12X BASE HI
*ROOKIES: 3X TO 8X BASE HI
STATED PRINT RUN 40 SER.#'d SETS
CARDS SERIALLY #'d TO 50
FIRST TEN #'s ARE GREEN
1 Kevin Garnett 150.00 400.00
2 LeBron James 20,000.00 40,000.00
4 Kobe Bryant 20,000.00 40,000.00
6 Tim Duncan 150.00 400.00
7 Yao Ming 150.00 400.00
8 Dwyane Wade 200.00 500.00
9 Dirk Nowitzki 150.00 400.00
10 Jason Kidd 60.00 150.00
11 Allen Iverson 200.00 500.00
12 Tracy McGrady 150.00 400.00
13 Steve Nash 200.00 500.00
14 Ray Allen 75.00 200.00
16 Vince Carter 125.00 300.00
17 Shaquille O'Neal 300.00 600.00
18 Chris Bosh 60.00 150.00
19 Gilbert Arenas 60.00 150.00
21 Paul Pierce 75.00 200.00
22 Chris Paul 75.00 200.00
23 Michael Jordan 30,000.00 60,000.00
25 Manu Ginobili 150.00 400.00
27 Tony Parker 75.00 200.00
30 Kevin Durant 10,000.00 20,000.00
31 Yi Jianlian 75.00 200.00
35 Grant Hill 125.00 300.00
44 Tayshaun Prince 60.00 150.00
71 Derrick Rose 300.00 600.00
74 Russell Westbrook 1,000.00 2,000.00
99 Marc Gasol 30.00 80.00

2008-09 SkyBox One on One Dual Memorabilia

COMBINED MEM ODDS 1:4
OOAH R.Hamilton/R.Allen 3.00 8.00
OOAJ G.Arenas/L.James 6.00 15.00
OOBA C.Anthony/K.Bryant 40.00 100.00
OOBB A.Bynum/C.Boozer 3.00 8.00
OOBG K.Garnett/K.Bryant 40.00 100.00
OOBH M.Bibby/K.Hinrich 3.00 8.00
OOBM K.Martin/E.Brand 3.00 8.00
OOBO S.O'Neal/K.Bryant 40.00 100.00
OOBP T.Parker/C.Billups 3.00 8.00
OOCI A.Iguodala/V.Carter 3.00 8.00
OODG P.Gasol/T.Duncan 4.00 10.00
OODM T.Duncan/Y.Ming 3.00 8.00
OOGW K.Garnett/R.Wallace 4.00 10.00
OOHB C.Bosh/D.Howard 3.00 8.00
OOHG M.Ginobili/R.Hamilton 3.00 8.00
OOJA C.Anthony/L.James 8.00 20.00
OOKC J.Kidd/V.Carter 4.00 10.00
OOMH S.Marion/J.Howard 3.00 8.00
OOMM C.Maggette/S.Marbury 3.00 8.00
OOMO Y.Ming/S.O'Neal 4.00 10.00
OOMW D.Williams/T.McGrady 3.00 8.00
OONG P.Gasol/D.Nowitzki 4.00 10.00
OONP S.Nash/T.Parker 4.00 10.00
OOPF J.Farmar/T.Parker 3.00 8.00
OOPJ P.Pierce/L.James 6.00 15.00
OOPP P.Pierce/T.Prince 3.00 8.00
OOPW C.Paul/D.Williams 4.00 10.00
OORR J.Richardson/Z.Randolph 3.00 8.00
OOSH D.Howard/A.Stoudemire 4.00 10.00
OOWR B.Roy/D.Williams 3.00 8.00

2008-09 SkyBox Paraph Signatures

COMBINED AUTOGRAPH ODDS 1:12
PSAM Alonzo Mourning 30.00 60.00
PSAT Alando Tucker 4.00 10.00
PSDH Dwight Howard 15.00 40.00
PSJK Jason Kidd 20.00 40.00
PSJN Joakim Noah 4.00 10.00
PSKD Michael Jordan 300.00 550.00
PSLA LaMarcus Aldridge 4.00 10.00
PSPP Paul Pierce 15.00 40.00
PSRJ Richard Jefferson 4.00 10.00
PSTP Tayshaun Prince 4.00 10.00

2008-09 SkyBox Rookie Prevue

COMBINED MEM ODDS 1:4
*RETAIL GREEN: .4X TO 1X HI COLUMN
RPAR Anthony Randolph 1.00 2.50
RPBL Brook Lopez 2.00 5.00
RPDA D.J. Augustin 1.50 4.00
RPDJ DeAndre Jordan 2.00 5.00
RPDR Derrick Rose 4.00 10.00
RPEG Eric Gordon 2.50 6.00
RPGH George Hill 1.50 4.00
RPJA Joe Alexander 1.00 2.50
RPJB Jerryd Bayless 1.25 3.00
RPJH J.J. Hickson 1.00 2.50
RPJT Jason Thompson 1.00 2.50
RPKK Kosta Koufos 1.00 2.50
RPKL Kevin Love 4.00 10.00
RPKW Kyle Weaver 1.00 2.50
RPMB Michael Beasley 1.50 4.00
RPMC Mario Chalmers 1.50 4.00
RPOM O.J. Mayo 1.25 3.00
RPRL Robin Lopez 1.25 3.00
RPSW Sonny Weems 1.00 2.50
RPWS Walter Sharpe 1.00 2.50

2008-09 SkyBox Signature Set Dual

STATED PRINT RUN 23 TO 25 SER.#'d SETS
SSAW Anderson/S.Williams/25 10.00 25.00
SSBW C.Watson/Belinelli/25 6.00 15.00
SSDG K.Durant/J.Green/25 50.00 125.00
SSFD R.Felton/J.Dudley/25 8.00 20.00
SSFR B.Roy/Fernandez/25 25.00 50.00
SSGA R.Gay/D.Arthur/25 8.00 20.00
SSGN B.Gordon/J.Noah/25 8.00 20.00
SSJB A.Jefferson/Brewer/25 8.00 20.00
SSJJ L.James/M.Jordan/23 2,500.00 5,000.00
SSJS Sessions/R.Jefferson/25 6.00 15.00
SSKJ D.Jordan/C.Kaman/25 8.00 20.00
SSPG K.Garnett/P.Pierce/25 100.00 200.00
SSPS T.Prince/Stuckey/25 10.00 25.00
SSSB J.Smith/R.Balkman/25 6.00 15.00
SSSW J.Smith/M.Speights/25 8.00 20.00
SSTS Tucker/Singletary/25 6.00 15.00
SSWC Chandler/D.West/25 8.00 20.00
SSWH M.Williams/Horford/25 8.00 20.00
SSWV S.Vujacic/L.Walton/25 10.00 25.00

2008-09 SkyBox Standouts

COMBINED MEM ODDS 1:4
*RETAIL GREEN: .4X TO 1X HI COLUMN
*PATCHES: .75X TO 2X HI COLUMN
PATCH PRINT RUN 25 SER.#'d SETS
SOAB Andrew Bynum 2.00 5.00
SOAK Andrei Kirilenko 2.50 6.00
SOBU Beno Udrih 2.00 5.00
SOCK Chris Kaman 2.00 5.00
SODW Deron Williams 2.50 6.00
SOFO Randy Foye 3.00 8.00
SOJC Jarron Collins 2.00 5.00
SOJH Josh Howard 2.50 6.00
SOJR Jason Richardson 3.00 8.00
SOLD Luol Deng 2.50 6.00
SOLH Luther Head 2.00 5.00
SOLR Luke Ridnour 2.50 6.00
SOME Monta Ellis 2.50 6.00
SOPD Paul Davis 2.00 5.00
SORF Raymond Felton 2.00 5.00
SORG Rudy Gay 3.00 8.00
SOSD Samuel Dalembert 2.00 5.00
SOSS Stromile Swift 2.00 5.00
SOUH Udonis Haslem 2.00 5.00
SOZR Zach Randolph 3.00 8.00

1999-00 SkyBox APEX

COMPLETE SET (163) 60.00 120.00
COMPLETE SET w/o RC (150) 10.00 25.00
151-163 STATED ODDS 1:13
1 Paul Pierce .60 1.50
2 Stephon Marbury .40 1.00
3 Chris Webber .40 1.00
4 Kobe Bryant 2.50 6.00
5 David Robinson .60 1.50
6 Gary Payton .50 1.25
7 Kornel David RC .20 .50
8 Glenn Robinson .25 .60
9 Nick Van Exel .25 .60
10 Jelani McCoy .20 .50
11 Charles Oakley .30 .75
12 Michael Finley .30 .75
13 Steve Smith .25 .60
14 Arvydas Sabonis .25 .60
15 Cuttino Mobley .20 .50
16 Eric Piatkowski .25 .60
17 Bobby Jackson .25 .60
18 Keith Van Horn .25 .60
19 Shaquille O'Neal 1.25 3.00
20 Karl Malone .60 1.50
21 Allan Houston .25 .60
22 Ron Mercer .25 .60
23 Vince Carter .75 2.00
24 Lindsey Hunter .20 .50
25 Scottie Pippen .75 2.00
26 Wesley Person .20 .50
27 Vitaly Potapenko .20 .50
28 Glen Rice .30 .75
29 Tyrone Nesby RC .20 .50
30 Detlef Schrempf .25 .60
31 Clifford Robinson .25 .60
32 Joe Smith .25 .60
33 P.J. Brown .20 .50
34 Christian Laettner .25 .60
35 Avery Johnson .25 .60
36 Kevin Garnett .75 2.00
37 Jason Kidd .50 1.25
38 Kenny Anderson .25 .60
39 Shawn Kemp .50 1.25
40 Bison Dele .20 .50
41 Rodney Rogers .20 .50
42 Jamal Mashburn .25 .60
43 Grant Hill .50 1.25
44 Larry Johnson .30 .75
45 Darrell Armstrong .20 .50
46 Shandon Anderson .20 .50
47 Kendall Gill .30 .75
48 Jason Williams .50 1.25
49 Tom Gugliotta .25 .60
50 Ray Allen .50 1.25
51 Sam Mitchell .20 .50
52 Brent Barry .25 .60
53 Antawn Jamison .30 .75
54 Chris Mullin .30 .75
55 Alan Henderson .20 .50
56 Derek Anderson .20 .50
57 Tim Thomas .25 .60
58 Anfernee Hardaway .75 2.00
59 Pat Garrity .20 .50
60 Corliss Williamson .20 .50
61 Gary Trent .20 .50
62 Greg Ostertag .20 .50
63 Vin Baker .25 .60
64 LaPhonso Ellis .20 .50
65 Brevin Knight .20 .50
66 Rick Fox .20 .50
67 Bryant Reeves .20 .50
68 Mark Jackson .25 .60
69 John Starks .30 .75
70 Robert Traylor .20 .50
71 Maurice Taylor .20 .50
72 Hersey Hawkins .20 .50
73 Zydrunas Ilgauskas .25 .60
74 Charles Barkley .75 2.00
75 Isaac Austin .20 .50
76 Mike Bibby .30 .75
77 Michael Olowokandi .20 .50
78 Brian Grant .20 .50
79 Felipe Lopez .20 .50
80 Chris Crawford .20 .50
81 Dee Brown .20 .50
82 Antoine Walker .30 .75
83 Vlade Divac .30 .75
84 Rod Strickland .25 .60
85 Dickey Simpkins .20 .50
86 Donyell Marshall .25 .60
87 Larry Hughes .25 .60
88 Rasheed Wallace .40 1.00
89 Erick Dampier .20 .50
90 Kerry Kittles .25 .60
91 Mitch Richmond .40 1.00
92 Isaiah Rider .25 .60
93 Bobby Phills .20 .50
94 Dirk Nowitzki 1.00 2.50
95 Cedric Henderson .20 .50
96 Howard Eisley .20 .50
97 Toni Kukoc .40 1.00
98 Jalen Rose .25 .60
99 Michael Doleac .20 .50
100 Matt Geiger .20 .50
101 Bryon Russell .20 .50
102 Alvin Williams .20 .50
103 Shawn Bradley .20 .50
104 Latrell Sprewell .40 1.00
105 Vernon Maxwell .20 .50
106 Tim Hardaway .40 1.00
107 Peja Stojakovic .30 .75
108 Tracy Murray .20 .50
109 Theo Ratliff .25 .60
110 Dikembe Mutombo .50 1.25
111 Alonzo Mourning .50 1.25
112 Raef LaFrentz .25 .60
113 Marcus Camby .25 .60
114 Eddie Jones .30 .75
115 Chauncey Billups .30 .75
116 Jayson Williams .20 .50
117 Anthony Mason .30 .75
118 Tracy McGrady .50 1.25
119 John Stockton .50 1.25
120 Matt Harpring .20 .50
121 Mario Elie .20 .50
122 Juwan Howard .25 .60
123 Antonio McDyess .25 .60
124 Ricky Davis .30 .75
125 Reggie Miller .60 1.50
126 Allen Iverson .75 2.00
127 Terrell Brandon .20 .50
128 Hakeem Olajuwon .60 1.50
129 Damon Stoudamire .30 .75
130 Randy Brown .20 .50
131 Cedric Ceballos .20 .50
132 Jerry Stackhouse .30 .75
133 Michael Dickerson .20 .50
134 Rik Smits .25 .60
135 Cherokee Parks .20 .50
136 Tim Duncan .75 2.00
137 Shareef Abdur-Rahim .30 .75
138 Derek Fisher .25 .60
139 Bo Outlaw .20 .50
140 Eric Snow .20 .50
141 Jaren Jackson .20 .50
142 Tony Battie .20 .50
143 Derrick Coleman .25 .60
144 Corey Benjamin .25 .60
145 Steve Nash .60 1.50
146 Mookie Blaylock .20 .50
147 Voshon Lenard .20 .50
148 Vinny Del Negro .20 .50
149 Jeff Hornacek .25 .60
150 Patrick Ewing .40 1.00
151 Elton Brand RC 1.25 3.00

152 Steve Francis RC 1.25 3.00
153 Baron Davis RC 1.50 4.00
154 Lamar Odom RC 1.25 3.00
155 Jonathan Bender RC .60 1.50
156 Wally Szczerbiak RC 1.00 2.50
157 Richard Hamilton RC 1.50 4.00
158 Andre Miller RC 1.25 3.00
159 Shawn Marion RC 1.25 3.00
160 Jason Terry RC 1.00 2.50
161 Trajan Langdon RC .50 1.25
162 A.Radojevic RC .40 1.00
163 Corey Maggette RC .75 2.00
P2 Stephon Marbury PROMO 1.00 2.50
NNO K.Van Horn AU JSY/50 30.00 80.00

1999-00 SkyBox APEX Xtra
*STARS: 25X TO 60X BASE CARD HI
*RCs: 3X TO 8X BASE HI
STATED PRINT RUN 50 SERIAL #'d SETS
4 Kobe Bryant 500.00 1,000.00
19 Shaquille O'Neal 150.00 400.00
20 Karl Malone 75.00 200.00
23 Vince Carter 125.00 300.00
94 Dirk Nowitzki 150.00 400.00
125 Reggie Miller 60.00 150.00
126 Allen Iverson 150.00 400.00
137 Shareef Abdur-Rahim 25.00 60.00
150 Patrick Ewing 30.00 80.00

1999-00 SkyBox APEX Allies
COMPLETE SET (15) 12.00 30.00
STATED ODDS 1:6 HOB/RET 1.00 2.50
1 K.Bryant/S.O'Neal 12.00 30.00
2 K.Van Horn/S.Marbury 1.25 3.00
3 J.Stockton/K.Malone 2.00 5.00
4 M.Bibby/S.Abdur-Rahim 1.00 2.50
5 A.Iverson/L.Hughes 2.50 6.00
6 M.Olowokandi/M.Taylor .60 1.50
7 V.Carter/T.McGrady 2.50 6.00
8 G.Hill/J.Stackhouse 1.50 4.00
9 J.Williams/C.Webber 1.50 4.00
10 T.Duncan/D.Robinson 2.50 6.00
11 J.Kidd/T.Gugliotta 1.50 4.00
12 V.Baker/G.Payton 1.50 4.00
13 A. Mourning/T. Hardaway 1.50 4.00
14 S.Kemp/B.Knight 1.50 4.00
15 A.McDyess/R.LaFrentz .40 1.00

1999-00 SkyBox APEX Cutting Edge
COMPLETE SET (15) 60.00 150.00
STATED ODDS 1:24 HOB/RET
*PLUS: 1.25X TO 3X HI COLUMN
PLUS: STATED ODDS 1:240 HOB/RET
*WARP TEK: 8X TO 20X VALUE
WARP TEK: PRINT RUN 25 SERIAL #'d SETS
1 Allen Iverson 25.00 60.00
2 Paul Pierce 8.00 20.00
3 Vince Carter 15.00 40.00
4 Jason Williams 5.00 12.00
5 Kobe Bryant 60.00 150.00
6 Kevin Garnett 15.00 40.00
7 Stephon Marbury 4.00 10.00
8 Jason Kidd 8.00 20.00
9 Tim Duncan 15.00 40.00
10 Mike Bibby 3.00 8.00
11 Marcus Camby 2.50 6.00
12 Michael Olowokandi 2.00 5.00
13 Antawn Jamison 3.00 8.00
14 Keith Van Horn 2.50 6.00
15 Raef LaFrentz 2.50 6.00

1999-00 SkyBox APEX Cutting Edge Plus
*PLUS: 1.25X TO 3X VALUE
1 Allen Iverson 100.00 250.00

1999-00 SkyBox APEX First Impressions
COMPLETE SET (20) 12.00 30.00
STATED ODDS 1:12 HOB/RET
1 Jonathan Bender 1.00 2.50
2 Steve Francis 2.00 5.00
3 Ron Artest 2.50 6.00
4 Baron Davis 2.50 6.00
5 Shawn Marion 2.00 5.00
6 Jason Terry 1.50 4.00
7 Elton Brand 2.00 5.00
8 Kenny Thomas 1.00 2.50
9 Trajan Langdon .75 2.00
10 Aleksandar Radojevic .60 1.50
11 Corey Maggette 1.25 3.00
12 Jeff Foster 1.00 2.50
13 Scott Padgett .75 2.00
14 Lamar Odom 2.00 5.00
15 William Avery .60 1.50
16 Andre Miller 2.00 5.00
17 Wally Szczerbiak 1.50 4.00
18 Richard Hamilton 2.50 6.00
19 James Posey 1.00 2.50
20 Jumaine Jones .60 1.50

1999-00 SkyBox APEX Jam Session
COMPLETE SET (15) 200.00 500.00
STATED ODDS 1:96 HOB/RET
1 Stephon Marbury 6.00 15.00
2 Paul Pierce 12.00 30.00
3 Kobe Bryant 200.00 500.00
4 Keith Van Horn 4.00 10.00
5 Shaquille O'Neal 50.00 120.00
6 Anfernee Hardaway 15.00 40.00
7 Grant Hill 12.00 30.00
8 Antonio McDyess 4.00 10.00
9 Kevin Garnett 25.00 60.00
10 Tracy McGrady 15.00 40.00
11 Shareef Abdur-Rahim 5.00 12.00
12 Shawn Kemp 12.00 30.00
13 Antoine Walker 5.00 12.00
14 Eddie Jones 5.00 12.00
15 Vin Baker 4.00 10.00

1999-00 SkyBox APEX Net Shredders
1 Vince Carter 150.00 400.00
2 Tracy McGrady 125.00 300.00
3 Allen Iverson 150.00 400.00
4 Larry Hughes 30.00 80.00
5 Glenn Robinson 30.00 80.00
6 Ray Allen 125.00 300.00
7 Jason Williams 125.00 300.00
8 Chris Webber 125.00 300.00
9 Tim Duncan 150.00 400.00
10 David Robinson 125.00 300.00

1999-00 SkyBox APEX Lamar Odom
NNO Lamar Odom 2.50 6.00

2003-04 SkyBox Autographics
COMP.SET w/o SP's (45) 12.50 30.00
46-90 RC PRINT RUN 1500 SER.#'d SETS
1 Vince Carter .75 2.00
2 Kobe Bryant 3.00 8.00
3 Tony Parker .60 1.50
4 Richard Hamilton .50 1.25
5 Jamal Mashburn .30 .75
6 Paul Pierce .60 1.50
7 Allan Houston .40 1.00
8 Carlos Boozer .30 .75
9 Michael Redd .40 1.00
10 Chris Webber .50 1.25
11 Yao Ming 1.00 2.50
12 Tracy McGrady .60 1.50
13 Zach Randolph .40 1.00
14 Ben Wallace .50 1.25
15 Kenyon Martin .40 1.00
16 Ray Allen .60 1.50
17 Jermaine O'Neal .40 1.00
18 Bonzi Wells .25 .60
19 Ron Artest .40 1.00
20 Peja Stojakovic .30 .75
21 Dirk Nowitzki 1.00 2.50
22 Desmond Mason .30 .75
23 Morris Peterson .25 .60
24 Eddy Curry .25 .60
25 Kevin Garnett 1.00 2.50
26 Rashard Lewis .30 .75
27 Jason Richardson .40 1.00
28 Amare Stoudemire .50 1.25
29 Steve Francis .40 1.00
30 Allen Iverson 1.00 2.50
31 Jason Terry .30 .75
32 Pau Gasol .60 1.50
33 Manu Ginobili .75 2.00
34 Reggie Miller .75 2.00
35 Cuttino Mobley .25 .60
36 Mike Bibby .40 1.00
37 Mike Dunleavy .30 .75
38 Jason Kidd .60 1.50
39 Shareef Abdur-Rahim .30 .75
40 Elton Brand .30 .75
41 Kwame Brown .25 .60
42 Shaquille O'Neal 1.50 4.00
43 Tim Duncan 1.00 2.50
44 Nene .30 .75
45 Baron Davis .40 1.00
46 Boris Diaw RC 1.50 4.00
47 Luke Walton RC 1.50 4.00
48 Willie Green RC 1.50 4.00
49 Marcus Banks RC 1.00 2.50
50 Dahntay Jones RC 1.25 3.00
51 Leandro Barbosa RC 1.50 4.00
52 Josh Howard RC 1.50 4.00
53 Ndudi Ebi RC 1.00 2.50
54 Chris Bosh RC 5.00 12.00
55 Carmelo Anthony RC 8.00 20.00
56 Zoran Planinic RC 1.00 2.50
57 Aleksandar Pavlovic RC 1.25 3.00
58 Marquis Daniels RC 1.25 3.00
59 Keith McLeod RC 1.00 2.50
60 Ben Handlogten RC 1.00 2.50
61 Francisco Elson RC 1.00 2.50
62 David West RC 2.00 5.00
63 Maurice Williams RC 1.50 4.00
64 Brian Cook RC 1.00 2.50
65 Keith Bogans RC 1.00 2.50
66 Kendrick Perkins RC 1.25 3.00
67 Troy Bell RC 1.00 2.50
68 Kyle Korver RC 2.00 5.00
69 Mickael Pietrus RC 1.25 3.00
70 Maciej Lampe RC 1.00 2.50
71 Steve Blake RC 1.25 3.00
72 Chris Kaman RC 1.50 4.00
73 Curtis Borchardt 1.25 3.00
74 Kirk Hinrich RC 1.50 4.00
75 Dwyane Wade RC 12.00 30.00
76 Zarko Cabarkapa RC 1.00 2.50
77 LeBron James RC 200.00 500.00
78 Jerome Beasley RC 1.00 2.50
79 Nick Collison RC 1.25 3.00
80 Linton Johnson RC 1.00 2.50
81 Udonis Haslem RC 2.00 5.00
82 Travis Outlaw RC 1.25 3.00
83 Jason Kapono RC 1.00 2.50
84 T.J. Ford RC 1.25 3.00
85 Luke Ridnour RC 1.50 4.00
86 Darko Milicic RC 1.25 3.00
87 Mike Sweetney RC 1.00 2.50
88 Jarvis Hayes RC 1.00 2.50
89 Josh Moore RC 1.00 2.50
90 Reece Gaines RC 1.00 2.50

2003-04 SkyBox Autographics Insignia Purple
*PURPLE STARS: 6X TO 15X BASE HI
*PURPLE RCs: 2X TO 5X BASE HI
38 Jason Kidd 20.00 50.00
77 LeBron James 6,000.00 12,000.00

2003-04 SkyBox Autographics Insignia Silver
*SILVER SINGLES: 2.5X TO 6X BASE HI
*SILVER RCs: 1X TO 2X BASE HI
SILVER PRINT RUN 150 SER.#'d SETS
77 LeBron James 1,500.00 3,000.00

2003-04 SkyBox Autographics Autoclassics
COMPLETE SET (15) 10.00 25.00
STATED ODDS 1:12
1 Vince Carter 1.50 4.00
2 Shawn Marion .75 2.00
3 Tracy McGrady 1.25 3.00
4 David Robinson 1.50 4.00
5 Paul Pierce 1.25 3.00
6 Carmelo Anthony 4.00 10.00
7 Stephon Marbury 1.00 2.50
8 Jason Richardson .75 2.00
9 Steve Francis .75 2.00
10 Chris Bosh 2.50 6.00
11 Dirk Nowitzki 2.00 5.00
12 Allen Iverson 2.00 5.00
13 Yao Ming 2.00 5.00
14 Shaquille O'Neal 3.00 8.00
15 Tim Duncan 2.00 5.00

2003-04 SkyBox Autographics Autoclassics Memorabilia
PRINT RUN 45 SER.#'d SETS
AI Allen Iverson 12.00 30.00
CA Carmelo Anthony 12.00 30.00
CB Chris Bosh 10.00 25.00
DN Dirk Nowitzki 20.00 50.00
DR David Robinson 15.00 40.00
JR Jason Richardson 8.00 20.00
PP Paul Pierce 12.00 30.00
SF Steve Francis 8.00 20.00
SM Stephon Marbury 10.00 25.00
SM Shawn Marion 8.00 20.00
SO Shaquille O'Neal 30.00 80.00
TD Tim Duncan 20.00 50.00
TM Tracy McGrady 12.00 30.00
VC Vince Carter 15.00 40.00
YM Yao Ming 20.00 50.00

2003-04 SkyBox Autographics Autoclassics Signatures
PRINT RUN 25 SER.#'d SETS
CA Carmelo Anthony 100.00 200.00
SM Shawn Marion 12.50 30.00
VC Vince Carter 20.00 50.00

2003-04 SkyBox Autographics Autographs
PRINT RUNS LISTED BELOW
AM Aaron McKie/300 2.50 6.00
AP Aleksandar Pavlovic/300 3.00 8.00
AW Antoine Walker/200 5.00 12.00
BD Boris Diaw/300 4.00 10.00
BM Brad Miller/250 3.00 8.00
CA Carmelo Anthony 15.00 40.00
DJ Dahntay Jones/450 3.00 8.00
DW1 Dwyane Wade/200 25.00 60.00
DW2 David West/350 5.00 12.00
DW3 Dajuan Wagner/200 4.00 10.00
JD Juan Dixon/300 4.00 10.00
JH Josh Howard/200 4.00 10.00
JK Jason Kapono/400 2.50 6.00
KK Kyle Korver/400 5.00 12.00
KR Kareem Rush/300 4.00 10.00
LR Luke Ridnour/500 4.00 10.00
LW Luke Walton/400 4.00 10.00
MB Marcus Banks/400 2.50 6.00
MG Manu Ginobili/200 15.00 40.00
MP Mickael Pietrus/300 3.00 8.00
NH Nene/250 4.00 10.00
PP Paul Pierce/200 20.00 50.00
PS Peja Stojakovic/200 6.00 15.00
RM Ronald Murray/250 4.00 10.00
SA Shareef Abdur-Rahim/250 4.00 10.00
SC Speedy Claxton/300 4.00 10.00
SM Shawn Marion/150 5.00 12.00
TC Tyson Chandler/400 5.00 12.00
TH Travis Hansen/400 2.50 6.00
TM Tracy McGrady/200 10.00 25.00
TP1 Tayshaun Prince/200 4.00 10.00
TP2 Tony Parker/200 8.00 20.00
UH Udonis Haslem/300 5.00 12.00
VC Vince Carter/600 8.00 20.00
WZ Wang Zhizhi/300 30.00 80.00
ZC Zarko Cabarkapa/300 2.50 6.00
ZP Zoran Planinic/300 2.50 6.00

2003-04 SkyBox Autographics Autographs Gold
*GOLD: .75X TO 2X BASE AU HI
PRINT RUN 50 SER.#'d SETS

2003-04 SkyBox Autographics Autographs Silver
*SILVER: .5X TO 1.25X BASE HI
PRINT RUN 150 SER.#'d SETS
SM Shawn Marion 5.00 12.00

2003-04 SkyBox Autographics Autographs on Location
PRINT RUN 99 SER.#'d SETS
AW Antoine Walker 8.00 20.00
CA Carmelo Anthony 30.00 80.00
DW Dwyane Wade 40.00 100.00
PP Paul Pierce 15.00 40.00
TM Tracy McGrady 15.00 40.00
VC Vince Carter 10.00 25.00

2003-04 SkyBox Autographics Autographs Jerseys
PRINT RUN 125 SER.#'d SETS
CA Carmelo Anthony 40.00 80.00
MP Mickael Pietrus 6.00 15.00
TM Tracy McGrady 15.00 40.00
TP Tony Parker 10.00 25.00
TP Tayshaun Prince 6.00 15.00

2003-04 SkyBox Autographics Autographs Patches
PRINT RUN 25 SER.#'d SETS
CA Carmelo Anthony 100.00 200.00
TM Tracy McGrady 30.00 80.00
TP Tayshaun Prince 12.50 30.00

2003-04 SkyBox Autographics Jerseygraphics
PRINT RUN 100 TO 350 SER.#'d SETS
*GOLD: .6X TO 1.5X BASE HI
GOLD PRINT RUN 50 SER.#'d SETS
AI Allen Iverson/350 6.00 15.00
AK Andrei Kirilenko/350 2.00 5.00
AS Amare Stoudemire/350 3.00 8.00
BD Baron Davis/350 2.50 6.00
BW1 Bonzi Wells/350 2.00 5.00
BW2 Ben Wallace/350 3.00 8.00
CA Carmelo Anthony/350 12.00 30.00
CB Chris Bosh/350 8.00 20.00
CK Chris Kaman/350 2.50 6.00
CW Chris Webber/220 3.00 8.00
DN Dirk Nowitzki/260 6.00 15.00
DW1 Dwyane Wade/350 20.00 50.00
DW2 David West/350 3.00 8.00
DW3 Dajuan Wagner/350 2.00 5.00
EB Elton Brand/350 2.00 5.00
EC Eddy Curry/350 1.50 4.00
GA Gilbert Arenas/350 2.50 6.00
GP Gary Payton/350 4.00 10.00
GR Glenn Robinson/350 2.00 5.00
JH Jarvis Hayes/350 1.50 4.00
JK Jason Kidd/350 4.00 10.00
JO Jermaine O'Neal/350 2.50 6.00
JR Jason Richardson/350 2.50 6.00
JS Jerry Stackhouse/350 3.00 8.00
KB Kwame Brown/350 2.00 5.00
KG Kevin Garnett/350 6.00 15.00
KM1 Karl Malone/350 5.00 12.00
KM2 Kenyon Martin/350 2.50 6.00
LS Latrell Sprewell/350 3.00 8.00
MB Marcus Banks/200 1.50 4.00
MB Mike Bibby/350 2.50 6.00
MD Mike Dunleavy/350 2.00 5.00
MF Michael Finley/160 2.50 6.00
MG Manu Ginobili/350 5.00 12.00
MP1 Mickael Pietrus/200 2.00 5.00
MP2 Morris Peterson/350 1.50 4.00
MR Michael Redd/350 2.50 6.00
MS Mike Sweetney/350 1.50 4.00
NH Nene/350 2.00 5.00
PG Pau Gasol/350 4.00 10.00
PP Paul Pierce/350 4.00 10.00
PS Peja Stojakovic/300 2.00 5.00
RA Ray Allen/350 4.00 10.00
RG Reece Gaines/350 1.50 4.00
RH Richard Hamilton/350 3.00 8.00
RM Reggie Miller/350 5.00 12.00
SA Shareef Abdur-Rahim/350 2.50 6.00
SF Steve Francis/350 2.50 6.00
SM1 Stephon Marbury/350 3.00 8.00
SM2 Shawn Marion/350 2.50 6.00
SO Shaquille O'Neal/350 10.00 25.00
SP Scottie Pippen/100 8.00 20.00
TC Tyson Chandler/350 2.00 5.00
TD Tim Duncan/350 6.00 15.00
TM Tracy McGrady/350 4.00 10.00
TO Travis Outlaw/350 2.00 5.00
TP1 Tayshaun Prince/350 2.50 6.00
TP2 Tony Parker/350 4.00 10.00
VC Vince Carter/350 5.00 12.00
YM Yao Ming/350 6.00 15.00

2003-04 SkyBox Autographics Jerseygraphics Silver
*SILVER: .5X TO 1.25X BASE JSY HI
PRINT RUN 150 SER.#'d SETS
SP Scottie Pippen 8.00 20.00

2003-04 SkyBox Autographics Rookies Affirmed
COMPLETE SET (15) 300.00 600.00
STATED ODDS 1:4
1 C.Anthony/T.McGrady 2.50 6.00
2 C.Bosh/V.Carter 1.50 4.00
3 D.West/J.Mashburn .60 1.50
4 T.Bell/P.Gasol .75 2.00
5 M.Pietrus/J.Richardson .50 1.25
6 D.Wade/J.Stackhouse 8.00 20.00
7 U.Haslem/S.Marbury .60 1.50
8 J.Hayes/R.Murray .30 .75
9 R.Gaines/T.Parker .75 2.00
10 M.Banks/P.Pierce .75 2.00
11 K.Hinrich/S.Nash 1.00 2.50
12 L.James/K.Bryant 150.00 400.00
13 C.Kaman/Y.Ming 1.25 3.00
14 T.Ford/A.Iverson 1.25 3.00
15 D.Milicic/D.Nowitzki 1.25 3.00

2003-04 SkyBox Autographics Rookies Affirmed Game-Used
PRINT RUN 500 SER.#'d SETS
*PATCH: 1X TO 2.5X BASE HI
PATCH PRINT RUN 50 SER.#'d SETS
CATM C.Anthony/T.McGrady 8.00 20.00
CBVC C.Bosh/V.Carter 6.00 15.00
DWAS D.West/J.Mashburn 4.00 10.00
DWRL D.Wade/J.Stackhouse 8.00 20.00
JHRM J.Hayes/R.Murray 4.00 10.00
MBPP M.Banks/P.Pierce 4.00 10.00
MPJR M.Pietrus/J.Richardson 4.00 10.00
RGTP R.Gaines/T.Parker 4.00 10.00
TBPG T.Bell/P.Gasol 4.00 10.00
UHBW U.Haslem/S.Marbury 4.00 10.00

2003-04 SkyBox Autographics Rookies Affirmed Game-Used Autographs
PRINT RUN 50 SER.#'d SETS
CATM C.Anthony/T.McGrady 125.00 300.00
DWRL D.Wade/J.Stackhouse 125.00 300.00
MBPP M.Banks/P.Pierce 20.00 50.00

2004-05 SkyBox Autographics
COMP.SET w/o SP's (60) 15.00 40.00
61-105 RC PRINT RUN 750 SER.#'d SETS
1 Dwyane Wade 1.50 4.00
2 Derek Fisher .30 .75
3 Latrell Sprewell .50 1.25
4 Peja Stojakovic .30 .75
5 LeBron James 8.00 20.00
6 Elton Brand .30 .75
7 Allan Houston .40 1.00
8 Chris Bosh .60 1.50
9 Carmelo Anthony .75 2.00
10 Shaquille O'Neal 1.50 4.00
11 Steve Nash .75 2.00
12 Antawn Jamison .30 .75
13 Darko Milicic .25 .60
14 Michael Redd .30 .75
15 Shawn Marion .40 1.00
16 Dirk Nowitzki 1.00 2.50
17 Kobe Bryant 3.00 8.00
18 Steve Francis .40 1.00
19 Carlos Boozer .30 .75
20 Karl Malone .75 2.00
21 T.J. Ford .25 .60
22 Darius Miles .25 .60
23 Paul Pierce .60 1.50
24 Jermaine O'Neal .40 1.00
25 Baron Davis .40 1.00
26 Tony Parker .60 1.50
27 Kirk Hinrich .40 1.00
28 Chris Kaman .25 .60
29 Stephon Marbury .50 1.25
30 Rashard Lewis .30 .75
31 Ben Wallace .50 1.25
32 Antoine Walker .40 1.00
33 Amare Stoudemire .40 1.00
34 Gary Payton .60 1.50
35 Yao Ming 1.00 2.50
36 Richard Jefferson .30 .75
37 Tim Duncan 1.00 2.50
38 Drew Gooden .25 .60
39 Lamar Odom .40 1.00
40 Grant Hill .50 1.25
41 Vince Carter .75 2.00
42 Michael Finley .40 1.00
43 Jason Williams .30 .75
44 Samuel Dalembert .25 .60
45 Andrei Kirilenko .30 .75
46 Jason Kapono .25 .60
47 Reggie Miller .75 2.00
48 Jamaal Magloire .25 .60
49 Ray Allen .60 1.50
50 Kenyon Martin .40 1.00
51 Pau Gasol .60 1.50
52 Allen Iverson 1.00 2.50
53 Gilbert Arenas .40 1.00
54 Jason Richardson .40 1.00
55 Kevin Garnett 1.00 2.50
56 Zach Randolph .40 1.00
57 Al Harrington .30 .75
58 Tracy McGrady .60 1.50
59 Jason Kidd .60 1.50
60 Chris Webber .50 1.25
61 Andris Biedrins RC 1.00 2.50
62 Robert Swift RC 1.00 2.50
63 Pavel Podkolzin RC 1.00 2.50
64 Kevin Martin RC 2.00 5.00
65 Beno Udrih RC 1.25 3.00
66 David Harrison RC 1.00 2.50
67 Andre Emmett RC 1.00 2.50
68 Emeka Okafor RC 1.25 3.00
69 Dwight Howard RC 5.00 12.00
70 Ben Gordon RC 1.50 4.00
71 Shaun Livingston RC 1.50 4.00
72 Devin Harris RC 1.25 3.00
73 Josh Childress RC 1.00 2.50
74 Luol Deng RC 1.50 4.00
75 Rafael Araujo RC 1.00 2.50
76 Andre Iguodala RC 2.50 6.00
77 Luke Jackson RC 1.00 2.50
78 Sebastian Telfair RC 1.25 3.00
79 Kris Humphries RC 1.25 3.00
80 Al Jefferson RC 1.50 4.00
81 Kirk Snyder RC 1.00 2.50
82 Josh Smith RC 1.50 4.00
83 J.R. Smith RC 1.50 4.00
84 Dorell Wright RC 1.25 3.00
85 Jameer Nelson RC 1.50 4.00
86 Delonte West RC 1.25 3.00
87 Tony Allen RC 1.50 4.00
88 Sasha Vujacic RC 1.25 3.00
89 Andres Nocioni RC 1.50 4.00
90 Royal Ivey RC 1.00 2.50
91 Trevor Ariza RC 1.50 4.00
92 Chris Duhon RC 1.25 3.00
93 John Edwards RC 1.00 2.50
94 Jackson Vroman RC 1.00 2.50
95 Quinton Ross 1.00 2.50
96 Erik Daniels RC 1.25 3.00
97 Anderson Varejao RC 1.50 4.00
98 Lionel Chalmers RC 1.25 3.00
99 Carlos Delfino 1.00 2.50
100 Jared Reiner RC 1.50 4.00
101 Bernard Robinson RC 1.00 2.50
102 Peter John Ramos RC 1.00 2.50
103 D.J. Mbenga RC 1.00 2.50
104 Mario Kasun RC 1.00 2.50
105 Nenad Krstic RC 1.25 3.00

2004-05 SkyBox Autographics Insignia
*1-60 INSIGNIA: 2.5X TO 6X BASE HI
*61-105 INSIGNIA: .5X TO 1.25X BASE HI
PRINT RUN 150 SER.#'d SETS

2004-05 SkyBox Autographics Insignia 25
*1-60 INSIGNIA: 6X TO 15X BASE HI
*61-105 INSIGNIA: 1.5X TO 4X BASE HI
PRINT RUN 25 SER.#'d SETS

2004-05 SkyBox Autographics Autographs Jerseys
STATED ODDS 1:20
*AU JSY 100: .5X TO 1.25X BASE AU JSY HI
BASE SER.#'d VER. DO NOT HAVE 100 AU
*AU JSY 30: .6X TO 1.5X BASE AU JSY HI
*EMBOSS: .5X TO 1.25X BASE AU JSY HI
*#'d VER.EMBOSS SAME VALUE AS BASE
EMBOSSED PRINT RUN 65 SER.#'d SETS
AJ Antawn Jamison/76 4.00 10.00
AK Andrei Kirilenko 4.00 10.00
BD Baron Davis/24 10.00 25.00
BD Boris Diaw 4.00 10.00
BW Ben Wallace 12.50 30.00
CA Carlos Arroyo 3.00 8.00
CB Carlos Boozer/29 8.00 20.00
CD Chris Duhon/47 4.00 10.00
CD Carlos Delfino 3.00 8.00
DH David Harrison 3.00 8.00
DW David West 4.00 10.00
JD Juan Dixon 3.00 8.00
JH Josh Howard 4.00 10.00
LW Luke Walton 4.00 10.00
MD Mike Dunleavy/20 3.00 8.00
MP Mickael Pietrus 3.00 8.00
NC Nick Collison/53 3.00 8.00
PS Peja Stojakovic/53 15.00 30.00
QR Quinton Ross 3.00 8.00
RH Richard Hamilton/90 10.00 25.00
TO Travis Outlaw 4.00 10.00
VC Vince Carter 12.50 30.00

2004-05 SkyBox Autographics Autographs Patches
PRINT RUN 75 SER.#'d SETS
*AU EMBOSSED: .4X TO 1X BASE HI
AU EMBOSS PRINT RUN 50 SER.#'d SETS
AK Andrei Kirilenko 15.00 40.00
AV Anderson Varejao 10.00 25.00
AW Antoine Walker 15.00 40.00
BD Boris Diaw 12.50 30.00
BW Ben Wallace 15.00 40.00
CA Carlos Arroyo 20.00 50.00
CB Carlos Boozer 10.00 25.00
GA Gilbert Arenas 10.00 25.00
JD Juan Dixon 10.00 25.00
LW Luke Walton 10.00 25.00
MD Mike Dunleavy 10.00 25.00
MP Mickael Pietrus 10.00 25.00
NC Nick Collison 10.00 25.00
QR Quinton Ross 10.00 25.00
RH Richard Hamilton 20.00 50.00

2004-05 SkyBox Autographics Future Signs
COMPLETE SET (20) 10.00 25.00
STATED ODDS 1:6 H, 1:12 R
1 Andris Biedrins .40 1.00
2 Robert Swift .40 1.00
3 Pavel Podkolzin .40 1.00
4 Ben Gordon .60 1.50
5 Shaun Livingston .60 1.50
6 Devin Harris .50 1.25
7 Josh Childress .40 1.00
8 Luol Deng .60 1.50
9 Rafael Araujo .40 1.00
10 Luke Jackson .40 1.00
11 Sebastian Telfair .50 1.25
12 Kris Humphries .50 1.25
13 Al Jefferson .60 1.50
14 Kirk Snyder .40 1.00
15 Josh Smith .60 1.50
16 J.R. Smith .60 1.50
17 Dorell Wright .50 1.25
18 Jameer Nelson .60 1.50
19 Delonte West .50 1.25
20 Tony Allen .60 1.50

2004-05 SkyBox Autographics Future Signs Autographs
STATED ODDS 1:19
*AUTO 100: .5X TO 1.25X BASE AU HI
*AUTO 50: .75X TO 2X BASE AU HI
*AUTO EMBOSS: .6X TO 1.5X BASE AU HI
AU EMBOSS PRINT RUN 85 SER.#'d SETS
*AUTO EMBOSS 20: 1X TO 2.5X BASE HI
AB Andris Biedrins 2.50 6.00
AJ Al Jefferson 4.00 10.00
BG Ben Gordon 4.00 10.00
DW Dorell Wright 3.00 8.00
DW2 Delonte West 3.00 8.00
JC Josh Childress 2.50 6.00
JS2 J.R. Smith 4.00 10.00
KH Kris Humphries 3.00 8.00
KS Kirk Snyder 2.50 6.00
LD Luol Deng 4.00 10.00
PP Pavel Podkolzin 2.50 6.00
RA Rafael Araujo 2.50 6.00

2004-05 SkyBox Autographics Future Signs Autographs Patches
PRINT RUN 70 SER.#'d SETS
JS2 J.R. Smith 10.00 25.00
KH Kris Humphries 8.00 20.00
RA Rafael Araujo 6.00 15.00

2004-05 SkyBox Autographics Jerseygraphics
STATED ODDS 1:40 RETAIL
AI Allen Iverson 6.00 15.00
AS Amare Stoudemire 2.50 6.00
BD Boris Diaw 2.00 5.00
CA Carmelo Anthony 5.00 12.00
CB Chris Bosh 4.00 10.00
DN Dirk Nowitzki 6.00 15.00
DW Dajuan Wagner 2.00 5.00
JD Juan Dixon 2.00 5.00
JO Jermaine O'Neal 2.00 5.00
KB Kevin Garnett 6.00 15.00
MD Mike Dunleavy 1.50 4.00
MG Manu Ginobili 5.00 12.00
MJ Marko Jaric 2.00 5.00
MS Mike Sweetney 2.00 5.00
SF Steve Francis 2.50 6.00
SM Stephon Marbury 3.00 8.00
VC Vince Carter 5.00 12.00

2004-05 SkyBox Autographics Master Collection
PRINT RUN 25 SER.#'d SETS
BW Ben Wallace 15.00 40.00
CB Charles Barkley 300.00 600.00
CB2 Carlos Boozer 15.00 40.00
DW Dwyane Wade 100.00 200.00
EB Elton Brand 15.00 40.00
GP Gary Payton 30.00 80.00
LD Luol Deng 30.00 80.00
PS Peja Stojakovic 20.00 50.00
SM Shawn Marion 15.00 40.00
TP Tony Parker 15.00 40.00
VC Vince Carter 30.00 80.00

2004-05 SkyBox Autographics Signature Moves
COMPLETE SET (10) 8.00 20.00
STATED ODDS 1:12 H, 1:24 R
1 Allen Iverson 1.50 4.00
2 LeBron James 5.00 12.00
3 Carmelo Anthony 1.25 3.00
4 Shaquille O'Neal 2.50 6.00
5 Kobe Bryant 5.00 12.00
6 Vince Carter 1.25 3.00
7 Tracy McGrady 1.00 2.50
8 Jason Kidd 1.00 2.50
9 Kevin Garnett 1.50 4.00
10 Tim Duncan 1.50 4.00

1990-91 SkyBox Broadcasters
COMPLETE SET (4) 100.00 250.00
1 Bob Costas 60.00 150.00
2 Julie Moran
(Michael Jordan on back) 100.00 250.00
3 Ahmad Rashad 60.00 150.00
4 Pat Riley 60.00 150.00

1991-92 SkyBox Canadian Minis
COMPLETE SET (50) 12.00 30.00
1 Kevin Willis .30 .75
2 Larry Bird 1.25 3.00
3 Kevin McHale .60 1.50
4 Robert Parish .50 1.25
5 Kendall Gill .40 1.00
6 J.R. Reid .25 .60
7 Michael Jordan 3.00 8.00
8 Scottie Pippen 1.00 2.50
9 Brad Daugherty .40 1.00
10 Larry Nance .40 1.00
11 Rolando Blackman .30 .75
12 Derek Harper .30 .75
13 Chris Jackson .30 .75
14 Jerome Lane .25 .60
15 Joe Dumars .50 1.25
16 Dennis Rodman .75 2.00
17 Tim Hardaway .50 1.25
18 Chris Mullin .50 1.25
19 Hakeem Olajuwon .75 2.00
20 Otis Thorpe .30 .75
21 Reggie Miller .60 1.50
22 Detlef Schrempf .30 .75
23 Danny Manning .30 .75
24 Charles Smith .30 .75
25 Magic Johnson 1.25 3.00
26 James Worthy .50 1.25
27 Sherman Douglas .30 .75
28 Rony Seikaly .30 .75
29 Alvin Robertson .30 .75
30 Tony Campbell .25 .60
31 Derrick Coleman .40 1.00
32 Charles Oakley .30 .75
33 Dennis Scott .30 .75
34 Scott Skiles .30 .75
35 Charles Barkley .75 2.00
36 Hersey Hawkins .30 .75
37 Jeff Hornacek .30 .75
38 Kevin Johnson .40 1.00
39 Clyde Drexler .60 1.50
40 Terry Porter .30 .75
41 Wayman Tisdale .30 .75
42 Terry Cummings .40 1.00
43 David Robinson .75 2.00
44 Shawn Kemp .60 1.50
45 Ricky Pierce .30 .75
46 Karl Malone .75 2.00
47 John Stockton .75 2.00
48 Harvey Grant .30 .75
49 Bernard King .50 1.25
50 Checklist Card .60 1.50

1999-00 SkyBox Dominion
COMPLETE SET (220) 25.00 60.00
1 Jason Williams .60 1.50
2 Isaiah Rider .30 .75
3 Tim Hardaway .50 1.25
4 Isaac Austin .25 .60
5 Joe Smith .30 .75
6 Mitch Richmond .50 1.25
7 Sam Mitchell .25 .60
8 Terrell Brandon .25 .60
9 Grant Long .25 .60
10 Shaquille O'Neal 1.50 4.00
11 Derrick Coleman .30 .75
12 Rod Strickland .30 .75
13 J.R. Reid .25 .60
14 Tyrone Corbin .25 .60
15 Jeff Hornacek .30 .75
16 Malik Rose .25 .60
17 Terry Davis .25 .60
18 Theo Ratliff .30 .75
19 Kevin Willis .25 .60
20 Raef LaFrentz .30 .75
21 Othella Harrington .25 .60
22 Marcus Camby .30 .75
23 Keon Clark .25 .60
24 Robert Pack .25 .60
25 Sam Mack .25 .60
26 Shawn Kemp .60 1.50
27 Nick Anderson .25 .60
28 Bill Wennington .25 .60
29 Steve Smith .30 .75
30 Kobe Bryant 3.00 8.00
31 Bobby Phills .25 .60
32 Cedric Ceballos .25 .60
33 Derek Fisher .30 .75
34 Doug Christie .30 .75
35 Danny Manning .30 .75
36 Eric Murdock .25 .60
37 Glen Rice .40 1.00
38 Dikembe Mutombo .60 1.50
39 Jason Kidd .60 1.50
40 Cedric Henderson .25 .60
41 Rasheed Wallace .50 1.25
42 Tim Duncan 1.00 2.50
43 John Stockton .60 1.50
44 Dell Curry .25 .60
45 Muggsy Bogues .30 .75
46 Danny Fortson .25 .60
47 Charles Oakley .40 1.00
48 Elden Campbell .25 .60
49 Tony Massenburg .25 .60
50 Kevin Garnett 1.00 2.50
51 Cherokee Parks .25 .60
52 LaPhonso Ellis .25 .60
53 Sam Cassell .30 .75
54 Shawn Bradley .30 .75
55 David Robinson .75 2.00
56 Juwan Howard .30 .75
57 Lindsey Hunter .25 .60
58 Mark Jackson .30 .75
59 Olden Polynice .25 .60
60 Tracy McGrady .60 1.50
61 Michael Finley .40 1.00
62 Matt Geiger .25 .60
63 Maurice Taylor .25 .60
64 Rex Chapman .25 .60
65 Chris Mullin .40 1.00
66 Ray Allen .60 1.50
67 Bison Dele .25 .60
68 Dickey Simpkins .25 .60
69 Alvin Williams .25 .60
70 Grant Hill .60 1.50
71 Mark Bryant .25 .60
72 Adam Keefe .25 .60
73 Alan Henderson .25 .60
74 Eric Snow .25 .60
75 Matt Harpring .25 .60
76 Jalen Rose .30 .75
77 Derek Harper .30 .75
78 Kerry Kittles .30 .75
79 Tony Battie .25 .60
80 Larry Hughes .30 .75
81 Arvydas Sabonis .30 .75
82 Allan Houston .30 .75
83 Tom Gugliotta .30 .75
84 Reggie Miller .75 2.00
85 Dejuan Wheat .25 .60
86 Pat Garrity .25 .60
87 Karl Malone .75 2.00

88 Sam Perkins .25 .60
89 Michael Olowokandi .25 .60
90 Anfernee Hardaway 1.00 2.50
91 Bryant Reeves .25 .60
92 Gary Trent .25 .60
93 George Lynch .25 .60
94 Scottie Pippen 1.00 2.50
95 Jerry Stackhouse .40 1.00
96 Kendall Gill .40 1.00
97 Vin Baker .30 .75
98 Dale Davis .25 .60
99 Charles Barkley 1.00 2.50
100 Allen Iverson 1.00 2.50
101 Keith Van Horn .30 .75
102 Andrew DeClercq .25 .60
103 Michael Doleac .25 .60
104 Chauncey Billups .40 1.00
105 Chris Mills .25 .60
106 Lamond Murray .25 .60
107 Glenn Robinson .30 .75
108 Brian Grant .25 .60
109 Christian Laettner .30 .75
110 Antawn Jamison .40 1.00
111 Erick Dampier .25 .60
112 Vernon Maxwell .25 .60
113 Kenny Anderson .30 .75
114 Clarence Weatherspoon .25 .60
115 Corliss Williamson .25 .60
116 Paul Pierce .75 2.00
117 Clifford Robinson .30 .75
118 Damon Stoudamire .40 1.00
119 Dana Barros .25 .60
120 Stephon Marbury .50 1.25
120B Stephon Marbury PROMO .60 1.50
121 Latrell Sprewell .50 1.25
122 Tyronn Lue .25 .60
123 Walt Williams .25 .60
124 P.J. Brown .25 .60
125 Gary Payton .60 1.50
126 Nick Van Exel .30 .75
127 Bryant Stith .25 .60
128 Eric Piatkowski .25 .60
129 Tyrone Nesby RC .25 .60
130 Ron Mercer .30 .75
131 Hersey Hawkins .25 .60
132 Vlade Divac .40 1.00
133 Darrick Martin .25 .60
134 Avery Johnson .30 .75
135 Jaren Jackson .25 .60
136 Brevin Knight .25 .60
137 Wesley Person .25 .60
138 Derek Anderson .25 .60
139 Tim Thomas .30 .75
140 Antonio McDyess .30 .75
141 A.C. Green .30 .75
142 Chris Webber .50 1.25
143 Scott Burrell .25 .60
144 John Starks .40 1.00
145 Howard Eisley .25 .60
146 Mike Bibby .40 1.00
147 Toni Kukoc .50 1.25
148 Eddie Jones .40 1.00
149 Otis Thorpe .25 .60
150 Shareef Abdur-Rahim .40 1.00
151 Calbert Cheaney .25 .60
152 Cuttino Mobley .25 .60
153 Michael Dickerson .25 .60
154 Sean Elliott .30 .75
155 Terry Porter .25 .60
156 Dean Garrett .25 .60
157 Charlie Ward .25 .60
158 Larry Johnson .40 1.00
159 Dan Majerle .40 1.00
160 Jayson Williams .25 .60
161 Anthony Peeler .25 .60
162 Ron Harper .30 .75
163 Darrell Armstrong .25 .60
164 Kurt Thomas .25 .60
165 Brent Barry .30 .75
166 Lawrence Funderburke .25 .60
167 Terry Cummings .30 .75
168 Jamal Mashburn .30 .75
169 Robert Traylor .25 .60
170 Greg Ostertag .25 .60
171 Brad Miller .30 .75
172 Mario Elie .25 .60
173 Antoine Walker .40 1.00
174 Ricky Davis .40 1.00
175 Vince Carter 1.00 2.50
176 Hakeem Olajuwon WT .75 2.00
177 Luc Longley WT .30 .75
178 Tim Duncan WT 1.00 2.50
179 Rick Fox WT .25 .60
180 Zydrunas Ilgauskas WT .30 .75
181 Toni Kukoc WT .50 1.25
182 Felipe Lopez WT .25 .60
183 Dikembe Mutombo WT .60 1.50
184 Steve Nash WT .75 2.00
185 Dirk Nowitzki WT 1.25 3.00
186 Vitaly Potapenko WT .25 .60
187 Detlef Schrempf WT .30 .75
188 Rik Smits WT .30 .75
189 Vladimir Stepania WT .25 .60
190 Peja Stojakovic WT .40 1.00
191 Donyell Marshall 3FA .30 .75
192 Shareef Abdur-Rahim 3FA .40 1.00
193 Michael Dickerson 3FA .25 .60
194 Damon Stoudamire 3FA .40 1.00
195 Allen Iverson 3FA 1.00 2.50
196 Grant Hill 3FA .60 1.50
197 Scottie Pippen 3FA 1.00 2.50
198 Bryon Russell 3FA .25 .60
199 Alonzo Mourning 3FA .60 1.50
200 Patrick Ewing 3FA .50 1.25
201 Ron Artest RC 1.00 2.50
202 William Avery RC .25 .60
203 Lamar Odom RC .75 2.00
204 Baron Davis RC 1.00 2.50
205 John Celestand RC .25 .60
206 Jumaine Jones RC .25 .60
207 Andre Miller RC .75 2.00
208 Elton Brand RC .75 2.00
209 James Posey RC .40 1.00
210 Jason Terry RC .60 1.50
211 Kenny Thomas RC .40 1.00
212 Steve Francis RC .75 2.00
213 Wally Szczerbiak RC .60 1.50
214 Richard Hamilton RC 1.00 2.50
215 Jonathan Bender RC .40 1.00
216 Shawn Marion RC .75 2.00
217 A.Radojevic RC .25 .60
218 Tim James RC .25 .60
219 Trajan Langdon RC .30 .75
220 Corey Maggette RC .50 1.25

1999-00 SkyBox Dominion 2 Point Play

COMPLETE SET (10) 5.00 12.00
STATED ODDS 1:9
*PLUS: .75X TO 2X HI COLUMN
PLUS: STATED ODDS 1:90
*WARP TEK: 12X TO 30X HI COLUMN
WARP TEK: STATED ODDS 1:900
1 K.Van Horn/G.Hill .75 2.00
2 P.Pierce/S.Pippen 1.25 3.00
3 T.Duncan/K.Garnett 1.25 3.00
4 K.Bryant/V.Carter 4.00 10.00
5 S.O'Neal/M.Olowokandi 2.00 5.00
6 C.Webber/S.Kemp .75 2.00
7 J.Williams/A.Iverson 1.25 3.00
8 S.Marbury/A.Hardaway 1.25 3.00
9 J.Kidd/M.Bibby .75 2.00
10 S.Abdur-Rahim/A.McDyess .50 1.25

1999-00 SkyBox Dominion Game Day 2K

COMPLETE SET (20) 4.00 10.00
STATED ODDS 1:3
*PLUS: 1.5X TO 4X HI COLUMN
PLUS: STATED ODDS 1:30
1 Vince Carter .75 2.00
2 Kobe Bryant 2.50 6.00
3 Dirk Nowitzki 1.00 2.50
4 Cuttino Mobley .20 .50
5 Kevin Garnett .75 2.00
6 Stephon Marbury .40 1.00
7 Shaquille O'Neal 1.25 3.00
8 Keith Van Horn .25 .60
9 Paul Pierce .60 1.50
10 Jason Williams .50 1.25
11 Mike Bibby .30 .75
12 Michael Dickerson .20 .50
13 Antawn Jamison .30 .75
14 Raef LaFrentz .25 .60
15 Tyrone Nesby .20 .50
16 Ron Mercer .25 .60
17 Tracy McGrady .50 1.25
18 Larry Hughes .25 .60
19 Robert Traylor .20 .50
20 Michael Doleac .20 .50

1999-00 SkyBox Dominion Game Day 2K Warp Tek

*WARP TEK: 15X TO 40X VALUE
STATED ODDS 1:300
1 Vince Carter 125.00 300.00
2 Kobe Bryant 300.00 600.00
3 Dirk Nowitzki 150.00 400.00
5 Kevin Garnett 125.00 300.00
7 Shaquille O'Neal 150.00 400.00
9 Paul Pierce 100.00 250.00
10 Jason Williams 100.00 250.00
17 Tracy McGrady 100.00 250.00

1999-00 SkyBox Dominion Hats Off

PRINT RUNS LISTED BELOW
1 Elton Brand/135 12.00 30.00
2 Steve Francis/170 12.00 30.00
3 Baron Davis/170 15.00 40.00
4 Wally Szczerbiak/140 10.00 25.00
5 Richard Hamilton/150 15.00 40.00
6 Andre Miller/140 12.00 30.00
7 Shawn Marion/150 12.00 30.00
8 Jason Terry/170 10.00 25.00
9 A.Radojevic/135 4.00 10.00
10 William Avery/185 4.00 10.00
11 Ron Artest/140 15.00 40.00
12 James Posey/170 6.00 15.00
13 Tim James/140 4.00 10.00
14 Jumaine Jones/135 4.00 10.00

1999-00 SkyBox Dominion Sky's the Limit

COMPLETE SET (15) 12.50 30.00
STATED ODDS 1:24
*PLUS: 1.5X TO 4X HI COLUMN
PLUS: STATED ODDS 1:240
*WARP TEK: 15X TO 40X VALUE
WARP TEK: PRINT RUN 25 SERIAL #'d SETS
1 Kevin Garnett 2.50 6.00
2 Jason Williams 1.50 4.00
3 Grant Hill 1.50 4.00
4 Keith Van Horn .75 2.00
5 Allen Iverson 2.50 6.00
6 Ron Mercer .75 2.00
7 Anfernee Hardaway 2.50 6.00
8 Kobe Bryant 12.00 30.00
9 Shareef Abdur-Rahim 1.00 2.50
10 Jason Kidd 1.50 4.00
11 Shaquille O'Neal 4.00 10.00
12 Stephon Marbury 1.25 3.00
13 Paul Pierce 2.00 5.00
14 Tim Duncan 2.50 6.00
15 Vince Carter 2.50 6.00

2000 SkyBox Dominion WNBA

COMPLETE SET (156) 10.00 25.00
SUBSET CARDS HALF VALUE OF BASE CARDS
1 Cynthia Cooper 1.25 3.00
2 Sue Wicks .30 .75
3 Clarisse Machanguana RC .20 .50
4 Adrienne Goodson .20 .50
5 Astou Ndiaye RC .60 1.50
6 Crystal Robinson .20 .50
7 Tora Suber .30 .75
8 Lady Hardmon .20 .50
9 Maria Stepanova .20 .50
10 Mwadi Mabika .20 .50
11 Rebecca Lobo .60 1.50
12 Ticha Penicheiro .50 1.25
13 Vicky Bullett .20 .50
14 Adia Barnes .20 .50
15 Andrea Stinson .40 1.00
16 Sheryl Swoopes 1.25 3.00
17 Heather Owen RC .20 .50
18 Andrea Congreaves .20 .50
19 Brandy Reed .30 .75
20 Dawn Staley .50 1.25
21 Jennifer Rizzotti RC 1.00 2.50
22 Latasha Byears .30 .75
23 Merlakia Jones .30 .75
24 Niesa Johnson RC .20 .50
25 Rushia Brown .20 .50
26 Taj McWilliams RC .20 .50
27 Wendy Palmer .50 1.25
28 Krystyna Lara RC .20 .50
29 Andrea Lloyd Curry RC .30 .75
30 Carla McGhee .20 .50
31 DeLisha Milton .20 .50
32 Katie Smith .60 1.50
33 Mery Andrade .20 .50
34 Nikki McCray .50 1.25
35 Ruthie Bolton-Holifield .60 1.50
36 Tamecka Dixon .30 .75
37 Tracy Henderson RC .20 .50
38 Yolanda Griffith .60 1.50
39 LaTonya Johnson .20 .50
40 Coquese Washington .20 .50
41 Chamique Holdsclaw 1.25 3.00
42 Dominique Canty RC .60 1.50
43 Kedra Holland-Corn RC .30 .75
44 Michele Timms .60 1.50
45 Nykesha Sales .30 .75
46 Shalonda Enis RC .20 .50
47 Tamika Whitmore RC .20 .50
48 Tracy Reid .30 .75
49 Kate Starbird .30 .75
50 Amanda Wilson RC .60 1.50
51 Sonia Chase RC .30 .75
52 Elaine Powell .20 .50
53 Michelle Edwards .40 1.00
54 Olympia Scott-Richardson .20 .50
55 Shannon Johnson .20 .50
56 Tammy Jackson .20 .50
57 Ukari Figgs .20 .50
58 Linda Burgess .20 .50
59 Angie Braziel RC .40 1.00
60 Tricia Bader RC .20 .50
61 Adrienne Johnson .30 .75
62 Chasity Melvin RC .20 .50
63 Korie Hlede .30 .75
64 Michelle Griffiths .20 .50
65 Penny Moore .20 .50
66 Sheri Sam .20 .50
67 Tangela Smith .20 .50
68 Val Whiting .20 .50
69 Angie Potthoff .20 .50
70 Cindy Brown .30 .75
71 Kristin Folkl .30 .75
72 Lisa Leslie 1.00 2.50
73 Monica Lamb .20 .50
74 Teresa Weatherspoon .75 2.00
75 Valerie Still RC .60 1.50
76 Tonya Edwards .20 .50
77 Heather Quella RC .30 .75
78 Cass Bauer RC .50 1.25
79 Bridget Pettis .20 .50
80 Cindy Blodgett .20 .50
81 Janeth Arcain .20 .50
82 Kym Hampton .20 .50
83 Margo Dydek .40 1.00
84 Murriel Page .25 .60
85 Sonja Tate .20 .50
86 Vickie Johnson .30 .75
87 Eva Nemcova .20 .50
88 Charlotte Smith .20 .50
89 Venus Lacy RC .20 .50
90 Polina Tzekova RC .20 .50
91 Dalma Ivanyi RC .20 .50
92 Allison Feaster .25 .60
93 Becky Hammon RC 8.00 20.00
94 Amaya Valdemoro RC .30 .75
95 Jennifer Gillom .50 1.25
96 La'Keshia Frett RC .20 .50
97 Markita Aldridge RC .20 .50
98 Natalie Williams .40 1.00
99 Rhonda Mapp .20 .50
100 Suzie McConnell-Serio .40 1.00
101 Tina Thompson .60 1.50
102 Wanda Guyton .20 .50
103 Lisa Harrison RC .50 1.25
104 Andrea Nagy RC .50 1.25
105 Edna Campbell ED .25 .60
106 Nina Bjedov ED RC .30 .75
107 Sonja Henning ED RC .30 .75
108 Toni Foster ED .20 .50
109 Angela Aycock ED RC .30 .75
110 Charmin Smith ED RC .50 1.25
111 Chantel Tremitiere ED .20 .50
112 Gordana Grubin ED RC .20 .50
113 Kara Wolters ED .25 .60
114 Rita Williams ED .25 .60
115 Stephanie McCarty ED .40 1.00
116 Monica Maxwell ED RC .25 .60
117 Debbie Black ED .30 .75
118 Elena Baranova ED .50 1.25
119 Sharon Manning ED .20 .50
120 Molly Goodenbour ED RC .20 .50
121 Alisa Burras ED RC .30 .75
122 Mila Nikolich ED RC .20 .50
123 Jamila Wideman ED .20 .50
124 Michele VanGorp ED .25 .60
125 Sophia Witherspoon ED .20 .50
126 Tari Phillips ED .20 .50
127 Sheri Sam SM .10 .25
128 Mwadi Mabika SM .10 .25
129 Murriel Page SM .12 .30
130 Latasha Byears SM .15 .40
131 Dominique Canty SM .30 .75
132 Crystal Robinson SM .10 .25
133 Cynthia Cooper SM .60 1.50
134 Ruthie Bolton-Holifield SM .30 .75
135 Cindy Brown SM .15 .40
136 Kristin Folkl SM .15 .40
137 Jennifer Gillom SM .25 .60
138 Adrienne Goodson SM .10 .25
139 Vickie Johnson SM .15 .40
140 Merlakia Jones SM .15 .40
141 Rebecca Lobo SM .30 .75
142 Nikki McCray SM .25 .60
143 Suzie McConnell-Serio SM .20 .50
144 DeLisha Milton SM .10 .25
145 Eva Nemcova SM .15 .40
146 Wendy Palmer SM .25 .60
147 Brandy Reed SM .15 .40
148 Nykesha Sales SM .15 .40
149 Andrea Stinson SM .20 .50
150 Michele Timms SM .30 .75
151 Valerie Still SM .30 .75
152 Andrea Nagy SM .25 .60
153 Tonya Edwards SM .10 .25
154 Taj McWilliams SM .15 .40
155 Kedra Holland-Corn SM .15 .40
156 Maria Stepanova SM .10 .25

2000 SkyBox Dominion WNBA Extra

COMPLETE SET (156) 75.00 150.00
*EXTRA: 1.5X TO 4X BASE CARD HI
STATED ODDS 1:3

2000 SkyBox Dominion WNBA All-WNBA

COMPLETE SET (10) 12.50 30.00
AW1 Sheryl Swoopes 4.00 10.00
AW2 Natalie Williams 1.25 3.00
AW3 Yolanda Griffith 2.00 5.00
AW4 Cynthia Cooper 4.00 10.00
AW5 Ticha Penicheiro 1.50 4.00
AW6 Chamique Holdsclaw 4.00 10.00
AW7 Tina Thompson 2.00 5.00
AW8 Lisa Leslie 3.00 8.00
AW9 Teresa Weatherspoon 2.50 6.00
AW10 Shannon Johnson .60 1.50

2000 SkyBox Dominion WNBA Autographics

STATED ODDS 1:144
NNO CARDS LISTED BELOW ALPHABETICALLY
1 Ruthie Bolton-Holifield 4.00 10.00
2 Cynthia Cooper 8.00 20.00
3 Jennifer Gillom 3.00 8.00
4 Yolanda Griffith 4.00 10.00
5 Chamique Holdsclaw 8.00 20.00
6 Kedra Holland-Corn 2.00 5.00
7 Lisa Leslie 6.00 15.00
8 Taj McWilliams 2.00 5.00
9 Ticha Penicheiro 3.00 8.00
10 Crystal Robinson 1.25 3.00
11 Kate Starbird 2.00 5.00
12 Andrea Stinson 2.50 6.00
13 Sue Wicks 2.00 5.00

2000 SkyBox Dominion WNBA Girls Rock

COMPLETE SET (10) 15.00 40.00
GR1 Sheryl Swoopes 5.00 12.00
GR2 Chamique Holdsclaw 5.00 12.00
GR3 Dawn Staley 2.00 5.00
GR4 Katie Smith 2.50 6.00
GR5 Yolanda Griffith 2.50 6.00
GR6 Ticha Penicheiro 2.00 5.00
GR7 Teresa Weatherspoon 3.00 8.00
GR8 Natalie Williams 1.50 4.00
GR9 Lisa Leslie 4.00 10.00
GR10 Cynthia Cooper 5.00 12.00

2000 SkyBox Dominion WNBA Supreme Court

COMPLETE SET (20) 12.50 30.00
SC1 Dawn Staley 1.50 4.00
SC2 Merlakia Jones 1.00 2.50
SC3 Eva Nemcova 1.00 2.50
SC4 Suzie McConnell-Serio 1.25 3.00
SC5 Cynthia Cooper 4.00 10.00
SC6 Brandy Reed 1.00 2.50
SC7 Katie Smith 2.00 5.00
SC8 Vickie Johnson 1.00 2.50
SC9 Rebecca Lobo 2.00 5.00
SC10 Shannon Johnson .60 1.50
SC11 Nykesha Sales 1.00 2.50
SC12 Jennifer Gillom 1.50 4.00
SC13 Nikki McCray 1.50 4.00
SC14 Michele Timms 2.00 5.00
SC15 Tina Thompson 2.00 5.00
SC16 Ruthie Bolton-Holifield 2.00 5.00
SC17 Wendy Palmer 1.50 4.00
SC18 DeLisha Milton .60 1.50
SC19 Andrea Stinson 1.25 3.00
SC20 Adrienne Goodson .60 1.50

2000 SkyBox Dominion WNBA The Cooper Collection

COMPLETE SET (8) 4.00 10.00
COMMON CARD (CC1-CC8) .75 2.00

1995-96 SkyBox Expansion Debut

COMPLETE SET (2) 2.00 5.00
1 Toronto Raptors
Grant Hill 1.25 3.00
2 Vancover Grizzlies
Grant Hill 1.25 3.00

2004-05 SkyBox Fresh Ink

COMP.SET w/o SP's (90) 15.00 40.00
RC PRINT RUN 499 SER.#'d SETS
1 T.J. Ford .20 .50
2 Pau Gasol .50 1.25
3 Kirk Hinrich .30 .75
4 Shawn Marion .30 .75
5 Darius Miles .20 .50
6 Dirk Nowitzki .75 2.00
7 Paul Pierce .50 1.25
8 Theron Smith .20 .50
9 Rasheed Wallace .40 1.00
10 Kobe Bryant 2.50 6.00
11 Kevin Garnett .75 2.00
12 Steve Nash .60 1.50
13 Gilbert Arenas .30 .75
14 Udonis Haslem .20 .50
15 Ben Wallace .40 1.00
16 Josh Howard .50 1.25
17 Elton Brand .50 1.25
18 Caron Butler .25 .60
19 Drew Gooden .20 .50
20 Richard Hamilton .40 1.00
21 Grant Hill .40 1.00
22 Jason Kapono .20 .50
23 Tony Parker .50 1.25
24 Jalen Rose .25 .60
25 Amare Stoudemire .30 .75
26 Gerald Wallace .25 .60
27 Jason Williams .20 .50
28 LeBron James 2.50 6.00
29 Jamal Crawford .30 .75
30 Earl Boykins .20 .50
31 Michael Finley .30 .75
32 Chris Kaman .25 .60
33 Stephon Marbury .40 1.00
34 Shaquille O'Neal 1.25 3.00
35 Antoine Walker .30 .75
36 Ron Artest .30 .75
37 Samuel Dalembert .20 .50
38 Reece Gaines .20 .50
39 Rashard Lewis .25 .60
40 Desmond Mason .25 .60
41 Jason Richardson .30 .75
42 Wally Szczerbiak .25 .60
43 Bonzi Wells .20 .50
44 Tim Duncan .75 2.00
45 Lamar Odom .30 .75
46 Jermaine O'Neal .25 .60
47 Mickael Pietrus .20 .50
48 Zach Randolph .30 .75
49 Joe Smith .25 .60
50 Allan Houston .30 .75
51 Carmelo Anthony .60 1.50
52 Manu Ginobili .60 1.50
53 Tyronn Lue .20 .50
54 Tayshaun Prince .30 .75
55 Luke Ridnour .25 .60
56 Peja Stojakovic .25 .60
57 Dwyane Wade 1.25 3.00
58 David West .25 .60
59 Allen Iverson .75 2.00
60 Richard Jefferson .25 .60
61 Andrei Kirilenko .25 .60
62 Latrell Sprewell .40 1.00
63 Jason Kidd .50 1.25
64 Baron Davis .30 .75
65 Al Harrington .25 .60
66 Jarvis Hayes .20 .50
67 Gary Payton .50 1.25
68 Chris Webber .40 1.00
69 Vince Carter .60 1.50
70 Eric Williams .20 .50
71 Nene .25 .60
72 Chris Bosh .50 1.25
73 Sam Cassell .25 .60
74 Mike Dunleavy .20 .50
75 Steve Francis .30 .75
76 Antawn Jamison .30 .75
77 Joe Johnson .25 .60
78 Corey Maggette .25 .60
79 Jamaal Magloire .20 .50
80 Kenyon Martin .30 .75
81 Reggie Miller .60 1.50
82 Yao Ming .75 2.00
83 Dajuan Wagner .20 .50
84 Willie Green .30 .75
85 Shareef Abdur-Rahim .30 .75
86 Tracy McGrady .50 1.25
87 Carlos Arroyo .20 .50
88 Michael Redd .25 .60
89 Alonzo Mourning .40 1.00
90 Mike Bibby .30 .75
91 Luke Jackson RC 1.00 2.50
92 Matt Freije RC 1.00 2.50
93 Kevin Martin RC 2.00 5.00
94 Josh Smith RC 1.50 4.00
95 Kris Humphries RC 1.25 3.00
96 Trevor Ariza RC 1.25 3.00
97 Shaun Livingston RC 1.50 4.00
98 Pavel Podkolzin RC 1.00 2.50
99 Kirk Snyder RC 1.00 2.50
100 Beno Udrih RC 1.25 3.00
101 Tony Allen RC 1.50 4.00
102 Chris Duhon RC 1.25 3.00
103 Josh Childress RC 1.00 2.50
104 David Harrison RC 1.00 2.50
105 Al Jefferson RC 1.50 4.00
106 Rafael Araujo RC 1.00 2.50
107 Andre Emmett RC 1.00 2.50
108 Devin Harris RC 1.25 3.00
109 Andre Iguodala RC 2.50 6.00
110 Emeka Okafor RC 1.25 3.00
111 Dorell Wright RC 1.25 3.00
112 Luol Deng RC 1.25 3.00
113 Dwight Howard RC 5.00 12.00
114 J.R. Smith RC 1.50 4.00
115 Sasha Vujacic RC 1.25 3.00
116 Jameer Nelson RC 1.50 4.00
117 Robert Swift RC 1.00 2.50
118 Sebastian Telfair RC 1.25 3.00
119 Andris Biedrins RC 1.25 3.00
120 Ben Gordon RC 1.50 4.00

2004-05 SkyBox Fresh Ink 50

*50 SINGLES: 3X TO 8X BASE HI
*50 RC's: 1.25X TO 3X BASE HI
PRINT RUN 50 SER.#'d SETS

2004-05 SkyBox Fresh Ink Autographs

PRINT RUN 199 SER.#'d SETS
*AUTO 99: .5X TO 1.25X BASE AU HI
*AUTO 25: .75X TO 2X BASE AU HI
*RED AUTO: .4X TO 1X BASE AU HI
N Nene 5.00 12.00
AJ Al Jefferson 5.00 12.00
AK Andrei Kirilenko 8.00 20.00
AV Anderson Varejao 4.00 10.00
BG Ben Gordon 5.00 12.00
BW Ben Wallace 8.00 20.00
CA Carmelo Anthony 15.00 30.00
CB Chris Bosh 10.00 25.00
CB Carlos Boozer 5.00 12.00
CD Carlos Delfino 5.00 12.00
CD2 Chris Duhon 4.00 10.00
DH David Harrison 3.00 8.00
DH Devin Harris 4.00 10.00
DW Dwyane Wade 30.00 80.00
DW David West 5.00 12.00
GA Gilbert Arenas 8.00 20.00
JC Josh Childress 3.00 8.00
JR Jason Richardson 5.00 12.00
JS Jerry Stackhouse 6.00 15.00
JS2 Josh Smith 5.00 12.00
KH2 K.Humphries Gophers 6.00 15.00
KM Kenyon Martin 8.00 20.00
KS Kirk Snyder 3.00 8.00
LC Lionel Chalmers 4.00 10.00
LD Luol Deng 5.00 12.00
LJ Luke Jackson 3.00 8.00
MB2 Matt Bonner 5.00 12.00
MP Mickael Pietrus 5.00 12.00
MS Mike Sweetney 5.00 12.00
NC Nick Collison 5.00 12.00
QR Quinton Ross 5.00 12.00
RH Richard Hamilton 8.00 20.00
RS Robert Swift 3.00 8.00
TA2 Tony Allen OK State 10.00 25.00
TO Travis Outlaw 5.00 12.00
VC Vince Carter 12.50 30.00

2004-05 SkyBox Fresh Ink Five on Five

STATED ODDS 1:432
6 Kings/Trailblazers 6.00 15.00
8 Suns/Jazz 8.00 20.00

2004-05 SkyBox Fresh Ink Five on Five Jerseys

PRINT RUN 199 SER.#'d SETS
1 Spurs/Mavericks 12.00 30.00
2 Pistons/Pacers 12.00 30.00
3 Timberwolves/Nuggets 12.00 30.00
4 Nets/Heat 12.00 30.00
5 Celtics/Knicks 12.00 30.00
6 Kings/Trailblazers 12.00 30.00
7 76ers/Wizards 12.00 30.00
9 Bucks/Hornets 12.00 30.00

2004-05 SkyBox Fresh Ink Game Breakers

COMPLETE SET (15) 30.00 80.00
STATED ODDS 1:18 H, 1:24 R
1 K.Garnett/T.Duncan 3.00 8.00
2 S.O'Neal/A.Mourning 2.50 6.00
3 S.Marbury/J.Kidd 2.50 6.00
4 L.Bird/M.Johnson 8.00 20.00
5 P.Pierce/A.Walker 2.50 6.00
6 L.James/K.Bryant 5.00 12.00
7 D.Nowitzki/S.Nash 3.00 8.00
8 I.Thomas/M.Cooper 4.00 10.00
9 C.Anthony/D.Wade 3.00 8.00
10 P.Gasol/A.Kirilenko 2.50 6.00
11 R.Miller/B.Davis 2.50 6.00
12 C.Barkley/S.Pippen 8.00 20.00
13 V.Carter/A.Jamison 2.50 6.00
14 T.McGrady/S.Francis 2.50 6.00
15 D.West/J.Nelson 2.00 5.00

2004-05 SkyBox Fresh Ink Game Breakers Jerseys

PRINT RUN 199 SER.#'d SETS
*PATCHES: .75X TO 2X BASE HI
PATCH PRINT RUN 49 SER.#'d SETS
1 K.Garnett/T.Duncan 6.00 15.00
3 S.Marbury/J.Kidd 4.00 10.00
5 P.Pierce/A.Walker 4.00 10.00
7 D.Nowitzki/S.Nash 6.00 15.00
9 C.Anthony/D.Wade 10.00 25.00
10 P.Gasol/A.Kirilenko 4.00 10.00
11 R.Miller/B.Davis 5.00 12.00
13 V.Carter/A.Jamison 5.00 12.00
14 T.McGrady/S.Francis 4.00 10.00
15 D.West/J.Nelson 3.00 8.00

2004-05 SkyBox Fresh Ink Game Breakers Patches

PRINT RUN 49 SER.#'d SETS

2004-05 SkyBox Fresh Ink Property Of

COMPLETE SET (30) 12.00 30.00
STATED ODDS 1:3 H, 1:6 R
1 Josh Childress .40 1.00
2 Kevin McHale .75 2.00
3 Emeka Okafor .50 1.25
4 Ben Gordon .50 1.25
5 LeBron James 5.00 12.00
6 Michael Finley .60 1.50
7 Carmelo Anthony 1.25 3.00
8 Ben Wallace .75 2.00
9 Rick Barry .50 1.25
10 Yao Ming 1.50 4.00
11 Jermaine O'Neal .50 1.25
12 Elton Brand .50 1.25
13 Kobe Bryant 5.00 12.00
14 Jason Williams .50 1.25
15 Dwyane Wade 2.50 6.00
16 Michael Redd .50 1.25
17 Latrell Sprewell .75 2.00
18 Richard Jefferson .50 1.25
19 Baron Davis .60 1.50
20 Walt Frazier .75 2.00
21 Dwight Howard 2.00 5.00
22 Allen Iverson 1.50 4.00
23 Kevin Johnson .60 1.50
24 Clyde Drexler 1.00 2.50
25 Peja Stojakovic .50 1.25
26 Manu Ginobili 1.25 3.00
27 Ray Allen 1.00 2.50
28 Chris Bosh 1.00 2.50
29 Andrei Kirilenko .50 1.25
30 Elvin Hayes .60 1.50

2004-05 SkyBox Fresh Ink Property Of Jerseys

PRINT RUN 199 SER.#'d SETS
*PATCHES: .75X TO 2X BASE HI
PATCH PRINT RUN 99 SER.#'d SETS
1 Josh Childress 2.00 5.00
6 Michael Finley 3.00 8.00
7 Carmelo Anthony 6.00 15.00
8 Ben Wallace 4.00 10.00
10 Yao Ming 8.00 20.00
11 Jermaine O'Neal 2.50 6.00
12 Elton Brand 2.50 6.00
14 Jason Williams 2.50 6.00
15 Dwyane Wade 8.00 20.00
16 Michael Redd 2.50 6.00
17 Latrell Sprewell 4.00 10.00
18 Richard Jefferson 2.50 6.00
19 Baron Davis 3.00 8.00
21 Dwight Howard 8.00 20.00
22 Allen Iverson 8.00 20.00
25 Peja Stojakovic 2.50 6.00
26 Manu Ginobili 6.00 15.00
27 Ray Allen 5.00 12.00
29 Andrei Kirilenko 2.50 6.00

2004-05 SkyBox Fresh Ink Teammate Tandems

COMPLETE SET (10) 20.00 50.00
STATED ODDS 1:108 H, 1:360 R
1 Y.Ming/T.McGrady 4.00 10.00
2 S.O'Neal/D.Wade 5.00 12.00
3 M.Finley/D.Nowitzki 4.00 10.00
4 R.Hamilton/B.Wallace 3.00 8.00
5 T.Ford/M.Redd 3.00 8.00
6 K.Garnett/L.Sprewell 4.00 10.00
7 R.Jefferson/J.Kidd 4.00 10.00
8 C.Bosh/J.Rose 3.00 8.00
9 M.Pietrus/J.Richardson 3.00 8.00
10 T.Duncan/T.Parker 4.00 10.00

2004-05 SkyBox Fresh Ink Teammate Tandems Jerseys

PRINT RUN 199 SER.#'d SETS
*RETAIL: .4X TO 1X HI COLUMN
RETAIL STATED ODDS 1:24 PACKS
*PATCHES: 1X TO 2.5X BASE HI
PATCH PRINT RUN 49 SER.#'d SETS
1 Y.Ming/T.McGrady 6.00 15.00
3 M.Finley/D.Nowitzki 8.00 20.00
4 R.Hamilton/B.Wallace 5.00 12.00
5 T.Ford/M.Redd 5.00 12.00
6 K.Garnett/L.Sprewell 6.00 15.00
7 R.Jefferson/J.Kidd 5.00 12.00
9 M.Pietrus/J.Richardson 5.00 12.00
10 T.Duncan/T.Parker 6.00 15.00

1999-00 SkyBox Impact

COMPLETE SET (200) 12.50 30.00
V.CARTER COMM: PRINT RUN #'d TO 2000
V.CARTER AU: PRINT RUN #'d TO 15
1 Tim Duncan .75 2.00
2 Doug Christie .25 .60
3 Mark Jackson .25 .60
4 Paul Pierce .60 1.50
5 James Posey RC .30 .75
6 Steve Smith .25 .60
7 Charlie Ward .20 .50
8 Elton Brand RC .60 1.50
9 Howard Eisley .20 .50
10 Grant Hill .50 1.25
11 Christian Laettner .25 .60
12 Corey Maggette RC .40 1.00
13 Scot Pollard .20 .50
14 Robert Traylor .20 .50
15 Nick Anderson .20 .50
16 Pat Garrity .20 .50
17 Hersey Hawkins .20 .50
18 Troy Hudson .30 .75
19 Charles Oakley .30 .75
20 Gary Payton .50 1.25
21 Rik Smits .25 .60
22 Muggsy Bogues .25 .60
23 Dale Davis .20 .50
24 Larry Johnson .30 .75
25 Antonio McDyess .25 .60
26 Alonzo Mourning .50 1.25
27 Scottie Pippen .75 2.00
28 Rod Strickland .25 .60
29 Antoine Walker .30 .75
30 Allen Iverson .75 2.00
31 Sam Cassell .25 .60
32 Mookie Blaylock .25 .60
33 Jim Jackson .20 .50
34 Brevin Knight .20 .50
35 Anthony Peeler .20 .50
36 Bryon Russell .20 .50
37 Maurice Taylor .20 .50
38 Elden Campbell .20 .50
39 Austin Croshere .20 .50
40 Keith Van Horn .25 .60
41 Raef LaFrentz .25 .60
42 Jamal Mashburn .25 .60
43 Jermaine O'Neal .25 .60
44 Glenn Robinson .25 .60
45 Mitch Richmond .40 1.00
46 Keon Clark .20 .50
47 Derrick Coleman .25 .60
48 Patrick Ewing .40 1.00
49 Brian Grant .20 .50
50 Kobe Bryant 2.50 6.00
51 Dan Majerle .30 .75
52 Ruben Patterson .20 .50
53 Walt Williams .20 .50
54 Chris Childs .20 .50
55 Baron Davis RC .75 2.00
56 Richard Hamilton RC .75 2.00
57 Voshon Lenard .20 .50
58 Vernon Maxwell .20 .50
59 Hakeem Olajuwon .60 1.50
60 Jason Williams .50 1.25
61 Gary Trent .20 .50
62 Kenny Anderson .25 .60
63 Shawn Bradley .20 .50
64 Obinna Ekezie RC .20 .50
65 Tom Gugliotta .25 .60
66 Ron Harper .25 .60
67 Corey Benjamin .20 .50
68 Donyell Marshall .25 .60
69 David Robinson .60 1.50
70 Stephon Marbury .40 1.00
71 Marcus Camby .25 .60
72 Horace Grant .25 .60
73 Tim Hardaway .40 1.00
74 Greg Foster .20 .50
75 Cuttino Mobley .25 .60
76 Rodney Buford RC .20 .50
77 Clifford Robinson .25 .60
78 Isaac Austin .20 .50
79 Robert Pack .20 .50
80 Eddie Jones .30 .75
81 Shawn Marion RC .60 1.50
82 Anthony Mason .30 .75
83 Oliver Miller .20 .50
84 Dirk Nowitzki 1.00 2.50
85 Jayson Williams .20 .50
86 Brent Barry .25 .60
87 P.J. Brown .20 .50
88 Kelvin Cato .20 .50
89 Jim McIlvaine .20 .50
90 Steve Francis RC .60 1.50
91 Bryant Reeves .20 .50
92 Jerry Stackhouse .30 .75
93 Allan Houston .25 .60

94 Kevin Garnett .75 2.00
95 Karl Malone .60 1.50
96 David Wesley .20 .50
97 Eddie Robinson RC .30 .75
98 Ben Wallace .25 .60
99 Chris Webber .40 1.00
100 Lamar Odom RC .60 1.50
101 Shandon Anderson .20 .50
102 Terrell Brandon .20 .50
103 Jeff Hornacek .25 .60
104 Terry Mills .20 .50
105 Tyrone Nesby RC .20 .50
106 Bo Outlaw .20 .50
107 Peja Stojakovic .30 .75
108 Ron Artest RC .75 2.00
109 Tony Battie .20 .50
110 Cedric Ceballos .20 .50
111 Anfernee Hardaway .75 2.00
112 Othella Harrington .20 .50
113 Dennis Rodman .60 1.50
114 Loy Vaught .20 .50
115 Malik Rose .20 .50
116 Vin Baker .25 .60
117 Charles Barkley .75 2.00
118 Michael Finley .30 .75
119 Adrian Griffin RC .25 .60
120 Jason Kidd .50 1.25
121 Gheorghe Muresan .20 .50
122 Cherokee Parks .20 .50
123 Glen Rice .30 .75
124 Bimbo Coles .20 .50
125 Andrew DeClercq .20 .50
126 Matt Geiger .20 .50
127 Bobby Jackson .25 .60
128 Michael Olowokandi .20 .50
129 Greg Ostertag .20 .50
130 Tracy McGrady .50 1.25
131 Rodney Rogers .20 .50
132 Juwan Howard .25 .60
133 Terry Cummings .25 .60
134 Mario Elie .20 .50
135 Trajan Langdon RC .25 .60
136 George Lynch .20 .50
137 Roshown McLeod .20 .50
138 Joe Smith .25 .60
139 John Stockton .50 1.25
140 Ray Allen .50 1.25
141 Vince Carter .75 2.00
142 Al Harrington .30 .75
143 Ron Mercer .25 .60
144 Vitaly Potapenko .20 .50
145 Arvydas Sabonis .25 .60
146 Latrell Sprewell .40 1.00
147 Aaron Williams .20 .50
148 Shareef Abdur-Rahim .30 .75
149 Vonteego Cummings RC .25 .60
150 Shaquille O'Neal 1.25 3.00
151 Derek Fisher .25 .60
152 Todd MacCulloch RC .25 .60
153 Andre Miller RC .60 1.50
154 Dikembe Mutombo .50 1.25
155 Ervin Johnson .20 .50
156 Michael Dickerson .20 .50
157 A.C. Green .25 .60
158 Kevin Willis .20 .50
159 Kerry Kittles .25 .60
160 Damon Stoudamire .30 .75
161 Eric Snow .20 .50
162 Bob Sura .20 .50
163 Jason Terry RC .50 1.25
164 Derek Anderson .20 .50
165 Randy Brown .20 .50
166 Vlade Divac .30 .75
167 Chris Gatling .20 .50
168 Lindsey Hunter .20 .50
169 Tim Thomas .25 .60
170 Antawn Jamison .30 .75
171 Alan Henderson .20 .50
172 Larry Hughes .25 .60
173 Shawn Kemp .50 1.25
174 Radoslav Nesterovic RC .30 .75
175 Scott Padgett .25 .60
176 Brian Skinner .20 .50
177 Jerome Williams .20 .50
178 Corliss Williamson .20 .50
179 Sean Elliott .25 .60
180 Wally Szczerbiak RC .50 1.25
181 Toni Kukoc .40 1.00
182 Chucky Atkins RC .25 .60
183 Jalen Rose .25 .60
184 Nick Van Exel .25 .60
185 Rasheed Wallace .40 1.00
186 Avery Johnson .25 .60
187 Jamie Feick RC .20 .50
188 Adonal Foyle .20 .50
189 Devean George RC .25 .60
190 Mike Bibby .30 .75
191 Lamond Murray .20 .50
192 Billy Owens .20 .50
193 Isaiah Rider .25 .60
194 Darrell Armstrong .20 .50
195 Antonio Davis .20 .50
196 Dale Ellis .20 .50
197 Tim Young RC .20 .50
198 Roy Rogers .20 .50
199 Terry Porter .20 .50
200 Reggie Miller .60 1.50
P141 Vince Carter PROMO .75 2.00
NNO V.Carter COMM 6.00 15.00

1999-00 SkyBox Impact Rewind '99

COMPLETE SET (40) 6.00 15.00
ONE PER PACK
RN1 Tim Duncan .60 1.50
RN2 David Robinson .50 1.25
RN3 Sean Elliott .20 .50
RN4 Mario Elie .15 .40
RN5 Avery Johnson .20 .50
RN6 Malik Rose .15 .40
RN7 Jaren Jackson .15 .40
RN8 Tim Duncan .60 1.50
RN9 Gerald King .15 .40
RN10 Jerome Kersey .15 .40
RN11 Steve Kerr .20 .50
RN12 Antonio Daniels .15 .40
RN13 Karl Malone .50 1.25
RN14 Vince Carter .60 1.50
RN15 Karl Malone .50 1.25
RN16 Tim Duncan .60 1.50
RN17 Alonzo Mourning .40 1.00
RN18 Allen Iverson .60 1.50
RN19 Jason Kidd .40 1.00
RN20 Chris Webber .30 .75
RN21 Grant Hill .40 1.00
RN22 Shaquille O'Neal 1.00 2.50
RN23 Gary Payton .40 1.00
RN24 Tim Hardaway .30 .75
RN25 Kevin Garnett .60 1.50
RN26 Antonio McDyess .20 .50
RN27 Hakeem Olajuwon .50 1.25
RN28 Kobe Bryant 2.00 5.00
RN29 John Stockton .40 1.00
RN30 Vince Carter .60 1.50
RN31 Paul Pierce .50 1.25
RN32 Jason Williams .40 1.00
RN33 Mike Bibby .25 .60
RN34 Matt Harpring .15 .40
RN35 Michael Dickerson .15 .40
RN36 Cuttino Mobley .15 .40
RN37 Michael Doleac .15 .40
RN38 Michael Olowokandi .15 .40
RN39 Antawn Jamison .25 .60
RN40 Vince Carter .60 1.50

1999-00 SkyBox Impact Tattoos

COMMON CARD (1-29) .40 1.00
2 Boston Celtics .75 2.00
4 Chicago Bulls .75 2.00
8 Detroit Pistons .50 1.25
13 Los Angeles Lakers .75 2.00
18 New York Knicks .75 2.00
24 San Antonio Spurs .50 1.25

1991 SkyBox Magic Johnson Video

NNO Magic Johnson 6.00 15.00

2003-04 SkyBox LE

COMP.SET w/o SP's (110) 12.50 30.00
PRINT RUN 399 SER.#'d SETS
1 Jason Terry .25 .60
2 Antoine Walker .30 .75
3 Paul Pierce .50 1.25
4 Eddy Curry .20 .50
5 Ricky Davis .25 .60
6 Jamal Crawford .30 .75
7 Raef LaFrentz .20 .50
8 Darius Miles .20 .50
9 Ray Allen .50 1.25
10 Sam Cassell .25 .60
11 Andre Miller .25 .60
12 Dirk Nowitzki .75 2.00
13 Zach Randolph .30 .75
14 Tim Duncan .75 2.00
15 Gary Payton .50 1.25
16 Ben Wallace .40 1.00
17 Michael Finley .30 .75
18 David Wesley .20 .50
19 Nick Van Exel .30 .75
20 Marcus Camby .25 .60
21 Gilbert Arenas .30 .75
22 Marcus Haislip .20 .50
23 Cuttino Mobley .20 .50
24 Tayshaun Prince .30 .75
25 Chris Webber .40 1.00
26 Reggie Miller .60 1.50
27 Chauncey Billups .40 1.00
28 Quentin Richardson .20 .50
29 Mike Dunleavy .25 .60
30 Karl Malone .60 1.50
31 Yao Ming .75 2.00
32 Tyson Chandler .25 .60
33 Jason Williams .50 1.25
34 Eddie Griffin .20 .50
35 Eddie Jones .30 .75
36 Jamaal Tinsley .20 .50
37 Michael Redd .30 .75
38 Elton Brand .25 .60
39 Rashard Lewis .25 .60
40 Vince Carter .60 1.50
41 Wally Szczerbiak .25 .60
42 Chris Wilcox .20 .50
43 Kenyon Martin .30 .75
44 Shaquille O'Neal 1.25 3.00
45 Baron Davis .30 .75
46 Pau Gasol .50 1.25
47 Dikembe Mutombo .40 1.00
48 Shane Battier .25 .60
49 Drew Gooden .25 .60
50 Lamar Odom .25 .60
51 Glenn Robinson .25 .60
52 Tim Thomas .20 .50
53 Shawn Marion .30 .75
54 Kevin Garnett .75 2.00
55 Stephon Marbury .40 1.00
56 Rasheed Wallace .40 1.00
57 Troy Hudson .20 .50
58 Mike Bibby .30 .75
59 Jason Kidd .50 1.25
60 Tony Parker .50 1.25
61 Andrei Kirilenko .30 .75
62 Manu Ginobili .60 1.50
63 Kerry Kittles .25 .60
64 Brent Barry .25 .60
65 Allan Houston .30 .75
66 Morris Peterson .20 .50
67 Tracy McGrady .50 1.25
68 Matt Harpring .25 .60
69 Erick Dampier .20 .50
70 Jerry Stackhouse .40 1.00
71 John Salmons .25 .60
72 Stephen Jackson .25 .60
73 Scottie Pippen .75 2.00
74 Dajuan Wagner .20 .50
75 Keon Clark .20 .50
76 Carlos Boozer .25 .60
77 Steve Nash .60 1.50
78 Nene .25 .60
79 Keith Van Horn .30 .75
80 Earl Boykins .20 .50
81 Richard Hamilton .40 1.00
82 Jason Richardson .30 .75
83 Steve Francis .30 .75
84 Jermaine O'Neal .30 .75
85 Ron Artest .30 .75
86 Corey Maggette .25 .60
87 Kwame Brown .20 .50
88 Kobe Bryant 2.50 6.00
89 Mike Miller .25 .60
90 Caron Butler .25 .60
91 Desmond Mason .25 .60
92 Latrell Sprewell .40 1.00
93 Richard Jefferson .25 .60
94 Jamal Mashburn .25 .60
95 Troy Murphy .20 .50
96 Peja Stojakovic .25 .60
97 Allen Iverson .75 2.00
98 Amare Stoudemire .40 1.00
99 Rasho Nesterovic .20 .50
100 Bonzi Wells .20 .50
101 Bobby Jackson .25 .60
102 Anfernee Hardaway .75 2.00
103 Larry Hughes .25 .60
104 Shareef Abdur-Rahim .30 .75
105 Hedo Turkoglu .25 .60
106 Alvin Williams .20 .50
107 Qyntel Woods .20 .50
108 Brad Miller .25 .60
109 Jalen Rose .25 .60
110 Antonio Davis .25 .60
111 David West RC 3.00 8.00
112 Boris Diaw RC 2.50 6.00
113 Travis Hansen RC 1.50 4.00
114 Marcus Banks RC 1.50 4.00
115 Kendrick Perkins RC 2.00 5.00
116 Darius Songaila 1.50 4.00
117 Kirk Hinrich/99 RC 8.00 20.00
118 LeBron James/99 RC 1,500.00 3,000.00
119 Jason Kapono RC 1.50 4.00
120 Josh Howard RC 2.50 6.00
121 Marquis Daniels RC 2.00 5.00
122 Carmelo Anthony/99 RC 50.00 120.00
123 Darko Milicic/99 RC 6.00 15.00
124 Zaur Pachulia RC 2.50 6.00
125 Mickael Pietrus RC 2.00 5.00
126 Ben Handlogten RC 1.50 4.00
127 James Jones RC 1.50 4.00
128 Chris Kaman RC 2.50 6.00
129 Josh Moore RC 1.50 4.00
130 Brian Cook RC 1.50 4.00
131 Luke Walton RC 2.50 6.00
132 Troy Bell RC 1.50 4.00
133 Dahntay Jones RC 2.00 5.00
134 Dwyane Wade/99 RC 60.00 150.00
135 Udonis Haslem RC 3.00 8.00
136 T.J. Ford/99 RC 6.00 15.00
137 Ndudi Ebi RC 1.50 4.00
138 Zoran Planinic RC 1.50 4.00
139 Raul Lopez 2.50 6.00
140 Francisco Elson RC 1.50 4.00
141 Mike Sweetney RC 1.50 4.00
142 Maciej Lampe RC 1.50 4.00
143 Slavko Vranes RC 1.50 4.00
144 Keith Bogans/99 RC 5.00 12.00
145 Reece Gaines RC 1.50 4.00
146 Willie Green RC 2.50 6.00
147 Kyle Korver RC 3.00 8.00
148 Zarko Cabarkapa RC 1.50 4.00
149 Leandro Barbosa RC 2.50 6.00
150 Travis Outlaw RC 2.00 5.00
151 Curtis Borchardt 2.00 5.00
152 Alex Garcia RC 1.50 4.00
153 Richie Frahm RC 2.50 6.00
154 Nick Collison RC 2.00 5.00
155 Luke Ridnour/99 RC 8.00 20.00
156 Chris Bosh/99 RC 25.00 60.00
157 Aleksandar Pavlovic RC 2.00 5.00
158 Maurice Williams RC 2.00 5.00
159 Jarvis Hayes/99 RC 5.00 12.00
160 Steve Blake RC 2.00 5.00

2003-04 SkyBox LE Retail

COMPLETE SET (160) 30.00 60.00
*VETS: SAME PRICE AS HOBBY
111 David West RC 1.00 2.50
112 Boris Diaw RC .75 2.00
113 Travis Hansen RC .50 1.25
114 Marcus Banks RC .50 1.25
115 Kendrick Perkins RC .60 1.50
116 Darius Songaila .50 1.25
117 Kirk Hinrich RC .75 2.00
118 LeBron James RC 8.00 20.00
119 Jason Kapono RC .50 1.25
120 Josh Howard RC .75 2.00
121 Marquis Daniels RC .60 1.50
122 Carmelo Anthony RC 4.00 10.00
123 Darko Milicic RC .60 1.50
124 Zaur Pachulia RC .75 2.00
125 Mickael Pietrus RC .60 1.50
126 Ben Handlogten RC .50 1.25
127 James Jones RC .50 1.25
128 Chris Kaman RC .75 2.00
129 Josh Moore RC .50 1.25
130 Brian Cook RC .50 1.25
131 Luke Walton RC .75 2.00
132 Troy Bell RC .50 1.25
133 Dahntay Jones RC .60 1.50
134 Dwyane Wade RC 6.00 15.00
135 Udonis Haslem RC 1.00 2.50
136 T.J. Ford RC .60 1.50
137 Ndudi Ebi RC .60 1.50
138 Zoran Planinic RC .60 1.50
139 Raul Lopez .75 2.00
140 Francisco Elson RC .50 1.25
141 Mike Sweetney RC .50 1.25
142 Maciej Lampe RC .50 1.25
143 Slavko Vranes RC .50 1.25
144 Keith Bogans RC .50 1.25
145 Reece Gaines RC .50 1.25
146 Willie Green RC .75 2.00
147 Kyle Korver RC 1.00 2.50
148 Zarko Cabarkapa RC .50 1.25
149 Leandro Barbosa RC .75 2.00
150 Travis Outlaw RC .60 1.50
151 Curtis Borchardt .60 1.50
152 Alex Garcia RC .50 1.25
153 Richie Frahm RC .75 2.00
154 Nick Collison RC .60 1.50
155 Luke Ridnour RC .75 2.00
156 Chris Bosh RC 2.50 6.00
157 Aleksandar Pavlovic RC .60 1.50
158 Maurice Williams RC .75 2.00
159 Jarvis Hayes RC .50 1.25
160 Steve Blake RC .60 1.50

2003-04 SkyBox LE Artist Proofs

*AP SINGLES: 5X TO 12X BASE HI
*AP RCs: .75X TO 2X BASE HI
*AP RCs/99: .25X TO .6X BASE HI
PRINT RUN 50 SER.#'d SETS

2003-04 SkyBox LE Gold Proofs

*GOLD SINGLES: 4X TO 10X BASE HI
*GOLD RC's: .6X TO 1.5X BASE HI
*GOLD RC's/99: .2X TO .5X BASE HI
PRINT RUN 150 SER.#'d SETS

2003-04 SkyBox LE Photographer Proofs

*PP SINGLES: 8X TO 20X BASE HI
*PP RCs: 1X TO 2.5 BASE HI
*PP RCs/99: .4X TO 1X BASE HI
PHOTO.PROOF PRINT RUN 25 SER.#'d SETS

2003-04 SkyBox LE Championship MettLE

STATED PRINT RUN 99 SER.#'d SETS
LARRY BROWN DOES NOT HAVE JSY
RGAI Allen Iverson 40.00 100.00
RGJK Jason Kidd 15.00 40.00
RGJO Jermaine O'Neal 10.00 25.00
RGLB Larry Brown 30.00 80.00
RGMB Mike Bibby 10.00 25.00
RGRA Ray Allen 15.00 40.00
RGTD Tim Duncan 40.00 100.00
RGTM Tracy McGrady 25.00 60.00

2003-04 SkyBox LE History of the Draft Autographs

1 Vince Carter 50.00 120.00
2 Manu Ginobili 40.00 100.00
3 Shawn Marion 8.00 20.00

2003-04 SkyBox LE History of the Draft Autographs 99

PRINT RUN 99 SER.#'d SETS
*AUTO 50: .5X TO 1.25X AUTO 99
1 Vince Carter 60.00 150.00
2 Manu Ginobili 50.00 120.00
3 Shawn Marion 10.00 25.00
4 Paul Pierce 40.00 100.00
5 Mike Bibby 8.00 20.00
6 Tracy McGrady 40.00 100.00

2003-04 SkyBox LE History of the Draft The 90s

CARDS #'d TO PLAYER'S DRAFT YEAR
*PAR.50 SINGLES: .5X TO 1.2X BASE JSY HI
HDAI Allen Iverson/96 10.00 25.00
HDAJ Antawn Jamison/98 4.00 10.00
HDAW Antoine Walker/96 4.00 10.00
HDBD Baron Davis/99 4.00 10.00
HDBW Bonzi Wells/98 2.50 6.00
HDCM Corey Maggette/99 3.00 8.00
HDCW Chris Webber/93 5.00 12.00
HDDN Dirk Nowitzki/98 10.00 25.00
HDEB Elton Brand/99 3.00 8.00
HDGP Gary Payton/90 6.00 15.00
HDGR Glenn Robinson/94 3.00 8.00
HDJK Jason Kidd/94 6.00 15.00
HDJM Jamal Mashburn/93 3.00 8.00
HDJO Jermaine O'Neal/96 4.00 10.00
HDJR Jalen Rose/94 3.00 8.00
HDJS Jerry Stackhouse/95 5.00 12.00
HDJT Jason Terry/99 3.00 8.00
HDKG Kevin Garnett/95 10.00 25.00
HDKV Keith Van Horn/97 3.00 8.00
HDLO Lamar Odom/99 3.00 8.00
HDLS Latrell Sprewell/92 5.00 12.00
HDMB Mike Bibby/98 4.00 10.00
HDMF Michael Finley/95 4.00 10.00
HDMG Manu Ginobili/99 8.00 20.00
HDPP Paul Pierce/98 6.00 15.00
HDPS Peja Stojakovic/96 3.00 8.00
HDRA Ray Allen/96 6.00 15.00
HDRD Ricky Davis/98 3.00 8.00
HDRH Richard Hamilton/99 5.00 12.00
HDRL Rashard Lewis/98 3.00 8.00
HDRW Rasheed Wallace/95 5.00 12.00
HDSA Shareef Abdur-Rahim/96 4.00 10.00
HDSF Steve Francis/99 4.00 10.00
HDSM Stephon Marbury/96 5.00 12.00
HDSM Shawn Marion/99 4.00 10.00
HDSN Steve Nash/96 8.00 20.00
HDSO Shaquille O'Neal/92 15.00 40.00
HDTD Tim Duncan/97 10.00 25.00
HDTM Tracy McGrady/97 6.00 15.00
HDVC Vince Carter/98 8.00 20.00

2003-04 SkyBox LE Jersey Proofs

PRINT RUN 399 SER.#'d SETS
*PAR.50 SINGLES: .6X TO 1.5X BASE JSY HI
3 Paul Pierce 4.00 10.00
4 Eddy Curry 1.50 4.00
9 Ray Allen 4.00 10.00
12 Dirk Nowitzki 6.00 15.00
14 Tim Duncan 6.00 15.00
16 Ben Wallace 3.00 8.00
24 Tayshaun Prince 2.50 6.00
25 Chris Webber 3.00 8.00
26 Reggie Miller 5.00 12.00
29 Mike Dunleavy 2.00 5.00
30 Karl Malone 5.00 12.00
31 Yao Ming 6.00 15.00
32 Tyson Chandler 2.00 5.00
37 Michael Redd 2.50 6.00
38 Elton Brand 2.00 5.00
40 Drew Gooden 2.00 5.00
43 Kenyon Martin 2.50 6.00
44 Shaquille O'Neal 10.00 25.00
45 Baron Davis 2.50 6.00
46 Pau Gasol 4.00 10.00
48 Shane Battier 2.00 5.00
50 Lamar Odom 2.00 5.00
53 Shawn Marion 2.50 6.00
54 Kevin Garnett 6.00 15.00
55 Stephon Marbury 3.00 8.00
56 Rasheed Wallace 3.00 8.00
58 Mike Bibby 2.50 6.00
59 Jason Kidd 4.00 10.00
60 Tony Parker 4.00 10.00
61 Andrei Kirilenko 2.00 5.00
67 Tracy McGrady 4.00 10.00
70 Jerry Stackhouse 2.00 5.00
73 Scottie Pippen 6.00 15.00
77 Steve Nash 5.00 12.00
78 Nene 2.00 5.00
81 Richard Hamilton 3.00 8.00
82 Jason Richardson 2.50 6.00
83 Steve Francis 2.50 6.00
84 Jermaine O'Neal 2.50 6.00
87 Kwame Brown 2.00 5.00
90 Caron Butler 2.00 5.00
92 Latrell Sprewell 3.00 8.00
93 Richard Jefferson 2.00 5.00
96 Peja Stojakovic 2.00 5.00
97 Allen Iverson 6.00 15.00
98 Amare Stoudemire 3.00 8.00
100 Bonzi Wells 2.00 5.00
104 Shareef Abdur-Rahim 2.50 6.00
109 Jalen Rose 2.00 5.00

2003-04 SkyBox LE League Leaders

COMPLETE SET (9) 5.00 12.00
STATED ODDS 1:1E
1 Tracy McGrady 1.00 2.50
2 Ben Wallace .75 2.00
3 Jason Kidd 1.00 2.50
4 Allen Iverson 1.50 4.00
5 Eddy Curry .40 1.00
6 Kevin Garnett 1.50 4.00
7 Caron Butler .50 1.25
8 Amare Stoudemire .75 2.00
9 Yao Ming 1.50 4.00

2003-04 SkyBox LE League Leaders Game-Used

PRINT RUN 75 SER.#'d SETS
*PAR.50 SINGLES: .5X TO 1.25X BASE JSY HI
LLAI Allen Iverson 8.00 20.00
LLAS Amare Stoudemire 4.00 10.00
LLBW Ben Wallace 4.00 10.00
LLCB Caron Butler 2.50 6.00
LLEC Eddy Curry 2.00 5.00
LLJK Jason Kidd 5.00 12.00
LLKG Kevin Garnett 8.00 20.00
LLTM Tracy McGrady 8.00 20.00
LLYM Yao Ming 8.00 20.00

2003-04 SkyBox LE Rare Form

STATED ODDS 1:28
1 Vince Carter 6.00 15.00
2 Carmelo Anthony 15.00 40.00
3 Dwyane Wade 40.00 100.00
4 Dajuan Wagner 2.00 5.00
5 Tony Parker 5.00 12.00
6 Caron Butler 2.50 6.00
7 Tyson Chandler 2.50 6.00
8 Chris Bosh 10.00 25.00
9 Jason Richardson 3.00 8.00
10 Jerry Stackhouse 4.00 10.00

2003-04 SkyBox LE Rare Form Autographs

OVERALL AUTOGRAPH ODDS 1:18
1 Vince Carter/259 40.00 100.00
2 Carmelo Anthony/490 75.00 200.00
3 Tony Parker/260 20.00 50.00
5 Tyson Chandler 5.00 12.00
6 Troy Bell/350 4.00 10.00
7 Boris Diaw/275 6.00 15.00
8 Mickael Pietrus/280 5.00 12.00
9 Josh Howard/880 6.00 15.00
13 Travis Outlaw 5.00 12.00
15 Brian Cook/490 4.00 10.00
17 Dahntay Jones/350 5.00 12.00
19 Zaur Pachulia/75 6.00 15.00
20 Kendrick Perkins/395 5.00 12.00
21 Tayshaun Prince/100 20.00 50.00
22 Mike Sweetney/180 4.00 10.00
23 Maurice Williams/425 6.00 15.00
24 Travis Hansen/330 4.00 10.00

2003-04 SkyBox LE Rare Form Autographs 150

PRINT RUN 150 SER.#'d SETS
*AU 50 SINGLES: .5X TO 1.25X AU 150 HI
1 Vince Carter 40.00 100.00
2 Carmelo Anthony 75.00 200.00
3 Tony Parker 20.00 50.00
4 Caron Butler 5.00 12.00
5 Tyson Chandler 5.00 12.00
6 Troy Bell 4.00 10.00
7 Boris Diaw 6.00 15.00
8 Mickael Pietrus 5.00 12.00
9 Josh Howard 6.00 15.00
10 David West 8.00 20.00
11 Luke Walton 6.00 15.00
13 Travis Outlaw 5.00 12.00
15 Brian Cook 4.00 10.00
17 Dahntay Jones 5.00 12.00
19 Zaur Pachulia 6.00 15.00
20 Kendrick Perkins 5.00 12.00
21 Tayshaun Prince 20.00 50.00
22 Mike Sweetney 4.00 10.00
23 Maurice Williams 6.00 15.00
24 Travis Hansen 4.00 10.00

2003-04 SkyBox LE Rare Form Game-Used

PRINT RUN 99 SER.#'d SETS
*PAR.50 SINGLES: .5X TO 1.25X BASE JSY HI
RFCA Carmelo Anthony 20.00 50.00
RFCB Chris Bosh 12.00 30.00
RFCB Caron Butler 3.00 8.00
RFDW Dajuan Wagner 2.50 6.00
RFDW Dwyane Wade 30.00 80.00
RFJR Jason Richardson 4.00 10.00
RFJS Jerry Stackhouse 5.00 12.00
RFTC Tyson Chandler 3.00 8.00
RFTP Tony Parker 6.00 15.00
RFVC Vince Carter 8.00 20.00

2003-04 SkyBox LE Sky's the Limit

COMPLETE SET (20) 60.00 150.00
STATED ODDS 1:6
1 Baron Davis .60 1.50
2 Dirk Nowitzki 1.50 4.00
3 Tayshaun Prince .60 1.50
4 Caron Butler .50 1.25
5 Steve Nash 1.25 3.00
6 Shawn Marion .60 1.50
7 Scottie Pippen 1.50 4.00
8 Kobe Bryant 5.00 12.00
9 Tony Parker 1.00 2.50
10 Amare Stoudemire .75 2.00
11 Jason Richardson .60 1.50
12 Manu Ginobili 1.25 3.00
13 Drew Gooden .50 1.25
14 Paul Pierce 1.00 2.50
15 Yao Ming 1.50 4.00
16 LeBron James 30.00 80.00
17 Darko Milicic .50 1.25
18 Carmelo Anthony 3.00 8.00
19 Chris Bosh 2.00 5.00
20 Dwyane Wade 5.00 12.00

2003-04 SkyBox LE Sky's the Limit Game-Used

PRINT RUN 99 SER.#'d SETS
*PAR.50 SINGLES: .5X TO 1.25X BASE JSY HI
SLBD Baron Davis 4.00 10.00
SLCA Carmelo Anthony 20.00 50.00
SLCB Chris Bosh 12.00 30.00
SLCB Caron Butler 3.00 8.00
SLDG Drew Gooden 3.00 8.00
SLDN Dirk Nowitzki 10.00 25.00
SLDW Dwyane Wade 30.00 80.00
SLJR Jason Richardson 4.00 10.00
SLMG Manu Ginobili 8.00 20.00
SLPP Paul Pierce 6.00 15.00
SLSM Shawn Marion 4.00 10.00
SLSN Steve Nash 8.00 20.00
SLSP Scottie Pippen 10.00 25.00
SLTD Amare Stoudemire 5.00 12.00
SLTP Tayshaun Prince 4.00 10.00
SLTP Tony Parker 6.00 15.00
SLYM Yao Ming 10.00 25.00

2004-05 SkyBox LE

COMP.SET w/o SP's (75) 20.00 40.00
1 Tony Parker .50 1.25
2 Vince Carter .60 1.50
3 Al Harrington .25 .60
4 Dwyane Wade 1.25 3.00
5 Latrell Sprewell .40 1.00
6 Michael Finley .30 .75
7 Caron Butler .25 .60
8 Zach Randolph .30 .75
9 Peja Stojakovic .25 .60
10 Eddy Curry .20 .50
11 Allen Iverson .75 2.00
12 Kirk Hinrich .30 .75
13 Jason Williams .25 .60
14 Hedo Turkoglu .25 .60
15 Manu Ginobili .60 1.50
16 Eddie House .20 .50
17 Reggie Miller .60 1.50
18 Steve Francis .30 .75
19 LeBron James 2.50 6.00
20 Dirk Nowitzki .75 2.00
21 Stephon Marbury .40 1.00
22 Ray Allen .50 1.25
23 Carmelo Anthony .60 1.50
24 Lamar Odom .25 .60
25 Jamaal Magloire .20 .50
26 Shareef Abdur-Rahim .30 .75
27 Chris Webber .40 1.00
28 Jason Richardson .30 .75
29 Richard Jefferson .25 .60
30 Richard Hamilton .40 1.00
31 Alonzo Mourning .40 1.00
32 Chris Bosh .50 1.25
33 Mike Dunleavy .25 .60
34 Andrei Kirilenko .25 .60
35 Tracy McGrady .50 1.25
36 T.J. Ford .25 .60
37 Jason Kidd .50 1.25
38 Carlos Arroyo .50 1.25
39 Rasheed Wallace .40 1.00
40 Gilbert Arenas .30 .75
41 Kenyon Martin .30 .75
42 Tim Duncan .75 2.00
43 Yao Ming .75 2.00
44 Carlos Boozer .25 .60
45 Michael Redd .25 .60
46 Larry Hughes .25 .60
47 Antoine Walker .30 .75
48 Kevin Garnett .75 2.00
49 Willie Green .30 .75
50 Tyson Chandler .30 .75
51 Elton Brand .25 .60
52 Allan Houston .30 .75
53 Shawn Marion .30 .75
54 Ricky Davis .30 .75
55 Shaquille O'Neal 1.25 3.00
56 Steve Nash .60 1.50
57 Jarvis Hayes .20 .50
58 Zydrunas Ilgauskas .25 .60
59 Corey Maggette .25 .60
60 Ben Wallace .40 1.00
61 Darius Miles .20 .50
62 Drew Gooden .20 .50
63 Pau Gasol .50 1.25
64 Jamal Crawford .30 .75
65 Gary Payton .50 1.25
66 Jermaine O'Neal .25 .60
67 Jason Kapono .20 .50
68 Marquis Daniels .20 .50
69 Kobe Bryant 2.50 6.00
70 Baron Davis .30 .75
71 Mike Bibby .30 .75
72 Rashard Lewis .25 .60
73 Paul Pierce .50 1.25
74 Sam Cassell .25 .60
75 Amare Stoudemire .50 1.25
76 Dwight Howard/99 RC 12.00 30.00
77 Emeka Okafor/99 RC 3.00 8.00
78 Ben Gordon/99 RC 4.00 10.00
79 Shaun Livingston/99 RC 4.00 10.00
80 Devin Harris/99 RC 3.00 8.00
81 Josh Childress/99 RC 2.50 6.00
82 Luol Deng/99 RC 4.00 10.00
83 Rafael Araujo/99 RC 2.50 6.00
84 Andre Iguodala/99 RC 6.00 15.00
85 Luke Jackson/99 RC 2.50 6.00
86 Andris Biedrins/99 RC 2.50 6.00
87 Robert Swift RC 1.25 3.00
88 Sebastian Telfair/99 RC 3.00 8.00
89 Kris Humphries RC 1.50 4.00
90 Al Jefferson RC 2.00 5.00
91 Kirk Snyder RC 1.25 3.00
92 Josh Smith/99 RC 4.00 10.00
93 J.R. Smith/99 RC 4.00 10.00
94 Dorell Wright RC 1.50 4.00
95 Jameer Nelson/99 RC 4.00 10.00
96 Pavel Podkolzin RC 1.25 3.00
97 Nenad Krstic RC 1.50 4.00
98 Andres Nocioni/99 RC 4.00 10.00
99 Delonte West RC 1.50 4.00
100 Tony Allen RC 2.00 5.00
101 Kevin Martin RC 2.50 6.00
102 Sasha Vujacic/99 RC 3.00 8.00
103 Beno Udrih RC 1.50 4.00
104 David Harrison RC 1.25 3.00
105 Anderson Varejao/99 RC 3.00 8.00
106 Jackson Vroman RC 1.25 3.00
107 Peter John Ramos RC 1.25 3.00
108 Lionel Chalmers RC 1.50 4.00
109 Donta Smith RC 1.25 3.00
110 Andre Emmett RC 1.25 3.00
111 Antonio Burks RC 1.25 3.00
112 Royal Ivey RC 1.25 3.00
113 Chris Duhon/99 RC 3.00 8.00
114 Erik Daniels RC 1.50 4.00
115 Justin Reed RC 1.25 3.00
116 Horace Jenkins RC 1.50 4.00
117 D.J. Mbenga RC 1.25 3.00
118 Trevor Ariza RC 2.00 5.00
119 Tim Pickett RC 1.50 4.00
120 Bernard Robinson RC 1.25 3.00
121 Ibrahim Kutluay RC 2.00 5.00
122 Romain Sato RC 1.25 3.00
123 Luis Flores RC 1.50 4.00
124 Damien Wilkins RC 1.50 4.00
125 Yuta Tabuse/99 RC 4.00 10.00

2004-05 SkyBox LE Retail

COMPLETE SET (125) 20.00 50.00
*VETS: SAME PRICE AS HOBBY
76 Dwight Howard RC 2.50 6.00
77 Emeka Okafor RC .60 1.50
78 Ben Gordon RC .75 2.00
79 Shaun Livingston RC .75 2.00
80 Devin Harris RC .60 1.50
81 Josh Childress RC .50 1.25
82 Luol Deng RC .75 2.00
83 Rafael Araujo RC .50 1.25
84 Andre Iguodala RC 1.25 3.00
85 Luke Jackson RC .50 1.25
86 Andris Biedrins RC .50 1.25
87 Robert Swift RC .50 1.25
88 Sebastian Telfair RC .60 1.50
89 Kris Humphries RC .60 1.50
90 Al Jefferson RC .75 2.00
91 Kirk Snyder RC .50 1.25
92 Josh Smith RC .75 2.00
93 J.R. Smith RC .75 2.00
94 Dorell Wright RC .60 1.50
95 Jameer Nelson RC .75 2.00
96 Pavel Podkolzin RC .50 1.25
97 Nenad Krstic RC .60 1.50
98 Andres Nocioni RC .75 2.00
99 Delonte West RC .60 1.50
100 Tony Allen RC .75 2.00
101 Kevin Martin RC 1.00 2.50
102 Sasha Vujacic RC .60 1.50
103 Beno Udrih RC .60 1.50
104 David Harrison RC .50 1.25
105 Anderson Varejao RC .60 1.50
106 Jackson Vroman RC .50 1.25
107 Peter John Ramos RC .50 1.25
108 Lionel Chalmers RC .60 1.50
109 Donta Smith RC .50 1.25
110 Andre Emmett RC .50 1.25
111 Antonio Burks RC .50 1.25
112 Royal Ivey RC .50 1.25
113 Chris Duhon RC .60 1.50
114 Erik Daniels RC .60 1.50
115 Justin Reed RC .50 1.25
116 Horace Jenkins RC .60 1.50
117 D.J. Mbenga RC .50 1.25
118 Trevor Ariza RC .75 2.00
119 Tim Pickett RC .60 1.50
120 Bernard Robinson RC .50 1.25
121 Ibrahim Kutluay RC .75 2.00
122 Romain Sato RC .60 1.50
123 Luis Flores RC .60 1.50
124 Damien Wilkins RC .60 1.50
125 Yuta Tabuse RC .75 2.00

2004-05 SkyBox LE 150

*LE 150 1-75 SINGLES: 2X TO 5X BASE HI
*LE 150 RC/499 SINGLES: .6X TO 1.5X BASE HI
19 LeBron James 40.00 100.00

2004-05 SkyBox LE 50

*LE 50 1-75 STARS: 3X TO 8X BASE HI
*LE 50 RCs/99: .5X TO 1.25X BASE HI
*LE 50 RCs/499: 1X TO 2.5X BASE HI
19 LeBron James 75.00 200.00

2004-05 SkyBox LE 35

*1-75 SINGLES: 4X TO 10X BASE HI
*RCs/99: .6X TO 1.5X BASE HI
*RCs/499: 1.25X TO 3X BASE HI
19 LeBron James 100.00 250.00

2004-05 SkyBox LE Jersey Proofs

STATED ODDS 1:60
*JSY 99 SINGLES: .5X TO 1.25X BASE JSY HI
*PATCH SINGLES: 1X TO 2.5X BASE JSY HI
PATCH PRINT RUN 50 SER.#'d SETS
1 Tony Parker 4.00 10.00
2 Vince Carter 5.00 12.00
3 Al Harrington 2.00 5.00
4 Dwyane Wade 10.00 25.00
5 Latrell Sprewell 3.00 8.00
7 Caron Butler 2.00 5.00
8 Zach Randolph 2.50 6.00
9 Peja Stojakovic 2.00 5.00
10 Eddy Curry 1.50 4.00
11 Allen Iverson 6.00 15.00
12 Kirk Hinrich 2.50 6.00
13 Jason Williams 2.00 5.00
15 Manu Ginobili 5.00 12.00
17 Reggie Miller 5.00 12.00
18 Steve Francis 2.50 6.00
21 Stephon Marbury 3.00 8.00
22 Ray Allen 4.00 10.00
23 Carmelo Anthony 5.00 12.00
24 Lamar Odom 2.50 6.00
26 Shareef Abdur-Rahim 2.50 6.00

28 Jason Richardson 2.50 6.00
32 Chris Bosh 4.00 10.00
33 Mike Dunleavy 1.50 4.00
34 Andrei Kirilenko 2.00 5.00
35 Tracy McGrady 4.00 10.00
36 T.J. Ford 1.50 4.00
39 Rasheed Wallace 3.00 8.00
40 Gilbert Arenas 2.50 6.00
42 Tim Duncan 6.00 15.00
43 Yao Ming 6.00 15.00
44 Carlos Boozer 2.00 5.00
46 Larry Hughes 2.00 5.00
48 Kevin Garnett 6.00 15.00
50 Tyson Chandler 2.00 5.00
51 Elton Brand 2.00 5.00
52 Allan Houston 2.50 6.00
53 Shawn Marion 2.50 6.00
55 Shaquille O'Neal 10.00 25.00
56 Steve Nash 5.00 12.00
59 Corey Maggette 2.00 5.00
60 Ben Wallace 3.00 8.00
61 Darius Miles 2.00 5.00
63 Pau Gasol 4.00 10.00
65 Gary Payton 4.00 10.00
71 Mike Bibby 2.50 6.00
72 Rashard Lewis 2.00 5.00
73 Paul Pierce 4.00 10.00
75 Amare Stoudemire 2.50 6.00

2004-05 SkyBox LE Future Legends

COMPLETE SET (24) 20.00 50.00
STATED ODDS 1:12
1 Dwight Howard 3.00 8.00
2 Jameer Nelson 1.00 2.50
3 Shaun Livingston 1.00 2.50
4 Sebastian Telfair .75 2.00
5 Ben Gordon 1.00 2.50
6 Luol Deng 1.00 2.50
7 Josh Childress .60 1.50
8 Josh Smith 1.00 2.50
9 Andre Iguodala 1.50 4.00
10 J.R. Smith 1.00 2.50
11 Kris Humphries .75 2.00
12 Kirk Snyder .60 1.50
13 Devin Harris .75 2.00
14 Pavel Podkolzin .60 1.50
15 Rafael Araujo .60 1.50
16 Robert Swift .60 1.50
17 Andris Biedrins .60 1.50
18 Luke Jackson .60 1.50
19 Chris Duhon .75 2.00
20 Dorell Wright .75 2.00
21 Tony Allen 1.00 2.50
22 Delonte West .75 2.00
23 Yuta Tabuse 1.00 2.50
24 Emeka Okafor .75 2.00

2004-05 SkyBox LE Future Legends Jerseys

PRINT RUN 75 SER.#'d SETS
*JERSEY 50 SINGLES: .5X TO 1.25X BASE HI
*PATCH: 1X TO 2.5X BASE HI
PATCH PRINT RUN 25 SER.#'d SETS
AB Andris Biedrins 1.50 4.00
AI Andre Iguodala 4.00 10.00
AJ Al Jefferson 2.50 6.00
BG Ben Gordon 2.50 6.00
DH Dwight Howard 8.00 20.00
DH2 Devin Harris 2.00 5.00
DW Dorell Wright 2.00 5.00
DW2 Delonte West 2.00 5.00
FL Sasha Vujacic 2.00 5.00
JC Josh Childress 1.50 4.00
JN Jameer Nelson 2.50 6.00
JS Josh Smith 2.50 6.00
JS J.R. Smith 2.50 6.00
KH Kris Humphries 2.00 5.00
KS Kirk Snyder 1.50 4.00
LD Luol Deng 2.50 6.00
LJ Luke Jackson 1.50 4.00
RA Rafael Araujo 1.50 4.00
SL Shaun Livingston 2.50 6.00
ST Sebastian Telfair 2.50 6.00
TA Tony Allen 2.50 6.00
YT Yuta Tabuse 2.50 6.00

2004-05 SkyBox LE Future Legends of the Draft Patches Autographs

PRINT RUN 25 SER.#'d SETS
AB Andris Biedrins 5.00 12.00
AJ Al Jefferson 8.00 20.00
BG Ben Gordon 20.00 50.00
DH2 Devin Harris 6.00 15.00
JS J.R. Smith 8.00 20.00
JS Josh Smith 8.00 20.00
KH Kris Humphries 6.00 15.00
KS Kirk Snyder 5.00 12.00
LJ Luke Jackson 5.00 12.00
RA Rafael Araujo 5.00 12.00
ST Sebastian Telfair 6.00 15.00
YT Yuta Tabuse 8.00 20.00

2004-05 SkyBox LE Legends of the Draft

COMPLETE SET (20) 15.00 40.00
STATED ODDS 1:4 H, 1:8 R
1 Oscar Robertson 2.50 6.00
2 Walt Bellamy 1.00 2.50
3 Elgin Baylor 1.25 3.00
4 Cazzie Russell 1.00 2.50
5 Bob Lanier 1.00 2.50
6 Kevin McHale 1.50 4.00
7 Bill Walton 1.25 3.00
8 John Havlicek 1.25 3.00
9 Robert Parish 1.25 3.00
10 Isiah Thomas 2.00 5.00
11 Walt Frazier 1.50 4.00
12 George Gervin 1.25 3.00
13 Nate Archibald 1.00 2.50
14 Bob Cousy 2.00 5.00
15 Rick Barry 1.00 2.50
16 Earl Monroe 1.25 3.00
17 Willis Reed 2.00 5.00
18 Darryl Dawkins .75 2.00
19 Wes Unseld 1.25 3.00
20 Pat Riley 1.50 4.00

2004-05 SkyBox LE Legends of the Draft Jerseys

PRINT RUN 50 SER.#'d SETS
*PATCH: .6X TO 1.5X BASE HI
PATCH PRINT RUN 25 SER.#'d SETS
AH Anfernee Hardaway 10.00 25.00
AI Allen Iverson 10.00 25.00
AK Andrei Kirilenko 3.00 8.00
AS Amare Stoudemire 4.00 10.00
AW Antoine Walker 4.00 10.00
BD Baron Davis 4.00 10.00
CA Carmelo Anthony 8.00 20.00
CM Corey Maggette 3.00 8.00
CW Chris Webber 5.00 12.00
DN Dirk Nowitzki 10.00 25.00
DW Dwyane Wade 15.00 40.00
EB Elton Brand 3.00 8.00
JK Jason Kidd 6.00 15.00
JO Jermaine O'Neal 3.00 8.00
JR Jason Richardson 4.00 10.00
KM Kenyon Martin 4.00 10.00
LO Lamar Odom 4.00 10.00
MB Mike Bibby 4.00 10.00
PG Pau Gasol 6.00 15.00
PP Paul Pierce 6.00 15.00
RA Ray Allen 6.00 15.00
RH Richard Hamilton 5.00 12.00
RM Reggie Miller 8.00 20.00
RW Rasheed Wallace 5.00 12.00
SF Steve Francis 4.00 10.00
SM Stephon Marbury 5.00 12.00
SM2 Shawn Marion 4.00 10.00
SO Shaquille O'Neal 15.00 40.00
SP Scottie Pippen 20.00 50.00
TD Tim Duncan 10.00 25.00
TP Tony Parker 6.00 15.00
TW Tracy McGrady 6.00 15.00
VC Vince Carter 8.00 20.00
YM Yao Ming 10.00 25.00

2004-05 SkyBox LE Legends of the Draft Jerseys Year

JSY #'d TO PLAYER DRAFT YEAR
AI Allen Iverson/96 8.00 20.00
AK Andrei Kirilenko/99 2.50 6.00
AS Amare Stoudemire/102 3.00 8.00
AW Antoine Walker/96 3.00 8.00
BD Baron Davis/99 3.00 8.00
CA Carmelo Anthony/103 6.00 15.00
CM Corey Maggette/99 2.50 6.00
CW Chris Webber/93 4.00 10.00
DN Dirk Nowitzki/98 8.00 20.00
DW Dwyane Wade/103 12.00 30.00
EB Elton Brand/99 2.50 6.00
JK Jason Kidd/94 5.00 12.00
JO Jermaine O'Neal/96 2.50 6.00
JR Jason Richardson/101 3.00 8.00
JS Jerry Stackhouse/95 3.00 8.00
KG Kevin Garnett/95 8.00 20.00
KM Kenyon Martin/100 3.00 8.00
LO Lamar Odom/99 3.00 8.00
MB Mike Bibby/98 3.00 8.00
PG Pau Gasol/101 5.00 12.00
PJ Peja Stojakovic/96 2.50 6.00
PP Paul Pierce/98 5.00 12.00
RA Ray Allen/96 5.00 12.00
RH Richard Hamilton/99 4.00 10.00
RM Reggie Miller/87 6.00 15.00
RW Rasheed Wallace/95 4.00 10.00
SF Steve Francis/99 3.00 8.00
SM2 Shawn Marion/99 3.00 8.00
SN Steve Nash/96 6.00 15.00
SP Scottie Pippen/87 15.00 40.00
TD Tim Duncan/97 8.00 20.00
TP Tony Parker/101 5.00 12.00
TW Tracy McGrady/97 5.00 12.00
VC Vince Carter/98 6.00 15.00

2004-05 SkyBox LE Legends of the Draft Patches Autographs

PRINT RUN 25 SER.#'d SETS
BD Baron Davis 15.00 40.00
CA Carmelo Anthony 30.00 80.00
CM Corey Maggette 12.00 30.00
DW Dwyane Wade 100.00 200.00
EB Elton Brand 12.00 30.00
JK Jason Kidd 30.00 80.00
JS Jerry Stackhouse 20.00 50.00
KM Kenyon Martin 20.00 50.00
RJ Richard Jefferson 12.00 30.00
SM Stephon Marbury 20.00 50.00
TM Tracy McGrady 25.00 60.00
VC Vince Carter 30.00 80.00

2004-05 SkyBox LE Rare Form

COMPLETE SET (10) 60.00 150.00
STATED ODDS 1:576 RETAIL
1 Shaquille O'Neal 15.00 40.00
2 Dwyane Wade 15.00 40.00
3 Carmelo Anthony 8.00 20.00
4 Kenyon Martin 4.00 10.00
5 Allen Iverson 8.00 20.00
6 Vince Carter 8.00 20.00
7 Kevin Garnett 8.00 20.00
8 Tim Duncan 8.00 20.00
9 LeBron James 50.00 120.00
10 Kobe Bryant 30.00 80.00

2004-05 SkyBox LE Rare Form Jerseys

PRINT RUN 50 SER.#'d SETS
AI Allen Iverson 10.00 25.00
AS Amare Stoudemire 4.00 10.00
CA Carmelo Anthony 8.00 20.00
DW Dwyane Wade 15.00 40.00
KG Kevin Garnett 10.00 25.00
KM Kenyon Martin 4.00 10.00
SN Steve Nash 8.00 20.00
SO Shaquille O'Neal 15.00 40.00
TD Tim Duncan 10.00 25.00
VC Vince Carter 8.00 20.00

2004-05 SkyBox LE Rare Form Jerseys Numbers

STATED PRINT RUN 3 TO 32 SETS
AS Amare Stoudemire/32 5.00 12.00
KG Kevin Garnett/21 12.00 30.00
SO Shaquille O'Neal/32 20.00 50.00
VC Vince Carter/15 12.00 30.00

2004-05 SkyBox LE Sky's the Limit Jerseys

PRINT RUN 50 SER.#'d SETS
*JSY 50 SINGLES: .5X TO 1.25X BASE JSY
PATCH PRINT RUN 25 SER.#'d SETS
AI Allen Iverson 8.00 20.00
AI2 Andre Iguodala 5.00 12.00
BD Baron Davis 3.00 8.00
BG Ben Gordon 3.00 8.00
DH Dwight Howard 10.00 25.00
DH Devin Harris 2.50 6.00
DN Dirk Nowitzki 8.00 20.00
DW Dwyane Wade 12.00 30.00
DW2 Dorell Wright 2.50 6.00
EB Elton Brand 2.50 6.00
JK Jason Kidd 5.00 12.00
JN Jameer Nelson 3.00 8.00
JS J.R. Smith 3.00 8.00
KH Kirk Hinrich 3.00 8.00
RJ Richard Jefferson 2.50 6.00
SF Steve Francis 3.00 8.00
SL Shaun Livingston 3.00 8.00
ST Sebastian Telfair 2.50 6.00
TM Tracy McGrady 5.00 12.00
YM Yao Ming 8.00 20.00

1991-92 SkyBox Mark and See Minis

COMPLETE SET (14) 20.00 50.00
530 Charles Barkley 2.50 6.00
531 Larry Bird 4.00 10.00
532 Patrick Ewing 1.50 4.00
533 Magic Johnson 1.50 4.00
534 Michael Jordan 10.00 25.00
535 Karl Malone 3.00 8.00
536 Chris Mullin 1.50 4.00
537 Scottie Pippen 2.50 6.00
538 David Robinson 2.50 6.00
539 John Stockton 3.00 8.00
544 Team USA Card 1 .75 2.00
545 Team USA Card 2 2.50 6.00
546 Team USA Card 3 1.25 3.00
NNO Team Photo 1.50 4.00

1993 SkyBox Milestone Promos

COMPLETE SET (2) 2.50 6.00
1 Magic
(Magic Johnson) 1.50 4.00
2 The Admiral
(David Robinson 1.50 4.00

1998-99 SkyBox Molten Metal

COMPLETE SET (150) 20.00 50.00
CARDS 1-100 INSERTED 4:1 PACKS
CARDS 101-130 INSERTED 1:1 PACKS
CARDS 131-150 INSERTED 1:2 PACKS
1 Maurice Taylor .30 .75
2 Bison Dele .30 .75
3 Anthony Mason .40 1.00
4 John Starks .50 1.25
5 Anthony Johnson .30 .75
6 Calbert Cheaney .30 .75
7 Roshown McLeod RC .30 .75
8 Jalen Rose .40 1.00
9 Kelvin Cato .30 .75
10 Walter McCarty .30 .75
11 Isaac Austin .30 .75
12 Arvydas Sabonis .50 1.25
13 David Wesley .30 .75
14 Jim Jackson .30 .75
15 Elden Campbell .30 .75
16 Michael Doleac RC .40 1.00
17 Chris Webber .60 1.50
18 Mitch Richmond .60 1.50
19 Johnny Newman .30 .75
20 Jayson Williams .30 .75
21 George Lynch .30 .75
22 Ron Harper .50 1.25
23 Donyell Marshall .30 .75
24 Derek Fisher .40 1.00
25 Matt Harpring RC .50 1.25
26 Jason Williams RC 1.50 4.00
27 Toni Kukoc .50 1.25
28 Clarence Weatherspoon .30 .75
29 Eddie Jones .50 1.25
30 Bo Outlaw .30 .75
31 Zydrunas Ilgauskas .50 1.25
32 Michael Dickerson RC .50 1.25
33 Tyronn Lue RC .60 1.50
34 Theo Ratliff .40 1.00
35 Dirk Nowitzki RC 10.00 25.00
36 Robert Traylor RC .50 1.25
37 Gary Trent .30 .75
38 Wesley Person .30 .75
39 Bryce Drew RC .30 .75
40 P.J. Brown .30 .75
41 Joe Smith .40 1.00
42 Avery Johnson .40 1.00
43 Chris Anstey .30 .75
44 Mario Elie .30 .75
45 Voshon Lenard .30 .75
46 Rex Chapman .40 1.00
47 Hersey Hawkins .30 .75
48 Shawn Bradley .30 .75
49 Matt Maloney .30 .75
50 Dan Majerle .50 1.25
51 Pat Garrity RC .40 1.00
52 Sam Perkins .50 1.25
53 Mookie Blaylock .40 1.00
54 Al Harrington RC .60 1.50
55 Clifford Robinson .30 .75
56 Alan Henderson .30 .75
57 Chris Mullin .60 1.50
58 Dennis Scott .30 .75
59 A.C. Green .40 1.00
60 Tyrone Hill .30 .75
61 Chauncey Billups .60 1.50
62 Michael Finley .50 1.25
63 Terrell Brandon .40 1.00
64 Detlef Schrempf .50 1.25
65 Bonzi Wells RC .50 1.25
66 Larry Johnson .75 2.00
67 Bryant Reeves .30 .75
68 Raef LaFrentz RC .60 1.50
69 Kendall Gill .40 1.00
70 Bryon Russell .30 .75
71 Bobby Phills .30 .75
72 Tony Delk .30 .75
73 Lorenzen Wright .30 .75
74 Keon Clark RC .50 1.25
75 Billy Owens .40 1.00
76 Tracy Murray .30 .75
77 Bobby Jackson .40 1.00
78 Sam Cassell .40 1.00
79 Corliss Williamson .30 .75
80 Jeff Hornacek .40 1.00
81 LaPhonso Ellis .30 .75
82 Sam Mitchell .30 .75
83 Sean Elliott .50 1.25
84 John Wallace .30 .75
85 Dikembe Mutombo .75 2.00
86 Rik Smits .40 1.00
87 Isaiah Rider .40 1.00
88 Joe Dumars .50 1.25
89 Allan Houston .50 1.25
90 Sam Mack .30 .75
91 Paul Pierce RC 2.00 5.00
92 Lamond Murray .30 .75
93 Rasheed Wallace .60 1.50
94 Danny Fortson .30 .75
95 Cherokee Parks .30 .75
96 Antonio Daniels .30 .75
97 Shandon Anderson .30 .75
98 Ricky Davis RC .75 2.00
99 Rodney Rogers .30 .75
100 Tariq Abdul-Wahad .30 .75
101 Glenn Robinson .50 1.25
102 Ron Mercer .40 1.00
103 Alonzo Mourning .75 2.00
104 Marcus Camby .40 1.00
105 Steve Smith .40 1.00
106 Tim Hardaway .60 1.50
107 Rod Strickland .40 1.00
108 Reggie Miller 1.00 2.50
109 Juwan Howard .40 1.00
110 Hakeem Olajuwon 1.00 2.50
111 John Stockton 1.00 2.50
112 Antonio McDyess .40 1.00
113 Charles Barkley 1.25 3.00
114 Karl Malone 1.00 2.50
115 Jerry Stackhouse .50 1.25
116 Tracy McGrady .75 2.00
117 Brevin Knight .30 .75
118 Gary Payton .75 2.00
119 Derek Anderson .40 1.00
120 Glen Rice .50 1.25
121 David Robinson 1.00 2.50
122 Vin Baker .40 1.00
123 Tom Gugliotta .40 1.00
124 Patrick Ewing .75 2.00
125 Ray Allen .75 2.00
126 Anfernee Hardaway 1.25 3.00
127 Jason Kidd .75 2.00
128 Kenny Anderson .40 1.00
129 Kerry Kittles .40 1.00
130 Tim Thomas .40 1.00
131 Shareef Abdur-Rahim .50 1.25
132 Mike Bibby RC 1.50 4.00
133 Kobe Bryant 8.00 20.00
134 Vince Carter RC 4.00 10.00
135 Tim Duncan 1.25 3.00
136 Kevin Garnett 1.25 3.00
137 Grant Hill .75 2.00
138 Larry Hughes RC 1.25 3.00
139 Allen Iverson 1.25 3.00
140 Antawn Jamison RC 1.25 3.00
141 Michael Jordan 12.00 30.00
142 Shawn Kemp .75 2.00
143 Stephon Marbury .60 1.50
144 Michael Olowokandi RC 1.00 2.50
145 Shaquille O'Neal 2.00 5.00
146 Scottie Pippen 1.25 3.00
147 Dennis Rodman 1.25 3.00
148 Damon Stoudamire .50 1.25
149 Keith Van Horn .50 1.25
150 Antoine Walker .50 1.25

1998-99 SkyBox Molten Metal Xplosion

COMPLETE SET (150) 175.00 350.00
*1-100 STARS/RCs: 1X TO 2.5X BASE HI
1-100 STATED ODDS 1:2.5
*101-130 STARS: 2.5X TO 6X BASE HI
101-130 STATED ODDS 1:18
*131-150 STARS: 5X TO 12X BASE HI
*131-150 RCs: 1.5X TO 4X BASE HI
131-150 STATED ODDS 1:60
134 Vince Carter 20.00 50.00
141 Michael Jordan 500.00 1,000.00
147 Dennis Rodman 12.00 30.00

1998-99 SkyBox Molten Metal Fusion

1-30 STATED ODDS 1:16
31-50: PRINT RUN 40 SERIAL #'d SETS
36/37/39/41-43: PRINT RUN 250 #'d SETS
1 Glenn Robinson 6.00 15.00
2 Ron Mercer 5.00 12.00
3 Alonzo Mourning 30.00 80.00
4 Marcus Camby 5.00 12.00
5 Steve Smith 5.00 12.00
6 Tim Hardaway 8.00 20.00
7 Rod Strickland 5.00 12.00
8 Reggie Miller 40.00 100.00
9 Juwan Howard 5.00 12.00
10 Hakeem Olajuwon 40.00 100.00
11 John Stockton 40.00 100.00
12 Antonio McDyess 5.00 12.00
13 Charles Barkley 50.00 120.00
14 Karl Malone 40.00 100.00
15 Jerry Stackhouse 6.00 15.00
16 Tracy McGrady 40.00 100.00
17 Brevin Knight 4.00 10.00
18 Gary Payton 30.00 80.00
19 Derek Anderson 5.00 12.00
20 Glen Rice 6.00 15.00
21 David Robinson 40.00 100.00
22 Vin Baker 5.00 12.00
23 Tom Gugliotta 5.00 12.00
24 Patrick Ewing 40.00 100.00
25 Ray Allen 40.00 100.00
26 Anfernee Hardaway 50.00 120.00
27 Jason Kidd 40.00 100.00
28 Kenny Anderson 5.00 12.00
29 Kerry Kittles 5.00 12.00
30 Tim Thomas 5.00 12.00
31 Shareef Abdur-Rahim 125.00 300.00
32 Mike Bibby 125.00 300.00
33 Kobe Bryant 6,000.00 12,000.00
34 Vince Carter 1,500.00 3,000.00
35 Tim Duncan 1,500.00 3,000.00
36 Kevin Garnett 400.00 800.00
37 Grant Hill 300.00 600.00
38 Larry Hughes 125.00 300.00
39 Allen Iverson 400.00 800.00
40 Antawn Jamison 125.00 300.00
41 Michael Jordan 4,000.00 8,000.00
42 Shawn Kemp 200.00 500.00
43 Stephon Marbury 125.00 300.00
44 Michael Olowokandi 125.00 300.00
45 Shaquille O'Neal 1,500.00 3,000.00
46 Scottie Pippen 1,500.00 3,000.00
47 Dennis Rodman 1,500.00 3,000.00
48 Damon Stoudamire 200.00 500.00
49 Keith Van Horn 125.00 300.00
50 Antoine Walker 125.00 300.00

1998-99 SkyBox Molten Metal Fusion Titanium

1-30 STATED ODDS 1:96
31-50: PRINT RUN 250 SERIAL #'d SETS
36/37/39/41-43: PRINT RUN 40 #'d SETS
1 Glenn Robinson 12.00 30.00
2 Ron Mercer 10.00 25.00
3 Alonzo Mourning 150.00 400.00
4 Marcus Camby 40.00 100.00
5 Steve Smith 40.00 100.00
6 Tim Hardaway 40.00 100.00
7 Rod Strickland 40.00 100.00
8 Reggie Miller 200.00 500.00
9 Juwan Howard 60.00 150.00
10 Hakeem Olajuwon 200.00 500.00
11 John Stockton 200.00 500.00
12 Antonio McDyess 10.00 25.00
13 Charles Barkley 150.00 400.00
14 Karl Malone 125.00 300.00
15 Jerry Stackhouse 60.00 150.00
16 Tracy McGrady 125.00 300.00
17 Brevin Knight 8.00 20.00
18 Gary Payton 100.00 250.00
19 Derek Anderson 10.00 25.00
20 Glen Rice 12.00 30.00
21 David Robinson 125.00 300.00
22 Vin Baker 10.00 25.00
23 Tom Gugliotta 10.00 25.00
24 Patrick Ewing 125.00 300.00
25 Ray Allen 125.00 300.00
26 Anfernee Hardaway 200.00 500.00
27 Jason Kidd 125.00 300.00
28 Kenny Anderson 30.00 80.00
29 Kerry Kittles 30.00 80.00
30 Tim Thomas 30.00 80.00
31 Shareef Abdur-Rahim 40.00 100.00
32 Mike Bibby 40.00 100.00
33 Kobe Bryant 3,000.00 6,000.00
34 Vince Carter 500.00 1,000.00
35 Tim Duncan 400.00 800.00
36 Kevin Garnett 1,500.00 3,000.00
37 Grant Hill 1,000.00 2,000.00
38 Larry Hughes 40.00 100.00
39 Allen Iverson 1,500.00 3,000.00
40 Antawn Jamison 40.00 100.00
41 Michael Jordan 10,000.00 20,000.00
42 Shawn Kemp 600.00 1,200.00
43 Stephon Marbury 500.00 1,000.00
44 Michael Olowokandi 40.00 100.00
45 Shaquille O'Neal 400.00 800.00
46 Scottie Pippen 400.00 800.00
47 Dennis Rodman 400.00 800.00
48 Damon Stoudamire 60.00 150.00
49 Keith Van Horn 40.00 100.00
50 Antoine Walker 40.00 100.00

1992-93 SkyBox Nestle

COMPLETE SET (50) 60.00 150.00
1 Michael Adams .75 2.00
2 Rolando Blackman 1.00 2.50
3 Manute Bol 1.25 3.00
4 Dee Brown .75 2.00
5 Tony Campbell .75 2.00
6 Derrick Coleman 1.25 3.00
7 Brad Daugherty .75 2.00
8 Clyde Drexler 4.00 10.00
9 Joe Dumars 2.00 5.00
10 Sean Elliott 2.00 5.00
11 Pervis Ellison .75 2.00
12 Kendall Gill 1.25 3.00
13 Tim Hardaway 2.00 5.00
14 Derek Harper 1.25 3.00
15 Hersey Hawkins 1.25 3.00
16 Chris Jackson 1.00 2.50
17 Mark Jackson 1.50 4.00
18 Kevin Johnson 1.50 4.00
19 Shawn Kemp 3.00 8.00
20 Reggie Lewis 1.25 3.00
21 Dan Majerle 1.50 4.00
22 Karl Malone 4.00 10.00
23 Danny Manning 1.25 3.00
24 Reggie Miller 4.00 10.00
25 Chris Mullin 2.50 6.00
26 Dikembe Mutombo 1.50 4.00
27 Charles Oakley 1.25 3.00
28 John Paxson 1.25 3.00
29 Sam Perkins 1.25 3.00
30 Drazen Petrovic 3.00 8.00
31 Ricky Pierce .75 2.00
32 Scottie Pippen 8.00 20.00
33 Terry Porter .75 2.00
34 Mark Price 1.25 3.00
35 J.R. Reid .75 2.00
36 Glen Rice 2.50 6.00
37 Alvin Robertson .75 2.00
38 David Robinson 4.00 10.00
39 Dennis Rodman 4.00 10.00
40 Detlef Schrempf 1.25 3.00
41 Dennis Scott 1.25 3.00
42 Rony Seikaly .75 2.00
43 Scott Skiles 1.25 3.00
44 Charles Smith .75 2.00
45 Kenny Smith .75 2.00
46 John Stockton 8.00 20.00
47 Otis Thorpe 1.25 3.00
48 Wayman Tisdale .75 2.00
49 Dominique Wilkins 3.00 8.00
50 James Worthy 2.50 6.00

1993-94 SkyBox Premium Promos

COMPLETE SET (6) 10.00 25.00
1 Michael Jordan 8.00 20.00
2 Christian Laettner .50 1.25
3 Dan Majerle .50 1.25
4 Alonzo Mourning
Patrick Ewing .75 2.00
5 Shaquille O'Neal 2.50 6.00
6 David Robinson 1.00 2.50

1993-94 SkyBox Premium

COMPLETE SET (341) 20.00 50.00
COMPLETE SERIES 1 (191) 10.00 25.00
COMPLETE SERIES 2 (150) 10.00 25.00
DP4/DP17: SER.1 STATED ODDS 1:36
HOC EXCH: SER.1 STATED ODDS 1:360
1 Checklist .20 .50
2 Checklist .20 .50
3 Checklist .20 .50
4 Larry Johnson PO .50 1.25
5 Alonzo Mourning PO .60 1.50
6 Hakeem Olajuwon PO .75 2.00
7 Brad Daugherty PO .30 .75
8 Oliver Miller PO .25 .60
9 David Robinson PO .75 2.00
10 Patrick Ewing PO .60 1.50
11 Ricky Pierce PO .30 .75
12 Sam Perkins PO .30 .75
13 John Starks PO .40 1.00
14 Michael Jordan PO 4.00 10.00
15 Dan Majerle PO .40 1.00
16 Scottie Pippen PO 1.00 2.50
17 Shawn Kemp PO .60 1.50
18 Charles Barkley PO 1.00 2.50
19 Horace Grant PO .40 1.00
20 K.Johnson/M.Jordan PO 4.00 10.00
21 John Paxson PO .40 1.00
22 David Robinson IS .75 2.00
23 NBA On NBC .20 .50
24 Stacey Augmon .30 .75
25 Mookie Blaylock .40 1.00
26 Craig Ehlo .25 .60
27 Adam Keefe .25 .60
28 Dominique Wilkins .60 1.50
29 Kevin Willis .30 .75
30 Dee Brown .30 .75
31 Sherman Douglas .25 .60
32 Rick Fox .30 .75
33 Kevin Gamble .25 .60
34 Xavier McDaniel .40 1.00
35 Robert Parish .50 1.25
36 Muggsy Bogues .40 1.00
37 Dell Curry .40 1.00
38 Kendall Gill .30 .75
39 Larry Johnson .50 1.25
40 Alonzo Mourning .60 1.50
41 Johnny Newman .25 .60
42 B.J. Armstrong .40 1.00
43 Bill Cartwright .30 .75
44 Horace Grant .40 1.00
45 Michael Jordan 4.00 10.00
46 John Paxson .40 1.00
47 Scottie Pippen 1.00 2.50
48 Scott Williams .25 .60
49 Terrell Brandon .30 .75
50 Brad Daugherty .30 .75
51 Larry Nance .30 .75
52 Mark Price .40 1.00
53 Gerald Wilkins .30 .75
54 John Williams .25 .60
55 Terry Davis .25 .60
56 Derek Harper .30 .75
57 Jim Jackson .30 .75
58 Sean Rooks .25 .60
59 Doug Smith .25 .60
60 Mahmoud Abdul-Rauf .30 .75
61 LaPhonso Ellis .30 .75
62 Mark Macon .25 .60
63 Dikembe Mutombo .60 1.50
64 Bryant Stith .25 .60
65 Reggie Williams .25 .60
66 Joe Dumars .50 1.25
67 Bill Laimbeer .40 1.00
68 Terry Mills .25 .60
69 Alvin Robertson .30 .75
70 Dennis Rodman 1.00 2.50
71 Isiah Thomas .60 1.50
72 Victor Alexander .25 .60
73 Tim Hardaway .50 1.25
74 Tyrone Hill .25 .60
75 Sarunas Marciulionis .40 1.00
76 Chris Mullin .50 1.25
77 Billy Owens .30 .75
78 Latrell Sprewell .60 1.50
79 Robert Horry .40 1.00
80 Vernon Maxwell .30 .75
81 Hakeem Olajuwon .75 2.00
82 Kenny Smith .30 .75
83 Otis Thorpe .40 1.00
84 Dale Davis .30 .75
85 Reggie Miller .75 2.00
86 Pooh Richardson .30 .75
87 Detlef Schrempf .40 1.00
88 Malik Sealy .25 .60
89 Rik Smits .30 .75
90 Ron Harper .40 1.00
91 Mark Jackson .30 .75
92 Danny Manning .30 .75
93 Stanley Roberts .25 .60
94 Loy Vaught .25 .60
95 Randy Woods .25 .60
96 Sam Bowie .30 .75
97 Doug Christie .30 .75
98 Vlade Divac .40 1.00
99 Anthony Peeler .25 .60
100 Sedale Threatt .25 .60
101 James Worthy .50 1.25
102 Grant Long .25 .60
103 Harold Miner .30 .75
104 Glen Rice .40 1.00
105 John Salley .30 .75
106 Rony Seikaly .30 .75
107 Steve Smith .30 .75
108 Anthony Avent .25 .60
109 Jon Barry .25 .60
110 Frank Brickowski .25 .60
111 Blue Edwards .25 .60
112 Todd Day .25 .60
113 Lee Mayberry .25 .60
114 Eric Murdock .25 .60
115 Thurl Bailey .25 .60
116 Christian Laettner .40 1.00
117 Chuck Person .30 .75
118 Doug West .25 .60
119 Micheal Williams .25 .60
120 Kenny Anderson .30 .75
121 Benoit Benjamin .25 .60
122 Derrick Coleman .40 1.00
123 Chris Morris .25 .60
124 Rumeal Robinson .25 .60
125 Rolando Blackman .30 .75
126 Patrick Ewing .60 1.50
127 Anthony Mason .30 .75
128 Charles Oakley .40 1.00
129 Doc Rivers .30 .75
130 Charles Smith .25 .60
131 John Starks .40 1.00
132 Nick Anderson .30 .75
133 Shaquille O'Neal 2.00 5.00
134 Donald Royal .25 .60
135 Dennis Scott .25 .60
136 Scott Skiles .25 .60
137 Brian Williams .25 .60
138 Johnny Dawkins .30 .75
139 Hersey Hawkins .30 .75
140 Jeff Hornacek .30 .75
141 Andrew Lang .25 .60
142 Tim Perry .25 .60
143 Clarence Weatherspoon .25 .60
144 Danny Ainge .40 1.00
145 Charles Barkley 1.00 2.50
146 Cedric Ceballos .30 .75
147 Kevin Johnson .40 1.00
148 Oliver Miller .25 .60
149 Dan Majerle .40 1.00
150 Clyde Drexler .60 1.50
151 Harvey Grant .30 .75
152 Jerome Kersey .30 .75
153 Terry Porter .30 .75
154 Clifford Robinson .40 1.00
155 Rod Strickland .30 .75
156 Buck Williams .30 .75
157 Mitch Richmond .50 1.25
158 Lionel Simmons .25 .60
159 Wayman Tisdale .30 .75
160 Spud Webb .30 .75
161 Walt Williams .40 1.00
162 Antoine Carr .25 .60
163 Lloyd Daniels .25 .60
164 Sean Elliott .40 1.00
165 Dale Ellis .25 .60
166 Avery Johnson .30 .75
167 J.R. Reid .30 .75
168 David Robinson .75 2.00
169 Shawn Kemp .60 1.50
170 Derrick McKey .30 .75
171 Nate McMillan .30 .75
172 Gary Payton .50 1.25
173 Sam Perkins .30 .75
174 Ricky Pierce .30 .75
175 Tyrone Corbin .25 .60
176 Jay Humphries .30 .75
177 Jeff Malone .30 .75
178 Karl Malone .75 2.00
179 John Stockton .75 2.00
180 Michael Adams .30 .75
181 Kevin Duckworth .30 .75
182 Pervis Ellison .25 .60
183 Tom Gugliotta .30 .75
184 Don MacLean .25 .60
185 Brent Price .25 .60
186 George Lynch RC .40 1.00
187 Rex Walters RC .30 .75
188 Shawn Bradley RC .40 1.00
189 Ervin Johnson RC .40 1.00
190 Luther Wright RC .25 .60
191 Calbert Cheaney RC .40 1.00
192 Craig Ehlo .25 .60
193 Duane Ferrell .25 .60
194 Paul Graham .25 .60
195 Andrew Lang .25 .60
196 Chris Corchiani .25 .60
197 Acie Earl RC .40 1.00
198 Dino Radja RC .40 1.00
199 Ed Pinckney .25 .60
200 Tony Bennett .25 .60
201 Scott Burrell RC .40 1.00
202 Kenny Gattison .25 .60
203 Hersey Hawkins .30 .75
204 Eddie Johnson .25 .60
205 Corie Blount RC .40 1.00
206 Steve Kerr .30 .75
207 Toni Kukoc RC 1.00 2.50
208 Pete Myers .25 .60
209 Danny Ferry .25 .60
210 Tyrone Hill .25 .60
211 Gerald Madkins RC .40 1.00
212 Chris Mills RC .40 1.00
213 Lucious Harris RC .40 1.00
214 Popeye Jones RC .40 1.00
215 Jamal Mashburn RC .75 2.00
216 Darnell Mee RC .25 .60
217 Rodney Rogers RC .40 1.00
218 Brian Williams .25 .60
219 Greg Anderson .25 .60
220 Sean Elliott .40 1.00
221 Allan Houston RC .75 2.00
222 Lindsey Hunter RC .40 1.00
223 Chris Gatling .25 .60
224 Josh Grant RC .30 .75
225 Keith Jennings .25 .60
226 Avery Johnson .30 .75
227 Chris Webber RC 2.00 5.00
228 Sam Cassell RC .75 2.00
229 Mario Elie .25 .60
230 Richard Petruska RC .40 1.00
231 Eric Riley RC .40 1.00
232 Antonio Davis RC .50 1.25
233 Scott Haskin RC .25 .60
234 Derrick McKey .30 .75
235 Mark Aguirre .30 .75
236 Terry Dehere RC .40 1.00
237 Gary Grant .25 .60
238 Randy Woods .25 .60
239 Sam Bowie .30 .75

240 Elden Campbell .25 .60
241 Nick Van Exel RC 1.00 2.50
242 Manute Bol .25 .60
243 Brian Shaw .25 .60
244 Vin Baker RC .60 1.50
245 Brad Lohaus .25 .60
246 Ken Norman .25 .60
247 Derek Strong RC .30 .75
248 Danny Schayes .25 .60
249 Mike Brown .25 .60
250 Luc Longley .30 .75
251 Isaiah Rider RC .60 1.50
252 Kevin Edwards .25 .60
253 Armon Gilliam .25 .60
254 Greg Anthony .25 .60
255 Anthony Bonner .25 .60
256 Tony Campbell .25 .60
257 Hubert Davis .30 .75
258 Litterial Green .25 .60
259 Anfernee Hardaway RC 2.00 5.00
260 Larry Krystkowiak .25 .60
261 Todd Lichti .25 .60
262 Dana Barros .25 .60
263 Greg Graham RC .25 .60
264 Warren Kidd RC .25 .60
265 Moses Malone .60 1.50
266 A.C. Green .30 .75
267 Joe Kleine .25 .60
268 Malcolm Mackey RC .25 .60
269 Mark Bryant .25 .60
270 Chris Dudley .25 .60
271 Harvey Grant .30 .75
272 James Robinson RC .40 1.00
273 Duane Causwell .25 .60
274 Bobby Hurley RC .40 1.00
275 Jim Les .25 .60
276 Willie Anderson .25 .60
277 Terry Cummings .30 .75
278 Vinny Del Negro .25 .60
279 Sleepy Floyd .30 .75
280 Dennis Rodman 1.00 2.50
281 Vincent Askew .25 .60
282 Kendall Gill .30 .75
283 Steve Scheffler .25 .60
284 Detlef Schrempf .40 1.00
285 David Benoit .25 .60
286 Tom Chambers .40 1.00
287 Felton Spencer .25 .60
288 Rex Chapman .25 .60
289 Kevin Duckworth .30 .75
290 Gheorghe Muresan RC .40 1.00
291 Kenny Walker .25 .60
292 A.Lang/C.Ehlo CF .25 .60
293 D.Radja/A.Earl CF .40 1.00
294 E.Johnson/H.Hawkins CF .30 .75
295 T.Kukoc/C.Blount CF 1.00 2.50
296 T.Hill/C.Mills CF .40 1.00
297 J.Mashburn/P.Jones CF .75 2.00
298 D.Mee/R.Rogers CF .40 1.00
299 L.Hunter/A.Houston CF .75 2.00
300 C.Webber/A.Johnson CF 2.00 5.00
301 S.Cassell/M.Elie CF .75 2.00
302 D.McKey/A.Davis CF .50 1.25
303 T.Dehere/M.Aguirre CF .40 1.00
304 N.Van Exel/G.Lynch CF 1.00 2.50
305 H.Miner/S.Smith CF .30 .75
306 K.Norman/V.Baker CF .60 1.50
307 M.Brown/I.Rider CF .60 1.50
308 K.Edwards/R.Walters CF .30 .75
309 H.Davis/A.Bonner CF .30 .75
310 A.Hardaway/Kryst CF 2.00 5.00
311 M.Malone/S.Bradley CF .60 1.50
312 J.Kleine/A.C. Green CF .30 .75
313 H.Grant/C.Dudley CF .30 .75
314 B.Hurley/M.Richmond CF .50 1.25
315 S.Floyd/D.Rodman CF 1.00 2.50
316 K.Gill/D.Schrempf CF .40 1.00
317 F.Spencer/L.Wright CF .25 .60
318 C.Cheaney/Duckworth CF .40 1.00
319 Karl Malone PC .75 2.00
320 Alonzo Mourning PC .60 1.50
321 Scottie Pippen PC 1.00 2.50
322 Mark Price PC .40 1.00
323 LaPhonso Ellis PC .30 .75
324 Joe Dumars PC .50 1.25
325 Chris Mullin PC .50 1.25
326 Ron Harper PC .40 1.00
327 Glen Rice PC .40 1.00
328 Christian Laettner PC .40 1.00
329 Kenny Anderson PC .30 .75
330 John Starks PC .40 1.00
331 Shaquille O'Neal PC 2.00 5.00
332 Charles Barkley PC 1.00 2.50
333 Clifford Robinson PC .40 1.00
334 Clyde Drexler PC .60 1.50
335 Mitch Richmond PC .50 1.25
336 David Robinson PC .75 2.00
337 Shawn Kemp PC .60 1.50
338 John Stockton PC .75 2.00
339 Checklist 4 .20 .50
340 Checklist 5 .20 .50
341 Checklist 6 .20 .50
DP4 Jim Jackson 1992 .40 1.00
DP17 Doug Christie 1992 .30 .75
NNO Expired HOC Exchange .60 1.50
NNO Head of Class Card 12.00 30.00

1993-94 SkyBox Premium All-Rookies

COMPLETE SET (5) 4.00 10.00
SER.1 STATED ODDS 1:36
AR1 Shaquille O'Neal 3.00 8.00
AR2 Alonzo Mourning 1.00 2.50
AR3 Christian Laettner .60 1.50
AR4 Tom Gugliotta .50 1.25
AR5 LaPhonso Ellis .50 1.25

1993-94 SkyBox Premium Center Stage

COMPLETE SET (9) 12.00 30.00
SER.1 STATED ODDS 1:12
CS1 Michael Jordan 10.00 25.00
CS2 Shaquille O'Neal 3.00 8.00
CS3 Charles Barkley 1.50 4.00
CS4 John Starks .60 1.50
CS5 Larry Johnson .75 2.00
CS6 Hakeem Olajuwon 1.25 3.00
CS7 Kenny Anderson .50 1.25
CS8 Mahmoud Abdul-Rauf .50 1.25
CS9 Clifford Robinson .60 1.50

1993-94 SkyBox Premium Draft Picks

COMPLETE SET (26) 12.00 30.00
COMPLETE SERIES 1 (9) 3.00 8.00
COMPLETE SERIES 2 (17) 10.00 25.00
SER.1/2 STATED ODDS 1:12
DP1 Chris Webber 2.50 6.00
DP2 Shawn Bradley .50 1.25
DP3 Anfernee Hardaway 2.50 6.00
DP4 Jamal Mashburn 1.00 2.50
DP5 Isaiah Rider .75 2.00
DP6 Calbert Cheaney .50 1.25
DP7 Bobby Hurley .50 1.25
DP8 Vin Baker .75 2.00
DP9 Rodney Rogers .50 1.25
DP10 Lindsey Hunter .50 1.25
DP11 Allan Houston 1.00 2.50
DP12 George Lynch .50 1.25
DP13 Terry Dehere .50 1.25
DP14 Scott Haskin .30 .75
DP15 Doug Edwards .50 1.25
DP16 Rex Walters .40 1.00
DP17 Greg Graham .30 .75
DP18 Luther Wright .30 .75
DP19 Acie Earl .50 1.25
DP20 Scott Burrell .50 1.25
DP21 James Robinson .50 1.25
DP22 Chris Mills .50 1.25
DP23 Ervin Johnson .50 1.25
DP24 Sam Cassell 1.00 2.50
DP25 Corie Blount .50 1.25
DP27 Malcolm Mackey .30 .75

1993-94 SkyBox Premium Dynamic Dunks

COMPLETE SET (9) 8.00 20.00
SER.2 STATED ODDS 1:36
D1 Nick Anderson .50 1.25
D2 Charles Barkley 1.50 4.00
D3 Robert Horry .60 1.50
D4 Michael Jordan 8.00 20.00
D5 Shawn Kemp 1.00 2.50
D6 Anthony Mason .50 1.25
D7 Alonzo Mourning 1.00 2.50
D8 Hakeem Olajuwon 1.25 3.00
D9 Dominique Wilkins 1.00 2.50

1993-94 SkyBox Premium Shaq Talk

COMPLETE SET (10) 12.50 30.00
COMPLETE SERIES 1 (5) 6.00 15.00
COMPLETE SERIES 2 (5) 6.00 15.00
COMMON SHAQ (1-10) 2.00 5.00
SER.1/2 STATED ODDS 1:36

1993-94 SkyBox Premium Showdown Series

COMPLETE SET (12) 6.00 15.00
COMPLETE SERIES 1 (6) 2.00 5.00
COMPLETE SERIES 2 (6) 4.00 10.00
SER.1/2 STATED ODDS 1:6
SS1 A.Mourning/P.Ewing .60 1.50
SS2 S.O'Neal/P.Ewing 2.00 5.00
SS3 A.Mourning/S.O'Neal 2.00 5.00
SS4 H.Olajuwon/D.Mutombo .75 2.00
SS5 D.Robinson/H.Olajuwon .75 2.00
SS6 D.Robinson/D.Mutombo .75 2.00
SS7 S.Kemp/K.Malone .75 2.00
SS8 L.Johnson/C.Barkley 1.00 2.50
SS9 D.Wilkins/S.Pippen 1.00 2.50
SS10 R.Miller/J.Dumars .75 2.00
SS11 C.Drexler/M.Jordan 4.00 10.00
SS12 M.Johnson/L.Bird 1.50 4.00

1993-94 SkyBox Premium Thunder and Lightning

COMPLETE SET (9) 5.00 12.00
SER.2 STATED ODDS 1:12
TL1 J.Mashburn/J.Jackson .75 2.00
TL2 H.Miner/S.Smith .30 .75
TL3 I.Rider/M.Williams .60 1.50
TL4 D.Coleman/K.Anderson .40 1.00
TL5 P.Ewing/J.Starks .60 1.50
TL6 S.O'Neal/A.Hardaway 2.00 5.00
TL7 S.Bradley/J.Hornacek .40 1.00
TL8 W.Williams/B.Hurley .40 1.00
TL9 D.Rodman/D.Robinson 1.00 2.50

1993-94 SkyBox Premium USA Tip-Off

COMPLETE SET (14) 12.00 30.00
EXCH.CARD: SER.2 STATED ODDS 1:240
1 S.Smith/M.Johnson 1.50 4.00
2 L.Johnson/C.Barkley 1.50 4.00
3 P.Ewing/A.Mourning 1.00 2.50
4 S.Kemp/K.Malone 1.25 3.00
5 C.Mullin/D.Majerle .75 2.00
6 J.Stockton/M.Price 1.25 3.00
7 C.Laettner/D.Coleman .60 1.50
8 D.Wilkins/C.Drexler 1.00 2.50
9 J.Dumars/S.Pippen 1.50 4.00
10 D.Robinson/S.O'Neal 3.00 8.00
11 R.Miller/L.Bird 2.50 6.00
12 Tim Hardaway .75 2.00
13 Isiah Thomas 1.00 2.50
NNO Expired USA Exchange .60 1.50

1993-94 SkyBox Premium USA Tip-Off Gold

*GOLD: 1.25X TO 3X BASIC

1994-95 SkyBox Premium Promo Sheet

COMPLETE SET (6) .75 2.00
255 Glenn Robinson .40 1.00
295 Scott Skiles .08 .25
R3 Jamal Mashburn .15 .40
DP12 Khalid Reeves .08 .25
SF14 Danny Manning .15 .40
SU21 Isaiah Rider .15 .40

1994-95 SkyBox Premium

COMPLETE SET (350) 15.00 30.00
COMPLETE SERIES 1 (200) 7.50 15.00
COMPLETE SERIES 2 (150) 7.50 15.00
EMOTION SHEETS A/B/C EXP: 3/1/95
THIRD PRIZE GAME CARD EXP: 6/30/95
OLAJ.GLD: SER.1 STATED ODDS 1:360 RET
DUAL AU: SER.2 STATED ODDS 1:15,000
GHO: SER.2 STATED ODDS 1:360 RETAIL
1 Stacey Augmon .12 .30
2 Mookie Blaylock .15 .40
3 Doug Edwards .10 .25
4 Craig Ehlo .10 .25
5 Adam Keefe .10 .25
6 Danny Manning .12 .30
7 Kevin Willis .12 .30
8 Dee Brown .12 .30
9 Sherman Douglas .10 .25
10 Acie Earl .10 .25
11 Kevin Gamble .10 .25
12 Xavier McDaniel .10 .25
13 Dino Radja .10 .25
14 Muggsy Bogues .12 .30
15 Scott Burrell .10 .25
16 Dell Curry .10 .25
17 LeRon Ellis .10 .25
18 Hersey Hawkins .10 .25
19 Larry Johnson .20 .50
20 Alonzo Mourning .25 .60
21 B.J. Armstrong .15 .40
22 Corie Blount .10 .25
23 Horace Grant .15 .40
24 Toni Kukoc .20 .50
25 Luc Longley .12 .30
26 Scottie Pippen .40 1.00
27 Scott Williams .10 .25
28 Terrell Brandon .10 .25
29 Brad Daugherty .12 .30
30 Tyrone Hill .10 .25
31 Chris Mills .12 .30
32 Bobby Phills .10 .25
33 Mark Price .15 .40
34 Gerald Wilkins .12 .30
35 Lucious Harris .10 .25
36 Jim Jackson .12 .30
37 Popeye Jones .10 .25
38 Jamal Mashburn .15 .40
39 Sean Rooks .10 .25
40 Mahmoud Abdul-Rauf .10 .25
41 LaPhonso Ellis .10 .25
42 Dikembe Mutombo .25 .60
43 Robert Pack .12 .30
44 Rodney Rogers .10 .25
45 Bryant Stith .10 .25
46 Reggie Williams .10 .25
47 Joe Dumars .15 .40
48 Sean Elliott .12 .30
49 Allan Houston .15 .40
50 Lindsey Hunter .10 .25
51 Terry Mills .10 .25
52 Victor Alexander .10 .25
53 Tim Hardaway .20 .50
54 Chris Mullin .20 .50
55 Billy Owens .10 .25
56 Latrell Sprewell .20 .50
57 Chris Webber .30 .75
58 Sam Cassell .15 .40
59 Carl Herrera .10 .25
60 Robert Horry .15 .40
61 Vernon Maxwell .10 .25
62 Hakeem Olajuwon .30 .75
63 Kenny Smith .12 .30
64 Otis Thorpe .10 .25
65 Antonio Davis .12 .30
66 Dale Davis .10 .25
67 Derrick McKey .10 .25
68 Reggie Miller .30 .75
69 Pooh Richardson .10 .25
70 Rik Smits .12 .30
71 Haywoode Workman .10 .25
72 Terry Dehere .10 .25
73 Harold Ellis .10 .25
74 Ron Harper .12 .30
75 Mark Jackson .12 .30
76 Loy Vaught .10 .25
77 Dominique Wilkins .25 .60
78 Elden Campbell .10 .25
79 Doug Christie .12 .30
80 Vlade Divac .15 .40
81 George Lynch .10 .25
82 Anthony Peeler .10 .25
83 Sedale Threatt .10 .25
84 Nick Van Exel .15 .40
85 Harold Miner .10 .25
86 Glen Rice .15 .40
87 John Salley .10 .25
88 Rony Seikaly .10 .25
89 Brian Shaw .10 .25
90 Steve Smith .12 .30
91 Vin Baker .15 .40
92 Jon Barry .10 .25
93 Todd Day .10 .25
94 Blue Edwards .10 .25
95 Lee Mayberry .10 .25
96 Eric Murdock .10 .25
97 Mike Brown .10 .25
98 Stacey King .10 .25
99 Christian Laettner .12 .30
100 Isaiah Rider .15 .40
101 Doug West .10 .25
102 Micheal Williams .10 .25
103 Kenny Anderson .12 .30
104 P.J. Brown .10 .25
105 Derrick Coleman .15 .40
106 Kevin Edwards .10 .25
107 Chris Morris .10 .25
108 Rex Walters .10 .25
109 Hubert Davis .10 .25
110 Patrick Ewing .25 .60
111 Derek Harper .12 .30
112 Anthony Mason .12 .30
113 Charles Oakley .15 .40
114 Charles Smith .10 .25
115 John Starks .15 .40
116 Nick Anderson .15 .40
117 Anfernee Hardaway .30 .75
118 Shaquille O'Neal .60 1.50
119 Donald Royal .10 .25
120 Dennis Scott .12 .30
121 Scott Skiles .10 .25
122 Dana Barros .10 .25
123 Shawn Bradley .10 .25
124 Johnny Dawkins .10 .25
125 Greg Graham .10 .25
126 Clarence Weatherspoon .10 .25
127 Danny Ainge .15 .40
128 Charles Barkley .40 1.00
129 Cedric Ceballos .12 .30
130 A.C. Green .12 .30
131 Kevin Johnson .15 .40
132 Dan Majerle .15 .40
133 Oliver Miller .10 .25
134 Clyde Drexler .25 .60
135 Harvey Grant .10 .25
136 Tracy Murray .10 .25
137 Terry Porter .10 .25
138 Clifford Robinson .12 .30
139 James Robinson .10 .25
140 Rod Strickland .10 .25
141 Bobby Hurley .10 .25
142 Olden Polynice .10 .25
143 Mitch Richmond .20 .50
144 Lionel Simmons .10 .25
145 Wayman Tisdale .10 .25
146 Spud Webb .12 .30
147 Walt Williams .10 .25
148 Willie Anderson .10 .25
149 Vinny Del Negro .10 .25
150 Dale Ellis .10 .25
151 J.R. Reid .10 .25
152 David Robinson .30 .75
153 Dennis Rodman .40 1.00
154 Kendall Gill .10 .25
155 Shawn Kemp .25 .60
156 Nate McMillan .12 .30
157 Gary Payton .25 .60
158 Sam Perkins .10 .25
159 Ricky Pierce .10 .25
160 Detlef Schrempf .15 .40
161 David Benoit .10 .25
162 Tyrone Corbin .10 .25
163 Jeff Hornacek .12 .30
164 Jay Humphries .10 .25
165 Karl Malone .30 .75
166 Bryon Russell .10 .25
167 Felton Spencer .10 .25
168 John Stockton .30 .75
169 Michael Adams .10 .25
170 Rex Chapman .10 .25
171 Calbert Cheaney .12 .30
172 Pervis Ellison .10 .25
173 Tom Gugliotta .10 .25
174 Don MacLean .10 .25
175 Gheorghe Muresan .10 .25
176 Charles Barkley NBC .40 1.00
177 Charles Oakley NBC .15 .40
178 Hakeem Olajuwon NBC .30 .75
179 Dikembe Mutombo NBC .25 .60
180 Scottie Pippen NBC .40 1.00
181 Sam Cassell NBC .15 .40
182 Karl Malone NBC .30 .75
183 Reggie Miller PO .30 .75
184 Patrick Ewing NBC .25 .60
185 Vernon Maxwell NBC .10 .25
186 A.Hardaway/S.Smith DD .30 .75
187 S.O'Neal/C.Webber DD .60 1.50
188 R.Rogers/J.Mashburn DD .15 .40
189 T.Kukoc/D.Radja DD .20 .50
190 L.Hunter/K.Anderson DD .12 .30
191 L.Sprewell/J.Jackson DD .20 .50
192 C.Weatherspoon/V.Baker DD .15 .40
193 C.Cheaney/C.Mills DD .12 .30
194 I.Rider/R.Horry DD .15 .40
195 S.Cassell/Van Exel DD .15 .40
196 G.Muresan/S.Bradley DD .10 .25
197 L.Ellis/T.Gugliotta DD .10 .25
198 USA Basketball Card .10 .25
199 Checklist .10 .25
200 Checklist .10 .25
201 Sergei Bazarevich RC .15 .40
202 Tyrone Corbin .10 .25
203 Grant Long .10 .25
204 Ken Norman .10 .25
205 Steve Smith .12 .30
206 Blue Edwards .10 .25
207 Greg Minor RC .15 .40
208 Eric Montross RC .12 .30
209 Dominique Wilkins .25 .60
210 Michael Adams .10 .25
211 Kenny Gattison .10 .25
212 Darrin Hancock .12 .30
213 Robert Parish .15 .40
214 Ron Harper .12 .30
215 Steve Kerr .12 .30
216 Will Perdue .10 .25
217 Dickey Simpkins RC .12 .30
218 John Battle .10 .25
219 Michael Cage .10 .25
220 Tony Dumas RC .12 .30
221 Jason Kidd RC .75 2.00
222 Roy Tarpley .10 .25
223 Dale Ellis .10 .25
224 Jalen Rose RC .40 1.00
225 Bill Curley RC .10 .25
226 Grant Hill RC .75 2.00
227 Oliver Miller .10 .25
228 Mark West .10 .25
229 Tom Gugliotta .10 .25
230 Ricky Pierce .10 .25
231 Carlos Rogers RC .12 .30
232 Clifford Rozier RC .10 .25
233 Rony Seikaly .10 .25
234 Tim Breaux .10 .25
235 Duane Ferrell .10 .25
236 Mark Jackson .12 .30
237 Byron Scott .12 .30
238 John Williams .10 .25
239 Lamond Murray RC .15 .40
240 Eric Piatkowski RC .15 .40
241 Pooh Richardson .10 .25
242 Malik Sealy .10 .25
243 Cedric Ceballos .12 .30
244 Eddie Jones RC .50 1.25
245 Anthony Miller RC .15 .40
246 Tony Smith .10 .25
247 Kevin Gamble .10 .25
248 Brad Lohaus .10 .25
249 Billy Owens .10 .25
250 Khalid Reeves RC .12 .30
251 Kevin Willis .12 .30
252 Eric Mobley RC .10 .25
253 Johnny Newman .10 .25
254 Ed Pinckney .10 .25
255 Glenn Robinson RC .30 .75
256 Howard Eisley .15 .40
257 Donyell Marshall RC .15 .40
258 Yinka Dare RC .10 .25
259 Sean Higgins .10 .25
260 Jayson Williams .10 .25
261 Charlie Ward RC .15 .40
262 Monty Williams RC .20 .50
263 Horace Grant .15 .40
264 Brian Shaw .10 .25
265 Brooks Thompson RC .12 .30
266 Derrick Alston RC .10 .25
267 B.J. Tyler RC .10 .25
268 Scott Williams .10 .25
269 Sharone Wright RC .12 .30
270 Antonio Lang RC .15 .40
271 Danny Manning .12 .30
272 Wesley Person RC .15 .40
273 Trevor Ruffin RC .10 .25
274 Wayman Tisdale .10 .25
275 Jerome Kersey .10 .25
276 Aaron McKie RC .15 .40
277 Frank Brickowski .10 .25
278 Brian Grant RC .25 .60
279 Michael Smith RC .10 .25
280 Terry Cummings .12 .30
281 Sean Elliott .12 .30
282 Avery Johnson .12 .30
283 Moses Malone .15 .40
284 Chuck Person .12 .30
285 Vincent Askew .10 .25
286 Bill Cartwright .12 .30
287 Sarunas Marciulionis .10 .25
288 Dontonio Wingfield RC .15 .40
289 Jay Humphries .10 .25
290 Adam Keefe .10 .25
291 Jamie Watson RC .10 .25
292 Kevin Duckworth .10 .25
293 Juwan Howard RC .25 .60
294 Jim McIlvaine RC .12 .30
295 Scott Skiles .12 .30
296 Anthony Tucker RC .10 .25
297 Chris Webber .30 .75
298 Checklist 201-265 .10 .25
299 Checklist 266-345 .10 .25
300 Checklist 346-350/Inserts .10 .25
301 Vin Baker SSL .15 .40
302 Charles Barkley SSL .40 1.00
303 Derrick Coleman SSL .15 .40
304 Clyde Drexler SSL .25 .60
305 LaPhonso Ellis SSL .10 .25
306 Larry Johnson SSL .20 .50
307 Shawn Kemp SSL .25 .60
308 Karl Malone SSL .30 .75
309 Jamal Mashburn SSL .15 .40
310 Scottie Pippen SSL .40 1.00
311 Dominique Wilkins SSL .25 .60
312 Walt Williams SSL .10 .25
313 Sharone Wright SSL .07 .20
314 B.J. Armstrong SSH .15 .40
315 Joe Dumars SSH .15 .40
316 Tony Dumas SSH .07 .20
317 Tim Hardaway SSH .20 .50
318 Toni Kukoc SSH .20 .50
319 Danny Manning SSH .12 .30
320 Reggie Miller SSH .30 .75
321 Chris Mullin SSH .30 .75
322 Wesley Person SSH .10 .25
323 John Starks SSH .15 .40
324 John Stockton SSH .30 .75
325 Clarence Weatherspoon SSH .10 .25
326 Shawn Bradley SSW .10 .25
327 Vlade Divac SSW .15 .40
328 Patrick Ewing SSW .25 .60
329 Christian Laettner SSW .12 .30
330 Eric Montross SSW .07 .20
331 Gheorghe Muresan SSW .10 .25
332 Dikembe Mutombo SSW .25 .60
333 Hakeem Olajuwon SSW .30 .75
334 Robert Parish SSW .15 .40
335 David Robinson SSW .30 .75
336 Dennis Rodman SSW .40 1.00
337 Rony Seikaly SSW .10 .25
338 Rik Smits SSW .12 .30
339 Kenny Anderson SPI .12 .30
340 Dee Brown SPI .12 .30
341 Bobby Hurley SPI .10 .25
342 Kevin Johnson SPI .15 .40
343 Jason Kidd SPI .50 1.25
344 Gary Payton SPI .25 .60
345 Mark Price SPI .15 .40
346 Khalid Reeves SPI .07 .20
347 Jalen Rose SPI .25 .60
348 Latrell Sprewell SPI .25 .60
349 B.J. Tyler SPI .05 .15
350 Charlie Ward SPI .10 .25
PR Hakeem Olajuwon PROMO .40 1.00
PR Hakeem Olajuwon JUMBO PROMO .40 1.00
GHO Grant Hill Gold 5.00 12.00
NNO Grant Hill SkyBox JUMBO 2.50 6.00
NNO Grant Hill Slammin' Univ. JUMBO 2.50 6.00
NNO Grant Hill Hoops JUMBO 2.50 6.00
NNO H.Olajuwon Gold 4.00 10.00
NNO Emotion Sheet A 15.00 30.00
NNO Emotion Sheet B 15.00 30.00
NNO Emotion Exchange A Expired .40 1.00
NNO Emotion Exchange B Expired .40 1.00
NNO Emotion Exchange C Expired .40 1.00
NNO 3rd Prize Game Card Expired .08 .25
NNO H.Olajuwon/D.Robinson AU 150.00 400.00
NNO Magic Johnson Exchange Card 2.00 5.00
NNO 3 Card Panel Exchange Magic Johnson Hakeem Olajuwon David Robinson 1.50 4.00

1994-95 SkyBox Premium Center Stage

COMPLETE SET (9) 20.00 50.00
SER.1 STATED ODDS 1:72
CS1 Hakeem Olajuwon 4.00 10.00
CS2 Shaquille O'Neal 6.00 15.00
CS3 Anfernee Hardaway 4.00 10.00
CS4 Chris Webber 4.00 10.00
CS5 Scottie Pippen 5.00 12.00
CS6 David Robinson 4.00 10.00
CS7 Latrell Sprewell 2.50 6.00
CS8 Charles Barkley 5.00 12.00
CS9 Alonzo Mourning 3.00 8.00

1994-95 SkyBox Premium Draft Picks

COMPLETE SET (27) 15.00 40.00
COMPLETE SERIES 1 (5) 8.00 20.00
COMPLETE SERIES 2 (22) 10.00 25.00
SER.1 ODDS 1:45; SER.2 ODDS 1:18
DP1 Glenn Robinson 1.25 3.00
DP2 Jason Kidd 3.00 8.00
DP3 Grant Hill 3.00 8.00
DP4 Donyell Marshall .60 1.50
DP5 Juwan Howard 1.00 2.50
DP6 Sharone Wright .50 1.25
DP7 Lamond Murray .60 1.50
DP8 Brian Grant 1.00 2.50
DP9 Eric Montross .50 1.25
DP10 Eddie Jones 2.00 5.00
DP11 Carlos Rogers .50 1.25
DP12 Khalid Reeves .50 1.25
DP13 Jalen Rose 1.50 4.00
DP14 Yinka Dare .40 1.00
DP15 Eric Piatkowski .60 1.50
DP16 Clifford Rozier .40 1.00
DP17 Aaron McKie .60 1.50
DP18 Eric Mobley .40 1.00
DP19 Tony Dumas .50 1.25
DP20 B.J. Tyler .40 1.00
DP21 Dickey Simpkins .50 1.25
DP22 Bill Curley .40 1.00
DP23 Wesley Person .60 1.50
DP24 Monty Williams .75 2.00
DP25 Greg Minor .60 1.50
DP26 Charlie Ward .60 1.50
DP27 Brooks Thompson .50 1.25

1994-95 SkyBox Premium Grant Hill

COMPLETE SET (5) 10.00 25.00
COMMON HILL (GH1-GH5) 3.00 8.00
SER.2 STATED ODDS 1:36 HOBBY

1994-95 SkyBox Premium Head of the Class

COMPLETE SET (6) 8.00 20.00
EXCH.CARD: SER.1 STATED ODDS 1:480
1 Grant Hill 4.00 10.00
2 Juwan Howard 1.25 3.00
3 Jason Kidd 4.00 10.00
4 Donyell Marshall .75 2.00
5 Glenn Robinson 1.50 4.00
6 Sharone Wright .60 1.50
NNO HOC Exchange Card Expired .75 2.00
NNO Checklist Card .40 1.00

1994-95 SkyBox Premium Ragin' Rookies Promos

COMPLETE SET (7) 1.50 4.00
RR8 Lindsey Hunter .30 .75
RR10 Sam Cassell .50 1.25
RR13 Nick Van Exel .50 1.25
RR15 Vin Baker .50 1.25
RR16 Isaiah Rider .50 1.25
RR19 Shawn Bradley .30 .75
RR23 Bryon Russell .30 .75

1994-95 SkyBox Premium Ragin' Rookies

COMPLETE SET (24) 10.00 25.00
SER.1 STATED ODDS 1:5
RR1 Dino Radja .60 1.50
RR2 Corie Blount .60 1.50
RR3 Toni Kukoc 1.25 3.00
RR4 Chris Mills .75 2.00
RR5 Jamal Mashburn 1.00 2.50
RR6 Rodney Rogers .60 1.50
RR7 Allan Houston 1.00 2.50
RR8 Lindsey Hunter .60 1.50
RR9 Chris Webber 2.00 5.00
RR10 Sam Cassell 1.00 2.50
RR11 Antonio Davis .75 2.00
RR12 Terry Dehere .60 1.50
RR13 Nick Van Exel 1.00 2.50
RR14 George Lynch .60 1.50
RR15 Vin Baker 1.00 2.50
RR16 Isaiah Rider 1.00 2.50
RR17 P.J. Brown .60 1.50
RR18 Anfernee Hardaway 2.00 5.00
RR19 Shawn Bradley .60 1.50
RR20 James Robinson .60 1.50
RR21 Bobby Hurley .60 1.50
RR22 Ervin Johnson .60 1.50
RR23 Bryon Russell .60 1.50
RR24 Calbert Cheaney .75 2.00

1994-95 SkyBox Premium Revolution

COMPLETE SET (10) 20.00 50.00
SER.2 STATED ODDS 1:72
R1 Patrick Ewing 3.00 8.00
R2 Grant Hill 5.00 12.00
R3 Jamal Mashburn 2.00 5.00
R4 Alonzo Mourning 3.00 8.00
R5 Dikembe Mutombo 3.00 8.00
R6 Shaquille O'Neal 8.00 20.00
R7 Scottie Pippen 5.00 12.00
R8 Glenn Robinson 2.00 5.00
R9 Latrell Sprewell 2.50 6.00
R10 Chris Webber 4.00 10.00

1994-95 SkyBox Premium SkyTech Force

COMPLETE SET (30) 4.00 10.00
SER.2 STATED ODDS 1:2
SF1 Kenny Anderson .20 .50
SF2 B.J. Armstrong .25 .60
SF3 Charles Barkley .60 1.50
SF4 Shawn Bradley .15 .40
SF5 LaPhonso Ellis .15 .40
SF6 Anfernee Hardaway .50 1.25
SF7 Bobby Hurley .15 .40
SF8 Kevin Johnson .25 .60
SF9 Larry Johnson .30 .75
SF10 Shawn Kemp .40 1.00
SF11 Jason Kidd 1.25 3.00
SF12 Christian Laettner .20 .50
SF13 Karl Malone .50 1.25
SF14 Danny Manning .20 .50
SF15 Chris Mills .20 .50
SF16 Chris Mullin .30 .75
SF17 Lamond Murray .25 .60
SF18 Charles Oakley .25 .60
SF19 Hakeem Olajuwon .50 1.25
SF20 Gary Payton .40 1.00
SF21 Mark Price .25 .60
SF22 Dino Radja .15 .40
SF23 Mitch Richmond .30 .75
SF24 Clifford Robinson .20 .50
SF25 David Robinson .50 1.25
SF26 Dennis Rodman .60 1.50
SF27 Dickey Simpkins .20 .50
SF28 John Starks .25 .60
SF29 John Stockton .50 1.25
SF30 Charlie Ward .25 .60

1994-95 SkyBox Premium Slammin' Universe

COMPLETE SET (30) 4.00 10.00
SER.2 STATED ODDS 1:2
SU1 Vin Baker .25 .60
SU2 Dee Brown .20 .50
SU3 Derrick Coleman .25 .60
SU4 Clyde Drexler .40 1.00
SU5 Joe Dumars .25 .60
SU6 Tony Dumas .20 .50
SU7 Patrick Ewing .40 1.00
SU8 Horace Grant .25 .60
SU9 Tom Gugliotta .15 .40
SU10 Grant Hill 1.25 3.00
SU11 Jim Jackson .20 .50
SU12 Toni Kukoc .30 .75
SU13 Donyell Marshall .25 .60
SU14 Jamal Mashburn .25 .60
SU15 Reggie Miller .50 1.25
SU16 Eric Montross .20 .50
SU17 Alonzo Mourning .40 1.00
SU18 Dikembe Mutombo .40 1.00
SU19 Shaquille O'Neal 1.00 2.50
SU20 Glen Rice .25 .60
SU21 Isaiah Rider .25 .60
SU22 Glenn Robinson .50 1.25
SU23 Jalen Rose .60 1.50
SU24 Detlef Schrempf .25 .60
SU25 Steve Smith .25 .60
SU26 Latrell Sprewell .30 .75
SU27 Rod Strickland .15 .40
SU28 B.J. Tyler .15 .40
SU29 Nick Van Exel .25 .60
SU30 Dominique Wilkins .40 1.00

1995-96 SkyBox Premium Promo Sheet

COMPLETE SET (8) 3.00 8.00
153 Dana Barros .40 1.00
182 Alonzo Mourning .75 2.00
229 Brent Barry .40 1.00
235 Jerry Stackhouse .75 2.00
255 Tim Hardaway .60 1.50
283 Grant Hill .75 2.00
285 Clyde Drexler .75 2.00
HH13 Michael Finley .60 1.50
S7 Anfernee Hardaway .60 1.50

1995-96 SkyBox Premium

COMPLETE SET (301) 17.50 35.00
COMPLETE SERIES 1 (150) 7.50 15.00
COMPLETE SERIES 2 (151) 10.00 20.00
SUBSET SAME VALUE AS BASE CARDS
MELTDOWN WRAPPER EXCH.EXP: 12/31/96
1 Stacey Augmon .15 .40
2 Mookie Blaylock .15 .40
3 Grant Long .12 .30
4 Steve Smith .15 .40
5 Dee Brown .15 .40
6 Sherman Douglas .12 .30
7 Eric Montross .12 .30
8 Dino Radja .12 .30
9 Dominique Wilkins .30 .75
10 Muggsy Bogues .12 .30
11 Scott Burrell .12 .30
12 Dell Curry .20 .50
13 Larry Johnson .25 .60
14 Alonzo Mourning .30 .75
15 Michael Jordan UER 2.00 5.00
16 Steve Kerr .20 .50
17 Toni Kukoc .25 .60
18 Scottie Pippen .50 1.25
19 Terrell Brandon .15 .40
20 Tyrone Hill .12 .30
21 Chris Mills .12 .30
22 Mark Price .12 .30
23 John Williams .12 .30
24 Tony Dumas .12 .30
25 Jim Jackson .15 .40
26 Popeye Jones .12 .30
27 Jason Kidd .30 .75
28 Jamal Mashburn .20 .50
29 LaPhonso Ellis .15 .40
30 Dikembe Mutombo .30 .75
31 Robert Pack .12 .30
32 Jalen Rose .25 .60
33 Bryant Stith .12 .30
34 Joe Dumars .20 .50
35 Grant Hill .30 .75
36 Allan Houston .15 .40
37 Lindsey Hunter .12 .30
38 Chris Gatling .12 .30
39 Tim Hardaway .25 .60
40 Donyell Marshall .12 .30
41 Chris Mullin .20 .50
42 Carlos Rogers .12 .30
43 Latrell Sprewell .20 .50
44 Sam Cassell .20 .50
45 Clyde Drexler .30 .75
46 Robert Horry .20 .50
47 Hakeem Olajuwon .40 1.00
48 Kenny Smith .15 .40
49 Dale Davis .12 .30
50 Mark Jackson .15 .40
51 Reggie Miller .40 1.00
52 Rik Smits .15 .40
53 Lamond Murray .12 .30

54 Eric Piatkowski .12 .30
55 Pooh Richardson .12 .30
56 Rodney Rogers .15 .40
57 Loy Vaught .12 .30
58 Elden Campbell .12 .30
59 Cedric Ceballos .15 .40
60 Vlade Divac .20 .50
61 Eddie Jones .20 .50
62 Anthony Peeler .12 .30
63 Nick Van Exel .20 .50
64 Bimbo Coles .12 .30
65 Billy Owens .12 .30
66 Khalid Reeves .12 .30
67 Glen Rice .20 .50
68 Kevin Willis .12 .30
69 Vin Baker .15 .40
70 Todd Day .12 .30
71 Eric Murdock .12 .30
72 Glenn Robinson .20 .50
73 Tom Gugliotta .12 .30
74 Christian Laettner .15 .40
75 Isaiah Rider .20 .50
76 Doug West .12 .30
77 Kenny Anderson .15 .40
78 P.J. Brown .12 .30
79 Derrick Coleman .15 .40
80 Armon Gilliam .12 .30
81 Patrick Ewing .30 .75
82 Derek Harper .15 .40
83 Anthony Mason .12 .30
84 Charles Oakley .15 .40
85 John Starks .20 .50
86 Nick Anderson .15 .40
87 Horace Grant .15 .40
88 Anfernee Hardaway .50 1.25
89 Shaquille O'Neal .75 2.00
90 Dana Barros .15 .40
91 Shawn Bradley .12 .30
92 Clarence Weatherspoon .12 .30
93 Sharone Wright .12 .30
94 Charles Barkley .50 1.25
95 Kevin Johnson .20 .50
96 Dan Majerle .20 .50
97 Danny Manning .15 .40
98 Wesley Person .12 .30
99 Clifford Robinson .20 .50
100 Rod Strickland .12 .30
101 Otis Thorpe .15 .40
102 Buck Williams .12 .30
103 Brian Grant .15 .40
104 Olden Polynice .12 .30
105 Mitch Richmond .25 .60
106 Walt Williams .12 .30
107 Vinny Del Negro .12 .30
108 Sean Elliott .15 .40
109 Avery Johnson .12 .30
110 David Robinson .40 1.00
111 Dennis Rodman .40 1.00
112 Shawn Kemp .30 .75
113 Gary Payton .30 .75
114 Sam Perkins .12 .30
115 Detlef Schrempf .20 .50
116 David Benoit .12 .30
117 Jeff Hornacek .15 .40
118 Karl Malone .40 1.00
119 John Stockton .40 1.00
120 Calbert Cheaney .12 .30
121 Juwan Howard .20 .50
122 Don MacLean .12 .30
123 Gheorghe Muresan .12 .30
124 Chris Webber .25 .60
125 Robert Horry FC .12 .30
126 Mark Jackson FC .15 .40
127 Steve Smith FC .15 .40
128 Lamond Murray FC .12 .30
129 Christian Laettner FC .12 .30
130 Kenny Anderson FC .15 .40
131 Anthony Mason FC .12 .30
132 Kevin Johnson FC .20 .50
133 Jeff Hornacek FC .15 .40
134 Larry Johnson TP .25 .60
135 Popeye Jones TP .12 .30
136 Allan Houston TP .15 .40
137 Chris Gatling TP .12 .30
138 Sam Cassell TP .20 .50
139 Anthony Peeler TP .12 .30
140 Vin Baker TP .15 .40
141 Dana Barros TP .15 .40
142 Gheorghe Muresan TP .12 .30
143 Toronto Raptors .12 .30
144 Vancouver Grizzlies .12 .30
145 G.Rice/M.Bogues EXP .20 .50
146 N.Anderson/C.Laettner EXP .15 .40
147 John Salley TF .12 .30
148 Greg Anthony TF .12 .30
149 Checklist #1 .12 .30
150 Checklist #2 .12 .30
151 Craig Ehlo .12 .30
152 Spud Webb .20 .50
153 Dana Barros .15 .40
154 Rick Fox .15 .40
155 Kendall Gill .12 .30
156 Khalid Reeves .12 .30
157 Glen Rice .20 .50
158 Luc Longley .15 .40
159 Dennis Rodman .40 1.00
160 Dickey Simpkins .12 .30
161 Danny Ferry .12 .30
162 Dan Majerle .20 .50
163 Bobby Phills .15 .40
164 Loucious Harris .12 .30
165 George McCloud .12 .30
166 Mahmoud Abdul-Rauf .15 .40
167 Don MacLean .12 .30
168 Reggie Williams .12 .30
169 Terry Mills .12 .30
170 Otis Thorpe .15 .40
171 B.J. Armstrong .20 .50
172 Rony Seikaly .12 .30
173 Chucky Brown .12 .30
174 Mario Elie .12 .30
175 Antonio Davis .12 .30
176 Ricky Pierce .12 .30
177 Terry Dehere .12 .30
178 Rodney Rogers .15 .40
179 Malik Sealy .12 .30
180 Brian Williams .12 .30
181 Sedale Threatt .12 .30
182 Alonzo Mourning .30 .75
183 Lee Mayberry .12 .30
184 Sean Rooks .12 .30
185 Shawn Bradley .12 .30
186 Kevin Edwards .12 .30
187 Hubert Davis .12 .30
188 Charles Smith .12 .30
189 Charlie Ward .15 .40
190 Dennis Scott .12 .30
191 Brian Shaw .12 .30
192 Derrick Coleman .15 .40
193 Richard Dumas .12 .30
194 Vernon Maxwell .12 .30
195 A.C. Green .15 .40
196 Elliot Perry .12 .30
197 John Williams .12 .30
198 Aaron McKie .12 .30
199 Bobby Hurley .12 .30
200 Michael Smith UER .12 .30
201 J.R. Reid .12 .30
202 Hersey Hawkins .15 .40
203 Willie Anderson .12 .30
204 Oliver Miller .12 .30
205 Tracy Murray .12 .30
206 Alvin Robertson .12 .30
207 Carlos Rogers UER .12 .30
208 John Salley .12 .30
209 Zan Tabak .12 .30
210 Adam Keefe .12 .30
211 Chris Morris .12 .30
212 Greg Anthony .12 .30
213 Blue Edwards .12 .30
214 Kenny Gattison .12 .30
215 Antonio Harvey .12 .30
216 Chris King .12 .30
217 Byron Scott .20 .50
218 Robert Pack .12 .30
219 Alan Henderson RC .20 .50
220 Eric Williams RC .20 .50
221 George Zidek RC .20 .50
222 Jason Caffey RC .20 .50
223 Bob Sura RC .15 .40
224 Cherokee Parks RC .15 .40
225 Antonio McDyess RC .25 .60
226 Theo Ratliff RC .20 .50
227 Joe Smith RC .25 .60
228 Travis Best RC .20 .50
229 Brent Barry RC .30 .75
230 Sasha Danilovic RC .20 .50
231 Kurt Thomas RC .20 .50
232 Shawn Respert RC .15 .40
233 Kevin Garnett RC 1.50 4.00
234 Ed O'Bannon RC .15 .40
235 Jerry Stackhouse RC .60 1.50
236 Michael Finley RC .60 1.50
237 Mario Bennett RC .15 .40
238 Randolph Childress RC .15 .40
239 Arvydas Sabonis RC .40 1.00
240 Gary Trent RC .30 .75
241 Tyus Edney RC .20 .50
242 Corliss Williamson RC .20 .50
243 Cory Alexander RC .20 .50
244 Damon Stoudamire RC .50 1.25
245 Greg Ostertag RC .20 .50
246 Lawrence Moten RC .20 .50
247 Bryant Reeves RC .15 .40
248 Rasheed Wallace RC .60 1.50
249 Muggsy Bogues HR .20 .50
250 Dell Curry HR .20 .50
251 Scottie Pippen HR .50 1.25
252 Danny Ferry HR .12 .30
253 Mahmoud Abdul-Rauf HR .15 .40
254 Joe Dumars HR .20 .50
255 Tim Hardaway HR .25 .60
256 Chris Mullin HR .20 .50
257 Hakeem Olajuwon HR .40 1.00
258 Kenny Smith HR .15 .40
259 Reggie Miller HR .40 1.00
260 Rik Smits HR .20 .50
261 Vlade Divac HR .20 .50
262 Doug West HR .12 .30
263 Patrick Ewing HR .30 .75
264 Charles Oakley HR .15 .40
265 Nick Anderson HR .15 .40
266 Dennis Scott HR .12 .30
267 Jeff Turner HR .12 .30
268 Charles Barkley HR .50 1.25
269 Kevin Johnson HR .20 .50
270 Clifford Robinson HR .20 .50
271 Buck Williams HR .12 .30
272 Lionel Simmons HR .12 .30
273 David Robinson HR .40 1.00
274 Gary Payton HR .30 .75
275 Karl Malone HR .40 1.00
276 John Stockton HR .40 1.00
277 Steve Smith ELE .15 .40
278 Michael Jordan ELE 2.00 5.00
279 Jim Jackson ELE .15 .40
280 Jason Kidd ELE .30 .75
281 Jamal Mashburn ELE .20 .50
282 Dikembe Mutombo ELE .30 .75
283 Grant Hill ELE .30 .75
284 Tim Hardaway ELE .25 .60
285 Clyde Drexler ELE .30 .75
286 Cedric Ceballos ELE .15 .40
287 Gary Payton ELE .30 .75
288 Billy Owens ELE .12 .30
289 Vin Baker ELE .15 .40
290 Glenn Robinson ELE .20 .50
291 Kenny Anderson ELE .15 .40
292 Anfernee Hardaway ELE .50 1.25
293 Shaquille O'Neal ELE .75 2.00
294 Charles Barkley ELE .50 1.25
295 Rod Strickland ELE .12 .30
296 Mitch Richmond ELE .25 .60
297 Juwan Howard ELE .15 .40
298 Chris Webber ELE .25 .60
299 Checklist #1 .12 .30
300 Checklist #2 .12 .30
301 Magic Johnson .60 1.50
PR Grant Hill JUMBO 2.50 6.00
NNO G.Hill Meltdown 10.00 25.00
NNO J.Stackhouse Meltdown 12.50 30.00

1995-96 SkyBox Premium Atomic

COMPLETE SET (15) 2.50 6.00
SER.1 STATED ODDS 1:4 HOBBY/RETAIL
A1 Eric Montross .25 .60
A2 Charles Oakley .30 .75
A3 Rik Smits .30 .75
A4 Vlade Divac .40 1.00
A5 Buck Williams .25 .60
A6 Vin Baker .30 .75
A7 Glenn Robinson .40 1.00
A8 Isaiah Rider .40 1.00
A9 Derrick Coleman .30 .75
A10 Clarence Weatherspoon .25 .60
A11 Sharone Wright .25 .60
A12 Brian Grant .30 .75
A13 Jim Jackson .30 .75
A14 Clyde Drexler .60 1.50
A15 Anfernee Hardaway 1.00 2.50

1995-96 SkyBox Premium Close-Ups

COMPLETE SET (9) 10.00 25.00
SER.1 STATED ODDS 1:9 RETAIL
ONE PER SPECIAL SER.1 RETAIL PACK
C1 Scottie Pippen 3.00 8.00
C2 Grant Hill 2.00 5.00
C3 Clyde Drexler 2.00 5.00
C4 Nick Van Exel 1.25 3.00
C5 Tom Gugliotta .75 2.00
C6 Patrick Ewing 2.00 5.00
C7 Charles Barkley 3.00 8.00
C8 Karl Malone 2.50 6.00
C9 Juwan Howard 1.25 3.00

1995-96 SkyBox Premium Dynamic

COMPLETE SET (12) 2.50 6.00
SER.1 STATED ODDS 1:4 HOBBY/RETAIL
D1 Larry Johnson .50 1.25
D2 Alonzo Mourning .60 1.50
D3 Dikembe Mutombo .60 1.50
D4 Jalen Rose .50 1.25
D5 Grant Hill .60 1.50
D6 Latrell Sprewell .40 1.00
D7 Reggie Miller .75 2.00
D8 John Starks .40 1.00
D9 Calbert Cheaney .25 .60
D10 Dennis Rodman .75 2.00
D11 Detlef Schrempf .40 1.00
D12 Chris Webber .50 1.25

1995-96 SkyBox Premium High Hopes

COMPLETE SET (20) 15.00 40.00
SER.2 STATED ODDS 1:18 H/R, 1:12 JUM
HH1 Alan Henderson .75 2.00
HH2 Eric Williams .75 2.00
HH3 George Zidek .60 1.50
HH4 Bob Sura .60 1.50
HH5 Cherokee Parks .60 1.50
HH6 Antonio McDyess 1.00 2.50
HH7 Joe Smith 1.00 2.50
HH8 Brent Barry 1.25 3.00
HH9 Shawn Respert .60 1.50
HH10 Kevin Garnett 6.00 15.00
HH11 Ed O'Bannon .60 1.50
HH12 Jerry Stackhouse 2.50 6.00
HH13 Michael Finley 2.00 5.00
HH14 Arvydas Sabonis 1.50 4.00
HH15 Gary Trent .60 1.50
HH16 Tyus Edney .75 2.00
HH17 Damon Stoudamire 2.00 5.00
HH18 Greg Ostertag .75 2.00
HH19 Bryant Reeves .60 1.50
HH20 Rasheed Wallace 2.50 6.00

1995-96 SkyBox Premium Hot Sparks

COMPLETE SET (11) 8.00 20.00
SER.2 STATED ODDS 1:12 HOBBY
HS1 Mookie Blaylock 1.00 2.50
HS2 Jason Kidd 1.50 4.00
HS3 Tim Hardaway 1.25 3.00
HS4 Nick Van Exel 1.00 2.50
HS5 Kenny Anderson .75 2.00
HS6 Anfernee Hardaway 2.50 6.00
HS7 Rod Strickland .60 1.50
HS8 Gary Payton 1.50 4.00
HS9 Damon Stoudamire 1.50 4.00
HS10 John Stockton 2.00 5.00
HS11 Magic Johnson 3.00 8.00

1995-96 SkyBox Premium Kinetic

COMPLETE SET (9) 1.25 3.00
SER.1 STATED ODDS 1:4 HOBBY/RETAIL
K1 Mookie Blaylock .40 1.00
K2 Tim Hardaway .50 1.25
K3 Lamond Murray UER .25 .60
K4 Stacey Augmon .30 .75
K5 Nick Van Exel .40 1.00
K6 Khalid Reeves .25 .60
K7 Kenny Anderson .30 .75
K8 Rod Strickland .25 .60
K9 Gary Payton .60 1.50

1995-96 SkyBox Premium Larger Than Life

COMPLETE SET (10) 15.00 40.00
SER.1 STATED ODDS 1:48 HOBBY/RETAIL
L1 Michael Jordan 100.00 250.00
L2 Jason Kidd 2.00 5.00
L3 Grant Hill 2.00 5.00
L4 Hakeem Olajuwon 2.50 6.00
L5 Glenn Robinson 1.25 3.00
L6 Patrick Ewing 2.00 5.00
L7 Shaquille O'Neal 5.00 12.00
L8 Charles Barkley 3.00 8.00
L9 David Robinson 2.50 6.00
L10 John Stockton 2.50 6.00

1995-96 SkyBox Premium Lottery Exchange

COMPLETE SET (13) 15.00 40.00
ONE SET PER THREE EXCH.CARDS BY MAIL
EXCH.CARDS: SER.1 STATED ODDS 1:40
1 Joe Smith 1.00 2.50
2 Antonio McDyess 1.00 2.50
3 Jerry Stackhouse 2.50 6.00
4 Rasheed Wallace 2.50 6.00
5 Kevin Garnett 4.00 10.00
6 Bryant Reeves .60 1.50
7 Damon Stoudamire 2.00 5.00
8 Shawn Respert .60 1.50
9 Ed O'Bannon .60 1.50
10 Kurt Thomas .75 2.00
11 Gary Trent .60 1.50
12 Cherokee Parks .60 1.50
13 Corliss Williamson .75 2.00
NNO Exchange Card 3 .40 1.00
NNO Exchange Card 1 .40 1.00
NNO Exchange Card 2 .40 1.00

1995-96 SkyBox Premium Meltdown

COMPLETE SET (10) 300.00 600.00
SER.2 STATED ODDS 1:54 H/R, 1:42 JUM
M1 Michael Jordan 200.00 500.00
M2 Dan Majerle 4.00 10.00
M3 Jason Kidd 6.00 15.00
M4 Antonio McDyess 5.00 12.00
M5 Grant Hill 6.00 15.00
M6 Joe Smith 5.00 12.00
M7 Hakeem Olajuwon 8.00 20.00
M8 Shaquille O'Neal 15.00 40.00
M9 Jerry Stackhouse 12.00 30.00
M10 David Robinson 8.00 20.00

1995-96 SkyBox Premium Rookie Prevue

COMPLETE SET (20) 20.00 50.00
SER.1 STATED ODDS 1:9 HOBBY/RETAIL
RP1 Joe Smith 1.25 3.00
RP2 Antonio McDyess 1.25 3.00
RP3 Jerry Stackhouse 3.00 8.00
RP4 Rasheed Wallace 3.00 8.00
RP5 Bryant Reeves .75 2.00
RP6 Damon Stoudamire 2.50 6.00
RP7 Shawn Respert .75 2.00
RP8 Ed O'Bannon .75 2.00
RP9 Kurt Thomas 1.00 2.50
RP10 Gary Trent .75 2.00
RP11 Cherokee Parks .75 2.00
RP12 Corliss Williamson 1.00 2.50
RP13 Eric Williams 1.00 2.50
RP14 Brent Barry 1.50 4.00
RP15 Alan Henderson 1.00 2.50
RP16 Bob Sura .75 2.00
RP17 Theo Ratliff 1.50 4.00
RP18 Randolph Childress .75 2.00
RP19 Michael Finley 2.50 6.00
RP20 George Zidek .75 2.00

1995-96 SkyBox Premium Standouts

COMPLETE SET (12) 15.00 30.00
SER.1 STATED ODDS 1:18 H/R, 1:36 JUM
S1 Alonzo Mourning 3.00 8.00
S2 Scottie Pippen 5.00 12.00
S3 Danny Manning 1.50 4.00
S4 Jamal Mashburn 2.00 5.00
S5 Latrell Sprewell 2.00 5.00
S6 Reggie Miller 4.00 10.00
S7 Anfernee Hardaway 5.00 12.00
S8 Brian Grant 1.50 4.00
S9 Shawn Kemp 3.00 8.00
S10 Clifford Robinson 2.00 5.00
S11 Joe Dumars 2.00 5.00
S12 Chris Webber 2.50 6.00

1995-96 SkyBox Premium Standouts Hobby

COMPLETE SET (6) 40.00 100.00
SER.1 STATED ODDS 1:18 HOBBY
SH1 Michael Jordan 40.00 100.00
SH2 Jason Kidd 4.00 10.00
SH3 Hakeem Olajuwon 5.00 12.00
SH4 Eddie Jones 2.50 6.00
SH5 Shaquille O'Neal 10.00 25.00
SH6 Grant Hill 4.00 10.00

1995-96 SkyBox Premium USA Basketball

COMPLETE SET (10) 8.00 20.00
SER.2 STATED ODDS 1:12 RETAIL
ONE PER SPECIAL SER.2 RETAIL PACK
U1 Anfernee Hardaway 2.00 5.00
U2 Grant Hill 1.25 3.00
U3 Karl Malone 1.50 4.00
U4 Reggie Miller 1.50 4.00
U5 Scottie Pippen 2.00 5.00
U6 Hakeem Olajuwon 1.50 4.00
U7 Shaquille O'Neal 3.00 8.00
U8 David Robinson 1.50 4.00
U9 Glenn Robinson .75 2.00
U10 John Stockton 1.50 4.00

1996-97 SkyBox Premium

COMPLETE SET (281) 20.00 35.00
COMPLETE SERIES 1 (131) 12.50 25.00
COMPLETE SERIES 2 (150) 7.50 15.00
PM/DT SUBSET CARDS SAME VALUE AS BASE
1 Mookie Blaylock .40 1.00
2 Alan Henderson .25 .60
3 Christian Laettner .40 1.00
4 Dikembe Mutombo .60 1.50
5 Steve Smith .40 1.00
6 Dana Barros .25 .60
7 Rick Fox .25 .60
8 Dino Radja .25 .60
9 Antoine Walker RC .60 1.50
10 Eric Williams .25 .60
11 Dell Curry .40 1.00
12 Tony Delk RC .40 1.00
13 Matt Geiger .25 .60
14 Glen Rice .40 1.00
15 Ron Harper .30 .75
16 Michael Jordan 6.00 15.00
17 Toni Kukoc .40 1.00
18 Scottie Pippen 1.00 2.50
19 Dennis Rodman 1.00 2.50
20 Terrell Brandon .30 .75
21 Danny Ferry .25 .60
22 Chris Mills .25 .60
23 Bobby Phills .25 .60
24 Vitaly Potapenko RC .30 .75
25 Jim Jackson .25 .60
26 Jason Kidd .60 1.50
27 Jamal Mashburn .40 1.00
28 George McCloud .25 .60
29 Samaki Walker RC .30 .75
30 LaPhonso Ellis .25 .60
31 Antonio McDyess .40 1.00
32 Bryant Stith .25 .60
33 Joe Dumars .50 1.25
34 Grant Hill .60 1.50
35 Lindsey Hunter .25 .60
36 Theo Ratliff .25 .60
37 Otis Thorpe .30 .75
38 Todd Fuller RC .25 .60
39 Chris Mullin .50 1.25
40 Joe Smith .30 .75
41 Latrell Sprewell .40 1.00
42 Charles Barkley 1.00 2.50
43 Clyde Drexler .60 1.50
44 Mario Elie .25 .60
45 Hakeem Olajuwon .75 2.00
46 Erick Dampier RC .40 1.00
47 Dale Davis .25 .60
48 Derrick McKey .25 .60
49 Reggie Miller .75 2.00
50 Rik Smits .30 .75
51 Brent Barry .30 .75
52 Rodney Rogers .25 .60
53 Loy Vaught .25 .60
54 Lorenzen Wright RC .30 .75
55 Kobe Bryant RC 40.00 100.00
56 Cedric Ceballos .30 .75
57 Eddie Jones .40 1.00
58 Shaquille O'Neal 1.50 4.00
59 Nick Van Exel .40 1.00
60 Tim Hardaway .50 1.25
61 Alonzo Mourning .60 1.50
62 Kurt Thomas .25 .60
63 Ray Allen RC 2.00 5.00
64 Vin Baker .30 .75
65 Shawn Respert .25 .60
66 Glenn Robinson .40 1.00
67 Kevin Garnett 1.25 3.00
68 Tom Gugliotta .25 .60
69 Stephon Marbury RC 1.25 3.00
70 Sam Mitchell .25 .60
71 Shawn Bradley .25 .60
72 Kendall Gill .40 1.00
73 Kerry Kittles RC .40 1.00
74 Ed O'Bannon .25 .60
75 Patrick Ewing .60 1.50
76 Larry Johnson .50 1.25
77 Charles Oakley .40 1.00
78 John Starks .40 1.00
79 John Wallace RC .40 1.00
80 Nick Anderson .30 .75
81 Horace Grant .40 1.00
82 Anfernee Hardaway 1.00 2.50
83 Dennis Scott .30 .75
84 Derrick Coleman .30 .75
85 Allen Iverson RC 3.00 8.00
86 Jerry Stackhouse .50 1.25
87 Clarence Weatherspoon .25 .60
88 Michael Finley .40 1.00
89 Robert Horry .40 1.00
90 Kevin Johnson .40 1.00
91 Steve Nash RC 2.50 6.00
92 Wesley Person .25 .60
93 Aaron McKie .25 .60
94 Jermaine O'Neal RC .60 1.50
95 Clifford Robinson .40 1.00
96 Arvydas Sabonis .40 1.00
97 Gary Trent .25 .60
98 Tyus Edney .25 .60
99 Brian Grant .30 .75
100 Mitch Richmond .50 1.25
101 Billy Owens .25 .60
102 Corliss Williamson .25 .60
103 Vinny Del Negro .25 .60
104 Sean Elliott .40 1.00
105 Avery Johnson .30 .75
106 Chuck Person .30 .75
107 David Robinson .75 2.00
108 Hersey Hawkins .30 .75
109 Shawn Kemp .60 1.50
110 Gary Payton .60 1.50
111 Sam Perkins .30 .75
112 Detlef Schrempf .40 1.00
113 Marcus Camby RC .60 1.50
114 Carlos Rogers .25 .60
115 Damon Stoudamire .40 1.00
116 Zan Tabak .25 .60
117 Antoine Carr .25 .60
118 Jeff Hornacek .30 .75
119 Karl Malone .75 2.00
120 Chris Morris .25 .60
121 John Stockton .75 2.00
122 Shareef Abdur-Rahim RC .60 1.50
123 Greg Anthony .25 .60
124 Bryant Reeves .25 .60
125 Roy Rogers RC .25 .60
126 Calbert Cheaney .25 .60
127 Juwan Howard .40 1.00
128 Gheorghe Muresan .25 .60
129 Chris Webber .50 1.25
130 Checklist .12 .30
131 Checklist .12 .30
132 Jon Barry .25 .60
133 Christian Laettner .40 1.00
134 Dikembe Mutombo .60 1.50
135 Dee Brown .25 .60
136 Todd Day .25 .60
137 David Wesley .25 .60
138 Vlade Divac .40 1.00
139 Anthony Goldwire .25 .60
140 Anthony Mason .40 1.00
141 Jason Caffey .25 .60
142 Luc Longley .30 .75
143 Tyrone Hill .25 .60
144 Antonio Lang .25 .60
145 Sam Cassell .50 1.25
146 Chris Gatling .25 .60
147 Eric Montross .25 .60
148 Ervin Johnson .25 .60
149 Sarunas Marciulionis .25 .60
150 Stacey Augmon .30 .75
151 Grant Long .25 .60
152 Terry Mills .25 .60
153 Kenny Smith .30 .75
154 B.J. Armstrong .30 .75
155 Bimbo Coles .25 .60
156 Charles Barkley 1.00 2.50
157 Brent Price .25 .60
158 Duane Ferrell .25 .60
159 Jalen Rose .30 .75
160 Terry Dehere .25 .60
161 Bo Outlaw .25 .60
162 Corie Blount .25 .60
163 Shaquille O'Neal 1.50 4.00
164 Rumeal Robinson .25 .60
165 P.J. Brown .25 .60
166 Ronnie Grandison .25 .60
167 Sherman Douglas .25 .60
168 Johnny Newman .25 .60
169 James Robinson .25 .60
170 Doug West .25 .60
171 Robert Pack .25 .60
172 Khalid Reeves .25 .60
173 Chris Childs .25 .60
174 Allan Houston .40 1.00
175 Charlie Ward .25 .60
176 Darrell Armstrong RC .60 1.50
177 Gerald Wilkins .30 .75
178 Lucious Harris .30 .75
179 Robert Horry .40 1.00
180 Danny Manning .30 .75
181 Kenny Anderson .30 .75
182 Isaiah Rider .30 .75
183 Rasheed Wallace .50 1.25
184 Mahmoud Abdul-Rauf .30 .75
185 Cory Alexander .25 .60
186 Vernon Maxwell .25 .60
187 Dominique Wilkins .60 1.50
188 Nate McMillan .25 .60
189 Larry Stewart .25 .60
190 Doug Christie .25 .60
191 Hubert Davis .25 .60
192 Walt Williams .25 .60
193 Adam Keefe .25 .60
194 Greg Ostertag .25 .60
195 John Stockton .75 2.00
196 George Lynch .25 .60
197 Lee Mayberry .25 .60
198 Tracy Murray .25 .60
199 Rod Strickland .40 1.00
200 Shareef Abdur-Rahim ROO .60 1.50
201 Ray Allen ROO 2.00 5.00
202 Shandon Anderson ROO RC .30 .75
203 Kobe Bryant ROO 20.00 50.00
204 Marcus Camby ROO .60 1.50
205 Erick Dampier ROO .40 1.00
206 Emanual Davis ROO RC .30 .75
207 Tony Delk ROO .30 .75
208 Brian Evans ROO RC .25 .60
209 Derek Fisher ROO RC .50 1.25
210 Todd Fuller ROO .25 .60
211 Dean Garrett ROO RC .40 1.00
212 Reggie Geary ROO RC .40 1.00
213 Darvin Ham ROO RC .75 2.00
214 Othella Harrington ROO RC .30 .75
215 Shane Heal ROO RC .40 1.00
216 Allen Iverson ROO 3.00 8.00
217 Dontae' Jones ROO RC .30 .75
218 Kerry Kittles ROO .40 1.00
219 Priest Lauderdale ROO RC .25 .60
220 Randy Livingston ROO RC .40 1.00
221 Matt Maloney ROO RC .30 .75
222 Stephon Marbury ROO 1.25 3.00
223 Walter McCarty ROO RC .40 1.00
224 Amal McCaskill ROO RC .40 1.00
225 Jeff McInnis ROO RC .40 1.00
226 Martin Muursepp ROO RC .25 .60
227 Steve Nash ROO 2.50 6.00
228 Ruben Nembhard ROO RC .40 1.00
229 Jermaine O'Neal ROO .60 1.50
230 Vitaly Potapenko ROO .30 .75
231 Virginius Praskevicius ROO RC .40 1.00
232 Roy Rogers ROO .30 .75
233 Malik Rose ROO RC .50 1.25
234 Antoine Walker ROO .60 1.50
235 Samaki Walker ROO .30 .75
236 Ben Wallace ROO RC 2.00 5.00
237 John Wallace ROO .40 1.00
238 Jerome Williams ROO RC .30 .75
239 Lorenzen Wright ROO .30 .75
240 Sam Cassell PM .50 1.25
241 Anfernee Hardaway PM 1.00 2.50
242 Tim Hardaway PM .50 1.25
243 Grant Hill PM .60 1.50
244 Allan Houston PM .40 1.00
245 Juwan Howard PM .40 1.00
246 Kevin Johnson PM .40 1.00
247 Michael Jordan PM 4.00 10.00
248 Jason Kidd PM .60 1.50
249 Karl Malone PM .75 2.00
250 Reggie Miller PM .75 2.00
251 Gary Payton PM .60 1.50
252 Wesley Person PM .25 .60
253 Glen Rice PM .40 1.00
254 David Robinson PM .75 2.00
255 Steve Smith PM .40 1.00
256 Latrell Sprewell PM .40 1.00
257 Jerry Stackhouse PM .50 1.25
258 Rod Strickland PM .40 1.00
259 Nick Van Exel PM .40 1.00
260 Charles Barkley DT 1.00 2.50
261 Dale Davis DT .25 .60
262 Patrick Ewing DT .60 1.50
263 Michael Finley DT .40 1.00
264 Chris Gatling DT .25 .60
265 Armon Gilliam DT .25 .60
266 Tyrone Hill DT .25 .60
267 Robert Horry DT .40 1.00
268 Mark Jackson DT .30 .75
269 Shawn Kemp DT .60 1.50
270 Jamal Mashburn DT .40 1.00
271 Anthony Mason DT .30 .75
272 Alonzo Mourning DT .60 1.50
273 Dikembe Mutombo DT .60 1.50
274 Shaquille O'Neal DT 1.50 4.00
275 Isaiah Rider DT .30 .75
276 Dennis Rodman DT 1.00 2.50
277 Damon Stoudamire DT .40 1.00
278 Chris Webber DT .50 1.25
279 Jayson Williams DT .25 .60
280 Checklist (132-239) .12 .30
281 Checklist (240-281/inserts) .12 .30
NNO Jerry Stackhouse PROMO .75 2.00

1996-97 SkyBox Premium Rubies

*RUBIES: 8X TO 20X BASE HI
ONE PER SER.1/2 HOBBY BOX
16 Michael Jordan 600.00 1,200.00
18 Scottie Pippen 15.00 40.00
19 Dennis Rodman 25.00 60.00
55 Kobe Bryant 2,000.00 4,000.00
82 Anfernee Hardaway 25.00 60.00
85 Allen Iverson 100.00 250.00
203 Kobe Bryant ROO 1,500.00 3,000.00
216 Allen Iverson ROO 20.00 50.00
227 Steve Nash ROO 10.00 25.00
247 Michael Jordan PM 125.00 300.00

1996-97 SkyBox Premium Autographics

STATED ODDS 1:72 FLEER/SKYBOX PROD.
SET INCLUDES #'s 22A, 61 AND 68
CARDS LISTED BELOW ALPHABETICALLY
BEWARE COUNTERFEITS
1 Ray Allen 75.00 200.00
2 Kenny Anderson 5.00 12.00
3 Nick Anderson 10.00 25.00
4 B.J. Armstrong 6.00 15.00
5 Vincent Askew 5.00 12.00
6 Dana Barros 5.00 12.00
7 Brent Barry 5.00 12.00
8 Travis Best 5.00 12.00
9 Muggsy Bogues 6.00 15.00
10 P.J. Brown 5.00 12.00
11 Randy Brown 6.00 15.00
12 Marcus Camby 20.00 50.00
13 Chris Childs 5.00 12.00
14 Dell Curry 5.00 12.00
15 Andrew DeClercq 5.00 12.00
16 Tony Delk 8.00 20.00
17 Sherman Douglas 5.00 12.00
18 Clyde Drexler 60.00 150.00
19 Tyus Edney 5.00 12.00
20 Michael Finley 8.00 20.00
21 Rick Fox 6.00 15.00
22 Kevin Garnett 200.00 500.00
23 Matt Geiger 5.00 12.00
24 Kendall Gill 6.00 15.00
25 Brian Grant 5.00 12.00
26 Tim Hardaway 25.00 60.00
27 Grant Hill 100.00 250.00
28 Tyrone Hill 5.00 12.00
29 Allan Houston 12.00 30.00
30 Juwan Howard 30.00 80.00
31 Zydrunas Ilgauskas 6.00 15.00
32 Jim Jackson 5.00 12.00
33 Mark Jackson 6.00 15.00
34 Eddie Jones 20.00 50.00
35 Adam Keefe 5.00 12.00
36 Steve Kerr 40.00 100.00
37 Kerry Kittles 8.00 20.00
38 Toni Kukoc 25.00 60.00
39 Andrew Lang 5.00 12.00
40 Voshon Lenard 5.00 12.00
41 Grant Long 5.00 12.00
42 Luc Longley 15.00 40.00
43 George Lynch 5.00 12.00
44 Don MacLean 5.00 12.00
45 Stephon Marbury 75.00 200.00
46 Lee Mayberry 5.00 12.00
47 Walter McCarty 5.00 12.00
48 George McCloud 75.00 200.00
49 Antonio McDyess 15.00 40.00
50 Nate McMillan 5.00 12.00
51 Chris Mills 5.00 12.00
52 Sam Mitchell 5.00 12.00
53 Eric Montross 5.00 12.00
54 Chris Morris 5.00 12.00
55 Lawrence Moten 5.00 12.00
56 Alonzo Mourning 100.00 250.00
57 Gheorghe Muresan 6.00 15.00
58 Steve Nash 200.00 500.00
59 Ed O'Bannon 5.00 12.00
60 Charles Oakley 10.00 25.00
62 Greg Ostertag 5.00 12.00
63 Billy Owens 5.00 12.00
64 Sam Perkins 5.00 12.00
65 Chuck Person 5.00 12.00
66 Wesley Person 5.00 12.00
67 Bobby Phills 5.00 12.00
69 Theo Ratliff 5.00 12.00
70 Glen Rice 5.00 12.00
71 Rodney Rogers 5.00 12.00
72 Byron Scott 5.00 12.00
73 Dennis Scott 5.00 12.00
74 Joe Smith 10.00 25.00
75 Kenny Smith 6.00 15.00
76 Rik Smits 5.00 12.00
77 Eric Snow 5.00 12.00
78 Latrell Sprewell 15.00 40.00
79 Jerry Stackhouse 15.00 40.00
80 John Starks 12.00 30.00
81 Bryant Stith 5.00 12.00
82 Damon Stoudamire 75.00 200.00
83 Rod Strickland 50.00 120.00
84 Bob Sura 5.00 12.00
85 Zan Tabak 5.00 12.00
86 Loy Vaught 6.00 15.00
87 Antoine Walker 25.00 60.00
88 Samaki Walker 6.00 15.00
89 John Wallace 6.00 15.00
90 Bill Wennington 6.00 15.00
91 David Wesley 5.00 12.00
92 Doug West 5.00 12.00
93 Monty Williams 5.00 12.00
94 Joe Wolf 5.00 12.00
95 Sharone Wright 5.00 12.00

1996-97 SkyBox Premium Autographics Blue

*BLUE: .75X TO 2X VALUE
ALL OLAJUWON CARDS SIGNED IN BLUE
ALL PIPPEN CARDS SIGNED IN BLUE
GARNETT BLUE CARDS 2:1 VERSUS BLACK
NO JOHN WALLACE BLUE AU's EXIST
22 Kevin Garnett 200.00 500.00
61 Hakeem Olajuwon 125.00 300.00
68 Scottie Pippen 150.00 400.00
82 Damon Stoudamire 100.00 250.00

1996-97 SkyBox Premium Close-Ups

COMPLETE SET (9) 8.00 20.00
SER.1 STATED ODDS 1:24 HOBBY/RETAIL
CU1 Anfernee Hardaway 3.00 8.00
CU2 Grant Hill 2.00 5.00
CU3 Juwan Howard 1.25 3.00

CU4 Jason Kidd 2.00 5.00
CU5 Shawn Kemp 2.00 5.00
CU6 Alonzo Mourning 2.00 5.00
CU7 Hakeem Olajuwon 2.50 6.00
CU8 Jerry Stackhouse 1.50 4.00
CU9 Damon Stoudamire 1.25 3.00

1996-97 SkyBox Premium Emerald Autographs
SER.2 STATED ODDS 1:20 HOBBY BOXES
E1 Ray Allen 75.00 200.00
E2 Marcus Camby 10.00 25.00
E3 Grant Hill 100.00 200.00
E4 Kerry Kittles 6.00 15.00
E5 Jerry Stackhouse 10.00 25.00
NNO Expired Trade Cards .40 1.00

1996-97 SkyBox Premium Golden Touch
COMPLETE SET (10) 1,000.00 2,000.00
SER.2 STATED ODDS 1:240 HOBBY/RETAIL
1 Vin Baker 10.00 25.00
2 Terrell Brandon 10.00 25.00
3 Allan Houston 12.00 30.00
4 Allen Iverson 125.00 300.00
5 Michael Jordan 800.00 1,500.00
6 Shawn Kemp 30.00 80.00
7 Karl Malone 40.00 100.00
8 Stephon Marbury 40.00 100.00
9 Latrell Sprewell 12.00 30.00
10 Damon Stoudamire 12.00 30.00

1996-97 SkyBox Premium Intimidators
COMPLETE SET (20) 12.00 30.00
SER.2 STATED ODDS 1:8 HOBBY/RETAIL
1 Shareef Abdur-Rahim 1.50 4.00
2 Charles Barkley 2.50 6.00
3 Marcus Camby 1.50 4.00
4 Elden Campbell .60 1.50
5 Derrick Coleman .75 2.00
6 Patrick Ewing 1.50 4.00
7 Michael Finley 1.00 2.50
8 Kevin Garnett 3.00 8.00
9 Jim Jackson .60 1.50
10 Anthony Mason .75 2.00
11 Antonio McDyess 1.00 2.50
12 Alonzo Mourning 1.50 4.00
13 Gheorghe Muresan .60 1.50
14 Dikembe Mutombo 1.50 4.00
15 Shaquille O'Neal 4.00 10.00
16 Isaiah Rider .75 2.00
17 Clifford Robinson 1.00 2.50
18 David Robinson 2.00 5.00
19 Dennis Rodman 2.50 6.00
20 Clarence Weatherspoon .60 1.50

1996-97 SkyBox Premium Larger Than Life
COMPLETE SET (18) 350.00 700.00
SER.1 STATED ODDS 1:180 HOBBY
B1 Shareef Abdur-Rahim 5.00 12.00
B2 Marcus Camby 5.00 12.00
B3 Kevin Garnett 25.00 60.00
B4 Anfernee Hardaway 30.00 80.00
B5 Grant Hill 12.00 30.00
B6 Allen Iverson 75.00 200.00
B7 Michael Jordan 500.00 1,000.00
B8 Shawn Kemp 12.00 30.00
B9 Stephon Marbury 15.00 40.00
B10 Jamal Mashburn 8.00 20.00
B11 Antonio McDyess 8.00 20.00
B12 Alonzo Mourning 12.00 30.00
B13 Dikembe Mutombo 12.00 30.00
B14 Hakeem Olajuwon 15.00 40.00
B15 Shaquille O'Neal 40.00 100.00
B16 Dennis Rodman 20.00 50.00
B17 Jerry Stackhouse 10.00 25.00
B18 Damon Stoudamire 8.00 20.00

1996-97 SkyBox Premium Net Sets
COMPLETE SET (20) 75.00 200.00
SER.2 STATED ODDS 1:48 HOBBY
1 Vin Baker 2.00 5.00
2 Clyde Drexler 4.00 10.00
3 Patrick Ewing 4.00 10.00
4 Anfernee Hardaway 6.00 15.00
5 Grant Hill 4.00 10.00
6 Juwan Howard 2.50 6.00
7 Allen Iverson 20.00 50.00
8 Michael Jordan 75.00 200.00
9 Shawn Kemp 4.00 10.00
10 Jason Kidd 4.00 10.00
11 Karl Malone 5.00 12.00
12 Stephon Marbury 8.00 20.00
13 Alonzo Mourning 4.00 10.00
14 Hakeem Olajuwon 5.00 12.00
15 Shaquille O'Neal 10.00 25.00
16 Scottie Pippen 6.00 15.00
17 David Robinson 5.00 12.00
18 Joe Smith 2.00 5.00
19 Damon Stoudamire 2.50 6.00
20 Chris Webber 3.00 8.00

1996-97 SkyBox Premium New Editions
COMPLETE SET (10) 200.00 500.00
SER.2 STATED ODDS 1:36 RETAIL
1 Shareef Abdur-Rahim 2.50 6.00
2 Ray Allen 15.00 40.00
3 Kobe Bryant 150.00 400.00
4 Marcus Camby 2.50 6.00
5 Allen Iverson 30.00 80.00
6 Kerry Kittles 1.50 4.00
7 Matt Maloney 1.25 3.00
8 Stephon Marbury 10.00 25.00
9 Steve Nash 15.00 40.00
10 Samaki Walker 1.25 3.00

1996-97 SkyBox Premium Rookie Prevue
COMPLETE SET (18) 125.00 300.00
SER.1 STATED ODDS 1:54 HOBBY/RETAIL
R1 Shareef Abdur-Rahim 2.50 6.00
R2 Ray Allen 8.00 20.00
R3 Kobe Bryant 100.00 250.00
R4 Marcus Camby 2.50 6.00
R5 Erick Dampier 1.50 4.00
R6 Tony Delk 1.50 4.00
R7 Brian Evans 1.00 2.50
R8 Todd Fuller 1.00 2.50
R9 Allen Iverson 20.00 50.00
R10 Kerry Kittles 1.50 4.00
R11 Stephon Marbury 5.00 12.00
R12 Steve Nash 10.00 25.00
R13 Vitaly Potapenko 1.25 3.00
R14 Roy Rogers 1.25 3.00
R15 Antoine Walker 2.50 6.00
R16 Samaki Walker 1.25 3.00
R17 John Wallace 1.25 3.00
R18 Lorenzen Wright 1.25 3.00

1996-97 SkyBox Premium Standouts
COMPLETE SET (9) 50.00 120.00
SER.1 STATED ODDS 1:180 RETAIL
SO1 Grant Hill 10.00 25.00
SO2 Juwan Howard 6.00 15.00
SO3 Jason Kidd 10.00 25.00
SO4 Reggie Miller 12.00 30.00
SO5 Shaquille O'Neal 25.00 60.00
SO6 Gary Payton 10.00 25.00
SO7 Scottie Pippen 15.00 40.00
SO8 Mitch Richmond 8.00 20.00
SO9 Joe Smith 5.00 12.00

1996-97 SkyBox Premium Thunder and Lightning
COMPLETE SET (10) 40.00 100.00
SER.2 STATED ODDS 1:144 HOBBY/RETAIL
1 M.Jordan/S.Pippen 40.00 100.00
2 K.Johnson/D.Manning 2.00 5.00
3 G.Hill/J.Dumars 3.00 8.00
4 L.Sprewell/J.Smith 2.00 5.00
5 C.Barkley/H.Olajuwon 5.00 12.00
6 V.Baker/G.Robinson 2.00 5.00
7 P.Ewing/L.Johnson 3.00 8.00
8 S.Kemp/G.Payton 3.00 8.00
9 K.Malone/J.Stockton 4.00 10.00
10 J.Howard/C.Webber 2.50 6.00

1996-97 SkyBox Premium Triple Threats
COMPLETE SET (9) 60.00 150.00
SPs: SER.1 STATED
ODDS 1:720 HOB/RET 1.50 4.00
*RUBY: 10X TO 25X BASE HI
SPs DO NOT HAVE RUBY PARALLEL
TT1 Chris Mullin 2.00 5.00
TT2 Joe Smith 1.25 3.00
TT3 Latrell Sprewell 1.50 4.00
TT4 Avery Johnson 1.25 3.00
TT5 Sean Elliott 1.50 4.00
TT6 David Robinson 3.00 8.00
TT7 John Stockton 3.00 8.00
TT8 Karl Malone 3.00 8.00
TT9 Jeff Hornacek 1.25 3.00
TT10 Dennis Rodman SP 4.00 10.00
TT11 Michael Jordan SP 60.00 150.00
TT12 Scottie Pippen SP 4.00 10.00

1997-98 SkyBox Premium
COMPLETE SET (250) 50.00 90.00
COMPLETE SERIES 1 (125) 12.50 25.00
COMPLETE SERIES 2 (125) 40.00 70.00
TS SUBSET 1:4 HOB/RET
1 Grant Hill .40 1.00
2 Matt Maloney .15 .40
3 Vinny Del Negro .20 .50
4 Kevin Willis .20 .50
5 Mark Jackson .20 .50
6 Ray Allen .50 1.25
7 Derrick Coleman .20 .50
8 Isaiah Rider .20 .50
9 Rod Strickland .20 .50
10 Danny Ferry .15 .40
11 Antonio Davis .20 .50
12 Glenn Robinson .25 .60
13 Cedric Ceballos .20 .50
14 Sean Elliott .20 .50
15 Walt Williams .20 .50
16 Glen Rice .25 .60
17 Clyde Drexler .40 1.00
18 Sherman Douglas .15 .40
19 Othella Harrington .15 .40
20 John Stockton .50 1.25
21 Priest Lauderdale .15 .40
22 Khalid Reeves .15 .40
23 Kobe Bryant 2.50 6.00
24 Vin Baker UER .20 .50
25 Steve Nash .60 1.50
26 Jeff Hornacek .25 .60
27 Tyrone Corbin .15 .40
28 Charles Barkley .60 1.50
29 Michael Jordan 2.50 6.00
30 Latrell Sprewell .30 .75
31 Anfernee Hardaway .60 1.50
32 Steve Kerr .30 .75
33 Joe Smith .20 .50
34 Jermaine O'Neal .30 .75
35 Ron Mercer RC .30 .75
36 Antonio McDyess .25 .60
37 Patrick Ewing .40 1.00
38 Avery Johnson .20 .50
39 Toni Kukoc .30 .75
40 Sam Perkins .20 .50
41 Voshon Lenard .15 .40
42 Detlef Schrempf .20 .50
43 Horace Grant .25 .60
44 Luc Longley .25 .60
45 Todd Fuller .15 .40
46 Tim Hardaway .30 .75
47 Nick Anderson .20 .50
48 Scottie Pippen .60 1.50
49 Lindsey Hunter .15 .40
50 Shawn Kemp .40 1.00
51 Larry Johnson .30 .75
52 Shawn Bradley .15 .40
53 Martin Muursepp .20 .50
54 Jamal Mashburn .20 .50
55 John Starks .25 .60
56 Rony Seikaly .20 .50
57 Gary Payton .40 1.00
58 Juwan Howard .20 .50
59 Vitaly Potapenko .15 .40
60 Reggie Miller .50 1.25
61 Alonzo Mourning .40 1.00
62 Roy Rogers .15 .40
63 Antoine Walker .25 .60
64 Joe Dumars .30 .75
65 Allan Houston .25 .60
66 Hersey Hawkins .20 .50
67 Dell Curry .20 .50
68 Tony Delk .20 .50
69 Mookie Blaylock .25 .60
70 Derek Harper .20 .50
71 Loy Vaught .20 .50
72 Tom Gugliotta .20 .50
73 Mitch Richmond .30 .75
74 Dikembe Mutombo .40 1.00
75 Tony Battie RC .25 .60
76 Derek Fisher .25 .60
77 Jason Kidd .40 1.00
78 Shareef Abdur-Rahim .25 .60
79 Tracy McGrady RC 1.25 3.00
80 Anthony Mason .20 .50
81 Mario Elie .15 .40
82 Karl Malone .50 1.25
83 Mark Price .25 .60
84 Steve Smith .20 .50
85 LaPhonso Ellis .20 .50
86 Robert Horry .25 .60
87 Wesley Person .20 .50
88 Marcus Camby .25 .60
89 Antonio Daniels RC .25 .60
90 Eddie Jones .25 .60
91 Gary Trent .15 .40
92 Danny Fortson RC .25 .60
93 Chris Childs .15 .40
94 David Robinson .50 1.25
95 Bryant Reeves .15 .40
96 Chris Webber .30 .75
97 P.J. Brown .15 .40
98 Tyrone Hill .20 .50
99 Dale Davis .20 .50
100 Allen Iverson .75 2.00
101 Jerry Stackhouse .25 .60
102 Arvydas Sabonis .30 .75
103 Damon Stoudamire .25 .60
104 Tim Thomas RC .30 .75
105 Christian Laettner .25 .60
106 Robert Pack .15 .40
107 Lorenzen Wright .15 .40
108 Olden Polynice .15 .40
109 Terrell Brandon .20 .50
110 Theo Ratliff .20 .50
111 Kevin Garnett .60 1.50
112 Tim Duncan RC 1.50 4.00
113 Bryon Russell .15 .40
114 Chauncey Billups RC .75 2.00
115 Dale Ellis .20 .50
116 Shaquille O'Neal .75 2.00
117 Keith Van Horn RC .40 1.00
118 Kenny Anderson .20 .50
119 Dennis Rodman .60 1.50
120 Hakeem Olajuwon .50 1.25
121 Stephon Marbury .30 .75
122 Kendall Gill .20 .50
123 Kerry Kittles .20 .50
124 Checklist .15 .40
125 Checklist .15 .40
126 Anthony Johnson RC .25 .60
127 Chris Anstey RC .15 .40
128 Dean Garrett .15 .40
129 Rik Smits .20 .50
130 Tracy Murray .15 .40
131 Charles O'Bannon RC .20 .50
132 Eldridge Recasner .15 .40
133 Johnny Taylor RC .15 .40
134 Priest Lauderdale .15 .40
135 Rod Strickland .20 .50
136 Alan Henderson .20 .50
137 Austin Croshere RC .20 .50
138 Buck Williams .15 .40
139 Clifford Robinson .20 .50
140 Darrell Armstrong .15 .40
141 Dennis Scott .20 .50
142 Carl Herrera .15 .40
143 Maurice Taylor RC .20 .50
144 Chris Gatling .15 .40
145 Alvin Williams RC .25 .60
146 Antonio McDyess .25 .60
147 Chauncey Billups .40 1.00
148 George McCloud .15 .40
149 George Lynch .15 .40
150 John Thomas RC .15 .40
151 Jayson Williams .15 .40
152 Otis Thorpe .20 .50
153 Serge Zwikker RC .15 .40
154 Chris Crawford RC .25 .60
155 Muggsy Bogues .20 .50
156 Mark Jackson .20 .50
157 Dontonio Wingfield .15 .40
158 Rodrick Rhodes RC .20 .50
159 Sam Cassell .20 .50
160 Hubert Davis .15 .40
161 Clarence Weatherspoon .15 .40
162 Eddie Johnson .15 .40
163 Jacque Vaughn RC .20 .50
164 Mark Price .25 .60
165 Terry Dehere .15 .40
166 Travis Knight .15 .40
167 Charles Smith RC .20 .50
168 David Wesley .20 .50
169 David Wingate .15 .40
170 Todd Day .20 .50
171 Adonal Foyle RC .20 .50
172 Chris Mills .15 .40
173 Paul Grant RC .15 .40
174 Adam Keefe .15 .40
175 Erick Dampier UER .20 .50
176 Ervin Johnson .15 .40
177 Lamond Murray .15 .40
178 Vlade Divac .25 .60
179 Bobby Phills .20 .50
180 Brian Williams .20 .50
181 Chris Dudley .15 .40
182 Tyrone Hill .20 .50
183 Donyell Marshall .15 .40
184 Kevin Gamble .15 .40
185 Scot Pollard RC .20 .50
186 Cherokee Parks .15 .40
187 Terry Mills .15 .40
188 Glen Rice .25 .60
189 Shawn Respert .15 .40
190 Terrell Brandon .20 .50
191 Keith Closs RC .25 .60
192 Tariq Abdul-Wahad RC .20 .50
193 Wesley Person .20 .50
194 Chuck Person .20 .50
195 Derek Anderson RC .25 .60
196 Jon Barry .15 .40
197 Chris Mullin .30 .75
198 Ed Gray RC .20 .50
199 Charlie Ward .20 .50
200 Kelvin Cato RC .20 .50
201 Michael Finley .25 .60
202 Rick Fox .25 .60
203 Scott Burrell .15 .40
204 Vin Baker .20 .50
205 Eric Snow .15 .40
206 Isaac Austin .15 .40
207 Keith Booth RC .20 .50
208 Brian Grant .20 .50
209 Chris Webber .30 .75
210 Eric Williams .15 .40
211 Jim Jackson .20 .50
212 Anthony Parker RC .20 .50
213 Brevin Knight RC .25 .60
214 Cory Alexander .15 .40
215 James Robinson .15 .40
216 Bobby Jackson RC .30 .75
217 Bo Outlaw .15 .40
218 God Shammgod RC .25 .60
219 James Cotton RC .25 .60
220 Jud Buechler .15 .40
221 Shandon Anderson .15 .40
222 Kevin Johnson .25 .60
223 Chris Morris .15 .40
224 Shareef Abdur-Rahim TS .50 1.25
225 Ray Allen TS 1.00 2.50
226 Kobe Bryant TS 5.00 12.00
227 Marcus Camby TS .50 1.25
228 Antonio Daniels TS .50 1.25
229 Tim Duncan TS 3.00 8.00
230 Kevin Garnett TS 1.25 3.00
231 Anfernee Hardaway TS 1.25 3.00
232 Grant Hill TS .75 2.00
233 Allen Iverson TS 1.50 4.00
234 Bobby Jackson TS .60 1.50
235 Michael Jordan TS 5.00 12.00
236 Shawn Kemp TS .75 2.00
237 Karl Malone TS .75 2.00
238 Stephon Marbury TS .60 1.50
239 Hakeem Olajuwon TS 1.00 2.50
240 Shaquille O'Neal TS 1.50 4.00
241 Gary Payton TS .75 2.00
242 Scottie Pippen TS 1.25 3.00
243 David Robinson TS 1.00 2.50
244 Dennis Rodman TS 1.25 3.00
245 Jerry Stackhouse TS .50 1.25
246 Damon Stoudamire TS .50 1.25
247 Keith Van Horn TS .75 2.00
248 Antoine Walker TS .50 1.25
249 Grant Hill CL .40 1.00
250 Hakeem Olajuwon CL .50 1.25
NNO A.Iverson Shoe Bronze .50 1.25
NNO A.Iverson Shoe Gold 1.50 4.00
NNO A.Iverson Shoe Emerald 12.00 30.00
NNO A.Iverson Shoe Ruby 5.00 12.00
NNO A.Iverson Shoe Silver .75 2.00

1997-98 SkyBox Premium Star Rubies
*STARS: 100X TO 250X BASE CARD HI
*RCs: 50X TO 100X BASE HI
*TS: SAME VALUE AS BASE RUBY
STATED PRINT RUN 50 SERIAL #'d SETS
1 Grant Hill 300.00 600.00
6 Ray Allen 150.00 400.00
12 Glenn Robinson 75.00 200.00
17 Clyde Drexler 125.00 250.00
20 John Stockton 300.00 600.00
23 Kobe Bryant 15,000.00 30,000.00
25 Steve Nash 300.00 600.00
28 Charles Barkley 2,000.00 4,000.00
29 Michael Jordan 40,000.00 60,000.00
30 Latrell Sprewell 200.00 500.00
31 Anfernee Hardaway 600.00 1,200.00
32 Steve Kerr 75.00 200.00
36 Antonio McDyess 100.00 250.00
37 Patrick Ewing 500.00 1,000.00
46 Tim Hardaway 75.00 150.00
48 Scottie Pippen 600.00 1,200.00
50 Shawn Kemp 200.00 500.00
51 Larry Johnson 100.00 250.00
54 Jamal Mashburn 60.00 150.00
57 Gary Payton 200.00 500.00
58 Juwan Howard 100.00 250.00
60 Reggie Miller 400.00 800.00
63 Antoine Walker 75.00 200.00
72 Tom Gugliotta 60.00 150.00
77 Jason Kidd 125.00 300.00
79 Tracy McGrady 500.00 1,000.00
82 Karl Malone 300.00 600.00
90 Eddie Jones 100.00 250.00
94 David Robinson 500.00 1,000.00
96 Chris Webber 400.00 800.00
100 Allen Iverson 2,000.00 4,000.00
101 Jerry Stackhouse 125.00 300.00
102 Arvydas Sabonis 125.00 300.00
103 Damon Stoudamire 75.00 200.00
111 Kevin Garnett 500.00 1,000.00
112 Tim Duncan 3,000.00 6,000.00
114 Chauncey Billups 125.00 300.00
116 Shaquille O'Neal 500.00 1,000.00
117 Keith Van Horn 100.00 250.00
119 Dennis Rodman 2,000.00 4,000.00
120 Hakeem Olajuwon 400.00 800.00
121 Stephon Marbury 150.00 400.00
146 Antonio McDyess 100.00 250.00
147 Chauncey Billups 125.00 300.00
201 Michael Finley 75.00 200.00
209 Chris Webber 400.00 800.00

1997-98 SkyBox Premium And One
COMPLETE SET (10) 20.00 50.00
SER.1 STATED ODDS 1:96 HOB/RET
1 Shawn Kemp 2.50 6.00
2 Hakeem Olajuwon 3.00 8.00
3 Charles Barkley 4.00 10.00
4 Antoine Walker 1.50 4.00
5 Dennis Rodman 4.00 10.00
6 Tim Duncan 10.00 25.00
7 Marcus Camby 1.50 4.00
8 Keith Van Horn 2.50 6.00
9 Shareef Abdur-Rahim 1.50 4.00
10 Michael Jordan 20.00 50.00

1997-98 SkyBox Premium And One Wrappers
*WRAPPERS: .4X TO 1X BASIC

1997-98 SkyBox Premium Autographics
ALL MCGRADY CARDS ARE CEN.MARKS
ALL R.WALLACE CARDS ARE CEN.MARKS
STATED ODDS 1:24 HOOPS 1; 1:144 HOOPS 2
STATED ODDS 1:96 METAL; 1:72 MET.CHAMP
STATED ODDS 1:72 SKYBOX; 1:60 E-X
STATED ODDS 1:120 Z-FORCE 1,2
CARDS LISTED BELOW ALPHABETICALLY
1 Shareef Abdur-Rahim 10.00 25.00
2 Cory Alexander 3.00 8.00
3 Kenny Anderson 5.00 12.00
4 Nick Anderson 4.00 10.00
5 Stacey Augmon 6.00 15.00
6 Isaac Austin 3.00 8.00
7 Vin Baker 10.00 25.00
8 Charles Barkley 800.00 1,500.00
9 Dana Barros 4.00 10.00
10 Brent Barry 4.00 10.00
11 Tony Battie 5.00 12.00
12 Travis Best 4.00 10.00
13 Corie Blount 3.00 8.00
14 P.J. Brown 4.00 10.00
15 Randy Brown 5.00 12.00
16 Jud Buechler 10.00 25.00
17 Marcus Camby 8.00 20.00
18 Elden Campbell 5.00 12.00
19 Chris Carr 4.00 10.00
20 Kelvin Cato 5.00 12.00
21 Duane Causwell 4.00 10.00
22 Rex Chapman 10.00 25.00
23 Calbert Cheaney 4.00 10.00
24 Randolph Childress 4.00 10.00
25 Derrick Coleman 10.00 25.00
26 Austin Croshere 5.00 12.00
27 Dell Curry 5.00 12.00
28 Ben Davis 8.00 20.00
29 Mark Davis 4.00 10.00
30 Andrew DeClercq 3.00 8.00
31 Tony Delk 4.00 10.00
32 Vlade Divac 8.00 25.00
33 Clyde Drexler 40.00 100.00
34 Joe Dumars 15.00 40.00
35 Howard Eisley 4.00 10.00
36 Danny Ferry 4.00 10.00
37 Michael Finley 12.00 30.00
38 Derek Fisher 10.00 25.00
39 Danny Fortson 8.00 20.00
40 Todd Fuller 4.00 10.00
41 Chris Gatling 4.00 10.00
42 Matt Geiger 4.00 10.00
43 Brian Grant 4.00 10.00
44 Tom Gugliotta 6.00 15.00
45 Tim Hardaway 20.00 50.00
46 Ron Harper 30.00 80.00
47 Othella Harrington 4.00 10.00
48 Grant Hill 100.00 250.00
49 Tyrone Hill 4.00 10.00
50 Allan Houston 15.00 40.00
51 Juwan Howard 10.00 25.00
52 Lindsey Hunter 8.00 20.00
53 Bobby Hurley 6.00 15.00
54 Jim Jackson 5.00 12.00
55 Avery Johnson 4.00 10.00
56 Eddie Johnson 4.00 10.00
57 Ervin Johnson 4.00 10.00
58 Larry Johnson 30.00 80.00
59 Popeye Jones 4.00 10.00
60 Adam Keefe 4.00 10.00
61 Steve Kerr 20.00 50.00
62 Kerry Kittles 10.00 25.00
63 Brevin Knight 5.00 12.00
64 Travis Knight 4.00 10.00
65 George Lynch 4.00 10.00
66 Don MacLean 4.00 10.00
67 Stephon Marbury 40.00 100.00
68 Donny Marshall 5.00 12.00
69 Walter McCarty 5.00 12.00
70 Antonio McDyess 12.00 30.00
72 Ron Mercer 8.00 20.00
73 Reggie Miller 200.00 500.00
74 Chris Mills 4.00 10.00
75 Sam Mitchell 5.00 12.00
76 Chris Morris 4.00 10.00
77 Alonzo Mourning 50.00 120.00
78 Chris Mullin 15.00 40.00
79 Dikembe Mutombo 40.00 100.00
80 Anthony Parker 5.00 12.00
81 Sam Perkins 5.00 12.00
82 Elliot Perry 4.00 10.00
83 Bobby Phills 6.00 15.00
84 Eric Piatkowski 4.00 10.00
85 Scottie Pippen 200.00 500.00
86 Vitaly Potapenko 4.00 10.00
87 Brent Price 4.00 10.00
88 Theo Ratliff 4.00 10.00
89 Glen Rice 10.00 25.00
90 Glenn Robinson 8.00 20.00
91 Dennis Rodman 200.00 500.00
92 Roy Rogers 4.00 10.00
93 Malik Rose 4.00 10.00
94 Joe Smith 10.00 25.00
95 Tony Smith 3.00 8.00
96 Eric Snow 5.00 12.00
97 Jerry Stackhouse Pistons 12.00 30.00
98 Jerry Stackhouse Sixers 12.00 30.00
99 John Starks 15.00 40.00
100 Bryant Stith 4.00 10.00
101 Erick Strickland 4.00 10.00
102 Rod Strickland 15.00 40.00
103 Nick Van Exel 20.00 50.00
104 Keith Van Horn 10.00 25.00
105 David Vaughn 3.00 8.00
106 Jacque Vaughn 4.00 10.00
107 Antoine Walker 6.00 15.00
108 Samaki Walker 4.00 10.00
109 Clarence Weatherspoon 4.00 10.00
110 David Wesley 4.00 10.00
111 Dominique Wilkins 25.00 60.00
112 Gerald Wilkins 4.00 10.00
113 Eric Williams 4.00 10.00
114 John Williams 4.00 10.00
115 Lorenzo Williams 3.00 8.00
116 Monty Williams 3.00 8.00
117 Scott Williams 4.00 10.00
118 Walt Williams 4.00 10.00
119 Lorenzen Wright 4.00 10.00

1997-98 SkyBox Premium Autographics Century Marks
*CENTURY MARKS: 1.25X TO 3X VALUE
STATED PRINT RUN 100 HAND #'d SETS
1 Shareef Abdur-Rahim 60.00 150.00
4 Nick Anderson 125.00 300.00
7 Vin Baker 60.00 150.00
8 Charles Barkley 2,500.00 5,000.00
14 P.J. Brown 40.00 100.00
22 Rex Chapman 75.00 200.00
23 Calbert Cheaney 40.00 100.00
27 Dell Curry 150.00 400.00
32 Vlade Divac 60.00 150.00
33 Clyde Drexler 200.00 500.00
34 Joe Dumars 75.00 200.00
37 Michael Finley 60.00 150.00
38 Derek Fisher 60.00 150.00
42 Matt Geiger 40.00 100.00
44 Tom Gugliotta 25.00 60.00
45 Tim Hardaway 75.00 200.00
46 Ron Harper 100.00 250.00
48 Grant Hill 500.00 1,000.00
50 Allan Houston 90.00 175.00
53 Bobby Hurley 20.00 50.00
58 Larry Johnson 75.00 200.00
61 Steve Kerr 100.00 250.00
62 Kerry Kittles 25.00 60.00
67 Stephon Marbury 300.00 600.00
69 Walter McCarty 20.00 50.00
70 Antonio McDyess 50.00 120.00
71 Tracy McGrady 600.00 1,200.00
73 Reggie Miller 1,500.00 3,000.00
77 Alonzo Mourning 300.00 600.00
78 Chris Mullin 300.00 600.00
79 Dikembe Mutombo 200.00 500.00
85 Scottie Pippen 800.00 1,500.00
89 Glen Rice 60.00 150.00
90 Glenn Robinson 25.00 60.00
91 Dennis Rodman 500.00 1,000.00
96 Eric Snow 25.00 60.00
97 Jerry Stackhouse Pistons 75.00 200.00
98 Jerry Stackhouse Sixers 75.00 200.00
102 Rod Strickland 60.00 150.00
103 Nick Van Exel 125.00 300.00
104 Keith Van Horn 75.00 200.00
107 Antoine Walker 40.00 100.00
108 Rasheed Wallace 500.00 1,000.00
111 Dominique Wilkins 75.00 200.00

1997-98 SkyBox Premium Competitive Advantage
COMPLETE SET (15) 800.00 1,500.00
SER.2 STATED ODDS 1:96 HOB/RET
CA1 Allen Iverson 50.00 120.00
CA2 Kobe Bryant 300.00 600.00
CA3 Michael Jordan 500.00 1,000.00
CA4 Shaquille O'Neal 50.00 120.00
CA5 Stephon Marbury 15.00 40.00
CA6 Shareef Abdur-Rahim 12.00 30.00
CA7 Marcus Camby 10.00 25.00
CA8 Kevin Garnett 30.00 80.00
CA9 Dennis Rodman 40.00 100.00
CA10 Anfernee Hardaway 30.00 80.00
CA11 Ray Allen 25.00 60.00
CA12 Scottie Pippen 30.00 80.00
CA13 Shawn Kemp 15.00 40.00
CA14 Hakeem Olajuwon 25.00 60.00
CA15 John Stockton 30.00 80.00

1997-98 SkyBox Premium Golden Touch
SER.2 STATED ODDS 1:360 HOB/RET
GT1 Michael Jordan 2,000.00 4,000.00
GT2 Allen Iverson 150.00 400.00
GT3 Kobe Bryant 1,000.00 2,000.00
GT4 Shaquille O'Neal 150.00 400.00
GT5 Stephon Marbury 75.00 200.00
GT6 Marcus Camby 40.00 100.00
GT7 Anfernee Hardaway 150.00 400.00
GT8 Kevin Garnett 150.00 400.00
GT9 Shareef Abdur-Rahim 60.00 150.00
GT10 Dennis Rodman 150.00 400.00
GT11 Grant Hill 150.00 400.00
GT12 Kerry Kittles 30.00 80.00
GT13 Antoine Walker 60.00 150.00
GT14 Scottie Pippen 150.00 400.00
GT15 Damon Stoudamire 60.00 150.00

1997-98 SkyBox Premium Jam Pack
COMPLETE SET (15) 20.00 40.00
SER.2 STATED ODDS 1:18 HOB/RET
JP1 Ray Allen 4.00 10.00
JP2 Damon Stoudamire 2.00 5.00
JP3 Shawn Kemp 3.00 8.00
JP4 Hakeem Olajuwon 4.00 10.00
JP5 Jerry Stackhouse 2.00 5.00
JP6 John Wallace 1.25 3.00
JP7 Juwan Howard 1.50 4.00
JP8 David Robinson 4.00 10.00
JP9 Gary Payton 3.00 8.00
JP10 Joe Smith 1.50 4.00
JP11 Charles Barkley 5.00 12.00
JP12 Terrell Brandon 1.50 4.00
JP13 Vin Baker 1.50 4.00
JP14 Antonio McDyess 2.00 5.00
JP15 Tim Duncan 5.00 12.00

1997-98 SkyBox Premium Next Game
COMPLETE SET (15) 5.00 12.00
SER.1 STATED ODDS 1:6 HOB/RET
1 Derek Anderson .30 .75
2 Tony Battie .30 .75
3 Chauncey Billups 1.00 2.50
4 Kelvin Cato .25 .60
5 Austin Croshere .25 .60
6 Antonio Daniels .30 .75
7 Tim Duncan 2.00 5.00
8 Danny Fortson .30 .75
9 Adonal Foyle .25 .60
10 Tracy McGrady 1.50 4.00
11 Ron Mercer .40 1.00
12 Olivier Saint-Jean .25 .60
13 Maurice Taylor .25 .60
14 Tim Thomas .40 1.00
15 Keith Van Horn .50 1.25

1997-98 SkyBox Premium Premium Players
COMPLETE SET (15) 300.00 700.00
SER 1 STATED ODDS 1:192 HOB/RET
1 Michael Jordan 1,000.00 2,000.00
2 Allen Iverson 20.00 50.00
3 Kobe Bryant 400.00 800.00
4 Shaquille O'Neal 20.00 50.00
5 Stephon Marbury 6.00 15.00
6 Marcus Camby 5.00 12.00
7 Anfernee Hardaway 20.00 50.00
8 Kevin Garnett 20.00 50.00
9 Shareef Abdur-Rahim 5.00 12.00
10 Dennis Rodman 20.00 50.00
11 Ray Allen 12.00 30.00
12 Grant Hill 15.00 40.00
13 Kerry Kittles 5.00 12.00
14 Karl Malone 10.00 25.00
15 Scottie Pippen 20.00 50.00

1997-98 SkyBox Premium Reebok Chase Bronze
COMPLETE SET (15) 2.00 5.00
*GOLD: 12.5X TO 3X BRONZE
*SILVER: .5X TO 1.25X BRONZE
ONE PER SER.1 PACK
3 Vinny Del Negro .20 .50
5 Mark Jackson .20 .50
12 Glenn Robinson .25 .60
13 Cedric Ceballos .20 .50
17 Clyde Drexler .40 1.00
38 Avery Johnson .20 .50
41 Voshon Lenard .15 .40
50 Shawn Kemp .40 1.00
81 Mario Elie .15 .40
84 Steve Smith .20 .50
98 Tyrone Hill .20 .50
100 Allen Iverson .75 2.00
106 Robert Pack .15 .40
116 Shaquille O'Neal .75 2.00
118 Kenny Anderson .20 .50

1997-98 SkyBox Premium Rock 'n Fire
COMPLETE SET (10) 20.00 50.00
SER 1 STATED ODDS 1:18 HOB/RET
1 Allen Iverson 5.00 12.00
2 Kobe Bryant 15.00 40.00
3 Shaquille O'Neal 5.00 12.00
4 Stephon Marbury 2.00 5.00
5 Marcus Camby 1.50 4.00
6 Anfernee Hardaway 4.00 10.00
7 Kevin Garnett 4.00 10.00
8 Shareef Abdur-Rahim 1.50 4.00
9 Damon Stoudamire 1.50 4.00
10 Grant Hill 2.50 6.00

1997-98 SkyBox Premium Silky Smooth
COMPLETE SET (10) 300.00 600.00
SER.1 STATED ODDS 1:360 HOB/RET
1 Michael Jordan 200.00 500.00
2 Allen Iverson 15.00 40.00
3 Kobe Bryant 30.00 80.00
4 Shaquille O'Neal 15.00 40.00
5 Stephon Marbury 6.00 15.00
6 Gary Payton 8.00 20.00
7 Anfernee Hardaway 12.00 30.00
8 Kevin Garnett 15.00 40.00
9 Scottie Pippen 20.00 50.00
10 Grant Hill 8.00 20.00

1997-98 SkyBox Premium Star Search
COMPLETE SET (15) 5.00 12.00
SER.2 STATED ODDS 1:6 HOB/RET
SS1 Tim Duncan 2.00 5.00
SS2 Tony Battie .30 .75
SS3 Keith Van Horn .50 1.25
SS4 Antonio Daniels .30 .75
SS5 Chauncey Billups 1.00 2.50
SS6 Ron Mercer .40 1.00
SS7 Tracy McGrady 1.50 4.00
SS8 Danny Fortson .30 .75
SS9 Brevin Knight .30 .75
SS10 Derek Anderson .30 .75
SS11 Bobby Jackson .40 1.00
SS12 Jacque Vaughn .25 .60
SS13 Tim Thomas .40 1.00
SS14 Austin Croshere .25 .60
SS15 Kelvin Cato .25 .60

1997-98 SkyBox Premium Thunder and Lightning
COMPLETE SET (15) 1,250.00 2,500.00
SER.2 STATED ODDS 1:192 HOB/RET
TL1 Stephon Marbury 12.00 30.00
TL2 Shareef Abdur-Rahim 10.00 25.00
TL3 Shaquille O'Neal 50.00 120.00
TL4 Scottie Pippen 50.00 120.00
TL5 Michael Jordan 1,000.00 2,000.00
TL6 Marcus Camby 10.00 25.00
TL7 Kobe Bryant 400.00 800.00
TL8 Kevin Garnett 50.00 120.00
TL9 Kerry Kittles 8.00 20.00
TL10 Grant Hill 15.00 40.00
TL11 Dennis Rodman 50.00 120.00
TL12 Damon Stoudamire 10.00 25.00
TL13 Antoine Walker 10.00 25.00
TL14 Anfernee Hardaway 40.00 100.00
TL15 Allen Iverson 50.00 120.00

1998-99 SkyBox Premium
COMPLETE SET (265) 60.00 150.00
COMPLETE SET w/o SP (225) 20.00 50.00
COMPLETE SERIES 1 (125) 12.00 30.00
COMPLETE SERIES 2 (140) 50.00 120.00
RC STATED ODDS 1:4 PACKS
1 Tim Duncan 1.00 2.50
2 Voshon Lenard .25 .60
3 John Starks .40 1.00
4 Juwan Howard .30 .75
5 Michael Finley .40 1.00
6 Bobby Jackson .30 .75
7 Glenn Robinson .40 1.00

8 Antonio McDyess .30 .75
9 Eric Williams .25 .60
10 Zydrunas Ilgauskas .40 1.00
11 Terrell Brandon .30 .75
12 Shandon Anderson .25 .60
13 Rod Strickland .30 .75
14 Dennis Rodman 1.00 2.50
15 Clarence Weatherspoon .25 .60
16 P.J. Brown .25 .60
17 Anfernee Hardaway 1.00 2.50
18 Dikembe Mutombo .60 1.50
19 Patrick Ewing .60 1.50
20 Scottie Pippen 1.00 2.50
21 Shaquille O'Neal 1.50 4.00
22 Donyell Marshall .25 .60
23 Michael Jordan 4.00 10.00
24 Mark Price .40 1.00
25 Jim Jackson .25 .60
26 Isaiah Rider .30 .75
27 Eddie Jones .40 1.00
28 Detlef Schrempf .40 1.00
29 Corliss Williamson .25 .60
30 Bo Outlaw .25 .60
31 Allen Iverson 1.00 2.50
32 Luc Longley .30 .75
33 Theo Ratliff .30 .75
34 Antoine Walker .40 1.00
35 Lamond Murray .25 .60
36 Avery Johnson .30 .75
37 John Stockton .75 2.00
38 David Wesley .25 .60
39 Elden Campbell .25 .60
40 Grant Hill .60 1.50
41 Sam Cassell .30 .75
42 Tracy McGrady .60 1.50
43 Glen Rice .40 1.00
44 Kobe Bryant 3.00 8.00
45 John Wallace .25 .60
46 Bobby Phills .25 .60
47 Jerry Stackhouse .40 1.00
48 Stephon Marbury .50 1.25
49 Jeff Hornacek .30 .75
50 Tom Gugliotta .30 .75
51 Joe Dumars .40 1.00
52 Johnny Newman .25 .60
53 Kevin Garnett 1.00 2.50
54 Dennis Scott .25 .60
55 Anthony Mason .30 .75
56 Rodney Rogers .25 .60
57 Bryon Russell .25 .60
58 Maurice Taylor .25 .60
59 Mookie Blaylock .30 .75
60 Shawn Bradley .25 .60
61 Matt Maloney .25 .60
62 Karl Malone .75 2.00
63 Larry Johnson .60 1.50
64 Calbert Cheaney .25 .60
65 Steve Smith .30 .75
66 Toni Kukoc .40 1.00
67 Reggie Miller .75 2.00
68 Jayson Williams .25 .60
69 Gary Payton .60 1.50
70 Sean Elliott .40 1.00
71 Charles Barkley 1.00 2.50
72 Tim Hardaway .50 1.25
73 Rasheed Wallace .50 1.25
74 Tariq Abdul-Wahad .25 .60
75 Kenny Anderson .30 .75
76 Chris Mullin .50 1.25
77 Keith Van Horn .40 1.00
78 Hersey Hawkins .25 .60
79 Ron Mercer .30 .75
80 Rik Smits .30 .75
81 David Robinson .75 2.00
82 Derek Anderson .30 .75
83 Danny Fortson .25 .60
84 Jason Kidd .60 1.50
85 Chauncey Billups .50 1.25
86 Chris Anstey .25 .60
87 Hakeem Olajuwon .75 2.00
88 Bryant Reeves .25 .60
89 Anthony Johnson .25 .60
90 Shawn Kemp .60 1.50
91 Brevin Knight .25 .60
92 Ray Allen .60 1.50
93 Tim Thomas .30 .75
94 Jalen Rose .30 .75
95 Kerry Kittles .30 .75
96 Vin Baker .30 .75
97 Shareef Abdur-Rahim .40 1.00
98 Alonzo Mourning .60 1.50
99 Joe Smith .30 .75
100 Damon Stoudamire .40 1.00
101 Alan Henderson .25 .60
102 Walter McCarty .25 .60
103 Vlade Divac .40 1.00
104 Wesley Person .25 .60
105 A.C. Green .30 .75
106 Malik Sealy .25 .60
107 Carl Thomas .25 .60
108 Brent Price .25 .60
109 Mark Jackson .30 .75
110 Lorenzen Wright .25 .60
111 Derek Fisher .30 .75
112 Michael Smith .25 .60
113 Tyrone Hill .25 .60
114 Cherokee Parks .25 .60
115 Kendall Gill .30 .75
116 Darrell Armstrong .25 .60
117 Derrick Coleman .30 .75
118 Rex Chapman .30 .75
119 Arvydas Sabonis .40 1.00
120 Billy Owens .30 .75
121 Sam Perkins .25 .60
122 Gary Trent .25 .60
123 Sam Mack .25 .60
124 Tracy Murray .25 .60
125 Allan Houston .40 1.00
126 Mitch Richmond .50 1.25
127 Carl Herrera .25 .60
128 Ron Harper .40 1.00
129 Gary Trent .25 .60
130 Chris Webber .50 1.25
131 Antonio Daniels .25 .60
132 Charles Oakley .30 .75
133 Marcus Camby .30 .75
134 Tony Battie .25 .60
135 Otis Thorpe .25 .60
136 Dale Davis .25 .60
137 Chuck Person .30 .75
138 Ervin Johnson .25 .60
139 Jamal Mashburn .40 1.00
140 Brian Grant .25 .60
141 Chris Mills .25 .60
142 Doug Christie .30 .75
143 George McCloud .25 .60
144 Todd Fuller .25 .60
145 Jerome Williams .25 .60
146 Chauncey Billups .50 1.25
147 Dean Garrett .25 .60
148 Robert Pack .25 .60
149 Clarence Weatherspoon .25 .60
150 Tim Legler .25 .60
151 Bob Sura .25 .60
152 B.J. Armstrong .25 .60
153 Charlie Ward .25 .60
154 Rony Seikaly .25 .60
155 Chris Carr .25 .60
156 Eldridge Recasner .25 .60
157 Michael Stewart .25 .60
158 Jim McIlvaine .25 .60
159 Adam Keefe .25 .60
160 Antonio Davis .25 .60
161 Lawrence Funderburke .25 .60
162 Greg Ostertag .25 .60
163 Dan Majerle .40 1.00
164 Dale Ellis .25 .60
165 Greg Anthony .25 .60
166 Chris Whitney .25 .60
167 Eric Piatkowski .25 .60
168 Tom Gugliotta .30 .75
169 Luc Longley .30 .75
170 Antonio McDyess .30 .75
171 George Lynch .25 .60
172 Dell Curry .25 .60
173 Johnny Newman .25 .60
174 Christian Laettner .30 .75
175 Steve Kerr .30 .75
176 Popeye Jones .25 .60
177 Brent Barry .30 .75
178 Billy Owens .30 .75
179 Cherokee Parks .25 .60
180 Derek Harper .30 .75
181 Howard Eisley .25 .60
182 Matt Geiger .25 .60
183 Darrick Martin .25 .60
184 Isaac Austin .25 .60
185 Dennis Scott .25 .60
186 Derrick Coleman .30 .75
187 Sam Perkins .25 .60
188 Latrell Sprewell .50 1.25
189 Jud Buechler .25 .60
190 Jason Caffey .25 .60
191 Vlade Divac .40 1.00
192 Travis Best .25 .60
193 Loy Vaught .25 .60
194 Mario Elie .25 .60
195 Ed Gray .25 .60
196 Joe Smith .30 .75
197 John Starks .40 1.00
198 Anthony Johnson .25 .60
199 Kurt Thomas .25 .60
200 Chris Dudley .25 .60
201 Shareef Abdur-Rahim NF .40 1.00
202 Ray Allen NF .60 1.50
203 Vin Baker NF .30 .75
204 Charles Barkley NF 1.00 2.50
205 Kobe Bryant NF 3.00 8.00
206 Tim Duncan NF 1.00 2.50
207 Anfernee Hardaway NF 1.00 2.50
208 Grant Hill NF .60 1.50
209 Allen Iverson NF 1.00 2.50
210 Jason Kidd NF .60 1.50
211 Shawn Kemp NF .60 1.50
212 Shaquille O'Neal NF 1.50 4.00
213 Kerry Kittles NF .30 .75
214 Karl Malone NF .75 2.00
215 Stephon Marbury NF .50 1.25
216 Ron Mercer NF .30 .75
217 Reggie Miller NF .75 2.00
218 Kevin Garnett NF 1.00 2.50
219 Gary Payton NF .60 1.50
220 Scottie Pippen NF 1.00 2.50
221 David Robinson NF .75 2.00
222 Hakeem Olajuwon NF .75 2.00
223 Damon Stoudamire NF .40 1.00
224 Keith Van Horn NF .40 1.00
225 Antoine Walker NF .40 1.00
226 Cory Carr RC .60 1.50
227 Cuttino Mobley RC 1.25 3.00
228 Miles Simon RC .75 2.00
229 J.R. Henderson RC .60 1.50
230 Jason Williams RC 2.50 6.00
231 Felipe Lopez RC .50 1.25
232 Shammond Williams RC .60 1.50
233 Ricky Davis RC 1.25 3.00
234 Vince Carter RC 4.00 10.00
235 Antawn Jamison RC 1.25 3.00
236 Ryan Stack RC .25 .60
237 Nazr Mohammed RC .75 2.00
238 Sam Jacobson RC .50 1.25
239 Larry Hughes RC 1.25 3.00
240 Ruben Patterson RC .75 2.00
241 Al Harrington RC 1.00 2.50
242 Ansu Sesay RC .60 1.50
243 Vladimir Stepania RC .75 2.00
244 Matt Harpring RC .75 2.00
245 Andrae Patterson RC .60 1.50
246 Pat Garrity RC .60 1.50
247 Bonzi Wells RC .75 2.00
248 Bryce Drew RC .50 1.25
249 Toby Bailey RC .60 1.50
250 Michael Doleac RC .60 1.50
251 Michael Dickerson RC .75 2.00
252 Peja Stojakovic RC 1.50 4.00
253 Robert Traylor RC .75 2.00
254 Tyronn Lue RC 1.00 2.50
255 Dirk Nowitzki RC 5.00 12.00
256 Raef LaFrentz RC 1.00 2.50
257 Jelani McCoy RC .60 1.50
258 Michael Olowokandi RC 1.00 2.50
259 Brian Skinner RC .60 1.50
260 Keon Clark RC .60 1.50
261 Roshown McLeod RC .50 1.25
262 Mike Bibby RC 1.50 4.00
263 Paul Pierce RC 3.00 8.00
264 Tyson Wheeler RC .60 1.50
265 Corey Benjamin RC .50 1.25

1998-99 SkyBox Premium Star Rubies

*STARS: 60X TO 150X BASE CARD HI
*RCs: 8X TO 20X BASE HI
VETS: STATED PRINT RUN 50 SERIAL #'d SETS
RC's: STATED PRINT RUN 25 SERIAL #'d SETS
M.JORDAN #266 RUBY DOES NOT EXIST

1 Tim Duncan 1,500.00 3,000.00
14 Dennis Rodman 1,500.00 3,000.00
17 Anfernee Hardaway 1,500.00 3,000.00
20 Scottie Pippen 1,500.00 3,000.00
21 Shaquille O'Neal 1,500.00 3,000.00
23 Michael Jordan 20,000.00 40,000.00
27 Eddie Jones 75.00 150.00
31 Allen Iverson 1,500.00 3,000.00
37 John Stockton 200.00 500.00
40 Grant Hill 400.00 800.00
42 Tracy McGrady 600.00 1,200.00
44 Kobe Bryant 15,000.00 30,000.00
51 Joe Dumars 125.00 300.00
53 Kevin Garnett 1,500.00 3,000.00
63 Larry Johnson 75.00 200.00
67 Reggie Miller 200.00 500.00
71 Charles Barkley 300.00 600.00
84 Jason Kidd 150.00 300.00
85 Chauncey Billups 60.00 150.00
87 Hakeem Olajuwon 125.00 250.00
90 Shawn Kemp 500.00 1,000.00
92 Ray Allen 150.00 400.00
98 Alonzo Mourning 125.00 250.00
126 Mitch Richmond 100.00 250.00
130 Chris Webber 200.00 500.00
188 Latrell Sprewell 50.00 120.00
202 Ray Allen NF 150.00 400.00
204 Charles Barkley NF 400.00 800.00
205 Kobe Bryant NF 750.00 1,500.00
206 Tim Duncan NF 80.00 200.00
207 Anfernee Hardaway NF 100.00 200.00
208 Grant Hill NF 100.00 250.00
209 Allen Iverson NF 80.00 200.00
210 Jason Kidd NF 150.00 300.00
211 Shawn Kemp NF 300.00 600.00
212 Shaquille O'Neal NF 150.00 300.00
217 Reggie Miller NF 50.00 120.00
218 Kevin Garnett NF 400.00 800.00
220 Scottie Pippen NF 200.00 400.00
222 Hakeem Olajuwon NF 50.00 120.00
230 Jason Williams 1,500.00 3,000.00
234 Vince Carter 8,000.00 15,000.00
252 Peja Stojakovic 150.00 400.00
254 Tyronn Lue 20.00 50.00
255 Dirk Nowitzki 10,000.00 20,000.00
262 Mike Bibby 125.00 300.00
263 Paul Pierce 3,000.00 6,000.00

1998-99 SkyBox Premium 3D's

COMPLETE SET (15) 2,000.00 4,000.00
SER.1 STATED ODDS 1:96

1 Kobe Bryant 600.00 1,200.00
2 Anfernee Hardaway 100.00 250.00
3 Allen Iverson 125.00 300.00
4 Michael Jordan 2,000.00 4,000.00
5 Stephon Marbury 40.00 100.00
6 Ron Mercer 20.00 50.00
7 Shareef Abdur-Rahim 30.00 80.00
8 Tim Duncan 100.00 250.00
9 Damon Stoudamire 40.00 100.00
10 Kevin Garnett 100.00 250.00
11 Grant Hill 75.00 200.00
12 Scottie Pippen 100.00 250.00
13 Keith Van Horn 20.00 50.00
14 Dennis Rodman 150.00 400.00
15 Shaquille O'Neal 150.00 400.00

1998-99 SkyBox Premium Autographics

STATED ODDS 1:18 E-X; 1:144 HOOPS
STATED ODDS 1:68 METAL; 1:24 MOLTEN
STATED ODDS 1:68 SKYBOX 1; 1:24 SKYBOX 2
STATED ODDS 1:112 THUNDER
IVERSON SIGNED EQUAL BLACK/BLUE

1 Tariq Abdul-Wahad 5.00 12.00
2 Shareef Abdur-Rahim 8.00 20.00
3 Cory Alexander 4.00 10.00
4 Ray Allen 20.00 50.00
5 Kenny Anderson 6.00 15.00
6 Nick Anderson 5.00 12.00
7 Chris Anstey 4.00 10.00
8 Isaac Austin 4.00 10.00
9 Vin Baker 10.00 25.00
10 Dana Barros 4.00 10.00
11 Tony Battie 4.00 10.00
12 Corey Benjamin 4.00 10.00
13 Travis Best 4.00 10.00
14 Mike Bibby 20.00 50.00
15 Chauncey Billups 30.00 80.00
16 Corie Blount 4.00 10.00
17 Terrell Brandon 6.00 15.00
18 P.J. Brown 4.00 10.00
19 Scott Burrell 5.00 12.00
20 Jason Caffey 4.00 10.00
21 Marcus Camby 8.00 20.00
22 Elden Campbell 8.00 20.00
23 Chris Carr 4.00 10.00
24 Cory Carr 4.00 10.00
25 Vince Carter 300.00 600.00
26 Kelvin Cato 4.00 10.00
27 Calbert Cheaney 4.00 10.00
28 Keith Closs 4.00 10.00
29 Antonio Daniels 4.00 10.00
30 Dale Davis 8.00 20.00
31 Ricky Davis 10.00 25.00
32 Andrew DeClercq 4.00 10.00
33 Tony Delk 5.00 12.00
34 Michael Dickerson 6.00 15.00
35 Michael Doleac 5.00 12.00
36 Bryce Drew 4.00 10.00
37 Tim Duncan 1,000.00 2,000.00
38 Howard Eisley 4.00 10.00
39 Danny Ferry 5.00 12.00
40 Derek Fisher 6.00 15.00
41 Danny Fortson 4.00 10.00
42 Adonal Foyle 4.00 10.00
43 Todd Fuller 4.00 10.00
44 Kevin Garnett 400.00 800.00
45 Pat Garrity 5.00 12.00
46 Brian Grant 5.00 12.00
47 Tom Gugliotta 6.00 15.00
48 Tom Hammonds 4.00 10.00
49 Tim Hardaway 20.00 50.00
50 Matt Harpring 6.00 15.00
51 Othella Harrington 4.00 10.00
52 Hersey Hawkins 8.00 20.00
53 Cedric Henderson 4.00 10.00
54 Grant Hill 250.00 500.00
55 Tyrone Hill 4.00 10.00
56 Allan Houston 20.00 50.00
57 Juwan Howard 10.00 25.00
58 Larry Hughes 40.00 100.00
59 Zydrunas Ilgauskas 15.00 30.00
60 Allen Iverson 400.00 800.00
61 Bobby Jackson 4.00 10.00
62 Antawn Jamison 8.00 20.00
63 Anthony Johnson 4.00 10.00
64 Ervin Johnson 4.00 10.00
65 Larry Johnson 30.00 80.00
66 Eddie Jones 20.00 50.00
67 Adam Keefe 4.00 10.00
68 Shawn Kemp 100.00 250.00
69 Steve Kerr 8.00 20.00
70 Jason Kidd 100.00 250.00
71 Kerry Kittles 6.00 15.00
72 Brevin Knight 5.00 12.00
73 Raef LaFrentz 6.00 15.00
74 Felipe Lopez 4.00 10.00
75 George Lynch 4.00 10.00
76 Karl Malone 200.00 500.00
77 Danny Manning 10.00 25.00
78 Stephon Marbury 40.00 100.00
79 Donyell Marshall 5.00 12.00
80 Tony Massenburg 4.00 10.00
81 Walter McCarty 4.00 10.00
82 Jelani McCoy 4.00 10.00
83 Antonio McDyess 8.00 20.00
84 Tracy McGrady 125.00 300.00
85 Ron Mercer 6.00 15.00
86 Sam Mitchell 4.00 10.00
87 Nazr Mohammed 5.00 12.00
88 Alonzo Mourning 100.00 250.00
89 Chris Mullin 40.00 100.00
90 Dikembe Mutombo 60.00 150.00
91 Hakeem Olajuwon 300.00 600.00
92 Michael Olowokandi 6.00 15.00
93 Elliot Perry 4.00 10.00
94 Bobby Phills 4.00 10.00
95 Eric Piatkowski 4.00 10.00
96 Scottie Pippen 500.00 1,000.00
97 Scot Pollard 5.00 12.00
98 Vitaly Potapenko 4.00 10.00
99 Brent Price 4.00 10.00
100 Theo Ratliff 5.00 12.00
101 Eldridge Recasner 4.00 10.00
102 Bryant Reeves 5.00 12.00
103 Glen Rice 8.00 20.00
104 Chris Robinson 4.00 10.00
105 David Robinson 300.00 600.00
106 Glenn Robinson 5.00 12.00
107 Dennis Rodman 400.00 800.00
108 Bryon Russell 5.00 12.00
109 Danny Schayes 4.00 10.00
110 Detlef Schrempf 10.00 25.00
111 Rony Seikaly 5.00 12.00
112 Brian Skinner 4.00 10.00
113 Reggie Slater 4.00 10.00
114 Joe Smith 6.00 15.00
115 Steve Smith 8.00 20.00
116 Rik Smits 6.00 15.00
117 Jerry Stackhouse 12.00 30.00
118 John Starks 5.00 12.00
119 Bryant Stith 4.00 10.00
120 Damon Stoudamire 20.00 50.00
121 Mark Strickland 4.00 10.00
122 Rod Strickland 6.00 15.00
123 Bob Sura 4.00 10.00
124 Tim Thomas 5.00 12.00
125 Robert Traylor 5.00 12.00
126 Gary Trent 4.00 10.00
127 Keith Van Horn 6.00 15.00
128 Jacque Vaughn 4.00 10.00
129 Antoine Walker 6.00 15.00
130 Eric Washington 4.00 10.00
131 Clarence Weatherspoon 4.00 10.00
132 Bonzi Wells 8.00 20.00
133 David Wesley 4.00 10.00
134 Eric Williams 4.00 10.00
135 Jason Williams 125.00 300.00
136 Jayson Williams 4.00 10.00
137 Monty Williams 4.00 10.00
138 Walt Williams 4.00 10.00
139 Lorenzen Wright 4.00 10.00

1998-99 SkyBox Premium Autographics Blue

*BLUE: .75X TO 2X VALUE
STATED PRINT RUN 50 SERIAL #'d SETS

25 Vince Carter 1,000.00 2,000.00
37 Tim Duncan 2,000.00 4,000.00
44 Kevin Garnett 1,000.00 2,000.00
76 Karl Malone 400.00 800.00
84 Tracy McGrady 400.00 800.00
107 Dennis Rodman 1,000.00 2,000.00

1998-99 SkyBox Premium B.P.O.

COMPLETE SET (15) 6.00 15.00
SER.2 STATED ODDS 1:6 HOB/RET

1 Ron Mercer .50 1.25
2 Shareef Abdur-Rahim .60 1.50
3 Stephon Marbury .60 1.50
4 Tim Thomas .50 1.25
5 Tim Duncan 1.50 4.00
6 Mike Bibby 1.25 3.00
7 Ray Allen 1.00 2.50
8 Shawn Kemp 1.00 2.50
9 Vince Carter 3.00 8.00
10 Antoine Walker .60 1.50
11 Raef LaFrentz .75 2.00
12 Damon Stoudamire .60 1.50
13 Keith Van Horn .60 1.50
14 Kerry Kittles .50 1.25
15 Allen Iverson 1.50 4.00

1998-99 SkyBox Premium Fresh Faces

COMPLETE SET (10) 10.00 25.00
SER.2 STATED ODDS 1:36 HOB/RET

1 Mike Bibby 1.25 3.00
2 Vince Carter 3.00 8.00
3 Al Harrington .75 2.00
4 Larry Hughes 1.00 2.50
5 Antawn Jamison 1.00 2.50
6 Raef LaFrentz .75 2.00
7 Michael Olowokandi .75 2.00
8 Paul Pierce 2.50 6.00
9 Robert Traylor .60 1.50
10 Bonzi Wells .60 1.50

1998-99 SkyBox Premium Intimidation Nation

COMPLETE SET (10) 600.00 1,000.00
SER.1 STATED ODDS 1:360

1 Shaquille O'Neal 150.00 400.00
2 Kobe Bryant 500.00 1,000.00
3 Kevin Garnett 100.00 250.00
4 Grant Hill 60.00 150.00
5 Shawn Kemp 50.00 120.00
6 Keith Van Horn 20.00 50.00
7 Antoine Walker 20.00 50.00
8 Michael Jordan 2,000.00 4,000.00
9 Gary Payton 60.00 150.00
10 Tim Duncan 100.00 250.00

1998-99 SkyBox Premium Just Cookin'

COMPLETE SET (10) 2.50 6.00
SER.1 STATED ODDS 1:12

1 Maurice Taylor .40 1.00
2 Brevin Knight .40 1.00
3 Tim Thomas .50 1.25
4 Chauncey Billups .75 2.00
5 Chris Anstey .40 1.00
6 Tracy McGrady 1.00 2.50
7 Zydrunas Ilgauskas .60 1.50
8 Antonio Daniels .40 1.00
9 Bobby Jackson .50 1.25
10 Derek Anderson .50 1.25

1998-99 SkyBox Premium Mod Squad

COMPLETE SET (16) 15.00 40.00
SER.2 STATED ODDS 1:18 HOB/RET

1 Tim Thomas .75 2.00
2 Shaquille O'Neal 4.00 10.00
3 Scottie Pippen 2.50 6.00
4 Kobe Bryant 12.00 30.00
5 Kevin Garnett 2.50 6.00
6 Grant Hill 1.50 4.00
7 Anfernee Hardaway 2.50 6.00
8 Antoine Walker 1.00 2.50
9 Stephon Marbury 1.25 3.00
10 Kerry Kittles .75 2.00
11 Allen Iverson 2.50 6.00
12 Gary Payton 1.50 4.00
13 Damon Stoudamire 1.00 2.50
14 Marcus Camby .75 2.00
15 Shareef Abdur-Rahim 1.00 2.50
16 Michael Jordan 12.00 30.00

1998-99 SkyBox Premium Net Set

COMPLETE SET (15) 25.00 50.00
SER.1 STATED ODDS 1:36

1 Ron Mercer 1.50 4.00
2 Shawn Kemp 3.00 8.00
3 Brevin Knight 1.25 3.00
4 Maurice Taylor 1.25 3.00
5 Ray Allen 3.00 8.00
6 Dennis Rodman 5.00 12.00
7 Kerry Kittles 1.50 4.00
8 Tim Thomas 1.50 4.00
9 Gary Payton 3.00 8.00
10 Marcus Camby 1.50 4.00
11 Karl Malone 4.00 10.00
12 Juwan Howard 1.50 4.00
13 Zydrunas Ilgauskas 2.00 5.00
14 Scottie Pippen 5.00 12.00
15 Anfernee Hardaway 5.00 12.00

1998-99 SkyBox Premium Slam Funk

COMPLETE SET (10) 400.00 800.00
SER.2 STATED ODDS 1:360 HOB/RET

1 Kobe Bryant 350.00 700.00
2 Kevin Garnett 100.00 250.00
3 Grant Hill 75.00 200.00
4 Shaquille O'Neal 150.00 400.00
5 Michael Olowokandi 40.00 100.00
6 Tim Duncan 100.00 250.00
7 Antawn Jamison 50.00 120.00
8 Keith Van Horn 50.00 120.00
9 Ron Mercer 50.00 120.00
10 Scottie Pippen 75.00 200.00

1998-99 SkyBox Premium Smooth

COMPLETE SET (15) 4.00 10.00
SER.1 STATED ODDS 1:6

1 Stephon Marbury .60 1.50
2 Shareef Abdur-Rahim .50 1.25
3 Keith Van Horn .50 1.25
4 Marcus Camby .40 1.00
5 Ray Allen .75 2.00
6 Allen Iverson 1.25 3.00
7 Kerry Kittles .40 1.00
8 Tim Thomas .40 1.00
9 Damon Stoudamire .50 1.25
10 Antoine Walker .50 1.25
11 Brevin Knight .30 .75
12 Zydrunas Ilgauskas .50 1.25
13 Ron Mercer .40 1.00
14 Maurice Taylor .30 .75
15 Tim Duncan 1.25 3.00

1998-99 SkyBox Premium Soul of the Game

COMPLETE SET (15) 400.00 800.00
SER.1 STATED ODDS 1:18

1 Michael Jordan 400.00 800.00
2 Antoine Walker 8.00 20.00
3 Scottie Pippen 30.00 80.00
4 Grant Hill 15.00 40.00
5 Dennis Rodman 30.00 80.00
6 Kobe Bryant 125.00 300.00
7 Kevin Garnett 30.00 80.00
8 Shaquille O'Neal 40.00 100.00
9 Stephon Marbury 10.00 25.00
10 Kerry Kittles 6.00 15.00
11 Anfernee Hardaway 25.00 60.00
12 Allen Iverson 40.00 100.00
13 Damon Stoudamire 8.00 20.00
14 Marcus Camby 8.00 20.00
15 Shareef Abdur-Rahim 10.00 25.00

1998-99 SkyBox Premium That's Jam

COMPLETE SET (15) 100.00 250.00
SER.2 STATED ODDS 1:96 HOB/RET

1 Tim Duncan 100.00 250.00
2 Stephon Marbury 40.00 100.00
3 Shareef Abdur-Rahim 30.00 80.00
4 Shaquille O'Neal 125.00 300.00
5 Ron Mercer 15.00 40.00
6 Scottie Pippen 50.00 120.00
7 Antawn Jamison 30.00 80.00
8 Anfernee Hardaway 75.00 200.00
9 Damon Stoudamire 20.00 50.00
10 Allen Iverson 125.00 300.00
11 Keith Van Horn 20.00 50.00
12 Grant Hill 60.00 150.00
13 Kevin Garnett 100.00 250.00
14 Kobe Bryant 500.00 1,000.00
15 Antoine Walker 30.00 80.00

1999-00 SkyBox Premium

COMPLETE SET (150) 50.00 120.00
COMPLETE SET w/o SP (125) 15.00 40.00
101-125 SP's STATED ODDS 1:8

1 Vince Carter 1.00 2.50
2 Nick Anderson .25 .60
3 Isaiah Rider .30 .75
4 Mitch Richmond .50 1.25
5 Danny Fortson .25 .60
6 Kenny Anderson .30 .75
7 Reggie Miller .75 2.00
8 Tracy McGrady .60 1.50
9 Steve Nash .75 2.00
10 Robert Traylor .25 .60
11 Tom Gugliotta .30 .75
12 Steve Smith .30 .75
13 Jalen Rose .30 .75
14 Kerry Kittles .30 .75
15 Nick Van Exel .30 .75
16 Raef LaFrentz .30 .75
17 Damon Stoudamire .40 1.00
18 Gary Trent .25 .60
19 Jayson Williams .25 .60
20 Brian Grant .25 .60
21 Rod Strickland .30 .75
22 Larry Hughes .30 .75
23 Derek Anderson .25 .60
24 Hakeem Olajuwon .75 2.00
25 Ray Allen .60 1.50
26 Gary Payton .60 1.50
27 Michael Finley .30 .75
28 Keith Van Horn .30 .75
29 Clifford Robinson .25 .60
30 Shawn Kemp .60 1.50
31 Glenn Robinson .30 .75
32 Theo Ratliff .30 .75
33 Lindsey Hunter .25 .60
34 Chris Webber .50 1.25
35 Grant Hill .60 1.50
36 Vlade Divac .40 1.00
37 Paul Pierce .75 2.00
38 Tyrone Nesby RC .25 .60
39 Larry Johnson .40 1.00
40 Bryon Russell .25 .60
41 Antoine Walker .40 1.00
42 Michael Olowokandi .30 .75
43 John Stockton .60 1.50
44 Elden Campbell .25 .60
45 Christian Laettner .30 .75
46 Maurice Taylor .25 .60
47 Shareef Abdur-Rahim .40 1.00
48 Ricky Davis .40 1.00
49 Jerry Stackhouse .40 1.00
50 Kobe Bryant 3.00 8.00
51 Jason Williams .60 1.50
52 Mike Bibby .40 1.00
53 Eddie Jones .40 1.00
54 Antawn Jamison .40 1.00
55 Shaquille O'Neal 1.50 4.00
56 Tim Duncan 1.00 2.50
57 Cherokee Parks .25 .60
58 Antonio McDyess .30 .75
59 Rasheed Wallace .50 1.25
60 Anthony Mason .30 .75
61 Chris Mills .25 .60
62 Glen Rice .40 1.00
63 Latrell Sprewell .50 1.25
64 Darrell Armstrong .25 .60
65 Sean Elliott .30 .75
66 Juwan Howard .30 .75
67 Brent Barry .30 .75
68 John Starks .40 1.00
69 Tim Hardaway .50 1.25
70 Marcus Camby .30 .75
71 Anfernee Hardaway 1.00 2.50
72 Avery Johnson .30 .75
73 Tariq Abdul-Wahad .25 .60
74 Charles Barkley 1.00 2.50
75 Stephon Marbury .50 1.25
76 Jamal Mashburn .30 .75
77 Matt Harpring .25 .60
78 David Robinson .75 2.00
79 Cedric Ceballos .25 .60
80 Terrell Brandon .25 .60
81 Jason Kidd .60 1.50
82 Toni Kukoc .50 1.25
83 Michael Dickerson .25 .60
84 Alonzo Mourning .60 1.50
85 Kevin Garnett 1.00 2.50
86 Matt Geiger .25 .60
87 Vin Baker .30 .75
88 Dikembe Mutombo .60 1.50
89 Hersey Hawkins .25 .60
90 Joe Smith .30 .75
91 Charles Oakley .40 1.00
92 Ron Mercer .30 .75
93 Rik Smits .30 .75
94 Patrick Ewing .50 1.25
95 Karl Malone .75 2.00
96 Scottie Pippen 1.00 2.50
97 Zydrunas Ilgauskas .30 .75
98 Sam Cassell .30 .75
99 Detlef Schrempf .30 .75
100 Allen Iverson 1.00 2.50
101 Elton Brand RC .75 2.00
101A Elton Brand SP 1.50 4.00
102 Steve Francis RC .75 2.00
102A Steve Francis SP 1.50 4.00
103 Baron Davis RC 1.00 2.50
103A Baron Davis SP 2.00 5.00
104 Lamar Odom RC .75 2.00
104A Lamar Odom SP 1.50 4.00
105 Jonathan Bender RC .40 1.00
105A Jonathan Bender SP .75 2.00
106 Wally Szczerbiak RC .60 1.50
106A Wally Szczerbiak SP 1.25 3.00
107 Richard Hamilton RC 1.00 2.50
107A Richard Hamilton SP 2.00 5.00
108 Andre Miller RC .75 2.00
108A Andre Miller SP 1.50 4.00
109 Shawn Marion RC .75 2.00
109A Shawn Marion SP 1.50 4.00
110 Jason Terry RC .60 1.50
110A Jason Terry SP 1.25 3.00
111 Trajan Langdon RC .30 .75
111A Trajan Langdon SP .60 1.50
112 A.Radojevic RC .25 .60
112A A.Radojevic SP .50 1.25
113 Corey Maggette RC .50 1.25
113A Corey Maggette SP 1.00 2.50
114 William Avery RC .25 .60
114A William Avery SP .50 1.25
115 Vonteego Cummings RC .25 .60
115A Vonteego Cummings SP .50 1.25
116 Ron Artest RC 1.00 2.50
116A Ron Artest SP 2.00 5.00
117 Cal Bowdler RC .25 .60
117A Cal Bowdler SP .50 1.25
118 James Posey RC .40 1.00
118A James Posey SP .75 2.00
119 Quincy Lewis RC .25 .60
119A Quincy Lewis SP .50 1.25
120 Dion Glover RC .25 .60
120A Dion Glover SP .50 1.25
121 Jeff Foster RC .40 1.00
121A Jeff Foster SP .75 2.00
122 Kenny Thomas RC .40 1.00
122A Kenny Thomas SP .75 2.00
123 Devean George RC .30 .75
123A Devean George SP .60 1.50
124 Scott Padgett RC .30 .75
124A Scott Padgett SP .60 1.50
125 Tim James RC .25 .60
125A Tim James SP .50 1.25

1999-00 SkyBox Premium Star Rubies

*STARS: 40X TO 100X HI COLUMN
*RCs: 12X TO 30X HI
*SPs: 8X TO 20X HI
STARS/RC's: PRINT RUN 45 SERIAL #'d SETS
SPs: PRINT RUN 25 SERIAL #'d SETS

24 Hakeem Olajuwon 40.00 100.00
26 Gary Payton 200.00 500.00
30 Shawn Kemp 125.00 300.00
35 Grant Hill 75.00 200.00
50 Kobe Bryant 250.00 500.00
55 Shaquille O'Neal 150.00 300.00
56 Tim Duncan 200.00 500.00
63 Latrell Sprewell 75.00 200.00
71 Anfernee Hardaway 200.00 500.00
74 Charles Barkley 300.00 600.00
78 David Robinson 150.00 400.00
82 Toni Kukoc 50.00 120.00
84 Alonzo Mourning 150.00 400.00
85 Kevin Garnett 200.00 500.00
96 Scottie Pippen 150.00 400.00
102 Steve Francis 50.00 120.00
102A Steve Francis SP 75.00 200.00
103 Baron Davis 50.00 120.00
103A Baron Davis SP 75.00 200.00
110 Jason Terry 20.00 50.00
110A Jason Terry SP 30.00 80.00

1999-00 SkyBox Premium Autographics

STATED ODDS 1:68/1:144 HOO DECADE
STATED ODDS 1:96 METAL
STATED ODDS 1:288 IMPACT

NNO Cory Alexander 2.00 5.00
NNO Ray Allen 60.00 150.00
NNO Darrell Armstrong 3.00 8.00
NNO Ron Artest 3.00 8.00
NNO William Avery 2.00 5.00
NNO Charles Barkley 800.00 1,200.00
NNO Dana Barros 2.00 5.00
NNO Corey Benjamin 2.00 5.00
NNO Travis Best 3.00 8.00
NNO Mike Bibby 10.00 25.00
NNO Calvin Booth 3.00 8.00
NNO Cal Bowdler 3.00 8.00
NNO Bruce Bowen 6.00 15.00
NNO P.J. Brown 3.00 8.00
NNO Jud Buechler 3.00 8.00
NNO Marcus Camby 8.00 20.00
NNO Elden Campbell 4.00 10.00
NNO Cory Carr 2.00 5.00
NNO Vince Carter 30.00 80.00
NNO John Celestand 2.00 5.00
NNO Dell Curry 3.00 8.00
NNO Baron Davis 12.00 30.00
NNO Andrew DeClercq 2.00 5.00
NNO Tony Delk 4.00 10.00
NNO Michael Dickerson 3.00 8.00
NNO Michael Doleac 2.00 5.00
NNO Bryce Drew 2.00 5.00
NNO Obinna Ekezie 2.00 5.00
NNO Evan Eschmeyer 4.00 10.00
NNO Michael Finley 10.00 25.00
NNO Greg Foster 2.00 5.00
NNO Jeff Foster 3.00 8.00
NNO Steve Francis 10.00 25.00
NNO Todd Fuller 2.00 5.00
NNO Lawrence Funderburke 3.00 8.00
NNO Dean Garrett 3.00 8.00
NNO Pat Garrity 3.00 8.00
NNO Devean George 4.00 10.00
NNO Kendall Gill 5.00 12.00

NNO Dion Glover 2.00 5.00
NNO Brian Grant 3.00 8.00
NNO Paul Grant 2.00 5.00
NNO Tom Gugliotta 8.00 20.00
NNO Richard Hamilton 6.00 15.00
NNO Tim Hardaway 10.00 25.00
NNO Matt Harpring 2.00 5.00
NNO Al Harrington 3.00 8.00
NNO Othella Harrington 2.00 5.00
NNO Troy Hudson 3.00 8.00
NNO Larry Hughes 8.00 20.00
NNO Tim James 2.00 5.00
NNO Antawn Jamison 6.00 15.00
NNO Anthony Johnson 3.00 8.00
NNO Avery Johnson 6.00 15.00
NNO Ervin Johnson 2.00 5.00
NNO Eddie Jones 6.00 15.00
NNO Jumaine Jones 2.00 5.00
NNO Adam Keefe 2.00 5.00
NNO Shawn Kemp 50.00 120.00
NNO Kerry Kittles 6.00 15.00
NNO Raef LaFrentz 5.00 12.00
NNO Trajan Langdon 5.00 12.00
NNO Quincy Lewis 2.00 5.00
NNO Felipe Lopez 3.00 8.00
NNO Tyronn Lue 3.00 8.00
NNO George Lynch 3.00 8.00
NNO Sam Mack 2.00 5.00
NNO Stephon Marbury 12.00 30.00
NNO Shawn Marion 8.00 20.00
NNO Tony Massenburg 2.00 5.00
NNO Jelani McCoy 2.00 5.00
NNO Antonio McDyess 8.00 20.00
NNO Tracy McGrady 40.00 100.00
NNO Roshown McLeod 2.00 5.00
NNO Brad Miller 5.00 12.00
NNO Sam Mitchell 3.00 8.00
NNO Nazr Mohammed 6.00 15.00
NNO Alonzo Mourning 50.00 120.00
NNO Tyrone Nesby 2.00 5.00
NNO Shaquille O'Neal 125.00 250.00
NNO Lamar Odom 12.00 30.00
NNO Hakeem Olajuwon 30.00 80.00
NNO Michael Olowokandi 2.00 5.00
NNO Andrae Patterson 2.00 5.00
NNO Eric Piatkowski 2.00 5.00
NNO Scottie Pippen 75.00 200.00
NNO Scot Pollard 2.00 5.00
NNO James Posey 6.00 15.00
NNO Brent Price 2.00 5.00
NNO Aleksandar Radojevic 3.00 8.00
NNO Theo Ratliff 3.00 8.00
NNO J.R. Reid 2.00 5.00
NNO David Robinson 125.00 300.00
NNO Glenn Robinson 3.00 8.00
NNO Jalen Rose 8.00 20.00
NNO Michael Ruffin 2.00 5.00
NNO Wally Szczerbiak 6.00 15.00
NNO Joe Smith 8.00 20.00
NNO Jerry Stackhouse 8.00 20.00
NNO John Starks 8.00 20.00
NNO Vladimir Stepania 3.00 8.00
NNO Damon Stoudamire 6.00 15.00
NNO Maurice Taylor 3.00 8.00
NNO Jason Terry 8.00 20.00
NNO Kenny Thomas 3.00 8.00
NNO Robert Traylor 3.00 8.00
NNO Gary Trent 2.00 5.00
NNO Antoine Walker 10.00 25.00
NNO Chris Webber 500.00 800.00
NNO David Wesley 3.00 8.00
NNO Aaron Williams 2.00 5.00
NNO Jerome Williams 2.00 5.00
NNO Haywoode Workman 3.00 8.00
NNO Scott Padgett 2.50 6.00

1999-00 SkyBox Premium Autographics Blue

*BLUE: .75X TO 2X VALUE
STATED PRINT RUN 50 SERIAL #'d SETS
NNO Darrell Armstrong 10.00 25.00
NNO Charles Barkley 1,500.00 2,500.00
NNO Bruce Bowen 15.00 40.00
NNO Elden Campbell 10.00 25.00
NNO Vince Carter 200.00 400.00
NNO Baron Davis 40.00 100.00
NNO Alonzo Mourning 100.00 250.00
NNO Lamar Odom 50.00 120.00
NNO Hakeem Olajuwon 125.00 300.00
NNO Jalen Rose 25.00 60.00
NNO Wally Szczerbiak 20.00 50.00
NNO John Starks 30.00 80.00

1999-00 SkyBox Premium Back for More

COMPLETE SET (15) 5.00 12.00
STATED ODDS 1:6 HOB/RET
1 Mike Bibby .75 2.00
2 Tyrone Nesby .50 1.25
3 Ricky Davis .75 2.00
4 Michael Dickerson .50 1.25
5 Michael Doleac .50 1.25
6 Antawn Jamison .75 2.00
7 Larry Hughes .60 1.50
8 Matt Harpring .50 1.25
9 Peja Stojakovic .75 2.00
10 Raef LaFrentz .60 1.50
11 Michael Olowokandi .50 1.25
12 Robert Traylor .50 1.25
13 Paul Pierce 1.50 4.00
14 Kornel David .50 1.25
15 Jason Williams 1.25 3.00

1999-00 SkyBox Premium Club Vertical

STATED PRINT RUN 100 SERIAL #'d SETS
1 Vince Carter 400.00 800.00
2 Tim Duncan 400.00 800.00
3 Shaquille O'Neal 500.00 1,000.00
4 Paul Pierce 300.00 600.00
5 Kobe Bryant 1,500.00 3,000.00
6 Kevin Garnett 400.00 800.00
7 Keith Van Horn 100.00 250.00
8 Jason Williams 150.00 400.00
9 Grant Hill 300.00 600.00
10 Allen Iverson 400.00 800.00

1999-00 SkyBox Premium Genuine Coverage

STATED PRINT RUN 275 TO 450 SETS
1 Kobe Bryant/340 200.00 500.00
2 Vince Carter/355 75.00 200.00
3 Patrick Ewing/450 20.00 50.00
4 Grant Hill/370 60.00 150.00
5 Allen Iverson/275 125.00 300.00
6 Alonzo Mourning/360 25.00 60.00

1999-00 SkyBox Premium Good Stuff

COMPLETE SET (10) 10.00 25.00
STATED ODDS 1:36 HOB/RET
*PARALLEL: 8X TO 20X HI COLUMN
PARALLEL: PRINT RUN 99 SERIAL #'d SETS
1 Kobe Bryant 12.00 30.00
2 Vince Carter 2.50 6.00
3 Jason Williams 1.50 4.00
4 Paul Pierce 2.00 5.00
5 Tim Duncan 2.50 6.00
6 Kevin Garnett 2.50 6.00
7 Grant Hill 1.50 4.00
8 Keith Van Horn .75 2.00
9 Allen Iverson 2.50 6.00
10 Shaquille O'Neal 4.00 10.00

1999-00 SkyBox Premium Majestic

COMPLETE SET (15) 10.00 25.00
STATED ODDS 1:12 HOB/RET
1 Antawn Jamison 1.00 2.50
2 Jason Kidd 1.50 4.00
3 Ron Mercer .75 2.00
4 Shawn Kemp 1.50 4.00
5 Stephon Marbury 1.00 2.50
6 Shaquille O'Neal 4.00 10.00
7 Larry Hughes .75 2.00
8 Kevin Garnett 2.50 6.00
9 Antoine Walker 1.00 2.50
10 Keith Van Horn .75 2.00
11 Anfernee Hardaway 2.50 6.00
12 Tim Duncan 2.50 6.00
13 Scottie Pippen 2.50 6.00
14 Shareef Abdur-Rahim 1.00 2.50
15 Chris Webber 1.25 3.00

1999-00 SkyBox Premium Prime Time Rookies

COMPLETE SET (15) 25.00 60.00
STATED ODDS 1:96 HOB/RET
PT1 Elton Brand 3.00 8.00
PT2 Steve Francis 3.00 8.00
PT3 Baron Davis 4.00 10.00
PT4 Lamar Odom 3.00 8.00
PT5 Jonathan Bender 1.50 4.00
PT6 Wally Szczerbiak 2.50 6.00
PT7 Richard Hamilton 4.00 10.00
PT8 Andre Miller 3.00 8.00
PT9 Shawn Marion 3.00 8.00
PT10 Jason Terry 2.50 6.00
PT11 Trajan Langdon 1.25 3.00
PT12 Dion Glover 1.00 2.50
PT13 Corey Maggette 2.00 5.00
PT14 William Avery 1.00 2.50
PT15 Tim James 1.00 2.50

1999-00 SkyBox Premium Prime Time Rookies Autographs

STATED PRINT RUN 25 SERIAL #'d SETS
PT1 Elton Brand 30.00 80.00
PT2 Steve Francis 30.00 80.00
PT3 Baron Davis 40.00 100.00
PT4 Lamar Odom 30.00 80.00
PT5 Jonathan Bender 15.00 40.00
PT6 Wally Szczerbiak 25.00 60.00
PT7 Richard Hamilton 40.00 100.00
PT8 Andre Miller 30.00 80.00
PT9 Shawn Marion 30.00 80.00
PT10 Jason Terry 20.00 50.00
PT11 Trajan Langdon 12.00 30.00
PT12 Dion Glover 10.00 25.00
PT13 Corey Maggette 20.00 50.00
PT14 William Avery 10.00 25.00
PT15 Tim James 10.00 25.00

2004-05 SkyBox Premium

COMP.SET w/o SP's (75) 15.00 40.00
76-100 RC PRINT RUN 999 SER.#'d SETS
1 Dwyane Wade 1.50 4.00
2 Rashard Lewis .30 .75
3 Jermaine O'Neal .30 .75
4 Ben Wallace .50 1.25
5 Steve Francis .40 1.00
6 Lamar Odom .40 1.00
7 Jason Richardson .40 1.00
8 Jarvis Hayes .25 .60
9 Carmelo Anthony .75 2.00
10 Tony Parker .60 1.50
11 Eddy Curry .25 .60
12 Nene .25 .60
13 Kevin Garnett 1.00 2.50
14 Darius Miles .25 .60
15 Elton Brand .25 .60
16 Zach Randolph .40 1.00
17 Mike Dunleavy .25 .60
18 Dajuan Wagner .25 .60
19 Steve Nash .75 2.00
20 Ron Artest .40 1.00
21 Ricky Davis .30 .75
22 Antawn Jamison .30 .75
23 Jamal Mashburn .30 .75
24 T.J. Ford .25 .60
25 Amare Stoudemire .40 1.00
26 Jason Kapono .25 .60
27 Shawn Marion .30 .75
28 Corliss Williamson .25 .60
29 Reggie Miller .75 2.00
30 Desmond Mason .30 .75
31 Pau Gasol .60 1.50
32 Baron Davis .40 1.00
33 Allen Iverson 1.00 2.50
34 Darko Milicic .25 .60
35 Ray Allen .60 1.50
36 Jason Williams .30 .75
37 Michael Redd .30 .75
38 Yao Ming 1.00 2.50
39 Antoine Walker .40 1.00
40 Jason Terry .30 .75
41 Sam Cassell .30 .75
42 Richard Jefferson .30 .75
43 Manu Ginobili .75 2.00
44 Dirk Nowitzki 1.00 2.50
45 Peja Stojakovic .30 .75
46 Samuel Dalembert .25 .60
47 Latrell Sprewell .50 1.25
48 Gerald Wallace .30 .75
49 Andrei Kirilenko .30 .75
50 Nick Van Exel .40 1.00
51 Jalen Rose .30 .75
52 Shaquille O'Neal 1.50 4.00
53 Shareef Abdur-Rahim .40 1.00
54 Tracy McGrady .60 1.50
55 Rasheed Wallace .50 1.25
56 Cuttino Mobley .30 .75
57 Jason Kidd .60 1.50
58 Chris Webber .50 1.25
59 Paul Pierce .60 1.50
60 Mike Bibby .40 1.00
61 Allan Houston .40 1.00
62 Kobe Bryant 3.00 8.00
63 Kenyon Martin .40 1.00
64 LeBron James 3.00 8.00
65 Tim Duncan 1.00 2.50
66 Stephon Marbury .50 1.25
67 Kirk Hinrich .40 1.00
68 Chris Bosh .60 1.50
69 Corey Maggette .30 .75
70 Vince Carter .75 2.00
71 Caron Butler .30 .75
72 Stephen Jackson .30 .75
73 Carlos Boozer .30 .75
74 Michael Finley .40 1.00
75 Jamal Crawford .40 1.00
76 Dwight Howard RC 5.00 12.00
77 Emeka Okafor RC 1.25 3.00
78 Ben Gordon RC 1.50 4.00
79 Shaun Livingston RC 1.50 4.00
80 Devin Harris RC 1.25 3.00
81 Josh Childress RC 1.00 2.50
82 Luol Deng RC 1.50 4.00
83 Rafael Araujo RC 1.00 2.50
84 Andre Iguodala RC 2.50 6.00
85 Luke Jackson RC 1.00 2.50
86 Andris Biedrins RC 1.00 2.50
87 Robert Swift RC 1.00 2.50
88 Sebastian Telfair RC 1.25 3.00
89 Kris Humphries RC 1.25 3.00
90 Al Jefferson RC 1.50 4.00
91 Kirk Snyder RC 1.00 2.50
92 Josh Smith RC 1.50 4.00
93 J.R. Smith RC 1.50 4.00
94 Dorell Wright RC 1.25 3.00
95 Jameer Nelson RC 1.50 4.00
96 Bernard Robinson RC 1.00 2.50
97 Andre Emmett RC 1.00 2.50
98 Delonte West RC 1.25 3.00
99 Tony Allen RC 1.50 4.00
100 Kevin Martin RC 2.00 5.00

2004-05 SkyBox Premium Ruby

*1-75 RUBY: 2.5X TO 6X BASE HI
*76-100 RUBY RC's: 1X TO 2.5X BASE HI
PRINT RUN 75 SER.#'d SETS
64 LeBron James 50.00 120.00

2004-05 SkyBox Premium Autographs

PRINT RUN 100 SER.#'d SETS
*DIE CUTS: .4X TO 1X BASE AU HI
6 Lamar Odom 6.00 15.00
12 Nene 6.00 15.00
22 Antawn Jamison 6.00 15.00
49 Andrei Kirilenko 6.00 15.00
70 Vince Carter 15.00 40.00
78 Ben Gordon 6.00 15.00
82 Luol Deng 6.00 15.00
83 Rafael Araujo 4.00 10.00
85 Luke Jackson 4.00 10.00
86 Andris Biedrins 4.00 10.00
87 Robert Swift 4.00 10.00
89 Kris Humphries 5.00 12.00
91 Kirk Snyder 4.00 10.00
93 J.R. Smith 6.00 15.00
94 Dorell Wright 5.00 12.00
97 Andre Emmett 4.00 10.00
98 Delonte West 5.00 12.00

2004-05 SkyBox Premium Hometown Shout Outs

COMPLETE SET (12) 10.00 25.00
PRINT RUNS LISTED IN CHECKLIST
1 Carmelo Anthony/410 1.50 4.00
2 Dwyane Wade/708 3.00 8.00
3 Rasheed Wallace/215 1.00 2.50
4 Allen Iverson/757 2.00 5.00
5 Paul Pierce/510 1.25 3.00
6 Richard Jefferson/602 .60 1.50
7 Tim Duncan/340 2.00 5.00
8 Michael Redd/614 .60 1.50
9 Elton Brand/914 .60 1.50
10 LeBron James/330 6.00 15.00
11 Vince Carter/386 1.50 4.00
12 Kobe Bryant/610 6.00 15.00

2004-05 SkyBox Premium Hometown Shout Outs Autographs

PRINT RUNS LISTED IN CHECKLIST
CA Carmelo Anthony/25 30.00 80.00
CA Carlos Arroyo/250 15.00 40.00
CD Carlos Delfino/250 4.00 10.00
DH David Harrison/250 4.00 10.00
DW Dwyane Wade/50 20.00 50.00
HS Ha Seung-Jin/250 4.00 10.00
JJ Joe Johnson/250 5.00 12.00
NC Nick Collison/150 4.00 10.00
PP Paul Pierce 6.00 15.00
RJ Richard Jefferson/75 6.00 15.00
VC Vince Carter 15.00 40.00

2004-05 SkyBox Premium Hometown Shout Outs Jerseys

OVERALL GAME USED ODDS 1:6 H, 1:48 R
*JERSEY 75 SINGLES: .6X TO 1.5X BASE HI
AI Allen Iverson 6.00 15.00
CA Carmelo Anthony 5.00 12.00
DW Dwyane Wade 10.00 25.00
EB Elton Brand 2.00 5.00
MR Michael Redd 2.00 5.00
PP Paul Pierce 4.00 10.00
RJ Richard Jefferson 2.00 5.00
RW Rasheed Wallace 3.00 8.00
TD Tim Duncan 6.00 15.00
VC Vince Carter 5.00 12.00

2004-05 SkyBox Premium Parquet Performers

STATED ODDS 1:12
1 Danny Ainge 6.00 15.00
2 Nate Archibald 6.00 15.00
3 Larry Bird 15.00 40.00
4 Kevin McHale 6.00 15.00
5 K.C. Jones 6.00 15.00
7 Pete Maravich 20.00 50.00
8 Jo Jo White 12.00 30.00
9 Robert Parish 10.00 25.00
10 John Havlicek 6.00 15.00
11 Bob Cousy 20.00 50.00
12 Tom Heinsohn 6.00 15.00
13 Dave Cowens 6.00 15.00
14 Bill Sharman 10.00 25.00
15 Sam Jones 6.00 15.00

2004-05 SkyBox Premium Parquet Performers Autographs

STATED ODDS 1:144
BC Bob Cousy 15.00 40.00
BS Bill Sharman 12.00 30.00
DA Danny Ainge 20.00 50.00
DC Dave Cowens 20.00 50.00
KM Kevin McHale 75.00 150.00
NA Nate Archibald 15.00 40.00
RP Robert Parish 15.00 40.00
SJ Sam Jones 12.00 30.00
TH Tom Heinsohn 15.00 40.00

2004-05 SkyBox Premium Performers

COMPLETE SET (20) 10.00 25.00
STATED ODDS 1:6
1 Tracy McGrady .75 2.00
2 Kenyon Martin .50 1.25
3 Chris Webber .60 1.50
4 Kevin Garnett 1.25 3.00
5 Shaquille O'Neal 2.00 5.00
6 Allen Iverson 1.25 3.00
7 Steve Francis .50 1.25
8 Manu Ginobili 1.00 2.50
9 Paul Pierce .75 2.00
10 Ben Wallace .60 1.50
11 Carmelo Anthony 1.00 2.50
12 Peja Stojakovic .40 1.00
13 Richard Hamilton .40 1.00
14 Stephon Marbury .60 1.50
15 Vince Carter 1.00 2.50
16 Kobe Bryant 4.00 10.00
17 LeBron James 4.00 10.00
18 Dirk Nowitzki 1.25 3.00
19 Jermaine O'Neal .40 1.00
20 Dwyane Wade 2.00 5.00

2004-05 SkyBox Premium Performers Autographs

PRINT RUNS LISTED IN CHECKLIST
BW Ben Wallace/25 15.00 40.00
CA Carmelo Anthony/25 30.00 80.00
DW Dwyane Wade/50 40.00 100.00
JO Jermaine O'Neal/50 12.00 30.00
KM Kenyon Martin/50 8.00 20.00
MG Manu Ginobili/41 20.00 50.00
PS Peja Stojakovic/100 8.00 20.00
RH Richard Hamilton/78 8.00 20.00
SM Stephon Marbury/50 8.00 20.00
TM Tracy McGrady/43 20.00 50.00
VC Vince Carter 15.00 40.00

2004-05 SkyBox Premium Performers Jerseys

OVERALL GAME USED ODDS 1:6 H, 1:48 R
*JERSEY 75 SINGLES: .5X TO 1.25X BASE HI
AI Allen Iverson 6.00 15.00
BW Ben Wallace 3.00 8.00
CA Carmelo Anthony 5.00 12.00
CW Chris Webber 3.00 8.00
DN Dirk Nowitzki 6.00 15.00
DW Dwyane Wade 10.00 25.00
JO Jermaine O'Neal 2.00 5.00
KG Kevin Garnett 6.00 15.00
KM Kenyon Martin 2.50 6.00
MG Manu Ginobili 5.00 12.00
PP Paul Pierce 4.00 10.00
PS Peja Stojakovic 2.00 5.00
RH Richard Hamilton 3.00 8.00
SF Steve Francis 2.50 6.00
SM Stephon Marbury 3.00 8.00
SO Shaquille O'Neal 10.00 25.00
TM Tracy McGrady 4.00 10.00
VC Vince Carter 5.00 12.00

2004-05 SkyBox Premium Proven Performers

COMPLETE SET (15) 15.00 40.00
STATED ODDS 1:24
1 Nate Archibald 1.50 4.00
2 Darryl Dawkins 1.25 3.00
3 Walt Frazier 2.50 6.00
4 George Gervin 2.00 5.00
5 John Havlicek 2.00 5.00
6 Robert Parish 2.00 5.00
7 Isiah Thomas 3.00 8.00
8 Earl Monroe 2.00 5.00
9 Oscar Robertson 4.00 10.00
10 Charles Barkley 3.00 8.00
11 Dave Bing 2.00 5.00
12 Magic Johnson 8.00 20.00
13 Bob Cousy 3.00 8.00
14 Bernard King 2.50 6.00
15 Kevin McHale 2.50 6.00

2004-05 SkyBox Premium Proven Performers Autographs

PRINT RUNS LISTED IN CHECKLIST
EM Earl Monroe 10.00 25.00
EM2 Earl Monroe JSY 12.00 30.00
GG George Gervin/100 12.00 30.00
MJ Magic Johnson/25 50.00 120.00
NA Nate Archibald 10.00 25.00
RP Robert Parish 12.00 30.00
WF Walt Frazier 10.00 25.00
WF2 Walt Frazier JSY 15.00 40.00

2004-05 SkyBox Premium Proven Performers Jerseys

OVERALL GAME USED ODDS 1:6 H, 1:48 R
CB Charles Barkley 20.00 50.00
IT Isiah Thomas 6.00 15.00
KM Kevin McHale 6.00 15.00
RP Robert Parish 6.00 15.00

2004-05 SkyBox Premium Proven Performers Jerseys 75

*75 SINGLES: .5X TO 1.25X BASE JSY HI
PRINT RUN 75 SER.#'d SETS

1994 SkyBox Premium Blue Chips Prototypes

COMPLETE SET (3) 1.50 4.00
1 Title card (Mail-in offer) .20 .50
2 Pete Pep Talk 1 (Nick Nolte and team) .40 1.00
3 A Few Tips (Nick Nolte and Shaquille O'Neal) 1.50 4.00

1994 SkyBox Premium Blue Chips

COMPLETE SET (90) 3.00 8.00
1 Pete Pep Talk 1 .05 .15
2 Thousands Cheer .05 .15
3 Stacking Hands .05 .15
4 Two More Points .05 .15
5 You're Outta Here .05 .15
6 Pete Punts .05 .15
7 Q and A .05 .15
8 Pete's Nemesis .05 .15
9 Sympathetic Ear (Bob Cousy listening to Nick Nolte) .15 .40
10 Pete's Dolphin Tank .05 .15
11 Film at 11 .05 .15
12 Gotta Have Heart .05 .15
13 Pete Pep Talk 2 .05 .15
14 Another Game Another Loss .05 .15
15 Scouting at St. Joe's .05 .15
16 At Home With Butch (Hardaway at home with mother) .20 .50
17 Let's Make A Deal .05 .15
18 Uncle Phil's Big Score .05 .15
19 The First Sighting .05 .15
20 The First Dunk (O'Neal slam dunking) .20 .50
21 Hiring the Tutor (O'Neal introduced to Mary McDonnell) .20 .50
22 A Tutor with Class .05 .15
23 Hometown Parade (Matt Nover) .08 .25
24 Back Home in Indiana .05 .15
25 The Hard Sell (Nolte recruiting Matt Nover) .05 .15
26 Varsity vs. Blue Chips .05 .15
27 Ed Smells Something .05 .15
28 Unfinished Business .05 .15
29 On Campus (Shaquille O'Neal Penny Hardaway Matt Nover girl watching) .20 .50
30 News Crew (O'Neal with microphone in hand) .20 .50
31 Rick's on the Air .08 .25
32 Secret is Revealed .05 .15
33 Unhappy Seeing Happy .05 .15
34 Butch at Practice (Hardaway kneeling, basketball in hand) .20 .50
35 A Few Tips (Nolte coaching O'Neal in practice) .20 .50
36 More Preparation .05 .15
37 Two Old Friends (Nick Nolte, Bob Cousy) .20 .50
38 Pete Challenges Tony .05 .15
39 We want Indiana (O'Neal in huddle) .20 .50
40 Taking the Lead (O'Neal shooting) .20 .50
41 Job Well Done (O'Neal onbench) .20 .50
42 On the Move (O'Neal establishing position) .20 .50
43 Fans Go Wild .05 .15
44 The Celebration (O'Neal and Hardaway celebrating) .20 .50
45 Victory Returns .05 .15
46 Ed's Full-Court Press .05 .15
47 Happy's Last Hurrah .05 .15
48 No Longer the Coach .05 .15
49 Always the Teacher .05 .15
50 Coach Bell .05 .15
51 Pete's Assistants .05 .15
52 Vic Roker (Bob Cousy) .15 .40
53 Happy Kuykendall .05 .15
54 Uncle Phil .05 .15
55 Jenny Bell .05 .15
56 Butch McRae (Anfernee Hardaway) .20 .50
57 Neon Bodeaux (Shaquille O'Neal) .20 .50
58 Billy Friedkin (Movie Director) .05 .15
59 Tony .05 .15
60 The Dolphin Girl .05 .15
61 Team 1 .05 .15
62 Team 2 .05 .15
63 Lavada McRae .05 .15
64 Ed Axelby .05 .15
65 Ricky Roe (Matt Nover) .08 .25
66 Under the Hoop (O'Neal playing defense) .20 .50
67 Precision Pass (Hardaway passing) .20 .50
68 Up and In .05 .15
69 Foul .05 .15
70 Out of My Way (O'Neal establishing position) .20 .50
71 Taking a Breather (O'Neal taking breather during timeout) .20 .50
72 Neon at the Line (O'Neal shooting free throw) .20 .50
73 Give Neon the Ball .20 .50
74 Mary McDonnell .05 .15
75 Standing Tall (O'Neal holding net) .20 .50
76 Nick and Rob (Nolte and Cousy conversing on campus) .15 .40
77 Roll Camera (O'Neal joking during filming) .20 .50
78 Nick Nolte and the Crew .05 .15
79 Pre-school with Shaq (O'Neal with pre-school kids) .20 .50
80 Piling On .05 .15
81 Mary Up in Arms (Mary McDonnell in O'Neal's arms) .20 .50
82 Five Blue-Chippers (Penny Hardaway Shaquille O'Neal Matt Nover Nick Nolte William Friedkin) .20 .50
83 The Exorcist (O'Neal making face) .20 .50
84 Checking the Stats (O'Neal reading sports magazine) .20 .50
85 Anfernee's Tricks (Hardaway holding two basketballs) .20 .50
86 The Legendary .05 .15
87 Shaq at Practice (O'Neal holding ball over head) .20 .50
88 Shaq Rehearses (O'Neal posed with basketball in hand) .20 .50
89 Checklist A .05 .15
90 Checklist B .05 .15

1994 SkyBox Premium Blue Chips Foil

COMPLETE SET (7) 20.00 50.00
F1 Getting to Know Butch McRae Anfernee Hardaway 5.00 12.00
F2 Butch Up Close Anfernee Hardaway 5.00 12.00
F3 Getting to Know Neon Shaquille O'Neal 5.00 12.00
F4 Neon Takes Charge Shaquille O'Neal 5.00 12.00
F5 Getting to Know Ricky Roe, Matt Nover 1.50 4.00
F6 Ricky on the Line Matt Nover 1.50 4.00
SP Neon's game-winner (O'Neal Mail-away) 5.00 12.00

1993-94 SkyBox Premium Pepsi Shaq Attaq

COMPLETE SET (5) 10.00 25.00
COMMON CARD (1-4) 3.00 8.00
5 Cover Card 5.00 12.00

1993-94 SkyBox Schick

COMPLETE SET (52) 60.00 150.00
1 Kenny Anderson 1.25 3.00
2 Greg Anthony 1.00 2.50
3 Vin Baker 2.50 6.00
4 Stacey Augmon 1.25 3.00
5 Corie Blount 1.50 4.00
6 Shawn Bradley 1.50 4.00
7 Terrell Brandon 1.25 3.00
8 P.J. Brown 1.50 4.00
9 Scott Burrell 1.50 4.00
10 Sam Cassell 3.00 8.00
11 Calbert Cheaney 1.50 4.00
12 Doug Christie 1.25 3.00
13 Lloyd Daniels 1.00 2.50
14 Hubert Davis 1.25 3.00
15 Todd Day 1.00 2.50
16 Terry Dehere 1.50 4.00
17 Acie Earl 1.50 4.00
18 LaPhonso Ellis 1.25 3.00
19 Tom Gugliotta 1.25 3.00
20 Anfernee Hardaway 8.00 20.00
21 Scott Haskin 1.00 2.50
22 Robert Horry 1.50 4.00
23 Allan Houston 3.00 8.00
24 Lindsey Hunter 1.50 4.00
25 Bobby Hurley 1.50 4.00
26 Jim Jackson 1.25 3.00
27 Ervin Johnson 1.50 4.00
28 Adam Keefe 1.00 2.50
29 Toni Kukoc 4.00 10.00
30 Christian Laettner 1.50 4.00
31 Malcolm Mackey 1.00 2.50
32 Jamal Mashburn 3.00 8.00
33 Oliver Miller 1.00 2.50
34 Chris Mills 1.50 4.00
35 Harold Miner 1.25 3.00
36 Alonzo Mourning 2.50 6.00
37 Tracy Murray 1.00 2.50
38 Shaquille O'Neal 8.00 20.00
39 Anthony Peeler 1.00 2.50
40 Dino Radja 1.50 4.00
41 Isaiah Rider 2.50 6.00
42 James Robinson 1.50 4.00
43 Rodney Rogers 1.50 4.00
44 Malik Sealy 1.00 2.50
45 Steve Smith 1.25 3.00
46 Elmore Spencer 1.00 2.50
47 Latrell Sprewell 2.50 6.00
48 Rex Walters 1.25 3.00
49 Clarence Weatherspoon 1.00 2.50
50 Chris Webber 8.00 20.00
51 Walt Williams 1.50 4.00
52 Luther Wright 1.00 2.50

1993-94 SkyBox Sportslook Promo

RR8 Magic Johnson 1.25 3.00

1993 SkyBox Story-of-a-Game

COMPLETE SET (3) 4.00 10.00
COMMON CARD (1-3) 1.50 4.00

1998-99 SkyBox Thunder

COMPLETE SET (127) 20.00 50.00
CARDS 1-50 INSERTED 4:1
CARDS 51-100 INSERTED 3:1
CARDS 101-125 INSERTED 1:1
1 Kerry Kittles .40 1.00
2 Larry Johnson .75 2.00
3 Hakeem Olajuwon 1.00 2.50
4 Glenn Robinson .50 1.25
5 Alonzo Mourning .75 2.00
6 Reggie Miller 1.00 2.50
7 Toni Kukoc .50 1.25
8 Corliss Williamson .30 .75
9 Nick Van Exel .50 1.25
10 Mookie Blaylock .40 1.00
11 Michael Smith .30 .75
12 Avery Johnson .40 1.00
13 Brian Williams .30 .75
14 Doug Christie .40 1.00
15 Danny Fortson .30 .75
16 Michael Stewart .30 .75
17 Anthony Peeler .30 .75
18 Cedric Henderson .30 .75
19 Lamond Murray .30 .75
20 Walt Williams .30 .75
21 Samaki Walker .30 .75
22 David Wesley .30 .75
23 Maurice Taylor .30 .75
24 Todd Fuller .30 .75
25 Jeff Hornacek .40 1.00
26 Danny Manning .40 1.00
27 Detlef Schrempf .50 1.25
28 Nick Anderson .30 .75
29 Ron Harper .50 1.25
30 Brian Shaw .30 .75
31 Bryant Stith .30 .75
32 Chris Whitney .30 .75
33 Patrick Ewing .75 2.00
34 Travis Knight .30 .75
35 Tracy McGrady .75 2.00
36 Dan Majerle .50 1.25
37 Dale Davis .30 .75
38 Kelvin Cato .30 .75
39 Zydrunas Ilgauskas .50 1.25
40 Sean Elliott .50 1.25
41 Tony Delk .30 .75
42 Bobby Phills .30 .75
43 Clifford Robinson .30 .75
44 Shawn Bradley .30 .75
45 Aaron McKie .30 .75
46 Mark Jackson .40 1.00
47 P.J. Brown .30 .75
48 Armon Gilliam .30 .75
49 Ed Gray .30 .75
50 Olden Polynice .30 .75
51 Kendall Gill .40 1.00
52 Bryon Russell .30 .75
53 Dale Ellis .30 .75
54 Mark Price .50 1.25
55 Donyell Marshall .30 .75
56 John Starks .50 1.25
57 Jerome Williams .30 .75
58 Rodney Rogers .30 .75
59 Michael Finley .50 1.25
60 Marcus Camby .40 1.00
61 Chris Anstey .30 .75
62 Rodrick Rhodes .30 .75
63 Derek Anderson .40 1.00
64 Jermaine O'Neal .50 1.25
65 Glen Rice .50 1.25
66 Bryant Reeves .30 .75
67 Jalen Rose .40 1.00
68 Calbert Cheaney .30 .75
69 Steve Smith .40 1.00
70 Shandon Anderson .30 .75
71 Tony Battie .30 .75
72 Kenny Anderson .40 1.00
73 Tim Hardaway .60 1.50
74 Antonio Daniels .30 .75
75 Charles Barkley 1.25 3.00
76 Chauncey Billups .60 1.50
77 Lindsey Hunter .30 .75
78 Terrell Brandon .40 1.00
79 Anthony Mason .40 1.00
80 Elden Campbell .30 .75
81 Rasheed Wallace .60 1.50
82 Erick Dampier .30 .75
83 Tracy Murray .30 .75
84 Sam Cassell .40 1.00
85 Bobby Jackson .40 1.00
86 Horace Grant .50 1.25
87 Brent Price .30 .75
88 Allan Houston .50 1.25
89 Brevin Knight .30 .75
90 Steve Nash 1.00 2.50
91 Lorenzen Wright .30 .75
92 Hubert Davis .30 .75
93 Walter McCarty .30 .75
94 Jamal Mashburn .50 1.25
95 Dikembe Mutombo .75 2.00
96 Chris Carr .30 .75
97 Tariq Abdul-Wahad .30 .75
98 Chris Mullin .60 1.50
99 Charlie Ward .30 .75
100 Tim Thomas .40 1.00
101 Tim Duncan 1.25 3.00
102 Antoine Walker .50 1.25
103 Stephon Marbury .60 1.50
104 Ray Allen .75 2.00
105 Shawn Kemp .75 2.00
106 Michael Jordan 5.00 12.00
107 Gary Payton .75 2.00
108 Kobe Bryant 4.00 10.00
109 Karl Malone 1.00 2.50
110 Kevin Garnett 1.25 3.00
111 Jason Kidd .75 2.00
112 Dennis Rodman 1.25 3.00
113 Grant Hill .75 2.00
114 Keith Van Horn .50 1.25
115 Shareef Abdur-Rahim .50 1.25
116 Ron Mercer .40 1.00
117 Allen Iverson 1.25 3.00
118 Shaquille O'Neal 2.00 5.00
119 Anfernee Hardaway 1.25 3.00
120 Scottie Pippen 1.25 3.00
121 David Robinson 1.00 2.50
122 Vin Baker .40 1.00

123 John Stockton 1.00 2.50
124 Eddie Jones .50 1.25
125 Juwan Howard .40 1.00
126 Checklist .12 .30
127 Checklist .12 .30
NNO Grant Hill SAMPLE .75 2.00

1998-99 SkyBox Thunder Rave

*STARS: 12X TO 30X BASE CARD HI
STATED PRINT RUN 150 SERIAL #'d SETS
3 Hakeem Olajuwon 100.00 250.00
5 Alonzo Mourning 75.00 200.00
6 Reggie Miller 125.00 300.00
7 Toni Kukoc 40.00 100.00
33 Patrick Ewing 100.00 250.00
35 Tracy McGrady 125.00 300.00
75 Charles Barkley 150.00 400.00
76 Chauncey Billups 60.00 150.00
90 Steve Nash 125.00 300.00
101 Tim Duncan 200.00 500.00
103 Stephon Marbury 60.00 150.00
104 Ray Allen 75.00 200.00
105 Shawn Kemp 75.00 200.00
106 Michael Jordan 1,500.00 3,000.00
107 Gary Payton 75.00 200.00
108 Kobe Bryant 600.00 1,200.00
109 Karl Malone 100.00 250.00
110 Kevin Garnett 200.00 500.00
111 Jason Kidd 60.00 150.00
112 Dennis Rodman 150.00 400.00
113 Grant Hill 75.00 200.00
117 Allen Iverson 200.00 500.00
118 Shaquille O'Neal 200.00 500.00
119 Anfernee Hardaway 150.00 400.00
120 Scottie Pippen 150.00 400.00
121 David Robinson 125.00 300.00
123 John Stockton 100.00 250.00

1998-99 SkyBox Thunder Super Rave

*STARS: 60X TO 150X BASE CARD HI
STATED PRINT RUN 25 SERIAL #'d SETS
3 Hakeem Olajuwon 600.00 1,200.00
6 Reggie Miller 800.00 1,500.00
7 Toni Kukoc 200.00 500.00
33 Patrick Ewing 600.00 1,200.00
35 Tracy McGrady 800.00 1,500.00
75 Charles Barkley 1,000.00 2,000.00
76 Chauncey Billups 300.00 600.00
90 Steve Nash 800.00 1,500.00
101 Tim Duncan 1,500.00 3,000.00
103 Stephon Marbury 300.00 600.00
104 Ray Allen 500.00 1,000.00
105 Shawn Kemp 500.00 1,000.00
106 Michael Jordan 20,000.00 40,000.00
107 Gary Payton 500.00 1,000.00
108 Kobe Bryant 15,000.00 30,000.00
109 Karl Malone 600.00 1,200.00
110 Kevin Garnett 1,500.00 3,000.00
111 Jason Kidd 300.00 600.00
112 Dennis Rodman 1,000.00 2,000.00
113 Grant Hill 500.00 2,000.00
117 Allen Iverson 1,500.00 3,000.00
118 Shaquille O'Neal 1,500.00 3,000.00
119 Anfernee Hardaway 1,500.00 3,000.00
120 Scottie Pippen 1,500.00 3,000.00
121 David Robinson 800.00 1,500.00
123 John Stockton 500.00 1,000.00

1998-99 SkyBox Thunder Boss

COMPLETE SET (20) 75.00 200.00
STATED ODDS 1:16 HOB/RET
1 Shareef Abdur-Rahim 1.25 3.00
2 Vin Baker 1.00 2.50
3 Tim Duncan 3.00 8.00
4 Kevin Garnett 3.00 8.00
5 Tim Hardaway 1.50 4.00
6 Grant Hill 2.00 5.00
7 Michael Jordan 75.00 200.00
8 Shawn Kemp 2.00 5.00
9 Jason Kidd 2.00 5.00
10 Karl Malone 2.50 6.00
11 Stephon Marbury 1.50 4.00
12 Ron Mercer 1.00 2.50
13 Shaquille O'Neal 5.00 12.00
14 Gary Payton 2.00 5.00
15 Scottie Pippen 3.00 8.00
16 Glenn Robinson 1.25 3.00
17 John Stockton 2.50 6.00
18 Damon Stoudamire 1.25 3.00
19 Keith Van Horn 1.25 3.00
20 Antoine Walker 1.25 3.00

1998-99 SkyBox Thunder Bringin' It

COMPLETE SET (10) 8.00 20.00
STATED ODDS 1:8 HOB/RET
1 Charles Barkley 2.00 5.00
2 Anfernee Hardaway 2.00 5.00
3 Eddie Jones .75 2.00
4 Karl Malone 1.50 4.00
5 Hakeem Olajuwon 1.50 4.00
6 Shaquille O'Neal 3.00 8.00
7 Scottie Pippen 2.00 5.00
8 Glen Rice .75 2.00
9 David Robinson 1.50 4.00
10 Dennis Rodman 2.00 5.00

1998-99 SkyBox Thunder Flight School

COMPLETE SET (12) 100.00 250.00
STATED ODDS 1:96 HOBBY
1 Ray Allen 4.00 10.00
2 Kobe Bryant 50.00 120.00
3 Michael Finley 1.50 4.00
4 Kevin Garnett 8.00 20.00
5 Anfernee Hardaway 8.00 20.00
6 Grant Hill 2.50 6.00
7 Allen Iverson 8.00 20.00
8 Eddie Jones 1.50 4.00
9 Michael Jordan 75.00 200.00
10 Shawn Kemp 8.00 20.00
11 Antonio McDyess 1.25 3.00
12 Ron Mercer 1.25 3.00

1998-99 SkyBox Thunder Lift Off

COMPLETE SET (10) 75.00 200.00
STATED ODDS 1:56 HOB/RET 1.50 4.00
1 Shareef Abdur-Rahim 1.50 4.00
2 Ray Allen 5.00 12.00
3 Kobe Bryant 75.00 200.00
4 Tim Duncan 12.00 30.00
5 Allen Iverson 12.00 30.00
6 Kerry Kittles 1.25 3.00
7 Stephon Marbury 2.00 5.00
8 Ron Mercer 1.25 3.00
9 Keith Van Horn 1.50 4.00
10 Antoine Walker 1.50 4.00

1998-99 SkyBox Thunder Noyz Boyz

COMPLETE SET (15)
STATED ODDS 1:300 HOB/RET
1 Shareef Abdur-Rahim 75.00 200.00
2 Ray Allen 125.00 300.00
3 Kobe Bryant 1,500.00 3,000.00
4 Tim Duncan 300.00 600.00
5 Kevin Garnett 300.00 600.00
6 Anfernee Hardaway 300.00 600.00
7 Grant Hill 125.00 300.00
8 Allen Iverson 400.00 800.00
9 Michael Jordan 3,000.00 6,000.00
10 Stephon Marbury 100.00 250.00
11 Shaquille O'Neal 300.00 600.00
12 Scottie Pippen 300.00 600.00
13 Dennis Rodman 300.00 600.00
14 Keith Van Horn 60.00 150.00
15 Antoine Walker 75.00 200.00

1992 SkyBox USA

COMPLETE SET (110) 12.00 30.00
1 Charles Barkley NBA Update .50 1.25
2 Charles Barkley NBA Rookie .50 1.25
3 Charles Barkley Game Strategy .50 1.25
4 Charles Barkley NBA Best Game .50 1.25
5 Charles Barkley Off the Court .50 1.25
6 Charles Barkley NBA Playoffs .50 1.25
7 Charles Barkley NBA All-Star Record .50 1.25
8 Charles Barkley NBA Shooting .50 1.25
9 Charles Barkley NBA Rebounds .50 1.25
10 Larry Bird NBA Update .75 2.00
11 Larry Bird NBA Rookie .75 2.00
12 Larry Bird Game Strategy .75 2.00
13 Larry Bird NBA Best Game .75 2.00
14 Larry Bird Off the Court .75 2.00
15 Larry Bird NBA Playoffs .75 2.00
16 Larry Bird NBA All-Star Record .75 2.00
17 Larry Bird NBA Shooting .75 2.00
18 Larry Bird NBA Rebounds .75 2.00
19 Patrick Ewing NBA Update .40 1.00
20 Patrick Ewing NBA Rookie .40 1.00
21 Patrick Ewing Game Strategy .40 1.00
22 Patrick Ewing NBA Best Game .40 1.00
23 Patrick Ewing Off the Court .40 1.00
24 Patrick Ewing NBA Playoffs .40 1.00
25 Patrick Ewing NBA All-Star Record .40 1.00
26 Patrick Ewing NBA Shooting .40 1.00
27 Patrick Ewing NBA Rebounds .40 1.00
28 Magic Johnson NBA Update .75 2.00
29 Magic Johnson NBA Rookie .75 2.00
30 Magic Johnson Game Strategy .75 2.00
31 Magic Johnson NBA Best Game .75 2.00
32 Magic Johnson Off the Court .75 2.00
33 Magic Johnson NBA Playoffs .75 2.00
34 Magic Johnson NBA All-Star Record .75 2.00
35 Magic Johnson NBA Shooting .75 2.00
36 Magic Johnson NBA Assists .75 2.00
37 Michael Jordan NBA Update 2.00 5.00
38 Michael Jordan NBA Rookie 5.00 12.00
39 Michael Jordan Game Strategy 2.00 5.00
40 Michael Jordan NBA Best Game 2.00 5.00
41 Michael Jordan Off the Court 2.00 5.00
42 Michael Jordan NBA Playoffs 2.00 5.00
43 Michael Jordan NBA All-Star Record 2.00 5.00
44 Michael Jordan NBA Shooting 2.00 5.00
45 Michael Jordan NBA All-Time Records 2.00 5.00
46 Karl Malone NBA Update .50 1.25
47 Karl Malone NBA Rookie .50 1.25
48 Karl Malone Game Strategy .50 1.25
49 Karl Malone NBA Best Game .50 1.25
50 Karl Malone Off the Court .50 1.25
51 Karl Malone NBA Playoffs .50 1.25
52 Karl Malone NBA All-Star Record .50 1.25
53 Karl Malone NBA Shooting .50 1.25
54 Karl Malone NBA Rebounds .50 1.25
55 Chris Mullin NBA Update .30 .75
56 Chris Mullin NBA Rookie .30 .75
57 Chris Mullin Game Strategy .30 .75
58 Chris Mullin NBA Best Game .30 .75
59 Chris Mullin Off the Court .30 .75
60 Chris Mullin NBA Playoffs .30 .75
61 Chris Mullin NBA All-Star Record .30 .75
62 Chris Mullin NBA Shooting .30 .75
63 Chris Mullin NBA Minutes .30 .75
64 Scottie Pippen NBA Update .60 1.50
65 Scottie Pippen NBA Rookie .60 1.50
66 Scottie Pippen Game Strategy .60 1.50
67 Scottie Pippen NBA Best Game .60 1.50
68 Scottie Pippen Off the Court .60 1.50
69 Scottie Pippen NBA Playoffs .60 1.50
70 Scottie Pippen NBA All-Star Record .60 1.50
71 Scottie Pippen NBA Shooting .60 1.50
72 Scottie Pippen NBA Steals and Blocks .60 1.50
73 David Robinson NBA Update .50 1.25
74 David Robinson NBA Rookie .50 1.25
75 David Robinson Game Strategy .50 1.25
76 David Robinson NBA Best Game .50 1.25
77 David Robinson Off the Court .50 1.25
78 David Robinson NBA Playoffs .50 1.25
79 David Robinson NBA All-Star .50 1.25
80 David Robinson NBA Shooting .50 1.25
81 David Robinson NBA All-Around .50 1.25
82 John Stockton NBA Update .50 1.25
83 John Stockton NBA Rookie .50 1.25
84 John Stockton Game Strategy .50 1.25
85 John Stockton NBA Best Game .50 1.25
86 John Stockton Off the Court .50 1.25
87 John Stockton NBA Playoffs .50 1.25
88 John Stockton NBA All-Star Record .50 1.25
89 John Stockton NBA Shooting .50 1.25
90 John Stockton NBA Assists .50 1.25
91 P.J. Carlesimo CO College Coaching .20 .50
92 P.J. Carlesimo CO NCAA Coaching Record .08 .25
93 Chuck Daly CO NBA Coaching .50 1.25
94 Chuck Daly CO NCAA Coaching Record .50 1.25
95 Mike Krzyzewski CO College Coaching .60 1.50
96 Mike Krzyzewski CO College Coaching Record .60 1.50
97 Lenny Wilkens CO NBA Coaching .40 1.00
98 Lenny Wilkens CO NBA Coaching Record .40 1.00
99 Checklist 1-54 .08 .25
100 Checklist 55-110 .08 .25
101 Magic on Barkley .75 2.00
102 Magic on Bird .75 2.00
103 Magic on Ewing .75 2.00
104 Magic on Magic .75 2.00
105 Magic on Jordan 2.00 5.00
106 Magic on Malone .75 2.00
107 Magic on Mullin .75 2.00
108 Magic on Pippen .75 2.00
109 Magic on Robinson .75 2.00
110 Magic on Stockton .75 2.00
NNO Plastic Team Card 12.00 30.00

1994 SkyBox USA Prototypes

COMPLETE SET (8) 1.25 3.00
1 Derrick Coleman .25 .60
2 Joe Dumars .30 .75
3 Magic Johnson .60 1.50
4 Larry Johnson .30 .75
5 Shawn Kemp .30 .75
6 Alonzo Mourning .30 .75
7 Isiah Thomas .40 1.00
8 Dominique Wilkins .40 1.00

1994 SkyBox USA

COMPLETE SET (89) 6.00 15.00
1 Alonzo Mourning .20 .50
2 Alonzo Mourning .20 .50
3 Alonzo Mourning .20 .50
4 Alonzo Mourning .20 .50
5 Alonzo Mourning .20 .50
6 Alonzo Mourning .20 .50
7 Larry Johnson .20 .50
8 Larry Johnson .20 .50
9 Larry Johnson .20 .50
10 Larry Johnson .20 .50
11 Larry Johnson .20 .50
12 Larry Johnson .20 .50
13 Shawn Kemp .20 .50
14 Shawn Kemp .20 .50
15 Shawn Kemp .20 .50
16 Shawn Kemp .20 .50
17 Shawn Kemp .20 .50
18 Shawn Kemp .20 .50
19 Mark Price .15 .40
20 Mark Price .15 .40
21 Mark Price .15 .40
22 Mark Price .15 .40
23 Mark Price .15 .40
24 Mark Price .15 .40
25 Steve Smith .12 .30
26 Steve Smith .12 .30
27 Steve Smith .12 .30
28 Steve Smith .12 .30
29 Steve Smith .12 .30
30 Steve Smith .12 .30
31 Dominique Wilkins .25 .60
32 Dominique Wilkins .25 .60
33 Dominique Wilkins .25 .60
34 Dominique Wilkins .25 .60
35 Dominique Wilkins .25 .60
36 Dominique Wilkins .25 .60
37 Derrick Coleman .15 .40
38 Derrick Coleman .15 .40
39 Derrick Coleman .15 .40
40 Derrick Coleman .15 .40
41 Derrick Coleman .15 .40
42 Derrick Coleman .15 .40
43 Isiah Thomas .25 .60
44 Isiah Thomas .25 .60
45 Isiah Thomas .25 .60
46 Isiah Thomas .25 .60
47 Isiah Thomas .25 .60
48 Isiah Thomas .25 .60
49 Joe Dumars .20 .50
50 Joe Dumars .20 .50
51 Joe Dumars .20 .50
52 Joe Dumars .20 .50
53 Joe Dumars .20 .50
54 Joe Dumars .20 .50
55 Dan Majerle .15 .40
56 Dan Majerle .15 .40
57 Dan Majerle .15 .40
58 Dan Majerle .15 .40
59 Dan Majerle .15 .40
60 Dan Majerle .15 .40
61 Tim Hardaway .20 .50
62 Tim Hardaway .20 .50
63 Tim Hardaway .20 .50
64 Tim Hardaway .20 .50
65 Tim Hardaway .20 .50
66 Tim Hardaway .20 .50
67 Shaquille O'Neal .50 1.25
68 Shaquille O'Neal .50 1.25
69 Shaquille O'Neal .50 1.25
70 Shaquille O'Neal .50 1.25
71 Shaquille O'Neal .50 1.25
72 Shaquille O'Neal .50 1.25
73 Reggie Miller .25 .60
74 Reggie Miller .25 .60
75 Reggie Miller .25 .60
76 Reggie Miller .25 .60
77 Reggie Miller .25 .60
78 Reggie Miller .25 .60
79 Don Chaney CO .15 .40
80 Pete Gillen CO .15 .40
81 Rick Majerus CO .15 .40
82 Don Nelson CO .15 .40
83 '94 USA Team .15 .40
84 International Rules Time .15 .40
85 International Rules Court Dimensions .15 .40
86 International Rules Rules .15 .40
87 Magic Johnson Passing the Torch .40 1.00
88 David Robinson Passing the Torch .25 .60
89 Checklist .08 .25
NNO Expired T-Shirt Exch. .08 .25

1994 SkyBox USA Gold

COMPLETE SET (89) 25.00 60.00
*GOLD: 1.25X TO 3X HI COLUMN

1994 SkyBox USA Autographs

COMPLETE SET (7) 300.00 600.00
11A Larry Johnson 25.00 60.00
17A Shawn Kemp 50.00 125.00
35A Dominique Wilkins 40.00 100.00
47A Isiah Thomas 50.00 125.00
53A Joe Dumars 40.00 100.00
59A Dan Majerle 40.00 100.00
65A Tim Hardaway 30.00 80.00

1994 SkyBox USA Dream Play

COMPLETE SET (13) 4.00 10.00
DP1 Alonzo Mourning .60 1.50
DP2 Larry Johnson .60 1.50
DP3 Shawn Kemp .60 1.50
DP4 Mark Price .50 1.25
DP5 Steve Smith .40 1.00
DP6 Dominique Wilkins .60 1.50
DP7 Derrick Coleman .50 1.25
DP8 Isiah Thomas .75 2.00
DP9 Joe Dumars .60 1.50
DP10 Dan Majerle .50 1.25
DP11 Tim Hardaway .60 1.50
DP12 Shaquille O'Neal 1.50 4.00
DP13 Reggie Miller .75 2.00

1994 SkyBox USA Kevin Johnson

COMPLETE SET (14) 10.00 25.00
90G Kevin Johnson International .75 2.00
90S Kevin Johnson International .20 .50
91G Kevin Johnson NBA Rookie .75 2.00
91S Kevin Johnson NBA Rookie .20 .50
92G Kevin Johnson Best Game .75 2.00
92S Kevin Johnson Best Game .20 .50
93G Kevin Johnson NBA Update .75 2.00
93S Kevin Johnson NBA Update .20 .50
94G Kevin Johnson Trademark Move .75 2.00
94S Kevin Johnson Trademark Move .20 .50
95G Kevin Johnson Magic on Johnson .75 2.00
95S Kevin Johnson Magic on Johnson .20 .50
DP14 Kevin Johnson Dream Play 1.25 3.00
PT14 Kevin Johnson Portrait 5.00 12.00

1994 SkyBox USA On The Court

COMPLETE SET (14) 6.00 15.00
1 Isiah Thomas 1.25 3.00
2 Tim Hardaway 1.00 2.50
3 Reggie Miller 1.25 3.00
4 Steve Smith .60 1.50
5 Joe Dumars 1.00 2.50
6 Shawn Kemp 1.00 2.50
7 Mark Price .75 2.00
8 Dan Majerle .75 2.00
9 Kevin Johnson .75 2.00
10 Derrick Coleman .75 2.00
11 Alonzo Mourning 1.00 2.50
12 Dominique Wilkins 1.25 3.00
13 Larry Johnson 1.00 2.50
14 Shaquille O'Neal 2.50 6.00
NNO Exp.On The Court Exch. .20 .50

1994 SkyBox USA Portraits

COMPLETE SET (13) 40.00 80.00
PT1 Alonzo Mourning 6.00 15.00
PT2 Larry Johnson 6.00 15.00
PT3 Shawn Kemp 6.00 15.00
PT4 Mark Price 5.00 12.00
PT5 Steve Smith 4.00 10.00
PT6 Dominique Wilkins 8.00 20.00
PT7 Derrick Coleman 5.00 12.00
PT8 Isiah Thomas 8.00 20.00
PT9 Joe Dumars 6.00 15.00
PT10 Dan Majerle 5.00 12.00
PT11 Tim Hardaway 6.00 15.00
PT12 Shaquille O'Neal 15.00 40.00
PT13 Reggie Miller 8.00 20.00

1996 SkyBox USA

COMPLETE SET (60) 5.00 12.00
1 Anfernee Hardaway GS .25 .60
2 Grant Hill GS .25 .60
3 Karl Malone GS .20 .50
4 Reggie Miller GS .25 .60
5 Scottie Pippen GS .25 .60
6 Hakeem Olajuwon GS .25 .60
7 Shaquille O'Neal GS .40 1.00
8 David Robinson GS .25 .60
9 Glenn Robinson GS .12 .30
10 John Stockton GS .20 .50
11 Anfernee Hardaway .25 .60
12 Grant Hill .25 .60
13 Karl Malone .20 .50
14 Reggie Miller .25 .60
15 Scottie Pippen .25 .60
16 Hakeem Olajuwon .25 .60
17 Shaquille O'Neal .40 1.00
18 David Robinson .25 .60
19 Glenn Robinson .12 .30
20 John Stockton .20 .50
21 Anfernee Hardaway .25 .60
22 Grant Hill .25 .60
23 Karl Malone .20 .50
24 Reggie Miller .25 .60
25 Scottie Pippen .25 .60
26 Hakeem Olajuwon .25 .60
27 Shaquille O'Neal .40 1.00
28 David Robinson .25 .60
29 Glenn Robinson .12 .30
30 John Stockton .20 .50
31 Anfernee Hardaway .25 .60
32 Grant Hill .25 .60
33 Karl Malone .20 .50
34 Reggie Miller .25 .60
35 Scottie Pippen .25 .60
36 Hakeem Olajuwon .25 .60
37 Shaquille O'Neal .40 1.00
38 David Robinson .25 .60
39 Glenn Robinson .12 .30
40 John Stockton .20 .50
41 Anfernee Hardaway .25 .60
42 Grant Hill .25 .60
43 Karl Malone .20 .50
44 Reggie Miller .25 .60
45 Scottie Pippen .25 .60
46 Hakeem Olajuwon .20 .50
47 Shaquille O'Neal .40 1.00
48 David Robinson .25 .60
49 Glenn Robinson .12 .30
50 John Stockton .20 .50
51 Lenny Wilkens CO .15 .40
52 Bobby Cremins .15 .40
53 Clem Haskins .15 .40
54 Jerry Sloan .15 .40
55 Shaquille O'Neal Anfernee Hardaway AD .30 .75
56 Karl Malone John Stockton AD .15 .40
57 David Robinson Hakeem Olajuwon AD .15 .40
58 Scottie Pippen Grant Hill AD .15 .40
59 Reggie Miller Glenn Robinson AD .15 .40
60 Checklist .08 .25
NNO Grant Hill Promo Sheet 1.25 3.00

1996 SkyBox USA Bronze

COMPLETE SET (10) 8.00 20.00
*SPARKLE: .5X TO 1.25X VALUE
SPARKLE: STATED ODDS 1:18 HOBBY
B1 Anfernee Hardaway 1.50 4.00
B2 Grant Hill 1.50 4.00
B3 Karl Malone 1.25 3.00
B4 Reggie Miller 1.50 4.00
B5 Scottie Pippen 1.50 4.00
B6 Hakeem Olajuwon 1.25 3.00
B7 Shaquille O'Neal 2.50 6.00
B8 David Robinson 1.50 4.00
B9 Glenn Robinson .75 2.00
B10 John Stockton 1.25 3.00

1996 SkyBox USA Gold

COMPLETE SET (10) 40.00 100.00
*SPARKLE: .5X TO 1.25X VALUE
SPARKLE: STATED ODDS 1:180 HOBBY
G1 Anfernee Hardaway 8.00 20.00
G2 Grant Hill 8.00 20.00
G3 Karl Malone 6.00 15.00
G4 Reggie Miller 8.00 20.00
G5 Scottie Pippen 8.00 20.00
G6 Hakeem Olajuwon 6.00 15.00
G7 Shaquille O'Neal 12.00 30.00
G8 David Robinson 8.00 20.00
G9 Glenn Robinson 4.00 10.00
G10 John Stockton 6.00 15.00

1996 SkyBox USA Quads

COMPLETE SET (15) 5.00 12.00
Q1 Anfernee Hardaway .75 2.00
Q2 Grant Hill .75 2.00
Q3 Karl Malone .60 1.50
Q4 Reggie Miller .75 2.00
Q5 Scottie Pippen .75 2.00
Q6 Hakeem Olajuwon .60 1.50
Q7 Shaquille O'Neal 1.25 3.00
Q8 David Robinson .75 2.00
Q9 Glenn Robinson .40 1.00
Q10 John Stockton .60 1.50
Q11 Power Quad .40 1.00
Q12 Versatility Quad .40 1.00
Q13 Passing Quad .40 1.00
Q14 Defensive Quad .40 1.00
Q15 Scorers Quad .40 1.00

1996 SkyBox USA Silver

COMPLETE SET (10) 20.00 50.00
*SPARKLE: .5X TO 1.25X VALUE
SPARKLE: STATED ODDS 1:72 HOBBY
S1 Anfernee Hardaway 4.00 10.00
S2 Grant Hill 4.00 10.00
S3 Karl Malone 3.00 8.00
S4 Reggie Miller 4.00 10.00
S5 Scottie Pippen 4.00 10.00
S6 Hakeem Olajuwon 3.00 8.00
S7 Shaquille O'Neal 6.00 15.00
S8 David Robinson 4.00 10.00
S9 Glenn Robinson 2.00 5.00
S10 John Stockton 3.00 8.00

1996 SkyBox USA Wrapper Exchange

COMPLETE SET (25) 5.00 12.00
61 Charles Barkley GS .25 .60
62 Mitch Richmond GS .15 .40
63 Charles Barkley BB .25 .60
64 Mitch Richmond BB .15 .40
65 Charles Barkley PP .25 .60
66 Mitch Richmond PP .15 .40
67 Charles Barkley CON .25 .60
68 Mitch Richmond CON .15 .40
69 Charles Barkley CON .25 .60
70 Mitch Richmond CON .15 .40
71 Charles Barkley Mitch Richmond AD .15 .40
B11 Charles Barkley Bronze .60 1.50
B12 Mitch Richmond Bronze .40 1.00
G11 Charles Barkley Gold 1.50 4.00
G12 Mitch Richmond Gold 1.00 2.50
Q16 Charles Barkley Quad 1.00 2.50
Q17 Mitch Richmond Quad .60 1.50
S11 Charles Barkley Silver 1.00 2.50
S12 Mitch Richmond Silver .60 1.50
BS11 Charles Barkley Bronze Sparkle .60 1.50
BS12 Mitch Richmond Bronze Sparkle .40 1.00
GS11 Charles Barkley Gold Sparkle 1.50 4.00
GS12 Mitch Richmond Gold Sparkle 1.00 2.50
SS11 Charles Barkley Silver Sparkle 1.00 2.50
SS12 Mitch Richmond Silver Sparkle .60 1.50

1996 SkyBox USA Texaco

COMPLETE SET (14) 2.50 6.00
1 Charles Barkley .50 1.25
2 Anfernee Hardaway .50 1.25
3 Grant Hill .50 1.25
4 Karl Malone .40 1.00
5 Reggie Miller .50 1.25
6 Hakeem Olajuwon .50 1.25
7 Shaquille O'Neal .75 2.00
8 Scottie Pippen .50 1.25
9 Mitch Richmond .30 .75
10 David Robinson .50 1.25
11 Glenn Robinson .25 .60
12 John Stockton .40 1.00
13 Lenny Wilkens CO .30 .75
14 Team Card .30 .75

1991 Smokey's Larry Johnson

COMPLETE SET (7) 2.00 5.00
COMMON CARD (1-7) .40 1.00
PR Larry Johnson PROMO .50 1.25

2001 Sol Fleer WNBA

COMPLETE SET (9) 4.00 10.00
1 Debbie Black .40 1.00
2 Katrina Colleton .40 1.00
3 Tracy Reid .40 1.00
4 Kisha Ford .40 1.00
5 Kristen Rasmussen .40 1.00
6 Sandy Brondello 1.50 4.00
7 Marlies Askamp .40 1.00
8 Ron Rothstein .40 1.00
9 Sheri Sam .40 1.00

1994-95 SP

COMPLETE SET (165) 30.00 80.00
MJ1R: STATED ODDS 1:30
MJ1S: STATED ODDS 1:192
1 Glenn Robinson FOIL RC .75 2.00
2 Jason Kidd FOIL RC 2.00 5.00
3 Grant Hill FOIL RC 2.00 5.00
4 Donyell Marshall FOIL RC .40 1.00
5 Juwan Howard FOIL RC .60 1.50
6 Sharone Wright FOIL RC .30 .75
7 Lamond Murray FOIL RC .40 1.00
8 Brian Grant FOIL RC .60 1.50
9 Eric Montross FOIL RC .30 .75
10 Eddie Jones FOIL RC 1.25 3.00
11 Carlos Rogers FOIL RC .30 .75
12 Khalid Reeves FOIL RC .30 .75
13 Jalen Rose FOIL RC 1.00 2.50
14 Eric Piatkowski FOIL RC .40 1.00
15 Clifford Rozier FOIL RC .25 .60
16 Aaron McKie FOIL RC .40 1.00
17 Eric Mobley FOIL RC .25 .60
18 Tony Dumas FOIL RC .30 .75
19 B.J. Tyler FOIL RC .25 .60
20 Dickey Simpkins FOIL RC .30 .75
21 Bill Curley FOIL RC .25 .60
22 Wesley Person FOIL RC .40 1.00
23 Monty Williams FOIL RC .50 1.25
24 Greg Minor FOIL RC .40 1.00
25 Charlie Ward FOIL RC .40 1.00
26 Brooks Thompson FOIL RC .30 .75
27 Trevor Ruffin FOIL RC .25 .60
28 Derrick Alston FOIL RC .25 .60
29 Michael Smith FOIL RC .25 .60
30 Dontonio Wingfield FOIL RC .40 1.00
31 Stacey Augmon .30 .75
32 Steve Smith .30 .75
33 Mookie Blaylock .40 1.00
34 Grant Long .25 .60
35 Ken Norman .25 .60
36 Dominique Wilkins .60 1.50
37 Dino Radja .25 .60
38 Dee Brown .30 .75
39 David Wesley .25 .60
40 Rick Fox .25 .60
41 Alonzo Mourning .60 1.50
42 Larry Johnson .50 1.25
43 Hersey Hawkins .25 .60
44 Scott Burrell .25 .60
45 Muggsy Bogues .30 .75
46 Scottie Pippen 1.00 2.50
47 Toni Kukoc .50 1.25
48 B.J. Armstrong .40 1.00
49 Will Perdue .25 .60
50 Ron Harper .30 .75
51 Mark Price .25 .60
52 Tyrone Hill .25 .60
53 Chris Mills .30 .75
54 John Williams .25 .60
55 Bobby Phills .25 .60
56 Jim Jackson .30 .75
57 Jamal Mashburn .40 1.00
58 Popeye Jones .25 .60
59 Roy Tarpley .25 .60
60 Lorenzo Williams .25 .60
61 Mahmoud Abdul-Rauf .25 .60
62 Rodney Rogers .25 .60
63 Bryant Stith .25 .60
64 Dikembe Mutombo .60 1.50
65 Robert Pack .30 .75
66 Joe Dumars .40 1.00
67 Terry Mills .25 .60
68 Oliver Miller .25 .60
69 Lindsey Hunter .25 .60
70 Mark West .25 .60
71 Latrell Sprewell .50 1.25
72 Tim Hardaway .50 1.25
73 Ricky Pierce .25 .60
74 Rony Seikaly .25 .60
75 Tom Gugliotta .25 .60
76 Hakeem Olajuwon .75 2.00
77 Clyde Drexler .60 1.50
78 Vernon Maxwell .25 .60
79 Robert Horry .40 1.00
80 Sam Cassell .40 1.00
81 Reggie Miller .75 2.00
82 Rik Smits .30 .75
83 Derrick McKey .25 .60
84 Mark Jackson .30 .75
85 Dale Davis .25 .60
86 Loy Vaught .25 .60
87 Terry Dehere .25 .60
88 Malik Sealy .25 .60
89 Pooh Richardson .25 .60
90 Tony Massenburg .25 .60
91 Cedric Ceballos .30 .75
92 Nick Van Exel .40 1.00
93 George Lynch .25 .60
94 Vlade Divac .40 1.00
95 Elden Campbell .25 .60
96 Glen Rice .40 1.00
97 Kevin Willis .30 .75
98 Billy Owens .25 .60
99 Bimbo Coles .25 .60
100 Harold Miner .25 .60
101 Vin Baker .40 1.00
102 Todd Day .25 .60
103 Marty Conlon .25 .60
104 Lee Mayberry .25 .60
105 Eric Murdock .25 .60
106 Isaiah Rider .40 1.00
107 Doug West .25 .60
108 Christian Laettner .30 .75
109 Sean Rooks .25 .60
110 Stacey King .25 .60
111 Derrick Coleman .40 1.00
112 Kenny Anderson .30 .75
113 Chris Morris .25 .60
114 Armon Gilliam .25 .60
115 Benoit Benjamin .25 .60
116 Patrick Ewing .60 1.50
117 Charles Oakley .40 1.00
118 John Starks .40 1.00
119 Derek Harper .30 .75
120 Charles Smith .25 .60
121 Shaquille O'Neal 1.50 4.00
122 Anfernee Hardaway .75 2.00
123 Nick Anderson .25 .60
124 Horace Grant .40 1.00
125 Donald Royal .25 .60
126 Clarence Weatherspoon .25 .60
127 Dana Barros .25 .60
128 Jeff Malone .25 .60

129 Willie Burton .25 .60
130 Shawn Bradley .25 .60
131 Charles Barkley 1.00 2.50
132 Kevin Johnson .40 1.00
133 Danny Manning .30 .75
134 Dan Majerle .40 1.00
135 A.C. Green .30 .75
136 Otis Thorpe .25 .60
137 Clifford Robinson .30 .75
138 Rod Strickland .25 .60
139 Buck Williams .25 .60
140 James Robinson .25 .60
141 Mitch Richmond .50 1.25
142 Walt Williams .25 .60
143 Olden Polynice .25 .60
144 Spud Webb .30 .75
145 Duane Causwell .25 .60
146 David Robinson .75 2.00
147 Dennis Rodman 1.00 2.50
148 Sean Elliott .30 .75
149 Avery Johnson .30 .75
150 J.R. Reid .25 .60
151 Shawn Kemp .60 1.50
152 Gary Payton .60 1.50
153 Detlef Schrempf .40 1.00
154 Nate McMillan .30 .75
155 Kendall Gill .25 .60
156 Karl Malone .75 2.00
157 John Stockton .75 2.00
158 Jeff Hornacek .30 .75
159 Felton Spencer .25 .60
160 David Benoit .25 .60
161 Chris Webber .75 2.00
162 Rex Chapman .25 .60
163 Don MacLean .25 .60
164 Calbert Cheaney .30 .75
165 Scott Skiles .25 .60
P23 M.Jordan Promo 4.00 10.00
MJ1R M.Jordan Red 2.50 6.00
MJ1S M.Jordan Silver 8.00 20.00

1994-95 SP Die Cuts
COMPLETE SET (165) 20.00 50.00
*STARS: 1X TO 2.5X BASE CARD HI
*RCs: .75X TO 2X BASE HI
ONE PER PACK

1994-95 SP Holoviews
COMPLETE SET (36) 12.00 30.00
STATED ODDS 1:5
*DIE CUTS: 1X TO 2.5X HI COLUMN
DIE CUTS: STATED ODDS 1:75
PC1 Eric Montross .40 1.00
PC2 Dominique Wilkins 1.25 3.00
PC3 Larry Johnson 1.00 2.50
PC4 Dickey Simpkins .40 1.00
PC5 Jalen Rose 1.25 3.00
PC6 Latrell Sprewell 1.00 2.50
PC7 Carlos Rogers .40 1.00
PC8 Lamond Murray .50 1.25
PC9 Eddie Jones 1.50 4.00
PC10 Cedric Ceballos .40 1.00
PC11 Khalid Reeves .40 1.00
PC12 Glenn Robinson 1.00 2.50
PC13 Christian Laettner .60 1.50
PC14 Derrick Coleman .75 2.00
PC15 Vin Baker .50 1.25
PC16 Donyell Marshall .50 1.25
PC17 Kenny Anderson .60 1.50
PC18 Sharone Wright .40 1.00
PC19 Wesley Person .50 1.25
PC20 Brian Grant .75 2.00
PC21 Mitch Richmond 1.00 2.50
PC22 Shawn Kemp 1.25 3.00
PC23 Gary Payton 1.25 3.00
PC24 Juwan Howard .75 2.00
PC25 Stacey Augmon .60 1.50
PC26 Aaron McKie .50 1.25
PC27 Clifford Rozier .30 .75
PC28 Eric Piatkowski .50 1.25
PC29 Shaquille O'Neal 3.00 8.00
PC30 Charlie Ward .50 1.25
PC31 Monty Williams .60 1.50
PC32 Jason Kidd 2.50 6.00
PC33 Bill Curley .30 .75
PC34 Grant Hill 2.50 6.00
PC35 Jamal Mashburn .75 2.00
PC36 Nick Van Exel .75 2.00

1995 SP
COMPLETE SET (150) 10.00 25.00
CB1 E.Ivan
Michael Jordan 8.00 20.00

1995-96 SP
COMPLETE SET (167) 12.00 30.00
C1: STATED ODDS 1:359
1 Stacey Augmon .20 .50
2 Mookie Blaylock .25 .60
3 Andrew Lang .15 .40
4 Steve Smith .20 .50
5 Spud Webb .20 .50
6 Dana Barros .20 .50
7 Dee Brown .20 .50
8 Todd Day .15 .40
9 Rick Fox .15 .40
10 Eric Montross .15 .40
11 Dino Radja .15 .40
12 Kenny Anderson .20 .50
13 Scott Burrell .15 .40
14 Dell Curry .25 .60
15 Matt Geiger .15 .40
16 Larry Johnson .30 .75
17 Glen Rice .25 .60
18 Steve Kerr .25 .60
19 Toni Kukoc .30 .75
20 Luc Longley .20 .50
21 Scottie Pippen .60 1.50
22 Dennis Rodman .50 1.25
23 Michael Jordan 2.50 6.00
24 Terrell Brandon .20 .50
25 Michael Cage .15 .40
26 Danny Ferry .15 .40
27 Chris Mills .15 .40
28 Bobby Phills .20 .50
29 Tony Dumas .15 .40
30 Jim Jackson .20 .50
31 Popeye Jones .15 .40
32 Jason Kidd .40 1.00
33 Jamal Mashburn .25 .60
34 Mahmoud Abdul-Rauf .20 .50
35 LaPhonso Ellis .20 .50
36 Dikembe Mutombo .40 1.00
37 Jalen Rose .30 .75
38 Bryant Stith .15 .40
39 Joe Dumars .25 .60
40 Grant Hill .40 1.00
41 Lindsey Hunter .15 .40
42 Allan Houston .20 .50
43 Otis Thorpe .20 .50
44 B.J. Armstrong .25 .60
45 Tim Hardaway .30 .75
46 Chris Mullin .25 .60
47 Latrell Sprewell .25 .60
48 Rony Seikaly .15 .40
49 Sam Cassell .25 .60
50 Clyde Drexler .40 1.00
51 Robert Horry .25 .60
52 Hakeem Olajuwon .50 1.25
53 Kenny Smith .20 .50
54 Dale Davis .15 .40
55 Derrick McKey .15 .40
56 Reggie Miller .50 1.25
57 Ricky Pierce .15 .40
58 Rik Smits .20 .50
59 Lamond Murray .15 .40
60 Rodney Rogers .20 .50
61 Malik Sealy .15 .40
62 Loy Vaught .15 .40
63 Brian Williams .15 .40
64 Elden Campbell .15 .40
65 Cedric Ceballos .20 .50
66 Magic Johnson .75 2.00
67 Eddie Jones .25 .60
68 Nick Van Exel .25 .60
69 Bimbo Coles .15 .40
70 Alonzo Mourning .40 1.00
71 Billy Owens .15 .40
72 Kevin Willis .15 .40
73 Vin Baker .20 .50
74 Benoit Benjamin .15 .40
75 Sherman Douglas .15 .40
76 Lee Mayberry .15 .40
77 Glenn Robinson .25 .60
78 Tom Gugliotta .20 .50
79 Christian Laettner .20 .50
80 Sam Mitchell .15 .40
81 Terry Porter .15 .40
82 Isaiah Rider .25 .60
83 Shawn Bradley .15 .40
84 P.J. Brown .15 .40
85 Kendall Gill .15 .40
86 Armon Gilliam .15 .40
87 Jayson Williams .15 .40
88 Patrick Ewing .40 1.00
89 Derek Harper .20 .50
90 Anthony Mason .15 .40
91 Charles Oakley .20 .50
92 John Starks .25 .60
93 Nick Anderson .20 .50
94 Horace Grant .20 .50
95 Anfernee Hardaway .60 1.50
96 Shaquille O'Neal 1.00 2.50
97 Dennis Scott .15 .40
98 Derrick Coleman .20 .50
99 Vernon Maxwell .15 .40
100 Trevor Ruffin .15 .40
101 Clarence Weatherspoon .15 .40
102 Sharone Wright .15 .40
103 Charles Barkley .60 1.50
104 A.C. Green .20 .50
105 Kevin Johnson .25 .60
106 Wesley Person .20 .50
107 John Williams .15 .40
108 Chris Dudley .15 .40
109 Harvey Grant .15 .40
110 Aaron McKie .15 .40
111 Clifford Robinson .25 .60
112 Rod Strickland .20 .50
113 Brian Grant .20 .50
114 Sarunas Marciulionis .25 .60
115 Olden Polynice .15 .40
116 Mitch Richmond .30 .75
117 Walt Williams .15 .40
118 Vinny Del Negro .15 .40
119 Sean Elliott .20 .50
120 Avery Johnson .20 .50
121 Chuck Person .20 .50
122 David Robinson .50 1.25
123 Hersey Hawkins .20 .50
124 Shawn Kemp .40 1.00
125 Gary Payton .40 1.00
126 Sam Perkins .15 .40
127 Detlef Schrempf .25 .60
128 Oliver Miller .15 .40
129 Tracy Murray .15 .40
130 Ed Pinckney .15 .40
131 Alvin Robertson .15 .40
132 Zan Tabak .15 .40
133 Jeff Hornacek .20 .50
134 Adam Keefe .15 .40
135 Karl Malone .50 1.25
136 Chris Morris .15 .40
137 John Stockton .50 1.25
138 Greg Anthony .15 .40
139 Blue Edwards .15 .40
140 Kenny Gattison .15 .40
141 Chris King .15 .40
142 Byron Scott .25 .60
143 Calbert Cheaney .15 .40
144 Juwan Howard .25 .60
145 Gheorghe Muresan .15 .40
146 Robert Pack .15 .40
147 Chris Webber .30 .75
148 Alan Henderson RC .25 .60
149 Eric Williams RC .25 .60
150 George Zidek RC .20 .50
151 Bob Sura RC .20 .50
152 Antonio McDyess RC .40 1.00
153 Theo Ratliff RC .40 1.00
154 Joe Smith RC .30 .75
155 Brent Barry RC .40 1.00
156 Sasha Danilovic RC .25 .60
157 Kurt Thomas RC .25 .60
158 Shawn Respert RC .20 .50
159 Kevin Garnett RC 5.00 12.00
160 Ed O'Bannon RC .20 .50
161 Jerry Stackhouse RC 1.50 4.00
162 Michael Finley RC .60 1.50
163 Arvydas Sabonis RC .50 1.25
164 Cory Alexander RC .25 .60
165 Damon Stoudamire RC .60 1.50
166 Bryant Reeves RC .20 .50
167 Rasheed Wallace RC .75 2.00
C1 H.Olajuwon Comm. 5.00 12.00
P23 Michael Jordan PROMO 4.00 10.00

1995-96 SP All-Stars
COMPLETE SET (30) 15.00 40.00
STATED ODDS 1:5
*GOLD: 2.5X TO 6X HI COLUMN
GOLD: STATED ODDS 1:61
AS1 Anfernee Hardaway 1.50 4.00
AS2 Michael Jordan 6.00 15.00
AS3 Grant Hill 1.00 2.50
AS4 Scottie Pippen 1.50 4.00
AS5 Shaquille O'Neal 2.50 6.00
AS6 Vin Baker .50 1.25
AS7 Terrell Brandon .50 1.25
AS8 Patrick Ewing 1.00 2.50
AS9 Juwan Howard .60 1.50
AS10 Reggie Miller 1.25 3.00
AS11 Alonzo Mourning 1.00 2.50
AS12 Glen Rice .60 1.50
AS13 Clyde Drexler 1.00 2.50
AS14 Jason Kidd 1.00 2.50
AS15 Charles Barkley 1.50 4.00
AS16 Shawn Kemp 1.00 2.50
AS17 Hakeem Olajuwon 1.25 3.00
AS18 Sean Elliott .50 1.25
AS19 Karl Malone 1.25 3.00
AS20 Dikembe Mutombo 1.00 2.50
AS21 Gary Payton 1.00 2.50
AS22 Mitch Richmond .75 2.00
AS23 David Robinson 1.25 3.00
AS24 John Stockton 1.25 3.00
AS25 Jerry Stackhouse 1.00 2.50
AS26 Damon Stoudamire .75 2.00
AS27 Rasheed Wallace .75 2.00
AS28 Kevin Garnett 2.50 6.00
AS29 Antonio McDyess .40 1.00
AS30 Joe Smith .40 1.00

1995-96 SP Holoviews
COMPLETE SET (40) 40.00 100.00
STATED ODDS 1:7
PC1 Mookie Blaylock 1.50 4.00
PC2 Eric Williams .75 2.00
PC3 Larry Johnson 2.00 5.00
PC4 George Zidek .60 1.50
PC5 Michael Jordan 30.00 80.00
PC6 Bob Sura .60 1.50
PC7 Jason Kidd 2.50 6.00
PC8 Cherokee Parks .60 1.50
PC9 Antonio McDyess 1.00 2.50
PC10 Grant Hill 2.50 6.00
PC11 Theo Ratliff 1.25 3.00
PC12 Joe Smith 1.00 2.50
PC13 Latrell Sprewell 1.50 4.00
PC14 Hakeem Olajuwon 3.00 8.00
PC15 Travis Best .75 2.00
PC16 Brent Barry 1.25 3.00
PC17 Nick Van Exel 1.50 4.00
PC18 Kurt Thomas .75 2.00
PC19 Shawn Respert .60 1.50
PC20 Glenn Robinson 1.50 4.00
PC21 Christian Laettner 1.25 3.00
PC22 Ed O'Bannon .60 1.50
PC23 Patrick Ewing 2.50 6.00
PC24 Anfernee Hardaway 4.00 10.00
PC25 Shaquille O'Neal 6.00 15.00
PC26 Jerry Stackhouse 2.50 6.00
PC27 Mario Bennett .60 1.50
PC28 Michael Finley 2.00 5.00
PC29 Randolph Childress .60 1.50
PC30 Brian Grant 1.25 3.00
PC31 Mitch Richmond 2.00 5.00
PC32 Cory Alexander .75 2.00
PC33 David Robinson 3.00 8.00
PC34 Sherrell Ford .60 1.50
PC35 Shawn Kemp 2.50 6.00
PC36 Damon Stoudamire 2.00 5.00
PC37 Greg Ostertag .75 2.00
PC38 Bryant Reeves .60 1.50
PC39 Juwan Howard 1.50 4.00
PC40 Rasheed Wallace 2.50 6.00

1995-96 SP Holoviews Die Cuts
*DIE CUTS: 1.5X TO 4X HI COLUMN
STATED ODDS 1:76
PC13 Latrell Sprewell 8.00 20.00

1995-96 SP Jordan Collection
COMPLETE SET (4) 12.00 30.00
COMMON CARD (JC17-JC20) 4.00 10.00

1996-97 SP
COMPLETE SET (146) 50.00 120.00
RC's CONDITION SENSITIVE
1 Mookie Blaylock .40 1.00
2 Christian Laettner .40 1.00
3 Dikembe Mutombo .60 1.50
4 Steve Smith .30 .75
5 Dana Barros .25 .60
6 Rick Fox .25 .60
7 Dino Radja .25 .60
8 Eric Williams .25 .60
9 Dell Curry .40 1.00
10 Vlade Divac .40 1.00
11 Anthony Mason .30 .75
12 Glen Rice .40 1.00
13 Scottie Pippen 1.00 2.50
14 Toni Kukoc .40 1.00
15 Luc Longley .30 .75
16 Michael Jordan 4.00 10.00
17 Dennis Rodman 1.00 2.50
18 Terrell Brandon .30 .75
19 Tyrone Hill .25 .60
20 Bobby Phills .25 .60
21 Bob Sura .25 .60
22 Chris Gatling .25 .60
23 Jim Jackson .25 .60
24 Sam Cassell .30 .75
25 Jamal Mashburn .40 1.00
26 Dale Ellis .30 .75
27 LaPhonso Ellis .25 .60
28 Mark Jackson .30 .75
29 Antonio McDyess .40 1.00
30 Bryant Stith .25 .60
31 Joe Dumars .50 1.25
32 Grant Hill .60 1.50
33 Lindsey Hunter .25 .60
34 Otis Thorpe .30 .75
35 Chris Mullin .50 1.25
36 Mark Price .40 1.00
37 Joe Smith .30 .75
38 Latrell Sprewell .40 1.00
39 Charles Barkley 1.00 2.50
40 Clyde Drexler .60 1.50
41 Mario Elie .25 .60
42 Hakeem Olajuwon .75 2.00
43 Travis Best .25 .60
44 Dale Davis .25 .60
45 Reggie Miller .75 2.00
46 Rik Smits .30 .75
47 Pooh Richardson .25 .60
48 Rodney Rogers .25 .60
49 Malik Sealy .25 .60
50 Loy Vaught .25 .60
51 Elden Campbell .25 .60
52 Robert Horry .40 1.00
53 Eddie Jones .40 1.00
54 Shaquille O'Neal 1.50 4.00
55 Nick Van Exel .40 1.00
56 Sasha Danilovic .25 .60
57 Tim Hardaway .50 1.25
58 Dan Majerle .40 1.00
59 Alonzo Mourning .60 1.50
60 Vin Baker .30 .75
61 Sherman Douglas .25 .60
62 Armon Gilliam .25 .60
63 Glenn Robinson .40 1.00
64 Kevin Garnett 1.25 3.00
65 Tom Gugliotta .25 .60
66 Terry Porter .25 .60
67 Doug West .25 .60
68 Shawn Bradley .25 .60
69 Kendall Gill .40 1.00
70 Robert Pack .25 .60
71 Jayson Williams .25 .60
72 Chris Childs .25 .60
73 Patrick Ewing .60 1.50
74 Allan Houston .40 1.00
75 Larry Johnson .50 1.25
76 John Starks .40 1.00
77 Nick Anderson .25 .60
78 Horace Grant .40 1.00
79 Anfernee Hardaway 1.00 2.50
80 Dennis Scott .30 .75
81 Derrick Coleman .30 .75
82 Mark Davis .25 .60
83 Jerry Stackhouse .50 1.25
84 Clarence Weatherspoon .25 .60
85 Cedric Ceballos .30 .75
86 Kevin Johnson .40 1.00
87 Jason Kidd .60 1.50
88 Danny Manning .30 .75
89 Wesley Person .25 .60
90 Kenny Anderson .30 .75
91 Isaiah Rider .30 .75
92 Clifford Robinson .40 1.00
93 Arvydas Sabonis .40 1.00
94 Rasheed Wallace .50 1.25
95 Mahmoud Abdul-Rauf .30 .75
96 Brian Grant .30 .75
97 Olden Polynice .25 .60
98 Mitch Richmond .50 1.25
99 Corliss Williamson .25 .60
100 Sean Elliott .40 1.00
101 Avery Johnson .30 .75
102 David Robinson .75 2.00
103 Dominique Wilkins .60 1.50
104 Hersey Hawkins .25 .60
105 Jim McIlvaine .25 .60
106 Shawn Kemp .60 1.50
107 Gary Payton .60 1.50
108 Detlef Schrempf .25 .60
109 Doug Christie .25 .60
110 Popeye Jones .25 .60
111 Damon Stoudamire .40 1.00
112 Walt Williams .25 .60
113 Jeff Hornacek .30 .75
114 Karl Malone .75 2.00
115 Greg Ostertag .25 .60
116 Bryon Russell .25 .60
117 John Stockton .75 2.00
118 Greg Anthony .25 .60
119 Blue Edwards .25 .60
120 Anthony Peeler .25 .60
121 Bryant Reeves .25 .60
122 Calbert Cheaney .25 .60
123 Juwan Howard .40 1.00
124 Gheorghe Muresan .25 .60
125 Rod Strickland .40 1.00
126 Chris Webber .50 1.25
127 Antoine Walker RC 1.00 2.50
128 Tony Delk RC .60 1.50
129 Vitaly Potapenko RC .50 1.25
130 Samaki Walker RC .50 1.25
131 Todd Fuller RC .40 1.00
132 Erick Dampier RC .60 1.50
133 Lorenzen Wright RC .60 1.50
134 Kobe Bryant RC 40.00 100.00
135 Derek Fisher RC .75 2.00
136 Ray Allen RC 2.00 5.00
137 Stephon Marbury RC 2.00 5.00
138 Kerry Kittles RC .60 1.50
139 Walter McCarty RC .60 1.50
140 John Wallace RC .50 1.25
141 Allen Iverson RC 2.50 6.00
142 Steve Nash RC 3.00 8.00
143 Jermaine O'Neal RC 1.00 2.50
144 Marcus Camby RC 1.00 2.50
145 Shareef Abdur-Rahim RC 1.00 2.50
146 Roy Rogers RC .50 1.25
S16 Michael Jordan Sample 3.00 8.00

1996-97 SP Game Film
COMPLETE SET (10) 75.00 200.00
STATED ODDS 1:120
GF1 Michael Jordan 60.00 150.00
GF2 Kevin Garnett 10.00 25.00
GF3 Charles Barkley 12.00 30.00
GF4 Anfernee Hardaway 12.00 30.00
GF5 Shaquille O'Neal 12.00 30.00
GF6 Jim Jackson 3.00 8.00
GF7 Dennis Rodman 12.00 30.00
GF8 Alonzo Mourning 8.00 20.00
GF9 Grant Hill 8.00 20.00
GF10 Shawn Kemp 6.00 15.00

1996-97 SP Holoviews
COMPLETE SET (40) 75.00 150.00
STATED ODDS 1:10
PC1 Mookie Blaylock 1.50 4.00
PC2 Antoine Walker 1.50 4.00
PC3 Eric Williams 1.00 2.50
PC4 Tony Delk 1.00 2.50
PC5 Michael Jordan 125.00 300.00
PC6 Dennis Rodman 4.00 10.00
PC7 Vitaly Potapenko .75 2.00
PC8 Bob Sura 1.00 2.50
PC9 Jamal Mashburn 1.50 4.00
PC10 Antonio McDyess 1.50 4.00
PC11 Grant Hill 2.50 6.00
PC12 Joe Smith 1.25 3.00
PC13 Latrell Sprewell 1.50 4.00
PC14 Charles Barkley 4.00 10.00
PC15 Hakeem Olajuwon 3.00 8.00
PC16 Erick Dampier 1.00 2.50
PC17 Lorenzen Wright .75 2.00
PC18 Kobe Bryant 200.00 500.00
PC19 Shaquille O'Neal 6.00 15.00
PC20 Alonzo Mourning 2.50 6.00
PC21 Ray Allen 5.00 12.00
PC22 Kevin Garnett 5.00 12.00
PC23 Stephon Marbury 3.00 8.00
PC24 Kerry Kittles 1.00 2.50
PC25 Walter McCarty 1.00 2.50
PC26 John Wallace .75 2.00
PC27 Anfernee Hardaway 4.00 10.00
PC28 Allen Iverson 8.00 20.00
PC29 Jerry Stackhouse 2.00 5.00
PC30 Steve Nash 6.00 15.00
PC31 Jermaine O'Neal 1.50 4.00
PC32 Brian Grant 1.25 3.00
PC33 Mitch Richmond 2.00 5.00
PC34 David Robinson 3.00 8.00
PC35 Shawn Kemp 2.50 6.00
PC36 Marcus Camby 1.50 4.00
PC37 Damon Stoudamire 1.50 4.00
PC38 John Stockton 3.00 8.00
PC39 Shareef Abdur-Rahim 1.50 4.00
PC40 Juwan Howard 1.50 4.00

1996-97 SP Inside Info
COMPLETE SET (17) 50.00 120.00
ONE PER BOX
*GOLD: 1.5X TO 4X HI COLUMN
IN1 Charles Barkley 6.00 15.00
IN2 Kevin Garnett 8.00 20.00
IN3 Anfernee Hardaway 6.00 15.00
IN4 Grant Hill 4.00 10.00
IN5 Allen Iverson 10.00 25.00
IN6 Jason Kidd 4.00 10.00
IN7 Shawn Kemp 4.00 10.00
IN8 Antonio McDyess 2.50 6.00
IN9 Dikembe Mutombo 4.00 10.00
IN10 Shaquille O'Neal 10.00 25.00
IN11 Hakeem Olajuwon 5.00 12.00
IN12 Dennis Rodman 6.00 15.00
IN13 Jerry Stackhouse 3.00 8.00
IN14 John Stockton 4.00 10.00
IN15 Damon Stoudamire 2.50 6.00
IN16 Chris Webber 3.00 8.00
IN17 Michael Jordan 25F 20.00 50.00

1996-97 SP Rookie Jumbos
COMPLETE SET (20) 12.00 30.00
1 Antoine Walker 1.00 2.50
2 Tony Delk .60 1.50
3 Vitaly Potapenko .50 1.25
4 Samaki Walker .50 1.25
5 Todd Fuller .40 1.00
6 Erick Dampier .60 1.50
7 Lorenzen Wright .50 1.25
8 Kobe Bryant 20.00 50.00
9 Derek Fisher .75 2.00
10 Ray Allen 3.00 8.00
11 Stephon Marbury 2.00 5.00
12 Kerry Kittles .60 1.50
13 Walter McCarty .60 1.50
14 John Wallace .50 1.25
15 Allen Iverson 5.00 12.00
16 Steve Nash 4.00 10.00
17 Jermaine O'Neal 1.00 2.50
18 Marcus Camby 1.00 2.50
19 Shareef Abdur-Rahim 1.00 2.50
20 Roy Rogers .50 1.25

1996-97 SP SPx Force
STATED ODDS 1:360
F1 MJ/Stack/Mitch/Spree 30.00 80.00
F2 Kemp/Rod/Barkley/Juwan 15.00 40.00
F3 Blay/VanX/Marbury/Stoud 10.00 25.00
F4 Camby/Damp/Penny/McD 10.00 25.00
F5 MJ/Penny/Kemp/Stoud 40.00 100.00
A1 Anfernee Hardaway AU 125.00 250.00
A2 Michael Jordan AU 7,000.00 10,000.00
A3 Shawn Kemp AU 175.00 350.00
A4 Damon Stoudamire AU 75.00 150.00

2012 SP
COMP.SET w/o SP's (50) 8.00 20.00
51-80 STATED ODDS 1:4
61 Michael Jordan PS 3.00 8.00

2012 SP Blue
*BLUE: .5X TO 1.2X BASIC CARDS
*BLUE PS (51-80): 1.5X TO 4X BASIC CARDS
STATED ODDS 1:2 RETAIL
PS (51-80) STATED ODDS 1:48 RETAIL

2014 SP
COMP.SET w/o SPs (50) 8.00 20.00
*1-50 RETAIL: .4X TO 1X SP AUTH.
*51-75 AM RETAIL: .4X TO 1X SP AUTH.

2014 SP Blue
*1-50 BLUE: .6X TO 1.5X SP AUTHENTIC
1-50 STATED ODDS 1:3
*1-50 BLUE: .6X TO 1.5X SP AUTHENTIC
51-68 STATED ODDS 1:33
*69-75 BLUE: .6X TO 1.5X SP AUTHENTIC
69-75 STATED ODDS 1:86
69 Tiger Woods AM
Michael Jordan 200.00 500.00

1997-98 SP Authentic
COMPLETE SET (176) 60.00 120.00
RCs CONDITION SENSITIVE!
1 Steve Smith .30 .75
2 Dikembe Mutombo .60 1.50
3 Christian Laettner .40 1.00
4 Mookie Blaylock .40 1.00
5 Alan Henderson .25 .60
6 Antoine Walker .40 1.00
7 Ron Mercer RC 1.00 2.50
8 Walter McCarty .25 .60
9 Kenny Anderson .30 .75
10 Travis Knight .25 .60
11 Dana Barros .25 .60
12 Glen Rice .40 1.00
13 Vlade Divac .40 1.00
14 Dell Curry .30 .75
15 David Wesley .30 .75
16 Bobby Phills .30 .75
17 Anthony Mason .30 .75
18 Toni Kukoc .50 1.25
19 Dennis Rodman 1.00 2.50
20 Ron Harper .40 1.00
21 Steve Kerr .50 1.25
22 Scottie Pippen 1.00 2.50
23 Michael Jordan 6.00 15.00
24 Shawn Kemp .60 1.50
25 Wesley Person .25 .60
26 Derek Anderson RC .75 2.00
27 Zydrunas Ilgauskas .40 1.00
28 Brevin Knight RC .75 2.00
29 Michael Finley .40 1.00
30 Shawn Bradley .25 .60
31 A.C. Green .30 .75
32 Hubert Davis .25 .60
33 Dennis Scott .30 .75
34 Tony Battie RC .75 2.00
35 Bobby Jackson RC 1.00 2.50
36 LaPhonso Ellis .30 .75
37 Bryant Stith .25 .60
38 Dean Garrett .25 .60
39 Danny Fortson RC .75 2.00
40 Grant Hill .60 1.50
41 Brian Williams .30 .75
42 Lindsey Hunter .25 .60
43 Malik Sealy .30 .75
44 Jerry Stackhouse .40 1.00
45 Muggsy Bogues .30 .75
46 Joe Smith .30 .75
47 Donyell Marshall .25 .60
48 Erick Dampier .30 .75
49 Bimbo Coles .25 .60
50 Charles Barkley 1.00 2.50
51 Hakeem Olajuwon .60 1.50
52 Clyde Drexler .60 1.50
53 Kevin Willis .30 .75
54 Mario Elie .25 .60
55 Reggie Miller .75 2.00
56 Rik Smits .30 .75
57 Chris Mullin .50 1.25
58 Antonio Davis .30 .75
59 Dale Davis .30 .75
60 Mark Jackson .30 .75
61 Brent Barry .30 .75
62 Loy Vaught .30 .75
63 Rodney Rogers .30 .75
64 Lamond Murray .25 .60
65 Maurice Taylor RC .60 1.50
66 Shaquille O'Neal 1.25 3.00
67 Eddie Jones .40 1.00
68 Kobe Bryant 4.00 10.00
69 Nick Van Exel .40 1.00
70 Robert Horry .40 1.00
71 Tim Hardaway .50 1.25
72 Jamal Mashburn .40 1.00
73 Alonzo Mourning .60 1.50
74 Isaac Austin .25 .60
75 P.J. Brown .25 .60
76 Ray Allen .75 2.00
77 Glenn Robinson .40 1.00
78 Ervin Johnson .25 .60
79 Terrell Brandon .30 .75
80 Tyrone Hill .25 .60
81 Stephon Marbury .50 1.25
82 Kevin Garnett 1.00 2.50
83 Tom Gugliotta .30 .75
84 Chris Carr .25 .60
85 Cherokee Parks .25 .60
86 Sam Cassell .30 .75
87 Chris Gatling .25 .60
88 Kendall Gill .25 .60
89 Keith Van Horn RC 1.25 3.00
90 Jayson Williams .25 .60
91 Kerry Kittles .25 .60
92 Patrick Ewing .60 1.50
93 Larry Johnson .50 1.25
94 Chris Childs .25 .60
95 John Starks .40 1.00
96 Charles Oakley .30 .75
97 Allan Houston .40 1.00
98 Mark Price .40 1.00
99 Anfernee Hardaway 1.00 2.50
100 Rony Seikaly .25 .60
101 Horace Grant .40 1.00
102 Bo Outlaw .25 .60
103 Clarence Weatherspoon .25 .60
104 Allen Iverson 1.25 3.00
105 Jim Jackson .30 .75
106 Theo Ratliff .30 .75
107 Tim Thomas RC 1.00 2.50
108 Danny Manning .30 .75
109 Jason Kidd .60 1.50
110 Kevin Johnson .40 1.00
111 Rex Chapman .25 .60
112 Clifford Robinson .30 .75
113 Antonio McDyess .40 1.00
114 Damon Stoudamire .40 1.00
115 Isaiah Rider .30 .75
116 Arvydas Sabonis .50 1.25
117 Rasheed Wallace .50 1.25
118 Brian Grant .30 .75
119 Gary Trent .25 .60
120 Mitch Richmond .50 1.25
121 Corliss Williamson .25 .60
122 Lawrence Funderburke RC .60 1.50
123 Olden Polynice .25 .60
124 Billy Owens .25 .60
125 Avery Johnson .30 .75
126 Sean Elliott .30 .75
127 David Robinson .75 2.00
128 Tim Duncan RC ! 12.00 30.00
129 Jaren Jackson .25 .60
130 Detlef Schrempf .40 1.00
131 Gary Payton .60 1.50
132 Vin Baker .30 .75
133 Hersey Hawkins .30 .75
134 Dale Ellis .30 .75
135 Sam Perkins .30 .75
136 Marcus Camby .40 1.00
137 John Wallace .25 .60
138 Doug Christie .25 .60
139 Chauncey Billups RC 2.00 5.00
140 Walt Williams .30 .75
141 Karl Malone .75 2.00
142 Bryon Russell .25 .60
143 Jeff Hornacek .40 1.00
144 Greg Ostertag .25 .60
145 John Stockton .75 2.00
146 Shandon Anderson .25 .60
147 Shareef Abdur-Rahim .40 1.00
148 Bryant Reeves .25 .60
149 Antonio Daniels RC .75 2.00
150 Otis Thorpe .30 .75
151 Blue Edwards .25 .60
152 Chris Webber .50 1.25
153 Juwan Howard .30 .75
154 Rod Strickland .30 .75
155 Calbert Cheaney .30 .75
156 Tracy Murray .25 .60
157 Chauncey Billups FW 1.25 3.00
158 Ed Gray FW RC .75 2.00
159 Tony Battie FW .40 1.00
160 Keith Van Horn FW .60 1.50
161 Cedric Henderson FW RC .60 1.50
162 Kelvin Cato FW RC .60 1.50
163 Tariq Abdul-Wahad FW RC .60 1.50
164 Derek Anderson FW .40 1.00
165 Tim Duncan FW 2.50 6.00
166 Tracy McGrady FW RC 4.00 10.00
167 Ron Mercer FW .50 1.25
168 Bobby Jackson FW .50 1.25
169 Antonio Daniels FW .40 1.00
170 Zydrunas Ilgauskas FW .40 1.00
171 Maurice Taylor FW .30 .75
172 Tim Thomas FW .50 1.25
173 Brevin Knight FW .40 1.00
174 Lawrence Funderburke FW .40 1.00
175 Jacque Vaughn FW RC .60 1.50
176 Danny Fortson FW .60 1.50
SPA23 Michael Jordan PROMO 3.00 8.00

1997-98 SP Authentic Authentics
OVERALL STATED ODDS 1:288
A1 Jordan/AU Game/23 10,000.00 20,000.00
J1 Jordan/Game/100 150.00 400.00
J2 Michael Jordan 150.00 400.00
J3 Michael Jordan 150.00 400.00
J4 Michael Jordan 150.00 400.00
J5 Michael Jordan 150.00 400.00
J6 Michael Jordan
Unsigned Game Night Card/100 150.00 400.00
AH1 Hard/AU Blk.Jsy/100 200.00 500.00
AH2 Hard/AU Blue Jsy/190 125.00 300.00
AH3 Hard/AU SI Cover/300 75.00 200.00
AH4 Hard/8x10 Photo/300 15.00 30.00
MJ2 Jordan/AU 16x20/100 400.00 800.00
MJ3 Jordan/2-card/500 35.00 60.00
MJ4 Jordan/8x10/400 35.00 60.00
MJ5 Jordan/Gold Card/250 15.00 40.00
MJ7 Jordan/Poster/200 30.00 80.00
NNO SP Uncut Sheet/200 90.00 150.00
SK1 Kemp/AU Jersey/35 300.00 600.00
SK2 Kemp/AU Photo/104 40.00 100.00
SK3 Kemp/AU Mini-ball/100 40.00 100.00

1997-98 SP Authentic BuyBack
STATED ODDS 1:309 PACKS
CARDS NUMBERED BELOW ALPHABETICALLY
PRINT RUNS PROVIDED BY UD
1 S.Abdur-Rahim 96-7/192 20.00 50.00
2 Vin Baker 94-5/17 12.00 30.00
3 Vin Baker 95-6/71 12.00 30.00
4 Vin Baker 95-6AS/83 12.00 30.00
5 Clyde Drexler 94-5/141 40.00 100.00
6 Clyde Drexler 95-6/200 40.00 100.00
7 Clyde Drexler 96-7/63 40.00 100.00
8 A.Hardaway 94-5/77 75.00 200.00
9 A.Hardaway 95-6/100 75.00 200.00
10 A.Hardaway 96-7/31 100.00 250.00
11 Tim Hardaway 94-5/126 30.00 80.00
12 Tim Hardaway 95-6/84 30.00 80.00
13 Tim Hardaway 96-7/43 20.00 50.00
14 Juwan Howard 94-5/50 15.00 40.00
15 Juwan Howard 95-6/300 12.00 30.00
16 Juwan Howard 95-6AS/50 12.00 30.00
17 Juwan Howard 96-7/33 12.00 30.00
18 Eddie Jones 94-5/50 25.00 60.00
19 Eddie Jones 95-6/87 20.00 50.00
20 Eddie Jones 96-7/18 20.00 50.00
21 M.Jordan 94-5MJ1R/55 10,000.00 20,000.00
22 Jason Kidd 94-5/50 75.00 200.00
23 Jason Kidd 95-6/300 50.00 120.00
24 Jason Kidd 95-6AS/43 50.00 120.00
25 Jason Kidd 96-7/43 50.00 120.00
26 Kerry Kittles 96-7/201 12.00 30.00
27 Karl Malone 94-5/187 60.00 150.00
28 Karl Malone 95-6/36 60.00 150.00
29 Glen Rice 95-6AS78 12.00 30.00
30 Glen Rice 96-7/47 12.00 30.00
31 Mitch Richmond 94-5/95 20.00 50.00
32 Mitch Richmond 95-6/83 20.00 50.00
33 Mitch Richmond 96-7/39 20.00 50.00
34 D.Stoudamire 95-6/35 40.00 100.00
35 D.Stoudamire 96-7/36 40.00 100.00
36 Antoine Walker 96-7/32 15.00 40.00

1997-98 SP Authentic Premium Portraits
STATED ODDS 1:1,528
DP Damon Stoudamire 60.00 150.00
EP Eddie Jones 40.00 100.00
JP Jason Kidd 100.00 250.00
KP Kerry Kittles 15.00 40.00
MP Dikembe Mutombo 30.00 80.00
RP Glen Rice 40.00 100.00
TP Tim Hardaway 15.00 40.00

1997-98 SP Authentic Profiles 1

COMPLETE SET (40) 30.00 60.00
STATED ODDS 1:3
*PRO.2: 1.25X TO 3X HI COLUMN
PRO.2: STATED ODDS 1:12
P1 Michael Jordan 20.00 50.00
P2 Glen Rice .50 1.25
P3 Brent Barry .40 1.00
P4 LaPhonso Ellis .40 1.00
P5 Allen Iverson 6.00 15.00
P6 Dikembe Mutombo .75 2.00
P7 Charles Barkley 1.25 3.00
P8 Antoine Walker .50 1.25
P9 Karl Malone 1.00 2.50
P10 Jason Kidd .75 2.00
P11 Gary Payton .75 2.00
P12 Kevin Garnett 1.25 3.00
P13 Keith Van Horn .75 2.00
P14 Glenn Robinson .50 1.25
P15 Michael Finley .50 1.25
P16 Hakeem Olajuwon 1.00 2.50
P17 Chris Webber .60 1.50
P18 Mitch Richmond .60 1.50
P19 Marcus Camby .50 1.25
P20 Tim Hardaway .60 1.50
P21 Shawn Kemp .75 2.00
P22 Reggie Miller 1.00 2.50
P23 Shaquille O'Neal 1.50 4.00
P24 Chauncey Billups 1.50 4.00
P25 Grant Hill .75 2.00
P26 Shareef Abdur-Rahim .50 1.25
P27 David Robinson 1.00 2.50
P28 Scottie Pippen 1.25 3.00
P29 Juwan Howard .40 1.00
P30 Anfernee Hardaway 1.25 3.00
P31 Jerry Stackhouse .50 1.25
P32 Kobe Bryant 10.00 25.00
P33 Patrick Ewing .75 2.00
P34 Alonzo Mourning .75 2.00
P35 John Stockton 1.00 2.50
P36 Kenny Anderson .40 1.00
P37 Tim Duncan 6.00 15.00
P38 Stephon Marbury .60 1.50
P39 Dennis Rodman 1.25 3.00
P40 Joe Smith .40 1.00

1997-98 SP Authentic Profiles 3

*STARS: 12X TO 30X VALUE
*RCs: 10X TO 25X VALUE
STATED PRINT RUN 100 SERIAL #'d SETS
P1 Michael Jordan 1,500.00 3,000.00
P5 Allen Iverson 400.00 800.00
P7 Charles Barkley 150.00 400.00
P9 Karl Malone 150.00 400.00
P11 Gary Payton 75.00 200.00
P12 Kevin Garnett 300.00 600.00
P16 Hakeem Olajuwon 150.00 400.00
P18 Mitch Richmond 40.00 100.00
P20 Tim Hardaway 60.00 150.00
P21 Shawn Kemp 125.00 300.00
P22 Reggie Miller 150.00 400.00
P23 Shaquille O'Neal 300.00 600.00
P24 Chauncey Billups 75.00 200.00
P25 Grant Hill 100.00 250.00
P26 Shareef Abdur-Rahim 30.00 80.00
P27 David Robinson 150.00 400.00
P28 Scottie Pippen 200.00 500.00
P30 Anfernee Hardaway 300.00 600.00
P31 Jerry Stackhouse 20.00 50.00
P32 Kobe Bryant 1,000.00 2,000.00
P33 Patrick Ewing 125.00 300.00
P34 Alonzo Mourning 100.00 250.00
P37 Tim Duncan 800.00 1,500.00
P39 Dennis Rodman 200.00 500.00

1997-98 SP Authentic Sign of the Times

STATED ODDS 1:42
AH Allan Houston 10.00 25.00
AJ Avery Johnson 8.00 20.00
BB Brent Barry 6.00 15.00
BW Brian Williams 15.00 40.00
CM Chris Mullin 15.00 40.00
DM Dikembe Mutombo 40.00 100.00
DS Damon Stoudamire 15.00 40.00
EJ Eddie Jones 20.00 50.00
GM Gheorghe Muresan 6.00 15.00
GP Gary Payton 60.00 150.00
GR Glen Rice 8.00 20.00
HW Juwan Howard 8.00 20.00
KJ Kevin Johnson 20.00 50.00
KK Kerry Kittles 8.00 20.00
LH Lindsey Hunter 5.00 12.00
MB Mookie Blaylock 10.00 25.00
MR Mitch Richmond 15.00 40.00
SC Sam Cassell 8.00 20.00
SE Sean Elliott 10.00 25.00
TE Terrell Brandon 5.00 12.00
TG Tom Gugliotta 8.00 20.00
TH Tim Hardaway 20.00 50.00
VB Vin Baker 8.00 20.00

1997-98 SP Authentic Sign of the Times Stars and Rookies

STATED ODDS 1:113
AW Antoine Walker 8.00 20.00
CD Clyde Drexler 75.00 200.00
CH Chauncey Billups 60.00 150.00
JK Jason Kidd 60.00 150.00
JS John Stockton TRADE 25.00 50.00
KM Karl Malone 125.00 300.00
KV Keith Van Horn 10.00 25.00
MJ Michael Jordan 60,000.00 100,000.00
RO Ron Mercer 10.00 25.00
SA Shareef Abdur-Rahim 20.00 50.00
TB Tony Battie 5.00 12.00

1998-99 SP Authentic

COMPLETE SET w/o RC (90) 20.00 50.00
RC PRINT RUN 3500 SERIAL #'d SETS
1 Michael Jordan 4.00 10.00
2 Michael Jordan 6.00 15.00
3 Michael Jordan 4.00 10.00
4 Michael Jordan 4.00 10.00
5 Michael Jordan 4.00 10.00
6 Michael Jordan 4.00 10.00
7 Michael Jordan 4.00 10.00
8 Michael Jordan 4.00 10.00
9 Michael Jordan 4.00 10.00
10 Michael Jordan 4.00 10.00
11 Steve Smith .30 .75
12 Dikembe Mutombo .60 1.50
13 Alan Henderson .25 .60
14 Antoine Walker .40 1.00
15 Ron Mercer .30 .75
16 Kenny Anderson .30 .75
17 Derrick Coleman .30 .75
18 David Wesley .25 .60
19 Glen Rice .40 1.00
20 Toni Kukoc .40 1.00
21 Ron Harper .40 1.00
22 Brent Barry .30 .75
23 Shawn Kemp .60 1.50
24 Zydrunas Ilgauskas .40 1.00
25 Brevin Knight .25 .60
26 Michael Finley .40 1.00
27 Steve Nash .75 2.00
28 Cedric Ceballos .30 .75
29 Antonio McDyess .30 .75
30 Nick Van Exel .40 1.00
31 Grant Hill .60 1.50
32 Jerry Stackhouse .40 1.00
33 Bison Dele .25 .60
34 John Starks .40 1.00
35 Chris Mills .25 .60
36 Hakeem Olajuwon .75 2.00
37 Charles Barkley 1.00 2.50
38 Scottie Pippen 1.00 2.50
39 Reggie Miller .75 2.00
40 Chris Mullin .50 1.25
41 Rik Smits .30 .75
42 Lamond Murray .25 .60
43 Maurice Taylor .25 .60
44 Kobe Bryant 3.00 8.00
45 Dennis Rodman 1.00 2.50
46 Shaquille O'Neal 1.50 4.00
47 Alonzo Mourning .60 1.50
48 Tim Hardaway .50 1.25
49 Jamal Mashburn .40 1.00
50 Ray Allen .60 1.50
51 Glenn Robinson .40 1.00
52 Terrell Brandon .30 .75
53 Kevin Garnett 1.00 2.50
54 Stephon Marbury .50 1.25
55 Joe Smith .30 .75
56 Keith Van Horn .40 1.00
57 Kendall Gill .30 .75
58 Jayson Williams .25 .60
59 Patrick Ewing .60 1.50
60 Allan Houston .40 1.00
61 Larry Johnson .60 1.50
62 Anfernee Hardaway 1.00 2.50
63 Horace Grant .40 1.00
64 Allen Iverson 1.00 2.50
65 Tim Thomas .30 .75
66 Jason Kidd .60 1.50
67 Tom Gugliotta .30 .75
68 Rex Chapman .30 .75
69 Damon Stoudamire .40 1.00
70 Isaiah Rider .30 .75
71 Rasheed Wallace .50 1.25
72 Chris Webber .50 1.25
73 Vlade Divac .40 1.00
74 Corliss Williamson .25 .60
75 Tim Duncan 1.00 2.50
76 David Robinson .75 2.00
77 Sean Elliott .40 1.00
78 Detlef Schrempf .40 1.00
79 Vin Baker .30 .75
80 Gary Payton .60 1.50
81 Doug Christie .30 .75
82 Tracy McGrady .60 1.50
83 Karl Malone .75 2.00
84 John Stockton .75 2.00
85 Jeff Hornacek .30 .75
86 Shareef Abdur-Rahim .40 1.00
87 Bryant Reeves .25 .60
88 Juwan Howard .30 .75
89 Mitch Richmond .50 1.25
90 Rod Strickland .30 .75
91 Michael Olowokandi RC 3.00 8.00
92 Mike Bibby RC 8.00 20.00
93 Raef LaFrentz RC 3.00 8.00
94 Antawn Jamison RC 4.00 10.00
95 Vince Carter RC 100.00 250.00
96 Robert Traylor RC 2.50 6.00
97 Jason Williams RC 30.00 80.00
98 Larry Hughes RC 4.00 10.00
99 Dirk Nowitzki RC 100.00 250.00
100 Paul Pierce RC 30.00 80.00
101 Bonzi Wells RC 2.50 6.00
102 Michael Doleac RC 2.00 5.00
103 Keon Clark RC 2.50 6.00
104 Michael Dickerson RC 2.50 6.00
105 Matt Harpring RC 2.50 6.00
106 Bryce Drew RC 1.50 4.00
107 Pat Garrity RC 2.00 5.00
108 Roshown McLeod RC 1.50 4.00
109 Ricky Davis RC 4.00 10.00
110 Brian Skinner RC 2.00 5.00
111 Tyronn Lue RC 3.00 8.00
112 Felipe Lopez RC 3.00 8.00
113 Al Harrington RC 3.00 8.00
114 Sam Jacobson RC 1.50 4.00
115 Cory Carr RC 2.00 5.00
116 Corey Benjamin RC 1.50 4.00
117 Nazr Mohammed RC 2.50 6.00
118 Rashard Lewis RC 6.00 15.00
119 Peja Stojakovic RC 8.00 20.00
120 Andrae Patterson RC 2.00 5.00
23P Michael Jordan PROMO 3.00 8.00

1998-99 SP Authentic Authentics

STATED ODDS 1:864
T1 L.Bird Ball/10 400.00 600.00
T2 J.Erving/SI Cover/25 125.00 250.00
T3 A.Hard/SI Cover/200 25.00 50.00
T4 A.Hard/8x10/200 25.00 50.00
T5 T.Hard/Mini-ball/125 20.00 40.00
T6 T.Hard/8x10/150 12.50 25.00
T7 T.Hard/8x10/75 20.00 40.00
T8 J.Howard/Mini-ball/150 12.50 25.00
T9 E.Jones/Mini-ball/50 20.00 40.00
T10 E.Jones/8x10/100 15.00 30.00
T11 M.Jordan/Blk.Jersey/23 1,500.00 3,000.00
T12 M.Jordan/Wht.Jersey/23 1,500.00 3,000.00
T13 S.Kemp/8x10/150 20.00 40.00
T14 S.Kemp/Jersey/30 200.00 500.00
T15 G.Payton/SI Cover/75 50.00 120.00
T16 S.Pippen/Ball/25 150.00 400.00
T17 Forum Floor Pieces/23 125.00 300.00

1998-99 SP Authentic First Class

COMPLETE SET (30) 15.00 40.00
STATED ODDS 1:7
FC1 Michael Jordan 15.00 40.00
FC2 Dikembe Mutombo 1.00 2.50
FC3 Antoine Walker .60 1.50
FC4 Glen Rice .60 1.50
FC5 Toni Kukoc .60 1.50
FC6 Shawn Kemp 1.00 2.50
FC7 Michael Finley .60 1.50
FC8 Raef LaFrentz .75 2.00
FC9 Grant Hill 1.00 2.50
FC10 Antawn Jamison 1.00 2.50
FC11 Scottie Pippen 1.50 4.00
FC12 Reggie Miller 1.25 3.00
FC13 Michael Olowokandi .60 1.50
FC14 Kobe Bryant 8.00 20.00
FC15 Tim Hardaway .75 2.00
FC16 Ray Allen 1.00 2.50
FC17 Kevin Garnett 1.50 4.00
FC18 Keith Van Horn .60 1.50
FC19 Allan Houston .60 1.50
FC20 Anfernee Hardaway 1.50 4.00
FC21 Allen Iverson 1.50 4.00
FC22 Jason Kidd 1.00 2.50
FC23 Damon Stoudamire .60 1.50
FC24 Jason Williams 2.00 5.00
FC25 Tim Duncan 1.50 4.00
FC26 Gary Payton 1.00 2.50
FC27 Vince Carter 8.00 20.00
FC28 Karl Malone 1.25 3.00
FC29 Mike Bibby 1.25 3.00
FC30 Mitch Richmond .75 2.00

1998-99 SP Authentic MICHAEL

COMPLETE SET (15) 300.00 600.00
COMMON CARD (M1-15) 25.00 60.00
STATED ODDS 1:144

1998-99 SP Authentic NBA 2K

COMPLETE SET (20) 25.00 60.00
STATED ODDS 1:23
2K1 Michael Olowokandi 1.25 3.00
2K2 Mike Bibby 2.00 5.00
2K3 Raef LaFrentz 1.25 3.00
2K4 Antawn Jamison 1.50 4.00
2K5 Vince Carter 12.00 30.00
2K6 Robert Traylor 1.00 2.50
2K7 Jason Williams 3.00 8.00
2K8 Larry Hughes 1.50 4.00
2K9 Dirk Nowitzki 20.00 50.00
2K10 Paul Pierce 5.00 12.00
2K11 Cuttino Mobley 1.50 4.00
2K12 Michael Doleac .75 2.00
2K13 Corey Benjamin .60 1.50
2K14 Michael Dickerson 1.00 2.50
2K15 Allen Iverson 2.50 6.00
2K16 Kobe Bryant 8.00 20.00
2K17 Tim Duncan 2.50 6.00
2K18 Keith Van Horn 1.00 2.50
2K19 Kevin Garnett 2.50 6.00
2K20 Grant Hill 1.50 4.00

1998-99 SP Authentic Sign of the Times Bronze

STATED ODDS 1:23
AM Antonio McDyess 8.00 20.00
AV Avery Johnson 8.00 20.00
BE Blue Edwards 6.00 15.00
BG Brian Grant 6.00 15.00
BK Brevin Knight 6.00 15.00
BL Mookie Blaylock 12.00 30.00
BP Bobby Phills 12.00 30.00
BR Bryon Russell 6.00 15.00
CB Chauncey Billups 20.00 50.00
CC Chris Carr 6.00 15.00
CH Calbert Cheaney 6.00 15.00
DA Derek Anderson 8.00 20.00
DC Doug Christie 8.00 20.00
DK Derek Fisher 10.00 25.00
DM Donyell Marshall 6.00 15.00
DN Danny Manning 12.00 30.00
DT Detlef Schrempf 10.00 25.00
DV David Wesley 6.00 15.00
ED Erick Dampier 6.00 15.00
EG Ed Gray 6.00 15.00
GR Glen Rice 10.00 25.00
HG Horace Grant 10.00 25.00
HW Juwan Howard 10.00 25.00
JH Jeff Hornacek 12.00 30.00
JR Jalen Rose 8.00 20.00
JW Jerome Williams 6.00 15.00
JY Jayson Williams 6.00 15.00
KA Kenny Anderson 10.00 25.00
LH Lindsey Hunter 6.00 15.00
LJ Larry Johnson 25.00 60.00
MG Tracy McGrady 100.00 250.00
MI Michael Finley 12.00 30.00
MK Mark Jackson 6.00 15.00
NA Nick Anderson 6.00 15.00
OH Othella Harrington 6.00 15.00
PJ P.J. Brown 6.00 15.00
RH Ron Harper 20.00 50.00
RR Rodrick Rhodes 6.00 15.00
SE Sean Elliott 8.00 20.00
TB Terrell Brandon 8.00 20.00
TK Toni Kukoc 20.00 50.00
TQ Tariq Abdul-Wahad 6.00 15.00
TR Theo Ratliff 8.00 20.00
TY Maurice Taylor 6.00 15.00
WM Walter McCarty 8.00 20.00

1998-99 SP Authentic Sign of the Times Gold

STATED ODDS 1:864
AI Allen Iverson 1,000.00 2,000.00
AW Antoine Walker 40.00 100.00
MJ M.Jordan 25,000.00 50,000.00
TH Tim Hardaway 100.00 250.00

1998-99 SP Authentic Sign of the Times Silver

STATED ODDS 1:115
AJ Antawn Jamison 15.00 40.00
DR Dennis Rodman 200.00 500.00
HO Hakeem Olajuwon 100.00 250.00
LR Larry Hughes 12.00 30.00
MB Mike Bibby 20.00 50.00
MO Michael Olowokandi 6.00 15.00
MT Dikembe Mutombo 40.00 100.00
PN Anfernee Hardaway 300.00 600.00
RL Raef LaFrentz 10.00 25.00
RM Ron Mercer 12.00 30.00
RT Robert Traylor 6.00 15.00
SH Shawn Kemp 60.00 150.00
VC Vince Carter 400.00 800.00

1999-00 SP Authentic

COMPLETE SET (135) 200.00 400.00
COMPLETE SET w/o RC (90) 15.00 40.00
91-135 PRINT RUN 1500 SERIAL #'d SETS
1 Dikembe Mutombo .60 1.50
2 Jim Jackson .25 .60
3 Alan Henderson .25 .60
4 Antoine Walker .40 1.00
5 Paul Pierce .75 2.00
6 Kenny Anderson .30 .75
7 Eddie Jones .40 1.00
8 Derrick Coleman .30 .75
9 Anthony Mason .40 1.00
10 Chris Carr .25 .60
11 Hersey Hawkins .25 .60
12 B.J. Armstrong .25 .60
13 Shawn Kemp .60 1.50
14 Bob Sura .25 .60
15 Lamond Murray .25 .60
16 Michael Finley .40 1.00
17 Cedric Ceballos .25 .60
18 Dirk Nowitzki 1.25 3.00
19 Erick Strickland .25 .60
20 Antonio McDyess .30 .75
21 Nick Van Exel .30 .75
22 Grant Hill .60 1.50
23 Jerry Stackhouse .40 1.00
24 Lindsey Hunter .25 .60
25 Christian Laettner .30 .75
26 Antawn Jamison .40 1.00
27 Chris Mills .25 .60
28 Larry Hughes .30 .75
29 Charles Barkley 1.00 2.50
30 Hakeem Olajuwon .75 2.00
31 Cuttino Mobley .30 .75
32 Reggie Miller .75 2.00
33 Jalen Rose .30 .75
34 Rik Smits .30 .75
35 Maurice Taylor .25 .60
36 Derek Anderson .25 .60
37 Tyrone Nesby RC .25 .60
38 Kobe Bryant 3.00 8.00
39 Shaquille O'Neal 1.50 4.00
40 Glen Rice .40 1.00
41 Tim Hardaway .50 1.25
42 Alonzo Mourning .60 1.50
43 Jamal Mashburn .30 .75
44 Ray Allen .60 1.50
45 Sam Cassell .30 .75
46 Glenn Robinson .30 .75
47 Kevin Garnett 1.00 2.50
48 Terrell Brandon .25 .60
49 Joe Smith .25 .60
50 Stephon Marbury .50 1.25
51 Keith Van Horn .30 .75
52 Jamie Feick RC .25 .60
53 Kerry Kittles .30 .75
54 Allan Houston .30 .75
55 Latrell Sprewell .50 1.25
56 Patrick Ewing .50 1.25
57 Darrell Armstrong .25 .60
58 Ron Mercer .30 .75
59 Michael Doleac .25 .60
60 Allen Iverson 1.00 2.50
61 Toni Kukoc .50 1.25
62 Eric Snow .25 .60
63 Anfernee Hardaway 1.00 2.50
64 Jason Kidd .60 1.50
65 Tom Gugliotta .30 .75
66 Scottie Pippen 1.00 2.50
67 Steve Smith .30 .75
68 Damon Stoudamire .40 1.00
69 Jason Williams .60 1.50
70 Peja Stojakovic .50 1.25
71 Chris Webber .50 1.25
72 Vlade Divac .40 1.00
73 Tim Duncan 1.00 2.50
74 David Robinson .75 2.00
75 Avery Johnson .30 .75
76 Gary Payton .60 1.50
77 Vin Baker .30 .75
78 Vernon Maxwell .25 .60
79 Vince Carter 1.00 2.50
80 Tracy McGrady .60 1.50
81 Doug Christie .30 .75
82 Karl Malone .75 2.00
83 John Stockton .60 1.50
84 Jeff Hornacek .30 .75
85 Mike Bibby .40 1.00
86 Shareef Abdur-Rahim .40 1.00
87 Othella Harrington .25 .60
88 Mitch Richmond .50 1.25
89 Juwan Howard .30 .75
90 Rod Strickland .30 .75
91 Elton Brand RC 6.00 15.00
92 Steve Francis RC 6.00 15.00
93 Baron Davis RC 12.00 30.00
94 Lamar Odom RC 6.00 15.00
95 Jonathan Bender RC 3.00 8.00
96 Wally Szczerbiak RC 5.00 12.00
97 Richard Hamilton RC 8.00 20.00
98 Andre Miller RC 6.00 15.00
99 Shawn Marion RC 6.00 15.00
100 Jason Terry RC 5.00 12.00
101 Trajan Langdon RC 2.50 6.00
102 A.Radojevic RC 2.00 5.00
103 Corey Maggette RC 10.00 25.00
104 William Avery RC 2.00 5.00
105 Ron Artest RC 8.00 20.00
106 James Posey RC 3.00 8.00
107 Quincy Lewis RC 2.00 5.00
108 Dion Glover RC 2.00 5.00
109 Kenny Thomas RC 3.00 8.00
110 Devean George RC 2.50 6.00
111 Tim James RC 2.00 5.00
112 Vonteego Cummings RC 2.00 5.00
113 Jumaine Jones RC 2.00 5.00
114 Scott Padgett RC 2.50 6.00
115 Adrian Griffin RC 2.50 6.00
116 Anthony Carter RC 2.50 6.00
117 Todd MacCulloch RC 2.50 6.00
118 Chucky Atkins RC 2.50 6.00
119 Obinna Ekezie RC 2.00 5.00
120 Eddie Robinson RC 3.00 8.00
121 Michael Ruffin RC 2.00 5.00
122 Laron Profit RC 2.00 5.00
123 Cal Bowdler RC 2.00 5.00
124 Chris Herren RC 2.50 6.00
125 Milt Palacio RC 2.50 6.00
126 Jeff Foster RC 3.00 8.00
127 Ryan Bowen RC 2.50 6.00
128 Tim Young RC 2.00 5.00
129 Derrick Dial RC 2.50 6.00
130 Greg Buckner RC 3.00 8.00
131 Rodney Buford RC 3.00 8.00
132 Evan Eschmeyer RC 2.50 6.00
133 Jermaine Jackson RC 3.00 8.00
134 John Celestand RC 2.00 5.00
135 Ryan Robertson RC 2.00 5.00
KG Kevin Garnett PROMO 1.00 2.50

1999-00 SP Authentic Athletic

COMPLETE SET (12) 8.00 20.00
STATED ODDS 1:12
A1 Grant Hill 1.00 2.50
A2 Shareef Abdur-Rahim .60 1.50
A3 Jason Kidd 1.00 2.50
A4 Vince Carter 1.50 4.00
A5 Steve Francis 1.25 3.00
A6 Scottie Pippen 1.50 4.00
A7 Paul Pierce 1.25 3.00
A8 Kobe Bryant 5.00 12.00
A9 Stephon Marbury .75 2.00
A10 Michael Finley .60 1.50
A11 Eddie Jones .60 1.50
A12 Kevin Garnett 1.50 4.00

1999-00 SP Authentic BuyBack

STATED ODDS 1:288
PRINT RUNS LISTED BELOW
2 M.Bibby 98-9SPA2K/42 20.00 50.00
3A K.Bryant Redemption 40.00 100.00
8 K.Bryant 98-9SPA/132 300.00 600.00
9 K.Garnett 95-6SP/21 125.00 300.00
11 K.Garnett 96-7SP/21 125.00 300.00
15 K.Garnett 98-9SPA/NNO 75.00 200.00
18 B.Grant 94-5SP/NNO 6.00 15.00
22 B.Grant 95-6SP/NNO 6.00 15.00
25 B.Grant 96-7SP/16 15.00 40.00
26 B.Grant 97-8SPA/16 15.00 40.00
27 T.Gugliotta 94-5SP/24 10.00 25.00
29 T.Gugliotta 95-6SP/24 10.00 25.00
30 T.Gugliotta 96-7SP/24 10.00 25.00
32 T.Gugliotta 98-9SPA/110 6.00 15.00
33 A.Hard 94-5SP/30 100.00 250.00
35 A.Hard 95-6SP/30 100.00 250.00
40 A.Hard 98-9SPA/32 100.00 250.00
43 L.Hughes 98-9SPA2K/90 12.00 30.00
44 M.Jackson 94-5SP/NNO 6.00 15.00
48 A.Jmsn 98-9SPAFC/NNO 6.00 15.00
50 E.Jones 94-5SP/NNO 30.00 80.00
52 E.Jones 95-6SP/NNO 10.00 25.00
54 E.Jones 96-7SP/NNO 10.00 25.00
60 B.Knight 97-8SPA/24 10.00 25.00
61 B.Knight 98-9SPA/NNO 6.00 15.00
63 R.LaFrentz 98-9SPAFC/NNO 6.00 15.00
64 R.LaFrentz 98-9SPA2K/NNO 6.00 15.00
65 K.Malone 94-5SP/NNO 30.00 80.00
74 J.O'Neal 96-7SP/170 40.00 100.00
77 G.Rice 94-5SP/41 15.00 40.00
79 G.Rice 95-6SP/NNO 8.00 20.00
82 G.Rice 96-7SP/41 15.00 40.00
85 G.Rice 98-9SPA/NNO 8.00 20.00
87 J.Rose 94-5SP/100 25.00 60.00
88 J.Rose 95-6SP/120 12.00 30.00
89 J.Stack 95-6SP/NNO 25.00 60.00
94 J.Stack 96-7SP/16 40.00 100.00
96 J.Stack 97-8SPA/25 40.00 100.00
97 J.Stack 98-9SPA/NNO 12.00 30.00
98 D.Stoud 95-6SP/NNO 10.00 25.00
100 D.Stoud 95-6SPHo/35 25.00 60.00
102 D.Stoud 96-7SP/31 25.00 60.00
105 D.Stoud 98-9SPA/NNO 10.00 25.00
108 M.Taylor 97-8SPA/20 12.00 30.00
109 M.Taylor 98-9SPA/NNO 6.00 15.00
111 R.Traylor 98-9SPA2K/NNO 6.00 15.00
112 A.Walker 96-7SP/NNO 15.00 40.00
114 A.Walker 97-8SPA/19 25.00 60.00
115 A.Walker 98-9SPA/NNO 12.00 30.00
117 Jay.Will 95-6SP/NNO 6.00 15.00
118 Jay.Will 96-7SP/33 8.00 20.00
120 Jay.Will 98-9SPA/NNO 6.00 15.00

1999-00 SP Authentic First Class

COMPLETE SET (12) 6.00 15.00
STATED ODDS 1:12
FC1 Kevin Garnett 1.50 4.00
FC2 Kobe Bryant 5.00 12.00
FC3 Gary Payton 1.00 2.50
FC4 Tim Hardaway .75 2.00
FC5 Antonio McDyess .50 1.25
FC6 Allan Houston .50 1.25
FC7 Jason Kidd 1.00 2.50
FC8 Reggie Miller 1.25 3.00
FC9 Jason Williams 1.00 2.50
FC10 Allen Iverson 1.50 4.00
FC11 David Robinson 1.25 3.00
FC12 Shaquille O'Neal 2.50 6.00

1999-00 SP Authentic Maximum Force

COMPLETE SET (15) 4.00 10.00
STATED ODDS 1:4
M1 Karl Malone .75 2.00
M2 Antawn Jamison .40 1.00
M3 Shareef Abdur-Rahim .40 1.00
M4 Tim Duncan 1.00 2.50
M5 Allen Iverson 1.00 2.50
M6 Michael Finley .40 1.00
M7 Kevin Garnett 1.00 2.50
M8 Kobe Bryant 3.00 8.00
M9 Gary Payton .60 1.50
M10 Keith Van Horn .30 .75
M11 Chris Webber .50 1.25
M12 Glenn Robinson .30 .75
M13 Alonzo Mourning .60 1.50
M14 Antoine Walker .40 1.00
M15 Antonio McDyess .30 .75

1999-00 SP Authentic Premier Powers

COMPLETE SET (9) 20.00 50.00
STATED ODDS 1:72
P1 Kobe Bryant 12.00 30.00
P2 Kevin Garnett 4.00 10.00
P3 Tim Duncan 4.00 10.00
P4 Elton Brand 3.00 8.00
P5 Vince Carter 4.00 10.00
P6 Lamar Odom 3.00 8.00
P7 Grant Hill 2.50 6.00
P8 Shaquille O'Neal 6.00 15.00
P9 Allen Iverson 4.00 10.00

1999-00 SP Authentic Sign of the Times

STATED ODDS 1:23
AC Anthony Carter 4.00 10.00
AD Antonio Davis 4.00 10.00
AG Adrian Griffin 4.00 10.00
AH Al Harrington 4.00 10.00
AJ Antawn Jamison 5.00 12.00
AL Alan Henderson 4.00 10.00
AM Andre Miller 4.00 10.00
AN Anfernee Hardaway 75.00 200.00
AW Antoine Walker 5.00 12.00
BD Baron Davis 6.00 15.00
BG Brian Grant 4.00 10.00
BR Brevin Knight 4.00 10.00
BW Bonzi Wells 4.00 10.00
CA Chucky Atkins 4.00 10.00
CM Corey Maggette 4.00 10.00
CR Austin Croshere 4.00 10.00
CT Cuttino Mobley 4.00 10.00
DA Darrell Armstrong 4.00 10.00
DG Dion Glover 4.00 10.00
DN Dirk Nowitzki 75.00 200.00
DS Damon Stoudamire 5.00 12.00
EJ Eddie Jones 10.00 25.00
GR Glen Rice 6.00 15.00
JB Jonathan Bender 4.00 10.00
JO Jermaine O'Neal 4.00 10.00
JP James Posey 4.00 10.00
JR Jalen Rose 8.00 20.00
JS Jerry Stackhouse 6.00 15.00
JT Jason Terry 5.00 12.00
JY Jayson Williams 4.00 10.00
KB Kobe Bryant 2,500.00 5,000.00
KG Kevin Garnett 75.00 200.00
KM Karl Malone 75.00 200.00
LH Larry Hughes 8.00 20.00
LM Lamond Murray 4.00 10.00
MB Mike Bibby 4.00 10.00
MD Antonio McDyess 8.00 20.00
ME Mario Elie 8.00 20.00
MI Michael Dickerson 4.00 10.00
MJ Michael Jordan 5,000.00 10,000.00
MK Mark Jackson 4.00 10.00
MT Maurice Taylor 4.00 10.00
QL Quincy Lewis 4.00 10.00
RA Ron Artest 8.00 20.00
RH Richard Hamilton 5.00 12.00
RL Raef LaFrentz 4.00 10.00
RP Ruben Patterson 4.00 10.00
RT Robert Traylor 4.00 10.00
SF Steve Francis 6.00 15.00
SH Shawn Marion 5.00 12.00
SM Sam Mack 4.00 10.00
SU Bob Sura 4.00 10.00
TG Tom Gugliotta 4.00 10.00
TL Trajan Langdon 4.00 10.00
TN Tyrone Nesby 4.00 10.00
TR Tracy McGrady 25.00 60.00
WA William Avery 4.00 10.00
WS Wally Szczerbiak 4.00 10.00

1999-00 SP Authentic Sign of the Times Gold

*GOLD: 1.5X TO 4X BASE AUTO
STATED PRINT RUN 25 SERIAL #'d SETS
DN Dirk Nowitzki 1,000.00 3,000.00
KB Kobe Bryant 6,000.00 10,000.00
KG Kevin Garnett 1,000.00 3,000.00
KM Karl Malone 500.00 1,000.00
ME Mario Elie 20.00 50.00
RA Ron Artest 75.00 200.00
SF Steve Francis 40.00 100.00
TR Tracy McGrady 150.00 400.00

1999-00 SP Authentic Supremacy

COMPLETE SET (9) 8.00 20.00
STATED ODDS 1:24
S1 Vince Carter 2.00 5.00
S2 Shaquille O'Neal 3.00 8.00
S3 Tim Duncan 2.00 5.00
S4 Kevin Garnett 2.00 5.00
S5 Jason Williams 1.25 3.00
S6 Stephon Marbury 1.00 2.50
S7 Gary Payton 1.25 3.00
S8 Kobe Bryant 6.00 15.00
S9 Grant Hill 1.25 3.00

2000-01 SP Authentic

COMP.SET w/o SP's (90) 10.00 25.00
1 Jason Terry .40 1.00
2 Alan Henderson .25 .60
3 Lorenzen Wright .25 .60
4 Paul Pierce .60 1.50
5 Antoine Walker .40 1.00
6 Bryant Stith .25 .60
7 Jamal Mashburn .30 .75
8 Baron Davis .40 1.00
9 David Wesley .30 .75
10 Elton Brand .40 1.00
11 Ron Artest .40 1.00
12 Ron Mercer .30 .75
13 Andre Miller .30 .75
14 Lamond Murray .25 .60
15 Jim Jackson .25 .75
16 Michael Finley .40 1.00
17 Dirk Nowitzki 1.00 2.50
18 Steve Nash .60 1.50
19 Antonio McDyess .30 .75
20 Nick Van Exel .40 1.00
21 Raef LaFrentz .30 .75
22 Jerry Stackhouse .40 1.00
23 Chucky Atkins .25 .60
24 Joe Smith .30 .75
25 Antawn Jamison .40 1.00
26 Larry Hughes .40 1.00
27 Mookie Blaylock .40 1.00
28 Steve Francis .40 1.00
29 Hakeem Olajuwon .75 2.00
30 Cuttino Mobley .30 .75
31 Reggie Miller .75 2.00
32 Jermaine O'Neal .30 .75
33 Jalen Rose .30 .75
34 Travis Best .25 .60
35 Lamar Odom .40 1.00
36 Corey Maggette .30 .75
37 Eric Piatkowski .25 .60
38 Shaquille O'Neal 1.50 4.00
39 Kobe Bryant 3.00 8.00
40 Isaiah Rider .30 .75
41 Horace Grant .40 1.00
42 Eddie Jones .40 1.00
43 Brian Grant .30 .75
44 Tim Hardaway .50 1.25
45 Ray Allen .60 1.50
46 Glenn Robinson .40 1.00
47 Sam Cassell .30 .75
48 Kevin Garnett 1.00 2.50
49 Terrell Brandon .30 .75
50 Chauncey Billups .50 1.25
51 Wally Szczerbiak .30 .75
52 Stephon Marbury .50 1.25
53 Keith Van Horn .30 .75
54 Aaron Williams .25 .60
55 Latrell Sprewell .50 1.25
56 Allan Houston .40 1.00
57 Glen Rice .40 1.00
58 Tracy McGrady .75 2.00
59 Grant Hill .60 1.50
60 Darrell Armstrong .25 .60
61 Allen Iverson 1.00 2.50
62 Dikembe Mutombo .60 1.50
63 Aaron McKie .25 .60
64 Jason Kidd .60 1.50
65 Clifford Robinson .40 1.00
66 Shawn Marion .40 1.00
67 Damon Stoudamire .40 1.00
68 Steve Smith .40 1.00
69 Rasheed Wallace .50 1.25
70 Chris Webber .50 1.25
71 Jason Williams .60 1.50
72 Peja Stojakovic .30 .75
73 Tim Duncan 1.00 2.50
74 David Robinson .75 2.00
75 Derek Anderson .30 .75
76 Gary Payton .60 1.50
77 Rashard Lewis .30 .75
78 Patrick Ewing .60 1.50
79 Vince Carter .75 2.00
80 Charles Oakley .40 1.00
81 Antonio Davis .30 .75
82 Karl Malone .75 2.00
83 John Stockton .75 2.00
84 John Starks .40 1.00
85 Shareef Abdur-Rahim .40 1.00
86 Mike Bibby .40 1.00
87 Michael Dickerson .25 .60
88 Richard Hamilton .50 1.25
89 Mitch Richmond .50 1.25
90 Christian Laettner .40 1.00
91 Kenyon Martin AU/500 RC 10.00 25.00
92 Stromile Swift AU/500 RC 4.00 10.00
93 Darius Miles AU/500 RC 6.00 15.00
94 Marcus Fizer/1250 RC 2.00 5.00
95 Mike Miller AU/500 RC 8.00 20.00
96 DerMarr Johnson AU/500 RC 3.00 8.00
97 Chris Mihm/1250 RC 1.50 4.00
98 Jamal Crawford/1250 RC 6.00 15.00
99 Joel Przybilla/2000 RC 1.50 4.00
100 Keyon Dooling/1250 RC 2.00 5.00
101 Jerome Moiso/1250 RC 1.50 4.00
102 Etan Thomas/2000 RC 1.50 4.00
103 Courtney Alexander/1250 RC 1.50 4.00
104 Mateen Cleaves/1250 RC 2.00 5.00
105 Jason Collier/2000 RC 2.00 5.00
106 Hedo Turkoglu/1250 RC 4.00 10.00
107 Desmond Mason/1250 RC 3.00 8.00
108 Q.Richardson/1250 RC 2.00 5.00
109 Jamaal Magloire/1250 RC 2.50 6.00
110 Speedy Claxton/2000 RC 2.00 5.00
111 M.Peterson AU/500 RC 5.00 12.00
112 Donnell Harvey/2000 RC 1.50 4.00
113 D.Stevenson/1250 RC 2.50 6.00
114 Jake Tsakalidis/2000 RC 1.25 3.00
115 S.Samake/2000 RC 1.25 3.00
116 Erick Barkley/2000 RC 1.25 3.00
117 Mark Madsen/2000 RC 2.00 5.00
118 A.J. Guyton/1250 RC 1.50 4.00
119 O.Oyedeji/2000 RC 1.25 3.00
120 Eddie House/1250 RC 2.00 5.00
121 Eduardo Najera/2000 RC 2.00 5.00
122 Lavor Postell/2000 RC 1.25 3.00
123 Hanno Mottola/1250 RC 1.50 4.00
124 Ira Newble/2000 RC 1.50 4.00
125 Chris Porter/1250 RC 1.50 4.00
126 R.Wolkowyski/2000 RC 1.25 3.00
127 Pepe Sanchez/2000 RC 1.50 4.00
128 S.Jackson/1250 RC 5.00 12.00
129 Marc Jackson/1250 RC 2.00 5.00
130 Dragan Tarlac/2000 RC 1.25 3.00
131 Lee Nailon/2000 1.25 3.00
132 Mike Penberthy/1250 RC 2.50 6.00
133 Mark Blount/2000 RC 1.50 4.00
134 Dan Langhi/2000 RC 1.25 3.00
135 Daniel Santiago/2000 RC 2.00 5.00
136 Wang Zhizhi AU/500 RC 75.00 200.00
S1 Kobe Bryant PROMO 1.00 2.50

2000-01 SP Authentic Athletic

COMPLETE SET (7) 5.00 12.00
STATED ODDS 1:24
A1 Allen Iverson 1.50 4.00
A2 Elton Brand .60 1.50
A3 Antonio McDyess .50 1.25
A4 Vince Carter 1.25 3.00
A5 Kobe Bryant 5.00 12.00
A6 Grant Hill 1.00 2.50
A7 Kevin Garnett 1.50 4.00

2000-01 SP Authentic BuyBack
STATED ODDS 1:2500
20 K.Garnett 95-6SP/21 150.00 300.00
45 T.Hardaway 98-9SPA/40 15.00 40.00
47 T.Hardaway 99-0SPA/17 20.00 50.00
61 M.Jordan 94-5SP/23 2,500.00 5,000.00
84 T.McGrady 98-9SPA/20 75.00 150.00
85 T.McGrady 99-0SPA/17 50.00 100.00
105 J.Stack 95-6SP/22 40.00 100.00
110 A.Walker 96-7SP/24 30.00 80.00

2000-01 SP Authentic First Class
COMPLETE SET (7) 20.00 50.00
STATED ODDS 1:24
FC1 Shareef Abdur-Rahim .75 2.00
FC2 Kevin Garnett 2.00 5.00
FC3 Baron Davis .75 2.00
FC4 Shaquille O'Neal 3.00 8.00
FC5 Rashard Lewis .60 1.50
FC6 Paul Pierce 1.25 3.00
FC7 Kobe Bryant 15.00 40.00

2000-01 SP Authentic Premier Powers
COMPLETE SET (7) 6.00 15.00
STATED ODDS 1:24
P1 Chris Webber .75 2.00
P2 Allen Iverson 1.50 4.00
P3 Kobe Bryant 5.00 12.00
P4 Rasheed Wallace .75 2.00
P5 Tracy McGrady 1.25 3.00
P6 Kevin Garnett 1.50 4.00
P7 Tim Duncan 1.50 4.00

2000-01 SP Authentic Sign of the Times
STATED ODDS 1:23
AC Austin Croshere 3.00 8.00
AJ Antawn Jamison 5.00 12.00
AM Antonio McDyess 4.00 10.00
AR Darrell Armstrong 3.00 8.00
AW Antoine Walker 5.00 12.00
CA Courtney Alexander 3.00 8.00
CM Chris Mihm 3.00 8.00
DA Darius Miles 5.00 12.00
DE Desmond Mason 6.00 15.00
DH Donnell Harvey 4.00 10.00
DJ DerMarr Johnson 3.00 8.00
DN Dirk Nowitzki 100.00 250.00
DS DeShawn Stevenson 5.00 12.00
EB Erick Barkley 3.00 8.00
EJ Eddie Jones 10.00 25.00
ET Etan Thomas 4.00 10.00
FI Marcus Fizer 4.00 10.00
GP Gary Payton 20.00 50.00
JA Jamaal Magloire 5.00 12.00
JB Jonathan Bender 3.00 8.00
JC Jamal Crawford 12.00 30.00
JM Jerome Moiso 3.00 8.00
JO Jermaine O'Neal 6.00 15.00
JP Joel Przybilla 4.00 10.00
JR Jalen Rose 10.00 25.00
JS Jerry Stackhouse 10.00 25.00
KB Kobe Bryant SP 2,500.00 5,000.00
KG Kevin Garnett SP 400.00 800.00
KM Kenyon Martin 6.00 15.00
MA Corey Maggette 4.00 10.00
MB Mike Bibby 6.00 15.00
MC Mateen Cleaves 4.00 10.00
MF Michael Finley 8.00 20.00
MK Mike Miller 6.00 15.00
MM Mark Madsen 8.00 20.00
MN Mamadou N'Diaye 3.00 8.00
MP Mike Penberthy 5.00 12.00
MP Morris Peterson 5.00 12.00
QR Quentin Richardson 4.00 10.00
RH Richard Hamilton 6.00 15.00
RM Reggie Miller 150.00 400.00
SC Speedy Claxton 5.00 12.00
SF Steve Francis 5.00 12.00
SJ Stephen Jackson 10.00 25.00
SM Shawn Marion 10.00 25.00
SS Stromile Swift 4.00 10.00
TM Tracy McGrady 75.00 200.00
TT Tim Thomas 3.00 8.00

2000-01 SP Authentic Sign of the Times Platinum
*PLATINUM: .6X TO 1.5X BASIC SIGN
STATED ODDS 1:287
PRINT RUN 200 SETS UNLESS NOTED
DH Donnell Harvey/200 5.00 12.00
DS DeShawn Stevenson/200 6.00 15.00
ET Etan Thomas/200 5.00 12.00
JA Jamaal Magloire/200 6.00 15.00
JP Joel Przybilla/200 5.00 12.00
KG Kevin Garnett/21 400.00 800.00
MJ Michael Jordan/23 2,000.00 4,000.00

2000-01 SP Authentic Sign of the Times Double
STATED ODDS 1:287
CADH C.Alexander/D.Harvey 5.00 12.00
DADS D.Miles/D.Stevenson 12.00 30.00
DAQR D.Miles/Q.Richardson 12.00 30.00
FJC M.Fizer/J.Crawford 6.00 15.00
JCDS J.Crawford/D.Stevenson 12.00 30.00
KBKG K.Bryant/K.Garnett 2,500.00 5,000.00
KBKM K.Bryant/K.Martin 500.00 1,000.00
KBSF K.Bryant/S.Francis 1,000.00 2,000.00
KBTM K.Bryant/T.McGrady 2,000.00 4,000.00
KGKM K.Garnett/K.Martin 100.00 250.00
KMDA K.Martin/D.Miles 15.00 40.00
KMDJ K.Martin/D.Johnson 12.00 30.00
KMFI K.Martin/M.Fizer 15.00 40.00
KMSJ K.Martin/S.Jackson 20.00 50.00
KMSS K.Martin/S.Swift 12.00 30.00
MCMP M.Cleaves/M.Peterson 6.00 15.00
MJDR M.Jordan/J.Erving 4,000.00 8,000.00
MJKB M.Jordan/K.Bryant 10,000.00 20,000.00

2000-01 SP Authentic Sign of the Times Triple
STATED PRINT RUN 25 SERIAL #'d SETS
DRMGLB Erving/Magic/Bird 1,500.00 3,000.00
KBKGKM Kobe/Garnett/Martin 1,000.00 2,000.00
KBMJKG Kobe/Jordan/Garnett 10,000.00 20,000.00
KBMJMG Kobe/Jordan/Magic 10,000.00 20,000.00
KMSJMJ Martin/S.Jcksn/M.Jcksn 40.00 100.00
KMSSDA Martin/Swift/Miles 40.00 100.00

2000-01 SP Authentic Special Forces
COMPLETE SET (7) 5.00 12.00
STATED ODDS 1:24
SF1 Kobe Bryant 5.00 12.00
SF2 Steve Francis .60 1.50
SF3 Eddie Jones .60 1.50
SF4 Shaquille O'Neal 2.50 6.00
SF5 Stephon Marbury .75 2.00
SF6 Lamar Odom .60 1.50
SF7 Kevin Garnett 1.50 4.00

2000-01 SP Authentic Spectacular
COMPLETE SET (7) 5.00 12.00
STATED ODDS 1:24
SP1 Kobe Bryant 5.00 12.00
SP2 Chris Webber .75 2.00
SP3 Latrell Sprewell .75 2.00
SP4 Vince Carter 1.25 3.00
SP5 Rashard Lewis .50 1.25
SP6 Tim Duncan 1.50 4.00
SP7 Karl Malone 1.25 3.00

2000-01 SP Authentic Supremacy
COMPLETE SET (7) 6.00 15.00
STATED ODDS 1:24
S1 Shaquille O'Neal 2.50 6.00
S2 Tim Duncan 1.50 4.00
S3 Kevin Garnett 1.50 4.00
S4 Allen Iverson 1.50 4.00
S5 Kobe Bryant 5.00 12.00
S6 Vince Carter 1.25 3.00
S7 Jason Kidd 1.00 2.50

2001-02 SP Authentic
COMP.SET w/o SP's (90) 20.00 40.00
91-106 PRINT RUN 1600 SER.#'d SETS
107-115 PRINT RUN 550 SER.#'d SETS
116-131 PRINT RUN 1525 SER.#'d SETS
132-140 PRINT RUN 750 SER.#'d SETS
141-159 PRINT RUN 2000 SER.#'d SETS
160-165 PRINT RUN 1000 SER.#'d SETS
1 Shareef Abdur-Rahim .30 .75
2 Jason Terry .40 1.00
3 Dion Glover .25 .60
4 Paul Pierce .60 1.50
5 Antoine Walker .30 .75
6 Kenny Anderson .30 .75
7 Baron Davis .40 1.00
8 David Wesley .25 .60
9 Jamal Mashburn .30 .75
10 Jalen Rose .30 .75
11 Fred Hoiberg .25 .60
12 Marcus Fizer .25 .60
13 Andre Miller .30 .75
14 Lamond Murray .25 .60
15 Chris Mihm .25 .60
16 Dirk Nowitzki 1.00 2.50
17 Steve Nash .75 2.00
18 Michael Finley .40 1.00
19 Nick Van Exel .40 1.00
20 Antonio McDyess .30 .75
21 Juwan Howard .30 .75
22 James Posey .25 .60
23 Jerry Stackhouse .40 1.00
24 Clifford Robinson .25 .60
25 Ben Wallace .50 1.25
26 Antawn Jamison .30 .75
27 Larry Hughes .30 .75
28 Danny Fortson .25 .60
29 Steve Francis .40 1.00
30 Cuttino Mobley .30 .75
31 Reggie Miller .75 2.00
32 Al Harrington .30 .75
33 Jermaine O'Neal .30 .75
34 Darius Miles .25 .60
35 Elton Brand .30 .75
36 Lamar Odom .30 .75
37 Corey Maggette .30 .75
38 Kobe Bryant 3.00 8.00
39 Shaquille O'Neal 1.50 4.00
40 Rick Fox .30 .75
41 Lindsey Hunter .25 .60
42 Stromile Swift .25 .60
43 Michael Dickerson .25 .60
44 Jason Williams .60 1.50
45 Alonzo Mourning .60 1.50
46 Eddie Jones .40 1.00
47 Anthony Carter .25 .60
48 Ray Allen .60 1.50
49 Glenn Robinson .40 1.00
50 Sam Cassell .30 .75
51 Kevin Garnett 1.00 2.50
52 Terrell Brandon .30 .75
53 Wally Szczerbiak .30 .75
54 Joe Smith .25 .60
55 Jason Kidd .60 1.50
56 Kenyon Martin .40 1.00
57 Mark Jackson .30 .75
58 Allan Houston .40 1.00
59 Latrell Sprewell .50 1.25
60 Marcus Camby .30 .75
61 Tracy McGrady .60 1.50
62 Grant Hill .60 1.50
63 Mike Miller .30 .75
64 Allen Iverson 1.00 2.50
65 Dikembe Mutombo .60 1.50
66 Aaron McKie .25 .60
67 Stephon Marbury .50 1.25
68 Shawn Marion .40 1.00
69 Anfernee Hardaway 1.00 2.50
70 Rasheed Wallace .50 1.25
71 Bonzi Wells .25 .60
72 Derek Anderson .25 .60
73 Chris Webber .50 1.25
74 Mike Bibby .40 1.00
75 Peja Stojakovic .30 .75
76 Tim Duncan 1.00 2.50
77 David Robinson .75 2.00
78 Antonio Daniels .25 .60
79 Gary Payton .60 1.50
80 Rashard Lewis .30 .75
81 Desmond Mason .30 .75
82 Vince Carter .75 2.00
83 Morris Peterson .25 .60
84 Antonio Davis .30 .75
85 Karl Malone .75 2.00
86 John Stockton .75 2.00
87 Donyell Marshall .25 .60
88 Richard Hamilton .50 1.25
89 Courtney Alexander .25 .60
90 Michael Jordan 6.00 15.00
91 Tierre Brown RC 2.00 5.00
92 Damone Brown RC 1.25 3.00
93 Michael Bradley RC 1.25 3.00
94 Kedrick Brown RC 1.25 3.00
95 Alton Ford RC 2.00 5.00
96 Jason Collins RC 1.50 4.00
97 Antonis Fotsis RC 1.25 3.00
98 Mengke Bateer RC 15.00 40.00
99 Trenton Hassell RC 1.25 3.00
100 Jamison Brewer RC 2.00 5.00
101 Bobby Simmons RC 2.00 5.00
102 Mike James RC 2.00 5.00
103 Oscar Torres RC 2.00 5.00
104 Brandon Armstrong RC 1.25 3.00
105 Will Solomon RC 1.50 4.00
106 Vladimir Radmanovic RC 1.50 4.00
107 Kirk Haston RC 2.00 5.00
108 Gerald Wallace RC 4.00 10.00
109 Andrei Kirilenko RC 5.00 12.00
110 Joseph Forte RC 2.00 5.00
111 Brendan Haywood RC 2.50 6.00
112 Zach Randolph RC 6.00 15.00
113 DeSagana Diop RC 2.00 5.00
114 Shane Battier RC 6.00 15.00
115 Pau Gasol RC 12.00 30.00
116 Alvin Jones AU RC 2.00 5.00
117 Zeljko Rebraca AU RC 3.00 8.00
118 Kenny Satterfield AU RC 2.00 5.00
119 Jarron Collins AU RC 3.00 8.00
120 Ruben Boumtje-Boumtje AU RC 2.50 6.00
121 Loren Woods AU RC 2.00 5.00
122 Earl Watson AU RC 2.50 6.00
123 Jeff Trepagnier AU RC 2.00 5.00
124 Brian Scalabrine AU RC 3.00 8.00
125 Terence Morris AU RC 2.00 5.00
126 Gilbert Arenas AU RC 8.00 20.00
127 S.Dalembert AU RC 3.00 8.00
128 Jeryl Sasser AU RC 2.00 5.00
129 Rodney White AU RC 2.00 5.00
130 Eddie Griffin AU RC 2.50 6.00
131 Tyson Chandler AU RC 5.00 12.00
132 Steven Hunter AU RC 2.50 6.00
133 Troy Murphy AU RC 3.00 8.00
134 Richard Jefferson AU RC 5.00 12.00
135 Joe Johnson AU RC 6.00 15.00
136 Eddy Curry AU RC 4.00 10.00
137 J.Richardson AU RC 6.00 15.00
138 Tony Parker AU RC 75.00 200.00
139 Jamaal Tinsley AU RC 3.00 8.00
140 Kwame Brown AU RC 4.00 10.00
141 Paul Pierce SPEC 2.00 5.00
142 Tim Duncan SPEC 3.00 8.00
143 Stephon Marbury SPEC 1.50 4.00
144 Shareef Abdur-Rahim SPEC 1.00 2.50
145 Ray Allen SPEC 2.00 5.00
146 Bonzi Wells SPEC .75 2.00
147 Kenyon Martin SPEC 1.25 3.00
148 Darius Miles SPEC .75 2.00
149 Baron Davis SPEC 1.25 3.00
150 Dirk Nowitzki SPEC 3.00 8.00
151 Antoine Walker SPEC 1.00 2.50
152 Mike Miller SPEC 1.00 2.50
153 Shawn Marion SPEC 1.25 3.00
154 Jason Kidd SPEC 2.00 5.00
155 Elton Brand SPEC 1.25 3.00
156 Antawn Jamison SPEC 1.00 2.50
157 Rashard Lewis SPEC 1.00 2.50
158 Steve Francis SPEC 1.25 3.00
159 Tracy McGrady SPEC 2.00 5.00
160 Kobe Bryant SPEC 12.00 30.00
161 Allen Iverson SPEC 4.00 10.00
162 Vince Carter SPEC 3.00 8.00
163 Shaquille O'Neal SPEC 6.00 15.00
164 Kevin Garnett SPEC 4.00 10.00
165 Michael Jordan SPEC 12.00 30.00
PROMO Michael Jordan PROMO 4.00 10.00

2001-02 SP Authentic Dual Signatures
PRINT RUN 50 SER.#'d SETS
DR/LB J.Erving/L.Bird 400.00 800.00
KB/MG K.Bryant/M.Johnson 1,500.00 3,000.00
MG/LB M.Johnson/L.Bird 600.00 1,200.00
MJ/DR M.Jordan/J.Erving 2,000.00 4,000.00
MJ/KB M.Jordan/K.Bryant 8,000.00 15,000.00
TC/EC T.Chandler/E.Curry 10.00 25.00

2001-02 SP Authentic Rookie Authentics
PRINT RUN 1275 SER.#'d SETS
RAAK Andrei Kirilenko 3.00 8.00
RABA Brandon Armstrong 1.25 3.00
RAEC Eddy Curry 2.00 5.00
RAEG Eddie Griffin 1.50 4.00
RAGW Gerald Wallace 2.50 6.00
RAJA Jarron Collins 2.00 5.00
RAJC Jason Collins 1.50 4.00
RAJF Joseph Forte 1.25 3.00
RAJJ Joe Johnson 3.00 8.00
RAJR Jason Richardson 3.00 8.00
RAJS Jeryl Sasser 1.25 3.00
RAKB Kedrick Brown 1.25 3.00
RAKW Kwame Brown 2.00 5.00
RAMB Michael Bradley 1.25 3.00
RARJ Richard Jefferson 2.50 6.00
RARW Rodney White 1.25 3.00
RASD Samuel Dalembert 2.00 5.00
RASH Steven Hunter 1.25 3.00
RATC Tyson Chandler 3.00 8.00
RATH Trenton Hassell 1.25 3.00
RATM Terence Morris 1.25 3.00
RATP Tony Parker 10.00 25.00
RAVR Vladimir Radmanovic 1.50 4.00

2001-02 SP Authentic Signatures
PRINT RUN 390 SER.#'d SETS
AJ Alvin Jones 2.50 6.00
DJ DerMarr Johnson 4.00 10.00
EG Eddie Griffin 3.00 8.00
GA Gilbert Arenas 8.00 20.00
GW Gerald Wallace 5.00 12.00
JC Jason Collins 8.00 20.00
JJ Joe Johnson 6.00 15.00
JR Jason Richardson 6.00 15.00
JS Jeryl Sasser 2.50 6.00
JT Jamaal Tinsley 3.00 8.00
KM Kenyon Martin 6.00 15.00
KS Kenny Satterfield 2.50 6.00
KW Kwame Brown 4.00 10.00
LW Loren Woods 2.50 6.00
MM Mike Miller 5.00 12.00
MP Morris Peterson 4.00 10.00
QR Quentin Richardson 2.50 6.00
RJ Richard Jefferson 5.00 12.00
RW Rodney White 2.50 6.00
SH Steven Hunter 2.50 6.00
TC Tyson Chandler 6.00 15.00
TM Troy Murphy 3.00 8.00
TP Tony Parker 30.00 80.00
VR Vladimir Radmanovic 3.00 8.00

2001-02 SP Authentic Star Signatures
PRINT RUN 75 SER.#'d SETS
DMS Darius Miles 15.00 30.00
JKS Jason Kidd 25.00 60.00
KBS Kobe Bryant 150.00 400.00
KGS Kevin Garnett 40.00 100.00
MJS Michael Jordan 1,500.00 3,000.00
SAS Shareef Abdur-Rahim 15.00 30.00

2001-02 SP Authentic Superstar Authentics
PRINT RUN 200 SER.#'d SETS
SAAI Allen Iverson 12.00 30.00
SACW Chris Webber 8.00 20.00
SAJK Jason Kidd 8.00 20.00
SAKB Kobe Bryant 75.00 200.00
SAKG Kevin Garnett 12.00 30.00
SAMJ Michael Jordan 30.00 80.00
SATM Tracy McGrady 8.00 20.00

2002-03 SP Authentic
COMP.SET w/o SP's (100) 15.00 40.00
101-142 PRINT RUN 2000 SER.#'d SETS
143-174 PRINT RUN 1500 SER.#'d SETS
175-203 PRINT RUN 1500 SER.#'d SETS
1 Glenn Robinson .40 1.00
2 Shareef Abdur-Rahim .40 1.00
3 Jason Terry .30 .75
4 Theo Ratliff .25 .60
5 Paul Pierce .60 1.50
5A Paul Pierce AU 15.00 40.00
6 Antoine Walker .30 .75
6A Antoine Walker AU 8.00 20.00
7 Tony Delk .25 .60
8 Vin Baker .30 .75
9 Jalen Rose .30 .75
10 Eddy Curry .25 .60
11 Tyson Chandler .40 1.00
11A Tyson Chandler AU 5.00 12.00
12 Marcus Fizer .25 .60
12A Marcus Fizer AU 5.00 12.00
13 Darius Miles .25 .60
14 Zydrunas Ilgauskas .30 .75
15 Dirk Nowitzki 1.00 2.50
16 Michael Finley .40 1.00
17 Steve Nash .75 2.00
18 Raef LaFrentz .25 .60
19 Juwan Howard .30 .75
20 Rodney White .25 .60
21 Ben Wallace .50 1.25
22 Richard Hamilton .50 1.25
23 Chauncey Billups .40 1.00
24 Chucky Atkins .25 .60
25 Jason Richardson .40 1.00
26 Antawn Jamison .30 .75
27 Gilbert Arenas .40 1.00
28 Steve Francis .40 1.00
29 Cuttino Mobley .25 .60
30 Jermaine O'Neal .30 .75
30A Jermaine O'Neal AU 8.00 20.00
31 Jamaal Tinsley .25 .60
32 Reggie Miller .75 2.00
33 Ron Artest .30 .75
34 Elton Brand .30 .75
35 Andre Miller .30 .75
36 Michael Olowokandi .25 .60
37 Kobe Bryant 3.00 8.00
38 Shaquille O'Neal 1.50 4.00
39 Robert Horry .40 1.00
40 Derek Fisher .40 1.00
41 Pau Gasol .60 1.50
42 Shane Battier .40 1.00
43 Eddie Jones .40 1.00
44 Brian Grant .25 .60
45 Malik Allen .25 .60
46 Gary Payton .60 1.50
47 Sam Cassell .30 .75
48 Kevin Garnett 1.00 2.50
49 Wally Szczerbiak .30 .75
50 Troy Hudson .25 .60
51 Radoslav Nesterovic .25 .60
52 Jason Kidd .60 1.50
53 Richard Jefferson .30 .75
54 Kenyon Martin .40 1.00
54A Kenyon Martin AU 8.00 20.00
55 Kerry Kittles .25 .60
56 Baron Davis .40 1.00
57 Jamal Mashburn .30 .75
58 David Wesley .25 .60
59 P.J. Brown .25 .60
60 Jamaal Magloire .25 .60
60A Jamaal Magloire AU 5.00 12.00
61 Allan Houston .40 1.00
62 Kurt Thomas .25 .60
63 Latrell Sprewell .40 1.00
64 Clarence Weatherspoon .25 .60
65 Tracy McGrady .60 1.50
66 Grant Hill .60 1.50
67 Mike Miller .30 .75
67A Mike Miller AU 8.00 20.00
68 Allen Iverson 1.00 2.50
69 Keith Van Horn .30 .75
70 Stephon Marbury .50 1.25
71 Shawn Marion .40 1.00
72 Anfernee Hardaway 1.00 2.50
73 Rasheed Wallace .50 1.25
74 Derek Anderson .25 .60
75 Scottie Pippen 1.00 2.50
76 Bonzi Wells .25 .60
77 Chris Webber .50 1.25
78 Mike Bibby .40 1.00
78A Mike Bibby AU 6.00 15.00
79 Peja Stojakovic .30 .75
80 Hedo Turkoglu .30 .75
81 Vlade Divac .30 .75
82 Tim Duncan 1.00 2.50
83 David Robinson .75 2.00
84 Tony Parker .60 1.50
85 Steve Smith .30 .75
86 Ray Allen .60 1.50
87 Rashard Lewis .30 .75
88 Brent Barry .25 .60
89 Elden Campbell .25 .60
90 Vince Carter .75 2.00
91 Morris Peterson .30 .75
92 Antonio Davis .30 .75
93 Alvin Williams .25 .60
94 Karl Malone .75 2.00
95 John Stockton .75 2.00
96 Andrei Kirilenko .30 .75
97 DeShawn Stevenson .25 .60
97A DeShawn Stevenson AU 5.00 12.00
98 Jerry Stackhouse .40 1.00
99 Michael Jordan 4.00 10.00
100 Kwame Brown .25 .60
101 Kobe Bryant SPEC 8.00 20.00
102 Allen Iverson SPEC 2.50 6.00
103 Pau Gasol SPEC 1.50 4.00
104 Antoine Walker SPEC .75 2.00
105 Jermaine O'Neal SPEC .75 2.00
106 Ray Allen SPEC 1.50 4.00
107 Baron Davis SPEC 1.00 2.50
108 Tim Duncan SPEC 2.50 6.00
109 Rashard Lewis SPEC .75 2.00
110 Michael Jordan SPEC 12.00 30.00
111 Stephon Marbury SPEC 1.25 3.00
112 Shareef Abdur-Rahim SPEC 1.00 2.50
113 Vince Carter SPEC 2.00 5.00
114 Allan Houston SPEC 1.00 2.50
115 Dirk Nowitzki SPEC 2.50 6.00
116 Grant Hill SPEC 1.50 4.00
117 Mike Bibby SPEC 1.00 2.50
118 Derek Anderson SPEC .60 1.50
119 Shaquille O'Neal SPEC 4.00 10.00
120 Steve Francis SPEC 1.00 2.50
121 Richard Jefferson SPEC .75 2.00
122 Ben Wallace SPEC 1.25 3.00
123 Jason Kidd SPEC 1.50 4.00
124 Jalen Rose SPEC .75 2.00
125 Paul Pierce SPEC 1.50 4.00
126 Michael Finley SPEC 1.00 2.50
127 Jamal Mashburn SPEC .75 2.00
128 Elton Brand SPEC .75 2.00
129 Rasheed Wallace SPEC 1.25 3.00
130 Gary Payton SPEC 1.50 4.00
131 Tracy McGrady SPEC 1.50 4.00
132 Richard Hamilton SPEC 1.25 3.00
133 Chris Webber SPEC 1.25 3.00
134 Karl Malone SPEC 2.00 5.00
135 Darius Miles SPEC .60 1.50
136 Shawn Marion SPEC 1.00 2.50
137 Kevin Garnett SPEC 2.50 6.00
138 Eddie Jones SPEC 1.00 2.50
139 Jason Richardson SPEC 1.00 2.50
140 Glenn Robinson SPEC 1.00 2.50
141 Jerry Stackhouse SPEC 1.00 2.50
142 Shane Battier SPEC 1.00 2.50
143 Yao Ming AU RC 200.00 500.00
144 Jay Williams AU RC 2.50 6.00
145 Drew Gooden AU RC 3.00 8.00
146 N.Tskitishvili AU RC 2.00 5.00
147 DaJuan Wagner AU RC 2.50 6.00
148 Nene Hilario AU RC 3.00 8.00
149 Chris Wilcox AU RC 2.50 6.00
150 Amare Stoudemire AU RC 12.00 30.00
151 Caron Butler AU RC 3.00 8.00
152 Jared Jeffries AU RC 2.50 6.00
153 Melvin Ely AU RC 2.50 6.00
154 Marcus Haislip AU RC 2.00 5.00
155 Fred Jones AU RC 2.50 6.00
156 Bostjan Nachbar AU RC 2.50 6.00
157 Jiri Welsch AU RC 2.50 6.00
158 Juan Dixon AU RC 2.50 6.00
159 Curtis Borchardt AU RC 2.50 6.00
160 Ryan Humphrey AU RC 2.50 6.00
161 Kareem Rush AU RC 2.50 6.00
162 Qyntel Woods AU RC 2.50 6.00
163 Casey Jacobsen AU RC 2.50 6.00
164 Tayshaun Prince AU RC 6.00 15.00
165 Frank Williams AU RC 2.00 5.00
166 John Salmons AU RC 3.00 8.00
167 Chris Jefferies AU RC 2.00 5.00
168 Dan Dickau AU RC 2.00 5.00
169 Carlos Boozer AU RC 3.00 8.00
170 Marko Jaric AU 3.00 8.00
171 Sam Clancy AU RC 2.50 6.00
172 Manu Ginobili AU RC 100.00 250.00
173 V.Yarbrough AU RC 2.00 5.00
174 Gordan Giricek AU RC 3.00 8.00
175 Predrag Savovic RC 1.25 3.00
176 Mike Dunleavy RC 1.50 4.00
177 Tamar Slay RC 1.00 2.50
178 Rasual Butler RC 1.25 3.00
179 Reggie Evans RC 1.25 3.00
180 Igor Rakocevic RC 1.00 2.50
181 Juaquin Hawkins RC 1.00 2.50
182 J.R. Bremer RC 1.00 2.50
183 Cezary Trybanski RC 1.50 4.00
184 Junior Harrington RC 1.00 2.50
185 Efthimios Rentzias RC 1.00 2.50
186 Smush Parker RC 1.50 4.00
187 Jamal Sampson RC 1.00 2.50
188 Roger Mason RC 1.25 3.00
189 Robert Archibald RC 1.00 2.50
190 Mehmet Okur RC 1.50 4.00
191 Dan Gadzuric RC 1.00 2.50
192 Pat Burke RC 1.00 2.50
193 Lonny Baxter RC 1.00 2.50
194 Tito Maddox RC 1.00 2.50
195 Jannero Pargo RC 1.00 2.50
196 Ronald Murray RC 1.50 4.00
197 Mike Wilks RC 1.50 4.00
198 Mike Batiste RC 1.00 2.50
199 Chris Owens RC 1.00 2.50
200 Raul Lopez RC 1.50 4.00
201 Antoine Rigaudeau RC 1.00 2.50
202 Ken Johnson 1.25 3.00
203 Maceo Baston RC 1.50 4.00
NNO Michael Jordan PROMO 10.00 25.00

2002-03 SP Authentic Limited
*1-100 STARS: 3X TO 8X BASE CARD HI
*1-100 AU's: .75X TO 2X BASE CARD HI
*101-142 SPEC: 1.25X TO 3X BASE CARD HI
1-142 PRINT RUN 100 SER.#'d SETS
*RCs: 1.5X TO 4X BASE CARD HI
143-203 RC PRINT RUN 50 SER.#'d SETS
150 Amare Stoudemire AU 60.00 150.00

2002-03 SP Authentic Dual Excellence Signatures
PRINT RUN 25 SER.#'d SETS
JEKA J.Erving/K.Abdul-Jabbar 300.00 600.00
KBJK K.Bryant/J.Kidd 600.00 1,200.00
KBMB K.Bryant/M.Bibby 500.00 1,000.00
MJLB M.Jordan/L.Bird 2,500.00 5,000.00

2002-03 SP Authentic Marks of Distinction
PRINT RUN 50 SER.#'d SETS
BRM Bill Russell 2,000.00 4,000.00
DRM Julius Erving 150.00 400.00
JKM Jason Kidd 75.00 200.00
JRM Jason Richardson 20.00 50.00
JWM Jay Williams 20.00 50.00
KAM Kareem Abdul-Jabbar 150.00 400.00
KBM Kobe Bryant 2,000.00 4,000.00
KGM Kevin Garnett 150.00 400.00
LBM Larry Bird 200.00 500.00
MJM Michael Jordan 3,000.00 6,000.00

2002-03 SP Authentic SP Dual Signatures
ONE SINGLE SIG OR DUAL SIG PER BOX
ASCJ A.Stoudemire/C.Jacobsen 8.00 20.00
CWME C.Wilcox/M.Ely 6.00 15.00
DRKA J.Erving/Kareem SP 200.00 500.00
DWCB D.Wagner/C.Boozer 6.00 15.00
EGMJ M.Ginobili/M.Jaric 25.00 60.00
JJJD J.Dixon/J.Jeffries 6.00 15.00
JKKM J.Kidd/K.Marton 20.00 50.00
JWTC JayWill/Chandler SP 8.00 20.00
KBKA Bryant/Kareem SP 3,000.00 6,000.00
MJKB Jordan/Bryant SP 6,000.00 12,000.00
PPAW P.Pierce/A.Walker 40.00 100.00
YMJW Y.Ming/J.Williams 150.00 400.00

2002-03 SP Authentic SP Signatures
ONE SINGLE SIG OR DUAL SIG PER BOX
AW Antoine Walker 8.00 20.00
BN Bostjan Nachbar 3.00 8.00
CA Carlos Boozer 4.00 10.00
CB Chauncey Billups 12.00 30.00
CU Curtis Borchardt 2.50 6.00
CW Chris Wilcox 3.00 8.00
DD Dan Dickau 2.50 6.00
DG Dan Gadzuric 3.00 8.00
DR Julius Erving SP 200.00 500.00
DS DeShawn Stevenson 2.50 6.00
DW DaJuan Wagner 3.00 8.00
EG Manu Ginobili 60.00 150.00
ET Etan Thomas 3.00 8.00
FW Frank Williams 2.50 6.00
GW Gerald Wallace 6.00 15.00
JD Juan Dixon 3.00 8.00
JK Jason Kidd 25.00 60.00
JM Jamaal Magloire 3.00 8.00
JO Jermaine O'Neal 4.00 10.00
JR Jason Richardson 4.00 10.00
JS John Salmons 4.00 10.00
JW Jay Williams 6.00 15.00
KA Kareem Abdul-Jabbar 125.00 300.00
KB Kobe Bryant SP 3,000.00 6,000.00
KG Kevin Garnett SP 150.00 400.00
KM Kenyon Martin 8.00 20.00
KR Kareem Rush 3.00 8.00
LB Larry Bird 125.00 300.00
MB Mike Bibby 8.00 20.00
MF Marcus Fizer 3.00 8.00
MJ Michael Jordan SP 4,000.00 8,000.00
MM Mike Miller 5.00 12.00
MO Jerome Moiso 4.00 10.00
PP Paul Pierce 15.00 40.00
PS Peja Stojakovic 8.00 20.00
SC Sam Clancy 3.00 8.00
SM Shawn Marion SP 8.00 20.00
TC Tyson Chandler 5.00 12.00
WE Jiri Welsch 3.00 8.00
YM Yao Ming 400.00 800.00

2002-03 SP Authentic Beckett.com Samples
SAMPLES: .75X TO 2X BASE HI

2003-04 SP Authentic
COMP.SET w/o SP's (90) 15.00 40.00
154-189 PRINT RUN 1250 SER.#'d SETS
HASLEM ON 138 NO RC AND 188 AU RC
1 Shareef Abdur-Rahim .40 1.00
2 Theo Ratliff .25 .60
3 Jason Terry .30 .75
4 Raef LaFrentz .25 .60
5 Vin Baker .25 .60
6 Paul Pierce .60 1.50
7 Antonio Davis .30 .75
8 Scottie Pippen 1.00 2.50
9 Tyson Chandler .30 .75
10 Dajuan Wagner .25 .60
11 Carlos Boozer .30 .75
12 Zydrunas Ilgauskas .30 .75
13 Dirk Nowitzki 1.00 2.50
14 Antoine Walker .40 1.00
15 Steve Nash .75 2.00
16 Michael Finley .40 1.00
17 Earl Boykins .25 .60
18 Andre Miller .30 .75
19 Nene .30 .75
20 Chauncey Billups .50 1.25
21 Richard Hamilton .50 1.25
22 Ben Wallace .50 1.25
23 Clifford Robinson .25 .60
24 Jason Richardson .40 1.00
25 Nick Van Exel .40 1.00
26 Yao Ming 1.00 2.50
27 Cuttino Mobley .25 .60
28 Steve Francis .40 1.00
29 Jermaine O'Neal .40 1.00
30 Reggie Miller .75 2.00
31 Ron Artest .30 .75
32 Elton Brand .30 .75
33 Corey Maggette .30 .75
34 Quentin Richardson .25 .60
35 Kobe Bryant 3.00 8.00
36 Karl Malone .75 2.00
37 Gary Payton .60 1.50
38 Shaquille O'Neal 1.50 4.00
39 Pau Gasol .60 1.50
40 Bonzi Wells .25 .60
41 Mike Miller .30 .75
42 Lamar Odom .30 .75
43 Eddie Jones .40 1.00
44 Caron Butler .30 .75
45 Toni Kukoc .40 1.00
46 Desmond Mason .30 .75
47 Michael Redd .40 1.00
48 Latrell Sprewell .50 1.25
49 Kevin Garnett 1.00 2.50
50 Sam Cassell .30 .75
51 Richard Jefferson .30 .75
52 Kenyon Martin .40 1.00
53 Jason Kidd .60 1.50
54 Jamal Mashburn .30 .75
55 Baron Davis .40 1.00
56 David Wesley .25 .60
57 Allan Houston .40 1.00
58 Stephon Marbury .50 1.25
59 Keith Van Horn .30 .75
60 Gordan Giricek .25 .60
61 Drew Gooden .30 .75
62 Tracy McGrady .60 1.50
63 Glenn Robinson .30 .75
64 Allen Iverson 1.00 2.50
65 Eric Snow .25 .60
66 Amare Stoudemire .50 1.25
67 Antonio McDyess .30 .75
68 Shawn Marion .40 1.00
69 Zach Randolph .40 1.00
70 Damon Stoudamire .30 .75
71 Rasheed Wallace .50 1.25
72 Peja Stojakovic .30 .75
73 Chris Webber .50 1.25
74 Mike Bibby .40 1.00
75 Brad Miller .30 .75
76 Tony Parker .60 1.50
77 Tim Duncan 1.00 2.50
78 Manu Ginobili .75 2.00
79 Vladimir Radmanovic .25 .60
80 Ray Allen .60 1.50
81 Rashard Lewis .30 .75
82 Morris Peterson .25 .60
83 Vince Carter .75 2.00
84 Jalen Rose .30 .75
85 Andrei Kirilenko .30 .75
86 Matt Harpring .25 .60
87 Carlos Arroyo .30 .75
88 Gilbert Arenas .40 1.00
89 Larry Hughes .30 .75
90 Jerry Stackhouse .50 1.25
91 Kobe Bryant SPEC 8.00 20.00
92 Jason Kidd SPEC 1.50 4.00
93 Rasheed Wallace SPEC 1.25 3.00
94 Jalen Rose SPEC .75 2.00
95 Tim Duncan SPEC 2.50 6.00
96 Shareef Abdur-Rahim SPEC 1.00 2.50
97 Baron Davis SPEC 1.00 2.50
98 Pau Gasol SPEC 1.50 4.00
99 Allen Iverson SPEC 2.50 6.00
100 Yao Ming SPEC 2.50 6.00
101 Gary Payton SPEC 1.50 4.00
102 Ray Allen SPEC 1.50 4.00
103 Tracy McGrady SPEC 1.50 4.00
104 Amare Stoudemire SPEC 1.25 3.00
105 Tony Parker SPEC 1.50 4.00
106 Stephon Marbury SPEC 1.25 3.00
107 Richard Hamilton SPEC 1.25 3.00
108 Chris Webber SPEC 1.25 3.00
109 Elton Brand SPEC .75 2.00
110 Jerry Stackhouse SPEC 1.25 3.00
111 Andre Miller SPEC .75 2.00
112 Kevin Garnett SPEC 2.50 6.00
113 Jason Richardson SPEC 1.00 2.50
114 Allan Houston SPEC 1.00 2.50
115 Dajuan Wagner SPEC .60 1.50
116 Richard Jefferson SPEC .75 2.00
117 Shaquille O'Neal SPEC 4.00 10.00
118 Latrell Sprewell SPEC 1.25 3.00
119 Rashard Lewis SPEC .75 2.00
120 Steve Nash SPEC 2.00 5.00
121 Desmond Mason SPEC .75 2.00
122 Mike Bibby SPEC 1.00 2.50
123 Shawn Marion SPEC 1.00 2.50
124 Vince Carter SPEC 2.00 5.00
125 Caron Butler SPEC .75 2.00
126 Gilbert Arenas SPEC 1.00 2.50
127 Dirk Nowitzki SPEC 2.50 6.00
128 Paul Pierce SPEC 1.50 4.00
129 Jermaine O'Neal SPEC 1.00 2.50
130 Andrei Kirilenko SPEC .75 2.00
131 Michael Jordan SPEC 10.00 25.00
132 Steve Francis SPEC 1.00 2.50
133 T.J. Ford RC 2.00 5.00
134 Kirk Hinrich RC 2.50 6.00
135 Nick Collison RC 2.00 5.00
136 Maurice Carter RC 2.50 6.00
137 Francisco Elson RC 1.00 2.50
138 Udonis Haslem 3.00 8.00
139 Jon Stefansson RC 1.50 4.00
140 Richie Frahm RC 2.50 6.00
141 Ronald Dupree RC 1.50 4.00
142 Josh Moore RC 1.50 4.00
143 Alex Garcia RC 1.50 4.00
144 Zach Randolph SPEC 1.00 2.50
145 Ben Handlogten RC 1.50 4.00
146 Devin Brown RC 1.50 4.00
147 Marquis Daniels RC 2.00 5.00
148 LeBron James AU RC 8,000.00 15,000.00
149 Darko Milicic AU RC 5.00 12.00
150 Carmelo Anthony AU RC 125.00 300.00
151 Chris Bosh AU RC 50.00 120.00
152 Dwyane Wade AU RC 150.00 400.00
153 Jarvis Hayes AU RC 4.00 10.00
154 Mickael Pietrus AU RC 3.00 8.00
155 Chris Kaman AU RC 4.00 10.00
156 Dahntay Jones AU RC 3.00 8.00
157 Marcus Banks AU RC 3.00 8.00
158 Luke Ridnour AU RC 4.00 10.00
159 Reece Gaines AU RC 2.50 6.00

160 Troy Bell AU RC 2.50 6.00
161 Mike Sweetney AU RC 2.50 6.00
162 David West AU RC 5.00 12.00
163 Aleksandar Pavlovic AU RC 3.00 8.00
164 Steve Blake AU RC 3.00 8.00
165 Boris Diaw AU RC 4.00 10.00
166 Zoran Planinic AU RC 3.00 8.00
167 Travis Outlaw AU RC 3.00 8.00
168 Brian Cook AU RC 2.50 6.00
169 Jerome Beasley AU RC 2.50 6.00
170 Ndudi Ebi AU RC 2.50 6.00
171 Kendrick Perkins AU RC 3.00 8.00
172 Leandro Barbosa AU RC 4.00 10.00
173 Josh Howard AU RC 4.00 10.00
174 Maciej Lampe AU RC 2.50 6.00
175 Jason Kapono AU RC 2.50 6.00
176 Luke Walton AU RC 4.00 10.00
177 Slavko Vranes AU RC 2.50 6.00
178 Zarko Cabarkapa AU RC 2.50 6.00
179 Zaur Pachulia AU RC 4.00 10.00
180 Maurice Williams AU RC 4.00 10.00
181 Brandon Hunter AU RC 2.50 6.00
182 Keith Bogans AU RC 2.50 6.00
183 Travis Hansen AU RC 2.50 6.00
184 Theron Smith AU RC 2.50 6.00
185 Willie Green AU RC 4.00 10.00
186 James Jones AU RC 2.50 6.00
187 Kyle Korver AU RC 5.00 12.00
188 Udonis Haslem AU RC 5.00 12.00
189 James Lang AU RC 2.50 6.00

2003-04 SP Authentic Limited

*1-90 SINGLES: 2X TO 5X BASE HI
*91-132 SPEC: .75X TO 2X BASE HI
*133-147 RCs: .75X TO 2X BASE HI
1-147 PRINT RUN 100 SER.#'d SETS
148-153 PRINT RUN 50 SER.#'d SETS
*154-189 AU RCs: .6X TO 1.5X BASE HI
154-189 PRINT RUN 100 SER.#'d SETS
35 Kobe Bryant 12.00 30.00
91 Kobe Bryant SPEC 12.00 30.00
152 Dwyane Wade AU 800.00 1,500.00

2003-04 SP Authentic Limited Extra

*1-90 SINGLES: 6X TO 15X BASE HI
*91-132 SPEC: 2.5X TO 6X BASE HI
*133-147 RCs: 1.25X TO 3X BASE HI
1-147 PRINT RUN 25 SER.#'d SETS
*154-189 AU RCs: 1X TO 2.5X BASE HI
154-189 PRINT RUN 25 SER.#'d SETS
35 Kobe Bryant 40.00 100.00
37 Gary Payton 10.00 25.00
131 Michael Jordan SPEC 75.00 150.00
180 Maurice Williams AU 30.00 80.00

2003-04 SP Authentic Signatures

ALL SIG STATED ODDS 1:24
ADA Antonio McDyess 3.00 8.00
AJA Antawn Jamison 4.00 10.00
AMJ Andre Miller 3.00 8.00
CAA Corey Maggette 3.00 8.00
CBA Chauncey Billups 8.00 20.00
CHA Chris Bosh 10.00 25.00
CKA Chris Kaman 4.00 10.00
COA Carlos Boozer 3.00 8.00
CYA Carmelo Anthony SP 25.00 60.00
DAA Darius Miles 2.50 6.00
DEA Desmond Mason 3.00 8.00
DJA Dahntay Jones 3.00 8.00
DMA Darko Milicic 3.00 8.00
DRA David Robinson 15.00 40.00
DWA Dajuan Wagner 2.50 6.00
DYA Dwyane Wade 60.00 150.00
ECA Eddy Curry 2.50 6.00
EGA Manu Ginobili 75.00 200.00
GAA Gilbert Arenas 8.00 20.00
GGA Gordan Giricek 4.00 10.00
GPA Gary Payton 25.00 60.00
GWA Gerald Wallace 4.00 10.00
JAA Jarvis Hayes 2.50 6.00
JEA Julius Erving 40.00 100.00
JHA Josh Howard 4.00 10.00
JKA Jason Kidd 12.00 30.00
JOA Jason Kapono 2.50 6.00
JRA Jason Richardson SP 6.00 15.00
JSA Jerry Stackhouse 5.00 12.00
KBA Kobe Bryant SP 500.00 1,000.00
KGA Kevin Garnett SP 150.00 400.00
KKA Kyle Korver 5.00 12.00
KOA Keith Bogans 2.50 6.00
LBA Larry Bird 60.00 120.00
LJA LeBron James SP 3,000.00 6,000.00
LOA Lamar Odom 3.00 8.00
LWA Luke Walton 4.00 10.00
MAA Marcus Banks 2.50 6.00
MBA Mike Bibby 4.00 10.00
MJA Michael Jordan SP 1,500.00 3,000.00
MOA Morris Peterson 4.00 10.00
MPA Mickael Pietrus 3.00 8.00
MSA Mike Sweetney 2.50 6.00
MWA Maurice Williams 4.00 10.00
NEA Ndudi Ebi 2.50 6.00
PEA Patrick Ewing 125.00 300.00
PPA Paul Pierce 20.00 50.00
PSA Peja Stojakovic 8.00 20.00
RHA Richard Hamilton 12.00 30.00
SAA Shareef Abdur-Rahim 4.00 10.00
SBA Shane Battier 4.00 10.00
SMA Shawn Marion 6.00 15.00
SVA Slavko Vranes 2.50 6.00
TBA Troy Bell 2.50 6.00
TMA Tracy McGrady 30.00 80.00
TPA Tony Parker 25.00 60.00
YMA Yao Ming 100.00 250.00
ZOA Alonzo Mourning 20.00 50.00
ZPA Zoran Planinic 2.50 6.00

2003-04 SP Authentic Signatures Dual

STATED ODDS 1:288
AKA S.Abdur-R/J.Kidd 12.00 30.00
ASA G.Arenas/J.Stackhouse 8.00 20.00
BBA T.Bell/S.Battier 8.00 20.00
BMA L.Bird/A.Mourning SP 150.00 400.00
BRA B.Barry/L.Ridnour 4.00 10.00
BSA M.Bibby/P.Stojakovic 15.00 40.00
CRA E.Curry/J.Rose 8.00 20.00
CWA B.Cook/L.Walton 4.00 10.00
ESA J.Erving/A.Stoudemire SP 60.00 150.00
GBA K.Garnett/K.Bryant SP 2,000.00 4,000.00
HAD R.Hamilton/C.Billups 40.00 100.00
HPA B.Hunter/P.Pierce 15.00 40.00
JAA L.James/C.Anthony SP 5,000.00 10,000.00
JJA M.Jordan/L.James SP 25,000.00 50,000.00
KJA J.Kidd/R.Jefferson SP 25.00 60.00
MDA S.Marion/L.Barbosa 8.00 20.00
MGA T.McGrady/R.Gaines SP 15.00 40.00
MIA D.Milicic/C.Billups SP 8.00 20.00
MLA A.McDyess/M.Lampe 8.00 20.00
MSA A.Miller/R.Gaines 8.00 20.00
NAA Nene/C.Anthony SP 50.00 120.00
OPA T.Outlaw/K.Perkins 8.00 20.00
OWA L.Odom/D.Wade 125.00 300.00
PBA M.Peterson/C.Bosh 15.00 40.00
PGA T.Parker/M.Ginobili 100.00 250.00
PKA G.Payton/K.Bryant SP 1,500.00 3,000.00
RPA J.Richardson/M.Pietrus 8.00 20.00
SRA J.Stockton/D.Robinson 75.00 200.00
WMA D.Wagner/D.Miles 8.00 20.00

2003-04 SP Authentic Signatures Triple

COMMON CARD 20.00 50.00
PRINT RUN 15 SER.#'d SETS
AMN Carmelo/A.Miller/Nene 60.00 150.00
HPW Hayes/Pietrus/West 20.00 50.00
KPB Kidd/Parker/Banks 100.00 250.00
MBK Darko/Bosh/Kaman 50.00 120.00
MRP McGrady/J.Rich/Pierce 200.00 500.00
PBJ Payton/Kobe/Magic 2,000.00 4,000.00
SMB Amare/Marion/Barb 30.00 80.00

2003-04 SP Authentic SPGU Authentic Fabrics Dual

PRINT RUN 50 SER.#'d SETS
AMJ C.Anthony/A.Miller 20.00 40.00
BGJ T.Bell/P.Gasol 6.00 15.00
BOJ K.Bryant/L.Walton 12.00 30.00
GMJ R.Gaines/T.McGrady 8.00 20.00
HSJ J.Hayes/J.Stackhouse 6.00 15.00
HTJ T.Hansen/J.Terry 6.00 15.00
KBJ C.Kaman/E.Brand 6.00 15.00
MSJ D.Milicic/A.Stoudemire 8.00 20.00
PRJ M.Pietrus/J.Richardson 6.00 15.00
SHJ M.Sweetney/A.Houston 6.00 15.00
WBJ D.Wade/C.Butler 25.00 60.00

2003-04 SP Authentic SPGU Authentic Fabrics Triple

PRINT RUN 25 SER.#'d SETS
CCP Chandler/Curry/Pip 50.00 120.00
DMW B.Davis/Mash/West 12.00 30.00
GSE KG/Sprewell/Ebi 20.00 50.00
JJM LeBron/MJ/McGrady 1,500.00 3,000.00
JMW LeBron/Darko/Wade 500.00 1,000.00
MBJ M.Miller/Battier/Jones 12.00 30.00
MML McDyess/Marion/Lampe 12.00 30.00
MRK D.Mason/Redd/Kukoc 30.00 80.00
POB Payton/Shaq/Kobe 75.00 200.00
VRP Van Exel/J-Rich/Pietrus 12.00 30.00

2003-04 SP Authentic SPGU Rookie Authentic Fabrics

PRINT RUN 150 SER.#'d SETS
APJ Aleksandar Pavlovic 3.00 8.00
BDJ Boris Diaw 4.00 10.00
CHJ Chris Bosh 12.00 30.00
CKJ Chris Kaman 4.00 10.00
CYJ Carmelo Anthony 12.00 30.00
DEJ David West 5.00 12.00
DJJ Dahntay Jones 3.00 8.00
DMJ Darko Milicic 3.00 8.00
DYJ Dwyane Wade 20.00 50.00
JHJ Jarvis Hayes 2.50 6.00
JKJ Jason Kapono 2.50 6.00
JOJ Josh Howard 4.00 10.00
KOJ Keith Bogans 2.50 6.00
KPJ Zoran Planinic 2.50 6.00
KPJ Kendrick Perkins 3.00 8.00
LBJ Leandro Barbosa 4.00 10.00
LJJ LeBron James 200.00 500.00
LRJ Luke Ridnour 4.00 10.00
LWJ Luke Walton 4.00 10.00
MAJ Marcus Banks 2.50 6.00
MIJ Mike Sweetney 2.50 6.00
MLJ Maciej Lampe 2.50 6.00
MPJ Mickael Pietrus 3.00 8.00
NEJ Ndudi Ebi 2.50 6.00
RGJ Reece Gaines 2.50 6.00
SBJ Steve Blake 3.00 8.00
TBJ Troy Bell 2.50 6.00
THJ Travis Hansen 2.50 6.00
TOJ Travis Outlaw 3.00 8.00
ZCJ Zarko Cabarkapa 2.50 6.00

2003-04 SP Authentic SPGU Rookie Authentic Patches

*PATCHES: 1X TO 2.5X BASE FAB HI
PRINT RUN 50 SER.#'d SETS
DYP Dwyane Wade 100.00 250.00
LJP LeBron James 1,000.00 2,000.00

2003-04 SP Authentic SPGU Rookie Exclusive Autographs Update

PRINT RUN 100 SER.#'d SETS
R43 Mike Sweetney 5.00 12.00
R44 Francisco Elson 5.00 12.00
R45 Marquis Daniels 6.00 15.00
R46 Theron Smith 5.00 12.00
R47 Willie Green 8.00 20.00
R48 Udonis Haslem 10.00 25.00
R50 James Jones 5.00 12.00

2004-05 SP Authentic

COMP.SET w/o SP's (90)
91-130 ESS PRINT RUN 2999 SER.#'d SETS
131-140 RC PRINT RUN 999 SER.#'d SETS
141-180 RC PRINT RUN 1499 SER.#'d SETS
SIX AU VERSIONS FOR CARD #146
181-186 RC PRINT RUN 999 SER.#'d SETS
1 Al Harrington .30 .75
2 Antoine Walker .40 1.00
3 Tony Delk .25 .60
4 Gary Payton .60 1.50
5 Mark Blount .25 .60
6 Paul Pierce .60 1.50
7 Kareem Rush .25 .60
8 Gerald Wallace .30 .75
9 Jason Kapono .25 .60
10 Eddy Curry .25 .60
11 Kirk Hinrich .40 1.00
12 Tyson Chandler .30 .75
13 Drew Gooden .25 .60
14 LeBron James 12.00 30.00
15 Zydrunas Ilgauskas .30 .75
16 Dirk Nowitzki 1.00 2.50
17 Jason Terry .30 .75
18 Michael Finley .40 1.00
19 Carmelo Anthony .75 2.00
20 Kenyon Martin .40 1.00
21 Andre Miller .30 .75
22 Ben Wallace .50 1.25
23 Chauncey Billups .50 1.25
24 Rasheed Wallace .50 1.25
25 Derek Fisher .30 .75
26 Jason Richardson .40 1.00
27 Speedy Claxton .25 .60
28 Juwan Howard .30 .75
29 Tracy McGrady .60 1.50
30 Yao Ming 1.00 2.50
31 Jermaine O'Neal .30 .75
32 Reggie Miller .75 2.00
33 Fred Jones .25 .60
34 Corey Maggette .30 .75
35 Elton Brand .30 .75
36 Kerry Kittles .30 .75
37 Caron Butler .30 .75
38 Kobe Bryant 3.00 8.00
39 Lamar Odom .40 1.00
40 Bonzi Wells .25 .60
41 Jason Williams .30 .75
42 Pau Gasol .60 1.50
43 Dwyane Wade 1.50 4.00
44 Eddie Jones .40 1.00
45 Shaquille O'Neal 1.50 4.00
46 Desmond Mason .30 .75
47 Keith Van Horn .30 .75
48 Michael Redd .30 .75
49 Kevin Garnett 1.00 2.50
50 Latrell Sprewell .50 1.25
51 Sam Cassell .30 .75
52 Vince Carter .75 2.00
53 Jason Kidd .60 1.50
54 Richard Jefferson .30 .75
55 Baron Davis .40 1.00
56 Jamaal Magloire .25 .60
57 P.J. Brown .25 .60
58 Allan Houston .40 1.00
59 Jamal Crawford .40 1.00
60 Stephon Marbury .50 1.25
61 Hedo Turkoglu .30 .75
62 Grant Hill .50 1.25
63 Steve Francis .40 1.00
64 Allen Iverson 1.00 2.50
65 Glenn Robinson .30 .75
66 Kyle Korver .30 .75
67 Amare Stoudemire .40 1.00
68 Shawn Marion .40 1.00
69 Steve Nash .75 2.00
70 Darius Miles .25 .60
71 Shareef Abdur-Rahim .40 1.00
72 Zach Randolph .40 1.00
73 Chris Webber .50 1.25
74 Mike Bibby .40 1.00
75 Peja Stojakovic .30 .75
76 Manu Ginobili .75 2.00
77 Tim Duncan 1.00 2.50
78 Tony Parker .60 1.50
79 Rashard Lewis .30 .75
80 Ray Allen .60 1.50
81 Ronald Murray .25 .60
82 Donyell Marshall .25 .60
83 Jalen Rose .30 .75
84 Chris Bosh .60 1.50
85 Andrei Kirilenko .30 .75
86 Carlos Boozer .30 .75
87 Matt Harpring .25 .60
88 Antawn Jamison .30 .75
89 Gilbert Arenas .40 1.00
90 Larry Hughes .30 .75
91 Bill Russell ESS 2.00 5.00
92 Larry Bird ESS 5.00 12.00
93 Paul Pierce ESS 2.00 5.00
94 Michael Jordan ESS 10.00 25.00
95 LeBron James ESS 10.00 25.00
96 Dirk Nowitzki ESS 3.00 8.00
97 Carmelo Anthony ESS 2.50 6.00
98 Ben Wallace ESS 1.50 4.00
99 Isiah Thomas ESS 2.00 5.00
100 Tracy McGrady ESS 2.00 5.00
101 Yao Ming ESS 3.00 8.00
102 Jermaine O'Neal ESS 1.00 2.50
103 Reggie Miller ESS 2.50 6.00
104 Elton Brand ESS 1.00 2.50
105 Kareem Abdul-Jabbar ESS 2.00 5.00
106 Kobe Bryant ESS 10.00 25.00
107 Magic Johnson ESS 5.00 12.00
108 Wilt Chamberlain ESS 2.50 6.00
109 Pau Gasol ESS 2.00 5.00
110 Dwyane Wade ESS 5.00 12.00
111 Shaquille O'Neal ESS 5.00 12.00
112 Michael Redd ESS 1.00 2.50
113 Oscar Robertson ESS 2.50 6.00
114 Kevin Garnett ESS 3.00 8.00
115 Sam Cassell ESS 1.00 2.50
116 Jason Kidd ESS 2.00 5.00
117 Baron Davis ESS 1.25 3.00
118 Stephon Marbury ESS 1.50 4.00
119 Steve Francis ESS 1.25 3.00
120 Allen Iverson ESS 3.00 8.00
121 Julius Erving ESS 3.00 8.00
122 Amare Stoudemire ESS 1.25 3.00
123 Shawn Marion ESS 1.25 3.00
124 Chris Webber ESS 1.50 4.00
125 Peja Stojakovic ESS 1.00 2.50
126 Tim Duncan ESS 3.00 8.00
127 Ray Allen ESS 2.00 5.00
128 Vince Carter ESS 2.50 6.00
129 Andrei Kirilenko ESS 1.00 2.50
130 John Stockton ESS 2.50 6.00
131 Emeka Okafor RC 1.50 4.00
132 Mario Kasun RC 1.50 4.00
133 Andre Barrett RC 1.25 3.00
134 Ha Seung-Jin RC 2.00 5.00
135 Horace Jenkins RC 1.50 4.00
136 Tony Bobbitt RC 2.00 5.00
137 Luis Flores RC 1.50 4.00
138 John Edwards RC 1.25 3.00
139 Beno Udrih RC 1.50 4.00
140 Erik Daniels RC 1.50 4.00
141 Nenad Krstic AU RC 3.00 8.00
142 Yuta Tabuse AU RC 4.00 10.00
143 Pape Sow AU RC 2.50 6.00
144 Andres Nocioni AU RC 4.00 10.00
145 Bernard Robinson AU RC 2.50 6.00
147 Trevor Ariza AU RC 4.00 10.00
148 Damien Wilkins AU RC 3.00 8.00
149 Justin Reed AU RC 2.50 6.00
150 Chris Duhon AU RC 3.00 8.00
151 Royal Ivey AU RC 2.50 6.00
152 Antonio Burks AU RC 2.50 6.00
153 Andre Emmett AU RC 2.50 6.00
154 Donta Smith AU RC 2.50 6.00
155 Lionel Chalmers AU RC 3.00 8.00
156 P.J. Ramos AU RC 2.50 6.00
157 Jackson Vroman AU RC 2.50 6.00
158 Anderson Varejao AU RC 3.00 8.00
159 David Harrison AU RC 3.00 8.00
160 D.J. Mbenga AU RC 2.50 6.00
161 Sasha Vujacic AU RC 3.00 8.00
162 Kevin Martin AU RC 5.00 12.00
163 Tony Allen AU RC 4.00 10.00
164 Delonte West AU RC 3.00 8.00
165 Romain Sato AU RC 2.50 6.00
166 Viktor Khryapa AU RC 2.50 6.00
167 Pavel Podkolzin AU RC 2.50 6.00
168 Jameer Nelson AU RC 4.00 10.00
169 Dorell Wright AU RC 3.00 8.00
170 J.R. Smith AU RC 4.00 10.00
171 Josh Smith AU RC 4.00 10.00
172 Kirk Snyder AU RC 2.50 6.00
173 Al Jefferson AU RC 4.00 10.00
174 Kris Humphries AU RC 3.00 8.00
175 Sebastian Telfair AU RC 3.00 8.00
176 Robert Swift AU RC 2.50 6.00
177 Andris Biedrins AU RC 2.50 6.00
178 Luke Jackson AU RC 2.50 6.00
179 Andre Iguodala AU RC 12.00 30.00
180 Rafael Araujo AU RC 2.50 6.00
181 Luol Deng AU RC 6.00 15.00
182 Josh Childress AU RC 4.00 10.00
183 Devin Harris AU RC 5.00 12.00
184 Shaun Livingston AU RC 8.00 20.00
185 Ben Gordon AU RC 6.00 15.00
186 Dwight Howard AU RC 25.00 60.00

2004-05 SP Authentic Limited

*1-90: 2.5X TO 6X BASE HI
*91-130 ESS: .75X TO 2X BASE HI
*131-140 RC: 1X TO 2.5X BASE HI
*141-180 AU RC: .6X TO 1.5X BASE HI
*181-186 AU RC: .5X TO 1.25X BASE HI
STATED PRINT RUN 100 SER.#'d SETS
186 Dwight Howard AU 40.00 100.00

2004-05 SP Authentic Limited Extra

*1-90: 6X TO 15X BASE HI
*91-130 ESS: 2X TO 5X BASE HI
*131-140 RC: 1.25X TO 3X BASE HI
*141-180 AU RC: 1X TO 2.5X BASE HI
*181-186 AU RC: .6X TO 1.5X BASE HI
STATED PRINT RUN 25 SER.#'d SETS
CARD 146 NOT ISSUED
142 Yuta Tabuse AU 10.00 25.00
186 Dwight Howard AU 60.00 150.00

2004-05 SP Authentic Fabrics Dual

PRINT RUN 100 SER.#'d SETS
AH T.Ariza/A.Houston 3.00 8.00
AM R.Araujo/D.Marshall 2.00 5.00
BJ K.Bryant/L.James 125.00 300.00
BO C.Butler/L.Odom 3.00 8.00
BS A.Biedrins/K.Snyder 2.00 5.00
CW J.Childress/A.Walker 3.00 8.00
DB L.Deng/E.Brand 3.00 8.00
DP C.Duhon/S.Pippen 8.00 20.00
HB K.Humphries/C.Boozer 2.50 6.00
HF D.Howard/S.Francis 10.00 25.00
HO D.Harrison/J.O'Neal 2.50 6.00
HS D.Harris/J.Stackhouse 3.00 8.00
HW R.Hamilton/R.Wallace 4.00 10.00
IR A.Iguodala/G.Robinson 5.00 12.00
JA A.Jamison/G.Arenas 3.00 8.00
JJ L.James/M.Jordan 125.00 300.00
JP A.Jefferson/G.Payton 5.00 12.00
KB A.Kirilenko/C.Boozer 2.50 6.00
KJ N.Krstic/R.Jefferson 2.50 6.00
LM S.Livingston/C.Maggette 3.00 8.00
MM K.Martin/A.Miller 3.00 8.00
MW K.Martin/C.Webber 4.00 10.00
SM J.R.Smith/J.Mashburn 3.00 8.00
SR H.Seung-Jin/Z.Randolph 3.00 8.00
TM S.Telfair/D.Miles 2.50 6.00

2004-05 SP Authentic Fabrics Triple

PRINT RUN 25 SER.#'d SETS
AJB Araujo/L.Jackson/Biedrins 15.00 40.00
BSA Bird/Peja/Ray Allen 30.00 80.00
GBR Gordon/Kobe/O.Robertson 50.00 120.00
JAJ Jordan/Carmelo/LeBron 100.00 250.00
JBJ Jordan/Kobe/LeBron 500.00 1,000.00
JSC Magic/Stockton/Cousy 40.00 100.00
JSG LeBron/Amare/Gasol 25.00 60.00
NFT Dirk/Finley/J.Terry 15.00 40.00
OMT J.O'Neal/R.Miller/Tinsley 15.00 40.00
ROO Admiral/Hakeem/Shaq 40.00 100.00

2004-05 SP Authentic Fabrics Patches

PRINT RUN 50 SER.#'d SETS
AI Andre Iguodala 10.00 25.00
AJ Al Jefferson 6.00 15.00
AK Andrei Kirilenko 5.00 12.00
AR Rafael Araujo 4.00 10.00
AS Amare Stoudemire 6.00 15.00
BD Baron Davis 6.00 15.00
BG Ben Gordon 6.00 15.00
BI Andris Biedrins 4.00 10.00
CA Carmelo Anthony 12.00 30.00
DE Devin Harris 5.00 12.00
DH Dwight Howard 20.00 50.00
DN Dirk Nowitzki 15.00 40.00
DW Dorell Wright 5.00 12.00
JC Josh Childress 4.00 10.00
JE Julius Erving 15.00 40.00
JK Jason Kidd 10.00 25.00
JN Jameer Nelson 6.00 15.00
JR J.R. Smith 6.00 15.00
JS Josh Smith 6.00 15.00
KB Kobe Bryant 125.00 300.00
KG Kevin Garnett 15.00 40.00
KH Kris Humphries 5.00 12.00
KS Kirk Snyder 4.00 10.00
LB Larry Bird 30.00 80.00
LD Luol Deng 6.00 15.00
LJ LeBron James 100.00 250.00
LU Luke Jackson 4.00 10.00
MA Magic Johnson 30.00 80.00
MJ Michael Jordan 150.00 400.00
PP Paul Pierce 10.00 25.00
PS Peja Stojakovic 5.00 12.00
RA Ray Allen 12.00 30.00
SH Shawn Marion 6.00 15.00
SL Shaun Livingston 6.00 15.00
SM Stephon Marbury 8.00 20.00
SO Shaquille O'Neal 40.00 80.00
ST Sebastian Telfair 5.00 12.00
TD Tim Duncan 15.00 40.00
TM Tracy McGrady 10.00 25.00
TP Tony Parker 10.00 25.00
YM Yao Ming 15.00 40.00

2004-05 SP Authentic Fabrics Autographs

PRINT RUN 50 SER.#'d SETS
AI Andre Iguodala 12.00 30.00
AJ Al Jefferson 8.00 20.00
AK Andrei Kirilenko 8.00 20.00
AR Rafael Araujo 5.00 12.00
AS Amare Stoudemire 12.00 30.00
BD Baron Davis 20.00 50.00
BG Ben Gordon 8.00 20.00
BI Andris Biedrins 5.00 12.00
BW Ben Wallace 15.00 40.00
CA Carmelo Anthony 40.00 100.00
DE Devin Harris 6.00 15.00
DH Dwight Howard 60.00 150.00
DW Dorell Wright 6.00 15.00
JC Josh Childress 5.00 12.00
JE Julius Erving 125.00 300.00
JK Jason Kidd 20.00 50.00
JN Jameer Nelson 8.00 20.00
JR J.R. Smith 25.00 60.00
JS Josh Smith 8.00 20.00
JW Jason Williams 75.00 200.00
KB Kobe Bryant 1,250.00 2,500.00
KG Kevin Garnett 200.00 500.00
KH Kris Humphries 6.00 15.00
KS Kirk Snyder 5.00 12.00
LB Larry Bird 125.00 300.00
LD Luol Deng 8.00 20.00
LJ LeBron James 1,500.00 3,000.00
LU Luke Jackson 5.00 12.00
MA Magic Johnson 125.00 300.00
MJ Michael Jordan 2,500.00 5,000.00
PG Pau Gasol 12.00 30.00
PP Paul Pierce 40.00 100.00
PS Peja Stojakovic 12.00 30.00
RA Ray Allen 40.00 100.00
SH Shawn Marion 12.00 30.00
SL Shaun Livingston 8.00 20.00
SM Stephon Marbury 15.00 40.00
ST Sebastian Telfair 6.00 15.00
TM Tracy McGrady 60.00 150.00
YM Yao Ming 75.00 200.00

2004-05 SP Authentic Fabrics Rookies

COMBINED ODDS FOR MEMORABILIA 1:24
AB Antonio Burks SP 1.50 4.00
AE Andre Emmett 1.50 4.00
AI Andre Iguodala 4.00 10.00
AJ Al Jefferson 2.50 6.00
AV Anderson Varejao 2.00 5.00
BG Ben Gordon 2.50 6.00
BI Andris Biedrins 1.50 4.00
BR Bernard Robinson 1.50 4.00
CD Chris Duhon 2.00 5.00
DA David Harrison 1.50 4.00
DE Devin Harris 2.00 5.00
DH Dwight Howard 8.00 20.00
DS Donta Smith 1.50 4.00
DW Dorell Wright 2.00 5.00
HS Ha Seung-Jin 2.50 6.00
JC Josh Childress 1.50 4.00
JN Jameer Nelson 2.50 6.00
JR J.R. Smith 2.50 6.00
JS Josh Smith SP 3.00 8.00
JV Jackson Vroman 1.50 4.00
KH Kris Humphries 2.00 5.00
KM Kevin Martin 3.00 8.00
KS Kirk Snyder 1.50 4.00
LC Lionel Chalmers 2.00 5.00
LD Luol Deng 2.50 6.00
LU Luke Jackson 1.50 4.00
MF Matt Freije 1.50 4.00
NK Nenad Krstic 2.00 5.00
PR Peter John Ramos 1.50 4.00
RA Rafael Araujo 1.50 4.00
RS Robert Swift SP 1.50 4.00
SL Shaun Livingston 2.50 6.00
ST Sebastian Telfair 2.00 5.00
SV Sasha Vujacic 2.00 5.00
TA Tony Allen 2.50 6.00
TR Trevor Ariza 2.50 6.00
WE Delonte West 2.00 5.00

2004-05 SP Authentic Signatures

ALL SIGNATURE STATED ODDS 1:24
SINGLE AND DUAL COMBINED ODDS 1:288
AB Antonio Burks 2.50 6.00
AE Andre Emmett 2.50 6.00
AH Al Harrington 3.00 8.00
AI Andre Iguodala 8.00 20.00
AJ Antawn Jamison 5.00 12.00
AK Andrei Kirilenko 4.00 10.00
AL Al Jefferson 10.00 25.00
AM Andre Miller 4.00 10.00
AN Antonio McDyess 5.00 12.00
AR Rafael Araujo 2.50 6.00
AS Amare Stoudemire 6.00 15.00
AV Anderson Varejao 3.00 8.00
AY Carlos Arroyo 15.00 40.00
BD Baron Davis 5.00 12.00
BE Ben Wallace 15.00 40.00
BG Ben Gordon 10.00 25.00
BI Andris Biedrins 2.50 6.00
BK Bernard King 8.00 20.00
BO Carlos Boozer 4.00 10.00
BR Bill Russell 1,500.00 3,000.00
BU Beno Udrih 3.00 8.00
BW Bill Walton 4.00 10.00
CA Carmelo Anthony 20.00 50.00
CD Chris Duhon 3.00 8.00
CH Chauncey Billups 6.00 15.00
CL Clyde Drexler 15.00 40.00
CM Corey Maggette 4.00 10.00
CR Jamal Crawford 4.00 10.00
DE Devin Harris 3.00 8.00
DF Derek Fisher 5.00 12.00
DH Dwight Howard 20.00 50.00
DM Desmond Mason 4.00 10.00
DR David Robinson 30.00 60.00
DS Donta Smith 2.50 6.00
DW Dorell Wright 3.00 8.00
GA Gilbert Arenas 6.00 15.00
GP Gary Payton 8.00 20.00
HA David Harrison 2.50 6.00
HO Hakeem Olajuwon 20.00 50.00
JA Jason Richardson 4.00 10.00
JC Josh Childress 2.50 6.00
JE Julius Erving 40.00 100.00
JH Josh Howard 4.00 10.00
JK Jason Kidd 15.00 40.00
JN Jameer Nelson 4.00 10.00
JO John Stockton 50.00 120.00
JR J.R. Smith 8.00 20.00
JS Josh Smith 8.00 20.00
JV Jackson Vroman 2.50 6.00
JW Jason Williams 40.00 100.00
KB Kobe Bryant 200.00 500.00
KE Kevin Martin 5.00 12.00
KG Kevin Garnett 25.00 60.00
KH Kris Humphries 3.00 8.00
KI Kirk Hinrich 10.00 25.00
KS Kirk Snyder 2.50 6.00
LB Larry Bird 50.00 120.00
LC Lionel Chalmers 3.00 8.00
LD Luol Deng 4.00 10.00
LJ LeBron James 1,000.00 2,000.00
LO Lamar Odom 5.00 12.00
LU Luke Jackson 2.50 6.00
MA Magic Johnson 75.00 150.00
MB Mike Bibby 4.00 10.00
MD Marquis Daniels 4.00 10.00
MJ Michael Jordan 2,000.00 4,000.00
MR Michael Redd 4.00 10.00
NK Nenad Krstic 3.00 8.00
NO Andres Nocioni 4.00 10.00
PA Pavel Podkolzin 2.50 6.00
PE Peter John Ramos 2.50 6.00
PG Pau Gasol 10.00 25.00
PP Paul Pierce 25.00 60.00
PR Pat Riley 12.00 30.00
PS Peja Stojakovic 5.00 12.00
RH Richard Hamilton 6.00 15.00
RI Royal Ivey 2.50 6.00
RJ Richard Jefferson 4.00 10.00
RN Dennis Rodman 50.00 120.00
RO Jalen Rose 6.00 15.00
RS Robert Swift 2.50 6.00
RY Ray Allen 15.00 40.00
SA Shareef Abdur-Rahim 4.00 10.00
SC Sam Cassell 4.00 10.00
SH Shawn Marion 6.00 15.00
SM Stephon Marbury 8.00 20.00
ST Sebastian Telfair 3.00 8.00
SV Sasha Vujacic 3.00 8.00
TA Tony Allen 2.50 6.00
TM Tracy McGrady 15.00 40.00
TP Tony Parker 12.00 30.00
WE Delonte West 3.00 8.00
WF Walt Frazier 10.00 25.00
WR Willis Reed 40.00 100.00
YM Yao Ming 40.00 100.00
ZR Zach Randolph 4.00 10.00

2004-05 SP Authentic Signatures Dual

SINGLE AND DUAL COMBINED ODDS 1:288
AB C.Arroyo/C.Boozer 10.00 25.00
AJ T.Allen/A.Jefferson 12.00 30.00
AM C.Anthony/A.Miller SP 75.00 200.00
AR S.Abdur-R/Z.Randolph 12.00 30.00
AT S.Abdur-Rahim/S.Telfair 12.00 30.00
BB B.Wallace/C.Billups 75.00 200.00
BE L.Bird/J.Erving 600.00 1,200.00
BJ L.Bird/M.Johnson 1,000.00 2,000.00
BO K.Bryant/L.Odom SP 600.00 1,200.00
CA J.Crawford/T.Ariza 12.00 30.00
CB S.Cassell/M.Bibby 12.00 30.00
CL Chalmers/Livingston 12.00 30.00
CS J.Childress/D.Smith 8.00 20.00
CT C.Anthony/T.McGrady 200.00 500.00
DH L.Deng/K.Hinrich 12.00 30.00
DJ D.Howard/J.R.Smith 40.00 100.00
DM B.Davis/J.Magloire 12.00 30.00
DS B.Davis/J.R.Smith 12.00 30.00
EB A.Emmett/A.Burks 8.00 20.00
GC Garnett/Cassell SP 60.00 150.00
GD B.Gordon/L.Deng 12.00 30.00
GH B.Gordon/R.Hamilton 15.00 40.00
GM K.Garnett/T.McGrady 150.00 400.00
HD D.Harris/M.Daniels 10.00 25.00
HG D.Howard/B.Gordon 25.00 60.00
HJ D.Harris/J.Stackhouse 12.00 30.00
HN D.Howard/J.Nelson 25.00 60.00
HR H.Olajuwon/D.Robinson 125.00 300.00
HS A.Harrington/Josh Smith 12.00 30.00
IS A.Iguodala/J.R.Smith 20.00 50.00
JA A.Jamison/G.Arenas 12.00 30.00
JC J.Stockton/C.Arroyo 60.00 150.00
JJ M.Jordan/L.James 15,000.00 20,000.00
JK R.Jefferson/N.Krstic 10.00 25.00
JW A.Jefferson/D.West 12.00 30.00
KD K.Garnett/D.Howard 125.00 300.00
KH Kirilenko/Humphries 10.00 25.00
KJ J.Kidd/R.Jefferson 20.00 50.00
KK J.Kidd/N.Krstic 20.00 50.00
KR B.King/W.Reed 125.00 300.00
LC L.James/C.Anthony 1,500.00 3,000.00
LK L.James/K.Bryant 5,000.00 10,000.00
LL L.James/L.Jackson 800.00 1,500.00
MB K.Martin/M.Bibby 15.00 40.00
MC S.Marbury/J.Crawford 15.00 40.00
MJ M.Daniels/J.Howard 10.00 25.00
ML C.Maggette/S.Livingston 12.00 30.00
MM T.McGrady/Y.Ming 150.00 400.00
MP A.Miller/T.Parker 20.00 50.00
NW J.Nelson/DelWest 12.00 30.00
OR L.Odom/K.Rush 12.00 30.00
PH Podkolzin/Harris 10.00 25.00
PM G.Payton/S.Marbury 40.00 100.00
PU T.Parker/B.Udrih 20.00 50.00
RB J.Richardson/A.Biedrins 12.00 30.00
RD R.Swift/Dam.Wilkins 10.00 25.00
RF J.Richardson/D.Fisher 12.00 30.00
RL R.Allen/L.Ridnour 40.00 100.00
RM M.Redd/D.Mason SP 10.00 25.00
RO B.Russell/H.Olajuwon 1,500.00 3,000.00
SA J.Stockton/A.Kirilenko 75.00 200.00
SB P.Stojakovic/M.Bibby SP 30.00 80.00
SD Stoudemire/Deng 12.00 30.00
SH Snyder/Humphries 10.00 25.00
SK J.Stockton/J.Kidd 100.00 250.00
SM A.Stoudemire/S.Marion SP 25.00 60.00
SW J.R.Smith/D.Wright 12.00 30.00
TN S.Telfair/J.Nelson 12.00 30.00
WB J.Williams/S.Battier 40.00 100.00

2005-06 SP Authentic

COMP.SET w/o SP's (90) 15.00 40.00
91-132 PRINT RUN 1299 SER.#'d SETS
133-157 PRINT RUN 999 SER.#'d SETS
1 Boris Diaw .30 .75
2 Josh Childress .25 .60
3 Josh Smith .30 .75
4 Antoine Walker .30 .75
5 Al Jefferson .25 .60
6 Paul Pierce .60 1.50
7 Kareem Rush .25 .60
8 Emeka Okafor .30 .75
9 Gerald Wallace .30 .75
10 Ben Gordon .30 .75
11 Kirk Hinrich .30 .75
12 Michael Jordan 3.00 8.00
13 Drew Gooden .30 .75
14 LeBron James 3.00 8.00
15 Luke Jackson .25 .60
16 Dirk Nowitzki 1.00 2.50
17 Jason Terry .30 .75
18 Josh Howard .30 .75
19 Nene Hilario .30 .75
20 Carmelo Anthony .60 1.50
21 Kenyon Martin .30 .75
22 Ben Wallace .50 1.25
23 Chauncey Billups .50 1.25
24 Rasheed Wallace .40 1.00
25 Baron Davis .40 1.00
26 Jason Richardson .40 1.00
27 Mike Dunleavy .25 .60
28 David Wesley .25 .60
29 Tracy McGrady .60 1.50
30 Yao Ming .75 2.00
31 Jamaal Tinsley .25 .60
32 Jermaine O'Neal .30 .75
33 Fred Jones .25 .60
34 Corey Maggette .30 .75
35 Elton Brand .30 .75
36 Shaun Livingston .30 .75
37 Caron Butler .30 .75
38 Kobe Bryant 3.00 8.00
39 Wilt Chamberlain .75 2.00
40 Jason Williams .60 1.50
41 Pau Gasol .60 1.50
42 Shane Battier .30 .75
43 Udonis Haslem .25 .60
44 Dwyane Wade .75 2.00
45 Shaquille O'Neal 1.25 3.00
46 Desmond Mason .25 .60
47 T.J. Ford .25 .60
48 Michael Redd .30 .75
49 Kevin Garnett 1.00 2.50
50 Wally Szczerbiak .30 .75
51 Ndudi Ebi .25 .60
52 Jason Kidd .60 1.50
53 Richard Jefferson .30 .75
54 Vince Carter .75 2.00
55 Lee Nailon .25 .60
56 J.R. Smith .40 1.00
57 Jamaal Magloire .25 .60
58 Jamal Crawford .40 1.00
59 Stephon Marbury .50 1.25
60 Quentin Richardson .25 .60
61 Dwight Howard .50 1.25
62 Grant Hill .60 1.50
63 Steve Francis .40 1.00
64 Allen Iverson .75 2.00
65 Andre Iguodala .40 1.00
66 Chris Webber .50 1.25
67 Amare Stoudemire .40 1.00
68 Shawn Marion .30 .75
69 Steve Nash .75 2.00
70 Sebastian Telfair .30 .75
71 Darius Miles .25 .60
72 Zach Randolph .40 1.00
73 Brad Miller .30 .75
74 Mike Bibby .40 1.00
75 Peja Stojakovic .30 .75
76 Manu Ginobili .75 2.00
77 Tim Duncan 1.00 2.50
78 Tony Parker .60 1.50
79 Luke Ridnour .30 .75
80 Rashard Lewis .30 .75
81 Ray Allen .60 1.50
82 Chris Bosh .50 1.25
83 Morris Peterson .25 .60
84 Jalen Rose .30 .75
85 Andrei Kirilenko .30 .75
86 Carlos Boozer .30 .75
87 John Stockton .75 2.00
88 Antawn Jamison .30 .75
89 Gilbert Arenas .40 1.00
90 Brendan Haywood .25 .60
91 Andrew Bogut AU RC 6.00 15.00
92 Marvin Williams AU RC 5.00 12.00
93 Deron Williams AU RC 8.00 20.00
94 Chris Paul AU RC 75.00 200.00

95 Raymond Felton AU RC 4.00 10.00
96 Martell Webster AU RC 4.00 10.00
97 Charlie Villanueva AU RC 4.00 10.00
98 Channing Frye AU RC 4.00 10.00
99 Brandon Bass AU RC 4.00 10.00
100 Travis Diener AU RC 3.00 8.00
101 Andray Blatche AU RC 5.00 12.00
102 Monta Ellis AU RC 6.00 15.00
103 Sean May AU RC 3.00 8.00
104 Rashad McCants AU RC 3.00 8.00
105 Antoine Wright AU RC 4.00 10.00
106 Joey Graham AU RC 4.00 10.00
107 Danny Granger AU RC 5.00 12.00
108 Gerald Green AU RC 5.00 12.00
109 Hakim Warrick AU RC 4.00 10.00
110 Julius Hodge AU RC 3.00 8.00
111 Sarunas Jasikevicius AU RC 5.00 12.00
112 M.Andriuskevicius AU RC 3.00 8.00
113 Francisco Garcia AU RC 3.00 8.00
114 Luther Head AU RC 3.00 8.00
115 Nate Robinson AU RC 5.00 12.00
116 Jason Maxiell AU RC 4.00 10.00
117 Wayne Simien AU RC 3.00 8.00
118 David Lee AU RC 5.00 12.00
119 Daniel Ewing AU RC 4.00 10.00
120 Louis Williams AU RC 12.00 30.00
121 Salim Stoudamire AU RC 4.00 10.00
122 Jarrett Jack AU RC 5.00 12.00
123 Andrew Bynum AU RC 4.00 10.00
124 C.J. Miles AU RC 4.00 10.00
125 Ersan Ilyasova AU RC 4.00 10.00
126 Will Bynum AU RC 4.00 10.00
127 Lawrence Roberts AU RC 3.00 8.00
128 Dijon Thompson AU RC 3.00 8.00
129 Johan Petro AU RC 3.00 8.00
130 Bracey Wright AU RC 3.00 8.00
131 Ike Diogu AU RC 3.00 8.00
132 Ryan Gomes AU RC 4.00 10.00
133 Ronnie Price RC 1.50 4.00
134 Alan Anderson RC 1.25 3.00
135 Esteban Batista RC 1.25 3.00
136 Linas Kleiza RC 1.50 4.00
137 Eddie Basden RC 1.25 3.00
138 Josh Powell RC 1.50 4.00
139 Kevin Burleson RC 2.00 5.00
140 Von Wafer RC 1.25 3.00
141 Rawle Marshall RC 1.25 3.00
142 Gerald Fitch RC 1.25 3.00
143 Robert Whaley RC 1.25 3.00
144 Orien Greene RC 1.50 4.00
145 Fabricio Oberto RC 1.50 4.00
146 Amir Johnson RC 2.00 5.00
147 Shavlik Randolph RC 1.25 3.00
148 Arvydas Macijauskas RC 1.25 3.00
149 Alex Acker RC 1.25 3.00
150 James Singleton RC 1.25 3.00
151 Anthony Roberson RC 1.50 4.00
152 Earl Barron RC 1.25 3.00
153 Dwayne Jones RC 1.25 3.00
154 Sean Banks RC 1.25 3.00
155 Sharrod Ford RC 1.25 3.00
156 Andre Owens RC 1.25 3.00
157 Donell Taylor RC 1.25 3.00

2005-06 SP Authentic Limited Extra Autographs

PRINT RUN 9 TO 25 SER.#'d SETS
5 Al Jefferson/25 8.00 20.00
9 Gerald Wallace/25 8.00 20.00
14 LeBron James/25 2,500.00 5,000.00
29 Tracy McGrady/25 125.00 300.00
30 Yao Ming/25 200.00 500.00
65 Andre Iguodala/25 8.00 20.00
70 Sebastian Telfair/25 8.00 20.00
82 Chris Bosh/25 40.00 100.00
84 Jalen Rose/25 12.00 30.00
88 Antawn Jamison/25 12.00 30.00

2005-06 SP Authentic Limited Extra Patches

*PATCH: 8X TO 20X BASE HI
PRINT RUN 25 SER.#'d SETS
38 Kobe Bryant 125.00 300.00
39 Wilt Chamberlain 100.00 200.00
47 Oscar Robertson 60.00 120.00
62 Grant Hill 12.50 30.00
66 Chris Webber 12.50 30.00
76 Manu Ginobili 12.50 30.00
87 John Stockton 50.00 100.00

2005-06 SP Authentic Limited Extra Rookie Autographs

PRINT RUN 25 SER.#'d SETS
91 Andrew Bogut JSY 15.00 40.00
92 Marvin Williams JSY 12.00 30.00
93 Deron Williams JSY 20.00 50.00
94 Chris Paul JSY 250.00 500.00
95 Raymond Felton JSY 10.00 25.00
96 Martell Webster JSY 10.00 25.00
97 Charlie Villanueva JSY 10.00 25.00
98 Channing Frye JSY 10.00 25.00
99 Brandon Bass JSY 10.00 25.00
100 Travis Diener JSY 8.00 20.00
101 Andray Blatche JSY 12.00 30.00
102 Monta Ellis JSY 15.00 40.00
103 Sean May JSY 8.00 20.00
104 Rashad McCants JSY 8.00 20.00
105 Antoine Wright JSY 10.00 25.00
106 Joey Graham JSY 10.00 25.00
107 Danny Granger JSY 12.00 30.00
108 Gerald Green JSY 12.00 30.00
109 Hakim Warrick JSY 10.00 25.00
110 Julius Hodge JSY 8.00 20.00
111 Sarunas Jasikevicius JSY 12.00 30.00
112 Martynas Andriuskevicius JSY 8.00 20.00
113 Francisco Garcia JSY 8.00 20.00
114 Luther Head JSY 8.00 20.00
115 Nate Robinson JSY 12.00 30.00
116 Jason Maxiell JSY 10.00 25.00
117 Wayne Simien JSY 8.00 20.00
118 David Lee JSY 12.00 30.00
119 Daniel Ewing JSY 10.00 25.00
120 Louis Williams JSY 30.00 80.00
121 Salim Stoudamire JSY 10.00 25.00
122 Jarrett Jack JSY 12.00 30.00
123 Andrew Bynum JSY 10.00 25.00
124 C.J. Miles JSY 10.00 25.00
125 Ersan Ilyasova JSY 10.00 25.00
126 Will Bynum 8.00 20.00
127 Lawrence Roberts 6.00 15.00
128 Dijon Thompson 6.00 15.00
129 Johan Petro 6.00 15.00
130 Bracey Wright 6.00 15.00
131 Ike Diogu 6.00 15.00
132 Ryan Gomes 8.00 20.00

2005-06 SP Authentic Limited Rookie Autographs

PRINT RUN 100 SER.#'d SETS
91 Andrew Bogut 10.00 25.00
92 Marvin Williams 8.00 20.00
93 Deron Williams 12.00 30.00
94 Chris Paul 125.00 300.00
95 Raymond Felton 6.00 15.00
96 Martell Webster 6.00 15.00
97 Charlie Villanueva 6.00 15.00
98 Channing Frye 6.00 15.00
99 Brandon Bass 6.00 15.00
100 Travis Diener 5.00 12.00
101 Andray Blatche 8.00 20.00
102 Monta Ellis 10.00 25.00
103 Sean May 5.00 12.00
104 Rashad McCants 5.00 12.00
105 Antoine Wright 6.00 15.00
106 Joey Graham 6.00 15.00
107 Danny Granger 8.00 20.00
108 Gerald Green 8.00 20.00
109 Hakim Warrick 6.00 15.00
110 Julius Hodge 5.00 12.00
111 Sarunas Jasikevicius 8.00 20.00
112 Martynas Andriuskevicius 5.00 12.00
113 Francisco Garcia 5.00 12.00
114 Luther Head 5.00 12.00
115 Nate Robinson 8.00 20.00
116 Jason Maxiell 6.00 15.00
117 Wayne Simien 5.00 12.00
118 David Lee 8.00 20.00
119 Daniel Ewing 6.00 15.00
120 Louis Williams 20.00 50.00
121 Salim Stoudamire 6.00 15.00
122 Jarrett Jack 8.00 20.00
123 Andrew Bynum 6.00 15.00
124 C.J. Miles 6.00 15.00
125 Ersan Ilyasova 6.00 15.00
126 Will Bynum 6.00 15.00
127 Lawrence Roberts 5.00 12.00
128 Dijon Thompson 5.00 12.00
129 Johan Petro 5.00 12.00
130 Bracey Wright 5.00 12.00
131 Ike Diogu 5.00 12.00
132 Ryan Gomes 6.00 15.00

2005-06 SP Authentic Limited Rookie Patches

PRINT RUN 100 SER.#'d SETS
SER.#'s 1/1299 THROUGH 100/1299
91 Andrew Bogut 10.00 25.00
92 Marvin Williams 8.00 20.00
93 Deron Williams 12.00 30.00
94 Chris Paul 150.00 400.00
95 Raymond Felton 6.00 15.00
96 Martell Webster 6.00 15.00
97 Charlie Villanueva 6.00 15.00
98 Channing Frye 6.00 15.00
99 Brandon Bass 6.00 15.00
100 Travis Diener 5.00 12.00
101 Andray Blatche 8.00 20.00
102 Monta Ellis 10.00 25.00
103 Sean May 5.00 12.00
104 Rashad McCants 5.00 12.00
105 Antoine Wright 6.00 15.00
106 Joey Graham 6.00 15.00
107 Danny Granger 8.00 20.00
108 Gerald Green 8.00 20.00
109 Hakim Warrick 6.00 15.00
110 Julius Hodge 6.00 15.00
111 Sarunas Jasikevicius 8.00 20.00
112 Martynas Andriuskevicius 5.00 12.00
113 Francisco Garcia 5.00 12.00
114 Luther Head 5.00 12.00
115 Nate Robinson 8.00 20.00
116 Jason Maxiell 6.00 15.00
117 Wayne Simien 5.00 12.00
118 David Lee 8.00 20.00
119 Daniel Ewing 6.00 15.00
120 Louis Williams 20.00 50.00
121 Salim Stoudamire 6.00 15.00
122 Jarrett Jack 8.00 20.00
123 Andrew Bynum 6.00 15.00
124 C.J. Miles 6.00 15.00

2005-06 SP Authentic Limited Rookies

*LIMITED: 1X TO 2.5X BASE HI
PRINT RUN 100 SER.#'d SETS
*EXTRA: 1.5X TO 4X BASE HI
EXTRA PRINT RUN 25 SER.#'d SETS

2005-06 SP Authentic Limited Warm Ups

PRINT RUN 100 SER.#'d SETS
3 Josh Smith 2.50 6.00
4 Antoine Walker 2.50 6.00
7 Kareem Rush 2.00 5.00
13 Drew Gooden 2.50 6.00
15 Luke Jackson 2.00 5.00
16 Dirk Nowitzki 8.00 20.00
17 Jason Terry 2.50 6.00
18 Josh Howard 2.50 6.00
19 Nene Hilario 2.50 6.00
21 Kenyon Martin 2.50 6.00
24 Rasheed Wallace 3.00 8.00
26 Jason Richardson 3.00 8.00
27 Mike Dunleavy 2.00 5.00
28 David Wesley 2.00 5.00
31 Jamaal Tinsley 2.00 5.00
32 Jermaine O'Neal 2.50 6.00
33 Fred Jones 2.00 5.00
34 Corey Maggette 2.50 6.00
35 Elton Brand 2.50 6.00
36 Shaun Livingston 2.50 6.00
37 Caron Butler 2.50 6.00
38 Kobe Bryant 50.00 120.00
39 Wilt Chamberlain 20.00 50.00
40 Jason Williams 5.00 12.00
43 Udonis Haslem 2.00 5.00
45 Shaquille O'Neal 10.00 25.00
46 Desmond Mason 2.00 5.00
50 Wally Szczerbiak 2.50 6.00
51 Ndudi Ebi 2.00 5.00
53 Richard Jefferson 2.50 6.00
55 Lee Nailon 2.00 5.00
58 Jamal Crawford 3.00 8.00
60 Quentin Richardson 2.00 5.00
62 Grant Hill 5.00 12.00
63 Steve Francis 3.00 8.00
66 Chris Webber 4.00 10.00
67 Amare Stoudemire 3.00 8.00
71 Darius Miles 2.00 5.00
72 Zach Randolph 3.00 8.00
73 Brad Miller 2.50 6.00
74 Mike Bibby 3.00 8.00
75 Peja Stojakovic 2.50 6.00
76 Manu Ginobili 6.00 15.00
77 Tim Duncan 8.00 20.00
78 Tony Parker 5.00 12.00
79 Luke Ridnour 2.50 6.00
80 Rashard Lewis 2.50 6.00
81 Ray Allen 5.00 12.00
83 Morris Peterson 2.00 5.00
86 Carlos Boozer 2.50 6.00
87 John Stockton 6.00 15.00
89 Gilbert Arenas 3.00 8.00
90 Brendan Haywood 2.00 5.00

2005-06 SP Authentic Limited Warm Ups Autographs

PRINT RUN 100 SER.#'d SETS
2 Josh Childress 6.00 15.00
5 Al Jefferson 8.00 20.00
6 Paul Pierce 50.00 120.00
9 Gerald Wallace 6.00 15.00
10 Ben Gordon 12.00 30.00
12 Michael Jordan 5,000.00 10,000.00
14 LeBron James 3,000.00 6,000.00
20 Carmelo Anthony 75.00 200.00
22 Ben Wallace 75.00 200.00
23 Chauncey Billups 30.00 80.00
25 Baron Davis 20.00 50.00
29 Tracy McGrady 100.00 250.00
30 Yao Ming 150.00 400.00
41 Pau Gasol 75.00 200.00
49 Kevin Garnett 125.00 300.00
52 Jason Kidd 50.00 120.00
56 J.R. Smith 15.00 40.00
57 Jamaal Magloire 6.00 15.00
59 Stephon Marbury 40.00 100.00
61 Dwight Howard 40.00 100.00
65 Andre Iguodala 20.00 50.00
69 Steve Nash 100.00 250.00
70 Sebastian Telfair 6.00 15.00
82 Chris Bosh 30.00 80.00
84 Jalen Rose 10.00 25.00
85 Andrei Kirilenko 10.00 25.00
88 Antawn Jamison 10.00 25.00

2005-06 SP Authentic Sensational Sigs

AB Andray Blatche 6.00 15.00
AL Al Jefferson 4.00 10.00
AN Martynas Andriuskevicius 4.00 10.00
AW Antoine Wright 5.00 12.00
BB Brandon Bass 5.00 12.00
BK Bernard King 8.00 20.00
CJ C.J. Miles 5.00 12.00
CM Cuttino Mobley 4.00 10.00
CO Corey Maggette 5.00 12.00
CT Chris Taft 4.00 10.00
CV Charlie Villanueva 5.00 12.00
CW Chris Wilcox 4.00 10.00
DE Daniel Ewing 5.00 12.00
DG Danny Granger 6.00 15.00
DT Dijon Thompson 4.00 10.00
EI Ersan Ilyasova 5.00 12.00
GG Gerald Green 6.00 15.00
GW Gerald Wallace 5.00 12.00
HW Hakim Warrick 5.00 12.00
ID Ike Diogu 4.00 10.00
JA Jason Maxiell 5.00 12.00
JH Julius Hodge 4.00 10.00
JR Jalen Rose 5.00 12.00
KK Kyle Korver 5.00 12.00
LJ LeBron James SP 2,000.00 4,000.00
LR Lawrence Roberts 4.00 10.00
LW Louis Williams 15.00 40.00
MA Martell Webster 5.00 12.00
MD Marquis Daniels 4.00 10.00
ME Monta Ellis 8.00 20.00
MJ Michael Jordan SP 3,000.00 6,000.00
MP Morris Peterson 4.00 10.00
MW Maurice Williams 5.00 12.00
RF Raymond Felton 5.00 12.00
RG Ryan Gomes 5.00 12.00
RM Rashad McCants 4.00 10.00
SB Shane Battier 5.00 12.00
SJ Sarunas Jasikevicius 6.00 15.00
SM Sean May 4.00 10.00
TA Tony Allen 4.00 10.00
UH Udonis Haslem 4.00 10.00
WB Will Bynum 5.00 12.00

2005-06 SP Authentic Sign of the Times All-Stars

PRINT RUN 50 SER.#'d SETS
AJ Antawn Jamison 6.00 15.00
AK Andrei Kirilenko 6.00 15.00
AM Antonio McDyess 6.00 15.00
BL Bill Laimbeer 15.00 40.00
BM Brad Miller 6.00 15.00
GA Gilbert Arenas 6.00 15.00
GP Gary Payton 15.00 40.00
GR Glenn Robinson 10.00 25.00
JK Jason Kidd 15.00 40.00
JM Jamaal Magloire 6.00 15.00
KG Kevin Garnett 25.00 60.00
LJ LeBron James 2,000.00 4,000.00
PP Paul Pierce 12.50 30.00
SA Shareef Abdur-Rahim 6.00 15.00
SC Sam Cassell 6.00 15.00
SM Stephon Marbury 8.00 20.00
SN Steve Nash 40.00 100.00
ST Jerry Stackhouse 12.00 30.00
TM Tracy McGrady 40.00 100.00
WA Ben Wallace 12.50 30.00
YM Yao Ming 20.00 50.00

2005-06 SP Authentic Sign of the Times Dual

PRINT RUN 50 SER.#'d SETS
BF A.Bogut/C.Frye 12.00 30.00
BH C.Bosh/D.Howard 20.00 50.00
BW A.Bogut/M.Williams 10.00 25.00
CB C.Billups/B.Wallace 20.00 50.00
FL C.Frye/D.Lee 10.00 25.00
FM R.Felton/S.May 10.00 25.00
GB F.Garcia/M.Bibby 10.00 25.00
GJ D.Granger/S.Jasikevicius 10.00 25.00
GM G.Green/T.McGrady 20.00 50.00
GW P.Gasol/H.Warrick 10.00 25.00
HK J.Hodge/L.Kleiza 10.00 25.00
HR L.Head/N.Robinson 10.00 25.00
JG A.Jefferson/G.Green 10.00 25.00
JH L.James/D.Howard 1,000.00 2,000.00
JJ L.James/M.Jordan 2,500.00 5,000.00
MF R.McCants/R.Felton 10.00 25.00
MO Y.Ming/H.Olajuwon 25.00 60.00
NL C.Neal/M.Lemon 40.00 80.00
PW C.Paul/D.Williams 50.00 120.00
VG C.Villanueva/J.Graham 10.00 25.00
WB M.Webster/A.Bynum 10.00 25.00
WJ M.Webster/J.Jack 10.00 25.00
WP M.Williams/C.Paul 40.00 100.00
WS M.Williams/S.Stoudamire 10.00 25.00

2005-06 SP Authentic Sign of the Times Legends

PRINT RUN 25 SER.#'d SETS
BK Bob Knight 200.00 500.00
BR Bill Russell 100.00 250.00
BW Bill Walton 20.00 50.00
DR Dennis Rodman 75.00 200.00
EH Elvin Hayes 15.00 40.00
GG George Gervin 15.00 40.00
HO Hakeem Olajuwon 20.00 50.00
IT Isiah Thomas 15.00 40.00
JE Julius Erving 20.00 50.00
JH John Stockton 100.00 250.00
JW John Wooden 75.00 200.00
KA Kareem Abdul-Jabbar 50.00 120.00
LB Larry Bird 100.00 250.00
LW Lenny Wilkens 15.00 40.00
LY Larry Brown 20.00 50.00
MA Magic Johnson 75.00 200.00
MJ Michael Jordan 2,500.00 5,000.00
PR Pat Riley 15.00 40.00
RP Robert Parish 15.00 40.00
SP Scottie Pippen 150.00 300.00
WF Walt Frazier 15.00 40.00
WR Willis Reed 60.00 150.00

2005-06 SP Authentic Sign of the Times Rookies

PRINT RUN 100 SER.#'d SETS
AB Andrew Bogut 8.00 20.00
AN Andrew Bynum 5.00 12.00
CF Channing Frye 5.00 12.00
CP Chris Paul 100.00 250.00
CV Charlie Villanueva 5.00 12.00
DG Danny Granger 6.00 15.00
DT Dijon Thompson 4.00 10.00
DW Deron Williams 8.00 20.00
FG Francisco Garcia 4.00 10.00
GE Gerald Green 4.00 10.00
HW Hakim Warrick 5.00 12.00
ID Ike Diogu 4.00 10.00
JA Jason Maxiell 4.00 10.00
JG Joey Graham 5.00 12.00
JJ Jarrett Jack 6.00 15.00
JP Johan Petro 4.00 10.00
JU Julius Hodge 4.00 10.00
LH Luther Head 4.00 10.00
MW Marvin Williams 6.00 15.00
NR Nate Robinson 6.00 15.00
RF Raymond Felton 4.00 10.00
RM Rashad McCants 4.00 10.00
SE Sean May 4.00 10.00
SS Salim Stoudamire 5.00 12.00
WE Martell Webster 5.00 12.00

2005-06 SP Authentic Sign of the Times Veterans

PRINT RUN 75 SER.#'d SETS
AH Al Harrington 6.00 15.00
AL Al Jefferson 6.00 15.00
CA Carlos Boozer 6.00 15.00
CB Chauncey Billups 10.00 25.00
CH Chris Bosh 10.00 25.00
CM Cuttino Mobley 6.00 15.00
DH Dwight Howard 15.00 40.00
DS Damon Stoudamire 6.00 15.00
GW Gerald Wallace 6.00 15.00
JC Josh Childress 6.00 15.00
JN Jameer Nelson 6.00 15.00
JR Jalen Rose 8.00 20.00
KH Kirk Hinrich 6.00 15.00
KK Kyle Korver 6.00 15.00
LO Lamar Odom 8.00 20.00
MD Marquis Daniels 6.00 15.00
MP Morris Peterson 6.00 15.00
PG Pau Gasol 10.00 25.00
RH Richard Hamilton 10.00 25.00
RJ Richard Jefferson 6.00 15.00
SB Shane Battier 6.00 15.00
SI J.R. Smith 6.00 15.00
TA Trevor Ariza 6.00 15.00
UH Udonis Haslem 6.00 15.00

2006-07 SP Authentic

COMP.SET w/o SP's (100) 15.00 35.00
101-122 AU RC PRINT RUN 999 SER.#'d SETS
123-132 AU RC PRINT RUN 299 SER.#'d SETS
1 Joe Johnson .50 1.25
2 Marvin Williams .30 .75
3 Josh Childress .30 .75
4 Paul Pierce .75 2.00
5 Sebastian Telfair .30 .75
6 Gerald Green .40 1.00
7 Emeka Okafor .40 1.00
8 Raymond Felton .30 .75
9 Gerald Wallace .40 1.00
10 Ben Wallace .60 1.50
11 Ben Gordon .40 1.00
12 Kirk Hinrich .40 1.00
13 LeBron James 4.00 10.00
14 Zydrunas Ilgauskas .40 1.00
15 Drew Gooden .40 1.00
16 Jason Terry .40 1.00
17 Dirk Nowitzki 1.25 3.00
18 Devin Harris .30 .75
19 Carmelo Anthony .75 2.00
20 Kenyon Martin .40 1.00
21 Andre Miller .40 1.00
22 Chauncey Billups .60 1.50
23 Richard Hamilton .50 1.25
24 Rasheed Wallace .60 1.50
25 Jason Richardson .50 1.25
26 Baron Davis .50 1.25
27 Troy Murphy .30 .75
28 Tracy McGrady .75 2.00
29 Yao Ming 1.25 3.00
30 Shane Battier .40 1.00
31 Jermaine O'Neal .50 1.25
32 Sarunas Jasikevicius .40 1.00
33 Al Harrington .40 1.00
34 Elton Brand .40 1.00
35 Sam Cassell .40 1.00
36 Chris Kaman .30 .75
37 Kobe Bryant 4.00 10.00
38 Lamar Odom .40 1.00
39 Vladimir Radmanovic .30 .75
40 Pau Gasol .75 2.00
41 Hakim Warrick .30 .75
42 Damon Stoudamire .40 1.00
43 Shaquille O'Neal 2.00 5.00
44 Dwyane Wade 1.00 2.50
45 Alonzo Mourning .75 2.00
46 Andrew Bogut .40 1.00
47 Charlie Villanueva .30 .75
48 Michael Redd .40 1.00
49 Kevin Garnett 1.25 3.00
50 Ricky Davis .40 1.00
51 Rashad McCants .30 .75
52 Vince Carter 1.00 2.50
53 Jason Kidd .75 2.00
54 Richard Jefferson .40 1.00
55 Chris Paul 1.00 2.50
56 Peja Stojakovic .40 1.00
57 Tyson Chandler .40 1.00
58 Stephon Marbury .60 1.50
59 Channing Frye .30 .75
60 Nate Robinson .40 1.00
61 Grant Hill .75 2.00
62 Dwight Howard .60 1.50
63 Jameer Nelson .30 .75
64 Allen Iverson 1.25 3.00
65 Andre Iguodala .50 1.25
66 Kyle Korver .40 1.00
67 Steve Nash 1.00 2.50
68 Amare Stoudemire .50 1.25
69 Shawn Marion .50 1.25
70 Jamaal Magloire .30 .75
71 Martell Webster .40 1.00
72 Jarrett Jack .40 1.00
73 Mike Bibby .50 1.25
74 Ron Artest .50 1.25
75 Brad Miller .40 1.00
76 Tony Parker .75 2.00
77 Tim Duncan 1.25 3.00
78 Manu Ginobili 1.00 2.50
79 Ray Allen .75 2.00
80 Rashard Lewis .40 1.00
81 Luke Ridnour .40 1.00
82 Chris Bosh .60 1.50
83 T.J. Ford .30 .75
84 Joey Graham .30 .75
85 Carlos Boozer .40 1.00
86 Andrei Kirilenko .40 1.00
87 Deron Williams .75 2.00
88 Gilbert Arenas .50 1.25
89 Antawn Jamison .40 1.00
90 Andray Blatche .30 .75
91 Adam Morrison RC 1.50 4.00
92 Alexander Johnson RC 1.25 3.00
93 J.J. Redick RC 4.00 10.00
94 Vassilis Spanoulis RC 1.25 3.00
95 Jorge Garbajosa RC 1.50 4.00
96 Leon Powe RC 1.25 3.00
97 Chris Quinn RC 1.25 3.00
98 Terence Kinsey RC 1.25 3.00
99 Yakhouba Diawara RC 1.25 3.00
100 Robert Hite RC 1.25 3.00
101 Thabo Sefolosha AU RC 5.00 12.00
102 Ronnie Brewer AU RC 6.00 15.00
103 Cedric Simmons AU RC 4.00 10.00
104 Dee Brown AU RC 4.00 10.00
105 Craig Smith AU RC 5.00 12.00
106 Rodney Carney AU RC 4.00 10.00
107 Pops Mensah-Bonsu AU RC 4.00 10.00
108 Shawne Williams AU RC 4.00 10.00
109 Quincy Douby AU RC 4.00 10.00
110 Renaldo Balkman AU RC 5.00 12.00
111 Rajon Rondo AU RC 25.00 60.00
112 Marcus Williams AU RC 4.00 10.00
113 Josh Boone AU RC 4.00 10.00
114 Kyle Lowry AU RC 20.00 50.00
115 Shannon Brown AU RC 6.00 15.00
116 Jordan Farmar AU RC 5.00 12.00
117 Sergio Rodriguez AU RC 5.00 12.00
118 Maurice Ager AU RC 4.00 10.00
119 Mardy Collins AU RC 4.00 10.00
120 James White AU RC 4.00 10.00
121 Steve Novak AU RC 5.00 12.00
122 Solomon Jones AU RC 4.00 10.00
123 Andrea Bargnani AU RC 8.00 20.00
124 L.Aldridge AU RC 20.00 50.00
125 Tyrus Thomas AU RC 6.00 15.00
126 Shelden Williams AU RC 6.00 15.00
127 Brandon Roy AU RC 15.00 40.00
128 Randy Foye AU RC 6.00 15.00
129 Rudy Gay AU RC 10.00 25.00
130 Patrick O'Bryant AU RC 5.00 12.00
131 Saer Sene AU RC 5.00 12.00
132 Hilton Armstrong AU RC 5.00 12.00

2006-07 SP Authentic Gold

*1-90 GOLD: 4X TO 10X BASE HI
*91-100 GOLD RCs: 1X TO 2.5X BASE HI
*101-122 GOLD AU RCs: 1X TO 2.5X BASE HI
*123-132 GOLD AU RCs: .75X TO 2X BASE HI
GOLD PRINT RUN 25 SER.#'d SETS
124 LaMarcus Aldridge AU 40.00 100.00
127 Brandon Roy AU 40.00 100.00
129 Rudy Gay AU 40.00 100.00

2006-07 SP Authentic Autographed Jerseys

PRINT RUN 50 SER.#'d SETS
AI Andre Iguodala 6.00 15.00
AJ Al Jefferson 8.00 20.00
AM Alonzo Mourning 40.00 80.00
AR Allan Ray 5.00 12.00
BD Baron Davis 10.00 25.00
BG Ben Gordon 10.00 25.00
BI Chauncey Billups 6.00 15.00
CB Chris Bosh 12.00 30.00
CM Corey Maggette 5.00 12.00
CP Chris Paul 25.00 60.00
CS Craig Smith 5.00 12.00
DI Boris Diaw 5.00 12.00
DN David Noel 5.00 12.00
DW Deron Williams 12.00 30.00
JK Jason Kidd 15.00 40.00
JS J.R. Smith 5.00 12.00
KD Keyon Dooling 5.00 12.00
KH Kirk Hinrich 10.00 25.00
KK Kyle Korver 5.00 12.00
LB Leandro Barbosa 6.00 15.00
LH Larry Hughes 6.00 15.00
LR Luke Ridnour 5.00 12.00
MA Maurice Ager 5.00 12.00
MB Mike Bibby 6.00 15.00
MD Marquis Daniels 5.00 12.00
MJ Mike James 5.00 12.00
QD Quincy Douby 5.00 12.00
RB Raja Bell 12.50 30.00
RF Raymond Felton 6.00 15.00
RJ Richard Jefferson 5.00 12.00
RM Rashad McCants 5.00 12.00
SM Sean May 5.00 12.00
TC Tyson Chandler 5.00 12.00
TF T.J. Ford 5.00 12.00
TP Tayshaun Prince 6.00 15.00

2006-07 SP Authentic Autographed Jerseys Dual

PRINT RUN 25 SER.#'d SETS
DBD M.Bibby/Q.Douby 12.00 30.00
DBH C.Billups/R.Hamilton 12.00 30.00
DCP C.Paul/T.Chandler 20.00 40.00
DCR M.Collins/Q.Richardson 8.00 20.00
DDH C.Duhon/K.Hinrich 12.00 30.00
DDO B.Davis/P.O'Bryant 8.00 20.00
DFB C.Frye/R.Balkman 8.00 20.00
DHB L.Hughes/S.Brown 8.00 20.00
DKI K.Korver/A.Iguodala 12.00 30.00
DKJ J.Kidd/R.Jefferson 25.00 60.00
DNM D.Noel/R.McCants 8.00 20.00

2006-07 SP Authentic Autographed Jerseys Triple

PRINT RUN 15 SER.#'d SETS
CFR Collins/Frye/Richardson 20.00 50.00
HBP Billups/Hamilton/Prince 20.00 50.00
JEJ Jordan/James/Erving 2,500.00 5,000.00
MMD McGrady/Ming/Drexler 100.00 200.00
NDP Paul/Nash/Davis 100.00 200.00

2006-07 SP Authentic Chirography

APPROXIMATE ODDS 1:30
*GOLD: .6X TO 1.5X BASE HI
PRINT RUN 25 SER.#'d SETS
AI Andre Iguodala 6.00 15.00
BE Charlie Bell 4.00 10.00
BG Ben Gordon 6.00 15.00
BM Brad Miller 4.00 10.00
BO Chris Bosh 12.00 30.00
BR Brandon Roy 10.00 25.00
CB Chauncey Billups 5.00 12.00
CM Corey Maggette 4.00 10.00
DG Danny Granger 4.00 10.00
DM Damir Markota 4.00 10.00
DW Deron Williams 10.00 25.00
FG Francisco Garcia 4.00 10.00
GG Gerald Green 4.00 10.00
HW Hakim Warrick 4.00 10.00
IU Ime Udoka 10.00 25.00
JA Antawn Jamison 5.00 12.00
JG Joey Graham 4.00 10.00
JJ Jarrett Jack 4.00 10.00
JK Jason Kapono 4.00 10.00
JS J.R. Smith 5.00 12.00
KI Jason Kidd 10.00 25.00
KK Kyle Korver 4.00 10.00
LA LaMarcus Aldridge 12.00 30.00
LB Leandro Barbosa 4.00 10.00
LR Luke Ridnour 4.00 10.00
MI Mile Ilic 4.00 10.00
MW Martell Webster 4.00 10.00
NO Steve Novak 5.00 12.00
NR Nate Robinson 6.00 15.00
PA Paul Millsap 5.00 12.00
PM Pops Mensah-Bonsu 4.00 10.00
QR Quentin Richardson 4.00 10.00
RB Raja Bell 8.00 20.00
RH Ryan Hollins 4.00 10.00
RJ Richard Jefferson 4.00 10.00
RM Rashad McCants 4.00 10.00
RR Rajon Rondo 12.00 30.00
RT Ronny Turiaf 5.00 12.00
SA Shareef Abdur-Rahim 4.00 10.00
SB Shannon Brown 4.00 10.00
SJ Solomon Jones 4.00 10.00
SK Steve Kerr 6.00 15.00
SM Sean May 4.00 10.00
SN Steve Nash 25.00 60.00
SR Sergio Rodriguez 4.00 10.00
SW Shawne Williams 4.00 10.00
TC Tyson Chandler 5.00 12.00
TF T.J. Ford 4.00 10.00
TM Tracy McGrady 10.00 25.00
TP Tayshaun Prince 5.00 12.00
TS Thabo Sefolosha 6.00 15.00
TT Tyrus Thomas 6.00 15.00
VC Vince Carter 12.00 30.00
WI Shelden Williams 4.00 10.00

2006-07 SP Authentic Fabrics

APPROXIMATE ODDS 1:24
AB Andrew Bogut 2.00 5.00
AI Andre Iguodala 2.50 6.00
AJ Antawn Jamison 2.00 5.00
AM Alonzo Mourning 4.00 10.00
AW Antoine Walker 2.50 6.00
BL Bill Laimbeer 4.00 10.00
BW Ben Wallace 3.00 8.00
CA Carmelo Anthony 4.00 10.00
CB Chauncey Billups 3.00 8.00
CM Corey Maggette 2.00 5.00
CP Chris Paul 5.00 12.00
DM Darko Milicic 2.00 5.00
DN Dirk Nowitzki 6.00 15.00
DR David Robinson 4.00 10.00
GG George Gervin 4.00 10.00
GP Gary Payton 3.00 8.00
HO Hakeem Olajuwon 5.00 12.00
JC Josh Childress 1.50 4.00
JK Jason Kidd 4.00 10.00
KA Kareem Abdul-Jabbar 8.00 20.00
KB Kobe Bryant 8.00 20.00
KH Kirk Hinrich 2.00 5.00
LH Larry Hughes 2.00 5.00
LJ LeBron James 10.00 25.00
LO Lamar Odom 2.00 5.00
MA Donyell Marshall 2.00 5.00
MJ Michael Jordan 20.00 50.00
MW Marvin Williams 1.50 4.00
NR Nate Robinson 2.00 5.00
PP Paul Pierce 4.00 10.00
RW Rasheed Wallace 3.00 8.00
SE Sean Elliott 2.00 5.00
SO Shaquille O'Neal 10.00 25.00
TC Tyson Chandler 2.00 5.00
TM Tracy McGrady 4.00 10.00
TP Tayshaun Prince 2.50 6.00
VC Vince Carter 5.00 12.00
WF Walt Frazier 3.00 8.00
YM Yao Ming 6.00 15.00
ZI Zydrunas Ilgauskas 2.00 5.00

2006-07 SP Authentic Fabrics Dual

PRINT RUN 100 SER.#'d SETS
BI K.Bryant/A.Iverson 75.00 200.00
DR D.Robinson/T.Duncan 12.50 30.00
GM K.Garnett/R.McCants 5.00 12.00
GW P.Gasol/H.Warrick 5.00 12.00
JJ M.Jordan/L.James 50.00 120.00
JP C.Paul/L.James 12.00 30.00
KC V.Carter/J.Kidd 10.00 25.00
MA C.Anthony/K.Martin 5.00 12.00
MF S.Marbury/W.Frazier 5.00 12.00
MJ T.McGrady/L.James 15.00 40.00
MM M.Jordan/M.Johnson 40.00 100.00
NH D.Nowitzki/D.Harris 5.00 12.00
NS S.Nash/A.Stoudemire 8.00 20.00
PB L.Bird/P.Pierce 20.00 40.00

2006-07 SP Authentic Fabrics Triple

PRINT RUN 50 SER.#'d SETS
BOF Bryant/Odom/Farmar 15.00 40.00
DMO O'Neal/Ming/Duncan 15.00 40.00
GFR Foye/Gay/Redick 10.00 25.00
JEB Jordan/Bird/Erving 60.00 150.00
MMN McGrady/Ming/Novak 12.50 30.00
NMS Nash/Stoudemire/Marion 15.00 40.00

2006-07 SP Authentic Fabrics Quad

PRINT RUN 25 SER.#'d SETS
ARSA Aldridge/Roy/Arm/Simmons 25.00 60.00
IGJB James/Ilgauski/Gden/Brown 30.00 80.00
KCJW Jefferson/Carter/Kidd/Williams 20.00 50.00
WHGT Gordon/Hinrich/Wallace/Thomas 20.00 50.00
WWMO Shaq/Walker/J.Will/Zo 30.00 80.00

2006-07 SP Authentic Rookie Autographed Patches

PRINT RUN 30 SER.#'d SETS
AB Andrea Bargnani 50.00 100.00
BJ Bobby Jones 8.00 20.00
BR Brandon Roy 100.00 200.00
HA Hilton Armstrong 8.00 20.00
JB Josh Boone 8.00 20.00
JF Jordan Farmar 10.00 25.00
JG Jorge Garbajosa 10.00 25.00
JW James White 8.00 20.00
LA LaMarcus Aldridge 60.00 150.00
MA Maurice Ager 8.00 20.00
MW Marcus Williams 8.00 20.00
PD Paul Davis 8.00 20.00
PO Patrick O'Bryant 8.00 20.00
PT P.J. Tucker 12.00 30.00
RB Ronnie Brewer 12.00 30.00
RC Rodney Carney 8.00 20.00
RF Randy Foye 10.00 25.00
RG Rudy Gay 12.00 30.00
RR Rajon Rondo 150.00 300.00
SB Shannon Brown 8.00 20.00
SN Steve Novak 10.00 25.00
SS Saer Sene 8.00 20.00
SW Shelden Williams 8.00 20.00
WI Shawne Williams 8.00 20.00

2006-07 SP Authentic Rookie Exclusives Jerseys

APPROXIMATE ODDS 1:30
*PATCH: 1.5X TO 4X BASE HI
PATCH PRINT RUN 25 SER.#'d SETS
AB Andrea Bargnani 2.00 5.00
AR Allan Ray 1.50 4.00
BR Brandon Roy 5.00 12.00
CS Cedric Simmons 1.50 4.00
DE Dee Brown 1.50 4.00
DN David Noel 1.50 4.00
JB Josh Boone 1.50 4.00
JF Jordan Farmar 2.00 5.00
JG Jorge Garbajosa 1.50 4.00
JW James White 1.50 4.00
MA Maurice Ager 1.50 4.00
MC Mardy Collins 1.50 4.00
MW Marcus Williams 1.50 4.00
PD Paul Davis 1.50 4.00
PO Patrick O'Bryant 1.50 4.00
QD Quincy Douby 1.50 4.00
RB Renaldo Balkman 2.00 5.00
RC Rodney Carney 1.50 4.00
RF Randy Foye 2.00 5.00
RG Rudy Gay 3.00 8.00
RO Ronnie Brewer 2.50 6.00
RR Rajon Rondo 8.00 20.00
SB Shannon Brown 1.50 4.00
SJ Solomon Jones 1.50 4.00
SM Craig Smith 2.00 5.00
SN Steve Novak 2.00 5.00
SS Saer Sene 1.50 4.00

TS Thabo Sefolosha 2.00 5.00
TT Tyrus Thomas 2.00 5.00
WI Shawne Williams 1.50 4.00

2006-07 SP Authentic Rookie Exclusives Jerseys Autographs

PRINT RUN 60 SER.#'d SETS
AB Andrea Bargnani 6.00 15.00
BR Brandon Roy 20.00 50.00
DE Dee Brown 5.00 12.00
DN David Noel 5.00 12.00
JB Josh Boone 5.00 12.00
JF Jordan Farmar 6.00 15.00
JG Jorge Garbajosa 6.00 15.00
JW James White 5.00 12.00
MA Maurice Ager 5.00 12.00
MC Mardy Collins 5.00 12.00
MW Marcus Williams 5.00 12.00
PD Paul Davis 5.00 12.00
PO Patrick O'Bryant 5.00 12.00
QD Quincy Douby 5.00 12.00
RB Renaldo Balkman 6.00 15.00
RC Rodney Carney 5.00 12.00
RF Randy Foye 6.00 15.00
RG Rudy Gay 10.00 25.00
RO Ronnie Brewer 8.00 20.00
RR Rajon Rondo 30.00 80.00
SB Shannon Brown 5.00 12.00
SJ Solomon Jones 5.00 12.00
SM Craig Smith 6.00 15.00
SN Steve Novak 6.00 15.00
SS Saer Sene 5.00 12.00
TS Thabo Sefolosha 6.00 15.00
TT Tyrus Thomas 6.00 15.00
WI Shawne Williams 5.00 12.00

2006-07 SP Authentic Sign of the Times All-Stars

PRINT RUN 50 SER.#'d SETS
AD Adrian Dantley 6.00 15.00
AJ Antawn Jamison 6.00 15.00
BD Baron Davis 6.00 15.00
BL Bill Laimbeer 15.00 40.00
BM Brad Miller 6.00 15.00
CB Chris Bosh 10.00 25.00
CD Clyde Drexler 15.00 40.00
CH Connie Hawkins 8.00 20.00
DA Brad Daugherty 6.00 15.00
DR David Robinson 40.00 80.00
JK Jason Kidd 20.00 50.00
JM Jamaal Magloire 6.00 15.00
MR Michael Ray Richardson 6.00 15.00
PP Paul Pierce 15.00 40.00
PS Peja Stojakovic 6.00 15.00
RH Richard Hamilton 8.00 20.00
RO Dennis Rodman 30.00 80.00
SE Sean Elliott 12.50 30.00
SN Steve Nash 50.00 100.00
TM Tracy McGrady 15.00 40.00
VC Vince Carter 40.00 100.00
YM Yao Ming 15.00 40.00

2006-07 SP Authentic Sign of the Times Legends

PRINT RUN 25 SER.#'d SETS
BK Bernard King 8.00 20.00
BW Bill Walton 20.00 50.00
CM Cedric Maxwell 8.00 20.00
FR World B. Free 10.00 25.00
HO Hakeem Olajuwon 20.00 40.00
JE Julius Erving 50.00 100.00
LB Larry Bird 60.00 120.00
MA Magic Johnson 60.00 120.00
ME Mark Eaton 8.00 20.00
MJ Michael Jordan 300.00 600.00
NA Nate Archibald 8.00 20.00
PW Paul Westphal 8.00 20.00
SP Sam Perkins 8.00 20.00
TC Tom Chambers 8.00 20.00
WF Walt Frazier 15.00 40.00

2006-07 SP Authentic Sign of the Times Rookies

PRINT RUN 100 SER.#'d SETS
AB Andrea Bargnani 12.00 30.00
AR Allan Ray 2.50 6.00
BR Brandon Roy 12.00 30.00
CS Cedric Simmons 2.50 6.00
HA Hassan Adams 2.50 6.00
HI Hilton Armstrong 2.50 6.00
JB Josh Boone 2.50 6.00
KL Kyle Lowry 12.00 30.00
LA LaMarcus Aldridge 15.00 40.00
MC Mardy Collins 2.50 6.00
PM Pops Mensah-Bonsu 2.50 6.00
PO Patrick O'Bryant 2.50 6.00
QD Quincy Douby 2.50 6.00
RB Renaldo Balkman 3.00 8.00
RC Rodney Carney 2.50 6.00
RF Randy Foye 3.00 8.00
RG Rudy Gay 5.00 12.00
RH Ryan Hollins 2.50 6.00
RR Rajon Rondo 25.00 60.00
SB Shannon Brown 2.50 6.00
SS Saer Sene 2.50 6.00
SW Shelden Williams 2.50 6.00
TS Thabo Sefolosha 3.00 8.00
TT Tyrus Thomas 3.00 8.00
WB Will Blalock 2.50 6.00

2006-07 SP Authentic Sign of the Times Veterans

PRINT RUN 75 SER.#'d SETS
BG Ben Gordon 12.00 30.00
BM Brad Miller 4.00 10.00
BO Chris Bosh 12.00 30.00
CB Chauncey Billups 6.00 15.00
CM Corey Maggette 4.00 10.00
DG Danny Granger 4.00 10.00
DS DeShawn Stevenson 4.00 10.00
DW Deron Williams 10.00 25.00
GG Gerald Green 4.00 10.00
HW Hakim Warrick 4.00 10.00
JJ Jarrett Jack 4.00 10.00
KH Kirk Hinrich 12.00 30.00
LB Leandro Barbosa 4.00 10.00
MJ Mike James 4.00 10.00
MW Marvin Williams 4.00 10.00
RB Raja Bell 8.00 20.00
RJ Richard Jefferson 4.00 10.00
TF T.J. Ford 4.00 10.00

2006-07 SP Authentic Sign of the Times Dual

PRINT RUN 100 SER.#'d SETS
UNLESS LISTED IN CHECKLIST
SDAB Bargnani/Aldridge/15 12.00 30.00
SDAM Ager/Mnsh-Bsu/15 12.00 30.00
SDAR A.Ray/R.Rondo/15 30.00 80.00
SDBA H.Adams/J.Boone 10.00 25.00
SDBB D.Brown/R.Brewer 10.00 25.00
SDBF C.Bosh/T.J. Ford 12.00 30.00
SDCN R.Carney/S.Novak 10.00 25.00
SDFB C.Frye/R.Balkman 10.00 25.00
SDGB D.Gibson/S.Brown 10.00 25.00
SDHA J.Augustine/Hollins/15 10.00 25.00
SDHB R.Hamilton/Billups/15 12.00 30.00
SDHG B.Gordon/K.Hinrich 20.00 50.00
SDIJ A.Iguodala/B.Jones 20.00 40.00
SDJJ M.Jordan/L.James 3,000.00 6,000.00
SDKD B.Davis/J.Kidd 20.00 50.00
SDKN J.Kidd/S.Nash/15 40.00 100.00
SDMA Carmelo/McGrady/15 60.00 150.00
SDMD B.Miller/P.Davis/15 10.00 25.00
SDOH R.Felton/E.Okafor 10.00 25.00
SDPB W.Blalock/T.Prince/15 10.00 25.00
SDPJ P.Pierce/R.Jefferson 20.00 50.00
SDRJ Rondo/Jefferson/15 30.00 80.00
SDRK K.Korver/Q.Rich/15 15.00 40.00
SDRR B.Roy/S.Rdrgz/15 15.00 40.00
SDSA C.Simmons/H.Armstrong 10.00 25.00
SDSJ D.Stevenson/A.Jamison/15 10.00 25.00
SDTS T.Sefolosha/T.Thomas/15 10.00 25.00
SDWA D.West/T.Allen/15 10.00 25.00
SDWG H.Warrick/R.Gay/15 15.00 40.00
SDWJ S.Williams/S.Jones/15 10.00 25.00
SDWR B.Wallace/D.Rodman/15 60.00 120.00
SDWW S.Williams/J.White 10.00 25.00

2007-08 SP Authentic

COMP.SET w/o SP's (100) 25.00 50.00
1 Brandon Roy .60 1.50
2 Channing Frye .30 .75
3 Jarrett Jack .40 1.00
4 LaMarcus Aldridge .50 1.25
5 Delonte West .30 .75
6 Johan Petro .30 .75
7 Nick Collison .30 .75
8 Joe Johnson .40 1.00
9 Josh Smith .30 .75
10 Marvin Williams .30 .75
11 Hakim Warrick .30 .75
12 Pau Gasol .75 2.00
13 Rudy Gay .40 1.00
14 Al Jefferson .30 .75
15 Paul Pierce .75 2.00
16 Ray Allen .75 2.00
17 Andrew Bogut .40 1.00
18 Charlie Villanueva .30 .75
19 Maurice Williams .40 1.00
20 Michael Redd .40 1.00
21 Kevin Garnett 1.25 3.00
22 Randy Foye .40 1.00
23 Ricky Davis .40 1.00
24 Emeka Okafor .40 1.00
25 Gerald Wallace .40 1.00
26 Jason Richardson .50 1.25
27 David Lee .30 .75
28 Eddy Curry .30 .75
29 Stephon Marbury .60 1.50
30 Zach Randolph .50 1.25
31 Brad Miller .40 1.00
32 Kevin Martin .40 1.00
33 Mike Bibby .50 1.25
34 Ron Artest .50 1.25
35 Jamaal Tinsley .30 .75
36 Jermaine O'Neal .50 1.25
37 Mike Dunleavy .30 .75
38 Andre Iguodala .50 1.25
39 Andre Miller .40 1.00
40 Rodney Carney .30 .75
41 Chris Paul 1.00 2.50
42 David West .40 1.00
43 Tyson Chandler .50 1.25
44 Corey Maggette .40 1.00
45 Cuttino Mobley .40 1.00
46 Elton Brand .40 1.00
47 Darko Milicic .30 .75
48 Dwight Howard .60 1.50
49 Hedo Turkoglu .40 1.00
50 Rashard Lewis .40 1.00
51 Antawn Jamison .40 1.00
52 Caron Butler .40 1.00
53 Gilbert Arenas .50 1.25
54 Jason Kidd .75 2.00
55 Richard Jefferson .40 1.00
56 Vince Carter 1.00 2.50
57 Baron Davis .40 1.00
58 Monta Ellis .40 1.00
59 Stephen Jackson .40 1.00
60 Jordan Farmar .30 .75
61 Kobe Bryant 4.00 10.00
62 Lamar Odom .40 1.00
63 Alonzo Mourning .75 2.00
64 Dwyane Wade 1.00 2.50
65 Shaquille O'Neal 2.00 5.00
66 Allen Iverson 1.25 3.00
67 Carmelo Anthony .75 2.00
68 Marcus Camby .40 1.00
69 Andrea Bargnani .30 .75
70 Chris Bosh .60 1.50
71 Jose Calderon .30 .75
72 T.J. Ford .30 .75
73 Ben Gordon .60 1.50
74 Ben Wallace .60 1.50
75 Kirk Hinrich .50 1.25
76 Luol Deng .40 1.00
77 Larry Hughes .40 1.00
78 LeBron James 4.00 10.00
79 Zydrunas Ilgauskas .40 1.00
80 Andrei Kirilenko .40 1.00
81 Carlos Boozer .40 1.00
82 Deron Williams .40 1.00
83 Mehmet Okur .30 .75
84 Luther Head .30 .75
85 Tracy McGrady .75 2.00
86 Yao Ming 1.25 3.00
87 Chauncey Billups .60 1.50
88 Rasheed Wallace .60 1.50
89 Richard Hamilton .60 1.50
90 Tayshaun Prince .50 1.25
91 Manu Ginobili 1.00 2.50
92 Tim Duncan 1.25 3.00
93 Tony Parker .75 2.00
94 Amare Stoudemire .50 1.25
95 Grant Hill .75 2.00
96 Shawn Marion .50 1.25
97 Steve Nash 1.00 2.50
98 Dirk Nowitzki 1.25 3.00
99 Jason Terry .40 1.00
100 Josh Howard .40 1.00
101 Greg Oden/299 RC 4.00 10.00
102 Yi Jianlian/299 RC 5.00 12.00
103 Brandan Wright/299 RC 3.00 8.00
104 Thaddeus Young/299 RC 4.00 10.00
105 Nick Young/299 RC 4.00 10.00
106 Jamario Moon/299 RC 3.00 8.00
106B Guillermo Diaz/299 4.00 10.00
107 Marco Belinelli AU/999 RC 4.00 10.00
108 Darryl Watkins AU/999 RC 3.00 8.00
109 Oleksiy Pecherov AU/999 RC 5.00 12.00
110 Juan Carlos Navarro AU/999 RC 4.00 10.00
111 JamesOn Curry AU/999 RC 3.00 8.00
112 Demetris Nichols AU/999 RC 3.00 8.00
113 Herbert Hill AU/999 RC 3.00 8.00
114 Coby Karl/299 RC 2.50 6.00
115 Darius Washington/299 4.00 10.00
116 Glen Davis AU/999 RC 4.00 10.00
117 Cheikh Samb/299 RC 2.50 6.00
118 Ramon Sessions AU/999 RC 4.00 10.00
119 Luis Scola AU/999 RC 5.00 12.00
122 Spencer Hawes JSY AU/599 RC 4.00 10.00
123 Acie Law JSY AU/599 RC 4.00 10.00
124 Julian Wright JSY AU/599 RC 4.00 10.00
125 Al Thornton JSY AU/599 RC 4.00 10.00
126 R.Stuckey JSY AU/599 RC 4.00 10.00
127 Sean Williams JSY AU/599 RC 4.00 10.00
128 J.Crittenton JSY AU/599 RC 4.00 10.00
129 Jason Smith JSY AU/599 RC 4.00 10.00
130 D.Cook JSY AU/599 RC 5.00 12.00
131 Jared Dudley JSY AU/599 RC 5.00 12.00
132 W.Chandler JSY AU/599 RC 5.00 12.00
133 Morris Almond JSY AU/599 RC 4.00 10.00
134 Arron Afflalo JSY AU/599 RC 5.00 12.00
135 Alando Tucker JSY AU/599 RC 4.00 10.00
136 Carl Landry JSY AU/599 RC 4.00 10.00
137 Gabe Pruitt JSY AU/599 RC 4.00 10.00
138 Aaron Brooks/299 RC 3.00 8.00
139 Nick Fazekas JSY AU/599 RC 4.00 10.00
140 J.Davidson JSY AU/599 RC 4.00 10.00
141 J.McRoberts JSY AU/599 RC 4.00 10.00
142 Glen Davis/299 RC 3.00 8.00
143 Adam Haluska JSY AU/599 RC 4.00 10.00
147 D.McGuire JSY AU/599 RC 4.00 10.00
148 Aaron Gray JSY AU/599 RC 4.00 10.00
149 Taurean Green JSY AU/599 RC 4.00 10.00
150 D.J. Strawberry JSY AU/599 RC 4.00 10.00
151 Chris Richard JSY AU/399 RC 4.00 10.00
152 K.Durant JSY AU/299 RC 1,500.00 3,000.00
153 Al Horford JSY AU/299 RC 25.00 60.00
154 M.Conley Jr. JSY AU/299 RC 25.00 60.00
155 Jeff Green JSY AU/299 RC 8.00 20.00
156 Corey Brewer JSY AU/299 RC 8.00 20.00
157 J.Noah JSY AU/299 RC 10.00 25.00

2007-08 SP Authentic By The Number Career Points

PRINT RUN 75 SER.#'d SETS
*JERSEY NUMB: .5X TO 1.25X BASE HI
JSY NUM PRINT RUN 25 SER.#'d SETS
*RC YEAR SAME VALUE AS POINTS
RC YEAR PRINT RUN 50 SER.#'d SETS
EXCH EXPIRE DATE 1/28/10
BNAD Adrian Dantley 8.00 20.00
BNAH Al Harrington 8.00 20.00
BNAJ Al Jefferson 8.00 20.00
BNAM Alonzo Mourning 20.00 50.00
BNAU James Augustine 8.00 20.00
BNBA Leandro Barbosa 8.00 20.00
BNBD Baron Davis 15.00 30.00
BNBJ Bobby Jackson 8.00 20.00
BNBM Brad Miller 8.00 20.00
BNBR Brandon Roy 12.00 30.00
BNBW Bill Walton 20.00 50.00
BNCA Carmelo Anthony 40.00 100.00
BNCB Chris Bosh 15.00 40.00
BNCH Tom Chambers 8.00 20.00
BNDA Brad Daugherty 8.00 20.00
BNDG Daniel Gibson 8.00 20.00
BNDH Dwight Howard 40.00 100.00
BNDM Donyell Marshall 8.00 20.00
BNDW Deron Williams 8.00 20.00
BNHA Hilton Armstrong 8.00 20.00
BNHO Hakeem Olajuwon 40.00 100.00
BNJA Antawn Jamison 10.00 25.00
BNJJ Jarrett Jack 8.00 20.00
BNJO Michael Jordan/23 3,000.00 6,000.00
BNJW Jamaal Wilkes 15.00 40.00
BNKB Kobe Bryant/24 1,500.00 3,000.00
BNKH Kirk Hinrich 10.00 25.00
BNLA LaMarcus Aldridge 20.00 50.00
BNLB Larry Bird 150.00 400.00
BNLJ LeBron James 1,500.00 3,000.00
BNMJ Magic Johnson 150.00 400.00
BNPE Morris Peterson 8.00 20.00
BNPM Paul Millsap 8.00 20.00
BNPP Paul Pierce 40.00 100.00
BNQR Quentin Richardson 8.00 20.00
BNRB Rick Barry 15.00 40.00
BNRG Rudy Gay 15.00 40.00
BNRR Rajon Rondo 60.00 150.00
BNSA Shareef Abdur-Rahim 10.00 25.00
BNSH Spencer Haywood 8.00 20.00
BNSK Steve Kerr 15.00 40.00
BNSM Sidney Moncrief 8.00 20.00
BNSP Sam Perkins 8.00 20.00
BNTC Terry Cummings 8.00 20.00
BNTM Tracy McGrady 75.00 200.00
BNTP Tayshaun Prince 8.00 20.00
BNTT Tyrus Thomas 8.00 20.00
BNTY Tyson Chandler 8.00 20.00
BNVC Vince Carter 75.00 200.00
BNWF Walt Frazier 25.00 60.00
BNYM Yao Ming 300.00 600.00

2007-08 SP Authentic Chirography

EXCH.EXPIRE DATE 1/28/10
CRAD Adrian Dantley 6.00 15.00
CRAJ Antawn Jamison 4.00 10.00
CRAM Alonzo Mourning 20.00 50.00
CRBD Baron Davis 6.00 15.00
CRCM Chris Mihm 4.00 10.00
CRDR Dennis Rodman 20.00 50.00
CRDW Deron Williams 10.00 25.00
CRFG Francisco Garcia 4.00 10.00
CRGI Artis Gilmore 6.00 15.00
CRJO Magic Johnson 40.00 100.00
CRLJ LeBron James 1,000.00 2,000.00
CRRO Brandon Roy 10.00 25.00
CRRP Robert Parish 6.00 15.00
CRSA Shareef Abdur-Rahim 5.00 12.00
CRSN Steve Nash 40.00 100.00
CRSP Sam Perkins 6.00 15.00
CRTP Tayshaun Prince 6.00 15.00
CRWE Jerry West 40.00 100.00
CRWF Walt Frazier 15.00 40.00

2007-08 SP Authentic Chirography Gold

STATED PRINT RUN 5 TO 25 SER.#'d SETS
EXCHANGE EXPIRATION 1/28/10
CRAB Andrea Bargnani 8.00 20.00
CRAD Adrian Dantley 15.00 40.00
CRAM Alonzo Mourning 60.00 150.00
CRBD Baron Davis 15.00 40.00
CRBJ Bobby Jackson 8.00 20.00
CRBW Bill Walton 15.00 40.00
CRCD Chuck Daly 50.00 120.00
CRCH Connie Hawkins 20.00 40.00
CRDA Brad Daugherty 15.00 30.00
CRDG Daniel Gibson 15.00 30.00
CRDN Don Nelson 20.00 40.00
CRDR Dennis Rodman 25.00 60.00
CRDT David Thompson 15.00 30.00
CRDW Deron Williams 20.00 50.00
CRFG Francisco Garcia 8.00 20.00
CRHO Hakeem Olajuwon 25.00 60.00
CRJK Jason Kidd 20.00 50.00
CRJO Magic Johnson 60.00 150.00
CRJW Jamaal Wilkes 10.00 25.00
CRLB Leandro Barbosa 12.00 30.00
CRMB Mike Bibby 8.00 20.00
CRMI Andre Miller 8.00 20.00
CRMP Mark Price 20.00 50.00
CRPA Tony Parker 20.00 40.00
CRPP Paul Pierce 25.00 50.00
CRRB Rick Barry 8.00 20.00
CRRO Brandon Roy 25.00 60.00
CRRP Robert Parish 20.00 40.00
CRSA Shareef Abdur-Rahim 10.00 25.00
CRSB Shannon Brown 12.00 30.00
CRSN Steve Nash 100.00 250.00
CRSP Sam Perkins 15.00 30.00
CRST John Stockton 40.00 80.00
CRTC Tom Chambers 8.00 20.00
CRTY Tyson Chandler 15.00 30.00
CRWA Don Slick Watts 8.00 20.00
CRWE Jerry West 100.00 250.00
CRWF Walt Frazier 20.00 50.00

2007-08 SP Authentic Destination Stardom

COMPLETE SET (30) 20.00 40.00
DS1 Kevin Durant 8.00 20.00
DS2 Al Horford 2.00 5.00
DS3 Mike Conley Jr. 2.00 5.00
DS4 Jeff Green .60 1.50
DS5 Corey Brewer .60 1.50
DS6 Joakim Noah .75 2.00
DS7 Spencer Hawes .50 1.25
DS8 Acie Law .50 1.25
DS9 Julian Wright .50 1.25
DS10 Al Thornton .50 1.25
DS11 Rodney Stuckey .50 1.25
DS12 Sean Williams .50 1.25
DS13 Marco Belinelli .60 1.50
DS14 Javaris Crittenton .50 1.25
DS15 Jason Smith .50 1.25
DS16 Daequan Cook .60 1.50
DS17 Jared Dudley .60 1.50
DS18 Wilson Chandler .60 1.50
DS19 Morris Almond .50 1.25
DS20 Arron Afflalo .60 1.50
DS21 Alando Tucker .50 1.25
DS22 Glen Davis .60 1.50
DS23 Carl Landry .50 1.25
DS24 Gabe Pruitt .50 1.25
DS25 Luis Scola .75 2.00
DS26 Nick Fazekas .50 1.25
DS27 Jermareo Davidson .50 1.25
DS28 Josh McRoberts .50 1.25
DS29 Kyrylo Fesenko .50 1.25
DS30 Aaron Gray .50 1.25

2007-08 SP Authentic Profiles

COMPLETE SET (60) 25.00 50.00
AP1 Acie Law .60 1.50
AP2 Al Horford 2.50 6.00
AP3 Al Thornton .60 1.50
AP4 Arron Afflalo .75 2.00
AP5 Corey Brewer .75 2.00
AP6 Daequan Cook .75 2.00
AP7 Jared Dudley .60 1.50
AP8 Jason Smith .60 1.50
AP9 Javaris Crittenton .60 1.50
AP10 Jeff Green .75 2.00
AP11 Joakim Noah 1.00 2.50
AP12 Julian Wright .60 1.50
AP13 Kevin Durant 10.00 25.00
AP14 Marco Belinelli .75 2.00
AP15 Mike Conley Jr. 2.50 6.00
AP16 Morris Almond .60 1.50
AP17 Rodney Stuckey .60 1.50
AP18 Sean Williams .60 1.50
AP19 Spencer Hawes .60 1.50
AP20 Wilson Chandler .75 2.00
AP21 Allen Iverson 2.50 6.00
AP22 Carlos Boozer .75 2.00
AP23 Carmelo Anthony 1.50 4.00
AP24 Chauncey Billups 1.25 3.00
AP25 Chris Bosh 1.25 3.00
AP26 Dirk Nowitzki 2.50 6.00
AP27 Dwyane Wade 2.00 5.00
AP28 Gilbert Arenas 1.00 2.50
AP29 Jason Kidd 1.50 4.00
AP30 Kevin Garnett 2.50 6.00
AP31 Kobe Bryant 8.00 20.00
AP32 LeBron James 8.00 20.00
AP33 Ray Allen 1.50 4.00
AP34 Shaquille O'Neal 4.00 10.00
AP35 Steve Nash 2.00 5.00
AP36 Tim Duncan 2.50 6.00
AP37 Tony Parker 1.50 4.00
AP38 Tracy McGrady 1.50 4.00
AP39 Vince Carter 2.00 5.00
AP40 Yao Ming 2.50 6.00
AP41 Adrian Dantley .75 2.00
AP42 Bill Walton 1.25 3.00
AP43 Chris Mullin 1.25 3.00
AP44 David Robinson 2.00 5.00
AP45 Elvin Hayes 1.00 2.50
AP46 George Gervin 1.25 3.00
AP47 Hakeem Olajuwon 2.00 5.00
AP48 Jerry West 2.50 6.00
AP49 John Stockton 2.00 5.00
AP50 Julius Erving 2.50 6.00
AP51 Kareem Abdul-Jabbar 3.00 8.00
AP52 Karl Malone 1.25 3.00
AP53 Larry Bird 4.00 10.00
AP54 Magic Johnson 4.00 10.00
AP55 Michael Jordan 10.00 25.00
AP56 Moses Malone 1.50 4.00
AP57 Oscar Robertson 1.00 2.50
AP58 Rick Barry .75 2.00
AP59 Robert Parish 1.00 2.50
AP60 Wilt Chamberlain 3.00 8.00

2007-08 SP Authentic Recruiting Class 2007

STATED PRINT RUN 60 TO 75 SER.#'d SETS
*CITY NAME: SAME VALUE AS BASE
CITY NAME STATED PRINT RUN 50 SETS
*TEAM NAME: .5X TO 1.25X BASE HI
TEAM NAME STATED PRINT RUN 25 SETS
EXCH EXPIRE DATE 1/28/10
RCAA Arron Afflalo/75 5.00 12.00
RCAB Aaron Brooks/75 5.00 12.00
RCAH Al Horford/75 10.00 25.00
RCAL Acie Law/75 4.00 10.00
RCAT Al Thornton/75 4.00 10.00
RCCB Corey Brewer/75 5.00 12.00
RCCL Carl Landry/75 5.00 12.00
RCDC Daequan Cook/75 5.00 12.00
RCDM Dominic McGuire/75 4.00 10.00
RCDU Jared Dudley/75 5.00 12.00
RCGD Glen Davis/75 5.00 12.00
RCGP Gabe Pruitt/75 4.00 10.00
RCJC Javaris Crittenton/75 4.00 10.00
RCJD Jermareo Davidson/75 4.00 10.00
RCJG Jeff Green/75 5.00 12.00
RCJM Josh McRoberts/75 4.00 10.00
RCJN Joakim Noah/75 30.00 80.00
RCJS Jason Smith/75 4.00 10.00
RCJW Julian Wright/75 4.00 10.00
RCKD Kevin Durant/60 150.00 300.00
RCMA Morris Almond/75 4.00 10.00
RCMB Marco Belinelli/75 5.00 12.00
RCMC Mike Conley Jr./75 15.00 40.00
RCNF Nick Fazekas/75 4.00 10.00
RCRS Rodney Stuckey/75 4.00 10.00
RCSH Spencer Hawes/75 4.00 10.00
RCSW Sean Williams/75 4.00 10.00
RCTG Taurean Green/75 4.00 10.00
RCTU Alando Tucker/75 4.00 10.00
RCWC Wilson Chandler/75 5.00 12.00

2007-08 SP Authentic Sign of the Times Dual

PRINT RUN 16 TO 50 SER.#'d SETS
EXCH EXPIRE DATE 1/28/10
STAJ A.Bargnani/J.Garbajosa 8.00 20.00
STAL K.Lowry/J.Augustine 8.00 20.00
STAR L.Aldridge/B.Roy 20.00 50.00
STAW D.Williams/J.Augustine 8.00 20.00
STBD P.Davis/S.Brown 8.00 20.00
STBG M.Bibby/F.Garcia 8.00 20.00
STBM J.Boone/R.Mahorn 8.00 20.00
STDB B.Diaw/L.Barbosa 8.00 20.00
STDG K.Durant/J.Green 100.00 250.00
STDH B.Davis/A.Harrington 10.00 25.00
STDM M.Jordan/D.Rodman 1,000.00 2,000.00
STFB T.Ford/J.Boone 8.00 20.00
STGC R.Gay/M.Conley Jr. 10.00 25.00
STGH H.Grant/D.Howard 10.00 25.00
STGM D.Marshall/D.Gibson 8.00 20.00
STGN A.Gray/J.Noah 8.00 20.00
STGR R.Rondo/D.Gibson 10.00 25.00
STHM A.Harrington/P.Millsap 8.00 20.00
STIB M.Bibby/A.Iguodala 8.00 20.00
STIC A.Iguodala/J.Augustine 8.00 20.00
STJA S.Jones/J.Augustine 8.00 20.00
STJC A.Jefferson/R.Carney 8.00 20.00
STJR M.Johnson/P.Riley 40.00 100.00
STJS A.Jamison/D.Stevenson 8.00 20.00
STLA M.Ager/K.Lowry 8.00 20.00
STMD C.Mihm/P.Davis 8.00 20.00
STMG H.Greer/A.Miller 8.00 20.00
STMN S.May/D.Noel/31 8.00 20.00
STMP P.Millsap/L.Powe 8.00 20.00
STMS M.Ager/S.Brown 8.00 20.00
STMT A.Mourning/T.Thomas 12.00 30.00
STOA P.O'Bryant/M.Ager 8.00 20.00
STOP P.O'Bryant/P.Davis 8.00 20.00
STOS H.Olajuwon/R.Sampson 25.00 50.00
STPD T.Prince/A.Dantley 12.00 30.00
STPJ T.Prince/L.James 1,000.00 2,000.00
STPW T.Parker/D.Williams 15.00 40.00
STRP R.Rondo/H.Armstrong 20.00 40.00
STSA C.Simmons/H.Armstrong 8.00 20.00
STSJ S.May/J.Dudley 8.00 20.00
STWA B.Walton/L.Aldridge 12.00 30.00
STWD D.Wilkins/Y.Diawara 8.00 20.00
STWJ S.Williams/S.Jones 8.00 20.00
STWP B.Walton/R.Parish 15.00 40.00

2008-09 SP Authentic

COMP.SET w/o SP's (100) 25.00 50.00
1 Dwyane Wade 1.00 2.50
2 Alonzo Mourning .60 1.50
3 Daequan Cook .30 .75
4 Kevin Durant 2.00 5.00
5 Jeff Green .40 1.00
6 Chris Wilcox .30 .75
7 Al Jefferson .30 .75
8 Corey Brewer .40 1.00
9 Randy Foye .50 1.25
10 Rudy Gay .50 1.25
11 Mike Conley Jr. .40 1.00
12 Mike Miller .40 1.00
13 Jamal Crawford .50 1.25
14 Eddy Curry .30 .75
15 Quentin Richardson .30 .75
16 Stephon Marbury .50 1.25
17 Chris Kaman .30 .75
18 Marcus Camby .40 1.00
19 Baron Davis .50 1.25
20 Michael Redd .40 1.00
21 Richard Jefferson .40 1.00
22 Mo Williams .40 1.00
23 Emeka Okafor .30 .75
24 Gerald Wallace .40 1.00
25 Jason Richardson .50 1.25
26 Joakim Noah .30 .75
27 Luol Deng .40 1.00
28 Ben Gordon .40 1.00
29 Michael Jordan 4.00 10.00
30 Vince Carter 1.00 2.50
31 Yi Jianlian .60 1.50
32 Devin Harris .30 .75
33 T.J. Ford .30 .75
34 Danny Granger .40 1.00
35 Mike Dunleavy .30 .75
36 Ron Artest .50 1.25
37 Kevin Martin .40 1.00
38 Brad Miller .40 1.00
39 Brandon Roy .40 1.00
40 LaMarcus Aldridge .50 1.25
41 Greg Oden .30 .75
42 Corey Maggette .40 1.00
43 Al Harrington .40 1.00
44 Monta Ellis .40 1.00
45 Al Horford .50 1.25
46 Joe Johnson .50 1.25
47 Josh Smith .30 .75
48 Mike Bibby .50 1.25
49 Andre Iguodala .40 1.00
50 Andre Miller .40 1.00
51 Thaddeus Young .40 1.00
52 Chris Bosh .60 1.50
53 Jermaine O'Neal .50 1.25
54 Jose Calderon .30 .75
55 Antawn Jamison .40 1.00
56 Caron Butler .40 1.00
57 Gilbert Arenas .50 1.25
58 LeBron James 4.00 10.00
59 Daniel Gibson .30 .75
60 Anderson Varejao .30 .75
61 Allen Iverson 1.00 2.50
62 Carmelo Anthony .60 1.50
63 Elton Brand .40 1.00
64 Jason Kidd .75 2.00
65 Dirk Nowitzki 1.25 3.00
66 Josh Howard .40 1.00
67 Dwight Howard .60 1.50
68 Hedo Turkoglu .40 1.00
69 Rashard Lewis .40 1.00
70 Deron Williams .40 1.00
71 Carlos Boozer .40 1.00
72 Andrei Kirilenko .40 1.00
73 Ronnie Brewer .30 .75
74 Shaquille O'Neal 1.50 4.00
75 Steve Nash 1.00 2.50
76 Amare Stoudemire .50 1.25
77 Leandro Barbosa .40 1.00
78 Yao Ming 1.25 3.00
79 Tracy McGrady .75 2.00
80 Shane Battier .40 1.00
81 Luis Scola .40 1.00
82 Tim Duncan 1.25 3.00
83 Tony Parker .60 1.50
84 Manu Ginobili 1.00 2.50
85 Chris Paul 1.00 2.50
86 David West .40 1.00
87 Tyson Chandler .40 1.00
88 Peja Stojakovic .40 1.00
89 Kobe Bryant 4.00 10.00
90 Pau Gasol .60 1.50
91 Lamar Odom .40 1.00
92 Andrew Bynum .30 .75
93 Chauncey Billups .60 1.50
94 Richard Hamilton .50 1.25
95 Rasheed Wallace .60 1.50
96 Tayshaun Prince .50 1.25
97 Kevin Garnett 1.25 3.00
98 Paul Pierce .75 2.00
99 Ray Allen .75 2.00
100 Rajon Rondo .60 1.50
101 Alexis Ajinca AU/199 RC 5.00 12.00
102 Joe Alexander JSY AU/499 RC 5.00 12.00
103 R.Anderson JSY AU/499 RC 6.00 15.00
104 Darrell Arthur JSY AU/499 RC 6.00 15.00
105 D.J. Augustin JSY AU/299 RC 8.00 20.00
106 J.Bayless JSY AU/299 RC 6.00 15.00
107 M.Beasley JSY AU/299 RC 8.00 20.00
108 M.Chalmers JSY AU/499 RC 8.00 20.00
109 Joe Crawford AU/199 RC 5.00 12.00
110 Joey Dorsey JSY AU/499 RC 5.00 12.00
111 C.D-Roberts JSY AU/499 RC 5.00 12.00
112 Patrick Ewing Jr. JSY AU/499 RC 5.00 12.00
113 D.Gallinari AU/199 RC 12.00 30.00
114 J.R. Giddens JSY AU/499 RC 5.00 12.00
115 E.Gordon JSY AU/299 RC 12.00 30.00
116 Donte Greene JSY AU/499 RC 5.00 12.00
117 Malik Hairston AU/199 RC 5.00 12.00
118 Roy Hibbert JSY AU/499 RC 6.00 15.00
119 J.J. Hickson JSY AU/499 RC 5.00 12.00
120 George Hill JSY AU/499 RC 8.00 20.00
121 D.Jordan JSY AU/499 RC 20.00 50.00
122 Kosta Koufos JSY AU/499 RC 5.00 12.00
123 Courtney Lee JSY AU/499 RC 6.00 15.00
124 B.Lopez JSY AU/299 RC 10.00 25.00
125 Robin Lopez JSY AU/499 RC 6.00 15.00
126 Kevin Love JSY AU/299 RC 40.00 100.00
127 O.J. Mayo JSY AU/299 RC 6.00 15.00
128 J.McGee JSY AU/499 RC 8.00 20.00
129 A.Randolph JSY AU/499 RC 5.00 12.00
130 D.Rose JSY AU/299 RC 200.00 500.00
131 Brandon Rush JSY AU/299 RC 5.00 12.00
132 Walter Sharpe JSY AU/499 RC 5.00 12.00
133 Sean Singletary AU/199 RC 5.00 12.00
134 M.Speights JSY AU/499 RC 6.00 15.00
135 Mike Taylor AU/199 RC 5.00 12.00
136 J.Thompson JSY AU/499 RC 5.00 12.00
137 Kyle Weaver JSY AU/499 RC 5.00 12.00
138 Sonny Weems JSY AU/499 RC 5.00 12.00
139 Westbrook JSY AU/299 RC 400.00 800.00
140 D.J. White JSY AU/499 RC 5.00 12.00
147 R.Fernandez JSY AU/499 RC 6.00 15.00

2008-09 SP Authentic Chirography

COMBINED AUTO ODDS 1:12
CAD Adrian Dantley 5.00 12.00
CAE Alex English 5.00 12.00
CAG Artis Gilmore 5.00 12.00
CBD Brad Daugherty 5.00 12.00
CBL Bob Lanier 5.00 12.00
CBS Bill Sharman 8.00 20.00
CBW Buck Williams 5.00 12.00
CDD Darryl Dawkins 6.00 15.00
CDR Dennis Rodman 20.00 50.00
CDT David Thompson 6.00 15.00
CDW Don Watts 5.00 12.00
CGG George Gervin 8.00 20.00
CGM George McGinnis 5.00 12.00
CGO Gail Goodrich 10.00 25.00
CGR Glen Rice 15.00 30.00
CJE Julius Erving 40.00 100.00
CJH John Havlicek 30.00 80.00
CJS John Salley 6.00 15.00
CLB Larry Bird 50.00 100.00
CMC Maurice Cheeks 5.00 12.00
CMJ Michael Jordan 350.00 550.00
CNT Nate Thurmond 6.00 15.00
CRB Rick Barry 8.00 20.00
CRO David Robinson 40.00 80.00
CRP Robert Parish 10.00 25.00
CSJ Sam Jones 12.00 30.00
CSK Steve Kerr 8.00 20.00
CTH Tom Heinsohn 15.00 40.00
CTS Tom Sanders 8.00 20.00
CVD Vlade Divac 15.00 40.00
CWF Walt Frazier 12.00 30.00
CWI Dominique Wilkins 15.00 30.00
CXM Xavier McDaniel 6.00 15.00

2008-09 SP Authentic Destination Stardom

COMPLETE SET (30) 15.00 40.00
STATED ODDS 1:3
DS1 Derrick Rose 6.00 15.00
DS2 Michael Beasley .75 2.00
DS3 O.J. Mayo .60 1.50
DS4 Russell Westbrook 10.00 25.00
DS5 Kevin Love 1.50 4.00
DS6 Danilo Gallinari 1.25 3.00
DS7 Eric Gordon 1.25 3.00
DS8 Joe Alexander .50 1.25
DS9 D.J. Augustin .75 2.00
DS10 Brook Lopez 1.00 2.50
DS11 Jerryd Bayless .60 1.50
DS12 Jason Thompson .50 1.25
DS13 Brandon Rush .50 1.25
DS14 Anthony Randolph .50 1.25
DS15 Robin Lopez .60 1.50
DS16 Marreese Speights .60 1.50
DS17 Roy Hibbert .60 1.50
DS18 Javale McGee .75 2.00
DS19 J.J. Hickson .50 1.25
DS20 Alexis Ajinca .50 1.25
DS21 Courtney Lee .60 1.50
DS22 D.J. White .50 1.25
DS23 J.R. Giddens .50 1.25
DS24 Joey Dorsey .50 1.25
DS25 Sonny Weems .50 1.25
DS26 Mario Chalmers .75 2.00
DS27 Sun Yue 1.00 2.50
DS28 Rudy Fernandez .60 1.50
DS29 Marc Gasol 1.50 4.00
DS30 Hamed Haddadi .75 2.00

2008-09 SP Authentic Limited Memorabilia

SPLAD Darrell Arthur 2.00 5.00
SPLAR Anthony Randolph 1.50 4.00
SPLBL Brook Lopez 3.00 8.00
SPLBR Brandon Rush 1.50 4.00
SPLCD Chris Douglas-Roberts 1.50 4.00
SPLDA D.J. Augustin 2.50 6.00
SPLDG Donte Greene 1.50 4.00
SPLDJ DeAndre Jordan 3.00 8.00
SPLDR Derrick Rose 15.00 40.00
SPLEG Eric Gordon 4.00 10.00
SPLGH George Hill 2.50 6.00
SPLJA Joe Alexander 1.50 4.00
SPLJB Jerryd Bayless 2.00 5.00
SPLJD Joey Dorsey 1.50 4.00
SPLJG J.R. Giddens 1.50 4.00
SPLJH J.J. Hickson 1.50 4.00
SPLJM Javale McGee 2.50 6.00
SPLJT Jason Thompson 1.50 4.00
SPLKK Kosta Koufos 1.50 4.00
SPLKL Kevin Love 5.00 12.00
SPLKW Kyle Weaver 1.50 4.00
SPLMB Michael Beasley 2.50 6.00
SPLMC Mario Chalmers 2.50 6.00
SPLMS Marreese Speights 2.00 5.00
SPLOM O.J. Mayo 2.00 5.00
SPLRA Ryan Anderson 2.00 5.00
SPLRF Rudy Fernandez 2.00 5.00
SPLRL Robin Lopez 2.00 5.00
SPLSW Sonny Weems 1.50 4.00
SPLWS Walter Sharpe 1.50 4.00

2008-09 SP Authentic Profiles

COMPLETE SET (60) 30.00 60.00
STATED ODDS 1:3
AP1 Charles Oakley .75 2.00
AP2 Dominique Wilkins 1.25 3.00
AP3 James Worthy .75 2.00
AP4 Joe Dumars .75 2.00
AP5 Julius Erving 2.00 5.00
AP6 Kareem Abdul-Jabbar 2.00 5.00
AP7 Larry Bird 2.50 6.00
AP8 Larry Johnson .75 2.00
AP9 Magic Johnson 2.50 6.00
AP10 Michael Jordan 6.00 15.00
AP11 Muggsy Bogues .60 1.50
AP12 Oscar Robertson .75 2.00

AP13 Rick Mahorn .50 1.25
AP14 Spud Webb .60 1.50
AP15 Vlade Divac .75 2.00
AP16 Al Horford .75 2.00
AP17 Amare Stoudemire .75 2.00
AP18 Carlos Boozer .60 1.50
AP19 Chris Bosh 1.00 2.50
AP20 David West .60 1.50
AP21 Dirk Nowitzki 2.00 5.00
AP22 Dwight Howard 1.00 2.50
AP23 Kevin Garnett 2.00 5.00
AP24 LeBron James 6.00 15.00
AP25 Pau Gasol 1.00 2.50
AP26 Rasheed Wallace 1.00 2.50
AP27 Shaquille O'Neal 2.50 6.00
AP28 Shawn Marion .75 2.00
AP29 Tim Duncan 2.00 5.00
AP30 Yao Ming 2.00 5.00
AP31 Allen Iverson 1.50 4.00
AP32 Baron Davis .75 2.00
AP33 Carmelo Anthony 1.00 2.50
AP34 Chauncey Billups 1.00 2.50
AP35 Chris Paul 1.50 4.00
AP36 Deron Williams .60 1.50
AP37 Dwyane Wade 1.50 4.00
AP38 Joe Johnson .75 2.00
AP39 Kevin Durant 3.00 8.00
AP40 Kobe Bryant 6.00 15.00
AP41 Paul Pierce 1.25 3.00
AP42 Steve Nash 1.50 4.00
AP43 Tony Parker 1.00 2.50
AP44 Tracy McGrady 1.25 3.00
AP45 Vince Carter 1.50 4.00
AP46 Derrick Rose 3.00 8.00
AP47 Michael Beasley .75 2.00
AP48 O.J. Mayo .60 1.50
AP49 Russell Westbrook 4.00 10.00
AP50 Kevin Love 1.50 4.00
AP51 Danilo Gallinari 1.25 3.00
AP52 Sun Yue 1.00 2.50
AP53 Jason Thompson .50 1.25
AP54 Eric Gordon 1.25 3.00
AP55 Rudy Fernandez .60 1.50
AP56 Marc Gasol 1.50 4.00
AP57 D.J. Augustin .75 2.00
AP58 Jerryd Bayless .60 1.50
AP59 Luc Richard Mbah A Moute .60 1.50
AP60 Hamed Haddadi .75 2.00

2008-09 SP Authentic Recruiting Class City Name

TOTAL PRINT RUNS LISTED
RCCBL Brook Lopez/13 30.00 80.00
RCCBW Bill Walker/26 8.00 20.00
RCCDA Darrell Arthur/34 8.00 20.00
RCCDG Danilo Gallinari/13 15.00 40.00
RCCDJ D.J. Augustin/16 10.00 25.00
RCCDR Derrick Rose/23 200.00 500.00
RCCDW D.J. White/38 8.00 20.00
RCCEG Eric Gordon/17 25.00 60.00
RCCGH George Hill/40 20.00 50.00
RCCJA Joe Alexander/24 8.00 20.00
RCCJB Jerryd Bayless/20 8.00 20.00
RCCJC Joe Crawford/34 8.00 20.00
RCCJG J.R. Giddens/26 8.00 20.00
RCCJH J.J. Hickson/36 8.00 20.00
RCCJM Javale McGee/31 25.00 60.00
RCCJT Jason Thompson/25 8.00 20.00
RCCKL Kevin Love/48 75.00 200.00
RCCMB Michael Beasley/17 12.00 30.00
RCCMS Marreese Speights/30 8.00 20.00
RCCOM O.J. Mayo/35 10.00 25.00
RCCPE Patrick Ewing Jr./37 8.00 20.00
RCCRA Ryan Anderson/29 8.00 20.00
RCCRH Roy Hibbert/37 10.00 25.00
RCCRL Robin Lopez/27 12.00 30.00
RCCRW Russell Westbrook/19 200.00 500.00
RCCSS Sean Singletary/27 8.00 20.00
RCCWS Walter Sharpe/14 8.00 20.00

2008-09 SP Authentic Recruiting Class Full Name

TOTAL PRINT RUNS LISTED
RCNAR Anthony Randolph/75 8.00 20.00
RCNBR Brandon Rush/66 8.00 20.00
RCNBW Bill Walker/80 8.00 20.00
RCNDA Darrell Arthur/78 8.00 20.00
RCNDJ D.J. Augustin/80 8.00 20.00
RCNDR Derrick Rose/66 200.00 500.00
RCNDW D.J. White/77 8.00 20.00
RCNGH George Hill/80 15.00 40.00
RCNJA Joe Alexander/72 8.00 20.00
RCNJB Jerryd Bayless/65 8.00 20.00
RCNJC Joe Crawford/77 8.00 20.00
RCNJG J.R. Giddens/81 8.00 20.00
RCNJM Javale McGee/77 15.00 40.00
RCNJT Jason Thompson/65 8.00 20.00
RCNKL Kevin Love/18 75.00 200.00
RCNMB Michael Beasley/70 10.00 25.00
RCNMS Marreese Speights/80 8.00 20.00
RCNOM O.J. Mayo/30 10.00 25.00
RCNPE Patrick Ewing Jr./84 8.00 20.00
RCNRA Ryan Anderson/84 8.00 20.00
RCNRH Roy Hibbert/70 10.00 25.00
RCNRL Robin Lopez/80 12.00 30.00
RCNRW Russell Westbrook/84 200.00 500.00
RCNSS Sean Singletary/84 8.00 20.00
RCNWS Walter Sharpe/84 8.00 20.00

2008-09 SP Authentic Sign of the Times Dual

PRINT RUN 50 SER.#'d SETS
SDAR L.Aldridge/B.Roy 15.00 40.00
SDAS L.Amundson/J.Smith 6.00 15.00
SDBB S.Battier/R.Brewer 6.00 15.00
SDBW M.Belinelli/C.Watson 6.00 15.00
SDCC Conley Jr./Conley Sr. 8.00 20.00
SDCO E.Okafor/T.Chandler 6.00 15.00
SDDG K.Durant/J.Green 40.00 100.00
SDFF R.Felton/R.Foye 6.00 15.00
SDGC R.Gay/M.Conley 6.00 15.00
SDGH A.Horford/K.Garnett 25.00 50.00
SDHA W.Herrmann/A.Afflalo 6.00 15.00
SDHM A.Horford/J.Moon 6.00 15.00
SDIS R.Stuckey/A.Iguodala 10.00 25.00
SDJS J.Boone/S.Williams 6.00 15.00
SDJW R.Jefferson/M.Williams 6.00 15.00
SDKB C.Billups/J.Kidd 15.00 30.00
SDKJ C.Kaman/A.Jefferson 6.00 15.00
SDKK C.Karl/G.Karl 6.00 15.00
SDMI A.Iguodala/A.Miller 6.00 15.00
SDOB L.Odom/C.Boozer 8.00 20.00
SDPA R.Allen/P.Pierce 60.00 150.00
SDPH T.Price/D.Howard 20.00 40.00
SDPP T.Parker/C.Paul 75.00 200.00
SDSB A.Bynum/A.Stoudemire 12.00 30.00
SDSV J.Smith/S.Vujacic 6.00 15.00
SDTS A.Thornton/L.Scola 6.00 15.00
SDVR S.Vujacic/R.Rondo 15.00 40.00
SDWG D.West/R.Gay 10.00 25.00
SDWL L.Walton/C.Landry 6.00 15.00

2008-09 SP Authentic Varsity Letters Legends City Name

TOTAL PRINT RUNS LISTED
VLBD Brad Daugherty/18* 15.00 40.00
VLBL Bob Lanier/14* 30.00 60.00
VLBR Bill Russell/13* 500.00 1,000.00
VLDR Dennis Rodman/12* 200.00 400.00
VLDW Don Watts/13* 15.00 40.00
VLMP Mark Price/18* 150.00 300.00
VLRB Rick Barry/19* 40.00 80.00
VLRM Rick Mahorn/14* 25.00 60.00
VLRO David Robinson/15* 100.00 200.00
VLSJ Sam Jones/13* 50.00 120.00
VLTC Tom Chambers/11* 25.00 50.00

2008-09 SP Authentic Varsity Letters Legends Full Name

TOTAL PRINT RUNS LISTED
VLBD Brad Daugherty/39* 10.00 25.00
VLBL Bob Lanier/18* 20.00 40.00
VLBR Bill Russell/22* 500.00 1,000.00
VLDR Dennis Rodman/24* 25.00 60.00
VLDW Don Watts/39* 12.00 30.00
VLGR Glen Rice/24* 75.00 150.00
VLLJ Larry Johnson/24* 100.00 200.00
VLMB Muggsy Bogues/36* 60.00 150.00
VLMJ Michael Jordan/26* 900.00 1,500.00
VLMP Mark Price/36* 125.00 250.00
VLRB Rick Barry/27* 30.00 60.00
VLRO David Robinson/26* 75.00 150.00
VLSJ Sam Jones/24* 60.00 120.00
VLTC Tom Chambers/33* 15.00 40.00

2008-09 SP Authentic Varsity Letters Veterans City Name

TOTAL PRINT RUNS LISTED
VVAB Andrew Bogut/14* 15.00 30.00
VVAH Al Horford/39* 15.00 30.00
VVAM Alonzo Mourning/27* 100.00 200.00
VVAT Alando Tucker/48* 15.00 30.00
VVBG Ben Gordon/23* 25.00 50.00
VVCK Chris Kaman/17* 15.00 30.00
VVCL Carl Landry/14* 25.00 60.00
VVCP Chris Paul/10* 150.00 400.00
VVDC Daequan Cook/42* 15.00 30.00
VVDH Dwight Howard/22* 50.00 120.00
VVJA Antawn Jamison/17* 30.00 60.00
VVJF Jordan Farmar/28* 15.00 30.00
VVKB Kobe Bryant/16* 500.00 1,000.00
VVKD Kevin Durant/19* 150.00 300.00
VVKG Kevin Garnett/13* 75.00 150.00
VVLJ LeBron James/18* 1,000.00 2,000.00
VVLW Luke Walton/28* 15.00 30.00
VVMC Mike Conley Jr./16* 20.00 50.00
VVMW Mario West/32* 15.00 30.00
VVQR Quentin Richardson/42* 15.00 30.00
VVRJ Richard Jefferson/29* 15.00 30.00
VVRS Ramon Sessions/39* 15.00 30.00
VVST Rodney Stuckey/21* 20.00 50.00
VVSV Sasha Vujacic/44* 20.00 40.00

2008-09 SP Authentic Varsity Letters Veterans Full Name

TOTAL PRINT RUN LISTED
VVAH Al Horford/81* 6.00 15.00
VVAM Alonzo Mourning/56* 75.00 150.00
VVAT Alando Tucker/84* 6.00 15.00
VVBD Baron Davis/60* 6.00 15.00
VVBG Ben Gordon/63* 20.00 40.00
VVBY Andrew Bynum/55* 15.00 40.00
VVCK Chris Kaman/60* 6.00 15.00
VVCL Carl Landry/90* 15.00 30.00
VVCP Chris Paul/54* 60.00 150.00
VVDC Daequan Cook/88* 6.00 15.00
VVDH Dwight Howard/60* 30.00 80.00
VVDW David West/72* 6.00 15.00
VVJA Antawn Jamison/65* 15.00 30.00
VVJF Jordan Farmar/84* 20.00 40.00
VVKB Kobe Bryant/20* 500.00 1,000.00
VVKD Kevin Durant/22* 200.00 350.00
VVKG Kevin Garnett/24* 75.00 150.00
VVLJ LeBron James/22* 1,000.00 2,000.00
VVLW Luke Walton/60* 6.00 15.00
VVMC Mike Conley Jr./60* 15.00 40.00
VVMW Mario West/72* 6.00 15.00
VVQR Quentin Richardson/85* 6.00 15.00
VVRJ Richard Jefferson/60* 6.00 15.00
VVRS Ramon Sessions/91* 6.00 15.00
VVST Rodney Stuckey/78* 12.00 30.00
VVSV Sasha Vujacic/84* 6.00 15.00

2008-09 SP Authentic Vital Signs

COMBINED AUTO ODDS 1:12
VSAH Al Horford 8.00 20.00
VSBG Ben Gordon 5.00 12.00
VSDF Derek Fisher 5.00 12.00
VSDH Dwight Howard 15.00 40.00
VSDL David Lee 4.00 10.00
VSDW David West 5.00 12.00
VSJB Josh Boone 4.00 10.00
VSJG Jeff Green 5.00 12.00
VSKB Kobe Bryant 800.00 1,500.00
VSKD Kevin Durant 100.00 250.00
VSKG Kevin Garnett 100.00 200.00
VSLJ LeBron James 800.00 1,500.00
VSLW Luke Walton 4.00 10.00
VSRF Rudy Fernandez 10.00 25.00
VSRG Rudy Gay 5.00 12.00
VSRS Rodney Stuckey 4.00 10.00
VSSE Ramon Sessions 4.00 10.00
VSTC Tyson Chandler 5.00 12.00

2010-11 SP Authentic

COMP.SET w/o RCs (100) 8.00 20.00
AU PRINT RUN 149 TO 299 SER.#'d SETS
MOST AU PRINT RUNS BASED ON LAST NAME
TOTAL PRINT RUN LISTED WITH ASTERISK
1 Michael Jordan 2.50 6.00
2 Jerry West .60 1.50
3 Bill Walton .50 1.25
4 Bill Russell 1.00 2.50
5 David Robinson .50 1.25
6 Hakeem Olajuwon .60 1.50
7 Alonzo Mourning .50 1.25
8 Christian Laettner .30 .75
9 Magic Johnson 1.25 3.00
10 George Gervin .50 1.25
11 Clyde Drexler .50 1.25
12 Dominique Wilkins .50 1.25
13 John Stockton .60 1.50
14 Larry Bird 1.25 3.00
15 James Worthy .40 1.00
16 Julius Erving .60 1.50
17 Bruce Bowen .20 .50
18 Phil Ford .30 .75
19 Bobby Jones .25 .60
20 B.J. Armstrong .30 .75
21 Rick Barry .40 1.00
22 Elgin Baylor .60 1.50
23 LeBron James 2.50 6.00
24 Jim Jackson .20 .50
25 Larry Brown .30 .75
26 Bill Cartwright .30 .75
27 Cynthia Cooper .40 1.00
28 Walter Davis .20 .50
29 Adrian Dantley .30 .75
30 Brad Daugherty .25 .60
31 Hubert Davis .20 .50
32 Vlade Divac .30 .75
33 Rick Fox .25 .60
34 Walt Frazier .50 1.25
35 Gail Goodrich .30 .75
36 Darrell Griffith .20 .50
37 Anfernee Hardaway .75 2.00
38 James Harden .75 2.00
39 Robert Horry .30 .75
40 John Havlicek .60 1.50
41 Steve Alford .30 .75
42 Rod Hundley .30 .75
43 Lauren Jackson .40 1.00
44 Mark Jackson .25 .60
45 Avery Johnson .25 .60
46 Larry Johnson .40 1.00
47 Rex Walters .20 .50
48 Shawn Kemp .50 1.25
49 Toni Kukoc .30 .75
50 Bill Laimbeer .25 .60
51 Lonnie Shelton .20 .50
52 Freddie Lewis .20 .50
53 George Lynch .30 .75
54 Danny Manning .25 .60
55 Sam Perkins .25 .60
56 Greg Anthony .20 .50
57 Bill Sharman .30 .75
58 Candace Parker .75 2.00
59 Terry Porter .20 .50
60 Glen Rice .30 .75
61 Micheal Ray Richardson .25 .60
62 Mateen Cleaves .25 .60
63 Dennis Rodman .60 1.50
64 Derrick Rose .60 1.50
65 Pat Riley .30 .75
66 Calbert Cheaney .25 .60
67 Cazzie Russell .25 .60
68 Bobby Hurley .30 .75
69 Jack Sikma .25 .60
70 Sam Cassell .25 .60
71 Jerry Sloan .30 .75
72 Kenny Smith .25 .60
73 J.R. Reid .20 .50
74 Tim Hardaway .40 1.00
75 David Thompson .30 .75
76 Reggie Theus .30 .75
77 Rudy Tomjanovich .25 .60
78 Chet Walker .25 .60
79 Russell Westbrook .50 1.25
80 Marion Jones .40 1.00
81 Steve Fisher .40 1.00
82 Tom Izzo .30 .75
83 Roy Williams .60 1.50
84 Bill Self .40 1.00
85 Jim Boeheim .40 1.00
86 Gary Williams .40 1.00
87 Mike Montgomery .30 .75
88 Jim Calhoun .40 1.00
89 Billy Donovan .30 .75
90 Mark Few .30 .75
91 Ben Howland .30 .75
92 Thad Matta .30 .75
93 Bruce Pearl 2.00 5.00
94 Bob Huggins .30 .75
95 Bo Ryan .30 .75
96 Tubby Smith .30 .75
97 Sean Miller .30 .75
98 Rick Majerus .30 .75
99 Jay Wright .30 .75
100 Jamie Dixon .30 .75
201 Hassan Whiteside AU/2691* 15.00 40.00
202 Terrico White AU/1495* 6.00 15.00
203 Andy Rautins AU/1794* 6.00 15.00
204 Derrick Favors AU/894* 12.00 30.00
205 Al-Farouq Aminu AU/745* 6.00 15.00
206 Cole Aldrich AU/1043* 10.00 25.00
207 D.Cousins AU/1043* 20.00 50.00
208 Ed Davis AU/745* 4.00 10.00
209 H.N'Diaye AU/1794* 5.00 12.00
210 Greg Monroe AU/894* 8.00 20.00
211 Brian Zoubek AU/894* 8.00 20.00
212 Manny Harris AU/1794* 5.00 12.00
213 Damion James AU/745* 3.00 8.00
214 S.Robinson AU/1192* 3.00 8.00
215 Armon Johnson AU/2093* 3.00 8.00
216 Craig Brackins AU/2093* 3.00 8.00
217 Gani Lawal AU/1495* 3.00 8.00
218 Luke Babbitt AU/2093* 3.00 8.00
219 D.Jones AU/1495* 3.00 8.00
220 Xavier Henry AU/745* 3.00 8.00
221 Solomon Alabi AU/1794* 3.00 8.00
222 J.Crawford AU/2392* 3.00 8.00
223 Eric Bledsoe AU/1043* 20.00 50.00
224 Jerome Jordan AU/894* 5.00 12.00
225 J.Anderson AU/2392* 3.00 8.00
226 Dexter Pittman AU/2093* 3.00 8.00
227 Da'Sean Butler AU/894* 8.00 20.00
228 Trevor Booker AU/1794* 6.00 15.00
229 Ekpe Udoh AU/596* 3.00 8.00
230 Sherron Collins AU/2093* 3.00 8.00
231 Deon Thompson AU/1192* 5.00 12.00
232 Gordon Hayward AU/1043* 25.00 60.00
233 Scottie Reynolds AU/1192* 5.00 12.00
234 J.Varnado AU/1043* EXCH 3.00 8.00
235 Q.Pondexter AU/2691* 8.00 20.00
236 Luke Harangody AU/2691* 3.00 8.00
237 Paul George AU/894* 30.00 80.00
238 Greivis Vasquez AU/2093* 6.00 15.00
239 Aubrey Coleman AU/1043* 5.00 12.00
240 Lazar Hayward AU/1794* 3.00 8.00
241 Elliot Williams AU/2392* 3.00 8.00
242 Devin Ebanks AU/1794* 3.00 8.00

2010-11 SP Authentic By The Letter Legend Last Name

STATED PRINT RUN 30 TO 149 SER.#'d SETS
MOST PRINT RUNS BASED ON LAST NAME
TOTAL PRINT RUN LISTED WITH ASTERISK
LAJ Avery Johnson/525* 10.00 25.00
LAM Alonzo Mourning/240* 50.00 125.00
LBC Bill Cartwright/300* 10.00 25.00
LBJ B.J. Armstrong/1341* 10.00 25.00
LBL Bill Laimbeer/1192* 10.00 25.00
LBS Bill Sharman/210* 15.00 40.00
LBW Bill Walton/180* 15.00 40.00
LCA Sam Cassell/1043* 10.00 25.00
LCC Cynthia Cooper/180* 10.00 25.00
LCL Christian Laettner/600* 10.00 25.00
LCP Candace Parker/894* 20.00 50.00
LCW Chet Walker/450* 10.00 25.00
LDA Danny Manning/210* 30.00 80.00
LDR Derrick Rose/596* 75.00 150.00
LDT David Thompson/240* 10.00 25.00
LEB Elgin Baylor/180* 15.00 40.00
LGG Gail Goodrich/240* 15.00 40.00
LHO Hakeem Olajuwon/240* 30.00 80.00
LJE Julius Erving/180* 50.00 120.00
LJH James Harden/180* 20.00 50.00
LJJ Jim Jackson/894* 10.00 25.00
LJR J.R. Reid/596* 10.00 25.00
LJS Jerry Sloan/375* 12.00 30.00
LKS Kenny Smith/150* 10.00 25.00
LLB Larry Bird/120* 50.00 120.00
LLJ LeBron James/150* 800.00 1,500.00
LMJ Michael Jordan/180* 500.00 1,000.00
LRF Rick Fox/90* 20.00 50.00
LRI Glen Rice/120* 30.00 80.00
LRO David Robinson/240* 60.00 150.00
LRU Bill Russell/210* 500.00 1,000.00
LRW R.Westbrook/1341* 40.00 100.00
LRY Robert Horry/894* 15.00 40.00
LSA Steve Alford/894* 10.00 25.00
LSC Sidney Crosby/180* 150.00 300.00
LTP Terry Porter/450* 12.00 30.00

2010-11 SP Authentic Chirography

STATED ODDS 1:128 PACKS
CAH Anfernee Hardaway 50.00 120.00
CCP Candace Parker 10.00 25.00
CDE DeMarcus Cousins 20.00 50.00
CDF Derrick Favors 15.00 40.00
CHR Robert Horry 10.00 25.00
CJJ Jim Jackson 8.00 20.00
CRF Rick Fox 8.00 20.00

2010-11 SP Authentic Holo F/X

COMPLETE SET (42) 30.00 80.00
STATED ODDS 1:6 PACKS
1 Derrick Rose 2.00 5.00
2 Walt Frazier 1.50 4.00
3 Christian Laettner 1.00 2.50
4 Robert Horry 1.00 2.50
5 Anfernee Hardaway 2.50 6.00
6 Julius Erving 2.00 5.00
7 Larry Bird 4.00 10.00
8 Jim Jackson .60 1.50
9 Elgin Baylor 2.00 5.00
10 Tim Hardaway 1.25 3.00
11 Dennis Rodman 2.00 5.00
12 Kenny Smith .75 2.00
13 Jerry West 2.00 5.00
14 Bill Russell 3.00 8.00
15 Xavier Henry .60 1.50
16 Greg Anthony .60 1.50
17 Magic Johnson 4.00 10.00
18 George Gervin 1.50 4.00
19 Hakeem Olajuwon 2.00 5.00
20 David Robinson 2.00 5.00
21 LeBron James 8.00 20.00
22 Ed Davis .75 2.00
23 Michael Jordan 12.00 30.00
24 Greg Monroe .75 2.00
25 Bill Walton 1.50 4.00
26 Cazzie Russell .75 2.00
27 Alonzo Mourning 1.50 4.00
28 Rick Fox .75 2.00
29 Candace Parker 2.50 6.00
30 Danny Manning .75 2.00
31 Clyde Drexler 1.50 4.00
32 Derrick Favors 1.00 2.50
33 Al-Farouq Aminu .75 2.00
34 DeMarcus Cousins 2.00 5.00
35 Larry Johnson 1.00 2.50
36 James Worthy 1.25 3.00
37 David Thompson 1.00 2.50
38 Jim Boeheim 1.25 3.00
39 Bill Self 1.00 2.50
40 Roy Williams 2.00 5.00
41 Ben Howland 1.00 2.50
42 Tom Izzo 1.00 2.50

2010-11 SP Authentic Holo F/X Die Cuts

*HOLO DC: 2X TO 5X BASE HI
STATED ODDS 1:144 PACKS
11 Dennis Rodman 12.50 30.00
21 LeBron James 50.00 120.00
23 Michael Jordan 100.00 200.00
27 Alonzo Mourning 15.00 40.00

2010-11 SP Authentic Jordan Brand Classic

JCDA Ed Davis 1.50 4.00
JCDE Devin Ebanks 1.25 3.00
JCEB Devin Ebanks 1.25 3.00
JCED Ed Davis 1.50 4.00
JCGM Greg Monroe 1.50 4.00
JCMG Greg Monroe 1.50 4.00
JCMO Greg Monroe 1.50 4.00

2010-11 SP Authentic Michael Jordan Supreme Court Floor

COMMON FLOOR (1-10) 12.00 30.00
UNCOMMON FLOOR (11-20) 15.00 40.00
RARE FLOOR (21-30) 20.00 50.00
ULTRA RARE FLOOR (31-40) 40.00 100.00
COMBINED ODDS 1:48 PACKS

2010-11 SP Authentic Sign of the Times

STATED ODDS 1:12 PACKS
SAD Adrian Dantley 6.00 15.00
SBC Bobby Cremins 6.00 15.00
SBD Billy Donovan 40.00 100.00
SBH Bob Huggins 30.00 80.00
SBW Bill Walton 30.00 80.00
SCB Craig Brackins 3.00 8.00
SDM Danny Manning 8.00 20.00
SDR Derrick Rose 75.00 200.00
SDW Donald Williams 3.00 8.00
SEB Elgin Baylor 20.00 50.00
SFL Freddie Lewis 3.00 8.00
SGE George Gervin 20.00 50.00
SGL Gani Lawal 3.00 8.00
SHA John Havlicek 100.00 250.00
SJA James Anderson 3.00 8.00
SJD Jamie Dixon 8.00 20.00
SJE Julius Erving 125.00 300.00
SJO Magic Johnson 125.00 300.00
SJS Jack Sikma 3.00 8.00
SLB Larry Bird 150.00 400.00
SLE LeBron James 1,500.00 3,000.00
SLJ LeBron James 1,500.00 3,000.00
SMC Michael Cooper 8.00 20.00
SMF Mark Few 40.00 100.00
SMI Michael Jordan 2,500.00 5,000.00
SMJ Michael Jordan 2,500.00 5,000.00
SMM Mike Montgomery 3.00 8.00
SMR Micheal Ray Richardson 3.00 8.00
SRM Rick Majerus 20.00 50.00
SRW Russell Westbrook 100.00 250.00
SRX Rex Walters 3.00 8.00
SSC Sam Cassell 3.00 8.00
SSK Shawn Kemp 30.00 80.00
SSP Sam Perkins 6.00 15.00
STB Trevor Booker 3.00 8.00
STK Toni Kukoc 12.00 30.00
STS Tubby Smith 12.00 30.00
SWE Bruce Weber 5.00 12.00
SWF Walt Frazier 20.00 50.00

2011-12 SP Authentic

COMPLETE SET (100) 40.00 100.00
1 Michael Jordan 2.00 5.00
2 LeBron James 2.50 6.00
3 Grant Hill .50 1.25
4 Walt Frazier .50 1.25
5 Anfernee Hardaway .75 2.00
6 Alonzo Mourning .50 1.25
7 Julius Erving .75 2.00
8 David Robinson .60 1.50
9 Russell Westbrook .50 1.25
10 Magic Johnson 1.25 3.00
11 Derrick Rose .60 1.50
12 Hakeem Olajuwon .60 1.50
13 Clyde Drexler .50 1.25
14 James Worthy .50 1.25
15 Larry Bird 1.25 3.00
16 Tristan Thompson .30 .75
17 Jimmer Fredette .30 .75
18 Alec Burks .30 .75
19 Bismack Biyombo .25 .60
20 Justin Harper .20 .50
21 Demetri McCamey .25 .60
22 Nolan Smith .30 .75
23 Klay Thompson 8.00 20.00
24 Nikola Vucevic .30 .75
25 JaJuan Johnson .20 .50
26 Reggie Jackson .25 .60
27 Kawhi Leonard 8.00 20.00
28 Tobias Harris .50 1.25
29 MarShon Brooks .25 .60
30 Tyler Honeycutt .20 .50
31 Marcus Morris .30 .75
32 Markieff Morris .30 .75
33 Norris Cole .25 .60
34 Cory Joseph .25 .60
35 Shelvin Mack .20 .50
36 Jordan Williams .20 .50
37 Chandler Parsons .25 .60
38 Chris Singleton .25 .60
39 Jonas Valanciunas .40 1.00
40 Donatas Motiejunas .25 .60
41 Jon Leuer .25 .60
42 Malcolm Lee .25 .60
43 Charles Jenkins .25 .60
44 Travis Leslie .25 .60
45 Josh Selby .25 .60
46 Keith Benson .25 .60
47 E'Twaun Moore .40 1.00
48 Matt Howard .30 .75
49 Scotty Hopson .20 .50
50 Durrell Summers .20 .50
51 LeBron James FX 5.00 12.00
52 Michael Jordan FX 5.00 12.00
53 Alonzo Mourning FX 1.00 2.50
54 Larry Johnson FX .75 2.00
55 Magic Johnson FX 2.50 6.00
56 Clyde Drexler FX 1.00 2.50
57 Hakeem Olajuwon FX 1.25 3.00
58 John Havlicek FX 1.25 3.00
59 David Robinson FX 1.25 3.00
60 Julius Erving FX 1.50 4.00
61 Mark Jackson FX .50 1.25
62 Adrian Dantley FX .50 1.25
63 Dennis Rodman FX 1.50 4.00
64 Danny Manning FX .50 1.25
65 Gail Goodrich FX .60 1.50
66 Anfernee Hardaway FX 1.50 4.00
67 Glen Rice FX .60 1.50
68 Hal Greer FX .60 1.50
69 Derrick Rose FX 1.00 2.50
70 Grant Hill FX 1.00 2.50
71 Russell Westbrook FX 1.00 2.50
72 Bill Laimbeer FX .60 1.50
73 Walt Frazier FX 1.00 2.50
74 Bill Russell FX 2.00 5.00
75 James Worthy FX 1.00 2.50
76 Rick Barry FX .75 2.00
77 Jerry West FX 1.25 3.00
78 Larry Bird FX 2.50 6.00
79 Bill Walton FX 1.00 2.50
80 Elgin Baylor FX 1.00 2.50
81 David Thompson FX .60 1.50
82 Tim Hardaway FX .75 2.00
83 Jack Sikma FX .60 1.50
84 Chet Walker FX .50 1.25
85 Tristan Thompson FX .75 2.00
86 Jonas Valanciunas FX 1.00 2.50
87 Jimmer Fredette FX .75 2.00
88 Kawhi Leonard FX 75.00 200.00
89 Bismack Biyombo FX .60 1.50
90 Klay Thompson FX 25.00 60.00
91 Alec Burks FX .75 2.00
92 Markieff Morris FX .75 2.00
93 Marcus Morris FX .75 2.00
94 Nikola Vucevic FX .75 2.00
95 Chris Singleton FX .50 1.25
96 Tobias Harris FX 1.25 3.00
97 Nolan Smith FX .50 1.25
98 Reggie Jackson FX .60 1.50
99 JaJuan Johnson FX .50 1.25
100 Cory Joseph FX .60 1.50

2011-12 SP Authentic Autographs

FB FX PRINT RUN 3 TO 50 SER.#'d SETS
1 Michael Jordan 1,000.00 2,000.00
2 LeBron James 1,000.00 2,000.00
3 Grant Hill 100.00 200.00
4 Walt Frazier 12.00 30.00
5 Anfernee Hardaway 40.00 100.00
6 Alonzo Mourning 30.00 80.00
7 Julius Erving 40.00 100.00
8 David Robinson 30.00 80.00
9 Russell Westbrook 50.00 120.00
10 Magic Johnson 50.00 120.00
11 Derrick Rose 75.00 150.00
12 Hakeem Olajuwon 30.00 80.00
13 Clyde Drexler 40.00 100.00
14 James Worthy 15.00 40.00
15 Larry Bird 50.00 125.00
16 Tristan Thompson 6.00 15.00
17 Jimmer Fredette 6.00 15.00
18 Alec Burks 6.00 15.00
19 Bismack Biyombo 5.00 12.00
20 Justin Harper 4.00 10.00
21 Demetri McCamey 5.00 12.00
22 Nolan Smith 4.00 10.00
23 Klay Thompson 125.00 300.00
24 Nikola Vucevic 6.00 15.00
25 JaJuan Johnson 4.00 10.00
26 Reggie Jackson 5.00 12.00
27 Kawhi Leonard 125.00 300.00
28 Tobias Harris 10.00 25.00
29 MarShon Brooks 5.00 12.00
30 Tyler Honeycutt 4.00 10.00
31 Marcus Morris 6.00 15.00
32 Markieff Morris 6.00 15.00
33 Norris Cole 5.00 12.00
34 Cory Joseph 5.00 12.00
35 Shelvin Mack 4.00 10.00
36 Jordan Williams 4.00 10.00
37 Chandler Parsons 5.00 12.00
38 Chris Singleton 5.00 12.00
39 Jonas Valanciunas 8.00 20.00
41 Jon Leuer 5.00 12.00
42 Malcolm Lee 5.00 12.00
43 Charles Jenkins 5.00 12.00
44 Travis Leslie 5.00 12.00
45 Josh Selby 5.00 12.00
46 Keith Benson 5.00 12.00
47 E'Twaun Moore 8.00 20.00
48 Matt Howard 4.00 10.00
49 Scotty Hopson 4.00 10.00
50 Durrell Summers 4.00 10.00
62 Adrian Dantley FX/50 5.00 12.00
72 Bill Laimbeer FX/50 6.00 15.00
82 Tim Hardaway FX/50 10.00 25.00
83 Jack Sikma FX/50 5.00 12.00
84 Chet Walker FX/50 5.00 12.00
85 Tristan Thompson FX/50 8.00 20.00
86 Jonas Valanciunas FX/50 10.00 25.00
87 Jimmer Fredette FX/50 8.00 20.00
88 Kawhi Leonard FX/50 150.00 400.00
89 Bismack Biyombo FX/50 6.00 15.00
90 Klay Thompson FX/50 75.00 200.00
91 Alec Burks FX/50 8.00 20.00
92 Markieff Morris FX/50 8.00 20.00
93 Marcus Morris FX/50 8.00 20.00
95 Chris Singleton FX/50 5.00 12.00
96 Tobias Harris FX/50 12.00 30.00
97 Nolan Smith FX/50 6.00 15.00
98 Reggie Jackson FX/50 6.00 15.00
99 JaJuan Johnson FX/50 5.00 12.00
100 Cory Joseph FX/50 6.00 15.00

2011-12 SP Authentic Autographs Gold

STATED PRINT RUN 3 TO 25 SER.#'d SETS
27 Kawhi Leonard/25 1,000.00 2,000.00
28 Tobias Harris/25 25.00 60.00

2011-12 SP Authentic By The Letter

STATED PRINT RUN 5 TO 100 SER.#'d SETS
TOTAL PRINT RUN LISTED WITH ASTERISK
BLAH Anfernee Hardaway/35* 40.00 80.00
BLAM Alonzo Mourning/50* 40.00 100.00
BLBD Billy Donovan/210* 10.00 25.00
BLBL Bill Laimbeer/675* 6.00 15.00
BLBR Bill Russell/15* 1,000.00 2,000.00
BLCD Clyde Drexler/35* 40.00 100.00
BLCL Christian Laettner/400* 12.00 30.00
BLDM Danny Manning/150* 8.00 20.00
BLDR Derrick Rose/35* 60.00 120.00
BLDT David Thompson/175* 10.00 25.00
BLGA Greg Anthony/400* 6.00 15.00
BLGG Gail Goodrich/40* 12.00 30.00
BLGH Grant Hill/60* 50.00 120.00
BLHO Hakeem Olajuwon/35* 40.00 100.00
BLJE Julius Erving/25* 50.00 120.00
BLJW Jay Wright/135* 8.00 20.00
BLLB Larry Bird/60* 75.00 150.00
BLLJ LeBron James/345* 1,000.00 2,000.00
BLMB Mike Brey/225* 8.00 20.00
BLMF Mark Few/245* 12.00 30.00
BLMG Magic Johnson/65* 60.00 120.00
BLMJ Michael Jordan/299* 400.00 800.00
BLRB Rick Barry/50* 20.00 50.00
BLRO David Robinson/20* 60.00 150.00
BLRW Russell Westbrook/300* 60.00 150.00
BLRY Bo Ryan/225* 20.00 50.00
BLSF Steve Fisher/200* 6.00 15.00
BLTH Tim Hardaway/400* 10.00 25.00
BLWA Bill Walton/40* 20.00 50.00
BLWE Jerry West/60* 50.00 125.00
BLWF Walt Frazier/80* 12.00 30.00
BLAD1 Adrian Dantley D,N/50* 6.00 15.00
BLAD2 A.Dantley A,E,M,O,R,T/350* 6.00 15.00
BLBC1 B.Cartwright A,C,R,N,S/225* 6.00 15.00
BLBC2 B.Cartwright F,O,I/150* 6.00 15.00
BLBH1 Ben Howland U/15* 8.00 20.00
BLBH2 B.Howland A,C,L/90* 6.00 15.00
BLCR1 Cazzie Russell M/25* 6.00 15.00
BLCR2 C.Russell A,C,G,H,I,N/250* 6.00 15.00
BLCW1 Chet Walker B,Y/20* 6.00 15.00
BLCW2 C.Walker A,D,E,L,R/125* 6.00 15.00
BLDG1 Darrell Griffith V/25* 8.00 20.00
BLDG2 D.Griffith E,I,L,O,S,U/675* 6.00 15.00
BLEB1 Elgin Baylor E,T/100* 12.00 30.00
BLEB2 Elgin Baylor A,L,S/225* 12.00 30.00
BLFL1 Freddie Lewis/100* 6.00 15.00
BLFL2 F.Lewis A,E,I,N,O,R,S,T/550* 6.00 15.00
BLGR1 Glen Rice/25* 6.00 15.00
BLGR2 G.Rice A,C,G,H,I,N/525* 6.00 15.00
BLGW1 Gary Williams M,Y/30* 25.00 60.00
BLGW2 G.Williams A,D,L,N,R/150* 12.00 30.00
BLJC1 Jim Calhoun N/50* 15.00 40.00
BLJC2 J.Calhoun C,O,U/150* 6.00 15.00
BLJD1 Jamie Dixon P,T/30* 6.00 15.00
BLJD2 J.Dixon B,G,H,I,R,S,U/245* 6.00 15.00
BLJJ1 J.Jackson H,I,O/50* 6.00 15.00
BLJJ2 J.Jackson A,E,S,T/250* 8.00 20.00
BLJR1 J.R. Reid C,N/30* 10.00 25.00
BLJR2 J.Reid A,H,I,L,O,R,T/150* 10.00 25.00
BLLS1 L.Shelton A,E,T/250* 6.00 15.00
BLLS2 L.Shelton G,N,O,R,S/450* 6.00 15.00
BLRH1 Robert Horry B/50* 6.00 15.00
BLRH2 R.Horry A,L,M/600* 6.00 15.00
BLSC1 Sam Cassell A,E,T/125* 6.00 15.00
BLSC2 S.Cassell D,I,L,O,R,S/450* 6.00 15.00
BLSC3 Sam Cassell F/100* 6.00 15.00
BLTM1 Thad Matta O/40* 12.00 30.00
BLTM2 T.Matta A,H,I,S,T/245* 8.00 20.00
BLTS1 Tubby Smith M/10* 8.00 20.00
BLTS2 Tubby Smith N/30* 8.00 20.00
BLTS3 T.Smith A,E,I,O,S,T/150* 6.00 15.00

2011-12 SP Authentic College Pride Autographs

STATED PRINT RUN 5 TO 40 SER.#'d SETS
CJAL Solomon Alabi/40 6.00 15.00
CJBA B.J. Armstrong/40 20.00 50.00
CJBD Billy Donovan/40 15.00 40.00
CJBH Ben Howland/40 8.00 20.00
CJBL Bill Laimbeer/40 8.00 20.00
CJBS Bill Self/40 30.00 80.00
CJBW Bill Walton/40 15.00 40.00
CJCL Christian Laettner/40 15.00 40.00
CJCR Cazzie Russell/40 10.00 25.00
CJDC DeMarcus Cousins/40 30.00 80.00
CJDM Danny Manning/40 20.00 50.00
CJDT David Thompson/40 12.50 30.00
CJEB Elgin Baylor/40 6.00 15.00
CJFL Freddie Lewis/40 6.00 15.00
CJGR Glen Rice/40 12.00 30.00
CJHU Bobby Hurley/40 30.00 80.00
CJJB Jim Boeheim/40 40.00 100.00
CJJO Michael Jordan/40 400.00 800.00
CJKS Kenny Smith/40 6.00 15.00
CJLJ LeBron James/40 1,500.00 3,000.00
CJLS Lonnie Shelton/40 8.00 20.00
CJLU Luke Babbitt/40 6.00 15.00
CJRT Reggie Theus/40 10.00 25.00
CJRU Russell Westbrook/40 50.00 120.00
CJSA Steve Alford/40 15.00 40.00
CJSC Sam Cassell/40 6.00 15.00
CJSH Bill Sharman/40 8.00 20.00
CJTH Tim Hardaway/40 15.00 40.00
CJTI T.Izzo/40 25.00 60.00
CJTS Tubby Smith/40 6.00 15.00
CJWR Jay Wright/40 12.50 30.00

2011-12 SP Authentic Home Court Signatures

HCAD Adrian Dantley 4.00 10.00
HCAH Anfernee Hardaway 50.00 120.00
HCAM Alonzo Mourning 12.00 30.00
HCBC Bill Cartwright 4.00 10.00
HCBD Brad Daugherty 4.00 10.00
HCBH Bobby Hurley 6.00 15.00
HCBL Bill Laimbeer 4.00 10.00
HCBM Bob McAdoo 4.00 10.00
HCBR Bill Russell 500.00 1,000.00
HCBW Bill Walton 10.00 25.00
HCCD Clyde Drexler 4.00 10.00
HCCL Christian Laettner 25.00 60.00
HCCR Cazzie Russell 4.00 10.00
HCDG Darrell Griffith 4.00 10.00
HCDM Danny Manning 4.00 10.00
HCDR David Robinson 40.00 100.00
HCDT David Thompson 12.00 30.00
HCEB Elgin Baylor 8.00 20.00
HCGH Grant Hill 75.00 200.00
HCGO Gail Goodrich 10.00 25.00
HCGR Glen Rice 4.00 10.00
HCHO Hakeem Olajuwon 15.00 40.00
HCJA Jim Jackson 6.00 15.00
HCJE Julius Erving 50.00 120.00
HCJH John Havlicek 20.00 50.00
HCJJ JaJuan Johnson 4.00 10.00
HCJW James Worthy 20.00 50.00
HCLB Larry Bird 100.00 250.00
HCLJ LeBron James 1,250.00 2,500.00
HCLO Brook Lopez 4.00 10.00
HCMA Magic Johnson 40.00 100.00
HCMJ Michael Jordan 400.00 800.00
HCNS Nolan Smith 4.00 10.00
HCRB Rick Barry 4.00 10.00
HCRF Rick Fox 4.00 10.00
HCRH Robert Horry 4.00 10.00
HCRT Reggie Theus 4.00 10.00
HCSC Sam Cassell 4.00 10.00

HCSM Kenny Smith 4.00 10.00
HCSP Sam Perkins 4.00 10.00
HCSW S.Williams 4.00 10.00
HCTO Rudy Tomjanovich 10.00 25.00
HCWE Jerry West 50.00 125.00
HCWF Walt Frazier 4.00 10.00

2011-12 SP Authentic Jordan Brand Classic

JCHO Scotty Hopson 1.00 2.50
JCLE Malcolm Lee 1.25 3.00
JCML Malcolm Lee 1.25 3.00
JCSH Scotty Hopson 1.00 2.50
JBCCJ Cory Joseph 1.25 3.00
JBCSE Josh Selby 1.25 3.00
JBCTH Tobias Harris 2.50 6.00
JBCTT Tristan Thompson 1.50 4.00

2011-12 SP Authentic Jordan Brand Classic Autographs

JBCCJ Cory Joseph 6.00 15.00
JBCSE Josh Selby 6.00 15.00
JBCTH Tobias Harris 10.00 25.00
JBCTT Tristan Thompson 8.00 20.00

2011-12 SP Authentic North Carolina Floor

UNCBD Brad Daugherty 4.00 10.00
UNCBP Buzz Peterson 4.00 10.00
UNCJO Michael Jordan 10.00 25.00
UNCJR J.R. Reid 4.00 10.00
UNCJW James Worthy 5.00 12.00
UNCKS Kenny Smith 4.00 10.00
UNCMI Michael Jordan 10.00 25.00
UNCMJ Michael Jordan 10.00 25.00
UNCPE Sam Perkins 4.00 10.00
UNCRE J.R. Reid 4.00 10.00
UNCSM Kenny Smith 4.00 10.00
UNCSP Sam Perkins 4.00 10.00
UNCWF Joe Wolf 4.00 10.00
UNCWO James Worthy 5.00 12.00

2011-12 SP Authentic North Carolina Floor Autographs

STATED PRINT RUN 10 TO 75 SER.#'d SETS
UNCBD Brad Daugherty/75 10.00 25.00
UNCBP Buzz Peterson/75 10.00 25.00
UNCJO Michael Jordan/23 400.00 600.00
UNCJR J.R. Reid/75 10.00 25.00
UNCMI Michael Jordan/23 400.00 600.00
UNCMJ Michael Jordan/23 400.00 600.00
UNCPE Sam Perkins/75 12.00 30.00
UNCRE J.R. Reid/75 10.00 25.00
UNCSP Sam Perkins/75 10.00 25.00
UNCWF Joe Wolf/75 10.00 25.00

2011-12 SP Authentic Sign of the Times Dual

COMMON CARD 8.00 20.00
STATED PRINT RUN ONE TO 30 SETS
S2LD A.Dantley/Laimbeer/30 8.00 20.00
S2PD S.Perkins/Daugherty/30 12.00 30.00
S2SP S.Perkins/K.Smith/30 12.00 30.00

2011-12 SP Authentic Sign of the Times Triple

STATED PRINT RUN ONE TO 25 SETS
S3BCH Calhoun/Donvn/Hwlnd/25 12.00 30.00
S3SPD Smith/Daugherty/Perkins/25 15.00 40.00

2012 SP Authentic

COMP. SET w/o SP's (50) 8.00 20.00
51-80 STATED ODDS 1:2.5
EXCHANGE DEADLINE 9/4/2014
61 Michael Jordan PS 3.00 8.00

2012 SP Authentic Limited Parade of Stars Autographs

STATED PRINT RUN 10-25
NO PRICING ON CARDS #'d UNDER 25
EXCHANGE DEADLINE 9/4/2014
61 Michael Jordan/25 1,500.00 3,000.00

2012 SP Authentic Sign of the Times

GROUP A ODDS 1:2,714
GROUP B ODDS 1:1,403
GROUP C ODDS 1:424
GROUP D ODDS 1:275
GROUP E ODDS 1:31
GROUP F ODDS 1:28
EXCHANGE DEADLINE 9/5/2014
STMJ Michael Jordan A 300.00 550.00

2012 SP Authentic Sign of the Times Duals

GROUP A ODDS 1:53,664
GROUP B ODDS 1:6,240
GROUP C ODDS 1:2,199
GROUP D ODDS 1:596
GROUP E ODDS 1:539
EXCHANGE DEADLINE 9/4/2014

2012-13 SP Authentic

COMPLETE SET (100) 30.00 60.00
COMP.SET w/o FB (50) 6.00 15.00
FLASHBACK ODDS 1:4
1 Michael Jordan 2.00 5.00
2 Dominique Wilkins .30 .75
3 Larry Bird .75 2.00
4 Magic Johnson .75 2.00
5 David Robinson .40 1.00
6 Hakeem Olajuwon .50 1.25
7 Allen Iverson .40 1.00
8 Anfernee Hardaway .60 1.50
9 Dennis Rodman .60 1.50
10 Isiah Thomas .50 1.25
11 Bill Russell .75 2.00
12 Larry Johnson .30 .75
13 Julius Erving .60 1.50
14 Ray Allen .40 1.00
15 Gary Payton .30 .75
16 Karl Malone .40 1.00
17 LeBron James 2.00 5.00
18 Jason Kidd .40 1.00
19 Chris Paul .50 1.25
20 Grant Hill .40 1.00
21 Meyers Leonard .20 .50
22 Jeremy Lamb .25 .60
23 Kendall Marshall .15 .40
24 Moe Harkless .20 .50
25 Tyler Zeller .15 .40
26 Andrew Nicholson .15 .40
27 Evan Fournier .25 .60
28 Jared Cunningham .15 .40
29 Miles Plumlee .15 .40
30 Arnett Moultrie .15 .40
31 Bernard James .15 .40
32 Jae Crowder .30 .75
33 Draymond Green 1.00 2.50
34 Quincy Acy .15 .40
35 Khris Middleton .75 2.00
36 Will Barton .30 .75
37 Tyshawn Taylor .15 .40
38 Darius Miller .20 .50
39 Kevin Murphy .15 .40
40 Kris Joseph .15 .40
41 Darius Johnson-Odom .15 .40
42 Robbie Hummel .15 .40
43 Robert Sacre .15 .40
44 William Buford .15 .40
45 John Shurna .15 .40
46 Wesley Witherspoon .15 .40
47 Ricardo Ratliffe .15 .40
48 Tomas Satoransky .25 .60
49 Justin Hamilton .15 .40
50 JaMychal Green .20 .50
51 Alonzo Mourning FB 1.00 2.50
52 Anfernee Hardaway FB 1.50 4.00
53 Bill Russell FB 2.00 5.00
54 Chris Paul FB 1.25 3.00
55 Clyde Drexler FB 1.00 2.50
56 David Robinson FB 1.00 2.50
57 Dominique Wilkins FB .75 2.00
58 Grant Hill FB 1.00 2.50
59 Hakeem Olajuwon FB 1.25 3.00
60 Cheryl Miller FB .60 1.50
61 Jason Kidd FB 1.00 2.50
62 Julius Erving FB 1.50 4.00
63 Larry Bird FB 2.00 5.00
64 Larry Johnson FB .75 2.00
65 LeBron James FB 5.00 12.00
66 Magic Johnson FB 2.00 5.00
67 Michael Jordan FB 5.00 12.00
68 Bernard King FB .75 2.00
69 Derrick Coleman FB .60 1.50
70 Gary Payton FB .75 2.00
71 Karl Malone FB 1.00 2.50
72 Eddie Jones FB .50 1.25
73 Spud Webb FB .50 1.25
74 Antoine Walker FB .50 1.25
75 Ray Allen FB 1.00 2.50
76 Jeff Hornacek FB .50 1.25
77 John Havlicek FB 1.25 3.00
78 Allen Iverson FB 1.00 2.50
79 Connie Hawkins FB .60 1.50
80 Dennis Rodman FB 1.50 4.00
81 Muggsy Bogues FB .50 1.25
82 Isiah Thomas FB 1.25 3.00
83 Walt Frazier FB 1.00 2.50
84 Jamal Mashburn FB .50 1.25
85 Bill Walton FB 1.00 2.50
86 Meyers Leonard FB .50 1.25
87 Jeremy Lamb FB .60 1.50
88 Kendall Marshall FB .40 1.00
89 Moe Harkless FB .50 1.25
90 Tyler Zeller FB .40 1.00
91 Evan Fournier FB .60 1.50
92 Jared Cunningham FB .40 1.00
93 Miles Plumlee FB .40 1.00
94 Arnett Moultrie FB .40 1.00
95 Bernard James FB .40 1.00
96 Draymond Green FB 2.50 6.00
97 Darius Johnson-Odom FB .40 1.00
98 Darius Miller FB .50 1.25
99 Tyshawn Taylor FB .40 1.00
100 Andrew Nicholson FB .40 1.00

2012-13 SP Authentic Autographs

GROUP A ODDS 1:2228 HOBBY
GROUP B ODDS 1:1574 HOBBY
GROUP C ODDS 1:217 HOBBY
GROUP D ODDS 1:101 HOBBY
GROUP E ODDS 1:51 HOBBY
GROUP A FX ODDS 1:3009 HOBBY
GROUP B FX ODDS 1:2217 HOBBY
GROUP C FX ODDS 1:759 HOBBY
GROUP D FX ODDS 1:290 HOBBY
1 Michael Jordan A 1,000.00 2,000.00
2 Dominique Wilkins A 6.00 15.00
6 Hakeem Olajuwon A 12.00 30.00
7 Allen Iverson A 25.00 60.00
13 Julius Erving B 20.00 50.00
16 Karl Malone B 15.00 40.00
17 LeBron James A 1,000.00 2,000.00
19 Chris Paul C EXCH 25.00 60.00
20 Grant Hill B 12.00 30.00
21 Meyers Leonard B 5.00 12.00
23 Kendall Marshall C 4.00 10.00
24 Moe Harkless C 4.00 10.00
25 Tyler Zeller C 4.00 10.00
26 Andrew Nicholson C 4.00 10.00
27 Evan Fournier C 5.00 12.00
28 Jared Cunningham E 4.00 10.00
29 Miles Plumlee E 4.00 10.00
30 Arnett Moultrie E 4.00 10.00
31 Bernard James E 4.00 10.00
32 Jae Crowder D 4.00 10.00
33 Draymond Green E 15.00 40.00
34 Quincy Acy E 4.00 10.00
35 Khris Middleton D 8.00 20.00
36 Will Barton E 5.00 12.00
37 Tyshawn Taylor C 4.00 10.00
38 Darius Miller D 4.00 10.00
39 Kevin Murphy E 4.00 10.00
40 Kris Joseph E 4.00 10.00
41 Darius Johnson-Odom E 4.00 10.00
42 Robbie Hummel D 4.00 10.00
43 Robert Sacre D 4.00 10.00
44 William Buford D 4.00 10.00
46 Wesley Witherspoon D 4.00 10.00
48 Tomas Satoransky D 4.00 10.00
49 Justin Hamilton E 4.00 10.00
50 JaMychal Green D 4.00 10.00
53 Bill Russell FX B 400.00 800.00
54 Chris Paul FX C EXCH 25.00 60.00
60 Cheryl Miller FX B 8.00 20.00
66 Magic Johnson FX A 40.00 80.00
67 Michael Jordan FX B 1,000.00 2,000.00
73 Spud Webb FX C 6.00 15.00
76 Jeff Hornacek FX B 10.00 25.00
79 Connie Hawkins FX B 6.00 15.00
80 Dennis Rodman FX A 12.00 30.00
81 Muggsy Bogues FX C 6.00 15.00
82 Isiah Thomas FX B 12.00 30.00
83 Walt Frazier FX B 6.00 15.00
84 Jamal Mashburn FX B 8.00 20.00
86 Meyers Leonard FX C 5.00 12.00
88 Kendall Marshall FX C 6.00 15.00
89 Moe Harkless FX D 4.00 10.00
90 Tyler Zeller FX C 6.00 15.00
91 Evan Fournier FX D 5.00 12.00
92 Jared Cunningham FX D 4.00 10.00
93 Miles Plumlee FX D 4.00 10.00
94 Arnett Moultrie FX D 4.00 10.00
95 Bernard James FX C 4.00 10.00
96 Draymond Green FX D 15.00 40.00
97 Darius Johnson-Odom FX D 4.00 10.00
98 Darius Miller FX D 4.00 10.00
99 Tyshawn Taylor FX D 6.00 15.00
100 Andrew Nicholson FX D 4.00 10.00

2012-13 SP Authentic Autographs Gold

PRINT RUNS B/WN 5-30 COPIES PER
EXCHANGE DEADLINE 4/23/2015
21 Meyers Leonard/30 10.00 25.00
24 Moe Harkless/30 20.00 50.00
25 Tyler Zeller/30 6.00 15.00
27 Evan Fournier/30 10.00 25.00
28 Jared Cunningham/30 6.00 15.00
29 Miles Plumlee/30 8.00 20.00
30 Arnett Moultrie/30 8.00 20.00
31 Bernard James/30 6.00 15.00
32 Jae Crowder/30 10.00 25.00
33 Draymond Green/30 30.00 80.00
34 Quincy Acy/30 6.00 15.00
35 Khris Middleton/30 15.00 40.00
36 Will Barton/30 8.00 20.00
38 Darius Miller/30 10.00 25.00
39 Kevin Murphy/30 6.00 15.00
48 Tomas Satoransky/30 8.00 20.00
49 Justin Hamilton/30 6.00 15.00
50 JaMychal Green/30 6.00 15.00

2012-13 SP Authentic By The Letter Signatures

COMMON CARD 6.00 15.00
SERIAL NUMBERS B/WN 3-100 COPIES PER
TOTAL PRINT RUNS B/WN 9-700 COPIES PER
NO PRICING ON TOTAL 21 OR LESS
EXCHANGE DEADLINE 4/23/2015
AD Adrian Dantley/90* 10.00 25.00
AG A.C. Green/550* 6.00 15.00
AH Anfernee Hardaway/35* 75.00 150.00
AI Allen Iverson/30* 100.00 200.00
AL Allan Houston/450* 8.00 20.00
AM Alonzo Mourning/30* 40.00 80.00
AW Antoine Walker/600* 8.00 20.00
BD Brad Daugherty/650* 6.00 15.00
BH Bobby Hurley/400* 12.00 30.00
BK Bernard King/675* 8.00 20.00
BL Bill Laimbeer/675* 6.00 15.00
BM Bob McAdoo/650* 6.00 15.00
BO Muggsy Bogues/250* 6.00 15.00
CH Connie Hawkins/350* 6.00 15.00
CL Christian Laettner/400* 20.00 50.00
CO Derrick Coleman/400* 6.00 15.00
CP Chris Paul/30* 40.00 100.00
DC Dave Cowens/36* 8.00 20.00
DM Danny Manning/150* 10.00 25.00
DR David Robinson/20* 25.00 60.00
DW Dominique Wilkins/70* 20.00 50.00
EJ Eddie Jones/600* 6.00 15.00
FL Fat Lever/600* 6.00 15.00
GP Gary Payton/33* 40.00 80.00
GR Glen Rice/400* 6.00 15.00
HG Hal Greer/400* 6.00 15.00
HM Harold Miner/300* 8.00 20.00
HO Hakeem Olajuwon/35* 30.00 60.00
JH Jeff Hornacek/450* 8.00 20.00
JJ Jim Jackson/675* 10.00 25.00
JK Jason Kidd/30* 50.00 100.00
JO Magic Johnson/39* 75.00 150.00
KM Karl Malone/39* 75.00 150.00
LA Larry Bird/36* 75.00 150.00
LB LeBron James/75* 1,500.00 3,000.00
LH Lou Hudson/675* 6.00 15.00
MA Mark A. Jackson/175* 6.00 15.00
MB Mookie Blaylock/600* 6.00 15.00
MC Michael Cooper/675* 6.00 15.00
MJ Michael Jordan/299* 200.00 400.00
MP Mark Price/55* 25.00 60.00
MR M.Ray Richardson/700* 6.00 15.00
MW1 Mark West/350* 6.00 15.00
MW2 Mark West/150* 10.00 25.00
MW3 Mark West/200* 10.00 25.00
NV Nick Van Exel/500* 10.00 25.00
RA Ray Allen/25* 60.00 120.00
RM Reggie Miller/40* 100.00 200.00
RO Dennis Rodman/33* 50.00 100.00
RT Reggie Theus/400* 6.00 15.00
SB Shawn Bradley/225* 6.00 15.00
SE Sean Elliott/700* 8.00 20.00
SH Spencer Haywood/700* 6.00 15.00
SW Spud Webb/525* 6.00 15.00
TH Tim Hardaway/400* 6.00 15.00
VN Vinny Del Negro/525* 6.00 15.00
WF Walt Frazier/400* 10.00 25.00

2012-13 SP Authentic Canvas Collection

STATED ODDS 1:8
*GOLD: 1.5X TO 4X BASIC
STATED GOLD ODDS 1:72
CC1 Alonzo Mourning 1.00 2.50
CC2 Anfernee Hardaway 1.50 4.00
CC3 Bill Russell 2.00 5.00
CC4 Clyde Drexler 1.00 2.50
CC5 David Robinson 1.00 2.50
CC6 Dominique Wilkins .75 2.00
CC7 Hakeem Olajuwon 1.25 3.00
CC8 Sean Elliott .50 1.25
CC9 Julius Erving 1.50 4.00
CC10 Larry Bird 2.00 5.00
CC11 Larry Johnson .75 2.00
CC12 Magic Johnson 2.00 5.00
CC13 Michael Jordan 5.00 12.00
CC14 Dennis Rodman 1.50 4.00
CC15 Walt Frazier 1.00 2.50
CC16 John Havlicek 1.25 3.00
CC17 Isiah Thomas 1.25 3.00
CC18 Tim Hardaway .75 2.00
CC19 Bill Walton 1.00 2.50
CC20 Shawn Bradley .40 1.00
CC21 Bob McAdoo .50 1.25
CC22 Gary Payton .75 2.00
CC23 Rod Strickland .40 1.00
CC24 Karl Malone 1.00 2.50
CC25 Allen Iverson 1.00 2.50
CC26 Antoine Walker .50 1.25
CC27 Derrick Coleman .60 1.50
CC28 Vinny Del Negro .40 1.00
CC29 Mookie Blaylock .40 1.00
CC30 Cheryl Miller .60 1.50
CC31 Ray Allen 1.00 2.50
CC32 Jason Kidd 1.00 2.50
CC33 LeBron James 5.00 12.00
CC34 Chris Paul 1.25 3.00
CC35 Grant Hill 1.00 2.50
CC36 Meyers Leonard .50 1.25
CC37 Jeremy Lamb 1.00 2.50
CC38 Kendall Marshall .40 1.00
CC39 Moe Harkless .50 1.25
CC40 Tyler Zeller .40 1.00
CC41 Andrew Nicholson .40 1.00
CC42 Evan Fournier .60 1.50
CC43 Jared Cunningham .40 1.00
CC44 Miles Plumlee .40 1.00
CC45 Arnett Moultrie .40 1.00

2012-13 SP Authentic Canvas Collection Autographs

GROUP A ODDS 1:8301
GROUP B ODDS 1:3024
GROUP C ODDS 1:1160
GROUP D ODDS 1:706
GROUP E ODDS 1:154
EXCHANGE DEADLINE 4/23/2015
CC1 Alonzo Mourning B 75.00 150.00
CC6 Dominique Wilkins E 6.00 15.00
CC7 Hakeem Olajuwon C 6.00 15.00
CC8 Sean Elliott E 4.00 10.00
CC18 Tim Hardaway D 4.00 10.00
CC21 Bob McAdoo D 10.00 25.00
CC23 Rod Strickland E 4.00 10.00
CC26 Antoine Walker C 8.00 20.00
CC34 Chris Paul C 40.00 100.00
CC35 Grant Hill C 20.00 50.00
CC36 Meyers Leonard D 6.00 15.00
CC38 Kendall Marshall D 6.00 15.00
CC39 Moe Harkless E 4.00 10.00
CC40 Tyler Zeller E 6.00 15.00
CC41 Andrew Nicholson E 4.00 10.00
CC42 Evan Fournier E 4.00 10.00
CC43 Jared Cunningham E 4.00 10.00
CC44 Miles Plumlee E 4.00 10.00
CC45 Arnett Moultrie E 4.00 10.00

2012-13 SP Authentic College Pride Autographs

PRINT RUNS B/WN 10-75 COPIES PER
NO PRICING ON QTY 10
EXCHANGE DEADLINE 4/23/2015
BD Brad Daugherty/75 6.00 15.00
BK Bernard King/75 12.00 30.00
BM Bob McAdoo/75 10.00 25.00
CW Chet Walker/75 6.00 15.00
HG Hal Greer/75 6.00 15.00
HM Harold Miner/75 6.00 15.00
JJ Jim Jackson/75 6.00 15.00
JO Michael Jordan/23 1,500.00 3,000.00
LJ LeBron James/23 1,500.00 3,000.00
MB Mookie Blaylock/75 10.00 25.00
MC Michael Cooper/75 8.00 20.00
MP Mark Price/75 8.00 20.00
MR Micheal Ray Richardson/75 6.00 15.00
RH Robert Horry/75 8.00 20.00
SB Shawn Bradley/75 8.00 20.00
SW Spud Webb/75 6.00 15.00
WF Walt Frazier/75 8.00 20.00

2012-13 SP Authentic Final Floor Dual Signatures

GROUP A ODDS 1:7697
GROUP B ODDS 1: 2861
EXCHANGE DEADLINE 4/23/2015
HH G.Hill/B.Hurley B 30.00 80.00
HL G.Hill/C.Laettner B 40.00 80.00
WN Bill Walton/Swen Nater A 12.00 30.00

2012-13 SP Authentic Final Floor Signatures

GROUP A ODDS 1:42,336
GROUP B ODDS 1:3849
GROUP C ODDS 1:420
EXCHANGE DEADLINE 4/23/2015
AR Antoine Walker C 6.00 15.00
CD Clyde Drexler C 6.00 15.00
CL Clyde Lovellette C 10.00 25.00
CM Cheryl Miller C 6.00 15.00
DM Danny Manning C 8.00 20.00
DT David Thompson C 10.00 25.00
GR Glen Rice C 6.00 15.00
HO Hakeem Olajuwon B 25.00 60.00
JO Michael Jordan B 1,000.00 2,000.00
LJ Larry Johnson B 40.00 80.00
MB Mookie Blaylock C 10.00 25.00
SN Swen Nater B 10.00 25.00

2012-13 SP Authentic Home Court Signatures

GROUP A ODDS 1:3334
GROUP B ODDS 1:2447
GROUP C ODDS 1:1411
GROUP D ODDS 1:295
GROUP E ODDS 1:161
EXCHANGE DEADLINE 4/23/2015
AH Anfernee Hardaway B 30.00 80.00
AM Alonzo Mourning B 15.00 40.00
AW Antoine Walker D 6.00 15.00
BK Bernard King D 8.00 20.00
BO Muggsy Bogues D 6.00 15.00
CD Clyde Drexler A 15.00 40.00
DR Dennis Rodman B 15.00 40.00
DW Dominique Wilkins B 12.00 30.00
GH Grant Hill B 25.00 60.00
GP Gary Payton A 20.00 50.00
HM Harold Miner E 6.00 15.00
IT Isiah Thomas C 10.00 25.00
JA LeBron James D 1,500.00 3,000.00
JM Jamal Mashburn C 6.00 15.00
JO Michael Jordan E 1,000.00 2,000.00
LB Larry Bird A 75.00 150.00
LH Lou Hudson D 6.00 15.00
LS Lonnie Shelton E 6.00 15.00
MB Mookie Blaylock E 6.00 15.00
MI Michael Jordan E 1,000.00 2,000.00
MR Micheal Ray Richardson C 10.00 25.00
NV Nick Van Exel E 6.00 15.00
RM Reggie Miller B 100.00 250.00
SB Shawn Bradley E 6.00 15.00
SE Sean Elliott E 6.00 15.00
SH Spencer Haywood D 6.00 15.00
SW Spud Webb D 6.00 15.00
TH Tim Hardaway E 6.00 15.00
VN V.Del Negro 6.00 15.00

2012-13 SP Authentic Jordan Brand Classic Jerseys 09

BU William Buford 2.50 6.00
GR JaMychal Green 2.50 6.00
JG JaMychal Green 2.50 6.00
WB William Buford 2.50 6.00
WE Wesley Witherspoon 3.00 8.00
WI Wesley Witherspoon 3.00 8.00

2012-13 SP Authentic Jordan Brand Classic Jerseys 13

BA Will Barton 2.50 6.00
KM Kendall Marshall 2.50 6.00
MA Kendall Marshall 2.50 6.00
WB Will Barton 2.50 6.00

2012-13 SP Authentic Jordan Brand Classic Jerseys 13 Autographs

GROUP A ODDS 1:8467
GROUP B ODDS 1: 2822
BA Will Barton B 6.00 15.00
KM Kendall Marshall A 12.00 30.00
MA Kendall Marshall A 12.00 30.00
WB Will Barton B 6.00 15.00

2012-13 SP Authentic Nicknames Signatures

GROUP A ODDS 1:211,680 HOBBY
GROUP B ODDS 1:10,326 HOBBY
GROUP C ODDS 1:4704 HOBBY
GROUP D ODDS 1:3681 HOBBY
GROUP E ODDS 1:1291 HOBBY
EXCHANGE DEADLINE 4/23/2015
AG A.C. Green E 10.00 25.00
BR Bryant Reeves E 8.00 20.00
CH Connie Hawkins E 6.00 15.00
DR David Robinson
The Admiral C 25.00 60.00
DT David Thompson
Skywalker D 10.00 25.00
HM Harold Miner E 15.00 40.00
HO Hakeem Olajuwon
The Dream B 25.00 60.00
JM Jamal Mashburn E 12.00 30.00
RA Ray Allen
Ray Ray C 50.00 120.00
WF Walt Frazier
Clyde D 10.00 25.00

2012-13 SP Authentic Sign of the Times

COMMON CARD 4.00 10.00
GROUP A ODDS 1:4923
GROUP B ODDS 1:4234
GROUP C ODDS 1:1058
GROUP D ODDS 1:736
GROUP E ODDS 1:97
EXCHANGE DEADLINE 4/23/2015
BD Brad Daugherty E 4.00 10.00
BK Bernard King C 6.00 15.00
BL Bill Laimbeer E 4.00 10.00
BM Bob McAdoo E 8.00 20.00
BO Muggsy Bogues E 6.00 15.00
EJ Eddie Jones D 5.00 12.00
HM Harold Miner E 8.00 20.00
HO Jeff Hornacek C 6.00 15.00
IT Isiah Thomas A 12.00 30.00
JJ Jim Jackson D 5.00 12.00
LB Larry Bird A 25.00 60.00
LS Lonnie Shelton E 4.00 10.00
MB Mookie Blaylock B 10.00 25.00
MC Michael Cooper D 4.00 10.00
MW Mark West E 4.00 10.00
NV Nick Van Exel E 3.00 8.00
PR Pooh Richardson E 4.00 10.00
SB Shawn Bradley E 4.00 10.00
SE Sean Elliott E 4.00 10.00
SH Spencer Haywood E 4.00 10.00
SW Spud Webb C 4.00 10.00
TH Tim Hardaway E 5.00 12.00
TK Toni Kukoc C 6.00 15.00

2013-14 SP Authentic

F/X ODDS 1:4 HOBBY
1 Dominique Wilkins .50 1.25
2 Karl Malone .60 1.50
3 Allen Iverson .60 1.50
4 Grant Hill .50 1.25
5 Isiah Thomas .50 1.25
6 Reggie Miller .50 1.25
7 Glenn Robinson .25 .60
8 David Robinson .60 1.50
9 Anfernee Hardaway .75 2.00
10 Larry Bird 1.25 3.00
11 Magic Johnson 1.25 3.00
12 Julius Erving .75 2.00
13 Chris Paul .60 1.50
14 LeBron James 2.50 6.00
15 Michael Jordan 2.50 6.00
16 Jay Williams .20 .50
17 Keith Smart .30 .75
18 Paul George .50 1.25
19 Rajon Rondo .40 1.00
20 Joe Smith .25 .60
21 Archie Goodwin .40 1.00
22 Sergey Karasev .40 1.00
23 Tony Snell .50 1.25
24 Solomon Hill .50 1.25
25 Ryan Kelly .40 1.00
26 Seth Curry 1.00 2.50
27 Andre Roberson .50 1.25
28 Shane Larkin .40 1.00
29 Lucas Nogueira .40 1.00
30 Livio Jean-Charles .40 1.00
31 Isaiah Canaan .40 1.00
32 Tim Hardaway Jr. .75 2.00
33 Nemanja Nedovic .40 1.00
34 Mason Plumlee .50 1.25
35 Grant Jerrett .40 1.00
36 Giannis Antetokounmpo 20.00 50.00
37 Ricardo Ledo .40 1.00
38 Dennis Schroeder 1.25 3.00
39 Erick Green .50 1.25
40 Deshaun Thomas .40 1.00
41 Mike Muscala .60 1.50
42 C.J. Leslie .40 1.00
43 Lorenzo Brown .40 1.00
44 Reggie Bullock .50 1.25
45 Peyton Siva .40 1.00
46 Skylar Diggins 2.00 5.00
47 Allen Crabbe .40 1.00
48 Jamaal Franklin .40 1.00
49 Rudy Gobert 1.50 4.00
50 Pierre Jackson .40 1.00
51 Dominique Wilkins F/X .75 2.00
52 Karl Malone F/X 1.00 2.50
53 Bill Walton F/X .75 2.00
54 Allen Iverson F/X 1.00 2.50
55 Grant Hill F/X .75 2.00
56 Hakeem Olajuwon F/X 1.00 2.50
57 Isiah Thomas F/X .75 2.00
58 Dennis Rodman F/X 1.25 3.00
59 Reggie Miller F/X .75 2.00
60 Rajon Rondo F/X .60 1.50
61 David Robinson F/X 1.00 2.50
62 Larry Johnson F/X .60 1.50
63 Alonzo Mourning F/X .75 2.00
64 Anfernee Hardaway F/X 1.25 3.00
65 Kenny Anderson F/X .40 1.00
66 Larry Bird F/X 2.00 5.00
67 Magic Johnson F/X 2.00 5.00
68 Julius Erving F/X 1.25 3.00
69 Chris Paul F/X 1.00 2.50
70 Jason Kidd F/X .75 2.00
71 LeBron James F/X 4.00 10.00
72 Michael Jordan F/X 4.00 10.00
73 Jay Williams F/X .30 .75
74 Keith Smart F/X .50 1.25
75 Donyell Marshall F/X .30 .75
76 Glenn Robinson F/X .40 1.00
77 Allan Houston F/X .50 1.25
78 Paul George F/X .75 2.00
79 Joe Smith F/X .40 1.00
80 Jerry Lucas F/X .50 1.25
81 Micheal Ray Richardson F/X .40 1.00
82 John Havlicek F/X 1.25 3.00
83 Terrell Brandon F/X .30 .75
84 Cheryl Miller F/X .50 1.25
85 Glen Rice F/X .40 1.00
86 Mason Plumlee F/X .75 2.00
87 Shane Larkin F/X .60 1.50
88 Lucas Nogueira F/X .60 1.50
89 Dennis Schroeder F/X 2.00 5.00
90 Tim Hardaway Jr. F/X 1.25 3.00
91 G.Antetokounmpo F/X 30.00 80.00
92 Andre Roberson F/X .75 2.00
93 Archie Goodwin F/X .60 1.50
94 Livio Jean-Charles F/X .60 1.50
95 Sergey Karasev F/X .60 1.50
96 Skylar Diggins F/X 3.00 8.00
97 Reggie Bullock F/X .75 2.00
98 Solomon Hill F/X .75 2.00
99 Tony Snell F/X .75 2.00
100 Allen Crabbe F/X .60 1.50

2013-14 SP Authentic Rookie Film F/X

STATED ODDS 1:72 HOBBY
51 Dominique Wilkins 3.00 8.00
52 Karl Malone 4.00 10.00
53 Bill Walton 3.00 8.00
54 Allen Iverson 5.00 12.00
55 Grant Hill 6.00 15.00
56 Hakeem Olajuwon 6.00 15.00
57 Isiah Thomas 3.00 8.00
58 Dennis Rodman 5.00 12.00
59 Reggie Miller 3.00 8.00
60 Rajon Rondo 2.50 6.00
61 David Robinson 8.00 20.00
62 Larry Johnson 2.50 6.00
63 Alonzo Mourning 8.00 20.00
64 Anfernee Hardaway 8.00 20.00
65 Kenny Anderson 1.50 4.00
66 Larry Bird 8.00 20.00
67 Magic Johnson 8.00 20.00
68 Julius Erving 8.00 20.00
69 Chris Paul 4.00 10.00
70 Jason Kidd 3.00 8.00
71 LeBron James 10.00 25.00
72 Michael Jordan 25.00 60.00
73 Jay Williams 1.25 3.00
74 Keith Smart 2.00 5.00
75 Donyell Marshall 1.25 3.00
76 Glenn Robinson 1.50 4.00
77 Allan Houston 2.00 5.00
78 Paul George 3.00 8.00
79 Joe Smith 1.50 4.00
80 Jerry Lucas 2.00 5.00
81 Micheal Ray Richardson 1.50 4.00
82 John Havlicek 5.00 12.00
83 Terrell Brandon 1.25 3.00
84 Cheryl Miller 2.00 5.00
85 Glen Rice 1.50 4.00
86 Mason Plumlee 1.50 4.00
87 Shane Larkin 1.25 3.00
88 Lucas Nogueira 1.25 3.00
89 Dennis Schroeder 4.00 10.00
90 Tim Hardaway Jr. 2.50 6.00
91 Giannis Antetokounmpo 25.00 60.00
92 Andre Roberson 1.50 4.00
93 Archie Goodwin 1.25 3.00
94 Livio Jean-Charles 1.25 3.00
95 Sergey Karasev 1.25 3.00
96 Skylar Diggins 6.00 15.00
97 Reggie Bullock 1.50 4.00
98 Solomon Hill 1.50 4.00
99 Tony Snell 1.50 4.00
100 Allen Crabbe 1.25 3.00

2013-14 SP Authentic Rookie FX Film Autographs

GROUP A ODDS 1:4050 HOBBY
GROUP B ODDS 1:360 HOBBY
NO GROUP A PRICING AVAILABLE
EXCHANGE DEADLINE 3/13/2016
73 Jay Williams B 10.00 25.00
74 Keith Smart B 6.00 15.00
79 Joe Smith B 5.00 12.00
81 Micheal Ray Richardson B 8.00 20.00
86 Mason Plumlee B 5.00 12.00
91 Giannis Antetokounmpo B 150.00 400.00
93 Archie Goodwin B 4.00 10.00
94 Livio Jean-Charles B 4.00 10.00
96 Skylar Diggins B 20.00 50.00
97 Reggie Bullock B 5.00 12.00
98 Solomon Hill B 5.00 12.00

2013-14 SP Authentic Autographs

GROUP A ODDS 1:2642 HOBBY
GROUP B ODDS 1:1960 HOBBY
GROUP C ODDS 1:31 HOBBY
F/X GROUP A ODDS 1:1215 HOBBY
F/X GROUP B ODDS 1:124 HOBBY
EXCHANGE DEADLINE 3/13/2016
4 Grant Hill A 12.00 30.00
7 Glenn Robinson B 5.00 12.00
8 David Robinson A 30.00 80.00
9 Anfernee Hardaway B 12.00 30.00
10 Larry Bird A 75.00 200.00
15 Michael Jordan B 1,500.00 3,000.00
16 Jay Williams C 4.00 10.00
18 Paul George A 50.00 120.00
19 Rajon Rondo A 15.00 40.00
20 Joe Smith C 5.00 12.00
21 Archie Goodwin C 4.00 10.00
23 Tony Snell C 5.00 12.00
24 Solomon Hill C 5.00 12.00
25 Ryan Kelly C 4.00 10.00
26 Seth Curry C 10.00 25.00
27 Andre Roberson C 5.00 12.00
28 Shane Larkin C 4.00 10.00
29 Lucas Nogueira C 4.00 10.00
30 Livio Jean-Charles C 4.00 10.00
31 Isaiah Canaan C 4.00 10.00
32 Tim Hardaway Jr. C 8.00 20.00
33 Nemanja Nedovic C 4.00 10.00
34 Mason Plumlee C 5.00 12.00
35 Grant Jerrett C 4.00 10.00
36 Giannis Antetokounmpo C 400.00 800.00
39 Erick Green C 5.00 12.00
40 Deshaun Thomas C 4.00 10.00
41 Mike Muscala C 6.00 15.00
43 Lorenzo Brown C 4.00 10.00
44 Reggie Bullock C 5.00 12.00
45 Peyton Siva C 4.00 10.00
46 Skylar Diggins C 10.00 25.00
47 Allen Crabbe C 4.00 10.00
48 Jamaal Franklin C 4.00 10.00
49 Rudy Gobert C 15.00 40.00
50 Pierre Jackson C 4.00 10.00
53 Bill Walton F/X A 8.00 20.00
55 Grant Hill F/X A 15.00 40.00
56 Hakeem Olajuwon F/X A 20.00 50.00
57 Isiah Thomas F/X A 10.00 25.00
58 Dennis Rodman F/X A 15.00 40.00
60 Rajon Rondo F/X A 10.00 25.00
61 David Robinson F/X A 8.00 20.00
62 Larry Johnson F/X A 12.00 30.00
63 Alonzo Mourning F/X A 20.00 50.00
64 Anfernee Hardaway F/X A 20.00 50.00
65 Kenny Anderson F/X B 5.00 12.00
67 Magic Johnson F/X A 30.00 80.00
68 Julius Erving F/X A 30.00 60.00
70 Jason Kidd F/X A 12.00 30.00
73 Jay Williams F/X B 4.00 10.00
74 Keith Smart F/X B 6.00 15.00
75 Donyell Marshall F/X B 4.00 10.00
76 Glenn Robinson F/X B 5.00 12.00
77 Allan Houston F/X A 8.00 20.00
78 Paul George F/X A 15.00 40.00
79 Joe Smith F/X B 5.00 12.00
81 Micheal Ray Richardson F/X B 5.00 12.00
82 John Havlicek F/X A 100.00 250.00
84 Cheryl Miller F/X B 6.00 15.00
85 Glen Rice F/X A 5.00 12.00
86 Mason Plumlee F/X B 5.00 12.00
87 Shane Larkin F/X B 4.00 10.00
90 Tim Hardaway Jr. F/X B 10.00 25.00
91 G.Antetokounmpo F/X B 400.00 800.00
93 Archie Goodwin F/X B 4.00 10.00
94 Livio Jean-Charles F/X B 4.00 10.00
96 Skylar Diggins F/X B 20.00 50.00
97 Reggie Bullock F/X B 5.00 12.00
98 Solomon Hill F/X B 5.00 12.00

2013-14 SP Authentic By the Letter Signatures

OVERALL ODDS ONE PER BOX
SERIAL NUMBERS B/WN 3-75 PER
TOTAL PRINT RUNS B/WN 9-455 PER
EXCHANGE DEADLINE 3/13/2016
BLAC A.C. Green/385* 8.00 20.00
BLAE Alex English/455* 12.00 30.00
BLAH Allan Houston/315* 15.00 40.00
BLAM Alonzo Mourning/30* 75.00 200.00
BLAW Antoine Walker/400* 10.00 25.00
BLBD Brad Daugherty/455* 12.00 30.00
BLBL Bill Laimbeer/450* 12.00 30.00
BLBR Bryant Reeves/455* 6.00 15.00
BLBU Buck Williams/400* 12.00 30.00
BLBW Bill Walton/40* 15.00 40.00
BLCC Calbert Cheaney/420* 10.00 25.00
BLCL Christian Laettner/40* 20.00 50.00
BLCM Cheryl Miller/105* 12.00 30.00
BLCW Corliss Williamson/400* 6.00 15.00
BLDB Drew Barry/110* 6.00 15.00
BLDC Dave Cowens/180* 10.00 25.00
BLDR David Robinson/40* 40.00 100.00
BLDW Dominique Wilkins/70* 40.00 100.00
BLGH Grant Hill/40* 75.00 200.00
BLGL Glenn Robinson/450* 40.00 100.00
BLGR Glen Rice/80* 10.00 25.00
BLHA Anfernee Hardaway/21* 75.00 200.00
BLIT Isiah Thomas/35* 40.00 100.00
BLJE Julius Erving/15* 75.00 200.00
BLJK Jason Kidd/30* 40.00 100.00
BLJL Jerry Lucas/135* 40.00 100.00

2013-14 SP Authentic By the Letter Signatures

BLJM Jamal Mashburn/400* 12.00 30.00
BLJO Magic Johnson/39* 100.00 250.00
BLJS Joe Smith/400* 8.00 20.00
BLJW Jay Williams/200* 15.00 40.00
BLKA Kenny Anderson/385* 12.00 30.00
BLKG Kendall Gill/400* 10.00 25.00
BLKK Kerry Kittles/450* 10.00 25.00
BLKM Karl Malone/39* 60.00 150.00
BLKS Keith Smart/420* 10.00 25.00
BLLA Larry Johnson/20* 40.00 100.00
BLLB Larry Bird/36* 100.00 250.00
BLLE LaPhonso Ellis/450* 6.00 15.00
BLLJ LeBron James/150* 1,000.00 2,000.00
BLMA Donyell Marshall/375* 6.00 15.00
BLMJ Michael Jordan/299* 1,500.00 3,000.00
BLOB Otis Birdsong/420* 6.00 15.00
BLPG Paul George/110* 40.00 100.00
BLRH Robert Horry/350* 12.00 30.00
BLRM Ron Mercer/400* 6.00 15.00
BLRO Dennis Rodman/36* 75.00 200.00
BLRR Rajon Rondo/80* 40.00 100.00
BLRS Rod Strickland/450* 10.00 25.00
BLSB Shawn Bradley/420* 8.00 20.00
BLSC Detlef Schrempf/350* 10.00 25.00
BLSE Sean Elliott/420* 10.00 25.00
BLSN Swen Nater/300* 6.00 15.00
BLSP Sam Perkins/455* 6.00 15.00
BLTB Terrell Brandon/450* 8.00 20.00
BLTG Tony Gwynn/60* 40.00 100.00
BLTH Tim Hardaway/140* 20.00 50.00

2013-14 SP Authentic Canvas

CC1 Dominique Wilkins 1.00 2.50
CC2 Karl Malone 1.25 3.00
CC3 Allen Iverson 1.25 3.00
CC4 Grant Hill 1.25 3.00
CC5 Hakeem Olajuwon 1.25 3.00
CC6 Isiah Thomas 1.00 2.50
CC7 Dennis Rodman 1.50 4.00
CC8 Reggie Miller 1.00 2.50
CC9 Paul George 1.00 2.50
CC10 David Robinson 1.25 3.00
CC11 Anfernee Hardaway 1.50 4.00
CC12 Larry Bird 2.50 6.00
CC13 Magic Johnson 2.50 6.00
CC14 Julius Erving 1.50 4.00
CC15 Chris Paul 1.25 3.00
CC16 Derrick Coleman .60 1.50
CC17 LeBron James 5.00 12.00
CC18 Michael Jordan 5.00 12.00
CC19 Larry Johnson .75 2.00
CC20 Jay Williams .40 1.00
CC21 Glenn Robinson .50 1.25
CC22 Jerry Lucas .60 1.50
CC23 Dave Cowens .60 1.50
CC24 Joe Smith .50 1.25
CC25 John Havlicek 1.50 4.00
CC26 Kenny Anderson .50 1.25
CC27 Glen Rice .50 1.25
CC28 Cheryl Miller .60 1.50
CC29 Rajon Rondo .75 2.00
CC30 Alonzo Mourning 1.00 2.50
CC31 Archie Goodwin .40 1.00
CC32 Sergey Karasev .40 1.00
CC33 Tony Snell .50 1.25
CC34 Peyton Siva .40 1.00
CC35 Ryan Kelly .40 1.00
CC36 Seth Curry 1.00 2.50
CC37 Erick Green .50 1.25
CC38 Shane Larkin .40 1.00
CC39 Lucas Nogueira .40 1.00
CC40 Solomon Hill .50 1.25
CC41 Isaiah Canaan .40 1.00
CC42 Tim Hardaway Jr. .75 2.00
CC43 Andre Roberson .50 1.25
CC44 Mason Plumlee .50 1.25
CC45 Livio Jean-Charles .40 1.00
CC46 Giannis Antetokounmpo 30.00 80.00
CC47 Deshaun Thomas .40 1.00
CC48 Dennis Schroeder 1.25 3.00
CC49 Nemanja Nedovic .40 1.00
CC50 Lorenzo Brown .40 1.00
CC51 Grant Jerrett .40 1.00
CC52 C.J. Leslie .40 1.00
CC53 Reggie Bullock .50 1.25
CC54 Mike Muscala .60 1.50
CC55 Ricardo Ledo .40 1.00
CC56 Skylar Diggins 2.00 5.00
CC57 Allen Crabbe .40 1.00
CC58 Jamaal Franklin .40 1.00
CC59 Rudy Gobert 1.50 4.00
CC60 Pierre Jackson .40 1.00

2013-14 SP Authentic Canvas Autographs

GROUP A ODDS 1:2000 HOBBY
GROUP B ODDS 1:1333 HOBBY
GROUP C ODDS 1:80 HOBBY
EXCHANGE DEADLINE 3/13/2016
CC2 Karl Malone A 40.00 100.00
CC6 Isiah Thomas B 40.00 100.00
CC7 Dennis Rodman A 60.00 150.00
CC9 Paul George A 40.00 100.00
CC10 David Robinson A 50.00 120.00
CC11 Anfernee Hardaway A 75.00 200.00
CC12 Larry Bird A 100.00 250.00
CC13 Magic Johnson A 100.00 250.00
CC14 Julius Erving A 60.00 150.00
CC17 LeBron James B 1,000.00 2,000.00
CC18 Michael Jordan B 1,000.00 2,000.00
CC19 Larry Johnson A 20.00 50.00
CC20 Jay Williams C 10.00 25.00
CC21 Glenn Robinson C 5.00 12.00
CC22 Jerry Lucas C 6.00 15.00
CC23 Dave Cowens B 6.00 15.00
CC24 Joe Smith C 5.00 12.00
CC26 Kenny Anderson C 5.00 12.00
CC27 Glen Rice C 5.00 12.00
CC28 Cheryl Miller A 12.00 30.00
CC29 Rajon Rondo A 15.00 40.00
CC30 Alonzo Mourning A 40.00 100.00
CC31 Archie Goodwin C 4.00 10.00
CC34 Peyton Siva C 4.00 10.00
CC35 Ryan Kelly C 4.00 10.00
CC36 Seth Curry C 10.00 25.00
CC37 Erick Green C 5.00 12.00
CC38 Shane Larkin C 4.00 10.00
CC39 Lucas Nogueira C 4.00 10.00
CC40 Solomon Hill C 5.00 12.00
CC41 Isaiah Canaan C 4.00 10.00
CC42 Tim Hardaway Jr. C 15.00 40.00
CC43 Andre Roberson C 5.00 12.00
CC44 Mason Plumlee C 6.00 15.00
CC45 Livio Jean-Charles C 4.00 10.00
CC46 Giannis Antetokounmpo C 500.00 1,000.00
CC47 Deshaun Thomas C 4.00 10.00
CC49 Nemanja Nedovic C 4.00 10.00
CC50 Lorenzo Brown C 4.00 10.00
CC51 Grant Jerrett C 4.00 10.00
CC53 Reggie Bullock C 5.00 12.00
CC54 Mike Muscala C 6.00 15.00
CC56 Skylar Diggins B 8.00 20.00
CC57 Allen Crabbe C 4.00 10.00
CC58 Jamaal Franklin C 4.00 10.00
CC59 Rudy Gobert B 15.00 40.00
CC60 Pierre Jackson C 4.00 10.00

2013-14 SP Authentic LeBron James Supreme Court

COMMON ODDS 1:44 HOBBY
UNCOMMON ODDS 1:216 HOBBY
RARE ODDS 1:432 HOBBY
EXCHANGE DEADLINE 3/13/2016
SC1 LeBron James C 25.00 60.00
SC2 LeBron James C 25.00 60.00
SC3 LeBron James C 25.00 60.00
SC4 LeBron James C 25.00 60.00
SC5 LeBron James C 25.00 60.00
SC6 LeBron James U 25.00 60.00
SC7 LeBron James U 25.00 60.00
SC8 LeBron James U 25.00 60.00
SC9 LeBron James U 25.00 60.00
SC10 LeBron James U 25.00 60.00
SC11 LeBron James R 30.00 80.00
SC12 LeBron James R 30.00 80.00
SC13 LeBron James R 30.00 80.00
SC14 LeBron James R 30.00 80.00
SC15 LeBron James R 30.00 80.00
SC16 LeBron James AU/10 1,000.00 2,000.00
SC17 LeBron James AU/10 1,000.00 2,000.00
SC18 LeBron James AU/10 1,000.00 2,000.00
SC19 LeBron James AU/10 1,000.00 2,000.00
SC20 LeBron James AU/10 1,000.00 2,000.00

2013-14 SP Authentic On Court Authentics

STATED ODDS 1:72 HOBBY
OCAAH Allan Houston 4.00 10.00
OCABL Bill Laimbeer 4.00 10.00
OCABW Bill Walton 6.00 15.00
OCACL Christian Laettner 4.00 10.00
OCACP Chris Paul 8.00 20.00
OCADC Derrick Coleman 4.00 10.00
OCADM Danny Manning 3.00 8.00
OCADW Dominique Wilkins 6.00 15.00
OCAEH Elvin Hayes 5.00 12.00
OCAGH Grant Hill 6.00 15.00
OCAHO Hakeem Olajuwon 8.00 20.00
OCAIT Isiah Thomas 6.00 15.00
OCAJE Julius Erving 10.00 25.00
OCAJK Jason Kidd 6.00 15.00
OCAJO Michael Jordan 100.00 250.00
OCAJS Joe Smith 3.00 8.00
OCAKM Karl Malone 8.00 20.00
OCAKS Keith Smart 4.00 10.00
OCALA Larry Johnson 5.00 12.00
OCALB Larry Bird 15.00 40.00
OCALJ LeBron James 30.00 80.00
OCAMI Michael Jordan 30.00 80.00
OCAMJ Magic Johnson 15.00 40.00
OCAMR Micheal Ray Richardson 3.00 8.00
OCAPG Paul George 6.00 15.00
OCARH Robert Horry 4.00 10.00
OCARR Rajon Rondo 5.00 12.00
OCASB Shawn Bradley 2.50 6.00

2013-14 SP Authentic On Court Authentics Signatures

GROUP A ODDS 1:10,128 HOBBY
GROUP B ODDS 1:4535 HOBBY
GROUP C ODDS 1:616 HOBBY
EXCHANGE DEADLINE 3/13/2016
OCASBW Bill Walton C 15.00 40.00
OCASCL Christian Laettner C 20.00 50.00
OCASIT Isiah Thomas C 12.00 30.00
OCASJO Michael Jordan B 1,500.00 3,000.00
OCASLJ LeBron James B EXCH 1,000.00 2,000.00
OCASSB Shawn Bradley C 5.00 12.00

2013-14 SP Authentic Sign of the Times

GROUP A ODDS 1:2267 HOBBY
GROUP B ODDS 1:646 HOBBY
GROUP C ODDS 1:69 HOBBY
EXCHANGE DEADLINE 3/13/2016
SAW Antoine Walker B 5.00 12.00
SBD Brad Daugherty C 6.00 15.00
SBL Bill Laimbeer C 6.00 15.00
SBO Muggsy Bogues C 6.00 15.00
SCC Calbert Cheaney C 4.00 10.00
SCL Christian Laettner B 6.00 15.00
SDB Drew Barry C 4.00 10.00
SDO Donyell Marshall C 4.00 10.00
SDS Detlef Schrempf C 6.00 15.00
SEH Elvin Hayes B 8.00 20.00
SEJ Eddie Jones C 5.00 12.00
SEL Sean Elliott C 6.00 15.00
SGR Glenn Robinson C 5.00 12.00
SHM Harold Miner C 4.00 10.00
SJL Jerry Lucas B 6.00 15.00
SJM Jamal Mashburn B 6.00 15.00
SJS Joe Smith C 5.00 12.00
SKA Kenny Anderson C 5.00 12.00
SKG Kendall Gill C 8.00 20.00
SKK Kerry Kittles C 4.00 10.00
SKS Keith Smart C 6.00 15.00
SLS Lonnie Shelton C 4.00 10.00
SMA Danny Manning A 20.00 50.00
SMJ Magic Johnson A 30.00 60.00
SOB Otis Birdsong C 5.00 12.00
SRH Robert Horry B 6.00 15.00
SRS Rod Strickland C 5.00 12.00
SSB Shawn Bradley C 4.00 10.00
STR Theo Ratliff C 4.00 10.00

2013-14 SP Authentic Sign of the Times Dual

GROUP A ODDS 1:10,128 HOBBY
GROUP B ODDS 1:5840 HOBBY
GROUP C ODDS 1:1380 HOBBY
EXCHANGE DEADLINE 3/13/2016
S2BR B.Reeves/S.Bradley C 6.00 15.00
S2GC R.Gobert/L.Charles C 15.00 40.00
S2GS G.Jerrett/S.Hill C 8.00 20.00
S2MW J.Mashburn/A.Walker C 20.00 50.00
S2PK M.Plumlee/R.Kelly C 8.00 20.00
S2SR J.Smith/G.Robinson C 20.00 50.00
S2TT T.Hardaway/T.Hardaway Jr. C 20.00 50.00

2014 SP Authentic

COMP.SET w/o SP's (50) 6.00 15.00
51-68 STATED ODDS 1:4
69-75 STATED ODDS 1:9
23 Michael Jordan 1.25 3.00
69 T.Woods/M.Jordan AM 12.00 30.00

2014 SP Authentic Green

*GREEN/99: 6X TO 15X BASIC CARDS

2014 SP Authentic Limited Autographs

STATED PRINT RUN 10-100

2014 SP Authentic Sign of the Times

GROUP A ODDS 1:8,123
GROUP B ODDS 1:1,408
GROUP C ODDS 1:1,067
GROUP D ODDS 1:413
GROUP E ODDS 1:353
GROUP F ODDS 1:64
GROUP G ODDS 1:55
GROUP H ODDS 1:35

2014-15 SP Authentic

STATED PRINT RUN B/WN 175-475 COPIES PER
1 Alex English .50 1.25
2 Alonzo Mourning .60 1.50
3 Anfernee Hardaway 1.00 2.50
4 Antonio McDyess .30 .75
5 Bill Russell 1.25 3.00
6 Bill Walton .60 1.50
7 Brad Daugherty .30 .75
8 Lonnie Shelton .30 .75
9 Byron Scott .40 1.00
10 Tracy McGrady .60 1.50
11 Christian Laettner .40 1.00
12 Danny Manning .30 .75
13 David Robinson .75 2.00
14 Bo Kimble .30 .75
15 Allan Houston .40 1.00
16 Fat Lever .40 1.00
17 Doc Rivers .40 1.00
18 Buck Williams .40 1.00
19 Eric Piatkowski .25 .60
20 Grant Hill .60 1.50
21 Chauncey Billups .40 1.00
22 Dave Cowens .50 1.25
23 Elvin Hayes .60 1.50
24 James Harden .75 2.00
25 James Worthy .60 1.50
26 Jerry West 1.00 2.50
27 John Stockton .75 2.00
28 Julius Erving 1.00 2.50
29 Harold Miner .40 1.00
30 Jerry Lucas .50 1.25
31 Bo Outlaw .25 .60
32 Larry Bird 1.50 4.00
33 Nick Van Exel .40 1.00
34 LeBron James 3.00 8.00
35 Magic Johnson 1.50 4.00
36 Michael Jordan 2.00 5.00
37 Micheal Ray Richardson .30 .75
38 John Salley .30 .75
39 Shaquille O'Neal 1.50 4.00
40 Jay Williams .30 .75
41 Pervis Ellison .25 .60
42 Reggie Theus .30 .75
43 Donyell Marshall .25 .60
44 Robert Horry .40 1.00
45 Stephen Curry 3.00 8.00
46 Larry Johnson .50 1.25
47 Sleepy Floyd .30 .75
48 Yao Ming 1.00 2.50
49 Vinny Del Negro .30 .75
50 Kendall Gill .40 1.00
51 Keith Smart AM 1.50 4.00
52 Bill Russell AM 5.00 12.00
53 Bill Walton AM 2.50 6.00
54 Sam Perkins AM 1.25 3.00
55 Christian Laettner AM 1.50 4.00
56 Danny Manning AM 1.25 3.00
57 David Robinson AM 3.00 8.00
58 Grant Hill AM 2.50 6.00
59 Glen Rice AM 1.50 4.00
60 Shaquille O'Neal AM 6.00 15.00
61 James Worthy AM 2.50 6.00
62 Jerry West AM 4.00 10.00
63 Julius Erving AM 4.00 10.00
64 Larry Bird AM 6.00 15.00
65 Yao Ming AM 4.00 10.00
66 LeBron James AM 12.00 30.00
67 Magic Johnson AM 6.00 15.00
68 Michael Jordan AM 12.00 30.00
69 Pervis Ellison AM 1.00 2.50
70 Corliss Williamson AM 1.00 2.50
71 M.Johnson/L.Bird AM 6.00 15.00
72 M.Jordan/J.Worthy AM 12.00 30.00
73 D.Daniels/S.Napier AM 1.25 3.00
74 S.Napier/J.Young AM 1.25 3.00
75 G.Hill/C.Laettner AM 2.50 6.00
76 Jordan Adams AU/475 3.00 8.00
77 Joe Harris AU/475 5.00 12.00
78 Spencer Dinwiddie AU/475 5.00 12.00
79 Mitch McGary AU/475 3.00 8.00
80 Dwight Powell AU/475 4.00 10.00
81 Clint Capela AU/475 12.00 30.00
82 P.J. Hairston AU/475 3.00 8.00
83 Dario Saric AU/475 6.00 15.00
84 Alessandro Gentile AU/475 3.00 8.00
85 Thanasis Antetokounmpo AU/475 6.00 15.00
86 Zach LaVine AU/475 20.00 50.00
87 Josh Huestis AU/475 3.00 8.00
88 Doug McDermott AU/475 5.00 12.00
89 Nikola Mirotic AU/475 5.00 12.00
90 Jusuf Nurkic AU/475 10.00 25.00
91 James Young AU/475 3.00 8.00
92 C.J. Wilcox AU/475 3.00 8.00
93 Jordan Clarkson AU/475 12.00 30.00
94 DeAndre Daniels AU/475 3.00 8.00
95 Adreian Payne AU/475 3.00 8.00
96 Rodney Hood AU/475 4.00 10.00
97 Cleanthony Early AU/475 3.00 8.00
98 Shabazz Napier AU/475 4.00 10.00
99 Glenn Robinson III AU/475 4.00 10.00
100 James Michael McAdoo AU/475 3.00 8.00
101 Elfrid Payton AU/175 5.00 12.00
102 Nik Stauskas AU/175 3.00 8.00
103 T.J. Warren AU/175 5.00 12.00
104 Gary Harris AU/175 5.00 12.00
105 Aaron Gordon AU/175 15.00 40.00

2014-15 SP Authentic Authentic Moments Autographs

LACK OF PRICING DUE TO MARKET INFO
51 Keith Smart 5.00 12.00
53 Bill Walton 8.00 20.00
54 Sam Perkins 4.00 10.00
55 Christian Laettner 10.00 25.00
56 Danny Manning 4.00 10.00
58 Grant Hill 25.00 60.00
59 Glen Rice 5.00 12.00
65 Yao Ming 100.00 250.00
66 LeBron James 1,000.00 2,000.00
68 Michael Jordan 1,500.00 3,000.00
69 Pervis Ellison 3.00 8.00
70 Corliss Williamson 3.00 8.00
73 D.Daniels/S.Napier 4.00 10.00
74 S.Napier/J.Young 4.00 10.00
75 G.Hill/C.Laettner 20.00 50.00

2014-15 SP Authentic Autographs Emerald

STATED PRINT RUN B/WN 5-75 COPIES PER
NO PRICING ON QTY 5 OR LESS
1 Alex English/75 6.00 15.00
6 Bill Walton/75 6.00 15.00
12 Danny Manning/75 12.00 30.00
14 Bo Kimble/75 3.00 8.00
16 Fat Lever/75 4.00 10.00
17 Doc Rivers/75 4.00 10.00
22 Dave Cowens/75 5.00 12.00
37 Micheal Ray Richardson/75 3.00 8.00
41 Pervis Ellison/75 2.50 6.00
43 Donyell Marshall/75 2.50 6.00
49 Vinny Del Negro/75 3.00 8.00
50 Kendall Gill/75 8.00 20.00

2014-15 SP Authentic Chirography

STATED PRINT RUN B/WN 3-75 COPIES PER
NO PRICING ON QTY 10 OR LESS
CEP Eric Piatkowski/75 4.00 10.00
CKG Kendall Gill/75 6.00 15.00
CMJ Michael Jordan/23 400.00 800.00

2014-15 SP Authentic Flair Showcase Row 1 Autographs

STATED PRINT RUN X SER.#'d SETS
91 Harold Miner
G 5.00 12.00
92 Allan Houston
F 5.00 12.00
95 Antonio McDyess
G 4.00 10.00
97 Bill Walton
E 8.00 20.00
99 Christian Laettner
F 5.00 12.00
101 Danny Manning
E 4.00 10.00
102 Dave Cowens
F 6.00 15.00
104 John Salley
D 4.00 10.00
106 Vinny Del Negro
C 4.00 10.00
107 A.C. Green
C 5.00 12.00
108 Jay Williams
C 4.00 10.00
109 David Thompson
C 5.00 12.00
116 Doc Rivers
A 5.00 12.00
117 Kenny Anderson
C 4.00 10.00
119 Byron Scott
C 5.00 12.00
122 Michael Jordan
E 1,000.00 2,000.00
123 Larry Johnson
B 10.00 25.00
125 Sleepy Floyd
G 4.00 10.00
127 Bill Laimbeer
B 6.00 15.00
129 Reggie Theus
E 4.00 10.00
130 Micheal Ray Richardson
D 4.00 10.00
131 P.J. Hairston
G 3.00 8.00
132 Josh Huestis
E 3.00 8.00
133 Clint Capela
F 12.00 30.00
134 Dario Saric
C 6.00 15.00
135 Elfrid Payton
F 5.00 12.00
136 T.J. Warren
D 5.00 12.00
137 Mitch McGary
D 3.00 8.00
138 C.J. Wilcox
E 3.00 8.00
139 Shabazz Napier
D 4.00 10.00
140 Aaron Gordon
E 15.00 40.00
141 Jusuf Nurkic
F 10.00 25.00
142 Nikola Mirotic
E 5.00 12.00
143 Gary Harris
F 5.00 12.00
144 Doug McDermott
E 5.00 12.00
145 Rodney Hood
E 4.00 10.00
146 James Young
F 3.00 8.00
147 Jordan Adams
F 3.00 8.00
148 Nik Stauskas
D 3.00 8.00
149 Zach LaVine
G 15.00 40.00
150 Adreian Payne
C 3.00 8.00

2014-15 SP Authentic Limited Autographs

PRINT RUNS B/WN 5-75 COPIES PER
NO PRICING ON QTY 10 OR LESS
1 Alex English AU/75 10.00 25.00
4 Antonio McDyess AU/75 6.00 15.00
7 Brad Daugherty AU/75 6.00 15.00
8 Lonnie Shelton AU/75 6.00 15.00
14 Bo Kimble AU/75 6.00 15.00
15 Allan Houston AU/75 8.00 20.00
16 Fat Lever AU/75 8.00 20.00
18 Buck Williams AU/75 8.00 20.00
19 Eric Piatkowski AU/75 5.00 12.00
29 Harold Miner AU/75 8.00 20.00
31 Bo Outlaw AU/75 5.00 12.00
33 Nick Van Exel AU/75 8.00 20.00
37 Micheal Ray Richardson AU/75 6.00 15.00
38 John Salley AU/75 6.00 15.00
40 Jay Williams AU/75 6.00 15.00
42 Reggie Theus AU/75 6.00 15.00
43 Donyell Marshall AU/75 5.00 12.00
47 Sleepy Floyd AU/25 6.00 15.00
50 Kendall Gill AU/75 8.00 20.00

2014-15 SP Authentic Limited Patch Autographs

STATED PRINT RUN B/WN 25-50 COPIES PER
76 Jordan Adams/50 4.00 10.00
77 Joe Harris/50 6.00 15.00
78 Spencer Dinwiddie/50 10.00 25.00
80 Dwight Powell/50 5.00 12.00
81 Clint Capela/50 40.00 100.00
82 P.J. Hairston/50 4.00 10.00
85 Thanasis Antetokounmpo/50 8.00 20.00
86 Nikola Mirotic/50 12.00 30.00
87 Josh Huestis/50 4.00 10.00
88 Doug McDermott/50 15.00 40.00
89 Zach LaVine/50 20.00 50.00
91 James Young/50 4.00 10.00
93 Jordan Clarkson/50 40.00 100.00
95 Adreian Payne/50 4.00 10.00
96 Rodney Hood/50 20.00 50.00
98 Shabazz Napier/50 5.00 12.00
99 Glenn Robinson III/50 25.00 60.00
100 James Michael McAdoo/50 4.00 10.00
101 Elfrid Payton/25 50.00 120.00
102 Nik Stauskas/25 12.00 30.00
103 T.J. Warren/25 30.00 80.00
104 Gary Harris/25 6.00 15.00
105 Aaron Gordon/25 30.00 80.00

2014-15 SP Authentic Marks of Distinction

COMMON CARD 4.00 10.00
SEMISTARS 5.00 12.00
UNLISTED STARS 6.00 15.00
STATED PRINT RUN B/WN 3-50 COPIES PER
NO PRICING ON QTY 3 OR LESS
MDBO Bo Outlaw/50 4.00 10.00
MDBS Byron Scott/50 6.00 15.00
MDBW Bill Walton/50 10.00 25.00
MDDR Doc Rivers/50 6.00 15.00
MDLJ LeBron James/23 EXCH 1,500.00 3,000.00

2014-15 SP Authentic Rookie Chirography

STATED PRINT RUN B/WN 10-99 COPIES PER
NO PRICING ON QTY 10 OR LESS
RCCW C.J. Wilcox/99 3.00 8.00
RCJA Jordan Adams/99 3.00 8.00
RCMM Mitch McGary/99 EXCH 3.00 8.00
RCSN Shabazz Napier/99 4.00 10.00

2014-15 SP Authentic Rookie Extended

R1 Clint Capela 4.00 10.00
R2 P.J. Hairston 1.00 2.50
R3 Dario Saric 2.00 5.00
R4 DeAndre Daniels 1.00 2.50
R5 Glenn Robinson III 1.25 3.00
R6 Shabazz Napier 1.25 3.00
R7 Cleanthony Early 1.00 2.50
R8 Rodney Hood 1.25 3.00
R9 Jordan Adams 1.00 2.50
R10 Jusuf Nurkic 3.00 8.00
R11 Thanasis Antetokounmpo 2.00 5.00
R12 Josh Huestis 1.00 2.50
R13 Doug McDermott 1.50 4.00
R14 Zach LaVine 6.00 15.00
R15 Mitch McGary 1.00 2.50
R16 James Young 1.00 2.50
R17 Nikola Mirotic 1.50 4.00
R18 C.J. Wilcox 1.00 2.50
R19 Joe Harris 1.50 4.00
R20 Adreian Payne 1.00 2.50
R21 T.J. Warren 1.50 4.00
R22 Gary Harris 1.50 4.00
R23 Nik Stauskas 1.00 2.50
R24 Elfrid Payton 1.50 4.00
R25 Aaron Gordon 5.00 12.00

2014-15 SP Authentic Rookie Extended Autographs Emerald

STATED PRINT RUN 25-225 COPIES PER
R1 Clint Capela/225 12.00 30.00
R2 P.J. Hairston/225 6.00 15.00
R3 Dario Saric/225 10.00 25.00
R6 Shabazz Napier/225 4.00 10.00
R7 Cleanthony Early/225 3.00 8.00
R8 Rodney Hood/225 4.00 10.00
R9 Jordan Adams/225 3.00 8.00
R10 Jusuf Nurkic/225 10.00 25.00
R11 Thanasis Antetokounmpo/225 6.00 15.00
R12 Josh Huestis/225 3.00 8.00
R13 Doug McDermott/225 5.00 12.00
R14 Zach LaVine/225 10.00 25.00
R15 Mitch McGary/225 3.00 8.00
R16 James Young/225 3.00 8.00
R17 Nikola Mirotic/225 20.00 50.00
R18 C.J. Wilcox/225 3.00 8.00
R19 Joe Harris/225 5.00 12.00
R20 Adreian Payne/225 3.00 8.00
R21 T.J. Warren/150 8.00 20.00
R22 Gary Harris/150 5.00 12.00
R23 Nik Stauskas/150 5.00 12.00
R24 Elfrid Payton/25 12.00 30.00
R25 Aaron Gordon/25 12.00 30.00

2014-15 SP Authentic Rookie Extended Autographs Red

*RED: 1X TO 2.5X EMERALD HI
STATED PRINT RUN B/WN 5-50 COPIES PER
NO PRICING ON QTY 10 OR LESS

2014-15 SP Authentic Sign of the Times

SOTAE Alex English 5.00 12.00
SOTAG A.C. Green 4.00 10.00
SOTAH Anfernee Hardaway 12.00 30.00
SOTAM Antonio McDyess 3.00 8.00
SOTAP Adreian Payne 2.50 6.00
SOTBD Brad Daugherty 3.00 8.00
SOTBS Byron Scott 4.00 10.00
SOTBW Bill Walton 8.00 20.00
SOTCB Chauncey Billups 4.00 10.00
SOTCE Cleanthony Early 2.50 6.00
SOTCW C.J. Wilcox 2.50 6.00
SOTDC Dave Cowens 5.00 12.00
SOTGH Grant Hill 12.00 30.00
SOTGO Aaron Gordon 12.00 30.00
SOTHA Gary Harris 4.00 10.00
SOTJM James Michael McAdoo 2.50 6.00
SOTKG Kendall Gill 5.00 12.00
SOTKS Keith Smart 4.00 10.00
SOTMM Mitch McGary 2.50 6.00
SOTMR Micheal Ray Richardson 3.00 8.00
SOTNS Nik Stauskas 2.50 6.00
SOTPE Pervis Ellison 2.50 6.00
SOTPY Patric Young 2.50 6.00
SOTRI Doc Rivers 4.00 10.00
SOTRT Reggie Theus 3.00 8.00
SOTSC Stephen Curry 300.00 600.00
SOTSF Sleepy Floyd 3.00 8.00
SOTSN Shabazz Napier 3.00 8.00
SOTWI Jay Williams 3.00 8.00
SOTYM Yao Ming 15.00 40.00

2014-15 SP Authentic Sign of the Times Triple

STATED PRINT RUN B/WN 3-20 COPIES PER
NO PRICING ON QTY 3 OR LESS
SOT3HHM Mourning/Hardaway/Hill/20 40.00 100.00

2007-08 SP Authentic Retail

COMPLETE SET (153) 30.00 80.00
*VETS: .25X TO .6X HOBBY SP
101 Greg Oden RC 1.25 3.00
102 Yi Jianlian RC 1.50 4.00
103 Brandan Wright RC 1.00 2.50
104 Thaddeus Young RC 1.25 3.00
105 Nick Young RC 1.25 3.00
106 Jamario Moon RC 1.00 2.50
106B Guillermo Diaz 1.25 3.00
107 Marco Belinelli RC 1.00 2.50
108 Darryl Watkins RC .75 2.00
109 Oleksiy Pecherov RC 1.25 3.00
110 Juan Carlos Navarro RC 1.00 2.50
111 JamesOn Curry RC .75 2.00
112 Demetris Nichols RC .75 2.00
113 Herbert Hill RC .75 2.00
114 Coby Karl RC .75 2.00
115 Darius Washington 1.25 3.00
116 Louis Amundson RC .75 2.00
117 Cheikh Samb RC .75 2.00
118 Ramon Sessions RC 1.00 2.50
119 Luis Scola RC 1.25 3.00
120 Sean Williams RC .75 2.00
122 Spencer Hawes RC .75 2.00
123 Acie Law RC .75 2.00
124 Julian Wright RC .75 2.00
125 Al Thornton RC .75 2.00
126 Rodney Stuckey RC .75 2.00
127 Sean Williams RC .75 2.00
128 Javaris Crittenton RC .75 2.00
129 Jason Smith RC .75 2.00
130 Daequan Cook RC 1.00 2.50
131 Jared Dudley RC 1.00 2.50
132 Wilson Chandler RC 1.00 2.50
133 Morris Almond RC .75 2.00
134 Arron Afflalo RC 1.00 2.50
135 Alando Tucker RC .75 2.00
136 Carl Landry RC .75 2.00
137 Gabe Pruitt RC .75 2.00
138 Aaron Brooks RC 1.00 2.50
139 Nick Fazekas RC .75 2.00
140 Jermareo Davidson RC .75 2.00
141 Josh McRoberts RC .75 2.00
142 Glen Davis RC 1.00 2.50
143 Adam Haluska RC .75 2.00
147 Dominic McGuire RC .75 2.00
148 Aaron Gray RC .75 2.00
149 Taurean Green RC .75 2.00
150 D.J. Strawberry RC .75 2.00
151 Chris Richard RC .75 2.00
152 Kevin Durant RC 12.00 30.00
153 Al Horford RC 3.00 8.00
154 Mike Conley Jr. RC 3.00 8.00
155 Jeff Green RC 1.00 2.50
156 Corey Brewer RC 1.00 2.50
157 Joakim Noah RC 1.25 3.00

2007-08 SP Authentic Retail Rookie Autographs

PRINT RUNS LISTED IN CHECKLIST
INSERTED INTO RETAIL SP PACKS
122 Spencer Hawes/599 4.00 10.00
123 Acie Law/100 4.00 10.00
124 Julian Wright/100 4.00 10.00
125 Al Thornton/599 4.00 10.00
126 Rodney Stuckey/599 4.00 10.00
127 Sean Williams/100 4.00 10.00
128 Javaris Crittenton/100 4.00 10.00
129 Jason Smith/100 4.00 10.00
130 Daequan Cook/100 5.00 12.00
131 Jared Dudley/100 5.00 12.00
132 Wilson Chandler/599 5.00 12.00
133 Morris Almond/100 4.00 10.00
134 Arron Afflalo/599 5.00 12.00
135 Alando Tucker/100 4.00 10.00
136 Carl Landry/100 4.00 10.00
137 Gabe Pruitt/100 4.00 10.00
138 Aaron Brooks/599 5.00 12.00
139 Nick Fazekas/599 4.00 10.00
140 Jermareo Davidson/100 4.00 10.00
141 Josh McRoberts/599 4.00 10.00
142 Glen Davis/599 5.00 12.00
143 Adam Haluska/599 4.00 10.00
147 Dominic McGuire/100 4.00 10.00
148 Aaron Gray/100 4.00 10.00
149 Taurean Green/599 4.00 10.00
150 D.J. Strawberry/599 4.00 10.00
151 Chris Richard/100 4.00 10.00
152 Kevin Durant/399 800.00 1,500.00
153 Al Horford/399 15.00 40.00
154 Mike Conley Jr./100 15.00 40.00
155 Jeff Green/399 5.00 12.00
156 Corey Brewer/100 5.00 12.00
157 Joakim Noah/100 6.00 15.00

2008-09 SP Authentic Retail

COMP.SET w/o RCs (100) 10.00 25.00
*VETS: .25X TO .6X BASE HOBBY
50 Andre Miller .25 .60
101 Alexis Ajinca AU RC 4.00 10.00
102 Joe Alexander AU RC 4.00 10.00
103 Ryan Anderson AU RC 5.00 12.00
104 Darrell Arthur AU RC 5.00 12.00
106 Jerryd Bayless AU RC 5.00 12.00
107 Michael Beasley AU RC 6.00 15.00
108 Mario Chalmers AU RC 6.00 15.00
109 Joe Crawford AU RC 4.00 10.00
110 Joey Dorsey AU RC 4.00 10.00
112 Patrick Ewing Jr. AU RC 4.00 10.00
113 Danilo Gallinari AU RC 10.00 25.00
114 J.R. Giddens AU RC 4.00 10.00
115 Eric Gordon AU RC 10.00 25.00
116 Donte Greene AU RC 4.00 10.00
118 Roy Hibbert AU RC 5.00 12.00
119 J.J. Hickson AU RC 4.00 10.00
121 DeAndre Jordan AU RC 15.00 40.00
122 Kosta Koufos AU RC 4.00 10.00
123 Courtney Lee AU RC 5.00 12.00
125 Robin Lopez AU RC 5.00 12.00
126 Kevin Love AU RC 12.00 30.00
127 O.J. Mayo AU RC 5.00 12.00
128 Javale McGee AU RC 6.00 15.00
129 Anthony Randolph AU RC 4.00 10.00
130 Derrick Rose AU RC 100.00 250.00
131 Brandon Rush AU RC 4.00 10.00
132 Walter Sharpe AU RC 4.00 10.00
133 Sean Singletary AU RC 4.00 10.00
134 Marreese Speights AU RC 5.00 12.00
135 Mike Taylor AU RC 4.00 10.00
136 Jason Thompson AU RC 4.00 10.00
137 Kyle Weaver AU RC 4.00 10.00
138 Sonny Weems AU RC 4.00 10.00
139 Russell Westbrook AU RC 200.00 500.00
140 D.J. White AU RC 4.00 10.00
147 Rudy Fernandez AU RC 5.00 12.00

1994-95 SP Championship

COMPLETE SET (135) 15.00 30.00
1 Mookie Blaylock RF .15 .40
2 Dominique Wilkins RF .25 .60
3 Alonzo Mourning RF .25 .60
4 Michael Jordan RF 1.50 4.00
5 Mark Price RF .15 .40
6 Jamal Mashburn RF .15 .40
7 Dikembe Mutombo RF .25 .60
8 Grant Hill RF .40 1.00
9 Latrell Sprewell RF .20 .50
10 Hakeem Olajuwon RF .30 .75
11 Reggie Miller RF .30 .75
12 Loy Vaught RF .10 .25
13 Nick Van Exel RF .15 .40
14 Glen Rice RF .15 .40
15 Glenn Robinson RF .15 .40
16 Isaiah Rider RF .15 .40
17 Kenny Anderson RF .12 .30
18 Patrick Ewing RF .25 .60
19 Shaquille O'Neal RF .60 1.50
20 Dana Barros RF .10 .25
21 Charles Barkley RF .40 1.00
22 Clifford Robinson RF .12 .30
23 Mitch Richmond RF .20 .50
24 David Robinson RF .30 .75
25 Shawn Kemp RF .25 .60
26 Karl Malone RF .30 .75
27 Chris Webber RF .30 .75
28 Stacey Augmon .12 .30
29 Mookie Blaylock .15 .40
30 Grant Long .10 .25
31 Steve Smith .12 .30
32 Dee Brown .12 .30
33 Eric Montross RC .12 .30
34 Dino Radja .10 .25
35 Dominique Wilkins .25 .60
36 Muggsy Bogues .12 .30
37 Scott Burrell .10 .25
38 Larry Johnson .20 .50
39 Alonzo Mourning .25 .60
40 B.J. Armstrong .15 .40
41 Michael Jordan 3.00 8.00
42 Toni Kukoc .20 .50
43 Scottie Pippen .40 1.00
44 Tyrone Hill .10 .25
45 Chris Mills .12 .30
46 Mark Price .15 .40
47 John Williams .10 .25
48 Jim Jackson .12 .30
49 Jason Kidd RC .75 2.00
50 Jamal Mashburn .15 .40
51 Roy Tarpley .10 .25
52 Mahmoud Abdul-Rauf .10 .25
53 Dikembe Mutombo .25 .60
54 Rodney Rogers .10 .25
55 Bryant Stith .10 .25
56 Joe Dumars .15 .40
57 Grant Hill RC .75 2.00
58 Lindsey Hunter .10 .25
59 Terry Mills .10 .25
60 Tim Hardaway .20 .50
61 Donyell Marshall RC .15 .40

62 Chris Mullin .20 .50
63 Latrell Sprewell .20 .50
64 Sam Cassell .15 .40
65 Clyde Drexler .25 .60
66 Vernon Maxwell .10 .25
67 Hakeem Olajuwon .30 .75
68 Dale Davis .10 .25
69 Mark Jackson .12 .30
70 Reggie Miller .30 .75
71 Rik Smits .12 .30
72 Terry Dehere .10 .25
73 Lamond Murray RC .15 .40
74 Pooh Richardson .10 .25
75 Loy Vaught .10 .25
76 Cedric Ceballos .12 .30
77 Vlade Divac .15 .40
78 Eddie Jones RC .50 1.25
79 Nick Van Exel .15 .40
80 Bimbo Coles .10 .25
81 Billy Owens .10 .25
82 Glen Rice .15 .40
83 Kevin Willis .12 .30
84 Vin Baker .15 .40
85 Marty Conlon .10 .25
86 Eric Murdock .10 .25
87 Glenn Robinson RC .30 .75
88 Tom Gugliotta .10 .25
89 Christian Laettner .12 .30
90 Isaiah Rider .15 .40
91 Doug West .10 .25
92 Kenny Anderson .12 .30
93 Benoit Benjamin .10 .25
94 Derrick Coleman .15 .40
95 Armon Gilliam .10 .25
96 Patrick Ewing .25 .60
97 Derek Harper .12 .30
98 Charles Oakley .15 .40
99 John Starks .15 .40
100 Nick Anderson .10 .25
101 Horace Grant .15 .40
102 Anfernee Hardaway .30 .75
103 Shaquille O'Neal .60 1.50
104 Dana Barros .10 .25
105 Shawn Bradley .10 .25
106 Clarence Weatherspoon .10 .25
107 Sharone Wright RC .12 .30
108 Charles Barkley .40 1.00
109 Kevin Johnson .15 .40
110 Dan Majerle .15 .40
111 Wesley Person RC .15 .40
112 Terry Porter .10 .25
113 Clifford Robinson .12 .30
114 Rod Strickland .10 .25
115 Buck Williams .10 .25
116 Brian Grant RC .25 .60
117 Mitch Richmond .20 .50
118 Spud Webb .12 .30
119 Walt Williams .10 .25
120 Vinny Del Negro .10 .25
121 Sean Elliott .12 .30
122 David Robinson .30 .75
123 Dennis Rodman .40 1.00
124 Kendall Gill .10 .25
125 Shawn Kemp .25 .60
126 Gary Payton .25 .60
127 Detlef Schrempf .15 .40
128 David Benoit .10 .25
129 Jeff Hornacek .12 .30
130 Karl Malone .30 .75
131 John Stockton .30 .75
132 Rex Chapman .10 .25
133 Calbert Cheaney .12 .30
134 Juwan Howard RC .25 .60
135 Chris Webber .30 .75

1994-95 SP Championship Die Cuts

COMPLETE SET (135) 30.00 60.00
*DIE CUT: 1X TO 2.5X BASE CARD HI

1994-95 SP Championship Future Playoff Heroes

COMPLETE SET (10) 15.00 40.00
STATED ODDS 1:40
*DIE CUTS: 2.5X TO 6X HI COLUMN
DIE CUTS: STATED ODDS 1:300
F1 Brian Grant 1.25 3.00
F2 Anfernee Hardaway 3.00 8.00
F3 Grant Hill 4.00 10.00
F4 Eddie Jones 2.50 6.00
F5 Jamal Mashburn 1.50 4.00
F6 Shaquille O'Neal 6.00 15.00
F7 Isaiah Rider 1.50 4.00
F8 Glenn Robinson 1.50 4.00
F9 Latrell Sprewell 2.00 5.00
F10 Chris Webber 3.00 8.00

1994-95 SP Championship Playoff Heroes

COMPLETE SET (10) 10.00 25.00
STATED ODDS 1:15
*DIE CUTS: 2X TO 5X HI COLUMN
DIE CUTS: STATED ODDS 1:225
P1 Charles Barkley 2.00 5.00
P2 Michael Jordan 6.00 15.00
P3 Shawn Kemp 1.25 3.00
P4 Moses Malone .75 2.00
P5 Reggie Miller 1.50 4.00
P6 Alonzo Mourning 1.25 3.00
P7 Dikembe Mutombo 1.25 3.00
P8 Hakeem Olajuwon 1.50 4.00
P9 Robert Parish .75 2.00
P10 John Stockton 1.50 4.00

1995-96 SP Championship

COMPLETE SET (146) 20.00 50.00
1 Stacey Augmon .30 .75
2 Mookie Blaylock .40 1.00
3 Alan Henderson RC .40 1.00
4 Steve Smith .30 .75
5 Dana Barros .30 .75
6 Dee Brown .30 .75
7 Eric Montross .25 .60
8 Dino Radja .25 .60
9 Eric Williams RC .40 1.00
10 Kenny Anderson .30 .75
11 Larry Johnson .50 1.25
12 Glen Rice .40 1.00
13 George Zidek RC .30 .75
14 Toni Kukoc .50 1.25
15 Scottie Pippen 1.00 2.50
16 Dennis Rodman .75 2.00
17 Michael Jordan 4.00 10.00
18 Terrell Brandon .30 .75
19 Danny Ferry .25 .60
20 Chris Mills .25 .60
21 Bobby Phills .30 .75
22 Jim Jackson .30 .75
23 Popeye Jones .25 .60
24 Jason Kidd .60 1.50
25 Jamal Mashburn .40 1.00
26 Mahmoud Abdul-Rauf .30 .75
27 Dale Ellis .30 .75
28 Antonio McDyess RC .50 1.25
29 Dikembe Mutombo .60 1.50
30 Joe Dumars .40 1.00
31 Grant Hill .60 1.50
32 Allan Houston .30 .75
33 Otis Thorpe .30 .75
34 Tim Hardaway .50 1.25
35 Chris Mullin .40 1.00
36 Latrell Sprewell .40 1.00
37 Joe Smith RC .50 1.25
38 Sam Cassell .40 1.00
39 Clyde Drexler .60 1.50
40 Robert Horry .40 1.00
41 Hakeem Olajuwon .75 2.00
42 Dale Davis .25 .60
43 Derrick McKey .25 .60
44 Reggie Miller .75 2.00
45 Rik Smits .30 .75
46 Brent Barry RC .60 1.50
47 Lamond Murray .25 .60
48 Loy Vaught .25 .60
49 Brian Williams .25 .60
50 Cedric Ceballos .30 .75
51 Magic Johnson 1.25 3.00
52 Eddie Jones .40 1.00
53 Nick Van Exel .40 1.00
54 Sasha Danilovic RC .40 1.00
55 Alonzo Mourning .60 1.50
56 Billy Owens .25 .60
57 Kevin Willis .25 .60
58 Vin Baker .30 .75
59 Sherman Douglas .25 .60
60 Lee Mayberry .25 .60
61 Glenn Robinson .40 1.00
62 Kevin Garnett RC 2.50 6.00
63 Tom Gugliotta .25 .60
64 Christian Laettner .30 .75
65 Isaiah Rider .40 1.00
66 Chris Childs .25 .60
67 Kendall Gill .25 .60
68 Armon Gilliam .25 .60
69 Ed O'Bannon RC .30 .75
70 Patrick Ewing .60 1.50
71 Derek Harper .30 .75
72 Charles Oakley .30 .75
73 John Starks .40 1.00
74 Horace Grant .30 .75
75 Anfernee Hardaway 1.00 2.50
76 Shaquille O'Neal 1.50 4.00
77 Dennis Scott .25 .60
78 Derrick Coleman .30 .75
79 Trevor Ruffin .25 .60
80 Jerry Stackhouse RC 1.25 3.00
81 Clarence Weatherspoon .25 .60
82 Charles Barkley 1.00 2.50
83 Michael Finley RC 1.00 2.50
84 Kevin Johnson .40 1.00
85 Danny Manning .30 .75
86 Randolph Childress RC .30 .75
87 Clifford Robinson .40 1.00
88 Arvydas Sabonis RC .75 2.00
89 Rod Strickland .25 .60
90 Tyus Edney RC .40 1.00
91 Brian Grant .30 .75
92 Mitch Richmond .50 1.25
93 Walt Williams .25 .60
94 Sean Elliott .30 .75
95 Avery Johnson .30 .75
96 Chuck Person .30 .75
97 David Robinson .75 2.00
98 Shawn Kemp .60 1.50
99 Gary Payton .60 1.50
100 Sam Perkins .25 .60
101 Detlef Schrempf .40 1.00
102 Ed Pinckney .25 .60
103 Tracy Murray .25 .60
104 Alvin Robertson .25 .60
105 Damon Stoudamire RC 1.00 2.50
106 Jeff Hornacek .30 .75
107 Karl Malone .75 2.00
108 Chris Morris .25 .60
109 John Stockton .75 2.00
110 Greg Anthony .25 .60
111 Blue Edwards .25 .60
112 Bryant Reeves RC .30 .75
113 Byron Scott .40 1.00
114 Juwan Howard .40 1.00
115 Gheorghe Muresan .25 .60
116 Rasheed Wallace RC 1.25 3.00
117 Chris Webber .50 1.25
118 Mookie Blaylock RP .40 1.00
119 Dana Barros RP .30 .75
120 Larry Johnson RP .30 .75
121 Michael Jordan RP 4.00 10.00
122 Terrell Brandon RP .30 .75
123 Jason Kidd RP .60 1.50
124 Mahmoud Abdul-Rauf RP .30 .75
125 Grant Hill RP .60 1.50
126 Latrell Sprewell RP .40 1.00
127 Hakeem Olajuwon RP .75 2.00
128 Reggie Miller RP .75 2.00
129 Loy Vaught RP .25 .60
130 Magic Johnson RP 1.25 3.00
131 Alonzo Mourning RP .60 1.50
132 Vin Baker RP .30 .75
133 Tom Gugliotta RP .25 .60
134 Ed O'Bannon RP .30 .75
135 Patrick Ewing RP .60 1.50
136 Anfernee Hardaway RP 1.00 2.50
137 Jerry Stackhouse RP 1.25 3.00
138 Charles Barkley RP 1.00 2.50
139 Clifford Robinson RP .40 1.00
140 Mitch Richmond RP .50 1.25
141 David Robinson RP .75 2.00
142 Shawn Kemp RP .60 1.50
143 Damon Stoudamire RP 1.00 2.50
144 John Stockton RP .75 2.00
145 Bryant Reeves RP .30 .75
146 Juwan Howard RP .40 1.00

1995-96 SP Championship Champions of the Court

COMPLETE SET (30) 30.00 80.00
STATED ODDS 1:6
*DIE CUTS: 2.5X TO 6X HI COLUMN
DIE CUTS: STATED ODDS 1:75
C1 Steve Smith .75 2.00
C2 Dino Radja .60 1.50
C3 Glen Rice 1.00 2.50
C4 Scottie Pippen 2.50 6.00
C5 Terrell Brandon .75 2.00
C6 Jason Kidd 1.50 4.00
C7 Dikembe Mutombo 1.50 4.00
C8 Grant Hill 1.50 4.00
C9 Joe Smith 1.25 3.00
C10 Hakeem Olajuwon 2.00 5.00
C11 Reggie Miller 2.00 5.00
C12 Loy Vaught .60 1.50
C13 Magic Johnson 3.00 8.00
C14 Alonzo Mourning 1.50 4.00
C15 Vin Baker .75 2.00
C16 Kevin Garnett 8.00 20.00
C17 Ed O'Bannon .75 2.00
C18 Patrick Ewing 1.50 4.00
C19 Shaquille O'Neal 4.00 10.00
C20 Jerry Stackhouse 3.00 8.00
C21 Charles Barkley 2.50 6.00
C22 Clifford Robinson .60 1.50
C23 Mitch Richmond 1.25 3.00
C24 David Robinson 2.00 5.00
C25 Shawn Kemp 1.50 4.00
C26 Damon Stoudamire 2.50 6.00
C27 John Stockton 2.00 5.00
C28 Bryant Reeves .75 2.00
C29 Juwan Howard 1.00 2.50
C30 Michael Jordan 20.00 50.00

1995-96 SP Championship Championship Shots

COMPLETE SET (20) 10.00 25.00
STATED ODDS 1:3
ONE PER SPECIAL RETAIL PACK
*GOLD: 3X TO 8X HI COLUMN
GOLD: STATED ODDS 1:62
S1 Antonio McDyess .60 1.50
S2 Nick Van Exel .50 1.25
S3 Michael Finley 1.25 3.00
S4 Anfernee Hardaway 1.25 3.00
S5 Latrell Sprewell .50 1.25
S6 Brian Grant .40 1.00
S7 Juwan Howard .50 1.25
S8 Ed O'Bannon .40 1.00
S9 Kevin Garnett 4.00 10.00
S10 Charles Barkley 1.25 3.00
S11 Joe Smith .60 1.50
S12 Patrick Ewing .75 2.00
S13 Brent Barry .75 2.00
S14 Dennis Rodman 1.00 2.50
S15 Jerry Stackhouse 1.50 4.00
S16 Michael Jordan 8.00 20.00
S17 Jalen Rose .60 1.50
S18 Jamal Mashburn .50 1.25
S19 Theo Ratliff .75 2.00
S20 Shaquille O'Neal 2.00 5.00

1995-96 SP Championship Jordan Collection

COMPLETE SET (4) 15.00 40.00
COMMON CARD (JC21-JC24) 5.00 12.00

2000-01 SP Game Floor

61-100 PRINT RUN 300 SERIAL #'d SETS
1 Jason Terry 1.00 2.50
2 Toni Kukoc 1.25 3.00
3 Antoine Walker 1.00 2.50
4 Paul Pierce 1.50 4.00
5 Jamal Mashburn .75 2.00
6 Baron Davis 1.00 2.50
7 Elton Brand 1.00 2.50
8 Ron Mercer .75 2.00
9 Andre Miller .75 2.00
10 Lamond Murray .60 1.50
11 Michael Finley 1.00 2.50
12 Dirk Nowitzki 2.50 6.00
13 Antonio McDyess .75 2.00
14 Nick Van Exel 1.00 2.50
15 Jerry Stackhouse 1.00 2.50
16 Joe Smith .75 2.00
17 Antawn Jamison 1.00 2.50
18 Larry Hughes 1.00 2.50
19 Steve Francis 1.00 2.50
20 Maurice Taylor .60 1.50
21 Jalen Rose .75 2.00
22 Reggie Miller 2.00 5.00
23 Lamar Odom 1.00 2.50
24 Corey Maggette .75 2.00
25 Kobe Bryant 8.00 20.00
26 Shaquille O'Neal 4.00 10.00
27 Horace Grant 1.00 2.50
28 Eddie Jones 1.00 2.50
29 Tim Hardaway 1.00 2.50
30 Glenn Robinson 1.00 2.50
31 Ray Allen 1.50 4.00
32 Kevin Garnett 2.50 6.00
33 Terrell Brandon .75 2.00
34 Wally Szczerbiak .75 2.00
35 Stephon Marbury 1.25 3.00
36 Keith Van Horn .75 2.00
37 Latrell Sprewell 1.25 3.00
38 Allan Houston 1.00 2.50
39 Tracy McGrady 2.00 5.00
40 Darrell Armstrong .60 1.50
41 Allen Iverson 2.50 6.00
42 Dikembe Mutombo 1.50 4.00
43 Jason Kidd 2.50 6.00
44 Shawn Marion 1.00 2.50
45 Rasheed Wallace 1.25 3.00
46 Damon Stoudamire 1.00 2.50
47 Chris Webber 1.25 3.00
48 Jason Williams 1.50 4.00
49 Tim Duncan 2.50 6.00
50 David Robinson 2.00 5.00
51 Gary Payton 1.50 4.00
52 Rashard Lewis .75 2.00
53 Vince Carter 2.00 5.00
54 Charles Oakley 1.00 2.50
55 Karl Malone 2.00 5.00
56 John Stockton 2.00 5.00
57 Shareef Abdur-Rahim 1.00 2.50
58 Mike Bibby 1.00 2.50
59 Richard Hamilton 1.25 3.00
60 Mitch Richmond 1.25 3.00
61 Kenyon Martin RC 5.00 12.00
62 Marc Jackson RC 2.00 5.00
63 Darius Miles RC 2.50 6.00
64 Morris Peterson RC 2.50 6.00
65 Mike Miller RC 4.00 10.00
66 Quentin Richardson RC 2.00 5.00
67 DerMarr Johnson RC 1.50 4.00
68 Chris Mihm RC 1.50 4.00
69 Jamal Crawford RC 6.00 15.00
70 Joel Przybilla RC 2.00 5.00
71 Keyon Dooling RC 2.00 5.00
72 Jerome Moiso RC 1.50 4.00
73 Mike Penberthy RC 2.50 6.00
74 Courtney Alexander RC 1.50 4.00
75 Mateen Cleaves RC 2.00 5.00
76 Wang Zhizhi RC 30.00 80.00
77 Hedo Turkoglu RC 4.00 10.00
78 Desmond Mason RC 3.00 8.00
79 Marcus Fizer RC 2.00 5.00
80 Jamaal Magloire RC 2.50 6.00
81 Stromile Swift RC 2.00 5.00
82 DeShawn Stevenson RC 2.50 6.00
83 Stephen Jackson RC 5.00 12.00
84 Erick Barkley RC 1.50 4.00
85 Mark Madsen RC 2.50 6.00
86 Dan Langhi RC 1.50 4.00
87 Hanno Mottola RC 1.50 4.00
88 Paul McPherson RC 1.50 4.00
89 Eddie House RC 2.00 5.00
90 Chris Porter RC 1.50 4.00
91 Jason Collier RC 2.50 6.00
92 Speedy Claxton RC 2.50 6.00
93 Ruben Wolkowyski RC 1.50 4.00
94 A.J. Guyton RC 1.50 4.00
95 Donnell Harvey RC 2.00 5.00
96 Ira Newble RC 2.00 5.00
97 Lee Nailon 1.50 4.00
98 Pepe Sanchez RC 2.00 5.00
99 Eduardo Najera RC 2.50 6.00
100 David Vanterpool RC 2.50 6.00

2000-01 SP Game Floor Authentic Fabric/Floor Combos

STATED ODDS 1:10
*GOLD: 2.5X TO 6X HI
GOLD PRINT RUN 25 SER.#'d SETS
AIC Allen Iverson 20.00 50.00
DMC Darius Miles 3.00 8.00
JKC Jason Kidd 15.00 40.00
JMC Jamal Mashburn 2.50 6.00
KAC Karl Malone 15.00 40.00
KBC Kobe Bryant 100.00 250.00
KGC Kevin Garnett 20.00 50.00
MAC Marc Jackson 2.50 6.00
MDC Antonio McDyess 2.50 6.00
PPC Paul Pierce 15.00 40.00
RLC Rashard Lewis 2.50 6.00
SMC Stephon Marbury 4.00 10.00
SOC Shaquille O'Neal 25.00 60.00
TMC Tracy McGrady 20.00 50.00

2000-01 SP Game Floor Authentic Floor

STATED ODDS 1:1
AH Allan Houston AS 2.50 6.00
AH2 Allan Houston 2.50 6.00
AI Allen Iverson 6.00 15.00
AM Andre Miller 2.00 5.00
BD Baron Davis 2.50 6.00
CA Courtney Alexander 1.50 4.00
CP Chris Porter 1.50 4.00
CW Chris Webber 3.00 8.00
DE Desmond Mason 3.00 8.00
DJ DerMarr Johnson 1.50 4.00
DM Darius Miles 2.00 5.00
DS DeShawn Stevenson 2.00 5.00
DV David Robinson 5.00 12.00
EJ Eddie Jones 2.50 6.00
FI Marcus Fizer 2.00 5.00
GP Gary Payton 4.00 10.00
GR Glenn Robinson 2.50 6.00
JK Jason Kidd 4.00 10.00
JM Jamaal Magloire 2.50 6.00
JP Joel Przybilla 2.00 5.00
JS Jerry Stackhouse 2.50 6.00
JT Jason Terry 2.50 6.00
JW Jason Williams 4.00 10.00
KA Karl Malone 5.00 12.00
KB Kobe Bryant AS 40.00 100.00
KB2 Kobe Bryant 25.00 60.00
KE Khalid El-Amin 1.50 4.00
KG Kevin Garnett AS 6.00 15.00
KG2 Kevin Garnett 6.00 15.00
KM Kenyon Martin 5.00 12.00
LS Latrell Sprewell AS 3.00 8.00
LS2 Latrell Sprewell 3.00 8.00
MA Marc Jackson 2.00 5.00
MC Mateen Cleaves 2.00 5.00
MD Antonio McDyess AS 2.00 5.00
MD2 Antonio McDyess 2.00 5.00
MF Michael Finley 2.50 6.00
MJ Michael Jordan 40.00 100.00
MM Mike Miller 4.00 10.00
MP Morris Peterson 2.50 6.00
MT Dikembe Mutombo 4.00 10.00
PP Paul Pierce 4.00 10.00
PS Peja Stojakovic 2.00 5.00
QR Quentin Richardson 2.00 5.00
RA Ray Allen 4.00 10.00
RA2 Ray Allen AS 4.00 10.00
RL Rashard Lewis 2.00 5.00
RW Rasheed Wallace AS 3.00 8.00
RW2 Rasheed Wallace 3.00 8.00
SA Shareef Abdur-Rahim 2.50 6.00
SF Steve Francis 2.50 6.00
SH Shawn Marion 2.50 6.00
SJ Stephen Jackson 5.00 12.00
SM Stephon Marbury AS 3.00 8.00
SM2 Stephon Marbury 3.00 8.00
SO Shaquille O'Neal 10.00 25.00
SP Scottie Pippen 6.00 15.00
SS Stromile Swift 2.00 5.00
TM Tracy McGrady 5.00 12.00
WS Wally Szczerbiak 2.00 5.00

2000-01 SP Game Floor Authentic Floor Autographs

STATED PRINT RUN 200 SERIAL #'d SETS
CAA Courtney Alexander/200 3.00 8.00
DJA DerMarr Johnson/200 3.00 8.00
DMA Darius Miles/200 5.00 12.00
DSA DeShawn Stevenson/200 5.00 12.00
FIA Marcus Fizer/200 4.00 10.00
JPA Joel Przybilla/200 4.00 10.00
JSA Jerry Stackhouse/200 12.00 30.00
KGA Kevin Garnett/21 150.00 400.00
KMA Kenyon Martin/200 8.00 20.00
MAA Marc Jackson/200 4.00 10.00
MJA Michael Jordan/23 10,000.00 20,000.00
MMA Mike Miller/200 8.00 20.00
MPA Morris Peterson/200 5.00 12.00
SFA Steve Francis/200 12.00 30.00
SJA Stephen Jackson/200 10.00 25.00
SSA Stromile Swift/200 4.00 10.00

2000-01 SP Game Floor Authentic Floor Combos

STATED ODDS 1:10
*GOLD: .75X TO 2X BASE COMBO HI
GOLD PRINT RUN 100 SER.#'d SETS
C1 A.Iverson/S.O'Neal 25.00 60.00
C2 M.Jackson/S.Jackson 4.00 10.00
C3 S.Marbury/S.Francis 5.00 12.00
C4 C.Webber/J.Williams 5.00 12.00
C5 D.Miles/M.Jackson 4.00 10.00
C6 M.Jordan/L.Bird 200.00 500.00
C7 K.Martin/C.Webber 5.00 12.00
C8 K.Martin/D.Johnson 4.00 10.00
C9 K.Martin/M.Jackson 4.00 10.00
C10 K.Martin/S.Jackson 4.00 10.00
C11 K.Garnett/C.Webber 8.00 20.00
C12 K.Garnett/T.McGrady 12.00 30.00
C13 K.Bryant/A.Iverson 100.00 250.00
C14 K.Bryant/C.Webber 50.00 120.00
C15 K.Bryant/D.Miles 40.00 100.00
C16 K.Bryant/J.Kidd 100.00 250.00
C17 M.Jordan/K.Malone 100.00 250.00
C18 K.Malone/J.Stockton 15.00 40.00
C19 K.Bryant/K.Martin 40.00 100.00
C20 K.Bryant/K.Garnett 100.00 250.00
C21 K.Bryant/K.Garnett 100.00 250.00
C22 K.Bryant/L.Bird 125.00 300.00
C23 J.Williams/P.Stojakovic 5.00 12.00
C24 K.Bryant/M.Jordan 200.00 500.00
C25 K.Bryant/S.O'Neal 125.00 300.00
C26 K.Bryant/S.Francis 40.00 100.00
C27 K.Bryant/T.McGrady 100.00 250.00
C28 J.Kidd/S.Marion 8.00 20.00
C29 M.Cleaves/M.Peterson 4.00 10.00
C30 K.Garnett/R.Wallace 10.00 25.00

2002-03 SP Game Used

OVERALL ODDS JSY/AU's 1:1
103-144 PRINT RUN 900 SER.#'d SETS
1 Shareef Abdur-Rahim JSY 3.00 8.00
2 DerMarr Johnson JSY 2.50 6.00
3 Jason Terry JSY 2.50 6.00
4 Antoine Walker JSY 2.50 6.00
5 Paul Pierce SP JSY 10.00 25.00
6 Kedrick Brown JSY 2.00 5.00
7 Tony Battie 1.25 3.00
8 Jamal Mashburn JSY 2.50 6.00
9 Baron Davis 2.00 5.00
10 David Wesley 1.25 3.00
11 Jalen Rose 1.50 4.00
12 Eddy Curry JSY 2.50 6.00
13 Tyson Chandler JSY 3.00 8.00
14 Marcus Fizer JSY 2.00 5.00
15 Lamond Murray 1.25 3.00
16 Andre Miller JSY 2.50 6.00
17 Chris Mihm JSY 2.00 5.00
18 Ricky Davis 1.50 4.00
19 Dirk Nowitzki 5.00 12.00
20 Michael Finley 2.00 5.00
21 Steve Nash 4.00 10.00
22 Nick Van Exel 2.00 5.00
23 Antonio McDyess JSY 2.50 6.00
24 Juwan Howard 1.50 4.00
25 James Posey 1.25 3.00
26 Jerry Stackhouse 2.00 5.00
27 Clifford Robinson 2.00 5.00
28 Ben Wallace 2.50 6.00
29 Antawn Jamison 1.50 4.00
30 Jason Richardson SP JSY 3.00 8.00
31 Gilbert Arenas 2.00 5.00
32 Steve Francis 2.00 5.00
33 Cuttino Mobley 1.25 3.00
34 Eddie Griffin JSY 2.00 5.00
35 Reggie Miller JSY 6.00 15.00
36 Jermaine O'Neal 1.50 4.00
37 Jamaal Tinsley JSY 2.50 6.00
38 Elton Brand 1.50 4.00
39 Darius Miles JSY 3.00 8.00
40 Lamar Odom JSY 3.00 8.00
41 Corey Maggette JSY 2.50 6.00
42 Kobe Bryant SP JSY 75.00 200.00
43 Shaquille O'Neal 8.00 20.00
44 Derek Fisher 2.00 5.00
45 Devean George 1.25 3.00
46 Pau Gasol 1.50 4.00
47 Jason Williams 2.50 6.00
48 Shane Battier 2.00 5.00
49 Stromile Swift 1.25 3.00
50 Alonzo Mourning 3.00 8.00
51 Eddie Jones 2.00 5.00
52 Brian Grant 1.25 3.00
53 Ray Allen 3.00 8.00
54 Glenn Robinson 2.00 5.00
55 Sam Cassell 2.00 5.00
56 Kevin Garnett SP JSY 12.00 30.00
57 Wally Szczerbiak JSY 2.50 6.00
58 Terrell Brandon JSY 2.50 6.00
59 Chauncey Billups JSY 3.00 8.00
60 Jason Kidd SP JSY 8.00 20.00
61 Richard Jefferson 1.50 4.00
62 Kenyon Martin JSY 3.00 8.00
63 Brandon Armstrong JSY 2.50 6.00
64 Keith Van Horn 1.50 4.00
65 Allan Houston 2.00 5.00
66 Latrell Sprewell 2.00 5.00
67 Kurt Thomas 1.25 3.00
68 Tracy McGrady 3.00 8.00
69 Mike Miller JSY 2.50 6.00
70 Darrell Armstrong JSY 2.00 5.00
71 Allen Iverson SP JSY 8.00 20.00
72 Dikembe Mutombo JSY 5.00 12.00
73 Aaron McKie 1.25 3.00
74 Stephon Marbury 2.50 6.00
75 Shawn Marion 2.00 5.00
76 Joe Johnson JSY 2.50 6.00
77 Anfernee Hardaway 5.00 12.00
78 Rasheed Wallace 2.50 6.00
79 Damon Stoudamire 2.00 5.00
80 Scottie Pippen 5.00 12.00
81 Chris Webber 2.50 6.00
82 Peja Stojakovic 1.50 4.00
83 Mike Bibby JSY 3.00 8.00
84 Gerald Wallace JSY 2.50 6.00
85 Tim Duncan 5.00 12.00
86 David Robinson 4.00 10.00
87 Tony Parker JSY 5.00 12.00
88 Gary Payton 3.00 8.00
89 Rashard Lewis 1.50 4.00
90 Desmond Mason 1.50 4.00
91 V.Radmanovic JSY 2.00 5.00
92 Morris Peterson 1.50 4.00
93 Antonio Davis 1.50 4.00
94 Vince Carter 4.00 10.00
95 Karl Malone 4.00 10.00
96 John Stockton JSY 6.00 15.00
97 Donyell Marshall 1.25 3.00
98 Andrei Kirilenko 1.50 4.00
99 Richard Hamilton 2.50 6.00
100 Michael Jordan SP JSY 125.00 300.00
101 Courtney Alexander JSY 2.00 5.00
102 Kwame Brown JSY 2.00 5.00
103 Jay Williams RC 3.00 8.00
104 Yao Ming RC 20.00 50.00
105 Drew Gooden RC 4.00 10.00
106 DaJuan Wagner RC 3.00 8.00
107 Curtis Borchardt RC 2.50 6.00
108 Amare Stoudemire RC 10.00 25.00
109 Caron Butler RC 4.00 10.00
110 Jared Jeffries RC 3.00 8.00
111 Chris Wilcox RC 3.00 8.00
112 Qyntel Woods RC 2.50 6.00
113 Casey Jacobsen RC 3.00 8.00
114 Melvin Ely RC 3.00 8.00
115 Kareem Rush RC 3.00 8.00
116 Mike Dunleavy RC 4.00 10.00
117 Dan Dickau RC 2.50 6.00
118 Juan Dixon RC 3.00 8.00
119 Sam Clancy RC 3.00 8.00
120 Tayshaun Prince RC 8.00 20.00
121 Dan Gadzuric RC 3.00 8.00
122 Chris Jefferies RC 2.50 6.00
123 Steve Logan RC 4.00 10.00
124 Vincent Yarbrough RC 2.50 6.00
125 Fred Jones RC 3.00 8.00
126 Efthimios Rentzias RC 2.50 6.00
127 Nene Hilario RC 4.00 10.00
128 Rod Grizzard RC 2.50 6.00
129 Matt Barnes RC 5.00 12.00
130 Nikoloz Tskitishvili RC 2.50 6.00
131 Bostjan Nachbar RC 3.00 8.00
132 Marcus Haislip RC 2.50 6.00
133 Jamal Sampson RC 2.50 6.00
134 Frank Williams RC 2.50 6.00
135 Tito Maddox RC 2.50 6.00
136 Carlos Boozer RC 4.00 10.00
137 Jiri Welsch RC 3.00 8.00
138 John Salmons RC 4.00 10.00
139 Predrag Savovic RC 3.00 8.00
140 Marko Jaric 4.00 10.00
141 Robert Archibald RC 2.50 6.00
142 Manu Ginobili RC 20.00 50.00
143 Chris Owens RC 2.50 6.00
144 Ryan Humphrey RC 3.00 8.00

2002-03 SP Game Used Autographed Jerseys

PRINT RUN 100 SERIAL #'D SETS
1 Shareef Abdur-Rahim 8.00 20.00
2 DerMarr Johnson 5.00 12.00
4 Antoine Walker 10.00 25.00
6 Kedrick Brown 5.00 12.00
12 Eddy Curry 5.00 12.00
13 Tyson Chandler 10.00 25.00
14 Marcus Fizer 8.00 20.00
16 Andre Miller 10.00 25.00
34 Eddie Griffin 8.00 20.00
39 Darius Miles 5.00 12.00
40 Lamar Odom 8.00 20.00
41 Corey Maggette 8.00 20.00
57 Wally Szczerbiak 10.00 25.00
58 Terrell Brandon 5.00 12.00
61 Richard Jefferson 6.00 15.00
62 Kenyon Martin 15.00 40.00
63 Brandon Armstrong 5.00 12.00
69 Mike Miller 12.00 30.00
84 Gerald Wallace 12.00 30.00
87 Tony Parker 40.00 100.00
91 Vladimir Radmanovic 8.00 20.00
101 Courtney Alexander 5.00 12.00
102 Kwame Brown 5.00 12.00

2002-03 SP Game Used Autographed SP Jerseys

PRINT RUN 25 SERIAL #'D SETS
5 Paul Pierce 150.00 400.00
42 Kobe Bryant 3,000.00 6,000.00
56 Kevin Garnett 200.00 500.00
60 Jason Kidd 125.00 300.00
100 Michael Jordan 4,000.00 8,000.00

2002-03 SP Game Used Rookies Gold

*GOLD: 1.25X TO 3X BASE CARD HI
PRINT RUN 50 SER.#'d SETS

2002-03 SP Game Used All-Star Apparel

STATED OVERALL JSY ODDS 1:1
*GOLD: .75X TO 2X HI
GOLD: STATED PRINT RUN 100 SETS
AKAS Andrei Kirilenko 2.00 5.00
AMAS Alonzo Mourning 4.00 10.00
BHAS Brendan Haywood 1.50 4.00
CMAS Chris Mihm 1.50 4.00
DMAS Desmond Mason 2.00 5.00
DNAS Dirk Nowitzki 6.00 15.00
GIAS Gilbert Arenas 2.50 6.00
GPAS Gary Payton 4.00 10.00
GWAS Gerald Wallace 2.00 5.00
KBAS Kobe Bryant 40.00 100.00
KDAS Jason Kidd 4.00 10.00
KMAS Kenyon Martin 2.50 6.00
LNAS Lee Nailon 1.50 4.00
MFAS Marcus Fizer 1.50 4.00
MGAS Magic Johnson 6.00 15.00
MJAS Michael Jordan 125.00 300.00
MMAS Mike Miller 2.00 5.00
PGAS Pau Gasol 4.00 10.00
QRAS Quentin Richardson 1.50 4.00
SFAS Steve Francis 2.50 6.00
SNAS Steve Nash 5.00 12.00
SSAS Steve Smith 2.00 5.00
WSAS Wally Szczerbiak 2.00 5.00
ZRAS Zeljko Rebraca 1.50 4.00

2002-03 SP Game Used Authentic Fabrics Dual

PRINT RUN 100 SERIAL #'d SETS
AMCMJ A.Miller/C.Mihm 6.00 15.00
BDJMJ B.Davis/J.Mashburn 6.00 15.00
CMLOJ C.Maggette/L.Odom 6.00 15.00
CWPSJ C.Webber/P.Stojakovic 10.00 25.00
DNMFJ D.Nowitzki/M.Finley 15.00 40.00
DNSNJ D.Nowitzki/S.Nash 15.00 40.00
DRTPJ D.Robinson/T.Parker 10.00 25.00
EBKMJ E.Brand/K.Malone 12.00 30.00
ECTCJ E.Curry/T.Chandler 6.00 15.00
JPJHJ J.Posey/J.Howard 6.00 15.00
JTTPJ J.Tinsley/T.Parker 10.00 25.00
KBAIJ K.Bryant/A.Iverson 75.00 200.00
KBKGJ K.Bryant/K.Garnett 40.00 100.00
KGTBJ K.Garnett/T.Brandon 8.00 20.00
KGWSJ K.Garnett/W.Szczerbiak 8.00 20.00
KMJSJ K.Malone/J.Stockton 8.00 20.00
KMKVJ K.Martin/K.Van Horn 6.00 15.00
KWCAJ K.Brown/C.Alexander 6.00 15.00
MFTHJ M.Fizer/T.Hassell 6.00 15.00
MJKBJ M.Jordan/K.Bryant 200.00 500.00
MJMGJ M.Jordan/M.Johnson 50.00 120.00
PPAWJ P.Pierce/A.Walker 6.00 15.00
RAGRJ R.Allen/G.Robinson 12.00 30.00
RMJOJ R.Miller/J.O'Neal 15.00 40.00
RWDSJ R.Wallace/D.Stoudamire 12.00 30.00
SADJJ S.Abdur-Rahim/D.Johnson 6.00 15.00
SMSMJ S.Marbury/S.Marion 10.00 25.00
TMMMJ T.McGrady/M.Miller 12.00 30.00

2002-03 SP Game Used Authentic Fabrics Triple

PRINT RUN 25 SERIAL #'d SETS
1 Walker/Pierce/Anderson 30.00 80.00
2 Webber/Stojakovic/Bibby 30.00 80.00
3 Terry/Abdur-Rahim/Johnson 20.00 50.00
4 Bryant/Fox/Horry 100.00 250.00
5 Malone/Stockton/Kirilenko 25.00 60.00
6 McDyess/Howard/Posey 20.00 50.00
7 Jordan/Bryant/Garnett 300.00 600.00
8 Marbury/Marion/Hardaway 50.00 120.00

2002-03 SP Game Used Authentic Patches

PRINT RUN 100 SERIAL #'d SETS
AWP Antoine Walker 10.00 25.00
BDP Baron Davis 12.00 30.00
CMP Corey Maggette 10.00 25.00
DJP DerMarr Johnson 8.00 20.00
DMP Darius Miles 8.00 20.00
GWP Gerald Wallace 10.00 25.00
JRP Jason Richardson 12.00 30.00
KBP Kobe Bryant 75.00 200.00
KGP Kevin Garnett 30.00 80.00
KWP Kwame Brown 8.00 20.00
LSP Latrell Sprewell 15.00 40.00
MJP Michael Jordan 100.00 200.00
PPP Paul Pierce 20.00 50.00
QRP Quentin Richardson 8.00 20.00
SAP Shareef Abdur-Rahim 12.00 30.00
TBP Terrell Brandon 8.00 20.00
TPP Tony Parker 20.00 50.00
WSP Wally Szczerbiak 10.00 25.00

2002-03 SP Game Used Autographed Authentic Patches

PRINT RUN 50 SERIAL #'d SETS
AWAP Antoine Walker 30.00 80.00
CMAP Corey Maggette 15.00 40.00
DJAP DerMarr Johnson 15.00 40.00
DMAP Darius Miles 15.00 40.00
GWAP Gerald Wallace 30.00 80.00
KBAP Kobe Bryant 1,000.00 2,000.00
KGAP Kevin Garnett 125.00 250.00
KWAP Kwame Brown 15.00 40.00
MJAP Michael Jordan 2,500.00 5,000.00
PPAP Paul Pierce 40.00 100.00
QRAP Quentin Richardson 15.00 40.00
TBAP Terrell Brandon 15.00 40.00
TPAP Tony Parker 40.00 100.00
WSAP Wally Szczerbiak 15.00 40.00

2002-03 SP Game Used Dual Authentic Patches

PRINT RUN 25 SERIAL #'d SETS
KBJKP K.Bryant/J.Kidd 150.00 400.00
KBJRP K.Bryant/J.Richardson 125.00 300.00
KBKGP K.Bryant/K.Garnett 125.00 300.00
KBMGP K.Bryant/M.Johnson 100.00 200.00
MJKBP M.Jordan/K.Bryant 500.00 1,000.00
MJMGP M.Jordan/M.Johnson 300.00 500.00

2002-03 SP Game Used Extra SIGnificance

PRINT RUN 25 SERIAL #'D SETS
DMLO D.Miles/L.Odom 25.00 60.00
JKKM J.Kidd/K.Martin 75.00 200.00
JRJT J.Richardson/J.Tinsley 25.00 60.00
KBJK K.Bryant/J.Kidd 2,000.00 4,000.00
KBJR K.Bryant/J.Richardson 1,000.00 2,000.00
KBKG K.Bryant/K.Garnett 10,000.00 20,000.00
KBMA K.Bryant/M.Johnson 10,000.00 20,000.00
KGTC K.Garnett/T.Chandler 125.00 300.00
MJKB M.Jordan/K.Bryant 30,000.00 60,000.00
MJMA M.Jordan/M.Johnson 10,000.00 20,000.00

2002-03 SP Game Used SIGnificance
STATED PRINT RUN 100 SERIAL #'d SETS
*GOLD: .75X TO 2X SIGNIFICANCE HI
GOLD PRINT RUN 50 SER.#'d SETS
AW Antoine Walker 6.00 15.00
CM Corey Maggette 4.00 10.00
DJ DerMarr Johnson 4.00 10.00
DS DeShawn Stevenson 4.00 10.00
EG Eddie Griffin 4.00 10.00
HM Hanno Mottola 4.00 10.00
JA Jamaal Magloire 4.00 10.00
JS Jerry Stackhouse 6.00 15.00
JT Jamaal Tinsley 4.00 10.00
KE Kedrick Brown 4.00 10.00
KM Kenyon Martin 6.00 15.00
KW Kwame Brown 4.00 10.00
LH Larry Hughes 4.00 10.00
LM Lamond Murray 4.00 10.00
LW Loren Woods 4.00 10.00
MB Michael Bradley 4.00 10.00
MF Marcus Fizer 4.00 10.00
MK Mark Madsen 4.00 10.00
MM Mike Miller 4.00 10.00
MO Terence Morris 4.00 10.00
MP Morris Peterson 4.00 10.00
QR Quentin Richardson 4.00 10.00
RJ Richard Jefferson 5.00 12.00
RM Ron Mercer 4.00 10.00
RW Rodney White 4.00 10.00
SD Samuel Dalembert 4.00 10.00
TC Tyson Chandler 8.00 20.00
TM Troy Murphy 4.00 10.00
WS Wally Szczerbiak 4.00 10.00

2002-03 SP Game Used Special SIGnificance
STATED PRINT RUN 50 SERIAL #'d SETS
AM Andre Miller 10.00 25.00
DM Darius Miles 10.00 25.00
JK Jason Kidd 30.00 80.00
JR Jason Richardson 15.00 40.00
KB Kobe Bryant 200.00 500.00
KG Kevin Garnett 125.00 300.00
LO Lamar Odom 15.00 40.00
MJ Michael Jordan 1,500.00 3,000.00
PP Paul Pierce 60.00 150.00
SA Shareef Abdur-Rahim 10.00 25.00
TM Troy Murphy 10.00 25.00

2002-03 SP Game Used UD Rookie Exclusive Autographs
PRINT RUN 100 SERIAL #'d SETS
RKAS Amare Stoudemire 50.00 120.00
RKCA Caron Butler 6.00 15.00
RKCH Chris Jefferies 4.00 10.00
RKCJ Casey Jacobsen 5.00 12.00
RKCW Chris Wilcox 5.00 12.00
RKDD Dan Dickau 4.00 10.00
RKDG Drew Gooden 6.00 15.00
RKDW DaJuan Wagner 5.00 12.00
RKEL Melvin Ely 5.00 12.00
RKFJ Fred Jones 5.00 12.00
RKFW Frank Williams 4.00 10.00
RKJD Juan Dixon 5.00 12.00
RKJJ Jared Jeffries 5.00 12.00
RKJS John Salmons 6.00 15.00
RKJW Jay Williams 5.00 12.00
RKKR Kareem Rush 5.00 12.00
RKMH Marcus Haislip 4.00 10.00
RKNH Nene Hilario 6.00 15.00
RKNT Nikoloz Tskitishvili 4.00 10.00
RKQW Qyntel Woods 4.00 10.00
RKRH Ryan Humphrey 5.00 12.00
RKTP Tayshaun Prince 12.00 30.00
RKYM Yao Ming 50.00 120.00

2003-04 SP Game Used
OVERALL JSY STATED ODDS ONE PER PACK
95-106 MJ PRINT RUN 999 SER.#'d SETS
107-148 PRINT RUN 999 SER.#'d SETS
1 Shareef Abdur-Rahim 1.50 4.00
2 Glenn Robinson 1.25 3.00
3 Jason Terry JSY 2.50 6.00
4 Paul Pierce 2.50 6.00
5 Antoine Walker 1.50 4.00
6 Eddy Curry 1.00 2.50
7 Tyson Chandler JSY 2.50 6.00
8 Jalen Rose JSY 2.50 6.00
9 Jay Williams JSY 2.00 5.00
10 DaJuan Wagner JSY 2.00 5.00
11 Darius Miles JSY 2.00 5.00
12 Carlos Boozer JSY 2.50 6.00
13 Steve Nash 3.00 8.00
14 Michael Finley 1.50 4.00
15 Nick Van Exel 1.50 4.00
16 Dirk Nowitzki JSY 8.00 20.00
17 Rodney White 1.00 2.50
18 Marcus Camby 1.25 3.00
19 Nikoloz Tskitishvili 1.00 2.50
20 Nene Hilario JSY 2.50 6.00
21 Richard Hamilton 2.00 5.00
22 Chauncey Billups 2.00 5.00
23 Ben Wallace 2.00 5.00
24 Gilbert Arenas 1.50 4.00
25 Troy Murphy 1.00 2.50
26 Jason Richardson JSY 3.00 8.00
27 Antawn Jamison JSY 3.00 8.00
28 Cuttino Mobley 1.00 2.50
29 Steve Francis 1.50 4.00
30 Eddie Griffin 1.00 2.50
31 Jermaine O'Neal 1.50 4.00
32 Reggie Miller 3.00 8.00
33 Jamaal Tinsley JSY 2.00 5.00
34 Lamar Odom 1.25 3.00
35 Chris Wilcox 1.00 2.50
36 Marko Jaric 1.00 2.50
37 Elton Brand JSY 2.50 6.00
38 Andre Miller JSY 2.50 6.00
39 Kobe Bryant 12.00 30.00
40 Shaquille O'Neal 6.00 15.00
41 Gary Payton 2.50 6.00
42 Kareem Rush JSY 2.00 5.00
43 Mike Miller 1.25 3.00
44 Shane Battier JSY 2.50 6.00
45 Pau Gasol JSY 5.00 12.00
46 Eddie Jones 1.50 4.00
47 Brian Grant 1.00 2.50
48 Caron Butler JSY 2.50 6.00
49 Joe Smith 1.25 3.00
50 Desmond Mason 1.25 3.00
51 Toni Kukoc 1.50 4.00
52 Wally Szczerbiak 1.25 3.00
53 Kevin Garnett JSY 8.00 20.00
54 Alonzo Mourning 2.00 5.00
55 Kenyon Martin 1.50 4.00
56 Jason Kidd JSY 5.00 12.00
57 Richard Jefferson JSY 2.50 6.00
58 Baron Davis 1.50 4.00
59 Jamal Mashburn JSY 2.50 6.00
60 Latrell Sprewell 2.00 5.00
61 Allan Houston 1.50 4.00
62 Antonio McDyess 1.25 3.00
63 Juwan Howard 1.25 3.00
64 Drew Gooden JSY 2.50 6.00
65 Tracy McGrady JSY 5.00 12.00
66 Keith Van Horn 1.25 3.00
67 Aaron McKie 1.00 2.50
68 Allen Iverson JSY 8.00 20.00
69 Stephon Marbury 2.00 5.00
70 Shawn Marion 1.50 4.00
71 Anfernee Hardaway 4.00 10.00
72 Joe Johnson 1.25 3.00
73 Amare Stoudemire JSY 4.00 10.00
74 Rasheed Wallace 2.00 5.00
75 Scottie Pippen 4.00 10.00
76 Mike Bibby 1.50 4.00
77 Peja Stojakovic 1.25 3.00
78 Gerald Wallace 1.25 3.00
79 Chris Webber JSY 4.00 10.00
80 Tim Duncan 4.00 10.00
81 Manu Ginobili 3.00 8.00
82 Tony Parker JSY 5.00 12.00
83 Ray Allen 2.50 6.00
84 Rashard Lewis JSY 2.50 6.00
85 Morris Peterson 1.00 2.50
86 Antonio Davis 1.25 3.00
87 Vince Carter 3.00 8.00
88 John Stockton JSY 6.00 15.00
89 Karl Malone JSY 6.00 15.00
90 Jerry Stackhouse 2.00 5.00
91 Michael Jordan 12.00 30.00
92 Michael Jordan JSY 150.00 400.00
93 Kobe Bryant JSY 100.00 250.00
94 Yao Ming JSY 8.00 20.00
95 Michael Jordan Tribute 20.00 50.00
96 Michael Jordan Tribute 20.00 50.00
97 Michael Jordan Tribute 20.00 50.00
98 Michael Jordan Tribute 20.00 50.00
99 Michael Jordan Tribute 20.00 50.00
100 Michael Jordan Tribute 20.00 50.00
101 Michael Jordan Tribute 20.00 50.00
102 Michael Jordan Tribute 20.00 50.00
103 Michael Jordan Tribute 20.00 50.00
104 Michael Jordan Tribute 20.00 50.00
105 Michael Jordan Tribute 20.00 50.00
106 Michael Jordan Tribute 20.00 50.00
107 LeBron James RC 200.00 500.00
108 Darko Milicic RC 2.50 6.00
109 Carmelo Anthony RC 15.00 40.00
110 Chris Bosh RC 10.00 25.00
111 Dwyane Wade RC 25.00 60.00
112 Chris Kaman RC 3.00 8.00
113 Kirk Hinrich RC 3.00 8.00
114 T.J. Ford RC 2.50 6.00
115 Mike Sweetney RC 2.00 5.00
116 Jarvis Hayes RC 2.00 5.00
117 Mickael Pietrus RC 2.50 6.00
118 Nick Collison RC 2.50 6.00
119 Marcus Banks RC 2.00 5.00
120 Luke Ridnour RC 3.00 8.00
121 Reece Gaines RC 2.00 5.00
122 Troy Bell RC 2.00 5.00
123 Zarko Cabarkapa RC 2.00 5.00
124 David West RC 4.00 10.00
125 Aleksandar Pavlovic RC 2.50 6.00
126 Dahntay Jones RC 2.50 6.00
127 Boris Diaw RC 3.00 8.00
128 Zoran Planinic RC 2.00 5.00
129 Travis Outlaw RC 2.00 5.00
130 Brian Cook RC 2.00 5.00
131 Carlos Delfino RC 2.50 6.00
132 Ndudi Ebi RC 2.00 5.00
133 Kendrick Perkins RC 2.50 6.00
134 Leandro Barbosa RC 3.00 8.00
135 Josh Howard RC 3.00 8.00
136 Maciej Lampe RC 2.00 5.00
137 Jason Kapono RC 2.00 5.00
138 Luke Walton RC 3.00 8.00
139 Jerome Beasley RC 2.00 5.00
140 Sofoklis Schortsanitis RC 2.00 5.00
141 Mario Austin RC 2.00 5.00
142 Travis Hansen RC 2.00 5.00
143 Steve Blake RC 2.50 6.00
144 Slavko Vranes RC 2.00 5.00
145 Zaur Pachulia RC 3.00 8.00
146 Keith Bogans RC 2.00 5.00
147 Matt Bonner RC 3.00 8.00
148 Maurice Williams RC 3.00 8.00

2003-04 SP Game Used Gold
*1-94 SINGLES: .5X TO 1.25X BASE HI
*1-94 JSY SINGLES: .6X TO 1.5X BASE HI
1-94 PRINT RUN 100 SER.#'d SETS
1-94 JSY PRINT RUN 50 SER.#'d SETS
COMMON MJ TRIB (95-106) 80.00 200.00
95-106 MJ PRINT RUN 50 SER.#'d SETS
*107-148 RC SINGLES: 1X TO 2.5X BASE HI
107-148 RC PRINT RUN 50 SER.#'d SETS
91 Michael Jordan 60.00 150.00
92 Michael Jordan JSY 300.00 600.00
107 Lebron James 5,000.00 10,000.00
111 Dwyane Wade 60.00 150.00

2003-04 SP Game Used All Star Apparel
OVERALL JERSEY ODDS ONE PER PACK
*GOLD SINGLES: .75X TO 2X BASE CARD HI
GOLD PRINT RUN 100 SER.#'d SETS
AKAS Andrei Kirilenko 3.00 8.00
BWAS Ben Wallace 5.00 12.00
DGAS Drew Gooden 3.00 8.00
DMAS Desmond Mason 3.00 8.00
GAAS Gilbert Arenas 4.00 10.00
GGAS Gordan Giricek 2.50 6.00
JAAS Marko Jaric 2.50 6.00
JRAS Jason Richardson 4.00 10.00
JTAS Jamaal Tinsley 2.50 6.00
KBAS Kobe Bryant 100.00 250.00
NHAS Nene Hilario 3.00 8.00
RJAS Richard Jefferson 3.00 8.00
SMAS Shawn Marion 4.00 10.00
TDAS Tim Duncan 10.00 25.00
TMAS Troy Murphy 2.50 6.00
TPAS Tony Parker 6.00 15.00
YMAS Yao Ming 10.00 25.00
ZIAS Zydrunas Ilgauskas 3.00 8.00

2003-04 SP Game Used Authentic Fabrics
OVERALL JERSEY ODDS ONE PER PACK
*GOLD SINGLES/100: .75X TO 2X BASE HI
ADJ Antonio Davis 2.50 6.00
AHJ Allan Houston 3.00 8.00
AHJ Anfernee Hardaway 8.00 20.00
AMJ Aaron McKie 2.00 5.00
AMJ Alonzo Mourning 4.00 10.00
AWJ Antoine Walker 3.00 8.00
BDJ Baron Davis 3.00 8.00
BNJ Bostjan Nachbar 2.00 5.00
BWJ Ben Wallace 4.00 10.00
CBJ Chauncey Billups 4.00 10.00
CJD Chris Jefferies 2.00 5.00
CWJ Chris Wilcox 2.00 5.00
DDJ Dan Dickau 2.00 5.00
DGJ Devean George 2.00 5.00
DMJ Desmond Mason 2.50 6.00
DMJ Dikembe Mutombo 4.00 10.00
DRJ David Robinson 6.00 15.00
DWJ David Wesley 2.00 5.00
ECJ Eddy Curry 2.00 5.00
EGJ Manu Ginobili 6.00 15.00
EGJ Eddie Griffin 2.00 5.00
EJJ Eddie Jones 3.00 8.00
ESJ Eric Snow 2.00 5.00
FJJ Marcus Fizer 2.00 5.00
FJJ Fred Jones 2.00 5.00
FWJ Frank Williams 2.00 5.00
GGJ Gordan Giricek 2.00 5.00
GHJ Grant Hill 4.00 10.00
GPJ Gary Payton 5.00 12.00
GRJ Glenn Robinson 2.50 6.00
GWJ Gerald Wallace 2.50 6.00
JAJ Marko Jaric 2.00 5.00
JDJ Juan Dixon 2.00 5.00
JEJ Jared Jeffries 2.00 5.00
JJJ Joe Johnson 2.50 6.00
JOJ Jermaine O'Neal 3.00 8.00
JSJ John Salmons 2.50 6.00
JWJ Jiri Welsch 2.00 5.00
KBJ Kobe Bryant 100.00 250.00
KBJ Kwame Brown 2.00 5.00
KEJ Kedrick Brown 2.00 5.00
KMJ Kenyon Martin 3.00 8.00
KTJ Kurt Thomas 2.00 5.00
KVJ Keith Van Horn 2.50 6.00
LJJ LeBron James 200.00 500.00
LOJ Lamar Odom 2.50 6.00
LSJ Latrell Sprewell 4.00 10.00
MAJ Shawn Marion 3.00 8.00
MBJ Mike Bibby 3.00 8.00
MCJ Marcus Camby 2.50 6.00
MEJ Melvin Ely 2.00 5.00
MFJ Michael Finley 3.00 8.00
MHJ Marcus Haislip 2.00 5.00
MJJ Michael Jordan 200.00 500.00
MMJ Mike Miller 2.50 6.00
MPJ Morris Peterson 2.00 5.00
NTJ Nikoloz Tskitishvili 2.00 5.00
PPJ Paul Pierce 5.00 12.00
PSJ Peja Stojakovic 2.00 5.00
QRJ Quentin Richardson 2.00 5.00
QWJ Qyntel Woods 2.00 5.00
RAJ Ray Allen 5.00 12.00
RBJ Rasual Butler 2.00 5.00
RHJ Richard Hamilton 4.00 10.00
RMJ Reggie Miller 6.00 15.00
RWJ Rasheed Wallace 4.00 10.00
SAJ Shareef Abdur Rahim 3.00 8.00
SFJ Steve Francis 3.00 8.00
SMJ Stephon Marbury 4.00 10.00
SNJ Steve Nash 6.00 15.00
SPJ Scottie Pippen 8.00 20.00
STJ Jerry Stackhouse 4.00 10.00
TDJ Tim Duncan 8.00 20.00
TKJ Toni Kukoc 3.00 8.00
VBJ Vin Baker 2.00 5.00
WAJ Charlie Ward 2.00 5.00
WSJ Wally Szczerbiak 2.50 6.00

2003-04 SP Game Used Authentic Fabrics Autographs
PRINT RUN 100 SER.#'d SETS
AJAJ Antawn Jamison 10.00 25.00
ASAJ Amare Stoudemire 12.00 30.00
CMAJ Corey Maggette 8.00 20.00
DRAJ David Robinson 50.00 120.00
DWAJ DaJuan Wagner 6.00 15.00
EGAJ Manu Ginobili 50.00 120.00
ETAJ Etan Thomas 6.00 15.00
FJAJ Fred Jones 6.00 15.00
GAAJ Gilbert Arenas 10.00 25.00
GWAJ Gerald Wallace 8.00 20.00
JKAJ Jason Kidd 40.00 100.00
JMAJ Jerome Moiso 6.00 15.00
JOAJ Jermaine O'Neal 10.00 25.00
JRAJ Jason Richardson 10.00 25.00
JSAJ Jerry Stackhouse 12.00 30.00
JTAJ Jamaal Tinsley 6.00 15.00
JWAJ Jay Williams 6.00 15.00
KBAJ Kobe Bryant 1,500.00 3,000.00
LOAJ Lamar Odom 8.00 20.00
MBAJ Mike Bibby 10.00 25.00
PPAJ Paul Pierce 40.00 100.00
PSAJ Peja Stojakovic 8.00 20.00
RJAJ Richard Jefferson 8.00 20.00
RSAJ Jalen Rose 8.00 20.00
SFAJ Steve Francis 10.00 25.00
SMAJ Shawn Marion 10.00 25.00
TMAJ Tracy McGrady 100.00 250.00
TPAJ Tony Parker 40.00 100.00
YMAJ Yao Ming 150.00 400.00

2003-04 SP Game Used Authentic Fabrics Dual
PRINT RUN 100 SER.#'d SETS
AIKVJ Iverson/V.Horn 12.00 30.00
AMQRJ A.Miller/Q-Rich 4.00 10.00
ASCJJ Amare/C.Jacobsen 6.00 15.00
AWVBJ Walker/V.Baker 5.00 12.00
BDJMJ B.Davis/J-Mash 5.00 12.00
BWCBJ B.Wallace/Billups 6.00 15.00
CBDMJ Boozer/Miles 4.00 10.00
CBRBJ C.Butler/R.Butler 4.00 10.00
DMKMJ K-Mart/Mutombo 6.00 15.00
DNSNJ Nowitzki/Nash 12.00 30.00
EBMEJ Brand/M.Ely 4.00 10.00
EJAMJ E.Jones/Mourning 6.00 15.00
GAAJJ Arenas/Jamison 5.00 12.00
GHDGJ G.Hill/Gooden 6.00 15.00
GPTKJ Payton/Kukoc 8.00 20.00
JHMCJ Howard/Camby 4.00 10.00
JRECJ Rose/E.Curry 4.00 10.00
JSWZJ J.Smith/Szczerb 4.00 10.00
JTDDJ Terry/Dickau 4.00 10.00
JTJOJ Tinsley/J.O'Neal 5.00 12.00
KBDFJ Bryant/Fisher 60.00 150.00
KGTHJ Garnett/Hudson 12.00 30.00
KMJSJ Stockton/Malone 30.00 80.00
LSAHJ Spree/Houston 6.00 15.00
MFRLJ Finley/LaFrentz 5.00 12.00
MJKBJ Jordan/Bryant 400.00 800.00
MJMAJ Jordan/Magic 150.00 400.00
NHNTJ Nene/Tskitishvili 4.00 10.00
PGMMJ Gasol/M.Miller 8.00 20.00
PPKBJ Pierce/Ke.Brown 8.00 20.00
RJKJ R.Jefferson/Kidd 8.00 20.00
RMFJJ R.Miller/F.Jones 10.00 25.00
RWSPJ R.Wallace/Pippen 12.00 30.00
SAGRJ A-Rahim/G.Robinsn 5.00 12.00
SMAHJ Marbury/A.Hard 12.00 30.00
TMGGJ T-Mac/Giricek 8.00 20.00
TPRHJ Prince/R.Hamilton 6.00 15.00
WZCWJ Zhi Zhi/Wilcox 5.00 12.00

2003-04 SP Game Used Authentic Fabrics Dual Autographs
PRINT RUN 15 TO 50 SER.#'d SETS
1 A.Miller/J.Kidd 20.00 50.00
2 A.Miller/L.Odom 10.00 25.00
3 A.Miller/M.Jaric 10.00 25.00
4 C.Billups/T.Prince 40.00 100.00
5 C.Maggette/A.Miller 10.00 25.00
6 G.Giricek/D.Gooden 10.00 25.00
7 D.Gooden/P.Pierce 20.00 50.00
8 D.Wagner/C.Boozer 10.00 25.00
9 M.Ginobili/M.Jaric 25.00 60.00
10 E.Griffin/S.Francis 10.00 25.00
11 G.Arenas/J.Rich 12.00 30.00
12 G.Giricek/T.Parker 20.00 50.00
13 Stojakovic/Wallace 10.00 25.00
14 J.Kidd/J.Tinsley 20.00 50.00
15 M.Bibby/J.Kidd/15 50.00 120.00
16 J.Kidd/R.Jefferson 20.00 50.00
17 J.O'Neal/K.Garnett 75.00 200.00
18 J.Rose/M.Fizer 10.00 25.00
19 J-Rich/R.Jefferson 12.00 30.00
20 J-Rich/T.Parker 20.00 50.00
22 Stack/J.Dixon 15.00 40.00
23 J.Tinsley/T.Parker 20.00 50.00
24 J-Will/C.Boozer 10.00 25.00
25 J-Will/M.Fizer 8.00 20.00
26 K.Bryant/M.Bibby 1,250.00 2,500.00
28 L.Odom/C.Wilcox 10.00 25.00
29 Bibby/P.Stojakovic 12.00 30.00
30 M.Bibby/S.Francis/15 12.00 30.00
31 M.Ely/L.Odom 10.00 25.00
32 M.Pele/J.Richardson 12.00 30.00
33 R.Hamilton/C.Billups 15.00 40.00
34 R.Jefferson/M.Bibby 12.00 30.00
35 S.Francis/K.Bryant/15 1,250.00 2,500.00
36 S.Francis/Y.Ming 200.00 500.00
37 Marion/A.Stoudemire 25.00 60.00
39 T.McGrady/Garnett/15 150.00 400.00
41 T.Parker/M.Ginobili 100.00 250.00
42 T.Parker/M.Jaric 20.00 50.00

2003-04 SP Game Used Authentic Fabrics Triple
PRINT RUN 25 SER.#'d SETS
1 D.Rob/Ginobili/Parker 40.00 100.00
2 Wagner/Miles/Bzer 12.00 30.00
3 Rose/Chandler/Williams 15.00 40.00
4 Stockton/Malone/AK47 30.00 80.00
6 Jefferies/Peterson/Davis 12.00 30.00
8 Gasol/Battier/Miller 20.00 50.00
9 Allen/Lewis/Forte 15.00 40.00
10 A-Rahim/Terry/G.Rob 12.00 30.00

2003-04 SP Game Used Authentic Patches
PRINT RUN 100 SER.#'d SETS
AHP Allan Houston 25.00 60.00
AIP Allen Iverson 60.00 150.00
AJP Antawn Jamison 25.00 60.00
AMP Alonzo Mourning 30.00 80.00
ASP Amare Stoudemire 30.00 80.00
AWP Antoine Walker 25.00 60.00
BDP Baron Davis 25.00 60.00
CBP Caron Butler 20.00 50.00
CWP Chris Webber 30.00 80.00
DNP Dirk Nowitzki 60.00 150.00
DRP David Robinson 50.00 125.00
DWP DaJuan Wagner 15.00 40.00
EBP Elton Brand 20.00 50.00
EJP Eddie Jones 25.00 60.00
GAP Gilbert Arenas 25.00 60.00
GHP Grant Hill 30.00 80.00
GPP Gary Payton 40.00 100.00
HAP Anfernee Hardaway 60.00 150.00
HTP Hedo Turkoglu 20.00 50.00
JJP Jared Jeffries 15.00 40.00
JKP Jason Kidd 40.00 100.00
JMP Jamal Mashburn 20.00 50.00
JOP Jermaine O'Neal 25.00 60.00
JRP Jason Richardson 25.00 60.00
JSP John Stockton 50.00 125.00
JTP Jamaal Tinsley 15.00 40.00
JWP Jay Williams 15.00 40.00
KAP Karl Malone 50.00 125.00
KBP Kobe Bryant 400.00 800.00
KGP Kevin Garnett 60.00 150.00
KJP Kareem Abdul-Jabbar 40.00 100.00
KMP Kenyon Martin 25.00 60.00
KRP Kareem Rush 15.00 40.00
KVP Keith Van Horn 20.00 50.00
LOP Lamar Odom 20.00 50.00
LSP Latrell Sprewell 30.00 80.00
MAP Magic Johnson 60.00 150.00
MBP Mike Bibby 25.00 60.00
MCP Antonio McDyess 20.00 50.00
MIP Andre Miller 20.00 50.00
MJP Michael Jordan 500.00 1,000.00
NHP Nene Hilario 20.00 50.00
PGP Pau Gasol 40.00 100.00
PPP Paul Pierce 40.00 100.00
RAP Ray Allen 40.00 100.00
RHP Richard Hamilton 30.00 80.00
RJP Richard Jefferson 20.00 50.00
RLP Rashard Lewis 20.00 50.00
RMP Reggie Miller 50.00 125.00
RWP Rasheed Wallace 30.00 80.00
SBP Shane Battier 20.00 50.00
SFP Steve Francis 25.00 60.00
SHP Shawn Marion 25.00 60.00
SMP Stephon Marbury 30.00 80.00
SPP Scottie Pippen 60.00 150.00
TMP Tracy McGrady 40.00 100.00
WSP Wally Szczerbiak 20.00 50.00
WZP Wang Zhi Zhi 25.00 60.00
YMP Yao Ming 60.00 150.00

2003-04 SP Game Used Authentic Patches Autographs
PRINT RUN 50 SER.#'d SETS
AJAP Antawn Jamison 40.00 100.00
ASAP Amare Stoudemire 50.00 125.00
BIAP Chauncey Billups 75.00 200.00
BOAP Carlos Boozer 30.00 80.00
CBAP Caron Butler 30.00 80.00
DDAP Dan Dickau 25.00 60.00
DGAP Drew Gooden 30.00 80.00
DJAP DerMarr Johnson 25.00 60.00
DWAP DaJuan Wagner 25.00 60.00
EGAP Manu Ginobili 100.00 250.00
ETAP Etan Thomas 25.00 60.00
GAAP Gilbert Arenas 40.00 100.00
GWAP Gerald Wallace 30.00 80.00
JDAP Juan Dixon 25.00 60.00
JKAP Jason Kidd 75.00 200.00
JMAP Jerome Moiso 25.00 60.00
JOAP Jermaine O'Neal 40.00 100.00
JRAP Jason Richardson 40.00 100.00
JSAP Jerry Stackhouse 50.00 125.00
JWAP Jay Williams 25.00 60.00
KBAP Kobe Bryant 2,000.00 4,000.00
LOAP Lamar Odom 30.00 80.00
MBAP Mike Bibby 40.00 100.00
MJAP Michael Jordan 3,000.00 6,000.00
NHAP Nene Hilario 30.00 80.00
PPAP Paul Pierce 75.00 200.00
PSAP Peja Stojakovic 30.00 80.00
RHAP Richard Hamilton 50.00 125.00
RJAP Richard Jefferson 30.00 80.00
ROAP Jalen Rose 30.00 80.00
SFAP Steve Francis 40.00 100.00
SMAP Shawn Marion 40.00 100.00
TMAP Tracy McGrady 125.00 300.00
TPAP Tony Parker 75.00 200.00
YMAP Yao Ming 200.00 500.00

2003-04 SP Game Used Authentic Patches Dual
PRINT RUN 25 SER.#'d SETS
1 C.Wilcox/J.Dixon 20.00 50.00
2 J.Richardson/A.Jamison 40.00 100.00
3 K.Bryant/K.Rush 300.00 600.00
4 M.Jordan/K.Bryant 1,500.00 3,000.00
5 M.Jordan/L.Bird 1,000.00 2,000.00
6 P.Stojakovic/G.Giricek 25.00 60.00
7 S.Nash/R.Fox 40.00 100.00
8 T.McGrady/D.Miles 40.00 100.00

2003-04 SP Game Used Extra SIGnificance
PRINT RUN 25 SER.#'d SETS
ASMM Amare/M.Malone 75.00 200.00
ASTM Amare/T.McGrady 125.00 300.00
JEMM J.Erving/M.Malone 125.00 300.00
KAMJ Abdul-Jabbar/Magic 500.00 1,000.00
MJLB M.Jordan/L.Bird 3,000.00 6,000.00
MJLJ M.Jordan/L.James 15,000.00 30,000.00
PSMB Stojakovic/M.Bibby 60.00 150.00
TMKB T.McGrady/K.Bryant 2,000.00 4,000.00
YMKA Y.Ming/Abdul-Jabbar 400.00 800.00
YMMM Y.Ming/M.Malone 300.00 600.00

2003-04 SP Game Used Legendary Fabrics
OVERALL JERSEY ODDS ONE PER PACK
BRLO Bill Russell 20.00 50.00
DWL Dominique Wilkins 6.00 15.00
EJL Magic Johnson 12.00 30.00
JEL Julius Erving 8.00 20.00
KML Kevin McHale 6.00 15.00
LBL Larry Bird 12.00 30.00
MJL Michael Jordan 50.00 125.00
ORL Oscar Robertson 6.00 15.00
WCL Wilt Chamberlain 20.00 50.00

2003-04 SP Game Used Legendary Fabrics Autographs
PRINT RUN 100 SER.#'d SETS
2 Bill Russell 1,500.00 3,000.00
3 Larry Bird 80.00 200.00
4 Julius Erving 60.00 150.00
5 Magic Johnson 50.00 120.00
6 Kareem Abdul-Jabbar 50.00 120.00
7 Dominique Wilkins 40.00 100.00

2003-04 SP Game Used Rookie Exclusive Autographs
PRINT RUN 100 SER.#'d SETS
RE1 Lebron James 5,000.00 10,000.00
RE2 Darko Milicic 5.00 12.00
RE3 Carmelo Anthony 75.00 200.00
RE4 Chris Bosh 25.00 60.00
RE5 Chris Kaman 6.00 15.00
RE6 Reece Gaines 4.00 10.00
RE7 Mickael Pietrus 5.00 12.00
RE8 Marcus Banks 4.00 10.00
RE9 Troy Bell 4.00 10.00
RE10 Zarko Cabarkapa 4.00 10.00
RE11 David West 8.00 20.00
RE12 Aleksandar Pavlovic 5.00 12.00
RE13 Dahntay Jones 5.00 12.00
RE14 Boris Diaw 6.00 15.00
RE15 Zoran Planinic 4.00 10.00
RE16 Travis Outlaw 5.00 12.00
RE17 Brian Cook 4.00 10.00
RE18 Leandro Barbosa 6.00 15.00
RE19 Josh Howard 6.00 15.00
RE20 Maciej Lampe 4.00 10.00
RE21 Jason Kapono 4.00 10.00
RE22 Luke Walton 6.00 15.00
RE23 Jerome Beasley 4.00 10.00
RE24 Sofoklis Schortsanitis 4.00 10.00
RE25 Mario Austin 4.00 10.00
RE26 Travis Hansen 4.00 10.00
RE27 Steve Blake 5.00 12.00
RE28 Slavko Vranes 4.00 10.00
RE29 Zaur Pachulia 6.00 15.00
RE30 Keith Bogans 4.00 10.00
RE31 Matt Bonner 6.00 15.00
RE32 Maurice Williams 6.00 15.00
RE33 Kyle Korver 8.00 20.00
RE34 Rick Rickert 4.00 10.00
RE35 Brandon Hunter 4.00 10.00
RE36 Jarvis Hayes 4.00 10.00
RE37 Ndudi Ebi 4.00 10.00
RE38 Kendrick Perkins 5.00 12.00
RE39 Dwyane Wade 125.00 300.00
RE40 Luke Ridnour 6.00 15.00
RE41 James Lang 4.00 10.00
RE42 Carlos Delfino 5.00 12.00

2003-04 SP Game Used SIGnificance
PRINT RUN 23 TO 100 SER.#'d SETS
AJ Antawn Jamison 6.00 15.00
AM Andre Miller 4.00 10.00
AM Antonio McDyess 4.00 10.00
AS Amare Stoudemire 12.00 30.00
BI Chauncey Billups 8.00 20.00
BO Carlos Boozer 6.00 15.00
BW Bill Walton 8.00 20.00
CB Caron Butler 8.00 20.00
CJ Chris Jefferies 4.00 10.00
CM Corey Maggette 4.00 10.00
DA Dan Gadzuric 4.00 10.00
DD Dan Dickau 4.00 10.00
DG Drew Gooden 4.00 10.00
DJ DerMarr Johnson 4.00 10.00
DR David Robinson 30.00 80.00
DWO DaJuan Wagner 6.00 15.00
EGO Manu Ginobili 30.00 80.00
ET Etan Thomas 4.00 10.00
FJ Fred Jones 4.00 10.00
GA Gilbert Arenas 8.00 20.00
GG Gordan Giricek 4.00 10.00
GR Eddie Griffin 4.00 10.00
GW Gerald Wallace 6.00 15.00
HU Ryan Humphrey 4.00 10.00
IM George Gervin 10.00 25.00
JD Juan Dixon 4.00 10.00
JK Jason Kidd 20.00 50.00
JM Jerome Moiso 6.00 15.00
JO Jermaine O'Neal 8.00 20.00
JR Jason Richardson 6.00 15.00
JS Jerry Stackhouse 8.00 20.00
JT Jamaal Tinsley 6.00 15.00
JW Jay Williams 6.00 15.00
KA Kareem Abdul-Jabbar 30.00 80.00
KB Kobe Bryant 125.00 300.00
KG Kevin Garnett 60.00 150.00
LO Lamar Odom 8.00 20.00
MB Mike Bibby 8.00 20.00
MJ Michael Jordan/23 1,500.00 3,000.00
MP Morris Peterson 4.00 10.00
NH Nene Hilario 5.00 12.00
NW Dominique Wilkins 15.00 40.00
PP Paul Pierce 12.00 30.00
PS Peja Stojakovic 6.00 15.00
QW Qyntel Woods 4.00 10.00
RE Reggie Evans 4.00 10.00
RH Richard Hamilton 8.00 20.00
RJ Richard Jefferson 4.00 10.00
RO Jalen Rose 6.00 15.00
SF Steve Francis 8.00 20.00
SM Shawn Marion 8.00 20.00
TM Tracy McGrady 10.00 25.00
TP Tony Parker 15.00 40.00
WI Chris Wilcox 4.00 10.00
WZ Wang Zhi Zhi 100.00 250.00
YM Yao Ming 60.00 150.00
ZR Zack Randolph 4.00 10.00

2003-04 SP Game Used SIGnificant Marks
PRINT RUN 75 SER.#'d SETS
AJSM Antawn Jamison 10.00 25.00
AMSM Andre Miller 8.00 20.00
ANSM Antonio McDyess 8.00 20.00
ASSM Amare Stoudemire 12.00 30.00
BOSM Carlos Boozer 8.00 20.00
BWSM Bill Walton 15.00 40.00
CBSM Caron Butler 8.00 20.00
CMSM Corey Maggette 8.00 20.00
CWSM Chris Wilcox 6.00 15.00
DGSM Drew Gooden 8.00 20.00
DJSM DerMarr Johnson 6.00 15.00
DRSM David Robinson 40.00 100.00
DWSM DaJuan Wagner 6.00 15.00
EGSM Manu Ginobili 40.00 100.00
ETSM Etan Thomas 6.00 15.00
GASM Gilbert Arenas 10.00 25.00
GESM George Gervin 15.00 40.00
GGSM Gordan Giricek 6.00 15.00
GRSM Eddie Griffin 6.00 15.00
GWSM Gerald Wallace 8.00 20.00
JDSM Juan Dixon 6.00 15.00
JKSM Jason Kidd 40.00 100.00
JMSM Jerome Moiso 6.00 15.00
JOSM Jermaine O'Neal 10.00 25.00
JRSM Jason Richardson 10.00 25.00
JSSM Jerry Stackhouse 12.00 30.00
JWSM Jay Williams 6.00 15.00
LOSM Lamar Odom 8.00 20.00
MBSM Mike Bibby 10.00 25.00
MPSM Morris Peterson 6.00 15.00
PPSM Paul Pierce 40.00 100.00
PSSM Peja Stojakovic 8.00 20.00
RHSM Richard Hamilton 12.00 30.00
RJSM Richard Jefferson 8.00 20.00
ROSM Jalen Rose 8.00 20.00
SFSM Steve Francis 10.00 25.00
SMSM Shawn Marion 10.00 25.00
TMSM Tracy McGrady 100.00 250.00
TPSM Tony Parker 40.00 100.00
YMSM Yao Ming 125.00 300.00

2003-04 SP Game Used SIGnificant Numbers
PRINT RUNS LISTED IN CHECKLIST
AS32 Amare Stoudemire/32 60.00 150.00
JR23 Jason Richardson/23 40.00 100.00
KG21 Kevin Garnett/21 125.00 300.00
MJ23 Michael Jordan/23 5,000.00 10,000.00
PP34 Paul Pierce/34 100.00 250.00

2004-05 SP Game Used
ALL JSY's LISTED AT STATED ODDS 1:1
91-132 RC PRINT RUN 999 SER.#'d SETS
133-162 SIR PRINT RUN 999 SER.#'d SETS
1 Tony Delk .60 1.50
2 Boris Diaw .75 2.00
3 Ricky Davis .75 2.00
4 Gary Payton 1.50 4.00
5 Gerald Wallace .75 2.00
6 Jason Kapono .60 1.50
7 Tyson Chandler .75 2.00
8 Kirk Hinrich 1.00 2.50
9 DaJuan Wagner .60 1.50
10 Zydrunas Ilgauskas .75 2.00
11 Jerry Stackhouse 1.00 2.50
12 Michael Finley 1.00 2.50
13 Andre Miller .75 2.00
14 Nene .75 2.00
15 Richard Hamilton 1.25 3.00
16 Rasheed Wallace 1.25 3.00
17 Derek Fisher .75 2.00
18 Mike Dunleavy .60 1.50
19 Tracy McGrady 1.50 4.00
20 Jim Jackson .75 2.00
21 Reggie Miller 2.00 5.00
22 Jermaine O'Neal .75 2.00
23 Elton Brand .75 2.00
24 Corey Maggette .75 2.00
25 Lamar Odom 1.00 2.50
26 Caron Butler .75 2.00
27 Pau Gasol 1.50 4.00
28 Bonzi Wells .60 1.50
29 Dwyane Wade 4.00 10.00
30 Shaquille O'Neal 4.00 10.00
31 Michael Redd .75 2.00
32 T.J. Ford .60 1.50
33 Latrell Sprewell 1.25 3.00
34 Sam Cassell .75 2.00
35 Jason Kidd 1.50 4.00
36 Richard Jefferson .75 2.00
37 Baron Davis 1.00 2.50
38 Jamaal Magloire .60 1.50
39 Allan Houston .75 2.00
40 Stephon Marbury 1.25 3.00
41 Steve Francis 1.00 2.50
42 Cuttino Mobley .75 2.00
43 Glenn Robinson .75 2.00
44 Kenny Thomas .60 1.50
45 Shawn Marion 1.00 2.50
46 Amare Stoudemire 1.00 2.50
47 Zach Randolph 1.00 2.50
48 Damon Stoudamire 1.00 2.50
49 Chris Webber 1.25 3.00
50 Peja Stojakovic .75 2.00
51 Manu Ginobili 2.00 5.00
52 Tim Duncan 2.50 6.00
53 Rashard Lewis .75 2.00
54 Ray Allen 1.50 4.00
55 Jalen Rose .75 2.00
56 Vince Carter 2.00 5.00
57 Carlos Boozer .75 2.00
58 Andrei Kirilenko .75 2.00
59 Larry Hughes .75 2.00
60 Gilbert Arenas 1.00 2.50
61 Paul Pierce JSY 4.00 10.00
62 Eddy Curry JSY 1.50 4.00
63 LeBron James JSY 100.00 250.00
64 Antawn Jamison JSY 2.00 5.00
65 Dirk Nowitzki JSY 6.00 15.00
66 Antoine Walker JSY 2.50 6.00
67 Carmelo Anthony JSY 5.00 12.00
68 Ben Wallace JSY 3.00 8.00
69 Jason Richardson JSY 2.50 6.00
70 Yao Ming JSY 6.00 15.00
71 Michael Jordan JSY 150.00 400.00
72 Kobe Bryant JSY 100.00 250.00
73 Quentin Richardson JSY 1.50 4.00
74 Jason Williams JSY 1.50 4.00
75 Eddie Jones JSY 2.50 6.00
76 Keith Van Horn JSY 2.00 5.00
77 Kevin Garnett JSY 6.00 15.00
78 Kenyon Martin JSY 2.50 6.00
79 Jamal Mashburn JSY 2.00 5.00
80 Kurt Thomas JSY 1.50 4.00
81 Juwan Howard JSY 2.00 5.00
82 Allen Iverson JSY 6.00 15.00
83 Joe Johnson JSY 2.00 5.00
84 Shareef Abdur-Rahim JSY 2.50 6.00
85 Mike Bibby JSY 2.50 6.00
86 Tony Parker JSY 4.00 10.00
87 Luke Ridnour JSY 2.00 5.00
88 Jalen Rose JSY 2.00 5.00
89 Gordan Giricek JSY 1.50 4.00
90 Juan Dixon JSY 1.50 4.00
91 Emeka Okafor RC 2.50 6.00
92 Dwight Howard RC 10.00 25.00
93 Shaun Livingston RC 3.00 8.00
94 Luol Deng RC 3.00 8.00
95 Ben Gordon RC 3.00 8.00
96 Devin Harris RC 2.50 6.00
97 Andre Iguodala RC 5.00 12.00
98 Andris Biedrins RC 2.00 5.00
99 Josh Childress RC 2.00 5.00
100 Josh Smith RC 3.00 8.00
101 Jameer Nelson RC 3.00 8.00
102 J.R. Smith RC 3.00 8.00
103 Sergei Monia RC 2.00 5.00
104 Sebastian Telfair RC 2.50 6.00
105 Pavel Podkolzin RC 2.00 5.00
106 Luke Jackson RC 2.00 5.00
107 Dorell Wright RC 2.50 6.00
108 Robert Swift RC 2.00 5.00

109 Anderson Varejao RC 2.50 6.00
110 Sasha Vujacic RC 2.50 6.00
111 Rafael Araujo RC 2.00 5.00
112 Al Jefferson RC 3.00 8.00
113 Kris Humphries RC 2.50 6.00
114 Kirk Snyder RC 2.00 5.00
115 Peter John Ramos RC 2.00 5.00
116 Beno Udrih RC 2.50 6.00
117 Viktor Khryapa RC 2.00 5.00
118 David Harrison RC 2.00 5.00
119 Trevor Ariza RC 3.00 8.00
120 Ha Seung-Jin RC 3.00 8.00
121 Kevin Martin RC 4.00 10.00
122 Delonte West RC 2.50 6.00
123 Blake Stepp RC 3.00 8.00
124 Chris Duhon RC 2.50 6.00
125 Tony Allen RC 3.00 8.00
126 Donta Smith RC 2.00 5.00
127 Andre Emmett RC 2.00 5.00
128 Royal Ivey RC 2.00 5.00
129 Nenad Krstic RC 2.50 6.00
130 Romain Sato RC 2.00 5.00
131 Antonio Burks RC 2.00 5.00
132 Lionel Chalmers RC 2.50 6.00
133 LeBron James SIR 6.00 15.00
134 LeBron James SIR 6.00 15.00
135 LeBron James SIR 6.00 15.00
136 LeBron James SIR 6.00 15.00
137 LeBron James SIR 6.00 15.00
138 LeBron James SIR 6.00 15.00
139 LeBron James SIR 6.00 15.00
140 LeBron James SIR 6.00 15.00
141 LeBron James SIR 6.00 15.00
142 LeBron James SIR 6.00 15.00
143 LeBron James SIR 6.00 15.00
144 LeBron James SIR 6.00 15.00
145 LeBron James SIR 6.00 15.00
146 LeBron James SIR 6.00 15.00
147 LeBron James SIR 6.00 15.00
148 LeBron James SIR 6.00 15.00
149 LeBron James SIR 6.00 15.00
150 LeBron James SIR 6.00 15.00
151 LeBron James SIR 6.00 15.00
152 LeBron James SIR 6.00 15.00
153 LeBron James SIR 6.00 15.00
154 LeBron James SIR 6.00 15.00
155 LeBron James SIR 6.00 15.00
156 LeBron James SIR 6.00 15.00
157 LeBron James SIR 6.00 15.00
158 LeBron James SIR 6.00 15.00
159 LeBron James SIR 6.00 15.00
160 LeBron James SIR 6.00 15.00
161 LeBron James SIR 6.00 15.00
162 LeBron James SIR 6.00 15.00

2004-05 SP Game Used Parallel
*1-60: .75X TO 2X BASE HI
*61-90: .6X TO 1.5X BASE HI
1-90 PRINT RUN 100 SER.#'d SETS
*91-132: 1X TO 2.5X BASE HI
*133-162: 2.5X TO 6X BASE HI
91-162 PRINT RUN 50 SER.#'d SETS

2004-05 SP Game Used All-Star Apparel
ALL JSY's LISTED AT STATED ODDS 1:1
*GOLD SINGLES: .6X TO 1.5X BASE JSY HI
GOLD PRINT RUN 100 SER.#'d SETS
BO Carlos Boozer 2.00 5.00
CM Cuttino Mobley 2.00 5.00
MD Mike Dunleavy 1.50 4.00
NH Nene 2.00 5.00
RM Ronald Murray 2.00 5.00
UH Udonis Haslem 1.50 4.00

2004-05 SP Game Used All-Star Sigs
PRINT RUN 25 SER.#'d SETS
AK Andrei Kirilenko 12.00 30.00
BD Baron Davis 30.00 80.00
BM Brad Miller 10.00 25.00
BR Bill Russell 1,000.00 2,000.00
CD Clyde Drexler 40.00 100.00
DE Dennis Rodman 150.00 400.00
DR David Robinson 125.00 300.00
GP Gary Payton 40.00 100.00
JE Julius Erving 75.00 200.00
JK Jason Kidd 30.00 80.00
JS John Stockton 75.00 200.00
KB Kobe Bryant 1,000.00 2,000.00
KG Kevin Garnett 200.00 500.00
LB Larry Bird 125.00 300.00
MA Magic Johnson 125.00 300.00
MJ Michael Jordan 3,000.00 6,000.00
MR Michael Redd 10.00 25.00
PP Paul Pierce 40.00 100.00
RM Reggie Miller 100.00 250.00
RP Robert Parish 30.00 80.00
SA Shareef Abdur-Rahim 12.00 30.00
SM Stephon Marbury 20.00 50.00
WF Walt Frazier 20.00 50.00
YM Yao Ming 125.00 300.00
ZO Alonzo Mourning 60.00 150.00

2004-05 SP Game Used Authentic Fabrics
ALL JSY's LISTED AT STATED ODDS 1:1
SP INFO PROVIDED BY UPPER DECK
*GOLD SINGLES: .6X TO 1.5X BASE JSY HI
GOLD PRINT RUN 100 SER.#'d SETS
AH Anfernee Hardaway 6.00 15.00
AJ Antawn Jamison 2.00 5.00
AK Andrei Kirilenko 2.00 5.00
AM Aaron McKie 1.50 4.00
AN Andre Miller 2.00 5.00
AS Amare Stoudemire 2.50 6.00
BD Baron Davis 2.50 6.00
BO Boris Diaw 2.00 5.00
CA Carlos Boozer 2.00 5.00
CB Caron Butler 2.00 5.00
CH Chauncey Billups 3.00 8.00
CJ Casey Jacobsen SP 2.00 5.00
CM Corey Maggette 2.00 5.00
CW Chris Wilcox 1.50 4.00
DA Derek Anderson 2.00 5.00
DB Shane Battier 2.00 5.00
DF Derek Fisher 2.00 5.00
DG Drew Gooden 1.50 4.00
DI Dikembe Mutombo 2.50 6.00
DM Darius Miles 1.50 4.00
DW David Wesley 1.50 4.00
EB Elton Brand 2.00 5.00
EC Eddy Curry 1.50 4.00
EG Manu Ginobili 5.00 12.00
EJ Eddie Jones SP 2.50 6.00
FJ Fred Jones 1.50 4.00
GA Gilbert Arenas 2.50 6.00
GG Gordan Giricek SP 2.00 5.00
GR Glenn Robinson 2.00 5.00
JA Marko Jaric SP 2.00 5.00
JD Juan Dixon SP 2.00 5.00
JH Jarvis Hayes 1.50 4.00
JI Jiri Welsch 1.50 4.00
JJ Joe Johnson 2.00 5.00
JK Jason Kidd SP 4.00 10.00
JM Jamaal Magloire 1.50 4.00
JO Jermaine O'Neal 2.00 5.00
JR Jalen Rose 2.00 5.00
JS Jerry Stackhouse 2.50 6.00
JT Jason Terry 2.00 5.00
JW Jason Williams 2.00 5.00
KB Kobe Bryant SP 60.00 150.00
KK Kerry Kittles 2.00 5.00
KR Kareem Rush SP 2.00 5.00
KT Kurt Thomas SP 2.00 5.00
KV Keith Van Horn SP 2.00 5.00
LE Rashard Lewis 2.00 5.00
LH Larry Hughes SP 2.00 5.00
LJ LeBron James 40.00 100.00
LO Lamar Odom 2.50 6.00
LR Luke Ridnour 2.00 5.00
LS Latrell Sprewell 3.00 8.00
MA Jamal Mashburn 2.00 5.00
MB Mike Bibby 2.50 6.00
MD Antonio McDyess 2.00 5.00
MI Mike Dunleavy 1.50 4.00
MJ Michael Jordan SP 75.00 200.00
MM Mike Miller 2.00 5.00
MO Morris Peterson 1.50 4.00
MP Michael Pietrus 1.50 4.00
MR Michael Redd 2.00 5.00
NH Nene 2.00 5.00
NV Nick Van Exel 2.50 6.00
OL Michael Olowokandi 1.50 4.00
PG Pau Gasol 4.00 10.00
PR Tayshaun Prince 2.50 6.00
PS Peja Stojakovic 2.00 5.00
QR Quentin Richardson 1.50 4.00
RA Ray Allen 4.00 10.00
RH Richard Hamilton 3.00 8.00
RL Raef LaFrentz 2.00 5.00
RM Reggie Miller 3.00 8.00
SB Shane Battier 2.00 5.00
SJ Stephen Jackson 2.00 5.00
SM Shawn Marion SP 2.50 6.00
SS Stromile Swift SP 2.00 5.00
ST Stephon Marbury 3.00 8.00
TC Tyson Chandler 2.00 5.00
TD Tim Duncan 6.00 15.00
TK Toni Kukoc 2.50 6.00
TP Tony Parker 4.00 10.00
TR Theo Ratliff 1.50 4.00
WS Wally Szczerbiak 2.00 5.00
ZI Zydrunas Ilgauskas SP 2.00 5.00

2004-05 SP Game Used Authentic Fabrics Autographs
PRINT RUN 100 SER.#'d SETS
AJ Antawn Jamison 6.00 15.00
AK Andrei Kirilenko 6.00 15.00
AM Andre Miller 6.00 15.00
AN Antonio McDyess 6.00 15.00
AS Amare Stoudemire 8.00 20.00
BD Baron Davis 10.00 25.00
CA Carmelo Anthony 25.00 60.00
CM Corey Maggette 6.00 15.00
DW Dwyane Wade 200.00 500.00
GA Gilbert Arenas 6.00 15.00
GP Gary Payton 20.00 50.00
JC Jamal Crawford 6.00 15.00
JK Jason Kidd 25.00 60.00
JR Jason Richardson 10.00 25.00
KB Kobe Bryant 1,000.00 2,000.00
KG Kevin Garnett 200.00 500.00
LJ LeBron James 2,000.00 4,000.00
LO Lamar Odom 10.00 25.00
MB Mike Bibby 6.00 15.00
MJ Michael Jordan 2,000.00 4,000.00
PG Pau Gasol 20.00 50.00
PP Paul Pierce 40.00 100.00
RJ Richard Jefferson 6.00 15.00
RM Reggie Miller 125.00 300.00
SA Shareef Abdur-Rahim 6.00 15.00
SC Sam Cassell 6.00 15.00
SH Shawn Marion 6.00 15.00
SM Stephon Marbury 20.00 50.00
TM Tracy McGrady 40.00 100.00
YM Yao Ming 75.00 200.00
ZR Zach Randolph 10.00 25.00

2004-05 SP Game Used Authentic Fabrics Dual
PRINT RUN 100 SER.#'d SETS
AL R.Allen/R.Lewis 6.00 15.00
BJ K.Bryant/L.James 150.00 400.00
BM E.Brand/C.Maggette 3.00 8.00
BR C.Bosh/J.Rose 6.00 15.00
CB W.Chamberlain/Kobe 125.00 300.00
CC J.Crawford/T.Chandler 4.00 10.00
DM B.Davis/J.Mashburn 4.00 10.00
FM S.Francis/Y.Ming 10.00 25.00
GF D.George/D.Fisher 3.00 8.00
GP M.Ginobili/T.Parker 8.00 20.00
GW P.Gasol/J.Williams 12.00 30.00
HG J.Howard/R.Gaines 3.00 8.00
HH L.Hughes/J.Hayes 3.00 8.00
IS A.Iverson/E.Snow 10.00 25.00
JB M.Jordan/K.Bryant 200.00 500.00
JJ L.James/M.Jordan 300.00 600.00
JT M.Jordan/I.Thomas 125.00 300.00
KM J.Kidd/K.Martin 6.00 15.00
MA D.Miles/S.Abdur-Rahim 4.00 10.00
MB M.Miller/S.Battier 3.00 8.00
MT T.McGrady/A.Iverson 10.00 25.00
NN D.Nowitzki/S.Nash 10.00 25.00
OM S.O'Neal/K.Malone 15.00 40.00
PB P.Pierce/L.Bird 15.00 40.00
PS J.Posey/S.Swift 3.00 8.00
RA Z.Randolph/S.Abdur-Rahim 4.00 10.00
RD D.Robinson/T.Duncan 8.00 20.00
RJ J.Richardson/R.Jefferson 4.00 10.00
RK G.Robinson/K.Korver 3.00 8.00
RV M.Redd/K.Van Horn 3.00 8.00
RW K.Rush/L.Walton 3.00 8.00
SC L.Sprewell/S.Cassell 5.00 12.00
SK J.Stockton/A.Kirilenko 8.00 20.00
SM A.Stoudemire/S.Marion 4.00 10.00
SW P.Stojakovic/C.Webber 5.00 12.00
TS K.Thomas/M.Sweetney 2.50 6.00
WH B.Wallace/R.Hamilton 5.00 12.00
WO D.Wade/L.Odom 15.00 40.00

2004-05 SP Game Used Authentic Fabrics Dual Autographs
PRINT RUN 15 TO 50 SER.#'d SETS
AJ C.Anthony/L.James/15 2,000.00 4,000.00
AM C.Anthony/A.Miller 30.00 80.00
AR S.Abdur-R/Z.Randolph 12.00 30.00
AS G.Arenas/J.Stackhouse 12.00 30.00
BA M.Bibby/G.Arenas 12.00 30.00
BG C.Billups/K.Garnett 150.00 400.00
BH C.Billups/R.Hamilton 15.00 40.00
BJ M.Bibby/R.Jefferson 12.00 30.00
BM S.Battier/C.Maggette 12.00 30.00
BP K.Bryant/G.Payton 1,000.00 2,000.00
BS C.Bosh/S.Marbury 15.00 40.00
DM B.Davis/R.Miller 60.00 150.00
GB P.Gasol/S.Battier 12.00 30.00
GC K.Garnett/S.Cassell 50.00 120.00
GM K.Garnett/McGrady/15 300.00 600.00
JB L.James/C.Boozer 800.00 1,500.00
JJ M.Jordan/L.James/15 5,000.00 8,000.00
JM L.James/Y.Ming 1,000.00 2,000.00
KG A.Kirilenko/P.Gasol 20.00 50.00
KJ J.Kidd/R.Jefferson 25.00 60.00
MA D.Miles/S.Abdur-Rahim 12.00 30.00
MG T.McGrady/D.Gooden 20.00 50.00
MH A.Miller/Nene 12.00 30.00
MJ R.Miller/F.Jones 40.00 100.00
MK S.Marbury/J.Kidd 30.00 80.00
MM S.Marion/A.McDyess 12.00 30.00
MP T.McGrady/P.Pierce 40.00 100.00
MR A.Mourning/R.Jefferson 40.00 100.00
MW C.Maggette/C.Wilcox 12.00 30.00
PB P.Pierce/L.Bird/15 200.00 500.00
PF G.Payton/D.Fisher 40.00 100.00
PM P.Pierce.M.Banks 15.00 40.00
RJ J-Rich/F.Jones 12.00 30.00
RP J-Rich/M.Pietrus 12.00 30.00
RR Z.Randolph/J-Rich 12.00 30.00
SA S.Marion/Amare 25.00 60.00
SM A.Stoudemire/A.McDyess 25.00 60.00
WD C.Wilcox/J.Dixon 12.00 30.00
WH D.Wade/U.Haslem 100.00 250.00
WO D.Wade/L.Odom 100.00 250.00

2004-05 SP Game Used Authentic Fabrics Triple
PRINT RUN 25 SER.#'d SETS
JBJ Jordan/Kobe/LeBron 500.00 1,000.00
JBW LeBron/Boozer/Wagner 20.00 50.00
MKJ Martin/Kittles/Jefferson 10.00 25.00
PDW Pierce/Davis/Welsch 12.00 30.00
RSA Randolph/Stoud/Anderson 10.00 25.00
RVD JRich/Van Exel/Dunleavy 10.00 25.00

2004-05 SP Game Used Authentic Patches
PRINT RUN 100 SER.#'d SETS
AK Andrei Kirilenko 5.00 12.00
AL Ray Allen 10.00 25.00
AM Andre Miller 5.00 12.00
AS Amare Stoudemire 6.00 15.00
AW Antoine Walker 6.00 15.00
BW Ben Wallace 8.00 20.00
CA Carmelo Anthony 12.00 30.00
CB Chris Bosh 10.00 25.00
CH Chauncey Billups 8.00 20.00
CM Cuttino Mobley 5.00 12.00
CO Corey Maggette 5.00 12.00
CW Chris Webber 8.00 20.00
DG Drew Gooden 4.00 10.00
DM Darius Miles 4.00 10.00
DN Dirk Nowitzki 15.00 40.00
DW Dwyane Wade 25.00 60.00
EC Eddy Curry 4.00 10.00
EG Manu Ginobili 12.00 30.00
GA Gilbert Arenas 6.00 15.00
GP Gary Payton 8.00 20.00
JC Jamal Crawford 6.00 15.00
JH Jarvis Hayes 4.00 10.00
JR Jalen Rose 5.00 12.00
JS Jerry Stackhouse 6.00 15.00
JT Jason Terry 5.00 12.00
JW Jason Williams 15.00 40.00
KB Kobe Bryant 125.00 300.00
KE Kenyon Martin 6.00 15.00
KG Kevin Garnett 15.00 40.00
KM Karl Malone 6.00 15.00
LH Larry Hughes 5.00 12.00
LJ LeBron James 150.00 400.00
LO Lamar Odom 6.00 15.00
LS Latrell Sprewell 6.00 15.00
MB Mike Bibby 6.00 15.00
MF Michael Finley 6.00 15.00
MJ Michael Jordan 150.00 400.00
MP Morris Peterson 4.00 10.00
MR Michael Redd 5.00 12.00
NH Nene 5.00 12.00
NV Nick Van Exel 6.00 15.00
PG Pau Gasol 10.00 25.00
PP Paul Pierce 10.00 25.00
PS Peja Stojakovic 5.00 12.00
QR Quentin Richardson 4.00 10.00
RH Richard Hamilton 8.00 20.00
RJ Richard Jefferson 5.00 12.00
RL Rashard Lewis 5.00 12.00
RM Reggie Miller 15.00 40.00
SA Shareef Abdur-Rahim 6.00 15.00
SF Steve Francis 6.00 15.00
SH Shawn Marion 6.00 15.00
SM Stephon Marbury 8.00 20.00
SN Steve Nash 12.00 30.00
TM Tracy McGrady 10.00 25.00
TP Tony Parker 10.00 25.00
ZR Zach Randolph 6.00 15.00

*2004-05 SP Game Used Authentic Patches Autographs
PRINT RUN 50 SER.#'d SETS
AJ Antawn Jamison 15.00 40.00
AK Andrei Kirilenko 15.00 40.00
AM Andre Miller 15.00 40.00
AN Antonio McDyess 15.00 40.00
AS Amare Stoudemire 20.00 50.00
BD Baron Davis 15.00 40.00
CA Carmelo Anthony 75.00 200.00
CM Corey Maggette 15.00 40.00
DW Dwyane Wade 150.00 400.00
GA Gilbert Arenas 15.00 40.00
GP Gary Payton 40.00 100.00
JC Jamal Crawford 50.00 120.00
JK Jason Kidd 60.00 150.00
JR Jason Richardson 15.00 40.00
KB Kobe Bryant 1,500.00 3,000.00
KG Kevin Garnett 300.00 600.00
LJ LeBron James 2,000.00 4,000.00
LO Lamar Odom 20.00 50.00
MB Mike Bibby 20.00 50.00
PG Pau Gasol 40.00 100.00
PP Paul Pierce 75.00 200.00
RJ Richard Jefferson 15.00 40.00
RM Reggie Miller 200.00 500.00
SA Shareef Abdur-Rahim 15.00 40.00
SC Sam Cassell 15.00 40.00
SH Shawn Marion 15.00 40.00
SM Stephon Marbury 60.00 150.00
TM Tracy McGrady 150.00 400.00
YM Yao Ming 500.00 1,000.00
ZR Zach Randolph 20.00 50.00

2004-05 SP Game Used Authentic Patches Dual
PRINT RUN 25 SER.#'d SETS
AG A.Jamison/G.Arenas 40.00 100.00
BW M.Bibby/C.Webber 75.00 200.00
CR W.Chamberlain/B.Russell 1,000.00 2,000.00
JA L.James/C.Anthony 1,500.00 3,000.00
JB M.Jordan/K.Bryant 3,000.00 6,000.00
JR M.Jordan/D.Rodman 2,000.00 4,000.00
PM G.Payton/K.Malone 75.00 200.00
SW J.Stackhouse/A.Walker 40.00 100.00

2004-05 SP Game Used Endorsed Numbers
PRINT RUNS LISTED IN CHECKLIST
AJ Antawn Jamison/33 12.00 30.00
AK Andrei Kirilenko/47 20.00 50.00
AN Antonio McDyess/24 20.00 50.00
BB Brent Barry/31 15.00 40.00
BH Brandon Hunter/56 5.00 12.00
BM Brad Miller/52 10.00 25.00
CD Clyde Drexler/22 100.00 250.00
CK Chris Kaman/35 5.00 12.00
CM Cedric Maxwell/31 10.00 25.00
CW Chris Wilcox/54 5.00 12.00
DA David Robinson/50 75.00 200.00
DJ Dahntay Jones/30 5.00 12.00
DM Darko Milicic/31 15.00 40.00
DR Dennis Rodman/91 75.00 200.00
FE Francisco Elson/56 6.00 15.00
GP Gary Payton/20 75.00 200.00
GR Glenn Robinson/31 30.00 80.00
IT Isiah Thomas/11 125.00 300.00
JA Jason Kapono/24 5.00 12.00
JJ James Jones/33 6.00 15.00
KG Kevin Garnett/21 150.00 400.00
KK Kyle Korver/26 15.00 40.00
LB Larry Bird/33 100.00 250.00
LJ LeBron James/23 2,500.00 5,000.00
MA Magic Johnson/32 100.00 250.00
MJ Michael Jordan/23 5,000.00 10,000.00
ML Maciej Lampe/30 5.00 12.00
MR Michael Redd/22 12.00 30.00
MS Mike Sweetney/50 5.00 12.00
MW Maurice Williams/25 5.00 12.00
NH Nene/31 8.00 20.00
PG Pau Gasol/16 40.00 100.00
PP Paul Pierce/34 100.00 250.00
RH Richard Hamilton/32 20.00 50.00
RJ Richard Jefferson/24 10.00 25.00
RM Reggie Miller/31 150.00 400.00
SA Shareef Abdur-Rahim/33 15.00 40.00
SC Sam Cassell/19 15.00 40.00
SH Shawn Marion/31 15.00 40.00
TO Travis Outlaw/25 5.00 12.00
WG Willie Green/33 5.00 12.00
WZ Wang Zhizhi/15 150.00 400.00
ZO Alonzo Mourning/33 75.00 200.00
ZP Zaza Pachulia/27 5.00 12.00
ZR Zach Randolph/50 12.00 30.00

2004-05 SP Game Used Legendary Fabrics
ALL JSY'S LISTED AT STATED ODDS 1:1
BR Bill Russell 20.00 50.00
CD Clyde Drexler 8.00 20.00
DR Dennis Rodman 12.00 30.00
GG George Gervin 5.00 12.00
IT Isiah Thomas 8.00 20.00
JE Julius Erving 12.00 30.00
JS John Stockton 10.00 25.00
LB Larry Bird 20.00 50.00
MA Magic Johnson 20.00 50.00
MJ Michael Jordan 40.00 100.00
WF Walt Frazier 6.00 15.00

2004-05 SP Game Used Legendary Fabrics Autographs
PRINT RUN 100 SER.#'d SETS
BR Bill Russell 1,500.00 3,000.00
CD Clyde Drexler 75.00 200.00
DR Dennis Rodman 300.00 600.00
GG George Gervin 25.00 60.00
IT Isiah Thomas 25.00 60.00
JE Julius Erving 75.00 200.00
JS John Stockton 75.00 200.00
LB Larry Bird 125.00 300.00
MA Magic Johnson 125.00 300.00
MJ Michael Jordan 3,000.00 6,000.00
WF Walt Frazier 20.00 50.00

2004-05 SP Game Used Rookie Exclusive Autographs
PRINT RUN 100 SER.#'d SETS
RE1 Andre Emmett 4.00 10.00
RE2 Andre Iguodala 20.00 50.00
RE3 Al Jefferson 10.00 25.00
RE4 Anderson Varejao 12.00 30.00
RE5 Ben Gordon 15.00 40.00
RE6 Andris Biedrins 4.00 10.00
RE7 Blake Stepp 6.00 15.00
RE8 Antonio Burks 4.00 10.00
RE9 Beno Udrih 5.00 12.00
RE10 Chris Duhon 5.00 12.00
RE11 David Harrison 4.00 10.00
RE12 Delonte West 10.00 25.00
RE13 Dwight Howard 20.00 50.00
RE14 Dorell Wright 5.00 12.00
RE15 Donta Smith 4.00 10.00
RE16 Devin Harris 12.00 30.00
RE17 Ha Seung-Jin 10.00 25.00
RE18 Josh Childress 4.00 10.00
RE19 Jameer Nelson 10.00 25.00
RE20 J.R. Smith 6.00 15.00
RE21 Pape Sow 4.00 10.00
RE22 Jackson Vroman 4.00 10.00
RE23 Kris Humphries 5.00 12.00
RE24 Kevin Martin 25.00 60.00
RE25 Kirk Snyder 4.00 10.00
RE26 Lionel Chalmers 5.00 12.00
RE27 Luol Deng 12.00 30.00
RE28 Luke Jackson 4.00 10.00
RE29 Matt Freije 4.00 10.00
RE30 Pavel Podkolzin 4.00 10.00
RE31 Peter John Ramos 4.00 10.00
RE32 Rafael Araujo 4.00 10.00
RE33 Robert Swift 4.00 10.00
RE34 Romain Sato 4.00 10.00
RE35 Shaun Livingston 10.00 25.00
RE36 Sergei Monia 4.00 10.00
RE37 Sebastian Telfair 5.00 12.00
RE38 Sasha Vujacic 5.00 12.00
RE39 Tony Allen 6.00 15.00
RE40 Tim Pickett 5.00 12.00
RE41 Trevor Ariza 6.00 15.00
RE42 Viktor Khryapa 4.00 10.00
RE43 David Young 6.00 15.00
RE44 Royal Ivey 4.00 10.00
RE45 Christian Drejer 6.00 15.00
RE46 Bernard Robinson 4.00 10.00
RE48 Justin Reed 4.00 10.00
RE49 Darius Rice 6.00 15.00
RE50 Ricky Minard 5.00 12.00
RE51 Nenad Krstic 5.00 12.00
NNO Josh Smith 20.00 50.00

2004-05 SP Game Used SIGnificance
PRINT RUN 100 SER.#'d SETS
AJ Antawn Jamison 5.00 12.00
AK Andrei Kirilenko 6.00 15.00
AL Al Harrington 5.00 12.00
AM Andre Miller 5.00 12.00
AS Amare Stoudemire 12.00 30.00
BB Brent Barry 5.00 12.00
BC Bob Cousy 75.00 200.00
BD Baron Davis 5.00 12.00
BE Jerome Beasley 5.00 12.00
BH Brandon Hunter 5.00 12.00
BL Steve Blake 5.00 12.00
BM Brad Miller 6.00 15.00
BO Carlos Boozer 5.00 12.00
BR Bill Russell 1,000.00 2,000.00
BW Bill Walton 10.00 25.00
CA Carmelo Anthony 30.00 80.00
CD Clyde Drexler 12.00 30.00
CE Cedric Maxwell 5.00 12.00
CH Chauncey Billups 8.00 20.00
CK Chris Kaman 5.00 12.00
CM Corey Maggette 5.00 12.00
DA Chuck Daly 50.00 120.00
DD Darryl Dawkins 10.00 25.00
DF Derek Fisher 6.00 15.00
DG Drew Gooden 5.00 12.00
DI Dan Dickau 5.00 12.00
DM Darko Milicic 5.00 12.00
DR David Robinson 125.00 300.00
DT David Thompson 5.00 12.00
DW Dwyane Wade 125.00 300.00
DY Dahntay Jones 5.00 12.00
EC Eddy Curry 5.00 12.00
FE Francisco Elson 5.00 12.00
FJ Fred Jones 5.00 12.00
GA Gilbert Arenas 6.00 15.00
GG George Gervin 20.00 50.00
GO Gordan Giricek 5.00 12.00
GP Gary Payton 20.00 50.00
GR Glenn Robinson 5.00 12.00
GW Gerald Wallace 5.00 12.00
IT Isiah Thomas 20.00 50.00
JA Jamaal Wilkes 8.00 20.00
JB Jon Barry 5.00 12.00
JD Juan Dixon 5.00 12.00
JE Julius Erving 75.00 200.00
JH Josh Howard 5.00 12.00
JJ James Jones 5.00 12.00
JK Jason Kidd 12.00 30.00
JM Jerome Moiso 5.00 12.00
JO John Salley 8.00 20.00
JR Jalen Rose 6.00 15.00
JS John Stockton 75.00 200.00
JT Jamaal Tinsley 5.00 12.00
JW James Worthy 25.00 60.00
KA Jason Kapono 5.00 12.00
KB Kobe Bryant 1,500.00 3,000.00
KC K.C. Jones 8.00 20.00
KE Keith Bogans 5.00 12.00
KG Kevin Garnett 150.00 400.00
KK Kyle Korver 8.00 20.00
KR Kareem Rush 5.00 12.00
KU Kurt Rambis 5.00 12.00
LA Larry Bird 125.00 300.00
LB Leandro Barbosa 5.00 12.00
LJ LeBron James 2,000.00 4,000.00
LO Lamar Odom 6.00 15.00
LR Luke Ridnour 5.00 12.00
MA Magic Johnson 125.00 300.00
MB Mike Bibby 6.00 15.00
MI Mickael Pietrus 5.00 12.00
MJ Michael Jordan 3,000.00 6,000.00
MP Morris Peterson 5.00 12.00
MR Michael Redd 5.00 12.00
MS Mike Sweetney 5.00 12.00
MW Maurice Williams 5.00 12.00
NH Nene 5.00 12.00
PB Primoz Brezec 5.00 12.00
PG Pau Gasol 10.00 25.00
PL Zoran Planinic 5.00 12.00
PP Paul Pierce 30.00 80.00
PR Pat Riley 25.00 60.00
RG Reece Gaines 5.00 12.00
RH Richard Hamilton 6.00 15.00
RI Jason Richardson 5.00 12.00
RJ Richard Jefferson 5.00 12.00
RM Reggie Miller 125.00 300.00
RO Dennis Rodman 125.00 300.00
RP Robert Parish 8.00 20.00
SA Shareef Abdur-Rahim 5.00 12.00
SB Shane Battier 6.00 15.00
SC Sam Cassell 5.00 12.00
SH Shawn Marion 8.00 20.00
SM Stephon Marbury 12.00 30.00
ST Jerry Stackhouse 6.00 15.00
SW Spud Webb 8.00 20.00
TB Troy Bell 5.00 12.00
TM Tracy McGrady 20.00 50.00
TO Travis Outlaw 5.00 12.00
TP Tony Parker 6.00 15.00
TS Theron Smith 5.00 12.00
WF Walt Frazier 8.00 20.00
WG Willie Green 5.00 12.00
WR Willis Reed 60.00 150.00
WU Wes Unseld 8.00 20.00
WZ Wang Zhizhi 100.00 250.00
YM Yao Ming 125.00 300.00
ZC Zarko Cabarkapa 5.00 12.00
ZO Alonzo Mourning 20.00 50.00
ZP Zaza Pachulia 5.00 12.00
ZR Zach Randolph 6.00 15.00

2004-05 SP Game Used SIGnificance Duals
PRINT RUN 25 SER.#'d SETS
AJ C.Anthony/M.Jordan 800.00 1,500.00
BB B.Barry/J.Barry 15.00 40.00
BJ K.Bryant/M.Johnson 500.00 1,000.00
BK C.Boozer/A.Kirilenko 20.00 50.00
CC E.Curry/J.Crawford 20.00 50.00
DE D.Dawkins/J.Erving 60.00 150.00
DT B.Davis/I.Thomas 20.00 50.00
GC K.Garnett/S.Cassell 75.00 150.00
GR K.Garnett/B.Russell 1,500.00 3,000.00
JC K.C.Jones/B.Cousy 30.00 80.00
JJ L.James/M.Jordan 3,000.00 6,000.00
KS J.Kidd/J.Stockton 100.00 200.00
LK L.Bird/K.C.Jones 100.00 200.00
MD T.McGrady/C.Drexler 75.00 150.00
MJ C.Maxwell/K.C.Jones 15.00 40.00
MP C.Maxwell/R.Parish 40.00 100.00
MS S.Marbury/M.Sweetney 20.00 50.00
PB P.Pierce/L.Bird 75.00 150.00
RJ K.Rambis/M.Johnson 40.00 100.00
RP M.Redd/Z.Pachulia 15.00 40.00
RW K.Rush/L.Walton 15.00 40.00
SE A.Stoudemire/J.Erving 75.00 150.00
WE D.Wade/J.Erving 125.00 250.00

2004-05 SP Game Used SIGnificant Numbers
STATED PRINT RUN ONE TO 50 SETS
AK Andrei Kirilenko/47 25.00 60.00
AS Amare Stoudemire/32 12.00 30.00
CA Carmelo Anthony/15 30.00 80.00
DR David Robinson/50 125.00 300.00
LJ LeBron James/23 2,000.00 4,000.00
MA Magic Johnson/32 150.00 400.00
MJ Michael Jordan/23 3,000.00 6,000.00

2004-05 SP Game Used Wood Impressions
STATED PRINT RUN 75 SER.#'d SETS
AK Andrei Kirilenko 40.00 100.00
AM Andre Miller 10.00 25.00
AS Amare Stoudemire 15.00 40.00
BC Bob Cousy 125.00 300.00
BD Baron Davis 15.00 40.00
CA Carmelo Anthony 125.00 300.00
CD Clyde Drexler 75.00 200.00
CH Chauncey Billups 20.00 50.00
CM Corey Maggette 10.00 25.00
DR Dennis Rodman 125.00 300.00
DT David Thompson 15.00 40.00
DW Dwyane Wade 125.00 300.00
FE Francisco Elson 10.00 25.00
GG George Gervin 20.00 50.00
GP Gary Payton 75.00 200.00
IT Isiah Thomas 125.00 300.00
JC Jamal Crawford 12.00 30.00
JE Julius Erving 500.00 1,000.00
JH Josh Howard 10.00 25.00
JK Jason Kidd 50.00 120.00
JR Jason Richardson 10.00 25.00
JS John Stockton 125.00 300.00
JW James Worthy 60.00 150.00
KB Kobe Bryant 2,500.00 5,000.00
KG Kevin Garnett 500.00 1,000.00
KK Kyle Korver 75.00 200.00
LJ LeBron James 2,500.00 5,000.00
LO Lamar Odom 15.00 40.00
MA Magic Johnson 400.00 800.00
MD Marquis Daniels 10.00 25.00
MJ Michael Jordan 3,000.00 6,000.00
PG Pau Gasol 75.00 200.00
PP Paul Pierce 400.00 800.00
RJ Richard Jefferson 15.00 40.00
RM Reggie Miller 300.00 600.00
SA Shareef Abdur-Rahim 10.00 25.00
SM Shawn Marion 12.00 30.00
SW Spud Webb 20.00 50.00
TM Tracy McGrady 125.00 300.00
WR Willis Reed 60.00 150.00
YM Yao Ming 500.00 1,000.00
ZR Zach Randolph 10.00 25.00

2005-06 SP Game Used
1 Al Harrington .75 2.00
2 Josh Smith .75 2.00
3 Josh Childress .60 1.50
4 Joe Johnson .75 2.00
5 Paul Pierce 1.50 4.00
6 Antoine Walker .75 2.00
7 Gary Payton 1.50 4.00
8 Al Jefferson .60 1.50
9 Emeka Okafor .75 2.00
10 Primoz Brezec .60 1.50
11 Gerald Wallace .75 2.00
12 Michael Jordan 8.00 20.00
13 Ben Gordon .75 2.00
14 Luol Deng .75 2.00
15 Eddy Curry .60 1.50
16 LeBron James 8.00 20.00
17 Dajuan Wagner .60 1.50
18 Drew Gooden .75 2.00
19 Larry Hughes .75 2.00
20 Dirk Nowitzki 2.50 6.00
21 Marquis Daniels .60 1.50
22 Michael Finley 1.00 2.50
23 Jerry Stackhouse .75 2.00
24 Andre Miller .75 2.00
25 Carmelo Anthony 1.50 4.00
26 Kenyon Martin .75 2.00
27 Nene .75 2.00
28 Rasheed Wallace 1.00 2.50
29 Ben Wallace 1.25 3.00
30 Richard Hamilton 1.25 3.00
31 Chauncey Billups 1.25 3.00
32 Baron Davis 1.00 2.50
33 Derek Fisher 1.00 2.50
34 Jason Richardson 1.00 2.50
35 Tracy McGrady 1.50 4.00
36 Yao Ming 2.00 5.00
37 Juwan Howard .75 2.00
38 Jermaine O'Neal .75 2.00
39 Ron Artest .75 2.00
40 Jamaal Tinsley .60 1.50
41 Corey Maggette .75 2.00
42 Elton Brand .75 2.00
43 Shaun Livingston .75 2.00
44 Kobe Bryant 8.00 20.00
45 Brian Cook .60 1.50
46 Lamar Odom .75 2.00
47 Bonzi Wells .60 1.50
48 Pau Gasol 1.50 4.00
49 Shane Battier .75 2.00
50 Shaquille O'Neal 3.00 8.00
51 Dwyane Wade 2.00 5.00
52 Dorell Wright .60 1.50
53 Eddie Jones .75 2.00
54 Joe Smith .75 2.00
55 Michael Redd .75 2.00
56 Desmond Mason .60 1.50
57 Kevin Garnett 2.50 6.00
58 Wally Szczerbiak .75 2.00
59 Sam Cassell .75 2.00
60 Vince Carter 2.00 5.00
61 Jason Kidd 1.50 4.00
62 Richard Jefferson .75 2.00
63 Jamaal Magloire .60 1.50
64 J.R. Smith 1.00 2.50
65 Bostjan Nachbar .60 1.50
66 Allan Houston .75 2.00
67 Stephon Marbury 1.25 3.00
68 Jamal Crawford 1.00 2.50
69 Dwight Howard 1.25 3.00
70 Grant Hill 1.50 4.00
71 Jameer Nelson .60 1.50
72 Steve Francis 1.00 2.50
73 Allen Iverson 2.00 5.00
74 Andre Iguodala 1.00 2.50
75 Chris Webber 1.25 3.00
76 Samuel Dalembert .60 1.50
77 Amare Stoudemire 1.00 2.50
78 Steve Nash 2.00 5.00
79 Quentin Richardson .60 1.50
80 Shawn Marion .75 2.00
81 Darius Miles .60 1.50
82 Zach Randolph 1.00 2.50
83 Shareef Abdur-Rahim 1.00 2.50
84 Peja Stojakovic .75 2.00
85 Mike Bibby 1.00 2.50
86 Manu Ginobili 2.00 5.00
87 Tim Duncan 2.50 6.00
88 Tony Parker 1.50 4.00
89 Ray Allen 1.50 4.00
90 Rashard Lewis .75 2.00
91 Robert Swift .60 1.50
92 Ronald Murray .60 1.50
93 Chris Bosh 1.25 3.00
94 Morris Peterson .60 1.50
95 Rafael Araujo .60 1.50
96 Andrei Kirilenko .75 2.00
97 Raul Lopez .60 1.50
98 Carlos Boozer .75 2.00
99 Antawn Jamison .75 2.00
100 Gilbert Arenas 1.00 2.50
101 Andrew Bynum RC 2.00 5.00
102 Julius Hodge RC 1.50 4.00
103 David Lee RC 2.50 6.00
104 Sarunas Jasikevicius RC 2.50 6.00
105 Ike Diogu RC 1.50 4.00
106 Luther Head RC 1.50 4.00
107 Jason Maxiell RC 2.00 5.00
108 Linas Kleiza RC 2.00 5.00
109 Amir Johnson RC 2.50 6.00
110 Andray Blatche RC 2.50 6.00
111 Sean May RC 1.50 4.00
112 Alex Acker RC 1.50 4.00
113 Nate Robinson RC 2.50 6.00
114 Brandon Bass RC 2.00 5.00
115 Ricky Sanchez RC 2.50 6.00
116 Daniel Ewing RC 2.00 5.00
117 Salim Stoudamire RC 2.00 5.00
118 Dijon Thompson RC 1.50 4.00
119 Danny Granger RC 2.50 6.00
120 Raymond Felton RC 2.00 5.00
121 Louis Williams RC 6.00 15.00
122 Channing Frye RC 2.00 5.00
123 Francisco Garcia RC 1.50 4.00
124 Ryan Gomes RC 2.00 5.00
125 Ersan Ilyasova RC 2.00 5.00
126 Jarrett Jack RC 2.50 6.00
127 Lawrence Roberts RC 1.50 4.00
128 Bracey Wright RC 1.50 4.00
129 C.J. Miles RC 2.00 5.00
130 Will Bynum RC 2.00 5.00
131 Travis Diener RC 1.50 4.00
132 Monta Ellis RC 3.00 8.00
133 Martell Webster RC 2.00 5.00
134 Johan Petro RC 1.50 4.00
135 Uros Slokar RC 2.50 6.00
136 Von Wafer RC 1.50 4.00

137 Martynas Andriuskevicius RC 1.50 4.00
138 Charlie Villanueva RC 2.00 5.00
139 Antoine Wright RC 2.00 5.00
140 Joey Graham RC 2.00 5.00
141 Wayne Simien RC 1.50 4.00
142 Hakim Warrick RC 2.00 5.00
143 Gerald Green RC 2.50 6.00
144 Marvin Williams RC 2.50 6.00
145 Deron Williams RC 4.00 10.00
146 Rashad McCants RC 1.50 4.00
147 Robert Whaley RC 1.50 4.00
148 Chris Taft RC 1.50 4.00
149 Chris Paul RC 12.00 30.00
150 Andrew Bogut RC 3.00 8.00

2005-06 SP Game Used 100
*1-100 VETERANS: .75X TO 2X BASE HI
*101-150 RC's: .6X TO 1.5X BASE HI
PRINT RUN 100 SER.#'d SETS
12 Michael Jordan 40.00 100.00

2005-06 SP Game Used 50
*1-100 VETERANS: 1.25X TO 3X BASE HI
*101-150 RCs: .75X TO 2X BASE HI
PRINT RUN 50 SER.#'d SETS
12 Michael Jordan 60.00 150.00

2005-06 SP Game Used 25
*1-100 VETERANS: 2X TO 5X BASE HI
*101-150 RCs: .1X TO 2.5X BASE HI
PRINT RUN 25 SER.#'d SETS
12 Michael Jordan 75.00 200.00

2005-06 SP Game Used Jerseys
PRINT RUN 100 SER.#'d SETS
1J Al Harrington 2.50 6.00
2J Josh Smith 2.50 6.00
3J Josh Childress 2.00 5.00
4J Joe Johnson 2.50 6.00
5J Paul Pierce 5.00 12.00
6J Antoine Walker 2.50 6.00
7J Gary Payton 5.00 12.00
8J Al Jefferson 2.00 5.00
10J Primoz Brezec 2.00 5.00
11J Gerald Wallace 2.50 6.00
12J Michael Jordan 40.00 100.00
13J Ben Gordon 2.50 6.00
14J Luol Deng 2.50 6.00
15J Eddy Curry 2.00 5.00
16J LeBron James 15.00 40.00
17J Dajuan Wagner 2.00 5.00
18J Drew Gooden 2.50 6.00
19J Larry Hughes 2.50 6.00
20J Dirk Nowitzki 8.00 20.00
21J Marquis Daniels 2.00 5.00
22J Michael Finley 3.00 8.00
23J Jerry Stackhouse 2.50 6.00
24J Andre Miller 2.50 6.00
25J Carmelo Anthony 5.00 12.00
26J Kenyon Martin 2.50 6.00
27J Nene 2.50 6.00
28J Rasheed Wallace 3.00 8.00
29J Ben Wallace 4.00 10.00
30J Richard Hamilton 4.00 10.00
31J Chauncey Billups 4.00 10.00
32J Baron Davis 3.00 8.00
33J Derek Fisher 3.00 8.00
34J Jason Richardson 3.00 8.00
35J Tracy McGrady 5.00 12.00
36J Yao Ming 6.00 15.00
37J Juwan Howard 2.50 6.00
38J Jermaine O'Neal 2.50 6.00
39J Ron Artest 2.50 6.00
40J Jamaal Tinsley 2.00 5.00
41J Corey Maggette 2.50 6.00
42J Elton Brand 2.50 6.00
43J Shaun Livingston 2.50 6.00
44J Kobe Bryant 50.00 120.00
45J Brian Cook 2.00 5.00
46J Lamar Odom 2.50 6.00
47J Bonzi Wells 2.00 5.00
48J Pau Gasol 5.00 12.00
49J Shane Battier 2.50 6.00
50J Shaquille O'Neal 10.00 25.00
51J Dwyane Wade 6.00 15.00
52J Dorell Wright 2.00 5.00
53J Eddie Jones 2.50 6.00
54J Joe Smith 2.50 6.00
55J Michael Redd 2.50 6.00
56J Desmond Mason 2.00 5.00
57J Kevin Garnett 8.00 20.00
58J Wally Szczerbiak 2.50 6.00
59J Sam Cassell 2.50 6.00
61J Jason Kidd 5.00 12.00
62J Richard Jefferson 2.50 6.00
63J Jamaal Magloire 2.00 5.00
64J J.R. Smith 3.00 8.00
65J Bostjan Nachbar 2.00 5.00
66J Allan Houston 2.50 6.00
67J Stephon Marbury 4.00 10.00
68J Jamal Crawford 3.00 8.00
69J Dwight Howard 4.00 10.00
70J Grant Hill 5.00 12.00
71J Jameer Nelson 2.00 5.00
72J Steve Francis 3.00 8.00
74J Andre Iguodala 3.00 8.00
75J Chris Webber 4.00 10.00
76J Samuel Dalembert 2.00 5.00
77J Amare Stoudemire 3.00 8.00
78J Steve Nash 6.00 15.00
79J Quentin Richardson 2.00 5.00
80J Shawn Marion 2.50 6.00
81J Darius Miles 2.00 5.00
82J Zach Randolph 3.00 8.00
83J Shareef Abdur-Rahim 3.00 8.00
84J Peja Stojakovic 2.50 6.00
85J Mike Bibby 3.00 8.00
86J Manu Ginobili 6.00 15.00
87J Tim Duncan 8.00 20.00
88J Tony Parker 5.00 12.00
89J Ray Allen 5.00 12.00
90J Rashard Lewis 2.50 6.00
91J Robert Swift 2.00 5.00
92J Ronald Murray 2.00 5.00
93J Chris Bosh 4.00 10.00
94J Morris Peterson 2.00 5.00
95J Rafael Araujo 2.00 5.00
96J Andrei Kirilenko 2.50 6.00
97J Raul Lopez 2.00 5.00
98J Carlos Boozer 2.50 6.00
99J Antawn Jamison 2.50 6.00
100J Gilbert Arenas 3.00 8.00

2005-06 SP Game Used Authentic Fabrics
STATED ODDS ONE PER PACK
*GOLD: .5X TO 1.25X BASE FAB HI
GOLD PRINT RUN 100 SER.#'d SETS
AB Andris Biedrins 1.50 4.00
AE Andre Emmett 1.50 4.00
AH Anfernee Hardaway 6.00 15.00
AI Andre Iguodala 2.50 6.00
AJ Al Jefferson 1.50 4.00
AK Andrei Kirilenko 2.00 5.00
AM Antonio McDyess 2.00 5.00
AN Antawn Jamison 2.00 5.00
AR Ron Artest 2.00 5.00
AS Amare Stoudemire 2.50 6.00
BC Brian Cook 1.50 4.00
BD Baron Davis 2.50 6.00
BE Ben Wallace 3.00 8.00
BG Ben Gordon 2.00 5.00
BJ Bobby Jackson 2.00 5.00
BR Bernard Robinson 1.50 4.00
BW Bonzi Wells 1.50 4.00
CA Carmelo Anthony 4.00 10.00
CB Carlos Boozer 2.00 5.00
CD Carlos Delfino 1.50 4.00
CM Corey Maggette 2.00 5.00
CU Cuttino Mobley 1.50 4.00
CW Corliss Williamson 1.50 4.00
DE Devean George 1.50 4.00
DG Drew Gooden 2.00 5.00
DH Dwight Howard 3.00 8.00
DJ Damon Jones 1.50 4.00
DM Darius Miles 1.50 4.00
DN Dirk Nowitzki 6.00 15.00
DS Darius Songaila 1.50 4.00
EB Elton Brand 2.00 5.00
EC Eddy Curry 1.50 4.00
EJ Eddie Jones 2.00 5.00
GP Gary Payton 4.00 10.00
GR Glenn Robinson 2.00 5.00
GW Gerald Wallace 2.00 5.00
JA Jason Kapono 1.50 4.00
JD Juan Dixon 1.50 4.00
JH Jarvis Hayes 1.50 4.00
JJ Jim Jackson 1.50 4.00
JK Jason Kidd 4.00 10.00
JM Jamaal Magloire 1.50 4.00
JN Jameer Nelson 1.50 4.00
JO Jermaine O'Neal 2.00 5.00
JR Jason Richardson 2.50 6.00
JS Joe Smith 2.00 5.00
KB Kobe Bryant 40.00 100.00
KE Kevin Martin 2.00 5.00
KG Kevin Garnett 6.00 15.00
KH Kris Humphries 1.50 4.00
KM Kenyon Martin 2.00 5.00
KS Kirk Snyder 1.50 4.00
KW Kwame Brown 1.50 4.00
LA Larry Hughes 2.00 5.00
LD Luol Deng 2.00 5.00
LH Lucious Harris 1.50 4.00
LJ LeBron James 30.00 80.00
LO Raul Lopez 2.00 5.00
LU Luke Jackson 2.00 5.00
MA Malik Rose 2.00 5.00
MB Mike Bibby 2.50 6.00
MD Marquis Daniels 2.00 5.00
MG Manu Ginobili 5.00 12.00
MI Mike Dunleavy 1.50 4.00
MJ Michael Jordan 60.00 150.00
MP Morris Peterson SP 1.50 4.00
MR Michael Redd SP 2.00 5.00
MT Maurice Taylor 2.00 5.00
NK Nenad Krstic 2.00 5.00
NT Nikoloz Tskitishvili 2.00 5.00
PP Paul Pierce 4.00 10.00
PS Peja Stojakovic 2.00 5.00
QR Quentin Richardson 1.50 4.00
RA Ray Allen 4.00 10.00
RF Rafael Araujo 1.50 4.00
RG Reece Gaines 1.50 4.00
RH Richard Hamilton 3.00 8.00
RJ Richard Jefferson 2.00 5.00
RL Rashard Lewis 2.00 5.00
RM Ronald Murray 1.50 4.00
RR Rodney Rogers 1.50 4.00
SD Samuel Dalembert 1.50 4.00
SF Steve Francis 2.50 6.00
SM Stephon Marbury 3.00 8.00
SN Steve Nash 5.00 12.00
SO Shaquille O'Neal 8.00 20.00
ST Sebastian Telfair 2.00 5.00
SV Sasha Vujacic 2.00 5.00
TA Tony Allen SP 2.00 5.00
TC Tyson Chandler 2.00 5.00
TD Tim Duncan 6.00 15.00
TH Troy Hudson 1.50 4.00
TM Tracy McGrady 4.00 10.00
TP Tony Parker 4.00 10.00
UH Udonis Haslem 1.50 4.00
VR Vladimir Radmanovic 1.50 4.00
WG Willie Green 1.50 4.00
WI Kevin Willis 1.50 4.00
WS Wally Szczerbiak 2.00 5.00
YM Yao Ming 5.00 12.00

2005-06 SP Game Used Authentic Fabrics Patches
*PATCHES: 2X TO 5X BASE HI
PRINT RUN 75 SER.#'d SETS
KB Kobe Bryant 125.00 300.00
MJ Michael Jordan 200.00 500.00

2005-06 SP Game Used Authentic Fabrics Autographs
PRINT RUN 23 TO 100 SER.#'d SETS
AB Andris Biedrins/100 5.00 12.00
AH Al Harrington/100 5.00 12.00
AJ Antawn Jamison/100 5.00 12.00
AK Andrei Kirilenko/100 8.00 20.00
AR Carlos Arroyo/100 15.00 40.00
BD Baron Davis/100 5.00 12.00
BG Ben Gordon/100 5.00 12.00
BM Brad Miller/100 5.00 12.00
CM Corey Maggette/100 5.00 12.00
DG Drew Gooden/100 5.00 12.00
DH Dwight Howard/100 15.00 40.00
DM Desmond Mason/100 5.00 12.00
DS Damon Stoudamire/100 5.00 12.00
DW Dorell Wright/100 5.00 12.00
GA Gilbert Arenas/100 5.00 12.00
JM Jamaal Magloire/100 5.00 12.00
JW Jason Williams/100 15.00 40.00
KH Kirk Hinrich/100 5.00 12.00
LJ LeBron James/100 2,000.00 4,000.00
MB Mike Bibby/100 5.00 12.00
MJ Michael Jordan/23 2,500.00 5,000.00
MR Michael Redd/100 5.00 12.00
PP Paul Pierce/100 12.00 30.00
QR Quentin Richardson/100 5.00 12.00
RJ Richard Jefferson/100 5.00 12.00
SM Shawn Marion/100 6.00 15.00
SN Steve Nash/100 50.00 120.00
TM Tracy McGrady/100 20.00 50.00

2005-06 SP Game Used Authentic Fabrics Autographs Patches
PRINT RUN 10 TO 25 SER.#'d SETS
AB Andris Biedrins/25 15.00 40.00
AH Al Harrington/25 15.00 40.00
AJ Antawn Jamison/25 15.00 40.00
AK Andrei Kirilenko/25 15.00 40.00
AR Carlos Arroyo/25 20.00 50.00
BD Baron Davis/25 15.00 40.00
BG Ben Gordon/25 15.00 40.00
BM Brad Miller/25 15.00 40.00
CM Corey Maggette/25 15.00 40.00
DG Drew Gooden/25 15.00 40.00
DH Dwight Howard/25 25.00 60.00
DM Desmond Mason/25 15.00 40.00
DW Dorell Wright/25 15.00 40.00
GA Gilbert Arenas/25 15.00 40.00
JM Jamaal Magloire/25 15.00 40.00
JW Jason Williams/25 60.00 150.00
LJ LeBron James/25 3,000.00 6,000.00
MB Mike Bibby/25 15.00 40.00
MR Michael Redd/25 15.00 40.00
PP Paul Pierce/25 50.00 120.00
QR Quentin Richardson/25 15.00 40.00
RJ Richard Jefferson/25 15.00 40.00
SM Shawn Marion/25 15.00 40.00
SN Steve Nash/25 75.00 200.00
TM Tracy McGrady/25 60.00 150.00

2005-06 SP Game Used Authentic Fabrics Dual
PRINT RUN 100 SER.#'d SETS
*GOLD: .5X TO 1.25X BASE FAB HI
GOLD PRINT RUN 50 SER.#'d SETS
AL R.Allen/R.Lewis 8.00 20.00
AT A.Jefferson/T.Allen 5.00 12.00
BC B.Miller/C.Mobley 5.00 12.00
BJ K.Bryant/L.James 150.00 400.00
BL C.Boozer/R.Lopez 5.00 12.00
BO K.Bryant/L.Odom 50.00 120.00
BP C.Bosh/M.Peterson 5.00 12.00
CS S.Cassell/W.Szczerbiak 5.00 12.00
DH J.Dixon/J.Hayes 5.00 12.00
DS M.Daniels/J.Stackhouse 5.00 12.00
GJ D.Gooden/L.Jackson 5.00 12.00
GP M.Ginobili/T.Parker 8.00 20.00
GW P.Gasol/B.Wells 5.00 12.00
HB R.Hamilton/C.Billups 6.00 15.00
HC K.Hinrich/E.Curry 5.00 12.00
HN D.Howard/J.Nelson 5.00 12.00
HS K.Humphries/K.Snyder 5.00 12.00
JA A.Jamison/G.Arenas 5.00 12.00
JH D.Jones/U.Haslem 5.00 12.00
JJ L.James/M.Jordan 75.00 200.00
JS J.Johnson/S.Marion 5.00 12.00
KJ J.Kidd/R.Jefferson 6.00 15.00
MB C.Maggette/E.Brand 5.00 12.00
MC S.Marbury/J.Crawford 5.00 12.00
MM A.Miller/K.Martin 5.00 12.00
MR R.Murray/V.Radmanovic 5.00 12.00
MS J.Magloire/J.R.Smith 5.00 12.00
MT D.Miles/S.Telfair 5.00 12.00
NF D.Nowitzki/M.Finley 6.00 15.00
OA J.O'Neal/R.Artest 5.00 12.00
OJ S.O'Neal/E.Jones 6.00 15.00
RA Z.Randolph/S.Abdur-Rahim 5.00 12.00
RF J.Richardson/D.Fisher 5.00 12.00
RK B.Robinson/J.Kapono 5.00 12.00
RM M.Redd/D.Mason 5.00 12.00
RP D.Rodman/S.Pippen 30.00 80.00
SC Jsh.Smith/J.Childress 5.00 12.00
TS I.Thomas/J.Stockton 8.00 20.00
WI C.Webber/A.Iguodala 5.00 12.00
WP A.Walker/G.Payton 5.00 12.00
WW R.Wallace/B.Wallace 5.00 12.00

2005-06 SP Game Used Authentic Fabrics Dual Gold
*GOLD: .5X TO 1.25X BASE HI
PRINT RUN 50 SER.#'d SETS
JJ L.James/M.Jordan 150.00 400.00

2005-06 SP Game Used Authentic Fabrics Dual Autographs
PRINT RUN 50 SER.#'d SETS
AJ K.Abdul-Jabbar/M.Johnson 125.00 300.00
AM C.Anthony/A.Miller 20.00 50.00
AT A.Jefferson/T.Allen 12.00 30.00
BH C.Billups/R.Hamilton 15.00 40.00
BS M.Bibby/P.Stojakovic 12.00 30.00
CD E.Curry/L.Deng 12.00 30.00
CH Childress/Harrington 12.00 30.00
DD B.Davis/M.Dunleavy 12.00 30.00
GH B.Gordon/K.Hinrich 12.00 30.00
GW P.Gasol/J.Williams 40.00 100.00
HN D.Howard/J.Nelson 20.00 50.00
IK A.Iguodala/K.Korver 15.00 40.00
JA A.Jamison/G.Arenas 15.00 40.00
JJ L.James/M.Jordan 5,000.00 8,000.00
KB A.Kirilenko/C.Boozer 12.00 30.00
KJ J.Kidd/R.Jefferson 20.00 50.00
ML C.Maggette/S.Livingston 12.00 30.00
MW C.Maggette/C.Wilcox 12.00 30.00
MY T.McGrady/Y.Ming 40.00 100.00
PP P.Pierce/G.Payton 40.00 100.00
PR S.Pippen/D.Rodman 300.00 600.00
RM M.Redd/D.Mason 12.00 30.00
RP J.Rose/M.Peterson 12.00 30.00
SD J.Stackhouse/M.Daniels 12.00 30.00
SM J.R.Smith/J.Magloire 12.00 30.00
ST D.Stoudamire/Telfair 12.00 30.00
VO S.Vujacic/L.Odom 12.00 30.00
WB G.Wallace/P.Brezec 12.00 30.00

2005-06 SP Game Used Authentic Fabrics Triple
PRINT RUN 25 SER.#'d SETS
BML Brand/Maggette/Livingston 12.50 30.00
DIW Dalembert/Iggy/Webber 15.00 40.00
DPG Duncan/Parker/Ginobili 20.00 50.00
DRD B.Davis/J-Rich/Dunleavy 12.50 30.00
JAH Jamison/Arenas/Hayes 12.50 30.00
JJB LeBron/MJ/Kobe 500.00 1,000.00
NFD Nowitzki/Finley/Daniels 20.00 50.00
OAT J.O'Neal/Artest/Tinsley 12.50 30.00
PJA Pierce/Big Al/T.Allen 15.00 40.00

2005-06 SP Game Used Legendary Fabrics
BK Bernard King 6.00 15.00
BR Bill Russell 15.00 40.00
CD Clyde Drexler 6.00 15.00
DR Dennis Rodman 10.00 25.00
GG George Gervin 6.00 15.00
HO Hakeem Olajuwon 6.00 15.00
JS John Stockton 10.00 25.00
KA Kareem Abdul-Jabbar 8.00 20.00
LB Larry Bird 15.00 40.00
MJ Michael Jordan 125.00 300.00
MJ2 Magic Johnson 12.00 30.00
SP Scottie Pippen 15.00 40.00

2005-06 SP Game Used Legendary Fabrics Autographs
PRINT RUN 23 TO 50 SER.#'d SETS
BK Bernard King/50 12.00 30.00
BR Bill Russell/50 125.00 300.00
DR Dennis Rodman/50 75.00 200.00
GG George Gervin/50 15.00 40.00
HO Hakeem Olajuwon/50 30.00 80.00
JS John Stockton/50 60.00 150.00
KA Kareem Abdul-Jabbar/50 50.00 120.00
LB Larry Bird/50 60.00 150.00
MA Magic Johnson/50 50.00 125.00
MJ Michael Jordan/23 2,000.00 4,000.00
SP Scottie Pippen/50 100.00 250.00

2005-06 SP Game Used Rookie Exclusive Autographs
PRINT RUN 100 SER.#'d SETS
AA Alex Acker 5.00 12.00
AB Andray Blatche 8.00 20.00
AJ Amir Johnson 8.00 20.00
AN Andrew Bogut 10.00 25.00
AW Antoine Wright 6.00 15.00
BB Brandon Bass 6.00 15.00
BW Bracey Wright 5.00 12.00
BY Andrew Bynum 6.00 15.00
CF Channing Frye 6.00 15.00
CJ C.J. Miles 6.00 15.00
CP Chris Paul 50.00 100.00
CT Chris Taft 5.00 12.00
CV Charlie Villanueva 6.00 15.00
DE Daniel Ewing 6.00 15.00
DG Danny Granger 8.00 20.00
DL David Lee 8.00 20.00
DT Dijon Thompson 5.00 12.00
DW Deron Williams 40.00 100.00
EI Ersan Ilyasova 6.00 15.00
FG Francisco Garcia 5.00 12.00
GG Gerald Green 8.00 20.00
HW Hakim Warrick 6.00 15.00
ID Ike Diogu 5.00 12.00
JG Joey Graham 6.00 15.00
JH Julius Hodge 5.00 12.00
JJ Jarrett Jack 8.00 20.00
JM Jason Maxiell 6.00 15.00
JP Johan Petro 5.00 12.00
LH Luther Head 6.00 15.00
LK Linas Kleiza 6.00 15.00
LR Lawrence Roberts 5.00 12.00
LW Louis Williams 20.00 50.00
MA Martell Webster 6.00 15.00
ME Monta Ellis 20.00 50.00
MG Mickael Gelabale 8.00 20.00
MW Marvin Williams 8.00 20.00
MY Martynas Andriuskevicius 5.00 12.00
NR Nate Robinson 15.00 40.00
RA Rashad McCants 5.00 12.00
RF Raymond Felton 8.00 20.00
RG Ryan Gomes 6.00 15.00
RS Ricky Sanchez 8.00 20.00
RT Ronny Turiaf 8.00 20.00
RW Robert Whaley 5.00 12.00
SJ Sarunas Jasikevicius 5.00 12.00
SM Sean May 5.00 12.00
SS Salim Stoudamire 6.00 15.00
TD Travis Diener 8.00 20.00
US Uros Slokar 8.00 20.00
VW Von Wafer 5.00 12.00
WB Will Bynum 6.00 15.00
WS Wayne Simien 5.00 12.00

2005-06 SP Game Used Signature Numbers
CARDS #'d TO PLAYER JSY NUMBER
AKO Andrei Kirilenko/47 ERR 12.00 30.00
CA Carmelo Anthony/15 25.00 60.00
DR Dennis Rodman/91 50.00 100.00
HO Hakeem Olajuwon/34 20.00 50.00
JN Jameer Nelson/14 12.00 30.00
JR J.R. Smith/23 15.00 40.00
KK Kyle Korver/26 12.00 30.00
LB Larry Bird/33 100.00 250.00
LJ LeBron James/23 3,000.00 6,000.00
MA Magic Johnson/32 60.00 120.00
MJ Michael Jordan/23 2,500.00 5,000.00
MR Michael Redd/22 12.00 30.00
PG Pau Gasol/16 20.00 50.00
PP Paul Pierce/34 15.00 40.00
ST Sebastian Telfair/31 12.00 30.00
UH Udonis Haslem/40 12.00 30.00

2005-06 SP Game Used SIGnificance
PRINT RUN 100 SER.#'d SETS
*SIG 25: .75X TO 2X BASE HI
SIG 25 PRINT RUN 25 SER.#'d SETS
AB Andray Blatche 5.00 12.00
AH Al Harrington 4.00 10.00
AI Andre Iguodala 5.00 12.00
AJ Antawn Jamison 4.00 10.00
AKO Andrei Kirilenko ERR 8.00 20.00
AL Al Jefferson 3.00 8.00
AM Antonio McDyess 4.00 10.00
AN Martynas Andriuskevicius 3.00 8.00
AR Carlos Arroyo 3.00 8.00
AW Antoine Wright 4.00 10.00
BB Brandon Bass 4.00 10.00
BD Baron Davis 5.00 12.00
BE Bernard King 6.00 15.00
BG Ben Gordon 4.00 10.00
BK Bob Knight 150.00 400.00
BL Bill Laimbeer 6.00 15.00
BM Brad Miller 4.00 10.00
BO Andrew Bogut 6.00 15.00
BU Beno Udrih 3.00 8.00
BW Bracey Wright 3.00 8.00
BY Andrew Bynum 4.00 10.00
CB Carlos Boozer 4.00 10.00
CD Clyde Drexler 15.00 40.00
CF Channing Frye 4.00 10.00
CH Chauncey Billups 6.00 15.00
CJ C.J. Miles 4.00 10.00
CM Corey Maggette 4.00 10.00
CN Curly Neal 20.00 50.00
CO Michael Cooper 6.00 15.00
CP Chris Paul 30.00 80.00
CS Chris Bosh 6.00 15.00
CT Chris Taft 3.00 8.00
CV Charlie Villanueva 4.00 10.00
DA Daniel Ewing 4.00 10.00
DD Dan Dickau 3.00 8.00
DE Desmond Mason 3.00 8.00
DF Derek Fisher 5.00 12.00
DG Danny Granger 5.00 12.00
DH Dwight Howard 10.00 25.00
DL David Lee 5.00 12.00
DM Darko Milicic 3.00 8.00
DP Dan Patrick 15.00 40.00
DR Dennis Rodman 30.00 80.00
DS Damon Stoudamire 5.00 12.00
DT Dijon Thompson 3.00 8.00
DW Deron Williams 8.00 20.00
ED Erik Daniels 3.00 8.00
EH Elvin Hayes 6.00 15.00
EI Ersan Ilyasova 4.00 10.00
FG Francisco Garcia 3.00 8.00
GA Gilbert Arenas 5.00 12.00
GG George Gervin 10.00 25.00
GW Gerald Wallace 4.00 10.00
HO Hakeem Olajuwon 12.00 30.00
HW Hakim Warrick 4.00 10.00
ID Ike Diogu 3.00 8.00
IT Isiah Thomas 20.00 50.00
JA Jamal Crawford 5.00 12.00
JC Josh Childress 3.00 8.00
JD Juan Dixon 3.00 8.00
JG Joey Graham 4.00 10.00
JH Julius Hodge 3.00 8.00
JJ Jarrett Jack 5.00 12.00
JK Jason Kidd 12.00 30.00
JM Jamaal Magloire 3.00 8.00
JO John Edwards 3.00 8.00
JP Johan Petro 3.00 8.00
JR J.R. Smith 5.00 12.00
JV Jackson Vroman 3.00 8.00
JW John Wooden 50.00 120.00
KA Jason Kapono 3.00 8.00
KE Kevin Martin 4.00 10.00
KH Kris Humphries 3.00 8.00
KI Kirk Hinrich 4.00 10.00
KK Kyle Korver 4.00 10.00
KM Kenny Mayne 6.00 15.00
LA Larry Brown 5.00 12.00
LC Linda Cohn 10.00 25.00
LD Luol Deng 4.00 10.00
LF Luis Flores 3.00 8.00
LH Luther Head 3.00 8.00
LJ LeBron James 2,000.00 4,000.00
LO Lamar Odom 4.00 10.00
LR Lawrence Roberts 3.00 8.00
LU Louis Williams 6.00 15.00
LW Lenny Wilkens 10.00 25.00
MA Marvin Williams 5.00 12.00
MB Mike Bibby 5.00 12.00
MC Mark Cuban 30.00 80.00
MD Marquis Daniels 3.00 8.00
ME Monta Ellis 6.00 15.00
MI Andre Miller 4.00 10.00
MJ Michael Jordan 2,000.00 4,000.00
ML Meadowlark Lemon 12.50 30.00
MP Morris Peterson 3.00 8.00
MR Michael Redd 4.00 10.00
MW Maurice Williams 4.00 10.00
NR Nate Robinson 5.00 12.00
PG Pau Gasol 8.00 20.00
QR Quentin Richardson 3.00 8.00
RF Raymond Felton 4.00 10.00
RJ Richard Jefferson 4.00 10.00
RM Ronald Murray 3.00 8.00
RT Ronny Turiaf 5.00 12.00
SB Steve Blake 3.00 8.00
SH Shane Battier 4.00 10.00
SV Sasha Vujacic 4.00 10.00
TA Tony Allen 3.00 8.00
TD Travis Diener 3.00 8.00
TR Trevor Ariza 3.00 8.00
UH Udonis Haslem 3.00 8.00
VK Viktor Khryapa 3.00 8.00
VW Von Wafer 3.00 8.00
WE Martell Webster 4.00 10.00
WF Walt Frazier 10.00 25.00
WJ Jason Williams 30.00 80.00
WR Willis Reed 40.00 100.00
WS Wayne Simien 3.00 8.00
ZC Zarko Cabarkapa 3.00 8.00

2005-06 SP Game Used SIGnificance Dual
PRINT RUN 25 SER.#'d SETS
BW L.Brown/L.Wilkens 30.00 80.00
DO C.Drexler/H.Olajuwon 75.00 150.00
EI J.Erving/A.Iguodala 50.00 120.00
FR W.Frazier/W.Reed 125.00 300.00
FS C.Frye/S.Stoudamire 15.00 40.00
GH G.Green/H.Warrick 15.00 40.00
GW P.Gasol/J.Williams 30.00 80.00
HG K.Hinrich/B.Gordon 15.00 40.00
HH D.Harris/J.Howard 15.00 40.00
HN D.Howard/J.Nelson 20.00 50.00
IS A.Iguodala/J.R.Smith 50.00 100.00
JJ M.Jordan/L.James 4,000.00 8,000.00
KB A.Kirilenko/C.Boozer 15.00 40.00
KJ J.Kidd/R.Jefferson 30.00 80.00
KW B.Knight/J.Wooden 125.00 300.00
MA S.Marbury/T.Ariza 15.00 40.00
MM M.Johnson/M.Jordan 450.00 750.00
MP M.Bibby/P.Stojakovic 40.00 60.00
NL C.Neal/M.Lemon 75.00 150.00
NR S.Nash/Q.Richardson 60.00 150.00
PF C.Paul/R.Felton 60.00 150.00
PR S.Pippen/D.Rodman 250.00 500.00
RB B.Russell/L.Bird 200.00 350.00
TJ I.Thomas/M.Johnson 80.00 160.00
TL S.Telfair/S.Livingston 15.00 40.00
WH D.Williams/L.Head 60.00 120.00
WM M.Williams/S.May 15.00 40.00
YM Y.Ming/T.McGrady 150.00 300.00

2005-06 SP Game Used SIGnificant Numbers Autographs
CARDS #'d TO PLAYER JSY NUMBER
DR Dennis Rodman/91 50.00 120.00
KA Kareem Abdul-Jabbar/33 50.00 125.00
LB Larry Bird/33 80.00 200.00
LJ LeBron James/23 3,000.00 6,000.00
MA Magic Johnson/32 60.00 150.00
MJ Michael Jordan/23 2,500.00 5,000.00

2005-06 SP Game Used Superstar Exclusive Autographs
PRINT RUN 25 TO 100 SER.#'d SETS
AJ Antawn Jamison/25 10.00 25.00
BD Baron Davis/25 10.00 25.00
BG Ben Gordon/25 15.00 40.00
BK Bernard King/100 10.00 25.00
CB Chris Bosh/25 12.00 30.00
DE Devin Harris/25 10.00 25.00
DH Dwight Howard/25 35.00 70.00
JC Josh Childress/25 10.00 25.00
JK Jason Kidd/25 20.00 50.00
JN Jameer Nelson/25 10.00 25.00
JS John Salley/100 10.00 25.00
KH Kirk Hinrich/25 10.00 25.00
LD Luol Deng/25 12.00 30.00
LJ LeBron James/25 1,250.00 2,500.00
MB Mike Bibby/25 10.00 25.00
MJ Michael Jordan/25 2,000.00 4,000.00
MR Michael Redd/25 10.00 25.00
PG Pau Gasol/25 15.00 40.00
PS Peja Stojakovic/25 15.00 40.00
RH Richard Hamilton/25 12.00 30.00
RJ Richard Jefferson/25 10.00 25.00
SL Shaun Livingston/25 10.00 25.00
SN Stephon Marbury/25 15.00 40.00
SV Steve Nash/25 60.00 120.00
TM Tracy McGrady/25 30.00 80.00
WR Willis Reed/100 40.00 100.00
YM Yao Ming/25 25.00 60.00

2006-07 SP Game Used
COMP.SET w/o SP's (100) 25.00 60.00
JSY ODDS APPROXIMATELY ONE PER PACK
RC PRINT RUN 999 SER.#'d SETS
1 Al Harrington .60 1.50
2 Joe Johnson .75 2.00
3 Salim Stoudamire .50 1.25
4 Tony Allen .50 1.25
5 Dan Dickau .50 1.25
6 Gerald Green .60 1.50
7 Michael Olowokandi .50 1.25
8 Brevin Knight .50 1.25
9 Peja Stojakovic .60 1.50
10 Gerald Wallace .60 1.50
11 Luol Deng .60 1.50
12 Chris Duhon .50 1.25
13 Mike Sweetney .50 1.25
14 Drew Gooden .60 1.50
15 Luke Jackson .50 1.25
16 Damon Jones .50 1.25
17 Eric Snow .50 1.25
18 Erick Dampier .50 1.25
19 Marquis Daniels .50 1.25
20 Jerry Stackhouse .60 1.50
21 Jason Terry .60 1.50
22 Earl Boykins .60 1.50
23 Marcus Camby .60 1.50
24 Kenyon Martin .60 1.50
25 Andre Miller .60 1.50
26 Kelvin Cato .50 1.25
27 Lindsey Hunter .50 1.25
28 Antonio McDyess .50 1.25
29 Mike Dunleavy .50 1.25
30 Derek Fisher .75 2.00
31 Troy Murphy .60 1.50
32 Rafer Alston .50 1.25
33 Juwan Howard .60 1.50
34 Stromile Swift .50 1.25
35 Austin Croshere .50 1.25
36 Stephen Jackson .60 1.50
37 Jamaal Tinsley .50 1.25
38 Sam Cassell .60 1.50
39 Chris Kaman .50 1.25
40 Yaroslav Korolev .50 1.25
41 Cuttino Mobley .60 1.50
42 Devean George .50 1.25
43 Smush Parker .50 1.25
44 Ronny Turiaf .60 1.50
45 Shane Battier .60 1.50
46 Bobby Jackson .50 1.25
47 Mike Miller .60 1.50
48 Damon Stoudamire .60 1.50
49 Alonzo Mourning 1.25 3.00
50 Gary Payton 1.00 2.50
51 Dwyane Wade 1.50 4.00
52 Jason Williams 1.00 2.50
53 T.J. Ford .50 1.25
54 Jamaal Magloire .50 1.25
55 Maurice Williams .60 1.50
56 Marcus Banks .50 1.25
57 Eddie Griffin .50 1.25
58 Troy Hudson .50 1.25
59 Jason Collins .50 1.25
60 Nenad Krstic .50 1.25
61 Antoine Wright .50 1.25
62 P.J. Brown .50 1.25
63 Speedy Claxton .50 1.25
64 Marc Jackson .50 1.25
65 Jamal Crawford .75 2.00
66 Eddy Curry .60 1.50
67 Quentin Richardson .50 1.25
68 Carlos Arroyo .50 1.25
69 Keyon Dooling .50 1.25
70 Darko Milicic .50 1.25
71 Steven Hunter .50 1.25
72 Allen Iverson 2.00 5.00
73 Kyle Korver .60 1.50
74 Raja Bell .60 1.50
75 Boris Diaw .60 1.50
76 Kurt Thomas .50 1.25
77 Steve Blake .50 1.25
78 Darius Miles .50 1.25
79 Joel Przybilla .50 1.25
80 Ha Seung-Jin .50 1.25
81 Shareef Abdur-Rahim .75 2.00
82 Brad Miller .60 1.50
83 Kenny Thomas .50 1.25
84 Bonzi Wells .50 1.25
85 Brent Barry .50 1.25
86 Bruce Bowen .60 1.50
87 Michael Finley .75 2.00
88 Robert Horry .75 2.00
89 Luke Ridnour .60 1.50
90 Robert Swift .50 1.25
91 Chris Wilcox .50 1.25
92 Rafael Araujo .50 1.25
93 Jose Calderon .50 1.25
94 Mike James .50 1.25
95 Matt Harpring .50 1.25
96 Kris Humphries .50 1.25
97 Jason Richardson .75 2.00
98 Gilbert Arenas .75 2.00
99 Antonio Daniels .50 1.25
100 Brendan Haywood .50 1.25
101 Josh Childress JSY 1.50 4.00
102 Josh Smith JSY 1.50 4.00
103 Marvin Williams JSY 1.50 4.00
104 Al Jefferson JSY 1.50 4.00
105 Paul Pierce JSY 4.00 10.00
106 Wally Szczerbiak JSY 2.00 5.00
107 Raymond Felton JSY 1.50 4.00
108 Sean May JSY 1.50 4.00
109 Emeka Okafor JSY 2.00 5.00
110 Tyson Chandler JSY 2.00 5.00
111 Ben Gordon JSY 2.00 5.00
112 Kirk Hinrich JSY 2.00 5.00
113 Michael Jordan SP JSY 60.00 150.00
114 Larry Hughes JSY 2.00 5.00
115 Zydrunas Ilgauskas JSY 2.00 5.00
116 LeBron James JSY 50.00 120.00
117 Devin Harris JSY 1.50 4.00
118 Josh Howard JSY 2.00 5.00
119 Dirk Nowitzki JSY 6.00 15.00
120 Carmelo Anthony JSY 4.00 10.00
121 Julius Hodge JSY 1.50 4.00
122 Linas Kleiza JSY 1.50 4.00
123 Chauncey Billups JSY 3.00 8.00
124 Tayshaun Prince JSY 2.50 6.00
125 Ben Wallace JSY 3.00 8.00
126 Rasheed Wallace JSY 3.00 8.00
127 Baron Davis JSY 2.50 6.00
128 Ike Diogu JSY 1.50 4.00
129 Jason Richardson JSY 2.50 6.00
130 Chris Taft JSY 1.50 4.00
131 Luther Head JSY 1.50 4.00
132 Tracy McGrady JSY 4.00 10.00
133 Yao Ming JSY 6.00 15.00
134 Danny Granger JSY 1.50 4.00
135 Sarunas Jasikevicius JSY 2.00 5.00
136 Jermaine O'Neal JSY 2.50 6.00
137 Peja Stojakovic SP JSY 2.00 5.00
138 Elton Brand JSY 2.00 5.00
139 Shaun Livingston JSY 2.00 5.00
140 Corey Maggette JSY 2.00 5.00
141 Kwame Brown JSY 1.50 4.00
142 Kobe Bryant JSY 75.00 200.00
143 Andrew Bynum JSY 1.50 4.00
144 Lamar Odom JSY 2.00 5.00
145 Pau Gasol JSY 4.00 10.00
146 Eddie Jones JSY 2.50 6.00
147 Hakim Warrick JSY 1.50 4.00
148 Shaquille O'Neal JSY 10.00 25.00
149 Wayne Simien JSY 1.50 4.00
150 Antoine Walker JSY 2.50 6.00
151 Andrew Bogut JSY 2.00 5.00
152 Ersan Ilyasova JSY 1.50 4.00
153 Michael Redd JSY 2.00 5.00
154 Ricky Davis JSY 2.00 5.00
155 Kevin Garnett JSY 6.00 15.00
156 Rashad McCants JSY 1.50 4.00
157 Bracey Wright JSY 1.50 4.00
158 Vince Carter JSY 5.00 12.00
159 Richard Jefferson JSY 2.00 5.00
160 Jason Kidd JSY 4.00 10.00
161 Jeff McInnis JSY 1.50 4.00
163 Chris Paul JSY 5.00 12.00
164 J.R. Smith JSY 2.50 6.00
165 David West JSY 2.00 5.00
166 Steve Francis JSY 2.50 6.00
167 Channing Frye JSY 1.50 4.00
168 Stephon Marbury JSY 3.00 8.00
169 Nate Robinson JSY 2.00 5.00
170 Grant Hill JSY 4.00 10.00
171 Dwight Howard JSY 3.00 8.00
172 Jameer Nelson JSY 1.50 4.00
173 Samuel Dalembert JSY 1.50 4.00
174 Andre Iguodala JSY 2.50 6.00
175 Chris Webber JSY 3.00 8.00
176 Shawn Marion JSY 2.50 6.00
177 Steve Nash JSY 5.00 12.00
178 Amare Stoudemire JSY 2.50 6.00
179 Zach Randolph JSY 2.50 6.00
180 Sebastian Telfair JSY 1.50 4.00
181 Martell Webster JSY 2.00 5.00
182 Ron Artest JSY 2.50 6.00
183 Mike Bibby JSY 2.50 6.00
184 Francisco Garcia JSY 1.50 4.00
185 Tim Duncan JSY 6.00 15.00
186 Manu Ginobili JSY 5.00 12.00
187 Tony Parker JSY 4.00 10.00
188 Ray Allen JSY 4.00 10.00
189 Rashard Lewis JSY 2.00 5.00
190 Johan Petro JSY 1.50 4.00
191 Chris Bosh JSY 3.00 8.00
192 Joey Graham JSY 1.50 4.00

193 Charlie Villanueva JSY 1.50 4.00
194 Carlos Boozer JSY 2.00 5.00
195 Andrei Kirilenko JSY 2.00 5.00
196 C.J. Miles JSY 1.50 4.00
197 Deron Williams JSY 2.00 5.00
198 Andray Blatche JSY 1.50 4.00
199 Caron Butler JSY 2.00 5.00
200 Antawn Jamison JSY 2.00 5.00
201 Andrea Bargnani RC 2.00 5.00
202 LaMarcus Aldridge RC 6.00 15.00
203 Adam Morrison RC 2.00 5.00
204 Tyrus Thomas RC 2.00 5.00
205 Shelden Williams RC 1.50 4.00
206 Brandon Roy RC 5.00 12.00
207 Randy Foye RC 2.00 5.00
208 Rudy Gay RC 3.00 8.00
209 Patrick O'Bryant RC 1.50 4.00
210 Saer Sene RC 1.50 4.00
211 J.J. Redick RC 5.00 12.00
212 Hilton Armstrong RC 1.50 4.00
213 Thabo Sefolosha RC 2.00 5.00
214 Ronnie Brewer RC 2.50 6.00
215 Cedric Simmons RC 1.50 4.00
216 Rodney Carney RC 1.50 4.00
217 Shawne Williams RC 1.50 4.00
218 Hassan Adams RC 1.50 4.00
219 Quincy Douby RC 1.50 4.00
220 Renaldo Balkman RC 2.00 5.00
221 Rajon Rondo RC 8.00 20.00
222 Marcus Williams RC 1.50 4.00
223 Josh Boone RC 1.50 4.00
224 Kyle Lowry RC 8.00 20.00
225 Shannon Brown RC 1.50 4.00
226 Jordan Farmar RC 2.00 5.00
227 Maurice Ager RC 1.50 4.00
228 Mardy Collins RC 1.50 4.00
229 Will Blalock RC 1.50 4.00
230 James White RC 1.50 4.00
231 Steve Novak RC 2.00 5.00
232 Solomon Jones RC 1.50 4.00
233 Paul Davis RC 1.50 4.00
234 P.J. Tucker RC 2.50 6.00
235 Craig Smith RC 2.00 5.00
236 Bobby Jones RC 1.50 4.00
237 David Noel RC 1.50 4.00
238 Denham Brown RC 1.50 4.00
239 James Augustine RC 1.50 4.00
240 Daniel Gibson RC 2.00 5.00
241 Ryan Hollins RC 1.50 4.00
242 Alexander Johnson RC 1.50 4.00
243 Dee Brown RC 1.50 4.00
244 Paul Millsap RC 3.00 8.00
245 Leon Powe RC 1.50 4.00
246 Mike Gansey RC 1.50 4.00
247 Tarence Kinsey RC 1.50 4.00
248 Damir Markota RC 1.50 4.00
249 J.R. Pinnock RC 1.50 4.00
250 Kevin Pittsnogle RC 2.00 5.00

2006-07 SP Game Used Gold

*1-100 GOLD: .75X TO 2X BASE HI
*101-200 JSY GOLD: .5X TO 1.25X BASE HI
*201-249 RCs GOLD: .6X TO 1.5X BASE HI
PRINT RUN 100 SER.#'d SETS

2006-07 SP Game Used Patches

*PATCH: 1.25X TO 3X BASE HI
STATED PRINT RUN 25 SER.#'d SETS
170 Grant Hill 12.00 30.00
175 Chris Webber 15.00 40.00

2006-07 SP Game Used All-Star Memorabilia

PRINT RUN 100 SER.#'d SETS
*PATCHES: .75X TO 2X BASE HI
PATCH PRINT RUN 25 SER.#'d SETS
AB Andrew Bogut 3.00 8.00
AI Andre Iguodala 4.00 10.00
AN Andres Nocioni 2.50 6.00
BG Ben Gordon 3.00 8.00
BO Chris Bosh 5.00 12.00
BW Ben Wallace 5.00 12.00
CB Chauncey Billups 5.00 12.00
CF Channing Frye 2.50 6.00
CP Chris Paul 8.00 20.00
CV Charlie Villanueva 2.50 6.00
DG Danny Granger 2.50 6.00
DH Devin Harris 2.50 6.00
DJ Dahntay Jones 2.50 6.00
DN Dirk Nowitzki 10.00 25.00
DW Delonte West 2.50 6.00
EB Elton Brand 3.00 8.00
EO Emeka Okafor 3.00 8.00
GA Gilbert Arenas 4.00 10.00
HW Hakim Warrick 2.50 6.00
JS Josh Smith 2.50 6.00
JT Jason Terry 3.00 8.00
KB Kobe Bryant 50.00 120.00
LD Luol Deng 3.00 8.00
LH Luther Head 2.50 6.00
LJ LeBron James 15.00 40.00
NK Nenad Krstic 2.50 6.00
NR Nate Robinson 3.00 8.00
PG Pau Gasol 6.00 15.00
PP Paul Pierce 6.00 15.00
QR Quentin Richardson 2.50 6.00
RA Ray Allen 5.00 12.00
RH Richard Hamilton 4.00 10.00
RI Royal Ivey 2.50 6.00
RW Rasheed Wallace 5.00 12.00
SJ Sarunas Jasikevicius 3.00 8.00
SM Shawn Marion 4.00 10.00
SO Shaquille O'Neal 15.00 40.00
TD Tim Duncan 10.00 25.00
TF T.J. Ford 2.50 6.00
TP Tony Parker 6.00 15.00
VC Vince Carter 8.00 20.00
WI Deron Williams 3.00 8.00

2006-07 SP Game Used Authentic Fabrics Dual

PRINT RUN 100 SER.#'d SETS
AD R.Artest/Q.Douby 3.00 8.00
AI A.Iverson/A.Iguodala 6.00 15.00
AJ A.Jefferson/T.Allen 3.00 8.00
AR R.Jefferson/A.Wright 3.00 8.00
AW R.Allen/C.Wilcox 3.00 8.00
BF C.Bosh/T.J.Ford 3.00 8.00
BG C.Butler/B.Gordon 3.00 8.00
BM C.J.Miles/R.Brewer 3.00 8.00
CA T.Chandler/H.Armstrong 3.00 8.00
CJ J.Childress/S.Jones 3.00 8.00
CL L.James/C.Anthony 12.00 30.00
CM C.Maggette/S.Cassell 3.00 8.00
DI S.Dalembert/A.Iguodala 3.00 8.00
DM R.Davis/R.McCants 3.00 8.00
DR B.Davis/J.Richardson 3.00 8.00
DS D.Gooden/S.Brown 3.00 8.00
DT M.Dunleavy/C.Taft 3.00 8.00
FC E.Curry/C.Frye 3.00 8.00
FM S.Francis/S.Marbury 3.00 8.00
FR S.Francis/N.Robinson 3.00 8.00
FW R.Felton/Mv.Williams 3.00 8.00
GB M.Bibby/F.Garcia 3.00 8.00
GC J.Graham/J.Calderon 3.00 8.00
GW H.Warrick/R.Gay 3.00 8.00
HB R.Hamilton/C.Billups 4.00 10.00
HH J.Howard/D.Harris 3.00 8.00
HJ L.James/L.Hughes 8.00 20.00
HM A.Miller/J.Hodge 3.00 8.00
HS K.Hinrich/M.Sweetney 3.00 8.00
HT K.Hinrich/T.Thomas 3.00 8.00
IC A.Iverson/R.Carney 4.00 10.00
IJ Z.Ilgauskas/L.James 10.00 25.00
JA A.Jamison/G.Arenas 3.00 8.00
JB M.Johnson/L.Bird 20.00 50.00
JJ M.Jordan/L.James 75.00 200.00
JM J.Jack/M.Webster 3.00 8.00
JS J.Johnson/J.Smith 3.00 8.00
JW J.Johnson/Mv.Williams 3.00 8.00
KF B.King/W.Frazier 3.00 8.00
KW A.Kirilenko/D.Williams 3.00 8.00
LC S.Livingston/J.Childress 3.00 8.00
LP R.Lewis/J.Petro 3.00 8.00
MA J.Magloire/L.Aldridge 3.00 8.00
MF R.Felton/S.May 3.00 8.00
MH J.Howard/T.McGrady 4.00 10.00
ML C.Mobley/S.Livingston 3.00 8.00
MM C.Maggette/C.Mobley 3.00 8.00
NG D.Nowitzki/P.Gasol 5.00 12.00
NH G.Hill/J.Nelson 3.00 8.00
OD H.Olajuwon/C.Drexler 8.00 20.00
OF L.Odom/J.Farmar 3.00 8.00
OM E.Okafor/S.May 3.00 8.00
RA Z.Randolph/M.Ager 3.00 8.00
RJ L.Ridnour/L.Jackson 3.00 8.00
RP P.Pierce/R.Rondo 4.00 10.00
RR R.McCants/R.Foye 3.00 8.00
RV M.Redd/C.Villanueva 3.00 8.00
SA W.Szczerbiak/T.Allen 3.00 8.00
ST W.Szczerbiak/S.Telfair 3.00 8.00
SW J.Williams/W.Simien 3.00 8.00
TC M.Taylor/E.Curry 3.00 8.00
TD C.Taft/J.Diogu 3.00 8.00
TH J.Terry/J.Howard 3.00 8.00
TS K.Thomas/A.Stoudemire 4.00 10.00
TW J.Tinsley/S.Williams 3.00 8.00
WB D.Williams/D.Brown 3.00 8.00
WD J.Dixon/M.Webster 3.00 8.00
WK C.Webber/K.Korver 5.00 12.00
WS D.West/C.Simmons 3.00 8.00
WW Mv.Williams/S.Williams 3.00 8.00

2006-07 SP Game Used Authentic Fabrics Dual Autographs

STATED PRINT RUN 15 TO 50 SER.#'d SETS
AL R.Artest/B.Laimbeer 12.00 30.00
AP C.Paul/H.Armstrong 40.00 100.00
AS R.Artest/P.Stojakovic 10.00 25.00
BA M.Bibby/R.Artest 12.00 30.00
BC T.Chandler/A.Bogut 12.00 30.00
BG E.Brand/K.Garnett 25.00 60.00
BI A.Bogut/E.Ilyasova 8.00 20.00
BM M.Bibby/B.Miller 8.00 20.00
BP C.Billups/T.Prince 15.00 40.00
BR N.Robinson/R.Balkman 12.00 30.00
BW C.Boozer/D.Williams 20.00 50.00
CB T.Chandler/Kw.Brown 8.00 20.00
CJ V.Carter/R.Jefferson 15.00 40.00
DL M.Daniels/S.Livingston 8.00 20.00
DT B.Davis/C.Taft 8.00 20.00
FT T.J.Ford/P.J.Tucker 8.00 20.00
GB M.Bibby/F.Garcia 8.00 20.00
GH K.Garnett/D.Howard 50.00 120.00
GM K.Garnett/R.McCants 20.00 50.00
HG H.Warrick/R.Gay 12.00 30.00
HM L.Hughes/D.Marshall 8.00 20.00
IK K.Korver/A.Iguodala 12.00 30.00
IR A.Iguodala/N.Robinson 8.00 20.00
JA L.James/C.Anthony/15 2,000.00 4,000.00
JJ M.Jordan/L.James/15 4,000.00 8,000.00
JW J.Johnson/Mv.Williams 10.00 25.00
KC J.Kidd/V.Carter 25.00 60.00
KD J.Kidd/B.Davis 20.00 50.00
KF B.King/W.Frazier 20.00 50.00
KJ J.Kidd/R.Jefferson 12.00 30.00
KS K.Korver/P.Stojakovic 8.00 20.00
LS S.Livingston/J.R.Smith 8.00 20.00
MA Y.Ming/Abdul-Jabbar/15 50.00 120.00
MB D.Marshall/C.Boozer 8.00 20.00
MF R.McCants/R.Felton 10.00 25.00
MJ T.McGrady/L.James/15 1,500.00 3,000.00
ML C.Mobley/S.Livingston 8.00 20.00
MM C.Maggette/C.Mobley 8.00 20.00
NS S.Nash/C.Billups/15 50.00 120.00
OB L.Odom/Kw.Brown 8.00 20.00
OD Olajuwon/Drexler/15 75.00 150.00
OG L.Odom/J.Graham 8.00 20.00
OJ L.Odom/A.Jefferson 8.00 20.00
PJ P.Pierce/A.Jefferson 20.00 50.00
PT S.Telfair/K.Pittsnogle 8.00 20.00
RC Q.Richardson/E.Curry 8.00 20.00
RH L.Ridnour/K.Hinrich 8.00 20.00
RJ Q.Richardson/J.Johnson 8.00 20.00
SC T.Chandler/C.Simmons 8.00 20.00
TG C.Taft/F.Garcia 8.00 20.00
TR S.Telfair/N.Robinson 8.00 20.00
WB A.Bogut/Mv.Williams 12.00 30.00
WJ A.Jamison/Mv.Williams 8.00 20.00
WP C.Paul/D.Williams 40.00 100.00

2006-07 SP Game Used Authentic Fabrics Dual Patches

*PATCHES: 1X TO 2.5X BASE HI
PRINT RUN 25 SER.#'d SETS
CL L.James/C.Anthony 30.00 80.00

2006-07 SP Game Used Authentic Fabrics Dual Patches Autographs

STATED PRINT RUN 5 TO 25 SER.#'d SETS
AL R.Artest/B.Laimbeer/25 15.00 40.00
AP C.Paul/H.Armstrong/25 60.00 150.00
BC T.Chandler/A.Bogut/25 20.00 50.00
BM M.Bibby/B.Miller/25 20.00 50.00
BW C.Boozer/D.Williams/25 10.00 25.00
CB T.Chandler/Kw.Brown/25 10.00 25.00
CJ V.Carter/R.Jefferson/25 20.00 50.00
DL M.Daniels/S.Livingston/25 10.00 25.00
DT B.Davis/C.Taft/25 10.00 25.00
GM K.Garnett/R.McCants/25 25.00 60.00
HG H.Warrick/R.Gay/25 10.00 25.00
IK K.Korver/A.Iguodala/25 15.00 40.00
IR A.Iguodala/N.Robinson/25 10.00 25.00
KC J.Kidd/V.Carter/25 30.00 80.00
KD J.Kidd/B.Davis/25 15.00 40.00
KF B.King/W.Frazier/25 25.00 60.00
KJ J.Kidd/R.Jefferson/25 25.00 60.00
KS K.Korver/P.Stojakovic/25 10.00 25.00
MB D.Marshall/C.Boozer/25 10.00 25.00
MF R.McCants/R.Felton/25 12.00 30.00
MM C.Maggette/C.Mobley/25 10.00 25.00
OJ L.Odom/A.Jefferson/25 10.00 25.00
PT S.Telfair/K.Pittsnogle/25 10.00 25.00
RH L.Ridnour/K.Hinrich/25 10.00 25.00
TG C.Taft/F.Garcia/25 10.00 25.00
TR S.Telfair/N.Robinson/25 10.00 25.00
WP C.Paul/D.Williams/25 30.00 80.00

2006-07 SP Game Used Authentic Fabrics Triple

PRINT RUN 25 SER.#'d SETS
ASJ Szcz/A.Jefferson/T.Allen 12.00 30.00
BAJ Kobe/LeBron/Melo 200.00 500.00
BBB Brand/Battier/Boozer 12.00 30.00
BGF Bosh/T.J.Ford/Graham 12.00 30.00
BOV Odom/Kw.Brown/Vujacic 12.00 30.00
DMO Duncan/Olajuwon/Yao 20.00 50.00
DPG Duncan/Parker/Manu 25.00 60.00
DRD J-Rich/Dunleavy/Diogu 12.00 30.00
GHO KG/D.Howard/J.O'Neal 20.00 50.00
HBP Hamilton/Billups/Prince 15.00 40.00
HDG Hinrich/Deng/Gordon 15.00 40.00
IKB Ilgauskas/Krstic/Bogut 12.00 30.00
JMM Jamison/McInnis/May 12.00 30.00
KCJ Kidd/Vince/R.Jefferson 15.00 40.00
MRR Marbury/Q-Rich/N.Robinson 12.00 30.00
MWP Mason/West/Paul 15.00 40.00
NKS Nowitzki/Kirilenko/Peja 15.00 40.00
NMS Nash/Marion/Amare 20.00 50.00
WIK Webber/Iverson/Korver 15.00 40.00

2006-07 SP Game Used Legendary Fabrics

PRINT RUN 100 SER.#'d SETS
BK Bernard King 5.00 12.00
BL Bill Laimbeer 6.00 15.00
BR Bill Russell 15.00 40.00
CD Clyde Drexler 8.00 20.00
DR Dennis Rodman 8.00 20.00
GG George Gervin 8.00 20.00
HO Hakeem Olajuwon 8.00 20.00
JE Julius Erving 10.00 25.00
JH Jeff Hornacek 6.00 15.00
JS John Starks 5.00 12.00
KA Kareem Abdul-Jabbar 8.00 20.00
LB Larry Bird 10.00 25.00
MA Magic Johnson 10.00 25.00
MJ Michael Jordan 30.00 75.00
NA Nate Archibald 5.00 12.00
RP Robert Parish 5.00 12.00
SE Sean Elliott 5.00 12.00
SK Steve Kerr 5.00 12.00
ST John Stockton 8.00 20.00
WF Walt Frazier 5.00 12.00

2006-07 SP Game Used Legendary Fabrics Autographs

PRINT RUN 10 TO 50 SER.#'d SETS
BK Bernard King/50 10.00 25.00
BL Bill Laimbeer/50 10.00 25.00
CD Clyde Drexler/50 30.00 80.00
GG George Gervin/50 10.00 25.00
HO Hakeem Olajuwon/50 25.00 60.00
JE Julius Erving/10 75.00 150.00
JH Jeff Hornacek/50 20.00 50.00
JS John Starks/50 30.00 60.00
KA Kareem Abdul-Jabbar/10 60.00 120.00
LB Larry Bird/10 125.00 225.00
MA Magic Johnson/50 75.00 150.00
MJ Michael Jordan/50 1,500.00 3,000.00
NA Nate Archibald/50 12.00 30.00
RP Robert Parish/50 12.00 30.00
SK Steve Kerr/50 20.00 50.00
WF Walt Frazier/50 12.00 30.00

2006-07 SP Game Used Rookie Exclusive Autographs

PRINT RUN 100 SER.#'d SETS
AB Andrea Bargnani 5.00 12.00
AD Hassan Adams 4.00 10.00
AR Allan Ray 4.00 10.00
BA Renaldo Balkman 5.00 12.00
BJ Bobby Jones 4.00 10.00
BR Brandon Roy 12.00 30.00
CS Cedric Simmons 4.00 10.00
DB Denham Brown 4.00 10.00
DE Dee Brown 4.00 10.00
DG Daniel Gibson 5.00 12.00
DN David Noel 4.00 10.00
HA Hilton Armstrong 4.00 10.00
JA James Augustine 4.00 10.00
JB Josh Boone 4.00 10.00
JF Jordan Farmar 5.00 12.00
JW James White 4.00 10.00
KL Kyle Lowry 20.00 50.00
KP Kevin Pittsnogle 5.00 12.00
LA LaMarcus Aldridge 25.00 60.00
MA Maurice Ager 4.00 10.00
MC Mardy Collins 4.00 10.00
MG Mike Gansey 4.00 10.00
MW Marcus Williams 4.00 10.00
PD Paul Davis 4.00 10.00
PO Patrick O'Bryant 4.00 10.00
PT P.J. Tucker 6.00 15.00
QD Quincy Douby 4.00 10.00
RB Ronnie Brewer 6.00 15.00
RC Rodney Carney 4.00 10.00
RF Randy Foye 5.00 12.00
RG Rudy Gay 8.00 20.00
RH Ryan Hollins 4.00 10.00
RR Rajon Rondo 30.00 80.00
SB Shannon Brown 4.00 10.00
SJ Solomon Jones 4.00 10.00
SM Craig Smith 5.00 12.00
SN Steve Novak 5.00 12.00
SS Saer Sene 4.00 10.00
SW Shelden Williams 4.00 10.00
TT Tyrus Thomas 5.00 12.00
WI Shawne Williams 4.00 10.00

2006-07 SP Game Used SIGnificance

PRINT RUN 23 TO 100 SER.#'d SETS
AB Andrew Bogut/100 5.00 12.00
AH Hilton Armstrong/100 2.50 6.00
AI Andre Iguodala/100 4.00 10.00
AJ Al Jefferson/100 2.50 6.00
AU James Augustine/25 2.50 6.00
BA Andrea Bargnani/100 8.00 20.00
BB Brent Barry/100 4.00 10.00
BI Chauncey Billups/100 6.00 15.00
BJ Bobby Jackson/100 4.00 10.00
BK Bernard King/100 8.00 20.00
BM Brad Miller/100 3.00 8.00
BN Denham Brown/100 2.50 6.00
BR Brandon Roy/100 12.00 30.00
BW Bill Walton/100 12.00 30.00
CA Carmelo Anthony/50 30.00 80.00
CB Carlos Boozer/100 4.00 10.00
CD Clyde Drexler/100 15.00 40.00
CE Cedric Simmons/25 2.50 6.00
CM Cuttino Mobley/100 3.00 8.00
CS Craig Smith/100 3.00 8.00
CT Chris Taft/100 2.50 6.00
DB Dee Brown/100 2.50 6.00
DE Daniel Ewing/100 2.50 6.00
DG Daniel Gibson/100 3.00 8.00
DH Dwight Howard/100 12.00 30.00
DM Donyell Marshall/100 2.50 6.00
DN David Noel/100 2.50 6.00
DS DeShawn Stevenson/100 2.50 6.00
DW Deron Williams/100 3.00 8.00
EC Eddy Curry/100 3.00 8.00
EI Ersan Ilyasova/100 2.50 6.00
FG Francisco Garcia/100 2.50 6.00
FR Randy Foye/100 3.00 8.00
HA Hassan Adams/100 2.50 6.00
HW Hakim Warrick/100 2.50 6.00
JB Bobby Jones/100 2.50 6.00
JG Joey Graham/100 2.50 6.00
JK Jason Kapono/100 2.50 6.00
JW James White/100 2.50 6.00
KB Kwame Brown/100 4.00 10.00
KG Kevin Garnett/100 125.00 300.00
KH Kirk Hinrich/100 6.00 15.00
KK Kyle Korver/100 4.00 10.00
KL Kyle Lowry/100 12.00 30.00
LA LaMarcus Aldridge/100 15.00 40.00
LB Larry Bird/25 125.00 300.00
LH Larry Hughes/100 4.00 10.00
LJ LeBron James/23 1,500.00 3,000.00
LO Lamar Odom/100 5.00 12.00
LR Luke Ridnour/100 3.00 8.00
MA Maurice Ager/100 2.50 6.00
MB Mike Bibby/100 8.00 20.00
MD Marquis Daniels/100 2.50 6.00
MI Michael Jordan/23 2,000.00 4,000.00
MW Martell Webster/100 3.00 8.00
NR Nate Robinson/100 4.00 10.00
NS Steve Novak/100 3.00 8.00
PO Patrick O'Bryant/100 2.50 6.00
PP Paul Pierce/100 40.00 100.00
PS Peja Stojakovic/100 5.00 12.00
QD Quincy Douby/100 2.50 6.00
RB Renaldo Balkman/100 2.50 6.00
RC Rodney Carney/100 2.50 6.00
RF Raymond Felton/100 2.50 6.00
RG Rudy Gay/100 5.00 12.00
RH Ryan Hollins/100 2.50 6.00
RJ Richard Jefferson/100 4.00 10.00
RM Rashad McCants/100 2.50 6.00
RT Ronny Turiaf/100 3.00 8.00
SB Shannon Brown/100 2.50 6.00
SC Speedy Claxton/100 2.50 6.00
SL Shaun Livingston/100 6.00 15.00
SW Shelden Williams/100 2.50 6.00
TF T.J. Ford/100 2.50 6.00
TP Tayshaun Prince/100 6.00 15.00
TT Tyrus Thomas/100 3.00 8.00
VC Vince Carter/100 40.00 100.00
WI Marvin Williams/100 2.50 6.00
WM Marcus Williams/100 2.50 6.00
YK Yaroslav Korolev/100 2.50 6.00
YM Yao Ming/100 125.00 300.00

2006-07 SP Game Used SIGnificance Dual

PRINT RUN 10 TO 50 SER.#'d SETS
AL R.Artest/B.Laimbeer 20.00 50.00
AP C.Paul/H.Armstrong 40.00 100.00
AR L.Aldridge/B.Roy 40.00 100.00
AS R.Artest/P.Stojakovic 12.00 30.00
AT L.Aldridge/P.J.Tucker 20.00 50.00
BE C.Boozer/D.Ewing 8.00 20.00
BJ A.Johnson/W.Blalock 8.00 20.00
BP C.Billups/T.Prince 8.00 20.00
BR B.Barry/N.Robinson 8.00 20.00
BT Kw.Brown/R.Turiaf 8.00 20.00
BW A.Bogut/Mv.Williams 8.00 20.00
CB T.Chandler/A.Bogut 8.00 20.00
CJ V.Carter/R.Jefferson 10.00 25.00
DL M.Daniels/S.Livingston 8.00 20.00
EK D.Ewing/Y.Korolev 8.00 20.00
FO F.Garcia/D.Greene 8.00 20.00
FS R.Foye/C.Smith 8.00 20.00
FT T.J.Ford/P.J.Tucker 8.00 20.00
GG J.Graham/S.Graham 8.00 20.00
GH K.Garnett/D.Howard 75.00 200.00
GM K.Garnett/R.McCants 40.00 100.00
HR R.Jefferson/H.Adams 8.00 20.00
IR A.Iguodala/N.Robinson 8.00 20.00
JR A.Jefferson/R.Rondo 15.00 40.00
JS J.Johnson/S.Stoudamire 8.00 20.00
JW A.Jamison/Mv.Williams 8.00 20.00
KF B.King/W.Frazier 25.00 60.00
KS K.Korver/P.Stojakovic 8.00 20.00
LD S.Livingston/P.Davis 8.00 20.00
ME C.Mobley/D.Ewing 8.00 20.00
MF R.McCants/R.Felton 8.00 20.00
MK C.Mobley/C.Kaman 8.00 20.00
OJ L.Odom/A.Jefferson 8.00 20.00
OW L.Odom/V.Wafer 8.00 20.00
PJ P.Pierce/A.Jefferson 12.00 30.00
PR R.Rondo/K.Pittsnogle 8.00 20.00
RC Q.Richardson/E.Curry 8.00 20.00
RJ Q.Richardson/J.Johnson 8.00 20.00
RK Q.Richardson/B.King 10.00 25.00
SI B.Simmons/E.Ilyasova 8.00 20.00
TE C.Taft/M.Ellis 8.00 20.00
TH K.Hinrich/T.Thomas 8.00 20.00
TR S.Telfair/N.Robinson 8.00 20.00
WB Mar.Williams/J.Boone 8.00 20.00
WE D.Williams/D.Ewing 8.00 20.00
WJ B.Jackson/H.Warrick 8.00 20.00
WS S.Williams/S.Jones 8.00 20.00

2006-07 SP Game Used Significant Numbers

CARDS #'d TO PLAYER'S JSY NUMBER
BK Bernard King/30 15.00 40.00
BL Bill Laimbeer/40 30.00 80.00
BM Brad Miller/52 6.00 15.00
BO Bobby Jones/11 15.00 40.00
CA Carmelo Anthony/15 20.00 50.00
CD Clyde Drexler/22 40.00 100.00
CO Corey Maggette/50 8.00 20.00
CT Chris Taft/21 10.00 25.00
DM Donyell Marshall/24 6.00 15.00
DR Dennis Rodman/91 60.00 150.00
EC Eddy Curry/34 6.00 15.00
EI Ersan Ilyasova/23 6.00 15.00
FG Francisco Garcia/32 6.00 15.00
GG George Gervin/44 15.00 40.00
HA Hilton Armstrong/12 6.00 15.00
HO Hakeem Olajuwon/34 75.00 200.00
HW Hakim Warrick/21 10.00 25.00
JM Jamaal Magloire/20 8.00 20.00
JO Michael Jordan/23 2,500.00 5,000.00
JW James White/15 6.00 15.00
KA Kareem Abdul-Jabbar/33 200.00 500.00
KG Kevin Garnett/21 150.00 400.00
KK Kyle Korver/26 12.00 30.00
KW Kwame Brown/54 10.00 25.00
LA LaMarcus Aldridge/12 30.00 60.00
LB Larry Bird/33 125.00 250.00
LH Larry Hughes/32 15.00 40.00
LJ LeBron James/23 2,000.00 4,000.00
NS Steve Novak/20 10.00 25.00
PO Patrick O'Bryant/26 6.00 15.00
PP Paul Pierce/34 60.00 150.00
PS Peja Stojakovic/16 15.00 40.00
RC Rodney Carney/25 8.00 20.00
RE Renaldo Balkman/32 10.00 25.00
RF Raymond Felton/20 20.00 50.00
RG Rudy Gay/22 20.00 50.00
RJ Richard Jefferson/24 6.00 15.00
RP Robert Parish/00 12.00 30.00
SE Sean Elliott/32 15.00 40.00
SJ Solomon Jones/44 6.00 15.00
SK Steve Kerr/25 25.00 60.00
SL Shaun Livingston/14 20.00 50.00
SM J.R. Smith/23 12.00 30.00
SN Steve Nash/13 150.00 400.00
TE Sebastian Telfair/31 12.00 30.00
TP Tayshaun Prince/22 20.00 50.00
TT Tyrus Thomas/24 12.00 30.00
VC Vince Carter/15 75.00 200.00
WF Walt Frazier/10 25.00 60.00
WI Marvin Williams/24 12.00 30.00
YM Yao Ming/11 200.00 500.00

2007-08 SP Game Used

COMP.SET w/o SP's (100)
JSY APPROXIMATE ODDS ONE PER PACK
RC PRINT RUN 999 SER.#'d SETS
1 Joe Johnson .75 2.00
2 Marvin Williams .60 1.50
3 Josh Smith .60 1.50
4 Al Jefferson .60 1.50
5 Paul Pierce 1.50 4.00
6 Delonte West .60 1.50
7 Raymond Felton .75 2.00
8 Gerald Wallace .75 2.00
9 Emeka Okafor .75 2.00
10 Michael Jordan 25.00 60.00
11 Ben Gordon .75 2.00
12 Luol Deng .75 2.00
13 Kirk Hinrich 1.00 2.50
14 LeBron James 8.00 20.00
15 Larry Hughes .75 2.00
16 Zydrunas Ilgauskas .75 2.00
17 Dirk Nowitzki 2.50 6.00
18 Josh Howard .75 2.00
19 Jason Terry .75 2.00
20 Allen Iverson 2.50 6.00
21 Carmelo Anthony 1.50 4.00
22 Marcus Camby .75 2.00
23 J.R. Smith 1.00 2.50
24 Chauncey Billups 1.25 3.00
25 Rasheed Wallace 1.25 3.00
26 Richard Hamilton 1.25 3.00
27 Tayshaun Prince 1.00 2.50
28 Jason Richardson 1.00 2.50
29 Baron Davis .75 2.00
30 Monta Ellis .75 2.00
31 Tracy McGrady 1.50 4.00
32 Yao Ming 2.50 6.00
33 Rafer Alston 1.00 2.50
34 Jermaine O'Neal 1.25 3.00
35 Danny Granger .60 1.50
36 Jamaal Tinsley .60 1.50
37 Elton Brand .75 2.00
38 Corey Maggette .75 2.00
39 Cuttino Mobley .75 2.00
40 Kobe Bryant 8.00 20.00
41 Lamar Odom .75 2.00
42 Luke Walton .75 2.00
43 Kwame Brown .60 1.50
44 Pau Gasol 1.50 4.00
45 Mike Miller .75 2.00
46 Hakim Warrick .60 1.50
47 Dwyane Wade 2.00 5.00
48 Shaquille O'Neal 4.00 10.00
49 Jason Williams 1.50 4.00
50 Michael Redd .75 2.00
51 Mo Williams .75 2.00
52 Andrew Bogut .75 2.00
53 Kevin Garnett 2.50 6.00
54 Ricky Davis .75 2.00
55 Mike James .60 1.50
56 Vince Carter 2.00 5.00
57 Jason Kidd 1.50 4.00
58 Nenad Krstic .60 1.50
59 Richard Jefferson .75 2.00
60 Stephon Marbury 1.25 3.00
61 Eddy Curry .60 1.50
62 Jamal Crawford 1.00 2.50
63 David Lee .60 1.50
64 Chris Paul 2.00 5.00
65 Tyson Chandler 1.00 2.50
66 David West .75 2.00
67 Peja Stojakovic .75 2.00
68 Dwight Howard 1.25 3.00
69 Grant Hill 1.50 4.00
70 Jameer Nelson .60 1.50
71 Andre Miller .75 2.00
72 Andre Iguodala 1.00 2.50
73 Kyle Korver 1.00 2.50
74 Steve Nash 2.00 5.00
75 Amare Stoudemire 1.00 2.50
76 Shawn Marion 1.00 2.50
77 Leandro Barbosa .75 2.00
78 Brandon Roy 1.25 3.00
79 Zach Randolph 1.00 2.50
80 LaMarcus Aldridge 1.00 2.50
81 Mike Bibby 1.00 2.50
82 Kevin Martin .75 2.00
83 Ron Artest 1.00 2.50
84 Tony Parker 1.50 4.00
85 Manu Ginobili 2.00 5.00
86 Tim Duncan 2.50 6.00
87 Rashard Lewis .75 2.00
88 Ray Allen 1.50 4.00
89 Chris Wilcox .60 1.50
90 T.J. Ford .60 1.50
91 Chris Bosh 1.25 3.00
92 Juan Dixon .60 1.50
93 Andrea Bargnani .60 1.50
94 Carlos Boozer .75 2.00
95 Mehmet Okur .60 1.50
96 Deron Williams .75 2.00
97 Gilbert Arenas 1.00 2.50
98 Antawn Jamison .75 2.00
99 Caron Butler .75 2.00
100 DeShawn Stevenson .60 1.50
101 Al Jefferson JSY 2.00 5.00
102 Allen Iverson JSY 8.00 20.00
103 Amare Stoudemire JSY 3.00 8.00
104 Andre Iguodala JSY 3.00 8.00
105 Andre Miller JSY 2.50 6.00
106 Ben Gordon JSY 2.50 6.00
107 Bruce Bowen JSY 2.00 5.00
108 Carmelo Anthony JSY 5.00 12.00
109 Charlie Villanueva JSY 2.00 5.00
110 Corey Maggette JSY 2.50 6.00
111 Danny Granger JSY 2.00 5.00
112 Darko Milicic JSY 2.00 5.00
113 Devin Harris JSY 2.00 5.00
114 Dirk Nowitzki JSY 8.00 20.00
115 Donyell Marshall JSY 2.00 5.00
116 Drew Gooden JSY 2.50 6.00
117 Dwight Howard JSY 4.00 10.00
118 Elton Brand JSY 2.50 6.00
119 Gilbert Arenas JSY 3.00 8.00
120 Grant Hill JSY 5.00 12.00
121 Jason Kidd JSY 5.00 12.00
122 Jason Richardson JSY 3.00 8.00
123 Jermaine O'Neal JSY 3.00 8.00
124 Kevin Garnett JSY 8.00 20.00
125 Kobe Bryant JSY 60.00 150.00
126 LeBron James JSY 60.00 150.00
127 Luol Deng JSY 2.50 6.00
128 Manu Ginobili JSY 6.00 15.00
129 Mike Bibby JSY 2.00 5.00
130 Nenad Krstic JSY 2.00 5.00
131 Pau Gasol JSY 5.00 12.00
132 Paul Pierce JSY 5.00 12.00
133 Rashard Lewis JSY 2.50 6.00
134 Ray Allen JSY 2.50 6.00
135 Richard Jefferson JSY 2.50 6.00
136 Shaquille O'Neal JSY 12.00 30.00
137 Shaun Livingston JSY 2.50 6.00
138 Shawn Marion JSY 3.00 8.00
139 Tayshaun Prince JSY 3.00 8.00
140 Tim Duncan JSY 8.00 20.00
141 Greg Oden RC 2.00 5.00
142 Kevin Durant RC 20.00 50.00
143 Al Horford RC 5.00 12.00
144 Mike Conley Jr. RC 5.00 12.00
145 Jeff Green RC 1.50 4.00
146 Dominic McGuire RC 1.25 3.00
147 Corey Brewer RC 1.50 4.00
148 Brandan Wright RC 1.50 4.00
149 Joakim Noah RC 2.00 5.00
150 Spencer Hawes RC 1.25 3.00
151 Acie Law RC 1.25 3.00
152 Thaddeus Young RC 2.00 5.00
153 Julian Wright RC 1.25 3.00
154 Al Thornton RC 1.25 3.00
155 Rodney Stuckey RC 2.00 5.00
156 Nick Young RC 1.25 3.00
157 Sean Williams RC 1.25 3.00
158 Marco Belinelli RC 1.50 4.00
159 Javaris Crittenton RC 1.25 3.00
160 Jason Smith RC 1.25 3.00
161 Daequan Cook RC 1.50 4.00
162 Jared Dudley RC 1.50 4.00
163 Wilson Chandler RC 1.50 4.00
164 Morris Almond RC 1.25 3.00
165 Aaron Brooks RC 1.50 4.00
166 Arron Afflalo RC 1.50 4.00
167 Alando Tucker RC 1.25 3.00
168 Petteri Koponen RC 1.50 4.00
169 Carl Landry RC 1.25 3.00
170 Gabe Pruitt RC 1.25 3.00
171 Marcus Williams RC 1.25 3.00
172 Nick Fazekas RC 1.25 3.00
173 Glen Davis RC 1.50 4.00
174 Jermareo Davidson RC 1.25 3.00
175 Josh McRoberts RC 1.25 3.00
176 Chris Richard RC 1.25 3.00
177 Derrick Byars RC 1.25 3.00
178 Adam Haluska RC 1.25 3.00
179 Reyshawn Terry RC 1.25 3.00
180 Jared Jordan RC 1.25 3.00
181 Aaron Gray RC 1.25 3.00
182 JamesOn Curry RC 1.25 3.00
183 Taurean Green RC 1.25 3.00
184 Demetris Nichols RC 1.25 3.00
185 Herbert Hill RC 1.25 3.00
186 Brad Newley RC 2.00 5.00
187 Ramon Sessions RC 1.50 4.00
188 Sammy Mejia RC 1.25 3.00
189 D.J. Strawberry RC 1.25 3.00
190 Stephane Lasme RC 1.25 3.00

2007-08 SP Game Used Gold

*1-100 GOLD: 1.5X TO 4X BASE HI
*101-140 GOLD JSY: 1X TO 2.5X BASE HI
*141-190 GOLD RC: 1.5X TO 4X BASE HI
PRINT RUN 25 SER.#'d SETS
142 Kevin Durant 300.00 600.00

2007-08 SP Game Used All-Star Jersey

PRINT RUN 199 SER.#'d SETS
*PATCHES: 1.25X TO 3X BASE HI
PATCH PRINT RUN 50 SER.#'d SETS
ASAB Andrew Bogut 2.50 6.00
ASBG Ben Gordon 2.50 6.00
ASBO Carlos Boozer 2.50 6.00
ASBR Brandon Roy 4.00 10.00
ASBY Andrew Bynum 2.00 5.00
ASCB Chauncey Billups 4.00 10.00
ASCP Chris Paul 6.00 15.00
ASDH Dwight Howard 4.00 10.00
ASDJ Damon Jones 2.00 5.00
ASDL David Lee 2.00 5.00
ASDN Dirk Nowitzki 8.00 20.00
ASFE Raymond Felton 2.50 6.00
ASGA Gilbert Arenas 3.00 8.00
ASGG Gerald Green 2.50 6.00
ASJF Jordan Farmar 2.00 5.00
ASJG Jorge Garbajosa 2.50 6.00
ASJH Josh Howard 2.50 6.00
ASJJ Joe Johnson 2.50 6.00
ASJK Jason Kidd 5.00 12.00
ASJO Jermaine O'Neal 3.00 8.00
ASKB Kobe Bryant 100.00 250.00
ASLH Luther Head 2.00 5.00
ASLJ LeBron James 125.00 300.00
ASMM Mike Miller 2.50 6.00
ASMO Mehmet Okur 2.00 5.00
ASMW Marcus Williams 2.00 5.00
ASPM Paul Millsap 2.50 6.00
ASPP Paul Pierce 5.00 12.00
ASRA Ray Allen 5.00 12.00
ASRF Randy Foye 2.50 6.00
ASSN Steve Nash 6.00 15.00
ASSP Smush Parker 2.00 5.00
ASTP Tony Parker 5.00 12.00
ASTT Tyrus Thomas 2.00 5.00
ASYM Yao Ming 40.00 100.00

2007-08 SP Game Used Authentic Fabrics

APPROXIMATE ODDS ONE PER BOX
*PATCHES/25: 1.25X TO 3X BASE HI
PATCH PRINT RUN 25 SER.#'d SETS
AFAB Andrew Bynum 2.50 6.00
AFAI Allen Iverson 10.00 25.00
AFAJ Antawn Jamison 3.00 8.00
AFAM Alonzo Mourning 6.00 15.00
AFBR Brandon Roy 5.00 12.00
AFCB Chauncey Billups 5.00 12.00
AFCP Chris Paul 8.00 20.00
AFCW Chris Webber 5.00 12.00
AFDW Deron Williams 3.00 8.00
AFEB Elton Brand 3.00 8.00
AFGW Gerald Wallace 3.00 8.00
AFJO Jermaine O'Neal 4.00 10.00
AFJR Jason Richardson 4.00 10.00
AFLJ LeBron James 75.00 200.00
AFMG Manu Ginobili 8.00 20.00
AFMJ Michael Jordan 200.00 500.00
AFPG Pau Gasol 6.00 15.00
AFQD Quincy Douby 2.50 6.00
AFRW Rasheed Wallace 5.00 12.00
AFYM Yao Ming 20.00 50.00

2007-08 SP Game Used Authentic Fabrics Dual

PRINT RUN 99 SER.#'d SETS
*PATCH: .75X TO 2X BASE HI
PATCH PRINT RUN 50 SER.#'d SETS
AB G.Arenas/C.Butler 4.00 10.00
AI A.Iverson/C.Anthony 15.00 40.00
AW R.Artest/A.Walker 4.00 10.00
BJ M.Bibby/M.James 4.00 10.00
BS B.Bowen/J.Smith 4.00 10.00
BV A.Bogut/C.Villanueva 4.00 10.00
CJ V.Carter/R.Jefferson 6.00 15.00
CO M.Camby/M.Okur 4.00 10.00
DB A.Daniels/A.Blatche 4.00 10.00
DM R.Davis/K.Martin 4.00 10.00
DW L.Deng/M.Williams 4.00 10.00
FL R.Felton/S.Livingston 4.00 10.00
GD M.Ginobili/T.Duncan 15.00 40.00
GJ K.Garnett/M.James 6.00 15.00
HB B.Haywood/K.Brown 4.00 10.00
HD L.Hughes/M.Daniels 4.00 10.00
HJ A.Harrington/A.Jamison 4.00 10.00
HP R.Hamilton/T.Prince 6.00 15.00
HT D.Harris/J.Tinsley 4.00 10.00
HW R.Wallace/R.Hamilton 6.00 15.00
JJ L.James/M.Jordan 150.00 400.00
JK J.Williams/K.Hinrich 6.00 15.00
JP R.Jefferson/T.Prince 4.00 10.00
JS J.Smith/J.Childress 4.00 10.00
KN N.Krstic/Nene 4.00 10.00
KR K.Korver/M.Redd 4.00 10.00
LB D.Lee/C.Boozer 4.00 10.00
LP R.Lewis/M.Peterson 4.00 10.00
MD A.Miller/B.Davis 4.00 10.00
MG C.Maggette/D.Granger 4.00 10.00
MH S.May/J.Haslem 4.00 10.00
MI Y.Ming/Z.Ilgauskas 6.00 15.00
MK A.Mourning/A.Kirilenko 5.00 12.00
MN D.Milicic/J.Nelson 4.00 10.00

MT S.Marbury/J.Terry 5.00 12.00
OW L.Odom/L.Walton 4.00 10.00
PD M.Pietrus/M.Dunleavy 4.00 10.00
PS P.Pierce/P.Stojakovic 6.00 15.00
RB Z.Randolph/A.Bynum 4.00 10.00
RH J.Rose/G.Hill 8.00 20.00
RR N.Robinson/Q.Richardson 4.00 10.00
RW L.Ridnour/C.Wilcox 4.00 10.00
SK S.Swift/T.Kinsey 4.00 10.00
SR W.Szczerbiak/A.Ray 4.00 10.00
WA C.Webber/L.Aldridge 6.00 15.00
WB D.West/E.Boykins 4.00 10.00
WC D.Gooden/T.Chandler 4.00 10.00
WH G.Wallace/J.Howard 4.00 10.00
WM B.Wallace/B.Miller 4.00 10.00
WS D.West/J.Smith 4.00 10.00

2007-08 SP Game Used Authentic Fabrics Triple

PRINT RUN 50 SER.#'d SETS
*PATCHES: .75X TO 2X BASE HI
PATCH PRINT RUN 25 SER.#'d SETS
AMB Artest/Douby/Bibby 8.00 20.00
ASO Armstrong/Sene/O'Bryant 5.00 12.00
BBA Blatche/Bynum/Aldridge 8.00 20.00
BGM Bryant/Garnett/McGrady 125.00 300.00
BMK Udrih/Ginobili/Kerr 15.00 40.00
CBW Cook/Brown/Walton 6.00 15.00
FMW Felton/May/Wallace 6.00 15.00
HJB Harrington/Jamison/Boozer 6.00 15.00
HLN Harris/Livingston/Noel 6.00 15.00
ICA Iverson/Camby/Anthony 20.00 50.00
IKD Iguodala/Korver/Dalembert 8.00 20.00
JGC Jones/Green/Carter 15.00 40.00
JJJ James/Jordan/Johnson 150.00 400.00
KNM Krstic/Nene/Milicic 6.00 15.00
LAR Lewis/Allen/Ridnour 12.00 30.00
LRR Lee/Robinson/Richardson 8.00 20.00
MCI Mourning/Chandler/Ilgauskas 12.00 30.00
MHG Marshall/Hughes/Gooden 6.00 15.00
MHR Miller/Haslem/Randolph 8.00 20.00
MNS Marion/Nash/Stoudemire 15.00 40.00
MTW Miller/Tinsley/Williams 15.00 40.00
NBW Nelson/Boykins/West 5.00 12.00
PGD Parker/Ginobili/Duncan 20.00 50.00
PWH Prince/Webber/Hamilton 10.00 25.00
RSD Redick/Smith/Dunleavy 8.00 20.00
SKW Stockton/Kirilenko/Williams 15.00 40.00
SRC Smith/Richardson/Childress 8.00 20.00
WBB Wallace/Bowen/Battier 10.00 25.00
WGP Webster/Granger/Petro 6.00 15.00
WRR Webster/Roy/Randolph 10.00 25.00

2007-08 SP Game Used Authentic Fabrics Quad

PRINT RUN 25 SER.#'d SETS
ABPB Artest/Bowen/Pietrus/Butler 12.00 30.00
BHWR Brand/Hill/Wallace/Randolph 20.00 50.00
BTHW Boykins/Tinsley/Harris/West 12.00 30.00
CCIO Camby/Chandler/Ilgauskas/Okur 12.00 30.00
ESDO Eaton/Stock/Drexler/Olajuwn 40.00 100.00
GCMM KG/Carter/T-Mac/Marion 40.00 100.00
IWGS Iguodala/Wallace/Green/Swift 12.00 30.00
JDSH Jefferson/Davis/Smith/Hughes 15.00 40.00
JOHK James/O'Neal/Howard/Kidd 125.00 300.00
KDNF Kirilenko/Davis/Nene/Frye 12.00 30.00
LHWB Lewis/Harrington/Walton/Battier 12.00 30.00
MOVG May/Odom/Villanueva/Gooden 12.00 30.00
NDAS Dirk/Duncan/Anthony/Amare 25.00 60.00
RFSH Redd/Finley/Stojak/Rip 15.00 40.00
RMLC Ray/Steph/Lvngstn/Cssll 15.00 40.00
RZMP Richardson/Szczerbiak/
Stevenson/Peterson 12.00 30.00
TRJW Terry/Ridnour/James/Redick 12.00 30.00
WABG Williams/Aldridge/
Brown/Granger 12.00 30.00
WMMB BigBen/Miller/Darko/Brown 15.00 40.00

2007-08 SP Game Used Cut from the Cloth

APPROXIMATELY ONE PER BOX
*PATCHES: 1.25X TO 3X BASE HI
PATCH PRINT RUN 25 SER.#'d SETS
CCAB Andrew Bogut 2.00 5.00
CCAH Al Harrington 2.00 5.00
CCAK Andrei Kirilenko 2.00 5.00
CCAM Alonzo Mourning 6.00 15.00
CCBC Brian Cook 1.50 4.00
CCBH Brendan Haywood 1.50 4.00
CCBR Brandon Roy 3.00 8.00
CCCB Caron Butler 2.00 5.00
CCCH Chauncey Billups 5.00 12.00
CCCP Chris Paul 6.00 15.00
CCCR Charlie Villanueva 1.50 4.00
CCDW Deron Williams 2.00 5.00
CCEB Elton Brand 2.00 5.00
CCJH Josh Howard 2.00 5.00
CCJJ J.J. Redick 2.50 6.00
CCJR Jason Richardson 2.50 6.00
CCJS Josh Smith 1.50 4.00
CCKH Kirk Hinrich 2.50 6.00
CCLH Larry Hughes 2.00 5.00
CCLO Lamar Odom 2.00 5.00
CCMR Michael Redd 2.00 5.00
CCMW Martell Webster 2.00 5.00
CCNR Nate Robinson 2.50 6.00
CCPS Peja Stojakovic 2.00 5.00
CCRW Rasheed Wallace 6.00 15.00
CCSM Stephon Marbury 6.00 15.00
CCSN Steve Nash 6.00 15.00
CCTM Tracy McGrady 6.00 15.00
CCTP Tony Parker 6.00 15.00
CCVC Vince Carter 6.00 15.00

2007-08 SP Game Used Hardcourt Classics

PRINT RUN 199 SER.#'d SETS
*PATCH: 1X TO 2.5X BASE HI
PATCH PRINT RUN 25 SER.#'d SETS
HCAD Antonio Daniels 2.00 5.00
HCAS Amare Stoudemire 3.00 8.00
HCBC Brian Cardinal 2.00 5.00
HCBH Brendan Haywood 2.00 5.00
HCBL Andray Blatche 2.00 5.00
HCBW Ben Wallace 4.00 10.00
HCCD Chris Duhon 2.00 5.00
HCCF Channing Frye 2.00 5.00
HCCM Corey Maggette 2.50 6.00
HCDH Dwight Howard 4.00 10.00
HCDS Damon Stoudamire 3.00 8.00
HCDT Donell Taylor 2.00 5.00
HCDW Dorell Wright 2.00 5.00
HCEH Eddie House 2.00 5.00
HCEP Eric Piatkowski 2.00 5.00
HCGO Ben Gordon 2.50 6.00
HCHW Hakim Warrick 2.00 5.00
HCJC Jason Collins 2.00 5.00
HCJH Juwan Howard 3.00 8.00
HCJJ Jerome James 2.00 5.00
HCJK Jason Kapono 2.00 5.00
HCJM Jeff McInnis 2.00 5.00
HCJN Jameer Nelson 2.00 5.00
HCJP James Posey 2.00 5.00
HCJR Jalen Rose 2.50 6.00
HCJS James Singleton 2.00 5.00
HCJT Jake Tsakalidis 2.00 5.00
HCJW Jason Williams 12.00 30.00
HCKB Keith Bogans 2.00 5.00
HCKG Kevin Garnett 12.00 30.00
HCKH Kirk Hinrich 3.00 8.00
HCLA LeBron James 75.00 200.00
HCLD Luol Deng 2.50 6.00
HCLH Luther Head 2.00 5.00
HCLJ Linton Johnson 2.00 5.00
HCLW Lorenzen Wright 2.00 5.00
HCMJ Marc Jackson 2.00 5.00
HCMM Mikki Moore 2.00 5.00
HCMR Michael Redd 2.50 6.00
HCMS Mike Sweetney 2.00 5.00
HCMW Mike Wilks 2.00 5.00
HCNR Nate Robinson 3.00 8.00
HCOH Othella Harrington 2.00 5.00
HCPA Jannero Pargo 2.00 5.00
HCPB Pat Burke 2.00 5.00
HCPG Pau Gasol 5.00 12.00
HCQD Quincy Douby 2.00 5.00
HCQR Quentin Richardson 2.00 5.00
HCSB Shannon Brown 2.00 5.00
HCSM Shawn Marion 3.00 8.00
HCSO Shaquille O'Neal 15.00 40.00
HCST DeShawn Stevenson 2.00 5.00
HCTA Trevor Ariza 2.00 5.00
HCUH Udonis Haslem 2.00 5.00
HCWS Wally Szczerbiak 2.50 6.00

2007-08 SP Game Used Rookie Exclusives Autographs

PRINT RUN 100 SER.#'d SETS
REAA Arron Afflalo 5.00 12.00
REAB Aaron Brooks 5.00 12.00
REAG Aaron Gray 4.00 10.00
REAH Adam Haluska 4.00 10.00
REAL Acie Law 4.00 10.00
REAT Al Thornton 4.00 10.00
RECB Corey Brewer 5.00 12.00
RECL Carl Landry 4.00 10.00
RECU JamesOn Curry 4.00 10.00
REDA Jermareo Davidson 4.00 10.00
REDB Derrick Byars 4.00 10.00
REDC Daequan Cook 5.00 12.00
REDN Demetris Nichols 4.00 10.00
REDS D.J. Strawberry 4.00 10.00
REGD Glen Davis 5.00 12.00
REGP Gabe Pruitt 4.00 10.00
REHH Herbert Hill 4.00 10.00
REHO Al Horford 15.00 40.00
REJC Javaris Crittenton 4.00 10.00
REJD Jared Dudley 5.00 12.00
REJG Jeff Green 5.00 12.00
REJJ Jared Jordan 4.00 10.00
REJM Josh McRoberts 4.00 10.00
REJN Joakim Noah 6.00 15.00
REJS Jason Smith 4.00 10.00
REJW Julian Wright 4.00 10.00
REKD Kevin Durant 500.00 1,000.00
REMA Morris Almond 4.00 10.00
REMB Marco Belinelli 5.00 12.00
REMC Mike Conley Jr. 15.00 40.00
REMW Marcus Williams 4.00 10.00
RENF Nick Fazekas 4.00 10.00
REPK Petteri Koponen 5.00 12.00
RERS Rodney Stuckey 4.00 10.00
RERT Reyshawn Terry 4.00 10.00
RESB Stanko Barac 6.00 15.00
RESH Spencer Hawes 4.00 10.00
RESL Stephane Lasme 4.00 10.00
RESM Sammy Mejia 4.00 10.00
RETG Taurean Green 4.00 10.00
RETU Alando Tucker 4.00 10.00
REWC Wilson Chandler 5.00 12.00

2007-08 SP Game Used Signature Swatch

PRINT RUN 30 SER.#'d SETS
SSAH Al Harrington 6.00 15.00
SSAI Andre Iguodala 8.00 20.00
SSAJ Antawn Jamison 6.00 15.00
SSAM Alonzo Mourning 40.00 100.00
SSAR Allan Ray 5.00 12.00
SSBB Bruce Bowen 5.00 12.00
SSBD Baron Davis 15.00 40.00
SSBG Ben Gordon 6.00 15.00
SSBJ Bobby Jones 8.00 20.00
SSBM Brad Miller 5.00 12.00
SSBR Brandon Roy 10.00 25.00
SSCA Carmelo Anthony 50.00 120.00
SSCB Chris Bosh 20.00 50.00
SSCF Channing Frye 5.00 12.00
SSCM Corey Maggette 6.00 15.00
SSCP Chris Paul 75.00 200.00
SSCS Cedric Simmons 5.00 12.00
SSDN David Noel 5.00 12.00
SSDS DeShawn Stevenson 5.00 12.00
SSDW Deron Williams 6.00 15.00
SSEO Emeka Okafor 6.00 15.00
SSFO Randy Foye 6.00 15.00
SSGW Gerald Wallace 6.00 15.00
SSHA Hilton Armstrong 5.00 12.00
SSJK Jason Kidd 40.00 100.00
SSJM Jamaal Magloire 5.00 12.00
SSJO Jermaine O'Neal 8.00 20.00
SSJS J.R. Smith 8.00 20.00
SSKB Kobe Bryant 1,500.00 3,000.00
SSKH Kirk Hinrich 8.00 20.00
SSKK Kyle Korver 5.00 12.00
SSLA LaMarcus Aldridge 15.00 40.00
SSLH Larry Hughes 6.00 15.00
SSLJ LeBron James 2,000.00 4,000.00
SSMA Maurice Ager 5.00 12.00
SSMB Mike Bibby 8.00 20.00
SSMC Mardy Collins 5.00 12.00
SSMI Andre Miller 6.00 15.00
SSMJ Michael Jordan 3,000.00 6,000.00
SSNO Steve Novak 5.00 12.00
SSPA Tony Parker 20.00 50.00
SSPD Paul Davis 5.00 12.00
SSPP Paul Pierce 40.00 100.00
SSPS Peja Stojakovic 6.00 15.00
SSQD Quincy Douby 5.00 12.00
SSQR Quentin Richardson 5.00 12.00
SSRF Raymond Felton 6.00 15.00
SSRH Richard Hamilton 12.00 30.00
SSRJ Richard Jefferson 6.00 15.00
SSSA Sean May 5.00 12.00
SSSB Shannon Brown 5.00 12.00
SSSM Craig Smith 5.00 12.00
SSSN Steve Nash 50.00 120.00
SSSS Saer Sene 5.00 12.00
SSTM Tracy McGrady 75.00 200.00
SSTP Tayshaun Prince 8.00 20.00
SSVC Vince Carter 75.00 200.00
SSWB Will Blalock 5.00 12.00
SSYM Yao Ming 200.00 500.00

2007-08 SP Game Used Signature Swatch Patch

*PATCH: .75X TO 2X HI COLUMN
PATCH PRINT RUN 15 SER.#'d SETS
SSCP Chris Paul 150.00 400.00

2007-08 SP Game Used SIGnificance

APPROXIMATE ODDS ONE PER BOX
SIAI Andre Iguodala 8.00 20.00
SIAJ Antawn Jamison 4.00 10.00
SIAM Andre Miller 4.00 10.00
SIBA Leandro Barbosa 4.00 10.00
SIBD Baron Davis 4.00 10.00
SIBG Ben Gordon 4.00 10.00
SIBM Brad Miller 4.00 10.00
SIBR Brandon Roy 8.00 20.00
SICA Carmelo Anthony 25.00 60.00
SICB Chris Bosh 12.00 30.00
SICD Chris Duhon 3.00 8.00
SICM Corey Maggette 4.00 10.00
SICP Chris Paul 60.00 150.00
SICS Craig Smith 3.00 8.00
SIDB Dee Brown 3.00 8.00
SIDR Clyde Drexler 25.00 60.00
SIDW Deron Williams 4.00 10.00
SIHA Hassan Adams 3.00 8.00
SIHO Hakeem Olajuwon 40.00 100.00
SIHW Hakim Warrick 3.00 8.00
SIIU Ime Udoka 10.00 25.00
SIJA James Augustine 3.00 8.00
SIJE Julius Erving 50.00 120.00
SIJG Joey Graham 3.00 8.00
SIJJ Jarrett Jack 4.00 10.00
SIJK Jason Kidd 25.00 60.00
SIJS J.R. Smith 10.00 25.00
SIKB Kobe Bryant 1,000.00 2,000.00
SILA LaMarcus Aldridge 10.00 25.00
SILB Larry Bird 100.00 250.00
SILJ LeBron James 1,500.00 3,000.00
SIMC Mardy Collins 3.00 8.00
SIMI Michael Jordan 3,000.00 6,000.00
SIMJ Magic Johnson 100.00 250.00
SINO Steve Novak 3.00 8.00
SIPM Paul Millsap 4.00 10.00
SIPP Paul Pierce 25.00 60.00
SIRB Raja Bell 4.00 10.00
SIRG Rudy Gay 4.00 10.00
SIRO David Robinson 40.00 100.00
SISN Steve Nash 40.00 100.00
SIST John Stockton 40.00 100.00
SISW Shelden Williams 3.00 8.00
SITM Tracy McGrady 60.00 150.00
SITS Thabo Sefolosha 3.00 8.00
SIVC Vince Carter 60.00 150.00
SIVS Vassilis Spanoulis 3.00 8.00
SIWB Will Blalock 3.00 8.00

2007-08 SP Game Used SIGnificance Dual

PRINT RUN 50 SER.#'d SETS
SP PRINT RUN 25 SER.#'d SETS
UNLESS LISTED IN CHECKLIST
SDAR L.Aldridge/B.Roy 15.00 40.00
SDBA N.Archibald/M.Bogues 15.00 40.00
SDBB R.Bell/L.Barbosa 15.00 30.00
SDBJ K.Bryant/L.James SP 3,000.00 6,000.00
SDBM M.Bibby/B.Miller 12.00 30.00
SDBO J.O'Neal/K.Bryant SP 1,000.00 2,000.00
SDCL T.Chandler/D.Lee 10.00 25.00
SDCM V.Carter/McGrady SP 125.00 300.00
SDCO E.Curry/E.Okafor 10.00 25.00
SDCS T.Chandler/P.Stojakovic 10.00 25.00
SDDH A.Harrington/B.Davis 10.00 25.00
SDDS C.Duhon/T.Sefolosha 10.00 25.00
SDER J.Erving/W.Frazier SP 1,250.00 2,500.00
SDFC W.Frazier/M.Collins 10.00 25.00
SDFG J.Garbajosa/T.Ford 10.00 25.00
SDFR C.Russell/Frazier SP 40.00 100.00
SDFS C.Smith/R.Foye 10.00 25.00
SDGR R.Gay/B.Roy SP 25.00 60.00
SDHC C.Duhon/K.Hinrich/15 25.00 60.00
SDJI R.Jefferson/M.Ilic 10.00 25.00
SDJS A.Jamison/D.Stevenson 10.00 25.00
SDKC J.Kidd/V.Carter SP 75.00 200.00
SDKK S.Kerr/J.Kapono 6.00 15.00
SDKR D.Rodman/S.Kerr SP 75.00 200.00
SDLF C.Frye/D.Lee 10.00 25.00
SDLM Mahorn/Laimbeer SP 30.00 80.00
SDMI A.Miller/A.Iguodala 12.00 30.00
SDMM McGrady/Y.Ming SP 125.00 300.00
SDMW S.May/M.Williams 10.00 25.00
SDNB S.Novak/W.Blalock 10.00 25.00
SDOF R.Felton/E.Okafor 10.00 25.00
SDOM Murphy/Olajuwon/20 40.00 80.00
SDPB M.Bogues/R.Parish 20.00 50.00
SDPC V.Carter/P.Pierce SP 30.00 80.00
SDSP P.Stojakovic/C.Paul 40.00 100.00
SDSS Stockton/Nash SP 125.00 300.00
SDST T.Thomas/J.Smith 10.00 25.00
SDTB T.Prince/W.Blalock 10.00 25.00

2007-08 SP Game Used Significant Numbers Autographs

PRINT RUNS LISTED IN CHECKLIST
AM Alonzo Mourning/33 60.00 150.00
AR Allan Ray/20 8.00 20.00
BL Bill Laimbeer/40 20.00 50.00
BM Brad Miller/52 12.00 30.00
CA Carmelo Anthony/15 75.00 200.00
CD Clyde Drexler/22 60.00 150.00
CF Channing Frye/44 8.00 20.00
CM Corey Maggette/50 8.00 20.00
CS Cedric Simmons/15 8.00 20.00
DD Darryl Dawkins/53 20.00 50.00
DL David Lee/42 15.00 40.00
DM Donyell Marshall/24 8.00 20.00
DN David Noel/34 8.00 20.00
DW Delonte West/30 8.00 20.00
FE Raymond Felton/20 8.00 20.00
HW Hakim Warrick/21 8.00 20.00
KB Kobe Bryant/24 1,500.00 3,000.00
KK Kyle Korver/26 20.00 50.00
LA LaMarcus Aldridge/12 30.00 80.00
LB Larry Bird/33 150.00 400.00
LJ1 LeBron James/23 2,000.00 4,000.00
LJ2 LeBron James/23 2,000.00 4,000.00
MC Mardy Collins/25 8.00 20.00
ME Mark Eaton/53 15.00 40.00
MJ Michael Jordan/23 4,000.00 8,000.00
MP Morris Peterson/24 8.00 20.00
MS Saer Sene/18 8.00 20.00
MW Marvin Williams/24 8.00 20.00
NO Steve Novak/20 8.00 20.00
PD Paul Davis/40 8.00 20.00
PP Paul Pierce/34 75.00 200.00
PS Peja Stojakovic/16 20.00 50.00
QR Quentin Richardson/23 8.00 20.00
RC Rodney Carney/25 8.00 20.00
RG Rudy Gay/22 15.00 40.00
RH Richard Hamilton/32 15.00 40.00
SK Steve Kerr/25 15.00 40.00
SM Sean May/42 8.00 20.00
SN Steve Nash/13 50.00 120.00
ST John Stockton/12 100.00 200.00
TP Tayshaun Prince/22 20.00 50.00
TT Tyrus Thomas/24 12.00 30.00
YM Yao Ming/11 200.00 500.00

2007-08 SP Game Used Significant Numbers Non-Auto Patch

PRINT RUNS LISTED IN CHECKLIST
AG Maurice Ager/13 6.00 15.00
AM Alonzo Mourning/33 75.00 200.00
AR Allan Ray/20 60.00 150.00
BJ Bobby Jackson/35 6.00 15.00
BL Bill Laimbeer/40 12.00 30.00
BM Brad Miller/52 6.00 15.00
CA Carmelo Anthony/15 60.00 150.00
CF Channing Frye/44 6.00 15.00
CM Corey Maggette/50 6.00 15.00
CS Cedric Simmons/15 6.00 15.00
DD Darryl Dawkins/53 6.00 15.00
DH Dwight Howard/12 25.00 60.00
DM Donyell Marshall/24 6.00 15.00
DN David Noel/34 6.00 15.00
DR David Robinson/55 50.00 120.00
EB Elton Brand/42 6.00 15.00
HW Hakim Warrick/21 6.00 15.00
JN Jameer Nelson/14 6.00 15.00
JR Jason Richardson/23 20.00 50.00
KB Kobe Bryant/24 600.00 1,200.00
KH Kirk Hinrich/12 15.00 40.00
KK Kyle Korver/26 15.00 40.00
LA LaMarcus Aldridge/35 15.00 40.00
LB Larry Bird/33 75.00 200.00
LH Larry Hughes/32 6.00 15.00
LJ1 LeBron James/35 600.00 1,200.00
LJ2 LeBron James/23 600.00 1,200.00
MA Magic Johnson/32 75.00 200.00
MB Mike Bibby/10 15.00 40.00
MC Mardy Collins/25 6.00 15.00
ME Mark Eaton/53 15.00 40.00
MG Manu Ginobili/20 75.00 200.00
MJ Michael Jordan/23 1,000.00 2,000.00
MP Morris Peterson/35 6.00 15.00
MS Saer Sene/18 6.00 15.00
MW Marvin Williams/24 6.00 15.00
NO Steve Novak/20 6.00 15.00
PD Paul Davis/40 6.00 15.00
PP Paul Pierce/34 60.00 150.00
PS Peja Stojakovic/16 10.00 25.00
QR Quentin Richardson/23 6.00 15.00
RC Rodney Carney/25 6.00 15.00
RG Rudy Gay/22 12.00 30.00
RH Richard Hamilton/32 20.00 50.00
RJ Richard Jefferson/24 6.00 15.00
RO Dennis Rodman/91 50.00 120.00
SE Sean Elliott/32 10.00 25.00
SK Steve Kerr/25 40.00 100.00
SM Sean May/42 6.00 15.00
SN Steve Nash/13 75.00 200.00
ST John Stockton/12 60.00 150.00
TT Tyrus Thomas/24 6.00 15.00
VC Vince Carter/15 75.00 200.00
WF Walt Frazier/10 40.00 100.00
YM Yao Ming/11 125.00 300.00

2007-08 SP Game Used Swatch of Class

APPROXIMATE ODDS ONE PER BOX
*PATCHES: 1.5X TO 4X BASE HI
PATCH PRINT RUN 25 SER.#'d SETS
SCCD Clyde Drexler 8.00 20.00
SCDD Darryl Dawkins 4.00 10.00
SCDE Dennis Rodman 12.00 30.00
SCDR David Robinson 10.00 25.00
SCJE Julius Erving 15.00 40.00
SCJS John Stockton 10.00 25.00
SCLB Larry Bird 25.00 60.00
SCMA Magic Johnson 25.00 60.00
SCMJ Michael Jordan 125.00 300.00
SCRP Robert Parish 8.00 20.00

2009-10 SP Game Used

COMP. SET w/o SPs (100) 30.00 60.00
ROOKIE PRINT RUN 399 SER.#'d SETS
1 Al Harrington .75 2.00
2 Al Horford 1.00 2.50
3 Al Jefferson .60 1.50
4 Al Thornton .60 1.50
5 Allen Iverson 2.00 5.00
6 Andre Iguodala 1.00 2.50
7 Andre Miller 1.00 2.50
8 Andrea Bargnani .60 1.50
9 Antawn Jamison .75 2.00
10 Baron Davis .75 2.00
11 Ben Gordon .75 2.00
12 Ben Wallace 1.25 3.00
13 Beno Udrih .60 1.50
14 Brad Miller .75 2.00
15 Brandon Roy 1.25 3.00
16 Carlos Boozer .75 2.00
17 Carmelo Anthony 1.50 4.00
18 Chauncey Billups 1.25 3.00
19 Chris Bosh 1.25 3.00
20 Chris Duhon .60 1.50
21 Chris Paul 2.00 5.00
22 Courtney Lee .60 1.50
23 D.J. Augustin .60 1.50
24 Danny Granger .60 1.50
25 David Lee .60 1.50
26 David West .75 2.00
27 Derek Fisher 1.00 2.50
28 Deron Williams .75 2.00
29 Derrick Rose 1.50 4.00
30 DeShawn Stevenson .60 1.50
31 Devin Harris .60 1.50
32 Dirk Nowitzki 2.50 6.00
33 Dwight Howard 1.25 3.00
34 Dwyane Wade 2.00 5.00
35 Elton Brand .75 2.00
36 Eric Gordon .75 2.00
37 Gilbert Arenas .75 2.00
38 Hedo Turkoglu .75 2.00
39 Jamal Crawford 1.00 2.50
40 Jason Kidd 1.50 4.00
41 Jason Richardson 1.00 2.50
42 Jeff Green .75 2.00
43 Jermaine O'Neal 1.00 2.50
44 Jerryd Bayless .60 1.50
45 Joe Johnson 1.00 2.50
46 Jose Calderon .60 1.50
47 Josh Howard .75 2.00
48 Josh Smith .60 1.50
49 Kenyon Martin .75 2.00
50 Kevin Durant 4.00 10.00
51 Kevin Garnett 2.50 6.00
52 Kevin Love 1.00 2.50
53 Kevin Martin .75 2.00
54 Kobe Bryant 8.00 20.00
55 Lamar Odom .75 2.00
56 LaMarcus Aldridge 1.00 2.50
57 LeBron James 8.00 20.00
58 Luis Scola .75 2.00
59 Luke Ridnour .75 2.00
60 Luol Deng .75 2.00
61 Manu Ginobili 2.00 5.00
62 Marc Gasol 1.00 2.50
63 Mario Chalmers .75 2.00
64 Michael Beasley .60 1.50
65 Michael Redd .75 2.00
66 Mike Bibby 1.00 2.50
67 Mike Dunleavy .60 1.50
68 Mo Williams .75 2.00
69 Monta Ellis .75 2.00
70 O.J. Mayo .60 1.50
71 Pau Gasol 1.50 4.00
72 Paul Pierce 1.50 4.00
73 Peja Stojakovic .75 2.00
74 Quentin Richardson .60 1.50
75 Raja Bell .75 2.00
76 Ray Allen 1.50 4.00
77 Raymond Felton .60 1.50
78 Richard Hamilton 1.00 2.50
79 Richard Jefferson .75 2.00
80 Rodney Stuckey .60 1.50
81 Ron Artest 1.00 2.50
82 Ronnie Brewer .60 1.50
83 Rudy Fernandez .60 1.50
84 Rudy Gay 1.00 2.50
85 Russell Westbrook 2.00 5.00
86 Sebastian Telfair .60 1.50
87 Shaquille O'Neal 3.00 8.00
88 Shawn Marion 1.00 2.50
89 Stephen Jackson .75 2.00
90 Steve Nash 2.00 5.00
91 T.J. Ford .60 1.50
92 Tayshaun Prince 1.00 2.50
93 Thaddeus Young .60 1.50
94 Tim Duncan 2.50 6.00
95 Tony Parker 1.50 4.00
96 Tracy McGrady 2.00 5.00
97 Tyson Chandler .75 2.00
98 Vince Carter 2.00 5.00
99 Yao Ming 2.50 6.00
100 Yi Jianlian 1.25 3.00
101 A.J. Price RC 1.50 4.00
102 B.J. Mullens RC 1.50 4.00
103 Blake Griffin RC 10.00 25.00
104 Brandon Jennings RC 2.50 6.00
105 Chase Budinger RC 1.50 4.00
106 DaJuan Summers RC 1.50 4.00
107 Rodrigue Beaubois RC 1.50 4.00
108 Danny Green RC 2.50 6.00
109 Dante Cunningham RC 1.50 4.00
110 Darren Collison RC 2.50 6.00
111 DeJuan Blair RC 2.00 5.00
112 DeMar DeRozan RC 10.00 25.00
113 Derrick Brown RC 1.50 4.00
114 Earl Clark RC 1.50 4.00
115 Eric Maynor RC 1.50 4.00
116 Gerald Henderson RC 1.50 4.00
117 Hasheem Thabeet RC 1.50 4.00
118 James Harden RC 20.00 50.00
119 James Johnson RC 2.00 5.00
120 Jeff Pendergraph RC 1.50 4.00
121 Jeff Teague RC 2.00 5.00
122 Jonny Flynn RC 1.50 4.00
123 Jordan Hill RC 1.50 4.00
124 Austin Daye RC 1.50 4.00
125 Jrue Holiday RC 8.00 20.00
126 Marcus Thornton RC 2.00 5.00
127 Nick Calathes RC 1.50 4.00
128 Omri Casspi RC 1.50 4.00
129 Patrick Mills RC 4.00 10.00
130 Ricky Rubio RC 3.00 8.00
131 Sam Young RC 1.50 4.00
132 Sergio Llull RC 1.50 4.00
133 Stephen Curry RC 300.00 600.00
134 Taj Gibson RC 2.00 5.00
135 Terrence Williams RC 1.50 4.00
136 Toney Douglas RC 1.50 4.00
137 Ty Lawson RC 2.00 5.00
138 Tyler Hansbrough RC 2.00 5.00
139 Jermaine Taylor RC 1.50 4.00
140 Tyreke Evans RC 2.00 5.00
141 DeMarre Carroll RC 2.00 5.00
142 Wayne Ellington RC 2.00 5.00

2009-10 SP Game Used 3 Star Swatches

PRINT RUN 299 SER.#'d SETS
*SWATCH 125: .5X TO 1.25X BASE HI
*SWATCH 50: .6X TO 1.5X BASE HI
*SWATCH 35: .75X TO 2X BASE HI
3SAGA Arenas/Allen/Garnett 8.00 20.00
3SAHW Allen/Gordon/Hamilton 6.00 15.00
3SARB Roy/Aldridge/Bayless 5.00 12.00
3SASY O'Neal/Bynum/Ming 12.00 30.00
3SAWI Walton/Iguodala/Arenas 4.00 10.00
3SBAH Bryant/Artest/Howard 25.00 60.00
3SBFR Foye/Bogans/Rush 4.00 10.00
3SBGJ James/Bryant/Garnett 100.00 250.00
3SBHM Howard/Butler/Millsap 4.00 10.00
3SBIM Malone/Iguodala/Brand 8.00 20.00
3SBJD Bryant/James/Durant 125.00 300.00
3SBMH Bryant/Howard/McGrady 50.00 120.00
3SBMJ Bryant/James/Robertson 125.00 300.00
3SBOB Bargnani/Bosh/O'Neal 5.00 12.00
3SBOF Bryant/Grant/O'Neal 40.00 100.00
3SBWC Wright/Brown/Chandler 4.00 10.00
3SBWM Millsap/Williams/Boozer 4.00 10.00
3SCFM Carter/Felton/May 8.00 20.00
3SCGM Carter/McGrady/Gervin 10.00 25.00
3SCMA Anthony/Marion/Carter 12.00 30.00
3SCMP Carter/McGrady/Pippen 15.00 40.00
3SDFA Farmar/Davis/Afflalo 4.00 10.00
3SDGP Gervin/Duncan/Parker 12.00 30.00
3SDGR Duncan/Gervin/Robinson 12.00 30.00
3SDHP Duncan/Howard/Paul 8.00 20.00
3SDMF Davis/Farmar/Webb 5.00 12.00
3SDMO Duncan/Ming/O'Neal 12.00 30.00
3SDPR Duncan/Parker/Robinson 12.00 30.00
3SDWC Chalmers/D-Roberts/White 4.00 10.00
3SEFC Ellis/Crittenton/Farmar 4.00 10.00
3SEGH Ewing/Hibbert/Green 6.00 15.00
3SEHO O'Neal/Ewing/Howard 8.00 20.00
3SELR Ewing/Robinson/Lee 8.00 20.00
3SGAS Greene/Sharpe/Alexander 4.00 10.00
3SGCH Carter/Hill/Garnett 12.00 30.00
3SGCO Garnett/O'Neal/Carter 12.00 30.00
3SGMN Garnett/Nowitzki/Marion 12.00 30.00
3SGMO Ming/Gasol/O'Neal 15.00 40.00
3SGNA Garnett/Nowitzki/Anthony 15.00 40.00
3SGNB Nowitzki/Garnett/Bosh 15.00 40.00
3SGPA Garnett/Anthony/Prince 12.00 30.00
3SGYL Lopez/Gray/Young 4.00 10.00
3SHAR Allen/Redick/Hornacek 8.00 20.00
3SHBA Hamilton/Arenas/Billups 8.00 20.00
3SHDP Pippen/Rose/Deng 8.00 20.00
3SHFT Fernandez/Hamilton/Tucker 4.00 10.00
3SHHL Head/Landry/Howard 4.00 10.00
3SHIP Hamilton/Iverson/Prince 8.00 20.00
3SHIW Iverson/Hamilton/Wallace 8.00 20.00
3SHJK Jordan/Hibbert/Koufos 4.00 10.00
3SHMS Hornacek/Stockton/Malone 8.00 20.00
3SHWD Walton/Douby/Harrington 4.00 10.00
3SIBJ Johnson/Billups/Iverson 12.00 30.00
3SJBJ James/Jordan/Bryant 800.00 1,500.00
3SJGP Grant/Jordan/Pippen 100.00 250.00
3SJMJ Jordan/Johnson/Malone 200.00 500.00
3SJWS Stockton/Williams/Johnson 12.00 30.00
3SKPS Kidd/Stockton/Paul 10.00 25.00
3SLGH Grant/Lewis/Howard 6.00 15.00
3SLHD Lee/Haslem/Davis 4.00 10.00
3SMBD Maggette/Boozer/Deng 4.00 10.00
3SMBO Ming/Bynum/O'Neal 12.00 30.00
3SMBR Mayo/Rose/Beasley 5.00 12.00
3SMCD Cooper/Drexler/Malone 8.00 20.00
3SMCK Malone/Boozer/Okur 6.00 15.00
3SMDO Maggette/Davis/Odom 5.00 12.00
3SMER Maggette/Ellis/Randolph 4.00 10.00
3SMGP Malone/Pippen/Gervin 10.00 25.00
3SMHH Howard/Hughes/Maggette 4.00 10.00
3SMHL Landry/Scola/McGrady 6.00 15.00
3SMME Maggette/Ellis/Mullin 5.00 12.00
3SMMO Marion/O'Neal/Martin 6.00 15.00
3SMPT Pippen/Thomas/Maggette 6.00 15.00
3SMSM Stoudemire/Malone/Ming 10.00 25.00
3SMTO Harrington/O'Neal/Tinsley 4.00 10.00
3SMUW Williams/Udrih/Miller 4.00 10.00
3SMWH O'Neal/Haslem/Wade 8.00 20.00
3SNAK Anderson/Koufos/Novak 4.00 10.00
3SNAR Roy/Arenas/Nash 8.00 20.00
3SNGM Nash/Ming/Garnett 15.00 40.00
3SNHB Noah/Horford/Brewer 4.00 10.00
3SNIM Nash/Iverson/Marbury 12.00 30.00
3SNKP Parker/Kidd/Nash 10.00 25.00
3SOJC Odom/Cooper/Johnson 6.00 15.00
3SPAG Garnett/Allen/Pierce 60.00 150.00
3SPMG Robinson/Grant/Malone 10.00 25.00
3SRBG Rush/Giddens/Beasley 5.00 12.00
3SSJC Kidd/Nash/Paul 10.00 25.00
3SSMR Szczerbiak/Ridnour/Miller 4.00 10.00
3SSOT Swift/O'Neal/Thomas 6.00 15.00
3STBS Thomas/Brewer/Simmons 4.00 10.00
3STFP Tinsley/Ford/Paul 5.00 12.00
3STGW Gordon/Thomas/White 6.00 15.00
3STRC Crittenton/Tinsley/Robinson 4.00 10.00
3STSN Thomas/Noah/Deng 4.00 10.00
3STUW Tinsley/Udrih/Williams 4.00 10.00
3STWB Tinsley/West/Felton 4.00 10.00
3SWDG Durant/Green/Westbrook 10.00 25.00
3SWTR Thornton/Randolph/Thompson 4.00 10.00
3SWWH Wallace/Wallace/Howard 6.00 15.00

2009-10 SP Game Used 4 on 4 Fabrics

STATED PRINT RUN 99 SER.#'d SETS
*SWATCH 65: .4X TO 1X BASE HI
FFGUARD Guard Legends 60.00 150.00
FFSTARS NBA All-Stars 12.00 30.00
FF01CFINL 2001 NBA Playoffs 60.00 150.00
FF02CFINL 2002 NBA Playoffs 60.00 150.00
FF03FINL 2003 NBA Finals 20.00 50.00
FF04FINL 2004 NBA Finals 60.00 150.00
FF05FINL 2005 NBA Finals 20.00 50.00
FF06FINL 2006 NBA Finals 25.00 60.00
FF07FINL 2007 NBA Finals 60.00 150.00
FF2009AS 2009 NBA All-Stars 60.00 150.00
FF80STAR 1980s Stars 30.00 80.00
FF90EAST 1990s E.Conf.Stars 60.00 150.00
FF90STAR 1990s Stars 60.00 150.00
FF90WEST 1990s W.Conf.Stars 30.00 80.00
FF91FINL 1991 NBA Finals 60.00 150.00
FFATLCHA Hawks/Bobcats 8.00 20.00
FFATLDAL Hawks/Mavericks 20.00 50.00
FFATLMIA Hawks/Heat 15.00 40.00
FFATLORL Hawks/Magic 10.00 25.00
FFATLWAS Hawks/Wizards 8.00 20.00
FFBOSLAL Celtics/Lakers 60.00 150.00
FFBOSNET Celtics/Nets 20.00 50.00
FFBOSNYK Celtics/Knicks 20.00 50.00
FFBOSPHI Celtics/76ers 20.00 50.00
FFBOSTOR Celtics/Raptors 20.00 50.00
FFCENTER Center Legends 30.00 80.00
FFCHAMIA Bobcats/Heat 8.00 20.00
FFCHAORL Bobcats/Magic 10.00 25.00
FFCHAWAS Bobcats/Wizards 6.00 15.00
FFCHICLE Bulls/Cavaliers 60.00 150.00
FFCHIDET Bulls/Pistons 15.00 40.00
FFCHIIND Bulls/Pacers 12.00 30.00
FFCHIMIL Bulls/Bucks 12.00 30.00
FFCLEDET Cavaliers/Pistons 60.00 150.00
FFCLEIND Cavaliers/Pacers 60.00 150.00
FFCLEMIL Cavaliers/Bucks 60.00 150.00
FFCLEPHO Cavaliers/Suns 60.00 150.00
FFDALHOU Mavericks/Rockets 20.00 50.00
FFDALMEM Mavericks/Grizzlies 20.00 50.00
FFDALNEW Mavericks/Hornets 20.00 50.00
FFDALSAN Mavericks/Spurs 20.00 50.00
FFDENMIN Nuggets/Timberwolves 12.00 30.00
FFDENOKL Nuggets/Thunder 15.00 40.00
FFDENPOR Nuggets/Trail Blazers 10.00 25.00
FFDENUTA Nuggets/Jazz 12.00 30.00
FFDETIND Pistons/Pacers 6.00 15.00
FFDETMIL Pistons/Bucks 15.00 40.00
FFDETNEW Pistons/Hornets 15.00 40.00
FFEAST6M E.Conference 6th Men 8.00 20.00
FFEASTAS E.Conference All-Stars 60.00 150.00
FFEASTCE E.Conference Centers 10.00 25.00
FFEASTPF E.Conference PF 20.00 50.00
FFEASTPG E.Conference PG 12.00 30.00
FFEASTSF E.Conference SF 60.00 150.00
FFEASTSG E.Conference SG 15.00 40.00
FFEASVWES East vs West 60.00 150.00
FFFORWRD Forward Legends 30.00 80.00
FFGOLLAC Warriors/Clippers 6.00 15.00
FFGOLLAL Warriors/Lakers 60.00 150.00
FFGOLPHO Warriors/Suns 15.00 40.00
FFGOLSAC Warriors/Kings 6.00 15.00
FFHOUMEM Rockets/Grizzlies 20.00 50.00
FFHOUNEW Rockets/Hornets 15.00 40.00
FFHOUSAN Rockets/Spurs 20.00 50.00
FFINDMIL Pacers/Bucks 6.00 15.00
FFLACLAL Clippers/Lakers 60.00 150.00
FFLACPHO Clippers/Suns 8.00 20.00
FFLACSAC Clippers/Kings 8.00 20.00
FFLALPHO Lakers/Suns 60.00 150.00
FFLALSAC Lakers/Kings 60.00 150.00
FFMEMNEW Grizzlies/Hornets 15.00 40.00
FFMEMSAN Grizzlies/Spurs 20.00 50.00
FFMIAORL Heat/Magic 15.00 40.00
FFMIAUTA Heat/Jazz 15.00 40.00
FFMIAWAS Heat/Wizards 6.00 15.00
FFMINOKL Timberwolves/Thunder 30.00 80.00
FFMINPOR Timberwolves/Blazers 10.00 25.00
FFMINUTA Timberwolves/Jazz 8.00 20.00
FFNETNYK Nets/Knicks 15.00 40.00
FFNETPHI Nets/76ers 15.00 40.00
FFNETTOR Nets/Raptors 15.00 40.00
FFNEWMEM Hornets/Grizzlies 8.00 20.00
FFNEWSAN Hornets/Spurs 15.00 40.00
FFNYKPHI Knicks/76ers 8.00 20.00
FFNYKTOR Knicks/Raptors 10.00 25.00
FFOKLPOR Thunder/Trail Blazers 30.00 80.00
FFOKLUTA Thunder/Jazz 6.00 15.00
FFORLPOR Magic/Trail Blazers 10.00 25.00
FFORLWAS Magic/Wizards 10.00 25.00
FFPHITOR 76ers/Raptors 10.00 25.00
FFPHOSAC Suns/Kings 25.00 60.00
FFPORUTA Trail Blazers/Jazz 10.00 25.00
FFSACLAC Kings/Clippers 6.00 15.00
FFWEST6M W.Conference 6th Men 15.00 40.00
FFWESTAS W.Conference All-Stars 60.00 150.00
FFWESTCE W.Conference Centers 25.00 60.00
FFWESTPF W.Conference PF 20.00 50.00
FFWESTPG W.Conference PG 15.00 40.00
FFWESTSF W.Conference SF 30.00 80.00
FFWESTSG W.Conference SG 60.00 150.00

2009-10 SP Game Used Combo Materials

STATED PRINT RUN 499 SER.#'d SETS
*MATERIAL 155: .5X TO 1.25X BASE HI
*MATERIAL 50: .6X TO 1.5X BASE HI
*MATERIAL 35: .6X TO 1.5X BASE HI
CM23 L.James/M.Jordan 600.00 1,200.00
CMAA C.Anthony/G.Arenas 6.00 15.00
CMAB G.Arenas/C.Butler 3.00 8.00
CMAG K.Garnett/R.Allen 8.00 20.00
CMAN R.Allen/D.Nowitzki 8.00 20.00
CMAP T.Parker/G.Arenas 6.00 15.00
CMAT C.Anthony/T.Thomas 5.00 12.00
CMBA C.Billups/G.Arenas 4.00 10.00
CMBH U.Haslem/E.Brand 3.00 8.00
CMBJ K.Bryant/L.James 300.00 600.00
CMBL C.Boozer/D.Lee 3.00 8.00
CMBM A.Bargnani/Y.Ming 8.00 20.00
CMBO K.Bryant/L.Odom 25.00 60.00
CMBP C.Billups/T.Parker 8.00 20.00
CMBS K.Bryant/S.O'Neal 60.00 150.00
CMCA V.Carter/C.Anthony 10.00 25.00
CMCB C.Bosh/V.Carter 8.00 20.00
CMCG R.Gay/M.Cooper 4.00 10.00
CMCH V.Carter/G.Hill 8.00 20.00
CMCJ C.Maggette/J.Howard 3.00 8.00
CMCN D.Nowitzki/V.Carter 8.00 20.00
CMCR C.Maggette/R.Gay 3.00 8.00
CMCS C.Bosh/S.Marion 4.00 10.00
CMCT T.Thomas/V.Carter 6.00 15.00
CMDB B.Davis/C.Billups 5.00 12.00

CMDD B.Davis/C.Kaman 3.00 8.00
CMDG H.Grant/V.Divac 4.00 10.00
CMDH D.Howard/T.Duncan 8.00 20.00
CMDJ M.Johnson/B.Davis 8.00 20.00
CMDO J.O'Neal/L.Deng 3.00 8.00
CMDR D.Howard/R.Wallace 6.00 15.00
CMDT T.McGrady/D.Wade 10.00 25.00
CMDW B.Davis/D.Williams 4.00 10.00
CMFB J.Farmar/K.Bryant 15.00 40.00
CMFF T.Ford/R.Felton 3.00 8.00
CMGA G.Arenas/K.Garnett 8.00 20.00
CMGB K.Garnett/C.Bosh 10.00 25.00
CMGD K.Garnett/D.Nowitzki 10.00 25.00
CMGO K.Garnett/S.O'Neal 10.00 25.00
CMGP H.Grant/S.Pippen 8.00 20.00
CMGS S.Pippen/G.Gervin 10.00 25.00
CMHB C.Billups/R.Hamilton 6.00 15.00
CMHD L.Deng/L.Hughes 3.00 8.00
CMHG R.Hamilton/R.Gay 4.00 10.00
CMHI L.Hughes/A.Iguodala 4.00 10.00
CMHJ J.Johnson/G.Hill 6.00 15.00
CMHM J.Hornacek/K.Malone 6.00 15.00
CMHO G.Hill/S.O'Neal 8.00 20.00
CMHS J.Hornacek/J.Stockton 6.00 15.00
CMHT J.Tinsley/L.Hughes 3.00 8.00
CMIB C.Billups/A.Iverson 12.00 30.00
CMIM Z.Ilgauskas/Y.Ming 8.00 20.00
CMIP A.Iverson/C.Paul 25.00 60.00
CMIT A.Thornton/A.Iguodala 3.00 8.00
CMIW A.Iverson/D.Williams 8.00 20.00
CMJA M.Jordan/R.Allen 125.00 300.00
CMJB K.Bryant/M.Jordan 600.00 1,200.00
CMJD M.Johnson/C.Drexler 12.00 30.00
CMJJ M.Johnson/M.Jordan 200.00 500.00
CMJK J.Johnson/K.Bryant 25.00 60.00
CMJL L.Odom/J.O'Neal 4.00 10.00
CMJM J.Howard/S.Marion 3.00 8.00
CMJP M.Jordan/S.Pippen 150.00 400.00
CMKK K.Garnett/K.Malone 10.00 25.00
CMKM J.Kidd/T.McGrady 10.00 25.00
CMKP K.Garnett/P.Pierce 12.00 30.00
CMKT J.Kidd/J.Tinsley 5.00 12.00
CMLG R.Lewis/J.Green 3.00 8.00
CMLM M.Johnson/L.James 75.00 200.00
CMLO M.Okur/R.Lewis 3.00 8.00
CMLS S.Pippen/L.James 75.00 200.00
CMMB Y.Ming/A.Bargnani 8.00 20.00
CMMC M.Cooper/K.Malone 6.00 15.00
CMMD M.Miller/D.Gooden 3.00 8.00
CMMG M.Miller/R.Gay 3.00 8.00
CMMH J.Howard/S.Marion 3.00 8.00
CMMJ L.James/K.Malone 40.00 100.00
CMMN D.Majerle/S.Nash 8.00 20.00
CMMO S.O'Neal/Y.Ming 10.00 25.00
CMMP S.Pippen/K.Malone 8.00 20.00
CMMS K.Malone/J.Stockton 8.00 20.00
CMMT A.Thornton/D.Mason 3.00 8.00
CMMW K.Martin/L.Walton 3.00 8.00
CMNS J.Stockton/S.Nash 8.00 20.00
CMOC V.Carter/L.Odom 6.00 15.00
CMOG L.Odom/P.Gasol 5.00 12.00
CMOO M.Okur/S.O'Neal 6.00 15.00
CMPG C.Anthony/P.Pierce 8.00 20.00
CMPI P.Pierce/A.Iguodala 6.00 15.00
CMPR C.Paul/B.Roy 8.00 20.00
CMRE L.Ridnour/M.Ellis 3.00 8.00
CMRJ J.Farmar/R.Felton 3.00 8.00
CMSA S.Marbury/A.Iverson 10.00 25.00
CMSM W.Szczerbiak/C.Mullin 5.00 12.00
CMSO S.O'Neal/A.Stoudemire 8.00 20.00
CMSS S.Swift/W.Szczerbiak 3.00 8.00
CMUS J.Stockton/B.Udrih 5.00 12.00
CMWG B.Wallace/P.Gasol 8.00 20.00
CMWH L.Head/D.Williams 4.00 10.00
CMWM S.Williams/J.McGee 3.00 8.00

2009-10 SP Game Used Combo Patches
STATED PRINT RUN 99 SER.#'d SETS
CPR Nene/Z.Randolph 8.00 20.00
CPAA J.Alexander/R.Anderson 5.00 12.00
CPAB B.Wallace/A.McDyess 10.00 25.00
CPAG T.Ariza/J.Green 6.00 15.00
CPAH A.Gray/H.Armstrong 5.00 12.00
CPAL A.Thornton/A.Tucker 5.00 12.00
CPAM M.Camby/A.McDyess 6.00 15.00
CPAT A.Afflalo/A.Tucker 5.00 12.00
CPAW R.Anderson/S.Williams 5.00 12.00
CPBB B.Cardinal/B.Wallace 10.00 25.00
CPBC R.Carney/S.Battier 8.00 20.00
CPBF M.Bibby/R.Felton 8.00 20.00
CPBJ J.Collins/B.Wright 5.00 12.00
CPBW B.Wright/B.Wallace 10.00 25.00
CPBY T.Young/S.Brown 5.00 12.00
CPCC M.Conley/J.Crittenton 6.00 15.00
CPCE T.Chandler/M.Camby 6.00 15.00
CPCH B.Haywood/B.Cardinal 5.00 12.00
CPCI J.Crawford/A.Iverson 15.00 40.00
CPCM J.Crittenton/D.McGuire 5.00 12.00
CPCS R.Stuckey/S.Claxton 5.00 12.00
CPCW W.Chandler/S.Williams 6.00 15.00
CPDA R.Anderson/S.Dalembert 5.00 12.00
CPDG K.Durant/J.Green 30.00 80.00
CPDH V.Divac/S.Hawes 8.00 20.00
CPDW J.Wright/K.Durant 30.00 80.00
CPEM K.Malone/P.Ewing 12.00 30.00
CPER R.Lewis/E.Gordon 6.00 15.00
CPFD M.Finley/K.Durant 30.00 80.00
CPFG M.Finley/M.Ginobili 15.00 40.00
CPGA C.Anthony/K.Garnett 20.00 50.00
CPGB M.Ginobili/J.Bayless 15.00 40.00
CPGC A.Gray/W.Chandler 6.00 15.00
CPGF M.Ginobili/R.Fernandez 15.00 40.00
CPGG K.Garnett/P.Gasol 20.00 50.00
CPGH M.Ginobili/G.Hill 15.00 40.00
CPGK M.Ginobili/J.Kapono 15.00 40.00
CPGL D.Lee/D.Gooden 6.00 15.00
CPGM M.Ginobili/A.Morrison 15.00 40.00
CPGO P.Gasol/J.O'Neal 12.00 30.00
CPGS G.Green/W.Szczerbiak 6.00 15.00
CPHG K.Hinrich/M.Ginobili 15.00 40.00
CPHW B.Haywood/B.Wright 5.00 12.00
CPID A.Iverson/K.Durant 30.00 80.00
CPIS A.Iverson/R.Stuckey 15.00 40.00
CPIW A.Iverson/R.Wallace 15.00 40.00
CPJB K.Bogans/R.Jefferson 6.00 15.00
CPJC J.Collins/J.Smith 5.00 12.00
CPJG M.Ginobili/R.Jefferson 15.00 40.00
CPJL R.Lopez/D.Jordan 6.00 15.00
CPJR J.Tinsley/B.Udrih 5.00 12.00
CPJT R.Jefferson/A.Tucker 6.00 15.00
CPKG M.Ginobili/S.Kerr 15.00 40.00
CPKJ K.Martin/J.Bayless 6.00 15.00
CPKK K.Malone/K.McHale 12.00 30.00
CPMA S.Marion/R.Artest 8.00 20.00
CPMB J.Bayless/D.Miles 5.00 12.00
CPMC D.Milicic/M.Conley 6.00 15.00
CPMD M.Almond/M.Dunleavy 5.00 12.00
CPMG J.McRoberts/J.Green 6.00 15.00
CPMI Z.Ilgauskas/M.Moore 6.00 15.00
CPMK K.Koufos/K.Malone 10.00 25.00
CPMN J.McRoberts/J.Noah 5.00 12.00
CPMP S.Pippen/K.Malone 20.00 50.00
CPMT J.Thompson/J.McGee 6.00 15.00
CPMW J.Wright/J.McRoberts 5.00 12.00
CPMY J.McRoberts/T.Young 5.00 12.00
CPNB M.Bibby/N.Young 8.00 20.00
CPND J.Noah/K.Durant 30.00 80.00
CPNJ J.Green/J.Noah 6.00 15.00
CPNH G.Hill/S.Nash 15.00 40.00
CPNI S.Nash/A.Iverson 15.00 40.00
CPNL R.Lopez/J.Noah 5.00 12.00
CPNW J.Noah/J.Wright 5.00 12.00
CPOB J.Bayless/T.Outlaw 5.00 12.00
CPOD C.Kaman/P.O'Bryant 6.00 15.00
CPPC J.Crittenton/O.Pecherov 5.00 12.00
CPPK K.Malone/P.Gasol 12.00 30.00
CPPM G.Pruitt/D.McGuire 5.00 12.00
CPRH G.Hill/D.Robinson 15.00 40.00
CPRP D.Robinson/R.Parish 15.00 40.00
CPRR Z.Randolph/J.Richardson 8.00 20.00
CPRS A.Randolph/W.Sharpe 5.00 12.00
CPSB J.Bayless/J.Smith 8.00 20.00
CPSG A.Gray/C.Simmons 5.00 12.00
CPSR J.Richardson/W.Szczerbiak 8.00 20.00
CPST T.Chandler/S.Williams 6.00 15.00
CPSW B.Wright/J.Smith 5.00 12.00
CPTC J.Tinsley/M.Conley 6.00 15.00
CPTL R.Lopez/J.Thompson 5.00 12.00
CPTS J.Thompson/M.Speights 5.00 12.00
CPTT J.Terry/A.Tucker 6.00 15.00
CPTY N.Young/R.Theus 6.00 15.00
CPWA S.Williams/R.Anderson 5.00 12.00
CPWB L.Wright/K.Brown 5.00 12.00
CPWH S.Hawes/B.Wright 5.00 12.00
CPWM M.Speights/W.Chandler 6.00 15.00
CPWR B.Wright/A.Randolph 5.00 12.00
CPWB B.Wright/H.Warrick 5.00 12.00
CPYW S.Williams/T.Young 5.00 12.00

2009-10 SP Game Used Fabric Foursomes
PRINT RUN 199 SER.#'d SETS
*MATERIAL 125: SAME VALUE
*MATERIAL 50: .75X TO 2X HI
*MATERIAL 35: .75X TO 2X HI
F4AATB Brks/Affl/Almnd/Tckr 4.00 10.00
F4AHLB Brks/Lndry/Artest/Ming 15.00 40.00
F4ALAH Lee/Hill/Anderson/Arthur 5.00 12.00
F4ALTB Bylss/Agstn/Lpz/Thmpsn 5.00 12.00
F4AWDA D-Rbrts/Andrsn/Wllms/Agr 4.00 10.00
F4BDGP Duncn/Pippen/KG/Kobe 50.00 120.00
F4BGBR Kobe/Ice/Rbinsn/Bird 50.00 120.00
F4BJJO Kobe/Shaq/Al/LeBron 50.00 125.00
F4BJWL Law/Wllms/Jhnsn/Bbby 6.00 15.00
F4BMCS Smith/Kobe/Crtr/Mson 50.00 120.00
F4BMDI Iggy/Miller/Dlmbrt/Brnd 6.00 15.00
F4BMGS Brnd/Pau/Amare/Miller 10.00 25.00
F4BMMJ James/Yao/Brnd/Martin 50.00 120.00
F4BNGN Kobe/KG/Dirk/Nash 50.00 120.00
F4BOGB Byum/Odom/Kobe/Pau 50.00 120.00
F4BOWB Bozer/Okur/Wllms/Brwr 5.00 12.00
F4CGAW Artest/KG/Wllce/Cmby 15.00 40.00
F4CHBL Crtr/Boone/Lpez/Hrris 12.00 30.00
F4DBCM Dxn/McGee/Crttntn/Btler 5.00 12.00
F4DBPH Hill/Dncn/Bwn/Prkr 15.00 40.00
F4DDFG Grngr/Ford/Dniels/Dnlvy 4.00 10.00
F4DFPG Prkr/Ginbili/Dncn/Fnly 15.00 40.00
F4DGNR Grdn/Deng/Noah/Rose 10.00 25.00
F4DHGC Hrfrd/Conly/Drnt/Green 25.00 60.00
F4DIOR Al/Shaq/Dncn/Rbnsn 20.00 50.00
F4DKIC Dncn/Kidd/Crtr/Al 15.00 40.00
F4DMBA Agstn/May/Diaw/Wllce 5.00 12.00
F4DMIO Al/Malone/Shaq/Dncn 20.00 50.00
F4DTGJ Davis/Jrdn/Grdn/Thrntn 5.00 12.00
F4EMHO Shaq/Yao/Hwrd/Ewng 20.00 50.00
F4FCDC Chndlr/Cook/Ddly/Frnndz 5.00 12.00
F4GCGM Gsol/Mayo/Cnly/Gay 6.00 15.00
F4GCKS Chmbrs/Stcktn/King/KG 15.00 40.00
F4GFRW Wllms/Foye/Roy/Gay 8.00 20.00
F4GGLA Grdn/Alxndr/Love/Lopz 5.00 12.00
F4GHTG Gray/Thms/Deng/Hnrch 5.00 12.00
F4HAPD Pruitt/Dvis/Alln/House 4.00 10.00
F4HBAS Rip/Afflo/Shrp/Brwn 6.00 15.00
F4HBYM Hywd/Bltch/Yung/McGuir 4.00 10.00
F4HCRG Curry/Rbnsn/Hrrngtn/Richrdsn 5.00 12.00
F4HEOR Ewing/Rbnsn/Shaq/Hill 20.00 50.00
F4HMHA Hib/JVle/J.J./Ajinca 5.00 12.00
F4HNSS Smmns/Nconi/Hghs/Thabo 5.00 12.00
F4HOBA Hwrd/Wllce/Okfr/Agstin 5.00 12.00
F4HSGR Rbnsn/Hwrd/Green/Smith 8.00 20.00
F4IDPD Parish/Dnkr/Al/Dntley 12.00 30.00
F4IWJW LB/J.Wllce/Ilgask/West 50.00 120.00
F4IWPS Prince/Al/Wllce/Stcky 12.00 30.00
F4JASB Btlr/Amas/Jmison/Stvnsn 5.00 12.00
F4JBVA Alxndr/Bogut/Vllnva/Rjeff 5.00 12.00
F4JDWC Jrdn/Drsy/Chlmrs/Wewr 5.00 12.00
F4JMCA Jrdn/Wilt/Kareem/Mail 50.00 120.00
F4JOMR Mail/Olaj/Jordan/Rbnsn 50.00 120.00
F4JORD LBJ/Roy/Okfr/Durant 50.00 120.00
F4JPST Paul/Isiah/Stock/Jhnsn 25.00 60.00
F4JRRB Rjeff/Bgut/Ridnur/Redd 5.00 12.00
F4JSWH Smith/Wllms/Hrfrd/Jhnsn 6.00 15.00
F4KBCB Brgnni/Cldrn/Kpno/Bosh 8.00 20.00
F4KKMM Miles/Millsp/AK47/Krvr 5.00 12.00
F4KNHW Wrght/Kidd/Hwrd/Dirk 15.00 40.00
F4LHBR Lewis/Nlsn/Rdck/Hwrd 8.00 20.00
F4LHNL Hwrd/Lee/Nlsn/Lewis 8.00 20.00
F4MBAN Mtrn/Melo/Billups/Nene 10.00 25.00
F4MBMS TMac/Battier/Yao/Scola 15.00 40.00
F4MBRW Beasly/Rose/Mayo/Wstbrk 12.00 30.00
F4MDGW Wstbrk/Masn/Green/Durnt 25.00 60.00
F4MEWR Rndlph/Wrght/Mgott/Ellis 5.00 12.00
F4MMBL Love/Brewr/Miller/Jfrsn 6.00 15.00
F4MMMD Drsey/Yao/TMac/Mtmbo 15.00 40.00
F4MNDG Mllsp/Gay/Nvk/Gbsn 6.00 15.00
F4MUDT Nconi/Hws/Udrih/Thmpsn 4.00 10.00
F4MWCB Bsley/Cook/Wrght/Mglore 4.00 10.00
F4MWHC Wade/Hslm/Shaq/Chlmrs 12.00 30.00
F4MYSS Smth/Spights/Mrshll/Yng 5.00 12.00
F4NHSO Hill/Shaq/Amare/Nash 20.00 50.00
F4NKMW Nash/Wllms/Miller/Kidd 12.00 30.00
F4NWBL Law/Noah/Wright/Brwr 4.00 10.00
F4ODRB Outlw/Rdrgz/Roy/Bylss 8.00 20.00
F4ORMW Mlne/Rbrtsn/Wlkns/Olaj 10.00 25.00
F4PAGR KG/Allen/Rnd/Pierce 15.00 40.00
F4PCSP Chndlr/Paul/Ptrsn/Stojak 12.00 30.00
F4POMR Shaq/Rbnsn/Zo/Olaj 20.00 50.00
F4SJMG Miller/Jmisn/Grdn/Strks 5.00 12.00
F4SKBW Blkmn/Weems/Klz/Smth 6.00 15.00
F4SWGH Gbsn/Wrght/Hcksn/Szcz 5.00 12.00
F4TAMB Aldrdg/Tyrs/Brgn/Mrrsn 6.00 15.00
F4TGSW Grg/Snglein/Wllms/Jet 5.00 12.00
F4TJFS BigAl/Tlfr/Foye/Smth 4.00 10.00
F4TMRH Rush/Hbbrt/McRob/Tinsl 5.00 12.00
F4TYSW Wright/Thmtn/Stcky/Yng 4.00 10.00
F4WARF Wbstr/Frndz/Aldrdg/Roy 8.00 20.00
F4WBOF Okfr/Wllce/Bell/Felfn 5.00 12.00
F4WGGS Wite/Shrp/Green/Gddns 4.00 10.00
F4WKWW White/Weav/Wstbrk/Krstc 12.00 30.00
F4WMEO West/Ewing/Mail/Shaq 20.00 50.00
F4YCSW Wllms/Yng/Crttntn/Smth 4.00 10.00

2009-10 SP Game Used Logo Men
STATED PRINT RUN ONE TO 18 SER.#'d SETS
LOGOBI Chauncey Billups/16 150.00 400.00
LOGODN Dirk Nowitzki/14 800.00 1,500.00
LOGOJO Jermaine O'Neal/15 75.00 200.00
LOGOKG Kevin Garnett/18 800.00 1,500.00
LOGOPP Paul Pierce/14 800.00 1,500.00

2009-10 SP Game Used Multi Marks Dual
MDAA A.Biedrins/A.Blatche 5.00 12.00
MDAB C.Brewer/R.Artest 8.00 20.00
MDAD A.Horford/D.Arthur 8.00 20.00
MDAG D.Augustin/E.Gordon 6.00 15.00
MDAH L.Aldridge/A.Horford 8.00 20.00
MDAN J.Noah/L.Aldridge 8.00 20.00
MDAT T.Chandler/A.Bynum 6.00 15.00
MDAW S.Webb/K.Anderson 6.00 15.00
MDBA J.Boone/R.Anderson 5.00 12.00
MDBB C.Brewer/B.Brown 5.00 12.00
MDBC M.Conley/A.Bynum 6.00 15.00
MDBG A.Bynum/M.Gasol 8.00 20.00
MDBJ B.Brown/J.Barea 8.00 20.00
MDBL B.Bass/R.Lopez 5.00 12.00
MDBM T.McGrady/M.Beasley 60.00 150.00
MDBN J.Noah/A.Blatche 5.00 12.00
MDBR B.Rush/C.Bosh 10.00 25.00
MDBS M.Speights/A.Blatche 6.00 15.00
MDBT A.Thornton/A.Bynum 5.00 12.00
MDBW B.Brown/K.Weaver 5.00 12.00
MDCA T.Chandler/H.Armstrong 6.00 15.00
MDCB V.Carter/M.Beasley 60.00 150.00
MDCG A.Gilmore/T.Chambers 10.00 25.00
MDCH T.Chandler/D.Howard 10.00 25.00
MDCM O.Mayo/M.Conley 6.00 15.00
MDCT M.Conley/M.Taylor 6.00 15.00
MDDA A.Afflalo/K.Dooling 5.00 12.00
MDDE E.Gordon/B.Diaw 6.00 15.00
MDDM D.Gallinari/M.Bibby 8.00 20.00
MDDW M.Williams/K.Durant 100.00 250.00
MDDX W.Bynum/M.Almond 5.00 12.00
MDEB L.Bird/J.Erving 125.00 300.00
MDEW J.Erving/D.Wilkins 75.00 200.00
MDFB R.Fernandez/N.Batum 6.00 15.00
MDFM P.Millsap/R.Felton 6.00 15.00
MDGA A.Bogut/K.Garnett 100.00 250.00
MDGD G.Goodrich/K.Durant 100.00 250.00
MDGL C.Landry/A.Gray 5.00 12.00
MDGM J.Nelson/P.Gasol 12.00 30.00
MDGP K.Garnett/T.Parker 100.00 250.00
MDGR D.Granger/B.Rush 5.00 12.00
MDGT J.Thompson/E.Gordon 6.00 15.00
MDGW E.Gordon/R.Westbrook 75.00 200.00
MDHA D.Augustin/J.Hornacek 6.00 15.00
MDHG S.Haywood/J.Green 6.00 15.00
MDHM Y.Ming/D.Howard 100.00 250.00
MDHR M.Redd/J.Hornacek 6.00 15.00
MDJB A.Jamison/C.Bosh 10.00 25.00
MDJD C.Duhon/B.Jackson 5.00 12.00
MDJK K.Love/J.Wright 8.00 20.00
MDJM J.Wright/M.Beasley 5.00 12.00
MDJS D.Jordan/W.Sharpe 6.00 15.00
MDJW M.Williams/L.James 1,000.00 2,000.00
MDKD A.Dantley/B.King 10.00 25.00
MDKT J.Kidd/I.Thomas 40.00 100.00
MDLB K.Love/C.Brewer 8.00 20.00
MDLF J.Lucas/W.Frazier 30.00 80.00
MDLM L.James/M.Williams 1,000.00 2,000.00
MDLP T.Prince/B.Lanier 10.00 25.00
MDLS R.Sessions/A.Law 6.00 15.00
MDLW B.Lopez/S.Williams 8.00 20.00
MDMB O.Mayo/M.Beasley 12.00 30.00
MDMC M.Conley/C.Brewer 6.00 15.00
MDMD C.Drexler/Y.Ming 125.00 300.00
MDMH J.McRoberts/S.Hawes 5.00 12.00
MDML K.Love/O.Mayo 8.00 20.00
MDMR Y.Ming/D.Robinson 125.00 300.00
MDMY Y.Ming/S.Nash 125.00 300.00
MDNS D.Wilkins/M.Jordan 1,500.00 3,000.00
MDNT D.West/A.Jamison 6.00 15.00
MDPB C.Brewer/T.Parker 12.00 30.00
MDPH A.Horford/B.Pettit 10.00 25.00
MDPS T.Prince/R.Stuckey 8.00 20.00
MDRA D.Augustin/M.Richardson 6.00 15.00
MDRB J.Bayless/B.Roy 10.00 25.00
MDRM D.Rose/O.Mayo 12.00 30.00
MDRN J.Noah/D.Rodman 40.00 100.00
MDRS B.Roy/R.Stuckey 10.00 25.00
MDSA J.Alexander/J.Smith 5.00 12.00
MDSC D.Stoudamire/S.Cassell 6.00 15.00
MDSN B.Bowen/J.Bayless 6.00 15.00
MDSR R.Stuckey/D.Rose 12.00 30.00
MDSS K.Smith/B.Scott 6.00 15.00
MDSW C.Walker/J.Stockton 12.00 30.00
MDTG A.Thornton/D.Gallinari 6.00 15.00
MDTR D.Rose/T.Thomas 12.00 30.00
MDVB M.Beasley/Vandeweghe 6.00 15.00
MDVF J.Farmar/S.Vujacic 5.00 12.00
MDVP K.Vandeweghe/R.Parish 10.00 25.00
MDWA A.Ajinca/S.Williams 5.00 12.00
MDWB J.Wright/J.Bayless 5.00 12.00
MDWC M.Conley/M.Williams 6.00 15.00
MDWD J.Dorsey/C.Wilcox 5.00 12.00
MDWJ D.Jackson/J.Wright 5.00 12.00
MDWL B.Lopez/S.Williams 8.00 20.00
MDWR M.Williams/R.Rondo 10.00 25.00
MDWW L.Williams/J.Wright 5.00 12.00

2009-10 SP Game Used Multi Marks Triple
STATED PRINT RUN 4 TO 100 SER.#'d SETS
MTAAG Gasol/Aldridge/Amundson/75 12.00 30.00
MTARB Brewer/Roy/Armstrong/50 8.00 20.00
MTARC Armstrong/Roy/Conley/75 8.00 20.00
MTBAT Aldridge/Thrntn/Bosh/60 12.00 30.00
MTBBC Conley/Brewer/Brown/100 8.00 20.00
MTBBS Boone/Batum/Speights/75 8.00 20.00
MTBCT Conley/Taylor/Brewer/100 8.00 20.00
MTBMG McRob/Bosh/Glinri/50 8.00 20.00
MTBNT Thornton/Boone/Noah/100 8.00 20.00
MTBWJ Jordan/Wright/Balkman/75 8.00 20.00
MTDLW Deng/Lee/Westbrook/75 40.00 100.00
MTFBA Barea/Afflalo/Foye/75 12.00 30.00
MTFBG Brown/Gordon/Fernandez/100 8.00 20.00
MTFHS Fernandez
Singletary/Hickson/75 8.00 20.00
MTFNC Conley/Fernandez/Noah/100 8.00 20.00
MTGAW Gervin/Wright/Almond/50 10.00 25.00
MTGNW Noah/Gay/Wright/50 8.00 20.00
MTGWA Wright/Alexander/Garcia/75 8.00 20.00
MTHAB Hrnck/Bylss/Allen/14 25.00 60.00
MTHGM Horford/McGee/Green/75 8.00 20.00
MTHWB Wright/Horford/Beasley/100 8.00 20.00
MTJGJ LJ/Garnett/Jordan/25 3,000.00 6,000.00
MTJWJ LJ/Jackson/Williams/75 1,000.00 2,000.00
MTMBH Marshall/Horford/Biedrins/50 8.00 20.00
MTMHT Thomas/Howard/Yao/18 150.00 400.00
MTMLW Mayo/Love/Westbrk/100 60.00 150.00
MTMNW McRob/Wright/Noah/25 8.00 20.00
MTMRG Rose/Gallinari/Rush/75 15.00 40.00
MTMWH Ming/Walton/Horford/40 125.00 300.00
MTMWS West/McRoberts/Sharpe/50 8.00 20.00
MTNBC Conley/Brewer/Noah/100 8.00 20.00
MTNSB Smith/Noah/Brown/75 8.00 20.00
MTNTB Batum/Thornton/Noah/75 8.00 20.00
MTOBG Odom/Gordon/Brown/75 8.00 20.00
MTOMM Ming/McGrady/Olaj/25 150.00 400.00
MTPBG Bynum/Peterson/Green/75 8.00 20.00
MTRWK Riley/Karl/Westphal/14 40.00 100.00
MTSCC Chalmers/Stuckey/Conley/75 8.00 20.00
MTWGB Byls/Gordon/Webb/75 10.00 25.00
MTWGK Williams/Gay/Koufos/100 8.00 20.00
MTWMG McRoberts/West/Green/50 8.00 20.00
MTWRP Porter/Walton/Roy/75 12.00 30.00
MTWTC Conley/Williams/Tucker/75 8.00 20.00

2009-10 SP Game Used Multi Marks Quad
STATED PRINT RUN 5 TO 99 SER.#'d SETS
MQBBMG Brwn/Brwr/Myo/Gnari/25 10.00 25.00
MQBBRW Brwn/Bsly/Rose/Wstbrk/25 75.00 200.00
MQBCMG Brwn/Myo/Cnly/Grdn/25 15.00 40.00
MQBHHS Sharp/Jcksn/Hbbrt/Brwn/99 10.00 25.00
MQBLGA Brwn/Gay/Lpz/Ajnc/99 10.00 25.00
MQBRBG Bwn/Roy/Grdn/Brwn/50 10.00 25.00
MQBRRB Andrs/Rndp/Roy/Bylss/50 10.00 25.00
MQCBWL VC/Wllms/Brwr/Lve/50 60.00 150.00
MQCMRB Bls/Cnly/Myo/Rose/50 20.00 50.00
MQDCMW Myo/Cnly/Drnt/Wstbrk/50 150.00 400.00
MQDHBG Durant/Green
Brewer/Horford/50 100.00 250.00
MQDHGM Hrfrd/Myo/Grn/Drant/50 100.00 250.00
MQGBNG Noah/Gal/Bosh/KG/50 75.00 200.00
MQGJNB Gasol/Nelson
Bsly/LJ/25 1,000.00 2,000.00
MQGMHB Bsly/Hrfrd/KG/Yao/50 150.00 400.00
MQGNBH Bosh/Garnett
Nance/Haywood/50 40.00 100.00
MQGNMB Nance/Garnett
Bosh/Ming/25 150.00 400.00
MQGTGW Gib/EG/Thrtn/Wstb/50 30.00 80.00
MQHGWD Wright/Douglas-
Roberts/Harrington/Gordon/50 10.00 25.00
MQHJWH Hinrich/Hill/Jack/Weaver/99 10.00 25.00
MQHNCL Lopez/Noah
Harrington/Chandler/50 10.00 25.00
MQHNHL DH/Noah/Hrfrd/Lve/50 20.00 50.00
MQJBRW LJ/Rose/Bsly
Wstbrk/25 1,500.00 3,000.00
MQJMBR Noah/Blch/Jmsn/Rndph/50 10.00 25.00
MQJWWW Williams/Williams
Jamison/Wright/32 10.00 25.00
MQKBPW Kidd/Bllps/Prkr/Wllms/50 60.00 150.00
MQMBRW Bea/Ros/May/Wst/50 75.00 200.00
MQMDMH Divac/Hws/Yao/McG/50 125.00 300.00
MQMDSF Frazier/Zo/Stock/Dghty/15 75.00 200.00
MQMMBO Zo/Shaq/Yao/Bynm/25 125.00 300.00
MQMPBR Balkman/Marshall
Prince/Randolph/99 10.00 25.00
MQMSCM McCants/Mbah a
Moute/Stuckey/Conley/50 10.00 25.00
MQNBRL Brwr/Lve/Rose/Noah/50 50.00 120.00
MQOCHL DH/Odom/Love/VC/50 75.00 200.00
MQPBMG Gallinari/Pruitt
Mayo/Brewer/50 10.00 25.00
MQRCMR Mayo/Cnly/Roy/Rose/50 40.00 100.00
MQTCMG Cnly/Myo/Thrtn/Grdn/50 10.00 25.00
MQTHLA Ajinca/Lopez
Hawes/Thomas/50 10.00 25.00
MQWPBB Prin/West/Brew/Bosh/50 12.00 30.00

2009-10 SP Game Used Retro Rookie Exclusives
STATED PRINT RUN 5 TO 300 SER.#'d SETS
RRAE Alex English/180 10.00 25.00
RRAM Alonzo Mourning/25 50.00 120.00
RRAR B.J. Armstrong/278 8.00 20.00
RRAS Amare Stoudemire/15 20.00 50.00
RRBC Bill Cartwright/150 6.00 15.00
RRBD Brad Daugherty/300 8.00 20.00
RRBK Bernard King/250 10.00 25.00
RRBM Bob McAdoo/300 10.00 25.00
RRBP Bob Pettit/70 15.00 40.00
RRBR Brandon Roy/50 10.00 25.00
RRBS Bill Sharman/100 12.00 30.00
RRBW Bill Walton/100 10.00 25.00
RRCB Chauncey Billups/100 10.00 25.00
RRCD Clyde Drexler/25 25.00 60.00
RRCR Cazzie Russell/75 8.00 20.00
RRDH Dwight Howard/25 12.00 30.00
RRDN Don Nelson/100 12.00 30.00
RRDR Dennis Rodman/35 25.00 60.00
RRDW Dominique Wilkins/50 15.00 40.00
RREB Elgin Baylor/50 40.00 100.00
RREC Eddy Curry/100 5.00 12.00
RRGG George Gervin/75 15.00 40.00
RRGO Gail Goodrich/100 8.00 20.00
RRGR Glen Rice/55 12.00 30.00
RRHA Connie Hawkins/20 20.00 50.00
RRHG Horace Grant/50 8.00 20.00
RRHL Hal Greer/50 10.00 25.00
RRJA LeBron James/23 4,000.00 8,000.00
RRJK Jason Kidd/25 15.00 40.00
RRJO Jermaine O'Neal/60 8.00 20.00
RRJW James Worthy/25 20.00 50.00
RRKA Kareem Abdul-Jabbar/25 40.00 100.00
RRKD Kevin Durant/25 75.00 200.00
RRKG Kevin Garnett/25 60.00 150.00
RRKV Kiki Vandeweghe/170 6.00 15.00
RRLA LaMarcus Aldridge/50 15.00 40.00
RRLD Luol Deng/100 6.00 15.00
RRLJ Larry Johnson/25 25.00 60.00
RRLO Lamar Odom/100 6.00 15.00
RRMJ Michael Jordan/23 6,000.00 12,000.00
RRMP Mark Price/300 8.00 20.00
RROR Oscar Robertson/25 30.00 80.00
RRPA Tony Parker/25 15.00 30.00
RRPR Pat Riley/25 15.00 30.00
RRQR Quentin Richardson/250 5.00 12.00
RRRB Rick Barry/75 15.00 40.00
RRRG Rudy Gay/100 8.00 20.00
RRRM Rick Mahorn/80 5.00 12.00
RRRO Rolondo Blackman/165 6.00 15.00
RRSC Bill Laimbeer/260 8.00 20.00
RRTC Tom Chambers/100 8.00 20.00
RRTM Tracy McGrady/25 25.00 60.00
RRVC Vince Carter/25 20.00 50.00
RRYM Yao Ming/25 50.00 120.00

2009-10 SP Game Used Rookie Exclusive Signatures
STATED PRINT RUN 100 SER.#'d SETS
READ Austin Daye 4.00 10.00
REAP A.J. Price 4.00 10.00
REBM B.J. Mullens 4.00 10.00
REBR Derrick Brown 4.00 10.00
REBU Chase Budinger 8.00 20.00
RECA DeMarre Carroll 5.00 12.00
RECU Dante Cunningham 4.00 10.00
REDC Darren Collison 6.00 15.00
REDG Danny Green 6.00 15.00
REDS DaJuan Summers 4.00 10.00
REEC Earl Clark 4.00 10.00
REEM Eric Maynor 5.00 12.00
REGH Gerald Henderson 4.00 10.00
REGR Taylor Griffin 4.00 10.00
REGS Goran Suton 4.00 10.00
REHA James Harden 200.00 500.00
REJB Jon Brockman 4.00 10.00
REJE Jonas Jerebko 5.00 12.00
REJF Jonny Flynn 4.00 10.00
REJH Jrue Holiday 20.00 50.00
REJJ James Johnson 5.00 12.00
REJM Jack McClinton 4.00 10.00
REJP Jeff Pendergraph 4.00 10.00
REJT Jeff Teague 5.00 12.00
RELH Lester Hudson 4.00 10.00
REMT Marcus Thornton 5.00 12.00
RENC Nick Calathes 4.00 10.00
REOC Omri Casspi 4.00 10.00
REPB Patrick Beverley 6.00 15.00
RERB Rodrigue Beaubois 4.00 10.00
RERR Ricky Rubio 25.00 60.00
RERV Robert Vaden 4.00 10.00
RESC Stephen Curry 2,000.00 4,000.00
RESL Sergio Llull 4.00 10.00
RESY Sam Young 4.00 10.00
RETA Jermaine Taylor 4.00 10.00
RETD Toney Douglas 4.00 10.00
RETG Taj Gibson 5.00 12.00
RETL Ty Lawson 5.00 12.00
REWE Wayne Ellington 5.00 12.00

2009-10 SP Game Used Signature Fabrics
SFAA Arron Afflalo 4.00 10.00
SFAB Andrew Bogut 5.00 12.00
SFAJ Al Jefferson 4.00 10.00
SFAL Morris Almond 4.00 10.00
SFAM Alonzo Mourning 25.00 60.00
SFAR Anthony Randolph 4.00 10.00
SFAT Al Thornton 4.00 10.00
SFBD Boris Diaw 5.00 12.00
SFBL Brook Lopez 8.00 20.00
SFBO Bruce Bowen 5.00 12.00
SFBR Brandon Roy 5.00 12.00
SFBY Andrew Bynum 5.00 12.00
SFCB Chauncey Billups 8.00 20.00
SFCD Clyde Drexler 30.00 80.00
SFCH Chris Bosh 12.00 30.00
SFCJ C.J. Miles 4.00 10.00
SFCL Carl Landry 4.00 10.00
SFCO Corey Brewer 4.00 10.00
SFCR Javaris Crittenton 4.00 10.00
SFDC Daequan Cook 4.00 10.00
SFDE Derrick Rose 40.00 100.00
SFDG Chris Douglas-Roberts 4.00 10.00
SFDH Dwight Howard 12.00 30.00
SFDM Desmond Mason 4.00 10.00
SFDO Donyell Marshall 4.00 10.00
SFDR David Robinson 40.00 100.00
SFDS DeShawn Stevenson 5.00 12.00
SFDW Dominique Wilkins 15.00 40.00
SFEC Eddy Curry 5.00 12.00
SFEG Eric Gordon 5.00 12.00
SFGR Jeff Green 5.00 12.00
SFHA Spencer Hawes 4.00 10.00
SFJA Antawn Jamison 5.00 12.00
SFJC Javaris Crittenton 4.00 10.00
SFJD Joey Dorsey 4.00 10.00
SFJF Jordan Farmar 5.00 12.00
SFJG Jeff Green 5.00 12.00
SFJH J.J. Hickson 5.00 12.00
SFJK Jason Kidd 15.00 40.00
SFJM Javale McGee 5.00 12.00
SFJN Joakim Noah 5.00 12.00
SFJO DeAndre Jordan 6.00 15.00
SFJR J.R. Giddens 4.00 10.00
SFJS Jason Smith 4.00 10.00
SFJW Julian Wright 4.00 10.00
SFJY Jared Dudley 4.00 10.00
SFKD Kevin Durant 125.00 300.00
SFKG Kevin Garnett 75.00 200.00
SFKK Kosta Koufos 4.00 10.00
SFKL Kevin Love 10.00 25.00
SFKW Kyle Weaver 4.00 10.00
SFLB Larry Bird 125.00 300.00
SFLD Luol Deng 4.00 10.00
SFLE Courtney Lee 4.00 10.00
SFLJ LeBron James 3,000.00 6,000.00
SFLK Linas Kleiza 4.00 10.00
SFLO Lamar Odom 5.00 12.00
SFLS Luis Scola 5.00 12.00
SFMA Mario Chalmers 4.00 10.00
SFMB Michael Beasley 4.00 10.00
SFMC Mike Conley Jr. 6.00 15.00
SFMD Marquis Daniels 4.00 10.00
SFMI Mike Conley Jr. 6.00 15.00
SFMJ Michael Jordan 3,000.00 6,000.00
SFMO Jamario Moon 4.00 10.00
SFMP Morris Peterson 4.00 10.00
SFMS Josh McRoberts 5.00 12.00
SFMW Marvin Williams 5.00 12.00
SFNE Donte Greene 4.00 10.00
SFNO Joakim Noah 4.00 10.00
SFON Jermaine O'Neal 5.00 12.00
SFPA Tony Parker 12.00 30.00
SFPG Pau Gasol 20.00 50.00
SFQR Quentin Richardson 4.00 10.00
SFRA Ron Artest 10.00 25.00
SFRB Renaldo Balkman 4.00 10.00
SFRF Rudy Fernandez 6.00 15.00
SFRG Rudy Gay 6.00 15.00
SFRJ Richard Jefferson 4.00 10.00
SFRO Dennis Rodman 60.00 150.00
SFRS Ramon Sessions 4.00 10.00
SFRU Brandon Rush 4.00 10.00
SFRW Russell Westbrook 60.00 150.00
SFSH Shelden Williams 4.00 10.00
SFSM Josh Smith 5.00 12.00
SFST Rodney Stuckey 4.00 10.00
SFSW Sean Williams 4.00 10.00
SFTA Trevor Ariza 8.00 20.00
SFTM Tracy McGrady 60.00 150.00
SFTP Tayshaun Prince 8.00 20.00
SFTT Tyrus Thomas 4.00 10.00
SFTU Alando Tucker 4.00 10.00
SFVC Vince Carter 60.00 150.00
SFWI Mo Williams 5.00 12.00
SFWR Julian Wright 5.00 12.00
SFWS Walter Sharpe 4.00 10.00
SFYM Yao Ming 125.00 300.00

2009-10 SP Game Used SIGnificance
SAA Alexis Ajinca 3.00 8.00
SAB Andrew Bogut 4.00 10.00
SAG Aaron Gray 3.00 8.00
SAJ Al Jefferson 3.00 8.00
SAL Acie Law 3.00 8.00
SAN Ryan Anderson 3.00 8.00
SAR Darrell Arthur 3.00 8.00
SAT Al Thornton 3.00 8.00
SAV Anderson Varejao 3.00 8.00
SBB Bobby Brown 3.00 8.00
SBC Corey Brewer 3.00 8.00
SBD Boris Diaw 4.00 10.00
SBJ Josh Boone 3.00 8.00
SBL Brook Lopez 5.00 12.00
SBP Bob Pettit 12.00 30.00
SBR Bobby Brown 3.00 8.00
SBU Beno Udrih 3.00 8.00
SBW Bill Walker 3.00 8.00
SBY Andrew Bynum 5.00 12.00
SCA M.L. Carr 6.00 15.00
SCB Chauncey Billups 8.00 20.00
SCD Chris Duhon 3.00 8.00
SCH Chris Bosh 12.00 30.00
SCL Carl Landry 3.00 8.00
SCM Chris Mihm 3.00 8.00
SCO Corey Brewer 3.00 8.00
SCR Caron Butler 4.00 10.00
SDA D.J. Augustin 3.00 8.00
SDC Daequan Cook 3.00 8.00
SDE DeAndre Jordan 4.00 10.00
SDG Danilo Gallinari 4.00 10.00
SDJ Darnell Jackson 3.00 8.00
SDO Joey Dorsey 3.00 8.00
SDR Derrick Rose 40.00 100.00
SDW Dominique Wilkins 15.00 40.00
SEG Eric Gordon 4.00 10.00
SGA Danilo Gallinari 4.00 10.00
SGI Artis Gilmore 6.00 15.00
SGP Gabe Pruitt 3.00 8.00
SJA Antawn Jamison 4.00 10.00
SJB Jerryd Bayless 3.00 8.00
SJC Javaris Crittenton 3.00 8.00
SJD Jared Dudley 3.00 8.00
SJF Jordan Farmar 4.00 10.00
SJG Jeff Green 3.00 8.00
SJH J.J. Hickson 3.00 8.00
SJJ Jarrett Jack 3.00 8.00
SJM Javale McGee 4.00 10.00
SJN Joakim Noah 3.00 8.00
SJO Joe Alexander 3.00 8.00
SJS Jason Smith 3.00 8.00
SJT Jason Thompson 3.00 8.00
SKD Kevin Durant 125.00 300.00
SKG Kevin Garnett 75.00 200.00
SKK Kosta Koufos 3.00 8.00
SKL Kevin Love 15.00 40.00
SKW Kyle Weaver 3.00 8.00
SLA Louis Amundson 3.00 8.00
SLD Luol Deng 4.00 10.00
SLE Courtney Lee 3.00 8.00
SLM Luc Mbah A Moute 3.00 8.00
SLO Kyle Lowry 12.00 30.00
SMA Morris Almond 3.00 8.00
SMJ Josh McRoberts 3.00 8.00
SMK Maurice Cheeks 4.00 10.00
SMS Marreese Speights 3.00 8.00
SMT Mike Taylor 3.00 8.00
SMW Mo Williams 4.00 10.00
SNO Joakim Noah 3.00 8.00
SOD Lamar Odom 4.00 10.00
SOM O.J. Mayo 5.00 12.00
SOR Oscar Robertson 75.00 200.00
SPA Tony Parker 12.00 30.00
SPM Paul Millsap 4.00 10.00
SQR Quentin Richardson 3.00 8.00
SRA Ron Artest 8.00 20.00
SRJ Richard Jefferson 4.00 10.00
SRL Robin Lopez 3.00 8.00
SRM Rashad McCants 3.00 8.00
SRS Ramon Sessions 3.00 8.00
SRU Brandon Rush 3.00 8.00
SRW Russell Westbrook 60.00 150.00
SSH Spencer Hawes 3.00 8.00
SSJ Josh Smith 3.00 8.00
SSM Jason Smith 3.00 8.00
SSS Sean Singletary 3.00 8.00
SST Rodney Stuckey 3.00 8.00
SSV Sasha Vujacic 3.00 8.00
SSW Spud Webb 8.00 20.00
STC Tom Chambers 5.00 12.00
STY Tyson Chandler 4.00 10.00
SWA Walter Sharpe 3.00 8.00
SWI Deron Williams 4.00 10.00
SWS Shelden Williams 3.00 8.00
SYM Yao Ming 125.00 300.00

2009-10 SP Game Used Six Star Swatches 65
STATED PRINT RUN 65 SER.#'d SETS
*BASE SIX STAR: .4X TO 1X BASE HI
BASE SIX STAR PRINT RUN 99 SETS
6SAGWMHM OM/DW/AH/CA/BG/AM 10.00 25.00
6SAIDENO KB/MJ/KG/DH/MJ/SO 200.00 500.00
6SAJBWHO GA/LJ/DW/JO/DH/CB 100.00 250.00
6SALLBWS CL/MS/JB/DA/BL/KW 8.00 20.00
6SAMNDSG MA/PM/CS/DG/SN/SB 8.00 20.00
6SAWGGDS JD/JG/WS/DA/DG/DW 8.00 20.00
6SBAGCPR VC/TP/RA/DR/KG/KB 100.00 250.00
6SBAMMDL CL/SM/RA/MB/CM/MD 10.00 25.00
6SBAMPSA AS/RA/TP/CA/SM/KB 100.00 250.00
6SBDGJJO KB/KG/TD/SO/LJ/AI 100.00 250.00
6SBDKGWW LJ/RW/TD/KG/KB/JK 100.00 250.00
6SBDNGIN DN/KB/KG/TD/AI/SN 100.00 250.00
6SBISHOP SO/GG/LB/MJ/MJ/DH 200.00 500.00
6SBJKAHD BK/CD/DH/KB/CA/RJ 100.00 250.00
6SBLHAKH KK/RA/JH/MC/GH/CL 8.00 20.00
6SBMDMFV AB/CF/ID/RM/CV/SM 8.00 20.00
6SBNAIMI SN/ZI/AI/KB/SM/RA 100.00 250.00
6SBNAMIJ RA/KB/MJ/AI/CP/SN 100.00 250.00
6SBPCJHN VC/AJ/DN/LH/PP/MB 20.00 50.00
6SBPFWWW MW/CP/MW/DW/AB/RF 12.00 30.00
6SBROCKR MJ/SK/SP/MJ/VD/JW 200.00 500.00
6SBSWDSB QD/RB/SW/CS/RB/TS 8.00 20.00
6SCBCRBG JR/KB/TC/SB/EC/PG 8.00 20.00
6SCBKFCS JK/TM/MB/TC/MC/SS 12.00 30.00
6SCBRKSO AK/PP/CB/DW/SO/SB 8.00 20.00
6SCJMGGP BG/MG/AJ/KM/VC/MM 12.00 30.00
6SCMGMAW MC/BW/AM/DM/RA/KG 12.00 30.00
6SCMSOSB AB/DM/JS/PS/EO/TC 8.00 20.00
6SDACKSC DA/SW/CB/AH/CD/KD 12.00 30.00
6SDBICMG PG/TD/EB/MM/VC/AI 12.00 30.00
6SDBJBPS TP/CB/JD/CB/CB/LS 8.00 20.00
6SDGMKGS PG/KG/KM/TD/AK/AS 12.00 30.00
6SDGMNOH MO/TD/KG/JH/DN/TM 12.00 30.00
6SDHCBRW AH/MB/DR/MC/KD/RW 12.00 30.00
6SDICBMC MC/AI/BD/SN/AM/CB 12.00 30.00
6SDIHSHJ TD/DH/AS/AJ/ZI/BH 12.00 30.00
6SDIMJHR AI/LJ/DH/YM/TD/DR 100.00 250.00
6SDKMNPM TD/TP/YM/TM/DN/JK 15.00 40.00
6SDNSAPR DN/TD/CA/BR/CP/AS 15.00 40.00
6SDSHBOM RH/WS/BD/AM/EB/LO 8.00 20.00
6SDWHBGC AK/MC/CB/BW/KD/JG 12.00 30.00
6SEGMBJB CB/LJ/LB/GG/JE/SM 25.00 60.00
6SFACDCB WC/AC/DC/RF/MA/JD 8.00 20.00
6SFRLBRB JB/SR/RR/KL/JF/SB 8.00 20.00
6SGAALBT EG/JA/JB/DA/BL/JT 8.00 20.00
6SGFOARS RF/KA/RG/MS/JR/PO 8.00 20.00
6SGGMBPO CB/YM/KG/PG/JO/CP 20.00 50.00
6SGWGWGR HW/DG/GG/AW/JG/NR 8.00 20.00
6SHCBJBO JJ/CB/SO/VC/CB/RH 12.00 30.00
6SHCNAGH RH/GA/VC/BG/DH/DN 12.00 30.00
6SHKSAPT LH/GP/JT/KK/MA/RS 8.00 20.00
6SJAHPGG DG/RG/CP/LJ/CA/DH 100.00 250.00
6SJMAKBW CB/CA/DW/LJ/CK/DM 100.00 250.00
6SKJABWH LJ/DW/RA/CB/DH/JK 100.00 250.00
6SKASCDY KB/YM/AI/DW/SN/CB 100.00 250.00
6SKJEMCA MO/EO/JM/CF/KG/AH 12.00 30.00
6SLADKAY YM/DH/AB/KB/LJ/AB 100.00 250.00
6SLILYRO JS/KM/IT/MJ/MJ/SP 200.00 500.00
6SLKJGHM LH/LK/DL/ME/FG/JJ 8.00 20.00
6SLOGANO MJ/KB/KG/DR/MJ/RW 200.00 500.00
6SMASONC MJ/DR/MJ/HO/SO/KM 200.00 500.00
6SMBRGLW KL/EG/OM/DR/MB/RW 10.00 25.00
6SMGSADR CA/DR/CD/KG/AS/KM 12.00 30.00
6SMGSWDN AS/MD/YM/CW/DW/NH 10.00 25.00
6SMJSSRN NH/JS/KM/JS/RJ/BR 8.00 20.00
6SMMMGEK KM/GG/AM/BK/PE/HO 12.00 30.00
6SMMMMCS KM/JC/SS/MM/DM/DM 8.00 20.00
6SMOWADB KD/DM/EO/LA/MB/MW 12.00 30.00
6SMTMAGK RA/SM/JT/DG/CM/AK 8.00 20.00
6SNBKDBP SN/CP/BD/JK/MB/CB 12.00 30.00
6SNOAHLU MJ/JE/KG/KB/LJ/KD 200.00 500.00
6SNTHMWG RH/DG/SN/DW/JT/AM 10.00 25.00
6SNTYHWL JN/AL/TY/SH/AT/JW 8.00 20.00
6SNWVUMD KM/BU/DW/JN/SV/CD 8.00 20.00
6SOBPTCW CB/LO/TT/CP/MC/RW 10.00 25.00
6SOHDGHI EO/BG/LD/AI/DH/DH 8.00 20.00
6SOMNJHP HO/TM/DW/DN/RP/LJ 15.00 40.00
6SPBMFGO VD/KM/SO/HG/DR/KB 15.00 40.00
6SPEJBMB PP/LB/JE/MB/LJ/OM 100.00 250.00
6SPHJWBJ AJ/RH/RW/CB/PP/JJ 10.00 25.00
6SPNCJRM PP/ND/LJ/OM/RJ/MR 100.00 250.00
6SPWSDFA AS/MP/JA/BW/LD/RF 10.00 25.00
6SRAGDRL AC/GH/DS/RJ/LR/RM 8.00 20.00
6SRHMRLS AR/RL/BR/RH/JM/MS 8.00 20.00
6SRHOWHF KH/LW/JH/TO/LR/TF 8.00 20.00
6SRHSPWD MR/DW/CP/DH/JS/KD 10.00 25.00
6SRWJJCH GW/JJ/BH/ZR/RJ/JC 8.00 20.00
6SSJOPRD AS/LJ/MC/GA/SD/TP 100.00 250.00
6SSKWRGC WS/DG/AK/MW/RR/WC 8.00 20.00
6SSLRADS RA/RL/JS/JR/MD/WS 8.00 20.00
6SSOHSBO EO/SS/JS/JO/AB/DH 8.00 20.00
6SSSTSJH JS/JS/RR/AJ/SB/RS 8.00 20.00
6STADCPO JT/MO/JC/GA/SD/TP 10.00 25.00
6STAMBRW TT/AB/AM/BR/LA/SW 8.00 20.00
6STEAKKS SO/AI/KB/EB/KM/TD 12.00 30.00
6STORGER MJ/KA/WC/HO/MM/KM 200.00 500.00
6SWAPDTL AT/AA/CL/WC/GP/GD 8.00 20.00
6SWBRSOH WO/RB/AH/DL/CD/KW 8.00 20.00

6SWHFWGL JG/RF/SW/KL/DW/DH 10.00 25.00
6SYCSSBW JS/SW/MB/RS/JC/NY 8.00 20.00

2009-10 SP Game Used Triple Patch

STATED PRINT RUN 60 SER.#'d SETS
TPADD Douby/Allen/Dunleavy 10.00 25.00
TPAMS Stojakovic/Allen/Ginobili 10.00 25.00
TPASG Allen/KG/Szczerbiak 12.00 30.00
TPASR Stojakovic/Randolph/Artest 8.00 20.00
TPAWA Anderson/Arthur/Weaver 8.00 20.00
TPAYS Young/Stuckey/Archibald 8.00 20.00
TPBDL Bryant/Love/Durant 25.00 60.00
TPBFC Conley/Bibby/Hinrich 8.00 20.00
TPBGW Gray/Blatche/Wright 8.00 20.00
TPBHG Haywood/Brand/Gooden 8.00 20.00
TPBLM McGuire/Brewer/Landry 8.00 20.00
TPBMN Noah/McRob/Brown 12.00 30.00
TPBRJ Brown/James/Rose 8.00 20.00
TPBSW Battier/Swift/Williams 8.00 20.00
TPCCD Collins/Collins/Davis 8.00 20.00
TPCMB Davis/Marion/Bayless 8.00 20.00
TPCOY Chambers/Outlaw/Young 8.00 20.00
TPDAD Davis/Armstrong/Diogu 8.00 20.00
TPDBM Duncan/Brand/Zo 15.00 40.00
TPDCC Daniels/Crittenton/Collins 8.00 20.00
TPDCO O'Neal/Collins/Dalembert 12.00 30.00
TPDCS Davis/Chandler/Sefolosha 8.00 20.00
TPDMD Douglas-Roberts Deng/Morrison 8.00 20.00
TPDSB Brown/Stojakovic/Davis 8.00 20.00
TPDSG Peja/Dunleavy/Ginobili 8.00 20.00
TPDWA Wright/Daniels/Afflalo 8.00 20.00
TPDYC Dixon/Crittenton/Young 8.00 20.00
TPFRT Rodriguez/Tucker/Foye 8.00 20.00
TPFRY Rndlph/Thornton/Young 8.00 20.00
TPGCN Nene/Garnett/Chandler 15.00 30.00
TPGHT Gray/Horford/Thompson 8.00 20.00
TPGKS Sene/Krstic/Gasol 12.50 30.00
TPGPD Davis/Pruitt/Garnett 10.00 25.00
TPGRA KG/Robinson/Arthur 12.50 30.00
TPGRB Randolph/Biedrins/KG 10.00 25.00
TPHAW Wright/Afflalo/Haywood 8.00 20.00
TPHCY Chandler/Hrrngtn/Yng 10.00 25.00
TPHGC Ginobili/Hughes/Collins 8.00 20.00
TPHGF Fernandez/Garcia/Howard 8.00 20.00
TPIAG Iverson/Gordon/Agstn 10.00 25.00
TPICG Iverson/Gibson/Rondo 25.00 60.00
TPIMR Rose/Iverson/Mayo 25.00 60.00
TPITF Iverson/Telfair/Felton 10.00 25.00
TPJLB Brooks/Law/Jackson 8.00 20.00
TPJRB Barry/Dirk/Dunleavy 8.00 20.00
TPJSC Dunleavy/Simmons/Cook 8.00 20.00
TPKKM Beasley/KG/Malone 25.00 50.00
TPKSN Sene/Krstic/Nene 8.00 20.00
TPLAR Rondo/Artest/Lewis 8.00 20.00
TPLGB Lowry/Giddens/Bayless 8.00 20.00
TPLGR Gay/Rondo/Lewis 10.00 25.00
TPLJA Lewis/Almond/Jefferson 8.00 20.00
TPMCT Tlfr/Chndlr/Marion 8.00 20.00
TPMCY Marion/Young/Chandler 8.00 20.00
TPMGB Brewer/George/Mason 8.00 20.00
TPMGF Garnett/Reed/Malone 20.00 50.00
TPMGK Malone/King/Garnett 20.00 40.00
TPMJG James/Gay/Garnett 25.00 60.00
TPMMM Malone/Ewing/Mutombo 20.00 50.00
TPMMS Smith/Jefferson/Mason 8.00 20.00
TPMNG Green/McRob/Noah 8.00 20.00
TPMRH Rose/Hill/Mayo 20.00 50.00
TPMRW Maggette/Wade/Rich 10.00 25.00
TPMWW Miller/Wright/Williams 8.00 20.00
TPNFT Hinrich/Telfair/Nash 8.00 20.00
TPNGD Nash/Garnett/Durant 15.00 40.00
TPOWD Davis/Williams/Okur 8.00 20.00
TPPFF Farmar/Brown/Ariza 8.00 20.00
TPPSW Wright/Smith/Petro 8.00 20.00
TPRAW Richardson/Wright/Aldridge 8.00 20.00
TPRDS Dixon/Richardson/Smith 8.00 20.00
TPRGB Giddens/Randolph/Bayless 8.00 20.00
TPSAY Young/Stojakovic/Almons 8.00 20.00
TPSDG Davis/Smith/Green 8.00 20.00
TPSIA Aldridge/Szczerbiak/Ilgauskas 8.00 20.00
TPSRD Redd/Dunleavy/Szczerbiak 8.00 20.00
TPSSW Szczerbiak/Stojakovic/Williams 8.00 20.00
TPSWB Brewer/Stevenson/West 8.00 20.00
TPSYC Szczerbiak/Young/Chandler 8.00 20.00
TPSYW Young/Swift/Williams 8.00 20.00
TPTFD Dudley/Tinsley/Farmar 8.00 20.00
TPTNS Nelson/Tinsley/Singleton 8.00 20.00
TPVSG Villanueva/Simmons/Giddens 8.00 20.00
TPWAJ Dorsey/Randolph/Szczerbiak 8.00 20.00
TPWAT Afflalo/Conley/Tucker 8.00 20.00
TPWMD Wallace/Thornton/May 8.00 20.00
TPWRW Walton/Malone/Rodman 20.00 50.00
TPYHS Horford/Young/Sharpe 8.00 20.00

2012 SP Game Used

COMP.SET w/o SP's (30) 20.00 40.00
SP1 STATED ODDS 1:72
23 Michael Jordan 4.00 10.00

2012 SP Game Used Inked Drivers Black

STATED PRINT RUN 3-25

2012 SP Game Used Inked Drivers Light Orange

*LT.ORANGE/15-35: .5X TO 1.2X SILVER
STATED PRINT RUN 5-35

2012 SP Game Used Scorecard Signatures

STATED ODDS 1:15
GROUP A STATED ODDS 1:1,790
GROUP B STATED ODDS 1:203
GROUP C STATED ODDS 1:63
GROUP D STATED ODDS 1:23
SSMJ Michael Jordan A 300.00 500.00

2012 SP Game Used Spectrum Autographs

STATED PRINT RUN 5-100

2014 SP Game Used

COMP.SET w/o SP's (30) 25.00 50.00
OVERALL RC SHIRT AU ODDS 1:3 PACKS
23 Michael Jordan 4.00 10.00

2014 SP Game Used Inked Drivers

*BLONDE/35: .5X TO 1.2X BASIC DRIVER

2014 SP Game Used Inked Drivers Black

*BLACK/25: .5X TO 1.2X BASIC DRIVER
STATED PRINT RUN 3-25

2014 SP Game Used Leader Board Letter Marks

SERIAL NUMBERS B/WN 2-35 COPIES PER
ALL VERSIONS OF PLAYERS EQUALLY PRICED

2014 SP Game Used Spectrum Autographs

STATED PRINT RUN 10-100

2007-08 SP Rookie Edition

61-104 RC ODDS THREE PER PACK
105-120 ODDS ONE PER PACK
121-150 STATED ODDS 1:12
151-180 STATED ODDS 1:12
181-210 STATED ODDS 1:12
1 Andre Iguodala .50 1.25
2 Andre Miller .40 1.00
3 Gerald Wallace .40 1.00
4 Jason Richardson .50 1.25
5 Andrew Bogut .40 1.00
6 Michael Redd .40 1.00
7 Ben Gordon .40 1.00
8 Ben Wallace .60 1.50
9 LeBron James 4.00 10.00
10 Larry Hughes .40 1.00
11 Paul Pierce .75 2.00
12 Ray Allen .75 2.00
13 Elton Brand .40 1.00
14 Pau Gasol .75 2.00
15 Kyle Lowry .50 1.25
16 Joe Johnson .40 1.00
17 Josh Smith .30 .75
18 Dwyane Wade 1.00 2.50
19 Shaquille O'Neal 1.00 2.50
20 Chris Paul 1.00 2.50
21 Morris Peterson .30 .75
22 Carlos Boozer .40 1.00
23 Michael Jordan 5.00 12.00
24 Deron Williams .40 1.00
25 Mehmet Okur .30 .75
26 Ron Artest .50 1.25
27 Mike Bibby .50 1.25
28 Eddy Curry .30 .75
29 Zach Randolph .50 1.25
30 Kobe Bryant 4.00 10.00
31 Lamar Odom .40 1.00
32 Dwight Howard .60 1.50
33 Rashard Lewis .40 1.00
34 Dirk Nowitzki 1.25 3.00
35 Josh Howard .40 1.00
36 Jason Kidd .75 2.00
37 Vince Carter 1.00 2.50
38 Allen Iverson 1.25 3.00
39 Carmelo Anthony .75 2.00
40 Jermaine O'Neal .50 1.25
41 Tayshaun Prince .50 1.25
42 Chauncey Billups .60 1.50
43 Richard Hamilton .60 1.50
44 T.J. Ford .30 .75
45 Chris Bosh .60 1.50
46 Tracy McGrady .75 2.00
47 Yao Ming 1.25 3.00
48 Tim Duncan 1.25 3.00
49 Tony Parker .75 2.00
50 Amare Stoudemire .50 1.25
51 Shawn Marion .50 1.25
52 Steve Nash 1.00 2.50
53 Chris Wilcox .30 .75
54 Kevin Garnett 1.25 3.00
55 Brandon Roy .60 1.50
56 LaMarcus Aldridge .50 1.25
57 Baron Davis .40 1.00
58 Caron Butler .40 1.00
59 Gilbert Arenas .50 1.25
60 Antawn Jamison .40 1.00
61 Kevin Durant RC 6.00 15.00
62 Al Horford RC 1.50 4.00
63 Mike Conley Jr. RC 1.50 4.00
64 Jeff Green RC .50 1.25
65 Corey Brewer RC .50 1.25
66 Joakim Noah RC .60 1.50
67 Spencer Hawes RC .40 1.00
68 Acie Law RC .40 1.00
69 Julian Wright RC .40 1.00
70 Al Thornton RC .40 1.00
71 Rodney Stuckey RC .40 1.00
72 Sean Williams RC .40 1.00
73 Marco Belinelli RC .50 1.25
74 Javaris Crittenton RC .40 1.00
75 Jason Smith RC .40 1.00
76 Daequan Cook RC .50 1.25
77 Jared Dudley RC .50 1.25
78 Wilson Chandler RC .50 1.25
79 Morris Almond RC .40 1.00
80 Aaron Brooks RC .50 1.25
81 Arron Afflalo RC .50 1.25
82 Alando Tucker RC .40 1.00
83 Carl Landry RC .40 1.00
84 Gabe Pruitt RC .40 1.00
85 Juan Carlos Navarro RC .50 1.25
86 Yi Jianlian RC .75 2.00
87 Glen Davis RC .50 1.25
88 Jermareo Davidson RC .40 1.00
89 Thaddeus Young RC .60 1.50
90 Brandan Wright RC .50 1.25
91 Luis Scola RC .60 1.50
92 Chris Richard RC .40 1.00
93 Adam Haluska RC .40 1.00
94 D.J. Strawberry RC .40 1.00
95 Darryl Watkins RC .40 1.00
96 Cheikh Samb RC .40 1.00
97 Greg Oden RC .60 1.50
98 Aaron Gray RC .40 1.00
99 JamesOn Curry RC .40 1.00
100 Taurean Green RC .40 1.00
101 Demetris Nichols RC .40 1.00
102 Nick Young RC .60 1.50
103 Ramon Sessions RC .50 1.25
104 Coby Karl RC .40 1.00
105 Jason Smith 96-97 .50 1.25
106 Kevin Durant 96-97 8.00 20.00
107 Al Horford 96-97 2.00 5.00
108 Mike Conley Jr. 96-97 2.00 5.00
109 Jeff Green 96-97 .60 1.50
110 Corey Brewer 96-97 .60 1.50
111 Joakim Noah 96-97 .75 2.00
112 Spencer Hawes 96-97 .50 1.25
113 Acie Law 96-97 .50 1.25
114 Julian Wright 96-97 .50 1.25
115 Al Thornton 96-97 .50 1.25
116 Rodney Stuckey 96-97 .50 1.25
117 Sean Williams 96-97 .50 1.25
118 Marco Belinelli 96-97 .60 1.50
119 Javaris Crittenton 96-97 .50 1.25
120 Jason Smith 96-97 .50 1.25
121 Kevin Durant 97-98 15.00 40.00
122 Al Horford 97-98 4.00 10.00
123 Mike Conley Jr. 97-98 4.00 10.00
124 Jeff Green 97-98 1.25 3.00
125 Corey Brewer 97-98 1.25 3.00
126 Joakim Noah 97-98 1.50 4.00
127 Spencer Hawes 97-98 1.00 2.50
128 Acie Law 97-98 1.00 2.50
129 Julian Wright 97-98 1.00 2.50
130 Al Thornton 97-98 1.00 2.50
131 Rodney Stuckey 97-98 1.00 2.50
132 Sean Williams 97-98 1.00 2.50
133 Marco Belinelli 97-98 1.25 3.00
134 Javaris Crittenton 97-98 1.00 2.50
135 Jason Smith 97-98 1.00 2.50
136 Daequan Cook 97-98 1.25 3.00
137 Jared Dudley 97-98 1.25 3.00
138 Wilson Chandler 97-98 1.25 3.00
139 Brandan Wright 97-98 1.25 3.00
140 Aaron Brooks 97-98 1.25 3.00
141 Alando Tucker 97-98 1.00 2.50
142 Carl Landry 97-98 1.00 2.50
143 Gabe Pruitt 97-98 1.00 2.50
144 D.J. Strawberry 97-98 1.00 2.50
145 Yi Jianlian 97-98 2.00 5.00
146 Glen Davis 97-98 1.25 3.00
147 Greg Oden 97-98 1.50 4.00
148 Aaron Gray 97-98 1.00 2.50
149 Taurean Green 97-98 1.00 2.50
150 D.J. Strawberry 97-98 1.00 2.50
151 Kevin Durant 94-95 15.00 40.00
152 Al Horford 94-95 4.00 10.00
153 Mike Conley Jr. 94-95 4.00 10.00
154 Jeff Green 94-95 1.25 3.00
155 Corey Brewer 94-95 1.25 3.00
156 Joakim Noah 94-95 1.50 4.00
157 Spencer Hawes 94-95 1.00 2.50
158 Acie Law 94-95 1.00 2.50
159 Julian Wright 94-95 1.00 2.50
160 Al Thornton 94-95 1.00 2.50
161 Rodney Stuckey 94-95 1.00 2.50
162 Sean Williams 94-95 1.00 2.50
163 Marco Belinelli 94-95 1.25 3.00
164 Javaris Crittenton 94-95 1.00 2.50
165 Jason Smith 94-95 1.00 2.50
166 Daequan Cook 94-95 1.25 3.00
167 Jared Dudley 94-95 1.25 3.00
168 Wilson Chandler 94-95 1.25 3.00
169 Morris Almond 94-95 1.00 2.50
170 Aaron Brooks 94-95 1.25 3.00
171 Arron Afflalo 94-95 1.25 3.00
172 Alando Tucker 94-95 1.00 2.50
173 Carl Landry 94-95 1.00 2.50
174 Gabe Pruitt 94-95 1.00 2.50
175 Ramon Sessions 94-95 1.25 3.00
176 Oleksiy Pecherov 94-95 1.50 4.00
177 Luis Scola 94-95 1.50 4.00
178 Greg Oden 94-95 1.50 4.00
179 Dominique Wilkins 94-95 2.50 6.00
180 Yi Jianlian 94-95 2.00 5.00
181 Carmelo Anthony 98-99 2.00 5.00
182 B.J. Armstrong 98-99 2.00 5.00
183 Larry Bird 98-99 8.00 20.00
184 Steve Novak 98-99 1.25 3.00
185 Kobe Bryant 98-99 60.00 150.00
186 Vince Carter 98-99 4.00 10.00
187 Tom Chambers 98-99 2.00 5.00
188 Baron Davis 98-99 1.50 4.00
189 Boris Diaw 98-99 1.50 4.00
190 Hilton Armstrong 98-99 1.50 4.00
191 Hal Greer 98-99 2.50 6.00
192 Keyon Dooling 98-99 1.25 3.00
193 LeBron James 98-99 60.00 150.00
194 Antawn Jamison 98-99 1.50 4.00
195 Magic Johnson 98-99 8.00 20.00
196 Michael Jordan 98-99 125.00 300.00
197 Danny Manning 98-99 1.50 4.00
198 Tracy McGrady 98-99 3.00 8.00
199 Chris Mihm 98-99 1.25 3.00
200 Yao Ming 98-99 5.00 12.00
201 Steve Nash 98-99 4.00 10.00
202 Hakeem Olajuwon 98-99 4.00 10.00
203 Tony Parker 98-99 3.00 8.00
204 Paul Pierce 98-99 3.00 8.00
205 Quentin Richardson 98-99 1.25 3.00
206 Dennis Rodman 98-99 5.00 12.00
207 DeShawn Stevenson 98-99 1.25 3.00
208 John Stockton 98-99 4.00 10.00
209 Shelden Williams 98-99 1.25 3.00
210 Dominique Wilkins 98-99 3.00 8.00

2007-08 SP Rookie Edition 1994-95 SP Rookie Autographs

OVERALL AUTO ODDS 1:7
151 Kevin Durant 300.00 600.00
152 Al Horford 12.00 30.00
153 Mike Conley Jr. 12.00 30.00
154 Jeff Green 4.00 10.00
155 Corey Brewer 4.00 10.00
156 Joakim Noah 5.00 12.00
157 Spencer Hawes 3.00 8.00
158 Acie Law 3.00 8.00
159 Julian Wright 3.00 8.00
160 Al Thornton 3.00 8.00
161 Rodney Stuckey 3.00 8.00
162 Sean Williams 3.00 8.00
163 Marco Belinelli 4.00 10.00
164 Javaris Crittenton 3.00 8.00
165 Jason Smith 3.00 8.00
166 Daequan Cook 4.00 10.00
167 Jared Dudley 4.00 10.00
168 Wilson Chandler 4.00 10.00
169 Morris Almond 3.00 8.00
170 Aaron Brooks 4.00 10.00
171 Arron Afflalo 4.00 10.00
172 Alando Tucker 3.00 8.00
173 Carl Landry 3.00 8.00
174 Gabe Pruitt 3.00 8.00
175 Ramon Sessions 4.00 10.00
176 Oleksiy Pecherov 5.00 12.00
179 Ramon Sessions 4.00 10.00

2007-08 SP Rookie Edition 1996-97 SP Rookie Autographs

OVERALL AUTO ODDS 1:7
106 Kevin Durant 300.00 600.00
107 Al Horford 12.00 30.00
108 Mike Conley Jr. 12.00 30.00
109 Jeff Green 4.00 10.00
110 Corey Brewer 4.00 10.00
111 Joakim Noah 5.00 12.00
112 Spencer Hawes 3.00 8.00
113 Acie Law 3.00 8.00
114 Julian Wright 3.00 8.00
115 Al Thornton 3.00 8.00
116 Rodney Stuckey 3.00 8.00
117 Sean Williams 3.00 8.00
118 Marco Belinelli 4.00 10.00
119 Javaris Crittenton 3.00 8.00
120 Jason Smith 3.00 8.00

2007-08 SP Rookie Edition 1997-98 SP Rookie Autographs

OVERALL AUTO ODDS 1:7
121 Kevin Durant 300.00 600.00
122 Al Horford 12.00 30.00
123 Mike Conley Jr. 12.00 30.00
124 Jeff Green 4.00 10.00
125 Corey Brewer 4.00 10.00
126 Joakim Noah 5.00 12.00
127 Spencer Hawes 3.00 8.00
128 Acie Law 3.00 8.00
129 Julian Wright 3.00 8.00
130 Al Thornton 3.00 8.00
131 Rodney Stuckey 3.00 8.00
132 Sean Williams 3.00 8.00
133 Marco Belinelli 4.00 10.00
134 Javaris Crittenton 3.00 8.00
135 Jason Smith 3.00 8.00
136 Daequan Cook 4.00 10.00
137 Jared Dudley 4.00 10.00
138 Wilson Chandler 4.00 10.00
140 Aaron Brooks 4.00 10.00
141 Alando Tucker 3.00 8.00
142 Carl Landry 3.00 8.00
143 Gabe Pruitt 3.00 8.00
146 Glen Davis 4.00 10.00
148 Aaron Gray 3.00 8.00
149 Taurean Green 3.00 8.00
144 D.J. Strawberry 3.00 8.00

2007-08 SP Rookie Edition 1998-99 SP Autographs

OVERALL AUTO ODDS 1:7
181 Carmelo Anthony 75.00 200.00
182 B.J. Armstrong 6.00 15.00
183 Larry Bird 125.00 300.00
184 Steve Novak 5.00 12.00
185 Kobe Bryant 2,000.00 4,000.00
186 Vince Carter 100.00 250.00
187 Tom Chambers 5.00 12.00
188 Baron Davis 6.00 15.00
189 Boris Diaw 5.00 12.00
190 Hilton Armstrong 5.00 12.00
191 Hal Greer 12.00 30.00
193 LeBron James 2,000.00 4,000.00
194 Antawn Jamison 6.00 15.00
195 Magic Johnson 125.00 300.00
196 Michael Jordan 3,000.00 6,000.00
197 Danny Manning 8.00 20.00
198 Tracy McGrady 100.00 250.00
199 Chris Mihm 5.00 12.00
200 Yao Ming 150.00 400.00
201 Steve Nash 75.00 200.00
202 Hakeem Olajuwon 40.00 100.00
203 Tony Parker 25.00 60.00
204 Paul Pierce 40.00 100.00
205 Quentin Richardson 5.00 12.00
206 Dennis Rodman 25.00 60.00
207 DeShawn Stevenson 5.00 12.00
208 John Stockton 75.00 200.00
209 Shelden Williams 5.00 12.00

2007-08 SP Rookie Edition Rookie Autographs

OVERALL AUTO ODDS 1:7
61 Kevin Durant 400.00 800.00
62 Al Horford 12.00 30.00
63 Mike Conley Jr. 12.00 30.00
64 Jeff Green 4.00 10.00
65 Corey Brewer 4.00 10.00
66 Joakim Noah 5.00 12.00
67 Spencer Hawes 3.00 8.00
68 Acie Law 3.00 8.00
69 Julian Wright 3.00 8.00
70 Al Thornton 3.00 8.00
71 Rodney Stuckey 3.00 8.00
72 Sean Williams 3.00 8.00
73 Marco Belinelli 4.00 10.00
74 Javaris Crittenton 3.00 8.00
75 Jason Smith 3.00 8.00
76 Daequan Cook 4.00 10.00
77 Jared Dudley 4.00 10.00
78 Wilson Chandler 4.00 10.00
79 Morris Almond 3.00 8.00
80 Aaron Brooks 4.00 10.00
81 Arron Afflalo 4.00 10.00
82 Alando Tucker 3.00 8.00
83 Carl Landry 3.00 8.00
84 Gabe Pruitt 3.00 8.00
85 Juan Navarro 4.00 10.00
87 Glen Davis 4.00 10.00
88 Jermareo Davidson 3.00 8.00
92 Chris Richard 3.00 8.00
93 Adam Haluska 3.00 8.00
94 D.J. Strawberry 3.00 8.00
96 Cheikh Samb 3.00 8.00
98 Aaron Gray 3.00 8.00
99 JamesOn Curry 3.00 8.00
100 Taurean Green 3.00 8.00
101 Demetris Nichols 3.00 8.00
103 Ramon Sessions 4.00 10.00
104 Coby Karl 3.00 8.00
105 D.J. Strawberry 3.00 8.00

2007-08 SP Rookie Edition SP Limited Jerseys

SPAB Andrea Bargnani 2.00 5.00
SPAH Al Horford 8.00 20.00
SPAJ Antawn Jamison 2.50 6.00
SPAL Acie Law 2.00 5.00
SPAS Amare Stoudemire 3.00 8.00
SPAT Al Thornton 2.00 5.00
SPBI Chauncey Billups 4.00 10.00
SPBO Chris Bosh 4.00 10.00
SPBW Brandan Wright 2.50 6.00
SPCA Carmelo Anthony 5.00 12.00
SPCB Corey Brewer 2.50 6.00
SPCP Chris Paul 6.00 15.00
SPDC Daequan Cook 2.50 6.00
SPDH Dwight Howard 4.00 10.00
SPDW Deron Williams 2.50 6.00
SPEO Emeka Okafor 2.50 6.00
SPGD Glen Davis 2.50 6.00
SPJC Javaris Crittenton 2.00 5.00
SPJD Jared Dudley 2.50 6.00
SPJG Jeff Green 2.50 6.00
SPJN Joakim Noah 3.00 8.00
SPJS Jason Smith 2.00 5.00
SPJW Julian Wright 2.00 5.00
SPKB Kobe Bryant 75.00 200.00
SPKD Kevin Durant 40.00 100.00
SPKG Kevin Garnett 8.00 20.00
SPLA LaMarcus Aldridge 3.00 8.00
SPLJ LeBron James 75.00 200.00
SPMC Mike Conley Jr. 8.00 20.00
SPNY Nick Young 3.00 8.00
SPRG Rudy Gay 2.50 6.00
SPRS Rodney Stuckey 2.50 6.00
SPSH Spencer Hawes 2.00 5.00
SPSO Shaquille O'Neal 12.00 30.00
SPSW Sean Williams 2.00 5.00
SPTD Tim Duncan 8.00 20.00
SPTM Tracy McGrady 5.00 12.00
SPTP Tayshaun Prince 3.00 8.00
SPTT Tyrus Thomas 2.00 5.00
SPTY Thaddeus Young 3.00 8.00
SPVC Vince Carter 6.00 15.00
SPYM Yao Ming 8.00 20.00

2007-08 SP Rookie Threads

COMP.SET w/o SP's (42) 12.00 30.00
43-48 RC PRINT RUN 199 SER.#'d SETS
49-60 AU RC PRINT RUN 199 SER.#'d SETS
61-83 AU RC PRINT RUN 799 SER.#'d SETS
1 Allen Iverson 1.25 3.00
2 Amare Stoudemire .50 1.25
3 Andre Iguodala .50 1.25
4 Andrea Bargnani .30 .75
5 Baron Davis .40 1.00
6 Ben Gordon .40 1.00
7 Brandon Roy .60 1.50
8 Carmelo Anthony .75 2.00
9 Chauncey Billups .60 1.50
10 Chris Bosh .60 1.50
11 Chris Paul 1.00 2.50
12 David Lee .30 .75
13 Deron Williams .40 1.00
14 Dirk Nowitzki 1.25 3.00
15 Dwight Howard .60 1.50
16 Dwyane Wade 1.00 2.50
17 Elton Brand .40 1.00
18 Emeka Okafor .40 1.00
19 Gilbert Arenas .50 1.25
20 Jason Kidd .75 2.00
21 Jermaine O'Neal .50 1.25
22 Kevin Garnett 1.25 3.00
23 Kirk Hinrich .50 1.25
24 Kobe Bryant 4.00 10.00
25 LaMarcus Aldridge .50 1.25
26 LeBron James 4.00 10.00
27 Luke Ridnour .40 1.00
28 Marvin Williams .30 .75
29 Michael Jordan 5.00 12.00
30 Michael Redd .40 1.00
31 Mike Bibby .50 1.25
32 Paul Pierce .75 2.00
33 Randy Foye .40 1.00
34 Rudy Gay .40 1.00
35 Shaquille O'Neal 2.00 5.00
36 Stephon Marbury .60 1.50
37 Steve Nash 1.00 2.50
38 Tim Duncan 1.25 3.00
39 Tony Parker .75 2.00
40 Tracy McGrady .75 2.00
41 Vince Carter 1.00 2.50
42 Yao Ming 1.25 3.00
43 Greg Oden RC 1.50 4.00
44 Yi Jianlian RC 2.00 5.00
45 Brandan Wright RC 1.25 3.00
46 Thaddeus Young RC 1.50 4.00
47 Nick Young RC 1.50 4.00
48 Juan Carlos Navarro RC 1.25 3.00
49 Kevin Durant JSY AU RC 800.00 1,500.00
50 Al Horford JSY AU RC 12.00 30.00
51 M.Conley Jr. JSY AU RC 12.00 30.00
52 Jeff Green JSY AU RC 4.00 10.00
53 Corey Brewer JSY AU RC 4.00 10.00
54 Joakim Noah JSY AU RC 5.00 12.00
55 Spencer Hawes JSY AU RC 3.00 8.00
56 Acie Law JSY AU RC 3.00 8.00
57 Julian Wright JSY AU RC 3.00 8.00
58 Al Thornton JSY AU RC 3.00 8.00
59 Rodney Stuckey JSY AU RC 3.00 8.00
60 Jason Smith JSY AU RC 3.00 8.00
61 Taurean Green JSY AU RC 1.50 4.00
62 Javaris Crittenton JSY AU RC 1.50 4.00
63 Sean Williams JSY AU RC 1.50 4.00
64 Daequan Cook JSY AU RC 2.00 5.00
65 Jared Dudley JSY AU RC 2.00 5.00
66 W.Chandler JSY AU RC 2.00 5.00
67 Morris Almond JSY AU RC 1.50 4.00
68 Aaron Brooks JSY AU RC 2.00 5.00
69 Arron Afflalo JSY AU RC 2.00 5.00
70 Alando Tucker JSY AU RC 1.50 4.00
71 Aaron Gray JSY AU RC 1.50 4.00
72 Carl Landry JSY AU RC 1.50 4.00
73 Gabe Pruitt JSY AU RC 1.50 4.00
74 Nick Fazekas JSY AU RC 1.50 4.00
75 Adam Haluska JSY AU RC 1.50 4.00
76 Glen Davis JSY AU RC 2.00 5.00
77 Josh McRoberts JSY AU RC 1.50 4.00
78 Herbert Hill JSY AU RC 1.50 4.00
79 Jermareo Davidson JSY AU RC 1.50 4.00
80 Chris Richard JSY AU RC 1.50 4.00
81 Dominic McGuire JSY AU RC 1.50 4.00
83 Demetris Nichols JSY AU RC 1.50 4.00
84 D.J. Strawberry JSY AU RC 1.50 4.00

2007-08 SP Rookie Threads Maximum Threads

PRINT RUN 25 SER.#'d SETS
MTAB Andrea Bargnani 4.00 10.00
MTAJ Antawn Jamison 5.00 12.00
MTAS Amare Stoudemire 6.00 15.00
MTBG Ben Gordon 5.00 12.00
MTBI Chauncey Billups 8.00 20.00
MTBO Carlos Boozer 5.00 12.00
MTBW Ben Wallace 8.00 20.00
MTCA Carmelo Anthony 10.00 25.00
MTCB Chris Bosh 8.00 20.00
MTCM Corey Maggette 5.00 12.00
MTDH Dwight Howard 8.00 20.00
MTDN Dirk Nowitzki 10.00 25.00
MTDR David Robinson 12.00 30.00
MTDW Deron Williams 5.00 12.00
MTEO Emeka Okafor 5.00 12.00
MTHO Hakeem Olajuwon 12.00 30.00
MTJE Al Jefferson 4.00 10.00
MTJK Jason Kidd 10.00 25.00
MTJO Jermaine O'Neal 6.00 15.00
MTJS John Stockton 12.00 30.00
MTKA Kareem Abdul-Jabbar 20.00 50.00
MTKB Kobe Bryant 75.00 200.00
MTKG Kevin Garnett 15.00 40.00
MTLA LaMarcus Aldridge 6.00 15.00
MTLB Larry Bird 25.00 60.00
MTLJ LeBron James 60.00 150.00
MTLO Lamar Odom 5.00 12.00
MTMC Marcus Camby 5.00 12.00
MTRA Ray Allen 10.00 25.00
MTRH Richard Hamilton 8.00 20.00
MTRL Rashard Lewis 5.00 12.00
MTRW Rasheed Wallace 8.00 20.00
MTSL Shaun Livingston 5.00 12.00
MTSO Shaquille O'Neal 25.00 60.00
MTSW Shelden Williams 4.00 10.00
MTTC Tom Chambers 6.00 15.00
MTTM Tracy McGrady 10.00 25.00
MTTP Tayshaun Prince 6.00 15.00
MTTS Thabo Sefolosha 4.00 10.00
MTTT Tyrus Thomas 4.00 10.00
MTVC Vince Carter 12.00 30.00
MTYM Yao Ming 15.00 40.00

2007-08 SP Rookie Threads Portraits Autographs

STATED COMBINED AUTO ODDS 1:1.2
POAJ Al Jefferson 5.00 12.00
POBG Ben Gordon 5.00 12.00
POCA Carmelo Anthony 15.00 30.00
PODR David Robinson 25.00 60.00
POHO Hakeem Olajuwon 15.00 40.00
POJE Julius Erving 25.00 60.00
POJO Michael Jordan 1,000.00 2,000.00
POKB Kobe Bryant 75.00 150.00
POLB Larry Bird 40.00 80.00
POLJ LeBron James 300.00 600.00
POMB Mike Bibby 5.00 12.00
POMJ Magic Johnson 30.00 80.00
POSN Steve Nash 20.00 50.00
POTP Tayshaun Prince 6.00 15.00
POVC Vince Carter 10.00 25.00

2007-08 SP Rookie Threads Rookie Threads

ONE MEMORABILIA CARD PER PACK
*PARALLEL: .5X TO 1.25X BASE HI
PRINT RUN 199 SER.#'d SETS
RTAA Arron Afflalo 2.00 5.00
RTAB Aaron Brooks 2.00 5.00
RTAG Aaron Gray 1.50 4.00
RTAH Al Horford 6.00 15.00
RTAL Acie Law 1.50 4.00
RTAT Al Thornton 1.50 4.00
RTBW Brandan Wright 2.00 5.00
RTCB Corey Brewer 2.00 5.00
RTCL Carl Landry 1.50 4.00
RTCR Chris Richard 1.50 4.00
RTDA Jermareo Davidson 1.50 4.00
RTDC Daequan Cook 2.00 5.00
RTDM Dominic McGuire 1.50 4.00
RTDN Demetris Nichols 1.50 4.00
RTDS D.J. Strawberry 1.50 4.00
RTGD Glen Davis 2.00 5.00
RTGP Gabe Pruitt 1.50 4.00
RTHA Adam Haluska 1.50 4.00
RTHH Herbert Hill 1.50 4.00
RTJC Javaris Crittenton 1.50 4.00
RTJD Jared Dudley 2.00 5.00
RTJG Jeff Green 2.00 5.00
RTJM Josh McRoberts 1.50 4.00
RTJN Joakim Noah 2.50 6.00
RTJS Jason Smith 1.50 4.00
RTJW Julian Wright 1.50 4.00
RTKD Kevin Durant 20.00 50.00
RTMA Morris Almond 1.50 4.00
RTMC Mike Conley Jr. 6.00 15.00
RTNF Nick Fazekas 1.50 4.00
RTNY Nick Young 2.50 6.00
RTRS Rodney Stuckey 1.50 4.00
RTSH Spencer Hawes 1.50 4.00
RTSW Sean Williams 1.50 4.00
RTTG Taurean Green 1.50 4.00
RTTU Alando Tucker 1.50 4.00
RTTY Thaddeus Young 2.50 6.00
RTWC Wilson Chandler 2.00 5.00

2007-08 SP Rookie Threads Rookie Threads Patch

*PATCH: .6X TO 1.5X BASE HI
PATCH PRINT RUN 50 SER.#'d SETS
RTKD Kevin Durant 50.00 120.00

2007-08 SP Rookie Threads Rookie Threads Dual

ONE MEMORABILIA CARD PER PACK
*PARALLEL: .5X TO 1.25X BASE HI
PARALLEL PRINT RUN 99 SER.#'d SETS
AS M.Almond/R.Stuckey 3.00 8.00
BR C.Brewer/C.Richard 3.00 8.00
CC M.Conley/D.Cook 3.00 8.00
CM J.Crittenton/D.McGuire 3.00 8.00
DD J.Dudley/J.Davidson 3.00 8.00
DG K.Durant/J.Green 40.00 100.00
DH K.Durant/A.Horford 6.00 15.00
DR C.Richard/G.Davis 3.00 8.00
DW S.Williams/J.Dudley 3.00 8.00
HB A.Horford/C.Brewer 3.00 8.00
HL A.Horford/A.Law 3.00 8.00
HS H.Hill/J.Smith 3.00 8.00
LB A.Brooks/C.Landry 3.00 8.00
MD G.Davis/J.McRoberts 3.00 8.00
NB C.Brewer/J.Noah 3.00 8.00
NC W.Chandler/D.Nichols 3.00 8.00
SA A.Afflalo/R.Stuckey 3.00 8.00
SH S.Hawes/R.Stuckey 3.00 8.00
TS A.Tucker/D.Strawberry 3.00 8.00
TW J.Wright/A.Thornton 3.00 8.00
WW B.Wright/J.Wright 3.00 8.00
WY B.Wright/T.Young 3.00 8.00
YC T.Young/J.Crittenton 3.00 8.00
YP N.Young/G.Pruitt 3.00 8.00
YY N.Young/T.Young 3.00 8.00

2007-08 SP Rookie Threads Rookie Threads Patch Dual

PRINT RUN 25 SER.#'d SETS
AS M.Almond/R.Stuckey 4.00 10.00
BR C.Brewer/C.Richard 5.00 12.00
CC D.Cook/M.Conley 6.00 15.00
DG K.Durant/J.Green 75.00 200.00
DH K.Durant/A.Horford 75.00 200.00
HB A.Horford/C.Brewer 6.00 15.00
HL A.Horford/A.Law 6.00 15.00
LB C.Landry/A.Brooks 5.00 12.00
MD J.McRoberts/G.Davis 5.00 12.00
NB J.Noah/C.Brewer 6.00 15.00
SA A.Afflalo/R.Stuckey 5.00 12.00
SH R.Stuckey/S.Hawes 4.00 10.00
TS A.Tucker/D.Strawberry 4.00 10.00
TW A.Thornton/J.Wright 4.00 10.00
WW B.Wright/J.Wright 5.00 12.00
YT T.Young/B.Wright 6.00 15.00
YC T.Young/J.Crittenton 6.00 15.00
YP N.Young/G.Pruitt 6.00 15.00
YY T.Young/N.Young 6.00 15.00

2007-08 SP Rookie Threads Rookie Threads Triple

MEMORABILIA ODDS ON PER PACK
*PARALLEL: .5X TO 1.25X BASE HI
PARALLEL PRINT RUN 50 SER.#'d SETS
ACB Afflalo/Brooks/Cook 5.00 12.00
DCW Williams/Chandler/Davis 4.00 10.00
DGW Durant/Green/Wright 10.00 25.00
DHC Horford/Conley/Durant 10.00 25.00
DYW Durant/Young/Wright 10.00 25.00
GSP Pruitt/Green/Strawberry 4.00 10.00
GYC Gray/Young/Crittenton 4.00 10.00
NDS Strawberry/Davis/Noah 5.00 12.00
NGR Richard/Green/Noah 5.00 12.00
NHB Noah/Brewer/Horford 5.00 12.00
PLC Pruitt/Conley/Law 4.00 10.00
SHW Smith/Williams/Hawes 4.00 10.00
TCB Thornton/Cook/Brewer 4.00 10.00
TLC Tucker/Landry/Conley 4.00 10.00
TYW Young/Wright/Thornton 4.00 10.00
YCS Young/Crittenton/Stuckey 4.00 10.00
YYW Young/Wright/Young 4.00 10.00

2007-08 SP Rookie Threads Rookie Threads Patch Triple

PRINT RUN 15 SER.#'d SETS
ACB Afflalo/Cook/Brooks 8.00 20.00
DCW Davis/Chandler/Williams 8.00 20.00
DGW Durant/Green/Wright 50.00 100.00
DHC Durant/Horford/Conley 50.00 100.00
GSP Pruitt/Green/Strawberry 8.00 20.00
GYC Gray/Young/Crittenton 8.00 20.00
NDS Noah/Davis/Strawberry 8.00 20.00
NGR Noah/Green/Richard 8.00 20.00
NHB Noah/Horford/Brewer 12.00 30.00
PLC Pruitt/Law/Conley 8.00 20.00
SHW Smith/Hawes/Williams 8.00 20.00
TCB Thornton/Cook/Brewer 8.00 20.00
TLC Tucker/Landry/Conley 8.00 20.00
TYW Thornton/Young/Wright 8.00 20.00
YCS Young/Crittenton/Stuckey 8.00 20.00
YYW Young/Young/Wright 8.00 20.00

2007-08 SP Rookie Threads Rookie Threads Patch Autographs

PRINT RUN 25 SER.#'d SETS
RTAA Arron Afflalo 8.00 20.00
RTAB Aaron Brooks 8.00 20.00
RTAG Aaron Gray 6.00 15.00
RTAH Al Horford 25.00 60.00
RTAL Acie Law 6.00 15.00
RTAT Al Thornton 6.00 15.00
RTCB Corey Brewer 8.00 20.00
RTCL Carl Landry 6.00 15.00
RTCR Chris Richard 6.00 15.00
RTDA Jermareo Davidson 6.00 15.00
RTDC Daequan Cook 8.00 20.00
RTDM Dominic McGuire 6.00 15.00
RTDN Demetris Nichols 6.00 15.00
RTDS D.J. Strawberry 6.00 15.00
RTGD Glen Davis 8.00 20.00
RTGP Gabe Pruitt 6.00 15.00
RTHA Adam Haluska 6.00 15.00
RTHH Herbert Hill 6.00 15.00
RTJC Javaris Crittenton 6.00 15.00
RTJD Jared Dudley 8.00 20.00
RTJG Jeff Green 8.00 20.00
RTJM Josh McRoberts 6.00 15.00
RTJN Joakim Noah 10.00 25.00
RTJS Jason Smith 6.00 15.00
RTJW Julian Wright 6.00 15.00
RTKD Kevin Durant 400.00 800.00
RTMA Morris Almond 6.00 15.00
RTMC Mike Conley Jr. 25.00 60.00
RTNF Nick Fazekas 6.00 15.00
RTNY Nick Young 6.00 15.00
RTRS Rodney Stuckey 6.00 15.00
RTSH Spencer Hawes 6.00 15.00
RTSW Sean Williams 6.00 15.00
RTTG Taurean Green 6.00 15.00
RTTU Alando Tucker 6.00 15.00
RTWC Wilson Chandler 8.00 20.00

2007-08 SP Rookie Threads Rookie Threads Patch Dual Autographs

PRINT RUN 15 SER.#'d SETS
AS M.Almond/R.Stuckey 12.00 30.00
BR C.Brewer/C.Richard 12.00 30.00
CC D.Cook/M.Conley 15.00 40.00
CM J.Crittenton/D.McGuire 12.00 30.00
DD J.Dudley/J.Davidson 12.00 30.00
DH K.Durant/A.Horford 400.00 800.00
DR G.Davis/C.Richard 12.00 30.00
DW J.Dudley/S.Williams 12.00 30.00
HB A.Horford/C.Brewer 15.00 40.00
HL A.Horford/A.Law 15.00 40.00
HS J.Smith/H.Hill 12.00 30.00
LB C.Landry/A.Brooks 12.00 30.00
MD J.McRoberts/G.Davis 12.00 30.00
NB J.Noah/C.Brewer 12.00 30.00
NC D.Nichols/W.Chandler 12.00 30.00
SA A.Affalo/R.Stuckey 12.00 30.00
SH R.Stuckey/S.Hawes 12.00 30.00
TS A.Tucker/D.Strawberry 12.00 30.00
TW A.Thornton/J.Wright 12.00 30.00

2007-08 SP Rookie Threads Rookies Gold

*43-48 GOLD: .75X TO 2X BASE HI
*49-60 GOLD: SAME VALUE AS BASE
*61-84 GOLD: .75X TO 2X BASE HI
GOLD PRINT RUN 50 SER.#'d SETS
49 Kevin Durant JSY AU 3,000.00 6,000.00

2007-08 SP Rookie Threads Scripted in Time

COMBINED AUTO ODDS 1:1.2
AJ Al Jefferson 4.00 10.00
BB Bruce Bowen 4.00 10.00
BD Baron Davis 6.00 15.00
CP Chris Paul 100.00 250.00
DG Daniel Gibson 5.00 12.00
DH Dwight Howard 20.00 40.00
DL David Lee 4.00 10.00
EO Emeka Okafor 4.00 10.00
GR Danny Granger 5.00 12.00
JO Jermaine O'Neal 4.00 10.00
KH Kirk Hinrich 4.00 10.00
KK Kyle Korver 4.00 10.00
KL Kyle Lowry 4.00 10.00
LA LaMarcus Aldridge 6.00 15.00
LB Leandro Barbosa 4.00 10.00
LH Larry Hughes 4.00 10.00
LP Leon Powe 5.00 12.00
PO Patrick O'Bryant 4.00 10.00
PP Paul Pierce 10.00 25.00
RC Rodney Carney 4.00 10.00
RR Rajon Rondo 8.00 20.00
SB Shannon Brown 4.00 10.00
TF T.J. Ford 4.00 10.00
TM Tracy McGrady 10.00 25.00
TT Tyrus Thomas 4.00 10.00
YM Yao Ming 15.00 30.00

2007-08 SP Rookie Threads Signing Day

COMBINED AUTO ODDS 1:1.2
SDAA Arron Afflalo 2.50 6.00
SDAB Aaron Brooks 2.50 6.00
SDAG Aaron Gray 2.00 5.00
SDAH Al Horford 6.00 15.00
SDAL Acie Law 2.00 5.00
SDAT Al Thornton 2.00 5.00
SDCB Corey Brewer 2.50 6.00
SDCK Coby Karl 2.00 5.00
SDCL Carl Landry 2.00 5.00
SDCR Chris Richard 2.00 5.00
SDDA Jermareo Davidson 2.00 5.00
SDDC Daequan Cook 2.50 6.00
SDDN Demetris Nichols 2.00 5.00
SDDS D.J. Strawberry 2.00 5.00
SDGD Glen Davis 2.50 6.00
SDGP Gabe Pruitt 2.00 5.00
SDHA Adam Haluska 2.00 5.00
SDHH Herbert Hill 2.00 5.00
SDJC Javaris Crittenton 2.00 5.00
SDJD Jared Dudley 2.50 6.00
SDJG Jeff Green 2.50 6.00
SDJM Josh McRoberts 2.00 5.00
SDJN Joakim Noah 3.00 8.00
SDJS Jason Smith 2.00 5.00
SDJW Julian Wright 2.00 5.00
SDKD Kevin Durant 150.00 300.00
SDLS Luis Scola 3.00 8.00
SDMA Morris Almond 2.00 5.00
SDMB Marco Belinelli 2.50 6.00
SDMC Mike Conley Jr. 8.00 20.00
SDNF Nick Fazekas 2.00 5.00
SDRS Ramon Sessions 2.50 6.00
SDRS Rodney Stuckey 2.00 5.00
SDSH Spencer Hawes 2.00 5.00
SDSW Sean Williams 2.00 5.00
SDTG Taurean Green 2.00 5.00
SDTU Alando Tucker 2.00 5.00
SDWC Wilson Chandler 2.50 6.00

2007-08 SP Rookie Threads SP Marks Dual

PRINT RUN 50 SER.#'d SETS
MDAR L.Aldridge/B.Roy 20.00 40.00
MDAS A.Affalo/R.Stuckey 10.00 25.00
MDCJ V.Carter/A.Jamison 20.00 40.00
MDCM V.Carter/T.McGrady 25.00 60.00
MDDA A.Mourning/D.Cook 20.00 40.00
MDDB B.Davis/M.Belinelli 15.00 40.00
MDDG K.Durant/J.Green 125.00 250.00
MDDH B.Davis/A.Harrington 10.00 25.00
MDGC R.Gay/M.Conley 8.00 20.00
MDHB S.Hawes/M.Bibby 8.00 20.00
MDHD H.Grant/D.Howard 10.00 25.00
MDHG K.Hinrich/B.Gordon 12.50 30.00
MDJP T.Prince/R.Jefferson 8.00 20.00
MDKA S.Kerr/B.Armstrong 20.00 40.00
MDKP J.Kidd/T.Parker 20.00 50.00
MDLG D.Lee/R.Gay 8.00 20.00
MDMW Y.Ming/B.Walton 20.00 40.00
MDOM Y.Ming/H.Olajuwon 30.00 60.00
MDPD P.Pierce/A.Dantley/26 20.00 40.00
MDPS R.Stuckey/T.Prince 12.00 30.00
MDPW C.Paul/D.Williams 50.00 120.00
MDRG T.Green/B.Roy 10.00 25.00
MDRR D.Robinson/D.Rodman 40.00 80.00
MDTM A.Thornton/D.Manning 20.00 40.00
MDTN T.Thomas/J.Noah 15.00 30.00
MDWH A.Horford/D.Wilkins 25.00 50.00

2007-08 SP Rookie Threads SP Marks Triple

PRINT RUN 25 SER.#'d SETS
ARM Aldridge/Roy/McRoberts 12.00 30.00
CAW Chandler/Armstrong/Wright 10.00 25.00
CBP Carney/Boone/Powe 10.00 25.00
CRA Collins/Rondo/Afflalo 10.00 25.00
FFR Foye/Rondo/Felton 20.00 40.00
GGP Garcia/Gibson/Pruitt 10.00 25.00
GIS Gordon/Iguodala/Stuckey 10.00 25.00
JBJ Bryant/James/Jordan 40,000.00 80,000.00
JFB Foye/Brewer/Jefferson 15.00 30.00
JGH Gordon/Haluska/Jamison 20.00 40.00
JMN Jamison/May/Noel 10.00 25.00
MRC Mourning/Riley/Cook 50.00 100.00
OMM Mourning/Ming/Olajuwon 50.00 100.00
PAJ Anthony/Jefferson/Prince 20.00 50.00
PDB Peterson/Brown/Davis 10.00 25.00
PJH Jamison/Harrington/Pierce 12.00 30.00
PRM Rondo/Morris/Prince 12.00 30.00

2007-08 SP Rookie Threads SP Threads

SPAG Maurice Ager 2.50 6.00
SPAI Andre Iguodala 4.00 10.00
SPAK Andrei Kirilenko 3.00 8.00
SPAS Amare Stoudemire 4.00 10.00
SPBB Bruce Bowen 2.50 6.00
SPBL Bill Laimbeer 3.00 8.00
SPBW Ben Wallace 5.00 12.00
SPCA Carmelo Anthony 6.00 15.00
SPCD Clyde Drexler 6.00 15.00
SPCF Channing Frye 2.50 6.00
SPCK Chris Kaman 3.00 8.00
SPCM Corey Maggette 3.00 8.00
SPCP Chris Paul 8.00 20.00
SPDG Drew Gooden 3.00 8.00
SPDH Dwight Howard 5.00 12.00
SPDM Donyell Marshall 2.50 6.00
SPDN Dirk Nowitzki 10.00 25.00
SPDR David Robinson 8.00 20.00
SPDW Deron Williams 3.00 8.00
SPEB Elton Brand 3.00 8.00
SPEL Sean Elliott 3.00 8.00
SPEO Emeka Okafor 3.00 8.00
SPGA Gilbert Arenas 4.00 10.00
SPGH Grant Hill 6.00 15.00
SPIV Allen Iverson 10.00 25.00
SPJA LeBron James 15.00 40.00
SPJC Josh Childress 2.50 6.00
SPJH Josh Howard 3.00 8.00
SPJK Jason Kidd 6.00 15.00
SPJO Jermaine O'Neal 4.00 10.00
SPJT Jamaal Tinsley 2.50 6.00
SPKB Kobe Bryant 125.00 300.00
SPKG Kevin Garnett 10.00 25.00
SPLA LaMarcus Aldridge 4.00 10.00
SPLH Larry Hughes 3.00 8.00
SPLJ LeBron James 15.00 40.00
SPLO Lamar Odom 3.00 8.00
SPMA Desmond Mason 2.50 6.00
SPMB Mike Bibby 4.00 10.00
SPMJ Michael Jordan 40.00 100.00
SPMW Martell Webster 3.00 8.00
SPN Nene 3.00 8.00
SPPD Paul Davis 2.50 6.00
SPPR Tayshaun Prince 4.00 10.00
SPRH Richard Hamilton 5.00 12.00
SPRL Rashard Lewis 3.00 8.00
SPRO Dennis Rodman 10.00 25.00
SPRW Rasheed Wallace 5.00 12.00
SPSE Sean May 2.50 6.00
SPSL Shaun Livingston 3.00 8.00
SPSM Shawn Marion 4.00 10.00
SPSN Steve Nash 8.00 20.00
SPSO Shaquille O'Neal 15.00 40.00
SPST Stephon Marbury 5.00 12.00
SPTD Tim Duncan 10.00 25.00
SPTP Tony Parker 6.00 15.00
SPVC Vince Carter 8.00 20.00
SPWS Wally Szczerbiak 3.00 8.00
SPYM Yao Ming 10.00 25.00
SPZI Zydrunas Ilgauskas 3.00 8.00

2007-08 SP Rookie Threads SP Threads Patch

*PATCH: .75X TO 2X BASE HI
ONE MEMORABILIA CARD PER PACK
SPJA LeBron James 60.00 150.00
SPKB Kobe Bryant 300.00 600.00
SPLJ LeBron James 60.00 150.00
SPMJ Michael Jordan 125.00 300.00

2008-09 SP Rookie Threads

COMP.SET w/o SPs (60) 20.00 50.00
61-66 RC PRINT RUN 99 SER.#'d SETS
67-94 JSY AU RC PRINT RUN 599 SETS
95-100 JSY AU RC PRINT RUN 399 SETS
1 Antawn Jamison .50 1.25
2 Gilbert Arenas .60 1.50
3 Carlos Boozer .50 1.25
4 Deron Williams .50 1.25
5 Jermaine O'Neal .60 1.50
6 Chris Bosh .75 2.00
7 Jeff Green .75 2.00
8 Kevin Durant 2.50 6.00
9 Tim Duncan 1.50 4.00
10 Tony Parker .75 2.00
11 Beno Udrih .40 1.00
12 Kevin Martin .50 1.25
13 Brandon Roy .50 1.25
14 Greg Oden .40 1.00
15 Amare Stoudemire .60 1.50
16 Steve Nash 1.25 3.00
17 Thaddeus Young .50 1.25
18 Andre Iguodala .50 1.25
19 Hedo Turkoglu .50 1.25
20 Dwight Howard .75 2.00
21 Jamal Crawford .60 1.50
22 Stephon Marbury .60 1.50
23 David West .50 1.25
24 Chris Paul 1.25 3.00
25 Yi Jianlian .75 2.00
26 Vince Carter 1.25 3.00
27 Al Jefferson .40 1.00
28 Corey Brewer .50 1.25
29 Richard Jefferson .50 1.25
30 Michael Redd .50 1.25
31 Dwyane Wade 1.25 3.00
32 Shawn Marion .60 1.50
33 Mike Conley Jr. .50 1.25
34 Rudy Gay .60 1.50
35 Pau Gasol .75 2.00
36 Kobe Bryant 5.00 12.00
37 Al Thornton .40 1.00
38 Baron Davis .60 1.50
39 Danny Granger .50 1.25
40 T.J. Ford .50 1.25
41 Tracy McGrady 1.00 2.50
42 Yao Ming 1.50 4.00
43 Stephen Jackson .50 1.25
44 Monta Ellis .50 1.25
45 Richard Hamilton .60 1.50
46 Chauncey Billups .75 2.00
47 Allen Iverson 1.25 3.00
48 Carmelo Anthony .75 2.00
49 Jason Kidd 1.00 2.50
50 Dirk Nowitzki 1.50 4.00
51 LeBron James 5.00 12.00
52 Ben Wallace .75 2.00
53 Ben Gordon .50 1.25
54 Joakim Noah .40 1.00
55 Gerald Wallace .50 1.25
56 Jason Richardson .60 1.50
57 Kevin Garnett 1.50 4.00
58 Paul Pierce 1.00 2.50
59 Al Horford .60 1.50
60 Joe Johnson .60 1.50
61 James Gist RC 1.25 3.00
62 Danilo Gallinari RC 3.00 8.00
63 Malik Hairston RC 1.25 3.00
64 Mike Taylor RC 1.25 3.00
65 Joe Crawford RC 1.25 3.00
66 Trent Plaisted RC 1.25 3.00
67 R. Westbrook JSY AU RC 200.00 500.00
68 Sonny Weems JSY AU RC 3.00 8.00
69 Joe Alexander JSY AU RC 3.00 8.00
70 D.J. Augustin JSY AU RC 5.00 12.00
71 Brook Lopez JSY AU RC 6.00 15.00
72 Jason Thompson JSY AU RC 3.00 8.00
73 Brandon Rush JSY AU RC 3.00 8.00
74 Anthony Randolph JSY AU RC 3.00 8.00
75 Robin Lopez JSY AU RC 4.00 10.00
76 Marreese Speights JSY AU RC 4.00 10.00
77 Roy Hibbert JSY AU RC 4.00 10.00
78 JaVale McGee JSY AU RC 5.00 12.00
79 J.J. Hickson JSY AU RC 3.00 8.00
80 Kyle Weaver JSY AU RC 3.00 8.00
81 Ryan Anderson JSY AU RC 4.00 10.00
82 Courtney Lee JSY AU RC 4.00 10.00
83 Kosta Koufos JSY AU RC 3.00 8.00
84 George Hill JSY AU RC 5.00 12.00
85 Darrell Arthur JSY AU RC 4.00 10.00
86 Donte Greene JSY AU RC 3.00 8.00
87 D.J. White JSY AU RC 3.00 8.00
88 J.R. Giddens JSY AU RC 3.00 8.00
89 Walter Sharpe JSY AU RC 3.00 8.00
90 Joey Dorsey JSY AU RC 3.00 8.00
91 Mario Chalmers JSY AU RC 5.00 12.00
92 DeAndre Jordan JSY AU RC 6.00 15.00
93 C.Douglas-Roberts JSY AU RC 3.00 8.00
94 Patrick Ewing Jr. JSY AU RC 3.00 8.00
95 Derrick Rose JSY AU RC 75.00 200.00
96 Michael Beasley JSY AU RC 6.00 15.00
97 O.J. Mayo JSY AU RC 8.00 20.00
98 Kevin Love JSY AU RC 12.00 30.00
99 Eric Gordon JSY AU RC 10.00 25.00
100 Jerryd Bayless JSY AU RC 5.00 12.00

2008-09 SP Rookie Threads Authorization

APPROXIMATE ODDS 1:12
AUAB Andrew Bynum 2.50 6.00
AUAH Al Horford 4.00 10.00
AUBR Bill Russell 400.00 800.00
AUBW Bill Walton 12.00 30.00
AUCB Chauncey Billups 5.00 12.00
AUCP Chris Paul 25.00 60.00
AUCW Chris Wilcox 2.50 6.00
AUDH Dwight Howard 10.00 25.00
AUJA LeBron James 1,000.00 2,000.00
AUJM Jamario Moon 2.50 6.00
AUJP John Paxson 3.00 8.00
AUKA Kareem Abdul-Jabbar 50.00 120.00
AUKB Kobe Bryant 400.00 800.00
AUKD Kevin Durant 75.00 200.00
AULJ Larry Johnson 25.00 60.00
AULS Luis Scola 3.00 8.00
AUMJ Michael Jordan 500.00 1,000.00
AUMW Maurice Williams 3.00 8.00
AURG Rudy Gay 4.00 10.00
AUTC Tom Chambers 3.00 8.00
AUWF Walt Frazier 4.00 10.00

2008-09 SP Rookie Threads Letters of Introduction

CARDS #'d TO LETTERS IN FULL NAME
LICD Chris Douglas-Roberts/19* 8.00 20.00
LIJB Jerryd Bayless/13* 10.00 25.00
LIMB Michael Beasley/14* 12.00 30.00
LIMS Marreese Speights/16* 10.00 25.00

2008-09 SP Rookie Threads Rookie Threads

APPROXIMATE ODDS 1:3
*PARALLEL 125: .4X TO 1X BASE HI
PARALLEL PRINT RUN 125 SER.#'d SETS
*PATCH: 1X TO 2.5X HI COLUMN
PATCH PRINT RUN 35 SER.#'d SETS
RTAR Anthony Randolph 1.25 3.00
RTBR Brandon Rush 1.25 3.00
RTCL Courtney Lee 1.50 4.00
RTDA D.J. Augustin 2.00 5.00
RTDR Derrick Rose 8.00 20.00
RTEG Eric Gordon 3.00 8.00
RTGH George Hill 2.00 5.00
RTGR Donte Greene 1.25 3.00
RTJA Joe Alexander 1.25 3.00
RTJB Jerryd Bayless 1.50 4.00
RTJD Joey Dorsey 1.25 3.00
RTJG J.R. Giddens 1.25 3.00
RTJH J.J. Hickson 1.25 3.00
RTJT Jason Thompson 1.25 3.00
RTKL Kevin Love 4.00 10.00
RTMB Michael Beasley 2.00 5.00
RTMC Mario Chalmers 2.00 5.00
RTMS Marreese Speights 1.50 4.00
RTOM O.J. Mayo 1.50 4.00
RTSW Sonny Weems 1.25 3.00

2008-09 SP Rookie Threads Rookie Threads Dual

APPROXIMATE ODDS 1:6
RTDAB D.Augustin/J.Bayless 2.50 6.00
RTDAL K.Love/J.Alexander 3.00 8.00
RTDBC M.Beasley/M.Chalmers 2.50 6.00
RTDBH J.Bayless/G.Hill 2.50 6.00
RTDBR D.Rose/M.Beasley 3.00 8.00
RTDDD J.Dorsey/C.Douglas-Roberts 2.50 6.00
RTDGA E.Gordon/J.Alexander 2.50 6.00
RTDGD D.Greene/J.Dorsey 2.50 6.00
RTDGW E.Gordon/D.White 2.50 6.00
RTDLL B.Lopez/R.Lopez 2.50 6.00
RTDLW R.Westbrook/K.Love 8.00 20.00
RTDMR O.Mayo/D.Rose 3.00 8.00
RTDRC B.Rush/M.Chalmers 2.50 6.00
RTDWH S.Weems/G.Hill 2.50 6.00

2008-09 SP Rookie Threads Rookie Threads Dual Parallel

*PARALLEL: .5X TO 1.25X BASE HI
PRINT RUN 50 SER.#'d SETS
RTDAM O.Mayo/D.Arthur 3.00 8.00
RTDAW D.Augustin/K.Weaver 3.00 8.00
RTDDA R.Anderson/Douglas-Roberts 3.00 8.00
RTDGJ E.Gordon/D.Jordan 5.00 12.00
RTDHM R.Hibbert/J.McGee 3.00 8.00
RTDRL B.Rush/C.Lee 3.00 8.00
RTDTE J.Thompson/Ewing Jr. 3.00 8.00
RTDTS J.Thompson/Speights 3.00 8.00
RTDWW R.Westbrook/D.White 5.00 12.00

2008-09 SP Rookie Threads Rookie Threads Dual Patch

*PATCH: 1X TO 2.5X BASE HI
PRINT RUN 25 SER.#'d SETS
RTDAM O.Mayo/D.Arthur 6.00 15.00
RTDAW D.Augustin/K.Weaver 6.00 15.00
RTDDA R.Anderson/Douglas-Roberts 6.00 15.00
RTDGJ E.Gordon/D.Jordan 10.00 25.00
RTDHM R.Hibbert/J.McGee 6.00 15.00
RTDRL B.Rush/C.Lee 6.00 15.00
RTDTE J.Thompson/Ewing Jr. 6.00 15.00
RTDTS J.Thompson/Speights 6.00 15.00
RTDWW R.Westbrook/D.White 10.00 25.00

2008-09 SP Rookie Threads Rookie Threads Triple

APPROXIMATE ODDS 1:6
*PARALLEL: .75X TO 2X BASE HI
PARALLEL PRINT RUN 15 SER.#'d SETS
*PATCH: 1.25X TO 3X BASE HI
PATCH PRINT RUN 15 SER.#'d SETS
RTTAGH Hill/Arthur/Greene 2.50 6.00
RTTAGW Westbrook/Gordon/Augustin 8.00 20.00
RTTALA Lopez/Alexander/Augustin 2.50 6.00
RTTARW Rose/Westbrook/Augustin 8.00 20.00
RTTBLA Beasley/Love/Alexander 3.00 8.00
RTTDWE Weems/Douglas-Roberts/Ewing Jr. 2.50 6.00
RTTGWH Weems/Hill/Greene 2.50 6.00
RTTHGS Giddens/Sharpe/Hickson 2.50 6.00
RTTMHH Hickson/Hibbert/McGee 2.50 6.00
RTTJLK Jordan/Koufos/Lopez 3.00 8.00
RTTJWC Chalmers/Jordan/Weaver 3.00 8.00
RTTLAK Anderson/Lee/Koufos 2.50 6.00
RTTLDA Lopez/Anderson/Douglas-Roberts 2.50 6.00
RTTMBR Rose/Beasley/Mayo 3.00 8.00
RTTMGB Mayo/Gordon/Bayless 2.50 6.00
RTTMRG Rose/Mayo/Gordon 3.00 8.00
RTTRAC Rush/Arthur/Chalmers 2.50 6.00
RTTRDD Rose/Dorsey/Douglas-Roberts 3.00 8.00
RTTRLS Speights/Randolph/Lopez 2.50 6.00
RTTRSC Chalmers/Speights/Rush 2.50 6.00
RTTRTB Rush/Bayless/Thompson 2.50 6.00
RTTWES Ewing Jr./Sharpe/White 2.50 6.00
RTTWGD White/Giddens/Dorsey 2.50 6.00

2008-09 SP Rookie Threads Rookies Parallel

PRINT RUNS LISTED IN CHECKLIST
61 James Gist/59 2.00 5.00
63 Malik Hairston/47 2.00 5.00
64 Mike Taylor/55 2.00 5.00
65 Joe Crawford/58 2.00 5.00
66 Trent Plaisted/37 2.00 5.00
68 Sonny Weems JSY AU/39 6.00 15.00
73 Brandon Rush JSY AU/13 6.00 15.00
74 A. Randolph JSY AU/14 6.00 15.00
75 Robin Lopez JSY AU/15 8.00 20.00
76 M. Speights JSY AU/16 8.00 20.00
77 Roy Hibbert JSY AU/17 8.00 20.00
78 Javale McGee JSY AU/18 10.00 25.00
79 J.J. Hickson JSY AU/19 6.00 15.00
80 Kyle Weaver JSY AU/38 6.00 15.00
81 Ryan Anderson JSY AU/21 8.00 20.00
82 Courtney Lee JSY AU/22 8.00 20.00
83 Kosta Koufos JSY AU/23 6.00 15.00
84 George Hill JSY AU/26 10.00 25.00
85 Darrell Arthur JSY AU/27 8.00 20.00
86 Donte Greene JSY AU/28 6.00 15.00
87 D.J. White JSY AU/29 6.00 15.00
88 J.R. Giddens JSY AU/30 6.00 15.00
89 Walter Sharpe JSY AU/32 6.00 15.00
90 Joey Dorsey JSY AU/33 6.00 15.00
91 Mario Chalmers JSY AU/34 10.00 25.00
92 DeAndre Jordan JSY AU/35 12.00 30.00
93 Chris Douglas-Roberts JSY AU/40 6.00 15.00
94 Patrick Ewing Jr. JSY AU/43 6.00 15.00

2008-09 SP Rookie Threads Scripted in Time

SITAB Andrew Bynum 2.50 6.00
SITAJ Al Jefferson 2.50 6.00
SITBB Bruce Bowen 3.00 8.00
SITBD Baron Davis 4.00 10.00
SITBG Ben Gordon 3.00 8.00
SITDF Derek Fisher 3.00 8.00
SITDH Dwight Howard 5.00 12.00
SITEO Emeka Okafor 2.50 6.00
SITGR Danny Granger 3.00 8.00
SITHA Hilton Armstrong 2.50 6.00
SITHE Luther Head 2.50 6.00
SITJG Jeff Green 3.00 8.00
SITJS Jason Smith 2.50 6.00
SITKA Kelenna Azubuike 2.50 6.00
SITKL Kyle Lowry 4.00 10.00
SITLA LaMarcus Aldridge 6.00 15.00
SITLH Larry Hughes 3.00 8.00
SITLP Leon Powe 2.50 6.00
SITPM Paul Millsap 3.00 8.00
SITPP Paul Pierce 15.00 40.00
SITRA Ray Allen 12.00 30.00
SITRC Rodney Carney 2.50 6.00
SITRJ Richard Jefferson 3.00 8.00
SITRS Rodney Stuckey 2.50 6.00
SITSB Shane Battier 3.00 8.00
SITTF T.J. Ford 2.50 6.00
SITTM Tracy McGrady 12.00 30.00
SITTP Tayshaun Prince 4.00 10.00
SITTT Tyrus Thomas 2.50 6.00
SITYM Yao Ming 20.00 50.00

2008-09 SP Rookie Threads Signing Day

APPROXIMATE ODDS 1:6
SDAR Anthony Randolph 2.50 6.00
SDBL Brook Lopez 5.00 12.00
SDBR Brandon Rush 2.50 6.00
SDCD Chris Douglas-Roberts 2.50 6.00
SDDA D.J. Augustin 4.00 10.00
SDDG Danilo Gallinari 6.00 15.00
SDDR Derrick Rose 20.00 50.00
SDDW D.J. White 2.50 6.00
SDEG Eric Gordon 6.00 15.00
SDGH George Hill 4.00 10.00
SDGR Donte Greene 2.50 6.00
SDJA Joe Alexander 2.50 6.00
SDJB Jerryd Bayless 3.00 8.00
SDJC Joe Crawford 2.50 6.00
SDJD Joey Dorsey 2.50 6.00
SDJG J.R. Giddens 2.50 6.00
SDJH J.J. Hickson 2.50 6.00
SDJT Jason Thompson 2.50 6.00
SDKK Kosta Koufos 2.50 6.00
SDKL Kevin Love 12.00 30.00
SDMB Michael Beasley 4.00 10.00
SDMC Mario Chalmers 4.00 10.00
SDMH Malik Hairston 2.50 6.00
SDMS Marreese Speights 3.00 8.00
SDOM O.J. Mayo 3.00 8.00
SDPE Patrick Ewing Jr. 2.50 6.00
SDRH Roy Hibbert 3.00 8.00
SDRL Robin Lopez 3.00 8.00
SDRW Russell Westbrook 125.00 300.00
SDSW Sonny Weems 2.50 6.00

2008-09 SP Rookie Threads SP Threads

APPROXIMATE ODDS 1:4
TAB Andrea Bargnani 2.00 5.00
TAI Allen Iverson 5.00 12.00
TAK Andrei Kirilenko 2.00 5.00
TAS Amare Stoudemire 2.50 6.00
TBO Andrew Bogut 2.00 5.00
TCB Caron Butler 2.00 5.00
TCH Chris Bosh 3.00 8.00
TDG Daniel Gibson 1.50 4.00
TDH Devin Harris 1.50 4.00
TDN Dirk Nowitzki 6.00 15.00
TEB Elton Brand 2.00 5.00
TGH Grant Hill 4.00 10.00
THO Dwight Howard 3.00 8.00
TJG Jeff Green 2.00 5.00
TJH Josh Howard 2.00 5.00
TJJ Joe Johnson 2.50 6.00
TJK Jason Kidd 4.00 10.00
TJR Jason Richardson 2.50 6.00
TJS Josh Smith 1.50 4.00
TKD Kevin Durant 12.00 30.00
TKG Kevin Garnett 6.00 15.00
TKH Kirk Hinrich 2.00 5.00
TLD Luol Deng 2.00 5.00
TLJ LeBron James 15.00 40.00
TMG Manu Ginobili 5.00 12.00
TPG Pau Gasol 3.00 8.00
TRA Ray Allen 4.00 10.00
TRH Richard Hamilton 2.50 6.00
TSL Shaun Livingston 1.50 4.00
TSM Shawn Marion 2.50 6.00
TTD Tim Duncan 6.00 15.00

2008-09 SP Rookie Threads SP Threads Patch

*PATCH: 1X TO 2.5X BASE HI
TGH Grant Hill 20.00 50.00

2008-09 SP Rookie Threads SP Threads Dual

APPROXIMATE ODDS 1:5
TDAP S.Pippen/C.Anthony 15.00 40.00
TDBJ K.Bryant/M.Jordan 400.00 800.00
TDDD C.Drexler/K.Durant 10.00 25.00
TDEA J.Erving/G.Arenas 5.00 12.00
TDEJ P.Ewing/A.Jefferson 6.00 15.00
TDGM K.McHale/K.Garnett 6.00 15.00
TDHK J.Hornacek/K.Korver 6.00 15.00
TDHO S.O'Neal/D.Howard 8.00 20.00
TDIR A.Iverson/B.Roy 6.00 15.00
TDJB L.Bird/L.James 12.00 30.00
TDKJ M.Johnson/J.Kidd 8.00 20.00
TDMB C.Boozer/K.Malone 5.00 12.00
TDMW A.Mourning/S.Williams 5.00 12.00
TDPT I.Thomas/C.Paul 5.00 12.00
TDRM D.Majerle/M.Redd 5.00 12.00
TDSP J.Starks/T.Parker 5.00 12.00
TDSR D.Robinson/A.Stoudemire 6.00 15.00
TDWL B.Laimbeer/R.Wallace 5.00 12.00
TDWS D.Williams/J.Stockton 5.00 12.00

2008-09 SP Rookie Threads SP Threads Dual Patch

TDAP C.Anthony/S.Pippen 30.00 80.00
TDBJ M.Jordan/K.Bryant 1,000.00 2,000.00
TDDD C.Drexler/K.Durant 12.00 30.00
TDEA J.Erving/G.Arenas 15.00 40.00
TDEJ P.Ewing/A.Jefferson 10.00 25.00
TDGM K.Garnett/K.McHale 15.00 40.00
TDHK J.Hornacek/K.Korver 10.00 25.00
TDHO D.Howard/S.O'Neal 12.00 30.00
TDIR A.Iverson/B.Roy 12.00 30.00
TDJB L.James/L.Bird 20.00 50.00
TDKJ J.Kidd/M.Johnson 15.00 40.00
TDMW S.Williams/A.Mourning 12.50 30.00
TDPT I.Thomas/C.Paul 12.50 30.00
TDRM M.Redd/D.Majerle 10.00 25.00
TDSP J.Starks/T.Parker 15.00 30.00
TDWL R.Wallace/B.Laimbeer 10.00 25.00

2003-04 SP Signature Edition

COMP.SET w/o SP's (100) 30.00 80.00
143-222 SER.#'d TO PLAYER JERSEY #
223-225 PRINT RUN 250 SER.#'d SETS
1 Shareef Abdur-Rahim .60 1.50
2 Jason Terry .50 1.25
3 Theo Ratliff .40 1.00
4 Raef LaFrentz .40 1.00
5 Paul Pierce 1.00 2.50
6 Larry Bird 1.50 4.00
7 Jalen Rose .50 1.25
8 Scottie Pippen 1.50 4.00
9 Michael Jordan 12.00 30.00
10 Dennis Rodman 1.25 3.00
11 Dajuan Wagner .40 1.00
12 Darius Miles .40 1.00
13 Carlos Boozer .50 1.25
14 Zydrunas Ilgauskas .50 1.25
15 Dirk Nowitzki 1.50 4.00
16 Steve Nash 1.25 3.00
17 Antoine Walker .60 1.50
18 Antawn Jamison .60 1.50
19 Andre Miller .50 1.25
20 Nene .50 1.25
21 Nikoloz Tskitishvili .40 1.00
22 Ben Wallace .75 2.00
23 Richard Hamilton .75 2.00
24 Chauncey Billups .75 2.00
25 Nick Van Exel .60 1.50
26 Jason Richardson .60 1.50
27 Mike Dunleavy .50 1.25
28 Yao Ming 1.50 4.00
29 Steve Francis .60 1.50
30 Cuttino Mobley .40 1.00
31 Reggie Miller 1.25 3.00
32 Jermaine O'Neal .60 1.50
33 Jamaal Tinsley .40 1.00
34 Chris Wilcox .40 1.00
35 Elton Brand .50 1.25
36 Wang Zhizhi .60 1.50
37 Corey Maggette .50 1.25
38 Kobe Bryant 5.00 12.00
39 Shaquille O'Neal 2.50 6.00
40 Gary Payton 1.00 2.50
41 Karl Malone 1.25 3.00
42 Pau Gasol 1.00 2.50
43 Shane Battier .50 1.25
44 Mike Miller .50 1.25
45 Caron Butler .50 1.25
46 Eddie Jones .60 1.50
47 Lamar Odom .50 1.25
48 Brian Grant .40 1.00
49 Desmond Mason .50 1.25
50 Michael Redd .60 1.50
51 Tim Thomas .40 1.00
52 Wally Szczerbiak .50 1.25
53 Kevin Garnett 1.50 4.00
54 Latrell Sprewell .75 2.00
55 Sam Cassell .50 1.25
56 Richard Jefferson .50 1.25
57 Kenyon Martin .60 1.50
58 Jason Kidd 1.00 2.50
59 Alonzo Mourning .75 2.00
60 Jamal Mashburn .50 1.25
61 Baron Davis .60 1.50
62 David Wesley .40 1.00
63 Allan Houston .60 1.50
64 Keith Van Horn .50 1.25
65 Antonio McDyess .50 1.25
66 Gordan Giricek .40 1.00
67 Tracy McGrady 1.00 2.50
68 Drew Gooden .50 1.25
69 Grant Hill .75 2.00
70 Glenn Robinson .50 1.25
71 Allen Iverson 1.50 4.00
72 Julius Erving 1.00 2.50
73 Eric Snow .40 1.00
74 Shawn Marion .60 1.50
75 Amare Stoudemire .75 2.00
76 Stephon Marbury .75 2.00
77 Bonzi Wells .40 1.00
78 Rasheed Wallace .75 2.00
79 Derek Anderson .50 1.25
80 Zach Randolph .60 1.50
81 Mike Bibby .60 1.50
82 Chris Webber .75 2.00
83 Peja Stojakovic .50 1.25
84 Brad Miller .50 1.25
85 Tony Parker 1.00 2.50
86 Tim Duncan 1.50 4.00
87 Manu Ginobili 1.25 3.00
88 David Robinson 1.25 3.00
89 Rashard Lewis .50 1.25
90 Ray Allen 1.00 2.50
91 Vladimir Radmanovic .40 1.00
92 Morris Peterson .40 1.00
93 Vince Carter 1.25 3.00
94 Antonio Davis .50 1.25
95 Andrei Kirilenko .50 1.25
96 Matt Harpring .40 1.00
97 Jarron Collins .40 1.00
98 Gilbert Arenas .60 1.50
99 Jerry Stackhouse .75 2.00
100 Kwame Brown .40 1.00
101 LeBron James RC 800.00 1,500.00
102 Darko Milicic RC 3.00 8.00
103 Carmelo Anthony RC 20.00 50.00
104 Chris Bosh RC 12.00 30.00
105 Dwyane Wade RC 12.00 30.00
106 Chris Kaman RC 4.00 10.00
107 Kirk Hinrich RC 4.00 10.00
108 T.J. Ford RC 3.00 8.00
109 Mike Sweetney RC 2.50 6.00
110 Jarvis Hayes RC 2.50 6.00
111 Mickael Pietrus RC 3.00 8.00
112 Nick Collison RC 3.00 8.00
113 Marcus Banks RC 2.50 6.00
114 Luke Ridnour RC 4.00 10.00
115 Reece Gaines RC 2.50 6.00
116 Troy Bell RC 2.50 6.00
117 Zarko Cabarkapa RC 2.50 6.00
118 David West RC 5.00 12.00
119 Aleksandar Pavlovic RC 3.00 8.00
120 Dahntay Jones RC 3.00 8.00
121 Boris Diaw RC 4.00 10.00
122 Zoran Planinic RC 2.50 6.00
123 Travis Outlaw RC 3.00 8.00
124 Brian Cook RC 2.50 6.00
125 James Lang RC 2.50 6.00
126 Ndudi Ebi RC 2.50 6.00
127 Kendrick Perkins RC 3.00 8.00
128 Leandro Barbosa RC 4.00 10.00
129 Josh Howard RC 4.00 10.00
130 Maciej Lampe RC 2.50 6.00
131 Jason Kapono RC 2.50 6.00
132 Luke Walton RC 4.00 10.00
133 Jerome Beasley RC 2.50 6.00
134 Willie Green RC 4.00 10.00
135 James Jones RC 2.50 6.00
136 Travis Hansen RC 2.50 6.00
137 Steve Blake RC 3.00 8.00
138 Slavko Vranes RC 2.50 6.00
139 Zaur Pachulia RC 4.00 10.00
140 Keith Bogans RC 2.50 6.00
141 Kyle Korver RC 5.00 12.00
142 Brandon Hunter RC 2.50 6.00
144 LeBron James/23 3,000.00 6,000.00
145 Michael Jordan/23 75.00 150.00
146 Darius Miles/21 6.00 15.00
148 Gary Payton/20 12.50 30.00
152 Ray Allen/34 10.00 25.00
153 Paul Pierce/34 12.50 30.00
154 Carmelo Anthony/15 25.00 60.00
160 Andrei Kirilenko/47 6.00 15.00
162 Nene/31 6.00 15.00
163 Elton Brand/42 6.00 15.00
168 Jerry Stackhouse/42 8.00 20.00
171 Darko Milicic/31 15.00 40.00
174 Glenn Robinson/31 6.00 15.00
175 Tim Duncan/21 25.00 60.00
177 Scottie Pippen/33 50.00 120.00
178 Richard Hamilton/32 8.00 20.00
179 Corey Maggette/50 6.00 15.00
182 Amare Stoudemire/32 12.50 30.00
185 Dirk Nowitzki/41 12.50 30.00
187 Magic Johnson/32 25.00 60.00
188 Michael Redd/22 6.00 15.00
190 Rasheed Wallace/30 6.00 15.00
192 Jason Terry/31 6.00 15.00
196 Kevin Garnett/21 25.00 60.00
203 Mike Miller/33 6.00 15.00
207 Morris Peterson/24 6.00 15.00
209 Jason Richardson/23 6.00 15.00
210 Shaquille O'Neal/34 15.00 40.00
211 Desmond Mason/24 6.00 15.00
212 Jamal Mashburn/24 6.00 15.00
213 Shawn Marion/31 8.00 20.00
214 Manu Ginobili/20 10.00 25.00
215 Larry Bird/33 60.00 150.00
216 Antawn Jamison/33 6.00 15.00
217 Reggie Miller/31 30.00 80.00
218 Pau Gasol/16 10.00 25.00
222 Vince Carter/15 20.00 50.00
223 Spike Lee 1.50 4.00
224 Summer Sanders 1.25 3.00
225 Cheryl Miller .75 2.00

2003-04 SP Signature Edition Gold

*GOLD SINGLES: 2X TO 5X BASE HI
GOLD PRINT RUN 100 SER.#'d SETS
GOLD PARALLEL FOR 1-100 ONLY
9 Michael Jordan 75.00 200.00
36 Wang Zhizhi 20.00 50.00
38 Kobe Bryant 20.00 50.00

2003-04 SP Signature Edition Autographed Parallel

1-100 SER.#'d TO PLAYER JERSEY #
RC AU PRINT RUN 25 SER.#'d SETS
SKIP-NUMBERED PARALLEL SET
A5 Paul Pierce/34 50.00 120.00
A6 Larry Bird/33 125.00 250.00
A9 Michael Jordan/23 1,500.00 3,000.00
A10 Dennis Rodman/91 60.00 150.00
A12 Darius Miles/21 10.00 25.00
A18 Antawn Jamison/33 15.00 40.00
A20 Nene/31 15.00 40.00
A23 Richard Hamilton/32 15.00 40.00
A26 Jason Richardson/23 15.00 40.00
A31 Reggie Miller/31 125.00 300.00
A34 Chris Wilcox/54 10.00 25.00
A36 Wang Zhizhi/16 15.00 40.00
A37 Corey Maggette/50 10.00 25.00
A40 Gary Payton/20 30.00 80.00
A43 Shane Battier/31 15.00 40.00
A53 Kevin Garnett/21 100.00 250.00
A56 Richard Jefferson/24 15.00 40.00
A65 Antonio McDyess/34 20.00 40.00
A74 Shawn Marion/31 12.00 30.00
A83 Peja Stojakovic/16 50.00 120.00
A87 Manu Ginobili/20 75.00 200.00
A92 Morris Peterson/24 10.00 25.00
A99 Jerry Stackhouse/42 15.00 40.00
A101 LeBron James 15,000.00 30,000.00
A102 Darko Milicic 10.00 25.00
A103 Carmelo Anthony 150.00 300.00
A104 Chris Bosh 100.00 200.00
A105 Dwyane Wade 2,000.00 4,000.00
A106 Chris Kaman 12.00 30.00
A107 Kirk Hinrich 12.00 30.00
A108 T.J. Ford 10.00 25.00
A109 Mike Sweetney 8.00 20.00
A110 Jarvis Hayes 8.00 20.00
A111 Mickael Pietrus 10.00 25.00
A112 Nick Collison 10.00 25.00
A113 Marcus Banks 8.00 20.00
A114 Luke Ridnour 12.00 30.00
A115 Reece Gaines 8.00 20.00
A116 Troy Bell 8.00 20.00
A117 Zarko Cabarkapa 8.00 20.00
A118 David West 20.00 50.00
A119 Aleksandar Pavlovic 10.00 25.00
A120 Dahntay Jones 10.00 25.00
A121 Boris Diaw 12.00 30.00
A122 Zoran Planinic 8.00 20.00
A123 Travis Outlaw 10.00 25.00
A124 Brian Cook 8.00 20.00
A125 James Lang 8.00 20.00
A126 Ndudi Ebi 8.00 20.00
A127 Kendrick Perkins 10.00 25.00

A128 Leandro Barbosa 12.00 30.00
A129 Josh Howard 12.00 30.00
A130 Maciej Lampe 8.00 20.00
A131 Jason Kapono 8.00 20.00
A132 Luke Walton 12.00 30.00
A133 Jerome Beasley 8.00 20.00
A134 Willie Green 12.00 30.00
A135 James Jones 8.00 20.00
A136 Travis Hansen 8.00 20.00
A137 Steve Blake 10.00 25.00
A138 Slavko Vranes 8.00 20.00
A139 Zaur Pachulia 12.00 30.00
A140 Keith Bogans 8.00 20.00
A141 Kyle Korver 15.00 40.00
A142 Brandon Hunter 8.00 20.00

2003-04 SP Signature Edition Alumni Associates Signatures

PRINT RUN 100 SER.#'d SETS
AK S.A-Rahim/J.Kidd 15.00 40.00
AW G.Arenas/L.Walton 10.00 25.00
BJ M.Bibby/R.Jefferson 10.00 25.00
DB M.Dunleavy/S.Battier 15.00 40.00
FD S.Francis/J.Dixon 10.00 25.00
MJ C.Maggette/D.Jones 10.00 25.00
MW A.McDyess/G.Wallace 10.00 25.00
PG Pierce/Gooden 20.00 50.00
PR M.Peterson/J.Richardson 10.00 25.00
SJ J.Stack/A.Jamison 10.00 25.00
WM B.Walton/R.Miller 50.00 125.00

2003-04 SP Signature Edition Celebrity Signings

*GOLD: .6X TO 1.5X BASE AU HI
GOLD PRINT RUN 15 TO 50 SER.#'d SETS
CM Cheryl Miller 12.50 30.00
SL Spike Lee/32 100.00 200.00
SS Summer Sanders 20.00 50.00

2003-04 SP Signature Edition Famous Nicknames

PRINT RUN 25 TO 100 SER.#'d SETS
AS Amare Stoudemire/25 75.00 150.00
BB Brent Barry/25 25.00 60.00
CA Carmelo Anthony/25 300.00 600.00
CB Chauncey Billups/25 25.00 60.00
CM Cuttino Mobley/25 25.00 60.00
DM Desmond Mason/25 25.00 60.00
DR Dennis Rodman/100 150.00 400.00
EG Manu Ginobili/25 125.00 300.00
GA Gilbert Arenas/25 50.00 120.00
GG George Gervin/25 40.00 100.00
GP Gary Payton/25 50.00 120.00
GR Glenn Robinson/25 25.00 60.00
JE Julius Erving/25 150.00 400.00
JR Jason Richardson/25 25.00 60.00
KG1 Kevin Garnett/25 125.00 250.00
KG2 Kevin Garnett/25 125.00 250.00
LJ1 L.James King/25 15,000.00 30,000.00
LJ2 L.James Bron/25 15,000.00 30,000.00
LJ3 L.James Chosen/25 15,000.00 30,000.00
LO Lamar Odom/25 25.00 60.00
MB Mike Bibby/25 40.00 100.00
NH Nene/25 25.00 60.00
PP Paul Pierce/25 200.00 500.00
RH Richard Hamilton/25 25.00 60.00
RO David Robinson/100 100.00 250.00
SF Steve Francis/25 40.00 100.00
SL Spike Lee/25 150.00 300.00
SM Shawn Marion/25 40.00 100.00
TM Tracy McGrady/25 150.00 400.00
YM Yao Ming/25 150.00 400.00

2003-04 SP Signature Edition INKcredible INKscriptions

PRINT RUN 25 SER.#'d SETS
BW Bill Walton 20.00 50.00
CA Carmelo Anthony 150.00 300.00
DM Darko Milicic 15.00 40.00
GG George Gervin 40.00 100.00
GP Gary Payton 30.00 80.00
JE Julius Erving 75.00 200.00
JK Jason Kidd 50.00 120.00
JR1 Jason Richardson 20.00 50.00
JR2 Jason Richardson 20.00 50.00
KG Kevin Garnett 125.00 300.00
LJ LeBron James 20,000.00 40,000.00
PS Peja Stojakovic 40.00 100.00

2003-04 SP Signature Edition Marquee Marks

PRINT RUN 100 SER.#'d SETS
AN C.Anthony/Nene/75 25.00 60.00
BP K.Bryant/G.Payton/100 125.00 300.00
DD Dunleavy Sr./Dunleavy Jr./100 12.00 30.00
JMO L.James/D.Miles/100 2,000.00 4,000.00
JS Magic/J.Stockton/75 125.00 300.00
LM Spike Lee/R.Miller/25 250.00 500.00
MM C.Miller/R.Miller/100 75.00 200.00
MS C.Miller/S.Sanders/100 15.00 40.00
WW B.Walton/L.Walton/100 15.00 40.00

2003-04 SP Signature Edition National Treasures

PRINT RUN 100 SER.#'d SETS
NT1 L.Barbosa/Nene 12.50 30.00
NT2 Z.Cabarkapa/P.Stojakovic 12.50 30.00
NT3 M.Pietrus/B.Diaw 12.50 30.00
NT4 Y.Ming/W.Zhi Zhi 1,500.00 4,000.00
NT5 T.Parker/M.Pietrus 20.00 50.00
NT6 Planinic/Milicic 12.50 30.00

2003-04 SP Signature Edition Rookie INKorporated

PRINT RUN 100 SER.#'d SETS
AP Aleksandar Pavlovic 4.00 10.00
BC Brian Cook 3.00 8.00
BD Boris Diaw 5.00 12.00
CA Carmelo Anthony 50.00 120.00
CB Chris Bosh 25.00 60.00
CK Chris Kaman 5.00 12.00
DJ Dahntay Jones 4.00 10.00
DM Darko Milicic 4.00 10.00
DY Dwyane Wade 150.00 400.00
HO Josh Howard 5.00 12.00
JH Jarvis Hayes 3.00 8.00
JK Jason Kapono 3.00 8.00
KP Kendrick Perkins 4.00 10.00
LB Leandro Barbosa 5.00 12.00
LJ LeBron James 10,000.00 20,000.00
LR Luke Ridnour 5.00 12.00
LW Luke Walton 5.00 12.00
MB Marcus Banks 3.00 8.00
ML Maciej Lampe 3.00 8.00
MP Mickael Pietrus 4.00 10.00
MS Mike Sweetney 3.00 8.00
NE Ndudi Ebi 3.00 8.00
RG Reece Gaines 3.00 8.00
TB Troy Bell 3.00 8.00
TO Travis Outlaw 4.00 10.00
WE David West 6.00 15.00
ZC Zarko Cabarkapa 3.00 8.00
ZP Zoran Planinic 3.00 8.00

2003-04 SP Signature Edition Scripts for Success

PRINT RUN 250 SER.#'d SETS
AP Aleksandar Pavlovic 3.00 8.00
BC Brian Cook 2.50 6.00
BD Boris Diaw 4.00 10.00
CB Chris Bosh 12.00 30.00
CK Chris Kaman 4.00 10.00
DJ Dahntay Jones 3.00 8.00
DM Darko Milicic 3.00 8.00
DY Dwyane Wade 100.00 250.00
HO Josh Howard 4.00 10.00
JH Jarvis Hayes 2.50 6.00
JK Jason Kapono 2.50 6.00
KP Kendrick Perkins 3.00 8.00
LB Leandro Barbosa 4.00 10.00
LR Luke Ridnour 4.00 10.00
LW Luke Walton 4.00 10.00
MB Marcus Banks 2.50 6.00
ML Maciej Lampe 2.50 6.00
MP Mickael Pietrus 3.00 8.00
MS Mike Sweetney 2.50 6.00
MW Maurice Williams 4.00 10.00
NE Ndudi Ebi 2.50 6.00
RG Reece Gaines 2.50 6.00
TB Troy Bell 2.50 6.00
TO Travis Outlaw 3.00 8.00
WE David West 5.00 12.00
ZA Zaur Pachulia 4.00 10.00
ZC Zarko Cabarkapa 2.50 6.00
ZP Zoran Planinic 2.50 6.00

2003-04 SP Signature Edition Signatures

STATED ODDS FOR ANY AUTOGRAPH 1:1
AJ Antawn Jamison 4.00 10.00
AM Antonio McDyess SP 5.00 12.00
AP Aleksandar Pavlovic 2.50 6.00
BA Marcus Banks 2.00 5.00
BD Boris Diaw 3.00 8.00
BO Carlos Boozer 3.00 8.00
CA Carmelo Anthony SP 40.00 80.00
CB Chauncey Billups 4.00 10.00
CH Chris Bosh 8.00 20.00
CK Chris Kaman 3.00 8.00
CM Corey Maggette 3.00 8.00
CW Chris Wilcox 3.00 8.00
DA Darius Miles SP 2.00 5.00
DG Drew Gooden 3.00 8.00
DJ Dahntay Jones 2.50 6.00
DM Darko Milicic 2.50 6.00
DR Dennis Rodman SP 40.00 100.00
DU Mike Dunleavy Sr. 3.00 8.00
DY Dwyane Wade 40.00 100.00
EG Manu Ginobili 40.00 100.00
GA Gilbert Arenas 3.00 8.00
GG George Gervin 8.00 20.00
GP Gary Payton SP 8.00 20.00
HW Josh Howard 3.00 8.00
JD Juan Dixon 3.00 8.00
JE Julius Erving SP 30.00 80.00
JH Jarvis Hayes 2.00 5.00
JK Jason Kidd 12.00 30.00
JL James Lang 2.00 5.00
JR Jason Richardson 6.00 15.00
JS Jerry Stackhouse 6.00 15.00
KB Kobe Bryant 500.00 1,000.00
KG Kevin Garnett 125.00 300.00
KO Jason Kapono 2.00 5.00
KP Kendrick Perkins 2.50 6.00
LB Larry Bird SP 75.00 150.00
LE Leandro Barbosa 3.00 8.00
LJ LeBron James 10,000.00 15,000.00
LO Lamar Odom SP 6.00 15.00
LR Luke Ridnour 3.00 8.00
LW Luke Walton 5.00 12.00
MA Magic Johnson SP 75.00 200.00
MB Mike Bibby 3.00 8.00
MD Mike Dunleavy 5.00 12.00
MI Andre Miller 3.00 8.00
MJ Michael Jordan 3,000.00 6,000.00
MK Mickael Pietrus 2.50 6.00
ML Maciej Lampe 2.00 5.00
MP Morris Peterson 3.00 8.00
MS Mike Sweetney SP 2.00 5.00
MW Maurice Williams 3.00 8.00
NE Ndudi Ebi 2.00 5.00
NH Nene 3.00 8.00
PE Patrick Ewing 125.00 300.00
PP Paul Pierce 20.00 50.00
PS Peja Stojakovic 8.00 20.00
RG Reece Gaines 2.00 5.00
RH Richard Hamilton 6.00 15.00
RJ Richard Jefferson 2.50 6.00
RL Rashard Lewis SP 6.00 15.00
RM Reggie Miller 75.00 200.00
RO Jalen Rose 6.00 15.00
SA Shareef Abdur-Rahim SP 6.00 15.00
SF Steve Francis 6.00 15.00
SM Shawn Marion SP 6.00 15.00
ST John Stockton SP 50.00 120.00
TB Troy Bell 2.00 5.00
TM Tracy McGrady 15.00 40.00
TO Travis Outlaw 2.50 6.00
TP Tony Parker 15.00 40.00
WA Bill Walton SP 12.00 30.00
WE David West 4.00 10.00
WG Dajuan Wagner SP 3.00 8.00
WZ Wang Zhizhi SP 100.00 250.00
YM Yao Ming 25.00 60.00
ZC Zarko Cabarkapa 2.00 5.00
ZP Zoran Planinic 2.00 5.00

2003-04 SP Signature Edition Signatures Gold

*GOLD SINGLES: .75X TO 2X BASE AU HI
GOLD PRINT RUN 50 SER.#'d SETS
CA Carmelo Anthony 100.00 200.00
CH Chris Bosh 40.00 100.00
DM Darko Milicic 5.00 12.00
DR Dennis Rodman 100.00 250.00
DY Dwyane Wade 150.00 300.00
GP Gary Payton 12.00 30.00
JK Jason Kidd 40.00 100.00
LB Larry Bird 80.00 200.00
MA Magic Johnson 100.00 200.00
PE Patrick Ewing 200.00 400.00
RM Reggie Miller 250.00 500.00
WA Bill Walton 15.00 40.00
YM Yao Ming 60.00 150.00

2003-04 SP Signature Edition Signatures Triple

PRINT RUN 25 SER.#'d SETS
BPG Kobe/Payton/KG 600.00 1,200.00
BSW Bibby/Peja/Wallace 100.00 200.00
JJM LeBron/MJ/McGrady 20,000.00 40,000.00
JMA LeBron/Darko/Carmelo 1,500.00 3,000.00
KJP Kidd/Jefferson/Zoran 75.00 150.00
MGG McGrady/Gaines/Gooden 75.00 150.00
MGJ McGrady/KG/LeBron 4,000.00 8,000.00
MHB Darko/Hamilton/Billups 75.00 150.00
MJM A.Miller/Rose/R.Miller 200.00 500.00
RJP J-Rich/Jamison/Pietrus 30.00 80.00

2003-04 SP Signature Edition Tins

COMPLETE SET 6.00 15.00
*BLACK TINS: .6X TO 1.5X BASE HI
NNO Darko Milicic .25 .60
NNO LeBron James 3.00 8.00
NNO Tracy McGrady .50 1.25
NNO Kobe Bryant 2.50 6.00
NNO Carmelo Anthony 1.50 4.00
NNO Michael Jordan 3.00 8.00

2004-05 SP Signature Edition

101-142 PRINT RUN 499 SER.#'d SETS
143-242 #'d TO PLAYER JSY NUMBER
1 Antoine Walker .60 1.50
2 Al Harrington .50 1.25
3 Boris Diaw .50 1.25
4 Paul Pierce 1.00 2.50
5 Ricky Davis .50 1.25
6 Gary Payton 1.00 2.50
7 Gerald Wallace .50 1.25
8 Emeka Okafor RC 1.50 4.00
9 Jahidi White .40 1.00
10 Eddy Curry .40 1.00
11 Kirk Hinrich .60 1.50
12 Michael Jordan 5.00 12.00
13 LeBron James 5.00 12.00
14 Dajuan Wagner .40 1.00
15 Jeff McInnis .40 1.00
16 Drew Gooden .40 1.00
17 Dirk Nowitzki 1.50 4.00
18 Michael Finley .60 1.50
19 Jerry Stackhouse .60 1.50
20 Jason Terry .60 1.50
21 Kenyon Martin .60 1.50
22 Andre Miller .50 1.25
23 Carmelo Anthony 1.25 3.00
24 Nene .50 1.25
25 Chauncey Billups .75 2.00
26 Rasheed Wallace .75 2.00
27 Ben Wallace .75 2.00
28 Richard Hamilton .75 2.00
29 Derek Fisher .50 1.25
30 Jason Richardson .60 1.50
31 Mike Dunleavy .40 1.00
32 Yao Ming 1.50 4.00
33 Tracy McGrady 1.50 4.00
34 Juwan Howard .50 1.25
35 Jermaine O'Neal .50 1.25
36 Reggie Miller 1.25 3.00
37 Ron Artest .60 1.50
38 Jamaal Tinsley .40 1.00
39 Elton Brand .50 1.25
40 Corey Maggette .50 1.25
41 Marko Jaric .40 1.00
42 Kerry Kittles .50 1.25
43 Kobe Bryant 5.00 12.00
44 Chucky Atkins .40 1.00
45 Lamar Odom .60 1.50
46 Caron Butler .50 1.25
47 Pau Gasol 1.00 2.50
48 Jason Williams .50 1.25
49 Bonzi Wells .40 1.00
50 Shaquille O'Neal 2.50 6.00
51 Dwyane Wade 2.50 6.00
52 Eddie Jones .60 1.50
53 Michael Redd .50 1.25
54 Desmond Mason .50 1.25
55 T.J. Ford .40 1.00
56 Latrell Sprewell .75 2.00
57 Kevin Garnett 1.50 4.00
58 Sam Cassell .50 1.25
59 Troy Hudson .40 1.00
60 Vince Carter 1.25 3.00
61 Richard Jefferson .50 1.25
62 Jason Kidd 1.00 2.50
63 Lee Nailon .40 1.00
64 Baron Davis .60 1.50
65 Jamaal Magloire .40 1.00
66 Allan Houston .60 1.50
67 Jamal Crawford .60 1.50
68 Stephon Marbury .75 2.00
69 Grant Hill .75 2.00
70 Cuttino Mobley .50 1.25
71 Steve Francis .60 1.50
72 Glenn Robinson .50 1.25
73 Allen Iverson 1.50 4.00
74 Kyle Korver .60 1.50
75 Amare Stoudemire .60 1.50
76 Steve Nash 1.25 3.00
77 Quentin Richardson .40 1.00
78 Shawn Marion .60 1.50
79 Shareef Abdur-Rahim .60 1.50
80 Damon Stoudamire .60 1.50
81 Zach Randolph .60 1.50
82 Darius Miles .40 1.00
83 Peja Stojakovic .50 1.25
84 Chris Webber .75 2.00
85 Mike Bibby .60 1.50
86 Tony Parker 1.00 2.50
87 Tim Duncan 1.50 4.00
88 Manu Ginobili 1.25 3.00
89 Ronald Murray .40 1.00
90 Ray Allen 1.00 2.50
91 Rashard Lewis .50 1.25
92 Chris Bosh 1.00 2.50
93 Jalen Rose .50 1.25
94 Rafer Alston .40 1.00
95 Andrei Kirilenko .50 1.25
96 Matt Harpring .40 1.00
97 Carlos Boozer .50 1.25
98 Gilbert Arenas .60 1.50
99 Jarvis Hayes .40 1.00
100 Antawn Jamison .50 1.25
101 Dwight Howard JSY RC 10.00 25.00
102 Ben Gordon JSY RC 3.00 8.00
103 Shaun Livingston JSY RC 3.00 8.00
104 Devin Harris JSY RC 2.50 6.00
105 Josh Childress JSY RC 2.00 5.00
106 Luol Deng JSY RC 3.00 8.00
107 Rafael Araujo JSY RC 2.00 5.00
108 Andre Iguodala JSY RC 5.00 12.00
109 Luke Jackson JSY RC 2.00 5.00
110 Sebastian Telfair JSY RC 2.50 6.00
111 Kris Humphries JSY RC 2.50 6.00
112 Al Jefferson JSY RC 3.00 8.00
113 Kirk Snyder JSY RC 2.00 5.00
114 Josh Smith JSY RC 3.00 8.00
115 J.R. Smith JSY RC 3.00 8.00
116 Dorell Wright JSY RC 2.50 6.00
117 Jameer Nelson JSY RC 3.00 8.00
118 Delonte West JSY RC 2.50 6.00
119 Tony Allen JSY RC 3.00 8.00
120 Kevin Martin JSY RC 4.00 10.00
121 David Harrison JSY RC 2.00 5.00
122 Anderson Varejao JSY RC 2.50 6.00
123 Jackson Vroman JSY RC 2.00 5.00
124 Lionel Chalmers JSY RC 2.00 5.00
125 Andre Emmett JSY RC 2.00 5.00
126 Chris Duhon JSY RC 2.50 6.00
127 Bernard Robinson JSY RC 2.00 5.00
128 Tim Pickett RC 1.50 4.00
129 Nenad Krstic JSY RC 2.50 6.00
130 Andris Biedrins JSY RC 2.50 6.00
131 Robert Swift RC 2.00 5.00
132 Andres Nocioni RC 2.00 5.00
133 Justin Reed RC 1.25 3.00
134 Romain Sato RC 1.25 3.00
135 Sasha Vujacic JSY RC 2.50 6.00
136 Beno Udrih RC 1.50 4.00
137 Peter John Ramos JSY RC 2.00 5.00
138 Donta Smith JSY RC 2.00 5.00
139 Antonio Burks RC 1.25 3.00
140 Yuta Tabuse JSY RC 3.00 8.00
141 Trevor Ariza JSY RC 3.00 8.00
142 Matt Freije JSY RC 2.00 5.00
143 Drew Gooden/90 4.00 10.00
144 Elton Brand/42 4.00 10.00
145 Shawn Marion/31 6.00 15.00
146 Dirk Nowitzki/41 6.00 15.00
149 Pau Gasol/16 6.00 15.00
152 Devin Harris/34 6.00 15.00
165 Shaquille O'Neal/32 12.50 30.00
166 Shareef Abdur-Rahim/33 4.00 10.00
167 Jason Terry/31 4.00 10.00
171 Zach Randolph/50 5.00 12.00
172 Dave DeBusschere/22 10.00 25.00
176 Gary Payton/20 8.00 20.00
180 Michael Redd/22 4.00 10.00
181 Peja Stojakovic/16 8.00 20.00
183 Luke Jackson/33 4.00 10.00
184 Richard Hamilton/32 6.00 15.00
185 Kevin Garnett/21 12.00 30.00
188 Sebastian Telfair/31 4.00 10.00
191 David Robinson/50 10.00 25.00
192 Jerry Stackhouse/42 4.00 10.00
193 Kris Humphries/43 4.00 10.00
194 Dennis Rodman/91 6.00 15.00
199 Michael Jordan/23 75.00 150.00
200 Magic Johnson/32 15.00 40.00
207 George Gervin/44 6.00 15.00
212 Bernard King/30 4.00 10.00
214 Grant Hill/33 8.00 20.00
215 J.R. Smith/23 8.00 20.00
216 LeBron James/23 25.00 60.00
218 Amare Stoudemire/32 8.00 20.00
221 Larry Bird/33 15.00 40.00
222 Reggie Miller/31 12.00 30.00
224 Andrei Kirilenko/47 6.00 15.00
228 Corey Maggette/50 4.00 10.00
233 Hakeem Olajuwon/34 6.00 15.00
234 Richard Jefferson/24 4.00 10.00
235 Tim Duncan/21 12.00 30.00
236 Ray Allen/34 10.00 25.00
238 Paul Pierce/34 8.00 20.00
240 Willis Reed/19 5.00 12.00
242 Manu Ginobili/20 6.00 15.00

2004-05 SP Signature Edition 25

PRINT RUN 25 SER.#'d SETS
MOST RC PLAYERS ARE AUTOGRAPHED
12 Michael Jordan 100.00 250.00
13 LeBron James 75.00 200.00
69 Grant Hill 12.00 30.00
101 Dwight Howard JSY AU 175.00 350.00
102 Ben Gordon JSY AU 20.00 50.00
104 Devin Harris JSY AU 20.00 50.00
108 Andre Iguodala JSY AU 40.00 100.00
112 Al Jefferson JSY AU 10.00 25.00
117 Jameer Nelson JSY AU 10.00 25.00
118 Delonte West JSY AU 8.00 20.00
119 Tony Allen JSY AU 8.00 20.00
122 Anderson Varejao JSY AU 8.00 20.00
126 Chris Duhon JSY AU 8.00 20.00
129 Nenad Krstic JSY AU 8.00 20.00
130 Andris Biedrins JSY AU 6.00 15.00
141 Trevor Ariza JSY AU 10.00 25.00

2004-05 SP Signature Edition Autographed Parallel

CARDS #'d TO PLAYER JSY NUMBER
CARDS WITH ASTERISK ISSUED AS EXCH
A4 Paul Pierce/34* 100.00 250.00
A6 Gary Payton/20 100.00 250.00
A12 Michael Jordan/23* 5,000.00 10,000.00
A13 LeBron James/23 4,000.00 8,000.00
A19 Jerry Stackhouse/42 60.00 150.00
A22 Andre Miller/24 20.00 50.00
A23 Carmelo Anthony/15 125.00 300.00
A28 Richard Hamilton/32 60.00 150.00
A30 Jason Richardson/23 40.00 100.00
A36 Reggie Miller/31 200.00 500.00
A40 Corey Maggette/50 15.00 40.00
A47 Pau Gasol/16 75.00 200.00
A53 Michael Redd/22 20.00 50.00
A57 Kevin Garnett/21 300.00 600.00
A65 Jamaal Magloire/21 12.00 30.00
A75 Amare Stoudemire/32 30.00 80.00
A78 Shawn Marion/31 30.00 80.00
A79 Shareef Abdur-Rahim/33 40.00 100.00
A81 Zach Randolph/50 30.00 80.00
A95 Andrei Kirilenko/47 30.00 80.00

2004-05 SP Signature Edition AKA Autographs

PRINT RUNS LISTED IN CHECKLIST
PRINT RUNS LISTED IN CHECKLIST
AL A.Jefferson Big Al/100 10.00 25.00
AM A.McDyess/100 10.00 25.00
AR R.Araujo Hoffa/100 6.00 15.00
AS A.Stoudemire Future/50 40.00 100.00
BC Bob Cousy Cooz/50 150.00 400.00
BG B.Gordon M.S.G./50 20.00 50.00
BW B.Wallace Big Ben/50 75.00 200.00
CA C.Arroyo New Maestro/100 25.00 60.00
CD C.Drexler The Glide/50 75.00 200.00
CH C.Duhon C-Doo/100 8.00 20.00
DF Derek Fisher Fish/100 60.00 150.00
DG Drew Gooden Truth/100 10.00 25.00
DH D.Howard DeBo/100 40.00 100.00
DR D.Rodman The Worm/50 200.00 500.00
DS D.Stoud ROY 96/100 75.00 200.00
DW Delonte West Recz/100 8.00 20.00
EC Eddy Curry ECity/100 6.00 15.00
GP Gary Payton 100.00 250.00
GW Gerald Wallace 10.00 25.00
HO H.Olajuwon The Dream/50 500.00 1,000.00
JA Jason Williams JW/100 150.00 400.00
JC J.Childress Real Deal/50 6.00 15.00
JM J.Magloire Big Cat/100 10.00 25.00
JS Josh Smith JSmoove/100 10.00 25.00
JV J.Vroman Jax/100 6.00 15.00
JW John Wooden 125.00 300.00
KA Kenny Anderson 10.00 25.00
KE Kv.Martin K-Mart/100 6.00 15.00
KG Kevin Garnett KG/100 300.00 600.00
KH K.Hinrich Capt. Kirk/50 25.00 60.00
LJ LeBron James Bron/100 2,500.00 5,000.00
LO Lamar Odom/50 15.00 40.00
MB Mike Bibby 25.00 60.00
MR Michael Redd Silky/50 15.00 40.00
PP Paul Pierce Truth/50 100.00 250.00
RH R.Hamilton RIP/50 40.00 100.00
RM R.Murray Flip/100 10.00 25.00
RT R.Traylor Tractor/100 10.00 25.00
RY Ray Allen 20.00 50.00
SA S.Abdur-Rahim Reef/50 30.00 80.00
SE S.Telfair Bassy/50 8.00 20.00
SM Shawn Marion Matrix/50 15.00 40.00
ST Stephon Marbury 40.00 100.00
TK1 Kukoc Croat. Sensation/100 125.00 300.00
TK2 Kukoc Pink Panther/100 125.00 300.00
TM Tracy McGrady T-Mac/50 200.00 500.00
AU S.Augmon Plastic Man/100 12.00 30.00

2004-05 SP Signature Edition Alumni Associates

PRINT RUN 100 SER.#'d SETS
AB G.Arenas/M.Bibby 40.00 100.00
BO C.Boozer/C.Duhon 20.00 50.00
CS L.Chalmers/R.Sato 12.00 30.00
DA B.Davis/T.Ariza 40.00 100.00
HG R.Hamilton/B.Gordon 40.00 100.00
JI R.Jefferson/A.Iguodala 40.00 100.00
JJ F.Jones/L.Jackson 12.00 30.00
KD K.Hinrich/D.Gooden 40.00 100.00
MD C.Maggette/L.Deng 20.00 50.00
NW J.Nelson/Del.West 20.00 50.00
RR J.Richardson/Z.Randolph 40.00 100.00

2004-05 SP Signature Edition INKredible INKscriptions

PRINT RUN 25 SER.#'d SETS
AK Andrei Kirilenko 40.00 100.00
AL Ray Allen 200.00 500.00
AS Amare Stoudemire 40.00 100.00
BD B.Davis Bdiddy 200.00 500.00
BG B.Gordon 04 NCAA Champ 40.00 100.00
BG2 B.Gordon Draft Pick #3 40.00 100.00
BK Bob Knight 125.00 300.00
CA1 C.Anthony Final 4 MVP 400.00 800.00
CA2 Anthony 03 NCAA Champ 400.00 800.00
CA3 Carmelo Anthony Melo 500.00 1,000.00
CD Drexler Phi Slamma Jamma 400.00 800.00
CH C.Billups 04 Finals MVP 200.00 500.00
DE Devin Harris Big 10 POY 30.00 80.00
DE2 Devin Harris Draft Pick #5 30.00 80.00
DH D.Howard 04 Naismith AW 150.00 400.00
DH2 D.Howard Draft Pick #1 150.00 400.00
DH3 Dwight Howard 100.00 250.00
DR D.Robinson The Admiral 500.00 1,000.00
HO Olajuwon Phi Slamma Jamma 500.00 1,000.00
JA Jalen Rose Fab Five 125.00 300.00
JC J.Childress 04 Pac 10 POY 40.00 100.00
JE Julius Erving Dr. J 500.00 1,000.00
JH Josh Howard 15.00 40.00
JN J.Nelson John Wooden AW 40.00 100.00
JR J.R.Smith McDonald's MVP 125.00 300.00
JR2 J.R. Smith 40.00 100.00
KG Kevin Garnett 2004 MVP 500.00 1,000.00
KS Kirk Snyder 04 WAC POY 30.00 80.00
LJ1 LeBron James King James 10,000.00 20,000.00
LJ2 L.James 04 Naismith AW 8,000.00 15,000.00
LJ3 LeBron James 04 ROY 8,000.00 15,000.00
MA Magic Johnson 300.00 600.00
PS P.Stojakovic 3 Time All-Star 75.00 200.00
RA1 Araujo 04 Mount.West POY 20.00 50.00
RH R.Hamilton 04 NBA Champs 200.00 500.00
SL1 S.Livingston Draft Pick #4 100.00 250.00
SL2 Shaun Livingston Geezy 100.00 250.00
ST1 Telfair 3 Time PSAL Champ 40.00 100.00
TA1 Tony Allen 2004 Big 12 POY 40.00 100.00
TA2 Tony Allen 15.00 40.00
TM T.McGrady 5 Time All-Star 400.00 800.00
WJ J.Williams White Chocolate 400.00 800.00

2004-05 SP Signature Edition Marks of Distinction

PRINT RUN 25 SER.#'d SETS
AK Andrei Kirilenko 15.00 40.00
BD Baron Davis 25.00 60.00
BK Bernard King 40.00 100.00
BR Bill Russell 1,500.00 3,000.00
BW Ben Wallace 75.00 200.00
CA Carmelo Anthony 125.00 300.00
CD Clyde Drexler 125.00 300.00
DH Dwight Howard 150.00 400.00
DR David Robinson 150.00 400.00
HO Hakeem Olajuwon 150.00 400.00
IT Isiah Thomas 75.00 200.00
JE Julius Erving 150.00 400.00
JK Jason Kidd 100.00 250.00
JR Jason Richardson 40.00 100.00
JS John Stockton 150.00 400.00
KB Kobe Bryant 2,500.00 5,000.00
KG Kevin Garnett 300.00 600.00
KH Kirk Hinrich 30.00 80.00
LB Larry Bird 400.00 800.00
LJ LeBron James 4,000.00 8,000.00
MA Magic Johnson 400.00 800.00
MJ Michael Jordan 4,000.00 8,000.00
PG Pau Gasol 100.00 250.00
PP Paul Pierce 100.00 250.00
PS Peja Stojakovic 40.00 100.00
RA Ray Allen 150.00 400.00
SM Stephon Marbury 100.00 250.00
TM Tracy McGrady 150.00 400.00
YM Yao Ming 400.00 800.00

2004-05 SP Signature Edition Marquee Marks

PRINT RUN 100 SER.#'d SETS
JB M.Johnson/K.Bryant 1,500.00 3,000.00
KR B.King/W.Reed 75.00 200.00
MM Y.Ming/T.McGrady 500.00 1,000.00
MT S.Marbury/S.Telfair 20.00 50.00
NL C.Neal/M.Lemon 200.00 500.00
SB P.Stojakovic/M.Bibby 40.00 100.00
SH J.R.Smith/D.Howard 75.00 200.00

2004-05 SP Signature Edition Pride of a Nation

PRINT RUN 100 SER.#'d SETS
BV P.Brezec/S.Vujacic 10.00 25.00
KG T.Kukoc/G.Giricek 15.00 40.00
KK V.Khryapa/A.Kirilenko 10.00 25.00
KP A.Kirilenko/P.Podkolzin 10.00 25.00
VU S.Vujacic/B.Udrih 10.00 25.00

2004-05 SP Signature Edition Quadruple Authentic Signatures

PRINT RUN 15 SER.#'d SETS
BJJB Kobe/Magic/LeBron/Bird 8,000.00 15,000.00
CBPP Cousy/Bird/Pierce/Payton* 1,000.00 2,000.00
KSJM Kidd/Stckn/Magic/Mrbry* 300.00 600.00
SMGK Peja/Yao/Gasol/Kirilenko 300.00 600.00
WOMR Wallace/Hakeem/Yao/D.Rob 500.00 1,000.00

2004-05 SP Signature Edition Rookie Auto Drafts

CARDS #'D TO DRAFT POSITION
AE Andre Emmett/35 4.00 10.00
AN Antonio Burks/36 4.00 10.00
AV Anderson Varejao/30 5.00 12.00
BR Bernard Robinson/45 4.00 10.00
BU Beno Udrih/28 5.00 12.00
CD Chris Duhon/38 5.00 12.00
DA David Harrison/29 4.00 10.00
DW Dorell Wright/19 5.00 12.00
JN Jameer Nelson/20 6.00 15.00
JR J.R. Smith/18 15.00 40.00
JS Josh Smith/17 6.00 15.00
JU Justin Reed/40 4.00 10.00
KM Kevin Martin/26 8.00 20.00
KS Kirk Snyder/16 4.00 10.00
LC Lionel Chalmers/33 5.00 12.00
LF Luis Flores/55 5.00 12.00
MF Matt Freije/53 4.00 10.00
NK Nenad Krstic/24 5.00 12.00
PP Pavel Podkolzin/21 4.00 10.00
PR Peter John Ramos/32 4.00 10.00
PS Pape Sow/47 4.00 10.00
RI Royal Ivey/37 4.00 10.00
RO Romain Sato/52 4.00 10.00
SV Sasha Vujacic/27 5.00 12.00
TP Tim Pickett/44 5.00 12.00
TR Trevor Ariza/43 6.00 15.00
WE Delonte West/24 5.00 12.00

2004-05 SP Signature Edition Rookie GRAPHiti

PRINT RUN 200 SER.#'d SETS
AB Andris Biedrins 4.00 10.00
AE Andre Emmett 4.00 10.00
AI Andre Iguodala 10.00 25.00
AJ Al Jefferson 6.00 15.00
AN Andres Nocioni 6.00 15.00
AV Anderson Varejao 6.00 15.00
BG Ben Gordon 6.00 15.00
BR Bernard Robinson 4.00 10.00
BU Beno Udrih 5.00 12.00
CD Chris Duhon 5.00 12.00
DA David Harrison 4.00 10.00
DE Devin Harris 5.00 12.00
DH Dwight Howard 20.00 50.00
DW Dorell Wright 5.00 12.00
JC Josh Childress 4.00 10.00
JN Jameer Nelson 6.00 15.00
JR J.R. Smith 6.00 15.00
JS Josh Smith 6.00 15.00
JU Justin Reed 4.00 10.00
JV Jackson Vroman 4.00 10.00
KH Kris Humphries 5.00 12.00
KM Kevin Martin 8.00 20.00
KS Kirk Snyder 4.00 10.00
LC Lionel Chalmers 5.00 12.00
LD Luol Deng 6.00 15.00
LF Luis Flores 5.00 12.00
LJ Luke Jackson 4.00 10.00
MF Matt Freije 4.00 10.00
NK Nenad Krstic 5.00 12.00
PR Peter John Ramos 4.00 10.00
RA Rafael Araujo 4.00 10.00
RS Robert Swift 4.00 10.00
SL Shaun Livingston 6.00 15.00
ST Sebastian Telfair 5.00 12.00
SV Sasha Vujacic 5.00 12.00
TA Tony Allen 6.00 15.00
TP Tim Pickett 5.00 12.00
TR Trevor Ariza 6.00 15.00
WE Delonte West 5.00 12.00
YT Yuta Tabuse 12.00 30.00

2004-05 SP Signature Edition Rookies INKorporated

PRINT RUN 100 SER.#'d SET
AB Andris Biedrins 4.00 10.00
AE Andre Emmett 4.00 10.00
AI Andre Iguodala 10.00 25.00
AJ Al Jefferson 6.00 15.00
AN Andres Nocioni 6.00 15.00
AV Anderson Varejao 5.00 12.00
BG Ben Gordon 6.00 15.00
BR Bernard Robinson 4.00 10.00
BU Beno Udrih 5.00 12.00
CD Chris Duhon 5.00 12.00
DA David Harrison 4.00 10.00
DE Devin Harris 5.00 12.00
DH Dwight Howard 30.00 80.00
DW Dorell Wright 5.00 12.00
JC Josh Childress 4.00 10.00
JN Jameer Nelson 6.00 15.00
JR J.R. Smith 6.00 15.00
JS Josh Smith 6.00 15.00
JV Jackson Vroman 4.00 10.00
KH Kris Humphries 5.00 12.00
KM Kevin Martin 8.00 20.00
KS Kirk Snyder 4.00 10.00
LC Lionel Chalmers 5.00 12.00
LD Luol Deng 6.00 15.00
LF Luis Flores 5.00 12.00
LJ Luke Jackson 4.00 10.00
MF Matt Freije 4.00 10.00
NK Nenad Krstic 5.00 12.00
PR Peter John Ramos 4.00 10.00
RA Rafael Araujo 4.00 10.00
RS Robert Swift 4.00 10.00
SL Shaun Livingston 6.00 15.00
ST Sebastian Telfair 5.00 12.00
SV Sasha Vujacic 5.00 12.00
TA Tony Allen 6.00 15.00
TP Tim Pickett 5.00 12.00
TR Trevor Ariza 6.00 15.00
WE Delonte West 5.00 12.00
YT Yuta Tabuse 12.00 30.00

2004-05 SP Signature Edition Scripts for Success

PRINT RUN 25 SER.#'d SETS
AB Andris Biedrins 5.00 12.00
AE Andre Emmett 5.00 12.00
AI Andre Iguodala 12.00 30.00
AJ Al Jefferson 8.00 20.00
AN Andres Nocioni 8.00 20.00
AV Anderson Varejao 6.00 15.00
BG Ben Gordon 8.00 20.00
BR Bernard Robinson 5.00 12.00
BU Beno Udrih 6.00 15.00
CD Chris Duhon 6.00 15.00
DA David Harrison 5.00 12.00
DE Devin Harris 6.00 15.00
DH Dwight Howard 50.00 120.00
DW Dorell Wright 6.00 15.00
JC Josh Childress 5.00 12.00
JN Jameer Nelson 8.00 20.00
JR J.R. Smith 8.00 20.00
JS Josh Smith 8.00 20.00
JU Justin Reed 5.00 12.00
JV Jackson Vroman 5.00 12.00
KH Kris Humphries 6.00 15.00
KM Kevin Martin 10.00 25.00
KS Kirk Snyder 5.00 12.00
LC Lionel Chalmers 6.00 15.00
LD Luol Deng 8.00 20.00
LF Luis Flores 6.00 15.00
LJ Luke Jackson 5.00 12.00
MF Matt Freije 5.00 12.00
NK Nenad Krstic 6.00 15.00
PR Peter John Ramos 5.00 12.00
RA Rafael Araujo 5.00 12.00
RS Robert Swift 5.00 12.00
SL Shaun Livingston 8.00 20.00
ST Sebastian Telfair 6.00 15.00
SV Sasha Vujacic 6.00 15.00
TA Tony Allen 8.00 20.00
TP Tim Pickett 6.00 15.00
TR Trevor Ariza 8.00 20.00
WE Delonte West 6.00 15.00
YT Yuta Tabuse 20.00 50.00

2004-05 SP Signature Edition Signatures

OVERALL AUTOGRAPH ODDS 1:1
AB Andris Biedrins 3.00 8.00
AE Andre Emmett 3.00 8.00
AH Al Harrington 4.00 10.00
AI Andre Iguodala 10.00 25.00
AJ Al Jefferson 6.00 15.00
AK Andrei Kirilenko 8.00 20.00
AL Ray Allen 40.00 100.00
AN Antawn Jamison 4.00 10.00
AR Carlos Arroyo 6.00 15.00
AS Amare Stoudemire 8.00 20.00
AV Anderson Varejao 4.00 10.00
BC Bob Cousy 100.00 250.00
BD Baron Davis 8.00 20.00
BE Beno Udrih 4.00 10.00
BG Ben Gordon 5.00 12.00
BK Bernard King 10.00 25.00
BM Brad Miller 4.00 10.00
BO Carlos Boozer 4.00 10.00
BR Bill Russell SP 1,500.00 3,000.00
BU Antonio Burks 3.00 8.00
BW Ben Wallace 40.00 100.00
CA Carmelo Anthony SP 100.00 250.00
CD Chris Duhon 4.00 10.00
CL Clyde Drexler 40.00 100.00
CM Corey Maggette 3.00 8.00
CR Jamal Crawford SP 10.00 25.00
DA David Harrison 3.00 8.00
DE Dennis Rodman 60.00 150.00
DF Derek Fisher 12.00 30.00
DH Dwight Howard 30.00 80.00
DM Desmond Mason 4.00 10.00
DR David Robinson SP 100.00 250.00

DS Donta Smith 3.00 8.00
GG George Gervin 12.00 30.00
HA Devin Harris 4.00 10.00
HO Hakeem Olajuwon SP 100.00 250.00
IT Isiah Thomas SP 40.00 100.00
IV Royal Ivey 3.00 8.00
JA Jason Richardson 8.00 20.00
JC Josh Childress SP 8.00 20.00
JE Julius Erving SP 100.00 250.00
JH Josh Howard 4.00 10.00
JK Jason Kidd SP 20.00 50.00
JN Jameer Nelson 5.00 12.00
JR J.R. Smith 5.00 12.00
JS John Stockton SP 75.00 200.00
JV Jackson Vroman 3.00 8.00
JW Jason Williams SP 75.00 200.00
KB Kobe Bryant SP 2,000.00 4,000.00
KG Kevin Garnett SP 100.00 250.00
KH Kris Humphries 4.00 10.00
KI Kirk Hinrich 5.00 12.00
KM Kevin Martin 6.00 15.00
KR Kareem Rush 3.00 8.00
KS Kirk Snyder 3.00 8.00
LB Larry Bird SP 100.00 250.00
LC Lionel Chalmers 4.00 10.00
LD Luol Deng 5.00 12.00
LF Luis Flores 4.00 10.00
LJ LeBron James 2,000.00 4,000.00
LO Lamar Odom SP 20.00 50.00
LU Luke Jackson 3.00 8.00
MA Magic Johnson SP 100.00 250.00
MB Mike Bibby SP 10.00 25.00
MD Marquis Daniels 3.00 8.00
MJ Michael Jordan SP 3,000.00 6,000.00
MR Michael Redd 4.00 10.00
NH Nene 4.00 10.00
NK Nenad Krstic 4.00 10.00
NO Andres Nocioni 5.00 12.00
PG Pau Gasol 25.00 60.00
PP Paul Pierce SP 25.00 60.00
PR Peter John Ramos 3.00 8.00
PS Peja Stojakovic 4.00 10.00
RA Rafael Araujo 3.00 8.00
RE Justin Reed 3.00 8.00
RH Richard Hamilton 12.00 30.00
RJ Richard Jefferson 4.00 10.00
RM Reggie Miller SP 100.00 250.00
RO Bernard Robinson 3.00 8.00
RS Robert Swift 3.00 8.00
SA Romain Sato 3.00 8.00
SC Sam Cassell 4.00 10.00
SF Shareef Abdur-Rahim 5.00 12.00
SH Shawn Marion 5.00 12.00
SL Shaun Livingston 5.00 12.00
SM Josh Smith 5.00 12.00
ST Stephon Marbury 15.00 40.00
SV Sasha Vujacic 4.00 10.00
TA Tony Allen 5.00 12.00
TE Sebastian Telfair SP 4.00 10.00
TM Tracy McGrady SP 75.00 200.00
TP Tony Parker 20.00 50.00
TP2 T.Parker AU Both Sides 25.00 60.00
TR Trevor Ariza 5.00 12.00
WE Delonte West 4.00 10.00
WR Dorell Wright 4.00 10.00
YM Yao Ming SP 125.00 300.00
ZO Alonzo Mourning SP 75.00 200.00
ZR Zach Randolph 12.00 30.00

2004-05 SP Signature Edition Signatures Dual

PRINT RUN 100 SER.#'d SETS
SP PRINT RUN 25 SER.#'d SETS
AA A.Emmett/A.Burks 8.00 20.00
AM C.Anthony/T.McGrady SP 50.00 120.00
AT S.Abdur-Rahim/S.Telfair 8.00 20.00
BH C.Billups/R.Hamilton 40.00 100.00
BJ K.Bryant/M.Jordan SP 6,000.00 12,000.00
BM M.Bibby/Kv.Martin 12.00 30.00
BS C.Boozer/K.Snyder 8.00 20.00
CS J.Childress/Josh Smith* 10.00 25.00
DH M.Daniels/D.Harris 10.00 25.00
DP B.Davis/T.Parker 25.00 60.00
DS B.Davis/J.R.Smith 20.00 50.00
DT Del.West/T.Allen 10.00 25.00
EJ J.Erving/M.Jordan SP* 2,000.00 4,000.00
GC K.Garnett/S.Cassell* 125.00 300.00
GD B.Gordon/L.Deng 12.00 30.00
GH K.Garnett/D.Howard SP 150.00 400.00
HN D.Howard/J.Nelson 40.00 100.00
JB L.James/K.Bryant SP 4,000.00 8,000.00
JH L.James/D.Howard SP 1,000.00 2,000.00
JJ M.Jordan/L.James SP 6,000.00 12,000.00
JR A.Jamison/P.J.Ramos 8.00 20.00
JV L.Jackson/A.Varejao 8.00 20.00
KH Kirilenko/Humphries 8.00 20.00
KJ J.Kidd/R.Jefferson 20.00 50.00
KM B.King/S.Marbury SP 20.00 50.00
LC S.Livingston/L.Chalmers 8.00 20.00
LM L.Bird/M.Johnson SP* 500.00 1,000.00
MG T.McGrady/K.Garnett SP 350.00 700.00
MH R.Miller/D.Harrison 75.00 200.00
OM Olajuwon/Y.Ming SP 500.00 1,000.00
OR L.Odom/K.Rush 8.00 20.00
PA M.Peterson/R.Araujo* 8.00 20.00
PP P.Pierce/G.Payton* 125.00 300.00
RB B.Russell/L.Bird SP 2,000.00 4,000.00
RS Z.Randolph/D.Stoudamire 12.00 30.00
SM A.Stoudamire/S.Marion* 15.00 40.00
VM J.Vroman/S.Marion 8.00 20.00
WR B.Wallace/D.Rodman SP 125.00 300.00

2004-05 SP Signature Edition SP Signs

PRINT RUN 50 TO 100 SER.#'d SETS
AE Andre Emmett/100 4.00 10.00
AH Al Harrington/100 5.00 12.00
AI Andre Iguodala/50 12.00 30.00
AJ Al Jefferson/100 6.00 15.00
AK Andrei Kirilenko/50 5.00 12.00
AL Ray Allen/100 40.00 100.00
AM Andre Miller/100 5.00 12.00
AN Antawn Jamison/100 5.00 12.00
AR Carlos Arroyo/100 4.00 10.00
AS Amare Stoudemire/100 8.00 20.00
AV Anderson Varejao/100 5.00 12.00
BC Bob Cousy/50 75.00 200.00
BD Baron Davis/50 10.00 25.00
BE Beno Udrih/100 5.00 12.00
BG Ben Gordon/50 6.00 15.00
BI Bill Walton/100 12.00 30.00
BK Bernard King/50 12.00 30.00
BM Brad Miller/100 5.00 12.00
BO Carlos Boozer/100 5.00 12.00
BR Bill Russell/50 1,000.00 2,000.00
BU Antonio Burks/100 4.00 10.00
BW Ben Wallace/50 30.00 80.00
CA Carmelo Anthony/50 40.00 100.00
CB Chauncey Billups/100 12.00 30.00
CD Chris Duhon/100 5.00 12.00
CL Clyde Drexler/50 40.00 100.00
CM Corey Maggette/100 5.00 12.00
DA David Harrison/100 4.00 10.00
DE Dennis Rodman/50 60.00 150.00
DG Drew Gooden/100 4.00 10.00
DH Dwight Howard/100 12.00 30.00
DW Dorell Wright/100 5.00 12.00
ED Erik Daniels/100 5.00 12.00
GG George Gervin/100 12.00 30.00
HA Devin Harris/50 5.00 12.00
HO Hakeem Olajuwon/50 50.00 120.00
HS Ha Seung-Jin/100 6.00 15.00
IT Isiah Thomas/100 20.00 50.00
JC Josh Childress/50 4.00 10.00
JE Julius Erving/50 75.00 200.00
JH Josh Howard/100 5.00 12.00
JK Jason Kidd/50 20.00 50.00
JM Jamaal Magloire/100 4.00 10.00
JN Jameer Nelson/100 6.00 15.00
JR J.R. Smith/100 6.00 15.00
JS John Stockton/50 60.00 150.00
JU Justin Reed/100 4.00 10.00
JV Jackson Vroman/100 4.00 10.00
JW Jason Williams/100 50.00 120.00
KB Kobe Bryant/50 800.00 1,500.00
KH Kris Humphries/100 5.00 12.00
KI Kirk Hinrich/50 6.00 15.00
KM Kevin Martin/100 8.00 20.00
KS Kirk Snyder/100 4.00 10.00
LB Larry Bird/50 100.00 250.00
LC Lionel Chalmers/100 5.00 12.00
LD Luol Deng/50 6.00 15.00
LF Luis Flores/100 5.00 12.00
LJ LeBron James/50 1,000.00 2,000.00
LO Lamar Odom/50 6.00 15.00
LU Luke Jackson/100 4.00 10.00
MA Magic Johnson/100 75.00 200.00
MB Mike Bibby/100 10.00 25.00
MC Michael Cooper/100 10.00 25.00
MJ Michael Jordan/100 2,000.00 4,000.00
MR Michael Redd/50 5.00 12.00
NO Andres Nocioni/100 6.00 15.00
PA Pape Sow/100 4.00 10.00
PG Pau Gasol/100 25.00 60.00
PP Paul Pierce/50 30.00 80.00
PR Pat Riley/50 25.00 60.00
PS Peja Stojakovic/50 5.00 12.00
RA Rafael Araujo/100 4.00 10.00
RH Richard Hamilton/50 12.00 30.00
RJ Richard Jefferson/100 5.00 12.00
SA Romain Sato/100 4.00 10.00
SC Sam Cassell/100 5.00 12.00
SF Shareef Abdur-Rahim/100 6.00 15.00
SL Shaun Livingston/50 6.00 15.00
SM Josh Smith/50 6.00 15.00
SP Scottie Pippen/100 125.00 300.00
ST Stephon Marbury/100 12.00 30.00
TA Tony Allen/100 6.00 15.00
TE Sebastian Telfair/100 5.00 12.00
TM Tracy McGrady/100 40.00 100.00
TP Tony Parker/100 20.00 50.00
TR Trevor Ariza/100 6.00 15.00
WE Delonte West/100 5.00 12.00
WF Walt Frazier/100 12.00 30.00
YM Yao Ming/50 150.00 400.00

2004-05 SP Signature Edition Triple Authentic Signatures

PRINT RUN 25 SER.#'d SETS
ARD Shareef/Randolph/Drexler* 50.00 120.00
BJA Kobe/Magic/Kareem* 2,000.00 4,000.00
BJE Bird/Magic/Erving* 1,000.00 2,000.00
BPJ Bird/Pierce/A.Jefferson* 200.00 500.00
DMS Baron/Magloire/J.R.Smith 40.00 100.00
GDH Gordon/Deng/Hinrich 40.00 100.00
GMH KG/McGrady/D.Howard 400.00 800.00
HBW Hamilton/Billups/Wallace 200.00 500.00
JAJ LeBron/Carmelo/Jordan* 6,000.00 12,000.00
JBJ Jordan/Kobe/LeBron 10,000.00 20,000.00
JHA LeBron/Howard/Carmelo* 1,000.00 2,000.00
LTH Livingston/Telfair/D.Harris 12.00 30.00
OMM Olajuwon/Yao/McGrady 600.00 1,200.00
SCS Jo.Smith/Childress/D.Smith 12.00 30.00
SKH Stockton/Kirilenko/Humph 75.00 200.00

2005-06 SP Signature Edition

COMP.SET w/o SP's (100) 50.00 100.00
1 Josh Smith .50 1.25
2 Josh Childress .40 1.00
3 Joe Johnson .50 1.25
4 Paul Pierce 1.00 2.50
5 Ricky Davis .50 1.25
6 Al Jefferson .40 1.00
7 Emeka Okafor .50 1.25
8 Kareem Rush .40 1.00
9 Gerald Wallace .50 1.25
10 Michael Jordan 5.00 12.00
11 Ben Gordon .50 1.25
12 Luol Deng .50 1.25
13 Kirk Hinrich .50 1.25
14 LeBron James 5.00 12.00
15 Larry Hughes .50 1.25
16 Zydrunas Ilgauskas .50 1.25
17 Donyell Marshall .40 1.00
18 Dirk Nowitzki 1.50 4.00
19 Jason Terry .50 1.25
20 Josh Howard .50 1.25
21 Devin Harris .40 1.00
22 Carmelo Anthony 1.00 2.50
23 Marcus Camby .50 1.25
24 Andre Miller .50 1.25
25 Kenyon Martin .50 1.25
26 Chauncey Billups .75 2.00
27 Ben Wallace .75 2.00
28 Richard Hamilton .75 2.00
29 Jason Richardson .60 1.50
30 Troy Murphy .40 1.00
31 Baron Davis .60 1.50
32 Tracy McGrady 1.00 2.50
33 Yao Ming 1.25 3.00
34 Stromile Swift .40 1.00
35 Jermaine O'Neal .50 1.25
36 Ron Artest .50 1.25
37 Stephen Jackson .50 1.25
38 Corey Maggette .50 1.25
39 Shaun Livingston .50 1.25
40 Chris Wilcox .40 1.00
41 Elton Brand .50 1.25
42 Kobe Bryant 5.00 12.00
43 Kwame Brown .40 1.00
44 Lamar Odom .50 1.25
45 Pau Gasol 1.00 2.50
46 Damon Stoudamire .60 1.50
47 Lorenzen Wright .40 1.00
48 Shaquille O'Neal 2.00 5.00
49 Dwyane Wade 1.25 3.00
50 Antoine Walker .50 1.25
51 Jason Williams 1.00 2.50
52 Desmond Mason .40 1.00
53 Michael Redd .50 1.25
54 Maurice Williams .50 1.25
55 Kevin Garnett 1.50 4.00
56 Marko Jaric .40 1.00
57 Wally Szczerbiak .50 1.25
58 Jason Kidd 1.00 2.50
59 Richard Jefferson .50 1.25
60 Vince Carter 1.25 3.00
61 Jamaal Magloire .40 1.00
62 J.R. Smith .60 1.50
63 Speedy Claxton .40 1.00
64 Stephon Marbury .75 2.00
65 Quentin Richardson .40 1.00
66 Mike Sweetney .40 1.00
67 Grant Hill 1.00 2.50
68 Dwight Howard .75 2.00
69 Steve Francis .60 1.50
70 Allen Iverson 1.25 3.00
71 Samuel Dalembert .40 1.00
72 Kyle Korver .50 1.25
73 Chris Webber .75 2.00
74 Steve Nash 1.25 3.00
75 Amare Stoudemire .60 1.50
76 Shawn Marion .60 1.50
77 Sebastian Telfair .50 1.25
78 Zach Randolph .60 1.50
79 Juan Dixon .40 1.00
80 Mike Bibby .60 1.50
81 Peja Stojakovic .50 1.25
82 Brad Miller .50 1.25
83 Tim Duncan 1.50 4.00
84 Manu Ginobili 1.25 3.00
85 Robert Horry .60 1.50
86 Tony Parker 1.00 2.50
87 Ray Allen 1.00 2.50
88 Rashard Lewis .50 1.25
89 Vladimir Radmanovic .40 1.00
90 Chris Bosh .75 2.00
91 Rafer Alston .50 1.25
92 Jalen Rose .50 1.25
93 Andrei Kirilenko .50 1.25
94 Matt Harpring .40 1.00
95 Carlos Boozer .50 1.25
96 Mehmet Okur .40 1.00
97 Gilbert Arenas .60 1.50
98 Antawn Jamison .50 1.25
99 Caron Butler .50 1.25
100 Antonio Daniels .40 1.00
101 Andrew Bogut RC 3.00 8.00
102 Marvin Williams RC 2.50 6.00
103 Deron Williams RC 4.00 10.00
104 Chris Paul RC 40.00 100.00
105 Raymond Felton RC 2.00 5.00
106 Martell Webster RC 2.00 5.00
107 Charlie Villanueva RC 2.00 5.00
108 Channing Frye RC 2.00 5.00
109 Ike Diogu RC 1.50 4.00
110 Andrew Bynum RC 2.00 5.00
111 Sean May RC 1.50 4.00
112 Rashad McCants RC 1.50 4.00
113 Antoine Wright RC 2.00 5.00
114 Joey Graham RC 2.00 5.00
115 Danny Granger RC 2.50 6.00
116 Gerald Green RC 2.50 6.00
117 Hakim Warrick RC 2.00 5.00
118 Julius Hodge RC 1.50 4.00
119 Nate Robinson RC 2.50 6.00
120 Jarrett Jack RC 2.50 6.00
121 Francisco Garcia RC 1.50 4.00
122 Luther Head RC 1.50 4.00
123 Johan Petro RC 1.50 4.00
124 Jason Maxiell RC 2.00 5.00
125 Linas Kleiza RC 2.00 5.00
126 Wayne Simien RC 1.50 4.00
127 David Lee RC 2.50 6.00
128 Salim Stoudamire RC 2.00 5.00
129 Daniel Ewing RC 2.00 5.00
130 Brandon Bass RC 2.00 5.00
131 C.J. Miles RC 2.00 5.00
132 Ersan Ilyasova RC 2.00 5.00
133 Travis Diener RC 1.50 4.00
134 Monta Ellis RC 3.00 8.00
135 Chris Taft RC 1.50 4.00
136 Martynas Andriuskevicius RC 1.50 4.00
137 Louis Williams RC 6.00 15.00
138 Bracey Wright RC 1.50 4.00
139 Robert Whaley RC 1.50 4.00
140 Andray Blatche RC 2.50 6.00
141 Ryan Gomes RC 2.00 5.00
142 Sarunas Jasikevicius RC 2.50 6.00

2005-06 SP Signature Edition Gold

*1-100 GOLD: 3X TO 8X BASE HI
*101-142 GOLD: 1.25X TO 3X BASE HI
GOLD PRINT RUN 25 SER.#'d SETS
10 Michael Jordan 100.00 250.00
104 Chris Paul 150.00 400.00

2005-06 SP Signature Edition INKredible INKscriptions

PRINT RUNS 50 TO 100 SER.#'d SETS
AB Andrew Bogut/50 25.00 60.00
AJ Al Jefferson/100 10.00 25.00
AK Andrei Kirilenko/50 15.00 40.00
BB Brent Barry/100 20.00 50.00
BI Bill Walton/100 40.00 100.00
BJ Bobby Jackson/100 20.00 50.00
BK Bob Knight/50 200.00 500.00
BL Bill Laimbeer/100 40.00 100.00
BR Brandon Bass/100 6.00 15.00
CB Chris Bosh/50 40.00 100.00
CH Chauncey Billups/100 40.00 100.00
CP Chris Paul/50 500.00 1,000.00
DA David Robinson/50 100.00 250.00
DR Dennis Rodman/50 150.00 400.00
EB Elton Brand/50 20.00 50.00
EH Elvin Hayes/100 40.00 100.00
EO Emeka Okafor/100 6.00 15.00
GE George Gervin/100 25.00 60.00
GG Gerald Green/100 8.00 20.00
HO Hakeem Olajuwon/50 100.00 250.00
HW Hakim Warrick/100 12.00 30.00
IT Isiah Thomas/50 40.00 100.00
JE Julius Erving/50 150.00 400.00
JG Joey Graham/100 6.00 15.00
JH Julius Hodge/100 6.00 15.00
KA Kareem Abdul-Jabbar/50 300.00 600.00
KW Kwame Brown/100 20.00 50.00
LB LeBron James/50 3,000.00 6,000.00
LH Larry Hughes/100 15.00 40.00
LW Louis Williams/100 15.00 40.00
MJ Magic Johnson/50 200.00 500.00
MW Marvin Williams/50 10.00 25.00
NR Nate Robinson/100 40.00 100.00
PP Paul Pierce/50 150.00 400.00
QR Quentin Richardson/100 6.00 15.00
RA Ron Artest/50 20.00 50.00
RF Raymond Felton/100 6.00 15.00
RM Rashad McCants/100 6.00 15.00
RP Robert Parish/50 20.00 50.00
SE Sean May/100 6.00 15.00
SM Stephon Marbury/50 20.00 50.00
SN Steve Nash/50 125.00 300.00
SP Scottie Pippen/50 200.00 500.00
SS Salim Stoudamire/100 6.00 15.00
TM Tracy McGrady/50 125.00 300.00
WS Wayne Simien/100 6.00 15.00
YM Yao Ming/50 300.00 600.00

2005-06 SP Signature Edition Marks of Distinction

PRINT RUN 40 SER.#'d SETS
AB Andrew Bogut 8.00 20.00
AJ Antawn Jamison 8.00 20.00
AN Andrew Bynum 8.00 20.00
AW Antoine Wright 8.00 20.00
CB Chris Bosh 8.00 20.00
CF Channing Frye 8.00 20.00
CH Chauncey Billups 10.00 25.00
CM Cuttino Mobley 8.00 20.00
CP Chris Paul 400.00 800.00
CV Charlie Villanueva 8.00 20.00
DG Danny Granger 8.00 20.00
DH Dwight Howard 12.00 30.00
DR Dennis Rodman 20.00 50.00
DW Deron Williams 8.00 20.00
FG Francisco Garcia 8.00 20.00
GG Gerald Green 8.00 20.00
HO Hakeem Olajuwon 20.00 50.00
HW Hakim Warrick 8.00 20.00
IT Isiah Thomas 20.00 50.00
JG Joey Graham 8.00 20.00
JH Julius Hodge 8.00 20.00
JJ Jarrett Jack 8.00 20.00
JK Jason Kidd 15.00 40.00
JS J.R. Smith 8.00 20.00
LB Larry Bird 50.00 120.00
LJ LeBron James 2,000.00 4,000.00
LO Lamar Odom 8.00 20.00
MA Magic Johnson 50.00 120.00
MJ Michael Jordan 2,500.00 5,000.00
MR Michael Redd 8.00 20.00
MV Marvin Williams 8.00 20.00
MW Martell Webster 8.00 20.00
NR Nate Robinson 8.00 20.00
PP Paul Pierce 12.00 30.00
RF Raymond Felton 8.00 20.00
RM Rashad McCants 8.00 20.00
SM Sean May 8.00 20.00
ST Stephon Marbury 12.00 30.00
TC Tyson Chandler 8.00 20.00
TM Tracy McGrady 20.00 50.00
YM Yao Ming 20.00 50.00

2005-06 SP Signature Edition Rookie GRAPHiti

PRINT RUN 100 SER.#'d SETS
AB Andray Blatche 6.00 15.00
AW Antoine Wright 5.00 12.00
BB Brandon Bass 5.00 12.00
BW Bracey Wright 4.00 10.00
CT Chris Taft 4.00 10.00
DE Daniel Ewing 5.00 12.00
DL David Lee 6.00 15.00
DT Dijon Thompson 4.00 10.00
EI Ersan Ilyasova 5.00 12.00
GG Gerald Green 6.00 15.00
HW Hakim Warrick 5.00 12.00
JG Joey Graham 5.00 12.00
JH Julius Hodge 4.00 10.00
JM Jason Maxiell 5.00 12.00
LK Linas Kleiza 5.00 12.00
LR Lawrence Roberts 4.00 10.00
LW Louis Williams 15.00 40.00
MA Martynas Andriuskevicius 4.00 10.00
ME Monta Ellis 15.00 40.00
NR Nate Robinson 15.00 40.00
RG Ryan Gomes 5.00 12.00
SJ Sarunas Jasikevicius 6.00 15.00
SM Sean May 4.00 10.00
SS Salim Stoudamire 5.00 12.00
TD Travis Diener 4.00 10.00

2005-06 SP Signature Edition Rookies INKorporated

PRINT RUN 50 SER.#'d SETS
AB Andrew Bogut 12.50 30.00
AN Andrew Bynum 5.00 12.00
AW Antoine Wright 5.00 12.00
CF Channing Frye 5.00 12.00
CP Chris Paul 400.00 800.00
CV Charlie Villanueva 5.00 12.00
DG Danny Granger 6.00 15.00
DW Deron Williams 10.00 25.00
FG Francisco Garcia 4.00 10.00
GG Gerald Green 6.00 15.00
HW Hakim Warrick 5.00 12.00
ID Ike Diogu 4.00 10.00
JG Joey Graham 5.00 12.00
JH Julius Hodge 4.00 10.00
JJ Jarrett Jack 6.00 15.00
JM Jason Maxiell 5.00 12.00
JP Johan Petro 4.00 10.00
LH Luther Head 4.00 10.00
MA Marvin Williams 6.00 15.00
MW Martell Webster 5.00 12.00
NR Nate Robinson 20.00 50.00
RF Raymond Felton 5.00 12.00
RM Rashad McCants 4.00 10.00
SM Sean May 4.00 10.00
WS Wayne Simien 4.00 10.00

2005-06 SP Signature Edition Scripts for Success

PRINT RUN 200 SER.#'d SETS
*SILVER: .6X TO 1.5X BASE HI
SILVER PRINT RUN 50 SER.#'d SETS
*GOLD: .75X TO 2X BASE HI
GOLD PRINT RUN 25 SER.#'d SETS
AB Andrew Bogut 5.00 12.00
AD Andray Blatche 4.00 10.00
AL Al Jefferson 4.00 10.00
AN Andrew Bynum 3.00 8.00
AW Antoine Wright 3.00 8.00
BB Brandon Bass 3.00 8.00
BR Bruce Bowen 5.00 12.00
BW Bracey Wright 2.50 6.00
CF Channing Frye 3.00 8.00
CP Chris Paul 300.00 600.00
CT Chris Taft 2.50 6.00
CV Charlie Villanueva 3.00 8.00
DD Dan Dickau 3.00 8.00
DE Daniel Ewing 3.00 8.00
DG Danny Granger 4.00 10.00
DH Dwight Howard 12.00 30.00
DL David Lee 4.00 10.00
DS Damon Stoudamire 4.00 10.00
DT Dijon Thompson 2.50 6.00
DW Deron Williams 6.00 15.00
EI Ersan Ilyasova 3.00 8.00
FG Francisco Garcia 2.50 6.00
GG Gerald Green 4.00 10.00
HW Hakim Warrick 3.00 8.00
ID Ike Diogu 2.50 6.00
IT Isiah Thomas 10.00 25.00
JA Jamaal Magloire 4.00 10.00
JG Joey Graham 3.00 8.00
JH Julius Hodge 2.50 6.00
JJ Jarrett Jack 3.00 8.00
JM Jason Maxiell 3.00 8.00
JP Johan Petro 2.50 6.00
JR J.R. Smith 3.00 8.00
KK Kyle Korver 4.00 10.00
LH Luther Head 2.50 6.00
LK Linas Kleiza 3.00 8.00
LO Lamar Odom 5.00 12.00
LR Lawrence Roberts 2.50 6.00
MA Martynas Andriuskevicius 2.50 6.00
MD Marquis Daniels 4.00 10.00
ME Monta Ellis 12.00 30.00
MV Marvin Williams 4.00 10.00
PP Paul Pierce 30.00 80.00
QR Quentin Richardson 4.00 10.00
RF Raymond Felton 3.00 8.00
RG Ryan Gomes 3.00 8.00
RM Rashad McCants 3.00 8.00
RP Robert Parish 8.00 20.00
SA Shareef Abdur-Rahim 4.00 10.00
SJ Sarunas Jasikevicius 4.00 10.00
SM Sean May 2.50 6.00
SS Salim Stoudamire 3.00 8.00
TD Travis Diener 2.50 6.00
WS Wayne Simien 2.50 6.00

2005-06 SP Signature Edition Signatures

*GOLD: .75X TO 2X BASE AU HI
GOLD PRINT RUN 25 SER.#'d SETS
AB Andrew Bogut 6.00 15.00
AD Andre Miller 4.00 10.00
AJ Antawn Jamison 4.00 10.00
AK Andrei Kirilenko 4.00 10.00
AL Al Jefferson 3.00 8.00
AN Andrew Bynum 4.00 10.00
AR Andris Biedrins 3.00 8.00
AR Amir Johnson 5.00 12.00
AW Antoine Wright 3.00 8.00
AY Carlos Arroyo 15.00 40.00
BA Bracey Wright 3.00 8.00
BB Brent Barry 4.00 10.00
BD Baron Davis 5.00 12.00
BJ Bobby Jackson 4.00 10.00
BK Bernard King 12.00 30.00
BL Bill Laimbeer 12.00 30.00
BM Brad Miller 4.00 10.00
BO Bob Knight SP 60.00 150.00
BR Brandon Bass 4.00 10.00
BS Bobby Simmons 3.00 8.00
BT Andray Blatche 3.00 8.00
CA Carmelo Anthony SP 75.00 200.00
CB Carlos Boozer SP 4.00 10.00
CD Chris Duhon 3.00 8.00
CF Channing Frye 3.00 8.00
CH Chauncey Billups 12.00 30.00
CJ C.J. Miles 3.00 8.00
CM Corey Maggette 4.00 10.00
CP Chris Paul 150.00 400.00
CR Chris Bosh 12.00 30.00
CT Chris Taft 3.00 8.00
CU Cuttino Mobley 3.00 8.00
CV Charlie Villanueva 4.00 10.00
CW Chris Wilcox 3.00 8.00
DA Darko Milicic 3.00 8.00
DD Dan Dickau 3.00 8.00
DE Daniel Ewing 4.00 10.00
DG Danny Granger 5.00 12.00
DH David Harrison 3.00 8.00
DL David Lee 5.00 12.00
DM Desmond Mason 3.00 8.00
DO Donyell Marshall 3.00 8.00
DR Dennis Rodman 125.00 300.00
DS Damon Stoudamire 5.00 12.00
DW Deron Williams 8.00 20.00
EB Elton Brand SP 4.00 10.00
EH Elvin Hayes 10.00 25.00
EO Emeka Okafor 4.00 10.00
ES Ersan Ilyasova 4.00 10.00
FG Francisco Garcia 3.00 8.00
GE George Gervin 10.00 25.00
GG Gerald Green 5.00 12.00
GO Gordan Giricek 3.00 8.00
GP Gary Payton 20.00 50.00
GW Gerald Wallace 4.00 10.00
HA Josh Howard 4.00 10.00
HD Dwight Howard 20.00 50.00
HO Hakeem Olajuwon SP 40.00 100.00
HW Hakim Warrick 4.00 10.00
ID Ike Diogu 3.00 8.00
IT Isiah Thomas 20.00 50.00
JA Jason Kidd 20.00 50.00
JC Josh Childress 3.00 8.00
JG Joey Graham 4.00 10.00
JH Julius Hodge 3.00 8.00
JJ Jarrett Jack 5.00 12.00
JK Jason Kapono 3.00 8.00
JM Jason Maxiell 4.00 10.00
JO Joe Johnson 4.00 10.00
JP Johan Petro 4.00 10.00
JR J.R. Smith 5.00 12.00
JS James Singleton 3.00 8.00
KA Kareem Abdul-Jabbar SP 125.00 300.00
KB Kwame Brown 3.00 8.00
KD Keyon Dooling 3.00 8.00
KH Kirk Hinrich 4.00 10.00
KK Kyle Korver 4.00 10.00
KR Kris Humphries 3.00 8.00
LE Luke Jackson 3.00 8.00
LH Larry Hughes 4.00 10.00
LJ LeBron James 1,000.00 2,000.00
LK Linas Kleiza 4.00 10.00
LO Lamar Odom 10.00 25.00
LR Lawrence Roberts 3.00 8.00
LU Luther Head 3.00 8.00
LW Louis Williams 12.00 30.00
MA Martynas Andriuskevicius 3.00 8.00
MC Antonio McDyess 4.00 10.00
MD Marquis Daniels 3.00 8.00
ME Monta Ellis 6.00 15.00
MJ Michael Jordan SP 2,000.00 4,000.00
ML Jamaal Magloire 3.00 8.00
MP Morris Peterson 3.00 8.00
MR Michael Redd 4.00 10.00
MW Marvin Williams 5.00 12.00
NR Nate Robinson 5.00 12.00
OG Orien Greene 4.00 10.00
PP Paul Pierce 20.00 50.00
RA Ron Artest 4.00 10.00
RF Raymond Felton 4.00 10.00
RG Ryan Gomes 3.00 8.00
RH Richard Hamilton 10.00 25.00
RI Luke Ridnour 4.00 10.00
RM Rashad McCants 3.00 8.00
RP Robert Parish 10.00 25.00
SA Shareef Abdur-Rahim 8.00 20.00
SE Sean May 3.00 8.00
SI Scottie Pippen 125.00 300.00
SJ Sarunas Jasikevicius 5.00 12.00
SK Steve Kerr 20.00 50.00
SM Stephon Marbury 12.00 30.00
SP Speedy Claxton 3.00 8.00
SS Salim Stoudamire 4.00 10.00
ST Stromile Swift 3.00 8.00
TA Tony Allen 3.00 8.00
TC Tyson Chandler 4.00 10.00
TD Travis Diener 3.00 8.00
TM Tracy McGrady 50.00 120.00
TP Tayshaun Prince 8.00 20.00
VC Vince Carter 60.00 150.00
VR Vladimir Radmanovic 3.00 8.00
VW Von Wafer 3.00 8.00
WA Bill Walton 12.00 30.00
WS Wayne Simien 3.00 8.00
YM Yao Ming 200.00 500.00

2005-06 SP Signature Edition Signatures Dual

PRINT RUN 25 SER.#'d SETS
AH C.Anthony/J.Hodge 15.00 40.00
BA A.Bogut/A.Bynum 10.00 25.00
BI A.Bogut/E.Ilyasova 10.00 25.00
BJ L.Bird/M.Johnson 150.00 400.00
BM E.Brand/C.Maggette 10.00 25.00
BP C.Billups/T.Prince 20.00 50.00
DD I.Diogu/B.Davis 10.00 25.00
FM R.Felton/S.May 10.00 25.00
FR C.Frye/N.Robinson 10.00 25.00
GS B.Gordon/J.R.Smith 10.00 25.00
GW P.Gasol/H.Warrick 10.00 25.00
GJ A.Jefferson/G.Green 10.00 25.00
JH L.James/L.Hughes 1,000.00 2,000.00
MK S.Marbury/J.Kidd 30.00 80.00
MM Y.Ming/T.McGrady 75.00 200.00
MR S.Marbury/N.Robinson 10.00 25.00
MS T.McGrady/S.Swift 12.00 30.00
NB S.Nash/C.Billups 30.00 80.00
PG P.Pierce/G.Green 20.00 50.00
PS C.Paul/J.R.Smith 125.00 300.00
RP D.Rodman/S.Pippen 200.00 500.00
SW B.Simmons/M.Williams 10.00 25.00
TS I.Thomas/J.Stockton 100.00 250.00
VG C.Villanueva/J.Graham 10.00 25.00
WD H.Warrick/I.Diogu 10.00 25.00
WJ M.Webster/J.Jack 10.00 25.00
WM D.Williams/C.J.Miles 15.00 40.00
WP Mv.Williams/C.Paul 125.00 300.00
WS Mv.Williams/S.Stoudamire 10.00 25.00

2006-07 SP Signature Edition

1-100 PRINT RUN 499 SER.#'d SETS
1 Josh Childress .60 1.50
2 Joe Johnson 1.00 2.50
3 Marvin Williams .60 1.50
4 Al Jefferson .60 1.50
5 Paul Pierce 1.50 4.00
6 Sebastian Telfair .60 1.50
7 Raymond Felton .60 1.50
8 Emeka Okafor .75 2.00
9 Gerald Wallace .75 2.00
10 Ben Gordon .75 2.00
11 Kirk Hinrich .75 2.00
12 Ben Wallace 1.25 3.00
13 Drew Gooden .75 2.00
14 LeBron James 8.00 20.00
15 Donyell Marshall .60 1.50
16 Devin Harris .60 1.50
17 Josh Howard .75 2.00
18 Dirk Nowitzki 2.50 6.00
19 Jason Terry .75 2.00
20 Carmelo Anthony 1.50 4.00
21 Kenyon Martin .75 2.00
22 J.R. Smith 1.00 2.50
23 Chauncey Billups 1.25 3.00
24 Richard Hamilton 1.00 2.50
25 Rasheed Wallace 1.25 3.00
26 Baron Davis 1.00 2.50
27 Troy Murphy .60 1.50
28 Jason Richardson 1.00 2.50
29 Rafer Alston .75 2.00
30 Shane Battier .75 2.00
31 Tracy McGrady 1.50 4.00
32 Yao Ming 2.50 6.00
33 Marquis Daniels .60 1.50
34 Al Harrington .75 2.00
35 Jermaine O'Neal 1.00 2.50
36 Elton Brand .75 2.00
37 Sam Cassell .75 2.00
38 Chris Kaman .60 1.50
39 Corey Maggette .75 2.00
40 Kobe Bryant 8.00 20.00
41 Lamar Odom .75 2.00
42 Kwame Brown .60 1.50
43 Eddie Jones 1.00 2.50
44 Mike Miller .75 2.00
45 Hakim Warrick .60 1.50
46 Pau Gasol 1.50 4.00
47 Alonzo Mourning 1.50 4.00
48 Shaquille O'Neal 4.00 10.00
49 Dwyane Wade 2.00 5.00
50 Jason Williams 1.25 3.00
51 Andrew Bogut .75 2.00
52 Michael Redd .75 2.00
53 Charlie Villanueva .60 1.50
54 Kevin Garnett 2.50 6.00
55 Mike James .60 1.50
56 Rashad McCants .60 1.50
57 Vince Carter 2.00 5.00
58 Richard Jefferson .75 2.00
59 Nate Robinson 1.50 4.00
60 Tyson Chandler .75 2.00
61 Desmond Mason .60 1.50
62 Chris Paul 2.00 5.00
63 Peja Stojakovic .75 2.00
64 Steve Francis 1.00 2.50
65 Stephon Marbury 1.25 3.00
66 Quentin Richardson .60 1.50
67 Nate Robinson .75 2.00
68 Carlos Arroyo .60 1.50
69 Dwight Howard 1.25 3.00
70 Darko Milicic .60 1.50
71 Andre Iguodala 1.00 2.50
72 Allen Iverson 2.50 6.00
73 Kyle Korver .75 2.00
74 Chris Webber 1.25 3.00
75 Boris Diaw .75 2.00
76 Shawn Marion 1.00 2.50
77 Steve Nash 1.50 4.00
78 Amare Stoudemire 1.00 2.50
79 Jamaal Magloire .60 1.50
80 Zach Randolph 1.00 2.50
81 Martell Webster .75 2.00
82 Ron Artest 1.00 2.50
83 Brad Miller .75 2.00
84 Mike Bibby .75 2.00
85 Tim Duncan 2.50 6.00
86 Michael Finley 1.00 2.50
87 Manu Ginobili 2.00 5.00
88 Tony Parker 1.50 4.00
89 Ray Allen 1.50 4.00
90 Rashard Lewis .75 2.00
91 Luke Ridnour .75 2.00
92 Chris Bosh 1.25 3.00
93 T.J. Ford .60 1.50
94 Joey Graham .60 1.50
95 Carlos Boozer .75 2.00
96 Andrei Kirilenko .75 2.00
97 Deron Williams .75 2.00
98 Gilbert Arenas 1.00 2.50
99 Caron Butler .75 2.00
100 Antawn Jamison .75 2.00
101 Andrea Bargnani RC 2.00 5.00
102 LaMarcus Aldridge RC 6.00 15.00
103 Adam Morrison RC 2.00 5.00
104 Tyrus Thomas RC 2.00 5.00
105 Shelden Williams RC 1.50 4.00
106 Brandon Roy RC 5.00 12.00
107 Randy Foye RC 2.00 5.00
108 Rudy Gay RC 3.00 8.00
109 Patrick O'Bryant RC 1.50 4.00
110 Saer Sene RC 1.50 4.00
111 J.J. Redick RC 5.00 12.00
112 Hilton Armstrong RC 1.50 4.00
113 Thabo Sefolosha RC 2.00 5.00
114 Ronnie Brewer RC 2.50 6.00
115 Cedric Simmons RC 1.50 4.00
116 Rodney Carney RC 1.50 4.00
117 Shawne Williams RC 1.50 4.00
118 Quincy Douby RC 1.50 4.00
119 Renaldo Balkman RC 2.00 5.00
120 Rajon Rondo RC 8.00 20.00
121 Marcus Williams RC 1.50 4.00
122 Josh Boone RC 1.50 4.00
123 Kyle Lowry RC 8.00 20.00
124 Shannon Brown RC 1.50 4.00
125 Jordan Farmar RC 2.00 5.00
126 Sergio Rodriguez RC 2.00 5.00
127 Maurice Ager RC 1.50 4.00
128 Mardy Collins RC 1.50 4.00
129 James White RC 1.50 4.00
130 Steve Novak RC 2.00 5.00
131 Solomon Jones RC 1.50 4.00
132 Paul Davis RC 1.50 4.00
133 P.J. Tucker RC 2.50 6.00
134 Craig Smith RC 2.00 5.00
135 Bobby Jones RC 1.50 4.00
136 David Noel RC 1.50 4.00
137 James Augustine RC 1.50 4.00

138 Daniel Gibson RC 2.00 5.00
139 Marcus Vinicius RC 1.50 4.00
140 Dee Brown RC 1.50 4.00
141 Ryan Hollins RC 1.50 4.00
142 Hassan Adams RC 1.50 4.00

2006-07 SP Signature Edition Gold

*1-100 GOLD: 2.5X TO 6X BASE HI
*101-142 GOLD: 1.25X TO 3X BASE HI
PRINT RUN 25 SER.#'d SETS

2006-07 SP Signature Edition AKA Signings

PRINT RUN 25 TO 50 SER.#'d SETS
AB Andrea Bargnani/25 4.00 10.00
AD Adrian Dantley/50 8.00 20.00
BB Brent Barry/50 8.00 20.00
BG Ben Gordon/25 4.00 10.00
BL Bill Laimbeer/50 20.00 50.00
BR Bill Russell/25 1,500.00 3,000.00
BS Byron Scott/50 12.00 30.00
CA Carmelo Anthony/25 75.00 200.00
CB Chauncey Billups/50 20.00 50.00
CD Clyde Drexler/25 100.00 250.00
CS Cedric Simmons/50 3.00 8.00
DD Darryl Dawkins/50 20.00 50.00
DN David Noel/50 3.00 8.00
DR Dennis Rodman/25 125.00 300.00
EH Elvin Hayes/25 15.00 40.00
GG George Gervin/50 20.00 50.00
HA Hilton Armstrong/50 3.00 8.00
HO Hakeem Olajuwon/25 100.00 250.00
JB Josh Boone/50 3.00 8.00
JE Julius Erving/25 100.00 250.00
JF Jordan Farmar/50 4.00 10.00
JK Jason Kidd/25 20.00 50.00
JW James White/50 3.00 8.00
KH Kirk Hinrich/25 25.00 60.00
LA LaMarcus Aldridge/25 30.00 80.00
LJ LeBron James/25 2,000.00 4,000.00
MA Maurice Ager/25 3.00 8.00
MJ Magic Johnson/25 125.00 300.00
MP Morris Peterson/50 3.00 8.00
NA Nate Archibald/50 12.00 30.00
PD Paul Davis/50 3.00 8.00
PO Patrick O'Bryant/50 3.00 8.00
PP Paul Pierce/25 125.00 300.00
QD Quincy Douby/50 3.00 8.00
QR Quentin Richardson/50 3.00 8.00
RB Renaldo Balkman/50 4.00 10.00
RF Randy Foye/50 4.00 10.00
RH Richard Hamilton/50 20.00 50.00
RJ Richard Jefferson/25 4.00 10.00
RR Rajon Rondo/50 25.00 60.00
SM Craig Smith/50 4.00 10.00
ST Sebastian Telfair/50 3.00 8.00
SW Shelden Williams/50 3.00 8.00
TM Tracy McGrady/25 100.00 250.00
TT Tyrus Thomas/25 4.00 10.00
VC Vince Carter/25 125.00 300.00

2006-07 SP Signature Edition Alumni Associations

PRINT RUN 50 SER.#'d SETS
AB H.Armstrong/J.Boone 6.00 15.00
AF L.Aldridge/T.Ford 12.00 30.00
AJ H.Adams/R.Jefferson 8.00 20.00
BA M.Ager/S.Brown 6.00 15.00
BJ C.Bosh/J.Jack 12.00 30.00
BT B.Bass/T.Thomas 10.00 25.00
BW E.Brand/S.Williams 8.00 20.00
DF B.Davis/J.Farmar 10.00 25.00
DJ D.Brown/J.Augustine 6.00 15.00
GG B.Gordon/R.Gay 12.00 30.00
GT D.Gibson/P.Tucker 10.00 25.00
JB J.Johnson/R.Brewer 10.00 25.00
JR B.Jones/B.Roy 20.00 50.00
KA J.Kidd/S.Abdur-Rahim 15.00 40.00
MF R.McCants/R.Felton 6.00 15.00
NM D.Noel/S.May 6.00 15.00
RF A.Ray/R.Foye 8.00 20.00
RP R.Rondo/T.Prince 30.00 80.00
WC M.Williams/V.Carter 20.00 50.00
WO M.Williams/E.Okafor 8.00 20.00

2006-07 SP Signature Edition Five Star Autographs

PRINT RUN 10 SER.#'d SETS
BATFR Barg/Aldrd/Tyrus/Foye/Roy 40.00 100.00
DWEHF BD/Walton/Eat/Hllins/Frmr 25.00 60.00
HGDTS Kirk/Grdn/Dhn/Tyrus/Thbo 25.00 60.00
WDWAR Wltn/Glide/Wbstr/Aldr/Roy 125.00 300.00

2006-07 SP Signature Edition Four Star Autographs

PRINT RUN 15 SER.#'d SETS
APMJ Melo/Pierce/T-Mac/James 1,000.00 2,000.00
BATW Bargn/Aldrdg/Tyrus/Wllms 20.00 50.00
DWAR Glide/Wltn/Aldrdg/Roy 60.00 150.00
GHST Gordon/Hinrich
Sefolosha/Thomas 20.00 50.00
JEBJ Jordan/Erving/Bird/Johnson 1,000.00 3,000.00
KICJ Korver/Iggy/Cmy/Jones 20.00 50.00
ODMM Olaj/Glide/Ming/TMac 150.00 400.00
OGGH Okfr/Gordon/Gay/Rip 40.00 100.00
PKNB Paul/Kidd/Nash/Billups 150.00 400.00

2006-07 SP Signature Edition Hoops Inc. Autographs

PRINT RUN 50 SER.#'d SETS
*GOLD: .5X TO 1.25X BASE HI
GOLD PRINT RUN 25 SER.#'d SETS
AD Adrian Dantley 8.00 20.00
CH Connie Hawkins 8.00 20.00
DJ Dennis Johnson 25.00 60.00
EH Elvin Hayes 6.00 15.00
FW Walt Frazier 8.00 20.00
GG George Gervin 12.00 30.00
HG Hal Greer 6.00 15.00
JS Jack Sikma 6.00 15.00
MB Muggsy Bogues 8.00 20.00
MC Michael Cooper 8.00 20.00
ME Mark Eaton 6.00 15.00
MR Micheal Ray Richardson 6.00 15.00
NA Nate Archibald 8.00 20.00
NT Nate Thurmond 6.00 15.00
PW Paul Westphal 8.00 20.00
RP Robert Parish 10.00 25.00
RS Ralph Sampson 8.00 20.00
RT Reggie Theus 6.00 15.00
SK Steve Kerr 8.00 20.00
SP Sam Perkins 8.00 20.00
SW Spud Webb 10.00 25.00
WT Wayman Tisdale 6.00 15.00

2006-07 SP Signature Edition INKredible INKscriptions

PRINT RUN 50 TO 100 SER.#'d SETS
AB Andrea Bargnani/50 25.00 60.00
AJ Antawn Jamison/100 8.00 20.00
AR Allan Ray/50 3.00 8.00
BG Ben Gordon/50 8.00 20.00
BJ Bobby Jones/100 3.00 8.00
BM Brad Miller/100 5.00 12.00
BR Brandon Roy/50 20.00 50.00
CE Cedric Simmons/50 3.00 8.00
CS Craig Smith/100 4.00 10.00
DG Daniel Gibson/50 4.00 10.00
DM Damir Markota/100 3.00 8.00
DN David Noel/100 3.00 8.00
DW Deron Williams/50 25.00 60.00
GW Gerald Wallace/50 8.00 20.00
HA Hassan Adams/100 3.00 8.00
HI Hilton Armstrong/100 3.00 8.00
JA James Augustine/100 3.00 8.00
JB Josh Boone/50 3.00 8.00
JF Jordan Farmar/100 4.00 10.00
JW James White/100 3.00 8.00
KK Kyle Korver/50 15.00 40.00
LA LaMarcus Aldridge/50 15.00 40.00
LB Leandro Barbosa/100 5.00 12.00
MJ Mike James/100 5.00 12.00
NO Steve Novak/100 5.00 12.00
NR Nate Robinson/100 10.00 25.00
PD Paul Davis/50 3.00 8.00
PM Pops Mensah-Bonsu/100 3.00 8.00
PT P.J. Tucker/100 5.00 12.00
QD Quincy Douby/100 3.00 8.00
RB Raja Bell/50 15.00 40.00
RE Renaldo Balkman/100 4.00 10.00
RF Raymond Felton/100 12.00 30.00
RG Rudy Gay/50 20.00 50.00
RJ Richard Jefferson/50 6.00 15.00
SB Shannon Brown/50 12.00 30.00
SJ Solomon Jones/100 3.00 8.00
SN Steve Nash/50 300.00 600.00
SR Sergio Rodriguez/50 6.00 15.00
SS Saer Sene/100 3.00 8.00
SW Shelden Williams/50 3.00 8.00
TF T.J. Ford/100 5.00 12.00
TP Tayshaun Prince 12.00 30.00
TS Thabo Sefolosha/50 12.00 30.00
TT Tyrus Thomas/50 4.00 10.00
WB Will Blalock/100 3.00 8.00
WI Shawne Williams/50 3.00 8.00

2006-07 SP Signature Edition Marks of Distinction

PRINT RUN 50 SER.#'d SETS
AB Andrea Bargnani 4.00 10.00
AH Al Harrington 4.00 10.00
AI Andre Iguodala 5.00 12.00
AJ Antawn Jamison 4.00 10.00
AR Hilton Armstrong 3.00 8.00
BA Renaldo Balkman 4.00 10.00
BD Baron Davis 5.00 12.00
BG Ben Gordon 4.00 10.00
BM Brad Miller 4.00 10.00
BR Brandon Roy 10.00 25.00
CB Chauncey Billups 8.00 20.00
CH Chris Bosh 6.00 15.00
CM Corey Maggette 4.00 10.00
CS Cedric Simmons 3.00 8.00
DB Dee Brown 3.00 8.00
EB Elton Brand 4.00 10.00
EO Emeka Okafor 4.00 10.00
HA Hassan Adams 3.00 8.00
JA James Augustine 3.00 8.00
JB Josh Boone 3.00 8.00
JF Jordan Farmar 4.00 10.00
JJ Jarrett Jack 4.00 10.00
JO Joe Johnson 5.00 12.00
KL Kyle Lowry 15.00 40.00
LB Leandro Barbosa 4.00 10.00
MA Maurice Ager 3.00 8.00
MB Mike Bibby 5.00 12.00
MC Mardy Collins 3.00 8.00
MJ Michael Jordan 1,000.00 2,000.00
MW Marcus Williams 3.00 8.00
ON Jermaine O'Neal 5.00 12.00
PO Patrick O'Bryant 3.00 8.00
PP Paul Pierce 15.00 40.00
PS Peja Stojakovic 4.00 10.00
QD Quincy Douby 3.00 8.00
RB Raja Bell 4.00 10.00
RC Rodney Carney 3.00 8.00
RF Randy Foye 4.00 10.00
RG Rudy Gay 6.00 15.00
RH Richard Hamilton 8.00 20.00
RJ Richard Jefferson 4.00 10.00
RO Ronnie Brewer 5.00 12.00
RR Rajon Rondo 12.00 30.00
SN Steve Novak 4.00 10.00
SR Sergio Rodriguez 4.00 10.00
SS Saer Sene 3.00 8.00
SW Shawne Williams 3.00 8.00
TP Tayshaun Prince 5.00 12.00
TS Thabo Sefolosha 4.00 10.00
WI Shelden Williams 3.00 8.00

2006-07 SP Signature Edition Rookie GRAPHiti

PRINT RUN 50 SER.#'d SETS
*GOLD: .5X TO 1.25X BASE HI
GOLD PRINT RUN 25 SER.#'d SETS
AB Andrea Bargnani 4.00 10.00
BR Brandon Roy 10.00 25.00
CS Cedric Simmons 3.00 8.00
HA Hilton Armstrong 3.00 8.00
JB Josh Boone 3.00 8.00
JF Jordan Farmar 4.00 10.00
KL Kyle Lowry 10.00 25.00
LA LaMarcus Aldridge 12.00 30.00
MA Maurice Ager 3.00 8.00
MW Marcus Williams 3.00 8.00
PO Patrick O'Bryant 3.00 8.00
QD Quincy Douby 3.00 8.00
RB Renaldo Balkman 4.00 10.00
RC Rodney Carney 3.00 8.00
RF Randy Foye 4.00 10.00
RG Rudy Gay 6.00 15.00
RO Ronnie Brewer 5.00 12.00
RR Rajon Rondo 12.00 30.00
SB Shannon Brown 3.00 8.00
SR Sergio Rodriguez 4.00 10.00
SS Saer Sene 3.00 8.00
SW Shelden Williams 3.00 8.00
TS Thabo Sefolosha 4.00 10.00
TT Tyrus Thomas 4.00 10.00
WI Shawne Williams 3.00 8.00

2006-07 SP Signature Edition Signature Style

PRINT RUN 25 SER.#'d SETS
AI Andre Iguodala 10.00 25.00
BB Bruce Bowen 8.00 20.00
BG Ben Gordon 8.00 20.00
BL Bill Laimbeer 15.00 40.00
BM Brad Miller 8.00 20.00
CB Chris Bosh 12.00 30.00
CD Clyde Drexler 50.00 120.00
CP Chris Paul 30.00 80.00
DR David Robinson 60.00 150.00
GG George Gervin 20.00 50.00
HO Hakeem Olajuwon 60.00 150.00
JE Julius Erving 75.00 200.00
JK Jason Kidd 20.00 50.00
JS John Stockton 60.00 150.00
KA Kareem Abdul-Jabbar 125.00 300.00
KK Kyle Korver 10.00 25.00
LB Larry Bird 125.00 300.00
LJ LeBron James 1,250.00 2,500.00
MA Magic Johnson 125.00 300.00
MB Mike Bibby 8.00 20.00
MJ Michael Jordan 2,000.00 4,000.00
PS Peja Stojakovic 8.00 20.00
RO Dennis Rodman 75.00 200.00
RP Robert Parish 12.00 30.00
SK Steve Kerr 25.00 60.00
SN Steve Nash 75.00 200.00
SW Spud Webb 12.00 30.00
TM Tracy McGrady 75.00 200.00
VC Vince Carter 100.00 250.00
YM Yao Ming 125.00 300.00

2006-07 SP Signature Edition Signatures

APPROXIMATE ODDS ONE PER PACK
AB Andrea Bargnani 3.00 8.00
AH Al Harrington 3.00 8.00
AJ Al Jefferson 2.50 6.00
AM Maurice Ager 2.50 6.00
AR Hilton Armstrong 2.50 6.00
BA Leandro Barbosa 3.00 8.00
BB Brent Barry 2.50 6.00
BD Baron Davis 4.00 10.00
BO Chris Bosh 5.00 12.00
BR Ronnie Brewer 3.00 8.00
CA Carmelo Anthony 40.00 100.00
CB Chauncey Billups 12.00 30.00
CD Clyde Drexler 30.00 80.00
CM Corey Maggette 3.00 8.00
CP Chris Paul 40.00 100.00
CS Cedric Simmons 2.50 6.00
DB Dee Brown 2.50 6.00
DG Daniel Gibson 3.00 8.00
DM Damir Markota 2.50 6.00
DN David Noel 2.50 6.00
DR David Robinson 40.00 100.00
DS DeShawn Stevenson 2.50 6.00
EB Elton Brand 3.00 8.00
EO Emeka Okafor 3.00 8.00
FO Randy Foye 3.00 8.00
GD Gerald Green 3.00 8.00
GG George Gervin 12.00 30.00
GR Danny Granger 2.50 6.00
HA Hassan Adams 2.50 6.00
HO Hakeem Olajuwon 40.00 100.00
IU Ime Udoka 10.00 25.00
JA James Augustine 2.50 6.00
JB Josh Boone 2.50 6.00
JC Josh Childress 2.50 6.00
JE Julius Erving 60.00 150.00
JF Jordan Farmar 3.00 8.00
JG Jorge Garbajosa 3.00 8.00
JJ Jarrett Jack 3.00 8.00
JK Jason Kidd 15.00 40.00
JM Mike James 2.50 6.00
JN Antawn Jamison 3.00 8.00
JO Avery Johnson 5.00 12.00
JS J.R. Smith 4.00 10.00
JW James White 2.50 6.00
KA Kareem Abdul-Jabbar 75.00 200.00
KK Kyle Korver 6.00 15.00
KL Kyle Lowry 15.00 40.00
LA LaMarcus Aldridge 12.00 30.00
LB Larry Bird 75.00 200.00
LJ LeBron James 1,000.00 2,000.00
LR Luke Ridnour 3.00 8.00
MA Magic Johnson 75.00 200.00
MC Mardy Collins 2.50 6.00
ME Pops Mensah-Bonsu 2.50 6.00
MI Mile Ilic 2.50 6.00
MJ Michael Jordan 2,000.00 4,000.00
MO Cuttino Mobley 3.00 8.00
MP Morris Peterson 2.50 6.00
MW Marvin Williams 2.50 6.00
NO Steve Novak 2.50 6.00
NR Nate Robinson 3.00 8.00
OG Orien Greene 2.50 6.00
PD Paul Davis 2.50 6.00
PM Paul Millsap 5.00 12.00
PO Patrick O'Bryant 2.50 6.00
PT P.J. Tucker 4.00 10.00
QD Quincy Douby 2.50 6.00
RA Allan Ray 2.50 6.00
RB Raja Bell 3.00 8.00
RC Rodney Carney 2.50 6.00
RE Renaldo Balkman 3.00 8.00
RF Raymond Felton 2.50 6.00
RG Rudy Gay 5.00 12.00
RH Ryan Hollins 2.50 6.00
RM Rashad McCants 2.50 6.00
RO Dennis Rodman 75.00 200.00
RR Rajon Rondo 15.00 40.00
RT Reggie Theus 3.00 8.00
RU Bill Russell 600.00 1,200.00
RY Brandon Roy 8.00 20.00
SB Shannon Brown 2.50 6.00
SJ Solomon Jones 2.50 6.00
SK Steve Kerr 15.00 40.00
SM Craig Smith 3.00 8.00
SN Steve Nash 60.00 150.00
SR Sergio Rodriguez 3.00 8.00
SS Saer Sene 2.50 6.00
ST John Stockton 30.00 80.00
SW Shawne Williams 2.50 6.00
TF T.J. Ford 2.50 6.00
TM Tracy McGrady 60.00 150.00
TS Thabo Sefolosha 3.00 8.00
TT Tyrus Thomas 3.00 8.00
VC Vince Carter 75.00 200.00
WB Will Blalock 2.50 6.00
WE Spud Webb 10.00 25.00
WI Shelden Williams 2.50 6.00
WT Wayman Tisdale 10.00 25.00
YK Yaroslav Korolev 2.50 6.00
YM Yao Ming 125.00 300.00

2006-07 SP Signature Edition Signs of Success

PRINT RUN 25 SER.#'d SETS
AB Andrea Bargnani 4.00 10.00
AI Andre Iguodala 8.00 20.00
AR Allan Ray 3.00 8.00
BA Renaldo Balkman 4.00 10.00
BJ Bobby Jones 3.00 8.00
BR Brandon Roy 6.00 15.00
CS Cedric Simmons 3.00 8.00
DB Dee Brown 3.00 8.00
DG Danny Granger 3.00 8.00
DM Damir Markota 3.00 8.00
DN David Noel 3.00 8.00
GG Gerald Green 5.00 12.00
HA Hassan Adams 3.00 8.00
HI Hilton Armstrong 3.00 8.00
JB Josh Boone 3.00 8.00
JC Josh Childress 3.00 8.00
JF Jordan Farmar 4.00 10.00
JS J.R. Smith 5.00 12.00
KL Kyle Lowry 15.00 40.00
LA LaMarcus Aldridge 15.00 40.00
LB Leandro Barbosa 4.00 10.00
LR Luke Ridnour 4.00 10.00
MA Maurice Ager 3.00 8.00
ME Pops Mensah-Bonsu 3.00 8.00
MJ Mike James 3.00 8.00
MW Marcus Williams 3.00 8.00
OG Orien Greene 3.00 8.00
PM Paul Millsap 6.00 15.00
PO Patrick O'Bryant 3.00 8.00
PT P.J. Tucker 5.00 12.00
QD Quincy Douby 3.00 8.00
RB Raja Bell 4.00 10.00
RC Rodney Carney 3.00 8.00
RF Randy Foye 4.00 10.00
RG Rudy Gay 6.00 15.00
RH Ryan Hollins 3.00 8.00
RO Ronnie Brewer 5.00 12.00
RR Rajon Rondo 15.00 40.00
SB Shannon Brown 3.00 8.00
SJ Solomon Jones 3.00 8.00
SM Craig Smith 4.00 10.00
SN Steve Novak 4.00 10.00
SR Sergio Rodriguez 4.00 10.00
SS Saer Sene 3.00 8.00
SW Shawne Williams 3.00 8.00
TS Thabo Sefolosha 4.00 10.00
TT Tyrus Thomas 4.00 10.00
WB Will Blalock 3.00 8.00
WE Martell Webster 4.00 10.00
WI Shelden Williams 3.00 8.00

2006-07 SP Signature Edition Three Star Autographs

PRINT RUN 25 SER.#'d SETS
ATG Aldridge/Tucker/Gibson 15.00 40.00
BBF Bargnani/Bosh/Ford 15.00 40.00
BBM Brewer/Brown/Millsap 15.00 40.00
BCF Balkman/Collins/Frye 12.00 30.00
BDM Bibby/Douby/Miller 12.00 30.00
BPB Billups/Prince/Blalock 15.00 40.00
CKJ Carter/Kidd/Jefferson 30.00 80.00
CWJ Childress/Williams/Jones 12.00 30.00
DFH Davis/Farmar/Hollins 15.00 40.00
GGW Granger/Greene/Williams 12.00 30.00
GLW Gay/Lowry/Warrick 15.00 40.00
JKC Jones/Korver/Carney 12.00 30.00
JMS James/McCants/Smith 12.00 30.00
MMN Ming/McGrady/Novak 50.00 120.00
NDA Nelson/Dooling/Augustine 12.00 30.00
OBM Okafor/Boone/Marshall 12.00 30.00
PRR Pierce/Rondo/Ray 50.00 120.00
PWF Paul/Williams/Felton 40.00 100.00
RFW Roy/Foye/Williams 12.00 30.00
SAC Simmons/Armstrong/Chandler 12.00 30.00
SSR Sene/Sefolosha/Rodriguez 12.00 30.00
TSG Thomas/Sefolosha/Gordon 12.00 30.00
WBA Williams/Boone/Adams 12.00 30.00

2006-07 SP Signature Edition Two Star Autographs

PRINT RUN 25 SER.#'d SETS
AI H.Adams/M.Ilic 8.00 20.00
AM M.Ager/P.Mensah-Bonsu 8.00 20.00
AN J.Augustine/J.Nelson 8.00 20.00
BB L.Barbosa/R.Bell 8.00 20.00
BC R.Balkman/M.Collins 8.00 20.00
BG A.Bargnani/J.Garbajosa 8.00 20.00
BM R.Brewer/P.Millsap 8.00 20.00
BS S.Swift/B.Bass 8.00 20.00
BW B.Brown/J.White 8.00 20.00
CJ R.Carney/B.Jones 8.00 20.00
CS S.Stoudamire/S.Claxton 8.00 20.00
DA C.Duhon/B.Armstrong 8.00 20.00
FJ R.Foye/M.James 8.00 20.00
FT T.J. Ford/P.Tucker 8.00 20.00
GB S.Brown/D.Gibson 8.00 20.00
GG D.Granger/O.Greene 8.00 20.00
GL R.Gay/K.Lowry 10.00 25.00
HF R.Hollins/J.Farmar 8.00 20.00
HW C.Hawkins/P.Westphal 10.00 25.00
IR A.Iguodala/N.Robinson 12.00 30.00
JC J.Johnson/J.Childress 8.00 20.00
JD A.Jamison/B.Daugherty 10.00 25.00
JG A.Jefferson/G.Green 8.00 20.00
JS A.Jamison/D.Stevenson 8.00 20.00
JW J.Jack/M.Webster 8.00 20.00
KN K.Korver/S.Novak 8.00 20.00
MA B.Miller/S.Abdur-Rahim 8.00 20.00
MB E.Brand/C.Maggette 8.00 20.00
MC D.Markota/C.Bell 8.00 20.00
MD C.Maggette/P.Davis 8.00 20.00
MJ M.Williams/J.Boone 8.00 20.00
NB D.Noel/A.Bogut 8.00 20.00
OD P.O'Bryant/I.Diogu 8.00 20.00
OG E.Okafor/B.Gordon 8.00 20.00
PB T.Prince/W.Blalock 8.00 20.00
PG M.Peterson/J.Graham 8.00 20.00
RG S.Rodriguez/S.Graham 8.00 20.00
RR R.Rondo/A.Ray 10.00 25.00
RS L.Ridnour/S.Sene 8.00 20.00
SA C.Simmons/H.Armstrong 8.00 20.00
SF B.Scott/J.Farmar 8.00 20.00
SJ C.Smith/M.James 8.00 20.00
SS S.Williams/S.Jones 8.00 20.00
TT T.Thomas/T.Sefolosha 8.00 20.00
WB D.Brown/D.Williams 8.00 20.00
WH A.Harrington/S.Williams 8.00 20.00
WJ H.Warrick/R.Jefferson 8.00 20.00

2009-10 SP Signature Edition

COMPLETE SET (100) 30.00 60.00
1 Al Harrington .75 2.00
2 Al Horford 1.00 2.50
3 Al Jefferson .60 1.50
4 Al Thornton .60 1.50
5 Allen Iverson 2.00 5.00
6 Andre Iguodala 1.00 2.50
7 Andre Miller 1.00 2.50
8 Andrea Bargnani .60 1.50
9 Antawn Jamison .75 2.00
10 Baron Davis .75 2.00
11 Ben Gordon .75 2.00
12 Ben Wallace 1.25 3.00
13 Beno Udrih .60 1.50
14 Brad Miller .75 2.00
15 Brandon Roy 1.25 3.00
16 Carlos Boozer .75 2.00
17 Carmelo Anthony 1.50 4.00
18 Chauncey Billups 1.25 3.00
19 Chris Bosh 1.25 3.00
20 Chris Duhon .60 1.50
21 Chris Paul 2.00 5.00
22 Courtney Lee .60 1.50
23 D.J. Augustin .60 1.50
24 Danny Granger .60 1.50
25 David Lee .60 1.50
26 David West .75 2.00
27 Derek Fisher 1.00 2.50
28 Deron Williams .75 2.00
29 Derrick Rose 1.50 4.00
30 DeShawn Stevenson .60 1.50
31 Devin Harris .60 1.50
32 Dirk Nowitzki 2.50 6.00
33 Dwight Howard 1.25 3.00
34 Dwyane Wade 2.00 5.00
35 Elton Brand .75 2.00
36 Eric Gordon .75 2.00
37 Gilbert Arenas .75 2.00
38 Hedo Turkoglu .75 2.00
39 Jamal Crawford 1.00 2.50
40 Jason Kidd 1.50 4.00
41 Jason Richardson 1.00 2.50
42 Jeff Green .75 2.00
43 Jermaine O'Neal 1.00 2.50
44 Jerryd Bayless .60 1.50
45 Joe Johnson 1.00 2.50
46 Jose Calderon .60 1.50
47 Josh Howard .75 2.00
48 Josh Smith .60 1.50
49 Kenyon Martin .75 2.00
50 Kevin Durant 4.00 10.00
51 Kevin Garnett 2.50 6.00
52 Kevin Love 1.00 2.50
53 Kevin Martin .75 2.00
54 Kobe Bryant 8.00 20.00
55 Lamar Odom .75 2.00
56 LaMarcus Aldridge 1.00 2.50
57 LeBron James 8.00 20.00
58 Luis Scola .75 2.00
59 Luke Ridnour .75 2.00
60 Luol Deng .75 2.00
61 Manu Ginobili 2.00 5.00
62 Marc Gasol 1.00 2.50
63 Mario Chalmers .75 2.00
64 Michael Beasley .60 1.50
65 Michael Redd .60 1.50
66 Mike Bibby 1.00 2.50
67 Mike Dunleavy .60 1.50
68 Mo Williams .75 2.00
69 Monta Ellis .75 2.00
70 O.J. Mayo .60 1.50
71 Pau Gasol 1.50 4.00
72 Paul Pierce 1.50 4.00
73 Peja Stojakovic .75 2.00
74 Quentin Richardson .60 1.50
75 Raja Bell .75 2.00
76 Ray Allen 1.50 4.00
77 Raymond Felton .60 1.50
78 Richard Hamilton 1.00 2.50
79 Richard Jefferson .75 2.00
80 Rodney Stuckey .60 1.50
81 Ron Artest 1.00 2.50
82 Ronnie Brewer .60 1.50
83 Rudy Fernandez .60 1.50
84 Rudy Gay 1.00 2.50
85 Russell Westbrook 2.00 5.00
86 Sebastian Telfair .60 1.50
87 Shaquille O'Neal 3.00 8.00
88 Shawn Marion 1.00 2.50
89 Stephen Jackson .75 2.00
90 Steve Nash 2.00 5.00
91 T.J. Ford .60 1.50
92 Tayshaun Prince 1.00 2.50
93 Thaddeus Young .60 1.50
94 Tim Duncan 2.50 6.00
95 Tony Parker 1.50 4.00
96 Tracy McGrady 2.00 5.00
97 Tyson Chandler .75 2.00
98 Vince Carter 2.00 5.00
99 Yao Ming 2.50 6.00
100 Yi Jianlian 1.25 3.00

2009-10 SP Signature Edition 2 Star Signatures

STATED PRINT RUN 23 TO 299 SER.#'d SETS
2SAB M.Almond/A.Brooks/99 6.00 15.00
2SAH G.Hill/K.Azubuike/199 6.00 15.00
2SAJ L.Amundson/D.Jackson/149 6.00 15.00
2SBA N.Batum/A.Ajinca/199 6.00 15.00
2SBG F.Brown/H.Greer/60 6.00 15.00
2SBJ D.Byars/B.Brown/299 6.00 15.00
2SBO K.Brown/P.O'Bryant/65 6.00 15.00
2SBS J.Barea/R.Sessions/99 6.00 15.00
2SBT M.Taylor/B.Brown/299 6.00 15.00
2SBW F.Brown/L.Wilkens/60 6.00 15.00
2SCV E.Vandeweghe/A.Cervi/60 6.00 15.00
2SDD K.Dooling/C.Douglas-Roberts/99 6.00 15.00
2SDL D.Byars/J.Jordan/299 6.00 15.00
2SDS B.Davis/R.Stuckey/99 6.00 15.00
2SFB R.Fernandez/N.Batum/199 6.00 15.00
2SFJ J.Jack/R.Felton/60 6.00 15.00
2SFL C.Lee/R.Fernandez/199 6.00 15.00
2SFR R.Fernandez/Rondo/199 8.00 20.00
2SGB C.Boozer/H.Grant/49 10.00 25.00
2SGD P.Gasol/Daugherty/60 8.00 20.00
2SGS P.Gasol/J.Smith/30 8.00 20.00
2SGT J.Gist/R.Terry/299 6.00 15.00
2SHC E.Curry/A.Harrington/99 6.00 15.00
2SHP T.Porter/R.Harper/99 8.00 20.00
2SJA A.Afflalo/J.Barea/99 6.00 15.00
2SJB D.Jackson/N.Batum/249 6.00 15.00
2SJJ L.James/Jordan/23 10,000.00 20,000.00
2SJR J.Paxson/R.Harper/35 40.00 100.00
2SKD Donovan/Knight/60 40.00 100.00
2SLB Sharman/L.Wilkens/30 15.00 40.00
2SLD Daugherty/Laimbeer/60 10.00 25.00
2SLG C.Lee/J.Giddens/199 6.00 15.00
2SLH G.Hill/C.Lee/199 6.00 15.00
2SLS J.Sikma/B.Laimbeer/65 6.00 15.00
2SMB C.Maggette/S.Battier/30 6.00 15.00
2SMD M.Bibby/D.Augustin/99 6.00 15.00
2SMS T.Sanders/McAdoo/89 12.00 30.00
2SMW B.Miller/C.Wilcox/119 6.00 15.00
2SND B.Daugherty/L.Nance/60 6.00 15.00
2SNH L.Nance/S.Haywood/60 6.00 15.00
2SPH Heinsohn/Parish/79 25.00 60.00
2SPS J.Smith/M.Peterson/40 6.00 15.00
2SRA M.Ray Richardson/K.Anderson/60 6.00 15.00
2SRB Rondo/A.Brooks/199 8.00 20.00
2SRL R.Rondo/C.Lee/199 8.00 20.00
2SSA J.Smith/R.Anderson/60 6.00 15.00
2SSB J.Sikma/F.Brown/69 6.00 15.00
2SSD C.Daly/J.Sloan/40 100.00 250.00
2SSG J.Sloan/Goodrich/60 40.00 100.00
2SSM R.Sessions/L.Moute/99 6.00 15.00
2SSR S.Haywood/Parish/99 8.00 20.00
2SSS J.Smith/Stoudemire/40 8.00 20.00
2SSW S.Swift/S.Williams/60 6.00 15.00
2STS D.Thomp/J.Smith/30 6.00 15.00
2STT J.Thompson/A.Thornton/99 6.00 15.00
2SWA S.Webb/K.Anderson/60 6.00 15.00
2SWF S.Webb/D.Fisher/99 10.00 25.00
2SWI Iguodala/G.Wallace/30 6.00 15.00
2SWL S.Lasme/D.Washington/299 6.00 15.00
2SWS J.Sloan/C.Walker/60 25.00 60.00

2009-10 SP Signature Edition 3 Star Signatures

STATED PRINT RUN 10 TO 199 SER.#'d SETS
3SABA Batum/Ajinca/Amundson/199 6.00 15.00
3SABM Armst/Btum/McGee/199 6.00 15.00
3SACG Giddens/Crittenton/Augustin/99 6.00 15.00
3SADW Arthur/Dudley/White/99 6.00 15.00
3SALH Lee/Azubuike/Hill/199 6.00 15.00
3SBBG Gddns/Brks/Barea/199 6.00 15.00
3SBBW Bowen/Williams/Brewer/99 6.00 15.00
3SBDA Boone/Douglas-
Roberts/Anderson/199 6.00 15.00
3SBDS Bibby/Stuckey/Davis/49 10.00 25.00
3SBGA Gsol/Batum/Andrsn/199 10.00 25.00
3SBSC Brooks/Chalmers/Sessions/199 6.00 15.00
3SBSJ Jordan/Brown/Sessions/149 6.00 15.00
3SBWJ Williams/Jordan/Byars/199 6.00 15.00
3SCBW Curry/Wilcox/Boozer/49 6.00 15.00
3SCHV Crry/Hywd/Vndwgh/35 10.00 25.00
3SDSG Glmre/Skma/Dghty/35 10.00 25.00
3SDWL Wllms/Lee/Dling/35 6.00 15.00
3SDWP Wltn/Prtr/Drxlr/49 25.00 60.00
3SESL Smmr/Ellngtn/Lwsn/99 6.00 15.00
3SFAH Frndz/Hllns/Andrsn/35 10.00 25.00
3SFBS Frndz/Sessns/Barea/199 10.00 25.00
3SFCH Cook/Hill/Fernandez/49 6.00 15.00
3SFRB Brks/Rondo/Frndz/199 8.00 20.00
3SFRS Sessions/Ford/Rondo/39 12.00 30.00
3SFWP Webb/Fisher/Porter/49 8.00 20.00
3SFWR Wllms/Fshr/Rndo/99 15.00 40.00
3SGRD Gmt/Rbnsn/Dnvn/25 40.00 100.00
3SGSM Greer/Sndrs/Mrtn/40 15.00 40.00
3SHBG Brwn/Hvlck/Gdrch/10 25.00 60.00
3SHHR Rubio/Hndrsn/Hrdn/99 75.00 200.00
3SHKH Hywd/King/Hrmgtn/35 8.00 20.00
3SHWB Hrmgtn/Bosh/Wllc/35 8.00 20.00
3SITL Terry/Ray/Gist/299 6.00 15.00
3SJFB Barea/Jcksn/Felton/49 6.00 15.00
3SLGM Landry/Greene
Mbah A Moute/99 6.00 15.00
3SLMO Laimbeer/Miller/O'Neal/25 10.00 25.00
3SMGP Gasol/Miller/Parish/25 12.00 30.00
3SMIM Iggy/Mggs/Mllsp/35 10.00 25.00
3SMPA Amundson
Pecherov/Marshall/95 6.00 15.00
3SMSW West/Stevenson/Maggette/120 6.00 15.00
3SOAI Iggy/Anthony/Odom/25 25.00 50.00
3SODO Odom/O'Bryant/Deng/15 6.00 15.00
3SOMH Zo/Hwrd/Olaj/35 75.00 200.00
3SOTW Thms/Okfr/Wrght/50 6.00 15.00
3SPPS Parish/Sanders/Pierce/49 25.00 60.00
3SPRP Parker/Redd/Paul/20 75.00 200.00
3SPTR Rdmn/Pxn/Theus/25 40.00 100.00
3SRAH Hill/Rondo/Almond/99 10.00 25.00
3SRSB Stcky/Rndo/Brks/49 8.00 20.00
3SRSC Rndo/Chlmrs/Sessns/99 8.00 20.00
3SSDG Gasol/Davis/Smith/40 8.00 20.00
3SSHG Haywd/Sikma/Green/49 10.00 25.00
3SSSB Amare/Smith/Bass/30 8.00 20.00
3SSWS Sndrs/Wlkr/Sloan/55 30.00 80.00
3STMB Tmpsn/Buse/McAd/55 12.00 30.00
3SWAP Andrsn/Prtr/Webb/35 12.00 30.00
3SWHW West/Wlkns/Hagan/30 30.00 80.00
3SWML McGee/Wilcox/Lopez/99 6.00 15.00
3SWMS Mbah/Shrp/Wlkr/199 6.00 15.00
3SWRP Riley/Wilkes/Price/35 20.00 50.00

2009-10 SP Signature Edition 4 Star Signatures

STATED PRINT RUN 10 TO 99 SER.#'d SETS
4SBCHH CB/GH/EC/JH/99 30.00 80.00
4SBDDV TB/AD/BD/JV/39 10.00 25.00
4SBPGG PP/KB/PG/KG/25 3,000.00 6,000.00
4SBWKO PO/CW/KB/CK/39 10.00 25.00
4SCMBK CK/CB/EC/BM/75 10.00 25.00
4SGBLL MB/BL/KL/MG/75 20.00 50.00
4SGCRV HG/EV/AR/AC/39 25.00 60.00
4SGLDG PG/HG/BL/BD/39 25.00 60.00
4SHHME GH/WE/EM/JH/99 12.00 30.00
4SJDFR BJ/KD/RR/RF/99 15.00 40.00
4SKDAP JK/KA/BD/TP/39 30.00 80.00
4SKPAH RH/SK/BA/JP/99 40.00 100.00
4SMESC DS/WE/EC/BM/99 10.00 25.00
4SMRGW RW/EG/OM/DR/75 125.00 300.00
4SNDSG PG/BD/JS/LN/39 15.00 40.00
4SOWMI LO/AI/DM/GW/39 10.00 25.00
4SPKJA PP/CA/BK/LJ/25 1,000.00 2,000.00
4SPLHR TH/JL/RP/DR/39 25.00 60.00
4SRBBS RR/AB/JB/RS/99 20.00 50.00
4SSSNK JS/DN/BS/GK/39 75.00 200.00
4SSWSG JS/TS/CW/GG/39 30.00 80.00
4STDJW LJ/DD/DT/DW/39 2,000.00 4,000.00
4SWFMG RF/PM/GW/JG/39 12.00 30.00
4SWGBS GW/CB/JS/PG/39 12.00 30.00
4SWRAP SW/RR/KA/TP/39 25.00 60.00
4SWSCM SM/DC/BS/JW/39 50.00 120.00

2009-10 SP Signature Edition INKcredible

STATED PRINT RUN 15 TO 499 SER.#'d SETS
IAA Alexis Ajinca/499 3.00 8.00
IAB Aaron Brooks/399 3.00 8.00
IAC Al Cervi/99 8.00 20.00
IAF Arron Afflalo/399 3.00 8.00
IAJ Al Jefferson/32 3.00 8.00
IAM Alonzo Mourning/49 20.00 50.00
IAR Anthony Randolph/169 3.00 8.00
IAU D.J. Augustin/199 3.00 8.00
IBA Jose Barea/199 10.00 25.00
IBB Bobby Brown/499 3.00 8.00
IBC Bill Cartwright/99 8.00 20.00
IBD Baron Davis/75 4.00 10.00
IBE Michael Beasley/99 3.00 8.00
IBI Mike Bibby/50 4.00 10.00
IBL Andray Blatche/99 3.00 8.00
IBR Brad Davis/99 3.00 8.00
IBW Bill Walker/499 3.00 8.00
ICA Carmelo Anthony/49 15.00 40.00
ICB Corey Brewer/99 3.00 8.00
ICD Chris Douglas-Roberts/499 3.00 8.00
ICL Clyde Lovellette/99 6.00 15.00
ICM Corey Maggette/75 4.00 10.00
ICO Mike Conley Jr./99 4.00 10.00
ICW Chet Walker/99 6.00 15.00
IDA Brad Daugherty/139 5.00 12.00
IDB Derrick Byars/499 3.00 8.00
IDF Derek Fisher/149 4.00 10.00
IDG Daniel Gibson/50 3.00 8.00
IDJ Darnell Jackson/499 3.00 8.00
IDM Donyell Marshall/199 3.00 8.00
IDO Billy Donovan/49 15.00 40.00
IDR Derrick Rose/99 30.00 80.00
IDW D.J. White/399 3.00 8.00
IEG Eric Gordon/99 4.00 10.00
IFG Francisco Garcia/129 3.00 8.00
IGA Danilo Gallinari/199 4.00 10.00
IGD Glen Davis/499 3.00 8.00
IGG George Gervin/149 6.00 15.00
IGH George Hill/399 4.00 10.00
IGP Gabe Pruitt/499 3.00 8.00
IGR Donte Greene/399 3.00 8.00
IGW Gerald Wallace/99 4.00 10.00
IJB Jerryd Bayless/199 3.00 8.00
IJD Joey Dorsey/499 3.00 8.00
IJG Jeff Green/99 4.00 10.00
IJL Jim Loscutoff/99 5.00 12.00
IJN Joakim Noah/149 3.00 8.00
IJO DeAndre Jordan/499 6.00 15.00
IJP Jim Price/99 3.00 8.00
IJS Jack Sikma/399 4.00 10.00
IJW Jerry West/49 25.00 60.00
IKA Kenny Anderson/99 4.00 10.00
IKL Kevin Love/199 8.00 20.00
ILA Louis Amundson/199 3.00 8.00
ILB Larry Bird/25 50.00 120.00
ILE Courtney Lee/99 3.00 8.00
ILJ LeBron James/23 2,000.00 4,000.00
ILM Luc Mbah A Moute/499 3.00 8.00
ILN Larry Nance/99 5.00 12.00
ILO Brook Lopez/199 5.00 12.00
IMA Morris Almond/99 3.00 8.00
IMB Marco Belinelli/399 3.00 8.00
IMC Mario Chalmers/499 3.00 8.00
IMJ Michael Jordan/23 1,000.00 3,000.00
IML Meadowlark Lemon/65 25.00 60.00
IMR Micheal Ray Richardson/149 4.00 10.00
IMT Mike Taylor/499 3.00 8.00
IMW Marvin Williams/99 3.00 8.00
INB Nicolas Batum/499 4.00 10.00
IOM O.J. Mayo/99 3.00 8.00
IPE Patrick Ewing Jr./249 3.00 8.00
IPG Pau Gasol/75 12.00 30.00
IRA Ray Allen/25 20.00 50.00
IRB Renaldo Balkman/50 3.00 8.00
IRH Roy Hibbert/149 4.00 10.00
IRJ Richard Jefferson/115 4.00 10.00
IRP Robert Parish/149 6.00 15.00
IRR Rajon Rondo/299 6.00 15.00
IRS Ramon Sessions/199 3.00 8.00
IRU Brandon Rush/99 3.00 8.00
IRW Russell Westbrook/149 50.00 120.00
ISH Spencer Haywood/299 4.00 10.00
ISI James Silas/99 6.00 15.00
ISJ Sam Jones/35 20.00 40.00
ISL Jerry Sloan/99 8.00 20.00
ISM Josh Smith/119 3.00 8.00
ISO Sonny Weems/499 3.00 8.00
ISS Sean Singletary/499 3.00 8.00
ISW Spud Webb/299 5.00 12.00
ITS Tom Sanders/149 8.00 20.00
IWA Darrell Walker/99 4.00 10.00

2006-07 SP Signature Edition Gold

IWE David West/149 4.00 10.00
IWI Chris Wilcox/279 3.00 8.00
IYM Yao Ming/49 20.00 50.00

2009-10 SP Signature Edition Signature Rookies

STATED PRINT RUN 199 SER.#'d SETS
RAD Austin Daye 3.00 8.00
RAJ A.J. Price 3.00 8.00
RBM B.J. Mullens 3.00 8.00
RBR Derrick Brown 3.00 8.00
RBU Chase Budinger 3.00 8.00
RCU Dante Cunningham 3.00 8.00
RDC Darren Collison 5.00 12.00
RDG Danny Green 5.00 12.00
RDS DaJuan Summers 3.00 8.00
REC Earl Clark 3.00 8.00
REM Eric Maynor 3.00 8.00
RGH Gerald Henderson 3.00 8.00
RGI Taylor Griffin 3.00 8.00
RHA James Harden 200.00 500.00
RHO Jrue Holiday 15.00 40.00
RJE Jonas Jerebko 4.00 10.00
RJF Jonny Flynn 3.00 8.00
RJJ James Johnson 4.00 10.00
RJP Jeff Pendergraph 3.00 8.00
RJT Jeff Teague 4.00 10.00
RMT Marcus Thornton 4.00 10.00
ROC Omri Casspi 3.00 8.00
RPB Patrick Beverley 5.00 12.00
RRR Ricky Rubio 25.00 60.00
RSC Stephen Curry 1,500.00 3,000.00
RSY Sam Young 3.00 8.00
RTA Jermaine Taylor 3.00 8.00
RTD Toney Douglas 3.00 8.00
RTG Taj Gibson 4.00 10.00
RTL Ty Lawson 4.00 10.00
RWE Wayne Ellington 4.00 10.00

2009-10 SP Signature Edition SIGnificance

STATED PRINT RUN 25 TO 499 SER.#'d SETS
SAA Alexis Ajinca/399 3.00 8.00
SAG Aaron Gray/499 3.00 8.00
SAJ Al Jefferson/249 3.00 8.00
SAL Acie Law/99 3.00 8.00
SAN Ryan Anderson/399 3.00 8.00
SAR Darrell Arthur/399 3.00 8.00
SAT Al Thornton/299 3.00 8.00
SAV Anderson Varejao/99 4.00 10.00
SBB Bobby Brown/499 3.00 8.00
SBC Corey Brewer/49 3.00 8.00
SBD Boris Diaw/109 4.00 10.00
SBJ Josh Boone/399 3.00 8.00
SBL Brook Lopez/199 5.00 12.00
SBR Bobby Brown/499 3.00 8.00
SBU Beno Udrih/99 3.00 8.00
SBW Bill Walker/499 3.00 8.00
SBY Andrew Bynum/199 3.00 8.00
SCA M.L. Carr/99 5.00 12.00
SCB Chauncey Billups/89 6.00 15.00
SCD Chris Duhon/99 3.00 8.00
SCH Chris Bosh/45 6.00 15.00
SCL Carl Landry/249 3.00 8.00
SCO Corey Brewer/49 3.00 8.00
SCR Caron Butler/99 4.00 10.00
SDA D.J. Augustin/199 4.00 10.00
SDC Daequan Cook/149 3.00 8.00
SDE DeAndre Jordan/499 6.00 15.00
SDG Danilo Gallinari/149 4.00 10.00
SDH Dwight Howard/49 10.00 25.00
SDJ Darnell Jackson/499 3.00 8.00
SDO Joey Dorsey/499 3.00 8.00
SDR Derrick Rose/49 30.00 80.00
SEG Eric Gordon/99 6.00 15.00
SGA Danilo Gallinari/149 4.00 10.00
SGI Artis Gilmore/25 10.00 25.00
SGP Gabe Pruitt/499 3.00 8.00
SJA Antawn Jamison/149 4.00 10.00
SJB Jerryd Bayless/199 3.00 8.00
SJC Javaris Crittenton/105 3.00 8.00
SJD Jared Dudley/99 3.00 8.00
SJF Jordan Farmar/99 4.00 10.00
SJG Jeff Green/99 4.00 10.00
SJH J.J. Hickson/249 3.00 8.00
SJJ Jarrett Jack/30 4.00 10.00
SJM Javale McGee/399 4.00 10.00
SJN Joakim Noah/125 3.00 8.00
SJO Joe Alexander/249 3.00 8.00
SJS Jason Smith/399 3.00 8.00
SJT Jason Thompson/249 3.00 8.00
SKK Kosta Koufos/399 3.00 8.00
SKL Kevin Love/149 8.00 20.00
SKW Kyle Weaver/499 3.00 8.00
SLA Louis Amundson/349 3.00 8.00
SLD Luol Deng/40 4.00 10.00
SLE Courtney Lee/399 4.00 10.00
SLM Luc Mbah A Moute/499 3.00 8.00
SLO Kyle Lowry/99 5.00 12.00
SMA Morris Almond/199 3.00 8.00
SMB Michael Beasley/49 3.00 8.00
SMC Mario Chalmers 4.00 10.00
SMC Mike Conley Jr./49 6.00 15.00
SMI Mike Conley Jr./49 6.00 15.00
SMJ Josh McRoberts/99 3.00 8.00
SMK Maurice Cheeks/99 4.00 10.00
SMS Marreese Speights/249 4.00 10.00
SMT Mike Taylor/499 3.00 8.00
SMW Mo Williams/299 4.00 10.00
SJO Joakim Noah/125 3.00 8.00
SOD Lamar Odom/149 8.00 20.00
SOM O.J. Mayo/99 3.00 8.00
SOR Oscar Robertson/25 40.00 100.00
SPA Tony Parker/65 10.00 25.00
SQR Quentin Richardson/379 4.00 10.00
SRA Ron Artest/25 6.00 15.00
SRJ Richard Jefferson/75 4.00 10.00
SRL Robin Lopez/249 3.00 8.00
SRM Rashad McCants/99 3.00 8.00
SRS Ramon Sessions/199 3.00 8.00
SRU Brandon Rush/299 3.00 8.00
SRW Russell Westbrook/199 50.00 120.00
SSH Spencer Hawes/199 3.00 8.00
SSJ Josh Smith/99 3.00 8.00
SSM Jason Smith/399 3.00 8.00
SSS Sean Singletary/499 3.00 8.00
SST Rodney Stuckey/125 3.00 8.00
SSV Sasha Vujacic/99 3.00 8.00
SSW Spud Webb/199 4.00 10.00
STC Tom Chambers/99 5.00 12.00
STY Tyson Chandler/139 3.00 8.00
SWI Deron Williams/50 4.00 10.00
SWS Shelden Williams/199 3.00 8.00
SYM Yao Ming/49 20.00 50.00

1972-73 Spalding

COMPLETE SET (7) 150.00 300.00
1 Rick Barry 40.00 100.00
2 Rick Barry
(Action Shot) 40.00 100.00
3 Wilt Chamberlain
(Philadelphia) 100.00 250.00
4 Wilt Chamberlain
(San Francisco) 100.00 250.00
5 Julius Erving 150.00 400.00
6 Gail Goodrich 30.00 80.00
7 Luke Jackson 20.00 50.00

2001 Sparks Fleer WNBA

COMPLETE SET (9) 5.00 12.00
1 Temecka Dixon .40 1.00
2 Lisa Leslie 2.50 6.00
3 Ukari Figgs .40 1.00
4 Delisha Milton .40 1.00
5 L.A. Sparks
Melissa's .40 1.00
6 Mwadi Mabika .40 1.00
7 Rhonda Mapp .40 1.00
8 Michael Cooper .40 1.00
9 Latasha Byears .40 1.00

1996 Sported/Match

COMPLETE SET (15) 10.00 25.00
2 Michael Jordan BK 8.00 20.00
7 Shaquille O'Neal BK 3.00 8.00

2012 Sportkings Double Memorabilia Silver

ANNOUNCED PRINT RUN 60
DM5 D.Robinson/B.Walton 10.00 20.00

2013 Sportkings Autograph Memorabilia Silver

PRINT RUN 20-50
AMCD1 Clyde Drexler/50* 12.00 30.00
AMCD2 Clyde Drexler/50* 12.00 30.00
AMSO1 Shaquille O'Neal/20* 40.00 80.00
AMSO2 Shaquille O'Neal/30* 40.00 80.00
AMSO3 Shaquille O'Neal/30* 40.00 80.00
AMSP1 Scottie Pippen/40* 40.00 80.00
AMSP2 Scottie Pippen/40* 40.00 80.00
AMSP3 Scottie Pippen/40* 40.00 80.00

2013 Sportkings Cityscapes Double Silver

ANNOUNCED PRINT RUN 40
CSD1 S.Pippen/B.Hull 10.00 25.00
CSD4 F.Valenzuela/S.O'Neal 6.00 15.00
CSD5 G.Howe/C.Drexler 8.00 20.00

2013 Sportkings Cityscapes Triple Silver

ANNOUNCED PRINT RUN 30
CST2 Thomas/Pippen/Hull 10.00 25.00

2013 Sportkings Double Memorabilia Silver

ANNOUNCED PRINT RUN 60
DM4 D.Robinson/S.O'Neal 6.00 15.00
DM6 S.Pippen/S.O'Neal 6.00 15.00

2013 Sportkings Quad Memorabilia Silver

ANNOUNCED PRINT RUN 40
QM2 Shaq/Drex/Pipp/Robin 12.00 30.00

2013 Sportkings Triple Memorabilia Silver

ANNOUNCED PRINT RUN 40
TM1 Shaq/Pippen/Robinson 8.00 20.00

1994-95 Sports Action Basket

COMPLETE SET (172) 200.00 500.00
5301 Dan Majerle 2.00 5.00
5302 Ron Harper 2.00 5.00
5303 Muggsy Bogues 1.50 4.00
5304 Shaquille O'Neal 8.00 20.00
5305 Larry Johnson 1.50 4.00
5306 Jalen Rose 3.00 8.00
5307 Nate McMillan 1.25 3.00
5308 Clippers Cheerleaders .40 1.00
5309 Kenny Smith 1.25 3.00
5310 Gorilla Mascot .60 1.50
5311 Michael Young 1.25 3.00
5312 David Robinson 5.00 12.00
5313 Jason Kidd 6.00 15.00
5314 Richard Dacoury 1.25 3.00
5315 Damon Bailey 1.50 4.00
5316 Dennis Rodman 3.00 8.00
5317 Michael Jordan 20.00 50.00
5318 B.J. Armstrong 1.25 3.00
5501 Billy Owens 1.25 3.00
5502 Alonzo Mourning 3.00 8.00
5503 Yann Bonato 1.25 3.00
5504 Isiah Thomas 2.50 6.00
5505 Glenn Robinson 3.00 8.00
5506 Karl Malone 5.00 12.00
5507 Dikembe Mutombo 2.50 6.00
5508 Hakeem Olajuwon 3.00 8.00
5509 Rony Seikaly 1.25 3.00
5510 Vernon Maxwell 1.25 3.00
5511 Stephane Ostrowski 1.25 3.00
5512 Arvydas Sabonis 3.00 8.00
5513 Yinka Dare 1.25 3.00
5514 Jamal Mashburn 3.00 8.00
5515 Buck Williams 1.50 4.00
5516 Mookie Blaylock 1.25 3.00
5517 Charles Barkley 5.00 12.00
5518 Patrick Ewing 3.00 8.00
5601 Scott Skiles 1.50 4.00
5602 Terry Porter 1.25 3.00
5603 Dominique Wilkins 3.00 8.00
5604 Stuff Mascot .40 1.00
5605 Anthony Peeler 1.25 3.00
5606 Donyell Marshall 1.50 4.00
5607 Chris Webber 3.00 8.00
5608 Alexander Volkov 2.00 5.00
5609 Pooh Richardson 1.25 3.00
5610 Robert Parish 1.50 4.00
5611 Isaiah Rider 1.50 4.00
5612 Steve Smith 1.50 4.00
5613 Michael Adams 1.25 3.00
5614 John Lucas Foundation .75 2.00
5615 Michael Jordan 20.00 50.00
5616 Sarunas Marciulionis 2.00 5.00
5617 Gerald Wilkins 1.50 4.00
5618 Miami Cheerleader .75 2.00
5701 Charlotte Mascot .40 1.00
5702 Brad Daugherty 1.25 3.00
5703 Chris Mullin 3.00 8.00
5704 Don MacLean 1.25 3.00
5705 Vlade Divac 1.50 4.00
5706 Danny Ainge 2.00 5.00
5707 Mark Jackson 2.00 5.00
5708 Lakers Cheerleaders 1.25 3.00
5709 B.J. Armstrong 1.50 4.00
5710 Nikos Gallis 2.00 5.00
5711 Joe Dumars 2.50 6.00
5712 Antoine Rigaudeau 2.00 5.00
5713 Rik Smits 1.25 3.00
5714 Charles Oakley 1.25 3.00
5715 Shawn Kemp 2.00 5.00
5716 Chris Webber 3.00 8.00
5717 Bill Varner 1.25 3.00
5718 Christian Laettner 2.00 5.00
5801 John Stockton 6.00 15.00
5802 Mitch Richmond 2.50 6.00
5803 Charles Barkley 5.00 12.00
5804 Latrell Sprewell 2.50 6.00
5805 Danny Manning 1.50 4.00
5806 Miami Mascot .40 1.00
5807 Bulls Mascot .40 1.00
5808 Kevin Willis 1.25 3.00
5809 Micheal Williams 1.25 3.00
5810 Magic Johnson 6.00 15.00
5811 Kevin Johnson 1.50 4.00
5812 Dennis Rodman 3.00 8.00
5813 John Starks 1.50 4.00
5814 Gheorghe Muresan 1.25 3.00
5815 Orlando Cheerleader 1.25 3.00
5816 Jeff Hornacek 2.00 5.00
5817 Clyde Drexler 4.00 10.00
5818 Dell Curry 1.25 3.00
5901 Jimmy Jackson 1.50 4.00
5902 Byron Scott 2.00 5.00
5903A Sam Cassell 2.00 5.00
5903B Otis Thorpe UER
Should have been numbered 5904 1.25 3.00
5905 San Antonio Mascot .40 1.00
5906 James Worthy 2.50 6.00
5907 A.C. Green 2.00 5.00
5908 Cleveland Cheerleader 1.25 3.00
5909 John Paxson 1.50 4.00
5910 Doug Christie 1.25 3.00
5911 Derrick Coleman 1.25 3.00
5912 Sean Rooks 1.25 3.00
5913 Turbo Mascot .40 1.00
5914 Charles Smith 1.25 3.00
5915 Derrick McKey 1.25 3.00
5916 Cherokee Parks 1.25 3.00
5917 Felton Spencer 1.25 3.00
5918 Derrick Phelps 1.25 3.00
6001 Steve Smith 1.50 4.00
6002 Tim Hardaway 2.00 5.00
6003 Dee Brown 1.25 3.00
6004 Reggie Miller 4.00 10.00
6005 Mark Price 2.00 5.00
6006 Jack Nicholson 2.00 5.00
6007 Kenny Anderson 1.25 3.00
6008 Jimmy Jackson 1.50 4.00
6009 Dikembe Mutombo 2.50 6.00
6010 Charles Oakley 1.25 3.00
6011 Muggsy Bogues 1.50 4.00
6012 Dan Majerle 2.00 5.00
6013 Mahmoud Abdul-Rauf .75 2.00
6014 B.J. Armstrong 1.50 4.00
6015 Nick Van Exel 2.50 6.00
6016 Kevin Johnson 1.50 4.00
6017 John Stockton 6.00 15.00
6018 Detlef Schrempf 1.50 4.00
6101 Scottie Pippen 5.00 12.00
6102 LaPhonso Ellis 1.25 3.00
6103 Sherman Douglas 1.25 3.00
6104 Isaiah Rider 1.50 4.00
6105 Vinny Del Negro 1.25 3.00
6106 Gary Payton 3.00 8.00
6107 Mookie Blaylock 1.25 3.00
6108 Christian Laettner 2.00 5.00
6109 Kevin Willis 1.25 3.00
6110 Harold Miner 1.25 3.00
6111 Chris Webber 3.00 8.00
6112 Rod Strickland 1.25 3.00
6113 Derrick Coleman 1.25 3.00
6114 Larry Johnson 1.50 4.00
6115 Rony Seikaly 1.25 3.00
6116 Derrick Coleman 1.25 3.00
6117 Larry Johnson 1.50 4.00
6118 Karl Malone 5.00 12.00
6201 Dell Curry 1.25 3.00
6202 Joe Dumars 2.50 6.00
6203 Robert Horry 2.00 5.00
6204 Glen Rice 2.00 5.00
6205 Hakeem Olajuwon 3.00 8.00
6206 Danny Ainge 1.50 4.00
6207 Oklahoma Cheerleader .75 2.00
6208 J.R. Reid 1.25 3.00
6209 Derrick McKey 1.25 3.00
6210 Shaquille O'Neal 6.00 15.00
6211 Christian Laettner 2.00 5.00
6212 John Starks 1.50 4.00
6213 Vernon Maxwell 1.25 3.00
6214 Charles Barkley 5.00 12.00
6215 Clyde Drexler 4.00 10.00
6216 Doug Smith 1.25 3.00
6217 Gators Cheerleader 1.25 3.00
6218 David Robinson 4.00 10.00
5406 Detlef Schrempf 1.50 4.00
5407 Anfernee Hardaway 3.00 8.00
5409 Reggie Miller 4.00 10.00
5410 Spud Webb 1.50 4.00
5412 Eric Montross 1.25 3.00
5415 Hakeem Olajuwon 3.00 8.00
5417 Glen Rice 2.00 5.00
5418 Kenny Anderson 1.25 3.00
6302 Craig Ehlo 1.25 3.00
6306 Jamal Mashburn 3.00 8.00

1995 Sports Action Basket

COMPLETE SET (41) 150.00 300.00
1 Charles Barkley SN 2.50 6.00
2 Larry Bird LN 4.00 10.00
3 Dee Brown SN 1.00 2.50
4 Sam Cassell SN 1.50 4.00
5 Vlade Divac ES 1.50 4.00
6 Patrick Ewing SN 2.00 5.00
7 Horace Grant SN 1.25 3.00
8 Anfernee Hardaway ES 2.50 6.00
9 Anfernee Hardaway SN 2.50 6.00
10 Grant Hill ES 2.50 6.00
11 Jeff Hornacek SN 1.25 3.00
12 Bobby Hurley SN 1.00 2.50
13 Jim Jackson SN 1.00 2.50
14 Magic Johnson LN 4.00 10.00
15 Vinnie Johnson SN 1.50 4.00
16 Michael Jordan SN 12.00 30.00
17 Michael Jordan HOME UER ES 12.00 30.00
18 Michael Jordan AWAY ES 12.00 30.00
19 Shawn Kemp SN 1.50 4.00
20 Shawn Kemp BC 1.50 4.00
21 Jason Kidd SN 2.50 6.00
22 Toni Kukoc SN 1.50 4.00
23 Christian Laettner ES 1.25 3.00
24 Karl Malone HOME ES 2.00 5.00
25 Karl Malone AWAY UER ES 2.00 5.00
26 Anthony Mason SN 1.00 2.50
27 Antonio McDyess SN 2.00 5.00
28 Nate McMillan SN 1.00 2.50
29 Reggie Miller SN 2.00 5.00
30 Chris Mullin SN 1.50 4.00
31 Alonzo Mourning ES 2.00 5.00
32 Shaquille O'Neal ES 4.00 10.00
33 Hakeem Olajuwon UER ES 2.00 5.00
34 Hakeem Olajuwon SN 2.00 5.00
35 Gary Payton SN 1.50 4.00
36 Mitch Richmond SN 1.50 4.00
37 Mitch Richmond ES 1.50 4.00
38 Isaiah Rider SN 1.50 4.00
39 Dennis Rodman SN 3.00 8.00
40 Arvydas Sabonis SN 3.00 8.00
41 Nick Van Exel SN 1.50 4.00

1995 Sports Action Basket Sticker Panels

COMPLETE SET (7) 25.00 60.00
1 Hakeem Olajuwon
Michael Jordan
Jalen Rose
Charles Barkley
Chris Webber
Magic Cheerleader
Reggie Miller
Georgia Tech
Shawn Kemp 8.00 20.00
2 Miami Hurricanes
The Intimidator
Rebels Logo
Grant Hill
Dennis Rodman
Anfernee Hardaway
Lakers Cheerleader
Muggsy Bogues
Shaquille O'Neal
Scottie Pippen 3.00 8.00
3 Clyde Drexler
Robert Horry
Mitch Richmond
Mortal Kombat
Jimmy Jackson
Derek Harper
Mookie Blaylock
Vinny Del Negro
Dee Brown 3.00 8.00
4 Gorilla Mascot
Space Player
Horace Grant
James Robinson
Danny Ferry
David Robinson
Doug Smith
Kendall Gill
Mahmoud Abdul-Rauf
Mitch Richmond 3.00 8.00
5 Mitch Richmond
Dennis Rodman
Shaquille O'Neal
Jason Kidd
Knicks Cheerleader
Penny Hardaway
Larry Johnson
Charles Smith
Isaiah Rider 4.00 10.00
6 Dee Brown
Karl Malone
Rik Smits
Chris Mullin
Joe Dumars
Shaquille O'Neal
Sean Elliott
John Starks
Pedrag Danilovic 3.00 8.00
7 KO
Playground Attitude
Dennis Rodman
Pacers Mascot
Charles Barkley
John Stockton
Don MacLean
Billy Owens
Coach Attitude 4.00 10.00

1996 Sports Action Basket Punch Outs

COMPLETE SET (10) 50.00 125.00
1 Michael Jordan 25.00 60.00
2 Steve Kerr 2.00 5.00
3 Toni Kukoc 3.00 8.00
4 Scottie Pippen 5.00 12.00
5 Dennis Rodman 5.00 12.00
6 Frank Brickowski 2.00 5.00
7 Hersey Hawkins 2.00 5.00
8 Shawn Kemp 4.00 10.00
9 Gary Payton 4.00 10.00
10 Detlef Schrempf 2.00 5.00

1978 Sports I.D. Patches

COMPLETE SET (6) 60.00 120.00
1 Darryl Dawkins 5.00 10.00
2 Julius Erving 20.00 40.00
3 Dan Issel 12.50 25.00
4 Bobby Jones 7.50 15.00
5 Nuggets Team Photo 7.50 15.00
6 Spurs Team Photo 7.50 15.00
7 David Thompson 7.50 15.00

1997 Sports Time USBL

COMPLETE SET (50) 8.00 20.00
1 Norris Coleman .08 .25
2 Anthony Mason 1.25 3.00
3 Michael Anderson .08 .25
4 Dallas Comegys .20 .50
5 Anthony Pullard .08 .25
6 Darrell Armstrong .08 .25
7 Kermit Holmes .08 .25
8 Lloyd Daniels .30 .75
9 Roy Tarpley .40 1.00
10 Paul Graham .20 .50
11 Nantambu Willingham .08 .25
12 Michael Ray Richardson
World B. Free .40 1.00
13 Richard Dumas .20 .50
14 International All-Star Tour .08 .25
15 Keith Jennings .20 .50
16 Duane Washington .20 .50
17 Wes Matthews .20 .50
18 Michael Adams .40 1.00
19 First USBL Game
John Hot Rod Williams .30 .75
20 Chuck Nevitt .20 .50
21 The Awards
Muggsy Bogues .40 1.00
22 The First Game
Michael Adams .08 .25
23 The Beginning
Daniel T. Meisenheimer .08 .25
24 Charlie Ward .75 2.00
25 Oliver Lee .08 .25
26 Greg Sutton .08 .25
27 1991 USBL Championship
Paul Graham .08 .25
28 Miami Tropics .08 .25
29 New Haven Skyhawks .08 .25
30 Back to Back Champions
Miami Tropics .08 .25
31 Springfield Fame .08 .25
32 Nate Johnson .08 .25
33 Muggsy Bogues 1.25 3.00
34 Chris Collier .08 .25
35 Sandhi Ortiz-Delvalle .08 .25
36 Henri Abrams .08 .25
37 Dan Cyrulik .08 .25
38 Charles Smith .30 .75
39 Mark Boyd .08 .25
40 Tim Legler .40 1.00
41 Jerry Ice Reynolds .20 .50
42 Road to the NBA
Richard Dumas .08 .25
43 Anthony Mason CL .40 1.00
44 Richard Dumas CL .08 .25
45 Atlanta Trojans
Atlantic City Seagulls .08 .25
46 Connecticut Skyhawks
Florida Sharks .08 .25
47 Jacksonville Barracudas
Long Island Surf .08 .25
48 New Hampshire Thunder Loons
Philadelphia Power .08 .25
49 Portland Wave
Raleigh Cougars .08 .25
50 Tampa Bay Windjammers
Westchester Kings .08 .25

1997 Sports Weekly Michael Jordan Promo

13 Michael Jordan 2.00 5.00

1998 Sports Weekly Michael Jordan Promo

23 Michael Jordan 2.00 5.00

1977-79 Sportscaster Series 4

COMPLETE SET (24) 15.00 30.00
412 Bill Russell 3.00 6.00
414 Dave Cowens 1.00 2.00
415 Rick Barry 1.00 2.00

1977-79 Sportscaster Series 14

COMPLETE SET (24) 17.50 35.00
1412 Emil Zatopek .50 1.00
1418 Oscar Robertson 2.00 4.00

1977-79 Sportscaster Series 18

COMPLETE SET (24) 12.50 25.00
1820 Jackie Chazalon .50 1.00

1977-79 Sportscaster Series 19

COMPLETE SET (24) 25.00 50.00
1914 Bob Pettit 1.00 2.00

1977-79 Sportscaster Series 30

COMPLETE SET (24) 12.50 25.00
3010 Fouls and Penalties .50 1.00
3012 Podoloff Cup 1.50 3.00
3013 NBA All-Star Game 1.00 2.00

1977-79 Sportscaster Series 52

COMPLETE SET (24) 10.00 20.00
5224 Hank Luisetti 1.25 2.50

1977-79 Sportscaster Series 74

COMPLETE SET (24) 200.00 400.00
7407 A Pro Oddity 2.00 4.00
7418 Larry Bird 125.00 250.00

1977-79 Sportscaster Series 77

COMPLETE SET (24) 150.00 300.00
7705 Kevin Porter 2.50 5.00
7721 Nat Holman 4.00 8.00

1977-79 Sportscaster Series 84

COMPLETE SET (24) 60.00 120.00
8409 United Basketball 3.00 6.00

1972 Sportscope Arena Great Moments in Basketball

1 Lew Alcindor/Wilt Chamberlain 40.00 75.00
2 Lew Alcindor/Bob Lanier 40.00 75.00
3 Lew Alcindor/Willis Reed/Bill Bradley 40.00 75.00
4 Dave Bing/Oscar Robertson 25.00 50.00
5 Austin Carr 15.00 30.00
6 Wilt Chamberlain/Lew Alcindor 50.00 100.00
7 Wilt Chamberlain/Jerry Lucas 75.00 150.00
8 Dave Cowens 25.00 50.00
9 Billy Cunningham/Phil Jackson 25.00 50.00
10 Dave DeBusschere 25.00 50.00
11 Walt Frazier 25.00 50.00
12 Gail Goodrich 20.00 40.00
13 John Havlicek 25.00 50.00
14 Pete Maravich 75.00 150.00
15 Jack Marin 15.00 30.00
16 Jack Newman 15.00 30.00
17 Unidentified Chicago Bulls #18 15.00 30.00
18 Dick VanArsdale/Walt Frazier 20.00 40.00
19 Lenny Wilkens 25.00 50.00

1976 Sportstix

1 Dave DeBusschere 7.50 15.00

1996 SPx

COMPLETE SET (50) 20.00 50.00
R1: STATED ODDS 1:75
T1: STATED ODDS 1:95
1 Stacey Augmon .75 2.00
2 Mookie Blaylock .60 1.50
3 Eric Montross .60 1.50
4 Eric Williams .60 1.50
5 Larry Johnson 1.00 2.50
6 George Zidek .60 1.50
7 Jason Caffey .60 1.50
8 Michael Jordan 15.00 40.00
9 Chris Mills .60 1.50
10 Bob Sura .60 1.50
11 Jason Kidd 1.50 4.00
12 Jamal Mashburn .75 2.00
13 Antonio McDyess 1.00 2.50
14 Jalen Rose .75 2.00
15 Grant Hill 1.50 4.00
16 Theo Ratliff .75 2.00
17 Joe Smith .75 2.00
18 Latrell Sprewell 1.00 2.50
19 Hakeem Olajuwon 1.25 3.00
20 Reggie Miller 1.50 4.00
21 Rik Smits .75 2.00
22 Brent Barry .75 2.00
23 Lamond Murray .60 1.50
24 Magic Johnson 2.50 6.00
25 Eddie Jones 1.00 2.50
26 Nick Van Exel 1.00 2.50
27 Alonzo Mourning 1.25 3.00
28 Kurt Thomas .60 1.50
29 Vin Baker .75 2.00
30 Glenn Robinson .75 2.00
31 Kevin Garnett 2.50 6.00
32 Ed O'Bannon .60 1.50
33 Patrick Ewing 1.25 3.00
34 Anfernee Hardaway 1.50 4.00
35 Shaquille O'Neal 2.50 6.00
36 Jerry Stackhouse 1.25 3.00
37 Charles Barkley 1.50 4.00
38 Michael Finley 1.25 3.00
39 Randolph Childress 1.00 2.50
40 Gary Trent .60 1.50
41 Brian Grant .75 2.00
42 Mitch Richmond 1.00 2.50
43 David Robinson 1.50 4.00
44 Shawn Kemp 1.00 2.50
45 Gary Payton 1.00 2.50
46 Damon Stoudamire .75 2.00
47 Karl Malone 1.25 3.00
48 John Stockton 1.25 3.00
49 Bryant Reeves .60 1.50
50 Rasheed Wallace 1.25 3.00
R1 Michael Jordan RB 15.00 40.00
T1 A.Hardaway COR TRIB 1.50 4.00
NNO Anfernee Hardaway AU 40.00 100.00
NNO A.Hardaway Expired 15.00 30.00
NNO Michael Jordan AU 6,000.00 10,000.00
NNO M.Jordan Expired 300.00 600.00

1996 SPx Gold

COMPLETE SET (50) 50.00 120.00
*GOLD: .75X TO 2X BASE CARD HI
STATED ODDS 1:7
8 Michael Jordan 60.00 150.00

1996 SPx Holoview Heroes

COMPLETE SET (10) 40.00 100.00
STATED ODDS 1:24
H1 Michael Jordan 50.00 120.00
H2 Jason Kidd 2.50 6.00
H3 Grant Hill 2.50 6.00
H4 Joe Smith 1.25 3.00
H5 Magic Johnson 4.00 10.00
H6 Antonio McDyess 1.50 4.00
H7 Anfernee Hardaway 2.50 6.00
H8 Jerry Stackhouse 2.00 5.00
H9 Damon Stoudamire 1.25 3.00
H10 Shaquille O'Neal 8.00 20.00

1997 SPx

COMPLETE SET (50) 50.00 120.00
1 Mookie Blaylock .75 2.00
2 Antoine Walker 1.00 2.50
3 Eric Williams .60 1.50
4 Tony Delk .75 2.00
5 Michael Jordan 20.00 50.00
6 Dennis Rodman 2.50 6.00
7 Vitaly Potapenko .60 1.50
8 Bob Sura .60 1.50
9 Jamal Mashburn .75 2.00
10 Samaki Walker .60 1.50
11 Antonio McDyess .75 2.00
12 Joe Dumars 1.00 2.50
13 Grant Hill 1.50 4.00
14 Joe Smith .75 2.00
15 Latrell Sprewell 1.25 3.00
16 Charles Barkley 2.50 6.00
17 Hakeem Olajuwon 2.00 5.00
18 Erick Dampier .60 1.50
19 Reggie Miller 2.00 5.00
20 Brent Barry .75 2.00
21 Lorenzen Wright .60 1.50
22 Kobe Bryant 40.00 100.00
23 Eddie Jones 1.00 2.50
24 Shaquille O'Neal 3.00 8.00
25 Alonzo Mourning 1.50 4.00
26 Kurt Thomas .60 1.50
27 Vin Baker .75 2.00
28 Glenn Robinson 1.00 2.50
29 Kevin Garnett 2.00 5.00
30 Stephon Marbury 1.25 3.00
31 Kerry Kittles .75 2.00
32 Patrick Ewing 1.50 4.00
33 Larry Johnson 1.25 3.00
34 Anfernee Hardaway 2.50 6.00
35 Allen Iverson 2.50 6.00
36 Jerry Stackhouse 1.00 2.50
37 Kevin Johnson 1.00 2.50
38 Steve Nash 2.00 5.00
39 Jermaine O'Neal 1.25 3.00
40 Mitch Richmond 1.25 3.00
41 David Robinson 2.00 5.00
42 Shawn Kemp 1.50 4.00
43 Gary Payton 1.50 4.00
44 Marcus Camby 1.00 2.50
45 Damon Stoudamire 1.25 3.00
46 Karl Malone 2.00 5.00
47 John Stockton 2.00 5.00
48 Shareef Abdur-Rahim 1.00 2.50
49 Bryant Reeves .60 1.50
50 Juwan Howard .75 2.00
SPX5 Michael Jordan PROMO 20.00 50.00

1997 SPx Gold

*STARS: .75X TO 2X BASE CARD HI
STATED ODDS 1:9
22 Kobe Bryant 125.00 300.00

1997 SPx Holoview Heroes

COMPLETE SET (20) 200.00 500.00
STATED ODDS 1:75
H1 Michael Jordan 150.00 400.00
H2 Grant Hill 15.00 40.00
H3 Reggie Miller 20.00 50.00
H4 Joe Smith 8.00 20.00
H5 Kevin Garnett 20.00 50.00
H6 Mitch Richmond 12.00 30.00
H7 Allen Iverson 40.00 100.00
H8 Patrick Ewing 15.00 40.00
H9 Hakeem Olajuwon 20.00 50.00
H10 David Robinson 20.00 50.00
H11 Anfernee Hardaway 25.00 60.00
H12 Juwan Howard 8.00 20.00
H13 Gary Payton 15.00 40.00
H14 Dennis Rodman 25.00 60.00
H15 Shaquille O'Neal 40.00 100.00
H16 Charles Barkley 25.00 60.00
H17 Damon Stoudamire 12.00 30.00
H18 Shawn Kemp 15.00 40.00
H19 Glenn Robinson 10.00 25.00
H20 John Stockton 20.00 50.00

1997 SPx ProMotion

COMPLETE SET (5) 600.00 1,200.00
STATED ODDS 1:430
1 Michael Jordan 500.00 1,000.00
2 Damon Stoudamire 40.00 100.00
3 Anfernee Hardaway 75.00 200.00
4 Shawn Kemp 75.00 200.00
5 Antonio McDyess 40.00 100.00

1997 SPx ProMotion Autographs

1 Michael Jordan 6,000.00 12,000.00
2 Damon Stoudamire 100.00 250.00
3 Anfernee Hardaway 300.00 600.00
4 Shawn Kemp 150.00 400.00
5 Antonio McDyess 75.00 200.00

1997-98 SPx

COMPLETE SET (50) 20.00 50.00
1 Mookie Blaylock .60 1.50
2 Dikembe Mutombo 1.00 2.50
3 Chauncey Billups RC 2.50 6.00
4 Antoine Walker .60 1.50
5 Glen Rice .60 1.50
6 Michael Jordan 6.00 15.00
7 Scottie Pippen 1.50 4.00
8 Dennis Rodman 1.50 4.00
9 Shawn Kemp 1.00 2.50
10 Michael Finley .60 1.50
11 Tony Battie RC .75 2.00
12 LaPhonso Ellis .50 1.25
13 Grant Hill 1.00 2.50
14 Joe Dumars .75 2.00
15 Joe Smith .50 1.25
16 Clyde Drexler 1.00 2.50
17 Charles Barkley 1.50 4.00
18 Hakeem Olajuwon 1.25 3.00
19 Reggie Miller 1.25 3.00
20 Brent Barry .50 1.25
21 Kobe Bryant 6.00 15.00
22 Shaquille O'Neal 2.00 5.00
23 Alonzo Mourning 1.25 3.00
24 Glenn Robinson .60 1.50
25 Kevin Garnett 1.50 4.00
26 Stephon Marbury .75 2.00
27 Keith Van Horn RC 1.25 3.00
28 Patrick Ewing 1.00 2.50
29 Anfernee Hardaway 1.50 4.00
30 Allen Iverson 2.00 5.00
31 Kevin Johnson .60 1.50
32 Antonio McDyess .60 1.50
33 Jason Kidd 1.00 2.50
34 Kenny Anderson .50 1.25
35 Rasheed Wallace .75 2.00
36 Mitch Richmond .75 2.00
37 Tim Duncan RC 5.00 12.00
38 David Robinson 1.25 3.00
39 Vin Baker .50 1.25
40 Gary Payton 1.00 2.50
41 Marcus Camby .60 1.50
42 Tracy McGrady RC 4.00 10.00
43 Damon Stoudamire .60 1.50
44 Karl Malone 1.25 3.00
45 John Stockton 1.25 3.00
46 Shareef Abdur-Rahim .60 1.50
47 Antonio Daniels RC .75 2.00
48 Bryant Reeves .40 1.00
49 Juwan Howard .60 1.50
50 Chris Webber .75 2.00
T1 Piece of History Trade 4.00 10.00

1997-98 SPx Sky

COMPLETE SET (50) 30.00 80.00
*STARS: .5X TO 1.25X BASE CARD HI
*RCs: .4X TO 1X BASE HI
ONE PER PACK
6 Michael Jordan 10.00 25.00

1997-98 SPx Bronze

COMPLETE SET (50) 25.00 60.00
*STARS: .75X TO 2X BASE CARD HI
*RCs: .6X TO 1.5X BASE HI
STATED ODDS 1:3

1997-98 SPx Silver

*STARS: 1X TO 2.5X BASE CARD HI
*RCs: .75X TO 2X BASE HI

STATED ODDS 1:6
6 Michael Jordan 30.00 80.00

1997-98 SPx Gold
*STARS: 4X TO 10X BASE CARD HI
*RCs: 2X TO 5X BASE HI
STATED ODDS 1:17
6 Michael Jordan 200.00 500.00
37 Tim Duncan 30.00 80.00

1997-98 SPx Grand Finale
*STARS: 50X TO 120X BASE CARD HI
*RCs: 20X TO 50X BASE HI
STATED PRINT RUN 50 SERIAL #'d SETS
6 Michael Jordan 8,000.00 12,000.00
7 Scottie Pippen 200.00 400.00
8 Dennis Rodman 300.00 600.00
9 Shawn Kemp 100.00 200.00
13 Grant Hill 600.00 1,000.00
16 Clyde Drexler 125.00 225.00
17 Charles Barkley 150.00 300.00
18 Hakeem Olajuwon 600.00 1,200.00
19 Reggie Miller 125.00 250.00
21 Kobe Bryant 2,500.00 5,000.00
22 Shaquille O'Neal 500.00 1,000.00
23 Alonzo Mourning 150.00 400.00
25 Kevin Garnett 400.00 800.00
37 Tim Duncan 1,000.00 2,000.00
38 David Robinson 1,000.00 2,000.00
42 Tracy McGrady 500.00 1,000.00
43 Damon Stoudamire 150.00 400.00
44 Karl Malone 150.00 400.00
45 John Stockton 150.00 400.00
50 Chris Webber 100.00 250.00

1997-98 SPx Hardcourt Holoview
COMPLETE SET (20) 350.00 700.00
STATED ODDS 1:54
HH1 Michael Jordan 200.00 500.00
HH2 Allen Iverson 15.00 40.00
HH3 Antoine Walker 6.00 15.00
HH4 Chris Webber 8.00 20.00
HH5 Glenn Robinson 6.00 15.00
HH6 Kevin Garnett 15.00 40.00
HH7 Shareef Abdur-Rahim 6.00 15.00
HH8 Keith Van Horn 4.00 10.00
HH9 Kobe Bryant 40.00 100.00
HH10 Glen Rice 6.00 15.00
HH11 Damon Stoudamire 6.00 15.00
HH12 Hakeem Olajuwon 12.00 30.00
HH13 Mookie Blaylock 6.00 15.00
HH14 Shaquille O'Neal 20.00 50.00
HH15 Stephon Marbury 8.00 20.00
HH16 Chauncey Billups 8.00 20.00
HH17 Anfernee Hardaway 15.00 40.00
HH18 Tim Duncan 20.00 50.00
HH19 Mitch Richmond 8.00 20.00
HH20 Grant Hill 10.00 25.00

1997-98 SPx ProMotion
COMPLETE SET (10) 1,500.00 3,000.00
STATED ODDS 1:252
PM1 Michael Jordan 1,250.00 2,500.00
PM2 Shaquille O'Neal 100.00 250.00
PM3 Tim Duncan 300.00 600.00
PM4 Shareef Abdur-Rahim 60.00 150.00
PM5 Grant Hill 75.00 200.00
PM6 Karl Malone 75.00 200.00
PM7 Anfernee Hardaway 75.00 200.00
PM8 Keith Van Horn 20.00 50.00
PM9 Kevin Garnett 100.00 250.00
PM10 Damon Stoudamire 12.00 30.00

1999-00 SPx
COMPLETE SET w/o RC (90) 18.00 30.00
91-120 UNSIGNED #'d TO 3500
91-120 SIGNED #'d TO 2500 UNLESS NOTED
1 Dikembe Mutombo .75 2.00
2 Alan Henderson .30 .75
3 Antoine Walker .50 1.25
4 Paul Pierce 1.00 2.50
5 Kenny Anderson .40 1.00
6 Eddie Jones .50 1.25
7 David Wesley .30 .75
8 Elden Campbell .30 .75
9 Toni Kukoc .60 1.50
10 Dickey Simpkins .30 .75
11 Shawn Kemp .75 2.00
12 Brevin Knight .30 .75
13 Michael Finley .50 1.25
14 Cedric Ceballos .30 .75
15 Dirk Nowitzki 1.50 4.00
16 Antonio McDyess .40 1.00
17 Nick Van Exel .40 1.00
18 Chauncey Billups .50 1.25
19 Grant Hill .75 2.00
20 Jerry Stackhouse .50 1.25
21 Bison Dele .30 .75
22 Lindsey Hunter .30 .75
23 Antawn Jamison .50 1.25
24 Donyell Marshall .40 1.00
25 John Starks .50 1.25
26 Chris Mills .30 .75
27 Hakeem Olajuwon 1.00 2.50
28 Scottie Pippen 1.25 3.00
29 Charles Barkley 1.25 3.00
30 Reggie Miller 1.00 2.50
31 Rik Smits .40 1.00
32 Jalen Rose .40 1.00
33 Chris Mullin .50 1.25
34 Maurice Taylor .30 .75
35 Michael Olowokandi .30 .75
36 Shaquille O'Neal 2.00 5.00
37 Kobe Bryant 4.00 10.00
38 Glen Rice .50 1.25
39 Tim Hardaway .60 1.50
40 Alonzo Mourning .75 2.00
41 Dan Majerle .50 1.25
42 P.J. Brown .30 .75
43 Glenn Robinson .40 1.00
44 Ray Allen .75 2.00
45 Sam Cassell .40 1.00
46 Tim Thomas .40 1.00
47 Kevin Garnett 1.25 3.00
48 Bobby Jackson .40 1.00
49 Joe Smith .40 1.00
50 Stephon Marbury .60 1.50
51 Keith Van Horn .60 1.50
52 Jayson Williams .30 .75
53 Patrick Ewing .60 1.50
54 Latrell Sprewell .60 1.50
55 Allan Houston .40 1.00
56 Marcus Camby .40 1.00
57 Bo Outlaw .30 .75
58 Darrell Armstrong .30 .75
59 Allen Iverson 1.25 3.00
60 Theo Ratliff .40 1.00
61 Larry Hughes .40 1.00
62 Jason Kidd .75 2.00
63 Tom Gugliotta .40 1.00
64 Clifford Robinson .40 1.00
65 Brian Grant .30 .75
66 Jermaine O'Neal .40 1.00
67 Rasheed Wallace .60 1.50
68 Damon Stoudamire .50 1.25
69 Jason Williams .75 2.00
70 Chris Webber .60 1.50
71 Vlade Divac .50 1.25
72 Avery Johnson .40 1.00
73 Tim Duncan 1.25 3.00
74 David Robinson 1.00 2.50
75 Sean Elliott .40 1.00
76 Gary Payton .75 2.00
77 Vin Baker .40 1.00
78 Jelani McCoy .30 .75
79 Charles Oakley .50 1.25
80 Vince Carter 1.25 3.00
81 Tracy McGrady .75 2.00
82 Doug Christie .40 1.00
83 Karl Malone 1.00 2.50
84 John Stockton .75 2.00
85 Shareef Abdur-Rahim .50 1.25
86 Bryant Reeves .30 .75
87 Mike Bibby .50 1.25
88 Juwan Howard .40 1.00
89 Mitch Richmond .60 1.50
90 Rod Strickland .40 1.00
91 Elton Brand RC 4.00 10.00
92 Steve Francis AU/500 RC 15.00 40.00
93 Baron Davis AU/500 RC 25.00 60.00
94 Lamar Odom/3500 RC 4.00 10.00
95 Jonathan Bender/3500 RC 2.00 5.00
96 W.Szczerbiak AU/500 RC 5.00 12.00
97 R.Hamilton AU/2500 RC 5.00 12.00
98 Andre Miller AU/500 RC 6.00 15.00
99 Shawn Marion AU/2500 RC 4.00 10.00
100 Jason Terry AU/2500 RC 3.00 8.00
101 T.Langdon AU/2500 RC 1.50 4.00
102 Venson Hamilton/3500 RC 2.00 5.00
103 Corey Maggette AU/500 RC 4.00 10.00
104 William Avery AU/2500 RC 1.25 3.00
105 Dion Glover/3500 RC 1.25 3.00
106 Ron Artest AU RC 5.00 12.00
107 Cal Bowdler/3500 RC 1.25 3.00
108 James Posey AU/2500 RC 2.00 5.00
109 Quincy Lewis AU/2500 RC 1.25 3.00
110 D.George AU/2500 RC 1.50 4.00
111 Tim James AU/2500 RC 1.25 3.00
112 V.Cummings/3500 RC 1.25 3.00
113 Jumaine Jones AU/2500 RC 1.25 3.00
114 Scott Padgett AU/2500 RC 1.50 4.00
115 Kenny Thomas/3500 RC 2.00 5.00
116 Jeff Foster/3500 RC 2.00 5.00
117 Ryan Robertson/3500 RC 1.25 3.00
118 Chris Herren AU/2500 RC 6.00 15.00
119 E.Eschmeyer AU/2500 RC 1.50 4.00
120 A.J. Bramlett AU/2500 RC 2.00 5.00
P32 Karl Malone PROMO .75 2.00

1999-00 SPx Radiance
*STARS: 8X TO 20X BASE CARD HI
STATED PRINT RUN 100 SERIAL #'d SETS
4 Paul Pierce 15.00 40.00
11 Shawn Kemp 20.00 50.00
19 Grant Hill 20.00 50.00
28 Scottie Pippen 25.00 60.00
29 Charles Barkley 20.00 50.00
37 Kobe Bryant 60.00 150.00
59 Allen Iverson 40.00 100.00
81 Tracy McGrady 30.00 80.00
91 Elton Brand 15.00 40.00
92 Steve Francis 15.00 40.00
93 Baron Davis 20.00 50.00
94 Lamar Odom 15.00 40.00
95 Jonathan Bender 8.00 20.00
96 Wally Szczerbiak 12.00 30.00
97 Richard Hamilton 20.00 50.00
98 Andre Miller 15.00 40.00
99 Shawn Marion 15.00 40.00
100 Jason Terry 12.00 30.00
101 Trajan Langdon 6.00 15.00
102 Venson Hamilton 8.00 20.00
103 Corey Maggette 10.00 25.00
104 William Avery 5.00 12.00
105 Dion Glover 5.00 12.00
106 Ron Artest 20.00 50.00
107 Cal Bowdler 5.00 12.00
108 James Posey 8.00 20.00
109 Quincy Lewis 5.00 12.00
110 Devean George 6.00 15.00
111 Tim James 5.00 12.00
112 Vonteego Cummings 5.00 12.00
113 Jumaine Jones 5.00 12.00
114 Scott Padgett 6.00 15.00
115 Kenny Thomas 8.00 20.00
116 Jeff Foster 8.00 20.00
117 Ryan Robertson 5.00 12.00
118 Chris Herren 6.00 15.00
119 Evan Eschmeyer 6.00 15.00
120 A.J. Bramlett 8.00 20.00

1999-00 SPx Decade of Jordan
COMPLETE SET (10) 15.00 30.00
COMMON CARD (J1-J10) 2.00 5.00
STATED ODDS 1:9

1999-00 SPx Masters
COMPLETE SET (15) 15.00 40.00
STATED ODDS 1:17
M1 Michael Jordan 15.00 40.00
M2 Vince Carter 2.50 6.00
M3 Tim Duncan 2.50 6.00
M4 Allen Iverson 2.50 6.00
M5 Gary Payton 1.50 4.00
M6 Shareef Abdur-Rahim 1.00 2.50
M7 Keith Van Horn .75 2.00
M8 Grant Hill 1.50 4.00
M9 Kobe Bryant 8.00 20.00
M10 Kevin Garnett 2.50 6.00
M11 Karl Malone 2.00 5.00
M12 Allan Houston .75 2.00
M13 Jason Kidd 1.50 4.00
M14 Antoine Walker 1.00 2.50
M15 Jason Williams 1.50 4.00

1999-00 SPx Prolifics
COMPLETE SET (15) 12.50 25.00
STATED ODDS 1:17
P1 Michael Jordan 40.00 100.00
P2 Karl Malone 1.50 4.00
P3 Jason Kidd 1.25 3.00
P4 Reggie Miller 1.50 4.00
P5 Glen Rice .75 2.00
P6 Hakeem Olajuwon 1.50 4.00
P7 Mitch Richmond 1.00 2.50
P8 Shawn Kemp 1.25 3.00
P9 Patrick Ewing 1.00 2.50
P10 Dikembe Mutombo 1.25 3.00
P11 Scottie Pippen 2.00 5.00
P12 John Stockton 1.25 3.00
P13 David Robinson 1.50 4.00
P14 Tim Hardaway 1.00 2.50
P15 Charles Barkley 2.00 5.00

1999-00 SPx Spxcitement
COMPLETE SET (20) 15.00 40.00
STATED ODDS 1:3
S1 Antoine Walker .40 1.00
S2 Antonio McDyess .30 .75
S3 Antawn Jamison .40 1.00
S4 Vin Baker .30 .75
S5 Juwan Howard .30 .75
S6 Brian Grant .25 .60
S7 Brevin Knight .25 .60
S8 Glenn Robinson .30 .75
S9 Stephon Marbury .50 1.25
S10 Reggie Miller .75 2.00
S11 Nick Van Exel .30 .75
S12 Alonzo Mourning .60 1.50
S13 David Robinson .75 2.00
S14 Hakeem Olajuwon .75 2.00
S15 Toni Kukoc .50 1.25
S16 Maurice Taylor .25 .60
S17 Darrell Armstrong .25 .60
S18 Latrell Sprewell .50 1.25
S19 Tom Gugliotta .30 .75
S20 Michael Jordan 25.00 60.00

1999-00 SPx Spxtreme
COMPLETE SET (20) 75.00 200.00
STATED ODDS 1:6
X1 Michael Jordan 75.00 200.00
X2 Tim Hardaway 1.25 3.00
X3 Marcus Camby .75 2.00
X4 Jason Williams 1.50 4.00
X5 Shareef Abdur-Rahim 1.00 2.50
X6 Keith Van Horn .75 2.00
X7 Glen Rice 1.00 2.50
X8 Gary Payton 1.50 4.00
X9 Grant Hill 1.50 4.00
X10 Allan Houston .75 2.00
X11 Ray Allen 1.50 4.00
X12 Michael Finley 1.00 2.50
X13 Shawn Kemp 1.50 4.00
X14 Shaquille O'Neal 8.00 20.00
X15 Paul Pierce 2.00 5.00
X16 Mike Bibby 1.00 2.50
X17 Michael Olowokandi .60 1.50
X18 Damon Stoudamire 1.00 2.50
X19 Mitch Richmond 1.25 3.00
X20 Eddie Jones 1.00 2.50

1999-00 SPx Starscape
COMPLETE SET (10) 12.00 30.00
STATED ODDS 1:9
ST1 Michael Jordan 25.00 60.00
ST2 John Stockton 1.00 2.50
ST3 Antonio McDyess .50 1.25
ST4 Alonzo Mourning .60 1.50
ST5 Shaquille O'Neal 2.50 6.00
ST6 Stephon Marbury .75 2.00
ST7 Chris Webber .75 2.00
ST8 Charles Barkley 1.50 4.00
ST9 Antawn Jamison .60 1.50
ST10 Scottie Pippen 1.50 4.00

1999-00 SPx Winning Materials
STATED ODDS 1:252
CARDS WM3 AND WM7 DO NOT EXIST
WM1 Michael Jordan 800.00 1,500.00
WM1A M.Jordan AU/23 2,000.00 5,000.00
WM2 Karl Malone 20.00 50.00
WM2A K.Malone AU/32 100.00 250.00
WM4 Kobe Bryant 60.00 150.00
WM5 Paul Pierce 12.00 30.00
WM6 Kevin Garnett 15.00 40.00
WM8 Shaquille O'Neal 20.00 50.00
WM9 David Robinson 12.00 30.00
WM10 Charles Barkley 20.00 50.00

2000-01 SPx
COMPLETE SET w/o RC (90) 20.00 50.00
1 Dikembe Mutombo .75 2.00
2 Jim Jackson .40 1.00
3 Jason Terry .50 1.25
4 Paul Pierce .75 2.00
5 Kenny Anderson .40 1.00
6 Antoine Walker .50 1.25
7 Derrick Coleman .40 1.00
8 Baron Davis .50 1.25
9 David Wesley .40 1.00
10 Elton Brand .50 1.25
11 Ron Artest .50 1.25
12 Corey Benjamin .30 .75
13 Trajan Langdon .30 .75
14 Lamond Murray .30 .75
15 Andre Miller .40 1.00
16 Michael Finley .50 1.25
17 Gary Trent .30 .75
18 Dirk Nowitzki 1.25 3.00
19 Antonio McDyess .40 1.00
20 Nick Van Exel .50 1.25
21 Raef LaFrentz .40 1.00
22 Jerry Stackhouse .50 1.25
23 Michael Curry .30 .75
24 Jerome Williams .30 .75
25 Larry Hughes .50 1.25
26 Antawn Jamison .50 1.25
27 Mookie Blaylock .50 1.25
28 Hakeem Olajuwon 1.00 2.50
29 Steve Francis .50 1.25
30 Shandon Anderson .30 .75
31 Reggie Miller 1.00 2.50
32 Jalen Rose .40 1.00
33 Austin Croshere .30 .75
34 Lamar Odom .50 1.25
35 Michael Olowokandi .30 .75
36 Tyrone Nesby .30 .75
37 Shaquille O'Neal 2.00 5.00
38 Kobe Bryant 4.00 10.00
39 Robert Horry .50 1.25
40 Ron Harper .50 1.25
41 Alonzo Mourning .75 2.00
42 Eddie Jones .50 1.25
43 Tim Hardaway .60 1.50
44 Glenn Robinson .50 1.25
45 Sam Cassell .40 1.00
46 Ray Allen .75 2.00
47 Tim Thomas .30 .75
48 Kevin Garnett 1.25 3.00
49 Terrell Brandon .40 1.00
50 Wally Szczerbiak .40 1.00
51 Keith Van Horn .40 1.00
52 Stephon Marbury .60 1.50
53 Jamie Feick .30 .75
54 Latrell Sprewell .60 1.50
55 Marcus Camby .40 1.00
56 Allan Houston .50 1.25
57 Grant Hill .75 2.00
58 Tracy McGrady 1.00 2.50
59 Darrell Armstrong .30 .75
60 Allen Iverson 1.25 3.00
61 Toni Kukoc .60 1.50
62 Theo Ratliff .30 .75
63 Anfernee Hardaway .75 2.00
64 Jason Kidd .75 2.00
65 Shawn Marion .50 1.25
66 Steve Smith .50 1.25
67 Rasheed Wallace .60 1.50
68 Scottie Pippen 1.25 3.00
69 Bonzi Wells .30 .75
70 Jason Williams .75 2.00
71 Vlade Divac .50 1.25
72 Chris Webber .60 1.50
73 David Robinson 1.00 2.50
74 Sean Elliott .40 1.00
75 Tim Duncan 1.25 3.00
76 Gary Payton .75 2.00
77 Rashard Lewis .40 1.00
78 Vin Baker .40 1.00
79 Vince Carter 1.00 2.50
80 Muggsy Bogues .50 1.25
81 Antonio Davis .40 1.00
82 Karl Malone 1.00 2.50
83 John Stockton 1.00 2.50
84 Bryon Russell .30 .75
85 Shareef Abdur-Rahim .50 1.25
86 Michael Dickerson .30 .75
87 Mike Bibby .50 1.25
88 Mitch Richmond .60 1.50
89 Richard Hamilton .60 1.50
90 Juwan Howard .40 1.00
91 Lavor Postell RC .60 1.50
92 Mark Madsen JSY AU RC 3.00 8.00
93 Soumaila Samake RC .60 1.50
94 Michael Redd RC 2.50 6.00
95 Paul McPherson RC .60 1.50
96 Ruben Wolkowyski RC .60 1.50
97 Daniel Santiago RC 1.00 2.50
98 Pepe Sanchez RC .75 2.00
99 Marc Jackson RC 1.25 3.00
100 Khalid El-Amin RC 1.00 2.50
101 Iakovos Tsakalidis RC 1.00 2.50
102 Jabari Smith RC 1.00 2.50
103 Jason Hart RC 1.50 4.00
104 Stephen Jackson RC 3.00 8.00
105 Eduardo Najera RC 2.50 6.00
106 Hanno Mottola RC 1.50 4.00
107 Eddie House RC 2.00 5.00
108 Dan Langhi RC 1.50 4.00
109 A.J. Guyton RC 1.50 4.00
110 Chris Porter RC 1.50 4.00
111 Mike Miller JSY AU RC 5.00 12.00
112 Keyon Dooling JSY AU RC 2.50 6.00
113 C.Alexander JSY AU RC 2.00 5.00
114 Desmond Mason JSY AU RC 4.00 10.00
115 Jamaal Magloire JSY AU RC 3.00 8.00
116 D.Stevenson JSY AU RC 3.00 8.00
117 Dermarr Johnson JSY AU RC 2.00 5.00
118 Mateen Cleaves JSY AU RC 2.50 6.00
119 Morris Peterson JSY AU RC 3.00 8.00
120 Jerome Moiso JSY AU RC 2.00 5.00
121 Donnell Harvey JSY AU RC 2.50 6.00
122 Q.Richardson JSY AU RC 2.50 6.00
123 Jamal Crawford JSY AU RC 12.00 30.00
124 Erick Barkley JSY AU RC 2.00 5.00
125 Hedo Turkoglu JSY AU RC 5.00 12.00
126 Etan Thomas JSY AU RC 2.50 6.00
127 Mamadou N'Diaye JSY AU RC 2.00 5.00
128 Joel Przybilla JSY AU RC 2.50 6.00
129 Jason Collier JSY AU RC 3.00 8.00
130 Speedy Claxton JSY AU RC 3.00 8.00
131 Kenyon Martin JSY AU RC 12.00 30.00
132 Stromile Swift JSY AU RC 3.00 8.00
133 Darius Miles JSY AU RC 4.00 10.00
134 Marcus Fizer JSY AU RC 3.00 8.00
135 Chris Mihm JSY AU RC 2.50 6.00
136 Jake Voskuhl JSY AU RC 2.00 5.00
137 Pete Mickeal JSY AU RC 2.50 6.00
138 Dalibor Bagaric RC .75 2.00

2000-01 SPx Spectrum
*STARS: 25X TO 60X BASE CARD HI
STATED PRINT RUN 25 SERIAL #'d SETS
91 Lavor Postell 6.00 15.00
92 Mark Madsen JSY AU 20.00 50.00
93 Soumaila Samake 6.00 15.00
94 Michael Redd 25.00 60.00
95 Paul McPherson 6.00 15.00
96 Ruben Wolkowyski 6.00 15.00
97 Daniel Santiago 10.00 25.00
98 Pepe Sanchez 8.00 20.00
99 Marc Jackson 8.00 20.00
100 Khalid El-Amin 6.00 15.00
101 Iakovos Tsakalidis 6.00 15.00
102 Jabari Smith 6.00 15.00
103 Jason Hart 10.00 25.00
104 Stephen Jackson 20.00 50.00
105 Eduardo Najera 10.00 25.00
106 Hanno Mottola 6.00 15.00
107 Eddie House 8.00 20.00
108 Dan Langhi 6.00 15.00
109 A.J. Guyton 6.00 15.00
110 Chris Porter 6.00 15.00
111 Mike Miller JSY AU 30.00 80.00
112 Keyon Dooling JSY AU 15.00 40.00
113 Courtney Alexander JSY AU 12.00 30.00
114 Desmond Mason JSY AU 25.00 60.00
115 Jamaal Magloire JSY AU 20.00 50.00
116 DeShawn Stevenson JSY AU 20.00 50.00
117 Dermarr Johnson JSY AU 12.00 30.00
118 Mateen Cleaves JSY AU 15.00 40.00
119 Morris Peterson JSY AU 20.00 50.00
120 Jerome Moiso JSY AU 12.00 30.00
121 Donnell Harvey JSY AU 15.00 40.00
122 Quentin Richardson JSY AU 15.00 40.00
123 Jamal Crawford JSY AU 75.00 200.00
124 Erick Barkley JSY AU 12.00 30.00
125 Hedo Turkoglu JSY AU 30.00 80.00
126 Etan Thomas JSY AU 15.00 40.00
127 Mamadou N'Diaye JSY AU 12.00 30.00
128 Joel Przybilla JSY AU 15.00 40.00
129 Jason Collier JSY AU 20.00 50.00
130 Speedy Claxton JSY AU 20.00 50.00
131 Kenyon Martin JSY AU 75.00 200.00
132 Stromile Swift JSY AU 15.00 40.00
133 Darius Miles JSY AU 20.00 50.00
134 Marcus Fizer JSY AU 15.00 40.00
135 Chris Mihm JSY AU 12.00 30.00
136 Jake Voskuhl JSY AU 12.00 30.00
137 Pete Mickeal JSY AU 15.00 40.00
138 Dalibor Bagaric 8.00 20.00

2000-01 SPx Masters
COMPLETE SET (11) 25.00 60.00
STATED ODDS 1:8
M1 Michael Jordan 20.00 50.00
M2 Kobe Bryant 12.00 30.00
M3 Steve Francis .60 1.50
M4 Elton Brand .60 1.50
M5 Tim Duncan 1.50 4.00
M6 Jason Kidd 1.00 2.50
M7 Kevin Garnett 1.50 4.00
M8 Karl Malone 1.25 3.00
M9 Shaquille O'Neal 2.50 6.00
M10 Gary Payton 1.00 2.50
M11 Vince Carter 1.25 3.00

2000-01 SPx Spxcitement
COMPLETE SET (20) 12.00 30.00
STATED ODDS 1:5
S1 Kobe Bryant 8.00 20.00
S2 Gary Payton .75 2.00
S3 Rasheed Wallace .60 1.50
S4 Jason Williams .75 2.00
S5 Ray Allen .75 2.00
S6 Tim Duncan 1.25 3.00
S7 Stephon Marbury .60 1.50
S8 Allen Iverson 1.25 3.00
S9 Jerry Stackhouse .50 1.25
S10 Kevin Garnett 1.25 3.00
S11 Antawn Jamison .50 1.25
S12 Paul Pierce .75 2.00
S13 Lamar Odom .50 1.25
S14 Elton Brand .50 1.25
S15 Vince Carter 1.00 2.50
S16 Antonio McDyess .40 1.00
S17 Michael Finley .50 1.25
S18 Jalen Rose .40 1.00
S19 Richard Hamilton .60 1.50
S20 Jason Kidd .75 2.00

2000-01 SPx Spxtreme
COMPLETE SET (11) 10.00 25.00
STATED ODDS 1:8
X1 Kevin Garnett 1.25 3.00
X2 Steve Francis .50 1.25
X3 Chris Webber .60 1.50
X4 Elton Brand .50 1.25
X5 Shareef Abdur-Rahim .50 1.25
X6 Larry Hughes .50 1.25
X7 Vince Carter 1.00 2.50
X8 Kobe Bryant 8.00 20.00
X9 Scottie Pippen 1.25 3.00
X10 Anfernee Hardaway .75 2.00
X11 Shaquille O'Neal 2.00 5.00

2000-01 SPx UD Authentics Rookie Exclusives
DM Darius Miles 8.00 20.00
KM Kenyon Martin 15.00 40.00
MF Marcus Fizer 6.00 15.00
MI Mike Miller 12.00 30.00
SS Stromile Swift 6.00 15.00

2000-01 SPx Winning Materials
STATED ODDS 1:72
AU STATED ODDS 1:252
BR1 Bryon Russell 3.00 8.00
CM1 Chris Mihm 2.50 6.00
DM1 DerMarr Johnson 2.50 6.00
JS1 John Stockton 10.00 25.00
KB1 K.Bryant JSY/WM 40.00 100.00
KB2 K.Bryant JSY/Shoe 75.00 200.00
KB3 K.Bryant WM/Shoe 75.00 200.00
KG1 K.Garnett JSY/WM 6.00 15.00
KG2 K.Garnett JSY/SS 6.00 15.00
KG3 K.Garnett JSY/Shorts 6.00 15.00
KM1 Kenyon Martin 8.00 20.00
MF1 Marcus Fizer 3.00 8.00
MM1 K.Malone JSY/Shorts 10.00 25.00
MM3 K.Malone JSY/Shoe 10.00 25.00
TB1 Terrell Brandon JSY/WM 4.00 10.00
WS1 W.Szczerbiak JSY/WM 4.00 10.00
WS2 W.Szczerbiak JSY/SS 4.00 10.00
DMA1 DerMarr Johnson AU 4.00 10.00
KBA1 K.Bryant JSY/WM AU 150.00 400.00
KBA2 K.Bryant JSY/Shoe AU 150.00 400.00
KBA3 K.Bryant WM/Shoe AU 150.00 400.00
KGA1 K.Garnett JSY/WM AU 50.00 120.00
KGA2 K.Garnett JSY/SS AU 60.00 150.00
KMA1 Kenyon Martin AU 8.00 20.00
MFA1 Marcus Fizer AU 5.00 12.00
MJA1 M.Jordan JSY/WM AU 1,500.00 3,000.00
MJA2 M.Jordan WM/Sh AU 1,500.00 3,000.00

2001-02 SPx
COMP.SET w/o SP's (90) 15.00 40.00
91-105 THREE VERSIONS SER.#'d TO 800
106-111 THREE VERSIONS SER.#'d TO 250
121-140 PRINT RUN 1999 SER.#'d SETS
THREE VERSIONS OF EACH JSY AU RC EXIST
1 Jason Terry .50 1.25
2 Shareef Abdur-Rahim .40 1.00
3 DerMarr Johnson .30 .75
4 Paul Pierce .75 2.00
5 Antoine Walker .40 1.00
6 Kenny Anderson .40 1.00
7 Baron Davis .50 1.25
8 Jamal Mashburn .40 1.00
9 David Wesley .30 .75
10 Ron Mercer .30 .75
11 Ron Artest .40 1.00
12 Marcus Fizer .30 .75
13 Andre Miller .40 1.00
14 Lamond Murray .30 .75
15 Chris Mihm .30 .75
16 Michael Finley .50 1.25
17 Dirk Nowitzki 1.25 3.00
18 Steve Nash 1.00 2.50
19 Antonio McDyess .40 1.00
20 Nick Van Exel .50 1.25
21 Raef LaFrentz .30 .75
22 Jerry Stackhouse .50 1.25
23 Chucky Atkins .30 .75
24 Corliss Williamson .30 .75
25 Antawn Jamison .40 1.00
26 Larry Hughes .40 1.00
27 Chris Porter .30 .75
28 Steve Francis .50 1.25
29 Cuttino Mobley .40 1.00
30 Maurice Taylor .30 .75
31 Reggie Miller 1.00 2.50
32 Jalen Rose .40 1.00
33 Jermaine O'Neal .40 1.00
34 Darius Miles .30 .75
35 Elton Brand .40 1.00
36 Lamar Odom .40 1.00
37 Quentin Richardson .30 .75
38 Kobe Bryant 4.00 10.00
39 Shaquille O'Neal 2.00 5.00
40 Rick Fox .40 1.00
41 Derek Fisher .40 1.00
42 Stromile Swift .30 .75
43 Jason Williams .75 2.00
44 Michael Dickerson .30 .75
45 Alonzo Mourning .75 2.00
46 Eddie Jones .50 1.25
47 Anthony Carter .30 .75
48 Glenn Robinson .50 1.25
49 Ray Allen .75 2.00
50 Sam Cassell .40 1.00
51 Kevin Garnett 1.25 3.00
52 Wally Szczerbiak .40 1.00
53 Terrell Brandon .40 1.00
54 Chauncey Billups .60 1.50
55 Kenyon Martin .50 1.25
56 Keith Van Horn .40 1.00
57 Jason Kidd .75 2.00
58 Latrell Sprewell .60 1.50
59 Allan Houston .50 1.25
60 Marcus Camby .40 1.00
61 Tracy McGrady .75 2.00
62 Mike Miller .40 1.00
63 Grant Hill .75 2.00
64 Allen Iverson 1.25 3.00
65 Dikembe Mutombo .75 2.00
66 Aaron McKie .30 .75
67 Stephon Marbury .60 1.50
68 Shawn Marion .50 1.25
69 Tom Gugliotta .30 .75
70 Rasheed Wallace .60 1.50
71 Damon Stoudamire .50 1.25
72 Bonzi Wells .30 .75
73 Chris Webber .60 1.50
74 Peja Stojakovic .60 1.50
75 Mike Bibby .50 1.25
76 Tim Duncan 1.25 3.00
77 David Robinson 1.00 2.50
78 Antonio Daniels .30 .75
79 Gary Payton .75 2.00
80 Rashard Lewis .40 1.00
81 Desmond Mason .40 1.00
82 Vince Carter 1.00 2.50
83 Morris Peterson .30 .75
84 Antonio Davis .40 1.00
85 Karl Malone 1.00 2.50
86 John Stockton 1.00 2.50
87 Donyell Marshall .30 .75
88 Richard Hamilton .60 1.50
89 Courtney Alexander .30 .75
90 Michael Jordan 8.00 20.00
91A Tony Parker JSY AU RC 30.00 80.00
91B Tony Parker JSY AU RC 30.00 80.00
91C Tony Parker JSY AU RC 30.00 80.00
92A Jamaal Tinsley JSY AU RC 2.50 6.00
92B Jamaal Tinsley JSY AU RC 2.50 6.00
92C Jamaal Tinsley JSY AU RC 2.50 6.00
93A S.Dalembert JSY AU RC 3.00 8.00
93B S.Dalembert JSY AU RC 3.00 8.00
93C S.Dalembert JSY AU RC 3.00 8.00
94A Gerald Wallace JSY AU RC 4.00 10.00
94B Gerald Wallace JSY AU RC 4.00 10.00
94C Gerald Wallace JSY AU RC 4.00 10.00
95A B.Armstrong JSY AU RC 2.00 5.00
95B B.Armstrong JSY AU RC 2.00 5.00
95C B.Armstrong JSY AU RC 2.00 5.00
96A Jeryl Sasser JSY AU RC 2.00 5.00
96B Jeryl Sasser JSY AU RC 2.00 5.00
96C Jeryl Sasser JSY AU RC 2.00 5.00
97A Jason Collins JSY AU RC 2.50 6.00
97B Jason Collins JSY AU RC 2.50 6.00
97C Jason Collins JSY AU RC 2.50 6.00
98A M.Bradley JSY AU RC 2.00 5.00
98B M.Bradley JSY AU RC 2.00 5.00
98C M.Bradley JSY AU RC 2.00 5.00
99A Steven Hunter JSY AU RC 2.00 5.00
99B Steven Hunter JSY AU RC 2.00 5.00
99C Steven Hunter JSY AU RC 2.00 5.00
100A Troy Murphy JSY AU RC 2.50 6.00
100B Troy Murphy JSY AU RC 2.50 6.00
100C Troy Murphy JSY AU RC 2.50 6.00
101A R.Jefferson JSY AU RC 4.00 10.00
101B R.Jefferson JSY AU RC 4.00 10.00
101C R.Jefferson JSY AU RC 4.00 10.00
102A V.Radmanov JSY AU RC 2.50 6.00
102B V.Radmanov JSY AU RC 2.50 6.00
102C V.Radmanov JSY AU RC 2.50 6.00
103A Kedrick Brown JSY AU RC 2.00 5.00
103B Kedrick Brown JSY AU RC 2.00 5.00
103C Kedrick Brown JSY AU RC 2.00 5.00
104A J.Johnson JSY AU ERR RC 5.00 12.00
104B J.Johnson JSY AU ERR RC 5.00 12.00
104C J.Johnson JSY AU ERR RC 5.00 12.00
104D J.Johnson JSY AU COR RC 5.00 12.00
104E J.Johnson JSY AU COR RC 5.00 12.00
104F J.Johnson JSY AU COR RC 5.00 12.00
105A Kirk Haston JSY AU RC 2.00 5.00
105B Kirk Haston JSY AU RC 2.00 5.00
105C Kirk Haston JSY AU RC 2.00 5.00
106A Rodney White JSY AU RC 3.00 8.00
106B Rodney White JSY AU RC 3.00 8.00
106C Rodney White JSY AU RC 3.00 8.00
107A Eddie Griffin JSY AU RC 4.00 10.00
107B Eddie Griffin JSY AU RC 4.00 10.00
107C Eddie Griffin JSY AU RC 4.00 10.00
108A J.Richardson JSY AU RC 15.00 40.00
108B J.Richardson JSY AU RC 15.00 40.00
108C J.Richardson JSY AU RC 15.00 40.00
109A Eddy Curry JSY AU RC 5.00 12.00
109B Eddy Curry JSY AU RC 5.00 12.00
109C Eddy Curry JSY AU RC 5.00 12.00
110A T.Chandler JSY AU RC 8.00 20.00
110B T.Chandler JSY AU RC 8.00 20.00
110C T.Chandler JSY AU RC 8.00 20.00
111A Kwame Brown JSY AU RC 5.00 12.00
111B Kwame Brown JSY AU RC 5.00 12.00
111C Kwame Brown JSY AU RC 5.00 12.00
121 Shane Battier RC 4.00 10.00
122 Brendan Haywood RC 1.50 4.00
123 Joseph Forte RC 1.25 3.00
124 Zach Randolph RC 4.00 10.00
125 DeSagana Diop RC 1.25 3.00
126 Damone Brown RC 1.25 3.00
127 Andrei Kirilenko RC 3.00 8.00
128 Trenton Hassell RC 1.25 3.00
129 Gilbert Arenas RC 5.00 12.00
130 Earl Watson RC 1.50 4.00
131 Kenny Satterfield RC 1.25 3.00
132 Will Solomon RC 1.50 4.00
133 Bobby Simmons RC 2.00 5.00
134 Brian Scalabrine RC 2.00 5.00
135 Charlie Bell RC 2.00 5.00
136 Zeljko Rebraca RC 2.00 5.00
137 Loren Woods RC 1.25 3.00
138 Terence Morris RC 1.25 3.00
139 Jamison Brewer RC 2.00 5.00
140 Pau Gasol RC 8.00 20.00
NNO Kobe Bryant PROMO 4.00 10.00

2001-02 SPx Spectrum
*1-90 STARS: 12X TO 30X BASE CARD HI
*91-105 RCs: 1.5X TO 4X HI
*106-111 RCs: 1X TO 2.5X HI
*121-140 RCs: 2X TO 5X HI
STATED PRINT RUN 25 SERIAL #'d SETS
91-111 HAS THREE VERSIONS ALL EQUAL
91A Tony Parker JSY AU 150.00 400.00
140 Pau Gasol 60.00 150.00

2001-02 SPx Winning Materials
STATED ODDS 1:18
AH Anfernee Hardaway Shorts/WU 10.00 25.00
AI Allen Iverson JSY/Shorts 10.00 25.00
CB Chauncey Billups JSY/WU 5.00 12.00
KB Kobe Bryant JSY/WU 50.00 120.00
KE Kenyon Martin Shorts/Shirt 4.00 10.00
KG Kevin Garnett JSY/WU 10.00 25.00
KG2 Kevin Garnett WU/Shirt 10.00 25.00
KM Karl Malone JSY/JSY 8.00 20.00
KM2 Karl Malone WU/Shorts 8.00 20.00
KV Keith Van Horn WU/JSY 3.00 8.00
LP Lavor Postell Shirt/Pr.JSY 2.50 6.00
MM Mike Miller WU/Shirt 3.00 8.00
MO Michael Olowokandi Shirt/WU 2.50 6.00
RH Richard Hamilton WU/Shirt 5.00 12.00
SM Shawn Marion WU/Shirt 4.00 10.00
SS Stromile Swift WU/Shirt 2.50 6.00
ST John Stockton JSY/Pr.JSY 8.00 20.00
ST2 John Stockton JSY/Shirt 8.00 20.00
TB Terrell Brandon WU/Shirt 3.00 8.00
WS Wally Szczerbiak WU/Shirt 3.00 8.00

2002-03 SPx
COMP.SET w/o SP's (90) 12.00 30.00
111-132 PRINT RUN 999 SER.#'d SETS
133-138 PRINT RUN 1599 SER.#'d SETS
137-147 PRINT RUN 2599 SER.#'d SETS
148-162 PRINT RUN 2999 SER.#'d SETS
1 Shareef Abdur-Rahim .50 1.25
2 Jason Terry .40 1.00
3 Glenn Robinson .50 1.25
4 Paul Pierce .75 2.00
5 Antoine Walker .40 1.00
6 Kedrick Brown .30 .75
7 Vin Baker .40 1.00
8 Jalen Rose .40 1.00
9 Tyson Chandler .50 1.25
10 Eddy Curry .30 .75
11 Ricky Davis .40 1.00
12 Chris Mihm .30 .75
13 Darius Miles .30 .75
14 Dirk Nowitzki 1.25 3.00
15 Michael Finley .50 1.25
16 Steve Nash 1.00 2.50
17 Raef LaFrentz .30 .75
18 James Posey .30 .75
19 Juwan Howard .40 1.00
20 Richard Hamilton .60 1.50
21 Ben Wallace .60 1.50
22 Chauncey Billups .50 1.25
23 Antawn Jamison .40 1.00
24 Jason Richardson .50 1.25
25 Steve Francis .50 1.25
26 Eddie Griffin .30 .75
27 Cuttino Mobley .30 .75
28 Reggie Miller 1.00 2.50
29 Jamaal Tinsley .30 .75
30 Jermaine O'Neal .40 1.00
31 Elton Brand .40 1.00
32 Andre Miller .40 1.00
33 Lamar Odom .50 1.25
34 Kobe Bryant 4.00 10.00
35 Shaquille O'Neal 2.00 5.00
36 Robert Horry .50 1.25

37 Devean George .30 .75
38 Pau Gasol .75 2.00
39 Shane Battier .50 1.25
40 Jason Williams .60 1.50
41 Alonzo Mourning .75 2.00
42 Eddie Jones .50 1.25
43 Brian Grant .30 .75
44 Ray Allen .75 2.00
45 Tim Thomas .30 .75
46 Kevin Garnett 1.25 3.00
47 Terrell Brandon .30 .75
48 Wally Szczerbiak .40 1.00
49 Jason Kidd .75 2.00
50 Richard Jefferson .40 1.00
51 Kenyon Martin .50 1.25
52 Baron Davis .50 1.25
53 Jamal Mashburn .40 1.00
54 David Wesley .30 .75
55 P.J. Brown .30 .75
56 Allan Houston .50 1.25
57 Antonio McDyess .40 1.00
58 Latrell Sprewell .50 1.25
59 Tracy McGrady .75 2.00
60 Mike Miller .40 1.00
61 Darrell Armstrong .30 .75
62 Allen Iverson 1.25 3.00
63 Keith Van Horn .40 1.00
64 Stephon Marbury .60 1.50
65 Shawn Marion .50 1.25
66 Anfernee Hardaway 1.25 3.00
67 Rasheed Wallace .60 1.50
68 Damon Stoudamire .50 1.25
69 Scottie Pippen 1.25 3.00
70 Chris Webber .60 1.50
71 Mike Bibby .50 1.25
72 Peja Stojakovic .40 1.00
73 Hedo Turkoglu .40 1.00
74 Tim Duncan 1.25 3.00
75 David Robinson 1.00 2.50
76 Tony Parker .75 2.00
77 Steve Smith .40 1.00
78 Gary Payton .75 2.00
79 Rashard Lewis .40 1.00
80 Brent Barry .30 .75
81 Desmond Mason .40 1.00
82 Vince Carter 1.00 2.50
83 Morris Peterson .40 1.00
84 Antonio Davis .40 1.00
85 Karl Malone 1.00 2.50
86 John Stockton 1.00 2.50
87 Andrei Kirilenko .40 1.00
88 Jerry Stackhouse .50 1.25
89 Michael Jordan 8.00 20.00
90 Kwame Brown .30 .75
91 Jason Richardson JSY AU 6.00 15.00
92 Tyson Chandler JSY AU 6.00 15.00
93 Kenyon Martin JSY AU 12.00 30.00
94 Gerald Wallace JSY AU SP 6.00 15.00
95 K.Abdul-Jabbar JSY AU SP 125.00 300.00
96 Morris Peterson JSY AU SP 6.00 15.00
97 Andre Miller JSY AU 6.00 15.00
98 Quentin Richardson JSY AU 6.00 15.00
99 Mike Miller JSY AU 6.00 15.00
100 Jer. O'Neal JSY AU SP 12.00 30.00
101 Marcus Fizer JSY AU 6.00 15.00
102 Mike Bibby JSY AU 12.00 30.00
103 C. Billups JSY AU SP 15.00 40.00
104 Lamar Odom JSY AU SP 12.00 30.00
105 Antoine Walker JSY AU 10.00 25.00
106 Paul Pierce JSY AU 30.00 80.00
107 Jason Kidd JSY AU SP 20.00 50.00
108 Kevin Garnett JSY AU SP 125.00 300.00
109 Kobe Bryant JSY AU SP 500.00 1,000.00
110 M. Jordan JSY AU SP 2,000.00 4,000.00
111 Chris Jefferies JSY AU RC 2.50 6.00
112 John Salmons JSY AU RC 4.00 10.00
113 Tayshaun Prince JSY AU RC 15.00 40.00
114 Casey Jacobsen JSY AU RC 3.00 8.00
115 Qyntel Woods JSY AU RC 2.50 6.00
116 Kareem Rush JSY AU RC 3.00 8.00
117 Ryan Humphrey JSY AU RC 3.00 8.00
118 Carlos Boozer JSY AU RC 4.00 10.00
119 Sam Clancy JSY AU RC 3.00 8.00
120 Fred Jones JSY AU RC 3.00 8.00
121 Marcus Haislip JSY AU RC 2.50 6.00
122 Melvin Ely JSY AU RC 3.00 8.00
123 Jared Jeffries JSY AU RC 3.00 8.00
124 Dan Gadzuric JSY AU RC 3.00 8.00
125 A.Stoudemire JSY AU RC 15.00 40.00
126 Caron Butler JSY AU RC 4.00 10.00
127 Nene Hilario JSY AU RC 4.00 10.00
128 DaJuan Wagner JSY AU RC 3.00 8.00
129 N.Tskitishvili JSY AU RC 2.50 6.00
130 Drew Gooden JSY AU RC 4.00 10.00
131 Jay Williams JSY AU RC 3.00 8.00
132 Yao Ming JSY AU RC 125.00 300.00
133 Mike Dunleavy RC 1.50 4.00
134 Frank Williams RC 1.00 2.50
135 Jiri Welsch RC 1.25 3.00
136 Dan Dickau RC 1.00 2.50
137 Efthimios Rentzias RC 1.00 2.50
138 Chris Wilcox RC 1.25 3.00
139 Curtis Borchardt RC 1.00 2.50
140 Predrag Savovic RC 1.25 3.00
141 Tito Maddox RC 1.00 2.50
142 Roger Mason RC 1.25 3.00
143 Juan Dixon RC 1.25 3.00
144 Pat Burke RC 1.00 2.50
145 Marko Jaric 1.50 4.00
146 Gordan Giricek RC 1.50 4.00
147 Juaquin Hawkins RC 1.00 2.50
148 Vincent Yarbrough RC 1.00 2.50
149 Robert Archibald RC 1.00 2.50
150 Bostjan Nachbar RC 1.25 3.00
151 Jamal Sampson RC 1.00 2.50
152 Lonny Baxter RC 1.00 2.50
153 J.R. Bremer RC 1.00 2.50
154 Cezary Trybanski RC 1.50 4.00
155 Manu Ginobili RC 8.00 20.00
156 Raul Lopez RC 1.00 2.50
157 Rasual Butler RC 1.25 3.00
158 Tamar Slay RC 1.00 2.50
159 Ronald Murray RC 1.50 4.00
160 Igor Rakocevic RC 1.00 2.50
161 Reggie Evans RC 1.25 3.00
162 Jannero Pargo RC 1.00 2.50

2002-03 SPx Spectrum

*1-90 STARS: 10X TO 25X BASE CARD HI
*111-132 RCs: 1.5X TO 4X HI
*133-162 RCs: 3X TO 8X HI
STATED PRINT RUN 25 SER.#'d SETS
89 Michael Jordan 200.00 500.00

2002-03 SPx Winning Combos

STATED ODDS 1:18
AIJK A.Iverson/J.Kidd SP 6.00 15.00
BDJM B.Davis/J.Mashburn 2.50 6.00
BHKW B.Haywood/K.Brown 1.50 4.00
CWPS C.Webber/P.Stojakovic 3.00 8.00
ECTC E.Curry/T.Chandler 2.50 6.00
JTJO J.Tinsley/J.O'Neal 2.00 5.00
KBAI Bryant/Iverson SP 60.00 150.00
KBJK K.Bryant/J.Kidd 60.00 150.00
KBTM K.Bryant/T.McGrady SP 60.00 150.00
KGWS K.Garnett/W.Szczerbiak 6.00 15.00
KMJS K.Malone/J.Stockton 5.00 12.00
KMRJ K.Martin/R.Jefferson 2.50 6.00
MJKB M.Jordan/K.Bryant SP 150.00 400.00
PPAW P.Pierce/A.Walker 4.00 10.00
QRLO Q.Richardson/L.Odom 2.50 6.00
SADJ S.Abdur-Rahim/D.Johnson 2.50 6.00
SMSM S.Marbury/S.Marion 3.00 8.00
TMMM T.McGrady/M.Miller SP 4.00 10.00
WCKB Chamberlain/Bryant SP 125.00 300.00
WCMJ Chamberlain/Jordan SP 150.00 400.00

2002-03 SPx Winning Materials

STATED ODDS 1:18
AMW A.McDyess JSY/WU 3.00 8.00
BDW Baron Davis JSY/WU 4.00 10.00
CWW Chris Webber JSY/WU 5.00 12.00
DNW D.Nowitzki Shorts/WU 10.00 25.00
DRW D.Robinson JSY/WU 8.00 20.00
EBW Elton Brand Shorts/WU 3.00 8.00
JKW Jason Kidd Shirt/WU 6.00 15.00
KBW K.Bryant Shorts/WU 50.00 120.00
KGW K.Garnett Shorts/WU 10.00 25.00
KMW K.Martin Shirt/WU 4.00 10.00
MJW M.Jordan Shirt/JSY SP 125.00 300.00
MMW Mike Miller JSY/Shirt 3.00 8.00
PPW Paul Pierce Shirt/WU 6.00 15.00
PSW P.Stojakovic JSY/WU 3.00 8.00
RHW R.Hamilton Shirt/WU 5.00 12.00
RJW R.Jefferson Shirt/WU 3.00 8.00
SHW S.Marion Shirt/WU 4.00 10.00
SMW S.Marbury Shirt/WU 5.00 12.00
TMW T.McGrady Shirt/WU SP 6.00 15.00

2002-03 SPx Winning Materials Autographs

PRINT RUN 23 TO 100 SER.#'d SETS
AMA Andre Miller/100 6.00 15.00
JKA Jason Kidd/100 20.00 50.00
JWA Jay Williams/100 6.00 15.00
KBA Kobe Bryant/100 1,000.00 2,000.00
KGA Kevin Garnett/100 125.00 300.00
KMA Kenyon Martin/100 12.00 30.00
MBA Mike Bibby/100 12.00 30.00
MJA Michael Jordan/23 3,000.00 6,000.00
MMA Mike Miller/100 6.00 15.00
PPA Paul Pierce/100 40.00 100.00
QRA Quentin Richardson/100 6.00 15.00
TCA Tyson Chandler/100 6.00 15.00

2003-04 SPx

COMP.SET w/o SP's (90) 25.00 60.00
91-132 PRINT RUN 3999 SER.#'d SETS
151-156 RC PRINT RUN 750 SER.#'d SETS
157-165 PRINT RUN 1250 SER.#'d SETS
166-185 RC PRINT RUN 1999 SER.#'d SETS
186-206 PRINT RUNS LISTED BELOW
1 Shafreef Abdur-Rahim .50 1.25
2 Jason Terry .40 1.00
3 Theo Ratliff .30 .75
4 Paul Pierce .75 2.00
5 Raef LaFrentz .30 .75
6 Vin Baker .30 .75
7 Jalen Rose .40 1.00
8 Tyson Chandler .30 .75
9 Michael Jordan 10.00 25.00
10 Dajuan Wagner .30 .75
11 Darius Miles .30 .75
12 Carlos Boozer .40 1.00
13 Dirk Nowitzki 1.25 3.00
14 Antoine Walker .50 1.25
15 Steve Nash 1.00 2.50
16 Nene .40 1.00
17 Marcus Camby .40 1.00
18 Andre Miller .40 1.00
19 Richard Hamilton .60 1.50
20 Ben Wallace .60 1.50
21 Chauncey Billups .60 1.50
22 Nick Van Exel .50 1.25
23 Jason Richardson .50 1.25
24 Speedy Claxton .30 .75
25 Steve Francis .50 1.25
26 Yao Ming 1.25 3.00
27 Cuttino Mobley .30 .75
28 Reggie Miller 1.00 2.50
29 Jamaal Tinsley .30 .75
30 Jermaine O'Neal .50 1.25
31 Elton Brand .40 1.00
32 Corey Maggette .40 1.00
33 Quentin Richardson .30 .75
34 Kobe Bryant 8.00 20.00
35 Karl Malone 1.00 2.50
36 Shaquille O'Neal 2.00 5.00
37 Gary Payton .75 2.00
38 Pau Gasol .75 2.00
39 Shane Battier .40 1.00
40 Mike Miller .40 1.00
41 Eddie Jones .50 1.25
42 Lamar Odom .40 1.00
43 Caron Butler .40 1.00
44 Michael Redd .50 1.25
45 Joe Smith .40 1.00
46 Desmond Mason .40 1.00
47 Kevin Garnett 1.25 3.00
48 Latrell Sprewell .50 1.25
49 Michael Olowokandi .30 .75
50 Jason Kidd .75 2.00
51 Richard Jefferson .40 1.00
52 Kenyon Martin .50 1.25
53 Baron Davis .50 1.25
54 Jamal Mashburn .40 1.00
55 David Wesley .30 .75
56 Allan Houston .50 1.25
57 Antonio McDyess .40 1.00
58 Keith Van Horn .40 1.00
59 Tracy McGrady .75 2.00
60 Grant Hill .60 1.50
61 Drew Gooden .40 1.00
62 Juwan Howard .40 1.00
63 Allen Iverson 1.25 3.00
64 Glenn Robinson .40 1.00
65 Eric Snow .30 .75
66 Stephon Marbury .60 1.50
67 Shawn Marion .50 1.25
68 Amare Stoudemire 1.25 3.00
69 Rasheed Wallace .60 1.50
70 Bonzi Wells .30 .75
71 Damon Stoudamire .40 1.00
72 Chris Webber .60 1.50
73 Mike Bibby .60 1.50
74 Peja Stojakovic .40 1.00
75 Brad Miller .40 1.00
76 Tim Duncan 1.25 3.00
77 Tony Parker .75 2.00
78 Manu Ginobili 1.00 2.50
79 Ray Allen .75 2.00
80 Rashard Lewis .40 1.00
81 Vladimir Radmanovic .30 .75
82 Vince Carter 1.00 2.50
83 Morris Peterson .30 .75
84 Antonio Davis .40 1.00
85 Raul Lopez .50 1.25
86 Matt Harpring .30 .75
87 Andrei Kirilenko .40 1.00
88 Jerry Stackhouse .60 1.50
89 Gilbert Arenas .50 1.25
90 Larry Hughes .40 1.00
91 Allen Iverson 2.50 6.00
92 Dirk Nowitzki 2.50 6.00
93 Kobe Bryant 12.00 30.00
94 Michael Jordan 15.00 40.00
95 Vince Carter 2.00 5.00
96 Shaquille O'Neal 4.00 10.00
97 Yao Ming 2.50 6.00
98 Amare Stoudemire 1.25 3.00
99 Paul Pierce 1.50 4.00
100 Jason Richardson 1.00 2.50
101 Steve Francis 1.00 2.50
102 Jermaine O'Neal 1.00 2.50
103 Karl Malone 2.00 5.00
104 Tracy McGrady 1.50 4.00
105 Stephon Marbury 1.25 3.00
106 Chris Webber 1.25 3.00
107 Tim Duncan 2.50 6.00
108 Ray Allen 1.50 4.00
109 Antoine Walker 1.00 2.50
110 Steve Nash 2.00 5.00
111 Elton Brand .75 2.00
112 Rashard Lewis .75 2.00
113 Jerry Stackhouse 1.25 3.00
114 Shawn Marion 1.00 2.50
115 Mike Bibby 1.00 2.50
116 Tony Parker 1.50 4.00
117 Michael Finley 1.00 2.50
118 Allan Houston 1.00 2.50
119 Richard Hamilton 1.25 3.00
120 Ben Wallace 1.25 3.00
121 Reggie Miller 2.00 5.00
122 Richard Jefferson .75 2.00
123 Glenn Robinson .75 2.00
124 Rasheed Wallace 1.25 3.00
125 Gilbert Arenas 1.00 2.50
126 Jason Kidd 1.50 4.00
127 Latrell Sprewell 1.25 3.00
128 Kevin Garnett 2.50 6.00
129 Caron Butler .75 2.00
130 Pau Gasol 1.50 4.00
131 Alonzo Mourning 1.25 3.00
132 Gary Payton 1.50 4.00
133 Kirk Hinrich RC 3.00 8.00
134 T.J. Ford RC 2.00 5.00
135 Nick Collison RC 2.00 5.00
136 Keith McLeod RC 2.00 5.00
137 Jon Stefansson RC 2.00 5.00
138 Britton Johnsen RC 2.00 5.00
139 Matt Carroll RC 2.00 5.00
140 Linton Johnson RC 2.00 5.00
141 Francisco Elson RC 2.00 5.00
142 Willie Green RC 3.00 8.00
143 Kyle Korver RC 4.00 10.00
144 Theron Smith RC 2.00 5.00
145 Brandon Hunter RC 2.00 5.00
146 Josh Moore RC 2.00 5.00
147 Marquis Daniels RC 2.50 6.00
148 James Lang RC 2.00 5.00
149 Udonis Haslem RC 4.00 10.00
150 Alex Garcia RC 2.00 5.00
151 L. James JSY AU RC 3,000.00 6,000.00
152 Darko Milicic JSY AU RC 2.50 6.00
153 C. Anthony JSY AU RC 100.00 250.00
154 Chris Bosh JSY AU RC 30.00 80.00
155 Dwyane Wade JSY AU RC 125.00 300.00
156 Chris Kaman JSY AU RC 6.00 15.00
157 Jarvis Hayes JSY AU RC 5.00 12.00
158 Mickael Pietrus JSY AU RC 4.00 10.00
159 Dahntay Jones JSY AU RC 4.00 10.00
160 Marcus Banks JSY AU RC 4.00 10.00
161 Luke Ridnour JSY AU RC 5.00 12.00
162 Reece Gaines JSY AU RC 3.00 8.00
163 Troy Bell JSY AU RC 3.00 8.00
164 Mike Sweetney JSY AU RC 3.00 8.00
165 David West JSY AU RC 6.00 15.00
166 Aleksandar Pavlovic JSY AU RC 3.00 8.00
167 Mo Williams JSY AU RC 4.00 10.00
168 Boris Diaw JSY AU RC 4.00 10.00
169 Zoran Planinic JSY AU RC 2.50 6.00
170 Travis Outlaw JSY AU RC 3.00 8.00
171 Brian Cook JSY AU RC 2.50 6.00
172 Jerome Beasley JSY AU RC 2.50 6.00
173 Ndudi Ebi JSY AU RC 2.50 6.00
174 Kendrick Perkins JSY AU RC 4.00 10.00
175 Leandro Barbosa JSY AU RC 4.00 10.00
176 Josh Howard JSY AU RC 4.00 10.00
177 Maciej Lampe JSY AU RC 2.50 6.00
178 Jason Kapono JSY AU RC 2.50 6.00
179 Luke Walton JSY AU RC 4.00 10.00
180 Slavko Vranes JSY AU RC 2.00 5.00
181 Zarko Cabarkapa JSY AU RC 2.50 6.00
182 Travis Hansen JSY AU RC 2.50 6.00
183 Steve Blake JSY AU RC 3.00 8.00
184 Zaur Pachulia JSY AU RC 4.00 10.00
185 Keith Bogans JSY AU RC 2.50 6.00
186 M. Jordan JSY AU/23 4,000.00 8,000.00
187 Kobe Bryant JSY AU/25 1,500.00 3,000.00
188 Kevin Garnett JSY AU/150 125.00 300.00
189 Richard Jefferson JSY AU/215 8.00 20.00
190 Gilbert Arenas JSY AU/215 10.00 25.00
191 Antawn Jamison JSY AU/215 8.00 20.00
192 Tracy McGrady JSY AU/50 125.00 300.00
193 Steve Francis JSY AU/100 15.00 40.00
194 Yao Ming JSY AU/100 125.00 300.00
195 A.Stoudemire JSY AU/215 10.00 25.00
196 S.Abdur-Rahim JSY AU/342 8.00 20.00
197 Shane Battier JSY AU/280 8.00 20.00
198 Tony Parker JSY AU/200 20.00 50.00
199 Andre Miller JSY AU/215 8.00 20.00
200 Shawn Marion JSY AU/265 8.00 20.00
201 Richard Hamilton JSY AU/215 12.00 30.00
202 Lamar Odom JSY AU/215 10.00 25.00
203 Jerry Stackhouse JSY AU/215 12.00 30.00
204 Antonio McDyess JSY AU/230 8.00 20.00
205 Manu Ginobili JSY AU/215 40.00 100.00
206 Drew Gooden JSY AU/215 8.00 20.00

2003-04 SPx Spectrum

*1-90 SINGLES: 8X TO 20X BASE HI
*91-132 SINGLES: 4X TO 10X BASE HI
*133-150 RCs: 1X TO 2.5X BASE HI
*151-156 RCs: .75X TO 2X BASE HI
*157-165 RCs: 1X TO 2.5X BASE HI
*166-185 RCs: 1.25X TO 3X BASE HI
1-185 PRINT RUN 25 SER.#'d SETS
9 Michael Jordan 300.00 600.00
93 Kobe Bryant 150.00 400.00
94 Michael Jordan 200.00 500.00
151 LeBron James JSY AU 30,000.00 60,000.00
153 Carmelo Anthony JSY AU 300.00 600.00
154 Chris Bosh JSY AU 150.00 300.00
155 Dwyane Wade JSY AU 400.00 800.00

2003-04 SPx Winning Materials

STATED ODDS 1:18
WM1 Shaquille O'Neal SP 15.00 40.00
WM2 Paul Pierce 6.00 15.00
WM3 Anfernee Hardaway 10.00 25.00
WM4 Nene 3.00 8.00
WM5 Jay Williams 2.50 6.00
WM6 Tony Parker 6.00 15.00
WM7 Stephon Marbury 5.00 12.00
WM8 Gary Payton 6.00 15.00
WM9 Vlade Divac 4.00 10.00
WM10 Reggie Miller SP 8.00 20.00
WM11 Jermaine O'Neal 4.00 10.00
WM12 Baron Davis 4.00 10.00
WM13 Jamal Mashburn 4.00 10.00
WM14 Darius Miles 2.50 6.00
WM15 David Robinson 8.00 20.00
WM16 Kwame Brown 2.50 6.00
WM17 Karl Malone 8.00 20.00
WM18 Joe Smith 3.00 8.00
WM19 Steve Nash 8.00 20.00
WM20 Richard Jefferson 3.00 8.00
WM21 Antonio McDyess 3.00 8.00
WM22 Caron Butler 3.00 8.00
WM23 Andre Miller 3.00 8.00
WM24 Shane Battier 3.00 8.00
WM25 Steve Francis 4.00 10.00
WM26 Elton Brand 3.00 8.00
WM27 Lamar Odom 3.00 8.00
WM28 Jason Richardson 4.00 10.00
WM29 Antawn Jamison 4.00 10.00
WM30 Kurt Thomas 2.50 6.00
WM31 Pau Gasol 6.00 15.00
WM32 Allen Iverson 10.00 25.00
WM33 Jason Kidd 6.00 15.00
WM34 Dirk Nowitzki 10.00 25.00
WM35 Chris Webber 5.00 12.00
WM36 Amare Stoudemire 5.00 12.00
WM37 Tracy McGrady 6.00 15.00
WM38 Tim Duncan 10.00 25.00
WM39 Kevin Garnett 10.00 25.00
WM40 LeBron James SP 200.00 500.00
WM41 Kobe Bryant SP 50.00 120.00
WM42 Michael Jordan SP 125.00 300.00

2003-04 SPx Winning Materials Autographs

PRINT RUN 100 SERIAL #'d SETS
AJ Antawn Jamison 8.00 20.00
AM Andre Miller 6.00 15.00
CB Caron Butler 6.00 15.00
DW Dajuan Wagner 5.00 12.00
JM Jerome Moiso 5.00 12.00
JT Jamaal Tinsley 5.00 12.00
KB Kobe Bryant 1,000.00 2,000.00
MA Marko Jaric 5.00 12.00
MB Mike Bibby 8.00 20.00
NH Nene 6.00 15.00
PS Peja Stojakovic 6.00 15.00
RH Richard Hamilton 10.00 25.00
RJ Richard Jefferson 6.00 15.00
SF Steve Francis 15.00 40.00
YM Yao Ming 125.00 300.00

2003-04 SPx Winning Materials Combos

STATED ODDS 1:18
WC1 P.Gasol/S.Swift 4.00 10.00
WC2 M.Jaric/A.Miller 2.00 5.00
WC3 P.Stojakovic/M.Bibby 2.50 6.00
WC4 R.Jefferson/J.Kidd 4.00 10.00
WC5 G.Arenas/J.Richardson 2.50 6.00
WC6 T.Parker/R.Nesterovic 4.00 10.00
WC7 M.Fizer/T.Chandler 2.00 5.00
WC8 T.McGrady/A.Stoudemire 4.00 10.00
WC9 K.Garnett/W.Szczerbiak 6.00 15.00
WC10 B.Miller/R.Miller 5.00 12.00
WC11 C.Mobley/S.Francis 2.50 6.00
WC12 M.Finley/S.Nash 5.00 12.00
WC13 D.Nowitzki/E.Najera 6.00 15.00
WC14 D.Mason/G.Payton 4.00 10.00
WC15 J.Erving/M.Johnson 6.00 15.00
WC16 A.Kirilenko/K.Malone 5.00 12.00
WC17 J.Rose/E.Curry 2.00 5.00
WC18 J.Howard/Nene 2.00 5.00
WC19 K.Van Horn/A.McKie 2.00 5.00
WC20 C.Boozer/C.Mihm 2.00 5.00
WC21 C.Maggette/M.Olowokandi 2.00 5.00
WC22 D.Fisher/K.Bryant 40.00 100.00
WC23 L.Hughes/Kw.Brown 2.00 5.00
WC24 M.Miller/S.Battier 2.00 5.00
WC25 Q.Richardson/L.Odom 2.00 5.00
WC26 T.Ratliff/J.Terry 2.00 5.00
WC27 S.Abdur-Rahim/J.Terry 2.50 6.00
WC28 P.Stojakovic/B.Miller 2.00 5.00
WC29 D.Mutombo/B.Armstrong 3.00 8.00
WC30 D.Miles/C.Boozer 2.00 5.00
WC31 B.Davis/D.Wesley 2.50 6.00
WC32 E.Brand/C.Maggette 2.00 5.00
WC33 R.Allen/R.Lewis 4.00 10.00
WC34 K.Martin/D.Mutombo 3.00 8.00
WC35 A.Kirilenko/D.Stevenson 2.00 5.00
WC36 A.Hardaway/J.Johnson 6.00 15.00
WC37 C.Billups/R.Hamilton 3.00 8.00
WC38 C.Webber/H.Turkoglu 3.00 8.00
WC39 J.Magloire/J.Mashburn 2.00 5.00
WC40 D.Johnson/J.Terry 2.00 5.00
WC41 L.James/D.Milicic SP 75.00 200.00
WC42 K.Bryant/M.Jordan SP 125.00 300.00

2004-05 SPx

COMP.SET w/o SP's (90) 15.00 40.00
91-111 PRINT RUN 1999 SER.#'d SETS
112-117 PRINT RUN 99 SER.#'d SETS
108, 118-139 PRINT RUN 1999 #'d SETS
140-147 PRINT RUN 750 SER.#'d SETS
148-168 STATED ODDS
1 Antoine Walker .50 1.25
2 Al Harrington .40 1.00
3 Boris Diaw .40 1.00
4 Paul Pierce .75 2.00
5 Ricky Davis .40 1.00
6 Gary Payton .75 2.00
7 Jahidi White .30 .75
8 Jason Kapono .30 .75
9 Gerald Wallace .40 1.00
10 Eddy Curry .30 .75
11 Kirk Hinrich .50 1.25
12 Tyson Chandler .40 1.00
13 LeBron James 8.00 20.00
14 Drew Gooden .30 .75
15 Dajuan Wagner .30 .75
16 Dirk Nowitzki 1.25 3.00
17 Michael Finley .50 1.25
18 Jerry Stackhouse .50 1.25
19 Carmelo Anthony 1.00 2.50
20 Kenyon Martin .50 1.25
21 Nene .40 1.00
22 Chauncey Billups .60 1.50
23 Richard Hamilton .60 1.50
24 Ben Wallace .60 1.50
25 Mike Dunleavy .30 .75
26 Jason Richardson .50 1.25
27 Derek Fisher .40 1.00
28 Yao Ming 1.25 3.00
29 Jim Jackson .40 1.00
30 Tracy McGrady .75 2.00
31 Jermaine O'Neal .40 1.00
32 Reggie Miller 1.00 2.50
33 Stephen Jackson .40 1.00
34 Elton Brand .40 1.00
35 Corey Maggette .40 1.00
36 Chris Kaman .40 1.00
37 Kobe Bryant 8.00 20.00
38 Chris Mihm .30 .75
39 Lamar Odom .50 1.25
40 Pau Gasol .75 2.00
41 Jason Williams .40 1.00
42 Bonzi Wells .30 .75
43 Shaquille O'Neal 2.00 5.00
44 Dwyane Wade 2.00 5.00
45 Eddie Jones .50 1.25
46 Michael Redd .50 1.25
47 Desmond Mason .40 1.00
48 T.J. Ford .30 .75
49 Latrell Sprewell .60 1.50
50 Kevin Garnett 1.25 3.00
51 Sam Cassell .40 1.00
52 Richard Jefferson .40 1.00
53 Alonzo Mourning .60 1.50
54 Jason Kidd .75 2.00
55 Jamal Mashburn .40 1.00
56 Baron Davis .50 1.25
57 Jamaal Magloire .30 .75
58 Allan Houston .50 1.25
59 Jamal Crawford .50 1.25
60 Stephon Marbury .60 1.50
61 Cuttino Mobley .40 1.00
62 Hedo Turkoglu .40 1.00
63 Steve Francis .50 1.25
64 Glenn Robinson .40 1.00
65 Allen Iverson 1.25 3.00
66 Aaron McKie .30 .75
67 Amare Stoudemire .50 1.25
68 Steve Nash 1.00 2.50
69 Shawn Marion .50 1.25
70 Shareef Abdur-Rahim .50 1.25
71 Damon Stoudamire .50 1.25
72 Zach Randolph .50 1.25
73 Peja Stojakovic .50 1.25
74 Chris Webber .60 1.50
75 Mike Bibby .50 1.25
76 Tony Parker .75 2.00
77 Tim Duncan 1.25 3.00
78 Manu Ginobili .75 2.00
79 Ronald Murray .30 .75
80 Ray Allen .75 2.00
81 Rashard Lewis .40 1.00
82 Chris Bosh .75 2.00
83 Vince Carter 1.00 2.50
84 Jalen Rose .40 1.00
85 Andrei Kirilenko .40 1.00
86 Carlos Boozer .40 1.00
87 Carlos Arroyo .30 .75
88 Gilbert Arenas .50 1.25
89 Jarvis Hayes .30 .75
90 Antawn Jamison .40 1.00
91 Matt Freije RC 1.50 4.00
92 Horace Jenkins RC 2.00 5.00
93 Luis Flores RC 2.00 5.00
94 Jared Reiner RC 2.50 6.00
95 D.J. Mbenga RC 1.50 4.00
96 Pape Sow RC 1.50 4.00
97 Erik Daniels RC 2.00 5.00
98 Arthur Johnson RC 2.00 5.00
99 John Edwards RC 1.50 4.00
100 Andre Barrett RC 1.50 4.00
101 Romain Sato RC 1.50 4.00
102 Tim Pickett RC 2.00 5.00
103 Bernard Robinson RC 1.50 4.00
104 Justin Reed RC 1.50 4.00
105 Andres Nocioni RC 2.50 6.00
106 Awvee Storey RC 2.50 6.00
107 Damien Wilkins RC 2.00 5.00
108 Nenad Krstic JSY AU RC 3.00 8.00
109 Viktor Khryapa RC 1.50 4.00
110 Royal Ivey RC 1.50 4.00
111 Antonio Burks RC 1.50 4.00
112 Robert Swift RC 8.00 20.00
113 Trevor Ariza RC 12.00 30.00
114 Chris Duhon RC 10.00 25.00
115 Beno Udrih RC 10.00 25.00
116 Pavel Podkolzin RC 8.00 20.00
117 Emeka Okafor RC 10.00 25.00
118 Yuta Tabuse JSY AU RC 4.00 10.00
119 Andre Emmett JSY AU RC 2.50 6.00
120 Sasha Vujacic JSY AU RC 3.00 8.00
121 Lionel Chalmers JSY AU RC 3.00 8.00
122 J.R. Smith JSY AU RC 4.00 10.00
123 Dorell Wright JSY AU RC 3.00 8.00
124 Jameer Nelson JSY AU RC 4.00 10.00
125 Andris Biedrins JSY AU RC 2.50 6.00
126 Jackson Vroman JSY AU RC 2.50 6.00
127 A.Varejao JSY AU RC 3.00 8.00
128 Delonte West JSY AU RC 3.00 8.00
129 Tony Allen JSY AU RC 4.00 10.00
130 Kevin Martin JSY AU RC 5.00 12.00
131 Rafael Araujo JSY AU RC 2.50 6.00
132 David Harrison JSY AU RC 2.50 6.00
133 Kris Humphries JSY AU RC 3.00 8.00
134 Al Jefferson JSY AU RC 4.00 10.00
135 Kirk Snyder JSY AU RC 2.50 6.00
136 Peter J.Ramos JSY AU RC 2.50 6.00
137 Luke Jackson JSY AU RC 2.50 6.00
138 Donta Smith JSY AU RC 2.50 6.00
139 Josh Smith JSY AU RC 4.00 10.00
140 Sebastian Telfair JSY AU RC 5.00 12.00
141 Andre Iguodala JSY AU RC 20.00 50.00
142 Luol Deng JSY AU RC 6.00 15.00
143 Josh Childress JSY AU RC 4.00 10.00
144 Devin Harris JSY AU RC 5.00 12.00
145 S.Livingston JSY AU RC 6.00 15.00
146 Ben Gordon JSY AU RC 6.00 15.00
147 Dwight Howard JSY AU RC 50.00 120.00
148 Kobe Bryant AU SP 800.00 1,500.00
149 Pau Gasol AU 20.00 50.00
150 Jason Kidd AU 20.00 50.00
151 Richard Hamilton AU 12.00 30.00
152 Amare Stoudemire AU 15.00 40.00
153 Chauncey Billups AU 12.00 30.00
154 Mike Bibby AU 12.00 30.00
155 Jason Richardson AU 12.00 30.00
156 LeBron James AU SP 2,000.00 4,000.00
157 Larry Bird AU SP 75.00 200.00
158 Reggie Miller AU 75.00 200.00
159 Kevin Garnett AU 75.00 200.00
160 Baron Davis AU 12.00 30.00
161 Carmelo Anthony AU 60.00 150.00
162 Magic Johnson AU SP 75.00 200.00
163 Tracy McGrady AU 40.00 100.00
164 Yao Ming AU 60.00 150.00
165 Michael Jordan AU SP 2,000.00 4,000.00
166 Andrei Kirilenko AU 12.00 30.00
167 Stephon Marbury AU 12.00 30.00
168 Shawn Marion AU 12.00 30.00

2004-05 SPx Spectrum

*1-90: 8X TO 20X BASE HI
*91-111: 1.25X TO 3X BASE HI
*112-117: .25X TO .6X BASE HI
*108, 118-139: 1.5X TO 4X BASE HI
*140-147: 1X TO 2.5X BASE HI
1-147 PRINT RUN 25 SER.#'d SETS
148-168 PRINT RUN ONE SET

2004-05 SPx Throwback

*1-90 THROW: .75X TO 2X BASE HI
1-90 PRINT RUN 500 SER.#'d SETS
*118-139 JSY RCs: .75X TO 2X BASE HI
*140-147 JSY RCs: .5X TO 1.25X BASE HI

2004-05 SPx Winning Materials

STATED ODDS 1:15
AI Allen Iverson 8.00 20.00
AK Andrei Kirilenko 2.50 6.00
AS Amare Stoudemire 3.00 8.00
BD Baron Davis 3.00 8.00
BM Brad Miller 2.50 6.00
BW Ben Wallace 4.00 10.00
CA Carmelo Anthony 6.00 15.00
CB Carlos Boozer 2.50 6.00
DA David Wesley 2.00 5.00
DH Dwight Howard 10.00 25.00
DM Darius Miles 2.00 5.00
DN Dirk Nowitzki 8.00 20.00
DS DeShawn Stevenson 2.00 5.00
DW Dajuan Wagner 2.00 5.00
EB Elton Brand 2.50 6.00
EC Eddy Curry 2.00 5.00
JC Jamal Crawford 3.00 8.00
JK Jason Kidd 5.00 12.00
JM Jamaal Magloire 2.00 5.00
JO Jermaine O'Neal 2.50 6.00
KB Kobe Bryant 75.00 200.00
KG Kevin Garnett 8.00 20.00
LJ LeBron James SP 100.00 250.00
MB Mike Bibby 3.00 8.00
MJ Michael Jordan SP 200.00 500.00
PG Pau Gasol 5.00 12.00
PP Paul Pierce 5.00 12.00
PS Peja Stojakovic 2.50 6.00
RA Ray Allen 5.00 12.00
RJ Richard Jefferson 2.00 5.00
RM Reggie Miller 6.00 15.00
SA Shareef Abdur-Rahim 3.00 8.00
SM Shawn Marion 3.00 8.00
SN Steve Nash 6.00 15.00
SO Shaquille O'Neal 12.00 30.00
ST Stephon Marbury 4.00 10.00
TD Tim Duncan 8.00 20.00
TM Tracy McGrady 5.00 12.00
WS Wally Szczerbiak 2.50 6.00
YM Yao Ming 8.00 20.00

2004-05 SPx Winning Materials Autographs

PRINT RUN 100 SER.#'d SETS
AI Andre Iguodala 20.00 50.00
AK Andrei Kirilenko 20.00 50.00
AS Amare Stoudemire 20.00 50.00
BD Baron Davis 20.00 50.00
BG Ben Gordon 15.00 40.00
BM Brad Miller 10.00 25.00
CA Carmelo Anthony 100.00 250.00
CB Carlos Boozer 8.00 20.00
DE Devin Harris 8.00 20.00
DF Derek Fisher 15.00 40.00
DH Dwight Howard 25.00 60.00
JA Jason Richardson 12.00 30.00
JC Jamal Crawford 15.00 40.00
JK Jason Kidd 40.00 100.00
JR Jalen Rose 8.00 20.00
JS John Stockton 75.00 200.00
KB Kobe Bryant 1,500.00 3,000.00
KG Kevin Garnett 125.00 300.00
LB Larry Bird 125.00 300.00
LD Luol Deng 10.00 25.00
LJ0 LeBron James 1,500.00 3,000.00
LO Lamar Odom 15.00 40.00
MA Magic Johnson 125.00 300.00
MJ Michael Jordan 3,000.00 6,000.00
PP Paul Pierce 100.00 250.00
RJ Richard Jefferson 12.00 30.00
RM Reggie Miller 125.00 300.00
SA Shareef Abdur-Rahim 20.00 50.00
SL Shaun Livingston 20.00 50.00
SM Shawn Marion 20.00 50.00
ST Stephon Marbury 50.00 120.00
TE Sebastian Telfair 8.00 20.00
TM Tracy McGrady 125.00 300.00
YM Yao Ming 125.00 300.00

2004-05 SPx Winning Materials Combos

STATED ODDS 1:15
AJ A.Walker/Josh Smith 3.00 8.00
AK A.Jamison/K.Brown 2.50 6.00
AM C.Anthony/A.Miller 6.00 15.00
BA C.Bosh/R.Araujo 5.00 12.00
BJ K.Bryant/L.James 125.00 300.00
BO K.Bryant/L.Odom 40.00 100.00
BP M.Banks/G.Payton 5.00 12.00
DG L.Deng/B.Gordon 3.00 8.00
DM B.Davis/J.Magloire 3.00 8.00
DP T.Duncan/T.Parker 8.00 20.00
ES A.Emmett/S.Swift 2.00 5.00
FM S.Francis/C.Mobley 3.00 8.00
GC K.Garnett/S.Cassell 8.00 20.00
GD M.Ginobili/T.Duncan 8.00 20.00
GM K.Garnett/T.McGrady 8.00 20.00
II A.Iverson/A.Iguodala 8.00 20.00
JB M.Jordan/K.Bryant 150.00 400.00
JC J.Stockton/C.Boozer 6.00 15.00
JJ L.James/M.Jordan SP 150.00 400.00
JS L.James/E.Snow 40.00 100.00
KA K.Martin/A.Miller 3.00 8.00
KB A.Kirilenko/C.Boozer SP 2.50 6.00
KC K.Malone/C.Butler 6.00 15.00
KJ J.Kidd/R.Jefferson 5.00 12.00
LA L.James/C.Anthony SP 40.00 100.00
MB C.Maggette/E.Brand 2.50 6.00
MC S.Marbury/J.Crawford 4.00 10.00
MH S.Marbury/A.Houston 4.00 10.00
MY Y.Ming/T.McGrady 8.00 20.00
MS S.Marion/A.Stoudemire 3.00 8.00
MT D.Miles/S.Telfair 2.50 6.00
NH D.Nowitzki/D.Harris 8.00 20.00
NW J.Nelson/Del.West 3.00 8.00
OH S.O'Neal/D.Howard 12.00 30.00
OM J.O'Neal/R.Miller 6.00 15.00
PJ P.Pierce/A.Jefferson 5.00 12.00
PM P.Gasol/M.Miller 5.00 12.00
RD J.Richardson/M.Dunleavy 3.00 8.00
SB P.Stojakovic/M.Bibby 3.00 8.00
SD S.Abdur-R/D.Miles 3.00 8.00
SN A.Stoudemire/S.Nash 6.00 15.00
TH J.Tinsley/D.Harrison 2.00 5.00

2005-06 SPx

COMP.SET w/o SP's (90) 20.00 50.00
91-120 RC PRINT RUN 1499 SER.#'d SETS
UNLESS LISTED IN CHECKLIST
147-154 RC PRINT RUN 750 SER.#'d SETS
1 Josh Childress .30 .75
2 Josh Smith .40 1.00
3 Al Harrington .40 1.00
4 Antoine Walker .40 1.00
5 Gary Payton .75 2.00
6 Paul Pierce .75 2.00
7 Kareem Rush .30 .75
8 Emeka Okafor .40 1.00
9 Gerald Wallace .40 1.00
10 Michael Jordan 4.00 10.00
11 Kirk Hinrich .40 1.00
12 Ben Gordon .40 1.00
13 Drew Gooden .40 1.00
14 Larry Hughes .40 1.00
15 LeBron James 4.00 10.00
16 Zydrunas Ilgauskas .40 1.00
17 Dirk Nowitzki 1.25 3.00
18 Jason Terry .40 1.00
19 Michael Finley .50 1.25
20 Carmelo Anthony .75 2.00
21 Kenyon Martin .40 1.00
22 Andre Miller .40 1.00
23 Ben Wallace .60 1.50
24 Chauncey Billups .60 1.50
25 Richard Hamilton .60 1.50
26 Troy Murphy .30 .75
27 Jason Richardson .50 1.25
28 Baron Davis .50 1.25
29 Tracy McGrady .75 2.00
30 Yao Ming 1.00 2.50
31 David Wesley .30 .75
32 Jermaine O'Neal .40 1.00
33 Jamaal Tinsley .30 .75
34 Ron Artest .40 1.00
35 Corey Maggette .40 1.00
36 Elton Brand .40 1.00
37 Bobby Simmons .30 .75
38 Caron Butler .40 1.00
39 Kobe Bryant 4.00 10.00

Card	Low	High
40 Lamar Odom	.40	1.00
41 Mike Miller	.40	1.00
42 Jason Williams	.75	2.00
43 Pau Gasol	.75	2.00
44 Dwyane Wade	1.00	2.50
45 Eddie Jones	.40	1.00
46 Shaquille O'Neal	1.50	4.00
47 Desmond Mason	.30	.75
48 Keith Van Horn	.40	1.00
49 Michael Redd	.40	1.00
50 Kevin Garnett	1.25	3.00
51 Latrell Sprewell	.50	1.25
52 Sam Cassell	.40	1.00
53 Vince Carter	1.00	2.50
54 Jason Kidd	.75	2.00
55 Richard Jefferson	.40	1.00
56 Dan Dickau	.30	.75
57 Jamaal Magloire	.30	.75
58 J.R. Smith	.50	1.25
59 Jamal Crawford	.50	1.25
60 Stephon Marbury	.60	1.50
61 Quentin Richardson	.30	.75
62 Dwight Howard	.60	1.50
63 Grant Hill	.75	2.00
64 Steve Francis	.50	1.25
65 Allen Iverson	1.00	2.50
66 Andre Iguodala	.50	1.25
67 Chris Webber	.60	1.50
68 Amare Stoudemire	.60	1.50
69 Shawn Marion	.40	1.00
70 Steve Nash	1.00	2.50
71 Damon Stoudamire	.50	1.25
72 Shareef Abdur-Rahim	.50	1.25
73 Zach Randolph	.50	1.25
74 Brad Miller	.40	1.00
75 Mike Bibby	.50	1.25
76 Peja Stojakovic	.40	1.00
77 Manu Ginobili	1.00	2.50
78 Tim Duncan	1.25	3.00
79 Tony Parker	.75	2.00
80 Rashard Lewis	.40	1.00
81 Ray Allen	.75	2.00
82 Luke Ridnour	.40	1.00
83 Rafer Alston	.40	1.00
84 Jalen Rose	.40	1.00
85 Chris Bosh	.60	1.50
86 Andrei Kirilenko	.60	1.50
87 Carlos Boozer	.40	1.00
88 Matt Harpring	.30	.75
89 Antawn Jamison	.40	1.00
90 Gilbert Arenas	.50	1.25
91 Bracey Wright RC	1.25	3.00
92 Chris Taft RC	1.25	3.00
93 Jose Calderon RC	2.00	5.00
94 Dijon Thompson RC	1.25	3.00
95 Esteban Batista RC	1.25	3.00
96 Linas Kleiza RC	1.50	4.00
97 Earl Barron RC	1.25	3.00
98 Ike Diogu RC	1.25	3.00
99 Alan Anderson RC	1.25	3.00
100 Shavlik Randolph RC	1.25	3.00
101 Eddie Basden RC	1.25	3.00
102 Johan Petro RC	1.25	3.00
103 Ersan Ilyasova RC	1.50	4.00
104 Dwayne Jones RC	1.25	3.00
105 Aaron Miles RC	1.50	4.00
106 James Singleton RC	1.50	4.00
107 Von Wafer RC	1.25	3.00
108 Josh Powell RC	1.50	4.00
109 Yaroslav Korolev RC	1.25	3.00
110 Ronnie Price RC	1.50	4.00
111 Andray Blatche RC	2.00	5.00
112 Robert Whaley RC	1.25	3.00
113 Donell Taylor RC	1.25	3.00
114 Orien Greene RC	1.50	4.00
115 Lawrence Roberts RC	1.25	3.00
116 Amir Johnson RC	2.00	5.00
117 Matt Walsh RC	2.00	5.00
118 Fabricio Oberto RC	1.50	4.00
119 Arvydas Macijauskas RC	1.25	3.00
120 Alex Acker RC	1.25	3.00
121 Salim Stoudamire JSY AU RC	3.00	8.00
122 Francisco Garcia JSY AU RC	2.50	6.00
123 Daniel Ewing JSY AU RC	3.00	8.00
124 N.Robinson JSY AU/199 RC	4.00	10.00
125 Luther Head JSY AU RC	2.50	6.00
126 Louis Williams JSY AU RC	10.00	25.00
127 Jarrett Jack JSY AU RC	4.00	10.00
128 J.Maxiell JSY AU/1453 RC	3.00	8.00
129 Wayne Simien JSY AU RC	2.50	6.00
130 Julius Hodge JSY AU RC	2.50	6.00
131 C.J. Miles JSY AU RC	3.00	8.00
132 Andrew Bynum JSY AU RC	30.00	80.00
133 Monta Ellis JSY AU/99 RC	10.00	25.00
134 Joey Graham JSY AU RC	3.00	8.00
135 Antoine Wright JSY AU RC	3.00	8.00
136 Sean May JSY AU/1458 RC	2.50	6.00
137 Channing Frye JSY AU RC	3.00	8.00
138 Gerald Green JSY AU RC	4.00	10.00
139 S.Jasikevicius JSY AU RC	4.00	10.00
140 Danny Granger JSY AU RC	4.00	10.00
141 H.Warrick JSY AU/99 RC	3.00	8.00
142 David Lee JSY AU RC	4.00	10.00
143 Brandon Bass JSY AU RC	3.00	8.00
144 Ryan Gomes JSY AU RC	3.00	8.00
145 M.Andriuskevicius JSY AU RC	2.50	6.00
146 Travis Diener JSY AU RC	2.50	6.00
147 Martell Webster JSY AU RC	5.00	12.00
148 Rashad McCants JSY AU RC	4.00	10.00
149 Deron Williams JSY AU RC	10.00	25.00
150 Charlie Villanueva JSY AU RC	5.00	12.00
151 Raymond Felton JSY AU RC	5.00	12.00
152 Andrew Bogut JSY AU RC	8.00	20.00
153 Chris Paul JSY AU RC	100.00	250.00
154 Marvin Williams JSY AU RC	6.00	15.00

2005-06 SPx Spectrum

*1-90 SPECTRUM: 6X TO 15X BASE HI
*91-120 RCs: 1.25X TO 3X BASE HI
*121-146 RCs: 1.5X TO 4X BASE HI
*147-154 RCs: 1X TO 2.5X BASE HI
*124, 133, 141 RC SP: .75X TO 2X BASE HI
PRINT RUN 25 SER.#'d SETS

Card	Low	High
10 Michael Jordan	200.00	500.00
15 LeBron James	125.00	300.00
39 Kobe Bryant	125.00	300.00

2005-06 SPx Flashback Fabrics

Card	Low	High
AK Andrei Kirilenko	8.00	20.00
BD Baron Davis	8.00	20.00
BG Ben Gordon	8.00	20.00
BO Carlos Boozer	8.00	20.00
BW Ben Wallace	20.00	50.00
CA Carmelo Anthony	60.00	150.00
CB Chauncey Billups	10.00	25.00
CH Chris Bosh	12.00	30.00
DH Dwight Howard	12.00	30.00
DR David Robinson	30.00	80.00
GA Gilbert Arenas	10.00	25.00
HO Hakeem Olajuwon	30.00	80.00
IT Isiah Thomas	20.00	50.00
JC Josh Childress	8.00	20.00
JK Jason Kidd	25.00	60.00
JR J.R. Smith	12.00	30.00
JS John Stockton	40.00	100.00
KH Kirk Hinrich	10.00	25.00
LB Larry Bird	75.00	200.00
LD Luol Deng	8.00	20.00
LJ LeBron James SP	800.00	1,500.00
LO Lamar Odom	10.00	25.00
MA Magic Johnson	50.00	120.00
MB Mike Bibby	8.00	20.00
MJ Michael Jordan SP	2,000.00	4,000.00
PG Pau Gasol	8.00	20.00
PP Paul Pierce	12.00	30.00
PS Peja Stojakovic	8.00	20.00
QR Quentin Richardson	8.00	20.00
RH Richard Hamilton	8.00	20.00
RJ Richard Jefferson	8.00	20.00
SE Sean May	8.00	20.00
SL Shaun Livingston	10.00	25.00
SN Steve Nash	60.00	150.00
ST Stephon Marbury	12.00	30.00
TM Tracy McGrady	60.00	150.00
UH Udonis Haslem	8.00	20.00
VC Vince Carter	60.00	150.00
WF Walt Frazier	15.00	40.00
YM Yao Ming	75.00	200.00

2005-06 SPx SPxcitement Rookies

PRINT RUN 1999 SER.#'d SETS
*SPECTRUM: 1.25X TO 3X BASE HI
SPECTRUM PRINT RUN 99 SER.#'d SETS

Card	Low	High
XCR1 Chris Paul	5.00	12.00
XCR2 Marvin Williams	1.00	2.50
XCR3 Andrew Bogut	1.25	3.00
XCR4 Hakim Warrick	.75	2.00
XCR5 Rashad McCants	.60	1.50
XCR6 Raymond Felton	.75	2.00
XCR7 Sean May	.60	1.50
XCR8 Charlie Villanueva	.75	2.00
XCR9 Gerald Green	1.00	2.50
XCR10 Danny Granger	1.00	2.50
XCR11 Deron Williams	1.50	4.00
XCR12 Martell Webster	.75	2.00
XCR13 Andrew Bynum	.75	2.00
XCR14 Channing Frye	.75	2.00
XCR15 Joey Graham	.75	2.00
XCR16 Ike Diogu	.60	1.50
XCR17 Antoine Wright	.75	2.00
XCR18 Julius Hodge	.60	1.50
XCR19 Nate Robinson	1.00	2.50
XCR20 Jarrett Jack	1.00	2.50

2005-06 SPx SPxcitement Veterans

PRINT RUN 999 SER.#'d SETS
*SPECTRUM: 1X TO 2.5X BASE HI
SPECTRUM PRINT RUN 99 SER.#'d SETS

Card	Low	High
XCV1 Gary Payton	2.00	5.00
XCV2 Paul Pierce	2.00	5.00
XCV3 Michael Jordan	30.00	80.00
XCV4 Ben Gordon	1.00	2.50
XCV5 Kirk Hinrich	1.00	2.50
XCV6 LeBron James	10.00	25.00
XCV7 Carmelo Anthony	2.00	5.00
XCV8 Ben Wallace	1.50	4.00
XCV9 Chauncey Billups	1.50	4.00
XCV10 Richard Hamilton	1.50	4.00
XCV11 Baron Davis	1.25	3.00
XCV12 Tracy McGrady	2.00	5.00
XCV13 Yao Ming	2.50	6.00
XCV14 Kobe Bryant	10.00	25.00
XCV15 Lamar Odom	1.00	2.50
XCV16 Pau Gasol	2.00	5.00
XCV17 Jason Williams	1.00	2.50
XCV18 Michael Redd	1.00	2.50
XCV19 Jason Kidd	2.00	5.00
XCV20 Richard Jefferson	1.00	2.50
XCV21 J.R. Smith	1.25	3.00
XCV22 Stephon Marbury	1.50	4.00
XCV23 Dwight Howard	1.50	4.00
XCV24 Jameer Nelson	.75	2.00
XCV25 Andre Iguodala	1.25	3.00
XCV26 Kyle Korver	1.00	2.50
XCV27 Quentin Richardson	.75	2.00
XCV28 Steve Nash	2.50	6.00
XCV29 Damon Stoudamire	1.25	3.00
XCV30 Mike Bibby	1.25	3.00
XCV31 Peja Stojakovic	1.00	2.50
XCV32 Chris Bosh	1.50	4.00
XCV33 Andrei Kirilenko	1.00	2.50
XCV34 Antawn Jamison	1.00	2.50
XCV35 Carlos Boozer	1.00	2.50
XCV36 Hakeem Olajuwon	2.50	6.00
XCV37 Isiah Thomas	2.00	5.00
XCV38 Dennis Rodman	2.50	6.00
XCV39 Scottie Pippen	2.50	6.00
XCV40 John Stockton	2.50	6.00

2005-06 SPx Winning Materials

STATED ODDS 1:18
*SPECTRUM: 1X TO 2.5X BASE HI
SPECTRUM PRINT RUN 25 SER.#'d SETS

Card	Low	High
AB Andrew Bogut	3.00	8.00
AS Amare Stoudemire	2.50	6.00
BD Baron Davis	2.50	6.00
CA Carmelo Anthony	4.00	10.00
CB Chris Bosh	3.00	8.00
CP Chris Paul	12.00	30.00
CW Chris Webber	3.00	8.00
DE Deron Williams	4.00	10.00
DN Dirk Nowitzki	6.00	15.00
EB Elton Brand	2.00	5.00
GA Gilbert Arenas	2.50	6.00
GG Gerald Green	2.50	6.00
GH Grant Hill	4.00	10.00
JK Jason Kidd	4.00	10.00
JO Jermaine O'Neal	2.00	5.00
JR Jason Richardson	2.50	6.00
KB Kobe Bryant	60.00	150.00
KG Kevin Garnett	6.00	15.00
KM Kenyon Martin	2.00	5.00
LJ LeBron James	60.00	150.00
MF Michael Finley	2.50	6.00
MG Manu Ginobili	5.00	12.00
MJ Michael Jordan	125.00	300.00
MW Marvin Williams	2.50	6.00
PG Pau Gasol	4.00	10.00
PP Paul Pierce	4.00	10.00
PS Peja Stojakovic	2.00	5.00
QR Quentin Richardson	1.50	4.00
RA Ray Allen	4.00	10.00
RL Rashard Lewis	2.00	5.00
SF Steve Francis	2.50	6.00
SM Shawn Marion	2.00	5.00
SN Steve Nash	5.00	12.00
SO Shaquille O'Neal	8.00	20.00
ST Stephon Marbury	3.00	8.00
TD Tim Duncan	6.00	15.00
TM Tracy McGrady	4.00	10.00
TP Tony Parker	4.00	10.00
VC Vince Carter	5.00	12.00
YM Yao Ming	5.00	12.00
ZI Zydrunas Ilgauskas	2.00	5.00

2005-06 SPx Winning Materials Autographs

PRINT RUN 25 TO 50 SER.#'d SETS

Card	Low	High
AB Andrew Bogut/50	8.00	20.00
BG Ben Gordon/50	6.00	15.00
CA Carmelo Anthony/25	100.00	250.00
CB Chauncey Billups/50	20.00	50.00
CH Chris Bosh/50	15.00	40.00
CP Chris Paul/50	75.00	200.00
DE Deron Williams/50	8.00	20.00
GG Gerald Green/50	6.00	15.00
KH Kirk Hinrich/50	12.00	30.00
LJ LeBron James/25	2,500.00	5,000.00
MB Mike Bibby/50	10.00	25.00
MJ Michael Jordan/25	3,000.00	6,000.00
MW Marvin Williams/50	6.00	15.00
PS Peja Stojakovic/50	12.00	30.00
QR Quentin Richardson/50	6.00	15.00
SN Steve Nash/25	75.00	200.00
TM Tracy McGrady/50	75.00	200.00
YM Yao Ming/25	125.00	300.00

2005-06 SPx Winning Materials Combos

STATED ODDS 1:18
*SPECTRUM: 1X TO 2.5X BASE HI
SPECTRUM PRINT RUN 25 SER.#'d SETS

Card	Low	High
AL R.Allen/R.Lewis	4.00	10.00
AN C.Anthony/Nene	4.00	10.00
BB K.Bryant/C.Butler	40.00	100.00
BH C.Billups/R.Hamilton	3.00	8.00
BP B.Miller/P.Stojakovic	2.00	5.00
BS R.Bowen/S.Swift	1.50	4.00
CL S.Cassell/S.Livingston	2.00	5.00
DC L.Deng/T.Chandler	2.00	5.00
DG T.Duncan/M.Ginobili	6.00	15.00
DW S.Dalembert/C.Webber	3.00	8.00
FN S.Francis/J.Nelson	2.50	6.00
GC D.George/B.Cook	1.50	4.00
GH B.Gordon/K.Hinrich	2.00	5.00
GS K.Garnett/W.Szczerbiak	6.00	15.00
HH D.Howard/G.Hill	4.00	10.00
HM A.Houston/S.Marbury	3.00	8.00
HW U.Haslem/D.Wright	1.50	4.00
JA A.Jamison/G.Arenas	2.50	6.00
JI L.James/Z.Ilgauskas	40.00	100.00
JJ M.Jordan/L.James SP	150.00	400.00
KB A.Kirilenko/C.Boozer	2.00	5.00
KJ J.Kidd/R.Jefferson	4.00	10.00
KM L.Kleiza/K.Martin	2.00	5.00
MB C.Maggette/E.Brand	2.00	5.00
MS S.Marion/A.Stoudemire	2.50	6.00
MY T.McGrady/Y.Ming	12.00	30.00
NR S.Nash/S.Marion	5.00	12.00
NT D.Nowitzki/J.Terry	6.00	15.00
OT J.O'Neal/J.Tinsley	2.00	5.00
PJ P.Pierce/A.Jefferson	4.00	10.00
PU T.Parker/B.Udrih	4.00	10.00
RA J.Rose/R.Araujo	2.00	5.00
RD J.Richardson/B.Davis	2.50	6.00
RM Z.Randolph/D.Miles	2.50	6.00
RR L.Ridnour/V.Radmanovic	2.00	5.00
RW K.Rush/G.Wallace	2.00	5.00
SM J.R.Smith/J.Magloire	2.50	6.00
TH J.Terry/D.Harris	2.00	5.00
WP A.Walker/G.Payton	4.00	10.00
WS D.Wagner/E.Snow	1.50	4.00
WW D.Wesley/C.Ward	1.50	4.00
YO Y.Ming/S.O'Neal	12.00	30.00

2006-07 SPx

COMP.SET w/o RC's (100) 25.00 60.00
122-127 RC PRINT RUN 299 SER.#'d SETS
128-152 RC PRINT RUN 1199 SER.#'d SETS

Card	Low	High
1 Joe Johnson	.50	1.25
2 Salim Stoudamire	.30	.75
3 Marvin Williams	.30	.75
4 Tony Allen	.30	.75
5 Al Jefferson	.30	.75
6 Paul Pierce	.75	2.00
7 Raymond Felton	.30	.75
8 Emeka Okafor	.40	1.00
9 Gerald Wallace	.40	1.00
10 Tyson Chandler	.40	1.00
11 Ben Gordon	.40	1.00
12 Michael Jordan	4.00	10.00
13 Drew Gooden	.40	1.00
14 Zydrunas Ilgauskas	.40	1.00
15 LeBron James	4.00	10.00
16 Devin Harris	.30	.75
17 Dirk Nowitzki	1.25	3.00
18 Jason Terry	.40	1.00
19 Carmelo Anthony	.75	2.00
20 Andre Miller	.40	1.00
21 Eduardo Najera	.30	.75
22 Chauncey Billups	.60	1.50
23 Richard Hamilton	.50	1.25
24 Ben Wallace	.60	1.50
25 Rasheed Wallace	.60	1.50
26 Baron Davis	.50	1.25
27 Troy Murphy	.30	.75
28 Jason Richardson	.50	1.25
29 Rafer Alston	.40	1.00
30 Tracy McGrady	.75	2.00
31 Yao Ming	1.25	3.00
32 Sarunas Jasikevicius	.40	1.00
33 Jermaine O'Neal	.50	1.25
34 Peja Stojakovic	.40	1.00
35 Elton Brand	.40	1.00
36 Sam Cassell	.40	1.00
37 Chris Kaman	.30	.75
38 Shaun Livingston	.40	1.00
39 Kobe Bryant	4.00	10.00
40 Lamar Odom	.40	1.00
41 Ronny Turiaf	.40	1.00
42 Pau Gasol	.75	2.00
43 Mike Miller	.40	1.00
44 Damon Stoudamire	.40	1.00
45 Shaquille O'Neal	2.00	5.00
46 Wayne Simien	.30	.75
47 Dwyane Wade	1.00	2.50
48 Jason Williams	.60	1.50
49 Andrew Bogut	.40	1.00
50 T.J. Ford	.30	.75
51 Jamaal Magloire	.30	.75
52 Michael Redd	.40	1.00
53 Ricky Davis	.40	1.00
54 Kevin Garnett	1.25	3.00
55 Rashad McCants	.30	.75
56 Vince Carter	1.00	2.50
57 Richard Jefferson	.40	1.00
58 Jason Kidd	.75	2.00
59 Speedy Claxton	.30	.75
60 Desmond Mason	.30	.75
61 Chris Paul	1.00	2.50
62 Steve Francis	.50	1.25
63 Channing Frye	.30	.75
64 Stephon Marbury	.60	1.50
65 Nate Robinson	.40	1.00
66 Carlos Arroyo	.30	.75
67 Grant Hill	.75	2.00
68 Dwight Howard	.60	1.50
69 Jameer Nelson	.30	.75
70 Andre Iguodala	.50	1.25
71 Allen Iverson	1.25	3.00
72 Chris Webber	.60	1.50
73 Boris Diaw	.40	1.00
74 Shawn Marion	.50	1.25
75 Steve Nash	1.00	2.50
76 Amare Stoudemire	.50	1.25
77 Zach Randolph	.50	1.25
78 Sebastian Telfair	.30	.75
79 Martell Webster	.40	1.00
80 Shareef Abdur-Rahim	.50	1.25
81 Ron Artest	.50	1.25
82 Mike Bibby	.50	1.25
83 Brad Miller	.40	1.00
84 Tim Duncan	1.25	3.00
85 Michael Finley	.50	1.25
86 Manu Ginobili	1.00	2.50
87 Tony Parker	.75	2.00
88 Ray Allen	.75	2.00
89 Rashard Lewis	.40	1.00
90 Chris Wilcox	.30	.75
91 Chris Bosh	.60	1.50
92 Joey Graham	.30	.75
93 Charlie Villanueva	.30	.75
94 Carlos Boozer	.40	1.00
95 Andrei Kirilenko	.40	1.00
96 C.J. Miles	.30	.75
97 Deron Williams	.40	1.00
98 Gilbert Arenas	.50	1.25
99 Caron Butler	.40	1.00
100 Antawn Jamison	.40	1.00
101 Adam Morrison RC	1.50	4.00
102 Alexander Johnson RC	1.25	3.00
103 Damir Markota RC	1.25	3.00
104 J.J. Redick RC	4.00	10.00
105 Will Blalock RC	1.25	3.00
106 Leon Powe RC	1.25	3.00
107 Thabo Sefolosha RC	1.50	4.00
108 Pops Mensah-Bonsu RC	1.25	3.00
109 Robert Hite RC	1.25	3.00
110 Tarence Kinsey RC	1.25	3.00
111 Vassilis Spanoulis RC	1.25	3.00
112 Yakhouba Diawara RC	1.25	3.00
113 Daniel Gibson RC	1.50	4.00
114 Hassan Adams RC	1.25	3.00
115 James Augustine RC	1.25	3.00
116 Chris Quinn RC	1.25	3.00
117 Mardy Collins RC	1.25	3.00
118 Paul Millsap RC	2.50	6.00
119 P.J. Tucker RC	2.00	5.00
120 Ryan Hollins RC	1.25	3.00
121 Saer Sene RC	1.25	3.00
122 Andrea Bargnani JSY AU RC	6.00	15.00
123 LaMarcus Aldridge JSY AU RC	30.00	80.00
124 Tyrus Thomas JSY AU RC	6.00	15.00
125 Shelden Williams JSY AU RC	5.00	12.00
126 Brandon Roy JSY AU RC	15.00	40.00
127 Randy Foye JSY AU RC	6.00	15.00
128 Paul Davis JSY AU RC	3.00	8.00
129 Solomon Jones JSY AU RC	3.00	8.00
130 David Noel JSY AU RC	3.00	8.00
131 Alan Ray JSY AU RC	3.00	8.00
132 Bobby Jones JSY AU RC	3.00	8.00
133 Cedric Simmons JSY AU RC	3.00	8.00
134 Dee Brown JSY AU RC	3.00	8.00
135 Shawne Williams JSY AU RC	3.00	8.00
136 Hilton Armstrong JSY AU RC	3.00	8.00
137 James White JSY AU RC	3.00	8.00
138 Jordan Farmar JSY AU RC	4.00	10.00
139 Josh Boone JSY AU RC	3.00	8.00
140 Kyle Lowry JSY AU RC	15.00	40.00
141 Marcus Williams JSY AU RC	3.00	8.00
142 Maurice Ager JSY AU RC	3.00	8.00
143 Patrick O'Bryant JSY AU RC	3.00	8.00
144 Quincy Douby JSY AU RC	3.00	8.00
145 Rajon Rondo JSY AU RC	15.00	40.00
146 Renaldo Balkman JSY AU RC	4.00	10.00
147 Rodney Carney JSY AU RC	3.00	8.00
148 Ronnie Brewer JSY AU RC	5.00	12.00
149 Rudy Gay JSY AU RC	6.00	15.00
150 Shannon Brown JSY AU RC	3.00	8.00
151 Steve Novak JSY AU RC	4.00	10.00
152 Craig Smith JSY AU RC	4.00	10.00

2006-07 SPx Spectrum

*1-100 SPECTRUM: 4X TO 10X BASE HI
*101-121 RCs: 1.25X TO 3X BASE HI
*122-127 RCs: 1.25X TO 3X BASE HI
*128-152 RCs: 1.25X TO 3X BASE HI
SPECTRUM PRINT RUN 25 SER.#'d SETS

Card	Low	High
12 Michael Jordan	60.00	150.00
39 Kobe Bryant	30.00	80.00
71 Allen Iverson	10.00	25.00
126 Brandon Roy JSY AU	100.00	250.00

2006-07 SPx Flashback Fabrics

APPROXIMATE ODDS 1:72

Card	Low	High
FFAB Andrew Bynum	2.00	5.00
FFAI Allen Iverson	8.00	20.00
FFAJ Antawn Jamison	2.50	6.00
FFAK Andrei Kirilenko	2.50	6.00
FFAW Antoine Walker	3.00	8.00
FFBB Bruce Bowen	2.50	6.00
FFBG Ben Gordon	2.50	6.00
FFBM Brad Miller	2.50	6.00
FFCB Carlos Boozer	2.50	6.00
FFCF Channing Frye	2.00	5.00
FFCW Chris Webber	4.00	10.00
FFDG Drew Gooden	2.50	6.00
FFDH Devin Harris	2.00	5.00
FFDM Desmond Mason	2.00	5.00
FFDR Dennis Rodman	10.00	25.00
FFGA Gilbert Arenas	3.00	8.00
FFGE Devean George	2.00	5.00
FFGG George Gervin	5.00	12.00
FFGH Grant Hill	5.00	12.00
FFID Ike Diogu	2.00	5.00
FFJC Jamal Crawford	3.00	8.00
FFJN Jameer Nelson	2.00	5.00
FFJR Jason Richardson	3.00	8.00
FFJS John Stockton	8.00	20.00
FFJT Jason Terry	2.50	6.00
FFLD Luol Deng	2.50	6.00
FFLH Luther Head	2.00	5.00
FFLO Lamar Odom	2.50	6.00
FFMG Manu Ginobili	6.00	15.00
FFMJ Magic Johnson	8.00	20.00
FFQR Quentin Richardson	2.00	5.00
FFRJ Richard Jefferson	2.50	6.00
FFRO David Robinson	6.00	15.00
FFRW Rasheed Wallace	4.00	10.00
FFSD Samuel Dalembert	2.00	5.00
FFSE Sean Elliott	2.50	6.00
FFSJ Sarunas Jasikevicius	2.50	6.00
FFSM Sean May	2.00	5.00
FFWF Walt Frazier	5.00	12.00
FFWR Antoine Wright	2.00	5.00
FFWS Wally Szczerbiak	2.50	6.00

2006-07 SPx Flashback Fabrics Autographs

APPROXIMATE ODDS 1:144

Card	Low	High
FFBD Baron Davis	6.00	15.00
AFFAB Andrew Bogut	6.00	15.00
AFFAI Andre Iguodala	8.00	20.00
AFFAJ Al Jefferson	6.00	15.00
AFFBK Bernard King	10.00	25.00
AFFBL Bill Laimbeer	10.00	25.00
AFFCA Carmelo Anthony	20.00	50.00
AFFCB Chris Bosh	10.00	25.00
AFFCD Clyde Drexler	25.00	60.00
AFFCM Corey Maggette	6.00	15.00
AFFDG Danny Granger	6.00	15.00
AFFDW Deron Williams	6.00	15.00
AFFFG Francisco Garcia	6.00	15.00
AFFHO Hakeem Olajuwon	20.00	50.00
AFFHW Hakim Warrick	6.00	15.00
AFFJG Joey Graham	6.00	15.00
AFFJS J.R. Smith	6.00	15.00
AFFKK Kyle Korver	8.00	20.00
AFFLB Larry Bird	75.00	200.00
AFFLH Larry Hughes	8.00	20.00
AFFLJ LeBron James	1,000.00	2,000.00
AFFMD Marquis Daniels	6.00	15.00
AFFMJ Michael Jordan	400.00	800.00
AFFMW Marvin Williams	6.00	15.00
AFFNR Nate Robinson	6.00	15.00
AFFPP Paul Pierce	10.00	25.00
AFFPS Peja Stojakovic	8.00	20.00
AFFRA Ron Artest	8.00	20.00
AFFRF Raymond Felton	6.00	15.00
AFFRP Robert Parish	10.00	25.00
AFFSK Steve Kerr	20.00	50.00
AFFSL Shaun Livingston	6.00	15.00
AFFSN Steve Nash	30.00	80.00
AFFST Sebastian Telfair	6.00	15.00
AFFTC Tyson Chandler	6.00	15.00
AFFTM Tracy McGrady	30.00	80.00
AFFVC Vince Carter	30.00	80.00
AFFWE Martell Webster	6.00	15.00
AFFYK Yaroslav Korolev	6.00	15.00
AFFYM Yao Ming	15.00	40.00

2006-07 SPx SPxcitement

COMPLETE SET 25.00 60.00
APPROXIMATE ODDS ONE PER PACK

Card	Low	High
SPX1 Andrea Bargnani	.50	1.25
SPX2 LaMarcus Aldridge	1.50	4.00
SPX3 Adam Morrison	.50	1.25
SPX4 Tyrus Thomas	.50	1.25
SPX5 Shelden Williams	.40	1.00
SPX6 Brandon Roy	1.25	3.00
SPX7 Rudy Gay	.75	2.00
SPX8 Saer Sene	.40	1.00
SPX9 Hilton Armstrong	.40	1.00
SPX10 Thabo Sefolosha	.50	1.25
SPX11 Ronnie Brewer	.60	1.50
SPX12 Cedric Simmons	.40	1.00
SPX13 Rodney Carney	.40	1.00
SPX14 Quincy Douby	.40	1.00
SPX15 Rajon Rondo	2.00	5.00
SPX16 Renaldo Balkman	.50	1.25
SPX17 Steve Novak	.50	1.25
SPX18 Maurice Ager	.40	1.00
SPX19 Mardy Collins	.40	1.00
SPX20 James White	.40	1.00
SPX21 Craig Smith	.50	1.25
SPX22 Bobby Jones	.40	1.00
SPX23 Dee Brown	.40	1.00
SPX24 Will Blalock	.40	1.00
SPX25 Daniel Gibson	.50	1.25
SPX26 Michael Jordan	15.00	40.00
SPX27 Larry Bird	2.00	5.00
SPX28 Bill Russell	2.00	5.00
SPX29 Julius Erving	1.25	3.00
SPX30 Moses Malone	1.00	2.50
SPX31 Robert Parish	.75	2.00
SPX32 Magic Johnson	2.00	5.00
SPX33 Walt Frazier	.75	2.00
SPX34 Dennis Rodman	1.25	3.00
SPX35 Kareem Abdul-Jabbar	2.00	5.00
SPX36 Hakeem Olajuwon	1.25	3.00
SPX37 Zach Randolph	.60	1.50
SPX38 Clyde Drexler	.75	2.00
SPX39 David Robinson	1.00	2.50
SPX40 John Stockton	1.00	2.50
SPX41 Marvin Williams	.40	1.00
SPX42 Joe Johnson	.60	1.50
SPX43 Paul Pierce	1.00	2.50
SPX44 Emeka Okafor	.50	1.25
SPX45 Raymond Felton	.40	1.00
SPX46 Ben Gordon	.50	1.25
SPX47 Kirk Hinrich	.50	1.25
SPX48 LeBron James	10.00	25.00
SPX49 Zydrunas Ilgauskas	.50	1.25
SPX50 Dirk Nowitzki	1.50	4.00
SPX51 Jason Terry	.50	1.25
SPX52 Carmelo Anthony	1.00	2.50
SPX53 Kenyon Martin	.50	1.25
SPX54 Chauncey Billups	.75	2.00
SPX55 Richard Hamilton	.60	1.50
SPX56 Ben Wallace	.75	2.00
SPX57 Baron Davis	.60	1.50
SPX58 Jason Richardson	.60	1.50
SPX59 Tracy McGrady	1.00	2.50
SPX60 Yao Ming	1.50	4.00
SPX61 Jermaine O'Neal	.60	1.50
SPX62 Peja Stojakovic	.50	1.25
SPX63 Elton Brand	.50	1.25
SPX64 Sam Cassell	.50	1.25
SPX65 Kobe Bryant	10.00	25.00
SPX66 Pau Gasol	1.00	2.50
SPX67 Shaquille O'Neal	2.50	6.00
SPX68 Dwyane Wade	1.25	3.00
SPX69 Gary Payton	.75	2.00
SPX70 Kevin Garnett	1.50	4.00
SPX71 Vince Carter	1.25	3.00
SPX72 Jason Kidd	1.00	2.50
SPX73 Chris Paul	1.25	3.00
SPX74 Stephon Marbury	.75	2.00
SPX75 Grant Hill	1.00	2.50
SPX76 Dwight Howard	.75	2.00
SPX77 Allen Iverson	1.50	4.00
SPX78 Chris Webber	.75	2.00
SPX79 Shawn Marion	.60	1.50
SPX80 Amare Stoudemire	.60	1.50
SPX81 Steve Nash	1.25	3.00
SPX82 Ron Artest	.60	1.50
SPX83 Tim Duncan	1.50	4.00
SPX84 Manu Ginobili	1.25	3.00
SPX85 Tony Parker	1.00	2.50
SPX86 Ray Allen	1.00	2.50
SPX87 Chris Bosh	.75	2.00
SPX88 Charlie Villanueva	.40	1.00
SPX89 Andrei Kirilenko	.50	1.25
SPX90 Gilbert Arenas	.60	1.50
SPX91 Antawn Jamison	.50	1.25
SPX92 Carlos Boozer	.50	1.25
SPX93 Deron Williams	.50	1.25
SPX94 Rashard Lewis	.50	1.25
SPX95 Michael Finley	.60	1.50
SPX96 Josh Howard	.50	1.25
SPX97 Boris Diaw	.50	1.25
SPX98 Andre Iguodala	.60	1.50
SPX99 Mike Bibby	.60	1.50

2006-07 SPx Winning Combos

APPROXIMATE ODDS 1:20

Card	Low	High
WCAP R.Allen/J.Petro	6.00	15.00
WCBB K.Brown/A.Bynum	2.50	6.00
WCBG M.Bibby/F.Garcia	4.00	10.00
WCBM K.Bryant/T.McGrady	75.00	200.00
WCBV C.Bosh/C.Villanueva	5.00	12.00
WCCD T.Chandler/L.Deng	3.00	8.00
WCCF E.Curry/C.Frye	3.00	8.00
WCCR J.Crawford/N.Robinson	4.00	10.00
WCDG L.Deng/B.Gordon	3.00	8.00
WCDH M.Daniels/D.Harris	2.50	6.00
WCDI S.Dalembert/A.Iguodala	4.00	10.00
WCDP T.Duncan/T.Parker	5.00	12.00
WCDR B.Davis/J.Richardson	4.00	10.00
WCGH K.Garnett/D.Howard	6.00	15.00
WCGJ D.Granger/S.Jasikevicius	3.00	8.00
WCGW D.George/L.Walton	2.50	6.00
WCHB R.Hamilton/C.Billups	5.00	12.00
WCHG L.Hughes/D.Gooden	3.00	8.00
WCHN G.Hill/J.Nelson	6.00	15.00
WCHS K.Hinrich/W.Simien	3.00	8.00
WCIK Z.Ilgauskas/N.Krstic	3.00	8.00
WCJA A.Jefferson/T.Allen	2.50	6.00
WCJB A.Jamison/C.Butler	3.00	8.00
WCJG E.Jones/P.Gasol	6.00	15.00
WCJJ M.Jordan/L.James	125.00	300.00
WCJW R.Jefferson/A.Wright	3.00	8.00
WCKC J.Kidd/V.Carter	8.00	20.00
WCKW A.Kirilenko/D.Williams	3.00	8.00
WCMB C.Maggette/E.Brand	3.00	8.00
WCMI J.Magloire/E.Ilyasova	2.50	6.00
WCMO Y.Ming/S.O'Neal	15.00	40.00
WCMR S.Marbury/Q.Richardson	5.00	12.00
WCNS S.Nash/A.Stoudemire	5.00	12.00
WCOM E.Okafor/S.May	3.00	8.00
WCPD D.West/P.Stojakovic	3.00	8.00
WCPM P.Pierce/S.Marion	6.00	15.00
WCRB M.Redd/A.Bogut	3.00	8.00
WCRD Z.Randolph/J.Dixon	4.00	10.00
WCSA A.Stoudemire/C.Anthony	5.00	12.00
WCSH S.Swift/L.Head	2.50	6.00
WCSP J.Smith/C.Paul	3.00	8.00
WCSW W.Szczerbiak/D.West	3.00	8.00
WCTN J.Terry/D.Nowitzki	5.00	12.00
WCTO J.Tinsley/J.O'Neal	4.00	10.00
WCTW S.Telfair/M.Webster	3.00	8.00
WCWJ D.Jones/H.Warrick	2.50	6.00
WCWK C.Webber/K.Korver	5.00	12.00
WCWM R.McCants/B.Wright	2.50	6.00
WCWS A.Walker/W.Simien	4.00	10.00
WCWW R.Wallace/B.Wallace	5.00	12.00

2006-07 SPx Winning Materials

Card	Low	High
WMAI Andre Iguodala	3.00	8.00
WMAJ Al Jefferson	2.00	5.00
WMBD Baron Davis	3.00	8.00
WMBO Chris Bosh	4.00	10.00
WMBW Ben Wallace	4.00	10.00
WMCA Carmelo Anthony	5.00	12.00
WMCB Chauncey Billups	4.00	10.00
WMCF Channing Frye	2.00	5.00
WMCM Corey Maggette	2.50	6.00
WMCP Chris Paul	6.00	15.00
WMCV Charlie Villanueva	2.00	5.00
WMDG Drew Gooden	2.50	6.00
WMDH Dwight Howard	4.00	10.00
WMDJ Dahntay Jones	2.00	5.00
WMDN Dirk Nowitzki	8.00	20.00
WMDW Delonte West	2.00	5.00
WMEB Elton Brand	2.50	6.00
WMEO Emeka Okafor	2.50	6.00
WMGA Gilbert Arenas	3.00	8.00
WMGR Danny Granger	2.00	5.00
WMID Ike Diogu	2.00	5.00
WMJH Josh Howard	2.50	6.00
WMJK Jason Kidd	5.00	12.00
WMJO Jermaine O'Neal	3.00	8.00
WMKB Kobe Bryant	75.00	200.00
WMKG Kevin Garnett	8.00	20.00
WMLD Luol Deng	2.50	6.00
WMLH Luther Head	2.00	5.00
WMLJ LeBron James	25.00	60.00
WMMA Shawn Marion	3.00	8.00
WMMJ Michael Jordan	50.00	120.00
WMMR Michael Redd	2.50	6.00
WMNK Nenad Krstic	2.00	5.00
WMPG Pau Gasol	5.00	12.00
WMPP Paul Pierce	5.00	12.00
WMRA Ray Allen	5.00	12.00
WMRH Richard Hamilton	3.00	8.00
WMRW Rasheed Wallace	4.00	10.00
WMSD Samuel Dalembert	2.00	5.00
WMSL Shaun Livingston	2.50	6.00
WMSM Stephon Marbury	4.00	10.00
WMSN Steve Nash	6.00	15.00
WMSO Shaquille O'Neal	12.00	30.00
WMTD Tim Duncan	8.00	20.00
WMTM Tracy McGrady	5.00	12.00
WMTP Tony Parker	5.00	12.00
WMVC Vince Carter	6.00	15.00
WMWS Wally Szczerbiak	2.50	6.00
WMYM Yao Ming	8.00	20.00
WMZI Zydrunas Ilgauskas	2.50	6.00

2007-08 SPx

COMP.SET w/o SP's (90) 15.00 40.00
101-110 PRINT RUN 299 SER.#'d SETS
111-140 PRINT RUN 825 SER.#'d SETS

Card	Low	High
1 Chauncey Billups	.60	1.50
2 Tayshaun Prince	.50	1.25
3 Richard Hamilton	.60	1.50
4 Rasheed Wallace	.60	1.50
5 Zydrunas Ilgauskas	.40	1.00
6 Larry Hughes	.40	1.00
7 LeBron James	4.00	10.00
8 T.J. Ford	.30	.75
9 Andrea Bargnani	.30	.75
10 Chris Bosh	.60	1.50
11 Shaquille O'Neal	2.00	5.00
12 Dwyane Wade	1.00	2.50
13 Udonis Haslem	.30	.75
14 Ben Wallace	.60	1.50
15 Ben Gordon	.40	1.00
16 Luol Deng	.40	1.00
17 Kirk Hinrich	.50	1.25
18 Vince Carter	1.00	2.50
19 Richard Jefferson	.40	1.00
20 Jason Kidd	.75	2.00
21 Gilbert Arenas	.50	1.25
22 Caron Butler	.40	1.00
23 Antawn Jamison	.40	1.00
24 Dwight Howard	.60	1.50
25 Jameer Nelson	.40	1.00
26 Jermaine O'Neal	.50	1.25
27 Danny Granger	.30	.75
28 Mike Dunleavy	.30	.75
29 Andre Iguodala	.50	1.25
30 Kyle Korver	.50	1.25
31 Gerald Wallace	.40	1.00
32 Emeka Okafor	.40	1.00
33 Jason Richardson	.50	1.25
34 Eddy Curry	.40	1.00
35 Stephon Marbury	.60	1.50
36 Quentin Richardson	.30	.75
37 David Lee	.30	.75
38 Marvin Williams	.30	.75
39 Josh Smith	.30	.75
40 Joe Johnson	.40	1.00
41 Michael Redd	.40	1.00
42 Andrew Bogut	.40	1.00
43 Paul Pierce	.75	2.00
44 Al Jefferson	.30	.75
45 Ray Allen	.75	2.00
46 Dirk Nowitzki	1.25	3.00
47 Jerry Stackhouse	.50	1.25
48 Jason Terry	.40	1.00
49 Josh Howard	.40	1.00
50 Amare Stoudemire	.50	1.25
51 Steve Nash	1.00	2.50
52 Leandro Barbosa	.40	1.00
53 Shawn Marion	.50	1.25
54 Tony Parker	.75	2.00
55 Tim Duncan	1.25	3.00
56 Manu Ginobili	1.00	2.50
57 Michael Finley	.50	1.25
58 Andrei Kirilenko	.40	1.00
59 Carlos Boozer	.40	1.00
60 Deron Williams	.40	1.00
61 Mehmet Okur	.30	.75
62 Tracy McGrady	.75	2.00
63 Yao Ming	1.25	3.00
64 Carmelo Anthony	.75	2.00
65 Allen Iverson	1.25	3.00
66 Marcus Camby	.40	1.00
67 Kobe Bryant	4.00	10.00
68 Lamar Odom	.40	1.00
69 Baron Davis	.40	1.00
70 Al Harrington	.40	1.00
71 Stephen Jackson	.40	1.00
72 Elton Brand	.40	1.00

73 Corey Maggette .40 1.00
74 Shaun Livingston .40 1.00
75 David West .40 1.00
76 Chris Paul 1.00 2.50
77 Tyson Chandler .50 1.25
78 Kevin Garnett 1.25 3.00
79 Ricky Davis .40 1.00
80 Randy Foye .40 1.00
81 Kevin Martin .40 1.00
82 Ron Artest .50 1.25
83 Mike Bibby .50 1.25
84 Steve Francis .40 1.00
85 Brandon Roy .60 1.50
86 Jarrett Jack .40 1.00
87 Delonte West .30 .75
88 Rashard Lewis .40 1.00
89 Pau Gasol .75 2.00
90 Mike Miller .40 1.00
91 Greg Oden RC 3.00 8.00
92 Thaddeus Young RC 3.00 8.00
93 Brandan Wright RC 2.50 6.00
94 Yi Jianlian RC 4.00 10.00
95 Nick Young RC 3.00 8.00
96 Chris Richard RC 2.00 5.00
97 Marco Belinelli RC 2.50 6.00
98 Juan Carlos Navarro RC 2.50 6.00
99 Sammy Mejia RC 2.00 5.00
100 Kyrylo Fesenko RC 2.00 5.00
101 Kevin Durant JSY AU RC 600.00 1,200.00
102 Al Horford JSY AU RC 15.00 40.00
103 Mike Conley Jr. JSY AU RC 15.00 40.00
104 Jeff Green JSY AU RC 5.00 12.00
105 Corey Brewer JSY AU RC 5.00 12.00
106 Joakim Noah JSY AU RC 6.00 15.00
107 Spencer Hawes JSY AU RC 4.00 10.00
108 Acie Law JSY AU RC 4.00 10.00
109 Julian Wright JSY AU RC 4.00 10.00
110 Al Thornton JSY AU RC 4.00 10.00
111 Javaris Crittenton JSY AU RC 3.00 8.00
112 Daequan Cook JSY AU RC 4.00 10.00
113 Jared Dudley JSY AU RC 4.00 10.00
114 Wilson Chandler JSY AU RC 4.00 10.00
115 Morris Almond JSY AU RC 3.00 8.00
116 Arron Afflalo JSY AU RC 4.00 10.00
117 Alando Tucker JSY AU RC 3.00 8.00
118 Carl Landry JSY AU RC 3.00 8.00
119 Gabe Pruitt JSY AU RC 3.00 8.00
120 Marcus Williams JSY AU RC 3.00 8.00
121 Nick Fazekas JSY AU RC 3.00 8.00
122 Jermareo Davidson JSY AU RC 3.00 8.00
123 Josh McRoberts JSY AU RC 3.00 8.00
124 Glen Davis JSY AU RC 4.00 10.00
125 Adam Haluska JSY AU RC 3.00 8.00
126 Reyshawn Terry JSY AU RC 3.00 8.00
127 Jared Jordan JSY AU RC 3.00 8.00
128 Stephane Lasme JSY AU RC 3.00 8.00
129 Aaron Gray JSY AU RC 3.00 8.00
130 Taurean Green JSY AU RC 3.00 8.00
131 Demetris Nichols JSY AU RC 3.00 8.00
132 Herbert Hill JSY AU RC 3.00 8.00
133 Aaron Brooks JSY AU RC 4.00 10.00
134 D.J. Strawberry JSY AU RC 3.00 8.00
135 Dominic McGuire JSY AU RC 3.00 8.00
136 Jason Smith JSY AU RC 3.00 8.00
137 Sean Williams JSY AU RC 3.00 8.00
138 Derrick Byars JSY AU RC 3.00 8.00
139 Ramon Sessions JSY AU RC 4.00 10.00
140 Rodney Stuckey JSY AU RC 3.00 8.00

2007-08 SPx Radiance

*1-90 RADIANCE: 3X TO 8X BASE HI
*91-10 RC RAD: 1X TO 2.5X BASE HI
*101-110 RC RAD: 1.25X TO 3X BASE HI
*111-140 RC RAD: 1.5X TO 4X BASE HI
RADIANCE PRINT RUN 25 SER.#'d SETS

2007-08 SPx Duel Scripts

PRINT RUN 10 TO 25 SER.#'d SETS
BB B.Bowen/Barbosa/25 12.00 30.00
BJ L.James/K.Bryant/10 2,500.00 5,000.00
CJ C.Brewer/J.Noah/25 20.00 50.00
EB L.Bird/J.Erving/25 400.00 800.00
GD C.Drexler/G.Gervin/25 60.00 150.00
HG R.Hamilton/Gibson/25 12.00 30.00
HH R.Hamilton/Hughes/25 20.00 50.00
IJ A.Jefferson/Iguodala/25 20.00 50.00
JA L.James/C.Anthony/25 1,500.00 3,000.00
JE M.Jordan/J.Erving/25 2,000.00 4,000.00
LM L.Bird/M.Johnson/25 800.00 1,500.00
NA N.Nixon/Archibald/25 20.00 50.00
NP S.Nash/T.Parker/25 100.00 250.00
SJ M.Johnson/Stockton/25 125.00 300.00
TC Thornton/Crittenton/25 12.00 30.00
WR B.Russell/J.West/25 600.00 1,200.00

2007-08 SPx Endorsements

AA Arron Afflalo 2.50 6.00
AH Al Horford 10.00 25.00
AI Andre Iguodala 4.00 10.00
AL Acie Law 2.50 6.00
BR Bill Russell 300.00 600.00
BW Bill Walton 8.00 20.00
CA Carmelo Anthony 15.00 30.00
CB Corey Brewer 3.00 8.00
CD Clyde Drexler 15.00 40.00
DH Dwight Howard 10.00 25.00
GG George Gervin 8.00 20.00
HO Hakeem Olajuwon 15.00 40.00
JG Jeff Green 3.00 8.00
JN Joakim Noah 4.00 10.00
JO Jermaine O'Neal 4.00 10.00
KB Kobe Bryant 125.00 300.00
KD Kevin Durant 500.00 1,000.00
LB Larry Bird 50.00 120.00
LJ LeBron James 1,000.00 2,000.00
MC Mike Conley Jr. 10.00 25.00
MJ Michael Jordan 1,000.00 2,000.00
RJ Richard Jefferson 3.00 8.00
SH Spencer Hawes 2.50 6.00
TM Tracy McGrady 10.00 25.00
TP Tony Parker 8.00 20.00
VC Vince Carter 15.00 40.00
WF Walt Frazier 10.00 25.00
YM Yao Ming 20.00 40.00

2007-08 SPx Flashback Fabrics

*PARALLEL: 1X TO 2.5X BASE HI
PARALLEL PRINT RUN 25 SER.#'d SETS
AW Antoine Walker 2.50 6.00
BB Bruce Bowen 2.00 5.00
BD Boris Diaw 2.00 5.00
BU Caron Butler 2.00 5.00
CB Carlos Boozer 2.00 5.00
CV Charlie Villanueva 1.50 4.00
CW Chris Webber 3.00 8.00
DG Danny Granger 1.50 4.00
DN Dirk Nowitzki 6.00 15.00
DW Deron Williams 2.00 5.00
EO Emeka Okafor 2.00 5.00
GA Gilbert Arenas 2.50 6.00
JK Jason Kidd 4.00 10.00
JR Jason Richardson 2.50 6.00
JT Jason Terry 2.00 5.00
JW Jason Williams 4.00 10.00
KA Jason Kapono 2.00 5.00
KG Kevin Garnett 6.00 15.00
KM Kenyon Martin 2.00 5.00
LJ LeBron James 12.00 30.00
LO Lamar Odom 2.00 5.00
MA Stephon Marbury 3.00 8.00
MB Mike Bibby 2.50 6.00
MC Marcus Camby 2.00 5.00
MF Michael Finley 2.50 6.00
MO Alonzo Mourning 6.00 15.00
N Nene 2.00 5.00
PG Pau Gasol 4.00 10.00
PP Paul Pierce 4.00 10.00
PS Peja Stojakovic 2.00 5.00
RA Ray Allen 4.00 10.00
RL Rashard Lewis 2.00 5.00
RW Rasheed Wallace 3.00 8.00
SC Sam Cassell 2.00 5.00
SF Steve Francis 2.00 5.00
SM Shawn Marion 2.50 6.00
SO Shaquille O'Neal 10.00 25.00
TC Tyson Chandler 2.50 6.00
TD Tim Duncan 6.00 15.00
UH Udonis Haslem 1.50 4.00
ZR Zach Randolph 2.50 6.00

2007-08 SPx Flashback Fabrics Autographs

STATED PRINT RUN 10 TO 25 SER.#'d SETS
AD Adrian Dantley/25 8.00 20.00
AH Al Harrington/25 8.00 20.00
AI Andre Iguodala/25 8.00 20.00
AJ Al Jefferson/25 8.00 20.00
BD Baron Davis/25 12.00 30.00
BG Ben Gordon/25 12.00 30.00
BO Chris Bosh/25 15.00 40.00
BR Bill Russell/25 600.00 1,200.00
CD Clyde Drexler/25 25.00 50.00
CP Chris Paul/25 75.00 200.00
DH Dwight Howard/25 40.00 80.00
GG George Gervin/25 12.00 30.00
HO Hakeem Olajuwon/25 25.00 60.00
JA Antawn Jamison/25 8.00 20.00
JE Julius Erving/25 40.00 100.00
JO Jermaine O'Neal/25 8.00 20.00
JS John Stockton/25 50.00 100.00
LB Larry Bird/25 75.00 150.00
LJ LeBron James/25 1,500.00 3,000.00
MI Michael Jordan/25 1,500.00 3,000.00
MJ Magic Johnson/25 40.00 100.00
MR Michael Ray Richardson/25 8.00 20.00
NA Nate Archibald/25 15.00 30.00
PA Tony Parker/25 15.00 30.00
QR Quentin Richardson/25 8.00 20.00
RH Richard Hamilton/25 15.00 30.00
RJ Richard Jefferson/25 8.00 20.00
RO Brandon Roy/25 15.00 30.00
RT Reggie Theus/25 15.00 30.00
SK Steve Kerr/25 15.00 30.00
SN Steve Nash/25 40.00 100.00
TC Tyson Chandler/25 8.00 20.00
TM Tracy McGrady/25 20.00 50.00
TP Tayshaun Prince/25 8.00 20.00
VC Vince Carter/25 15.00 40.00
WF Walt Frazier/25 15.00 40.00
YM Yao Ming/25 25.00 60.00

2007-08 SPx Freshman Orientation

APPROXIMATE ODDS TWO PER BOX
*PATCHES: 1X TO 2.5X BASE HI
PATCH PRINT RUN 25 SER.#'d SETS
AA Arron Afflalo 2.00 5.00
AB Aaron Brooks 2.00 5.00
AH Al Horford 6.00 15.00
AL Acie Law 1.50 4.00
AT Al Thornton 1.50 4.00
BW Brandan Wright 2.00 5.00
CB Corey Brewer 2.00 5.00
CL Carl Landry 1.50 4.00
DC Daequan Cook 2.00 5.00
GD Glen Davis 2.00 5.00
GP Gabe Pruitt 1.50 4.00
JC Javaris Crittenton 1.50 4.00
JD Jared Dudley 2.00 5.00
JG Jeff Green 2.00 5.00
JM Josh McRoberts 1.50 4.00
JN Joakim Noah 2.50 6.00
JS Jason Smith 1.50 4.00
JW Julian Wright 1.50 4.00
KD Kevin Durant 40.00 100.00
MA Morris Almond 1.50 4.00
MC Mike Conley Jr. 6.00 15.00
MW Marcus Williams 1.50 4.00
NF Nick Fazekas 1.50 4.00
NY Nick Young 2.50 6.00
RS Rodney Stuckey 1.50 4.00
SH Spencer Hawes 1.50 4.00
SW Sean Williams 1.50 4.00
TU Alando Tucker 1.50 4.00
TY Thaddeus Young 2.50 6.00
WC Wilson Chandler 2.00 5.00

2007-08 SPx Freshman Orientation Autographs

PRINT RUN 25 TO 50 SER.#'d SETS
AA Arron Afflalo/50 5.00 12.00
AB Aaron Brooks/25 5.00 12.00
AH Al Horford/25 15.00 40.00
AL Acie Law/25 4.00 10.00
AT Al Thornton/25 4.00 10.00
BW Brandan Wright/25 5.00 12.00
CB Corey Brewer/25 5.00 12.00
CL Carl Landry/50 4.00 10.00
DC Daequan Cook/25 5.00 12.00
GD Glen Davis/50 5.00 12.00
GP Gabe Pruitt/50 4.00 10.00
JC Javaris Crittenton/25 4.00 10.00
JD Jared Dudley/25 5.00 12.00
JG Jeff Green/25 5.00 12.00
JM Josh McRoberts/50 4.00 10.00
JN Joakim Noah/25 6.00 15.00
JS Jason Smith/25 4.00 10.00
JW Julian Wright/25 4.00 10.00
KD Kevin Durant/25 500.00 1,000.00
MA Morris Almond/50 4.00 10.00
MC Mike Conley Jr./25 15.00 40.00
MW Marcus Williams/50 4.00 10.00
NF Nick Fazekas/50 4.00 10.00
NY Nick Young/25 6.00 15.00
RS Rodney Stuckey/25 4.00 10.00
SH Spencer Hawes/25 4.00 10.00
SW Sean Williams/25 4.00 10.00
TU Alando Tucker/25 4.00 10.00
TY Thaddeus Young/25 6.00 15.00
WC Wilson Chandler/50 5.00 12.00

2007-08 SPx Freshman Orientation Tandems

*PATCHES: .75X TO 2X BASE HI
PATCH PRINT RUN 15 SER.#'d SETS
AA A.Brooks/A.Afflalo 4.00 10.00
AB M.Almond/A.Brooks 3.00 8.00
AS R.Stuckey/A.Afflalo 4.00 10.00
CW S.Williams/W.Chandler 3.00 8.00
DD J.Dudley/J.Davidson 3.00 8.00
DG K.Durant/J.Green 20.00 50.00
DH K.Durant/A.Horford 40.00 10.00
DW S.Williams/J.Dudley 3.00 8.00
HB A.Horford/C.Brewer 5.00 12.00
HS S.Hawes/J.Smith 3.00 8.00
LC M.Conley/A.Law 3.00 8.00
NB C.Brewer/J.Noah 5.00 12.00
PD G.Davis/G.Pruitt 4.00 10.00
TC A.Thornton/J.Crittenton 3.00 8.00
TL A.Tucker/C.Landry 3.00 8.00
WW J.Wright/B.Wright 3.00 8.00
YC T.Young/J.Crittenton 3.00 8.00
YP N.Young/G.Pruitt 3.00 8.00
YS T.Young/J.Smith 3.00 8.00

2007-08 SPx Freshman Orientation Triples

ACC Cook/Crittenton/Almond 3.00 8.00
DGC Durant/Green/Conley 10.00 25.00
DLC Landry/Chandler/Davis 3.00 8.00
NHB Horford/Brewer/Noah 6.00 15.00
SLC Conley/Law/Stuckey 4.00 10.00
STW Williams/Smith/Tucker 3.00 8.00
TYD Young/Thornton/Dudley 3.00 8.00
WGW Green/Wright/Wright 4.00 10.00
YAB Young/Brooks/Afflalo 4.00 10.00

2007-08 SPx Super Scripts

APPROXIMATELY ONE PER BOX
AB Andrea Bargnani 2.50 6.00
AH Al Horford 10.00 25.00
AI Andre Iguodala 4.00 10.00
AJ Antawn Jamison 3.00 8.00
AL Acie Law 2.50 6.00
AT Al Thornton 2.50 6.00
BD Boris Diaw 3.00 8.00
BI Chauncey Billups 5.00 12.00
BO Chris Bosh 8.00 20.00
BR Brandon Roy 5.00 12.00
CA Carmelo Anthony 15.00 40.00
CP Chris Paul 30.00 80.00
DA Baron Davis 6.00 15.00
DG Daniel Gibson 2.50 6.00
DH Dwight Howard 8.00 20.00
DJ D.J. Strawberry 2.50 6.00
EO Emeka Okafor 3.00 8.00
JE Al Jefferson 2.50 6.00
JG Jeff Green 3.00 8.00
JJ Jarrett Jack 3.00 8.00
JN Joakim Noah 4.00 10.00
KB Kobe Bryant 125.00 300.00
KD Kevin Durant 400.00 800.00
KK Kyle Korver 4.00 10.00
LB Leandro Barbosa 3.00 8.00
LH Larry Hughes 3.00 8.00
LJ LeBron James 1,000.00 2,000.00
MC Mike Conley Jr. 10.00 25.00
PR Tayshaun Prince 4.00 10.00
QR Quentin Richardson 2.50 6.00
RF Randy Foye 3.00 8.00
RH Richard Hamilton 5.00 12.00
RJ Richard Jefferson 3.00 8.00
RM Rashad McCants 2.50 6.00
SH Spencer Hawes 2.50 6.00
SM Sean May 2.50 6.00
TC Tyson Chandler 4.00 10.00
TF T.J. Ford 2.50 6.00
TP Tony Parker 8.00 20.00
VC Vince Carter 8.00 20.00

2007-08 SPx Winning Materials Jersey Numbers

APPROXIMATELY TWO PER BOX
*STAT JSY: SAME VALUE
APPROXIMATELY TWO PER BOX
AB Andrea Bargnani 1.50 4.00
AH Al Harrington 2.00 5.00
AJ Al Jefferson 1.50 4.00
AK Andrei Kirilenko 2.00 5.00
AM Alonzo Mourning 5.00 12.00
AR Ron Artest 2.50 6.00
AS Amare Stoudemire 2.50 6.00
AW Antoine Walker 2.50 6.00
BB Bruce Bowen 2.00 5.00
BD Baron Davis 2.00 5.00
BG Ben Gordon 2.00 5.00
BI Chauncey Billups 3.00 8.00
BM Brad Miller 2.00 5.00
BO Andrew Bogut 2.00 5.00
BR Brandon Roy 3.00 8.00
BU Caron Butler 2.00 5.00
BY Andrew Bynum 1.50 4.00
CA Carmelo Anthony 4.00 10.00
CB Carlos Boozer 2.00 5.00
CH Chris Bosh 3.00 8.00
CM Corey Maggette 2.00 5.00
CP Chris Paul 5.00 12.00
CV Charlie Villanueva 1.50 4.00
CW Chris Webber 3.00 8.00
DE Deron Williams 2.00 5.00
DG Danny Granger 1.50 4.00
DH Dwight Howard 3.00 8.00
DI Boris Diaw 2.00 5.00
DW Delonte West 1.50 4.00
EC Eddy Curry 2.00 5.00
GG Gerald Green 2.00 5.00
GH Grant Hill 4.00 10.00
GO Drew Gooden 2.00 5.00
GP Gary Payton 4.00 10.00
HA Devin Harris 1.50 4.00
IG Andre Iguodala 2.50 6.00
JA Antawn Jamison 2.00 5.00
JH Josh Howard 2.00 5.00
JJ Joe Johnson 2.00 5.00
JK Jarrett Jack 2.00 5.00
JO Jermaine O'Neal 2.50 6.00
JR Jason Richardson 2.50 6.00
JS J.R. Smith 2.50 6.00
JT Jason Terry 2.00 5.00
JW Jason Williams 4.00 10.00
KB Kobe Bryant 60.00 150.00
KG Kevin Garnett 6.00 15.00
KH Kirk Hinrich 2.50 6.00
KM Kenyon Martin 2.00 5.00
LD Luol Deng 2.00 5.00
LH Larry Hughes 2.00 5.00
LJ LeBron James 10.00 25.00
LO Lamar Odom 2.00 5.00
MA Sean May 2.00 5.00
MB Mike Bibby 2.50 6.00
MC Antonio McDyess 2.00 5.00
MF Michael Finley 2.50 6.00
MG Manu Ginobili 5.00 12.00
MI Andre Miller 2.00 5.00
MR Michael Redd 2.00 5.00
MW Marvin Williams 1.50 4.00
NH Nene 2.00 5.00
PG Pau Gasol 4.00 10.00
PS Peja Stojakovic 2.00 5.00
QR Quentin Richardson 1.50 4.00
RA Ray Allen 4.00 10.00
RF Raymond Felton 2.00 5.00
RG Rudy Gay 2.00 5.00
RH Richard Hamilton 3.00 8.00
RJ Richard Jefferson 2.00 5.00
RL Rashard Lewis 2.00 5.00
RW Rasheed Wallace 3.00 8.00
SC Sam Cassell 2.00 5.00
SH Shawn Marion 2.50 6.00
SL Shaun Livingston 2.00 5.00
SM Josh Smith 1.50 4.00
SN Steve Nash 5.00 12.00
SO Shaquille O'Neal 10.00 25.00
ST Stephon Marbury 3.00 8.00
TD Tim Duncan 6.00 15.00
TJ T.J. Ford 1.50 4.00
TM Tracy McGrady 4.00 10.00
TP Tayshaun Prince 2.50 6.00
VC Vince Carter 5.00 12.00
WE David West 2.00 5.00
WI Chris Wilcox 2.00 5.00
WS Wally Szczerbiak 2.00 5.00
YM Yao Ming 6.00 15.00
ZI Zydrunas Ilgauskas 2.00 5.00
ZR Zach Randolph 2.50 6.00

2007-08 SPx Winning Materials Combos

*PATCHES: 1X TO 2.5X BASE HI
PATCH PRINT RUN 50 SER.#'d SETS
AA A.Iverson/A.Mourning 6.00 15.00
BA R.Artest/M.Bibby 3.00 8.00
BF C.Bosh/T.Ford 4.00 10.00
BO C.Bosh/J.O'Neal 3.00 8.00
BP C.Billups/T.Prince 3.00 8.00
CL E.Curry/D.Lee 3.00 8.00
DH B.Davis/A.Harrington 3.00 8.00
DP T.Duncan/T.Parker 4.00 10.00
FM R.Felton/S.May 3.00 8.00
GF K.Garnett/R.Foye 4.00 10.00
GG P.Gasol/R.Gay 3.00 8.00
GH D.Gooden/K.Hinrich 3.00 8.00
GO J.O'Neal/D.Granger 3.00 8.00
HB R.Hamilton/C.Billups 4.00 10.00
HH D.Howard/G.Hill 5.00 12.00
HJ L.James/L.Hughes 6.00 15.00
JA G.Arenas/A.Jamison 3.00 8.00
JG A.Jefferson/G.Green 3.00 8.00
KB C.Boozer/A.Kirilenko 3.00 8.00
KC V.Carter/J.Kidd 4.00 10.00
KL K.Bryant/L.Odom 40.00 100.00
LW R.Lewis/C.Wilcox 3.00 8.00
MA C.Anthony/K.Martin 4.00 10.00
MB E.Brand/C.Maggette 3.00 8.00
MI A.Iguodala/A.Miller 3.00 8.00
MM Y.Ming/T.McGrady 5.00 12.00
MR S.Marbury/Z.Randolph 3.00 8.00
NH D.Nowitzki/J.Howard 4.00 10.00
NJ Nene/J.Smith 3.00 8.00
PA R.Allen/P.Pierce 5.00 12.00
RB A.Bogut/M.Redd 3.00 8.00
RO E.Okafor/J.Richardson 3.00 8.00
SD A.Stoudemire/B.Diaw 4.00 10.00
SW M.Williams/J.Smith 3.00 8.00
WG B.Gordon/B.Wallace 3.00 8.00
WM D.Williams/P.Millsap 4.00 10.00
WP J.Williams/G.Payton 4.00 10.00
WW C.Webber/R.Wallace 4.00 10.00

2007-08 SPx Winning Materials Combos Patches Autographs

PRINT RUN 8 TO 25 SER.#'d SETS
BP C.Billups/T.Prince/15 25.00 60.00
GG P.Gasol/R.Gay/25 30.00 60.00
SD A.Stoudemire/B.Diaw/25 30.00 80.00
SW M.Williams/J.Smith/25 12.00 30.00
WM D.Williams/P.Millsap/25 30.00 60.00

2007-08 SPx Winning Materials Triples

*PATCHES: .75X TO 2X BASE HI
PATCH PRINT RUN 25 SER.#'d SETS
AMN Anthony/Martin/Nene 6.00 15.00
BMJ Bryant/James/McGrady 125.00 300.00
CAW Camby/Wallace/Artest 4.00 10.00
HPM Hamilton/Prince/McDyess 5.00 12.00
JAB Arenas/Butler/Jamison 4.00 10.00
JSW Johnson/Williams/Smith 4.00 10.00
KCJ Carter/Kidd/Jefferson 5.00 12.00
MBL Brand/Maggette/Livingston 4.00 10.00
NIP Nash/Parker/Iverson 6.00 15.00
NMS Nash/Stoudemire/Marion 5.00 12.00
PAG Pierce/Jefferson/Green 4.00 10.00
PGB Parker/Ginobili/Bowen 5.00 12.00
PMO O'Neal/Mourning/Payton 8.00 20.00
RBV Bogut/Redd/Villanueva 4.00 10.00
RMF Okafor/May/Felton 4.00 10.00
TNH Nowitzki/Howard/Terry 5.00 12.00
WDG Wallace/Deng/Gordon 4.00 10.00
WHR Webber/Howard/Rose 4.00 10.00
ZGJ Ilgauskas/Hughes/Gooden 4.00 10.00

2008-09 SPx

COMP.SET w/o SP's (90) 60.00 150.00
131-178 RC PRINT RUN 599 SER.#'d SETS
1 Kevin Garnett 2.00 5.00
2 Ray Allen 1.25 3.00
3 Paul Pierce 1.25 3.00
4 Chauncey Billups 1.00 2.50
5 Rasheed Wallace 1.00 2.50
6 Richard Hamilton .75 2.00
7 Tayshaun Prince .75 2.00
8 Dwight Howard 1.00 2.50
9 Hedo Turkoglu .60 1.50
10 Rashard Lewis .60 1.50
11 Daniel Gibson .50 1.25
12 Ben Wallace 1.00 2.50
13 LeBron James 20.00 50.00
14 Antawn Jamison .60 1.50
15 Caron Butler .60 1.50
16 Gilbert Arenas .75 2.00
17 Chris Bosh 1.00 2.50
18 Jamario Moon .50 1.25
19 T.J. Ford .50 1.25
20 Andre Iguodala .60 1.50
21 Andre Miller .60 1.50
22 Thaddeus Young .60 1.50
23 Al Horford .75 2.00
24 Joe Johnson .75 2.00
25 Josh Smith .50 1.25
26 Danny Granger .60 1.50
27 Jermaine O'Neal .75 2.00
28 Devin Harris .50 1.25
29 Richard Jefferson .60 1.50
30 Vince Carter 1.50 4.00
31 Ben Gordon .60 1.50
32 Joakim Noah .50 1.25
33 Luol Deng .60 1.50
34 Emeka Okafor .50 1.25
35 Gerald Wallace .60 1.50
36 Jason Richardson .75 2.00
37 Andrew Bogut .60 1.50
38 Michael Redd .60 1.50
39 Yi Jianlian 1.00 2.50
40 Eddy Curry .50 1.25
41 Jamal Crawford .75 2.00
42 Stephon Marbury .75 2.00
43 Zach Randolph .75 2.00
44 Daequan Cook .50 1.25
45 Dwyane Wade 1.50 4.00
46 Shawn Marion .75 2.00
47 Jordan Farmar .50 1.25
48 Kobe Bryant 30.00 80.00
49 Pau Gasol 1.00 2.50
50 Lamar Odom .60 1.50
51 Chris Paul 1.50 4.00
52 David West .60 1.50
53 Peja Stojakovic .60 1.50
54 Manu Ginobili 1.50 4.00
55 Tim Duncan 2.00 5.00
56 Tony Parker 1.00 2.50
57 Carlos Boozer .60 1.50
58 Deron Williams .60 1.50
59 Mehmet Okur .50 1.25
60 Luis Scola .60 1.50
61 Tracy McGrady 1.25 3.00
62 Yao Ming 2.00 5.00
63 Amare Stoudemire .75 2.00
64 Shaquille O'Neal 2.50 6.00
65 Steve Nash 1.50 4.00
66 Jason Kidd 1.25 3.00
67 Dirk Nowitzki 2.00 5.00
68 Josh Howard .60 1.50
69 Allen Iverson 1.50 4.00
70 Carmelo Anthony 1.00 2.50
71 Kenyon Martin .60 1.50
72 Baron Davis .75 2.00
73 Monta Ellis .60 1.50
74 Stephen Jackson .60 1.50
75 Brandon Roy .60 1.50
76 Greg Oden .50 1.25
77 LaMarcus Aldridge .75 2.00
78 Francisco Garcia .50 1.25
79 Kevin Martin .60 1.50
80 Ron Artest .75 2.00
81 Al Thornton .50 1.25
82 Chris Kaman .50 1.25
83 Elton Brand .60 1.50
84 Al Jefferson .50 1.25
85 Corey Brewer .60 1.50
86 Mike Conley Jr. .60 1.50
87 Rudy Gay .75 2.00
88 Damien Wilkins .50 1.25
89 Jeff Green .60 1.50
90 Kevin Durant 3.00 8.00
91 Danilo Gallinari RC 5.00 12.00
92 Rudy Fernandez RC 2.50 6.00
93 Sean Singletary RC 2.00 5.00
94 Othello Hunter RC 3.00 8.00
95 Shan Foster RC 2.00 5.00
96 Mike Taylor RC 2.00 5.00
97 Joe Crawford RC 2.00 5.00
98 Thomas Gardner RC 3.00 8.00
99 Nicolas Batum RC 4.00 10.00
100 Malik Hairston RC 2.00 5.00
101 Danilo Gallinari RC 5.00 12.00
102 Rudy Fernandez RC 2.50 6.00
103 Sean Singletary RC 2.00 5.00
104 Othello Hunter RC 3.00 8.00
105 Shan Foster RC 2.00 5.00
106 Mike Taylor RC 2.00 5.00
107 Joe Crawford RC 2.00 5.00
108 Thomas Gardner RC 3.00 8.00
109 Nicolas Batum RC 4.00 10.00
110 Malik Hairston RC 2.00 5.00
111 Derrick Rose JSY AU RC 125.00 300.00
112 Michael Beasley JSY AU RC 8.00 20.00
113 O.J. Mayo JSY AU RC 6.00 15.00
114 R.Westbrook JSY AU RC 150.00 400.00
115 Kevin Love JSY AU RC 15.00 40.00
116 Eric Gordon JSY AU RC 12.00 30.00
117 D.J. Augustin JSY AU RC 8.00 20.00
118 Jerryd Bayless JSY AU RC 6.00 15.00
119 Brook Lopez JSY AU RC 10.00 25.00
120 Brandon Rush JSY AU RC 5.00 12.00
121 Derrick Rose JSY AU RC 125.00 300.00
122 Michael Beasley JSY AU RC 8.00 20.00
123 O.J. Mayo JSY AU RC 6.00 15.00
124 R. Westbrook JSY AU RC 150.00 400.00
125 Kevin Love JSY AU RC 15.00 40.00
126 Eric Gordon JSY AU RC 12.00 30.00
127 D.J. Augustin JSY AU RC 8.00 20.00
128 Jerryd Bayless JSY AU RC 6.00 15.00
129 Brook Lopez JSY AU RC 10.00 25.00
130 Brandon Rush JSY AU RC 5.00 12.00
131 Joe Alexander JSY AU RC 3.00 8.00
132 Jason Thompson JSY AU RC 3.00 8.00
133 Anthony Randolph JSY AU RC 3.00 8.00
134 Robin Lopez JSY AU RC 4.00 10.00
135 Marreese Speights JSY AU RC 4.00 10.00
136 Roy Hibbert JSY AU RC 4.00 10.00
137 Javale McGee JSY AU RC 5.00 12.00
138 J.J. Hickson JSY AU RC 3.00 8.00
139 Ryan Anderson JSY AU RC 4.00 10.00
140 Courtney Lee JSY AU RC 4.00 10.00
141 Kosta Koufos JSY AU RC 3.00 8.00
142 George Hill JSY AU RC 5.00 12.00
143 Darrell Arthur JSY AU RC 4.00 10.00
144 Donte Greene JSY AU RC 3.00 8.00
145 D.J. White JSY AU RC 3.00 8.00
146 J.R. Giddens JSY AU RC 3.00 8.00
147 Walter Sharpe JSY AU RC 3.00 8.00
148 Joey Dorsey JSY AU RC 3.00 8.00
149 Mario Chalmers JSY AU RC 5.00 12.00
150 DeAndre Jordan JSY AU RC 6.00 15.00
151 Kyle Weaver JSY AU RC 3.00 8.00
152 Sonny Weems JSY AU RC 3.00 8.00
153 C.Douglas-Roberts JSY AU RC 3.00 8.00
154 Patrick Ewing Jr. JSY AU RC 3.00 8.00
155 Joe Alexander JSY AU RC 3.00 8.00
156 Jason Thompson JSY AU RC 3.00 8.00
157 Anthony Randolph JSY AU RC 3.00 8.00
158 Robin Lopez JSY AU RC 4.00 10.00
159 Marreese Speights JSY AU RC 4.00 10.00
160 Roy Hibbert JSY AU RC 4.00 10.00
161 Javale McGee JSY AU RC 5.00 12.00
162 J.J. Hickson JSY AU RC 3.00 8.00
163 Ryan Anderson JSY AU RC 4.00 10.00
164 Courtney Lee JSY AU RC 4.00 10.00
165 Kosta Koufos JSY AU RC 3.00 8.00
166 George Hill JSY AU RC 5.00 12.00
167 Darrell Arthur JSY AU RC 4.00 10.00
168 Donte Greene JSY AU RC 3.00 8.00
169 D.J. White JSY AU RC 3.00 8.00
170 J.R. Giddens JSY AU RC 3.00 8.00
171 Walter Sharpe JSY AU RC 3.00 8.00
172 Joey Dorsey JSY AU RC 3.00 8.00
173 Mario Chalmers JSY AU RC 5.00 12.00
174 DeAndre Jordan JSY AU RC 6.00 15.00
175 Kyle Weaver JSY AU RC 3.00 8.00
176 Sonny Weems JSY AU RC 3.00 8.00
177 Chris Douglas-Roberts JSY AU RC 3.00 8.00
178 Patrick Ewing Jr. JSY AU RC 3.00 8.00

2008-09 SPx Radiance

*1-90 RADIANCE: 5X TO 12X BASE HI
*91-110 RAD: .6X TO 1.5X BASE HI
*111-178 RAD: .75X TO 2X BASE HI
PRINT RUN 25 SER.#'d SETS

2008-09 SPx Dual Scripts

STATED PRINT RUN 25 TO 50 SER.#'d SETS
DSAB Almond/A.Brooks/50 5.00 12.00
DSAG E.Gordon/Augustin/50 8.00 20.00
DSAT Tucker/Azubuike/50 5.00 12.00
DSBA A.Afflalo/M.Bibby/50 5.00 12.00
DSBG C.Brewer/J.Green/50 5.00 12.00
DSBM C.Billups/A.Miller/50 5.00 12.00
DSBR D.Rose/Beasley/50 100.00 250.00
DSBT Thornton/Bynum/50 10.00 25.00
DSCB Crittenton/Brooks/50 5.00 12.00
DSCP P.Pierce/V.Carter/50 30.00 80.00
DSEE Ewing/Ewing Jr./25 60.00 120.00
DSFL A.Law/R.Felton/50 6.00 15.00
DSFS Strawberry/Farmar/50 5.00 12.00
DSGL K.Love/Gallinari/50 30.00 80.00
DSGS Sessions/Gibson/50 5.00 12.00
DSGW J.Wright/R.Gay/50 5.00 12.00
DSIM Moon/Iguodala/50 5.00 12.00
DSKH Hawes/Kaman/50 6.00 15.00
DSLL B.Lopez/R.Lopez/50 10.00 25.00
DSMW Mayo/Westbrook/50 75.00 200.00
DSPC M.Conley/C.Paul/50 40.00 100.00
DSPN J.Noah/T.Prince/50 15.00 40.00
DSPS G.Pruitt/Sessions/50 6.00 15.00
DSPW S.Williams/Powe/50 5.00 12.00
DSRB Bayless/B.Rush/50 6.00 15.00
DSSS J.Smith/Stuckey/50 6.00 15.00
DSTA Alexander/Thompson/50 5.00 12.00
DSWL D.West/C.Landry/50 5.00 12.00

2008-09 SPx Endorsements

STATED PRINT RUN 12 TO 25 SER.#'d SETS
SPXBR Bill Russell/25 400.00 800.00
SPXCP Chris Paul/25 60.00 150.00
SPXDR David Robinson/25 75.00 200.00
SPXJE Julius Erving/25 100.00 250.00
SPXJS John Stockton/12 75.00 200.00
SPXKB Kobe Bryant/24 1,000.00 2,000.00
SPXKD Kevin Durant/25 125.00 300.00
SPXKG Kevin Garnett/25 100.00 250.00
SPXLB Larry Bird/25 100.00 200.00
SPXLJ LeBron James/23 800.00 1,500.00
SPXMJ Magic Johnson/25 100.00 250.00
SPXOR Oscar Robertson/25 60.00 150.00
SPXSN Steve Nash/25 50.00 120.00
SPXYM Yao Ming/25 125.00 300.00

2008-09 SPx Freshman Orientation

STATED ODDS 1:1.5
*PATCH: 1.25X TO 3X BASE HI
PATCH PRINT RUN 25 SER.#'d SETS
FOAD Darrell Arthur 2.00 5.00
FOAR Anthony Randolph 1.50 4.00
FOBL Brook Lopez 3.00 8.00
FOBR Brandon Rush 1.50 4.00
FOCD Chris Douglas-Roberts 1.50 4.00
FODA D.J. Augustin 2.50 6.00
FODG Donte Greene 1.50 4.00
FODR Derrick Rose 12.00 30.00
FODW D.J. White 1.50 4.00
FOEG Eric Gordon 4.00 10.00
FOGH George Hill 2.50 6.00
FOJA Joe Alexander 1.50 4.00
FOJB Jerryd Bayless 2.00 5.00
FOJG J.R. Giddens 1.50 4.00
FOJH J.J. Hickson 1.50 4.00
FOJM Javale McGee 2.50 6.00
FOJT Jason Thompson 1.50 4.00
FOKK Kosta Koufos 1.50 4.00
FOKL Kevin Love 5.00 12.00
FOMB Michael Beasley 2.50 6.00
FOMC Mario Chalmers 2.50 6.00
FOMS Marreese Speights 2.00 5.00
FOOM O.J. Mayo 2.00 5.00
FOPE Patrick Ewing Jr. 1.50 4.00
FORA Ryan Anderson 2.00 5.00
FORH Roy Hibbert 2.00 5.00
FORL Robin Lopez 2.00 5.00
FORW Russell Westbrook 15.00 40.00
FOSW Sonny Weems 1.50 4.00
FOWS Walter Sharpe 1.50 4.00

2008-09 SPx Signature Block

COMBINED AUTO/MEM ODDS 1:10
SBAJ Antawn Jamison 4.00 10.00
SBAM Alonzo Mourning 40.00 100.00
SBBA B.J. Armstrong 4.00 10.00
SBCM Chris Mullin 10.00 25.00
SBDF Derek Fisher 8.00 20.00
SBDH Dwight Howard 12.00 30.00
SBDM Danny Manning 5.00 12.00
SBDW Dominique Wilkins 15.00 30.00
SBFG Francisco Garcia 4.00 10.00
SBKG Kevin Garnett 30.00 80.00
SBLH Larry Hughes 4.00 10.00
SBLO Lamar Odom 8.00 20.00
SBLS Luis Scola 4.00 10.00
SBMC Maurice Cheeks 5.00 12.00
SBMJ Michael Jordan 400.00 800.00
SBMR Micheal Ray Richardson 4.00 10.00
SBPO Patrick O'Bryant 4.00 10.00
SBQR Quentin Richardson 4.00 10.00
SBSM Sidney Moncrief 4.00 10.00
SBSP Sam Perkins 4.00 10.00
SBTC Tom Chambers 4.00 10.00
SBVC Vince Carter 12.00 30.00

2008-09 SPx Super Scripts

COMBINED AUTO/MEM ODDS 1:10
SSAL Acie Law 3.00 8.00
SSBI Chauncey Billups 4.00 10.00
SSBO Chris Bosh 8.00 20.00
SSCM Chris Mihm 3.00 8.00
SSDH Dwight Howard 10.00 25.00
SSDS D.J. Strawberry 3.00 8.00
SSFG Francisco Garcia 3.00 8.00
SSJC Javaris Crittenton 3.00 8.00
SSJD Jared Dudley 3.00 8.00
SSJF Jordan Farmar 5.00 12.00
SSJN Joakim Noah 8.00 20.00
SSJS Jason Smith 3.00 8.00
SSJW Julian Wright 3.00 8.00
SSKB Kobe Bryant 500.00 1,000.00
SSKD Kevin Durant 40.00 100.00
SSKG Kevin Garnett 30.00 80.00
SSKK Kyle Korver 3.00 8.00
SSMA Morris Almond 3.00 8.00
SSMW Mario West 3.00 8.00
SSRS Ramon Sessions 4.00 10.00
SSSH Spencer Hawes 3.00 8.00
SSSW Sean Williams 3.00 8.00
SSWI Shelden Williams 3.00 8.00

2008-09 SPx Triple Scripts

PRINT RUN 25 SER.#'d SETS
TSBWA Bryant/Kareem/West 500.00 1,000.00
TSMMS McGrady/Ming/Scola 40.00 100.00
TSNKP Parker/Kidd/Nash 100.00 250.00
TSPAG Garnett/Pierce/Allen 300.00 600.00
TSPWR Paul/Williams/Roy 50.00 120.00
TSRBM Rose/Beasley/Mayo 50.00 120.00
TSSHB Howard/Stoudemire/Bynum 40.00 100.00
TSWJA James/Anthony/West 1,000.00 2,000.00

2008-09 SPx Winning Materials Initials

STATED ODDS 1:1.5
*JSY NUM: .4X TO 1X BASE HI
*PATCHES: 1X TO 2.5X BASE HI
PATCH PRINT RUN 25 SER.#'d SETS
WMIAB Andrew Bynum 1.50 4.00
WMIAI Allen Iverson 5.00 12.00
WMIAJ Antawn Jamison 2.00 5.00
WMIAM Andre Miller 2.00 5.00
WMIAS Amare Stoudemire 2.50 6.00
WMIAT Al Thornton 1.50 4.00
WMIBG Ben Gordon 2.00 5.00
WMIBR Brandon Roy 2.00 5.00
WMICA Carmelo Anthony 3.00 8.00
WMICB Chris Bosh 3.00 8.00
WMICM Corey Maggette 2.00 5.00
WMICP Chris Paul 5.00 12.00
WMIDG Daniel Gibson 1.50 4.00
WMIDH Dwight Howard 3.00 8.00
WMIDN Dirk Nowitzki 6.00 15.00
WMIEB Elton Brand 2.00 5.00
WMIEO Emeka Okafor 1.50 4.00
WMIGD Glen Davis 1.50 4.00
WMIHA Hilton Armstrong 1.50 4.00
WMIIG Andre Iguodala 2.00 5.00
WMIJF Jordan Farmar 1.50 4.00
WMIJG Jeff Green 2.00 5.00
WMIJH Josh Howard 2.00 5.00
WMIJK Jason Kidd 6.00 15.00
WMIJO Jermaine O'Neal 2.50 6.00
WMIJS J.R. Smith 2.50 6.00
WMIKB Kobe Bryant 60.00 150.00
WMIKD Kevin Durant 10.00 25.00
WMIKG Kevin Garnett 6.00 15.00
WMIKH Kirk Hinrich 2.00 5.00
WMILA LaMarcus Aldridge 2.50 6.00
WMILH Larry Hughes 2.00 5.00
WMILJ LeBron James 60.00 150.00
WMILO Lamar Odom 2.00 5.00

WMIPP Paul Pierce 4.00 10.00
WMIRA Ray Allen 4.00 10.00
WMIRF Raymond Felton 1.50 4.00
WMIRG Rudy Gay 2.50 6.00
WMIRL Rashard Lewis 2.00 5.00
WMISO Shaquille O'Neal 8.00 20.00
WMISW Shelden Williams 1.50 4.00
WMITM Tracy McGrady 4.00 10.00
WMITP Tayshaun Prince 2.50 6.00
WMIVC Vince Carter 5.00 12.00
WMIYM Yao Ming 6.00 15.00

2008-09 SPx Winning Materials Patches SPx

*PATCHES: 1X TO 2.5X HI COLUMN
STATED PRINT RUN 25 SER.#'d SETS
SPXLJ LeBron James 40.00 100.00

2008-09 SPx Winning Materials Combos

COMMON CARD 3.00 8.00
STATED ODDS 1:1.5
*PATCHES: 1.25X TO 3X HI COLUMN
PATCH PRINT RUN 25 SER.#'d SETS
WMCAD K.Durant/C.Anthony 8.00 20.00
WMCAG R.Allen/K.Garnett 6.00 15.00
WMCAB B.Roy/L.Aldridge 3.00 8.00
WMCBB A.Bargnani/C.Bosh 3.00 8.00
WMCBF J.Farmer/A.Bynum 3.00 8.00
WMCBG K.Bryant/P.Gasol 40.00 100.00
WMCBJ L.James/K.Bryant 200.00 500.00
WMCBL A.Law/M.Bibby 3.00 8.00
WMCBM R.Brewer/P.Millsap 3.00 8.00
WMCBO A.Bargnani/J.O'Neal 3.00 8.00
WMCBW D.Williams/C.Boozer 3.00 8.00
WMCCH D.Harris/V.Carter 3.00 8.00
WMCCL S.Livingston/M.Camby 3.00 8.00
WMCCN K.Martin/Nene 3.00 8.00
WMCCT A.Thornton/M.Camby 3.00 8.00
WMCDG J.Green/K.Durant 6.00 15.00
WMCDM M.Ginobili/T.Duncan 4.00 10.00
WMCEJ M.Johnson/J.Erving 6.00 15.00
WMCEW B.Wright/M.Ellis 3.00 8.00
WMCFD R.Felton/J.Davidson 3.00 8.00
WMCFW M.Webster/C.Frye 3.00 8.00
WMCGD B.Gordon/L.Deng 3.00 8.00
WMCGP P.Pierce/K.Garnett 6.00 15.00
WMCHB C.Billups/R.Hamilton 3.00 8.00
WMCHG D.Gooden/L.Hughes 3.00 8.00
WMCHN D.Nowitzki/J.Howard 3.00 8.00
WMCIA C.Anthony/A.Iverson 4.00 10.00
WMCIY A.Iguodala/T.Young 3.00 8.00
WMCJB A.Jamison/C.Butler 3.00 8.00
WMCJF R.Foye/A.Jefferson 3.00 8.00
WMCJH J.Johnson/A.Horford 3.00 8.00
WMCJP M.Jordan/S.Pippen 40.00 100.00
WMCJS J.Smith/J.Johnson 3.00 8.00
WMCKN D.Nowitzki/J.Kidd 4.00 10.00
WMCKO A.Kirilenko/M.Okur 3.00 8.00
WMCLH D.Howard/R.Lewis 3.00 8.00
WMCMB E.Brand/A.Miller 3.00 8.00
WMCMD K.Martin/Q.Douby 3.00 8.00
WMCMH S.Marion/U.Haslem 3.00 8.00
WMCMM T.McGrady/Y.Ming 4.00 10.00
WMCMR N.Robinson/S.Marbury 3.00 8.00
WMCMS J.Stockton/K.Malone 4.00 10.00
WMCNH S.Nash/G.Hill 6.00 15.00
WMCPG T.Parker/M.Ginobili 4.00 10.00
WMCPM D.Majerle/M.Price 3.00 8.00
WMCPW C.Paul/D.Williams 3.00 8.00
WMCPY N.Young/O.Pecherov 3.00 8.00
WMCRB A.Bogut/M.Redd 3.00 8.00
WMCRP G.Pruitt/R.Rondo 3.00 8.00
WMCRR Q.Richardson/Z.Randolph 3.00 8.00
WMCRT I.Thomas/D.Rodman 5.00 12.00
WMCRW J.Richardson/G.Wallace 3.00 8.00
WMCSE J.Starks/P.Ewing 4.00 10.00
WMCSH D.Howard/A.Stoudemire 3.00 8.00
WMCSO A.Stoudemire/S.O'Neal 4.00 10.00
WMCSP P.Stojakovic/C.Paul 4.00 10.00
WMCTN J.Noah/T.Thomas 3.00 8.00
WMCWJ B.Wallace/L.James 6.00 15.00
WMCWO E.Okafor/G.Wallace 3.00 8.00
WMCWP T.Prince/R.Wallace 4.00 10.00

2008-09 SPx Winning Materials Trios

COMBINED MEM STATED ODDS 1:1.5
*PATCH: 1.5X TO 4X BASE HI
PATCH PRINT RUN 15 SER.#'d SETS
WMTBBG Bargnani/Bosh/Graham 4.00 10.00
WMTBGB Bryant/Gasol/Bynum 40.00 100.00
WMTBJS Smith/Johnson/Bibby 4.00 10.00
WMTBLS Scola/Landry/Battier 4.00 10.00
WMTBWB Williams/Boozer/Brewer 5.00 12.00
WMTCBH Boone/Carter/Harris 4.00 10.00
WMTCKT Thornton/Camby/Kaman 4.00 10.00
WMTCSP Stojakovic/Paul/Chandler 5.00 12.00
WMTDMG Martin/Douby/Garcia 4.00 10.00
WMTDPG Parker/Duncan/Ginobili 15.00 40.00
WMTGFW Granger/Ford/Williams 4.00 10.00
WMTHDG Gordon/Deng/Hinrich 4.00 10.00
WMTHWS Stuckey/Hamilton/Wallace 4.00 10.00
WMTJBY Jamison/Butler/Young 4.00 10.00
WMTJMF Foye/Jefferson/McCants 4.00 10.00
WMTKIA Anthony/Iverson/Martin 6.00 15.00
WMTKNH Nowitzki/Howard/Kidd 5.00 12.00
WMTLAH Howard/Lewis/Arroyo 4.00 10.00
WMTMEW Wright/Ellis/Maggette 4.00 10.00
WMTMIY Iguodala/Miller/Young 4.00 10.00
WMTMMH Marion/Haslem/Mourning 5.00 12.00
WMTMRC Crawford/Marbury/Randolph 4.00 10.00
WMTNSO Stoudemire/O'Neal/Nash 6.00 15.00
WMTPAG Allen/Garnett/Pierce 25.00 60.00
WMTPDG Green/Durant/Petro 12.00 30.00
WMTRRB Bogut/Redd/Ridnour 4.00 10.00
WMTRWO Okafor/Wallace/Richardson 4.00 10.00
WMTTGF Gay/Thomas/Farmar 4.00 10.00
WMTWAR Roy/Aldridge/Webster 4.00 10.00
WMTWJG Wallace/James/Gibson 25.00 60.00

2014-15 SPx

JSY AU PRINT RUN B/WN 250-499 COPIES PER
1 Pervis Ellison .60 1.50
2 Alonzo Mourning 1.50 4.00
3 Anfernee Hardaway 2.50 6.00
4 Antonio McDyess .75 2.00
5 Bill Russell 3.00 8.00
6 Bill Walton 1.50 4.00
7 Shaquille O'Neal 4.00 10.00
8 A.C. Green 1.00 2.50
9 Christian Laettner 1.00 2.50
10 Alex English 1.25 3.00
11 Danny Manning .75 2.00
12 Bo Kimble SP .75 2.00
13 David Robinson 2.00 5.00
14 Doc Rivers 1.00 2.50
15 Dave Cowens 1.25 3.00
16 Grant Hill 1.50 4.00
17 David Thompson 1.00 2.50
18 Kenny Anderson .75 2.00
19 Vinny Del Negro .75 2.00
20 Allan Houston 1.00 2.50
21 James Harden 2.00 5.00
22 James Worthy 1.50 4.00
23 Jerry West 2.50 6.00
24 Jerry Lucas 1.25 3.00
25 Byron Scott 1.00 2.50
26 John Stockton 2.00 5.00
27 John Salley .75 2.00
28 Julius Erving 2.50 6.00
29 Elvin Hayes 1.50 4.00
30 Eric Piatkowski .60 1.50
31 Micheal Ray Richardson .75 2.00
32 Larry Bird 4.00 10.00
33 Joe Smith .75 2.00
34 LeBron James 8.00 20.00
35 Magic Johnson 4.00 10.00
36 Michael Jordan 8.00 20.00
37 Harold Miner 1.00 2.50
38 Bo Outlaw .60 1.50
39 Donyell Marshall .60 1.50
40 Jay Williams .75 2.00
41 Reggie Theus .75 2.00
42 Keith Smart 1.00 2.50
43 Stacey Augmon .60 1.50
44 Nick Van Exel 1.00 2.50
45 Sleepy Floyd .75 2.00
46 Stephen Curry 8.00 20.00
47 Bill Laimbeer 1.00 2.50
48 Brad Daugherty .75 2.00
49 Yao Ming 2.50 6.00
50 Jerry Stackhouse 1.00 2.50
51 Clint Capela 3.00 8.00
52 P.J. Hairston .75 2.00
53 Dario Saric 1.50 4.00
54 Kyle Anderson 1.25 3.00
55 Joe Harris 1.25 3.00
56 Elfrid Payton 1.25 3.00
57 Josh Huestis .75 2.00
58 Aaron Gordon 4.00 10.00
59 Jordan Adams .75 2.00
60 Jusuf Nurkic 2.50 6.00
61 C.J. Wilcox .75 2.00
62 Gary Harris 1.25 3.00
63 Doug McDermott 1.25 3.00
64 Zach LaVine 5.00 12.00
65 Mitch McGary .75 2.00
66 James Young .75 2.00
67 T.J. Warren 1.25 3.00
68 Nik Stauskas .75 2.00
69 Nikola Mirotic 1.25 3.00
70 Adreian Payne .75 2.00
71 Rodney Hood 1.00 2.50
72 Cleanthony Early .75 2.00
73 Shabazz Napier 1.00 2.50
74 Glenn Robinson III 1.00 2.50
75 Thanasis Antetokounmpo 1.25 3.00
76 Clint Capela JSY AU/499 12.00 30.00
77 P.J. Hairston JSY AU/499 3.00 8.00
79 C.J. Wilcox JSY AU/499 3.00 8.00
80 Josh Huestis JSY AU/499 3.00 8.00
81 T.J. Warren JSY AU/499 5.00 12.00
82 Jordan Adams JSY AU/499 3.00 8.00
83 Joe Harris JSY AU/499 3.00 8.00
84 Nikola Mirotic JSY AU/499 5.00 12.00
85 Gary Harris JSY AU/499 5.00 12.00
86 Doug McDermott JSY AU/499 5.00 12.00
87 Zach LaVine JSY AU/499 12.00 30.00
88 Mitch McGary JSY AU/499 3.00 8.00
89 James Young JSY AU/499 3.00 8.00
90 Elfrid Payton JSY AU/499 5.00 12.00
91 Nik Stauskas JSY AU/499 3.00 8.00
92 Jusuf Nurkic JSY AU/499 10.00 25.00
93 Adreian Payne JSY AU/499 3.00 8.00
94 Rodney Hood JSY AU/499 4.00 10.00
96 Shabazz Napier JSY AU/499 4.00 10.00
97 Glenn Robinson III JSY AU/499 4.00 10.00
98 Thanasis Antetokounmpo
JSY AU/499 6.00 15.00
99 Kyle Anderson JSY AU/250 5.00 12.00
100 Aaron Gordon JSY AU/250 15.00 40.00

2014-15 SPx Rookie Patch Autographs

*RK PATCH AUTO: 1.5X TO 4X BASE HI
STATED PRINT RUN 30 SER.#'d SETS

2014-15 SPx '96 Inserts

STATED ODDS 1:7 PACKS
961 Yao Ming 6.00 15.00
962 Jerry Stackhouse 2.00 5.00
963 Alonzo Mourning 4.00 10.00
964 Anfernee Hardaway 3.00 8.00
965 Bill Russell 8.00 20.00
966 Doc Rivers 2.00 5.00
967 Christian Laettner 2.50 6.00
968 Stephen Curry 20.00 50.00
969 David Robinson 5.00 12.00
9610 Grant Hill 4.00 10.00
9611 Antonio McDyess 2.00 5.00
9612 Bill Walton 4.00 10.00
9613 Shaquille O'Neal 10.00 25.00
9614 James Harden 5.00 12.00
9615 James Worthy 4.00 10.00
9616 Jerry West 6.00 15.00
9617 John Stockton 5.00 12.00
9618 Julius Erving 6.00 15.00
9619 Kenny Anderson 2.00 5.00
9620 John Salley 2.00 5.00
9621 Joe Smith 2.00 5.00
9622 Larry Bird 10.00 25.00
9623 Dave Cowens 3.00 8.00
9624 LeBron James 20.00 50.00
9625 Magic Johnson 10.00 25.00
9626 Michael Jordan 20.00 50.00
9627 A.C. Green 2.50 6.00
9628 Jay Williams 2.00 5.00
9629 Aaron Gordon 8.00 20.00
9630 Elfrid Payton 2.50 6.00

2014-15 SPx '97 Inserts

STATED ODDS 1:7 PACKS
971 Alonzo Mourning 2.50 6.00
972 Anfernee Hardaway 4.00 10.00
973 Antonio McDyess 1.25 3.00
974 Bill Russell 5.00 12.00
975 Bill Walton 2.50 6.00
976 Doc Rivers 1.50 4.00
977 Byron Scott 1.50 4.00
978 Christian Laettner 1.50 4.00
979 Danny Manning 1.25 3.00
9710 David Robinson 3.00 8.00
9711 John Salley 1.50 4.00
9712 Grant Hill 3.00 8.00
9713 Jerry Stackhouse 3.00 8.00
9714 Donyell Marshall 1.00 2.50
9715 Shabazz Napier 1.25 3.00
9716 James Worthy 2.50 6.00
9717 Jerry West 4.00 10.00
9718 John Stockton 3.00 8.00
9719 Julius Erving 4.00 10.00
9720 Jerry Lucas 2.00 5.00
9721 Larry Bird 6.00 15.00
9722 Stephen Curry 12.00 30.00
9723 LeBron James 12.00 30.00
9724 Magic Johnson 8.00 20.00
9725 Michael Jordan 20.00 50.00
9726 Tracy McGrady 2.50 6.00
9727 Harold Miner 1.50 4.00
9728 Yao Ming 4.00 10.00
9729 Aaron Gordon 5.00 12.00
9730 T.J. Warren 1.50 4.00

2014-15 SPx Autographs

GROUP A ODDS 1:4,870 PACKS
GROUP B ODDS 1:1,723 PACKS
GROUP C ODDS 1:200 PACKS
GROUP D ODDS 1:85 PACKS
GROUP E ODDS 1:25 PACKS
GROUP F ODDS 1:20 PACKS
1 Pervis Ellison D 5.00 12.00
3 Anfernee Hardaway C 30.00 80.00
4 Antonio McDyess D 4.00 10.00
5 Bill Russell A 400.00 800.00
6 Bill Walton C 25.00 60.00
9 Christian Laettner C 5.00 12.00
10 Alex English B 8.00 20.00
12 Bo Kimble D 4.00 10.00
14 Doc Rivers D 5.00 12.00
15 Dave Cowens C 8.00 20.00
18 Kenny Anderson D 4.00 10.00
20 Allan Houston C 5.00 12.00
24 Jerry Lucas C 6.00 15.00
26 John Stockton D 20.00 50.00
29 Elvin Hayes B 8.00 20.00
30 Eric Piatkowski C 3.00 8.00
33 Joe Smith B 10.00 25.00
34 LeBron James C EXCH 1,000.00 2,000.00
36 Michael Jordan C 1,000.00 2,000.00
37 Harold Miner D 6.00 15.00
38 Bo Outlaw C 3.00 8.00
40 Jay Williams D 10.00 25.00
41 Reggie Theus C 4.00 10.00
42 Keith Smart B 5.00 12.00
43 Stacey Augmon D 3.00 8.00
44 Nick Van Exel D 5.00 12.00
45 Sleepy Floyd D 4.00 10.00
46 Stephen Curry C 300.00 600.00
47 Bill Laimbeer B 5.00 12.00
48 Brad Daugherty D 4.00 10.00
50 Jerry Stackhouse C 4.00 10.00
51 Clint Capela F 15.00 40.00
52 P.J. Hairston F 3.00 8.00
53 Dario Saric E 10.00 25.00
54 Kyle Anderson E 5.00 12.00
55 Joe Harris F 5.00 12.00
56 Elfrid Payton E 5.00 12.00
57 Josh Huestis E 3.00 8.00
58 Aaron Gordon E 15.00 40.00
59 Jordan Adams E 3.00 8.00
60 Jusuf Nurkic E 10.00 25.00
61 C.J. Wilcox E 3.00 8.00
62 Gary Harris E 5.00 12.00
63 Doug McDermott E 5.00 12.00
64 Zach LaVine E 8.00 20.00
65 Mitch McGary F EXCH 3.00 8.00
66 James Young E 3.00 8.00
67 T.J. Warren E 5.00 12.00
68 Nik Stauskas E 3.00 8.00
69 Nikola Mirotic E 8.00 20.00
70 Adreian Payne E 3.00 8.00
71 Rodney Hood F 4.00 10.00
73 Shabazz Napier F 4.00 10.00
74 Glenn Robinson III F 4.00 10.00
75 Thanasis Antetokounmpo F 6.00 15.00

2014-15 SPx Finite Legends

STATED PRINT RUN 799 SER.#'d SETS
FAH Allan Houston 2.00 5.00
FAM Alonzo Mourning 3.00 8.00
FBD Brad Daugherty 1.50 4.00
FBR Bill Russell 6.00 15.00
FBS Byron Scott 2.00 5.00
FBW Bill Walton 3.00 8.00
FDM Danny Manning 1.50 4.00
FDR David Robinson 4.00 10.00
FEH Elvin Hayes 3.00 8.00
FGH Grant Hill 4.00 10.00
FHA Anfernee Hardaway 5.00 12.00
FJA LeBron James 2.50 6.00
FJE Julius Erving 5.00 12.00
FJH James Harden 4.00 10.00
FJO Michael Jordan 8.00 20.00
FJS John Salley 1.50 4.00
FJW Jay Williams 1.50 4.00
FKA Kenny Anderson 1.50 4.00
FLB Larry Bird 3.00 8.00
FMJ Magic Johnson 8.00 20.00
FMR Micheal Ray Richardson 1.50 4.00
FNE Nick Van Exel 2.00 5.00
FRI Doc Rivers 2.00 5.00
FRT Reggie Theus 1.50 4.00
FSC Stephen Curry 15.00 40.00
FSM Joe Smith 1.50 4.00
FST John Stockton 2.00 5.00
FWE Jerry West 5.00 12.00
FWO James Worthy 3.00 8.00
FYM Yao Ming 5.00 12.00

2014-15 SPx Finite Legends Radiance

*RADIANCE: .5X TO 1.2X BASE HI
STATED PRINT RUN 99 SER.#'d SETS
FJA LeBron James 20.00 50.00
FJO Michael Jordan 25.00 60.00
FMJ Magic Johnson 10.00 25.00

2014-15 SPx Finite Rookies

*RADIANCE: .5X TO 1.2X BASE HI
STATED PRINT RUN 499 SER.#'d SETS
FIAG Aaron Gordon 3.00 8.00
FIAP Adreian Payne 2.50 6.00
FIDM Doug McDermott 4.00 10.00
FIEP Elfrid Payton 4.00 10.00
FIGH Gary Harris 4.00 10.00
FIJN Dario Saric 5.00 12.00
FIJY James Young 2.50 6.00
FIMM Mitch McGary 2.50 6.00
FINS Nik Stauskas 2.50 6.00
FISN Shabazz Napier 2.50 6.00
FITW T.J. Warren 4.00 10.00
FIZL Zach LaVine 8.00 20.00

2014-15 SPx Signatures

GROUP A ODDS 1:2,760 PACKS
GROUP B ODDS 1:1,258 PACKS
GROUP C ODDS 1:1,500 PACKS
GROUP D ODDS 1:250 PACKS
GROUP E ODDS 1:150 PACKS
SAD Jordan Adams D 4.00 10.00
SAG Aaron Gordon B 20.00 50.00
SBK Bo Kimble E 5.00 12.00
SCW Corliss Williamson E 4.00 10.00
SDR David Robinson A 15.00 40.00
SGH Grant Hill A 15.00 40.00
SHA Gary Harris C 6.00 15.00
SJA LeBron James C 1,000.00 2,000.00
SJH James Harden A 8.00 20.00
SJS Jerry Stackhouse D 12.00 30.00
SJW James Worthy A 10.00 25.00
SLB Larry Bird A 125.00 300.00
SLO Lute Olson B 20.00 50.00
SMC Doug McDermott B 6.00 15.00
SMJ Michael Jordan C 1,500.00 3,000.00
SMM Mitch McGary D 8.00 20.00
SPE Pervis Ellison E 4.00 10.00
SSA Stacey Augmon E 4.00 10.00
SSF Sleepy Floyd E 5.00 12.00
STW T.J. Warren B 10.00 25.00
SVD Vinny Del Negro D 5.00 12.00
SZL Zach LaVine C 50.00 120.00

2014-15 SPx Super Scripts Autographs

GROUP A ODDS 1:5,900 PACKS
GROUP B ODDS 1:2,800 PACKS
GROUP C ODDS 1:1,244 PACKS
GROUP D ODDS 1:300 PACKS
GROUP E ODDS 1:120 PACKS
SSAG A.C. Green E 4.00 10.00
SSBK Bo Kimble E 5.00 12.00
SSBR Bill Russell A 400.00 800.00
SSBW Bill Walton C 10.00 25.00
SSCE Cleanthony Early D 4.00 10.00
SSGH Grant Hill C 20.00 50.00
SSGO Aaron Gordon D 20.00 50.00
SSJO Michael Jordan D 200.00 300.00
SSJS Jerry Stackhouse C 8.00 20.00
SSMC Antonio McDyess E 5.00 12.00
SSPE Pervis Ellison E 8.00 20.00
SSRH Rodney Hood E 5.00 12.00
SSRI Doc Rivers C 6.00 15.00
SSSA Stacey Augmon E 4.00 10.00
SSSN Shabazz Napier D 5.00 12.00

2014-15 SPx UD Premier Jersey Autographs

STATED PRINT RUN B/WN 15-80 COPIES PER
NO PRICING ON QTY 15 OR LESS
1 T.J. Warren/80 8.00 20.00
2 Kyle Anderson/80 12.00 30.00
3 DeAndre Daniels/80 8.00 20.00
4 Thanasis Antetokounmpo/80 10.00 25.00
5 Dwight Powell/80 6.00 15.00
6 Clint Capela/80 20.00 50.00
7 P.J. Hairston/80 5.00 12.00
9 Josh Huestis/80 5.00 12.00
10 Jordan Clarkson/80 20.00 50.00
11 Jusuf Nurkic/80 20.00 50.00
12 Jordan Adams/80 8.00 20.00
13 Nikola Mirotic/80 40.00 100.00
14 Gary Harris/80 8.00 20.00
15 Doug McDermott/80 25.00 60.00
16 Zach LaVine/80 30.00 80.00
17 Mitch McGary/80 5.00 12.00
18 James Young/80 5.00 12.00
19 C.J. Wilcox/80 5.00 12.00
20 Joe Harris/80 8.00 20.00
21 Spencer Dinwiddie/80 8.00 20.00
22 Adreian Payne/80 5.00 12.00
23 Rodney Hood/80 6.00 15.00
25 Shabazz Napier/80 6.00 15.00
26 Glenn Robinson III/80 6.00 15.00
27 James Michael McAdoo/80 6.00 15.00
28 Elfrid Payton/30 8.00 20.00
30 Nik Stauskas/30 5.00 12.00

2014-15 SPx UD Premier Jersey Autographs Patch

*PATCH: .6X TO 1.5X BASE HI
STATED PRINT RUN B/WN 3-30 COPIES PER
NO PRICING ON QTY 10 OR LESS
LACK OF PRICING DUE TO MARKET INFO

2014-15 SPx Winning Big Materials

STATED ODDS 1:9 PACKS
WMAG A.C. Green 3.00 8.00
WMAH Allan Houston 3.00 8.00
WMAM Alonzo Mourning 5.00 12.00
WMAP Adreian Payne 3.00 8.00
WMBD Brad Daugherty 2.50 6.00
WMBW Bill Walton 5.00 12.00
WMCJ C.J. Wilcox 2.00 5.00
WMCL Christian Laettner 3.00 8.00
WMCW Corliss Williamson 2.00 5.00
WMDM Donyell Marshall 2.00 5.00
WMEP Elfrid Payton 2.50 6.00
WMGH Gary Harris 3.00 8.00
WMGO Aaron Gordon 10.00 25.00
WMHA Anfernee Hardaway 5.00 12.00
WMJA Jordan Adams 2.00 5.00
WMJH James Harden 5.00 12.00
WMJN Jusuf Nurkic 6.00 15.00
WMJS Joe Smith 2.50 6.00
WMJW Jay Williams 10.00 25.00
WMJY James Young 2.00 5.00
WMKS Keith Smart 3.00 8.00
WMLJ LeBron James 10.00 25.00
WMMA Danny Manning 2.50 6.00
WMMC Doug McDermott 3.00 8.00
WMMM Mitch McGary 2.00 5.00
WMMR Micheal Ray Richardson 2.50 6.00
WMNM Nikola Mirotic 3.00 8.00
WMNS Nik Stauskas 2.00 5.00
WMPH P.J. Hairston 2.00 5.00
WMRH Rodney Hood 2.50 6.00
WMSC Stephen Curry 40.00 100.00
WMSN Shabazz Napier 2.50 6.00
WMTW T.J. Warren 3.00 8.00
WMWE Jerry West 8.00 20.00
WMWI Buck Williams 3.00 8.00
WMZL Zach LaVine 12.00 30.00

2014-15 SPx Winning Big Materials Patch

*PATCH: 1X TO 2.5X BASE HI
STATED PRINT RUN B/WN 5-25 COPIES PER
NO PRICING ON QTY 5 OR LESS
WMJH James Harden/25 20.00 50.00
WMMA Danny Manning/25 12.00 30.00
WMPH P.J. Hairston/25 5.00 12.00
WMRH Rodney Hood/25 6.00 15.00
WMSC Stephen Curry/25 125.00 300.00

2014-15 SPx Winning Materials Combos

STATED ODDS 1:45 PACKS
WM2CJ C.Laettner/J.Williams 10.00 25.00
WM2GS A.Gordon/N.Stauskas 4.00 10.00
WM2HH A.Houston/A.Hardaway 6.00 15.00
WM2HP A.Payne/G.Harris 6.00 15.00
WM2JC L.James/S.Curry 50.00 120.00
WM2LS K.Smart/C.Laettner 5.00 12.00
WM2MF A.Mourning/S.Floyd 4.00 10.00
WM2ML J.Johnson/A.Mourning 5.00 12.00
WM2ND D.Daniels/S.Napier 5.00 12.00
WM2SG L.Shelton/A.Green 6.00 15.00
WM2SM N.Stauskas/M.McGary 4.00 10.00
WM2SW B.Williams/J.Smith 10.00 25.00
WM2WL C.Laettner/E.Walton 4.00 10.00

2014-15 SPx Winning Materials Trios

STATED ODDS 1:160 PACKS
WMTGLW Warren/LaVine/Gordon 5.00 12.00
WMTGSP Gordon/Payton/Stauskas 3.00 8.00
WMTHSH Smith/Houston/Hardaway 5.00 12.00

1998-99 SPx Finite

BASE CARD PRINT RUN 10000 SERIAL #'d SETS
SP PRINT RUN 5400 SERIAL #'d SETS
SPx STATED PRINT RUN 4050 SERIAL #'d SETS
TF STATED PRINT RUN 3390 SERIAL #'d SETS
FE STATED PRINT RUN 1770 SERIAL #'d SETS
RC STATED PRINT RUN 2500 SERIAL #'d SETS
RCs DISTRIBUTED IN UD 2 BOXES
1 Michael Jordan 8.00 20.00
2 Hakeem Olajuwon 1.50 4.00
3 Keith Van Horn .75 2.00
4 Rasheed Wallace 1.00 2.50
5 Mookie Blaylock .60 1.50
6 Bobby Jackson .60 1.50
7 Detlef Schrempf .75 2.00
8 Antonio McDyess .60 1.50
9 Lamond Murray .50 1.25
10 Chris Mullin 1.00 2.50
11 Zydrunas Ilgauskas .75 2.00
12 Tracy Murray .50 1.25
13 Jerry Stackhouse .75 2.00
14 Avery Johnson .60 1.50
15 Larry Johnson 1.25 3.00
16 Alan Henderson .50 1.25
17 David Wesley .50 1.25
18 Kevin Willis .50 1.25
19 Eddie Jones .75 2.00
20 Horace Grant .75 2.00
21 Ray Allen 1.25 3.00
22 Derrick Coleman .60 1.50
23 Derek Anderson .60 1.50
24 Tim Hardaway 1.00 2.50
25 Danny Fortson .50 1.25
26 Tariq Abdul-Wahad .50 1.25
27 Charles Barkley 2.00 5.00
28 Sam Cassell .60 1.50
29 Kevin Garnett 2.00 5.00
30 Jeff Hornacek .60 1.50
31 Isaac Austin .50 1.25
32 Allan Houston .75 2.00
33 David Robinson 1.50 4.00
34 Tracy McGrady 1.25 3.00
35 LaPhonso Ellis .50 1.25
36 Shawn Kemp 1.25 3.00
37 Glenn Robinson .75 2.00
38 Shareef Abdur-Rahim .75 2.00
39 Vin Baker .60 1.50
40 Rik Smits .60 1.50
41 Jason Kidd 1.25 3.00
42 Erick Dampier .50 1.25
43 Shawn Bradley .50 1.25
44 Anfernee Hardaway 2.00 5.00
45 John Stockton 1.50 4.00
46 Calbert Cheaney .50 1.25
47 Terrell Brandon .60 1.50
48 Hubert Davis .50 1.25
49 Patrick Ewing 1.25 3.00
50 Kobe Bryant 6.00 15.00
51 Gary Payton 1.25 3.00
52 Marcus Camby .60 1.50
53 Bryant Reeves .50 1.25
54 Reggie Miller 1.50 4.00
55 Antoine Walker .75 2.00
56 Scottie Pippen 2.00 5.00
57 Hersey Hawkins .50 1.25
58 John Starks .75 2.00
59 Dikembe Mutombo 1.25 3.00
60 Damon Stoudamire .75 2.00
61 Rodney Rogers .50 1.25
62 Nick Anderson .50 1.25
63 Brian Williams .50 1.25
64 Ron Mercer .60 1.50
65 Donyell Marshall .50 1.25
66 Glen Rice .75 2.00
67 Michael Finley .75 2.00
68 Tim Duncan 2.00 5.00
69 Stephon Marbury 1.00 2.50
70 Antonio Daniels .50 1.25
71 Chauncey Billups 1.00 2.50
72 Kerry Kittles .60 1.50
73 Brian Grant .50 1.25
74 Anthony Mason .60 1.50
75 Allen Iverson 2.00 5.00
76 Juwan Howard .60 1.50
77 Grant Hill 1.25 3.00
78 Tony Delk .50 1.25
79 Olden Polynice .50 1.25
80 Alonzo Mourning 1.25 3.00
81 Karl Malone 1.50 4.00
82 Isaiah Rider .60 1.50
83 Shaquille O'Neal 3.00 8.00
84 Steve Smith .60 1.50
85 Kenny Anderson .60 1.50
86 Toni Kukoc .75 2.00
87 Anthony Peeler .50 1.25
88 Tim Thomas .60 1.50
89 Nick Van Exel .75 2.00
90 Jamal Mashburn .75 2.00
91 Reggie Miller SP 2.50 6.00
92 Juwan Howard SP 1.00 2.50
93 Glen Rice SP 1.25 3.00
94 Grant Hill SP 2.00 5.00
95 Maurice Taylor SP .75 2.00
96 Vin Baker SP 1.00 2.50
97 Tim Thomas SP 1.00 2.50
98 Bobby Jackson SP 1.00 2.50
99 Damon Stoudamire SP 1.25 3.00
100 Michael Jordan SP 12.00 30.00
101 Eddie Jones SP 1.25 3.00
102 Keith Van Horn SP 1.25 3.00
103 Dikembe Mutombo SP 2.00 5.00
104 Brevin Knight SP .75 2.00
105 Shawn Bradley SP .75 2.00
106 Lamond Murray SP .75 2.00
107 Tim Duncan SP 3.00 8.00
108 Bryant Reeves SP .75 2.00
109 Antoine Walker SP 1.25 3.00
110 John Stockton SP 2.50 6.00
111 Nick Anderson SP .75 2.00
112 Chris Mullin SP 1.50 4.00
113 Glenn Robinson SP 1.25 3.00
114 Kevin Garnett SP 3.00 8.00
115 Michael Stewart SP .75 2.00
116 Antonio McDyess SP 1.00 2.50
117 Jim Jackson SP .75 2.00
118 Chauncey Billups SP 1.50 4.00
119 Sam Cassell SP 1.00 2.50
120 Dennis Rodman SP 3.00 8.00
121 Rasheed Wallace SP 1.50 4.00
122 Brian Williams SP .75 2.00
123 Anfernee Hardaway SP 3.00 8.00
124 Scottie Pippen SP 3.00 8.00
125 Terrell Brandon SP 1.00 2.50
126 Michael Finley SP 1.25 3.00
127 Kerry Kittles SP 1.00 2.50
128 Toni Kukoc SP 1.25 3.00
129 Hakeem Olajuwon SP 2.50 6.00
130 Tim Hardaway SP 1.50 4.00
131 Shareef Abdur-Rahim SP 1.25 3.00
132 Donyell Marshall SP .75 2.00
133 David Robinson SP 2.50 6.00
134 LaPhonso Ellis SP .75 2.00
135 Ray Allen SP 2.00 5.00
136 Nick Van Exel SP 1.25 3.00
137 Patrick Ewing SP 2.00 5.00
138 Anthony Mason SP 1.00 2.50
139 Shaquille O'Neal SP 5.00 12.00
140 Shawn Kemp SP 2.00 5.00
141 Stephon Marbury SP 1.50 4.00
142 Karl Malone SP 2.50 6.00
143 Allen Iverson SP 3.00 8.00
144 Kenny Anderson SP 1.00 2.50
145 Marcus Camby SP 1.00 2.50
146 Steve Smith SP 1.00 2.50
147 Gary Payton SP 2.00 5.00
148 Jason Kidd SP 2.00 5.00
149 Alonzo Mourning SP 2.00 5.00
150 Charles Barkley SP 3.00 8.00
151 Kobe Bryant SPx 15.00 40.00
152 Ron Mercer SPx 1.50 4.00
153 Maurice Taylor SPx 1.25 3.00
154 Tim Duncan SPx 5.00 12.00
155 Shareef Abdur-Rahim SPx 2.00 5.00
156 Eddie Jones SPx 2.00 5.00
157 Chauncey Billups SPx 2.50 6.00
158 Derek Anderson SPx 1.50 4.00
159 Bobby Jackson SPx 1.50 4.00
160 Stephon Marbury SPx 2.50 6.00
161 Anfernee Hardaway SPx 5.00 12.00
162 Zydrunas Ilgauskas SPx 2.00 5.00
163 Allen Iverson SPx 5.00 12.00
164 Antoine Walker SPx 2.00 5.00
165 Tracy McGrady SPx 3.00 8.00
166 Rasheed Wallace SPx 2.50 6.00
167 Jason Kidd SPx 3.00 8.00
168 Kevin Garnett SPx 5.00 12.00
169 Damon Stoudamire SPx 2.00 5.00
170 Brevin Knight SPx 1.25 3.00
171 Tim Thomas SPx 1.50 4.00
172 Danny Fortson SPx 1.25 3.00
173 Jermaine O'Neal SPx 2.00 5.00
174 Keith Van Horn SPx 2.00 5.00
175 Ray Allen SPx 3.00 8.00
176 Kerry Kittles SPx 1.50 4.00
177 Vin Baker SPx 1.50 4.00
178 Allan Houston SPx 2.00 5.00
179 Alan Henderson SPx 1.25 3.00
180 Bryon Russell SPx 1.25 3.00
181 Michael Jordan TF 25.00 60.00
182 Maurice Taylor TF 1.50 4.00
183 Isaiah Rider TF 2.00 5.00
184 Antonio McDyess TF 2.00 5.00
185 Anfernee Hardaway TF 6.00 15.00
186 Glenn Robinson TF 2.50 6.00
187 Dikembe Mutombo TF 4.00 10.00
188 Shawn Kemp TF 4.00 10.00
189 Tracy McGrady TF 4.00 10.00
190 Reggie Miller TF 5.00 12.00
191 Derek Anderson TF 2.00 5.00
192 Allan Houston TF 2.50 6.00
193 Michael Finley TF 2.50 6.00
194 Nick Van Exel TF 2.50 6.00
195 Juwan Howard TF 2.00 5.00
196 LaPhonso Ellis TF 1.50 4.00
197 Ron Mercer TF 2.00 5.00
198 Glen Rice TF 2.50 6.00
199 Joe Smith TF 2.00 5.00
200 Kobe Bryant TF 20.00 50.00
201 Michael Jordan FE 20.00 50.00
202 Karl Malone FE 8.00 20.00
203 Hakeem Olajuwon FE 8.00 20.00
204 David Robinson FE 8.00 20.00
205 Shaquille O'Neal FE 15.00 40.00
206 John Stockton FE 8.00 20.00
207 Grant Hill FE 6.00 15.00
208 Tim Hardaway FE 5.00 12.00
209 Scottie Pippen FE 10.00 25.00
210 Gary Payton FE 6.00 15.00
211 Michael Olowokandi RC 3.00 8.00
212 Mike Bibby RC 5.00 12.00
213 Raef LaFrentz RC 3.00 8.00
214 Antawn Jamison RC 4.00 10.00
215 Vince Carter RC 30.00 80.00
216 Robert Traylor RC 2.50 6.00
217 Jason Williams RC 8.00 20.00
218 Larry Hughes RC 4.00 10.00
219 Dirk Nowitzki RC 40.00 100.00
220 Paul Pierce RC 10.00 25.00
221 Bonzi Wells RC 2.50 6.00
222 Michael Doleac RC 2.00 5.00
223 Keon Clark RC 2.50 6.00
224 Michael Dickerson RC 2.50 6.00
225 Matt Harpring RC 2.50 6.00
226 Bryce Drew RC 1.50 4.00
229 Pat Garrity RC 2.00 5.00
230 Roshown McLeod RC 1.50 4.00
231 Ricky Davis RC 4.00 10.00
232 Brian Skinner RC 2.00 5.00
233 Tyronn Lue RC 3.00 8.00
234 Felipe Lopez RC 1.50 4.00
235 Al Harrington RC 3.00 8.00
236 Ruben Patterson RC 2.50 6.00
237 Jelani McCoy RC 2.00 5.00
238 Corey Benjamin RC 1.50 4.00
239 Nazr Mohammed RC 2.50 6.00
240 Rashard Lewis RC 4.00 10.00
S1 Michael Jordan PROMO 5.00 12.00

1998-99 SPx Finite Radiance

*1-90 STARS: .6X TO 1.5X BASE HI
1-90 PRINT RUN 5000 SERIAL #'d SETS
*91-150 STARS: .6X TO 1.5X BASE HI
91-150 PRINT RUN 2700 SERIAL #'d SETS
*151-180 STARS: .6X TO 1.5X BASE HI
151-180 PRINT RUN 2025 SERIAL #'d SETS
*181-200 STARS: .75X TO 2X BASE HI
181-200 PRINT RUN 1130 SERIAL #'d SETS
*201-210 STARS: .75X TO 2X BASE HI
201-210 PRINT RUN 590 SERIAL #'d SETS
211-240 RCs: .4X TO 1X BASE HI
211-240 RC PRINT RUN 1500 SERIAL #'d SETS
215 Vince Carter 15.00 40.00
219 Dirk Nowitzki 25.00 60.00

1998-99 SPx Finite Spectrum

*1-90 STARS: 3X TO 8X BASE HI
1-90 PRINT RUN 350 SERIAL #'d SETS
*91-150 STARS: 2.5X TO 6X BASE HI
91-150 PRINT RUN 250 SERIAL #'d SETS
*151-180 STARS: 2.5X TO 6X BASE HI
151-180 PRINT RUN 75 SERIAL #'d SETS
*181-200 STARS: 3X TO 8X BASE HI
181-200 PRINT RUN 50 SERIAL #'d SETS
*201-210 STARS: 5X TO 12X BASE HI
201-210 PRINT RUN 25 SERIAL #'d SETS
*211-240 RCs: 8X TO 20X BASE HI
211-240 PRINT RUN 25 SERIAL #'d SETS
1 Michael Jordan 200.00 500.00
100 Michael Jordan SP 300.00 600.00
143 Allen Iverson SP 25.00 60.00
151 Kobe Bryant SPx 150.00 400.00
163 Allen Iverson SPx 75.00 200.00
181 Michael Jordan TF 750.00 1,500.00
185 Anfernee Hardaway TF 50.00 120.00
188 Shawn Kemp TF 40.00 100.00
200 Kobe Bryant TF 300.00 600.00
201 Michael Jordan FE 3,000.00 6,000.00
209 Scottie Pippen FE 100.00 250.00
215 Vince Carter 500.00 1,000.00
219 Dirk Nowitzki 600.00 1,200.00
240 Rashard Lewis 80.00 200.00

1979-80 Spurs Police

COMPLETE SET (15) 3.00 6.00
1 Bob Bass .25 .60
2 Mike Evans .25 .60
3 Mike Gale .25 .60
4 George Gervin 1.50 4.00
5 Paul Griffin .25 .60
6 George Karl ACO .40 1.00
7 Larry Kenon .30 .75
8 Irv Kiffin .25 .60
9 Bernie LaReau .25 .60
10 Doug Moe CO .40 1.00
11 Mark Olberding .25 .60
12 Billy Paultz .30 .75
13 Wiley Peck .25 .60
14 Kevin Restani .25 .60
15 James Silas .30 .75

1988-89 Spurs Police/Diamond Shamrock

COMPLETE SET (8) 4.00 10.00
1 Greg Anderson 33 .40 1.00
2 Willie Anderson 40 .40 1.00
3 Frank Brickowski 43 .40 1.00
4 Larry Brown CO .75 2.00
5 Dallas Comegys 22 .40 .40
6 Johnny Dawkins 24 .40 .40
7 Alvin Robertson 21 .40 .40
8 David Robinson 50 3.00 8.00

1976-77 Spurs Team Issue

COMPLETE SET (8) 12.50 25.00
1 Mike D'Antoni 2.00 5.00
2 Louie Dampier 2.00 5.00

3 Coby Dietrick 1.25 3.00
4 Mike Gale 1.25 3.00
5 Billy Paultz 1.50 4.00
6 James Silas 1.50 4.00
7 Ken Smith 1.25 3.00
8 Henry Ward 1.25 3.00

2007 Spurs Upper Deck

COMPLETE SET (27) 10.00 20.00
1 Tony Parker .75 2.00
2 Brent Barry .40 1.00
3 Tony Parker .75 2.00
4 Jackie Butler .40 1.00
5 2007 NBA Champions .40 1.00
6 Matt Bonner .40 1.00
7 Bruce Bowen .40 1.00
8 Gregg Popovich CO 15.00 40.00
9 Bruce Bowen/Michael Finley .60 1.50
10 Manu Ginobili .75 2.00
11 Francisco Elson .40 1.00
12 Manu Ginobili .75 2.00
13 James White .40 1.00
14 4 Time NBA Champions .40 1.00
15 Melvin Ely .40 1.00
16 Michael Finley .75 2.00
17 The Coyote .40 1.00
18 Fabricio Oberto/Brent Barry .40 1.00
19 Tim Duncan 1.00 2.50
20 Jacque Vaughn .40 1.00
21 Tim Duncan 1.00 2.50
22 Fabricio Oberto .40 1.00
23 2007 Conference Champs .40 1.00
24 Beno Udrih .40 1.00
25 Robert Horry .75 2.00
26 Tim Duncan/Tony Parker CL 1.00 2.50
27 Robert Horry .75 2.00

1971-72 Squires Virginia Team Issue

COMPLETE SET (2) 25.00 50.00
1 Bill Bunting
Jim Eakins
Julius Erving
George Irvine
Neil Johnson
Mike Maloy
Doug Moe
Dana Pagett 20.00 40.00
2 Al Bianchi CO
Earl M. Foreman PRES
Charlie Scott
Ray Scott
Willie Sojourner
Adrian Smith
Roland Taylor 7.50 15.00

2000 St. Vincent Stamps

NNO1 Michael Jordan 2.00 5.00
NNO2 Michael Jordan Full Sheet 8.00 20.00

1992-93 Stadium Club

COMPLETE SET (400) 12.50 30.00
COMPLETE SERIES 1 (200) 6.00 15.00
COMPLETE SERIES 2 (200) 6.00 15.00
1 Michael Jordan 6.00 15.00
2 Greg Anthony .02 .10
3 Otis Thorpe .10 .30
4 Jim Les .02 .10
5 Kevin Willis .02 .10
6 Derek Harper .10 .30
7 Elden Campbell .10 .30
8 A.J. English .02 .10
9 Kenny Gattison .02 .10
10 Drazen Petrovic .02 .10
11 Chris Mullin .25 .60
12 Mark Price .02 .10
13 Karl Malone .40 1.00
14 Gerald Glass .02 .10
15 Negele Knight .02 .10
16 Mark Macon .02 .10
17 Michael Cage .02 .10
18 Kevin Edwards .02 .10
19 Sherman Douglas .02 .10
20 Ron Harper .10 .30
21 Clifford Robinson .10 .30
22 Byron Scott .10 .30
23 Antoine Carr .02 .10
24 Greg Dreiling .02 .10
25 Bill Laimbeer .10 .30
26 Hersey Hawkins .10 .30
27 Will Perdue .02 .10
28 Todd Lichti .02 .10
29 Gary Grant .02 .10
30 Sam Perkins .10 .30
31 Jayson Williams .10 .30
32 Magic Johnson .75 2.00
33 Larry Bird 1.00 2.50
34 Chris Morris .02 .10
35 Nick Anderson .10 .30
36 Scott Hastings .02 .10
37 Ledell Eackles .02 .10
38 Robert Pack .02 .10
39 Dana Barros .02 .10
40 Anthony Bonner .02 .10
41 J.R. Reid .02 .10
42 Tyrone Hill .02 .10
43 Rik Smits .10 .30
44 Kevin Duckworth .02 .10
45 LaSalle Thompson .02 .10
46 Brian Williams .02 .10
47 Willie Anderson .02 .10
48 Ken Norman .02 .10
49 Mike Iuzzolino .02 .10
50 Isiah Thomas .25 .60
51 Alec Kessler .02 .10
52 Johnny Dawkins .02 .10
53 Avery Johnson .02 .10
54 Stacey Augmon .10 .30
55 Charles Oakley .10 .30
56 Rex Chapman .02 .10
57 Charles Shackleford .02 .10
58 Jeff Ruland .02 .10
59 Craig Ehlo .02 .10
60 Jon Koncak .02 .10
61 Danny Schayes .02 .10
62 David Benoit .02 .10
63 Robert Parish .10 .30
64 Mookie Blaylock .10 .30
65 Sean Elliott .10 .30
66 Mark Aguirre .02 .10
67 Scott Williams .02 .10
68 Doug West .02 .10
69 Kenny Anderson .25 .60
70 Randy Brown .02 .10
71 Muggsy Bogues .10 .30
72 Spud Webb .10 .30
73 Sedale Threatt .02 .10
74 Chris Gatling .02 .10
75 Derrick McKey .02 .10
76 Sleepy Floyd .02 .10
77 Chris Jackson .02 .10
78 Thurl Bailey .02 .10
79 Steve Smith .30 .75
80 Cedric Ceballos .02 .10
81 Anthony Bowie .02 .10
82 John Williams .02 .10
83 Paul Graham .02 .10
84 Willie Burton .02 .10
85 Vernon Maxwell .02 .10
86 Stacey King .02 .10
87 B.J. Armstrong .02 .10
88 Kevin Gamble .02 .10
89 Terry Catledge .02 .10
90 Jeff Malone .02 .10
91 Sam Bowie .02 .10
92 Orlando Woolridge .02 .10
93 Steve Kerr .10 .30
94 Eric Leckner .02 .10
95 Loy Vaught .02 .10
96 Jud Buechler .02 .10
97 Doug Smith .02 .10
98 Sidney Green .02 .10
99 Jerome Kersey .02 .10
100 Patrick Ewing .25 .60
101 Ed Nealy .02 .10
102 Shawn Kemp .50 1.25
103 Luc Longley .10 .30
104 George McCloud .02 .10
105 Ron Anderson .02 .10
106 Moses Malone UER .25 .60
107 Tony Smith .02 .10
108 Terry Porter .02 .10
109 Blair Rasmussen .02 .10
110 Bimbo Coles .02 .10
111 Grant Long .02 .10
112 John Battle .02 .10
113 Brian Oliver .02 .10
114 Tyrone Corbin .02 .10
115 Benoit Benjamin .02 .10
116 Rick Fox .10 .30
117 Rafael Addison .02 .10
118 Danny Young .02 .10
119 Fat Lever .02 .10
120 Terry Cummings .10 .30
121 Felton Spencer .02 .10
122 Joe Kleine .02 .10
123 Johnny Newman .02 .10
124 Gary Payton .50 1.25
125 Kurt Rambis .02 .10
126 Vlade Divac .10 .30
127 John Paxson .02 .10
128 Lionel Simmons .02 .10
129 Randy Wittman .02 .10
130 Winston Garland .02 .10
131 Jerry Reynolds .02 .10
132 Dell Curry .02 .10
133 Fred Roberts .02 .10
134 Michael Adams .02 .10
135 Charles Jones .02 .10
136 Frank Brickowski .02 .10
137 Alton Lister .02 .10
138 Horace Grant .10 .30
139 Greg Sutton .02 .10
140 John Starks .10 .30
141 Detlef Schrempf .10 .30
142 Rodney Monroe .02 .10
143 Pete Chilcutt .02 .10
144 Mike Brown .02 .10
145 Rony Seikaly .02 .10
146 Donald Hodge .02 .10
147 Kevin McHale .25 .60
148 Ricky Pierce .02 .10
149 Brian Shaw .02 .10
150 Reggie Williams .02 .10
151 Kendall Gill .10 .30
152 Tom Chambers .02 .10
153 Jack Haley .02 .10
154 Terrell Brandon .25 .60
155 Dennis Scott .10 .30
156 Mark Randall .02 .10
157 Kenny Payne .02 .10
158 Bernard King .02 .10
159 Tate George .02 .10
160 Scott Skiles .02 .10
161 Pervis Ellison .02 .10
162 Marcus Liberty .02 .10
163 Rumeal Robinson .02 .10
164 Anthony Mason .25 .60
165 Les Jepsen .02 .10
166 Kenny Smith .02 .10
167 Randy White .02 .10
168 Dee Brown .02 .10
169 Chris Dudley .02 .10
170 Armon Gilliam .02 .10
171 Eddie Johnson .02 .10
172 A.C. Green .10 .30
173 Darrell Walker .02 .10
174 Bill Cartwright .02 .10
175 Mike Gminski .02 .10
176 Tom Tolbert .02 .10
177 Buck Williams .10 .30
178 Mark Eaton .02 .10
179 Danny Manning .10 .30
180 Glen Rice .25 .60
181 Sarunas Marciulionis .02 .10
182 Danny Ferry .02 .10
183 Chris Corchiani .02 .10
184 Dan Majerle .10 .30
185 Alvin Robertson .02 .10
186 Vern Fleming .02 .10
187 Kevin Lynch .02 .10
188 John Williams .02 .10
189 Checklist 1-100 .02 .10
190 Checklist 101-200 .02 .10
191 David Robinson MC .25 .60
192 Larry Johnson MC .10 .30
193 Derrick Coleman MC .02 .10
194 Larry Bird MC .50 1.25
195 Billy Owens MC .02 .10
196 Dikembe Mutombo MC .25 .60
197 Charles Barkley MC .25 .60
198 Scottie Pippen MC .40 1.00
199 Clyde Drexler MC .10 .30
200 John Stockton MC .10 .30
201 Shaquille O'Neal MC 3.00 8.00
202 Chris Mullin MC .10 .30
203 Glen Rice MC .10 .30
204 Isiah Thomas MC .10 .30
205 Karl Malone MC .25 .60
206 Christian Laettner MC .25 .60
207 Patrick Ewing MC .10 .30
208 Dominique Wilkins MC .10 .30
209 Alonzo Mourning MC .50 1.25
210 Michael Jordan MC 6.00 15.00
211 Tim Hardaway .30 .75
212 Rodney McCray .02 .10
213 Larry Johnson .30 .75
214 Charles Smith .02 .10
215 Kevin Brooks .02 .10
216 Kevin Johnson .25 .60
217 Duane Cooper RC .02 .10
218 Christian Laettner UER RC .50 1.25
219 Tim Perry .02 .10
220 Hakeem Olajuwon .40 1.00
221 Lee Mayberry RC .02 .10
222 Mark Bryant .02 .10
223 Robert Horry RC .25 .60
224 Tracy Murray UER RC .10 .30
225 Greg Grant .02 .10
226 Rolando Blackman .02 .10
227 James Edwards UER .02 .10
228 Sean Green .02 .10
229 Buck Johnson .02 .10
230 Andrew Lang .02 .10
231 Tracy Moore RC .02 .10
232 Adam Keefe UER RC .02 .10
233 Tony Campbell .02 .10
234 Rod Strickland .25 .60
235 Terry Mills .02 .10
236 Billy Owens .10 .30
237 Bryant Stith UER RC .10 .30
238 Tony Bennett UER RC .02 .10
239 David Wood .02 .10
240 Jay Humphries .02 .10
241 Doc Rivers .10 .30
242 Wayman Tisdale .02 .10
243 Litterial Green RC .02 .10
244 Jon Barry .10 .30
245 Brad Daugherty .02 .10
246 Nate McMillan .02 .10
247 Shaquille O'Neal RC 4.00 10.00
248 Chris Smith RC .02 .10
249 Duane Ferrell .02 .10
250 Anthony Peeler RC .10 .30
251 Gundars Vetra RC .02 .10
252 Danny Ainge .10 .30
253 Mitch Richmond .25 .60
254 Malik Sealy RC .10 .30
255 Brent Price RC .10 .30
256 Xavier McDaniel .02 .10
257 Bobby Phills RC .25 .60
258 Donald Royal .02 .10
259 Olden Polynice .02 .10
260 Dominique Wilkins UER .25 .60
261 Larry Krystkowiak .02 .10
262 Duane Causwell .02 .10
263 Todd Day RC .10 .30
264 Sam Mack RC .10 .30
265 John Stockton .25 .60
266 Eddie Lee Wilkins .02 .10
267 Gerald Glass .02 .10
268 Robert Pack .02 .10
269 Gerald Wilkins .02 .10
270 Reggie Lewis .10 .30
271 Scott Brooks .02 .10
272 Randy Woods UER RC .02 .10
273 Dikembe Mutombo .30 .75
274 Kiki Vandeweghe .02 .10
275 Rich King .02 .10
276 Jeff Turner .02 .10
277 Vinny Del Negro .02 .10
278 Marlon Maxey RC .02 .10
279 Elmore Spencer UER RC .02 .10
280 Cedric Ceballos .10 .30
281 Alex Blackwell RC .02 .10
282 Terry Davis .02 .10
283 Morlon Wiley .02 .10
284 Trent Tucker .02 .10
285 Carl Herrera .02 .10
286 Eric Anderson RC .02 .10
287 Clyde Drexler .25 .60
288 Tom Gugliotta RC .75 2.00
289 Dale Ellis .02 .10
290 Lance Blanks .02 .10
291 Tom Hammonds .02 .10
292 Eric Murdock .02 .10
293 Walt Williams RC .25 .60
294 Gerald Paddio .02 .10
295 Brian Howard RC .02 .10
296 Ken Williams .02 .10
297 Alonzo Mourning RC 1.50 4.00
298 Larry Nance .02 .10
299 Jeff Grayer .02 .10
300 Dave Johnson RC .02 .10
301 Bob McCann RC .02 .10
302 Bart Kofoed .02 .10
303 Anthony Cook .02 .10
304 Radisav Curcic RC .02 .10
305 John Crotty RC .02 .10
306 Brad Sellers .02 .10
307 Marcus Webb RC .02 .10
308 Winston Garland .02 .10
309 Walter Palmer .02 .10
310 Rod Higgins .02 .10
311 Travis Mays .02 .10
312 Alex Stivrins RC .02 .10
313 Greg Kite .02 .10
314 Dennis Rodman .50 1.25
315 Mike Sanders .02 .10
316 Ed Pinckney .02 .10
317 Harold Miner RC .10 .30
318 Pooh Richardson .02 .10
319 Oliver Miller RC .10 .30
320 Latrell Sprewell RC 2.00 5.00
321 Anthony Pullard RC .02 .10
322 Mark Randall .02 .10
323 Jeff Hornacek .10 .30
324 Rick Mahorn UER .02 .10
325 Sean Rooks RC .02 .10
326 Paul Pressey .02 .10
327 James Worthy .25 .60
328 Matt Bullard .02 .10
329 Reggie Smith RC .02 .10
330 Don MacLean UER RC .02 .10
331 John Williams UER .02 .10
332 Frank Johnson .02 .10
333 Hubert Davis UER RC .10 .30
334 Lloyd Daniels RC .02 .10
335 Steve Bardo RC .02 .10
336 Jeff Sanders .02 .10
337 Tree Rollins .02 .10
338 Micheal Williams .02 .10
339 Lorenzo Williams RC .02 .10
340 Harvey Grant .02 .10
341 Avery Johnson .02 .10
342 Bo Kimble .02 .10
343 LaPhonso Ellis UER RC .25 .60
344 Mookie Blaylock .10 .30
345 Isaiah Morris UER RC .02 .10
346 Clarence Weatherspoon RC .25 .60
347 Manute Bol .02 .10
348 Victor Alexander .02 .10
349 Corey Williams RC .02 .10
350 Byron Houston RC .02 .10
351 Stanley Roberts .02 .10
352 Anthony Avent RC .02 .10
353 Vincent Askew .02 .10
354 Herb Williams .02 .10
355 J.R. Reid .02 .10
356 Brad Lohaus .02 .10
357 Reggie Miller .25 .60
358 Blue Edwards .02 .10
359 Tom Tolbert .02 .10
360 Charles Barkley .40 1.00
361 David Robinson .40 1.00
362 Dale Davis .02 .10
363 Robert Werdann UER RC .02 .10
364 Chuck Person .02 .10
365 Alaa Abdelnaby .02 .10
366 Dave Jamerson .02 .10
367 Scottie Pippen .75 2.00
368 Mark Jackson .10 .30
369 Keith Askins .02 .10
370 Marty Conlon .02 .10
371 Chucky Brown .02 .10
372 LaBradford Smith .02 .10
373 Tim Kempton .02 .10
374 Sam Mitchell .02 .10
375 John Salley .02 .10
376 Mario Elie .10 .30
377 Mark West .02 .10
378 David Wingate .02 .10
379 Jaren Jackson RC .10 .30
380 Rumeal Robinson .02 .10
381 Kennard Winchester .02 .10
382 Walter Bond RC .02 .10
383 Isaac Austin RC .10 .30
384 Derrick Coleman .10 .30
385 Larry Smith .02 .10
386 Joe Dumars .25 .60
387 Matt Geiger UER RC .10 .30
388 Stephen Howard RC .02 .10
389 William Bedford .02 .10
390 Jayson Williams .10 .30
391 Kurt Rambis .02 .10
392 Keith Jennings RC .02 .10
393 Steve Kerr UER .10 .30
394 Larry Stewart .02 .10
395 Danny Young .02 .10
396 Doug Overton .02 .10
397 Mark Acres .02 .10
398 John Bagley .02 .10
399 Checklist 201-300 .02 .10
400 Checklist 301-400 .02 .10

1992-93 Stadium Club Beam Team

COMPLETE SET (21) 600.00 1,200.00
SER.2 STATED ODDS 1:36
1 Michael Jordan 250.00 600.00
2 Dominique Wilkins 8.00 20.00
3 Shawn Kemp 8.00 20.00
4 Clyde Drexler 8.00 20.00
5 Scottie Pippen 12.00 30.00
6 Chris Mullin 6.00 15.00
7 Reggie Miller 10.00 25.00
8 Glen Rice 3.00 8.00
9 Jeff Hornacek 4.00 10.00
10 Jeff Malone 4.00 10.00
11 John Stockton 8.00 20.00
12 Kevin Johnson 4.00 10.00
13 Mark Price 4.00 10.00
14 Tim Hardaway 4.00 10.00
15 Charles Barkley 12.00 30.00
16 Hakeem Olajuwon 12.00 30.00
17 Karl Malone 8.00 20.00
18 Patrick Ewing 8.00 20.00
19 Dennis Rodman 12.00 30.00
20 David Robinson 12.00 30.00
21 Shaquille O'Neal 250.00 600.00

1993-94 Stadium Club

COMPLETE SET (360) 20.00 50.00
COMPLETE SERIES 1 (180) 10.00 25.00
COMPLETE SERIES 2 (180) 10.00 25.00
NUMBER 345 NEVER ISSUED
KUKOC AND CORCHIANI NUMBERED 336
1 Michael Jordan TD 3.00 8.00
2 Kenny Anderson TD .25 .60
3 Steve Smith TD .25 .60
4 Kevin Gamble TD .20 .50
5 Detlef Schrempf TD .30 .75
6 Larry Johnson TD .40 1.00
7 Brad Daugherty TD .25 .60
8 Rumeal Robinson TD .20 .50
9 Micheal Williams TD .20 .50
10 David Robinson TD .60 1.50
11 Sam Perkins TD .25 .60
12 Thurl Bailey .20 .50
13 Sherman Douglas .20 .50
14 Larry Stewart .20 .50
15 Kevin Johnson .30 .75
16 Bill Cartwright .25 .60
17 Larry Nance .25 .60
18 P.J. Brown RC .30 .75
19 Tony Bennett .20 .50
20 Robert Parish .40 1.00
21 David Benoit .20 .50
22 Detlef Schrempf .30 .75
23 Hubert Davis .25 .60
24 Donald Hodge .20 .50
25 Hersey Hawkins .25 .60
26 Mark Jackson .25 .60
27 Reggie Williams .20 .50
28 Lionel Simmons .20 .50
29 Ron Harper .30 .75
30 Chris Mills RC .30 .75
31 Danny Schayes .20 .50
32 J.R. Reid .25 .60
33 Willie Burton .20 .50
34 Greg Anthony .20 .50
35 Elden Campbell .20 .50
36 Ervin Johnson RC .30 .75
37 Scott Brooks .20 .50
38 Johnny Newman .20 .50
39 Rex Chapman .20 .50
40 Chuck Person .25 .60
41 John Williams .20 .50
42 Anthony Bowie .20 .50
43 Negele Knight .20 .50
44 Tyrone Corbin .20 .50
45 Jud Buechler .20 .50
46 Adam Keefe .20 .50
47 Glen Rice .30 .75
48 Tracy Murray .20 .50
49 Rick Mahorn .25 .60
50 Vlade Divac .30 .75
51 Eric Murdock .20 .50
52 Isaiah Morris .20 .50
53 Bobby Hurley RC .30 .75
54 Mitch Richmond .40 1.00
55 Danny Ainge .30 .75
56 Dikembe Mutombo .50 1.25
57 Jeff Hornacek .25 .60
58 Tony Campbell .20 .50
59 Vinny Del Negro .20 .50
60 Xavier McDaniel HC .30 .75
61 Scottie Pippen HC .75 2.00
62 Larry Nance HC .25 .60
63 Dikembe Mutombo HC .50 1.25
64 Hakeem Olajuwon HC .60 1.50
65 Dominique Wilkins HC .50 1.25
66 Clarence Weatherspoon HC .20 .50
67 Chris Morris HC .20 .50
68 Patrick Ewing HC .50 1.25
69 Kevin Willis HC .25 .60
70 Jon Barry .20 .50
71 Jerry Reynolds .20 .50
72 Sarunas Marciulionis .30 .75
73 Mark West .20 .50
74 B.J. Armstrong .30 .75
75 Greg Kite .20 .50
76 LaSalle Thompson .20 .50
77 Randy White .20 .50
78 Alaa Abdelnaby .20 .50
79 Kevin Brooks .20 .50
80 Vern Fleming .25 .60
81 Doc Rivers .25 .60
82 Shawn Bradley RC .30 .75
83 Wayman Tisdale .25 .60
84 Olden Polynice .20 .50
85 Michael Cage .25 .60
86 Harold Miner .25 .60
87 Doug Smith .20 .50
88 Tom Gugliotta .25 .60
89 Hakeem Olajuwon .60 1.50
90 Loy Vaught .20 .50
91 James Worthy .40 1.00
92 John Paxson .30 .75
93 Jon Koncak .20 .50
94 Lee Mayberry .20 .50
95 Clarence Weatherspoon .20 .50
96 Mark Eaton .30 .75
97 Rex Walters RC .25 .60
98 Alvin Robertson .25 .60
99 Dan Majerle .30 .75
100 Shaquille O'Neal 1.50 4.00
101 Derrick Coleman TD .30 .75
102 Hersey Hawkins TD .25 .60
103 Scottie Pippen TD .75 2.00
104 Scott Skiles TD .20 .50
105 Rod Strickland TD .25 .60
106 Pooh Richardson TD .25 .60
107 Tom Gugliotta TD .25 .60
108 Mark Jackson TD .25 .60
109 Dikembe Mutombo TD .50 1.25
110 Charles Barkley TD .75 2.00
111 Otis Thorpe TD .30 .75
112 Malik Sealy .20 .50
113 Mark Macon .20 .50
114 Dee Brown .25 .60
115 Nate McMillan .25 .60
116 John Starks 2.00 5.00
117 Clyde Drexler .50 1.25
118 Antoine Carr .20 .50
119 Doug West .20 .50
120 Victor Alexander .20 .50
121 Kenny Gattison .20 .50
122 Spud Webb .25 .60
123 Rumeal Robinson .20 .50
124 Tim Kempton .20 .50
125 Karl Malone .60 1.50
126 Randy Woods .20 .50
127 Calbert Cheaney RC .30 .75
128 Johnny Dawkins .25 .60
129 Dominique Wilkins .50 1.25
130 Horace Grant .30 .75
131 Bill Laimbeer .30 .75
132 Kenny Smith .25 .60
133 Sedale Threatt .20 .50
134 Brian Shaw .20 .50
135 Dennis Scott .20 .50
136 Mark Bryant .20 .50
137 Xavier McDaniel .30 .75
138 David Wood .20 .50
139 Luther Wright RC .20 .50
140 Lloyd Daniels .20 .50
141 Marlon Maxey UER .20 .50
142 Pooh Richardson .25 .60
143 Jeff Grayer .20 .50
144 LaPhonso Ellis .25 .60
145 Gerald Wilkins .25 .60
146 Dell Curry .30 .75
147 Duane Causwell .20 .50
148 Tim Hardaway .40 1.00
149 Isiah Thomas .50 1.25
150 Doug Edwards RC .30 .75
151 Anthony Peeler .20 .50
152 Tate George .20 .50
153 Terry Davis .20 .50
154 Sam Perkins .25 .60
155 John Salley .25 .60
156 Vernon Maxwell .25 .60
157 Anthony Avent .20 .50
158 Clifford Robinson .30 .75
159 Corie Blount RC .30 .75
160 Gerald Paddio .20 .50
161 Blair Rasmussen .20 .50
162 Carl Herrera .20 .50
163 Chris Smith .20 .50
164 Pervis Ellison .20 .50
165 Rod Strickland .25 .60
166 Jeff Malone .25 .60
167 Danny Ferry .20 .50
168 Kevin Lynch .20 .50
169 Michael Jordan 3.00 8.00
170 Derrick Coleman HC .30 .75
171 Jerome Kersey HC .25 .60
172 David Robinson HC .60 1.50
173 Shawn Kemp HC .50 1.25
174 Karl Malone HC .60 1.50
175 Shaquille O'Neal HC 1.50 4.00
176 Alonzo Mourning HC .50 1.25
177 Charles Barkley HC .75 2.00
178 Larry Johnson HC .40 1.00
179 Checklist 1-90 .20 .50
180 Checklist 91-180 .20 .50
181 Michael Jordan FF 3.00 8.00
182 Dominique Wilkins FF .50 1.25
183 Dennis Rodman FF .75 2.00
184 Scottie Pippen FF .75 2.00
185 Larry Johnson FF .40 1.00
186 Karl Malone FF .60 1.50
187 Clarence Weatherspoon FF .20 .50
188 Charles Barkley FF .75 2.00
189 Patrick Ewing FF .50 1.25
190 Derrick Coleman FF .30 .75
191 LaBradford Smith .20 .50
192 Derek Harper .25 .60
193 Ken Norman .20 .50
194 Rodney Rogers RC .30 .75
195 Chris Dudley .20 .50
196 Gary Payton .40 1.00
197 Andrew Lang .20 .50
198 Billy Owens .25 .60
199 Bryon Russell RC .30 .75
200 Patrick Ewing .50 1.25
201 Stacey King .20 .50
202 Grant Long .20 .50
203 Sean Elliott .30 .75
204 Muggsy Bogues .30 .75
205 Kevin Edwards .20 .50
206 Dale Davis .25 .60
207 Dale Ellis .20 .50
208 Terrell Brandon .25 .60
209 Kevin Gamble .20 .50
210 Robert Horry .30 .75
211 Moses Malone UER .50 1.25
212 Gary Grant .20 .50
213 Bobby Hurley .30 .75
214 Larry Krystkowiak .20 .50
215 A.C. Green .25 .60
216 Christian Laettner .30 .75
217 Orlando Woolridge .20 .50
218 Craig Ehlo .20 .50
219 Terry Porter .25 .60
220 Jamal Mashburn RC .60 1.50
221 Kevin Duckworth .25 .60
222 Shawn Kemp .50 1.25
223 Frank Brickowski .20 .50
224 Chris Webber RC 1.50 4.00
225 Charles Oakley .30 .75
226 Jay Humphries .25 .60
227 Steve Kerr .25 .60
228 Tim Perry .20 .50
229 Sleepy Floyd .25 .60
230 Bimbo Coles .20 .50
231 Eddie Johnson .20 .50
232 Terry Mills .20 .50
233 Danny Manning .25 .60
234 Isaiah Rider RC .50 1.25
235 Darnell Mee RC .20 .50
236 Haywoode Workman .20 .50
237 Scott Skiles .20 .50
238 Otis Thorpe .30 .75
239 Mike Peplowski RC .20 .50
240 Eric Leckner .20 .50
241 Johnny Newman .20 .50
242 Benoit Benjamin .20 .50
243 Doug Christie .25 .60
244 Acie Earl RC .30 .75
245 Luc Longley .25 .60
246 Tyrone Hill .20 .50
247 Allan Houston RC .60 1.50
248 Joe Kleine .20 .50
249 Mookie Blaylock .30 .75
250 Anthony Bonner .20 .50
251 Luther Wright .20 .50
252 Todd Day .20 .50
253 Kendall Gill .25 .60
254 Mario Elie .25 .60
255 Pete Myers UER .20 .50
256 Jim Les .20 .50
257 Stanley Roberts .20 .50
258 Michael Adams .25 .60
259 Hersey Hawkins .25 .60
260 Shawn Bradley .30 .75
261 Scott Haskin RC .20 .50
262 Corie Blount .30 .75
263 Charles Smith .20 .50
264 Armon Gilliam .20 .50
265 Jamal Mashburn NW .60 1.50
266 Anfernee Hardaway NW 1.50 4.00
267 Shawn Bradley NW .30 .75
268 Chris Webber NW 1.50 4.00
269 Bobby Hurley NW .30 .75
270 Isaiah Rider NW .50 1.25
271 Dino Radja NW .30 .75
272 Chris Mills NW .30 .75
273 Nick Van Exel NW .75 2.00
274 Lindsey Hunter NW .30 .75
275 Toni Kukoc NW .75 2.00
276 Popeye Jones NW .30 .75
277 Chris Mills .30 .75
278 Ricky Pierce .25 .60
279 Negele Knight .20 .50
280 Kenny Walker .20 .50
281 Nick Van Exel RC .75 2.00
282 Derrick Coleman UER .30 .75
283 Popeye Jones RC .30 .75
284 Derrick McKey .25 .60
285 Rick Fox .25 .60
286 Jerome Kersey .25 .60
287 Steve Smith .25 .60
288 Brian Williams .20 .50
289 Chris Mullin .40 1.00
290 Terry Cummings .25 .60
291 Donald Royal .20 .50
292 Alonzo Mourning .50 1.25
293 Mike Brown .20 .50
294 Latrell Sprewell .50 1.25
295 Oliver Miller .20 .50
296 Terry Dehere RC .30 .75
297 Detlef Schrempf .30 .75
298 Sam Bowie UER .25 .60
299 Chris Morris .20 .50
300 Scottie Pippen .75 2.00
301 Warren Kidd RC .20 .50
302 Don MacLean .20 .50
303 Sean Rooks .20 .50
304 Matt Geiger .20 .50
305 Dennis Rodman .75 2.00
306 Reggie Miller .60 1.50
307 Vin Baker RC .50 1.25
308 Anfernee Hardaway RC 1.50 4.00
309 Lindsey Hunter RC .30 .75
310 Stacey Augmon .25 .60
311 Randy Brown .20 .50
312 Anthony Mason .25 .60
313 John Stockton .60 1.50
314 Sam Cassell RC .60 1.50
315 Buck Williams .25 .60
316 Bryant Stith .20 .50
317 Brad Daugherty .25 .60
318 Dino Radja RC .30 .75
319 Rony Seikaly .25 .60
320 Charles Barkley .75 2.00
321 Avery Johnson .25 .60
322 Mahmoud Abdul-Rauf .25 .60
323 Larry Johnson .40 1.00
324 Micheal Williams .20 .50
325 Mark Aguirre .25 .60
326 Jim Jackson .25 .60
327 Antonio Harvey RC .30 .75
328 David Robinson .60 1.50
329 Calbert Cheaney .30 .75
330 Kenny Anderson .25 .60
331 Walt Williams .30 .75
332 Kevin Willis .25 .60
333 Nick Anderson .25 .60
334 Rik Smits .25 .60
335 Joe Dumars .40 1.00
336 Toni Kukoc RC .75 2.00
337 Harvey Grant .25 .60
338 Tom Chambers .30 .75
339 Blue Edwards .20 .50
340 Mark Price .30 .75
341 Ervin Johnson .30 .75
342 Rolando Blackman .25 .60
343 Scott Burrell RC .30 .75
344 Gheorghe Muresan RC .30 .75
345 Chris Corchiani UER 336 .20 .50
346 Richard Petruska RC .30 .75
347 Dana Barros .20 .50
348 Hakeem Olajuwon FF .60 1.50
349 Dee Brown FF .25 .60
350 John Starks FF .30 .75
351 Ron Harper FF .30 .75
352 Chris Webber FF 1.50 4.00
353 Dan Majerle FF .30 .75
354 Clyde Drexler FF .50 1.25
355 Shawn Kemp FF .50 1.25
356 David Robinson FF .60 1.50
357 Chris Morris FF .20 .50
358 Shaquille O'Neal FF 1.50 4.00
359 Checklist .20 .50
360 Checklist .20 .50

1993-94 Stadium Club First Day Issue

*FDI: 4X TO 10X BASE CARD HI
SER.1/2 STATED ODDS 1:24
1 Michael Jordan TD 150.00 400.00
169 Michael Jordan 150.00 400.00
181 Michael Jordan FF 150.00 400.00

1993-94 Stadium Club Beam Team

COMPLETE SET (27) 25.00 60.00
COMPLETE SERIES 1 (13) 15.00 40.00
COMPLETE SERIES 2 (14) 8.00 20.00
SER.1/2 STATED ODDS 1:24
1 Shaquille O'Neal 12.00 30.00
2 Mark Price .75 2.00
3 Patrick Ewing 1.25 3.00
4 Michael Jordan 75.00 200.00
5 Charles Barkley 2.00 5.00
6 Reggie Miller 1.50 4.00
7 Derrick Coleman .75 2.00
8 Dominique Wilkins 1.25 3.00
9 Karl Malone 1.50 4.00
10 Alonzo Mourning 1.25 3.00
11 Tim Hardaway 1.00 2.50
12 Hakeem Olajuwon 1.50 4.00
13 David Robinson 1.50 4.00
14 Dan Majerle .75 2.00
15 Larry Johnson 1.00 2.50
16 LaPhonso Ellis .60 1.50
17 Nick Van Exel 2.00 5.00
18 Scottie Pippen 2.00 5.00
19 John Stockton 1.50 4.00
20 Bobby Hurley .75 2.00
21 Chris Webber 4.00 10.00
22 Jamal Mashburn 1.50 4.00

23 Anfernee Hardaway 6.00 15.00
24 Isaiah Rider 1.25 3.00
25 Ken Norman .50 1.25
26 Danny Manning .60 1.50
27 Calbert Cheaney .75 2.00

1993-94 Stadium Club Big Tips

COMPLETE SET (27) 5.00 12.00
COMMON CARD (1-27) .40 1.00

1993-94 Stadium Club Frequent Flyer Points

COMPLETE SET (100) 12.00 30.00
1 Charles Barkley 1.50 4.00
2 Dee Brown .50 1.25
3 Derrick Coleman .60 1.50
4 Clyde Drexler 1.00 2.50
5 Patrick Ewing 1.00 2.50
6 Ron Harper .60 1.50
7 Larry Johnson .75 2.00
8 Shawn Kemp 1.00 2.50
9 Dan Majerle .60 1.50
10 Karl Malone 1.25 3.00
11 Chris Morris .40 1.00
12 Hakeem Olajuwon 1.25 3.00
13 Shaquille O'Neal 3.00 8.00
14 Scottie Pippen 1.50 4.00
15 David Robinson 1.25 3.00
16 Dennis Rodman 1.50 4.00
17 John Starks .60 1.50
18 Clarence Weatherspoon .40 1.00
19 Chris Webber 3.00 8.00
20 Dominique Wilkins 1.00 2.50

1993-94 Stadium Club Frequent Flyer Upgrades

COMPLETE SET (20) 25.00 60.00
POINT CARDS: SER.2 STATED ODDS 1:6
182 Dominique Wilkins 2.50 6.00
183 Dennis Rodman 4.00 10.00
184 Scottie Pippen 4.00 10.00
185 Larry Johnson 2.00 5.00
186 Karl Malone 3.00 8.00
187 Clarence Weatherspoon 1.00 2.50
188 Charles Barkley 4.00 10.00
189 Patrick Ewing 2.50 6.00
190 Derrick Coleman 1.50 4.00
348 Hakeem Olajuwon 3.00 8.00
349 Dee Brown 1.25 3.00
350 John Starks 1.50 4.00
351 Ron Harper 1.50 4.00
352 Chris Webber 8.00 20.00
353 Dan Majerle 4.00 10.00
354 Clyde Drexler 2.50 6.00
355 Shawn Kemp 2.50 6.00
356 David Robinson 3.00 8.00
357 Chris Morris 1.00 2.50
358 Shaquille O'Neal 8.00 20.00

1993-94 Stadium Club Rim Rockers

COMPLETE SET (6) 4.00 10.00
SER.2 STATED ODDS 1:24
1 Shaquille O'Neal 3.00 8.00
2 Harold Miner .50 1.25
3 Charles Barkley 1.50 4.00
4 Dominique Wilkins 1.00 2.50
5 Shawn Kemp 1.00 2.50
6 Robert Horry .60 1.50

1993-94 Stadium Club Super Teams

COMPLETE SET (27) 7.50 15.00
SER.1 STATED ODDS 1:24
1 Atlanta/D.Wilkins WD .50 1.25
2 Boston Celtics
(Xavier McDaniel
Robert Parish) .40 1.00
3 Charlotte/LJ/Mourning .50 1.25
4 Chicago Bulls
(Horace Grant) .75 2.00
5 Cleveland Cavaliers
(Brad Daugherty
John Williams) .25 .60
6 Dallas Mavericks
(Group photo) .40 1.00
7 Denver Nuggets
(Dikembe Mutombo
Kevin Brooks) .50 1.25
8 Detroit Pistons
(Group photo) .40 1.00
9 Golden State Warriors
(Group photo) .40 1.00
10 Houston/Group WCDF 2.50 6.00
11 Indiana Pacers
(Group photo) .40 1.00
12 Los Angeles Clippers
(Danny Manning
Ron Harper) .30 .75
13 Los Angeles Lakers
(Group photo) .75 2.00
14 Miami Heat
(John Salley
Willie Burton) .25 .60
15 Milwaukee Bucks
(Group photo) .40 1.00
16 Minnesota Timberwolves
(Christian Laettner
Felton Spencer) .30 .75
17 New Jersey Nets
(Derrick Coleman) .30 .75
18 New York/P.Ewing WCD 1.00 2.50
19 Orlando/S.O'Neal 2.50 6.00
20 Philadelphia 76ers
(Clarence Weatherspoon
Jeff Hornacek) .25 .60
21 Phoenix/C.Barkley .75 2.00
22 Portland Trail Blazers
(Buck Williams) .25 .60
23 Sacramento Kings
(Lionel Simmons) .20 .50
24 San Antonio/D.Robinson .60 1.50
25 Seattle/S.Kemp WD .75 2.00
26 Utah Jazz
(Group photo) .40 1.00
27 Washington Bullets
(Group photo) .40 1.00

1993-94 Stadium Club Super Teams Division Winners

COMPLETE BAG HAWKS (11) 2.00 5.00
COMPLETE BAG KNICKS (11) 3.00 6.00
COMPLETE BAG ROCKETS (11) 5.00 10.00
COMPLETE BAG SONICS (11) 5.00 10.00
H46 Adam Keefe .40 1.00
H93 Jon Koncak .40 1.00
H129 Dominique Wilkins 1.00 2.50
H150 Doug Edwards .60 1.50
H197 Andrew Lang .40 1.00
H218 Craig Ehlo .40 1.00
H233 Danny Manning .50 1.25
H249 Mookie Blaylock .60 1.50
H310 Stacey Augmon .50 1.25
H332 Kevin Willis .50 1.25
K23 Hubert Davis .50 1.25
K34 Greg Anthony .40 1.00
K81 Doc Rivers .50 1.25
K116 John Starks .60 1.50
K192 Derek Harper .50 1.25
K200 Patrick Ewing 1.00 2.50
K225 Charles Oakley .60 1.50
K250 Anthony Bonner .40 1.00
K263 Charles Smith .40 1.00
K312 Anthony Mason .50 1.25
R37 Scott Brooks .40 1.00
R89 Hakeem Olajuwon 2.50 6.00
R132 Kenny Smith .50 1.25
R156 Vernon Maxwell .50 1.25
R162 Carl Herrera .40 1.00
R210 Robert Horry .60 1.50
R238 Otis Thorpe .60 1.50
R254 Mario Elie .50 1.25
R314 Sam Cassell 1.25 3.00
R346 Richard Petruska .60 1.50
S85 Michael Cage .50 1.25
S115 Nate McMillan .50 1.25
S154 Sam Perkins .50 1.25
S173 Shawn Kemp HC 1.00 2.50
S196 Gary Payton 2.50 6.00
S222 Shawn Kemp 2.50 6.00
S253 Kendall Gill .50 1.25
S278 Ricky Pierce .50 1.25
S297 Detlef Schrempf .60 1.50
S341 Ervin Johnson .60 1.50
HD1 Hawks DW Super Team .60 1.50
KD18 Knicks DW Super Team .40 1.00
RD10 Rocket DW Super Team .40 1.00
SD25 Sonics DW Super Team .40 1.00

1993-94 Stadium Club Super Teams Master Photos

COMPLETE BAG KNICKS (11) 5.00 10.00
COMPLETE BAG ROCKETS (11) 7.50 15.00
K1 Greg Anthony .60 1.50
K2 Anthony Bonner .60 1.50
K3 Hubert Davis .75 2.00
K4 Patrick Ewing 1.50 4.00
K5 Derek Harper .75 2.00
K6 Anthony Mason .75 2.00
K7 Charles Oakley 1.00 2.50
K8 Doc Rivers .75 2.00
K9 Charles Smith .60 1.50
K10 John Starks 1.00 2.50
KMP Knicks MP Superteam .40 1.00
R1 Scott Brooks .60 1.50
R2 Sam Cassell 2.00 5.00
R3 Mario Elie .75 2.00
R4 Carl Herrera .60 1.50
R5 Robert Horry 1.00 2.50
R6 Vernon Maxwell .75 2.00
R7 Hakeem Olajuwon 4.00 10.00
R8 Richard Petruska .75 2.00
R9 Kenny Smith .75 2.00
R10 Otis Thorpe 1.00 2.50
RMP Rockets MP Superteam .40 1.00

1993-94 Stadium Club Super Teams NBA Finals

COMPLETE SET (361) 20.00 50.00
*STARS: .75X TO 2X HI COLUMN
*RCs: .6X TO 1.5X HI
169 Michael Jordan 12.00 30.00

1994-95 Stadium Club

COMPLETE SET (362) 30.00 80.00
COMPLETE SERIES 1 (182) 8.00 20.00
COMPLETE SERIES 2 (180) 8.00 20.00
1 Patrick Ewing .60 1.50
2 Patrick Ewing TG .60 1.50
3 Bimbo Coles .25 .60
4 Elden Campbell .25 .60
5 Brent Price .25 .60
6 Hubert Davis .25 .60
7 Donald Royal .25 .60
8 Tim Perry .25 .60
9 Chris Webber .75 2.00
10 Chris Webber TG .75 2.00
11 Brad Daugherty .30 .75
12 P.J. Brown .25 .60
13 Charles Barkley 1.00 2.50
14 Mario Elie .25 .60
15 Tyrone Hill .25 .60
16 Anfernee Hardaway .75 2.00
17 Anfernee Hardaway TG .75 2.00
18 Toni Kukoc .50 1.25
19 Chris Morris .25 .60
20 Gerald Wilkins .30 .75
21 David Benoit .25 .60
22 Kevin Duckworth .25 .60
23 Derrick Coleman .40 1.00
24 Adam Keefe .25 .60
25 Marlon Maxey .25 .60
26 Vern Fleming .25 .60
27 Jeff Malone .25 .60
28 Rodney Rogers .25 .60
29 Terry Mills .25 .60
30 Doug West .25 .60
31 Doug West TTG .25 .60
32 Shaquille O'Neal 1.50 4.00
33 Scottie Pippen 1.00 2.50
34 Lee Mayberry .25 .60
35 Dale Ellis .25 .60
36 Cedric Ceballos .30 .75
37 Lionel Simmons .25 .60
38 Kenny Gattison .25 .60
39 Popeye Jones .25 .60
40 Jerome Kersey .25 .60
41 Jerome Kersey TTG .25 .60
42 Larry Stewart .25 .60
43 Rod Strickland .25 .60
44 Chris Mills .30 .75
45 Latrell Sprewell .50 1.25
46 Haywoode Workman .25 .60
47 Charles Smith .25 .60
48 Detlef Schrempf .40 1.00
49 Gary Grant .25 .60
50 Gary Grant TTG .25 .60
51 Tom Chambers .30 .75
52 J.R. Reid .25 .60
53 Mookie Blaylock .40 1.00
54 Mookie Blaylock TTG .40 1.00
55 Rony Seikaly .25 .60
56 Isaiah Rider .40 1.00
57 Isaiah Rider TTG .40 1.00
58 Nick Anderson .25 .60
59 Victor Alexander .25 .60
60 Lucious Harris .25 .60
61 Mark Macon .25 .60
62 Otis Thorpe .25 .60
63 Randy Woods .25 .60
64 Clyde Drexler .60 1.50
65 Dikembe Mutombo .60 1.50
66 Todd Day .25 .60
67 Greg Anthony .25 .60
68 Sherman Douglas .25 .60
69 Chris Mullin .50 1.25
70 Kevin Johnson .40 1.00
71 Kendall Gill .25 .60
72 Dennis Rodman 1.00 2.50
73 Dennis Rodman TG 1.00 2.50
74 Jeff Turner .25 .60
75 John Stockton .75 2.00
76 John Stockton TTG .75 2.00
77 Doug Edwards .25 .60
78 Jim Jackson .30 .75
79 Hakeem Olajuwon .75 2.00
80 Glen Rice .40 1.00
81 Christian Laettner .30 .75
82 Terry Porter .25 .60
83 Joe Dumars .40 1.00
84 David Wingate .25 .60
85 B.J. Armstrong .40 1.00
86 Derrick McKey .25 .60
87 Elmore Spencer .25 .60
88 Walt Williams .25 .60
89 Shawn Bradley .25 .60
90 Acie Earl .25 .60
91 Acie Earl TTG .25 .60
92 Randy Brown .25 .60
93 Grant Long .25 .60
94 Terry Dehere .25 .60
95 Spud Webb .30 .75
96 Lindsey Hunter .25 .60
97 Blair Rasmussen .25 .60
98 Tim Hardaway .50 1.25
99 Kevin Edwards .25 .60
100 P.Ewing/R.Williams CT .60 1.50
101 C.Person/C.Barkley CT 1.00 2.50
102 Abdul-Rauf/S.O'Neal CT 1.50 4.00
103 R.Seikaly/D.Coleman CT .40 1.00
104 H.Olajuwon/C.Drexler CT .75 2.00
105 C.Mullin/M.Jackson CT .50 1.25
106 R.Horry/L.Sprewell CT .50 1.25
107 P.Richardson/R.Miller CT .75 2.00
108 D.Scott/K.Anderson CT .30 .75
109 K.Gill/K.Norman CT .25 .60
110 S.Skiles/K.Willis CT .30 .75
111 T.Mills/G.Rice CT .40 1.00
112 C.Laettner/B.Hurley CT .30 .75
113 S.Augmon/L.Johnson CT .50 1.25
114 S.Perkins/J.Worthy CT .50 1.25
115 Carl Herrera .25 .60
116 Sam Bowie .25 .60
117 Gary Payton .60 1.50
118 Danny Ainge .40 1.00
119 Danny Ainge TTG .40 1.00
120 Luc Longley .30 .75
121 Antonio Davis .30 .75
122 Terry Cummings .30 .75
123 Terry Cummings TTG .30 .75
124 Mark Price .40 1.00
125 Jamal Mashburn .40 1.00
126 Mahmoud Abdul-Rauf .25 .60
127 Charles Oakley .40 1.00
128 Steve Smith .30 .75
129 Vin Baker .40 1.00
130 Robert Horry .40 1.00
131 Doug Christie .30 .75
132 Wayman Tisdale .25 .60
133 Wayman Tisdale TTG .25 .60
134 Muggsy Bogues .30 .75
135 Dino Radja .25 .60
136 Jeff Hornacek .30 .75
137 Gheorghe Muresan .25 .60
138 Loy Vaught .25 .60
139 Loy Vaught TTG .25 .60
140 Benoit Benjamin .25 .60
141 Johnny Dawkins .25 .60
142 Allan Houston .40 1.00
143 Jon Barry .25 .60
144 Reggie Miller .75 2.00
145 Kevin Willis .30 .75
146 James Worthy .50 1.25
147 James Worthy TTG .50 1.25
148 Scott Burrell .25 .60
149 Tom Gugliotta .30 .75
150 LaPhonso Ellis .25 .60
151 Doug Smith .25 .60
152 A.C. Green .30 .75
153 A.C. Green TTG .30 .75
154 George Lynch .25 .60
155 Sam Perkins .25 .60
156 Corie Blount .25 .60
157 Xavier McDaniel .25 .60
158 Xavier McDaniel TTG .25 .60
159 Eric Murdock .25 .60
160 David Robinson .75 2.00
161 Karl Malone .75 2.00
162 Karl Malone TTG .75 2.00
163 Clarence Weatherspoon .25 .60
164 Calbert Cheaney .30 .75
165 Tom Hammonds .25 .60
166 Tom Hammonds TTG .25 .60
167 Alonzo Mourning .60 1.50
168 Clifford Robinson .30 .75
169 Micheal Williams .25 .60
170 Ervin Johnson .25 .60
171 Mike Gminski .25 .60
172 Jason Kidd RC 2.00 5.00
173 Anthony Bonner .25 .60
174 Stacey King .25 .60
175 Rex Chapman .25 .60
176 Greg Graham .25 .60
177 Stanley Roberts .25 .60
178 Mitch Richmond .50 1.25
179 Eric Montross RC .30 .75
180 Eddie Jones RC 1.25 3.00
181 Grant Hill RC 2.00 5.00
182 Donyell Marshall RC .40 1.00
183 Glenn Robinson RC .75 2.00
184 Dominique Wilkins .60 1.50
185 Mark Price .40 1.00
186 Anthony Mason .30 .75
187 Tyrone Corbin .25 .60
188 Dale Davis .25 .60
189 Nate McMillan .30 .75
190 Jason Kidd 2.00 5.00
191 John Salley .25 .60
192 Keith Jennings .25 .60
193 Mark Bryant .25 .60
194 Sleepy Floyd .25 .60
195 Grant Hill 2.00 5.00
196 Joe Kleine .25 .60
197 Anthony Peeler .25 .60
198 Malik Sealy .25 .60
199 Kenny Walker .25 .60
200 Donyell Marshall .40 1.00
201 Vlade Divac AI .40 1.00
202 Dino Radja AI .25 .60
203 Carl Herrera AI .25 .60
204 Olden Polynice AI .25 .60
205 Patrick Ewing AI .60 1.50
206 Willie Anderson .25 .60
207 Mitch Richmond .50 1.25
208 John Crotty .25 .60
209 Tracy Murray .25 .60
210 Juwan Howard RC .60 1.50
211 Robert Parish .40 1.00
212 Steve Kerr .30 .75
213 Anthony Bowie .25 .60
214 Tim Breaux .25 .60
215 Sharone Wright RC .30 .75
216 Brian Williams .25 .60
217 Rick Fox .25 .60
218 Harold Miner .25 .60
219 Duane Ferrell .25 .60
220 Lamond Murray RC .40 1.00
221 Blue Edwards .25 .60
222 Bill Cartwright .30 .75
223 Sergei Bazarevich RC .40 1.00
224 Herb Williams .25 .60
225 Brian Grant RC .60 1.50
226 D.Harper/J.Starks BCT .60 1.50
227 R.Strickland/C.Drexler BCT .60 1.50
228 K.Johnson/D.Majerle BCT .40 1.00
229 L.Hunter/J.Dumars BCT .40 1.00
230 T.Hardaway/L.Sprewell BCT .50 1.25
231 Bill Wennington .25 .60
232 Brian Shaw .25 .60
233 Jamie Watson RC .25 .60
234 Chris Whitney .25 .60
235 Eric Montross .30 .75
236 Kenny Smith .30 .75
237 Andrew Lang .25 .60
238 Lorenzo Williams .25 .60
239 Dana Barros .25 .60
240 Eddie Jones 1.25 3.00
241 Harold Ellis .25 .60
242 James Edwards .25 .60
243 Don MacLean .25 .60
244 Ed Pinckney .25 .60
245 Carlos Rogers RC .30 .75
246 Michael Adams .25 .60
247 Rex Walters .25 .60
248 John Starks .40 1.00
249 Terrell Brandon .40 1.00
250 Khalid Reeves RC .30 .75
251 Dominique Wilkins AI .60 1.50
252 Toni Kukoc AI .50 1.25
253 Rick Fox AI .25 .60
254 Detlef Schrempf AI .40 1.00
255 Rik Smits AI .30 .75
256 Johnny Dawkins .25 .60
257 Dan Majerle .40 1.00
258 Mike Brown .25 .60
259 Byron Scott .30 .75
260 Jalen Rose RC 1.00 2.50
261 Byron Houston .25 .60
262 Frank Brickowski .25 .60
263 Vernon Maxwell .25 .60
264 Craig Ehlo .25 .60
265 Yinka Dare RC .25 .60
266 Dee Brown .30 .75
267 Felton Spencer .25 .60
268 Harvey Grant .25 .60
269 Nick Van Exel .40 1.00
270 Bob Martin .25 .60
271 Hersey Hawkins .30 .75
272 Scott Williams .25 .60
273 Sarunas Marciulionis .25 .60
274 Kevin Gamble .25 .60
275 Clifford Rozier RC .25 .60
276 B.J. Armstrong/R.Harper BCT .40 1.00
277 J.Stockton/J.Hornacek BCT .75 2.00
278 B.Hurley/M.Richmond BCT .50 1.25
279 A.Hardaway/D.Scott BCT .75 2.00
280 J.Kidd/J.Jackson BCT 2.00 5.00
281 Ron Harper .30 .75
282 Chuck Person .30 .75
283 John Williams .25 .60
284 Robert Pack .30 .75
285 Aaron McKie RC .40 1.00
286 Chris Smith .25 .60
287 Horace Grant .40 1.00
288 Oliver Miller .25 .60
289 Derek Harper .30 .75
290 Eric Mobley RC .25 .60
291 Scott Skiles .25 .60
292 Olden Polynice .25 .60
293 Mark Jackson .25 .60
294 Wayman Tisdale .25 .60
295 Tony Dumas RC .30 .75
296 Bryon Russell .25 .60
297 Vlade Divac .40 1.00
298 David Wesley .25 .60
299 Askia Jones RC .40 1.00
300 B.J. Tyler RC .25 .60
301 Hakeem Olajuwon AI .75 2.00
302 Luc Longley AI .30 .75
303 Rony Seikaly AI .25 .60
304 Sarunas Marciulionis AI .25 .60
305 Dikembe Mutombo AI .60 1.50
306 Ken Norman .25 .60
307 Dell Curry .25 .60
308 Danny Ferry .25 .60
309 Shawn Kemp .60 1.50
310 Dickey Simpkins RC .30 .75
311 Johnny Newman .25 .60
312 Dwayne Schintzius .25 .60
313 Sean Elliott .30 .75
314 Sean Rooks .25 .60
315 Bill Curley RC .25 .60
316 Bryant Stith .25 .60
317 Pooh Richardson .25 .60
318 Jim McIlvaine RC .30 .75
319 Dennis Scott .30 .75
320 Wesley Person RC .40 1.00
321 Bobby Hurley .25 .60
322 Armon Gilliam .25 .60
323 Rik Smits .30 .75
324 Tony Smith .25 .60
325 Monty Williams RC .50 1.25
326 G.Payton/K.Gill BCT .60 1.50
327 M.Blaylock/S.Augmon BCT .40 1.00
328 M.Jackson/R.Miller BCT .75 2.00
329 S.Cassell/V.Maxwell BCT .40 1.00
330 H.Miner/K.Reeves BCT .30 .75
331 Vinny Del Negro .25 .60
332 Billy Owens .25 .60
333 Mark West .25 .60
334 Matt Geiger .25 .60
335 Greg Minor RC .40 1.00
336 Larry Johnson .50 1.25
337 Donald Hodge .25 .60
338 Aaron Williams RC .40 1.00
339 Jay Humphries .25 .60
340 Charlie Ward RC .40 1.00
341 Scott Brooks .25 .60
342 Stacey Augmon .30 .75
343 Will Perdue .25 .60
344 Dale Ellis .25 .60
345 Brooks Thompson RC .30 .75
346 Manute Bol .25 .60
347 Kenny Anderson .30 .75
348 Willie Burton .25 .60
349 Michael Cage .25 .60
350 Danny Manning .30 .75
351 Ricky Pierce .25 .60
352 Sam Cassell .40 1.00
353 Reggie Miller FG .75 2.00
354 David Robinson FG .75 2.00
355 Shaquille O'Neal FG 1.50 4.00
356 Scottie Pippen FG 1.00 2.50
357 Alonzo Mourning FG .60 1.50
358 Clarence Weatherspoon FG .25 .60
359 Derrick Coleman FG .40 1.00
360 Charles Barkley FG 1.00 2.50
361 Karl Malone FG .75 2.00
362 Chris Webber FG .75 2.00
NNO Reggie Miller AU 50.00 120.00

1994-95 Stadium Club First Day Issue

*STARS: 2.5X TO 6X BASE CARD HI
*RCs: 2.5X TO 6X BASE HI
SER.1/2 STATED ODDS 1:24

1994-95 Stadium Club Beam Team

COMPLETE SET (27) 25.00 60.00
SER.2 STATED ODDS 1:24
1 Mookie Blaylock 1.50 4.00
2 Dominique Wilkins 2.50 6.00
3 Alonzo Mourning 2.50 6.00
4 Toni Kukoc 2.00 5.00
5 Mark Price 1.50 4.00
6 Jason Kidd 8.00 20.00
7 Jalen Rose 4.00 10.00
8 Grant Hill 8.00 20.00
9 Latrell Sprewell 2.00 5.00
10 Hakeem Olajuwon 3.00 8.00
11 Reggie Miller 3.00 8.00
12 Lamond Murray 1.50 4.00
13 George Lynch 1.00 2.50
14 Khalid Reeves 1.25 3.00
15 Glenn Robinson 3.00 8.00
16 Donyell Marshall 1.50 4.00
17 Derrick Coleman 1.50 4.00
18 Patrick Ewing 2.50 6.00
19 Shaquille O'Neal 6.00 15.00
20 Clarence Weatherspoon 1.00 2.50
21 Charles Barkley 4.00 10.00
22 Clifford Robinson 1.25 3.00
23 Bobby Hurley 1.00 2.50
24 David Robinson 3.00 8.00
25 Shawn Kemp 2.50 6.00
26 Karl Malone 3.00 8.00
27 Chris Webber 3.00 8.00

1994-95 Stadium Club Clear Cut

COMPLETE SET (27) 12.00 30.00
SER.1 STATED ODDS 1:12
1 Stacey Augmon .60 1.50
2 Dino Radja .50 1.25
3 Alonzo Mourning 1.25 3.00
4 Scottie Pippen 2.00 5.00
5 Gerald Wilkins .60 1.50
6 Jamal Mashburn .75 2.00
7 Dikembe Mutombo 1.25 3.00
8 Lindsey Hunter .50 1.25
9 Chris Mullin 1.00 2.50
10 Hakeem Olajuwon 1.50 4.00
11 Reggie Miller 1.50 4.00
12 Gary Grant .50 1.25
13 Doug Christie .60 1.50
14 Steve Smith .60 1.50
15 Vin Baker .75 2.00
16 Christian Laettner .60 1.50
17 Derrick Coleman .75 2.00
18 Charles Oakley .75 2.00
19 Dennis Scott .60 1.50
20 Clarence Weatherspoon .50 1.25
21 Charles Barkley 2.00 5.00
22 Clifford Robinson .60 1.50
23 Mitch Richmond 1.00 2.50
24 David Robinson 1.50 4.00
25 Shawn Kemp 1.25 3.00
26 Karl Malone 1.50 4.00
27 Don MacLean .50 1.25

1994-95 Stadium Club Dynasty and Destiny

COMPLETE SET (20) 4.00 10.00
SER.1 STATED ODDS 1:6
1A Mark Price .40 1.00
1B Kenny Anderson .30 .75
2A Karl Malone .75 2.00
2B Derrick Coleman .40 1.00
3A John Stockton .75 2.00
3B Anfernee Hardaway .75 2.00
4A Mitch Richmond .50 1.25
4B Jim Jackson .30 .75
5A James Worthy .50 1.25
5B Jamal Mashburn .40 1.00
6A Patrick Ewing .60 1.50
6B Alonzo Mourning .60 1.50
7A Hakeem Olajuwon .75 2.00
7B Shaquille O'Neal 1.50 4.00
8A Clyde Drexler .60 1.50
8B Isaiah Rider .40 1.00
9A Scottie Pippen 1.00 2.50
9B Latrell Sprewell .50 1.25
10A Charles Barkley 1.00 2.50
10B Chris Webber .75 2.00

1994-95 Stadium Club Rising Stars

COMPLETE SET (12) 20.00 50.00
SER.1 STATED ODDS 1:24
1 Kenny Anderson 1.25 3.00
2 Latrell Sprewell 2.00 5.00
3 Jamal Mashburn 1.50 4.00
4 Alonzo Mourning 2.50 6.00
5 Shaquille O'Neal 6.00 15.00
6 LaPhonso Ellis 1.00 2.50
7 Chris Webber 3.00 8.00
8 Isaiah Rider 1.50 4.00
9 Dikembe Mutombo 2.50 6.00
10 Anfernee Hardaway 3.00 8.00
11 Antonio Davis 1.25 3.00
12 Robert Horry 1.50 4.00

1994-95 Stadium Club Super Skills

COMPLETE SET (25) 12.00 30.00
SER.2 STATED ODDS 1:24
1 Mark Price .60 1.50
2 Tim Hardaway .75 2.00
3 Kevin Johnson .60 1.50
4 John Stockton 1.25 3.00
5 Mookie Blaylock .60 1.50
6 Reggie Miller 1.25 3.00
7 Jeff Hornacek .50 1.25
8 Latrell Sprewell .75 2.00
9 John Starks .60 1.50
10 Nate McMillan .50 1.25
11 Chris Mullin .75 2.00
12 Toni Kukoc .75 2.00
13 Anthony Mason .50 1.25
14 Robert Horry .60 1.50
15 Scottie Pippen 1.50 4.00
16 Charles Barkley 1.50 4.00
17 Dennis Rodman 1.50 4.00
18 Karl Malone 1.25 3.00
19 Chris Webber 1.25 3.00
20 Charles Oakley .60 1.50
21 Patrick Ewing 1.00 2.50
22 Shaquille O'Neal 2.50 6.00
23 Dikembe Mutombo 1.00 2.50
24 David Robinson 1.25 3.00
25 Hakeem Olajuwon 1.25 3.00

1994-95 Stadium Club Super Teams

COMPLETE SET (27) 12.00 30.00
SER.1 STATED ODDS 1:24
1 Atlanta Hawks
Kevin Willis .40 1.00
2 Boston/Group .40 1.00
3 Charlotte Hornets
Muggsy Bogues .40 1.00
4 Chicago Bulls
Group .40 1.00
5 Cleveland Cavaliers
Danny Ferry .40 1.00
6 Dallas/J.Jackson .40 1.00
7 Denver/R.Rogers .40 1.00
8 Detroit/J.Dumars .40 1.00
9 Golden State/C.Webber 2.00 5.00
10 Houston/Olajuwon WCF 4.00 10.00
11 Indiana/Group WD .40 1.00
12 LA Clippers
Group .40 1.00
13 L.A.Lakers/N.Van Exel .40 1.00
14 Miami/G.Rice .40 1.00
15 Milwaukee/V.Baker .40 1.00
16 Minnesota/Laettner .40 1.00
17 New Jersey/C.Morris .40 1.00
18 New York Knicks
Group .40 1.00
19 Orlando/S.O'Neal WCD 6.00 15.00
20 Philadelphia/D.Barros .40 1.00
21 Phoenix/C.Barkley WD 2.00 5.00
22 Portland Trail Blazers
Group .40 1.00
23 Sacramento Kings
Olden Polynice .40 1.00
24 San Antonio/Group WD .40 1.00
25 Seattle Supersonics
Group .40 1.00
26 Utah/J.Stockton 1.00 2.50
27 Washington/Group .40 1.00

1994-95 Stadium Club Super Teams Division Winners

COMP.BAG MAGIC (11) 6.00 12.00
COMP.BAG PACERS (11) 1.50 3.00
COMP.BAG SPURS (11) 2.50 5.00
COMP.BAG SUNS (11) 3.00 6.00
M7 Donald Royal .20 .50
M16 Anfernee Hardaway 1.50 4.00
M32 Shaquille O'Neal 2.50 6.00
M58 Nick Anderson .20 .50
M74 Jeff Turner .20 .50
M213 Anthony Bowie .20 .50
M232 Brian Shaw .20 .50
M287 Horace Grant .30 .75
M319 Dennis Scott .25 .60
M345 Brooks Thompson .25 .60
MD19 Magic DW Super Team .40 1.00
P26 Vern Fleming .20 .50
P46 Haywoode Workman .20 .50
P86 Derrick McKey .20 .50
P121 Antonio Davis .25 .60
P144 Reggie Miller .60 1.50
P188 Dale Davis .20 .50
P219 Duane Ferrell .20 .50
P259 Byron Scott .25 .60
P293 Mark Jackson .25 .60
P323 Rik Smits .25 .60
PD11 Pacers DW Super Team .40 1.00
SP52 J.R. Reid .20 .50
SP72 Dennis Rodman 1.00 2.50
SP73 Dennis Rodman TG 1.00 2.50
SP122 Terry Cummings .25 .60
SP160 David Robinson .75 2.00
SP206 Willie Anderson .20 .50
SP282 Chuck Person .25 .60
SP313 Sean Elliott .25 .60
SP331 Vinny Del Negro .20 .50
SP354 David Robinson FG .75 2.00
SPD24 Spurs DW Super Team .40 1.00
SU13 Charles Barkley 1.00 2.50
SU70 Kevin Johnson .30 .75
SU118 Danny Ainge .30 .75
SU152 A.C. Green .25 .60
SU196 Joe Kleine .20 .50
SU257 Dan Majerle .30 .75
SU294 Wayman Tisdale .20 .50
SU320 Wesley Person .30 .75
SU350 Danny Manning .25 .60
SU360 Charles Barkley FG 1.00 2.50
SUD21 Suns DW Super Team .40 1.00

1994-95 Stadium Club Super Teams Master Photos

COMP.BAG MAGIC (11) 7.50 15.00
COMP.BAG ROCKETS (11) 4.00 8.00
M1 Nick Anderson .30 .75
M2 Anthony Bowie .30 .75
M3 Jeff Turner .30 .75
M4 Dennis Scott .40 1.00
M5 Horace Grant .50 1.25
M6 Shaquille O'Neal 4.00 10.00
M7 Brooks Thompson .40 1.00
M8 Anfernee Hardaway 2.00 5.00
M9 Donald Royal .30 .75
M10 Brian Shaw .30 .75
MM19 Magic MP Super Team .40 1.00
R1 Tim Breaux .30 .75
R2 Scott Brooks .30 .75
R3 Clyde Drexler
Hakeem Olajuwon CT 1.25 3.00
R4 Hakeem Olajuwon 1.50 4.00
R5 Sam Cassell .50 1.25
R6 Vernon Maxwell .30 .75
R7 Mario Elie .30 .75
R8 Carl Herrera .30 .75
R9 Kenny Smith .40 1.00
R10 Robert Horry .50 1.25
MR10 Rockets MP Super Team .40 1.00

1994-95 Stadium Club Super Teams NBA Finals

COMPLETE SET (363) 20.00 50.00
*FINALS: .75X TO 2X HI COLUMN

1994-95 Stadium Club Team of the Future

COMPLETE SET (10) 12.00 30.00
SER.2 STATED ODDS 1:24
1 Anfernee Hardaway 2.50 6.00
2 Latrell Sprewell 1.50 4.00
3 Grant Hill 6.00 15.00
4 Chris Webber 2.50 6.00
5 Shaquille O'Neal 5.00 12.00
6 Jason Kidd 6.00 15.00
7 Jim Jackson 1.00 2.50
8 Jamal Mashburn 1.25 3.00
9 Glenn Robinson 2.50 6.00
10 Alonzo Mourning 2.00 5.00

1995-96 Stadium Club

COMPLETE SET (361) 15.00 40.00
COMPLETE SERIES 1 (180) 15.00 25.00
COMPLETE SERIES 2 (181) 10.00 25.00
1 Michael Jordan 4.00 10.00
2 Glenn Robinson .40 1.00
3 Jason Kidd .60 1.50
4 Clyde Drexler .60 1.50
5 Horace Grant .30 .75
6 Allan Houston .30 .75
7 Xavier McDaniel .25 .60
8 Jeff Hornacek .30 .75
9 Vlade Divac .40 1.00
10 Juwan Howard .40 1.00
11B Keith Jennings EXP Blue .25 .60
11R Keith Jennings EXP Red .25 .60
12 Grant Long .25 .60
13 Jalen Rose .50 1.25
14 Malik Sealy .25 .60
15 Gary Payton .60 1.50
16 Danny Ferry .25 .60
17 Glen Rice .40 1.00
18 Randy Brown .25 .60
19 Greg Graham .25 .60
20 Kenny Anderson UER .30 .75
21 Aaron McKie .25 .60
22 John Salley EXP .25 .60
23 Darrin Hancock .25 .60
24 Carlos Rogers .25 .60
25 Vin Baker .30 .75
26 Bill Wennington .25 .60
27 Kenny Smith .30 .75
28 Sherman Douglas .25 .60
29 Terry Davis .25 .60
30 Grant Hill .60 1.50
31 Reggie Miller .75 2.00
32 Anfernee Hardaway 1.00 2.50
33 Patrick Ewing .60 1.50

34 Charles Barkley 1.00 2.50
35 Eddie Jones .40 1.00
36 Kevin Duckworth .25 .60
37 Tom Hammonds .25 .60
38 Craig Ehlo .25 .60
39 Micheal Williams .25 .60
40 Alonzo Mourning .60 1.50
41 John Williams .25 .60
42 Felton Spencer .25 .60
43 Lamond Murray .25 .60
44B Dontonio Wingfield EXP Blue .25 .60
44R Dontonio Wingfield EXP Red .25 .60
45 Rik Smits .30 .75
46 Donyell Marshall .25 .60
47 Clarence Weatherspoon .25 .60
48 Kevin Edwards .25 .60
49 Charlie Ward .30 .75
50 David Robinson .75 2.00
51 James Robinson .25 .60
52 Bill Cartwright .30 .75
53 Bobby Hurley .25 .60
54 Kevin Gamble .25 .60
55B B.J. Tyler EXP Blue .25 .60
55R B.J. Tyler EXP Red .25 .60
56 Chris Smith .25 .60
57 Wesley Person .25 .60
58 Tim Breaux .25 .60
59 Mitchell Butler .25 .60
60 Toni Kukoc .50 1.25
61 Roy Tarpley .30 .75
62 Todd Day .25 .60
63 Anthony Peeler .25 .60
64 Brian Williams .25 .60
65 Muggsy Bogues .40 1.00
66B Jerome Kersey EXP Blue .25 .60
66R Jerome Kersey EXP Red .25 .60
67 Eric Piatkowski .25 .60
68 Tim Perry .25 .60
69 Chris Gatling .25 .60
70 Mark Price .40 1.00
71 Terry Mills .25 .60
72 Anthony Avent .25 .60
73 Matt Geiger .25 .60
74 Walt Williams .25 .60
75 Sean Elliott .30 .75
76 Ken Norman .25 .60
77B Kendall Gill TA Blue .25 .60
77R Kendall Gill TA Red .25 .60
78 Byron Houston .25 .60
79 Rick Fox .25 .60
80 Derek Harper .30 .75
81 Rod Strickland .30 .75
82 Bryon Russell .25 .60
83 Antonio Davis .25 .60
84 Isaiah Rider .40 1.00
85 Kevin Johnson .40 1.00
86 Derrick Coleman .30 .75
87 Doug Overton .25 .60
88B Hersey Hawkins TA Blue .30 .75
88R Hersey Hawkins TA Red .30 .75
89 Popeye Jones .25 .60
90 Dickey Simpkins .25 .60
91B Rodney Rogers TA Blue .30 .75
91R Rodney Rogers TA Red .30 .75
92B Rex Chapman TA Blue .25 .60
92R Rex Chapman TA Red .25 .60
93B Spud Webb TA Blue .40 1.00
93R Spud Webb TA Red .40 1.00
94 Lee Mayberry .25 .60
95 Cedric Ceballos .30 .75
96 Tyrone Hill .25 .60
97 Bill Curley .25 .60
98 Jeff Turner .25 .60
99B Tyrone Corbin TA Blue .25 .60
99R Tyrone Corbin TA Red .25 .60
100 John Stockton .75 2.00
101B Mookie Blaylock EC Blue .40 1.00
101R Mookie Blaylock EC Red .40 1.00
102B Dino Radja EC Blue .25 .60
102R Dino Radja EC Red .25 .60
103B Alonzo Mourning EC Blue .60 1.50
103R Alonzo Mourning EC Red .60 1.50
104B Scottie Pippen EC Blue 1.00 2.50
104R Scottie Pippen EC Red 1.00 2.50
105B Terrell Brandon EC Blue .30 .75
105R Terrell Brandon EC Red .30 .75
106B Jim Jackson EC Blue .30 .75
106R Jim Jackson EC Red .30 .75
107B Mahmoud Abdul-Rauf EC Blue .30 .75
107R Mahmoud Abdul-Rauf EC Red .30 .75
108B Grant Hill EC Blue .60 1.50
108R Grant Hill EC Red .60 1.50
109B Tim Hardaway EC Blue .50 1.25
109R Tim Hardaway EC Red .50 1.25
110B Hakeem Olajuwon EC Blue .75 2.00
110R Hakeem Olajuwon EC Red .75 2.00
111B Rik Smits EC Blue .30 .75
111R Rik Smits EC Red .30 .75
112B Loy Vaught EC Blue .25 .60
112R Loy Vaught EC Red .25 .60
113B Vlade Divac EC Blue .40 1.00
113R Vlade Divac EC Red .40 1.00
114B Kevin Willis EC Blue .25 .60
114R Kevin Willis EC Red .25 .60
115B Glenn Robinson EC Blue .40 1.00
115R Glenn Robinson EC Red .40 1.00
116B Christian Laettner EC Blue .30 .75
116R Christian Laettner EC Red .30 .75
117B Derrick Coleman EC Blue .30 .75
117R Derrick Coleman EC Red .30 .75
118B Patrick Ewing EC Blue .60 1.50
118R Patrick Ewing EC Red .60 1.50
119B Shaquille O'Neal EC Blue 1.50 4.00
119R Shaquille O'Neal EC Red 1.50 4.00
120B Dana Barros EC Blue .30 .75
120R Dana Barros EC Red .30 .75
121B Charles Barkley EC Blue 1.00 2.50
121R Charles Barkley EC Red 1.00 2.50
122B Rod Strickland EC Blue .25 .60
122R Rod Strickland EC Red .25 .60
123B Brian Grant EC Blue .30 .75
123R Brian Grant EC Red .30 .75
124B David Robinson EC Blue .75 2.00
124R David Robinson EC Red .75 2.00
125B Shawn Kemp EC Blue .60 1.50
125R Shawn Kemp EC Red .60 1.50
126B Oliver Miller EC Blue .25 .60
126R Oliver Miller EC Red .25 .60
127B Karl Malone EC Blue .75 2.00
127R Karl Malone EC Red .75 2.00
128B Benoit Benjamin EC Blue .25 .60
128R Benoit Benjamin EC Red .25 .60
129B Chris Webber EC Blue .50 1.25
129R Chris Webber EC Red .50 1.25
130 Dan Majerle .40 1.00
131 Calbert Cheaney .25 .60
132 Mark Jackson .30 .75
133B Greg Anthony EXP Blue .25 .60
133R Greg Anthony EXP Red .25 .60
134 Scott Burrell .25 .60
135 Detlef Schrempf .40 1.00
136 Marty Conlon .25 .60
137 Rony Seikaly .25 .60
138 Olden Polynice .25 .60
139 Terry Cummings .30 .75
140 Stacey Augmon .30 .75
141 Bryant Stith .25 .60
142 Sean Higgins .25 .60
143 Antoine Carr .25 .60
144B Blue Edwards EXP Blue .25 .60
144R Blue Edwards EXP Red .25 .60
145 A.C. Green .30 .75
146 Bobby Phills .30 .75
147 Terry Dehere .25 .60
148 Sharone Wright .25 .60
149 Nick Anderson .30 .75
150 Jim Jackson .30 .75
151 Eric Montross .25 .60
152 Doug West .25 .60
153 Charles Smith .25 .60
154 Will Perdue .30 .75
155B Gerald Wilkins EXP Blue .25 .60
155R Gerald Wilkins EXP Red .25 .60
156 Robert Horry .40 1.00
157 Robert Parish .50 1.25
158 Lindsey Hunter .25 .60
159 Harvey Grant .40 1.00
160 Tim Hardaway .50 1.25
161 Sarunas Marciulionis .40 1.00
162 Khalid Reeves .25 .60
163 Bo Outlaw .25 .60
164 Dale Davis .25 .60
165 Nick Van Exel .40 1.00
166B Byron Scott EXP Blue .40 1.00
166R Byron Scott EXP Red .40 1.00
167 Steve Smith .30 .75
168 Brian Grant .30 .75
169 Avery Johnson .30 .75
170 Dikembe Mutombo .60 1.50
171 Tom Gugliotta .25 .60
172 Armon Gilliam .25 .60
173 Shawn Bradley .25 .60
174 Herb Williams .25 .60
175 Dino Radja .25 .60
176 Billy Owens .25 .60
177B Kenny Gattison EXP Blue .25 .60
177R Kenny Gattison EXP Red .25 .60
178 J.R. Reid .25 .60
179 Otis Thorpe .30 .75
180 Sam Cassell .40 1.00
181 Sam Cassell .40 1.00
182 Pooh Richardson .25 .60
183 Johnny Newman .25 .60
184 Dennis Scott .25 .60
185 Will Perdue .30 .75
186 Andrew Lang .25 .60
187 Karl Malone .75 2.00
188 Buck Williams .25 .60
189 P.J. Brown .25 .60
190 Khalid Reeves .25 .60
191 Kevin Willis .25 .60
192 Robert Pack .25 .60
193 Joe Dumars .40 1.00
194 Sam Perkins .25 .60
195 Dan Majerle .40 1.00
196 John Williams .25 .60
197 Reggie Williams .25 .60
198 Greg Anthony .25 .60
199 Steve Kerr .40 1.00
200 Richard Dumas .25 .60
201 Dee Brown .30 .75
202 Zan Tabak .25 .60
203 David Wood .25 .60
204 Duane Causwell .25 .60
205 Sedale Threatt .25 .60
206 Hubert Davis .25 .60
207 Donald Hodge .25 .60
208 Duane Ferrell .25 .60
209 Sam Mitchell .25 .60
210 Adam Keefe .25 .60
211 Clifford Robinson .40 1.00
212 Rodney Rogers .30 .75
213 Jayson Williams .25 .60
214 Brian Shaw .25 .60
215 Luc Longley .30 .75
216 Don MacLean .25 .60
217 Rex Chapman .25 .60
218 Wayman Tisdale .25 .60
219 Shawn Kemp .60 1.50
220 Chris Webber .50 1.25
221 Antonio Harvey .25 .60
222 Sarunas Marciulionis .40 1.00
223 Jeff Malone .25 .60
224 Chucky Brown .25 .60
225 Greg Minor .25 .60
226 Clifford Rozier .25 .60
227 Derrick McKey .25 .60
228 Tony Dumas .25 .60
229 Oliver Miller .25 .60
230 Charles Oakley .30 .75
231 Fred Roberts .25 .60
232 Glen Rice .40 1.00
233 Terry Porter .25 .60
234 Mark Macon .25 .60
235 Michael Cage .25 .60
236 Eric Murdock .25 .60
237 Vinny Del Negro .25 .60
238 Spud Webb .40 1.00
239 Mario Elie .25 .60
240 Blue Edwards .25 .60
241 Dontonio Wingfield .25 .60
242 Brooks Thompson .25 .60
243 Alonzo Mourning .60 1.50
244 Dennis Rodman .75 2.00
245 Lorenzo Williams .25 .60
246 Haywoode Workman .25 .60
247 Loy Vaught .25 .60
248 Vernon Maxwell .25 .60
249 Lionel Simmons .25 .60
250 Chris Childs .25 .60
251 Mahmoud Abdul-Rauf .30 .75
252 Vincent Askew .25 .60
253 Chris Morris .25 .60
254 Elliot Perry .25 .60
255 Dell Curry .40 1.00
256 Dana Barros .30 .75
257 Terrell Brandon .30 .75
258 Monty Williams .25 .60
259 Corie Blount .25 .60
260 B.J. Armstrong .40 1.00
261 Jim McIlvaine .25 .60
262 Otis Thorpe .30 .75
263 Sean Rooks .25 .60
264 Tony Massenburg .25 .60
265 Steve Smith .30 .75
266 Ron Harper .30 .75
267 Dale Ellis .30 .75
268 Clyde Drexler .60 1.50
269 Jamie Watson .25 .60
270 Doc Rivers .30 .75
271 Derrick Alston .25 .60
272 Eric Mobley .25 .60
273 Ricky Pierce .25 .60
274 David Wesley .25 .60
275 John Starks .40 1.00
276 Chris Mullin .40 1.00
277 Ervin Johnson .25 .60
278 Jamal Mashburn .40 1.00
279 Joe Kleine .25 .60
280 Mitch Richmond .50 1.25
281 Chris Mills .25 .60
282 Bimbo Coles .25 .60
283 Larry Johnson .50 1.25
284 Stanley Roberts .25 .60
285 Rex Walters .25 .60
286 Donald Royal .25 .60
287 Benoit Benjamin .25 .60
288 Chris Dudley .25 .60
289 Elden Campbell .25 .60
290 Mookie Blaylock .40 1.00
291 Hersey Hawkins .30 .75
292 Anthony Mason .25 .60
293 Latrell Sprewell .40 1.00
294 Harold Miner .25 .60
295 Scott Williams .25 .60
296 David Benoit .25 .60
297 Christian Laettner .30 .75
298 LaPhonso Ellis .30 .75
299 Gheorghe Muresan .25 .60
300 Kendall Gill .25 .60
301 Eddie Johnson .25 .60
302 Terry Cummings .30 .75
303 Chuck Person .30 .75
304 Michael Smith .25 .60
305 Mark West .25 .60
306 Willie Anderson .25 .60
307 Pervis Ellison .40 1.00
308 Brian Williams .25 .60
309 Danny Manning .30 .75
310 Hakeem Olajuwon .75 2.00
311 Scottie Pippen 1.00 2.50
312 Jon Koncak .25 .60
313 Sasha Danilovic RC .40 1.00
314 Lucious Harris .25 .60
315 Yinka Dare .25 .60
316 Eric Williams RC .40 1.00
317 Gary Trent RC .30 .75
318 Theo Ratliff RC .60 1.50
319 Lawrence Moten RC .40 1.00
320 Jerome Allen RC .40 1.00
321 Tyus Edney RC .40 1.00
322 Loren Meyer RC .25 .60
323 Michael Finley RC 1.00 2.50
324 Alan Henderson RC .60 1.50
325 Bob Sura RC .40 1.00
326 Joe Smith RC .50 1.25
327 Damon Stoudamire RC 1.00 2.50
328 Sherrell Ford RC .30 .75
329 Jerry Stackhouse RC 1.25 3.00
330 George Zidek RC .30 .75
331 Brent Barry RC .60 1.50
332 Shawn Respert RC .30 .75
333 Rasheed Wallace RC 1.25 3.00
334 Antonio McDyess RC .50 1.25
335 David Vaughn RC .40 1.00
336 Cory Alexander RC .40 1.00
337 Jason Caffey RC .40 1.00
338 Frankie King RC .40 1.00
339 Travis Best RC .40 1.00
340 Greg Ostertag RC .30 .75
341 Ed O'Bannon RC .30 .75
342 Kurt Thomas RC .40 1.00
343 Kevin Garnett RC 3.00 8.00
344 Bryant Reeves RC .30 .75
345 Corliss Williamson RC .40 1.00
346 Cherokee Parks RC .30 .75
347 Junior Burrough RC .30 .75
348 Randolph Childress RC .30 .75
349 Lou Roe RC .40 1.00
350 Mario Bennett RC .30 .75
351 Dikembe Mutombo XP .60 1.50
352 Larry Johnson XP .50 1.25
353 Vlade Divac XP .60 1.50
354 Karl Malone XP .75 2.00
355 John Stockton XP .75 2.00
356 Alonzo Mourning TA .60 1.50
357 Glen Rice TA .40 1.00
358 Dan Majerle TA .40 1.00
359 John Williams TA .25 .60
360 Mark Price TA .40 1.00
361 Magic Johnson 1.25 3.00

1995-96 Stadium Club Retail Orange

*ORANGE: 3X TO 8X BASE HI

1995-96 Stadium Club Beam Team

COMPLETE SET (20) 200.00 500.00
COMPLETE SERIES 1 (10) 40.00 100.00
COMPLETE SERIES 2 (10) 150.00 400.00
SER.1 STATED ODDS 1:18 HOB/RET, 1:9 JUM
SER.2 STATED ODDS 1:36 HOB, 1:144 JUM
SER.2 STATED ODDS 1:72 RETAIL
B1 David Robinson 6.00 15.00
B2 Juwan Howard 3.00 8.00
B3 Mitch Richmond 4.00 10.00
B4 Reggie Miller 6.00 15.00
B5 Glenn Robinson 3.00 8.00
B6 Shaquille O'Neal 12.00 30.00
B7 Shawn Kemp 5.00 12.00
B8 Karl Malone 6.00 15.00
B9 Jamal Mashburn 3.00 8.00
B10 Alonzo Mourning 5.00 12.00
B11 Charles Barkley 8.00 20.00
B12 Hakeem Olajuwon 6.00 15.00
B13 Kenny Anderson 2.50 6.00
B14 Michael Jordan 200.00 500.00
B15 Dikembe Mutombo 5.00 12.00
B16 Rod Strickland 2.00 5.00
B17 Patrick Ewing 5.00 12.00
B18 Latrell Sprewell 3.00 8.00
B19 Grant Hill 5.00 12.00
B20 Cedric Ceballos 2.50 6.00

1995-96 Stadium Club Draft Picks

COMPLETE SET (15) 6.00 15.00
SKIP-NUMBERED SET
2 Antonio McDyess .60 1.50
3 Jerry Stackhouse 1.50 4.00
4 Rasheed Wallace 1.50 4.00
5 Kevin Garnett 4.00 10.00
6 Bryant Reeves .40 1.00
8 Shawn Respert .40 1.00
9 Ed O'Bannon .40 1.00
11 Gary Trent .40 1.00
12 Cherokee Parks .40 1.00
15 Brent Barry .75 2.00
16 Alan Henderson .50 1.25
17 Bob Sura .40 1.00
18 Theo Ratliff .75 2.00
19 Randolph Childress .40 1.00
22 George Zidek .40 1.00

1995-96 Stadium Club Extreme

13 Jalen Rose .50 1.25
26 Bill Wennington .25 .60
31 Reggie Miller .75 2.00
34 Charles Barkley 1.00 2.50
41 John Williams .25 .60
49 Charlie Ward .30 .75
56 Chris Smith .25 .60
64 Brian Williams .25 .60
65 Muggsy Bogues .40 1.00
72 Anthony Avent .25 .60
96 Tyrone Hill .25 .60
117 Derrick Coleman .30 .75
125 Shawn Kemp .60 1.50
143 Antoine Carr .25 .60
147 Terry Dehere .25 .60
148 Sharone Wright .25 .60
149 Nick Anderson .30 .75
153 Charles Smith .25 .60
168 Brian Grant .30 .75
179 Otis Thorpe .30 .75

1995-96 Stadium Club Intercontinental

COMPLETE SET (10) 4.00 10.00
IC1 Hakeem Olajuwon 2.00 5.00
IC2 Dikembe Mutombo 1.50 4.00
IC3 Bill Wennington .60 1.50
IC4 Rick Fox .60 1.50
IC5 Carl Herrera .60 1.50
IC6 Rony Seikaly .60 1.50
IC7 Rik Smits .75 2.00
IC8 Dino Radja .60 1.50
IC9 Sarunas Marciulionis 1.00 2.50
IC10 Luc Longley .75 2.00

1995-96 Stadium Club Nemeses

COMPLETE SET (10) 20.00 50.00
SER.1 STATED ODDS 1:18 HOB/RET, 1:9 JUM
N1 H.Olajuwon/D.Robinson 2.00 5.00
N2 P.Ewing/R.Smits 1.50 4.00
N3 J.Stockton/K.Johnson 2.00 5.00
N4 S.O'Neal/A.Mourning 4.00 10.00
N5 C.Barkley/K.Malone 2.50 6.00
N6 S.Pippen/G.Hill 2.50 6.00
N7 A.Hardaway/K.Anderson 2.50 6.00
N8 R.Miller/J.Starks 2.00 5.00
N9 T.Kukoc/D.Radja 1.25 3.00
N10 M.Jordan/J.Dumars 15.00 40.00

1995-96 Stadium Club Power Zone

COMPLETE SET (12) 8.00 20.00
COMPLETE SERIES 1 (6) 4.00 10.00
COMPLETE SERIES 2 (6) 4.00 10.00
SER.1 STATED ODDS 1:36 H/R, 1:18 JUM
SER.2 STATED ODDS 1:48 HOB/JUM/RET
PZ1 Shaquille O'Neal 4.00 10.00
PZ2 Charles Barkley 2.50 6.00
PZ3 Patrick Ewing 1.50 4.00
PZ4 Karl Malone 2.00 5.00
PZ5 Larry Johnson 1.25 3.00
PZ6 Derrick Coleman .75 2.00
PZ7 Hakeem Olajuwon 2.00 5.00
PZ8 David Robinson 2.00 5.00
PZ9 Shawn Kemp 1.50 4.00
PZ10 Dennis Rodman 2.00 5.00
PZ11 Alonzo Mourning 1.50 4.00
PZ12 Vin Baker .75 2.00

1995-96 Stadium Club Reign Men

COMPLETE SET (10) 20.00 50.00
SER.2 STATED ODDS 1:48 HOB, 1:96 JUM
SER.2 STATED ODDS 1:24 RETAIL
RM1 Shawn Kemp 2.50 6.00
RM2 Michael Jordan 30.00 80.00
RM3 Larry Johnson 2.00 5.00
RM4 Grant Hill 2.50 6.00
RM5 Isaiah Rider 1.50 4.00
RM6 Sean Elliott 1.25 3.00
RM7 Scottie Pippen 4.00 10.00
RM8 Robert Horry 1.50 4.00
RM9 Kendall Gill 1.00 2.50
RM10 Jerry Stackhouse 5.00 12.00

1995-96 Stadium Club Spike Says

COMPLETE SET (10) 8.00 20.00
SER.2 STATED ODDS 1:24 HOB, 1:12 RET
SS1 Michael Jordan 8.00 20.00
SS2 Alonzo Mourning 1.25 3.00
SS3 Reggie Miller 1.50 4.00
SS4 Patrick Ewing 1.25 3.00
SS5 Charles Barkley 2.00 5.00
SS6 Kenny Anderson .60 1.50
SS7 Scottie Pippen 2.00 5.00
SS8 Jerry Stackhouse 2.50 6.00
SS9 Shaquille O'Neal 3.00 8.00
SS10 John Starks .75 2.00

1995-96 Stadium Club Warp Speed

COMPLETE SET (12) 150.00 400.00
COMPLETE SERIES 1 (6) 125.00 300.00
COMPLETE SERIES 2 (6) 20.00 50.00
SER.1 STATED ODDS 1:36 H/R, 1:18 JUM
SER.2 STATED ODDS 1:48 H/R, 1:48 JUM
WS1 Michael Jordan 150.00 400.00
WS2 Kevin Johnson 2.00 5.00
WS3 Gary Payton 3.00 8.00
WS4 Anfernee Hardaway 5.00 12.00
WS5 Mookie Blaylock 2.00 5.00
WS6 Tim Hardaway 2.50 6.00
WS7 Scottie Pippen 5.00 12.00
WS8 Jason Kidd 3.00 8.00
WS9 Grant Hill 3.00 8.00
WS10 Nick Van Exel 2.00 5.00
WS11 Kenny Anderson 1.50 4.00
WS12 Latrell Sprewell 2.00 5.00

1995-96 Stadium Club Wizards

COMPLETE SET (10) 12.50 30.00
SER.1 STATED ODDS 1:24 HOB, 1:9 JUM
W1 Nick Van Exel 2.00 5.00
W2 Tim Hardaway 2.50 6.00
W3 Mookie Blaylock 2.00 5.00
W4 Gary Payton 3.00 8.00
W5 Jason Kidd 3.00 8.00
W6 Kenny Anderson 1.50 4.00
W7 John Stockton 4.00 10.00
W8 Kevin Johnson 2.00 5.00
W9 Muggsy Bogues 2.00 5.00
W10 Anfernee Hardaway 5.00 12.00

1995-96 Stadium Club X-2

COMPLETE SET (10) 10.00 25.00
SER.2 STATED ODDS 1:24 HOB, 1:96 JUM
SER.2 STATED ODDS 1:48 RETAIL
X1 Hakeem Olajuwon 3.00 8.00
X2 Shaquille O'Neal 6.00 15.00
X3 David Robinson 3.00 8.00
X4 Patrick Ewing 2.50 6.00
X5 Charles Barkley 4.00 10.00
X6 Karl Malone 3.00 8.00
X7 Derrick Coleman 1.25 3.00
X8 Shawn Kemp 2.50 6.00
X9 Vin Baker 1.25 3.00
X10 Vlade Divac 1.50 4.00

1996-97 Stadium Club Promos

COMPLETE SET (6) 1.50 4.00
1 Scottie Pippen 1.00 2.50
33 Arvydas Sabonis .40 1.00
46 Damon Stoudamire .40 1.00
47 Elden Campbell .25 .60
77 Nick Anderson .25 .60
78 David Robinson .75 2.00

1996-97 Stadium Club

COMPLETE SET (180) 15.00 40.00
COMPLETE SERIES 1 (90) 8.00 20.00
COMPLETE SERIES 2 (90) 8.00 20.00
1 Scottie Pippen 1.00 2.50
2 Dale Davis .25 .60
3 Horace Grant .40 1.00
4 Gheorghe Muresan .25 .60
5 Elliot Perry .25 .60
6 Carlos Rogers .25 .60
7 Glenn Robinson .40 1.00
8 Avery Johnson .30 .75
9 Dee Brown .25 .60
10 Grant Hill .60 1.50
11 Tyus Edney .25 .60
12 Patrick Ewing .60 1.50
13 Jason Kidd .60 1.50
14 Clifford Robinson .40 1.00
15 Robert Horry .40 1.00
16 Dell Curry .40 1.00
17 Terry Porter .25 .60
18 Shaquille O'Neal 1.50 4.00
19 Bryant Stith .25 .60
20 Shawn Kemp .60 1.50
21 Kurt Thomas .25 .60
22 Pooh Richardson .25 .60
23 Bob Sura .25 .60
24 Olden Polynice .25 .60
25 Lawrence Moten .25 .60
26 Kendall Gill .40 1.00
27 Cedric Ceballos .30 .75
28 Latrell Sprewell .40 1.00
29 Christian Laettner .40 1.00
30 Jamal Mashburn .40 1.00
31 Jerry Stackhouse .50 1.25
32 John Stockton .75 2.00
33 Arvydas Sabonis .40 1.00
34 Detlef Schrempf .40 1.00
35 Toni Kukoc .40 1.00
36 Sasha Danilovic .25 .60
37 Dana Barros .25 .60
38 Loy Vaught .25 .60
39 John Starks .40 1.00
40 Marty Conlon .25 .60
41 Antonio McDyess .40 1.00
42 Michael Finley .40 1.00
43 Tom Gugliotta .25 .60
44 Terrell Brandon .30 .75
45 Derrick McKey .25 .60
46 Damon Stoudamire .40 1.00
47 Elden Campbell .25 .60
48 Luc Longley .30 .75
49 B.J. Armstrong .30 .75
50 Lindsey Hunter .25 .60
51 Glen Rice .40 1.00
52 Shawn Respert .25 .60
53 Cory Alexander .25 .60
54 Tim Legler .25 .60
55 Bryant Reeves .25 .60
56 Anfernee Hardaway 1.00 2.50
57 Charles Barkley 1.00 2.50
58 Mookie Blaylock .40 1.00
59 Kevin Garnett 1.25 3.00
60 Hersey Hawkins .25 .60
61 Ed O'Bannon .25 .60
62 George Zidek .25 .60
63 Mitch Richmond .50 1.25
64 Derrick Coleman .30 .75
65 Chris Webber .50 1.25
66 Bobby Phills .25 .60
67 Rik Smits .30 .75
68 Jeff Hornacek .30 .75
69 Sam Cassell .30 .75
70 Gary Trent .25 .60
71 LaPhonso Ellis .25 .60
72 Oliver Miller .25 .60
73 Rex Chapman .25 .60
74 Jim Jackson .25 .60
75 Eric Williams .25 .60
76 Brent Barry .30 .75
77 Nick Anderson .30 .75
78 David Robinson .75 2.00
79 Calbert Cheaney .25 .60
80 Joe Smith .30 .75
81 Steve Kerr .30 .75
82 Wayman Tisdale .25 .60
83 Steve Smith .30 .75
84 Clyde Drexler .60 1.50
85 Theo Ratliff .25 .60
86 Charlie Ward .25 .60
87 Karl Malone .75 2.00
88 Clarence Weatherspoon .25 .60
89 Greg Anthony .25 .60
90 Shawn Bradley .25 .60
91 Otis Thorpe .30 .75
92 Larry Johnson .50 1.25
93 Sharone Wright .25 .60
94 Charles Barkley 1.00 2.50
95 Wesley Person .25 .60
96 Dikembe Mutombo .60 1.50
97 Eddie Jones .40 1.00
98 Juwan Howard .40 1.00
99 Grant Hill .60 1.50
100 Chris Carr RC .40 1.00
101 Michael Jordan 4.00 10.00
102 Vincent Askew .25 .60
103 Gary Payton .60 1.50
104 Chris Mills .25 .60
105 Reggie Miller .75 2.00
106 Don MacLean .25 .60
107 John Stockton .75 2.00
108 Mahmoud Abdul-Rauf .30 .75
109 P.J. Brown .25 .60
110 Kenny Anderson .30 .75
111 Mark Price .40 1.00
112 Derek Harper .30 .75
113 Dino Radja .25 .60
114 Terry Dehere .25 .60
115 Mark Jackson .30 .75
116 Vin Baker .30 .75
117 Dennis Scott .25 .60
118 Sean Elliott .40 1.00
119 Lee Mayberry .25 .60
120 Vlade Divac .40 1.00
121 Joe Dumars .50 1.25
122 Isaiah Rider .30 .75
123 Hakeem Olajuwon .75 2.00
124 Robert Pack .25 .60
125 Jalen Rose .30 .75
126 Allan Houston .40 1.00
127 Nate McMillan .25 .60
128 Rod Strickland .40 1.00
129 Sean Rooks .25 .60
130 Dennis Rodman 1.00 2.50
131 Alonzo Mourning .60 1.50
132 Danny Ferry .25 .60
133 Sam Cassell .30 .75
134 Brian Grant .30 .75
135 Karl Malone .75 2.00
136 Chris Gatling .25 .60
137 Tom Gugliotta .25 .60
138 Hubert Davis .25 .60
139 Lucious Harris .25 .60
140 Rony Seikaly .30 .75
141 Alan Henderson .25 .60
142 Mario Elie .25 .60
143 Vinny Del Negro .25 .60
144 Harvey Grant .25 .60
145 Muggsy Bogues .40 1.00
146 Rodney Rogers .25 .60
147 Kevin Johnson .40 1.00
148 Anthony Peeler .25 .60
149 Jon Koncak .25 .60
150 Ricky Pierce .30 .75
151 Todd Day .25 .60
152 Tyrone Hill .25 .60
153 Nick Van Exel .40 1.00
154 Rasheed Wallace .50 1.25
155 Jayson Williams .25 .60
156 Sherman Douglas .25 .60
157 Bryon Russell .25 .60
158 Ron Harper .30 .75
159 Stacey Augmon .30 .75
160 Antonio Davis .25 .60
161 Tim Hardaway .50 1.25
162 Charles Oakley .40 1.00
163 Billy Owens .25 .60
164 Sam Perkins .30 .75
165 Chris Whitney .25 .60
166 Matt Geiger .25 .60
167 Andrew Lang .25 .60
168 Danny Manning .30 .75
169 Doug Christie .25 .60
170 George Lynch .25 .60
171 Malik Sealy .25 .60
172 Eric Montross .25 .60
173 Rick Fox .25 .60
174 Chris Mullin .50 1.25
175 Ken Norman .25 .60
176 Sarunas Marciulionis .25 .60
177 Kevin Garnett 1.25 3.00
178 Brian Shaw .25 .60
179 Will Perdue .25 .60
180 Scott Williams .25 .60
NNO Checklist .20 .50

1996-97 Stadium Club Matrix

*STARS: 3X TO 8X BASE CARD HI
SER.1 STATED ODDS 1:12 H, 1:10 R

1996-97 Stadium Club Class Acts

COMPLETE SET (10) 10.00 25.00
SER.2 STATED ODDS 1:24 HOBBY/RETAIL
*ATO.REF: 5X TO 12X HI
ATO.REF: SER.2 STATED ODDS 1:192 H/R
*REF: 1.5X TO 4X HI COLUMN
REF: SER.2 STATED ODDS 1:96 H/R
CA1 M.Jordan/J.Stackhouse 25.00 60.00
CA2 P.Ewing/A.Mourning 1.00 2.50
CA3 G.Payton/B.Barry 1.00 2.50
CA4 C.Webber/J.Howard .75 2.00
CA5 C.Laettner/G.Hill 1.00 2.50
CA6 S.Abdur-Rahim/J.Kidd 1.00 2.50
CA7 C.Drexler/H.Olajuwon 1.25 3.00
CA8 S.Marbury/K.Anderson 2.00 5.00
CA9 A.Hardaway/L.Wright 1.50 4.00
CA10 A.Iverson/D.Mutombo 5.00 12.00

1996-97 Stadium Club Finest Reprints

SER.1 STATED ODDS 1:24 HOB, 1:20 RET
*REF: 2X TO 5X BASE
2 Nate Archibald 2.00 5.00
4 Charles Barkley 4.00 10.00
5 Rick Barry 2.00 5.00
6 Elgin Baylor 3.00 8.00
7 Dave Bing 2.00 5.00
8 Bird/Erving/Johnson 30.00 80.00
10 Bob Cousy 4.00 10.00
12 Billy Cunningham 2.00 5.00
13 Dave DeBusschere 2.00 5.00
15 Julius Erving 4.00 10.00
17 Walt Frazier 2.50 6.00
18 George Gervin 2.50 6.00
19 Hal Greer 2.00 5.00
24 Michael Jordan 150.00 400.00
26 Karl Malone 3.00 8.00
28 Pete Maravich 5.00 12.00
29 Kevin McHale 2.50 6.00
34 Robert Parish 2.00 5.00
35 Bob Pettit 2.00 5.00
36 Scottie Pippen 4.00 10.00
41 Dolph Schayes 1.50 4.00
44 Isiah Thomas 2.50 6.00
48 Jerry West 3.00 8.00
49 Lenny Wilkens UER 2.00 5.00
50 James Worthy 2.50 6.00

1996-97 Stadium Club Fusion

COMPLETE SET (32) 70.00 140.00
COMPLETE SERIES 1 (16) 50.00 100.00
COMPLETE SERIES 2 (16) 25.00 50.00
SER.1/2 STATED ODDS 1:24 HOBBY
F1 Michael Jordan 75.00 200.00
F2 Chris Webber 2.50 6.00
F3 Glenn Robinson 2.00 5.00
F4 Glen Rice 2.00 5.00
F5 Gary Payton 3.00 8.00
F6 Rik Smits 1.50 4.00
F7 Grant Hill 3.00 8.00
F8 Horace Grant 2.00 5.00
F9 Scottie Pippen 5.00 12.00
F10 Gheorghe Muresan 1.25 3.00
F11 Vin Baker 1.50 4.00
F12 Dell Curry 2.00 5.00
F13 Shawn Kemp 3.00 8.00
F14 Reggie Miller 4.00 10.00
F15 Joe Dumars 2.50 6.00
F16 Anfernee Hardaway 5.00 12.00
F17 Charles Barkley 5.00 12.00
F18 Juwan Howard 2.00 5.00
F19 Patrick Ewing 3.00 8.00
F20 John Stockton 4.00 10.00
F21 David Robinson 4.00 10.00
F22 Cedric Ceballos 1.50 4.00
F23 Alonzo Mourning 3.00 8.00
F24 Mookie Blaylock 2.00 5.00
F25 Clyde Drexler 3.00 8.00
F26 Rod Strickland 2.00 5.00
F27 Larry Johnson 2.50 6.00
F28 Karl Malone 4.00 10.00
F29 Sean Elliott 2.00 5.00
F30 Shaquille O'Neal 8.00 20.00
F31 Tim Hardaway 2.50 6.00
F32 Dikembe Mutombo 3.00 8.00

1996-97 Stadium Club Gallery Player's Private Issue

COMPLETE SET (18) 200.00 400.00

1996-97 Stadium Club Golden Moments

COMPLETE SET (5) 5.00 12.00
GM1 Robert Parish .60 1.50
GM2 John Stockton 1.00 2.50
GM3 M.Jordan/D.Rodman 5.00 12.00
GM4 Dennis Scott .40 1.00
GM5 Hakeem Olajuwon 1.00 2.50

1996-97 Stadium Club High Risers

COMPLETE SET (15) 75.00 200.00
SER.2 STATED ODDS 1:36 HOBBY/RETAIL
HR1 Scottie Pippen 4.00 10.00
HR2 Anfernee Hardaway 4.00 10.00
HR3 Vin Baker 1.25 3.00
HR4 Brent Barry 1.25 3.00
HR5 Clyde Drexler 2.50 6.00
HR6 Kevin Garnett 5.00 12.00
HR7 Grant Hill 2.50 6.00
HR8 Michael Finley 1.50 4.00
HR9 Jerry Stackhouse 2.00 5.00
HR10 Isaiah Rider 1.25 3.00
HR11 Shaquille O'Neal 6.00 15.00
HR12 Antonio McDyess 1.50 4.00
HR13 Shawn Kemp 2.50 6.00
HR14 Michael Jordan 100.00 250.00
HR15 Juwan Howard 1.50 4.00

1996-97 Stadium Club Mega Heroes

COMPLETE SET (9) 8.00 20.00
SER.2 STATED ODDS 1:20 RETAIL
MH1 Dennis Rodman 8.00 20.00
MH2 David Robinson 3.00 8.00
MH3 Karl Malone 3.00 8.00
MH4 Clyde Drexler 2.50 6.00
MH5 Anfernee Hardaway 4.00 10.00
MH6 Hakeem Olajuwon 3.00 8.00
MH7 Charles Oakley 1.50 4.00
MH8 Joe Smith 1.25 3.00
MH9 Glenn Robinson 1.50 4.00

1996-97 Stadium Club Rookie Showcase
COMPLETE SET (25) 20.00 50.00
SER.2 STATED ODDS 1:12 HOBBY/RETAIL
RS1 Marcus Camby 1.50 4.00
RS2 Shareef Abdur-Rahim 1.50 4.00
RS3 Stephon Marbury 3.00 8.00
RS4 Ray Allen 5.00 12.00
RS5 Antoine Walker 1.50 4.00
RS6 Lorenzen Wright .75 2.00
RS7 Kerry Kittles 1.00 2.50
RS8 Samaki Walker .75 2.00
RS9 Erick Dampier 1.00 2.50
RS10 Todd Fuller .60 1.50
RS11 Kobe Bryant 60.00 150.00
RS12 Steve Nash 6.00 15.00
RS13 Tony Delk 1.00 2.50
RS14 Jermaine O'Neal 1.50 4.00
RS15 John Wallace .75 2.00
RS16 Walter McCarty 1.00 2.50
RS17 Dontae' Jones .75 2.00
RS18 Roy Rogers .75 2.00
RS19 Derek Fisher 1.25 3.00
RS20 Martin Muursepp .60 1.50
RS21 Jerome Williams .75 2.00
RS22 Brian Evans .60 1.50
RS23 Priest Lauderdale .60 1.50
RS24 Travis Knight .75 2.00
RS25 Allen Iverson 8.00 20.00

1996-97 Stadium Club Rookies 1
COMPLETE SET (25) 15.00 40.00
R1 Allen Iverson 5.00 12.00
R2 Marcus Camby .40 1.00
R3 Shareef Abdur-Rahim .40 1.00
R4 Stephon Marbury .75 2.00
R5 Ray Allen 1.25 3.00
R6 Antoine Walker .40 1.00
R7 Lorenzen Wright .20 .50
R8 Kerry Kittles .25 .60
R9 Samaki Walker .20 .50
R10 Erick Dampier .25 .60
R11 Todd Fuller .15 .40
R12 Kobe Bryant 20.00 50.00
R13 Steve Nash 1.50 4.00
R14 Tony Delk .25 .60
R15 Jermaine O'Neal .40 1.00
R16 John Wallace .20 .50
R17 Walter McCarty .25 .60
R18 Dontae Jones .20 .50
R19 Roy Rogers .20 .50
R20 Derek Fisher .30 .75
R21 Martin Muursepp .15 .40
R22 Jerome Williams .20 .50
R23 Brian Evans .15 .40
R24 Priest Lauderdale .15 .40
R25 Travis Knight .20 .50

1996-97 Stadium Club Rookies 2
COMPLETE SET (20) 15.00 40.00
R1 Shareef Abdur-Rahim .40 1.00
R2 Tony Delk .25 .60
R3 Priest Lauderdale .15 .40
R4 Roy Rogers .20 .50
R5 Lorenzen Wright .20 .50
R6 Stephon Marbury .75 2.00
R7 Derek Fisher .30 .75
R8 John Wallace .20 .50
R9 Kobe Bryant 20.00 50.00
R10 Kerry Kittles .25 .60
R11 Antoine Walker .40 1.00
R12 Steve Nash 1.50 4.00
R13 Erick Dampier .25 .60
R14 Walter McCarty .25 .60
R15 Vitaly Potapenko .20 .50
R16 Allen Iverson 5.00 12.00
R17 Marcus Camby .40 1.00
R18 Todd Fuller .15 .40
R19 Ray Allen 1.25 3.00
R20 Jermaine O'Neal .40 1.00

1996-97 Stadium Club Shining Moments
COMPLETE SET (15) 5.00 12.00
SM1 Charles Barkley 1.00 2.50
SM2 Michael Jordan 6.00 15.00
SM3 Karl Malone .75 2.00
SM4 Hakeem Olajuwon .75 2.00
SM5 John Stockton .75 2.00
SM6 Patrick Ewing .60 1.50
SM7 Reggie Miller .75 2.00
SM8 David Robinson .75 2.00
SM9 Dennis Rodman 1.00 2.50
SM10 Damon Stoudamire .40 1.00
SM11 Brent Barry .30 .75
SM12 Tim Legler .25 .60
SM13 Jason Kidd .60 1.50
SM14 Terrell Brandon .30 .75
SM15 Allen Iverson 3.00 8.00

1996-97 Stadium Club Special Forces
COMPLETE SET (10) 60.00 150.00
SER.1 STATED ODDS 1:20 RETAIL
SF1 Anfernee Hardaway 4.00 10.00
SF2 Grant Hill 2.50 6.00
SF3 Shawn Kemp 2.50 6.00
SF4 Michael Jordan 100.00 250.00
SF5 Shaquille O'Neal 6.00 15.00
SF6 Scottie Pippen 4.00 10.00
SF7 Damon Stoudamire 1.50 4.00
SF8 Jerry Stackhouse 2.00 5.00
SF9 Gary Payton 2.50 6.00
SF10 Dennis Rodman 4.00 10.00

1996-97 Stadium Club Top Crop
COMPLETE SET (12) 50.00 120.00
SER.1 STATED ODDS 1:24 HOB, 1:20 RET
TC1 S.O'Neal/H.Olajuwon 8.00 20.00
TC2 A.Mourning/D.Mutombo 1.50 4.00
TC3 P.Ewing/D.Robinson 2.00 5.00
TC4 G.Hill/S.Elliott 1.50 4.00
TC5 S.Pippen/S.Kemp 8.00 20.00
TC6 V.Baker/K.Malone 2.00 5.00
TC7 J.Howard/C.Barkley 2.50 6.00
TC8 G.Rice/C.Drexler 1.50 4.00
TC9 M.Jordan/G.Payton 50.00 120.00
TC10 T.Brandon/J.Stockton 2.00 5.00
TC11 R.Miller/M.Richmond 1.50 4.00
TC12 A.Hardaway/J.Kidd 2.50 6.00

1996-97 Stadium Club Welcome Additions
COMPLETE SET (25) 4.00 10.00
WA1 Charles Barkley .75 2.00
WA2 Armon Gilliam .20 .50
WA3 Larry Johnson .40 1.00
WA4 Felton Spencer .20 .50
WA5 Isaiah Rider .25 .60
WA6 Kevin Willis .25 .60
WA7 Mahmoud Abdul-Rauf .25 .60
WA8 Chris Childs .20 .50
WA9 Robert Horry .30 .75
WA10 Dan Majerle .30 .75
WA11 Robert Pack .20 .50
WA12 Rod Strickland .30 .75
WA13 Tyrone Corbin .20 .50
WA14 Anthony Mason .25 .60
WA15 Derek Harper .25 .60
WA16 Kenny Anderson .25 .60
WA17 Hubert Davis .20 .50
WA18 Allan Houston .30 .75
WA19 Shaquille O'Neal 1.25 3.00
WA20 Brent Price .20 .50
WA21 Ervin Johnson .20 .50
WA22 Craig Ehlo .20 .50
WA23 Jalen Rose .25 .60
WA24 Oliver Miller .20 .50
WA25 Mark West .20 .50

1997-98 Stadium Club Promos
COMPLETE SET (6) 2.00 5.00
21 Glen Rice .50 1.25
41 Reggie Miller 1.00 2.50
87 Patrick Ewing .75 2.00
95 Antoine Walker .50 1.25
115 Karl Malone 1.00 2.50
169 Kenny Anderson .40 1.00

1997-98 Stadium Club
COMPLETE SET (240) 30.00 80.00
COMPLETE SERIES 1 (120) 15.00 40.00
COMPLETE SERIES 2 (120) 15.00 40.00
1 Scottie Pippen 1.00 2.50
2 Bryon Russell .25 .60
3 Muggsy Bogues .30 .75
4 Gary Payton .60 1.50
5 Bulls - Team of the 90s 4.00 10.00
6 Corliss Williamson .25 .60
7 Samaki Walker .25 .60
8 Allan Houston .40 1.00
9 Ray Allen .75 2.00
10 Nick Van Exel .40 1.00
11 Chris Mullin .50 1.25
12 Popeye Jones .25 .60
13 Horace Grant .40 1.00
14 Rik Smits .30 .75
15 Wayman Tisdale .25 .60
16 Donny Marshall .25 .60
17 Rod Strickland .30 .75
18 Rod Strickland .30 .75
19 Greg Anthony .30 .75
20 Lindsey Hunter .25 .60
21 Glen Rice .40 1.00
22 Anthony Goldwire .25 .60
23 Mahmoud Abdul-Rauf .25 .60
24 Sean Elliott .30 .75
25 Cory Alexander .25 .60
26 Tyrone Corbin .25 .60
27 Sam Perkins .30 .75
28 Brian Shaw .25 .60
29 Doug Christie .25 .60
30 Mark Jackson .30 .75
31 Christian Laettner .40 1.00
32 Damon Stoudamire .40 1.00
33 Eric Williams .25 .60
34 Glenn Robinson .40 1.00
35 Brooks Thompson .25 .60
36 Derrick Coleman .40 1.00
37 Theo Ratliff .30 .75
38 Ron Harper .40 1.00
39 Hakeem Olajuwon .75 2.00
40 Mitch Richmond .50 1.25
41 Reggie Miller .75 2.00
42 Reggie Miller .75 2.00
43 Shaquille O'Neal 1.25 3.00
44 Zydrunas Ilgauskas .40 1.00
45 Jamal Mashburn .30 .75
46 Isaiah Rider .30 .75
47 Tom Gugliotta .30 .75
48 Rex Chapman .25 .60
49 Lorenzen Wright .25 .60
50 Pooh Richardson .25 .60
51 Armon Gilliam .25 .60
52 Kevin Johnson .40 1.00
53 Kerry Kittles .30 .75
54 Kerry Kittles .30 .75
55 Charles Oakley .30 .75
56 Dennis Rodman 1.00 2.50
57 Greg Ostertag .25 .60
58 Todd Fuller .25 .60
59 Mark Davis .25 .60
60 Erick Strickland RC .25 .60
61 Clifford Robinson .30 .75
62 Nate McMillan .25 .60
63 Steve Kerr .50 1.25
64 Bob Sura .25 .60
65 Danny Ferry .25 .60
66 Loy Vaught .30 .75
67 A.C. Green .30 .75
68 John Stockton .75 2.00
69 Terry Mills .25 .60
70 Voshon Lenard .25 .60
71 Matt Maloney .25 .60
72 Charlie Ward .30 .75
73 Brent Barry .30 .75
74 Chris Webber .50 1.25
75 Stephon Marbury .50 1.25
76 Bryant Stith .25 .60
77 Shareef Abdur-Rahim .40 1.00
78 Sean Rooks .25 .60
79 Rony Seikaly .30 .75
80 Brent Price .25 .60
81 Wesley Person .30 .75
82 Michael Smith .25 .60
83 Gary Trent .25 .60
84 Dan Majerle .40 1.00
85 Rex Walters .25 .60
86 Clarence Weatherspoon .25 .60
87 Patrick Ewing .60 1.50
88 B.J. Armstrong .25 .60
89 Travis Best .25 .60
90 Steve Smith .30 .75
91 Vitaly Potapenko .25 .60
92 Derek Strong .25 .60
93 Michael Finley .40 1.00
94 Will Perdue .25 .60
95 Antoine Walker .40 1.00
96 Chuck Person .30 .75
97 Mookie Blaylock .40 1.00
98 Eric Snow .25 .60
99 Tony Delk .30 .75
100 Mario Elie .25 .60
101 Terrell Brandon .30 .75
102 Shawn Bradley .25 .60
103 Latrell Sprewell .50 1.25
104 Latrell Sprewell .50 1.25
105 Tim Hardaway .50 1.25
106 Terry Porter .25 .60
107 Darrell Armstrong .25 .60
108 Rasheed Wallace .50 1.25
109 Vinny Del Negro .30 .75
110 Tracy Murray .25 .60
111 Lawrence Moten .25 .60
112 Lamond Murray .25 .60
113 Juwan Howard .30 .75
114 Juwan Howard .30 .75
115 Karl Malone .75 2.00
116 Aaron McKie .25 .60
117 Shawn Respert .25 .60
118 Michael Jordan 6.00 15.00
119 Shawn Kemp .60 1.50
120 Arvydas Sabonis .50 1.25
121 Tyus Edney .25 .60
122 Bryant Reeves .25 .60
123 Jason Kidd .60 1.50
124 Dikembe Mutombo .60 1.50
125 Allen Iverson 1.25 3.00
126 Allen Iverson 1.25 3.00
127 Larry Johnson .50 1.25
128 Jerry Stackhouse .40 1.00
129 Kendall Gill .30 .75
130 Kendall Gill .30 .75
131 Vin Baker .30 .75
132 Joe Dumars .50 1.25
133 Calbert Cheaney .25 .60
134 Alonzo Mourning .60 1.50
135 Isaac Austin .25 .60
136 Joe Smith .30 .75
137 Elden Campbell .25 .60
138 Kevin Garnett 1.00 2.50
139 Malik Sealy .30 .75
140 John Starks .40 1.00
141 Clyde Drexler .60 1.50
142 Matt Geiger .25 .60
143 Mark Price .40 1.00
144 Buck Williams .25 .60
145 Grant Hill .60 1.50
146 Kobe Bryant 4.00 10.00
147 Dale Ellis .30 .75
148 Jason Caffey .25 .60
149 Toni Kukoc .50 1.25
150 Avery Johnson .30 .75
151 Alan Henderson .25 .60
152 Walt Williams .30 .75
153 Greg Minor .25 .60
154 Calbert Cheaney .30 .75
155 Vlade Divac .40 1.00
156 Greg Foster .25 .60
157 LaPhonso Ellis .30 .75
158 Charles Barkley 1.00 2.50
159 Antonio Davis .30 .75
160 Roy Rogers .25 .60
161 Robert Horry .40 1.00
162 Sam Cassell .40 1.00
163 Chris Carr .25 .60
164 Robert Pack .25 .60
165 Sam Cassell .30 .75
166 Rodney Rogers .25 .60
167 Chris Childs .25 .60
168 Shandon Anderson .30 .75
169 Kenny Anderson .30 .75
170 Anthony Mason .30 .75
171 Olden Polynice .25 .60
172 David Wingate .25 .60
173 David Robinson .75 2.00
174 Billy Owens .25 .60
175 Detlef Schrempf .40 1.00
176 Carlos Rogers .25 .60
177 Marcus Camby .40 1.00
178 Dana Barros .25 .60
179 Shandon Anderson .25 .60
180 Jayson Williams .30 .75
181 Eldridge Recasner .25 .60
182 Doug West .25 .60
183 Kevin Willis .30 .75
184 Eddie Johnson .25 .60
185 Derek Fisher .40 1.00
186 Eddie Jones .40 1.00
187 Sherman Douglas .25 .60
188 Anthony Peeler .25 .60
189 Danny Manning .30 .75
190 Stacey Augmon .30 .75
191 Hersey Hawkins .30 .75
192 Micheal Williams .25 .60
193 Jeff Hornacek .40 1.00
194 Anfernee Hardaway 1.00 2.50
195 Harvey Grant .25 .60
196 Nick Anderson .30 .75
197 Luc Longley .40 1.00
198 Andrew Lang .25 .60
199 P.J. Brown .30 .75
200 Cedric Ceballos .30 .75
201 Tim Duncan RC 2.50 6.00
202 Ervin Johnson TRAN .25 .60
203 Keith Van Horn RC .60 1.50
204 David Wesley TRAN .25 .60
205 Chauncey Billups RC 1.25 3.00
206 Jim Jackson TRAN .30 .75
207 Antonio Daniels RC .40 1.00
208 Travis Knight TRAN .25 .60
209 Tony Battie RC .40 1.00
210 Bobby Phills TRAN .25 .60
211 Bobby Jackson RC .50 1.25
212 Otis Thorpe TRAN .30 .75
213 Tim Thomas RC .50 1.25
214 Chris Mullin TRAN .50 1.25
215 Adonal Foyle RC .30 .75
216 Brian Williams TRAN .30 .75
217 Tracy McGrady RC 2.00 5.00
218 Tyus Edney TRAN .25 .60
219 Danny Fortson RC .40 1.00
220 Clifford Robinson TRAN .30 .75
221 Olivier Saint-Jean RC .30 .75
222 Vin Baker TRAN .30 .75
223 Austin Croshere RC .30 .75
224 John Wallace TRAN .25 .60
225 Derek Anderson RC .40 1.00
226 Kelvin Cato RC .30 .75
227 Maurice Taylor RC .30 .75
228 Scot Pollard RC .30 .75
229 John Thomas RC .25 .60
230 Dean Garrett TRAN .25 .60
231 Brevin Knight RC .40 1.00
232 Ron Mercer RC .50 1.25
233 Johnny Taylor RC .25 .60
234 Antonio McDyess TRAN .40 1.00
235 Ed Gray RC .40 1.00
236 Terrell Brandon TRAN .30 .75
237 Anthony Parker RC .40 1.00
238 Shawn Kemp TRAN .60 1.50
239 Paul Grant RC .25 .60
240 Dennis Scott TRAN .30 .75

1997-98 Stadium Club First Day Issue
*STARS: 10X TO 25X BASE CARD HI
*RCs: 5X TO 12X BASE HI
STATED PRINT RUN 200 SETS
5 Bulls - Team of the 90's 150.00 400.00
118 Michael Jordan 100.00 200.00

1997-98 Stadium Club One Of A Kind
*STARS: 25X TO 60X BASE CARD HI
*RCs: 12.5X TO 30X BASE HI
STATED PRINT RUN 150 SERIAL #'d SETS
5 Bulls - Team of the 90s 300.00 600.00
118 Michael Jordan 450.00 750.00
146 Kobe Bryant 100.00 250.00

1997-98 Stadium Club Bowman's Best Previews
SER.1/2 STATED ODDS 1:24 HOB/RET
*ATO.REF: 2X TO 5X HI
ATO.REF: SER.1/2 STATED ODDS 1:192 H/R
*REF: 1.25X TO 3X HI COLUMN
REF: SER.1/2 STATED ODDS 1:96 H/R
BBP1 Allen Iverson 3.00 8.00
BBP2 Gary Payton 1.50 4.00
BBP3 Grant Hill 1.50 4.00
BBP4 Anfernee Hardaway 2.50 6.00
BBP5 Karl Malone 2.00 5.00
BBP6 Glen Rice 1.00 2.50
BBP7 Antoine Walker 1.00 2.50
BBP8 Alonzo Mourning 1.50 4.00
BBP9 Shareef Abdur-Rahim 1.00 2.50
BBP10 Shaquille O'Neal 3.00 8.00
BBP11 Maurice Taylor .40 1.00
BBP12 Chauncey Billups 1.50 4.00
BBP13 Paul Grant .30 .75
BBP14 Tony Battie .50 1.25
BBP15 Austin Croshere .60 1.50
BBP16 Brevin Knight .50 1.25
BBP17 Bobby Jackson .60 1.50
BBP18 Johnny Taylor .30 .75
BBP19 Scot Pollard .40 1.00
BBP20 Tariq Abdul-Wahad .40 1.00

1997-98 Stadium Club Co-Signers
SER.1 STATED ODDS 1:387 HOB
SER.2 STATED ODDS 1:309 HOB
CO1 K.Malone/K.Bryant 1,500.00 3,000.00
CO2 J.Howard/H.Olajuwon 125.00 300.00
CO3 J.Starks/J.Smith 25.00 60.00
CO4 C.Drexler/T.Hardaway 75.00 200.00
CO5 K.Bryant/J.Starks 1,000.00 2,000.00
CO6 H.Olajuwon/C.Drexler 200.00 500.00
CO7 T.Hardaway/J.Howard 12.00 30.00
CO8 J.Smith/K.Malone 40.00 100.00
CO9 J.Howard/C.Drexler 30.00 80.00
CO10 H.Olajuwon/T.Hardaway 75.00 200.00
CO11 J.Smith/K.Bryant 1,000.00 2,000.00
CO12 K.Malone/J.Starks 40.00 100.00
CO13 D.Mutombo/C.Billups 50.00 120.00
CO14 K.Van Horn/C.Webber 75.00 200.00
CO15 K.Malone/K.Kittles 40.00 100.00
CO16 R.Mercer/A.Walker 25.00 60.00
CO17 C.Webber/K.Malone 125.00 300.00
CO18 A.Walker/D.Mutombo 30.00 80.00
CO19 K.Kittles/K.Van Horn 12.00 30.00
CO20 C.Billups/R.Mercer 12.00 30.00
CO21 A.Walker/C.Billups 20.00 50.00
CO22 D.Mutombo/R.Mercer 25.00 60.00
CO23 K.Van Horn/K.Malone 40.00 100.00
CO24 C.Webber/K.Kittles 75.00 200.00

1997-98 Stadium Club Hardcourt Heroics
COMPLETE SET (10) 10.00 25.00
SER.1 STATED ODDS 1:12 HOB/RET
H1 Michael Jordan 40.00 100.00
H2 Gary Payton 1.25 3.00
H3 Charles Barkley 2.00 5.00
H4 Mitch Richmond 1.00 2.50
H5 Shawn Kemp 1.25 3.00
H6 Anfernee Hardaway 2.00 5.00
H7 Vin Baker .60 1.50
H8 Shaquille O'Neal 2.50 6.00
H9 Scottie Pippen 2.00 5.00
H10 Grant Hill 1.25 3.00

1997-98 Stadium Club Hardwood Hopefuls
COMPLETE SET (10) 6.00 15.00
SER.1 STATED ODDS 1:36 HOB/RET
HH1 Brevin Knight .50 1.25
HH2 Adonal Foyle .40 1.00
HH3 Keith Van Horn .75 2.00
HH4 Tim Duncan 3.00 8.00
HH5 Danny Fortson .50 1.25
HH6 Tracy McGrady 2.50 6.00
HH7 Tony Battie .50 1.25
HH8 Chauncey Billups 1.50 4.00
HH9 Austin Croshere .40 1.00
HH10 Antonio Daniels .50 1.25

1997-98 Stadium Club Hoop Screams
COMPLETE SET (10) 6.00 15.00
SER.1 STATED ODDS 1:12 HOB/RET
HS1 Shaquille O'Neal 1.50 4.00
HS2 Cedric Ceballos .40 1.00
HS3 Kevin Garnett 1.25 3.00
HS4 Shawn Kemp .75 2.00
HS5 Jerry Stackhouse .50 1.25
HS6 Grant Hill .75 2.00
HS7 Patrick Ewing .75 2.00
HS8 Marcus Camby .50 1.25
HS9 Kobe Bryant 5.00 12.00
HS10 Michael Jordan 15.00 40.00

1997-98 Stadium Club Never Compromise
COMPLETE SET (20) 30.00 80.00
SER.2 STATED ODDS 1:36 HOB/RET
NC1 Michael Jordan 60.00 150.00
NC2 Karl Malone 3.00 8.00
NC3 Hakeem Olajuwon 3.00 8.00
NC4 Kevin Garnett 4.00 10.00
NC5 Dikembe Mutombo 2.50 6.00
NC6 Gary Payton 2.50 6.00
NC7 Grant Hill 2.50 6.00
NC8 Charles Barkley 4.00 10.00
NC9 Shaquille O'Neal 5.00 12.00
NC10 Anfernee Hardaway 4.00 10.00
NC11 Tim Duncan 5.00 12.00
NC12 Keith Van Horn 1.25 3.00
NC13 Tracy McGrady 4.00 10.00
NC14 Tim Thomas 1.00 2.50
NC15 Austin Croshere .60 1.50
NC16 Maurice Taylor .60 1.50
NC17 Chauncey Billups 2.50 6.00
NC18 Adonal Foyle .60 1.50
NC19 Tony Battie .75 2.00
NC20 Bobby Jackson 1.00 2.50

1997-98 Stadium Club Royal Court
COMPLETE SET (20) 20.00 50.00
SER.2 STATED ODDS 1:12 HOB/RET
RC1 Scottie Pippen 2.50 6.00
RC2 Karl Malone 2.00 5.00
RC3 Gary Payton 1.50 4.00
RC4 Kobe Bryant 20.00 50.00
RC5 Antoine Walker 1.00 2.50
RC6 Michael Jordan 40.00 100.00
RC7 Shaquille O'Neal 3.00 8.00
RC8 Dikembe Mutombo 1.50 4.00
RC9 Hakeem Olajuwon 2.00 5.00
RC10 Grant Hill 1.50 4.00
RC11 Tim Duncan 6.00 15.00
RC12 Keith Van Horn .75 2.00
RC13 Chauncey Billups 1.50 4.00
RC14 Antonio Daniels .50 1.25
RC15 Tony Battie .50 1.25
RC16 Bobby Jackson .60 1.50
RC17 Tim Thomas .60 1.50
RC18 Adonal Foyle .40 1.00
RC19 Tracy McGrady 4.00 10.00
RC20 Danny Fortson .50 1.25

1997-98 Stadium Club Triumvirate
SER.1/2 STATED ODDS 1:48 RETAIL
*LUM.CARDS: 1.25X TO 3X BASE TRIUMV.
LUM: SER.1/2 STATED ODDS 1:192 RET
*ILLUM.CARDS: 2X TO 5X BASE TRIUMV.
ILLUM: SER.1/2 STATED ODDS 1:384 RET
T1A Scottie Pippen 8.00 20.00
T1B Michael Jordan 500.00 1,000.00
T1C Dennis Rodman 10.00 25.00
T2A Ray Allen 6.00 15.00
T2B Vin Baker 2.50 6.00
T2C Glenn Robinson 3.00 8.00
T3A Juwan Howard 2.50 6.00
T3B Chris Webber 4.00 10.00
T3C Rod Strickland 2.50 6.00
T4A Christian Laettner 3.00 8.00
T4B Dikembe Mutombo 5.00 12.00
T4C Steve Smith 2.50 6.00
T5A Tom Gugliotta 2.50 6.00
T5B Kevin Garnett 8.00 20.00
T5C Stephon Marbury 4.00 10.00
T6A Charles Barkley 8.00 20.00
T6B Hakeem Olajuwon 6.00 15.00
T6C Clyde Drexler 5.00 12.00
T7A John Stockton 6.00 15.00
T7B Karl Malone 6.00 15.00
T7C Bryon Russell 2.00 5.00
T8A Larry Johnson 4.00 10.00
T8B Patrick Ewing 5.00 12.00
T8C Allan Houston 3.00 8.00
T9A Tim Hardaway 4.00 10.00
T9B Michael Jordan 500.00 1,000.00
T9C Anfernee Hardaway 8.00 20.00
T10A Glen Rice 3.00 8.00
T10B Scottie Pippen 8.00 20.00
T10C Grant Hill 5.00 12.00
T11A Dikembe Mutombo 5.00 12.00
T11B Patrick Ewing 5.00 12.00
T11C Alonzo Mourning 5.00 12.00
T12A Ron Mercer 2.00 5.00
T12B Keith Van Horn 2.50 6.00
T12C Tracy McGrady 8.00 20.00
T13A Gary Payton 5.00 12.00
T13B John Stockton 6.00 15.00
T13C Stephon Marbury 4.00 10.00
T14A Karl Malone 6.00 15.00
T14B Charles Barkley 8.00 20.00
T14C Kevin Garnett 8.00 20.00
T15A David Robinson 6.00 15.00
T15B Hakeem Olajuwon 6.00 15.00
T15C Shaquille O'Neal 10.00 25.00
T16A Antonio Daniels 1.50 4.00
T16B Tim Duncan 10.00 25.00
T16C Adonal Foyle 1.25 3.00

1998-99 Stadium Club Promos
COMPLETE SET (6) 2.00 5.00
PP1 Shareef Abdur-Rahim .40 1.00
PP2 Shaquille O'Neal 1.50 4.00
PP3 Keith Van Horn .40 1.00
PP4 Kevin Garnett 1.00 2.50
PP5 Tracy McGrady .60 1.50
PP6 Tim Hardaway .50 1.25

1998-99 Stadium Club
COMPLETE SET (240) 75.00 200.00
COMPLETE SERIES 1 (120) 60.00 150.00
COMP.SERIES 1 w/o RC (100) 12.00 30.00
COMPLETE SERIES 2 (120) 20.00 50.00
SER.1 ROOKIE REDEMPTION ODDS 1:6
1 Eddie Jones .40 1.00
2 Matt Geiger .25 .60
3 Ray Allen .60 1.50
4 Billy Owens .30 .75
5 Larry Johnson .60 1.50
6 Jerry Stackhouse .40 1.00
7 Travis Best .25 .60
8 Sam Cassell .30 .75
9 Isaiah Rider .30 .75
10 Walter McCarty .25 .60
11 Hakeem Olajuwon .75 2.00
12 Detlef Schrempf .40 1.00
13 Chris Garner .25 .60
14 Voshon Lenard .25 .60
15 Kevin Garnett 1.00 2.50
16 Doug Christie .30 .75
17 Dikembe Mutombo .60 1.50
18 Terrell Brandon .30 .75
19 Brevin Knight .25 .60
20 Dan Majerle .40 1.00
21 Keith Van Horn .40 1.00
22 Jim Jackson .25 .60
23 Theo Ratliff .30 .75
24 Anthony Peeler .25 .60
25 Tim Hardaway .50 1.25
26 Bo Outlaw .25 .60
27 Blue Edwards .25 .60
28 Khalid Reeves .25 .60
29 David Wesley .25 .60
30 Toni Kukoc .40 1.00
31 Jaren Jackson .25 .60
32 Mario Elie .25 .60
33 Nick Anderson .25 .60
34 Derek Anderson .30 .75
35 Rodney Rogers .25 .60
36 Jalen Rose .30 .75
37 Corliss Williamson .25 .60
38 Tyrone Corbin .25 .60
39 Antonio Davis .25 .60
40 Chris Mills .25 .60
41 Clarence Weatherspoon .25 .60
42 George Lynch .25 .60
43 Kelvin Cato .25 .60
44 Anthony Mason .30 .75
45 Tracy McGrady .60 1.50
46 Lamond Murray .25 .60
47 Mookie Blaylock .30 .75
48 Tracy Murray .25 .60
49 Ron Harper .40 1.00
50 Tom Gugliotta .30 .75
51 Allan Houston .40 1.00
52 Arvydas Sabonis .40 1.00
53 Brian Williams .25 .60
54 Brian Shaw .25 .60
55 John Stockton .75 2.00
56 Rick Fox .25 .60
57 Hersey Hawkins .25 .60
58 Danny Manning .30 .75
59 Chris Carr .25 .60
60 Lindsey Hunter .25 .60
61 Donyell Marshall .25 .60
62 Michael Jordan 4.00 10.00
63 Mark Strickland .25 .60
64 LaPhonso Ellis .25 .60
65 Rod Strickland .30 .75
66 David Robinson .75 2.00
67 Cedric Ceballos .30 .75
68 Christian Laettner .30 .75
69 Anthony Goldwire .25 .60
70 Armon Gilliam .25 .60
71 Shaquille O'Neal 1.50 4.00
72 Sherman Douglas .25 .60
73 Kendall Gill .30 .75
74 Charlie Ward .25 .60
75 Allen Iverson 1.00 2.50
76 Shawn Kemp .60 1.50
77 Travis Knight .25 .60
78 Gary Payton .60 1.50
79 Cedric Henderson .25 .60
80 Matt Bullard .25 .60
81 Steve Kerr .30 .75
82 Shawn Bradley .25 .60
83 Antonio McDyess .30 .75
84 Robert Horry .30 .75
85 Darrick Martin .25 .60
86 Derek Strong .25 .60
87 Shandon Anderson .25 .60
88 Lawrence Funderburke .25 .60
89 Brent Price .25 .60
90 Reggie Miller .75 2.00
91 Shareef Abdur-Rahim .40 1.00
92 Jeff Hornacek .30 .75
93 Antoine Carr .25 .60
94 Greg Anthony .25 .60
95 Rex Chapman .30 .75
96 Antoine Walker .40 1.00
97 Bobby Jackson .30 .75
98 Calbert Cheaney .25 .60
99 Avery Johnson .30 .75
100 Jason Kidd .60 1.50
101 Michael Olowokandi RC .60 1.50
102 Mike Bibby RC 1.00 2.50
103 Raef LaFrentz RC .60 1.50
104 Antawn Jamison RC .75 2.00
105 Vince Carter RC 2.50 6.00
106 Robert Traylor RC .50 1.25
107 Jason Williams RC 1.50 4.00
108 Larry Hughes RC .75 2.00
109 Dirk Nowitzki RC 3.00 8.00
110 Paul Pierce RC 2.00 5.00
111 Bonzi Wells RC .50 1.25
112 Michael Doleac RC .40 1.00
113 Keon Clark RC .50 1.25
114 Michael Dickerson RC .50 1.25
115 Matt Harpring RC .50 1.25
116 Bryce Drew RC .30 .75
117 Pat Garrity RC .40 1.00
118 Roshown McLeod RC .30 .75
119 Ricky Davis RC .75 2.00
120 Brian Skinner RC .40 1.00
121 Dee Brown .25 .60
122 Hubert Davis .25 .60
123 Vitaly Potapenko .25 .60
124 Ervin Johnson .25 .60
125 Chris Gatling .25 .60
126 Darrell Armstrong .25 .60
127 Glen Rice .40 1.00
128 Ben Wallace .30 .75
129 Sam Mitchell .25 .60
130 Joe Dumars .40 1.00
131 Terry Davis .25 .60
132 A.C. Green .30 .75
133 Alan Henderson .25 .60
134 Ron Mercer .30 .75
135 Brian Grant .25 .60
136 Chris Childs .25 .60
137 Rony Seikaly .25 .60
138 Pete Chilcutt .25 .60
139 Anfernee Hardaway 1.00 2.50
140 Bryon Russell .25 .60
141 Tim Thomas .30 .75
142 Erick Dampier .25 .60
143 Charles Barkley 1.00 2.50
144 Mark Jackson .30 .75
145 Bryant Reeves .25 .60
146 Tyrone Hill .25 .60
147 Rasheed Wallace .50 1.25
148 Tim Duncan 1.00 2.50
149 Steve Smith .30 .75
150 Alonzo Mourning .60 1.50
151 Danny Fortson .25 .60
152 Aaron Williams .25 .60
153 Andrew DeClercq .25 .60
154 Elden Campbell .25 .60
155 Don Reid .25 .60
156 Rik Smits .30 .75
157 Adonal Foyle .25 .60
158 Muggsy Bogues .30 .75
159 Chris Mullin .50 1.25
160 Randy Brown .25 .60
161 Kenny Anderson .30 .75
162 Tariq Abdul-Wahad .25 .60
163 P.J. Brown .25 .60
164 Jayson Williams .25 .60
165 Grant Hill .60 1.50
166 Clifford Robinson .25 .60
167 Damon Stoudamire .40 1.00
168 Aaron McKie .25 .60
169 Erick Strickland .25 .60
170 Kobe Bryant 3.00 8.00
171 Karl Malone .75 2.00
172 Eric Piatkowski .25 .60
173 Rodrick Rhodes .25 .60
174 Sean Elliott .40 1.00
175 John Wallace .25 .60
176 Derek Fisher .30 .75
177 Maurice Taylor .25 .60
178 Wesley Person .25 .60
179 Jamal Mashburn .40 1.00
180 Patrick Ewing .60 1.50
181 Howard Eisley .25 .60
182 Michael Finley .40 1.00
183 Juwan Howard .30 .75
184 Matt Maloney .25 .60
185 Glenn Robinson .40 1.00
186 Zydrunas Ilgauskas .40 1.00
187 Dana Barros .25 .60
188 Stacey Augmon .30 .75
189 Bobby Phills .25 .60
190 Kerry Kittles .30 .75
191 Vin Baker .30 .75
192 Stephon Marbury .50 1.25
193 Peja Stojakovic RC .75 2.00
194 Michael Olowokandi .50 1.25
195 Mike Bibby .75 2.00
196 Raef LaFrentz .50 1.25
197 Antawn Jamison .60 1.50
198 Vince Carter 2.00 5.00
199 Robert Traylor .40 1.00
200 Jason Williams 1.25 3.00
201 Larry Hughes .60 1.50
202 Dirk Nowitzki 2.50 6.00
203 Paul Pierce 1.50 4.00
204 Bonzi Wells .40 1.00
205 Michael Doleac .30 .75
206 Keon Clark .40 1.00
207 Michael Dickerson .40 1.00
208 Matt Harpring .40 1.00
209 Bryce Drew .25 .60
210 Pat Garrity .30 .75
211 Roshown McLeod .25 .60
212 Ricky Davis .60 1.50
213 Brian Skinner .30 .75
214 Tyronn Lue RC .50 1.25
215 Felipe Lopez RC .25 .60
216 Al Harrington RC .50 1.25
217 Sam Jacobson RC .25 .60
218 Vladimir Stepania RC .40 1.00
219 Corey Benjamin RC .25 .60
220 Nazr Mohammed RC .40 1.00
221 Tom Gugliotta TRAN .30 .75
222 Derrick Coleman TRAN .30 .75
223 Mitch Richmond TRAN .50 1.25
224 John Starks TRAN .40 1.00
225 Antonio McDyess TRAN .30 .75
226 Joe Smith TRAN .30 .75
227 Bobby Jackson TRAN .30 .75
228 Luc Longley TRAN .30 .75
229 Isaac Austin TRAN .25 .60
230 Chris Webber TRAN .50 1.25
231 Chauncey Billups TRAN .50 1.25
232 Sam Perkins TRAN .25 .60
233 Loy Vaught TRAN .30 .75
234 Antonio Daniels TRAN .25 .60
235 Brent Barry TRAN .30 .75
236 Latrell Sprewell TRAN .50 1.25
237 Vlade Divac TRAN .40 1.00
238 Marcus Camby TRAN .30 .75
239 Charles Oakley TRAN .30 .75
240 Scottie Pippen TRAN 1.00 2.50

1998-99 Stadium Club First Day Issue
*STARS: 12.5X TO 30X BASE CARD HI
*SER.1 RCs: 1X TO 2.5X BASE HI
*SER.2 RCs: 6X TO 15X BASE HI
STATED PRINT RUN 200 SERIAL #'d SETS
62 Michael Jordan 400.00 800.00
105 Vince Carter 40.00 100.00

109 Dirk Nowitzki 50.00 120.00
198 Vince Carter 25.00 60.00
202 Dirk Nowitzki 30.00 80.00
203 Paul Pierce 25.00 60.00

1998-99 Stadium Club One Of A Kind

*STARS: 12X TO 30X BASE CARD HI
*SER.1 RCs: 1.25X TO 3X BASE HI
*SER.2 RCs: 8X TO 20X BASE HI
SER.1 STATED ODDS 1:56 HOBBY
SER.2 STATED ODDS 1:55 HOBBY
STATED PRINT RUN 150 SERIAL #'d SETS
62 Michael Jordan 500.00 1,000.00
105 Vince Carter 125.00 300.00
109 Dirk Nowitzki 150.00 400.00
170 Kobe Bryant 300.00 600.00
198 Vince Carter 75.00 200.00
202 Dirk Nowitzki 100.00 250.00

1998-99 Stadium Club Chrome

COMPLETE SET (40) 20.00 50.00
COMPLETE SERIES 1 (20) 10.00 25.00
COMPLETE SERIES 2 (20) 10.00 25.00
SER.1/2 STATED ODDS 1:12 HOB/RET
*REF: 1X TO 2.5X HI COLUMN
REF: SER.1/2 STATED ODDS 1:48 H/R
SCC1 Alonzo Mourning 1.25 3.00
SCC2 Scottie Pippen 2.00 5.00
SCC3 Patrick Ewing 1.25 3.00
SCC4 Vin Baker .60 1.50
SCC5 Glenn Robinson .75 2.00
SCC6 Kobe Bryant 15.00 40.00
SCC7 Charles Barkley 2.00 5.00
SCC8 Chris Mullin 1.00 2.50
SCC9 Steve Smith .60 1.50
SCC10 Stephon Marbury 1.00 2.50
SCC11 Zydrunas Ilgauskas .75 2.00
SCC12 Jayson Williams .50 1.25
SCC13 Juwan Howard .60 1.50
SCC14 Grant Hill 1.25 3.00
SCC15 Damon Stoudamire .75 2.00
SCC16 Ron Mercer .60 1.50
SCC17 Tim Duncan 2.00 5.00
SCC18 Michael Finley .75 2.00
SCC19 Glen Rice .75 2.00
SCC20 Karl Malone 1.50 4.00
SCC21 Eddie Jones .75 2.00
SCC22 Dikembe Mutombo 1.25 3.00
SCC23 Keith Van Horn .75 2.00
SCC24 Jason Kidd 1.25 3.00
SCC25 Shaquille O'Neal 3.00 8.00
SCC26 Kevin Garnett 2.00 5.00
SCC27 Allen Iverson 2.00 5.00
SCC28 Shawn Kemp 1.25 3.00
SCC29 Gary Payton 1.25 3.00
SCC30 Shareef Abdur-Rahim .75 2.00
SCC31 Mike Bibby 1.25 3.00
SCC32 Raef LaFrentz .75 2.00
SCC33 Jason Williams 2.00 5.00
SCC34 Paul Pierce 2.50 6.00
SCC35 Michael Doleac .50 1.25
SCC36 Michael Dickerson .60 1.50
SCC37 Bryce Drew .40 1.00
SCC38 Roshown McLeod .40 1.00
SCC39 Felipe Lopez .40 1.00
SCC40 Al Harrington .75 2.00

1998-99 Stadium Club Chrome Refractors

*REF: 1.25X TO 3X BASE CARD HI
SCC6 Kobe Bryant 75.00 200.00
SCC17 Tim Duncan 12.00 30.00
SCC25 Shaquille O'Neal 12.00 30.00
SCC27 Allen Iverson 12.00 30.00
SCC33 Jason Williams 15.00 40.00
SCC34 Paul Pierce 15.00 40.00

1998-99 Stadium Club Co-Signers

SER.1 STATED OVERALL ODDS 1:209 HOB
SER.2 STATED OVERALL ODDS 1:290 HOB
CO1 T.Duncan/K.Bryant 3,000.00 6,000.00
CO2 L.Johnson/D.Stoudamire 75.00 200.00
CO3 A.Walker/J.Kidd 75.00 200.00
CO4 G.Payton/S.Abdur-Rahim 20.00 50.00
CO5 K.Bryant/L.Johnson 1,500.00 3,000.00
CO6 T.Duncan/D.Stoudamire 200.00 500.00
CO7 S.Abdur-Rahim/A.Walker 15.00 40.00
CO8 G.Payton/J.Kidd 75.00 200.00
CO9 D.Stoudamire/K.Bryant 1,500.00 3,000.00
CO10 L.Johnson/T.Duncan 300.00 600.00
CO11 J.Kidd/S.Abdur-Rahim 40.00 100.00
CO12 A.Walker/G.Payton 25.00 60.00
CO13 T.Duncan/E.Jones 300.00 600.00
CO14 J.Williams/V.Baker 15.00 40.00
CO15 E.Jones/J.Williams 15.00 40.00
CO16 V.Baker/T.Duncan 300.00 600.00
CO17 E.Jones/V.Baker 15.00 40.00
CO18 T.Duncan/J.Williams 200.00 500.00
CO19 A.Jamison/M.Olowo. 15.00 40.00
CO20 V.Carter/M.Bibby 125.00 300.00
CO21 M.Olowokandi/V.Carter 75.00 200.00
CO22 M.Bibby/A.Jamison 40.00 100.00
CO23 A.Jamison/V.Carter 100.00 250.00
CO24 M.Bibby/M.Olowo. 25.00 60.00

1998-99 Stadium Club Never Compromise

COMPLETE SET (20) 12.00 30.00
COMPLETE SERIES 1 (10) 6.00 15.00
COMPLETE SERIES 2 (10) 6.00 15.00
SER.1/2 STATED ODDS 1:12 HOB/RET
NC1 Michael Jordan 20.00 50.00
NC2 Kobe Bryant 4.00 10.00
NC3 Vin Baker .40 1.00
NC4 Tim Duncan 1.25 3.00
NC5 Eddie Jones .50 1.25
NC6 Shawn Kemp .75 2.00
NC7 Grant Hill .75 2.00
NC8 Antoine Walker .50 1.25
NC9 Karl Malone 1.00 2.50
NC10 Scottie Pippen 1.25 3.00
NC11 Michael Olowokandi .50 1.25
NC12 Mike Bibby .75 2.00
NC13 Raef LaFrentz .50 1.25
NC14 Antawn Jamison .60 1.50
NC15 Vince Carter 2.00 5.00
NC16 Robert Traylor .40 1.00
NC17 Jason Williams 1.25 3.00
NC18 Bryce Drew .25 .60
NC19 Paul Pierce 1.50 4.00
NC20 Felipe Lopez .25 .60

1998-99 Stadium Club Never Compromise Oversized

1 Kobe Bryant 5.00 12.00
2 Vin Baker .50 1.25
3 Tim Duncan 1.50 4.00
4 Eddie Jones .60 1.50
5 Shawn Kemp 1.00 2.50
6 Antoine Walker .60 1.50
7 Karl Malone 1.25 3.00
8 Scottie Pippen 1.50 4.00

1998-99 Stadium Club Prime Rookies

COMPLETE SET (10) 30.00 80.00
SER.1 STATED ODDS 1:16 HOB/RET
P1 Michael Olowokandi 2.00 5.00
P2 Mike Bibby 3.00 8.00
P3 Raef LaFrentz 2.00 5.00
P4 Antawn Jamison 2.50 6.00
P5 Vince Carter 10.00 25.00
P6 Robert Traylor 1.50 4.00
P7 Jason Williams 5.00 12.00
P8 Larry Hughes 2.50 6.00
P9 Dirk Nowitzki 15.00 40.00
P10 Paul Pierce 6.00 15.00

1998-99 Stadium Club Royal Court

COMPLETE SET (15) 75.00 200.00
SER.2 STATED ODDS 1:16 HOB/RET
RC1 Gary Payton 1.50 4.00
RC2 Kobe Bryant 25.00 60.00
RC3 Tim Duncan 2.50 6.00
RC4 Scottie Pippen 2.50 6.00
RC5 Allen Iverson 2.50 6.00
RC6 Shaquille O'Neal 4.00 10.00
RC7 Stephon Marbury 1.25 3.00
RC8 Antoine Walker 1.00 2.50
RC9 Michael Jordan 75.00 200.00
RC10 Keith Van Horn 1.00 2.50
RC11 Michael Olowokandi 1.25 3.00
RC12 Mike Bibby 2.00 5.00
RC13 Antawn Jamison 1.50 4.00
RC14 Robert Traylor 1.00 2.50
RC15 Roshown McLeod .60 1.50

1998-99 Stadium Club Statliners

COMPLETE SET (20) 25.00 60.00
SER.1 STATED ODDS 1:8 HOB/RET
S1 Karl Malone 1.25 3.00
S2 Michael Jordan 15.00 40.00
S3 Antoine Walker .60 1.50
S4 Tim Duncan 1.50 4.00
S5 Grant Hill 1.00 2.50
S6 Allen Iverson 1.50 4.00
S7 Kevin Garnett 1.50 4.00
S8 Gary Payton 1.00 2.50
S9 Shareef Abdur-Rahim .60 1.50
S10 Shawn Kemp 1.00 2.50
S11 Stephon Marbury .75 2.00
S12 Vin Baker .50 1.25
S13 Ray Allen 1.00 2.50
S14 Glen Rice .60 1.50
S15 Dikembe Mutombo 1.00 2.50
S16 Shaquille O'Neal 2.50 6.00
S17 Kobe Bryant 12.00 30.00
S18 Scottie Pippen 1.50 4.00
S19 Keith Van Horn .60 1.50
S20 David Robinson 1.25 3.00

1998-99 Stadium Club Triumvirate

SER.1/2 STATED ODDS 1:24 HOBBY
*LUMINESCENT: 1X TO 2.5X HI COLUMN
LUM: SER.1/2 STATED ODDS 1:96 HOB
*ILLUMINATOR: 2X TO 5X HI
ILLUM: SER.1/2 STATED ODDS 1:192 HOB
T1A Kenny Anderson 1.00 2.50
T1B Antoine Walker 1.25 3.00
T1C Ron Mercer 1.00 2.50
T2A Kobe Bryant 8.00 20.00
T2B Shaquille O'Neal 5.00 12.00
T2C Eddie Jones 1.25 3.00
T3A Stephon Marbury 1.50 4.00
T3B Kevin Garnett 3.00 8.00
T3C Tom Gugliotta 1.00 2.50
T4A Jayson Williams .75 2.00
T4B Keith Van Horn 1.25 3.00
T4C Kerry Kittles 1.00 2.50
T5A Kevin Johnson 1.25 3.00
T5B Antonio McDyess 1.50 4.00
T5C Jason Kidd 2.00 5.00
T6A Avery Johnson 1.00 2.50
T6B David Robinson 2.50 6.00
T6C Tim Duncan 3.00 8.00
T7A Vin Baker 1.00 2.50
T7B Gary Payton 2.00 5.00
T7C Detlef Schrempf 1.25 3.00
T8A John Stockton 2.50 6.00
T8B Karl Malone 2.50 6.00
T8C Jeff Hornacek 1.00 2.50
T9A Shaquille O'Neal 5.00 12.00
T9B David Robinson 2.50 6.00
T9C Hakeem Olajuwon 2.50 6.00
T10A Dikembe Mutombo 2.00 5.00
T10B Alonzo Mourning 2.00 5.00
T10C Patrick Ewing 2.00 5.00
T11A Tim Duncan 3.00 8.00
T11B Kevin Garnett 3.00 8.00
T11C Shareef Abdur-Rahim 1.25 3.00
T12A Shawn Kemp 2.00 5.00
T12B Grant Hill 2.00 5.00
T12C Antoine Walker 1.25 3.00
T13A Kobe Bryant 10.00 25.00
T13B Gary Payton 2.00 5.00
T13C Stephon Marbury 1.50 4.00
T14A Ray Allen 2.00 5.00
T14B Allen Iverson 3.00 8.00
T14C Anfernee Hardaway 3.00 8.00
T15A Antawn Jamison 2.00 5.00
T15B Michael Olowokandi 1.50 4.00
T15C Raef LaFrentz 1.50 4.00
T16A Robert Traylor 1.25 3.00
T16B Larry Hughes 2.00 5.00
T16C Vince Carter 6.00 15.00

1998-99 Stadium Club Wing Men

COMPLETE SET (20) 20.00 50.00
SER.2 STATED ODDS 1:8 HOB/RET
W1 Kobe Bryant 12.00 30.00
W2 Tim Duncan 2.00 5.00
W3 Michael Finley .75 2.00
W4 Kevin Garnett 2.00 5.00
W5 Shawn Kemp 1.25 3.00
W6 Grant Hill 1.25 3.00
W7 Eddie Jones .75 2.00
W8 Tim Thomas .60 1.50
W9 Vin Baker .60 1.50
W10 Antoine Walker .75 2.00
W11 Steve Smith .60 1.50
W12 Glen Rice .75 2.00
W13 Ron Mercer .60 1.50
W14 Allen Iverson 2.00 5.00
W15 Ray Allen 1.25 3.00
W16 Glenn Robinson .75 2.00
W17 Kerry Kittles .60 1.50
W18 Vince Carter 6.00 15.00
W19 Larry Hughes 1.25 3.00
W20 Paul Pierce 3.00 8.00

1999-00 Stadium Club

COMPLETE SET (201) 25.00 60.00
COMPLETE SET w/o RC (175) 12.50 30.00
RC SUBSET STATED ODDS 1:3
1 Allen Iverson .60 1.50
2 Chris Crawford .15 .40
3 Chris Webber .30 .75
4 Antawn Jamison .25 .60
5 Karl Malone .50 1.25
6 Sam Cassell .20 .50
7 Kerry Kittles .20 .50
8 Tim Thomas .20 .50
9 Chauncey Billups .25 .60
10 Shawn Bradley .15 .40
11 Alan Henderson .15 .40
12 David Wesley .15 .40
13 Glenn Robinson .20 .50
14 Mitch Richmond .30 .75
15 Luc Longley .20 .50
16 Shareef Abdur-Rahim .25 .60
17 Christian Laettner .20 .50
18 Anthony Mason .25 .60
19 Randy Brown .15 .40
20 Charles Barkley .60 1.50
21 Bob Sura .15 .40
22 Bobby Jackson .20 .50
23 Arvydas Sabonis .20 .50
24 Tracy Murray .15 .40
25 Matt Harpring .15 .40
26 Shawn Kemp .40 1.00
27 Travis Best .15 .40
28 Ruben Patterson .15 .40
29 Mike Bibby .25 .60
30 Vlade Divac .25 .60
31 Tyrone Hill .15 .40
32 David Robinson .50 1.25
33 Keith Van Horn .20 .50
34 Alvin Williams .15 .40
35 Juwan Howard .20 .50
36 Shaquille O'Neal 1.00 2.50
37 Dale Davis .15 .40
38 Alonzo Mourning .40 1.00
39 Michael Olowokandi .15 .40
40 Jason Caffey .15 .40
41 Andrew DeClercq .15 .40
42 Jud Buechler .15 .40
43 Toni Kukoc .30 .75
44 Dikembe Mutombo .40 1.00
45 Steve Nash .50 1.25
46 Eddie Jones .25 .60
47 Reggie Miller .50 1.25
48 Rick Fox .15 .40
49 Larry Hughes .20 .50
50 Tim Duncan .60 1.50
51 Jerome Williams .15 .40
52 Rod Strickland .20 .50
53 Anthony Peeler .15 .40
54 Greg Ostertag .15 .40
55 Patrick Ewing .30 .75
56 Grant Hill .40 1.00
57 Derrick Coleman .20 .50
58 Raef LaFrentz .20 .50
59 Mark Bryant .15 .40
60 Rik Smits .20 .50
61 Latrell Sprewell .30 .75
62 John Starks .25 .60
63 Brevin Knight .15 .40
64 Cuttino Mobley .15 .40
65 Clarence Weatherspoon .15 .40
66 Marcus Camby .20 .50
67 Stephon Marbury .30 .75
68 Tom Gugliotta .20 .50
69 Vince Carter .60 1.50
70 Vladimir Stepania .15 .40
71 Chris Mullin .25 .60
72 Tyrone Nesby RC .15 .40
73 Kornel David RC .15 .40
74 Elden Campbell .15 .40
75 Lindsey Hunter .15 .40
76 Chris Childs .15 .40
77 Ervin Johnson .15 .40
78 Rasheed Wallace .30 .75
79 Jeff Hornacek .20 .50
80 Matt Geiger .15 .40
81 Antoine Walker .25 .60
82 Jason Williams .40 1.00
83 Robert Horry .20 .50
84 Jaren Jackson .15 .40
85 Kendall Gill .25 .60
86 Dan Majerle .25 .60
87 Bobby Phills .15 .40
88 Eric Piatkowski .15 .40
89 Robert Traylor .15 .40
90 Cory Carr .15 .40
91 P.J. Brown .15 .40
92 Terrell Brandon .15 .40
93 Corliss Williamson .15 .40
94 Bryant Reeves .15 .40
95 Larry Johnson .25 .60
96 Keith Closs .15 .40
97 Gary Trent .15 .40
98 Walter McCarty .15 .40
99 Wesley Person .15 .40
100 Chris Mills .15 .40
101 Glen Rice .25 .60
102 Peja Stojakovic .25 .60
103 Jason Kidd .40 1.00
104 Dirk Nowitzki .75 2.00
105 Bryon Russell .15 .40
106 Vin Baker .20 .50
107 Darrell Armstrong .15 .40
108 Eric Snow .15 .40
109 Hakeem Olajuwon .50 1.25
110 Tracy McGrady .40 1.00
111 Kenny Anderson .20 .50
112 Jalen Rose .20 .50
113 Greg Anthony .15 .40
114 Tim Hardaway .30 .75
115 Doug Christie .20 .50
116 Allan Houston .20 .50
117 Kobe Bryant 2.00 5.00
118 Kevin Garnett .60 1.50
119 Vitaly Potapenko .15 .40
120 Steve Kerr .20 .50
121 Nick Van Exel .20 .50
122 Jerry Stackhouse .25 .60
123 Derek Fisher .20 .50
124 Donyell Marshall .20 .50
125 Mark Jackson .20 .50
126 Ray Allen .40 1.00
127 Avery Johnson .20 .50
128 Michael Doleac .15 .40
129 Charles Oakley .25 .60
130 Gary Payton .40 1.00
131 Theo Ratliff .20 .50
132 Cedric Ceballos .15 .40
133 Paul Pierce .50 1.25
134 Michael Finley .25 .60
135 Malik Sealy .15 .40
136 Brian Grant .15 .40
137 John Stockton .40 1.00
138 Chris Whitney .15 .40
139 Maurice Taylor .15 .40
140 Antonio McDyess .20 .50
141 Adrian Griffin RC .20 .50
142 Vernon Maxwell .15 .40
143 Jamal Mashburn .20 .50
144 Jayson Williams .15 .40
145 Joe Smith .20 .50
146 Clifford Robinson .20 .50
147 Mario Elie .15 .40
148 Damon Stoudamire .25 .60
149 Felipe Lopez .15 .40
150 Rex Chapman .15 .40
151 Antonio Davis TRAN .15 .40
152 Mookie Blaylock TRAN .15 .40
153 Ron Mercer TRAN .20 .50
154 Horace Grant TRAN .20 .50
155 Steve Smith TRAN .20 .50
156 Isaiah Rider TRAN .20 .50
157 Tariq Abdul-Wahad TRAN .15 .40
158 Michael Dickerson TRAN .15 .40
159 Nick Anderson TRAN .15 .40
160 Jim Jackson TRAN .15 .40
161 Hersey Hawkins TRAN .15 .40
162 Brent Barry TRAN .20 .50
163 Shandon Anderson TRAN .15 .40
164 Scottie Pippen TRAN .60 1.50
165 Isaac Austin TRAN .15 .40
166 Anfernee Hardaway TRAN .60 1.50
167 Natalie Williams USA .30 .75
168 Teresa Edwards USA .30 .75
169 Yolanda Griffith USA .40 1.00
170 Nikki McCray USA .30 .75
171 Katie Smith USA .50 1.25
172 Chamique Holdsclaw USA 1.50 4.00
173 Dawn Staley USA .40 1.00
174 R.Bolton-Holifield USA .30 .75
175 Lisa Leslie USA .75 2.00
176 Elton Brand RC 1.00 2.50
177 Steve Francis RC 1.00 2.50
178 Baron Davis RC 1.25 3.00
179 Lamar Odom RC 1.00 2.50
180 Jonathan Bender RC .50 1.25
181 Wally Szczerbiak RC .75 2.00
182 Richard Hamilton RC 1.25 3.00
183 Andre Miller RC 1.00 2.50
184 Shawn Marion RC 1.00 2.50
185 Jason Terry RC .75 2.00
186 Trajan Langdon RC .40 1.00
187 A.Radojevic RC .30 .75
188 Corey Maggette RC .60 1.50
189 William Avery RC .30 .75
190 DeMarco Johnson RC .50 1.25
191 Ron Artest RC 1.25 3.00
192 Cal Bowdler RC .30 .75
193 James Posey RC .50 1.25
194 Quincy Lewis RC .30 .75
195 Scott Padgett RC .40 1.00
196 Jeff Foster RC .50 1.25
197 Kenny Thomas RC .50 1.25
198 Devean George RC .40 1.00
199 Tim James RC .30 .75
200 Vonteego Cummings RC .30 .75
201 Jumaine Jones RC .30 .75

1999-00 Stadium Club First Day Issue

*STARS: 10X TO 25X BASE CARD HI
*RCs: 2X TO 5X BASE HI
STATED ODDS 1:26 RETAIL
STATED PRINT RUN 150 SERIAL #'d SETS

1999-00 Stadium Club One of a Kind

*STARS: 10X TO 25X BASE CARD HI
*RCs: 2X TO 5X BASE HI
STATED ODDS 1:22 HOBBY, 1:9 HTA
STATED PRINT RUN 150 SERIAL #'d SETS

1999-00 Stadium Club 3x3

COMPLETE SET (30) 50.00 120.00
STATED ODDS 1:27 H/R, 1:14 HTA
*LUMINESCENT: .75X TO 2X HI COLUMN
LUM: STATED ODDS 1:108 H/R, 1:54 HTA
ILLUMINATOR: 1.5X TO 4X HI COLUMN
ILLUM: STATED ODDS 1:216 H/R, 1:108 HTA
1A Vince Carter 4.00 10.00
1B Shareef Abdur-Rahim 1.50 4.00
1C Grant Hill 2.50 6.00
2A Allen Iverson 4.00 10.00
2B Stephon Marbury 2.00 5.00
2C Jason Williams 2.50 6.00
3A Kevin Garnett 4.00 10.00
3B Antoine Walker 1.50 4.00
3C Scottie Pippen 4.00 10.00
4A Kobe Bryant 20.00 50.00
4B Eddie Jones 1.50 4.00
4C Michael Finley 1.50 4.00
5A Tim Duncan 4.00 10.00
5B Keith Van Horn 1.25 3.00
5C Antonio McDyess 1.25 3.00
6A Shaquille O'Neal 6.00 15.00
6B Alonzo Mourning 2.50 6.00
6C Dikembe Mutombo 2.50 6.00
7A Karl Malone 3.00 8.00
7B Chris Webber 2.00 5.00
7C Shawn Kemp 2.50 6.00
8A John Stockton 2.50 6.00
8B Gary Payton 2.50 6.00
8C Jason Kidd 2.50 6.00
9A Elton Brand 2.00 5.00
9B Lamar Odom 2.00 5.00
9C Wally Szczerbiak 1.50 4.00
10A Steve Francis 2.00 5.00
10B Baron Davis 2.50 6.00
10C Jason Terry 1.50 4.00

1999-00 Stadium Club Chrome Previews

COMPLETE SET (20) 15.00 40.00
STATED ODDS 1:24 H/R, 1:12 HTA
*REF: 1.25X TO 3X HI COLUMN
REF: STATED ODDS 1:120 H/R, 1:60 HTA
*JUMBO: .4X TO 1X HI
JUMBO: ONE PER HOB/HTA BOX
*JUMBO.REF: 1.5X TO 4X HI
JUMBO.REF: STATED ODDS 1:12 H, 1:8 HTA
SCC1 Kevin Garnett 2.00 5.00
SCC2 Grant Hill 1.25 3.00
SCC3 Vince Carter 2.00 5.00
SCC4 Allen Iverson 2.00 5.00
SCC5 Shareef Abdur-Rahim .75 2.00
SCC6 Stephon Marbury 1.00 2.50
SCC7 Kobe Bryant 6.00 15.00
SCC8 Keith Van Horn .60 1.50
SCC9 Tim Duncan 2.00 5.00
SCC10 Shaquille O'Neal 3.00 8.00
SCC11 Jason Williams 1.25 3.00
SCC12 Scottie Pippen 2.00 5.00
SCC13 Gary Payton 1.25 3.00
SCC14 Karl Malone 1.50 4.00
SCC15 Elton Brand 1.50 4.00
SCC16 Steve Francis 1.50 4.00
SCC17 Baron Davis 2.00 5.00
SCC18 Lamar Odom 1.50 4.00
SCC19 Ron Artest 2.00 5.00
SCC20 Corey Maggette 1.00 2.50

1999-00 Stadium Club Co-Signers

OVERALL STATED ODDS 1:254 H, 1:102 HTA
CS1 T.Duncan/T.McGrady 600.00 1,200.00
CS2 T.Duncan/M.Camby 400.00 800.00
CS3 T.Duncan/E.Brand 400.00 800.00
CS4 T.Duncan/S.Francis 400.00 800.00
CS5 T.Duncan/S.Marion 400.00 800.00
CS6 T.Duncan/J.Bender 300.00 600.00
CS7 T.Duncan/W.Szcz 400.00 800.00
CS8 T.Duncan/C.Maggette 400.00 800.00
CS9 T.McGrady/S.Francis 75.00 200.00
CS10 C.Maggette/S.Marion 15.00 40.00
CS11 M.Camby/G.Payton 25.00 60.00
CS12 E.Brand/S.A-Rahim 20.00 50.00
CS13 P.Pierce/J.Bender 75.00 200.00
CS14 T.Gugliotta/W.Szcz 10.00 25.00
CS15 T.McGrady/C.Maggette 75.00 200.00
CS16 S.Francis/S.Marion 25.00 60.00
CS17 G.Payton/J.Bender 25.00 60.00
CS18 P.Pierce/M.Camby 75.00 200.00
CS19 E.Brand/T.Gugliotta 10.00 25.00
CS20 W.Szcz/S.A-Rahim 15.00 40.00
CS21 T.McGrady/S.Marion 75.00 200.00
CS22 S.Francis/C.Maggette 10.00 25.00
CS23 G.Payton/P.Pierce 150.00 400.00
CS24 J.Bender/M.Camby 10.00 25.00
CS25 E.Brand/W.Szcz 15.00 40.00
CS26 T.Gugliotta/S.A-Rahim 10.00 25.00

1999-00 Stadium Club Lone Star Signatures

OVERALL STATED ODDS 1:389 H, 1:156 HTA
LS1 Tim Duncan 400.00 800.00
LS2 Shawn Marion 8.00 20.00
LS3 Jonathan Bender 6.00 15.00
LS4 Wally Szczerbiak 8.00 20.00
LS5 Corey Maggette 10.00 25.00
LS6 Gary Payton 15.00 40.00
LS7 Tom Gugliotta 20.00 40.00
LS8 Steve Francis 8.00 20.00
LS9 Elton Brand 8.00 20.00
LS10 Tracy McGrady 25.00 60.00
LS11 Paul Pierce 15.00 40.00
LS12 Shareef Abdur-Rahim 6.00 15.00
LS13 Marcus Camby 6.00 15.00

1999-00 Stadium Club Never Compromise

COMPLETE SET (30) 15.00 40.00
*GAME-VIEW STARS: 8X TO 20X HI COLUMN
*GAME-VIEW RCs: 5X TO 12X HI COLUMN
GAME-VIEW: STATED ODDS 1:220 H, 1:88 HTA
GAME-VIEW: PRINT RUN 100 SERIAL #'d SETS
NC1 Elton Brand .75 2.00
NC2 Steve Francis .75 2.00
NC3 Baron Davis 1.00 2.50
NC4 Lamar Odom .75 2.00
NC5 Jonathan Bender .40 1.00
NC6 Wally Szczerbiak .60 1.50
NC7 Richard Hamilton 1.00 2.50
NC8 Andre Miller .75 2.00
NC9 Corey Maggette .50 1.25
NC10 Jason Terry .60 1.50
NC11 Kevin Garnett 1.50 4.00
NC12 Grant Hill 1.00 2.50
NC13 Vince Carter 1.50 4.00
NC14 Allen Iverson 1.50 4.00
NC15 Shareef Abdur-Rahim .60 1.50
NC16 Stephon Marbury .75 2.00
NC17 Kobe Bryant 5.00 12.00
NC18 Keith Van Horn .50 1.25
NC19 Tim Duncan 1.50 4.00
NC20 Shaquille O'Neal 2.50 6.00
NC21 Karl Malone 1.25 3.00
NC22 Scottie Pippen 1.50 4.00
NC23 David Robinson 1.25 3.00
NC24 John Stockton 1.00 2.50
NC25 Charles Barkley 1.50 4.00
NC26 Gary Payton 1.00 2.50
NC27 Shawn Kemp 1.00 2.50
NC28 Alonzo Mourning 1.00 2.50
NC29 Reggie Miller 1.25 3.00
NC30 Mitch Richmond .75 2.00

1999-00 Stadium Club Onyx Extreme

COMPLETE SET (10) 3.00 8.00
STATED ODDS 1:8 H/R, 1:6 HTA
*DIE CUTS: 1.25X TO 3X HI COLUMN
DIE CUTS: STATED ODDS 1:40 H/R, 1:30 HTA
OE1 Antonio McDyess .40 1.00
OE2 Antoine Walker .50 1.25
OE3 Jason Williams .75 2.00
OE4 Chris Webber .60 1.50
OE5 David Robinson 1.00 2.50
OE6 Wally Szczerbiak .75 2.00
OE7 Jason Kidd .75 2.00
OE8 Shawn Kemp .75 2.00
OE9 Aleksandar Radojevic .30 .75
OE10 Tim Duncan 1.25 3.00

1999-00 Stadium Club Picture Ending

COMPLETE SET (10) 2.50 6.00
STATED ODDS 1:12 H/R, 1:6 HTA
PE1 Allan Houston .40 1.00
PE2 John Stockton .75 2.00
PE3 Sean Elliott .40 1.00
PE4 Latrell Sprewell .60 1.50
PE5 Darrell Armstrong .30 .75
PE6 Marcus Camby .40 1.00
PE7 Keith Van Horn .40 1.00
PE8 Antoine Walker .50 1.25
PE9 Larry Johnson .50 1.25
PE10 Avery Johnson .40 1.00

1999-00 Stadium Club Pieces of Patriotism

STATED ODDS 1:147 HOB, 1:59 HTA
P1 Allan Houston 6.00 15.00
P2 Kevin Garnett 10.00 25.00
P3 Gary Payton 8.00 20.00
P4 Steve Smith 6.00 15.00
P5 Tim Hardaway 6.00 15.00
P6 Tim Duncan 12.00 30.00
P7 Jason Kidd 8.00 20.00
P8 Tom Gugliotta 6.00 15.00
P9 Vin Baker 6.00 15.00

2000-01 Stadium Club Promos

COMPLETE SET (6) 2.00 5.00
PP1 Shaquille O'Neal 2.00 5.00
PP2 Latrell Sprewell .60 1.50
PP3 Ray Allen .75 2.00
PP4 Clifford Robinson .50 1.25
PP5 Corey Maggette .40 1.00
PP6 John Stockton 1.00 2.50

2000-01 Stadium Club

COMPLETE SET (175) 30.00 60.00
COMPLETE SET w/o RC (150) 10.00 25.00
151-175 STATED ODDS 1:4 H, 1:1 HTA
1 Baron Davis .25 .60
2 Adrian Griffin .15 .40
3 Dikembe Mutombo .40 1.00
4 Andre Miller .20 .50
5 Kenny Anderson .20 .50
6 Keon Clark .15 .40
7 Larry Hughes .25 .60
8 Ruben Patterson .15 .40
9 Shandon Anderson .15 .40
10 Reggie Miller .50 1.25
11 Lamar Odom .25 .60
12 John Stockton .50 1.25
13 Rod Strickland .15 .40
14 Michael Dickerson .15 .40
15 Quincy Lewis .15 .40
16 Vin Baker .20 .50
17 Vince Carter .50 1.25
18 Avery Johnson .20 .50
19 Michael Finley .25 .60
20 Eric Snow .15 .40
21 Kevin Garnett .60 1.50
22 Rodney Rogers .15 .40
23 Bonzi Wells .15 .40
24 Jason Kidd .40 1.00
25 Toni Kukoc .30 .75
26 Darrell Armstrong .15 .40
27 Larry Johnson .30 .75
28 Kendall Gill .25 .60
29 Wally Szczerbiak .20 .50
30 Tim Thomas .15 .40
31 Dan Majerle .25 .60
32 Karl Malone .50 1.25
33 Juwan Howard .20 .50
34 Kobe Bryant 2.00 5.00
35 Bryant Reeves .15 .40
36 Cuttino Mobley .20 .50
37 Mookie Blaylock .25 .60
38 Jerome Williams .15 .40
39 James Posey .15 .40
40 Shawn Bradley .15 .40
41 Tim Hardaway .30 .75
42 Theo Ratliff .15 .40
43 Damon Stoudamire .25 .60
44 Derrick Coleman .25 .60
45 Ron Artest .25 .60
46 Antoine Walker .25 .60
47 Jason Terry .25 .60
48 Antonio McDyess .20 .50
49 Jonathan Bender .15 .40
50 Shaquille O'Neal 1.00 2.50
51 Anthony Carter .15 .40
52 Ray Allen .40 1.00
53 Joe Smith .20 .50
54 Marcus Camby .20 .50
55 Keith Van Horn .20 .50
56 Charlie Ward .20 .50
57 John Amaechi .15 .40
58 Tom Gugliotta .20 .50
59 Allan Houston .25 .60
60 Anfernee Hardaway .40 1.00
61 Scottie Pippen .60 1.50
62 Jason Williams .40 1.00
63 Steve Smith .25 .60
64 David Robinson .50 1.25
65 Gary Payton .40 1.00
66 Robert Horry .25 .60
67 Greg Ostertag .15 .40
68 Mike Bibby .25 .60
69 Tim Duncan .60 1.50
70 Richard Hamilton .30 .75
71 Bryon Russell .15 .40
72 Charles Oakley .15 .40
73 Rashard Lewis .20 .50
74 Chris Webber .30 .75
75 Arvydas Sabonis .25 .60
76 Allen Iverson .60 1.50
77 Bo Outlaw .15 .40
78 Elden Campbell .15 .40
79 Dirk Nowitzki .60 1.50
80 Elton Brand .25 .60
81 Brevin Knight .15 .40
82 David Wesley .20 .50
83 Raef LaFrentz .20 .50
84 Antawn Jamison .25 .60
85 Hakeem Olajuwon .50 1.25
86 Jamie Feick .15 .40
87 Jalen Rose .20 .50
88 Michael Olowokandi .15 .40
89 Rick Fox .20 .50
90 Austin Croshere .15 .40
91 Glenn Robinson .25 .60
92 Stephon Marbury .30 .75
93 Clifford Robinson .25 .60
94 Derek Fisher .25 .60
95 Vlade Divac .25 .60
96 Jim Jackson .25 .60
97 Paul Pierce .40 1.00
98 Corey Benjamin .15 .40
99 Lamond Murray .15 .40
100 Steve Francis .25 .60
101 Mitch Richmond .30 .75
102 Othella Harrington .15 .40
103 Nick Anderson .20 .50
104 Antonio Davis .20 .50
105 Ervin Johnson .15 .40
106 Rasheed Wallace .30 .75
107 Shawn Marion .25 .60
108 Latrell Sprewell .30 .75
109 Terrell Brandon .20 .50
110 Sam Cassell .20 .50
111 Shareef Abdur-Rahim .25 .60
112 Travis Best .15 .40
113 Tyrone Nesby .15 .40
114 Alan Henderson .15 .40
115 Vonteego Cummings .15 .40
116 Kelvin Cato .15 .40
117 Jerry Stackhouse .25 .60
118 Nick Van Exel .25 .60
119 Corliss Williamson TRAN .15 .40
120 Doug Christie TRAN .20 .50
121 Horace Grant TRAN .20 .50
122 Glen Rice TRAN .25 .60
123 Patrick Ewing TRAN .40 1.00
124 Dale Davis TRAN .20 .50
125 Brian Grant TRAN .20 .50
126 Shawn Kemp TRAN .40 1.00
127 Cedric Ceballos TRAN .20 .50
128 Christian Laettner TRAN .25 .60
129 Lindsey Hunter TRAN .15 .40
130 Donyell Marshall TRAN .25 .60
131 Robert Pack TRAN .15 .40
132 Danny Fortson TRAN .20 .50
133 Howard Eisley TRAN .15 .40
134 Andrew DeClercq TRAN .15 .40
135 Mark Jackson TRAN .20 .50
136 Grant Hill TRAN .40 1.00
137 Tracy McGrady TRAN .50 1.25
138 Maurice Taylor TRAN .15 .40
139 Derek Anderson TRAN .20 .50
140 Corey Maggette TRAN .20 .50
141 Jermaine O'Neal TRAN .20 .50
142 Ben Wallace TRAN .30 .75
143 Ron Mercer TRAN .20 .50
144 John Starks TRAN .20 .50
145 Erick Strickland TRAN .15 .40
146 Isaiah Rider TRAN .20 .50
147 Eddie Jones TRAN .25 .60
148 Anthony Mason TRAN .25 .60
149 P.J. Brown TRAN .15 .40
150 Jamal Mashburn TRAN .20 .50
151 Kenyon Martin RC .75 2.00
152 Stromile Swift RC .30 .75
153 Darius Miles RC .40 1.00
154 Marcus Fizer RC .30 .75
155 Mike Miller RC .60 1.50
156 DerMarr Johnson RC .25 .60
157 Chris Mihm RC .25 .60
158 Jamal Crawford RC 1.00 2.50
159 Joel Przybilla RC .30 .75
160 Keyon Dooling RC .30 .75
161 Jerome Moiso RC .25 .60
162 Etan Thomas RC .30 .75
163 Courtney Alexander RC .25 .60
164 Mateen Cleaves RC .30 .75
165 Jason Collier RC .40 1.00
166 Desmond Mason RC .50 1.25
167 Quentin Richardson RC .30 .75
168 Jamaal Magloire RC .40 1.00
169 Speedy Claxton RC .40 1.00
170 Morris Peterson RC .40 1.00
171 Donnell Harvey RC .30 .75
172 DeShawn Stevenson RC .40 1.00
173 Mamadou N'Diaye RC .25 .60
174 Erick Barkley RC .25 .60
175 Mark Madsen RC .40 1.00

2000-01 Stadium Club 11 x 14 Autographs

NNO CARDS LISTED BELOW ALPHABETICALLY
IVERSON WAS NEVER REDEEMED
STATED ODDS 1:1675 H/R 1:656 HTA
1 Ron Artest 8.00 20.00
2 Elton Brand 8.00 20.00
3 Mateen Cleaves 8.00 20.00
4 Jamal Crawford 8.00 20.00
5 Tim Duncan 60.00 120.00
6 Steve Francis 8.00 20.00
7 Larry Hughes 8.00 20.00
9 Magic Johnson 60.00 120.00
10 Tracy McGrady 20.00 50.00

11 Shaquille O'Neal 60.00 120.00
12 Latrell Sprewell 30.00 80.00

2000-01 Stadium Club Beam Team

STATED PRINT RUN 500 SERIAL #'d SETS
STATED ODDS 1:67 H/R, 1:26 HTA
BT1 Tim Duncan 25.00 60.00
BT2 Shaquille O'Neal 25.00 60.00
BT3 Kevin Garnett 20.00 50.00
BT4 Vince Carter 20.00 50.00
BT5 Kobe Bryant 75.00 200.00
BT6 Allen Iverson 20.00 50.00
BT7 Steve Francis 5.00 12.00
BT8 Chris Webber 20.00 50.00
BT9 Elton Brand 5.00 12.00
BT10 Larry Hughes 5.00 12.00
BT11 Lamar Odom 5.00 12.00
BT12 Shareef Abdur-Rahim 5.00 12.00
BT13 Jason Kidd 8.00 20.00
BT14 Gary Payton 12.00 30.00
BT15 Antonio McDyess 4.00 10.00
BT16 Jason Williams 20.00 50.00
BT17 Karl Malone 10.00 25.00
BT18 Eddie Jones 5.00 12.00
BT19 Scottie Pippen 12.00 30.00
BT20 Latrell Sprewell 12.00 30.00
BT21 Paul Pierce 12.00 30.00
BT22 Michael Finley 5.00 12.00
BT23 Jerry Stackhouse 5.00 12.00
BT24 Jalen Rose 4.00 10.00
BT25 Antoine Walker 5.00 12.00
BT26 Anfernee Hardaway 12.00 30.00
BT27 Mike Bibby 5.00 12.00
BT28 Kenyon Martin 10.00 25.00
BT29 Stromile Swift 4.00 10.00
BT30 Darius Miles 5.00 12.00

2000-01 Stadium Club Capture the Action

COMPLETE SET (14) 8.00 20.00
STATED ODDS 1:8 H/R, 1:2 HTA
CA1 Shaquille O'Neal 2.00 5.00
CA2 Kobe Bryant 3.00 8.00
CA3 Vince Carter 1.00 2.50
CA4 Kevin Garnett 1.25 3.00
CA5 Allen Iverson 1.25 3.00
CA6 Steve Francis .50 1.25
CA7 Tracy McGrady 1.00 2.50
CA8 Tim Duncan 1.25 3.00
CA9 Elton Brand .50 1.25
CA10 Lamar Odom .50 1.25
CA11 Larry Hughes .50 1.25
CA12 Chris Webber .60 1.50
CA13 Antonio McDyess .40 1.00
CA14 Gary Payton .75 2.00

2000-01 Stadium Club Capture the Action Game View

*GAME VIEW: 5X TO 12X BASE HI
STATED PRINT RUN 100 SERIAL #'d SETS
STATED ODDS 1:278 H/R, 1:108 HTA
CA2 Kobe Bryant 100.00 200.00

2000-01 Stadium Club Co-Signers

OVERALL STATED ODDS 1:649 H, 1:252 HTA
CS1 M.Johnson/S.O'Neal 300.00 600.00
CS2 M.Johnson/M.Cleaves 75.00 200.00
CS3 S.O'Neal/T.Duncan 800.00 1,500.00
CS4 T.Duncan/E.Brand 400.00 800.00
CS5 E.Brand/R.Artest 20.00 50.00
CS6 A.Iverson/S.Francis 150.00 400.00
CS7 S.Francis/M.Cleaves 12.00 30.00
CS9 T.McGrady/L.Sprewell 75.00 200.00
CS10 A.Iverson/J.Crawford 150.00 400.00
CS11 T.McGrady/E.Jones 100.00 250.00
CS12 R.Artest/J.Crawford 20.00 50.00

2000-01 Stadium Club Game Jerseys

OVERALL STATED ODDS 1:20 H/R 1:8 HTA
SCAH1 Dikembe Mutombo 5.00 12.00
SCAH2 Jason Terry 3.00 8.00
SCAH3 Jim Jackson 2.50 6.00
SCAH4 Alan Henderson 2.00 5.00
SCAH5 Cal Bowdler 2.00 5.00
SCAH6 DerMarr Johnson 1.25 3.00
SCAH7 Chris Crawford 2.00 5.00
SCAH8 Lorenzen Wright 2.00 5.00
SCAH9 Roshown McLeod 2.00 5.00
SCAH10 Dion Glover 2.00 5.00
SCAH11 Anthony Johnson 2.00 5.00
SCAH12 Hanno Mottola 1.25 3.00
SCBC1 Antoine Walker 3.00 8.00
SCBC2 Paul Pierce 5.00 12.00
SCBC3 Kenny Anderson 2.50 6.00
SCBC4 Adrian Griffin 2.00 5.00
SCBC5 Vitaly Potapenko 2.00 5.00
SCBC6 Walter McCarty 2.00 5.00
SCBC7 Tony Battie 2.00 5.00
SCLC1 Jeff McInnis 2.00 5.00
SCLC2 Michael Olowokandi 2.00 5.00
SCLC3 Tyrone Nesby 2.00 5.00
SCLC4 Derek Strong 2.00 5.00
SCLC5 Corey Maggette 2.50 6.00
SCLC6 Eric Piatkowski 2.00 5.00
SCLC7 Brian Skinner 2.00 5.00
SCLC8 Darius Miles 2.00 5.00
SCLC9 Keyon Dooling 2.50 6.00
SCLC10 Quentin Richardson 1.50 4.00
SCLC11 Sean Rooks 2.00 5.00
SCLL1 Shaquille O'Neal 12.00 30.00
SCLL2 Horace Grant 3.00 8.00
SCLL3 Robert Horry 3.00 8.00
SCLL4 Rick Fox 2.50 6.00
SCLL5 Brian Shaw 2.00 5.00
SCLL6 Ron Harper 3.00 8.00
SCLL7 Tyronn Lue 2.00 5.00
SCLL8 Isaiah Rider 2.50 6.00
SCLL9 Greg Foster 2.00 5.00
SCLL10 Mark Madsen 2.00 5.00
SCLL11 Devean George 2.00 5.00
SCNJ1 Stephon Marbury 4.00 10.00
SCNJ2 Keith Van Horn 2.50 6.00
SCNJ3 Kendall Gill 3.00 8.00
SCNJ4 Evan Eschmeyer 2.00 5.00
SCNJ5 Soumaila Samake 1.25 3.00
SCNJ6 Stephen Jackson 4.00 10.00
SCNJ7 Johnny Newman 2.00 5.00
SCNJ8 Jim McIlvaine 2.00 5.00
SCNJ9 Lucious Harris 2.00 5.00
SCNJ10 Sherman Douglas 2.00 5.00
SCNJ11 Kenyon Martin 4.00 10.00
SCNJ12 Aaron Williams 2.00 5.00
SCOM1 Grant Hill 5.00 12.00
SCOM2 Tracy McGrady 6.00 15.00
SCOM3 Darrell Armstrong 2.00 5.00
SCOM4 Michael Doleac 2.00 5.00
SCOM5 Pat Garrity 2.00 5.00
SCOM6 Dee Brown 2.00 5.00
SCOM7 Bo Outlaw 2.00 5.00
SCOM8 John Amaechi 2.00 5.00
SCOM9 Mike Miller 3.00 8.00
SCOM10 Monty Williams 2.50 6.00
SCOM11 Andrew DeClercq 2.00 5.00
SCOM12 Don Reid 2.00 5.00
SCPS1 Jason Kidd 5.00 12.00
SCPS2 Anfernee Hardaway 5.00 12.00
SCPS3 Tom Gugliotta 2.50 6.00
SCPS4 Shawn Marion 3.00 8.00
SCPS5 Clifford Robinson 3.00 8.00
SCPS6 Rodney Rogers 2.00 5.00
SCPS7 Chris Dudley 2.00 5.00
SCPS8 Rex Chapman 2.50 6.00
SCPS9 Iakovos Tsakalidis 1.25 3.00
SCPS10 Tony Delk 2.00 5.00
SCPS11 Mario Elie 2.00 5.00
SCPS12 Corie Blount 2.00 5.00
SCVG1 Shareef Abdur-Rahim 3.00 8.00
SCVG2 Mike Bibby 3.00 8.00
SCVG3 Michael Dickerson 2.00 5.00
SCVG4 Othella Harrington 2.00 5.00
SCVG5 Bryant Reeves 2.00 5.00
SCVG6 Damon Jones 3.00 8.00
SCVG7 Brent Price 2.00 5.00
SCVG8 Stromile Swift 1.50 4.00
SCVG9 Grant Long 2.00 5.00
SCVG10 Doug West 2.00 5.00
SCVG11 Tony Massenburg 2.00 5.00
SCVG12 Isaac Austin 2.00 5.00
SCWW1 Mitch Richmond 4.00 10.00
SCWW2 Juwan Howard 2.50 6.00
SCWW3 Rod Strickland 2.00 5.00
SCWW4 Richard Hamilton 4.00 10.00
SCWW5 Jahidi White 2.00 5.00
SCWW6 Michael Smith 2.00 5.00
SCWW7 Chris Whitney 2.00 5.00

2000-01 Stadium Club Head to Head Game Jerseys

STATED ODDS 1:96 HTA
HH1 K.Martin/A.Walker 5.00 12.00
HH2 S.Swift/D.Miles 5.00 12.00
HH3 G.Hill/S.Abdur-Rahim 6.00 15.00
HH4 J.Howard/K.Van Horn 5.00 12.00
HH5 K.Dooling/J.Kidd 6.00 15.00
HH6 D.Johnson/P.Pierce 5.00 12.00
HH7 Q.Richardson/S.Marion 5.00 12.00
HH8 S.Marbury/K.Anderson 5.00 12.00
HH9 T.McGrady/A.Hardaway 15.00 40.00
HH10 J.Terry/M.Bibby 5.00 12.00

2000-01 Stadium Club Lone Star Signatures

OVERALL STATED ODDS 1:237 H/R 1:92 HTA
LSAI Allen Iverson 150.00 400.00
LSEB Elton Brand 6.00 15.00
LSEJ Eddie Jones 8.00 20.00
LSJC Jamal Crawford 20.00 50.00
LSLS Latrell Sprewell 25.00 60.00
LSMC Mateen Cleaves 6.00 15.00
LSMJ Magic Johnson 40.00 100.00
LSRA Ron Artest 6.00 15.00
LSSF Steve Francis 8.00 20.00
LSSO Shaquille O'Neal 60.00 120.00
LSTD Tim Duncan 400.00 800.00
LSTM Tracy McGrady 25.00 60.00

2000-01 Stadium Club Starting Five Game Jerseys

STATED ODDS 1:2234 H, 1:858 HTA
SFAH Atlanta Hawks 15.00 40.00
SFBC Boston Celtics 50.00 120.00
SFNJN New Jersey Nets 40.00 80.00
SFOM Orlando Magic 40.00 80.00
SFPS Phoenix Suns 75.00 150.00
SFVG Vancouver Grizzlies 30.00 80.00
SFWW Washington Wizards 30.00 80.00

2000-01 Stadium Club Striking Distance

COMPLETE SET (20) 15.00 30.00
STATED ODDS 1:8 H/R, 1:3 HTA
SD1 Reggie Miller 1.25 3.00
SD2 Tim Duncan 1.50 4.00
SD3 Allen Iverson 1.50 4.00
SD4 Kevin Garnett 1.50 4.00
SD5 Vince Carter 1.25 3.00
SD6 Kobe Bryant 5.00 12.00
SD7 Shaquille O'Neal 2.50 6.00
SD8 Chris Webber .75 2.00
SD9 Elton Brand .60 1.50
SD10 Steve Francis .60 1.50
SD11 Lamar Odom .60 1.50
SD12 Gary Payton 1.00 2.50
SD13 Karl Malone 1.25 3.00
SD14 Latrell Sprewell .75 2.00
SD15 Ray Allen 1.00 2.50
SD16 Stephon Marbury .75 2.00
SD17 Rasheed Wallace .75 2.00
SD18 Jason Williams 1.00 2.50
SD19 Scottie Pippen 1.50 4.00
SD20 Eddie Jones .60 1.50

2001-02 Stadium Club

COMP.SET w/o SP's (101) 12.50 25.00
RC STATED ODDS 1:4, 1:1 HTA
1 Dikembe Mutombo .40 1.00
2 Clifford Robinson .25 .60
3 Bonzi Wells .15 .40
4 Peja Stojakovic .20 .50
5 Gary Payton .40 1.00
6 Morris Peterson .15 .40
7 Patrick Ewing .40 1.00
8 Terrell Brandon .20 .50
9 Tim Thomas .15 .40
10 Kobe Bryant 2.00 5.00
11 Hakeem Olajuwon .50 1.25
12 Marc Jackson .15 .40
13 Wang Zhizhi .25 .60
14 Andre Miller .20 .50
15 Elton Brand .20 .50
16 Eddie Robinson .15 .40
17 Jason Terry .25 .60
18 Allan Houston .25 .60
19 Grant Hill .40 1.00
20 Tim Duncan .60 1.50
21 Kevin Garnett .60 1.50
22 Jahidi White .15 .40
23 Michael Dickerson .15 .40
24 Karl Malone .50 1.25
25 Chris Webber .30 .75
26 Scottie Pippen .60 1.50
27 Latrell Sprewell .30 .75
28 Keith Van Horn .30 .75
29 Ray Allen .40 1.00
30 Alonzo Mourning .40 1.00
31 Lamar Odom .20 .50
32 Jalen Rose .20 .50
33 Ben Wallace .30 .75
34 Shaquille O'Neal 1.00 2.50
35 Antonio McDyess .20 .50
36 Dirk Nowitzki .60 1.50
37 Marcus Fizer .15 .40
38 Jamal Mashburn .20 .50
39 Paul Pierce .40 1.00
40 DerMarr Johnson .15 .40
41 Steve Nash .50 1.25
42 Jerry Stackhouse .25 .60
43 Larry Hughes .20 .50
44 Cuttino Mobley .20 .50
45 Horace Grant .20 .50
46 Eddie Jones .25 .60
47 Wally Szczerbiak .20 .50
48 Marcus Camby .20 .50
49 Jamal Crawford .25 .60
50 Vince Carter .50 1.25
51 Donyell Marshall .15 .40
52 Shareef Abdur-Rahim .20 .50
53 Courtney Alexander .15 .40
54 Kenny Anderson .20 .50
55 Ron Mercer .15 .40
56 Lamond Murray .15 .40
57 Michael Finley .25 .60
58 Raef LaFrentz .15 .40
59 Reggie Miller .50 1.25
60 Steve Francis .25 .60
61 Rick Fox .20 .50
62 Tim Hardaway .30 .75
63 Glenn Robinson .25 .60
64 LaPhonso Ellis .20 .50
65 Kenyon Martin .25 .60
66 Jason Williams .40 1.00
67 Derek Anderson .15 .40
68 Eric Snow .15 .40
69 Darius Miles .15 .40
70 Antawn Jamison .20 .50
71 Mateen Cleaves .15 .40
72 Jason Kidd .40 1.00
73 Rasheed Wallace .30 .75
74 Chris Porter .15 .40
75 Tracy McGrady .40 1.00
76 Aaron McKie .15 .40
77 Baron Davis .25 .60
78 Toni Kukoc .30 .75
79 Antoine Walker .20 .50
80 Shawn Marion .25 .60
81 Mike Miller .25 .60
82 Stephon Marbury .30 .75
83 Glen Rice .25 .60
84 David Robinson .50 1.25
85 Rashard Lewis .20 .50
86 John Stockton .50 1.25
87 Stromile Swift .15 .40
88 Richard Hamilton .30 .75
89 Desmond Mason .20 .50
90 Brian Grant .15 .40
91 Keyon Dooling .15 .40
92 Jermaine O'Neal .20 .50
93 Nick Van Exel .25 .60
94 Tom Gugliotta .15 .40
95 Darrell Armstrong .15 .40
96 Sam Cassell .20 .50
97 Mike Bibby .25 .60
98 DeShawn Stevenson .15 .40
99 Antonio Davis .20 .50
100 Allen Iverson .60 1.50
101 Kwame Brown RC .75 2.00
102 Tyson Chandler RC 1.25 3.00
103 Pau Gasol RC 3.00 8.00
104 Eddy Curry RC .75 2.00
105 Jason Richardson RC 1.25 3.00
106 Shane Battier RC 1.50 4.00
107 Eddie Griffin RC .60 1.50
108 DeSagana Diop RC .50 1.25
109 Rodney White RC .50 1.25
110 Joe Johnson RC 1.25 3.00
111 Kedrick Brown RC .50 1.25
112 Vladimir Radmanovic RC .60 1.50
113 Richard Jefferson RC 1.00 2.50
114 Troy Murphy RC .60 1.50
115 Steven Hunter RC .50 1.25
116 Kirk Haston RC .50 1.25
117 Michael Bradley RC .50 1.25
118 Jason Collins RC .60 1.50
119 Zach Randolph RC 1.50 4.00
120 Brendan Haywood RC .60 1.50
121 Joseph Forte RC .50 1.25
122 Jeryl Sasser RC .50 1.25
123 Brandon Armstrong RC .50 1.25
124 Gerald Wallace RC 1.00 2.50
125 Samuel Dalembert RC .75 2.00
126 Jamaal Tinsley RC .60 1.50
127 Tony Parker RC 3.00 8.00
128 Trenton Hassell RC .50 1.25
129 Gilbert Arenas RC 2.00 5.00
130 Omar Cook RC .75 2.00
131 Jeff Trepagnier RC .50 1.25
132 Loren Woods RC .50 1.25
133 Terence Morris RC .50 1.25
134 Michael Jordan 6.00 15.00

2001-02 Stadium Club Parallel

1-100 STATED ODDS 1:4
101-133 STATED ODDS 1:12
134 Michael Jordan 15.00 40.00

2001-02 Stadium Club Co-Signers

DUAL STAT.ODDS 1:1647 HOBBY
TRIPLE STAT.ODDS 1:10168 HOBBY
CS2 S.O'Neal/Abdul-Jabbar 300.00 600.00
CS3 B.Davis/J.Terry 25.00 60.00
SCATRI Magic/Kareem/Shaq 500.00 1,000.00

2001-02 Stadium Club Dunkus Colossus

COMPLETE SET (15) 10.00 25.00
STATED ODDS 1:4
DC1 Baron Davis .75 2.00
DC2 Vince Carter 1.50 4.00
DC3 Tracy McGrady 1.25 3.00
DC4 Shawn Marion .75 2.00
DC5 Kevin Garnett 2.00 5.00
DC6 Darius Miles .50 1.25
DC7 Steve Francis .75 2.00
DC8 Chris Webber 1.00 2.50
DC9 Alonzo Mourning 1.25 3.00
DC10 Rasheed Wallace 1.00 2.50
DC11 Tim Duncan 2.00 5.00
DC12 Antonio McDyess .60 1.50
DC13 Jerry Stackhouse .75 2.00
DC14 Jermaine O'Neal .60 1.50
DC15 Shaquille O'Neal 3.00 8.00

2001-02 Stadium Club Lone Star Signatures

STATED ODDS 1:18
LSAH Al Harrington 5.00 12.00
LSAJ Antawn Jamison 5.00 12.00
LSCA Courtney Alexander 5.00 12.00
LSEB Elton Brand 5.00 12.00
LSEMJ Magic Johnson 60.00 150.00
LSGA Gilbert Arenas 8.00 20.00
LSHT Hedo Turkoglu 5.00 12.00
LSIT Iakovos Tsakalidis 5.00 12.00
LSJF Joseph Forte 5.00 12.00
LSJT Jason Terry 8.00 20.00
LSKAJ Kareem Abdul-Jabbar 150.00 400.00
LSKS Kenny Satterfield 5.00 12.00
LSMJ Marc Jackson 5.00 12.00
LSPS Peja Stojakovic 8.00 20.00
LSSB Shane Battier 5.00 12.00
LSSM Shawn Marion 8.00 20.00
LSSO Shaquille O'Neal 75.00 200.00
LSTM Troy Murphy 6.00 15.00

2001-02 Stadium Club Maximus Rejectus

STATED ODDS 1:8
MR1 Chris Webber 1.00 2.50
MR2 Shaquille O'Neal 3.00 8.00
MR3 Tim Duncan 2.00 5.00
MR4 Kevin Garnett 2.00 5.00
MR5 Darius Miles .50 1.25
MR6 Theo Ratliff .50 1.25
MR7 Dikembe Mutombo 1.25 3.00
MR8 Jermaine O'Neal .60 1.50
MR9 Alonzo Mourning 1.25 3.00
MR10 Marcus Camby .60 1.50

2001-02 Stadium Club NBA Call Signs

COMPLETE SET (10) 12.00 30.00
STATED ODDS 1:24
CS1 Steve Francis 1.25 3.00
CS2 Shaquille O'Neal 5.00 12.00
CS3 Allen Iverson 3.00 8.00
CS4 Tracy McGrady 2.00 5.00
CS5 Vince Carter 2.50 6.00
CS6 Lamar Odom 1.00 2.50
CS7 Gary Payton 2.00 5.00
CS8 Stephon Marbury 1.50 4.00
CS9 Karl Malone 2.50 6.00
CS10 Glenn Robinson 1.25 3.00

2001-02 Stadium Club Stroke of Genius

STATED ODDS 1:40
SGAI Allen Iverson 8.00 20.00
SGBD Baron Davis 2.50 6.00
SGCW Chris Webber 3.00 8.00
SGDM Darius Miles 1.50 4.00
SGGP Gary Payton 4.00 10.00
SGGR Glenn Robinson 2.50 6.00
SGJK Jason Kidd 4.00 10.00
SGJS John Stockton 6.00 15.00
SGKM Karl Malone 6.00 15.00
SGKW Jason Williams 6.00 15.00
SGRM Reggie Miller 4.00 10.00
SGRW Rasheed Wallace 3.00 8.00
SGSM Shawn Marion 2.50 6.00
SGSO Shaquille O'Neal 10.00 25.00
SGSXM Stephon Marbury 3.00 8.00

2001-02 Stadium Club Stroke of Genius Autographs

PRINT RUNS LISTED BELOW
SGASM Shawn Marion/31 12.00 30.00
SGASO Shaquille O'Neal/34 125.00 300.00

2001-02 Stadium Club Touch of Class

STATED ODDS 1:40
TCAFM Antonio McDyess 3.00 8.00
TCAM Andre Miller 3.00 8.00
TCDN Dirk Nowitzki 10.00 25.00
TCEB Elton Brand 3.00 8.00
TCJS Jerry Stackhouse 4.00 10.00
TCJT Jason Terry 4.00 10.00
TCKM Kenyon Martin 4.00 10.00
TCMF Michael Finley 4.00 10.00
TCMJ Marc Jackson 2.50 6.00
TCMM Mike Miller 3.00 8.00
TCPP Paul Pierce 6.00 15.00
TCRA Ray Allen 6.00 15.00
TCSF Steve Francis 4.00 10.00
TCTD Tim Duncan 10.00 25.00
TCTM Tracy McGrady 6.00 15.00

2001-02 Stadium Club Touch of Class Autographs

PRINT RUNS LISTED BELOW
TCAAM Andre Miller/24 20.00 50.00
TCAEB Elton Brand/42 40.00 100.00
TCATD Tim Duncan/21 8,000.00 15,000.00

2001-02 Stadium Club Traction

STATED ODDS 1:844
TAJ Antawn Jamison 5.00 12.00
TBD Baron Davis 6.00 15.00
TEB Elton Brand 5.00 12.00
TJT Jason Terry 6.00 15.00
TPS Peja Stojakovic 5.00 12.00
TRH Richard Hamilton 8.00 20.00
TSM Shawn Marion 6.00 15.00
TSO Shaquille O'Neal 25.00 60.00
TTD Tim Duncan 15.00 40.00

2001-02 Stadium Club Traction Autographs

PRINT RUNS LISTED BELOW
TAJ Antawn Jamison/33 75.00 200.00
TEB Elton Brand/21 75.00 200.00
TJT Jason Terry/31 75.00 200.00
TPS Peja Stojakovic/16 100.00 250.00
TRH Richard Hamilton/16 200.00 500.00
TSM Shawn Marion/31 125.00 300.00

2002-03 Stadium Club

COMPLETE SET (133) 50.00 100.00
COMP.SET w/o SP's (100) 10.00 25.00
101-133 STATED ODDS 1:3
1 Shaquille O'Neal 1.00 2.50
2 Pau Gasol .40 1.00
3 Allen Iverson .60 1.50
4 Bonzi Wells .15 .40
5 Mike Bibby .25 .60
6 Rashard Lewis .20 .50
7 Aaron McKie .15 .40
8 Shane Battier .25 .60
9 Kenyon Martin .25 .60
10 Tim Duncan .60 1.50
11 Richard Jefferson .20 .50
12 Jalen Rose .20 .50
13 Antoine Walker .20 .50
14 Michael Finley .25 .60
15 Clifford Robinson .25 .60
16 Antawn Jamison .20 .50
17 Reggie Miller .50 1.25
18 Elton Brand .20 .50
19 Robert Horry .25 .60
20 Kevin Garnett .60 1.50
21 Baron Davis .25 .60
22 Latrell Sprewell .25 .60
23 Glenn Robinson .25 .60
24 Wally Szczerbiak .20 .50
25 Tracy McGrady .40 1.00
26 Stephon Marbury .30 .75
27 Rasheed Wallace .30 .75
28 Doug Christie .15 .40
29 Desmond Mason .20 .50
30 Vince Carter .50 1.25
31 Andrei Kirilenko .30 .75
32 Richard Hamilton .30 .75
33 Jamaal Tinsley .15 .40
34 Steve Francis .25 .60
35 Ben Wallace .30 .75
36 Juwan Howard .25 .60
37 Dirk Nowitzki .60 1.50
38 Andre Miller .20 .50
39 Elden Campbell .15 .40
40 Paul Pierce .40 1.00
41 Shareef Abdur-Rahim .25 .60
42 John Stockton .50 1.25
43 Gary Payton .40 1.00
44 David Robinson .50 1.25
45 Scottie Pippen .60 1.50
46 Morris Peterson .20 .50
47 Mike Miller .20 .50
48 Marcus Camby .20 .50
49 Joe Smith .20 .50
50 Kobe Bryant 2.00 5.00
51 Alonzo Mourning .40 1.00
52 Ray Allen .40 1.00
53 Keith Van Horn .20 .50
54 Grant Hill .40 1.00
55 Dikembe Mutombo .40 1.00
56 Shawn Marion .25 .60
57 Peja Stojakovic .25 .60
58 Tony Parker .40 1.00
59 Keon Clark .15 .40
60 Brendan Haywood .15 .40
61 Derek Anderson .15 .40
62 Allan Houston .25 .60
63 Brian Grant .15 .40
64 Lamar Odom .25 .60
65 Jermaine O'Neal .20 .50
66 Kenny Anderson .20 .50
67 Demarr Johnson .15 .40
68 Lamond Murray .15 .40
69 Jason Richardson .25 .60
70 Rodney Rogers .15 .40
71 Rick Fox .15 .40
72 Tim Thomas .15 .40
73 Darrell Armstrong .15 .40
74 Anfernee Hardaway .60 1.50
75 Chris Webber .30 .75
76 Derrick Coleman .20 .50
77 Karl Malone .50 1.25
78 Antonio Davis .20 .50
79 Jason Terry .20 .50
80 Wang Zhizhi .20 .50
81 Steve Nash .50 1.25
82 Eddy Curry UER .15 .40
83 Tim Hardaway .25 .60
84 Corliss Williamson .15 .40
85 Eddie Griffin .15 .40
86 Darius Miles .15 .40
87 Jason Williams .30 .75
88 Sam Cassell .20 .50
89 Kwame Brown .15 .40
90 Jason Kidd .40 1.00
91 Jamal Mashburn .20 .50
92 Jamal Magloire .15 .40
93 Tyson Chandler .25 .60
94 Jumaine Jones .15 .40
95 Antonio McDyess .20 .50
96 Jerry Stackhouse .25 .60
97 Gilbert Arenas .25 .60
98 Cuttino Mobley .15 .40
99 Eddie Jones .25 .60
100 Michael Jordan 2.50 6.00
101 Yao Ming RC 4.00 10.00
102 Jay Williams RC .60 1.50
103 Mike Dunleavy RC .75 2.00
104 Drew Gooden RC .75 2.00
105 Nikoloz Tskitishvili RC .50 1.25
106 DaJuan Wagner RC .60 1.50
107 Nene Hilario RC .75 2.00
108 Chris Wilcox RC .60 1.50
109 Amare Stoudemire RC 2.00 5.00
110 Caron Butler RC .75 2.00
111 Jared Jeffries RC .60 1.50
112 Melvin Ely RC .60 1.50
113 Marcus Haislip RC .50 1.25
114 Fred Jones RC .50 1.25
115 Bostjan Nachbar RC .60 1.50
116 Dan Dickau RC .50 1.25
117 Juan Dixon RC .60 1.50
118 Dan Gadzuric RC .60 1.50
119 Ryan Humphrey RC .60 1.50
120 Kareem Rush RC .60 1.50
121 Qyntel Woods RC .50 1.25
122 Casey Jacobsen RC .60 1.50
123 Tayshaun Prince RC 1.50 4.00
124 Frank Williams RC .50 1.25
125 John Salmons RC .75 2.00
126 Chris Jefferies RC .50 1.25
127 Sam Clancy RC .60 1.50
128 Ronald Murray RC .75 2.00
129 Roger Mason RC .60 1.50
130 Robert Archibald RC .50 1.25
131 Vincent Yarbrough RC .50 1.25
132 Darius Songaila RC .75 2.00
133 Carlos Boozer RC .75 2.00

2002-03 Stadium Club 10th Anniversary Parallel

*STARS: .5X TO 1.25X BASE CARD HI
*RCs: .75X TO 2X BASE CARD HI
ONE 10th ANNIV. OR INSERT PER PACK
101-133 PRINT RUN 1000 SER.#'d SETS
100 Michael Jordan 4.00 10.00

2002-03 Stadium Club Photo Proof Parallel

*STARS: 3X TO 8X BASE CARD HI
*RCs: 3X TO 8X BASE CARD HI
1-100 PRINT RUN 500 SER.#'d SETS
101-133 PRINT RUN 100 SER.#'d SETS
100 Michael Jordan 20.00 50.00

2002-03 Stadium Club All-Star Coverage Relics

PRINT RUN 700 SER.#'d SETS
ASAI Allen Iverson 8.00 20.00
ASBH Brendan Haywood 2.00 5.00
ASDLM Darius Miles 2.00 5.00
ASEB Elton Brand 2.50 6.00
ASJK Jason Kidd 5.00 12.00
ASJO Jermaine O'Neal 2.50 6.00
ASJR Jason Richardson 3.00 8.00
ASKM Kenyon Martin 3.00 8.00
ASPG Pau Gasol 5.00 12.00
ASPS Peja Stojakovic 2.50 6.00
ASSB Shane Battier 3.00 8.00
ASSF Steve Francis 3.00 8.00
ASTD Tim Duncan 8.00 20.00
ASTM Tracy McGrady 5.00 12.00
ASTP Tony Parker 5.00 12.00

2002-03 Stadium Club All-Star Coverage Relics Autographs

PRINT RUN 25 SER.#'d SETS
ASAEB Elton Brand 25.00 60.00
ASAJO Jermaine O'Neal 25.00 60.00
ASASB Shane Battier 25.00 60.00
ASATD Tim Duncan 125.00 250.00

2002-03 Stadium Club Beam Team

PRINT RUN 500 SER.#'d SETS
BT1 Shaquille O'Neal 75.00 200.00
BT2 Michael Jordan 800.00 1,500.00
BT3 Antoine Walker 4.00 10.00
BT4 Vince Carter 30.00 80.00
BT5 Darius Miles 3.00 8.00
BT6 Jerry Stackhouse 5.00 12.00
BT7 Kevin Garnett 75.00 200.00
BT8 Tim Duncan 75.00 200.00
BT9 Kobe Bryant 500.00 1,000.00
BT10 Steve Francis 5.00 12.00
BT11 Tony Parker 25.00 60.00
BT12 Richard Jefferson 4.00 10.00
BT13 Dirk Nowitzki 75.00 200.00
BT14 Antawn Jamison 4.00 10.00
BT15 DaJuan Wagner 4.00 10.00
BT16 Caron Butler 5.00 12.00
BT17 Mike Dunleavy 4.00 10.00
BT18 Kareem Rush 4.00 10.00
BT19 Amare Stoudemire 12.00 30.00
BT20 Drew Gooden 5.00 12.00

2002-03 Stadium Club Co-Signers

STATED ODDS 1:2224
CS1 S.O'Neal/T.Duncan 1,500.00 3,000.00
CS2 E.Brand/S.Marion 30.00 80.00

2002-03 Stadium Club Dual Relics

PRINT RUN 100 SER.#'d SETS
CC1 T.McGrady/S.Francis 20.00 50.00
CC2 S.O'Neal/T.Duncan 40.00 100.00
CC3 A.Iverson/S.O'Neal 40.00 100.00
CC4 T.Duncan JSY/WU 40.00 100.00
CC5 S.O'Neal JSY/WU 40.00 100.00
CC6 M.Finley/D.Nowitzki 20.00 50.00
CC7 J.Stockton/K.Malone 20.00 50.00
CC8 R.Allen/G.Robinson 15.00 40.00
CC9 C.Webber/P.Stojakovic 20.00 50.00
CC10 P.Pierce/B.Davis 20.00 50.00

2002-03 Stadium Club Frequent Flyers Relics

PRINT RUNS LISTED BELOW
FFAH Anfernee Hardaway/700 10.00 25.00
FFDN Dirk Nowitzki/700 10.00 25.00
FFJT Jason Terry/200 3.00 8.00
FFPP Paul Pierce/700 6.00 15.00
FFQR Quentin Richardson/350 2.50 6.00
FFRA Ray Allen/700 6.00 15.00
FFRL Raef Lafrentz/700 2.50 6.00
FFRW Rasheed Wallace/350 5.00 12.00
FFSM Stephon Marbury/700 5.00 12.00
FFSO Shaquille O'Neal/700 15.00 40.00
FFSDM Shawn Marion/700 4.00 10.00
FFTD Tim Duncan/700 10.00 25.00
FFTM Tracy McGrady/700 6.00 15.00

2002-03 Stadium Club Frequent Flyers Relics Autographs

PRINT RUN 25 SER.#'d SETS
FFAJT Jason Terry 25.00 60.00
FFARL Raef LaFrentz 20.00 50.00
FFASO Shaquille O'Neal 300.00 600.00
FFATD Tim Duncan 500.00 1,000.00
FFASDM Shawn Marion 40.00 100.00

2002-03 Stadium Club Lone Star Signatures

PRINT RUNS LISTED BELOW
LSAM Aaron McKie/250 5.00 12.00
LSDB Damone Brown/500 5.00 12.00
LSDG Drew Gooden/100 5.00 12.00
LSDW DaJuan Wagner/100 4.00 10.00
LSEB Elton Brand/100 8.00 20.00
LSFJ Fred Jones/100 4.00 10.00
LSFW Frank Williams/100 3.00 8.00
LSJF Joseph Forte/250 5.00 12.00
LSJT Jake Tsakalidis/500 5.00 12.00
LSKB Kwame Brown/250 5.00 12.00
LSKS Kenny Satterfield/250 5.00 12.00
LSLP Lavor Postell/1000 5.00 12.00
LSMB Mike Bibby/500 6.00 15.00
LSMD Mike Dunleavy/100 5.00 12.00
LSRH Richard Hamilton/500 6.00 15.00
LSSM Shawn Marion/200 8.00 20.00
LSSO Shaquille O'Neal/1000 100.00 250.00
LSTM Troy Murphy/250 5.00 12.00
LSYM Yao Ming/100 200.00 500.00

2002-03 Stadium Club Reprint Relics

PRINT RUN 700 SER.#'d SETS
SCCW Chris Webber 5.00 12.00
SCDM Darius Miles 2.50 6.00
SCDN Dirk Nowitzki 10.00 25.00
SCEB Elton Brand 3.00 8.00
SCJK Jason Kidd 6.00 15.00
SCMF Michael Finley 4.00 10.00
SCPG Pau Gasol 6.00 15.00
SCRA Ray Allen 6.00 15.00
SCSO Shaquille O'Neal 15.00 40.00
SCTD Tim Duncan 10.00 25.00

2002-03 Stadium Club The Hustlers

COMPLETE SET (20) 20.00 50.00
STATED ODDS 1:4
H1 Baron Davis .75 2.00
H2 Jamaal Tinsley .50 1.25
H3 Karl Malone 1.50 4.00
H4 Kevin Garnett 2.00 5.00
H5 Tim Duncan 2.00 5.00
H6 Kenyon Martin .75 2.00
H7 Michael Jordan 12.00 30.00
H8 Vince Carter 8.00 20.00
H9 Kobe Bryant 12.00 30.00
H10 Alonzo Mourning 1.25 3.00
H11 Shaquille O'Neal 3.00 8.00
H12 Chris Webber 1.00 2.50
H13 Paul Pierce 1.25 3.00
H14 Tony Parker 1.25 3.00
H15 Jason Kidd 1.25 3.00
H16 Antonio McDyess .60 1.50
H17 Eddie Jones .75 2.00
H18 Michael Finley .75 2.00
H19 Tracy McGrady 1.25 3.00
H20 Gary Payton 1.25 3.00

2002-03 Stadium Club Urban Legends

COMPLETE SET (10) 12.00 30.00
STATED ODDS 1:8
UL1 Allen Iverson 2.00 5.00
UL2 Kobe Bryant 12.00 30.00
UL3 Elton Brand .60 1.50
UL4 Jamaal Tinsley .50 1.25
UL5 Vince Carter 1.50 4.00
UL6 Kevin Garnett 2.00 5.00
UL7 Gary Payton 1.25 3.00
UL8 Ron Artest .60 1.50
UL9 Kenny Anderson .60 1.50
UL10 Stephon Marbury 1.00 2.50

2002-03 Stadium Club Beckett.com Samples

*SINGLES: .75X TO 2X BASE STADIUM HI

2007-08 Stadium Club Promos

PP1 Dwyane Wade .75 2.00
PP2 Carmelo Anthony .60 1.50
PP3 Larry Bird/Magic Johnson 1.50 4.00

2007-08 Stadium Club

COMP.SET w/o SP's (100) 20.00 50.00
RC PRINT RUN 1999 SER.#'d SETS
EXCH EXPIRE DATE 1/31/10
1 Amare Stoudemire .40 1.00
2 Baron Davis .30 .75
3 Dwyane Wade .75 2.00
4 Chris Bosh .50 1.25
5 Josh Smith .25 .60
6 Tyson Chandler .40 1.00
7 Al Jefferson .25 .60
8 Deron Williams .30 .75
9 Andre Iguodala .40 1.00
10 Jermaine O'Neal .40 1.00
11 Yao Ming 1.00 2.50
12 Kirk Hinrich .40 1.00
13 Steve Nash .75 2.00
14 Jameer Nelson .25 .60
15 Carmelo Anthony .60 1.50
16 Pau Gasol .60 1.50
17 Andrew Bynum .25 .60
18 Gerald Wallace .30 .75
19 Carlos Boozer .30 .75
20 Rasheed Wallace .50 1.25
21 Tim Duncan 1.00 2.50
22 Michael Redd .30 .75
23 LeBron James 3.00 8.00
24 Kobe Bryant 3.00 8.00
25 Richard Jefferson .30 .75
26 Mike Bibby .40 1.00
27 Ben Gordon .30 .75
28 Caron Butler .30 .75
29 Corey Maggette .30 .75
30 Kevin Garnett 1.00 2.50
31 Shawn Marion .40 1.00
32 Shaquille O'Neal 1.50 4.00

33 Allen Iverson 1.00 2.50
34 Eddy Curry .25 .60
35 Chris Wilcox .25 .60
36 T.J. Ford .25 .60
37 LaMarcus Aldridge .40 1.00
38 Drew Gooden .30 .75
39 Antawn Jamison .30 .75
40 Richard Hamilton .50 1.25
41 Dirk Nowitzki 1.00 2.50
42 Elton Brand .30 .75
43 Jason Richardson .40 1.00
44 Paul Pierce .60 1.50
45 Manu Ginobili .75 2.00
46 Danny Granger .25 .60
47 Andrei Kirilenko .30 .75
48 Jarrett Jack .30 .75
49 Andre Miller .30 .75
50 Gilbert Arenas .40 1.00
51 Mehmet Okur .25 .60
52 Rudy Gay .30 .75
53 Ben Wallace .50 1.25
54 Tayshaun Prince .40 1.00
55 Jason Kidd .60 1.50
56 Josh Howard .30 .75
57 Daniel Gibson .25 .60
58 Rafer Alston .40 1.00
59 Monta Ellis .30 .75
60 Dwight Howard .50 1.25
61 Chauncey Billups .50 1.25
62 Joe Johnson .30 .75
63 Kevin Martin .30 .75
64 Ray Allen .60 1.50
65 Luol Deng .30 .75
66 Raymond Felton .30 .75
67 Lamar Odom .30 .75
68 Mo Williams .30 .75
69 Tony Parker .60 1.50
70 Brandon Roy .50 1.25
71 Tracy McGrady .60 1.50
72 Marcus Camby .30 .75
73 Stephon Marbury .50 1.25
74 Jason Terry .30 .75
75 Randy Foye .30 .75
76 Vince Carter .75 2.00
77 Andrea Bargnani .25 .60
78 Chris Paul .75 2.00
79 Rashard Lewis .30 .75
80 Leandro Barbosa .30 .75
81 Larry Johnson 1.25 3.00
82 Patrick Ewing 1.25 3.00
83 Hakeem Olajuwon 2.00 5.00
84 Clyde Drexler 1.50 4.00
85 David Robinson 2.00 5.00
86 Bill Walton 1.25 3.00
87 Wilt Chamberlain 3.00 8.00
88 Bill Russell 3.00 8.00
89 Bob Lanier .75 2.00
90 Dennis Rodman 2.50 6.00
91 John Stockton 2.00 5.00
92 Isiah Thomas 1.00 2.50
93 Magic Johnson 4.00 10.00
94 Larry Bird 4.00 10.00
95 Elgin Baylor 1.00 2.50
96 Oscar Robertson 1.00 2.50
97 Joe Barry Carroll 1.00 2.50
98 James Worthy 1.50 4.00
99 Pete Maravich 2.50 6.00
100 Kenny Smith .75 2.00
101 Greg Oden RC 1.50 4.00
102 Kevin Durant RC 50.00 120.00
103 Al Horford RC 4.00 10.00
104 Mike Conley Jr. RC 4.00 10.00
105 Jeff Green RC 1.25 3.00
106 Yi Jianlian RC 2.00 5.00
107 Corey Brewer RC 1.25 3.00
108 Brandan Wright RC 1.25 3.00
109 Joakim Noah RC 1.50 4.00
110 Spencer Hawes RC 1.00 2.50
111 Acie Law RC 1.00 2.50
112 Thaddeus Young RC 1.50 4.00
113 Julian Wright RC 1.00 2.50
114 Al Thornton RC 1.00 2.50
115 Rodney Stuckey RC 1.00 2.50
116 Nick Young RC 1.50 4.00
117 Sean Williams RC 1.00 2.50
118 Marco Belinelli RC 1.25 3.00
119 Javaris Crittenton RC 1.00 2.50
120 Jason Smith RC 1.00 2.50
121 Daequan Cook RC 1.25 3.00
122 Jared Dudley RC 1.25 3.00
123 Wilson Chandler RC 1.25 3.00
124 D.J. Strawberry RC 1.00 2.50
125 Morris Almond RC 1.00 2.50
126 Aaron Brooks RC 1.25 3.00
127 Arron Afflalo RC 1.25 3.00
128 Luis Scola RC 1.50 4.00
129 Alando Tucker RC 1.00 2.50
130 Carl Landry RC 1.00 2.50
131 Gabe Pruitt RC 1.00 2.50
132 Marcus Williams RC 1.00 2.50
133 Nick Fazekas RC 1.00 2.50
134 Glen Davis RC 1.25 3.00
135 Jermareo Davidson RC 1.00 2.50
136 Josh McRoberts RC 1.00 2.50
137 Oleksiy Pecherov RC 1.50 4.00
138 Derrick Byars RC 1.00 2.50
139 Adam Haluska RC 1.00 2.50
140 Reyshawn Terry RC 1.00 2.50
141 Jared Jordan RC 1.00 2.50
142 Stephane Lasme RC 1.00 2.50
143 Dominic McGuire RC 1.00 2.50
144 Aaron Gray RC 1.00 2.50
145 JamesOn Curry RC 1.00 2.50
146 Taurean Green RC 1.00 2.50
147 Demetris Nichols RC 1.00 2.50
148 Herbert Hill RC 1.00 2.50
149 Ramon Sessions RC 1.25 3.00
150 Sammy Mejia RC 1.00 2.50
NNO G.Oden AU 8x10 100.00 200.00

2007-08 Stadium Club Chrome Rookie Refractors

*REFRACTORS: .5X TO 1.25X BASE HI
REF.PRINT RUN 999 SER.#'d SETS
102 Kevin Durant 125.00 300.00

2007-08 Stadium Club Chrome Rookie Refractors Gold

*REF.GOLD: 1.25X TO 3X BASE HI
PRINT RUN 99 SER.#'d SETS
102 Kevin Durant 1,000.00 2,000.00

2007-08 Stadium Club Chrome Rookie X-Fractors

*X-FRACTOR: 1.5X TO 4X BASE HI
PRINT RUN 50 SER.#'d SETS
102 Kevin Durant 1,500.00 3,000.00

2007-08 Stadium Club Chrome Rookie X-Fractors Autographs

GROUP A ODDS 1:66, GROUP B 1:30
GROUP C ODDS 1:9
101 Greg Oden B 5.00 12.00
106 Yi Jianlian A 6.00 15.00
108 Brandan Wright A 4.00 10.00
110 Spencer Hawes B 3.00 8.00
111 Acie Law B 3.00 8.00
112 Thaddeus Young C 5.00 12.00
115 Rodney Stuckey C 3.00 8.00
116 Nick Young A 5.00 12.00
117 Sean Williams C 3.00 8.00
118 Marco Belinelli C 4.00 10.00
119 Javaris Crittenton C 3.00 8.00
120 Jason Smith B 3.00 8.00
121 Daequan Cook C 4.00 10.00
122 Jared Dudley B 4.00 10.00
123 Wilson Chandler C 4.00 10.00
125 Morris Almond C 3.00 8.00
126 Aaron Brooks C 4.00 10.00
127 Arron Afflalo C 4.00 10.00
132 Marcus Williams C 3.00 8.00
133 Nick Fazekas C 3.00 8.00

2007-08 Stadium Club First Day Issue

*1-80 VETS: .6X TO 1.5X BASE HI
*81-100 RETIRED: .5X TO 1.25X BASE HI
PRINT RUN 1999 SER.#'d SETS

2007-08 Stadium Club Photographer's Proof Silver

*SILVER 1-80: .75X TO 2X BASE HI
*SILVER 81-100: .6X TO 1.5X BASE HI
SILVER PRINT RUN 199 SER.#'d SETS

2007-08 Stadium Club Beam Team Autographs

GROUP A ODDS 1:110, GROUP B 1:141
GROUP C ODDS 1:38, GROUP D 1:26
GROUP E ODDS 1:20, GROUP F 1:44
*AU GOLD: .5X TO 1.25X BASE HI
GOLD PRINT RUN 25 SER.#'d SETS
AB Andrea Bargnani A 5.00 12.00
ABY Andrew Bynum B 5.00 12.00
AI Andre Iguodala A 5.00 12.00
AM Adam Morrison A 5.00 12.00
BD Baron Davis C 5.00 12.00
BG Ben Gordon A 5.00 12.00
CA Carmelo Anthony A 20.00 50.00
CB Carlos Boozer A 5.00 12.00
CBI Chauncey Billups B 6.00 15.00
CBO Chris Bosh A 6.00 15.00
CD Chris Duhon D 5.00 12.00
CF Channing Frye D 5.00 12.00
CM Corey Maggette E 5.00 12.00
DG Danny Granger F 5.00 12.00
DL David Lee E 5.00 12.00
DW Dwyane Wade A 20.00 50.00
DWI Deron Williams C 5.00 12.00
EO Emeka Okafor A 5.00 12.00
GW Gerald Wallace C 5.00 12.00
HT Hedo Turkoglu E 5.00 12.00
JC Josh Childress C 5.00 12.00
JF Jordan Farmar A 6.00 15.00
JH Josh Howard B 5.00 12.00
JO Jermaine O'Neal A 5.00 12.00
KH Kirk Hinrich B 5.00 12.00
MJ Mike James E 5.00 12.00
MW Marcus Williams D 5.00 12.00
MWE Martell Webster D 5.00 12.00
RA Ray Allen A 15.00 40.00
RB Raja Bell E 5.00 12.00
RF Raymond Felton C 5.00 12.00
SC Speedy Claxton F 5.00 12.00
SD Samuel Dalembert E 5.00 12.00
SO Shaquille O'Neal A 60.00 150.00
TJF T.J. Ford C 5.00 12.00
TP Tony Parker A 12.00 30.00
UH Udonis Haslem D 5.00 12.00
VC Vince Carter A 15.00 40.00

2007-08 Stadium Club Beam Team Relics

GROUP A ODDS 1:30, GROUP B 1:40
GROUP C ODDS 1:6, GROUP D 1:6
*GOLD: .6X TO 1.5X BASE HI
GOLD PRINT RUN 99 SER.#'d SETS
AB Andrea Bargnani D 2.00 5.00
AI Allen Iverson A 8.00 20.00
AIG Andre Iguodala C 3.00 8.00
AS Amare Stoudemire A 3.00 8.00
BD Baron Davis B 2.50 6.00
BG Ben Gordon A 2.50 6.00
CA Carmelo Anthony A 5.00 12.00
CB Carlos Boozer A 2.50 6.00
CBI Chauncey Billups C 4.00 10.00
CBO Chris Bosh C 4.00 10.00
DH Dwight Howard C 4.00 10.00
DN Dirk Nowitzki D 8.00 20.00
DW Dwyane Wade D 3.00 8.00
DWI Deron Williams D 2.50 6.00
JK Jason Kidd A 5.00 12.00
JO Jermaine O'Neal D 3.00 8.00
KB Kobe Bryant C 150.00 400.00
LD Luol Deng D 2.50 6.00
SN Steve Nash C 2.00 5.00
SO Shaquille O'Neal D 4.00 10.00
TD Tim Duncan C 8.00 20.00
TM Tracy McGrady C 5.00 12.00
TP Tony Parker C 6.00 15.00
VC Vince Carter B 6.00 15.00
YM Yao Ming C 8.00 20.00

2007-08 Stadium Club Full Court Press Relics

PRINT RUN 499 SER.#'d SETS
*GOLD: .5X TO 1.25X BASE HI
GOLD PRINT RUN 50 SER.#'d SETS
*DUAL: SAME VALUE AS BASE
DUAL PRINT RUN 199 SER.#'d SETS
*DUAL GOLD: .6X TO 1.5X BASE HI
DUAL GOLD PRINT RUN 25 SER.#'d SETS
*TRIPLE: .5X TO 1.25X BASE HI
TRIPLE PRINT RUN 99 SER.#'d SETS
AA Arron Afflalo 2.00 5.00
AB Aaron Brooks 2.00 5.00
AH Al Horford 6.00 15.00
AJ Al Jefferson 1.50 4.00
AL Acie Law 1.50 4.00
AS Amare Stoudemire 2.50 6.00
AT Al Thornton 1.50 4.00
ATU Alando Tucker 1.50 4.00
BD Baron Davis 2.00 5.00
BW Brandan Wright 2.00 5.00
BWA Ben Wallace 3.00 8.00
CA Carmelo Anthony 4.00 10.00
CB Corey Brewer 2.00 5.00
CBO Chris Bosh 3.00 8.00
CP Chris Paul 5.00 12.00
DC Daequan Cook 2.00 5.00
DH Dwight Howard 3.00 8.00
DN Dirk Nowitzki 6.00 15.00
DR David Robinson 5.00 12.00
DW Dwyane Wade 5.00 12.00
DWI Dominique Wilkins 4.00 10.00
EB Elton Brand 2.00 5.00
GD Glen Davis 2.00 5.00
GO Greg Oden 2.50 6.00
IT Isiah Thomas 2.50 6.00
JC Javaris Crittenton 1.50 4.00
JD Jared Dudley 2.00 5.00
JG Jeff Green 2.00 5.00
JK Jason Kidd 4.00 10.00
JM Josh McRoberts 1.50 4.00
JN Joakim Noah 2.50 6.00
JS Jason Smith 1.50 4.00
JW Julian Wright 1.50 4.00
KB Kobe Bryant 60.00 150.00
LB Larry Bird 10.00 25.00
MC Mike Conley Jr. 6.00 15.00
MJ Magic Johnson 10.00 25.00
NY Nick Young 2.50 6.00
RJ Richard Jefferson 2.00 5.00
RS Rodney Stuckey 1.50 4.00
SH Spencer Hawes 1.50 4.00
SN Steve Nash 5.00 12.00
SO Shaquille O'Neal 10.00 25.00
SW Sean Williams 1.50 4.00
TD Tim Duncan 6.00 15.00
TM Tracy McGrady 4.00 10.00
TY Thaddeus Young 2.50 6.00
VC Vince Carter 5.00 12.00
WC Wilson Chandler 2.00 5.00
YM Yao Ming 6.00 15.00

2007-08 Stadium Club Future Foundation Autographs Relics Dual

GROUP A ODDS 1:2050, GROUP B 1:1175
GROUP C ODDS 1:176
AW C.Anthony/M.Williams B 15.00 40.00
BL C.Billups/A.Law C 15.00 40.00
BW C.Bosh/B.Wright B 20.00 50.00
DC B.Davis/J.Crittenton C 12.00 30.00
IY A.Iguodala/T.Young C 12.00 30.00
OH J.O'Neal/S.Hawes C 12.00 30.00
RO B.Russell/G.Oden A 600.00 1,200.00
RW D.Rodman/S.Williams C 15.00 40.00
WT D.Wilkins/A.Thornton C 15.00 40.00
WY D.Wade/N.Young A 30.00 80.00

2007-08 Stadium Club Super Teams

PRINT RUN 50 SER.#'d SETS
ATL Atlanta Hawks 5.00 12.00
BOS Boston Celtics 10.00 25.00
CHA Charlotte Bobcats 5.00 12.00
CHI Chicago Bulls 6.00 15.00
CLE Cleveland Cavaliers 10.00 25.00
DAL Dallas Mavericks 6.00 15.00
DEN Denver Nuggets 6.00 15.00
DET Detroit Pistons 5.00 12.00
GST Golden State Warriors 5.00 12.00
HOU Houston Rockets 5.00 12.00
IND Indiana Pacers 5.00 12.00
LAC Los Angeles Clippers 5.00 12.00
LAL Los Angeles Lakers 10.00 25.00
MEM Memphis Grizzlies 5.00 12.00
MIA Miami Heat 6.00 15.00
MIL Milwaukee Bucks 5.00 12.00
MIN Minnesota Timberwolves 5.00 12.00
NJE New Jersey Nets 5.00 12.00
NOR New Orleans Hornets 5.00 12.00
NYC New York Knicks 6.00 15.00
ORL Orlando Magic 6.00 15.00
PHI Philadelphia 76ers 5.00 12.00
PHO Phoenix Suns 6.00 15.00
POR Portland Trail Blazers 5.00 12.00
SAC Sacramento Kings 5.00 12.00
SAN San Antonio Spurs 6.00 15.00
SEA Seattle SuperSonics 6.00 15.00
TOR Toronto Raptors 5.00 12.00
UTA Utah Jazz 5.00 12.00
WAS Washington Wizards 5.00 12.00

2007-08 Stadium Club Super Teams Rookie Black Refractors

COMPLETE SET (50) 100.00 200.00
SET AVAILABLE VIA DIVISON ST WINNER
101 Greg Oden 2.00 5.00
102 Kevin Durant 400.00 800.00
103 Al Horford 5.00 12.00
104 Mike Conley Jr. 5.00 12.00
105 Jeff Green 1.50 4.00
106 Yi Jianlian 2.50 6.00
107 Corey Brewer 1.50 4.00
108 Brandan Wright 1.50 4.00
109 Joakim Noah 2.00 5.00
110 Spencer Hawes 1.25 3.00
111 Acie Law 1.25 3.00
112 Thaddeus Young 2.00 5.00
113 Julian Wright 1.25 3.00
114 Al Thornton 1.25 3.00
115 Rodney Stuckey 1.25 3.00
116 Nick Young 2.00 5.00
117 Sean Williams 1.25 3.00
118 Marco Belinelli 1.50 4.00
119 Javaris Crittenton 1.25 3.00
120 Jason Smith 1.25 3.00
121 Daequan Cook 1.50 4.00
122 Jared Dudley 1.50 4.00
123 Wilson Chandler 1.50 4.00
124 D.J. Strawberry 1.25 3.00
125 Morris Almond 1.25 3.00
126 Aaron Brooks 1.50 4.00
127 Arron Afflalo 1.50 4.00
128 Luis Scola 2.00 5.00
129 Alando Tucker 1.25 3.00
130 Carl Landry 1.25 3.00
131 Gabe Pruitt 1.25 3.00
132 Marcus Williams 1.25 3.00
133 Nick Fazekas 1.25 3.00
134 Glen Davis 1.50 4.00
135 Jermareo Davidson 1.25 3.00
136 Josh McRoberts 1.25 3.00
137 Oleksiy Pecherov 2.00 5.00
138 Derrick Byars 1.25 3.00
139 Adam Haluska 1.25 3.00
140 Reyshawn Terry 1.25 3.00
141 Jared Jordan 1.25 3.00
142 Stephane Lasme 1.25 3.00
143 Dominic McGuire 1.25 3.00
144 Aaron Gray 1.25 3.00
145 JamesOn Curry 1.25 3.00
146 Taurean Green 1.25 3.00
147 Demetris Nichols 1.25 3.00
148 Herbert Hill 1.25 3.00
149 Ramon Sessions 1.50 4.00
150 Sammy Mejia 1.25 3.00

1999-00 Stadium Club Chrome

COMPLETE SET (150) 25.00 60.00
1 Allen Iverson .75 2.00
2 Chris Webber .40 1.00
3 Antawn Jamison .30 .75
4 Karl Malone .60 1.50
5 Sam Cassell .25 .60
6 Kerry Kittles .25 .60
7 Tim Thomas .25 .60
8 Shawn Bradley .20 .50
9 David Wesley .20 .50
10 Glenn Robinson .25 .60
11 Mitch Richmond .40 1.00
12 Shareef Abdur-Rahim .30 .75
13 Christian Laettner .25 .60
14 Anthony Mason .30 .75
15 Randy Brown .20 .50
16 Charles Barkley .75 2.00
17 Bobby Jackson .20 .50
18 Matt Harpring .20 .50
19 Shawn Kemp .50 1.25
20 Ruben Patterson .20 .50
21 Mike Bibby .30 .75
22 Vlade Divac .30 .75
23 David Robinson .60 1.50
24 Keith Van Horn .25 .60
25 Juwan Howard .25 .60
26 Shaquille O'Neal 1.25 3.00
27 Alonzo Mourning .50 1.25
28 Michael Olowokandi .20 .50
29 Andrew DeClercq .20 .50
30 Toni Kukoc .40 1.00
31 Dikembe Mutombo .50 1.25
32 Steve Nash .60 1.50
33 Eddie Jones .30 .75
34 Reggie Miller .60 1.50
35 Larry Hughes .25 .60
36 Tim Duncan .75 2.00
37 Jerome Williams .20 .50
38 Rod Strickland .20 .50
39 Patrick Ewing .40 1.00
40 Grant Hill .50 1.25
41 Derrick Coleman .25 .60
42 Raef LaFrentz .25 .60
43 Rik Smits .25 .60
44 Latrell Sprewell .40 1.00
45 John Starks .30 .75
46 Cuttino Mobley .20 .50
47 Marcus Camby .25 .60
48 Stephon Marbury .40 1.00
49 Tom Gugliotta .20 .50
50 Vince Carter .75 2.00
51 Chris Mullin .30 .75
52 Tyrone Nesby RC .20 .50
53 Elden Campbell .20 .50
54 Lindsey Hunter .20 .50
55 Rasheed Wallace .40 1.00
56 Jeff Hornacek .25 .60
57 Matt Geiger .20 .50
58 Antoine Walker .30 .75
59 Jason Williams .50 1.25
60 Robert Horry .25 .60
61 Kendall Gill .30 .75
62 Dan Majerle .30 .75
63 Robert Traylor .20 .50
64 P.J. Brown .20 .50
65 Terrell Brandon .20 .50
66 Corliss Williamson .20 .50
67 Bryant Reeves .20 .50
68 Larry Johnson .30 .75
69 Keith Closs .20 .50
70 Walter McCarty .20 .50
71 Wesley Person .20 .50
72 Chris Mills .20 .50
73 Glen Rice .30 .75
74 Jason Kidd .50 1.25
75 Dirk Nowitzki 1.00 2.50
76 Bryon Russell .20 .50
77 Vin Baker .25 .60
78 Darrell Armstrong .25 .60
79 Eric Snow .25 .60
80 Hakeem Olajuwon .60 1.50
81 Tracy McGrady .50 1.25
82 Kenny Anderson .25 .60
83 Jalen Rose .25 .60
84 Tim Hardaway .40 1.00
85 Doug Christie .25 .60
86 Allan Houston .25 .60
87 Kobe Bryant 2.50 6.00
88 Kevin Garnett .75 2.00
89 Steve Kerr .25 .60
90 Nick Van Exel .25 .60
91 Jerry Stackhouse .30 .75
92 Derek Fisher .25 .60
93 Donyell Marshall .25 .60
94 Mark Jackson .25 .60
95 Ray Allen .50 1.25
96 Avery Johnson .25 .60
97 Michael Doleac .20 .50
98 Charles Oakley .30 .75
99 Gary Payton .50 1.25
100 Theo Ratliff .25 .60
101 Cedric Ceballos .20 .50
102 Paul Pierce .60 1.50
103 Michael Finley .30 .75
104 Brian Grant .20 .50
105 John Stockton .50 1.25
106 Maurice Taylor .20 .50
107 Antonio McDyess .25 .60
108 Adrian Griffin RC .40 1.00
109 Jamal Mashburn .25 .60
110 Jayson Williams .20 .50
111 Joe Smith .25 .60
112 Clifford Robinson .25 .60
113 Mario Elie .20 .50
114 Damon Stoudamire .30 .75
115 Felipe Lopez .20 .50
116 Antonio Davis TRAN .20 .50
117 Mookie Blaylock TRAN .20 .50
118 Ron Mercer TRAN .25 .60
119 Horace Grant TRAN .25 .60
120 Steve Smith TRAN .25 .60
121 Isaiah Rider TRAN .25 .60
122 Tariq Abdul-Wahad TRAN .20 .50
123 Michael Dickerson TRAN .20 .50
124 Nick Anderson TRAN .20 .50
125 Jim Jackson TRAN .20 .50
126 Hersey Hawkins TRAN .20 .50
127 Brent Barry TRAN .25 .60
128 Shandon Anderson TRAN .20 .50
129 Scottie Pippen TRAN .75 2.00
130 Isaac Austin TRAN .20 .50
131 Anfernee Hardaway TRAN .75 2.00
132 Elton Brand RC 1.00 2.50
133 Steve Francis RC 1.00 2.50
134 Baron Davis RC 1.25 3.00
135 Lamar Odom RC 1.00 2.50
136 Jonathan Bender RC .50 1.25
137 Wally Szczerbiak RC .75 2.00
138 Richard Hamilton RC 1.25 3.00
139 Andre Miller RC 1.00 2.50
140 Shawn Marion RC 1.00 2.50
141 Jason Terry RC .75 2.00
142 Trajan Langdon RC .40 1.00
143 A.Radojevic RC .30 .75
144 Corey Maggette RC .60 1.50
145 William Avery RC .30 .75
146 Ron Artest RC 1.25 3.00
147 Cal Bowdler RC .30 .75
148 James Posey RC .50 1.25
149 Quincy Lewis RC .30 .75
150 Scott Padgett RC .40 1.00

1999-00 Stadium Club Chrome First Day Issue

*STARS: 10X TO 25X BASE CARD HI
*RCs: 3X TO 8X BASE HI
STATED PRINT RUN 100 SERIAL #'d SETS
STATED ODDS 1:47

1999-00 Stadium Club Chrome First Day Issue Refractors

*STARS: 30X TO 80X BASE CARD HI
*RCs: 8X TO 20X BASE HI
STATED PRINT RUN 25 SERIAL #'d SETS
STATED ODDS 1:186
87 Kobe Bryant 250.00 500.00

1999-00 Stadium Club Chrome Refractors

*STARS: 2X TO 5X BASE CARD HI
*RCs: 1.25X TO 3X BASE HI
STATED ODDS 1:12

1999-00 Stadium Club Chrome Clear Shots

COMPLETE SET (10) 4.00 10.00
STATED ODDS 1:16
*REF: 1X TO 2.5X HI COLUMN
REF: STATED ODDS 1:80
CS1 Lamar Odom .60 1.50
CS2 Elton Brand .60 1.50
CS3 Steve Francis .60 1.50
CS4 Shawn Marion .60 1.50
CS5 Wally Szczerbiak .60 1.50
CS6 Richard Hamilton .75 2.00
CS7 Andre Miller .60 1.50
CS8 Jason Terry .50 1.25
CS9 Baron Davis .75 2.00
CS10 Jonathan Bender .30 .75

1999-00 Stadium Club Chrome Eyes of the Game

COMPLETE SET (10) 20.00 50.00
STATED ODDS 1:24
*REF: 1.25X TO 3X HI COLUMN
REF: STATED ODDS 1:120
EG1 Jason Kidd 2.00 5.00
EG2 Jason Williams 2.00 5.00
EG3 Gary Payton 2.00 5.00
EG4 Kevin Garnett 3.00 8.00
EG5 Vince Carter 3.00 8.00
EG6 Kobe Bryant 10.00 25.00
EG7 Stephon Marbury 1.50 4.00
EG8 Allen Iverson 3.00 8.00
EG9 Alonzo Mourning 2.00 5.00
EG10 John Stockton 2.00 5.00

1999-00 Stadium Club Chrome True Colors

COMPLETE SET (10) 5.00 12.00
STATED ODDS 1:8
*REF: 1X TO 2.5X HI COLUMN
REF: STATED ODDS 1:40
TC1 Gary Payton .75 2.00
TC2 Stephon Marbury .60 1.50
TC3 Karl Malone 1.00 2.50
TC4 Kevin Garnett 1.25 3.00
TC5 Allen Iverson 1.25 3.00
TC6 Vince Carter 1.25 3.00
TC7 Grant Hill .75 2.00
TC8 Shaquille O'Neal 2.00 5.00
TC9 Reggie Miller 1.00 2.50
TC10 Tim Duncan 1.25 3.00

1999-00 Stadium Club Chrome Visionaries

COMPLETE SET (10) 12.50 30.00
STATED ODDS 1:32
*REF: 1X TO 2.5X HI COLUMN
REF: STATED ODDS 1:160
V1 Vince Carter 3.00 8.00
V2 Tim Duncan 3.00 8.00
V3 Jason Williams 2.00 5.00
V4 Lamar Odom 2.50 6.00
V5 Steve Francis 2.50 6.00
V6 Paul Pierce 2.50 6.00
V7 Tracy McGrady 2.00 5.00
V8 Elton Brand 2.50 6.00
V9 Shawn Marion 2.50 6.00
V10 Antawn Jamison 1.25 3.00

1994-95 Stadium Club Members Only 50

COMP.FACT SET (50) 25.00 60.00
1 Shaquille O'Neal 4.00 10.00
2 Charles Oakley 1.00 2.50
3 Chris Webber 2.00 5.00
4 Dominique Wilkins 1.50 4.00
5 Kenny Anderson .75 2.00
6 Kevin Willis .75 2.00
7 Anfernee Hardaway 2.00 5.00
8 Derrick Coleman 1.00 2.50
9 Clarence Weatherspoon .60 1.50
10 Glen Rice 1.00 2.50
11 Patrick Ewing 1.50 4.00
12 Reggie Miller 2.00 5.00
13 Scottie Pippen 2.50 6.00
14 Steve Smith .75 2.00
15 Alonzo Mourning 1.50 4.00
16 Vin Baker 1.00 2.50
17 Tyrone Hill .60 1.50
18 Joe Dumars 1.00 2.50
19 Mookie Blaylock 1.00 2.50
20 Michael Jordan 8.00 20.00
21 Larry Johnson 1.25 3.00
22 Mark Price 1.00 2.50
23 Rik Smits .75 2.00
24 Hakeem Olajuwon 2.00 5.00
25 Karl Malone 2.00 5.00
26 Jamal Mashburn 1.00 2.50
27 Sean Elliott .75 2.00
28 Christian Laettner .75 2.00
29 Dikembe Mutombo 1.50 4.00
30 John Stockton 2.00 5.00
31 Clyde Drexler 1.50 4.00
32 Tom Gugliotta .60 1.50
33 Mahmoud Abdul-Rauf .60 1.50
34 David Robinson 2.00 5.00
35 Chris Mullin 1.25 3.00
36 Shawn Kemp 1.50 4.00
37 Mitch Richmond 1.25 3.00
38 Clifford Robinson .75 2.00
39 Cedric Ceballos .75 2.00
40 Charles Barkley 2.50 6.00
41 Loy Vaught .60 1.50
42 Gary Payton 1.50 4.00
43 Walt Williams .60 1.50
44 Nick Van Exel 1.00 2.50
45 Kevin Johnson 1.00 2.50
46 Glenn Robinson TRP 1.25 3.00
47 Jason Kidd TRP 5.00 12.00
48 Grant Hill TRP 5.00 12.00
49 Donyell Marshall TRP 1.00 2.50
50 Juwan Howard TRP 1.50 4.00

1995-96 Stadium Club Members Only 50

COMP.FACT SET (50) 10.00 25.00
1 Magic Johnson 1.00 2.50
2 Steve Smith .25 .60
3 Scottie Pippen .75 2.00
4 David Robinson .60 1.50
5 Jason Kidd .50 1.25
6 Dikembe Mutombo .50 1.25
7 Sean Elliott .25 .60
8 Rik Smits .25 .60
9 Brian Grant .25 .60
10 Hakeem Olajuwon .60 1.50
11 Greg Anthony .20 .50
12 Mitch Richmond .40 1.00
13 Clyde Drexler .50 1.25
14 Mahmoud Abdul-Rauf .25 .60
15 Larry Johnson .40 1.00
16 Mookie Blaylock .25 .60
17 Clarence Weatherspoon .20 .50
18 Grant Hill .50 1.25
19 Vin Baker .25 .60
20 Patrick Ewing .50 1.25
21 Charles Barkley .75 2.00
22 Glenn Robinson .30 .75
23 Dino Radja .20 .50
24 Charles Oakley .25 .60
25 Anfernee Hardaway .75 2.00
26 Jamal Mashburn .30 .75
27 John Stockton .60 1.50
28 Isaiah Rider .20 .50
29 Cedric Ceballos .25 .60
30 Shaquille O'Neal 1.25 3.00
31 Shawn Kemp .50 1.25
32 Juwan Howard .30 .75
33 Alonzo Mourning .50 1.25
34 Tom Gugliotta .30 .75
35 Karl Malone .60 1.50
36 Clifford Robinson .30 .75
37 Chris Webber .40 1.00
38 Latrell Sprewell .30 .75
39 Loy Vaught .20 .50
40 Michael Jordan 8.00 20.00
41 Reggie Miller .60 1.50
42 Terrell Brandon .25 .60
43 Armon Gilliam .20 .50
44 Gary Payton .50 1.25
45 Glen Rice .30 .75
46 Jerry Stackhouse FIN 2.00 5.00
47 Michael Finley FIN 1.50 4.00
48 Joe Smith FIN .75 2.00
49 Damon Stoudamire FIN 1.50 4.00
50 Brent Barry FIN 1.00 2.50

1996-97 Stadium Club Members Only 55

COMP.FACT SET (55) 125.00 300.00
1 Scottie Pippen 1.25 3.00
2 Dikembe Mutombo .75 2.00
3 Antonio McDyess .50 1.25
4 Mark Jackson .40 1.00
5 Vin Baker .40 1.00
6 Kendall Gill .50 1.25
7 Kenny Anderson .40 1.00
8 Karl Malone 1.00 2.50
9 Chris Webber .60 1.50
10 David Robinson 1.00 2.50
11 Cedric Ceballos .40 1.00
12 Patrick Ewing .75 2.00
13 Alonzo Mourning .75 2.00
14 Latrell Sprewell .50 1.25
15 Terrell Brandon .40 1.00
16 Anthony Mason .40 1.00
17 Joe Dumars .60 1.50
18 Hakeem Olajuwon 1.00 2.50
19 Brent Barry .40 1.00
20 Shaquille O'Neal 2.00 5.00
21 Kevin Garnett 1.50 4.00
22 Anfernee Hardaway 1.25 3.00
23 Jerry Stackhouse .60 1.50
24 Mitch Richmond .60 1.50
25 Gary Payton .75 2.00
26 Damon Stoudamire .50 1.25
27 Christian Laettner .50 1.25
28 Dino Radja .30 .75
29 Shawn Bradley .30 .75
30 John Stockton 1.00 2.50
31 Sean Elliott .50 1.25
32 Jason Kidd .75 2.00
33 Allan Houston .50 1.25
34 Glenn Robinson .50 1.25
35 Tim Hardaway .60 1.50
36 Reggie Miller 1.00 2.50
37 Charles Barkley 1.25 3.00
38 Joe Smith .40 1.00
39 Grant Hill .75 2.00
40 LaPhonso Ellis .30 .75
41 Michael Jordan 25.00 60.00
42 Glen Rice .50 1.25
43 Rony Seikaly .40 1.00
44 Shawn Kemp .75 2.00
45 Juwan Howard .50 1.25
46 Tyrone Hill .30 .75
47 Michael Finley .50 1.25
48 Loy Vaught .30 .75
49 Arvydas Sabonis .50 1.25
50 Brian Grant .40 1.00
51 Kerry Kittles Finest 3.00 8.00
52 Kobe Bryant Finest 125.00 300.00
53 Stephon Marbury Finest 10.00 25.00
54 Allen Iverson Finest 25.00 60.00
55 Shareef Abdur-Rahim Finest 5.00 12.00

1992-93 Stadium Club Members Only Parallel

COMPLETE SET (421) 100.00 250.00
1 Michael Jordan 30.00 80.00
2 Greg Anthony .10 .30
3 Otis Thorpe .20 .50
4 Jim Les .10 .30
5 Kevin Willis .10 .30
6 Derek Harper .25 .60
7 Elden Campbell .20 .50
8 A.J. English .10 .30
9 Kenny Gattison .10 .30
10 Drazen Petrovic 1.50 4.00
11 Chris Mullin .75 2.00
12 Mark Price .60 1.50
13 Karl Malone 1.50 4.00
14 Gerald Glass .10 .30
15 Negele Knight .10 .30
16 Mark Macon .10 .30
17 Michael Cage .10 .30
18 Kevin Edwards .10 .30
19 Sherman Douglas .10 .30
20 Ron Harper .40 1.00
21 Clifford Robinson .20 .50
22 Byron Scott .40 1.00
23 Antoine Carr .10 .30
24 Greg Dreiling .10 .30
25 Bill Laimbeer .40 1.00
26 Hersey Hawkins .20 .50
27 Will Perdue .10 .30
28 Todd Lichti .10 .30
29 Gary Grant .10 .30
30 Sam Perkins .40 1.00
31 Jayson Williams .20 .50
32 Magic Johnson 2.50 6.00
33 Larry Bird 3.00 8.00
34 Chris Morris .10 .30
35 Nick Anderson .20 .50
36 Scott Hastings .10 .30
37 Ledell Eackles .10 .30
38 Robert Pack .10 .30
39 Dana Barros .10 .30
40 Anthony Bonner .10 .30
41 J.R. Reid .10 .30
42 Tyrone Hill .10 .30
43 Rik Smits .30 .75
44 Kevin Duckworth .10 .30
45 LaSalle Thompson .10 .30
46 Brian Williams .10 .30
47 Willie Anderson .10 .30
48 Ken Norman .10 .30
49 Mike Iuzzolino .10 .30
50 Isiah Thomas .75 2.00
51 Alec Kessler .10 .30
52 Johnny Dawkins .10 .30
53 Avery Johnson .40 1.00
54 Stacey Augmon .20 .50
55 Charles Oakley .20 .50
56 Rex Chapman .40 1.00
57 Charles Shackleford .10 .30
58 Jeff Ruland .10 .30
59 Craig Ehlo .10 .30
60 John Koncak .10 .30
61 Danny Schayes .10 .30
62 David Benoit .10 .30
63 Robert Parish .40 1.00
64 Mookie Blaylock .20 .50
65 Sean Elliott .40 1.00
66 Mark Aguirre .30 .75
67 Scott Williams .10 .30
68 Doug West .10 .30
69 Kenny Anderson .30 .75
70 Randy Brown .10 .30

71 Muggsy Bogues .40 1.00
72 Spud Webb .40 1.00
73 Sedale Threatt .10 .30
74 Chris Gatling .10 .30
75 Derrick McKey .10 .30
76 Sleepy Floyd .10 .30
77 Chris Jackson .10 .30
78 Thurl Bailey .10 .30
79 Steve Smith .60 1.50
80 Cedric Ceballos .10 .30
81 Anthony Bowie .10 .30
82 John Williams .10 .30
83 Paul Graham .10 .30
84 Willie Burton .10 .30
85 Vernon Maxwell .10 .30
86 Stacey King .10 .30
87 B.J. Armstrong .20 .50
88 Kevin Gamble .10 .30
89 Terry Catledge .10 .30
90 Jeff Malone .20 .50
91 Sam Bowie .30 .75
92 Orlando Woolridge .10 .30
93 Steve Kerr .40 1.00
94 Eric Leckner .10 .30
95 Loy Vaught .10 .30
96 Jud Buechler .10 .30
97 Doug Smith .10 .30
98 Sidney Green .10 .30
99 Jerome Kersey .10 .30
100 Patrick Ewing 1.00 2.50
101 Ed Nealy .10 .30
102 Shawn Kemp 1.00 2.50
103 Luc Longley .30 .75
104 George McCloud .10 .30
105 Ron Anderson .10 .30
106 Moses Malone UER
(Rookie Card is 1975-76, not 1976-77) .40 1.00
107 Tony Smith .10 .30
108 Terry Porter .20 .50
109 Blair Rasmussen .10 .30
110 Bimbo Coles .10 .30
111 Grant Long .10 .30
112 John Battle .10 .30
113 Brian Oliver .10 .30
114 Tyrone Corbin .10 .30
115 Benoit Benjamin .10 .30
116 Rick Fox .30 .75
117 Rafael Addison .10 .30
118 Danny Young .10 .30
119 Fat Lever .10 .30
120 Terry Cummings .20 .50
121 Felton Spencer .10 .30
122 Joe Kleine .10 .30
123 Johnny Newman .10 .30
124 Gary Payton 1.50 4.00
125 Kurt Rambis .10 .30
126 Vlade Divac .30 .75
127 John Paxson .40 1.00
128 Lionel Simmons .10 .30
129 Randy Wittman .10 .30
130 Winston Garland .10 .30
131 Jerry Reynolds .10 .30
132 Dell Curry .10 .30
133 Fred Roberts .10 .30
134 Michael Adams .10 .30
135 Charles Jones .10 .30
136 Frank Brickowski .10 .30
137 Alton Lister .10 .30
138 Horace Grant .40 1.00
139 Greg Sutton .10 .30
140 John Starks .30 .75
141 Detlef Schrempf .30 .75
142 Rodney Monroe .10 .30
143 Pete Chilcutt .10 .30
144 Mike Brown .10 .30
145 Rony Seikaly .10 .30
146 Donald Hodge .10 .30
147 Kevin McHale .60 1.50
148 Ricky Pierce .10 .30
149 Brian Shaw .10 .30
150 Reggie Williams .10 .30
151 Kendall Gill .30 .75
152 Tom Chambers .10 .30
153 Jack Haley .10 .30
154 Terrell Brandon .30 .75
155 Dennis Scott .20 .50
156 Mark Randall .10 .30
157 Kenny Payne .10 .30
158 Bernard King .30 .75
159 Tate George .10 .30
160 Scott Skiles .40 1.00
161 Pervis Ellison .10 .30
162 Marcus Liberty .10 .30
163 Rumeal Robinson .10 .30
164 Anthony Mason .30 .75
165 Les Jepsen .10 .30
166 Kenny Smith .20 .50
167 Randy White .10 .30
168 Dee Brown .10 .30
169 Chris Dudley .10 .30
170 Armon Gilliam .10 .30
171 Eddie Johnson .10 .30
172 A.C. Green .40 1.00
173 Darrell Walker .10 .30
174 Bill Cartwright .20 .50
175 Mike Gminski .10 .30
176 Tom Tolbert .10 .30
177 Buck Williams .20 .50
178 Mark Eaton .10 .30
179 Danny Manning .30 .75
180 Glen Rice .40 1.00
181 Sarunas Marciulionis .30 .75
182 Danny Ferry .10 .30
183 Chris Corchiani .10 .30
184 Dan Majerle .50 1.25
185 Alvin Robertson .10 .30
186 Vern Fleming .10 .30
187 Kevin Lynch .10 .30
188 John Williams .10 .30
189 Checklist 1-100 .10 .30
190 Checklist 101-200 .10 .30
191 David Robinson MC .75 2.00
192 Larry Johnson MC .30 .75
193 Derrick Coleman MC .10 .30
194 Larry Bird MC 1.50 4.00
195 Billy Owens MC .10 .30
196 Dikembe Mutombo MC .40 1.00
197 Charles Barkley MC .75 2.00
198 Scottie Pippen MC 1.00 2.50
199 Clyde Drexler MC .75 2.00
200 John Stockton MC 1.00 2.50
201 Shaquille O'Neal MC 4.00 10.00
202 Chris Mullin MC .40 1.00
203 Glen Rice MC .30 .75
204 Isiah Thomas MC .50 1.25
205 Karl Malone MC .75 2.00
206 Christian Laettner MC 1.00 2.50
207 Patrick Ewing MC .50 1.25
208 Dominique Wilkins MC .60 1.50
209 Alonzo Mourning MC 2.00 5.00
210 Michael Jordan MC 30.00 80.00
211 Tim Hardaway MC .60 1.50
212 Rodney McCray .10 .30
213 Larry Johnson .30 .75
214 Charles Smith .10 .30
215 Kevin Brooks .10 .30
216 Kevin Johnson .30 .75
217 Duane Cooper .10 .30
218 Christian Laettner UER
(Missing '92 Draft Pick logo) 2.00 5.00
219 Tim Perry .10 .30
220 Hakeem Olajuwon 1.25 3.00
221 Lee Mayberry .10 .30
222 Mark Bryant .10 .30
223 Robert Horry 1.50 4.00
224 Tracy Murray UER
(Missing '92 Draft Pick logo) .20 .50
225 Greg Grant .10 .30
226 Rolando Blackman .30 .75
227 James Edwards UER
(Rookie Card is 1978-79, not 1980-81) .10 .30
228 Sean Green .10 .30
229 Buck Johnson .10 .30
230 Andrew Lang .10 .30
231 Tracy Moore .10 .30
232 Adam Keefe UER
(Missing '92 Draft Pick logo) .20 .50
233 Tony Campbell .10 .30
234 Rod Strickland .20 .50
235 Terry Mills .10 .30
236 Billy Owens .20 .50
237 Bryant Stith UER
(Missing '92 Draft Pick logo) .20 .50
238 Tony Bennett UER
(Missing '92 Draft Pick logo) .10 .30
239 David Wood .10 .30
240 Jay Humphries .10 .30
241 Doc Rivers .30 .75
242 Wayman Tisdale .10 .30
243 Litterial Green .10 .30
244 Jon Barry .30 .75
245 Brad Daugherty .10 .30
246 Nate McMillan .20 .50
247 Shaquille O'Neal 10.00 25.00
248 Chris Smith .10 .30
249 Duane Ferrell .10 .30
250 Anthony Peeler .30 .75
251 Gundars Vetra .10 .30
252 Danny Ainge .40 1.00
253 Mitch Richmond .60 1.50
254 Malik Sealy .40 1.00
255 Brent Price .20 .50
256 Xavier McDaniel .10 .30
257 Bobby Phills .30 .75
258 Donald Royal .10 .30
259 Olden Polynice .10 .30
260 Dominique Wilkins UER
(Scoring 10,000th point &
should be 20,000th) 1.00 2.50
261 Larry Krystkowiak .10 .30
262 Duane Causwell .10 .30
263 Todd Day .20 .50
264 Sam Mack .20 .50
265 John Stockton 1.50 4.00
266 Eddie Lee Wilkins .10 .30
267 Gerald Glass .10 .30
268 Robert Pack .10 .30
269 Gerald Wilkins .10 .30
270 Reggie Lewis .20 .50
271 Scott Brooks .10 .30
272 Randy Woods UER
(Missing '92 Draft Pick logo) .10 .30
273 Dikembe Mutombo .60 1.50
274 Kiki Vandeweghe .40 1.00
275 Rich King .10 .30
276 Jeff Turner .20 .50
277 Vinny Del Negro .10 .30
278 Marlon Maxey .10 .30
279 Elmore Spencer UER
(Missing '92 Draft Pick logo) .10 .30
280 Cedric Ceballos .20 .50
281 Alex Blackwell .10 .30
282 Terry Davis .10 .30
283 Morlon Wiley .10 .30
284 Trent Tucker .10 .30
285 Carl Herrera .10 .30
286 Eric Anderson .10 .30
287 Clyde Drexler 1.25 3.00
288 Tom Gugliotta 2.50 6.00
289 Dale Ellis .10 .30
290 Lance Blanks .10 .30
291 Tom Hammonds .10 .30
292 Eric Murdock .10 .30
293 Walt Williams .30 .75
294 Gerald Paddio .10 .30
295 Brian Howard .10 .30
296 Ken Williams .10 .30
297 Alonzo Mourning 4.00 10.00
298 Larry Nance .30 .75
299 Jeff Grayer .10 .30
300 Dave Johnson .10 .30
301 Bob McCann .10 .30
302 Bart Kofoed .10 .30
303 Anthony Cook .10 .30
304 Radisav Curcic .10 .30
305 John Crotty .10 .30
306 Brad Sellers .10 .30
307 Marcus Webb .10 .30
308 Winston Garland .10 .30
309 Walter Palmer .10 .30
310 Rod Higgins .10 .30
311 Travis Mays .10 .30
312 Alex Stivrins .10 .30
313 Greg Kite .10 .30
314 Dennis Rodman 1.25 3.00
315 Mike Sanders .10 .30
316 Ed Pinckney .10 .30
317 Harold Miner .20 .50
318 Pooh Richardson .10 .30
319 Oliver Miller .20 .50
320 Latrell Sprewell 2.00 5.00
321 Anthony Pullard .50 1.25
322 Mark Randall .10 .30
323 Jeff Hornacek .40 1.00
324 Rick Mahorn UER
(Rookie Card is 1981-82, not 1992-93) .10 .30
325 Sean Rooks .10 .30
326 Paul Pressey .10 .30
327 James Worthy .60 1.50
328 Matt Bullard .10 .30
329 Reggie Smith .10 .30
330 Don MacLean UER
(Missing '92 Draft Pick logo) .20 .50
331 John Williams UER
(Rookie Card erroneously
shows Hot Rod) .10 .30
332 Frank Johnson .10 .30
333 Hubert Davis UER
(Missing '92 Draft Pick logo) .20 .50
334 Lloyd Daniels .10 .30
335 Steve Bardo .10 .30
336 Jeff Sanders .10 .30
337 Tree Rollins .10 .30
338 Micheal Williams .10 .30
339 Lorenzo Williams .10 .30
340 Harvey Grant .10 .30
341 Avery Johnson .40 1.00
342 Bo Kimble .10 .30
343 LaPhonso Ellis UER
(Missing '92 Draft Pick logo) .30 .75
344 Mookie Blaylock .20 .50
345 Isaiah Morris UER
(Missing '92 Draft Pick logo) .10 .30
346 Clarence Weatherspoon .30 .75
347 Manute Bol .10 .30
348 Victor Alexander .10 .30
349 Corey Williams .10 .30
350 Byron Houston .10 .30
351 Stanley Roberts .10 .30
352 Anthony Avent .10 .30
353 Vincent Askew .10 .30
354 Herb Williams .10 .30
355 J.R. Reid .10 .30
356 Brad Lohaus .10 .30
357 Reggie Miller 1.00 2.50
358 Blue Edwards .10 .30
359 Tony Campbell .20 .50
360 Charles Barkley 1.25 3.00
361 David Robinson 1.25 3.00
362 Dale Davis .20 .50
363 Robert Werdann UER
(Missing '92 Draft Pick logo) .10 .30
364 Chuck Person .10 .30
365 Alaa Abdelnaby .10 .30
366 Dave Jamerson .10 .30
367 Scottie Pippen 2.00 5.00
368 Mark Jackson .50 1.25
369 Keith Askins .10 .30
370 Marty Conlon .10 .30
371 Chucky Brown .10 .30
372 LaBradford Smith .10 .30
373 Tim Kempton .10 .30
374 Sam Mitchell .10 .30
375 John Salley .20 .50
376 Mario Elie .20 .50
377 Mark West .10 .30
378 David Wingate .10 .30
379 Jaren Jackson .20 .50
380 Rumeal Robinson .10 .30
381 Kennard Winchester .10 .30
382 Walter Bond .10 .30
383 Isaac Austin .20 .50
384 Derrick Coleman .20 .50
385 Larry Smith .10 .30
386 Joe Dumars .60 1.50
387 Matt Geiger UER
(Missing '92 Draft Pick logo) .10 .30
388 Stephen Howard .10 .30
389 William Bedford .10 .30
390 Jayson Williams .20 .50
391 Kurt Rambis .30 .75
392 Keith Jennings .10 .30
393 Steve Kerr UER
(The words key stat are
repeated on back) .30 .75
394 Larry Stewart .10 .30
395 Danny Young .10 .30
396 Doug Overton .10 .30
397 Mark Acres .10 .30
398 John Bagley .10 .30
399 Checklist 201-300 .10 .30
400 Checklist 301-400 .10 .30
BT1 Michael Jordan 400.00 800.00
BT2 Dominique Wilkins 2.50 6.00
BT3 Shawn Kemp 1.50 4.00
BT4 Clyde Drexler 2.50 6.00
BT5 Scottie Pippen 2.50 6.00
BT6 Chris Mullin 1.50 4.00
BT7 Reggie Miller 2.00 5.00
BT8 Glen Rice 1.25 3.00
BT9 Jeff Hornacek 1.25 3.00
BT10 Jeff Malone .75 2.00
BT11 John Stockton 3.00 8.00
BT12 Kevin Johnson 1.00 2.50
BT13 Mark Price 1.00 2.50
BT14 Tim Hardaway 1.50 4.00
BT15 Charles Barkley 2.50 6.00
BT16 Hakeem Olajuwon 2.00 5.00
BT17 Karl Malone 2.50 6.00
BT18 Patrick Ewing 1.50 4.00
BT19 Dennis Rodman 2.00 5.00
BT20 David Robinson 2.50 6.00
BT21 Shaquille O'Neal 200.00 500.00

1993-94 Stadium Club Members Only Parallel

COMPLETE SET (414) 40.00 100.00
1 Michael Jordan TD 10.00 25.00
2 Kenny Anderson TD .75 2.00
3 Steve Smith TD .75 2.00
4 Kevin Gamble TD .60 1.50
5 Detlef Schrempf TD 1.00 2.50
6 Larry Johnson TD 1.25 3.00
7 Brad Daugherty TD .75 2.00
8 Rumeal Robinson TD .60 1.50
9 Micheal Williams TD .60 1.50
10 David Robinson TD 2.00 5.00
11 Sam Perkins TD .75 2.00
12 Thurl Bailey .60 1.50
13 Sherman Douglas .60 1.50
14 Larry Stewart .60 1.50
15 Kevin Johnson 1.00 2.50
16 Bill Cartwright .75 2.00
17 Larry Nance .75 2.00
18 P.J. Brown 1.00 2.50
19 Tony Bennett .60 1.50
20 Robert Parish 1.25 3.00
21 David Benoit .60 1.50
22 Detlef Schrempf 1.00 2.50
23 Hubert Davis .75 2.00
24 Donald Hodge .60 1.50
25 Hersey Hawkins .75 2.00
26 Mark Jackson .75 2.00
27 Reggie Williams .60 1.50
28 Lionel Simmons .60 1.50
29 Ron Harper 1.00 2.50
30 Chris Mills 1.00 2.50
31 Danny Schayes .60 1.50
32 J.R. Reid .75 2.00
33 Willie Burton .60 1.50
34 Greg Anthony .60 1.50
35 Elden Campbell .60 1.50
36 Ervin Johnson 1.00 2.50
37 Scott Brooks .60 1.50
38 Johnny Newman .60 1.50
39 Rex Chapman .60 1.50
40 Chuck Person .75 2.00
41 John Williams .60 1.50
42 Anthony Bowie .60 1.50
43 Negele Knight .60 1.50
44 Tyrone Corbin .60 1.50
45 Jud Buechler .60 1.50
46 Adam Keefe .60 1.50
47 Glen Rice 1.00 2.50
48 Tracy Murray .60 1.50
49 Rick Mahorn .75 2.00
50 Vlade Divac 1.00 2.50
51 Eric Murdock .60 1.50
52 Isaiah Morris .60 1.50
53 Bobby Hurley 1.00 2.50
54 Mitch Richmond 1.25 3.00
55 Danny Ainge 1.00 2.50
56 Dikembe Mutombo 1.50 4.00
57 Jeff Hornacek .75 2.00
58 Tony Campbell .60 1.50
59 Vinny Del Negro .60 1.50
60 Xavier McDaniel HC 1.00 2.50
61 Scottie Pippen HC 2.50 6.00
62 Larry Nance HC .75 2.00
63 Dikembe Mutombo HC 1.50 4.00
64 Hakeem Olajuwon HC 2.00 5.00
65 Dominique Wilkins HC 1.50 4.00
66 Clarence Weatherspoon HC .60 1.50
67 Chris Morris HC .60 1.50
68 Patrick Ewing HC 1.50 4.00
69 Kevin Willis HC .75 2.00
70 Jon Barry .60 1.50
71 Jerry Reynolds .60 1.50
72 Sarunas Marciulionis 1.00 2.50
73 Mark West .60 1.50
74 B.J. Armstrong 1.00 2.50
75 Greg Kite .60 1.50
76 LaSalle Thompson .60 1.50
77 Randy White .60 1.50
78 Alaa Abdelnaby .60 1.50
79 Kevin Brooks .60 1.50
80 Vern Fleming .75 2.00
81 Doc Rivers .75 2.00
82 Shawn Bradley 1.00 2.50
83 Wayman Tisdale .75 2.00
84 Olden Polynice .60 1.50
85 Michael Cage .75 2.00
86 Harold Miner .75 2.00
87 Doug Smith .60 1.50
88 Tom Gugliotta .75 2.00
89 Hakeem Olajuwon 2.00 5.00
90 Loy Vaught .60 1.50
91 James Worthy 1.25 3.00
92 John Paxson 1.00 2.50
93 Jon Koncak .60 1.50
94 Lee Mayberry .60 1.50
95 Clarence Weatherspoon .60 1.50
96 Mark Eaton 1.00 2.50
97 Rex Walters .75 2.00
98 Alvin Robertson .75 2.00
99 Dan Majerle 1.00 2.50
100 Shaquille O'Neal 5.00 12.00
101 Derrick Coleman TD 1.00 2.50
102 Hersey Hawkins TD .75 2.00
103 Scottie Pippen TD 2.50 6.00
104 Scott Skiles TD .60 1.50
105 Rod Strickland TD .75 2.00
106 Pooh Richardson TD .75 2.00
107 Tom Gugliotta TD .75 2.00
108 Mark Jackson TD .75 2.00
109 Dikembe Mutombo TD 1.50 4.00
110 Charles Barkley TD 2.50 6.00
111 Otis Thorpe TD 1.00 2.50
112 Malik Sealy .60 1.50
113 Mark Macon .60 1.50
114 Dee Brown .75 2.00
115 Nate McMillan .75 2.00
116 John Starks 1.00 2.50
117 Clyde Drexler 1.50 4.00
118 Antoine Carr .60 1.50
119 Doug West .60 1.50
120 Victor Alexander .60 1.50
121 Kenny Gattison .60 1.50
122 Spud Webb .75 2.00
123 Rumeal Robinson .60 1.50
124 Tim Kempton .60 1.50
125 Karl Malone 2.00 5.00
126 Randy Woods .60 1.50
127 Calbert Cheaney 1.00 2.50
128 Johnny Dawkins .75 2.00
129 Dominique Wilkins 1.50 4.00
130 Horace Grant 1.00 2.50
131 Bill Laimbeer 1.00 2.50
132 Kenny Smith .75 2.00
133 Sedale Threatt .60 1.50
134 Brian Shaw .60 1.50
135 Dennis Scott .60 1.50
136 Mark Bryant .60 1.50
137 Xavier McDaniel 1.00 2.50
138 David Wood .60 1.50
139 Luther Wright .60 1.50
140 Lloyd Daniels .60 1.50
141 Marlon Maxey UER .60 1.50
142 Pooh Richardson .75 2.00
143 Jeff Grayer .60 1.50
144 LaPhonso Ellis .75 2.00
145 Gerald Wilkins .75 2.00
146 Dell Curry 1.00 2.50
147 Duane Causwell .60 1.50
148 Tim Hardaway 1.25 3.00
149 Isiah Thomas 1.50 4.00
150 Doug Edwards 1.00 2.50
151 Anthony Peeler .60 1.50
152 Tate George .60 1.50
153 Terry Davis .60 1.50
154 Sam Perkins .75 2.00
155 John Salley .60 1.50
156 Vernon Maxwell .75 2.00
157 Anthony Avent .60 1.50
158 Clifford Robinson 1.00 2.50
159 Corie Blount 1.00 2.50
160 Gerald Paddio .60 1.50
161 Blair Rasmussen .60 1.50
162 Carl Herrera .60 1.50
163 Chris Smith .60 1.50
164 Pervis Ellison .60 1.50
165 Rod Strickland .75 2.00
166 Jeff Malone .75 2.00
167 Danny Ferry .60 1.50
168 Kevin Lynch .60 1.50
169 Michael Jordan 10.00 25.00
170 Derrick Coleman HC 1.00 2.50
171 Jerome Kersey HC .75 2.00
172 David Robinson HC 2.00 5.00
173 Shawn Kemp HC 1.50 4.00
174 Karl Malone HC 2.00 5.00
175 Shaquille O'Neal HC 5.00 12.00
176 Alonzo Mourning HC 1.50 4.00
177 Charles Barkley HC 2.50 6.00
178 Larry Johnson HC 1.25 3.00
179 Checklist 1-90 .40 1.00
180 Checklist 91-180 .40 1.00
181 Michael Jordan FF 10.00 25.00
182 Dominique Wilkins FF 1.50 4.00
183 Dennis Rodman FF 2.50 6.00
184 Scottie Pippen FF 2.50 6.00
185 Larry Johnson FF 1.25 3.00
186 Karl Malone FF 2.00 5.00
187 Clarence Weatherspoon FF .60 1.50
188 Charles Barkley FF 2.50 6.00
189 Patrick Ewing FF 1.50 4.00
190 Derrick Coleman FF 1.00 2.50
191 LaBradford Smith .60 1.50
192 Derek Harper .75 2.00
193 Ken Norman .60 1.50
194 Rodney Rogers 1.00 2.50
195 Chris Dudley .60 1.50
196 Gary Payton 1.25 3.00
197 Andrew Lang .60 1.50
198 Billy Owens .75 2.00
199 Bryon Russell 1.00 2.50
200 Patrick Ewing 1.50 4.00
201 Stacey King .60 1.50
202 Grant Long .60 1.50
203 Sean Elliott 1.00 2.50
204 Muggsy Bogues 1.00 2.50
205 Kevin Edwards .60 1.50
206 Dale Davis .75 2.00
207 Dale Ellis .60 1.50
208 Terrell Brandon .75 2.00
209 Kevin Gamble .60 1.50
210 Robert Horry 1.00 2.50
211 Moses Malone UER 1.50 4.00
212 Gary Grant .60 1.50
213 Bobby Hurley 1.00 2.50
214 Larry Krystkowiak .60 1.50
215 A.C. Green .75 2.00
216 Christian Laettner 1.00 2.50
217 Orlando Woolridge .60 1.50
218 Craig Ehlo .60 1.50
219 Terry Porter .75 2.00
220 Jamal Mashburn 2.00 5.00
221 Kevin Duckworth .75 2.00
222 Shawn Kemp 1.50 4.00
223 Frank Brickowski .60 1.50
224 Chris Webber 5.00 12.00
225 Charles Oakley 1.00 2.50
226 Jay Humphries .75 2.00
227 Steve Kerr .75 2.00
228 Tim Perry .60 1.50
229 Sleepy Floyd .75 2.00
230 Bimbo Coles .60 1.50
231 Eddie Johnson .60 1.50
232 Terry Mills .75 2.00
233 Danny Manning .75 2.00
234 Isaiah Rider 1.50 4.00
235 Darnell Mee .60 1.50
236 Haywoode Workman .60 1.50
237 Scott Skiles .60 1.50
238 Otis Thorpe 1.00 2.50
239 Mike Peplowski .60 1.50
240 Eric Leckner .60 1.50
241 Johnny Newman .60 1.50
242 Benoit Benjamin .60 1.50
243 Doug Christie .75 2.00
244 Acie Earl 1.00 2.50
245 Luc Longley .75 2.00
246 Tyrone Hill .60 1.50
247 Allan Houston 2.00 5.00
248 Joe Kleine .60 1.50
249 Mookie Blaylock 1.00 2.50
250 Anthony Bonner .60 1.50
251 Luther Wright .60 1.50
252 Todd Day .60 1.50
253 Kendall Gill .75 2.00
254 Mario Elie .75 2.00
255 Pete Myers .60 1.50
256 Jim Les .60 1.50
257 Stanley Roberts .60 1.50
258 Michael Adams .60 1.50
259 Hersey Hawkins .75 2.00
260 Shawn Bradley 1.00 2.50
261 Scott Haskin .60 1.50
262 Corie Blount 1.00 2.50
263 Charles Smith .60 1.50
264 Armon Gilliam .60 1.50
265 Jamal Mashburn NW 2.00 5.00
266 Anfernee Hardaway NW 5.00 12.00
267 Shawn Bradley NW 1.00 2.50
268 Chris Webber NW 5.00 12.00
269 Bobby Hurley NW 1.00 2.50
270 Isaiah Rider NW 1.50 4.00
271 Dino Radja NW 1.00 2.50
272 Chris Mills NW 1.00 2.50
273 Nick Van Exel NW 2.50 6.00
274 Lindsey Hunter NW 1.00 2.50
275 Toni Kukoc NW 2.50 6.00
276 Popeye Jones NW 1.00 2.50
277 Chris Mills 1.00 2.50
278 Ricky Pierce .75 2.00
279 Negele Knight .60 1.50
280 Kenny Walker .60 1.50
281 Nick Van Exel 2.50 6.00
282 Derrick Coleman UER 1.00 2.50
283 Popeye Jones 1.00 2.50
284 Derrick McKey .75 2.00
285 Rick Fox .75 2.00
286 Jerome Kersey .75 2.00
287 Steve Smith .75 2.00
288 Brian Williams .60 1.50
289 Chris Mullin 1.25 3.00
290 Terry Cummings .75 2.00
291 Donald Royal .60 1.50
292 Alonzo Mourning 1.50 4.00
293 Mike Brown .60 1.50
294 Latrell Sprewell 1.50 4.00
295 Oliver Miller .60 1.50
296 Terry Dehere 1.00 2.50
297 Detlef Schrempf 1.00 2.50
298 Sam Bowie UER .75 2.00
299 Chris Morris .60 1.50
300 Scottie Pippen 2.50 6.00
301 Warren Kidd .60 1.50
302 Don MacLean .60 1.50
303 Sean Rooks .60 1.50
304 Matt Geiger .60 1.50
305 Dennis Rodman 2.50 6.00
306 Reggie Miller 2.00 5.00
307 Vin Baker 1.50 4.00
308 Anfernee Hardaway 5.00 12.00
309 Lindsey Hunter 1.00 2.50
310 Stacey Augmon .75 2.00
311 Randy Brown .60 1.50
312 Anthony Mason .75 2.00
313 John Stockton 2.00 5.00
314 Sam Cassell 2.00 5.00
315 Buck Williams .75 2.00
316 Bryant Stith .60 1.50
317 Brad Daugherty .75 2.00
318 Dino Radja 1.00 2.50
319 Rony Seikaly .75 2.00
320 Charles Barkley 2.50 6.00
321 Avery Johnson .75 2.00
322 Mahmoud Abdul-Rauf .75 2.00
323 Larry Johnson 1.25 3.00
324 Micheal Williams .60 1.50
325 Mark Aguirre .75 2.00
326 Jim Jackson .75 2.00
327 Antonio Harvey 1.00 2.50
328 David Robinson 2.00 5.00
329 Calbert Cheaney 1.00 2.50
330 Kenny Anderson .75 2.00
331 Walt Williams 1.00 2.50
332 Kevin Willis .75 2.00
333 Nick Anderson .75 2.00
334 Rik Smits .75 2.00
335 Joe Dumars 1.25 3.00
336 Toni Kukoc 2.50 6.00
337 Harvey Grant .75 2.00
338 Tom Chambers 1.00 2.50
339 Blue Edwards .60 1.50
340 Mark Price 1.00 2.50
341 Ervin Johnson 1.00 2.50
342 Rolando Blackman .75 2.00
343 Scott Burrell 1.00 2.50
344 Gheorghe Muresan 1.00 2.50
345 Chris Corchiani .60 1.50
346 Richard Petruska 1.00 2.50
347 Dana Barros .75 2.00
348 Hakeem Olajuwon FF 2.00 5.00
349 Dee Brown FF .75 2.00
350 John Starks FF 1.00 2.50
351 Ron Harper FF 1.00 2.50
352 Chris Webber FF 5.00 12.00
353 Dan Majerle FF 1.00 2.50
354 Clyde Drexler FF 1.50 4.00
355 Shawn Kemp FF 1.50 4.00
356 David Robinson FF 2.00 5.00
357 Chris Morris FF .60 1.50
358 Shaquille O'Neal FF 5.00 12.00
359 Checklist .40 1.00
360 Checklist .40 1.00
BT1 Shaquille O'Neal 20.00 50.00
BT2 Mark Price 1.25 3.00
BT3 Patrick Ewing 2.00 5.00
BT4 Michael Jordan 100.00 250.00
BT5 Charles Barkley 3.00 8.00
BT6 Reggie Miller 2.50 6.00
BT7 Derrick Coleman 1.25 3.00
BT8 Dominique Wilkins 2.00 5.00
BT9 Karl Malone 2.50 6.00
BT10 Alonzo Mourning 2.00 5.00
BT11 Tim Hardaway 1.50 4.00
BT12 Hakeem Olajuwon 2.50 6.00
BT13 David Robinson 2.50 6.00
BT14 Dan Majerle 1.25 3.00
BT15 Larry Johnson 1.50 4.00
BT16 LaPhonso Ellis 1.00 2.50
BT17 Nick Van Exel 2.50 6.00
BT18 Scottie Pippen 3.00 8.00
BT19 John Stockton 3.00 8.00
BT20 Bobby Hurley 1.25 3.00
BT21 Chris Webber 6.00 15.00
BT22 Jamal Mashburn 2.50 6.00
BT23 Anfernee Hardaway 20.00 50.00
BT24 Isaiah Rider 2.50 6.00
BT25 Ken Norman .75 2.00
BT26 Danny Manning 1.00 2.50
BT27 Calbert Cheaney 1.25 3.00
ST1 Atlanta
Dominique Wilkins 1.50 4.00
ST2 Boston
Robert Parish 1.25 3.00
ST3 Charlotte
Larry Johnson
Alonzo Mourning 1.50 4.00
ST4 Chicago
Horace Grant 2.50 6.00
ST5 Cleveland
Brad Daugherty .75 2.00
ST6 Dallas
Group 1.25 3.00
ST7 Denver
Dikembe Mutombo 1.50 4.00
ST8 Detroit
Group 1.25 3.00
ST9 Golden State
Group 1.25 3.00
ST10 Houston
Group 1.25 3.00
ST11 Indiana
Group 1.25 3.00
ST12 L.A.Clippers
Danny Manning .75 2.00
ST13 L.A.Lakers
Group 2.50 6.00
ST14 Miami
John Salley 1.25 3.00
ST15 Milwaukee
Group 1.25 3.00
ST16 Minnesota
Christian Laettner 1.00 2.50
ST17 New Jersey
Derrick Coleman 1.00 2.50
ST18 New York
Patrick Ewing 1.50 4.00
ST19 Orlando
Shaquille O'Neal 5.00 12.00
ST20 Philadelphia
Clarence Weatherspoon 1.25 3.00
ST21 Phoenix
Charles Barkley 2.50 6.00
ST22 Portland
Buck Williams 1.25 3.00
ST23 Sacramento
Lionel Simmons 1.25 3.00
ST24 San Antonio
David Robinson 2.00 5.00
ST25 Seattle
Shawn Kemp 1.50 4.00
ST26 Utah
Group 1.25 3.00
ST27 Washington
Group 1.25 3.00

1994-95 Stadium Club Members Only Parallel

COMPLETE SET (509) 125.00 300.00
1 Patrick Ewing 1.25 3.00
2 Patrick Ewing TG 1.25 3.00
3 Bimbo Coles .50 1.25
4 Elden Campbell .50 1.25
5 Brent Price .50 1.25
6 Hubert Davis .50 1.25
7 Donald Royal .50 1.25
8 Tim Perry .50 1.25
9 Chris Webber 1.50 4.00
10 Chris Webber TG 1.50 4.00
11 Brad Daugherty .60 1.50
12 P.J. Brown .50 1.25
13 Charles Barkley 2.00 5.00
14 Mario Elie .50 1.25
15 Tyrone Hill .50 1.25
16 Anfernee Hardaway 1.50 4.00
17 Anfernee Hardaway TG 1.50 4.00
18 Toni Kukoc 1.00 2.50
19 Chris Morris .50 1.25
20 Gerald Wilkins .60 1.50
21 David Benoit .50 1.25
22 Kevin Duckworth .50 1.25
23 Derrick Coleman .75 2.00
24 Adam Keefe .50 1.25
25 Marlon Maxey .50 1.25
26 Vern Fleming .50 1.25
27 Jeff Malone .50 1.25
28 Rodney Rogers .50 1.25
29 Terry Mills .50 1.25
30 Doug West .50 1.25
31 Doug West TG .50 1.25
32 Shaquille O'Neal 3.00 8.00
33 Scottie Pippen 2.00 5.00
34 Lee Mayberry .50 1.25
35 Dale Ellis .50 1.25
36 Cedric Ceballos .60 1.50
37 Lionel Simmons .50 1.25
38 Kenny Gattison .50 1.25
39 Popeye Jones .50 1.25
40 Jerome Kersey .50 1.25
41 Jerome Kersey TG .50 1.25
42 Larry Stewart .50 1.25
43 Rod Strickland .50 1.25
44 Chris Mills .60 1.50
45 Latrell Sprewell 1.00 2.50
46 Haywoode Workman .50 1.25
47 Charles Smith .50 1.25
48 Detlef Schrempf .75 2.00
49 Gary Grant .50 1.25
50 Gary Grant TG .50 1.25
51 Tom Chambers .60 1.50
52 J.R. Reid .50 1.25
53 Mookie Blaylock .75 2.00
54 Mookie Blaylock TG .75 2.00
55 Rony Seikaly .50 1.25
56 Isaiah Rider .75 2.00
57 Isaiah Rider TG .75 2.00
58 Nick Anderson .50 1.25
59 Victor Alexander .50 1.25
60 Lucious Harris .50 1.25
61 Mark Macon .50 1.25
62 Otis Thorpe .50 1.25
63 Randy Woods .50 1.25
64 Clyde Drexler 1.25 3.00
65 Dikembe Mutombo 1.25 3.00
66 Todd Day .50 1.25
67 Greg Anthony .50 1.25
68 Sherman Douglas .50 1.25

69 Chris Mullin 1.00 2.50
70 Kevin Johnson .75 2.00
71 Kendall Gill .50 1.25
72 Dennis Rodman 2.00 5.00
73 Dennis Rodman TG 2.00 5.00
74 Jeff Turner .50 1.25
75 John Stockton 1.50 4.00
76 John Stockton TG 1.50 4.00
77 Doug Edwards .50 1.25
78 Jim Jackson .60 1.50
79 Hakeem Olajuwon 1.50 4.00
80 Glen Rice .75 2.00
81 Christian Laettner .60 1.50
82 Terry Porter .50 1.25
83 Joe Dumars .75 2.00
84 David Wingate .50 1.25
85 B.J. Armstrong .75 2.00
86 Derrick McKey .50 1.25
87 Elmore Spencer .50 1.25
88 Walt Williams .50 1.25
89 Shawn Bradley .50 1.25
90 Acie Earl .50 1.25
91 Acie Earl TTG .50 1.25
92 Randy Brown .50 1.25
93 Grant Long .50 1.25
94 Terry Dehere .50 1.25
95 Spud Webb .60 1.50
96 Lindsey Hunter .50 1.25
97 Blair Rasmussen .50 1.25
98 Tim Hardaway 1.00 2.50
99 Kevin Edwards .50 1.25
100 Patrick Ewing CT
Reggie Williams CT 1.25 3.00
101 Chuck Person CT
Charles Barkley CT 2.00 5.00
102 Mahmoud Abdul-Rauf CT
Shaquille O'Neal CT 3.00 8.00
103 Rony Seikaly CT
Derrick Coleman CT .75 2.00
104 Hakeem Olajuwon CT
Clyde Drexler CT 1.50 4.00
105 Chris Mullin CT
Mark Jackson CT 1.00 2.50
106 Robert Horry CT
Latrell Sprewell CT 1.00 2.50
107 Pooh Richardson CT
Reggie Miller CT 1.50 4.00
108 Dennis Scott CT
Kenny Anderson CT .60 1.50
109 Kendall Gill CT
Ken Norman CT .50 1.25
110 Scott Skiles CT
Kevin Willis CT .60 1.50
111 Terry Mills CT
Glen Rice CT .75 2.00
112 Christian Laettner CT
Bobby Hurley CT .60 1.50
113 Stacey Augmon CT
Larry Johnson CT 1.00 2.50
114 Sam Perkins CT
James Worthy CT 1.00 2.50
115 Carl Herrera .50 1.25
116 Sam Bowie .50 1.25
117 Gary Payton 1.25 3.00
118 Danny Ainge .75 2.00
119 Danny Ainge TG .75 2.00
120 Luc Longley .60 1.50
121 Antonio Davis .60 1.50
122 Terry Cummings .60 1.50
123 Terry Cummings TG .60 1.50
124 Mark Price .75 2.00
125 Jamal Mashburn .75 2.00
126 Mahmoud Abdul-Rauf .50 1.25
127 Charles Oakley .75 2.00
128 Steve Smith .60 1.50
129 Vin Baker .75 2.00
130 Robert Horry .75 2.00
131 Doug Christie .60 1.50
132 Wayman Tisdale .50 1.25
133 Wayman Tisdale TG .50 1.25
134 Muggsy Bogues .60 1.50
135 Dino Radja .50 1.25
136 Jeff Hornacek .60 1.50
137 Gheorghe Muresan .50 1.25
138 Loy Vaught .50 1.25
139 Loy Vaught TG .50 1.25
140 Benoit Benjamin .50 1.25
141 Johnny Dawkins .50 1.25
142 Allan Houston .75 2.00
143 Jon Barry .50 1.25
144 Reggie Miller 1.50 4.00
145 Kevin Willis .60 1.50
146 James Worthy 1.00 2.50
147 James Worthy TG 1.00 2.50
148 Scott Burrell .50 1.25
149 Tom Gugliotta .50 1.25
150 LaPhonso Ellis .50 1.25
151 Doug Smith .50 1.25
152 A.C. Green .60 1.50
153 A.C. Green TG .60 1.50
154 George Lynch .50 1.25
155 Sam Perkins .50 1.25
156 Corie Blount .50 1.25
157 Xavier McDaniel .50 1.25
158 Xavier McDaniel TG .50 1.25
159 Eric Murdock .50 1.25
160 David Robinson 1.50 4.00
161 Karl Malone 1.50 4.00
162 Karl Malone TG 1.50 4.00
163 Clarence Weatherspoon .50 1.25
164 Calbert Cheaney .60 1.50
165 Tom Hammonds .50 1.25
166 Tom Hammonds TG .50 1.25
167 Alonzo Mourning 1.25 3.00
168 Clifford Robinson .60 1.50
169 Micheal Williams .50 1.25
170 Ervin Johnson .50 1.25
171 Mike Gminski .50 1.25
172 Jason Kidd 4.00 10.00
173 Anthony Bonner .50 1.25
174 Stacey King .50 1.25
175 Rex Chapman .50 1.25
176 Greg Graham .50 1.25
177 Stanley Roberts .50 1.25
178 Mitch Richmond 1.00 2.50
179 Eric Montross .60 1.50
180 Eddie Jones 2.50 6.00
181 Grant Hill 4.00 10.00
182 Donyell Marshall .75 2.00
183 Glenn Robinson 1.50 4.00
184 Dominique Wilkins 1.25 3.00
185 Mark Price .75 2.00
186 Anthony Mason .60 1.50
187 Tyrone Corbin .50 1.25
188 Dale Davis .50 1.25
189 Nate McMillan .60 1.50
190 Jason Kidd 4.00 10.00
191 John Salley .50 1.25
192 Keith Jennings .50 1.25
193 Mark Bryant .50 1.25
194 Sleepy Floyd .50 1.25
195 Grant Hill 4.00 10.00
196 Joe Kleine .50 1.25
197 Anthony Peeler .50 1.25
198 Malik Sealy .50 1.25
199 Kenny Walker .50 1.25
200 Donyell Marshall .75 2.00
201 Vlade Divac AI .75 2.00
202 Dino Radja AI .50 1.25
203 Carl Herrera AI .50 1.25
204 Olden Polynice AI .50 1.25
205 Patrick Ewing AI 1.25 3.00
206 Willie Anderson .50 1.25
207 Mitch Richmond 1.00 2.50
208 John Crotty .50 1.25
209 Tracy Murray .50 1.25
210 Juwan Howard 1.25 3.00
211 Robert Parish .75 2.00
212 Steve Kerr .60 1.50
213 Anthony Bowie .50 1.25
214 Tim Breaux .50 1.25
215 Sharone Wright .60 1.50
216 Brian Williams .50 1.25
217 Rick Fox .50 1.25
218 Harold Miner .50 1.25
219 Duane Ferrell .50 1.25
220 Lamond Murray .75 2.00
221 Blue Edwards .50 1.25
222 Bill Cartwright .60 1.50
223 Sergei Bazarevich .75 2.00
224 Herb Williams .50 1.25
225 Brian Grant 1.25 3.00
226 Derek Harper BCT
John Starks .75 2.00
227 Rod Strickland BCT
Clyde Drexler 1.25 3.00
228 Kevin Johnson BCT
Dan Majerle .75 2.00
229 Lindsey Hunter BCT
Joe Dumars .75 2.00
230 Tim Hardaway BCT
Latrell Sprewell 1.00 2.50
231 Bill Wennington .50 1.25
232 Brian Shaw .50 1.25
233 Jamie Watson .50 1.25
234 Chris Whitney .50 1.25
235 Eric Montross .60 1.50
236 Kenny Smith .60 1.50
237 Andrew Lang .50 1.25
238 Lorenzo Williams .50 1.25
239 Dana Barros .50 1.25
240 Eddie Jones 2.50 6.00
241 Harold Ellis .50 1.25
242 James Edwards .50 1.25
243 Don MacLean .50 1.25
244 Ed Pinckney .50 1.25
245 Carlos Rogers .60 1.50
246 Michael Adams .50 1.25
247 Rex Walters .50 1.25
248 John Starks .75 2.00
249 Terrell Brandon .50 1.25
250 Khalid Reeves .60 1.50
251 Dominique Wilkins AI 1.25 3.00
252 Toni Kukoc AI 1.00 2.50
253 Rick Fox AI .50 1.25
254 Detlef Schrempf AI .75 2.00
255 Rik Smits AI .60 1.50
256 Johnny Dawkins .50 1.25
257 Dan Majerle .75 2.00
258 Mike Brown .50 1.25
259 Byron Scott .60 1.50
260 Jalen Rose 2.00 5.00
261 Byron Houston .50 1.25
262 Frank Brickowski .50 1.25
263 Vernon Maxwell .50 1.25
264 Craig Ehlo .50 1.25
265 Yinka Dare .50 1.25
266 Dee Brown .60 1.50
267 Felton Spencer .50 1.25
268 Harvey Grant .50 1.25
269 Nick Van Exel .75 2.00
270 Bob Martin .50 1.25
271 Hersey Hawkins .50 1.25
272 Scott Williams .50 1.25
273 Sarunas Marciulionis .50 1.25
274 Kevin Gamble .50 1.25
275 Clifford Robinson .50 1.25
276 B.J. Armstrong BCT
Ron Harper .75 2.00
277 John Stockton BCT
Jeff Hornacek 1.50 4.00
278 Bobby Hurley BCT
Mitch Richmond 1.00 2.50
279 Anfernee Hardaway BCT
Dennis Scott 1.50 4.00
280 Jason Kidd BCT
Jim Jackson 4.00 10.00
281 Ron Harper .60 1.50
282 Chuck Person .60 1.50
283 John Williams .50 1.25
284 Robert Pack .50 1.25
285 Aaron McKie .75 2.00
286 Chris Smith .50 1.25
287 Horace Grant .60 1.50
288 Oliver Miller .50 1.25
289 Derek Harper .60 1.50
290 Eric Mobley .50 1.25
291 Scott Skiles .50 1.25
292 Olden Polynice .50 1.25
293 Mark Jackson .60 1.50
294 Wayman Tisdale .50 1.25
295 Tony Dumas .60 1.50
296 Bryon Russell .60 1.50
297 Vlade Divac .75 2.00
298 David Wesley .50 1.25
299 Askia Jones .75 2.00
300 B.J. Tyler .50 1.25
301 Hakeem Olajuwon AI 1.50 4.00
302 Luc Longley AI .60 1.50
303 Rony Seikaly AI .60 1.50
304 Sarunas Marciulionis AI .50 1.25
305 Dikembe Mutombo AI 1.25 3.00
306 Ken Norman .50 1.25
307 Dell Curry .50 1.25
308 Danny Ferry .50 1.25
309 Shawn Kemp 1.25 3.00
310 Dickey Simpkins .60 1.50
311 Johnny Newman .50 1.25
312 Dwayne Schintzius .50 1.25
313 Sean Elliott .60 1.50
314 Sean Rooks .50 1.25
315 Bill Curley .50 1.25
316 Bryant Stith .50 1.25
317 Pooh Richardson .50 1.25
318 Jim McIlvaine .60 1.50
319 Dennis Scott .60 1.50
320 Wesley Person .75 2.00
321 Bobby Hurley .50 1.25
322 Armon Gilliam .50 1.25
323 Rik Smits .60 1.50
324 Tony Smith .50 1.25
325 Monty Williams 1.00 2.50
326 Gary Payton BCT
Kendall Gill 1.25 3.00
327 Mookie Blaylock BCT
Stacey Augmon .75 2.00
328 Mark Jackson BCT
Reggie Miller 1.50 4.00
329 Sam Cassell BCT
Vernon Maxwell .75 2.00
330 Harold Miner BCT
Khalid Reeves .60 1.50
331 Vinny Del Negro .50 1.25
332 Billy Owens .50 1.25
333 Mark West .50 1.25
334 Matt Geiger .50 1.25
335 Greg Minor .75 2.00
336 Larry Johnson 1.00 2.50
337 Donald Hodge .50 1.25
338 Aaron Williams .75 2.00
339 Jay Humphries .50 1.25
340 Charlie Ward .75 2.00
341 Scott Brooks .50 1.25
342 Stacey Augmon .60 1.50
343 Will Perdue .50 1.25
344 Dale Ellis .50 1.25
345 Brooks Thompson .60 1.50
346 Manute Bol .50 1.25
347 Kenny Anderson .60 1.50
348 Willie Burton .50 1.25
349 Michael Cage .50 1.25
350 Danny Manning .60 1.50
351 Ricky Pierce .50 1.25
352 Sam Cassell .75 2.00
353 Reggie Miller FG 1.50 4.00
354 David Robinson FG 1.50 4.00
355 Shaquille O'Neal FG 3.00 8.00
356 Scottie Pippen FG 2.00 5.00
357 Alonzo Mourning FG 1.25 3.00
358 Clarence Weatherspoon FG .50 1.25
359 Derrick Coleman FG .75 2.00
360 Charles Barkley FG 2.00 5.00
361 Karl Malone FG 1.50 4.00
362 Chris Webber FG 1.50 4.00
BT1 Mookie Blaylock .75 2.00
BT2 Dominique Wilkins 1.25 3.00
BT3 Alonzo Mourning 1.25 3.00
BT4 Toni Kukoc 1.00 2.50
BT5 Mark Price .75 2.00
BT6 Jason Kidd 4.00 10.00
BT7 Jalen Rose 2.00 5.00
BT8 Grant Hill 4.00 10.00
BT9 Latrell Sprewell 1.00 2.50
BT10 Hakeem Olajuwon 1.50 4.00
BT11 Reggie Miller 1.50 4.00
BT12 Lamond Murray .75 2.00
BT13 George Lynch .50 1.25
BT14 Khalid Reeves .60 1.50
BT15 Glenn Robinson 1.50 4.00
BT16 Donyell Marshall .75 2.00
BT17 Derrick Coleman .75 2.00
BT18 Patrick Ewing 1.25 3.00
BT19 Shaquille O'Neal 3.00 8.00
BT20 Clarence Weatherspoon .50 1.25
BT21 Charles Barkley 2.00 5.00
BT22 Clifford Robinson .60 1.50
BT23 Bobby Hurley .50 1.25
BT24 David Robinson 1.50 4.00
BT25 Shawn Kemp 1.25 3.00
BT26 Karl Malone 1.50 4.00
BT27 Chris Webber 1.50 4.00
CC1 Stacey Augmon .60 1.50
CC2 Dino Radja .50 1.25
CC3 Alonzo Mourning 1.25 3.00
CC4 Scottie Pippen 2.00 5.00
CC5 Gerald Wilkins .60 1.50
CC6 Jamal Mashburn .75 2.00
CC7 Dikembe Mutombo 1.25 3.00
CC8 Lindsey Hunter .50 1.25
CC9 Chris Mullin 1.00 2.50
CC10 Hakeem Olajuwon 1.50 4.00
CC11 Reggie Miller 1.50 4.00
CC12 Gary Grant .50 1.25
CC13 Doug Christie .60 1.50
CC14 Steve Smith .60 1.50
CC15 Vin Baker .75 2.00
CC16 Christian Laettner .60 1.50
CC17 Derrick Coleman .75 2.00
CC18 Charles Oakley .75 2.00
CC19 Dennis Scott .60 1.50
CC20 Clarence Weatherspoon .50 1.25
CC21 Charles Barkley 2.00 5.00
CC22 Clifford Robinson .60 1.50
CC23 Mitch Richmond 1.00 2.50
CC24 David Robinson 1.50 4.00
CC25 Shawn Kemp 1.25 3.00
CC26 Karl Malone 1.50 4.00
CC27 Don MacLean .50 1.25
DD1A Mark Price .75 2.00
DD1B Kenny Anderson .60 1.50
DD2A Karl Malone 1.50 4.00
DD2B Derrick Coleman .75 2.00
DD3A John Stockton 1.50 4.00
DD3B Anfernee Hardaway 1.50 4.00
DD4A Mitch Richmond 1.00 2.50
DD4B Jim Jackson .60 1.50
DD5A James Worthy 1.00 2.50
DD5B Jamal Mashburn .75 2.00
DD6A Patrick Ewing 1.25 3.00
DD6B Alonzo Mourning 1.25 3.00
DD7A Hakeem Olajuwon 1.50 4.00
DD7B Shaquille O'Neal 3.00 8.00
DD8A Clyde Drexler 1.25 3.00
DD8B Isaiah Rider .75 2.00
DD9A Scottie Pippen 2.00 5.00
DD9B Latrell Sprewell 1.00 2.50
DD10A Charles Barkley 2.00 5.00
DD10B Chris Webber 1.50 4.00
RS1 Kenny Anderson .60 1.50
RS2 Latrell Sprewell 1.00 2.50
RS3 Jamal Mashburn .75 2.00
RS4 Alonzo Mourning 1.25 3.00
RS5 Shaquille O'Neal 3.00 8.00
RS6 LaPhonso Ellis .50 1.25
RS7 Chris Webber 1.50 4.00
RS8 Isaiah Rider .75 2.00
RS9 Dikembe Mutombo 1.25 3.00
RS10 Anfernee Hardaway 1.50 4.00
RS11 Antonio Davis .60 1.50
RS12 Robert Horry .75 2.00
SS1 Mark Price .75 2.00
SS2 Tim Hardaway 1.00 2.50
SS3 Kevin Johnson .75 2.00
SS4 John Stockton 1.50 4.00
SS5 Mookie Blaylock .75 2.00
SS6 Reggie Miller 1.50 4.00
SS7 Jeff Hornacek .60 1.50
SS8 Latrell Sprewell 1.00 2.50
SS9 John Starks .75 2.00
SS10 Nate McMillan .60 1.50
SS11 Chris Mullin 1.00 2.50
SS12 Toni Kukoc 1.00 2.50
SS13 Anthony Mason .60 1.50
SS14 Robert Horry .75 2.00
SS15 Scottie Pippen 2.00 5.00
SS16 Charles Barkley 2.00 5.00
SS17 Dennis Rodman 2.00 5.00
SS18 Karl Malone 1.50 4.00
SS19 Chris Webber 1.50 4.00
SS20 Charles Oakley .75 2.00
SS21 Patrick Ewing 1.25 3.00
SS22 Shaquille O'Neal 3.00 8.00
SS23 Dikembe Mutombo 1.25 3.00
SS24 David Robinson 1.50 4.00
SS25 Hakeem Olajuwon 1.50 4.00
ST1 Atlanta Hawks
Craig Ehlo .50 1.25
ST2 Boston Celtics
Group .40 1.00
ST3 Charlotte Hornets
Group .40 1.00
ST4 Chicago Bulls
Group .40 1.00
ST5 Cleveland Cavaliers
Group .40 1.00
ST6 Dallas Mavericks
Jim Jackson .60 1.50
ST7 Denver Nuggets
Group .40 1.00
ST8 Detroit Pistons
Joe Dumars .40 1.00
ST9 Golden State Warriors
Chris Webber 1.50 4.00
ST10 Houston Rockets
Hakeem Olajuwon 1.50 4.00
ST11 Indiana Pacers
Rik Smits .60 1.50
ST12 Los Angeles Clippers
Group .40 1.00
ST13 Los Angeles Lakers
Nick Van Exel .75 2.00
ST14 Miami Heat
Group .40 1.00
ST15 Milwaukee Bucks
Vin Baker .75 2.00
ST16 Minnesota Timberwolves
Group .40 1.00
ST17 New Jersey Nets
Group .40 1.00
ST18 New York Knicks
Group .40 1.00
ST19 Orlando Magic
Shaquille O'Neal 3.00 8.00
ST20 Philadelphia 76ers
Group .40 1.00
ST21 Phoenix Suns
Group .40 1.00
ST22 Portland Trail Blazers
Group .40 1.00
ST23 Sacramento Kings
Olden Polynice .50 1.25
ST24 San Antonio Spurs
Group .40 1.00
ST25 Seattle Supersonics
Group .40 1.00
ST26 Utah Jazz
John Stockton 1.50 4.00
ST27 Washington Bullets
Group .40 1.00
TF1 Anfernee Hardaway 1.50 4.00
TF2 Latrell Sprewell 1.00 2.50
TF3 Grant Hill 4.00 10.00
TF4 Chris Webber 1.50 4.00
TF5 Shaquille O'Neal 3.00 8.00
TF6 Jason Kidd 4.00 10.00
TF7 Jim Jackson .60 1.50
TF8 Jamal Mashburn .75 2.00
TF9 Glenn Robinson 1.50 4.00
TF10 Alonzo Mourning 1.25 3.00
0 Reggie Miller AU 50.00 120.00

1995-96 Stadium Club Members Only Parallel I

COMPLETE SET (292) 120.00 300.00
1 Michael Jordan 10.00 25.00
2 Glenn Robinson .75 2.00
3 Jason Kidd 1.25 3.00
4 Clyde Drexler 1.25 3.00
5 Horace Grant .60 1.50
6 Allan Houston .60 1.50
7 Xavier McDaniel .50 1.25
8 Jeff Hornacek .60 1.50
9 Vlade Divac .75 2.00
10 Juwan Howard .75 2.00
11B Keith Jennings EXP Blue .50 1.25
11R Keith Jennings EXP Red .50 1.25
12 Grant Long .50 1.25
13 Jalen Rose 1.00 2.50
14 Malik Sealy .50 1.25
15 Gary Payton 1.25 3.00
16 Danny Ferry .50 1.25
17 Glen Rice .75 2.00
18 Randy Brown .50 1.25
19 Greg Graham .50 1.25
20 Kenny Anderson .60 1.50
21 Aaron McKie .50 1.25
22B John Salley EXP Blue .50 1.25
22R John Salley EXP Red .50 1.25
23 Darrin Hancock .50 1.25
24 Carlos Rogers .50 1.25
25 Vin Baker .60 1.50
26 Bill Wennington .50 1.25
27 Kenny Smith .60 1.50
28 Sherman Douglas .50 1.25
29 Terry Davis .50 1.25
30 Grant Hill 1.25 3.00
31 Reggie Miller 1.50 4.00
32 Anfernee Hardaway 2.00 5.00
33 Patrick Ewing 1.25 3.00
34 Charles Barkley 2.00 5.00
35 Eddie Jones .75 2.00
36 Kevin Duckworth .50 1.25
37 Tom Hammonds .50 1.25
38 Craig Ehlo .50 1.25
39 Micheal Williams .50 1.25
40 Alonzo Mourning 1.25 3.00
41 John Williams .50 1.25
42 Felton Spencer .50 1.25
43 Lamond Murray .50 1.25
44B Dontonio Wingfield EXP Blue .50 1.25
44R Dontonio Wingfield EXP Red .50 1.25
45 Rik Smits .60 1.50
46 Donyell Marshall .50 1.25
47 Clarence Weatherspoon .50 1.25
48 Kevin Edwards .50 1.25
49 Charlie Ward .60 1.50
50 David Robinson 1.50 4.00
51 James Robinson .50 1.25
52 Bill Cartwright .60 1.50
53 Bobby Hurley .50 1.25
54 Kevin Gamble .50 1.25
55B B.J. Tyler EXP Blue .50 1.25
55R B.J. Tyler EXP Red .50 1.25
56 Chris Smith .50 1.25
57 Wesley Person .50 1.25
58 Tim Breaux .50 1.25
59 Mitchell Butler .50 1.25
60 Toni Kukoc 1.00 2.50
61 Roy Tarpley .60 1.50
62 Todd Day .50 1.25
63 Anthony Peeler .50 1.25
64 Brian Williams .50 1.25
65 Muggsy Bogues .75 2.00
66B Jerome Kersey EXP Blue .50 1.25
66R Jerome Kersey EXP Red .50 1.25
67 Eric Piatkowski .50 1.25
68 Tim Perry .50 1.25
69 Chris Gatling .50 1.25
70 Mark Price .75 2.00
71 Terry Mills .50 1.25
72 Anthony Avent .50 1.25
73 Matt Geiger .50 1.25
74 Walt Williams .50 1.25
75 Sean Elliott .60 1.50
76 Ken Norman .50 1.25
77B Kendall Gill TA Blue .50 1.25
77R Kendall Gill TA Red .50 1.25
78 Byron Houston .50 1.25
79 Rick Fox .50 1.25
80 Derek Harper .60 1.50
81 Rod Strickland .60 1.50
82 Bryon Russell .50 1.25
83 Antonio Davis .50 1.25
84 Isaiah Rider .75 2.00
85 Kevin Johnson .75 2.00
86 Derrick Coleman .60 1.50
87 Doug Overton .50 1.25
88B Hersey Hawkins TA Blue .60 1.50
88R Hersey Hawkins TA Red .60 1.50
89 Popeye Jones .50 1.25
90 Dickey Simpkins .50 1.25
91B Rodney Rogers TA Blue .60 1.50
91R Rodney Rogers TA Red .60 1.50
92B Rex Chapman TA Blue .50 1.25
92R Rex Chapman TA Red .50 1.25
93B Spud Webb TA Blue .75 2.00
93R Spud Webb TA Red .75 2.00
94 Lee Mayberry .50 1.25
95 Cedric Ceballos .60 1.50
96 Tyrone Hill .50 1.25
97 Bill Curley .50 1.25
98 Jeff Turner .50 1.25
99B Tyrone Corbin TA Blue .50 1.25
99R Tyrone Corbin TA Red .50 1.25
100 John Stockton 1.50 4.00
101B Mookie Blaylock EC Blue .75 2.00
101R Mookie Blaylock EC Red .75 2.00
102B Dino Radja EC Blue .50 1.25
102R Dino Radja EC Red .50 1.25
103B Alonzo Mourning EC Blue 1.25 3.00
103R Alonzo Mourning EC Red 1.25 3.00
104B Scottie Pippen EC Blue 2.00 5.00
104R Scottie Pippen EC Red 2.00 5.00
105B Terrell Brandon EC Blue .60 1.50
105R Terrell Brandon EC Red .60 1.50
106B Jim Jackson EC Blue .60 1.50
106R Jim Jackson EC Red .60 1.50
107B Mahmoud Abdul-Rauf EC Blue .60 1.50
107R Mahmoud Abdul-Rauf EC Red .60 1.50
108B Grant Hill EC Blue 1.25 3.00
108R Grant Hill EC Red 1.25 3.00
109B Tim Hardaway EC Blue 1.00 2.50
109R Tim Hardaway EC Red 1.00 2.50
110B Hakeem Olajuwon EC Blue 1.50 4.00
110R Hakeem Olajuwon EC Red 1.50 4.00
111B Rik Smits EC Blue .60 1.50
111R Rik Smits EC Red .60 1.50
112B Loy Vaught EC Blue .50 1.25
112R Loy Vaught EC Red .50 1.25
113B Vlade Divac EC Blue .75 2.00
113R Vlade Divac EC Red .75 2.00
114B Kevin Willis EC Blue .50 1.25
114R Kevin Willis EC Red .50 1.25
115B Glenn Robinson EC Blue .75 2.00
115R Glenn Robinson EC Red .75 2.00
116B Christian Laettner EC Blue .60 1.50
116R Christian Laettner EC Red .60 1.50
117B Derrick Coleman EC Blue .60 1.50
117R Derrick Coleman EC Red .60 1.50
118B Patrick Ewing EC Blue 1.25 3.00
118R Patrick Ewing EC Red 1.25 3.00
119B Shaquille O'Neal EC Blue 3.00 8.00
119R Shaquille O'Neal EC Red 3.00 8.00
120B Dana Barros EC Blue .60 1.50
120R Dana Barros EC Red .60 1.50
121B Charles Barkley EC Blue 2.00 5.00
121R Charles Barkley EC Red 2.00 5.00
122B Rod Strickland EC Blue .50 1.25
122R Rod Strickland EC Red .50 1.25
123B Brian Grant EC Blue .60 1.50
123R Brian Grant EC Red .60 1.50
124B David Robinson EC Blue 1.50 4.00
124R David Robinson EC Red 1.50 4.00
125B Shawn Kemp EC Blue 1.25 3.00
125R Shawn Kemp EC Red 1.25 3.00
126B Oliver Miller EC Blue .50 1.25
126R Oliver Miller EC Red .50 1.25
127B Karl Malone EC Blue 1.50 4.00
127R Karl Malone EC Red 1.50 4.00
128B Benoit Benjamin EC Blue .50 1.25
128R Benoit Benjamin EC Red .50 1.25
129B Chris Webber EC Blue 1.00 2.50
129R Chris Webber EC Red 1.00 2.50
130 Dan Majerle .75 2.00
131 Calbert Cheaney .50 1.25
132 Mark Jackson .60 1.50
133B Greg Anthony EXP Blue .50 1.25
133R Greg Anthony EXP Red .50 1.25
134 Scott Burrell .50 1.25
135 Detlef Schrempf .75 2.00
136 Marty Conlon .50 1.25
137 Rony Seikaly .50 1.25
138 Olden Polynice .50 1.25
139 Terry Cummings .60 1.50
140 Stacey Augmon .60 1.50
141 Bryant Stith .50 1.25
142 Sean Higgins .50 1.25
143 Antoine Carr .50 1.25
144B Blue Edwards EXP Blue .50 1.25
144R Blue Edwards EXP Red .50 1.25
145 A.C. Green .60 1.50
146 Bobby Phills .60 1.50
147 Terry Dehere .50 1.25
148 Sharone Wright .50 1.25
149 Nick Anderson .60 1.50
150 Jim Jackson .60 1.50
151 Eric Montross .50 1.25
152 Doug West .50 1.25
153 Charles Smith .50 1.25
154 Will Perdue .60 1.50
155B Gerald Wilkins EXP Blue .50 1.25
155R Gerald Wilkins EXP Red .50 1.25
156 Robert Horry .75 2.00
157 Robert Parish 1.00 2.50
158 Lindsey Hunter .50 1.25
159 Harvey Grant .75 2.00
160 Tim Hardaway 1.00 2.50
161 Sarunas Marciulionis .75 2.00
162 Khalid Reeves .50 1.25
163 Bo Outlaw .50 1.25
164 Dale Davis .50 1.25
165 Nick Van Exel .75 2.00
166B Byron Scott EXP Blue .75 2.00
166R Byron Scott EXP Red .75 2.00
167 Steve Smith .60 1.50
168 Brian Grant .60 1.50
169 Avery Johnson .60 1.50
170 Dikembe Mutombo 1.25 3.00
171 Tom Gugliotta .50 1.25
172 Armon Gilliam .50 1.25
173 Shawn Bradley .50 1.25
174 Herb Williams .50 1.25
175 Dino Radja .50 1.25
176 Billy Owens .50 1.25
177B Kenny Gattison EXP Blue .50 1.25
177R Kenny Gattison EXP Red .50 1.25
178 J.R. Reid .50 1.25
179 Otis Thorpe .60 1.50
180 Sam Cassell .75 2.00
N1 Hakeem Olajuwon
David Robinson 3.00 8.00
N2 Patrick Ewing
Rik Smits 2.50 6.00
N3 John Stockton
Kevin Johnson 3.00 8.00
N4 Shaquille O'Neal
Alonzo Mourning 6.00 15.00
N5 Charles Barkley
Karl Malone 4.00 10.00
N6 Scottie Pippen
Grant Hill 4.00 10.00
N7 Anfernee Hardaway
Kenny Anderson 4.00 10.00
N8 Reggie Miller
John Starks 3.00 8.00
N9 Toni Kukoc
Dino Radja 2.00 5.00
N10 Michael Jordan
Joe Dumars 30.00 80.00
BT1 David Robinson 3.00 8.00
BT2 Juwan Howard 1.50 4.00
BT3 Mitch Richmond 2.00 5.00
BT4 Reggie Miller 3.00 8.00
BT5 Vin Baker 1.25 3.00
BT6 Shaquille O'Neal 6.00 15.00
BT7 Shawn Kemp 2.50 6.00
BT8 Karl Malone 3.00 8.00
BT9 Jamal Mashburn 1.50 4.00
BT10 Alonzo Mourning 2.50 6.00
DP2 Antonio McDyess 1.25 3.00
DP3 Jerry Stackhouse 3.00 8.00
DP4 Rasheed Wallace 3.00 8.00
DP5 Kevin Garnett 8.00 20.00
DP6 Bryant Reeves .75 2.00
DP8 Shawn Respert .75 2.00
DP9 Ed O'Bannon .75 2.00
DP11 Gary Trent .75 2.00
DP12 Cherokee Parks .75 2.00
DP15 Brent Barry 1.50 4.00
DP16 Alan Henderson 1.00 2.50
DP17 Bob Sura .75 2.00
DP18 Theo Ratliff 1.50 4.00
DP19 Randolph Childress .75 2.00
DP22 George Zidek .75 2.00
IC1 Hakeem Olajuwon 3.00 8.00
IC2 Dikembe Mutombo 2.50 6.00
IC3 Bill Wennington 1.00 2.50
IC4 Rick Fox 1.00 2.50
IC5 Carl Herrera 1.00 2.50
IC6 Rony Seikaly 1.00 2.50
IC7 Rik Smits 1.25 3.00
IC8 Dino Radja 1.00 2.50
IC9 Sarunas Marciulionis 1.50 4.00
IC10 Luc Longley 1.25 3.00
PZ1 Shaquille O'Neal 6.00 15.00
PZ2 Charles Barkley 4.00 10.00
PZ3 Patrick Ewing 2.50 6.00
PZ4 Karl Malone 3.00 8.00
PZ5 Larry Johnson 2.00 5.00
PZ6 Derrick Coleman 1.25 3.00
WS1 Michael Jordan 125.00 300.00
WS2 Kevin Johnson 1.50 4.00
WS3 Gary Payton 2.50 6.00
WS4 Anfernee Hardaway 4.00 10.00
WS5 Mookie Blaylock 1.50 4.00
WS6 Tim Hardaway 2.00 5.00
WZ1 Nick Van Exel 1.50 4.00
WZ2 Tim Hardaway 2.00 5.00
WZ3 Mookie Blaylock 1.50 4.00
WZ4 Gary Payton 2.50 6.00
WZ5 Jason Kidd 2.50 6.00
WZ6 Kenny Anderson 1.25 3.00
WZ7 John Stockton 3.00 8.00
WZ8 Kevin Johnson 1.50 4.00
WZ9 Muggsy Bogues 1.50 4.00
WZ10 Anfernee Hardaway 4.00 10.00

1995-96 Stadium Club Members Only Parallel II

COMPLETE SET (233) 120.00 300.00
181 Sam Cassell .75 2.00
182 Pooh Richardson .50 1.25
183 Johnny Newman .50 1.25
184 Dennis Scott .50 1.25
185 Will Perdue .60 1.50
186 Andrew Lang .50 1.25
187 Karl Malone 1.50 4.00
188 Buck Williams .50 1.25
189 P.J. Brown .50 1.25
190 Khalid Reeves .50 1.25
191 Kevin Willis .50 1.25
192 Robert Pack .50 1.25
193 Joe Dumars .75 2.00
194 Sam Perkins .50 1.25
195 Dan Majerle .75 2.00
196 John Williams .50 1.25
197 Reggie Williams .50 1.25
198 Greg Anthony .50 1.25
199 Steve Kerr .75 2.00
200 Richard Dumas .50 1.25
201 Dee Brown .60 1.50
202 Zan Tabak .50 1.25
203 David Wood .50 1.25
204 Duane Causwell .50 1.25
205 Sedale Threatt .50 1.25
206 Hubert Davis .50 1.25
207 Donald Hodge .50 1.25
208 Duane Ferrell .50 1.25
209 Sam Mitchell .50 1.25
210 Adam Keefe .50 1.25
211 Clifford Robinson .75 2.00
212 Rodney Rogers .60 1.50
213 Jayson Williams .50 1.25
214 Brian Shaw .50 1.25
215 Luc Longley .60 1.50
216 Don MacLean .50 1.25
217 Rex Chapman .50 1.25
218 Wayman Tisdale .50 1.25
219 Shawn Kemp 1.25 3.00
220 Chris Webber 1.00 2.50
221 Antonio Harvey .50 1.25
222 Sarunas Marciulionis .75 2.00
223 Jeff Malone .50 1.25
224 Chucky Brown .50 1.25
225 Greg Minor .50 1.25
226 Clifford Rozier .50 1.25
227 Derrick McKey .50 1.25
228 Tony Dumas .50 1.25
229 Oliver Miller .50 1.25
230 Charles Oakley .60 1.50
231 Fred Roberts .50 1.25
232 Glen Rice .75 2.00
233 Terry Porter .50 1.25
234 Mark Macon .50 1.25
235 Michael Cage .50 1.25
236 Eric Murdock .50 1.25
237 Vinny Del Negro .50 1.25
238 Spud Webb .75 2.00
239 Mario Elie .50 1.25
240 Blue Edwards .50 1.25
241 Dontonio Wingfield .50 1.25
242 Brooks Thompson .50 1.25
243 Alonzo Mourning 1.25 3.00
244 Dennis Rodman 1.50 4.00
245 Lorenzo Williams .50 1.25
246 Haywoode Workman .50 1.25
247 Loy Vaught .50 1.25
248 Vernon Maxwell .50 1.25
249 Lionel Simmons .50 1.25
250 Chris Childs .50 1.25
251 Mahmoud Abdul-Rauf .60 1.50
252 Vincent Askew .50 1.25
253 Chris Morris .50 1.25
254 Elliot Perry .50 1.25
255 Dell Curry .75 2.00
256 Dana Barros .60 1.50
257 Terrell Brandon .60 1.50
258 Monty Williams .50 1.25
259 Corie Blount .50 1.25
260 B.J. Armstrong .75 2.00
261 Jim McIlvaine .50 1.25

262 Otis Thorpe .60 1.50
263 Sean Rooks .50 1.25
264 Tony Massenburg .50 1.25
265 Steve Smith .60 1.50
266 Ron Harper .60 1.50
267 Dale Ellis .60 1.50
268 Clyde Drexler 1.25 3.00
269 Jamie Watson .50 1.25
270 Doc Rivers .60 1.50
271 Derrick Alston .50 1.25
272 Eric Mobley .50 1.25
273 Ricky Pierce .50 1.25
274 David Wesley .50 1.25
275 John Starks .75 2.00
276 Chris Mullin .75 2.00
277 Ervin Johnson .50 1.25
278 Jamal Mashburn .75 2.00
279 Joe Kleine .50 1.25
280 Mitch Richmond 1.00 2.50
281 Chris Mills .50 1.25
282 Bimbo Coles .50 1.25
283 Larry Johnson 1.00 2.50
284 Stanley Roberts .50 1.25
285 Rex Walters .50 1.25
286 Donald Royal .50 1.25
287 Benoit Benjamin .50 1.25
288 Chris Dudley .50 1.25
289 Elden Campbell .50 1.25
290 Mookie Blaylock .75 2.00
291 Hersey Hawkins .60 1.50
292 Anthony Mason .50 1.25
293 Latrell Sprewell .75 2.00
294 Harold Miner .50 1.25
295 Scott Williams .50 1.25
296 David Benoit .50 1.25
297 Christian Laettner .60 1.50
298 LaPhonso Ellis .60 1.50
299 Gheorghe Muresan .50 1.25
300 Kendall Gill .50 1.25
301 Eddie Johnson .50 1.25
302 Terry Cummings .60 1.50
303 Chuck Person .60 1.50
304 Michael Smith .50 1.25
305 Mark West .50 1.25
306 Willie Anderson .50 1.25
307 Pervis Ellison .50 1.25
308 Brian Williams .50 1.25
309 Danny Manning .60 1.50
310 Hakeem Olajuwon 1.50 4.00
311 Scottie Pippen 2.00 5.00
312 Jon Koncak .50 1.25
313 Sasha Danilovic .75 2.00
314 Lucious Harris .50 1.25
315 Yinka Dare .50 1.25
316 Eric Williams .75 2.00
317 Gary Trent .60 1.50
318 Theo Ratliff 1.25 3.00
319 Lawrence Moten .75 2.00
320 Jerome Allen .75 2.00
321 Tyus Edney .75 2.00
322 Loren Meyer .50 1.25
323 Michael Finley 2.00 5.00
324 Alan Henderson .75 2.00
325 Bob Sura .60 1.50
326 Joe Smith 1.00 2.50
327 Damon Stoudamire 2.00 5.00
328 Sherrell Ford .60 1.50
329 Jerry Stackhouse 2.50 6.00
330 George Zidek .60 1.50
331 Brent Barry 1.25 3.00
332 Shawn Respert .60 1.50
333 Rasheed Wallace 2.50 6.00
334 Antonio McDyess 1.00 2.50
335 David Vaughn .75 2.00
336 Cory Alexander .75 2.00
337 Jason Caffey .75 2.00
338 Frankie King .75 2.00
339 Travis Best .75 2.00
340 Greg Ostertag .75 2.00
341 Ed O'Bannon .60 1.50
342 Kurt Thomas .75 2.00
343 Kevin Garnett 12.00 30.00
344 Bryant Reeves .60 1.50
345 Corliss Williamson .75 2.00
346 Cherokee Parks .60 1.50
347 Junior Burrough .75 2.00
348 Randolph Childress .60 1.50
349 Lou Roe .75 2.00
350 Mario Bennett .60 1.50
351 Dikembe Mutombo 1.25 3.00
352 Larry Johnson 1.00 2.50
353 Vlade Divac .75 2.00
354 Karl Malone 1.50 4.00
355 John Stockton 1.50 4.00
356 Alonzo Mourning 1.25 3.00
357 Glen Rice .75 2.00
358 Dan Majerle .75 2.00
359 John Williams .50 1.25
360 Mark Price .75 2.00
361 Magic Johnson 2.50 6.00
B11 Charles Barkley 4.00 10.00
B12 Hakeem Olajuwon 3.00 8.00
B13 Kenny Anderson 1.25 3.00
B14 Michael Jordan 20.00 50.00
B15 Dikembe Mutombo 2.50 6.00
B16 Rod Strickland 1.00 2.50
B17 Patrick Ewing 2.50 6.00
B18 Latrell Sprewell 1.50 4.00
B19 Grant Hill 2.50 6.00
B20 Cedric Ceballos 1.25 3.00
X1 Hakeem Olajuwon 3.00 8.00
X2 Shaquille O'Neal 6.00 15.00
X3 David Robinson 3.00 8.00
X4 Patrick Ewing 2.50 6.00
X5 Charles Barkley 4.00 10.00
X6 Karl Malone 3.00 8.00
X7 Derrick Coleman 1.25 3.00
X8 Shawn Kemp 2.50 6.00
X9 Vin Baker 1.25 3.00
X10 Vlade Divac 1.50 4.00
PZ7 Hakeem Olajuwon 3.00 8.00
PZ8 David Robinson 3.00 8.00
PZ9 Shawn Kemp 2.50 6.00
PZ10 Dennis Rodman 3.00 8.00
PZ11 Alonzo Mourning 2.50 6.00
PZ12 Vin Baker 1.25 3.00
RM1 Shawn Kemp 2.50 6.00
RM2 Michael Jordan 60.00 150.00
RM3 Larry Johnson 2.00 5.00
RM4 Grant Hill 2.50 6.00
RM5 Isaiah Rider 1.50 4.00
RM6 Sean Elliott 1.25 3.00
RM7 Scottie Pippen 4.00 10.00
RM8 Robert Horry 1.50 4.00
RM9 Kendall Gill 1.00 2.50
RM10 Jerry Stackhouse 5.00 12.00
SS1 Michael Jordan 20.00 50.00
SS2 Alonzo Mourning 2.50 6.00
SS3 Reggie Miller 3.00 8.00
SS4 Patrick Ewing 2.50 6.00
SS5 Charles Barkley 4.00 10.00
SS6 Kenny Anderson 1.25 3.00
SS7 Scottie Pippen 4.00 10.00
SS8 Jerry Stackhouse 5.00 12.00
SS9 Shaquille O'Neal 6.00 15.00
SS10 John Starks 1.50 4.00
WS7 Scottie Pippen 4.00 10.00
WS8 Jason Kidd 2.50 6.00
WS9 Grant Hill 2.50 6.00
WS10 Nick Van Exel 1.50 4.00
WS11 Kenny Anderson 1.25 3.00
WS12 Latrell Sprewell 1.50 4.00

1996-97 Stadium Club Members Only Parallel I

COMPLETE SET (173) 150.00 400.00
1 Scottie Pippen 2.50 6.00
2 Dale Davis .60 1.50
3 Horace Grant 1.00 2.50
4 Gheorghe Muresan .60 1.50
5 Elliot Perry .60 1.50
6 Carlos Rogers .60 1.50
7 Glenn Robinson 1.00 2.50
8 Avery Johnson .75 2.00
9 Dee Brown .60 1.50
10 Grant Hill 1.50 4.00
11 Tyus Edney .60 1.50
12 Patrick Ewing 1.50 4.00
13 Jason Kidd 1.50 4.00
14 Clifford Robinson 1.00 2.50
15 Robert Horry 1.00 2.50
16 Dell Curry 1.00 2.50
17 Terry Porter .60 1.50
18 Shaquille O'Neal 4.00 10.00
19 Bryant Stith .60 1.50
20 Shawn Kemp 1.50 4.00
21 Kurt Thomas .60 1.50
22 Pooh Richardson .60 1.50
23 Bob Sura .60 1.50
24 Olden Polynice .60 1.50
25 Lawrence Moten .60 1.50
26 Kendall Gill 1.00 2.50
27 Cedric Ceballos .75 2.00
28 Latrell Sprewell 1.00 2.50
29 Christian Laettner 1.00 2.50
30 Jamal Mashburn 1.00 2.50
31 Jerry Stackhouse 1.25 3.00
32 John Stockton 2.00 5.00
33 Arvydas Sabonis 1.00 2.50
34 Detlef Schrempf 1.00 2.50
35 Toni Kukoc .60 1.50
36 Sasha Danilovic .60 1.50
37 Dana Barros .60 1.50
38 Loy Vaught .60 1.50
39 John Starks 1.00 2.50
40 Marty Conlon .60 1.50
41 Antonio McDyess 1.00 2.50
42 Michael Finley 1.00 2.50
43 Tom Gugliotta .60 1.50
44 Terrell Brandon .75 2.00
45 Derrick McKey .60 1.50
46 Damon Stoudamire 1.00 2.50
47 Elden Campbell .60 1.50
48 Luc Longley .75 2.00
49 B.J. Armstrong .75 2.00
50 Lindsey Hunter .60 1.50
51 Glen Rice 1.00 2.50
52 Shawn Respert .60 1.50
53 Cory Alexander .60 1.50
54 Tim Legler .60 1.50
55 Bryant Reeves .60 1.50
56 Anfernee Hardaway 2.50 6.00
57 Charles Barkley 2.50 6.00
58 Mookie Blaylock 1.00 2.50
59 Kevin Garnett 3.00 8.00
60 Hersey Hawkins .60 1.50
61 Ed O'Bannon .60 1.50
62 George Zidek .60 1.50
63 Mitch Richmond 1.25 3.00
64 Derrick Coleman .75 2.00
65 Chris Webber 1.25 3.00
66 Bobby Phills .75 2.00
67 Rik Smits .75 2.00
68 Jeff Hornacek .75 2.00
69 Sam Cassell .75 2.00
70 Gary Trent .60 1.50
71 LaPhonso Ellis .60 1.50
72 Oliver Miller .60 1.50
73 Rex Chapman .60 1.50
74 Jim Jackson .60 1.50
75 Eric Williams .60 1.50
76 Brent Barry .75 2.00
77 Nick Anderson .60 1.50
78 David Robinson 2.00 5.00
79 Calbert Cheaney .60 1.50
80 Joe Smith .75 2.00
81 Steve Kerr .75 2.00
82 Wayman Tisdale .75 2.00
83 Steve Smith .75 2.00
84 Clyde Drexler 1.50 4.00
85 Theo Ratliff .60 1.50
86 Charlie Ward .60 1.50
87 Karl Malone 2.00 5.00
88 Clarence Weatherspoon .60 1.50
89 Greg Anthony .60 1.50
90 Shawn Bradley .60 1.50
F1 Michael Jordan 125.00 300.00
F2 Chris Webber 2.00 5.00
F3 Glenn Robinson 1.50 4.00
F4 Glen Rice 1.50 4.00
F5 Gary Payton 2.50 6.00
F6 Rik Smits 1.25 3.00
F7 Grant Hill 2.50 6.00
F8 Horace Grant 1.50 4.00
F9 Scottie Pippen 4.00 10.00
F10 Gheorghe Muresan 1.00 2.50
F11 Vin Baker 1.25 3.00
F12 Dell Curry 1.50 4.00
F13 Shawn Kemp 2.50 6.00
F14 Reggie Miller 3.00 8.00
F15 Joe Dumars 2.00 5.00
F16 Anfernee Hardaway 4.00 10.00
R1 Allen Iverson 30.00 80.00
R2 Marcus Camby 6.00 15.00
R3 Shareef Abdur-Rahim 6.00 15.00
R4 Stephon Marbury 12.00 30.00
R5 Ray Allen 20.00 50.00
R6 Antoine Walker 6.00 15.00
R7 Lorenzen Wright 3.00 8.00
R8 Kerry Kittles 4.00 10.00
R9 Samaki Walker 3.00 8.00
R10 Erick Dampier 4.00 10.00
R11 Todd Fuller 2.50 6.00
R12 Kobe Bryant 75.00 200.00
R13 Steve Nash 25.00 60.00
R14 Tony Delk 4.00 10.00
R15 Jermaine O'Neal 6.00 15.00
R16 John Wallace 3.00 8.00
R17 Walter McCarty 4.00 10.00
R18 Dontae' Jones 3.00 8.00
R19 Roy Rogers 3.00 8.00
R20 Derek Fisher 5.00 12.00
R21 Martin Muursepp 2.50 6.00
R22 Jerome Williams 3.00 8.00
R23 Brian Evans 2.50 6.00
R24 Priest Lauderdale 2.50 6.00
R25 Travis Knight 3.00 8.00
GM1 Robert Parish 1.25 3.00
GM2 John Stockton 2.00 5.00
GM3 Michael Jordan
Toni Kukoc
Dennis Rodman 10.00 25.00
GM4 Dennis Scott .75 2.00
GM5 Hakeem Olajuwon 2.00 5.00
SF1 Anfernee Hardaway 4.00 10.00
SF2 Grant Hill 2.50 6.00
SF3 Shawn Kemp 2.50 6.00
SF4 Michael Jordan 125.00 300.00
SF5 Shaquille O'Neal 6.00 15.00
SF6 Scottie Pippen 4.00 10.00
SF7 Damon Stoudamire 1.50 4.00
SF8 Jerry Stackhouse 2.00 5.00
SF9 Gary Payton 2.50 6.00
SF10 Dennis Rodman 4.00 10.00
SM1 Charles Barkley 2.50 6.00
SM2 Michael Jordan 15.00 40.00
SM3 Karl Malone 2.00 5.00
SM4 Hakeem Olajuwon 2.00 5.00
SM5 John Stockton 2.00 5.00
SM6 Patrick Ewing 1.50 4.00
SM7 Reggie Miller 2.00 5.00
SM8 David Robinson 2.00 5.00
SM9 Dennis Rodman 2.50 6.00
SM10 Damon Stoudamire 1.00 2.50
SM11 Brent Barry .75 2.00
SM12 Tim Legler .60 1.50
SM13 Jason Kidd 1.50 4.00
SM14 Terrell Brandon .75 2.00
SM15 Allen Iverson 8.00 20.00
TC1 Hakeem Olajuwon
Shaquille O'Neal 6.00 15.00
TC2 Dikembe Mutombo
Alonzo Mourning 2.50 6.00
TC3 David Robinson
Patrick Ewing 3.00 8.00
TC4 Sean Elliott
Grant Hill 2.50 6.00
TC5 Shawn Kemp
Scottie Pippen 4.00 10.00
TC6 Karl Malone
Vin Baker 3.00 8.00
TC7 Charles Barkley
Juwan Howard 4.00 10.00
TC8 Clyde Drexler
Glen Rice 2.50 6.00
TC9 Gary Payton
Michael Jordan 150.00 400.00
TC10 John Stockton
Terrell Brandon 3.00 8.00
TC11 Mitch Richmond
Reggie Miller 3.00 8.00
TC12 Jason Kidd
Anfernee Hardaway 4.00 10.00

1996-97 Stadium Club Members Only Parallel II

COMPLETE SET (210) 200.00 500.00
91 Otis Thorpe .75 2.00
92 Larry Johnson 1.25 3.00
93 Sharone Wright .60 1.50
94 Charles Barkley 2.50 6.00
95 Wesley Person .60 1.50
96 Dikembe Mutombo 1.50 4.00
97 Eddie Jones 1.00 2.50
98 Juwan Howard 1.00 2.50
99 Grant Hill 1.50 4.00
100 Chris Carr 1.00 2.50
101 Michael Jordan 10.00 25.00
102 Vincent Askew .60 1.50
103 Gary Payton 1.50 4.00
104 Chris Mills .60 1.50
105 Reggie Miller 2.00 5.00
106 Don MacLean .60 1.50
107 John Stockton 2.00 5.00
108 Mahmoud Abdul-Rauf .75 2.00
109 P.J. Brown .60 1.50
110 Kenny Anderson .60 1.50
111 Mark Price 1.00 2.50
112 Derek Harper .60 1.50
113 Dino Radja .60 1.50
114 Terry Dehere .60 1.50
115 Mark Jackson .75 2.00
116 Vin Baker .75 2.00
117 Dennis Scott .75 2.00
118 Sean Elliott 1.00 2.50
119 Lee Mayberry .60 1.50
120 Vlade Divac 1.00 2.50
121 Joe Dumars 1.25 3.00
122 Isaiah Rider .75 2.00
123 Hakeem Olajuwon 2.00 5.00
124 Robert Pack .60 1.50
125 Jalen Rose .75 2.00
126 Allan Houston 1.00 2.50
127 Nate McMillan .60 1.50
128 Rod Strickland 1.00 2.50
129 Sean Rooks .60 1.50
130 Dennis Rodman 2.50 6.00
131 Alonzo Mourning 1.50 4.00
132 Danny Ferry .60 1.50
133 Sam Cassell .75 2.00
134 Brian Grant .75 2.00
135 Karl Malone 2.00 5.00
136 Chris Gatling .60 1.50
137 Tom Gugliotta .60 1.50
138 Hubert Davis .60 1.50
139 Lucious Harris .60 1.50
140 Rony Seikaly .75 2.00
141 Alan Henderson .60 1.50
142 Mario Elie .60 1.50
143 Vinny Del Negro .60 1.50
144 Harvey Grant .60 1.50
145 Muggsy Bogues 1.00 2.50
146 Rodney Rogers .60 1.50
147 Kevin Johnson 1.00 2.50
148 Anthony Peeler .60 1.50
149 Jon Koncak .60 1.50
150 Ricky Pierce .75 2.00
151 Todd Day .60 1.50
152 Tyrone Hill .60 1.50
153 Nick Van Exel 1.00 2.50
154 Rasheed Wallace 1.25 3.00
155 Jayson Williams .60 1.50
156 Sherman Douglas .60 1.50
157 Bryon Russell .60 1.50
158 Loy Vaught .75 2.00
159 Stacey Augmon .75 2.00
160 Antonio Davis .60 1.50
161 Tim Hardaway 1.25 3.00
162 Charles Oakley 1.00 2.50
163 Billy Owens .60 1.50
164 Sam Perkins .75 2.00
165 Chris Whitney .60 1.50
166 Matt Geiger .60 1.50
167 Andrew Lang .60 1.50
168 Danny Manning .75 2.00
169 Doug Christie .60 1.50
170 George Lynch .60 1.50
171 Malik Sealy .60 1.50
172 Eric Montross .60 1.50
173 Rick Fox .60 1.50
174 Chris Mullin 1.25 3.00
175 Ken Norman .60 1.50
176 Sarunas Marciulionis .60 1.50
177 Kevin Garnett 3.00 8.00
178 Brian Shaw .60 1.50
179 Will Perdue .60 1.50
180 Scott Williams .60 1.50
F17 Charles Barkley 4.00 10.00
F18 Juwan Howard 1.50 4.00
F19 Patrick Ewing 2.50 6.00
F20 John Stockton 3.00 8.00
F21 David Robinson 3.00 8.00
F22 Cedric Ceballos 1.25 3.00
F23 Alonzo Mourning 2.50 6.00
F24 Mookie Blaylock 1.50 4.00
F25 Clyde Drexler 2.50 6.00
F26 Rod Strickland 1.50 4.00
F27 Larry Johnson 2.00 5.00
F28 Karl Malone 3.00 8.00
F29 Sean Elliott 1.50 4.00
F30 Shaquille O'Neal 6.00 15.00
F31 Tim Hardaway 2.00 5.00
F32 Dikembe Mutombo 2.50 6.00
R1 Shareef Abdur-Rahim 6.00 15.00
R2 Tony Delk 4.00 10.00
R3 Priest Lauderdale 2.50 6.00
R4 Roy Rogers 3.00 8.00
R5 Lorenzen Wright 3.00 8.00
R6 Stephon Marbury 12.00 30.00
R7 Derek Fisher 5.00 12.00
R8 John Wallace 3.00 8.00
R9 Kobe Bryant 75.00 200.00
R10 Kerry Kittles 4.00 10.00
R11 Antoine Walker 6.00 15.00
R12 Steve Nash 25.00 60.00
R13 Erick Dampier 4.00 10.00
R14 Walter McCarty 4.00 10.00
R15 Vitaly Potapenko 3.00 8.00
R16 Allen Iverson 30.00 80.00
R17 Marcus Camby 6.00 15.00
R18 Todd Fuller 2.50 6.00
R19 Ray Allen 20.00 50.00
R20 Jermaine O'Neal 6.00 15.00
CA1 Michael Jordan
Jerry Stackhouse 40.00 100.00
CA2 Patrick Ewing
Alonzo Mourning 2.50 6.00
CA3 Brent Barry
Gary Payton 2.50 6.00
CA4 Chris Webber
Juwan Howard 2.00 5.00
CA5 Christian Laettner
Grant Hill 2.50 6.00
CA6 Jason Kidd
Shareef Abdur-Rahim 2.50 6.00
CA7 Clyde Drexler
Hakeem Olajuwon 3.00 8.00
CA8 Kenny Anderson
Stephon Marbury 5.00 12.00
CA9 Anfernee Hardaway
Lorenzen Wright 4.00 10.00
CA10 Dikembe Mutombo
Allen Iverson 12.00 30.00
HR1 Scottie Pippen 4.00 10.00
HR2 Anfernee Hardaway 4.00 10.00
HR3 Vin Baker 1.25 3.00
HR4 Brent Barry 1.25 3.00
HR5 Clyde Drexler 2.50 6.00
HR6 Kevin Garnett 5.00 12.00
HR7 Grant Hill 2.50 6.00
HR8 Michael Finley 1.50 4.00
HR9 Jerry Stackhouse 2.00 5.00
HR10 Isaiah Rider 1.25 3.00
HR11 Shaquille O'Neal 6.00 15.00
HR12 Antonio McDyess 1.50 4.00
HR13 Shawn Kemp 2.50 6.00
HR14 Michael Jordan 125.00 300.00
HR15 Juwan Howard 1.50 4.00
MH1 Dennis Rodman 4.00 10.00
MH2 David Robinson 3.00 8.00
MH3 Karl Malone 3.00 8.00
MH4 Clyde Drexler 2.50 6.00
MH5 Anfernee Hardaway 4.00 10.00
MH6 Hakeem Olajuwon 3.00 8.00
MH7 Charles Oakley 1.50 4.00
MH8 Joe Smith 1.25 3.00
MH9 Glenn Robinson 1.50 4.00
RS1 Marcus Camby 2.50 6.00
RS2 Shareef Abdur-Rahim 2.50 6.00
RS3 Stephon Marbury 5.00 12.00
RS4 Ray Allen 8.00 20.00
RS5 Antoine Walker 2.50 6.00
RS6 Lorenzen Wright 1.25 3.00
RS7 Kerry Kittles 1.50 4.00
RS8 Samaki Walker 1.25 3.00
RS9 Erick Dampier 1.50 4.00
RS10 Todd Fuller 1.00 2.50
RS11 Kobe Bryant 300.00 600.00
RS12 Steve Nash 10.00 25.00
RS13 Tony Delk 1.50 4.00
RS14 Jermaine O'Neal 2.50 6.00
RS15 John Wallace 1.25 3.00
RS16 Walter McCarty 1.50 4.00
RS17 Dontae' Jones 1.25 3.00
RS18 Roy Rogers 1.25 3.00
RS19 Derek Fisher 2.00 5.00
RS20 Martin Muursepp 1.00 2.50
RS21 Jerome Williams 1.25 3.00
RS22 Brian Evans 1.00 2.50
RS23 Priest Lauderdale 1.00 2.50
RS24 Travis Knight 1.25 3.00
RS25 Allen Iverson 12.00 30.00
WA1 Charles Barkley 2.50 6.00
WA2 Armon Gilliam .60 1.50
WA3 Larry Johnson 1.25 3.00
WA4 Felton Spencer .60 1.50
WA5 Isaiah Rider .75 2.00
WA6 Kevin Willis .75 2.00
WA7 Mahmoud Abdul-Rauf .75 2.00
WA8 Chris Childs .60 1.50
WA9 Robert Horry 1.00 2.50
WA10 Dan Majerle 1.00 2.50
WA11 Robert Pack .60 1.50
WA12 Rod Strickland 1.00 2.50
WA13 Tyrone Corbin .60 1.50
WA14 Anthony Mason .75 2.00
WA15 Derek Harper .75 2.00
WA16 Kenny Anderson .75 2.00
WA17 Hubert Davis .60 1.50
WA18 Allan Houston 1.00 2.50
WA19 Shaquille O'Neal 4.00 10.00
WA20 Brent Price .60 1.50
WA21 Ervin Johnson .60 1.50
WA22 Craig Ehlo .60 1.50
WA23 Jalen Rose .75 2.00
WA24 Oliver Miller .60 1.50
WA25 Mark West .60 1.50

1997-98 Stadium Club Members Only Parallel I

COMPLETE SET (184) 200.00 400.00
1 Scottie Pippen 3.00 8.00
3 Muggsy Bogues 1.00 2.50
5 Bulls - Team of the 90s
Ron Harper
Michael Jordan
Scottie Pippen
Dennis Rodman 40.00 100.00
7 Samaki Walker .75 2.00
9 Ray Allen 2.50 6.00
11 Chris Mullin 1.50 4.00
13 Horace Grant 1.25 3.00
15 Wayman Tisdale .75 2.00
17 Rod Strickland 1.00 2.50
19 Greg Anthony 1.00 2.50
21 Glen Rice 1.25 3.00
23 Mahmoud Abdul-Rauf .75 2.00
25 Cory Alexander .75 2.00
27 Sam Perkins 1.00 2.50
29 Doug Christie .75 2.00
31 Christian Laettner 1.25 3.00
33 Eric Williams .75 2.00
35 Brooks Thompson .75 2.00
37 Theo Ratliff 1.00 2.50
39 Hakeem Olajuwon 2.50 6.00
41 Reggie Miller 2.50 6.00
43 Shaquille O'Neal 4.00 10.00
45 Jamal Mashburn 1.00 2.50
47 Tom Gugliotta 1.00 2.50
49 Lorenzen Wright .75 2.00
51 Armon Gilliam .75 2.00
53 Kerry Kittles 1.00 2.50
55 Bo Outlaw .75 2.00
57 Greg Ostertag .75 2.00
59 Mark Davis .75 2.00
61 Clifford Robinson 1.00 2.50
63 Steve Kerr 1.50 4.00
65 Danny Ferry .75 2.00
67 A.C. Green 1.00 2.50
69 Terry Mills .75 2.00
71 Matt Maloney .75 2.00
73 Brent Barry 1.00 2.50
75 Stephon Marbury 1.50 4.00
77 Shareef Abdur-Rahim 1.50 4.00
79 Rony Seikaly 1.00 2.50
81 Wesley Person 1.00 2.50
83 Gary Trent .75 2.00
85 Rex Walters .75 2.00
87 Patrick Ewing 2.00 5.00
89 Travis Best .75 2.00
91 Vitaly Potapenko .75 2.00
93 Michael Finley 1.25 3.00
95 Antoine Walker 1.25 3.00
97 Mookie Blaylock 1.25 3.00
99 Tony Delk 1.00 2.50
101 Terrell Brandon 1.00 2.50
103 Latrell Sprewell 1.50 4.00
105 Tim Hardaway 1.50 4.00
107 Darrell Armstrong .75 2.00
109 Vinny Del Negro .75 2.00
111 Lawrence Moten .75 2.00
113 Juwan Howard 1.00 2.50
115 Karl Malone 2.50 6.00
117 Shawn Respert .75 2.00
119 Shawn Kemp 2.00 5.00
121 Tyus Edney .75 2.00
123 Jason Kidd 2.00 5.00
125 Allen Iverson 4.00 10.00
127 Larry Johnson 1.50 4.00
129 Kendall Gill 1.00 2.50
131 Vin Baker 1.00 2.50
133 Calbert Cheaney 1.00 2.50
135 Isaac Austin .75 2.00
137 Elden Campbell .75 2.00
139 Malik Sealy 1.00 2.50
141 Clyde Drexler 2.00 5.00
143 Mark Price 1.25 3.00
145 Grant Hill 2.00 5.00
147 Dale Ellis 1.00 2.50
149 Toni Kukoc 1.50 4.00
151 Alan Henderson .75 2.00
153 Greg Minor .75 2.00
155 Vlade Divac 1.25 3.00
157 LaPhonso Ellis 1.00 2.50
159 Antonio Davis 1.00 2.50
161 Robert Horry 1.25 3.00
163 Chris Carr .75 2.00
165 Sam Cassell 1.00 2.50
167 Chris Childs .75 2.00
169 Kenny Anderson 1.00 2.50
171 Olden Polynice .75 2.00
173 David Robinson 2.50 6.00
175 Detlef Schrempf 1.25 3.00
177 Marcus Camby 1.25 3.00
179 Shandon Anderson .75 2.00
181 Eldridge Recasner .75 2.00
183 Kevin Willis 1.00 2.50
185 Derek Fisher 1.25 3.00
187 Sherman Douglas .75 2.00
189 Danny Manning 1.00 2.50
191 Hersey Hawkins 1.00 2.50
193 Jeff Hornacek 1.25 3.00
195 Harvey Grant .75 2.00
197 Luc Longley 1.25 3.00
199 P.J. Brown .75 2.00
201 Tim Duncan 8.00 20.00
203 Keith Van Horn 2.00 5.00
205 Chauncey Billups 4.00 10.00
207 Antonio Daniels 1.25 3.00
209 Tony Battie 1.25 3.00
211 Bobby Jackson 1.50 4.00
213 Tim Thomas 1.50 4.00
215 Adonal Foyle 1.00 2.50
217 Tracy McGrady 6.00 15.00
219 Danny Fortson 1.25 3.00
221 Olivier Saint-Jean 1.00 2.50
223 Austin Croshere 1.00 2.50
225 Derek Anderson 1.25 3.00
227 Maurice Taylor 1.00 2.50
229 John Thomas .75 2.00
231 Brevin Knight 1.25 3.00
233 Johnny Taylor .75 2.00
235 Ed Gray 1.25 3.00
237 Anthony Parker 1.25 3.00
239 Paul Grant .75 2.00
H1 Michael Jordan 15.00 40.00
H2 Gary Payton 2.50 6.00
H3 Charles Barkley 4.00 10.00
H4 Mitch Richmond 2.00 5.00
H5 Shawn Kemp 2.50 6.00
H6 Anfernee Hardaway 4.00 10.00
H7 Vin Baker 1.25 3.00
H8 Shaquille O'Neal 5.00 12.00
H9 Scottie Pippen 4.00 10.00
H10 Grant Hill 2.50 6.00
T1A Scottie Pippen 4.00 10.00
T1B Michael Jordan 15.00 40.00
T1C Dennis Rodman 4.00 10.00
T2A Ray Allen 3.00 8.00
T2B Vin Baker 1.25 3.00
T2C Glenn Robinson 1.50 4.00
T3A Juwan Howard 1.25 3.00
T3B Chris Webber 2.00 5.00
T3C Rod Strickland 1.25 3.00
T4A Christian Laettner 1.50 4.00
T4B Dikembe Mutombo 2.50 6.00
T4C Steve Smith 1.25 3.00
T5A Tom Gugliotta 1.25 3.00
T5B Kevin Garnett 4.00 10.00
T5C Stephon Marbury 2.00 5.00
T6A Charles Barkley 4.00 10.00
T6B Hakeem Olajuwon 3.00 8.00
T6C Clyde Drexler 2.50 6.00
T7A John Stockton 3.00 8.00
T7B Karl Malone 3.00 8.00
T7C Bryon Russell 1.00 2.50
T8A Larry Johnson 2.00 5.00
T8B Patrick Ewing 2.50 6.00
T8C Allan Houston 1.50 4.00
HH1 Brevin Knight .75 2.00
HH2 Adonal Foyle .60 1.50
HH3 Keith Van Horn 1.25 3.00
HH4 Tim Duncan 5.00 12.00
HH5 Danny Fortson .75 2.00
HH6 Tracy McGrady 4.00 10.00
HH7 Tony Battie .75 2.00
HH8 Chauncey Billups 2.50 6.00
HH9 Austin Croshere .60 1.50
HH10 Antonio Daniels .75 2.00
HS1 Shaquille O'Neal 5.00 12.00
HS2 Cedric Ceballos 1.25 3.00
HS3 Kevin Garnett 4.00 10.00
HS4 Shawn Kemp 2.50 6.00
HS5 Jerry Stackhouse 1.50 4.00
HS6 Grant Hill 2.50 6.00
HS7 Patrick Ewing 2.50 6.00
HS8 Marcus Camby 1.50 4.00
HS9 Kobe Bryant 15.00 40.00
HS10 Michael Jordan 50.00 120.00
BBP1 Allen Iverson 5.00 12.00
BBP2 Gary Payton 2.50 6.00
BBP3 Grant Hill 2.50 6.00
BBP4 Anfernee Hardaway 4.00 10.00
BBP5 Karl Malone 3.00 8.00
BBP6 Glen Rice 1.50 4.00
BBP7 Antoine Walker 1.50 4.00
BBP8 Alonzo Mourning 2.50 6.00
BBP9 Shareef Abdur-Rahim 1.50 4.00
BBP10 Shaquille O'Neal 5.00 12.00

1997-98 Stadium Club Members Only Parallel II

COMPLETE SET (194) 200.00 400.00
2 Bryon Russell .75 2.00
4 Gary Payton 2.00 5.00
6 Corliss Williamson .75 2.00
8 Allan Houston 1.25 3.00
10 Nick Van Exel 1.25 3.00
12 Popeye Jones .75 2.00
14 Rik Smits 1.00 2.50
16 Donny Marshall .75 2.00
18 Rod Strickland 1.00 2.50
20 Lindsey Hunter .75 2.00
22 Anthony Goldwire .75 2.00
24 Tyrone Corbin .75 2.00
26 Sean Elliott 1.00 2.50
28 Brian Shaw 1.00 2.50
30 Mark Jackson 1.00 2.50
32 Damon Stoudamire 1.25 3.00
34 Glenn Robinson 1.25 3.00
36 Derrick Coleman 1.25 3.00
38 Ron Harper 1.25 3.00
40 Mitch Richmond 1.50 4.00
42 Reggie Miller 2.50 6.00
44 Zydrunas Ilgauskas 1.25 3.00
46 Isaiah Rider 1.00 2.50
48 Rex Chapman .75 2.00
50 Pooh Richardson .75 2.00
52 Kevin Johnson 1.25 3.00
54 Kerry Kittles 1.00 2.50
56 Dennis Rodman 3.00 8.00
58 Todd Fuller .75 2.00
60 Erick Strickland .75 2.00
62 Nate McMillan .75 2.00
64 Bob Sura .75 2.00
66 Loy Vaught 1.00 2.50
68 John Stockton 2.50 6.00
70 Voshon Lenard .75 2.00
72 Charlie Ward 1.00 2.50
74 Chris Webber 1.50 4.00
76 Bryant Stith .75 2.00
78 Sean Rooks .75 2.00
80 Brent Price .75 2.00
82 Michael Smith .75 2.00
84 Dan Majerle 1.25 3.00
86 Clarence Weatherspoon .75 2.00
88 B.J. Armstrong .75 2.00
90 Steve Smith 1.00 2.50
92 Derek Strong .75 2.00
94 Will Perdue .75 2.00
96 Chuck Person 1.00 2.50
98 Eric Snow .75 2.00
100 Mario Elie .75 2.00
102 Shawn Bradley .75 2.00
104 Latrell Sprewell 1.50 4.00
106 Terry Porter .75 2.00
108 Rasheed Wallace 1.50 4.00
110 Tracy Murray .75 2.00
112 Lamond Murray .75 2.00
114 Juwan Howard 1.00 2.50
116 Aaron McKie .75 2.00
118 Michael Jordan 12.00 30.00
120 Arvydas Sabonis 1.50 4.00
122 Bryant Reeves .75 2.00
124 Dikembe Mutombo 2.00 5.00
126 Allen Iverson 4.00 10.00
128 Jerry Stackhouse 1.25 3.00
130 Kendall Gill 1.00 2.50
132 Joe Dumars 1.50 4.00
134 Alonzo Mourning 2.00 5.00
136 Joe Smith 1.00 2.50
138 Kevin Garnett 3.00 8.00
140 John Starks 1.25 3.00
142 Matt Geiger .75 2.00
144 Buck Williams .75 2.00
146 Kobe Bryant 12.00 30.00
148 Jason Caffey .75 2.00
150 Avery Johnson 1.00 2.50
152 Walt Williams 1.00 2.50
154 Calbert Cheaney 1.00 2.50
156 Greg Foster .75 2.00
158 Charles Barkley 3.00 8.00
160 Roy Rogers .75 2.00
162 Sam Cassell 1.00 2.50
164 Robert Pack .75 2.00
166 Rodney Rogers 1.00 2.50
168 Shandon Anderson .75 2.00
170 Anthony Mason 1.00 2.50
172 David Wingate .75 2.00
174 Billy Owens .75 2.00
176 Carlos Rogers .75 2.00
178 Dana Barros .75 2.00
180 Jayson Williams .75 2.00
182 Doug West .75 2.00
184 Eddie Johnson 1.00 2.50
186 Eddie Jones 1.25 3.00
188 Anthony Peeler .75 2.00
190 Stacey Augmon 1.00 2.50
192 Micheal Williams .75 2.00
194 Anfernee Hardaway 3.00 8.00
196 Nick Anderson 1.00 2.50
198 Andrew Lang .75 2.00
200 Cedric Ceballos 1.00 2.50
202 Ervin Johnson TRAN 1.00 2.50
204 David Wesley TRAN 1.00 2.50
206 Jim Jackson TRAN .75 2.00
208 Travis Knight TRAN .75 2.00
210 Bobby Phills TRAN 1.00 2.50
212 Otis Thorpe TRAN 1.00 2.50
214 Chris Mullin TRAN 1.50 4.00
216 Brian Williams TRAN 1.00 2.50
218 Tyus Edney TRAN .75 2.00
220 Clifford Robinson TRAN 1.00 2.50
222 Vin Baker TRAN 1.00 2.50
224 John Wallace TRAN .75 2.00
226 Kelvin Cato 1.00 2.50
228 Scot Pollard 1.00 2.50
230 Dean Garrett TRAN .75 2.00
232 Ron Mercer 1.50 4.00
234 Antonio McDyess TRAN 1.25 3.00
236 Terrell Brandon TRAN 1.00 2.50
238 Shawn Kemp TRAN 2.00 5.00
240 Dennis Scott TRAN 1.00 2.50
T9A Tim Hardaway 2.00 5.00
T9B Michael Jordan 15.00 40.00
T9C Anfernee Hardaway 4.00 10.00
T10A Glen Rice 1.50 4.00
T10B Scottie Pippen 4.00 10.00
T10C Grant Hill 2.50 6.00
T11A Dikembe Mutombo 2.50 6.00
T11B Patrick Ewing 2.50 6.00
T11C Alonzo Mourning 2.50 6.00
T12A Ron Mercer 1.00 2.50

T12B Keith Van Horn 1.25 3.00
T12C Tracy McGrady 4.00 10.00
T13A Gary Payton 2.50 6.00
T13B John Stockton 3.00 8.00
T13C Stephon Marbury 2.00 5.00
T14A Karl Malone 3.00 8.00
T14B Charles Barkley 4.00 10.00
T14C Kevin Garnett 4.00 10.00
T15A David Robinson 3.00 8.00
T15B Hakeem Olajuwon 3.00 8.00
T15C Shaquille O'Neal 5.00 12.00
T16A Antonio Daniels .75 2.00
T16B Tim Duncan 5.00 12.00
T16C Adonal Foyle .60 1.50
NC1 Michael Jordan 60.00 150.00
NC2 Karl Malone 3.00 8.00
NC3 Hakeem Olajuwon 3.00 8.00
NC4 Kevin Garnett 4.00 10.00
NC5 Dikembe Mutombo 2.50 6.00
NC6 Gary Payton 2.50 6.00
NC7 Grant Hill 2.50 6.00
NC8 Charles Barkley 4.00 10.00
NC9 Shaquille O'Neal 5.00 12.00
NC10 Anfernee Hardaway 4.00 10.00
NC11 Tim Duncan 5.00 12.00
NC12 Keith Van Horn 1.25 3.00
NC13 Tracy McGrady 4.00 10.00
NC14 Tim Thomas 1.00 2.50
NC15 Austin Croshere .60 1.50
NC16 Maurice Taylor .60 1.50
NC17 Chauncey Billups 2.50 6.00
NC18 Adonal Foyle .60 1.50
NC19 Tony Battie .75 2.00
NC20 Bobby Jackson 1.00 2.50
RC1 Scottie Pippen 4.00 10.00
RC2 Karl Malone 3.00 8.00
RC3 Gary Payton 2.50 6.00
RC4 Kobe Bryant 15.00 40.00
RC5 Antoine Walker 1.50 4.00
RC6 Michael Jordan 60.00 150.00
RC7 Shaquille O'Neal 5.00 12.00
RC8 Dikembe Mutombo 2.50 6.00
RC9 Hakeem Olajuwon 3.00 8.00
RC10 Grant Hill 2.50 6.00
RC11 Tim Duncan 5.00 12.00
RC12 Keith Van Horn 1.25 3.00
RC13 Chauncey Billups 2.50 6.00
RC14 Antonio Daniels .75 2.00
RC15 Tony Battie .75 2.00
RC16 Bobby Jackson 1.00 2.50
RC17 Tim Thomas 1.00 2.50
RC18 Adonal Foyle .60 1.50
RC19 Tracy McGrady 4.00 10.00
RC20 Danny Fortson .75 2.00
BBP11 Maurice Taylor .60 1.50
BBP12 Chauncey Billups 2.50 6.00
BBP13 Paul Grant .50 1.25
BBP14 Tony Battie .75 2.00
BBP15 Austin Croshere .60 1.50
BBP16 Brevin Knight .75 2.00
BBP17 Bobby Jackson 1.00 2.50
BBP18 Johnny Taylor .50 1.25
BBP19 Scot Pollard .60 1.50
BBP20 Tariq Abdul-Wahad .60 1.50

1983 Star All-Star Game

COMPLETE SET (32) 100.00 250.00
1 Julius Erving CL ! 3.00 8.00
2 Larry Bird 20.00 50.00
3 Maurice Cheeks 2.00 5.00
4 Julius Erving 5.00 12.00
5 Marques Johnson 1.25 3.00
6 Bill Laimbeer 2.50 6.00
7 Moses Malone 2.50 6.00
8 Sidney Moncrief 2.00 5.00
9 Robert Parish 2.50 6.00
10 Reggie Theus 2.50 6.00
11 Isiah Thomas 15.00 40.00
12 Andrew Toney 1.25 3.00
13 Buck Williams 1.25 3.00
14 Kareem Abdul-Jabbar 3.00 8.00
15 Alex English 2.50 6.00
16 George Gervin 2.50 6.00
17 Artis Gilmore 2.50 6.00
18 Magic Johnson 12.00 30.00
19 Maurice Lucas 1.25 3.00
20 Jim Paxson 1.25 3.00
21 Jack Sikma 1.25 3.00
22 David Thompson 2.00 5.00
23 Kiki Vandeweghe 2.50 6.00
24 Jamaal Wilkes 1.25 3.00
25 Gus Williams 1.25 3.00
26 Julius Erving MVP 4.00 10.00
27 R.Theus/M.Malone 2.50 6.00
28 All-Star ATL 1.25 3.00
29 L.Bird/R.Parish 5.00 12.00
30 Sidney Moncrief IA 1.25 3.00
xx A.Gilmore/A.English 2.50 6.00
xx Kareem Abdul-Jabbar 3.00 8.00
BAG Complete sealed bag (32) 30.00 80.00

1983-84 Star

COMPLETE SET (275) 1,500.00 3,000.00
1 Julius Erving SP ! 25.00 60.00
2 Maurice Cheeks SP 6.00 15.00
3 Franklin Edwards SP 1.50 4.00
4 Marc Iavaroni SP 2.50 6.00
5 Clemon Johnson SP 2.00 5.00
6 Bobby Jones SP 8.00 20.00
7 Moses Malone SP 8.00 20.00
8 Leo Rautins SP 1.50 4.00
9 Clint Richardson SP 1.50 4.00
10 Sedale Threatt SP XRC 4.00 10.00
11 Andrew Toney SP XRC 6.00 15.00
12 Sam Williams SP 1.50 4.00
13 Magic Johnson SP ! 40.00 100.00
14 Kareem Abdul-Jabbar SP 25.00 60.00
15 Michael Cooper SP 10.00 25.00
16 Calvin Garrett SP 1.50 4.00
17 Mitch Kupchak SP 2.50 6.00
18 Bob McAdoo SP 5.00 12.00
19 Mike McGee SP 1.50 4.00
20 Swen Nater SP 1.50 4.00
21 Kurt Rambis SP XRC 15.00 40.00
22 Byron Scott SP XRC 12.00 30.00
23 Larry Spriggs SP 1.50 4.00
24 Jamaal Wilkes SP 5.00 12.00
25 James Worthy SP XRC 50.00 120.00
26 Larry Bird SP ! 125.00 300.00
27 Danny Ainge SP XRC 20.00 50.00
28 Quinn Buckner SP 4.00 10.00
29 M.L. Carr SP 4.00 10.00
30 Carlos Clark SP 4.00 10.00
31 Gerald Henderson SP 8.00 20.00
32 Dennis Johnson SP 12.00 30.00
33 Cedric Maxwell SP 8.00 20.00
34 Kevin McHale SP ! 20.00 50.00
35 Robert Parish SP ! 10.00 25.00
36 Scott Wedman SP 4.00 10.00
37 Greg Kite SP XRC 4.00 10.00
38 Sidney Moncrief SP 5.00 12.00
39A Sidney Moncrief SP 8.00 20.00
39B Nate Archibald SP 6.00 15.00
40 Randy Breuer SP XRC 2.00 5.00
41 Junior Bridgeman SP 1.50 4.00
42 Harvey Catchings SP 4.00 10.00
43 Kevin Grevey SP 1.50 4.00
44A Marques Johnson SP UER
Bob Lanier pictured 4.00 10.00
44B Marques Johnson SP 4.00 10.00
45 Bob Lanier SP 6.00 15.00
46 Alton Lister SP XRC 1.50 4.00
47 Paul Mokeski SP XRC 1.50 4.00
48 Paul Pressey SP XRC 1.50 4.00
49 Mark Aguirre SP XRC 60.00 150.00
50 Rolando Blackman SP XRC 25.00 60.00
51 Pat Cummings SP 40.00 100.00
52 Brad Davis SP XRC 40.00 100.00
53 Dale Ellis SP XRC 25.00 60.00
54 Bill Garnett SP 12.00 30.00
55 Derek Harper SP XRC 25.00 60.00
56 Kurt Nimphius SP 12.00 30.00
57 Jim Spanarkel SP 12.00 30.00
58 Elston Turner SP 6.00 15.00
59 Jay Vincent SP XRC 15.00 40.00
60 Mark West SP XRC 8.00 20.00
61 Bernard King 8.00 20.00
62 Bill Cartwright 2.50 6.00
63 Len Elmore 1.25 3.00
64 Eric Fernsten 1.25 3.00
65 Ernie Grunfeld 1.25 3.00
66 Louis Orr 1.25 3.00
67 Leonard Robinson 1.25 3.00
68 Rory Sparrow XRC 1.50 4.00
69 Trent Tucker XRC 1.50 4.00
70 Darrell Walker XRC 1.50 4.00
71 Marvin Webster 1.25 3.00
72 Ray Williams 1.25 3.00
73 Ralph Sampson XRC 5.00 12.00
74 James Bailey 1.25 3.00
75 Phil Ford 1.25 3.00
76 Elvin Hayes 4.00 10.00
77 Caldwell Jones 1.25 3.00
78 Major Jones 1.25 3.00
79 Allen Leavell 1.25 3.00
80 Lewis Lloyd 1.25 3.00
81 Rodney McCray XRC 4.00 10.00
82 Robert Reid 1.50 4.00
83 Terry Teagle XRC 4.00 10.00
84 Wally Walker 1.25 3.00
85 Kelly Tripucka XRC 1.50 4.00
86 Kent Benson 1.25 3.00
87 Earl Cureton 1.25 3.00
88 Lionel Hollins 1.25 3.00
89 Vinnie Johnson 1.50 4.00
90 Bill Laimbeer 2.50 6.00
91 Cliff Levingston XRC 1.50 4.00
92 John Long 1.25 3.00
93 David Thirdkill 1.25 3.00
94 Isiah Thomas XRC 125.00 300.00
95 Ray Tolbert 2.00 5.00
96 Terry Tyler 2.00 5.00
97 Jim Paxson 6.00 15.00
98 Kenny Carr 1.25 3.00
99 Wayne Cooper 1.25 3.00
100 Clyde Drexler XRC 200.00 500.00
101 Jeff Lamp XRC 2.50 6.00
102 Lafayette Lever XRC 6.00 15.00
103 Calvin Natt 1.25 3.00
104 Audie Norris 1.25 3.00
105 Tom Piotrowski 1.25 3.00
106 Mychal Thompson 1.25 3.00
107 Darnell Valentine XRC 1.50 4.00
108 Pete Verhoeven 1.25 3.00
109 Walter Davis 2.50 6.00
110 Alvan Adams 4.00 10.00
111 James Edwards 1.50 4.00
112 Rod Foster XRC 1.50 4.00
113 Maurice Lucas 1.50 4.00
114 Kyle Macy 1.50 4.00
115 Larry Nance XRC 12.00 30.00
116 Charles Pittman 1.25 3.00
117 Rick Robey 1.25 3.00
118 Mike Sanders XRC 1.50 4.00
119 Alvin Scott 1.25 3.00
120 Paul Westphal 2.50 6.00
121 Bill Walton 6.00 15.00
122 Michael Brooks 1.25 3.00
123 Terry Cummings XRC 6.00 15.00
124 James Donaldson XRC 1.50 4.00
125 Craig Hodges XRC 1.50 4.00
126 Greg Kelser XRC 1.50 4.00
127 Hank McDowell 1.25 3.00
128 Billy McKinney 1.25 3.00
129 Norm Nixon 1.25 3.00
130 Ricky Pierce UER XRC 2.50 6.00
131 Derek Smith XRC 1.50 4.00
132 Jerome Whitehead 2.50 6.00
133 Adrian Dantley 5.00 12.00
134 Mitchell Anderson 1.25 3.00
135 Thurl Bailey XRC 2.50 6.00
136 Tom Boswell 1.25 3.00
137 John Drew 1.25 3.00
138 Mark Eaton XRC 10.00 25.00
139 Jerry Eaves 1.25 3.00
140 Rickey Green XRC 1.50 4.00
141 Darrell Griffith 1.25 3.00
142 Bobby Hansen XRC 1.50 4.00
143 Rich Kelley 1.25 3.00
144 Jeff Wilkins 1.25 3.00
145 Buck Williams XRC 10.00 25.00
146 Otis Birdsong 1.25 3.00
147 Darwin Cook 1.25 3.00
148 Darryl Dawkins 4.00 10.00
149 Mike Gminski 1.25 3.00
150 Reggie Johnson 1.25 3.00
151 Albert King XRC 1.50 4.00
152 Mike O'Koren 1.25 3.00
153 Kelvin Ransey 1.25 3.00
154 Micheal Ray Richardson 1.25 3.00
155 Clarence Walker 4.00 10.00
156 Bill Willoughby 1.25 3.00
157 Steve Stipanovich XRC 1.50 4.00
158 Butch Carter 1.25 3.00
159 Edwin Leroy Combs 1.25 3.00
160 George L. Johnson 1.25 3.00
161 Clark Kellogg XRC 2.50 6.00
162 Sidney Lowe XRC 3.00 8.00
163 Kevin McKenna 1.25 3.00
164 Jerry Sichting XRC 1.50 4.00
165 Brook Steppe 1.25 3.00
166 Jimmy Thomas 1.25 3.00
167 Granville Waiters 1.25 3.00
168 Herb Williams XRC 1.50 4.00
169 Tom Sluby 1.25 3.00
170 Wallace Bryant 1.25 3.00
171 Quintin Dailey XRC 1.50 4.00
172 Sidney Green XRC 1.50 4.00
173 David Greenwood 1.25 3.00
174 Rod Higgins XRC 1.50 4.00
175 Clarence Johnson 5.00 12.00
176 Ronnie Lester 2.50 6.00
177 Jawann Oldham 1.25 3.00
178 Ennis Whatley XRC 4.00 10.00
179 Mitchell Wiggins XRC 1.50 4.00
180 Orlando Woolridge XRC 10.00 25.00
181 Kiki Vandeweghe XRC 6.00 15.00
182 Richard Anderson 1.25 3.00
183 Howard Carter 1.25 3.00
184 T.R. Dunn 1.25 3.00
185 Keith Edmonson 1.25 3.00
186 Alex English 5.00 12.00
187 Mike Evans 1.25 3.00
188 Bill Hanzlik XRC 1.50 4.00
189 Dan Issel 5.00 12.00
190 Anthony Roberts 1.25 3.00
191 Danny Schayes XRC 3.00 8.00
192 Rob Williams 1.25 3.00
193 Jack Sikma 5.00 12.00
194 Fred Brown 2.00 5.00
195 Tom Chambers XRC 12.00 30.00
196 Steve Hawes 1.25 3.00
197 Steve Hayes 2.50 6.00
198 Reggie King 1.25 3.00
199 Scooter McCray 1.25 3.00
200 Jon Sundvold XRC 8.00 20.00
201 Danny Vranes 1.25 3.00
202 Gus Williams 4.00 10.00
203 Al Wood 1.25 3.00
204 Jeff Ruland XRC 1.50 4.00
205 Greg Ballard 1.25 3.00
206 Charles Davis 1.25 3.00
207 Darren Daye 1.25 3.00
208 Michael Gibson 1.25 3.00
209 Frank Johnson XRC 2.50 6.00
210 Joe Kopicki 1.25 3.00
211 Rick Mahorn 1.50 4.00
212 Jeff Malone XRC 2.50 6.00
213 Tom McMillen 1.25 3.00
214 Ricky Sobers 1.25 3.00
215 Bryan Warrick 1.25 3.00
216 Billy Knight 1.25 3.00
217 Don Buse 2.50 6.00
218 Larry Drew XRC 1.50 4.00
219 Eddie Johnson XRC 4.00 10.00
220 Joe Meriweather 1.25 3.00
221 Larry Micheaux 1.25 3.00
222 Ed Nealy XRC 3.00 8.00
223 Mark Olberding 2.00 5.00
224 Dave Robisch 2.00 5.00
225 Reggie Theus 2.50 6.00
226 LaSalle Thompson XRC 1.50 4.00
227 Mike Woodson 1.25 3.00
228 World B. Free 2.00 5.00
229 John Bagley XRC 1.50 4.00
230 Jeff Cook 1.25 3.00
231 Geoff Crompton 1.25 3.00
232 John Garris 1.25 3.00
233 Stewart Granger 1.25 3.00
234 Roy Hinson XRC 1.50 4.00
235 Phil Hubbard 1.25 3.00
236 Geoff Huston 1.25 3.00
237 Ben Poquette 1.25 3.00
238 Cliff Robinson 2.00 5.00
239 Lonnie Shelton 1.25 3.00
240 Paul Thompson 1.25 3.00
241 George Gervin 8.00 20.00
242 Gene Banks 3.00 8.00
243 Ron Brewer 1.25 3.00
244 Artis Gilmore 4.00 10.00
245 Edgar Jones 1.25 3.00
246 John Lucas 2.00 5.00
247A Mike Mitchell ERR 1.25 3.00
247B Mike Mitchell ERR 2.50 6.00
248A M.McNamara ERR XRC 1.50 4.00
248B M.McNamara ERR XRC 2.50 6.00
249 Johnny Moore 2.00 5.00
250 John Paxson XRC 8.00 20.00
251 Fred Roberts XRC 1.50 4.00
252 Joe Barry Carroll 1.25 3.00
253 Mike Bratz 3.00 8.00
254 Don Collins 1.25 3.00
255 Lester Conner 1.25 3.00
256 Chris Engler 3.00 8.00
257 Sleepy Floyd XRC 4.00 10.00
258 Wallace Johnson 1.25 3.00
259 Pace Mannion 1.25 3.00
260 Purvis Short 1.25 3.00
261 Larry Smith 1.25 3.00
262 Darren Tillis 1.25 3.00
263 Dominique Wilkins XRC 300.00 600.00
264 Rickey Brown 1.25 3.00
265 Johnny Davis 1.25 3.00
266 Mike Glenn XRC 1.50 4.00
267 Scott Hastings XRC 1.50 4.00
268 Eddie Johnson 1.25 3.00
269 Mark Landsberger 2.50 6.00
270 Billy Paultz 2.50 6.00
271 Doc Rivers XRC 12.00 30.00
272 Tree Rollins 1.50 4.00
273 Dan Roundfield 1.25 3.00
274 Sly Williams 1.25 3.00
275 Randy Wittman XRC 1.50 4.00
BAG1 76ers sealed bag (12) 400.00 800.00
BAG2 Blazers sealed bag (12) 500.00 1,000.00
BAG3 Bucks sealed bag (11) 125.00 300.00
BAG4 Bullets sealed bag (12) 100.00 250.00
BAG5 Bulls sealed bag (12) 60.00 150.00
BAG6 Cavs sealed bag (13) 40.00 100.00
BAG7 Celtics sealed bag (12) 1,000.00 2,000.00
BAG8 Clippers sealed bag (12) 50.00 120.00
BAG9 Hawks sealed bag (14) 1,000.00 2,000.00
BAG10 Jazz sealed bag (12) 125.00 300.00
BAG11 Kings sealed bag (12) 125.00 300.00
BAG12 Knicks sealed bag (12) 125.00 300.00
BAG13 Lakers sealed bag (13) 500.00 1,000.00
BAG14 Mavs sealed bag (12) 200.00 500.00
BAG15 Nets sealed bag (12) 75.00 200.00
BAG16 Nuggets sealed bag (12) 75.00 200.00
BAG17 Pacers sealed bag (12) 75.00 200.00
BAG18 Pistons sealed bag (12) 500.00 1,000.00
BAG19 Rockets sealed bag (12) 30.00 80.00
BAG20 Sonics sealed bag (11) 75.00 200.00
BAG21 Spurs sealed bag (11) 40.00 100.00
BAG22 Suns sealed bag (12) 100.00 250.00
BAG23 Warriors sealed bag (11) 50.00 120.00

1983-84 Star All-Rookies

COMPLETE SET (10) 30.00 80.00
1 Terry Cummings 4.00 10.00
2 Quintin Dailey 2.00 5.00
3 Rod Higgins 2.00 5.00
4 Clark Kellogg 2.50 6.00
5 Lafayette Lever 2.50 6.00
6 Paul Pressey 2.50 6.00
7 Trent Tucker 2.00 5.00
8 Dominique Wilkins ! 25.00 60.00
9 Rob Williams 1.25 3.00
10 James Worthy 12.00 30.00
BAG Complete sealed bag (10) 75.00 200.00

1983-84 Star Sixers Champs

COMPLETE SET (25) 30.00 80.00
1 Moses Malone CL 5.00 12.00
2 Billy Cunningham CO 2.00 5.00
3 M.Malone/Abdul-Jabbar 8.00 20.00
4 Julius Erving IA 8.00 20.00
5 Clint Richardson IA 1.50 4.00
6 Andrew Toney IA 3.00 8.00
7 Phila. 113, LA 107
Game 1 Boxscore 2.00 5.00
8 Bobby Jones IA 3.00 8.00
9 Maurice Cheeks IA 2.00 5.00
10 Julius Erving IA 12.00 30.00
11 Andrew Toney IA 2.00 5.00
12 Phila. 103, LA 93
Game 2 Boxscore 1.50 4.00
13 Serious Sixers 2.50 6.00
14 Moses Malone IA 5.00 12.00
15 Clemon Johnson IA 1.50 4.00
16 Maurice Cheeks IA 2.00 5.00
17 Phila. 111, LA 94
Game 3 Boxscore 2.00 5.00
18 Julius Erving IA 8.00 20.00
19 Bobby Jones 6M 2.00 5.00
20 Moses Malone IA 5.00 12.00
21 World Champs 2.50 6.00
22 Julius Erving COMM 8.00 20.00
23 Moses Malone COMM 5.00 12.00
24 Julius Erving COMM 8.00 20.00
25 Moses Malone MVP 5.00 12.00
BAG Complete sealed bag (25) 50.00 120.00

1984 Star All-Star Game

COMPLETE SET (25) 30.00 80.00
1 Isiah Thomas CL 4.00 10.00
2 Larry Bird 12.00 30.00
3 Otis Birdsong .75 2.00
4 Julius Erving 8.00 20.00
5 Bernard King 1.25 3.00
6 Bill Laimbeer 2.50 6.00
7 Kevin McHale 3.00 8.00
8 Sidney Moncrief 2.00 5.00
9 Robert Parish 1.25 3.00
10 Jeff Ruland 1.00 2.50
11 Isiah Thomas 5.00 12.00
12 Andrew Toney 1.00 2.50
13 Kelly Tripucka 1.00 2.50
14 Kareem Abdul-Jabbar 8.00 20.00
15 Mark Aguirre .75 2.00
16 Adrian Dantley 1.25 3.00
17 Walter Davis .75 2.00
18 Alex English 1.50 4.00
19 George Gervin 2.50 6.00
20 Rickey Green .75 2.00
21 Magic Johnson 12.00 30.00
22 Jim Paxson 1.25 3.00
23 Ralph Sampson 1.50 4.00
24 Jack Sikma 2.00 5.00
25 Kiki Vandeweghe 1.50 4.00
BAG Complete sealed bag (25) 125.00 300.00

1984 Star All-Star Game Denver Police

COMPLETE SET (34) 75.00 200.00
1 Isiah Thomas CL 3.00 8.00
2 Larry Bird 20.00 50.00
3 Otis Birdsong 2.00 5.00
4 Julius Erving 12.00 30.00
5 Bernard King 2.50 6.00
6 Bill Laimbeer 2.50 6.00
7 Kevin McHale 4.00 10.00
8 Sidney Moncrief 2.50 6.00
9 Robert Parish 5.00 12.00
10 Jeff Ruland 1.25 3.00
11 Isiah Thomas w/Magic 10.00 25.00
12 Andrew Toney 2.00 5.00
13 Kelly Tripucka 2.00 5.00
14 Kareem Abdul-Jabbar 12.00 30.00
15 Mark Aguirre 2.00 5.00
16 Adrian Dantley 2.00 5.00
17 Walter Davis 2.00 5.00
18 Alex English 2.50 6.00
19 George Gervin 4.00 10.00
20 Rickey Green 1.25 3.00
21 Magic Johnson 15.00 40.00
22 Jim Paxson 2.50 6.00
23 Ralph Sampson 2.00 5.00
24 Jack Sikma 2.50 6.00
25 Kiki Vandeweghe 2.00 5.00
26 Michael Cooper SD 6.00 15.00
27 Clyde Drexler SD 12.00 30.00
28 Julius Erving SD 12.00 30.00
29 Darrell Griffith SD 2.50 6.00
30 Edgar Jones SD 2.00 5.00
31 Larry Nance SD 4.00 10.00
32 Ralph Sampson SD 4.00 10.00
33 Dominique Wilkins SD 20.00 50.00
34 Orlando Woolridge SD 4.00 10.00

1984 Star Award Banquet

COMPLETE SET (24) 60.00 150.00
1 1984 Award Winners .75 2.00
2 Frank Layden CO .75 2.00
3 Ralph Sampson ROY .75 2.00
4 Adrian Dantley POY .75 2.00
5 Kevin McHale 6M 1.25 3.00
6 Magic Johnson POY 5.00 12.00
7 Sidney Moncrief DEF .75 2.00
8 Larry Bird MVP 6.00 15.00
9 Larry Nance SD 1.25 3.00
10 Bird/Griff/Gilm/Dant LL 4.00 10.00
11 Magic/Green/Eat/Moses LL 3.00 8.00
12 Isiah Thomas AS MVP 2.50 6.00
13 Adrian Dantley LL .75 2.00
14 Artis Gilmore LL .75 2.00
15 Larry Bird LL 6.00 15.00
16 Darrell Griffith LL .75 2.00
17 Magic Johnson LL 5.00 12.00
18 Rickey Green LL .75 2.00
19 Mark Eaton LL .75 2.00
20 Moses Malone LL 1.25 3.00
21 Abdul-Jabbar w/D.Stern 4.00 10.00
22 All-Defensive Team 1.25 3.00
23 All-Rookie Team 1.25 3.00
24 All-NBA Team 6.00 15.00
BAG Complete sealed bag (24) 125.00 300.00

1984 Star Larry Bird

COMPLETE SET (18) 125.00 300.00
COMMON L.BIRD (1-18) 8.00 20.00
BAG Complete sealed bag (18) 125.00 300.00

1984 Star Celtics Champs

COMPLETE SET (25) 100.00 200.00
1 Auerbach/B.Musburger CL 6.00 15.00
2 Abdul-Jabbar/Parish IA 6.00 15.00
3 Kevin McHale IA 5.00 12.00
4 Larry Bird IA 12.00 30.00
5 Magic Johnson IA 10.00 25.00
6 D.Ainge/K.C.Jones 3.00 8.00
7 Larry Bird IA 10.00 25.00
8 Abdul-Jabbar/McHale IA 6.00 15.00
9 James Worthy IA 4.00 10.00
10 Magic Johnson IA 10.00 25.00
11 Magic/Bird IA 25.00 50.00
12 Worthy/Ainge IA 5.00 12.00
13 Boston 129& LA 125 .75 2.00
14 Larry Bird IA 12.00 30.00
15 Pat Riley CO IA 3.00 8.00
16 Kareem Abdul-Jabbar 8.00 20.00
17 Robert Parish IA 1.25 3.00
18 Kareem Abdul-Jabbar IA 8.00 20.00
19 Dennis Johnson IA 3.00 8.00
20 Kareem Abdul-Jabbar IA 8.00 20.00
21 K.C. Jones CO 1.25 3.00
22 M.L. Carr IA .75 2.00
23 Red Auerbach ! 3.00 8.00
24 Larry Bird MVP ! 15.00 40.00
25 Boston Garden ! 4.00 10.00
BAG Complete sealed bag (25) 100.00 250.00

1984 Star Slam Dunk

COMPLETE SET (11) 60.00 150.00
1 Group Photo CL 12.00 30.00
2 Michael Cooper 3.00 8.00
3 Clyde Drexler 12.00 30.00
4 Julius Erving 8.00 20.00
5 Darrell Griffith 2.00 5.00
6 Edgar Jones .75 2.00
7 Larry Nance 3.00 8.00
8 Ralph Sampson 2.50 6.00
9 Dominique Wilkins UER 25.00 60.00
10 Orlando Woolridge 2.00 5.00
11 Larry Nance Champion 3.00 8.00
BAG Complete sealed bag (11) 100.00 250.00

1984-85 Star

COMPLETE SET (288) 20,000.00 40,000.00
CONDITION SENSITIVE SET
BEWARE JORDAN COUNTERFEITS
1 Larry Bird 60.00 150.00
2 Danny Ainge 6.00 15.00
3 Quinn Buckner 2.00 5.00
4 Rick Carlisle 10.00 25.00
5 M.L. Carr 2.00 5.00
6 Dennis Johnson 4.00 10.00
7 Greg Kite 2.00 5.00
8 Cedric Maxwell 6.00 15.00
9 Kevin McHale 8.00 20.00
10 Robert Parish 6.00 15.00
11 Scott Wedman 2.00 5.00
12 Larry Bird MVP ! 20.00 50.00
13 Marques Johnson 2.00 5.00
14 Junior Bridgeman 2.00 5.00
15 Michael Cage XRC 4.00 10.00
16 Harvey Catchings 2.00 5.00
17 James Donaldson 2.00 5.00
18 Lancaster Gordon 2.00 5.00
19 Jay Murphy 2.00 5.00
20 Norm Nixon 2.00 5.00
21 Derek Smith 2.00 5.00
22 Bill Walton 10.00 25.00
23 Bryan Warrick 2.00 5.00
24 Rory White 2.00 5.00
25 Bernard King 8.00 20.00
26 James Bailey 2.00 5.00
27 Ken Bannister 2.00 5.00
28 Butch Carter 2.00 5.00
29 Bill Cartwright 2.50 6.00
30 Pat Cummings 2.00 5.00
31 Ernie Grunfeld 2.00 5.00
32 Louis Orr 2.00 5.00
33 Leonard Robinson 2.00 5.00
34 Rory Sparrow 2.00 5.00
35 Trent Tucker 2.00 5.00
36 Darrell Walker 2.00 5.00
37 Eddie Lee Wilkins XRC 2.00 5.00
38 Alvan Adams 2.00 5.00
39 Walter Davis 2.00 5.00
40 James Edwards 2.00 5.00
41 Rod Foster 2.00 5.00
42 Michael Holton 2.00 5.00
43 Jay Humphries XRC 2.00 5.00
44 Charles Jones 2.00 5.00
45 Maurice Lucas 2.00 5.00
46 Kyle Macy 4.00 10.00
47 Larry Nance 6.00 15.00
48 Charles Pittman 2.00 5.00
49 Rick Robey 2.00 5.00
50 Mike Sanders 2.00 5.00
51 Alvin Scott 2.00 5.00
52 Clark Kellogg 2.00 5.00
53 Tony Brown 2.00 5.00
54 Devin Durrant 2.00 5.00
55 Vern Fleming XRC 2.00 5.00
56 Bill Garnett 2.00 5.00
57 Stuart Gray UER 2.00 5.00
58 Jerry Sichting 2.00 5.00
59 Terence Stansbury 2.00 5.00
60 Steve Stipanovich 2.00 5.00
61 Jimmy Thomas 2.00 5.00
62 Granville Waiters 2.00 5.00
63 Herb Williams 2.50 6.00
64 Artis Gilmore 5.00 12.00
65 Gene Banks 2.00 5.00
66 Ron Brewer 2.00 5.00
67 George Gervin 10.00 25.00
68 Edgar Jones 2.00 5.00
69 Ozell Jones 2.00 5.00
70 Mark McNamara 2.00 5.00
71 Mike Mitchell 2.00 5.00
72 Johnny Moore 2.00 5.00
73 John Paxson 4.00 10.00
74 Fred Roberts 4.00 10.00
75 Alvin Robertson XRC 4.00 10.00
76 Dominique Wilkins 60.00 150.00
77 Rickey Brown 2.00 5.00
78 Antoine Carr XRC 2.00 5.00
79 Mike Glenn 2.00 5.00
80 Scott Hastings 2.00 5.00
81 Eddie Johnson 2.00 5.00
82 Cliff Levingston 2.00 5.00
83 Leo Rautins 2.00 5.00
84 Doc Rivers 4.00 10.00
85 Tree Rollins 2.00 5.00
86 Randy Wittman 2.00 5.00
87 Sly Williams 2.00 5.00
88 Darryl Dawkins 2.00 5.00
89 Otis Birdsong 2.00 5.00
90 Darwin Cook 2.00 5.00
91 Mike Gminski 2.00 5.00
92 George L. Johnson 2.00 5.00
93 Albert King 2.00 5.00
94 Mike O'Koren 2.00 5.00
95 Kelvin Ransey 2.00 5.00
96 M.R. Richardson 2.00 5.00
97 Wayne Sappleton 2.00 5.00
98 Jeff Turner XRC 2.00 5.00
99 Buck Williams 4.00 10.00
100 Michael Wilson 3.00 8.00
101 Michael Jordan XRC 20,000.00 40,000.00
102 Dave Corzine 5.00 12.00
103 Quintin Dailey 5.00 12.00
104 Sidney Green 5.00 12.00
105 David Greenwood 2.00 5.00
106 Rod Higgins 5.00 12.00
107 Steve Johnson XRC 2.00 5.00
108 Caldwell Jones 2.50 6.00
109 Wes Matthews 2.00 5.00
110 Jawann Oldham 2.50 6.00
111 Ennis Whatley 2.00 5.00
112 Orlando Woolridge 6.00 15.00
113 Tom Chambers 6.00 15.00
114 Cory Blackwell 2.00 5.00
115 Frank Brickowski XRC 8.00 20.00
116 Gerald Henderson 2.00 5.00
117 Reggie King 2.00 5.00
118 Tim McCormick XRC 2.00 5.00
119 John Schweitz 2.00 5.00
120 Jack Sikma 4.00 10.00
121 Ricky Sobers 2.00 5.00
122 Jon Sundvold 2.00 5.00
123 Danny Vranes 2.00 5.00
124 Al Wood 2.00 5.00
125 Terry Cummings UER 4.00 10.00
126 Randy Breuer 2.00 5.00
127 Charles Davis 2.00 5.00
128 Mike Dunleavy 2.50 6.00
129 Kenny Fields 2.00 5.00
130 Kevin Grevey 2.00 5.00
131 Craig Hodges 2.00 5.00
132 Alton Lister 2.00 5.00
133 Larry Micheaux 2.00 5.00
134 Paul Mokeski 2.00 5.00
135 Sidney Moncrief 4.00 10.00
136 Paul Pressey 2.00 5.00
137 Alex English 4.00 10.00
138 Wayne Cooper 2.00 5.00
139 T.R. Dunn 2.00 5.00
140 Mike Evans 2.00 5.00
141 Bill Hanzlik 2.00 5.00
142 Dan Issel 6.00 15.00
143 Joe Kopicki 2.00 5.00
144 Lafayette Lever 4.00 10.00
145 Calvin Natt 2.00 5.00
146 Danny Schayes 2.00 5.00
147 Elston Turner 2.00 5.00
148 Willie White 2.00 5.00
149 Purvis Short 2.00 5.00
150 Chuck Aleksinas 2.00 5.00
151 Mike Bratz 2.00 5.00
152 Steve Burtt 2.00 5.00
153 Lester Conner 2.00 5.00
154 Sleepy Floyd 4.00 10.00
155 Mickey Johnson 2.00 5.00
156 Gary Plummer 2.00 5.00
157 Larry Smith 2.00 5.00
158 Peter Thibeaux 2.00 5.00
159 Jerome Whitehead 2.00 5.00
160 Othell Wilson 2.00 5.00
161 Kiki Vandeweghe 4.00 10.00
162 Sam Bowie XRC 4.00 10.00
163 Kenny Carr 3.00 8.00
164 Steve Colter 2.00 5.00
165 Clyde Drexler ! 30.00 80.00
166 Audie Norris 2.00 5.00
167 Jim Paxson 2.00 5.00
168 Tom Scheffler 2.00 5.00
169 Bernard Thompson 2.00 5.00
170 Mychal Thompson 2.00 5.00
171 Darnell Valentine 2.00 5.00
172 Magic Johnson ! 50.00 120.00
173 Kareem Abdul-Jabbar 20.00 50.00
174 Michael Cooper 4.00 10.00
175 Earl Jones 2.00 5.00
176 Mitch Kupchak 2.00 5.00
177 Ronnie Lester 2.50 6.00
178 Bob McAdoo 4.00 10.00
179 Mike McGee 2.00 5.00
180 Kurt Rambis 4.00 10.00
181 Byron Scott 4.00 10.00
182 Larry Spriggs 2.00 5.00
183 Jamaal Wilkes 4.00 10.00
184 James Worthy 12.00 30.00
185 Gus Williams 2.00 5.00
186 Greg Ballard 2.00 5.00
187 Dudley Bradley 2.00 5.00
188 Darren Daye 2.00 5.00
189 Frank Johnson 2.00 5.00
190 Charles Jones XRC 2.00 5.00
191 Rick Mahorn 2.00 5.00
192 Jeff Malone 2.00 5.00
193 Tom McMillen 2.50 6.00
194 Jeff Ruland 2.00 5.00
195 Michael Jordan OLY ! 2,500.00 5,000.00
196 Vern Fleming OLY 2.00 5.00
197 Sam Perkins OLY 4.00 10.00
198 Alvin Robertson OLY 2.00 5.00
199 Jeff Turner OLY 2.00 5.00
200 Leon Wood OLY 2.00 5.00
201 Moses Malone 10.00 25.00
202 Charles Barkley XRC 300.00 600.00
203 Maurice Cheeks 4.00 10.00
204 Julius Erving 20.00 50.00
205 Clemon Johnson 2.00 5.00
206 George L. Johnson 2.00 5.00
207 Bobby Jones 8.00 20.00
208 Clint Richardson 2.00 5.00
209 Sedale Threatt 2.00 5.00
210 Andrew Toney 2.00 5.00
211 Sam Williams 2.00 5.00
212 Leon Wood XRC 2.00 5.00
213 Mel Turpin XRC 2.00 5.00
214 Ron Anderson XRC 2.00 5.00
215 John Bagley 2.00 5.00
216 Johnny Davis 2.00 5.00
217 World B. Free 2.00 5.00
218 Roy Hinson 2.00 5.00
219 Phil Hubbard 2.00 5.00
220 Edgar Jones 2.00 5.00
221 Ben Poquette 2.00 5.00
222 Lonnie Shelton 2.00 5.00
223 Mark West 2.00 5.00
224 Kevin Williams 2.00 5.00
225 Mark Eaton 2.00 5.00
226 Mitchell Anderson 2.00 5.00
227 Thurl Bailey 2.00 5.00
228 Adrian Dantley 4.00 10.00
229 Rickey Green 2.00 5.00
230 Darrell Griffith 4.00 10.00
231 Rich Kelley 2.00 5.00
232 Pace Mannion 2.00 5.00
233 Billy Paultz 2.00 5.00
234 Fred Roberts 2.00 5.00
235 John Stockton XRC 300.00 600.00
236 Jeff Wilkins 2.00 5.00
237 Hakeem Olajuwon XRC ! 600.00 1,200.00
238 Craig Ehlo XRC 6.00 15.00
239 Lionel Hollins 2.00 5.00
240 Allen Leavell 2.00 5.00
241 Lewis Lloyd 2.00 5.00
242 John Lucas 2.00 5.00
243 Rodney McCray 2.00 5.00
244 Hank McDowell 2.00 5.00
245 Larry Micheaux 2.00 5.00
246 Jim Petersen XRC 2.00 5.00
247 Robert Reid 2.00 5.00
248 Ralph Sampson 6.00 15.00
249 Mitchell Wiggins 2.00 5.00
250 Mark Aguirre 2.00 5.00
251 Rolando Blackman 2.00 5.00
252 Wallace Bryant 2.00 5.00
253 Brad Davis 2.00 5.00
254 Dale Ellis 2.00 5.00
255 Derek Harper 2.00 5.00
256 Kurt Nimphius 2.00 5.00
257 Sam Perkins XRC 6.00 15.00
258 Charlie Sitton 2.00 5.00
259 Tom Sluby 2.00 5.00
260 Jay Vincent 2.00 5.00
261 Isiah Thomas 30.00 80.00
262 Kent Benson 2.00 5.00
263 Earl Cureton 2.00 5.00
264 Vinnie Johnson 2.00 5.00
265 Bill Laimbeer 4.00 10.00
266 John Long 2.00 5.00
267 Dan Roundfield 2.00 5.00
268 Kelly Tripucka 2.00 5.00
269 Terry Tyler 2.00 5.00
270 Reggie Theus 2.00 5.00
271 Don Buse 2.00 5.00
272 Larry Drew 2.00 5.00
273 Eddie Johnson 2.50 6.00
274 Billy Knight 2.00 5.00
275 Joe Meriweather 2.00 5.00
276 Mark Olberding 2.00 5.00
277 LaSalle Thompson 2.00 5.00
278 Otis Thorpe XRC 8.00 20.00
279 Pete Verhoeven 2.00 5.00
280 Mike Woodson 2.00 5.00
281 Julius Erving SPEC ! 30.00 80.00
282 K.Abdul-Jabbar SPEC ! 30.00 80.00
283 Dan Issel SPEC ! 6.00 15.00
284 Bernard King SPEC ! 6.00 15.00
285 Moses Malone SPEC ! 8.00 20.00
286 Mark Eaton SPEC ! 4.00 10.00
287 Isiah Thomas SPEC ! 25.00 60.00
288 Michael Jordan SPEC ! 2,500.00 5,000.00
BAG1 76ers sealed bag (12) 1,000.00 2,000.00
BAG2 Blazers sealed bag (11) 100.00 250.00
BAG3 Bucks sealed bag (12) 60.00 150.00
BAG4 Bullets sealed bag (10) 40.00 100.00
BAG5 Bulls sealed bag (12) 20,000.00 40,000.00
BAG6 Cavs sealed bag (12) 40.00 100.00
BAG7 Celtics sealed bag (12) 300.00 600.00

BAG8 Clippers sealed bag (12) 40.00 100.00
BAG9 Hawks sealed bag (12) 125.00 300.00
BAG10 Jazz sealed bag (12) 400.00 800.00
BAG11 Kings sealed bag (11) 60.00 150.00
BAG12 Knicks sealed bag (13) 50.00 120.00
BAG13 Lakers sealed bag (13) 300.00 600.00
BAG14 Mavs sealed bag (11) 15.00 40.00
BAG15 Nets sealed bag (13) 30.00 80.00
BAG16 Nuggets sealed bag (12) 30.00 80.00
BAG17 Pacers sealed bag (12) 40.00 100.00
BAG18 Pistons sealed bag (9) 150.00 400.00
BAG19 Rockets sealed bag (13) 1,000.00 2,000.00
BAG20 Sonics sealed bag (12) 100.00 250.00
BAG21 Spurs sealed bag (12) 40.00 100.00
BAG22 Suns sealed bag (14) 60.00 150.00
BAG23 Warriors sealed bag (12) 50.00 120.00
BAG24 Olympic sealed bag (14) 1,000.00 2,000.00

1984-85 Star Arena

COMPLETE SET (48) 125.00 300.00
COMPLETE SET (49) w/Lanier 250.00 500.00
1 Larry Bird 20.00 50.00
2 Danny Ainge 4.00 10.00
3 Rick Carlisle 8.00 20.00
4 Dennis Johnson 6.00 15.00
5 Cedric Maxwell 4.00 10.00
6 Kevin McHale 6.00 15.00
7 Robert Parish 6.00 15.00
8 Scott Wedman 1.50 4.00
9 Parr/Bird/McHa/Coaches 15.00 40.00
1 Mark Aguirre UER 2.00 5.00
2 Rolando Blackman 1.50 4.00
3 Brad Davis 1.00 2.50
4 Dale Ellis 2.00 5.00
5 Bill Garnett 1.50 4.00
6 Derek Harper UER 1.50 4.00
7 Kurt Nimphius 1.00 2.50
8 Jim Spanarkel 1.00 2.50
9 Elston Turner 1.00 2.50
10 Jay Vincent 1.50 4.00
11 Mark West 1.50 4.00
1 Nate Archibald 3.00 8.00
2 Junior Bridgeman 1.00 2.50
3 Mike Dunleavy 1.50 4.00
4 Kevin Grevey 1.00 2.50
5 Marques Johnson 1.50 4.00
6 Bob Lanier SP 125.00 250.00
7 Alton Lister 1.00 2.50
8 Sidney Moncrief 1.50 4.00
9 Paul Pressey 1.50 4.00
1 Kareem Abdul-Jabbar 12.00 30.00
2 Michael Cooper 3.00 8.00
3 Magic Johnson 20.00 50.00
4 Mike McGee 2.00 5.00
5 Swen Nater 2.00 5.00
6 Kurt Rambis 4.00 10.00
7 Byron Scott 4.00 10.00
8 James Worthy 8.00 20.00
9 Magic Johnson/Kareem 20.00 50.00
10 Kareem Abdul-Jabbar LL 8.00 20.00
1 Julius Erving 8.00 20.00
2 Maurice Cheeks 1.00 2.50
3 Franklin Edwards 1.00 2.50
4 Marc Iavaroni 1.00 2.50
5 Clemon Johnson 1.00 2.50
6 Bobby Jones 1.50 4.00
7 Moses Malone 3.00 8.00
8 Clint Richardson 1.00 2.50
9 Andrew Toney 2.50 6.00
10 Sam Williams 1.00 2.50
BAG1 76ers sealed bag (10) 25.00 60.00
BAG2 Bucks sealed bag (8) 40.00 100.00
BAG3 Celtics sealed bag (9) 60.00 150.00
BAG4 Lakers sealed bag (10) 60.00 150.00
BAG5 Mavs sealed bag (11) 15.00 40.00

1984-85 Star Court Kings 5x7

COMPLETE SET (50) 4,000.00 8,000.00
1 Kareem Abdul-Jabbar 30.00 80.00
2 Jeff Ruland 3.00 8.00
3 Mark Aguirre 5.00 12.00
4 Julius Erving 30.00 80.00
5 Kelly Tripucka 5.00 12.00
6 Buck Williams 5.00 12.00
7 Sidney Moncrief 5.00 12.00
8 World B. Free 5.00 12.00
9 Bill Walton 15.00 40.00
10 Purvis Short 2.50 6.00
11 Rickey Green 2.50 6.00
12 Dominique Wilkins 40.00 100.00
13 Jim Paxson 5.00 12.00
14 Ralph Sampson 5.00 12.00
15 Magic Johnson 40.00 100.00
16 Reggie Theus 4.00 10.00
17 Moses Malone 12.00 30.00
18 Larry Bird 40.00 100.00
19 Larry Nance 6.00 15.00
20 Clark Kellogg 2.50 6.00
21 Jack Sikma 4.00 10.00
22 Alex English 12.00 30.00
23 Bernard King 15.00 40.00
24 Dave Corzine 2.50 6.00
25 George Gervin 12.00 30.00
26 Michael Jordan 2,500.00 5,000.00
27 Rolando Blackman 5.00 12.00
28 Dan Issel 8.00 20.00
29 Maurice Cheeks 10.00 25.00
30 Isiah Thomas 25.00 60.00
31 Robert Parish 12.00 30.00
32 Mark Eaton 5.00 12.00
33 Sam Perkins 5.00 12.00
34 Artis Gilmore 8.00 20.00
35 Andrew Toney 5.00 12.00
36 Adrian Dantley 5.00 12.00
37 Terry Cummings 5.00 12.00
38 Orlando Woolridge 5.00 12.00
39 Tom Chambers 6.00 15.00
40 Gus Williams 5.00 12.00
41 Charles Barkley 125.00 300.00
42 Kevin McHale 12.00 30.00
43 Otis Birdsong 2.50 6.00
44 Sam Bowie 5.00 12.00
45 Darrell Griffith 5.00 12.00
46 Kiki Vandeweghe 4.00 10.00
47 Hakeem Olajuwon 125.00 300.00
48 Marques Johnson 6.00 15.00
49 James Worthy 12.00 30.00
50 Mel Turpin 5.00 12.00
BAG1 Series 1 sealed bag (25) 300.00 600.00
BAG2 Series 2 sealed bag (25) 3,000.00 6,000.00

1984-85 Star Julius Erving

COMPLETE SET (18) 75.00 200.00
COMMON J.ERVING (1-18) 8.00 20.00
1 Julius Erving CL 8.00 20.00
18 Julius Erving TF 8.00 20.00
BAG1 Complete sealed bag (19) 100.00 250.00

1985 Star Kareem Abdul-Jabbar

COMPLETE SET (18) 30.00 80.00
COMMON JABBAR (1-18) 5.00 12.00
BAG1 Complete sealed bag (18) 50.00 120.00

1985 Star Coaches

COMPLETE SET (10) 12.00 30.00
1 John Bach 2.00 5.00
2 Hubie Brown 3.00 8.00
3 Cotton Fitzsimmons 2.00 5.00
4 Kevin Loughery 2.00 5.00
5 John MacLeod 2.00 5.00
6 Doug Moe 2.00 5.00
7 Don Nelson 3.00 8.00
8 Jack Ramsay 3.00 8.00
9 Pat Riley 5.00 12.00
10 Lenny Wilkens UER 2.00 5.00
BAG1 Complete sealed bag (10) 20.00 50.00

1985 Star Crunch'n'Munch All-Stars

COMPLETE SET (11) 500.00 1,000.00
1 All-Star CL 20.00 50.00
2 Larry Bird 40.00 100.00
3 Julius Erving 15.00 40.00
4 Michael Jordan ! 600.00 1,200.00
5 Moses Malone 10.00 25.00
6 Isiah Thomas 15.00 40.00
7 Kareem Abdul-Jabbar 25.00 60.00
8 Adrian Dantley 8.00 20.00
9 George Gervin 10.00 25.00
10 Magic Johnson 30.00 80.00
11 Ralph Sampson 8.00 20.00
BAG1 Complete sealed bag (11) 1,500.00 3,000.00

1985 Star Gatorade Slam Dunk

COMPLETE SET (9) 800.00 1,500.00
1 Slam Dunk CL 20.00 50.00
2 Larry Nance 8.00 20.00
3 Terence Stansbury 8.00 20.00
4 Clyde Drexler 20.00 50.00
5 Julius Erving 30.00 80.00
6 Darrell Griffith 8.00 20.00
7 Michael Jordan 800.00 1,500.00
8 Dominique Wilkins 20.00 50.00
9 Orlando Woolridge 4.00 10.00
BAG1 Complete sealed bag (11) 1,500.00 3,000.00
NNO Charles Barkley SP 60.00 150.00

1985 Star Last 11 ROY's

COMPLETE SET (11) 1,000.00 2,000.00
1 Michael Jordan 800.00 1,500.00
2 Ralph Sampson 5.00 12.00
3 Terry Cummings 5.00 12.00
4 Buck Williams 5.00 12.00
5 Darrell Griffith 5.00 12.00
6 Larry Bird 25.00 60.00
7 Phil Ford 4.00 10.00
8 Walter Davis 4.00 10.00
9 Adrian Dantley 5.00 12.00
10 Alvan Adams 4.00 10.00
11 Jamaal Wilkes 4.00 10.00
BAG1 Complete sealed bag (11) 1,500.00 3,000.00

1985 Star Lite All-Stars

COMPLETE SET (13) 500.00 1,000.00
1 1985 NBA All-Stars 10.00 25.00
2 Larry Bird 30.00 80.00
3 Julius Erving 12.00 30.00
4 Michael Jordan ! 600.00 1,200.00
5 Moses Malone 5.00 12.00
6 Isiah Thomas 8.00 20.00
7 K.C. Jones CO 4.00 10.00
8 Kareem Abdul-Jabbar 12.00 30.00
9 Adrian Dantley 5.00 12.00
10 George Gervin 6.00 15.00
11 Magic Johnson 25.00 60.00
12 Ralph Sampson 5.00 12.00
13 Pat Riley CO 5.00 12.00
BAG1 Complete sealed bag (13) 1,500.00 3,000.00

1985 Star Schick Legends

COMPLETE SET (25) 30.00 80.00
1 Schick NBA Legends CL 3.00 8.00
2 Rick Barry 3.00 8.00
3 Zelmo Beaty 3.00 8.00
4 Walt Bellamy 3.00 8.00
5 Dave Bing 3.00 8.00
6 Roger Brown 3.00 8.00
7 Bob Cousy 4.00 10.00
8 Mel Daniels 3.00 8.00
9 Bob Davies 3.00 8.00
10 Dave DeBusschere 3.00 8.00
11 Walt Frazier 4.00 10.00
12 John Havlicek 5.00 12.00
13 Connie Hawkins 3.00 8.00
14 Tom Heinsohn 3.00 8.00
15 Red Holzman CO 3.00 8.00
16 Johnny Kerr 3.00 8.00
17 Bobby Leonard 3.00 8.00
18 Pete Maravich 15.00 40.00
19 Earl Monroe 4.00 10.00
20 Bob Pettit 3.00 8.00
21 Oscar Robertson 5.00 12.00
22 Nate Thurmond 3.00 8.00
23 Dick Van Arsdale 3.00 8.00
24 Tom Van Arsdale 3.00 8.00
25 George Yardley 3.00 8.00
BAG1 Complete sealed bag (25) 125.00 300.00

1985 Star Slam Dunk Supers 5x7

COMPLETE SET (10) 1,000.00 2,000.00
1 Group Photo CL 300.00 600.00
2 Clyde Drexler 20.00 50.00
3 Julius Erving 30.00 80.00
4 Darrell Griffith 6.00 15.00
5 Michael Jordan 800.00 1,500.00
6 Larry Nance 8.00 20.00
7 Terence Stansbury 8.00 20.00
8 Dominique Wilkins 25.00 60.00
9 Orlando Woolridge 8.00 20.00
10 D.Wilkins Champion 25.00 60.00
BAG1 Complete sealed bag (10) 1,500.00 3,000.00

1985 Star Team Supers 5x7

COMPLETE SET (40) 500.00 1,000.00
BC1 Larry Bird 20.00 50.00
BC2 Robert Parish 10.00 25.00
BC3 Kevin McHale 12.00 30.00
BC4 Dennis Johnson 6.00 15.00
BC5 Danny Ainge 4.00 10.00
CB1 Michael Jordan 500.00 1,000.00
CB2 Orlando Woolridge 2.50 6.00
CB3 Quintin Dailey 2.00 5.00
CB4 Dave Corzine 2.00 5.00
CB5 Steve Johnson 2.00 5.00
DP1 Isiah Thomas 12.00 30.00
DP2 Kelly Tripucka 2.50 6.00
DP3 Vinnie Johnson 2.50 6.00
DP4 Bill Laimbeer 5.00 12.00
DP5 John Long 2.00 5.00
HR1 Ralph Sampson 4.00 10.00
HR2 Hakeem Olajuwon 40.00 100.00
HR3 Lewis Lloyd 2.00 5.00
HR4 Rodney McCray 2.00 5.00
HR5 Lionel Hollins 2.00 5.00
LA1 Kareem Abdul-Jabbar 15.00 40.00
LA2 Magic Johnson 20.00 50.00
LA3 James Worthy 6.00 15.00
LA4 Byron Scott 2.50 6.00
LA5 Bob McAdoo 5.00 12.00
MB1 Terry Cummings 3.00 8.00
MB2 Sidney Moncrief 3.00 8.00
MB3 Paul Pressey 2.50 6.00
MB4 Mike Dunleavy 2.50 6.00
MB5 Alton Lister 2.00 5.00
PS1 Julius Erving 15.00 40.00
PS2 Maurice Cheeks 3.00 8.00
PS3 Bobby Jones 3.00 8.00
PS4 Clemon Johnson 2.00 5.00
PS5 Leon Wood 2.50 6.00
PS6 Moses Malone 6.00 15.00
PS7 Andrew Toney 2.00 5.00
PS8 Charles Barkley 50.00 120.00
PS9 Clint Richardson 2.00 5.00
PS10 Sedale Threatt 2.00 5.00
BAG1a 76ers sealed blue bag (5) 20.00 50.00
BAG1b 76ers sealed white bag (5) 40.00 100.00
BAG2 Bucks sealed bag (5) 15.00 40.00
BAG3 Bulls sealed bag (5) 600.00 1,200.00
BAG4 Celtics sealed bag (5) 125.00 300.00
BAG5 Lakers sealed bag (5) 125.00 300.00
BAG6 Pistons sealed bag (5) 25.00 60.00
BAG7 Rockets sealed bag (5) 40.00 100.00

1985-86 Star

COMPLETE SET (172) 500.00 1,000.00
1 Maurice Cheeks ! 3.00 8.00
2 Charles Barkley ! 50.00 120.00
3 Julius Erving ! 20.00 50.00
4 Clemon Johnson 1.25 3.00
5 Bobby Jones ! 3.00 8.00
6 Moses Malone ! 8.00 20.00
7 Sedale Threatt ! 1.25 3.00
8 Andrew Toney 2.00 5.00
9 Leon Wood 1.25 3.00
10 Isiah Thomas UER 15.00 40.00
11 Kent Benson 1.00 2.50
12 Earl Cureton 1.00 2.50
13 Vinnie Johnson 1.25 3.00
14 Bill Laimbeer 2.50 6.00
15 John Long 1.00 2.50
16 Rick Mahorn 1.00 2.50
17 Kelly Tripucka 1.00 2.50
18 Hakeem Olajuwon ! 50.00 120.00
19 Allen Leavell 1.00 2.50
20 Lewis Lloyd 1.00 2.50
21 John Lucas 1.00 2.50
22 Rodney McCray 1.00 2.50
23 Robert Reid 1.00 2.50
24 Ralph Sampson 1.00 2.50
25 Mitchell Wiggins 1.00 2.50
26 Kareem Abdul-Jabbar 15.00 40.00
27 Michael Cooper 3.00 8.00
28 Magic Johnson 30.00 80.00
29 Mitch Kupchak 1.50 4.00
30 Maurice Lucas 1.50 4.00
31 Kurt Rambis 3.00 8.00
32 Byron Scott 3.00 8.00
33 James Worthy 8.00 20.00
34 Larry Nance 1.50 4.00
35 Alvan Adams 1.25 3.00
36 Walter Davis 1.25 3.00
37 James Edwards 1.00 2.50
38 Jay Humphries 1.00 2.50
39 Charles Pittman 1.00 2.50
40 Rick Robey 1.00 2.50
41 Mike Sanders 1.00 2.50
42 Dominique Wilkins 25.00 60.00
43 Scott Hastings 1.00 2.50
44 Eddie Johnson 1.00 2.50
45 Cliff Levingston 1.00 2.50
46 Tree Rollins 1.00 2.50
47 Doc Rivers UER 1.50 4.00
48 Kevin Willis XRC 5.00 12.00
49 Randy Wittman 1.00 2.50
50 Alex English 3.00 8.00
51 Wayne Cooper 1.00 2.50
52 T.R. Dunn 1.00 2.50
53 Mike Evans 1.00 2.50
54 Lafayette Lever 1.25 3.00
55 Calvin Natt 1.00 2.50
56 Danny Schayes 1.00 2.50
57 Elston Turner 1.00 2.50
58 Buck Williams 1.50 4.00
59 Otis Birdsong 1.00 2.50
60 Darwin Cook 1.00 2.50
61 Darryl Dawkins 1.25 3.00
62 Mike Gminski 1.00 2.50
63 Mickey Johnson 1.00 2.50
64 Mike O'Koren 1.00 2.50
65 Micheal Ray Richardson 1.00 2.50
66 Tom Chambers 4.00 10.00
67 Gerald Henderson 1.00 2.50
68 Tim McCormick 1.00 2.50
69 Jack Sikma 1.25 3.00
70 Ricky Sobers 1.00 2.50
71 Danny Vranes 1.00 2.50
72 Al Wood 1.00 2.50
73 Danny Young XRC 1.25 3.00
74 Reggie Theus 1.25 3.00
75 Larry Drew 1.00 2.50
76 Eddie Johnson 1.25 3.00
77 Mark Olberding 1.00 2.50
78 LaSalle Thompson 1.00 2.50
79 Otis Thorpe 2.00 5.00
80 Mike Woodson 1.25 3.00
81 Clark Kellogg 1.25 3.00
82 Quinn Buckner 1.00 2.50
83 Vern Fleming 1.00 2.50
84 Bill Garnett 1.00 2.50
85 Terence Stansbury 1.00 2.50
86 Steve Stipanovich 1.00 2.50
87 Herb Williams 1.00 2.50
88 Marques Johnson 1.25 3.00
89 Michael Cage 1.25 3.00
90 Franklin Edwards 1.00 2.50
91 Cedric Maxwell 1.00 2.50
92 Derek Smith 1.00 2.50
93 Rory White 1.00 2.50
94 Jamaal Wilkes 1.25 3.00
95G Larry Bird Green 30.00 80.00
95W Larry Bird White 50.00 120.00
96G Danny Ainge Green 4.00 10.00
96W Danny Ainge White 6.00 15.00
97G Dennis Johnson Green 3.00 8.00
98G Kevin McHale Green 6.00 15.00
98W Kevin McHale White 8.00 20.00
99G Robert Parish Green 6.00 15.00
99W Robert Parish White 8.00 20.00
100G Jerry Sichting Green 1.00 2.50
101G Bill Walton Green 6.00 12.00
102G Scott Wedman Green 1.00 2.50
103 Kiki Vandeweghe 1.25 3.00
104 Sam Bowie 1.25 3.00
105 Kenny Carr 1.00 2.50
106 Clyde Drexler ! 30.00 80.00
107 Jerome Kersey XRC 3.00 8.00
108 Jim Paxson 1.25 3.00
109 Mychal Thompson 1.25 3.00
110 Gus Williams 1.25 3.00
111 Darren Daye 1.00 2.50
112 Jeff Malone 1.25 3.00
113 Tom McMillen 1.25 3.00
114 Cliff Robinson 1.00 2.50
115 Dan Roundfield 1.00 2.50
116 Jeff Ruland 1.25 3.00
117 Michael Jordan ! 600.00 1,200.00
118 Gene Banks 1.25 3.00
119 Dave Corzine 1.25 3.00
120 Quintin Dailey 1.25 3.00
121 George Gervin 8.00 20.00
122 Jawann Oldham 1.25 3.00
123 Orlando Woolridge 1.25 3.00
124 Terry Cummings 1.50 4.00
125 Craig Hodges 1.00 2.50
126 Alton Lister 1.00 2.50
127 Paul Mokeski 1.00 2.50
128 Sidney Moncrief 1.50 4.00
129 Ricky Pierce 1.25 3.00
130 Paul Pressey 1.00 2.50
131 Purvis Short 1.00 2.50
132 Joe Barry Carroll 1.00 2.50
133 Lester Conner 1.00 2.50
134 Sleepy Floyd 1.25 3.00
135 Geoff Huston 1.00 2.50
136 Larry Smith 1.00 2.50
137 Jerome Whitehead 1.00 2.50
138 Adrian Dantley 1.50 4.00
139 Mitchell Anderson 1.00 2.50
140 Thurl Bailey 1.25 3.00
141 Mark Eaton 1.25 3.00
142 Rickey Green 1.00 2.50
143 Darrell Griffith 1.25 3.00
144 John Stockton 30.00 80.00
145 Artis Gilmore 1.50 4.00
146 Marc Iavaroni 1.25 3.00
147 Steve Johnson 1.00 2.50
148 Mike Mitchell 1.00 2.50
149 Johnny Moore 1.00 2.50
150 Alvin Robertson 1.00 2.50
151 Jon Sundvold 1.00 2.50
152 World B. Free 1.25 3.00
153 John Bagley 1.00 2.50
154 Johnny Davis 1.00 2.50
155 Roy Hinson 1.00 2.50
156 Phil Hubbard 1.00 2.50
157 Ben Poquette 1.00 2.50
158 Mel Turpin 1.00 2.50
159 Rolando Blackman 1.50 4.00
160 Mark Aguirre 1.50 4.00
161 Brad Davis 1.25 3.00
162 Dale Ellis 1.25 3.00
163 Derek Harper 1.50 4.00
164 Sam Perkins 1.50 4.00
165 Jay Vincent 1.00 2.50
166 Patrick Ewing XRC 100.00 250.00
167 Bill Cartwright 1.25 3.00
168 Pat Cummings 1.00 2.50
169 Ernie Grunfeld 1.25 3.00
170 Rory Sparrow 1.00 2.50
171 Trent Tucker 1.00 2.50
172 Darrell Walker 1.25 3.00
97W Dennis Johnson White 4.00 10.00
100W Jerry Sichting White 1.00 2.50
101W Bill Walton White 6.00 15.00
102W Scott Wedman White 1.25 3.00
BAG1 76ers sealed bag (9) 75.00 200.00
BAG2 Blazers sealed bag (7) 75.00 200.00
BAG3 Bucks sealed bag (7) 30.00 80.00
BAG4 Bullets sealed bag (7) 20.00 50.00
BAG5 Bulls sealed bag (7) 400.00 800.00
BAG6 Cavs sealed bag (7) 25.00 60.00
BAG7 Celtics grn sealed bag (8) 60.00 150.00
BAG8 Celtics wht sealed bag (8) 75.00 200.00
BAG9 Clippers sealed bag (7) 20.00 50.00
BAG10 Hawks sealed bag (8) 75.00 200.00
BAG11 Jazz sealed bag (8) 100.00 250.00
BAG12 Kings sealed bag (7) 30.00 80.00
BAG13 Knicks sealed bag (7) 300.00 600.00
BAG14 Lakers sealed bag (8) 75.00 200.00
BAG15 Mavs sealed bag (8) 30.00 80.00
BAG16 Nets sealed bag (7) 25.00 60.00
BAG17 Nuggets sealed bag (8) 30.00 80.00
BAG18 Pacers sealed bag (7) 25.00 60.00
BAG19 Pistons sealed bag (8) 50.00 120.00
BAG20 Rockets sealed bag (8) 60.00 150.00
BAG21 Sonics sealed bag (8) 40.00 100.00
BAG22 Spurs sealed bag (7) 40.00 100.00
BAG23 Suns sealed bag (8) 25.00 60.00
BAG24 Warriors sealed bag (7) 20.00 50.00

1985-86 Star All-Rookie Team

COMPLETE SET (11) 800.00 1,500.00
1 Hakeem Olajuwon 40.00 100.00
2 Michael Jordan 800.00 1,500.00
3 Charles Barkley 40.00 100.00
4 Sam Bowie 5.00 12.00
5 Sam Perkins 8.00 20.00
6 Vern Fleming 6.00 15.00
7 Otis Thorpe 8.00 20.00
8 John Stockton 40.00 100.00
9 Kevin Willis 6.00 15.00
10 Tim McCormick 3.00 8.00
11 Alvin Robertson 8.00 20.00
BAG1 Complete sealed bag (11) 1,500.00 3,000.00

1986 Star Best of the Best

COMPLETE SET (15) 500.00 1,000.00
1 Kareem Abdul-Jabbar 20.00 50.00
2 Charles Barkley 25.00 60.00
3 Larry Bird 20.00 50.00
4 Tom Chambers 4.00 10.00
5 Terry Cummings 4.00 10.00
6 Julius Erving 20.00 50.00
7 Patrick Ewing 10.00 25.00
8 Magic Johnson 20.00 50.00
9 Michael Jordan 500.00 1,000.00
10 Moses Malone 10.00 25.00
11 Hakeem Olajuwon 25.00 60.00
12 John Stockton 15.00 40.00
13 Isiah Thomas 12.00 30.00
14 Dominique Wilkins 15.00 40.00
15 James Worthy 10.00 25.00

1986 Star Best of the New/Old

COMPLETE SET (8) 400.00 800.00
COMPLETE NEW SET (4) 75.00 200.00
COMPLETE OLD SET (4) 200.00 500.00
1 Patrick Ewing 15.00 40.00
2 Michael Jordan 300.00 600.00
3 Hakeem Olajuwon 25.00 60.00
4 Ralph Sampson 5.00 12.00
5 Kareem Abdul-Jabbar 60.00 150.00
6 Julius Erving 60.00 150.00
7 George Gervin 30.00 80.00
8 Bill Walton 30.00 80.00
BAG1 Complete old sealed bag (4) 400.00 800.00
BAG2 Complete new sealed bag (4) 300.00 600.00

1986 Star Court Kings

COMPLETE SET (33) 200.00 500.00
1 Mark Aguirre 4.00 10.00
2 Kareem Abdul-Jabbar 12.00 30.00
3 Charles Barkley ! 20.00 50.00
4 Larry Bird ! 15.00 40.00
5 Rolando Blackman 4.00 10.00
6 Tom Chambers 4.00 10.00
7 Maurice Cheeks 4.00 10.00
8 Terry Cummings 4.00 10.00
9 Adrian Dantley 3.00 8.00
10 Darryl Dawkins 3.00 8.00
11 Mark Eaton 4.00 10.00
12 Alex English 4.00 10.00
13 Julius Erving 15.00 40.00
14 Patrick Ewing ! 15.00 40.00
15 George Gervin 4.00 10.00
16 Darrell Griffith 4.00 10.00
17 Magic Johnson 15.00 40.00
18 Michael Jordan 200.00 500.00
19 Clark Kellogg 3.00 8.00
20 Bernard King 3.00 8.00
21 Moses Malone 5.00 12.00
22 Kevin McHale 5.00 12.00
23 Sidney Moncrief 3.00 8.00
24 Larry Nance 3.00 8.00
25 Hakeem Olajuwon 20.00 50.00
26 Robert Parish 5.00 12.00
27 Ralph Sampson 4.00 10.00
28 Isiah Thomas 15.00 40.00
29 Andrew Toney 4.00 10.00
30 Kelly Tripucka 4.00 10.00
31 Kiki Vandeweghe 3.00 8.00
32 Dominique Wilkins UER 12.00 30.00
33 James Worthy 8.00 20.00
BAG1 Complete sealed bag (33) 300.00 600.00

1986 Star Magic Johnson

COMPLETE SET (10) 75.00 200.00
COMMON CARD (1-10) 10.00 25.00

1986 Star Michael Jordan

COMPLETE SET (10) 1,500.00 3,000.00
COMMON CARD (1-10) 150.00 400.00
BAG1 Complete sealed bag (10) 2,000.00 4,000.00

1990 Star Charles Barkley

COMPLETE SET (11) 1.25 3.00
COMMON CARD (1-11) .20 .50

1990 Star Dee Brown

COMPLETE SET (11) .75 2.00
COMMON CARD (1-11) .10 .25

1990 Star Tom Chambers

COMPLETE SET (11) .75 2.00
COMMON CARD (1-11) .12 .30

1990 Star Derrick Coleman I

COMPLETE SET (11) .75 2.00
COMMON CARD (1-11) .12 .30

1990 Star Derrick Coleman II

COMPLETE SET (11) .75 2.00
COMMON CARD (1-11) .12 .30

1990 Star Clyde Drexler

COMPLETE SET (11) 1.25 3.00
COMMON CARD (1-11) .25 .60

1990 Star Patrick Ewing

COMPLETE SET (11) 1.25 3.00
COMMON CARD (1-11) .15 .40

1990 Star Tim Hardaway

COMPLETE SET (11) .75 2.00
COMMON CARD (1-11) .15 .40

1990 Star Kevin Johnson

COMPLETE SET (11) .75 2.00
COMMON CARD (1-11) .10 .25

1990 Star Karl Malone

COMPLETE SET (11) 1.25 3.00
COMMON CARD (1-11) .20 .50

1990 Star Hakeem Olajuwon

COMPLETE SET (11) 1.25 3.00
COMMON CARD (1-11) .20 .50

1990 Star David Robinson I

COMPLETE SET (11) 2.00 5.00
COMMON CARD (1-11) .30 .75

1990 Star David Robinson II

COMPLETE SET (11) 1.50 4.00
COMMON CARD (1-11) .25 .60

1990 Star David Robinson III

COMPLETE SET (11) 1.50 4.00
COMMON CARD (1-11) .30 .75

1990 Star John Stockton

COMPLETE SET (11) 1.50 4.00
COMMON CARD (1-11) .20 .50

1990 Star Isiah Thomas

COMPLETE SET (11) 1.25 3.00
COMMON CARD (1-11) .20 .50

1990 Star Dominique Wilkins

COMPLETE SET (11) 1.25 3.00
COMMON CARD (1-11) .20 .50

1990 Star James Worthy

COMPLETE SET (11) 1.25 3.00
COMMON CARD (1-11) .15 .40

1990-91 Star Promos

COMPLETE SET (18) 16.00 40.00
1 Charles Barkley 2.50 6.00
2 Dee Brown .40 1.00
3 Tom Chambers .40 1.00
4 Derrick Coleman I .60 1.50
5 Derrick Coleman II .40 1.00
6 Clyde Drexler 1.25 3.00
7 Patrick Ewing 1.25 3.00
8 Tim Hardaway 1.50 4.00
9 Kevin Johnson .75 2.00
10 Karl Malone 3.00 8.00
11 Hakeem Olajuwon 2.00 5.00
12 David Robinson I 2.00 5.00
13 David Robinson II 2.00 5.00
14 David Robinson III 2.00 5.00
15 John Stockton 2.00 5.00
16 Isiah Thomas .75 2.00
17 Dominique Wilkins .75 2.00
18 James Worthy .75 2.00

1993-94 Star

COMPLETE SET (100) 6.00 15.00
1 Larry Bird Career Stats 1979-1987 .50 1.25
2 Chris Mullin Pro Season Stats .15 .40
3 Harold Miner Collegiate Record .10 .25
4 Tom Gugliotta UER Personal Data/(Misspelled Guggliotta on front and back) .10 .25
5 Christian Laettner College and NBA Record .12 .30
6 Tim Hardaway Collegiate Stats .15 .40
7 Shawn Kemp NBA Regular Season Stats .20 .50
8 Walt Frazier Collegiate Record .12 .30
9 John Starks Career Highlights .12 .30
10 Charles Barkley Collegiate Stats .30 .75
11 Robert Parish Pro Stats 1 .15 .40
12 Chris Mullin Playoff Stats .15 .40
13 Kevin McHale Collegiate Stats .15 .40
14 Scott Burrell Career Stats .12 .30
15 Harold Miner 1992/93 Season 1 .10 .25
16 Richard Dumas Career Stats .07 .20
17 Larry Bird Career Stats 1988-1992 .50 1.25
18 Xavier McDaniel Collegiate Stats .12 .30
19 Christian Laettner 1992-93 Season 1 .12 .30
20 Shawn Kemp NBA Playoff Stats .20 .50
21 Tom Gugliotta UER Collegiate Record/(Misspelled Guggliotta on front and back) .10 .25
22 Walt Frazier Career Stats 1 .12 .30
23 Tim Hardaway Regular Season Stats .15 .40
24 John Starks Personal Info .12 .30
25 Charles Barkley Pro Season Stats .30 .75
26 Robert Parish Pro Stats 2 .15 .40
27 Bill Walton Collegiate Stats .12 .30
28 Xavier McDaniel Regular Season Stats .12 .30
29 Chris Mullin All-Star Stats .15 .40
30 Scott Burrell 1992/93 Season .12 .30
31 Shawn Kemp 1992/93 Season .20 .50
32 Oliver Miller Career Stats .07 .20
33 Larry Bird All-Star Stats .50 1.25
34 Richard Dumas 1992/93 Season .07 .20
35 Kevin McHale Pro Stats .15 .40
36 Oliver Miller Collegiate Info .07 .20
37 Harold Miner 1992/93 Season 2 .10 .25
38 Christian Laettner 1992/93 Season 2 .12 .30
39 Charles Barkley Pro Season Stats .30 .75
40 Tom Gugliotta UER Career Highs/(Misspelled Guggliotta on front and back) .10 .25
41 John Starks 1992/93 Season 1 .12 .30
42 Tim Hardaway Playoff All-Star Stats .15 .40
43 Robert Parish All-Star Stats .15 .40
44 Scott Burrell Collegiate Info 1 .12 .30
45 Bill Walton Regular Season Stats .12 .30
46 Xavier McDaniel Playoff Stats .12 .30
47 Richard Dumas Career Highs .07 .20
48 Walt Frazier Career Stats 2 .12 .30
49 Oliver Miller 1992/93 Season 1 .07 .20
50 Charles Barkley All-Star Stats .30 .75
51 Larry Bird Playoff Stats .50 1.25
52 Chris Mullin Career Best .15 .40
53 Shawn Kemp Pro Info .20 .50
54 Christian Laettner College Info .12 .30
55 Robert Parish Playoff Stats .15 .40
56 John Starks 1992/93 Season 2 .12 .30
57 Xavier McDaniel Pro Info .12 .30
58 Bill Walton Playoff All-Star Stats .12 .30
59 Harold Miner Personal Info .10 .25
60 Richard Dumas Collegiate Info .07 .20
61 Oliver Miller 1992/93 Season 2 .07 .20
62 Tom Gugliotta UER Collegiate Info/(Misspelled Guggliotta on front and back) .10 .25
63 Scott Burrell Collegiate Info 2 .12 .30
64 Tim Hardaway Pro Info 1 .15 .40
65 Walt Frazier NBA Playoff Record .12 .30
66 Larry Bird Career Highlights .50 1.25
67 Shawn Kemp Personal Info .20 .50
68 Kevin McHale All-Star Stats .15 .40
69 Xavier McDaniel Personal Data .12 .30
70 John Starks NBA Regular Season and Playoff Record .12 .30
71 Bill Walton Career Info 1 .12 .30
72 Christian Laettner Personal Data and Collegiate Record .12 .30
73 Chris Mullin 1992/93 Season .15 .40
74 Walt Frazier NBA All-Star Game Record .12 .30
75 Charles Barkley Playoff Stats .30 .75
76 Oliver Miller Personal Info .07 .20
77 Kevin McHale Playoff Stats .15 .40
78 Robert Parish Career Highs .15 .40
79 Larry Bird All-Time Standings .50 1.25
80 Harold Miner Collegiate Info .10 .25
81 Kevin McHale Career Highs .15 .40
82 Tim Hardaway Pro Info 2 .15 .40
83 Tom Gugliotta UER Personal Data and 1992/93 Stats (Misspelled Guggliotta on front and back) .10 .25
84 Bill Walton Career Info 2 .12 .30
85 Shawn Kemp Personal Data .20 .50
86 Scott Burrell Personal Data .12 .30
87 Richard Dumas Personal Info .07 .20
88 Charles Barkley Pro Info .30 .75
89 Bill Walton Personal Info .12 .30
90 Kevin McHale Personal Data .15 .40
91 Christian Laettner Personal Info .12 .30
92 Walt Frazier Personal Data .12 .30
93 John Starks Collegiate and CBA Regular Season Record .12 .30
94 Harold Miner Personal Data and NBA Regular Season Record .10 .25
95 Robert Parish Personal Info .15 .40
96 Tim Hardaway Personal Data .15 .40

97 Tom Gugliotta UER
1992/93 Season
Misspelled Guggliotta
on front and back) .10 .25
98 Larry Bird
Personal Data .50 1.25
99 Chris Mullin
Personal Info .15 .40
100 Charles Barkley
Personal Info .30 .75

2009-10 Studio

COMPLETE SET (150) 30.00 60.00
COMMON ROOKIE (121-150) 1.00 2.50
1 Andrew Bynum .30 .75
2 Derek Fisher .50 1.25
3 Kobe Bryant 4.00 10.00
4 Lamar Odom .40 1.00
5 Carmelo Anthony .75 2.00
6 Chauncey Billups .60 1.50
7 Chris Andersen .50 1.25
8 Brandon Roy .60 1.50
9 LaMarcus Aldridge .50 1.25
10 Rudy Fernandez .30 .75
11 Manu Ginobili 1.00 2.50
12 Tim Duncan 1.25 3.00
13 Tony Parker .75 2.00
14 Luis Scola .40 1.00
15 Shane Battier .50 1.25
16 Tracy McGrady 1.00 2.50
17 Dirk Nowitzki 1.25 3.00
18 Jason Kidd .75 2.00
19 Jason Terry .40 1.00
20 Josh Howard .40 1.00
21 Chris Paul 1.00 2.50
22 David West .40 1.00
23 Peja Stojakovic .40 1.00
24 Rasual Butler .30 .75
25 Andrei Kirilenko .40 1.00
26 Carlos Boozer .40 1.00
27 Deron Williams .40 1.00
28 Amare Stoudemire .40 1.00
29 Grant Hill .75 2.00
30 Jason Richardson .50 1.25
31 Steve Nash 1.00 2.50
32 Anthony Randolph .30 .75
33 Corey Maggette .40 1.00
34 Monta Ellis .40 1.00
35 Raja Bell .40 1.00
36 Marc Gasol .50 1.25
37 Mike Conley Jr. .40 1.00
38 O.J. Mayo .30 .75
39 Rudy Gay .50 1.25
40 Al Jefferson .30 .75
41 Kevin Love .50 1.25
42 Ryan Gomes .30 .75
43 Jeff Green .40 1.00
44 Kevin Durant 2.00 5.00
45 Russell Westbrook 1.00 2.50
46 Al Thornton .30 .75
47 Chris Kaman .40 1.00
48 Eric Gordon .40 1.00
49 Andres Nocioni .30 .75
50 Francisco Garcia .30 .75
51 Kevin Martin .40 1.00
52 LeBron James 4.00 10.00
53 Mo Williams .40 1.00
54 Shaquille O'Neal 1.50 4.00
55 Kevin Garnett 1.25 3.00
56 Paul Pierce .75 2.00
57 Rajon Rondo .60 1.50
58 Ray Allen .75 2.00
59 Dwight Howard .60 1.50
60 Jameer Nelson .30 .75
61 Rashard Lewis .40 1.00
62 Al Horford .50 1.25
63 Joe Johnson .50 1.25
64 Josh Smith .30 .75
65 Mike Bibby .50 1.25
66 Dwyane Wade 1.00 2.50
67 Jermaine O'Neal .50 1.25
68 Michael Beasley .30 .75
69 Derrick Rose .75 2.00
70 Joakim Noah .30 .75
71 John Salmons .40 1.00
72 Andre Iguodala .50 1.25
73 Elton Brand .40 1.00
74 Thaddeus Young .30 .75
75 Ben Gordon .40 1.00
76 Richard Hamilton .50 1.25
77 Tayshaun Prince .50 1.25
78 Danny Granger .30 .75
79 Mike Dunleavy .30 .75
80 T.J. Ford .30 .75
81 Troy Murphy .30 .75
82 Boris Diaw .40 1.00
83 Gerald Wallace .40 1.00
84 Stephen Jackson .40 1.00
85 Raymond Felton .30 .75
86 Andrew Bogut .40 1.00
87 Luke Ridnour .40 1.00
88 Michael Redd .40 1.00
89 Brook Lopez .50 1.25
90 Devin Harris .30 .75
91 Yi Jianlian .60 1.50
92 Andrea Bargnani .50 1.25
93 Chris Bosh .60 1.50
94 Jose Calderon .30 .75
95 Al Harrington .40 1.00
96 David Lee .30 .75
97 Wilson Chandler .40 1.00
98 Antawn Jamison .40 1.00
99 Caron Butler .40 1.00
100 Mike Miller .40 1.00
101 Wes Unseld .50 1.25
102 Arnie Risen .50 1.25
103 Bailey Howell .50 1.25
104 Bill Cartwright .40 1.00
105 Byron Scott .40 1.00
106 Darryl Dawkins .50 1.25
107 Jeff Hornacek .40 1.00
108 Jerry Lucas .50 1.25
109 Kelly Tripucka .30 .75
110 Manute Bol .50 1.25
111 Mark Eaton .30 .75
112 Michael Cage .30 .75
113 Mitch Richmond .50 1.25
114 Norm Nixon .50 1.25
115 Paul Westphal .50 1.25
116 Rick Barry .40 1.00
117 Ron Harper .50 1.25
118 Spencer Haywood .30 .75
119 Dennis Rodman 1.00 2.50
120 Anfernee Hardaway 1.25 3.00
121 Ty Lawson RC .75 2.00
122 Jeff Pendergraph RC .60 1.50
123 DeJuan Blair RC .75 2.00
124 Jermaine Taylor RC .60 1.50
125 Rodrigue Beaubois RC .60 1.50
126 Darren Collison RC 1.00 2.50
127 Eric Maynor RC .60 1.50
128 Earl Clark RC .60 1.50
129 Stephen Curry RC 100.00 250.00
130 DeMarre Carroll RC .75 2.00
131 Hasheem Thabeet RC .60 1.50
132 Jonny Flynn RC .60 1.50
133 Wayne Ellington RC .75 2.00
134 B.J. Mullens RC .60 1.50
135 James Harden RC 15.00 40.00
136 Blake Griffin RC 4.00 10.00
137 Omri Casspi RC .60 1.50
138 Tyreke Evans RC .75 2.00
139 Jeff Teague RC .75 2.00
140 James Johnson RC .75 2.00
141 Taj Gibson RC .75 2.00
142 Jrue Holiday RC 3.00 8.00
143 Austin Daye RC .60 1.50
144 Tyler Hansbrough RC .75 2.00
145 Gerald Henderson RC .60 1.50
146 Brandon Jennings RC 1.00 2.50
147 Terrence Williams RC .60 1.50
148 DeMar DeRozan RC 6.00 15.00
149 Jordan Hill RC .60 1.50
150 Toney Douglas RC .60 1.50

2009-10 Studio Proofs Bronze

*BRONZE: .6X TO 1.5X BASE HI
STATED PRINT RUN 199 SER.#'d SETS
148 DeMar DeRozan 15.00 40.00

2009-10 Studio Proofs Gold

*GOLD: 1.5X TO 4X BASE HI
STATED PRINT RUN 49 SER.#'d SETS
44 Kevin Durant 8.00 20.00
148 DeMar DeRozan 30.00 80.00

2009-10 Studio Proofs Gold Signatures

STATED PRINT RUN 5 TO 25 SER.#'d SETS
3 Kobe Bryant/25 800.00 1,500.00
13 Tony Parker/25 10.00 25.00
41 Kevin Love/25 15.00 40.00
48 Eric Gordon/25 8.00 20.00
57 Rajon Rondo/25 20.00 40.00
80 T.J. Ford/25 8.00 15.00
101 Wes Unseld/25 10.00 25.00
105 Byron Scott/25 8.00 20.00
107 Jeff Hornacek/25 10.00 25.00
121 Ty Lawson/25 15.00 40.00
122 Jeff Pendergraph/25 5.00 12.00
123 DeJuan Blair/25 6.00 15.00
124 Jermaine Taylor/25 5.00 12.00
125 Rodrigue Beaubois/25 5.00 12.00
126 Darren Collison/25 8.00 20.00
127 Eric Maynor/25 5.00 12.00
128 Earl Clark/25 5.00 12.00
129 Stephen Curry/25 1,500.00 3,000.00
130 DeMarre Carroll/25 6.00 15.00
131 Hasheem Thabeet/25 5.00 12.00
132 Jonny Flynn/25 5.00 12.00
133 Wayne Ellington/25 6.00 15.00
134 B.J. Mullens/25 5.00 12.00
135 James Harden/25 125.00 300.00
136 Blake Griffin/25 75.00 200.00
137 Omri Casspi/25 5.00 12.00
138 Tyreke Evans/25 6.00 15.00
139 Jeff Teague/25 6.00 15.00
140 James Johnson/25 6.00 15.00
141 Taj Gibson/25 6.00 15.00
142 Jrue Holiday/25 20.00 50.00
143 Austin Daye/25 6.00 15.00
144 Tyler Hansbrough/25 6.00 15.00
145 Gerald Henderson/25 5.00 12.00
146 Brandon Jennings/25 8.00 20.00
147 Terrence Williams/25 5.00 12.00
149 Jordan Hill/25 5.00 12.00
150 Toney Douglas/25 5.00 12.00

2009-10 Studio Proofs Silver

*SILVER: .75X TO 2X BASE HI
STATED PRINT RUN 99 SER.#'d SETS
148 DeMar DeRozan 20.00 50.00

2009-10 Studio Proofs Silver Signatures

STATED PRINT RUN ONE TO 49 SER.#'d SETS
3 Kobe Bryant/49 600.00 1,200.00
13 Tony Parker/49 12.50 30.00
41 Kevin Love/49 10.00 25.00
42 Ryan Gomes/25 5.00 12.00
45 Russell Westbrook/25 60.00 150.00
47 Chris Kaman/25 6.00 15.00
48 Eric Gordon/49 5.00 12.00
57 Rajon Rondo/49 12.00 30.00
58 Ray Allen/25 20.00 40.00
67 Jermaine O'Neal/25 6.00 15.00
68 Michael Beasley/25 8.00 20.00
78 Danny Granger/25 10.00 25.00
80 T.J. Ford/49 4.00 10.00
90 Devin Harris/25 8.00 20.00
96 David Lee/25 8.00 20.00
101 Wes Unseld/49 8.00 20.00
103 Bailey Howell/25 10.00 25.00
105 Byron Scott/49 6.00 15.00
107 Jeff Hornacek/49 6.00 15.00
110 Manute Bol/25 30.00 80.00
119 Dennis Rodman/25 20.00 50.00
121 Ty Lawson/49 5.00 12.00
122 Jeff Pendergraph/49 4.00 10.00
123 DeJuan Blair/49 5.00 12.00
124 Jermaine Taylor/49 4.00 10.00
125 Rodrigue Beaubois/49 4.00 10.00
126 Darren Collison/49 6.00 15.00
127 Eric Maynor/49 4.00 10.00
128 Earl Clark/49 4.00 10.00
129 Stephen Curry/49 1,000.00 2,000.00
130 DeMarre Carroll/49 5.00 12.00
131 Hasheem Thabeet/49 4.00 10.00
132 Jonny Flynn/49 4.00 10.00
133 Wayne Ellington/49 5.00 12.00
134 B.J. Mullens/49 4.00 10.00
135 James Harden/49 75.00 200.00
136 Blake Griffin/49 30.00 80.00
137 Omri Casspi/49 4.00 10.00
138 Tyreke Evans/49 5.00 12.00
139 Jeff Teague/49 5.00 12.00
140 James Johnson/49 5.00 12.00
141 Taj Gibson/49 5.00 12.00
142 Jrue Holiday/49 15.00 40.00
143 Austin Daye/49 4.00 10.00
144 Tyler Hansbrough/49 5.00 12.00
145 Gerald Henderson/49 4.00 10.00
146 Brandon Jennings/49 6.00 15.00
147 Terrence Williams/49 4.00 10.00
149 Jordan Hill/49 4.00 10.00
150 Toney Douglas/49 4.00 10.00

2009-10 Studio Essence

COMPLETE SET (15) 7.50 15.00
*PROOF: .75X TO 2X BASE HI
PROOF PRINT RUN 199 SER.#'d SETS
1 Al Jefferson .50 1.25
2 Andre Iguodala .75 2.00
3 Andrew Bynum .50 1.25
4 Baron Davis .60 1.50
5 Charlie Villanueva .50 1.25
6 Chris Bosh 1.00 2.50
7 Chris Kaman .60 1.50
8 Devin Harris .50 1.25
9 Emeka Okafor .60 1.50
10 Josh Howard .60 1.50
11 Rajon Rondo 1.00 2.50
12 Randy Foye .50 1.25
13 Ronnie Brewer .50 1.25
14 Rudy Fernandez .50 1.25
15 Trevor Ariza .50 1.25

2009-10 Studio Essence Materials

STATED PRINT RUN 149 TO 249 SER.#'d SETS
1 Al Jefferson/249 2.00 5.00
2 Andre Iguodala/249 3.00 8.00
3 Andrew Bynum/149 2.00 5.00
4 Baron Davis/249 2.50 6.00
5 Charlie Villanueva/249 2.00 5.00
6 Chris Bosh/249 4.00 10.00
7 Chris Kaman/149 2.50 6.00
10 Josh Howard/249 2.50 6.00

2009-10 Studio Essence Signatures

STATED PRINT RUN 49 TO 99 SER.#'d SETS
ASTERISK CARDS FROM PANINI UPDATE
2 Andre Iguodala/49 6.00 15.00
3 Andrew Bynum/49* 8.00 20.00
4 Baron Davis/49* 5.00 12.00
7 Chris Kaman/99 4.00 10.00
8 Devin Harris/99 4.00 10.00
10 Josh Howard/49 4.00 10.00
11 Rajon Rondo/49* 15.00 40.00
12 Randy Foye/99 4.00 10.00
13 Ronnie Brewer/99 4.00 10.00

2009-10 Studio Heritage

COMPLETE SET (20) 20.00 40.00
*PROOFS: .6X TO 1.5X BASE HI
PROOF PRINT RUN 199 SER.#'d SETS
1 Elvin Hayes 2.00 5.00
2 Jerry West 2.00 5.00
3 Spencer Haywood .75 2.00
4 Sidney Moncrief 1.00 2.50
5 Sam Perkins .75 2.00
6 Robert Parish 1.50 4.00
7 Rick Barry 1.00 2.50
8 Paul Westphal 1.25 3.00
9 Nate Archibald 1.50 4.00
10 Moses Malone 2.00 5.00
11 Magic Johnson 5.00 12.00
12 Lou Hudson 1.25 3.00
13 Lenny Wilkens 1.25 3.00
14 Isiah Thomas 1.25 3.00
15 George Gervin 1.50 4.00
16 Frank Ramsey 1.25 3.00
17 Dolph Schayes 1.25 3.00
18 David Thompson 1.00 2.50
19 Darryl Dawkins 1.25 3.00
20 Connie Hawkins 1.50 4.00

2009-10 Studio Heritage Materials

STATED PRINT RUN 99 TO 249 SER.#'d SETS
2 Jerry West/99 6.00 15.00
6 Robert Parish/249 5.00 12.00
10 Moses Malone/99 6.00 15.00
11 Magic Johnson/249 8.00 20.00
14 Isiah Thomas/249 4.00 10.00
15 George Gervin/99 5.00 12.00

2009-10 Studio Heritage Signatures

STATED PRINT RUN 49 TO 99 SER.#'d SETS
1 Elvin Hayes/99 8.00 20.00
2 Jerry West/49 30.00 80.00
3 Spencer Haywood/99 8.00 20.00
4 Sidney Moncrief/99 8.00 20.00
5 Sam Perkins/99 8.00 20.00
6 Robert Parish/99 8.00 20.00
7 Rick Barry/99 8.00 20.00
8 Paul Westphal/99 8.00 20.00
9 Nate Archibald/99 8.00 20.00
11 Magic Johnson/49 40.00 100.00
13 Lenny Wilkens/99 8.00 20.00
14 Isiah Thomas/93 10.00 25.00
15 George Gervin/99 8.00 20.00
16 Frank Ramsey/99 8.00 20.00
17 Dolph Schayes/99 8.00 20.00
18 David Thompson/99 8.00 20.00

2009-10 Studio Masterstrokes

COMPLETE SET (20) 20.00 40.00
*PROOFS: .6X TO 1.5X BASE HI
PROOF PRINT RUN 199 SER.#'d SETS
1 Al Jefferson .60 1.50
2 Andre Iguodala 1.00 2.50
3 Carlos Boozer .75 2.00
4 Carmelo Anthony 1.50 4.00
5 Danilo Gallinari .75 2.00
6 Dwight Howard 1.25 3.00
7 Jason Kidd 1.50 4.00
8 Joe Johnson 1.00 2.50
9 Kevin Martin .75 2.00
10 Kobe Bryant 8.00 20.00
11 LeBron James 8.00 20.00
12 Manu Ginobili 2.00 5.00
13 O.J. Mayo .60 1.50
14 Paul Pierce 1.50 4.00
15 Kevin Durant 4.00 10.00
16 Tracy McGrady 2.00 5.00
17 Dwyane Wade 2.00 5.00
18 Chris Bosh 1.25 3.00
19 Stephen Jackson .75 2.00
20 Tayshaun Prince 1.00 2.50

2009-10 Studio Masterstrokes Materials

STATED PRINT RUN 50 TO 249 SER.#'d SETS
1 Al Jefferson/249 2.00 5.00
2 Andre Iguodala/249 3.00 8.00
3 Carlos Boozer/249 2.50 6.00
4 Carmelo Anthony/249 5.00 12.00
5 Danilo Gallinari/249 2.50 6.00
6 Dwight Howard/249 4.00 10.00
8 Joe Johnson/50 3.00 8.00
10 Kobe Bryant/249 12.00 30.00
11 LeBron James/249 10.00 25.00
12 Manu Ginobili/249 6.00 15.00
14 Paul Pierce/199 5.00 12.00
16 Tracy McGrady/199 6.00 15.00
17 Dwyane Wade/249 6.00 15.00
18 Chris Bosh/249 4.00 10.00
20 Tayshaun Prince/249 3.00 8.00

2009-10 Studio Masterstrokes Signatures

STATED PRINT RUN 49 TO 99 SER.#'d SETS
2 Andre Iguodala/81 8.00 20.00
3 Carlos Boozer/99 6.00 15.00
7 Jason Kidd/49 10.00 25.00
10 Kobe Bryant/99 500.00 1,000.00
16 Tracy McGrady/49 15.00 40.00
18 Chris Bosh/99 8.00 20.00

2009-10 Studio Materials

STATED PRINT RUN 10 TO 249 SER.#'d SETS
1 Andrew Bynum/249 2.00 5.00
3 Kobe Bryant/249 8.00 20.00
5 Carmelo Anthony/249 5.00 12.00
6 Chauncey Billups/249 4.00 10.00
7 Chris Andersen/249 3.00 8.00
8 Brandon Roy/249 4.00 10.00
9 LaMarcus Aldridge/249 3.00 8.00
11 Manu Ginobili/249 6.00 15.00
12 Tim Duncan/249 8.00 20.00
13 Tony Parker/249 5.00 12.00
14 Luis Scola/249 2.50 6.00
15 Shane Battier/249 3.00 8.00
16 Tracy McGrady/249 6.00 15.00
17 Dirk Nowitzki/249 8.00 20.00
18 Jason Kidd/249 5.00 12.00
19 Jason Terry/249 2.50 6.00
20 Josh Howard/249 2.50 6.00
21 Chris Paul/249 6.00 15.00
22 David West/249 2.50 6.00
25 Andrei Kirilenko/149 2.50 6.00
26 Carlos Boozer/249 2.50 6.00
27 Deron Williams/249 2.50 6.00
28 Amare Stoudemire/249 2.50 6.00
34 Monta Ellis/249 2.50 6.00
37 Mike Conley Jr./249 2.50 6.00
40 Al Jefferson/249 2.00 5.00
41 Kevin Love/249 3.00 8.00
42 Ryan Gomes/249 2.00 5.00
46 Al Thornton/249 2.00 5.00
47 Chris Kaman/149 2.50 6.00
49 Andres Nocioni/249 2.00 5.00
52 LeBron James/249 8.00 20.00
53 Mo Williams/249 2.50 6.00
54 Shaquille O'Neal/249 10.00 25.00
55 Kevin Garnett/249 8.00 20.00
56 Paul Pierce/199 5.00 12.00
58 Ray Allen/249 5.00 12.00
59 Dwight Howard/249 4.00 10.00
60 Jameer Nelson/249 2.00 5.00
61 Rashard Lewis/249 2.50 6.00
62 Al Horford/249 3.00 8.00
63 Joe Johnson/50 3.00 8.00
64 Josh Smith/249 2.00 5.00
65 Mike Bibby/50 3.00 8.00
66 Dwyane Wade/249 6.00 15.00
67 Jermaine O'Neal/50 3.00 8.00
68 Michael Beasley/249 3.00 8.00
69 Derrick Rose/50 5.00 12.00
70 Joakim Noah/249 2.00 5.00
72 Andre Iguodala/249 3.00 8.00
73 Elton Brand/249 2.50 6.00
74 Thaddeus Young/249 2.00 5.00
75 Ben Gordon/199 2.00 5.00
76 Richard Hamilton/249 3.00 8.00
77 Tayshaun Prince/249 3.00 8.00
82 Boris Diaw/249 2.50 6.00
83 Gerald Wallace/249 2.50 6.00
85 Raymond Felton/249 2.00 5.00
92 Andrea Bargnani/100 2.00 5.00
93 Chris Bosh/249 4.00 10.00
94 Jose Calderon/249 2.00 5.00
95 Al Harrington/25 2.50 6.00
96 David Lee/249 2.00 5.00
98 Antawn Jamison/249 2.50 6.00
113 Mitch Richmond/249 6.00 15.00
116 Rick Barry/199 2.50 6.00
117 Ron Harper/249 8.00 20.00
120 Anfernee Hardaway/249 10.00 25.00
121 Ty Lawson/249 1.50 4.00
122 Jeff Pendergraph/249 1.25 3.00
123 DeJuan Blair/249 1.50 4.00
124 Jermaine Taylor/249 1.25 3.00
125 Rodrigue Beaubois/249 1.25 3.00
126 Darren Collison/249 2.00 5.00
127 Eric Maynor/249 1.25 3.00
128 Earl Clark/249 1.25 3.00
129 Stephen Curry/249 75.00 200.00
130 DeMarre Carroll/249 1.50 4.00
131 Hasheem Thabeet/249 1.25 3.00
132 Jonny Flynn/249 1.25 3.00
133 Wayne Ellington/249 1.50 4.00
134 B.J. Mullens/249 1.25 3.00
135 James Harden/249 12.00 30.00
136 Blake Griffin/249 8.00 20.00
137 Omri Casspi/249 1.25 3.00
138 Tyreke Evans/249 1.50 4.00
139 Jeff Teague/249 1.50 4.00
140 James Johnson/249 1.50 4.00
141 Taj Gibson/249 1.50 4.00
142 Jrue Holiday/249 6.00 15.00
143 Austin Daye/249 1.25 3.00
144 Tyler Hansbrough/249 1.50 4.00
145 Gerald Henderson/249 1.25 3.00
146 Brandon Jennings/249 2.00 5.00
147 Terrence Williams/249 1.25 3.00
148 DeMar DeRozan/249 15.00 40.00
149 Jordan Hill/249 1.25 3.00
150 Toney Douglas/249 1.25 3.00

2009-10 Studio Signatures

STATED PRINT RUN 5 TO 199 SER.#'d SETS
3 Kobe Bryant/49 500.00 1,000.00
13 Tony Parker/25 10.00 25.00
15 Shane Battier/50 5.00 12.00
41 Kevin Love/25 15.00 40.00
45 Russell Westbrook/99 50.00 120.00
47 Chris Kaman/99 5.00 12.00
48 Eric Gordon/99 6.00 15.00
57 Rajon Rondo/50 15.00 40.00
58 Ray Allen/25 25.00 60.00
67 Jermaine O'Neal/25 6.00 15.00
68 Michael Beasley/50 6.00 15.00
78 Danny Granger/25 6.00 15.00
80 T.J. Ford/99 5.00 10.00
90 Devin Harris/49 5.00 10.00
93 Chris Bosh/25 20.00 40.00
96 David Lee/25 8.00 20.00
101 Wes Unseld/50 8.00 20.00
103 Bailey Howell/49 10.00 25.00
110 Manute Bol/50 20.00 40.00
116 Rick Barry/25 10.00 25.00
119 Dennis Rodman/25 20.00 50.00
121 Ty Lawson/199 4.00 10.00
122 Jeff Pendergraph/199 3.00 8.00
123 DeJuan Blair/199 4.00 10.00
124 Jermaine Taylor/199 3.00 8.00
125 Rodrigue Beaubois/199 3.00 8.00
126 Darren Collison/199 5.00 12.00
127 Eric Maynor/199 3.00 8.00
128 Earl Clark/199 3.00 8.00
129 Stephen Curry/199 1,000.00 2,000.00
130 DeMarre Carroll/199 4.00 10.00
131 Hasheem Thabeet/199 3.00 8.00
132 Jonny Flynn/199 3.00 8.00
133 Wayne Ellington/199 4.00 10.00
134 B.J. Mullens/199 3.00 8.00
135 James Harden/199 60.00 150.00
136 Blake Griffin/199 20.00 50.00
137 Omri Casspi/199 3.00 8.00
138 Tyreke Evans/199 4.00 10.00
139 Jeff Teague/199 4.00 10.00
140 James Johnson/199 4.00 10.00
141 Taj Gibson/199 4.00 10.00
142 Jrue Holiday/199 12.00 30.00
143 Austin Daye/199 3.00 8.00
144 Tyler Hansbrough/199 4.00 10.00
145 Gerald Henderson/199 3.00 8.00
146 Brandon Jennings/199 5.00 12.00
147 Terrence Williams/199 3.00 8.00
149 Jordan Hill/199 3.00 8.00
150 Toney Douglas/199 3.00 8.00

2009-10 Studio Skylines

COMPLETE SET (30) 25.00 50.00
*PROOFS: .6X TO 1.5X BASE HI
PROOF PRINT RUN 199 SER.#'d SETS
1 Mike Bibby 1.00 2.50
2 Rajon Rondo 1.25 3.00
3 Gerald Henderson .60 1.50
4 Derrick Rose 1.50 4.00
5 LeBron James 8.00 20.00
6 Jason Terry .75 2.00
7 Chauncey Billups 1.25 3.00
8 Ben Gordon .75 2.00
9 Stephen Curry 75.00 200.00
10 Tracy McGrady 2.00 5.00
11 Danny Granger .60 1.50
12 Blake Griffin 4.00 10.00
13 Kobe Bryant 8.00 20.00
14 O.J. Mayo .60 1.50
15 Dwyane Wade 2.00 5.00
16 Andrew Bogut .75 2.00
17 Kevin Love 1.00 2.50
18 Devin Harris .60 1.50
19 Chris Paul 2.00 5.00
20 Nate Robinson .75 2.00
21 Russell Westbrook 2.00 5.00
22 Dwight Howard 1.25 3.00
23 Elton Brand .75 2.00
24 Steve Nash 2.00 5.00
25 Brandon Roy 1.25 3.00
26 Kevin Martin .75 2.00
27 Tim Duncan 2.50 6.00
28 Chris Bosh 1.25 3.00
29 Deron Williams .75 2.00
30 Gilbert Arenas .75 2.00

2009-10 Studio Skylines Materials

STATED PRINT RUN 50 TO 249 SER.#'d SETS
1 Mike Bibby/50 3.00 8.00
3 Gerald Henderson/249 1.50 4.00
4 Derrick Rose/50 5.00 12.00
5 LeBron James/249 8.00 20.00
6 Jason Terry/249 2.50 6.00
7 Chauncey Billups/249 4.00 10.00
8 Ben Gordon/199 2.50 6.00
9 Stephen Curry/249 200.00 500.00
10 Tracy McGrady/249 6.00 15.00
12 Blake Griffin/249 10.00 25.00
13 Kobe Bryant/249 12.00 30.00
15 Dwyane Wade/249 6.00 15.00
17 Kevin Love/249 3.00 8.00
19 Chris Paul/249 6.00 15.00
20 Nate Robinson/249 2.50 6.00
22 Dwight Howard/249 4.00 10.00
23 Elton Brand/249 2.50 6.00
25 Brandon Roy/249 4.00 10.00
27 Tim Duncan/249 8.00 20.00
28 Chris Bosh/249 4.00 10.00
29 Deron Williams/249 2.50 6.00
30 Gilbert Arenas/249 2.50 6.00

2009-10 Studio Skylines Signatures

STATED PRINT RUN 49 TO 99 SER.#'d SETS
ASTERISK CARDS FROM PANINI UPDATE
1 Mike Bibby/99 6.00 15.00
2 Rajon Rondo/99* 15.00 40.00
3 Gerald Henderson/99 6.00 15.00
7 Chauncey Billups/99 8.00 20.00
9 Stephen Curry/99 1,500.00 3,000.00
10 Tracy McGrady/49 10.00 25.00
11 Danny Granger/99* 6.00 15.00
12 Blake Griffin/99 50.00 120.00
13 Kobe Bryant/99 500.00 1,000.00
17 Kevin Love/99 15.00 40.00
18 Devin Harris/99 6.00 15.00
21 Russell Westbrook/99 60.00 150.00
28 Chris Bosh/99 10.00 25.00
29 Deron Williams/92 10.00 25.00

2009-10 Studio Team Studio

COMPLETE SET (15) 10.00 25.00
*PROOFS: .75X TO 2X BASE HI
PROOF PRINT RUN 199 SER.#'d SETS
1 K.Bryant/P.Gasol 6.00 15.00
2 D.Howard/R.Lewis 1.00 2.50
3 T.Duncan/T.Parker 2.00 5.00
4 K.Garnett/R.Allen 2.00 5.00
5 D.Nowitzki/J.Howard 2.00 5.00
6 L.James/S.O'Neal 6.00 15.00
7 D.Wade/D.Cook 1.50 4.00
8 C.Anthony/C.Billups 1.25 3.00
9 C.Boozer/A.Kirilenko .60 1.50
10 A.Harrington/D.Lee .60 1.50
11 C.Bosh/A.Bargnani 1.00 2.50
12 B.Laimbeer/J.Dumars 1.00 2.50
13 L.Bird/K.McHale 3.00 8.00
14 M.Johnson/K.Abdul-Jabbar 3.00 8.00
15 G.McGinnis/M.Malone 1.25 3.00

2009-10 Studio Team Studio Materials

STATED PRINT RUN 25 TO 249 SER.#'d SETS
1 K.Bryant/P.Gasol/249 10.00 25.00
2 D.Howard/R.Lewis/249 4.00 10.00
3 T.Duncan/T.Parker/249 6.00 15.00
4 K.Garnett/R.Allen/249 6.00 15.00
5 D.Nowitzki/J.Howard/249 6.00 15.00
6 L.James/S.O'Neal/249 12.50 30.00
7 D.Wade/D.Cook/249 4.00 10.00
8 C.Anthony/C.Billups/249 5.00 12.00
9 C.Boozer/A.Kirilenko/249 4.00 10.00
10 A.Harrington/D.Lee/25 6.00 15.00
11 C.Bosh/A.Bargnani/249 4.00 10.00
13 L.Bird/K.McHale/249 10.00 25.00
14 Magic/Abdul-Jabbar/249 10.00 25.00
15 G.McGinnis/M.Malone/249 4.00 10.00

2016-17 Studio

1 Stephen Curry 4.00 10.00
2 Blake Griffin .50 1.25
3 Kyrie Irving 1.00 2.50
4 John Wall .60 1.50
5 Kevin Durant 2.00 5.00
6 Anthony Davis 1.50 4.00
7 Russell Westbrook .75 2.00
8 James Harden 1.00 2.50
9 Dirk Nowitzki 1.25 3.00
10 Carmelo Anthony .75 2.00
11 Dwyane Wade 1.00 2.50
12 Giannis Antetokounmpo 2.50 6.00
13 Chris Paul .75 2.00
14 Mike Conley .40 1.00
15 Kawhi Leonard 1.25 3.00
16 Jordan Clarkson .50 1.25
17 Aaron Gordon .50 1.25
18 LeBron James 4.00 10.00
19 Jahlil Okafor .30 .75
20 Devin Booker 2.00 5.00
21 Emmanuel Mudiay .30 .75
22 LaMarcus Aldridge .50 1.25
23 Paul George .75 2.00
24 DeMar DeRozan .60 1.50
25 Kemba Walker .40 1.00
26 Kyle Lowry .50 1.25
27 Eric Gordon .40 1.00
28 Pau Gasol .75 2.00
29 Jimmy Butler 1.00 2.50
30 Karl-Anthony Towns 1.00 2.50
31 Gordon Hayward .50 1.25
32 Dwight Howard .60 1.50
33 DeMarcus Cousins .40 1.00
34 Justise Winslow .40 1.00
35 Harrison Barnes .40 1.00
36 Damian Lillard 1.25 3.00
37 Klay Thompson 1.25 3.00
38 Tyson Chandler .40 1.00
39 Isaiah Thomas .40 1.00
40 Jabari Parker .30 .75
41 Joel Embiid 1.25 3.00
42 Andre Drummond .50 1.25
43 Elfrid Payton .40 1.00
44 Zach LaVine 1.00 2.50
45 Kenneth Faried .40 1.00
46 Steven Adams .40 1.00
47 Derrick Rose .75 2.00
48 DeAndre Jordan .40 1.00
49 Andrew Wiggins .60 1.50
50 Marc Gasol .50 1.25
51 Magic Johnson 2.00 5.00
52 Larry Bird 2.00 5.00
53 Julius Erving 1.25 3.00
54 Kareem Abdul-Jabbar 1.50 4.00
55 Pete Maravich 1.00 2.50
56 Scottie Pippen 1.00 2.50
57 Clyde Drexler .75 2.00
58 David Robinson 1.00 2.50
59 John Stockton .75 2.00
60 Wilt Chamberlain 1.50 4.00
61 Patrick Ewing .60 1.50
62 George Gervin .75 2.00
63 Drazen Petrovic .50 1.25
64 Jerry West 1.25 3.00
65 Jason Kidd .75 2.00
66 Karl Malone .75 2.00
67 Bill Russell 1.50 4.00
68 Oscar Robertson 1.25 3.00
69 Isiah Thomas .75 2.00
70 Hakeem Olajuwon 1.00 2.50
71 John Havlicek 1.25 3.00
72 Tim Duncan 1.00 2.50
73 Shaquille O'Neal 1.50 4.00
74 Allen Iverson .75 2.00
75 Kobe Bryant 4.00 10.00
76 Brandon Ingram RC 2.00 5.00
77 Malcolm Brogdon RC 1.50 4.00
78 Domantas Sabonis RC 3.00 8.00
79 Denzel Valentine RC .50 1.25
80 Buddy Hield RC 1.50 4.00
81 Juan Hernangomez RC 1.00 2.50
82 Wade Baldwin IV RC .50 1.25
83 Malik Beasley RC 1.00 2.50
84 Ben Simmons RC 1.50 4.00
85 Henry Ellenson RC .50 1.25
86 Jamal Murray RC 4.00 10.00
87 T. Luwawu-Cabarrot RC .75 2.00
88 Jaylen Brown RC 12.00 30.00
89 Patrick McCaw RC .50 1.25
90 Taurean Prince RC .60 1.50
91 Marquese Chriss RC .60 1.50
92 DeAndre' Bembry RC .75 2.00
93 Malachi Richardson RC .50 1.25
94 Dragan Bender RC .50 1.25
95 Isaiah Whitehead RC .50 1.25
96 Dejounte Murray RC 2.50 6.00
97 Jakob Poeltl RC 1.00 2.50
98 Kris Dunn RC .75 2.00
99 Pascal Siakam RC 3.00 8.00
100 Thon Maker RC .60 1.50
101 Stephen Curry SE 5.00 12.00
102 Giannis Antetokounmpo SE 3.00 8.00
103 James Harden SE 1.25 3.00
104 Mike Conley SE .50 1.25
105 Russell Westbrook SE 1.00 2.50
106 Brook Lopez SE .50 1.25
107 Damian Lillard SE 1.50 4.00
108 Jahlil Okafor SE .40 1.00
109 Stanley Johnson SE .40 1.00
110 Pau Gasol SE 1.00 2.50
111 Goran Dragic SE .60 1.50
112 Thaddeus Young SE .40 1.00
113 Rudy Gay SE .60 1.50
114 Dwight Howard SE .75 2.00
115 Elfrid Payton SE .50 1.25
116 Devin Booker SE 2.50 6.00
117 Michael Kidd-Gilchrist SE .40 1.00
118 Nerlens Noel SE .40 1.00
119 Chris Paul SE 1.00 2.50
120 Tony Parker SE 1.00 2.50
121 Dwyane Wade SE 1.25 3.00
122 Julius Randle SE .75 2.00
123 Jonas Valanciunas SE .50 1.25
124 Blake Griffin SE .60 1.50
125 Avery Bradley SE .40 1.00
126 Victor Oladipo SE .50 1.25
127 Dirk Nowitzki SE 1.50 4.00
128 Rodney Hood SE .50 1.25
129 Carmelo Anthony SE 1.00 2.50
130 Kenneth Faried SE .50 1.25
131 Eric Gordon SE .50 1.25
132 Zach Randolph SE .60 1.50
133 Dennis Schroder SE .60 1.50
134 Gordon Hayward SE .60 1.50
135 Joel Embiid SE 1.50 4.00
136 LeBron James SE 5.00 12.00
137 Kyle Korver SE .50 1.25
138 Harrison Barnes SE .50 1.25
139 Derrick Rose SE 1.00 2.50
140 Dion Waiters SE .40 1.00
141 Jeremy Lin SE 1.25 3.00
142 Willie Cauley-Stein SE .50 1.25
143 Andre Drummond SE .60 1.50
144 C.J. McCollum SE .60 1.50
145 Danilo Gallinari SE .50 1.25
146 Al Horford SE .60 1.50
147 J.J. Redick SE .60 1.50
148 Paul Millsap SE .50 1.25
149 Cody Zeller SE .40 1.00
150 Kevin Durant SE 2.50 6.00
151 George Hill SE .50 1.25
152 Greg Monroe SE .40 1.00
153 Wesley Matthews SE .40 1.00
154 Paul George SE 1.00 2.50
155 Draymond Green SE .75 2.00
156 Kemba Walker SE .50 1.25
157 DeMar DeRozan SE .75 2.00
158 Anthony Davis SE 2.00 5.00
159 Patrick Beverley SE .40 1.00
160 Kawhi Leonard SE 1.50 4.00
161 Jimmy Butler SE 1.25 3.00
162 DeMarcus Cousins SE .50 1.25
163 Steven Adams SE .50 1.25
164 Kevin Love SE .60 1.50
165 LaMarcus Aldridge SE .60 1.50
166 Brandon Knight SE .50 1.25
167 Isaiah Thomas SE .50 1.25
168 Aaron Gordon SE .60 1.50
169 Kristaps Porzingis SE 1.00 2.50
170 Kyrie Irving SE 1.25 3.00
171 E'Twaun Moore SE .40 1.00
172 Myles Turner SE .60 1.50
173 Marcus Smart SE .75 2.00
174 Nick Young SE .40 1.00
175 Andre Iguodala SE .60 1.50
176 Brandon Ingram SE 2.50 6.00
177 Malcolm Brogdon SE 2.00 5.00
178 Domantas Sabonis SE 4.00 10.00
179 Denzel Valentine SE .60 1.50
180 Buddy Hield SE 2.00 5.00
181 Juan Hernangomez SE 1.25 3.00
182 Wade Baldwin IV SE .60 1.50
183 Malik Beasley SE 1.25 3.00
184 Ben Simmons SE 2.00 5.00
185 Henry Ellenson SE .60 1.50
186 Jamal Murray SE 5.00 12.00
187 T. Luwawu-Cabarrot SE 1.00 2.50
188 Jaylen Brown SE 15.00 40.00
189 Patrick McCaw SE .60 1.50
190 Taurean Prince SE .75 2.00
191 Marquese Chriss SE .75 2.00
192 DeAndre' Bembry SE 1.00 2.50
193 Malachi Richardson SE .60 1.50
194 Dragan Bender SE .60 1.50
195 Isaiah Whitehead SE .60 1.50
196 Dejounte Murray SE 3.00 8.00
197 Jakob Poeltl SE 1.25 3.00
198 Kris Dunn SE 1.00 2.50

199 Pascal Siakam SE 4.00 10.00
200 Thon Maker SE .75 2.00
201 Stephen Curry SK 40.00 100.00
202 Blake Griffin SK 5.00 12.00
203 Kyrie Irving SK 10.00 25.00
204 John Wall SK 6.00 15.00
205 Kevin Durant SK 20.00 50.00
206 Anthony Davis SK 15.00 40.00
207 Russell Westbrook SK 8.00 20.00
208 James Harden SK 10.00 25.00
209 Dirk Nowitzki SK 12.00 30.00
210 Carmelo Anthony SK 8.00 20.00
211 Dwyane Wade SK 10.00 25.00
212 G. Antetokounmpo SK 25.00 60.00
213 Chris Paul SK 8.00 20.00
214 Mike Conley SK 4.00 10.00
215 Kawhi Leonard SK 12.00 30.00
216 Jordan Clarkson SK 5.00 12.00
217 Aaron Gordon SK 5.00 12.00
218 LeBron James SK 40.00 100.00
219 Jahlil Okafor SK 3.00 8.00
220 Devin Booker SK 20.00 50.00
221 Emmanuel Mudiay SK 3.00 8.00
222 LaMarcus Aldridge SK 5.00 12.00
223 Paul George SK 8.00 20.00
224 DeMar DeRozan SK 6.00 15.00
225 Kemba Walker SK 4.00 10.00
226 Kyle Lowry SK 5.00 12.00
227 Eric Gordon SK 4.00 10.00
228 Pau Gasol SK 8.00 20.00
229 Jimmy Butler SK 10.00 25.00
230 Karl-Anthony Towns SK 10.00 25.00
231 Gordon Hayward SK 5.00 12.00
232 Dwight Howard SK 6.00 15.00
233 DeMarcus Cousins SK 4.00 10.00
234 Justise Winslow SK 4.00 10.00
235 Harrison Barnes SK 4.00 10.00
236 Damian Lillard SK 12.00 30.00
237 Klay Thompson SK 12.00 30.00
238 Tyson Chandler SK 4.00 10.00
239 Isaiah Thomas SK 4.00 10.00
240 Jabari Parker SK 3.00 8.00
241 Joel Embiid SK 12.00 30.00
242 Andre Drummond SK 5.00 12.00
243 Elfrid Payton SK 4.00 10.00
244 Zach LaVine SK 10.00 25.00
245 Kenneth Faried SK 4.00 10.00
246 Steven Adams SK 4.00 10.00
247 Derrick Rose SK 8.00 20.00
248 DeAndre Jordan SK 4.00 10.00
249 Andrew Wiggins SK 6.00 15.00
250 Marc Gasol SK 5.00 12.00
251 Magic Johnson SK 20.00 50.00
252 Larry Bird SK 20.00 50.00
253 Julius Erving SK 12.00 30.00
254 Kareem Abdul-Jabbar SK 15.00 40.00
255 Pete Maravich SK 8.00 20.00
256 Scottie Pippen SK 10.00 25.00
257 Clyde Drexler SK 8.00 20.00
258 David Robinson SK 10.00 25.00
259 John Stockton SK 8.00 20.00
260 Wilt Chamberlain SK 15.00 40.00
261 Patrick Ewing SK 6.00 15.00
262 George Gervin SK 8.00 20.00
263 Drazen Petrovic SK 5.00 12.00
264 Jerry West SK 12.00 30.00
265 Jason Kidd SK 8.00 20.00
266 Karl Malone SK 8.00 20.00
267 Bill Russell SK 15.00 40.00
268 Oscar Robertson SK 12.00 30.00
269 Isiah Thomas SK 8.00 20.00
270 Hakeem Olajuwon SK 10.00 25.00
271 John Havlicek SK 12.00 30.00
272 Tim Duncan SK 10.00 25.00
273 Shaquille O'Neal SK 15.00 40.00
274 Allen Iverson SK 8.00 20.00
275 Kobe Bryant SK 40.00 100.00
276 Brandon Ingram SK 12.00 30.00
277 Malcolm Brogdon SK 10.00 25.00
278 Domantas Sabonis SK 20.00 50.00
279 Denzel Valentine SK 3.00 8.00
280 Buddy Hield SK 10.00 25.00
281 Juan Hernangomez SK 6.00 15.00
282 Wade Baldwin IV SK 3.00 8.00
283 Malik Beasley SK 6.00 15.00
284 Ben Simmons SK 10.00 25.00
285 Henry Ellenson SK 3.00 8.00
286 Jamal Murray SK 25.00 60.00
287 T. Luwawu-Cabarrot SK 5.00 12.00
288 Jaylen Brown SK 25.00 60.00
289 Patrick McCaw SK 3.00 8.00
290 Taurean Prince SK 4.00 10.00
291 Marquese Chriss SK 4.00 10.00
292 DeAndre' Bembry SK 5.00 12.00
293 Malachi Richardson SK 3.00 8.00
294 Dragan Bender SK 3.00 8.00
295 Isaiah Whitehead SK 3.00 8.00
296 Dejounte Murray SK 15.00 40.00
297 Jakob Poeltl SK 6.00 15.00
298 Kris Dunn SK 5.00 12.00
299 Pascal Siakam SK 20.00 50.00
300 Thon Maker SK 4.00 10.00

2016-17 Studio Glossy

*GLOSSY 101-175: .75X TO 2X BASIC
*GLOSSY 176-200: .75X TO 2X BASIC
176 Brandon Ingram SE 12.00 30.00
184 Ben Simmons SE 4.00 10.00

2016-17 Studio Breakout Signatures

PRINT RUNS B/WN 49-299 COPIES PER
*MAGENTA/30: .6X TO 1.5X BASIC
1 Buddy Hield/299 10.00 25.00
2 Denzel Valentine/299 3.00 8.00
3 Kyle Wiltjer/299 3.00 8.00
4 Marshall Plumlee/299 3.00 8.00
5 Juan Hernangomez/299 6.00 15.00
6 Jake Layman/299 4.00 10.00
7 Malcolm Brogdon/299 10.00 25.00
8 Willy Hernangomez/299 4.00 10.00
9 Domantas Sabonis/299 20.00 50.00
10 Jaylen Brown/299 125.00 300.00
11 Wade Baldwin IV/299 3.00 8.00
12 Marquese Chriss/199 4.00 10.00
13 Kris Dunn/199 5.00 12.00
14 Kay Felder/199 3.00 8.00
15 Pascal Siakam/299 20.00 50.00
16 Dario Saric/299 5.00 12.00
17 Brandon Ingram/99 12.00 30.00
18 Malcolm Delaney/299 3.00 8.00
21 James Ennis/299 3.00 8.00
22 Trey Lyles/299 4.00 10.00
23 C.J. McCollum/299 5.00 12.00
24 Larry Nance Jr./299 3.00 8.00
25 Sean Kilpatrick/299 3.00 8.00
26 Justin Anderson/299 3.00 8.00
27 Rodney McGruder/299 4.00 10.00
28 Josh Richardson/299 4.00 10.00
29 Norman Powell/299 5.00 12.00
30 Mario Hezonja/299 3.00 8.00
31 Brandon Knight/199 4.00 10.00
32 Maurice Harkless/299 3.00 8.00
33 Karl-Anthony Towns/49 20.00 50.00
34 Stephen Curry/49 300.00 600.00
35 Clint Capela/249 4.00 10.00
36 Michael Carter-Williams/199 3.00 8.00
37 Zach LaVine/99 10.00 25.00
38 Kyrie Irving/99 15.00 40.00
39 Anthony Davis/49 20.00 50.00
40 Andrew Wiggins/99 6.00 15.00

2016-17 Studio Celebrated Signatures

STATED PRINT RUN 49 SER.#'d SETS
*MAGENTA/30: .6X TO 1.5X BASIC
1 Magic Johnson 25.00 60.00
2 Kyrie Irving 25.00 60.00
3 Dennis Rodman 20.00 50.00
5 Oscar Robertson 25.00 60.00
6 Patrick Ewing 40.00 100.00
7 Kareem Abdul-Jabbar 20.00 50.00
8 Shaquille O'Neal 30.00 80.00
9 Scottie Pippen 30.00 80.00
10 Kobe Bryant 400.00 800.00
11 Nate Thurmond 8.00 20.00
12 Larry Bird 25.00 60.00
13 Pat Riley 20.00 50.00
15 Stephen Curry 300.00 600.00

2016-17 Studio Defying Gravity Die Cut

1 Blake Griffin 2.50 6.00
2 Zach LaVine 5.00 12.00
3 LeBron James 20.00 50.00
4 Kevin Durant 10.00 25.00
5 Aaron Gordon 2.50 6.00
6 Giannis Antetokounmpo 12.00 30.00
7 Russell Westbrook 4.00 10.00
8 Andrew Wiggins 3.00 8.00
9 John Wall 3.00 8.00
10 Jaylen Brown 5.00 12.00
11 Tracy McGrady 4.00 10.00
12 Clyde Drexler 4.00 10.00
13 Julius Erving 6.00 15.00
14 Dominique Wilkins 3.00 8.00
15 Shawn Kemp 4.00 10.00
16 Kobe Bryant 8.00 20.00

2016-17 Studio Driven

1 Russell Westbrook 1.25 3.00
2 Isaiah Thomas .60 1.50
3 Paul George 1.25 3.00
4 Mike Conley .60 1.50
5 Giannis Antetokounmpo 4.00 10.00
6 Kristaps Porzingis 1.25 3.00
7 Elfrid Payton .60 1.50
8 Rudy Gay .75 2.00
9 Kawhi Leonard 2.00 5.00
10 LeBron James 6.00 15.00
11 James Harden 1.50 4.00
12 Kemba Walker .60 1.50
13 Stephen Curry 6.00 15.00
14 D'Angelo Russell 1.00 2.50
15 Josh Richardson .60 1.50
16 Karl-Anthony Towns 1.50 4.00
17 Devin Booker 3.00 8.00
18 C.J. McCollum .75 2.00
19 Kyle Lowry .75 2.00
20 John Wall 1.00 2.50
21 Dennis Schroder .75 2.00
22 Dwyane Wade 1.50 4.00
23 Kevin Durant 3.00 8.00
24 Chris Paul 1.25 3.00
25 Jabari Parker .50 1.25
26 Andrew Wiggins 1.00 2.50
27 Dario Saric .75 2.00
28 Damian Lillard 2.00 5.00
29 Gordon Hayward .75 2.00
30 Bradley Beal 1.00 2.50

2016-17 Studio First Impact Memorabilia

*MAGENTA/23-30: 1X TO 2.5X BASIC
1 Brandon Ingram 5.00 12.00
2 Jaylen Brown 10.00 25.00
3 Dragan Bender 1.25 3.00
4 Kris Dunn 2.00 5.00
5 Buddy Hield 4.00 10.00
6 Jamal Murray 10.00 25.00
7 Marquese Chriss 1.50 4.00
8 Jakob Poeltl 2.50 6.00
9 Thon Maker 1.50 4.00
10 Domantas Sabonis 8.00 20.00
11 Taurean Prince 1.50 4.00
12 Denzel Valentine 1.25 3.00
13 Juan Hernangomez 2.50 6.00
14 Georgios Papagiannis 1.25 3.00
15 Wade Baldwin IV 1.25 3.00
16 Henry Ellenson 1.25 3.00
17 Malik Beasley 2.50 6.00
18 Caris LeVert 3.00 8.00
19 Malachi Richardson 1.25 3.00
20 Malcolm Brogdon 4.00 10.00
21 Dejounte Murray 6.00 15.00
22 Kay Felder 1.25 3.00
23 Patrick McCaw 1.25 3.00
24 Timothe Luwawu-Cabarrot 2.00 5.00
25 Isaiah Whitehead 1.25 3.00

2016-17 Studio From Downtown

1 Stephen Curry 800.00 1,500.00
2 James Harden 125.00 300.00
3 Karl-Anthony Towns 75.00 200.00
4 Yogi Ferrell 20.00 50.00
5 Russell Westbrook 75.00 200.00
6 Damian Lillard 150.00 400.00
7 LeBron James 1,500.00 3,000.00
8 Jimmy Butler 75.00 200.00
9 Kristaps Porzingis 50.00 120.00
10 Ben Simmons 60.00 150.00
11 Isaiah Thomas 40.00 100.00
12 Kyrie Irving 125.00 300.00
13 Kevin Durant 800.00 1,500.00
14 Devin Booker 300.00 600.00
15 Andrew Wiggins 60.00 150.00
16 Dirk Nowitzki 200.00 500.00
17 J.J. Redick 40.00 100.00
18 Kobe Bryant 1,500.00 3,000.00
19 Gary Payton 75.00 200.00
20 Allen Iverson 150.00 400.00

2016-17 Studio Gamers Memorabilia

*MAGENTA/30: 1X TO 2.5X BASIC
1 Steven Adams 1.50 4.00
2 LaMarcus Aldridge 2.00 5.00
3 Justin Anderson 1.25 3.00
4 Harrison Barnes 1.50 4.00
5 Nicolas Batum 1.50 4.00
6 Bradley Beal 2.50 6.00
7 Patrick Beverley 1.25 3.00
8 Devin Booker 8.00 20.00
9 Jordan Clarkson 2.00 5.00
10 Goran Dragic 2.00 5.00
11 Andre Drummond 2.00 5.00
12 Joel Embiid 5.00 12.00
13 Kenneth Faried 1.50 4.00
14 Marc Gasol 2.00 5.00
15 Pau Gasol 3.00 8.00
16 Rudy Gay 2.00 5.00
17 Taj Gibson 1.25 3.00
18 Rudy Gobert 2.50 6.00
19 Aaron Gordon 2.00 5.00
20 Draymond Green 2.50 6.00
21 Gordon Hayward 2.00 5.00
22 Al Horford 2.00 5.00
23 Dwight Howard 2.50 6.00
24 Reggie Jackson 1.50 4.00
25 DeAndre Jordan 1.50 4.00
26 Enes Kanter 1.25 3.00
27 Zach LaVine 4.00 10.00
28 Brook Lopez 1.50 4.00
29 Kevin Love 2.00 5.00
30 Wesley Matthews 1.25 3.00
31 C.J. McCollum 2.00 5.00
32 Emmanuel Mudiay 1.25 3.00
33 Joakim Noah 1.25 3.00
34 Victor Oladipo 1.50 4.00
35 Jabari Parker 1.25 3.00
36 Kristaps Porzingis 3.00 8.00
37 Julius Randle 2.50 6.00
38 J.J. Redick 2.00 5.00
39 D'Angelo Russell 2.50 6.00
40 Dennis Schroder 2.00 5.00
41 Marcus Smart 2.50 6.00
42 Isaiah Thomas 1.50 4.00
43 Tristan Thompson 1.50 4.00
44 Myles Turner 2.00 5.00
45 Hassan Whiteside 1.50 4.00
46 Andrew Wiggins 2.50 6.00

2016-17 Studio Rising to the Occasion

1 James Harden 1.50 4.00
2 Russell Westbrook 1.25 3.00
3 Kyrie Irving 1.50 4.00
4 Stephen Curry 6.00 15.00
5 DeMarcus Cousins .60 1.50
6 Damian Lillard 2.00 5.00
7 Kenneth Faried .60 1.50
8 Karl-Anthony Towns 1.50 4.00
9 Jimmy Butler 1.50 4.00
10 Kentavious Caldwell-Pope .60 1.50
11 Dirk Nowitzki 2.00 5.00
12 Kawhi Leonard 2.00 5.00
13 LeBron James 6.00 15.00
14 John Wall 1.00 2.50
15 Giannis Antetokounmpo 4.00 10.00
16 Aaron Gordon .75 2.00
17 Dennis Schroder .75 2.00
18 Jordan Clarkson .75 2.00
19 Isaiah Thomas .60 1.50
20 Carmelo Anthony 1.25 3.00
21 Blake Griffin .75 2.00
22 Devin Booker 3.00 8.00
23 DeMar DeRozan 1.00 2.50
24 Paul George 1.25 3.00
25 George Hill .60 1.50
26 Clyde Drexler 1.25 3.00
27 Tim Duncan 1.50 4.00
28 Tracy McGrady 1.25 3.00
29 Chauncey Billups 1.00 2.50
30 Robert Horry .75 2.00
31 Larry Bird 3.00 8.00
32 Shaquille O'Neal 2.50 6.00
33 John Havlicek 2.00 5.00
34 Steve Nash 1.25 3.00
35 Kobe Bryant 6.00 15.00

2016-17 Studio Rock Solid Die Cut

1 Ben Wallace 8.00 20.00
2 Jae Crowder 4.00 10.00
3 Jimmy Butler 8.00 20.00
4 James Harden 12.00 30.00
5 Russell Westbrook 12.00 30.00
6 LeBron James 30.00 80.00
7 Shaquille O'Neal 10.00 25.00
8 Kyle Lowry 6.00 15.00
9 Kobe Bryant 50.00 120.00
10 Draymond Green 10.00 25.00
11 Joel Embiid 8.00 20.00
12 Eric Bledsoe 5.00 12.00
13 Karl-Anthony Towns 12.00 30.00
14 DeAndre Jordan 5.00 12.00

2016-17 Studio Signatures

PRINT RUNS B/WN 49-299 COPIES PER
*MAGENTA/30: .6X TO 1.5X BASIC
1 Trey Lyles/299 4.00 10.00
2 C.J. McCollum/299 5.00 12.00
3 Jason Terry/299 4.00 10.00
4 Justin Anderson/299 3.00 8.00
5 Josh Richardson/299 4.00 10.00
6 Mario Hezonja/299 3.00 8.00
7 Brandon Knight/299 4.00 10.00
8 Maurice Harkless/299 3.00 8.00
9 Jrue Holiday/299 6.00 15.00
10 Karl-Anthony Towns/60 10.00 25.00
11 Al Horford/249 5.00 12.00
12 Khris Middleton/199 5.00 12.00
13 Kobe Bryant/49 800.00 1,500.00
14 Evan Turner/165 3.00 8.00
15 J.J. Barea/125 12.00 30.00
16 Luol Deng/125 4.00 10.00
17 Andre Drummond/249 5.00 12.00
18 Alec Burks/299 4.00 10.00
20 Marcin Gortat/299 3.00 8.00
21 Cody Zeller/299 3.00 8.00
22 Devin Harris/299 3.00 8.00
23 Taurean Prince/299 4.00 10.00
24 Buddy Hield/299 10.00 25.00
25 Denzel Valentine/299 3.00 8.00
26 Joel Bolomboy/299 3.00 8.00
27 Diamond Stone/299 3.00 8.00
28 Deyonta Davis/299 3.00 8.00
29 DeAndre' Bembry/299 5.00 12.00
30 Demetrius Jackson/299 3.00 8.00
32 Cheick Diallo/299 3.00 8.00
33 Damian Jones/299 3.00 8.00
34 Brice Johnson/299 3.00 8.00
35 Ivica Zubac/299 8.00 20.00
36 Jaylen Brown/99 125.00 300.00
37 Wade Baldwin IV/299 3.00 8.00
38 Marquese Chriss/249 4.00 10.00
39 Kris Dunn/175 5.00 12.00
40 Kristaps Porzingis/199 15.00 40.00
41 Larry Nance Jr./299 3.00 8.00
42 Brandon Ingram/99 30.00 80.00
43 Domantas Sabonis/299 20.00 50.00
44 Jamal Murray/199 40.00 100.00
45 Thon Maker/125 4.00 10.00

2016-17 Studio The Influencers Memorabilia

*MAGENTA/30: 1X TO 2.5X BASIC
1 Stephen Curry 25.00 60.00
2 LeBron James 40.00 100.00
3 Kevin Durant 8.00 20.00
4 James Harden 4.00 10.00
5 Russell Westbrook 3.00 8.00
6 Damian Lillard 5.00 12.00
7 DeMarcus Cousins 1.50 4.00
8 Dwyane Wade 4.00 10.00
9 Carmelo Anthony 3.00 8.00
10 Paul George 3.00 8.00
11 Anthony Davis 6.00 15.00
12 Dirk Nowitzki 5.00 12.00
13 Kyrie Irving 4.00 10.00
14 Karl-Anthony Towns 4.00 10.00
15 Chris Paul 3.00 8.00
16 Andre Drummond 2.00 5.00
17 Jimmy Butler 4.00 10.00
18 Isaiah Thomas 1.50 4.00
19 Kawhi Leonard 5.00 12.00
20 John Wall 2.50 6.00
21 C.J. McCollum 2.00 5.00
22 Giannis Antetokounmpo 10.00 25.00
23 DeMar DeRozan 2.50 6.00
24 Gordon Hayward 2.00 5.00
25 Klay Thompson 5.00 12.00
26 Dwight Howard 2.50 6.00
27 Hassan Whiteside 1.50 4.00
28 Kemba Walker 1.50 4.00
29 Julius Randle 2.50 6.00

2016-17 Studio Top Five

TOP1 Dario Saric 15.00 40.00
TOP2 Malcolm Brogdon 30.00 80.00
TOP3 Brandon Ingram 50.00 120.00
TOP4 Jaylen Brown 40.00 100.00
TOP5 Jamal Murray 12.00 30.00

1992-93 Suns 25th

COMPLETE SET (26) 6.00 15.00
1 Gail Goodrich .75 2.00
2 Connie Hawkins .75 2.00
3 Dick Van Arsdale .40 1.00
4 Paul Silas .40 1.00
5 Neil Walk .20 .50
6 Charlie Scott .25 .60
7 Curtis Perry .20 .50
8 Curtis Perry .20 .50
9 Alvan Adams .25 .60
10 Garfield Heard .20 .50
11 Walter Davis .40 1.00
12 Paul Westphal .40 1.00
13 Don Buse .20 .50
14 Truck Robinson .25 .60
15 Kyle Macy .40 1.00
16 Dennis Johnson .50 1.25
17 Maurice Lucas .40 1.00
18 Larry Nance .40 1.00
19 Walter Davis .40 1.00
20 Jeff Hornacek .40 1.00
21 Eddie Johnson .30 .75
22 Tyrone Corbin .20 .50
23 Tom Chambers .30 .75
24 Kevin Johnson .40 1.00
25 Dan Majerle .40 1.00
26 Charles Barkley 1.25 3.00

1976-77 Suns 8 x 10

COMPLETE SET (9) 25.00 50.00
1 Dennis Awtrey 1.25 3.00
2 Al Bianchi CO 1.50 4.00
3 Jerry Colangelo GM 1.25 3.00
4 Keith Erickson 1.25 3.00
5 Butch Feher 1.25 3.00
6 Garfield Heard 2.00 5.00
7 Ron Lee 1.25 3.00
8 John McLeod CO 1.25 3.00
9 Curtis Perry 1.25 3.00
10 Joe Proski TR 1.25 3.00
11 Ricky Sobers 1.25 3.00
12 Ira Terrell 1.25 3.00
13 Dick Van Arsdale 2.00 5.00
14 Tom Van Arsdale 1.50 4.00
15 Dick Van Arsdale
Tom Van Arsdale 2.00 5.00
16 Paul Westphal 2.50 6.00

1970-71 Suns A1 Premium Beer

COMPLETE SET (13) 900.00 1,700.00
1A Mel Counts
(95 cents) 50.00 100.00
1B Mel Counts
(98 cents) 60.00 120.00
2 Lamar Green 40.00 85.00
3 Clem Haskins 75.00 150.00
4 Connie Hawkins
(98 cents) 250.00 450.00
5 Greg Howard 40.00 85.00
6 Paul Silas 125.00 225.00
7 Fred Taylor CO 40.00 85.00
8A Dick Van Arsdale ERR 100.00 175.00
8B Dick Van Arsdale COR 75.00 150.00
9A Neal Walk
(95 cents) 50.00 100.00
9B Neal Walk
(No price) 60.00 120.00
10 John Wetzel
(No price) 50.00 100.00

1968-69 Suns Carnation Milk

COMPLETE SET (12) 800.00 1,400.00
1 Jim Fox 60.00 125.00
2 Gail Goodrich 200.00 400.00
3 Gary Gregor 50.00 100.00
4 Neil Johnson 60.00 125.00
5 John Kerr CO 90.00 170.00
6 Dave Lattin 60.00 125.00
7 Stan McKenzie 40.00 80.00
8 McCoy McLemore 40.00 80.00
9 Dick Snyder 40.00 80.00
10 Dick Van Arsdale 75.00 150.00
11 Bob Warlick 60.00 125.00
12 George Wilson 40.00 80.00

1969-70 Suns Carnation Milk

COMPLETE SET (10) 700.00 1,100.00
1 Jerry Chambers 35.00 70.00
2 Jim Fox 35.00 70.00
3 Gail Goodrich 100.00 200.00
4 Connie Hawkins 200.00 400.00
5 Stan McKenzie 35.00 70.00
6 Paul Silas 100.00 200.00
7 Dick Snyder 35.00 70.00
8 Dick Van Arsdale 50.00 100.00
9 Neal Walk 60.00 120.00
10 Gene Williams 35.00 70.00

1970-71 Suns Carnation Milk

COMPLETE SET (10) 400.00 800.00
1 Mel Counts 30.00 60.00
2 Lamar Green 25.00 50.00
3 Art Harris 25.00 50.00
4 Clem Haskins 40.00 80.00
5 Connie Hawkins 125.00 250.00
6 Gus Johnson 60.00 120.00
7 Otto Moore 25.00 50.00
8 Paul Silas 60.00 120.00
9 Dick Van Arsdale 40.00 80.00
10 Neal Walk 30.00 60.00

1971-72 Suns Carnation Milk

COMPLETE SET (5) 200.00 400.00
1 Connie Hawkins 100.00 200.00
2 Otto Moore 25.00 50.00
3 Fred Taylor CO 25.00 50.00
4 Neal Walk 30.00 60.00
5 John Wetzel 30.00 60.00

1972-73 Suns Carnation Milk

COMPLETE SET (12) 400.00 800.00
1 Mel Counts 30.00 60.00
2 Lamar Green 25.00 50.00
3 Clem Haskins 40.00 80.00
4 Connie Hawkins 100.00 200.00
5 Gus Johnson 50.00 100.00
6 Dennis Layton 30.00 60.00
7 Otto Moore 25.00 50.00
8 Fred Taylor CO 25.00 50.00
9 Dick Van Arsdale 40.00 80.00
10 Bill VanBredaKolff CO 25.00 50.00
11 Neal Walk 30.00 60.00
12 John Wetzel 30.00 60.00

1987-88 Suns Circle K

COMPLETE SET (15) 15.00 40.00
1 Alvan Adams 1.25 3.00
2 Herb Brown ACO .75 2.00
3 Jeff Cook .75 2.00
4 Winston Crite .60 1.50
5 Walter Davis 1.50 4.00
6 James Edwards 1.00 2.50
7 Armon Gilliam 2.50 6.00
8 Jeff Hornacek 4.00 10.00
9 Jay Humphries 1.00 2.50
10 Eddie Johnson 1.50 4.00
11 Larry Nance 2.00 5.00
12 Joe Proski TR .60 1.50
13 Mike Sanders .60 1.50
14 Bernard Thompson .60 1.50
15 John Wetzel CO .60 1.50

1975-76 Suns Fan Grabber

COMPLETE SET (16) 10.00 25.00
1 Alvan Adams 2.00 5.00
2 Dennis Awtrey .60 1.50
3 Al Bianchi GM .60 1.50
4 Jerry Colangelo VP 1.00 2.50
5 Keith Erickson 1.25 3.00
6 Nate Hawthorne .60 1.50
7 Garfield Heard 1.00 2.50
8 Phil Lumpkin .60 1.50
9 John MacLeod CO .75 2.00
10 Curtis Perry .75 2.00
11 Joe Proski TR .60 1.50
12 Pat Riley 7.50 15.00
13 Ricky Sobers 1.00 2.50
14 Dick Van Arsdale 1.25 3.00
15 Paul Westphal 3.00 8.00
16 John Wetzel .40 1.00

1982-83 Suns Giant Service

COMPLETE SET (3) 8.00 20.00
1 Walter Davis
January 3.00 7.00
2 Maurice Lucas
February 2.00 5.00
3 Larry Nance
March 4.00 9.00

1972-73 Suns Holsum

COMPLETE SET (9) 100.00 175.00
1 Corky Calhoun 8.00 20.00
2 Lamar Green 8.00 20.00
3 Clem Haskins 15.00 30.00
4 Connie Hawkins 60.00 120.00
5 Dennis Layton 8.00 20.00
6 Charlie Scott 25.00 50.00
7 Dick Van Arsdale 15.00 30.00
8 Neal Walk 10.00 20.00
9 Walt Wesley 8.00 20.00

1977-78 Suns Humpty Dumpty Discs

COMPLETE SET (12) 15.00 30.00
1 Alvan Adams 1.25 3.00
2 Dennis Awtrey .75 2.00
3 Mike Bratz 1.00 2.50
4 Don Buse 1.00 2.50
5 Walter Davis 7.50 15.00
6 Bayard Forrest .75 2.00
7 Garfield Heard 1.25 3.00
8 Ron Lee .75 2.00
9 Curtis Perry .75 2.00
10 Alvin Scott .75 2.00
11 Ira Terrell 1.00 2.50
12 Paul Westphal 2.50 6.00

1980-81 Suns Pepsi

COMPLETE SET (12) 5.00 10.00
1 Walter Davis 1.25 3.00
2 Alvin Scott .30 .75
3 Johnny High .30 .75
4 Dennis Johnson 1.25 3.00
5 Alvan Adams .75 2.00
6 Rich Kelley .30 .75
7 Truck Robinson .60 1.50
8 Joel Kramer .50 1.25
9 Jeff Cook .30 .75
10 Mike Niles .30 .75
11 Kyle Macy .60 1.50
12 John MacLeod CO .30 .75

1981-82 Suns Pepsi

COMPLETE SET (12) 20.00 50.00
1 Alvan Adams 2.00 5.00
2 Dudley Bradley 1.25 3.00
3 Jeff Cooke 1.25 3.00
4 Walter Davis 4.00 10.00
5 The Gorilla 2.00 5.00
6 Dennis Johnson 4.00 10.00
7 Joel Kramer 1.50 4.00
8 John MacLeod CO 1.50 4.00
9 Kyle Macy 2.00 5.00
10 Larry Nance 6.00 15.00
11 Truck Robinson 2.00 5.00
12 Alvin Scott 1.25 3.00

1984-85 Suns Police

COMPLETE SET (16) 20.00 40.00
4 Kyle Macy 1.50 4.00
6 Walter Davis 3.00 8.00
7 Mike Sanders .75 2.00
8 Rick Robey 1.50 4.00
10 Rod Foster .75 2.00
14 Alvin Scott .75 2.00
20 Maurice Lucas 1.50 4.00
22 Larry Nance 4.00 10.00
32 Charles Pittman .75 2.00
33 Alvan Adams 1.50 4.00
44 Paul Westphal 2.50 6.00
53 James Edwards 1.50 4.00
NNO Suns Mascot 1.50 4.00
NNO John MacLeod CO .75 2.00
NNO Al Bianchi ACO .75 2.00
NNO Joe Proski TR .75 2.00

1990-91 Suns Smokey

COMPLETE SET (5) 9.00 18.00
1 Tom Chambers 1.50 4.00
2 Jeff Hornacek 1.50 4.00
3 Eddie Johnson SP 2.50 6.00
4 Kevin Johnson 2.50 6.00
5 Dan Majerle 2.00 5.00

1972-73 Suns Team Issue

COMPLETE SET (10) 25.00 50.00
1 Corky Calhoun 1.25 3.00
2 Mel Counts 1.25 3.00
3 Lamar Green 1.25 3.00
4 Clem Haskins 2.50 6.00
5 Connie Hawkins 7.50 15.00
6 Gus Johnson 2.00 5.00
7 Dennis Mo Layton 1.25 3.00
8 Charlie Scott 3.00 8.00
9 Dick Van Arsdale 2.00 5.00
10 Neal Walk 1.50 4.00

1973-74 Suns Team Issue

COMPLETE SET 15.00 30.00
1 Dick Van Arsdale 1.50 4.00
2 Neal Walk 1.25 3.00
3 Dennis Scott 1.50 4.00
4 Lamar Green 1.25 3.00
5 Clem Haskins 1.25 3.00
6 Mike Bantom 1.25 3.00
7 Jim Owens 1.25 3.00
8 Bob Christian 1.25 3.00
9 Corky Calhoun 1.25 3.00
10 Gary Melchionni 1.25 3.00
11 Keith Erickson 1.25 3.00
12 Bill Chamberlain 1.25 3.00

1974-75 Suns Team Issue

COMPLETE SET (11) 17.50 35.00
1 Dennis Awtrey 1.25 3.00
2 Mike Bantom 1.25 3.00
3 Keith Erickson 1.50 4.00
4 Nate Hawthorne 1.25 3.00
5 Gary Melchionni 1.25 3.00
6 Jim Owens 1.25 3.00
7 Curtis Perry 1.25 3.00
8 Fred Saunders 1.25 3.00
9 Charlie Scott 2.50 6.00
10 Dick Van Arsdale 1.50 4.00
11 Earl Williams 1.25 3.00

1975-76 Suns Team Issue

COMPLETE SET (14) 12.00 30.00
1 Alvan Adams 1.50 4.00
2 Dennis Awtrey .75 2.00
3 Keith Erickson 1.25 3.00
4 Nate Hawthorne .75 2.00
5 Phil Lumpkin .75 2.00
6 John MacLeod CO 1.25 3.00
7 Curtis Perry .75 2.00
8 Joe Proski TR .75 2.00
9 Pat Riley 5.00 10.00
10 Fred Saunders .75 2.00
11 John Shumate 1.25 3.00
12 Ricky Sobers .75 2.00
13 Paul Westphal 2.00 5.00
14 John Wetzel .75 2.00

1977-78 Suns Team Issue

COMPLETE SET (12) 20.00 40.00
1 Alvan Adams 2.00 5.00
2 Dennis Awtrey 1.25 3.00
3 Mike Bratz 1.25 3.00
4 Don Buse 1.25 3.00
5 Walter Davis 3.00 8.00
6 Bayard Forrest 1.25 3.00
7 Greg Griffin 1.25 3.00
8 Garfield Heard 1.50 4.00
9 Ron Lee 1.25 3.00
10 Curtis Perry 1.25 3.00
11 Alvin Scott 1.25 3.00
12 Paul Westphal 2.00 5.00

1988-89 Suns Team Issue

COMPLETE SET (7) 10.00 25.00
1 Tyrone Corbin 1.50 4.00
2 Kenny Gattison 1.00 2.50
3 Armon Gilliam 1.50 4.00
4 Jeff Hornacek 2.00 5.00
5 Eddie Johnson 1.25 3.00
6 Kevin Johnson 5.00 12.00
7 Mark West 1.00 2.50

2001-02 Suns Topps

COMPLETE SET (9) 2.00 5.00
PS1 Jason Kidd .75 2.00
PS2 Anfernee Hardaway 1.25 3.00
PS3 Tom Gugliotta .30 .75
PS5 Clifford Robinson .50 1.25
PS6 Rodney Rogers .30 .75
PS7 Chris Dudley .30 .75
PS8 Scott Skiles CO .30 .75
PS9 The Gorilla MASCOT .25 .60
NNO Phoenix Suns .25 .60

1992-93 Suns Topps/Circle K Stickers

COMPLETE SET (12) 4.00 10.00
1 Danny Ainge S1 .60 1.50
2 Charles Barkley S3 1.50 4.00
3 Cedric Ceballos S3 .30 .75
4 Tom Chambers S4 .60 1.50
5 Frank Johnson S1 .20 .50
6 Kevin Johnson S1 .60 1.50
7 Tom Kempton S4 .08 .25
8 Negele Knight S2 .08 .25
9 Dan Majerle S2 .60 1.50
10 Oliver Miller S3 .20 .50
11 Jerrod Mustaf S4 .08 .25
12 Mark West S2 .08 .25

1976-77 Suns

COMPLETE SET (12) 6.00 15.00
1 Alvan Adams 1.25 3.00
2 Dennis Awtrey .60 1.50
3 Keith Erickson 1.25 3.00
4 Butch Feher .60 1.50
5 Garfield Heard 1.00 2.50
6 Ron Lee .60 1.50
7 Curtis Perry .60 1.50
8 Ricky Sobers 1.00 2.50
9 Ira Terrell .75 2.00
10 Dick Van Arsdale 1.25 3.00
11 Tom Van Arsdale 1.25 3.00
12 Paul Westphal 2.00 5.00

1987-88 Suns Wendy's

COMPLETE SET (4) 6.00 15.00
1 Jay Humphries 2.00 5.00
2 Larry Nance 4.00 10.00
3 Mike Sanders 1.25 3.00
4 Bernard Thompson 1.25 3.00

1974-75 Supersonics KTW-1250 Milk Cartons

COMPLETE SET (2) 60.00 120.00
1 Wayne Cody ANN 10.00 20.00
2 Bill Russell GM 50.00 100.00

1990-91 Supersonics Kayo

COMPLETE SET (14) 3.00 8.00
1 Shawn Kemp 1.00 2.50
2 Scott Meents .15 .40
3 Derrick McKey .25 .60
4 Michael Cage .25 .60
5 Benoit Benjamin .08 .25
6 Dave Corzine .08 .25
7 K.C. Jones CO .30 .75
8 Quintin Dailey .08 .25
9 Ricky Pierce .25 .60
10 Eddie Johnson .25 .60
11 Nate McMillan .40 1.00
12 Gary Payton 1.50 4.00
13 Sedale Threatt .08 .25
14 Dana Barros .20 .50

1993-94 Supersonics Playoff Taco Time

COMPLETE SET (4) 2.00 5.00
COMMON CARD (1-4) .50 1.25

1978-79 Supersonics Police

COMPLETE SET (16) 10.00 20.00
1 Fred Brown .75 2.00
2 Joe Hassett .30 .75
3 Dennis Johnson 1.50 4.00
4 John Johnson .30 .75
5 Tom LaGarde .40 1.00
6 Lonnie Shelton .50 1.25
7 Jack Sikma 1.00 2.50
8 Paul Silas 1.00 2.50
9 Dick Snyder .30 .75
10 Wally Walker .30 .75
11 Gus Williams .75 2.00
12 Len Wilkens CO 1.50 4.00
13 Les Habegger ACO .30 .75
14 Frank Furtado TR .30 .75
15 T. Wheedle
mascot .30 .75
16 Team Photo .75 2.00

1979-80 Supersonics Police

COMPLETE SET (16) 7.50 15.00
1 Gus Williams .60 1.50
2 James Bailey .30 .75
3 Jack Sikma .60 1.50
4 Tom LaGarde .30 .75

5 Paul Silas .75 2.00
6 Lonnie Shelton .40 1.00
7 T. Wheedle (Mascot) .20 .50
8 Vinnie Johnson 1.25 3.00
9 Dennis Johnson 1.00 2.50
10 Wally Walker .40 1.00
11 Les Habegger ACO .25 .60
12 Frank Furtado TR .25 .60
13 Fred Brown .60 1.50
14 John Johnson .30 .75
15 Team Photo 1.00 2.50
16 Len Wilkens CO 1.00 2.50

1983-84 Supersonics Police

COMPLETE SET (16) 3.00 8.00
1 Reggie King .30 .75
2 Frank Furtado TR .25 .60
3 Tom Chambers 1.25 3.00
4 Dave Harshman ACO .25 .60
5 Gus Williams .40 1.00
6 T. Wheedle (Mascot) .25 .60
7 Scooter McCray .30 .75
8 Jack Sikma .40 1.00
9 Al Wood .25 .60
10 Bob Blackburn ANN .25 .60
11 Danny Vranes .30 .75
12 Charles Bradley .25 .60
13 Steve Hawes .30 .75
14 Jon Sundvold .30 .75
15 Fred Brown .40 1.00
16 Lenny Wilkens CO .75 2.00

1979-80 Supersonics Portfolio

COMPLETE SET (11) 22.50 45.00
1 Dennis Awtrey 1.25 3.00
2 Fred Brown 3.00 8.00
3 Dennis Johnson 5.00 10.00
4 John Johnson 1.25 3.00
5 Tom LaGarde 1.25 3.00
6 Lonnie Shelton 1.50 4.00
7 Jack Sikma 3.00 8.00
8 Paul Silas 3.00 8.00
9 Dick Snyder 1.25 3.00
10 Wally Walker 1.50 4.00
11 Gus Williams 2.50 6.00

1971-72 Supersonics Reed

COMPLETE SET (13) 25.00 50.00
1 Fred Brown 2.50 6.00
2 Barry Clemens 1.25 3.00
3 Pete Cross 1.25 3.00
4 Jake Ford 1.25 3.00
5 Spencer Haywood 3.00 8.00
6 Garfield Heard 1.50 4.00
7 Don Kojis 1.25 3.00
8 Bob Rule 1.25 3.00
9 Don Smith 1.25 3.00
10 Dick Snyder 1.25 3.00
11 Rod Thorn ACO 1.50 4.00
12 Lenny Wilkens 5.00 10.00
13 Lee Winfield 1.25 3.00

1973-74 Supersonics Shur-Fresh

COMPLETE SET (12) 50.00 100.00
1 John Brisker 5.00 10.00
2 Fred Brown 10.00 20.00
3 Emmette Bryant ACO 3.00 8.00
4 Jim Fox 5.00 10.00
5 Dick Gibbs 3.00 8.00
6 Spencer Haywood 6.00 15.00
7 Bill Russell CO 30.00 60.00
8 Jim McDaniels 6.00 12.00
9 Kennedy McIntosh 3.00 8.00
10 Dick Snyder 3.00 8.00
11 Bud Stallworth 3.00 8.00
12 Lee Winfield 3.00 8.00

1990-91 Supersonics Smokey

COMPLETE SET (16) 6.00 15.00
1 Dana Barros .60 1.50
2 Michael Cage .60 1.50
3 Dave Corzine .40 1.00
4 Quintin Dailey .40 1.00
5 Dale Ellis .60 1.50
6 K.C. Jones CO .60 1.50
7 Shawn Kemp 1.50 4.00
8 Bob Kloppenburg CO .40 1.00
9 Xavier McDaniel .40 1.00
10 Derrick McKey .60 1.50
11 Nate McMillan .75 2.00
12 Scott Meents .40 1.00
13 Kip Motta CO .40 1.00
14 Gary Payton 3.00 8.00
15 Olden Polynice .40 1.00
16 Sedale Threatt .40 1.00

1969-70 Supersonics Sunbeam Bread

COMPLETE SET (11) 50.00 100.00
1 Lucius Allen 10.00 20.00
2 Bob Boozer 6.00 12.00
3 Barry Clemens 5.00 10.00
4 Art Harris 5.00 10.00
5 Tom Meschery SP 7.50 15.00
6 Erwin Mueller 5.00 10.00
7 Dorie Murrey 5.00 10.00
8 Bob Rule 6.00 12.00
9 John Tresvant 5.00 10.00
10 Len Wilkens P/CO SP 20.00 40.00
11 Seattle Coliseum DP 5.00 10.00

1970-71 Supersonics Sunbeam Bread

COMPLETE SET (11) 50.00 100.00
1 Tom Black 5.00 10.00
2 Barry Clemens 5.00 10.00
3 Pete Cross 5.00 10.00
4 Jake Ford 5.00 10.00
5 Garfield Heard 6.00 15.00
6 Don Kojis 6.00 12.00
7 Tom Meschery SP 6.00 15.00
8 Dick Snyder 5.00 10.00
9 Len Wilkens P/CO SP 20.00 40.00
10 Lee Winfield 5.00 10.00
11 Seattle Coliseum 5.00 10.00

1971-72 Supersonics Sunbeam Bread

COMPLETE SET (11) 50.00 100.00
1 Pete Cross 5.00 10.00
2 Jake Ford 5.00 10.00
3 Spencer Haywood 10.00 20.00
4 Garfield Heard 7.50 15.00
5 Don Kojis 6.00 12.00
6 Bob Rule 6.00 12.00
7 Don Smith 5.00 10.00
8 Dick Snyder 5.00 10.00
9 Len Wilkens P/CO 15.00 30.00
10 Lee Winfield 5.00 10.00
11 Sonics Coliseum 5.00 10.00

1993-94 Supersonics Taco Time

COMPLETE SET (9) 9.00 18.00
1 Nate McMillan 1.25 3.00
2 Sam Perkins 1.25 3.00
3 Gary Payton 2.50 6.00
4 Ricky Pierce .75 2.00
5A Derrick McKey .75 2.00
5B Detlef Schrempf 1.25 3.00
6 Shawn Kemp 1.50 4.00
7 George Karl CO .75 2.00
8 Kendall Gill 1.00 2.50
9 Michael Cage .75 2.00

1967-68 Supersonics Team Issue

COMPLETE SET (12) 100.00 200.00
1 Henry Akin 7.50 15.00
2 Walt Hazzard 15.00 30.00
3 Tommy Kron 7.50 15.00
4 Plummer Lott 7.50 15.00
5 Tom Meschery 10.00 20.00
6 Dorie Murrey 7.50 15.00
7 Bud Olsen 7.50 15.00
8 Bob Rule 10.00 20.00
9 Rod Thorn 10.00 20.00
10 Al Tucker 7.50 15.00
11 Bob Weiss 10.00 20.00
12 George Wilson 7.50 15.00

1968-69 Supersonics Team Issue

COMPLETE SET (12) 60.00 120.00
1 Dorie Murrey 5.00 10.00
2 Tom Meschery 6.00 12.00
3 Len Wilkens 12.50 25.00
4 Al Hairston 5.00 10.00
5 Art Harris 5.00 10.00
6 Bob Kauffman 5.00 10.00
7 Rod Thorn 6.00 12.00
8 Al Tucker 5.00 10.00
9 Bob Rule 6.00 12.00
10 Plummer Lott 5.00 10.00
11 Tommy Kron 5.00 10.00
12 Joe Kennedy 5.00 10.00

1975-76 Supersonics Team Issue

COMPLETE SET (8) 10.00 20.00
1 Mike Bantom 1.25 3.00
2 Rod Derline 1.25 3.00
3 Herm Gilliam 1.25 3.00
4 Leonard Gray 1.25 3.00
5 Willie Norwood 1.25 3.00
6 Frank Oleynick 1.25 3.00
7 Bruce Seals 1.25 3.00
8 Talvin Skinner 1.25 3.00

1976-77 Supersonics Team Issue

COMPLETE SET (9) 12.50 25.00
1 Mike Bantom 1.25 3.00
2 Tommy Burleson 1.50 4.00
3 Leonard Gray 1.25 3.00
4 Mike Green 1.25 3.00
5 Willie Norwood 1.25 3.00
6 Frank Oleynick 1.25 3.00
7 Bruce Seals 1.25 3.00
8 Slick Watts 1.25 3.00
9 Bob Wilkerson 1.50 4.00

1978-79 Supersonics Team Issue

COMPLETE SET (11) 17.50 35.00
1 Fred Brown 2.50 6.00
2 Al Fleming .75 2.00
3 Joe Hassett .75 2.00
4 Dennis Johnson 3.00 8.00
5 John Johnson .75 2.00
6 Jack Sikma 2.50 6.00
7 Paul Silas 2.50 6.00
8 Wally Walker 1.00 2.50
9 Marvin Webster 1.25 3.00
10 Gus Williams 2.00 5.00
11 Cover Photo (Smaller versions of all ten photos) 2.00 5.00

1978-79 Supersonics Team Issue 8 X 10

COMPLETE SET (7) 12.50 25.00
1 Fred Brown 2.00 5.00
2 Dennis Johnson 2.00 5.00
3 John Johnson 1.50 4.00
4 Lonnie Shelton 1.25 3.00
5 Jack Sikma 2.00 5.00
6 Wally Walker 1.50 4.00
7 Gus Williams 1.25 3.00

1983-84 Supersonics Team Issue

COMPLETE SET (12) 12.00 30.00
1 Fred Brown 1.50 4.00
2 Al Wood .75 2.00
3 David Thompson 1.50 4.00
4 Scooter McCray .75 2.00
5 Jack Sikma 1.50 4.00
6 Gus Williams 1.25 3.00
7 Lenny Wilkens CO 1.50 4.00
8 Tom Chambers 1.50 4.00
9 Steve Hawes .75 2.00
10 Steve Hayes .75 2.00
11 Clay Johnson .75 2.00
12 Danny Vranes .75 2.00

1990-91 Supersonics Team Issue

COMPLETE SET (6) 10.00 25.00
1 Benoit Benjamin 1.25 3.00
2 Eddie Johnson 1.50 4.00
3 K.C. Jones CO 1.50 4.00
4 Shawn Kemp 3.00 8.00
5 Derrick McKey 1.50 4.00
6 Gary Payton 5.00 12.00

1980 Superstar Matchbook

COMPLETE SET 30.00 60.00
2 Larry Bird 5.00 10.00

1975 SuperStar Sock Wrappers

1 Kareem Abdul-Jabbar 200.00 400.00
2 Lucius Allen 100.00 200.00
3 Nate Archibald 125.00 250.00
4 Rick Barry 125.00 250.00
5 Doug Collins 125.00 250.00
6 Elvin Hayes 150.00 300.00
7 Spencer Haywood 100.00 200.00
8 Bob Lanier 150.00 300.00
9 Pete Maravich 500.00 1,000.00

2001-02 Sweet Shot

COMP.SET w/o SP's 20.00 40.00
91-110 PRINT RUN 1200 SER.#'d SETS
110-120 PRINT RUN 600 SER.#'d SETS
1 Jason Terry .30 .75
2 Shareef Abdur-Rahim .25 .60
3 Toni Kukoc .40 1.00
4 Paul Pierce .50 1.25
5 Antoine Walker .25 .60
6 Kenny Anderson .25 .60
7 Baron Davis .25 .60
8 Jamal Mashburn .25 .60
9 David Wesley .20 .50
10 Ron Mercer .20 .50
11 Ron Artest .25 .60
12 A.J. Guyton .20 .50
13 Andre Miller .25 .60
14 Lamond Murray .20 .50
15 Chris Mihm .20 .50
16 Michael Finley .30 .75
17 Dirk Nowitzki .75 2.00
18 Steve Nash .60 1.50
19 Antonio McDyess .25 .60
20 Nick Van Exel .30 .75
21 Raef LaFrentz .20 .50
22 Jerry Stackhouse .30 .75
23 Chucky Atkins .20 .50
24 Corliss Williamson .20 .50
25 Antawn Jamison .25 .60
26 Marc Jackson .20 .50
27 Larry Hughes .25 .60
28 Steve Francis .30 .75
29 Cuttino Mobley .25 .60
30 Maurice Taylor .20 .50
31 Reggie Miller .60 1.50
32 Jalen Rose .25 .60
33 Jermaine O'Neal .25 .60
34 Darius Miles .20 .50
35 Elton Brand .25 .60
36 Corey Maggette .25 .60
37 Quentin Richardson .20 .50
38 Kobe Bryant 2.50 6.00
39 Shaquille O'Neal 1.25 3.00
40 Rick Fox .25 .60
41 Derek Fisher .25 .60
42 Stromile Swift .20 .50
43 Jason Williams .50 1.25
44 Michael Dickerson .20 .50
45 Alonzo Mourning .50 1.25
46 Eddie Jones .30 .75
47 Anthony Carter .20 .50
48 Glenn Robinson .30 .75
49 Ray Allen .50 1.25
50 Sam Cassell .30 .75
51 Kevin Garnett .75 2.00
52 Chauncey Billups .40 1.00
53 Terrell Brandon .25 .60
54 Joe Smith .25 .60
55 Kenyon Martin .30 .75
56 Keith Van Horn .25 .60
57 Jason Kidd .50 1.25
58 Latrell Sprewell .40 1.00
59 Allan Houston .25 .60
60 Marcus Camby .25 .60
61 Tracy McGrady .50 1.25
62 Mike Miller .25 .60
63 Grant Hill .50 1.25
64 Allen Iverson .75 2.00
65 Dikembe Mutombo .50 1.25
66 Aaron McKie .20 .50
67 Stephon Marbury .40 1.00
68 Shawn Marion .30 .75
69 Tom Gugliotta .20 .50
70 Rasheed Wallace .40 1.00
71 Damon Stoudamire .25 .60
72 Bonzi Wells .20 .50
73 Chris Webber .40 1.00
74 Peja Stojakovic .25 .60
75 Mike Bibby .30 .75
76 Tim Duncan .75 2.00
77 David Robinson .60 1.50
78 Antonio Daniels .20 .50
79 Gary Payton .50 1.25
80 Rashard Lewis .25 .60
81 Desmond Mason .20 .50
82 Vince Carter .60 1.50
83 Morris Peterson .20 .50
84 Antonio Davis .25 .60
85 Karl Malone .60 1.50
86 John Stockton .60 1.50
87 Donyell Marshall .20 .50
88 Richard Hamilton .40 1.00
89 Courtney Alexander .20 .50
90 Michael Jordan 6.00 15.00
91 Zach Randolph RC 3.00 8.00
92 Troy Murphy RC 1.25 3.00
93 Michael Bradley RC 1.00 2.50
94 Vladimir Radmanovic RC 1.25 3.00
95 Kirk Haston RC 1.00 2.50
96 Joseph Forte RC 1.00 2.50
97 Jamaal Tinsley RC 1.25 3.00
98 Jason Collins RC 1.25 3.00
99 Brendan Haywood RC 1.25 3.00
100 Richard Jefferson RC 2.00 5.00
101 Gerald Wallace RC 2.00 5.00
102 Jeryl Sasser RC 1.00 2.50
103 Samuel Dalembert RC 1.00 2.50
104 Tony Parker RC 6.00 15.00
105 Kedrick Brown RC 1.00 2.50
106 Brandon Armstrong RC 1.00 2.50
107 Steven Hunter RC 1.00 2.50
108 Andrei Kirilenko RC 2.50 6.00
109 Primoz Brezec RC 1.50 4.00
110 Terence Morris RC 1.00 2.50
111 Eddie Griffin RC 1.50 4.00
112 DeSagana Diop RC 1.25 3.00
113 Tyson Chandler RC 3.00 8.00
114 Joe Johnson RC 3.00 8.00
115 Rodney White RC 1.25 3.00
116 Eddy Curry RC 2.50 6.00
117 Shane Battier RC 4.00 10.00
118 Jason Richardson RC 3.00 8.00
119 Kwame Brown RC 2.00 5.00
120 Pau Gasol RC 8.00 20.00

2001-02 Sweet Shot Rookie Memorabilia

91-110 PRINT RUN 1200 SER.#'d SETS
110-120 PRINT RUN 600 SER.#'d SETS
91 Zach Randolph 5.00 12.00
92 Troy Murphy 2.00 5.00
93 Michael Bradley 1.50 4.00
94 Vladimir Radmanovic 2.00 5.00
95 Kirk Haston 1.50 4.00
96 Joseph Forte 1.50 4.00
97 Jamaal Tinsley 2.00 5.00
98 Jason Collins 2.00 5.00
99 Brendan Haywood 2.00 5.00
100 Richard Jefferson 3.00 8.00
101 Gerald Wallace 3.00 8.00
102 Jeryl Sasser 1.50 4.00
104 Tony Parker 10.00 25.00
106 Brandon Armstrong 1.50 4.00
107 Steven Hunter 1.50 4.00
108 Andrei Kirilenko 4.00 10.00
109 Primoz Brezec 2.50 6.00
110 Terence Morris 1.50 4.00
111 Eddie Griffin 3.00 8.00
112 DeSagana Diop 2.50 6.00
113 Tyson Chandler 6.00 15.00
114 Joe Johnson 6.00 15.00
115 Rodney White 2.50 6.00
116 Eddy Curry 4.00 10.00
117 Shane Battier 8.00 20.00
118 Jason Richardson 6.00 15.00
119 Kwame Brown 4.00 10.00
120 Pau Gasol 15.00 40.00

2001-02 Sweet Shot Game Jerseys

STATED ODDS 1:18
AI Allen Iverson 8.00 20.00
AJ Antawn Jamison 2.50 6.00
AW Antoine Walker 2.50 6.00
BD Baron Davis 3.00 8.00
CM Corey Maggette 2.50 6.00
CW Chris Webber 5.00 12.00
DJ DerMarr Johnson 2.00 5.00
DM Darius Miles 2.00 5.00
JM Jamal Mashburn 2.50 6.00
JT Jason Terry 3.00 8.00
KB Kobe Bryant 60.00 150.00
KE Kenyon Martin 3.00 8.00
KG Kevin Garnett 8.00 20.00
KM Karl Malone 6.00 15.00
KV Keith Van Horn 2.50 6.00
LH Larry Hughes 2.50 6.00
MF Marcus Fizer 2.00 5.00
MM Mike Miller 2.50 6.00
RM Ron Mercer 2.00 5.00
SM Shawn Marion 3.00 8.00
ST John Stockton 6.00 15.00
TB Terrell Brandon 2.50 6.00
TK Toni Kukoc 4.00 10.00
TM Tracy McGrady 5.00 12.00
WS Wally Szczerbiak 2.50 6.00

2001-02 Sweet Shot Hot Spot Floor

STATED ODDS 1:18
AHF Allan Houston 3.00 8.00
AMF Andre Miller 2.50 6.00
BWF Bonzi Wells 2.00 5.00
DEF Desmond Mason 2.50 6.00
DVF David Robinson 6.00 15.00
EJF Eddie Jones 3.00 8.00
JKF Jason Kidd 5.00 12.00
JMF Jamal Mashburn 2.50 6.00
JOF Jermaine O'Neal 2.50 6.00
JSF Jerry Stackhouse 3.00 8.00
JTF Jason Terry 3.00 8.00
KBF Kobe Bryant 40.00 100.00
KGF Kevin Garnett 8.00 20.00
LSF Latrell Sprewell 4.00 10.00
MAF Marc Jackson 2.00 5.00
MJF Michael Jordan 75.00 200.00
QRF Quentin Richardson 2.00 5.00
RAF Ray Allen 5.00 12.00
RHF Richard Hamilton 4.00 10.00
RLF Rashard Lewis 2.50 6.00
RMF Reggie Miller 5.00 12.00
RWF Rasheed Wallace 4.00 10.00
SFF Steve Francis 3.00 8.00
SHF Shawn Marion 3.00 8.00
SMF Stephon Marbury 4.00 10.00
SPF Scottie Pippen 8.00 20.00
TMF Tracy McGrady 5.00 12.00
WSF Wally Szczerbiak 2.50 6.00

2001-02 Sweet Shot Network Executives

STATED ODDS 1:108
AGN A.J. Guyton 6.00 15.00
AJN Antawn Jamison 8.00 20.00
DJN DerMarr Johnson 6.00 15.00
DMN Darius Miles 6.00 15.00
JAN Jason Terry 10.00 25.00
QRN Quentin Richardson 6.00 15.00
RHN Richard Hamilton 12.00 30.00
RMN Ron Mercer 6.00 15.00

2001-02 Sweet Shot Signature Shots

STATED ODDS 1:18
AWS Antoine Walker 5.00 12.00
DAS Darrell Armstrong 5.00 12.00
DES Desmond Mason 5.00 12.00
DJS DerMarr Johnson 5.00 12.00
ECS Eddy Curry 5.00 12.00
EGS Eddie Griffin 5.00 12.00
HUS Steven Hunter 5.00 12.00
JJS Joe Johnson 8.00 20.00
JMS Jamal Mashburn 5.00 12.00
JPS Joel Przybilla 5.00 12.00
JRS Jason Richardson 6.00 15.00
JSS Jerry Stackhouse 6.00 15.00
KBS Kobe Bryant 125.00 300.00
KES Kenyon Martin 6.00 15.00
KGS Kevin Garnett 40.00 100.00
KWS Kwame Brown 5.00 12.00
LHS Larry Hughes 5.00 12.00
MJS Michael Jordan 1,500.00 3,000.00
PPS Paul Pierce 12.00 30.00
RJS Richard Jefferson 5.00 12.00
SSS Stromile Swift 5.00 12.00
TCS Tyson Chandler 6.00 15.00
TMS Troy Murphy 6.00 15.00
WSS Wally Szczerbiak 6.00 15.00

2001-02 Sweet Shot Three-point Shots

NUMBERED TO PLAYER JSY
DE Desmond Mason/24 30.00 80.00
DM Darius Miles/21 20.00 50.00
JM Jamal Mashburn/24 30.00 80.00
JS Jerry Stackhouse/42 60.00 150.00
KG Kevin Garnett/21 100.00 250.00
MJ Michael Jordan/23 2,000.00 4,000.00
MM Mike Miller/50 40.00 100.00
PP Paul Pierce/34 75.00 200.00

2002-03 Sweet Shot

COMP.SET w/o SP's (90) 15.00 40.00
91-123 PRINT RUN 999 SER.#'d SETS
124-132 PRINT RUN 499 SER.#'d SETS
1 Shareef Abdur-Rahim .30 .75
2 Jason Terry .25 .60
3 Glenn Robinson .30 .75
4 Paul Pierce .50 1.25
5 Antoine Walker .25 .60
6 Kedrick Brown .20 .50
7 Vin Baker .25 .60
8 Jalen Rose .25 .60
9 Eddy Curry .20 .50
10 Tyson Chandler .30 .75
11 Zydrunas Ilgauskas .25 .60
12 Chris Mihm .20 .50
13 Darius Miles .25 .60
14 Dirk Nowitzki .75 2.00
15 Michael Finley .30 .75
16 Steve Nash .60 1.50
17 Raef LaFrentz .20 .50
18 James Posey .20 .50
19 Juwan Howard .25 .60
20 Richard Hamilton .40 1.00
21 Ben Wallace .40 1.00
22 Chauncey Billups .30 .75
23 Jason Richardson .30 .75
24 Antawn Jamison .25 .60
25 Steve Francis .30 .75
26 Eddie Griffin .20 .50
27 Cuttino Mobley .20 .50
28 Reggie Miller .60 1.50
29 Jamaal Tinsley .20 .50
30 Jermaine O'Neal .25 .60
31 Elton Brand .25 .60
32 Lamar Odom .30 .75
33 Andre Miller .25 .60
34 Kobe Bryant 2.50 6.00
35 Shaquille O'Neal 1.25 3.00
36 Devean George .20 .50
37 Pau Gasol .50 1.25
38 Shane Battier .25 .60
39 Jason Williams .40 1.00
40 Eddie House .20 .50
41 Eddie Jones .30 .75
42 Brian Grant .20 .50
43 Ray Allen .50 1.25
44 Tim Thomas .20 .50
45 Kevin Garnett .75 2.00
46 Terrell Brandon .25 .60
47 Wally Szczerbiak .25 .60
48 Joe Smith .25 .60
49 Jason Kidd .50 1.25
50 Richard Jefferson .25 .60
51 Kenyon Martin .30 .75
52 Dikembe Mutombo .50 1.25
53 Jamal Mashburn .25 .60
54 Baron Davis .30 .75
55 David Wesley .20 .50
56 Allan Houston .30 .75
57 Antonio McDyess .25 .60
58 Latrell Sprewell .40 1.00
59 Tracy McGrady .50 1.25
60 Mike Miller .25 .60
61 Darrell Armstrong .20 .50
62 Allen Iverson .75 2.00
63 Keith Van Horn .25 .60
64 Stephon Marbury .40 1.00
65 Shawn Marion .30 .75
66 Anfernee Hardaway .75 2.00
67 Rasheed Wallace .40 1.00
68 Bonzi Wells .20 .50
69 Scottie Pippen .75 2.00
70 Chris Webber .40 1.00
71 Mike Bibby .30 .75
72 Peja Stojakovic .25 .60
73 Hedo Turkoglu .20 .50
74 Tim Duncan .75 2.00
75 David Robinson .60 1.50
76 Tony Parker .50 1.25
77 Steve Smith .25 .60
78 Gary Payton .50 1.25
79 Rashard Lewis .25 .60
80 Desmond Mason .20 .50
81 Brent Barry .20 .50
82 Vince Carter .60 1.50
83 Morris Peterson .20 .50
84 Antonio Davis .25 .60
85 Karl Malone .60 1.50
86 John Stockton .60 1.50
87 Andrei Kirilenko .25 .60
88 Jerry Stackhouse .30 .75
89 Michael Jordan 3.00 8.00
90 Kwame Brown .20 .50
91 Efthimios Rentzias RC 1.25 3.00
92 Marko Jaric 2.00 5.00
93 Rasual Butler RC 1.50 4.00
94 Predrag Savovic RC 1.50 4.00
95 Sam Clancy RC 1.50 4.00
96 Lonny Baxter RC 1.25 3.00
97 Raul Lopez RC 2.00 5.00
98 Rod Grizzard RC 1.25 3.00
99 Tito Maddox RC 1.25 3.00
100 Carlos Boozer RC 2.00 5.00
101 Dan Gadzuric RC 1.50 4.00
102 Vincent Yarbrough RC 1.25 3.00
103 Robert Archibald RC 1.25 3.00
104 Roger Mason RC 1.50 4.00
105 Ronald Murray RC 2.00 5.00
106 Dan Dickau RC 1.25 3.00
107 Chris Jefferies RC 1.25 3.00
108 John Salmons RC 2.00 5.00
109 Frank Williams RC 1.25 3.00
110 Tayshaun Prince RC 4.00 10.00
111 Casey Jacobsen RC 1.50 4.00
112 Qyntel Woods RC 1.25 3.00
113 Kareem Rush RC 1.50 4.00
114 Ryan Humphrey RC 1.50 4.00
115 Curtis Borchardt RC 1.25 3.00
116 Juan Dixon RC 1.50 4.00
117 Jiri Welsch RC 1.50 4.00
118 Bostjan Nachbar RC 1.50 4.00
119 Fred Jones RC 1.50 4.00
120 Marcus Haislip RC 1.25 3.00
121 Melvin Ely RC 1.50 4.00
122 Jared Jeffries RC 1.50 4.00
123 Caron Butler RC 2.00 5.00
124 Amare Stoudemire RC 8.00 20.00
125 Chris Wilcox RC 2.50 6.00
126 Nene Hilario RC 3.00 8.00
127 DaJuan Wagner RC 2.50 6.00
128 Nikoloz Tskitishvili RC 2.00 5.00
129 Drew Gooden RC 3.00 8.00
130 Mike Dunleavy RC 3.00 8.00
131 Jay Williams RC 2.50 6.00
132 Yao Ming RC 15.00 40.00

2002-03 Sweet Shot Jerseys

STATED ODDS 1:12
*GOLD: .75X TO 2X JERSEYS HI
GOLD PRINT RUN 50 SER.#'d SETS
AIJ Allen Iverson 8.00 20.00
AJJ Antawn Jamison 2.50 6.00
BDJ Baron Davis 3.00 8.00
DJJ DerMarr Johnson 2.00 5.00
HTJ Hedo Turkoglu 2.50 6.00
JMJ Jamal Mashburn 2.50 6.00
JOJ Jermaine O'Neal 2.50 6.00
JSJ Joe Smith 2.50 6.00
KBJ Kobe Bryant 40.00 100.00
KGJ Kevin Garnett 8.00 20.00
KVJ Keith Van Horn 2.50 6.00
MCJ Antonio McDyess 2.50 6.00
MJJ Michael Jordan 30.00 80.00
PPJ Paul Pierce 5.00 12.00
RHJ Richard Hamilton 4.00 10.00
SFJ Steve Francis 3.00 8.00
SMJ Stephon Marbury 4.00 10.00
SNJ Steve Nash 6.00 15.00
WSJ Wally Szczerbiak 2.50 6.00

2002-03 Sweet Shot Off the Glass

STATED ODDS 1:84
G1 Michael Jordan 40.00 100.00
G2 Kobe Bryant 30.00 80.00
G3 Kevin Garnett 10.00 25.00
G4 Allen Iverson 10.00 25.00
G5 Shaquille O'Neal 15.00 40.00
G6 Vince Carter 8.00 20.00
G7 Paul Pierce 6.00 15.00
G8 Jason Kidd 6.00 15.00
G9 Steve Francis 4.00 10.00
G10 Tim Duncan 10.00 25.00
G11 Jay Williams 3.00 8.00
G12 Yao Ming 20.00 50.00

2002-03 Sweet Shot Signature Shots

STATED ODDS 1:24
AS Amare Stoudemire 12.00 30.00
AW Antoine Walker 8.00 20.00
CB Caron Butler 5.00 12.00
CW Chris Wilcox 4.00 10.00
DG Drew Gooden 5.00 12.00
DS DeShawn Stevenson 3.00 8.00
DW DaJuan Wagner 4.00 10.00
JE Julius Erving SP 60.00 150.00
JJ Jared Jeffries 4.00 10.00
JK Jason Kidd 25.00 60.00
JR Jason Richardson 5.00 12.00
JW Jay Williams 4.00 10.00
KB Kobe Bryant SP 150.00 400.00
KM Kenyon Martin 5.00 12.00
LB Larry Bird 40.00 100.00
LO Lamar Odom 5.00 12.00
ME Melvin Ely 4.00 10.00
MF Marcus Fizer 3.00 8.00
MG Magic Johnson 40.00 100.00
MJ Michael Jordan SP 1,500.00 3,000.00
MP Morris Peterson 4.00 10.00
NH Nene Hilario 5.00 12.00
NT Nikoloz Tskitishvili 3.00 8.00
PP Paul Pierce 40.00 100.00
QR Quentin Richardson 3.00 8.00
RJ Richard Jefferson 4.00 10.00
RM Ron Mercer/34 6.00 15.00
SA Shareef Abdur-Rahim 5.00 12.00
TC Tyson Chandler 5.00 12.00
YM Yao Ming 40.00 100.00

2002-03 Sweet Shot Sweet Swatches

STATED ODDS 1:12
*GOLD: .6X TO 1.5X SWATCH HI
GOLD PRINT RUN 100 SER.#'d SETS
AMS Andre Miller 2.50 6.00
AWS Antoine Walker 2.50 6.00
BDS Baron Davis 3.00 8.00
CWS Chris Webber 4.00 10.00
DMS Darius Miles 2.00 5.00
DNS Dirk Nowitzki 8.00 20.00
ECS Eddy Curry 2.00 5.00
JMS Jamal Mashburn 2.50 6.00
KBS Kobe Bryant 40.00 100.00
KES Kenyon Martin 3.00 8.00
KGS Kevin Garnett 8.00 20.00
KMS Karl Malone 6.00 15.00
KWS Kwame Brown 2.00 5.00
LOS Lamar Odom 3.00 8.00
MMS Mike Miller 2.50 6.00
RHS Robert Horry 3.00 8.00
SMS Shawn Marion 3.00 8.00
TBS Terrell Brandon 2.00 5.00
TMS Tracy McGrady 5.00 12.00
WSS Wally Szczerbiak 2.50 6.00

2002-03 Sweet Shot Three-Point Shots

CARDS NUMBERED TO PLAYER JERSEY
MFA Marcus Fizer/21 20.00 50.00
MGA Magic Johnson/32 150.00 300.00
MJA Michael Jordan/23 2,500.00 5,000.00
MMA Mike Miller/50 20.00 50.00
MPA Morris Peterson/24 20.00 50.00
PPA Paul Pierce/34 75.00 150.00

2003-04 Sweet Shot

COMP.SET w/o SP's (90) 15.00 40.00
91-96 PRINT RUN 799 SERIAL #'d SETS
97-132 PRINT RUN 999 SERIAL #'d SETS
MJ STATED PRINT RUN 799 SERIAL #'d SETS
1 Shareef Abdur-Rahim .30 .75
2 Jason Terry .25 .60
3 Theo Ratliff .20 .50
4 Paul Pierce .50 1.25
5 Antoine Walker .30 .75
6 Vin Baker .20 .50
7 Jalen Rose .25 .60
8 Tyson Chandler .25 .60
9 Jay Williams .20 .50
10 Dajuan Wagner .20 .50
11 Zydrunas Ilgauskas .25 .60
12 Darius Miles .20 .50
13 Dirk Nowitzki .75 2.00
14 Antawn Jamison .30 .75
15 Steve Nash .60 1.50
16 Nene Hilario .25 .60
17 Marcus Camby .25 .60
18 Andre Miller .25 .60
19 Richard Hamilton .40 1.00
20 Ben Wallace .40 1.00
21 Chauncey Billups .40 1.00
22 Nick Van Exel .30 .75
23 Jason Richardson .30 .75
24 Erick Dampier .20 .50
25 Steve Francis .30 .75
26 Yao Ming .75 2.00
27 Cuttino Mobley .20 .50
28 Reggie Miller .60 1.50
29 Jamaal Tinsley .20 .50
30 Jermaine O'Neal .30 .75
31 Elton Brand .25 .60
32 Corey Maggette .25 .60
33 Marko Jaric .20 .50
34 Kobe Bryant 2.50 6.00
35 Gary Payton .50 1.25
36 Shaquille O'Neal 1.25 3.00
37 Karl Malone .60 1.50
38 Pau Gasol .50 1.25
39 Shane Battier .25 .60
40 Mike Miller .25 .60
41 Eddie Jones .30 .75
42 Lamar Odom .25 .60
43 Caron Butler .25 .60
44 Michael Redd .30 .75
45 Joe Smith .25 .60
46 Desmond Mason .25 .60
47 Kevin Garnett .75 2.00
48 Wally Szczerbiak .25 .60
49 Latrell Sprewell .40 1.00
50 Jason Kidd .50 1.25
51 Richard Jefferson .25 .60
52 Kenyon Martin .30 .75
53 Baron Davis .30 .75
54 Jamal Mashburn .25 .60
55 David Wesley .20 .50
56 Allan Houston .30 .75
57 Antonio McDyess .25 .60
58 Keith Van Horn .25 .60
59 Tracy McGrady .50 1.25
60 Grant Hill .40 1.00
61 Drew Gooden .25 .60
62 Allen Iverson .75 2.00
64 Eric Snow .20 .50
64A Glenn Robinson .25 .60
65 Stephon Marbury .40 1.00
66 Shawn Marion .30 .75
67 Amare Stoudemire .40 1.00
68 Rasheed Wallace .40 1.00
69 Bonzi Wells .20 .50
70 Damon Stoudamire .25 .60
71 Chris Webber .40 1.00
72 Mike Bibby .30 .75
73 Peja Stojakovic .25 .60
74 Vlade Divac .30 .75
75 Tim Duncan .75 2.00
76 David Robinson .60 1.50
77 Tony Parker .50 1.25
78 Manu Ginobili .60 1.50
79 Ray Allen .50 1.25
80 Rashard Lewis .25 .60
81 Vladimir Radmanovic .20 .50
82 Vince Carter .60 1.50
83 Morris Peterson .20 .50
84 Antonio Davis .25 .60
85 Keon Clark .20 .50
86 John Stockton .60 1.50
87 Andrei Kirilenko .25 .60
88 Jerry Stackhouse .40 1.00
89 Kwame Brown .20 .50
90 Larry Hughes .25 .60
91 LeBron James RC 200.00 500.00
92 Darko Milicic RC 3.00 8.00
93 Carmelo Anthony RC 20.00 50.00
94 Chris Bosh RC 12.00 30.00
95 Dwyane Wade RC 30.00 80.00
96 Chris Kaman RC 4.00 10.00
97 Kirk Hinrich RC 3.00 8.00
98 T.J. Ford RC 2.50 6.00
99 Mike Sweetney RC 2.00 5.00
100 Jarvis Hayes RC 2.00 5.00
101 Mickael Pietrus RC 2.50 6.00
102 Nick Collison RC 2.50 6.00
103 Marcus Banks RC 2.00 5.00
104 Luke Ridnour RC 3.00 8.00
105 Reece Gaines RC 2.00 5.00
106 Troy Bell RC 2.00 5.00
107 Zarko Cabarkapa RC 2.00 5.00
108 David West RC 4.00 10.00
109 Aleksandar Pavlovic RC 2.50 6.00
110 Dahntay Jones RC 2.50 6.00
111 Boris Diaw RC 3.00 8.00
112 Zoran Planinic RC 2.00 5.00

113 Travis Outlaw RC 2.50 6.00
114 Brian Cook RC 2.00 5.00
115 Carlos Delfino RC 2.50 6.00
116 Ndudi Ebi RC 2.00 5.00
117 Kendrick Perkins RC 2.50 6.00
118 Leandro Barbosa RC 3.00 8.00
119 Josh Howard RC 3.00 8.00
120 Jason Kapono RC 2.00 5.00
121 Luke Walton RC 3.00 8.00
122 Jerome Beasley RC 2.00 5.00
123 Kyle Korver RC 4.00 10.00
124 Maciej Lampe RC 2.00 5.00
125 Travis Hansen RC 2.00 5.00
126 Steve Blake RC 2.50 6.00
127 Willie Green RC 3.00 8.00
128 Slavko Vranes RC 2.00 5.00
129 Keith Bogans RC 2.00 5.00
130 Maurice Williams RC 3.00 8.00
131 Matt Bonner RC 3.00 8.00
132 Zaur Pachulia RC 3.00 8.00
133 Michael Jordan 12.00 30.00
134 Michael Jordan 12.00 30.00
135 Michael Jordan 12.00 30.00
136 Michael Jordan 12.00 30.00
137 Michael Jordan 12.00 30.00
138 Michael Jordan 12.00 30.00
139 Michael Jordan 12.00 30.00
140 Michael Jordan 12.00 30.00
141 Michael Jordan 12.00 30.00
142 Michael Jordan 12.00 30.00
143 Michael Jordan 12.00 30.00
144 Michael Jordan 12.00 30.00

2003-04 Sweet Shot Jerseys

STATED ODDS 1:12
AHJ Allan Houston 2.50 6.00
AIJ Allen Iverson 10.00 25.00
ASJ Amare Stoudemire 3.00 8.00
AWJ Antoine Walker 2.50 6.00
BDJ Baron Davis 2.50 6.00
CWJ Chris Webber 3.00 8.00
DNJ Dirk Nowitzki 6.00 15.00
DRJ David Robinson 5.00 12.00
DWJ DaJuan Wagner 1.50 4.00
GAJ Gilbert Arenas 2.50 6.00
GHJ Grant Hill 3.00 8.00
JKJ Jason Kidd 4.00 10.00
JOJ Jermaine O'Neal 2.50 6.00
JSJ John Stockton 5.00 12.00
KBJ Kobe Bryant SP 60.00 150.00
KGJ Kevin Garnett 6.00 15.00
KMJ Kenyon Martin 2.50 6.00
LJJ LeBron James 125.00 300.00
LSJ Latrell Sprewell 3.00 8.00
MAJ Shawn Marion 2.50 6.00
MJJ Michael Jordan SP 150.00 400.00
PPJ Paul Pierce 4.00 10.00
RAJ Ray Allen 4.00 10.00
SFJ Steve Francis 2.50 6.00
SMJ Stephon Marbury 3.00 8.00
SNJ Steve Nash 5.00 12.00
SPJ Scottie Pippen 6.00 15.00
TDJ Tim Duncan 6.00 15.00
TMJ Tracy McGrady 4.00 10.00
YMJ Yao Ming 6.00 15.00

2003-04 Sweet Shot Signature Shots

STATED ODDS 1:24
AJ Antawn Jamison 5.00 12.00
AM Antonio McDyess 4.00 10.00
AS Amare Stoudemire 6.00 15.00
BA Marcus Banks 3.00 8.00
BI Chauncey Billups 12.00 30.00
BW Bill Walton 12.00 30.00
CA Carmelo Anthony 125.00 300.00
CB Caron Butler 4.00 10.00
CK Chris Kaman 5.00 12.00
DJ DerMarr Johnson 3.00 8.00
DM Darko Milicic 4.00 10.00
DR David Robinson SP 50.00 120.00
DW DaJuan Wagner 3.00 8.00
EG Manu Ginobili 75.00 200.00
GA Gilbert Arenas 5.00 12.00
JE Julius Erving SP 150.00 400.00
JK Jason Kidd SP 75.00 200.00
JR Jason Richardson 12.00 30.00
JS Jerry Stackhouse 8.00 20.00
KA Kareem Abdul-Jabbar SP 300.00 600.00
KB Kobe Bryant SP 1,500.00 3,000.00
LB Larry Bird SP 300.00 600.00
LJ LeBron James 4,000.00 8,000.00
LR Luke Ridnour 5.00 12.00
MA Magic Johnson SP 300.00 600.00
MB Mike Bibby SP 20.00 50.00
MI Andre Miller 4.00 10.00
MJ Michael Jordan SP 4,000.00 8,000.00
MP Mickael Pietrus 4.00 10.00
PP Paul Pierce 40.00 100.00
PS Peja Stojakovic 4.00 10.00
RG Reece Gaines 3.00 8.00
RH Richard Hamilton 12.00 30.00
RJ Richard Jefferson 4.00 10.00
RO Jalen Rose SP 6.00 15.00
SB Shane Battier 4.00 10.00
SF Steve Francis 5.00 12.00
SM Shawn Marion 6.00 15.00
TM Tracy McGrady SP 75.00 200.00
TO Travis Outlaw 4.00 10.00
TP Tony Parker 20.00 50.00
YM Yao Ming 200.00 500.00

2003-04 Sweet Shot Sweet Spot Signatures

STATED ODDS 1:168
AJA Antawn Jamison/49 6.00 15.00
AMA Antonio McDyess 5.00 12.00
ASA Amare Stoudemire 8.00 20.00
BAA Marcus Banks/49 4.00 10.00
BIA Chauncey Billups 20.00 50.00
BWA Bill Walton 15.00 40.00
CAA Carmelo Anthony/49 300.00 600.00
CBA Caron Butler 5.00 12.00
CKA Chris Kaman/49 6.00 15.00
DJA DerMarr Johnson 4.00 10.00
DMA Darko Milicic/49 5.00 12.00
DRA David Robinson/49 75.00 200.00
EGA Manu Ginobili 100.00 250.00
GAA Gilbert Arenas 6.00 15.00
JEA Julius Erving 150.00 400.00
JKA Jason Kidd/44 75.00 200.00
JRA Jason Richardson 12.00 30.00
JSA Jerry Stackhouse/49 6.00 15.00
KAA Kareem Abdul-Jabbar/49 200.00 500.00
KBA Kobe Bryant/50 1,000.00 2,000.00
LBA Larry Bird/50 200.00 500.00
LJA LeBron James/49 5,000.00 10,000.00
LRA Luke Ridnour/49 6.00 15.00
MAA Magic Johnson/49 200.00 500.00
MBA Mike Bibby/39 20.00 50.00
MIA Andre Miller 5.00 12.00
MJA Michael Jordan/23 5,000.00 10,000.00
MPA Mickael Pietrus/49 5.00 12.00
PPA Paul Pierce 75.00 200.00
PSA Peja Stojakovic 6.00 15.00
RGA Reece Gaines 4.00 10.00
RHA Richard Hamilton 20.00 50.00
RJA Richard Jefferson/49 5.00 12.00
ROA Jalen Rose/44 6.00 15.00
SBA Shane Battier 6.00 15.00
SFA Steve Francis/40 20.00 50.00
SMA Shawn Marion 6.00 15.00
TMA Tracy McGrady/49 125.00 300.00
TOA Travis Outlaw/49 5.00 12.00
TPA Tony Parker 75.00 200.00
YMA Yao Ming 200.00 500.00

2003-04 Sweet Shot Sweet Swatches

STATED ODDS 1:12
AHSS Allan Houston 2.50 6.00
AISS Allen Iverson 6.00 15.00
ASSS Amare Stoudemire 3.00 8.00
BDSS Baron Davis 2.50 6.00
CWSS Chris Webber SP 10.00 25.00
DNSS Dirk Nowitzki 6.00 15.00
DSSS Damon Stoudamire SP 8.00 20.00
ECSS Eddy Curry 1.50 4.00
JKSS Jason Kidd 4.00 10.00
JOSS Jermaine O'Neal 2.50 6.00
JRSS Jalen Rose 2.00 5.00
JSSS Joe Smith 2.00 5.00
JTSS Jamaal Tinsley 1.50 4.00
JWSS Jay Williams 1.50 4.00
KBSS Kobe Bryant SP 75.00 200.00
KGSS Kevin Garnett 6.00 15.00
LOSS Lamar Odom 2.00 5.00
LSSS Latrell Sprewell 3.00 8.00
MCSS Marcus Camby 2.00 5.00
MJSS Michael Jordan SP 200.00 500.00
MMSS Mike Miller 2.00 5.00
PPSS Paul Pierce 4.00 10.00
RISS Jason Richardson 2.50 6.00
RMSS Reggie Miller 5.00 12.00
SBSS Shane Battier 2.00 5.00
SFSS Steve Francis 2.50 6.00
SHSS Shawn Marion 2.50 6.00
SMSS Stephon Marbury 3.00 8.00
TBSS Terrell Brandon 1.50 4.00
TCSS Tyson Chandler 2.00 5.00
TMSS Tracy McGrady 4.00 10.00
WSSS Wally Szczerbiak 2.00 5.00
YMSS Yao Ming SP 20.00 50.00

2003-04 Sweet Shot Three-Point Shots

AJ3 Antawn Jamison/33 12.00 30.00
AM3 Antonio McDyess/34 12.00 30.00
AS3 Amare Stoudemire/32 20.00 50.00
CA3 Carmelo Anthony/15 150.00 400.00
DR3 David Robinson/50 60.00 150.00
EG3 Manu Ginobili/20 100.00 250.00
JA3 Marko Jaric/20 12.00 30.00
JR3 Jason Richardson/23 40.00 100.00
JS3 Jerry Stackhouse/42 20.00 50.00
KA3 K.Abdul-Jabbar/33 125.00 300.00
LB3 Larry Bird/33 125.00 300.00
LJ3 LeBron James/23 15,000.00 30,000.00
MA3 Magic Johnson/32 125.00 300.00
MI3 Andre Miller/24 12.00 30.00
MJ3 Michael Jordan/23 10,000.00 15,000.00
MP3 Morris Peterson/24 12.00 30.00
PP3 Paul Pierce/34 60.00 150.00
PS3 Peja Stojakovic/16 40.00 100.00
RH3 Richard Hamilton/32 25.00 60.00
RJ3 Richard Jefferson/24 12.00 30.00
SB3 Shane Battier/31 12.00 30.00
SM3 Shawn Marion/31 30.00 60.00

2004-05 Sweet Shot

COMP.SET w/o SP's (90) 15.00 40.00
91-130 PRINT RUN 1250 SER.#'d SETS
131-136 PRINT RUN 499 SER.#'d SETS
1 Antoine Walker .30 .75
2 Al Harrington .25 .60
3 Boris Diaw .25 .60
4 Paul Pierce .50 1.25
5 Ricky Davis .25 .60
6 Gary Payton .50 1.25
7 Gerald Wallace .25 .60
8 Jason Kapono .20 .50
9 Jahidi White .20 .50
10 Eddy Curry .20 .50
11 Kirk Hinrich .30 .75
12 Antonio Davis .20 .50
13 LeBron James 2.50 6.00
14 Dajuan Wagner .20 .50
15 Jeff McInnis .20 .50
16 Dirk Nowitzki .75 2.00
17 Michael Finley .30 .75
18 Jerry Stackhouse .30 .75
19 Kenyon Martin .30 .75
20 Andre Miller .25 .60
21 Carmelo Anthony .60 1.50
22 Chauncey Billups .40 1.00
23 Rasheed Wallace .40 1.00
24 Ben Wallace .40 1.00
25 Derek Fisher .25 .60
26 Jason Richardson .30 .75
27 Mike Dunleavy .20 .50
28 Yao Ming .75 2.00
29 Tracy McGrady .50 1.25
30 Juwan Howard .25 .60
31 Jermaine O'Neal .25 .60
32 Reggie Miller .60 1.50
33 Ron Artest .30 .75
34 Elton Brand .25 .60
35 Corey Maggette .25 .60
36 Marko Jaric .20 .50
37 Kobe Bryant 2.50 6.00
38 Karl Malone .60 1.50
39 Lamar Odom .30 .75
40 Pau Gasol .50 1.25
41 Jason Williams .25 .60
42 Bonzi Wells .20 .50
43 Shaquille O'Neal 1.25 3.00
44 Dwyane Wade 1.25 3.00
45 Eddie Jones .30 .75
46 Michael Redd .25 .60
47 Desmond Mason .25 .60
48 T.J. Ford .20 .50
49 Latrell Sprewell .40 1.00
50 Kevin Garnett .75 2.00
51 Sam Cassell .25 .60
52 Aaron Williams .20 .50
53 Richard Jefferson .25 .60
54 Jason Kidd .50 1.25
55 Jamal Mashburn .25 .60
56 Baron Davis .30 .75
57 Jamaal Magloire .20 .50
58 Allan Houston .30 .75
59 Jamal Crawford .30 .75
60 Stephon Marbury .40 1.00
61 Keith Bogans .20 .50
62 Cuttino Mobley .25 .60
63 Steve Francis .30 .75
64 Glenn Robinson .25 .60
65 Allen Iverson .75 2.00
66 Kenny Thomas .20 .50
67 Amare Stoudemire .30 .75
68 Steve Nash .60 1.50
69 Quentin Richardson .20 .50
70 Shareef Abdur-Rahim .30 .75
71 Damon Stoudamire .30 .75
72 Zach Randolph .30 .75
73 Peja Stojakovic .25 .60
74 Chris Webber .40 1.00
75 Mike Bibby .30 .75
76 Tony Parker .50 1.25
77 Tim Duncan .75 2.00
78 Manu Ginobili .60 1.50
79 Ronald Murray .20 .50
80 Ray Allen .50 1.25
81 Rashard Lewis .25 .60
82 Chris Bosh .50 1.25
83 Vince Carter .60 1.50
84 Jalen Rose .25 .60
85 Andrei Kirilenko .25 .60
86 Matt Harpring .20 .50
87 Carlos Boozer .20 .50
88 Gilbert Arenas .30 .75
89 Jarvis Hayes .20 .50
90 Antawn Jamison .25 .60
91 Anderson Varejao RC 1.50 4.00
92 Jackson Vroman RC 1.25 3.00
93 Peter John Ramos RC 1.25 3.00
94 Lionel Chalmers RC 1.50 4.00
95 Donta Smith RC 1.25 3.00
96 Andre Emmett RC 1.25 3.00
97 Antonio Burks RC 1.25 3.00
98 Royal Ivey RC 1.25 3.00
99 Chris Duhon RC 1.50 4.00
100 Albert Miralles RC 2.00 5.00
101 Justin Reed RC 1.25 3.00
102 David Young RC 2.00 5.00
103 Trevor Ariza RC 2.00 5.00
104 Luol Deng RC 2.00 5.00
105 Rafael Araujo RC 1.25 3.00
106 Andre Iguodala RC 3.00 8.00
107 Luke Jackson RC 1.25 3.00
108 Andris Biedrins RC 1.25 3.00
109 Robert Swift RC 1.25 3.00
110 Sebastian Telfair RC 1.50 4.00
111 Kris Humphries RC 1.50 4.00
112 Al Jefferson RC 2.00 5.00
113 Kirk Snyder RC 1.25 3.00
114 Josh Smith RC 2.00 5.00
115 J.R. Smith RC 2.00 5.00
116 Dorell Wright RC 1.50 4.00
117 Jameer Nelson RC 2.00 5.00
118 Pavel Podkolzin RC 1.25 3.00
119 Viktor Khryapa RC 1.25 3.00
120 Sergei Monia RC 1.25 3.00
121 Nenad Krstic RC 1.50 4.00
122 Tim Pickett RC 1.50 4.00
123 Bernard Robinson RC 1.25 3.00
124 Yuta Tabuse RC 2.00 5.00
125 Delonte West RC 1.50 4.00
126 Tony Allen RC 2.00 5.00
127 Kevin Martin RC 2.50 6.00
128 Sasha Vujacic RC 1.50 4.00
129 Beno Udrih RC 1.50 4.00
130 David Harrison RC 1.25 3.00
131 Dwight Howard RC 10.00 25.00
132 Emeka Okafor RC 2.50 6.00
133 Ben Gordon RC 3.00 8.00
134 Shaun Livingston RC 3.00 8.00
135 Devin Harris RC 2.50 6.00
136 Josh Childress RC 2.00 5.00

2004-05 Sweet Shot Jerseys

STATED ODDS 1:12
AI Allen Iverson 6.00 15.00
AJ Antawn Jamison SP 2.00 5.00
AK Andrei Kirilenko 2.00 5.00
AN Andre Iguodala 4.00 10.00
BG Ben Gordon 2.50 6.00
CA Carmelo Anthony 5.00 12.00
CB Chris Bosh 4.00 10.00
CW Chris Webber 3.00 8.00
DE Devin Harris 2.00 5.00
DH Dwight Howard 8.00 20.00
EB Elton Brand 2.00 5.00
GM Manu Ginobili SP 5.00 12.00
IT Isiah Thomas 4.00 10.00
JC Josh Childress 1.50 4.00
JK Jason Kidd 4.00 10.00
JN Jameer Nelson 2.50 6.00
JO Jermaine O'Neal 2.00 5.00
JR J.R. Smith 2.50 6.00
JS Josh Smith 2.50 6.00
KB Kobe Bryant 40.00 100.00
KG Kevin Garnett 6.00 15.00
KM Kenyon Martin 2.50 6.00
LB Larry Bird 10.00 25.00
LD Luol Deng 2.50 6.00
LJ LeBron James 10.00 25.00
LS Latrell Sprewell 3.00 8.00
LU Luke Jackson 1.50 4.00
MJ Michael Jordan SP 40.00 100.00
MR Michael Redd 2.00 5.00
PP Paul Pierce 4.00 10.00
PS Peja Stojakovic 2.00 5.00
RA Rafael Araujo 1.50 4.00
RH Richard Hamilton 3.00 8.00
RJ Richard Jefferson 2.00 5.00
SF Steve Francis 2.50 6.00
SL Shaun Livingston 2.50 6.00
SN Dirk Nowitzki 6.00 15.00
SN Steve Nash 5.00 12.00
SO Shaquille O'Neal 10.00 25.00
ST Sebastian Telfair 2.00 5.00
TD Tim Duncan 6.00 15.00
TM Tracy McGrady 4.00 10.00

2004-05 Sweet Shot Signature Shots

STATED ODDS 1:12
*COLOR PARALLEL: 1X TO 2.5X BASE HI
*SP COLOR PARALLEL: .6X TO 1.5X BASE HI
WHITE/BLUE/RED STATED ODDS 1:360
AI Andre Iguodala 4.00 10.00
AK Andrei Kirilenko 5.00 12.00
AS Amare Stoudemire 10.00 25.00
BG Ben Gordon 4.00 10.00
BK Bernard King 8.00 20.00
BM Brad Miller 4.00 10.00
CA Carmelo Anthony 20.00 50.00
CB Carlos Boozer 4.00 10.00
CD Clyde Drexler 12.00 30.00
CH Josh Childress 2.50 6.00
DE Devin Harris 3.00 8.00
DH Dwight Howard 15.00 40.00
DR Dennis Rodman 25.00 60.00
DW Dwyane Wade SP 40.00 100.00
HO Hakeem Olajuwon 20.00 50.00
JC Jamal Crawford SP 8.00 20.00
JE Julius Erving SP 40.00 100.00
JH Josh Howard 4.00 10.00
JK Jason Kidd 12.00 30.00
JN Jameer Nelson 4.00 10.00
JO John Stockton SP 50.00 120.00
JR J.R. Smith 4.00 10.00
JS Josh Smith 4.00 10.00
JW Jamaal Wilkes 8.00 20.00
KB Kobe Bryant SP 125.00 300.00
KG Kevin Garnett 60.00 150.00
LB Larry Bird SP 60.00 150.00
LD Luol Deng 4.00 10.00
LJ LeBron James 1,000.00 2,000.00
LU Luke Jackson 2.50 6.00
MA Magic Johnson SP 40.00 100.00
MD Marquis Daniels 4.00 10.00
MJ Michael Jordan SP 1,500.00 3,000.00
PR Pat Riley 8.00 20.00
RA Rafael Araujo 2.50 6.00
SE Sebastian Telfair 3.00 8.00
SL Shaun Livingston 4.00 10.00
SM Shawn Marion 4.00 10.00
ST Stephon Marbury 6.00 15.00
TM Tracy McGrady 12.00 30.00
WF Walt Frazier SP 12.00 30.00
YM Yao Ming SP 20.00 50.00

2004-05 Sweet Shot Swatches

STATED ODDS 1:12
AH Allan Houston 2.50 6.00
AI Allen Iverson 6.00 15.00
AK Andrei Kirilenko 2.00 5.00
AM Andre Miller 2.00 5.00
AS Amare Stoudemire 2.50 6.00
AW Antoine Walker 2.50 6.00
BD Baron Davis 2.50 6.00
CA Carmelo Anthony 5.00 12.00
CB Carlos Boozer 2.00 5.00
CM Corey Maggette 2.00 5.00
DN Dirk Nowitzki 6.00 15.00
DR David Robinson 5.00 12.00
EC Eddy Curry 1.50 4.00
EG Manu Ginobili 5.00 12.00
GA Gilbert Arenas 2.50 6.00
GP Gary Payton 4.00 10.00
JA Jalen Rose 2.00 5.00
JO Jermaine O'Neal 2.00 5.00
JR Jason Richardson 2.00 5.00
JT Jason Terry 2.00 5.00
KB Kobe Bryant 40.00 100.00
KG Kevin Garnett 6.00 15.00
KM Kenyon Martin 2.50 6.00
LJ LeBron James 15.00 40.00
LO Lamar Odom 2.50 6.00
MF Michael Finley 2.50 6.00
MJ Michael Jordan SP 60.00 120.00
NH Nene 2.00 5.00
PP Paul Pierce 4.00 10.00
PS Peja Stojakovic 2.00 5.00
QR Quentin Richardson 1.50 4.00
RJ Richard Jefferson 2.00 5.00
RM Reggie Miller 5.00 12.00
RW Rasheed Wallace 3.00 8.00
SC Sam Cassell 2.00 5.00
SH Shawn Marion 2.50 6.00
SM Stephon Marbury 3.00 8.00
SO Shaquille O'Neal 10.00 25.00
TD Tim Duncan 6.00 15.00
TM Tracy McGrady 4.00 10.00
TP Tony Parker 4.00 10.00
YM Yao Ming 6.00 15.00

2004-05 Sweet Shot Sweet Spot Signatures

STATED ODDS 1:180
AI Andre Iguodala 10.00 25.00
AK Andrei Kirilenko 15.00 40.00
AS Amare Stoudemire 20.00 50.00
BG Ben Gordon 6.00 15.00
BK Bernard King 25.00 60.00
BM Brad Miller 8.00 20.00
CA Carmelo Anthony 75.00 200.00
CB Carlos Boozer 8.00 20.00
CD Clyde Drexler 50.00 120.00
CH Josh Childress 4.00 10.00
CK Chris Kaman 8.00 20.00
DE Devin Harris 5.00 12.00
DH Dwight Howard 30.00 80.00
DR Dennis Rodman 75.00 200.00
DW Dwyane Wade 125.00 300.00
JC Jamal Crawford 12.00 30.00
JE Julius Erving 125.00 300.00
JH Josh Howard 8.00 20.00
JK Jason Kidd 40.00 100.00
JN Jameer Nelson 6.00 15.00
JO John Stockton 100.00 250.00
JR J.R. Smith 12.00 30.00
JS Josh Smith 6.00 15.00
JW Jamaal Wilkes 20.00 50.00
KB Kobe Bryant 1,000.00 2,000.00
KG Kevin Garnett 300.00 600.00
LB Larry Bird 300.00 600.00
LD Luol Deng 6.00 15.00
LJ LeBron James 1,500.00 3,000.00
LU Luke Jackson 4.00 10.00
MA Magic Johnson 300.00 600.00
MD Marquis Daniels 8.00 20.00
MJ Michael Jordan 3,000.00 6,000.00
PR Pat Riley 40.00 100.00
RA Rafael Araujo 4.00 10.00
SE Sebastian Telfair 5.00 12.00
SL Shaun Livingston 6.00 15.00
SM Shawn Marion 12.00 30.00
ST Stephon Marbury 20.00 50.00
TM Tracy McGrady 150.00 400.00
WF Walt Frazier 40.00 100.00

2004-05 Sweet Shot Three Point Shots

CARDS #'d TO PLAYER JERSEY
AK Andrei Kirilenko/47 15.00 40.00
AS Amare Stoudemire/32 75.00 150.00
BM Brad Miller/52 15.00 40.00
CA Carmelo Anthony/15 100.00 200.00
CD Clyde Drexler/22 75.00 150.00
DE Devin Harris/34 20.00 50.00
DR Dennis Rodman/91 50.00 120.00
JA Jason Richardson/23 15.00 40.00
JR J.R. Smith/23 25.00 60.00
KG Kevin Garnett/21 75.00 150.00
LB Larry Bird/33 150.00 300.00
LJ LeBron James/23 2,000.00 4,000.00
LU Luke Jackson/33 15.00 40.00
MA Magic Johnson/32 100.00 200.00
MR Michael Redd/22 15.00 40.00
RA Rafael Araujo/55 10.00 25.00
RH Richard Hamilton/32 40.00 100.00
RJ Richard Jefferson/24 15.00 40.00
SM Shawn Marion/31 40.00 100.00

2005-06 Sweet Shot

COMP.SET w/o SP's (100) 15.00 40.00
143-150 RC PRINT RUN 499 SER.#'d SETS
1 Al Harrington .30 .75
2 Josh Smith .30 .75
3 Josh Childress .25 .60
4 Tyronn Lue .25 .60
5 Paul Pierce .60 1.50
6 Antoine Walker .30 .75
7 Gary Payton .60 1.50
8 Al Jefferson .25 .60
9 Emeka Okafor .30 .75
10 Primoz Brezec .25 .60
11 Gerald Wallace .30 .75
12 Michael Jordan 3.00 8.00
13 Ben Gordon .30 .75
14 Luol Deng .30 .75
15 Kirk Hinrich .30 .75
16 LeBron James 3.00 8.00
17 Luke Jackson .25 .60
18 Drew Gooden .30 .75
19 Larry Hughes .30 .75
20 Dirk Nowitzki 1.00 2.50
21 Jason Terry .30 .75
22 Michael Finley .40 1.00
23 Jerry Stackhouse .30 .75
24 Andre Miller .30 .75
25 Carmelo Anthony .60 1.50
26 Kenyon Martin .30 .75
27 Earl Boykins .25 .60
28 Rasheed Wallace .40 1.00
29 Ben Wallace .50 1.25
30 Richard Hamilton .50 1.25
31 Chauncey Billups .50 1.25
32 Baron Davis .40 1.00
33 Derek Fisher .40 1.00
34 Jason Richardson .40 1.00
35 Tracy McGrady .60 1.50
36 Yao Ming .75 2.00
37 Juwan Howard .30 .75
38 Jermaine O'Neal .30 .75
39 Ron Artest .30 .75
40 Jamaal Tinsley .25 .60
41 Corey Maggette .30 .75
42 Elton Brand .30 .75
43 Shaun Livingston .30 .75
44 Kobe Bryant 3.00 8.00
45 Brian Cook .25 .60
46 Lamar Odom .30 .75
47 Mike Miller .30 .75
48 Pau Gasol .60 1.50
49 Shane Battier .30 .75
50 Shaquille O'Neal 1.25 3.00
51 Dwyane Wade .75 2.00
52 Udonis Haslem .25 .60
53 Joe Smith .25 .60
54 Michael Redd .30 .75
55 Desmond Mason .25 .60
56 Kevin Garnett 1.00 2.50
57 Wally Szczerbiak .30 .75
58 Sam Cassell .30 .75
59 Vince Carter .75 2.00
60 Jason Kidd .60 1.50
61 Richard Jefferson .30 .75
62 Jamaal Magloire .25 .60
63 J.R. Smith .40 1.00
64 Speedy Claxton .25 .60
65 Allan Houston .30 .75
66 Stephon Marbury .50 1.25
67 Jamal Crawford .40 1.00
68 Dwight Howard .50 1.25
69 Grant Hill .60 1.50
70 Jameer Nelson .40 1.00
71 Steve Francis .40 1.00
72 Allen Iverson .75 2.00
73 Andre Iguodala .40 1.00
74 Chris Webber .50 1.25
75 Kyle Korver .30 .75
76 Amare Stoudemire .40 1.00
77 Steve Nash .75 2.00
78 Quentin Richardson .25 .60
79 Shawn Marion .30 .75
80 Damon Stoudamire .40 1.00
81 Zach Randolph .40 1.00
82 Sebastian Telfair .30 .75
83 Peja Stojakovic .30 .75
84 Mike Bibby .40 1.00
85 Cuttino Mobley .25 .60
86 Manu Ginobili .75 2.00
87 Tim Duncan 1.00 2.50
88 Tony Parker .60 1.50
89 Ray Allen .60 1.50
90 Rashard Lewis .30 .75
91 Luke Ridnour .30 .75
92 Ronald Murray .25 .60
93 Chris Bosh .50 1.25
94 Morris Peterson .25 .60
95 Jalen Rose .30 .75
96 Andrei Kirilenko .30 .75
97 Raul Lopez .25 .60
98 Carlos Boozer .30 .75
99 Antawn Jamison .30 .75
100 Gilbert Arenas .40 1.00
101 Ike Diogu RC 1.25 3.00
102 Julius Hodge RC 1.25 3.00
103 David Lee RC 2.00 5.00
104 Linas Kleiza RC 1.50 4.00
105 Jason Maxiell RC 1.50 4.00
106 Luther Head RC 1.25 3.00
107 Jose Calderon RC 2.00 5.00
108 Brandon Bass RC 1.50 4.00
109 Ricky Sanchez RC 2.00 5.00
110 Andray Blatche RC 2.00 5.00
111 Sean May RC 1.25 3.00
112 Travis Diener RC 1.25 3.00
113 Nate Robinson RC 2.00 5.00
114 Von Wafer RC 1.25 3.00
115 James Singleton RC 1.25 3.00
116 Daniel Ewing RC 1.50 4.00
117 Salim Stoudamire RC 1.50 4.00
118 Dijon Thompson RC 1.25 3.00
119 Danny Granger RC 2.00 5.00
120 Will Bynum RC 1.50 4.00
121 Louis Williams RC 5.00 12.00
122 Channing Frye RC 1.50 4.00
123 Francisco Garcia RC 1.25 3.00
124 Ryan Gomes RC 1.50 4.00
125 Ronnie Price RC 1.50 4.00
126 Jarrett Jack RC 2.00 5.00
127 Alan Anderson RC 1.25 3.00
128 Ersan Ilyasova RC 1.50 4.00
129 C.J. Miles RC 1.50 4.00
130 Arvydas Macijauskas RC 1.25 3.00
131 Bracey Wright RC 1.25 3.00
132 Monta Ellis RC 2.50 6.00
133 Chris Taft RC 1.25 3.00
134 Johan Petro RC 1.25 3.00
135 Yaroslav Korolev RC 1.25 3.00
136 Andrew Bynum RC 1.50 4.00
137 Martynas Andriuskevicius RC 1.25 3.00
138 Charlie Villanueva RC 1.50 4.00
139 Antoine Wright RC 1.50 4.00
140 Joey Graham RC 1.50 4.00
141 Wayne Simien RC 1.25 3.00
142 Hakim Warrick RC 1.50 4.00
143 Gerald Green RC 3.00 8.00
144 Marvin Williams RC 3.00 8.00
145 Deron Williams RC 5.00 12.00
146 Rashad McCants RC 2.00 5.00
147 Raymond Felton RC 2.50 6.00
148 Martell Webster RC 2.50 6.00
149 Chris Paul RC 15.00 40.00
150 Andrew Bogut RC 4.00 10.00

2005-06 Sweet Shot Gold

*GOLD STARS: 1.25X TO 3X BASE HI
1-100 PRINT RUN 199 SER.#'d SETS
*GOLD RCs 101-142: .75X TO 2X BASE HI
*GOLD RCs 143-150: .5X TO 1.25X BASE HI

2005-06 Sweet Shot Spectrum

*SPEC STARS: 2X TO 5X BASE HI
1-100 PRINT RUN 75 SER.#'d SETS
*SPEC RCs 101-142: 1X TO 2.5X BASE HI
*SPEC RCs 143-150: .6X TO 1.5X BASE HI
101-150 PRINT RUN 50 SER.#'d SETS
12 Michael Jordan 25.00 60.00
16 LeBron James 20.00 50.00

2005-06 Sweet Shot Jerseys

*GOLD: .6X TO 1.5X BASE HI
GOLD PRINT RUN 50 TO 99 SER.#'d SETS
AB Andrew Bogut/125 4.00 10.00
AK Andrei Kirilenko/125 2.50 6.00
AN Andris Biedrins/125 2.00 5.00
AR Rafael Araujo/250 2.00 5.00
AS Amare Stoudemire/125 3.00 8.00
AT Antoine Wright/250 2.50 6.00
AW Antoine Walker/250 2.50 6.00
BB Bruce Bowen/125 2.50 6.00
BD Baron Davis/125 3.00 8.00
BG Ben Gordon/125 3.00 8.00
CA Carmelo Anthony/125 5.00 12.00
CB Caron Butler/250 2.50 6.00
CM Corey Maggette/125 2.50 6.00
CP Chris Paul/125 8.00 20.00
CV Charlie Villanueva/125 2.50 6.00
CW Chris Webber/250 4.00 10.00
DA Dajuan Wagner/250 2.00 5.00
DE Devin Harris/100 2.00 5.00
DF Derek Fisher/125 3.00 8.00
DG Devean George/125 2.50 6.00
DH Dwight Howard/125 4.00 10.00
DI Dikembe Mutombo/125 4.00 10.00
DM Darius Miles/250 2.00 5.00
DN Dirk Nowitzki/125 8.00 20.00
DO Dorell Wright/125 2.00 5.00
DR Dennis Rodman/125 6.00 15.00
DS DeShawn Stevenson/125 2.00 5.00
DW Deron Williams/125 5.00 12.00
EB Elton Brand/125 2.50 6.00
EC Eddy Curry/250 2.00 5.00
GA Gilbert Arenas/125 4.00 10.00
GG Gerald Green/250 3.00 8.00
GH Grant Hill/125 5.00 12.00
GR Danny Granger/250 3.00 8.00
HW Hakim Warrick/125 2.50 6.00
JA Jamal Crawford/125 3.00 8.00
JC Jason Collins/125 2.00 5.00
JH Josh Howard/50 2.50 6.00
JJ Jarrett Jack/250 3.00 8.00
JK Jason Kidd/125 5.00 12.00
JO Jermaine O'Neal/250 2.50 6.00
JR Jalen Rose/250 2.50 6.00
JS J.R. Smith/125 3.00 8.00
JT Jason Terry/250 2.50 6.00
JU Julius Hodge/125 2.00 5.00
KB Kobe Bryant/125 50.00 120.00
KD Keyon Dooling/250 2.00 5.00
KG Kevin Garnett/125 8.00 20.00
KM Kenyon Martin/250 2.50 6.00
KR Kareem Rush/250 2.00 5.00
KT Kurt Thomas/125 2.00 5.00
KW Kwame Brown/250 2.00 5.00
LB Larry Bird/125 10.00 25.00
LD Luol Deng/125 2.50 6.00
LH Larry Hughes/125 2.50 6.00
LJ LeBron James/125 15.00 40.00
LU Luke Jackson/125 2.00 5.00
LW Luke Walton/125 2.00 5.00
MA Magic Johnson/125 8.00 20.00
MD Mike Dunleavy/250 2.00 5.00
MG Manu Ginobili/250 6.00 15.00
MI Michael Finley/250 3.00 8.00
MJ Michael Jordan/125 40.00 100.00
MK Marko Jaric/125 2.00 5.00
MS Mike Sweetney/125 2.00 5.00
MW Marvin Williams/125 3.00 8.00
NH Nene/125 2.50 6.00
NR Nate Robinson/125 3.00 8.00
PG Pau Gasol/125 5.00 12.00
PP Paul Pierce/125 5.00 12.00
PS Peja Stojakovic/125 2.50 6.00
QR Quentin Richardson/125 2.50 6.00
RA Ray Allen/125 5.00 12.00
RD Ricky Davis/250 2.50 6.00
RF Raymond Felton/125 2.50 6.00
RI Jason Richardson/125 3.00 8.00
RJ Richard Jefferson/125 2.50 6.00
RL Rashard Lewis/125 2.50 6.00
RM Rashad McCants/125 2.50 6.00
RS Robert Swift/125 2.00 5.00
RW Rasheed Wallace/250 3.00 8.00
SC Sam Cassell/250 2.50 6.00
SD Samuel Dalembert/250 2.00 5.00
SF Steve Francis/250 3.00 8.00
SH Shawn Marion/125 2.50 6.00
SJ Sarunas Jasikevicius/125 3.00 8.00
SM Sean May/125 2.50 6.00
SN Steve Nash/125 6.00 15.00
SO Shaquille O'Neal/125 10.00 25.00
ST Stephon Marbury/125 4.00 10.00
TC Tyson Chandler/250 2.50 6.00
TD Tim Duncan/125 8.00 20.00
TM Tracy McGrady/250 5.00 12.00
WA Charlie Ward/250 2.00 5.00
WE Martell Webster/125 2.50 6.00
WI Chris Wilcox/125 2.00 5.00
WS Wayne Simien/250 2.00 5.00
YM Yao Ming/125 6.00 15.00
ZI Zydrunas Ilgauskas/125 2.50 6.00
ZR Zach Randolph/250 3.00 8.00

2005-06 Sweet Shot Signature Shots

SP INFO PROVIDED BY UPPER DECK
AB Andrew Bogut 4.00 10.00
AI Andre Iguodala 12.00 30.00
AK Andrei Kirilenko 5.00 12.00
BG Ben Gordon 6.00 15.00
BK Bob Knight SP 150.00 400.00
BM Brad Miller 4.00 10.00
CD Clyde Drexler 20.00 50.00
CF Channing Frye 4.00 10.00
CP Chris Paul 125.00 300.00
CV Charlie Villanueva 4.00 10.00
DE Devin Harris 3.00 8.00
DH Dwight Howard 30.00 80.00
DW Deron Williams 8.00 20.00
HW Hakim Warrick 4.00 10.00
ID Ike Diogu 3.00 8.00
JA Jamaal Wilkes 6.00 15.00
JC Josh Childress 3.00 8.00
JG Joey Graham 4.00 10.00
JN Jameer Nelson 5.00 12.00
JR J.R. Smith 8.00 20.00
JW John Wooden SP 100.00 250.00
KA Kareem Abdul-Jabbar SP 125.00 300.00
LA Larry Brown 20.00 50.00
LB Larry Bird SP 125.00 300.00
LD Luol Deng 4.00 10.00
LJ LeBron James 2,000.00 4,000.00
MA Magic Johnson SP 150.00 400.00
MJ Michael Jordan SP 3,000.00 6,000.00
MW Marvin Williams 5.00 12.00
RM Rashad McCants 3.00 8.00
SH Shawn Marion 4.00 10.00
SL Shaun Livingston 4.00 10.00
SM Sean May 3.00 8.00
SN Steve Nash SP 60.00 150.00
ST Sebastian Telfair 4.00 10.00
WE Martell Webster 4.00 10.00

2005-06 Sweet Shot Signature Shots Acetate

PRINT RUN 25 TO 75 SER.#'d SETS
AB Andrew Bogut/75 12.00 30.00
AN Andrew Bynum/75 8.00 20.00
CA Carmelo Anthony/25 100.00 250.00
CF Channing Frye/75 8.00 20.00
CP Chris Paul/75 125.00 300.00
DH Dwight Howard/75 30.00 80.00
DR Dennis Rodman/75 100.00 250.00
DW Deron Williams/75 15.00 40.00
GE Gerald Green/75 10.00 25.00
HW Hakim Warrick/75 8.00 20.00
ID Ike Diogu/75 6.00 15.00
IT Isiah Thomas/75 30.00 80.00
JG Joey Graham/75 8.00 20.00
JK Jason Kidd/75 25.00 60.00
JW John Wooden/75 125.00 300.00
LB Larry Bird/25 150.00 400.00
LJ LeBron James/25 2,000.00 4,000.00

MJ Michael Jordan/25 3,000.00 6,000.00
MW Marvin Williams/75 10.00 25.00
RF Raymond Felton/75 8.00 20.00
RJ Richard Jefferson/75 8.00 20.00
RM Rashad McCants/75 6.00 15.00
SM Sean May/75 6.00 15.00
SN Steve Nash/75 75.00 200.00
SP Scottie Pippen/75 100.00 250.00
TM Tracy McGrady/75 75.00 200.00
WE Martell Webster/75 8.00 20.00
YM Yao Ming/75 125.00 300.00

2005-06 Sweet Shot Signature Shots Wood

PRINT RUN 15 TO 30 SER.#'d SETS
AB Andrew Bogut/35 15.00 40.00
AN Andrew Bynum/35 10.00 25.00
CF Channing Frye/35 10.00 25.00
CP Chris Paul/35 150.00 400.00
DH Dwight Howard/35 40.00 100.00
DR Dennis Rodman/35 125.00 300.00
DW Deron Williams/35 20.00 50.00
GE Gerald Green/35 12.00 30.00
HW Hakim Warrick/35 10.00 25.00
ID Ike Diogu/35 8.00 20.00
IT Isiah Thomas/35 60.00 150.00
JE Julius Erving/35 125.00 300.00
JG Joey Graham/35 10.00 25.00
JK Jason Kidd/35 20.00 50.00
JW John Wooden/35 150.00 400.00
LA Larry Brown/35 25.00 60.00
MW Marvin Williams/35 12.00 30.00
RF Raymond Felton/35 10.00 25.00
RJ Richard Jefferson/35 10.00 25.00
RM Rashad McCants/35 8.00 20.00
SM Sean May/35 8.00 20.00
SN Steve Nash/35 100.00 250.00
SP Scottie Pippen/35 125.00 300.00
TM Tracy McGrady/35 125.00 300.00
WE Martell Webster/35 10.00 25.00
YM Yao Ming/35 150.00 400.00

2005-06 Sweet Shot Sweet Swatches

PRINT RUN 125 TO 250 SER.#'d SETS
*GOLD: .6X TO 1.5X BASE HI
GOLD PRINT RUN 50 TO 99 SETS
AB Andrew Bogut/125 4.00 10.00
AK Andrei Kirilenko/125 2.50 6.00
AN Andris Biedrins/125 2.00 5.00
AR Rafael Araujo/125 2.00 5.00
AS Amare Stoudemire/125 3.00 8.00
AT Antoine Wright/250 2.50 6.00
AW Antoine Walker/250 2.50 6.00
BB Bruce Bowen/125 2.50 6.00
BD Baron Davis/125 3.00 8.00
BG Ben Gordon/125 2.50 6.00
CA Carmelo Anthony/125 5.00 12.00
CB Caron Butler/250 2.50 6.00
CM Corey Maggette/125 2.50 6.00
CP Chris Paul/125 15.00 40.00
CV Charlie Villanueva/125 2.50 6.00
CW Chris Webber/250 4.00 10.00
DA Dajuan Wagner/250 2.00 5.00
DE Devin Harris/125 2.00 5.00
DF Derek Fisher/250 3.00 8.00
DG Devean George/125 2.00 5.00
DH Dwight Howard/125 4.00 10.00
DI Dikembe Mutombo/250 4.00 10.00
DM Darius Miles/250 2.00 5.00
DN Dirk Nowitzki/125 8.00 20.00
DO Dorell Wright/125 2.00 5.00
DS DeShawn Stevenson/250 2.00 5.00
DW Deron Williams/125 5.00 12.00
EB Elton Brand/125 2.50 6.00
EC Eddy Curry/250 2.50 6.00
GA Gilbert Arenas/125 3.00 8.00
GG Gerald Green/125 3.00 8.00
GH Grant Hill/125 5.00 12.00
GR Danny Granger/250 3.00 8.00
HW Hakim Warrick/250 2.50 6.00
JA Jamal Crawford/125 3.00 8.00
JC Jason Collins/125 2.00 5.00
JH Josh Howard/125 2.50 6.00
JK Jason Kidd/125 5.00 12.00
JL Jalen Rose/125 2.50 6.00
JO Jermaine O'Neal/125 2.50 6.00
JR J.R. Smith/125 3.00 8.00
JT Jason Terry/250 2.50 6.00
JU Julius Hodge/125 2.00 5.00
KB Kobe Bryant/125 50.00 120.00
KD Keyon Dooling/250 2.00 5.00
KG Kevin Garnett/125 8.00 20.00
KK Kyle Korver/125 2.50 6.00
KM Kenyon Martin/250 2.50 6.00
KR Kareem Rush/250 2.00 5.00
KT Kurt Thomas/250 2.50 6.00
KW Kwame Brown/250 2.00 5.00
LD Luol Deng/125 2.50 6.00
LH Larry Hughes/125 2.50 6.00
LJ LeBron James/125 30.00 80.00
LR Luke Ridnour/250 2.50 6.00
LU Luke Jackson/125 2.00 5.00
LW Luke Walton/125 2.00 5.00
MB Mike Bibby/125 3.00 8.00
MD Mike Dunleavy/125 2.00 5.00
MG Manu Ginobili/125 6.00 15.00
MI Michael Finley/250 3.00 8.00
MJ Michael Jordan/125 75.00 200.00
MK Marko Jaric/250 2.00 5.00
MS Mike Sweetney/125 2.00 5.00
MW Marvin Williams/125 3.00 8.00
NH Nene/125 2.50 6.00
NR Nate Robinson/125 3.00 8.00
PG Pau Gasol/250 5.00 12.00
PP Paul Pierce/125 5.00 12.00
PS Peja Stojakovic/125 2.50 6.00
QR Quentin Richardson/250 2.00 5.00
RA Ray Allen/125 5.00 12.00
RD Ricky Davis/250 2.50 6.00
RF Raymond Felton/250 2.50 6.00
RI Jason Richardson/125 3.00 8.00
RL Rashard Lewis/125 2.50 6.00
RM Rashad McCants/125 2.00 5.00
RN Ron Artest/125 2.50 6.00
RS Robert Swift/250 2.00 5.00
RW Rasheed Wallace/250 3.00 8.00
SC Sam Cassell/125 2.50 6.00
SD Samuel Dalembert/250 2.00 5.00
SH Shawn Marion/125 2.50 6.00
SJ Sarunas Jasikevicius/250 3.00 8.00
SM Sean May/125 2.00 5.00
SN Steve Nash/125 6.00 15.00
SO Shaquille O'Neal/125 10.00 25.00
ST Stephon Marbury/125 4.00 10.00
TC Tyson Chandler/250 2.50 6.00
TD Tim Duncan/125 8.00 20.00
TM Tracy McGrady/250 5.00 12.00
TP Tony Parker/125 5.00 12.00
WA Charlie Ward/250 2.00 5.00
WE Martell Webster/125 2.50 6.00
WI Chris Wilcox/250 2.00 5.00
WS Wayne Simien/125 2.00 5.00
YM Yao Ming/125 6.00 15.00
ZI Zydrunas Ilgauskas/125 2.50 6.00
ZR Zach Randolph/125 2.50 6.00

2005-06 Sweet Shot Three Point Shots

PRINT RUNS PROVIDED BY UPPER DECK
CARDS ARE NOT SERIAL #'d
CM Corey Maggette/50 10.00 25.00
DR Dennis Rodman/91 150.00 400.00
LB Larry Bird/33 150.00 400.00
LJ LeBron James/23 1,500.00 3,000.00
MJ Michael Jordan/23 2,500.00 5,000.00
PG Pau Gasol/16 40.00 100.00
PS Peja Stojakovic/16 20.00 50.00
RF Raymond Felton/20 10.00 25.00
RH Richard Hamilton/32 20.00 50.00
RJ Richard Jefferson/24 10.00 25.00
SM Sean May/42 10.00 25.00
SP Scottie Pippen/33 150.00 400.00

2006-07 Sweet Shot

COMP.SET w/o SP's (90) 15.00 40.00
91-115 AU RC PRINT RUN 799 SER.#'d SETS
116-135 AU RC PRINT RUN 250 SER.#'d SETS
133-140 AU RC PRINT RUN 99 SER.#'d SETS
1 Josh Childress .25 .60
2 Joe Johnson .40 1.00
3 Marvin Williams .25 .60
4 Al Jefferson .25 .60
5 Paul Pierce .60 1.50
6 Wally Szczerbiak .30 .75
7 Raymond Felton .25 .60
8 Emeka Okafor .30 .75
9 Gerald Wallace .30 .75
10 Ben Gordon .30 .75
11 Kirk Hinrich .30 .75
12 Michael Jordan 3.00 8.00
13 Larry Hughes .30 .75
14 Zydrunas Ilgauskas .30 .75
15 LeBron James 3.00 8.00
16 Marquis Daniels .25 .60
17 Dirk Nowitzki 1.00 2.50
18 Jason Terry .30 .75
19 Carmelo Anthony .60 1.50
20 Marcus Camby .30 .75
21 Kenyon Martin .30 .75
22 Chauncey Billups .50 1.25
23 Richard Hamilton .40 1.00
24 Ben Wallace .50 1.25
25 Baron Davis .40 1.00
26 Mike Dunleavy .25 .60
27 Jason Richardson .40 1.00
28 Rafer Alston .30 .75
29 Tracy McGrady .60 1.50
30 Yao Ming 1.00 2.50
31 Austin Croshere .25 .60
32 Jermaine O'Neal .40 1.00
33 Peja Stojakovic .30 .75
34 Elton Brand .30 .75
35 Sam Cassell .30 .75
36 Shaun Livingston .30 .75
37 Kwame Brown .25 .60
38 Kobe Bryant 3.00 8.00
39 Lamar Odom .30 .75
40 Pau Gasol .60 1.50
41 Bobby Jackson .25 .60
42 Hakim Warrick .25 .60
43 Shaquille O'Neal 1.50 4.00
44 Dwyane Wade .75 2.00
45 Jason Williams .50 1.25
46 Andrew Bogut .30 .75
47 T.J. Ford .25 .60
48 Jamaal Magloire .25 .60
49 Ricky Davis .30 .75
50 Kevin Garnett 1.00 2.50
51 Rashad McCants .25 .60
52 Vince Carter .75 2.00
53 Richard Jefferson .30 .75
54 Jason Kidd .60 1.50
55 Desmond Mason .25 .60
56 Chris Paul .75 2.00
57 J.R. Smith .40 1.00
58 Channing Frye .25 .60
59 Stephon Marbury .50 1.25
60 Quentin Richardson .25 .60
61 Carlos Arroyo .25 .60
62 Dwight Howard .50 1.25
63 Darko Milicic .25 .60
64 Andre Iguodala .40 1.00
65 Allen Iverson 1.00 2.50
66 Chris Webber .50 1.25
67 Boris Diaw .30 .75
68 Amare Stoudemire .40 1.00
69 Steve Nash .75 2.00
70 Juan Dixon .25 .60
71 Zach Randolph .40 1.00
72 Sebastian Telfair .25 .60
73 Ron Artest .40 1.00
74 Mike Bibby .40 1.00
75 Brad Miller .30 .75
76 Tim Duncan 1.00 2.50
77 Manu Ginobili .75 2.00
78 Tony Parker .60 1.50
79 Ray Allen .60 1.50
80 Rashard Lewis .30 .75
81 Luke Ridnour .30 .75
82 Chris Bosh .50 1.25
83 Joey Graham .25 .60
84 Charlie Villanueva .25 .60
85 Carlos Boozer .30 .75
86 Andrei Kirilenko .30 .75
87 Deron Williams .30 .75
88 Gilbert Arenas .40 1.00
89 Caron Butler .30 .75
90 Antawn Jamison .30 .75
91 David Noel AU RC 3.00 8.00
92 James Augustine AU RC 3.00 8.00
93 Kyle Lowry AU RC 15.00 40.00
94 Bobby Jones AU RC 3.00 8.00
95 Solomon Jones AU RC 3.00 8.00
96 Craig Smith AU RC 4.00 10.00
97 Josh Boone AU RC 3.00 8.00
98 Jordan Farmar AU RC 4.00 10.00
99 Marcus Williams AU RC 3.00 8.00
100 Hassan Adams AU RC 3.00 8.00
101 Dee Brown AU RC 3.00 8.00
102 Denham Brown AU RC 3.00 8.00
103 Steve Novak AU RC 4.00 10.00
104 James White AU RC 3.00 8.00
105 Daniel Gibson AU RC 4.00 10.00
106 Renaldo Balkman AU RC 4.00 10.00
107 P.J. Tucker AU RC 5.00 12.00
108 Saer Sene AU RC 3.00 8.00
109 Thabo Sefolosha AU RC 4.00 10.00
110 Maurice Ager AU RC 3.00 8.00
111 Rajon Rondo AU RC 10.00 25.00
112 Shawne Williams AU RC 3.00 8.00
113 Mardy Collins AU RC 3.00 8.00
114 Paul Davis AU RC 3.00 8.00
115 Quincy Douby AU RC 3.00 8.00
121 Rodney Carney AU RC 4.00 10.00
122 Randy Foye AU RC 5.00 12.00
123 Ronnie Brewer AU RC 6.00 15.00
124 Cedric Simmons AU RC 4.00 10.00
125 Andrea Bargnani AU RC 5.00 12.00
126 LaMarcus Aldridge AU RC 15.00 40.00
127 Tyrus Thomas AU RC 5.00 12.00
128 Rudy Gay AU RC 6.00 12.00
129 Shelden Williams AU RC 4.00 10.00
130 Patrick O'Bryant AU RC 4.00 10.00
131 Hilton Armstrong AU RC 4.00 10.00
132 Brandon Roy AU RC 12.00 30.00
133 Adam Morrison RC 4.00 10.00
134 J.J. Redick RC 10.00 25.00
135 Alexander Johnson RC 3.00 8.00
136 Damir Markota RC 3.00 8.00
137 Leon Powe RC 3.00 8.00
138 Ryan Hollins RC 3.00 8.00
139 Tarence Kinsey RC 3.00 8.00
140 Jorge Garbajosa RC 3.00 8.00

2006-07 Sweet Shot Gold

*1-90 GOLD: 1.25X TO 3X BASE HI
1-90 GOLD PRINT RUN 199 SER.#'d SETS
*91-115 AU RC GOLD: 1X TO 2.5X BASE HI
*116-132 AU RC GOLD: .75X TO 2X BASE HI
*133-140 ROOKIE GOLD: .75X TO 2X BASE HI
91-140 GOLD PRINT RUN 25 SER.#'d SETS
15 LeBron James 15.00 40.00

2006-07 Sweet Shot Signature Shots Acetate

PRINT RUN 25 SER.#'d SETS
BB Brent Barry 25.00 60.00
BD Baron Davis 10.00 25.00
CF Channing Frye 10.00 25.00
CP Chris Paul 125.00 300.00
DG Danny Granger 10.00 25.00
EI Ersan Ilyasova 10.00 25.00
GW Gerald Wallace 10.00 25.00
HW Hakim Warrick 12.00 30.00
JC Josh Childress 10.00 25.00
JJ Joe Johnson 10.00 25.00
JS J.R. Smith 10.00 25.00
KK Kyle Korver 10.00 25.00
KV Kiki Vandeweghe 10.00 25.00
LJ LeBron James 1,500.00 3,000.00
LW Louis Williams 10.00 25.00
MJ Michael Jordan 1,500.00 3,000.00
MW Marvin Williams 10.00 25.00
PP Paul Pierce 15.00 40.00
PS Peja Stojakovic 12.00 30.00
RF Raymond Felton 12.00 30.00
RM Rashad McCants 10.00 25.00
RT Ronny Turiaf 10.00 25.00
ST John Starks 20.00 50.00
TC Tyson Chandler 10.00 25.00
TP Tayshaun Prince 15.00 40.00
VC Vince Carter 40.00 80.00
WF Walt Frazier 12.00 30.00

2006-07 Sweet Shot Signature Shots Leather

APPROXIMATELY ONE PER BOX
AI Andre Iguodala 5.00 12.00
AU James Augustine 5.00 12.00
BB Brent Barry 6.00 15.00
BC Carlos Boozer 5.00 12.00
BJ Bobby Jones 5.00 12.00
BR Bill Russell SP 800.00 1,500.00
CA Carmelo Anthony 15.00 40.00
CB Chris Bosh SP 12.50 30.00
CD Chris Duhon 5.00 12.00
CF Channing Frye 5.00 12.00
CK Chris Kaman 5.00 12.00
CM Cuttino Mobley 5.00 12.00
CP Chris Paul SP 75.00 200.00
CT Chris Taft 5.00 12.00
DC Clyde Drexler 12.50 30.00
DG Danny Granger 5.00 12.00
DH Dwight Howard 12.50 30.00
DN David Noel 5.00 12.00
DR David Robinson SP 20.00 50.00
EC Eddy Curry 5.00 12.00
EI Ersan Ilyasova 5.00 12.00
FR Randy Foye 8.00 20.00
GW Gerald Wallace 5.00 12.00
HO Hakeem Olajuwon 15.00 40.00
HW Hakim Warrick 5.00 12.00
ID Ike Diogu 5.00 12.00
JA Al Jefferson 5.00 12.00
JB Josh Boone 5.00 12.00
JC Josh Childress 5.00 12.00
JE Julius Erving SP 25.00 60.00
JF Jordan Farmar 5.00 12.00
JJ Joe Johnson 6.00 15.00
JR Jalen Rose 5.00 12.00
JS J.R. Smith 5.00 12.00
KB Kwame Brown 5.00 12.00
KD Keyon Dooling 5.00 12.00
KK Kyle Korver 5.00 12.00
KL Kyle Lowry 6.00 15.00
KV Kiki Vandeweghe 6.00 15.00
LH Larry Hughes 5.00 12.00
LJ LeBron James SP 1,500.00 3,000.00
LR Luke Ridnour 5.00 12.00
LW Louis Williams 5.00 12.00
MC Corey Maggette 5.00 12.00
ME Monta Ellis 5.00 12.00
MW Marvin Williams 5.00 12.00
NR Nate Robinson 6.00 15.00
PS Peja Stojakovic SP 8.00 20.00
QR Quentin Richardson 5.00 12.00
RA Ron Artest SP 10.00 25.00
RB Ronnie Brewer 8.00 20.00
RC Rodney Carney 5.00 12.00
RF Raymond Felton 5.00 12.00
RJ Richard Jefferson 5.00 12.00
RM Rashad McCants 5.00 12.00
RT Ronny Turiaf 12.50 30.00
SC Craig Smith 5.00 12.00
SE Sean Elliott 8.00 20.00
SK Steve Kerr 8.00 20.00
SL Shaun Livingston 5.00 12.00
SO Solomon Jones 5.00 12.00
ST John Starks 20.00 50.00
SV Sasha Vujacic 5.00 12.00
TC Tyson Chandler 5.00 12.00
TM Tracy McGrady 10.00 25.00
TP Tayshaun Prince 6.00 15.00
TS Sebastian Telfair 5.00 12.00
VC Vince Carter SP 25.00 50.00
VW Von Wafer 5.00 12.00
WF Walt Frazier 6.00 15.00
WM Martell Webster 5.00 12.00
YK Yaroslav Korolev 5.00 12.00
YM Yao Ming 15.00 40.00

2006-07 Sweet Shot Stitches

APPROXIMATE ODDS ONE PER BOX
*GOLD: .6X TO 1.5X BASE HI
GOLD PRINT RUN 50 SER.#'d SETS
AK Andrei Kirilenko 2.00 5.00
AM Andre Miller 2.00 5.00
AS Amare Stoudemire 2.50 6.00
BD Baron Davis 2.50 6.00
CA Carmelo Anthony 4.00 10.00
CM Corey Maggette 2.00 5.00
DG Drew Gooden 2.00 5.00
DN Dirk Nowitzki 6.00 15.00
GA Gilbert Arenas 2.50 6.00
GH Grant Hill 4.00 10.00
JH Josh Howard 2.00 5.00
JK Jason Kidd 4.00 10.00
JM Jamaal Magloire 2.00 5.00
JO Jermaine O'Neal 2.50 6.00
JT Jamaal Tinsley 2.00 5.00
KG Kevin Garnett 6.00 15.00
KK Kyle Korver 2.00 5.00
LD Luol Deng 2.00 5.00
LJ LeBron James SP 10.00 25.00
MA Shawn Marion 2.50 6.00
MB Mike Bibby 2.50 6.00
MC Jeff McInnis 2.00 5.00
MJ Michael Jordan SP 40.00 80.00
MP Mickael Pietrus 2.00 5.00
PP Paul Pierce 4.00 10.00
RL Rashard Lewis 2.00 5.00
SD Samuel Dalembert 2.00 5.00
SF Steve Francis 2.50 6.00
SM Stephon Marbury 3.00 8.00
SO Shaquille O'Neal 10.00 25.00
SS Stromile Swift 2.00 5.00
TA Tony Allen 2.00 5.00
TC Tyson Chandler 2.00 5.00
TD Tim Duncan 6.00 15.00
TM Tracy McGrady 4.00 10.00
TP Tony Parker 4.00 10.00
VC Vince Carter 5.00 12.00
WS Wally Szczerbiak 2.00 5.00
YM Yao Ming 6.00 15.00
ZI Zydrunas Ilgauskas 2.00 5.00

2006-07 Sweet Shot Swatches Dual

PRINT RUN 199 SER.#'d SETS
*DUAL GOLD: .6X TO 1.5X BASE HI
GOLD PRINT RUN 25 SER.#'d SETS
AH R.Alston/L.Head 4.00 10.00
AK R.Allen/K.Korver 4.00 10.00
AL R.Allen/R.Lewis 4.00 10.00
AN C.Anthony/Nene 5.00 12.00
AT A.Jefferson/T.Allen 4.00 10.00
BB Kw.Brown/A.Bynum 4.00 10.00
BD A.Biedrins/I.Diogu 4.00 10.00
BG C.Bosh/J.Graham 4.00 10.00
BL E.Brand/S.Livingston 4.00 10.00
BM M.Bibby/B.Miller 4.00 10.00
BV A.Bogut/C.Villanueva 4.00 10.00
CH B.Haywood/C.Butler 4.00 10.00
CJ V.Carter/R.Jefferson 6.00 15.00
CP T.Chandler/C.Paul 5.00 12.00
CW Dv.West/T.Chandler 4.00 10.00
DB B.Davis/C.Billups 4.00 10.00
DG T.Duncan/M.Ginobili 6.00 15.00
DI S.Dalembert/A.Iguodala 4.00 10.00
DP T.Duncan/T.Parker 6.00 15.00
DW J.Dixon/M.Webster 4.00 10.00
FM S.Francis/S.Marbury 4.00 10.00
GJ D.Gooden/L.James 8.00 20.00
GM K.Garnett/S.Marion 5.00 12.00
GS P.Stojakovic/M.Ginobili 4.00 10.00
GW P.Gasol/H.Warrick 4.00 10.00
HB R.Hamilton/C.Billups 4.00 10.00
HG K.Hinrich/B.Gordon 4.00 10.00
HI L.Hughes/Z.Ilgauskas 4.00 10.00
JA A.Jamison/G.Arenas 4.00 10.00
JG D.Granger/S.Jasikevicius 4.00 10.00
JJ M.Jordan/L.James 75.00 200.00
JW J.Johnson/Mv.Williams 4.00 10.00
KJ J.Kidd/L.James 15.00 40.00
KW A.Kirilenko/D.Williams 4.00 10.00
LP R.Lewis/J.Petro 4.00 10.00
MB K.Bryant/T.McGrady 50.00 120.00
MD J.Magloire/J.Dixon 4.00 10.00
MH D.Milicic/D.Howard 4.00 10.00
MK J.McInnis/N.Krstic 4.00 10.00
MM T.McGrady/Y.Ming 6.00 15.00
MO Y.Ming/S.O'Neal 10.00 25.00
MR C.Maggette/M.Redd 4.00 10.00
MS A.Mourning/W.Simien 4.00 10.00
NH D.Nowitzki/J.Howard 6.00 15.00
NM S.Nash/S.Marion 6.00 15.00
OF E.Okafor/R.Felton 4.00 10.00
PP T.Parker/C.Paul 5.00 12.00
PS P.Pierce/W.Szczerbiak 4.00 10.00
RD J.Richardson/M.Dunleavy 4.00 10.00
RF N.Robinson/C.Frye 4.00 10.00
SD A.Stoudemire/B.Diaw 4.00 10.00
TC M.Taylor/E.Curry 4.00 10.00
TO J.Tinsley/J.O'Neal 4.00 10.00
TS K.Thomas/A.Stoudemire 4.00 10.00
UG B.Udrih/M.Ginobili 4.00 10.00
WC J.Childress/Mv.Williams 4.00 10.00
WD B.Wallace/L.Deng 4.00 10.00
WH R.Hamilton/B.Wallace 6.00 15.00
WK C.Webber/K.Korver 4.00 10.00
WP R.Wallace/T.Prince 6.00 15.00

2006-07 Sweet Shot Sweet Spot Signatures

AJ Antawn Jamison 10.00 25.00
BD Baron Davis 10.00 25.00
CA Carmelo Anthony 30.00 80.00
CD Clyde Drexler 40.00 80.00
CP Chris Paul 75.00 200.00
HO Hakeem Olajuwon 15.00 40.00
JC Josh Childress 10.00 25.00
JO Magic Johnson 30.00 80.00
KA Kareem Abdul-Jabbar 60.00 120.00
KK Kyle Korver 10.00 25.00
LB Larry Bird 50.00 125.00
LJ LeBron James SP 1,500.00 3,000.00
PP Paul Pierce 20.00 50.00
PS Peja Stojakovic 12.50 30.00
RA Ron Artest 15.00 40.00
RF Raymond Felton 15.00 40.00
RM Rashad McCants 10.00 25.00
TC Tyson Chandler 10.00 25.00
TP Tayshaun Prince 10.00 25.00
VC Vince Carter 20.00 50.00
YM Yao Ming 25.00 60.00

2007-08 Sweet Shot

1-90 PRINT RUN 350 SER.#'d SETS
103-132 AU RC PRINT RUN 699 SER.#'d SETS
1 Joe Johnson .75 2.00
2 Marvin Williams .60 1.50
3 Josh Smith .60 1.50
4 Al Jefferson .60 1.50
5 Paul Pierce 1.50 4.00
6 Ray Allen 1.50 4.00
7 Adam Morrison .60 1.50
8 Raymond Felton .75 2.00
9 Gerald Wallace .75 2.00
10 Jason Richardson 1.00 2.50
11 Ben Gordon .75 2.00
12 Luol Deng .75 2.00
13 Ben Wallace 1.25 3.00
14 Michael Jordan 10.00 25.00
15 Larry Hughes .75 2.00
16 LeBron James 8.00 20.00
17 Zydrunas Ilgauskas .75 2.00
18 Dirk Nowitzki 2.50 6.00
19 Josh Howard .75 2.00
20 Jason Terry .75 2.00
21 Allen Iverson 2.50 6.00
22 Nene .75 2.00
23 Carmelo Anthony 1.50 4.00
24 Chauncey Billups 1.25 3.00
25 Richard Hamilton 1.00 2.50
26 Tayshaun Prince 1.00 2.50
27 Baron Davis .75 2.00
28 Stephen Jackson .75 2.00
29 Brandan Wright RC 1.25 3.00
30 Tracy McGrady 1.50 4.00
31 Yao Ming 2.50 6.00
32 Shane Battier .75 2.00
33 Jermaine O'Neal .75 2.00
34 Danny Granger .60 1.50
35 Elton Brand .75 2.00
36 Corey Maggette .75 2.00
37 Kobe Bryant 8.00 20.00
38 Lamar Odom .75 2.00
39 Luke Walton .75 2.00
40 Rudy Gay .75 2.00
41 Pau Gasol 1.50 4.00
42 Dwyane Wade 2.00 5.00
43 Antoine Walker .75 2.00
44 Shaquille O'Neal 4.00 10.00
45 Michael Redd .75 2.00
46 Maurice Williams .75 2.00
47 Andrew Bogut .75 2.00
48 Yi Jianlian RC 2.00 5.00
49 Kevin Garnett 2.50 6.00
50 Ricky Davis .75 2.00
51 Randy Foye .75 2.00
52 Vince Carter 2.00 5.00
53 Jason Kidd 1.50 4.00
54 Richard Jefferson .75 2.00
55 Tyson Chandler 1.00 2.50
56 David West .75 2.00
57 Chris Paul 2.00 5.00
58 Eddy Curry .60 1.50
59 Jamal Crawford .75 2.00
60 Stephon Marbury 1.25 3.00
61 Zach Randolph 1.00 2.50
62 Dwight Howard 1.25 3.00
63 Grant Hill 1.50 4.00
64 Andre Miller .75 2.00
65 Thaddeus Young RC 1.50 4.00
66 Andre Iguodala 1.00 2.50
67 Steve Nash 2.00 5.00
68 Amare Stoudemire 1.00 2.50
69 Shawn Marion 1.00 2.50
70 Brandon Roy 1.25 3.00
71 Greg Oden RC 1.50 4.00
72 Ron Artest 1.00 2.50
73 Mike Bibby 1.00 2.50
74 Kevin Martin .75 2.00
75 Tim Duncan 2.50 6.00
76 Manu Ginobili 2.00 5.00
77 Tony Parker 1.50 4.00
78 Wally Szczerbiak .75 2.00
79 Delonte West .60 1.50
80 Rashard Lewis .75 2.00
81 T.J. Ford .60 1.50
82 Chris Bosh 1.25 3.00
83 Andrea Bargnani .60 1.50
84 Carlos Boozer .75 2.00
85 Mehmet Okur .60 1.50
86 Deron Williams .75 2.00
87 Gilbert Arenas 1.00 2.50
88 Antawn Jamison .75 2.00
89 Caron Butler .75 2.00
90 Nick Young RC 1.50 4.00
91 Al Horford AU RC 12.00 30.00
92 Acie Law AU RC 3.00 8.00
93 Joakim Noah AU RC 10.00 25.00
94 Marco Belinelli AU RC 4.00 10.00
95 Al Thornton AU RC 3.00 8.00
96 Javaris Crittenton AU RC 3.00 8.00
97 Mike Conley Jr. AU RC 12.00 30.00
98 Corey Brewer AU RC 4.00 10.00
99 Julian Wright AU RC 3.00 8.00
100 Spencer Hawes AU RC 3.00 8.00
101 Kevin Durant AU RC 400.00 800.00
102 Jeff Green AU RC 4.00 10.00
103 Daequan Cook AU RC 3.00 8.00
104 Jared Dudley AU RC 3.00 8.00
105 Wilson Chandler AU RC 3.00 8.00
106 Rodney Stuckey AU RC 2.50 6.00
107 Morris Almond AU RC 2.50 6.00
108 Arron Afflalo AU RC 3.00 8.00
109 Alando Tucker AU RC 2.50 6.00
110 Sean Williams AU RC 2.50 6.00
111 Carl Landry AU RC 2.50 6.00
112 Gabe Pruitt AU RC 2.50 6.00
113 Marcus Williams AU RC 2.50 6.00
114 Nick Fazekas AU RC 2.50 6.00
115 Jermareo Davidson AU RC 2.50 6.00
116 Josh McRoberts AU RC 2.50 6.00
117 Aaron Brooks AU RC 3.00 8.00
118 Derrick Byars AU RC 2.50 6.00
119 Adam Haluska AU RC 2.50 6.00
120 Reyshawn Terry AU RC 2.50 6.00
121 Jared Jordan AU RC 2.50 6.00
122 Stephane Lasme AU RC 2.50 6.00
123 Aaron Gray AU RC 2.50 6.00
124 Renaldas Seibutis AU RC 4.00 10.00
125 Taurean Green AU RC 2.50 6.00
126 Demetris Nichols AU RC 2.50 6.00
127 Herbert Hill AU RC 2.50 6.00
128 Sammy Mejia AU RC 2.50 6.00
129 D.J. Strawberry AU RC 2.50 6.00
130 Chris Richard AU RC 2.50 6.00
131 Glen Davis AU RC 3.00 8.00
132 Jason Smith AU RC 2.50 6.00

2007-08 Sweet Shot Rookie Stitches

PRINT RUN 99 SER.#'d SETS
*PATCHES: 1X TO 2.5X BASE HI
PATCH PRINT RUN 10 SER.#'d SETS
AH Al Horford 6.00 15.00
AL Acie Law 1.50 4.00
AT Al Thornton 1.50 4.00
BW Brandan Wright 2.00 5.00
CB Corey Brewer 2.00 5.00
DC Daequan Cook 1.50 4.00
JC Javaris Crittenton 1.50 4.00
JD Jared Dudley 2.00 5.00
JG Jeff Green 2.00 5.00
JN Joakim Noah 2.50 6.00
JS Jason Smith 1.50 4.00
JW Julian Wright 1.50 4.00
KD Kevin Durant 75.00 200.00
MC Mike Conley Jr. 6.00 15.00
NY Nick Young 2.50 6.00
RS Rodney Stuckey 1.50 4.00
SH Spencer Hawes 1.50 4.00
SW Sean Williams 1.50 4.00
TY Thaddeus Young 2.50 6.00
WC Wilson Chandler 2.00 5.00

2007-08 Sweet Shot Signature Kicks White Leather

PRINT RUN 24 TO 40 SER.#'d SETS
AA Arron Afflalo/40 6.00 15.00
AG Aaron Gray/40 5.00 12.00
AH Al Harrington/40 6.00 15.00
AJ Antawn Jamison/40 6.00 15.00
AL Morris Almond/40 5.00 12.00
BD Boris Diaw/40 6.00 15.00
BG Ben Gordon/40 6.00 15.00
BR Brandon Roy/40 10.00 25.00
CL Carl Landry/40 5.00 12.00
CS Craig Smith/40 5.00 12.00
DB Dee Brown/40 5.00 12.00
DG Daniel Gibson/40 5.00 12.00
DL David Lee/40 5.00 12.00
DN David Noel/40 5.00 12.00
DR Dennis Rodman/40 50.00 120.00
DW Deron Williams/40 6.00 15.00
HO Al Horford/40 20.00 50.00
JA James Augustine/40 5.00 12.00
JB Josh Boone/40 5.00 12.00
JC Javaris Crittenton/40 5.00 12.00
JG Jorge Garbajosa/40 6.00 15.00
JW Julian Wright/40 5.00 12.00
KB Kobe Bryant/24 1,500.00 3,000.00
KD Kevin Durant/40 500.00 1,000.00
KL Kyle Lowry/40 8.00 20.00
LA LaMarcus Aldridge/40 8.00 20.00
LB Leandro Barbosa/40 6.00 15.00
LJ LeBron James/40 1,000.00 2,000.00
LP Leon Powe/40 5.00 12.00
MA Maurice Ager/40 5.00 12.00
MB Marco Belinelli/40 6.00 15.00
MC Mardy Collins/40 5.00 12.00
MJ Michael Jordan/40 2,000.00 4,000.00
PM Paul Millsap/40 6.00 15.00
RF Randy Foye/40 6.00 15.00
RS Rodney Stuckey/40 6.00 15.00
SJ Solomon Jones/40 5.00 12.00
SK Steve Kerr/40 10.00 25.00
TF T.J. Ford/40 5.00 12.00
TG Taurean Green/40 5.00 12.00
TP Tayshaun Prince/40 8.00 20.00

2007-08 Sweet Shot Signature Shots

PRINT RUNS LISTED IN CHECKLIST
AB Andrea Bargnani/25 10.00 25.00
AD Adrian Dantley/98 10.00 25.00
AH Al Harrington/50 4.00 10.00
AI Andre Iguodala/50 6.00 15.00
AJ Antawn Jamison/50 5.00 12.00
AM Alonzo Mourning/25 60.00 120.00
BA B.J. Armstrong/98 8.00 20.00
BB Bruce Bowen/97 4.00 10.00
BD Baron Davis/50 8.00 20.00
BE Raja Bell/25 5.00 12.00
BG Ben Gordon/369 4.00 10.00
BI Larry Bird/50 40.00 100.00
BL Bill Laimbeer/197 6.00 15.00
BM Brad Miller/99 4.00 10.00
BS Bill Sharman/50 10.00 25.00
BW Bill Walton/25 15.00 40.00
CD Chris Duhon/297 4.00 10.00
CH Tyson Chandler/98 4.00 10.00
CR Cazzie Russell/25 10.00 25.00
CS Cedric Simmons/98 4.00 10.00
CW Shawne Williams/195 4.00 10.00
DB Dee Brown/195 4.00 10.00
DH Dwight Howard/50 6.00 15.00
DL David Lee/197 4.00 10.00
DN David Noel/150 4.00 10.00
DO Keyon Dooling/197 4.00 10.00
DR Dennis Rodman/25 50.00 120.00
DW Deron Williams/409 4.00 10.00
DX Clyde Drexler/25 40.00 80.00
EO Emeka Okafor/25 6.00 15.00
FG Francisco Garcia/97 4.00 10.00
GR Glen Rice/50 4.00 10.00
HA Hilton Armstrong/195 4.00 10.00
HG Horace Grant/50 15.00 40.00
HK Connie Hawkins/50 8.00 20.00
HO Hakeem Olajuwon/25 20.00 50.00
JA James Augustine/195 4.00 10.00
JB Josh Boone/195 4.00 10.00
JG Jorge Garbajosa/97 4.00 10.00
JK Jason Kidd/20 20.00 50.00
JM Magic Johnson/50 40.00 100.00
JO Avery Johnson/50 8.00 20.00
JR J.R. Smith/197 8.00 20.00
JW Jamaal Wilkes/98 6.00 15.00
KA Kareem Abdul-Jabbar/50 30.00 80.00
KD Kevin Durant/99 600.00 1,200.00
KL Kyle Lowry/189 4.00 10.00
LB Leandro Barbosa/197 4.00 10.00
LH Larry Hughes/50 4.00 10.00
LJ LeBron James/54 1,250.00 2,500.00
LP Leon Powe/197 4.00 10.00
MA Maurice Ager/225 4.00 10.00
MC Mardy Collins/195 4.00 10.00
MD Marquis Daniels/195 4.00 10.00
MI Mile Ilic/195 4.00 10.00
PD Paul Davis/195 4.00 10.00
PM Paul Millsap/97 4.00 10.00
PO Patrick O'Bryant/197 4.00 10.00
PP Paul Pierce/50 25.00 60.00
PR Pat Riley/25 25.00 60.00
QR Quentin Richardson/25 4.00 10.00
RB Ronnie Brewer/149 4.00 10.00
RC Rodney Carney/220 4.00 10.00
RF Raymond Felton/197 4.00 10.00
RH Ryan Hollins/219 4.00 10.00
RI Rick Mahorn/97 6.00 15.00
RR Rajon Rondo/97 12.00 30.00
RS Randolph Morris/195 4.00 10.00
RT Ronny Turiaf/195 4.00 10.00
SB Shannon Brown/195 4.00 10.00
SC Craig Smith/195 4.00 10.00
SF Stromile Swift/220 4.00 10.00
SJ Solomon Jones/195 4.00 10.00
SK Steve Kerr/50 15.00 40.00
SN Steve Nash/25 40.00 100.00
SP Sam Perkins/98 5.00 12.00
SR Sergio Rodriguez/195 4.00 10.00
SS Saer Sene/195 4.00 10.00
SW Shelden Williams/197 4.00 10.00
TC Tom Chambers/195 4.00 10.00
TF T.J. Ford/197 4.00 10.00
TM Tracy McGrady/50 10.00 25.00
TP Tayshaun Prince/25 8.00 20.00
TT Tyrus Thomas/25 6.00 15.00
VC Vince Carter/25 25.00 60.00
WD Walter Davis/32 5.00 12.00
WF Walt Frazier/25 12.00 30.00
WI Marvin Williams/399 4.00 10.00
WI2 Damien Wilkins/195 4.00 10.00
WO John Wooden/103 40.00 100.00
WT Wayman Tisdale/97 10.00 25.00
WU Wes Unseld/25 10.00 25.00
YD Yakhouba Diawara/195 4.00 10.00

2007-08 Sweet Shot Signature Shots Acetate

PRINT RUN 10 TO 25 SER.#'d SETS
BR Brandon Roy/25 30.00 60.00
CS Craig Smith/25 6.00 15.00
DG Daniel Gibson/25 6.00 15.00
DH Dwight Howard/25 25.00 60.00
JA James Augustine/25 6.00 15.00
JB Josh Boone/25 6.00 15.00
KD Kevin Durant/25 1,000.00 2,000.00
KL Kyle Lowry/25 6.00 15.00
LA LaMarcus Aldridge/25 10.00 25.00
LJ LeBron James/25 1,500.00 3,000.00
LP Leon Powe/25 6.00 15.00
LW Lenny Wilkens/25 12.00 30.00
MA Maurice Ager/25 6.00 15.00
MC Mardy Collins/25 6.00 15.00
PP Paul Pierce/25 40.00 100.00
RF Randy Foye/25 6.00 15.00
RG Rudy Gay/25 15.00 40.00
RM Randolph Morris/25 6.00 15.00
SI Cedric Simmons/25 6.00 15.00
SN Steve Nash/25 50.00 100.00
TT Tyrus Thomas/25 6.00 15.00
YM Yao Ming/25 25.00 60.00

2007-08 Sweet Shot Signature Shots Black Ink

PRINT RUNS LISTED IN CHECKLIST
AD Adrian Dantley/50 6.00 15.00
AJ Antawn Jamison/50 5.00 12.00
BA B.J. Armstrong/50 10.00 25.00
BB Bruce Bowen/97 4.00 10.00
BG Ben Gordon/92 6.00 15.00
BI Larry Bird/50 40.00 100.00
BL Bill Laimbeer/25 15.00 30.00
BS Bill Sharman/32 10.00 25.00

CH Tyson Chandler/25 6.00 15.00
CM Corey Maggette/50 6.00 15.00
CR Cazzie Russell/50 6.00 15.00
CS Cedric Simmons/98 4.00 10.00
CW Shawne Williams/195 4.00 10.00
DB Dee Brown/195 4.00 10.00
DG Daniel Gibson/97 6.00 15.00
DH Dwight Howard/45 15.00 40.00
DL David Lee/98 4.00 10.00
DN David Noel/69 4.00 10.00
DO Keyon Dooling/98 4.00 10.00
FG Francisco Garcia/97 4.00 10.00
FO Randy Foye/99 4.00 10.00
HA Hilton Armstrong/97 4.00 10.00
JA James Augustine/195 4.00 10.00
JB Josh Boone/195 4.00 10.00
JG Jorge Garbajosa/97 4.00 10.00
JO Avery Johnson/98 6.00 15.00
JR J.R. Smith/25 8.00 20.00
JW Jamaal Wilkes/25 15.00 30.00
KB Kobe Bryant/24 150.00 400.00
KD Kevin Durant/99 600.00 1,200.00
KL Kyle Lowry/189 4.00 10.00
LB Leandro Barbosa/197 4.00 10.00
LJ LeBron James/23 1,500.00 3,000.00
LP Leon Powe/100 4.00 10.00
LR Luke Ridnour/98 4.00 10.00
MA Maurice Ager/97 4.00 10.00
MC Mardy Collins/97 4.00 10.00
MD Marquis Daniels/97 4.00 10.00
MI Mile Ilic/97 4.00 10.00
PD Paul Davis/97 4.00 10.00
PM Paul Millsap/97 4.00 10.00
PO Patrick O'Bryant/98 4.00 10.00
RB Ronnie Brewer/97 4.00 10.00
RC Rodney Carney/98 4.00 10.00
RF Raymond Felton/98 5.00 12.00
RH Ryan Hollins/97 4.00 10.00
RI Rick Mahorn/97 6.00 15.00
RR Rajon Rondo/97 20.00 50.00
RS Randolph Morris/97 4.00 10.00
RT Ronny Turiaf/99 6.00 15.00
SB Shannon Brown/49 8.00 20.00
SC Craig Smith/195 4.00 10.00
SF Stromile Swift/98 4.00 10.00
SJ Solomon Jones/97 4.00 10.00
SP Sam Perkins/98 5.00 12.00
SR Sergio Rodriguez/97 4.00 10.00
SS Saer Sene/97 4.00 10.00
SW Shelden Williams/50 4.00 10.00
TC Tom Chambers/50 5.00 12.00
TF T.J. Ford/25 6.00 15.00
TM Tracy McGrady/41 12.50 30.00
WI Marvin Williams/25 8.00 20.00
WI2 Damien Wilkins/195 4.00 10.00
WT Wayman Tisdale/97 10.00 25.00
YD Yakhouba Diawara/99 4.00 10.00

2007-08 Sweet Shot Signature Shots White Ink
STATED PRINT RUN ONE TO 191 SER.#'d SETS
KK Kyle Korver/191 4.00 10.00

2007-08 Sweet Shot Sweet Spot Signatures
PRINT RUNS LISTED IN CHECKLIST
BR Brandon Roy/50 20.00 40.00
CS Craig Smith/50 6.00 15.00
DG Daniel Gibson/50 10.00 25.00
HG Horace Grant/25 15.00 40.00
HW Hakim Warrick/50 6.00 15.00
JN Joakim Noah/50 25.00 60.00
KD Kevin Durant/35 600.00 1,200.00
LA LaMarcus Aldridge/50 20.00 40.00
LJ LeBron James/25 150.00 300.00
MJ Michael Jordan/23 800.00 1,200.00
MO Randolph Morris/50 6.00 15.00
RG Rudy Gay/50 12.50 30.00
RM Rick Mahorn/50 12.50 30.00
SR Sergio Rodriguez/50 6.00 15.00
TG Taurean Green/50 6.00 15.00
TT Tyrus Thomas/25 30.00 60.00
WF Walt Frazier/50 15.00 40.00
YD Yakhouba Diawara/50 6.00 15.00

2007-08 Sweet Shot Sweet Spot Signatures Silver Stitch
PRINT RUNS LISTED IN CHECKLIST
CS Craig Smith/20 8.00 20.00
DG Daniel Gibson/20 8.00 20.00
JG Jorge Garbajosa/20 8.00 20.00
RM Rick Mahorn/20 20.00 40.00
SR Sergio Rodriguez/20 8.00 20.00

2007-08 Sweet Shot Sweet Stitches
*PATCHES: 1X TO 2.5X BASE HI
PATCH PRINT RUN 35 SER.#'d SETS
AI Allen Iverson 6.00 15.00
AR Ron Artest 2.50 6.00
BR Elton Brand 2.00 5.00
CA Carmelo Anthony 4.00 10.00
CM Corey Maggette 2.00 5.00
CW Chris Wilcox 2.00 5.00
DE Desmond Mason 2.00 5.00
DG Devean George 2.00 5.00
DH Devin Harris 1.50 4.00
DM Darko Milicic 2.00 5.00
DU Mike Dunleavy 1.50 4.00
FJ Fred Jones 2.00 5.00
GH Grant Hill 4.00 10.00
JO Jermaine O'Neal 2.50 6.00
JR Jason Richardson 2.50 6.00
JS J.R. Smith 2.50 6.00
KB Kobe Bryant 50.00 120.00
KG Kevin Garnett 6.00 15.00
LH Larry Hughes 2.00 5.00
LJ LeBron James 8.00 20.00
MA Martynas Andriuskevicius 2.00 5.00
MD Marquis Daniels 2.00 5.00
MG Manu Ginobili 5.00 12.00
PA Tony Parker 4.00 10.00
PG Pau Gasol 4.00 10.00
RA Ray Allen 4.00 10.00
RJ Richard Jefferson 2.00 5.00
RL Rashard Lewis 2.00 5.00
RW Rasheed Wallace 3.00 8.00
SD Samuel Dalembert 2.00 5.00
SF Steve Francis 2.00 5.00
SI Wayne Simien 2.00 5.00
SL Shaun Livingston 2.00 5.00
SM Sean May 2.00 5.00
SO Shaquille O'Neal 10.00 25.00
TD Tim Duncan 6.00 15.00
TP Tayshaun Prince 2.50 6.00
WS Wally Szczerbiak 2.00 5.00
ZI Zydrunas Ilgauskas 2.00 5.00
ZR Zach Randolph 2.50 6.00

2007-08 Sweet Shot Sweet Swatches Dual
*PATCHES: 1.25X TO 3X BASE HI
PATCH PRINT RUN 25 SER.#'d SETS
AG R.Allen/K.Garnett 6.00 15.00
AS M.Andriuskevicius/T.Selolosha 3.00 8.00
BB K.Brown/A.Bynum 3.00 8.00
BD E.Brand/P.Davis 3.00 8.00
BF K.Bryant/J.Farmar 40.00 100.00
BG M.Ginobili/B.Bowen 4.00 10.00
CJ R.Jefferson/V.Carter 5.00 12.00
CS T.Chandler/C.Simmons 3.00 8.00
DD M.Dunleavy/M.Daniels 3.00 8.00
DG L.Deng/B.Gordon 3.00 8.00
DP T.Duncan/T.Parker 5.00 12.00
DT R.Davis/S.Telfair 3.00 8.00
FB S.Battier/S.Francis 3.00 8.00
GH D.George/D.Harris 3.00 8.00
HB G.Hill/R.Bell 5.00 12.00
HJ L.James/L.Hughes 8.00 20.00
HW R.Hamilton/R.Wallace 3.00 8.00
IA A.Iverson/C.Anthony 6.00 15.00
IM D.Milicic/Z.Ilgauskas 3.00 8.00
JG L.Jackson/J.Graham 3.00 8.00
JJ M.Jordan/L.James 60.00 150.00
KB A.Kirilenko/C.Butler 3.00 8.00
LH D.Howard/R.Lewis 3.00 8.00
MC S.Marbury/M.Collins 3.00 8.00
MG D.Marshall/D.Gooden 3.00 8.00
MH Y.Ming/L.Head 4.00 10.00
ML C.Maggette/S.Livingston 3.00 8.00
MR D.Mason/M.Redd 3.00 8.00
MS A.Stoudemire/S.Marion 3.00 8.00
NA T.Ariza/J.Nelson 3.00 8.00
NH D.Nowitzki/J.Howard 4.00 10.00
PG K.Garnett/P.Pierce 5.00 12.00
RD R.Brewer/D.Brown 3.00 8.00
RF J.Richardson/R.Felton 3.00 8.00
SG P.Gasol/S.Swift 3.00 8.00
SP P.Stojakovic/C.Paul 4.00 10.00
SW W.Szczerbiak/D.West 3.00 8.00
TD I.Diogu/J.Tinsley 3.00 8.00
WR J.Rose/C.Webber 5.00 12.00
WW C.Wilcox/D.Wilkins 3.00 8.00

2009 Sweet Spot Signatures Red Stitch Blue Ink
OVERALL AUTO ODDS 1:3 HOBBY
PRINT RUNS B/WN 2-199 COPIES PER
NO PRICING ON QTY 25 OR LESS
EXCHANGE DEADLINE 10/7/2011
SLJ LeBron James/15 150.00 300.00

2009 Sweet Spot Signatures Red Stitch Green Ink
OVERALL AUTO ODDS 1:3 HOBBY
ANNOUNCED PRINT RUNS LISTED
PRINT RUN INFO PROVIDED BY UD
EXCHANGE DEADLINE 10/7/2011
SLJ LeBron James/25 * 125.00 250.00

1951 Syracuse National Glasses
COMPLETE SET (9) 500.00 850.00
1 Al Cervi 50.00 100.00
2 Billy Gabor 25.00 50.00
3 Alex Hannum 60.00 120.00
4 Noble Jorgensen 25.00 50.00
5 George Ratkovicz 25.00 50.00
6 Dolph Schayes 250.00 400.00
7 Paul Seymour 60.00 120.00
8 Front Office Personnel 25.00 50.00
9 Onodoga Cty War Memorial 25.00 50.00

1958-59 Syracuse Nationals
COMPLETE SET (11) 800.00 1,600.00
1 Al Bianchi 75.00 150.00
2 Ed Conlin 65.00 125.00
3 Larry Costello 75.00 150.00
4 Connie Dierking 75.00 150.00
5 Hal Greer 100.00 200.00
6 Bob Hopkins 65.00 125.00
7 John Kerr 100.00 200.00
8 Togo Palazzi 65.00 125.00
9 Dolph Schayes 150.00 300.00
10 Paul Seymour 65.00 125.00
11 Team Photo 75.00 150.00

1962-63 Syracuse Nationals
COMPLETE SET 400.00 800.00
1 Al Bianchi 30.00 60.00
2 Len Chappell 25.00 50.00
3 Larry Costello 40.00 80.00
4 Dave Gambee 25.00 50.00
5 Hal Greer 60.00 120.00
6 Alex Hannum 30.00 60.00
7 Swede Halbrook 25.00 50.00
8 John Kerr 50.00 100.00
9 Paul Neuman 25.00 50.00
10 Joe Roberts 25.00 50.00
11 Dolph Schayes 75.00 150.00
12 Lee Shaffer 25.00 50.00

1998 Taco Bell Shaquille O'Neal
1 Shaquille O'Neal 4.00 10.00

1984-85 Tampa Bay Thrillers
1 Jeff Rosenberg PRES
Bill Musselman CO
Charles Jones
James Banks
Les Craft
Marc Glass
Steve Hayes
Perry Moss
Freeman Williams
Ron Valentine 4.00 10.00

1980-81 TCMA CBA
COMPLETE SET (45) 40.00 80.00
1 Chubby Cox 1.25 3.00
2 Sylvester Cuyler 1.00 2.50
3 Harry Davis .75 2.00
4 Danny Salisbury .75 2.00
5 Cazzie Russell 4.00 10.00
6 Al Green 1.00 2.50
7 Rick Wilson .75 2.00
8 Jim Brogan .75 2.00
9 Andre McCarter 2.50 6.00
10 Jerry Baskerville 1.25 3.00
11 James Woods .75 2.00
12 Geoff Crompton 1.25 3.00
13 Korky Nelson .75 2.00
14 George Karl CO 7.50 15.00
15 Stan Pietkiewicz 1.25 3.00
16 Raymond Townsend 2.00 5.00
17 Lenny Horton .75 2.00
18 Carl Bailey .75 2.00
19 Ken Jones .75 2.00
20 Rory Sparrow 3.00 8.00
21 Mauro Panaggio CO 1.50 4.00
22 Glenn Hagan 1.25 3.00
23 Larry Fogle 1.25 3.00
24 Wayne Abrams .75 2.00
25 Jerry Christian .75 2.00
26 Edgar Jones 1.50 4.00
27 Jerry Radocha .75 2.00
28 Greg Jackson 1.00 2.50
29 Eddie Mast P/CO 1.25 3.00
30 Ron Davis 1.25 3.00
31 Tico Brown 1.00 2.50
32 Freeman Blade 1.00 2.50
33 Bill Klucas CO 1.00 2.50
34 Melvin Davis 1.00 2.50
35 James Hardy .75 2.00
36 Brad Davis 4.00 10.00
37 Andre Wakefield .75 2.00
38 Brett Vroman 1.25 3.00
39 Larry Knight .75 2.00
40 Mel Bennett .75 2.00
41 Stan Eckwood .75 2.00
42 Andrew Parker .75 2.00
43 Billy Ray (Dunk) Bates 1.50 4.00
44 Matt Teahan .75 2.00
45 Carlton Green .75 2.00

1981-82 TCMA CBA
COMPLETE SET (90) 60.00 150.00
1 1981 CBA Champions
Rochester Zeniths/(Previous champions
listed on back) 2.00 5.00
2 Wayne Abrams .75 2.00
3 Pete Taylor .75 2.00
4 George Torres .75 2.00
5 Henry Bibby 3.00 8.00
6 Rufus Harris .75 2.00
7 Donnie Koonce .75 2.00
8 Jeff Wilkins 1.50 4.00
9 Kurt Nimphius 1.25 3.00
10 Billy Ray(Dunk) Bates 1.50 4.00
11 James Lee 1.25 3.00
12 Marlon Redmond .75 2.00
13 Gary Mazza CO .75 2.00
14 Tony Fuller 1.25 3.00
15 Brad Davis 3.00 8.00
16 Joe Cooper 1.25 3.00
17 Andra Griffin .75 2.00
18 Rudy White 1.25 3.00
19 Ricky Williams .75 2.00
20 Glenn Hagan 1.25 3.00
21 Ernie Graham .75 2.00
22 Kevin Graham .75 2.00
23 Billy Reid .75 2.00
24 Mauro Panaggio CO 1.25 3.00
25 Bo Ellis 1.50 4.00
26 Ollie Matson 1.25 3.00
27 Tony Turner .75 2.00
28 Leo Papile CO .75 2.00
29 Larry Holmes .75 2.00
30 Steve Hayes 2.00 5.00
31 Carl Bailey .75 2.00
32 Tico Brown 1.25 3.00
33 Percy Davis .75 2.00
34 Al Leslie .75 2.00
35 Ken Dennard 1.50 4.00
36 Larry Spriggs 3.00 8.00
37 John Smith .75 2.00
38 Kenny Natt 1.25 3.00
39 Harry Heineken .75 2.00
40 Lowes Moore .75 2.00
41 Curtis Berry .75 2.00
42 Freeman Blade CO 1.25 3.00
43 Larry Lawrence .75 2.00
44 Purvis Miller .75 2.00
45 Ron Valentine .75 2.00
46 Charles Floyd .75 2.00
47 Greg Cornelius .75 2.00
48 Clay Johnson 2.00 5.00
49 Bill Klucas CO 1.25 3.00
50 Cazzie Russell P/CO 4.00 10.00
51 Craig Shelton 1.50 4.00
52 Dave Britton .75 2.00
53 Ken Green .75 2.00
54 Stan Pawlak CO 1.25 3.00
55 Rich Yonakor .75 2.00
56 Darryl Gladden .75 2.00
57 Norman Black .75 2.00
58 Pete Harris .75 2.00
59 Anthony Roberts .75 2.00
60 Jawann Oldham 1.50 4.00
61 Sam Clancy 2.00 5.00
62 Andre McCarter 2.00 5.00
63 Joe Merten .75 2.00
64 Eddie Moss .75 2.00
65 Brad Branson .75 2.00
66 Lenny Horton .75 2.00
67 Jerome Henderson .75 2.00
68 Terry Stotts 2.00 5.00
69 Tony Wells .75 2.00
70 Rickey Green 3.00 8.00
71 Don Newman .75 2.00
72 Randy Owens .75 2.00
73 Erv Giddings .75 2.00
74 Barry Young .75 2.00
75 Jim Brogan .75 2.00
76 Richard Johnson .75 2.00
77 George Karl CO 4.00 10.00
78 U.S. Reed 1.25 3.00
79 Fran Greenberg
(PR Director) .75 2.00
80 Ron Davis .75 2.00
81 Larry Fogle 1.00 2.50
82 Clarence Kea .75 2.00
83 Steve Craig 1.25 3.00
84 Harry Davis .75 2.00
85 Jacky Dorsey .75 2.00
86 Herb Gray .75 2.00
87 Randy Johnson .75 2.00
88 Jim Drucker COMM .75 2.00
89 Lynbert Johnson .75 2.00
90 Checklist 1-90 .75 2.00

1982-83 TCMA CBA
COMPLETE SET (90) 50.00 125.00
1 Cazzie Russell CO 3.00 8.00
2 Boot Bond .75 2.00
3 Ron Charles 1.00 2.50
4 Charles Pittman 1.50 4.00
5 Calvin Garrett 2.00 5.00
6 Willie Jones .60 1.50
7 Riley Clarida .60 1.50
8 Jim Johnstone .60 1.50
9 Bobby Potts .60 1.50
10 Lowes Moore .75 2.00
11 Dwight Anderson 2.50 6.00
12 John Coughran .60 1.50
13 Mike Evans 1.50 4.00
14 Alan Hardy .60 1.50
15 Willie Smith .60 1.50
16 Oliver Mack 2.00 5.00
17 Checklist 1-45 .60 1.50
18 Picture 1
(Action under basket) .60 1.50
19 James Lee 1.25 3.00
20 Kenny Natt 1.25 3.00
21 Cyrus Mann .60 1.50
22 Bobby Cattage .75 2.00
23 Garry Witts .60 1.50
24 Bill Klucas CO .60 1.50
25 Al Smith 1.00 2.50
26 B.B. Fontenet .60 1.50
27 Chris Giles .60 1.50
28 Barry Young .75 2.00
29 Horace Wyatt 1.00 2.50
30 Robert Smith .75 2.00
31 Ron Baxter 1.00 2.50
32 Charlie Jones .75 2.00
33 Tico Brown 1.00 2.50
34 John McCullough .60 1.50
35 Dan Callandrillo 1.00 2.50
36 John Leonard 1.00 2.50
37 Sam Worthen 1.00 2.50
38 Dale Wilkinson .75 2.00
39 Gary Johnson .60 1.50
40 Dean Meminger CO 1.25 3.00
41 Lloyd Terry .60 1.50
42 Mike Schultz .75 2.00
43 Darryl Gladden .60 1.50
44 Clarence Kea .75 2.00
45 Charlie Floyd .60 1.50
46 Skip Dillard 1.25 3.00
47 Craig Tucker .60 1.50
48 Gib Hinz .60 1.50
49 Tom Sienkiewicz .75 2.00
50 Larry Spriggs 2.00 5.00
51 Perry Moss .60 1.50
52 Gerald Sims .60 1.50
53 Alan Taylor .60 1.50
54 James Terry .60 1.50
55 John Nillen CO .60 1.50
56 Steve Burks .60 1.50
57 Anthony Martin .60 1.50
58 Purvis Miller .75 2.00
59 Kevin Smith .60 1.50
60 John Neumann CO 1.00 2.50
61 Mike Davis 1.25 3.00
62 Gary Carter 1.25 3.00
63 Checklist 46-90 .60 1.50
64 Picture 2
(Action under basket) .60 1.50
65 Charles Thompson .60 1.50
66 John Douglas .60 1.50
67 John Schweitz 1.25 3.00
68 Kevin Figaro .60 1.50
69 John Smith .60 1.50
70 Joe Cooper 1.00 2.50
71 Tony Brown 1.25 3.00
72 Mike Wilson .60 1.50
73 Wayne Abrams .60 1.50
74 T.X. Martin .60 1.50
75 Joe Merten .60 1.50
76 Joe Kopicki 1.00 2.50
77 Carl Nicks 1.00 2.50
78 Wayne Kreklow .60 1.50
79 Tony Guy .75 2.00
80 Dave Harshman CO .60 1.50
81 Bob Davis .60 1.50
82 Gary Mazza CO .60 1.50
83 Randy Owens .60 1.50
84 David Burns .60 1.50
85 Erv Giddings .60 1.50
86 JoJo Hunter 1.00 2.50
87 Frankie Sanders .60 1.50
88 Dave Richardson .60 1.50
89 Lionel Garrett .60 1.50
90 Marvin Barnes 3.00 8.00

1982-83 TCMA Lancaster CBA
COMPLETE SET (30) 14.00 35.00
1 Lightning Wins 1982
CBA Championship 1.25 3.00
2 1982-83 Lancaster
Lightning Team Picture .60 1.50
3 Dr. Seymour Kilstein PRES .40 1.00
4 Cazzie Russell CO 2.00 5.00
5 Cazzie Russell CO IA 2.00 5.00
6 Ed Koback
Operations 1.00 2.50
7 Bob Danforth
Marketing .40 1.00
8 Henry Bibby IA 1.25 3.00
9 Joe Cooper .75 2.00
10 Joe Cooper IA .60 1.50
11 Curtis Berry .75 2.00
12 Curtis Berry IA .60 1.50
13 James Lee 1.00 2.50
14 James Lee IA .75 2.00
15 Ed Sherod IA .60 1.50
16 Charlie Floyd .40 1.00
17 Charlie Floyd IA .40 1.00
18 Darryl Gladden .40 1.00
19 Darryl Gladden IA .40 1.00
20 Tom Sienkiewicz .75 2.00
21 Tom Sienkiewicz IA .60 1.50
22 Stan Williams .40 1.00
23 Willie Redden .40 1.00
24 Reginald Gaines .40 1.00
25 Gary (Cat) Johnson .75 2.00
26 Gary (Cat) Johnson IA .60 1.50
27 Keith Hilliard .40 1.00
28 Keith Hilliard IA .40 1.00
29 Donald Seals .40 1.00
30 Rufus Harris .75 2.00

1981 TCMA NBA
COMPLETE SET (44) 50.00 125.00
1 Alex Hannum .75 2.00
2 Larry Foust .40 1.00
3 George Mikan 5.00 12.00
4 Mel(Hutch) Hutchins .40 1.00
5 Bob Pettit 1.50 4.00
6 Willis Reed 1.25 3.00
7 Adolph Schayes 1.25 3.00
8 Vern Mikkelsen SP 5.00 12.00
9 Cazzie Russell .60 1.50
10 Dick Van Arsdale .60 1.50
11 Lenny Wilkens 1.25 3.00
12 Ray Felix .60 1.50
13 Ed Macauley 1.00 2.50
14 Clyde Lovellette .75 2.00
15 Slater(Dugie) Martin .75 2.00
16 Bill Russell 6.00 15.00
17 Oscar Robertson SP 6.00 15.00
18 Bill Bradley 2.00 5.00
19 Elgin Baylor 3.00 8.00
20 Bill Sharman 2.00 5.00
21 Tom(Satch) Sanders 1.00 2.50
22 Dave Bing .75 2.00
23 Carl Braun .75 2.00
24 Frank Selvy .75 2.00
25 George Yardley .60 1.50
26 Dick McGuire .60 1.50
27 Leroy Ellis .40 1.00
28 Jack Twyman .75 2.00
29 Nate Thurmond 1.25 3.00
30 Walt Frazier 1.50 4.00
31 John(Red) Kerr 1.25 3.00
32 Jerry West 4.00 10.00
33 John Egan SP 2.50 6.00
34 Jim Loscutoff 1.00 2.50
35 Bob Leonard .60 1.50
36 Rick Barry 1.25 3.00
37 Gene Shue .75 2.00
38 Jerry Lucas 1.25 3.00
39 Dave DeBusschere 1.25 3.00
40 Johnny Green
Charles Tyra
Carl Braun
Richie Guerin
John George 1.00 2.50
41 Bob Cousy 4.00 10.00
42 Walter Bellamy .60 1.50
43 Billy Cunningham 1.25 3.00
44 Wilt Chamberlain 6.00 15.00

1990 The National Michael Jordan Promo
NNO Michael Jordan 12.00 30.00

2008-09 Thunder Upper Deck
COMPLETE SET (14) 2.50 6.00
1 Kevin Durant 1.25 3.00
2 Earl Watson .20 .50
3 Nick Collison .20 .50
4 Jeff Green .25 .60
5 Chris Wilcox .20 .50
6 Damien Wilkins .20 .50
7 Johan Petro .20 .50
8 Robert Swift .20 .50
9 Mouhamed Sene .20 .50
10 Desmond Mason .20 .50
11 Russell Westbrook 8.00 20.00
12 D.J. White .20 .50
13 P.J. Carlesimo CO .20 .50
14 Kyle Weaver .20 .50

1989-90 Timberwolves Burger King
COMPLETE SET (7) 1.50 4.00
19 Tony Campbell .30 .75
23 Tyrone Corbin .40 1.00
24 Pooh Richardson .60 1.50
35 Sidney Lowe .30 .75
42 Sam Mitchell .40 1.00
45 Randy Breuer .30 .75
54 Brad Lohaus .30 .75

2009-10 Timeless Treasures
COMP.SET w/o SPs (100) 50.00 100.00
1-100 PRINT RUN 399 SER.#'d SETS
101-150 PRINT RUN 299 SER.#'d SETS
1 Kobe Bryant 8.00 20.00
2 LeBron James 8.00 20.00
3 Chris Paul 2.00 5.00
4 Dwight Howard 1.25 3.00
5 Dwyane Wade 2.00 5.00
6 Dirk Nowitzki 2.50 6.00
7 Danny Granger .60 1.50
8 Kevin Durant 4.00 10.00
9 Pau Gasol 1.50 4.00
10 Amare Stoudemire .75 2.00
11 Chris Bosh 1.25 3.00
12 Brandon Roy 1.25 3.00
13 Kevin Garnett 2.50 6.00
14 Al Jefferson .60 1.50
15 Deron Williams .75 2.00
16 Chauncey Billups 1.25 3.00
17 Steve Nash 2.00 5.00
18 Tim Duncan 2.50 6.00
19 Andre Iguodala 1.00 2.50
20 Jason Kidd 1.50 4.00
21 Devin Harris .60 1.50
22 Joe Johnson 1.00 2.50
23 Gerald Wallace .75 2.00
24 Vince Carter 2.00 5.00
25 Paul Pierce 1.50 4.00
26 Brook Lopez 1.00 2.50
27 Kevin Martin .75 2.00
28 Antawn Jamison .75 2.00
29 David West .75 2.00
30 Carmelo Anthony 1.50 4.00
31 Troy Murphy .60 1.50
32 Rashard Lewis .75 2.00
33 Elton Brand .75 2.00
34 Josh Smith .60 1.50
35 Baron Davis .75 2.00
36 Ray Allen 1.50 4.00
37 Carlos Boozer .75 2.00
38 David Lee .60 1.50
39 Derrick Rose 1.50 4.00
40 Rajon Rondo 1.25 3.00
41 O.J. Mayo .60 1.50
42 Nene .75 2.00
43 Andrea Bargnani .60 1.50
44 Charlie Villanueva .60 1.50
45 Ben Gordon .75 2.00
46 Mike Bibby 1.00 2.50
47 Tony Parker 1.50 4.00
48 Andrew Bynum .60 1.50
49 Russell Westbrook 2.00 5.00
50 Anthony Randolph .60 1.50
51 Eric Gordon .75 2.00
52 Jeff Green .75 2.00
53 Shaquille O'Neal 3.00 8.00
54 Aaron Brooks .60 1.50
55 Chris Kaman .75 2.00
56 D.J. Augustin .60 1.50
57 Emeka Okafor .75 2.00
58 Derek Fisher 1.00 2.50
59 Jermaine O'Neal 1.00 2.50
60 Josh Howard .75 2.00
61 Kevin Love 1.00 2.50
62 Lamar Odom .75 2.00
63 Michael Beasley .60 1.50
64 Richard Hamilton 1.00 2.50
65 Ron Artest 1.00 2.50
66 Ronnie Brewer .60 1.50
67 Rudy Fernandez .60 1.50
68 Ryan Gomes .60 1.50
69 Shane Battier 1.00 2.50
70 T.J. Ford .60 1.50
71 Tracy McGrady 2.00 5.00
72 Trevor Ariza .60 1.50
73 Greg Oden .60 1.50
74 Nate Archibald 1.25 3.00
75 Al Cervi 1.00 2.50
76 Bob Cousy 2.50 6.00
77 Harry Gallatin 1.00 2.50
78 Gail Goodrich 1.00 2.50
79 Hal Greer 1.25 3.00
80 John Havlicek 2.50 6.00
81 Connie Hawkins 1.25 3.00
82 Elvin Hayes 1.50 4.00
83 Bob McAdoo 1.25 3.00
84 Pete Maravich 3.00 8.00
85 Bill Russell 3.00 8.00
86 Dolph Schayes 1.00 2.50
87 Bill Sharman 1.25 3.00
88 David Thompson .75 2.00
89 Nate Thurmond .75 2.00
90 Jack Twyman 1.00 2.50
91 Wes Unseld 1.00 2.50
92 Bill Walton 1.50 4.00
93 Bobby Wanzer .60 1.50
94 Frank Ramsey 1.00 2.50
95 Willis Reed 1.50 4.00
96 Pat Riley 1.00 2.50
97 Xavier McDaniel .60 1.50
98 Oscar Robertson 1.25 3.00
99 Lenny Wilkens 1.00 2.50
100 James Worthy 1.25 3.00
101 Blake Griffin AU RC 20.00 50.00
102 Hasheem Thabeet AU RC 3.00 8.00
103 James Harden AU RC 75.00 200.00
104 Tyreke Evans AU RC 4.00 10.00
105 Jonny Flynn AU RC 3.00 8.00
106 Stephen Curry AU RC 500.00 1,000.00
107 Jordan Hill AU RC 3.00 8.00
108 Ricky Rubio AU RC 15.00 40.00
109 Brandon Jennings AU RC 5.00 12.00
110 Terrence Williams AU RC 3.00 8.00
111 Gerald Henderson AU RC 3.00 8.00
112 Tyler Hansbrough AU RC 4.00 10.00
113 Earl Clark AU RC 3.00 8.00
114 Austin Daye AU RC 3.00 8.00
115 James Johnson AU RC 4.00 10.00
116 Jrue Holiday AU RC 15.00 40.00
117 Ty Lawson AU RC 4.00 10.00
118 Jeff Teague AU RC 4.00 10.00
119 Eric Maynor AU RC 3.00 8.00
120 Darren Collison AU RC 5.00 12.00
121 Omri Casspi AU RC 3.00 8.00
122 B.J. Mullens AU RC 3.00 8.00
123 Rodrigue Beaubois AU RC 3.00 8.00
124 Taj Gibson AU RC 4.00 10.00
125 DeMarre Carroll AU RC 4.00 10.00
126 Wayne Ellington AU RC 4.00 10.00
127 Toney Douglas AU RC 3.00 8.00
128 Jeff Pendergraph AU RC 3.00 8.00
129 Jermaine Taylor AU RC 3.00 8.00
130 DaJuan Summers AU RC 3.00 8.00
131 Sam Young AU RC 3.00 8.00
132 DeJuan Blair AU RC 4.00 10.00
133 Jodie Meeks AU RC 3.00 8.00
134 Chase Budinger AU RC 3.00 8.00
135 Taylor Griffin AU RC 3.00 8.00
136 Marcus Thornton AU RC 4.00 10.00
137 Danny Green AU RC 6.00 15.00
138 Derrick Brown AU RC 3.00 8.00
139 Jonas Jerebko AU RC 4.00 10.00
140 Sergio Ibaka AU RC 12.00 30.00
141 Jon Brockman AU RC 3.00 8.00
142 Dante Cunningham AU RC 3.00 8.00
143 Wesley Matthews AU RC 5.00 12.00
144 A.J. Price AU RC 3.00 8.00
145 Lester Hudson AU RC 3.00 8.00
146 Marcus Landry AU RC 3.00 8.00
147 Sundiata Gaines AU RC 3.00 8.00
148 David Andersen AU RC 3.00 8.00
149 Patrick Mills AU RC 12.00 30.00
150 DeMar DeRozan AU RC 75.00 200.00

2009-10 Timeless Treasures Silver
*SILVER 1-100: 1.5X TO 4X BASE HI
SILVER 1-100 PRINT RUN 25 SER.#'d SETS
*SILVER RC/25: .6X TO 1.5X BASE HI
106 Stephen Curry AU/25 1,500.00 3,000.00
116 Jrue Holiday AU/25 20.00 50.00

2009-10 Timeless Treasures Championship Season Combos Materials
STATED PRINT RUN 25 SER.#'d SETS
1 K.Garnett/R.Allen 10.00 25.00
2 K.Garnett/R.Rondo 8.00 20.00
3 R.Rondo/R.Allen 10.00 25.00
4 K.Bryant/P.Gasol 15.00 40.00

2009-10 Timeless Treasures Championship Season Materials
STATED PRINT RUN 50 TO 100 SER.#'d SETS
1 Kevin Garnett/100 8.00 20.00
2 Rajon Rondo/100 4.00 10.00
3 Ray Allen/100 5.00 12.00
4 Pau Gasol/50 5.00 12.00
5 Kobe Bryant/100 10.00 25.00
6 Dwyane Wade/100 6.00 15.00
7 Tim Duncan/100 8.00 20.00
8 Tony Parker/100 5.00 12.00
10 Tom Heinsohn/100 3.00 8.00
11 Kareem Abdul-Jabbar/100 10.00 25.00
12 Manu Ginobili/100 6.00 15.00

2009-10 Timeless Treasures Championship Season Materials Laundry Tags Signatures
STATED PRINT RUN ONE TO 12 SER.#'d SETS
3 Ray Allen/12 50.00 100.00

2009-10 Timeless Treasures Championship Season Materials Signatures
STATED PRINT RUN 5 TO 25 SER.#'d SETS
2 Rajon Rondo/25 40.00 70.00
3 Ray Allen/25 30.00 80.00
11 Kareem Abdul-Jabbar/25 40.00 80.00

2009-10 Timeless Treasures Championship Season Quad Materials
STATED PRINT RUN 25 TO 50 SER.#'d SETS
1 Wade/KG/Kobe/Duncan/50 10.00 25.00
2 Kareem/Kobe/Arch/Hnshn/25 20.00 50.00

2009-10 Timeless Treasures Championship Season Triple Materials
STATED PRINT RUN 25 SER.#'d SETS
1 Garnett/Rondo/Allen/25 15.00 40.00

2009-10 Timeless Treasures HOF Combos Materials
STATED PRINT RUN 10 TO 50 SER.#'d SETS
1 Kareem/G.Mikan/50 20.00 50.00
2 L.Bird/K.McHale/50 10.00 25.00
3 J.Dumars/I.Thomas/50 6.00 15.00
4 A.English/D.Issel/50 5.00 12.00
5 T.Heinsohn/D.Cowens/50 6.00 15.00
6 D.Cowens/J.Havlicek/50 6.00 15.00
7 H.Olajuwon/C.Drexler/50 10.00 25.00

2009-10 Timeless Treasures HOF Materials Jerseys
STATED PRINT RUN 5 TO 50 SER.#'d SETS
1 George Mikan/50 15.00 40.00
2 Kareem Abdul-Jabbar/50 12.00 30.00
3 John Stockton/50 6.00 15.00
4 Tom Heinsohn/50 5.00 12.00
5 Adrian Dantley/50 3.00 8.00
6 Alex English/50 5.00 12.00
7 Earl Monroe/50 5.00 12.00
8 George Gervin/50 5.00 12.00
9 Dominique Wilkins/50 6.00 15.00
10 Dave Cowens/50 5.00 12.00
11 Joe Dumars/50 5.00 12.00
12 Jerry West/50 6.00 15.00
13 Isiah Thomas/50 4.00 10.00
14 Walt Frazier/50 6.00 15.00
15 Robert Parish/50 5.00 12.00
16 Rick Barry/50 3.00 8.00
17 Moses Malone/50 6.00 15.00
18 Magic Johnson/50 8.00 20.00
21 Kevin McHale/50 5.00 12.00
22 Dan Issel/50 3.00 8.00
23 Bob Lanier/50 5.00 12.00
24 Clyde Drexler/50 6.00 15.00
25 Clyde Drexler/50 6.00 15.00
29 Hakeem Olajuwon/50 5.00 12.00
30 Patrick Ewing/50 8.00 20.00

2009-10 Timeless Treasures HOF Materials Jerseys Signatures
STATED PRINT RUN 5 TO 25 SER.#'d SETS
2 Kareem Abdul-Jabbar/25 50.00 120.00
8 George Gervin/25 12.50 30.00
9 Dominique Wilkins/25 12.50 30.00
10 Dave Cowens/25 12.50 30.00
13 Isiah Thomas/25 12.50 30.00
14 Walt Frazier/25 12.50 30.00
15 Robert Parish/25 12.50 30.00
18 Magic Johnson/25 50.00 100.00
19 Larry Bird/25 50.00 100.00
22 Dan Issel/25 12.50 30.00
24 Clyde Drexler/25 25.00 50.00
25 Clyde Drexler/25 25.00 50.00
26 John Havlicek/25 20.00 40.00

2009-10 Timeless Treasures HOF Quad Materials
STATED PRINT RUN 10 TO 50 SER.#'d SETS
1 Mikan/KAJ/West/Magic/50 30.00 80.00
2 Dant/Dumars/Isiah/Lanier/50 15.00 30.00
3 Hein/Cowns/Hav/Bird/50 20.00 40.00

2009-10 Timeless Treasures HOF Signatures Silver
STATED PRINT RUN 35 SER.#'d SETS
2 Kareem Abdul-Jabbar 40.00 80.00
8 George Gervin 10.00 25.00
10 Dave Cowens 8.00 20.00
13 Isiah Thomas 8.00 20.00
15 Robert Parish 8.00 20.00
18 Magic Johnson 40.00 80.00
19 Larry Bird 40.00 80.00
24 Clyde Drexler 25.00 50.00
25 Clyde Drexler 20.00 50.00
26 John Havlicek 20.00 40.00
31 Wes Unseld 12.50 30.00
32 Bob Cousy 20.00 50.00
33 Oscar Robertson 40.00 80.00
34 Bill Russell 500.00 1,000.00

2009-10 Timeless Treasures Home and Road Gamers

STATED PRINT RUN 25 TO 100 SER.#'d SETS
1 Kevin Garnett/50 10.00 25.00
2 Deron Williams/50 3.00 8.00
3 Tracy McGrady/50 8.00 20.00
4 Tim Duncan/50 10.00 25.00
5 Kevin McHale/50 6.00 15.00
6 Kobe Bryant/50 15.00 40.00
7 Kareem Abdul-Jabbar/25 8.00 20.00
8 LeBron James/100 12.00 30.00
9 Dwight Howard/100 5.00 12.00
10 Shaquille O'Neal/100 12.00 30.00
11 Vince Carter/100 8.00 20.00
12 Dirk Nowitzki/100 10.00 25.00
14 Jason Kidd/100 6.00 15.00
15 Dan Issel/50 3.00 8.00
16 Chris Paul/100 8.00 20.00
17 LaMarcus Aldridge/100 4.00 10.00
18 Karl Malone/50 5.00 12.00
19 Dwyane Wade/50 8.00 20.00
20 Dikembe Mutombo/100 6.00 15.00
21 Kevin Durant/100 10.00 25.00
22 Hakeem Olajuwon/100 5.00 12.00
23 Elton Brand/100 3.00 8.00
24 Isiah Thomas/50 4.00 10.00
26 Brandon Roy/100 5.00 12.00
27 David Lee/50 4.00 10.00
28 Al Jefferson/100 2.50 6.00
29 Brook Lopez/100 4.00 10.00

2009-10 Timeless Treasures Home and Road Gamers Signatures

STATED PRINT RUN ONE TO 25 SER.#'d SETS
2 Deron Williams/25 20.00 50.00
3 Tracy McGrady/25 20.00 40.00
6 Kobe Bryant/25 800.00 1,500.00
15 Dan Issel/25 12.00 30.00
20 Dikembe Mutombo/25 30.00 60.00
24 Isiah Thomas/25 20.00 40.00
27 David Lee/20 12.00 30.00

2009-10 Timeless Treasures Materials Jerseys

STATED PRINT RUN 50 TO 100 SER.#'d SETS
TAGS PRINT RUN ONE SER.#'d SET
TAGS INK PRINT RUN ONE SER.#'d SET
TAGS NBA LOGO PRINT RUN ONE SET
TAGS NBA LOGO INK PRINT RUN ONE SET
TAGS TEAM LOGO PRINT RUN ONE SET
TAGS TEAM LOGO INK PRINT RUN ONE SET
1 Kobe Bryant/100 8.00 20.00
2 LeBron James/100 8.00 20.00
3 Chris Paul/100 6.00 15.00
4 Dwight Howard/100 4.00 10.00
5 Dwyane Wade/100 6.00 15.00
6 Dirk Nowitzki/100 8.00 20.00
7 Danny Granger/100 2.00 5.00
8 Kevin Durant/100 8.00 20.00
9 Pau Gasol/100 5.00 12.00
10 Amare Stoudemire/100 2.50 6.00
11 Chris Bosh/100 4.00 10.00
12 Brandon Roy/100 4.00 10.00
13 Kevin Garnett/100 8.00 20.00
14 Al Jefferson/100 2.00 5.00
15 Deron Williams/100 2.50 6.00
16 Chauncey Billups/100 4.00 10.00
18 Tim Duncan/100 8.00 20.00
19 Andre Iguodala/100 3.00 8.00
20 Jason Kidd/100 5.00 12.00
21 Devin Harris/100 2.00 5.00
22 Joe Johnson/100 3.00 8.00
23 Gerald Wallace/100 2.50 6.00
24 Vince Carter/100 6.00 15.00
25 Paul Pierce/100 5.00 12.00
26 Brook Lopez/100 3.00 8.00
28 Antawn Jamison/100 2.50 6.00
29 David West/100 2.50 6.00
30 Carmelo Anthony/100 5.00 12.00
31 Troy Murphy/100 2.00 5.00
32 Rashard Lewis/100 2.50 6.00
33 Elton Brand/100 2.50 6.00
34 Josh Smith/100 2.00 5.00
35 Baron Davis/100 2.50 6.00
36 Ray Allen/100 5.00 12.00
37 Carlos Boozer/100 2.50 6.00
38 David Lee/100 2.00 5.00
40 Rajon Rondo/100 4.00 10.00
41 O.J. Mayo/100 2.00 5.00
42 Nene/100 2.50 6.00
43 Andrea Bargnani/100 2.00 5.00
44 Charlie Villanueva/100 2.00 5.00
45 Ben Gordon/100 2.50 6.00
46 Mike Bibby/100 3.00 8.00
48 Andrew Bynum/100 2.00 5.00
49 Russell Westbrook/100 6.00 15.00
50 Anthony Randolph/100 2.00 5.00
51 Eric Gordon/100 2.50 6.00
52 Jeff Green/100 2.50 6.00
53 Shaquille O'Neal/100 10.00 25.00
54 Aaron Brooks/100 2.00 5.00
55 Chris Kaman/100 2.50 6.00
56 D.J. Augustin/100 2.00 5.00
57 Emeka Okafor/100 2.50 6.00
61 Kevin Love/100 3.00 8.00
63 Michael Beasley/100 2.00 5.00
64 Richard Hamilton/100 3.00 8.00
67 Rudy Fernandez/100 2.00 5.00
68 Ryan Gomes/100 2.00 5.00
69 Shane Battier/100 3.00 8.00
70 T.J. Ford/100 2.00 5.00
71 Tracy McGrady/100 6.00 15.00
73 Greg Oden/100 2.00 5.00
80 John Havlicek/50 6.00 15.00
91 Wes Unseld/50 4.00 10.00

2009-10 Timeless Treasures Materials Jerseys Ink

STATED PRINT RUN ONE TO 100 SER.#'d SETS
1 Kobe Bryant/100 500.00 1,000.00
3 Danny Granger/50 8.00 20.00
5 Chris Bosh/50 10.00 25.00
7 Deron Williams/50 12.50 30.00
10 Jason Kidd/25 25.00 50.00
11 Devin Harris/50 8.00 20.00
15 Ray Allen/50 15.00 40.00
18 Rajon Rondo/50 25.00 50.00
20 Tony Parker/45 10.00 25.00
22 Russell Westbrook/50 40.00 100.00
23 Eric Gordon/50 12.50 30.00
25 Tracy McGrady/50 15.00 30.00
27 Tyreke Evans/50 12.00 30.00
28 Brandon Jennings/100 8.00 20.00
29 Blake Griffin/100 40.00 100.00
30 Omri Casspi/50 8.00 20.00

2009-10 Timeless Treasures Materials Jerseys Prime Ink

STATED PRINT RUN ONE TO 25 SER.#'d SETS
1 Kobe Bryant/25 800.00 1,500.00
3 Danny Granger/25 10.00 25.00
5 Chris Bosh/25 15.00 40.00
7 Deron Williams/25 15.00 40.00
11 Devin Harris/25 10.00 25.00
15 Ray Allen/25 30.00 60.00
16 Carlos Boozer/25 15.00 40.00
17 David Lee/25 10.00 25.00
18 Rajon Rondo/25 30.00 80.00
20 Tony Parker/25 20.00 40.00
22 Russell Westbrook/25 75.00 200.00
23 Eric Gordon/25 15.00 40.00
27 Tyreke Evans/25 75.00 150.00
28 Brandon Jennings/25 25.00 60.00
29 Blake Griffin/25 60.00 150.00
30 Omri Casspi/25 15.00 30.00

2009-10 Timeless Treasures MVP Materials

STATED PRINT RUN 10 TO 100 SER.#'d SETS
TAGS NBA LOGO PRINT RUN ONE TO TWO SETS
TAGS NBA LOGO SIGS PRINT RUN ONE SET
TAGS TEAM LOGO PRINT RUN 1 TO 2 SETS
TAGS SIGS PRINT RUN 1 TO 4 SETS
TAGS TEAM LOGO SIGS PRINT RUN ONE SET
1 Dirk Nowitzki/100 10.00 25.00
2 LeBron James/90 10.00 25.00
3 Kobe Bryant/100 15.00 40.00
6 Larry Bird/100 15.00 40.00
7 Karl Malone/100 5.00 12.00

2009-10 Timeless Treasures MVP Materials Prime

PRINT RUNS 10 TO 25 SER.#'d SETS
2 LeBron James/25 15.00 40.00
5 Tim Duncan/25 20.00 50.00
7 Karl Malone/25 10.00 25.00

2009-10 Timeless Treasures MVP Materials MVP

STATED PRINT RUN 5 TO 25 SER.#'d SETS
1 Dirk Nowitzki/25 8.00 20.00
2 LeBron James/25 15.00 40.00
3 Kobe Bryant/25 20.00 50.00
6 Larry Bird/25 15.00 40.00
7 Karl Malone/25 10.00 25.00

2009-10 Timeless Treasures MVP Materials MVP Prime

STATED PRINT RUN 5 TO 25 SER.#'d SETS
5 Tim Duncan/25 30.00 80.00
7 Karl Malone/25 15.00 40.00

2009-10 Timeless Treasures MVP Materials Quads

STATED PRINT RUN 25 SER.#'d SETS
1 Dirk/Kobe/LBJ/Nash/25 30.00 60.00

2009-10 Timeless Treasures MVP Materials Signatures

STATED PRINT RUN 25 SER.#'d SETS
1 Dirk Nowitzki/25 50.00 120.00
3 Kobe Bryant/25 800.00 1,500.00
6 Larry Bird/25 50.00 100.00

2009-10 Timeless Treasures NBA Apprentice Materials

STATED PRINT RUN 100 SER.#'d SETS
*PRIME: .75X TO 2X BASE HI
PRIME PRINT RUNS 1 TO 99 SER.#'d SETS
TAGS PRINT RUN ONE SET
TAGS NBA LOGO PRINT RUN ONE SET
TAGS NBA LOGO SIGS PRINT RUN ONE SET
TAGS SIGS PRINT RUN ONE SET
TAGS TEAM LOGO PRINT RUN ONE SET
TAGS TEAM LOGO SIGS PRINT RUN ONE SET
1 Blake Griffin 12.50 30.00
2 Hasheem Thabeet 1.50 4.00
3 James Harden 40.00 100.00
4 Tyreke Evans 2.00 5.00
5 Jonny Flynn 1.50 4.00
6 Stephen Curry 300.00 600.00
7 Jordan Hill 1.50 4.00
8 DeMar DeRozan 20.00 50.00
9 Brandon Jennings 2.50 6.00
10 Terrence Williams 1.50 4.00
11 Gerald Henderson 1.50 4.00
12 Tyler Hansbrough 2.00 5.00
13 Earl Clark 1.50 4.00
14 Austin Daye 1.50 4.00
15 James Johnson 2.00 5.00
16 Jrue Holiday 8.00 20.00
17 Ty Lawson 2.00 5.00
18 Jeff Teague 2.00 5.00
19 Eric Maynor 1.50 4.00
20 Darren Collison 2.50 6.00
21 Omri Casspi 1.50 4.00
22 B.J. Mullens 1.50 4.00
23 Rodrigue Beaubois 1.50 4.00
24 Taj Gibson 2.00 5.00
25 DeMarre Carroll 1.50 4.00
26 Wayne Ellington 2.00 5.00
27 Toney Douglas 1.50 4.00
28 Jeff Pendergraph 1.50 4.00
29 Jermaine Taylor 1.50 4.00
30 DaJuan Summers 1.50 4.00
31 Sam Young 2.00 5.00
32 DeJuan Blair 2.00 5.00
33 Jodie Meeks 1.50 4.00
34 Chase Budinger 1.50 4.00
35 Taylor Griffin 1.50 4.00

2009-10 Timeless Treasures NBA Apprentice Materials Signatures

STATED PRINT RUN 50 SER.#'d SETS
1 Blake Griffin 50.00 120.00
2 Hasheem Thabeet 3.00 8.00
3 James Harden 150.00 400.00
4 Tyreke Evans 4.00 10.00
5 Jonny Flynn 3.00 8.00
6 Stephen Curry 1,500.00 3,000.00
7 Jordan Hill 3.00 8.00
9 Brandon Jennings 5.00 12.00
10 Terrence Williams 3.00 8.00
11 Gerald Henderson 3.00 8.00
12 Tyler Hansbrough 4.00 10.00
13 Earl Clark 3.00 8.00
14 Austin Daye 3.00 8.00
16 Jrue Holiday 15.00 40.00
18 Jeff Teague 4.00 10.00
19 Eric Maynor 3.00 8.00
20 Darren Collison 5.00 12.00
21 Omri Casspi 3.00 8.00
22 B.J. Mullens 3.00 8.00
23 Rodrigue Beaubois 3.00 8.00
24 Taj Gibson 4.00 10.00
25 DeMarre Carroll 3.00 8.00
26 Wayne Ellington 4.00 10.00
27 Toney Douglas 3.00 8.00
28 Jeff Pendergraph 3.00 8.00
30 DaJuan Summers 3.00 8.00
31 Sam Young 3.00 8.00
32 DeJuan Blair 4.00 10.00
33 Jodie Meeks 3.00 8.00
34 Chase Budinger 3.00 8.00
35 Taylor Griffin 3.00 8.00

2009-10 Timeless Treasures NBA Apprentice Combo Materials

STATED PRINT RUN 100 SER.#'d SETS
1 B.Griffin/B.Jennings 8.00 20.00
2 B.Griffin/T.Evans 8.00 20.00
3 B.Jennings/T.Evans 2.00 5.00
4 J.Johnson/T.Gibson 1.50 4.00
5 H.Thabeet/S.Young 1.25 3.00
6 B.Jennings/J.Meeks 2.00 5.00
7 J.Flynn/W.Ellington 1.50 4.00
8 J.Hill/T.Douglas 1.25 3.00
9 J.Harden/B.Mullens 12.00 30.00
10 T.Evans/O.Casspi 1.25 3.00
11 T.Lawson/T.Evans 1.50 4.00
12 T.Lawson/B.Jennings 2.00 5.00
13 S.Curry/J.Flynn 40.00 100.00
14 J.Harden/S.Curry 150.00 400.00
15 O.Casspi/D.Blair 1.25 3.00

2009-10 Timeless Treasures NBA Apprentice Combo Signatures

STATED PRINT RUN 100 SER.#'d SETS
1 B.Griffin/T.Griffin 75.00 150.00
2 H.Thabeet/S.Young 8.00 20.00
3 J.Harden/B.Mullens 30.00 80.00
4 T.Evans/O.Casspi 30.00 80.00
5 J.Flynn/W.Ellington 8.00 20.00
6 J.Hill/T.Douglas 8.00 20.00
7 B.Jennings/J.Meeks 15.00 40.00
9 T.Hansbrough/A.Price 10.00 25.00
10 E.Clark/T.Griffin 8.00 20.00
12 J.Johnson/T.Gibson 10.00 25.00
13 D.Collison/M.Thornton 15.00 40.00
16 H.Thabeet/A.Price 8.00 20.00
19 D.Blair/S.Young 8.00 20.00
20 J.Hill/C.Budinger 8.00 20.00
21 E.Clark/T.Williams 10.00 25.00
22 J.Holiday/D.Collison 15.00 30.00
23 J.Harden/J.Pendergraph 20.00 50.00
24 B.Jennings/T.Evans 75.00 150.00
25 B.Griffin/T.Hansbrough 100.00 200.00

2009-10 Timeless Treasures NBA Apprentice Quad Materials

STATED PRINT RUN 100 SER.#'d SETS
1 Griffin/Thabeet/Harden/Evans 12.00 30.00
2 Flynn/Curry/Hill/DeRozan 200.00 500.00
3 Jennings/Wllms/Hndrsn/Hnsbrgh 5.00 12.00
4 Griffin/Hill/Blair/Hansbrgh 12.00 30.00
5 Evans/Flynn/Jennings/Lawson 6.00 15.00
6 Jennings/Evans/Harden/Lawson 8.00 20.00
7 Collisn/Blair/Flynn/Casspi 5.00 12.00
8 Blair/Casspi/Hnsbrgh/Griffin 12.50 30.00
9 Maynor/Collison/Curry/Douglas 100.00 250.00
10 Griffin/Harden/Evans/Jennings 12.00 30.00
11 DeRozan/Hill/Holiday/Wllms 12.00 30.00
12 Taj/Jennings/Hnsbrgh/Jhnsn 5.00 12.00
13 Ty/Ellngtn/Harden/Flynn 8.00 20.00
14 Blair/Budngr/Thabeet/Collison 5.00 12.00
15 Griffin/Casspi/Curry/Evans 40.00 100.00

2009-10 Timeless Treasures NBA Apprentice Triple Materials

STATED PRINT RUN 100 SER.#'d SETS
1 Hansbrough/Lawson/Ellington 5.00 12.00
2 Griffin/Thabeet/Harden 10.00 25.00
3 Evans/Flynn/Curry 125.00 300.00
4 Hill/DeRozan/Jennings 10.00 25.00
5 Williams/Henderson/Hansbrough 5.00 12.00
6 Griffin/Evans/Jennings 10.00 25.00
7 Evans/Flynn/Curry 5.00 12.00
8 Evans/Lawson/Jennings 5.00 12.00
9 Harden/Curry/Budinger 125.00 300.00
10 Griffin/Hansbrough/Blair 10.00 25.00
11 Casspi/Griffin/Blair 6.00 15.00
12 Lawson/Flynn/Curry 40.00 100.00
13 Evans/Jennings/Casspi 5.00 12.00
14 Evans/Lawson/Casspi 5.00 12.00
15 Griffin/Hansbrough/Casspi 10.00 25.00

2009-10 Timeless Treasures Private Signings

STATED PRINT RUN 20 TO 100 SER.#'d SETS
1 Kobe Bryant/100 500.00 1,000.00
2 Steve Nash/20 40.00 100.00
3 Tracy McGrady/25 12.00 30.00
4 Danny Granger/25 10.00 25.00
5 Carmelo Anthony/25 20.00 50.00
6 Bill Russell/25 500.00 1,000.00
7 Bill Walton/25 12.00 30.00
8 Bob Cousy/25 20.00 50.00
9 Chris Bosh/20 15.00 40.00
10 Dave Cowens/25 12.00 30.00
11 David Thompson/25 10.00 25.00
12 Dennis Rodman/25 50.00 100.00
13 Isiah Thomas/25 10.00 25.00
14 Jerry West/25 25.00 60.00
15 John Havlicek/25 20.00 50.00
16 Kareem Abdul-Jabbar/25 50.00 100.00
17 Kevin Love/25 20.00 50.00
18 Kevin McHale/25 25.00 60.00
19 Larry Bird/25 40.00 100.00
20 Magic Johnson/25 40.00 100.00
21 Dominique Wilkins/20 10.00 25.00
22 Nate Thurmond/25 10.00 25.00
23 Oscar Robertson/25 30.00 80.00
24 Pau Gasol/25 25.00 60.00
25 Rajon Rondo/25 20.00 50.00
26 Ray Allen/25 25.00 60.00
27 Rick Barry/25 10.00 25.00
28 Robert Parish/25 10.00 25.00
29 Scottie Pippen/25 60.00 150.00
30 Tony Parker/20 12.00 30.00

2009-10 Timeless Treasures Rookie Year Materials

STATED PRINT RUN 25 TO 100 SER.#'d SETS
*PRIME: 1X TO 2.5X BASE HI
PRIME PRINT RUN 25 SER.#'d SETS
TAGS PRINT RUN ONE TO 6 SETS
TAGS NBA LOGO PRINT RUN 1 TO 3 SETS
TAGS NBA LOGO SIG.PRINT RUN ONE TO 3 SETS
TAGS SIGS PRINT RUN ONE TO 9 SETS
TAGS TEAM LOGO PRINT RUN 1 TO 3 SETS
TAGS TEAM LOGO SIG.PRINT RUN 1 TO 3 SETS
NBA LOGO PRINT RUN ONE TO 4 SETS
NBA LOGO SIGS PRINT RUN ONE TO 4 SETS
1 Dwight Howard/50 4.00 10.00
2 Chris Paul/50 6.00 15.00
3 LeBron James/100 15.00 40.00
4 Kobe Bryant/100 10.00 25.00
5 Brandon Roy/100 4.00 10.00
6 Derrick Rose/50 5.00 12.00
7 Carmelo Anthony/100 5.00 12.00
8 Andre Iguodala/100 3.00 8.00
9 Shaquille O'Neal/100 10.00 25.00
10 Deron Williams/100 2.50 6.00
11 Kevin Garnett/100 8.00 20.00
12 Kevin Durant/100 12.00 30.00
13 Brandon Jennings/25 3.00 8.00
14 Dikembe Mutombo/100 6.00 15.00
15 Tracy McGrady/100 6.00 15.00

2009-10 Timeless Treasures Rookie Year Materials Signatures

STATED PRINT RUN ONE TO 50 SER.#'d SETS
4 Kobe Bryant/50 500.00 1,000.00
6 Derrick Rose/25 75.00 200.00
10 Deron Williams/25 8.00 20.00
13 Brandon Jennings/25 8.00 20.00
14 Dikembe Mutombo/25 25.00 60.00
15 Tracy McGrady/25 25.00 60.00

2009-10 Timeless Treasures Rookie Year Materials Prime Signatures

STATED PRINT RUN ONE TO 25 SER.#'d SETS
4 Kobe Bryant/25 800.00 1,500.00
6 Derrick Rose/25 100.00 250.00

2009-10 Timeless Treasures Rookie Year Materials Quads

STATED PRINT RUN 25 SER.#'d SETS
1 LBJ/Kobe/CP3/Dwight 25.00 50.00
2 KG/Shaq/Kobe/LBJ 40.00 100.00
3 LBJ/Dwight/Iggy/Melo 15.00 30.00
4 KG/Shaq/TMac/Kobe 25.00 60.00
5 KG/Howard/Mutmbo/Shaq 20.00 50.00

2009-10 Timeless Treasures Rookie Year Materials ROY

STATED PRINT RUN 25 TO 100 SER.#'d SETS
2 Chris Paul/25 12.00 30.00
3 LeBron James/100 25.00 60.00
5 Brandon Roy/25 6.00 15.00
9 Shaquille O'Neal/100 12.00 30.00
12 Kevin Durant/100 12.00 30.00

2009-10 Timeless Treasures Rookie Year Materials ROY Prime

STATED PRINT RUN ONE TO 25 SER.#'d SETS
2 Chris Paul/25 20.00 50.00
3 LeBron James/25 60.00 150.00
12 Kevin Durant/25 25.00 60.00

2009-10 Timeless Treasures Rookie Year Materials ROY Prime Signatures

STATED PRINT RUN 25 SER.#'d SETS
6 Derrick Rose/25 125.00 300.00

2009-10 Timeless Treasures Signatures Silver

STATED PRINT RUN 25 TO 100 SER.#'d SETS
1 Kobe Bryant 500.00 1,000.00
7 Danny Granger 5.00 12.00
9 Pau Gasol 25.00 50.00
11 Chris Bosh 12.50 30.00
15 Deron Williams 10.00 25.00
21 Devin Harris 5.00 12.00
36 Ray Allen 20.00 50.00
39 Derrick Rose 75.00 150.00
40 Rajon Rondo 20.00 40.00
41 O.J. Mayo 15.00 30.00
44 Charlie Villanueva 5.00 12.00
47 Tony Parker 8.00 20.00
49 Russell Westbrook 30.00 80.00
51 Eric Gordon 6.00 15.00
54 Aaron Brooks 5.00 12.00
56 D.J. Augustin 5.00 12.00
57 Emeka Okafor 6.00 15.00
59 Jermaine O'Neal 5.00 12.00
60 Josh Howard 5.00 12.00
61 Kevin Love 15.00 40.00
63 Michael Beasley 8.00 20.00
66 Ronnie Brewer 5.00 12.00
68 Ryan Gomes 8.00 20.00
69 Shane Battier 5.00 12.00
70 T.J. Ford 5.00 12.00
71 Tracy McGrady 15.00 40.00
72 Trevor Ariza 6.00 15.00
74 Nate Archibald 8.00 20.00
75 Al Cervi 6.00 15.00
76 Bob Cousy 20.00 50.00
77 Harry Gallatin 5.00 12.00
78 Gail Goodrich 8.00 20.00
79 Hal Greer 8.00 20.00
80 John Havlicek 15.00 30.00
82 Elvin Hayes 5.00 12.00
83 Bob McAdoo 10.00 25.00
86 Dolph Schayes 8.00 20.00
87 Bill Sharman 8.00 20.00
88 David Thompson 8.00 20.00
89 Nate Thurmond 8.00 20.00
91 Wes Unseld 6.00 15.00
92 Bill Walton 8.00 20.00
93 Bobby Wanzer 6.00 15.00
94 Frank Ramsey 10.00 25.00
95 Willis Reed 40.00 100.00
96 Pat Riley 15.00 30.00
98 Oscar Robertson 30.00 60.00
99 Lenny Wilkens 6.00 15.00
100 James Worthy 20.00 50.00

2009-10 Timeless Treasures Souvenir Cuts

STATED PRINT RUN ONE TO 25 SER.#'d SETS
1 George Mikan/25 100.00 200.00
8 Hank Luisetti/15 50.00 125.00
9 Andy Phillip/15 100.00 175.00
13 Paul Arizin/25 20.00 50.00

2009-10 Timeless Treasures Souvenir Cuts Materials

STATED PRINT RUN 25 SER.#'d SETS
1 George Mikan/25 125.00 250.00

2009-10 Timeless Treasures Statistical Champions Materials

STATED PRINT RUN 50 TO 100 SER.#'d SETS
1 George Gervin/50 5.00 12.00
2 John Stockton/50 6.00 15.00
3 Dwight Howard/100 5.00 12.00
4 Kobe Bryant/100 10.00 25.00
5 Chris Paul/100 5.00 12.00

2009-10 Timeless Treasures Statistical Champions Materials Signatures

STATED PRINT RUN 50 SER.#'d SETS
1 George Gervin/50 15.00 40.00
4 Kobe Bryant/50 500.00 1,000.00

2010-11 Timeless Treasures

COMP.SET w/o RCs (100) 50.00 100.00
1-100 STATED PRINT RUN 399 SER.#'d SETS
AU RC PRINT RUN 249 TO 299 SER.#'d SETS
1 Kobe Bryant 8.00 20.00
2 Pau Gasol 1.50 4.00
3 Derek Fisher 1.00 2.50
4 Andrew Bynum .60 1.50
5 Caron Butler .75 2.00
6 Dirk Nowitzki 2.50 6.00
7 Jason Kidd 1.50 4.00
8 Jason Terry .75 2.00
9 Grant Hill 1.50 4.00
10 Jason Richardson 1.00 2.50
11 Robin Lopez .60 1.50
12 Steve Nash 2.00 5.00
13 Carmelo Anthony 1.50 4.00
14 Chauncey Billups 1.25 3.00
15 Chris Andersen 1.00 2.50
16 Nene .75 2.00
17 Al Jefferson .60 1.50
18 Deron Williams .75 2.00
19 Mehmet Okur .60 1.50
20 Paul Millsap .75 2.00
21 Brandon Roy 1.25 3.00
22 Greg Oden .60 1.50
23 LaMarcus Aldridge 1.00 2.50
24 Marcus Camby .75 2.00
25 George Hill .75 2.00
26 Manu Ginobili 2.00 5.00
27 Tim Duncan 2.50 6.00
28 Tony Parker 1.50 4.00
29 James Harden 2.50 6.00
30 Jeff Green .75 2.00
31 Kevin Durant 4.00 10.00
32 Russell Westbrook 1.50 4.00
33 Aaron Brooks .60 1.50
34 Kevin Martin .75 2.00
35 Luis Scola .75 2.00
36 Yao Ming 2.00 5.00
37 Marc Gasol 1.00 2.50
38 Rudy Gay 1.00 2.50
39 Zach Randolph 1.00 2.50
40 Chris Paul 2.00 5.00
41 Marcus Thornton .60 1.50
42 Trevor Ariza .60 1.50
43 Chris Kaman .60 1.50
44 Eric Gordon .75 2.00
45 Baron Davis 1.00 2.50
46 David Lee .60 1.50
47 Monta Ellis .75 2.00
48 Stephen Curry 8.00 20.00
49 Carl Landry .60 1.50
50 Samuel Dalembert .60 1.50
51 Tyreke Evans .75 2.00
52 Kevin Love 1.00 2.50
53 Michael Beasley .60 1.50
54 Sebastian Telfair .60 1.50
55 Anderson Varejao .60 1.50
56 Antawn Jamison .75 2.00
57 Mo Williams .75 2.00
58 Dwight Howard 1.25 3.00
59 J.J. Redick 1.00 2.50
60 Vince Carter 2.00 5.00
61 Al Horford 1.00 2.50
62 Joe Johnson 1.00 2.50
63 Josh Smith .60 1.50
64 Kendrick Perkins .60 1.50
65 Paul Pierce 1.50 4.00
66 Rajon Rondo 1.25 3.00
67 Shaquille O'Neal 4.00 10.00
68 Chris Bosh 1.25 3.00
69 Dwyane Wade 2.00 5.00
70 LeBron James 8.00 20.00
71 Andrew Bogut .75 2.00
72 Brandon Jennings .60 1.50
73 Michael Redd .75 2.00
74 D.J. Augustin .60 1.50
75 Gerald Wallace .60 1.50
76 Stephen Jackson .75 2.00
77 Carlos Boozer .75 2.00
78 Derrick Rose 2.00 5.00
79 Luol Deng .75 2.00
80 Andrea Bargnani .60 1.50
81 DeMar DeRozan 1.50 4.00
82 Leandro Barbosa .75 2.00
83 Danny Granger .60 1.50
84 Darren Collison .60 1.50
85 Troy Murphy .60 1.50
86 Amare Stoudemire 1.00 2.50
87 Anthony Randolph .60 1.50
88 Danilo Gallinari .75 2.00
89 Ben Wallace .75 2.00
90 Richard Hamilton 1.25 3.00
91 Tracy McGrady 1.50 4.00
92 Andre Iguodala 1.00 2.50
93 Louis Williams .75 2.00
94 Thaddeus Young .60 1.50
95 Al Thornton .60 1.50
96 JaVale McGee .75 2.00
97 Josh Howard .75 2.00
98 Anthony Morrow .60 1.50
99 Brook Lopez .75 2.00
100 Devin Harris .60 1.50
101 John Wall AU/299 RC 25.00 60.00
102 Evan Turner AU/299 RC 3.00 8.00
103 Derrick Favors AU/299 RC 4.00 10.00
104 Wesley Johnson AU/299 RC 2.50 6.00
105 D.Cousins AU/299 RC 8.00 20.00
106 Ekpe Udoh AU/299 RC 2.50 6.00
107 Greg Monroe AU/299 RC 3.00 8.00
108 Al-Farouq Aminu AU/299 RC 3.00 8.00
109 Gordon Hayward AU/299 RC 12.00 30.00
110 Paul George AU/299 RC 20.00 50.00
111 Cole Aldrich AU/299 RC 2.50 6.00
112 Xavier Henry AU/299 RC 2.50 6.00
113 Ed Davis AU/298 RC 3.00 8.00
114 P.Patterson AU/299 RC 3.00 8.00
115 Larry Sanders AU/299 RC 2.50 6.00
116 Luke Babbitt AU/299 RC 2.50 6.00
117 Kevin Seraphin AU/299 RC 2.50 6.00
118 Eric Bledsoe AU/299 RC 5.00 12.00
119 Avery Bradley AU/299 RC 4.00 10.00
120 James Anderson AU/299 RC 2.50 6.00
121 Craig Brackins AU/299 RC 2.50 6.00
122 Elliot Williams AU/299 RC 2.50 6.00
123 Trevor Booker AU/299 RC 2.50 6.00
124 Damion James AU/299 RC 2.50 6.00
125 Dominique Jones AU/299 RC 2.50 6.00
126 Quincy Pondexter AU/299 RC 2.50 6.00
127 J.Crawford AU/299 RC 2.50 6.00
128 Greivis Vasquez AU/299 RC 2.50 6.00
129 Daniel Orton AU/299 RC 2.50 6.00
130 Lazar Hayward AU/299 RC 2.50 6.00
131 Jeremy Lin AU/299 RC 30.00 80.00
132 Dexter Pittman AU/299 RC 2.50 6.00
133 Hassan Whiteside AU/286 RC 20.00 50.00
134 Armon Johnson AU/299 RC 2.50 6.00
135 Terrico White AU/299 RC 2.50 6.00
136 Darington Hobson AU/298 RC 2.50 6.00
137 Andy Rautins AU/297 RC 2.50 6.00
138 Landry Fields AU/299 RC 2.50 6.00
139 Lance Stephenson AU/299 RC 4.00 10.00
140 Jarvis Varnado AU/299 RC 2.50 6.00
141 Sherron Collins AU/299 RC 2.50 6.00
142 Devin Ebanks AU/299 RC 2.50 6.00
143 Gani Lawal AU/249 RC 2.50 6.00
144 Timofey Mozgov AU/299 RC 3.00 8.00
145 Solomon Alabi AU/299 RC 2.50 6.00
146 L.Harangody AU/299 RC 2.50 6.00
147 Willie Warren AU/298 RC 2.50 6.00
148 Jeremy Evans AU/299 RC 2.50 6.00
149 Derrick Caracter AU/299 RC 2.50 6.00
150 Stanley Robinson AU/299 RC 2.50 6.00

2010-11 Timeless Treasures Silver

*1-100 SILVER: 1.5X TO 4X BASE HI
*101-150 SILVER: .6X TO 1.5X BASE HI
STATED PRINT RUN 25 SER.#'d SETS
9 Grant Hill 8.00 20.00

2010-11 Timeless Treasures Championship Season Materials

STATED PRINT RUN 10 TO 99 SER.#'d SETS
1 Andrew Bynum/99 2.50 6.00
2 Derek Fisher/99 4.00 10.00
3 Derek Fisher/99 4.00 10.00
4 Glen Davis/99 2.50 6.00
5 Hakeem Olajuwon/99 8.00 20.00
6 Joe Dumars/99 4.00 10.00
7 Kevin Garnett/99 10.00 25.00
8 Kobe Bryant/99 12.00 30.00
9 Lamar Odom/99 3.00 8.00
10 Luke Walton/99 2.50 6.00
12 Manu Ginobili/99 8.00 20.00
13 Pau Gasol/99 6.00 15.00
14 Pau Gasol/99 6.00 15.00
16 Ron Artest/99 4.00 10.00
17 Scottie Pippen/99 10.00 25.00
18 Tim Duncan/49 10.00 25.00
19 Tim Duncan/99 10.00 25.00
20 Tony Parker/49 6.00 15.00

2010-11 Timeless Treasures Championship Season Materials Combos

STATED PRINT RUN 10 TO 25 SER.#'d SETS
1 A.Bynum/P.Gasol/25 8.00 20.00
2 L.Odom/L.Walton/25 6.00 15.00
3 D.Fisher/P.Gasol/25 8.00 20.00
5 T.Duncan/T.Parker/25 8.00 20.00
7 H.Olajuwon/S.Pippen/25 15.00 40.00
8 D.Fisher/R.Artest/25 10.00 25.00

2010-11 Timeless Treasures Championship Season Materials Prime

*PRIME: .6X TO 1.5X BASE HI
STATED PRINT RUN 5 TO 25 SER.#'d SETS
6 Joe Dumars/25 8.00 20.00
13 Pau Gasol/25 8.00 20.00
14 Pau Gasol/25 8.00 20.00
15 Ray Allen/25 10.00 25.00

2010-11 Timeless Treasures Championship Season Materials Quads

STATED PRINT RUN 10 TO 25 SER.#'d SETS
1 Bynum/Fisher/Bryant/Odom/25 15.00 40.00
2 Walton/Gasol/Artest/Bryant/25 20.00 50.00

2010-11 Timeless Treasures Championship Season Materials Signatures

STATED PRINT RUN 10 TO 25 SER.#'d SETS
2 Derek Fisher/25 15.00 40.00
3 Derek Fisher/25 15.00 40.00
8 Kobe Bryant/25 1,500.00 3,000.00
16 Ron Artest/25 10.00 25.00
17 Scottie Pippen/25 75.00 150.00
20 Tony Parker/25 10.00 25.00

2010-11 Timeless Treasures Championship Season Materials Triple

STATED PRINT RUN 10 TO 25 SER.#'d SETS
1 Ginobili/Duncan/Parker/25 10.00 25.00
2 Davis/Garnett/Allen/25 10.00 25.00

2010-11 Timeless Treasures HOF Materials Combos

STATED PRINT RUN 25 TO 50 SER.#'d SETS
1 L.Bird/M.Johnson/50 15.00 40.00
2 J.Stockton/K.Malone/50 8.00 20.00
3 I.Thomas/J.Dumars/25 6.00 15.00
5 D.Cowens/R.Parish/50 6.00 15.00
6 S.Pippen/C.Drexler/50 8.00 20.00
7 M.Malone/K.Malone/25 6.00 15.00
9 D.Wilkins/S.Pippen/50 10.00 25.00
10 G.Mikan/Abdul-Jabbar/50 15.00 40.00

2010-11 Timeless Treasures HOF Materials Combos Prime

STATED PRINT RUN 10 TO 50 SER.#'d SETS
1 L.Bird/M.Johnson/50 25.00 60.00
2 J.Stockton/K.Malone/50 20.00 50.00
3 I.Thomas/J.Dumars/50 8.00 20.00
5 D.Cowens/R.Parish/25 8.00 20.00
7 M.Malone/K.Malone/50 10.00 25.00
8 R.Barry/D.Issel/45 8.00 20.00

2010-11 Timeless Treasures HOF Materials Jerseys

STATED PRINT RUN 5 TO 50 SER.#'d SETS
5 David Robinson/50 8.00 20.00
6 Dave Cowens/50 6.00 15.00
7 Magic Johnson/50 6.00 15.00
15 Dominique Wilkins/50 6.00 15.00
21 Wes Unseld/50 5.00 12.00
28 Bob Lanier/50 6.00 15.00
33 Karl Malone/50 8.00 20.00
34 Kevin McHale/50 6.00 15.00
35 Hakeem Olajuwon/50 8.00 20.00

2010-11 Timeless Treasures HOF Materials Jerseys Signatures

STATED PRINT RUN 5 TO 25 SER.#'d SETS
6 Dave Cowens/25 8.00 20.00
15 Dominique Wilkins/25 20.00 50.00
21 Wes Unseld/25 8.00 20.00
28 Bob Lanier/25 10.00 25.00
34 Kevin McHale/25 20.00 50.00

2010-11 Timeless Treasures HOF Materials Quads

STATED PRINT RUN 10 TO 50 SER.#'d SETS
1 Mikan/Lanier/Ewing/Olaj/50 20.00 50.00
2 Bird/DJ/Parish/Cowens/50 12.00 30.00
3 Wilkins/Eng/McH/Malone/50 8.00 20.00
5 Bird/Magic/Kareem/Parish/50 25.00 60.00

2010-11 Timeless Treasures HOF Materials Quads Prime

STATED PRINT RUN 5 TO 50 SER.#'d SETS
2 Bird/DJ/Parish/Cowens/50 20.00 50.00
5 Bird/Magic/Kareem/Parish/50 40.00 100.00

2010-11 Timeless Treasures HOF Signatures Silver

STATED PRINT RUN 10 TO 49 SER.#'d SETS
2 Bill Walton/25 25.00 60.00
3 Elgin Baylor/25 15.00 40.00
4 Calvin Murphy/25 6.00 15.00
6 Dave Cowens/25 10.00 25.00
9 James Worthy/25 25.00 60.00
10 Bobby Wanzer/25 6.00 15.00
11 David Thompson/25 10.00 25.00
12 Adrian Dantley/25 6.00 15.00
13 Clyde Drexler/25 25.00 60.00
17 Joe Dumars/25 12.00 30.00
18 Oscar Robertson/25 50.00 120.00
19 Rick Barry/25 10.00 25.00
20 Gail Goodrich/49 6.00 15.00
21 Wes Unseld/25 12.00 30.00
22 K.C. Jones/25 12.00 30.00
23 Bob McAdoo/25 15.00 40.00
24 Dolph Schayes/25 6.00 15.00
25 Lenny Wilkens/25 10.00 25.00
26 Jerry West/25 40.00 100.00
27 Elvin Hayes/25 12.00 30.00
28 Bob Lanier/25 10.00 25.00
29 Sam Jones/25 15.00 40.00
30 Connie Hawkins/25 15.00 40.00
31 Hal Greer/25 12.00 30.00
32 George Gervin/25 15.00 40.00
34 Kevin McHale/25 20.00 50.00

2010-11 Timeless Treasures Home and Road Gamers

STATED PRINT RUN 10 TO 99 SER.#'d SETS
1 Hakeem Olajuwon/99 8.00 20.00
3 Dominique Wilkins/99 6.00 15.00
4 Kevin McHale/99 6.00 15.00
5 Dikembe Mutombo/99 6.00 15.00
6 Sleepy Floyd/49 2.50 6.00
7 Gary Payton/99 6.00 15.00
8 Glen Rice/99 4.00 10.00
9 Patrick Ewing/99 6.00 15.00
11 Karl Malone/99 8.00 20.00
12 Joe Johnson/49 4.00 10.00
13 Mike Bibby/99 4.00 10.00
14 Paul Pierce/99 6.00 15.00
15 Boris Diaw/99 3.00 8.00
16 Joakim Noah/99 4.00 10.00
17 Dirk Nowitzki/99 10.00 25.00
18 Jason Terry/99 3.00 8.00
19 Chris Andersen/99 4.00 10.00
20 J.R. Smith/99 4.00 10.00
21 Jeff Foster/99 2.50 6.00
22 Eric Gordon/49 3.00 8.00
23 Pau Gasol/99 6.00 15.00
25 Michael Redd/99 3.00 8.00
26 David West/99 3.00 8.00
27 James Harden/99 25.00 60.00
28 Dwight Howard/99 5.00 12.00
29 Jameer Nelson/99 2.50 6.00
30 LaMarcus Aldridge/99 4.00 10.00

2010-11 Timeless Treasures Home and Road Gamers Signatures

STATED PRINT RUN 10 TO 25 SER.#'d SETS
3 Dominique Wilkins/25 20.00 50.00
4 Kevin McHale/25 25.00 60.00
5 Dikembe Mutombo/25 20.00 50.00

6 Sleepy Floyd/25 10.00 25.00
7 Gary Payton/25 20.00 50.00
12 Joe Johnson/25 12.00 30.00
16 Joakim Noah/25 20.00 50.00
19 Chris Andersen/25 20.00 50.00
20 J.R. Smith/25 8.00 20.00
27 James Harden/25 25.00 60.00
30 LaMarcus Aldridge/25 12.00 30.00

2010-11 Timeless Treasures Materials Jerseys

STATED PRINT RUN ONE TO 99 SER.#'d SETS
1 Kobe Bryant/99 12.00 30.00
2 Pau Gasol/49 5.00 12.00
5 Caron Butler/99 2.50 6.00
6 Dirk Nowitzki/99 8.00 20.00
7 Jason Kidd/99 5.00 12.00
8 Jason Terry/99 2.50 6.00
9 Grant Hill/99 5.00 12.00
10 Jason Richardson/99 3.00 8.00
12 Steve Nash/99 6.00 15.00
13 Carmelo Anthony/99 5.00 12.00
14 Chauncey Billups/99 4.00 10.00
16 Nene/99 2.50 6.00
17 Al Jefferson/99 2.00 5.00
18 Deron Williams/49 2.50 6.00
19 Mehmet Okur/99 2.00 5.00
21 Brandon Roy/99 4.00 10.00
22 Greg Oden/99 2.00 5.00
23 LaMarcus Aldridge/99 3.00 8.00
26 Manu Ginobili/99 6.00 15.00
27 Tim Duncan/99 8.00 20.00
28 Tony Parker/99 5.00 12.00
29 James Harden/99 8.00 20.00
32 Russell Westbrook/49 5.00 12.00
35 Luis Scola/99 2.50 6.00
37 Marc Gasol/99 3.00 8.00
38 Rudy Gay/35 3.00 8.00
39 Zach Randolph/99 3.00 8.00
40 Chris Paul/99 6.00 15.00
43 Chris Kaman/99 2.00 5.00
44 Eric Gordon/49 2.50 6.00
45 Baron Davis/99 3.00 8.00
48 Stephen Curry/30 20.00 50.00
50 Samuel Dalembert/99 2.00 5.00
51 Tyreke Evans/99 2.50 6.00
52 Kevin Love/99 3.00 8.00
56 Antawn Jamison/99 2.50 6.00
58 Dwight Howard/99 4.00 10.00
59 J.J. Redick/99 3.00 8.00
60 Vince Carter/99 6.00 15.00
61 Al Horford/99 3.00 8.00
62 Joe Johnson/99 3.00 8.00
63 Josh Smith/49 2.00 5.00
65 Paul Pierce/30 5.00 12.00
68 Chris Bosh/99 4.00 10.00
69 Dwyane Wade/99 6.00 15.00
70 LeBron James/99 10.00 25.00
72 Brandon Jennings/99 2.00 5.00
73 Michael Redd/99 2.50 6.00
74 D.J. Augustin/99 2.00 5.00
75 Gerald Wallace/25 2.50 6.00
78 Derrick Rose/99 6.00 15.00
79 Luol Deng/99 2.50 6.00
80 Andrea Bargnani/99 2.00 5.00
81 DeMar DeRozan/99 5.00 12.00
82 Leandro Barbosa/99 2.50 6.00
84 Darren Collison/49 2.00 5.00
86 Amare Stoudemire/49 3.00 8.00
88 Danilo Gallinari/99 2.50 6.00
92 Andre Iguodala/99 3.00 8.00
94 Thaddeus Young/99 2.00 5.00
97 Josh Howard/99 2.50 6.00
99 Brook Lopez/25 2.50 6.00

2010-11 Timeless Treasures Materials Jerseys Ink

STATED PRINT RUN ONE TO 99 SER.#'d SETS
1 Al Horford/49 6.00 15.00
3 Baron Davis/49 8.00 20.00
4 Brandon Jennings/99 6.00 15.00
5 Brook Lopez/25 8.00 20.00
7 Derrick Rose/25 40.00 100.00
8 J.J. Redick/49 10.00 25.00
9 Joakim Noah/49 6.00 15.00
10 Joe Johnson/25 10.00 25.00
11 J.R. Smith/49 10.00 25.00
12 Kevin Love/49 12.00 30.00
13 LaMarcus Aldridge/49 10.00 25.00
16 Ron Artest/25 15.00 40.00
17 Stephen Curry/35 500.00 1,000.00
18 Steve Nash/20 40.00 100.00
19 Tony Parker/99 20.00 50.00
20 Alex English/25 8.00 20.00
21 Alvan Adams/99 6.00 15.00
22 Chris Mullin/99 10.00 25.00
24 Danny Manning/99 6.00 15.00
26 Gary Payton/49 20.00 50.00
28 John Stockton/25 40.00 100.00
29 Mark Aguirre/99 6.00 15.00
30 Robert Parish/25 12.00 30.00

2010-11 Timeless Treasures Materials Jerseys Prime Ink

STATED PRINT RUN 2 TO 25 SER.#'d SETS
16 Ron Artest/20 20.00 50.00
17 Stephen Curry/25 600.00 1,200.00
19 Tony Parker/25 25.00 60.00
20 Alex English/25 10.00 25.00
21 Alvan Adams/25 10.00 25.00
30 Robert Parish/15 15.00 40.00

2010-11 Timeless Treasures MVP Materials

STATED PRINT RUN 10 TO 99 SER.#'d SETS
1 Allen Iverson/99 8.00 20.00
2 Karl Malone/99 8.00 20.00
3 Kobe Bryant/25 40.00 100.00
4 LeBron James/99 20.00 50.00
7 Tim Duncan/49 8.00 20.00

2010-11 Timeless Treasures MVP Materials MVP

STATED PRINT RUN 5 TO 25 SER.#'d SETS
1 Allen Iverson/25 15.00 40.00
2 Karl Malone/25 15.00 40.00
4 LeBron James/25 40.00 100.00

2010-11 Timeless Treasures MVP Materials MVP Prime

STATED PRINT RUN 5 TO 25 SER.#'d SETS
1 Allen Iverson/25 12.00 30.00
2 Karl Malone/25 15.00 40.00
4 LeBron James/25 30.00 80.00
5 LeBron James/25 30.00 80.00

2010-11 Timeless Treasures MVP Materials Prime

STATED PRINT RUN 5 TO 25 SER.#'d SETS
1 Allen Iverson/25 12.50 30.00
2 Karl Malone/25 15.00 40.00
4 LeBron James/25 50.00 120.00
5 LeBron James/25 25.00 60.00
7 Tim Duncan/25 12.50 30.00

2010-11 Timeless Treasures MVP Materials Quads

STATED PRINT RUN 25 SER.#'d SETS
1 Iverson/Malone/Magic/LJ 20.00 50.00
2 Iverson/Malone/Magic/Dncn 15.00 40.00

2010-11 Timeless Treasures MVP Materials Signatures

STATED PRINT RUN 10 TO 25 SER.#'d SETS
1 Allen Iverson/25 100.00 200.00
3 Kobe Bryant/25 1,500.00 3,000.00

2010-11 Timeless Treasures NBA Apprentice Materials

STATED PRINT RUN 99 SER.#'d SETS
*PRIME: .75X TO 2X BASE HI
PRIME PRINT RUN ONE TO 25 SETS
1 John Wall 6.00 15.00
2 Evan Turner 1.50 4.00
3 Derrick Favors 2.00 5.00
4 Wesley Johnson 1.25 3.00
5 DeMarcus Cousins 4.00 10.00
6 Ekpe Udoh 1.25 3.00
7 Greg Monroe 1.50 4.00
8 Al-Farouq Aminu 1.50 4.00
9 Gordon Hayward 5.00 12.00
10 299 8.00 20.00
11 Cole Aldrich 1.25 3.00
12 Xavier Henry 1.25 3.00
13 Ed Davis 1.50 4.00
14 Patrick Patterson 1.50 4.00
15 Larry Sanders 1.25 3.00
16 Luke Babbitt 1.25 3.00
17 Eric Bledsoe 2.50 6.00
18 Avery Bradley 2.00 5.00
19 James Anderson 1.25 3.00
20 Craig Brackins 1.25 3.00
21 Elliot Williams 1.25 3.00
22 Trevor Booker 1.25 3.00
23 Damion James 1.25 3.00
24 Dominique Jones 1.25 3.00
25 Quincy Pondexter 1.25 3.00
26 Jordan Crawford 1.25 3.00
27 Greivis Vasquez 1.25 3.00
28 Daniel Orton 1.25 3.00
29 Lazar Hayward 1.25 3.00
30 Dexter Pittman 1.25 3.00
31 Hassan Whiteside 2.50 6.00
32 Terrico White 1.25 3.00
33 Andy Rautins 1.25 3.00
34 Lance Stephenson 2.00 5.00
35 Timofey Mozgov 1.50 4.00
36 Devin Ebanks 1.25 3.00
37 Gani Lawal 1.25 3.00
38 Kevin Seraphin 1.25 3.00
39 Luke Harangody 1.25 3.00
40 Willie Warren 1.25 3.00

2010-11 Timeless Treasures NBA Apprentice Materials Combos

STATED PRINT RUN 99 SER.#'d SETS
1 J.Wall/E.Turner 8.00 20.00
2 J.Wall/D.Cousins 10.00 25.00
3 E.Turner/D.Favors 5.00 12.00
4 D.Favors/W.Johnson 4.00 10.00
5 W.Johnson/D.Cousins 5.00 12.00
6 G.Monroe/T.White 3.00 8.00
7 A.Aminu/E.Bledsoe 4.00 10.00
8 L.Harangody/A.Bradley 3.00 8.00
9 G.Vasquez/X.Henry 3.00 8.00
10 C.Aldrich/X.Henry 3.00 8.00
11 E.Udoh/G.Hayward 4.00 10.00
12 P.George/L.Stephenson 12.00 30.00
13 D.James/D.Pittman 3.00 8.00
14 E.Davis/P.Patterson 4.00 10.00
15 E.Bledsoe/D.Orton 4.00 10.00

2010-11 Timeless Treasures NBA Apprentice Materials Quads

STATED PRINT RUN 99 SER.#'d SETS
1 Wall/Turner/Favors/Johnson 10.00 25.00
2 Wall/Cousins/Pttrsn/Bledsoe 20.00 50.00
3 Cousins/Udoh/Monroe/Aminu 6.00 15.00
4 Hayward/George/Ald/Henry 4.00 10.00
5 Pittman/Whtsd/Aldrich/Orton 4.00 10.00
6 Udoh/Monroe/Pttrsn/Sanders 5.00 12.00
7 Davis/Vasquez/Aminu/Favors 5.00 12.00
8 Turner/Hrngdy/Davis/James 6.00 15.00
9 Sanders/George/Srphn/Monroe 4.00 10.00
10 Mozgov/Booker/Crwfrd/Pttmn 4.00 10.00
11 Williams/Jhnsn/Hywrd/Babbitt 5.00 12.00
12 Warren/Lawal/Whtsd/Ebanks 4.00 10.00
13 Jones/Pttrsn/Pndxtr/Anderson 5.00 12.00
14 Warren/Bradley/James/Srphn 4.00 10.00
15 Ebanks/Mzgv/Rautins/Johnson 4.00 10.00

2010-11 Timeless Treasures NBA Apprentice Materials Signatures

STATED PRINT RUN 50 SER.#'d SETS
1 John Wall 30.00 80.00
2 Evan Turner 15.00 40.00
3 Derrick Favors 5.00 12.00
4 Wesley Johnson 3.00 8.00
5 DeMarcus Cousins 20.00 50.00
6 Ekpe Udoh 3.00 8.00
7 Greg Monroe 4.00 10.00
8 Al-Farouq Aminu 4.00 10.00
9 Gordon Hayward 20.00 50.00
10 Paul George 25.00 60.00
11 Cole Aldrich 3.00 8.00
12 Xavier Henry 3.00 8.00
13 Ed Davis 4.00 10.00
14 Patrick Patterson 4.00 10.00
15 Larry Sanders 3.00 8.00
16 Luke Babbitt 3.00 8.00
17 Eric Bledsoe 6.00 15.00
18 Avery Bradley 5.00 12.00
19 James Anderson 3.00 8.00
20 Craig Brackins 3.00 8.00
21 Elliot Williams 3.00 8.00
22 Trevor Booker 3.00 8.00
23 Damion James 3.00 8.00
24 Dominique Jones 3.00 8.00
25 Quincy Pondexter 3.00 8.00
26 Jordan Crawford 3.00 8.00
27 Greivis Vasquez 3.00 8.00
28 Daniel Orton 3.00 8.00
29 Lazar Hayward 3.00 8.00
30 Dexter Pittman 3.00 8.00
31 Hassan Whiteside 6.00 15.00
32 Terrico White 3.00 8.00
33 Andy Rautins 3.00 8.00
34 Lance Stephenson 5.00 12.00
35 Timofey Mozgov 15.00 40.00
36 Devin Ebanks 3.00 8.00
37 Gani Lawal 3.00 8.00
38 Kevin Seraphin 8.00 20.00
39 Luke Harangody 3.00 8.00
40 Willie Warren 3.00 8.00

2010-11 Timeless Treasures NBA Apprentice Materials Triple

STATED PRINT RUN 99 SER.#'d SETS
1 Wall/Turner/Favors 8.00 20.00
2 Johnson/Cousins/Udoh 5.00 12.00
3 Monroe/Aminu/Hayward 4.00 10.00
4 George/Aldrich/Henry 3.00 8.00
5 Davis/Patterson/Sanders 4.00 10.00
6 Babbitt/Bledsoe/Bradley 4.00 10.00
7 Anderson/Brackins/Williams 3.00 8.00
8 Booker/James/Jones 3.00 8.00
9 Pondexter/Crawford/Vasquez 3.00 8.00
10 Orton/Hayward/Pittman 3.00 8.00
11 Whiteside/White/Rautins 3.00 8.00
12 Stephenson/Mozgov/Ebanks 3.00 8.00
13 Lawal/Seraphin/Harangody 3.00 8.00
14 Wall/Cousins/Patterson 12.00 30.00
15 Patterson/Bledsoe/Orton 5.00 12.00

2010-11 Timeless Treasures NBA Apprentice Signatures Combos

STATED PRINT RUN 25 SER.#'d SETS
1 J.Wall/E.Turner 50.00 125.00
2 J.Wall/D.Cousins 50.00 125.00
3 E.Turner/D.Favors 15.00 40.00
4 D.Favors/W.Johnson 8.00 20.00
5 W.Johnson/D.Cousins 10.00 25.00
6 G.Monroe/T.White 12.00 30.00
7 A.Aminu/E.Bledsoe 12.00 30.00
8 L.Harangody/A.Bradley 8.00 20.00
9 G.Vasquez/X.Henry 10.00 25.00
10 C.Aldrich/X.Henry 8.00 20.00
11 E.Udoh/G.Hayward 10.00 25.00
12 P.George/L.Stephenson 10.00 25.00
13 D.James/D.Pittman 8.00 20.00
14 E.Davis/P.Patterson 8.00 20.00
15 E.Bledsoe/D.Orton 12.00 30.00

2010-11 Timeless Treasures NBA Draft Lottery Patches

STATED PRINT RUN 10 TO 140 SER.#'d SETS
2 Evan Turner/20 25.00 60.00
3 Derrick Favors/30 15.00 40.00
4 Wesley Johnson/40 10.00 25.00
5 DeMarcus Cousins/50 20.00 50.00
6 Ekpe Udoh/60 6.00 15.00
7 Greg Monroe/70 6.00 15.00
8 Al-Faroug Aminu/80 6.00 15.00
9 Gordon Hayward/90 10.00 25.00
10 Paul George/100 30.00 60.00
11 Cole Aldrich/110 6.00 15.00
12 Xavier Henry/120 6.00 15.00
13 Ed Davis/130 6.00 15.00
14 Patrick Patterson/140 8.00 20.00

2010-11 Timeless Treasures Rookie Year Materials

STATED PRINT RUN ONE TO 99 SER.#'d SETS
1 Al Horford/99 4.00 10.00
2 Al Thornton/99 2.50 6.00
3 Andre Iguodala/99 4.00 10.00
4 Andrea Bargnani/49 2.50 6.00
5 Chris Paul/99 8.00 20.00
6 Daequan Cook/99 2.50 6.00
7 Deron Williams/99 3.00 8.00
8 Dikembe Mutombo/99 6.00 15.00
9 Dwight Howard/99 5.00 12.00
10 Jameer Nelson/99 2.50 6.00
11 Jeff Green/99 3.00 8.00
12 Joakim Noah/49 4.00 10.00
13 Kevin Durant/99 15.00 40.00
14 Kevin Garnett/99 10.00 25.00
15 LeBron James/99 30.00 80.00
16 Luis Scola/99 3.00 8.00
17 Mike Conley Jr./20 3.00 8.00
18 Nate Robinson/49 3.00 8.00
19 O.J. Mayo/99 2.50 6.00
20 Patrick Ewing/99 6.00 15.00
22 Paul Pierce/99 6.00 15.00
23 Rodney Stuckey/49 2.50 6.00
24 Shaquille O'Neal/99 15.00 40.00
25 Thaddeus Young/49 2.50 6.00
26 Zydrunas Ilgauskas/99 8.00 20.00
27 Andrew Bogut/99 3.00 8.00

2010-11 Timeless Treasures Rookie Year Materials Prime

PRIME: .75X TO 2X BASE HI
STATED PRINT RUN ONE TO 25 SER.#'d SETS

2010-11 Timeless Treasures Rookie Year Materials Prime Signatures

STATED PRINT RUN 5 TO 25 SER.#'d SETS
2 Al Thornton/25 10.00 25.00
3 Andre Iguodala/15 12.00 30.00
7 Deron Williams/25 10.00 25.00
8 Dikembe Mutombo/25 20.00 50.00
12 Joakim Noah/25 20.00 50.00
27 Andrew Bogut/25 8.00 20.00

2010-11 Timeless Treasures Rookie Year Materials Quads

STATED PRINT RUN 25 SER.#'d SETS
1 Paul/Rob/Williams/Bogut 12.00 30.00
2 Mutombo/Ewing/Shaq/Garnett 20.00 50.00
3 Pierce/James/Durant/Howard 25.00 60.00
4 Iguodala/Bargnani/Scola/Noah 6.00 15.00
5 Horford/Thornton/Conley/Stuckey 6.00 15.00

2010-11 Timeless Treasures Rookie Year Materials ROY

STATED PRINT RUN 99 SER.#'d SETS
*PRIME: .75X TO 2X BASE HI
PRIME PRINT RUN ONE TO 25 SETS
5 Chris Paul 8.00 20.00
13 Kevin Durant 15.00 40.00
15 LeBron James 30.00 80.00
20 Patrick Ewing 6.00 15.00
24 Shaquille O'Neal 15.00 40.00

2010-11 Timeless Treasures Rookie Year Materials ROY Signatures

STATED PRINT RUN 10 TO 25 SER.#'d SETS
13 Kevin Durant/25 300.00 600.00

2010-11 Timeless Treasures Rookie Year Materials Signatures

STATED PRINT RUN 10 TO 50 SER.#'d SETS
1 Al Horford/50 5.00 12.00
2 Al Thornton/50 5.00 12.00
3 Andre Iguodala/50 6.00 15.00
4 Andrea Bargnani/25 6.00 15.00
7 Deron Williams/50 5.00 12.00
8 Dikembe Mutombo/50 10.00 25.00
13 Kevin Durant/25 200.00 500.00
27 Andrew Bogut/50 8.00 20.00

2010-11 Timeless Treasures Signatures Silver

STATED PRINT RUN 10 TO 99 SER.#'d SETS
1 Kobe Bryant/99 1,000.00 2,000.00
7 Jason Kidd/25 12.00 30.00
11 Robin Lopez/25 5.00 12.00
17 Al Jefferson/49 5.00 12.00
23 LaMarcus Aldridge/25 12.00 30.00
28 Tony Parker/99 12.00 30.00
29 James Harden/25 75.00 200.00
32 Russell Westbrook/99 75.00 200.00
33 Aaron Brooks/99 5.00 12.00
37 Marc Gasol/49 8.00 20.00
41 Marcus Thornton/15 5.00 12.00
46 David Lee/49 6.00 15.00
48 Stephen Curry/20 600.00 1,200.00
49 Carl Landry/99 6.00 15.00
51 Tyreke Evans/99 10.00 25.00
52 Kevin Love/19 12.00 30.00
53 Michael Beasley/49 5.00 12.00
57 Mo Williams/49 5.00 12.00
64 Kendrick Perkins/25 6.00 15.00
66 Rajon Rondo/25 20.00 50.00
68 Chris Bosh/49 15.00 40.00
71 Andrew Bogut/49 5.00 12.00
74 D.J. Augustin/99 5.00 12.00
78 Derrick Rose/25 60.00 150.00
80 Andrea Bargnani/49 5.00 12.00
81 DeMar DeRozan/49 20.00 50.00
83 Danny Granger/99 5.00 12.00
84 Darren Collison/99 5.00 12.00
87 Anthony Randolph/99 5.00 12.00
88 Danilo Gallinari/49 5.00 12.00
90 Richard Hamilton/25 12.00 30.00
91 Tracy McGrady/40 40.00 100.00
92 Andre Iguodala/49 5.00 12.00
97 Josh Howard/25 5.00 12.00
99 Brook Lopez/25 8.00 20.00
100 Devin Harris/49 5.00 12.00

2010-11 Timeless Treasures Timeless Signatures Silver

STATED PRINT RUN 10 TO 25 SER.#'d SETS
10 John Stockton/25 40.00 100.00

2012-13 Timeless Treasures

COMP.SET w/o RCs (150) 40.00 100.00
AU RC PRINT RUN 188 TO 499 SER.#'d SETS
1 Rajon Rondo 1.25 3.00
2 Kevin Durant 4.00 10.00
3 Hakim Warrick .60 1.50
4 Tyreke Evans .75 2.00
5 Jrue Holiday 1.25 3.00
6 Kevin Garnett 2.50 6.00
7 Evan Turner .60 1.50
8 Paul Pierce 1.50 4.00
9 Serge Ibaka .75 2.00
10 LaMarcus Aldridge 1.00 2.50
11 Jason Terry .75 2.00
12 Russell Westbrook 1.50 4.00
13 Greivis Vasquez .60 1.50
14 Vince Carter 2.00 5.00
15 Grant Hill 1.50 4.00
16 Thabo Sefolosha .60 1.50
17 J.J. Hickson .60 1.50
18 Nick Young .60 1.50
19 Dorell Wright .60 1.50
20 Jeremy Lin 1.50 4.00
21 Kevin Martin .75 2.00
22 Stephen Curry 8.00 20.00
23 Nick Collison .60 1.50
24 Amare Stoudemire 1.00 2.50
25 Eric Gordon .75 2.00
26 Darren Collison .60 1.50
27 Raymond Felton .60 1.50
28 Ryan Anderson .60 1.50
29 Chris Kaman .75 2.00
30 Jason Thompson .60 1.50
31 Tyson Chandler .60 1.50
32 Al Horford 1.00 2.50
33 Ben Gordon .75 2.00
34 Carlos Boozer .75 2.00
35 Daniel Gibson .60 1.50
36 Emeka Okafor .75 2.00
37 George Hill .75 2.00
38 Brendan Haywood .60 1.50
39 Kevin Love 1.00 2.50
40 Kobe Bryant 8.00 20.00
41 Andrew Bynum .60 1.50
42 Chauncey Billups 1.25 3.00
43 Chris Paul 2.00 5.00
44 Dirk Nowitzki 2.50 6.00
45 Brandon Bass .60 1.50
46 Steve Nash 2.00 5.00
47 Wesley Matthews .60 1.50
48 James Harden 2.00 5.00
49 Patrick Patterson .60 1.50
50 Landry Fields .60 1.50
51 Manu Ginobili 2.00 5.00
52 Nate Robinson .60 1.50
53 Paul George 1.50 4.00
54 Ramon Sessions .60 1.50
55 Stephen Jackson .75 2.00
56 Wilson Chandler .75 2.00
57 Zach Randolph 1.00 2.50
58 Al Jefferson .60 1.50
59 Brandon Jennings .60 1.50
60 Jose Calderon .60 1.50
61 Danny Granger .60 1.50
62 Ersan Ilyasova .60 1.50
63 Gerald Henderson .60 1.50
64 Jameer Nelson .60 1.50
65 Kirk Hinrich .75 2.00
66 LeBron James 8.00 20.00
67 Marc Gasol 1.00 2.50
68 Nene .75 2.00
69 Paul Millsap .75 2.00
70 Rashard Lewis 1.00 2.50
71 Tayshaun Prince 1.00 2.50
72 O.J. Mayo .60 1.50
73 Shawn Marion 1.00 2.50
74 Jarrett Jack .75 2.00
75 Courtney Lee .60 1.50
76 J.R. Smith 1.00 2.50
77 Carl Landry .60 1.50
78 DeMarcus Cousins 1.00 2.50
79 Alonzo Gee .60 1.50
80 Brandon Roy .75 2.00
81 Chris Bosh 1.25 3.00
82 Danny Green .75 2.00
83 Gerald Wallace .75 2.00
84 Jason Richardson 1.00 2.50
85 Kris Humphries .60 1.50
86 Louis Williams .75 2.00
87 Marcin Gortat .60 1.50
88 Ray Allen 1.50 4.00
89 Tim Duncan 2.50 6.00
90 Jason Kidd 1.50 4.00
91 Antawn Jamison .75 2.00
92 Andrew Bogut .75 2.00
93 Marcus Thornton .60 1.50
94 Metta World Peace .75 2.00
95 Anderson Varejao .60 1.50
96 Brook Lopez .75 2.00
97 Glen Davis .60 1.50
98 JaVale McGee .75 2.00
99 Kyle Korver .75 2.00
100 Luc Mbah a Moute .60 1.50
101 Mario Chalmers .75 2.00
102 Ricky Rubio .75 2.00
103 Tony Allen .60 1.50
104 Blake Griffin 1.00 2.50
105 Andre Iguodala 1.00 2.50
106 Pau Gasol 1.50 4.00
107 Carmelo Anthony 1.50 4.00
108 Nicolas Batum .75 2.00
109 David Lee .60 1.50
110 DeAndre Jordan .75 2.00
111 Jamal Crawford 1.00 2.50
112 Andre Miller .75 2.00
113 Darrell Arthur .60 1.50
114 Goran Dragic 1.00 2.50
115 Jeff Teague .60 1.50
116 Kyle Lowry 1.00 2.50
117 Luis Scola .75 2.00
118 Michael Beasley .60 1.50
119 Rodney Stuckey .60 1.50
120 Tony Parker 1.50 4.00
121 Andrea Bargnani .60 1.50
122 David West .75 2.00
123 Dwyane Wade 2.00 5.00
124 Gordon Hayward 1.00 2.50
125 J.J. Barea .75 2.00
126 Luol Deng .75 2.00
127 Mike Conley .75 2.00
128 Roy Hibbert .75 2.00
129 DeJuan Blair .60 1.50
130 Dwight Howard 1.25 3.00
131 Derrick Rose 1.50 4.00
132 Greg Monroe .60 1.50
133 J.J. Redick 1.00 2.50
134 Josh Smith .60 1.50
135 Mike Miller .75 2.00
136 Rudy Gay 1.00 2.50
137 DeMar DeRozan 1.25 3.00
138 Joakim Noah .75 2.00
139 Mo Williams .75 2.00
140 Andrei Kirilenko .75 2.00
141 Deron Williams .75 2.00
142 Joe Johnson .75 2.00
143 Monta Ellis .75 2.00
144 Derrick Favors .75 2.00
145 Devin Harris .60 1.50
146 John Wall 1.25 3.00
147 Arron Afflalo .60 1.50
148 Drew Gooden .75 2.00
149 Trevor Ariza .60 1.50
150 Ty Lawson .60 1.50
151 Alec Burks AU/499 RC EXCH 4.00 10.00
152 A.Drummond AU/499 RC 6.00 15.00
153 A.Nicholson AU/499 RC 2.50 6.00
154 Anthony Davis AU/188 RC 100.00 250.00
155 Arnett Moultrie AU/476 RC 2.50 6.00
156 Austin Rivers AU/499 RC 4.00 10.00
157 Bernard James AU/499 RC 2.50 6.00
158 Bismack Biyombo AU/499 RC 3.00 8.00
159 Bradley Beal AU/499 RC 30.00 80.00
160 Brandon Knight AU/476 RC 3.00 8.00
161 Chandler Parsons AU/476 RC 3.00 8.00
162 Charles Jenkins AU/476 RC 2.50 6.00
163 Chris Singleton AU/499 RC 2.50 6.00
164 Cory Joseph AU/499 RC 3.00 8.00
165 DeQuan Jones AU/499 RC EXCH 2.50 6.00
166 D.Johnson-Odom AU/499 RC 2.50 6.00
167 Darius Miller AU/499 RC EXCH 3.00 8.00
168 Darius Morris AU/499 RC 3.00 8.00
169 Derrick Williams AU/499 RC 2.50 6.00
170 Dion Waiters AU/349 RC EXCH 3.00 8.00
171 Doron Lamb AU/499 RC 2.50 6.00
172 Dray Green AU/499 RC 40.00 100.00
173 Enes Kanter AU/499 RC 4.00 10.00
174 E'Twaun Moore AU/499 RC 3.00 8.00
175 Evan Fournier AU/499 RC 4.00 10.00
176 Fab Melo AU/499 RC 2.50 6.00
177 Festus Ezeli AU/499 RC 2.50 6.00
178 Greg Stiemsma AU/499 RC 2.50 6.00
179 Gustavo Ayon AU/499 RC EXCH 2.50 6.00
180 Harrison Barnes AU/499 RC 5.00 12.00
181 Iman Shumpert AU/499 RC 3.00 8.00
182 Isaiah Thomas AU/499 RC 5.00 12.00
183 Ivan Johnson AU/499 RC 2.50 6.00
184 Jae Crowder AU/499 RC 5.00 12.00
186 Jan Vesely AU/499 RC 2.50 6.00
187 J.Cunningham AU/499 RC 2.50 6.00
188 Jeff Taylor AU/499 RC 2.50 6.00
189 J.Sullinger AU/399 RC EXCH 2.50 6.00
190 J.Lamb AU/399 RC EXCH 4.00 10.00
191 Jeremy Tyler AU/499 RC EXCH 2.50 6.00
192 Jimmer Fredette AU/499 RC 4.00 10.00
193 Jimmy Butler AU/499 RC 75.00 200.00
194 John Henson AU/499 RC 3.00 8.00
195 John Jenkins AU/476 RC 2.50 6.00
196 Jon Leuer AU/499 RC 2.50 6.00
197 Jordan Hamilton AU/499 RC 2.50 6.00
198 Josh Harrellson AU/499 RC EXCH 2.50 6.00
199 Josh Selby AU/499 RC EXCH 2.50 6.00
200 N.Colo AU/499 RC EXCH 2.50 6.00
201 C.Copeland AU/499 RC EXCH 2.50 6.00
202 Kawhi Leonard AU/499 RC 125.00 300.00
203 K.Walker AU/349 RC EXCH 10.00 25.00
204 Kendall Marshall AU/499 RC 2.50 6.00
205 Kenneth Faried AU/499 RC 3.00 8.00
206 Kevin Murphy AU/499 RC 2.50 6.00
207 Khris Middleton AU/499 RC 12.00 30.00
208 Kim English AU/499 RC 2.50 6.00
209 Klay Thompson AU/499 RC 100.00 250.00
210 Kris Joseph AU/499 RC 2.50 6.00
211 Kyle O'Quinn AU/499 RC EXCH 3.00 8.00
212 Kyrie Irving AU/399 RC 75.00 200.00
213 Lance Thomas AU/499 RC 2.50 6.00
214 Lavoy Allen AU/499 RC 2.50 6.00
215 Malcolm Lee AU/499 RC 2.50 6.00
216 J.Valanciunas AU/499 RC 5.00 12.00
217 Marc.Morris AU/499 RC EXCH 4.00 10.00
218 Mark.Morris AU/499 RC EXCH 4.00 10.00
219 Marquis Teague AU/438 RC 2.50 6.00
220 MarShon Brooks AU/499 RC 2.50 6.00
221 Meyers Leonard AU/499 RC 3.00 8.00
222 M.Kidd-Gilchrist AU/316 RC 3.00 8.00
223 Mike Scott AU/499 RC 3.00 8.00
224 Miles Plumlee AU/499 RC EXCH 2.50 6.00
225 Maurice Harkless AU/499 RC 3.00 8.00
226 Nikola Vucevic AU/499 RC 10.00 25.00
227 Nolan Smith AU/499 RC 2.50 6.00
228 Norris Cole AU/499 RC 2.50 6.00
229 Orlando Johnson AU/499 RC 2.50 6.00
230 Perry Jones AU/499 RC 2.50 6.00
231 Quincy Acy AU/499 RC 2.50 6.00
232 Quincy Miller AU/475 RC 2.50 6.00
233 Reggie Jackson AU/499 RC 4.00 10.00
234 Kyle Singler AU/499 RC 2.50 6.00
235 Robert Sacre AU/499 RC 2.50 6.00
236 Royce White AU/476 RC 2.50 6.00
237 Shelvin Mack AU/499 RC 3.00 8.00
238 Terrence Jones AU/476 RC 2.50 6.00
239 Terrence Ross AU/499 RC 6.00 15.00
240 T.Robinson AU/349 RC 2.50 6.00
241 Tobias Harris AU/499 RC 8.00 20.00
242 Tony Wroten AU/499 RC EXCH 2.50 6.00
243 T.Shengelia AU/476 RC 2.50 6.00
245 Trey Thompkins AU/499 RC 2.50 6.00
246 T.Thompson AU/499 RC 4.00 10.00
247 Tyler Honeycutt AU/499 RC 2.50 6.00
248 Tyler Zeller AU/499 RC 2.50 6.00
249 Tyshawn Taylor AU/475 RC 2.50 6.00
250 Will Barton AU/499 RC 5.00 12.00

2012-13 Timeless Treasures Silver

*VETS: 1.5X TO 4X BASE HI
*ROOKIES: .75X TO 2X BASE HI
STATED PRINT RUN 25 SER.#'d SETS
154 Anthony Davis AU 200.00 500.00

2012-13 Timeless Treasures All-Star Materials

STATED PRINT RUN 149 SER.#'d SETS
1 Blake Griffin 4.00 10.00
2 Kobe Bryant 30.00 80.00
3 Dwight Howard 5.00 12.00
4 Carmelo Anthony 6.00 15.00
5 Chris Paul 8.00 20.00
6 Deron Williams 3.00 8.00
7 Derrick Rose 6.00 15.00
8 Dirk Nowitzki 10.00 25.00
9 Dwyane Wade 8.00 20.00
10 Joe Johnson 3.00 8.00
11 Kevin Durant 15.00 40.00
12 Kevin Garnett 10.00 25.00
13 Kevin Love 4.00 10.00
14 Pau Gasol 6.00 15.00
15 Manu Ginobili 8.00 20.00
16 Paul Pierce 6.00 15.00
17 Rajon Rondo 5.00 12.00
18 Ray Allen 6.00 15.00
19 Russell Westbrook 6.00 15.00
20 Tim Duncan 10.00 25.00

2012-13 Timeless Treasures All-Star Materials Prime

*PRIME: 1X TO 2.5X BASE HI
STATED PRINT RUN 25 TO 49 SER.#'d SETS

2012-13 Timeless Treasures Perennial Materials

STATED PRINT RUN 149 SER.#'d SETS
1 Patrick Ewing 8.00 20.00
2 Karl Malone 8.00 20.00
3 Shaquille O'Neal 15.00 40.00
4 Hakeem Olajuwon 10.00 25.00
5 Ron Harper 5.00 12.00
6 Sean Elliott 4.00 10.00
7 Chris Mullin 5.00 12.00
8 Clyde Drexler 8.00 20.00
9 Kevin McHale 6.00 15.00
10 Jeff Hornacek 4.00 10.00
11 Kenny Anderson 4.00 10.00
12 Alex English 4.00 10.00
13 Kareem Abdul-Jabbar 15.00 40.00
14 Chris Mullin 6.00 15.00
15 Reggie Lewis 10.00 25.00
16 Steve Smith 4.00 10.00
17 Dikembe Mutombo 8.00 20.00
18 Robert Parish 8.00 20.00
19 Manute Bol 10.00 25.00
20 Jalen Rose 4.00 10.00
21 Mark Price 5.00 12.00
22 Glen Rice 4.00 10.00
23 Kelly Tripucka 4.00 10.00
24 Lou Hudson 4.00 10.00
25 Shawn Kemp 15.00 40.00

2012-13 Timeless Treasures Promising Pros Materials

STATED PRINT RUN 99 TO 149 SER.#'d SETS
1 Kyrie Irving/149 12.00 30.00
2 Derrick Williams/149 1.25 3.00
3 Tristan Thompson/149 2.00 5.00
4 Klay Thompson/149 12.00 30.00
5 Kawhi Leonard/99 15.00 40.00
6 Derrick Favors/149 2.00 5.00
7 DeMarcus Cousins/149 2.50 6.00
8 Iman Shumpert/149 1.50 4.00
9 Brandon Knight/149 1.50 4.00
10 Markieff Morris/149 2.00 5.00
11 Evan Turner/149 1.50 4.00
12 Gordon Hayward/149 2.50 6.00
13 MarShon Brooks/149 1.25 3.00
14 Kemba Walker/149 5.00 12.00
15 Kenneth Faried/149 1.50 4.00
16 Norris Cole/149 1.25 3.00
17 Jimmer Fredette/149 2.00 5.00
18 John Wall/149 3.00 8.00
19 Tiago Splitter/149 1.50 4.00
20 Ivan Johnson/149 1.25 3.00

2012-13 Timeless Treasures Revolution Memorabilia

STATED PRINT RUN 75 SER.#'d SETS
1 K.Bryant/L.James 75.00 200.00
2 K.Faried/K.Love 3.00 8.00
3 B.Griffin/K.Love 3.00 8.00
4 D.Rose/C.Paul 6.00 15.00
5 R.Rondo/R.Westbrook 5.00 12.00
6 T.Chandler/K.Garnett 8.00 20.00
7 K.Irving/K.Walker 20.00 50.00
8 P.Pierce/C.Anthony 5.00 12.00
9 T.Parker/J.Kidd 5.00 12.00
10 Z.Randolph/C.Bosh 4.00 10.00
11 D.Nowitzki/T.Duncan 15.00 40.00
12 T.Evans/T.Lawson 2.50 6.00
13 J.Wall/T.Evans 4.00 10.00
14 P.Gasol/A.Stoudemire 5.00 12.00
15 M.Ginobili/C.Billups 6.00 15.00
16 M.Gasol/S.Ibaka 3.00 8.00
17 D.Granger/R.Gay 3.00 8.00
18 B.Jennings/S.Curry 25.00 60.00
19 A.Iguodala/L.Deng 3.00 8.00
20 K.Durant/L.James 40.00 100.00

2012-13 Timeless Treasures Rookie Matchups

STATED PRINT RUN 99 SER.#'d SETS
1 K.Irving/B.Knight 6.00 15.00
2 T.Robinson/A.Davis 8.00 20.00
3 T.Thompson/D.Williams 1.00 2.50
4 M.Kidd-Gilchrist/H.Barnes 1.25 3.00
5 A.Drummond/J.Lamb 1.50 4.00
6 Marc.Morris/Mark.Morris 1.00 2.50
7 J.Henson/T.Zeller .75 2.00
8 D.Waiters/J.Sullinger .75 2.00
9 D.Lillard/I.Shumpert 12.00 30.00
10 K.Thompson/I.Thomas 20.00 50.00

2012-13 Timeless Treasures Three-Piece Puzzles

STATED PRINT RUN 199 SER.#'d SETS
1A Derrick Rose 2.50 6.00
1B Joakim Noah 1.25 3.00
1C Luol Deng 1.25 3.00
2A Chris Bosh 2.00 5.00
2B Dwyane Wade 3.00 8.00
2C LeBron James 12.00 30.00
3A Manu Ginobili 3.00 8.00
3B Tim Duncan 4.00 10.00
3C Tony Parker 2.50 6.00
4A Russell Westbrook 2.50 6.00
4B Kevin Durant 6.00 15.00
4C Serge Ibaka 1.25 3.00
5A Kevin Garnett 4.00 10.00
5B Paul Pierce 2.50 6.00
5C Rajon Rondo 2.00 5.00
6A Goran Dragic 1.50 4.00
6B Marcin Gortat 1.00 2.50
6C Michael Beasley 1.00 2.50
7A Brook Lopez 1.25 3.00
7B Deron Williams 1.50 4.00
7C Joe Johnson 1.25 3.00
8A Kobe Bryant 12.00 30.00
8B Pau Gasol 2.50 6.00
8C Steve Nash 3.00 8.00
9A Amare Stoudemire 1.50 4.00
9B Carmelo Anthony 2.50 6.00
9C Tyson Chandler 1.25 3.00
10A Marc Gasol 1.50 4.00
10B Rudy Gay 1.50 4.00
10C Zach Randolph 1.50 4.00
11A Darren Collison 1.00 2.50
11B Dirk Nowitzki 4.00 10.00
11C O.J. Mayo 1.00 2.50
12A Dion Waiters 1.25 3.00
12B Kyrie Irving 10.00 25.00
12C Tristan Thompson 1.50 4.00
13A Anthony Davis 12.00 30.00
13B Austin Rivers 1.50 4.00
13C Darius Miller 1.25 3.00

2012-13 Timeless Treasures Time to Shine Autographs

STATED PRINT RUN 49 TO 199 SER.#'d SETS
1 MarShon Brooks/199 3.00 8.00
2 Brandon Knight/199 4.00 10.00
3 Norris Cole/199 3.00 8.00
4 Kyrie Irving/99 75.00 200.00
5 Klay Thompson/199 100.00 250.00
6 Iman Shumpert/199 4.00 10.00
7 Kenneth Faried/199 4.00 10.00
8 Kawhi Leonard/99 100.00 250.00
9 Chandler Parsons/199 4.00 10.00
10 Isaiah Thomas/199 6.00 15.00
11 Tristan Thompson/99 5.00 12.00
12 Anthony Davis/49 100.00 250.00
13 Thomas Robinson/49 3.00 8.00
14 Michael Kidd-Gilchrist/49 4.00 10.00
15 Bradley Beal/99 20.00 50.00
16 Austin Rivers/99 5.00 12.00

17 Dion Waiters/199 4.00 10.00
18 Andre Drummond/99 8.00 20.00
19 Jimmer Fredette/199 5.00 12.00
20 Harrison Barnes/99 6.00 15.00

2012-13 Timeless Treasures Timeless Signatures

STATED PRINT RUN 25 TO 199 SER.#'d SETS
1 Jeff Hornacek/199 EXCH 6.00 15.00
2 John Starks/199 8.00 20.00
3 Bob Love/199 5.00 12.00
4 Larry Johnson/199 10.00 25.00
5 Spud Webb/199 8.00 20.00
6 Steve Smith/199 6.00 15.00
7 Jalen Rose/199 EXCH 5.00 12.00
8 Elgin Baylor/49 20.00 50.00
9 Dan Majerle/199 8.00 20.00
10 Bob McAdoo/99 10.00 25.00
11 Larry Bird/25 125.00 300.00
13 World B. Free/49 5.00 12.00
14 Steve Kerr/49 40.00 100.00
15 Hal Greer/99 8.00 20.00
16 Alonzo Mourning/49 20.00 50.00
17 Willis Reed/49 40.00 100.00
18 Anfernee Hardaway/49 75.00 200.00
19 George Gervin/49 12.00 30.00
20 Kenny Smith/49 6.00 15.00
21 Bruce Bowen/199 4.00 10.00
22 Sleepy Floyd/199 4.00 10.00
23 Rex Chapman/199 6.00 15.00
24 Sean Elliott/199 EXCH 6.00 15.00
25 Paul Silas/199 6.00 15.00
26 Magic Johnson/25 125.00 300.00
27 Cazzie Russell/199 6.00 15.00
28 Vlade Divac/199 4.00 10.00
29 Dan Issel/199 6.00 15.00
30 James Worthy/49 30.00 80.00
31 John Paxson/199 4.00 10.00
32 Bill Russell/25 1,000.00 2,000.00
33 Jamal Mashburn/199 8.00 20.00
34 Dikembe Mutombo/99 12.00 30.00
35 Terry Porter/199 5.00 12.00
36 Antoine Walker/199 8.00 20.00
37 Ralph Sampson/199 6.00 15.00
38 Lenny Wilkens/99 4.00 10.00
39 Dennis Scott/199 4.00 10.00
40 Calvin Murphy/99 6.00 15.00
41 John Stockton/25 50.00 120.00
42 Walt Frazier/99 10.00 25.00
43 Bill Walton/99 15.00 40.00
44 Allan Houston/99 6.00 15.00
45 George McGinnis/199 10.00 25.00
46 John Havlicek/25 75.00 200.00
47 Adrian Dantley/99 6.00 15.00
48 Bob Dandridge/199 5.00 12.00
49 Alex English/49 10.00 25.00
50 Yao Ming/25 500.00 1,000.00

2012-13 Timeless Treasures Timeless Talents Signatures

STATED PRINT RUN 25 TO 199 SER.#'d SETS
1 Brandon Roy/25 10.00 25.00
2 Jason Richardson/99 6.00 15.00
3 Carlos Boozer/99 4.00 10.00
4 Chauncey Billups/99 EXCH 10.00 25.00
5 Kobe Bryant/99 1,500.00 3,000.00
6 Pau Gasol/25 20.00 50.00
7 Deron Williams/25 8.00 20.00
8 Kevin Love/25 10.00 25.00
9 Luis Scola/99 4.00 10.00
10 Ryan Anderson/199 4.00 10.00
11 Kevin Durant/49 300.00 600.00
12 Channing Frye/99 EXCH 4.00 10.00
13 Nick Young/199 4.00 10.00
14 Thabo Sefolosha/199 4.00 10.00
15 D.J. Augustin/99 4.00 10.00
16 Al Horford/49 8.00 20.00
17 David West/99 5.00 12.00
18 Monta Ellis/99 5.00 12.00
19 Mike Conley/99 5.00 12.00
20 Caron Butler/49 4.00 10.00
21 Roy Hibbert/199 4.00 10.00
22 Gerald Henderson/199 4.00 10.00
23 James Harden/99 EXCH 100.00 250.00
24 Blake Griffin/49 25.00 60.00
25 Jose Calderon/99 EXCH 5.00 12.00
26 LaMarcus Aldridge/49 8.00 20.00
27 Zach Randolph/49 5.00 12.00
28 Shane Battier/49 6.00 15.00
29 David Lee/49 EXCH 6.00 15.00
30 Chris Bosh/25 12.00 30.00
31 Juwan Howard/99 5.00 12.00
32 Gerald Wallace/49 5.00 12.00
33 Andre Iguodala/49 8.00 20.00
34 Ben Gordon/49 5.00 12.00
35 Josh Smith/99 4.00 10.00
36 Chris Kaman/99 4.00 10.00
37 Jameer Nelson/99 4.00 10.00
38 Kevin Martin/99 6.00 15.00
39 Kris Humphries/199 EXCH 4.00 10.00
40 Stephen Curry/99 800.00 1,500.00
41 Antawn Jamison/99 5.00 12.00
42 Brook Lopez/99 6.00 15.00
43 Danny Granger/49 4.00 10.00
44 Taj Gibson/99 4.00 10.00
45 Wesley Matthews/199 4.00 10.00
46 Goran Dragic/99 6.00 15.00
47 Mario Chalmers/99 5.00 12.00
48 Drew Gooden/199 EXCH 4.00 10.00
49 Marcus Camby/199 6.00 15.00
50 Tyson Chandler/49 6.00 15.00

2012-13 Timeless Treasures Treasured Ink

STATED PRINT RUN 10 TO 199 SER.#'d SETS
1 David Robinson/25 50.00 120.00
2 Dolph Schayes/99 6.00 15.00
3 Mark Eaton/199 6.00 15.00
4 Bernard King/199 6.00 15.00
5 Kevin Durant/25 300.00 600.00
6 Andre Iguodala/49 8.00 20.00
7 Tom Heinsohn/199 30.00 80.00
8 Bill Walton/99 15.00 40.00
9 Kobe Bryant/99 1,000.00 2,000.00
10 Michael Cooper/199 6.00 15.00
11 Larry Bird/25 125.00 300.00
12 Gail Goodrich/99 6.00 15.00
13 Chris Mullin/199 6.00 15.00
16 Gary Payton/25 40.00 100.00
17 Blake Griffin/49 15.00 40.00
18 Bill Russell/25 1,000.00 2,000.00
19 Tony Parker/49 20.00 50.00
20 Bill Sharman/49 20.00 50.00
21 LaMarcus Aldridge/49 8.00 20.00
22 Magic Johnson/25 125.00 300.00
23 Kevin Love/25 10.00 25.00
26 Jerry West/25 40.00 100.00
28 Jeff Hornacek/199 8.00 20.00
29 Julius Erving/25 75.00 200.00
30 Kevin Willis/199 5.00 12.00

2012-13 Timeless Treasures Treasured Threads

STATED PRINT RUN 25 TO 99 SER.#'d SETS
1 Tim Duncan/99 10.00 25.00
2 Jeff Hornacek/99 3.00 8.00
3 Chauncey Billups/99 5.00 12.00
4 Ben Wallace/99 3.00 8.00
5 Andre Miller/99 3.00 8.00
6 Vince Carter/99 8.00 20.00
7 Hedo Turkoglu/99 3.00 8.00
8 Tyson Chandler/99 3.00 8.00
9 Patrick Ewing/99 6.00 15.00
10 LeBron James/99 30.00 80.00
11 Dirk Nowitzki/99 10.00 25.00
12 Carmelo Anthony/99 6.00 15.00
13 Paul Pierce/99 6.00 15.00
14 Tayshaun Prince/99 4.00 10.00
15 Dwyane Wade/99 8.00 20.00
16 Amare Stoudemire/99 4.00 10.00
17 Alonzo Mourning/99 6.00 15.00
18 Kevin Durant/99 15.00 40.00
19 Chris Paul/99 8.00 20.00
20 Scottie Pippen/99 10.00 25.00
21 David Robinson/99 6.00 15.00
22 Jerry West/25 10.00 25.00
23 Julius Erving/25 10.00 25.00
24 Dennis Rodman/99 10.00 25.00
25 Gary Payton/25 5.00 12.00
26 Andre Iguodala/99 4.00 10.00
27 Derrick Rose/99 6.00 15.00
28 Pau Gasol/99 6.00 15.00
29 Hakeem Olajuwon/99 8.00 20.00
30 Blake Griffin/99 4.00 10.00

2012-13 Timeless Treasures Validating Marks Autographs

STATED PRINT RUN 49 TO 199 SER.#'d SETS
1 Brandon Bass/99 4.00 10.00
2 James Harden/49 200.00 500.00
3 Gordon Hayward/199 5.00 12.00
4 Paul George/199 40.00 100.00
5 Gary Neal/99 EXCH 4.00 10.00
6 Derrick Favors/99 4.00 10.00
7 Greg Monroe/99 4.00 10.00
8 Danny Green/199 5.00 12.00
9 Ersan Ilyasova/199 4.00 10.00
10 Brandon Jennings/49 EXCH 4.00 10.00
11 JaVale McGee/99 EXCH 4.00 10.00
12 Omri Casspi/199 EXCH 4.00 10.00
13 Omer Asik/199 EXCH 4.00 10.00
14 Landry Fields/199 4.00 10.00
15 Tiago Splitter/199 4.00 10.00
16 Greivis Vasquez/199 4.00 10.00
17 Patrick Patterson/199 4.00 10.00
18 Avery Bradley/199 EXCH 4.00 10.00
19 Ed Davis/199 4.00 10.00
20 Tyreke Evans/49 4.00 10.00
21 Al-Farouq Aminu/199 4.00 10.00
22 Ekpe Udoh/199 4.00 10.00
23 Quincy Pondexter/199 4.00 10.00
24 Jonas Jerebko/199 4.00 10.00
25 Jordan Crawford/199 EXCH 4.00 10.00
26 Jrue Holiday/99 10.00 25.00
27 Serge Ibaka/199 EXCH 5.00 12.00
28 Eric Gordon/49 5.00 12.00
29 Marcus Thornton/199 4.00 10.00
30 DeAndre Jordan/99 4.00 10.00
31 Ty Lawson/99 4.00 10.00
32 Elliott Williams/199 4.00 10.00
33 Stephen Curry/99 800.00 1,500.00
34 Gary Forbes/199 4.00 10.00
36 Xavier Henry/199 4.00 10.00
37 James Anderson/199 4.00 10.00
38 Nikola Pekovic/199 4.00 10.00
39 Eric Bledsoe/199 8.00 20.00
40 Devin Ebanks/199 4.00 10.00
41 DeMarcus Cousins/49 EXCH 10.00 25.00
42 Kyle Lowry/199 10.00 25.00
43 Ryan Anderson/199 EXCH 4.00 10.00
44 Timofey Mozgov/199 EXCH 4.00 10.00
45 Luke Babbitt/199 4.00 10.00
46 Luke Harangody/199 EXCH 4.00 10.00
47 Tyler Hansbrough/99 4.00 10.00
48 Jeff Teague/199 4.00 10.00
49 Austin Daye/199 4.00 10.00
50 Brandon Rush/199 4.00 10.00

2013-14 Timeless Treasures

1-100 PRINT RUN 299 SER.#'d SETS
EXCHANGE DEADLINE 6/11/2015
1 Kyrie Irving 4.00 10.00
2 Kobe Bryant 10.00 25.00
3 Kevin Durant 4.00 10.00
4 Kevin Love 1.25 3.00
5 Derrick Rose 2.00 5.00
6 Damian Lillard 4.00 10.00
7 Dirk Nowitzki 3.00 8.00
8 Blake Griffin 1.25 3.00
9 Anthony Davis 4.00 10.00
10 Deron Williams 1.00 2.50
11 Kenneth Faried 1.00 2.50
12 Jimmer Fredette 1.25 3.00
13 Al Horford 1.25 3.00
14 Marc Gasol 1.25 3.00
15 James Harden 2.50 6.00
16 Andre Drummond 1.25 3.00
17 Russell Westbrook 2.50 6.00
18 Carmelo Anthony 2.00 5.00
19 Tony Parker 2.00 5.00
20 Bradley Beal 2.00 5.00
21 Klay Thompson 4.00 10.00
22 Paul George 2.00 5.00
23 Tyreke Evans 1.00 2.50
24 Paul Pierce 2.00 5.00
25 Dwight Howard 1.50 4.00
26 LeBron James 10.00 25.00
27 Michael Kidd-Gilchrist .75 2.00
28 Jrue Holiday 1.50 4.00
29 Enes Kanter 1.00 2.50
30 LaMarcus Aldridge 1.25 3.00
31 Vince Carter 2.50 6.00
32 Monta Ellis 1.00 2.50
33 Isaiah Thomas 1.00 2.50
34 Ricky Rubio 1.00 2.50
35 Rudy Gay 1.00 2.50
36 Ty Lawson .75 2.00
37 MarShon Brooks .75 2.00
38 Roy Hibbert .75 2.00
39 Tim Duncan 3.00 8.00
40 Tristan Thompson .75 2.00
41 John Wall 1.50 4.00
42 Devin Harris .75 2.00
43 Goran Dragic 1.00 2.50
44 Zach Randolph 1.00 2.50
45 Joakim Noah 1.25 3.00
46 Dwyane Wade 2.50 6.00
47 Kemba Walker 1.25 3.00
48 Ersan Ilyasova .75 2.00
49 Greivis Vasquez .75 2.00
50 Amar'e Stoudemire 1.25 3.00
51 Steve Nash 2.50 6.00
52 Chandler Parsons .75 2.00
53 Danny Green 1.00 2.50
54 Rajon Rondo 1.50 4.00
55 DeMarcus Cousins 1.25 3.00
56 Jameer Nelson .75 2.00
57 Draymond Green 2.00 5.00
58 Brandon Knight 1.00 2.50
59 Gordon Hayward 1.00 2.50
60 Nick Young .75 2.00
61 Nene .75 2.00
62 Josh Smith .75 2.00
63 Joe Johnson 1.00 2.50
64 JaVale McGee 1.00 2.50
65 Kendall Marshall .75 2.00
66 Chris Bosh 1.50 4.00
67 Carlos Boozer 1.00 2.50
68 Stephen Curry 10.00 25.00
69 Gary Neal .75 2.00
70 Shawn Marion 1.00 2.50
71 Kyle Lowry 1.25 3.00
72 Chris Paul 2.50 6.00
73 Wesley Matthews .75 2.00
74 Lance Stephenson 1.00 2.50
75 Al Jefferson .75 2.00
76 Ray Allen 2.00 5.00
77 Ben Gordon 1.00 2.50
78 Brandon Jennings .75 2.00
79 Derrick Williams .75 2.00
80 Jeff Teague .75 2.00
81 Tyson Chandler 1.00 2.50
82 Austin Rivers 1.00 2.50
83 Greg Monroe 1.00 2.50
84 David West 1.00 2.50
85 Thaddeus Young .75 2.00
86 Kawhi Leonard 4.00 10.00
87 Brook Lopez 1.00 2.50
88 Marcin Gortat .75 2.00
89 Jimmy Butler 2.50 6.00
90 Metta World Peace 1.00 2.50
91 Andrea Bargnani .75 2.00
92 Jae Crowder .75 2.00
93 Kevin Garnett 3.00 8.00
94 Tobias Harris 1.25 3.00
95 DeAndre Jordan 1.00 2.50
96 Anderson Varejao .75 2.00
97 Jeremy Lin 2.00 5.00
98 Iman Shumpert .75 2.00
99 Harrison Barnes 1.25 3.00
100 Chris Andersen 1.00 2.50
101 Anthony Bennett JSY AU RC 3.00 8.00
102 Allen Crabbe JSY AU RC 3.00 8.00
103 Glen Rice Jr. JSY AU RC 3.00 8.00
104 Victor Oladipo JSY AU RC 10.00 25.00
105 Archie Goodwin JSY AU RC 3.00 8.00
106 Tony Mitchell JSY AU RC 3.00 8.00
107 Otto Porter JSY AU RC 5.00 12.00
108 Andre Roberson JSY AU RC 4.00 10.00
109 Nate Wolters JSY AU RC 3.00 8.00
110 Cody Zeller JSY AU RC 4.00 10.00
111 Reggie Bullock JSY AU RC 3.00 8.00
112 Jeff Withey JSY AU RC 3.00 8.00
113 Alex Len JSY AU RC 4.00 10.00
114 Tim Hardaway Jr. JSY AU RC 6.00 15.00
115 Grant Jerrett JSY AU RC 3.00 8.00
116 Nerlens Noel JSY AU RC 4.00 10.00
117 Solomon Hill JSY AU RC 4.00 10.00
118 Jamaal Franklin JSY AU RC 3.00 8.00
119 Ben McLemore JSY AU RC 4.00 10.00
120 Mason Plumlee JSY AU RC 4.00 10.00
121 Ryan Kelly JSY AU RC 3.00 8.00
122 Kentavious Caldwell-Pope JSY AU RC 5.00 12.00
123 Tony Snell JSY AU RC 4.00 10.00
124 Erik Murphy JSY AU RC 3.00 8.00
125 Trey Burke JSY AU RC 4.00 10.00
126 Shane Larkin JSY AU RC 3.00 8.00
127 Peyton Siva JSY AU RC 3.00 8.00
128 C.J. McCollum JSY AU RC 12.00 30.00
129 Antetokounmpo JSY AU RC 300.00 600.00
130 Ricky Ledo JSY AU RC 3.00 8.00
131 M.Carter-Williams JSY AU RC 4.00 10.00
132 Shabazz Muhammad JSY AU RC 3.00 8.00
133 Isaiah Canaan JSY AU RC 3.00 8.00
134 Steven Adams JSY AU RC 8.00 20.00
135 Kelly Olynyk JSY AU RC 4.00 10.00

2013-14 Timeless Treasures Every Player Every Game Jerseys

STATED PRINT RUN 49 SER.#'d SETS
MOST NOT PRICED DUE TO LACK OF INFO
3 Rodney Stuckey 2.50 6.00
4 Luol Deng 3.00 8.00
6 Jonas Valanciunas 3.00 8.00
7 Tracy McGrady 6.00 15.00
13 Jeremy Lin 6.00 15.00
14 Paul Pierce 6.00 15.00
17 Rajon Rondo 5.00 12.00
18 Tim Duncan 10.00 25.00
21 Omer Asik 2.50 6.00
22 Kent Bazemore 2.50 6.00
24 David Lee 2.50 6.00
28 Thaddeus Young 2.50 6.00
31 Joakim Noah 6.00 15.00
34 Harrison Barnes 4.00 10.00
35 Jimmer Fredette 4.00 10.00
36 Kemba Walker 4.00 10.00
40 Dirk Nowitzki 10.00 25.00
42 Jeff Green 2.50 6.00
45 Tristan Thompson 2.50 6.00
52 Carmelo Anthony 6.00 15.00
54 Greg Monroe 2.50 6.00
58 Marc Gasol 4.00 10.00
60 Bradley Beal 6.00 15.00
61 Jason Richardson 4.00 10.00
63 Dwight Howard 5.00 12.00
64 Brandon Jennings 2.50 6.00
65 Dwyane Wade 8.00 20.00
67 Jason Kidd 6.00 15.00
68 Serge Ibaka 3.00 8.00
69 Thomas Robinson 6.00 15.00
75 LeBron James 20.00 50.00
76 Jeff Teague 2.50 6.00
77 Chandler Parsons 2.50 6.00
80 James Harden 8.00 20.00
81 Avery Bradley 2.50 6.00
83 Eric Gordon 3.00 8.00
85 Danny Green 3.00 8.00
86 Amar'e Stoudemire 4.00 10.00
88 Eric Bledsoe 3.00 8.00
89 Orlando Johnson 2.50 6.00
91 Steve Nash 8.00 20.00
93 Chris Paul 8.00 20.00
94 Shane Battier 3.00 8.00
97 Brandan Wright 2.50 6.00
99 Kenneth Faried 3.00 8.00

2013-14 Timeless Treasures Lottery Winners

1 Anthony Bennett 1.25 3.00
2 Victor Oladipo 3.00 8.00
3 Otto Porter 2.00 5.00
4 Cody Zeller 1.50 4.00
5 Alex Len 1.50 4.00
6 Nerlens Noel 1.50 4.00
7 Ben McLemore 1.50 4.00
8 Kentavious Caldwell-Pope 2.00 5.00
9 Trey Burke 1.50 4.00
10 C.J. McCollum 6.00 15.00
11 Michael Carter-Williams 1.50 4.00
12 Steven Adams 3.00 8.00
13 Kelly Olynyk 1.50 4.00
14 Shabazz Muhammad 1.25 3.00

2013-14 Timeless Treasures Perennial Materials

1 Dwyane Wade 6.00 15.00
2 Tony Parker 5.00 12.00
3 Deron Williams 2.50 6.00
4 Kevin Garnett 8.00 20.00
5 John Wall 4.00 10.00
6 Robert Parish 4.00 10.00
7 Raymond Felton 2.00 5.00
8 Luol Deng 2.50 6.00
9 Larry Bird 10.00 25.00
10 Shaquille O'Neal 12.00 30.00
12 Dirk Nowitzki 8.00 20.00
13 Rajon Rondo 4.00 10.00
14 Blake Griffin 5.00 12.00
15 Danny Green 2.50 6.00
16 Kevin Durant 6.00 15.00
17 Brent Barry 2.00 5.00
18 J.R. Smith 3.00 8.00
20 Ty Lawson 2.00 5.00

2013-14 Timeless Treasures Perennial Materials Prime

*PRIME: .75X TO 2X BASIC
PRINT RUNS B/WN 7-25 COPIES PER
NO PRICING ON QTY 10 OR LESS
11 Anfernee Hardaway/25 30.00 80.00

2013-14 Timeless Treasures Promising Pros Materials

1 Kenneth Faried 3.00 8.00
2 Kawhi Leonard 12.00 30.00
3 Chandler Parsons 2.50 6.00
5 Anthony Davis 12.00 30.00
6 Bradley Beal 6.00 15.00
7 Klay Thompson 12.00 30.00
8 John Henson 2.50 6.00
9 Markieff Morris 2.50 6.00
10 Andre Drummond 4.00 10.00
11 Kyrie Irving 8.00 20.00
12 Iman Shumpert 2.50 6.00
13 Draymond Green 6.00 15.00
14 Dion Waiters 2.50 6.00
15 Michael Kidd-Gilchrist 2.50 6.00
16 Kemba Walker 4.00 10.00
18 Jimmer Fredette 4.00 10.00
19 Tristan Thompson 2.50 6.00
20 Isaiah Thomas 3.00 8.00
21 Nikola Vucevic 5.00 12.00
22 Jrue Holiday 5.00 12.00
24 Paul George 8.00 20.00
25 Jeff Teague 2.50 6.00

2013-14 Timeless Treasures Promising Pros Materials Prime

*PRIME p/r 15: .75X TO 2X BASIC
*PRIME p/r 25: .75X TO 2X BASIC
PRINT RUNS B/WN 7-25 COPIES PER
NO PRICING ON QTY 10 OR LESS

2013-14 Timeless Treasures Rookie Jersey Autographs Prime

*PRIME: .5X TO 1.2X BASIC
STATED PRINT RUN 49 SER.#'d SETS
EXCHANGE DEADLINE 6/11/2015
108 Andre Roberson 5.00 12.00
128 C.J. McCollum 20.00 50.00
134 Steven Adams 15.00 40.00

2013-14 Timeless Treasures Rookie Jersey Autographs Prime Ruby

*RUBY: .6X TO 1.5X BASIC
STATED PRINT RUN 25 SER.#'d SETS
EXCHANGE DEADLINE 6/11/2015
104 Victor Oladipo 30.00 80.00
125 Trey Burke 6.00 15.00
127 Peyton Siva 5.00 12.00
128 C.J. McCollum 25.00 60.00
131 Michael Carter-Williams 6.00 15.00
132 Shabazz Muhammad 5.00 12.00
133 Isaiah Canaan 5.00 12.00

2013-14 Timeless Treasures Three-Piece Puzzles

1A Tim Hardaway 2.50 6.00
1B Mitch Richmond 2.50 6.00
1C Chris Mullin 2.50 6.00
2A Bill Russell 6.00 15.00
2B Bob Cousy 5.00 12.00
2C Tom Heinsohn 2.00 5.00
3A Detlef Schrempf 2.00 5.00
3B Gary Payton 3.00 8.00
3C Shawn Kemp 3.00 8.00
4A Jeff Hornacek 1.50 4.00
4B Karl Malone 4.00 10.00
4C John Stockton 4.00 10.00
5A Dwight Howard 2.50 6.00
5B James Harden 4.00 10.00
5C Chandler Parsons 1.25 3.00
6A Carmelo Anthony 3.00 8.00
6B J.R. Smith 2.00 5.00
6C Tyson Chandler 1.50 4.00
7A Kobe Bryant 15.00 40.00
7B Pau Gasol 3.00 8.00
7C Steve Nash 4.00 10.00
8A Kevin Durant 6.00 15.00
8B Russell Westbrook 3.00 8.00
8C Serge Ibaka 1.50 4.00
9A Dion Waiters 1.25 3.00
9B Kyrie Irving 6.00 15.00
9C Anthony Bennett 1.25 3.00
10A Blake Griffin 2.00 5.00
10B Chris Paul 4.00 10.00
10C DeAndre Jordan 1.50 4.00
11A LeBron James 15.00 40.00
11B Dwyane Wade 4.00 10.00
11C Chris Bosh 2.50 6.00
12A Tony Parker 3.00 8.00
12B Tim Duncan 5.00 12.00
12C Manu Ginobili 4.00 10.00

2013-14 Timeless Treasures Time To Shine

PRINT RUNS B/WN 25-249 COPIES PER
EXCHANGE DEADLINE 6/11/2015
2 Ersan Ilyasova 4.00 10.00
3 Nicolas Batum 5.00 12.00
4 Joakim Noah EXCH 6.00 15.00
5 Maurice Harkless 4.00 10.00
7 Nikola Vucevic 8.00 20.00
8 J.R. Smith 6.00 15.00
11 Goran Dragic 15.00 40.00
13 Lance Stephenson 5.00 12.00
14 Alexey Shved 4.00 10.00
15 James Jones 4.00 10.00
16 Steve Blake 8.00 20.00
17 Jeff Green 8.00 20.00
18 Jonas Valanciunas 6.00 15.00
19 George Hill 6.00 15.00
21 Evan Fournier 5.00 12.00
22 E'Twaun Moore 4.00 10.00
23 Tyler Zeller 4.00 10.00
24 Kendall Marshall 4.00 10.00
25 Jerryd Bayless EXCH 4.00 10.00

2013-14 Timeless Treasures Timeless Signatures

PRINT RUNS B/WN 15-299 COPIES PER
EXCHANGE DEADLINE 6/11/2015
2 Norm Nixon/299 5.00 12.00
3 Nate Archibald/15 10.00 25.00
5 Scottie Pippen/25 100.00 200.00
6 Ralph Sampson/15 12.00 30.00
7 Reggie Theus/299 5.00 12.00
8 Bill Laimbeer/299 6.00 15.00
10 Spencer Haywood/299 6.00 15.00
11 Isiah Thomas/25 12.00 30.00
13 Paul Westphal/299 6.00 15.00
14 Bill Walton/15 8.00 20.00
15 Rod Strickland/299 5.00 12.00
16 Bob Dandridge/299 5.00 12.00
17 David Robinson/35 60.00 120.00
18 George Gervin/15 60.00 120.00
19 Kendall Gill/299 6.00 15.00
20 Scott Skiles/299 5.00 12.00
21 Bobby Jones/299 6.00 15.00
22 Rolando Blackman/299 5.00 12.00
23 Cedric Maxwell/299 5.00 12.00
24 Mark Aguirre/299 5.00 12.00
25 Maurice Cheeks/299 5.00 12.00
26 Gary Payton/25 12.00 30.00
27 Sidney Moncrief/299 6.00 15.00
28 Dominique Wilkins/25 10.00 25.00
29 Artis Gilmore/15 12.00 30.00
31 Jo Jo White/299 5.00 12.00
32 Sam Jones/15 15.00 40.00
34 Jason Kidd/25 40.00 80.00
35 Bailey Howell/15 6.00 15.00
36 Alonzo Mourning/25 30.00 60.00
37 Danny Manning/15 10.00 25.00
41 Kareem Abdul-Jabbar/25 50.00 100.00
42 Cazzie Russell/299 5.00 12.00
43 Jack Sikma/299 6.00 15.00
45 Lenny Wilkens/15 12.00 30.00
46 Kiki Vandeweghe/299 5.00 12.00
47 Hal Greer/15 10.00 25.00
50 Hakeem Olajuwon/25 30.00 60.00

2013-14 Timeless Treasures Timeless Talents

PRINT RUNS B/WN 23-49 COPIES PER
SOME CARDS NOT SERIAL #'d
EXCAHNGE DEADLINE 6/11/2015
3 Herb Williams 4.00 10.00
4 Michael Finley/25 15.00 40.00
9 Rick Barry/49 8.00 20.00
11 Steve Francis/25 5.00 12.00
14 Nick Van Exel/25 12.00 30.00
15 Maurice Cheeks 5.00 12.00
16 Luc Longley 5.00 12.00
17 Zydrunas Ilgauskas 5.00 12.00
18 Vin Baker 4.00 10.00
19 Tom Chambers/25 8.00 20.00
21 Jason Terry/25 5.00 12.00
23 B.J. Armstrong/25 10.00 25.00
24 Bruce Bowen 6.00 15.00
25 Grant Hill/49 10.00 25.00
26 Alonzo Mourning/25 10.00 25.00
27 Deron Williams/25 5.00 12.00
30 Harrison Barnes/25 6.00 15.00
31 Bradley Beal/25 12.00 30.00
32 Kyrie Irving/49 EXCH 50.00 120.00
34 Dan Issel 8.00 20.00
35 Joe Dumars/25 8.00 20.00
36 Sam Perkins/25 5.00 12.00
37 Len Elmore 5.00 12.00
38 Michael Cooper 6.00 15.00
39 Muggsy Bogues 6.00 15.00

2013-14 Timeless Treasures Timeless Talents Ruby

*RUBY p/r 20-25: .5X TO 1.2X BASIC
*RUBY p/r 99: .5X TO 1.2X BASIC
PRINT RUNS B/WN 10-99 COPIES PER
NO PRICING ON QTY 10
8 Dwight Howard/20 40.00 80.00

2013-14 Timeless Treasures Timeless Talents Sapphire

*SAPPHIRE 15: .5X TO 1.2X BASIC
*SAPPHIRE 75: .5X TO 1.2X BASIC
PRINT RUNS B/WN 3-75 COPIES PER
NO PRICING ON QTY 5 OR LESS

2013-14 Timeless Treasures Timeless Teams

1 Bill Laimbeer 2.00 5.00
2 Dennis Rodman 5.00 12.00
3 Isiah Thomas 3.00 8.00
4 Joe Dumars 2.50 6.00
5 Mark Aguirre 1.50 4.00
6 Danny Ainge 2.00 5.00
7 Dennis Johnson 1.50 4.00
8 Kevin McHale 3.00 8.00
9 Larry Bird 8.00 20.00
10 Robert Parish 2.50 6.00
11 A.C. Green 2.00 5.00
12 Byron Scott 2.00 5.00
13 James Worthy 2.50 6.00
14 Kareem Abdul-Jabbar 6.00 15.00
15 Magic Johnson 8.00 20.00
16 Bobby Jones 2.50 6.00
17 Julius Erving 5.00 12.00
18 Maurice Cheeks 1.50 4.00
19 Moses Malone 3.00 8.00
20 Clint Richardson 1.25 3.00
21 Ron Harper 2.00 5.00
22 Scottie Pippen 5.00 12.00
23 Steve Kerr 2.00 5.00
24 Toni Kukoc 2.50 6.00
25 Luc Longley 1.50 4.00
26 Dick Barnett 2.00 5.00
27 Walt Frazier 3.00 8.00
28 Willis Reed 3.00 8.00
29 Dave DeBusschere 2.00 5.00
30 Cazzie Russell 1.50 4.00
31 Bob Dandridge 1.50 4.00
32 Kareem Abdul-Jabbar 6.00 15.00
33 Lucius Allen 2.00 5.00
34 Oscar Robertson 3.00 8.00
35 Jon McGlocklin 1.50 4.00
36 Dwyane Wade 4.00 10.00
37 LeBron James 15.00 40.00
38 Mario Chalmers 1.50 4.00
39 Ray Allen 3.00 8.00
40 Chris Bosh 2.50 6.00
41 Bruce Bowen 1.50 4.00
42 Tim Duncan 5.00 12.00
43 Tony Parker 3.00 8.00
44 David Robinson 4.00 10.00
45 Manu Ginobili 4.00 10.00
46 Clyde Drexler 3.00 8.00
47 Hakeem Olajuwon 4.00 10.00
48 Robert Horry 2.00 5.00
49 Sam Cassell 1.50 4.00
50 Vernon Maxwell 1.50 4.00

2013-14 Timeless Treasures Treasured Ink

PRINT RUNS B/WN 15-299 COPIES PER
EXCHANGE DEADLINE 6/11/2015
1 Kobe Bryant/49 500.00 1,000.00
2 Kevin Durant/49 60.00 150.00
3 Kyrie Irving/49 30.00 80.00
4 Blake Griffin/49 12.00 30.00
5 Steve Smith/299 5.00 12.00
6 Stephen Curry/25 500.00 1,000.00
8 Nate Archibald/15 10.00 25.00
9 Karl Malone/25 15.00 40.00
10 Kareem Abdul-Jabbar/25 50.00 100.00
11 Jim Jackson/299 4.00 10.00
13 Bailey Howell/49 6.00 15.00
14 Rolando Blackman/49 5.00 12.00
15 Tom Heinsohn/49 20.00 50.00
16 Antoine Walker/299 5.00 12.00
17 Anthony Mason/299 6.00 15.00
18 Nick Van Exel/15 12.00 30.00
19 Chris Bosh/25 15.00 40.00
20 Tony Parker/15 10.00 25.00
21 Sam Jones/15 15.00 40.00
22 A.C. Green/49 6.00 15.00
23 Larry Bird/25 EXCH 40.00 100.00
24 Jerry West/25 30.00 80.00

2013-14 Timeless Treasures Treasured Picks Jerseys

1 Shane Larkin 2.00 5.00
2 Peyton Siva 2.00 5.00
3 Shabazz Muhammad 2.00 5.00
4 Kelly Olynyk 2.50 6.00
5 Anthony Bennett 2.00 5.00
6 Ryan Kelly 2.00 5.00
7 Jamaal Franklin 2.00 5.00
8 Michael Carter-Williams 2.50 6.00
9 Victor Oladipo 10.00 25.00
10 Andre Roberson 2.50 6.00
11 Mason Plumlee 2.50 6.00
12 C.J. McCollum 10.00 25.00
13 Otto Porter 3.00 8.00
14 Nate Wolters 2.00 5.00
15 Tim Hardaway Jr. 4.00 10.00
16 Trey Burke 2.50 6.00
17 Cody Zeller 2.50 6.00
18 Tony Mitchell 2.00 5.00
19 Archie Goodwin 2.00 5.00
20 Kentavious Caldwell-Pope 3.00 8.00
21 Alex Len 2.50 6.00
22 Glen Rice Jr. 2.00 5.00
23 Allen Crabbe 2.00 5.00
24 Ben McLemore 2.50 6.00
25 Nerlens Noel 2.50 6.00

2013-14 Timeless Treasures Treasured Picks Jerseys Prime

*PRIME: .75X TO 2X BASIC
STATED PRINT RUN 25 SER.#'d SETS

2013-14 Timeless Treasures Treasured Threads

1 Shaquille O'Neal 12.00 30.00
2 Grant Hill 5.00 12.00
3 Kiki Vandeweghe 2.50 6.00
4 Jeff Malone 2.50 6.00
5 Dee Brown 2.50 6.00
6 Jamal Mashburn 2.50 6.00
7 Gus Williams 2.00 5.00
8 Robert Horry 3.00 8.00
9 Mitch Richmond 4.00 10.00
10 Manute Bol 3.00 8.00
11 Karl Malone 6.00 15.00
12 Patrick Ewing 5.00 12.00
13 Tim Duncan 8.00 20.00
14 LeBron James 10.00 25.00
15 Kobe Bryant 10.00 25.00
16 Bernard King 4.00 10.00
17 Jeremy Lin 5.00 12.00
18 Reggie Lewis 10.00 25.00
19 Paul Westphal 3.00 8.00
20 Danny Manning 2.50 6.00
21 Paul Pierce 5.00 12.00
22 Manu Ginobili 6.00 15.00
23 Carmelo Anthony 5.00 12.00
24 Ray Allen 5.00 12.00
25 Dwyane Wade 6.00 15.00

2013-14 Timeless Treasures Treasured Threads Prime

*PRIME p/r 25: 1X TO 2.5X BASE
PRINT RUNS B/WN 5-25 COPIES PER
NO PRICING ON QTY 10 OR LESS

2013-14 Timeless Treasures Trophies

3 Karl Malone 60.00 150.00

2013-14 Timeless Treasures Validating Marks

KOBE PRINT RUN 75 SER.#'d SETS
EXCHANGE DEADLINE 6/11/2015
1 Kendall Marshall 4.00 10.00
2 Kenyon Martin 6.00 15.00
4 Maurice Harkless 4.00 10.00
7 Lou Amundson 4.00 10.00
12 J.J. Redick 10.00 25.00
13 Goran Dragic 5.00 12.00
15 Danny Green 5.00 12.00
16 Nikola Pekovic 4.00 10.00
17 Boris Diaw 12.00 30.00
19 Corey Brewer 4.00 10.00
21 Kendrick Perkins 4.00 10.00
22 Ekpe Udoh 4.00 10.00
23 Earl Clark 4.00 10.00
25 Mateen Cleaves 4.00 10.00
27 Kyle Lowry 6.00 15.00
29 Kevin Love 12.00 30.00
34 Nicolas Batum 8.00 20.00
35 Marcin Gortat 4.00 10.00
37 MarShon Brooks 4.00 10.00
38 Patrick Beverley 4.00 10.00
39 Eddie Johnson 4.00 10.00
40 Kobe Bryant/75 500.00 1,000.00
41 Willie Reed 4.00 10.00
42 Campy Russell 5.00 12.00
43 Justin Hamilton 4.00 10.00
44 Gus Williams 4.00 10.00
45 Kyrie Irving 30.00 80.00
46 Otis Birdsong 5.00 12.00
48 Will Bynum 4.00 10.00
49 James Johnson 4.00 10.00
50 Kevin Durant EXCH 60.00 150.00

2013-14 Timeless Treasures Validating Marks Ruby

*RUBY p/r 35-49: .5X TO 1.2X BASIC
*RUBY p/r 99: .5X TO 1.2X BASIC
PRINT RUNS B/WN 10-99 COPIES PER
NO PRICING ON QTY 10 OR LESS
EXCHANGE DEADLINE 6/11/2015

2013-14 Timeless Treasures Validating Marks Sapphire

*SAPPHIRE p/r 15-25: .5X TO 1.2X BASIC
*SAPPHIRE p/r 49: .5X TO 1.2X BASIC
PRINT RUNS B/WN 3-49 COPIES PER
NO PRICING ON QTY 5 OR LESS
EXCHANGE DEADLINE 6/11/2015
40 Kobe Bryant/25 600.00 1,200.00

1957-58 Topps

COMPLETE SET (80) 20,000.00 30,000.00
CONDITION SENSITIVE SET
CARDS PRICED IN EX-MT CONDITION
1 Nat Clifton DP RC 150.00 400.00
2 George Yardley DP RC 75.00 200.00
3 Neil Johnston DP RC 60.00 150.00
4 Carl Braun DP 30.00 50.00
5 Bill Sharman DP RC 75.00 200.00
6 George King DP RC 40.00 100.00
7 Kenny Sears DP RC 25.00 60.00
8 Dick Ricketts DP RC 15.00 40.00
9 Jack Nichols DP 15.00 40.00
10 Paul Arizin DP RC 50.00 120.00
11 Chuck Noble DP 30.00 80.00
12 Slater Martin DP RC 50.00 120.00
13 Dolph Schayes DP RC 125.00 300.00
14 Dick Atha DP 25.00 60.00
15 Frank Ramsey DP RC 40.00 100.00
16 Dick McGuire DP RC 40.00 100.00
17 Bob Cousy DP RC 800.00 1,500.00
18 Larry Foust DP RC 15.00 40.00
19 Tom Heinsohn RC 500.00 1,000.00
20 Bill Thieben DP 25.00 60.00
21 Don Meineke DP RC 15.00 40.00
22 Tom Marshall 40.00 100.00
23 Dick Garmaker 40.00 100.00
24 Bob Pettit DP RC 150.00 400.00
25 Jim Krebs DP RC 25.00 60.00
26 Gene Shue DP RC 25.00 60.00
27 Ed Macauley DP RC 50.00 120.00
28 Vern Mikkelsen RC 50.00 120.00
29 Willie Naulls RC 30.00 80.00
30 Walter Dukes DP RC 20.00 50.00
31 Dave Piontek DP 15.00 40.00

32 Johnny Red Kerr RC 50.00 120.00
33 Larry Costello DP RC 30.00 80.00
34 Woody Sauldsberry DP RC 15.00 40.00
35 Ray Felix RC 25.00 60.00
36 Ernie Beck 15.00 40.00
37 Cliff Hagan RC 60.00 150.00
38 Guy Sparrow DP 30.00 80.00
39 Jim Loscutoff RC 60.00 150.00
40 Arnie Risen DP 40.00 100.00
41 Joe Graboski 40.00 100.00
42 M.Stokes DP UER RC 60.00 150.00
43 Rod Hundley DP RC 50.00 120.00
44 Tom Gola DP RC 40.00 100.00
45 Med Park RC 20.00 50.00
46 Mel Hutchins DP 15.00 40.00
47 Larry Friend DP 12.00 30.00
48 Lennie Rosenbluth DP RC 40.00 100.00
49 Walt Davis 25.00 60.00
50 Richie Regan RC 25.00 60.00
51 Frank Selvy DP RC 40.00 100.00
52 Art Spoelstra DP 25.00 60.00
53 Bob Hopkins RC 15.00 40.00
54 Earl Lloyd RC 100.00 250.00
55 Phil Jordan DP 25.00 60.00
56 Bob Houbregs DP RC 25.00 60.00
57 Lou Tsioropoulos DP 25.00 60.00
58 Ed Conlin RC 25.00 60.00
59 Al Bianchi RC 30.00 80.00
60 George Dempsey RC 40.00 100.00
61 Chuck Share 25.00 60.00
62 Harry Gallatin DP RC 25.00 60.00
63 Bob Harrison 15.00 40.00
64 Bob Burrow DP 10.00 25.00
65 Win Wilfong DP 20.00 50.00
66 Jack McMahon DP RC 30.00 80.00
67 Jack George 40.00 100.00
68 Charlie Tyra DP 10.00 25.00
69 Ron Sobie 25.00 60.00
70 Jack Coleman 15.00 40.00
71 Jack Twyman DP RC 75.00 200.00
72 Paul Seymour RC 15.00 40.00
73 Jim Paxson DP RC 20.00 50.00
74 Bob Leonard RC 30.00 80.00
75 Andy Phillip 40.00 100.00
76 Joe Holup 25.00 60.00
77 Bill Russell RC 5,000.00 10,000.00
78 Clyde Lovellette DP RC 50.00 120.00
79 Ed Fleming DP 25.00 60.00
80 Dick Schnittker RC 40.00 100.00

1968-69 Topps Test

COMPLETE SET (22) 18,000.00 24,000.00
1 Wilt Chamberlain 3,000.00 4,000.00
2 Hal Greer 400.00 800.00
3 Chet Walker 250.00 500.00
4 Bill Russell 3,000.00 4,000.00
5 John Havlicek UER 1,600.00 2,200.00
6 Cazzie Russell 300.00 600.00
7 Willis Reed 500.00 850.00
8 Bill Bradley 500.00 850.00
9 Odie Smith 200.00 450.00
10 Dave Bing 500.00 850.00
11 Dave DeBusschere 500.00 850.00
12 Earl Monroe 500.00 850.00
13 Nate Thurmond 400.00 800.00
14 Jim King 200.00 450.00
15 Len Wilkens 500.00 900.00
16 Bill Bridges 250.00 500.00
17 Zelmo Beaty 300.00 600.00
18 Elgin Baylor 1,400.00 2,000.00
19 Jerry West 2,400.00 3,000.00
20 Jerry Sloan 600.00 900.00
21 Jerry Lucas 500.00 850.00
22 Oscar Robertson 1,500.00 2,000.00

1969-70 Topps

COMPLETE SET (99) 4,000.00 8,000.00
CONDITION SENSITIVE SET
CARDS PRICED IN EX-MT CONDITION
1 Wilt Chamberlain 200.00 500.00
2 Gail Goodrich RC 20.00 50.00
3 Cazzie Russell RC 20.00 50.00
4 Darrall Imhoff RC 6.00 15.00
5 Bailey Howell 6.00 16.00
6 Lucius Allen RC 10.00 25.00
7 Tom Boerwinkle RC 5.00 12.00
8 Jimmy Walker RC 5.00 12.00
9 John Block RC 5.00 12.00
10 Nate Thurmond RC 50.00 120.00
11 Gary Gregor 3.00 8.00
12 Gus Johnson RC 12.00 30.00
13 Luther Rackley 4.00 10.00
14 Jon McGlocklin RC 12.00 30.00
15 Connie Hawkins RC 25.00 60.00
16 Johnny Egan 8.00 20.00
17 Jim Washington 4.00 10.00
18 Dick Barnett RC 15.00 40.00
19 Tom Meschery 8.00 20.00
20 John Havlicek RC 75.00 200.00
21 Eddie Miles 10.00 25.00
22 Walt Wesley 3.00 8.00
23 Rick Adelman RC 5.00 12.00
24 Al Attles 3.00 8.00
25 Lew Alcindor RC 1,000.00 2,000.00
26 Jack Marin RC 3.00 8.00
27 Walt Hazzard RC 8.00 20.00
28 Connie Dierking 5.00 12.00
29 Keith Erickson RC 8.00 20.00
30 Bob Rule RC 8.00 20.00
31 Dick Van Arsdale RC 8.00 20.00
32 Archie Clark RC 4.00 10.00
33 Terry Dischinger RC 6.00 15.00
34 Henry Finkel RC 5.00 12.00
35 Elgin Baylor 30.00 80.00
36 Ron Williams 10.00 25.00
37 Loy Petersen 6.00 15.00
38 Guy Rodgers 3.00 8.00
39 Toby Kimball 6.00 15.00
40 Billy Cunningham RC 25.00 60.00
41 Joe Caldwell RC 5.00 12.00
42 Leroy Ellis RC 5.00 12.00
43 Bill Bradley RC 30.00 80.00
44 Len Wilkens UER 20.00 50.00
45 Jerry Lucas RC 50.00 120.00
46 Neal Walk RC 8.00 20.00
47 Emmette Bryant RC 2.50 6.00
48 Bob Kauffman RC 8.00 20.00
49 Mel Counts RC 4.00 10.00
50 Oscar Robertson 50.00 120.00
51 Jim Barnett RC 5.00 12.00
52 Don Smith 3.00 8.00
53 Jim Davis 5.00 12.00
54 Wally Jones RC 6.00 15.00
55 Dave Bing RC 25.00 60.00
56 Wes Unseld RC 25.00 60.00
57 Joe Ellis 3.00 8.00
58 John Tresvant 3.00 8.00
59 Larry Siegfried RC 5.00 12.00
60 Willis Reed RC 60.00 150.00
61 Paul Silas RC 8.00 20.00
62 Bob Weiss RC 8.00 20.00
63 Willie McCarter 1.50 4.00
64 Don Kojis RC 1.50 4.00
65 Lou Hudson RC 8.00 20.00
66 Jim King 1.50 4.00
67 Luke Jackson RC 2.50 6.00
68 Len Chappell RC 2.50 6.00
69 Ray Scott 2.50 6.00
70 Jeff Mullins RC 4.00 10.00
71 Howie Komives 1.50 4.00
72 Tom Sanders RC 5.00 12.00
73 Dick Snyder 8.00 20.00
74 Dave Stallworth RC 15.00 40.00
75 Elvin Hayes RC 50.00 120.00
76 Art Harris 1.50 4.00
77 Don Ohl 2.50 6.00
78 Bob Love RC 12.00 30.00
79 Tom Van Arsdale RC 12.00 30.00
80 Earl Monroe RC 40.00 100.00
81 Greg Smith 2.50 6.00
82 Don Nelson RC 15.00 40.00
83 Happy Hairston RC 6.00 15.00
84 Hal Greer 25.00 60.00
85 Dave DeBusschere RC 25.00 60.00
86 Bill Bridges RC 3.00 8.00
87 Herm Gilliam RC 2.50 6.00
88 Jim Fox 2.50 6.00
89 Bob Boozer 2.50 6.00
90 Jerry West 50.00 120.00
91 Chet Walker RC 6.00 15.00
92 Flynn Robinson RC 3.00 8.00
93 Clyde Lee 4.00 10.00
94 Kevin Loughery RC 8.00 20.00
95 Walt Bellamy 8.00 20.00
96 Art Williams 8.00 20.00
97 Adrian Smith RC 6.00 15.00
98 Walt Frazier RC 60.00 150.00
99 Checklist 1-99 60.00 150.00

1969-70 Topps Rulers

COMPLETE SET (23) 400.00 800.00
1 Walt Bellamy 20.00 50.00
2 Jerry West 75.00 200.00
3 Bailey Howell 20.00 50.00
4 Elvin Hayes 75.00 200.00
5 Bob Rule 15.00 40.00
6 Gail Goodrich 25.00 60.00
7 Jeff Mullins 8.00 20.00
9 John Havlicek 100.00 250.00
10 Lew Alcindor 400.00 800.00
11 Wilt Chamberlain 200.00 500.00
12 Nate Thurmond 20.00 50.00
13 Hal Greer 20.00 50.00
14 Lou Hudson 12.00 30.00
15 Jerry Lucas 15.00 40.00
16 Dave Bing 20.00 50.00
17 Walt Frazier 75.00 200.00
18 Gus Johnson 25.00 60.00
19 Willis Reed 40.00 100.00
20 Earl Monroe 40.00 100.00
21 Billy Cunningham 20.00 50.00
22 Wes Unseld 40.00 100.00
23 Bob Boozer 8.00 20.00
24 Oscar Robertson 100.00 250.00

1970-71 Topps

COMPLETE SET (175) 1,250.00 2,500.00
1 Alcind/West/Hayes LL ! 25.00 60.00
2 West/Alcin/Hayes LL SP 25.00 60.00
3 Green/Imhoff/Hudson LL 2.00 5.00
4 Rob/Walker/Mull LL SP ! 8.00 20.00
5 Hayes/Uns/Alcindor LL 25.00 60.00
6 Wilkens/Fraz/Hask LL SP 8.00 20.00
7 Bill Bradley 10.00 25.00
8 Ron Williams 1.50 4.00
9 Otto Moore 3.00 8.00
10 John Havlicek SP ! 25.00 60.00
11 George Wilson RC 5.00 12.00
12 John Trapp 1.00 2.50
13 Pat Riley RC 25.00 60.00
14 Jim Washington 1.50 4.00
15 Bob Rule 1.50 4.00
16 Bob Weiss 1.50 4.00
17 Neil Johnson 1.00 2.50
18 Walt Bellamy 5.00 12.00
19 McCoy McLemore 3.00 8.00
20 Earl Monroe 6.00 15.00
21 Wally Anderzunas 1.00 2.50
22 Guy Rodgers 1.50 4.00
23 Rick Roberson 1.00 2.50
24 Checklist 1-110 15.00 40.00
25 Jimmy Walker 4.00 10.00
26 Mike Riordan RC 4.00 10.00
27 Henry Finkel 1.00 2.50
28 Joe Ellis 1.00 2.50
29 Mike Davis 2.50 6.00
30 Lou Hudson 6.00 15.00
31 Lucius Allen SP 15.00 40.00
32 Toby Kimball SP 4.00 10.00
33 Luke Jackson SP 4.00 10.00
34 Johnny Egan 3.00 8.00
35 Leroy Ellis SP 4.00 10.00
36 Jack Marin SP 8.00 20.00
37 Joe Caldwell SP 4.00 10.00
38 Keith Erickson 2.50 6.00
39 Don Smith 1.00 2.50
40 Flynn Robinson 1.50 4.00
41 Bob Boozer 1.00 2.50
42 Howie Komives 4.00 10.00
43 Dick Barnett 3.00 8.00
44 Stu Lantz RC 1.50 4.00
45 Dick Van Arsdale 2.50 6.00
46 Jerry Lucas 6.00 15.00
47 Don Chaney RC 5.00 12.00
48 Ray Scott 1.00 2.50
49 Dick Cunningham SP 8.00 20.00
50 Wilt Chamberlain 75.00 200.00
51 Kevin Loughery 1.50 4.00
52 Stan McKenzie 1.00 2.50
53 Fred Foster 1.00 2.50
54 Jim Davis 1.00 2.50
55 Walt Wesley 1.00 2.50
56 Bill Hewitt 1.00 2.50
57 Darrall Imhoff 1.00 2.50
58 John Block 1.00 2.50
59 Al Attles SP 5.00 12.00
60 Chet Walker 2.50 6.00
61 Luther Rackley 1.00 2.50
62 Jerry Chambers SP RC 8.00 20.00
63 Bob Dandridge RC 15.00 40.00
64 Dick Snyder 1.00 2.50
65 Elgin Baylor 15.00 40.00
66 Connie Dierking 1.00 2.50
67 Steve Kuberski RC 1.00 2.50
68 Tom Boerwinkle 1.00 2.50
69 Paul Silas 3.00 8.00
70 Elvin Hayes 15.00 40.00
71 Bill Bridges 1.50 4.00
72 Wes Unseld 6.00 15.00
73 Herm Gilliam 1.00 2.50
74 Bobby Smith SP RC 4.00 10.00
75 Lew Alcindor 125.00 300.00
76 Jeff Mullins 5.00 12.00
77 Happy Hairston 1.50 4.00
78 Dave Stallworth SP 3.00 8.00
79 Fred Hetzel 1.00 2.50
80 Len Wilkens SP 10.00 25.00
81 Johnny Green RC 4.00 10.00
82 Erwin Mueller 1.00 2.50
83 Wally Jones 8.00 20.00
84 Bob Love 3.00 8.00
85 Dick Garrett RC 1.00 2.50
86 Don Nelson SP 10.00 25.00
87 Neal Walk SP 3.00 8.00
88 Larry Siegfried 1.00 2.50
89 Gary Gregor 1.00 2.50
90 Nate Thurmond 3.00 8.00
91 John Warren 2.00 5.00
92 Gus Johnson 6.00 15.00
93 Gail Goodrich 6.00 15.00
94 Dorie Murrey 1.00 2.50
95 Cazzie Russell SP 20.00 50.00
96 Terry Dischinger 1.00 2.50
97 Norm Van Lier SP RC 8.00 20.00
98 Jim Fox 1.00 2.50
99 Tom Meschery 2.00 5.00
100 Oscar Robertson 30.00 80.00
101A Checklist 111-175 12.00 30.00
101B Checklist 111-175 12.00 30.00
102 Rich Johnson 2.00 5.00
103 Mel Counts 1.50 4.00
104 Bill Hosket SP RC 12.00 30.00
105 Archie Clark 1.50 4.00
106 Walt Frazier AS 8.00 20.00
107 Jerry West AS 30.00 80.00
108 Billy Cunningham AS SP 5.00 12.00
109 Connie Hawkins AS 5.00 12.00
110 Willis Reed AS 8.00 20.00
111 Nate Thurmond AS 2.00 5.00
112 John Havlicek AS 12.00 30.00
113 Elgin Baylor AS 12.00 30.00
114 Oscar Robertson AS 15.00 40.00
115 Lou Hudson AS 1.25 3.00
116 Emmette Bryant 1.25 3.00
117 Greg Howard 1.25 3.00
118 Rick Adelman 3.00 8.00
119 Barry Clemens 1.25 3.00
120 Walt Frazier 15.00 40.00
121 Jim Barnes RC 1.25 3.00
122 Bernie Williams 1.25 3.00
123 Pete Maravich RC 300.00 600.00
124 Matt Guokas RC 3.00 8.00
125 Dave Bing 6.00 15.00
126 John Tresvant 1.25 3.00
127 Shaler Halimon 1.25 3.00
128 Don Ohl 1.25 3.00
129 Fred Carter RC 2.50 6.00
130 Connie Hawkins 8.00 20.00
131 Jim King 1.25 3.00
132 Ed Manning RC 2.50 6.00
133 Adrian Smith 1.25 3.00
134 Walt Hazzard 3.00 8.00
135 Dave DeBusschere 6.00 15.00
136 Don Kojis 1.25 3.00
137 Calvin Murphy RC 15.00 40.00
138 Nate Bowman 1.25 3.00
139 Jon McGlocklin 2.00 5.00
140 Billy Cunningham 10.00 25.00
141 Willie McCarter 1.25 3.00
142 Jim Barnett 1.25 3.00
143 Jo Jo White RC 25.00 60.00
144 Clyde Lee 1.25 3.00
145 Tom Van Arsdale 2.50 6.00
146 Len Chappell 2.00 5.00
147 Lee Winfield 1.25 3.00
148 Jerry Sloan RC 12.00 30.00
149 Art Harris 2.50 6.00
150 Willis Reed 12.00 30.00
151 Art Williams 1.25 3.00
152 Don May 2.00 5.00
153 Loy Petersen 2.00 5.00
154 Dave Gambee 2.00 5.00
155 Hal Greer 2.50 6.00
156 Dave Newmark 1.25 3.00
157 Jimmy Collins 1.25 3.00
158 Bill Turner 1.25 3.00
159 Eddie Miles 1.25 3.00
160 Jerry West 40.00 100.00
161 Bob Quick 1.25 3.00
162 Fred Crawford 1.25 3.00
163 Tom Sanders 2.50 6.00
164 Dale Schlueter 1.25 3.00
165 Clem Haskins RC 5.00 12.00
166 Greg Smith 1.25 3.00
167 Rod Thorn RC 3.00 8.00
168 Willis Reed PO 12.00 30.00
169 Dick Garrett PO 2.00 5.00
170 Dave DeBusschere PO 5.00 12.00
171 Jerry West PO 8.00 20.00
172 Bill Bradley PO 8.00 20.00
173 Wilt Chamberlain PO 12.00 30.00
174 Walt Frazier PO 5.00 12.00
175 Knicks Celebrate 8.00 20.00

1970-71 Topps Poster

COMPLETE SET (24) 100.00 250.00
1 Walt Frazier 10.00 25.00
2 Joe Caldwell 3.00 8.00
3 Willis Reed 8.00 20.00
4 Elvin Hayes 8.00 20.00
5 Jeff Mullins 3.00 8.00
6 Oscar Robertson 12.00 30.00
7 Dave Bing 8.00 20.00
8 Jerry Sloan 6.00 15.00
9 Leroy Ellis 4.00 10.00
10 Hal Greer 8.00 20.00
11 Emmette Bryant 3.00 8.00
12 Bob Rule 5.00 12.00
13 Lew Alcindor 20.00 50.00
14 Chet Walker 4.00 10.00
15 Jerry West 15.00 40.00
16 Billy Cunningham 6.00 15.00
17 Wilt Chamberlain 15.00 40.00
18 John Havlicek 12.00 30.00
19 Lou Hudson 3.00 8.00
20 Earl Monroe 8.00 20.00
21 Wes Unseld 6.00 15.00
22 Connie Hawkins 8.00 20.00
23 Tom Van Arsdale 4.00 10.00
24 Len Chappell 4.00 10.00

1971-72 Topps

COMPLETE SET (233) 2,000.00 4,000.00
CARDS PRICED IN NM CONDITION
1 Oscar Robertson ! 50.00 120.00
2 Bill Bradley 6.00 15.00
3 Jim Fox .60 1.50
4 John Johnson RC .75 2.00
5 Luke Jackson .75 2.00
6 Don May DP .60 1.50
7 Kevin Loughery .75 2.00
8 Terry Dischinger .60 1.50
9 Neal Walk .75 2.00
10 Elgin Baylor 8.00 20.00
11 Rick Adelman .75 2.00
12 Clyde Lee 1.25 3.00
13 Jerry Chambers .60 1.50
14 Fred Carter .75 2.00
15 Tom Boerwinkle DP 1.25 3.00
16 John Block .60 1.50
17 Dick Barnett .60 1.50
18 Henry Finkel .60 1.50
19 Norm Van Lier 4.00 10.00
20 Spencer Haywood RC 50.00 120.00
21 George Johnson .60 1.50
22 Bobby Lewis .60 1.50
23 Bill Hewitt 1.00 2.50
24 Walt Hazzard DP 1.50 4.00
25 Happy Hairston .75 2.00
26 George Wilson .60 1.50
27 Lucius Allen .75 2.00
28 Jim Washington .60 1.50
29 Nate Archibald RC 40.00 100.00
30 Willis Reed 12.00 30.00
31 Erwin Mueller .60 1.50
32 Art Harris .60 1.50
33 Pete Cross .75 2.00
34 Geoff Petrie RC 2.00 5.00
35 John Havlicek 15.00 40.00
36 Larry Siegfried .60 1.50
37 John Tresvant DP .60 1.50
38 Ron Williams .60 1.50
39 Lamar Green DP .75 2.00
40 Bob Rule DP .75 2.00
41 Jim McMillian RC .75 2.00
42 Wally Jones .75 2.00
43 Bob Boozer .60 1.50
44 Eddie Miles .60 1.50
45 Bob Love DP 2.00 5.00
46 Claude English .60 1.50
47 Dave Cowens RC 20.00 50.00
48 Emmette Bryant .60 1.50
49 Dave Stallworth .75 2.00
50 Jerry West 25.00 60.00
51 Joe Ellis .60 1.50
52 Walt Wesley DP .60 1.50
53 Howie Komives .60 1.50
54 Paul Silas 1.50 4.00
55 Pete Maravich DP 50.00 120.00
56 Gary Gregor .60 1.50
57 Sam Lacey RC 1.50 4.00
58 Calvin Murphy DP 2.50 6.00
59 Bob Dandridge .75 2.00
60 Hal Greer 1.50 4.00
61 Keith Erickson 1.50 4.00
62 Joe Cooke .60 1.50
63 Bob Lanier RC 20.00 50.00
64 Don Kojis 2.00 5.00
65 Walt Frazier 5.00 12.00
66 Chet Walker DP 1.50 4.00
67 Dick Garrett .60 1.50
68 John Trapp .75 2.00
69 Jo Jo White 3.00 8.00
70 Wilt Chamberlain 75.00 200.00
71 Dave Sorenson .60 1.50
72 Jim King .60 1.50
73 Cazzie Russell 2.00 5.00
74 Jon McGlocklin .75 2.00
75 Tom Van Arsdale 3.00 8.00
76 Dale Schlueter .60 1.50
77 Gus Johnson DP 1.50 4.00
78 Dave Bing 4.00 10.00
79 Billy Cunningham 3.00 8.00
80 Len Wilkens 12.00 30.00
81 Jerry Lucas DP 2.00 5.00
82 Don Chaney 1.50 4.00
83 McCoy McLemore .60 1.50
84 Bob Kauffman DP .60 1.50
85 Dick Van Arsdale 2.50 6.00
86 Johnny Green .75 2.00
87 Jerry Sloan 3.00 8.00
88 Luther Rackley DP .60 1.50
89 Shaler Halimon .60 1.50
90 Jimmy Walker .75 2.00
91 Rudy Tomjanovich RC 15.00 40.00
92 Levi Fontaine .60 1.50
93 Bobby Smith .75 2.00
94 Bob Arnzen .60 1.50
95 Wes Unseld DP 10.00 25.00
96 Clem Haskins DP 1.50 4.00
97 Jim Davis .60 1.50
98 Steve Kuberski .60 1.50
99 Mike Davis DP .60 1.50
100 Lew Alcindor 100.00 250.00
101 Willie McCarter .60 1.50
102 Charlie Paulk 1.25 3.00
103 Lee Winfield .60 1.50
104 Jim Barnett .60 1.50
105 Connie Hawkins DP 2.50 6.00
106 Archie Clark DP 2.50 6.00
107 Dave DeBusschere 2.50 6.00
108 Stu Lantz DP .75 2.00
109 Don Smith .60 1.50
110 Lou Hudson 4.00 10.00
111 Leroy Ellis .60 1.50
112 Jack Marin .75 2.00
113 Matt Guokas .75 2.00
114 Don Nelson 3.00 8.00
115 Jeff Mullins DP .75 2.00
116 Walt Bellamy 2.50 6.00
117 Bob Quick .60 1.50
118 John Warren .60 1.50
119 Barry Clemens .60 1.50
120 Elvin Hayes DP 3.00 8.00
121 Gail Goodrich 15.00 40.00
122 Ed Manning .75 2.00
123 Herm Gilliam DP .60 1.50
124 Dennis Awtrey RC .75 2.00
125 John Hummer DP .60 1.50
126 Mike Riordan .75 2.00
127 Mel Counts .60 1.50
128 Bob Weiss DP .60 1.50
129 Greg Smith DP .60 1.50
130 Earl Monroe 6.00 15.00
131 Nate Thurmond DP 1.50 4.00
132 Bill Bridges DP .75 2.00
133 Lew Alcindor PO 10.00 25.00
134 NBA Playoffs G2 1.50 4.00
135 Bob Dandridge PO 1.50 4.00
136 Oscar Robertson PO 2.50 6.00
137 Oscar Robertson PO 5.00 12.00
138 Alcind/Hayes/Havl LL 10.00 25.00
139 Alcind/Havl/Hayes LL 10.00 25.00
140 Green/Alcind/Wilt LL 10.00 25.00
141 Walker/Oscar/Williams LL 8.00 20.00
142 Wilt/Hayes/Alcind LL 10.00 25.00
143 Van Lier/Oscar/West LL 8.00 20.00
144A NBA Checklist 1-144 6.00 15.00
144B NBA Checklist 1-144 6.00 15.00
145 ABA Checklist 145-233 6.00 15.00
146 Issel/Brisker/Scott LL 2.50 6.00
147 Issel/Barry/Brisker LL 4.00 10.00
148 ABA 2pt FG Pct Leaders 1.50 4.00
149 Barry/Carrier/Keller LL 3.00 8.00
150 ABA Rebound Leaders 1.50 4.00
151 ABA Assist Leaders 1.50 4.00
152 Larry Brown RC 8.00 20.00
153 Bob Bedell .75 2.00
154 Merv Jackson .75 2.00
155 Joe Caldwell 1.00 2.50
156 Billy Paultz RC 2.00 5.00
157 Les Hunter 1.00 2.50
158 Charlie Williams .75 2.00
159 Stew Johnson .75 2.00
160 Mack Calvin RC 2.00 5.00
161 Don Sidle .75 2.00
162 Mike Barrett .75 2.00
163 Tom Workman .75 2.00
164 Joe Hamilton 1.00 2.50
165 Zelmo Beaty RC 4.00 10.00
166 Dan Hester .75 2.00
167 Bob Verga .75 2.00
168 Wilbert Jones .75 2.00
169 Skeeter Swift .75 2.00
170 Rick Barry RC 30.00 80.00
171 Billy Keller RC 1.50 4.00
172 Ron Franz .75 2.00
173 Roland Taylor RC 1.00 2.50
174 Julian Hammond .75 2.00
175 Steve Jones RC 2.50 6.00
176 Gerald Govan 1.00 2.50
177 Darel Carrier RC 1.00 2.50
178 Ron Boone RC 2.50 6.00
179 George Peeples .75 2.00
180 John Brisker 1.00 2.50
181 Doug Moe RC 2.50 6.00
182 Ollie Taylor .75 2.00
183 Bob Netolicky RC 1.00 2.50
184 Sam Robinson .75 2.00
185 James Jones 2.50 6.00
186 Julius Keye 1.00 2.50
187 Wayne Hightower .75 2.00
188 Warren Armstrong RC 1.00 2.50
189 Mike Lewis .75 2.00
190 Charlie Scott RC 25.00 60.00
191 Jim Ard .75 2.00
192 George Lehmann .75 2.00
193 Ira Harge .75 2.00
194 Willie Wise RC 2.00 5.00
195 Mel Daniels RC 8.00 20.00
196 Larry Cannon .75 2.00
197 Jim Eakins 1.00 2.50
198 Rich Jones 1.00 2.50
199 Bill Melchionni RC 1.50 4.00
200 Dan Issel RC 20.00 50.00
201 George Stone .75 2.00
202 George Thompson .75 2.00
203 Craig Raymond .75 2.00
204 Freddie Lewis RC 1.00 2.50
205 George Carter 1.00 2.50
206 Lonnie Wright .75 2.00
207 Cincy Powell 1.00 2.50
208 Larry Miller 1.00 2.50
209 Sonny Dove 1.00 2.50
210 Byron Beck RC 1.00 2.50
211 John Beasley .75 2.00
212 Lee Davis .75 2.00
213 Rick Mount RC 2.50 6.00
214 Walt Simon .75 2.00
215 Glen Combs 1.50 4.00
216 Neil Johnson .75 2.00
217 Manny Leaks 2.00 5.00
218 Chuck Williams 1.50 4.00
219 Warren Davis .75 2.00
220 Donnie Freeman RC 1.00 2.50
221 Randy Mahaffey .75 2.00
222 John Barnhill .75 2.00
223 Al Cueto .75 2.00
224 Louie Dampier RC 10.00 25.00
225 Roger Brown RC 12.00 30.00
226 Joe DePre .75 2.00
227 Ray Scott .75 2.00
228 Arvesta Kelly .75 2.00
229 Vann Williford .75 2.00
230 Larry Jones 1.00 2.50
231 Gene Moore .75 2.00
232 Ralph Simpson RC 1.50 4.00
233 Red Robbins RC 2.00 5.00

1971-72 Topps Trios

COMPLETE SET (26) 200.00 400.00
1 Hudson/Rule/Murphy 4.00 10.00
1A Jones/Wise/Issel SP 8.00 20.00
4 Wesley/White/Dand 3.00 8.00
4A Calvin/Brown/Verga SP 4.00 10.00
7 Thurm/Monroe/Hay 5.00 10.00
7A Melch/Daniels/Freem SP 4.00 10.00
10 DeBuss/Lanier/Van Ars 6.00 15.00
10A Cald/Dampier/Lewis SP 4.00 10.00
13 Greer/Green/Hayes 5.00 12.00
13A Barry/Jones/Keye SP 15.00 40.00
16 Walker/May/Clark 1.50 4.00
16A Cannon/Beaty/Scott SP 3.00 8.00
19 Hairston/Ellis/Sloan 4.00 10.00
19A Jones/Carter/Brisk SP 4.00 10.00
22 Maravich/Kauf/Hav 30.00 80.00
22A ABA Team DP 1.50 4.00
23A ABA Team SP 15.00 40.00
24A ABA Team SP 15.00 40.00
25 Frazier/Van Arsd/Bing 8.00 20.00
28 Love/Williams/Cowens 8.00 20.00
31 West/Reed/Walker 25.00 60.00
34 Rober/Unsel/Smith SP 15.00 40.00
37 Hawk/Mullins/Alcin 30.00 80.00
40 Cunn/Bellamy/Petrie SP 6.00 15.00
43 Cham/Johns/Van L SP 25.00 60.00
46 NBA Team OP 1.25 3.00

1972-73 Topps

COMPLETE SET (264) 1,000.00 2,000.00
CARDS PRICED IN NM CONDITION
1 Wilt Chamberlain ! 50.00 120.00
2 Stan Love 1.25 3.00
3 Geoff Petrie 1.25 3.00
4 Curtis Perry RC .40 1.00
5 Pete Maravich 40.00 100.00
6 Gus Johnson 1.25 3.00
7 Dave Cowens 6.00 15.00
8 Randy Smith RC 1.50 4.00
9 Matt Guokas .60 1.50
10 Spencer Haywood 1.50 4.00
11 Jerry Sloan 1.25 3.00
12 Dave Sorenson .40 1.00
13 Howie Komives .40 1.00
14 Joe Ellis .40 1.00
15 Jerry Lucas 2.00 5.00
16 Stu Lantz .60 1.50
17 Bill Bridges .60 1.50
18 Leroy Ellis .40 1.00
19 Art Williams .40 1.00
20 Sidney Wicks RC 3.00 8.00
21 Wes Unseld 2.50 6.00
22 Jim Washington .40 1.00
23 Fred Hilton .40 1.00
24 Curtis Rowe RC .60 1.50
25 Oscar Robertson 20.00 50.00
26 Larry Steele RC .60 1.50
27 Charlie Davis .40 1.00
28 Nate Thurmond 2.00 5.00
29 Fred Carter .60 1.50
30 Connie Hawkins 3.00 8.00
31 Calvin Murphy 2.00 5.00
32 Phil Jackson RC 40.00 100.00
33 Lee Winfield .40 1.00
34 Jim Fox .40 1.00
35 Dave Bing 2.50 6.00
36 Gary Gregor .40 1.00
37 Mike Riordan .60 1.50
38 George Trapp .40 1.00
39 Mike Davis .40 1.00
40 Bob Rule .40 1.00
41 John Block .40 1.00
42 Bob Dandridge .60 1.50
43 John Johnson .60 1.50
44 Rick Barry 8.00 20.00
45 Jo Jo White 1.50 4.00
46 Cliff Meely .40 1.00
47 Charlie Scott 1.25 3.00
48 Johnny Green .60 1.50
49 Pete Cross .40 1.00
50 Gail Goodrich 2.50 6.00
51 Jim Davis .40 1.00
52 Dick Barnett .60 1.50
53 Bob Christian .40 1.00
54 Jon McGlocklin .40 1.00
55 Paul Silas 1.25 3.00
56 Hal Greer 1.50 4.00
57 Barry Clemens .40 1.00
58 Nick Jones .40 1.00
59 Cornell Warner .40 1.00
60 Walt Frazier 12.00 30.00
61 Dorie Murrey .40 1.00
62 Dick Cunningham .40 1.00
63 Sam Lacey .60 1.50
64 John Warren .60 1.50
65 Tom Boerwinkle .60 1.50
66 Fred Foster .40 1.00
67 Mel Counts .40 1.00
68 Toby Kimball .40 1.00
69 Dale Schlueter .40 1.00
70 Jack Marin .60 1.50
71 Jim Barnett .40 1.00
72 Clem Haskins 1.25 3.00
73 Earl Monroe 8.00 20.00
74 Tom Sanders 2.00 5.00
75 Jerry West 30.00 80.00
76 Elmore Smith RC .60 1.50
77 Don Adams .60 1.50
78 Wally Jones .60 1.50
79 Tom Van Arsdale .60 1.50
80 Bob Lanier 8.00 20.00
81 Len Wilkens 4.00 10.00
82 Neal Walk .60 1.50
83 Kevin Loughery .60 1.50
84 Stan McKenzie .60 1.50
85 Jeff Mullins .60 1.50
86 Otto Moore .40 1.00
87 John Tresvant .40 1.00
88 Dean Meminger RC .40 1.00
89 Jim McMillian .60 1.50
90 Austin Carr RC 3.00 8.00
91 Clifford Ray RC .60 1.50
92 Don Nelson 1.50 4.00
93 Mahdi Abdul-Rahman .60 1.50
94 Willie Norwood .40 1.00
95 Dick Van Arsdale .60 1.50
96 Don May .40 1.00
97 Walt Bellamy 1.50 4.00
98 Garfield Heard RC 1.50 4.00
99 Dave Wohl .40 1.00
100 Kareem Abdul-Jabbar 60.00 150.00
101 Ron Knight .40 1.00
102 Phil Chenier RC 1.50 4.00
103 Rudy Tomjanovich 3.00 8.00
104 Flynn Robinson .40 1.00
105 Dave DeBusschere 2.50 6.00
106 Dennis Layton .40 1.00
107 Bill Hewitt .40 1.00
108 Dick Garrett .40 1.00
109 Walt Wesley .40 1.00
110 John Havlicek 15.00 40.00
111 Norm Van Lier 8.00 20.00
112 Cazzie Russell 1.25 3.00
113 Herm Gilliam 1.25 3.00
114 Greg Smith .40 1.00
115 Nate Archibald 8.00 20.00
116 Don Kojis .40 1.00
117 Rick Adelman .60 1.50
118 Luke Jackson .60 1.50
119 Lamar Green .40 1.00
120 Archie Clark .60 1.50
121 Happy Hairston .60 1.50
122 Bill Bradley 6.00 15.00
123 Ron Williams .40 1.00
124 Jimmy Walker .60 1.50
125 Bob Kauffman .40 1.00
126 Rick Roberson .60 1.50
127 Howard Porter RC .60 1.50
128 Mike Newlin RC .60 1.50
129 Willis Reed 8.00 20.00
130 Lou Hudson 1.25 3.00
131 Don Chaney 1.25 3.00
132 Dave Stallworth .40 1.00
133 Charlie Yelverton .40 1.00
134 Ken Durrett .40 1.00
135 John Brisker .60 1.50
136 Dick Snyder .40 1.00
137 Jim McDaniels .40 1.00
138 Clyde Lee .40 1.00
139 Dennis Awtrey UER .40 1.00
140 Keith Erickson .60 1.50
141 Bob Weiss .60 1.50
142 Butch Beard RC 1.25 3.00
143 Terry Dischinger .40 1.00
144 Pat Riley 12.00 30.00
145 Lucius Allen .60 1.50
146 John Mengelt RC .40 1.00
147 John Hummer .40 1.00
148 Bob Love 2.00 5.00
149 Bobby Smith .60 1.50
150 Elvin Hayes 6.00 15.00
151 Nate Williams .40 1.00
152 Chet Walker 1.25 3.00
153 Steve Kuberski .40 1.00
154 Earl Monroe PO 4.00 10.00
155 NBA Playoffs G2 1.25 3.00
156 NBA Playoffs G3 1.25 3.00
157 NBA Playoffs G4 1.25 3.00
158 Jerry West PO 6.00 15.00
159 Wilt Chamberlain PO 12.00 30.00
160 NBA Checklist 1-176 6.00 15.00
161 John Havlicek AS 5.00 12.00
162 Spencer Haywood AS 15.00 40.00
163 Kareem Abdul-Jabbar AS 15.00 40.00
164 Jerry West AS 10.00 25.00
165 Walt Frazier AS 2.00 5.00
166 Bob Love AS 1.25 3.00
167 Billy Cunningham AS 1.50 4.00
168 Wilt Chamberlain AS 30.00 80.00
169 Nate Archibald AS 2.00 5.00
170 Archie Clark AS 1.25 3.00
171 Jabbar/Havl/Arch LL 12.00 30.00
172 Jabbar/Arch/Havl LL 12.00 30.00
173 Wilt/Jabbar/Bell LL 12.00 30.00
174 Marin/Murphy/Goodr LL 3.00 8.00
175 Wilt/Jabbar/Unseld LL 15.00 40.00
176 Wilkens/West/Arch LL 8.00 20.00
177 Roland Taylor .60 1.50
178 Art Becker .60 1.50
179 Mack Calvin .75 2.00
180 Artis Gilmore RC 20.00 50.00
181 Collis Jones .60 1.50
182 John Roche RC .75 2.00
183 George McGinnis RC 30.00 80.00
184 Johnny Neumann .75 2.00
185 Willie Wise .75 2.00
186 Bernie Williams .60 1.50
187 Byron Beck .75 2.00
188 Larry Miller .75 2.00
189 Cincy Powell .60 1.50
190 Donnie Freeman .75 2.00
191 John Baum .60 1.50
192 Billy Keller .75 2.00
193 Wilbert Jones .60 1.50
194 Glen Combs .60 1.50
195 Julius Erving RC 300.00 600.00
196 Al Smith .60 1.50
197 George Carter .60 1.50
198 Louie Dampier 1.25 3.00
199 Rich Jones .60 1.50
200 Mel Daniels 1.25 3.00
201 Gene Moore .60 1.50
202 Randy Denton .60 1.50
203 Larry Jones .60 1.50
204 Jim Ligon .60 1.50
205 Warren Jabali .75 2.00
206 Joe Caldwell .75 2.00
207 Darel Carrier .75 2.00
208 Gene Kennedy .60 1.50
209 Ollie Taylor .60 1.50
210 Roger Brown .75 2.00
211 George Lehmann .60 1.50
212 Red Robbins .75 2.00
213 Jim Eakins .75 2.00

214 Willie Long .60 1.50
215 Billy Cunningham 4.00 10.00
216 Steve Jones .75 2.00
217 Les Hunter .60 1.50
218 Billy Paultz .75 2.00
219 Freddie Lewis .75 2.00
220 Zelmo Beaty .75 2.00
221 George Thompson .60 1.50
222 Neil Johnson .60 1.50
223 Dave Robisch RC 6.00 15.00
224 Walt Simon .60 1.50
225 Bill Melchionni .75 2.00
226 Wendell Ladner RC .75 2.00
227 Joe Hamilton 4.00 10.00
228 Bob Netolicky .75 2.00
229 James Jones .75 2.00
230 Dan Issel 8.00 20.00
231 Charlie Williams .60 1.50
232 Willie Sojourner .60 1.50
233 Merv Jackson .60 1.50
234 Mike Lewis .60 1.50
235 Ralph Simpson .75 2.00
236 Darnell Hillman .75 2.00
237 Rick Mount 1.25 3.00
238 Gerald Govan .60 1.50
239 Ron Boone .75 2.00
240 Tom Washington 2.00 5.00
241 ABA Playoffs G1 1.25 3.00
242 Rick Barry PO 8.00 20.00
243 George McGinnis PO 4.00 10.00
244 Rick Barry PO 8.00 20.00
245 Billy Keller PO 1.25 3.00
246 ABA Playoffs G6
Tight Defense 4.00 10.00
247 ABA Champs: Pacers 1.25 3.00
248 ABA Checklist 177-264 6.00 15.00
249 Dan Issel AS 2.50 6.00
250 Rick Barry AS 8.00 20.00
251 Artis Gilmore AS 4.00 10.00
252 Donnie Freeman AS 1.25 3.00
253 Bill Melchionni AS 1.25 3.00
254 Willie Wise AS 1.25 3.00
255 Julius Erving AS 60.00 150.00
256 Zelmo Beaty AS 1.25 3.00
257 Ralph Simpson AS 1.25 3.00
258 Charlie Scott AS 1.25 3.00
259 Scott/Barry/Issel LL 3.00 8.00
260 Gilmore/Wash/Jones LL 1.50 4.00
261 Combs/Damp/Jabali LL 1.25 3.00
262 Barry/Calvin/Jones LL 1.50 4.00
263 Gilmore/Erving/Dan LL 15.00 40.00
264 Melch/Brown/Damp LL! 2.50 6.00

1973-74 Topps

COMPLETE SET (264) 200.00 500.00
CONDITION SENSITIVE SET
CARDS PRICED IN NM CONDITION
1 Nate Archibald ! 5.00 12.00
2 Steve Kuberski .20 .50
3 John Mengelt .20 .50
4 Jim McMillian .75 2.00
5 Nate Thurmond 1.50 4.00
6 Dave Wohl .20 .50
7 John Brisker .20 .50
8 Charlie Davis .20 .50
9 Lamar Green .20 .50
10 Walt Frazier AS2 2.50 6.00
11 Bob Christian .20 .50
12 Cornell Warner .20 .50
13 Calvin Murphy 1.50 4.00
14 Dave Sorenson .75 2.00
15 Archie Clark .40 1.00
16 Clifford Ray .40 1.00
17 Terry Driscoll .20 .50
18 Matt Guokas .60 1.50
19 Elmore Smith .40 1.00
20 John Havlicek AS1 12.00 30.00
21 Pat Riley 4.00 10.00
22 George Trapp .20 .50
23 Ron Williams .20 .50
24 Jim Fox .20 .50
25 Dick Van Arsdale .40 1.00
26 John Tresvant .20 .50
27 Rick Adelman .40 1.00
28 Eddie Mast .20 .50
29 Jim Cleamons .40 1.00
30 Dave DeBusschere AS2 2.00 5.00
31 Norm Van Lier .40 1.00
32 Stan McKenzie .20 .50
33 Bob Dandridge .40 1.00
34 Leroy Ellis .40 1.00
35 Mike Riordan .40 1.00
36 Fred Hilton 1.25 3.00
37 Toby Kimball .75 2.00
38 Jim Price .20 .50
39 Willie Norwood .20 .50
40 Dave Cowens AS2 5.00 10.00
41 Cazzie Russell 1.25 3.00
42 Lee Winfield .20 .50
43 Connie Hawkins 3.00 8.00
44 Mike Newlin .40 1.00
45 Chet Walker .40 1.00
46 Walt Bellamy 1.50 4.00
47 John Johnson .40 1.00
48 Henry Bibby RC 2.50 6.00
49 Bobby Smith .75 2.00
50 Kareem Abdul-Jabbar AS1 25.00 60.00
51 Mike Price .20 .50
52 John Hummer .20 .50
53 Kevin Porter RC 2.00 5.00
54 Nate Williams .20 .50
55 Gail Goodrich 2.00 5.00
56 Fred Foster .20 .50
57 Don Chaney .40 1.00
58 Bud Stallworth .75 2.00
59 Clem Haskins .60 1.50
60 Bob Love AS2 1.25 3.00
61 Jimmy Walker .40 1.00
62 NBA Eastern Semis .40 1.00
63 NBA Eastern Semis .40 1.00
64 Wilt Chamberlain PO 5.00 12.00
65 NBA Western Semis .40 1.00
66 Willis Reed/H.Finkel PO 6.00 15.00
67 NBA Western Finals .40 1.00
68 W.Frazier/Erickson Champ 1.50 4.00
69 Larry Steele .40 1.00
70 Oscar Robertson 10.00 25.00
71 Phil Jackson 6.00 15.00
72 John Wetzel .20 .50
73 Steve Patterson RC .75 2.00
74 Manny Leaks .75 2.00
75 Jeff Mullins .40 1.00
76 Stan Love 3.00 8.00
77 Dick Garrett .75 2.00
78 Don Nelson 1.50 4.00
79 Chris Ford RC 1.25 3.00
80 Wilt Chamberlain 40.00 100.00
81 Dennis Layton .20 .50
82 Bill Bradley 6.00 15.00
83 Jerry Sloan .40 1.00
84 Cliff Meely .20 .50
85 Sam Lacey .20 .50
86 Dick Snyder .20 .50
87 Jim Washington .20 .50
88 Lucius Allen .40 1.00
89 LaRue Martin RC .20 .50
90 Rick Barry 4.00 10.00
91 Fred Boyd .20 .50
92 Barry Clemens .20 .50
93 Dean Meminger .20 .50
94 Henry Finkel .20 .50
95 Elvin Hayes 3.00 8.00
96 Stu Lantz .40 1.00
97 Bill Hewitt .75 2.00
98 Neal Walk .75 2.00
99 Garfield Heard .75 2.00
100 Jerry West AS1 25.00 60.00
101 Otto Moore .20 .50
102 Don Kojis .20 .50
103 Fred Brown RC 2.50 6.00
104 Dwight Davis .20 .50
105 Willis Reed 6.00 15.00
106 Herm Gilliam .20 .50
107 Mickey Davis .40 1.00
108 Jim Barnett .20 .50
109 Ollie Johnson .20 .50
110 Bob Lanier 2.50 6.00
111 Fred Carter .40 1.00
112 Paul Silas 1.25 3.00
113 Phil Chenier .40 1.00
114 Dennis Awtrey .20 .50
115 Austin Carr .40 1.00
116 Bob Kauffman .20 .50
117 Keith Erickson .40 1.00
118 Walt Wesley .20 .50
119 Steve Bracey .20 .50
120 Spencer Haywood AS1 1.25 3.00
121 NBA Checklist 1-176 5.00 12.00
122 Jack Marin .40 1.00
123 Jon McGlocklin .20 .50
124 Johnny Green .40 1.00
125 Jerry Lucas 1.25 3.00
126 Paul Westphal RC 8.00 20.00
127 Curtis Rowe .40 1.00
128 Mahdi Abdul-Rahman .40 1.00
129 Lloyd Neal RC .40 1.00
130 Pete Maravich AS1 25.00 60.00
131 Don May .20 .50
132 Bob Weiss .40 1.00
133 Dave Stallworth .20 .50
134 Dick Cunningham .20 .50
135 Bob McAdoo RC 25.00 60.00
136 Butch Beard .40 1.00
137 Happy Hairston .40 1.00
138 Bob Rule .60 1.50
139 Don Adams .20 .50
140 Charlie Scott .40 1.00
141 Ron Riley .20 .50
142 Earl Monroe 1.50 4.00
143 Clyde Lee .20 .50
144 Rick Roberson .20 .50
145 Rudy Tomjanovich 2.50 6.00
146 Tom Van Arsdale .40 1.00
147 Art Williams .20 .50
148 Curtis Perry .20 .50
149 Rich Rinaldi .20 .50
150 Lou Hudson .40 1.00
151 Mel Counts .20 .50
152 Jim McDaniels .20 .50
153 Arch/Jabbar/Hayw LL 5.00 12.00
154 Arch/Jabbar/Hayw LL 5.00 12.00
155 Wilt/Guokas/Jabbar LL 5.00 12.00
156 Barry/Murphy/Newlin LL 1.50 4.00
157 Wilt/Thurm/Cowens LL 3.00 8.00
158 Arch/Wilkens/Bing LL 1.50 4.00
159 Don Smith .20 .50
160 Sidney Wicks 1.25 3.00
161 Howie Komives .20 .50
162 John Gianelli .20 .50
163 Jeff Halliburton .20 .50
164 Kennedy McIntosh .20 .50
165 Len Wilkens 3.00 8.00
166 Corky Calhoun .20 .50
167 Howard Porter .40 1.00
168 Jo Jo White 1.25 3.00
169 John Block .20 .50
170 Dave Bing 1.50 4.00
171 Joe Ellis .20 .50
172 Chuck Terry .20 .50
173 Randy Smith .40 1.00
174 Bill Bridges .40 1.00
175 Geoff Petrie .40 1.00
176 Wes Unseld 1.50 4.00
177 Skeeter Swift .40 1.00
178 Jim Eakins .60 1.50
179 Steve Jones .60 1.50
180 George McGinnis AS1 1.25 3.00
181 Al Smith .40 1.00
182 Tom Washington .40 1.00
183 Louie Dampier .60 1.50
184 Simmie Hill .40 1.00
185 George Thompson .40 1.00
186 Cincy Powell .60 1.50
187 Larry Jones .75 2.00
188 Neil Johnson .40 1.00
189 Tom Owens .40 1.00
190 Ralph Simpson AS2 .60 1.50
191 George Carter .60 1.50
192 Rick Mount .60 1.50
193 Red Robbins .60 1.50
194 George Lehmann .40 1.00
195 Mel Daniels AS2 .60 1.50
196 Bob Warren .40 1.00
197 Gene Kennedy .40 1.00
198 Mike Barr .40 1.00
199 Dave Robisch .40 1.00
200 Billy Cunningham AS1 2.00 5.00
201 John Roche .60 1.50
202 ABA Western Semis 1.25 3.00
203 ABA Western Semis 1.25 3.00
204 Dan Issel PO 1.25 3.00
205 ABA Eastern Semis 1.25 3.00
206 ABA Western Finals 1.25 3.00
207 Artis Gilmore PO 1.25 3.00
208 George McGinnis PO 1.25 3.00
209 Glen Combs .75 2.00
210 Dan Issel AS2 2.50 6.00
211 Randy Denton .40 1.00
212 Freddie Lewis .60 1.50
213 Stew Johnson .40 1.00
214 Roland Taylor .40 1.00
215 Rich Jones .75 2.00
216 Billy Paultz .60 1.50
217 Ron Boone .60 1.50
218 Walt Simon .40 1.00
219 Mike Lewis .40 1.00
220 Warren Jabali AS1 .60 1.50
221 Wilbert Jones .40 1.00
222 Don Buse RC .60 1.50
223 Gene Moore .40 1.00
224 Joe Hamilton .60 1.50
225 Zelmo Beaty .60 1.50
226 Brian Taylor RC .60 1.50
227 Julius Keye .40 1.00
228 Mike Gale RC .60 1.50
229 Warren Davis .40 1.00
230 Mack Calvin AS2 .60 1.50
231 Roger Brown 5.00 12.00
232 Chuck Williams .60 1.50
233 Gerald Govan .60 1.50
234 Erving/McG/Issel LL 4.00 10.00
235 Gil/Kenn/Owens LL 1.25 3.00
236 Comb/Brwn/Damp LL 1.25 3.00
237 Kellr/Boone/War LL 1.25 3.00
238 Gilmore/Daniels/Paultz LL 1.25 3.00
239 Mel/Will/Jabali LL 1.25 3.00
240 Julius Erving AS2 40.00 100.00
241 Jimmy O'Brien .40 1.00
242 ABA Checklist 177-264 6.00 12.00
243 Johnny Neumann .40 1.00
244 Darnell Hillman .60 1.50
245 Willie Wise .60 1.50
246 Collis Jones .40 1.00
247 Ted McClain .40 1.00
248 George Irvine RC .40 1.00
249 Bill Melchionni .60 1.50
250 Artis Gilmore AS1 2.50 6.00
251 Willie Long .40 1.00
252 Larry Miller .40 1.00
253 Lee Davis .40 1.00
254 Donnie Freeman .60 1.50
255 Joe Caldwell .60 1.50
256 Bob Netolicky .60 1.50
257 Bernie Williams .40 1.00
258 Byron Beck .60 1.50
259 Jim Chones RC 3.00 8.00
260 James Jones AS1 .75 2.00
261 Wendell Ladner .40 1.00
262 Ollie Taylor .40 1.00
263 Les Hunter .40 1.00
264 Billy Keller ! 1.25 3.00

1973-74 Topps Team Stickers

COMPLETE SET (33) 125.00 300.00
1 Carolina Cougars
Stars 8.00 20.00
2 Denver Rockets
Spurs 8.00 20.00
3 Indiana Pacers
Squires 8.00 20.00
4 Kentucky Colonels
Tams 8.00 20.00
5 Memphis Tams
Cougars 8.00 20.00
6 New York Nets
Conquistadors 8.00 20.00
7 San Antonio Spurs
Nets 8.00 20.00
8 San Diego Conquistadors
Pacers 8.00 20.00
9 Utah Stars
Colonels 8.00 20.00
10 Virginia Squires
Rockets 8.00 20.00
11 Atlanta Hawks
Celtics 8.00 20.00
12 Atlanta Hawks
Supersonics 8.00 20.00
13 Boston Celtics
Braves 8.00 20.00
14 Boston Celtics/76ers 8.00 20.00
15 Buffalo Braves
Lakers 8.00 20.00
16 Buffalo Braves
Trail Blazers 8.00 20.00
17 Capitol Bullets
Knicks 8.00 20.00
18 Chicago Bulls
Pistons 8.00 20.00
19 Cleveland Cavaliers
Hawks 8.00 20.00
20 Detroit Pistons
Warriors 8.00 20.00
21 Golden State Warriors
Bucks 8.00 20.00
22 Golden State Warriors
Kings 8.00 20.00
23 Houston Rockets
Braves 8.00 20.00
24 Kansas City Kings
Lakers/76ers 8.00 20.00
25 Los Angeles Lakers
Bullets 8.00 20.00
26 Los Angeles Lakers
Celtics 8.00 20.00
27 Milwaukee Bucks
Knicks 8.00 20.00
28 New York Knicks
Bulls 8.00 20.00
29 New York Knicks
Warriors 8.00 20.00
30 Philadelphia 76ers
Hawks 8.00 20.00
31 Phoenix Suns
Cavaliers 8.00 20.00
32 Portland Trail Blazers
Rockets 8.00 20.00
33 Seattle Supersonics
Suns 8.00 20.00

1974-75 Topps

COMPLETE SET (264) 300.00 600.00
CARDS PRICED IN NM CONDITION
1 Kareem Abdul-Jabbar ! 30.00 80.00
2 Don May .20 .50
3 Bernie Fryer RC .40 1.00
4 Don Adams .20 .50
5 Herm Gilliam .20 .50
6 Jim Chones .40 1.00
7 Rick Adelman .40 1.00
8 Randy Smith .40 1.00
9 Paul Silas 1.25 3.00
10 Pete Maravich 15.00 40.00
11 Ron Behagen .20 .50
12 Kevin Porter .40 1.00
13 Bill Bridges .40 1.00
14 Charles Johnson RC 1.25 3.00
15 Bob Love .40 1.00
16 Henry Bibby .40 1.00
17 Neal Walk .20 .50
18 John Brisker .20 .50
19 Lucius Allen .20 .50
20 Tom Van Arsdale .40 1.00
21 Larry Steele .20 .50
22 Curtis Rowe .40 1.00
23 Dean Meminger .20 .50
24 Steve Patterson .20 .50
25 Earl Monroe 2.50 6.00
26 Jack Marin .20 .50
27 Jo Jo White 1.25 3.00
28 Rudy Tomjanovich 2.50 6.00
29 Otto Moore .20 .50
30 Elvin Hayes AS2 2.00 5.00
31 Pat Riley 4.00 10.00
32 Clyde Lee .20 .50
33 Bob Weiss .20 .50
34 Jim Fox .20 .50
35 Charlie Scott .40 1.00
36 Cliff Meely .20 .50
37 Jon McGlocklin .20 .50
38 Jim McMillian .40 1.00
39 Bill Walton RC 60.00 150.00
40 Dave Bing AS2 1.25 3.00
41 Jim Washington .20 .50
42 Jim Cleamons .40 1.00
43 Mel Davis .20 .50
44 Garfield Heard .40 1.00
45 Jimmy Walker .40 1.00
46 Don Nelson .40 1.00
47 Jim Barnett .20 .50
48 Manny Leaks .20 .50
49 Elmore Smith .40 1.00
50 Rick Barry AS1 2.50 6.00
51 Jerry Sloan 1.25 3.00
52 John Hummer .40 1.00
53 Keith Erickson .40 1.00
54 George E. Johnson .40 1.00
55 Oscar Robertson 10.00 25.00
56 Steve Mix RC .40 1.00
57 Rick Roberson .40 1.00
58 John Mengelt .40 1.00
59 Dwight Jones RC .40 1.00
60 Austin Carr .40 1.00
61 Nick Weatherspoon RC .40 1.00
62 Clem Haskins .40 1.00
63 Don Kojis .40 1.00
64 Paul Westphal 1.25 3.00
65 Walt Bellamy 1.50 4.00
66 John Johnson .40 1.00
67 Butch Beard .40 1.00
68 Happy Hairston .40 1.00
69 Tom Boerwinkle .20 .50
70 Spencer Haywood AS2 1.25 3.00
71 Gary Melchionni .20 .50
72 Ed Ratleff RC .40 1.00
73 Mickey Davis .40 1.00
74 Dennis Awtrey .40 1.00
75 Fred Carter .40 1.00
76 George Trapp .40 1.00
77 John Wetzel .40 1.00
78 Bobby Smith .40 1.00
79 John Gianelli .40 1.00
80 Bob McAdoo AS2 2.50 6.00
81 Hawks TL/Maravich/Bell 8.00 20.00
82 Celtics TL/John Havlicek 2.00 5.00
83 Buffalo Braves TL .40 1.00
84 Bulls TL/Love/Walker 1.25 3.00
85 Cleveland Cavs TL .40 1.00
86 Detroit Pistons TL .40 1.00
87 Warriors TL/Rick Barry 1.25 3.00
88 Houston Rockets TL .40 1.00
89 Kansas City Omaha TL .40 1.00
90 Lakers TL/Gail Goodrich .40 1.00
91 Bucks TL/Jabbar/Oscar 10.00 25.00
92 New Orleans Jazz .40 1.00
93 Knicks TL/Fraz/Brad/DeB 8.00 20.00
94 Philadelphia 76ers TL .40 1.00
95 Phoenix Suns TL .40 1.00
96 Trail Blazers TL .40 1.00
97 Seattle Supersonics TL .40 1.00
98 Capitol Bullets TL .40 1.00
99 Sam Lacey .20 .50
100 John Havlicek AS1 4.00 10.00
101 Stu Lantz .40 1.00
102 Mike Riordan .20 .50
103 Larry Jones .20 .50
104 Connie Hawkins 1.50 4.00
105 Nate Thurmond 1.25 3.00
106 Dick Gibbs .20 .50
107 Corky Calhoun .20 .50
108 Dave Wohl .20 .50
109 Cornell Warner .20 .50
110 Geoff Petrie UER .40 1.00
111 Leroy Ellis .40 1.00
112 Chris Ford .40 1.00
113 Bill Bradley 4.00 10.00
114 Clifford Ray .40 1.00
115 Dick Snyder .20 .50
116 Nate Williams .20 .50
117 Matt Guokas .40 1.00
118 Henry Finkel .20 .50
119 Curtis Perry .20 .50
120 Gail Goodrich AS1 1.25 3.00
121 Wes Unseld 1.25 3.00
122 Howard Porter .40 1.00
123 Jeff Mullins .20 .50
124 Mike Bantom RC .40 1.00
125 Fred Brown .75 2.00
126 Bob Dandridge .40 1.00
127 Mike Newlin .40 1.00
128 Greg Smith .20 .50
129 Doug Collins RC 6.00 15.00
130 Lou Hudson .40 1.00
131 Bob Lanier 2.00 5.00
132 Phil Jackson 4.00 10.00
133 Don Chaney .40 1.00
134 Jim Brewer RC .40 1.00
135 Ernie DiGregorio RC 1.25 3.00
136 Steve Kuberski .20 .50
137 Jim Price .20 .50
138 Mike D'Antoni .20 .50
139 John Brown .20 .50
140 Norm Van Lier AS2 .40 1.00
141 NBA Checklist 1-176 5.00 10.00
142 Slick Watts RC .40 1.00
143 Walt Wesley .20 .50
144 McAd/Jabbar/Marav LL 15.00 40.00
145 McAd/Marav/Jabbar LL 20.00 50.00
146 McAd/Jabbar/Tomjan LL 10.00 25.00
147 NBA F.T. Pct. Leaders 3.00 8.00
148 Hayes/Cowens/McAd LL 4.00 10.00
149 NBA Assist Leaders .40 1.00
150 Walt Frazier AS1 2.00 5.00
151 Cazzie Russell .40 1.00
152 Calvin Murphy 1.25 3.00
153 Bob Kauffman .20 .50
154 Fred Boyd .20 .50
155 Dave Cowens 2.50 6.00
156 Willie Norwood .20 .50
157 Lee Winfield .20 .50
158 Dwight Davis .20 .50
159 George T. Johnson .20 .50
160 Dick Van Arsdale .40 1.00
161 NBA Eastern Semis .40 1.00
162 NBA Western Semis .40 1.00
163 NBA Div. Finals .40 1.00
164 NBA Championship .60 1.50
165 Phil Chenier .40 1.00
166 Kermit Washington RC .40 1.00
167 Dale Schlueter .20 .50
168 John Block .20 .50
169 Don Smith .20 .50
170 Nate Archibald 1.50 4.00
171 Chet Walker .40 1.00
172 Archie Clark .40 1.00
173 Kennedy McIntosh .20 .50
174 George Thompson .20 .50
175 Sidney Wicks 1.25 3.00
176 Jerry West 12.00 30.00
177 Dwight Lamar .40 1.00
178 George Carter .60 1.50
179 Wil Robinson .40 1.00
180 Artis Gilmore AS1 1.50 4.00
181 Brian Taylor .60 1.50
182 Darnell Hillman .60 1.50
183 Dave Robisch .60 1.50
184 Gene Littles RC .60 1.50
185 Willie Wise AS2 .60 1.50
186 James Silas RC 3.00 8.00
187 Caldwell Jones RC 1.25 3.00
188 Roland Taylor .40 1.00
189 Randy Denton .40 1.00
190 Dan Issel AS2 2.00 5.00
191 Mike Gale .40 1.00
192 Mel Daniels 1.25 3.00
193 Steve Jones .60 1.50
194 Marv Roberts .40 1.00
195 Ron Boone AS2 .75 2.00
196 George Gervin RC 30.00 80.00
197 Flynn Robinson .40 1.00
198 Cincy Powell .40 1.00
199 Glen Combs .40 1.00
200 Julius Erving UER 15.00 40.00
201 Billy Keller .60 1.50
202 Willie Long .40 1.00
203 ABA Checklist 177-264 5.00 10.00
204 Joe Caldwell .60 1.50
205 Swen Nater RC .60 1.50
206 Rick Mount .60 1.50
207 Erving/McG/Issel LL 8.00 20.00
208 ABA Two-Point Field 1.25 3.00
209 ABA Three-Point Field 1.25 3.00
210 ABA Free Throw 1.25 3.00
211 Gil/McGinn/Jones LL 1.25 3.00
212 ABA Assist Leaders 1.25 3.00
213 Larry Miller .40 1.00
214 Stew Johnson .40 1.00
215 Larry Finch RC 3.00 8.00
216 Larry Kenon RC 1.25 3.00
217 Joe Hamilton .60 1.50
218 Gerald Govan .60 1.50
219 Ralph Simpson .60 1.50
220 George McGinnis AS1 1.25 3.00
221 Carolina Cougars TL 1.25 3.00
222 Denver Nuggets TL 1.25 3.00
223 Indiana Pacers TL 1.25 3.00
224 Colonels TL/Dan Issel 1.25 3.00
225 Memphis Sounds TL 1.25 3.00
226 Nets TL/Erving 4.00 10.00
227 Spurs TL/George Gervin 4.00 10.00
228 San Diego Conq. TL 1.25 3.00
229 Utah Stars TL 1.25 3.00
230 Virginia Squires TL 1.25 3.00
231 Bird Averitt .40 1.00
232 John Roche .40 1.00
233 George Irvine .40 1.00
234 John Williamson RC .60 1.50
235 Billy Cunningham 1.50 4.00
236 Jimmy O'Brien .40 1.00
237 Wilbert Jones .40 1.00
238 Johnny Neumann .40 1.00
239 Al Smith .40 1.00
240 Roger Brown .60 1.50
241 Chuck Williams .60 1.50
242 Rich Jones .60 1.50
243 Dave Twardzik RC .60 1.50
244 Wendell Ladner .60 1.50
245 Mack Calvin AS1 .60 1.50
246 ABA Eastern Semis 1.25 3.00
247 ABA Western Semis 1.25 3.00
248 ABA Div. Finals 1.25 3.00
249 Julius Erving PO 12.00 30.00
250 Wilt Chamberlain CO 40.00 100.00
251 Ron Robinson .40 1.00
252 Zelmo Beaty .60 1.50
253 Donnie Freeman .60 1.50
254 Mike Green .40 1.00
255 Louie Dampier AS2 .60 1.50
256 Tom Owens .40 1.00
257 George Karl RC 8.00 20.00
258 Jim Eakins .60 1.50
259 Travis Grant .75 2.00
260 James Jones AS1 .60 1.50
261 Mike Jackson .40 1.00
262 Billy Paultz .60 1.50
263 Freddie Lewis .60 1.50
264 Byron Beck ! 1.25 3.00

1975-76 Topps

COMPLETE SET (330) 300.00 600.00
CARDS PRICED IN NM CONDITION
1 McAd/Barry/Jabbar LL ! 6.00 15.00
2 Nelson/Beard/Tomj LL 1.50 4.00
3 Barry/Murphy/Bradley LL 2.00 5.00
4 Unseld/Cowens/Lacey LL 1.25 3.00
5 Porter/Bing/Arch LL 1.25 3.00
6 Barry/Frazier/Steele LL 1.50 4.00
7 Tom Van Arsdale .75 2.00
8 Paul Silas .75 2.00
9 Jerry Sloan 1.50 4.00
10 Bob McAdoo AS1 5.00 12.00
11 Dwight Davis .60 .15
12 John Mengelt .75 2.00
13 George Johnson .60 1.50
14 Ed Ratleff .60 1.50
15 Nate Archibald AS1 1.50 4.00
16 Elmore Smith .60 .15
17 Bob Dandridge .75 2.00
18 Louie Nelson RC .60 1.50
19 Neal Walk .60 1.50
20 Billy Cunningham 2.00 5.00
21 Gary Melchionni .60 1.50
22 Barry Clemens .60 1.50
23 Jimmy Jones .60 1.50
24 Tom Burleson RC .75 2.00
25 Lou Hudson .75 2.00
26 Henry Finkel .30 .75
27 Jim McMillian .75 2.00
28 Matt Guokas .75 2.00
29 Fred Foster DP .60 1.50
30 Bob Lanier 3.00 8.00
31 Jimmy Walker .75 2.00
32 Cliff Meely .60 1.50
33 Butch Beard .75 2.00
34 Cazzie Russell .75 2.00
35 Jon McGlocklin .60 1.50
36 Bernie Fryer .60 1.50
37 Bill Bradley 2.50 6.00
38 Fred Carter .75 2.00
39 Dennis Awtrey DP .60 1.50
40 Sidney Wicks .75 2.00
41 Fred Brown .75 2.00
42 Rowland Garrett .60 1.50
43 Herm Gilliam .60 1.50
44 Don Nelson .75 2.00
45 Ernie DiGregorio 1.25 3.00
46 Jim Brewer .60 1.50
47 Chris Ford 1.25 3.00
48 Nick Weatherspoon .75 2.00
49 Zaid Abdul-Aziz .60 1.50
50 Keith Wilkes RC 30.00 80.00
51 Ollie Johnson DP .60 1.50
52 Lucius Allen .75 2.00
53 Mickey Davis .60 1.50
54 Otto Moore .60 1.50
55 Walt Frazier AS1 2.50 6.00
56 Steve Mix .75 2.00
57 Nate Hawthorne .60 1.50
58 Lloyd Neal .60 1.50
59 Slick Watts .75 2.00
60 Elvin Hayes 2.00 5.00
61 Checklist 1-110 3.00 8.00
62 Mike Sojourner .60 .15
63 Randy Smith .75 2.00
64 John Block DP .60 .15
65 Charlie Scott .75 2.00
66 Jim Chones .75 2.00
67 Rick Adelman .75 2.00
68 Curtis Rowe .60 .15
69 Derrek Dickey RC .75 2.00
70 Rudy Tomjanovich 2.00 5.00
71 Pat Riley 2.50 6.00
72 Cornell Warner .60 1.50
73 Earl Monroe 2.00 5.00
74 Allan Bristow RC 1.25 3.00
75 Pete Maravich DP 8.00 20.00
76 Curtis Perry .60 1.50
77 Bill Walton 12.00 30.00
78 Leonard Gray .60 1.50
79 Kevin Porter .75 2.00
80 John Havlicek AS2 8.00 20.00
81 Dwight Jones .60 .15
82 Jack Marin .60 .15
83 Dick Snyder .60 .15
84 George Trapp .60 1.50
85 Nate Thurmond 3.00 8.00
86 Charles Johnson .60 1.50
87 Ron Riley .60 1.50
88 Stu Lantz .60 1.50
89 Scott Wedman RC 1.00 2.50
90 Kareem Abdul-Jabbar 40.00 100.00
91 Aaron James .60 1.50
92 Jim Barnett .60 1.50
93 Clyde Lee .60 1.50
94 Larry Steele .75 2.00
95 Mike Riordan .60 1.50
96 Archie Clark .75 2.00
97 Mike Bantom .60 1.50
98 Bob Kauffman .60 1.50
99 Kevin Stacom RC .60 1.50
100 Rick Barry AS1 2.50 6.00
101 Ken Charles .60 1.50
102 Tom Boerwinkle .60 1.50
103 Mike Newlin .75 2.00
104 Leroy Ellis .75 2.00
105 Austin Carr .75 2.00
106 Ron Behagen .60 1.50
107 Jim Price .60 1.50
108 Bud Stallworth .60 1.50
109 Earl Williams .60 1.50
110 Gail Goodrich 1.25 3.00
111 Phil Jackson 5.00 12.00
112 Rod Derline .60 .15
113 Keith Erickson .60 1.50
114 Phil Lumpkin .60 1.50
115 Wes Unseld 1.25 3.00
116 Atlanta Hawks TL .60 1.50
117 Cowens/White TL 2.50 6.00
118 Buffalo Braves TL 1.25 3.00
119 Love/Walk/Thur TL 1.25 3.00
120 Cleveland Cavs TL .60 1.50
121 Lanier/Bing TL 1.25 3.00
122 Rick Barry TL 1.25 3.00
123 Houston Rockets TL .75 2.00
124 Kansas City Kings TL .75 2.00
125 Los Angeles Lakers TL .60 1.50
126 K.Abdul-Jabbar TL 5.00 12.00
127 Pete Maravich TL 5.00 12.00
128 Frazier/Bradley TL DP 1.25 3.00
129 Car/Coll/Curn TL DP .75 2.00
130 Phoenix Suns TL DP .60 1.50
131 Portland Blazers TL DP .60 1.50
132 Seattle Sonics TL .75 2.00
133 Hayes/Unseld TL 1.25 3.00
134 John Drew RC .75 2.00
135 Jo Jo White AS2 1.25 3.00
136 Garfield Heard .75 2.00
137 Jim Cleamons .60 1.50
138 Howard Porter .75 2.00
139 Phil Smith RC .75 2.00
140 Bob Love .75 2.00
141 John Gianelli DP .60 1.50
142 Larry McNeill RC .60 1.50
143 Brian Winters RC 1.25 3.00
144 George Thompson .60 1.50
145 Kevin Kunnert .60 1.50
146 Henry Bibby .75 2.00
147 John Johnson .60 1.50
148 Doug Collins 3.00 8.00
149 John Brisker .60 1.50
150 Dick Van Arsdale .75 2.00
151 Leonard Robinson RC 2.00 5.00
152 Dean Meminger .60 1.50
153 Phil Hankinson .60 1.50
154 Dale Schlueter .60 1.50
155 Norm Van Lier .75 2.00
156 Campy Russell RC 4.00 10.00
157 Jeff Mullins .75 2.00
158 Sam Lacey .60 1.50
159 Happy Hairston .75 2.00
160 Dave Bing DP 1.50 4.00
161 Kevin Restani RC .60 1.50
162 Dave Wohl .60 1.50
163 E.C. Coleman .60 1.50
164 Jim Fox .60 1.50
165 Geoff Petrie .75 2.00
166 Hawthorne Wingo DP UER .60 1.50
167 Fred Boyd .60 1.50
168 Willie Norwood .60 1.50
169 Bob Wilson .60 1.50
170 Dave Cowens 2.50 6.00
171 Tom Henderson RC .60 1.50
172 Jim Washington .60 1.50
173 Clem Haskins .75 2.00
174 Jim Davis .60 1.50
175 Bobby Smith DP .60 1.50
176 Mike D'Antoni .60 1.50
177 Zelmo Beaty .75 2.00
178 Gary Brokaw RC .60 1.50
179 Mel Davis .60 1.50
180 Calvin Murphy 1.50 4.00
181 Checklist 111-220 DP 3.00 8.00
182 Nate Williams .60 1.50
183 LaRue Martin .60 1.50
184 George McGinnis 1.50 4.00
185 Clifford Ray .60 1.50
186 Paul Westphal 2.00 5.00
187 Talvin Skinner .60 1.50
188 NBA Playoff Semis DP 1.25 3.00
189 Clifford Ray PO 1.25 3.00
190 Phil Chenier AS2 DP .75 2.00
191 John Brown .60 1.50
192 Lee Winfield .60 1.50
193 Steve Patterson .60 1.50
194 Charles Dudley .60 1.50
195 Connie Hawkins DP 2.00 5.00
196 Leon Benbow .60 1.50
197 Don Kojis .60 .15
198 Ron Williams .60 1.50
199 Mel Counts .60 1.50
200 Spencer Haywood AS2 1.50 4.00
201 Greg Jackson .75 2.00
202 Tom Kozelko DP .75 2.00
203 Atlanta Hawks CL .60 1.50
204 Boston Celtics CL 1.25 3.00
205 Buffalo Braves CL .60 1.50
206 Chicago Bulls CL 1.25 3.00
207 Cleveland Cavs CL .60 1.50
208 Detroit Pistons CL .60 1.50
209 Golden State CL .60 1.50
210 Houston Rockets CL .60 1.50
211 Kansas City Kings CL DP .60 1.50
212 Los Angeles Lakers CL DP .60 1.50
213 Milwaukee Bucks CL .60 1.50
214 New Orleans Jazz CL 6.00 15.00
215 New York Knicks CL .60 1.50
216 Philadelphia 76ers CL .60 1.50
217 Phoenix Suns CL DP .60 1.50
218 Portland Blazers CL .60 1.50
219 Sonics/B.Russell DP 5.00 10.00
220 Washington Bullets CL .60 1.50
221 McGin/Erving/Boone LL 4.00 10.00
222 Jones/Gilmore/Malone LL 4.00 10.00
223 ABA 3 Pt. Field Goal .75 2.00
224 ABA Free Throw .75 2.00
225 ABA Rebounds Leaders .75 2.00
226 ABA Assists Leaders .75 2.00
227 Mack Calvin AS1 .75 2.00
228 Billy Knight RC 1.25 3.00
229 Bird Averitt .60 1.50
230 George Carter .60 1.50
231 Swen Nater AS2 .75 2.00
232 Steve Jones .75 2.00

233 George Gervin 8.00 20.00
234 Lee Davis .60 1.50
235 Ron Boone AS1 .75 2.00
236 Mike Jackson .60 1.50
237 Kevin Joyce RC .60 1.50
238 Marv Roberts .60 1.50
239 Tom Owens .60 1.50
240 Ralph Simpson .75 2.00
241 Gus Gerard .60 1.50
242 Brian Taylor AS2 .75 2.00
243 Rich Jones .60 1.50
244 John Roche .60 1.50
245 Travis Grant .75 2.00
246 Dave Twardzik .75 2.00
247 Mike Green .60 1.50
248 Billy Keller .75 2.00
249 Stew Johnson .60 1.50
250 Artis Gilmore AS1 5.00 12.00
251 John Williamson .75 2.00
252 Marvin Barnes RC 1.50 4.00
253 James Silas AS2 .75 2.00
254 Moses Malone RC 30.00 80.00
255 Willie Wise .75 2.00
256 Dwight Lamar .60 1.50
257 Checklist 221-330 3.00 8.00
258 Byron Beck .75 2.00
259 Len Elmore RC 1.25 3.00
260 Dan Issel 2.00 5.00
261 Rick Mount .60 1.50
262 Billy Paultz .75 2.00
263 Donnie Freeman .60 1.50
264 George Adams .60 1.50
265 Don Chaney .75 2.00
266 Randy Denton .60 1.50
267 Don Washington .60 1.50
268 Roland Taylor .60 1.50
269 Charlie Edge .60 1.50
270 Louie Dampier .75 2.00
271 Collis Jones .60 1.50
272 Al Skinner RC .60 1.50
273 Coby Dietrick .60 1.50
274 Tim Bassett .60 1.50
275 Freddie Lewis .75 2.00
276 Gerald Govan .60 1.50
277 Ron Thomas .60 1.50
278 Denver Nuggets TL .75 2.00
279 McGinnis/Keller TL 1.00 2.50
280 Gilmore/Dampier TL 1.00 2.50
281 Memphis Sounds TL .75 2.00
282 Julius Erving TL 6.00 15.00
283 Barnes/Lewis TL 1.00 2.50
284 George Gervin TL 2.00 5.00
285 San Diego Sails TL .75 2.00
286 Malone/Boone TL 3.00 8.00
287 Virginia Squires TL .75 2.00
288 Claude Terry .60 1.50
289 Wilbert Jones .60 1.50
290 Darnell Hillman .75 2.00
291 Bill Melchionni .75 2.00
292 Mel Daniels .75 2.00
293 Fly Williams RC .75 2.00
294 Larry Kenon .75 2.00
295 Red Robbins .75 2.00
296 Warren Jabali .75 2.00
297 Jim Eakins .75 2.00
298 Bobby Jones RC 12.00 30.00
299 Don Buse .75 2.00
300 Julius Erving AS1 40.00 100.00
301 Billy Shepherd .60 1.50
302 Maurice Lucas RC 2.50 6.00
303 George Karl 2.00 5.00
304 Jim Bradley .60 1.50
305 Caldwell Jones .75 2.00
306 Al Smith .60 1.50
307 Jan Van Breda Kolff RC .75 2.00
308 Darrell Elston .60 1.50
309 ABA Playoff Semifinals .75 2.00
310 Artis Gilmore PO 1.00 2.50
311 Ted McClain .60 1.50
312 Willie Sojourner .60 1.50
313 Bob Warren .60 1.50
314 Bob Netolicky .75 2.00
315 Chuck Williams .60 1.50
316 Gene Kennedy .60 1.50
317 Jimmy O'Brien .60 1.50
318 Dave Robisch .60 1.50
319 Wali Jones .60 1.50
320 George Irvine .60 1.50
321 Denver Nuggets CL .75 2.00
322 Indiana Pacers CL .75 2.00
323 Kentucky Colonels CL .75 2.00
324 Memphis Sounds CL .75 2.00
325 New York Nets CL 2.50 6.00
326 St. Louis Spirits CL
(Spirits of St. Louis on card back) .75 2.00
327 San Antonio Spurs CL .75 2.00
328 San Diego Sails CL .75 2.00
329 Utah Stars CL .75 2.00
330 Virginia Squires CL ! 1.50 4.00

1975-76 Topps Team Checklist

COMPLETE SET (27) 75.00 150.00
203 Atlanta Hawks 2.50 6.00
204 Boston Celtics 5.00 10.00
205 Buffalo Braves 2.50 6.00
206 Chicago Bulls 2.50 6.00
207 Cleveland Cavaliers 2.50 6.00
208 Detroit Pistons 2.50 6.00
209 Golden State Warriors 2.50 6.00
210 Houston Rockets 2.50 6.00
211 Kansas City Kings 2.50 6.00
212 Los Angeles Lakers 5.00 10.00
213 Milwaukee Bucks 2.50 6.00
214 New Orleans Jazz 2.50 6.00
215 New York Knicks 3.00 8.00
216 Philadelphia 76ers 2.50 6.00
217 Phoenix Suns 2.50 6.00
218 Portland Trail Blazers 3.00 8.00
219 Seattle SuperSonics 2.50 6.00
220 Washington Bullets 2.50 6.00
321 Denver Nuggets 3.00 8.00
322 Indiana Pacers 3.00 8.00
323 Kentucky Colonels 3.00 8.00
324 Memphis Sounds 3.00 8.00
325 New York Nets 3.00 8.00
326 Spirits of St. Louis 3.00 8.00
327 San Antonio Spurs 3.00 8.00
328 San Diego Sails 3.00 8.00
329 Utah Stars 3.00 8.00
330 Virginia Squires 2.50 6.00

1976-77 Topps

COMPLETE SET (144) 200.00 500.00
CONDITION SENSITIVE SET
CARDS PRICED IN NM CONDITION
1 Julius Erving ! 60.00 150.00
2 Dick Snyder .75 2.00
3 Paul Silas 6.00 15.00
4 Keith Erickson .75 2.00
5 Wes Unseld 10.00 25.00
6 Butch Beard 1.00 2.50
7 Lloyd Neal .75 2.00
8 Tom Henderson .75 2.00
9 Jim McMillian 5.00 12.00
10 Bob Lanier 3.00 8.00
11 Junior Bridgeman RC 1.00 2.50
12 Corky Calhoun .75 2.00
13 Billy Keller 1.00 2.50
14 Mickey Johnson RC .75 2.00
15 Fred Brown 1.00 2.50
16 Keith Wilkes 1.00 2.50
17 Louie Nelson .75 2.00
18 Ed Ratleff .75 2.00
19 Billy Paultz 6.00 15.00
20 Nate Archibald 2.00 5.00
21 Steve Mix 1.00 2.50
22 Ralph Simpson 1.00 2.50
23 Campy Russell 6.00 15.00
24 Charlie Scott 1.00 2.50
25 Artis Gilmore 8.00 20.00
26 Dick Van Arsdale 1.00 2.50
27 Phil Chenier 1.00 2.50
28 Spencer Haywood 2.00 5.00
29 Chris Ford 1.00 2.50
30 Dave Cowens 6.00 15.00
31 Sidney Wicks 1.00 2.50
32 Jim Price .75 2.00
33 Dwight Jones .75 2.00
34 Lucius Allen .75 2.00
35 Marvin Barnes 1.00 2.50
36 Henry Bibby 1.00 2.50
37 Joe Meriweather RC .75 2.00
38 Doug Collins 6.00 15.00
39 Garfield Heard 1.00 2.50
40 Randy Smith 6.00 15.00
41 Tom Burleson 1.00 2.50
42 Dave Twardzik 1.00 2.50
43 Bill Bradley 6.00 15.00
44 Calvin Murphy 5.00 12.00
45 Bob Love 3.00 8.00
46 Brian Winters 1.00 2.50
47 Glenn McDonald .75 2.00
48 Checklist 1-144 10.00 25.00
49 Bird Averitt .75 2.00
50 Rick Barry 5.00 12.00
51 Ticky Burden RC .75 2.00
52 Rich Jones .75 2.00
53 Austin Carr 1.00 2.50
54 Steve Kuberski .75 2.00
55 Paul Westphal 1.00 2.50
56 Mike Riordan .75 2.00
57 Bill Walton 12.00 30.00
58 Eric Money RC .75 2.00
59 John Drew 1.00 2.50
60 Pete Maravich 12.00 30.00
61 John Shumate RC 1.00 2.50
62 Mack Calvin 1.00 2.50
63 Bruce Seals .75 2.00
64 Walt Frazier 6.00 15.00
65 Elmore Smith .75 2.00
66 Rudy Tomjanovich 2.50 6.00
67 Sam Lacey .75 2.00
68 George Gervin 10.00 25.00
69 Gus Williams RC 2.00 5.00
70 George McGinnis 1.00 2.50
71 Len Elmore .75 2.00
72 Jack Marin .75 2.00
73 Brian Taylor .75 2.00
74 Jim Brewer .75 2.00
75 Alvan Adams RC 2.50 6.00
76 Dave Bing 2.00 5.00
77 Phil Jackson 8.00 20.00
78 Geoff Petrie 1.00 2.50
79 Mike Sojourner .75 2.00
80 James Silas 1.00 2.50
81 Bob Dandridge 1.00 2.50
82 Ernie DiGregorio 1.00 2.50
83 Cazzie Russell 1.00 2.50
84 Kevin Porter 1.00 2.50
85 Tom Boerwinkle .75 2.00
86 Darnell Hillman .75 2.00
87 Herm Gilliam .75 2.00
88 Nate Williams .75 2.00
89 Phil Smith 1.00 2.50
90 John Havlicek 6.00 15.00
91 Kevin Kunnert .75 2.00
92 Jimmy Walker 1.00 2.50
93 Billy Cunningham 5.00 12.00
94 Dan Issel 2.50 6.00
95 Ron Boone 1.00 2.50
96 Lou Hudson 1.00 2.50
97 Jim Chones 1.00 2.50
98 Earl Monroe 8.00 20.00
99 Tom Van Arsdale 1.00 2.50
100 Kareem Abdul-Jabbar 30.00 80.00
101 Moses Malone 12.00 30.00
102 Ricky Sobers RC .75 2.00
103 Swen Nater .75 2.00
104 Leonard Robinson 1.00 2.50
105 Slick Watts 1.00 2.50
106 Otto Moore .75 2.00
107 Maurice Lucas 1.00 2.50
108 Norm Van Lier 1.00 2.50
109 Clifford Ray .75 2.00
110 David Thompson RC 30.00 80.00
111 Fred Carter 1.00 2.50
112 Caldwell Jones 6.00 15.00
113 John Williamson 1.00 2.50
114 Bobby Smith 1.00 2.50
115 Jo Jo White 1.00 2.50
116 Curtis Perry .75 2.00
117 John Gianelli .75 2.00
118 Curtis Rowe .75 2.00
119 Lionel Hollins RC 1.00 2.50
120 Elvin Hayes 2.50 6.00
121 Ken Charles .75 2.00
122 Dave Meyers RC 1.00 2.50
123 Jerry Sloan 1.00 2.50
124 Billy Knight 1.00 2.50
125 Gail Goodrich 1.00 2.50
126 K. Abdul-Jabbar AS 20.00 50.00
127 Julius Erving AS 20.00 50.00
128 George McGinnis AS 10.00 25.00
129 Nate Archibald AS 1.00 2.50
130 Pete Maravich AS 20.00 50.00
131 Dave Cowens AS 2.00 5.00
132 Rick Barry AS 2.00 5.00
133 Elvin Hayes AS 2.00 5.00
134 James Silas AS .75 2.00
135 Randy Smith AS .75 2.00
136 Leonard Gray .75 2.00
137 Charles Johnson .75 2.00
138 Ron Behagen .75 2.00
139 Mike Newlin 1.00 2.50
140 Bob McAdoo 2.50 6.00
141 Mike Gale .75 2.00
142 Scott Wedman 5.00 12.00
143 Lloyd Free RC 20.00 50.00
144 Bobby Jones ! 3.00 8.00

1977-78 Topps

COMPLETE SET (132) 100.00 250.00
*GRAY AND WHITE BACKS: EQUAL VALUE
1 Kareem Abdul-Jabbar ! 25.00 60.00
2 Henry Bibby .75 2.00
3 Curtis Rowe .75 2.00
4 Norm Van Lier .75 2.00
5 Darnell Hillman .75 2.00
6 Earl Monroe .75 2.00
7 Leonard Gray .75 2.00
8 Bird Averitt .75 2.00
9 Jim Brewer .75 2.00
10 Paul Westphal .75 2.00
11 Bob Gross RC .75 2.00
12 Phil Smith .75 2.00
13 Dan Roundfield RC .75 2.00
14 Brian Taylor .75 2.00
15 Rudy Tomjanovich 1.25 3.00
16 Kevin Porter .75 2.00
17 Scott Wedman .75 2.00
18 Lloyd Free .75 2.00
19 Tom Boswell RC .75 2.00
20 Pete Maravich 10.00 25.00
21 Cliff Pondexter .75 2.00
22 Bubbles Hawkins .75 2.00
23 Kevin Grevey RC .75 2.00
24 Ken Charles .75 2.00
25 Bob Dandridge .75 2.00
26 Lonnie Shelton RC .75 2.00
27 Don Chaney .75 2.00
28 Larry Kenon .75 2.00
29 Checklist 1-132 .75 2.00
30 Fred Brown .75 2.00
31 John Gianelli UER .75 2.00
32 Austin Carr .75 2.00
33 Jamaal Wilkes 1.25 3.00
34 Caldwell Jones .75 2.00
35 Jo Jo White .75 2.00
36 Scott May RC .75 2.00
37 Mike Newlin .75 2.00
38 Mel Davis .75 2.00
39 Lionel Hollins .75 2.00
40 Elvin Hayes 1.50 4.00
41 Dan Issel .75 2.00
42 Ricky Sobers .75 2.00
43 Don Ford .75 2.00
44 John Williamson .75 2.00
45 Bob McAdoo .75 2.00
46 Geoff Petrie .75 2.00
47 M.L. Carr RC 5.00 12.00
48 Brian Winters .75 2.00
49 Sam Lacey .75 2.00
50 George McGinnis .75 2.00
51 Slick Watts .75 2.00
52 Sidney Wicks .75 2.00
53 Wilbur Holland .75 2.00
54 Tim Bassett .75 2.00
55 Phil Chenier .75 2.00
56 Adrian Dantley RC 12.00 30.00
57 Jim Chones .75 2.00
58 John Lucas RC 1.00 2.50
59 Cazzie Russell .75 2.00
60 David Thompson 2.00 5.00
61 Bob Lanier .75 2.00
62 Dave Twardzik .75 2.00
63 Wilbert Jones .75 2.00
64 Clifford Ray .75 2.00
65 Doug Collins .75 2.00
66 Tom McMillen RC 1.00 2.50
67 Rich Kelley RC .75 2.00
68 Mike Bantom .75 2.00
69 Tom Boerwinkle .75 2.00
70 John Havlicek 6.00 15.00
71 Marvin Webster RC .75 2.00
72 Curtis Perry .75 2.00
73 George Gervin 4.00 10.00
74 Leonard Robinson .75 2.00
75 Wes Unseld 1.00 2.50
76 Dave Meyers .75 2.00
77 Gail Goodrich 1.00 2.50
78 Richard Washington RC .75 2.00
79 Mike Gale .75 2.00
80 Maurice Lucas .75 2.00
81 Harvey Catchings RC .75 2.00
82 Randy Smith .75 2.00
83 Campy Russell .75 2.00
84 Kevin Kunnert .75 2.00
85 Lou Hudson .75 2.00
86 Mickey Johnson .75 2.00
87 Lucius Allen .75 2.00
88 Spencer Haywood .75 2.00
89 Gus Williams .75 2.00
90 Dave Cowens 1.25 3.00
91 Al Skinner .75 2.00
92 Swen Nater .75 2.00
93 Tom Henderson .75 2.00
94 Don Buse .75 2.00
95 Alvan Adams 1.25 3.00
96 Mack Calvin .75 2.00
97 Tom Burleson .75 2.00
98 John Drew .75 2.00
99 Mike Green .75 2.00
100 Julius Erving 15.00 40.00
101 John Mengelt .75 2.00
102 Howard Porter .75 2.00
103 Billy Paultz .75 2.00
104 John Shumate .75 2.00
105 Calvin Murphy 1.25 3.00
106 Elmore Smith .75 2.00
107 Jim McMillian .75 2.00
108 Kevin Stacom .75 2.00
109 Jan Van Breda Kolff .75 2.00
110 Billy Knight .75 2.00
111 Robert Parish RC 15.00 40.00
112 Larry Wright .75 2.00
113 Bruce Seals .75 2.00
114 Junior Bridgeman .75 2.00
115 Artis Gilmore .75 2.00
116 Steve Mix .75 2.00
117 Ron Lee .75 2.00
118 Bobby Jones .75 2.00
119 Ron Boone .75 2.00
120 Bill Walton 8.00 20.00
121 Chris Ford 2.00 5.00
122 Earl Tatum .75 2.00
123 E.C. Coleman .75 2.00
124 Moses Malone 6.00 15.00
125 Charlie Scott 1.00 2.50
126 Bobby Smith .75 2.00
127 Nate Archibald 1.00 2.50
128 Mitch Kupchak RC 1.00 2.50
129 Walt Frazier 3.00 8.00
130 Rick Barry 1.25 3.00
131 Ernie DiGregorio .75 2.00
132 Darryl Dawkins RC 8.00 20.00

1978-79 Topps

COMPLETE SET (132) 25.00 60.00
1 Bill Walton ! 8.00 20.00
2 Doug Collins .75 2.00
3 Jamaal Wilkes .75 2.00
4 Wilbur Holland .75 2.00
5 Bob McAdoo .75 2.00
6 Lucius Allen .75 2.00
7 Wes Unseld .75 2.00
8 Dave Meyers .75 2.00
9 Austin Carr .75 2.00
10 Walter Davis RC 3.00 8.00
11 John Williamson .75 2.00
12 E.C. Coleman .75 2.00
13 Calvin Murphy .75 2.00
14 Bobby Jones 1.25 3.00
15 Chris Ford .75 2.00
16 Kermit Washington .75 2.00
17 Butch Beard .75 2.00
18 Steve Mix .75 2.00
19 Marvin Webster .75 2.00
20 George Gervin 2.50 6.00
21 Steve Hawes .75 2.00
22 Johnny Davis RC .75 2.00
23 Swen Nater .75 2.00
24 Lou Hudson .75 2.00
25 Elvin Hayes .75 2.00
26 Nate Archibald .75 2.00
27 James Edwards RC 1.25 3.00
28 Howard Porter .75 2.00
29 Quinn Buckner RC .75 2.00
30 Leonard Robinson .75 2.00
31 Jim Cleamons .75 2.00
32 Campy Russell .75 2.00
33 Phil Smith 6.00 15.00
34 Darryl Dawkins .75 2.00
35 Don Buse .75 2.00
36 Mickey Johnson .75 2.00
37 Mike Gale .75 2.00
38 Moses Malone 1.50 4.00
39 Gus Williams .75 2.00
40 Dave Cowens .75 2.00
41 Bobby Wilkerson RC .75 2.00
42 Wilbert Jones .75 2.00
43 Charlie Scott .75 2.00
44 John Drew .75 2.00
45 Earl Monroe .75 2.00
46 John Shumate .75 2.00
47 Earl Tatum .75 2.00
48 Mitch Kupchak .75 2.00
49 Ron Boone .75 2.00
50 Maurice Lucas .75 2.00
51 Louie Dampier .75 2.00
52 Aaron James .75 2.00
53 John Mengelt .75 2.00
54 Garfield Heard .75 2.00
55 George Johnson .75 2.00
56 Junior Bridgeman .75 2.00
57 Elmore Smith .75 2.00
58 Rudy Tomjanovich .75 2.00
59 Fred Brown .75 2.00
60 Rick Barry UER 1.00 2.50
61 Dave Bing .75 2.00
62 Anthony Roberts .75 2.00
63 Norm Nixon RC .75 2.00
64 Leon Douglas RC .75 2.00
65 Henry Bibby .75 2.00
66 Lonnie Shelton .75 2.00
67 Checklist 1-132 .75 2.00
68 Tom Henderson .75 2.00
69 Dan Roundfield .75 2.00
70 Armond Hill RC .75 2.00
71 Larry Kenon .75 2.00
72 Billy Knight .75 2.00
73 Artis Gilmore .75 2.00
74 Lionel Hollins .75 2.00
75 Bernard King RC 12.00 30.00
76 Brian Winters .75 2.00
77 Alvan Adams .75 2.00
78 Dennis Johnson RC 10.00 25.00
79 Scott Wedman .75 2.00
80 Pete Maravich 10.00 25.00
81 Dan Issel .75 2.00
82 M.L. Carr .75 2.00
83 Walt Frazier .75 2.00
84 Dwight Jones .75 2.00
85 Jo Jo White 1.00 2.50
86 Robert Parish 2.00 5.00
87 Charlie Criss RC .75 2.00
88 Jim McMillian .75 2.00
89 Chuck Williams .75 2.00
90 George McGinnis .75 2.00
91 Billy Paultz .75 2.00
92 Bob Dandridge .75 2.00
93 Ricky Sobers .75 2.00
94 Paul Silas .75 2.00
95 Gail Goodrich .75 2.00
96 Tim Bassett .75 2.00
97 Ron Lee .75 2.00
98 Bob Gross .75 2.00
99 Sam Lacey .75 2.00
100 David Thompson 1.50 4.00
101 John Gianelli .75 2.00
102 Norm Van Lier .75 2.00
103 Caldwell Jones .75 2.00
104 Eric Money .75 2.00
105 Jim Chones .75 2.00
106 John Lucas .75 2.00
107 Spencer Haywood .75 2.00
108 Eddie Johnson FC .75 2.00
109 Sidney Wicks .75 2.00
110 Kareem Abdul-Jabbar 15.00 40.00
111 Sonny Parker RC .75 2.00
112 Randy Smith .75 2.00
113 Kevin Grevey .75 2.00
114 Rich Kelley .75 2.00
115 Scott May .75 2.00
116 Lloyd Free .75 2.00
117 Jack Sikma RC 1.25 3.00
118 Kevin Porter .75 2.00
119 Darnell Hillman .75 2.00
120 Paul Westphal .75 2.00
121 Richard Washington .75 2.00
122 Dave Twardzik .75 2.00
123 Mike Bantom .75 2.00
124 Mike Newlin .75 2.00
125 Bob Lanier .75 2.00
126 Marques Johnson RC 1.50 4.00
127 Foots Walker RC .75 2.00
128 Cedric Maxwell RC 3.00 8.00
129 Ray Williams RC .75 2.00
130 Julius Erving 12.00 30.00
131 Clifford Ray .75 2.00
132 Adrian Dantley ! 1.25 3.00

1979-80 Topps

COMPLETE SET (132 60.00 150.00
1 George Gervin ! 5.00 12.00
2 Mitch Kupchak .75 2.00
3 Henry Bibby 1.50 4.00
4 Bob Gross .75 2.00
5 Dave Cowens .75 2.00
6 Dennis Johnson 1.25 3.00
7 Scott Wedman .75 2.00
8 Earl Monroe .75 2.00
9 Mike Bantom .75 2.00
10 Kareem Abdul-Jabbar AS 12.00 30.00
11 Jo Jo White .75 2.00
12 Spencer Haywood .75 2.00
13 Kevin Porter .75 2.00
14 Bernard King .75 2.00
15 Mike Newlin .75 2.00
16 Sidney Wicks .75 2.00
17 Dan Issel .75 2.00
18 Tom Henderson .75 2.00
19 Jim Chones .75 2.00
20 Julius Erving 12.00 30.00
21 Brian Winters .75 2.00
22 Billy Paultz .75 2.00
23 Cedric Maxwell .75 2.00
24 Eddie Johnson .75 2.00
25 Artis Gilmore .75 2.00
26 Maurice Lucas .75 2.00
27 Gus Williams .75 2.00
28 Sam Lacey .75 2.00
29 Toby Knight .75 2.00
30 Paul Westphal AS1 .75 2.00
31 Alex English RC 8.00 20.00
32 Gail Goodrich .75 2.00
33 Caldwell Jones .75 2.00
34 Kevin Grevey .75 2.00
35 Jamaal Wilkes .75 2.00
36 Sonny Parker .75 2.00
37 John Gianelli .75 2.00
38 John Long RC .75 2.00
39 George Johnson .75 2.00
40 Lloyd Free AS2 .75 2.00
41 Rudy Tomjanovich .75 2.00
42 Foots Walker .75 2.00
43 Dan Roundfield .75 2.00
44 Reggie Theus RC 1.25 3.00
45 Bill Walton 8.00 20.00
46 Fred Brown .75 2.00
47 Darnell Hillman .75 2.00
48 Ray Williams .75 2.00
49 Larry Kenon .75 2.00
50 David Thompson .75 2.00
51 Billy Knight .75 2.00
52 Alvan Adams .75 2.00
53 Phil Smith .75 2.00
54 Adrian Dantley .75 2.00
55 John Williamson .75 2.00
56 Campy Russell .75 2.00
57 Armond Hill .75 2.00
58 Bob Lanier .75 2.00
59 Mickey Johnson .75 2.00
60 Pete Maravich 8.00 20.00
61 Nick Weatherspoon .75 2.00
62 Robert Reid RC .75 2.00
63 Mychal Thompson RC 1.00 2.50
64 Doug Collins 1.00 2.50
65 Wes Unseld 1.00 2.50
66 Jack Sikma .75 2.00
67 Bobby Wilkerson .75 2.00
68 Bill Robinzine .75 2.00
69 Joe Meriweather .75 2.00
70 Marques Johnson AS .75 2.00
71 Ricky Sobers .75 2.00
72 Clifford Ray .75 2.00
73 Tim Bassett .75 2.00
74 James Silas .75 2.00
75 Bob McAdoo .75 2.00
76 Austin Carr .75 2.00
77 Don Ford .75 2.00
78 Steve Hawes .75 2.00
79 Ron Brewer RC .75 2.00
80 Walter Davis .75 2.00
81 Calvin Murphy .75 2.00
82 Tom Boswell .75 2.00
83 Lonnie Shelton .75 2.00
84 Terry Tyler RC .75 2.00
85 Randy Smith .75 2.00
86 Rich Kelley .75 2.00
87 Otis Birdsong RC 1.00 2.50
88 Marvin Webster .75 2.00
89 Eric Money .75 2.00
90 Elvin Hayes AS1 1.25 3.00
91 Junior Bridgeman .75 2.00
92 Johnny Davis .75 2.00
93 Robert Parish 1.50 4.00
94 Eddie Jordan .75 2.00
95 Leonard Robinson .75 2.00
96 Rick Robey RC .75 2.00
97 Norm Nixon .75 2.00
98 Mark Olberding .75 2.00
99 Wilbur Holland .75 2.00
100 Moses Malone AS1 2.50 6.00
101 Checklist 1-132 .75 2.00
102 Tom Owens .75 2.00
103 Phil Chenier .75 2.00
104 John Johnson .75 2.00
105 Darryl Dawkins .75 2.00
106 Charlie Scott .75 2.00
107 M.L. Carr .75 2.00
108 Phil Ford RC 1.00 2.50
109 Swen Nater .75 2.00
110 Nate Archibald .75 2.00
111 Aaron James .75 2.00
112 Jim Cleamons .75 2.00
113 James Edwards .75 2.00
114 Don Buse .75 2.00
115 Steve Mix .75 2.00
116 Charles Johnson .75 2.00
117 Elmore Smith .75 2.00
118 John Drew .75 2.00
119 Lou Hudson .75 2.00
120 Rick Barry .75 2.00
121 Kent Benson RC 1.00 2.50
122 Mike Gale .75 2.00
123 Jan Van Breda Kolff .75 2.00
124 Chris Ford .75 2.00
125 George McGinnis .75 2.00
126 Leon Douglas .75 2.00
127 John Lucas .75 2.00
128 Kermit Washington .75 2.00
129 Lionel Hollins .75 2.00
130 Bob Dandridge AS2 1.25 3.00
131 James McElroy .75 2.00
132 Bobby Jones ! .75 2.00

1980-81 Topps

COMPLETE SET (176) 2,000.00 4,000.00
1 3/Erving/258 Brewer 2.00 5.00
2 7 Malone AS/185/Parish TL .60 1.50
3 12 Gus Williams AS .25 .60
4 24/32/248 Elvin Hayes .40 1.00
5 29 Dan Roundfield .40 1.00
6 34 Bird RC/Erving/Magic RC 800.00 1,500.00
7 36 Cowens/186/Wilkes .60 1.50
8 38 Maravich/264/194 DJ 2.50 6.00
9 40 Rick Robey .25 .60
10 47 Scott May .25 .60
11 55 Don Ford .20 .50
12 58 Campy Russell .20 .50
13 60 Foots Walker .20 .50
14 61/Jabbar AS/200 Natt 8.00 20.00
15 63 Jim Cleamons .25 .60
16 69 Tom LaGarde .20 .50
17 71 Jerome Whitehead .25 .60
18 74 John Roche TL .25 .60
19 75 English/2/68 .50 1.25
20 82 Terry Tyler TL .20 .50
21 84 Kent Benson .20 .50
22 86/Parish TL/126 .60 1.50
23 88/Erving AS/Sobers 6.00 15.00
24 90 Eric Money .20 .50
25 95 Wayne Cooper .20 .50
26 97 Parish/187/46 .75 2.00
27 98 Sonny Parker .20 .50
28 105 Barry/122/48 .40 1.00
29 106 Allen Leavell .25 .60
30 108/176 Cheeks TL/87 .25 .60
31 110 Robert Reid .25 .60
32 111 Rudy Tomjanovich .25 .60
33 112/28 Tree Rollins/15 .20 .50
34 115 Mike Bantom .20 .50
35 116 Dudley Bradley .20 .50
36 118 James Edwards .20 .50
37 119 Mickey Johnson .20 .50
38 120 Billy Knight .25 .60
39 121 George McGinnis .25 .60
40 124 Phil Ford TL .25 .60
41 127 Phil Ford .25 .60
42 131 Scott Wedman .20 .50
43 132 Jabbar TL/Mitch/81 8.00 20.00
44 135 Jabbar/79/216 8.00 20.00
45 137 Coop/Malone TL/148 .60 1.50
46 140/Lanier AS/Walton .60 1.50
47 141 Norm Nixon .25 .60
48 143/30 Bird TL/Sikma 20.00 50.00
49 146/31 Bird TL/Brewer 15.00 40.00
50 147/133 Jabbar TL/207 8.00 20.00
51 149/262 Erving SD/62 1.25 3.00
52 151 Moncrief/260/220 1.25 3.00
53 156 George Johnson .25 .60
54 158 Maurice Lucas .25 .60
55 159 Mike Newlin .20 .50
56 160 Roger Phegley .20 .50
57 161 Cliff Robinson .20 .50
58 162 Jan V.Breda Kolff .25 .60
59 165/214/Gilmore .25 .60
60 166 Cartwright/244/25 .60 1.50
61 168/14/Dantley .25 .60
62 169 Joe Meriweather .25 .60
63 170 Monroe/27/85 .25 .60
64 172 Marvin Webster .25 .60
65 173 Ray Williams .10 .30
66 178 Cheeks/Magic AS/237 20.00 50.00
67 183 Bobby Jones .40 1.00
68 189/163/Issel .40 1.00
69 190 Don Buse .25 .60
70 191 Davis/Gervin AS/136 .40 1.00
71 192/Malone TL/64 .40 1.00
72 201 Tom Owens .20 .50
73 208 Gervin/Issel TL/249 .60 1.50
74 217/263/107 Malone .60 1.50
75 219 Swen Nater .20 .50
76 221 Brian Taylor .20 .50
77 228 Fred Brown .20 .50
78 230/W.Davis AS/Archibald .40 1.00
79 231 Lonnie Shelton .25 .60
80 233 Gus Williams .20 .50
81 236 Allan Bristow TL .20 .50
82 238/109/Lanier .40 1.00
83 241 Ben Poquette .40 1.00
84 245 Greg Ballard .10 .30
85 246 Bob Dandridge .25 .60
86 250 Kevin Porter .20 .50
87 251 Unseld/195/78 .25 .60
88 257 Hayes SD/144/McAdoo .25 .60
89 3 Dan Roundfield .25 .60
90 7 Malone AS/247/52 .40 1.00
91 12 Gus Williams .20 .50
92 24 Steve Hawes .20 .50
93 29 Dan Roundfield .20 .50
94 34 Bird/Cartwright/23 25.00 60.00
95 36 Cowens/16/59 .40 1.00
96 38 Maravich/187/46 3.00 8.00
97 40 Rick Robey .25 .60
98 47/30 Bird TL/Sikma 15.00 40.00
99 55 Don Ford .40 1.00
100 58 Campy Russell .25 .60
101 60 Foots Walker .20 .50
102 61 Austin Carr .20 .50
103 63 Jim Cleamons .20 .50
104 69/109/Bob Lanier .40 1.00
105 71 Jerome Whitehead .25 .60
106 74/28 Tree Rollins/15 .20 .50
107 75 English/Malone TL/64 .60 1.50
108 82 Terry Tyler TL .25 .60
109 84 Kent Benson .25 .60
110 86 Phil Hubbard .20 .50
111 88/18 Magic AS/237 12.00 30.00
112 90 Eric Money .20 .50
113 95 Wayne Cooper .20 .50
114 97 Parish/Malone TL/148 .75 2.00
115 98 Sonny Parker .25 .60
116 105 Barry/123/54 .40 1.00
117 106 Allen Leavell .25 .60
118 108 Calvin Murphy .25 .60
119 110 Robert Reid .25 .60
120 111 Rudy Tomjanovich .40 1.00
121 112/264/D.Johnson .40 1.00
122 115 Mike Bantom .25 .60
123 116 Dudley Bradley .40 1.00
124 118/Archibald TL/Hayes .50 1.25
125 119 Mickey Johnson .40 1.00
126 120 Billy Knight .25 .60
127 121/Lanier AS/Walton .60 1.50
128 124 Phil Ford TL .25 .60
129 127 Phil Ford .25 .60
130 131 Scott Wedman .20 .50
131 132 Jabbar TL/Par.TL/126 1.50 4.00
132 135 Jabbar/253/167 2.00 5.00
133 137 M.Cooper/212/229 .50 1.25
134 140/214/Gilmore .25 .60
135 141 Norm Nixon .25 .60
136 143 Marq.Johnson TL .20 .50
137 146/Erving AS/Sobers 1.25 3.00
138 147 Quinn Buckner .25 .60
139 149 Marques Johnson .25 .60
140 151 Moncrief/Jabb.TL/207 1.50 4.00
141 156 George Johnson .20 .50
142 158/262 Erving SD/62 1.25 3.00
143 159 Mike Newlin .25 .60
144 160 Roger Phegley .20 .50
145 161 Cliff Robinson .20 .50
146 162/Erving SD/139 Magic 40.00 100.00
147 165/185/Parish TL .40 1.00
148 166 Cartwright/13/179 .40 1.00
149 168 Toby Knight .25 .60
150 169 Joe Meriweather .20 .50
151 170 Monroe/206/91 .20 .50
152 172 Marvin Webster .20 .50
153 173 Ray Williams .20 .50
154 178 Cheeks/Gervin AS/136 1.50 4.00
155 183 Bobby Jones .25 .60
156 189/14/Dantley .25 .60
157 190 Don Buse .20 .50
158 191 Walter Davis .25 .60
159 192/263/107 Malone .60 1.50
160 201 Tom Owens .25 .60
161 208 Gervin/53/223 .60 1.50
162 217/8 Jabbar AS/Natt 1.25 3.00
163 219 Swen Nater .20 .50
164 221 Brian Taylor .20 .50
165 228/31 Bird TL/Brewer 15.00 40.00
166 230/163/Issel .40 1.00
167 231 Lonnie Shelton .20 .50
168 233 Gus Williams .25 .60
169 236 Allan Bristow TL .20 .50
170 238 Tom Boswell .20 .50
171 241/Cheeks TL/51 .40 1.00
172 245/W.Davis AS/Archibald .40 1.00
173 246 Bob Dandridge .20 .50
174 250 Kevin Porter .20 .50
175 251 Unseld/67/5 .40 1.00
176 257 Hayes SD/Erving/258 2.00 5.00

1980-81 Topps Team Posters

COMPLETE SET (16) 12.00 30.00
1 Atlanta Hawks .40 1.00
2 Boston Celtics 3.00 8.00
3 Chicago Bulls .40 1.00
4 Cleveland Cavaliers .40 1.00
5 Detroit Pistons .40 1.00
6 Houston Rockets .40 1.00
7 Indiana Pacers .40 1.00
8 Los Angeles Lakers 2.50 6.00
9 Milwaukee Bucks .40 1.00
10 New Jersey Nets .40 1.00
11 New York Knicks .40 1.00
12 Philadelphia 76ers .75 2.00
13 Phoenix Suns .40 1.00
14 Portland Blazers .40 1.00
15 Seattle Sonics .40 1.00
16 Washington Bullets .40 1.00

1981-82 Topps

COMPLETE SET (198) 25.00 60.00
1 John Drew .07 .20
2 Dan Roundfield .07 .20
3 Nate Archibald .25 .60
4 Larry Bird ! 20.00 50.00
5 Cedric Maxwell .07 .20
6 Robert Parish .60 1.50
7 Artis Gilmore .25 .60
8 Ricky Sobers .02 .10
9 Mike Mitchell .07 .20
10 Tom LaGarde .02 .10
11 Dan Issel .30 .75
12 David Thompson .30 .75

13 Lloyd Free	.08	.25
14 Moses Malone	.60	1.50
15 Calvin Murphy	.08	.25
16 Johnny Davis	.02	.10
17 Otis Birdsong	.08	.25
18 Phil Ford	.07	.20
19 Scott Wedman	.02	.10
20 Kareem Abdul-Jabbar	8.00	20.00
21 Magic Johnson !	20.00	50.00
22 Norm Nixon	.08	.25
23 Jamaal Wilkes	.08	.25
24 Marques Johnson	.08	.25
25 Bob Lanier	.30	.75
26 Bill Cartwright	.20	.50
27 Michael Ray Richardson	.07	.20
28 Ray Williams	.07	.20
29 Darryl Dawkins	.08	.25
30 Julius Erving	4.00	10.00
31 Lionel Hollins	.02	.10
32 Bobby Jones	.08	.25
33 Walter Davis	.20	.50
34 Dennis Johnson	.20	.50
35 Leonard Robinson	.08	.25
36 Mychal Thompson	.08	.25
37 George Gervin	.75	2.00
38 Swen Nater	.02	.10
39 Jack Sikma	.08	.25
40 Adrian Dantley	.25	.60
41 Darrell Griffith RC	.40	1.00
42 Elvin Hayes	.30	.75
43 Fred Brown	.08	.25
44 Atlanta Hawks TL	.05	.15
45 Celtics TL/Bird/Arch	.75	2.00
46 Chicago Bulls TL	.08	.25
47 Cleveland Cavs TL	.05	.15
48 Dallas Mavericks TL	.05	.15
49 Denver Nuggets TL	.05	.15
50 Detroit Pistons TL	.05	.15
51 Golden State TL	.08	.25
52 Rockets TL/Malone	.15	.40
53 Indiana Pacers TL	.08	.25
54 Kansas City Kings TL	.05	.15
55 Lakers TL/Jabbar	.50	1.25
56 Milwaukee Bucks TL	.08	.25
57 New Jersey Nets TL	.05	.15
58 New York Knicks TL	.08	.25
59 76ers TL/Erving	.50	1.25
60 Phoenix Suns TL	.08	.25
61 Trail Blazers TL	.05	.15
62 San Antonio Spurs TL	.08	.25
63 San Diego Clippers TL	.05	.15
64 Seattle Sonics TL	.05	.15
65 Utah Jazz TL	.08	.25
66 Washington Bullets TL	.08	.25
E67 Charlie Criss	.08	.25
E68 Eddie Johnson	.05	.15
E69 Wes Matthews	.05	.15
E70 Tom McMillen	.15	.40
E71 Tree Rollins	.15	.40
E72 M.L. Carr	.08	.25
E73 Chris Ford	.08	.25
E74 Gerald Henderson RC	.15	.40
E75 Kevin McHale RC	8.00	20.00
E76 Rick Robey	.08	.25
E77 Darwin Cook RC	.05	.15
E78 Mike Gminski RC	.30	.75
E79 Maurice Lucas	.08	.25
E80 Mike Newlin	.08	.25
E81 Mike O'Koren RC	.08	.25
E82 Steve Hawes	.05	.15
E83 Foots Walker	.08	.25
E84 Campy Russell	.08	.25
E85 DeWayne Scales	.05	.15
E86 Randy Smith	.08	.25
E87 Marvin Webster	.08	.25
E88 Sly Williams	.05	.15
E89 Mike Woodson RC	.08	.25
E90 Maurice Cheeks	.60	1.50
E91 Caldwell Jones	.08	.25
E92 Steve Mix	.08	.25
E93A Checklist 1-110 ERR	.75	2.00
E93B Checklist 1-110 COR	.50	1.00
E94 Greg Ballard	.05	.15
E95 Don Collins	.05	.15
E96 Kevin Grevey	.08	.25
E97 Mitch Kupchak	.08	.25
E98 Rick Mahorn RC	.30	.75
E99 Kevin Porter	.08	.25
E100 Nate Archibald SA	.08	.25
E101 Larry Bird SA	15.00	40.00
E102 Bill Cartwright SA	.05	.15
E103 Darryl Dawkins SA	.08	.25
E104 Julius Erving SA	6.00	15.00
E105 Kevin Porter SA	.08	.25
E106 Bobby Jones SA	.08	.25
E107 Cedric Maxwell SA	.08	.25
E108 Robert Parish SA	.40	1.00
E109 M.R.Richardson SA	.08	.25
E110 Dan Roundfield SA	.08	.25
W67 T.R. Dunn RC	.20	.50
W68 Alex English	.60	1.50
W69 Billy McKinney RC	.08	.25
W70 Dave Robisch	.08	.25
W71 Joe Barry Carroll RC	.15	.40
W72 Bernard King	.40	1.00
W73 Sonny Parker	.05	.15
W74 Purvis Short	.08	.25
W75 Larry Smith RC	.15	.40
W76 Jim Chones	.08	.25
W77 Michael Cooper	.30	.75
W78 Mark Landsberger	.05	.15
W79 Alvan Adams	.08	.25
W80 Jeff Cook	.05	.15
W81 Rich Kelley	.05	.15
W82 Kyle Macy RC	.15	.40
W83 Billy Ray Bates RC	.20	.50
W84 Bob Gross	.08	.25
W85 Calvin Natt	.08	.25
W86 Lonnie Shelton	.08	.25
W87 Jim Paxson RC	.50	1.25
W88 Kelvin Ransey	.05	.15
W89 Kermit Washington	.08	.25
W90 Henry Bibby	.08	.25
W91 Michael Brooks RC	.05	.15
W92 Joe Bryant	.08	.25
W93 Phil Smith	.05	.15
W94 Brian Taylor	.05	.15
W95 Freeman Williams	.08	.25
W96 James Bailey	.05	.15
W97 Checklist 1-110	.50	1.00
W98 John Johnson	.05	.15
W99 Vinnie Johnson RC	2.00	5.00
W100 Wally Walker RC	.08	.25
W101 Paul Westphal	.08	.25
W102 Allan Bristow	.08	.25
W103 Wayne Cooper	.05	.15
W104 Carl Nicks	.05	.15
W105 Ben Poquette	.05	.15
W106 K.Abdul-Jabbar SA	8.00	20.00
W107 Dan Issel SA	.20	.50
W108 Dennis Johnson SA	.08	.25
W109 Magic Johnson SA !	20.00	50.00
W110 Jack Sikma SA	.08	.25
MW67 David Greenwood	.08	.25
MW68 Dwight Jones	.05	.15
MW69 Reggie Theus	.15	.40
MW70 Bobby Wilkerson	.05	.15
MW71 Mike Bratz	.05	.15
MW72 Kenny Carr	.05	.15
MW73 Geoff Huston	.05	.15
MW74 Bill Laimbeer RC	8.00	20.00
MW75 Roger Phegley	.05	.15
MW76 Checklist 1-110	.50	1.00
MW77 Abdul Jeelani	.05	.15
MW78 Bill Robinzine	.05	.15
MW79 Jim Spanarkel	.05	.15
MW80 Kent Benson	.08	.25
MW81 Keith Herron	.05	.15
MW82 Phil Hubbard	.05	.15
MW83 John Long	.05	.15
MW84 Terry Tyler	.05	.15
MW85 Mike Dunleavy RC	.30	.75
MW86 Tom Henderson	.05	.15
MW87 Billy Paultz	.05	.15
MW88 Robert Reid	.05	.15
MW89 Mike Bantom	.05	.15
MW90 James Edwards	.08	.25
MW91 Billy Knight	.08	.25
MW92 George McGinnis	.08	.25
MW93 Louis Orr	.05	.15
MW94 Ernie Grunfeld RC	.15	.40
MW95 Reggie King	.05	.15
MW96 Sam Lacey	.05	.15
MW97 Junior Bridgeman	.08	.25
MW98 Mickey Johnson	.05	.15
MW99 Sidney Moncrief	.30	.75
MW100 Brian Winters	.08	.25
MW101 Dave Corzine RC	.15	.40
MW102 Paul Griffin	.05	.15
MW103 Johnny Moore RC	.08	.25
MW104 Mark Olberding	.05	.15
MW105 James Silas	.08	.25
MW106 George Gervin SA	.30	.75
MW107 Artis Gilmore SA	.08	.25
MW108 Marques Johnson SA	.08	.25
MW109 Bob Lanier SA	.20	.50
MW110 Moses Malone SA	.40	1.00

1992-93 Topps

COMPLETE SET (396)	40.00	100.00
COMPLETE FACT. SET (408)	60.00	150.00
COMPLETE SERIES 1 (198)	10.00	25.00
COMPLETE SERIES 2 (198)	25.00	60.00
*GOLD: 1.25X TO 3X BASE CARD HI		
1 Larry Bird	1.50	4.00
2 Magic Johnson HL	1.50	4.00
3 Michael Jordan HL	3.00	8.00
4 David Robinson HL	.75	2.00
5 Johnny Newman	.25	.60
6 Mike Iuzzolino	.25	.60
7 Ken Norman	.25	.60
8 Chris Jackson	.30	.75
9 Duane Ferrell	.25	.60
10 Sean Elliott	.40	1.00
11 Bernard King	.50	1.25
12 Armon Gilliam	.25	.60
13 Reggie Williams	.25	.60
14 Steve Kerr	.30	.75
15 Anthony Bowie	.25	.60
16 Alton Lister	.25	.60
17 Dee Brown	.30	.75
18 Tom Chambers	.40	1.00
19 Otis Thorpe	.30	.75
20 Karl Malone	.75	2.00
21 Kenny Gattison	.25	.60
22 Lionel Simmons UER	.25	.60
23 Vern Fleming	.30	.75
24 John Paxson	.30	.75
25 Mitch Richmond	.50	1.25
26 Danny Schayes	.25	.60
27 Derrick McKey	.30	.75
28 Mark Randall	.25	.60
29 Bill Laimbeer	.40	1.00
30 Chris Morris	.30	.75
31 Alec Kessler	.25	.60
32 Vlade Divac	.40	1.00
33 Rick Fox	.40	1.00
34 Charles Shackleford	.25	.60
35 Dominique Wilkins	.60	1.50
36 Sleepy Floyd	.30	.75
37 Doug West	.30	.75
38 Pete Chilcutt	.25	.60
39 Orlando Woolridge	.40	1.00
40 Eric Leckner	.25	.60
41 Joe Kleine	.25	.60
42 Scott Skiles	.25	.60
43 Jerrod Mustaf	.25	.60
44 John Starks	.40	1.00
45 Sedale Threatt	.25	.60
46 Doug Smith	.25	.60
47 Byron Scott	.40	1.00
48 Willie Anderson	.30	.75
49 David Benoit	.25	.60
50 Scott Hastings	.25	.60
51 Terry Porter	.30	.75
52 Sidney Green	.25	.60
53 Danny Young	.25	.60
54 Magic Johnson	1.50	4.00
55 Brian Williams	.30	.75
56 Randy Wittman	.25	.60
57 Kevin McHale	.60	1.50
58 Dana Barros	.25	.60
59 Thurl Bailey	.30	.75
60 Kevin Duckworth	.30	.75
61 John Williams	.30	.75
62 Willie Burton	.25	.60
63 Spud Webb	.40	1.00
64 Detlef Schrempf	.40	1.00
65 Sherman Douglas	.30	.75
66 Patrick Ewing	.60	1.50
67 Michael Adams	.30	.75
68 Vernon Maxwell	.30	.75
69 Terrell Brandon	.30	.75
70 Terry Catledge	.25	.60
71 Mark Eaton	.40	1.00
72 Tony Smith	.25	.60
73 B.J. Armstrong	.40	1.00
74 Moses Malone	.40	1.00
75 Anthony Bonner	.25	.60
76 George McCloud	.25	.60
77 Glen Rice	.40	1.00
78 Jon Koncak	.25	.60
79 Michael Cage	.30	.75
80 Ron Harper	.40	1.00
81 Tom Tolbert	.30	.75
82 Brad Sellers	.30	.75
83 Winston Garland	.25	.60
84 Negele Knight	.25	.60
85 Ricky Pierce	.30	.75
86 Mark Aguirre	.30	.75
87 Ron Anderson	.25	.60
88 Loy Vaught	.30	.75
89 Luc Longley	.40	1.00
90 Jerry Reynolds	.25	.60
91 Terry Cummings	.30	.75
92 Rony Seikaly	.30	.75
93 Derek Harper	.30	.75
94 Clifford Robinson	.30	.75
95 Kenny Anderson	.30	.75
96 Chris Gatling	.25	.60
97 Stacey Augmon	.40	1.00
98 Chris Corchiani	.25	.60
99 Pervis Ellison	.25	.60
100 Larry Bird AS	1.50	4.00
101 John Stockton AS UER	.75	2.00
102 Clyde Drexler AS	.60	1.50
103 Scottie Pippen AS	1.00	2.50
104 Reggie Lewis AS	.40	1.00
105 Hakeem Olajuwon AS	.75	2.00
106 David Robinson AS	.75	2.00
107 Charles Barkley AS	1.00	2.50
108 James Worthy AS	.60	1.50
109 Kevin Willis AS	.30	.75
110 Dikembe Mutombo AS	.60	1.50
111 Joe Dumars AS	.50	1.25
112 Jeff Hornacek AS UER (5 or 7 shots should be 5 of 7 shots)	.30	.75
113 Mark Price AS	.40	1.00
114 Michael Adams AS	.30	.75
115 Michael Jordan AS	3.00	8.00
116 Brad Daugherty AS	.30	.75
117 Dennis Rodman AS	1.00	2.50
118 Isiah Thomas AS	.60	1.50
119 Tim Hardaway AS	.50	1.25
120 Chris Mullin AS	.50	1.25
121 Patrick Ewing AS	.60	1.50
122 Dan Majerle AS	.40	1.00
123 Karl Malone AS	.75	2.00
124 Otis Thorpe AS	.30	.75
125 Dominique Wilkins AS	.60	1.50
126 Magic Johnson AS	1.50	4.00
127 Charles Oakley	.40	1.00
128 Robert Pack	.25	.60
129 Billy Owens	.30	.75
130 Jeff Malone	.30	.75
131 Danny Ferry	.30	.75
132 Sam Bowie	.25	.60
133 Avery Johnson	.30	.75
134 Jayson Williams	.30	.75
135 Fred Roberts	.25	.60
136 Greg Sutton	.25	.60
137 Dennis Rodman	1.00	2.50
138 John Williams	.25	.60
139 Greg Dreiling	.25	.60
140 Rik Smits	.30	.75
141 Michael Jordan	3.00	8.00
142 Nick Anderson	.30	.75
143 Jerome Kersey	.25	.60
144 Fat Lever	.30	.75
145 Tyrone Corbin	.30	.75
146 Robert Parish	.50	1.25
147 Steve Smith	.40	1.00
148 Chris Dudley	.25	.60
149 Antoine Carr	.25	.60
150 Elden Campbell	.25	.60
151 Randy White	.25	.60
152 Felton Spencer	.25	.60
153 Cedric Ceballos	.30	.75
154 Mark Macon	.25	.60
155 Jack Haley	.25	.60
156 Bimbo Coles	.30	.75
157 A.J. English	.25	.60
158 Kendall Gill	.30	.75
159 A.C. Green	.30	.75
160 Mark West	.25	.60
161 Benoit Benjamin	.25	.60
162 Tyrone Hill	.25	.60
163 Larry Nance	.30	.75
164 Gary Grant	.25	.60
165 Bill Cartwright	.25	.60
166 Greg Anthony	.30	.75
167 Jim Les	.25	.60
168 Johnny Dawkins	.25	.60
169 Alvin Robertson	.25	.60
170 Kenny Smith	.30	.75
171 Gerald Glass	.25	.60
172 Harvey Grant	.25	.60
173 Paul Graham	.25	.60
174 Sam Perkins	.30	.75
175 Manute Bol	.40	1.00
176 Muggsy Bogues	.40	1.00
177 Mike Brown	.25	.60
178 Donald Hodge	.25	.60
179 Dave Jamerson	.25	.60
180 Mookie Blaylock	.40	1.00
181 Randy Brown	.25	.60
182 Todd Lichti	.25	.60
183 Kevin Gamble	.25	.60
184 Gary Payton	.60	1.50
185 Brian Shaw	.25	.60
186 Grant Long	.25	.60
187 Frank Brickowski	.25	.60
188 Tim Hardaway	.50	1.25
189 Danny Manning	.30	.75
190 Kevin Johnson	.40	1.00
191 Craig Ehlo	.30	.75
192 Dennis Scott	.30	.75
193 Reggie Miller	.75	2.00
194 Darrell Walker	.25	.60
195 Anthony Mason	.30	.75
196 Buck Williams	.30	.75
197 Checklist 1-99	.20	.50
198 Checklist 100-198	.20	.50
199 Karl Malone 50P	.75	2.00
200 Dominique Wilkins 50P	.60	1.50
201 Tom Chambers 50P	.40	1.00
202 Bernard King 50P	.50	1.25
203 Kiki Vandeweghe 50P	.25	.60
204 Dale Ellis 50P	.30	.75
205 Michael Jordan 50P	3.00	8.00
206 Michael Adams 50P	.30	.75
207 Charles Smith 50P	.30	.75
208 Moses Malone 50P	.40	1.00
209 Terry Cummings 50P	.30	.75
210 Vernon Maxwell 50P	.30	.75
211 Patrick Ewing 50P	.60	1.50
212 Clyde Drexler 50P	.60	1.50
213 Kevin McHale 50P	.60	1.50
214 Hakeem Olajuwon 50P	.75	2.00
215 Reggie Miller 50P	.75	2.00
216 Gary Grant 20A	.25	.60
217 Doc Rivers 20A	.40	1.00
218 Mark Price 20A	.40	1.00
219 Isiah Thomas 20A	.60	1.50
220 Nate McMillan 20A	.30	.75
221 Fat Lever 20A	.25	.60
222 Kevin Johnson 20A	.40	1.00
223 John Stockton 20A	.75	2.00
224 Scott Skiles 20A	.25	.60
225 Kevin Brooks	.25	.60
226 Bobby Phills RC	.30	.75
227 Oliver Miller RC	.30	.75
228 John Williams	.25	.60
229 Brad Lohaus	.25	.60
230 Derrick Coleman	.40	1.00
231 Ed Pinckney	.25	.60
232 Trent Tucker	.25	.60
233 Lance Blanks	.25	.60
234 Drazen Petrovic	.50	1.25
235 Mark Bryant	.25	.60
236 Lloyd Daniels RC	.30	.75
237 Dale Davis	.25	.60
238 Jayson Williams	.25	.60
239 Mike Sanders	.25	.60
240 Mike Gminski	.25	.60
241 William Bedford	.25	.60
242 Dell Curry	.30	.75
243 Gerald Paddio	.25	.60
244 Chris Smith RC	.25	.60
245 Jud Buechler	.25	.60
246 Walter Palmer	.25	.60
247 Larry Krystkowiak	.30	.75
248 Marcus Liberty	.25	.60
249 Sam Mitchell	.25	.60
250 Kiki Vandeweghe	.30	.75
251 Vincent Askew	.25	.60
252 Travis Mays	.25	.60
253 Charles Smith	.30	.75
254 John Bagley	.25	.60
255 James Worthy	.60	1.50
256 Paul Pressey P/CO	.30	.75
257 Rumeal Robinson	.30	.75
258 Tom Gugliotta RC	.40	1.00
259 Eric Anderson RC	.25	.60
260 Hersey Hawkins	.30	.75
261 Terry Davis	.25	.60
262 Rex Chapman	.30	.75
263 Chucky Brown	.25	.60
264 Danny Young	.25	.60
265 Olden Polynice	.25	.60
266 Kevin Willis	.30	.75
267 Shawn Kemp	.60	1.50
268 Mookie Blaylock	.40	1.00
269 Malik Sealy RC	.30	.75
270 Charles Barkley	1.00	2.50
271 Corey Williams RC	.30	.75
272 Stephen Howard RC	.25	.60
273 Keith Askins	.25	.60
274 Matt Bullard	.25	.60
275 John Battle	.25	.60
276 Andrew Lang	.25	.60
277 David Robinson	.75	2.00
278 Harold Miner RC	.50	1.25
279 Tracy Murray RC	.30	.75
280 Pooh Richardson	.25	.60
281 Dikembe Mutombo	.60	1.50
282 Wayman Tisdale	.40	1.00
283 Larry Johnson	.50	1.25
284 Todd Day RC	.25	.60
285 Stanley Roberts	.25	.60
286 Randy Woods UER RC	.25	.60
287 Avery Johnson	.25	.60
288 Anthony Peeler RC	.30	.75
289 Mario Elie	.30	.75
290 Doc Rivers	.40	1.00
291 Blue Edwards	.25	.60
292 Sean Rooks RC	.25	.60
293 Xavier McDaniel	.25	.60
294 C.Weatherspoon RC	.40	1.00
295 Morlon Wiley	.25	.60
296 LaBradford Smith	.25	.60
297 Reggie Lewis	.40	1.00
298 Chris Mullin	.50	1.25
299 Litterial Green RC	.25	.60
300 Elmore Spencer RC	.25	.60
301 John Stockton	.75	2.00
302 Walt Williams RC	.40	1.00
303 Anthony Pullard RC	.25	.60
304 Gundars Vetra RC	.25	.60
305 LaSalle Thompson	.25	.60
306 Nate McMillan	.30	.75
307 Steve Bardo RC	.25	.60
308 Robert Horry RC	1.00	2.50
309 Scott Williams	.25	.60
310 Bo Kimble	.30	.75
311 Tree Rollins	.30	.75
312 Tim Perry	.25	.60
313 Isaac Austin RC	.25	.60
314 Tate George	.25	.60
315 Kevin Lynch	.25	.60
316 Victor Alexander	.25	.60
317 Doug Overton	.30	.75
318 Tom Hammonds	.25	.60
319 LaPhonso Ellis RC	.40	1.00
320 Scott Brooks	.30	.75
321 Anthony Avent UER RC	.25	.60
322 Matt Geiger RC	.25	.60
323 Duane Causwell	.25	.60
324 Horace Grant	.40	1.00
325 Mark Jackson	.40	1.00
326 Dan Majerle	.40	1.00
327 Chuck Person	.30	.75
328 Buck Johnson	.25	.60
329 Duane Cooper RC	.25	.60
330 Rod Strickland	.30	.75
331 Isiah Thomas	.60	1.50
332 Greg Kite	.25	.60
333 Don MacLean RC	.30	.75
334 Christian Laettner RC	1.25	3.00
335 John Crotty RC	.25	.60
336 Tracy Moore RC	.25	.60
337 Hakeem Olajuwon	.75	2.00
338 Byron Houston RC	.25	.60
339 Walter Bond RC	.25	.60
340 Brent Price RC	.25	.60
341 Bryant Stith RC	.30	.75
342 Will Perdue	.25	.60
343 Jeff Hornacek	.30	.75
344 Adam Keefe RC	.25	.60
345 Rafael Addison	.25	.60
346 Marlon Maxey RC	.25	.60
347 Joe Dumars	.50	1.25
348 Jon Barry RC	.25	.60
349 Marty Conlon	.25	.60
350 Alaa Abdelnaby	.25	.60
351 Micheal Williams	.25	.60
352 Brad Daugherty	.30	.75
353 Tony Bennett RC	.25	.60
354 Clyde Drexler	.60	1.50
355 Rolando Blackman	.30	.75
356 Tom Tolbert	.30	.75
357 Sarunas Marciulionis	.40	1.00
358 Jaren Jackson RC	.25	.60
359 Stacey King	.25	.60
360 Danny Ainge	.40	1.00
361 Dale Ellis	.30	.75
362 Shaquille O'Neal RC	10.00	25.00
363 Bob McCann RC	.25	.60
364 Reggie Smith RC	.25	.60
365 Vinny Del Negro	.30	.75
366 Robert Pack	.25	.60
367 David Wood	.25	.60
368 Rodney McCray	.25	.60
369 Terry Mills	.30	.75
370 Eric Murdock UER	.25	.60
371 Alex Blackwell RC	.25	.60
372 Jay Humphries	.30	.75
373 Eddie Lee Wilkins	.25	.60
374 James Edwards	.25	.60
375 Tim Kempton	.25	.60
376 J.R. Reid	.30	.75
377 Sam Mack RC	.25	.60
378 Donald Royal	.25	.60
379 Mark Price	.40	1.00
380 Mark Acres	.25	.60
381 Hubert Davis RC	.30	.75
382 Dave Johnson RC	.25	.60
383 John Salley	.30	.75
384 Eddie Johnson	.30	.75
385 Brian Howard RC	.25	.60
386 Isaiah Morris RC	.30	.75
387 Frank Johnson UER	.30	.75
388 Rick Mahorn	.30	.75
389 Scottie Pippen	1.00	2.50
390 Lee Mayberry RC	.25	.60
391 Tony Campbell	.25	.60
392 Latrell Sprewell RC	1.25	3.00
393 Alonzo Mourning RC	2.00	5.00
394 Robert Werdann RC	.25	.60
395 Checklist 199-297 UER	.20	.50
396 Checklist 298-396	.20	.50

1992-93 Topps Beam Team

COMPLETE SET (7)	8.00	20.00
SER.2 STATED ODDS 1:18		
*GOLD: 1.25X TO 3X HI COLUMN		
ONE GOLD BT SET PER GOLD FACTORY SET		
1 R.Miller/Barkley/Drexler	1.25	3.00
2 Ewing/T.Hard/Mourning	.75	2.00
3 K.Johnson/Jordan/Rodman	4.00	10.00
4 Wilkins/Stockton/K.Malon	1.00	2.50
5 Olajuwon/M.Price/Kemp	1.00	2.50
6 Pippen/D.Robinson/J.Malone	1.25	3.00
7 Mullin/O'Neal/Rice	4.00	10.00

1993-94 Topps

COMPLETE SET (396)	10.00	25.00
COMPLETE FACT.SET (410)	12.00	30.00
COMPLETE SERIES 1 (198)	5.00	12.00
COMPLETE SERIES 2 (198)	5.00	12.00
SUBSET CARDS SAME VALUE AS BASE CARDS		
1 Charles Barkley HL	.40	1.00
2 Hakeem Olajuwon HL	.30	.75
3 Shaquille O'Neal HL	.75	2.00
4 Chris Jackson HL	.12	.30
5 Clifford Robinson HL	.15	.40
6 Donald Hodge	.10	.25
7 Victor Alexander	.10	.25
8 Chris Morris	.10	.25
9 Muggsy Bogues	.15	.40
10 Steve Smith UER	.12	.30
11 Dave Johnson	.10	.25
12 Tom Gugliotta	.12	.30
13 Doug Edwards RC	.15	.40
14 Vlade Divac	.15	.40
15 Corie Blount RC	.15	.40
16 Derek Harper	.12	.30
17 Matt Bullard	.10	.25
18 Terry Catledge	.10	.25
19 Mark Eaton	.15	.40
20 Mark Jackson	.12	.30
21 Terry Mills	.10	.25
22 Johnny Dawkins	.12	.30
23 Michael Jordan UER	1.50	4.00
24 Rick Fox UER	.12	.30
25 Charles Oakley	.15	.40
26 Derrick McKey	.12	.30
27 Christian Laettner	.15	.40
28 Todd Day	.10	.25
29 Danny Ferry	.10	.25
30 Kevin Johnson	.15	.40
31 Vinny Del Negro	.10	.25
32 Kevin Brooks	.10	.25
33 Pete Chilcutt	.10	.25
34 Larry Stewart	.10	.25
35 Dave Jamerson	.10	.25
36 Sidney Green	.10	.25
37 J.R. Reid	.12	.30
38 Jim Jackson	.12	.30
39 Micheal Williams UER	.10	.25
40 Rex Walters RC	.12	.30
41 Shawn Bradley RC	.15	.40
42 Jon Koncak	.10	.25
43 Byron Houston	.10	.25
44 Brian Shaw	.10	.25
45 Bill Cartwright	.12	.30
46 Jerome Kersey	.12	.30
47 Danny Schayes	.10	.25
48 Olden Polynice	.10	.25
49 Anthony Peeler	.10	.25
50 Nick Anderson 50P	.12	.30
51 David Benoit	.10	.25
52 David Robinson 50P	.30	.75
53 Greg Kite	.10	.25
54 Gerald Paddio	.10	.25
55 Don MacLean	.10	.25
56 Randy Woods	.10	.25
57 Reggie Miller 50P	.30	.75
58 Kevin Gamble	.10	.25
59 Sean Green	.10	.25
60 Jeff Hornacek	.12	.30
61 John Starks	.15	.40
62 Gerald Wilkins	.12	.30
63 Jim Les	.10	.25
64 Michael Jordan 50P	1.50	4.00
65 Alvin Robertson	.12	.30
66 Tim Kempton	.10	.25
67 Bryant Stith	.10	.25
68 Jeff Turner	.10	.25
69 Malik Sealy	.10	.25
70 Dell Curry	.15	.40
71 Brent Price	.10	.25
72 Kevin Lynch	.10	.25
73 Bimbo Coles	.10	.25
74 Larry Nance	.12	.30
75 Luther Wright RC	.10	.25
76 Willie Anderson	.10	.25
77 Dennis Rodman	.40	1.00
78 Anthony Mason	.12	.30
79 Chris Gatling	.10	.25
80 Antoine Carr	.10	.25
81 Kevin Willis	.12	.30
82 Thurl Bailey	.10	.25
83 Reggie Williams	.10	.25
84 Rod Strickland	.12	.30
85 Rolando Blackman	.15	.40
86 Bobby Hurley RC	.15	.40
87 Jeff Malone	.12	.30
88 James Worthy	.20	.50
89 Alaa Abdelnaby	.10	.25
90 Duane Ferrell	.10	.25
91 Anthony Avent	.10	.25
92 Scottie Pippen	.40	1.00
93 Ricky Pierce	.12	.30
94 P.J. Brown RC	.15	.40
95 Jeff Grayer	.10	.25
96 Jerrod Mustaf	.10	.25
97 Elmore Spencer	.10	.25
98 Walt Williams	.15	.40
99 Otis Thorpe	.15	.40
100 Patrick Ewing AS	.25	.60
101 Michael Jordan AS	1.50	4.00
102 John Stockton AS	.30	.75
103 Dominique Wilkins AS	.25	.60
104 Charles Barkley AS	.40	1.00
105 Lee Mayberry	.10	.25
106 James Edwards	.10	.25
107 Scott Brooks	.10	.25
108 John Battle	.10	.25
109 Kenny Gattison	.10	.25
110 Pooh Richardson	.10	.25
111 Rony Seikaly	.12	.30
112 Mahmoud Abdul-Rauf	.12	.30
113 Nick Anderson	.12	.30
114 Gundars Vetra	.10	.25
115 Joe Dumars AS	.20	.50
116 Hakeem Olajuwon AS	.30	.75
117 Scottie Pippen AS	.40	1.00
118 Mark Price AS	.15	.40
119 Karl Malone AS	.30	.75
120 Michael Cage	.10	.25
121 Ed Pinckney	.10	.25
122 Jay Humphries	.10	.25
123 Dale Davis	.12	.30
124 Sean Rooks	.10	.25
125 Mookie Blaylock	.15	.40
126 Buck Williams	.12	.30
127 John Williams	.10	.25
128 Stacey King	.10	.25
129 Tim Perry	.10	.25
130 Tim Hardaway AS	.20	.50
131 Larry Johnson AS	.20	.50
132 Detlef Schrempf AS	.15	.40
133 Reggie Miller AS	.30	.75
134 Shaquille O'Neal AS	.75	2.00
135 Dale Ellis	.10	.25
136 Duane Causwell	.10	.25
137 Rumeal Robinson	.10	.25
138 Billy Owens	.12	.30
139 Malcolm Mackey RC	.10	.25
140 Vernon Maxwell	.12	.30
141 LaPhonso Ellis	.12	.30
142 Robert Parish	.20	.50
143 LaBradford Smith	.10	.25
144 Charles Smith	.10	.25
145 Terry Porter	.10	.25
146 Elden Campbell	.15	.40
147 Bill Laimbeer	.15	.40
148 Chris Mills RC	.15	.40
149 Brad Lohaus	.10	.25
150 Jim Jackson ART	.12	.30
151 Tom Gugliotta ART	.12	.30
152 Shaquille O'Neal ART	.75	2.00
153 Latrell Sprewell ART	.25	.60
154 Walt Williams ART	.15	.40
155 Gary Payton	.20	.50
156 Orlando Woolridge	.10	.25
157 Adam Keefe	.10	.25
158 Calbert Cheaney RC	.15	.40
159 Rick Mahorn	.12	.30
160 Robert Horry	.15	.40
161 John Salley	.12	.30
162 Sam Mitchell	.10	.25
163 Stanley Roberts	.10	.25
164 Clarence Weatherspoon	.10	.25
165 Anthony Bowie	.10	.25
166 Derrick Coleman	.15	.40
167 Negele Knight	.10	.25
168 Marlon Maxey	.10	.25
169 Spud Webb UER	.12	.30
170 Alonzo Mourning	.25	.60
171 Ervin Johnson RC	.15	.40
172 Sedale Threatt	.10	.25
173 Mark Macon	.10	.25
174 B.J. Armstrong	.15	.40
175 Harold Miner ART	.12	.30
176 Anthony Peeler ART	.10	.25
177 Alonzo Mourning ART	.25	.60
178 Christian Laettner ART	.15	.40
179 Clarence Weatherspoon ART	.10	.25
180 Dee Brown	.12	.30
181 Shaquille O'Neal	.75	2.00
182 Loy Vaught	.10	.25
183 Terrell Brandon	.12	.30
184 Lionel Simmons	.10	.25
185 Mark Aguirre	.12	.30
186 Danny Ainge	.15	.40
187 Reggie Miller	.30	.75
188 Terry Davis	.10	.25
189 Mark Bryant	.10	.25
190 Tyrone Corbin	.10	.25
191 Chris Mullin	.20	.50
192 Johnny Newman	.10	.25
193 Doug West	.10	.25
194 Keith Askins	.10	.25
195 Bo Kimble	.10	.25
196 Sean Elliott	.15	.40
197 Checklist 1-99 UER	.05	.15
198 Checklist 100-198	.05	.15
199 Michael Jordan FPM	1.50	4.00
200 Patrick Ewing FPM	.25	.60
201 John Stockton FPM	.30	.75
202 Shawn Kemp FPM	.25	.60
203 Mark Price FPM	.15	.40
204 Charles Barkley FPM	.40	1.00
205 Hakeem Olajuwon FPM	.30	.75
206 Clyde Drexler FPM	.25	.60
207 Kevin Johnson FPM	.15	.40
208 John Starks FPM	.15	.40
209 Chris Mullin FPM	.20	.50
210 Doc Rivers	.12	.30
211 Kenny Walker	.10	.25
212 Doug Christie	.12	.30
213 James Robinson RC	.15	.40
214 Larry Krystkowiak	.10	.25
215 Manute Bol	.10	.25
216 Carl Herrera	.10	.25
217 Paul Graham	.10	.25
218 Jud Buechler	.10	.25
219 Mike Brown	.10	.25
220 Tom Chambers	.15	.40
221 Kendall Gill	.12	.30
222 Kenny Anderson	.12	.30
223 Larry Johnson	.20	.50
224 Chris Webber RC	.75	2.00
225 Randy White	.10	.25
226 Rik Smits	.12	.30
227 A.C. Green	.12	.30
228 David Robinson	.30	.75
229 Sean Elliott	.15	.40
230 Gary Grant	.10	.25
231 Dana Barros	.10	.25
232 Bobby Hurley	.15	.40
233 Blue Edwards	.10	.25
234 Tom Hammonds	.10	.25
235 Pete Myers UER	.10	.25
236 Acie Earl RC	.15	.40
237 Tony Smith	.10	.25
238 Bill Wennington	.10	.25
239 Andrew Lang	.10	.25
240 Ervin Johnson	.15	.40
241 Byron Scott	.15	.40
242 Eddie Johnson	.10	.25
243 Anthony Bonner	.10	.25
244 Luther Wright	.10	.25
245 LaSalle Thompson	.10	.25
246 Harold Miner	.12	.30
247 Chris Smith	.10	.25
248 John Williams	.10	.25
249 Clyde Drexler	.25	.60
250 Calbert Cheaney	.15	.40
251 Avery Johnson	.12	.30
252 Steve Kerr	.12	.30
253 Warren Kidd RC	.10	.25
254 Wayman Tisdale	.12	.30
255 Bob Martin RC	.15	.40
256 Popeye Jones RC	.15	.40
257 Jimmy Oliver	.10	.25
258 Kevin Edwards	.10	.25
259 Dan Majerle	.15	.40
260 Jon Barry	.10	.25
261 Allan Houston RC	.30	.75
262 Dikembe Mutombo	.25	.60
263 Sleepy Floyd	.12	.30
264 George Lynch RC	.15	.40
265 Stacey Augmon UER	.12	.30
266 Hakeem Olajuwon	.30	.75
267 Scott Skiles	.10	.25
268 Detlef Schrempf	.15	.40
269 Brian Davis RC	.15	.40
270 Tracy Murray	.10	.25
271 Gheorghe Muresan RC	.15	.40
272 Terry Dehere RC	.15	.40
273 Terry Cummings	.12	.30
274 Keith Jennings	.10	.25
275 Tyrone Hill	.10	.25
276 Hersey Hawkins	.12	.30
277 Grant Long	.10	.25
278 Herb Williams	.10	.25
279 Karl Malone	.30	.75
280 Mitch Richmond	.20	.50

281 Derek Strong RC .12 .30
282 Dino Radja RC .15 .40
283 Jack Haley .10 .25
284 Derek Harper .12 .30
285 Dwayne Schintzius .10 .25
286 Michael Curry RC .15 .40
287 Rodney Rogers RC .15 .40
288 Horace Grant .15 .40
289 Oliver Miller .10 .25
290 Luc Longley .12 .30
291 Walter Bond .10 .25
292 Dominique Wilkins .25 .60
293 Vern Fleming .12 .30
294 Mark Price .15 .40
295 Mark Aguirre .12 .30
296 Shawn Kemp .25 .60
297 Pervis Ellison .10 .25
298 Josh Grant RC .12 .30
299 Scott Burrell RC .15 .40
300 Patrick Ewing .25 .60
301 Sam Cassell RC .30 .75
302 Nick Van Exel RC .40 1.00
303 Clifford Robinson .15 .40
304 Frank Johnson .10 .25
305 Matt Geiger .10 .25
306 Vin Baker RC .25 .60
307 Benoit Benjamin .10 .25
308 Shawn Bradley .15 .40
309 Chris Whitney RC .12 .30
310 Eric Riley RC .15 .40
311 Isiah Thomas .25 .60
312 Jamal Mashburn RC .30 .75
313 Xavier McDaniel .15 .40
314 Mike Peplowski RC .10 .25
315 Darnell Mee RC .10 .25
316 Toni Kukoc RC .40 1.00
317 Felton Spencer .10 .25
318 Sam Bowie .12 .30
319 Mario Elie .12 .30
320 Tim Hardaway .20 .50
321 Ken Norman .10 .25
322 Isaiah Rider RC .25 .60
323 Rex Chapman .10 .25
324 Dennis Rodman .40 1.00
325 Derrick McKey .12 .30
326 Corie Blount .15 .40
327 Fat Lever .12 .30
328 Ron Harper .15 .40
329 Eric Anderson .10 .25
330 Armon Gilliam .10 .25
331 Lindsey Hunter RC .15 .40
332 Eric Leckner .10 .25
333 Chris Corchiani .10 .25
334 Anfernee Hardaway RC .75 2.00
335 Randy Brown .10 .25
336 Sam Perkins .12 .30
337 Glen Rice .15 .40
338 Orlando Woolridge .10 .25
339 Mike Gminski .10 .25
340 Latrell Sprewell .25 .60
341 Harvey Grant .10 .25
342 Doug Smith .10 .25
343 Kevin Duckworth .12 .30
344 Cedric Ceballos .12 .30
345 Chuck Person .12 .30
346 Scott Haskin RC .10 .25
347 Frank Brickowski .10 .25
348 Scott Williams .10 .25
349 Brad Daugherty .12 .30
350 Willie Burton .10 .25
351 Joe Dumars .20 .50
352 Craig Ehlo .10 .25
353 Lucious Harris RC .15 .40
354 Danny Manning .12 .30
355 Litterial Green .10 .25
356 John Stockton .30 .75
357 Nate McMillan .12 .30
358 Greg Graham RC .10 .25
359 Rex Walters .10 .25
360 Lloyd Daniels .10 .25
361 Antonio Harvey RC .15 .40
362 Brian Williams .10 .25
363 LeRon Ellis .10 .25
364 Chris Dudley .12 .30
365 Hubert Davis .12 .30
366 Evers Burns RC .15 .40
367 Sherman Douglas .10 .25
368 Sarunas Marciulionis .15 .40
369 Tom Tolbert .10 .25
370 Robert Pack .10 .25
371 Michael Adams .12 .30
372 Negele Knight .10 .25
373 Charles Barkley .40 1.00
374 Bryon Russell RC .15 .40
375 Greg Anthony .10 .25
376 Ken Williams .10 .25
377 John Paxson .15 .40
378 Corey Gaines .10 .25
379 Eric Murdock .10 .25
380 Kevin Thompson RC .10 .25
381 Moses Malone .25 .60
382 Kenny Smith .12 .30
383 Dennis Scott .10 .25
384 Michael Jordan FSL 1.50 4.00
385 Hakeem Olajuwon FSL .30 .75
386 Shaquille O'Neal FSL .75 2.00
387 David Robinson FSL .30 .75
388 Derrick Coleman FSL .15 .40
389 Karl Malone FSL .30 .75
390 Patrick Ewing FSL .25 .60
391 Scottie Pippen FSL .40 1.00
392 Dominique Wilkins FSL .25 .60
393 Charles Barkley FSL .40 1.00
394 Larry Johnson FSL .20 .50
395 Checklist .05 .15
396 Checklist .05 .15
NNO Expired Finest Redempt. .40 1.00

1993-94 Topps Gold

COMPLETE SET (396) 30.00 70.00
COMPLETE SERIES 1 (198) 12.00 30.00
COMPLETE SERIES 2 (198) 15.00 40.00
*STARS: .6X TO 1.5X BASE CARD HI
*RCs: .6X TO 1.5X BASE HI
ONE PER PACK
23 Michael Jordan UER 4.00 10.00
197 Frank Johnson .15 .40
198 David Wingate .15 .40
395 Will Perdue .15 .40
396 Mark West .15 .40

1993-94 Topps Black Gold

COMPLETE SET (25) 8.00 20.00
COMPLETE SERIES 1 (13) 2.00 5.00
COMPLETE SERIES 2 (12) 6.00 15.00
SER.1/2 STATED ODDS 1:72 HOB/RET
SER.1/2 STATED ODDS 1:18 JUM/RACK
1 Sean Elliott .30 .75
2 Dennis Scott .20 .50
3 Kenny Anderson .25 .60
4 Alonzo Mourning .50 1.25
5 Glen Rice .30 .75
6 Billy Owens .25 .60
7 Jim Jackson .25 .60
8 Derrick Coleman .30 .75
9 Larry Johnson .40 1.00
10 Gary Payton .40 1.00
11 Christian Laettner .30 .75
12 Dikembe Mutombo .50 1.25
13 Mahmoud Abdul-Rauf .25 .60
14 Isaiah Rider .60 1.50
15 Steve Smith .25 .60
16 LaPhonso Ellis .25 .60
17 Danny Ferry .20 .50
18 Shaquille O'Neal 1.50 4.00
19 Anfernee Hardaway 2.00 5.00
20 J.R. Reid .20 .50
21 Shawn Bradley .40 1.00
22 Pervis Ellison .20 .50
23 Chris Webber 2.00 5.00
24 Jamal Mashburn .75 2.00
25 Kendall Gill .15 .40
A1 Winner A 1-13 EXCH 2.00 5.00
A2 Winner A 1-13 Prize .20 .50
B1 Winner B 14-25 EXCH 2.00 5.00
B2 Winner B 14-25 Prize .20 .50
AB1 Winner AB 1-25 EXCH 3.00 8.00
AB2 Winner AB 1-25 Prize .40 1.00

1994-95 Topps

COMPLETE SET (396) 25.00 60.00
COMPLETE SERIES 1 (198) 12.00 30.00
COMPLETE SERIES 2 (198) 12.00 30.00
*SPECT: 2X TO 5X BASE CARD HI
1 Patrick Ewing AS .60 1.50
2 Mookie Blaylock AS .40 1.00
3 Charles Oakley AS .40 1.00
4 Mark Price AS .40 1.00
5 John Starks AS .40 1.00
6 Dominique Wilkins AS .60 1.50
7 Horace Grant AS .40 1.00
8 Alonzo Mourning AS .60 1.50
9 B.J. Armstrong AS .40 1.00
10 Kenny Anderson AS .30 .75
11 Scottie Pippen AS 1.00 2.50
12 Derrick Coleman AS .40 1.00
13 Shaquille O'Neal AS 1.50 4.00
14 Anfernee Hardaway AS .75 2.00
15 Isaiah Rider SPEC .40 1.00
16 John Williams .25 .60
17 Todd Day .25 .60
18 Dale Davis .25 .60
19 Sean Rooks .25 .60
20 George Lynch .25 .60
21 Mitchell Butler .25 .60
22 Stacey King .25 .60
23 Sherman Douglas .25 .60
24 Derrick McKey .25 .60
25 Joe Dumars .40 1.00
26 Scott Brooks .25 .60
27 Clarence Weatherspoon .25 .60
28 Jayson Williams .25 .60
29 Scottie Pippen 1.00 2.50
30 John Starks .40 1.00
31 Robert Pack .30 .75
32 Donald Royal .25 .60
33 Haywoode Workman .25 .60
34 Greg Graham .25 .60
35 Terry Cummings .30 .75
36 Andrew Lang .25 .60
37 Jason Kidd RC 2.00 5.00
38 Terry Mills .25 .60
39 Alonzo Mourning .60 1.50
40 Shawn Kemp .60 1.50
41 Kevin Willis .30 .75
42 Kevin Willis FTR .30 .75
43 Armon Gilliam .25 .60
44 Bobby Hurley .25 .60
45 Jerome Kersey .25 .60
46 Xavier McDaniel .25 .60
47 Chris Webber .75 2.00
48 Chris Webber FTR .75 2.00
49 Jeff Malone .25 .60
50 Dikembe Mutombo SPEC .60 1.50
51 Dan Majerle SPEC .40 1.00
52 Dee Brown SPEC .30 .75
53 John Stockton SPEC .75 2.00
54 Dennis Rodman SPEC 1.00 2.50
55 Eric Murdock SPEC .25 .60
56 Glen Rice .40 1.00
57 Glen Rice FTR .40 1.00
58 Dino Radja .25 .60
59 Billy Owens .25 .60
60 Doc Rivers .30 .75
61 Don MacLean .25 .60
62 Lindsey Hunter .25 .60
63 Sam Cassell .40 1.00
64 James Worthy .50 1.25
65 Christian Laettner .30 .75
66 Wesley Person RC .40 1.00
67 Rich King .25 .60
68 Jon Koncak .25 .60
69 Muggsy Bogues .30 .75
70 Jamal Mashburn .40 1.00
71 Gary Grant .25 .60
72 Eric Murdock .25 .60
73 Scott Burrell .25 .60
74 Scott Burrell FTR .25 .60
75 Anfernee Hardaway .75 2.00
76 Anfernee Hardaway FTR .75 2.00
77 Yinka Dare RC .25 .60
78 Anthony Avent .25 .60
79 Jon Barry .25 .60
80 Rodney Rogers .25 .60
81 Chris Mills .30 .75
82 Anthony Mason .30 .75
83 Steve Smith .30 .75
84 Buck Williams .25 .60
85 Spud Webb .30 .75
86 Stacey Augmon .30 .75
87 Allan Houston .40 1.00
88 Will Perdue .25 .60
89 Chris Gatling .25 .60
90 Danny Ainge .40 1.00
91 Rick Mahorn .25 .60
92 Elmore Spencer .25 .60
93 Vin Baker .40 1.00
94 Rex Chapman .25 .60
95 Dale Ellis .25 .60
96 Doug Smith .25 .60
97 Tim Perry .25 .60
98 Toni Kukoc .50 1.25
99 Terry Dehere .25 .60
100 Shaquille O'Neal PP 1.50 4.00
101 Shawn Kemp PP .60 1.50
102 Hakeem Olajuwon PP .75 2.00
103 Derrick Coleman PP .40 1.00
104 Alonzo Mourning PP .60 1.50
105 Dikembe Mutombo PP .60 1.50
106 Chris Webber PP .75 2.00
107 Dennis Rodman PP 1.00 2.50
108 David Robinson PP .75 2.00
109 Charles Barkley PP 1.00 2.50
110 Brad Daugherty .30 .75
111 Derek Harper .30 .75
112 Detlef Schrempf .40 1.00
113 Harvey Grant .25 .60
114 Vlade Divac .40 1.00
115 Isaiah Rider .40 1.00
116 Mitch Richmond .50 1.25
117 Tom Chambers .30 .75
118 Kenny Gattison .25 .60
119 Kenny Gattison FTR .25 .60
120 Vernon Maxwell .25 .60
121 Reggie Williams .25 .60
122 Chris Mullin .50 1.25
123 Harold Miner .25 .60
124 Harold Miner FTR .25 .60
125 Calbert Cheaney .25 .60
126 Randy Woods .25 .60
127 Mike Gminski .25 .60
128 Willie Anderson .25 .60
129 Mark Macon .25 .60
130 Avery Johnson .30 .75
131 Bimbo Coles .25 .60
132 Kenny Smith .30 .75
133 Dennis Scott .30 .75
134 Lionel Simmons .25 .60
135 Nate McMillan .30 .75
136 Eric Montross RC .30 .75
137 Sedale Threatt .25 .60
138 Kenny Anderson .30 .75
139 Micheal Williams .25 .60
140 Grant Long .25 .60
141 Grant Long FTR .25 .60
142 Tyrone Corbin .25 .60
143 Craig Ehlo .25 .60
144 Gerald Wilkins .30 .75
145 LaPhonso Ellis .25 .60
146 Reggie Miller .75 2.00
147 Tracy Murray .25 .60
148 Victor Alexander .25 .60
149 Victor Alexander FTR .25 .60
150 Clifford Robinson .30 .75
151 Anthony Mason FTR .30 .75
152 Anthony Mason .30 .75
153 Jim Jackson .30 .75
154 Jeff Hornacek .30 .75
155 Nick Anderson .25 .60
156 Mike Brown .25 .60
157 Kevin Johnson .40 1.00
158 John Paxson .25 .60
159 Loy Vaught .25 .60
160 Carl Herrera .25 .60
161 Shawn Bradley .25 .60
162 Hubert Davis .25 .60
163 David Benoit .25 .60
164 Dell Curry .25 .60
165 Dee Brown .30 .75
166 LaSalle Thompson .25 .60
167 Eddie Jones RC 1.25 3.00
168 Walt Williams .25 .60
169 A.C. Green .30 .75
170 Kendall Gill .25 .60
171 Kendall Gill FTR .25 .60
172 Danny Ferry .25 .60
173 Bryant Stith .25 .60
174 John Salley .25 .60
175 Cedric Ceballos .30 .75
176 Derrick Coleman .40 1.00
177 Tony Bennett .25 .60
178 Kevin Duckworth .25 .60
179 Jay Humphries .25 .60
180 Sean Elliott .30 .75
181 Sam Perkins .30 .75
182 Luc Longley .30 .75
183 Mitch Richmond AS .50 1.25
184 Clyde Drexler AS .60 1.50
185 Karl Malone AS .75 2.00
186 Shawn Kemp AS .60 1.50
187 Hakeem Olajuwon AS .75 2.00
188 Danny Manning AS .25 .60
189 Kevin Johnson AS .40 1.00
190 John Stockton AS .75 2.00
191 Latrell Sprewell AS .50 1.25
192 Gary Payton AS .60 1.50
193 Clifford Robinson AS .40 1.00
194 David Robinson AS .75 2.00
195 Charles Barkley AS 1.00 2.50
196 Mark Price SPEC .40 1.00
197 Checklist 1-99 .07 .20
198 Checklist 100-198 .07 .20
199 Patrick Ewing .60 1.50
200 Patrick Ewing FTR .60 1.50
201 Tracy Murray PP .25 .60
202 Craig Ehlo PP .25 .60
203 Nick Anderson PP .25 .60
204 John Starks PP .40 1.00
205 Rex Chapman PP .25 .60
206 Hersey Hawkins PP .25 .60
207 Glen Rice PP .40 1.00
208 Jeff Malone PP .25 .60
209 Dan Majerle PP .40 1.00
210 Chris Mullin PP .50 1.25
211 Grant Hill RC 2.00 5.00
212 Bobby Phills .25 .60
213 Dennis Rodman 1.00 2.50
214 Doug West .25 .60
215 Harold Ellis .25 .60
216 Kevin Edwards .25 .60
217 Lorenzo Williams .25 .60
218 Rick Fox .25 .60
219 Mookie Blaylock .40 1.00
220 Mookie Blaylock FTR .40 1.00
221 John Williams .25 .60
222 Keith Jennings .25 .60
223 Nick Van Exel .40 1.00
224 Gary Payton .60 1.50
225 John Stockton .75 2.00
226 Ron Harper .30 .75
227 Monty Williams RC .50 1.25
228 Marty Conlon .25 .60
229 Hersey Hawkins .25 .60
230 Rik Smits .30 .75
231 James Robinson .25 .60
232 Malik Sealy .25 .60
233 Sergei Bazarevich RC .40 1.00
234 Brad Lohaus .25 .60
235 Olden Polynice .25 .60
236 Brian Williams .25 .60
237 Tyrone Hill .25 .60
238 Jim McIlvaine RC .30 .75
239 Latrell Sprewell .50 1.25
240 Latrell Sprewell FTR .50 1.25
241 Popeye Jones .25 .60
242 Scott Williams .25 .60
243 Eddie Jones 1.25 3.00
244 Moses Malone .40 1.00
245 B.J. Armstrong .40 1.00
246 Jim Les .25 .60
247 Greg Grant .25 .60
248 Lee Mayberry .25 .60
249 Mark Jackson .30 .75
250 Larry Johnson .50 1.25
251 Terrell Brandon .25 .60
252 Ledell Eackles .25 .60
253 Yinka Dare .25 .60
254 Dontonio Wingfield RC .40 1.00
255 Clyde Drexler .60 1.50
256 Andres Guibert .25 .60
257 Gheorghe Muresan .25 .60
258 Tom Hammonds .25 .60
259 Charles Barkley 1.00 2.50
260 Charles Barkley FTR 1.00 2.50
261 Acie Earl .25 .60
262 Lamond Murray RC .40 1.00
263 Dana Barros .25 .60
264 Greg Anthony .25 .60
265 Dan Majerle .40 1.00
266 Zan Tabak .25 .60
267 Ricky Pierce .25 .60
268 Eric Leckner .25 .60
269 Duane Ferrell .25 .60
270 Mark Price .40 1.00
271 Anthony Peeler .25 .60
272 Adam Keefe .25 .60
273 Rex Walters .25 .60
274 Scott Skiles .25 .60
275 Glenn Robinson RC .75 2.00
276 Tony Dumas RC .30 .75
277 Elliot Perry .25 .60
278 Bo Outlaw RC .40 1.00
279 Karl Malone .75 2.00
280 Karl Malone FTR .75 2.00
281 Herb Williams .25 .60
282 Vincent Askew .25 .60
283 Askia Jones RC .40 1.00
284 Shawn Bradley .25 .60
285 Tim Hardaway .50 1.25
286 Mark West .25 .60
287 Chuck Person .30 .75
288 James Edwards .25 .60
289 Antonio Lang RC .40 1.00
290 Dominique Wilkins .60 1.50
291 Khalid Reeves RC .30 .75
292 Jamie Watson RC .25 .60
293 Darnell Mee .25 .60
294 Brian Grant RC .60 1.50
295 Hakeem Olajuwon .75 2.00
296 Dickey Simpkins RC .30 .75
297 Tyrone Corbin .25 .60
298 David Wingate .25 .60
299 Shaquille O'Neal 1.50 4.00
300 Shaquille O'Neal FR 1.50 4.00
301 B.J. Armstrong PP .40 1.00
302 Mitch Richmond PP .50 1.25
303 Jim Jackson PP .30 .75
304 Jeff Hornacek PP .30 .75
305 Mark Price PP .40 1.00
306 Kendall Gill PP .25 .60
307 Dale Ellis PP .25 .60
308 Vernon Maxwell PP .25 .60
309 Joe Dumars PP .40 1.00
310 Reggie Miller PP .75 2.00
311 Geert Hammink .25 .60
312 Charles Smith .25 .60
313 Bill Cartwright .30 .75
314 Aaron McKie RC .40 1.00
315 Tom Gugliotta .25 .60
316 P.J. Brown .25 .60
317 David Wesley .25 .60
318 Felton Spencer .25 .60
319 Robert Horry .40 1.00
320 Robert Horry FR .40 1.00
321 Larry Krystkowiak .25 .60
322 Eric Piatkowski RC .40 1.00
323 Anthony Bonner .25 .60
324 Keith Askins .25 .60
325 Mahmoud Abdul-Rauf .25 .60
326 Darrin Hancock RC .30 .75
327 Vern Fleming .25 .60
328 Wayman Tisdale .25 .60
329 Sam Bowie .25 .60
330 Billy Owens .25 .60
331 Donald Hodge .25 .60
332 Derrick Alston RC .25 .60
333 Doug Edwards .25 .60
334 Johnny Newman .25 .60
335 Otis Thorpe .25 .60
336 Bill Curley RC .25 .60
337 Michael Cage .25 .60
338 Chris Smith .25 .60
339 Dikembe Mutombo .60 1.50
340 Dikembe Mutombo FTR .60 1.50
341 Duane Causwell .25 .60
342 Sean Higgins .25 .60
343 Steve Kerr .30 .75
344 Eric Montross .30 .75
345 Charles Oakley .40 1.00
346 Brooks Thompson RC .30 .75
347 Rony Seikaly .25 .60
348 Chris Dudley .25 .60
349 Sharone Wright RC .30 .75
350 Sarunas Marciulionis .25 .60
351 Anthony Miller RC .40 1.00
352 Pooh Richardson .25 .60
353 Byron Scott .30 .75
354 Michael Adams .25 .60
355 Ken Norman .25 .60
356 Clifford Rozier RC .25 .60
357 Tim Breaux .25 .60
358 Derek Strong .25 .60
359 David Robinson .75 2.00
360 David Robinson FR .75 2.00
361 Benoit Benjamin .25 .60
362 Terry Porter .25 .60
363 Ervin Johnson .25 .60
364 Alaa Abdelnaby .25 .60
365 Robert Parish .40 1.00
366 Mario Elie .25 .60
367 Antonio Harvey .25 .60
368 Charlie Ward RC .40 1.00
369 Kevin Gamble .25 .60
370 Rod Strickland .25 .60
371 Jason Kidd 2.00 5.00
372 Oliver Miller .25 .60
373 Eric Mobley RC .25 .60
374 Brian Shaw .25 .60
375 Horace Grant .40 1.00
376 Corie Blount .25 .60
377 Sam Mitchell .25 .60
378 Jalen Rose RC 1.00 2.50
379 Elden Campbell .25 .60
380 Elden Campbell FTR .25 .60
381 Donyell Marshall RC .40 1.00
382 Frank Brickowski .25 .60
383 B.J. Tyler RC .25 .60
384 Bryon Russell .25 .60
385 Danny Manning .30 .75
386 Manute Bol .25 .60
387 Brent Price .25 .60
388 J.R. Reid .25 .60
389 Byron Houston .25 .60
390 Blue Edwards .25 .60
391 Adrian Caldwell .25 .60
392 Wesley Person .40 1.00
393 Juwan Howard RC .60 1.50
394 Chris Morris .25 .60
395 Checklist 199-296 .20 .50
396 Checklist 297-396 .20 .50

1994-95 Topps Franchise/Futures

COMPLETE SET (20) 8.00 20.00
SER.2 STATED ODDS 1:18
1 Mookie Blaylock .60 1.50
2 Stacey Augmon .50 1.25
3 Dominique Wilkins 1.00 2.50
4 Eric Montross .50 1.25
5 Dikembe Mutombo 1.00 2.50
6 Jalen Rose 1.50 4.00
7 Joe Dumars .60 1.50
8 Grant Hill 3.00 8.00
9 Chris Mullin .75 2.00
10 Latrell Sprewell .75 2.00
11 Glen Rice .60 1.50
12 Khalid Reeves .50 1.25
13 Derrick Coleman .60 1.50
14 Yinka Dare .40 1.00
15 Patrick Ewing 1.00 2.50
16 Monty Williams .75 2.00
17 Shaquille O'Neal 2.50 6.00
18 Anfernee Hardaway 1.25 3.00
19 Charles Barkley 1.50 4.00
20 Wesley Person .60 1.50

1994-95 Topps Own the Game

COMPLETE SET (50) 30.00 80.00
SER.1 STATED ODDS 1:18
1 Kenny Anderson PASS 1.00 2.50
2 Charles Barkley SCORE 3.00 8.00
3 Mookie Blaylock PASS 1.25 3.00
4 Mookie Blaylock STEAL 1.25 3.00
5 Muggsy Bogues PASS 1.00 2.50
6 Shawn Bradley SWAT .75 2.00
7 Derrick Coleman REB 1.25 3.00
8 Sherman Douglas PASS .75 2.00
9 Patrick Ewing REB 2.00 5.00
10 Patrick Ewing SCORE 2.00 5.00
11 Patrick Ewing SWAT 2.00 5.00
12 Tom Gugliotta STEAL .75 2.00
13 Anfernee Hardaway STEAL 2.50 6.00
14 Mark Jackson PASS 1.00 2.50
15 Kevin Johnson PASS 1.25 3.00
16 Karl Malone REB 2.50 6.00
17 Karl Malone SCORE 2.50 6.00
18 Nate McMillan STEAL 1.00 2.50
19 Oliver Miller SWAT .75 2.00
20 Alonzo Mourning SWAT 2.00 5.00
21 Eric Murdock STEAL .75 2.00
22 Dikembe Mutombo REB 2.00 5.00
23 Dikembe Mutombo SWAT 2.00 5.00
24 Charles Oakley REB 1.25 3.00
25 Hakeem Olajuwon REB 2.50 6.00
26 Hakeem Olajuwon SCORE 2.50 6.00
27 Hakeem Olajuwon SWAT 2.50 6.00
28 Shaquille O'Neal REB 5.00 12.00
29 Shaquille O'Neal SCORE W 5.00 12.00
30 Shaquille O'Neal SWAT 5.00 12.00
31 Gary Payton STEAL 2.00 5.00
32 Scottie Pippen SCORE 3.00 8.00
33 Scottie Pippen STEAL W 3.00 8.00
34 Mark Price PASS 1.25 3.00
35 Mitch Richmond SCORE 1.50 4.00
36 David Robinson SCORE 2.50 6.00
37 David Robinson SWAT 2.50 6.00
38 Dennis Rodman REB W 3.00 8.00
39 Latrell Sprewell STEAL 1.50 4.00
40 John Stockton PASS W 2.50 6.00
41 John Stockton STEAL 2.50 6.00
42 Rod Strickland PASS .75 2.00
43 Chris Webber SWAT 2.50 6.00
44 Kevin Willis REB 1.00 2.50
45 Dominique Wilkins SCORE 2.00 5.00
46 Passers Field Card .40 1.00
47 Rebounders Field Card .40 1.00
48 Scorers Field Card .40 1.00
49 Stealers Field Card .40 1.00
50 Swatters Field Card .40 1.00

1994-95 Topps Own the Game Redemption

COMPLETE SET (10) 2.50 6.00
1 Shaquille O'Neal 2.00 5.00
2 Hakeem Olajuwon 1.00 2.50
3 Dennis Rodman 1.25 3.00
4 Patrick Ewing .75 2.00
5 John Stockton 1.00 2.50
6 Kenny Anderson .40 1.00
7 Scottie Pippen 1.25 3.00
8 Mookie Blaylock .50 1.25
9 Dikembe Mutombo .75 2.00
10 Shawn Bradley .30 .75

1994-95 Topps Super Sophomores

COMPLETE SET (10) 6.00 15.00
SER.2 STATED ODDS 1:36
1 Chris Webber 2.00 5.00
2 Anfernee Hardaway 2.00 5.00
3 Vin Baker 1.00 2.50
4 Sam Cassell 1.00 2.50
5 Jamal Mashburn 1.00 2.50
6 Isaiah Rider 1.00 2.50
7 Chris Mills .75 2.00
8 Antonio Davis .75 2.00
9 Nick Van Exel 1.00 2.50
10 Lindsey Hunter .60 1.50

1995-96 Topps

COMPLETE SET (291) 30.00 80.00
COMPLETE SERIES 1 (181) 12.00 30.00
COMPLETE SERIES 2 (110) 20.00 50.00
1 Michael Jordan AL 3.00 8.00
2 Dennis Rodman AL .60 1.50
3 John Stockton AL .60 1.50
4 Michael Jordan AL 3.00 8.00
5 David Robinson AL .60 1.50
6 Shaquille O'Neal LL 1.25 3.00
7 Hakeem Olajuwon LL .60 1.50
8 David Robinson LL .60 1.50
9 Karl Malone LL .60 1.50
10 Jamal Mashburn LL .30 .75
11 Dennis Rodman LL .60 1.50
12 Dikembe Mutombo LL .50 1.25
13 Shaquille O'Neal LL 1.25 3.00
14 Patrick Ewing LL .50 1.25
15 Tyrone Hill LL .20 .50
16 John Stockton LL .60 1.50
17 Kenny Anderson LL .25 .60
18 Tim Hardaway LL .40 1.00
19 Rod Strickland LL .20 .50
20 Muggsy Bogues LL .20 .50
21 Scottie Pippen LL .75 2.00
22 Mookie Blaylock LL .30 .75
23 Gary Payton LL .50 1.25
24 John Stockton LL .60 1.50
25 Nate McMillan LL .20 .50
26 Dikembe Mutombo LL .50 1.25
27 Hakeem Olajuwon LL .60 1.50
28 Shawn Bradley LL .20 .50
29 David Robinson LL .60 1.50
30 Alonzo Mourning LL .50 1.25
31 Reggie Miller .60 1.50
32 Karl Malone .60 1.50
33 Grant Hill .50 1.25
34 Charles Barkley .75 2.00
35 Cedric Ceballos .25 .60
36 Gheorghe Muresan .20 .50
37 Doug West .20 .50
38 Tony Dumas .20 .50
39 Kenny Gattison .20 .50
40 Chris Mullin .30 .75
41 Pervis Ellison .20 .50
42 Vinny Del Negro .20 .50
43 Mario Elie .20 .50
44 Todd Day .20 .50
45 Scottie Pippen .75 2.00
46 Buck Williams .20 .50
47 P.J. Brown .20 .50
48 Bimbo Coles .20 .50
49 Terrell Brandon .25 .60
50 Charles Oakley .20 .50
51 Sam Perkins .25 .60
52 Dale Ellis .20 .50
53 Andrew Lang .20 .50
54 Harold Ellis .20 .50
55 Clarence Weatherspoon .20 .50
56 Bill Curley .20 .50
57 Robert Parish .40 1.00
58 David Benoit .20 .50
59 Anthony Avent .20 .50
60 Jamal Mashburn .30 .75
61 Duane Ferrell .20 .50
62 Elden Campbell .20 .50
63 Rex Chapman .20 .50
64 Wesley Person .20 .50
65 Mitch Richmond .40 1.00
66 Micheal Williams .20 .50
67 Clifford Rozier .20 .50
68 Eric Montross .20 .50
69 Dennis Rodman .60 1.50
70 Vin Baker .25 .60
71 Tyrone Hill .20 .50
72 Tyrone Corbin .20 .50
73 Chris Dudley .20 .50
74 Nate McMillan .20 .50
75 Kenny Anderson .25 .60
76 Monty Williams .20 .50
77 Kenny Smith .25 .60
78 Rodney Rogers .25 .60
79 Corie Blount .20 .50
80 Glen Rice .30 .75
81 Walt Williams .20 .50
82 Scott Williams .20 .50
83 Michael Adams .20 .50
84 Terry Mills .20 .50
85 Horace Grant .25 .60
86 Chuck Person .25 .60
87 Adam Keefe .20 .50
88 Scott Brooks .20 .50
89 George Lynch .20 .50
90 Kevin Johnson .30 .75
91 Armon Gilliam .20 .50
92 Greg Minor .20 .50
93 Derrick McKey .20 .50
94 Victor Alexander .20 .50
95 B.J. Armstrong .30 .75
96 Terry Dehere .20 .50
97 Christian Laettner .25 .60
98 Hubert Davis .20 .50
99 Aaron McKie .20 .50
100 Hakeem Olajuwon .60 1.50
101 Michael Cage .20 .50
102 Grant Long .20 .50
103 Calbert Cheaney .20 .50
104 Olden Polynice .20 .50
105 Sharone Wright .20 .50
106 Lee Mayberry .20 .50
107 Robert Pack .20 .50
108 Loy Vaught .20 .50
109 Khalid Reeves .20 .50
110 Shawn Kemp .50 1.25
111 Lindsey Hunter .20 .50
112 Dell Curry .30 .75
113 Dan Majerle .30 .75
114 Bryon Russell .20 .50
115 John Starks .30 .75
116 Roy Tarpley .25 .60
117 Dale Davis .20 .50
118 Nick Anderson .25 .60
119 Rex Walters .20 .50
120 Dominique Wilkins .50 1.25
121 Sam Cassell .30 .75
122 Sean Elliott .25 .60
123 B.J. Tyler .20 .50
124 Eric Mobley .20 .50
125 Toni Kukoc .40 1.00
126 Pooh Richardson .20 .50
127 Isaiah Rider .30 .75
128 Steve Smith .25 .60
129 Chris Mills .20 .50
130 Detlef Schrempf .30 .75
131 Donyell Marshall .20 .50
132 Eddie Jones .30 .75
133 Otis Thorpe .25 .60
134 Lionel Simmons .20 .50
135 Jeff Hornacek .25 .60
136 Jalen Rose .40 1.00
137 Kevin Willis .20 .50
138 Don MacLean .20 .50
139 Dee Brown .25 .60
140 Glenn Robinson .30 .75
141 Joe Kleine .20 .50
142 Ron Harper .25 .60
143 Antonio Davis .20 .50
144 Jeff Malone .20 .50
145 Joe Dumars .30 .75
146 Jason Kidd .50 1.25
147 J.R. Reid .20 .50
148 Lamond Murray .20 .50
149 Derrick Coleman .25 .60
150 Alonzo Mourning .50 1.25
151 Clifford Robinson .30 .75
152 Kendall Gill .20 .50
153 Doug Christie .20 .50
154 Stacey Augmon .25 .60
155 Anfernee Hardaway .75 2.00
156 Mahmoud Abdul-Rauf .25 .60
157 Latrell Sprewell .30 .75
158 Mark Price .30 .75
159 Brian Grant .25 .60
160 Clyde Drexler .50 1.25
161 Juwan Howard .30 .75
162 Tom Gugliotta .25 .60
163 Nick Van Exel .30 .75
164 Billy Owens .20 .50
165 Brooks Thompson .20 .50
166 Acie Earl .20 .50
167 Ed Pinckney .20 .50
168 Oliver Miller .20 .50
169 John Salley .20 .50
170 Jerome Kersey .20 .50
171 Willie Anderson .20 .50
172 Keith Jennings .20 .50
173 Doug Smith .20 .50
174 Gerald Wilkins .20 .50
175 Byron Scott .30 .75
176 Benoit Benjamin .20 .50
177 Blue Edwards .20 .50
178 Greg Anthony .20 .50
179 Trevor Ruffin .20 .50
180 Kenny Gattison .20 .50
181 Checklist 1-181 .07 .20
182 Cherokee Parks RC .40 1.00
183 Kurt Thomas RC .50 1.25
184 Ervin Johnson .20 .50
185 Chucky Brown .20 .50
186 Luc Longley .20 .50
187 Anthony Miller .20 .50
188 Ed O'Bannon RC .40 1.00
189 Bobby Hurley .20 .50
190 Dikembe Mutombo .50 1.25
191 Robert Horry .20 .50
192 George Zidek RC .40 1.00
193 Rasheed Wallace RC 1.50 4.00
194 Marty Conlon .20 .50
195 A.C. Green .25 .60
196 Mike Brown .20 .50
197 Oliver Miller .20 .50
198 Charles Smith .20 .50
199 Eric Williams RC .50 1.25
200 Rik Smits .25 .60
201 Donald Royal .20 .50
202 Bryant Reeves RC .40 1.00
203 Danny Ferry .20 .50
204 Brian Williams .20 .50
205 Joe Smith RC .60 1.50
206 Gary Trent RC .40 1.00
207 Greg Ostertag RC .50 1.25
208 Ken Norman .20 .50
209 Avery Johnson .25 .60
210 Theo Ratliff UER RC .75 2.00
211 Corie Blount .20 .50
212 Hersey Hawkins .25 .60
213 Loren Meyer RC .30 .75

214 Mario Bennett RC .40 1.00
215 Randolph Childress RC .40 1.00
216 Spud Webb .30 .75
217 Popeye Jones .20 .50
218 Shawn Respert RC .40 1.00
219 Malik Sealy .20 .50
220 Dino Radja .20 .50
221 James Robinson .20 .50
222 David Vaughn .30 .75
223 Michael Smith .20 .50
224 Jamie Watson .20 .50
225 LaPhonso Ellis .25 .60
226 Kevin Gamble .20 .50
227 Dennis Rodman .60 1.50
228 B.J. Armstrong .20 .50
229 Jerry Stackhouse RC 1.50 4.00
230 Muggsy Bogues .30 .75
231 Lawrence Moten RC .50 1.25
232 Cory Alexander RC .50 1.25
233 Carlos Rogers .20 .50
234 Tyus Edney RC .50 1.25
235 Doc Rivers .25 .60
236 Antonio Harvey .20 .50
237 Kevin Garnett RC 4.00 10.00
238 Derek Harper .25 .60
239 Kevin Edwards .20 .50
240 Chris Smith .20 .50
241 Haywoode Workman .20 .50
242 Bobby Phills .25 .60
243 Sherrell Ford RC .40 1.00
244 Corliss Williamson RC .50 1.25
245 Shawn Bradley .20 .50
246 Jason Caffey RC .30 .75
247 Bryant Stith .20 .50
248 Mark West .20 .50
249 Dennis Scott .20 .50
250 Jim Jackson .25 .60
251 Travis Best RC .50 1.25
252 Sean Rooks .20 .50
253 Yinka Dare .20 .50
254 Felton Spencer .20 .50
255 Vlade Divac .30 .75
256 Michael Finley RC 1.25 3.00
257 Damon Stoudamire RC 1.25 3.00
258 Mark Bryant .20 .50
259 Brent Barry RC .75 2.00
260 Rony Seikaly .20 .50
261 Alan Henderson RC .50 1.25
262 Kendall Gill .20 .50
263 Rex Chapman .20 .50
264 Eric Murdock .20 .50
265 Rodney Rogers .25 .60
266 Greg Graham .20 .50
267 Jayson Williams .20 .50
268 Antonio McDyess RC .60 1.50
269 Sedale Threatt .20 .50
270 Danny Manning .25 .60
271 Pete Chilcutt .20 .50
272 Bob Sura RC .40 1.00
273 Dana Barros .25 .60
274 Allan Houston .25 .60
275 Tracy Murray .20 .50
276 Anthony Mason .20 .50
277 Michael Jordan 3.00 8.00
278 Patrick Ewing .50 1.25
279 Shaquille O'Neal 1.25 3.00
280 Larry Johnson .40 1.00
281 Mark Jackson .25 .60
282 Chris Webber .40 1.00
283 David Robinson .60 1.50
284 John Stockton .60 1.50
285 Mookie Blaylock .30 .75
286 Mark Price .30 .75
287 Tim Hardaway .40 1.00
288 Rod Strickland .20 .50
289 Sherman Douglas .20 .50
290 Gary Payton .50 1.25
291 Checklist (182-291) .25 .60

1995-96 Topps Draft Redemption

COMPLETE SET (29) 100.00 200.00
EXCH.CARDS: SER.1 STATED ODDS 1:18
1 Joe Smith 3.00 8.00
2 Antonio McDyess 3.00 8.00
3 Jerry Stackhouse 8.00 20.00
4 Rasheed Wallace 8.00 20.00
5 Kevin Garnett 15.00 40.00
6 Bryant Reeves 2.00 5.00
7 Damon Stoudamire 6.00 15.00
8 Shawn Respert 2.00 5.00
9 Ed O'Bannon 2.00 5.00
10 Kurt Thomas 2.50 6.00
11 Gary Trent 2.00 5.00
12 Cherokee Parks 2.00 5.00
13 Corliss Williamson 2.50 6.00
14 Eric Williams 2.50 6.00
15 Brent Barry 4.00 10.00
16 Alan Henderson 2.50 6.00
17 Bob Sura 2.00 5.00
18 Theo Ratliff 4.00 10.00
19 Randolph Childress 2.00 5.00
20 Jason Caffey 2.50 6.00
21 Michael Finley 6.00 15.00
22 George Zidek 2.00 5.00
23 Travis Best 2.50 6.00
24 Loren Meyer 1.50 4.00
25 David Vaughn 2.50 6.00
26 Sherrell Ford 2.00 5.00
27 Mario Bennett 2.00 5.00
28 Greg Ostertag 2.50 6.00
29 Cory Alexander 2.50 6.00
NNO Expired Exchange Cards .40 1.00

1995-96 Topps Foreign Legion

COMPLETE SET (10) 6.00 15.00
FL1 Luc Longley 1.00 2.50
FL2 Rick Fox .75 2.00
FL3 Dikembe Mutombo 1.00 2.50
FL4 Gheorghe Muresan .75 2.00
FL5 Sarunas Marciulionis 1.25 3.00
FL6 Dino Radja .75 2.00
FL7 Detlef Schrempf 1.25 3.00
FL8 Rony Seikaly .75 2.00
FL9 Bill Wennington .75 2.00
FL10 Rik Smits 1.00 2.50

1995-96 Topps Mystery Finest

COMPLETE SET (22) 30.00 80.00
SER.2 STATED ODDS 1:36 HOBBY/RETAIL
M1 Michael Jordan 15.00 40.00
M2 Anfernee Hardaway 4.00 10.00
M3 Clyde Drexler 2.50 6.00
M4 Mark Price 1.50 4.00
M5 Steve Smith 1.25 3.00
M6 Jim Jackson 1.25 3.00
M7 Nick Anderson 1.25 3.00
M8 Kenny Anderson 1.25 3.00
M9 Mookie Blaylock 1.50 4.00
M10 Jason Kidd 2.50 6.00
M11 Tim Hardaway 2.00 5.00
M12 Kevin Johnson 1.50 4.00
M13 Gary Payton 2.50 6.00
M14 John Stockton 3.00 8.00
M15 Rod Strickland 1.00 2.50
M16 Jamal Mashburn 1.50 4.00
M17 Danny Manning 1.25 3.00
M18 Billy Owens 1.00 2.50
M19 Grant Hill 2.50 6.00
M20 Scottie Pippen 4.00 10.00
M21 Isaiah Rider 1.50 4.00
M22 Latrell Sprewell 1.50 4.00

1995-96 Topps Mystery Finest Refractors

*REF: 2X TO 5X BASE HI
SER.2 STATED ODDS 1:36 HOB, 1:216 RET
CONDITION SENSITIVE SET
M1 Michael Jordan 400.00 800.00

1995-96 Topps Pan For Gold

COMPLETE SET (15) 20.00 50.00
SER.1 STATED ODDS 1:4 JUM, 1:8 RET
PFG1 Vin Baker 2.00 5.00
PFG2 John Stockton 5.00 12.00
PFG3 Dan Majerle 2.50 6.00
PFG4 Joe Dumars 2.50 6.00
PFG5 Rik Smits 2.00 5.00
PFG6 Tim Hardaway 3.00 8.00
PFG7 Charles Oakley 2.00 5.00
PFG8 Cedric Ceballos 2.00 5.00
PFG9 Karl Malone 5.00 12.00
PFG10 Scottie Pippen 6.00 15.00
PFG11 David Robinson 5.00 12.00
PFG12 Gary Payton 4.00 10.00
PFG13 Mitch Richmond 3.00 8.00
PFG14 Antonio Davis 1.50 4.00
PFG15 Dennis Rodman 5.00 12.00

1995-96 Topps Power Boosters

COMPLETE SET (45) 150.00 400.00
COMPLETE SERIES 1 (30) 125.00 300.00
COMPLETE SERIES 2 (15) 40.00 100.00
SER.1/2 STATED ODDS 1:36 HOBBY/RETAIL
1 Michael Jordan 75.00 200.00
2 Dennis Rodman 4.00 10.00
3 John Stockton 4.00 10.00
4 Michael Jordan 30.00 80.00
5 David Robinson 4.00 10.00
6 Shaquille O'Neal 8.00 20.00
7 Hakeem Olajuwon 4.00 10.00
8 David Robinson 4.00 10.00
9 Karl Malone 4.00 10.00
10 Jamal Mashburn 2.00 5.00
11 Dennis Rodman 4.00 10.00
12 Dikembe Mutombo 3.00 8.00
13 Shaquille O'Neal 8.00 20.00
14 Patrick Ewing 3.00 8.00
15 Tyrone Hill 1.25 3.00
16 John Stockton 4.00 10.00
17 Kenny Anderson 1.50 4.00
18 Tim Hardaway 2.50 6.00
19 Rod Strickland 1.25 3.00
20 Muggsy Bogues 2.00 5.00
21 Scottie Pippen 5.00 12.00
22 Mookie Blaylock 2.00 5.00
23 Gary Payton 3.00 8.00
24 John Stockton 4.00 10.00
25 Nate McMillan 1.25 3.00
26 Dikembe Mutombo 3.00 8.00
27 Hakeem Olajuwon 4.00 10.00
28 Shawn Bradley 1.25 3.00
29 David Robinson 4.00 10.00
30 Alonzo Mourning 3.00 8.00
276 Anthony Mason 1.25 3.00
277 Michael Jordan 125.00 300.00
278 Patrick Ewing 3.00 8.00
279 Shaquille O'Neal 8.00 20.00
280 Larry Johnson 2.50 6.00
281 Mark Jackson 1.50 4.00
282 Chris Webber 2.50 6.00
283 David Robinson 4.00 10.00
284 John Stockton 4.00 10.00
285 Mookie Blaylock 2.00 5.00
286 Mark Price 2.00 5.00
287 Tim Hardaway 2.50 6.00
288 Rod Strickland 2.00 5.00
289 Sherman Douglas 1.25 3.00
290 Gary Payton 3.00 8.00

1995-96 Topps Rattle and Roll

COMPLETE SET (10) 5.00 12.00
SER.2 STATED ODDS 1:12 RETAIL
R1 Juwan Howard 1.00 2.50
R2 Glenn Robinson 1.00 2.50
R3 Grant Hill 1.50 4.00
R4 Sharone Wright .60 1.50
R5 Brian Grant .75 2.00
R6 Antonio McDyess .60 1.50
R7 Bryant Reeves .40 1.00
R8 Gary Trent .40 1.00
R9 Jerry Stackhouse 1.50 4.00
R10 Joe Smith .60 1.50

1995-96 Topps Show Stoppers

COMPLETE SET (10) 20.00 50.00
SER.1 STATED ODDS 1:24 HOBBY
SS1 Michael Jordan 15.00 40.00
SS2 Grant Hill 2.50 6.00
SS3 Glenn Robinson 1.50 4.00
SS4 Anfernee Hardaway 4.00 10.00
SS5 Charles Barkley 4.00 10.00
SS6 Patrick Ewing 2.50 6.00
SS7 Shaquille O'Neal 6.00 15.00
SS8 Jason Kidd 2.50 6.00
SS9 Glen Rice 1.50 4.00
SS10 Karl Malone 3.00 8.00

1995-96 Topps Spark Plugs

COMPLETE SET (10) 15.00 40.00
SER.2 STATED ODDS 1:8 HOBBY/RETAIL
SP1 Shaquille O'Neal 2.50 6.00
SP2 Michael Jordan 20.00 50.00
SP3 Reggie Miller 1.25 3.00
SP4 Anfernee Hardaway 1.50 4.00
SP5 John Stockton 1.25 3.00
SP6 David Robinson 1.25 3.00
SP7 Hakeem Olajuwon 1.25 3.00
SP8 Tim Hardaway .75 2.00
SP9 Grant Hill 1.00 2.50
SP10 Scottie Pippen 1.50 4.00

1995-96 Topps Sudden Impact

COMPLETE SET (10) 20.00 50.00
SER.2 STATED ODDS 1:72 HOBBY
S1 Damon Stoudamire 5.00 12.00
S2 Cherokee Parks 1.50 4.00
S3 Kurt Thomas 2.00 5.00
S4 Gary Trent 1.50 4.00
S5 Bryant Reeves 1.50 4.00
S6 Ed O'Bannon 1.50 4.00
S7 Shawn Respert 1.50 4.00
S8 Antonio McDyess 2.50 6.00
S9 Joe Smith 2.50 6.00
S10 Jerry Stackhouse 6.00 15.00

1995-96 Topps Top Flight

COMPLETE SET (20) 15.00 40.00
ONE PER SPECIAL SER.1 RETAIL PACK
TF1 Michael Jordan 25.00 60.00
TF2 Isaiah Rider 1.25 3.00
TF3 Harold Miner .75 2.00
TF4 Dominique Wilkins 2.00 5.00
TF5 Clyde Drexler 2.00 5.00
TF6 Scottie Pippen 3.00 8.00
TF7 Shawn Kemp 2.00 5.00
TF8 Chris Webber 1.50 4.00
TF9 Anfernee Hardaway 3.00 8.00
TF10 Grant Hill 2.00 5.00
TF11 Kevin Johnson 1.25 3.00
TF12 John Starks 1.25 3.00
TF13 Dan Majerle 1.25 3.00
TF14 Latrell Sprewell 1.25 3.00
TF15 Dee Brown 1.00 2.50
TF16 Stacey Augmon 1.00 2.50
TF17 David Benoit .75 2.00
TF18 Sean Elliott 1.00 2.50
TF19 Cedric Ceballos 1.00 2.50
TF20 Robert Horry 1.25 3.00

1995-96 Topps Whiz Kids

COMPLETE SET (12) 12.00 30.00
SER.1 STATED ODDS 1:24 HOBBY/RETAIL
WK1 Grant Hill 2.50 6.00
WK2 Nick Van Exel 1.50 4.00
WK3 Juwan Howard 1.50 4.00
WK4 Chris Webber 2.00 5.00
WK5 Brian Grant 1.25 3.00
WK6 Glenn Robinson 1.50 4.00
WK7 Donyell Marshall 1.00 2.50
WK8 Jason Kidd 2.50 6.00
WK9 Anfernee Hardaway 4.00 10.00
WK10 Jamal Mashburn 1.50 4.00
WK11 Vin Baker 1.25 3.00
WK12 Eddie Jones 1.50 4.00

1995-96 Topps World Class

COMPLETE SET (10) 15.00 40.00
WC1 Michael Jordan 15.00 40.00
WC2 Karl Malone 2.50 6.00
WC3 Shaquille O'Neal 5.00 12.00
WC4 Reggie Miller 2.50 6.00
WC5 Hakeem Olajuwon 2.50 6.00
WC6 Grant Hill 2.00 5.00
WC7 Anfernee Hardaway 3.00 8.00
WC8 Scottie Pippen 3.00 8.00
WC9 David Robinson 2.50 6.00
WC10 Clyde Drexler 2.00 5.00

1996-97 Topps

COMPLETE SET (221) 75.00 200.00
COMP.FACT.HOB.SET (227) 100.00 250.00
COMPLETE SERIES 1 (110) 20.00 50.00
COMPLETE SERIES 2 (111) 60.00 150.00
1 Patrick Ewing .60 1.50
2 Christian Laettner .40 1.00
3 Mahmoud Abdul-Rauf .30 .75
4 Chris Webber .50 1.25
5 Jason Kidd .60 1.50
6 Clifford Rozier .25 .60
7 Elden Campbell .25 .60
8 Chuck Person .30 .75
9 Jeff Hornacek .30 .75
10 Rik Smits .30 .75
11 Kurt Thomas .25 .60
12 Rod Strickland .40 1.00
13 Kendall Gill .40 1.00
14 Brian Williams .25 .60
15 Tom Gugliotta .25 .60
16 Ron Harper .30 .75
17 Eric Williams .25 .60
18 A.C. Green .30 .75
19 Scott Williams .25 .60
20 Damon Stoudamire .40 1.00
21 Bryant Reeves .25 .60
22 Bob Sura .25 .60
23 Mitch Richmond .50 1.25
24 Larry Johnson .50 1.25
25 Vin Baker .30 .75
26 Mark Bryant .25 .60
27 Horace Grant .40 1.00
28 Allan Houston .40 1.00
29 Sam Perkins .30 .75
30 Antonio McDyess .40 1.00
31 Rasheed Wallace .50 1.25
32 Malik Sealy .25 .60
33 Scottie Pippen 1.00 2.50
34 Charles Barkley 1.00 2.50
35 Hakeem Olajuwon .75 2.00
36 John Starks .40 1.00
37 Byron Scott .40 1.00
38 Arvydas Sabonis .40 1.00
39 Vlade Divac .40 1.00
40 Joe Dumars .50 1.25
41 Danny Ferry .25 .60
42 Jerry Stackhouse .75 2.00
43 B.J. Armstrong .30 .75
44 Shawn Bradley .25 .60
45 Kevin Garnett 1.25 3.00
46 Dee Brown .25 .60
47 Michael Smith .25 .60
48 Doug Christie .25 .60
49 Mark Jackson .30 .75
50 Shawn Kemp .60 1.50
51 Sasha Danilovic .25 .60
52 Nick Anderson .25 .60
53 Matt Geiger .25 .60
54 Charles Smith .25 .60
55 Mookie Blaylock .40 1.00
56 Johnny Newman .25 .60
57 George McCloud .25 .60
58 Greg Ostertag .25 .60
59 Reggie Williams .25 .60
60 Brent Barry .25 .60
61 Doug West .25 .60
62 Donald Royal .25 .60
63 Randy Brown .25 .60
64 Vincent Askew .25 .60
65 John Stockton .75 2.00
66 Joe Kleine .25 .60
67 Keith Askins .25 .60
68 Bobby Phills .25 .60
69 Chris Mullin .50 1.25
70 Nick Van Exel .40 1.00
71 Rick Fox .25 .60
72 Chicago Bulls - 72 Wins .60 1.50
73 Shawn Respert .25 .60
74 Hubert Davis .25 .60
75 Jim Jackson .25 .60
76 Olden Polynice .25 .60
77 Gheorghe Muresan .25 .60
78 Theo Ratliff .25 .60
79 Khalid Reeves .25 .60
80 David Robinson .75 2.00
81 Lawrence Moten .25 .60
82 Sam Cassell .30 .75
83 George Zidek .25 .60
84 Sharone Wright .25 .60
85 Clarence Weatherspoon .25 .60
86 Alan Henderson .25 .60
87 Chris Dudley .25 .60
88 Ed O'Bannon .25 .60
89 Calbert Cheaney .25 .60
90 Cedric Ceballos .30 .75
91 Michael Cage .25 .60
92 Ervin Johnson .25 .60
93 Gary Trent .25 .60
94 Sherman Douglas .25 .60
95 Joe Smith .30 .75
96 Dale Davis .25 .60
97 Tony Dumas .25 .60
98 Muggsy Bogues .40 1.00
99 Toni Kukoc .40 1.00
100 Grant Hill .60 1.50
101 Michael Finley .40 1.00
102 Isaiah Rider .30 .75
103 Bryant Stith .25 .60
104 Pooh Richardson .25 .60
105 Karl Malone .75 2.00
106 Brian Grant .30 .75
107 Sean Elliott .40 1.00
108 Charles Oakley .40 1.00
109 Pervis Ellison .25 .60
110 Anfernee Hardaway 1.00 2.50
111 Checklist SP .40 1.00
112 Dikembe Mutombo .60 1.50
113 Alonzo Mourning .60 1.50
114 Hubert Davis .25 .60
115 Rony Seikaly .30 .75
116 Danny Manning .30 .75
117 Donyell Marshall .25 .60
118 Gerald Wilkins .30 .75
119 Ervin Johnson .25 .60
120 Jalen Rose .30 .75
121 Dino Radja .25 .60
122 Glenn Robinson .40 1.00
123 John Stockton .75 2.00
124 Matt Maloney RC .40 1.00
125 Clifford Robinson .40 1.00
126 Steve Kerr .30 .75
127 Nate McMillan .25 .60
128 Shareef Abdur-Rahim RC .60 1.50
129 Loy Vaught .25 .60
130 Anthony Mason .30 .75
131 Kevin Garnett 1.25 3.00
132 Roy Rogers RC .30 .75
133 Erick Dampier RC .40 1.00
134 Tyus Edney .25 .60
135 Chris Mills .25 .60
136 Cory Alexander .25 .60
137 Juwan Howard .40 1.00
138 Kobe Bryant RC 60.00 150.00
139 Michael Jordan 6.00 15.00
140 Jayson Williams .25 .60
141 Rod Strickland .40 1.00
142 Lorenzen Wright RC .30 .75
143 Will Perdue .25 .60
144 Derek Harper .25 .60
145 Billy Owens .30 .75
146 Antoine Walker RC .60 1.50
147 P.J. Brown .25 .60
148 Terrell Brandon .30 .75
149 Larry Johnson .50 1.25
150 Steve Smith .30 .75
151 Eddie Jones .40 1.00
152 Detlef Schrempf .40 1.00
153 Dale Ellis .30 .75
154 Isaiah Rider .30 .75
155 Tony Delk RC .40 1.00
156 Adrian Caldwell .25 .60
157 Jamal Mashburn .40 1.00
158 Dennis Scott .30 .75
159 Dana Barros .25 .60
160 Martin Muursepp RC .25 .60
161 Marcus Camby RC .60 1.50
162 Jerome Williams RC .30 .75
163 Wesley Person .25 .60
164 Luc Longley .25 .60
165 Charlie Ward .25 .60
166 Mark Jackson .30 .75
167 Derrick Coleman .30 .75
168 Dell Curry .40 1.00
169 Armon Gilliam .25 .60
170 Vlade Divac .40 1.00
171 Allen Iverson RC 3.00 8.00
172 Vitaly Potapenko RC .30 .75
173 Jon Koncak .25 .60
174 Lindsey Hunter .25 .60
175 Kevin Johnson .40 1.00
176 Dennis Rodman 1.00 2.50
177 Stephon Marbury RC 1.25 3.00
178 Karl Malone .75 2.00
179 Charles Barkley 1.00 2.50
180 Popeye Jones .25 .60
181 Samaki Walker RC .30 .75
182 Steve Nash RC 2.50 6.00
183 Latrell Sprewell .40 1.00
184 Kenny Anderson .30 .75
185 Tyrone Hill .25 .60
186 Robert Pack .25 .60
187 Greg Anthony .30 .75
188 Derrick McKey .25 .60
189 John Wallace RC .30 .75
190 Bryon Russell .25 .60
191 Jermaine O'Neal RC .60 1.50
192 Clyde Drexler .60 1.50
193 Mahmoud Abdul-Rauf .30 .75
194 Eric Montross .25 .60
195 Allan Houston .40 1.00
196 Harvey Grant .25 .60
197 Rodney Rogers .25 .60
198 Kerry Kittles RC .40 1.00
199 Grant Hill .60 1.50
200 Lionel Simmons .25 .60
201 Reggie Miller .75 2.00
202 Avery Johnson .30 .75
203 LaPhonso Ellis .25 .60
204 Brian Shaw .25 .60
205 Priest Lauderdale RC .25 .60
206 Derek Fisher RC .50 1.25
207 Terry Porter .25 .60
208 Todd Fuller RC .25 .60
209 Hersey Hawkins .25 .60
210 Tim Legler .25 .60
211 Terry Dehere .25 .60
212 Gary Payton .60 1.50
213 Joe Dumars .50 1.25
214 Don MacLean .25 .60
215 Greg Minor .25 .60
216 Tim Hardaway .50 1.25
217 Ray Allen RC 2.00 5.00
218 Mario Elie .25 .60
219 Brooks Thompson .25 .60
220 Shaquille O'Neal 1.50 4.00

1996-97 Topps NBA at 50

*STARS: 2X TO 5X BASE CARD HI
*RCs: 1.5X TO 4X BASE HI
SER.1/2 STATED ODDS 1:3 HOB/RET
138 Kobe Bryant 200.00 500.00

1996-97 Topps Draft Redemption

EXCH.CARDS: SER.1 STATED ODDS 1:18 H/R
NNO Expired Trade Cards .20 .50
DP1 Allen Iverson 20.00 50.00
DP2 Marcus Camby 4.00 10.00
DP3 Shareef Abdur-Rahim 4.00 10.00
DP4 Stephon Marbury 8.00 20.00
DP5 Ray Allen 12.00 30.00
DP6 Antoine Walker 4.00 10.00
DP7 Lorenzen Wright 2.00 5.00
DP8 Kerry Kittles 2.50 6.00
DP9 Samaki Walker 2.00 5.00
DP10 Erick Dampier 2.50 6.00
DP11 Todd Fuller 1.50 4.00
DP12 Vitaly Potapenko 2.00 5.00
DP13 Kobe Bryant 600.00 1,200.00
DP15 Steve Nash 15.00 40.00
DP16 Tony Delk 2.50 6.00
DP17 Jermaine O'Neal 4.00 10.00
DP18 John Wallace 2.00 5.00
DP19 Walter McCarty 2.50 6.00
DP20 Zydrunas Ilgauskas 4.00 10.00
DP21 Dontae' Jones 2.00 5.00
DP22 Roy Rogers 2.00 5.00
DP24 Derek Fisher 3.00 8.00
DP25 Martin Muursepp 1.50 4.00
DP26 Jerome Williams 2.00 5.00
DP27 Brian Evans 1.50 4.00
DP28 Priest Lauderdale 1.50 4.00
DP29 Travis Knight 2.00 5.00

1996-97 Topps Finest Reprints

COMPLETE SERIES 2 (25) 60.00 120.00
SER.2 STATED ODDS 1:36 HOBBY/RETAIL
*REF: 1.25X TO 3X HI COLUMN
REF: SER.2 STATED ODDS 1:144 HOB/RET
1 Lew Alcindor 4.00 10.00
3 Paul Arizin 1.25 3.00
9 Wilt Chamberlain 5.00 12.00
11 Dave Cowens 1.50 4.00
14 Clyde Drexler 1.50 4.00
16 Patrick Ewing 2.00 5.00
20 John Havlicek 3.00 8.00
21 Elvin Hayes 1.50 4.00
22 Bird/Erving/Johnson 10.00 25.00
23 Sam Jones 1.50 4.00
25 Jerry Lucas 1.50 4.00
27 Moses Malone 2.00 5.00
30 George Mikan 2.50 6.00
31 Earl Monroe 2.00 5.00
32 Shaquille O'Neal 4.00 10.00
33 Hakeem Olajuwon 3.00 8.00
37 Willis Reed 2.00 5.00
38 Oscar Robertson 3.00 8.00
39 David Robinson 2.50 6.00
40 Bill Russell 4.00 10.00
42 Bill Sharman 1.50 4.00
43 John Stockton 4.00 10.00
45 Nate Thurmond 1.50 4.00
46 Wes Unseld 1.50 4.00
47 Bill Walton 2.00 5.00

1996-97 Topps Hobby Masters

COMPLETE SET (20) 50.00 120.00
COMPLETE SERIES 1 (10) 25.00 60.00
COMPLETE SERIES 2 (10) 25.00 60.00
SER.1/2 STATED ODDS 1:36 HOBBY
HM11 Shaquille O'Neal 12.00 30.00
HM12 Jerry Stackhouse 4.00 10.00
HM13 Dennis Rodman 8.00 20.00
HM14 Joe Smith 2.50 6.00
HM15 Damon Stoudamire 3.00 8.00
HM16 Gary Payton 5.00 12.00
HM17 Mitch Richmond 4.00 10.00
HM18 Reggie Miller 6.00 15.00
HM19 Chris Webber 4.00 10.00
HM20 Vin Baker 2.50 6.00
HM21 Grant Hill 5.00 12.00
HM22 Scottie Pippen 8.00 20.00
HM23 Karl Malone 6.00 15.00
HM24 Patrick Ewing 5.00 12.00
HM25 Shawn Kemp 5.00 12.00
HM26 Anfernee Hardaway 8.00 20.00
HM27 Charles Barkley 8.00 20.00
HM28 Jason Kidd 5.00 12.00
HM29 Hakeem Olajuwon 6.00 15.00
HM30 Larry Johnson 4.00 10.00

1996-97 Topps Holding Court

COMPLETE SET (15) 15.00 40.00
SER.1 ODDS 1:36 H/R, 1:24 JUMBO
*REF: 1.25X TO 3X HI COLUMN
REF: SER.1 ODDS 1:108 H/R, 1:72 JUMBO
HC1 Larry Johnson 1.25 3.00
HC2 Michael Jordan 40.00 100.00
HC3 Cedric Ceballos .75 2.00
HC4 Grant Hill 1.50 4.00
HC5 Anfernee Hardaway 2.50 6.00
HC6 Reggie Miller 2.00 5.00
HC7 Glenn Robinson 1.00 2.50
HC8 Patrick Ewing 1.50 4.00
HC9 Chris Webber 1.25 3.00
HC10 Shaquille O'Neal 4.00 10.00
HC11 John Stockton 2.00 5.00
HC12 Mitch Richmond 1.25 3.00
HC13 David Robinson 2.00 5.00
HC14 Gary Payton 1.50 4.00
HC15 Karl Malone 2.00 5.00

1996-97 Topps Mystery Finest

COMPLETE SET (22) 30.00 80.00
SER.2 STATED ODDS 1:36 HOBBY/RETAIL
*BORDERLESS: .6X TO 1.5X HI COLUMN
BDLS: SER.2 STATED ODDS 1:72 HOB/RET
M1 Scottie Pippen 4.00 10.00
M2 Jason Kidd 2.50 6.00
M3 Anfernee Hardaway 4.00 10.00
M4 Gary Payton 2.50 6.00
M5 Juwan Howard 1.50 4.00
M6 Sean Elliott 1.50 4.00
M7 Dennis Rodman 4.00 10.00
M8 Shawn Kemp 2.50 6.00
M9 David Robinson 3.00 8.00
M10 Alonzo Mourning 2.50 6.00
M11 Dikembe Mutombo 2.50 6.00
M12 Shaquille O'Neal 6.00 15.00
M13 Clyde Drexler 2.50 6.00
M14 Michael Jordan 15.00 40.00
M15 Damon Stoudamire 1.50 4.00
M16 Mitch Richmond 2.00 5.00
M17 Patrick Ewing 2.50 6.00
M18 Vin Baker 1.25 3.00
M19 Hakeem Olajuwon 3.00 8.00
M20 Joe Smith 1.25 3.00
M21 Charles Barkley 4.00 10.00
M22 Reggie Miller 3.00 8.00

1996-97 Topps Mystery Finest Bordered Refractors

COMPLETE SET (22) 125.00 300.00
*BORDERED REF: 1.25X TO 3X BASE HI
SER.2 STATED ODDS 1:66 HOBBY JUMBO
M14 Michael Jordan 60.00 150.00

1996-97 Topps Mystery Finest Borderless Refractors

*STARS: 1.5X TO 4X HI COLUMN
SER.2 STATED ODDS 1:216 HOBBY/RETAIL
M14 Michael Jordan 150.00 400.00

1996-97 Topps Pro Files

COMPLETE SET (20) 12.00 30.00
COMPLETE SERIES 1 (10) 10.00 25.00
COMPLETE SERIES 2 (10) 3.00 8.00
SER.1/2 STATED ODDS 1:12 H/R, 1:6 JUM
TWO PER FACTORY SET
PF1 Grant Hill .60 1.50
PF2 Shawn Kemp .60 1.50
PF3 Michael Jordan 6.00 15.00
PF4 Vin Baker .30 .75
PF5 Chris Webber .50 1.25
PF6 Joe Smith .30 .75
PF7 Shaquille O'Neal 1.50 4.00
PF8 Patrick Ewing .60 1.50
PF9 Scottie Pippen 1.00 2.50
PF10 Damon Stoudamire .40 1.00
PF11 Anfernee Hardaway 1.00 2.50
PF12 Juwan Howard .40 1.00
PF13 Dikembe Mutombo .60 1.50
PF14 Dennis Rodman 1.00 2.50
PF15 Kevin Garnett 1.25 3.00
PF16 Jerry Stackhouse .50 1.25
PF17 Alonzo Mourning .60 1.50
PF18 Karl Malone .75 2.00
PF19 Hakeem Olajuwon .75 2.00
PF20 Gary Payton .60 1.50

1996-97 Topps Season's Best

COMPLETE SET (25) 20.00 50.00
SER.1 STATED ODDS 1:8 HOB/RET, 1:4 JUM
TWO PER FACTORY SET
SB1 Michael Jordan 40.00 100.00
SB2 Hakeem Olajuwon 1.50 4.00
SB3 Shaquille O'Neal 3.00 8.00
SB4 Karl Malone 1.50 4.00
SB5 David Robinson 1.50 4.00
SB6 Dennis Rodman 2.00 5.00
SB7 David Robinson 1.50 4.00
SB8 Dikembe Mutombo 1.25 3.00
SB9 Charles Barkley 2.00 5.00
SB10 Shawn Kemp 1.25 3.00
SB11 John Stockton 1.50 4.00
SB12 Jason Kidd 1.25 3.00
SB13 Avery Johnson .60 1.50
SB14 Rod Strickland .75 2.00
SB15 Damon Stoudamire .75 2.00
SB16 Gary Payton 1.25 3.00
SB17 Mookie Blaylock .75 2.00
SB18 Michael Jordan 40.00 100.00
SB19 Jason Kidd 1.25 3.00
SB20 Alvin Robertson .50 1.25
SB21 Dikembe Mutombo 1.25 3.00
SB22 Shawn Bradley .50 1.25
SB23 David Robinson 1.50 4.00
SB24 Hakeem Olajuwon 1.50 4.00
SB25 Alonzo Mourning 1.25 3.00

1996-97 Topps Super Teams

COMPLETE SET (29) 30.00 60.00
SER.1 STATED ODDS 1:36 HOBBY/RETAIL
ST1 Atlanta Hawks 1.00 2.50
ST2 Boston Celtics 1.00 2.50
ST3 Charlotte Hornets 1.00 2.50
ST4 Chicago Bulls WCDF 10.00 25.00
ST5 Cleveland Cavaliers 1.00 2.50
ST6 Dallas Mavericks 1.00 2.50
ST7 Denver Nuggets 1.00 2.50
ST8 Detroit Pistons 1.00 2.50
ST9 Golden State Warriors 1.00 2.50
ST10 Houston Rockets 1.00 2.50
ST11 Indiana Pacers 1.00 2.50
ST12 Los Angeles Clippers 1.00 2.50
ST13 Los Angeles Lakers 1.50 4.00
ST14 Miami Heat WD 1.50 4.00
ST15 Milwaukee Bucks 1.00 2.50
ST16 Minnesota T'wolves 1.00 2.50
ST17 New Jersey Nets 1.00 2.50
ST18 New York Knicks 1.00 2.50
ST19 Orlando Magic 1.00 2.50
ST20 Philadelphia 76ers 1.00 2.50
ST21 Phoenix Suns 1.00 2.50
ST22 Portland Trail Blazers 1.00 2.50
ST23 Sacramento Kings 1.00 2.50
ST24 San Antonio Spurs W 5.00 12.00
ST25 Seattle Supersonics WD 1.00 2.50
ST26 Toronto Raptors 1.00 2.50
ST27 Utah Jazz WCD 5.00 12.00
ST28 Vancouver Grizzlies 1.00 2.50
ST29 Washington Bullets 1.00 2.50

1996-97 Topps Super Team Conference Winners

COMPLETE SET (22) 10.00 25.00
M1 Scottie Pippen 1.50 4.00
M2 Jason Kidd 1.00 2.50
M3 Anfernee Hardaway 1.50 4.00
M4 Gary Payton 1.00 2.50
M5 Juwan Howard .60 1.50
M6 Sean Elliott .60 1.50
M7 Dennis Rodman 1.50 4.00
M8 Shawn Kemp 1.00 2.50
M9 David Robinson 1.25 3.00
M10 Alonzo Mourning 1.00 2.50
M11 Dikembe Mutombo 1.00 2.50
M12 Shaquille O'Neal 2.50 6.00
M13 Clyde Drexler 1.00 2.50
M14 Michael Jordan 6.00 15.00
M15 Damon Stoudamire .60 1.50
M16 Mitch Richmond .75 2.00
M17 Patrick Ewing 1.00 2.50
M18 Vin Baker .50 1.25
M19 Hakeem Olajuwon 1.25 3.00
M20 Joe Smith .50 1.25
M21 Charles Barkley 1.50 4.00
M22 Reggie Miller 1.25 3.00

1996-97 Topps Super Team Division Winners

COMPLETE SET (22) 8.00 20.00
M1 Scottie Pippen 1.25 3.00
M2 Jason Kidd .75 2.00
M3 Anfernee Hardaway 1.25 3.00
M4 Gary Payton .75 2.00
M5 Juwan Howard .50 1.25
M6 Sean Elliott .50 1.25
M7 Dennis Rodman 1.25 3.00
M8 Shawn Kemp .75 2.00
M9 David Robinson 1.00 2.50
M10 Alonzo Mourning .75 2.00
M11 Dikembe Mutombo .75 2.00
M12 Shaquille O'Neal 2.00 5.00
M13 Clyde Drexler .75 2.00
M14 Michael Jordan 5.00 12.00
M15 Damon Stoudamire .50 1.25
M16 Mitch Richmond .60 1.50
M17 Patrick Ewing .75 2.00
M18 Vin Baker .40 1.00
M19 Hakeem Olajuwon 1.00 2.50
M20 Joe Smith .40 1.00
M21 Charles Barkley 1.25 3.00
M22 Reggie Miller 1.00 2.50

1996-97 Topps Super Team NBA Finals

COMPLETE SET (22) 40.00 100.00
M1 Scottie Pippen 6.00 15.00
M2 Jason Kidd 4.00 10.00
M3 Anfernee Hardaway 6.00 15.00
M4 Gary Payton 4.00 10.00
M5 Juwan Howard 2.50 6.00
M6 Sean Elliott 2.50 6.00
M7 Dennis Rodman 6.00 15.00
M8 Shawn Kemp 4.00 10.00
M9 David Robinson 5.00 12.00
M10 Alonzo Mourning 4.00 10.00
M11 Dikembe Mutombo 4.00 10.00
M12 Shaquille O'Neal 10.00 25.00
M13 Clyde Drexler 4.00 10.00
M14 Michael Jordan 40.00 100.00
M15 Damon Stoudamire 2.50 6.00
M16 Mitch Richmond 3.00 8.00
M17 Patrick Ewing 4.00 10.00
M18 Vin Baker 2.00 5.00
M19 Hakeem Olajuwon 5.00 12.00
M20 Joe Smith 2.00 5.00
M21 Charles Barkley 6.00 15.00
M22 Reggie Miller 5.00 12.00

1996-97 Topps Youthquake

COMPLETE SET (15) 75.00 200.00
SER.2 STATED ODDS 1:36 RETAIL
YQ1 Allen Iverson 25.00 60.00
YQ2 Samaki Walker .75 2.00
YQ3 Stephon Marbury 3.00 8.00
YQ4 Damon Stoudamire 1.00 2.50
YQ5 John Wallace .75 2.00
YQ6 Michael Finley 1.00 2.50
YQ7 Marcus Camby 1.50 4.00
YQ8 Kerry Kittles 1.00 2.50
YQ9 Ray Allen 5.00 12.00
YQ10 Jerry Stackhouse 1.25 3.00
YQ11 Shareef Abdur-Rahim 1.50 4.00
YQ12 Antonio McDyess 1.00 2.50
YQ13 Joe Smith .75 2.00
YQ14 Brent Barry .75 2.00
YQ15 Kobe Bryant 125.00 300.00

1997-98 Topps
COMPLETE SET (220) 15.00 40.00
COMPLETE SERIES 1 (110) 5.00 12.00
COMPLETE SERIES 2 (110) 10.00 25.00
1 Scottie Pippen 1.00 2.50
2 Nate McMillan .25 .60
3 Byron Scott .30 .75
4 Mark Davis .25 .60
5 Rod Strickland .30 .75
6 Brian Grant .30 .75
7 Damon Stoudamire .40 1.00
8 John Stockton .75 2.00
9 Grant Long .25 .60
10 Darrell Armstrong .25 .60
11 Anthony Mason .30 .75
12 Travis Best .25 .60
13 Stephon Marbury .50 1.25
14 Jamal Mashburn .30 .75
15 Detlef Schrempf .40 1.00
16 Terrell Brandon .30 .75
17 Charles Barkley 1.00 2.50
18 Vin Baker .30 .75
19 Gary Trent .25 .60
20 Vinny Del Negro .30 .75
21 Todd Day .25 .60
22 Malik Sealy .30 .75
23 Wesley Person .30 .75
24 Reggie Miller .75 2.00
25 Dan Majerle .40 1.00
26 Todd Fuller .25 .60
27 Juwan Howard .30 .75
28 Clarence Weatherspoon .25 .60
29 Grant Hill .60 1.50
30 John Williams .25 .60
31 Ken Norman .25 .60
32 Patrick Ewing .60 1.50
33 Bryon Russell .25 .60
34 Tony Smith .25 .60
35 Andrew Lang .25 .60
36 Rony Seikaly .25 .60
37 Billy Owens .25 .60
38 Dino Radja .25 .60
39 Chris Gatling .25 .60
40 Dale Davis .30 .75
41 Arvydas Sabonis .50 1.25
42 Chris Mills .25 .60
43 A.C. Green .30 .75
44 Tyrone Hill .30 .75
45 Tracy Murray .30 .75
46 David Robinson .75 2.00
47 Lee Mayberry .25 .60
48 Jayson Williams .25 .60
49 Jason Kidd .60 1.50
50 Bryant Stith .25 .60
51 Latrell Sprewell .50 1.25
52 Brent Barry .30 .75
53 Henry James .25 .60
54 Allen Iverson 1.25 3.00
55 Shandon Anderson .25 .60
56 Mitch Richmond .50 1.25
57 Allan Houston .40 1.00
58 Ron Harper .40 1.00
59 Gheorghe Muresan .25 .60
60 Vincent Askew .25 .60
61 Ray Allen .75 2.00
62 Kenny Anderson .30 .75
63 Dikembe Mutombo .60 1.50
64 Sam Perkins .30 .75
65 Walt Williams .30 .75
66 Chris Carr .25 .60
67 Vlade Divac .40 1.00
68 LaPhonso Ellis .30 .75
69 B.J. Armstrong .25 .60
70 Jim Jackson .30 .75
71 Clyde Drexler .60 1.50
72 Lindsey Hunter .25 .60
73 Sasha Danilovic .25 .60
74 Elden Campbell .25 .60
75 Robert Pack .25 .60
76 Dennis Scott .30 .75
77 Will Perdue .25 .60
78 Anthony Peeler .25 .60
79 Steve Smith .30 .75
80 Steve Kerr .50 1.25
81 Buck Williams .25 .60
82 Terry Mills .25 .60
83 Michael Smith .25 .60
84 Adam Keefe .25 .60
85 Kevin Willis .30 .75
86 David Wesley .30 .75
87 Muggsy Bogues .30 .75
88 Bimbo Coles .25 .60
89 Tom Gugliotta .30 .75
90 Jermaine O'Neal .30 .75
91 Cedric Ceballos .30 .75
92 Shawn Kemp .60 1.50
93 Horace Grant .30 .75
94 Shareef Abdur-Rahim .40 1.00
95 Robert Horry .40 1.00
96 Vitaly Potapenko .25 .60
97 Pooh Richardson .25 .60
98 Doug Christie .25 .60
99 Voshon Lenard .25 .60
100 Dominique Wilkins .50 1.25
101 Alonzo Mourning .60 1.50
102 Sam Cassell .30 .75
103 Sherman Douglas .25 .60
104 Shawn Bradley .25 .60
105 Mark Jackson .30 .75
106 Dennis Rodman 1.00 2.50
107 Charles Oakley .30 .75
108 Matt Maloney .25 .60
109 Shaquille O'Neal 1.25 3.00
110 Checklist .10 .25
111 Antonio McDyess .40 1.00
112 Bob Sura .25 .60
113 Terrell Brandon .30 .75
114 Tim Thomas RC .50 1.25
115 Tim Duncan RC 8.00 20.00
116 Antonio Daniels RC .40 1.00
117 Bryant Reeves .25 .60
118 Keith Van Horn RC .60 1.50
119 Loy Vaught .30 .75
120 Rasheed Wallace .50 1.25
121 Bobby Jackson RC .50 1.25
122 Kevin Johnson .40 1.00
123 Michael Jordan 4.00 10.00
124 Ron Mercer RC .50 1.25
125 Tracy McGrady RC 2.00 5.00
126 Antoine Walker .40 1.00
127 Carlos Rogers .25 .60
128 Isaac Austin .25 .60
129 Mookie Blaylock .40 1.00
130 Rodrick Rhodes RC .30 .75
131 Dennis Scott .30 .75
132 Chris Mullin .50 1.25
133 P.J. Brown .25 .60
134 Rex Chapman .25 .60
135 Sean Elliott .30 .75
136 Alan Henderson .25 .60
137 Austin Croshere RC .30 .75
138 Nick Van Exel .40 1.00
139 Derek Strong .25 .60
140 Glenn Robinson .40 1.00
141 Avery Johnson .30 .75
142 Calbert Cheaney .30 .75
143 Mahmoud Abdul-Rauf .25 .60
144 Stojko Vrankovic .25 .60
145 Chris Childs .25 .60
146 Danny Manning .30 .75
147 Jeff Hornacek .40 1.00
148 Kevin Garnett 1.00 2.50
149 Joe Dumars .50 1.25
150 Johnny Taylor RC .25 .60
151 Mark Price .40 1.00
152 Toni Kukoc .50 1.25
153 Erick Dampier .30 .75
154 Lorenzen Wright .25 .60
155 Matt Geiger .25 .60
156 Tim Hardaway .50 1.25
157 Charles Smith RC .30 .75
158 Hersey Hawkins .30 .75
159 Michael Finley .40 1.00
160 Tyus Edney .25 .60
161 Christian Laettner .40 1.00
162 Doug West .25 .60
163 Jim Jackson .30 .75
164 Larry Johnson .50 1.25
165 Vin Baker .30 .75
166 Karl Malone .75 2.00
167 Kelvin Cato RC .30 .75
168 Luc Longley .40 1.00
169 Dale Davis .30 .75
170 Joe Smith .30 .75
171 Kobe Bryant 8.00 20.00
172 Scot Pollard RC .30 .75
173 Derek Anderson RC .40 1.00
174 Erick Strickland RC .25 .60
175 Olden Polynice .25 .60
176 Chris Whitney .25 .60
177 Anthony Parker RC .40 1.00
178 Armon Gilliam .25 .60
179 Gary Payton .60 1.50
180 Glen Rice .40 1.00
181 Chauncey Billups RC 1.25 3.00
182 Derek Fisher .40 1.00
183 John Starks .40 1.00
184 Mario Elie .25 .60
185 Chris Webber .50 1.25
186 Shawn Kemp .60 1.50
187 Greg Ostertag .25 .60
188 Olivier Saint-Jean RC .30 .75
189 Eric Snow .25 .60
190 Isaiah Rider .30 .75
191 Paul Grant RC .25 .60
192 Samaki Walker .25 .60
193 Cory Alexander .25 .60
194 Eddie Jones .40 1.00
195 John Thomas RC .25 .60
196 Otis Thorpe .25 .60
197 Rod Strickland .30 .75
198 David Wesley .30 .75
199 Jacque Vaughn RC .25 .60
200 Rik Smits .30 .75
201 Brevin Knight RC .40 1.00
202 Clifford Robinson .25 .60
203 Hakeem Olajuwon .75 2.00
204 Jerry Stackhouse .30 .75
205 Tyrone Hill .30 .75
206 Kendall Gill .30 .75
207 Marcus Camby .40 1.00
208 Tony Battie RC .40 1.00
209 Brent Price .25 .60
210 Danny Fortson RC .40 1.00
211 Jerome Williams .25 .60
212 Maurice Taylor RC .30 .75
213 Brian Williams .30 .75
214 Keith Booth RC .30 .75
215 Nick Anderson .25 .60
216 Travis Knight .25 .60
217 Adonal Foyle RC .30 .75
218 Anfernee Hardaway 1.00 2.50
219 Kerry Kittles .30 .75
220 Checklist .10 .25

1997-98 Topps Minted in Springfield
*STARS: 3X TO 8X BASE CARD HI
*RCs: 3X TO 8X BASE HI
SER.1 STATED ODDS 1:6 HOBBY/RETAIL
SER.2 STATED ODDS 1:9 HOBBY/RETAIL
1 Scottie Pippen 8.00 20.00
54 Allen Iverson 8.00 20.00
115 Tim Duncan 75.00 200.00
123 Michael Jordan 125.00 300.00

1997-98 Topps Autographs
SER.1 STATED ODDS 1:212 HOBBY
1 John Starks 8.00 20.00
2 Juwan Howard 6.00 15.00
3 Mitch Richmond 8.00 20.00
4 Hakeem Olajuwon 15.00 40.00
5 Glenn Robinson 6.00 15.00
6 Steve Smith 5.00 12.00
7 Antoine Walker 6.00 15.00
8 Clyde Drexler 10.00 25.00

1997-98 Topps Bound for Glory
COMPLETE SET (15) 60.00 150.00
SER.1 STATED ODDS 1:36 HOBBY
BG1 Robert Parish 1.50 4.00
BG2 Grant Hill 2.50 6.00
BG3 Chris Mullin 2.00 5.00
BG4 Hakeem Olajuwon 3.00 8.00
BG5 Dennis Rodman 4.00 10.00
BG6 Patrick Ewing 2.50 6.00
BG7 Karl Malone 3.00 8.00
BG8 Charles Barkley 4.00 10.00
BG9 David Robinson 3.00 8.00
BG10 Michael Jordan 60.00 150.00
BG11 Dominique Wilkins 2.00 5.00
BG12 Shaquille O'Neal 5.00 12.00
BG13 Clyde Drexler 2.50 6.00
BG14 John Stockton 3.00 8.00
BG15 Scottie Pippen 8.00 20.00

1997-98 Topps Clutch Time
COMPLETE SET (20) 20.00 50.00
SER.2 STATED ODDS 1:36 HOBBY
CT1 Michael Jordan 25.00 60.00
CT2 Christian Laettner 1.50 4.00
CT3 Patrick Ewing 2.50 6.00
CT4 Glen Rice 1.50 4.00
CT5 Stephon Marbury 2.00 5.00
CT6 Tim Hardaway 2.00 5.00
CT7 Reggie Miller 3.00 8.00
CT8 Gary Payton 2.50 6.00
CT9 Charles Barkley 4.00 10.00
CT10 Grant Hill 2.50 6.00
CT11 Karl Malone 3.00 8.00
CT12 Dikembe Mutombo 2.50 6.00
CT13 Hakeem Olajuwon 3.00 8.00
CT14 Shawn Kemp 2.50 6.00
CT15 John Stockton 3.00 8.00
CT16 Anfernee Hardaway 4.00 10.00
CT17 Glenn Robinson 1.50 4.00
CT18 Chris Webber 2.00 5.00
CT19 Allen Iverson 5.00 12.00
CT20 Scottie Pippen 4.00 10.00

1997-98 Topps Destiny
COMPLETE SET (15) 20.00 50.00
SER.2 STATED ODDS 1:18 RETAIL
D1 Grant Hill 2.00 5.00
D2 Kevin Garnett 3.00 8.00
D3 Vin Baker 1.00 2.50
D4 Antoine Walker 1.25 3.00
D5 Kobe Bryant 12.00 30.00
D6 Tracy McGrady 3.00 8.00
D7 Keith Van Horn 1.00 2.50
D8 Tim Duncan 4.00 10.00
D9 Eddie Jones 1.25 3.00
D10 Stephon Marbury 1.50 4.00
D11 Marcus Camby 1.25 3.00
D12 Antonio McDyess 1.25 3.00
D13 Shareef Abdur-Rahim 1.25 3.00
D14 Allen Iverson 4.00 10.00
D15 Shaquille O'Neal 4.00 10.00

1997-98 Topps Draft Redemption
SER.1 STATED ODDS 1:12 HOB, 1:18 RET
DP1 Tim Duncan 25.00 60.00
DP2 Keith Van Horn 3.00 8.00
DP3 Chauncey Billups 6.00 15.00
DP4 Antonio Daniels 2.00 5.00
DP5 Tony Battie 2.00 5.00
DP6 Ron Mercer 2.50 6.00
DP7 Tim Thomas 2.50 6.00
DP8 Adonal Foyle 1.50 4.00
DP9 Tracy McGrady 10.00 25.00
DP10 Danny Fortson 2.00 5.00
DP11 Olivier Saint-Jean 1.50 4.00
DP12 Austin Croshere 1.50 4.00
DP13 Derek Anderson 2.00 5.00
DP14 Maurice Taylor 1.50 4.00
DP15 Kelvin Cato 1.50 4.00
DP16 Brevin Knight 2.00 5.00
DP17 Johnny Taylor 1.25 3.00
DP18 Chris Anstey 1.25 3.00
DP19 Scot Pollard 1.50 4.00
DP20 Paul Grant 1.25 3.00
DP21 Anthony Parker 2.00 5.00
DP22 Ed Gray 2.00 5.00
DP23 Bobby Jackson 2.50 6.00
DP24 Rodrick Rhodes 1.50 4.00
DP25 John Thomas 1.25 3.00
DP26 Charles Smith 1.50 4.00
DP27 Jacque Vaughn 1.50 4.00
DP28 Keith Booth 1.50 4.00
DP29 Serge Zwikker 1.50 4.00

1997-98 Topps Fantastic 15
COMPLETE SET (15) 20.00 50.00
SER.1 STATED ODDS 1:36 RETAIL
F1 Antoine Walker 1.50 4.00
F2 Damon Stoudamire 1.50 4.00
F3 Brent Barry 1.25 3.00
F4 Michael Finley 1.50 4.00
F5 Ray Allen 1.50 4.00
F6 Allen Iverson 5.00 12.00
F7 Stephon Marbury 2.00 5.00
F8 Kerry Kittles 1.25 3.00
F9 John Wallace 1.00 2.50
F10 Kevin Garnett 4.00 10.00
F11 Jerry Stackhouse 1.50 4.00
F12 Kobe Bryant 15.00 40.00
F13 Marcus Camby 1.50 4.00
F14 Joe Smith 1.25 3.00
F15 Shareef Abdur-Rahim 1.50 4.00

1997-98 Topps Generations
COMPLETE SET (30) 75.00 150.00
SER.2 STATED ODDS 1:36 HOBBY/RETAIL
G1 Clyde Drexler 3.00 8.00
G2 Michael Jordan 125.00 300.00
G3 Charles Barkley 5.00 12.00
G4 Hakeem Olajuwon 4.00 10.00
G5 John Stockton 4.00 10.00
G6 Patrick Ewing 3.00 8.00
G7 Karl Malone 4.00 10.00
G8 Dennis Rodman 5.00 12.00
G9 Scottie Pippen 5.00 12.00
G10 David Robinson 4.00 10.00
G11 Mitch Richmond 2.50 6.00
G12 Glen Rice 2.00 5.00
G13 Shawn Kemp 3.00 8.00
G14 Gary Payton 3.00 8.00
G15 Dikembe Mutombo 3.00 8.00
G16 Steve Smith 1.50 4.00
G17 Christian Laettner 2.00 5.00
G18 Shaquille O'Neal 6.00 15.00
G19 Alonzo Mourning 3.00 8.00
G20 Tom Gugliotta 1.50 4.00
G21 Anfernee Hardaway 5.00 12.00
G22 Grant Hill 3.00 8.00
G23 Kevin Garnett 5.00 12.00
G24 Kobe Bryant 20.00 50.00
G25 Stephon Marbury 2.50 6.00
G26 Antoine Walker 2.00 5.00
G27 Shareef Abdur-Rahim 2.00 5.00
G28 Tim Duncan 6.00 15.00
G29 Keith Van Horn 1.50 4.00
G30 Tracy McGrady 5.00 12.00

1997-98 Topps Generations Refractors
*REF: 1X TO 2.5X HI COLUMN
SER.2 STATED ODDS 1:144 HOBBY/RETAIL
G2 Michael Jordan 400.00 800.00
G5 John Stockton 8.00 20.00
G8 Dennis Rodman 15.00 40.00
G21 Anfernee Hardaway 12.00 30.00
G24 Kobe Bryant 400.00 800.00
G28 Tim Duncan 20.00 50.00

1997-98 Topps Inside Stuff
COMPLETE SET (10) 15.00 40.00
SER.2 STATED ODDS 1:36 HOBBY/RETAIL
IS1 Michael Jordan 12.00 30.00
IS2 Eddie Johnson 1.00 2.50
IS3 John Stockton 2.50 6.00
IS4 Patrick Ewing 2.00 5.00
IS5 Shaquille O'Neal 4.00 10.00
IS6 Ervin Johnson .75 2.00
IS7 Shawn Kemp 2.00 5.00
IS8 Scottie Pippen 3.00 8.00
IS9 Kobe Bryant 12.00 30.00
IS10 Anfernee Hardaway 3.00 8.00

1997-98 Topps New School
COMPLETE SET (15) 15.00 40.00
SER.2 STATED ODDS 1:36 HOBBY/RETAIL
NS1 Austin Croshere .60 1.50
NS2 Antonio Daniels .75 2.00
NS3 Tim Thomas 1.00 2.50
NS4 Keith Van Horn 1.25 3.00
NS5 Bobby Jackson 1.00 2.50
NS6 Derek Anderson .75 2.00
NS7 Adonal Foyle .60 1.50
NS8 Johnny Taylor .60 1.50
NS9 Jacque Vaughn .60 1.50
NS10 Chauncey Billups 2.50 6.00
NS11 Brevin Knight .75 2.00
NS12 Tracy McGrady 4.00 10.00
NS13 Tony Battie .75 2.00
NS14 Scot Pollard .60 1.50
NS15 Tim Duncan 5.00 12.00

1997-98 Topps Rock Stars
COMPLETE SET (20) 125.00 300.00
SER.1 STATED ODDS 1:36 HOBBY/RETAIL
*REF: 1.5X TO 4X BASE ROCK STARS
REF: SER.1 STATED ODDS 1:144 H/R
RS1 Michael Jordan 100.00 250.00
RS2 Jerry Stackhouse 5.00 12.00
RS3 Chris Webber 6.00 15.00
RS4 Charles Barkley 12.00 30.00
RS5 Dennis Rodman 12.00 30.00
RS6 Anfernee Hardaway 12.00 30.00
RS7 Juwan Howard 4.00 10.00
RS8 Tim Hardaway 6.00 15.00
RS9 Gary Payton 8.00 20.00
RS10 Dikembe Mutombo 8.00 20.00
RS11 Tom Gugliotta 4.00 10.00
RS12 Kevin Garnett 12.00 30.00
RS13 Shaquille O'Neal 15.00 40.00
RS14 Hakeem Olajuwon 10.00 25.00
RS15 Grant Hill 8.00 20.00
RS16 Karl Malone 10.00 25.00
RS17 Damon Stoudamire 5.00 12.00
RS18 Shawn Kemp 8.00 20.00
RS19 Alonzo Mourning 8.00 20.00
RS20 Scottie Pippen 12.00 30.00

1997-98 Topps Rock Stars Refractors
*REF: 1.5X TO 4X BASE ROCK STARS
SER.1 STATED ODDS 1:144 HOBBY/RETAIL
RS1 Michael Jordan 1,000.00 2,000.00

1997-98 Topps Season's Best
COMPLETE SET (30) 20.00 50.00
SER.1 STATED ODDS 1:16 HOBBY/RETAIL
SB1 Gary Payton 1.25 3.00
SB2 Kevin Johnson .75 2.00
SB3 Tim Hardaway 1.00 2.50
SB4 John Stockton 1.50 4.00
SB5 Damon Stoudamire .75 2.00
SB6 Michael Jordan 15.00 40.00
SB7 Mitch Richmond 1.00 2.50
SB8 Latrell Sprewell 1.00 2.50
SB9 Reggie Miller 1.50 4.00
SB10 Clyde Drexler 1.25 3.00
SB11 Grant Hill 1.25 3.00
SB12 Scottie Pippen 2.00 5.00
SB13 Kendall Gill .60 1.50
SB14 Glen Rice .75 2.00
SB15 LaPhonso Ellis .60 1.50
SB16 Karl Malone 1.50 4.00
SB17 Charles Barkley 2.00 5.00
SB18 Vin Baker .60 1.50
SB19 Chris Webber 1.00 2.50
SB20 Tom Gugliotta .60 1.50
SB21 Shaquille O'Neal 2.50 6.00
SB22 Patrick Ewing 1.25 3.00
SB23 Hakeem Olajuwon 1.50 4.00
SB24 Alonzo Mourning 1.25 3.00
SB25 Dikembe Mutombo 1.25 3.00
SB26 Allen Iverson 2.50 6.00
SB27 Antoine Walker .75 2.00
SB28 Shareef Abdur-Rahim .75 2.00
SB29 Stephon Marbury 1.00 2.50
SB30 Kerry Kittles .60 1.50

1997-98 Topps Topps 40
COMPLETE SET (40) 40.00 80.00
COMPLETE SERIES 1 (20) 15.00 40.00
COMPLETE SERIES 2 (20) 15.00 40.00
BOTH SERIES STATED ODDS 1:12 H/R
T1 Glen Rice 1.00 2.50
T2 Patrick Ewing 1.50 4.00
T3 Terrell Brandon .75 2.00
T4 Jerry Stackhouse 1.00 2.50
T5 Michael Jordan 10.00 25.00
T6 Christian Laettner 1.00 2.50
T7 Latrell Sprewell 1.00 2.50
T8 Reggie Miller 2.00 5.00
T9 Gary Payton 1.50 4.00
T10 Detlef Schrempf 1.00 2.50
T11 Kevin Garnett 2.50 6.00
T12 Eddie Jones 1.00 2.50
T13 Clyde Drexler 1.50 4.00
T14 Anfernee Hardaway 2.50 6.00
T15 Chris Webber 1.25 3.00
T16 Jayson Williams .60 1.50
T17 Joe Smith .75 2.00
T18 Karl Malone 2.00 5.00
T19 Tim Hardaway 1.25 3.00
T20 Vin Baker .75 2.00
T21 Tom Gugliotta .75 2.00
T22 Allen Iverson 3.00 8.00
T23 David Robinson 2.00 5.00
T24 Dikembe Mutombo 1.50 4.00
T25 John Stockton 2.00 5.00
T26 Charles Barkley 2.50 6.00
T27 Mitch Richmond 1.25 3.00
T28 Damon Stoudamire 1.00 2.50
T29 Anthony Mason .75 2.00
T30 Shaquille O'Neal 3.00 8.00
T31 Glenn Robinson 1.00 2.50
T32 Juwan Howard .75 2.00
T33 Shawn Kemp 1.50 4.00
T34 Dennis Rodman 2.50 6.00
T35 Grant Hill 1.50 4.00
T36 Kevin Johnson 1.00 2.50
T37 Alonzo Mourning 1.50 4.00
T38 Hakeem Olajuwon 2.00 5.00
T39 Joe Dumars 1.25 3.00
T40 Scottie Pippen 2.50 6.00

1998-99 Topps Promos
PP7 Kobe Bryant 5.00 12.00

1998-99 Topps
COMPLETE SET (220) 25.00 60.00
COMPLETE SERIES 1 (110) 8.00 20.00
COMPLETE SERIES 2 (110) 15.00 40.00
1 Scottie Pippen 1.00 2.50
2 Shareef Abdur-Rahim .40 1.00
3 Rod Strickland .30 .75
4 Keith Van Horn .40 1.00
5 Ray Allen .60 1.50
6 Chris Mullin .50 1.25
7 Anthony Parker .25 .60
8 Lindsey Hunter .25 .60
9 Mario Elie .25 .60
10 Jerry Stackhouse .40 1.00
11 Eldridge Recasner .25 .60
12 Jeff Hornacek .40 1.00
13 Chris Webber .50 1.25
14 Lee Mayberry .25 .60
15 Erick Strickland .25 .60
16 Arvydas Sabonis .40 1.00
17 Tim Thomas .30 .75
18 Luc Longley .30 .75
19 Detlef Schrempf .40 1.00
20 Alonzo Mourning .60 1.50
21 Adonal Foyle .25 .60
22 Tony Battie .25 .60
23 Robert Horry .40 1.00
24 Derek Harper .30 .75
25 Jamal Mashburn .40 1.00
26 Elliot Perry .25 .60
27 Jalen Rose .30 .75
28 Joe Smith .30 .75
29 Henry James .25 .60
30 Travis Knight .25 .60
31 Tom Gugliotta .30 .75
32 Chris Anstey .25 .60
33 Antonio Daniels .25 .60
34 Elden Campbell .25 .60
35 Charlie Ward .25 .60
36 Eddie Johnson .25 .60
37 John Wallace .25 .60
38 Antonio Davis .25 .60
39 Antoine Walker .40 1.00
40 Patrick Ewing .60 1.50
41 Doug Christie .30 .75
42 Andrew Lang .25 .60
43 Joe Dumars .40 1.00
44 Jaren Jackson .25 .60
45 Loy Vaught .25 .60
46 Allan Houston .40 1.00
47 Mark Jackson .30 .75
48 Tracy Murray .25 .60
49 Tim Duncan 1.00 2.50
50 Micheal Williams .25 .60
51 Steve Nash .75 2.00
52 Matt Maloney .25 .60
53 Sam Cassell .30 .75
54 Voshon Lenard .25 .60
55 Dikembe Mutombo .60 1.50
56 Malik Sealy .25 .60
57 Dell Curry .25 .60
58 Stephon Marbury .50 1.25
59 Tariq Abdul-Wahad .25 .60
60 Isaiah Rider .30 .75
61 Kelvin Cato .25 .60
62 LaPhonso Ellis .25 .60
63 Jim Jackson .25 .60
64 Greg Ostertag .25 .60
65 Glenn Robinson .40 1.00
66 Chris Carr .25 .60
67 Marcus Camby .30 .75
68 Kobe Bryant 3.00 8.00
69 Bobby Jackson .25 .60
70 B.J. Armstrong .25 .60
71 Alan Henderson .25 .60
72 Terry Davis .25 .60
73 John Stockton .75 2.00
74 Lamond Murray .25 .60
75 Mark Price .40 1.00
76 Rex Chapman .30 .75
77 Michael Jordan 4.00 10.00
78 Terry Cummings .30 .75
79 Dan Majerle .40 1.00
80 Bo Outlaw .25 .60
81 Michael Finley .40 1.00
82 Vin Baker .30 .75
83 Clifford Robinson .25 .60
84 Greg Anthony .25 .60
85 Brevin Knight .25 .60
86 Jacque Vaughn .25 .60
87 Bobby Phills .25 .60
88 Sherman Douglas .25 .60
89 Kevin Johnson .40 1.00
90 Mahmoud Abdul-Rauf .25 .60
91 Lorenzen Wright .25 .60
92 Eric Williams .25 .60
93 Will Perdue .25 .60
94 Charles Barkley 1.00 2.50
95 Kendall Gill .30 .75
96 Wesley Person .25 .60
97 Buck Williams .25 .60
98 Erick Dampier .30 .75
99 Nate McMillan .25 .60
100 Sean Elliott .40 1.00
101 Rasheed Wallace .50 1.25
102 Zydrunas Ilgauskas .40 1.00
103 Eddie Jones .40 1.00
104 Ron Mercer .30 .75
105 Horace Grant .30 .75
106 Corliss Williamson .25 .60
107 Anthony Mason .30 .75
108 Mookie Blaylock .30 .75
109 Dennis Rodman 1.00 2.50
110 Checklist .10 .25
111 Steve Smith .30 .75
112 Cedric Henderson .25 .60
113 Raef LaFrentz RC .50 1.25
114 Calbert Cheaney .25 .60
115 Rik Smits .30 .75
116 Rony Seikaly .25 .60
117 Lawrence Funderburke .25 .60
118 Ricky Davis RC .60 1.50
119 Howard Eisley .25 .60
120 Kenny Anderson .30 .75
121 Corey Benjamin RC .25 .60
122 Maurice Taylor .25 .60
123 Eric Murdock .25 .60
124 Derek Fisher .30 .75
125 Kevin Garnett 1.00 2.50
126 Walt Williams .25 .60
127 Bryce Drew RC .25 .60
128 A.C. Green .30 .75
129 Ervin Johnson .25 .60
130 Christian Laettner .30 .75
131 Chauncey Billups .50 1.25
132 Hakeem Olajuwon .75 2.00
133 Al Harrington RC .50 1.25
134 Danny Manning .30 .75
135 Paul Pierce RC 6.00 15.00
136 Terrell Brandon .30 .75
137 Bob Sura .25 .60
138 Chris Gatling .25 .60
139 Donyell Marshall .25 .60
140 Marcus Camby .30 .75
141 Brian Skinner RC .30 .75
142 Charles Oakley .30 .75
143 Antawn Jamison RC .60 1.50
144 Nazr Mohammed RC .40 1.00
145 Karl Malone .75 2.00
146 Chris Mills .25 .60
147 Bison Dele .25 .60
148 Gary Payton .60 1.50
149 Terry Porter .25 .60
150 Tim Hardaway .50 1.25
151 Larry Hughes RC .60 1.50
152 Derek Anderson .30 .75
153 Jason Williams RC 1.25 3.00
154 Dirk Nowitzki RC 12.00 30.00
155 Juwan Howard .30 .75
156 Avery Johnson .25 .60
157 Matt Harpring RC .40 1.00
158 Reggie Miller .75 2.00
159 Walter McCarty .25 .60
160 Allen Iverson 1.00 2.50
161 Felipe Lopez RC .25 .60
162 Tracy McGrady .60 1.50
163 Damon Stoudamire .40 1.00
164 Antonio McDyess .30 .75
165 Grant Hill .50 1.25
166 Tyronn Lue RC .50 1.25
167 P.J. Brown .25 .60
168 Antonio Daniels .25 .60
169 Mitch Richmond .50 1.25
170 David Robinson .75 2.00
171 Shawn Bradley .25 .60
172 Shandon Anderson .25 .60
173 Chris Childs .25 .60
174 Shawn Kemp .60 1.50
175 Shaquille O'Neal 1.50 4.00
176 John Starks .40 1.00
177 Tyrone Hill .25 .60
178 Jayson Williams .25 .60
179 Anfernee Hardaway 1.00 2.50
180 Chris Webber .50 1.25
181 Don Reid .25 .60
182 Stacey Augmon .25 .60
183 Hersey Hawkins .25 .60
184 Sam Mitchell .25 .60
185 Jason Kidd .60 1.50
186 Nick Van Exel .40 1.00
187 Larry Johnson .60 1.50
188 Bryant Reeves .25 .60
189 Glen Rice .40 1.00
190 Kerry Kittles .30 .75
191 Toni Kukoc .40 1.00
192 Ron Harper .40 1.00
193 Bryon Russell .25 .60
194 Vladimir Stepania RC .40 1.00
195 Michael Olowokandi RC .50 1.25
196 Mike Bibby RC .75 2.00
197 Dale Ellis .25 .60
198 Muggsy Bogues .30 .75
199 Vince Carter RC 6.00 15.00
200 Robert Traylor RC .75 2.00
201 Peja Stojakovic RC .75 2.00
202 Aaron McKie .40 1.00
203 Hubert Davis .25 .60
204 Dana Barros .25 .60
205 Bonzi Wells RC .40 1.00
206 Michael Doleac RC .30 .75
207 Keon Clark RC .40 1.00
208 Michael Dickerson RC .40 1.00
209 Nick Anderson .25 .60
210 Brent Price .25 .60
211 Cherokee Parks .25 .60
212 Sam Jacobson RC .25 .60
213 Pat Garrity RC .30 .75
214 Tyrone Corbin .25 .60
215 David Wesley .25 .60
216 Rodney Rogers .25 .60
217 Dean Garrett .25 .60
218 Roshown McLeod RC .25 .60
219 Dale Davis .25 .60
220 Checklist .10 .25

1998-99 Topps Apparitions
COMPLETE SET (15) 300.00 600.00
SER.1 STATED ODDS 1:36 RETAIL
A1 Kobe Bryant 40.00 100.00
A2 Stephon Marbury 2.50 6.00
A3 Brent Barry 1.50 4.00
A4 Karl Malone 4.00 10.00
A5 Shaquille O'Neal 8.00 20.00
A6 Chris Webber 2.50 6.00
A7 Shawn Kemp 3.00 8.00
A8 Hakeem Olajuwon 4.00 10.00
A9 Anfernee Hardaway 5.00 12.00
A10 Michael Finley 2.00 5.00
A11 Keith Van Horn 2.00 5.00
A12 Kevin Garnett 5.00 12.00
A13 Vin Baker 1.50 4.00
A14 Tim Duncan 5.00 12.00
A15 Michael Jordan 200.00 500.00

1998-99 Topps Autographs
STATED ODDS 1:329 SER.1; 1:378 SER.2
AG1 Joe Smith 6.00 15.00
AG2 Kobe Bryant 1,250.00 2,500.00
AG3 Stephon Marbury 12.00 30.00
AG4 Dikembe Mutombo 20.00 50.00
AG5 Shareef Abdur-Rahim 10.00 25.00
AG6 Eddie Jones 10.00 25.00
AG7 Keith Van Horn 8.00 20.00
AG8 Glen Rice 8.00 20.00
AG9 Kobe Bryant 1,250.00 2,500.00
AG10 Ron Mercer 5.00 12.00
AG11 Glen Rice 8.00 20.00
AG12 Stephon Marbury 12.00 30.00
AG13 Kerry Kittles 5.00 12.00
AG14 Michael Olowokandi 5.00 12.00
AG15 Antawn Jamison 8.00 20.00
AG16 Mike Bibby 10.00 25.00
AG17 Robert Traylor 5.00 12.00
AG18 Paul Pierce 50.00 120.00

1998-99 Topps Chrome Preview
COMPLETE SET (10) 30.00 60.00
SER.2 STATED ODDS 1:36 HOB/RET
6 Chris Mullin 4.00 10.00
10 Jerry Stackhouse 3.00 8.00
19 Detlef Schrempf 3.00 8.00
40 Patrick Ewing 5.00 12.00
43 Joe Dumars 3.00 8.00
60 Isaiah Rider 2.50 6.00
73 John Stockton 6.00 15.00
77 Michael Jordan 12.00 30.00
81 Michael Finley 3.00 8.00
100 Sean Elliott 3.00 8.00

1998-99 Topps Chrome Preview Refractors
REF: 2.5X TO 6X VALUE
SER.2 STATED ODDS 1:40 HCP
SKIP-NUMBERED SET
77 Michael Jordan 800.00 1,500.00

1998-99 Topps Classic Collection
COMPLETE SET (10) 6.00 15.00
SER.2 STATED ODDS 1:12 HOB/RET
CL1 Larry Bird 1.50 4.00
CL2 Magic Johnson 1.50 4.00
CL3 Kareem Abdul-Jabbar 1.25 3.00
CL4 Julius Erving 1.00 2.50
CL5 Bill Russell 1.25 3.00
CL6 Wilt Chamberlain 1.25 3.00
CL7 Oscar Robertson 1.00 2.50
CL8 Jerry West 1.00 2.50
CL9 Elgin Baylor .75 2.00
CL10 Bob Cousy 1.00 2.50

1998-99 Topps Coast to Coast
COMPLETE SET (15) 30.00 80.00
SER.2 STATED ODDS 1:36 RETAIL
CC1 Kobe Bryant 25.00 60.00
CC2 Scottie Pippen 5.00 12.00
CC3 Eddie Jones 2.00 5.00
CC4 Grant Hill 2.00 5.00
CC5 Jason Kidd 3.00 8.00
CC6 Antoine Walker 2.00 5.00
CC7 Michael Finley 2.00 5.00
CC8 Kevin Garnett 5.00 12.00
CC9 Allen Iverson 5.00 12.00
CC10 Shawn Kemp 3.00 8.00
CC11 Glenn Robinson 2.00 5.00
CC12 Anfernee Hardaway 5.00 12.00
CC13 Tim Hardaway 2.50 6.00
CC14 Ron Mercer 1.50 4.00
CC15 Kerry Kittles 1.50 4.00

1998-99 Topps Cornerstones
COMPLETE SET (15) 25.00 60.00
SER.1 STATED ODDS 1:36 HOBBY
C1 Keith Van Horn 1.25 3.00
C2 Kevin Garnett 3.00 8.00
C3 Shareef Abdur-Rahim 1.25 3.00
C4 Antoine Walker 1.25 3.00
C5 Allen Iverson 3.00 8.00
C6 Grant Hill 2.00 5.00
C7 Marcus Camby 1.00 2.50
C8 Stephon Marbury 1.50 4.00
C9 Kobe Bryant 25.00 60.00
C10 Bobby Jackson 1.00 2.50
C11 Kerry Kittles 1.00 2.50
C12 Ron Mercer 1.00 2.50
C13 Eddie Jones 1.25 3.00
C14 Tim Thomas 1.00 2.50
C15 Tim Duncan 3.00 8.00

1998-99 Topps Draft Redemption
SER.1 STATED ODDS 1:18 HOB/RET
RED.CARDS NOT AVAILABLE FOR 17/18
1 Michael Olowokandi 3.00 8.00
2 Mike Bibby 5.00 12.00
3 Raef LaFrentz 3.00 8.00
4 Antawn Jamison 4.00 10.00
5 Vince Carter 12.00 30.00
6 Robert Traylor 2.50 6.00
7 Jason Williams 8.00 20.00
8 Larry Hughes 4.00 10.00
9 Dirk Nowitzki 30.00 80.00
10 Paul Pierce 10.00 25.00
11 Bonzi Wells 2.50 6.00

12 Michael Doleac 2.00 5.00
13 Keon Clark 2.50 6.00
14 Michael Dickerson 2.50 6.00
15 Matt Harpring 2.50 6.00
16 Bryce Drew 1.50 4.00
19 Pat Garrity 2.00 5.00
20 Roshown McLeod 1.50 4.00
21 Ricky Davis 4.00 10.00
22 Brian Skinner 2.00 5.00
23 Tyronn Lue 3.00 8.00
24 Felipe Lopez 1.50 4.00
25 Al Harrington 3.00 8.00
26 Sam Jacobson 1.50 4.00
27 Vladimir Stepania 2.50 6.00
28 Corey Benjamin 1.50 4.00
29 Nazr Mohammed 2.50 6.00

1998-99 Topps East/West

COMPLETE SET (20) 40.00 80.00
SER.2 STATED ODDS 1:36 HOB/RET
*REF: 2X TO 5X HI COLUMN
REF: SER.2 STATED ODDS 1:144 H/R
EW1 A.Walker/S.Abdur-Rahim 2.00 5.00
EW2 A.Mourning/S.O'Neal 8.00 20.00
EW3 T.Hardaway/J.Stockton 4.00 10.00
EW4 S.Pippen/K.Garnett 5.00 12.00
EW5 M.Jordan/K.Bryant 600.00 1,200.00
EW6 G.Hill/M.Finley 3.00 8.00
EW7 D.Mutombo/H.Olajuwon 4.00 10.00
EW8 K.Van Horn/T.Duncan 5.00 12.00
EW9 A.Iverson/G.Payton 5.00 12.00
EW10 P.Ewing/D.Robinson 4.00 10.00
EW11 J.Howard/C.Webber 2.50 6.00
EW12 B.Knight/S.Marbury 2.50 6.00
EW13 S.Kemp/V.Baker 3.00 8.00
EW14 A.Mason/T.Gugliotta 1.50 4.00
EW15 A.Hardaway/D.Stoudamire 5.00 12.00
EW16 R.Mercer/E.Jones 2.00 5.00
EW17 R.Strickland/J.Kidd 3.00 8.00
EW18 T.Thomas/A.McDyess 1.50 4.00
EW19 J.Williams/K.Malone 4.00 10.00
EW20 R.Miller/J.Jackson 4.00 10.00

1998-99 Topps Emissaries

COMPLETE SET (20) 25.00 50.00
SER.1 STATED ODDS 1:24 HOB/RET
E1 Scottie Pippen 4.00 10.00
E2 Karl Malone 3.00 8.00
E3 Chris Webber 2.00 5.00
E4 Anfernee Hardaway 4.00 10.00
E5 Detlef Schrempf 1.50 4.00
E6 Mitch Richmond 2.00 5.00
E7 Vlade Divac 1.50 4.00
E8 Shaquille O'Neal 6.00 15.00
E9 Luc Longley 1.25 3.00
E10 Grant Hill 2.50 6.00
E11 Christian Laettner 1.25 3.00
E12 Gary Payton 2.50 6.00
E13 Patrick Ewing 2.50 6.00
E14 Shawn Kemp 2.50 6.00
E15 Toni Kukoc 1.50 4.00
E16 David Robinson 3.00 8.00
E17 Hakeem Olajuwon 3.00 8.00
E18 Charles Barkley 4.00 10.00
E19 John Stockton 3.00 8.00
E20 Arvydas Sabonis 1.50 4.00

1998-99 Topps Gold Label

COMPLETE SET (10) 60.00 150.00
SER.2 STATED ODDS 1:12 HOB/RET
*BLACK LABEL: .75X TO 2X HI COLUMN
BLACK: SER.2 STATED ODDS 1:96 H/R
*RED: 10X TO 25X HI
STATED PRINT RUN 100 SERIAL #'d SETS
GL1 Michael Jordan 40.00 100.00
GL2 Shaquille O'Neal 3.00 8.00
GL3 Kobe Bryant 25.00 60.00
GL4 Antoine Walker .75 2.00
GL5 Charles Barkley 2.00 5.00
GL6 Keith Van Horn .75 2.00
GL7 Tim Duncan 2.00 5.00
GL8 Stephon Marbury 1.00 2.50
GL9 Shareef Abdur-Rahim .75 2.00
GL10 Gary Payton 1.25 3.00

1998-99 Topps Gold Label Red Label

*RED: 15X TO 40X VALUE
SER.2 STATED ODDS 1:4967 HOB/RET
STATED PRINT RUN 100 SERIAL #'d SETS
GL1 Michael Jordan 6,000.00 10,000.00
GL2 Shaquille O'Neal 200.00 500.00
GL3 Kobe Bryant 3,000.00 6,000.00
GL5 Charles Barkley 200.00 500.00
GL7 Tim Duncan 200.00 500.00
GL10 Gary Payton 60.00 150.00

1998-99 Topps Kick Start

COMPLETE SET (15) 25.00 60.00
SER.2 STATED ODDS 1:12 HOB/RET
KS1 Tim Duncan 2.50 6.00
KS2 Kobe Bryant 25.00 60.00
KS3 Antoine Walker 1.00 2.50
KS4 Stephon Marbury 1.25 3.00
KS5 Allen Iverson 2.50 6.00
KS6 Shareef Abdur-Rahim 1.00 2.50
KS7 Keith Van Horn 1.00 2.50
KS8 Ray Allen 1.50 4.00
KS9 Vince Carter 5.00 12.00
KS10 Kevin Garnett 2.50 6.00
KS11 Kerry Kittles .75 2.00
KS12 Tim Thomas .75 2.00
KS13 Ron Mercer .75 2.00
KS14 Antawn Jamison 1.50 4.00
KS15 Mike Bibby 2.00 5.00

1998-99 Topps Legacies

COMPLETE SET (15) 300.00 600.00
SER.2 STATED ODDS 1:36 HOBBY
L1 Scottie Pippen 12.00 30.00
L2 Grant Hill 3.00 8.00
L3 Hakeem Olajuwon 4.00 10.00
L4 Alonzo Mourning 3.00 8.00
L5 Shaquille O'Neal 8.00 20.00
L6 Shawn Kemp 3.00 8.00
L7 Gary Payton 3.00 8.00
L8 Karl Malone 4.00 10.00
L9 Patrick Ewing 3.00 8.00
L10 Tim Hardaway 2.50 6.00
L11 Reggie Miller 4.00 10.00
L12 Glen Rice 2.00 5.00
L13 Dikembe Mutombo 3.00 8.00
L14 John Stockton 4.00 10.00
L15 Michael Jordan 300.00 600.00

1998-99 Topps Roundball Royalty

COMPLETE SET (20) 150.00 400.00
SER.1 STATED ODDS 1:36 HOB/RET
*REF: 2.5X TO 6X VALUE
R1 Michael Jordan 125.00 300.00
R2 Kevin Garnett 5.00 12.00
R3 David Robinson 4.00 10.00
R4 Allen Iverson 5.00 12.00
R5 Hakeem Olajuwon 4.00 10.00
R6 Anfernee Hardaway 5.00 12.00
R7 Gary Payton 3.00 8.00
R8 Scottie Pippen 5.00 12.00
R9 Shaquille O'Neal 8.00 20.00
R10 Mitch Richmond 2.50 6.00
R11 John Stockton 4.00 10.00
R12 Grant Hill 3.00 8.00
R13 Charles Barkley 5.00 12.00
R14 Dikembe Mutombo 3.00 8.00
R15 Karl Malone 4.00 10.00
R16 Shawn Kemp 3.00 8.00
R17 Patrick Ewing 3.00 8.00
R18 Kobe Bryant 40.00 100.00
R19 Terrell Brandon 1.50 4.00
R20 Vin Baker 1.50 4.00

1998-99 Topps Season's Best

COMPLETE SET (30) 150.00 400.00
SER.1 STATED ODDS 1:12 HOB/RET
SB1 Rod Strickland 1.00 2.50
SB2 Gary Payton 2.00 5.00
SB3 Tim Hardaway 1.50 4.00
SB4 Stephon Marbury 1.50 4.00
SB5 Sam Cassell 1.00 2.50
SB6 Michael Jordan 150.00 400.00
SB7 Mitch Richmond 1.50 4.00
SB8 Steve Smith 1.00 2.50
SB9 Ray Allen 2.00 5.00
SB10 Isaiah Rider 1.00 2.50
SB11 Grant Hill 2.00 5.00
SB12 Kevin Garnett 3.00 8.00
SB13 Shareef Abdur-Rahim 1.25 3.00
SB14 Glenn Robinson 1.25 3.00
SB15 Michael Finley 1.25 3.00
SB16 Karl Malone 2.50 6.00
SB17 Tim Duncan 3.00 8.00
SB18 Antoine Walker 1.25 3.00
SB19 Chris Webber 1.50 4.00
SB20 Vin Baker 1.00 2.50
SB21 Shaquille O'Neal 5.00 12.00
SB22 David Robinson 2.50 6.00
SB23 Alonzo Mourning 2.00 5.00
SB24 Dikembe Mutombo 2.00 5.00
SB25 Hakeem Olajuwon 2.50 6.00
SB26 Tim Duncan 3.00 8.00
SB27 Keith Van Horn 1.25 3.00
SB28 Zydrunas Ilgauskas 1.25 3.00
SB29 Brevin Knight .75 2.00
SB30 Bobby Jackson 1.00 2.50

1999-00 Topps

COMPLETE SET (257) 30.00 80.00
COMPLETE SERIES 1 (120) 12.00 30.00
COMPLETE SERIES 2 (137) 15.00 40.00
COMP.SERIES 1 w/o SP (110) 6.00 12.00
COMP.SERIES 2 w/o SP (110) 5.00 10.00
SER.1/2 RC STATED ODDS 1:5 HOB/RET
USA STATED ODDS 1:5 HOB/RET
1 Steve Smith .15 .40
2 Ron Harper .15 .40
3 Michael Dickerson .12 .30
4 LaPhonso Ellis .12 .30
5 Chris Webber .25 .60
6 Jason Caffey .12 .30
7 Bryon Russell .12 .30
8 Bison Dele .12 .30
9 Isaiah Rider .15 .40
10 Dean Garrett .12 .30
11 Eric Murdock .12 .30
12 Juwan Howard .15 .40
13 Latrell Sprewell .25 .60
14 Jalen Rose .15 .40
15 Larry Johnson .20 .50
16 Eric Williams .12 .30
17 Bryant Reeves .12 .30
18 Tony Battie .12 .30
19 Luc Longley .12 .30
20 Gary Payton .30 .75
21 Tariq Abdul-Wahad .12 .30
22 Armen Gilliam UER .12 .30
23 Shaquille O'Neal .75 2.00
24 Gary Trent .12 .30
25 John Stockton .30 .75
26 Mark Jackson .15 .40
27 Cherokee Parks .12 .30
28 Michael Olowokandi .12 .30
29 Rael LaFrentz .15 .40
30 Dell Curry .12 .30
31 Travis Best .12 .30
32 Shawn Kemp .12 .30
33 Voshon Lenard .12 .30
34 Brian Grant .12 .30
35 Alvin Williams .12 .30
36 Derek Fisher .12 .30
37 Allan Houston .15 .40
38 Arvydas Sabonis .15 .40
39 Terry Cummings .12 .30
40 Dale Ellis .12 .30
41 Maurice Taylor .12 .30
42 Grant Hill .30 .75
43 Anthony Mason .20 .50
44 John Wallace .12 .30
45 David Wesley .12 .30
46 Nick Van Exel .15 .40
47 Cuttino Mobley .12 .30
48 Anfernee Hardaway .50 1.25
49 Terry Porter .12 .30
50 Brent Barry .15 .40
51 Derek Harper .15 .40
52 Antoine Walker .20 .50
53 Karl Malone .40 1.00
54 Ben Wallace .15 .40
55 Vlade Divac .20 .50
56 Sam Mitchell .12 .30
57 Joe Smith .15 .40
58 Shawn Bradley .12 .30
59 Darrell Armstrong .12 .30
60 Kenny Anderson .15 .40
61 Jason Williams .30 .75
62 Alonzo Mourning .15 .40
63 Matt Harpring .12 .30
64 Antonio Davis .12 .30
65 Lindsey Hunter .12 .30
66 Allen Iverson .50 1.25
67 Mookie Blaylock .12 .30
68 Wesley Person .12 .30
69 Bobby Phills .12 .30
70 Theo Ratliff .15 .40
71 Antonio Daniels .12 .30
72 P.J. Brown .12 .30
73 David Robinson .40 1.00
74 Sean Elliott .15 .40
75 Zydrunas Ilgauskas .15 .40
76 Kerry Kittles .15 .40
77 Otis Thorpe .12 .30
78 John Starks .20 .50
79 Jaren Jackson .12 .30
80 Hersey Hawkins .12 .30
81 Glenn Robinson .15 .40
82 Paul Pierce .40 1.00
83 Glen Rice .20 .50
84 Charlie Ward .12 .30
85 Dee Brown .12 .30
86 Danny Fortson .12 .30
87 Billy Owens .12 .30
88 Jason Kidd .30 .75
89 Brent Price .12 .30
90 Don Reid .12 .30
91 Mark Bryant .12 .30
92 Vinny Del Negro .12 .30
93 Stephon Marbury .25 .60
94 Donyell Marshall .15 .40
95 Jim Jackson .12 .30
96 Horace Grant .15 .40
97 Calbert Cheaney .12 .30
98 Vince Carter .50 1.25
99 Bobby Jackson .15 .40
100 Alan Henderson .12 .30
101 Mike Bibby .20 .50
102 Cedric Henderson .12 .30
103 Lamond Murray .12 .30
104 A.C. Green .15 .40
105 Hakeem Olajuwon .40 1.00
106 George Lynch .12 .30
107 Kendall Gill .20 .50
108 Rex Chapman .12 .30
109 Eddie Jones .20 .50
110 Kornel David RC .20 .50
111 Jason Terry RC .50 1.25
112 Corey Maggette RC .40 1.00
113 Ron Artest RC .75 2.00
114 Richard Hamilton RC .75 2.00
115 Elton Brand RC .60 1.50
116 Baron Davis RC .75 2.00
117 Wally Szczerbiak RC .50 1.25
118 Steve Francis RC .60 1.50
119 James Posey RC .30 .75
120 Shawn Marion RC .60 1.50
121 Tim Duncan .50 1.25
122 Danny Manning .15 .40
123 Chris Mullin .20 .50
124 Antawn Jamison .20 .50
125 Kobe Bryant 1.50 4.00
126 Matt Geiger .12 .30
127 Rod Strickland .15 .40
128 Howard Eisley .12 .30
129 Steve Nash .40 1.00
130 Felipe Lopez .12 .30
131 Ron Mercer .15 .40
132 Ruben Patterson .12 .30
133 Dana Barros .12 .30
134 Dale Davis .12 .30
135 Bo Outlaw .12 .30
136 Shandon Anderson .12 .30
137 Mitch Richmond .25 .60
138 Doug Christie .15 .40
139 Rasheed Wallace .25 .60
140 Chris Childs .12 .30
141 Jamal Mashburn .15 .40
142 Terrell Brandon .12 .30
143 Jamie Feick RC .12 .30
144 Robert Traylor .12 .30
145 Rick Fox .12 .30
146 Charles Barkley .50 1.25
147 Tyrone Nesby RC .12 .30
148 Jerry Stackhouse .20 .50
149 Cedric Ceballos .12 .30
150 Dikembe Mutombo .30 .75
151 Anthony Peeler .12 .30
152 Larry Hughes .15 .40
153 Clifford Robinson .12 .30
154 Corliss Williamson .20 .50
155 Olden Polynice .12 .30
156 Avery Johnson .15 .40
157 Tracy Murray .12 .30
158 Tom Gugliotta .15 .40
159 Tim Thomas .15 .40
160 Reggie Miller .40 1.00
161 Tim Hardaway .25 .60
162 Dan Majerle .20 .50
163 Will Perdue .12 .30
164 Brevin Knight .12 .30
165 Elden Campbell .12 .30
166 Chris Gatling .12 .30
167 Walter McCarty .12 .30
168 Chauncey Billups .20 .50
169 Chris Mills .12 .30
170 Christian Laettner .15 .40
171 Robert Pack .12 .30
172 Rik Smits .15 .40
173 Tyrone Hill .12 .30
174 Damon Stoudamire .20 .50
175 Nick Anderson .12 .30
176 Peja Stojakovic .20 .50
177 Vladimir Stepania .12 .30
178 Tracy McGrady .30 .75
179 Adam Keefe .12 .30
180 Shareef Abdur-Rahim .20 .50
181 Isaac Austin .12 .30
182 Mario Elie .12 .30
183 Rashard Lewis .15 .40
184 Scott Burrell .12 .30
185 Othella Harrington .12 .30
186 Eric Piatkowski .12 .30
187 Bryant Stith .12 .30
188 Michael Finley .20 .50
189 Chris Crawford .12 .30
190 Toni Kukoc .25 .60
191 Danny Ferry .12 .30
192 Erick Dampier .12 .30
193 Clarence Weatherspoon .12 .30
194 Bob Sura .12 .30
195 Jayson Williams .12 .30
196 Kurt Thomas .12 .30
197 Greg Anthony .12 .30
198 Rodney Rogers .12 .30
199 Detlef Schrempf .15 .40
200 Keith Van Horn .15 .40
201 Robert Horry .15 .40
202 Sam Cassell .15 .40
203 Malik Sealy .12 .30
204 Kelvin Cato .12 .30
205 Antonio McDyess .15 .40
206 Andrew DeClercq .12 .30
207 Ricky Davis .20 .50
208 Vitaly Potapenko .12 .30
209 Loy Vaught .12 .30
210 Kevin Garnett .50 1.25
211 Eric Snow .12 .30
212 Anfernee Hardaway .50 1.25
213 Vin Baker .15 .40
214 Lawrence Funderburke .12 .30
215 Jeff Hornacek .15 .40
216 Doug West .12 .30
217 Michael Doleac .12 .30
218 Ray Allen .30 .75
219 Derek Anderson .12 .30
220 Jerome Williams .12 .30
221 Derrick Coleman .15 .40
222 Randy Brown .12 .30
223 Patrick Ewing .25 .60
224 Walt Williams .12 .30
225 Charles Oakley .20 .50
226 Steve Kerr .15 .40
227 Muggsy Bogues .15 .40
228 Kevin Willis .15 .40
229 Marcus Camby .15 .40
230 Scottie Pippen .50 1.25
231 Lamar Odom RC .60 1.50
232 Jonathan Bender RC .30 .75
233 Andre Miller RC .60 1.50
234 Trajan Langdon RC .25 .60
235 A.Radojevic RC .20 .50
236 William Avery RC .20 .50
237 Cal Bowdler RC .20 .50
238 Quincy Lewis RC .20 .50
239 Dion Glover RC .20 .50
240 Jeff Foster RC .20 .50
241 Kenny Thomas RC .30 .75
242 Devean George RC .25 .60
243 Tim James RC .20 .50
244 Vonteego Cummings RC .20 .50
245 Jumaine Jones RC .25 .60
246 Scott Padgett RC .25 .60
247 Adrian Griffin RC .25 .60
248 Chris Herren RC .25 .60
249 Allan Houston USA .20 .50
250 Kevin Garnett USA .60 1.50
251 Gary Payton USA .40 1.00
252 Steve Smith USA .20 .50
253 Tim Hardaway USA .30 .75
254 Tim Duncan USA .60 1.50
255 Jason Kidd USA .40 1.00
256 Tom Gugliotta USA .20 .50
257 Vin Baker USA .20 .50

1999-00 Topps MVP Promotion

*MVP STARS: 10X TO 25X BASE CARD HI
*MVP RCs: 6X TO 15X BASE HI
SER.1 STATED ODDS 1:336
SER.2 STATED ODDS 1:172
STATED PRINT RUN 100 SETS

1999-00 Topps MVP Promotion Exchange

COMPLETE SET (22) 25.00 60.00
ONE SET VIA MAIL PER MVP WINNER
MVP1 Allen Iverson 3.00 8.00
MVP2 Alonzo Mourning 2.00 5.00
MVP3 Anthony Mason 1.25 3.00
MVP4 Chris Webber 1.50 4.00
MVP5 Eddie Jones 1.25 3.00
MVP6 Grant Hill 2.00 5.00
MVP7 Jason Kidd 2.00 5.00
MVP8 Karl Malone 2.50 6.00
MVP9 Kevin Garnett 3.00 8.00
MVP10 Kobe Bryant 10.00 25.00
MVP11 Michael Finley 1.25 3.00
MVP12 Sam Cassell 1.00 2.50
MVP13 Shaquille O'Neal 5.00 12.00
MVP14 Stephon Marbury 1.50 4.00
MVP15 Terrell Brandon .75 2.00
MVP16 Tim Duncan 3.00 8.00
MVP17 Vince Carter 3.00 8.00
MVP18 Steve Francis 2.50 6.00
MVP19 E.Brand/S.Francis 2.50 6.00
MVP20 Shaquille O'Neal 5.00 12.00
MVP21 Reggie Miller 2.50 6.00
MVP22 Shaquille O'Neal 5.00 12.00

1999-00 Topps 21st Century Topps

COMPLETE SET (16) 6.00 15.00
SER.2 STATED ODDS 1:27 HOB/RET
C1 Jason Terry .50 1.25
C2 Baron Davis .75 2.00
C3 Lamar Odom .60 1.50
C4 Jonathan Bender .30 .75
C5 Ron Artest .75 2.00
C6 Richard Hamilton .75 2.00
C7 Andre Miller .60 1.50
C8 Shawn Marion .60 1.50
C9 Steve Francis .60 1.50
C10 Elton Brand .60 1.50
C11 Wally Szczerbiak .50 1.25
C12 Corey Maggette .40 1.00
C13 James Posey .30 .75
C14 Trajan Langdon .25 .60
C15 Tim James .20 .50
C16 Cal Bowdler .20 .50

1999-00 Topps All-Matrix

COMPLETE SET (30) 30.00 80.00
SER.1 STATED ODDS 1:15 HOB/RET
AM1 Karl Malone 2.50 6.00
AM2 Scottie Pippen 3.00 8.00
AM3 Grant Hill 2.00 5.00
AM4 Shawn Kemp 2.00 5.00
AM5 Shaquille O'Neal 5.00 12.00
AM6 Anfernee Hardaway 3.00 8.00
AM7 Chris Webber 1.50 4.00
AM8 Gary Payton 2.00 5.00
AM9 Jason Kidd 2.00 5.00
AM10 John Stockton 2.00 5.00
AM11 Kevin Garnett 3.00 8.00
AM12 Vince Carter 3.00 8.00
AM13 Shareef Abdur-Rahim 1.25 3.00
AM14 Antoine Walker 1.25 3.00
AM15 Kobe Bryant 10.00 25.00
AM16 Tim Duncan 3.00 8.00
AM17 Keith Van Horn 1.00 2.50
AM18 Allen Iverson 3.00 8.00
AM19 Jason Williams 2.00 5.00
AM20 Stephon Marbury 1.50 4.00
AM21 Elton Brand 1.50 4.00
AM22 Jason Terry 1.25 3.00
AM23 Steve Francis 1.50 4.00
AM24 Corey Maggette 1.00 2.50
AM25 Lamar Odom 1.50 4.00
AM26 Ron Artest 2.00 5.00
AM27 Baron Davis 2.00 5.00
AM28 Andre Miller 1.50 4.00
AM29 Shawn Marion 1.50 4.00
AM30 Wally Szczerbiak 1.25 3.00

1999-00 Topps Autographs

SER.1 STATED ODDS 1:877 (A) HOB
SER.1 STATED ODDS 1:351 (B) HOB
SER.2 STATED ODDS 1:196 (A/B) HOB
SER.2 OVERALL STATED ODDS 1:98 H
AM Antonio McDyess A 6.00 15.00
AM2 Antonio McDyess B 6.00 15.00
AW Antoine Walker A 6.00 15.00
BD Baron Davis A 8.00 20.00
CM Corey Maggette A 8.00 20.00
DS Damon Stoudamire A 6.00 15.00
EB Elton Brand B 6.00 15.00
GP Gary Payton B 15.00 40.00
GP2 Gary Payton A 12.00 30.00
JJ Jumaine Jones A 5.00 12.00
JK Jason Kidd A 20.00 50.00
MR Mitch Richmond A 6.00 15.00
PP Paul Pierce B 20.00 50.00
SF Steve Francis B 6.00 15.00
SP Scottie Pippen B 50.00 120.00
SS Steve Smith B 5.00 12.00
TD Tim Duncan A 300.00 600.00
TG Tom Gugliotta B 5.00 12.00
WA William Avery A 2.00 5.00
WS Wally Szczerbiak A 5.00 12.00
SAR Shareef Abdur-Rahim B 8.00 20.00

1999-00 Topps Highlight Reels

COMPLETE SET (15) 8.00 20.00
SER.1 STATED ODDS 1:14 RETAIL
HR1 Stephon Marbury 1.00 2.50
HR2 Vince Carter 2.00 5.00
HR3 Kevin Garnett 2.00 5.00
HR4 Kobe Bryant 6.00 15.00
HR5 Chris Webber 1.00 2.50
HR6 Allen Iverson 2.00 5.00
HR7 Grant Hill 1.25 3.00
HR8 Antoine Walker .75 2.00
HR9 Jason Williams 1.25 3.00
HR10 Tim Duncan 2.00 5.00
HR11 Shareef Abdur-Rahim .75 2.00
HR12 Keith Van Horn .60 1.50
HR13 Antonio McDyess .60 1.50
HR14 Jason Kidd 1.25 3.00
HR15 Ron Mercer .60 1.50

1999-00 Topps Impact

COMPLETE SET (20) 25.00 60.00
SER.2 STATED ODDS 1:24 HOB/RET
*REF: 1X TO 2.5X HI COLUMN
REF: SER.2 STATED ODDS 1:120 H/R
I1 Elton Brand 1.50 4.00
I2 Lamar Odom 1.50 4.00
I3 Wally Szczerbiak 1.25 3.00
I4 Jason Terry 1.25 3.00
I5 Baron Davis 2.00 5.00
I6 Ron Artest 2.00 5.00
I7 Steve Francis 1.50 4.00
I8 Andre Miller 1.50 4.00
I9 Allen Iverson 3.00 8.00
I10 Jason Williams 2.00 5.00
I11 Keith Van Horn 1.00 2.50
I12 Vince Carter 3.00 8.00
I13 Kobe Bryant 10.00 25.00
I14 Tim Duncan 3.00 8.00
I15 Scottie Pippen 3.00 8.00
I16 Kevin Garnett 3.00 8.00
I17 Shaquille O'Neal 5.00 12.00
I18 Gary Payton 2.00 5.00
I19 Karl Malone 2.50 6.00
I20 Grant Hill 2.00 5.00

1999-00 Topps Jumbos

COMPLETE SET (8) 2.00 5.00
ONE PER SER.1 HOBBY BOX
1 Gary Payton .50 1.25
2 Shaquille O'Neal 1.25 3.00
3 Antoine Walker .30 .75
4 Jason Williams .50 1.25
5 Alonzo Mourning .50 1.25
6 Allen Iverson .75 2.00
7 Stephon Marbury .40 1.00
8 Vince Carter .75 2.00

1999-00 Topps Own the Game

COMPLETE SET (10) 12.50 30.00
SER.2 STATED ODDS 1:44 HOB/RET
OTG1 Allen Iverson 3.00 8.00
OTG2 Shaquille O'Neal 5.00 12.00
OTG3 Jason Kidd 2.00 5.00
OTG4 Stephon Marbury 1.50 4.00
OTG5 Dikembe Mutombo 2.00 5.00
OTG6 Tim Duncan 3.00 8.00
OTG7 Wally Szczerbiak 2.00 5.00
OTG8 Quincy Lewis .75 2.00
OTG9 Elton Brand 2.50 6.00
OTG10 Aleksandar Radojevic .75 2.00

1999-00 Topps Patriarchs

COMPLETE SET (15) 10.00 25.00
SER.1 STATED ODDS 1:22 HOB/RET
P1 Patrick Ewing 1.25 3.00
P2 Reggie Miller 2.00 5.00
P3 Hakeem Olajuwon 2.00 5.00
P4 Scottie Pippen 2.50 6.00
P5 Grant Hill 1.50 4.00
P6 Shaquille O'Neal 4.00 10.00
P7 Mitch Richmond 1.25 3.00
P8 Glen Rice 1.00 2.50
P9 Charles Barkley 2.50 6.00
P10 Karl Malone 2.00 5.00
P11 John Stockton 1.50 4.00
P12 Gary Payton 1.50 4.00
P13 David Robinson 2.00 5.00
P14 Tim Hardaway 1.25 3.00
P15 Joe Dumars 1.00 2.50

1999-00 Topps Picture Perfect

COMPLETE SET (10) 2.00 5.00
SER.1 STATED ODDS 1:8 HOB/RET
PIC1 Shaquille O'Neal 1.25 3.00
PIC2 Alonzo Mourning .50 1.25
PIC3 Shareef Abdur-Rahim .30 .75
PIC4 Juwan Howard .25 .60
PIC5 Keith Van Horn .25 .60
PIC6 Ron Mercer .25 .60
PIC7 Tim Hardaway .40 1.00
PIC8 Kevin Garnett .75 2.00
PIC9 Charles Barkley .50 1.25
PIC10 Kerry Kittles .25 .60

1999-00 Topps Prodigy

COMPLETE SET (20) 30.00 80.00
SER.1 STATED ODDS 1:36 HOB/RET
PR1 Stephon Marbury 2.50 6.00
PR2 Jason Kidd 3.00 8.00
PR3 Kevin Garnett 5.00 12.00
PR4 Kobe Bryant 15.00 40.00
PR5 Antoine Walker 2.00 5.00
PR6 Ron Mercer 1.50 4.00
PR7 Shareef Abdur-Rahim 2.00 5.00
PR8 Tim Duncan 5.00 12.00
PR9 Keith Van Horn 1.50 4.00
PR10 Ray Allen 3.00 8.00
PR11 Michael Doleac 1.25 3.00
PR12 Jason Williams 3.00 8.00
PR13 Michael Dickerson 1.25 3.00
PR14 Mike Bibby 2.00 5.00
PR15 Paul Pierce 4.00 10.00
PR16 Michael Olowokandi 1.25 3.00
PR17 Vince Carter 5.00 12.00
PR18 Antawn Jamison 2.00 5.00
PR19 Felipe Lopez 1.25 3.00
PR20 Matt Harpring 1.25 3.00

1999-00 Topps Prodigy Refractors

*REF: .6X TO 1.5X HI COLUMN
SER.1 STATED ODDS 1:144 H/R
PR4 Kobe Bryant 25.00 60.00
PR12 Jason Williams 8.00 20.00

1999-00 Topps Record Numbers

COMPLETE SET (10) 2.00 5.00
SER.1 STATED ODDS 1:12 HOB/RET
RN1 Karl Malone .60 1.50
RN2 Kerry Kittles .25 .60
RN3 Reggie Miller .60 1.50
RN4 Hakeem Olajuwon .60 1.50
RN5 John Stockton .50 1.25
RN6 Dikembe Mutombo .50 1.25
RN7 Kobe Bryant 2.50 6.00
RN8 Tim Duncan .75 2.00
RN9 Allen Iverson .75 2.00
RN10 Patrick Ewing .40 1.00

1999-00 Topps Season's Best

COMPLETE SET (30) 15.00 40.00
SER.1 STATED ODDS 1:12 HOB/RET
SB1 David Robinson 1.50 4.00
SB2 Shaquille O'Neal 3.00 8.00
SB3 Patrick Ewing 1.00 2.50
SB4 Hakeem Olajuwon 1.50 4.00
SB5 Alonzo Mourning 1.25 3.00
SB6 Antonio McDyess .60 1.50
SB7 Tim Duncan 2.00 5.00
SB8 Keith Van Horn .60 1.50
SB9 Karl Malone 1.50 4.00
SB10 Chris Webber 1.00 2.50
SB11 Kevin Garnett 2.00 5.00
SB12 Juwan Howard .60 1.50
SB13 Shareef Abdur-Rahim .75 2.00
SB14 Glenn Robinson .60 1.50
SB15 Grant Hill 1.25 3.00
SB16 Michael Finley .75 2.00
SB17 Steve Smith .60 1.50
SB18 Mitch Richmond 1.00 2.50
SB19 Kobe Bryant 6.00 15.00
SB20 Ray Allen 1.25 3.00
SB21 Allen Iverson 2.00 5.00
SB22 Gary Payton 1.25 3.00
SB23 Stephon Marbury 1.00 2.50
SB24 Jason Kidd 1.25 3.00
SB25 Tim Hardaway 1.00 2.50
SB26 Jason Williams 1.25 3.00
SB27 Vince Carter 2.00 5.00
SB28 Paul Pierce 1.50 4.00
SB29 Mike Bibby .75 2.00
SB30 Michael Dickerson .50 1.25

1999-00 Topps Team Topps

COMPLETE SET (24) 25.00 60.00
SER.2 STATED ODDS 1:18 HOB/RET
TT1 Gary Payton 2.00 5.00
TT2 Jason Kidd 2.00 5.00
TT3 Kobe Bryant 10.00 25.00
TT4 Anfernee Hardaway 3.00 8.00
TT5 Kevin Garnett 3.00 8.00
TT6 Patrick Ewing 1.50 4.00
TT7 Tim Duncan 3.00 8.00
TT8 Karl Malone 2.50 6.00
TT9 Shaquille O'Neal 5.00 12.00
TT10 Charles Barkley 3.00 8.00
TT11 John Stockton 2.00 5.00
TT12 Tim Hardaway 1.50 4.00
TT13 Hakeem Olajuwon 2.50 6.00
TT14 Jayson Williams .75 2.00
TT15 Reggie Miller 2.50 6.00
TT16 David Robinson 2.50 6.00
TT17 Grant Hill 2.00 5.00
TT18 Scottie Pippen 3.00 8.00
TT19 Chris Webber 1.50 4.00
TT20 Shawn Kemp 2.00 5.00
TT21 Alonzo Mourning 2.00 5.00
TT22 Mitch Richmond 1.50 4.00
TT23 Antoine Walker 1.25 3.00
TT24 Tom Gugliotta 1.00 2.50

2000-01 Topps Promos

COMPLETE SET (2) 1.00 2.50
PP1 Elton Brand .40 1.00
PP2 Tim Duncan 1.00 2.50

2000-01 Topps

COMPLETE SET (295) 40.00 80.00
COMPLETE SERIES 1 (155) 30.00 60.00
COMP.SERIES 1 w/o RC (130) 7.50 15.00
COMPLETE SERIES 2 (140) 12.50 25.00
COMP.SERIES 2 w/o RC (120) 7.50 15.00
RC SUBSET: STATED ODDS 1:5 H/R, 1:1 HTA
SOME RCs AVAILABLE VIA REDEMPTION
1 Elton Brand .20 .50
2 Marcus Camby .15 .40
3 Jalen Rose .15 .40
4 Jamie Feick .12 .30
5 Toni Kukoc .25 .60
6 Todd MacCulloch .12 .30
7 Mario Elie .12 .30
8 Doug Christie .15 .40
9 Sam Cassell .15 .40
10 Shaquille O'Neal .75 2.00
11 Larry Hughes .20 .50
12 Jerry Stackhouse .20 .50
13 Rick Fox .15 .40
14 Clifford Robinson .20 .50
15 Felipe Lopez .12 .30
16 Dirk Nowitzki .50 1.25
17 Cuttino Mobley .15 .40
18 Latrell Sprewell .25 .60
19 Nick Anderson .15 .40
20 Kevin Garnett .50 1.25
21 Rik Smits .12 .30
22 Jerome Williams .12 .30
23 Chris Webber .25 .60
24 Jason Terry .20 .50
25 Elden Campbell .12 .30
26 Kelvin Cato .12 .30
27 Tyrone Nesby .12 .30
28 Jonathan Bender .12 .30
29 Otis Thorpe .15 .40
30 Scottie Pippen .50 1.25
31 Radoslav Nesterovic .12 .30
32 P.J. Brown .12 .30
33 Reggie Miller .40 1.00
34 Andre Miller .15 .40
35 Tariq Abdul-Wahad .12 .30
36 Michael Doleac .12 .30
37 Rashard Lewis .15 .40
38 Jacque Vaughn .12 .30
39 Larry Johnson .25 .60
40 Steve Francis .20 .50
41 Arvydas Sabonis .20 .50
42 Jaren Jackson .12 .30
43 Howard Eisley .12 .30
44 Rod Strickland .12 .30
45 Tim Thomas .15 .40
46 Robert Horry .20 .50
47 Kenny Thomas .12 .30
48 Anthony Peeler .12 .30
49 Darrell Armstrong .12 .30
50 Vince Carter .40 1.00
51 Othella Harrington .12 .30
52 Derek Anderson .15 .40
53 Anthony Carter .12 .30
54 Scott Burrell .12 .30
55 Ray Allen .30 .75
56 Jason Kidd .30 .75
57 Sean Elliott .15 .40
58 Muggsy Bogues .20 .50
59 LaPhonso Ellis .15 .40
60 Tim Duncan .50 1.25
61 Adrian Griffin .12 .30
62 Wally Szczerbiak .15 .40
63 Austin Croshere .12 .30
64 Wesley Person .12 .30
65 James Posey .15 .40
66 Alan Henderson .12 .30
67 Ruben Patterson .12 .30
68 Jahidi White .12 .30
69 Shawn Marion .20 .50
70 Lamar Odom .20 .50
71 Lindsey Hunter .12 .30
72 Keon Clark .15 .40
73 Gary Trent .12 .30
74 Lamond Murray .12 .30
75 Paul Pierce .30 .75
76 Charlie Ward .12 .30
77 Matt Geiger .12 .30
78 Greg Anthony .12 .30
79 Horace Grant .20 .50
80 John Stockton .40 1.00
81 Peja Stojakovic .15 .40
82 William Avery .12 .30
83 Dan Majerle .20 .50
84 Christian Laettner .15 .40
85 Dana Barros .12 .30
86 Corey Benjamin .12 .30
87 Keith Van Horn .15 .40
88 Patrick Ewing .30 .75
89 Steve Smith .15 .40
90 Antonio Davis .15 .40
91 Samaki Walker .12 .30
92 Mitch Richmond .25 .60
93 Michael Olowokandi .12 .30
94 Baron Davis .20 .50
95 Dikembe Mutombo .30 .75
96 Andrew DeClercq .12 .30
97 Raef LaFrentz .15 .40
98 Trajan Langdon .15 .40
99 Ervin Johnson .12 .30
100 Alonzo Mourning .30 .75
101 Kendall Gill .12 .30
102 George Lynch .12 .30
103 Detlef Schrempf .15 .40
104 Donyell Marshall .15 .40
105 Bo Outlaw .12 .30
106 Kenny Anderson .15 .40
107 Eddie Robinson .12 .30

108 Jermaine O'Neal .15 .40
109 John Amaechi .12 .30
110 Glen Rice .20 .50
111 Vlade Divac .20 .50
112 Vin Baker .15 .40
113 Mike Bibby .20 .50
114 Richard Hamilton .25 .60
115 Mookie Blaylock .20 .50
116 Vitaly Potapenko .12 .30
117 Anthony Mason .20 .50
118 Robert Pack .12 .30
119 Vonteego Cummings .12 .30
120 Michael Finley .20 .50
121 Ron Artest .20 .50
122 Tyrone Hill .12 .30
123 Rodney Rogers .12 .30
124 Quincy Lewis .12 .30
125 Kenyon Martin RC .75 2.00
126 Stromile Swift RC .30 .75
127 Darius Miles RC .40 1.00
128 Marcus Fizer RC .30 .75
129 Mike Miller RC .60 1.50
130 DerMarr Johnson RC .25 .60
131 Chris Mihm RC .25 .60
132 Jamal Crawford RC 1.00 2.50
133 Joel Przybilla RC .30 .75
134 Keyon Dooling RC .30 .75
135 Jerome Moiso RC .25 .60
136 Etan Thomas RC .30 .75
137 Courtney Alexander RC .25 .60
138 Mateen Cleaves RC .30 .75
139 Jason Collier RC .40 1.00
140 Desmond Mason RC .50 1.25
141 Quentin Richardson RC .30 .75
142 Jamaal Magloire RC .40 1.00
143 Speedy Claxton RC .40 1.00
144 Morris Peterson RC .40 1.00
145 Donnell Harvey RC .30 .75
146 DeShawn Stevenson RC .40 1.00
147 Mamadou N'Diaye RC .25 .60
148 Erick Barkley RC .25 .60
149 Mark Madsen RC .40 1.00
150 Shaq/Iverson/G.Hill SL .15 .40
151 Kidd/Cassell/Van Exel SL .20 .50
152 Mutombo/Shaq/Duncan SL .25 .60
153 E.Jones/Pierce/Armstrong SL .10 .30
154 Mourning/Mutombo/Shaq SL .20 .50
155 Team Championship SL .30 .75
156 Jason Williams .30 .75
157 David Robinson .40 1.00
158 Shammond Williams .12 .30
159 Charles Oakley .20 .50
160 Greg Ostertag .12 .30
161 Juwan Howard .15 .40
162 Antoine Walker .20 .50
163 Alan Henderson .12 .30
164 Eddie Jones .20 .50
165 Allen Iverson .50 1.25
166 Grant Hill .25 .60
167 Terrell Brandon .15 .40
168 Stephon Marbury .25 .60
169 Jason Caffey .12 .30
170 Sam Mitchell .12 .30
171 Jamal Mashburn .15 .40
172 Ron Harper .20 .50
173 Eric Piatkowski .12 .30
174 Sam Perkins .12 .30
175 Walt Williams .12 .30
176 Bob Sura .12 .30
177 Michael Curry .12 .30
178 Nick Van Exel .20 .50
179 Danny Ferry .12 .30
180 Randy Brown .12 .30
181 Danny Fortson .15 .40
182 Jim Jackson .15 .40
183 Brad Miller .15 .40
184 Shawn Bradley .12 .30
185 Voshon Lenard .12 .30
186 Erick Dampier .12 .30
187 Mark Jackson .15 .40
188 Maurice Taylor .12 .30
189 Kobe Bryant 1.50 4.00
190 Clarence Weatherspoon .12 .30
191 Bobby Jackson .15 .40
192 Eric Snow .12 .30
193 Allan Houston .20 .50
194 Kurt Thomas .12 .30
195 Chauncey Billups .25 .60
196 Tom Gugliotta .15 .40
197 Theo Ratliff .12 .30
198 Rasheed Wallace .25 .60
199 Jon Barry .12 .30
200 Malik Rose .12 .30
201 Vernon Maxwell .12 .30
202 Dee Brown .12 .30
203 Bryon Russell .12 .30
204 Brent Barry .15 .40
205 Tracy McGrady .40 1.00
206 Bryant Reeves .12 .30
207 Isaac Austin .12 .30
208 Damon Stoudamire .20 .50
209 Anfernee Hardaway .20 .50
210 Aaron McKie .12 .30
211 Johnny Newman .12 .30
212 Scott Williams .12 .30
213 Brian Shaw .12 .30
214 Corey Maggette .15 .40
215 Travis Best .12 .30
216 Hakeem Olajuwon .40 1.00
217 Antawn Jamison .20 .50
218 John Starks .20 .50
219 Antonio McDyess .15 .40
220 Cedric Ceballos .15 .40
221 Chris Carr .12 .30
222 Roshown McLeod .12 .30
223 Calbert Cheaney .12 .30
224 Gary Payton .30 .75
225 Karl Malone .40 1.00
226 Michael Dickerson .12 .30
227 Tracy Murray .12 .30
228 Chris Childs .12 .30
229 Pat Garrity .12 .30
230 Rex Chapman .15 .40
231 Jumaine Jones .12 .30
232 Fred Hoiberg .12 .30
233 Bimbo Coles .12 .30
234 Shawn Kemp .30 .75
235 David Wesley .15 .40
236 Tony Battie .12 .30
237 Ron Mercer .15 .40
238 John Wallace .12 .30
239 Robert Traylor .12 .30
240 Derrick Coleman .12 .30
241 Steve Nash .30 .75
242 Ben Wallace .25 .60
243 Brian Skinner .12 .30
244 Chris Gatling .12 .30
245 Dale Davis .15 .40
246 Joe Smith .15 .40
247 Glenn Robinson .20 .50
248 Kerry Kittles .15 .40
249 Erick Strickland .12 .30
250 Sam Cassell .15 .40
251 Chucky Atkins .12 .30
252 Brian Grant .15 .40
253 Bonzi Wells .12 .30
254 Corliss Williamson .12 .30
255 Shareef Abdur-Rahim .20 .50
256 Kevin Willis .12 .30
257 Scott Padgett .12 .30
258 Terry Porter .12 .30
259 Tony Delk .12 .30
260 Avery Johnson .15 .40
261 Tim Hardaway .25 .60
262 Derek Fisher .20 .50
263 Isaiah Rider .15 .40
264 Shandon Anderson .12 .30
265 Adonal Foyle .12 .30
266 Hedo Turkoglu RC .60 1.50
267 Brian Cardinal RC .25 .60
268 Iakovos Tsakalidis RC .25 .60
269 Dalibor Bagaric RC .30 .75
270 Marko Jaric RC .40 1.00
271 Dan Langhi RC .25 .60
272 A.J. Guyton RC .25 .60
273 Jake Voskuhl RC .25 .60
274 Khalid El-Amin RC .25 .60
275 Mike Smith RC .25 .60
276 Soumaila Samake RC .25 .60
277 Eddie House RC .30 .75
278 Eduardo Najera RC .40 1.00
279 Lavor Postell RC .25 .60
280 Hanno Mottola RC .25 .60
281 Chris Carrawell RC .25 .60
282 Olumide Oyedeji RC .25 .60
283 Michael Redd RC 1.00 2.50
284 Chris Porter RC .25 .60
285 Mark Karcher RC .25 .60
286 S.Francis/G.Payton SC .20 .50
287 D.Miles/K.Garnett SC .20 .50
288 L.Odom/Abdur-Rahim SC .15 .40
289 T.Duncan/A.Mourning SC .25 .60
290 E.Brand/K.Malone SC .20 .50
291 L.Hughes/A.Iverson SC .25 .60
292 K.Bryant/R.Miller SC .50 1.25
293 V.Carter/G.Hill SC .25 .60
294 T.McGrady/S.Pippen SC .40 1.00
295 K.Martin/M.Camby SC .60 1.50

2000-01 Topps MVP Promotion

*STARS: 20X TO 50X BASE CARD HI
*RCs: 2X TO 5X BASE CARD HI
SER.1 STATED ODDS 1:253 H/R, 1:51 HTA
SER.2 STATED ODDS 1:179 H/R, 1:41 HTA

2000-01 Topps Autographs

SER.1 STATED ODDS 1:580 H/R, 1:115 HTA
SER.2 STATED ODDS 1:465 H/R, 1:89 HTA
DUNCAN AU: STATED ODDS 1:1239 HTA
ROY AU: STATED ODDS 1:11584
TAAI Allen Iverson A 75.00 150.00
TAAJ Antawn Jamison A 5.00 12.00
TAAM Antonio McDyess B 4.00 10.00
TAAJG A.J. Guyton A 2.50 6.00
TACA Courtney Alexander C 2.50 6.00
TAEB Elton Brand B 5.00 12.00
TAEB Elton Brand C 5.00 12.00
TAEMJ Magic Johnson A 40.00 80.00
TAJC Jamal Crawford A 10.00 25.00
TAJR Jalen Rose D 5.00 12.00
TAKD Keyon Dooling A 3.00 8.00
TALH Larry Hughes A 4.00 10.00
TALS Latrell Sprewell A 25.00 60.00
TAMC Mateen Cleaves B 3.00 8.00
TAMDC Marcus Camby B 5.00 12.00
TARA Ron Artest B 5.00 12.00
TAROY E.Brand/S.Francis 15.00 40.00
TASC Sam Cassell B 4.00 10.00
TASE Sean Elliott B 3.00 8.00
TASF Steve Francis B 5.00 12.00
TASO Shaquille O'Neal B 50.00 100.00
TASP Scoonie Penn B 4.00 10.00
TATB Terrell Brandon B 4.00 10.00
TATD Tim Duncan HTA 300.00 600.00
TATM Tracy McGrady B 15.00 40.00

2000-01 Topps Cards That Never Were

COMPLETE SET (10) 15.00 30.00
COMMON CARD (MJ1-MJ10) 1.50 4.00
SER.2 STATED ODDS 1:18 H/R, 1:6 HTA

2000-01 Topps Chrome Previews

COMPLETE SET (20) 15.00 40.00
SER.1 STATED ODDS 1:18 H/R, 1:5 HTA
TCP1 Shaquille O'Neal 3.00 8.00
TCP2 Kevin Garnett 2.00 5.00
TCP3 Vince Carter 1.50 4.00
TCP4 Tim Duncan 2.00 5.00
TCP5 Elton Brand .75 2.00
TCP6 Jason Kidd 1.25 3.00
TCP7 Lamar Odom .75 2.00
TCP8 Marcus Camby .60 1.50
TCP9 Paul Pierce 1.25 3.00
TCP10 Steve Francis .75 2.00
TCP11 Chris Webber 1.00 2.50
TCP12 Jalen Rose .60 1.50
TCP13 John Stockton 1.50 4.00
TCP14 Larry Hughes .75 2.00
TCP15 Ray Allen 1.25 3.00
TCP16 Alonzo Mourning 1.25 3.00
TCP17 Keith Van Horn .60 1.50
TCP18 Scottie Pippen 2.00 5.00
TCP19 Jerry Stackhouse .75 2.00
TCP20 Andre Miller .60 1.50

2000-01 Topps Combos 1

COMPLETE SET (10) 6.00 15.00
SER.1 STATED ODDS 1:12 H/R, 1:4 HTA
TC1 S.O'Neal/K.Bryant 2.00 5.00
TC2 S.Marbury/A.Iverson .60 1.50
TC3 C.Webber/J.Williams .60 1.50
TC4 Ewing/Mutombo/Mourning .60 1.50
TC5 T.McGrady/V.Carter 2.00 5.00
TC6 T.Duncan/G.Hill 1.00 2.50
TC7 E.Brand/L.Odom/S.Francis .60 1.50
TC8 G.Payton/J.Kidd .75 2.00
TC9 Stoud/Pip/Smith/Wallace .75 2.00
TC10 T.Duncan/K.Garnett 1.25 3.00

2000-01 Topps Combos 2

COMPLETE SET (10) 4.00 10.00
SER.2 STATED ODDS 1:12 H/R, 1:4 HTA
TC1 Hakeem Olajuwon .40 1.00
TC2 Patrick Ewing .40 1.00
TC3 Karl Malone .40 1.00
TC4 Scottie Pippen .60 1.50
TC5 Reggie Miller .40 1.00
TC6 S.O'Neal/M.Johnson 1.50 4.00
TC7 Fizer/Swift/K.Martin .40 1.00
TC8 Claxton/Dooling/Crawford .40 1.00
TC9 M.Miller/D.John/Miles .40 1.00
TC10 M.Johnson/M.Cleaves .60 1.50

2000-01 Topps East Meets West Game Jerseys

SER.2 STATED ODDS 1:598 HTA
EMW1 S.O'Neal/R.Miller 50.00 100.00
EMW2 G.Rice/J.Rose 12.50 30.00

2000-01 Topps Final Piece Game Jerseys

GROUP A ODDS 1:528
GROUP B ODDS 1:23719
SER.2 STATED ODDS 1:517 H/R, 1:52 HTA
FP1 Shaquille O'Neal A 25.00 60.00
FP2 Glen Rice A 8.00 20.00
FP3 Robert Horry A 8.00 20.00
FP4 Rick Fox A 8.00 20.00
FP5 Brian Shaw A 5.00 12.00
FP6 Ron Harper A 8.00 20.00
FP7 Derek Fisher A 8.00 20.00
FP8 A.C. Green B 6.00 15.00
FP9 John Salley A 5.00 12.00
FP10 Travis Knight A 5.00 12.00
FP11 Devean George A 5.00 12.00
FP12 Reggie Miller A 25.00 60.00
FP13 Jalen Rose A 6.00 15.00
FP14 Dale Davis A 6.00 15.00
FP15 Rik Smits A 6.00 15.00
FP16 Mark Jackson A 8.00 20.00
FP17 Travis Best A 5.00 12.00
FP18 Austin Croshere A 5.00 12.00
FP19 Derrick McKey A 5.00 12.00
FP20 Sam Perkins A 5.00 12.00
FP21 Chris Mullin A 15.00 40.00
FP22 Jonathan Bender A 5.00 12.00
FP23 Zan Tabak A 5.00 12.00

2000-01 Topps Flight Club

COMPLETE SET (20) 15.00 30.00
SER.2 STATED ODDS 1:18 H/R, 1:6 HTA
FC1 Vince Carter 1.50 4.00
FC2 Larry Hughes .75 2.00
FC3 Steve Francis .75 2.00
FC4 Tracy McGrady 1.50 4.00
FC5 Jerry Stackhouse .75 2.00
FC6 Kobe Bryant 6.00 15.00
FC7 Kevin Garnett 2.00 5.00
FC8 Michael Finley .75 2.00
FC9 Latrell Sprewell 1.00 2.50
FC10 Antonio McDyess .60 1.50
FC11 Lamar Odom .75 2.00
FC12 Shareef Abdur-Rahim .75 2.00
FC13 Chris Webber 1.00 2.50
FC14 Eddie Jones .75 2.00
FC15 Scottie Pippen 2.00 5.00
FC16 Grant Hill 1.25 3.00
FC17 Paul Pierce 1.25 3.00
FC18 Shawn Marion .75 2.00
FC19 Rasheed Wallace 1.00 2.50
FC20 Tim Duncan 2.00 5.00

2000-01 Topps Game Jerseys

GROUP A ODDS 1:971 H/R, 1:151 HTA
GROUP B ODDS 1:946 H/R, 1:302 HTA
OVERALL ODDS 1:502 H/R, 1:101 HTA
TR1 Richard Hamilton A 4.00 10.00
TR2 Tracy Murray A 2.00 5.00
TR3 Chris Whitney B 2.00 5.00
TR4 Jahidi White A 2.00 5.00
TR5 Rod Strickland A 2.00 5.00
TR6 Mitch Richmond B 4.00 10.00
TR7 Juwan Howard B 2.50 6.00
TR8 Isaac Austin B 2.00 5.00
TR9 Michael Smith A 2.00 5.00
TR10 Lorenzo Williams B 2.00 5.00
TR11 Tony Battie B 2.00 5.00
TR12 Antoine Walker A 3.00 8.00
TR13 Adrian Griffin A 2.00 5.00
TR14 Vitaly Potapenko A 2.00 5.00
TR15 Pervis Ellison A 2.00 5.00
TR16 Paul Pierce B 5.00 12.00
TR17 Eric Williams B 2.00 5.00
TR18 Dana Barros B 2.00 5.00
TR19 Walter McCarty A 2.00 5.00
TR20 Danny Fortson B 2.50 6.00

2000-01 Topps Hidden Gems

COMPLETE SET (10) 2.50 6.00
SER.1 STATED ODDS 1:11 H/R, 1:3 HTA
HG1 Karl Malone .75 2.00
HG2 Latrell Sprewell .50 1.25
HG3 Kobe Bryant 3.00 8.00
HG4 Michael Finley .40 1.00
HG5 Jalen Rose .30 .75
HG6 Reggie Miller .75 2.00
HG7 John Stockton .75 2.00
HG8 Terrell Brandon .30 .75
HG9 Nick Van Exel .40 1.00
HG10 Allan Houston .40 1.00

2000-01 Topps Hobby Masters

COMPLETE SET (10) 8.00 20.00
SER.1 STATED ODDS 1:5 HTA
HM1 Kevin Garnett 1.50 4.00
HM2 Jason Williams 1.00 2.50
HM3 Tim Duncan 1.50 4.00
HM4 Tracy McGrady 1.25 3.00
HM5 Kobe Bryant 5.00 12.00
HM6 Allen Iverson 1.50 4.00
HM7 Elton Brand .60 1.50
HM8 Steve Francis .60 1.50
HM9 Vince Carter 1.25 3.00
HM10 Chris Webber .75 2.00

2000-01 Topps Magic Johnson Reprints

COMPLETE SET (7) 40.00 70.00
COMMON CARD (1-7) 5.00 12.00
COMMON AU (1-7) 60.00 150.00
SER.1 STATED ODDS 1:508 H/R, 1:108 HTA
AU: SER.1 ST.ODDS 1:7088 H/R, 1:1506 HTA

2000-01 Topps Jumbos

ONE PER SER.1 HOBBY BOX

2000-01 Topps No Limit

COMPLETE SET (20) 10.00 20.00
SER.2 STATED ODDS 1:6 H/R, 1:2 HTA
NL1 Kobe Bryant 3.00 8.00
NL2 Kevin Garnett 1.00 2.50
NL3 Vince Carter .75 2.00
NL4 Tracy McGrady .75 2.00
NL5 Tim Duncan 1.00 2.50
NL6 Elton Brand .40 1.00
NL7 Lamar Odom .40 1.00
NL8 Larry Hughes .40 1.00
NL9 Chris Webber .50 1.25
NL10 Shareef Abdur-Rahim .40 1.00
NL11 Jason Kidd .60 1.50
NL12 Gary Payton .60 1.50
NL13 Paul Pierce .60 1.50
NL14 Stromile Swift .30 .75
NL15 Darius Miles .40 1.00
NL16 Mike Miller .60 1.50
NL17 Jason Williams .60 1.50
NL18 Jamal Crawford 1.00 2.50
NL19 Marcus Fizer .30 .75
NL20 DerMarr Johnson .25 .60

2000-01 Topps Quantum Leaps

COMPLETE SET (10) 6.00 15.00
SER.1 STATED ODDS 1:22 H/R, 1:6 HTA
QL1 Chris Webber .75 2.00
QL2 Antonio McDyess .50 1.25
QL3 Stephon Marbury .75 2.00
QL4 Shareef Abdur-Rahim .60 1.50
QL5 Kobe Bryant 5.00 12.00
QL6 Jason Kidd 1.00 2.50
QL7 Elton Brand .60 1.50
QL8 Lamar Odom .60 1.50
QL9 Kevin Garnett 1.50 4.00
QL10 Jerry Stackhouse .60 1.50

2000-01 Topps Rise to Stardom

COMPLETE SET (10) 8.00 20.00
SER.2 STATED ODDS 1:36 H/R, 1:12 HTA
RS1 Elton Brand .75 2.00
RS2 Steve Francis .75 2.00
RS3 Vince Carter 1.50 4.00
RS4 Tim Duncan 2.00 5.00
RS5 Allen Iverson 2.00 5.00
RS6 Damon Stoudamire .75 2.00
RS7 Grant Hill 1.25 3.00
RS8 Jason Kidd 1.25 3.00
RS9 Chris Webber 1.00 2.50
RS10 Shaquille O'Neal 3.00 8.00

2001-02 Topps Promos

COMPLETE SET (2) 2.00 5.00
PP1 Shaquille O'Neal 2.50 6.00
PP2 Tim Duncan 1.50 4.00

2001-02 Topps

COMPLETE SET (257) 40.00 100.00
COMP.SET w/o RC (220) 15.00 40.00
221-256 STATED ODDS 1:4
1 Shaquille O'Neal 1.50 4.00
2 Travis Best .25 .60
3 Allen Iverson 1.00 2.50
4 Shawn Marion .40 1.00
5 Rasheed Wallace .50 1.25
6 Antonio Daniels .25 .60
7 Rashard Lewis .30 .75
8 John Starks .30 .75
9 Stromile Swift .25 .60
10 Vince Carter .75 2.00
11 George Lynch .25 .60
12 Kendall Gill .25 .60
13 Glen Rice .40 1.00
14 Glenn Robinson .40 1.00
15 Wally Szczerbiak .30 .75
16 Rick Fox .30 .75
17 Darius Miles .30 .75
18 Jermaine O'Neal .30 .75
19 Erick Dampier .25 .60
20 Tracy McGrady .60 1.50
21 Kevin Garnett 1.00 2.50
22 Tim Thomas .25 .60
23 Larry Hughes .30 .75
24 Jerry Stackhouse .40 1.00
25 Voshon Lenard .25 .60
26 Howard Eisley .25 .60
27 Clarence Weatherspoon .25 .60
28 Marcus Fizer .25 .60
29 Elden Campbell .25 .60
30 Tim Duncan 1.00 2.50
31 Doug Christie .25 .60
32 Keon Clark .25 .60
33 Patrick Ewing .60 1.50
34 Hakeem Olajuwon .75 2.00
35 Stephen Jackson .30 .75
36 Larry Johnson .40 1.00
37 Eric Snow .25 .60
38 Tom Gugliotta .25 .60
39 Scottie Pippen 1.00 2.50
40 Chris Webber .50 1.25
41 David Robinson .75 2.00
42 Elton Brand .30 .75
43 Theo Ratliff .30 .75
44 Paul Pierce .60 1.50
45 Jamal Mashburn .30 .75
46 Eric Williams .25 .60
47 DerMarr Johnson .25 .60
48 Andre Miller .25 .60
49 Dirk Nowitzki 1.00 2.50
50 Kobe Bryant 3.00 8.00
51 Keyon Dooling .25 .60
52 Brian Grant .25 .60
53 Ervin Johnson .25 .60
54 Anthony Peeler .25 .60
55 Dikembe Mutombo .60 1.50
56 Steve Smith .30 .75
57 Hedo Turkoglu .30 .75
58 Terry Porter .25 .60
59 Lorenzen Wright .25 .60
60 Jason Terry .40 1.00
61 Vitaly Potapenko .25 .60
62 Derrick Coleman .25 .60
63 Ron Artest .30 .75
64 Chris Gatling .25 .60
65 Chris Mihm .25 .60
66 Reggie Miller .75 2.00
67 Lamar Odom .30 .75
68 Ron Harper .30 .75
69 Baron Davis .40 1.00
70 Brad Miller .40 1.00
71 Shawn Bradley .25 .60
72 James Posey .25 .60
73 Ben Wallace .50 1.25
74 Marc Jackson .25 .60
75 Maurice Taylor .25 .60
76 Aaron McKie .25 .60
77 Grant Hill .60 1.50
78 Arvydas Sabonis .30 .75
79 Peja Stojakovic .30 .75
80 Jason Kidd .60 1.50
81 Vin Baker .30 .75
82 Morris Peterson .25 .60
83 Bryon Russell .25 .60
84 Michael Dickerson .25 .60
85 Christian Laettner .30 .75
86 Jerome Williams .25 .60
87 Desmond Mason .30 .75
88 Sean Elliott .30 .75
89 Marcus Camby .30 .75
90 Stephon Marbury .50 1.25
91 Joel Przybilla .25 .60
92 Alonzo Mourning .60 1.50
93 Brian Shaw .25 .60
94 Austin Croshere .25 .60
95 Mookie Blaylock .25 .60
96 Mateen Cleaves .25 .60
97 Nick Van Exel .40 1.00
98 Michael Finley .40 1.00
99 Jamal Crawford .40 1.00
100 Steve Francis .40 1.00
101 Tim Hardaway .50 1.25
102 Sam Cassell .30 .75
103 Shammond Williams .25 .60
104 DeShawn Stevenson .25 .60
105 Bryant Reeves .25 .60
106 Richard Hamilton .50 1.25
107 Antonio Davis .30 .75
108 Brent Barry .25 .60
109 Derek Anderson .25 .60
110 Kenny Anderson .30 .75
111 Brevin Knight .25 .60
112 Tyrone Nesby .25 .60
113 Erick Strickland .25 .60
114 Jacque Vaughn .25 .60
115 John Stockton .75 2.00
116 Alvin Williams .25 .60
117 Speedy Claxton .25 .60
118 Bo Outlaw .25 .60
119 Jahidi White .25 .60
120 Karl Malone .75 2.00
121 Charles Oakley .30 .75
122 Malik Rose .25 .60
123 Avery Johnson .30 .75
124 Toni Kukoc .50 1.25
125 Bryant Stith .25 .60
126 P.J. Brown .25 .60
127 Ron Mercer .25 .60
128 Lamond Murray .25 .60
129 Steve Nash .75 2.00
130 Raef LaFrentz .25 .60
131 Corliss Williamson .25 .60
132 Danny Fortson .25 .60
133 Chris Porter .25 .60
134 Shandon Anderson .25 .60
135 Jalen Rose .30 .75
136 Corey Maggette .30 .75
137 Horace Grant .30 .75
138 Eddie Jones .40 1.00
139 Chauncey Billups .50 1.25
140 Ray Allen .60 1.50
141 Terrell Brandon .30 .75
142 Keith Van Horn .30 .75
143 Allan Houston .40 1.00
144 Mark Jackson .30 .75
145 Pat Garrity .25 .60
146 Anfernee Hardaway 1.00 2.50
147 Iakovos Tsakalidis .25 .60
148 Damon Stoudamire .40 1.00
149 Bobby Jackson .25 .60
150 Antawn Jamison .30 .75
151 Kenny Thomas .25 .60
152 Jonathan Bender .25 .60
153 Jeff McInnis .25 .60
154 Robert Horry .40 1.00
155 Anthony Mason .40 1.00
156 Lindsey Hunter .25 .60
157 LaPhonso Ellis .30 .75
158 Jamie Feick .25 .60
159 Kurt Thomas .25 .60
160 Gary Payton .60 1.50
161 Rod Strickland .25 .60
162 Bonzi Wells .25 .60
163 Scot Pollard .25 .60
164 Raja Bell RC .50 1.25
165 Rodney Rogers .25 .60
166 John Amaechi .25 .60
167 Darrell Armstrong .25 .60
168 Aaron Williams .25 .60
169 Latrell Sprewell .50 1.25
170 Radoslav Nesterovic .25 .60
171 Anthony Carter .25 .60
172 Quentin Richardson .25 .60
173 Primoz Brezec RC .40 1.00
174 Michael Olowokandi .25 .60
175 Jason Williams .60 1.50
176 Ruben Patterson .25 .60
177 Chris Childs .25 .60
178 Greg Ostertag .25 .60
179 Mike Bibby .40 1.00
180 Mitch Richmond .50 1.25
181 Donyell Marshall .25 .60
182 Dale Davis .25 .60
183 Tony Delk .30 .75
184 Mike Miller .30 .75
185 Charlie Ward .25 .60
186 Kenyon Martin .40 1.00
187 Walt Williams .25 .60
188 Al Harrington .30 .75
189 Chucky Atkins .25 .60
190 Kevin Willis .25 .60
191 Juwan Howard .30 .75
192 Jim Jackson .25 .60
193 Antonio McDyess .30 .75
194 Jamaal Magloire .25 .60
195 Mark Blount .25 .60
196 Fred Hoiberg .25 .60
197 Nazr Mohammed .25 .60
198 Antoine Walker .30 .75
199 Wang Zhizhi .40 1.00
200 Shareef Abdur-Rahim .30 .75
201 Chris Whitney .25 .60
202 David Wesley .25 .60
203 Matt Harpring .25 .60
204 George McCloud .25 .60
205 Joe Smith .30 .75
206 Cuttino Mobley .30 .75
207 Tyrone Hill .25 .60
208 Clifford Robinson .40 1.00
209 Vlade Divac .30 .75
210 Eddie Robinson .25 .60
211 Michael Curry .25 .60
212 Courtney Alexander .25 .60
213 Grant Long .25 .60
214 Dan Majerle .40 1.00
215 Points Leaders 3.00 8.00
216 Rebounds Leaders 1.50 4.00
217 Assists Leaders .75 2.00
218 Steals Leaders 1.00 2.50
219 Blocks Leaders 1.50 4.00
220 Team Championship 2.00 5.00
221 Kwame Brown RC .60 1.50
222 Tyson Chandler RC 1.00 2.50
223 Pau Gasol RC 6.00 15.00
224 Eddy Curry RC .60 1.50
225 Jason Richardson RC 1.00 2.50
226 Shane Battier RC 1.25 3.00
227 Eddie Griffin RC .50 1.25
228 DeSagana Diop RC .40 1.00
229 Rodney White RC .40 1.00
230 Joe Johnson RC 1.00 2.50
231 Kedrick Brown RC .40 1.00
232 Vladimir Radmanovic RC .50 1.25
233 Richard Jefferson RC .75 2.00
234 Troy Murphy RC .50 1.25
235 Steven Hunter RC .40 1.00
236 Kirk Haston RC .40 1.00
237 Michael Bradley RC .40 1.00
238 Jason Collins RC .50 1.25
239 Zach Randolph RC 1.25 3.00
240 Brendan Haywood RC .50 1.25
241 Joseph Forte RC .40 1.00
242 Jeryl Sasser RC .40 1.00
243 Brandon Armstrong RC .40 1.00
244 Gerald Wallace RC .75 2.00
245 Samuel Dalembert RC .60 1.50
246 Jamaal Tinsley RC .50 1.25
247 Tony Parker RC 6.00 15.00
248 Trenton Hassell RC .40 1.00
249 Gilbert Arenas RC 1.50 4.00
250 Jeff Trepagnier RC .40 1.00
251 Damone Brown RC .40 1.00
252 Loren Woods RC .40 1.00
253 Ousmane Cisse RC .40 1.00
254 Ken Johnson RC .40 1.00
255 Kenny Satterfield RC .40 1.00
256 Alvin Jones RC .40 1.00
257 Pau Gasol Preseason 5.00 12.00
TRSC Shaq/Abdul-Jabbar JSY 75.00 200.00
NNO Gilbert Arenas SPEC AU 8.00 20.00

2001-02 Topps MVP Promotion

*MVP STARS: 12X TO 30X BASE CARD HI
*MVP RCs: 2X TO 5X BASE CARD HI
STATED ODDS 1:104 H, 1:80 R, 1:27 HTA
ANNOUNCED PRINT RUN 100 SETS
EXCHANGE DEADLINE 08/02/02
41 David Robinson 15.00 40.00
146 Anfernee Hardaway 15.00 40.00

2001-02 Topps All-Star Remnants

STATED ODDS 1:160 H, 1:123 R, 1:42 HTA
TRAH Allan Houston 4.00 10.00
TRAM Andre Miller 3.00 8.00
TRBD Baron Davis 4.00 10.00
TRCW Chris Webber 5.00 12.00
TRDM Darius Miles 2.50 6.00
TRDN Dirk Nowitzki 10.00 25.00
TREB Elton Brand 3.00 8.00
TRJS Jerry Stackhouse 4.00 10.00
TRJT Jason Terry 4.00 10.00
TRJW Jason Williams 6.00 15.00
TRLO Lamar Odom 3.00 8.00
TRMB Mike Bibby 4.00 10.00
TRQR Quentin Richardson 2.50 6.00
TRRA Ray Allen 6.00 15.00
TRRH Richard Hamilton 5.00 12.00
TRRL Raef LaFrentz 2.50 6.00
TRRW Rasheed Wallace 5.00 12.00
TRSF Steve Francis 4.00 10.00
TRSM Shawn Marion 4.00 10.00
TRSO Shaquille O'Neal 15.00 40.00
TRTD Tim Duncan 10.00 25.00

2001-02 Topps All-Star Remnants Autographs

GROUP A ODDS 1:5848 H, 1:1514 HTA
GROUP B ODDS 1:8506 H, 1:2297 HTA
GROUP C ODDS 1:17328 H, 1:4442 HTA
GROUP D ODDS 1:77976 H, 1:22208 HTA
TREB Elton Brand/42 B 20.00 50.00
TRJT Jason Terry/31 A 20.00 50.00
TRRH Richard Hamilton/32 A 20.00 50.00
TRRL Raef LaFrentz/45 B 10.00 25.00
TRSM Shawn Marion/32 A 50.00 100.00
TRSO Shaquille O'Neal/34 A 150.00 300.00
TRTD Tim Duncan/21 C 200.00 400.00

2001-02 Topps Autographs

GROUP A 1:2515 H, 1:1958 R, 1:660 HTA
GROUP B 1:1006 H, 1:766 R, 1:264 HTA
GROUP C 1:838 H, 1:647 R, 1:221 HTA
TAJB Jonathan Bender B 5.00 12.00
TAAJ Antawn Jamison C 5.00 12.00
TABD Baron Davis C 8.00 20.00
TADM Desmond Mason B 5.00 12.00
TAEB Elton Brand B 5.00 12.00
TAJT Jason Terry B 6.00 15.00
TAKAJ Kareem Abdul-Jabbar A 125.00 300.00
TALJ Larry Johnson A 30.00 80.00
TAMJ Magic Johnson A 75.00 200.00
TARH Richard Hamilton C 8.00 20.00
TASM Shawn Marion B 8.00 20.00
TASO Shaquille O'Neal A 125.00 300.00

2001-02 Topps Kareem Abdul-Jabbar Reprints

COMPLETE SET (13) 10.00 25.00
COMMON CARD (1-13) 1.25 3.00
STATED ODDS 1:14 H, 1:11 R, 1:4 HTA

2001-02 Topps Kareem Abdul-Jabbar Reprints Autographs

COMMON CARD (1-13) 50.00 120.00
STATED ODDS 1:9747
AU PROOF STATED ODDS 1:22208 HTA
1 Lew Alcindor 100.00 200.00

2001-02 Topps Lottery Legends

COMPLETE SET (13) 6.00 15.00
STATED ODDS 1:6 H, 1:5 R, 1:2 HTA
LL1 Shaquille O'Neal 2.00 5.00
LL2 Steve Francis .50 1.25
LL3 Darius Miles .30 .75
LL4 Stephon Marbury .60 1.50
LL5 Vince Carter 1.00 2.50
LL6 Antoine Walker .40 1.00
LL7 Jason Williams .75 2.00
LL8 Larry Hughes .40 1.00
LL9 Tracy McGrady .75 2.00
LL10 Paul Pierce .75 2.00
LL11 Allan Houston .50 1.25
LL12 Austin Croshere .30 .75
LL13 Kobe Bryant 4.00 10.00

2001-02 Topps Mad Game

COMPLETE SET (10) 10.00 25.00
STATED ODDS 1:38 H, 1:29 R, 1:10 HTA
MG1 Allen Iverson 2.00 5.00
MG2 Shaquille O'Neal 3.00 8.00
MG3 Tim Duncan 2.00 5.00
MG4 Vince Carter 1.50 4.00
MG5 Kevin Garnett 2.00 5.00
MG6 Kobe Bryant 6.00 15.00
MG7 Tracy McGrady 1.25 3.00
MG8 Steve Francis .75 2.00
MG9 Chris Webber 1.00 2.50
MG10 Darius Miles .50 1.25

2001-02 Topps NBA All-Star Jam Session

COMPLETE SET (9) 6.00 15.00
1 Shaquille O'Neal 3.00 8.00
2 Tim Duncan 2.00 5.00
3 Allen Iverson 2.00 5.00
4 Tracy McGrady 1.25 3.00
5 Steve Francis .75 2.00
6 Elton Brand .60 1.50
7 Jamaal Tinsley .60 1.50
8 Jamaal Tinsley .60 1.50
9 Chris Webber 1.00 2.50

2001-02 Topps Team Topps

COMPLETE SET (9) 4.00 10.00
STATED ODDS 1:8 H, 1:7 R, 1:2 HTA
TT1 Shaquille O'Neal 2.00 5.00
TT2 Tim Duncan 1.25 3.00
TT3 Antawn Jamison .40 1.00
TT4 Jason Terry .50 1.25
TT5 Baron Davis .50 1.25
TT6 Elton Brand .40 1.00
TT7 Peja Stojakovic .40 1.00
TT8 Richard Hamilton .60 1.50
TT9 Shawn Marion .50 1.25
TT10 Team Shot .75 2.00

2002-03 Topps Promos

COMPLETE SET (6) 3.00 8.00
PP1 Tim Duncan 1.25 3.00
PP2 Steve Francis .75 2.00
PP3 Ray Allen .75 2.00
PP4 Steve Nash 1.00 2.50
PP5 Kenyon Martin .75 2.00
PP6 Andre Miller .75 2.00

2002-03 Topps

COMPLETE SET (220) 25.00 60.00
1 Shaquille O'Neal .75 2.00
2 Pau Gasol .30 .75
3 Allen Iverson .50 1.25
4 Tom Gugliotta .12 .30
5 Rasheed Wallace .25 .60
6 Peja Stojakovic .15 .40
7 Jason Richardson .20 .50
8 Rashard Lewis .15 .40
9 Morris Peterson .15 .40
10 Michael Jordan 2.00 5.00
11 Matt Harpring .12 .30
12 Shareef Abdur-Rahim .20 .50
13 Antoine Walker .15 .40
14 Stephon Marbury .25 .60
15 Jamal Mashburn .15 .40
16 Eddy Curry .12 .30
17 Jumaine Jones .12 .30
18 Wang Zhizhi .12 .30
19 James Posey .12 .30
20 Jason Kidd .30 .75
21 Jerry Stackhouse .20 .50
22 Kenny Thomas .12 .30
23 Ron Mercer .12 .30
24 Jeff McInnis .12 .30
25 Kobe Bryant 1.50 4.00
26 Jason Williams .25 .60
27 Eddie Jones .20 .50
28 Anthony Mason .15 .40
29 Kenyon Martin .20 .50
30 Kevin Garnett .50 1.25
31 Kurt Thomas .12 .30
32 Karl Malone .40 1.00
33 Patrick Ewing .25 .60

34 Antonio McDyess .15 .40
35 Dirk Nowitzki .50 1.25
36 Wesley Person .12 .30
37 Theo Ratliff .12 .30
38 Jarron Collins .12 .30
39 Horace Grant .15 .40
40 Vince Carter .40 1.00
41 Desmond Mason .15 .40
42 Todd MacCulloch .12 .30
43 Bobby Jackson .12 .30
44 Vlade Divac .15 .40
45 Keith Van Horn .15 .40
46 Bo Outlaw .12 .30
47 Eric Snow .12 .30
48 Grant Hill .30 .75
49 Terrell Brandon .12 .30
50 Tracy McGrady .30 .75
51 Tim Thomas .12 .30
52 Loren Woods .12 .30
53 Michael Redd .15 .40
54 Stromile Swift .12 .30
55 Dikembe Mutombo .30 .75
56 Richard Jefferson .15 .40
57 Glenn Robinson .20 .50
58 Samaki Walker .12 .30
59 Quentin Richardson .12 .30
60 Elton Brand .15 .40
61 Reggie Miller .40 1.00
62 Eddie Griffin .12 .30
63 Gilbert Arenas .20 .50
64 Zeljko Rebraca .12 .30
65 Donnell Harvey .12 .30
66 Juwan Howard .15 .40
67 Nick Van Exel .20 .50
68 Donyell Marshall .12 .30
69 Tyson Chandler .20 .50
70 Baron Davis .20 .50
71 Nazr Mohammed .12 .30
72 Marcus Camby .15 .40
73 Jamaal Magloire .12 .30
74 Marcus Fizer .12 .30
75 Steve Francis .20 .50
76 Aaron Mckie .12 .30
77 Anfernee Hardaway .50 1.25
78 Scottie Pippen .50 1.25
79 Mike Bibby .20 .50
80 Paul Pierce .30 .75
81 Tony Delk .12 .30
82 Kwame Brown .12 .30
83 Andrei Kirilenko .15 .40
84 Keon Clark .12 .30
85 Alvin Williams .12 .30
86 Brent Barry .12 .30
87 David Robinson .40 1.00
88 Doug Christie .12 .30
89 Derek Anderson .12 .30
90 Chris Webber .25 .60
91 Speedy Claxton .12 .30
92 Robert Horry .20 .50
93 Allan Houston .20 .50
94 Kerry Kittles .12 .30
95 Wally Szczerbiak .15 .40
96 Jonathan Bender .12 .30
97 Sam Cassell .15 .40
98 Rod Strickland .12 .30
99 Shane Battier .20 .50
100 Tim Duncan .50 1.25
101 Jermaine O'Neal .15 .40
102 Cuttino Mobley .12 .30
103 Danny Fortson .12 .30
104 Clifford Robinson .20 .50
105 Tim Hardaway .20 .50
106 Steve Nash .40 1.00
107 Zydrunas Ilgauskas .15 .40
108 Travis Best .12 .30
109 Eddie Robinson .12 .30
110 David Wesley .12 .30
111 Kenny Anderson .15 .40
112 DerMarr Johnson .12 .30
113 Courtney Alexander .12 .30
114 Brian Grant .12 .30
115 Lorenzen Wright .12 .30
116 Corliss Williamson .12 .30
117 Malik Rose .12 .30
118 Tony Parker .30 .75
119 Vladimir Radmanovic .12 .30
120 Hedo Turkoglu .15 .40
121 Damon Stoudamire .20 .50
122 Brendan Haywood .12 .30
123 Jalen Rose .15 .40
124 Mike Miller .15 .40
125 Derrick Coleman .15 .40
126 Mark Jackson .12 .30
127 Raef Lafrentz .12 .30
128 Ben Wallace .25 .60
129 Larry Hughes .15 .40
130 Ray Allen .30 .75
131 Gary Payton .30 .75
132 P.J. Brown .12 .30
133 Derek Fisher .20 .50
134 Michael Olowokandi .12 .30
135 Jamaal Tinsley .12 .30
136 Moochie Norris .12 .30
137 Chris Mihm .12 .30
138 Antawn Jamison .15 .40
139 Chucky Atkins .12 .30
140 Mengke Bateer .20 .50
141 Brad Miller .15 .40
142 Michael Finley .20 .50
143 Andre Miller .15 .40
144 Michael Dickerson .12 .30
145 Elden Campbell .12 .30
146 Kedrick Brown .12 .30
147 Jason Terry .15 .40
148 Chris Whitney .12 .30
149 Bryon Russell .12 .30
150 Darius Miles .12 .30
151 Latrell Sprewell .20 .50
152 Darrell Armstrong .12 .30
153 Joe Johnson .15 .40
154 Bonzi Wells .12 .30
155 Jim Jackson .12 .30
156 Steve Smith .15 .40
157 Vin Baker .15 .40
158 Antonio Davis .15 .40
159 John Stockton .40 1.00
160 Shawn Marion .20 .50
161 Devean George .12 .30
162 Clarence Weatherspoon .12 .30
163 Rick Fox .12 .30
164 Chauncey Billups .20 .50
165 Joe Smith .15 .40
166 Laphonso Ellis .15 .40
167 Maurice Taylor .12 .30
168 Lamond Murray .12 .30
169 Lamar Odom .20 .50
170 Toni Kukoc .20 .50
171 Alonzo Mourning .30 .75
172 Antonio Daniels .12 .30
173 Troy Murphy .15 .40
174 Hakeem Olajuwon .25 .60
175 Richard Hamilton .25 .60
176 Rodney Rogers .12 .30
177 Ruben Patterson .12 .30
178 Dale Davis .12 .30
179 League Leaders .50 1.25
180 League Leaders .20 .50
181 League Leaders .20 .50
182 League Leaders .20 .50
183 League Leaders .20 .50
184 Team Championship Card .60 1.50
185 Yao Ming RC 4.00 10.00
186 Jay Williams RC .60 1.50
187 Mike Dunleavy RC .75 2.00
188 Drew Gooden RC .75 2.00
189 Nikoloz Tskitishvili RC .50 1.25
190 DaJuan Wagner RC .60 1.50
191 Nene Hilario RC .75 2.00
192 Chris Wilcox RC .60 1.50
193 Amare Stoudemire RC 2.00 5.00
194 Caron Butler RC .75 2.00
195 Jared Jeffries RC .60 1.50
196 Melvin Ely RC .60 1.50
197 Marcus Haislip RC .50 1.25
198 Fred Jones RC .60 1.50
199 Bostjan Nachbar RC .60 1.50
200 Jiri Welsch RC .60 1.50
201 Juan Dixon RC .60 1.50
202 Curtis Borchardt RC .50 1.25
203 Ryan Humphrey RC .60 1.50
204 Kareem Rush RC .60 1.50
205 Qyntel Woods RC .50 1.25
206 Casey Jacobsen RC .60 1.50
207 Tayshaun Prince RC 1.50 4.00
208 Frank Williams RC .50 1.25
209 John Salmons RC .75 2.00
210 Chris Jefferies ERR RC .50 1.25
211 Sam Clancy RC .60 1.50
212 Dan Gadzuric RC .60 1.50
213 Matt Barnes RC 1.00 2.50
214 Robert Archibald RC .50 1.25
215 Vincent Yarbrough RC .50 1.25
216 Dan Dickau RC .60 1.50
217 Carlos Boozer RC .75 2.00
218 Tito Maddox RC .50 1.25
219 Chris Owens RC .50 1.25
220 Ronald Murray RC .75 2.00

2002-03 Topps Black

*BLACK STARS: 5X TO 12X BASE CARD HI
*BLACK RCs: 1.5X TO 4X BASE CARD HI
BLACK PRINT RUN 500 SER.#'d SETS

2002-03 Topps All-Star Relic Remnants

STAT.ODDS 1:149 H 1:540 R, 1:40 HTA
TRAI Allen Iverson 10.00 25.00
TRAW Antoine Walker 3.00 8.00
TRCW Chris Webber 5.00 12.00
TREB Elton Brand 3.00 8.00
TRJK Jason Kidd 6.00 15.00
TRJO Jermaine O'Neal 3.00 8.00
TRPS Peja Stojakovic 3.00 8.00
TRRA Ray Allen 6.00 15.00
TRSF Steve Francis 4.00 10.00
TRSN Steve Nash 8.00 20.00
TRTD Tim Duncan 10.00 25.00
TRAEB Elton Brand AU 25.00 60.00
TRATD Tim Duncan AU/25 300.00 600.00

2002-03 Topps Around The World

COMPLETE SET (24) 12.00 30.00
GAME CARDS IN TOPPS PACKS
AW1 Tim Duncan 1.50 4.00
AW2 Dirk Nowitzki 1.50 4.00
AW3 Pau Gasol 1.00 2.50
AW4 Steve Nash 1.25 3.00
AW5 Peja Stojakovic .50 1.25
AW6 Tony Parker 1.00 2.50
AW7 Hedo Turkoglu .50 1.25
AW8 Andrei Kirilenko .50 1.25
AW9 Dikembe Mutombo 1.00 2.50
AW10 Wang ZhiZhi .60 1.50
AW11 Michael Olowokandi .40 1.00
AW12 Vladimir Radmanovic .40 1.00
AW13 Nikoloz Tskitishvili .40 1.00
AW14 Shaquille O'Neal 2.50 6.00
AW15 Tracy McGrady 1.00 2.50
AW16 Nene Hilario .60 1.50
AW17 Kevin Garnett 1.50 4.00
AW18 Yao Ming 3.00 8.00
AW19 DaJuan Wagner .50 1.25
AW20 Mike Dunleavy .60 1.50
AW21 Caron Butler .60 1.50
AW22 Qyntel Woods .40 1.00
AW23 Drew Gooden .60 1.50
AW24 Chris Wilcox .50 1.25

2002-03 Topps Autographs

STATED ODDS 1:303 H, 1:80 HTA
TAAH Al Harrington 4.00 10.00
TACA Courtney Alexander 4.00 10.00
TACB Chauncey Billups 6.00 15.00
TACM Corey Maggette 4.00 10.00
TADH Donnell Harvey 4.00 10.00
TAEB Erick Barkley 4.00 10.00
TAKA Kareem Abdul-Jabbar 125.00 300.00
TAMD Michael Doleac 4.00 10.00
TAMJ Marc Jackson 4.00 10.00
TARM Roshown McLeod 4.00 10.00
TASO Shaquille O'Neal 30.00 80.00

2002-03 Topps Coast to Coast

COMPLETE SET (20) 12.00 30.00
STAT.ODDS 1:13 H, 1:10 R, 1:2 HTA
CC1 Tracy McGrady 1.00 2.50
CC2 Jason Kidd 1.00 2.50
CC3 Mike Bibby .60 1.50
CC4 Baron Davis .60 1.50
CC5 Steve Francis .60 1.50
CC6 Vince Carter 1.25 3.00
CC7 Kobe Bryant 5.00 12.00
CC8 Michael Jordan 6.00 15.00
CC9 Paul Pierce 1.00 2.50
CC10 Stephon Marbury .75 2.00
CC11 Ray Allen 1.00 2.50
CC12 Gary Payton 1.00 2.50
CC13 Shawn Marion .60 1.50
CC14 Steve Nash 1.25 3.00
CC15 Andre Miller .50 1.25
CC16 Jerry Stackhouse .60 1.50
CC17 Latrell Sprewell .60 1.50
CC18 Jason Richardson .60 1.50
CC19 Jamaal Tinsley .40 1.00
CC20 Tony Parker 1.00 2.50

2002-03 Topps Rookie Autographs

ANNOUNCED PRINT RUN 50 SETS
1 Drew Gooden 25.00 60.00
2 Nikoloz Tskitishvili 6.00 15.00
3 Marcus Haislip 6.00 15.00
4 Melvin Ely 8.00 20.00
5 Tayshaun Prince 25.00 60.00
6 Sam Clancy 8.00 20.00
7 Dan Gadzuric 8.00 20.00
8 Ryan Humphrey 8.00 20.00
9 Jared Jeffries 8.00 20.00
10 Fred Jones 20.00 50.00
11 Kareem Rush 20.00 50.00
12 John Salmons 25.00 60.00
13 Amare Stoudemire 125.00 250.00
14 Vincent Yarbrough 6.00 15.00
15 Ronald Murray 10.00 25.00

2002-03 Topps Shaq Attack Relics

COMPLETE SET (5) 50.00 100.00
COMMON CARD (SA1-SA5) 12.00 30.00
STAT.ODDS 1:319 H, 1:451 R, 1:90 HTA

2002-03 Topps Shaq Attack Relics Autographs

SAA1 Shaquille O'Neal/72 75.00 200.00
SAA2 Shaquille O'Neal/33 150.00 300.00
SAA3 Shaquille O'Neal/92 75.00 200.00
SAA4 Shaquille O'Neal/32 150.00 300.00
SAA5 Shaquille O'Neal/34 150.00 300.00

2002-03 Topps Slam Duncan Relics

COMPLETE SET (5) 30.00 60.00
COMMON CARD (SD1-SD5) 8.00 20.00
STAT.ODDS 1:319 H, 1:451 R, 1:90 HTA

2002-03 Topps Slam Duncan Relics Autographs

SDA1 Tim Duncan/76 150.00 300.00
SDA2 Tim Duncan/97 100.00 200.00
SDA3 Tim Duncan/21 200.00 400.00
SDA4 Tim Duncan/21 200.00 400.00
SDA5 Tim Duncan/21 200.00 400.00

2002-03 Topps Top Tandems

COMPLETE SET (10) 6.00 15.00
STAT.ODDS 1:5 H, 1:10 R, 1:2 HTA
TT1 A.Walker/P.Pierce 1.00 2.50
TT2 S.O'Neal/K.Bryant 5.00 12.00
TT3 D.Coleman/A.Iverson 1.50 4.00
TT4 S.Marion/S.Marbury .75 2.00
TT5 D.Nowitzki/M.Finley 1.50 4.00
TT6 M.Jordan/R.Hamilton 6.00 15.00
TT7 C.Webber/P.Stojakovic .75 2.00
TT8 V.Carter/M.Peterson 1.25 3.00
TT9 R.Allen/G.Robinson 1.00 2.50
TT10 S.Francis/C.Mobley .60 1.50

2002-03 Topps Verticality

COMPLETE SET (15) 25.00 60.00
STAT.ODDS 1:10 H, 1:8 R, 1:3 HTA
V1 Shawn Marion .75 2.00
V2 Darius Miles .50 1.25
V3 Vince Carter 6.00 15.00
V4 Tracy McGrady 1.25 3.00
V5 Kobe Bryant 12.00 30.00
V6 Jason Richardson .75 2.00
V7 Steve Francis .75 2.00
V8 Michael Jordan 12.00 30.00
V9 Jerry Stackhouse .75 2.00
V10 Baron Davis .75 2.00
V11 Pau Gasol 1.25 3.00
V12 Kevin Garnett 2.00 5.00
V13 Kenyon Martin .75 2.00
V14 Shaquille O'Neal 3.00 8.00
V15 Jermaine O'Neal .60 1.50

2003-04 Topps Promos

COMPLETE SET (6) 5.00 12.00
PP1 Shaquille O'Neal 2.50 6.00
PP2 Tracy McGrady 1.00 2.50
PP3 Chris Webber .75 2.00
PP4 Kevin Garnett 1.50 4.00
PP5 Tim Duncan 1.50 4.00
PP6 Steve Nash 1.25 3.00

2003-04 Topps

COMPLETE SET (249) 300.00 600.00
1 Tracy McGrady .60 1.50
2 DaJuan Wagner .25 .60
3 Allen Iverson 1.00 2.50
4 Chris Webber .50 1.25
5 Jason Kidd .60 1.50
6 Stephon Marbury .50 1.25
7 Jermaine O'Neal .40 1.00
8 Antoine Walker .40 1.00
9 Tony Parker .60 1.50
10 Mike Bibby .40 1.00
11 Yao Ming 1.00 2.50
12 Walter McCarty 2.50 6.00
13 Steve Nash .75 2.00
14 Paul Pierce .60 1.50
15 Vince Carter .75 2.00
16 Peja Stojakovic .30 .75
17 Kenny Anderson .30 .75
18 Kenyon Martin .40 1.00
19 Pau Gasol .60 1.50
20 Gary Payton .60 1.50
21 Tim Duncan 1.00 2.50
22 Jay Williams .25 .60
23 Jason Richardson .40 1.00
24 Andre Miller .30 .75
25 Latrell Sprewell .50 1.25
26 Darius Miles .25 .60
27 Richard Jefferson .30 .75
28 Shawn Marion .40 1.00
29 Baron Davis .40 1.00
30 Ben Wallace .50 1.25
31 Reggie Miller .75 2.00
32 Karl Malone .75 2.00
33 Grant Hill .50 1.25
34 Shaquille O'Neal 1.50 4.00
35 Steve Francis .40 1.00
36 Kobe Bryant 3.00 8.00
37 Mike Dunleavy .30 .75
38 Glenn Robinson .30 .75
39 Allan Houston .40 1.00
40 Kevin Ollie .25 .60
41 Dirk Nowitzki 1.00 2.50
42 Elton Brand .30 .75
43 Juan Dixon .25 .60
44 Brian Grant .25 .60
45 Jason Terry .30 .75
46 Richard Hamilton .50 1.25
47 Morris Peterson .25 .60
48 Ray Allen .60 1.50
49 Scottie Pippen 1.00 2.50
50 David Robinson .75 2.00
51 Cuttino Mobley .25 .60
52 Jerry Stackhouse .50 1.25
53 Marcus Camby .30 .75
54 Jalen Rose .30 .75
55 Dikembe Mutombo .50 1.25
56 P.J. Brown .25 .60
57 Jumaine Jones .25 .60
58 Shawn Bradley .25 .60
59 Juwan Howard .30 .75
60 Clifford Robinson .25 .60
61 Antawn Jamison .40 1.00
62 Raef LaFrentz .25 .60
63 Kareem Rush .25 .60
64 LaPhonso Ellis .25 .60
65 Toni Kukoc .40 1.00
66 Mike Miller .30 .75
67 Aaron McKie .25 .60
68 Tom Gugliotta .25 .60
69 Dale Davis .25 .60
70 Jared Jeffries .25 .60
71 Alvin Williams .25 .60
72 DeShawn Stevenson .25 .60
73 Doug Christie .30 .75
74 Troy Hudson .25 .60
75 Jason Collins .25 .60
76 Eddie Griffin .25 .60
77 Vladimir Radmanovic .25 .60
78 Michael Olowokandi .25 .60
79 Michael Redd .40 1.00
80 Tim Thomas .30 .75
81 Ron Mercer .25 .60
82 Shareef Abdur-Rahim .40 1.00
83 Eduardo Najera .25 .60
84 Jon Barry .25 .60
85 Erick Dampier .25 .60
86 Derek Fisher .40 1.00
87 Drew Gooden .30 .75
88 Dan Gadzuric .25 .60
89 Antonio McDyess .30 .75
90 Derrick Coleman .40 1.00
91 Carlos Boozer .25 .60
92 Rasheed Wallace .50 1.25
93 Antonio Davis .25 .60
94 Kwame Brown .30 .75
95 Manu Ginobili .75 2.00
96 Eric Williams .25 .60
97 Trenton Hassell .25 .60
98 Chris Whitney .25 .60
99 Chauncey Billups .50 1.25
100 Kevin Garnett 1.00 2.50
101 Marko Jaric .25 .60
102 Rasual Butler .25 .60
103 Gilbert Arenas .40 1.00
104 Keith Van Horn .30 .75
105 Iakovos Tsakalidis .25 .60
106 Ruben Patterson .25 .60
107 Jarron Collins .25 .60
108 Rodney White .25 .60
109 Rashard Lewis .30 .75
110 Malik Rose .25 .60
111 Bobby Jackson .30 .75
112 Brendan Haywood .25 .60
113 Charlie Ward .25 .60
114 Courtney Alexander .25 .60
115 Kerry Kittles .30 .75
116 Wally Szczerbiak .30 .75
117 Darrell Armstrong .25 .60
118 Anfernee Hardaway 1.00 2.50
119 Qyntel Woods .25 .60
120 Quentin Richardson .25 .60
121 Jonathan Bender .25 .60
122 Robert Horry .40 1.00
123 Lorenzen Wright .25 .60
124 Malik Allen .25 .60
125 Sam Cassell .30 .75
126 Joe Smith .30 .75
127 Dion Glover .25 .60
128 Jamal Crawford .40 1.00
129 Ricky Davis .30 .75
130 Nikoloz Tskitishvili .25 .60
131 Tyronn Lue .25 .60
132 Scott Padgett .25 .60
133 Jerome James .25 .60
134 Hedo Turkoglu .30 .75
135 Jamal Mashburn .30 .75
136 Pat Burke .25 .60
137 Joe Johnson .25 .60
138 Anthony Peeler .25 .60
139 Ron Artest .40 1.00
140 Theo Ratliff .25 .60
141 Caron Butler .25 .60
142 Anthony Mason .25 .60
143 Vin Baker .25 .60
144 Donyell Marshall .25 .60
145 Nene .25 .60
146 Chucky Atkins .25 .60
147 Tyson Chandler .30 .75
148 Jason Williams .60 1.50
149 Larry Hughes .30 .75
150 Stephen Jackson .30 .75
151 Kurt Thomas .25 .60
152 Mehmet Okur .30 .75
153 Amare Stoudemire .50 1.25
154 Elden Campbell .25 .60
155 Jamaal Tinsley .25 .60
156 Chris Wilcox .25 .60
157 Rick Fox .30 .75
158 Gordan Giricek .25 .60
159 Voshon Lenard .25 .60
160 Brent Barry .25 .60
161 Dan Dickau .25 .60
162 Junior Harrington .25 .60
163 Jiri Welsch .25 .60
164 Vladimir Stepania .25 .60
165 Brad Miller .30 .75
166 Moochie Norris .25 .60
167 Wesley Person .25 .60
168 Greg Buckner .25 .60
169 Bonzi Wells .25 .60
170 Predrag Drobnjak .25 .60
171 Andrei Kirilenko .30 .75
172 Vlade Divac .40 1.00
173 Rodney Rogers .25 .60
174 Kendall Gill .40 1.00
175 Kenny Thomas .25 .60
176 Derek Anderson .30 .75
177 Steve Smith .30 .75
178 Christian Laettner .30 .75
179 Tony Delk .25 .60
180 Zydrunas Ilgauskas .30 .75
181 James Posey .25 .60
182 Tayshaun Prince .40 1.00
183 Devean George .25 .60
184 Eddie Jones .40 1.00
185 Corey Maggette .25 .60
186 Ira Newble .25 .60
187 Shane Battier .30 .75
188 Clarence Weatherspoon .25 .60
189 Eric Snow .25 .60
190 Damon Stoudamire .30 .75
191 Keon Clark .25 .60
192 Desmond Mason .30 .75
193 Matt Harpring .25 .60
194 Radoslav Nesterovic .25 .60
195 Jamaal Magloire .25 .60
196 Pat Garrity .25 .60
197 Fred Jones .25 .60
198 Tony Battie .25 .60
199 Tyrone Hill .25 .60
200 Adrian Griffin .25 .60
201 Nick Van Exel .40 1.00
202 Shammond Williams .25 .60
203 Corliss Williamson .25 .60
204 Lamar Odom .30 .75
205 Travis Best .25 .60
206 Howard Eisley .25 .60
207 Jerome Williams .25 .60
208 David Wesley .25 .60
209 Bostjan Nachbar .25 .60
210 Marcus Fizer .25 .60
211 Michael Finley .40 1.00
212 Troy Murphy .25 .60
213 Adonal Foyle .25 .60
214 Samaki Walker .25 .60
215 Lucious Harris .25 .60
216 Lindsey Hunter .25 .60
217 Stromile Swift .25 .60
218 Eddy Curry .25 .60
219 Kelvin Cato .25 .60
220 Chris Andersen .50 1.25
221 LeBron James RC 200.00 500.00
222 Darko Milicic RC .75 2.00
223 Carmelo Anthony RC 5.00 12.00
224 Chris Bosh RC 3.00 8.00
225 Dwyane Wade RC 8.00 20.00
226 Chris Kaman RC 1.00 2.50
227 Kirk Hinrich RC 1.00 2.50
228 T.J. Ford RC .75 2.00
229 Mike Sweetney RC .60 1.50
230 Jarvis Hayes RC .60 1.50
231 Mickael Pietrus RC .75 2.00
232 Nick Collison RC .75 2.00
233 Marcus Banks RC .60 1.50
234 Luke Ridnour RC 1.00 2.50
235 Reece Gaines RC .60 1.50
236 Troy Bell RC .60 1.50
237 Zarko Cabarkapa RC .60 1.50
238 David West RC 1.25 3.00
239 Aleksandar Pavlovic RC .75 2.00
240 Dahntay Jones RC .75 2.00
241 Boris Diaw RC 1.00 2.50
242 Zoran Planinic RC .60 1.50
243 Travis Outlaw RC .60 1.50
244 Brian Cook RC .60 1.50
245 Carlos Delfino RC .75 2.00
246 Ndudi Ebi RC .60 1.50
247 Kendrick Perkins RC .75 2.00
248 Leandro Barbosa RC 1.00 2.50
249 Josh Howard RC 1.00 2.50

2003-04 Topps Black

1-220 SINGLES: 4X TO 10X BASE CARD HI
221-249 RCs: 1.25X TO 3X BASE CARD HI
STATED PRINT RUN 500 SER.#'d SETS
STATED ODDS 1:29 H, 1:26 R, 1:9 HTA
221 LeBron James 3,000.00 6,000.00
224 Chris Bosh 40.00 100.00
225 Dwyane Wade 800.00 1,500.00

2003-04 Topps First Edition

1ST ED.SINGLES: .75X TO 2X BASE HI
1ST ED.RCs: 1X TO 2.5X BASE HI
BOXES DISTRIBUTED TO HTA DEALERS
221 LeBron James 800.00 1,500.00
224 Chris Bosh 25.00 60.00

2003-04 Topps Gold

*1-220 SINGLES: 4X TO 10X BASE CARD HI
*221-249 RCs: 1.25X TO 3X BASE CARD HI
STATED PRINT RUN 99 SER.#'d SETS
STATED ODDS 1:91 H, 1:25 HTA
221 LeBron James 15,000.00 30,000.00
224 Chris Bosh 200.00 500.00
225 Dwyane Wade 3,000.00 6,000.00

2003-04 Topps Highlight Zone

COMPLETE SET (20) 12.50 30.00
STATED ODDS 1:16 H, 1:18R, 1:6 HTA
HZ1 Paul Pierce 1.25 3.00
HZ2 Shaquille O'Neal 3.00 8.00
HZ3 Chris Webber 1.00 2.50
HZ4 Steve Francis .75 2.00
HZ5 Shawn Marion .75 2.00
HZ6 Elton Brand .60 1.50
HZ7 Peja Stojakovic .60 1.50
HZ8 Vince Carter 1.50 4.00
HZ9 Stephon Marbury 1.00 2.50
HZ10 Jerry Stackhouse 1.00 2.50
HZ11 Ray Allen 1.25 3.00
HZ12 Baron Davis .75 2.00
HZ13 Antoine Walker .75 2.00
HZ14 Jason Kidd 1.25 3.00
HZ15 Antawn Jamison .75 2.00
HZ16 Steve Nash 1.50 4.00
HZ17 Jason Richardson .75 2.00
HZ18 Ricky Davis .60 1.50
HZ19 Latrell Sprewell 1.00 2.50
HZ20 Kobe Bryant 6.00 15.00

2003-04 Topps Justice of the Court

COMPLETE SET (20) 8.00 20.00
STATED ODDS 1:8 H, 1:9 R, 1:3 HTA
JC1 Ben Wallace .60 1.50
JC2 Gary Payton .75 2.00
JC3 Shaquille O'Neal 2.00 5.00
JC4 Tim Duncan 1.25 3.00
JC5 Chris Webber .60 1.50
JC6 Dirk Nowitzki 1.25 3.00
JC7 Kevin Garnett 1.25 3.00
JC8 Shawn Marion .50 1.25
JC9 Karl Malone 1.00 2.50
JC10 Nene .40 1.00
JC11 Yao Ming 1.25 3.00
JC12 Kobe Bryant 4.00 10.00
JC13 Vince Carter 1.00 2.50
JC14 Elton Brand .40 1.00
JC15 Kenyon Martin .50 1.25
JC16 Amare Stoudemire .60 1.50
JC17 Pau Gasol .75 2.00
JC18 Derrick Coleman .50 1.25
JC19 Ron Artest .50 1.25
JC20 Rasheed Wallace .60 1.50

2003-04 Topps Love it Live

COMPLETE SET (20) 10.00 25.00
STATED ODDS 1:8 H, 1:9 R, 1:3 HTA
LLAI Allen Iverson 1.25 3.00
LLAS Amare Stoudemire .60 1.50
LLBD Baron Davis .50 1.25
LLCB Caron Butler .40 1.00
LLCW Chris Webber .60 1.50
LLDG Drew Gooden .40 1.00
LLDN Dirk Nowitzki 1.25 3.00
LLDW DaJuan Wagner .30 .75
LLGP Gary Payton .75 2.00
LLJO Jermaine O'Neal .50 1.25
LLJS Jerry Stackhouse .60 1.50
LLKB Kobe Bryant 4.00 10.00
LLKG Kevin Garnett 1.25 3.00
LLPP Paul Pierce .75 2.00
LLSF Steve Francis .50 1.25
LLSO Shaquille O'Neal 2.00 5.00
LLTD Tim Duncan 1.25 3.00
LLTM Tracy McGrady .75 2.00
LLVC Vince Carter 1.00 2.50
LLYM Yao Ming 1.25 3.00

2003-04 Topps Love it Live Relics

GROUP A 1:48614 H, 1:51840 R, 1:14090 HTA
GROUP B 1:2431 H, 1:2142 R, 1:733 HTA
GROUP C 1:10568 H, 1:9425 R, 1:3212 HTA
GROUP D 1:812 H, 1:711 R, 1:244 HTA
GROUP E 1:5675 H, 1:5040 R, 1:1712 HTS
AI Allen Iverson B 10.00 25.00
AS Amare Stoudemire D 5.00 12.00
CB Caron Butler B 3.00 8.00
DG Drew Gooden B 3.00 8.00
DN Dirk Nowitzki E 10.00 25.00
DW DaJuan Wagner B 2.50 6.00
GP Gary Payton D 6.00 15.00
JO Jermaine O'Neal D 4.00 10.00
PP Paul Pierce D 6.00 15.00
SF Steve Francis C 4.00 10.00
SO Shaquille O'Neal B 15.00 40.00
TD Tim Duncan D 10.00 25.00
YM Yao Ming D 10.00 25.00

2003-04 Topps Mark of Excellence Autographs

GROUP A 1:12256 H, 1:10961 R, 1:3663 HTA
GROUP B 1:4051 H, 1:3583 R, 1:221 HTA
GROUP C 1:1306 H, 1:1144 R, 1:391 HTA
GROUP D 1:1217 H, 1:1069 R, 1:366 HTA
GROUP E 1:522 H, 1:457 R, 1:157 HTA
BB Brent Barry E 2.50 6.00
CA Carmelo Anthony B 30.00 80.00
EB Elton Brand D 3.00 8.00
FW Frank Williams E 2.50 6.00
JH Jarvis Hayes C 2.50 6.00
JO Jermaine O'Neal 4.00 10.00
JW Jerome Williams B 2.50 6.00
KH Kirk Hinrich D 4.00 10.00
KJ Ken Johnson E 2.50 6.00
LR Luke Ridnour C 4.00 10.00
MB Marcus Banks C 2.50 6.00
MP Morris Peterson E 2.50 6.00
MR Michael Redd B 4.00 10.00
MS Mike Sweetney C 2.50 6.00
NC Nick Collison D 3.00 8.00
RG Reece Gaines A 2.50 6.00
RR Rick Rickert C 2.50 6.00
SO Shaquille O'Neal E 30.00 80.00
TF T.J. Ford D 3.00 8.00
CBO Chris Bosh A 10.00 25.00
DGE Devean George E 2.50 6.00
DWE David West C 5.00 12.00
DWY Dwyane Wade C 25.00 60.00

2003-04 Topps Piece of a Dream Relics

GROUP A 1:37396 H, 1:34560 R, 1:10775 HTA
GROUP B 1:27518 H, 1:25920 R, 1:8326 HTA
GROUP C 1:14882 H, 1:12960 R, 1:4361 HTA
GROUP D 1:1140 H, 1:1002 R, 1:343 HTA
GROUP E 1:1620 H, 1:1422 R, 1:487 HTA
PDBD Baron Davis C 4.00 10.00
PDCW Chris Webber D 5.00 12.00
PDEB Elton Brand A 3.00 8.00
PDGH Grant Hill C 5.00 12.00
PDJK Jason Kidd A 6.00 15.00
PDJR Jason Richardson C 4.00 10.00
PDLS Latrell Sprewell B 5.00 12.00
PDMD Mike Dunleavy C 3.00 8.00
PDMP Morris Peterson C 2.50 6.00
PDMR Michael Redd C 4.00 10.00
PDNT Nikoloz Tskitishvili C 2.50 6.00
PDSB Shawn Bradley D 2.50 6.00
PDSM Stephon Marbury D 5.00 12.00
PDSN Steve Nash C 8.00 20.00

2003-04 Topps Rookie Photo Shoot Autographs

STATED PRINT RUN 56 SETS
TABC Brian Cook 10.00 25.00
TACA Carmelo Anthony 175.00 350.00
TACB Chris Bosh 150.00 300.00
TADJ Dahntay Jones 12.00 30.00
TADW1 David West 20.00 50.00
TADW2 Dwyane Wade 400.00 600.00
TAJH1 Jarvis Hayes 10.00 25.00
TAJH2 Josh Howard 15.00 40.00
TAJK Jason Kapono 10.00 25.00
TAKB Keith Bogans 10.00 25.00
TAKH Kirk Hinrich 15.00 40.00
TAKP Kendrick Perkins 12.00 30.00
TALB Leandro Barbosa 15.00 40.00
TALW Luke Walton 15.00 40.00
TAMB1 Marcus Banks 10.00 25.00
TAMB2 Matt Bonner 15.00 40.00
TAMP Mickael Pietrus 12.00 30.00
TAMS Mike Sweetney 10.00 25.00
TAMW Maurice Williams 15.00 40.00
TANE Ndudi Ebi 10.00 25.00
TARG Reece Gaines 10.00 25.00
TASB Steve Blake 12.00 30.00
TASV Slavko Vranes 10.00 25.00
TATB Troy Bell 10.00 25.00
TATF T.J. Ford 12.00 30.00
TATO Travis Outlaw 12.00 30.00
THAT Travis Hansen 10.00 25.00

2003-04 Topps Welcome to Atlanta Dual Relics

WA1-WA10 GROUP A
WA11-WA20 GROUP B
GROUP A 1:1460 H, 1:1283 R, 1:439 HTA
GROUP B 1:1042 H, 1:1283 R, 1:190 HTA
WA1 A.Iverson/D.Wagner 10.00 25.00
WA2 S.O'Neal/A.Stoudemire 25.00 50.00
WA3 J.Kidd/T.Parker 10.00 25.00
WA4 T.McGrady/J-Rich 10.00 25.00
WA5 J.O'Neal/D.Gooden 8.00 20.00
WA6 S.Marion/R.Jefferson 8.00 20.00
WA7 P.Pierce/C.Butler 10.00 25.00
WA8 S.Marbury/G.Arenas 8.00 20.00
WA9 B.Wallace/C.Boozer 8.00 20.00
WA10 T.Duncan/Nene 10.00 25.00
WA11 A.Walker/D.Nowitzki 8.00 20.00
WA12 Nene/A.Kirilenko 8.00 20.00
WA13 P.Gasol/D.Gooden 8.00 20.00
WA14 J.Tinsley/D.Wagner 8.00 20.00
WA15 S.Marion/J.Mashburn 8.00 20.00
WA16 J.Kidd/G.Payton 10.00 25.00
WA17 Y.Ming/S.O'Neal 30.00 60.00
WA18 J.O'Neal/K.Garnett 8.00 20.00
WA19 T.McGrady/A.Iverson 10.00 25.00
WA20 S.Nash/S.Francis 10.00 25.00

2004-05 Topps

COMPLETE SET (249) 75.00 200.00
1 Allen Iverson 1.25 3.00
2 Eddy Curry .30 .75
3 Stephon Marbury .60 1.50
4 Chris Bosh .75 2.00
5 Jason Kidd .75 2.00
6 Bonzi Wells .30 .75
7 Fred Jones .30 .75
8 Kobe Bryant 6.00 15.00
9 Ben Wallace .60 1.50
10 Darrell Armstrong .30 .75
11 Yao Ming 1.25 3.00
12 Udonis Haslem .30 .75
13 Nene .40 1.00
14 Michael Redd .40 1.00
15 Carmelo Anthony 1.00 2.50
16 Gary Trent .30 .75
17 Larry Hughes .40 1.00
18 Kareem Rush .30 .75
19 Antonio McDyess .40 1.00
20 Drew Gooden .30 .75
21 Kevin Garnett 1.25 3.00
22 DeShawn Stevenson .30 .75
23 LeBron James 8.00 20.00
24 Robert Horry .40 1.00
25 Shareef Abdur-Rahim .50 1.25
26 Antonio Daniels .30 .75
27 Scottie Pippen 1.25 3.00
28 Mike Dunleavy .30 .75
29 Joe Smith .40 1.00
30 Vince Carter 1.00 2.50
31 Reggie Miller 1.00 2.50
32 Chris Wilcox .30 .75
33 Rasheed Wallace .60 1.50
34 Paul Pierce .75 2.00
35 Tayshaun Prince .50 1.25
36 Raja Bell .40 1.00
37 Stephen Jackson .40 1.00
38 Eric Snow .30 .75
39 Zydrunas Ilgauskas .40 1.00
40 Andre Miller .40 1.00
41 Dirk Nowitzki 1.25 3.00
42 Steve Francis .50 1.25
43 Ray Allen .75 2.00
44 Donyell Marshall .30 .75
45 Pau Gasol .75 2.00
46 T.J. Ford .30 .75
47 Andrei Kirilenko .40 1.00
48 Jamaal Tinsley .30 .75
49 Earl Boykins .30 .75
50 Tim Duncan 1.25 3.00
51 Erick Dampier .30 .75
52 Nazr Mohammed .30 .75
53 Tim Thomas .30 .75
54 Keyon Dooling .30 .75
55 Jason Kapono .30 .75
56 Kirk Hinrich .50 1.25
57 Aaron McKie .30 .75
58 Brad Miller .40 1.00

59 Al Harrington .40 1.00
60 Gary Payton .75 2.00
61 Nick Van Exel .50 1.25
62 Cuttino Mobley .40 1.00
63 Marcus Camby .40 1.00
64 Desmond Mason .40 1.00
65 Boris Diaw .40 1.00
66 Kenyon Martin .50 1.25
67 Mike Miller .40 1.00
68 Dwyane Wade 2.00 5.00
69 Allan Houston .50 1.25
70 Jermaine O'Neal .40 1.00
71 Travis Hansen .30 .75
72 Qyntel Woods .30 .75
73 Jamal Crawford .50 1.25
74 Bobby Jackson .40 1.00
75 Derrick Coleman .40 1.00
76 Brian Skinner .30 .75
77 Elton Brand .40 1.00
78 Rodney Rogers .30 .75
79 Zarko Cabarkapa .30 .75
80 Mike Bibby .50 1.25
81 Jim Jackson .40 1.00
82 Kurt Thomas .30 .75
83 Vin Baker .30 .75
84 Rodney White .30 .75
85 Gordan Giricek .30 .75
86 Jamal Mashburn .40 1.00
87 Kenny Thomas .30 .75
88 Antoine Walker .50 1.25
89 Rasho Nesterovic .30 .75
90 Shawn Marion .50 1.25
91 Shane Battier .40 1.00
92 Marquis Daniels .30 .75
93 Ruben Patterson .30 .75
94 Michael Olowokandi .30 .75
95 Bruce Bowen .40 1.00
96 Caron Butler .40 1.00
97 Corliss Williamson .30 .75
98 Jeff Foster .30 .75
99 Carlos Boozer .40 1.00
100 Tracy McGrady .75 2.00
101 Stromile Swift .30 .75
102 Keith Van Horn .40 1.00
103 Derek Fisher .40 1.00
104 Juwan Howard .40 1.00
105 Tony Parker .75 2.00
106 Jason Terry .40 1.00
107 Vlade Divac .50 1.25
108 Marcus Banks .30 .75
109 Derek Anderson .40 1.00
110 Karl Malone 1.00 2.50
111 Baron Davis .50 1.25
112 Chris Crawford .30 .75
113 Kwame Brown .30 .75
114 Jiri Welsch .30 .75
115 Maciej Lampe .30 .75
116 Josh Howard .40 1.00
117 Luke Walton .40 1.00
118 John Salmons .40 1.00
119 David West .40 1.00
120 Amare Stoudemire .50 1.25
121 Antawn Jamison .40 1.00
122 Clarence Weatherspoon .30 .75
123 Aleksandar Pavlovic .30 .75
124 Kerry Kittles .40 1.00
125 Rafer Alston .30 .75
126 Jarvis Hayes .30 .75
127 Toni Kukoc .50 1.25
128 Latrell Sprewell .60 1.50
129 Keith Bogans .30 .75
130 Jason Richardson .50 1.25
131 Brent Barry .30 .75
132 Darko Milicic .30 .75
133 Peja Stojakovic .40 1.00
134 Jerome Williams .30 .75
135 Malik Rose .30 .75
136 Quentin Richardson .30 .75
137 Wally Szczerbiak .40 1.00
138 Theo Ratliff .30 .75
139 Gilbert Arenas .50 1.25
140 Richard Hamilton .60 1.50
141 Rashard Lewis .40 1.00
142 Joe Johnson .40 1.00
143 P.J. Brown .30 .75
144 Jason Collins .30 .75
145 Chauncey Billups .60 1.50
146 Raef LaFrentz .30 .75
147 Mickael Pietrus .30 .75
148 Lamar Odom .50 1.25
149 Vladimir Radmanovic .30 .75
150 Chris Webber .60 1.50
151 Tony Delk .30 .75
152 Troy Hudson .30 .75
153 David Wesley .30 .75
154 Juan Dixon .30 .75
155 Darius Miles .30 .75
156 Gerald Wallace .40 1.00
157 Jalen Rose .40 1.00
158 Charlie Ward .30 .75
159 Michael Finley .50 1.25
160 Jonathan Bender .30 .75
161 Lorenzen Wright .30 .75
162 George Lynch .30 .75
163 Leandro Barbosa .40 1.00
164 Dajuan Wagner .30 .75
165 Francisco Elson .30 .75
166 Jerry Stackhouse .50 1.25
167 Manu Ginobili 1.00 2.50
168 Chris Kaman .40 1.00
169 James Posey .40 1.00
170 Doug Christie .40 1.00
171 Zoran Planinic .30 .75
172 Maurice Taylor .30 .75
173 Carlos Arroyo .30 .75
174 Damon Stoudamire .50 1.25
175 Brian Cardinal .30 .75
176 Devean George .30 .75
177 Hedo Turkoglu .40 1.00
178 Anfernee Hardaway 1.25 3.00
179 Tony Battie .30 .75
180 Steve Nash 1.00 2.50
181 Glenn Robinson .40 1.00
182 Morris Peterson .30 .75
183 Luke Ridnour .40 1.00
184 Mehmet Okur .40 1.00
185 Eddie Jones .50 1.25
186 Tyronn Lue .30 .75
187 Raul Lopez .30 .75
188 Lucious Harris .30 .75
189 Alvin Williams .30 .75
190 Zach Randolph .50 1.25
191 Steve Blake .30 .75
192 Marko Jaric .30 .75
193 Anthony Peeler .30 .75
194 Troy Murphy .30 .75
195 Jamaal Magloire .30 .75
196 Brandon Hunter .30 .75
197 Jason Williams .40 1.00
198 Corey Maggette .40 1.00
199 Ron Artest .50 1.25
200 Shaquille O'Neal 2.00 5.00
201 Richard Jefferson .40 1.00
202 Kelvin Cato .30 .75
203 Mark Blount .30 .75
204 Eric Williams .30 .75
205 Sam Cassell .40 1.00
206 Voshon Lenard .30 .75
207 Bob Sura .30 .75
208 Speedy Claxton .30 .75
209 Samuel Dalembert .30 .75
210 Tyson Chandler .40 1.00
211 Brian Grant .40 1.00
212 Stanislav Medvedenko .30 .75
213 Danny Fortson .30 .75
214 Chucky Atkins .30 .75
215 Matt Harpring .30 .75
216 Trenton Hassell .30 .75
217 Ronald Murray .30 .75
218 Jeff McInnis .30 .75
219 Primoz Brezec .30 .75
220 Ricky Davis .40 1.00
221 Dwight Howard RC 2.50 6.00
222 Emeka Okafor RC .60 1.50
223 Ben Gordon RC .75 2.00
224 Shaun Livingston RC .75 2.00
225 Devin Harris RC .60 1.50
226 Josh Childress RC .50 1.25
227 Luol Deng RC .75 2.00
228 Rafael Araujo RC .50 1.25
229 Andre Iguodala RC 1.25 3.00
230 Luke Jackson RC .50 1.25
231 Andris Biedrins RC .50 1.25
232 Robert Swift RC .50 1.25
233 Sebastian Telfair RC .60 1.50
234 Kris Humphries RC .50 1.25
235 Al Jefferson RC .75 2.00
236 Kirk Snyder RC .50 1.25
237 Josh Smith RC .75 2.00
238 J.R. Smith RC .75 2.00
239 Dorell Wright RC .60 1.50
240 Jameer Nelson RC .75 2.00
241 Pavel Podkolzin RC .50 1.25
242 Viktor Khryapa RC .50 1.25
243 Sergei Monia RC .50 1.25
244 Delonte West RC .60 1.50
245 Tony Allen RC .75 2.00
246 Kevin Martin RC 1.00 2.50
247 Sasha Vujacic RC .60 1.50
248 Beno Udrih RC .60 1.50
249 David Harrison RC .50 1.25

2004-05 Topps Black
*BLACK STARS: 1.5X TO 4X BASE HI
*BLACK RCs: 1.5X TO 4X BASE HI
BLACK PRINT RUN 500 SER.#'d SETS
8 Kobe Bryant 60.00 150.00
23 LeBron James 400.00 800.00

2004-05 Topps First Edition
*FIRST ED. STARS: 1.5X TO 4X BASE HI
*FIRST ED. RCs: .75X TO 2X BASE HI
BOXES DISTRIBUTED TO HTA DEALERS
23 LeBron James 150.00 400.00

2004-05 Topps Gold
*GOLD STARS: 5X TO 12X BASE HI
*GOLD RCs: 3X TO 8X BASE HI
PRINT RUN 99 SER.#'d SETS
8 Kobe Bryant 200.00 500.00
23 LeBron James 2,000.00 4,000.00

2004-05 Topps All-Star Support
COMPLETE SET (20) 15.00 40.00
STATED ODDS 1:18
ASAW R.Artest/B.Wallace 1.00 2.50
ASBD C.Boozer/M.Dunleavy 1.00 2.50
ASBF K.Bryant/S.Francis 2.00 5.00
ASBW C.Bosh/D.Wade 2.00 5.00
ASCA S.Cassell/R.Allen 1.00 2.50
ASCP V.Carter/P.Pierce 1.50 4.00
ASDR B.Davis/M.Redd 1.00 2.50
ASGD K.Garnett/T.Duncan 1.50 4.00
ASGP M.Ginobili/T.Prince 1.00 2.50
ASHH K.Hinrich/J.Hayes 1.00 2.50
ASIK A.Iverson/J.Kidd 1.50 4.00
ASJA L.James/C.Anthony 3.00 8.00
ASKH C.Kaman/J.Howard 1.00 2.50
ASMJ R.Murray/M.Jaric 1.00 2.50
ASMK B.Miller/A.Kirilenko 1.00 2.50
ASMM J.Magloire/K.Martin 1.00 2.50
ASMO T.McGrady/J.O'Neal 1.25 3.00
ASNS Nene/A.Stoudemire 1.00 2.50
ASOM S.O'Neal/Y.Ming 1.50 4.00
ASSN P.Stojakovic/D.Nowitzki 1.25 3.00

2004-05 Topps All-Star Support Relics
STATED ODDS 1:200
PRINT RUN 250 SER.#'d SETS
ASAW R.Artest/B.Wallace 5.00 12.00
ASBD C.Boozer/M.Dunleavy 8.00 20.00
ASBF Kobe NO JSY/S.Francis 8.00 20.00
ASBW C.Bosh/D.Wade 8.00 20.00
ASCA Cassell/R.Allen NO JSY 5.00 12.00
ASCP V.Carter NO JSY/P.Pierce 5.00 12.00
ASDR B.Davis/M.Redd 5.00 12.00
ASGD K.Garnett/T.Duncan 10.00 25.00
ASGP M.Ginobili/T.Prince 5.00 12.00
ASHH K.Hinrich/J.Hayes 5.00 12.00
ASIK A.Iverson NO JSY/Carmelo 8.00 20.00
ASKH C.Kaman/J.Howard 5.00 12.00
ASMJ R.Murray/M.Jaric 5.00 12.00
ASMK B.Miller/A.Kirilenko 5.00 12.00
ASMM J.Magloire/K.Martin 5.00 12.00
ASMO T.McGrady/J.O'Neal 6.00 15.00
ASNS Nene/A.Stoudemire 5.00 12.00
ASOM S.O'Neal/Y.Ming 10.00 25.00
ASSN P.Stojakovic/D.Nowitzki 5.00 12.00

2004-05 Topps Drive N Thrive Relics
STATED ODDS 1:318
N Nene 2.50 6.00
AI Allen Iverson 8.00 20.00
AK Andrei Kirilenko 2.50 6.00
BD Baron Davis 3.00 8.00
CM Corey Maggette 2.50 6.00
DM Desmond Mason 2.50 6.00
DW Dwyane Wade 8.00 20.00
EG Manu Ginobili 6.00 15.00
GP Gary Payton 5.00 12.00
JC Jamal Crawford 3.00 8.00
JH Jarvis Hayes 2.00 5.00
JR Jason Richardson 3.00 8.00
JS Jerry Stackhouse 3.00 8.00
JT Jason Terry 2.50 6.00
KH Kirk Hinrich 3.00 8.00
KR Kareem Rush 2.00 5.00
MT Maurice Taylor 2.00 5.00
QR Quentin Richardson 2.00 5.00
QW Qyntel Woods 2.00 5.00
RH Richard Hamilton 4.00 10.00
RJ Richard Jefferson 2.50 6.00
RL Rashard Lewis 2.50 6.00
SF Steve Francis 3.00 8.00
SM Shawn Marion 3.00 8.00
SN Steve Nash 6.00 15.00
TM Tracy McGrady 5.00 12.00
CBO Carlos Boozer 2.50 6.00
CBO2 Chris Bosh 5.00 12.00
CBU Caron Butler 2.50 6.00
SMA Stephon Marbury 4.00 10.00

2004-05 Topps Great Expectations
COMPLETE SET (20) 8.00 20.00
STATED ODDS 1:9
AS Amare Stoudemire .50 1.25
BD Boris Diaw .40 1.00
CA Carmelo Anthony 1.00 2.50
CB Chris Bosh .75 2.00
CK Chris Kaman .40 1.00
DW Dwyane Wade 2.00 5.00
JH Jarvis Hayes .30 .75
KH Kirk Hinrich .50 1.25
LJ LeBron James 4.00 10.00
MD Mike Dunleavy .30 .75
MG Manu Ginobili 1.00 2.50
MS Mike Sweetney .30 .75
RM Ronald Murray .30 .75
TP Tayshaun Prince .50 1.25
YM Yao Ming 1.25 3.00
ZR Zach Randolph .50 1.25
CAR Carlos Arroyo .30 .75
CBZ Carlos Boozer .40 1.00
JHO Josh Howard .40 1.00
TJF T.J. Ford .30 .75

2004-05 Topps Marks of Excellence
STATED ODDS: GROUP A 1:54432, GROUP B 1:2838, GROUP C 1:1531, GROUP D 1:548, GROUP E 1:2395
BD Baron Davis B 12.00 30.00
BG Ben Gordon D 5.00 12.00
CA Carmelo Anthony D 75.00 200.00
CD Chris Duhon C 4.00 10.00
DH Devin Harris D 4.00 10.00
EO Emeka Okafor E 8.00 20.00
FJ Fred Jones D 5.00 12.00
JC Josh Childress D 3.00 8.00
JK Jason Kidd C 30.00 80.00
JO Jermaine O'Neal B 5.00 12.00
KS Kirk Snyder C 3.00 8.00
LD Luol Deng D 5.00 12.00
LJ Luke Jackson D 3.00 8.00
LO Lamar Odom C 6.00 15.00
PS Peja Stojakovic C 6.00 15.00
RH Richard Hamilton B 12.00 30.00
SL Shaun Livingston D 6.00 15.00
SM Stephon Marbury C 20.00 50.00
SO Shaquille O'Neal B 125.00 300.00
ST Sebastian Telfair D 4.00 10.00
TA Tony Allen C 5.00 12.00
TD Tim Duncan B 1,000.00 2,000.00
TM Tracy McGrady B 125.00 300.00
RAL Rafer Alston B 25.00 50.00

2004-05 Topps Peak Performers Relics
STATED ODDS 1:399
AS Amare Stoudemire 3.00 8.00
AW Antoine Walker 3.00 8.00
BW Ben Wallace 4.00 10.00
CA Carmelo Anthony 6.00 15.00
EB Elton Brand 2.50 6.00
GR Glenn Robinson 2.50 6.00
JM Jamal Mashburn 2.50 6.00
KB Kwame Brown 2.00 5.00
KG Kevin Garnett 8.00 20.00
MB Mike Bibby 3.00 8.00
MR Michael Redd 2.50 6.00
PG Pau Gasol 5.00 12.00
PP Paul Pierce 5.00 12.00
PS Peja Stojakovic 2.50 6.00
SO Shaquille O'Neal 12.00 30.00
TD Tim Duncan 8.00 20.00
TP Tony Parker 5.00 12.00
TT Tim Thomas 2.00 5.00
YM Yao Ming 8.00 20.00
ZI Zydrunas Ilgauskas 2.50 6.00
KMA Kenyon Martin 3.00 8.00
RAL Ray Allen 5.00 12.00

2004-05 Topps Rock Rhythm
COMPLETE SET (15) 12.50 30.00
STATED ODDS 1:12
AI Allen Iverson 2.00 5.00
BD Baron Davis .75 2.00
BW Ben Wallace 1.00 2.50
CA Carmelo Anthony 1.50 4.00
JK Jason Kidd 1.25 3.00
JR Jason Richardson .75 2.00
KB Kobe Bryant 6.00 15.00
KG Kevin Garnett 2.00 5.00
LJ LeBron James 6.00 15.00
SM Stephon Marbury 1.00 2.50
SO Shaquille O'Neal 3.00 8.00
TD Tim Duncan 2.00 5.00
TM Tracy McGrady 1.25 3.00
VC Vince Carter 1.50 4.00
YM Yao Ming 2.00 5.00

2004-05 Topps Rookie Photo Shoot Autographs
STATED ODDS 1:721
STATED PRINT RUN 55 SETS
AE Andre Emmett 10.00 25.00
AJ Al Jefferson 50.00 125.00
AV Anderson Varejao 12.00 30.00
BG Ben Gordon 50.00 125.00
BR Bernard Robinson 10.00 25.00
CD Chris Duhon 12.00 30.00
DH Dwight Howard 200.00 400.00
DH2 David Harrison 10.00 25.00
DW Dorell Wright 12.00 30.00
DW Delonte West 12.00 30.00
EO Emeka Okafor 30.00 80.00
JC Josh Childress 10.00 25.00
JN Jameer Nelson 15.00 40.00
JS Josh Smith 30.00 80.00
JV Jackson Vroman 10.00 25.00
KH Kris Humphries 12.00 30.00
KM Kevin Martin 30.00 80.00
KS Kirk Snyder 10.00 25.00
LC Lionel Chalmers 12.00 30.00
LD Luol Deng 40.00 100.00
LJ Luke Jackson 10.00 25.00
RA Rafael Araujo 10.00 25.00
RP Rickey Paulding 10.00 25.00
SL Shaun Livingston 15.00 40.00
ST Sebastian Telfair 12.00 30.00
TA Tony Allen 15.00 40.00
TA2 Trevor Ariza 15.00 40.00
DHA Devin Harris 30.00 80.00
HSJ Ha Seung-Jin 15.00 40.00
JRS J.R. Smith 50.00 125.00

2005-06 Topps
COMPLETE SET (255) 20.00 50.00
1 Grant Hill .75 2.00
2 Keith Van Horn .40 1.00
3 Quentin Richardson .30 .75
4 Damon Jones .30 .75
5 Lamar Odom .40 1.00
6 Jamal Crawford .50 1.25
7 Ben Gordon .40 1.00
8 Zach Randolph .50 1.25
9 Rafer Alston .40 1.00
10 Gilbert Arenas .50 1.25
11 Yao Ming 1.00 2.50
12 Cuttino Mobley .30 .75
13 Josh Smith .30 .75
14 Ray Allen .75 2.00
15 Vince Carter 1.00 2.50
16 Kenyon Martin .40 1.00
17 Mark Blount .30 .75
18 Carlos Arroyo .30 .75
19 Lee Nailon .30 .75
20 Bobby Simmons .30 .75
21 Tim Duncan 1.25 3.00
22 Michael Redd .40 1.00
23 Antawn Jamison .40 1.00
24 Matt Bonner .30 .75
25 Shane Battier .40 1.00
26 Nick Van Exel .50 1.25
27 Jason Hart .30 .75
28 Nene .40 1.00
29 Fred Jones .30 .75
30 Baron Davis .50 1.25
31 Danny Fortson .30 .75
32 Caron Butler .40 1.00
33 Allen Iverson 1.00 2.50
34 Eddie Griffin .30 .75
35 Jameer Nelson .30 .75
36 Brent Barry .30 .75
37 Zydrunas Ilgauskas .40 1.00
38 Jason Terry .40 1.00
39 Mike Dunleavy .30 .75
40 Paul Pierce .75 2.00
41 Reggie Miller .75 2.00
42 Lorenzen Wright .30 .75
43 Peja Stojakovic .40 1.00
44 Zaza Pachulia .30 .75
45 Dan Dickau .30 .75
46 Andre Iguodala .50 1.25
47 Andrei Kirilenko .40 1.00
48 Nenad Krstic .30 .75
49 Damon Stoudamire .50 1.25
50 Emeka Okafor .40 1.00
51 Jalen Rose .40 1.00
52 Beno Udrih .30 .75
53 Jared Jeffries .30 .75
54 Ricky Davis .40 1.00
55 Jason Kidd .75 2.00
56 Eddy Curry .30 .75
57 Chauncey Billups .60 1.50
58 Eric Snow .30 .75
59 Derek Fisher .50 1.25
60 Amare Stoudemire .50 1.25
61 Josh Childress .30 .75
62 Juwan Howard .40 1.00
63 Mehmet Okur .30 .75
64 Jerome Williams .30 .75
65 Shaun Livingston .40 1.00
66 Stephen Jackson .40 1.00
67 Alonzo Mourning .60 1.50
68 J.R. Smith .50 1.25
69 Kobe Bryant 4.00 10.00
70 Dwight Howard .60 1.50
71 Manu Ginobili 1.00 2.50
72 Kyle Korver .40 1.00
73 Reggie Evans .30 .75
74 Shareef Abdur-Rahim .50 1.25
75 Rafael Araujo .30 .75
76 Kirk Snyder .30 .75
77 Jermaine O'Neal .40 1.00
78 Melvin Ely .30 .75
79 Chris Kaman .40 1.00
80 Stephon Marbury .60 1.50
81 Joe Smith .30 .75
82 Samuel Dalembert .30 .75
83 Luke Ridnour .40 1.00
84 Sebastian Telfair .40 1.00
85 Larry Hughes .40 1.00
86 Tyson Chandler .40 1.00
87 Michael Finley .50 1.25
88 Drew Gooden .40 1.00
89 Marcus Camby .40 1.00
90 Dwyane Wade 1.00 2.50
91 Troy Murphy .30 .75
92 David Wesley .30 .75
93 Stromile Swift .30 .75
94 Clifford Robinson .30 .75
95 Sam Cassell .40 1.00
96 Joe Johnson .40 1.00
97 Bobby Jackson .40 1.00
98 Derek Anderson .30 .75
99 Rashard Lewis .40 1.00
100 Shaquille O'Neal 1.50 4.00
101 Keith McLeod .30 .75
102 Keith Bogans .30 .75
103 Al Harrington .40 1.00
104 Anderson Varejao .30 .75
105 Al Jefferson .30 .75
106 Jerry Stackhouse .40 1.00
107 Chris Duhon .30 .75
108 Earl Boykins .30 .75
109 Tayshaun Prince .50 1.25
110 Carlos Boozer .40 1.00
111 Rasual Butler .30 .75
112 Bonzi Wells .30 .75
113 Chris Wilcox .30 .75
114 Latrell Sprewell .50 1.25
115 Richard Jefferson .40 1.00
116 Toni Kukoc .50 1.25
117 Doug Christie .40 1.00
118 Brad Miller .40 1.00
119 Antonio Daniels .30 .75
120 Richard Hamilton .60 1.50
121 Kevin Garnett 1.25 3.00
122 Tony Parker .75 2.00
123 Mike Sweetney .30 .75
124 Speedy Claxton .30 .75
125 Udonis Haslem .30 .75
126 Chucky Atkins .30 .75
127 David Harrison .30 .75
128 Jason Collier .30 .75
129 Pau Gasol .75 2.00
130 Chris Webber .60 1.50
131 Kelvin Cato .30 .75
132 Michael Olowokandi .30 .75
133 Ben Wallace .60 1.50
134 Antoine Walker .40 1.00
135 Marquis Daniels .40 1.00
136 Ira Newble .30 .75
137 Austin Croshere .30 .75
138 Mike James .30 .75
139 Michael Doleac .30 .75
140 Carmelo Anthony .75 2.00
141 Sasha Vujacic .40 1.00
142 Brian Cardinal .30 .75
143 Ron Mercer .30 .75
144 Tim Thomas .30 .75
145 Juan Dixon .30 .75
146 Rodney Rogers .30 .75
147 Hedo Turkoglu .40 1.00
148 Nazr Mohammed .30 .75
149 Gerald Wallace .40 1.00
150 Dirk Nowitzki 1.25 3.00
151 Tony Allen .30 .75
152 Adonal Foyle .30 .75
153 Corey Maggette .40 1.00
154 Rasheed Wallace .50 1.25
155 Andre Miller .40 1.00
156 Luol Deng .40 1.00
157 Mike Miller .40 1.00
158 Wally Szczerbiak .40 1.00
159 Maurice Williams .30 .75
160 Chris Bosh .60 1.50
161 Jamaal Magloire .30 .75
162 Leandro Barbosa .40 1.00
163 Kevin Martin .40 1.00
164 Jeff Foster .30 .75
165 Nick Collison .30 .75
166 Matt Harpring .40 1.00
167 Kirk Hinrich .40 1.00
168 Antonio McDyess .40 1.00
169 Josh Howard .40 1.00
170 Elton Brand .40 1.00
171 Kurt Thomas .30 .75
172 Tyronn Lue .30 .75
173 Bob Sura .30 .75
174 Chris Mihm .30 .75
175 Jason Williams .75 2.00
176 Jim Jackson .30 .75
177 Brevin Knight .30 .75
178 Eduardo Najera .30 .75
179 Jeff McInnis .30 .75
180 Jason Richardson .50 1.25
181 Vladimir Radmanovic .30 .75
182 Jamaal Tinsley .30 .75
183 Eddie Jones .40 1.00
184 P.J. Brown .30 .75
185 Troy Hudson .30 .75
186 Steve Francis .50 1.25
187 Marc Jackson .30 .75
188 Kenny Thomas .30 .75
189 Joel Przybilla .30 .75
190 Steve Nash 1.00 2.50
191 Devin Brown .30 .75
192 Donyell Marshall .30 .75
193 Raja Bell .40 1.00
194 Brendan Haywood .30 .75
195 Primoz Brezec .30 .75
196 Gary Payton .75 2.00
197 Devin Harris .30 .75
198 Predrag Drobnjak .30 .75
199 Dikembe Mutombo .60 1.50
200 LeBron James 4.00 10.00
201 Marko Jaric .30 .75
202 Mike Bibby .50 1.25
203 Desmond Mason .30 .75
204 Morris Peterson .30 .75
205 Jarvis Hayes .30 .75
206 Bruce Bowen .40 1.00
207 Trevor Ariza .30 .75
208 Raef LaFrentz .30 .75
209 Brian Grant .30 .75
210 Shawn Marion .40 1.00
211 Dan Gadzuric .30 .75
212 Andres Nocioni .30 .75
213 Tony Delk .30 .75
214 Darius Miles .30 .75
215 Gordan Giricek .30 .75
216 Rasho Nesterovic .30 .75
217 Jason Collins .30 .75
218 Mickael Pietrus .30 .75
219 Erick Dampier .30 .75
220 Tracy McGrady .75 2.00
221 Andrew Bogut RC 1.00 2.50
222 Marvin Williams RC .75 2.00
223 Deron Williams RC 1.25 3.00
224 Chris Paul RC 4.00 10.00
225 Raymond Felton RC .60 1.50
226 Martell Webster RC .60 1.50
227 Charlie Villanueva RC .60 1.50
228 Channing Frye RC .60 1.50
229 Ike Diogu RC .50 1.25
230 Andrew Bynum RC .60 1.50
231 Fran Vazquez RC .50 1.25
232 Daniel Ewing RC .60 1.50
233 Sean May RC .50 1.25
234 Rashad McCants RC .50 1.25
235 Antoine Wright RC .60 1.50
236 Joey Graham RC .60 1.50
237 Danny Granger RC .75 2.00
238 Gerald Green RC .75 2.00
239 Hakim Warrick RC .60 1.50
240 Julius Hodge RC .50 1.25
241 Nate Robinson RC .75 2.00
242 Jarrett Jack RC .75 2.00
243 Francisco Garcia RC .50 1.25
244 Luther Head RC .50 1.25
245 Johan Petro RC .50 1.25
246 Jason Maxiell RC .60 1.50
247 Linas Kleiza RC .60 1.50
248 Ryan Gomes RC .60 1.50
249 Wayne Simien RC .50 1.25
250 David Lee RC .75 2.00
251 Shannon Elizabeth 2.00 5.00
252 Carmen Electra 2.00 5.00
253 Jenny McCarthy 2.00 5.00
254 Christie Brinkley 2.00 5.00
255 Jay-Z 1.50 4.00

2005-06 Topps Black
*1-220 BLACK: 1.5X TO 4X BASE HI
*221-250 RC BLACK: 1X TO 2.5X BASE HI
*251-255 BLACK: 1X TO 2.5X BASE HI
PRINT RUN 500 SER.#'d SETS
200 LeBron James 30.00 80.00
224 Chris Paul 150.00 400.00
255 Jay-Z 20.00 50.00

2005-06 Topps First Edition
*1-220 1ST ED.: 1.5X TO 4X BASE HI
*221-255 1ST ED.: .75X TO 2X BASE HI
BOXES DISTRIBUTED TO HTA DEALERS

2005-06 Topps Gold
*1-220 GOLD: 5X TO 12X BASE HI
*221-250 RC GOLD: 2X TO 5X BASE HI
*251-255 GOLD: 1.5X TO 4X BASE HI
33 Allen Iverson 15.00 40.00
69 Kobe Bryant 200.00 500.00
200 LeBron James 200.00 500.00
224 Chris Paul 500.00 1,000.00
255 Jay-Z 40.00 100.00

2005-06 Topps All-Star Altitude
COMPLETE SET (25) 15.00 30.00
STATED ODDS 1:10
ASAI Allen Iverson 1.25 3.00
ASAJ Antawn Jamison .50 1.25
ASAS Amare Stoudemire .60 1.50
ASBW Ben Wallace .75 2.00
ASDN Dirk Nowitzki 1.50 4.00
ASDW Dwyane Wade 1.25 3.00
ASGA Gilbert Arenas .60 1.50
ASGH Grant Hill 1.00 2.50
ASJO Jermaine O'Neal .50 1.25
ASKB Kobe Bryant 5.00 12.00
ASKG Kevin Garnett 1.50 4.00
ASLJ LeBron James 5.00 12.00
ASMG Manu Ginobili 1.25 3.00
ASPP Paul Pierce 1.00 2.50
ASRA Ray Allen 1.00 2.50
ASRL Rashard Lewis .50 1.25
ASSM Shawn Marion .50 1.25
ASSN Steve Nash 1.25 3.00
ASSO Shaquille O'Neal 2.00 5.00
ASTD Tim Duncan 1.50 4.00
ASTM Tracy McGrady 1.00 2.50
ASVC Vince Carter 1.25 3.00
ASYM Yao Ming 1.25 3.00
ASZI Zydrunas Ilgauskas .50 1.25

2005-06 Topps All-Star Altitude Relics
PRINT RUN 250 SER.#'d SETS
BW Ben Wallace 3.00 8.00
DN Dirk Nowitzki 6.00 15.00
GA Gilbert Arenas 2.50 6.00
GH Grant Hill 4.00 10.00
JO Jermaine O'Neal 2.00 5.00
MG Manu Ginobili 5.00 12.00
RA Ray Allen 4.00 10.00
SM Shawn Marion 2.00 5.00
SN Steve Nash 5.00 12.00
SO Shaquille O'Neal 8.00 20.00
TD Tim Duncan 6.00 15.00
TM Tracy McGrady 4.00 10.00
YM Yao Ming 5.00 12.00
ZI Zydrunas Ilgauskas 2.00 5.00
JRS J.R. Smith 2.50 6.00

2005-06 Topps Celebrity Threads
STATED ODDS 1:2198
CB Christie Brinkley 15.00 40.00
JZ Jay-Z 40.00 100.00
SE Shannon Elizabeth 15.00 40.00
CAE Carmen Electra 25.00 60.00
JMC Jenny McCarthy 25.00 60.00

2005-06 Topps Critical Component
COMPLETE SET (15) 12.50 25.00
STATED ODDS 1:17
CC1 Ray Allen 1.25 3.00
CC2 Vince Carter 1.50 4.00
CC3 Tim Duncan 2.00 5.00
CC4 Steve Nash 1.50 4.00
CC5 Gilbert Arenas .75 2.00
CC6 Carmelo Anthony 1.25 3.00
CC7 Chris Bosh 1.00 2.50
CC8 Richard Hamilton 1.00 2.50
CC9 Tracy McGrady 1.25 3.00
CC10 Paul Pierce 1.25 3.00
CC11 Dirk Nowitzki 2.00 5.00
CC12 Amare Stoudemire .75 2.00
CC13 Kobe Bryant 6.00 15.00
CC14 Shaquille O'Neal 2.50 6.00
CC15 Mike Bibby .75 2.00

2005-06 Topps Finishing Touch Relics
STATED ODDS 1:246
BG Ben Gordon 2.00 5.00
CA Carmelo Anthony 4.00 10.00
CB Chris Bosh 3.00 8.00
JK Jason Kidd 4.00 10.00
MC Marcus Camby 2.00 5.00
PG Pau Gasol 4.00 10.00
PP Paul Pierce 4.00 10.00
RM Reggie Miller 3.00 8.00
RW Rasheed Wallace 2.50 6.00
SF Steve Francis 2.50 6.00
SM Stephon Marbury 3.00 8.00
SO Shaquille O'Neal 8.00 20.00
TD Tim Duncan 6.00 15.00
WS Wally Szczerbiak 2.00 5.00
YM Yao Ming 5.00 12.00

2005-06 Topps Marks of Excellence
GROUP A ODDS 1:835, GRP B ODDS 1:419
GROUP C ODDS 1:2016
AI Allen Iverson 40.00 100.00
AS Amare Stoudemire A 8.00 20.00
BD Baron Davis A 8.00 20.00
BU Beno Udrih A 3.00 8.00
CA Carmelo Anthony C 12.00 30.00
DE Daniel Ewing B 4.00 10.00
DG Danny Granger B 5.00 12.00
DW Dorell Wright A 5.00 12.00
EO Emeka Okafor C 4.00 10.00
FV Fran Vazquez B 3.00 8.00
GG Gerald Green B 5.00 12.00
HW Hakim Warrick B 4.00 10.00
JG Joey Graham B 4.00 10.00
JH Julius Hodge B 3.00 8.00
JK Jason Kidd A 8.00 20.00
JM Jason Maxiell B 4.00 10.00
JN Jameer Nelson A 5.00 12.00
JS Josh Smith A 4.00 10.00
LD Luol Deng A 4.00 10.00
LH Luther Head B 3.00 8.00
LO Lamar Odom A 4.00 10.00
PP Pavel Podkolzin A 5.00 12.00
PS Pape Sow A 5.00 12.00
QR Quentin Richardson A 3.00 8.00
RA Rafer Alston A 12.50 30.00
RF Raymond Felton B 4.00 10.00
RH Richard Hamilton A 6.00 15.00
RM Rashad McCants B 3.00 8.00
SL Shaun Livingston A 5.00 12.00
SM Shawn Marion A 10.00 25.00
SO Shaquille O'Neal A 30.00 80.00
TD Tim Duncan A 700.00 1,000.00
TM Tracy McGrady A 12.00 30.00
WS Wayne Simien B 3.00 8.00
ABO Andrew Bogut B 6.00 15.00
CTA Chris Taft B 3.00 8.00
DWI Deron Williams B 8.00 20.00
HSJ Ha Seung-Jin A 5.00 12.00
PST Peja Stojakovic A 6.00 15.00
SMA Stephon Marbury A 8.00 20.00
SMY Sean May B 3.00 8.00

2005-06 Topps Rise to the Occasion Relics
STATED ODDS 1:257
AH Al Harrington 2.00 5.00
AI Andre Iguodala 2.50 6.00
AS Amare Stoudemire 2.50 6.00
CW Chris Webber 3.00 8.00
DF Derek Fisher 2.50 6.00
DG Drew Gooden 2.00 5.00
EB Elton Brand 2.00 5.00
EO Emeka Okafor 2.00 5.00
JC Josh Childress 1.50 4.00
JS Josh Smith 2.00 5.00
KM Kenyon Martin 2.00 5.00
LO Lamar Odom 2.00 5.00
LW Luke Walton 2.00 5.00
RJ Richard Jefferson 2.00 5.00
TM Tracy McGrady 4.00 10.00
JRS J.R. Smith 2.50 6.00

2005-06 Topps Rookie Photo Shoot Autographs
STATED ODDS 1:619
BB Brandon Bass 12.00 30.00
CV Charlie Villanueva 12.00 30.00
DE Daniel Ewing 12.00 30.00
DG Danny Granger 15.00 40.00
DL David Lee 15.00 40.00
DW Deron Williams 75.00 150.00
EI Ersan Ilyasova 12.00 30.00
FG Francisco Garcia 10.00 25.00
GG Gerald Green 15.00 40.00
HW Hakim Warrick 12.00 30.00
JG Joey Graham 12.00 30.00
JH Julius Hodge 10.00 25.00
JJ Jarrett Jack 15.00 40.00
JM Jason Maxiell 12.00 30.00
LH Luther Head 10.00 25.00
LW Louis Williams 40.00 100.00
ME Monta Ellis 40.00 100.00
NR Nate Robinson 15.00 40.00
RF Raymond Felton 12.00 30.00
RG Ryan Gomes 12.00 30.00
RM Rashad McCants 10.00 25.00
SJ Sarunas Jasikevicius 15.00 40.00
SM Sean May 10.00 25.00
WS Wayne Simien 10.00 25.00
ABL Andray Blatche 15.00 40.00
MWE Martell Webster 12.00 30.00

2005-06 Topps Rookie Photo Shoot Autographs Dual
STATED ODDS 1:7998
FM R.Felton/S.May 30.00 80.00
GV Graham/Villanueva 20.00 50.00
GW G.Green/Webster 30.00 80.00
HJ J.Hodge/J.Jack 20.00 50.00
HW L.Head/D.Williams 30.00 80.00
MM S.May/R.McCants 30.00 80.00
WF D.Williams/R.Felton 30.00 80.00
FMC R.Felton/McCants 30.00 80.00
GWI F.Garcia/D.Williams 30.00 80.00

2005-06 Topps Signs of Stardom
STATED ODDS 1:7391
CB Christie Brinkley 40.00 100.00
JZ Jay-Z 500.00 1,000.00
SE Shannon Elizabeth 40.00 100.00
CAE Carmen Electra 20.00 50.00
JMC Jenny McCarthy 40.00 100.00

2005-06 Topps Target Hardwood Classics Jerseys
AF Adonal Foyle 1.50 4.00
AI Allen Iverson 5.00 12.00
AJ Antawn Jamison 2.00 5.00
AM Andre Miller 2.00 5.00
AV Anderson Varejao 1.50 4.00
BS Bob Sura 1.50 4.00
CM Chris Mihm 1.50 4.00
DH Devin Harris 1.50 4.00
DM Darko Milicic 1.50 4.00
EB Earl Boykins 1.50 4.00
LW Luke Walton 1.50 4.00
RW Rasheed Wallace 2.50 6.00
SD Samuel Dalembert 1.50 4.00
ST Sebastian Telfair 2.00 5.00
TO Travis Outlaw 2.00 5.00
WG Willie Green 1.50 4.00
DHA David Harrison 1.50 4.00
HSJ Ha Seung-Jin 1.50 4.00

2005-06 Topps Versatile Velocity
COMPLETE SET (10) 10.00 25.00
STATED ODDS 1:25
VV1 Stephon Marbury 1.25 3.00
VV2 Kevin Garnett 2.50 6.00
VV3 Dwyane Wade 2.00 5.00
VV4 Shawn Marion .75 2.00
VV5 Ben Gordon .75 2.00
VV6 Corey Maggette .75 2.00
VV7 LeBron James 8.00 20.00
VV8 Gilbert Arenas 1.00 2.50
VV9 Manu Ginobili 2.00 5.00
VV10 Steve Francis 1.00 2.50

2006-07 Topps
COMPLETE SET (275) 75.00 200.00
COMP.SET w/o SP's (215) 40.00 100.00
1 Elton Brand .40 1.00
2 Tim Duncan 1.25 3.00
3 Chris Paul 1.00 2.50
4 Joe Johnson .50 1.25
5 Chauncey Billups .60 1.50
6 Al Harrington .40 1.00
7 Andres Nocioni .30 .75
8 Kobe Bryant 8.00 20.00
9 Al Jefferson .30 .75
10 Gerald Wallace .40 1.00
11 Jason Terry .40 1.00
12 Dwight Howard .60 1.50
13 Larry Hughes .40 1.00
14 Sebastian Telfair .30 .75
15 Vince Carter 1.00 2.50
16 Mike Bibby .50 1.25
17 Ben Gordon .40 1.00
18 Desmond Mason .30 .75
19 Eddie Jones .50 1.25
20 Raymond Felton .30 .75
21 Paul Pierce .75 2.00
22 Eddy Curry .40 1.00
23 Jason Richardson .50 1.25
24 Rasheed Wallace .60 1.50
25 Andrew Bogut .40 1.00
26 Stromile Swift .30 .75
27 Peja Stojakovic .40 1.00
28 Deron Williams .40 1.00
29 Kwame Brown .30 .75
30 Michael Redd .40 1.00
31 Shawn Marion .50 1.25
32 Shaquille O'Neal 2.00 5.00
33A Larry Bird Green jersey, jumper with crowd in background 2.00 5.00
33B Larry Bird Green jersey, boxing out Magic 2.00 5.00
33C Larry Bird Green jersey, dribbling 2.00 5.00
33D Larry Bird Green jersey, driving on defender 2.00 5.00
33E Larry Bird Green jersey, free throw, ball above head 2.00 5.00
33F Larry Bird Green jersey, free throw, ball above team name 2.00 5.00
33G Larry Bird Green jersey, free throw, ball below team name 2.00 5.00
33H Larry Bird Green jersey, hands on legs 2.00 5.00
33I Larry Bird Green jersey, looking up 2.00 5.00
33J Larry Bird Green jersey, pullup on Hawks defender 2.00 5.00
33K Larry Bird Green jersey, shooting jumper, arms extended 2.00 5.00
33L Larry Bird Green jersey, shooting jumper, ball by face 2.00 5.00
33M Larry Bird Green jersey, shooting over Abdul-Jabbar 2.00 5.00
33N Larry Bird Green jersey, shooting over King 2.00 5.00
33O Larry Bird Green jersey, walking 2.00 5.00
33P Larry Bird White jersey, about to pullup 2.00 5.00
33Q Larry Bird White jersey, dribbling around defender 2.00 5.00
33R Larry Bird White jersey, fade away 2.00 5.00
33S Larry Bird White jersey, free throw, black background 2.00 5.00
33T Larry Bird White jersey, passing over shoulder 2.00 5.00
33U Larry Bird White jersey, rebounding vs Sonics 2.00 5.00
33V Larry Bird White jersey, scoop 2.00 5.00
33W Larry Bird White jersey, shooting over Dawkins 2.00 5.00
33X Larry Bird White jersey, shooting over Magic, close up 2.00 5.00
33Y Larry Bird White jersey, shooting over Magic, full body 2.00 5.00
33Z Larry Bird White jersey, with Bill Walton 2.00 5.00
33ZA Larry Bird Red All-Star jersey 2.00 5.00
33ZB Larry Bird Green warmups, ball in both hands 2.00 5.00
33ZC Larry Bird Green warmups, ball in right hand 2.00 5.00
33ZD Larry Bird Green warmups, released shot 2.00 5.00
33ZE Larry Bird White warmups, jogging out of tunnel 2.00 5.00
33ZF Larry Bird White warmups, walking 2.00 5.00
33ZG Larry Bird Gray warmups, shooting 2.00 5.00
33ZH Larry Bird Street clothes, driving truck 2.00 5.00
34 Ray Allen .75 2.00
35 Marko Jaric .30 .75
36 Luther Head .30 .75
37 Robert Horry .50 1.25
38 Jason Collins .30 .75
39 Cuttino Mobley .40 1.00
40 Donyell Marshall .30 .75
41 Dirk Nowitzki 1.25 3.00
42 Jermaine O'Neal .50 1.25
43 Kurt Thomas .30 .75
44 Gerald Green .40 1.00
45 Marvin Williams .30 .75
46 Bonzi Wells .30 .75
47 Andrei Kirilenko .40 1.00
48 J.R. Smith .50 1.25
49 Baron Davis .50 1.25
50 Tracy McGrady .75 2.00
51 Chris Kaman .30 .75
52 Luol Deng .40 1.00
53 Emeka Okafor .40 1.00
54 Grant Hill .75 2.00
55 Amare Stoudemire .50 1.25
56 Lamar Odom .40 1.00
57 Eric Snow .30 .75
58 Ike Diogu .30 .75
59 Alonzo Mourning .75 2.00
60 Maurice Evans .30 .75
61 Marcus Camby .40 1.00
62 Bobby Simmons .30 .75
63 Vladimir Radmanovic .30 .75
64 Ryan Gomes .30 .75
65 Fred Jones .30 .75
66 Kirk Snyder .30 .75
67 Flip Murray .30 .75
68 T.J. Ford .30 .75
69 DeSagana Diop .30 .75
70 Josh Smith .30 .75
71 Lorenzen Wright .30 .75
72 Nate Robinson .40 1.00
73 Brendan Haywood .30 .75
74 Darius Miles .30 .75
75 Keith Van Horn .40 1.00
76 Johan Petro .30 .75
77 Yao Ming 1.25 3.00
78 Darko Milicic .30 .75
79 Smush Parker .30 .75
80 Sarunas Jasikevicius .40 1.00
81 Mike Dunleavy .30 .75
82 Joey Graham .30 .75
83 Jason Williams .60 1.50
84 Melvin Ely .30 .75
85 Ricky Davis .40 1.00
86 Michael Finley .50 1.25
87 Steve Blake .30 .75
88 Nenad Krstic .30 .75
89 Earl Boykins .30 .75
90 Richard Hamilton .50 1.25
91 Chris Duhon .30 .75
92 Hakim Warrick .30 .75
93 Wally Szczerbiak .40 1.00
94 Corey Maggette .40 1.00
95 Leandro Barbosa .40 1.00
96 Jamaal Tinsley .30 .75
97 Kenyon Martin .40 1.00
98 Kyle Korver .40 1.00
99 Jason Kidd .75 2.00
100 Dwyane Wade 1.00 2.50
101 Ben Wallace .60 1.50
102 Mike James .30 .75
103 Josh Howard .40 1.00
104 Joe Smith .40 1.00
105 Josh Childress .30 .75
106 Eddie Griffin .30 .75
107 Richard Jefferson .40 1.00
108 Jalen Rose .40 1.00
109 Mickael Pietrus .40 1.00
110 Steve Nash 1.00 2.50
111 Juwan Howard .40 1.00
112 Drew Gooden .40 1.00
113 Eduardo Najera .30 .75
114 Chris Mihm .30 .75
115 Jose Calderon .30 .75
116 Kevin Garnett 1.25 3.00
117 Rafer Alston .40 1.00
118 Delonte West .30 .75
119 Jamaal Magloire .30 .75
120 Channing Frye .30 .75
121 Andre Iguodala .50 1.25
122 Pau Gasol .75 2.00
123 LeBron James 12.00 30.00
124 Antonio Daniels .30 .75
125 James Posey .30 .75
126 Devean George .30 .75
127 Linas Kleiza .30 .75
128 Brian Cook .30 .75
129 Sean May .30 .75
130 Sam Cassell .40 1.00
131 Mehmet Okur .30 .75
132 Bruce Bowen .40 1.00
133 Kirk Hinrich .40 1.00
134 Chris Wilcox .30 .75
135 Brad Miller .40 1.00
136 Erick Dampier .30 .75
137 Primoz Brezec .30 .75
138 Derek Fisher .50 1.25
139 Antonio McDyess .40 1.00
140 Chris Bosh .60 1.50
141 Jamal Crawford .50 1.25
142 Mike Miller .40 1.00
143 Danny Granger .30 .75
144 Quinton Ross .30 .75
145 Manu Ginobili 1.00 2.50
146 Udonis Haslem .30 .75
147 Marquis Daniels .30 .75
148 Maurice Williams .40 1.00
149 Viktor Khryapa .30 .75
150 Gilbert Arenas .50 1.25
151 Tony Parker .75 2.00
152 Carlos Boozer .40 1.00
153 Quentin Richardson .30 .75
154 Clifford Robinson .40 1.00
155 Speedy Claxton .30 .75
156 Charlie Villanueva .30 .75
157 Rashard Lewis .40 1.00
158 DeShawn Stevenson .30 .75
159 Boris Diaw .40 1.00
160 Francisco Garcia .30 .75
161 Zaza Pachulia .30 .75
162 Raja Bell .40 1.00
163 Juan Dixon .30 .75
164 Shaun Livingston .40 1.00
165 Shareef Abdur-Rahim .50 1.25
166 Devin Harris .30 .75
167 Brevin Knight .30 .75
168 Troy Murphy .30 .75
169 Antawn Jamison .40 1.00
170 Tyson Chandler .40 1.00
171 Stephen Jackson .40 1.00
172 Shane Battier .40 1.00
173 Chris Webber .60 1.50
174 Trenton Hassell .30 .75
175 Devin Brown .30 .75
176 Luke Ridnour .30 .75
177 Joel Przybilla .30 .75
178 David West .40 1.00
179 John Salmons .40 1.00
180 Nazr Mohammed .40 1.00
181 Caron Butler .40 1.00
182 Troy Hudson .30 .75
183 Zydrunas Ilgauskas .40 1.00
184 David Wesley .40 1.00
185 Andre Miller .40 1.00
186 Nick Collison .40 1.00
187 Ron Artest .50 1.25
188 Samuel Dalembert .40 1.00
189 Tayshaun Prince .50 1.25
190 Jameer Nelson .30 .75
191 Zach Randolph .50 1.25
192 Stephon Marbury .60 1.50
193 Steve Francis .50 1.25
194 Matt Harpring .50 1.25
195 Kevin Martin .40 1.00
196 Rashad McCants .30 .75
197 Carmelo Anthony .75 2.00
198 Morris Peterson .30 .75
199 Etan Thomas .30 .75
200 Allen Iverson 1.25 3.00
201 Antoine Walker .50 1.25
202 Eddie House .30 .75
203 Adrian Griffin .30 .75
204 Salim Stoudamire .30 .75
205 Raef LaFrentz .30 .75
206 Jared Jeffries .30 .75
207 Rasual Butler .30 .75
208 Damon Jones .30 .75
209 Chuck Hayes .30 .75
210 James Singleton .30 .75
211 Marcus Banks .30 .75
212 P.J. Brown .30 .75
213 Hedo Turkoglu .50 1.25
214 Jarrett Jack .40 1.00
215 Kendrick Perkins .30 .75
216A Adam Morrison RC .60 1.50
216B Adam Morrison Draft RC .60 1.50
217 Leon Powe RC .50 1.25
218A Shelden Williams RC .50 1.25
218B Shelden Williams Draft RC .50 1.25
219 Alexander Johnson RC .50 1.25
220 Will Blalock RC .50 1.25
221 Steve Novak RC .60 1.50
222 Shawne Williams RC .50 1.25
223 Guillermo Diaz RC .50 1.25
224 Mardy Collins RC .50 1.25
225 Ryan Hollins RC .50 1.25
226 Kyle Lowry RC 2.50 6.00
227 Craig Smith RC .60 1.50
228 Denham Brown RC .50 1.25
229 Dee Brown RC .50 1.25
230 Daniel Gibson RC .60 1.50
231A Tyrus Thomas RC .60 1.50
231B Tyrus Thomas Draft RC .60 1.50
232A Patrick O'Bryant RC .50 1.25
232B Patrick O'Bryant Draft RC .50 1.25
233 Cedric Simmons RC .50 1.25
234 P.J. Tucker RC .75 2.00
235 Hassan Adams RC .50 1.25
236 Hilton Armstrong RC .50 1.25
237 James Augustine RC .50 1.25
238 Josh Boone RC .50 1.25
239 James White RC .50 1.25
240A J.J. Redick RC 1.50 4.00
240B J.J. Redick Draft RC 1.50 4.00
241A LaMarcus Aldridge RC 2.00 5.00
241B LaMarcus Aldridge Draft RC 2.00 5.00
242 Maurice Ager RC .50 1.25
243A Marcus Williams RC .50 1.25
243B Marcus Williams Draft RC .50 1.25
244 Paul Davis RC .50 1.25
245 Jordan Farmar RC .60 1.50
246A Brandon Roy RC 1.50 4.00
246B Brandon Roy Draft RC 1.50 4.00
247 Quincy Douby RC .50 1.25
248 Ronnie Brewer RC .75 2.00
249 Rodney Carney RC .50 1.25
250A Randy Foye RC .60 1.50
250B Randy Foye Draft RC .60 1.50
251 Rajon Rondo RC 2.50 6.00
252 Rudy Gay RC 1.00 2.50
253 Paul Millsap RC 1.00 2.50
254 Saer Sene RC .50 1.25
255A Andrea Bargnani RC .60 1.50
255B Andrea Bargnani Draft RC .60 1.50
256 Allan Ray RC .50 1.25
257 Thabo Sefolosha RC .60 1.50
258 Darius Washington RC .50 1.25
259 Renaldo Balkman RC .60 1.50
260 Mike Gansey RC .50 1.25
261 Solomon Jones RC .50 1.25
262 Bobby Jones RC .50 1.25
263 David Noel RC .50 1.25
264 Kevin Pittsnogle RC .60 1.50
265 Shannon Brown RC .60 1.50

2006-07 Topps Black
*1-215 BLACK: 4X TO 10X BASE HI
*216-275 BLACK: 1.5X TO 4X BASE HI
PRINT RUN 99 SER.#'d SETS
8 Kobe Bryant 125.00 300.00
123 LeBron James 125.00 300.00
226 Kyle Lowry 20.00 50.00
251 Rajon Rondo 20.00 50.00

2006-07 Topps Gold
*1-215 GOLD: 1.5X TO 4X BASE HI
*216-275 GOLD: .75X TO 2X BASE HI
PRINT RUN 500 SER.#'d SETS
33A Larry Bird Green jersey, jumper with crowd in background 6.00 15.00
123 LeBron James 60.00 150.00

2006-07 Topps 2K7 Promotion
COMPLETE SET (12) 8.00 20.00
APPROXIMATE ODDS 1:12
1 Allen Iverson 1.50 4.00
2 Dwyane Wade 1.25 3.00
3 Dwight Howard .75 2.00
4 LeBron James 5.00 12.00
5 Yao Ming 1.50 4.00
6 Tim Duncan 1.50 4.00
7 Kobe Bryant 5.00 12.00
8 Steven Nash 1.25 3.00
9 Kevin Garnett 1.50 4.00
10 Ben Wallace .75 2.00
11 Shaquille O'Neal 2.50 6.00
12 Dirk Nowitzki 1.50 4.00

2006-07 Topps Clutch City Prospects
COMPLETE SET (18) 6.00 15.00
STATED ODDS 1:9
1 Andrew Bogut .60 1.50
2 Luther Head .50 1.25
3 Channing Frye .50 1.25
4 Danny Granger .50 1.25
5 Chris Paul 1.50 4.00
6 Sarunas Jasikevicius .60 1.50
7 Nate Robinson .60 1.50
8 Charlie Villanueva .50 1.25
9 Deron Williams .60 1.50
10 Luol Deng .60 1.50
11 T.J. Ford .50 1.25
12 Ben Gordon .60 1.50
13 Devin Harris .50 1.25
14 Dwight Howard 1.00 2.50
15 Andre Iguodala .75 2.00
16 Nenad Krstic .50 1.25
17 Andres Nocioni .50 1.25
18 Delonte West .50 1.25

2006-07 Topps Clutch City Prospects Relics
GROUP A ODDS 1:1500, GROUP B 1:707
*BLACK: .5X TO 1.25X BASE HI
BLACK PRINT RUN 99 SER.#'d SETS
*GOLD: .6X TO 1.5X BASE HI
GOLD PRINT RUN 25 SER.#'d SETS
AB Andrew Bogut B 2.50 6.00
AN Andres Nocioni B 2.00 5.00
BG Ben Gordon B 2.50 6.00
CF Channing Frye B 2.00 5.00
CP Chris Paul B 6.00 15.00
CV Charlie Villanueva B 2.00 5.00
DH Dwight Howard B 4.00 10.00
DW Deron Williams B 2.50 6.00
HW Hakim Warrick B 2.00 5.00
LD Luol Deng B 2.50 6.00
NK Nenad Krstic B 2.00 5.00
NR Nate Robinson B 2.50 6.00
SJ Sarunas Jasikevicius A 2.50 6.00
DWE Delonte West B 2.00 5.00
TJF T.J. Ford B 2.00 5.00

2006-07 Topps Clutch City Stars
COMPLETE SET (24) 12.50 30.00
STATED ODDS 1:7
1 Allen Iverson 1.50 4.00
2 Dwyane Wade 1.25 3.00
3 LeBron James 5.00 12.00
4 Vince Carter 1.25 3.00
5 Shaquille O'Neal 2.50 6.00
6 Ben Wallace .75 2.00
7 Chris Bosh .75 2.00
8 Rasheed Wallace .75 2.00
9 Paul Pierce 1.00 2.50
10 Richard Hamilton .60 1.50
11 Gilbert Arenas .60 1.50
12 Chauncey Billups .75 2.00
13 Kobe Bryant 5.00 12.00
14 Steve Nash 1.25 3.00
15 Tim Duncan 1.50 4.00
16 Tracy McGrady 1.00 2.50
17 Yao Ming 1.50 4.00
18 Tony Parker 1.00 2.50
19 Kevin Garnett 1.50 4.00
20 Ray Allen 1.00 2.50
21 Dirk Nowitzki 1.50 4.00
22 Shawn Marion .60 1.50
23 Elton Brand .50 1.25
24 Pau Gasol .60 1.50

2006-07 Topps Clutch City Stars Relics
GROUP A ODDS: 1:115000, GROUP B 1:8200
GROUP C ODDS 1:1400
*BLACK: .5X TO 1.25X BASE HI
BLACK PRINT RUN 99 SER.#'d SETS
*GOLD: .6X TO 1.5X BASE HI
GOLD PRINT RUN 25 SER.#'d SETS
AI Allen Iverson C 8.00 20.00
BW Ben Wallace C 4.00 10.00
DN Dirk Nowitzki C 8.00 20.00
DW Dwyane Wade C 6.00 15.00
GA Gilbert Arenas C 3.00 8.00
KB Kobe Bryant C 50.00 120.00
KG Kevin Garnett A 8.00 20.00
PP Paul Pierce B 5.00 12.00
RH Richard Hamilton B 3.00 8.00
SN Steve Nash C 6.00 15.00
SO Shaquille O'Neal B 12.00 30.00
TD Tim Duncan C 8.00 20.00
TP Tony Parker C 5.00 12.00
VC Vince Carter C 6.00 15.00
YM Yao Ming A 8.00 20.00
CBI Chauncey Billups B 4.00 10.00

2006-07 Topps Hobby Masters
COMPLETE SET (20) 12.50 30.00
STATED ODDS 1:8
HM1 Kobe Bryant 5.00 12.00
HM2 Shaquille O'Neal 2.50 6.00
HM3 LeBron James 5.00 12.00
HM4 Allen Iverson 1.50 4.00
HM5 Tracy McGrady 1.00 2.50
HM6 Dwyane Wade 1.25 3.00
HM7 Vince Carter 1.25 3.00
HM8 Tim Duncan 1.50 4.00
HM9 Kevin Garnett 1.50 4.00
HM10 Yao Ming 1.50 4.00
HM11 Steve Nash 1.25 3.00
HM12 Carmelo Anthony 1.00 2.50
HM13 Jason Kidd 1.00 2.50
HM14 Jerry West 1.00 2.50
HM15 George Gervin 1.00 2.50
HM16 Larry Bird 2.00 5.00
HM17 Pete Maravich 1.00 2.50
HM18 Wilt Chamberlain 2.00 5.00
HM19 Oscar Robertson 1.50 4.00
HM20 Earl Monroe .60 1.50

2006-07 Topps Larry Bird The Missing Years
COMPLETE SET (10) 25.00 60.00
COMMON CARD (LB82-LB91) 4.00 10.00
STATED ODDS 1:18

2006-07 Topps Marks of Excellence
GROUP A ODDS 1:30000, GROUP B 1:1800
GROUP C ODDS 1:1800, GROUP D 1:1144
AI Allen Iverson D 50.00 120.00
AM Adam Morrison D 8.00 20.00
BH Ben Howland C 6.00 15.00
CB Chris Bosh A 6.00 15.00
DR DaRoc D 5.00 12.00
DW Dwyane Wade B 15.00 40.00
EO Emeka Okafor D 5.00 12.00
FM Streetballer D 5.00 12.00
FT Future D 5.00 12.00
HS Hops D 5.00 12.00
HW Hakim Warrick B 5.00 12.00
JB Jim Boeheim D 10.00 25.00
JC Jim Calhoun C 10.00 25.00
JZ Jay-Z A 800.00 1,500.00
LB Larry Bird B 40.00 100.00
LR Luke Ridnour D 5.00 12.00
LS Lil Scrappy D 5.00 12.00
RC Rodney Carney B 5.00 12.00
SO Shaquille O'Neal B 30.00 80.00
SW Shelden Williams B 5.00 12.00
TE Too EZ D 5.00 12.00
TW The Wizard D 5.00 12.00
WC White Chocolate D 5.00 12.00
BMA Bird Man D 5.00 12.00
DWE Delonte West D 5.00 12.00
JFK JFK D 5.00 12.00
JJR J.J. Redick D 5.00 12.00
JWO John Wooden C 40.00 100.00
RWI Roy Williams C 20.00 50.00

2006-07 Topps Own the Game
COMPLETE SET (28) 15.00 40.00
STATED ODDS 1:6
1 Kobe Bryant 5.00 12.00
2 Allen Iverson 1.50 4.00
3 LeBron James 5.00 12.00
4 Gilbert Arenas .60 1.50
5 Dwyane Wade 1.25 3.00
6 Kevin Garnett 1.50 4.00
7 Dwight Howard .75 2.00
8 Shawn Marion .60 1.50
9 Ben Wallace .75 2.00
10 Tim Duncan 1.50 4.00
11 Steve Nash 1.25 3.00
12 Baron Davis .60 1.50
13 Brevin Knight .40 1.00
14 Chauncey Billups .75 2.00
15 Jason Kidd 1.00 2.50
16 Marcus Camby .50 1.25
17 Andrei Kirilenko .50 1.25
18 Alonzo Mourning 1.00 2.50
19 Josh Smith .40 1.00
20 Elton Brand .50 1.25
21 Gerald Wallace .50 1.25
22 Brevin Knight .40 1.00
23 Chris Paul 1.25 3.00
24 Gilbert Arenas .60 1.50
25 Shawn Marion .60 1.50
26 Chris Paul 1.25 3.00
27 Larry Bird 2.00 5.00
28 Steve Nash 1.25 3.00

2006-07 Topps Own the Game Relics
GROUP A ODDS 1:35000, GROUP B 1:8200
GROUP C ODDS 1:1202, GROUP D 1:658
*BLACK: .5X TO 1.25X BASE HI
BLACK PRINT RUN 99 SER.#'d SETS
*GOLD: .6X TO 1.5X BASE HI
GOLD PRINT RUN 25 SER.#'d SETS
AI Allen Iverson D 8.00 20.00
CP Chris Paul D 6.00 15.00
DH Dwight Howard C 4.00 10.00
DN Dirk Nowitzki C 8.00 20.00
DW Dwyane Wade D 6.00 15.00
EB Elton Brand A 2.50 6.00
JS Josh Smith B 2.00 5.00
KB Kobe Bryant D 50.00 120.00
KG Kevin Garnett D 8.00 20.00
SN Steve Nash D 6.00 15.00
SO Shaquille O'Neal D 12.00 30.00
TD Tim Duncan D 8.00 20.00
TP Tony Parker D 5.00 12.00

2006-07 Topps Pride of the Program
COMPLETE SET (10) 12.50 30.00
STATED ODDS 1:16
PP1 Sheed/Chauncey/Rip 2.00 5.00
PP2 LeBron/Ilgauskas/Hughes 3.00 8.00
PP3 Vince/Kidd/Jefferson 2.00 5.00
PP4 Carmelo/Boykins/Camby 2.00 5.00
PP5 Wade/Walker/Shaq 3.00 8.00
PP6 Iverson/Dalembert/Iggy 2.00 5.00
PP7 Dirk/Terry/Howard 2.00 5.00
PP8 T-Mac/Yao/Head 2.50 6.00
PP9 Kobe/Odom/Bynum 2.50 6.00
PP10 Parker/Ginobili/Duncan 2.50 6.00

2006-07 Topps Pride of the Program Relics
STATED PRINT RUN 99 SER.#'d SETS
BBW Bynum/Kobe/Worthy 50.00 120.00
JPC Big Al/Pierce/Cowens 12.00 30.00
KBM AK-47/Boozer/Malone 8.00 20.00
MMD Yao/T-Mac/Drexler 12.00 30.00
PDG Parker/Duncan/Gervin 15.00 40.00
RFM Robinson/Frye/The Pearl 12.00 30.00

2006-07 Topps Rookie Photo Shoot Autographs
STATED ODDS 1:358
AM Adam Morrison 10.00 25.00
AR Allan Ray 8.00 20.00
CS Craig Smith 10.00 25.00
DN David Noel 8.00 20.00
JB Josh Boone 8.00 20.00
JF Jordan Farmar 10.00 25.00
KL Kyle Lowry 40.00 100.00
MA Maurice Ager 8.00 20.00
MC Mardy Collins 8.00 20.00
MW Marcus Williams 8.00 20.00
PD Paul Davis 8.00 20.00
QD Quincy Douby 8.00 20.00
RB Ronnie Brewer 12.00 30.00
RC Rodney Carney 8.00 20.00
RF Randy Foye 10.00 25.00
RR Rajon Rondo 30.00 80.00
SB Shannon Brown 8.00 20.00
SJ Solomon Jones 8.00 20.00
SN Steve Novak 10.00 25.00
SW Shelden Williams 8.00 20.00
CSI Cedric Simmons 8.00 20.00
DBR Denham Brown 8.00 20.00
DEE Dee Brown 8.00 20.00
HAR Hilton Armstrong 8.00 20.00
JJR J.J. Redick 40.00 100.00
KPI Kevin Pittsnogle 10.00 25.00
RBA Renaldo Balkman 10.00 25.00
SWI Shawne Williams 8.00 20.00

2007-08 Topps
COMPLETE SET (135) 100.00 250.00
1 Amare Stoudemire .50 1.25
2 Joe Johnson .40 1.00
3 Dwyane Wade 1.00 2.50
4 Chris Bosh .60 1.50
5 Jason Kidd .75 2.00
6 Bill Russell 1.50 4.00
7 Jermaine O'Neal .50 1.25
8 Mike Miller .40 1.00
9 Ray Allen .75 2.00
10 Elton Brand .50 1.25
11 Yao Ming 1.25 3.00
12 Al Harrington .40 1.00
13 Steve Nash 1.00 2.50
14 Dwight Howard .60 1.50
15 Carmelo Anthony .75 2.00
16 Pau Gasol .75 2.00
17 Chauncey Billups .60 1.50
18 Antawn Jamison .40 1.00
19 Shane Battier .40 1.00
20 Kevin Garnett 1.25 3.00
21 Tim Duncan 1.25 3.00
22 Michael Redd .40 1.00
23 LeBron James 4.00 10.00
24 Kobe Bryant 4.00 10.00
25 Eddy Curry .30 .75
26 Peja Stojakovic .40 1.00
27 Andrew Bogut .40 1.00
28 Vince Carter 1.00 2.50
29 Corey Maggette .40 1.00
30 Rasheed Wallace .60 1.50
31 Shawn Marion .50 1.25
32 Shaquille O'Neal 2.00 5.00
33 Allen Iverson 1.25 3.00
34 Paul Pierce .75 2.00
35 Adam Morrison .30 .75
36 Tony Parker .75 2.00
37 Mike Bibby .50 1.25
38 Andrea Bargnani .30 .75
39 Luol Deng .40 1.00
40 Chris Paul 1.00 2.50
41 Dirk Nowitzki 1.25 3.00
42 David Lee .30 .75
43 Paul Millsap .40 1.00
44 Danny Granger .30 .75
45 Al Jefferson .30 .75
46 Rafer Alston .50 1.25
47 Andrei Kirilenko .40 1.00
48 Shaun Livingston .40 1.00
49 Chris Wilcox .30 .75
50 Emeka Okafor .40 1.00
51 Zach Randolph .50 1.25
52 Devin Harris .30 .75
53 Mo Williams .40 1.00
54 Leandro Barbosa .40 1.00
55 Smush Parker .30 .75
56 Andre Miller .40 1.00
57 Manu Ginobili 1.00 2.50
58 Jason Richardson .50 1.25
59 Jason Terry .40 1.00
60 Gerald Wallace .40 1.00
61 Richard Hamilton .60 1.50
62 Ricky Davis .40 1.00
63 Boris Diaw .40 1.00
64 Carlos Boozer .40 1.00
65 Rashard Lewis .40 1.00
66 Josh Childress .30 .75
67 Lamar Odom .40 1.00
68 Kyle Korver .50 1.25
69 Stephon Marbury .60 1.50
70 Luke Walton .40 1.00
71 Baron Davis .40 1.00
72 Larry Hughes .40 1.00
73 Jameer Nelson .30 .75
74 Caron Butler .40 1.00
75 Udonis Haslem .30 .75
76 Mike Dunleavy .30 .75
77 Ben Gordon .40 1.00
78 Andrew Bynum .30 .75
79 Hakim Warrick .30 .75
80 Josh Smith .30 .75
81 Mehmet Okur .30 .75
82 J.R. Smith .50 1.25
83 Raymond Felton .40 1.00
84 Chris Webber .60 1.50
85 Jamal Crawford .50 1.25
86 Jarrett Jack .40 1.00
87 Anderson Varejao .30 .75
88 Ryan Gomes .30 .75
89 Charlie Villanueva .30 .75
90 Marcus Camby .40 1.00
91 Kirk Hinrich .50 1.25
92 Tayshaun Prince .50 1.25
93 Ron Artest .50 1.25
94 T.J. Ford .30 .75
95 Richard Jefferson .40 1.00
96 Zydrunas Ilgauskas .40 1.00
97 Josh Howard .40 1.00
98 Monta Ellis .40 1.00
99 Deron Williams .40 1.00
100 Gilbert Arenas .50 1.25
101 Tracy McGrady .75 2.00
102 Steve Blake .30 .75
103 Ben Wallace .60 1.50
104 Kevin Martin .40 1.00
105 Marcus Williams .30 .75
106 J.J. Redick .50 1.25
107 Brandon Roy .60 1.50
108 Desmond Mason .30 .75
109 Randy Foye .40 1.00
110 Andre Iguodala .50 1.25
111 Greg Oden RC .60 1.50
112 Kevin Durant RC 12.00 30.00
113 Al Horford RC 2.00 5.00
114 Mike Conley Jr. RC 2.00 5.00
115 Jeff Green RC .60 1.50
116 Yi Jianlian RC 1.00 2.50
117 Corey Brewer RC .60 1.50
118 Brandan Wright RC .60 1.50
119 Joakim Noah RC .75 2.00
120 Spencer Hawes RC .50 1.25
121 Acie Law RC .50 1.25
122 Thaddeus Young RC .75 2.00
123 Julian Wright RC .50 1.25
124 Al Thornton RC .50 1.25
125 Rodney Stuckey RC .75 2.00
126 Nick Young RC .75 2.00
127 Sean Williams RC .50 1.25
128 Marco Belinelli RC .60 1.50
129 Javaris Crittenton RC .50 1.25
130 Jason Smith RC .50 1.25
131 Daequan Cook RC .60 1.50
132 Jared Dudley RC .60 1.50
133 Wilson Chandler RC .60 1.50
134 Morris Almond RC .50 1.25
135 Aaron Brooks RC .60 1.50

2007-08 Topps Copper
*1-110 COPPER: 5X TO 12X BASE HI
*111-135 COPPER RC: 2.5X TO 6X BASE HI
COPPER PRINT RUN 50 SER.#'d SETS
57 Manu Ginobili 5.00 12.00
101 Tracy McGrady 150.00 400.00
112 Kevin Durant 2,000.00 4,000.00

2007-08 Topps First Edition
*1-110 1st EDITION: 3X TO 8X BASE HI
*111-135 1st ED.RC: 1.5X TO 4X BASE HI
1st EDITION PRINT RUN 119 SER.#'d SETS
23 LeBron James 50.00 120.00
101 Tracy McGrady 100.00 250.00
112 Kevin Durant 1,500.00 3,000.00

2007-08 Topps Gold
*GOLD STARS: 1.25X TO 3X BASE HI
*GOLD RCs: .75X TO 2X BASE HI
PRINT RUN 2007 SER.#'d SETS
23 LeBron James 25.00 60.00
101 Tracy McGrady 20.00 50.00
112 Kevin Durant 800.00 1,500.00

2007-08 Topps 1957-58 Variations
COMPLETE SET (50) 15.00 40.00
ONE VARIATION CARD PER PACK
*1-110 COPPER: 1.25X TO 3X BASE HI
*COPPER RC: 2X TO 5X BASE HI
COPPER PRINT RUN 50 SER.#'d SETS
*1-110 1st ED: .6X TO 1.5X BASE HI
*1st ED.RC: 1.5X TO 4X BASE HI
1st EDITION PRINT RUN 119 SER.#'d SETS
*1-110 GOLD: SAME AS BASE
*GOLD RC: .75X TO 2X BASE HI
GOLD PRINT RUN 2007 SER.#'d SETS
1 Amare Stoudemire .75 2.00
3 Dwyane Wade 1.50 4.00
4 Chris Bosh 1.00 2.50
5 Jason Kidd 1.25 3.00
7 Jermaine O'Neal .75 2.00

11 Yao Ming 2.00 5.00
13 Steve Nash 1.50 4.00
14 Dwight Howard 1.00 2.50
15 Carmelo Anthony 1.25 3.00
17 Chauncey Billups 1.00 2.50
20 Kevin Garnett 2.00 5.00
21 Tim Duncan 2.00 5.00
23 LeBron James 6.00 15.00
24 Kobe Bryant 6.00 15.00
25 Eddy Curry .50 1.25
28 Vince Carter 1.50 4.00
31 Shawn Marion .75 2.00
32 Shaquille O'Neal 3.00 8.00
33 Allen Iverson 2.00 5.00
41 Dirk Nowitzki 2.00 5.00
100 Gilbert Arenas .75 2.00
101 Tracy McGrady 1.25 3.00
104 Kevin Martin .60 1.50
107 Brandon Roy 1.00 2.50
110 Andre Iguodala .75 2.00
111 Greg Oden .75 2.00
112 Kevin Durant 12.00 30.00
113 Al Horford 2.00 5.00
114 Mike Conley Jr. 2.00 5.00
115 Jeff Green .60 1.50
116 Yi Jianlian 1.00 2.50
117 Corey Brewer .60 1.50
118 Brandan Wright .60 1.50
119 Joakim Noah .75 2.00
120 Spencer Hawes .50 1.25
121 Acie Law .50 1.25
122 Thaddeus Young .75 2.00
123 Julian Wright .50 1.25
124 Al Thornton .50 1.25
125 Rodney Stuckey .50 1.25
126 Nick Young .75 2.00
127 Sean Williams .50 1.25
128 Marco Belinelli .60 1.50
129 Javaris Crittenton .50 1.25
130 Jason Smith .50 1.25
131 Daequan Cook .60 1.50
132 Jared Dudley .60 1.50
133 Wilson Chandler .60 1.50
134 Morris Almond .50 1.25
135 Aaron Brooks .60 1.50

2007-08 Topps 1957-58 Variations Autographs
GROUP A ODDS 1:1700; B ODDS 1:325
GROUP C ODDS 1:299; D ODDS 1:285
3 Dwyane Wade A 25.00 60.00
4 Chris Bosh A 10.00 25.00
9 Ray Allen A 10.00 25.00
12 Al Harrington B 4.00 10.00
17 Chauncey Billups B 8.00 20.00
27 Andrew Bogut C 4.00 10.00
28 Vince Carter A 15.00 40.00
29 Corey Maggette D 4.00 10.00
35 Adam Morrison B 4.00 10.00
42 David Lee D 4.00 10.00
43 Paul Millsap A 4.00 10.00
47 Andrei Kirilenko C 4.00 10.00
54 Leandro Barbosa B 4.00 10.00
55 Smush Parker C 4.00 10.00
63 Boris Diaw D 4.00 10.00
64 Carlos Boozer C 4.00 10.00
70 Luke Walton D 4.00 10.00
73 Jameer Nelson B 4.00 10.00
79 Hakim Warrick D 4.00 10.00
86 Jarrett Jack C 4.00 10.00
89 Charlie Villanueva C 4.00 10.00
91 Kirk Hinrich B 4.00 10.00
97 Josh Howard B 4.00 10.00
106 J.J. Redick C 6.00 15.00
110 Andre Iguodala B 5.00 12.00

2007-08 Topps 1957-58 Variations Relics
STATED ODDS 1:71
1 Amare Stoudemire 3.00 8.00
2 Joe Johnson 2.50 6.00
3 Dwyane Wade 6.00 15.00
4 Chris Bosh 4.00 10.00
5 Jason Kidd 5.00 12.00
7 Jermaine O'Neal 3.00 8.00
11 Yao Ming 8.00 20.00
13 Steve Nash 6.00 15.00
14 Dwight Howard 4.00 10.00
17 Chauncey Billups 4.00 10.00
20 Kevin Garnett 8.00 20.00
21 Tim Duncan 8.00 20.00
24 Kobe Bryant 50.00 120.00
28 Vince Carter 6.00 15.00
31 Shawn Marion 3.00 8.00
32 Shaquille O'Neal 12.00 30.00
33 Allen Iverson 8.00 20.00
35 Adam Morrison 2.00 5.00
41 Dirk Nowitzki 8.00 20.00
61 Richard Hamilton 3.00 8.00
74 Caron Butler 2.50 6.00
91 Kirk Hinrich 3.00 8.00
101 Tracy McGrady 5.00 12.00
104 Kevin Martin 2.50 6.00
107 Brandon Roy 4.00 10.00

2007-08 Topps 50th Anniversary
1 Tim Duncan .50 1.25
2 Dirk Nowitzki .50 1.25
3 Greg Oden .20 .50
4 Moses Malone .30 .75
5 Bill Walton .25 .60
6 Dwyane Wade .40 1.00
7 Carmelo Anthony .30 .75
8 Chris Bosh .25 .60
9 Clyde Drexler .30 .75
10 Kevin McHale .25 .60
11 James Worthy .30 .75
12 Bill Russell .60 1.50
13 David Robinson .40 1.00
14 Shaquille O'Neal .75 2.00
15 Dwight Howard .25 .60
16 Elgin Baylor .20 .50
17 Dominique Wilkins .30 .75
18 Isiah Thomas .20 .50
19 Magic Johnson .75 2.00
20 Larry Bird .75 2.00
21 Gilbert Arenas .20 .50
22 Kobe Bryant 1.50 4.00
23 Allen Iverson .50 1.25
24 Tom Chambers .20 .50
25 Mitch Richmond .20 .50
26 Chris Mullin .25 .60
27 Rick Barry .15 .40
28 John Stockton .40 1.00
29 Dennis Rodman .50 1.25
30 Jason Kidd .30 .75
31 Yao Ming .50 1.25
32 Steve Nash .40 1.00
33 Walt Frazier .30 .75
34 George Gervin .25 .60
35 Karl Malone .25 .60
36 Ray Allen .30 .75
37 Vince Carter .40 1.00
38 Paul Pierce .30 .75
39 Tracy McGrady .30 .75
40 Kevin Garnett .50 1.25
41 Amare Stoudemire .20 .50
42 Wes Unseld .25 .60
43 Oscar Robertson .20 .50
44 Earl Monroe .20 .50
45 Wilt Chamberlain .60 1.50
46 Hakeem Olajuwon .40 1.00
47 Patrick Ewing .25 .60
48 Jerry West .50 1.25
49 Julius Erving .50 1.25
50 Pete Maravich .50 1.25

2007-08 Topps Bill Russell The Missing Years
COMPLETE SET (11) 10.00 25.00
COMMON CARD (BR58-BR69) 2.00 5.00
STATED ODDS 1:9
AUTOGRAPH ODDS 1:90000

2007-08 Topps Generation Now
COMPLETE SET (30) 6.00 15.00
STATED ODDS 1:3
GN1 LeBron James 2.50 6.00
GN2 Carmelo Anthony .50 1.25
GN3 Dwyane Wade .60 1.50
GN4 Chris Bosh .40 1.00
GN5 Josh Howard .25 .60
GN6 Dwight Howard .40 1.00
GN7 Emeka Okafor .25 .60
GN8 Ben Gordon .25 .60
GN9 Andre Iguodala .30 .75
GN10 Josh Smith .20 .50
GN11 Kevin Martin .25 .60
GN12 Chris Paul .60 1.50
GN13 Deron Williams .25 .60
GN14 Raymond Felton .25 .60
GN15 Marvin Williams .25 .60
GN16 David Lee .20 .50
GN17 Andrew Bynum .20 .50
GN18 Monta Ellis .25 .60
GN19 Jarrett Jack .25 .60
GN20 Hakim Warrick .20 .50
GN21 Ryan Gomes .20 .50
GN22 Sean May .20 .50
GN23 Charlie Villanueva .20 .50
GN24 Luke Walton .20 .50
GN25 Boris Diaw .25 .60
GN26 Brandon Roy .40 1.00
GN27 Andrea Bargnani .20 .50
GN28 Randy Foye .25 .60
GN29 Marcus Williams .20 .50
GN30 Adam Morrison .20 .50

2007-08 Topps Generation Now Relics
STATED ODDS 1:71
GNRAB Andrew Bynum 2.00 5.00
GNRAI Andre Iguodala 3.00 8.00
GNRAM Adam Morrison 2.00 5.00
GNRBD Boris Diaw 2.50 6.00
GNRBG Ben Gordon 2.50 6.00
GNRBR Brandon Roy 4.00 10.00
GNRCA Carmelo Anthony 5.00 12.00
GNRCB Chris Bosh 4.00 10.00
GNRCP Chris Paul 6.00 15.00
GNRCV Charlie Villanueva 2.00 5.00
GNRDH Dwight Howard 4.00 10.00
GNRDW Dwyane Wade 6.00 15.00
GNREO Emeka Okafor 2.50 6.00
GNRHW Hakim Warrick 2.00 5.00
GNRJH Josh Howard 2.50 6.00
GNRJJ Jarrett Jack 2.50 6.00
GNRJS Josh Smith 2.00 5.00
GNRLW Luke Walton 2.50 6.00
GNRME Monta Ellis 2.50 6.00
GNRMW Marcus Williams 2.00 5.00
GNRRF Raymond Felton 2.50 6.00
GNRSM Sean May 2.00 5.00
GNRABA Andrea Bargnani 2.00 5.00
GNRDWI Deron Williams 2.50 6.00
GNRRFO Randy Foye 2.50 6.00

2007-08 Topps Mini Exclusives
ONE PER RIP CARD
MEAI Allen Iverson 8.00 20.00
MEBR Bill Russell 10.00 25.00
MEBW Bill Walton 4.00 10.00
MECA Carmelo Anthony 5.00 12.00
MECD Clyde Drexler 5.00 12.00
MECM Chris Mullin 4.00 10.00
MEDH Dwight Howard 4.00 10.00
MEDN Dirk Nowitzki 8.00 20.00
MEDR Dennis Rodman 8.00 20.00
MEEB Elgin Baylor 3.00 8.00
MEEM Earl Monroe 3.00 8.00
MEGA Gilbert Arenas 3.00 8.00
MEGG George Gervin 4.00 10.00
MEIT Isiah Thomas 3.00 8.00
MEJE Julius Erving 8.00 20.00
MEJH Josh Howard 3.00 8.00
MEJK Jason Kidd 5.00 12.00
MEJS John Stockton 6.00 15.00
MEJW James Worthy 5.00 12.00
MEKB Kobe Bryant 25.00 60.00
MEKG Kevin Garnett 8.00 20.00
MEKM Karl Malone 4.00 10.00
MELB Leandro Barbosa 3.00 8.00
MELB Larry Bird 12.00 30.00
MEOR Oscar Robertson 3.00 8.00
MERB Rick Barry 2.50 6.00
MESN Steve Nash 6.00 15.00
METD Tim Duncan 8.00 20.00
MEVC Vince Carter 6.00 15.00
MEWC Wilt Chamberlain 10.00 25.00
MEAIG Andre Iguodala 3.00 8.00
MEDWI Dominique Wilkins 5.00 12.00

2007-08 Topps Mini Exclusives Autographs
MEDR Dennis Rodman 75.00 150.00
MEEB Elgin Baylor 10.00 25.00
MEJH Josh Howard 8.00 20.00
MEAIG Andre Iguodala 10.00 25.00
MEDWI Dominique Wilkins 15.00 40.00

2007-08 Topps Own the Game
COMPLETE SET (9) 6.00 15.00
STATED ODDS 1:11
OTG1 Mikki Moore .60 1.50
OTG2 Kyle Korver 1.00 2.50
OTG3 Jason Kapono .60 1.50
OTG4 Kevin Garnett 2.50 6.00
OTG5 Steve Nash 2.00 5.00
OTG6 Baron Davis .75 2.00
OTG7 Marcus Camby .75 2.00
OTG8 Kobe Bryant 8.00 20.00
OTG9 Jason Kidd 1.50 4.00

2007-08 Topps Rip Card Combinations
*RIPPED CARDS: HALF VALUE
PRINT RUN 99 SER.#'d SETS
VALUES FOR UNRIPPED CARDS
RIP1 James/Anthony/Wade 20.00 50.00
RIP2 Arenas/Iverson/Bryant 20.00 40.00
RIP3 Nash/Maravich/Kidd 20.00 50.00
RIP4 Howard/Duncan/Garnett 20.00 40.00
RIP5 Nowitzki/Garnett/Brand 20.00 40.00
RIP6 Bird/Erving/Johnson 30.00 60.00
RIP8 Russell/O'Neal/Chamberlain 30.00 80.00
RIP9 Rodman/Artest/Wallace 20.00 40.00
RIP10 Walton/Ming/Robinson 20.00 40.00
RIP11 Wilkins/Carter/Drexler 20.00 40.00
RIP12 Johnson/Thomas/Stockton 25.00 50.00
RIP13 Allen/Mullin/Nowitzki 12.00 30.00
RIP14 Robinson/Stoudemire/Malone 12.00 30.00
RIP15 Bryant/McGrady/James 75.00 200.00
RIP16 Monroe/Iverson/Robertson 12.00 30.00
RIP17 Smith/Gervin/Marion 12.00 30.00
RIP18 O'Neal/Worthy/Garnett 20.00 40.00
RIP19 O'Neal/Rodman/Malone 25.00 50.00
RIP20 Erving/Wade/Johnson 20.00 40.00
RIP21 Hill/Williams/Jamison 12.00 30.00
RIP22 Paul/Gordon/Iverson 25.00 60.00
RIP23 Bird/Johnson/Wade 25.00 60.00
RIP24 Erving/Bryant/Robertson 25.00 60.00
RIP25 Kidd/Stockton/Nash 25.00 50.00
RIP26 Arenas/Anthony/Pierce 20.00 40.00
RIP27 Mullin/Barry/Bird 20.00 40.00
RIP28 Ellis/Felton/Johnson 12.00 30.00
RIP30 Camby/Okafor/O'Neal 12.00 30.00
RIP31 Williams/Maravich/Stockton 25.00 50.00
RIP32 Erving/James/Wilkins 30.00 60.00
RIP33 Redd/Allen/Pierce 20.00 40.00
RIP35 Smith/Richardson/Mason 12.00 30.00
RIP36 Stoudemire/Gasol/Brand 12.00 30.00
RIP37 Marbury/Wade/Kidd 20.00 40.00
RIP38 James/O'Neal/Bryant 30.00 80.00

2007-08 Topps Rookie Photo Shoot Autographs
STATED ODDS 1:381
AA Arron Afflalo 6.00 15.00
AB Aaron Brooks 6.00 15.00
AG Aaron Gray 5.00 12.00
AT Al Thornton 5.00 12.00
BW Brandan Wright 6.00 15.00
CL Carl Landry 5.00 12.00
DB Derrick Byars 5.00 12.00
DC Daequan Cook 6.00 15.00
DM Dominic McGuire 5.00 12.00
GD Glen Davis 6.00 15.00
GO Greg Oden 12.00 30.00
GP Gabe Pruitt 5.00 12.00
HH Herbert Hill 5.00 12.00
JC Javaris Crittenton 5.00 12.00
JD Jared Dudley 6.00 15.00
JJ Jared Jordan 5.00 12.00
JM Josh McRoberts 5.00 12.00
JS Jason Smith 5.00 12.00
MA Morris Almond 5.00 12.00
MW Marcus Williams 5.00 12.00
NF Nick Fazekas 5.00 12.00
NY Nick Young 8.00 20.00
RS Rodney Stuckey 8.00 20.00
RT Reyshawn Terry 5.00 12.00
SH Spencer Hawes 5.00 12.00
SL Stephane Lasme 5.00 12.00
SW Sean Williams 5.00 12.00
TG Taurean Green 5.00 12.00
TY Thaddeus Young 8.00 20.00
WC Wilson Chandler 6.00 15.00
AL4 Acie Law 5.00 12.00
ATU Alando Tucker 5.00 12.00
JDA Jermareo Davidson 5.00 12.00

2007-08 Topps Rookie Photo Shoot Autographs Dual
STATED ODDS 1:2500
BL A.Brooks/A.Law 15.00 40.00
DB G.Davis/D.Byars 15.00 40.00
MH J.McRoberts/S.Hawes 15.00 40.00
OW G.Oden/B.Wright 30.00 80.00
SA R.Stuckey/A.Afflalo 15.00 40.00
SF J.Smith/N.Fazekas 15.00 40.00
TC A.Thornton/W.Chandler 15.00 40.00
WD S.Williams/J.Dudley 15.00 40.00
YP N.Young/G.Pruitt 15.00 40.00

2007-08 Topps Rookie Photo Shoot Autographs Triple
STATED ODDS 1:26000
BCA Brooks/Crittenton/Afflalo 20.00 50.00
CLY Cook/Law/Young 20.00 50.00
HFS Hawes/Fazekas/Smith 20.00 50.00
OYW Oden/Young/Wright 40.00 100.00
WTD Williams/Thornton/Dudley 20.00 50.00

2007-08 Topps Rookie Set
COMPLETE SET (1-14) 30.00 80.00
1 Greg Oden .50 1.25
2 Kevin Durant 12.00 30.00
3 Al Horford 1.25 3.00
4 Mike Conley Jr. 1.25 3.00
5 Jeff Green .40 1.00
6 Yi Jianlian .60 1.50
7 Corey Brewer .40 1.00
8 Brandan Wright .40 1.00
9 Joakim Noah .50 1.25
10 Spencer Hawes .30 .75
11 Acie Law .30 .75
12 Thaddeus Young .50 1.25
13 Julian Wright .30 .75
14 Al Thornton .30 .75

2007-08 Topps Rookie Set Orange
COMPLETE SET (14) 60.00 150.00
*SAME VALUE AS REGULAR
2 Kevin Durant 100.00 250.00

2008-09 Topps Black
*1-195 BLACK: 40X TO 100X BASE HI
*196-220 RC BLACK: 25X TO 60X BASE HI
PRINT RUN 51 SER.#'d SETS

2008-09 Topps Gold Border
*GOLD BORDER: 1.25X TO 3X BASE HI
1-195 GOLD STATED ODDS 1:7
196-220 GOLD STATED ODDS 1:44

2008-09 Topps Gold Foil
*STARS: .75X TO 2X BASE HI
*RCs: .6X TO 1.5X BASE HI
1-195 GOLD FOIL ODDS 1:2
196-220 GOLD FOIL ODDS 1:11
23 LeBron James 60.00 150.00

2008-09 Topps Orange
*ORANGE: 1.5X TO 4X BASE HI
ORANGE PRINT RUN 1199 SETS

2008-09 Topps 1958-59 Variations
STATED ODDS 1:2
*GOLD: 1.5X TO 4X BASE HI
GOLD PRINT RUN 50 SER.#'d SETS
1 Chris Paul 1.50 4.00
5 Kevin Garnett 2.00 5.00
8 Carlos Boozer .60 1.50
10 Gilbert Arenas .75 2.00
12 Dwight Howard 1.00 2.50
15 Carmelo Anthony 1.00 2.50
23 LeBron James 8.00 20.00
24 Kobe Bryant 8.00 20.00
60 Baron Davis .75 2.00
100 Dwyane Wade 1.50 4.00
147 Brandon Roy .60 1.50
166 John Stockton 1.50 4.00
170 David Thompson .75 2.00
172 Larry Bird 2.50 6.00
173 Isiah Thomas 1.25 3.00
174 Magic Johnson 2.50 6.00
175 Bill Russell 2.50 6.00
179 David Robinson 1.50 4.00
180 Jerry West 1.50 4.00
183 Lenny Wilkens .75 2.00
196 Derrick Rose 6.00 15.00
197 Michael Beasley .75 2.00
198 O.J. Mayo .60 1.50
199 Russell Westbrook 8.00 20.00
200 Kevin Love 1.50 4.00
201 Danilo Gallinari 1.25 3.00
202 Eric Gordon 1.25 3.00
203 Joe Alexander .50 1.25
204 D.J. Augustin .75 2.00
205 Brook Lopez 1.00 2.50

2008-09 Topps 1958-59 Variations Gold
23 LeBron James 75.00 200.00
24 Kobe Bryant 75.00 200.00

2008-09 Topps 1958-59 Variations Autographs
GROUP A ODDS 1:3422; B ODDS 1:1665
GROUP C ODDS 1:846; D ODDS 1:1118
GROUP E ODDS 1:850; F ODDS 1:398
*GOLD: .5X TO 1.25X BASE HI
GOLD PRINT RUN 25 SER.#'d SETS
1 Chris Paul A 40.00 100.00
8 Carlos Boozer C 5.00 12.00
10 Gilbert Arenas C 8.00 20.00
12 Dwight Howard B 10.00 25.00
39 Daniel Gibson D 5.00 12.00
60 Baron Davis C 6.00 15.00
65 Rajon Rondo E 10.00 25.00
100 Dwyane Wade A 40.00 100.00
102 Ryan Gomes E 5.00 12.00
112 Mo Williams D 5.00 12.00
165 Greg Oden A 15.00 40.00
167 Tim Hardaway F 6.00 15.00
170 David Thompson F 5.00 12.00
171 Spencer Haywood B 6.00 15.00
172 Larry Bird A 50.00 120.00
174 Magic Johnson A 50.00 120.00
177 Sidney Moncrief F 5.00 12.00
182 Sam Perkins B 5.00 12.00
183 Lenny Wilkens B 8.00 20.00
184 Jo Jo White B 8.00 20.00
185 Elgin Baylor C 15.00 40.00
186 Micheal Ray Richardson B 5.00 12.00
187 Otis Birdsong B 5.00 12.00
188 Derrick Coleman F 5.00 12.00
189 Mark Eaton B 5.00 12.00

2008-09 Topps 1958-59 Variations Relics
GROUP A ODDS 1:5197; B ODDS 1:437
GROUP C ODDS 1:60
*GOLD: .6X TO 1.5X BASE HI
GOLD PRINT RUN 50 SER.#'d SETS
1 Chris Paul C 5.00 12.00
5 Kevin Garnett C 6.00 15.00
8 Carlos Boozer C 2.00 5.00
10 Gilbert Arenas B 2.50 6.00
12 Dwight Howard C 3.00 8.00
15 Carmelo Anthony C 3.00 8.00
24 Kobe Bryant C 40.00 100.00
39 Daniel Gibson C 1.50 4.00
60 Baron Davis C 2.50 6.00
65 Rajon Rondo C 3.00 8.00
100 Dwyane Wade C 5.00 12.00
102 Ryan Gomes C 2.00 5.00
112 Mo Williams C 2.00 5.00
147 Brandon Roy C 2.00 5.00
165 Greg Oden C 1.50 4.00
166 John Stockton C 5.00 12.00
170 David Thompson B 2.50 6.00
172 Larry Bird B 8.00 20.00
173 Isiah Thomas B 3.00 8.00
174 Magic Johnson C 8.00 20.00
175 Bill Russell A 8.00 20.00
178 George Gervin C 3.00 8.00
179 David Robinson C 5.00 12.00
180 Jerry West A 8.00 20.00

2008-09 Topps In the Genes
STATED ODDS 1:9
*GOLD: .75X TO 2X BASE HI
GOLD PRINT RUN 50 SER.#'d SETS
IG1 K.Bryant/J.Bryant 2.50 6.00
IG2 C.Karl/G.Karl 1.50 4.00
IG3 K.Love/S.Love 2.00 5.00
IG4 M.Dunleavy Jr./M.Dunleavy Sr. 1.50 4.00
IG5 S.May/S.May 1.50 4.00
IG6 B.Barry/R.Barry 1.50 4.00
IG7 M.Bibby/H.Bibby 1.50 4.00
IG8 D.Wilkins/D.Wilkins 1.50 4.00
IG9 L.Walton/B.Walton 2.00 5.00
IG10 T.Green/S.Green 1.50 4.00

2008-09 Topps McDonald's All American Autographs
STATED ODDS 1:5908
B13 Darrell Arthur 10.00 25.00
B14 D.J. Augustin 12.00 30.00
B22 Brook Lopez 20.00 50.00
B23 Robin Lopez 10.00 25.00
DG Donte Greene 8.00 20.00
DR Derrick Rose 350.00 700.00
EG Eric Gordon 50.00 125.00
JB Jerryd Bayless 10.00 25.00
JJH J.J. Hickson 8.00 20.00
KK Kosta Koufos 8.00 20.00
KL Kevin Love 125.00 250.00
MB Michael Beasley 40.00 100.00
OJM O.J. Mayo 40.00 100.00

2008-09 Topps Mini Exclusives
MINIS INSERTED IN RIP CARDS
MEAI Allen Iverson 2.00 5.00
MEAJ Al Jefferson .60 1.50
MEBG Ben Gordon .75 2.00
MEBR Brandon Roy .75 2.00
MECA Carmelo Anthony 1.25 3.00
MECB Carlos Boozer .75 2.00
MECBI Chauncey Billups 1.25 3.00
MECM Corey Maggette .75 2.00
MECP Chris Paul 2.00 5.00
MEDH Dwight Howard 1.25 3.00
MEDL David Lee .60 1.50
MEDN Dirk Nowitzki 2.50 6.00
MEDR Dennis Rodman 2.00 5.00
MEDW Dwyane Wade 2.00 5.00
MEGA Gilbert Arenas 1.00 2.50
MEGO Greg Oden .60 1.50
MEJR Jason Richardson 1.00 2.50
MEJW Jerry West 2.00 5.00
MEKB Kobe Bryant 8.00 20.00
MELB Larry Bird 3.00 8.00
MELJ LeBron James 8.00 20.00
MEMJ Magic Johnson 3.00 8.00
MEMR Michael Redd .75 2.00
MENY Nick Young .60 1.50
MERA Ray Allen 1.50 4.00
MESN Steve Nash 2.00 5.00
MESO Shaquille O'Neal 3.00 8.00
METP Tony Parker 1.25 3.00
MEYJ Yi Jianlian 1.25 3.00
MEYM Yao Ming 2.50 6.00

2008-09 Topps Mini Exclusives Autographs
MEACP Chris Paul 25.00 60.00

2008-09 Topps Own the Game
COMPLETE SET (20) 8.00 20.00
STATED ODDS 1:5
*GOLD: .75X TO 2X BASE HI
GOLD PRINT RUN 50 SER.#'d SETS
OTG1 Andris Biedrins .50 1.25
OTG2 Tyson Chandler .60 1.50
OTG3 Peja Stojakovic .60 1.50
OTG4 Chauncey Billups 1.00 2.50
OTG5 Jason Kapono .50 1.25
OTG6 Steve Nash 1.50 4.00
OTG7 Dwight Howard 1.00 2.50
OTG8 Marcus Camby .60 1.50
OTG9 Chris Paul 1.50 4.00
OTG10 Steve Nash 1.50 4.00
OTG11 Chris Paul 1.50 4.00
OTG12 Baron Davis .75 2.00
OTG13 Marcus Camby .60 1.50
OTG14 Josh Smith .50 1.25
OTG15 LeBron James 6.00 15.00
OTG16 Kobe Bryant 6.00 15.00
OTG17 Dwight Howard 1.00 2.50
OTG18 Chris Paul 1.50 4.00
OTG19 Allen Iverson 1.50 4.00
OTG20 Joe Johnson .75 2.00

2008-09 Topps Own the Game Relics
STATED ODDS 1:134
*GOLD: .5X TO 1.25X BASE HI
GOLD PRINT RUN 50 SER.#'d SETS
OTGR1 Andris Biedrins 2.00 5.00
OTGR2 Peja Stojakovic 2.00 5.00
OTGR3 Jason Kapono 2.00 5.00
OTGR4 Dwight Howard 3.00 8.00
OTGR5 Chris Paul 5.00 12.00
OTGR6 Baron Davis 2.50 6.00
OTGR7 Marcus Camby 2.00 5.00
OTGR8 Kobe Bryant 40.00 100.00
OTGR9 Dwight Howard 3.00 8.00
OTGR10 Allen Iverson 5.00 12.00

2008-09 Topps Retail Relics
TBKR1 Daequan Cook 2.00 5.00
TBKR2 Andrea Bargnani 2.00 5.00
TBKR3 LaMarcus Aldridge 2.50 6.00
TBKR4 Andrew Bynum 1.50 4.00
TBKR5 Caron Butler 2.00 5.00
TBKR6 Chris Bosh 3.00 8.00
TBKR7 Corey Brewer 2.00 5.00
TBKR8 Corey Maggette 2.00 5.00
TBKR9 Rashad McCants 2.00 5.00
TBKR10 Zach Randolph 2.50 6.00
TBKR11 Martell Webster 2.00 5.00
TBKR12 Dwight Howard 3.00 8.00
TBKR13 Eddy Curry 2.00 5.00
TBKR14 Gilbert Arenas 2.50 6.00
TBKR15 Greg Oden 1.50 4.00
TBKR16 Jamal Crawford 2.50 6.00
TBKR17 Ronnie Brewer 1.50 4.00
TBKR18 Juan Carlos Navarro 2.00 5.00
TBKR19 Joe Johnson 2.50 6.00
TBKR20 Brandan Wright 1.50 4.00
TBKR21 Kirk Hinrich 2.00 5.00
TBKR22 Lamar Odom 2.00 5.00
TBKR23 Mehmet Okur 2.00 5.00
TBKR24 Glen Davis 1.50 4.00
TBKR25 Monta Ellis 2.00 5.00
TBKR26 Paul Pierce 4.00 10.00
TBKR27 Peja Stojakovic 2.00 5.00
TBKR28 Yao Ming 6.00 15.00
TBKR29 Richard Hamilton 2.50 6.00
TBKR30 Ron Artest 2.50 6.00
TBKR31 Shawn Marion 2.50 6.00
TBKR32 Jarrett Jack 2.00 5.00
TBKR33 Tim Duncan 6.00 15.00
TBKR34 Vince Carter 5.00 12.00
TBKR35 Yi Jianlian 3.00 8.00

2008-09 Topps Rip Cards 99
PRINT RUN 99 SER.#'d SETS
*RIP 25: .5X TO 1.25X BASE HI
1 Chris Paul 10.00 25.00
2 Allen Iverson 10.00 25.00
3 Tony Parker 6.00 15.00
4 LeBron James 15.00 40.00
5 Kobe Bryant 10.00 25.00
6 Shaquille O'Neal 15.00 40.00
7 Larry Bird 15.00 40.00
8 Magic Johnson 10.00 25.00
9 Carlos Boozer 4.00 10.00
10 Jason Kidd 10.00 25.00
11 Chauncey Billups 6.00 15.00
12 Jason Richardson 5.00 12.00
13 Corey Maggette 4.00 10.00
14 David Lee 5.00 12.00
15 Dwyane Wade 10.00 25.00
16 Greg Oden 3.00 8.00
17 Yi Jianlian 6.00 15.00
18 Nick Young 5.00 12.00
19 Dennis Rodman 6.00 15.00
20 Ray Allen 6.00 15.00
21 Steve Nash 6.00 15.00
23 Michael Redd 4.00 10.00
24 Jerry West 10.00 25.00
25 Gilbert Arenas 5.00 12.00
26 Dwight Howard 6.00 15.00
27 Yao Ming 12.00 30.00
28 Carmelo Anthony 6.00 15.00
29 Ben Gordon 4.00 10.00
30 Dirk Nowitzki 12.00 30.00

2008-09 Topps Rookie Medallions
PRINT RUN 15 SER.#'d SETS
14KAR Anthony Randolph 12.00 30.00
14KBL Brook Lopez 25.00 60.00
14KBR Brandon Rush 12.00 30.00
14KDA Darrell Arthur 15.00 40.00
14KDG Danilo Gallinari 30.00 80.00
14KDJA D.J. Augustin 20.00 50.00
14KDR Derrick Rose 80.00 200.00
14KEG Eric Gordon 30.00 80.00
14KJA Joe Alexander 12.00 30.00
14KJB Jerryd Bayless 15.00 40.00
14KKL Kevin Love 40.00 100.00
14KMB Michael Beasley 20.00 50.00
14KOJM O.J. Mayo 15.00 40.00
14KRL Robin Lopez 15.00 40.00
14KRW Russell Westbrook 100.00 250.00

2008-09 Topps Rookie Photo Shoot Autographs
STATED ODDS 1:240 PACKS
*RED INK: .5X TO 1.25X BASE HI
RED INK STATED ODDS 1:243 PACKS
RPAR Anthony Randolph 4.00 10.00
RPBL Brook Lopez 8.00 20.00
RPBR Brandon Rush 4.00 10.00
RPCDR Chris Douglas-Roberts 4.00 10.00
RPCL Courtney Lee 5.00 12.00
RPDA Darrell Arthur 5.00 12.00
RPDGR Donte Greene 4.00 10.00
RPDJ DeAndre Jordan 12.00 30.00
RPDJA D.J. Augustin 6.00 15.00
RPDJW D.J. White 4.00 10.00
RPDR Derrick Rose 40.00 100.00
RPEG Eric Gordon 15.00 40.00
RPGH George Hill 6.00 15.00
RPJA Joe Alexander 4.00 10.00
RPJB Jerryd Bayless 5.00 12.00
RPJD Joey Dorsey 4.00 10.00
RPJH J.J. Hickson 4.00 10.00
RPJM JaVale McGee 6.00 15.00
RPJRG J.R. Giddens 4.00 10.00
RPJT Jason Thompson 4.00 10.00
RPKK Kosta Koufos 4.00 10.00
RPKL Kevin Love 40.00 100.00
RPKW Kyle Weaver 4.00 10.00
RPMB Michael Beasley 12.00 30.00
RPMC Mario Chalmers 6.00 15.00
RPMS Marreese Speights 5.00 12.00
RPOJM O.J. Mayo 15.00 40.00
RPPE Patrick Ewing Jr. 4.00 10.00
RPRA Ryan Anderson 5.00 12.00
RPRH Roy Hibbert 12.00 30.00
RPRL Robin Lopez 5.00 12.00
RPRW Russell Westbrook 400.00 800.00
RPSW Sonny Weems 4.00 10.00
RPWS Walter Sharpe 4.00 10.00

2008-09 Topps Rookie Photo Shoot Autographs Dual
STATED ODDS 1:1461
RPDAA R.Anderson/J.Alexander 12.00 30.00
RPDBL M.Beasley/K.Love 30.00 80.00
RPDGA E.Gordon/D.Augustin 12.00 30.00
RPDGB E.Gordon/J.Bayless 12.00 30.00
RPDGW E.Gordon/D.White 12.00 30.00
RPDHK J.Hickson/K.Koufos 12.00 30.00
RPDLL B.Lopez/R.Lopez 12.00 30.00
RPDMB O.Mayo/M.Beasley 15.00 40.00
RPDML O.Mayo/K.Love 30.00 80.00
RPDRB D.Rose/M.Beasley 40.00 100.00
RPDRC B.Rush/M.Chalmers 15.00 40.00
RPDRL D.Rose/K.Love 75.00 200.00
RPDRM D.Rose/O.Mayo 40.00 100.00
RPDTR J.Thompson/A.Randolph 12.00 30.00
RPDWB R.Westbrook/J.Bayless 50.00 125.00

2008-09 Topps Rookie Photo Shoot Autographs Dual Red
*RED: .5X TO 1.25X HI COLUMN
OVERALL STATED ODDS 1:243
RPDRL D.Rose/K.Love 200.00 350.00

2008-09 Topps Rookie Photo Shoot Autographs Triple
STATED ODDS 1:5908
RPTABS Alexander/Love/Speights 25.00 60.00
RPTBLR Beasley/Love/Rose 100.00 200.00
RPTDRD Dorsey/Rose/D-Roberts 60.00 150.00
RPTGBW Grdn/Bylss/Wstbrk 50.00 120.00
RPTLKL Lopez/Koufos/Lopez 10.00 25.00
RPTMBA Mayo/Bayless/Augustin 10.00 25.00
RPTRAC Rush/Arthur/Chalmers 10.00 25.00
RPTRBM Rose/Beasley/Mayo 125.00 250.00

2008-09 Topps Rookie Photo Shoot Autographs Triple Red
*RED: .4X TO 1X HI COLUMN
OVERALL STATED ODDS 1:5908

2009-10 Topps
COMPLETE SET (330) 600.00 1,200.00
COMP.SET w/o RCs (315) 40.00 100.00
1 Joe Johnson .50 1.25
2 Josh Smith .30 .75
3 Mike Bibby .50 1.25
4 Marvin Williams .30 .75
5 Al Horford .50 1.25
6 Ronald Murray .30 .75
7 Zaza Pachulia .30 .75
8 Acie Law .30 .75
9 Solomon Jones .30 .75
10 Maurice Evans .30 .75
11 Mario West .30 .75
12 Paul Pierce .75 2.00
13 Ray Allen .75 2.00
14 Kevin Garnett 1.25 3.00
15 Rajon Rondo .60 1.50
16 Eddie House .30 .75
17 Kendrick Perkins .30 .75
18 Tony Allen .30 .75
19 Leon Powe .30 .75
20 Glen Davis .30 .75
21 Brian Scalabrine .30 .75
22 Stephon Marbury .60 1.50
23 Gerald Wallace .40 1.00
24 Boris Diaw .40 1.00
25 Emeka Okafor .40 1.00
26 Raymond Felton .30 .75
27 Raja Bell .40 1.00
28 D.J. Augustin .30 .75
29 Vladimir Radmanovic .30 .75
30 Sean Singletary .30 .75
31 DeSagana Diop .30 .75
32 Ben Gordon .40 1.00
33 Derrick Rose .75 2.00
34 Luol Deng .40 1.00
35 John Salmons .40 1.00
36 Tim Thomas .30 .75
37 Brad Miller .40 1.00
38 Kirk Hinrich .40 1.00
39 Tyrus Thomas .30 .75
40 Joakim Noah .30 .75
41 Aaron Gray .30 .75
42 LeBron James 8.00 20.00
43 Mo Williams .40 1.00
44 Zydrunas Ilgauskas .40 1.00
45 Delonte West .30 .75
46 Anderson Varejao .30 .75
47 Daniel Gibson .30 .75
48 Ben Wallace .60 1.50
49 J.J. Hickson .30 .75
50 Wally Szczerbiak .40 1.00
51 Aleksandar Pavlovic .30 .75
52 Dirk Nowitzki 1.25 3.00
53 Jason Terry .40 1.00
54 Josh Howard .40 1.00
55 Jason Kidd .75 2.00
56 Brandon Bass .30 .75
57 Jose Barea .50 1.25
58 Antoine Wright .30 .75
59 Gerald Green .40 1.00
60 Erick Dampier .30 .75
61 Devean George .30 .75
62 Carmelo Anthony .75 2.00
63 Chauncey Billups .60 1.50
64 Nene .40 1.00
65 J.R. Smith .50 1.25
66 Kenyon Martin .40 1.00
67 Linas Kleiza .30 .75
68 Dahntay Jones .30 .75
69 Chris Andersen .50 1.25
70 Renaldo Balkman .30 .75
71 Anthony Carter .30 .75
72 Allen Iverson 1.00 2.50
73 Richard Hamilton .50 1.25
74 Tayshaun Prince .50 1.25
75 Rodney Stuckey .30 .75
76 Rasheed Wallace .60 1.50
77 Antonio McDyess .40 1.00
78 Jason Maxiell .30 .75
79 Arron Afflalo .30 .75
80 Amir Johnson .30 .75
81 Walter Herrmann .30 .75
82 Stephen Jackson .40 1.00
83 Corey Maggette .40 1.00
84 Jamal Crawford .50 1.25
85 Kelenna Azubuike .30 .75
86 Monta Ellis .40 1.00
87 Andris Biedrins .30 .75
88 Marco Belinelli .30 .75
89 C.J. Watson .30 .75
90 Anthony Morrow .30 .75
91 Brandan Wright .30 .75
92 Anthony Randolph .30 .75
93 Yao Ming 1.25 3.00
94 Ron Artest .50 1.25
95 Tracy McGrady 1.00 2.50
96 Luis Scola .40 1.00
97 Von Wafer .30 .75
98 Aaron Brooks .30 .75
99 Carl Landry .30 .75
100 Shane Battier .50 1.25
101 Kyle Lowry .50 1.25

102 Chuck Hayes .30 .75
103 Danny Granger .30 .75
104 Mike Dunleavy .30 .75
105 T.J. Ford .30 .75
106 Marquis Daniels .30 .75
107 Troy Murphy .30 .75
108 Jarrett Jack .40 1.00
109 Rasho Nesterovic .30 .75
110 Brandon Rush .30 .75
111 Roy Hibbert .40 1.00
112 Jeff Foster .30 .75
113 Zach Randolph .50 1.25
114 Al Thornton .30 .75
115 Baron Davis .40 1.00
116 Eric Gordon .40 1.00
117 Chris Kaman .40 1.00
118 Marcus Camby .40 1.00
119 Mardy Collins .30 .75
120 Ricky Davis .40 1.00
121 DeAndre Jordan .40 1.00
122 Steve Novak .30 .75
123 Kobe Bryant 8.00 20.00
124 Pau Gasol .75 2.00
125 Andrew Bynum .30 .75
126 Derek Fisher .50 1.25
127 Lamar Odom .40 1.00
128 Trevor Ariza .30 .75
129 Jordan Farmar .30 .75
130 Adam Morrison .30 .75
131 Sasha Vujacic .30 .75
132 Luke Walton .40 1.00
133 D.J. Mbenga .30 .75
134 O.J. Mayo .30 .75
135 Rudy Gay .50 1.25
136 Hakim Warrick .30 .75
137 Marc Gasol .50 1.25
138 Mike Conley Jr. .40 1.00
139 Darko Milicic .30 .75
140 Darrell Arthur .30 .75
141 Hamed Haddadi .30 .75
142 Quinton Ross .30 .75
143 Dwyane Wade 1.00 2.50
144 Michael Beasley .30 .75
145 Jermaine O'Neal .50 1.25
146 Udonis Haslem .30 .75
147 Daequan Cook .30 .75
148 Mario Chalmers .40 1.00
149 Chris Quinn .30 .75
150 Jamario Moon .30 .75
151 Joel Anthony RC .50 1.25
152 Luther Head .30 .75
153 Michael Redd .40 1.00
154 Richard Jefferson .40 1.00
155 Charlie Villanueva .30 .75
156 Andrew Bogut .40 1.00
157 Luke Ridnour .40 1.00
158 Ramon Sessions .30 .75
159 Luc Mbah a Moute .30 .75
160 Joe Alexander .30 .75
161 Charlie Bell .30 .75
162 Keith Bogans .30 .75
163 Shelden Williams .30 .75
164 Al Jefferson .30 .75
165 Randy Foye .30 .75
166 Ryan Gomes .30 .75
167 Kevin Love .50 1.25
168 Craig Smith .30 .75
169 Mike Miller .40 1.00
170 Sebastian Telfair .30 .75
171 Corey Brewer .30 .75
172 Brian Cardinal .30 .75
173 Rodney Carney .30 .75
174 Devin Harris .30 .75
175 Vince Carter 1.00 2.50
176 Brook Lopez .50 1.25
177 Yi Jianlian .60 1.50
178 Keyon Dooling .30 .75
179 Jarvis Hayes .30 .75
180 Bobby Simmons .30 .75
181 Ryan Anderson .30 .75
182 Josh Boone .30 .75
183 Chris Douglas-Roberts .30 .75
184 Sean Williams .30 .75
185 Chris Paul 1.00 2.50
186 David West .40 1.00
187 Peja Stojakovic .40 1.00
188 Rasual Butler .30 .75
189 James Posey .30 .75
190 Tyson Chandler .40 1.00
191 Devin Brown .30 .75
192 Morris Peterson .30 .75
193 Hilton Armstrong .30 .75
194 Julian Wright .30 .75
195 Antonio Daniels .30 .75
196 Chris Wilcox .30 .75
197 Al Harrington .40 1.00
198 David Lee .30 .75
199 Nate Robinson .40 1.00
200 Wilson Chandler .40 1.00
201 Chris Duhon .30 .75
202 Quentin Richardson .30 .75
203 Larry Hughes .40 1.00
204 Danilo Gallinari .40 1.00
205 Jared Jeffries .30 .75
206 Russell Westbrook 1.00 2.50
207 Earl Watson .30 .75
208 Robert Swift .30 .75
209 Joe Smith .40 1.00
210 Desmond Mason .30 .75
211 Kevin Durant 2.00 5.00
212 Jeff Green .40 1.00
213 Nick Collison .30 .75
214 Thabo Sefolosha .30 .75
215 Damien Wilkins .30 .75
216 Rafer Alston .30 .75
217 Dwight Howard .60 1.50
218 Rashard Lewis .40 1.00
219 Hedo Turkoglu .40 1.00
220 Jameer Nelson .30 .75
221 Mickael Pietrus .30 .75
222 Courtney Lee .30 .75
223 J.J. Redick .50 1.25
224 Tyronn Lue .50 1.25
225 Anthony Johnson .30 .75
226 Tony Battie .30 .75
227 Andre Iguodala .50 1.25
228 Andre Miller .50 1.25
229 Elton Brand .40 1.00
230 Thaddeus Young .30 .75
231 Louis Williams .50 1.25
232 Willie Green .30 .75
233 Marreese Speights .40 1.00
234 Samuel Dalembert .30 .75
235 Reggie Evans .30 .75
236 Donyell Marshall .30 .75
237 Amare Stoudemire .40 1.00
238 Shaquille O'Neal 1.50 4.00
239 Jason Richardson .50 1.25
240 Steve Nash 1.00 2.50
241 Leandro Barbosa .40 1.00
242 Grant Hill .75 2.00
243 Matt Barnes .30 .75
244 Alando Tucker .30 .75
245 Louis Amundson .30 .75
246 Robin Lopez .30 .75
247 Goran Dragic RC 1.25 3.00
248 Jared Dudley .30 .75
249 Brandon Roy .60 1.50
250 LaMarcus Aldridge .50 1.25
251 Travis Outlaw .30 .75
252 Steve Blake .30 .75
253 Rudy Fernandez .30 .75
254 Greg Oden .30 .75
255 Jerryd Bayless .30 .75
256 Joel Przybilla .30 .75
257 Nicolas Batum .40 1.00
258 Sergio Rodriguez .30 .75
259 Martell Webster .30 .75
260 Channing Frye .30 .75
261 Kevin Martin .40 1.00
262 Andres Nocioni .30 .75
263 Francisco Garcia .30 .75
264 Beno Udrih .30 .75
265 Jason Thompson .30 .75
266 Spencer Hawes .30 .75
267 Bobby Jackson .30 .75
268 Rashad McCants .30 .75
269 Donte Greene .30 .75
270 Quincy Douby .30 .75
271 Tony Parker .75 2.00
272 Tim Duncan 1.25 3.00
273 Manu Ginobili 1.00 2.50
274 Roger Mason .30 .75
275 Michael Finley .50 1.25
276 Matt Bonner .30 .75
277 George Hill .40 1.00
278 Kurt Thomas .30 .75
279 Bruce Bowen .40 1.00
280 Ime Udoka .50 1.25
281 Drew Gooden .40 1.00
282 Chris Bosh .60 1.50
283 Andrea Bargnani .30 .75
284 Shawn Marion .50 1.25
285 Jose Calderon .30 .75
286 Anthony Parker .30 .75
287 Jason Kapono .30 .75
288 Marcus Banks .30 .75
289 Joey Graham .30 .75
290 Roko Ukic .30 .75
291 Pops Mensah-Bonsu .30 .75
292 Kris Humphries .30 .75
293 Carlos Boozer .40 1.00
294 Deron Williams .40 1.00
295 Mehmet Okur .30 .75
296 Paul Millsap .40 1.00
297 Ronnie Brewer .30 .75
298 Andrei Kirilenko .40 1.00
299 C.J. Miles .30 .75
300 Ronnie Price .30 .75
301 Kyle Korver .40 1.00
302 Kosta Koufos .30 .75
303 Matt Harpring .30 .75
304 Brevin Knight .30 .75
305 Antawn Jamison .40 1.00
306 Caron Butler .40 1.00
307 Nick Young .30 .75
308 Andray Blatche .30 .75
309 DeShawn Stevenson .30 .75
310 JaVale McGee .40 1.00
311 Mike James .30 .75
312 Gilbert Arenas .40 1.00
313 Juan Dixon .30 .75
314 Dominic McGuire .30 .75
315 Darius Songaila .30 .75
316 Blake Griffin RC 3.00 8.00
317 Ricky Rubio RC 1.00 2.50
318 Hasheem Thabeet RC .50 1.25
319 James Harden RC 25.00 60.00
320 DeMar DeRozan RC 8.00 20.00
321 Stephen Curry RC 600.00 1,200.00
322 Brandon Jennings RC .75 2.00
323 Jordan Hill RC .50 1.25
324 Earl Clark RC .50 1.25
325 Gerald Henderson RC .50 1.25
326 Jonny Flynn RC .50 1.25
327 Tyreke Evans RC .60 1.50
328 Tyler Hansbrough RC .60 1.50
329 Terrence Williams RC .50 1.25
330 Jrue Holiday RC 10.00 25.00

2009-10 Topps Black

*BLACK: 15X TO 40X BASE HI
*BLACK RC: 10X TO 25X BASE HI
PRINT RUN 50 SER #'d SETS
42 LeBron James 1,250.00 2,500.00
123 Kobe Bryant 1,250.00 2,500.00
211 Kevin Durant 125.00 300.00
317 Ricky Rubio 25.00 60.00
319 James Harden 600.00 1,200.00
321 Stephen Curry 15,000.00 30,000.00
330 Jrue Holiday 150.00 400.00

2009-10 Topps Gold

*1-309 GOLD: 1.5X TO 4X BASE HI
*310-330 GOLD: 1X TO 2.5X BASE HI
GOLD PRINT RUN 2009 SER.#'d SETS
42 LeBron James 40.00 100.00
123 Kobe Bryant 40.00 100.00
316 Blake Griffin 15.00 40.00
320 DeMar DeRozan 40.00 100.00
321 Stephen Curry 1,500.00 3,000.00
330 Jrue Holiday 30.00 80.00

2009-10 Topps All-Star Relics Dual

STATED PRINT RUN 199 SER.#'d SETS
*QUAD: .6X TO 1.5X BASE HI
QUAD PRINT RUN 100 SER.#'d SETS
ASDAI Allen Iverson 6.00 15.00
ASDAS Amare Stoudemire 2.50 6.00
ASDCB Chris Bosh 4.00 10.00
ASDDW Dwyane Wade 8.00 20.00
ASDGA Gilbert Arenas 2.50 6.00
ASDKB Kobe Bryant 12.00 30.00
ASDKG Kevin Garnett 8.00 20.00
ASDPG Pau Gasol 5.00 12.00
ASDPP Paul Pierce 5.00 12.00
ASDRH Richard Hamilton 3.00 8.00
ASDSM Shawn Marion 3.00 8.00
ASDSN Steve Nash 6.00 15.00
ASDSO Shaquille O'Neal 10.00 25.00
ASDTD Tim Duncan 8.00 20.00
ASDTM Tracy McGrady 6.00 15.00
ASDTP Tony Parker 5.00 12.00
ASDVC Vince Carter 6.00 15.00
ASDYM Yao Ming 8.00 20.00
ASDCBI Chauncey Billups 4.00 10.00

2009-10 Topps Autograph Relics

STATED PRINT RUN 299 SER.#'d SETS
TARAB Andrea Bargnani 6.00 15.00
TARBG Ben Gordon 6.00 15.00
TARBR Brandon Roy 6.00 15.00
TARCB Carlos Boozer 6.00 15.00
TARDG Danny Granger 6.00 15.00
TARGO Greg Oden 6.00 15.00
TARJB Jerryd Bayless 6.00 15.00
TARLW Luke Walton 6.00 15.00
TARNY Nick Young 6.00 15.00
TARRM Rashad McCants 6.00 15.00

2009-10 Topps Championship Materials

GROUP A ODDS 1:94, GROUP B ODDS 1:320
GROUP C ODDS 1:425, GROUP D ODDS 1:235
*PATCHES: .75X TO 2X BASE HI
PATCH PRINT RUN 50 SER.#'d SETS
CMAB Andrew Bynum A 2.00 5.00
CMBB Brent Barry A 2.50 6.00
CMBR Bill Russell D 12.00 30.00
CMBW Ben Wallace A 4.00 10.00
CMCD Clyde Drexler B 6.00 15.00
CMDR David Robinson A 8.00 20.00
CMDW Dwyane Wade C 6.00 15.00
CMEB Elgin Baylor C 10.00 25.00
CMIT Isiah Thomas D 4.00 10.00
CMJE Julius Erving B 10.00 25.00
CMJH John Havlicek C 5.00 12.00
CMKB Kobe Bryant D 8.00 20.00
CMKG Kevin Garnett D 8.00 20.00
CMMG Manu Ginobili D 6.00 15.00
CMMJ Magic Johnson D 6.00 15.00
CMMM Moses Malone B 6.00 15.00
CMPG Pau Gasol D 5.00 12.00
CMPP Paul Pierce A 5.00 12.00
CMRA Ray Allen D 5.00 12.00
CMRH Richard Hamilton C 3.00 8.00
CMRW Rasheed Wallace D 4.00 10.00
CMSC Sam Cassell A 2.50 6.00
CMSO Shaquille O'Neal A 10.00 25.00
CMSP Scottie Pippen D 10.00 25.00
CMTD Tim Duncan A 8.00 20.00
CMTP Tayshaun Prince A 3.00 8.00
CMBWA Bill Walton D 6.00 15.00
CMCBI Chauncey Billups 4.00 10.00
CMDRO Dennis Rodman C 8.00 20.00
CMTPA Tony Parker D 5.00 12.00

2009-10 Topps Draft Snapshot

COMPLETE SET (50) 15.00 40.00
STATED ODDS 1:6
DSN Nene .50 1.25
DSAH Allan Houston .50 1.25
DSAI Allen Iverson 1.25 3.00
DSAS Amare Stoudemire .50 1.25
DSBD Baron Davis .50 1.25
DSBG Ben Gordon .50 1.25
DSCA Carmelo Anthony 1.00 2.50
DSCB Caron Butler .50 1.25
DSCJ V.Carter/A.Jamison 1.25 3.00
DSCP Chris Paul 1.25 3.00
DSCW Chris Webber .75 2.00
DSDH Dwight Howard .75 2.00
DSDM Dikembe Mutombo 1.00 2.50
DSDR Derrick Rose 1.00 2.50
DSDW Dwyane Wade 1.25 3.00
DSEB Elton Brand .50 1.25
DSEO Emeka Okafor .50 1.25
DSGH Grant Hill 1.00 2.50
DSHO Hakeem Olajuwon .75 2.00
DSJJ Joe Johnson .60 1.50
DSJK Jason Kidd 1.00 2.50
DSJR Jason Richardson .60 1.50
DSJS Joe Smith .50 1.25
DSKA Kenny Anderson .50 1.25
DSKB Kobe Bryant 5.00 12.00
DSKD Kevin Durant 2.50 6.00
DSKG Kevin Garnett 1.50 4.00
DSLJ LeBron James 5.00 12.00
DSMC Marcus Camby .50 1.25
DSMF Michael Finley .60 1.50
DSMM Mike Miller .60 1.50
DSPE Patrick Ewing 1.00 2.50
DSPG Pau Gasol 1.00 2.50
DSPH Penny Hardaway 1.50 4.00
DSPP Paul Pierce 1.00 2.50
DSRA Ray Allen 1.00 2.50
DSRS Ralph Sampson 1.00 2.50
DSSN Steve Nash 1.25 3.00
DSSO Shaquille O'Neal 2.00 5.00
DSSP Scottie Pippen 1.50 4.00
DSTD Tim Duncan 1.50 4.00
DSTM Tracy McGrady 1.25 3.00
DSYM Yao Ming 1.50 4.00
DSCBO Chris Bosh .75 2.00
DSDHA Devin Harris .40 1.00
DSDMI Darko Milicic .40 1.00
DSDWI Deron Williams .50 1.25
DSJST Jerry Stackhouse .50 1.25
DSLJO Larry Johnson .60 1.50
DSTJF T.J. Ford .40 1.00

2009-10 Topps Franchise Fabrics Autographs

PRINT RUNS LISTED IN CHECKLIST
FFBG Ben Gordon Number/149 8.00 20.00
FFCB Carlos Boozer Logo/41 8.00 20.00

2009-10 Topps McDonalds All-American Game Day Autographs

STATED ODDS 1:670
BG Blake Griffin 100.00 250.00
BJ Brandon Jennings 12.00 30.00
BM B.J. Mullens 8.00 20.00
CB Chase Budinger 8.00 20.00
DR DeMar DeRozan 100.00 250.00
EC Earl Clark 8.00 20.00
GH Gerald Henderson 8.00 20.00
JF Jonny Flynn 8.00 20.00
JH James Harden 500.00 1,000.00
JH Jrue Holiday 40.00 100.00
MC Mike Conley Jr. 40.00 100.00
TE Tyreke Evans 10.00 25.00
TL Ty Lawson 10.00 25.00
WE Wayne Ellington 10.00 25.00

2009-10 Topps Rookie Rewind Jumbo Jersey Autographs

STATED PRINT RUN 99 SER.#'d SETS
JJABL Brook Lopez 10.00 25.00
JJADG Donte Greene 8.00 20.00
JJAEG Eric Gordon 12.00 30.00
JJAGH George Hill 8.00 20.00
JJAKL Kevin Love 20.00 50.00
JJAMS Marreese Speights 10.00 25.00
JJARA Ryan Anderson 8.00 20.00
JJASW Sonny Weems 8.00 20.00
JJACDR Chris Douglas-Roberts 8.00 20.00
JJAJJH J.J. Hickson 8.00 20.00
JJAOJM O.J. Mayo 8.00 20.00

2009-10 Topps Roundball Remnants

GROUP A ODDS 1:65, GROUP B ODDS 1:33
GROUP C ODDS 1:166, GROUP D ODDS 1:955
*PATCHES: .75X TO 2X BASE HI
PATCH PRINT RUN 50 SER.#'d SETS
RRAA Arron Afflalo A 2.50 6.00
RRAB Aaron Brooks A 2.50 6.00
RRAG Aaron Gray B 2.50 6.00
RRAH Al Harrington B 2.50 6.00
RRAI Allen Iverson D 8.00 20.00
RRAJ Al Jefferson B 2.50 6.00
RRAK Andrei Kirilenko C 3.00 8.00
RRAL Acie Law A 2.50 6.00
RRAM Adam Morrison B 2.50 6.00
RRAS Amare Stoudemire D 3.00 8.00
RRAT Al Thornton B 2.50 6.00
RRAV Anderson Varejao D 2.50 6.00
RRBD Baron Davis C 3.00 8.00
RRBG Ben Gordon D 3.00 8.00
RRBM Brad Miller B 3.00 8.00
RRBR Brandon Roy D 5.00 12.00
RRBU Beno Udrih B 2.50 6.00
RRBW Brandan Wright A 2.50 6.00
RRCF Channing Frye B 2.50 6.00
RRCK Chris Kaman B 2.50 6.00
RRCL Carl Landry A 2.50 6.00
RRCM Corey Maggette D 3.00 8.00
RRCV Charlie Villanueva B 2.50 6.00
RRDC Daequan Cook B 2.50 6.00
RRDG Danny Granger B 3.00 8.00
RRDL David Lee B 2.50 6.00
RRDM Darko Milicic B 2.50 6.00
RRDW David West B 3.00 8.00
RRFG Francisco Garcia B 2.50 6.00
RRGD Glen Davis C 2.50 6.00
RRJC Jamal Crawford B 4.00 10.00
RRJH Josh Howard D 3.00 8.00
RRKM Kevin Martin B 3.00 8.00
RRLA LaMarcus Aldridge D 4.00 10.00
RRLB Leandro Barbosa B 3.00 8.00
RRLD Luol Deng B 3.00 8.00
RRMC Marcus Camby D 3.00 8.00
RRME Monta Ellis B 3.00 8.00
RRPG Pau Gasol D 6.00 15.00
RRRA Rafer Alston C 2.50 6.00
RRRB Ronnie Brewer B 2.50 6.00
RRRG Rudy Gay A 4.00 10.00
RRSB Shane Battier A 4.00 10.00
RRSD Samuel Dalembert C 2.50 6.00
RRSH Spencer Hawes C 2.50 6.00
RRTA Trevor Ariza B 2.50 6.00
RRTC Tyson Chandler B 3.00 8.00
RRTM Tracy McGrady C 8.00 20.00
RRUH Udonis Haslem A 2.50 6.00
RRVC Vince Carter C 8.00 20.00
RRWC Wilson Chandler B 3.00 8.00
RRYJ Yi Jianlian B 5.00 12.00
RRZI Zydrunas Ilgauskas B 3.00 8.00
RRABA Andrea Bargnani C 2.50 6.00
RRABI Andris Biedrins B 2.50 6.00
RRABO Andrew Bogut B 2.50 6.00
RRABY Andrew Bynum B 2.50 6.00
RRAIG Andre Iguodala C 4.00 10.00
RRAJA Antawn Jamison B 3.00 8.00
RRAMC Antonio McDyess B 3.00 8.00
RRAMI Andre Miller B 4.00 10.00
RRATU Alando Tucker A 2.50 6.00
RRBDI Boris Diaw B 3.00 8.00
RRCBH Chris Bosh C 5.00 12.00
RRCBO Carlos Boozer B 3.00 8.00
RRCBR Corey Brewer C 2.50 6.00
RRCBU Caron Butler B 3.00 8.00
RRMCO Mike Conley Jr. D 3.00 8.00
RRRAR Ron Artest C 4.00 10.00
RRTJF T.J. Ford D 2.50 6.00

2023-24 Topps 3

STATED PRINT RUN 49 SER.#'d SETS
*BRONZE/25: .5X TO 1.2X BASIC
*BLUE JSY AU/15: .6X TO 1.5X BASIC
1 Trae Young 4.00 10.00
2 Dejounte Murray 2.50 6.00
3 Dominique Wilkins 3.00 8.00
4 LaMelo Ball 5.00 12.00
5 Giannis Antetokounmpo 10.00 25.00
6 Larry Johnson 2.50 6.00
7 Tyler Herro 3.00 8.00
8 Dwyane Wade 4.00 10.00
9 Julius Randle 2.50 6.00
10 Franz Wagner 3.00 8.00
11 Markelle Fultz 1.50 4.00
12 Anfernee Hardaway 5.00 12.00
13 Kyle Kuzma 2.50 6.00
14 Corey Kispert 1.50 4.00
15 Elvin Hayes 2.50 6.00
16 Michael Porter Jr. 2.50 6.00
17 Aaron Gordon 2.00 5.00
18 Tracy McGrady 3.00 8.00
19 Alex English 2.50 6.00
20 Karl-Anthony Towns 3.00 8.00
21 Rudy Gobert 2.50 6.00
22 Kevin Garnett 5.00 12.00
23 Chet Holmgren 5.00 12.00
24 Jalen Williams 4.00 10.00
25 Alonzo Mourning 3.00 8.00
26 Anfernee Simons 2.50 6.00
27 Shaedon Sharpe 4.00 10.00
28 Clyde Drexler 3.00 8.00
29 Metta World-Peace 2.00 5.00
30 Lauri Markkanen 3.00 8.00
31 Collin Sexton 2.50 6.00
32 John Stockton 4.00 10.00
33 Kyrie Irving 4.00 10.00
34 Magic Johnson 8.00 20.00
35 Tim Hardaway Jr. 1.50 4.00
36 Dirk Nowitzki 5.00 12.00
37 Alperen Sengun 3.00 8.00
38 Jalen Green 3.00 8.00
39 Fred VanVleet 3.00 8.00
40 Hakeem Olajuwon 4.00 10.00
41 Jaren Jackson Jr. 3.00 8.00
42 Desmond Bane 2.50 6.00
43 Marcus Smart 2.50 6.00
44 CJ McCollum 2.00 5.00
45 Trey Murphy III 2.50 6.00
46 Brandon Ingram 2.50 6.00
47 Devin Vassell 2.50 6.00
48 Manu Ginobili 4.00 10.00
49 David Robinson 4.00 10.00
50 DeMar DeRozan 3.00 8.00
51 Zach LaVine 3.00 8.00
52 Pau Gasol 3.00 8.00
53 Dennis Rodman 5.00 12.00
54 Donovan Mitchell 4.00 10.00
55 Evan Mobley 3.00 8.00
56 Jarrett Allen 2.00 5.00
57 Cade Cunningham 5.00 12.00
58 Paul Pierce 3.00 8.00
59 Rip Hamilton 2.50 6.00
60 Myles Turner 2.00 5.00
61 Tyrese Haliburton 4.00 10.00
62 Vince Carter 4.00 10.00
63 Khris Middleton 2.00 5.00
64 Ray Allen 3.00 8.00
65 Stephen Curry 15.00 40.00
66 Klay Thompson 5.00 12.00
67 Chris Paul 4.00 10.00
68 Rick Barry 2.50 6.00
69 Paul George 3.00 8.00
70 Russell Westbrook 3.00 8.00
71 Bennedict Mathurin 3.00 8.00
72 Austin Reaves 5.00 12.00
73 D'Angelo Russell 2.00 5.00
74 Lebron James 15.00 40.00
75 Shaquille O'Neal 6.00 15.00
76 Devin Booker 5.00 12.00
77 Kevin Durant 6.00 15.00
78 Bradley Beal 2.50 6.00
79 De'Aaron Fox 4.00 10.00
80 Domantas Sabonis 3.00 8.00
81 Damian Lillard 5.00 12.00
82 Peja Stojakovic 2.00 5.00
83 Jayson Tatum 8.00 20.00
84 Jaylen Brown 4.00 10.00
85 Kristaps Porzingis 2.50 6.00
86 Jrue Holiday 2.50 6.00
87 Larry Bird 8.00 20.00
88 Mikal Bridges 2.50 6.00
89 Spencer Dinwiddie 1.50 4.00
90 Cameron Johnson 2.00 5.00
91 Bam Adebayo 3.00 8.00
92 Jalen Brunson 4.00 10.00
93 Immanuel Quickley 2.00 5.00
94 Carmelo Anthony 3.00 8.00
95 Joel Embiid 5.00 12.00
96 Tyrese Maxey 4.00 10.00
97 Allen Iverson 5.00 12.00
98 Pascal Siakam 3.00 8.00
99 Scottie Barnes 2.50 6.00
100 OG Anunoby 2.50 6.00
101 Victor Wembanyama JSY AU RC Vertical 800.00 1,500.00
101 Victor Wembanyama JSY AU RC Horizontal 800.00 1,500.00
102 Brandon Miller JSY AU RC Horizontal 80.00 200.00
102 Brandon Miller JSY AU RC Vertical 80.00 200.00
103 Scoot Henderson JSY AU RC Vertical 60.00 150.00
103 Scoot Henderson JSY AU RC Horizontal 60.00 150.00
104 Kobe Brown JSY AU RC Vertical 20.00 50.00
104 Kobe Brown JSY AU RC Horizontal 20.00 50.00
105 Bilal Coulibaly JSY AU RC Vertical 50.00 125.00
105 Bilal Coulibaly JSY AU RC Horizontal 50.00 125.00
106 Jarace Walker JSY AU RC Horizontal 40.00 100.00
106 Jarace Walker JSY AU RC Vertical 40.00 100.00
107 Leonard Miller JSY AU RC Horizontal 20.00 50.00
107 Leonard Miller JSY AU RC Vertical 20.00 50.00
108 Colby Jones JSY AU RC Vertical 20.00 50.00
108 Colby Jones JSY AU RC Horizontal 20.00 50.00
109 Julian Phillips JSY AU RC Vertical 20.00 50.00
109 Julian Phillips JSY AU RC Horizontal 20.00 50.00
110 Gradey Dick JSY AU RC Horizontal 40.00 100.00
110 Gradey Dick JSY AU RC Vertical 40.00 100.00
111 Jordan Hawkins JSY AU RC Vertical 30.00 80.00
111 Jordan Hawkins JSY AU RC Horizontal 30.00 80.00
112 Amari Bailey JSY AU RC Horizontal 20.00 50.00
112 Amari Bailey JSY AU RC Vertical 20.00 50.00
113 Rayan Rupert JSY AU RC Vertical 20.00 50.00
113 Rayan Rupert JSY AU RC Horizontal 20.00 50.00
114 Jaime Jaquez Jr. JSY AU RC Horizontal 30.00 80.00
114 Jaime Jaquez Jr. JSY AU RC Vertical 30.00 80.00
115 Sidy Cissoko JSY AU RC Horizontal 20.00 50.00
115 Sidy Cissoko JSY AU RC Vertical 20.00 50.00
116 GG Jackson JSY AU RC Horizontal 40.00 100.00
116 GG Jackson JSY AU RC Vertical 40.00 100.00
117 Noah Clowney JSY AU RC Horizontal 25.00 60.00
117 Noah Clowney JSY AU RC Vertical 25.00 60.00
118 Kris Murray JSY AU RC Vertical 20.00 50.00
118 Kris Murray JSY AU RC Horizontal 20.00 50.00
119 Keyontae Johnson JSY AU RC Horizontal 20.00 50.00
119 Keyontae Johnson JSY AU RC Vertical 20.00 50.00
120 Marcus Sasser JSY AU RC Horizontal 30.00 80.00
120 Marcus Sasser JSY AU RC Vertical 30.00 80.00
121 Ben Sheppard JSY AU RC Vertical 20.00 50.00
121 Ben Sheppard JSY AU RC Horizontal 20.00 50.00
122 Nick Smith Jr. JSY AU RC Horizontal 25.00 60.00
122 Nick Smith Jr. JSY AU RC Vertical 25.00 60.00
123 Jalen Wilson JSY AU RC Vertical 20.00 50.00
123 Jalen Wilson JSY AU RC Horizontal 20.00 50.00
124 Jaylen Clark JSY AU RC Vertical 20.00 50.00
124 Jaylen Clark JSY AU RC Horizontal 20.00 50.00
125 Terquavion Smith JSY AU RC Vertical 20.00 50.00
125 Terquavion Smith JSY AU RC Horizontal 20.00 50.00
126 Jacob Toppin JSY AU RC Vertical 15.00 40.00
126 Jacob Toppin JSY AU RC Horizontal 15.00 40.00
127 Isaiah Wong JSY AU RC Vertical 20.00 50.00
127 Isaiah Wong JSY AU RC Horizontal 20.00 50.00

2023-24 Topps 3 Architects

STATED PRINT RUN 49 SER.#'d SETS
*BLUE/15: .6X TO 1.5X BASIC
ARCH1 Nikola Jokic 10.00 25.00
ARCH2 Kevin Durant 6.00 15.00
ARCH3 Jayson Tatum 8.00 20.00
ARCH4 Stephen Curry 15.00 40.00
ARCH5 Joel Embiid 5.00 12.00
ARCH6 Tyrese Haliburton 4.00 10.00
ARCH7 Kyrie Irving 4.00 10.00
ARCH8 Jalen Green 3.00 8.00
ARCH9 Jimmy Butler 3.00 8.00
ARCH10 De'Aaron Fox 4.00 10.00
ARCH11 Magic Johnson 8.00 20.00
ARCH12 Dirk Nowitzki 5.00 12.00
ARCH13 Giannis Antetokounmpo 10.00 25.00
ARCH14 Larry Bird 8.00 20.00
ARCH15 Shaquille O'Neal 6.00 15.00
ARCH16 Victor Wembanyama 40.00 100.00
ARCH17 Scoot Henderson 6.00 15.00
ARCH18 Brandon Miller 8.00 20.00
ARCH19 Jaime Jaquez Jr. 3.00 8.00
ARCH20 Jordan Hawkins 3.00 8.00

2023-24 Topps 3 Full Court Signs

STATED PRINT RUN 49 SER.#'d SETS
*BRONZE/25: .5X TO 1.2X BASIC
FCSAB Anthony Black 20.00 50.00
FCSAC Alex Caruso 10.00 25.00
FCSAE Alex English 12.00 30.00
FCSAG Aaron Gordon 10.00 25.00
FCSAH Al Horford 10.00 25.00
FCSAR Austin Reaves 25.00 60.00
FCSAS Anfernee Simons 12.00 30.00
FCSAW Andrew Wiggins 12.00 30.00
FCSBC Bilal Coulibaly 25.00 60.00
FCSBH Bones Hyland 8.00 20.00
FCSBM Brandon Miller 40.00 100.00
FCSBP Brandin Podziemski 30.00 80.00
FCSBS Ben Sheppard 10.00 25.00
FCSBW Ben Wallace 12.00 30.00
FCSCC Clint Capela 8.00 20.00
FCSCD Clyde Drexler 15.00 40.00
FCSCJ Colby Jones 10.00 25.00
FCSCM CJ McCollum 10.00 25.00
FCSCW Cam Whitmore 25.00 60.00
FCSDA Deandre Ayton 10.00 25.00
FCSDF De'Aaron Fox 20.00 50.00
FCSDL Dereck Lively II 20.00 50.00
FCSDM Donovan Mitchell 40.00 100.00
FCSDN Dirk Nowitzki 60.00 150.00
FCSDR D'Angelo Russell 10.00 25.00
FCSDS Domantas Sabonis 15.00 40.00
FCSDW Dominique Wilkins 15.00 40.00
FCSFV Fred VanVleet 15.00 40.00
FCSFW Franz Wagner 15.00 40.00
FCSGD Gradey Dick 20.00 50.00
FCSGH Gordon Hayward 10.00 25.00
FCSGW Grant Williams 8.00 20.00
FCSHO Hakeem Olajuwon 20.00 50.00
FCSJB Jalen Brunson 40.00 100.00
FCSJH Jrue Holiday 12.00 30.00
FCSJK Jason Kidd 15.00 40.00
FCSJS Jeremy Sochan 12.00 30.00
FCSJT Jayson Tatum 60.00 150.00
FCSJW Jalen Williams 20.00 50.00
FCSKB Kobe Bufkin 12.00 30.00
FCSKD Kevin Durant 60.00 150.00
FCSKG Kevin Garnett 40.00 100.00
FCSKK Kyle Kuzma 12.00 30.00
FCSLB Larry Bird 60.00 150.00
FCSLM Lauri Markkanen 15.00 40.00
FCSLS Latrell Sprewell 12.00 30.00
FCSMG Manu Ginobili 20.00 50.00
FCSMJ Magic Johnson 60.00 150.00
FCSMP Michael Porter Jr. 12.00 30.00
FCSMS Max Strus 10.00 25.00
FCSMT Myles Turner 10.00 25.00
FCSMW Mark Williams 10.00 25.00
FCSNB Nicolas Batum 6.00 15.00
FCSNC Noah Clowney 12.00 30.00
FCSNR Naz Reid 10.00 25.00
FCSNS Nick Smith Jr. 12.00 30.00
FCSNV Nikola Vucevic 10.00 25.00
FCSOP Olivier-Maxence Prosper 10.00 25.00
FCSPS Pascal Siakam 15.00 40.00
FCSRJ Richard Jefferson 8.00 20.00
FCSRR Rayan Rupert 10.00 25.00
FCSSC Stephen Curry 200.00 500.00
FCSSH Scoot Henderson 30.00 80.00
FCSSO Shaquille O'Neal 75.00 200.00
FCSTH Tim Hardaway Jr. 8.00 20.00
FCSTM Trey Murphy III 12.00 30.00
FCSTP Tony Parker 15.00 40.00
FCSVC Vince Carter 40.00 100.00
FCSVW Victor Wembanyama 500.00 1,000.00
FCSABA Amari Bailey 10.00 25.00
FCSAHA Anfernee Hardaway 25.00 60.00
FCSBBE Bradley Beal 12.00 30.00
FCSBSE Brice Sensabaugh 15.00 40.00
FCSDER Dennis Rodman 50.00 120.00
FCSDRO David Robinson 20.00 50.00
FCSDWA Dwyane Wade 20.00 50.00
FCSGHI Grant Hill 15.00 40.00
FCSJHA Jordan Hawkins 15.00 40.00
FCSJHO Jett Howard 12.00 30.00
FCSJHS Jalen Hood-Schifino 10.00 25.00
FCSJJJ Jaime Jaquez Jr. 15.00 40.00
FCSJOW Jordan Walsh 10.00 25.00
FCSJRO Jalen Rose 10.00 25.00
FCSJST Julian Strawther 12.00 30.00
FCSJWA Jarace Walker 20.00 50.00
FCSKBR Kobe Brown 10.00 25.00
FCSKMU Kris Murray 10.00 25.00
FCSMSA Marcus Sasser 15.00 40.00
FCSMSM Marcus Smart 12.00 30.00
FCSPST Peja Stojakovic 10.00 25.00
FCSSCI Sidy Cissoko 10.00 25.00
FCSTAH Taylor Hendricks 10.00 25.00
FCSTHA Tyrese Haliburton 40.00 100.00
FCSTHE Tyler Herro 15.00 40.00
FCSTMA Tyrese Maxey 20.00 50.00

2023-24 Topps 3 Ice Water

*BLUE/15: .6X TO 1.5X BASIC
IW1 Stephen Curry 15.00 40.00
IW2 Kevin Durant 6.00 15.00
IW3 Tyrese Haliburton 4.00 10.00
IW4 Trae Young 4.00 10.00
IW5 Giannis Antetokounmpo 10.00 25.00
IW6 LaMelo Ball 5.00 12.00
IW7 Jimmy Butler 3.00 8.00
IW8 De'Aaron Fox 4.00 10.00
IW9 Paul George 3.00 8.00
IW10 Allen Iverson 5.00 12.00
IW11 Dirk Nowitzki 5.00 12.00
IW12 Donovan Mitchell 4.00 10.00
IW13 Jayson Tatum 8.00 20.00
IW14 Jalen Brunson 4.00 10.00
IW15 Kyrie Irving 4.00 10.00
IW16 Jordan Hawkins 3.00 8.00
IW17 Brandon Miller 8.00 20.00
IW18 Jaime Jaquez Jr. 3.00 8.00
IW19 Scoot Henderson 6.00 15.00
IW20 Victor Wembanyama 40.00 100.00

2023-24 Topps 3 Knockout

*BLUE/15: .6X TO 1.5X BASIC
KO1 Stephen Curry 15.00 40.00
KO2 Tyrese Haliburton 4.00 10.00
KO3 Trae Young 4.00 10.00
KO4 Jayson Tatum 8.00 20.00
KO5 Larry Bird 8.00 20.00
KO6 Donovan Mitchell 4.00 10.00
KO7 Kyrie Irving 4.00 10.00
KO8 Joel Embiid 5.00 12.00
KO9 Kevin Durant 6.00 15.00
KO10 Chet Holmgren 5.00 12.00
KO11 Victor Wembanyama 40.00 100.00
KO12 Brandon Miller 8.00 20.00
KO13 Scoot Henderson 6.00 15.00
KO14 Anthony Black 4.00 10.00
KO15 Bilal Coulibaly 5.00 12.00
KO16 Dereck Lively II 4.00 10.00
KO17 Jordan Hawkins 3.00 8.00
KO18 Jaime Jaquez Jr. 3.00 8.00
KO19 Brandin Podziemski 6.00 15.00
KO20 Marcus Sasser 3.00 8.00
KO21 Dennis Rodman 5.00 12.00
KO22 Allen Iverson 5.00 12.00
KO23 John Stockton 4.00 10.00
KO24 Magic Johnson 8.00 20.00
KO25 Giannis Antetokounmpo 10.00 25.00

2023-24 Topps 3 Monsters of the Deep

STATED PRINT RUN 49 SER.#'d SETS
*BLUE/15: .6X TO 1.5X BASIC
MD1 Klay Thompson 5.00 12.00
MD2 Trae Young 4.00 10.00
MD3 Jayson Tatum 8.00 20.00
MD4 Giannis Antetokounmpo 10.00 25.00
MD5 Damian Lillard 5.00 12.00
MD6 Donovan Mitchell 4.00 10.00

MD7 Kyrie Irving 4.00 10.00
MD8 James Harden 4.00 10.00
MD9 Tyrese Haliburton 4.00 10.00
MD10 Desmond Bane 2.50 6.00
MD11 Stephen Curry 15.00 40.00
MD12 Joel Embiid 5.00 12.00
MD13 Kevin Durant 6.00 15.00
MD14 Chet Holmgren 5.00 12.00
MD15 De'Aaron Fox 4.00 10.00
MD16 Ray Allen 3.00 8.00
MD17 Larry Bird 8.00 20.00
MD18 Vince Carter 4.00 10.00
MD19 Allen Iverson 5.00 12.00
MD20 Ray Allen 3.00 8.00
MD21 Victor Wembanyama 40.00 100.00
MD22 Scoot Henderson 6.00 15.00
MD23 Jaime Jaquez Jr. 3.00 8.00
MD24 Brandon Ingram 2.50 6.00
MD25 Brandon Miller 8.00 20.00

2023-24 Topps 3 Raindrops Signatures

*BRONZE/25: .5X TO 1.2X BASIC
RSAB Anthony Black 15.00 40.00
RSAC Alex Caruso 8.00 20.00
RSAE Alex English 10.00 25.00
RSAH Anfernee Hardaway 20.00 50.00
RSAW Andrew Wiggins 10.00 25.00
RSBB Bogdan Bogdanovic 8.00 20.00
RSBH Bones Hyland 6.00 15.00
RSBM Brandon Miller 30.00 80.00
RSBP Brandin Podziemski 25.00 60.00
RSCL Caris LeVert 8.00 20.00
RSCM CJ McCollum 8.00 20.00
RSCW Cam Whitmore 20.00 50.00
RSDB Dillon Brooks 8.00 20.00
RSDG Devonte' Graham 6.00 15.00
RSDW Deron Williams 6.00 15.00
RSGD Gradey Dick 15.00 40.00
RSJA Jarrett Allen 8.00 20.00
RSJP Jordan Poole 12.00 30.00
RSJR Jalen Rose 8.00 20.00
RSJS Jerry Stackhouse 8.00 20.00
RSKB Kobe Bufkin 10.00 25.00
RSKH Kevin Huerter 6.00 15.00
RSLB Larry Bird 60.00 150.00
RSLJ LeBron James 1,500.00 300.00
RSLM Lauri Markkanen 12.00 30.00
RSMG Manu Ginobili 20.00 50.00
RSMS Marcus Smart 10.00 25.00
RSOA OG Anunoby 10.00 25.00
RSPS Peja Stojakovic 8.00 20.00
RSRB Rick Barry 10.00 25.00
RSRJ Richard Jefferson 6.00 15.00
RSSC Seth Curry 8.00 20.00
RSSH Scoot Henderson 25.00 60.00
RSTH Tyler Herro 12.00 30.00
RSTM Tyrese Maxey 15.00 40.00
RSVW Victor Wembanyama 500.00 1,000.00
RSBBE Bradley Beal 10.00 25.00
RSBBR Bruce Brown Jr. 8.00 20.00
RSJHA Jordan Hawkins 12.00 30.00
RSJHS Jalen Hood-Schifino 8.00 20.00

2023-24 Topps 3 Re-Markable

*BRONZE/25: .5X TO 1.2X BASIC
RMAB Anthony Black 20.00 50.00
RMAS Alperen Sengun 15.00 40.00
RMBM Brandon Miller 40.00 100.00
RMBW Bill Walton 15.00 40.00
RMCA Carmelo Anthony 40.00 100.00
RMCP Chris Paul 20.00 50.00
RMCS Collin Sexton 12.00 30.00
RMDA Deandre Ayton 10.00 25.00
RMDL Dereck Lively II 20.00 50.00
RMDM Dejounte Murray 12.00 30.00
RMDR D'Angelo Russell 10.00 25.00
RMDW Dwyane Wade 30.00 80.00
RMGW Grant Williams 8.00 20.00
RMJB Jalen Brunson 40.00 100.00
RMJW Jalen Williams 20.00 50.00
RMKD Kevin Durant 75.00 200.00
RMKT Karl-Anthony Towns 15.00 40.00
RMLJ Larry Johnson 12.00 30.00
RMLM Lauri Markkanen 15.00 40.00
RMMB Mikal Bridges 12.00 30.00
RMMS Marcus Smart 12.00 30.00
RMMT Myles Turner 10.00 25.00
RMNV Nikola Vucevic 10.00 25.00
RMPG Pau Gasol 15.00 40.00
RMPP Paul Pierce 15.00 40.00
RMPS Pascal Siakam 15.00 40.00
RMRH Rip Hamilton 12.00 30.00
RMSH Scoot Henderson 30.00 80.00
RMSK Shawn Kemp 15.00 40.00
RMSO Shaquille O'Neal 75.00 200.00
RMTH Tyler Herro 15.00 40.00
RMTM Tyrese Maxey 20.00 50.00
RMTP Tony Parker 15.00 40.00
RMVW Victor Wembanyama 500.00 1,000.00
RMZL Zach Lavine 15.00 40.00

2023-24 Topps 3 Relics Autographs Prime

*BRONZE/25: .5X TO 1.2X BASIC
RPAG Aaron Gordon 12.00 30.00
RPAR Austin Reaves 30.00 80.00
RPAS Anfernee Simons 15.00 40.00
RPAW Andrew Wiggins 15.00 40.00
RPBB Bradley Beal 15.00 40.00
RPCB Christian Braun 12.00 30.00
RPCC Clint Capela 10.00 25.00
RPCJ Cameron Johnson 12.00 30.00
RPCM CJ McCollum 12.00 30.00
RPCS Collin Sexton 15.00 40.00
RPDB Desmond Bane 15.00 40.00
RPDD Donte DiVincenzo 12.00 30.00
RPDF De'Aaron Fox 25.00 60.00
RPDG Devonte' Graham 10.00 25.00
RPDH De'Andre Hunter 12.00 30.00
RPDM Dejounte Murray 15.00 40.00
RPDR D'Angelo Russell 12.00 30.00
RPDV Devin Vassell 15.00 40.00
RPDW Derrick White 15.00 40.00
RPIH Isaiah Hartenstein 12.00 30.00
RPIS Isaiah Stewart 12.00 30.00
RPJB Jalen Brunson 75.00 200.00
RPJC John Collins 12.00 30.00
RPJM Jamal Murray 25.00 60.00
RPJP Jordan Poole 20.00 50.00
RPJR Jalen Green 20.00 50.00
RPJT Jayson Tatum 100.00 250.00
RPKD Kevin Durant 100.00 250.00
RPKH Kevin Huerter 10.00 25.00
RPKK Kyle Kuzma 15.00 40.00
RPLD Luguentz Dort 12.00 30.00
RPLM Lauri Markkanen 20.00 50.00
RPMB Mikal Bridges 15.00 40.00
RPMM Malik Monk 15.00 40.00
RPMS Marcus Smart 15.00 40.00
RPMW Mark Williams 12.00 30.00
RPOA OG Anunoby 15.00 40.00
RPTH Tyler Herro 20.00 50.00
RPTM Tyrese Maxey 25.00 60.00
RPZL Zach Lavine 20.00 50.00
RPDMI Donovan Mitchell 40.00 100.00
RPKAT Karl-Anthony Towns 20.00 50.00

2023-24 Topps 3 Rookie Relics Autographs Prime

*BRONZE/25: .5X TO 1.2X BASIC
RRABC Bilal Coulibaly 50.00 125.00
RRABM Brandon Miller 80.00 200.00
RRABS Ben Sheppard 20.00 50.00
RRACJ Colby Jones 20.00 50.00
RRAGD Gradey Dick 40.00 100.00
RRAGJ GG Jackson 40.00 100.00
RRAIW Isaiah Wong 20.00 50.00
RRAJC Jaylen Clark 20.00 50.00
RRAJJ Jaime Jaquez Jr. 30.00 80.00
RRAJP Julian Phillips 20.00 50.00
RRAJT Jacob Toppin 15.00 40.00
RRAJW Jarace Walker 40.00 100.00
RRAKJ Keyontae Johnson 20.00 50.00
RRAKM Kris Murray 20.00 50.00
RRALM Leonard Miller 20.00 50.00
RRAMS Marcus Sasser 30.00 80.00
RRANC Noah Clowney 25.00 60.00
RRANS Nick Smith Jr. 25.00 60.00
RRARR Rayan Rupert 20.00 50.00
RRASC Sidy Cissoko 20.00 50.00
RRASH Scoot Henderson 60.00 150.00
RRATS Terquavion Smith 20.00 50.00
RRAVW Victor Wembanyama 800.00 1,500.00
RRAABA Amari Bailey 20.00 50.00
RRAJHA Jordan Hawkins 30.00 80.00
RRAJWI Jalen Wilson 20.00 50.00
RRAKBR Kobe Brown 20.00 50.00

2023-24 Topps 3 Serendipitous Sigs

*BRONZE/25: .5X TO 1.2X BASIC
SSAG Aaron Gordon 8.00 20.00
SSBW Ben Wallace 15.00 40.00
SSCH Chet Holmgren 40.00 100.00
SSCL Christian Laettner 8.00 20.00
SSDA Deandre Ayton 8.00 20.00
SSDD Donte DiVincenzo 8.00 20.00
SSDM Donovan Mitchell 20.00 50.00
SSDR David Robinson 20.00 50.00
SSDS Domantas Sabonis 12.00 30.00
SSDW Dominique Wilkins 12.00 30.00
SSGH Grant Hill 12.00 30.00
SSGW Grant Williams 6.00 15.00
SSHO Hakeem Olajuwon 20.00 50.00
SSJC John Collins 8.00 20.00
SSJW Jason Williams 20.00 50.00
SSLS Latrell Sprewell 10.00 25.00
SSMM Malik Monk 10.00 25.00
SSMW Metta World Peace 8.00 20.00
SSRG Rudy Gobert 10.00 25.00
SSSC Stephen Curry 200.00 500.00
SSSD Spencer Dinwiddie 6.00 15.00
SSTH Tyrese Haliburton 40.00 100.00
SSVC Vince Carter 40.00 100.00
SSJGR Jalen Green 12.00 30.00

2023-24 Topps 3 Triple Double

*BLUE/15: .6X TO 1.5X BASIC
TD1 Giannis Antetokounmpo 10.00 25.00
TD2 Russell Westbrook 3.00 8.00
TD3 LaMelo Ball 5.00 12.00
TD4 Domantas Sabonis 3.00 8.00
TD5 Alperen Sengun 3.00 8.00
TD6 Nikola Jokic 10.00 25.00
TD7 Stephen Curry 15.00 40.00
TD8 Kevin Durant 6.00 15.00
TD9 Magic Johnson 8.00 20.00
TD10 Jason Kidd 3.00 8.00

2023-24 Topps 3 Triple Relics Autographs Prime

*BRONZE/25: .5X TO 1.2X BASIC
TRAAB Amari Bailey 12.00 30.00
TRAAC Alex Caruso 12.00 30.00
TRAAG Aaron Gordon 12.00 30.00
TRAAN Aaron Nesmith 12.00 30.00
TRAAR Austin Reaves 30.00 80.00
TRAAS Anfernee Simons 15.00 40.00
TRAAW Andrew Wiggins 15.00 40.00
TRABB Bradley Beal 15.00 40.00
TRABC Bilal Coulibaly 30.00 80.00
TRABM Brandon Miller 50.00 120.00
TRABS Ben Sheppard 12.00 30.00
TRACB Christian Braun 12.00 30.00
TRACC Clint Capela 10.00 25.00
TRACJ Colby Jones 12.00 30.00
TRACS Collin Sexton 15.00 40.00
TRADB Desmond Bane 15.00 40.00
TRADD Donte DiVincenzo 12.00 30.00
TRADR D'Angelo Russell 12.00 30.00
TRADS Domantas Sabonis 20.00 50.00
TRADV Devin Vassell 15.00 40.00
TRADW Derrick White 15.00 40.00
TRAGD Gradey Dick 25.00 60.00
TRAIW Isaiah Wong 12.00 30.00
TRAJA Jarrett Allen 12.00 30.00
TRAJC Jaylen Clark 12.00 30.00
TRAJG Jalen Green 20.00 50.00
TRAJH Jordan Hawkins 20.00 50.00
TRAJJ Jaime Jaquez Jr. 20.00 50.00
TRAJM Jamal Murray 25.00 60.00
TRAJP Julian Phillips 12.00 30.00
TRAJT Jayson Tatum 100.00 250.00
TRAKB Kobe Brown 12.00 30.00
TRACJM CJ McCollum 12.00 30.00
TRADBR Dillon Brooks 12.00 30.00
TRAJCO John Collins 12.00 30.00
TRAJHA Josh Hart 12.00 30.00
TRAJJJ Jaren Jackson Jr. 20.00 50.00
TRAJWA Jarace Walker 25.00 60.00
TRAJWI Jalen Wilson 12.00 30.00

2008 Topps All-Star Booklet Cards

CA Carmelo Anthony 4.00 10.00
CP Chris Paul 4.00 10.00
DW Dwyane Wade 6.00 15.00
GA Gilbert Arenas 3.00 8.00
YJ Yi Jianlian 3.00 8.00

2006 Topps Allen and Ginter Autographs

GROUP A ODDS 1:2467 H, 1:3850 R
GROUP B ODDS 1:14,500 H, 1:32,000 R
GROUP C ODDS 1:2200 H, 1:4300 R
GROUP D ODDS 1:548 H, 1:1090 R
GROUP E ODDS 1:473 H, 1:1000 R
GROUP F ODDS 1:250 H, 1:520 R
GROUP G ODDS 1:158 H, 1:299 R
GROUP A PRINT RUN 50 CARDS PER
GROUP A BONDS PRINT RUN 25 CARDS
GROUP B PRINT RUN 75 CARDS PER
GROUP C PRINT RUN 100 CARDS PER
GROUP D PRINT RUN 200 CARDS PER
GROUP A-D ARE NOT SERIAL-NUMBERED
A-D PRINT RUNS PROVIDED BY TOPPS
JW John Wooden D/200 * 125.00 250.00

2014 Topps Allen and Ginter Autographs

AGFADM Doug McDermott 15.00 40.00

2002 Topps All-Star Game

COMPLETE SET (9) 8.00 20.00
1 Shaquille O'Neal 2.00 5.00
2 Tim Duncan 1.50 4.00
3 Allen Iverson 1.25 3.00
4 Tracy McGrady 1.00 2.50
5 Steve Francis .75 2.00
6 Elton Brand .75 2.00
7 Jason Richardson 1.25 3.00
8 Jamaal Tinsley .75 2.00
9 Chris Webber .75 2.00

2003 Topps All-Star Game

COMPLETE SET (8) 6.00 15.00
1 Shaquille O'Neal 1.50 4.00
2 Mike Dunleavy .75 2.00
3 Glenn Robinson .75 2.00
4 Tracy McGrady 1.50 4.00
5 Stephon Marbury .75 2.00
6 Allen Iverson 1.25 3.00
7 Dirk Nowitzki 1.00 2.50
8 Jason Kidd 1.00 2.50

1992-93 Topps Archives

COMPLETE SET (150) 6.00 15.00
*GOLD: .75X TO 2X BASE CARD HI
1 Mark Aguirre FDP .60 1.50
2 James Worthy FDP 1.25 3.00
3 Ralph Sampson FDP .60 1.50
4 Hakeem Olajuwon FDP 1.50 4.00
5 Patrick Ewing FDP 1.25 3.00
6 Brad Daugherty FDP .60 1.50
7 David Robinson FDP 1.50 4.00
8 Danny Manning FDP .60 1.50
9 Pervis Ellison FDP UER .50 1.25
10 Derrick Coleman FDP .75 2.00
11 Larry Johnson FDP 1.00 2.50
12 Mark Aguirre .60 1.50
13 Danny Ainge .75 2.00
14 Rolando Blackman .60 1.50
15 Tom Chambers .75 2.00
16 Eddie Johnson .60 1.50
17 Alton Lister .50 1.25
18 Larry Nance .60 1.50
19 Kurt Rambis .60 1.50
20 Isiah Thomas 1.25 3.00
21 Buck Williams .60 1.50
22 Orlando Woolridge .75 2.00
23 John Bagley .50 1.25
24 Terry Cummings .60 1.50
25 Mark Eaton .75 2.00
26 Sleepy Floyd .60 1.50
27 Fat Lever .60 1.50
28 Ricky Pierce .60 1.50
29 Trent Tucker .50 1.25
30 Dominique Wilkins 1.25 3.00
31 James Worthy 1.25 3.00
32 Thurl Bailey .60 1.50
33 Clyde Drexler 1.25 3.00
34 Dale Ellis .60 1.50
35 Sidney Green .50 1.25
36 Derek Harper .60 1.50
37 Jeff Malone .60 1.50
38 Rodney McCray .50 1.25
39 John Paxson .60 1.50
40 Doc Rivers .75 2.00
41 Byron Scott .75 2.00
42 Sedale Threatt .50 1.25
43 Ron Anderson .50 1.25
44 Charles Barkley 2.00 5.00
45 Sam Bowie .60 1.50
46 Michael Cage .60 1.50
47 Tony Campbell .50 1.25
48 Antoine Carr .60 1.50
49 Craig Ehlo .60 1.50
50 Vern Fleming .60 1.50
51 Jay Humphries .60 1.50
52 Michael Jordan 15.00 40.00
53 Jerome Kersey .60 1.50
54 Hakeem Olajuwon 1.50 4.00
55 Sam Perkins .60 1.50
56 Alvin Robertson .60 1.50
57 John Stockton 1.50 4.00
58 Otis Thorpe .60 1.50
59 Kevin Willis .60 1.50
60 Michael Adams .60 1.50
61 Benoit Benjamin .50 1.25
62 Terry Catledge .50 1.25
63 Joe Dumars 1.00 2.50
64 Patrick Ewing 1.25 3.00
65 A.C. Green .60 1.50
66 Karl Malone 1.50 4.00
67 Reggie Miller 1.50 4.00
68 Chris Mullin 1.00 2.50
69 Xavier McDaniel .60 1.50
70 Charles Oakley .75 2.00
71 Terry Porter .60 1.50
72 Jerry Reynolds .50 1.25
73 Detlef Schrempf .75 2.00
74 Wayman Tisdale .75 2.00
75 Spud Webb .75 2.00
76 Gerald Wilkins .60 1.50
77 Dell Curry .60 1.50
78 Brad Daugherty .60 1.50
79 Johnny Dawkins .60 1.50
80 Kevin Duckworth .60 1.50
81 Ron Harper .75 2.00
82 Jeff Hornacek .60 1.50
83 Johnny Newman .50 1.25
84 Chuck Person .60 1.50
85 Mark Price .75 2.00
86 Dennis Rodman 2.00 5.00
87 John Salley .60 1.50
88 Scott Skiles .60 1.50
89 Muggsy Bogues .75 2.00
90 Armon Gilliam .50 1.25
91 Horace Grant .75 2.00
92 Mark Jackson .75 2.00
93 Kevin Johnson .75 2.00
94 Reggie Lewis .75 2.00
95 Derrick McKey .60 1.50
96 Ken Norman .50 1.25
97 Scottie Pippen 2.00 5.00
98 Olden Polynice .50 1.25
99 Kenny Smith .60 1.50
100 John Williams .60 1.50
101 Willie Anderson .60 1.50
102 Rex Chapman .60 1.50
103 Harvey Grant .60 1.50
104 Hersey Hawkins .60 1.50
105 Dan Majerle .75 2.00
106 Danny Manning .60 1.50
107 Vernon Maxwell .60 1.50
108 Chris Morris .60 1.50
109 Mitch Richmond UER 1.00 2.50
110 Rony Seikaly .60 1.50
111 Brian Shaw .50 1.25
112 Charles Smith .60 1.50
113 Rod Strickland .60 1.50
114 Micheal Williams .50 1.25
115 Nick Anderson .60 1.50
116 B.J. Armstrong .75 2.00
117 Mookie Blaylock .75 2.00
118 Vlade Divac .75 2.00
119 Sherman Douglas .60 1.50
120 Blue Edwards .50 1.25
121 Sean Elliott .75 2.00
122 Pervis Ellison .50 1.25
123 Tim Hardaway 1.00 2.50
124 Sarunas Marciulionis .75 2.00
125 Drazen Petrovic 1.00 2.50
126 J.R. Reid .60 1.50
127 Glen Rice .75 2.00
128 Pooh Richardson .50 1.25
129 Clifford Robinson .60 1.50
130 David Robinson 1.50 4.00
131 Dee Brown .60 1.50
132 Cedric Ceballos .60 1.50
133 Derrick Coleman .75 2.00
134 Kendall Gill .60 1.50
135 Chris Jackson .60 1.50
136 Shawn Kemp 1.25 3.00
137 Gary Payton 1.25 3.00
138 Dennis Scott .60 1.50
139 Lionel Simmons .50 1.25
140 Kenny Anderson .60 1.50
141 Greg Anthony .60 1.50
142 Stacey Augmon .75 2.00
143 Rick Fox .75 2.00
144 Larry Johnson 1.00 2.50
145 Luc Longley .75 2.00
146 Dikembe Mutombo 1.25 3.00
147 Billy Owens .60 1.50
148 Steve Smith .75 2.00
149 Checklist 1-75 .40 1.00
150 Checklist 76-150 .40 1.00

1992-93 Topps Archives Gold

COMPLETE FACT.SET (150) 20.00 50.00
*GOLD: .75X TO 2X BASE CARD HI
149G Rumeal Robinson 1.00 2.50
150G Shaquille O'Neal 25.00 60.00

1992-93 Topps Archives Master Photos

COMPLETE SET (12) 8.00 20.00
1981 Mark Aguirre .75 2.00
1982 James Worthy 1.50 4.00
1983 Ralph Sampson .75 2.00
1984 Hakeem Olajuwon 2.00 5.00
1985 Patrick Ewing 1.50 4.00
1986 Brad Daugherty .75 2.00
1987 David Robinson 2.00 5.00
1988 Danny Manning .75 2.00
1989 Pervis Ellison .60 1.50
1990 Derrick Coleman 1.00 2.50
1991 Larry Johnson 1.25 3.00
NNO First Picks 1981-91 .40 1.00

2005-06 Topps Big Game

1-110 PRINT RUN 179 SER.#'d SETS
142-146 PRINT RUN 529 SER.#'d SETS
1 Vince Carter 2.00 5.00
2 Mehmet Okur .60 1.50
3 Andre Iguodala 1.00 2.50
4 Baron Davis 1.00 2.50
5 Drew Gooden .75 2.00
6 Yao Ming 2.00 5.00
7 Gary Payton 1.50 4.00
8 Shaun Livingston .75 2.00
9 Marcus Camby .75 2.00
10 Ben Wallace 1.25 3.00
11 Mike Miller .75 2.00
12 Steve Francis 1.00 2.50
13 Sam Cassell .75 2.00
14 Gilbert Arenas 1.00 2.50
15 Chris Bosh 1.25 3.00
16 Jamaal Magloire .60 1.50
17 Zach Randolph 1.00 2.50
18 Josh Childress .60 1.50
19 Kirk Hinrich .75 2.00
20 Dirk Nowitzki 2.50 6.00
21 Trevor Ariza .60 1.50
22 Primoz Brezec .60 1.50
23 LeBron James 8.00 20.00
24 Vladimir Radmanovic .60 1.50
25 Tim Duncan 2.50 6.00
26 Damon Jones .60 1.50
27 Rasheed Wallace 1.00 2.50
28 Corey Maggette .75 2.00
29 Stephen Jackson .75 2.00
30 Amare Stoudemire 1.00 2.50
31 Jason Richardson 1.00 2.50
32 Brad Miller .75 2.00
33 Kenyon Martin .75 2.00
34 Paul Pierce 1.50 4.00
35 Lamar Odom .75 2.00
36 Marquis Daniels .60 1.50
37 Shane Battier .75 2.00
38 Eddy Curry .60 1.50
39 Michael Redd .75 2.00
40 Ray Allen 1.50 4.00
41 Latrell Sprewell 1.00 2.50
42 Rafer Alston .75 2.00
43 Brendan Haywood .60 1.50
44 Al Harrington .75 2.00
45 Udonis Haslem .60 1.50
46 Chauncey Billups 1.25 3.00
47 Andrei Kirilenko .75 2.00
48 Chris Webber 1.25 3.00
49 Stephon Marbury 1.25 3.00
50 Emeka Okafor .75 2.00
51 Cuttino Mobley .60 1.50
52 Shawn Marion .75 2.00
53 Jamaal Tinsley .60 1.50
54 Nenad Krstic .60 1.50
55 Bob Sura .60 1.50
56 Manu Ginobili 2.00 5.00
57 Dan Dickau .60 1.50
58 Wally Szczerbiak .75 2.00
59 Mike Dunleavy .60 1.50
60 Carmelo Anthony 1.50 4.00
61 Zydrunas Ilgauskas .75 2.00
62 Elton Brand .75 2.00
63 Jamal Crawford 1.00 2.50
64 Grant Hill 1.50 4.00
65 Ben Gordon .75 2.00
66 Rashard Lewis .75 2.00
67 Josh Howard .75 2.00
68 Jalen Rose .75 2.00
69 Pau Gasol 1.50 4.00
70 Steve Nash 2.00 5.00
71 Larry Hughes .75 2.00
72 J.R. Smith 1.00 2.50
73 Jason Kidd 1.50 4.00
74 Mike Bibby 1.00 2.50
75 Josh Smith .75 2.00
76 Richard Hamilton 1.25 3.00
77 Caron Butler .75 2.00
78 Richard Jefferson .75 2.00
79 Mike Sweetney .60 1.50
80 Shaquille O'Neal 3.00 8.00
81 Dwight Howard 1.25 3.00
82 Allen Iverson 2.00 5.00
83 Luol Deng .75 2.00
84 Luke Ridnour .75 2.00
85 Desmond Mason .60 1.50
86 Gerald Wallace .75 2.00
87 Carlos Boozer .75 2.00
88 Antoine Walker .75 2.00
89 Tony Parker 1.50 4.00
90 Tracy McGrady 1.50 4.00
91 Jermaine O'Neal .75 2.00
92 Andre Miller .75 2.00
93 Quentin Richardson .60 1.50
94 Dwyane Wade 2.00 5.00
95 Kevin Garnett 2.50 6.00
96 Peja Stojakovic .75 2.00
97 Antawn Jamison .75 2.00
98 Devin Harris .60 1.50
99 Kobe Bryant 8.00 20.00
100 Sebastian Telfair .75 2.00
101 Samuel Dalembert .60 1.50
102 Darius Miles .60 1.50
103 Al Jefferson .60 1.50
104 Brevin Knight .60 1.50
105 Anderson Varejao .60 1.50
106 Troy Murphy .60 1.50
107 Mike James .60 1.50
108 Maurice Williams .75 2.00
109 Robert Horry 1.00 2.50
110 Bobby Simmons .60 1.50
111 Andrew Bogut RC 2.50 6.00
112 Gerald Green RC 2.00 5.00
113 Raymond Felton RC 1.50 4.00
114 Francisco Garcia RC 1.25 3.00
115 Hakim Warrick RC 1.50 4.00
116 Jarrett Jack RC 2.00 5.00
117 Wayne Simien RC 1.25 3.00
118 Nate Robinson RC 1.25 3.00
119 Julius Hodge RC 1.25 3.00
120 Chris Paul RC 3.00 8.00
121 Rashad McCants RC 1.25 3.00
122 Ike Diogu RC 1.25 3.00
123 Antoine Wright RC 1.50 4.00
124 Luther Head RC 1.25 3.00
125 Ryan Gomes RC 1.25 3.00
126 David Lee RC 1.50 4.00
127 Andrew Bynum RC 1.50 4.00
128 Salim Stoudamire RC 1.50 4.00
129 Sean May RC 1.25 3.00
130 Deron Williams RC 3.00 8.00
131 Joey Graham RC 1.50 4.00
132 Fran Vazquez RC 1.50 4.00
133 Brandon Bass RC 1.50 4.00
134 Jason Maxiell RC 1.50 4.00
135 Charlie Villanueva RC 1.50 4.00
136 Daniel Ewing RC 1.50 4.00
137 Channing Frye RC 1.50 4.00
138 Chris Taft RC 1.25 3.00
139 Marvin Williams RC 2.00 5.00
140 Danny Granger RC 2.00 5.00
141 Travis Diener RC 1.25 3.00
142 Shannon Elizabeth 2.50 6.00
143 Jenny McCarthy 2.50 6.00
144 Christie Brinkley 2.50 6.00
145 Jay-Z 15.00 40.00
146 Carmen Electra 2.50 6.00

2005-06 Topps Big Game 99

*1-110 GAME 99: .6X TO 1.5X BASE HI
*111-141 GAME 99: .75X TO 2X BASE HI
*142-146 GAME 99: .75X TO 2X BASE HI
STATED PRINT RUN 99 SER.#'d SETS
145 Jay-Z 25.00 60.00

2005-06 Topps Big Game 33

*1-110 GAME 33: 2X TO 5X BASE HI
*111-141 GAME 33: 1.25X TO 3X BASE HI
*142-146 GAME 33: 1.25X TO 3X BASE HI
64 Grant Hill 8.00 20.00
99 Kobe Bryant 30.00 80.00
145 Jay-Z 30.00 80.00

2005-06 Topps Big Game All-Star Rally Relics

PRINT RUN 79 SER.#'d SETS
AI Allen Iverson Shirt 10.00 25.00
AJ Al Jefferson RC Chall Shorts 2.00 5.00
AS Amare Stoudemire Warm 3.00 8.00
BW Ben Wallace Warm 4.00 10.00
CA C.Anthony RC Chall JSY 5.00 12.00
CB Chris Bosh Shorts 4.00 10.00
DH Dwight Howard Warm 4.00 10.00
EB Earl Boykins Warm 2.00 5.00
EO Emeka Okafor RC Chall JSY 2.50 6.00
GA Gilbert Arenas Shirt 3.00 8.00
GH Grant Hill Warm 5.00 12.00
MG Manu Ginobili Warm 6.00 15.00
RA Ray Allen JSY 5.00 12.00
RD Ronald Dupree JSY 2.00 5.00
SM Shawn Marion Warm 2.50 6.00
SN Steve Nash Warm 6.00 15.00
SO Shaquille O'Neal Warm 10.00 25.00
TM Tracy McGrady Shirt 5.00 12.00
UH U.Haslem RC Chall Shirt 2.00 5.00
YM Yao Ming Warm 6.00 15.00

2005-06 Topps Big Game All-Star Rally Relics Autographs

PRINT RUNS LISTED IN CHECKLIST
AS A.Stoudemire Shirt/57 12.50 30.00
BW Ben Wallace Pants/20 15.00 40.00
CA C.Anthony RC Chall JSY/199 20.00 50.00
DW Dwyane Wade Pants/199 30.00 80.00
EO E.Okafor RC Chall JSY/199 10.00 25.00
QR Q.Richardson Event Shirt/31 10.00 25.00
SN Steve Nash Pants/199 20.00 50.00
SO Shaquille O'Neal Shirt/199 20.00 50.00
TD Tim Duncan Shirt/111 100.00 250.00
TM Tracy McGrady Shirt/76 20.00 50.00
JRS J.R. Smith Event JSY/32 8.00 20.00

2005-06 Topps Big Game Draft Day Moments Relics

BALL PRINT RUN 75 SER.#'d SETS
HAT PRINT RUNS LISTED IN CHECKLIST
AB Andrew Bogut Hat/27 8.00 20.00
AB2 Andrew Bogut Ball/75 5.00 12.00
AW Antoine Wright Hat/27 5.00 12.00
AW2 Antoine Wright Ball/75 3.00 8.00
CF Channing Frye Hat/146 5.00 12.00
CF2 Channing Frye Ball/75 3.00 8.00
CP Chris Paul Hat/125 10.00 25.00
CP2 Chris Paul Ball/75 20.00 50.00
CV Charlie Villanueva Hat/33 5.00 12.00
CV2 Charlie Villanueva Ball/75 3.00 8.00
DG Danny Granger Hat/25 6.00 15.00
DG2 Danny Granger Ball/75 4.00 10.00
DW Deron Williams Hat/30 10.00 25.00
DW2 Deron Williams Ball/75 6.00 15.00
FV Fran Vazquez Hat/99 4.00 10.00
GG Gerald Green Hat/21 6.00 15.00
GG2 Gerald Green Ball/75 4.00 10.00
HW Hakim Warrick Hat/26 5.00 12.00
HW2 Hakim Warrick Ball/75 3.00 8.00
IM Ian Mahinmi Hat/124 6.00 15.00
IM2 Ian Mahinmi Ball/75 4.00 10.00
JH2 Julius Hodge Ball/75 2.50 6.00
JP Johan Petro Hat/34 8.00 20.00
JP2 Johan Petro Ball/75 2.50 6.00
RF Raymond Felton Hat/33 5.00 12.00
RF2 Raymond Felton Ball/75 3.00 8.00
RM2 Rashad McCants Ball/75 2.50 6.00
SM Sean May Hat/36 4.00 10.00
YK Yaroslav Korolev Hat/143 4.00 10.00
YK2 Yaroslav Korolev Ball/75 2.50 6.00
ABY Andrew Bynum Hat/30 5.00 12.00
ABY2 Andrew Bynum Ball/75 3.00 8.00
MWE2 Martell Webster Ball/75 3.00 8.00

2005-06 Topps Big Game Draft Day Moments Relics Autographs

AU BALL PRINT RUN 99 SER.#'d SETS
AU HAT PRINT RUN 129 SER.#'d SETS
AB Andrew Bogut Hat 6.00 15.00
AB2 Andrew Bogut Ball 8.00 20.00
AW Antoine Wright Hat 5.00 12.00
AW2 Antoine Wright Ball 5.00 12.00
CV Charlie Villanueva Hat 5.00 12.00
CV2 Charlie Villanueva Ball 5.00 12.00
DG Danny Granger Hat 6.00 15.00
DG2 Danny Granger Ball 6.00 15.00
DW Deron Williams Hat 10.00 25.00
DW2 Deron Williams Ball 10.00 25.00
FV Fran Vazquez Hat 4.00 10.00
FV2 Fran Vazquez Ball 4.00 10.00
GG Gerald Green Hat 6.00 15.00
GG2 Gerald Green Ball 6.00 15.00
HW Hakim Warrick Hat 5.00 12.00
HW2 Hakim Warrick Ball 5.00 12.00
JH Julius Hodge Hat 4.00 10.00
JH2 Julius Hodge Ball 4.00 10.00
JP Johan Petro Hat 4.00 10.00
JP2 Johan Petro Ball 4.00 10.00
RF Raymond Felton Hat 5.00 12.00
RF2 Raymond Felton Ball 5.00 12.00
RM Rashad McCants Hat 4.00 10.00
RM2 Rashad McCants Ball 4.00 10.00
SM Sean May Hat 4.00 10.00
SM2 Sean May Ball 4.00 10.00
ABY Andrew Bynum Hat 5.00 12.00
ABY2 Andrew Bynum Ball 5.00 12.00
MWE Martell Webster Hat 5.00 12.00
MWE2 Martell Webster Ball 5.00 12.00

2005-06 Topps Big Game Final Score Relics

PRINT RUN 133 SER.#'d SETS
AM Antonio McDyess 4.00 10.00
BB Brent Barry 4.00 10.00
BU Beno Udrih 3.00 8.00
BW Ben Wallace 12.00 30.00
CA Carlos Arroyo 6.00 15.00
CB Chauncey Billups 12.00 30.00
DB Devin Brown 3.00 8.00
DH Darvin Ham 6.00 15.00
DM Darko Milicic 3.00 8.00
EC Elden Campbell 3.00 8.00
GR Glenn Robinson 8.00 20.00
LH Lindsey Hunter 3.00 8.00
MG Manu Ginobili 15.00 40.00
NM Nazr Mohammed 3.00 8.00
RD Ronald Dupree 3.00 8.00
RH Robert Horry 8.00 20.00
RN Rasho Nesterovic 3.00 8.00
RW Rasheed Wallace 5.00 12.00
TD Tim Duncan 20.00 50.00
TM Tony Massenburg 3.00 8.00
TP Tony Parker 12.00 30.00
BBO Bruce Bowen 4.00 10.00
RHA Richard Hamilton 8.00 20.00
TPR Tayshaun Prince 5.00 12.00

2005-06 Topps Big Game Final Score Relics Autographs

PRINT RUNS LISTED IN CHECKLIST
BU Beno Udrih/50 6.00 15.00
BW Ben Wallace/30 75.00 200.00
RH Richard Hamilton/56 20.00 50.00
TD Tim Duncan/50 300.00 600.00

2005-06 Topps Big Game Picture Perfect Relics

PRINT RUN 129 SER.#'d SETS
BOTH VERSIONS SAME VALUE
AB Andray Blatche JSY 2.50 6.00
AB2 Andray Blatche Shorts 2.50 6.00
AW Antoine Wright JSY 2.00 5.00
AW2 Antoine Wright Shorts 2.00 5.00
BB Brandon Bass JSY 2.00 5.00
BB2 Brandon Bass Shorts 2.00 5.00
CF Channing Frye JSY 2.00 5.00
CF2 Channing Frye Shorts 2.00 5.00
CP Chris Paul JSY 12.00 30.00
CP2 Chris Paul Shorts 12.00 30.00
CV Charlie Villanueva JSY 2.00 5.00
CV2 Charlie Villanueva Shorts 2.00 5.00
DE Daniel Ewing JSY 2.00 5.00
DE2 Daniel Ewing Shorts 2.00 5.00
DG Danny Granger JSY 2.50 6.00
DG2 Danny Granger Shorts 2.50 6.00
DL David Lee JSY 2.50 6.00
DL2 David Lee Shorts 2.50 6.00
DW Deron Williams JSY 4.00 10.00
DW2 Deron Williams Shorts 4.00 10.00
EI Ersan Ilyasova JSY 2.00 5.00
EI2 Ersan Ilyasova Shorts 2.00 5.00
FG Francisco Garcia JSY 1.50 4.00
FG2 Francisco Garcia Shorts 1.50 4.00
GG Gerald Green JSY 2.50 6.00
GG2 Gerald Green Shorts 2.50 6.00
HW Hakim Warrick JSY 2.00 5.00
HW2 Hakim Warrick Shorts 2.00 5.00
JG Joey Graham JSY 2.00 5.00
JG2 Joey Graham Shorts 2.00 5.00
JH Julius Hodge JSY 1.50 4.00
JH2 Julius Hodge Shorts 1.50 4.00
JJ Jarrett Jack JSY 2.50 6.00
JJ2 Jarrett Jack Shorts 2.50 6.00
JM Jason Maxiell JSY 2.00 5.00
JM2 Jason Maxiell Shorts 2.00 5.00
LH Luther Head JSY 1.50 4.00
LH2 Luther Head Shorts 1.50 4.00
LW Louis Williams JSY 6.00 15.00
LW2 Louis Williams Shorts 6.00 15.00
MA Martynas Andriuskevicius JSY 1.50 4.00
MA2 Martynas Andriuskevicius Shorts 1.50 4.00
ME Monta Ellis JSY 3.00 8.00
ME2 Monta Ellis Shorts 3.00 8.00
MW Martell Webster JSY 2.00 5.00
MW2 Martell Webster Shorts 2.00 5.00
NR Nate Robinson JSY 2.50 6.00
NR2 Nate Robinson Shorts 2.50 6.00
RF Raymond Felton JSY 2.00 5.00
RF2 Raymond Felton Shorts 2.00 5.00
RG Ryan Gomes JSY 2.00 5.00
RG2 Ryan Gomes Shorts 2.00 5.00
RM Rashad McCants JSY 1.50 4.00
RM2 Rashad McCants Shorts 1.50 4.00
SJ Sarunas Jasikevicius JSY 2.50 6.00
SJ2 Sarunas Jasikevicius Shorts 2.50 6.00
SM Sean May JSY 1.50 4.00
SM2 Sean May Shorts 1.50 4.00
SS Salim Stoudamire JSY 2.00 5.00
SS2 Salim Stoudamire Shorts 2.00 5.00
TD Travis Diener JSY 1.50 4.00
TD2 Travis Diener Shorts 1.50 4.00
WS Wayne Simien JSY 1.50 4.00
WS2 Wayne Simien Shorts 1.50 4.00
ABO Andrew Bogut JSY 3.00 8.00
ABO2 Andrew Bogut Jacket 3.00 8.00
CJM C.J. Miles JSY 2.00 5.00
CJM2 C.J. Miles Shorts 2.00 5.00

2005-06 Topps Big Game Picture Perfect Relics Autographs

PRINT RUN 199 SER.#'d SETS
UNLESS NOTED IN CHECKLIST
BOTH VERSIONS SAME VALUE
AB Andray Blatche JSY/129 5.00 12.00
AB2 Andray Blatche Shorts/179 5.00 12.00
AW Antoine Wright JSY 4.00 10.00
AW2 Antoine Wright Shorts 4.00 10.00
BB Brandon Bass JSY 4.00 10.00
BB2 Brandon Bass Shorts 4.00 10.00
CV Charlie Villanueva JSY 4.00 10.00
CV2 Charlie Villanueva Shorts 4.00 10.00
DE Daniel Ewing JSY 4.00 10.00
DE2 Daniel Ewing Shorts 4.00 10.00
DG Danny Granger JSY 5.00 12.00
DG2 Danny Granger Shorts 5.00 12.00
DL David Lee JSY 5.00 12.00
DL2 David Lee Shorts 5.00 12.00
DW Deron Williams JSY 8.00 20.00
DW2 Deron Williams Shorts 8.00 20.00
FG Francisco Garcia JSY 3.00 8.00
FG2 Francisco Garcia Shorts 3.00 8.00
GG Gerald Green JSY 5.00 12.00
GG2 Gerald Green Shorts 5.00 12.00
HW Hakim Warrick JSY 4.00 10.00
HW2 Hakim Warrick Shorts 4.00 10.00
JG Joey Graham JSY 4.00 10.00
JG2 Joey Graham Shorts 4.00 10.00
JH Julius Hodge JSY 3.00 8.00

JH2 Julius Hodge Shorts 3.00 8.00
JJ Jarrett Jack JSY 5.00 12.00
JJ2 Jarrett Jack Shorts 5.00 12.00
JM Jason Maxiell JSY 4.00 10.00
JM2 Jason Maxiell Shorts 4.00 10.00
LH Luther Head JSY 3.00 8.00
LH2 Luther Head Shorts 3.00 8.00
ME Monta Ellis JSY 6.00 15.00
ME2 Monta Ellis Shorts 10.00 25.00
MW Martell Webster JSY 4.00 10.00
MW2 Martell Webster Shorts 4.00 10.00
RF Raymond Felton JSY 4.00 10.00
RF2 Raymond Felton Shorts 4.00 10.00
RG Ryan Gomes JSY 4.00 10.00
RG2 Ryan Gomes Shorts 4.00 10.00
RM Rashad McCants JSY 3.00 8.00
RM2 Rashad McCants Shorts 3.00 8.00
SJ Sarunas Jasikevicius JSY 5.00 12.00
SJ2 Sarunas Jasikevicius Shorts 5.00 12.00
SM Sean May JSY 3.00 8.00
SM2 Sean May Shorts 3.00 8.00
TD Travis Diener JSY 3.00 8.00
TD2 Travis Diener Shorts 3.00 8.00
WS Wayne Simien JSY 3.00 8.00
WS2 Wayne Simien Shorts 3.00 8.00
ABO Andrew Bogut JSY 6.00 15.00
ABO2 Andrew Bogut Jacket 6.00 15.00

2005-06 Topps Big Game Relics

PRINT RUN 99 SER.#'d SETS
AI Allen Iverson JSY 6.00 15.00
AJ Al Jefferson JSY 2.00 5.00
AN Andres Nocioni JSY 2.00 5.00
AS Amare Stoudemire Shirt 3.00 8.00
BG Ben Gordon JSY 2.50 6.00
BW Ben Wallace Warm 4.00 10.00
CA Carmelo Anthony JSY 5.00 12.00
CB Christie Brinkley Jeans 12.50 30.00
CE Carmen Electra Jeans 12.50 30.00
DH Devin Harris JSY 2.00 5.00
DN Dirk Nowitzki JSY 8.00 20.00
EB Earl Boykins Warm 2.00 5.00
EO Emeka Okafor JSY 2.50 6.00
JM Jenny McCarthy Jeans 10.00 25.00
JO Jermaine O'Neal Warm 2.50 6.00
JS Josh Smith JSY 2.50 6.00
JZ Jay-Z Jeans 40.00 100.00
KB Kobe Bryant JSY 50.00 120.00
KG Kevin Garnett JSY 8.00 20.00
KH Kirk Hinrich JSY 2.50 6.00
KM Kenyon Martin JSY 2.50 6.00
LR Luke Ridnour JSY 2.50 6.00
MG Manu Ginobili Warm 6.00 15.00
NK Nenad Krstic JSY 2.00 5.00
RA Ray Allen JSY 5.00 12.00
RM Reggie Miller Warm 5.00 12.00
RW Rasheed Wallace JSY 3.00 8.00
SE Shannon Elizabeth Jeans 10.00 25.00
SN Steve Nash JSY 6.00 15.00
SO Shaquille O'Neal JSY 10.00 25.00
TD Tim Duncan JSY 8.00 20.00
TM Tracy McGrady JSY 5.00 12.00
YM Yao Ming JSY 6.00 15.00
AJA Antawn Jamison JSY 2.50 6.00
DHO Dwight Howard JSY 4.00 10.00
JRS J.R. Smith JSY 3.00 8.00

2005-06 Topps Big Game Relics Autographs

PRINT RUNS LISTED IN CHECKLIST
AI Allen Iverson/129 60.00 150.00
AS Amare Stoudemire Shirt/99 20.00 50.00
BD Baron Davis/128 5.00 12.00
BG Ben Gordon/101 10.00 25.00
BR Bernard Robinson/21 5.00 12.00
BU Beno Udrih Shirt/78 5.00 12.00
BW Ben Wallace Warm/20 20.00 50.00
CA Carmelo Anthony/199 20.00 40.00
CB Christie Brinkley Jeans/50 150.00 275.00
CE Carmen Electra Jeans/50 100.00 250.00
DH Devin Harris/32 8.00 20.00
DW Dwyane Wade/199 20.00 50.00
EO Emeka Okafor/199 10.00 25.00
FJ Fred Jones/199 5.00 12.00
JC Josh Childress/27 8.00 20.00
JK Jason Kidd/199 12.50 30.00
JM Jenny McCarthy Jeans/50 75.00 200.00
JN Jameer Nelson/199 5.00 12.00
JS Josh Smith/86 6.00 15.00
JZ Jay-Z/50 500.00 1,000.00
KH Kris Humphries/57 5.00 12.00
KM Kevin Martin Event JSY/199 5.00 12.00
KS Kirk Snyder/115 5.00 12.00
LD Luol Deng/147 6.00 15.00
RA Rafael Araujo Event JSY/79 5.00 12.00
RH Richard Hamilton Event Warm/199 5.00 12.00
SE Shannon Elizabeth Jeans/50 75.00 200.00
SL Shaun Livingston/199 5.00 12.00
SM Stephon Marbury/199 6.00 15.00
SN Steve Nash/199 25.00 60.00
SO Shaquille O'Neal/199 30.00 80.00
ST Sebastian Telfair/55 5.00 12.00
TA Trevor Ariza/99 5.00 12.00
TM Tracy McGrady/99 15.00 40.00
DWE Delonte West/23 10.00 25.00
DWR Dorell Wright/199 5.00 12.00

2006-07 Topps Big Game

1-75 PRINT RUN 269 SER.#'d SETS
RC PRINT RUN 579 SER.#'d SETS
1 Dirk Nowitzki 4.00 10.00
2 Tracy McGrady 2.50 6.00
3 Elton Brand 1.25 3.00
4 Ricky Davis 1.25 3.00
5 Marcus Camby 1.25 3.00
6 Gilbert Arenas 1.50 4.00
7 Channing Frye 1.00 2.50
8 Chauncey Billups 2.00 5.00
9 Shaquille O'Neal 6.00 15.00
10 Lamar Odom 1.25 3.00
11 Pau Gasol 2.50 6.00
12 Charlie Villanueva 1.00 2.50
13 Larry Hughes 1.25 3.00
14 Peja Stojakovic 1.25 3.00
15 Andre Iguodala 1.50 4.00
16 Vince Carter 3.00 8.00
17 Jason Terry 1.25 3.00
18 Ron Artest 1.50 4.00
19 Luke Ridnour 1.25 3.00
20 Paul Pierce 2.50 6.00
21 Michael Redd 1.25 3.00
22 Rasheed Wallace 2.00 5.00
23 Baron Davis 1.50 4.00
24 Amare Stoudemire 1.50 4.00
25 Zach Randolph 1.50 4.00
26 Yao Ming 4.00 10.00
27 Raymond Felton 1.00 2.50
28 Stephon Marbury 2.00 5.00
29 Kirk Hinrich 1.25 3.00
30 Andre Miller 1.25 3.00
31 Jason Kidd 2.50 6.00
32 Tayshaun Prince 1.50 4.00
33 Antoine Walker 1.50 4.00
34 LeBron James 20.00 50.00
35 Brad Miller 1.25 3.00
36 Tim Duncan 4.00 10.00
37 Jermaine O'Neal 1.50 4.00
38 Josh Smith 1.00 2.50
39 Gerald Wallace 1.25 3.00
40 Delonte West 1.00 2.50
41 Darius Miles 1.00 2.50
42 Chris Paul 3.00 8.00
43 Mike Bibby 1.50 4.00
44 Sam Cassell 1.25 3.00
45 Josh Howard 1.25 3.00
46 Allen Iverson 4.00 10.00
47 Jameer Nelson 1.00 2.50
48 Mehmet Okur 1.00 2.50
49 Shawn Marion 1.50 4.00
50 Ray Allen 2.50 6.00
51 Joe Johnson 1.50 4.00
52 Richard Hamilton 1.50 4.00
53 Richard Jefferson 1.25 3.00
54 Kobe Bryant 12.00 30.00
55 Manu Ginobili 3.00 8.00
56 Carmelo Anthony 2.50 6.00
57 Ben Gordon 1.25 3.00
58 Andrew Bogut 1.25 3.00
59 Antawn Jamison 1.25 3.00
60 Chris Bosh 2.00 5.00
61 David West 1.25 3.00
62 Steve Nash 3.00 8.00
63 Ben Wallace 2.00 5.00
64 Chris Webber 2.00 5.00
65 Caron Butler 1.25 3.00
66 Danny Granger 1.00 2.50
67 Andrei Kirilenko 1.25 3.00
68 Kevin Garnett 4.00 10.00
69 Dwyane Wade 3.00 8.00
70 Tony Parker 2.50 6.00
71 Dwight Howard 2.00 5.00
72 Rashard Lewis 1.25 3.00
73 Mike Miller 1.25 3.00
74 Jason Richardson 1.50 4.00
75 T.J. Ford 1.00 2.50
76 J.J. Redick RC 3.00 8.00
77 Marcus Williams RC 1.00 2.50
78 Shelden Williams RC 1.00 2.50
79 Tyrus Thomas RC 1.25 3.00
80 LaMarcus Aldridge RC 4.00 10.00
81 Cedric Simmons RC 1.00 2.50
82 Saer Sene RC 1.00 2.50
83 Randy Foye RC 1.00 2.50
84 Patrick O'Bryant RC 1.00 2.50
85 Adam Morrison RC 1.25 3.00
86 Rudy Gay RC 2.00 5.00
87 Ronnie Brewer RC 1.50 4.00
88 Josh Boone RC 1.00 2.50
89 Maurice Ager RC 1.00 2.50
90 Shannon Brown RC 1.00 2.50
91 Renaldo Balkman RC 1.25 3.00
92 Thabo Sefolosha RC 1.25 3.00
93 Shawne Williams RC 1.00 2.50
94 Hilton Armstrong RC 1.00 2.50
95 Brandon Roy RC 3.00 8.00
96 Kyle Lowry RC 5.00 12.00
97 Steve Novak RC 1.25 3.00
98 Paul Davis RC 1.00 2.50
99 Solomon Jones RC 1.00 2.50
100 P.J. Tucker RC 1.50 4.00
101 Rajon Rondo RC 5.00 12.00
102 Dee Brown RC 1.00 2.50
103 Craig Smith RC 1.25 3.00
104 Bobby Jones RC 1.00 2.50
105 James White RC 1.00 2.50
106 Jordan Farmar RC 1.25 3.00
107 Mardy Collins RC 1.00 2.50
108 Quincy Douby RC 1.00 2.50
109 Rodney Carney RC 1.00 2.50
110 Andrea Bargnani RC 1.25 3.00

2006-07 Topps Big Game Blue

*BLUE: 1.25X TO 3X BASE HI
STATED PRINT RUN 59 SER.#'d SETS

2006-07 Topps Big Game Red

*1-75 RED: .5X TO 1.25X BASE HI
*76-110 RED: .5X TO 1.25X BASE HI
STATED PRINT RUN 129 SER.#'d SETS

2006-07 Topps Big Game All-Star Rally Relics Jerseys

PRINT RUN 99 SER.#'d SETS
AI Allen Iverson 8.00 20.00
AN Andres Nocioni 2.00 5.00
BW Ben Wallace 4.00 10.00
CB Chauncey Billups 4.00 10.00
CF Channing Frye 2.00 5.00
DN Dirk Nowitzki 8.00 20.00
DW Dwyane Wade 6.00 15.00
KB Kobe Bryant 50.00 120.00
KG Kevin Garnett 8.00 20.00
LH Luther Head 2.00 5.00
NK Nenad Krstic 2.00 5.00
PG Pau Gasol 5.00 12.00
RH Richard Hamilton 3.00 8.00
SM Shawn Marion 3.00 8.00
SN Steve Nash 6.00 15.00
SO Shaquille O'Neal 12.00 30.00
TD Tim Duncan 8.00 20.00
TM Tracy McGrady 5.00 12.00
TP Tony Parker 5.00 12.00
VC Vince Carter 6.00 15.00
AIG Andre Iguodala 3.00 8.00
CBO Chris Bosh 4.00 10.00

2006-07 Topps Big Game All-Star Rally Relics Jerseys Autographs

PRINT RUN 199 SER.#'d SETS
AI Allen Iverson 40.00 100.00
DW Dwyane Wade 20.00 50.00
SO Shaquille O'Neal 30.00 80.00
TP Tony Parker 12.00 30.00
VC Vince Carter 15.00 40.00
CBO Chris Bosh 10.00 25.00

2006-07 Topps Big Game All-Star Rally Relics Dual Autographs

PRINT RUN 25 SER.#'d SETS
AI Allen Iverson 50.00 120.00
DW Dwyane Wade 60.00 120.00
SO Shaquille O'Neal 50.00 100.00
TP Tony Parker 20.00 50.00
VC Vince Carter 30.00 60.00
CBO Chris Bosh 20.00 50.00

2006-07 Topps Big Game Draft Day Moments Jerseys

PRINT RUN 99 SER.#'d SETS
*JUMBO: .6X TO 1.5X BASE HI
JUMBO PRINT RUN 99 SER.#'d SETS
*BALL: 1X TO 2.5X BASE HI
BALL PRINT RUN 25 SER.#'d SETS
*BALL/HAT: 1X TO 2.5X BASE HI
BALL/HAT PRINT RUN 25 SER.#'d SETS
*BALL/JSY: .6X TO 1.5X BASE HI
BALL/JSY PRINT RUN 50 SER.#'d SETS
*HAT: .75X TO 2X BASE HI
HAT PRINT RUN 50 SER.#'d SETS
*HAT/JSY: 1X TO 2.5X BASE HI
HAT/JSY PRINT RUN 25 SER.#'d SETS
*PATCHES: 1X TO 2.5X BASE HI
PATCH PRINT RUN 25 SER.#'d SETS
AB Andrea Bargnani 2.00 5.00
AM Adam Morrison 2.00 5.00
BR Brandon Roy 5.00 12.00
CS Cedric Simmons 1.50 4.00
HA Hilton Armstrong 1.50 4.00
LA LaMarcus Aldridge 6.00 15.00
MA Maurice Ager 1.50 4.00
MW Marcus Williams 1.50 4.00
RB Ronnie Brewer 2.50 6.00
RC Rodney Carney 1.50 4.00
RF Randy Foye 2.00 5.00
RG Rudy Gay 3.00 8.00
SS Saer Sene 1.50 4.00
SW Shelden Williams 1.50 4.00
TS Thabo Sefolosha 2.00 5.00
JJR J.J. Redick 5.00 12.00
POB Patrick O'Bryant 1.50 4.00

2006-07 Topps Big Game Draft Day Moments Jerseys Autographs

PRINT RUN 199 SER.#'d SETS
AB Andrea Bargnani 12.50 30.00
AM Adam Morrison 3.00 8.00
CS Cedric Simmons 2.50 6.00
HA Hilton Armstrong 2.50 6.00
MA Maurice Ager 2.50 6.00
MW Marcus Williams 2.50 6.00
RB Ronnie Brewer 4.00 10.00
RC Rodney Carney 2.50 6.00
RF Randy Foye 3.00 8.00
SS Saer Sene 2.50 6.00
SW Shelden Williams 2.50 6.00
TS Thabo Sefolosha 3.00 8.00
JJR J.J. Redick 8.00 20.00
POB Patrick O'Bryant 2.50 6.00

2006-07 Topps Big Game Draft Day Moments Hat Autographs

PRINT RUN 25 SER.#'d SETS
AB Andrea Bargnani 25.00 60.00
AM Adam Morrison 6.00 15.00
CS Cedric Simmons 5.00 12.00
HA Hilton Armstrong 5.00 12.00
MA Maurice Ager 5.00 12.00
MW Marcus Williams 5.00 12.00
RB Ronnie Brewer 8.00 20.00
RC Rodney Carney 5.00 12.00
RF Randy Foye 6.00 15.00
SS Saer Sene 5.00 12.00
SW Shelden Williams 5.00 12.00
TS Thabo Sefolosha 6.00 15.00
JJR J.J. Redick 15.00 40.00
POB Patrick O'Bryant 5.00 12.00

2006-07 Topps Big Game Draft Day Moments Patches Autographs

PRINT RUN 25 SER.#'d SETS
AB Andrea Bargnani 25.00 60.00
AM Adam Morrison 6.00 15.00
CS Cedric Simmons 5.00 12.00
HA Hilton Armstrong 5.00 12.00
MA Maurice Ager 5.00 12.00
MW Marcus Williams 5.00 12.00
RB Ronnie Brewer 8.00 20.00
RC Rodney Carney 5.00 12.00
RF Randy Foye 6.00 15.00
SS Saer Sene 5.00 12.00
SW Shelden Williams 5.00 12.00
TS Thabo Sefolosha 6.00 15.00
JJR J.J. Redick 15.00 40.00
POB Patrick O'Bryant 5.00 12.00

2006-07 Topps Big Game Final Score Relics

PRINT RUN 99 SER.#'d SETS
*PATCHES: 1.25X TO 3X BASE HI
PATCH PRINT RUN 50 SER.#'d SETS
AM Alonzo Mourning 6.00 15.00
AW Antoine Walker 6.00 15.00
DW Dwyane Wade 8.00 20.00
GP Gary Payton 5.00 12.00
JK Jason Kapono 2.50 6.00
JP James Posey 2.50 6.00
JW Jason Williams 2.50 6.00
MD Michael Doleac 2.50 6.00
SA Shandon Anderson 2.50 6.00
SO Shaquille O'Neal 15.00 40.00
UH Udonis Haslem 2.50 6.00

2006-07 Topps Big Game Final Score Relics Autographs

PRINT RUN 199 SER.#'d SETS
DW Dwyane Wade 100.00 250.00
SO Shaquille O'Neal 125.00 300.00

2006-07 Topps Big Game Final Score Patches Autographs

PRINT RUN 50 SER.#'d SETS
DW Dwyane Wade 150.00 400.00
SO Shaquille O'Neal 200.00 500.00

2006-07 Topps Big Game Picture Perfect Jerseys

PRINT RUN 99 SER.#'d SETS
*JSY/SHORTS: .5X TO 1.25X BASE HI
JSY/SHRT PRINT RUN 99 SER.#'d SETS
*PATCHES: .75X TO 2X BASE HI
PATCH PRINT RUN 50 SER.#'d SETS
AM Adam Morrison 2.00 5.00
AR Allan Ray 1.50 4.00
BJ Bobby Jones 1.50 4.00
CS Cedric Simmons 1.50 4.00
DB Dee Brown 1.50 4.00
HA Hilton Armstrong 1.50 4.00
JB Josh Boone 1.50 4.00
JF Jordan Farmar 2.00 5.00
JW James White 1.50 4.00
KL Kyle Lowry 8.00 20.00
KP Kevin Pittsnogle 2.00 5.00
LA LaMarcus Aldridge 6.00 15.00
MA Maurice Ager 1.50 4.00
MC Mardy Collins 1.50 4.00
MW Marcus Williams 1.50 4.00
PD Paul Davis 1.50 4.00
PO Patrick O'Bryant 1.50 4.00
QD Quincy Douby 1.50 4.00
RB Renaldo Balkman 2.00 5.00
RC Rodney Carney 1.50 4.00
RF Randy Foye 2.00 5.00
RG Rudy Gay 3.00 8.00
RR Rajon Rondo 8.00 20.00
SB Shannon Brown 1.50 4.00
SN Steve Novak 2.00 5.00
SW Shelden Williams 1.50 4.00
CSM Craig Smith 2.00 5.00
JJR J.J. Redick 5.00 12.00
RBR Ronnie Brewer 2.50 6.00
SWI Shawne Williams 1.50 4.00

2006-07 Topps Big Game Picture Perfect Jerseys Autographs

PRINT RUN 199 SER.#'d SETS
*JSY/SHORTS: .4X TO 1X BASE HI
JSY/SHRT PRINT RUN 199 SER.#'d SETS
*PATCH AU: .6X TO 1.5X BASE HI
PATCH AU PRINT RUN 99 SETS
AM Adam Morrison 3.00 8.00
AR Allan Ray 2.50 6.00
BJ Bobby Jones 2.50 6.00
CS Cedric Simmons 2.50 6.00
DB Dee Brown 2.50 6.00
HA Hilton Armstrong 2.50 6.00
JB Josh Boone 2.50 6.00
JF Jordan Farmar 3.00 8.00
JW James White 2.50 6.00
KL Kyle Lowry 12.00 30.00
MA Maurice Ager 2.50 6.00
MC Mardy Collins 2.50 6.00
MW Marcus Williams 2.50 6.00
PO Patrick O'Bryant 2.50 6.00
QD Quincy Douby 2.50 6.00
RB Renaldo Balkman 3.00 8.00
RC Rodney Carney 2.50 6.00
RF Randy Foye 3.00 8.00
RR Rajon Rondo 12.00 30.00
SB Shannon Brown 2.50 6.00
SW Shelden Williams 2.50 6.00
CSM Craig Smith 3.00 8.00
JJR J.J. Redick 8.00 20.00
RBR Ronnie Brewer 4.00 10.00
SWI Shawne Williams 2.50 6.00

2006-07 Topps Big Game Relics

PRINT RUN 99 SER.#'d SETS
*PATCHES: .75X TO 2X BASE HI
PATCH PRINT RUN 25 SER.#'d SETS
AB Andrew Bogut 2.50 6.00
AI Allen Iverson 8.00 20.00
AM Adam Morrison 2.50 6.00
CA Carmelo Anthony 5.00 12.00
CB Chris Bosh 4.00 10.00
DE Daniel Ewing 2.00 5.00
DW Dwyane Wade 6.00 15.00
EO Emeka Okafor 2.50 6.00
HW Hakim Warrick 2.50 6.00
JC Josh Childress 2.00 5.00
KB Kobe Bryant 50.00 120.00
LD Luol Deng 2.50 6.00
PP Paul Pierce 5.00 12.00
RF Raymond Felton 2.00 5.00
SN Steve Nash 6.00 15.00
SO Shaquille O'Neal 12.00 30.00
TP Tony Parker 5.00 12.00
JJR J.J. Redick 5.00 12.00
TJF T.J. Ford 2.00 5.00

2006-07 Topps Big Game Relics Autographs

PRINT RUN 75 SER.#'d SETS
*PATCH AU: .6X TO 1.5X BASE HI
PATCH AU PRINT RUN 25 SER.#'d SETS
AB Andrew Bogut 8.00 20.00
AI Allen Iverson 40.00 100.00
AM Adam Morrison 8.00 20.00
CB Chris Bosh 10.00 25.00
DE Daniel Ewing 5.00 12.00
DW Dwyane Wade 30.00 80.00
EO Emeka Okafor 5.00 12.00
HW Hakim Warrick 5.00 12.00
JC Josh Childress 5.00 12.00
LD Luol Deng 5.00 12.00
RF Raymond Felton 5.00 12.00
SO Shaquille O'Neal 40.00 80.00
TP Tony Parker 10.00 25.00
JJR J.J. Redick 6.00 15.00
TJF T.J. Ford 5.00 12.00

2006-07 Topps Big Game Patches

*PATCHES: .75X TO 2X BASE HI
PRINT RUN 25 SER.#'d SETS
KB Kobe Bryant 100.00 250.00

1996-97 Topps Chrome

COMPLETE SET (220) 3,000.00 6,000.00
CONDITION SENSITIVE SET
BEWARE KOBE COUNTERFEITS
1 Patrick Ewing 1.00 2.50
2 Christian Laettner .60 1.50
3 Mahmoud Abdul-Rauf .50 1.25
4 Chris Webber .75 2.00
5 Jason Kidd 1.00 2.50
6 Clifford Rozier .40 1.00
7 Elden Campbell .40 1.00
8 Chuck Person .50 1.25
9 Jeff Hornacek .50 1.25
10 Rik Smits .50 1.25
11 Kurt Thomas .40 1.00
12 Rod Strickland .60 1.50
13 Kendall Gill .60 1.50
14 Brian Williams .40 1.00
15 Tom Gugliotta .40 1.00
16 Ron Harper .50 1.25
17 Eric Williams .40 1.00
18 A.C. Green .50 1.25
19 Scott Williams .40 1.00
20 Damon Stoudamire .60 1.50
21 Bryant Reeves .40 1.00
22 Bob Sura .40 1.00
23 Mitch Richmond .75 2.00
24 Larry Johnson .75 2.00
25 Vin Baker .50 1.25
26 Mark Bryant .40 1.00
27 Horace Grant .60 1.50
28 Allan Houston .60 1.50
29 Sam Perkins .50 1.25
30 Antonio McDyess .60 1.50
31 Rasheed Wallace .75 2.00
32 Malik Sealy .40 1.00
33 Scottie Pippen 8.00 20.00
34 Charles Barkley 1.50 4.00
35 Hakeem Olajuwon 1.25 3.00
36 John Starks .60 1.50
37 Byron Scott .60 1.50
38 Arvydas Sabonis .60 1.50
39 Vlade Divac .60 1.50
40 Joe Dumars .75 2.00
41 Danny Ferry .40 1.00
42 Jerry Stackhouse .75 2.00
43 B.J. Armstrong .50 1.25
44 Shawn Bradley .40 1.00
45 Kevin Garnett 4.00 10.00
46 Dee Brown .40 1.00
47 Michael Smith .40 1.00
48 Doug Christie .40 1.00
49 Mark Jackson .50 1.25
50 Shawn Kemp 1.00 2.50
51 Sasha Danilovic .40 1.00
52 Nick Anderson .40 1.00
53 Matt Geiger .40 1.00
54 Charles Smith .40 1.00
55 Mookie Blaylock .60 1.50
56 Johnny Newman .40 1.00
57 George McCloud .40 1.00
58 Greg Ostertag .40 1.00
59 Reggie Williams .40 1.00
60 Brent Barry .50 1.25
61 Doug West .40 1.00
62 Donald Royal .40 1.00
63 Randy Brown .40 1.00
64 Vincent Askew .40 1.00
65 John Stockton 1.25 3.00
66 Joe Kleine .40 1.00
67 Keith Askins .40 1.00
68 Bobby Phills .40 1.00
69 Chris Mullin .75 2.00
70 Nick Van Exel .60 1.50
71 Rick Fox .50 1.25
72 Chicago Bulls - 72 Wins 8.00 20.00
73 Shawn Respert .40 1.00
74 Hubert Davis .40 1.00
75 Jim Jackson .40 1.00
76 Olden Polynice .40 1.00
77 Gheorghe Muresan .40 1.00
78 Theo Ratliff .40 1.00
79 Khalid Reeves .40 1.00
80 David Robinson 1.25 3.00
81 Lawrence Moten .40 1.00
82 Sam Cassell .50 1.25
83 George Zidek .40 1.00
84 Sharone Wright .40 1.00
85 Clarence Weatherspoon .40 1.00
86 Alan Henderson .40 1.00
87 Chris Dudley .40 1.00
88 Ed O'Bannon .40 1.00
89 Calbert Cheaney .40 1.00
90 Cedric Ceballos .50 1.25
91 Michael Cage .40 1.00
92 Ervin Johnson .40 1.00
93 Gary Trent .40 1.00
94 Sherman Douglas .40 1.00
95 Joe Smith .50 1.25
96 Dale Davis .40 1.00
97 Tony Dumas .40 1.00
98 Muggsy Bogues .60 1.50
99 Toni Kukoc .60 1.50
100 Grant Hill 1.00 2.50
101 Michael Finley .60 1.50
102 Isaiah Rider .50 1.25
103 Bryant Stith .40 1.00
104 Pooh Richardson .40 1.00
105 Karl Malone 1.25 3.00
106 Brian Grant .50 1.25
107 Sean Elliott .50 1.25
108 Charles Oakley .60 1.50
109 Pervis Ellison .40 1.00
110 Anfernee Hardaway 1.50 4.00
111 Checklist (1-220) .40 1.00
112 Dikembe Mutombo 1.00 2.50
113 Alonzo Mourning 1.00 2.50
114 Hubert Davis .40 1.00
115 Rony Seikaly .50 1.25
116 Danny Manning .50 1.25
117 Donyell Marshall .50 1.25
118 Gerald Wilkins .40 1.00
119 Ervin Johnson .40 1.00
120 Jalen Rose .50 1.25
121 Dino Radja .40 1.00
122 Glenn Robinson .60 1.50
123 John Stockton 1.25 3.00
124 Matt Maloney RC 1.25 3.00
125 Clifford Robinson .60 1.50
126 Steve Kerr .60 1.50
127 Nate McMillan .40 1.00
128 Shareef Abdur-Rahim RC 6.00 15.00
129 Loy Vaught .40 1.00
130 Anthony Mason .50 1.25
131 Kevin Garnett 6.00 15.00
132 Roy Rogers RC 1.25 3.00
133 Erick Dampier RC 1.50 4.00
134 Tyus Edney .40 1.00
135 Chris Mills .40 1.00
136 Cory Alexander .40 1.00
137 Juwan Howard .60 1.50
138 Kobe Bryant RC 500.00 1,000.00
139 Michael Jordan 60.00 150.00
140 Jayson Williams .40 1.00
141 Rod Strickland .60 1.50
142 Lorenzen Wright RC 1.25 3.00
143 Will Perdue .40 1.00
144 Derek Harper .50 1.25
145 Billy Owens .40 1.00
146 Antoine Walker RC 3.00 8.00
147 P.J. Brown .40 1.00
148 Terrell Brandon .50 1.25
149 Larry Johnson .75 2.00
150 Steve Smith .50 1.25
151 Eddie Jones .60 1.50
152 Detlef Schrempf .60 1.50
153 Dale Ellis .50 1.25
154 Isaiah Rider .50 1.25
155 Tony Delk RC 1.50 4.00
156 Adrian Caldwell .40 1.00
157 Jamal Mashburn .60 1.50
158 Dennis Scott .50 1.25
159 Dana Barros .40 1.00
160 Martin Muursepp RC 1.00 2.50
161 Marcus Camby RC 2.50 6.00
162 Jerome Williams RC 1.25 3.00
163 Wesley Person .40 1.00
164 Luc Longley .50 1.25
165 Charlie Ward .40 1.00
166 Mark Jackson .50 1.25
167 Derrick Coleman .50 1.25
168 Dell Curry .60 1.50
169 Armon Gilliam .40 1.00
170 Vlade Divac .60 1.50
171 Allen Iverson RC 75.00 200.00
172 Vitaly Potapenko RC 1.25 3.00
173 Jon Koncak .40 1.00
174 Lindsey Hunter .40 1.00
175 Kevin Johnson .60 1.50
176 Dennis Rodman 8.00 20.00
177 Stephon Marbury RC 20.00 50.00
178 Karl Malone 1.25 3.00
179 Charles Barkley 1.50 4.00
180 Popeye Jones .40 1.00
181 Samaki Walker RC 1.25 3.00
182 Steve Nash RC 50.00 120.00
183 Latrell Sprewell .60 1.50
184 Kenny Anderson .50 1.25
185 Tyrone Hill .40 1.00
186 Robert Pack .40 1.00
187 Greg Anthony .40 1.00
188 Derrick McKey .40 1.00
189 John Wallace RC 1.25 3.00
190 Bryon Russell .40 1.00
191 Jermaine O'Neal RC 2.50 6.00
192 Clyde Drexler 1.00 2.50
193 Mahmoud Abdul-Rauf .50 1.25
194 Eric Montross .40 1.00
195 Allan Houston .60 1.50
196 Harvey Grant .40 1.00
197 Rodney Rogers .40 1.00
198 Kerry Kittles RC 1.50 4.00
199 Grant Hill 1.00 2.50
200 Lionel Simmons .40 1.00
201 Reggie Miller 1.25 3.00
202 Avery Johnson .50 1.25
203 LaPhonso Ellis .40 1.00
204 Brian Shaw .40 1.00
205 Priest Lauderdale RC 1.00 2.50
206 Derek Fisher RC 2.00 5.00
207 Terry Porter .40 1.00
208 Todd Fuller RC 1.00 2.50
209 Hersey Hawkins .40 1.00
210 Tim Legler .40 1.00
211 Terry Dehere .40 1.00
212 Gary Payton 1.00 2.50
213 Joe Dumars .75 2.00
214 Don MacLean .40 1.00
215 Greg Minor .40 1.00
216 Tim Hardaway .75 2.00
217 Ray Allen RC 25.00 60.00
218 Mario Elie .40 1.00
219 Brooks Thompson .40 1.00
220 Shaquille O'Neal 6.00 15.00

1996-97 Topps Chrome Refractors

*STARS: 6X TO 15X HI COLUMN
*RCs: 1.5X TO 4X HI
STATED ODDS 1:12
CONDITION SENSITIVE SET
4 Chris Webber 40.00 100.00
33 Scottie Pippen 40.00 100.00
45 Kevin Garnett 400.00 800.00
50 Shawn Kemp 40.00 100.00
72 Chicago Bulls - 72 Wins 400.00 800.00
80 David Robinson 60.00 150.00
100 Grant Hill 20.00 50.00
110 Anfernee Hardaway 75.00 200.00
128 Shareef Abdur-Rahim 40.00 100.00
131 Kevin Garnett 400.00 800.00
138 Kobe Bryant 15,000.00 30,000.00
139 Michael Jordan 6,000.00 12,000.00
146 Antoine Walker 25.00 60.00
171 Allen Iverson 4,000.00 8,000.00
176 Dennis Rodman 150.00 400.00
177 Stephon Marbury 125.00 300.00
182 Steve Nash 2,000.00 4,000.00
198 Kerry Kittles 20.00 50.00
199 Grant Hill 40.00 100.00
212 Gary Payton 20.00 50.00
217 Ray Allen 1,500.00 3,000.00
220 Shaquille O'Neal 500.00 1,000.00

1996-97 Topps Chrome Pro Files

COMPLETE SET (20) 15.00 40.00
STATED ODDS 1:8
PF1 Grant Hill 1.50 4.00
PF2 Shawn Kemp 1.50 4.00
PF3 Michael Jordan 10.00 25.00
PF4 Vin Baker .75 2.00
PF5 Chris Webber 1.25 3.00
PF6 Joe Smith .75 2.00
PF7 Shaquille O'Neal 4.00 10.00
PF8 Patrick Ewing 1.50 4.00
PF9 Scottie Pippen 2.50 6.00
PF10 Damon Stoudamire 1.00 2.50
PF11 Anfernee Hardaway 2.50 6.00
PF12 Juwan Howard 1.00 2.50
PF13 Dikembe Mutombo 1.50 4.00
PF14 Dennis Rodman 2.50 6.00
PF15 Kevin Garnett 3.00 8.00
PF16 Jerry Stackhouse 1.25 3.00
PF17 Alonzo Mourning 1.50 4.00
PF18 Karl Malone 2.00 5.00
PF19 Hakeem Olajuwon 2.00 5.00
PF20 Gary Payton 1.50 4.00

1996-97 Topps Chrome Season's Best

COMPLETE SET (25) 20.00 50.00
STATED ODDS 1:6
SB1 Michael Jordan 10.00 25.00
SB2 Hakeem Olajuwon 2.00 5.00
SB3 Shaquille O'Neal 4.00 10.00
SB4 Karl Malone 2.00 5.00
SB5 David Robinson 2.00 5.00
SB6 Dennis Rodman 2.50 6.00
SB7 David Robinson 2.00 5.00
SB8 Dikembe Mutombo 1.50 4.00
SB9 Charles Barkley 2.50 6.00
SB10 Shawn Kemp 1.50 4.00
SB11 John Stockton 2.00 5.00
SB12 Jason Kidd 1.50 4.00
SB13 Avery Johnson .75 2.00
SB14 Rod Strickland 1.00 2.50
SB15 Damon Stoudamire 1.00 2.50
SB16 Gary Payton 1.50 4.00
SB17 Mookie Blaylock 1.00 2.50
SB18 Michael Jordan 10.00 25.00
SB19 Jason Kidd 1.50 4.00
SB20 Alvin Robertson .60 1.50
SB21 Dikembe Mutombo 1.50 4.00
SB22 Shawn Bradley .60 1.50
SB23 David Robinson 2.00 5.00
SB24 Hakeem Olajuwon 2.00 5.00
SB25 Alonzo Mourning 1.50 4.00

1996-97 Topps Chrome Youthquake

COMPLETE SET (15) 300.00 600.00
STATED ODDS 1:12
YQ1 Allen Iverson 25.00 60.00
YQ2 Samaki Walker .75 2.00
YQ3 Stephon Marbury 3.00 8.00
YQ4 Damon Stoudamire 1.50 4.00
YQ5 John Wallace .75 2.00
YQ6 Michael Finley 1.50 4.00
YQ7 Marcus Camby 1.50 4.00
YQ8 Kerry Kittles 1.00 2.50
YQ9 Ray Allen 5.00 12.00
YQ10 Jerry Stackhouse 2.00 5.00
YQ11 Shareef Abdur-Rahim 1.50 4.00
YQ12 Antonio McDyess 1.00 2.50
YQ13 Joe Smith .75 2.00
YQ14 Brent Barry .75 2.00
YQ15 Kobe Bryant 200.00 500.00

1997-98 Topps Chrome

COMPLETE SET (220) 150.00 400.00
1 Scottie Pippen 8.00 20.00
2 Nate McMillan .40 1.00
3 Byron Scott .50 1.25
4 Mark Davis .40 1.00
5 Rod Strickland .50 1.25
6 Brian Grant .50 1.25
7 Damon Stoudamire .60 1.50
8 John Stockton 1.25 3.00
9 Grant Long .40 1.00
10 Darrell Armstrong .40 1.00
11 Anthony Mason .50 1.25
12 Travis Best .40 1.00
13 Stephon Marbury .75 2.00
14 Jamal Mashburn .50 1.25
15 Detlef Schrempf .60 1.50
16 Terrell Brandon .50 1.25
17 Charles Barkley 1.50 4.00
18 Vin Baker .50 1.25
19 Gary Trent .40 1.00
20 Vinny Del Negro .50 1.25
21 Todd Day .40 1.00
22 Malik Sealy .50 1.25
23 Wesley Person .50 1.25
24 Reggie Miller 1.25 3.00
25 Dan Majerle .60 1.50
26 Todd Fuller .40 1.00
27 Juwan Howard .50 1.25
28 Clarence Weatherspoon .40 1.00
29 Grant Hill 1.00 2.50
30 John Williams .40 1.00
31 Ken Norman .40 1.00
32 Patrick Ewing 1.00 2.50
33 Bryon Russell .40 1.00
34 Tony Smith .40 1.00
35 Andrew Lang .40 1.00
36 Rony Seikaly .50 1.25
37 Billy Owens .40 1.00
38 Dino Radja .40 1.00
39 Chris Gatling .40 1.00
40 Dale Davis .50 1.25
41 Arvydas Sabonis .75 2.00
42 Chris Mills .40 1.00
43 A.C. Green .50 1.25
44 Tyrone Hill .50 1.25
45 Tracy Murray .40 1.00
46 David Robinson 1.25 3.00
47 Lee Mayberry .40 1.00
48 Jayson Williams .40 1.00
49 Jason Kidd 1.00 2.50
50 Bryant Stith .40 1.00
51 CL/Bulls - Team of the 90s 40.00 100.00
52 Brent Barry .50 1.25
53 Henry James .40 1.00
54 Allen Iverson 40.00 100.00
55 Shandon Anderson .40 1.00
56 Mitch Richmond .75 2.00
57 Allan Houston .60 1.50
58 Ron Harper .60 1.50
59 Gheorghe Muresan .40 1.00

60 Vincent Askew .40 1.00
61 Ray Allen 1.25 3.00
62 Kenny Anderson .50 1.25
63 Dikembe Mutombo 1.00 2.50
64 Sam Perkins .50 1.25
65 Walt Williams .50 1.25
66 Chris Carr .40 1.00
67 Vlade Divac .60 1.50
68 LaPhonso Ellis .50 1.25
69 B.J. Armstrong .40 1.00
70 Jim Jackson .50 1.25
71 Clyde Drexler 1.00 2.50
72 Lindsey Hunter .40 1.00
73 Sasha Danilovic .40 1.00
74 Elden Campbell .40 1.00
75 Robert Pack .40 1.00
76 Dennis Scott .50 1.25
77 Will Perdue .40 1.00
78 Anthony Peeler .40 1.00
79 Steve Smith .50 1.25
80 Steve Kerr .75 2.00
81 Buck Williams .40 1.00
82 Terry Mills .40 1.00
83 Michael Smith .40 1.00
84 Adam Keefe .40 1.00
85 Kevin Willis .50 1.25
86 David Wesley .50 1.25
87 Muggsy Bogues .50 1.25
88 Bimbo Coles .40 1.00
89 Tom Gugliotta .50 1.25
90 Jermaine O'Neal .50 1.25
91 Cedric Ceballos .50 1.25
92 Shawn Kemp 1.00 2.50
93 Horace Grant .60 1.50
94 Shareef Abdur-Rahim .60 1.50
95 Robert Horry .60 1.50
96 Vitaly Potapenko .40 1.00
97 Pooh Richardson .40 1.00
98 Doug Christie .40 1.00
99 Voshon Lenard .40 1.00
100 Dominique Wilkins .75 2.00
101 Alonzo Mourning 1.00 2.50
102 Sam Cassell .40 1.00
103 Sherman Douglas .40 1.00
104 Shawn Bradley .40 1.00
105 Mark Jackson .50 1.25
106 Dennis Rodman 5.00 12.00
107 Charles Oakley .50 1.25
108 Matt Maloney .40 1.00
109 Shaquille O'Neal 2.00 5.00
110 K.Malone MVP CL 1.25 3.00
111 Antonio McDyess .60 1.50
112 Bob Sura .40 1.00
113 Terrell Brandon .50 1.25
114 Tim Thomas RC 1.25 3.00
115 Tim Duncan RC 25.00 60.00
116 Antonio Daniels RC 1.00 2.50
117 Bryant Reeves .40 1.00
118 Keith Van Horn RC 1.50 4.00
119 Loy Vaught .50 1.25
120 Rasheed Wallace .75 2.00
121 Bobby Jackson RC 1.25 3.00
122 Kevin Johnson .60 1.50
123 Michael Jordan 20.00 50.00
124 Ron Mercer RC 1.25 3.00
125 Tracy McGrady RC 6.00 15.00
126 Antoine Walker .60 1.50
127 Carlos Rogers .40 1.00
128 Isaac Austin .40 1.00
129 Mookie Blaylock .60 1.50
130 Rodrick Rhodes RC .75 2.00
131 Dennis Scott .50 1.25
132 Chris Mullin .75 2.00
133 P.J. Brown .40 1.00
134 Rex Chapman .40 1.00
135 Sean Elliott .50 1.25
136 Alan Henderson .40 1.00
137 Austin Croshere RC .75 2.00
138 Nick Van Exel .60 1.50
139 Derek Strong .40 1.00
140 Glenn Robinson .60 1.50
141 Avery Johnson .50 1.25
142 Calbert Cheaney .50 1.25
143 Mahmoud Abdul-Rauf .40 1.00
144 Stojko Vrankovic .40 1.00
145 Chris Childs .40 1.00
146 Danny Manning .50 1.25
147 Jeff Hornacek .60 1.50
148 Kevin Garnett 1.50 4.00
149 Joe Dumars .75 2.00
150 Johnny Taylor RC .60 1.50
151 Mark Price .60 1.50
152 Toni Kukoc .75 2.00
153 Erick Dampier .50 1.25
154 Lorenzen Wright .40 1.00
155 Matt Geiger .40 1.00
156 Tim Hardaway .75 2.00
157 Charles Smith RC .75 2.00
158 Hersey Hawkins .50 1.25
159 Michael Finley .60 1.50
160 Tyus Edney .40 1.00
161 Christian Laettner .60 1.50
162 Doug West .40 1.00
163 Jim Jackson .50 1.25
164 Larry Johnson .75 2.00
165 Vin Baker .50 1.25
166 Karl Malone 1.25 3.00
167 Kelvin Cato RC .75 2.00
168 Luc Longley .60 1.50
169 Dale Davis .50 1.25
170 Joe Smith .50 1.25
171 Kobe Bryant 20.00 50.00
172 Scot Pollard RC .75 2.00
173 Derek Anderson RC 1.00 2.50
174 Erick Strickland RC .60 1.50
175 Olden Polynice .40 1.00
176 Chris Whitney .40 1.00
177 Anthony Parker RC 1.00 2.50
178 Armon Gilliam .40 1.00
179 Gary Payton 1.00 2.50
180 Glen Rice .60 1.50
181 Chauncey Billups RC 3.00 8.00
182 Derek Fisher .60 1.50
183 John Starks .60 1.50
184 Mario Elie .40 1.00
185 Chris Webber .75 2.00
186 Shawn Kemp 1.00 2.50
187 Greg Ostertag .40 1.00
188 Olivier Saint-Jean RC .75 2.00
189 Eric Snow .40 1.00
190 Isaiah Rider .50 1.25
191 Paul Grant RC .60 1.50
192 Samaki Walker .40 1.00
193 Cory Alexander .40 1.00
194 Eddie Jones .60 1.50
195 John Thomas RC .60 1.50
196 Otis Thorpe .50 1.25
197 Rod Strickland .50 1.25
198 David Wesley .50 1.25
199 Jacque Vaughn RC .75 2.00
200 Rik Smits .50 1.25
201 Brevin Knight RC 1.00 2.50
202 Clifford Robinson .50 1.25
203 Hakeem Olajuwon 1.25 3.00
204 Jerry Stackhouse .60 1.50
205 Tyrone Hill .50 1.25
206 Kendall Gill .50 1.25
207 Marcus Camby .60 1.50
208 Tony Battie RC 1.00 2.50
209 Brent Price .40 1.00
210 Danny Fortson RC 1.00 2.50
211 Jerome Williams .40 1.00
212 Maurice Taylor RC .75 2.00
213 Brian Williams .50 1.25
214 Keith Booth RC .75 2.00
215 Nick Anderson .50 1.25
216 Travis Knight .40 1.00
217 Adonal Foyle RC .75 2.00
218 Anfernee Hardaway 1.50 4.00
219 Kerry Kittles .50 1.25
220 D.Mutombo POY CL 1.00 2.50

1997-98 Topps Chrome Refractors

*STARS: 3X TO 8X BASE CARD HI
*RCs: 2X TO 5X BASE HI
STATED ODDS 1:12
1 Scottie Pippen 40.00 100.00
21 Todd Day 25.00 60.00
51 CL/Bulls - Team of the 90s 200.00 500.00
54 Allen Iverson 75.00 200.00
106 Dennis Rodman 30.00 80.00
109 Shaquille O'Neal 75.00 200.00
115 Tim Duncan 600.00 1,200.00
123 Michael Jordan 600.00 1,200.00
125 Tracy McGrady 125.00 300.00
171 Kobe Bryant 500.00 1,000.00
181 Chauncey Billups 75.00 200.00

1997-98 Topps Chrome Destiny

COMPLETE SET (15) 12.00 30.00
STATED ODDS 1:12
*REF: 1.5X TO 4X BASE DESTINY
REF: STATED ODDS 1:48
D1 Grant Hill 1.25 3.00
D2 Kevin Garnett 2.00 5.00
D3 Vin Baker .60 1.50
D4 Antoine Walker .75 2.00
D5 Kobe Bryant 60.00 150.00
D6 Tracy McGrady 4.00 10.00
D7 Keith Van Horn 1.25 3.00
D8 Tim Duncan 3.00 8.00
D9 Eddie Jones .75 2.00
D10 Stephon Marbury 1.00 2.50
D11 Marcus Camby .75 2.00
D12 Antonio McDyess .75 2.00
D13 Shareef Abdur-Rahim .75 2.00
D14 Allen Iverson 2.50 6.00
D15 Shaquille O'Neal 2.50 6.00

1997-98 Topps Chrome Season's Best

COMPLETE SET (29) 20.00 50.00
STATED ODDS 1:8
*REF: 1.25X TO 3X BASE SEAS.BEST
REF: STATED ODDS 1:24
SB1 Gary Payton 1.50 4.00
SB2 Kevin Johnson 1.00 2.50
SB3 Tim Hardaway 1.25 3.00
SB4 John Stockton 2.00 5.00
SB5 Damon Stoudamire 1.00 2.50
SB6 Michael Jordan 60.00 150.00
SB7 Mitch Richmond 1.25 3.00
SB9 Reggie Miller 2.00 5.00
SB10 Clyde Drexler 1.50 4.00
SB11 Grant Hill 1.50 4.00
SB12 Scottie Pippen 2.50 6.00
SB13 Kendall Gill .75 2.00
SB14 Glen Rice 1.00 2.50
SB15 LaPhonso Ellis .75 2.00
SB16 Karl Malone 2.00 5.00
SB17 Charles Barkley 2.50 6.00
SB18 Vin Baker .75 2.00
SB19 Chris Webber 1.25 3.00
SB20 Tom Gugliotta .75 2.00
SB21 Shaquille O'Neal 3.00 8.00
SB22 Patrick Ewing 1.50 4.00
SB23 Hakeem Olajuwon 2.00 5.00
SB24 Alonzo Mourning 1.50 4.00
SB25 Dikembe Mutombo 1.50 4.00
SB26 Allen Iverson 3.00 8.00
SB27 Antoine Walker 1.00 2.50
SB28 Shareef Abdur-Rahim 1.00 2.50
SB29 Stephon Marbury 1.25 3.00
SB30 Kerry Kittles .75 2.00

1997-98 Topps Chrome Topps 40

COMPLETE SET (39) 30.00 60.00
STATED ODDS 1:6
*REF: 2X TO 5X BASE TOP 40
REF: STATED ODDS 1:18
CARD T-40 7 DOES NOT EXIST
T1 Glen Rice .60 1.50
T2 Patrick Ewing 1.00 2.50
T3 Terrell Brandon .50 1.25
T4 Jerry Stackhouse .60 1.50
T5 Michael Jordan 10.00 25.00
T6 Christian Laettner .60 1.50
T8 Reggie Miller 1.25 3.00
T9 Gary Payton 1.00 2.50
T10 Detlef Schrempf .60 1.50
T11 Kevin Garnett 1.50 4.00
T12 Eddie Jones .60 1.50
T13 Clyde Drexler 1.00 2.50
T14 Anfernee Hardaway 1.50 4.00
T15 Chris Webber .75 2.00
T16 Jayson Williams .40 1.00
T17 Joe Smith .50 1.25
T18 Karl Malone 1.25 3.00
T19 Tim Hardaway .75 2.00
T20 Vin Baker .50 1.25
T21 Tom Gugliotta .50 1.25
T22 Allen Iverson 2.00 5.00
T23 David Robinson 1.25 3.00
T24 Dikembe Mutombo 1.00 2.50
T25 John Stockton 1.25 3.00
T26 Charles Barkley 1.50 4.00
T27 Mitch Richmond .75 2.00
T28 Damon Stoudamire .60 1.50
T29 Anthony Mason .50 1.25
T30 Shaquille O'Neal 2.00 5.00
T31 Glenn Robinson .60 1.50
T32 Juwan Howard .50 1.25
T33 Shawn Kemp 1.00 2.50
T34 Dennis Rodman 1.50 4.00
T35 Grant Hill 1.00 2.50
T36 Kevin Johnson .60 1.50
T37 Alonzo Mourning 1.00 2.50
T38 Hakeem Olajuwon 1.25 3.00
T39 Joe Dumars .75 2.00
T40 Scottie Pippen 1.50 4.00

1998-99 Topps Chrome

COMPLETE SET (220) 150.00 400.00
COMP.SET W/PREV (230) 200.00 500.00
THE FOLLOWING CARDS ARE IN PREVIEW:
6/10/19/40/43/60/73/77/81/100
PREV.SET: INSERTED IN TOPPS 2 PACKS
1 Scottie Pippen 1.50 4.00
2 Shareef Abdur-Rahim .60 1.50
3 Rod Strickland .50 1.25
4 Keith Van Horn .60 1.50
5 Ray Allen 1.00 2.50
7 Anthony Parker .40 1.00
8 Lindsey Hunter .40 1.00
9 Mario Elie .40 1.00
11 Eldridge Recasner .40 1.00
12 Jeff Hornacek .50 1.25
13 Chris Webber .75 2.00
14 Lee Mayberry .40 1.00
15 Erick Strickland .40 1.00
16 Arvydas Sabonis .60 1.50
17 Tim Thomas .50 1.25
18 Luc Longley .50 1.25
20 Alonzo Mourning 1.00 2.50
21 Adonal Foyle .40 1.00
22 Tony Battie .40 1.00
23 Robert Horry .60 1.50
24 Derek Harper .50 1.25
25 Jamal Mashburn .60 1.50
26 Elliott Perry .40 1.00
27 Jalen Rose .60 1.50
28 Joe Smith .50 1.25
29 Henry James .40 1.00
30 Travis Knight .40 1.00
31 Tom Gugliotta .50 1.25
32 Chris Anstey .40 1.00
33 Antonio Daniels .40 1.00
34 Elden Campbell .40 1.00
35 Charlie Ward .40 1.00
36 Eddie Johnson .40 1.00
37 John Wallace .40 1.00
38 Antonio Davis .40 1.00
39 Antoine Walker .60 1.50
41 Doug Christie .50 1.25
42 Andrew Lang .40 1.00
44 Jaren Jackson .40 1.00
45 Loy Vaught .40 1.00
46 Allan Houston .60 1.50
47 Mark Jackson .50 1.25
48 Tracy Murray .40 1.00
49 Tim Duncan 1.50 4.00
50 Micheal Williams .40 1.00
51 Steve Nash 1.25 3.00
52 Matt Maloney .40 1.00
53 Sam Cassell .50 1.25
54 Voshon Lenard .40 1.00
55 Dikembe Mutombo 1.00 2.50
56 Malik Sealy .40 1.00
57 Dell Curry .40 1.00
58 Stephon Marbury .75 2.00
59 Tariq Abdul-Wahad .40 1.00
61 Kelvin Cato .40 1.00
62 LaPhonso Ellis .40 1.00
63 Jim Jackson .40 1.00
64 Greg Ostertag .40 1.00
65 Glenn Robinson .60 1.50
66 Chris Carr .40 1.00
67 Marcus Camby .50 1.25
68 Kobe Bryant 15.00 40.00
69 Bobby Jackson .50 1.25
70 B.J. Armstrong .40 1.00
71 Alan Henderson .40 1.00
72 Terry Davis .40 1.00
74 Lamond Murray .40 1.00
76 Rex Chapman .50 1.25
78 Terry Cummings .50 1.25
79 Dan Majerle .60 1.50
80 Bo Outlaw .40 1.00
82 Vin Baker .50 1.25
83 Clifford Robinson .40 1.00
84 Greg Anthony .40 1.00
85 Brevin Knight .40 1.00
86 Jacque Vaughn .40 1.00
87 Bobby Phills .40 1.00
88 Sherman Douglas .40 1.00
91 Lorenzen Wright .40 1.00
92 Eric Williams .40 1.00
93 Will Perdue .40 1.00
94 Charles Barkley 1.50 4.00
95 Kendall Gill .50 1.25
96 Wesley Person .40 1.00
98 Erick Dampier .40 1.00
101 Rasheed Wallace .75 2.00
102 Zydrunas Ilgauskas .60 1.50
103 Eddie Jones .60 1.50
104 Ron Mercer .60 1.50
105 Horace Grant .60 1.50
106 Corliss Williamson .60 1.50
107 Anthony Mason .50 1.25
108 Mookie Blaylock .50 1.25
109 Dennis Rodman 1.50 4.00
110 Checklist .25 .60
111 Steve Smith .50 1.25
112 Cedric Henderson .40 1.00
113 Raef LaFrentz RC 1.25 3.00
114 Calbert Cheaney .40 1.00
115 Rik Smits .50 1.25
116 Rony Seikaly .40 1.00
117 Lawrence Funderburke .40 1.00
118 Ricky Davis RC 1.50 4.00
119 Howard Eisley .40 1.00
120 Kenny Anderson .50 1.25
121 Corey Benjamin RC .60 1.50
122 Maurice Taylor .40 1.00
123 Eric Murdock .40 1.00
124 Derek Fisher .50 1.25
125 Kevin Garnett 1.50 4.00
126 Walt Williams .40 1.00
127 Bryce Drew RC .60 1.50
128 A.C. Green .60 1.50
129 Ervin Johnson .40 1.00
130 Christian Laettner .50 1.25
131 Chauncey Billups .75 2.00
132 Hakeem Olajuwon 1.25 3.00
133 Al Harrington RC 1.25 3.00
134 Danny Manning .50 1.25
135 Paul Pierce RC 8.00 20.00
136 Terrell Brandon .50 1.25
137 Bob Sura .40 1.00
138 Chris Gatling .40 1.00
139 Donyell Marshall .40 1.00
140 Marcus Camby .50 1.25
141 Brian Skinner RC .75 2.00
142 Charles Oakley .50 1.25
143 Antawn Jamison RC 1.50 4.00
144 Nazr Mohammed RC 1.00 2.50
145 Karl Malone 1.25 3.00
146 Chris Mills .40 1.00
147 Bison Dele .40 1.00
148 Gary Payton 1.00 2.50
149 Terry Porter .40 1.00
150 Tim Hardaway .75 2.00
151 Larry Hughes RC 1.50 4.00
152 Derek Anderson .50 1.25
153 Jason Williams RC 3.00 8.00
154 Dirk Nowitzki RC 30.00 80.00
155 Juwan Howard .50 1.25
156 Avery Johnson .50 1.25
157 Matt Harpring RC 1.00 2.50
158 Reggie Miller 1.25 3.00
159 Walter McCarty .40 1.00
160 Allen Iverson 1.50 4.00
161 Felipe Lopez RC .60 1.50
162 Tracy McGrady 1.00 2.50
163 Damon Stoudamire .60 1.50
164 Antonio McDyess .50 1.25
165 Grant Hill 1.00 2.50
166 Tyronn Lue RC 1.25 3.00
167 P.J. Brown .40 1.00
168 Antonio Daniels .40 1.00
169 Mitch Richmond .75 2.00
170 David Robinson 1.25 3.00
171 Shawn Bradley .40 1.00
172 Shandon Anderson .40 1.00
173 Chris Childs .40 1.00
174 Shawn Kemp 1.00 2.50
175 Shaquille O'Neal 2.50 6.00
176 John Starks .60 1.50
177 Tyrone Hill .40 1.00
178 Jayson Williams .40 1.00
179 Anfernee Hardaway 1.50 4.00
180 Chris Webber .75 2.00
181 Don Reid .40 1.00
182 Stacey Augmon .50 1.25
183 Hersey Hawkins .40 1.00
184 Sam Mitchell .40 1.00
185 Jason Kidd 1.00 2.50
186 Nick Van Exel .60 1.50
187 Larry Johnson 1.00 2.50
188 Bryant Reeves .40 1.00
189 Glen Rice .60 1.50
190 Kerry Kittles .50 1.25
191 Toni Kukoc .60 1.50
192 Ron Harper .60 1.50
193 Bryon Russell .40 1.00
194 Vladimir Stepania RC 1.00 2.50
195 Michael Olowokandi RC 1.25 3.00
196 Mike Bibby RC 2.00 5.00
197 Dale Ellis .40 1.00
198 Muggsy Bogues .50 1.25
199 Vince Carter RC 25.00 60.00
200 Robert Traylor RC 1.00 2.50
201 Peja Stojakovic RC 2.00 5.00
202 Aaron McKie .40 1.00
203 Hubert Davis .40 1.00
204 Dana Barros .40 1.00
205 Bonzi Wells RC 1.00 2.50
206 Michael Doleac RC .75 2.00
207 Keon Clark RC 1.00 2.50
208 Michael Dickerson RC 1.00 2.50
209 Nick Anderson .40 1.00
210 Brent Price .40 1.00
211 Cherokee Parks .40 1.00
212 Sam Jacobson RC .60 1.50
213 Pat Garrity RC .75 2.00
214 Tyrone Corbin .40 1.00
215 David Wesley .40 1.00
216 Rodney Rogers .40 1.00
217 Dean Garrett .40 1.00
218 Roshown McLeod RC .60 1.50
219 Dale Davis .40 1.00
220 Checklist .25 .60
221 Scottie Pippen MO 1.50 4.00
222 Antonio McDyess MO .50 1.25
223 Stephon Marbury MO .75 2.00
224 Tom Gugliotta MO .50 1.25
225 Chris Webber MO .75 2.00
226 Latrell Sprewell MO .75 2.00
227 Mitch Richmond MO .75 2.00
228 Joe Smith MO .50 1.25
229 John Starks MO .60 1.50
230 Charles Oakley MO .60 1.50
231 Dennis Rodman MO 1.50 4.00
232 Eddie Jones MO .60 1.50
233 Nick Van Exel MO .60 1.50
234 Bobby Jackson MO .50 1.25
235 Glen Rice MO .60 1.50

1998-99 Topps Chrome Refractors

*STARS: 5X TO 12X HI COLUMN
*RCs: 2X TO 5X HI
STATED ODDS 1:12
THE FOLLOWING CARDS DO NOT EXIST:
75/89/90/97/99
THE FOLLOWING CARDS ARE IN PREVIEW:
6/10/19/40/43/60/73/77/81/100
PREV.SET: INSERTED IN TOPPS 2 HCP
1 Scottie Pippen 20.00 50.00
49 Tim Duncan 25.00 60.00
51 Steve Nash 25.00 60.00
68 Kobe Bryant 600.00 1,200.00
109 Dennis Rodman 20.00 50.00
125 Kevin Garnett 30.00 80.00
132 Hakeem Olajuwon 12.00 30.00
135 Paul Pierce 300.00 600.00
151 Larry Hughes 15.00 40.00
153 Jason Williams 125.00 300.00
154 Dirk Nowitzki 600.00 1,200.00
162 Tracy McGrady 15.00 40.00
166 Tyronn Lue 12.00 30.00
199 Vince Carter 400.00 800.00
201 Peja Stojakovic 15.00 40.00

1998-99 Topps Chrome Apparitions

COMPLETE SET (14) 75.00 200.00
STATED ODDS 1:24
*REF: 12X TO 30X HI COLUMN
REF: STATED ODDS 1:1,015
REF: PRINT RUN 100 SERIAL #'d SETS
*REF/100: 12X TO 30X BASE CARD HI
A1 Kobe Bryant 60.00 150.00
A2 Stephon Marbury 2.50 6.00
A3 Brent Barry 1.50 4.00
A4 Karl Malone 4.00 10.00
A5 Shaquille O'Neal 8.00 20.00
A6 Chris Webber 2.50 6.00
A7 Shawn Kemp 3.00 8.00
A8 Hakeem Olajuwon 4.00 10.00
A9 Anfernee Hardaway 5.00 12.00
A10 Michael Finley 2.00 5.00
A11 Keith Van Horn 2.00 5.00
A12 Kevin Garnett 5.00 12.00
A13 Vin Baker 1.50 4.00
A14 Tim Duncan 5.00 12.00

1998-99 Topps Chrome Back 2 Back

COMPLETE SET (7) 15.00 40.00
STATED ODDS 1:12
B1 Michael Jordan 15.00 40.00
B2 Scottie Pippen 2.00 5.00
B3 Dennis Rodman 2.00 5.00
B4 Hakeem Olajuwon 1.50 4.00
B5 John Stockton 1.50 4.00
B6 Dikembe Mutombo 1.25 3.00
B7 Grant Hill 1.25 3.00

1998-99 Topps Chrome Champion Spirit

COMPLETE SET (7) 20.00 50.00
STATED ODDS 1:12
CS1 Michael Jordan 15.00 40.00
CS2 Grant Hill 1.25 3.00
CS3 Ron Mercer .60 1.50
CS4 Mike Bibby 1.50 4.00
CS5 Michael Dickerson .75 2.00
CS6 Patrick Ewing 1.25 3.00
CS7 Scottie Pippen 2.00 5.00

1998-99 Topps Chrome Coast to Coast

COMPLETE SET (15) 12.00 30.00
STATED ODDS 1:24
*REF: 1.25X TO 3X HI COLUMN
REF: STATED ODDS 1:96
CC1 Kobe Bryant 40.00 100.00
CC2 Scottie Pippen 2.50 6.00
CC3 Eddie Jones 1.00 2.50
CC4 Grant Hill 1.50 4.00
CC5 Jason Kidd 1.50 4.00
CC6 Antoine Walker 1.00 2.50
CC7 Michael Finley 1.00 2.50
CC8 Kevin Garnett 2.50 6.00
CC9 Allen Iverson 2.50 6.00
CC10 Shawn Kemp 1.50 4.00
CC11 Glenn Robinson 1.00 2.50
CC12 Anfernee Hardaway 2.50 6.00
CC13 Tim Hardaway 1.25 3.00
CC14 Ron Mercer .75 2.00
CC15 Kerry Kittles .75 2.00

1998-99 Topps Chrome Instant Impact

COMPLETE SET (10) 12.00 30.00
STATED ODDS 1:36
*REF: 1.25X TO 3X HI COLUMN
REF: STATED ODDS 1:144
I1 Tim Duncan 3.00 8.00
I2 Keith Van Horn 1.25 3.00
I3 Stephon Marbury 1.50 4.00
I4 Hakeem Olajuwon 2.50 6.00
I5 Shaquille O'Neal 5.00 12.00
I6 Michael Olowokandi 1.50 4.00
I7 Raef LaFrentz 1.50 4.00
I8 Vince Carter 6.00 15.00
I9 Jason Williams 4.00 10.00
I10 Paul Pierce 5.00 12.00

1998-99 Topps Chrome Season's Best

COMPLETE SET (29) 8.00 20.00
STATED ODDS 1:6
*REF: 1.25X TO 3X HI COLUMN
REF: STATED ODDS 1:24
SB1 Rod Strickland .50 1.25
SB2 Gary Payton 1.00 2.50
SB3 Tim Hardaway .75 2.00
SB4 Stephon Marbury .75 2.00
SB5 Sam Cassell .50 1.25
SB7 Mitch Richmond .75 2.00
SB8 Steve Smith .50 1.25
SB9 Ray Allen 1.00 2.50
SB10 Isaiah Rider .50 1.25
SB11 Grant Hill 1.00 2.50
SB12 Kevin Garnett 1.50 4.00
SB13 Shareef Abdur-Rahim .60 1.50
SB14 Glenn Robinson .60 1.50
SB15 Michael Finley .60 1.50
SB16 Karl Malone 1.25 3.00
SB17 Tim Duncan 1.50 4.00
SB18 Antoine Walker .60 1.50
SB19 Chris Webber .75 2.00
SB20 Vin Baker .50 1.25
SB21 Shaquille O'Neal 2.50 6.00
SB22 David Robinson 1.25 3.00
SB23 Alonzo Mourning 1.00 2.50
SB24 Dikembe Mutombo 1.00 2.50
SB25 Hakeem Olajuwon 1.25 3.00
SB26 Tim Duncan 1.50 4.00
SB27 Keith Van Horn .60 1.50
SB28 Zydrunas Ilgauskas .60 1.50
SB29 Brevin Knight .40 1.00
SB30 Bobby Jackson .50 1.25

1999-00 Topps Chrome

COMPLETE SET (257) 60.00 120.00
1 Steve Smith .50 1.25
2 Ron Harper .50 1.25
3 Michael Dickerson .40 1.00
4 LaPhonso Ellis .40 1.00
5 Chris Webber .75 2.00
6 Jason Caffey .40 1.00
7 Bryon Russell .40 1.00
8 Bison Dele .40 1.00
9 Isaiah Rider .50 1.25
10 Dean Garrett .40 1.00
11 Eric Murdock .40 1.00
12 Juwan Howard .50 1.25
13 Latrell Sprewell .75 2.00
14 Jalen Rose .50 1.25
15 Larry Johnson .60 1.50
16 Eric Williams .40 1.00
17 Bryant Reeves .40 1.00
18 Tony Battie .40 1.00
19 Luc Longley .50 1.25
20 Gary Payton 1.00 2.50
21 Tariq Abdul-Wahad .40 1.00
22 Armon Gilliam UER .40 1.00
23 Shaquille O'Neal 2.50 6.00
24 Gary Trent .40 1.00
25 John Stockton 1.00 2.50
26 Mark Jackson .50 1.25
27 Cherokee Parks .40 1.00
28 Michael Olowokandi .40 1.00
29 Raef LaFrentz .50 1.25
30 Dell Curry .40 1.00
31 Travis Best .40 1.00
32 Shawn Kemp 1.00 2.50
33 Voshon Lenard .40 1.00
34 Brian Grant .40 1.00
35 Alvin Williams .40 1.00
36 Derek Fisher .50 1.25
37 Allan Houston .50 1.25
38 Arvydas Sabonis .50 1.25
39 Terry Cummings .40 1.00
40 Dale Ellis .40 1.00
41 Maurice Taylor .40 1.00
42 Grant Hill 1.00 2.50
43 Anthony Mason .60 1.50
44 John Wallace .40 1.00
45 David Wesley .40 1.00
46 Nick Van Exel .60 1.50
47 Cuttino Mobley .40 1.00
48 Anfernee Hardaway 1.50 4.00
49 Terry Porter .40 1.00
50 Brent Barry .50 1.25
51 Derek Harper .50 1.25
52 Antoine Walker .60 1.50
53 Karl Malone 1.25 3.00
54 Ben Wallace .50 1.25
55 Vlade Divac .60 1.50
56 Sam Mitchell .40 1.00
57 Joe Smith .50 1.25
58 Shawn Bradley .40 1.00
59 Darrell Armstrong .40 1.00
60 Kenny Anderson .50 1.25
61 Jason Williams 1.00 2.50
62 Alonzo Mourning 1.00 2.50
63 Matt Harpring .40 1.00
64 Antonio Davis .40 1.00
65 Lindsey Hunter .40 1.00
66 Allen Iverson 1.50 4.00
67 Mookie Blaylock .40 1.00
68 Wesley Person .40 1.00
69 Bobby Phills .40 1.00
70 Theo Ratliff .40 1.00
71 Antonio Daniels .40 1.00
72 P.J. Brown .40 1.00
73 David Robinson 1.25 3.00
74 Sean Elliott .50 1.25
75 Zydrunas Ilgauskas .50 1.25
76 Kerry Kittles .50 1.25
77 Otis Thorpe .40 1.00
78 John Starks .60 1.50
79 Jaren Jackson .40 1.00
80 Hersey Hawkins .40 1.00
81 Glenn Robinson .60 1.50
82 Paul Pierce 1.25 3.00
83 Glen Rice .60 1.50
84 Charlie Ward .40 1.00
85 Dee Brown .40 1.00
86 Danny Fortson .40 1.00
87 Billy Owens .40 1.00
88 Jason Kidd 1.00 2.50
89 Brent Price .40 1.00
90 Don Reid .40 1.00
91 Mark Bryant .40 1.00
92 Vinny Del Negro .40 1.00
93 Stephon Marbury .75 2.00
94 Donyell Marshall .50 1.25
95 Jim Jackson .40 1.00
96 Horace Grant .50 1.25
97 Calbert Cheaney .40 1.00
98 Vince Carter 1.50 4.00
99 Bobby Jackson .50 1.25
100 Alan Henderson .40 1.00
101 Mike Bibby .60 1.50
102 Cedric Henderson .40 1.00
103 Lamond Murray .40 1.00
104 A.C. Green .50 1.25
105 Hakeem Olajuwon 1.25 3.00
106 George Lynch .40 1.00
107 Kendall Gill .60 1.50
108 Rex Chapman .40 1.00
109 Eddie Jones .60 1.50
110 Kornel David RC .40 1.00
111 Jason Terry RC 1.00 2.50
112 Corey Maggette RC .75 2.00
113 Ron Artest RC 1.50 4.00
114 Richard Hamilton RC 1.50 4.00
115 Elton Brand RC 1.25 3.00
116 Baron Davis RC 1.50 4.00
117 Wally Szczerbiak RC 1.00 2.50
118 Steve Francis RC 1.25 3.00
119 James Posey RC .60 1.50
120 Shawn Marion RC 1.25 3.00
121 Tim Duncan 1.50 4.00
122 Danny Manning .50 1.25
123 Chris Mullin .60 1.50
124 Antawn Jamison .60 1.50
125 Kobe Bryant 40.00 100.00
126 Matt Geiger .40 1.00
127 Rod Strickland .50 1.25
128 Howard Eisley .40 1.00
129 Steve Nash 1.25 3.00
130 Felipe Lopez .40 1.00
131 Ron Mercer .50 1.25
132 Ruben Patterson .40 1.00
133 Dana Barros .40 1.00
134 Dale Davis .40 1.00
135 Bo Outlaw .40 1.00
136 Shandon Anderson .40 1.00
137 Mitch Richmond .75 2.00
138 Doug Christie .50 1.25
139 Rasheed Wallace .75 2.00
140 Chris Childs .40 1.00
141 Jamal Mashburn .50 1.25
142 Terrell Brandon .40 1.00
143 Jamie Feick RC .40 1.00
144 Robert Traylor .40 1.00
145 Rick Fox .40 1.00
146 Charles Barkley 1.50 4.00
147 Tyrone Nesby RC .40 1.00
148 Jerry Stackhouse .60 1.50
149 Cedric Ceballos .40 1.00
150 Dikembe Mutombo 1.00 2.50
151 Anthony Peeler .40 1.00
152 Larry Hughes .50 1.25
153 Clifford Robinson .50 1.25
154 Corliss Williamson .40 1.00
155 Olden Polynice .40 1.00
156 Avery Johnson .50 1.25
157 Tracy Murray .40 1.00
158 Tom Gugliotta .50 1.25
159 Tim Thomas .50 1.25
160 Reggie Miller 1.25 3.00
161 Tim Hardaway .75 2.00
162 Dan Majerle .60 1.50
163 Will Perdue .40 1.00
164 Brevin Knight .40 1.00
165 Elden Campbell .40 1.00
166 Chris Gatling .40 1.00
167 Walter McCarty .40 1.00
168 Chauncey Billups .60 1.50
169 Chris Mills .40 1.00
170 Christian Laettner .50 1.25
171 Robert Pack .40 1.00
172 Rik Smits .50 1.25
173 Tyrone Hill .40 1.00
174 Damon Stoudamire .60 1.50
175 Nick Anderson .40 1.00
176 Peja Stojakovic .60 1.50
177 Vladimir Stepania .40 1.00
178 Tracy McGrady 1.00 2.50
179 Adam Keefe .40 1.00
180 Shareef Abdur-Rahim .60 1.50
181 Isaac Austin .40 1.00
182 Mario Elie .40 1.00
183 Rashard Lewis .50 1.25
184 Scott Burrell .40 1.00
185 Othella Harrington .40 1.00
186 Eric Piatkowski .40 1.00
187 Bryant Stith .40 1.00
188 Michael Finley .60 1.50
189 Chris Crawford .40 1.00
190 Toni Kukoc .75 2.00
191 Danny Ferry .40 1.00
192 Erick Dampier .40 1.00
193 Clarence Weatherspoon .40 1.00
194 Bob Sura .40 1.00
195 Jayson Williams .40 1.00
196 Kurt Thomas .40 1.00
197 Greg Anthony .40 1.00
198 Rodney Rogers .40 1.00
199 Detlef Schrempf .50 1.25
200 Keith Van Horn .50 1.25
201 Robert Horry .50 1.25
202 Sam Cassell .50 1.25
203 Malik Sealy .40 1.00
204 Kelvin Cato .40 1.00
205 Antonio McDyess .50 1.25
206 Andrew DeClercq .40 1.00
207 Ricky Davis .60 1.50
208 Vitaly Potapenko .40 1.00
209 Loy Vaught .40 1.00
210 Kevin Garnett 1.50 4.00
211 Eric Snow .40 1.00
212 Anfernee Hardaway 1.50 4.00
213 Vin Baker .50 1.25
214 Lawrence Funderburke .40 1.00
215 Jeff Hornacek .50 1.25
216 Doug West .40 1.00
217 Michael Doleac .40 1.00
218 Ray Allen 1.00 2.50
219 Derek Anderson .50 1.25
220 Jerome Williams .40 1.00
221 Derrick Coleman .50 1.25
222 Randy Brown .40 1.00
223 Patrick Ewing .75 2.00
224 Walt Williams .40 1.00
225 Charles Oakley .60 1.50
226 Steve Kerr .60 1.50
227 Muggsy Bogues .50 1.25
228 Kevin Willis .40 1.00
229 Marcus Camby .50 1.25
230 Scottie Pippen 1.50 4.00
231 Lamar Odom RC 1.50 4.00
232 Jonathan Bender RC .75 2.00
233 Andre Miller RC 1.50 4.00
234 Trajan Langdon RC .60 1.50
235 A.Radojevic RC .50 1.25
236 William Avery RC .50 1.25
237 Cal Bowdler RC .50 1.25
238 Quincy Lewis RC .50 1.25
239 Dion Glover RC .50 1.25
240 Jeff Foster RC .75 2.00
241 Kenny Thomas RC .75 2.00
242 Devean George RC .60 1.50

243 Tim James RC .50 1.25
244 Vonteego Cummings RC .50 1.25
245 Jumaine Jones RC .50 1.25
246 Scott Padgett RC .60 1.50
247 Adrian Griffin RC .60 1.50
248 Chris Herren RC .60 1.50
249 Allan Houston USA .60 1.50
250 Kevin Garnett USA 2.00 5.00
251 Gary Payton USA 1.25 3.00
252 Steve Smith USA .60 1.50
253 Tim Hardaway USA 1.00 2.50
254 Tim Duncan USA 2.00 5.00
255 Jason Kidd USA 1.25 3.00
256 Tom Gugliotta USA .60 1.50
257 Vin Baker USA .60 1.50

1999-00 Topps Chrome Refractors

*STARS: 2.5X TO 6X BASE CARD HI
*RCs: 2X TO 5X BASE HI
STATED ODDS 1:12
48 Anfernee Hardaway 10.00 25.00
61 Jason Williams 10.00 25.00
111 Jason Terry 12.00 30.00
121 Tim Duncan 60.00 150.00
125 Kobe Bryant 400.00 800.00

1999-00 Topps Chrome All-Etch

COMPLETE SET (30) 25.00 60.00
STATED ODDS 1:10
*REF.STARS: 1.5X TO 4X HI COLUMN
REF: STATED ODDS 1:100
AE1 Karl Malone 2.00 5.00
AE2 Scottie Pippen 2.50 6.00
AE3 Grant Hill 1.50 4.00
AE4 Shawn Kemp 1.50 4.00
AE5 Shaquille O'Neal 4.00 10.00
AE6 Anfernee Hardaway 2.50 6.00
AE7 Chris Webber 1.25 3.00
AE8 Gary Payton 1.50 4.00
AE9 Jason Kidd 1.50 4.00
AE10 John Stockton 1.50 4.00
AE11 Kevin Garnett 2.50 6.00
AE12 Vince Carter 2.50 6.00
AE13 Shareef Abdur-Rahim 1.00 2.50
AE14 Antoine Walker 1.00 2.50
AE15 Kobe Bryant 40.00 100.00
AE16 Tim Duncan 2.50 6.00
AE17 Keith Van Horn .75 2.00
AE18 Allen Iverson 2.50 6.00
AE19 Jason Williams 1.50 4.00
AE20 Stephon Marbury 1.25 3.00
AE21 Elton Brand 1.50 4.00
AE22 Jason Terry 1.25 3.00
AE23 Steve Francis 1.50 4.00
AE24 Corey Maggette 1.00 2.50
AE25 Lamar Odom 1.50 4.00
AE26 Ron Artest 2.00 5.00
AE27 Baron Davis 2.00 5.00
AE28 Andre Miller 1.50 4.00
AE29 Shawn Marion 1.50 4.00
AE30 Wally Szczerbiak 1.25 3.00

1999-00 Topps Chrome All-Stars

COMPLETE SET (10) 8.00 20.00
STATED ODDS 1:30
*REF: 1.5X TO 4X HI COLUMN
REF: STATED ODDS 1:300
AS1 Patrick Ewing 1.25 3.00
AS2 Karl Malone 2.00 5.00
AS3 Hakeem Olajuwon 2.00 5.00
AS4 Scottie Pippen 2.50 6.00
AS5 Gary Payton 1.50 4.00
AS6 John Stockton 1.50 4.00
AS7 Shaquille O'Neal 4.00 10.00
AS8 Charles Barkley 2.50 6.00
AS9 David Robinson 2.00 5.00
AS10 Grant Hill 1.50 4.00

1999-00 Topps Chrome Highlight Reels

COMPLETE SET (15) 8.00 20.00
STATED ODDS 1:10
*REF: 1.5X TO 4X HI COLUMN
REF: STATED ODDS 1:100
HR1 Stephon Marbury .75 2.00
HR2 Vince Carter 1.50 4.00
HR3 Kevin Garnett 1.50 4.00
HR4 Kobe Bryant 25.00 60.00
HR5 Chris Webber .75 2.00
HR6 Allen Iverson 1.50 4.00
HR7 Grant Hill 1.00 2.50
HR8 Antoine Walker .60 1.50
HR9 Jason Williams 1.00 2.50
HR10 Tim Duncan 1.50 4.00
HR11 Shareef Abdur-Rahim .60 1.50
HR12 Keith Van Horn .50 1.25
HR13 Antonio McDyess .50 1.25
HR14 Jason Kidd 1.00 2.50
HR15 Ron Mercer .50 1.25

1999-00 Topps Chrome Highlight Reels Refractors

COMPLETE SET (15)
*REFRACTORS: 2X TO 5X VALUE
HR4 Kobe Bryant 200.00 500.00

1999-00 Topps Chrome Instant Impact

COMPLETE SET (10) 2.50 6.00
STATED ODDS 1:15
*REF: 1.5X TO 4X HI COLUMN
REF: STATED ODDS 1:150
II1 Scottie Pippen 1.50 4.00
II2 Nick Anderson .40 1.00
II3 Isaiah Rider .50 1.25
II4 Antonio Davis .40 1.00
II5 Ron Mercer .50 1.25
II6 Anfernee Hardaway 1.50 4.00
II7 Isaac Austin .40 1.00
II8 Steve Smith .50 1.25
II9 Michael Dickerson .40 1.00
II10 Horace Grant .50 1.25

1999-00 Topps Chrome Keepers

COMPLETE SET (10) 5.00 12.00
STATED ODDS 1:30
*REF: 2X TO 5X HI COLUMN
REF: STATED ODDS 1:300
K1 Elton Brand .60 1.50
K2 Lamar Odom .60 1.50
K3 Steve Francis .60 1.50
K4 Shawn Marion .60 1.50
K5 Wally Szczerbiak .50 1.25
K6 Baron Davis .75 2.00
K7 Andre Miller .60 1.50
K8 Corey Maggette .40 1.00
K9 Jason Terry .50 1.25
K10 Richard Hamilton .75 2.00

2000-01 Topps Chrome

COMPLETE SET (200) 125.00 300.00
COMPLETE SET w/o SP's (150) 40.00 100.00
151-200 PRINT RUN 1999 SERIAL #'d SETS
1 Elton Brand .60 1.50
2 Marcus Camby .50 1.25
3 Jalen Rose .50 1.25
4 Jamie Feick .40 1.00
5 Toni Kukoc .75 2.00
6 Doug Christie .50 1.25
7 Sam Cassell .50 1.25
8 Shaquille O'Neal 2.50 6.00
9 Larry Hughes .60 1.50
10 Jerry Stackhouse .60 1.50
11 Rick Fox .50 1.25
12 Clifford Robinson .60 1.50
13 Dirk Nowitzki 1.50 4.00
14 Cuttino Mobley .50 1.25
15 Latrell Sprewell .75 2.00
16 Kevin Garnett 1.50 4.00
17 Jerome Williams .40 1.00
18 Chris Webber .75 2.00
19 Jason Terry .60 1.50
20 Elden Campbell .40 1.00
21 Jonathan Bender .40 1.00
22 Scottie Pippen 1.50 4.00
23 Radoslav Nesterovic .40 1.00
24 Reggie Miller 1.25 3.00
25 Andre Miller .50 1.25
26 Rashard Lewis .50 1.25
27 Larry Johnson .75 2.00
28 Steve Francis .60 1.50
29 Rod Strickland .40 1.00
30 Tim Thomas .40 1.00
31 Robert Horry .60 1.50
32 Darrell Armstrong .40 1.00
33 Vince Carter 1.25 3.00
34 Othella Harrington .40 1.00
35 Derek Anderson .50 1.25
36 Anthony Carter .40 1.00
37 Ray Allen 1.00 2.50
38 Jason Kidd 1.00 2.50
39 Sean Elliott .50 1.25
40 Tim Duncan 1.50 4.00
41 Adrian Griffin .40 1.00
42 Wally Szczerbiak .50 1.25
43 Austin Croshere .40 1.00
44 James Posey .40 1.00
45 Alan Henderson .40 1.00
46 Jahidi White .40 1.00
47 Shawn Marion .60 1.50
48 Lamar Odom .60 1.50
49 Keon Clark .40 1.00
50 Lamond Murray .40 1.00
51 Paul Pierce 1.00 2.50
52 Charlie Ward .50 1.25
53 Horace Grant .60 1.50
54 John Stockton 1.25 3.00
55 Peja Stojakovic .50 1.25
56 Christian Laettner .60 1.50
57 Keith Van Horn .50 1.25
58 Patrick Ewing 1.00 2.50
59 Steve Smith .60 1.50
60 Antonio Davis .50 1.25
61 Mitch Richmond .75 2.00
62 Michael Olowokandi .40 1.00
63 Baron Davis .60 1.50
64 Dikembe Mutombo 1.00 2.50
65 Raef LaFrentz .50 1.25
66 Ervin Johnson .40 1.00
67 Alonzo Mourning 1.00 2.50
68 Kendall Gill .60 1.50
69 George Lynch .40 1.00
70 Donyell Marshall .50 1.25
71 Bo Outlaw .40 1.00
72 Kenny Anderson .50 1.25
73 John Amaechi .40 1.00
74 Vlade Divac .60 1.50
75 Vin Baker .50 1.25
76 Mike Bibby .60 1.50
77 Richard Hamilton .75 2.00
78 Mookie Blaylock .60 1.50
79 Vitaly Potapenko .40 1.00
80 Anthony Mason .60 1.50
81 Vonteego Cummings .40 1.00
82 Michael Finley .60 1.50
83 Ron Artest .60 1.50
84 Rodney Rogers .40 1.00
85 Team Championship 4.00 10.00
86 Jason Williams 1.00 2.50
87 David Robinson 1.25 3.00
88 Charles Oakley .60 1.50
89 Juwan Howard .50 1.25
90 Antoine Walker .60 1.50
91 Roshown McLeod .40 1.00
92 Eddie Jones .60 1.50
93 Allen Iverson 4.00 10.00
94 Grant Hill 1.00 2.50
95 Terrell Brandon .50 1.25
96 Stephon Marbury .75 2.00
97 Jamal Mashburn .50 1.25
98 Ron Harper .60 1.50
99 Jermaine O'Neal .50 1.25
100 Nick Van Exel .60 1.50
101 Danny Fortson .50 1.25
102 Jim Jackson .50 1.25
103 Brad Miller .50 1.25
104 Shawn Bradley .40 1.00
105 Mark Jackson .50 1.25
106 Maurice Taylor .40 1.00
107 Kobe Bryant 12.00 30.00
108 Clarence Weatherspoon .40 1.00
109 Eric Snow .40 1.00
110 Allan Houston .60 1.50
111 Chauncey Billups .75 2.00
112 Tom Gugliotta .50 1.25
113 Theo Ratliff .40 1.00
114 Rasheed Wallace .75 2.00
115 Glen Rice .60 1.50
116 Bryon Russell .40 1.00
117 Tracy McGrady 1.25 3.00
118 Bryant Reeves .40 1.00
119 Damon Stoudamire .60 1.50
120 Anfernee Hardaway 1.00 2.50
121 Johnny Newman .40 1.00
122 Corey Maggette .50 1.25
123 Travis Best .40 1.00
124 Hakeem Olajuwon 1.25 3.00
125 Antawn Jamison .60 1.50
126 John Starks .60 1.50
127 Antonio McDyess .50 1.25
128 Gary Payton 1.00 2.50
129 Karl Malone 1.25 3.00
130 Michael Dickerson .40 1.00
131 Shawn Kemp 1.00 2.50
132 David Wesley .50 1.25
133 P.J. Brown .40 1.00
134 Ron Mercer .50 1.25
135 Robert Traylor .40 1.00
136 Derrick Coleman .60 1.50
137 Steve Nash 1.00 2.50
138 Ben Wallace .75 2.00
139 Brian Skinner .40 1.00
140 Chris Gatling .40 1.00
141 Dale Davis .50 1.25
142 Glenn Robinson .60 1.50
143 Chucky Atkins .40 1.00
144 Brian Grant .50 1.25
145 Corliss Williamson .40 1.00
146 Shareef Abdur-Rahim .60 1.50
147 Avery Johnson .50 1.25
148 Tim Hardaway .75 2.00
149 Isaiah Rider .50 1.25
150 Shandon Anderson .40 1.00
151 Kenyon Martin RC 3.00 8.00
152 Stromile Swift RC 1.25 3.00
153 Darius Miles RC 1.50 4.00
154 Marcus Fizer RC 1.25 3.00
155 Mike Miller RC 2.50 6.00
156 DerMarr Johnson RC 1.00 2.50
157 Chris Mihm RC 1.00 2.50
158 Jamal Crawford RC 4.00 10.00
159 Joel Przybilla RC 1.25 3.00
160 Keyon Dooling RC 1.25 3.00
161 Jerome Moiso RC 1.00 2.50
162 Etan Thomas RC 1.25 3.00
163 Courtney Alexander RC 1.00 2.50
164 Mateen Cleaves RC 1.25 3.00
165 Jason Collier RC 1.50 4.00
166 Desmond Mason RC 2.00 5.00
167 Quentin Richardson RC 1.25 3.00
168 Jamaal Magloire RC 1.50 4.00
169 Speedy Claxton RC 1.50 4.00
170 Morris Peterson RC 1.50 4.00
171 Donnell Harvey RC 1.25 3.00
172 DeShawn Stevenson RC 1.50 4.00
173 Mamadou N'Diaye RC 1.00 2.50
174 Erick Barkley RC 1.00 2.50
175 Mark Madsen RC 1.50 4.00
176 Hedo Turkoglu RC 2.50 6.00
177 Brian Cardinal RC 1.00 2.50
178 Iakovos Tsakalidis RC 1.00 2.50
179 Dalibor Bagaric RC 1.25 3.00
180 Dragan Tarlac RC 1.00 2.50
181 Dan Langhi RC 1.00 2.50
182 A.J. Guyton RC 1.00 2.50
183 Jake Voskuhl RC 1.00 2.50
184 Khalid El-Amin RC 1.00 2.50
185 Mike Smith RC 1.00 2.50
186 Soumaila Samake RC 1.00 2.50
187 Eddie House RC 1.25 3.00
188 Eduardo Najera RC 1.50 4.00
189 Lavor Postell RC 1.00 2.50
190 Hanno Mottola RC 1.00 2.50
191 Olumide Oyedeji RC 1.00 2.50
192 Michael Redd RC 4.00 10.00
193 Chris Porter RC 1.00 2.50
194 Jabari Smith RC 1.00 2.50
195 Marc Jackson RC 1.25 3.00
196 Stephen Jackson RC 3.00 8.00
197 Pepe Sanchez RC 1.25 3.00
198 Daniel Santiago RC 1.50 4.00
199 Paul McPherson RC 1.00 2.50
200 Mike Penberthy RC 1.50 4.00

2000-01 Topps Chrome Refractors

*STARS: 4X TO 10X BASE CARD HI
1-150 STATED ODDS 1:12
*ROOKIES 151-200: 2X TO 5X BASE CARD HI
151-200 STATED ODDS 1:118
151-200 PRINT RUN 199 SERIAL #'d SETS
33 Vince Carter 30.00 80.00
85 Team Championship 125.00 300.00
93 Allen Iverson 125.00 300.00
107 Kobe Bryant 200.00 500.00
151 Kenyon Martin 50.00 120.00
158 Jamal Crawford 30.00 80.00

2000-01 Topps Chrome Aptitude for Altitude

COMPLETE SET (10) 5.00 12.00
STATED ODDS 1:20
*REF: 1.25X TO 3X APTITUDE ALTITUDE HI
REF.STATED ODDS 1:200 PACKS
AA1 Larry Hughes .75 2.00
AA2 Steve Francis .75 2.00
AA3 Shawn Marion .75 2.00
AA4 Michael Finley .75 2.00
AA5 Allen Iverson 10.00 25.00
AA6 Jerry Stackhouse .75 2.00
AA7 Rashard Lewis .60 1.50
AA8 Tim Thomas .50 1.25
AA9 Baron Davis .75 2.00
AA10 Darius Miles .75 2.00

2000-01 Topps Chrome Cards That Never Were

COMPLETE SET (10) 15.00 40.00
COMMON CARD (MJ1-MJ10) 2.00 5.00
REF: 1.5X TO 4X HI COLUMN

2000-01 Topps Chrome Combos

COMPLETE SET (20) 25.00 60.00
STATED ODDS 1:30
*REF: 1.25X TO 3X COMBOS HI
REF.STATED ODDS 1:300
TC1 S.O'Neal/K.Bryant 40.00 100.00
TC2 S.Marbury/A.Iverson 2.00 5.00
TC3 C.Webber/J.Williams 1.25 3.00
TC4 Ewing/Mutombo/Mourning 1.25 3.00
TC5 T.McGrady/V.Carter 2.50 6.00
TC6 T.Duncan/G.Hill 2.00 5.00
TC7 E.Brand/L.Odom/S.Francis 1.25 3.00
TC8 G.Payton/J.Kidd 2.00 5.00
TC9 Stoud/Pip/Smith/Wallace 2.00 5.00
TC10 T.Duncan/K.Garnett 2.50 6.00
TC11 Hakeem Olajuwon 1.25 3.00
TC12 Patrick Ewing 1.25 3.00
TC13 Karl Malone 1.25 3.00
TC14 Scottie Pippen 2.00 5.00
TC15 Reggie Miller 1.25 3.00
TC16 S.O'Neal/M.Johnson 3.00 8.00
TC17 Fizer/Swift/K.Martin 1.25 3.00
TC18 Claxton/Dooling/Crawford 1.25 3.00
TC19 M.Miller/D.John/Miles 1.25 3.00
TC20 M.Johnson/M.Cleaves 2.00 5.00

2000-01 Topps Chrome Combos Refractors

COMPLETE SET (10)
*REF: 1.25X TO 3X COMBOS HI
TC1 S.O'Neal/K.Bryant 200.00 500.00
TC2 S.Marbury/A.Iverson 12.00 30.00
TC3 C.Webber/J.Williams 12.00 30.00
TC4 Ewing/Mutombo/Mourning 12.00 30.00
TC5 T.McGrady/V.Carter 25.00 60.00
TC6 T.Duncan/G.Hill 6.00 15.00
TC7 E.Brand/L.Odom/S.Francis 4.00 10.00
TC8 G.Payton/J.Kidd 6.00 15.00
TC9 Stoud/Pip/Smith/Wallace 6.00 15.00
TC10 T.Duncan/K.Garnett 12.00 30.00
TC11 Hakeem Olajuwon 4.00 10.00
TC12 Patrick Ewing 4.00 10.00
TC13 Karl Malone 4.00 10.00
TC14 Scottie Pippen 6.00 15.00
TC15 Reggie Miller 6.00 15.00
TC16 S.O'Neal/M.Johnson 20.00 50.00
TC17 Fizer/Swift/K.Martin 4.00 10.00
TC18 Claxton/Dooling/Crawford 4.00 10.00
TC19 M.Miller/D.John/Miles 4.00 10.00
TC20 M.Johnson/M.Cleaves 6.00 15.00

2000-01 Topps Chrome Final Piece Game Jerseys

STATED ODDS 1:2025
PRINT RUN 25 SERIAL #'d SETS
FP1 Shaquille O'Neal 150.00 400.00
FP2 Glen Rice 40.00 100.00
FP3 Robert Horry 40.00 100.00
FP4 Rick Fox 30.00 80.00
FP5 Brian Shaw 25.00 60.00
FP6 Ron Harper 40.00 100.00
FP7 Derek Fisher 40.00 100.00
FP8 A.C. Green 30.00 80.00
FP9 John Salley 25.00 60.00
FP10 Travis Knight 25.00 60.00
FP11 Devean George 25.00 60.00
FP12 Reggie Miller 75.00 200.00
FP13 Jalen Rose 30.00 80.00
FP14 Dale Davis 30.00 80.00
FP15 Rik Smits 25.00 60.00
FP16 Mark Jackson 30.00 80.00
FP17 Travis Best 25.00 60.00
FP18 Austin Croshere 25.00 60.00
FP19 Derrick McKey 25.00 60.00
FP20 Sam Perkins 25.00 60.00
FP21 Chris Mullin 50.00 120.00
FP22 Jonathan Bender 25.00 60.00
FP23 Zan Tabak 25.00 60.00

2000-01 Topps Chrome Hobby Masters

COMPLETE SET (10) 15.00 40.00
STATED ODDS 1:30 HOBBY
*REF: 3X TO 8X HOBBY MASTERS HI
REF.STATED ODDS 1:602 HOBBY
HM1 Kevin Garnett 3.00 8.00
HM2 Jason Williams 2.00 5.00
HM3 Tim Duncan 3.00 8.00
HM4 Tracy McGrady 2.50 6.00
HM5 Kobe Bryant 20.00 50.00
HM6 Allen Iverson 3.00 8.00
HM7 Elton Brand 1.25 3.00
HM8 Steve Francis 1.25 3.00
HM9 Vince Carter 2.50 6.00
HM10 Chris Webber 1.50 4.00

2000-01 Topps Chrome In The Paint

COMPLETE SET (10) 15.00 40.00
STATED ODDS 1:60
*REF: 2X TO 5X IN THE PAINT HI
REF.STATED ODDS 1:600
IP1 Elton Brand 3.00 8.00
IP2 Tim Duncan 8.00 20.00
IP3 Antonio McDyess 2.50 6.00
IP4 Karl Malone 6.00 15.00
IP5 Rasheed Wallace 4.00 10.00
IP6 Antoine Walker 3.00 8.00
IP7 Shareef Abdur-Rahim 3.00 8.00
IP8 Lamar Odom 3.00 8.00
IP9 Kenyon Martin 6.00 15.00
IP10 Stromile Swift 2.50 6.00

2000-01 Topps Chrome Magic Johnson Reprints

COMPLETE SET (7) 12.50 30.00
COMMON CARD (1-7) 2.00 5.00
STATED ODDS 1:10
REF.STATED ODDS 1:100

2000-01 Topps Chrome No Limit

COMPLETE SET (20) 20.00 50.00
STATED ODDS 1:15
*REF: 1.25X TO 3X NO LIMIT HI
REF.STATED ODDS 1:150
NL1 Kobe Bryant 20.00 50.00
NL2 Kevin Garnett 2.50 6.00
NL3 Vince Carter 2.00 5.00
NL4 Tracy McGrady 2.00 5.00
NL5 Tim Duncan 2.50 6.00
NL6 Elton Brand 1.00 2.50
NL7 Lamar Odom 1.00 2.50
NL8 Larry Hughes 1.00 2.50
NL9 Chris Webber 1.25 3.00
NL10 Shareef Abdur-Rahim 1.00 2.50
NL11 Jason Kidd 1.50 4.00
NL12 Gary Payton 1.50 4.00
NL13 Paul Pierce 1.50 4.00
NL14 Stromile Swift .75 2.00
NL15 Darius Miles 1.00 2.50
NL16 Mike Miller 1.50 4.00
NL17 Jason Williams 1.50 4.00
NL18 Jamal Crawford 2.50 6.00
NL19 Marcus Fizer .75 2.00
NL20 DerMarr Johnson .60 1.50

2000-01 Topps Chrome No Limit Refractors

NL1 Kobe Bryant 125.00 300.00
NL2 Kevin Garnett 30.00 80.00
NL3 Vince Carter 30.00 80.00
NL4 Tracy McGrady 25.00 60.00
NL5 Tim Duncan 30.00 80.00
NL6 Elton Brand 6.00 15.00
NL7 Lamar Odom 6.00 15.00
NL8 Larry Hughes 6.00 15.00
NL9 Chris Webber 8.00 20.00
NL10 Shareef Abdur-Rahim 6.00 15.00
NL11 Jason Kidd 15.00 40.00
NL12 Gary Payton 15.00 40.00
NL13 Paul Pierce 15.00 40.00
NL14 Stromile Swift 5.00 12.00
NL15 Darius Miles 6.00 15.00
NL16 Mike Miller 10.00 25.00
NL17 Jason Williams 12.00 30.00
NL18 Jamal Crawford 15.00 40.00
NL19 Marcus Fizer 5.00 12.00
NL20 DerMarr Johnson 4.00 10.00

2001-02 Topps Chrome

COMP.SET w/o RC's (129)
1 Shaquille O'Neal 2.50 6.00
2 Steve Nash 1.25 3.00
3 Allen Iverson 1.50 4.00
4 Shawn Marion .60 1.50
5 Rasheed Wallace .75 2.00
6 Antonio Daniels .40 1.00
7 Rashard Lewis .50 1.25
8 Raef LaFrentz .40 1.00
9 Stromile Swift .40 1.00
10 Vince Carter 1.25 3.00
11 Danny Fortson .40 1.00
12 Jalen Rose .50 1.25
13 Glen Rice .60 1.50
14 Glenn Robinson .60 1.50
15 Wally Szczerbiak .50 1.25
16 Rick Fox .50 1.25
17 Darius Miles .40 1.00
18 Jermaine O'Neal .50 1.25
19 Eddie Jones .60 1.50
20 Tracy McGrady 1.00 2.50
21 Kevin Garnett 1.50 4.00
22 Tim Thomas .40 1.00
23 Larry Hughes .50 1.25
24 Jerry Stackhouse .60 1.50
25 Ray Allen 1.00 2.50
26 Terrell Brandon .50 1.25
27 Keith Van Horn .50 1.25
28 Marcus Fizer .40 1.00
29 Elden Campbell .40 1.00
30 Tim Duncan 1.50 4.00
31 Doug Christie .40 1.00
32 Allan Houston .60 1.50
33 Patrick Ewing 1.00 2.50
34 Hakeem Olajuwon 1.25 3.00
35 Anfernee Hardaway 1.50 4.00
36 Clarence Weatherspoon .40 1.00
37 Eric Snow .40 1.00
38 Tom Gugliotta .40 1.00
39 Scottie Pippen 1.50 4.00
40 Chris Webber .75 2.00
41 David Robinson 1.25 3.00
42 Elton Brand .50 1.25
43 Theo Ratliff .40 1.00
44 Paul Pierce 1.00 2.50
45 Jamal Mashburn .50 1.25
46 Damon Stoudamire .60 1.50
47 DerMarr Johnson .40 1.00
48 Andre Miller .50 1.25
49 Dirk Nowitzki 1.50 4.00
50 Kobe Bryant 30.00 80.00
51 Keyon Dooling .40 1.00
52 Brian Grant .40 1.00
53 Antawn Jamison .50 1.25
54 Jonathan Bender .40 1.00
55 Dikembe Mutombo 1.00 2.50
56 Steve Smith .50 1.25
57 Hedo Turkoglu .50 1.25
58 Robert Horry .60 1.50
59 Kurt Thomas .40 1.00
60 Jason Terry .60 1.50
61 Vitaly Potapenko .40 1.00
62 Gary Payton 1.00 2.50
63 Bonzi Wells .40 1.00
64 Raja Bell RC 1.25 3.00
65 Chris Mihm .40 1.00
66 Reggie Miller 1.25 3.00
67 Lamar Odom .50 1.25
68 Darrell Armstrong .40 1.00
69 Baron Davis .60 1.50
70 Aaron Williams .40 1.00
71 Latrell Sprewell .75 2.00
72 James Posey .40 1.00
73 Ben Wallace .75 2.00
74 Marc Jackson .40 1.00
75 Maurice Taylor .40 1.00
76 Aaron McKie .40 1.00
77 Grant Hill 1.00 2.50
78 Anthony Carter .40 1.00
79 Peja Stojakovic .50 1.25
80 Jason Kidd 1.00 2.50
81 Vin Baker .50 1.25
82 Morris Peterson .40 1.00
83 Bryon Russell .40 1.00
84 Michael Dickerson .40 1.00
85 Quentin Richardson .40 1.00
86 Primoz Brezec RC 1.00 2.50
87 Desmond Mason .50 1.25
88 Jason Williams 1.00 2.50
89 Marcus Camby .50 1.25
90 Stephon Marbury .75 2.00
91 Mike Bibby .60 1.50
92 Alonzo Mourning 1.00 2.50
93 Mitch Richmond .75 2.00
94 Donyell Marshall .40 1.00
95 Michael Jordan 12.00 30.00
96 Mike Miller .50 1.25
97 Nick Van Exel .60 1.50
98 Michael Finley .60 1.50
99 Jamal Crawford .60 1.50
100 Steve Francis .60 1.50
101 Kenyon Martin .60 1.50
102 Sam Cassell .50 1.25
103 Chucky Atkins .40 1.00
104 Juwan Howard .50 1.25
105 Bryant Reeves .40 1.00
106 Richard Hamilton .75 2.00
107 Antonio Davis .50 1.25
108 Antonio McDyess .50 1.25
109 Derek Anderson .40 1.00
110 Kenny Anderson .50 1.25
111 Antoine Walker .50 1.25
112 Wang ZhiZhi .60 1.50
113 Shareef Abdur-Rahim .50 1.25
114 Chris Whitney .40 1.00
115 John Stockton 1.25 3.00
116 Alvin Williams .40 1.00
117 David Wesley .40 1.00
118 Joe Smith .50 1.25
119 Jahidi White .40 1.00
120 Karl Malone 1.25 3.00
121 Cuttino Mobley .50 1.25
122 Tyrone Hill .40 1.00
123 Clifford Robinson .60 1.50
124 Toni Kukoc .75 2.00
125 Eddie Robinson .40 1.00
126 Courtney Alexander .40 1.00
127 Ron Mercer .40 1.00
128 Lamond Murray .40 1.00
129 Rodney Rogers .40 1.00
130 Tyson Chandler RC 1.50 4.00
131 Pau Gasol RC 12.00 30.00
132 Eddy Curry RC 1.00 2.50
133 Jason Richardson RC 1.50 4.00
134 Shane Battier RC 2.00 5.00
135 Eddie Griffin RC .75 2.00
136 DeSagana Diop RC .60 1.50
137 Rodney White RC .60 1.50
138 Joe Johnson RC 1.50 4.00
139 Kedrick Brown RC .60 1.50
140 Vladimir Radmanovic RC .75 2.00
141 Richard Jefferson RC 1.25 3.00
142 Troy Murphy RC .75 2.00
143 Steven Hunter RC .60 1.50
144 Kirk Haston RC .60 1.50
145 Michael Bradley RC .60 1.50
146 Jason Collins RC .75 2.00
147 Zach Randolph RC 2.00 5.00
148 Brendan Haywood RC .75 2.00
149 Joseph Forte RC .60 1.50
150 Jeryl Sasser RC .60 1.50
151 Brandon Armstrong RC .60 1.50
152 Gerald Wallace RC 1.25 3.00
153 Samuel Dalembert RC 1.00 2.50
154 Jamaal Tinsley RC .75 2.00
155 Tony Parker RC 12.00 30.00
156 Trenton Hassell RC .60 1.50
157 Gilbert Arenas RC 2.50 6.00
158 Jeff Trepagnier RC .60 1.50
159 Damone Brown RC .60 1.50
160 Loren Woods RC .60 1.50
161 Andrei Kirilenko RC 1.50 4.00
162 Zeljko Rebraca RC 1.00 2.50
163 Kenny Satterfield RC .60 1.50
164 Alvin Jones RC .60 1.50
165 Kwame Brown RC 1.00 2.50

2001-02 Topps Chrome Refractors

*REF.STARS: 3X TO 8X BASE CARD HI
*REF.RCs: 2X TO 5X BASE CARD HI
REF.STATED ODDS 1:4
1 Shaquille O'Neal 25.00 60.00
3 Allen Iverson 20.00 50.00
10 Vince Carter 12.00 30.00
20 Tracy McGrady 12.00 30.00
21 Kevin Garnett 20.00 50.00
30 Tim Duncan 20.00 50.00
39 Scottie Pippen 15.00 40.00
49 Dirk Nowitzki 20.00 50.00
50 Kobe Bryant 125.00 300.00
95 Michael Jordan 150.00 400.00
112 Wang ZhiZhi 25.00 60.00
131 Pau Gasol 75.00 200.00
138 Joe Johnson 12.00 30.00
147 Zach Randolph 10.00 25.00
155 Tony Parker 75.00 200.00

2001-02 Topps Chrome Refractors Black Border

*REF.BLK.STRS:20X TO 50X BASE CARD HI
*REF.BLK.RCs: 6X TO 15X BASE CARD HI
REF.BLACK PRINT RUN 50 SER.#'d SETS
1 Shaquille O'Neal 150.00 400.00
3 Allen Iverson 125.00 300.00
10 Vince Carter 75.00 200.00
20 Tracy McGrady 75.00 200.00
21 Kevin Garnett 150.00 400.00
30 Tim Duncan 125.00 300.00
35 Anfernee Hardaway 125.00 300.00
39 Scottie Pippen 125.00 300.00
49 Dirk Nowitzki 125.00 300.00
50 Kobe Bryant 2,000.00 4,000.00
55 Dikembe Mutombo 60.00 150.00
73 Ben Wallace 50.00 120.00
95 Michael Jordan 200.00 500.00
106 Richard Hamilton 60.00 150.00
131 Pau Gasol 500.00 1,000.00
138 Joe Johnson 40.00 100.00
147 Zach Randolph 60.00 150.00
155 Tony Parker 500.00 1,000.00

2001-02 Topps Chrome Autographs

STATED ODDS 1:257
CARDS WITH "H" HOBBY PACKS ONLY
CAAD Antonio Daniels H 5.00 12.00
CAAJ Antawn Jamison 5.00 12.00
CABD Baron Davis H 10.00 25.00
CAEB Elton Brand H 5.00 12.00
CAJF Joseph Forte H 5.00 12.00
CAJJ Joe Johnson H 8.00 20.00
CAPS Peja Stojakovic 6.00 15.00
CASB Shane Battier 5.00 12.00
CASM Shawn Marion 5.00 12.00
CAZR Zach Randolph 8.00 20.00

2001-02 Topps Chrome Fast and Furious

COMPLETE SET (14) 20.00 50.00
STATED ODDS 1:6
*REF: 1X TO 2.5X BASE HI
REF STATED ODDS 1:30
FF1 Steve Francis .60 1.50
FF2 Allen Iverson 1.50 4.00
FF3 Tracy McGrady 1.00 2.50
FF4 Vince Carter 1.25 3.00
FF5 Michael Jordan 8.00 20.00
FF6 Kobe Bryant 25.00 60.00
FF7 Kevin Garnett 1.50 4.00
FF8 Shaquille O'Neal 2.50 6.00
FF9 Ray Allen 1.00 2.50
FF10 Paul Pierce 1.00 2.50
FF11 Jerry Stackhouse .60 1.50
FF12 Antoine Walker .50 1.25
FF13 Chris Webber .75 2.00
FF14 Jason Richardson 1.00 2.50

2001-02 Topps Chrome Kareem Abdul-Jabbar Reprints

COMPLETE SET (13) 20.00 40.00
COMMON CARD (1-13) 2.50 6.00
STATED ODDS 1:20
REFRACTOR STATED ODDS 1:100

2001-02 Topps Chrome Lacing Up

PRINT RUN 50 SER.#'d SETS
LUAJ Antawn Jamison 25.00 60.00
LUBD Baron Davis 25.00 60.00
LUEB Elton Brand 8.00 20.00
LUEC Eddy Curry 10.00 25.00
LUJF Joseph Forte 6.00 15.00
LUJT Jason Terry 10.00 25.00
LUKB Kwame Brown 10.00 25.00
LUPS Peja Stojakovic 15.00 40.00
LURH Richard Hamilton 20.00 50.00
LUSB Shane Battier 20.00 50.00
LUSM Shawn Marion 10.00 25.00
LUSO 50.00 120.00
LUTD Tim Duncan 50.00 120.00
LUVR Vladimir Radmanovic 8.00 20.00

2001-02 Topps Chrome Mad Game

COMPLETE SET (10) 12.50 30.00
STATED ODDS 1:13
*REF: 1.25X TO 3X MAD GAME HI
REF.STATED ODDS 1:65
MG1 Allen Iverson 2.50 6.00
MG2 Shaquille O'Neal 4.00 10.00
MG3 Tim Duncan 2.50 6.00
MG4 Vince Carter 2.00 5.00
MG5 Kevin Garnett 2.50 6.00
MG6 Kobe Bryant 30.00 80.00
MG7 Tracy McGrady 1.50 4.00
MG8 Steve Francis 1.00 2.50
MG9 Chris Webber 1.25 3.00
MG10 Darius Miles .60 1.50

2001-02 Topps Chrome Shorts Illustrated

STATED ODDS 1:180
*REF: 1.25X TO 3X SHORT ILLUSTRATED HI
REF.PRINT RUN 50 SER.#'d SETS
SIAH Allan Houston 4.00 10.00
SICM Cuttino Mobley 3.00 8.00
SIDF Derek Fisher 3.00 8.00
SIDN Dirk Nowitzki 10.00 25.00
SIDW David Wesley 2.50 6.00
SIGP Gary Payton 6.00 15.00
SIMF Michael Finley 4.00 10.00
SIRH Richard Hamilton 5.00 12.00
SITD Tim Duncan 10.00 25.00
SIWS Wally Szczerbiak 3.00 8.00

2001-02 Topps Chrome Team Topps

COMPLETE SET (12) 12.50 30.00
STATED ODDS 1:30
*REF: 1X TO 2.5X TEAM TOPPS HI
REF.STATED ODDS 1:55
TT1 Shaquille O'Neal 5.00 12.00
TT2 Tim Duncan 3.00 8.00
TT3 Antawn Jamison 1.00 2.50
TT4 Jason Terry 1.25 3.00
TT5 Baron Davis 1.25 3.00
TT6 Elton Brand 1.00 2.50
TT7 Peja Stojakovic 1.00 2.50
TT8 Richard Hamilton 1.50 4.00
TT9 Shawn Marion 1.25 3.00
TT10 Team Photo 1.00 2.50
TT11 Shane Battier 2.50 6.00
TT12 Joseph Forte .75 2.00

2001-02 Topps Chrome Team Topps Jerseys

STATED ODDS 1:109
*REF: 1.25X TO 3X HI
REF.PRINT RUN 50 SER.#'d SETS
TTAJ Antawn Jamison 1.50 4.00
TTBD Baron Davis 2.00 5.00
TTEB Elton Brand 1.50 4.00
TTJF Joseph Forte 1.25 3.00
TTJT Jason Terry 2.00 5.00
TTPS Peja Stojakovic 1.50 4.00
TTRH Richard Hamilton 2.50 6.00
TTSB Shane Battier 4.00 10.00
TTSM Shawn Marion 2.00 5.00
TTSO Shaquille O'Neal 8.00 20.00
TTTD Tim Duncan 5.00 12.00

2002-03 Topps Chrome

COMPLETE SET (175)
RC CARD B VER. NOT IN ENGLISH
1 Shaquille O'Neal 2.50 6.00
2 Pau Gasol 1.00 2.50
3 Allen Iverson 1.50 4.00
4 Tom Gugliotta .40 1.00
5 Rasheed Wallace .75 2.00
6 Peja Stojakovic .50 1.25
7 Jason Richardson .60 1.50
8 Rashard Lewis .50 1.25
9 Morris Peterson .50 1.25
10 Michael Jordan 6.00 15.00
11 Matt Harpring .40 1.00
12 Shareef Abdur-Rahim .60 1.50
13 Antoine Walker .50 1.25
14 Stephon Marbury .75 2.00
15 Jamal Mashburn .50 1.25
16 Eddy Curry .40 1.00
17 Jumaine Jones .40 1.00
18 Jason Kidd 1.00 2.50
19 Jerry Stackhouse .60 1.50

20 Kenny Thomas .40 1.00
21 Kobe Bryant 15.00 40.00
22 Jason Williams .75 2.00
23 Eddie Jones .60 1.50
24 Kenyon Martin .60 1.50
25 Kevin Garnett 1.50 4.00
26 Kurt Thomas .40 1.00
27 Karl Malone 1.25 3.00
28 Reggie Evans RC 1.25 3.00
29 Dirk Nowitzki 1.50 4.00
30 Vince Carter 1.25 3.00
31 Desmond Mason .50 1.25
32 Todd MacCulloch .40 1.00
33 Grant Hill 1.00 2.50
34 Terrell Brandon .40 1.00
35 Tracy McGrady 1.00 2.50
36 Tim Thomas .40 1.00
37 Loren Woods .40 1.00
38 Michael Redd .50 1.25
39 Stromile Swift .40 1.00
40 Dikembe Mutombo 1.00 2.50
41 Richard Jefferson .50 1.25
42 Glenn Robinson .60 1.50
43 Quentin Richardson .40 1.00
44 Elton Brand .50 1.25
45 Reggie Miller 1.25 3.00
46 Eddie Griffin .40 1.00
47 Gilbert Arenas .60 1.50
48 Zeljko Rebraca .40 1.00
49 Mark Jackson .50 1.25
50 Juwan Howard .50 1.25
51 Nick Van Exel .60 1.50
52 Donyell Marshall .40 1.00
53 Tyson Chandler .60 1.50
54 Baron Davis .60 1.50
55 Nate Huffman RC .40 1.00
56 Jamaal Magloire .40 1.00
57 Marcus Fizer .40 1.00
58 Steve Francis .60 1.50
59 Aaron McKie .40 1.00
60 Scottie Pippen 1.50 4.00
61 Mike Bibby .60 1.50
62 Paul Pierce 1.00 2.50
63 Kwame Brown .40 1.00
64 Andrei Kirilenko .50 1.25
65 Keon Clark .40 1.00
66 Alvin Williams .40 1.00
67 Brent Barry .40 1.00
68 Doug Christie .40 1.00
69 Chris Webber .75 2.00
70 Robert Horry .60 1.50
71 Allan Houston .60 1.50
72 Kerry Kittles .40 1.00
73 Wally Szczerbiak .50 1.25
74 Jonathan Bender .40 1.00
75 Sam Cassell .50 1.25
76 Rod Strickland .40 1.00
77 Shane Battier .60 1.50
78 Tim Duncan 1.50 4.00
79 Jermaine O'Neal .50 1.25
80 Cuttino Mobley .40 1.00
81 Clifford Robinson .60 1.50
82 Steve Nash 1.25 3.00
83 Dermarr Johnson .40 1.00
84 Courtney Alexander .40 1.00
85 Corliss Williamson .40 1.00
86 Tony Parker 1.00 2.50
87 Damon Stoudamire .60 1.50
88 Jalen Rose .50 1.25
89 Mike Miller .50 1.25
90 Raef Lafrentz .40 1.00
91 Ben Wallace .75 2.00
92 Ray Allen 1.00 2.50
93 Gary Payton 1.00 2.50
94 Derek Fisher .60 1.50
95 Michael Olowokandi .40 1.00
96 Jamaal Tinsley .60 1.50
97 Chris Mihm .40 1.00
98 Antawn Jamison .50 1.25
99 Mengke Bateer .60 1.50
100 Michael Finley .60 1.50
101 Andre Miller .50 1.25
102 Elden Campbell .40 1.00
103 Kedrick Brown .40 1.00
104 Jason Terry .50 1.25
105 Kenny Anderson .50 1.25
106 Darius Miles .50 1.25
107 Latrell Sprewell .60 1.50
108 Darrell Armstrong .40 1.00
109 Joe Johnson .50 1.25
110 Bonzi Wells .40 1.00
111 LaPhonso Ellis .50 1.25
112 Steve Smith .50 1.25
113 Vin Baker .50 1.25
114 Antonio Davis .50 1.25
115 John Stockton 1.25 3.00
116 Shawn Marion .60 1.50
117 Devean George .40 1.00
118 Joe Smith .50 1.25
119 Sean Lampley .40 1.00
120 Lamar Odom .60 1.50
121 Alonzo Mourning 1.00 2.50
122 Antonio Daniels .40 1.00
123 Troy Murphy .50 1.25
124A Manu Ginobili RC 30.00 80.00
124B Manu Ginobili RC 30.00 80.00
125 Richard Hamilton .50 1.25
126 Amare Stoudemire RC 4.00 10.00
127 Carlos Boozer RC 1.50 4.00
128 Casey Jacobsen RC 1.25 3.00
129 Juaquin Hawkins RC 1.00 2.50
130 Pat Burke RC 1.00 2.50
131 Dan Dickau RC 1.00 2.50
132 Drew Gooden RC 1.50 4.00
133 Fred Jones RC 1.25 3.00
134 Jared Jeffries RC 1.25 3.00
135A Jiri Welsch RC 1.25 3.00
135B Jiri Welsch RC 1.25 3.00
136 Juan Dixon RC 1.25 3.00
137 Marcus Haislip RC 1.00 2.50
138 Melvin Ely RC 1.25 3.00
139A Nene Hilario RC 1.50 4.00
139B Nene Hilario RC 1.50 4.00
140 Qyntel Woods RC 1.00 2.50
141 Lonny Baxter RC 1.00 2.50
142 Ryan Humphrey RC 1.25 3.00
143 Smush Parker RC 1.25 3.00
144 Tayshaun Prince RC 3.00 8.00
145 Vincent Yarbrough RC 1.00 2.50
146A Yao Ming RC 40.00 100.00
146B Yao Ming RC 40.00 100.00
147 Pete Mickeal .40 1.00
148 Tamar Slay RC 1.00 2.50
149A Efthimios Rentzias RC 1.00 2.50
149B Efthimios Rentzias RC 1.00 2.50
150A Igor Rakocevic RC 1.00 2.50
150B Igor Rakocevic RC 1.00 2.50
151A Gordan Giricek RC 1.50 4.00
151B Gordan Giricek RC 1.50 4.00
152A Nikoloz Tskitishvili RC 1.00 2.50
152B Nikoloz Tskitishvili RC 1.00 2.50
153 Mike Dunleavy RC 1.50 4.00
154A Marko Jaric 1.50 4.00
154B Marko Jaric 1.50 4.00
155 Kareem Rush RC 1.25 3.00
156 John Salmons RC 1.50 4.00
157 Jay Williams RC 1.25 3.00
158 J.R. Bremer RC 1.00 2.50
159 Frank Williams RC 1.00 2.50
160 Adam Harrington RC 1.00 2.50
161 DaJuan Wagner RC 1.25 3.00
162 Chris Wilcox RC 1.25 3.00
163 Chris Jefferies RC 1.00 2.50
164 Caron Butler RC 1.50 4.00
165A Bostjan Nachbar RC 1.25 3.00
165B Bostjan Nachbar RC 1.25 3.00

2002-03 Topps Chrome Refractors
*STARS: 2X TO 5X BASE CARD HI
*RCs: 1X TO 2.5X BASE CARD HI
STATED ODDS 1:4
10 Michael Jordan 300.00 600.00
21 Kobe Bryant 300.00 600.00
78 Tim Duncan 40.00 100.00
124A Manu Ginobili 150.00 400.00
124B Manu Ginobili 150.00 400.00
146A Yao Ming 200.00 500.00
146B Yao Ming 200.00 500.00

2002-03 Topps Chrome Refractors Black Border
*STARS: 10X TO 25X BASE CARD HI
*RCs: 3X TO 8X BASE CARD HI
STATED ODDS 1:29
STATED PRINT RUN 99 SER.#'d SETS
1 Shaquille O'Neal 125.00 300.00
3 Allen Iverson 125.00 300.00
10 Michael Jordan 1,500.00 3,000.00
21 Kobe Bryant 1,000.00 2,000.00
25 Kevin Garnett 75.00 200.00
29 Dirk Nowitzki 75.00 200.00
30 Vince Carter 60.00 150.00
35 Tracy McGrady 60.00 150.00
78 Tim Duncan 200.00 500.00
124A Manu Ginobili 800.00 1,500.00
124B Manu Ginobili 800.00 1,500.00
126 Amare Stoudemire 75.00 200.00
146A Yao Ming 1,000.00 2,000.00
146B Yao Ming 1,000.00 2,000.00

2002-03 Topps Chrome Refractors White Border
*STARS: 6X TO 15X BASE CARD HI
*RCs: 1.5X TO 4X BASE CARD HI
PRINT RUN 249 SER.#'d SETS
1 Shaquille O'Neal 75.00 200.00
3 Allen Iverson 75.00 200.00
10 Michael Jordan 600.00 1,200.00
21 Kobe Bryant 600.00 1,200.00
25 Kevin Garnett 50.00 120.00
29 Dirk Nowitzki 50.00 120.00
30 Vince Carter 40.00 100.00
35 Tracy McGrady 40.00 100.00
78 Tim Duncan 125.00 300.00
124A Manu Ginobili 400.00 800.00
124B Manu Ginobili 400.00 800.00
126 Amare Stoudemire 40.00 100.00
146A Yao Ming 500.00 1,000.00
146B Yao Ming 500.00 1,000.00

2002-03 Topps Chrome Autographs
GROUP A ODDS 1:3796; B ODDS 1:949
GROUP C ODDS 1:1130; D ODDS 1:862
TCAMD Mike Dunleavy/500 4.00 10.00
TCASO Shaquille O'Neal/850 50.00 120.00
TCATM Troy Murphy/500 4.00 10.00
TCATM Tito Maddox/1100 4.00 10.00
TCAYM Yao Ming/250 125.00 300.00

2002-03 Topps Chrome Coast to Coast
COMPLETE SET (20) 15.00 40.00
STATED ODDS 1:8
*REF: .75X TO 2X COAST TO COAST HI
REF. STATED ODDS 1:40
CC1 Tracy McGrady 1.25 3.00
CC2 Jason Kidd 1.25 3.00
CC3 Mike Bibby .75 2.00
CC4 Baron Davis .75 2.00
CC5 Steve Francis .75 2.00
CC6 Vince Carter 1.50 4.00
CC7 Kobe Bryant 40.00 100.00
CC8 Michael Jordan 8.00 20.00
CC9 Paul Pierce 1.25 3.00
CC10 Stephon Marbury 1.00 2.50
CC11 Ray Allen 1.25 3.00
CC12 Gary Payton 1.25 3.00
CC13 Shawn Marion .75 2.00
CC14 Steve Nash 1.50 4.00
CC15 Andre Miller .60 1.50
CC16 Jerry Stackhouse .75 2.00
CC17 Latrell Sprewell .75 2.00
CC18 Jason Richardson .75 2.00
CC19 Jamaal Tinsley .60 1.50
CC20 Tony Parker 1.25 3.00

2002-03 Topps Chrome Destination Relics
GROUP A ODDS 1:9310; B: 1:2373
GROUP C ODDS 1:1898; D: 1:422; E: 1:111
*REF: 1.25X TO 3X HI
REF.PRINT RUN 25 SER.#'d SETS
FDBH Brendan Haywood 2.00 5.00
FDDR David Robinson 6.00 15.00
FDJJ Joe Johnson 2.50 6.00
FDLO Lamar Odom 3.00 8.00
FDMO Michael Olowokandi 2.00 5.00
FDNV Nick Van Exel 3.00 8.00
FDPS Peja Stojakovic 2.50 6.00
FDRW Rasheed Wallace 4.00 10.00
FDSF Steve Francis 3.00 8.00
FDSN Steve Nash 6.00 15.00
FDSS Steve Smith 2.50 6.00
FDWS Wally Szczerbiak 2.50 6.00

2002-03 Topps Chrome Franchise Fabric Relics
GROUP A ODDS 1:11167; B ODDS 1:9099
GROUP C ODDS 1:316; D ODDS 1:135
*REF: 1.5X TO 4X HI
REF.PRINT RUN 25 SER.#'d SETS
FFCW Chris Webber 4.00 10.00
FFDW DaJuan Wagner 2.50 6.00
FFEB Elton Brand 2.50 6.00
FFJO Jermaine O'Neal 2.50 6.00
FFJR Jason Richardson 3.00 8.00
FFKG Kevin Garnett 8.00 20.00
FFKM Kenyon Martin 3.00 8.00
FFMD Mike Dunleavy 3.00 8.00
FFMO Michael Olowokandi 2.00 5.00
FFNH Nene Hilario 3.00 8.00
FFSO Shaquille O'Neal 12.00 30.00
FFTD Tim Duncan 8.00 20.00
FFYM Yao Ming 15.00 40.00

2002-03 Topps Chrome Shaq Attack Relics
COMMON CARD (1-5) 12.00 30.00
STATED ODDS 1:474
*REF: 1X TO 2.5X BASE HI
REF PRINT RUN 34 SER.#'d SETS

2002-03 Topps Chrome The Move
COMPLETE SET (20) 30.00 80.00
STATED ODDS 1:28
*REF: 1X TO 2.5X THE MOVE HI
REF.STATED ODDS 1:140
TM1 Shaquille O'Neal 5.00 12.00
TM2 Reggie Miller 2.50 6.00
TM3 Allen Iverson 3.00 8.00
TM4 Kobe Bryant 40.00 100.00
TM5 Jason Kidd 2.00 5.00
TM6 Michael Jordan 20.00 50.00
TM7 Vince Carter 2.50 6.00
TM8 Ray Allen 2.00 5.00
TM9 Gary Payton 2.00 5.00
TM10 Jason Richardson 1.25 3.00
TM11 Tim Duncan 3.00 8.00
TM12 Scottie Pippen 3.00 8.00
TM13 Paul Pierce 2.00 5.00
TM14 Dikembe Mutombo 2.00 5.00
TM15 Tracy McGrady 2.00 5.00
TM16 Chris Wilcox 1.00 2.50
TM17 Yao Ming 6.00 15.00
TM18 Jay Williams 1.00 2.50
TM19 Mike Dunleavy 1.25 3.00
TM20 DaJuan Wagner 1.00 2.50

2002-03 Topps Chrome Zone Busters
COMPLETE SET (15) 12.50 30.00
STATED ODDS 1:12
*REF: .75X TO 2X ZONE BUSTER HI
REF.STATED ODDS 1:60
ZB1 Shaquille O'Neal 3.00 8.00
ZB2 Kevin Garnett 2.00 5.00
ZB3 Peja Stojakovic .60 1.50
ZB4 Kenyon Martin .75 2.00
ZB5 Latrell Sprewell .75 2.00
ZB6 Michael Finley .75 2.00
ZB7 Shawn Marion .75 2.00
ZB8 Kobe Bryant 20.00 50.00
ZB9 Mike Bibby .75 2.00
ZB10 Tracy McGrady 1.25 3.00
ZB11 Tony Parker 1.25 3.00
ZB12 Vince Carter 1.50 4.00
ZB13 Michael Jordan 8.00 20.00
ZB14 Elton Brand .75 2.00
ZB15 Jamaal Tinsley .50 1.25

2002-03 Topps Chrome Zone Busters Refractors
*REF: 1.5X TO 4X ZONE BUSTER HI
REF.STATED ODDS 1:60
ZB1 Shaquille O'Neal 30.00 80.00
ZB2 Kevin Garnett 30.00 80.00
ZB8 Kobe Bryant 125.00 300.00
ZB10 Tracy McGrady 15.00 40.00
ZB12 Vince Carter 20.00 50.00
ZB13 Michael Jordan 150.00 400.00

2003-04 Topps Chrome
COMPLETE SET (165) 2,500.00 5,000.00
COMP.SET w/o RC's (110) 30.00 80.00
B VERSION FOR CARDS 112, 121, 127
129, 131, 132, 138, 140, 146, 147, 149, 154
CARD B VERSION FOREIGN, SAME VALUE
1 Tracy McGrady 1.25 3.00
2 Dajuan Wagner .50 1.25
3 Allen Iverson 2.00 5.00
4 Chris Webber 1.00 2.50
5 Jason Kidd 1.25 3.00
6 Stephon Marbury 1.00 2.50
7 Jermaine O'Neal .75 2.00
8 Antoine Walker .75 2.00
9 Tony Parker 1.25 3.00
10 Mike Bibby .75 2.00
11 Yao Ming 2.00 5.00
12 Bobby Jackson .60 1.50
13 Steve Nash 1.50 4.00
14 Paul Pierce 1.25 3.00
15 Vince Carter 1.50 4.00
16 Peja Stojakovic 1.25 3.00
17 Wally Szczerbiak .60 1.50
18 Kenyon Martin .75 2.00
19 Pau Gasol 1.25 3.00
20 Gary Payton 1.25 3.00
21 Tim Duncan 2.00 5.00
22 Anfernee Hardaway 2.00 5.00
23 Jason Richardson .75 2.00
24 Andre Miller .60 1.50
25 Latrell Sprewell 1.00 2.50
26 Darius Miles .50 1.25
27 Richard Jefferson .60 1.50
28 Shawn Marion .75 2.00
29 Baron Davis .75 2.00
30 Ben Wallace 1.00 2.50
31 Reggie Miller 1.50 4.00
32 Karl Malone 1.50 4.00
33 Jonathan Bender .50 1.25
34 Shaquille O'Neal 3.00 8.00
35 Steve Francis .75 2.00
36 Kobe Bryant 6.00 15.00
37 Mike Dunleavy .60 1.50
38 Glenn Robinson .60 1.50
39 Allan Houston .75 2.00
40 Sam Cassell .60 1.50
41 Dirk Nowitzki 2.00 5.00
42 Elton Brand .60 1.50
43 Joe Smith .60 1.50
44 Brian Grant .60 1.50
45 Jason Terry .60 1.50
46 Richard Hamilton 1.00 2.50
47 Morris Peterson .50 1.25
48 Ray Allen 1.25 3.00
49 Scottie Pippen 2.00 5.00
50 Jamal Crawford .75 2.00
51 Cuttino Mobley .50 1.25
52 Jerry Stackhouse 1.00 2.50
53 Marcus Camby .60 1.50
54 Jalen Rose .60 1.50
55 Ricky Davis .60 1.50
56 Jamal Mashburn .60 1.50
57 Ron Artest .75 2.00
58 Theo Ratliff .50 1.25
59 Juwan Howard .60 1.50
60 Caron Butler .60 1.50
61 Antawn Jamison .75 2.00
62 Nene .60 1.50
63 Tyson Chandler .60 1.50
64 Jason Williams 1.25 3.00
65 Kurt Thomas .50 1.25
66 Mike Miller .60 1.50
67 Amare Stoudemire 1.00 2.50
68 Jamaal Tinsley .50 1.25
69 Brent Barry .50 1.25
70 Brad Miller .60 1.50
71 Bonzi Wells .50 1.25
72 Andrei Kirilenko .60 1.50
73 Kenny Thomas .50 1.25
74 Derek Anderson .60 1.50
75 Zydrunas Ilgauskas .60 1.50
76 Eddie Griffin .50 1.25
77 Tayshaun Prince .75 2.00
78 Michael Olowokandi .50 1.25
79 Michael Redd .75 2.00
80 Tim Thomas .50 1.25
81 Eddie Jones .75 2.00
82 Shareef Abdur-Rahim .75 2.00
83 Corey Maggette .60 1.50
84 Eric Snow .50 1.25
85 Keon Clark .50 1.25
86 Desmond Mason .60 1.50
87 Drew Gooden .60 1.50
88 Matt Harpring .50 1.25
89 Antonio McDyess .60 1.50
90 Radoslav Nesterovic .50 1.25
91 Jamaal Magloire .50 1.25
92 Rasheed Wallace 1.00 2.50
93 Antonio Davis .60 1.50
94 Kwame Brown .50 1.25
95 Manu Ginobili 1.50 4.00
96 Eric Williams .50 1.25
97 Nick Van Exel .75 2.00
98 Lamar Odom .75 2.00
99 Chauncey Billups 1.00 2.50
100 Kevin Garnett 2.00 5.00
101 Marko Jaric .50 1.25
102 David Wesley .50 1.25
103 Gilbert Arenas .75 2.00
104 Keith Van Horn .60 1.50
105 Bostjan Nachbar .50 1.25
106 Michael Finley .75 2.00
107 Troy Murphy .50 1.25
108 Eddy Curry .50 1.25
109 Rashard Lewis .60 1.50
110 Tony Battie .50 1.25
111 LeBron James RC 600.00 1,200.00
112A Darko Milicic RC 1.50 4.00
112B Darko Milicic
Native language 1.50 4.00
113 Carmelo Anthony RC 12.00 30.00
114 Chris Bosh RC 6.00 15.00
115 Dwyane Wade RC 25.00 60.00
116 Chris Kaman RC 2.00 5.00
117 Kirk Hinrich RC 2.00 5.00
118 T.J. Ford RC 1.50 4.00
119 Mike Sweetney RC 1.25 3.00
120 Jarvis Hayes RC 1.25 3.00
121A Mickael Pietrus RC 1.50 4.00
121B Mickael Pietrus
Native language 1.50 4.00
122 Nick Collison RC 1.50 4.00
123 Marcus Banks RC 1.25 3.00
124 Luke Ridnour RC 2.00 5.00
125 Reece Gaines RC 1.25 3.00
126 Troy Bell RC 1.25 3.00
127A Zarko Cabarkapa RC 1.25 3.00
127B Zarko Cabarkapa
Native language 1.25 3.00
128 David West RC 2.50 6.00
129A Aleksandar Pavlovic RC 1.50 4.00
129B Aleksandar Pavlovic
Native language 1.50 4.00
130 Dahntay Jones RC 1.25 3.00
131A Boris Diaw RC 2.00 5.00
131B Boris Diaw
Native language 2.00 5.00
132A Zoran Planinic RC 1.25 3.00
132B Zoran Planinic
Native language 1.25 3.00
133 Travis Outlaw RC 1.50 4.00
134 Brian Cook RC 1.25 3.00
135 Matt Carroll RC 1.25 3.00
136 Ndudi Ebi RC 1.25 3.00
137 Kendrick Perkins RC 1.50 4.00
138A Leandro Barbosa RC 2.00 5.00
138B Leandro Barbosa
Native language 2.00 5.00
139 Josh Howard RC 2.00 5.00
140A Maciej Lampe RC 1.25 3.00
140B Maciej Lampe
Native language 1.25 3.00
141 Jason Kapono RC 1.25 3.00
142 Luke Walton RC 2.00 5.00
143 Jerome Beasley RC 1.25 3.00
144 Travis Hansen RC 1.25 3.00
145 Steve Blake RC 1.50 4.00
146A Slavko Vranes RC 1.25 3.00
146B Slavko Vranes
Native language 1.25 3.00
147A Francisco Elson RC 1.25 3.00
147B Francisco Elson
Native language 1.25 3.00
148 Willie Green RC 2.00 5.00
149A Zaur Pachulia RC 2.00 5.00
149B Zaur Pachulia
Native language 2.00 5.00
150 Keith Bogans RC 1.25 3.00
151 Maurice Williams RC 2.00 5.00
152 James Jones RC 1.25 3.00
153 Kyle Korver RC 2.50 6.00
154A Jon Stefansson RC 1.25 3.00
154B Jon Stefansson
Native language 1.25 3.00
155 Brandon Hunter RC 1.25 3.00
156 Josh Moore RC 1.25 3.00
157 Torraye Braggs RC 1.25 3.00
158 Devin Brown RC 1.25 3.00
159 James Lang RC 1.25 3.00
160 Theron Smith RC 1.25 3.00
161 Linton Johnson RC 1.25 3.00
162 Marquis Daniels RC 1.50 4.00
163 Keith McLeod RC 1.25 3.00
164 Udonis Haslem RC 2.50 6.00
165 Ben Handlogten RC 1.25 3.00

2003-04 Topps Chrome Refractors
*1-110 SINGLES: 1.25X TO 3X BASE HI
*111-165 RC SINGLES: 1X TO 2.5X BASE HI
1-110 STATED ODDS 1:6
111-165 STATED ODDS 1:12
1 Tracy McGrady 10.00 25.00
3 Allen Iverson 20.00 50.00
4 Chris Webber 10.00 25.00
9 Tony Parker 10.00 25.00
11 Yao Ming 20.00 50.00
13 Steve Nash 10.00 25.00
14 Paul Pierce 10.00 25.00
15 Vince Carter 20.00 50.00
19 Pau Gasol 10.00 25.00
21 Tim Duncan 20.00 50.00
22 Anfernee Hardaway 10.00 25.00
31 Reggie Miller 10.00 25.00
34 Shaquille O'Neal 60.00 150.00
36 Kobe Bryant 150.00 400.00
41 Dirk Nowitzki 20.00 50.00
48 Ray Allen 10.00 25.00
49 Scottie Pippen 20.00 50.00
95 Manu Ginobili 10.00 25.00
100 Kevin Garnett 20.00 50.00
111 LeBron James 4,000.00 8,000.00
113 Carmelo Anthony 100.00 250.00
114 Chris Bosh 50.00 120.00
115 Dwyane Wade 125.00 300.00

2003-04 Topps Chrome Refractors Black
*1-110 SINGLES: 2.5X TO 6X BASE HI
*111-165 RC SINGLES: 2X TO 5X BASE HI
1 Tracy McGrady 20.00 50.00
3 Allen Iverson 40.00 100.00
4 Chris Webber 20.00 50.00
9 Tony Parker 20.00 50.00
11 Yao Ming 40.00 100.00
13 Steve Nash 20.00 50.00
14 Paul Pierce 20.00 50.00
15 Vince Carter 40.00 100.00
19 Pau Gasol 20.00 50.00
21 Tim Duncan 40.00 100.00
22 Anfernee Hardaway 20.00 50.00
31 Reggie Miller 20.00 50.00
34 Shaquille O'Neal 125.00 300.00
36 Kobe Bryant 500.00 1,000.00
41 Dirk Nowitzki 40.00 100.00
48 Ray Allen 20.00 50.00
49 Scottie Pippen 40.00 100.00
95 Manu Ginobili 20.00 50.00
100 Kevin Garnett 40.00 100.00
111 LeBron James 10,000.00 20,000.00
113 Carmelo Anthony 600.00 1,200.00
114 Chris Bosh 125.00 300.00
115 Dwyane Wade 600.00 1,200.00

2003-04 Topps Chrome Refractors Gold
*1-110 SINGLES: 12X TO 30X BASE HI
*111-165 RC SINGLES: 5X TO 12X BASE HI
1-110 PRINT RUN 99 SER.#'d SETS
111-165 PRINT RUN 50 SER.#'d SETS
1 Tracy McGrady 125.00 300.00
3 Allen Iverson 150.00 400.00
4 Chris Webber 75.00 200.00
8 Antoine Walker 30.00 80.00
9 Tony Parker 100.00 250.00
10 Mike Bibby 30.00 80.00
11 Yao Ming 500.00 1,000.00
13 Steve Nash 75.00 200.00
14 Paul Pierce 75.00 200.00
15 Vince Carter 150.00 400.00
19 Pau Gasol 75.00 200.00
20 Gary Payton 25.00 60.00
21 Tim Duncan 150.00 400.00
22 Anfernee Hardaway 50.00 120.00
25 Latrell Sprewell 40.00 100.00
30 Ben Wallace 150.00 400.00
31 Reggie Miller 125.00 300.00
32 Karl Malone 100.00 250.00
34 Shaquille O'Neal 400.00 800.00
36 Kobe Bryant 2,500.00 5,000.00
39 Allan Houston 40.00 100.00
41 Dirk Nowitzki 150.00 400.00
46 Richard Hamilton 100.00 250.00
48 Ray Allen 100.00 250.00
49 Scottie Pippen 125.00 300.00
52 Jerry Stackhouse 40.00 100.00
54 Jalen Rose 40.00 100.00
64 Jason Williams 75.00 200.00
67 Amare Stoudemire 60.00 150.00
77 Tayshaun Prince 60.00 150.00
92 Rasheed Wallace 75.00 200.00
95 Manu Ginobili 100.00 250.00
99 Chauncey Billups 60.00 150.00
100 Kevin Garnett 125.00 300.00
103 Gilbert Arenas 40.00 100.00
109 Rashard Lewis 40.00 100.00
111 LeBron James 20,000.00 40,000.00
113 Carmelo Anthony 3,000.00 6,000.00
114 Chris Bosh 1,000.00 2,000.00
115 Dwyane Wade 5,000.00 10,000.00
117 Kirk Hinrich 60.00 150.00
164 Udonis Haslem 60.00 150.00

2003-04 Topps Chrome X-Fractors
*X-FRAC.SINGLES: 3X TO 8X BASE HI
*X-FRAC RC SINGLES: 2.5X TO 6X BASE HI
ONE PER BOX TOPPER
PRINT RUN 220 SER.#'d SETS
1 Tracy McGrady 25.00 60.00
3 Allen Iverson 50.00 120.00
4 Chris Webber 25.00 60.00
9 Tony Parker 25.00 60.00
11 Yao Ming 50.00 120.00
13 Steve Nash 25.00 60.00
14 Paul Pierce 25.00 60.00
15 Vince Carter 50.00 120.00
19 Pau Gasol 25.00 60.00
21 Tim Duncan 50.00 120.00
22 Anfernee Hardaway 25.00 60.00
31 Reggie Miller 25.00 60.00
34 Shaquille O'Neal 150.00 400.00
36 Kobe Bryant 600.00 1,200.00
41 Dirk Nowitzki 50.00 120.00
48 Ray Allen 25.00 60.00
49 Scottie Pippen 50.00 120.00
95 Manu Ginobili 25.00 60.00
100 Kevin Garnett 50.00 120.00
111 LeBron James 12,500.00 25,000.00
113 Carmelo Anthony 800.00 1,500.00
114 Chris Bosh 150.00 400.00
115 Dwyane Wade 800.00 1,500.00

2003-04 Topps Chrome Autographs
STATED ODDS GROUP A 1:300; GROUP B 1:622
STATED ODDS GROUP C 1:2329; GROUP D 1:595
*REFRACTORS: 1.25X TO 3X BASE HI
REFRACTORS PRINT RUN 25 SETS
CACA Carmelo Anthony A 30.00 80.00
CADW Dwyane Wade A 75.00 200.00
CAKB Kwame Brown A 2.50 6.00
CAKH Kirk Hinrich B 8.00 20.00
CALR Luke Ridnour A 4.00 10.00
CAMR Michael Redd 5.00 12.00
CANC Nick Collison B 3.00 8.00
CARA Ray Allen D 12.00 30.00
CASO Shaquille O'Neal C 40.00 100.00
CASV Slavko Vranes B 2.50 6.00
CATF T.J. Ford D 3.00 8.00

2003-04 Topps Chrome Autographs Refractors
STATED ODDS 1:3150
PRINT RUN 25 SER.#'d SETS
CACA Carmelo Anthony 300.00 600.00
CADW Dwyane Wade 500.00 1,000.00
CARA Ray Allen 75.00 200.00
CASO Shaquille O'Neal 150.00 400.00

2003-04 Topps Chrome Bonus Coverage Relics
STATED ODDS GROUP A 1:1214; B 1:484
STATED ODDS GROUP C 1:242; D 1:102
*REFRACTORS: 1.25X TO 3X BASE HI
REFRACTORS PRINT RUN 5 TO 25 SETS
AI Allen Iverson A 8.00 20.00
AW Antoine Walker D 3.00 8.00
BD Baron Davis A 3.00 8.00
CB Caron Butler B 2.50 6.00
CW Chris Webber D 4.00 10.00
DM Darius Miles B 2.00 5.00
DW Dajuan Wagner C 2.50 6.00
JM Jamal Mashburn C 2.50 6.00
JR Jason Richardson A 3.00 8.00
KB Kevin Garnett A 8.00 20.00
MD Mike Dunleavy A 2.50 6.00
MF Michael Finley A 3.00 8.00
PG Pau Gasol D 5.00 12.00
RJ Richard Jefferson C 2.50 6.00
SA Shareef Abdur-Rahim A 3.00 8.00
SF Steve Francis A 3.00 8.00
SM Shawn Marion C 3.00 8.00
SO Shaquille O'Neal D 12.00 30.00
TM Tracy McGrady D 5.00 12.00
SMA Stephon Marbury B 4.00 10.00

2003-04 Topps Chrome Cuts Relics
STATED ODDS GROUP A 1:1214; B 1:484
STATED ODDS GROUP C 1:242; D 1:102
*REFRACTORS: 1.25X TO 3X BASE HI
REFRACTORS PRINT RUN 5 TO 25 SETS
BH Brendan Haywood B 2.00 5.00
BM Brad Miller C 2.50 6.00
BW Ben Wallace D 4.00 10.00
DF Derek Fisher A 3.00 8.00
EC Elden Campbell B 2.00 5.00
EG Manu Ginobili A 6.00 15.00
HT Hedo Turkoglu C 2.50 6.00
JS Jerry Stackhouse B 4.00 10.00
KM Kenyon Martin A 3.00 8.00
MB Mike Bibby B 3.00 8.00
MR Michael Redd B 3.00 8.00
NH Nene C 2.50 6.00
NT Nikoloz Tskitishvili B 2.00 5.00
RW Rasheed Wallace D 4.00 10.00
TC Tyson Chandler D 2.50 6.00
TD Tim Duncan 8.00 20.00
VR Vladimir Radmanovic A 2.00 5.00
ZI Zydrunas Ilgauskas D 2.50 6.00
AHA Anfernee Hardaway A 8.00 20.00

2003-04 Topps Chrome Gametime Gear Relics
STATED ODDS GROUP A 1:1214; B 1:484
STATED ODDS GROUP C 1:242; D 1:102
*REFRACTORS: 1.25X TO 3X BASE HI
REFRACTORS PRINT RUN 5 TO 25 SETS
AK Andrei Kirilenko A 2.50 6.00
AS Amare Stoudemire C 4.00 10.00
CB Carlos Boozer D 2.50 6.00
CM Cuttino Mobley D 2.50 6.00
DG Devean George A 2.50 6.00
DN Dirk Nowitzki D 8.00 20.00
DW David Wesley D 2.00 5.00
JD Juan Dixon B 2.00 5.00
JK Jason Kidd B 5.00 12.00
JO Jermaine O'Neal A 3.00 8.00
JW Jerome Williams D 2.00 5.00
LO Lamar Odom C 2.50 6.00
MP Morris Peterson B 2.00 5.00
PP Paul Pierce C 5.00 12.00
PS Peja Stojakovic D 2.50 6.00
QW Qyntel Woods C 2.00 5.00
RA Ray Allen D 5.00 12.00
TM Troy Murphy A 2.00 5.00
TP Tayshaun Prince A 3.00 8.00
WS Wally Szczerbiak C 2.50 6.00
YM Yao Ming D 8.00 20.00
TPA Tony Parker D 5.00 12.00

2004-05 Topps Chrome
COMPLETE SET (220) 200.00 500.00
COMP.SET w/o RC's (165) 150.00 400.00
1 Allen Iverson 2.00 5.00
2 Eddy Curry .50 1.25
3 Stephon Marbury 1.00 2.50
4 Chris Bosh 1.25 3.00
5 Jason Kidd 1.25 3.00
6 Baron Davis .75 2.00
7 Kwame Brown .50 1.25
8 Kobe Bryant 12.00 30.00
9 Ben Wallace 1.00 2.50
10 Josh Howard .60 1.50
11 Yao Ming 2.00 5.00
12 Luke Walton .60 1.50
13 Nene .60 1.50
14 Michael Redd .60 1.50
15 Carmelo Anthony 1.50 4.00
16 Amare Stoudemire .75 2.00
17 Jarvis Hayes .50 1.25
18 Toni Kukoc .75 2.00
19 Latrell Sprewell 1.00 2.50
20 Jason Richardson .75 2.00
21 Kevin Garnett 2.00 5.00
22 Darko Milicic .50 1.25
23 LeBron James 25.00 60.00
24 Peja Stojakovic .60 1.50
25 Wally Szczerbiak .60 1.50
26 Theo Ratliff .50 1.25
27 Gilbert Arenas .75 2.00
28 Mike Dunleavy .50 1.25
29 Joe Smith .60 1.50
30 Vince Carter 1.50 4.00
31 Reggie Miller 1.50 4.00
32 Chris Wilcox .50 1.25
33 Rasheed Wallace 1.00 2.50
34 Paul Pierce 1.25 3.00
35 Tayshaun Prince .75 2.00
36 Richard Hamilton 1.00 2.50
37 Rashard Lewis .60 1.50
38 Joe Johnson .60 1.50
39 Zydrunas Ilgauskas .60 1.50
40 Andre Miller .60 1.50
41 Dirk Nowitzki 2.00 5.00
42 Chauncey Billups 1.00 2.50
43 Ray Allen 1.25 3.00
44 Raef LaFrentz .50 1.25
45 Mickael Pietrus .50 1.25
46 T.J. Ford .50 1.25
47 Chris Webber 1.00 2.50
48 Jamaal Tinsley .50 1.25
49 Earl Boykins .50 1.25
50 Tim Duncan 2.00 5.00
51 Troy Hudson .50 1.25
52 Juan Dixon .50 1.25
53 Tim Thomas .50 1.25
54 Darius Miles .50 1.25
55 Jalen Rose 8.00 20.00
56 Kirk Hinrich .75 2.00
57 Michael Finley .75 2.00
58 Brad Miller .60 1.50
59 Jonathan Bender .50 1.25
60 Manu Ginobili 1.50 4.00
61 Chris Kaman .60 1.50
62 Doug Christie .60 1.50
63 Marcus Camby .60 1.50
64 Desmond Mason .60 1.50
65 Boris Diaw .60 1.50
66 Maurice Taylor .50 1.25
67 Damon Stoudamire .75 2.00
68 Dwyane Wade 8.00 20.00
69 Allan Houston .75 2.00
70 Jermaine O'Neal .60 1.50
71 Glenn Robinson .60 1.50
72 Morris Peterson .50 1.25
73 Luke Ridnour .60 1.50
74 Bobby Jackson .60 1.50
75 Eddie Jones .75 2.00
76 Alvin Williams .50 1.25
77 Elton Brand .60 1.50
78 Zach Randolph .75 2.00
79 Marko Jaric .50 1.25
80 Mike Bibby .75 2.00
81 Jim Jackson .60 1.50
82 Kurt Thomas .50 1.25
83 Troy Murphy .60 1.50
84 Rodney White .50 1.25
85 Jamaal Magloire .50 1.25
86 Jamal Mashburn .60 1.50
87 Kenny Thomas .50 1.25
88 Corey Maggette .60 1.50
89 Rasho Nesterovic .50 1.25
90 Shawn Marion .75 2.00
91 Antonio Daniels .50 1.25
92 Marquis Daniels .50 1.25
93 Richard Jefferson .50 1.25
94 Michael Olowokandi .50 1.25
95 Bruce Bowen .60 1.50
96 Mark Blount .50 1.25
97 Sam Cassell .60 1.50
98 Voshon Lenard .50 1.25
99 Speedy Claxton .50 1.25
100 Samuel Dalembert .50 1.25
101 Tyson Chandler .60 1.50
102 Keith Van Horn .60 1.50
103 Udonis Haslem .60 1.50
104 Trenton Hassell .50 1.25
105 Tony Parker 1.25 3.00
106 Ronald Murray .50 1.25
107 Jeff McInnis .50 1.25
108 Marcus Banks .50 1.25
109 Ricky Davis .60 1.50

110 Karl Malone 1.50 4.00
111 Bonzi Wells .50 1.25
112 Antonio McDyess .60 1.50
113 Drew Gooden .50 1.25
114 Stephen Jackson .60 1.50
115 Eric Snow .50 1.25
116 Steve Francis .75 2.00
117 Pau Gasol 1.25 3.00
118 Andrei Kirilenko .60 1.50
119 Erick Dampier .50 1.25
120 Jason Kapono .50 1.25
121 Al Harrington .60 1.50
122 Gary Payton 1.25 3.00
123 Nick Van Exel .75 2.00
124 Cuttino Mobley .60 1.50
125 Kenyon Martin .75 2.00
126 Mike Miller .60 1.50
127 Jamal Crawford .75 2.00
128 Kerry Kittles .60 1.50
129 Derrick Coleman .60 1.50
130 Gordan Giricek .50 1.25
131 Antoine Walker .75 2.00
132 Shane Battier .60 1.50
133 Caron Butler .60 1.50
134 Corliss Williamson .50 1.25
135 Carlos Boozer .60 1.50
136 Tracy McGrady 1.25 3.00
137 Stromile Swift .50 1.25
138 Derek Fisher .60 1.50
139 Juwan Howard .60 1.50
140 Jason Terry .60 1.50
141 Vlade Divac .75 2.00
142 Antawn Jamison .60 1.50
143 Aleksandar Pavlovic .50 1.25
144 Rafer Alston .50 1.25
145 Brent Barry .50 1.25
146 Quentin Richardson .50 1.25
147 Lamar Odom .75 2.00
148 Gerald Wallace .60 1.50
149 Charlie Ward .50 1.25
150 Jerry Stackhouse .75 2.00
151 Carlos Arroyo .50 1.25
152 Hedo Turkoglu .60 1.50
153 Steve Nash 1.50 4.00
154 Mehmet Okur .60 1.50
155 Tyronn Lue .50 1.25
156 Bob Sura .50 1.25
157 Jason Williams .60 1.50
158 Shaquille O'Neal 3.00 8.00
159 Kelvin Cato .50 1.25
160 Eric Williams .50 1.25
161 Brian Grant .60 1.50
162 Danny Fortson .50 1.25
163 Chucky Atkins .50 1.25
164 Matt Harpring .50 1.25
165 Primoz Brezec .50 1.25
166 Dwight Howard RC 6.00 15.00
167 Emeka Okafor RC 1.25 3.00
168 Ben Gordon RC 1.50 4.00
169 Shaun Livingston RC 1.50 4.00
170 Devin Harris RC 1.25 3.00
171 Josh Childress RC 1.00 2.50
172 Luol Deng RC 1.50 4.00
173 Rafael Araujo RC 1.00 2.50
174 Andre Iguodala RC 2.50 6.00
175 Luke Jackson RC 1.00 2.50
176 Andris Biedrins RC 1.00 2.50
177 Robert Swift RC 1.00 2.50
178 Sebastian Telfair RC 1.25 3.00
179 Kris Humphries RC 1.25 3.00
180 Al Jefferson RC 1.50 4.00
181 Kirk Snyder RC 1.00 2.50
182 Josh Smith RC 1.50 4.00
183 J.R. Smith RC 1.50 4.00
184 Dorell Wright RC 1.25 3.00
185 Jameer Nelson RC 1.50 4.00
186 Pavel Podkolzin RC 1.00 2.50
187 Horace Jenkins RC 1.25 3.00
188 Luis Flores RC 1.25 3.00
189 Delonte West RC 1.25 3.00
190 Tony Allen RC 1.50 4.00
191 Kevin Martin RC 2.00 5.00
192 Sasha Vujacic RC 1.25 3.00
193 Beno Udrih RC 1.25 3.00
194 David Harrison RC 1.00 2.50
195 Yuta Tabuse RC 1.50 4.00
196 Peter John Ramos RC 1.00 2.50
197 Chris Duhon RC 1.25 3.00
198 Trevor Ariza RC 1.50 4.00
199 Bernard Robinson RC 1.00 2.50
200 Andre Emmett RC 1.00 2.50
201 Mario Kasun RC 1.00 2.50
202 Matt Freije RC 1.00 2.50
203 Maurice Evans RC 1.50 4.00
204 Erik Daniels RC 1.25 3.00
205 Lionel Chalmers RC 1.25 3.00
206 Jared Reiner RC 1.50 4.00
207 D.J. Mbenga RC 1.00 2.50
208 Antonio Burks RC 1.00 2.50
209 Justin Reed RC 1.00 2.50
210 Pape Sow RC 1.00 2.50
211 Jackson Vroman RC 1.00 2.50
212 Romain Sato RC 1.00 2.50
213 Nenad Krstic RC 1.25 3.00
214 Damien Wilkins RC 1.25 3.00
215 Arthur Johnson RC 1.25 3.00
216 Ibrahim Kutluay RC 1.50 4.00
217 Andres Nocioni RC 1.50 4.00
218 Josh Davis RC 1.50 4.00
219 Donta Smith RC 1.00 2.50
220 Anderson Varejao RC 1.25 3.00

2004-05 Topps Chrome Refractors

*1-165 REFRACTORS: 2X TO 5X BASE HI
*166-220 REF.RCs: .75X TO 2X BASE HI
STATED ODDS 1:4
1 Allen Iverson 20.00 50.00
4 Chris Bosh 15.00 40.00
8 Kobe Bryant 400.00 800.00
15 Carmelo Anthony 20.00 50.00
21 Kevin Garnett 15.00 40.00
23 LeBron James 300.00 600.00
30 Vince Carter 12.00 30.00
31 Reggie Miller 10.00 25.00
43 Ray Allen 12.00 30.00
55 Jalen Rose 30.00 80.00
60 Manu Ginobili 12.00 30.00
153 Steve Nash 15.00 40.00
158 Shaquille O'Neal 20.00 50.00

2004-05 Topps Chrome Refractors Black

*1-165 SINGLES: 3X TO 8X BASE HI
*166-220 RC SINGLES: 1.5X TO 4X BASE HI
PRINT RUN 500 SER.#'d SETS
1 Allen Iverson 30.00 80.00
8 Kobe Bryant 300.00 600.00
15 Carmelo Anthony 30.00 80.00
23 LeBron James 1,000.00 2,000.00
30 Vince Carter 25.00 60.00
31 Reggie Miller 20.00 50.00
55 Jalen Rose 40.00 100.00
68 Dwyane Wade 60.00 150.00
158 Shaquille O'Neal 40.00 100.00
166 Dwight Howard 100.00 250.00

2004-05 Topps Chrome Refractors Gold

*1-165 SINGLES: 10X TO 25X BASE HI
*166-220 RC SINGLES: 2.5X TO 6X BASE HI
PRINT RUN 99 SER.#'d SETS
1 Allen Iverson 300.00 600.00
3 Stephon Marbury 75.00 200.00
4 Chris Bosh 75.00 200.00
8 Kobe Bryant 3,000.00 6,000.00
9 Ben Wallace 60.00 150.00
11 Yao Ming 300.00 600.00
15 Carmelo Anthony 150.00 400.00
21 Kevin Garnett 150.00 400.00
23 LeBron James 6,000.00 12,000.00
30 Vince Carter 100.00 250.00
31 Reggie Miller 100.00 250.00
34 Paul Pierce 125.00 300.00
41 Dirk Nowitzki 200.00 500.00
43 Ray Allen 75.00 200.00
47 Chris Webber 100.00 250.00
50 Tim Duncan 200.00 500.00
55 Jalen Rose 300.00 600.00
60 Manu Ginobili 150.00 400.00
68 Dwyane Wade 500.00 1,000.00
105 Tony Parker 60.00 150.00
110 Karl Malone 150.00 400.00
136 Tracy McGrady 125.00 300.00
153 Steve Nash 100.00 250.00
157 Jason Williams 30.00 80.00
158 Shaquille O'Neal 300.00 600.00
166 Dwight Howard 300.00 600.00
174 Andre Iguodala 100.00 250.00

2004-05 Topps Chrome X-Fractors

*1-165 SINGLES: 4X TO 10X BASE HI
*166-220 RC SINGLES: 2.5X TO 6X BASE HI
PRINT RUN 110 SER.#'d SETS
ONE PER BOX AS A TOPPER
4 Chris Bosh 50.00 120.00
8 Kobe Bryant 3,000.00 6,000.00
23 LeBron James 8,000.00 15,000.00
30 Vince Carter 12.00 30.00
31 Reggie Miller 8.00 20.00
55 Jalen Rose 125.00 300.00
68 Dwyane Wade 300.00 600.00
166 Dwight Howard 125.00 300.00

2004-05 Topps Chrome Autographs

GROUP A STATED ODDS 1:1264
GROUP B STATED ODDS 1:1073
GROUP C STATED ODDS 1:205
AB Andris Biedrins C 3.00 8.00
AS Amare Stoudemire A 5.00 12.00
AV Anderson Varejao B 4.00 10.00
BG Ben Gordon C 5.00 12.00
CA Carmelo Anthony A 15.00 40.00
DH Devin Harris C 4.00 10.00
EO Emeka Okafor A 4.00 10.00
JC Josh Childress C 3.00 8.00
JK Jason Kidd A 15.00 40.00
JN Jameer Nelson C 3.00 8.00
JO Jermaine O'Neal A 4.00 10.00
JS Josh Smith C 5.00 12.00
LD Luol Deng A 5.00 12.00
LJ Luke Jackson B 3.00 8.00
RH Richard Hamilton A 6.00 15.00
RS Robert Swift B 3.00 8.00
SL Shaun Livingston C 5.00 12.00
SO Shaquille O'Neal A 30.00 80.00
ST Sebastian Telfair C 4.00 10.00
TM Tracy McGrady A 20.00 50.00
JRS J.R. Smith C 5.00 12.00
SMA Shawn Marion A 6.00 15.00

2004-05 Topps Chrome Chrome-Town Heroes

PRINT RUNS LISTED IN CHECKLIST
*REFRACTOR: 1.25X TO 3X BASE HI
REFRACTOR PRINT RUN 25 SETS
AK Andrei Kirilenko/272 2.00 5.00
AS Amare Stoudemire/885 2.50 6.00
BW Ben Wallace/206 3.00 8.00
CA Carmelo Anthony/1000 5.00 12.00
CB Chris Bosh/859 4.00 10.00
CM Corey Maggette 2.00 5.00
CW Chris Webber/500 3.00 8.00
DM Desmond Mason/500 2.00 5.00
DN Dirk Nowitzki/500 6.00 15.00
GA Gilbert Arenas/287 2.50 6.00
GW Gerald Wallace/287 2.00 5.00
JO Jermaine O'Neal/336 2.00 5.00
JT Jason Terry/500 2.00 5.00
KG Kevin Garnett/500 6.00 15.00
KH Kirk Hinrich/1000 2.50 6.00
MD Mike Dunleavy/985 1.50 4.00
PG Pau Gasol/500 4.00 10.00
RJ Richard Jefferson/1000 2.00 5.00
RL Rashard Lewis/500 2.00 5.00
SO Shaquille O'Neal B 10.00 25.00
TP Tony Parker/385 4.00 10.00
YM Yao Ming/467 6.00 15.00
ZR Zach Randolph/364 2.50 6.00
CHB Chauncey Billups/211 3.00 8.00

2004-05 Topps Chrome Refined Remnants

PRINT RUNS LISTED IN CHECKLIST
*REFRACTORS: 1.5X TO 4X BASE HI
REFRACTOR PRINT RUN 25 SETS
BD Baron Davis/780 2.50 6.00
EB Elton Brand/412 2.00 5.00
GP Gary Payton B 4.00 10.00
JK Jason Kidd/782 4.00 10.00
PP Paul Pierce/500 4.00 10.00
PS Peja Stojakovic/1000 2.00 5.00
RA Ray Allen/500 4.00 10.00
RM Reggie Miller/1000 5.00 12.00
SC Sam Cassell/385 2.00 5.00
SM Shawn Marion/332 2.50 6.00
TD Tim Duncan/939 6.00 15.00
TM Tracy McGrady/385 4.00 10.00

2004-05 Topps Chrome Slices of Success

PRINT RUNS LISTED IN CHECKLIST
*REFRACTORS: 1.25X TO 3X BASE HI
REFRACTOR PRINT RUN 25 SETS
AJ Al Jefferson/976 2.50 6.00
AW Antoine Walker/900 2.50 6.00
BG Ben Gordon/500 2.50 6.00
DH Devin Harris/1000 2.00 5.00
EO Emeka Okafor/1000 2.00 5.00
JC Josh Childress/500 1.50 4.00
JH Jarvis Hayes/200 2.00 5.00
JM Jamaal Magloire/900 2.00 5.00
JT Jamaal Tinsley/500 2.00 5.00
KR Kareem Rush/500 2.00 5.00
KS Kirk Snyder/500 1.50 4.00
LD Luol Deng/307 2.50 6.00
LR Luke Ridnour/249 2.00 5.00
MB Mike Bibby/500 2.50 6.00
MJ Marko Jaric/1000 1.50 4.00
RN Rasho Nesterovic/754 2.00 5.00
SB Shane Battier/332 2.00 5.00
SF Steve Francis/500 2.50 6.00
SL Shaun Livingston/500 2.50 6.00
TA Tony Allen/500 2.50 6.00
TC Tyson Chandler/500 2.00 5.00
TP Tayshaun Prince/500 2.50 6.00
JHO Josh Howard/500 2.00 5.00
SAR Shareef Abdur-Rahim/1000 2.50 6.00

2004-05 Topps Chrome Total Recall

PRINT RUN 100 SER.#'d SETS
*REFRACTORS: 1X TO 2.5X BASE HI
REFRACTOR PRINT RUN 25 SETS
DD M.Dunleavy/L.Deng 5.00 12.00
DG B.Davis/B.Gordon 5.00 12.00
JI R.Jefferson/A.Iguodala 8.00 20.00
KH J.Kidd/D.Harris 8.00 20.00
MA B.Miller/R.Araujo 5.00 12.00
MC R.Miller/J.Childress 8.00 20.00
MT S.Marbury/S.Telfair 5.00 12.00
PJ T.Prince/L.Jackson 5.00 12.00
WO B.Wallace/E.Okafor 5.00 12.00

2005-06 Topps Chrome

COMPLETE SET (274) 30.00 60.00
1 Grant Hill .60 1.50
2 Lamar Odom .30 .75
3 Jamal Crawford .40 1.00
4 Ben Gordon .30 .75
5 Zach Randolph .40 1.00
6 Chris Duhon .25 .60
7 Gilbert Arenas .40 1.00
8 Yao Ming .75 2.00
9 Josh Smith .30 .75
10 Ray Allen .60 1.50
11 Vince Carter .75 2.00
12 Kenyon Martin .30 .75
13 Tim Duncan 1.00 2.50
14 Michael Redd .30 .75
15 Antawn Jamison .30 .75
16 Shane Battier .30 .75
17 Baron Davis .40 1.00
18 Allen Iverson .75 2.00
19 Jameer Nelson .25 .60
20 Brent Barry .30 .75
21 Zydrunas Ilgauskas .30 .75
22 Jason Terry .30 .75
23 Mike Dunleavy .25 .60
24 Paul Pierce .60 1.50
25 Peja Stojakovic .30 .75
26 Andre Iguodala .40 1.00
27 Andrei Kirilenko .30 .75
28 Nenad Krstic .25 .60
29 Emeka Okafor .30 .75
30 Jalen Rose .30 .75
31 Ricky Davis .30 .75
32 Jason Kidd .60 1.50
33 Chauncey Billups .50 1.25
34 Amare Stoudemire .40 1.00
35 Josh Childress .25 .60
36 Mehmet Okur .25 .60
37 Shaun Livingston .30 .75
38 Bruce Bowen .30 .75
39 J.R. Smith .40 1.00
40 Kobe Bryant 40.00 100.00
41 Dwight Howard .50 1.25
42 Manu Ginobili .75 2.00
43 Keith Van Horn .30 .75
44 Stephon Marbury .50 1.25
45 Samuel Dalembert .25 .60
46 Luke Ridnour .30 .75
47 Sebastian Telfair .30 .75
48 Tyson Chandler .30 .75
49 Drew Gooden .30 .75
50 Marcus Camby .30 .75
51 Dwyane Wade .75 2.00
52 Troy Murphy .30 .75
53 Rashard Lewis .30 .75
54 Shaquille O'Neal 1.25 3.00
55 Al Harrington .30 .75
56 Al Jefferson .25 .60
57 Earl Boykins .25 .60
58 Tayshaun Prince .40 1.00
59 Carlos Boozer .30 .75
60 Richard Jefferson .30 .75
61 Toni Kukoc .40 1.00
62 Brad Miller .30 .75
63 Richard Hamilton .50 1.25
64 Kevin Garnett 1.00 2.50
65 Tony Parker .60 1.50
66 Udonis Haslem .25 .60
67 Dikembe Mutombo .50 1.25
68 Pau Gasol .60 1.50
69 Chris Webber .50 1.25
70 Ben Wallace .50 1.25
71 Carmelo Anthony .60 1.50
72 Dirk Nowitzki 1.00 2.50
73 Tony Allen .25 .60
74 Corey Maggette .30 .75
75 Rasheed Wallace .40 1.00
76 Andre Miller .30 .75
77 Luol Deng .30 .75
78 Mike Miller .30 .75
79 Wally Szczerbiak .30 .75
80 Chris Bosh .50 1.25
81 Marquis Daniels .25 .60
82 Nick Collison .25 .60
83 Matt Harpring .25 .60
84 Kirk Hinrich .30 .75
85 Josh Howard .30 .75
86 Elton Brand .30 .75
87 Tyronn Lue .25 .60
88 Bob Sura .25 .60
89 Chris Mihm .25 .60
90 Brevin Knight .25 .60
91 Jason Richardson .40 1.00
92 Vladimir Radmanovic .25 .60
93 Eddie Griffin .25 .60
94 P.J. Brown .25 .60
95 Troy Hudson .25 .60
96 Steve Francis .40 1.00
97 Joel Przybilla .25 .60
98 Steve Nash .75 2.00
99 Brendan Haywood .25 .60
100 Primoz Brezec .25 .60
101 Devin Harris .25 .60
102 Lebron James 20.00 50.00
103 Mike Bibby .40 1.00
104 Jared Jeffries .25 .60
105 Morris Peterson .25 .60
106 Trevor Ariza .25 .60
107 Shawn Marion .30 .75
108 Andres Nocioni .25 .60
109 Darius Miles .25 .60
110 Tracy Mcgrady .60 1.50
111 Stephen Jackson .30 .75
112 Joe Johnson .30 .75
113 Bonzi Wells .25 .60
114 Damon Jones .25 .60
115 Rafer Alston .30 .75
116 Cuttino Mobley .25 .60
117 Nick Van Exel .40 1.00
118 Jason Hart .25 .60
119 Fred Jones .25 .60
120 Dan Dickau .25 .60
121 Damon Stoudamire .40 1.00
122 Kirk Snyder .25 .60
123 Larry Hughes .30 .75
124 Michael Finley .40 1.00
125 Sam Cassell .30 .75
126 Bobby Jackson .30 .75
127 Austin Croshere .25 .60
128 Kwame Brown .25 .60
129 James Posey .25 .60
130 Antonio Daniels .25 .60
131 Eddy Curry .25 .60
132 Mike James .25 .60
133 Juan Dixon .25 .60
134 Jason Williams .60 1.50
135 Jeff Mcinnis .25 .60
136 Jamaal Tinsley .25 .60
137 Derek Anderson .25 .60
138 Devin Brown .25 .60
139 Raja Bell .30 .75
140 Gary Payton .60 1.50
141 Marko Jaric .25 .60
142 Ron Artest .30 .75
143 Zaza Pachulia .25 .60
144 Jermaine O'Neal .30 .75
145 Quentin Richardson .25 .60
146 Lee Nailon .25 .60
147 Bobby Simmons .25 .60
148 Caron Butler .30 .75
149 Shareef Abdur-Rahim .40 1.00
150 Stromile Swift .25 .60
151 Rasual Butler .25 .60
152 Mike Sweetney .25 .60
153 Antoine Walker .30 .75
154 Eddie Jones .30 .75
155 David Harrison .25 .60
156 Kurt Thomas .25 .60
157 Donyell Marshall .25 .60
158 Brian Grant .25 .60
159 Desmond Mason .25 .60
160 Tim Thomas .25 .60
161 Marc Jackson .25 .60
162 Chucky Atkins .25 .60
163 Jeff Foster .25 .60
164 Jamaal Magloire .25 .60
165 Desagana Diop .25 .60
166 Danny Granger RC 1.50 4.00
167 Hakim Warrick RC 1.25 3.00
168 Chris Paul RC 15.00 40.00
169 Marvin Williams RC 1.50 4.00
170 Ike Diogu RC 1.00 2.50
171 Wayne Simien RC 1.00 2.50
172 James Singleton RC 1.00 2.50
173 Robert Whaley RC 1.00 2.50
174 Arvydas Macijauskas RC 1.00 2.50
175 Linas Kleiza RC 1.25 3.00
176 Raymond Felton RC 1.25 3.00
177 Ersan Ilyasova RC 1.25 3.00
178 Jarrett Jack RC 1.50 4.00
179 Antoine Wright RC 1.25 3.00
180 David Lee RC 1.50 4.00
181 Esteban Batista RC 1.00 2.50
182 Sarunas Jasikevicius RC 1.50 4.00
183 Francisco Garcia RC 1.00 2.50
184 C.J. Miles RC 1.25 3.00
185 Ryan Gomes RC 1.25 3.00
186 Andrew Bynum RC 1.25 3.00
187 Sean May RC 1.00 2.50
188 Jose Calderon RC 1.50 4.00
189 Rashad McCants RC 1.00 2.50
190 Johan Petro RC 1.00 2.50
191 Jason Maxiell RC 1.25 3.00
192 Martell Webster RC 1.25 3.00
193 Nate Robinson RC 1.50 4.00
194 Daniel Ewing RC 1.25 3.00
195 Fabricio Oberto RC 1.25 3.00
196 Travis Diener RC 1.00 2.50
197 Salim Stoudamire RC 1.25 3.00
198 Charlie Villanueva RC 1.25 3.00
199 Orien Greene RC 1.25 3.00
200 Deron Williams RC 2.50 6.00
201 Bracey Wright RC 1.00 2.50
202 Lawrence Roberts RC 1.00 2.50
203 Eddie Basden RC 1.00 2.50
204 Brandon Bass RC 1.25 3.00
205 Martynas Andriuskevicius RC 1.00 2.50
206 Channing Frye RC 1.25 3.00
207 Julius Hodge RC 1.00 2.50
208 Luther Head RC 1.00 2.50
209 Chris Taft RC 1.00 2.50
210 Andrew Bogut RC 2.00 5.00
211 Gerald Green RC 1.50 4.00
212 Joey Graham RC 1.25 3.00
213 Louis Williams RC 4.00 10.00
214 Yaroslav Korolev RC 1.00 2.50
215 Monta Ellis RC 2.00 5.00
216 Christie Brinkley 4.00 10.00
217 Jay-Z 3.00 8.00
218 Shannon Elizabeth 1.50 4.00
219 Carmen Electra 1.50 4.00
220 Jenny McCarthy Cut Out 60.00 150.00
221 Joe Shipp DL RC .75 2.00
222 Dwayne Jones DL RC .60 1.50
223 Will Conroy DL RC 1.00 2.50
224 Darnell Miller DL RC 1.00 2.50
225 Will Bynum DL RC .75 2.00
226 Jamar Smith DL RC 1.00 2.50
227 Daryl Dorsey DL RC .75 2.00
228 Tony Bland DL RC .60 1.50
229 Hiram Fuller DL RC 1.00 2.50
230 Tyrone Sally DL RC 1.00 2.50
231 Clay Tucker DL RC 1.00 2.50
232 George Leach DL RC 1.00 2.50
233 Marcus Douthit DL RC .60 1.50
234 Carlos Hurt DL RC 1.00 2.50
235 Seamus Boxley DL RC 1.00 2.50
236 Ramel Curry DL RC .60 1.50
237 Andreas Glyniadakis DL RC 1.00 2.50
238 Kareem Reid DL RC 1.00 2.50
239 Austin Nichols DL RC .60 1.50
240 Chris Shumate DL RC 1.00 2.50
241 Brandon Robinson DL RC 1.00 2.50
242 Harvey Thomas DL RC 1.00 2.50
243 Desmon Farmer DL RC 1.00 2.50
244 Marcus Hill DL RC 1.00 2.50
245 Robb Dryden DL RC 1.00 2.50
246 Nate Daniels DL RC 1.00 2.50
247 James Lang DL RC 1.00 2.50
248 Anthony Terrell DL RC 1.00 2.50
249 Jeff Hagen DL RC 1.00 2.50
250 Kevin Owens DL RC .60 1.50
251 Myron Allen DL RC 1.00 2.50
252 Ayudeji Akindele DL RC 1.00 2.50
253 T.J. Cummings DL RC 1.00 2.50
254 Mike King DL RC .60 1.50
255 Otis George DL RC 1.00 2.50
256 Ezra Williams DL RC 1.00 2.50
257 Anthony Wilkins DL RC 1.00 2.50
258 Scott Merritt DL RC 1.00 2.50
259 Seth Doliboa DL RC 1.00 2.50
260 Anthony Fuqua DL RC 1.00 2.50
261 Malik Moore DL RC .60 1.50
262 Randall Orr DL RC .60 1.50
263 Ricky Shields DL RC .60 1.50
264 John Lucas III DL RC .75 2.00
265 Butter Johnson DL RC 1.00 2.50
266 Isiah Victor DL RC 1.00 2.50
267 Roderick Riley DL RC 1.00 2.50
268 Bernard King DL RC 1.00 2.50
269 E.J. Rowland DL RC .60 1.50
270 Anthony Grundy DL RC 1.00 2.50
271 Brian Jackson DL RC .60 1.50
272 Keith Langford DL RC .75 2.00
273 Chuck Hayes DL RC 1.00 2.50
274 Jonathan Moore DL RC .60 1.50

2005-06 Topps Chrome Refractors

*1-165 REF: 1.5X TO 4X BASE HI
*166-274 REF: 1X TO 2.5X BASE HI
REFRACTOR PRINT RUN 999 SER.#'d SETS
40 Kobe Bryant 400.00 800.00
102 LeBron James 125.00 300.00
168 Chris Paul 100.00 250.00
213 Louis Williams 30.00 80.00
217 Jay-Z 40.00 100.00

2005-06 Topps Chrome Refractors Black

*1-165 REF.BLACK: 2X TO 5X BASE HI
*166-274 REF.BLACK: 1.25X TO 3X BASE HI
PRINT RUN 399 SER.#'d SETS
18 Allen Iverson 12.00 30.00
40 Kobe Bryant 800.00 1,500.00
102 LeBron James 200.00 500.00
168 Chris Paul 300.00 600.00
213 Louis Williams 15.00 40.00
217 Jay-Z 60.00 150.00

2005-06 Topps Chrome Refractors Gold

*REF.GOLD: 6X TO 15X BASE HI
*166-274 REF.GOLD: 3X TO 8X BASE HI
PRINT RUN 99 SER.#'d SETS
1 Grant Hill 20.00 50.00
8 Yao Ming 30.00 80.00
10 Ray Allen 40.00 100.00
11 Vince Carter 100.00 250.00
13 Tim Duncan 150.00 400.00
18 Allen Iverson 30.00 80.00
24 Paul Pierce 75.00 200.00
40 Kobe Bryant 4,000.00 8,000.00
42 Manu Ginobili 20.00 50.00
51 Dwyane Wade 150.00 400.00
54 Shaquille O'Neal 125.00 300.00
64 Kevin Garnett 125.00 300.00
65 Tony Parker 30.00 80.00
69 Chris Webber 15.00 40.00
71 Carmelo Anthony 60.00 150.00
72 Dirk Nowitzki 50.00 120.00
80 Chris Bosh 25.00 60.00
98 Steve Nash 50.00 120.00
102 LeBron James 4,000.00 8,000.00
110 Tracy Mcgrady 50.00 120.00
134 Jason Williams 12.00 30.00
168 Chris Paul 3,000.00 6,000.00
213 Louis Williams 30.00 80.00
217 Jay-Z 250.00 600.00

2005-06 Topps Chrome Blue X-Fractors

*1-165 X-FRACTORS: 4X TO 10X BASE HI
*166-274 X-FRAC: 3X TO 8X BASE HI
PRINT RUN 90 SER.#'d SETS
INSERTED ONE PER BOX AS TOPPER
40 Kobe Bryant 2,000.00 4,000.00
102 Lebron James 500.00 1,000.00
168 Chris Paul 2,500.00 5,000.00
217 Jay-Z 250.00 600.00

2005-06 Topps Chrome Autographs

PRINT RUNS LISTED IN CHECKLIST
*REFRACTORS: .75X TO 2X BASE AU HI
REFRACTOR PRINT RUN 15 TO 25 SETS
AI Allen Iverson/162 40.00 100.00
CA Carmelo Anthony/82 20.00 40.00
CB Christie Brinkley/30 40.00 100.00
DE Daniel Ewing/208 6.00 15.00
DG Danny Granger/112 12.00 30.00
EO Emeka Okafor/162 6.00 15.00
GG Gerald Green/208 8.00 20.00
HW Hakim Warrick/162 8.00 20.00
JG Joey Graham/84 6.00 15.00
JH Julius Hodge/84 6.00 15.00
JZ Jay-Z/208 500.00 1,000.00
LH Luther Head/208 6.00 15.00
OG Orien Greene/162 6.00 15.00
RF Raymond Felton/58 10.00 25.00
RM Rashad McCants/208 6.00 15.00
SE Shannon Elizabeth/30 60.00 120.00
SL Shaun Livingston/179 6.00 15.00
SM Sean May/208 6.00 15.00
SO Shaquille O'Neal/89 40.00 100.00
ABO Andrew Bogut/162 10.00 25.00
CAE Carmen Electra/30 60.00 120.00
DWA Dwyane Wade/162 40.00 100.00
DWI Deron Williams/162 10.00 25.00
JMC Jenny McCarthy/30 50.00 120.00

2005-06 Topps Chrome Chosen One Relics

PRINT RUN 400 SER.#'d SETS
*REFRACTORS: .6X TO 1.5X BASE HI
REF.PRINT RUN 99 SER.#'d SETS
*X-FRACTORS: 1.5X TO 4X BASE HI
X-FRAC.PRINT RUN 25 SER.#'d SETS
AB Andrew Bogut 3.00 8.00
AI Allen Iverson 5.00 12.00
CA Carmelo Anthony 4.00 10.00
CB Chauncey Billups 3.00 8.00
CF Channing Frye 2.00 5.00
CP Chris Paul 12.00 30.00
DH Dwight Howard 3.00 8.00
DL David Lee 2.50 6.00
DN Dirk Nowitzki 6.00 15.00
DW Deron Williams 4.00 10.00
EB Elton Brand 2.00 5.00
EO Emeka Okafor 2.00 5.00
GG Gerald Green 2.50 6.00
HW Hakim Warrick 2.00 5.00
JM Jenny McCarthy 6.00 15.00
JO Jermaine O'Neal 2.00 5.00
JZ Jay-Z 40.00 100.00
PG Pau Gasol 4.00 10.00
RF Raymond Felton 2.00 5.00
SO Shaquille O'Neal 8.00 20.00
TD Tim Duncan 6.00 15.00
YM Yao Ming 5.00 12.00
CBR Christie Brinkley 6.00 15.00
DWA Dwyane Wade 5.00 12.00

2005-06 Topps Chrome Hardwood Heroics

PRINT RUN 400 SER.#'d SETS
*REFRACTORS: .75X TO 2X BASE HI
REF.PRINT RUN 99 SER.#'d SETS
*X-FRACTORS: 1.5X TO 4X BASE HI
X-FRAC.PRINT RUN 25 SER.#'d SETS
AS Amare Stoudemire 2.50 6.00
BG Ben Gordon 2.00 5.00
BW Ben Wallace 3.00 8.00
CB Chauncey Billups 3.00 8.00
DW Dwyane Wade 5.00 12.00
EO Emeka Okafor 2.00 5.00
GH Grant Hill 4.00 10.00
JK Jason Kidd 4.00 10.00
JO Jermaine O'Neal 2.00 5.00
KB Kobe Bryant 75.00 200.00
LH Larry Hughes 2.00 5.00
MB Mike Bibby 2.50 6.00
RA Ray Allen 4.00 10.00
RH Robert Horry 2.50 6.00
RL Rashard Lewis 2.00 5.00
SN Steve Nash 5.00 12.00
TD Tim Duncan 6.00 15.00
TM Tracy McGrady 4.00 10.00
VC Vince Carter 5.00 12.00

2005-06 Topps Chrome Hardwood Heroics Refractors

DW Dwyane Wade 20.00 50.00

2005-06 Topps Chrome Hardwood Heroics X-Fractors

DW Dwyane Wade 25.00 60.00

2005-06 Topps Chrome Premium Performers

PRINT RUN 400 SER.#'d SETS
*REFRACTORS: .6X TO 1.5X BASE HI
REFRACTOR PRINT RUN 99 SER.#'d SETS
*X-FRACTORS: 1.5X TO 4X BASE HI
X-FRAC.PRINT RUN 25 SER.#'d SETS
AB Andrew Bogut 3.00 8.00
CB Chris Bosh 3.00 8.00
CW Chris Webber 3.00 8.00
DN Dirk Nowitzki 6.00 15.00
EB Elton Brand 2.00 5.00
GG Gerald Green 2.50 6.00
JK Jason Kidd 4.00 10.00
JZ Jay-Z 40.00 100.00
KG Kevin Garnett 6.00 15.00
MB Mike Bibby 2.50 6.00
PG Pau Gasol 4.00 10.00
PP Paul Pierce 4.00 10.00
RM Rashad McCants 1.50 4.00
SM Shawn Marion 2.00 5.00
SN Steve Nash 5.00 12.00
SO Shaquille O'Neal 8.00 20.00
ST Sebastian Telfair 2.00 5.00
TD Tim Duncan 6.00 15.00
TM Tracy McGrady 4.00 10.00
TP Tony Parker 4.00 10.00

2005-06 Topps Chrome Second Unit

PRINT RUN 400 SER.#'d SETS
*REFRACTORS: .5X TO 1.25X BASE HI
REFRACTOR PRINT RUN 99 SER.#'d SETS
*X-FRACTORS: 1.25X TO 3X BASE HI
X-FRAC.PRINT RUN 25 SER.#'d SETS
AJ Al Jefferson 2.00 5.00
AV Anderson Varejao 2.00 5.00
BG Ben Gordon 2.50 6.00
BU Beno Udrih 2.00 5.00
CD Carlos Delfino 2.00 5.00
DF Derek Fisher 3.00 8.00
DH Devin Harris 2.00 5.00
DW Dorell Wright 2.00 5.00
FG Francisco Garcia 2.00 5.00
FJ Fred Jones 2.00 5.00
JH Jarvis Hayes 2.00 5.00
JJ Jim Jackson 2.00 5.00
JK Jason Kapono 2.00 5.00
KK Kyle Korver 2.50 6.00
LW Luke Walton 2.00 5.00
MD Marquis Daniels 2.00 5.00
MJ Marko Jaric 2.00 5.00
MO Mehmet Okur 2.00 5.00
NC Nick Collison 2.00 5.00
RA Rafer Alston 2.50 6.00
SM Sean May 2.00 5.00
WS Wayne Simien 2.00 5.00
JHO Josh Howard 2.50 6.00
JOJ Joe Johnson 2.50 6.00
RAR Rafael Araujo 2.00 5.00

2006-07 Topps Chrome

COMPLETE SET (210) 125.00 300.00
COMP.SET w/o SP's (160) 75.00 200.00
1 Elton Brand .50 1.25
2 Tim Duncan 1.50 4.00
3 Chris Paul 1.25 3.00
4 Joe Johnson .60 1.50
5 Chauncey Billups .75 2.00
6 Andres Nocioni .40 1.00
7 Al Jefferson .40 1.00
8 Gerald Wallace .50 1.25
9 Jason Terry .50 1.25
10 Dwight Howard .75 2.00
11 Larry Hughes .50 1.25
12 Vince Carter 1.25 3.00
13 Mike Bibby .60 1.50
14 Ben Gordon .60 1.50
15 Desmond Mason .40 1.00
16 Raymond Felton .40 1.00
17 Paul Pierce 1.00 2.50
18 Jason Richardson .60 1.50
19 Rasheed Wallace .75 2.00
20 Leandro Barbosa .50 1.25
21 Deron Williams .60 1.50
22 Kwame Brown .40 1.00
23 Josh Childress .40 1.00
24 Shawn Marion .60 1.50
25 Shaquille O'Neal 2.50 6.00
26 Ray Allen 1.00 2.50
27 Cuttino Mobley .50 1.25
28 Dirk Nowitzki 1.50 4.00
29 Jermaine O'Neal .60 1.50
30 Marvin Williams .40 1.00
31 Eddy Curry .50 1.25
32 Andrei Kirilenko .50 1.25
33 Baron Davis .60 1.50
34 Tracy McGrady 1.00 2.50
35 Chris Kaman .40 1.00
36 Luol Deng .50 1.25
37 Emeka Okafor .50 1.25
38 Lamar Odom .50 1.25
39 Alonzo Mourning 1.00 2.50
40 Marcus Camby .50 1.25
41 Ike Diogu .40 1.00
42 Josh Smith .40 1.00
43 Nate Robinson .50 1.25
44 Yao Ming 1.50 4.00
45 Darko Milicic .40 1.00
46 Smush Parker .40 1.00
47 Mike Dunleavy .40 1.00
48 Ricky Davis .50 1.25
49 Michael Finley .60 1.50
50 Nenad Krstic .40 1.00
51 Earl Boykins .40 1.00
52 Richard Hamilton .60 1.50
53 Hakim Warrick .40 1.00
54 Corey Maggette .50 1.25
55 Kenyon Martin .50 1.25
56 Jason Kidd 1.00 2.50
57 Dwyane Wade 1.25 3.00
58 Josh Howard .50 1.25
59 Richard Jefferson .50 1.25
60 Steve Nash 1.25 3.00
61 Drew Gooden .50 1.25
62 Kevin Garnett 1.50 4.00
63 Delonte West .40 1.00
64 Channing Frye .40 1.00
65 Andre Iguodala .60 1.50
66 Pau Gasol 1.00 2.50
67 LeBron James 30.00 80.00
68 Sam Cassell .50 1.25
69 Mehmet Okur .40 1.00
70 Bruce Bowen .40 1.00
71 Kirk Hinrich .50 1.25
72 Chris Wilcox .40 1.00
73 Brad Miller .50 1.25
74 Chris Bosh .75 2.00
75 Jamal Crawford .60 1.50
76 Mike Miller .50 1.25
77 Danny Granger .50 1.25
78 Manu Ginobili 1.25 3.00
79 Udonis Haslem .40 1.00
80 Gilbert Arenas .60 1.50
81 Tony Parker 1.00 2.50
82 Carlos Boozer .50 1.25
83 Rashard Lewis .50 1.25
84 Boris Diaw .50 1.25
85 Shaun Livingston .50 1.25
86 Shareef Abdur-Rahim .60 1.50
87 Devin Harris .40 1.00
88 Brevin Knight .40 1.00
89 Troy Murphy .40 1.00
90 Antawn Jamison .50 1.25
91 Stephen Jackson .50 1.25

92 Chris Webber .75 2.00
93 Luke Ridnour .50 1.25
94 Joel Przybilla .40 1.00
95 David West .50 1.25
96 Caron Butler .50 1.25
97 Andre Miller .50 1.25
98 Ron Artest .60 1.50
99 Samuel Dalembert .40 1.00
100 Tayshaun Prince .60 1.50
101 Jameer Nelson .40 1.00
102 Zach Randolph .60 1.50
103 Stephon Marbury .75 2.00
104 Steve Francis .60 1.50
105 Kevin Martin .50 1.25
106 Carmelo Anthony 1.00 2.50
107 Morris Peterson .40 1.00
108 Allen Iverson 1.50 4.00
109 Antoine Walker .60 1.50
110 Jarrett Jack .50 1.25
111 Ben Wallace .75 2.00
112 Vladimir Radmanovic .40 1.00
113 Andrew Bogut .50 1.25
114 Nazr Mohammed .40 1.00
115 Kirk Snyder .40 1.00
116 Marquis Daniels .40 1.00
117 T.J. Ford .40 1.00
118 Stromile Swift .40 1.00
119 Lorenzen Wright .40 1.00
120 Mike James .40 1.00
121 Amare Stoudemire .60 1.50
122 Raef LaFrentz .40 1.00
123 Adrian Griffin .40 1.00
124 Maurice Evans .40 1.00
125 David Wesley .40 1.00
126 J.R. Smith .60 1.50
127 Ronald Murray .40 1.00
128 Shane Battier .50 1.25
129 Kobe Bryant 40.00 100.00
130 Jamaal Magloire .40 1.00
131 Charlie Villanueva .40 1.00
132 Tyson Chandler .50 1.25
133 Eddie House .40 1.00
134 Marcus Banks .40 1.00
135 Derek Fisher .60 1.50
136 Bobby Simmons .40 1.00
137 Al Harrington .50 1.25
138 Speedy Claxton .40 1.00
139 Viktor Khryapa .40 1.00
140 Sean May .40 1.00
141 Devean George .40 1.00
142 Joe Smith .50 1.25
143 Peja Stojakovic .50 1.25
144 DeShawn Stevenson .40 1.00
145 Fred Jones .40 1.00
146 P.J. Brown .40 1.00
147 Sebastian Telfair .40 1.00
148 Bonzi Wells .40 1.00
149 Michael Redd .50 1.25
150 Jared Jeffries .40 1.00
151 Larry Bird 2.00 5.00
152 Dominique Wilkins 1.00 2.50
153 Isiah Thomas 1.00 2.50
154 Wilt Chamberlain 2.00 5.00
155 Bill Walton .75 2.00
156 Oscar Robertson 1.50 4.00
157 Walt Frazier .75 2.00
158 Elgin Baylor 1.25 3.00
159 George Gervin 1.00 2.50
160 Moses Malone 1.00 2.50
161 Solomon Jones RC .75 2.00
162 Kyle Lowry RC 15.00 40.00
163 Maurice Ager RC .75 2.00
164 Patrick O'Bryant RC .75 2.00
165 Marcus Vinicius RC .75 2.00
166 Jorge Garbajosa RC 1.00 2.50
167 Josh Boone RC .75 2.00
168 Mardy Collins RC .75 2.00
169 Rodney Carney RC .75 2.00
170 P.J. Tucker RC 1.25 3.00
171 Shelden Williams RC .75 2.00
172 Ryan Hollins RC .75 2.00
173 Pops Mensah-Bonsu RC .75 2.00
174 Steve Novak RC 1.00 2.50
175 Paul Davis RC .75 2.00
176 David Noel RC .75 2.00
177 Marcus Williams RC .75 2.00
178 Renaldo Balkman RC 1.00 2.50
179 Quincy Douby RC .75 2.00
180 Andrea Bargnani RC 1.00 2.50
181 Chris Quinn RC .75 2.00
182 Thabo Sefolosha RC 1.00 2.50
183 LaMarcus Aldridge RC 3.00 8.00
184 Rudy Gay RC 1.50 4.00
185 Jordan Farmar RC 1.00 2.50
186 Damir Markota RC .75 2.00
187 Mile Ilic RC .75 2.00
188 James Augustine RC .75 2.00
189 Tyrus Thomas RC 1.00 2.50
190 Brandon Roy RC 2.50 6.00
191 Allan Ray RC .75 2.00
192 Shannon Brown RC .75 2.00
193 Will Blalock RC .75 2.00
194 James White RC .75 2.00
195 Adam Morrison RC 1.00 2.50
196 Craig Smith RC 1.00 2.50
197 Cedric Simmons RC .75 2.00
198 J.J. Redick RC 2.50 6.00
199 Sergio Rodriguez RC 1.00 2.50
200 Ronnie Brewer RC 1.25 3.00
201 Rajon Rondo RC 8.00 20.00
202 Daniel Gibson RC 1.00 2.50
203 Hassan Adams RC .75 2.00
204 Shawne Williams RC .75 2.00
205 Alexander Johnson RC .75 2.00
206 Randy Foye RC 1.00 2.50
207 Hilton Armstrong RC .75 2.00
208 Bobby Jones RC .75 2.00
209 Saer Sene RC .75 2.00
210 Dee Brown RC .75 2.00

2006-07 Topps Chrome Refractors

*REF 1-160: 3X TO 8X BASE HI
1-160 STATED ODDS 1:4
*REF 161-210: 2X TO 5X BASE HI
161-210 REF PRINT RUN 199 SETS
67 LeBron James 200.00 500.00
129 Kobe Bryant 150.00 400.00
198 J.J. Redick 40.00 100.00
201 Rajon Rondo 75.00 200.00

2006-07 Topps Chrome Refractors Black

*1-160 REF.BLACK: 5X TO 12X BASE HI
*161-210 REF.BLACK: 2X TO 5X BASE HI
REF.BLACK PRINT RUN 99 SER.#'d SETS
67 LeBron James 1,500.00 3,000.00
129 Kobe Bryant 1,000.00 2,000.00
198 J.J. Redick 50.00 120.00
201 Rajon Rondo 100.00 250.00

2006-07 Topps Chrome Refractors Gold

*1-160 REF.GOLD: 12X TO 30X BASE HI
*161-210 REF.GOLD: 6X TO 15X BASE HI
REF.GOLD PRINT RUN 25 SER.#'d SETS
2 Tim Duncan 125.00 300.00
3 Chris Paul 1,000.00 2,000.00
12 Vince Carter 125.00 300.00
17 Paul Pierce 125.00 300.00
25 Shaquille O'Neal 400.00 800.00
28 Dirk Nowitzki 125.00 300.00
34 Tracy McGrady 125.00 300.00
39 Alonzo Mourning 20.00 50.00
44 Yao Ming 600.00 1,200.00
60 Steve Nash 60.00 150.00
62 Kevin Garnett 600.00 1,200.00
67 LeBron James 6,000.00 12,000.00
92 Chris Webber 75.00 200.00
108 Allen Iverson 150.00 400.00
129 Kobe Bryant 5,000.00 10,000.00
154 Wilt Chamberlain 500.00 1,000.00
162 Kyle Lowry 300.00 600.00
183 LaMarcus Aldridge 600.00 1,200.00
190 Brandon Roy 125.00 300.00
198 J.J. Redick 200.00 500.00
201 Rajon Rondo 400.00 800.00

2006-07 Topps Chrome 1996-97 Variations

COMPLETE SET (10) 30.00 80.00
STATED ODDS 1:4
*REFRACTORS: 1.25X TO 3X BASE HI
REF.PRINT RUN 199 SER.#'d SETS
*REF.BLACK: 2.5X TO 6X BASE HI
REF.BLACK PRINT RUN 99 SER.#'d SETS
*REF.GOLD: 4X TO 10X BASE HI
REF.GOLD PRINT RUN 25 SER.#'d SETS
171 Shelden Williams .75 2.00
177 Marcus Williams .75 2.00
180 Andrea Bargnani 1.00 2.50
183 LaMarcus Aldridge 3.00 8.00
184 Rudy Gay 1.50 4.00
189 Tyrus Thomas 1.00 2.50
190 Brandon Roy 2.50 6.00
195 Adam Morrison 1.00 2.50
198 J.J. Redick 2.50 6.00
200 Ronnie Brewer 1.25 3.00

2006-07 Topps Chrome Autographs Refractors Black

GROUP A ODDS 1:2575, GROUP B 1:590
GROUP C ODDS 1:1191
RC GROUP A ODDS 1:1295, GROUP B 1:1030
RC GROUP C ODDS 1:1192, GROUP D 1:161
RC GROUP E ODDS 1:113, GROUP F 1:73
*REF.GOLD: .75X TO 2X BASE HI
REF.GOLD PRINT RUN 25 SER.#'d SETS
12 Vince Carter B 125.00 300.00
14 Ben Gordon B 4.00 10.00
25 Shaquille O'Neal A 300.00 600.00
37 Emeka Okafor A 4.00 10.00
42 Smush Parker C 3.00 8.00
57 Dwyane Wade A 150.00 400.00
74 Chris Bosh B 20.00 50.00
108 Allen Iverson A 300.00 600.00
151 Larry Bird A 200.00 500.00
153 Isiah Thomas B 75.00 200.00
161 Solomon Jones D 3.00 8.00
162 Kyle Lowry C 75.00 200.00
163 Maurice Ager D 3.00 8.00
164 Patrick O'Bryant B 3.00 8.00
165 Marcus Vinicius F 3.00 8.00
166 Jorge Garbajosa C 4.00 10.00
167 Josh Boone C 3.00 8.00
168 Mardy Collins C 3.00 8.00
169 Rodney Carney C 3.00 8.00
170 P.J. Tucker D 5.00 12.00
171 Shelden Williams A 3.00 8.00
172 Ryan Hollins E 3.00 8.00
173 Pops Mensah-Bonsu F 3.00 8.00
174 Steve Novak E 4.00 10.00
175 Paul Davis D 3.00 8.00
176 David Noel E 3.00 8.00
177 Marcus Williams A 3.00 8.00
178 Renaldo Balkman B 4.00 10.00
179 Quincy Douby D 3.00 8.00
180 Andrea Bargnani A 4.00 10.00
181 Chris Quinn F 3.00 8.00
182 Thabo Sefolosha E 4.00 10.00
185 Jordan Farmar C 4.00 10.00
186 Damir Markota F 3.00 8.00
187 Mile Ilic F 3.00 8.00
188 James Augustine E 3.00 8.00
191 Allan Ray F 3.00 8.00
192 Shannon Brown C 3.00 8.00
193 Will Blalock F 3.00 8.00
194 James White F 3.00 8.00
195 Adam Morrison A 4.00 10.00
196 Craig Smith E 4.00 10.00
197 Cedric Simmons C 3.00 8.00
198 J.J. Redick A 100.00 250.00
199 Sergio Rodriguez C 4.00 10.00
200 Ronnie Brewer B 5.00 12.00
201 Rajon Rondo C 75.00 200.00
202 Daniel Gibson F 4.00 10.00
203 Hassan Adams F 3.00 8.00
204 Shawne Williams E 3.00 8.00
205 Alexander Johnson F 3.00 8.00
206 Randy Foye B 4.00 10.00
207 Hilton Armstrong B 3.00 8.00
208 Bobby Jones E 3.00 8.00
209 Saer Sene D 3.00 8.00
210 Dee Brown D 3.00 8.00

2007-08 Topps Chrome

COMPLETE SET (160) 200.00 500.00
1 Amare Stoudemire .60 1.50
2 Joe Johnson .50 1.25
3 Dwyane Wade 1.25 3.00
4 Chris Bosh .75 2.00
5 Jason Kidd 1.00 2.50
6 Bill Russell 2.00 5.00
7 Jermaine O'Neal .60 1.50
8 Mike Miller .50 1.25
9 Ray Allen 1.00 2.50
10 Elton Brand .50 1.25
11 Yao Ming 1.50 4.00
12 Al Harrington .50 1.25
13 Steve Nash 1.25 3.00
14 Dwight Howard .75 2.00
15 Carmelo Anthony 1.00 2.50
16 Pau Gasol 1.00 2.50
17 Chauncey Billups .75 2.00
18 Bob Pettit .60 1.50
19 Jason Kapono .40 1.00
20 Kevin Garnett 1.50 4.00
21 Tim Duncan 1.50 4.00
22 Michael Redd .50 1.25
23 LeBron James 20.00 50.00
24 Kobe Bryant 20.00 50.00
25 Eddy Curry .40 1.00
26 Gerald Green .50 1.25
27 Andrew Bogut .50 1.25
28 Vince Carter 1.25 3.00
29 Corey Maggette .50 1.25
30 Morris Peterson .40 1.00
31 Shawn Marion .60 1.50
32 Shaquille O'Neal 2.50 6.00
33 Allen Iverson 1.50 4.00
34 Paul Pierce 1.00 2.50
35 Bill Sharman .60 1.50
36 Tony Parker 1.00 2.50
37 Mike Bibby .60 1.50
38 Andrea Bargnani .40 1.00
39 Luol Deng .50 1.25
40 Chris Paul 1.25 3.00
41 Dirk Nowitzki 1.50 4.00
42 David Lee .40 1.00
43 Vern Mikkelsen .60 1.50
44 Darko Milicic .40 1.00
45 Al Jefferson .40 1.00
46 Bob Cousy 1.00 2.50
47 Andrei Kirilenko .50 1.25
48 Anfernee Hardaway 1.50 4.00
49 Chris Wilcox .40 1.00
50 Dolph Schayes .60 1.50
51 Zach Randolph .60 1.50
52 Grant Hill 1.00 2.50
53 Jim Loscutoff .60 1.50
54 Leandro Barbosa .50 1.25
55 Smush Parker .40 1.00
56 Sam Jones .75 2.00
57 Manu Ginobili 1.25 3.00
58 Jason Richardson .60 1.50
59 Jason Terry .50 1.25
60 Gerald Wallace .50 1.25
61 Richard Hamilton .75 2.00
62 Cliff Hagan .50 1.25
63 Tom Heinsohn .60 1.50
64 Carlos Boozer .50 1.25
65 Rashard Lewis .50 1.25
66 Josh Childress .40 1.00
67 Channing Frye .40 1.00
68 Mike James .40 1.00
69 Kurt Thomas .40 1.00
70 Mikki Moore .40 1.00
71 Baron Davis .50 1.25
72 Reggie Theus .50 1.25
73 Jameer Nelson .40 1.00
74 Caron Butler .50 1.25
75 Jamaal Magloire .40 1.00
76 Darryl Dawkins .40 1.00
77 Ben Gordon .50 1.25
78 Andrew Bynum .40 1.00
79 Oscar Robertson .60 1.50
80 Josh Smith .40 1.00
81 Spud Webb .50 1.25
82 Chris Mullin .75 2.00
83 Raymond Felton .50 1.25
84 Sebastian Telfair .40 1.00
85 Clyde Drexler 1.00 2.50
86 Jarrett Jack .50 1.25
87 Anderson Varejao .50 1.25
88 Ryan Gomes .40 1.00
89 Bill Walton .75 2.00
90 Marcus Camby .50 1.25
91 Kirk Hinrich .60 1.50
92 David Robinson 1.25 3.00
93 Dennis Rodman 1.50 4.00
94 Dominique Wilkins 1.00 2.50
95 Richard Jefferson .50 1.25
96 Isiah Thomas .60 1.50
97 Josh Howard .50 1.25
98 John Stockton 1.25 3.00
99 Deron Williams .50 1.25
100 Gilbert Arenas .60 1.50
101 Tracy McGrady 1.00 2.50
102 Steve Blake .40 1.00
103 Ben Wallace .50 1.25
104 Kevin Martin .50 1.25
105 Larry Bird 2.50 6.00
106 Magic Johnson 2.50 6.00
107 Brandon Roy .75 2.00
108 Desmond Mason .40 1.00
109 Rick Barry .50 1.25
110 Andre Iguodala .60 1.50
111 Mike Conley Jr. RC 3.00 8.00
112 Glen Davis RC 1.00 2.50
113 Julian Wright RC .75 2.00
114 Rodney Stuckey RC .75 2.00
115 Chris Richard RC .75 2.00
116 Coby Karl RC .75 2.00
117 Thaddeus Young RC 1.25 3.00
118 Spencer Hawes RC .75 2.00
119 Jermareo Davidson RC .75 2.00
120 Daequan Cook RC 1.00 2.50
121 Josh McRoberts RC .75 2.00
122 Aaron Gray RC .75 2.00
123 Wilson Chandler RC 1.00 2.50
124 Herbert Hill RC .75 2.00
125 Stephane Lasme RC .75 2.00
126 Cheikh Samb RC .75 2.00
127 Adam Haluska RC .75 2.00
128 Al Thornton RC .75 2.00
129 Corey Brewer RC 1.00 2.50
130 Ramon Sessions RC 1.00 2.50
131 Kevin Durant RC 60.00 150.00
132 Alando Tucker RC .75 2.00
133 Marco Belinelli RC 1.00 2.50
134 Nick Fazekas RC .75 2.00
135 Yi Jianlian RC 1.50 4.00
136 Luis Scola RC 1.25 3.00
137 Jared Dudley RC 1.00 2.50
138 Taurean Green RC .75 2.00
139 Kosta Perovic RC .75 2.00
140 Kyrylo Fesenko RC .75 2.00
141 JamesOn Curry RC .75 2.00
142 D.J. Strawberry RC .75 2.00
143 Javaris Crittenton RC .75 2.00
144 Acie Law RC .75 2.00
145 Nick Young RC 1.25 3.00
146 Joakim Noah RC 1.25 3.00
147 Dominic McGuire RC .75 2.00
148 Arron Afflalo RC 1.00 2.50
149 Gabe Pruitt RC .75 2.00
150 Carl Landry RC .75 2.00
151 Jeff Green RC 1.00 2.50
152 Greg Oden RC 1.25 3.00
153 Jason Smith RC .75 2.00
154 Morris Almond RC .75 2.00
155 Juan Carlos Navarro RC 1.00 2.50
156 Brandon Wallace RC .75 2.00
157 Aaron Brooks RC 1.00 2.50
158 Brandan Wright RC 1.00 2.50
159 Sean Williams RC .75 2.00
160 Al Horford RC 3.00 8.00

2007-08 Topps Chrome Refractors

1-110 REF.PRINT RUN 999 SER.#'d SETS
111-160 REF.PRINT RUN 1499 SER.#'d SETS
23 LeBron James 200.00 500.00
24 Kobe Bryant 200.00 500.00
101 Tracy McGrady 30.00 80.00
131 Kevin Durant 600.00 1,200.00
160 Al Horford 15.00 40.00

2007-08 Topps Chrome Refractors Orange

*1-110 REF.ORANGE: 4X TO 10X BASE HI
*111-160 RC REF.ORNG: 1.5X TO 4X BASE HI
PRINT RUN 199 SER.#'d SETS
23 LeBron James 500.00 1,000.00
24 Kobe Bryant 500.00 1,000.00
101 Tracy McGrady 50.00 120.00
131 Kevin Durant 1,000.00 2,000.00
160 Al Horford 25.00 60.00

2007-08 Topps Chrome Refractors White

*1-110 REF.WHITE: 5X TO 12X BASE HI
*111-160 RC.REF.WHT: 2X TO 5X BASE HI
REF.WHITE PRINT RUN 99 SER.#'d SETS
23 LeBron James 1,000.00 2,000.00
24 Kobe Bryant 1,000.00 2,000.00
101 Tracy McGrady 75.00 200.00
131 Kevin Durant 1,500.00 3,000.00
160 Al Horford 30.00 80.00

2007-08 Topps Chrome X-Fractors

*1-110 X-FRAC: 8X TO 20X BASE HI
*111-160 RC X-FRAC: 3X TO 8X BASE HI
X-FRAC PRINT RUN 50 SER.#'d SETS
101 Tracy McGrady 125.00 300.00
131 Kevin Durant 2,500.00 5,000.00
160 Al Horford 50.00 120.00

2007-08 Topps Chrome 1957-58 Variations

COMPLETE SET (50) 40.00 75.00
APPROXIMATE ODDS ONE PER PACK
*X-FRACTORS: 4X TO 10X BASE HI
X-FRAC.PRINT RUN 50 SER.#'d SETS
3 Dwyane Wade 1.25 3.00
6 Bill Russell 2.00 5.00
9 Ray Allen 1.00 2.50
11 Yao Ming 1.50 4.00
13 Steve Nash 1.25 3.00
15 Carmelo Anthony 1.00 2.50
18 Bob Pettit .60 1.50
20 Kevin Garnett 1.50 4.00
21 Tim Duncan 1.50 4.00
23 LeBron James 20.00 50.00
24 Kobe Bryant 20.00 50.00
28 Vince Carter 1.25 3.00
32 Shaquille O'Neal 2.50 6.00
33 Allen Iverson 1.50 4.00
35 Bill Sharman .60 1.50
36 Tony Parker 1.00 2.50
40 Chris Paul 1.25 3.00
41 Dirk Nowitzki 1.50 4.00
42 David Lee .40 1.00
43 Vern Mikkelsen .60 1.50
46 Bob Cousy 1.00 2.50
50 Dolph Schayes .60 1.50
53 Jim Loscutoff .60 1.50
54 Leandro Barbosa .50 1.25
56 Sam Jones .75 2.00
58 Jason Richardson .60 1.50
60 Gerald Wallace .50 1.25
62 Cliff Hagan .50 1.25
63 Tom Heinsohn .60 1.50
64 Carlos Boozer .50 1.25
71 Baron Davis .50 1.25
72 Reggie Theus .50 1.25
76 Darryl Dawkins .40 1.00
79 Oscar Robertson .60 1.50
81 Spud Webb .50 1.25
82 Chris Mullin .75 2.00
85 Clyde Drexler 1.00 2.50
89 Bill Walton .75 2.00
90 Marcus Camby .50 1.25
92 David Robinson 1.25 3.00
93 Dennis Rodman 1.50 4.00
94 Dominique Wilkins 1.00 2.50
96 Isiah Thomas .60 1.50
98 John Stockton 1.25 3.00
99 Deron Williams .50 1.25
100 Gilbert Arenas .60 1.50
103 Ben Wallace .75 2.00
105 Larry Bird 2.50 6.00
106 Magic Johnson 2.50 6.00
109 Rick Barry .50 1.25

2007-08 Topps Chrome 1957-58 Variations Refractors

*REFRACTORS: 2X TO 5X BASE HI
PRINT RUN 999 SER.#'d SETS
23 LeBron James 200.00 500.00
24 Kobe Bryant 200.00 500.00

2007-08 Topps Chrome 1957-58 Variations Refractors Orange

*REF.ORANGE: 3X TO 8X BASE HI
PRINT RUN 199 SER.#'d SETS
23 LeBron James 500.00 1,000.00
24 Kobe Bryant 500.00 1,000.00

2007-08 Topps Chrome 1957-58 Variations Refractors White

*REF.WHITE: 4X TO 10X BASE HI
PRINT RUN 99 SER.#'d SETS
23 LeBron James 1,000.00 2,000.00
24 Kobe Bryant 1,000.00 2,000.00

2007-08 Topps Chrome 1957-58 Variations X-Fractors

*X-FRACTORS: 6X TO 15X BASE HI
PRINT RUN 50 SER.#'d SETS
23 LeBron James 1,500.00 3,000.00
24 Kobe Bryant 1,500.00 3,000.00

2007-08 Topps Chrome 1957-58 Variations Autographs

PRINT RUN 29 TO 99 SER.#'d SETS
*REF.ORANGE: .5X TO 1.25X BASE HI
*REF.ORANGE SP's: SAME VALUE
PRINT RUN 25 SER.#'d SETS
EXCH.EXPIRATION DATE 1/31/10
3 Dwyane Wade/29 40.00 100.00
6 Bill Russell/29 800.00 1,500.00
9 Ray Allen/99 15.00 30.00
28 Vince Carter/99 15.00 40.00
32 Shaquille O'Neal/29 50.00 100.00
42 David Lee/99 6.00 15.00
54 Leandro Barbosa/99 6.00 15.00
60 Gerald Wallace/99 6.00 15.00
64 Carlos Boozer/99 6.00 15.00
71 Baron Davis/99 6.00 15.00
81 Spud Webb/99 8.00 20.00
89 Bill Walton/29 25.00 50.00
92 David Robinson/29 50.00 100.00
93 Dennis Rodman/29 25.00 50.00
94 Dominique Wilkins/99 15.00 30.00
96 Isiah Thomas/29 20.00 40.00
98 John Stockton/29 30.00 60.00
99 Deron Williams/99 20.00 40.00
105 Larry Bird/29 40.00 100.00
109 Rick Barry/99 12.50 30.00

2007-08 Topps Chrome Rookie Autographs

PRINT RUN 149 TO 999 SER.#'d SETS
*REF.ORANGE: .75X TO 2X BASE HI
REF.ORANGE PRINT RUN 25 SER.#'d SETS
EXCH.EXPIRATION DATE 1/31/10
112 Glen Davis/999 4.00 10.00
114 Rodney Stuckey/999 3.00 8.00
117 Thaddeus Young/149 5.00 12.00
118 Spencer Hawes/149 3.00 8.00
119 Jermareo Davidson/999 3.00 8.00
120 Daequan Cook/539 4.00 10.00
121 Josh McRoberts/999 3.00 8.00
122 Aaron Gray/539 3.00 8.00
123 Wilson Chandler/539 4.00 10.00
124 Herbert Hill/999 3.00 8.00
125 Stephane Lasme/999 3.00 8.00
127 Adam Haluska/999 3.00 8.00
128 Al Thornton/149 3.00 8.00
133 Marco Belinelli/539 4.00 10.00
134 Nick Fazekas/999 3.00 8.00
135 Yi Jianlian/149 12.00 30.00
137 Jared Dudley/539 4.00 10.00
138 Taurean Green/999 3.00 8.00
141 JamesOn Curry/999 3.00 8.00
142 D.J. Strawberry/999 3.00 8.00
143 Javaris Crittenton/999 3.00 8.00
144 Acie Law/149 3.00 8.00
145 Nick Young/149 5.00 12.00
147 Dominic McGuire/999 3.00 8.00
148 Arron Afflalo/539 4.00 10.00
149 Gabe Pruitt/999 3.00 8.00
150 Carl Landry/999 3.00 8.00
152 Greg Oden/149 5.00 12.00
153 Jason Smith/149 3.00 8.00
154 Morris Almond/539 3.00 8.00
155 Juan Carlos Navarro/539 4.00 10.00
157 Aaron Brooks/539 4.00 10.00
158 Brandan Wright/999 4.00 10.00
159 Sean Williams/539 3.00 8.00

2008-09 Topps Chrome

COMPLETE SET (255) 800.00 1,500.00
1 Chris Paul 1.25 3.00
2 Joe Johnson .60 1.50
3 Allen Iverson 1.25 3.00
4 Luis Scola .50 1.25
5 Kevin Garnett 1.50 4.00
6 Andrew Bogut .50 1.25
7 Ben Gordon .50 1.25
8 Carlos Boozer .50 1.25
9 Tony Parker .75 2.00
10 Gilbert Arenas .60 1.50
11 Yao Ming 1.50 4.00
12 Dwight Howard .75 2.00
13 Steve Nash 1.25 3.00
14 Daequan Cook .40 1.00
15 Carmelo Anthony .75 2.00
16 Pau Gasol .60 1.50
17 Mike Dunleavy .40 1.00
18 Jason Maxiell .40 1.00
19 Al Thornton .40 1.00
20 Ray Allen 1.00 2.50
21 Tim Duncan 1.50 4.00
22 Michael Redd .50 1.25
23 LeBron James 50.00 120.00
24 Kobe Bryant 100.00 250.00
25 Al Jefferson .40 1.00
26 Raymond Felton .40 1.00
27 LaMarcus Aldridge .60 1.50
28 Jose Calderon .40 1.00
29 Andris Biedrins .40 1.00
30 Rasheed Wallace .75 2.00
31 Shawn Marion .60 1.50
32 Shaquille O'Neal 2.00 5.00
33 Mike Miller .50 1.25
34 Paul Pierce 1.00 2.50
35 Brad Miller .50 1.25
36 Richard Jefferson .50 1.25
37 DeShawn Stevenson .50 1.25
38 Zach Randolph .60 1.50
39 Daniel Gibson .40 1.00
40 Nazr Mohammed .40 1.00
41 Dirk Nowitzki 1.50 4.00
42 Elton Brand .50 1.25
43 Linas Kleiza .40 1.00
44 Andrea Bargnani .40 1.00
45 Josh Smith .40 1.00
46 Luol Deng .50 1.25
47 Andrei Kirilenko .50 1.25
48 Danny Granger .50 1.25
49 Rashad McCants .40 1.00
50 Emeka Okafor .40 1.00
51 Kyle Korver .50 1.25
52 Jamario Moon .40 1.00
53 Nick Young .40 1.00
54 Rashard Lewis .50 1.25
55 Jason Kidd 1.00 2.50
56 Josh Howard .50 1.25
57 Desmond Mason .40 1.00
58 Andre Miller .50 1.25
59 Rafer Alston .40 1.00
60 Baron Davis .60 1.50
61 Zydrunas Ilgauskas .50 1.25
62 Marvin Williams .40 1.00
63 Manu Ginobili 1.25 3.00
64 David West .50 1.25
65 Rajon Rondo .75 2.00
66 Kenyon Martin .50 1.25
67 Josh Boone .40 1.00
68 Travis Outlaw .50 1.25
69 Andre Iguodala .50 1.25
70 Yi Jianlian .75 2.00
71 Jordan Farmar .40 1.00
72 Udonis Haslem .40 1.00
73 Caron Butler .50 1.25
74 Craig Smith .40 1.00
75 Tayshaun Prince .60 1.50
76 Rudy Gay .60 1.50
77 Jermaine O'Neal .60 1.50
78 Devin Harris .40 1.00
79 Fabricio Oberto .40 1.00
80 Hedo Turkoglu .50 1.25
81 James Posey .40 1.00
82 Corey Maggette .50 1.25
83 Ricky Davis .50 1.25
84 Grant Hill 1.00 2.50
85 Eddie House .40 1.00
86 Jeff Green .50 1.25
87 Lamar Odom .50 1.25
88 Brandan Wright .40 1.00
89 Sean Williams .40 1.00
90 Drew Gooden .50 1.25
91 Amare Stoudemire .60 1.50
92 Charlie Villanueva .40 1.00
93 Ron Artest .60 1.50
94 Derek Fisher .50 1.25
95 Willie Green .40 1.00
96 Kirk Hinrich .50 1.25
97 Jameer Nelson .40 1.00
98 Al Harrington .50 1.25
99 Ronnie Brewer .40 1.00
100 Dwyane Wade 1.25 3.00
101 Jamal Crawford .60 1.50
102 Ryan Gomes .40 1.00
103 Marcus Camby .50 1.25
104 Antawn Jamison .50 1.25
105 Cuttino Mobley .40 1.00
106 Tyson Chandler .50 1.25
107 Al Horford .60 1.50
108 Chris Wilcox .40 1.00
109 Gerald Wallace .50 1.25
110 Andrew Bynum .40 1.00
111 Tracy McGrady 1.00 2.50
112 Mo Williams .50 1.25
113 Nate Robinson .40 1.00
114 Wally Szczerbiak .50 1.25
115 Vince Carter 1.25 3.00
116 T.J. Ford .40 1.00
117 Kevin Martin .50 1.25
118 Steve Blake .40 1.00
119 Anderson Varejao .50 1.25
120 Mike Conley Jr. .50 1.25
121 Chris Kaman .40 1.00
122 Louis Williams .60 1.50
123 Jason Richardson .60 1.50
124 John Salmons .40 1.00
125 Martell Webster .50 1.25
126 Kurt Thomas .40 1.00
127 Raja Bell .50 1.25
128 Jason Terry .50 1.25
129 Corey Brewer .50 1.25
130 Bruce Bowen .50 1.25
131 Glen Davis .40 1.00
132 Richard Hamilton .60 1.50
133 Ben Wallace .75 2.00
134 Chris Bosh .75 2.00
135 Beno Udrih .40 1.00
136 Jarrett Jack .50 1.25
137 Stephen Jackson .50 1.25
138 Damien Wilkins .40 1.00
139 Jamaal Tinsley .40 1.00
140 Deron Williams .50 1.25
141 Andres Nocioni .40 1.00
142 David Lee .40 1.00
143 Rodney Stuckey .40 1.00
144 Luke Walton .50 1.25
145 Jerry Stackhouse .60 1.50
146 Samuel Dalembert .40 1.00
147 Brandon Roy .50 1.25
148 Chauncey Billups .75 2.00
149 Michael Finley .60 1.50
150 Leandro Barbosa .40 1.00
151 Keith Bogans .40 1.00
152 Mike Bibby .60 1.50
153 Troy Murphy .40 1.00
154 Eddy Curry .40 1.00
155 Anthony Parker .40 1.00
156 Kevin Durant 2.50 6.00
157 Larry Hughes .50 1.25
158 Peja Stojakovic .50 1.25
159 Shane Battier .50 1.25
160 Kendrick Perkins .40 1.00
161 Mehmet Okur .40 1.00
162 Brendan Haywood .40 1.00
163 Monta Ellis .50 1.25
164 J.R. Smith .60 1.50
165 Greg Oden .40 1.00
166 John Stockton 1.25 3.00
167 Dennis Rodman 1.25 3.00
168 Dominique Wilkins 1.00 2.50
169 Larry Bird 2.00 5.00
170 Isiah Thomas 1.00 2.50
171 Magic Johnson 2.00 5.00
172 Bill Russell 2.00 5.00
173 David Robinson 1.25 3.00
174 Jerry West 1.25 3.00
175 Micheal Ray Richardson .50 1.25
176 Jo Jo White .60 1.50
177 Pete Maravich 1.50 4.00
178 Wilt Chamberlain 2.00 5.00
179 Patrick Ewing 1.00 2.50
180 Julius Erving 1.50 4.00
181 Derrick Rose RC 20.00 50.00
182 Michael Beasley RC 1.25 3.00
183 O.J. Mayo RC 1.00 2.50
184 Russell Westbrook RC 25.00 60.00
185 Kevin Love RC 2.50 6.00
186 Danilo Gallinari RC 2.00 5.00
187 Eric Gordon RC 2.00 5.00
188 Joe Alexander RC .75 2.00
189 D.J. Augustin RC 1.25 3.00
190 Brook Lopez RC 1.50 4.00
191 Jerryd Bayless RC 1.00 2.50
192 Jason Thompson RC .75 2.00
193 Anthony Randolph RC .75 2.00
194 Robin Lopez RC 1.00 2.50
195 Marreese Speights RC 1.00 2.50
196 Roy Hibbert RC 1.00 2.50
197 JaVale McGee RC 1.25 3.00
198 J.J. Hickson RC .75 2.00
199 Alexis Ajinca RC .75 2.00
200 Ryan Anderson RC 1.00 2.50
201 Courtney Lee RC 1.00 2.50
202 Kosta Koufos RC .75 2.00
203 Donte Greene RC .75 2.00
204 George Hill RC 1.25 3.00
205 D.J. White RC .75 2.00
206 J.R. Giddens RC .75 2.00
207 Joey Dorsey RC .75 2.00
208 Mario Chalmers RC 1.25 3.00
209 DeAndre Jordan RC 1.50 4.00
210 Chris Douglas-Roberts RC .75 2.00
211 Malik Hairston RC .75 2.00
212 Marc Gasol RC 2.50 6.00
213 Kyle Weaver RC .75 2.00
214 Patrick Ewing Jr. RC .75 2.00
215 Walter Sharpe RC .75 2.00
216 Sonny Weems RC .75 2.00
217 Trent Plaisted RC .75 2.00
218 Nicolas Batum RC 1.50 4.00
219 Brandon Rush RC .75 2.00
220 Darrell Arthur RC 1.00 2.50

2008-09 Topps Chrome Refractors

*STARS: .75X TO 2X BASE HI
*RCs: 1.25X TO 3X BASE HI
REF.STATED ODDS 1:4
AUTO GRP.A PRINT RUN 145 SETS
AUTO GRP.B PRINT RUN 245 SETS
AUTO GRP.C PRINT RUN 476 SETS
AUTO GRP.D PRINT RUN 795 SETS
1 Chris Paul 40.00 100.00
3 Allen Iverson 40.00 100.00
5 Kevin Garnett 40.00 100.00
11 Yao Ming 50.00 120.00
12 Dwight Howard 12.00 30.00
13 Steve Nash 15.00 40.00
15 Carmelo Anthony 25.00 60.00
16 Pau Gasol 12.00 30.00
20 Ray Allen 15.00 40.00
21 Tim Duncan 40.00 100.00
23 LeBron James 1,500.00 3,000.00
24 Kobe Bryant 1,500.00 3,000.00
34 Paul Pierce 25.00 60.00
41 Dirk Nowitzki 25.00 60.00
55 Jason Kidd 15.00 40.00
63 Manu Ginobili 10.00 25.00
100 Dwyane Wade 40.00 100.00
111 Tracy McGrady 15.00 40.00
115 Vince Carter 20.00 50.00
156 Kevin Durant 25.00 60.00
166 John Stockton 10.00 25.00
167 Dennis Rodman 25.00 60.00
168 Dominique Wilkins 10.00 25.00
169 Larry Bird 20.00 50.00
171 Magic Johnson 20.00 50.00
172 Bill Russell 20.00 50.00
173 David Robinson 12.00 30.00
174 Jerry West 10.00 25.00
177 Pete Maravich 12.00 30.00
178 Wilt Chamberlain 40.00 100.00
179 Patrick Ewing 10.00 25.00
180 Julius Erving 20.00 50.00
181 Derrick Rose 75.00 200.00
186 Danilo Gallinari 15.00 40.00
221 Derrick Rose AU A 400.00 800.00
222 Michael Beasley AU A 10.00 25.00
223 O.J. Mayo AU A 12.00 30.00
224 Russell Westbrook AU A 1,000.00 2,000.00
225 Kevin Love AU A 75.00 150.00
226 Danilo Gallinari AU A 25.00 60.00
227 Eric Gordon AU A 20.00 50.00
228 Joe Alexander AU B 4.00 10.00
229 D.J. Augustin AU B 6.00 15.00
230 Brook Lopez AU B 15.00 40.00
231 Jerryd Bayless AU B 5.00 12.00
232 Jason Thompson AU B 4.00 10.00
233 Anthony Randolph AU B 10.00 25.00
234 Robin Lopez AU A 5.00 12.00
235 Marreese Speights AU C 5.00 12.00
236 Roy Hibbert AU B 12.00 30.00
237 JaVale McGee AU C 6.00 15.00
238 J.J. Hickson AU C 4.00 10.00
239 Sonny Weems AU C 4.00 10.00
240 Ryan Anderson AU C 5.00 12.00
241 Courtney Lee AU B 5.00 12.00
242 Kosta Koufos AU C 4.00 10.00
243 Donte Greene AU B 4.00 10.00
244 George Hill AU B 6.00 15.00
245 D.J. White AU C 4.00 10.00
246 J.R. Giddens AU B 4.00 10.00
247 Joey Dorsey AU B 4.00 10.00

248 Mario Chalmers AU B 6.00 15.00
249 DeAndre Jordan AU C 12.00 30.00
250 Chris Douglas-Roberts AU D 4.00 10.00
251 Kyle Weaver AU D 4.00 10.00
252 Patrick Ewing Jr. AU D 4.00 10.00
253 Walter Sharpe AU D 4.00 10.00
254 Brandon Rush AU B 4.00 10.00
255 Darrell Arthur AU B 5.00 12.00

2008-09 Topps Chrome Refractors Gold

*1-180 REF.GOLD: 10X TO 25X BASE HI
*181-220 REF.GOLD: 4X TO 10X BASE HI
181-220 PRINT RUN 50 SER.#'d SETS
1 Chris Paul 800.00 1,500.00
3 Allen Iverson 500.00 1,000.00
5 Kevin Garnett 600.00 1,200.00
9 Tony Parker 60.00 150.00
11 Yao Ming 600.00 1,200.00
12 Dwight Howard 125.00 300.00
13 Steve Nash 300.00 600.00
15 Carmelo Anthony 300.00 600.00
16 Pau Gasol 125.00 300.00
20 Ray Allen 150.00 400.00
21 Tim Duncan 500.00 1,000.00
23 LeBron James 20,000.00 40,000.00
24 Kobe Bryant 30,000.00 60,000.00
32 Shaquille O'Neal 75.00 200.00
34 Paul Pierce 400.00 800.00
41 Dirk Nowitzki 500.00 1,000.00
55 Jason Kidd 150.00 400.00
63 Manu Ginobili 125.00 300.00
65 Rajon Rondo 75.00 200.00
70 Yi Jianlian 30.00 80.00
94 Derek Fisher 15.00 40.00
100 Dwyane Wade 500.00 1,000.00
111 Tracy McGrady 150.00 400.00
115 Vince Carter 200.00 500.00
133 Ben Wallace 30.00 80.00
148 Chauncey Billups 40.00 100.00
156 Kevin Durant 3,000.00 6,000.00
166 John Stockton 100.00 250.00
167 Dennis Rodman 300.00 600.00
168 Dominique Wilkins 100.00 250.00
169 Larry Bird 200.00 500.00
171 Magic Johnson 200.00 500.00
172 Bill Russell 300.00 600.00
173 David Robinson 125.00 300.00
174 Jerry West 100.00 250.00
177 Pete Maravich 125.00 300.00
178 Wilt Chamberlain 600.00 1,200.00
179 Patrick Ewing 125.00 300.00
180 Julius Erving 200.00 500.00
181 Derrick Rose 500.00 1,000.00
184 Russell Westbrook 2,000.00 4,000.00
186 Danilo Gallinari 75.00 200.00
187 Eric Gordon 40.00 100.00
197 JaVale McGee 25.00 60.00
204 George Hill 25.00 60.00
209 DeAndre Jordan 40.00 100.00
212 Marc Gasol 60.00 150.00

2008-09 Topps Chrome Refractors Orange

*ORANGE STARS: 2X TO 5X BASE HI
*ORANGE RCs: 2X TO 5X BASE HI
PRINT RUN 499 SER.#'d SETS
3 Allen Iverson 75.00 200.00
5 Kevin Garnett 75.00 200.00
11 Yao Ming 100.00 250.00
12 Dwight Howard 25.00 60.00
13 Steve Nash 40.00 100.00
15 Carmelo Anthony 50.00 120.00
16 Pau Gasol 25.00 60.00
20 Ray Allen 30.00 80.00
21 Tim Duncan 75.00 200.00
23 LeBron James 4,000.00 8,000.00
24 Kobe Bryant 8,000.00 15,000.00
41 Dirk Nowitzki 75.00 200.00
55 Jason Kidd 30.00 80.00
63 Manu Ginobili 20.00 50.00
100 Dwyane Wade 75.00 200.00
111 Tracy McGrady 30.00 80.00
115 Vince Carter 40.00 100.00
156 Kevin Durant 1,000.00 2,000.00
166 John Stockton 20.00 50.00
167 Dennis Rodman 50.00 120.00
168 Dominique Wilkins 20.00 50.00
169 Larry Bird 40.00 100.00
171 Magic Johnson 40.00 100.00
172 Bill Russell 40.00 100.00
173 David Robinson 25.00 60.00
174 Jerry West 20.00 50.00
177 Pete Maravich 25.00 60.00
178 Wilt Chamberlain 75.00 200.00
179 Patrick Ewing 20.00 50.00
180 Julius Erving 40.00 100.00
186 Danilo Gallinari 25.00 60.00

2008-09 Topps Chrome X-Fractors

*X-FRACTOR STARS: 2X TO 5X BASE HI
*X-FRACTOR RCs: 2X TO 5X BASE HI
PRINT RUN 288 SER.#'d SETS
3 Allen Iverson 75.00 200.00
5 Kevin Garnett 75.00 200.00
11 Yao Ming 100.00 250.00
12 Dwight Howard 25.00 60.00
13 Steve Nash 40.00 100.00
15 Carmelo Anthony 50.00 120.00
16 Pau Gasol 25.00 60.00
20 Ray Allen 30.00 80.00
21 Tim Duncan 75.00 200.00
23 LeBron James 5,000.00 10,000.00
24 Kobe Bryant 15,000.00 30,000.00
41 Dirk Nowitzki 75.00 200.00
55 Jason Kidd 30.00 80.00
63 Manu Ginobili 20.00 50.00
100 Dwyane Wade 75.00 200.00
111 Tracy McGrady 30.00 80.00
115 Vince Carter 40.00 100.00
156 Kevin Durant 1,000.00 2,000.00
166 John Stockton 20.00 50.00
167 Dennis Rodman 50.00 120.00
168 Dominique Wilkins 20.00 50.00
169 Larry Bird 40.00 100.00
171 Magic Johnson 40.00 100.00
172 Bill Russell 40.00 100.00
173 David Robinson 25.00 60.00
174 Jerry West 20.00 50.00
177 Pete Maravich 25.00 60.00
178 Wilt Chamberlain 75.00 200.00
180 Julius Erving 40.00 100.00
184 Russell Westbrook 600.00 1,200.00
186 Danilo Gallinari 25.00 60.00

2008-09 Topps Chrome 1958-59 Variations Autographs Refractors

GROUP A PRINT RUN 20 SETS
GROUP B PRINT RUN 45 SETS
GROUP C PRINT RUN 60 SETS
GROUP D PRINT RUN 360 SETS
*X-FRAC: .6X TO 1.5X BASE HI
X-FRAC.PRINT RUN 15 SER.#'d SETS
1 Chris Paul A 75.00 200.00
7 Ben Gordon B 8.00 20.00
8 Carlos Boozer B 8.00 20.00
12 Dwight Howard B 12.00 30.00
15 Carmelo Anthony A 25.00 60.00
34 Paul Pierce B 15.00 40.00
46 Luol Deng C 5.00 12.00
48 Danny Granger C 8.00 20.00
60 Baron Davis B 10.00 25.00
76 Rudy Gay D 5.00 12.00
111 Tracy McGrady A 10.00 25.00
147 Brandon Roy B 15.00 40.00
165 Greg Oden A 12.00 30.00
172 Larry Bird A 50.00 120.00

2008-09 Topps Chrome Youthquake Autographs Refractors

STATED PRINT RUN 30 TO 165 SETS
*X-FRACTORS: .75X TO 2X BASE HI
X-FRACTORS PRINT RUN 15 SETS
YQA1 Michael Beasley/30 10.00 25.00
YQA2 Jerryd Bayless/30 10.00 25.00
YQA3 Danilo Gallinari/30 12.00 30.00
YQA4 Eric Gordon/30 15.00 40.00
YQA5 Robin Lopez/165 10.00 25.00
YQA6 Kevin Love/30 100.00 250.00
YQA7 Derrick Rose/30 300.00 600.00
YQA8 Anthony Randolph/165 10.00 25.00
YQA9 O.J. Mayo/30 10.00 25.00
YQA10 Russell Westbrook/30 600.00 1,200.00
YQA11 D.J. Augustin/45 10.00 25.00
YQA12 Brook Lopez/45 15.00 40.00
YQA13 Rudy Gay/165 10.00 25.00
YQA14 Al Thornton/45 6.00 15.00
YQA15 Thaddeus Young/30 10.00 25.00

2009-10 Topps Chrome

PRINT RUN 999 SER.#'d SETS
1 Joe Johnson 1.00 2.50
2 Josh Smith .60 1.50
3 Mike Bibby 1.00 2.50
4 Marvin Williams .60 1.50
5 Al Horford 1.00 2.50
6 Paul Pierce 1.50 4.00
7 Ray Allen 1.50 4.00
8 Kevin Garnett 2.50 6.00
9 Rajon Rondo 1.25 3.00
10 Glen Davis .60 1.50
11 Gerald Wallace .75 2.00
12 Raymond Felton .60 1.50
13 Ben Gordon .75 2.00
14 Derrick Rose 1.50 4.00
15 Luol Deng .75 2.00
16 LeBron James 60.00 150.00
17 Mo Williams .75 2.00
18 Anderson Varejao .60 1.50
19 Daniel Gibson .60 1.50
20 Ben Wallace 1.25 3.00
21 Dirk Nowitzki 2.50 6.00
22 Jason Terry .75 2.00
23 Josh Howard .75 2.00
24 Jason Kidd 1.50 4.00
25 Carmelo Anthony 1.50 4.00
26 Chauncey Billups 1.25 3.00
27 J.R. Smith 1.00 2.50
28 Allen Iverson 10.00 25.00
29 Richard Hamilton 1.00 2.50
30 Tayshaun Prince 1.00 2.50
31 Corey Maggette .75 2.00
32 Monta Ellis .75 2.00
33 Anthony Randolph .60 1.50
34 Yao Ming 2.50 6.00
35 Ron Artest 1.00 2.50
36 Tracy McGrady 2.00 5.00
37 Shane Battier 1.00 2.50
38 Danny Granger .60 1.50
39 T.J. Ford .60 1.50
40 Troy Murphy .60 1.50
41 Al Thornton .60 1.50
42 Baron Davis .75 2.00
43 Eric Gordon .75 2.00
44 Kobe Bryant 500.00 1,000.00
45 Pau Gasol 1.50 4.00
46 Andrew Bynum .60 1.50
47 Lamar Odom .75 2.00
48 O.J. Mayo .60 1.50
49 Rudy Gay 1.00 2.50
50 Marc Gasol 1.00 2.50
51 Dwyane Wade 2.00 5.00
52 Michael Beasley .60 1.50
53 Michael Redd .75 2.00
54 Richard Jefferson .75 2.00
55 Andrew Bogut .75 2.00
56 Al Jefferson .60 1.50
57 Kevin Love 1.00 2.50
58 Mike Miller .75 2.00
59 Devin Harris .60 1.50
60 Vince Carter 1.50 4.00
61 Brook Lopez 1.00 2.50
62 Yi Jianlian 1.25 3.00
63 Chris Paul 2.00 5.00
64 David West .60 1.50
65 David Lee .60 1.50
66 Nate Robinson .75 2.00
67 Russell Westbrook 12.00 30.00
68 Kevin Durant 40.00 100.00
69 Dwight Howard 1.25 3.00
70 Rashard Lewis .75 2.00
71 Hedo Turkoglu .75 2.00
72 Jameer Nelson .60 1.50
73 Andre Iguodala 1.00 2.50
74 Elton Brand .75 2.00
75 Thaddeus Young .60 1.50
76 Amare Stoudemire .75 2.00
77 Shaquille O'Neal 3.00 8.00
78 Jason Richardson 1.00 2.50
79 Steve Nash 2.00 5.00
80 Brandon Roy 1.25 3.00
81 LaMarcus Aldridge 1.00 2.50
82 Rudy Fernandez .60 1.50
83 Greg Oden .60 1.50
84 Kevin Martin .75 2.00
85 Tony Parker 1.50 4.00
86 Tim Duncan 2.50 6.00
87 Manu Ginobili 2.00 5.00
88 Chris Bosh 1.25 3.00
89 Andrea Bargnani .60 1.50
90 Shawn Marion 1.00 2.50
91 Jose Calderon .60 1.50
92 Carlos Boozer .75 2.00
93 Deron Williams .75 2.00
94 Antawn Jamison .75 2.00
95 Gilbert Arenas .75 2.00
96 Blake Griffin RC 25.00 60.00
97 Ricky Rubio RC 8.00 20.00
98 Hasheem Thabeet RC 4.00 10.00
99 James Harden RC 200.00 500.00
100 DeMar DeRozan RC 60.00 150.00
101 Stephen Curry RC 5,000.00 10,000.00
102 Brandon Jennings RC 6.00 15.00
103 Jordan Hill RC 4.00 10.00
104 Earl Clark RC 4.00 10.00
105 Gerald Henderson RC 4.00 10.00
106 Jonny Flynn RC 4.00 10.00
107 Tyreke Evans RC 5.00 12.00
108 Tyler Hansbrough RC 5.00 12.00
109 Terrence Williams RC 4.00 10.00
110 Jrue Holiday RC 60.00 150.00

2009-10 Topps Chrome Refractors

*REF 1-95 : 2X TO 5X BASE HI
*REF RC: .6X TO 1.5X BASE HI
REF PRINT RUN 500 SER.#'d SETS
6 Paul Pierce 20.00 50.00
7 Ray Allen 25.00 60.00
8 Kevin Garnett 25.00 60.00
14 Derrick Rose 60.00 150.00
16 LeBron James 1,000.00 2,000.00
21 Dirk Nowitzki 25.00 60.00
24 Jason Kidd 15.00 40.00
25 Carmelo Anthony 20.00 50.00
28 Allen Iverson 25.00 60.00
34 Yao Ming 20.00 50.00
36 Tracy McGrady 25.00 60.00
44 Kobe Bryant 600.00 1,200.00
50 Marc Gasol 15.00 40.00
51 Dwyane Wade 40.00 100.00
60 Vince Carter 20.00 50.00
62 Yi Jianlian 20.00 50.00
63 Chris Paul 20.00 50.00
66 Nate Robinson 15.00 40.00
67 Russell Westbrook 25.00 60.00
68 Kevin Durant 100.00 250.00
69 Dwight Howard 12.00 30.00
77 Shaquille O'Neal 40.00 100.00
79 Steve Nash 20.00 50.00
85 Tony Parker 10.00 25.00
86 Tim Duncan 25.00 60.00
87 Manu Ginobili 20.00 50.00
96 Blake Griffin 75.00 200.00
99 James Harden 500.00 1,000.00
100 DeMar DeRozan 300.00 600.00
101 Stephen Curry 15,000.00 30,000.00
110 Jrue Holiday 150.00 400.00

2009-10 Topps Chrome Refractors Gold

*REF.GOLD 1-95: 12X TO 30X BASE HI
*REF.GOLD RC 96-110: 1.5X TO 4X BASE HI
PRINT RUN 50 SER.#'d SETS
6 Paul Pierce 100.00 250.00
7 Ray Allen 150.00 400.00
8 Kevin Garnett 300.00 600.00
14 Derrick Rose 300.00 600.00
16 LeBron James 5,000.00 10,000.00
21 Dirk Nowitzki 300.00 600.00
24 Jason Kidd 75.00 200.00
25 Carmelo Anthony 150.00 400.00
28 Allen Iverson 125.00 300.00
34 Yao Ming 1,000.00 2,000.00
36 Tracy McGrady 125.00 300.00
44 Kobe Bryant 3,000.00 6,000.00
50 Marc Gasol 75.00 200.00
51 Dwyane Wade 300.00 600.00
60 Vince Carter 100.00 250.00
62 Yi Jianlian 100.00 250.00
63 Chris Paul 100.00 250.00
67 Russell Westbrook 300.00 600.00
68 Kevin Durant 600.00 1,200.00
69 Dwight Howard 60.00 150.00
79 Steve Nash 60.00 150.00
85 Tony Parker 15.00 40.00
86 Tim Duncan 125.00 300.00
87 Manu Ginobili 40.00 100.00
96 Blake Griffin 300.00 600.00
97 Ricky Rubio 150.00 400.00
99 James Harden 10,000.00 20,000.00
100 DeMar DeRozan 1,000.00 2,000.00
101 SCurry 60,000.00 100,000.00
110 Jrue Holiday 500.00 1,000.00

2023-24 Topps Chrome

1 Victor Wembanyama RC 6.00 15.00
2 Mikal Bridges .40 1.00
3 Kyrie Irving .60 1.50
4 Tyrese Haliburton .60 1.50
5 Dejounte Murray .40 1.00
6 Jett Howard RC .60 1.50
7 Markelle Fultz .25 .60
8 Peja Stojakovic .30 .75
9 Deron Williams .25 .60
10 Domantas Sabonis .50 1.25
11 Jalen Brunson .60 1.50
12 Jrue Holiday .40 1.00
13 Metta World Peace .30 .75
14 Tyler Herro .50 1.25
15 Giannis Antetokounmpo 1.50 4.00
16 Maxwell Lewis RC .40 1.00
17 Arvydas Sabonis .40 1.00
18 Kobe Brown RC .50 1.25
19 Rasheed Wallace .40 1.00
20 Scottie Barnes .40 1.00
21 Jimmy Butler .50 1.25
22 David Robinson .60 1.50
23 LeBron James 2.50 6.00
24 Tracy McGrady .50 1.25
25 Lenny Wilkens .40 1.00
26 Alex English .40 1.00
27 Carmelo Anthony .50 1.25
28 Andrew Wiggins .40 1.00
29 Pascal Siakam .50 1.25
30 Stephen Curry 2.50 6.00
31 James Harden .60 1.50
32 Larry Johnson .40 1.00
33 Tyrese Maxey .60 1.50
34 Maurice Cheeks .30 .75
35 Jalen Hood-Schifino RC .50 1.25
36 Christian Laettner .30 .75
37 Jalen Green .50 1.25
38 Rudy Gobert .40 1.00
39 Julian Phillips RC .50 1.25
40 Latrell Sprewell .40 1.00
41 LaMelo Ball .75 2.00
42 Alonzo Mourning .50 1.25
43 Anfernee Hardaway .75 2.00
44 Anfernee Hardaway .75 2.00
45 Donovan Mitchell .60 1.50
46 Chris Livingston RC .50 1.25
47 CJ McCollum .30 .75
49 Jaylen Clark RC .50 1.25
50 Kevin Durant 1.00 2.50
51 Leaky Black RC .40 1.00
52 Hakeem Olajuwon .60 1.50
53 Shai Gilgeous-Alexander 1.50 4.00
54 GG Jackson RC 1.00 2.50
55 Zach LaVine .50 1.25
57 Sidy Cissoko RC .50 1.25
58 D'Angelo Russell .30 .75
59 Jakob Poeltl .25 .60
60 Scoot Henderson RC 1.50 4.00
61 Jalen Wilson RC .50 1.25
62 Cole Anthony .30 .75
63 Jordan Hawkins RC .75 2.00
64 Kevin Garnett .75 2.00
65 Zach Collins .25 .60
66 Allen Iverson .75 2.00
67 Khris Middleton .30 .75
68 Daniel Gafford .30 .75
69 Clint Capela .25 .60
70 Tobias Harris .30 .75
71 Shaedon Sharpe .60 1.50
72 Clyde Drexler .50 1.25
73 Brice Sensabaugh RC .75 2.00
74 Josh Giddey .40 1.00
75 George Gervin .50 1.25
76 Bennedict Mathurin .50 1.25
77 Jason Kidd .50 1.25
78 Jaylen Brown .60 1.50
79 Franz Wagner .50 1.25
80 Isaiah Wong RC .50 1.25
82 Vince Carter .60 1.50
83 Ben Sheppard RC .50 1.25
84 Kris Murray RC .50 1.25
85 Draymond Green .40 1.00
86 Nick Smith Jr. RC .60 1.50
87 Dennis Rodman .75 2.00
88 Shawn Kemp .50 1.25
89 Jason Williams .50 1.25
90 Collin Sexton .40 1.00
91 Colby Jones RC .50 1.25
92 Dereck Lively II RC 1.00 2.50
93 Kawhi Leonard .75 2.00
94 Bill Walton .50 1.25
95 Aaron Gordon .30 .75
97 Magic Johnson 1.25 3.00
98 Dirk Nowitzki .75 2.00
99 Bam Adebayo .50 1.25
100 Joel Embiid .75 2.00
101 Juwan Howard .30 .75
102 John Collins .30 .75
103 Aaron Nesmith .30 .75
104 Tony Parker .50 1.25
105 Karl-Anthony Towns .50 1.25
106 Evan Fournier .25 .60
107 Cade Cunningham .75 2.00
108 Bradley Beal .40 1.00
109 Rip Hamilton .40 1.00
110 Russell Westbrook .50 1.25
111 Grant Hill .50 1.25
112 Jamaal Wilkes .30 .75
113 Nicolas Batum .20 .50
114 Tristan Vukcevic RC .50 1.25
115 Paul George .50 1.25
116 David Thompson .40 1.00
117 De'Aaron Fox .60 1.50
118 Zach Randolph .30 .75
119 Marcus Smart .40 1.00
120 Olivier-Maxence Prosper RC .50 1.25
121 Jaime Jaquez Jr. RC .75 2.00
122 Jonathan Kuminga .50 1.25
123 OG Anunoby .40 1.00
124 Talen Horton-Tucker .25 .60
125 Jerry West .60 1.50
126 Fred VanVleet .40 1.00
127 Brandon Miller RC 2.00 5.00
128 Jamal Murray .60 1.50
129 Julius Randle .40 1.00
130 Malik Monk .40 1.00
131 Immanuel Quickley .30 .75
132 Damian Lillard .75 2.00
133 Cam Whitmore RC 1.25 3.00
134 Julian Strawther RC .60 1.50
136 Desmond Bane .40 1.00
137 Michael Porter Jr. .40 1.00
138 Timmy Allen RC .50 1.25
139 Kyle Kuzma .40 1.00
140 Marcus Sasser RC .75 2.00
141 Derrick White .40 1.00
142 Brandon Clarke .25 .60
143 Anfernee Simons .40 1.00
144 Pete Nance RC .40 1.00
145 Jae'Sean Tate .30 .75
146 Paul Pierce .50 1.25
147 Taylor Hendricks RC .50 1.25
148 Shaquille O'Neal 1.00 2.50
149 John Stockton .60 1.50
150 Brandon Ingram .40 1.00
151 Jarace Walker RC 1.00 2.50
152 Devin Vassell .40 1.00
153 Keyonte George RC 1.50 4.00
154 Dwyane Wade .60 1.50
155 Rayan Rupert RC .50 1.25
156 Ayo Dosunmu .30 .75
157 Alperen Sengun .50 1.25
158 Leonard Miller RC .50 1.25
159 Jordan Clarkson .30 .75
160 Naz Reid .30 .75
161 Robert Parish .40 1.00
162 Manu Ginobili .60 1.50
163 Jarred Vanderbilt .25 .60
164 Jayson Tatum 1.25 3.00
165 Jalen Pickett RC .40 1.00
166 Dominique Wilkins .50 1.25
167 Precious Achiuwa .25 .60
168 Reggie Jackson .20 .50
169 Gradey Dick RC 1.00 2.50
171 Bilal Coulibaly RC 1.25 3.00
172 Amari Bailey RC .50 1.25
173 James Nnaji RC .40 1.00
174 Liam Robbins RC .40 1.00
175 Larry Bird 1.25 3.00
176 Trayce Jackson-Davis RC .60 1.50
177 Lonnie Walker IV .30 .75
178 Elvin Hayes .40 1.00
179 Pau Gasol .50 1.25
180 Noah Clowney RC .60 1.50
181 Devin Booker .75 2.00
182 Dan Issel .40 1.00
183 Jaren Jackson Jr. .50 1.25
184 Jalen Williams .60 1.50
185 Walker Kessler .30 .75
186 Anthony Black RC 1.00 2.50
187 Chris Paul .60 1.50
188 Tim Hardaway Jr. .25 .60
189 Jordan Walsh RC .50 1.25
190 Brandin Podziemski RC 1.50 4.00
192 Richard Jefferson .25 .60
193 Rick Barry .40 1.00
194 Jalen Rose .30 .75
195 Ben Wallace .40 1.00
196 Chet Holmgren .75 2.00
197 Kobe Bufkin RC .60 1.50
198 Ben Simmons .30 .75

2023-24 Topps Chrome Aqua Refractors

*AQUA REF: 2.5X TO 6X BASIC
STATED PRINT RUN 199 SER.#'d SETS
1 Victor Wembanyama 100.00 250.00

2023-24 Topps Chrome Blue Basketball Refractors

*BLUE BK REF: 1X TO 2.5X BASIC
1 Victor Wembanyama 20.00 50.00

2023-24 Topps Chrome Blue Lava Refractors

*BLUE LAVA REF: 3X TO 8X BASIC
STATED PRINT RUN 149 SER.#'d SETS
1 Victor Wembanyama 125.00 300.00

2023-24 Topps Chrome Blue Refractors

*BLUE REF: 4X TO 10X BASIC
STATED PRINT RUN 75 SER.#'d SETS

2023-24 Topps Chrome Gold Geometric Refractors

*GOLD GEO REF: 5X TO 12X BASIC
STATED PRINT RUN 50 SER.#'d SETS
1 Victor Wembanyama 300.00 600.00
23 LeBron James 600.00 1,200.00

2023-24 Topps Chrome Gold Refractors

*GOLD REF: 5X TO 12X BASIC
STATED PRINT RUN 50 SER.#'d SETS
1 Victor Wembanyama 300.00 600.00
23 LeBron James 600.00 1,200.00

2023-24 Topps Chrome Green Refractors

*GREEN REF: 3X TO 8X BASIC
STATED PRINT RUN 99 SER.#'d SETS
1 Victor Wembanyama 150.00 400.00
23 LeBron James 40.00 100.00

2023-24 Topps Chrome Green Topps Refractors

*GRN TOPPS REF: 1X TO 2.5X BASIC
1 Victor Wembanyama 25.00 60.00

2023-24 Topps Chrome Green Wave Refractors

*GRN WAVE REF: 4X TO 10X BASIC
STATED PRINT RUN 65 SER.#'d SETS
1 Victor Wembanyama 200.00 500.00
23 LeBron James 50.00 20.00

2023-24 Topps Chrome Magenta Refractors

*MAGENTA REF: 1.25X TO 3X BASIC
1 Victor Wembanyama 30.00 80.00

2023-24 Topps Chrome Negative Refractors

*NEGATIVE REF: 1.25X TO 3X BASIC
1 Victor Wembanyama 50.00 120.00

2023-24 Topps Chrome Orange Basketball Refractors

*ORNG BK REF: 1.25X TO 3X BASIC
1 Victor Wembanyama 30.00 80.00

2023-24 Topps Chrome Orange Geometric Refractors

*ORANGE GEO REF: 6X TO 15X BASIC
STATED PRINT RUN 25 SER.#'d SETS
1 Victor Wembanyama 400.00 800.00
23 LeBron James 800.00 1,500.00

2023-24 Topps Chrome Orange Refractors

*ORANGE REF: 6X TO 15X BASIC
STATED PRINT RUN 25 SER.#'d SETS
1 Victor Wembanyama 400.00 800.00
23 LeBron James 800.00 1,500.00

2023-24 Topps Chrome Pink Basketball Refractors

*PINK BK REF: 1.25X TO 3X BASIC
1 Victor Wembanyama 30.00 80.00

2023-24 Topps Chrome Pink Refractors

*PINK REF: .75X TO 2X BASIC
1 Victor Wembanyama 20.00 50.00

2023-24 Topps Chrome Prism Refractors

*PRISM REF: 1.25X TO 3X BASIC
1 Victor Wembanyama 30.00 80.00

2023-24 Topps Chrome Purple Geometric Refractors

*PRPL GEO REF: 3X TO 8X BASIC
STATED PRINT RUN 119 SER.#'d SETS
1 Victor Wembanyama 125.00 300.00

2023-24 Topps Chrome Purple Refractors

*PRPL REF: 1.5X TO 4X BASIC
STATED PRINT RUN 349 SER.#'d SETS
1 Victor Wembanyama 60.00 150.00

2023-24 Topps Chrome Refractors

*REF: .75X TO 2X BASIC
1 Victor Wembanyama 20.00 50.00

2023-24 Topps Chrome Speckle Refractors

*SPECKLE REF: 2X TO 5X BASIC
STATED PRINT RUN 299 SER.#'d SETS
1 Victor Wembanyama 75.00 200.00

2023-24 Topps Chrome '72 Topps Autographs

*REFRACTOR: .5X TO 1.25X BASIC
*PRPL GEO REF: .5X TO 1.25X BASIC
*GOLD REF/50: .6X TO 1.5X BASIC
*ORNG GEO REF/25: .75X TO 2X BASIC
TAAB Amari Bailey 6.00 15.00
TAAE Alex English 8.00 20.00
TAAG Artis Gilmore 8.00 20.00
TAAJ Andre Jackson Jr. 10.00 25.00
TAAS Alperen SengÃ¼n 10.00 25.00
TAAW Andrew Wiggins 8.00 20.00
TABC Brandon Clarke 5.00 12.00
TABS Brice Sensabaugh 10.00 25.00
TABW Bill Walton 15.00 40.00
TACC Clint Capela 5.00 12.00
TACL Chris Livingston 6.00 15.00
TACM Calvin Murphy 6.00 15.00
TADA Deandre Ayton 6.00 15.00
TADD Donte DiVincenzo 6.00 15.00
TADR David Robinson 30.00 80.00
TADS Domantas Sabonis 10.00 25.00
TADW Dominique Wilkins 15.00 40.00
TAFW Franz Wagner 10.00 25.00
TAGG George Gervin 10.00 25.00
TAGW Grant Williams 5.00 12.00
TAHO Hakeem Olajuwon 30.00 80.00
TAJB Jalen Brunson 40.00 100.00
TAJH Jrue Holiday 8.00 20.00
TAJS Jeremy Sochan 8.00 20.00
TAJT Jae'Sean Tate 6.00 15.00
TAJW Jerry West 30.00 80.00
TAKH Kevin Huerter 5.00 12.00
TAKM Kris Murray 6.00 15.00
TALB Larry Bird 60.00 150.00
TALM Leonard Miller 6.00 15.00
TALS Latrell Sprewell 8.00 20.00
TAMC Maurice Cheeks 6.00 15.00
TAMT Myles Turner 6.00 15.00
TAMW Mark Williams 6.00 15.00
TAOT Obi Toppin 6.00 15.00
TAPW Patrick Williams 5.00 12.00
TARA Ray Allen 10.00 25.00
TARB Rick Barry 8.00 20.00
TARG Rudy Gobert 8.00 20.00
TARH Rui Hachimura 6.00 15.00
TARR Rayan Rupert 6.00 15.00
TASC Seth Curry 6.00 15.00
TASL Seth Lundy 5.00 12.00
TATM Tyrese Maxey 30.00 80.00
TAVC Vince Carter 30.00 80.00
TAVW Victor Wembanyama 1,500.00 3,000.00
TAAAG Aaron Gordon 6.00 15.00
TABBO Bogdan Bogdanovic 6.00 15.00
TABRB Bradley Beal 8.00 20.00
TABWA Ben Wallace 8.00 20.00
TACJM CJ McCollum 6.00 15.00
TAGGJ GG Jackson 12.00 30.00
TAJAG Jalen Green 10.00 25.00
TAJAW Jamaal Wilkes 6.00 15.00
TAJHO Juwan Howard 6.00 15.00
TAJPO Jakob Poeltl 5.00 12.00
TAMWP Metta World Peace 6.00 15.00
TATHJ Tim Hardaway Jr. 5.00 12.00
TATMA Terance Mann 5.00 12.00

2023-24 Topps Chrome Autographs

*REFRACTOR: .5X TO 1.25X BASIC
*PRPL GEO REF: .5X TO 1.25X BASIC
*GOLD REF/50: .6X TO 1.5X BASIC
*ORNG GEO REF/25: .75X TO 2X BASIC
CGAB Anthony Black 12.00 30.00
CGAC Alex Caruso 6.00 15.00
CGAG Aaron Gordon 6.00 15.00
CGAR Austin Reaves 15.00 40.00
CGAS Alperen SengÃ¼n 10.00 25.00
CGAW Andrew Wiggins 8.00 20.00
CGBB Bogdan Bogdanovic 6.00 15.00
CGBC Brandon Clarke 5.00 12.00
CGBM Brandon Miller 50.00 120.00
CGBW Bill Walton 15.00 40.00
CGCK Corey Kispert 5.00 12.00
CGCL Caris LeVert 6.00 15.00
CGCP Chris Paul 20.00 50.00
CGCW Cam Whitmore 15.00 40.00
CGDA Deandre Ayton 6.00 15.00
CGDB Dillon Brooks 6.00 15.00
CGDF De'Aaron Fox 12.00 30.00
CGDG Devonte' Graham 5.00 12.00
CGDH De'Andre Hunter 6.00 15.00
CGDM Dejounte Murray 8.00 20.00
CGDR David Robinson 30.00 80.00
CGDS Domantas Sabonis 10.00 25.00
CGDW Dominique Wilkins 15.00 40.00
CGEH Elvin Hayes 8.00 20.00
CGFW Franz Wagner 10.00 25.00
CGGD Gradey Dick 12.00 30.00
CGGG George Gervin 10.00 25.00
CGGH Gordon Hayward 6.00 15.00
CGIH Isaiah Hartenstein 6.00 15.00
CGIQ Immanuel Quickley 6.00 15.00
CGJA Jarrett Allen 6.00 15.00
CGJH Jrue Holiday 8.00 20.00
CGJP Jonathan Kuminga 15.00 40.00
CGJR Jalen Rose 6.00 15.00
CGJS Jeremy Sochan 8.00 20.00
CGJT Jayson Tatum 60.00 150.00
CGJW Jalen Williams 12.00 30.00
CGKH Kevin Huerter 5.00 12.00
CGKK Kyle Kuzma 8.00 20.00
CGLB Larry Bird 60.00 150.00
CGLJ Larry Johnson 8.00 20.00
CGLM Lauri Markkanen 10.00 25.00
CGLS Latrell Sprewell 8.00 20.00
CGLW Lenny Wilkens 8.00 20.00
CGMB Mikal Bridges 8.00 20.00
CGMG Manu Ginobili 20.00 50.00
CGMS Max Strus 6.00 15.00
CGMT Myles Turner 6.00 15.00
CGMW Mark Williams 6.00 15.00
CGNB Nicolas Batum 4.00 10.00
CGNR Naz Reid 6.00 15.00
CGNV Nikola Vucevic 6.00 15.00
CGOB Oshae Brissett 5.00 12.00
CGPP Paul Pierce 15.00 40.00
CGPS Pascal Siakam 10.00 25.00
CGRG Rudy Gobert 8.00 20.00
CGRH Rui Hachimura 6.00 15.00
CGRP Robert Parish 8.00 20.00
CGSC Seth Curry 6.00 15.00
CGSD Spencer Dinwiddie 5.00 12.00
CGSH Scoot Henderson 30.00 80.00
CGSK Shawn Kemp 10.00 25.00
CGSO Shaquille O'Neal 100.00 250.00
CGSS Shaedon Sharpe 12.00 30.00
CGTH Tyrese Haliburton 12.00 30.00
CGTM Tyrese Maxey 30.00 80.00
CGVW Victor Wembanyama 1,500.00 3,000.00
CGWK Walker Kessler 6.00 15.00
CGAHA Anfernee Hardaway 40.00 100.00
CGBBE Bradley Beal 8.00 20.00
CGBWA Ben Wallace 8.00 20.00
CGCJM CJ McCollum 6.00 15.00
CGDGA Daniel Gafford 6.00 15.00
CGDHO Danuel House Jr. 4.00 10.00
CGDWH Derrick White 8.00 20.00
CGGTJ Gary Trent Jr. 6.00 15.00
CGJAB Jalen Brunson 40.00 100.00
CGJAW Jarace Walker 12.00 30.00
CGJGR Jalen Green 10.00 25.00
CGJHO Jett Howard 8.00 20.00
CGJJA Jaime Jaquez Jr. 10.00 25.00
CGJJJ Jaren Jackson Jr. 10.00 25.00
CGJPO Jakob Poeltl 5.00 12.00
CGKAT Karl-Anthony Towns 10.00 25.00
CGMPJ Michael Porter Jr. 8.00 20.00
CGMSM Marcus Smart 8.00 20.00
CGNSJ Nick Smith Jr. 8.00 20.00
CGOGA OG Anunoby 8.00 20.00
CGPST Peja Stojakovic 6.00 15.00
CGRIH Rip Hamilton 8.00 20.00
CGSBE Saddiq Bey 6.00 15.00
CGTAH Taylor Hendricks 10.00 25.00
CGTHE Tyler Herro 10.00 25.00
CGTHJ Tim Hardaway Jr. 5.00 12.00
CGTMA Terance Mann 5.00 12.00
CGTMI Trey Murphy III 8.00 20.00

2023-24 Topps Chrome Certified Autographs

*PINK BK REF/55: .6X TO 1.5X BASIC
*ORNG BK REF/25: .75X TO 2X BASIC
CAAC Alex Caruso 6.00 15.00
CAAE Alex English 8.00 20.00
CAAG Aaron Gordon 6.00 15.00
CAAH Al Horford 6.00 15.00
CAAR Austin Reaves 15.00 40.00
CAAS Alperen SengÃ¼n 10.00 25.00
CAAT Azuolas Tubelis 5.00 12.00
CABC Brandon Clarke 5.00 12.00
CABW Bill Walton 15.00 40.00
CACK Corey Kispert 5.00 12.00
CACL Caris LeVert 6.00 15.00
CACM Calvin Murphy 6.00 15.00
CACS Collin Sexton 6.00 15.00
CADF De'Aaron Fox 12.00 30.00
CADM Donovan Mitchell 12.00 30.00
CADW Deron Williams 5.00 12.00
CAGH Gordon Hayward 6.00 15.00
CAGK Gabe Kalscheur 5.00 12.00
CAIW Isaiah Wong 6.00 15.00
CAJC John Collins 6.00 15.00
CAJG Jalen Green 10.00 25.00
CAJH Juwan Howard 6.00 15.00
CAJK Jonathan Kuminga 15.00 40.00
CAJT Jayson Tatum 60.00 150.00
CAJW Jalen Williams 12.00 30.00
CAKH Kevin Huerter 5.00 12.00
CALB Leaky Black 5.00 12.00
CALJ Larry Johnson 8.00 20.00
CALR Liam Robbins 5.00 12.00
CAMB Mikal Bridges 8.00 20.00
CAMF Markelle Fultz 5.00 12.00
CAMS Marcus Smart 8.00 20.00
CAMW Mark Williams 6.00 15.00
CANB Nicolas Batum 4.00 10.00
CANR Naz Reid 6.00 15.00
CANV Nikola Vucevic 6.00 15.00
CAPN Pete Nance 5.00 12.00
CAPS Peja Stojakovic 6.00 15.00
CAPW Patrick Williams 5.00 12.00
CARG Rudy Gobert 8.00 20.00
CARP Robert Parish 8.00 20.00
CASC Stephen Curry 400.00 800.00
CASD Spencer Dinwiddie 5.00 12.00
CASK Shawn Kemp 10.00 25.00
CATA Timmy Allen 6.00 15.00
CATH Tyrese Haliburton 12.00 30.00
CATM Tyrese Maxey 30.00 80.00
CATS Terquavion Smith 6.00 15.00
CATV Tristan Vukcevic 6.00 15.00
CAZR Zach Randolph 6.00 15.00
CAASI Anfernee Simons 8.00 20.00
CABBE Bradley Beal 8.00 20.00
CABWA Ben Wallace 8.00 20.00
CACJM CJ McCollum 6.00 15.00
CADAM Davion Mitchell 5.00 12.00
CADEM Dejounte Murray 8.00 20.00
CADOS Domantas Sabonis 10.00 25.00
CAFVV Fred VanVleet 10.00 25.00
CAJAB Jalen Brunson 40.00 100.00

CAJCL Jaylen Clark 6.00 15.00
CAJES Jeremy Sochan 8.00 20.00
CAJJJ Jaren Jackson Jr. 10.00 25.00
CAJRH Jrue Holiday 8.00 20.00
CAJTO Jacob Toppin 5.00 12.00
CAJLO Logan Johnson 4.00 10.00
CAMPJ Michael Porter Jr. 8.00 20.00
CASCU Seth Curry 6.00 15.00
CATHE Tyler Herro 10.00 25.00
CATHJ Tim Hardaway Jr. 5.00 12.00

2023-24 Topps Chrome Coast to Coast

*REFRACTOR: .75X TO 2X BASIC
*PRPL GEO REF: .75X TO 2X BASIC
*GREEN REF/99: 3X TO 8X BASIC
*GOLD REF/50: 5X TO 12X BASIC
*ORNG GEO REF/25: 6X TO 15X BASIC
CC1 Trae Young .60 1.50
CC2 Jayson Tatum 1.25 3.00
CC3 Mikal Bridges .40 1.00
CC4 LaMelo Ball .75 2.00
CC5 DeMar DeRozan .50 1.25
CC6 Donovan Mitchell .60 1.50
CC7 Jaylen Brown .60 1.50
CC8 Kyrie Irving .60 1.50
CC9 Jalen Green .50 1.25
CC10 Michael Porter Jr. .40 1.00
CC11 Stephen Curry 2.50 6.00
CC12 Fred VanVleet .50 1.25
CC13 Tyrese Haliburton .60 1.50
CC14 Paul George .50 1.25
CC15 Devin Booker .75 2.00
CC16 Marcus Smart .40 1.00
CC17 Tyler Herro .50 1.25
CC18 Jrue Holiday .40 1.00
CC19 Lauri Markkanen .50 1.25
CC20 Jalen Brunson .60 1.50
CC21 Josh Giddey .40 1.00
CC22 Klay Thompson .75 2.00
CC23 Markelle Fultz .25 .60
CC24 Shai Gilgeous-Alexander 1.50 4.00
CC25 Devin Booker .75 2.00
CC26 Kevin Durant 1.00 2.50
CC27 Scottie Barnes .40 1.00
CC28 De'Aaron Fox .60 1.50
CC29 Pascal Siakam .50 1.25
CC30 Bradley Beal .40 1.00

2023-24 Topps Chrome Destiny

*REFRACTOR: .75X TO 2X BASIC
*PRPL GEO REF: .75X TO 2X BASIC
*GREEN REF/99: 3X TO 8X BASIC
D1 Victor Wembanyama 5.00 12.00
D2 Brandon Miller 1.50 4.00
D3 Scoot Henderson 1.25 3.00
D4 Anthony Black .75 2.00
D5 Bilal Coulibaly 1.00 2.50
D6 Taylor Hendricks .40 1.00
D7 Gradey Dick .75 2.00
D8 Jordan Hawkins .60 1.50
D9 Jalen Hood-Schifino .40 1.00
D10 Jaime Jaquez Jr. .60 1.50
D11 Cam Whitmore 1.00 2.50
D12 Noah Clowney .50 1.25
D13 Kris Murray .40 1.00
D14 Marcus Sasser .60 1.50
D15 Ben Sheppard .40 1.00
D16 Nick Smith Jr. .50 1.25
D17 Brice Sensabaugh .60 1.50
D18 Colby Jones .40 1.00
D19 Jordan Walsh .40 1.00
D20 Rayan Rupert .40 1.00

2023-24 Topps Chrome Destiny Gold Refractors

*GOLD REF: 5X TO 12X BASIC
STATED PRINT RUN 50 SER.#'d SETS
D1 Victor Wembanyama 60.00 150.00

2023-24 Topps Chrome Destiny Orange Refractors

*ORNG REF: 6X TO 15X BASIC
STATED PRINT RUN 25 SER.#'d SETS
D1 Victor Wembanyama 100.00 250.00

2023-24 Topps Chrome DNA

*BLUE BK REF: .6X TO 1.5X BASIC
*GRN TOPPS REF: .75X TO 2X BASIC
*PINK REF: .75X TO 2X BASIC
*ORNG BK REF: 1X TO 2.5X BASIC
*PINK BK REF: 1.25X TO 3X BASIC
DNA1 Stephen Curry
Seth Curry 2.50 6.00
DNA2 Tim Hardaway
Tim Hardaway Jr. .40 1.00
DNA3 Juwan Howard
Jett Howard .40 1.00
DNA4 Domantas Sabonis
Arvydas Sabonis .50 1.25
DNA5 Obi Toppin
Jacob Toppin .30 .75

2023-24 Topps Chrome Expose

EXP1 Dejounte Murray 6.00 15.00
EXP2 Jaylen Brown 10.00 25.00
EXP3 DeMar DeRozan 8.00 20.00
EXP4 Kawhi Leonard 12.00 30.00
EXP5 Kyrie Irving 10.00 25.00
EXP6 LaMelo Ball 12.00 30.00
EXP7 Cade Cunningham 12.00 30.00
EXP8 Karl-Anthony Towns 8.00 20.00
EXP9 Myles Turner 5.00 12.00
EXP10 Paul George 8.00 20.00
EXP11 Domantas Sabonis 8.00 20.00
EXP12 Tyrese Maxey 10.00 25.00
EXP13 Devin Booker 12.00 30.00
EXP14 Klay Thompson 12.00 30.00
EXP15 Jalen Brunson 10.00 25.00
EXP16 Josh Giddey 6.00 15.00
EXP17 Chet Holmgren 12.00 30.00
EXP18 Kevin Durant 15.00 40.00
EXP19 Anfernee Simons 6.00 15.00
EXP20 Scottie Barnes 6.00 15.00
EXP21 Mikal Bridges 6.00 15.00
EXP22 Giannis Antetokounmpo 25.00 60.00
EXP23 Victor Wembanyama 500.00 1,000.00
EXP24 Shai Gilgeous-Alexander 25.00 60.00
EXP25 Anthony Black 10.00 25.00

2023-24 Topps Chrome Film Study

*BLUE BK REF: .6X TO 1.5X BASIC
*GRN TOPPS REF: .75X TO 2X BASIC
*PINK REF: .75X TO 2X BASIC
*ORNG BK REF: 1X TO 2.5X BASIC
*PINK BK REF: 1.25X TO 3X BASIC
FS1 Dejounte Murray .40 1.00
FS2 Jayson Tatum 1.25 3.00
FS3 Mikal Bridges .40 1.00
FS4 Zach LaVine .50 1.25
FS5 Donovan Mitchell .60 1.50
FS6 Stephen Curry 2.50 6.00
FS7 Jalen Green .50 1.25
FS8 Klay Thompson .75 2.00
FS9 Myles Turner .30 .75
FS10 Paul George .50 1.25
FS11 Domantas Sabonis .50 1.25
FS12 Marcus Smart .40 1.00
FS13 Victor Wembanyama 2.50 6.00
FS14 Brandon Miller 1.25 3.00
FS15 Scoot Henderson 1.00 2.50
FS16 Jalen Brunson .60 1.50
FS17 Chet Holmgren .75 2.00
FS18 James Harden .60 1.50
FS19 Devin Booker .75 2.00
FS20 Anfernee Simons .40 1.00
FS21 Bam Adebayo .50 1.25
FS22 Scottie Barnes .40 1.00
FS23 Walker Kessler .30 .75
FS24 Giannis Antetokounmpo 1.50 4.00
FS25 Jrue Holiday .40 1.00

2023-24 Topps Chrome Finesse

*REFRACTOR: .75X TO 2X BASIC
*PRPL GEO REF: .75X TO 2X BASIC
*GREEN REF/99: 3X TO 8X BASIC
F1 Trae Young .75 2.00
F2 Jaylen Brown .75 2.00
F3 Giannis Antetokounmpo 2.00 5.00
F4 Zach LaVine .60 1.50
F5 Nikola Jokic 2.00 5.00
F6 Cade Cunningham 1.00 2.50
F7 Chris Paul .75 2.00
F8 Jalen Green .60 1.50
F9 Tyrese Haliburton .75 2.00
F10 Shai Gilgeous-Alexander 2.00 5.00
F11 Lebron James 3.00 8.00
F12 Tyler Herro .60 1.50
F13 CJ McCollum .40 1.00
F14 Jalen Brunson .75 2.00
F15 Jalen Williams .75 2.00
F16 Joel Embiid 1.00 2.50
F17 Kevin Durant 1.25 3.00
F18 Devin Booker 1.00 2.50
F19 Karl-Anthony Towns .60 1.50
F20 Jeremy Sochan .50 1.25
F21 Paul George .60 1.50
F22 Collin Sexton .50 1.25
F23 Kyle Kuzma .50 1.25
F24 Stephen Curry 3.00 8.00
F25 Kyrie Irving .75 2.00

2023-24 Topps Chrome Finesse Gold Refractors

*GOLD REF: 5X TO 12X BASIC
STATED PRINT RUN 50 SER.#'d SETS
F11 Lebron James 100.00 250.00

2023-24 Topps Chrome Finesse Orange Refractors

*ORNG REF: 6X TO 15X BASIC
STATED PRINT RUN 25 SER.#'d SETS
F11 Lebron James 125.00 300.00

2023-24 Topps Chrome Future Stars Autographs

*PINK BK REF/55: .6X TO 1.5X BASIC
*ORNG BK REF/25: .75X TO 2X BASIC
FSAAB Amari Bailey 6.00 15.00
FSABM Brandon Miller 50.00 120.00
FSABP Brandin Podziemski 20.00 50.00
FSACJ Colby Jones 6.00 15.00
FSACW Cam Whitmore 15.00 40.00
FSAGD Gradey Dick 12.00 30.00
FSAJJ Jaime Jaquez Jr. 10.00 25.00
FSAJN James Nnaji 5.00 12.00
FSAJP Julian Phillips 6.00 15.00
FSAJS Julian Strawther 8.00 20.00
FSAJW Jalen Wilson 6.00 15.00
FSAKB Kobe Brown 6.00 15.00
FSAML Maxwell Lewis 5.00 12.00
FSAMS Marcus Sasser 10.00 25.00
FSANC Noah Clowney 8.00 20.00
FSASC Sidy Cissoko 6.00 15.00
FSASH Scoot Henderson 30.00 80.00
FSATH Taylor Hendricks 6.00 15.00
FSAVW Victor Wembanyama 1,500.00 3,000.00
FSAANB Anthony Black 12.00 30.00
FSABES Ben Sheppard 6.00 15.00
FSABIC Bilal Coulibaly 15.00 40.00
FSADEL Dereck Lively II 12.00 30.00
FSAJAW Jarace Walker 12.00 30.00
FSAJHA Jordan Hawkins 10.00 25.00
FSAJHS Jalen Hood-Schifino 6.00 15.00
FSAJOW Jordan Walsh 6.00 15.00
FSAKOB Kobe Bufkin 8.00 20.00
FSAOMP Olivier-Maxence Prosper 6.00 15.00
FSATJD Trayce Jackson-Davis 8.00 20.00

2023-24 Topps Chrome Helix

*GEO GRN REF: .5X TO 1.2X BASIC
H1 Kawhi Leonard 20.00 50.00
H2 Jayson Tatum 30.00 80.00
H3 Jimmy Butler 12.00 30.00
H4 Zach Lavine 12.00 30.00
H5 Donovan Mitchel 15.00 40.00
H6 Cade Cunningham 20.00 50.00
H7 Nikola Jokic 40.00 100.00
H8 LaMelo Ball 20.00 50.00
H9 Tyrese Haliburton 15.00 40.00
H10 Paul George 12.00 30.00
H11 Lebron James 60.00 150.00
H12 Tyler Herro 12.00 30.00
H13 CJ McCollum 8.00 20.00
H14 Jaime Jaquez Jr. 12.00 30.00
H15 Chet Holmgren 20.00 50.00
H16 Joel Embiid 20.00 50.00
H17 Kevin Durant 25.00 60.00
H18 Devin Booker 20.00 50.00
H19 Karl-Anthony Towns 12.00 30.00
H20 Brandon Miller 30.00 80.00
H21 Anthony Davis 20.00 50.00
H22 Victor Wembanyama 200.00 500.00
H23 Scoot Henderson 25.00 60.00
H24 Stephen Curry 60.00 150.00
H25 Kyrie Irving 15.00 40.00

2023-24 Topps Chrome Let's Go

LG1 Trae Young 5.00 12.00
LG2 Jayson Tatum 10.00 25.00
LG3 Mikal Bridges 3.00 8.00
LG4 LaMelo Ball 6.00 15.00
LG5 Donovan Mitchell 5.00 12.00
LG6 Kevin Durant 8.00 20.00
LG7 Stephen Curry 20.00 50.00
LG8 Paul George 4.00 10.00
LG9 Shai Gilgeous-Alexander 12.00 30.00
LG10 Jaren Jackson Jr. 4.00 10.00
LG11 Chet Holmgren 6.00 15.00
LG12 Zach LaVine 4.00 10.00
LG13 Karl-Anthony Towns 4.00 10.00
LG14 Giannis Antetokounmpo 12.00 30.00
LG15 Kyrie Irving 5.00 12.00
LG16 Joel Embiid 6.00 15.00
LG17 Devin Booker 6.00 15.00
LG18 Jalen Brunson 5.00 12.00
LG19 Cade Cunningham 6.00 15.00
LG20 Tyrese Haliburton 5.00 12.00
LG21 Jimmy Butler 4.00 10.00
LG22 Damian Lillard 6.00 15.00
LG23 Victor Wembanyama 20.00 50.00
LG24 Brandon Miller 10.00 25.00
LG25 Scoot Henderson 8.00 20.00

2023-24 Topps Chrome Power Boosters

*BLUE BK REF: .6X TO 1.5X BASIC
*GRN TOPPS REF: .75X TO 2X BASIC
*PINK REF: .75X TO 2X BASIC
*ORNG BK REF: 1X TO 2.5X BASIC
*PINK BK REF: 1.25X TO 3X BASIC
PB1 Trae Young .60 1.50
PB2 Jalen Green .50 1.25
PB3 Zach LaVine .50 1.25
PB4 Donovan Mitchell .60 1.50
PB5 Kyrie Irving .60 1.50
PB6 Stephen Curry 2.50 6.00
PB7 Devin Booker .75 2.00
PB8 Russell Westbrook .50 1.25
PB9 Jaylen Brown .60 1.50
PB10 Jrue Holiday .40 1.00
PB11 Kawhi Leonard .75 2.00
PB12 Paul George .50 1.25
PB13 Shai Gilgeous-Alexander 1.50 4.00
PB14 Damian Lillard .75 2.00
PB15 Tyrese Maxey .60 1.50

2023-24 Topps Chrome Radiating Rookies

*GRN GEO REF: .4X TO 1X BASIC
RAR1 Victor Wembanyama 500.00 1,000.00
RAR2 Brandon Miller 100.00 250.00
RAR3 Scoot Henderson 100.00 250.00
RAR4 Anthony Black 20.00 50.00
RAR5 Bilal Coulibaly 25.00 60.00
RAR6 Taylor Hendricks 10.00 25.00
RAR7 Gradey Dick 20.00 50.00
RAR8 Jordan Hawkins 15.00 40.00
RAR9 Jalen Hood-Schifino 10.00 25.00
RAR10 Jaime Jaquez Jr. 15.00 40.00
RAR11 Cam Whitmore 25.00 60.00
RAR12 Noah Clowney 12.00 30.00
RAR13 Kris Murray 10.00 25.00
RAR14 Marcus Sasser 15.00 40.00
RAR15 Ben Sheppard 10.00 25.00
RAR16 Nick Smith Jr. 12.00 30.00
RAR17 Brice Sensabaugh 15.00 40.00
RAR18 Colby Jones 10.00 25.00
RAR19 Jordan Walsh 10.00 25.00
RAR20 Rayan Rupert 10.00 25.00
RAR21 Dereck Lively II 20.00 50.00
RAR22 Jarace Walker 20.00 50.00
RAR23 Kobe Bufkin 12.00 30.00
RAR24 Sidy Cissoko 10.00 25.00
RAR25 Jett Howard 12.00 30.00

2023-24 Topps Chrome Rock Stars

RS1 Brandon Miller 20.00 50.00
RS2 Cade Cunningham 12.00 30.00
RS3 Shai Gilgeous-Alexander 25.00 60.00
RS4 Giannis Antetokounmpo 25.00 60.00
RS5 Donovan Mitchell 10.00 25.00
RS6 Jaren Jackson Jr. 8.00 20.00
RS7 James Harden 10.00 25.00
RS8 Jalen Brunson 10.00 25.00
RS9 Jayson Tatum 20.00 50.00
RS10 Nikola Jokic 25.00 60.00
RS11 Joel Embiid 12.00 30.00
RS12 Karl-Anthony Towns 8.00 20.00
RS13 Jimmy Butler 8.00 20.00
RS14 Kevin Durant 15.00 40.00
RS15 Jamal Murray 10.00 25.00
RS16 Chet Holmgren 12.00 30.00
RS17 Mikal Bridges 6.00 15.00
RS18 Damian Lillard 12.00 30.00
RS19 Bam Adebayo 8.00 20.00
RS20 Scoot Henderson 40.00 100.00
RS21 Khris Middleton 5.00 12.00
RS22 Stephen Curry 40.00 100.00
RS23 Trae Young 10.00 25.00
RS24 Tyrese Haliburton 10.00 25.00
RS25 Victor Wembanyama 500.00 1,000.00

2023-24 Topps Chrome Rookie Autographs

*REFRACTOR: .5X TO 1.25X BASIC
*PRPL GEO REF: .5X TO 1.25X BASIC
*GOLD REF/50: .6X TO 1.5X BASIC
*ORNG GEO REF/25: .75X TO 2X BASIC
CRAAB Anthony Black 12.00 30.00
CRAAJ Andre Jackson Jr. 10.00 25.00
CRABC Bilal Coulibaly 15.00 40.00
CRABM Brandon Miller 50.00 120.00
CRABP Brandin Podziemski 20.00 50.00
CRABS Brice Sensabaugh 10.00 25.00
CRACJ Colby Jones 6.00 15.00
CRACL Chris Livingston 6.00 15.00
CRADL Dereck Lively II 12.00 30.00
CRAGD Gradey Dick 12.00 30.00
CRAJH Jett Howard 8.00 20.00
CRAJJ Jaime Jaquez Jr. 10.00 25.00
CRAJN James Nnaji 5.00 12.00
CRAJP Julian Phillips 6.00 15.00
CRAJS Julian Strawther 8.00 20.00
CRAJW Jalen Wilson 6.00 15.00
CRAKB Kobe Brown 6.00 15.00
CRAKM Kris Murray 6.00 15.00
CRALM Leonard Miller 6.00 15.00
CRAML Maxwell Lewis 5.00 12.00
CRAMS Marcus Sasser 10.00 25.00
CRANC Noah Clowney 8.00 20.00
CRANS Nick Smith Jr. 8.00 20.00
CRARR Rayan Rupert 6.00 15.00
CRASC Sidy Cissoko 6.00 15.00
CRASH Scoot Henderson 30.00 80.00
CRASL Seth Lundy 5.00 12.00
CRATH Taylor Hendricks 6.00 15.00
CRAVW Victor Wembanyama 1,500.00 3,000.00
CRABES Ben Sheppard 6.00 15.00
CRACAW Cam Whitmore 15.00 40.00
CRAGGJ GG Jackson 12.00 30.00
CRAJAW Jarace Walker 12.00 30.00
CRAJHS Jalen Hood-Schifino 6.00 15.00
CRAJOH Jordan Hawkins 10.00 25.00
CRAJOW Jordan Walsh 6.00 15.00
CRAKOB Kobe Bufkin 8.00 20.00
CRAOMP Olivier-Maxence Prosper 6.00 15.00
CRATJD Trayce Jackson-Davis 8.00 20.00

2023-24 Topps Chrome Roundball Royalty

*BLUE BK REF: .6X TO 1.5X BASIC
*GRN TOPPS REF: .75X TO 2X BASIC
*PINK REF: .75X TO 2X BASIC
*ORNG BK REF: 1X TO 2.5X BASIC
*PINK BK REF: 1.25X TO 3X BASIC
RR1 Larry Bird 1.25 3.00
RR2 De'Aaron Fox .60 1.50
RR3 Devin Booker .75 2.00
RR4 Dirk Nowitzki .75 2.00
RR5 Magic Johnson 1.25 3.00
RR6 Kevin Garnett .75 2.00
RR7 Jayson Tatum 1.25 3.00
RR8 David Robinson .60 1.50
RR9 Joel Embiid .75 2.00
RR10 Karl-Anthony Towns .50 1.25
RR11 Dwyane Wade .60 1.50
RR12 Kyrie Irving .60 1.50
RR13 Domantas Sabonis .50 1.25
RR14 Shaquille O'Neal 1.00 2.50
RR15 Mikal Bridges .40 1.00
RR16 Anthony Black .60 1.50
RR17 Gradey Dick .60 1.50
RR18 Pascal Siakam .50 1.25
RR19 Cam Whitmore .75 2.00
RR20 Stephen Curry 2.50 6.00
RR21 Trae Young .60 1.50
RR22 Bilal Coulibaly .75 2.00
RR23 Kevin Durant 1.00 2.50
RR24 James Harden .60 1.50
RR25 Jordan Hawkins .50 1.25
RR26 Victor Wembanyama 10.00 25.00
RR27 Brandon Miller 1.25 3.00
RR28 Scoot Henderson 1.00 2.50
RR29 Nikola Jokic 1.50 4.00
RR30 Jarace Walker .60 1.50

2023-24 Topps Chrome Season's Best

*REFRACTOR: .75X TO 2X BASIC
*PRPL GEO REF: .75X TO 2X BASIC
*GREEN REF/99: 3X TO 8X BASIC
*GOLD REF/50: 5X TO 12X BASIC
*ORNG GEO REF/25: 6X TO 15X BASIC
SB1 Jayson Tatum 1.25 3.00
SB2 Devin Booker .75 2.00
SB3 Donovan Mitchell .60 1.50
SB4 Kyrie Irving .60 1.50
SB5 Stephen Curry 2.50 6.00
SB6 Paul George .50 1.25
SB7 Domantas Sabonis .50 1.25
SB8 Tyrese Haliburton .60 1.50
SB9 Trae Young .60 1.50
SB10 Joel Embiid .75 2.00

2023-24 Topps Chrome Sudden Impact

*BLUE BK REF: .6X TO 1.5X BASIC
*GRN TOPPS REF: .75X TO 2X BASIC
*PINK REF: .75X TO 2X BASIC
*ORNG BK REF: 1X TO 2.5X BASIC
*PINK BK REF: 1.25X TO 3X BASIC
SI1 Victor Wembanyama 5.00 12.00
SI2 Brandon Miller 1.25 3.00
SI3 Scoot Henderson 1.00 2.50
SI4 Jordan Hawkins .50 1.25
SI5 Jarace Walker .60 1.50
SI6 LaMelo Ball .75 2.00
SI7 Jaime Jaquez Jr. .50 1.25
SI8 Anthony Black .60 1.50
SI9 Brandin Podziemski 1.00 2.50
SI10 Cam Whitmore .75 2.00
SI11 Grant Williams .25 .60
SI12 Josh Giddey .40 1.00
SI13 Cade Cunningham .75 2.00
SI14 Alperen SengA¼n .50 1.25
SI15 Tyrese Haliburton .60 1.50
SI16 Marcus Smart .40 1.00
SI17 Anfernee Simons .40 1.00
SI18 Jalen Williams .60 1.50
SI19 Mikal Bridges .40 1.00
SI20 Tyrese Maxey .60 1.50
SI21 Scottie Barnes .40 1.00
SI22 Walker Kessler .30 .75
SI23 Chet Holmgren .75 2.00
SI24 Franz Wagner .50 1.25
SI25 Bennedict Mathurin .50 1.25

2023-24 Topps Chrome Superfly

SF1 Dominique Wilkins 6.00 15.00
SF2 Vince Carter 8.00 20.00
SF3 Shaquille O'Neal 12.00 30.00
SF4 Larry Bird 15.00 40.00
SF5 Magic Johnson 15.00 40.00
SF6 Jayson Tatum 15.00 40.00
SF7 David Robinson 8.00 20.00
SF8 Jerry West 8.00 20.00
SF9 Stephen Curry 30.00 80.00
SF10 Shai Gilgeous-Alexander 20.00 50.00
SF11 Dirk Nowitzki 10.00 25.00
SF12 Damian Lillard 10.00 25.00
SF13 Joel Embiid 10.00 25.00
SF14 Kevin Durant 12.00 30.00
SF15 Giannis Antetokounmpo 20.00 50.00
SF16 Victor Wembanyama 350.00 700.00
SF17 Brandon Miller 15.00 40.00
SF18 Scoot Henderson 12.00 30.00
SF19 Jarace Walker 8.00 20.00
SF20 Cam Whitmore 10.00 25.00
SF21 Anthony Black 8.00 20.00
SF22 Jordan Hawkins 6.00 15.00
SF23 Gradey Dick 8.00 20.00
SF24 Brandin Podziemski 12.00 30.00
SF25 Jaime Jaquez Jr. 6.00 15.00

2023-24 Topps Chrome Youthquake

*REFRACTOR: .75X TO 2X BASIC
*PRPL GEO REF: .75X TO 2X BASIC
YQ1 Victor Wembanyama 10.00 25.00
YQ2 Brandon Miller 1.50 4.00
YQ3 Scoot Henderson 1.25 3.00
YQ4 Jaime Jaquez Jr. .60 1.50
YQ5 Jarace Walker .75 2.00
YQ6 Bilal Coulibaly 1.00 2.50
YQ7 Shai Gilgeous-Alexander 2.00 5.00
YQ8 Cam Whitmore 1.00 2.50
YQ9 Anthony Black .75 2.00
YQ10 Gradey Dick .75 2.00
YQ11 Jalen Williams .75 2.00
YQ12 Dereck Lively II .75 2.00
YQ13 Jaren Jackson Jr. .60 1.50
YQ14 Chet Holmgren 1.00 2.50
YQ15 Tyrese Haliburton .75 2.00

2023-24 Topps Chrome Youthquake Gold Refractors

*GOLD REF: 5X TO 12X BASIC
STATED PRINT RUN 50 SER.#'d SETS
YQ1 Victor Wembanyama 200.00 500.00

2023-24 Topps Chrome Youthquake Green Refractors

*GREEN REF: 3X TO 8X BASIC
STATED PRINT RUN 99 SER.#'d SETS
YQ1 Victor Wembanyama 125.00 300.00

2023-24 Topps Chrome Youthquake Orange Refractors

*ORNG REF: 6X TO 15X BASIC
STATED PRINT RUN 25 SER.#'d SETS
YQ1 Victor Wembanyama 300.00 600.00

2024-25 Topps Chrome

*BLUE BK REF: .75X TO 2X BASIC
*MAGENTA REF: .75X TO 2X BASIC
*PINK BK REF: .75X TO 2X BASIC
*PINK REF: .75X TO 2X BASIC
*PRISM REF: .75X TO 2X BASIC
*PURPLE REF: .75X TO 2X BASIC
*REFRACTOR: .75X TO 2X BASIC
*TOPPS GRN REF: .75X TO 2X BASIC
*MAGENTA SPEC REF/250: 1.25X TO 3X BASIC
*PRPL SPEC REF/299: 1.25X TO 3X BASIC
*PRPL SONAR REF/275: 1.25X TO 3X BASIC
*NEGATIVE REF: 1.5X TO 4X BASIC
*AQUA REF/199: 1.5X TO 4X BASIC
*BLUE REF/150: 1.5X TO 4X BASIC
*BLUE SONAR REF/125: 1.5X TO 4X BASIC
*GREEN GEO REF/99: 2X TO 5X BASIC
*GREEN REF/99: 2X TO 5X BASIC
*BLUE LAVA REF/75: 2X TO 5X BASIC
*GREEN WAVE REF/65: 2.5X TO 6X BASIC
*GOLD GEO REF/50: 2.5X TO 6X BASIC
*GOLD REF/50: 2.5X TO 6X BASIC
*ORNG GEO REF/25: 3X TO 8X BASIC
*ORNG REF/25: 3X TO 8X BASIC
1 Jett Howard .30 .75
2 Damian Lillard .75 2.00
3 LaMelo Ball .60 1.50
4 Latrell Sprewell .40 1.00
5 Tobias Harris .25 .60
6 Alex Caruso .30 .75
7 Brandin Podziemski .40 1.00
8 Jordan Poole .30 .75
9 Alonzo Mourning .50 1.25
10 Joel Embiid .60 1.50
11 Bilal Coulibaly .40 1.00
12 Michael Porter Jr. .30 .75
13 Dwyane Wade .60 1.50
14 Lenny Wilkens .30 .75
15 Kyle Kuzma .25 .60
16 Jimmy Butler .50 1.25
17 Jarrett Allen .30 .75
18 Cade Cunningham .75 2.00
19 Nick Smith Jr. .25 .60
20 Donte DiVincenzo .30 .75
21 Aaron Nesmith .25 .60
22 LeBron James 2.50 6.00
23 Rasheed Wallace .40 1.00
24 Scoot Henderson .40 1.00
25 Shaedon Sharpe .40 1.00
26 Eric Gordon .25 .60
27 Jarred Vanderbilt .25 .60
28 Jaylen Brown .50 1.25
29 Kobe Bufkin .25 .60
30 Clyde Drexler .50 1.25
31 Taylor Hendricks .30 .75
32 Larry Bird 1.00 2.50
33 Bam Adebayo .40 1.00
34 Jamal Murray .50 1.25
35 Collin Sexton .30 .75
36 Jaime Jaquez Jr. .30 .75
37 Lauri Markkanen .30 .75
38 Myles Turner .25 .60
39 Dominique Wilkins .50 1.25
40 Tyrese Maxey .50 1.25
41 Giannis Antetokounmpo 1.25 3.00
42 Tracy McGrady .60 1.50
43 Naz Reid .30 .75
44 Kevin Garnett .75 2.00
45 Derrick White .30 .75
46 John Stockton .60 1.50
47 Jalen Brunson .60 1.50
48 Anthony Black .40 1.00
49 Marcus Sasser .25 .60
50 Nikola Jokic 1.50 4.00
51 Jayson Tatum 1.00 2.50
52 Karl-Anthony Towns .50 1.25
53 Anfernee Simons .30 .75
54 Vince Carter .60 1.50
55 DeMar DeRozan .40 1.00
56 Caris LeVert .25 .60
57 Immanuel Quickley .25 .60
58 Ayo Dosunmu .25 .60
59 Magic Johnson 1.00 2.50
60 OG Anunoby .25 .60
61 Brandon Miller .50 1.25
62 Aaron Gordon .25 .60
63 Jalen Williams .60 1.50
64 Pascal Siakam .40 1.00
65 Rip Hamilton .40 1.00
66 Walker Kessler .30 .75
67 Jabari Walker .20 .50
68 Anfernee Hardaway .75 2.00
69 Donovan Mitchell .60 1.50
70 Chris Livingston .25 .60
71 Josh Hart .25 .60
72 Corey Kispert .25 .60
73 Dejounte Murray .30 .75
74 Luguentz Dort .25 .60
75 Khris Middleton .30 .75
76 Josh Giddey .40 1.00
77 Anthony Edwards 1.50 4.00
78 Mark Williams .25 .60
79 Tyler Herro .50 1.25
80 Jarace Walker .30 .75
81 Gary Trent Jr. .20 .50
82 Trae Young .60 1.50
83 Carmelo Anthony .50 1.25
84 Zach Lavine .50 1.25
85 Elvin Hayes .40 1.00
86 Anthony Davis .75 2.00
87 Austin Reaves .40 1.00
88 Paul Pierce .50 1.25
89 Scottie Barnes .40 1.00
90 Rudy Gobert .30 .75
91 Jonas Valanciunas .25 .60
92 Gradey Dick .40 1.00
93 Franz Wagner .50 1.25
94 Allen Iverson .75 2.00
95 Dennis Rodman .75 2.00
96 Bennedict Mathurin .30 .75
97 Nikola Vucevic .25 .60
98 Larry Johnson .40 1.00
99 Chet Holmgren .50 1.25
100 Tyrese Haliburton .60 1.50
101 Kevin Durant 1.00 2.50
102 KJ Simpson RC .50 1.25
103 Kel'el Ware RC 1.25 3.00
104 Jake LaRavia .25 .60
105 Terrence Shannon Jr. RC 1.00 2.50
106 Alperen Sengun .50 1.25
107 Anton Watson RC .40 1.00
108 Tristen Newton RC .50 1.25
109 De'Aaron Fox .60 1.50
110 Payton Pritchard .30 .75
111 Enrique Freeman RC .40 1.00
112 Isaiah Collier RC 1.00 2.50
113 Desmond Bane .30 .75
114 Dereck Lively II .30 .75
115 Hakeem Olajuwon .60 1.50
116 Isaiah Stewart .25 .60
117 Kyrie Irving .75 2.00
118 Noah Clowney .30 .75
119 Nikola Topic RC 1.50 4.00
120 Kawhi Leonard .60 1.50
121 Quinten Post RC 1.00 2.50
122 Stephon Castle RC 3.00 8.00
123 Draymond Green .40 1.00
124 Tristan da Silva RC 1.25 3.00
125 Russell Westbrook .50 1.25
126 Olivier-Maxence Prosper .25 .60
127 Kyle Filipowski RC 1.25 3.00
128 Davion Mitchell .25 .60
129 Jason Kidd .60 1.50
130 Cam Spencer RC .50 1.25
131 Antonio Reeves RC .50 1.25
132 Ajay Mitchell RC .75 2.00
133 Ron Holland II RC 1.00 2.50
134 Devin Carter RC .60 1.50
135 Paul George .50 1.25
136 Alexandre Sarr RC 1.50 4.00
137 Fred VanVleet .40 1.00
138 Tony Parker .50 1.25
139 Johnny Furphy RC .75 2.00
140 Cam Whitmore .30 .75
141 Malik Monk .30 .75
142 Calvin Murphy .25 .60
143 Baylor Scheierman RC .60 1.50
144 Trey Murphy III .40 1.00
145 AJ Johnson RC 1.00 2.50
146 Jalen Bridges RC .40 1.00
147 Marcus Smart .30 .75
148 Tidjane SalaA¼n RC .50 1.25
149 Bronny James Jr. RC 1.50 4.00
150 Kevin McCullar Jr. RC .40 1.00
151 Cam Christie RC .60 1.50
152 Zach Edey RC 1.50 4.00
153 Domantas Sabonis .50 1.25
154 Brandon Ingram .30 .75
155 Andrew Wiggins .30 .75
156 Yves Missi RC 1.25 3.00
157 CJ McCollum .25 .60
158 Kyshawn George RC .75 2.00
159 Cam Johnson .25 .60
160 Cody Williams RC .60 1.50
161 Justin Edwards RC .75 2.00
162 Chris Paul .50 1.25
163 Quentin Grimes .30 .75
164 Devin Booker .75 2.00
165 Rob Dillingham RC 1.25 3.00
166 Pelle Larsson RC .60 1.50
167 Tyler Kolek RC .75 2.00
168 Jaylon Tyson RC .50 1.25
169 Zaccharie Risacher RC 1.50 4.00
170 Bradley Beal .40 1.00
171 Shaquille O'Neal .75 2.00
172 Pacome Dadiet RC .60 1.50
173 Jaren Jackson Jr. .50 1.25
174 Jamal Shead RC .50 1.25
175 Spencer Dinwiddie .20 .50
176 Norman Powell .30 .75
177 Derrick Jones Jr. .20 .50
178 Klay Thompson .75 2.00
179 Harrison Ingram RC .50 1.25
180 Lonnie Walker IV .25 .60
181 Jeremy Sochan .30 .75
182 Ryan Dunn RC .60 1.50
183 Adem Bona RC .60 1.50
184 Oso Ighodaro RC .60 1.50
185 Jaylen Wells RC 1.50 4.00
186 Sandro Mamukelashvili .40 1.00
187 Stephen Curry 2.50 6.00
188 Ja Morant 1.00 2.50
189 Dillon Jones RC .50 1.25
190 Mikal Bridges .30 .75
191 Ulrich Chomche RC .40 1.00
192 Colby Jones .25 .60
193 Victor Wembanyama 2.50 6.00
194 Jonathan Mogbo RC .75 2.00
195 DaRon Holmes II RC .60 1.50
196 Tyler Smith RC .60 1.50
197 Dirk Nowitzki .75 2.00
198 James Harden .60 1.50
199 Jalen Green .60 1.50
200 Jordan Hawkins .25 .60

2024-25 Topps Chrome '73 Topps Autographs

*REFRACTOR: .5X TO 1.2X BASIC
*PRPL GEO REF: .5X TO 1.2X BASIC
*GOLD GEO REF/50: .6X TO 1.5X BASIC
*GOLD REF/50: .6X TO 1.5X BASIC
*ORNG GEO REF/25: .75X TO 2X BASIC
73TAAI Allen Iverson 60.00 150.00
73TAAJ Andre Jackson Jr. 4.00 10.00
73TAAS Anfernee Simons 5.00 12.00
73TABB Bradley Beal 6.00 15.00
73TABS Ben Sheppard 4.00 10.00
73TABW Ben Wallace 6.00 15.00
73TACH Chet Holmgren 8.00 20.00
73TACJ Colby Jones 4.00 10.00
73TACM CJ McCollum 4.00 10.00
73TACS Collin Sexton 5.00 12.00
73TADB Dillon Brooks 4.00 10.00
73TADF De'Aaron Fox 10.00 25.00
73TADM Dejounte Murray 5.00 12.00
73TADR D'Angelo Russell 4.00 10.00
73TAJK Jason Kidd 8.00 20.00
73TAJM Jamal Murray 8.00 20.00
73TAJS Julian Strawther 5.00 12.00
73TAKL Kevin Love 4.00 10.00
73TAKP Kristaps Porzingis 6.00 15.00
73TAKT Karl-Anthony Towns 8.00 20.00
73TALB Larry Bird 60.00 150.00
73TALM Leonard Miller 5.00 12.00
73TAMJ Magic Johnson 60.00 150.00
73TAML Maxwell Lewis 4.00 10.00
73TAOP Olivier-Maxence Prosper 4.00 10.00
73TAPS Peja Stojakovic 5.00 12.00
73TARA Ray Allen 20.00 50.00
73TARJ Richard Jefferson 4.00 10.00
73TARW Rasheed Wallace 6.00 15.00
73TASC Stephen Curry 400.00 800.00
73TASH Scoot Henderson 6.00 15.00
73TASO Shaquille O'Neal 12.00 30.00
73TATH Tyrese Haliburton 40.00 100.00
73TATM Tracy McGrady 20.00 50.00
73TATP Tony Parker 8.00 20.00
73TAVC Vince Carter 20.00 50.00
73TAWK Walker Kessler 4.00 10.00
73TAJTA Jae'Sean Tate 4.00 10.00
73TAPMI Patty Mills 5.00 12.00
73TASCI Sidy Cissoko 5.00 12.00

2024-25 Topps Chrome 451

4511 Giannis Antetokounmpo 40.00 100.00
4512 Kyrie Irving 25.00 60.00
4513 Joel Embiid 15.00 40.00
4514 Victor Wembanyama 80.00 200.00
4515 Kevin Durant 30.00 80.00
4516 Stephen Curry 80.00 200.00
4517 LeBron James 80.00 200.00
4518 Jayson Tatum 30.00 80.00
4519 Jalen Brunson 20.00 50.00
45110 Jimmy Butler 15.00 40.00
45111 Karl-Anthony Towns 15.00 40.00
45112 Damian Lillard 25.00 60.00
45113 Chet Holmgren 15.00 40.00
45114 LaMelo Ball 20.00 50.00
45115 Anthony Edwards 50.00 125.00
45116 Zaccharie Risacher 30.00 80.00
45117 Alexandre Sarr 30.00 80.00
45118 Stephon Castle 60.00 150.00
45119 Tidjane SalaA¼n 10.00 25.00
45120 Rob Dillingham 25.00 60.00

2024-25 Topps Chrome Advisory

A1 Zaccharie Risacher 20.00 50.00
A2 Alexandre Sarr 20.00 50.00
A3 Stephon Castle 40.00 100.00
A4 Ron Holland II 12.00 30.00
A5 Tidjane SalaA¼n 6.00 15.00
A6 Rob Dillingham 15.00 40.00
A7 Zach Edey 20.00 50.00
A8 Cody Williams 8.00 20.00
A9 Nikola Topic 20.00 50.00
A10 Devin Carter 8.00 20.00
A11 Kel'el Ware 15.00 40.00
A12 Tristan da Silva 15.00 40.00
A13 Jaylon Tyson 6.00 15.00
A14 Yves Missi 15.00 40.00
A15 DaRon Holmes II 8.00 20.00
A16 AJ Johnson 12.00 30.00
A17 Kyshawn George 10.00 25.00
A18 Dillon Jones 6.00 15.00
A19 Terrence Shannon Jr. 12.00 30.00
A20 Ryan Dunn 8.00 20.00
A21 Isaiah Collier 12.00 30.00
A22 Baylor Scheierman 8.00 20.00
A23 Bronny James Jr. 20.00 50.00
A24 Tyler Smith 8.00 20.00
A25 Johnny Furphy 10.00 25.00

2024-25 Topps Chrome Autographs

*REFRACTOR: .5X TO 1.2X BASIC
*PRPL GEO REF: .6X TO 1.5X BASIC
*GOLD GEO REF/50: .6X TO 1.5X BASIC
*GOLD REF/50: .6X TO 1.5X BASIC
*ORNG GEO REF/25: .75X TO 2X BASIC
TCAAG Aaron Gordon 5.00 12.00
TCAAI Allen Iverson 60.00 150.00
TCAAM Alonzo Mourning 8.00 20.00
TCAAW Andrew Wiggins 6.00 15.00
TCABB Bradley Beal 6.00 15.00
TCABC Bilal Coulibaly 6.00 15.00

TCABM Brandon Miller 8.00 20.00
TCABP Brandin Podziemski 6.00 15.00
TCACA Carmelo Anthony 20.00 50.00
TCACD Clyde Drexler 8.00 20.00
TCACH Chet Holmgren 8.00 20.00
TCADF De'Aaron Fox 10.00 25.00
TCADL Dereck Lively II 5.00 12.00
TCADW Dwyane Wade 10.00 25.00
TCAEG Eric Gordon 4.00 10.00
TCAFV Fred VanVleet 5.00 12.00
TCAGT Gary Trent Jr. 4.00 10.00
TCAHO Hakeem Olajuwon 20.00 50.00
TCAJA Jarrett Allen 4.00 10.00
TCAJB Jalen Brunson 20.00 50.00
TCAJJ Jaime Jaquez Jr. 5.00 12.00
TCAJS John Stockton 20.00 50.00
TCAKK Kyle Kuzma 4.00 10.00
TCAKM Khris Middleton 5.00 12.00
TCANC Noah Clowney 5.00 12.00
TCANS Nick Smith Jr. 4.00 10.00
TCAPP Paul Pierce 8.00 20.00
TCAQG Quentin Grimes 5.00 12.00
TCARG Rudy Gobert 5.00 12.00
TCARH Rip Hamilton 6.00 15.00
TCATM Tyrese Maxey 10.00 25.00
TCAVW Victor Wembanyama 400.00 800.00
TCAZL Zach LaVine 8.00 20.00
TCAADO Ayo Dosunmu 4.00 10.00
TCAANE Aaron Nesmith 4.00 10.00
TCAASA Alexandre Sarr 15.00 40.00
TCABJJ Bronny James Jr. 40.00 100.00
TCACWI Cody Williams 6.00 15.00
TCAIST Isaiah Stewart 4.00 10.00
TCAJAV Jarred Vanderbilt 4.00 10.00
TCAJLA Jake LaRavia 4.00 10.00
TCAJVA Jonas Valanciunas 4.00 10.00
TCAJWA Jabari Walker 3.00 8.00
TCALWI Lenny Wilkens 5.00 12.00
TCARHO Ron Holland II 10.00 25.00
TCASCA Stephon Castle 75.00 200.00
TCASMA Sandro Mamukelashvili 6.00 15.00
TCATMC Tracy McGrady 20.00 50.00
TCAZED Zach Edey 15.00 40.00
TCAZRI Zaccharie Risacher 15.00 40.00

2024-25 Topps Chrome Ball of Duty

*BLUE BK REF: .75X TO 2X BASIC
*PINK REF: .75X TO 2X BASIC
*REFRACTOR: .75X TO 2X BASIC
*TOPPS GRN REF: .75X TO 2X BASIC
BOD1 LeBron James 2.50 6.00
BOD2 Devin Booker .75 2.00
BOD3 Stephen Curry 2.50 6.00
BOD4 Jayson Tatum 1.00 2.50
BOD5 Jalen Brunson .60 1.50
BOD6 Joel Embiid .50 1.25
BOD7 Nikola Jokic 1.50 4.00
BOD8 Chet Holmgren .50 1.25
BOD9 Kevin Durant 1.00 2.50
BOD10 Kyrie Irving .75 2.00
BOD11 LaMelo Ball .60 1.50
BOD12 Giannis Antetokounmpo 1.25 3.00
BOD13 Victor Wembanyama 2.50 6.00
BOD14 Brandon Miller .50 1.25
BOD15 Jimmy Butler .50 1.25
BOD16 Dominique Wilkins .50 1.25
BOD17 Paul Pierce .50 1.25
BOD18 Dennis Rodman .75 2.00
BOD19 Carmelo Anthony .50 1.25
BOD20 Ben Wallace .40 1.00
BOD21 Hakeem Olajuwon .60 1.50
BOD22 Shaquille O'Neal .75 2.00
BOD23 Dwyane Wade .60 1.50
BOD24 Kevin Garnett .75 2.00
BOD25 David Robinson .60 1.50

2024-25 Topps Chrome Certified Autograph Issue

*PINK BK REF/55: .6X TO 1.5X BASIC
TCAIAB Anthony Black 6.00 15.00
TCAIAG Artis Gilmore 6.00 15.00
TCAIAS Alperen Sengun 8.00 20.00
TCAIBB Bruce Brown Jr. 4.00 10.00
TCAIBC Bilal Coulibaly 6.00 15.00
TCAIBH Bones Hyland 4.00 10.00
TCAIBP Brandin Podziemski 6.00 15.00
TCAICA Carmelo Anthony 20.00 50.00
TCAICC Clint Capela 4.00 10.00
TCAICL Christian Laettner 5.00 12.00
TCAICW Cam Whitmore 5.00 12.00
TCAIDD Donte DiVincenzo 5.00 12.00
TCAIDG Daniel Gafford 4.00 10.00
TCAIDH De'Andre Hunter 5.00 12.00
TCAIDL Dereck Lively II 5.00 12.00
TCAIDN Dirk Nowitzki 60.00 150.00
TCAIDT David Thompson 6.00 15.00
TCAIDW Dwyane Wade 20.00 50.00
TCAIGD Gradey Dick 6.00 15.00
TCAIGJ GG Jackson II 5.00 12.00
TCAIGW Grant Williams 3.00 8.00
TCAIIQ Immanuel Quickley 4.00 10.00
TCAIJB Jalen Brunson 20.00 50.00
TCAIJC Jaylen Clark 4.00 10.00
TCAIJH Jalen Hood-Schifino 4.00 10.00
TCAIJP Jakob Poeltl 4.00 10.00
TCAIJS Jerry Stackhouse 6.00 15.00
TCAIJT Jayson Tatum 60.00 150.00
TCAIKD Kevin Durant 60.00 150.00
TCAILJ Larry Johnson 6.00 15.00
TCAILS Latrell Sprewell 6.00 15.00
TCAILW Lonnie Walker IV 4.00 10.00
TCAIMB Mo Bamba 3.00 8.00
TCAIMF Markelle Fultz 3.00 8.00
TCAIMG Manu Ginobili 20.00 50.00
TCAIMJ Magic Johnson 60.00 150.00
TCAINB Nicolas Batum 3.00 8.00
TCAINC Noah Clowney 5.00 12.00
TCAINR Naz Reid 5.00 12.00
TCAIOO Onyeka Okongwu 5.00 12.00
TCAIPP Paul Pierce 20.00 50.00
TCAIPW Patrick Williams 4.00 10.00
TCAIQG Quentin Grimes 5.00 12.00
TCAIRB Rick Barry 6.00 15.00
TCAIRH Rui Hachimura 5.00 12.00
TCAIRP Robert Parish 6.00 15.00
TCAISB Saddiq Bey 4.00 10.00
TCAISC Stephen Curry 400.00 800.00
TCAISK Shawn Kemp 8.00 20.00
TCAISS Shaedon Sharpe 6.00 15.00
TCAITH Taylor Hendricks 5.00 12.00
TCAITM Trey Murphy III 6.00 15.00
TCAIVC Vince Carter 20.00 50.00
TCAIVW Victor Wembanyama 400.00 800.00
TCAIZR Zach Randolph 4.00 10.00
TCAIBBO Bogdan Bogdanovic 4.00 10.00
TCAIBCL Brandon Clarke 4.00 10.00
TCAIDSH Day'ron Sharpe 4.00 10.00
TCAIDWI Deron Williams 4.00 10.00
TCAIGTJ Gary Trent Jr. 4.00 10.00
TCAIJCO John Collins 4.00 10.00
TCAIJHO Jett Howard 5.00 12.00
TCAIJVA Jarred Vanderbilt 4.00 10.00
TCAIJWI Jason Williams 8.00 20.00
TCAILBJ Lebron James 1,500.00 3,000.00
TCAIMST Max Strus 4.00 10.00
TCAIPMI Patty Mills 5.00 12.00
TCAIRJA Reggie Jackson 3.00 8.00
TCAISMA Sandro Mamukelashvili 6.00 15.00
TCAITMA Terance Mann 3.00 8.00

2024-25 Topps Chrome Certified Autograph Issue Rookies

*PRPL GEO REF: .5X TO 1.2X BASIC
*REFRACTOR: .5X TO 1.2X BASIC
*GOLD GEO REF/50: .6X TO 1.5X BASIC
*GOLD REF/50: .6X TO 1.5X BASIC
*ORNG GEO REF/25: .75X TO 2X BASIC
TCRAAJ AJ Johnson 10.00 25.00
TCRAAS Alexandre Sarr 15.00 40.00
TCRABJ Bronny James Jr. 40.00 100.00
TCRABS Baylor Scheierman 6.00 15.00
TCRACW Cody Williams 6.00 15.00
TCRADH DaRon Holmes II 6.00 15.00
TCRADJ Dillon Jones 5.00 12.00
TCRAIC Isaiah Collier 10.00 25.00
TCRAJB Jalen Bridges 4.00 10.00
TCRAJE Justin Edwards 8.00 20.00
TCRAJF Johnny Furphy 8.00 20.00
TCRAJM Jonathan Mogbo 8.00 20.00
TCRAJS Jamal Shead 6.00 15.00
TCRAJT Jaylon Tyson 5.00 12.00
TCRAKF Kyle Filipowski 10.00 25.00
TCRAKG Kyshawn George 8.00 20.00
TCRAKW Kel'el Ware 12.00 30.00
TCRANT Nikola Topic 40.00 100.00
TCRAOI Oso Ighodaro 6.00 15.00
TCRARD Rob Dillingham 12.00 30.00
TCRARH Ron Holland II 10.00 25.00
TCRASC Stephon Castle 75.00 200.00
TCRATD Tristan da Silva 12.00 30.00
TCRATK Tyler Kolek 8.00 20.00
TCRATS Tidjane SalaÃ¼n 5.00 12.00
TCRAYM Yves Missi 12.00 30.00
TCRAZR Zaccharie Risacher 15.00 40.00
TCRARDU Ryan Dunn 6.00 15.00
TCRATSH Terrence Shannon Jr. 10.00 25.00
TCRATSM Tyler Smith 6.00 15.00

2024-25 Topps Chrome Chromographs

*PINK BK REF/55: .6X TO 1.5X BASIC
CAE Alex English 6.00 15.00
CAG Aaron Gordon 5.00 12.00
CAH Al Horford 5.00 12.00
CAM Alonzo Mourning 8.00 20.00
CAN Aaron Nesmith 4.00 10.00
CAR Logan Johnson 4.00 10.00
CAS Anfernee Simons 5.00 12.00
CAW Andrew Wiggins 6.00 15.00
CBB Bradley Beal 6.00 15.00
CBC Jacob Toppin 4.00 10.00
CBM Brandon Miller 8.00 20.00
CBS Brice Sensabaugh 4.00 10.00
CBW Blake Wesley 3.00 8.00
CCA Cole Anthony 5.00 12.00
CCB Leonard Miller 5.00 12.00
CCD Clyde Drexler 8.00 20.00
CCH Chet Holmgren 8.00 20.00
CCJ Cameron Johnson 4.00 10.00
CCL Chris Livingston 4.00 10.00
CCM CJ McCollum 4.00 10.00
CCS Collin Sexton 5.00 12.00
CDB Desmond Bane 5.00 12.00
CDG Daniel Gafford 4.00 10.00
CDM Donovan Mitchell 20.00 50.00
CDR D'Angelo Russell 4.00 10.00
CDS Domantas Sabonis 8.00 20.00
CDT David Thompson 6.00 15.00
CDV Andre Jackson Jr. 4.00 10.00
CEH Elvin Hayes 6.00 15.00
CFW Franz Wagner 8.00 20.00
CGG George Gervin 8.00 20.00
CHA Hakeem Olajuwon 20.00 50.00
CIH Jabari Walker 3.00 8.00
CIW Isaiah Wong 4.00 10.00
CJA Jarrett Allen 4.00 10.00
CJC Jordan Clarkson 5.00 12.00
CJG Jalen Green 10.00 25.00
CJH Jordan Hawkins 4.00 10.00
CJK Jason Kidd 8.00 20.00
CJL Jake LaRavia 4.00 10.00
CJM Jamal Murray 8.00 20.00
CJP Julian Phillips 4.00 10.00
CJS Leaky Black 4.00 10.00
CJW Jalen Wilson 4.00 10.00
CKB Kobe Bufkin 4.00 10.00
CKC Kentavious Caldwell-Pope 3.00 8.00
CKG Kevin Garnett 20.00 50.00
CKK Kyle Kuzma 4.00 10.00
CKL Kevon Looney 4.00 10.00
CKM GG Jackson II 5.00 12.00
CKP Kristaps Porzingis 6.00 15.00
CKT Karl-Anthony Towns 8.00 20.00
CLD Luguentz Dort 4.00 10.00
CLJ Larry Johnson 6.00 15.00
CLM Lauri Markkanen 5.00 12.00
CMB Mikal Bridges 5.00 12.00
CMG Manu Ginobili 20.00 50.00
CMM Malik Monk 5.00 12.00
CMS Trey Murphy III 6.00 15.00
CMW Metta World Peace 5.00 12.00
CNB Nicolas Batum 3.00 8.00
CNC Nic Claxton 4.00 10.00
CNR Naz Reid 5.00 12.00
CNS Nick Smith Jr. 4.00 10.00
COA Bruce Brown Jr. 4.00 10.00
COO Onyeka Okongwu 5.00 12.00
COP Olivier-Maxence Prosper 4.00 10.00
CPG Pau Gasol 8.00 20.00
CPS Pascal Siakam 6.00 15.00
CRA Ray Allen 20.00 50.00
CRJ Richard Jefferson 4.00 10.00
CRR Rayan Rupert 5.00 12.00
CSA Steven Adams 4.00 10.00
CSC Seth Curry 5.00 12.00
CSD Jonas Valanciunas 4.00 10.00
CSH Scoot Henderson 6.00 15.00
CSO Shaquille O'Neal 75.00 200.00
CTH Tyler Herro 8.00 20.00
CTM Tyrese Maxey 10.00 25.00
CBBO Bogdan Bogdanovic 4.00 10.00
CCLA Christian Laettner 5.00 12.00
CCMU Calvin Murphy 5.00 12.00
CDBR Dillon Brooks 4.00 10.00
CDER Dennis Rodman 20.00 50.00
CDRO David Robinson 20.00 50.00
CGHI Grant Hill 8.00 20.00
CGWI Grant Williams 3.00 8.00
CJAW Jason Williams 20.00 50.00
CJGR Jeff Green 4.00 10.00
CJHO Juwan Howard 4.00 10.00
CJOW Jordan Walsh 4.00 10.00
CJST John Stockton 20.00 50.00
CJTA Jae'Sean Tate 4.00 10.00
CJWA Jarace Walker 4.00 10.00
CJWE Jerry West 20.00 50.00
CJWI Jamal Wilkes 5.00 12.00
CKBR Kobe Brown 4.00 10.00
CPST Peja Stojakovic 5.00 12.00
CRJA Reggie Jackson 3.00 8.00
CSCI Sidy Cissoko 5.00 12.00

2024-25 Topps Chrome Countdown Complete

*BLUE BK REF: .75X TO 2X BASIC
*PINK REF: .75X TO 2X BASIC
*REFRACTOR: .75X TO 2X BASIC
*TOPPS GRN REF: .75X TO 2X BASIC
CC1 Victor Wembanyama 2.50 6.00
CC2 LaMelo Ball .60 1.50
CC3 Tyrese Haliburton .60 1.50
CC4 Chet Holmgren .50 1.25
CC5 Brandon Miller .50 1.25
CC6 Jaime Jaquez Jr. .30 .75
CC7 Brandin Podziemski .40 1.00
CC8 Jalen Green .60 1.50
CC9 Tyrese Maxey .60 1.50
CC10 Cade Cunningham .75 2.00
CC11 Zaccharie Risacher 1.00 2.50
CC12 Alexandre Sarr 1.00 2.50
CC13 Stephon Castle 2.00 5.00
CC14 Ron Holland II .60 1.50
CC15 Tidjane SalaÃ¼n .30 .75
CC16 Rob Dillingham .75 2.00
CC17 Zach Edey 1.00 2.50
CC18 Cody Williams .40 1.00
CC19 Nikola Topic 1.00 2.50
CC20 Devin Carter .40 1.00
CC21 Tristan da Silva .75 2.00
CC22 AJ Johnson .60 1.50
CC23 Isaiah Collier .60 1.50
CC24 Baylor Scheierman .40 1.00
CC25 Bronny James Jr. 1.00 2.50

2024-25 Topps Chrome Destiny

*PRPL GEO REF: .75X TO 2X BASIC
*REFRACTOR: .75X TO 2X BASIC
*GREEN REF/99: 2X TO 5X BASIC
*GOLD GEO REF/50: 2.5X TO 6X BASIC
*GOLD REF/50: 2.5X TO 6X BASIC
*ORNG REF/25: 3X TO 8X BASIC
*ORNG GEO REF/25: 3X TO 8X BASIC
D1 Zaccharie Risacher 1.00 2.50
D2 Alexandre Sarr 1.00 2.50
D3 Stephon Castle 2.00 5.00
D4 Ron Holland II .60 1.50
D5 Tidjane SalaÃ¼n .30 .75
D6 Rob Dillingham .75 2.00
D7 Zach Edey 1.00 2.50
D8 Cody Williams .40 1.00
D9 Nikola Topic 1.00 2.50
D10 Devin Carter .40 1.00
D11 Kel'el Ware .75 2.00
D12 Tristan da Silva .75 2.00
D13 Jaylon Tyson .30 .75
D14 Yves Missi .30 .75
D15 DaRon Holmes II .40 1.00
D16 AJ Johnson .60 1.50
D17 Kyshawn George .50 1.25
D18 Dillon Jones .30 .75
D19 Terrence Shannon Jr. .60 1.50
D20 Ryan Dunn .40 1.00
D21 Isaiah Collier .60 1.50
D22 Baylor Scheierman .40 1.00
D23 Tyler Kolek .50 1.25
D24 Bronny James Jr. 1.00 2.50
D25 Johnny Furphy .50 1.25

2024-25 Topps Chrome Dippers

D1 Tyrese Haliburton 12.00 30.00
D2 Zach Lavine 10.00 25.00
D3 Damian Lillard 15.00 40.00
D4 Joel Embiid 12.00 30.00
D5 LeBron James 50.00 125.00
D6 Kevin Durant 20.00 50.00
D7 Nikola Jokic 30.00 80.00
D8 Giannis Antetokounmpo 25.00 60.00
D9 Paul George 10.00 25.00
D10 Stephen Curry 50.00 125.00
D11 Jaylen Brown 10.00 25.00
D12 Jayson Tatum 20.00 50.00
D13 Chet Holmgren 12.00 30.00
D14 Jalen Brunson 12.00 30.00
D15 Jimmy Butler 12.00 30.00
D16 Kyrie Irving 15.00 40.00
D17 Victor Wembanyama 50.00 125.00
D18 Brandon Miller 10.00 25.00
D19 Scoot Henderson 8.00 20.00
D20 Donovan Mitchell 12.00 30.00
D21 Zaccharie Risacher 20.00 50.00
D22 Alexandre Sarr 20.00 50.00
D23 Stephon Castle 40.00 100.00
D24 Rob Dillingham 15.00 40.00
D25 Cody Williams 8.00 20.00

2024-25 Topps Chrome Film Study

*BLUE BK REF: .75X TO 2X BASIC
*PINK REF: .75X TO 2X BASIC
*REFRACTOR: .75X TO 2X BASIC
*TOPPS GRN REF: .75X TO 2X BASIC
FS1 Donovan Mitchell .60 1.50
FS2 Nikola Jokic 1.50 4.00
FS3 Giannis Antetokounmpo 1.25 3.00
FS4 Kevin Durant 1.00 2.50
FS5 Joel Embiid .60 1.50
FS6 LeBron James 2.50 6.00
FS7 Stephen Curry 2.50 6.00
FS8 Devin Booker .75 2.00
FS9 Damian Lillard .75 2.00
FS10 LaMelo Ball .60 1.50
FS11 Cade Cunningham .75 2.00
FS12 Chet Holmgren .50 1.25
FS13 Tyrese Haliburton .60 1.50
FS14 Jalen Brunson .60 1.50
FS15 Kawhi Leonard .60 1.50
FS16 Brandon Miller .50 1.25
FS17 Jimmy Butler .50 1.25
FS18 Kyrie Irving .75 2.00
FS19 Jalen Green .60 1.50
FS20 Jayson Tatum 1.00 2.50

2024-25 Topps Chrome Fresh Start

*BLUE BK REF: .75X TO 2X BASIC
*PINK REF: .75X TO 2X BASIC
*REFRACTOR: .75X TO 2X BASIC
*TOPPS GRN REF: .75X TO 2X BASIC
FS1 Zaccharie Risacher 1.00 2.50
FS2 Alexandre Sarr 1.00 2.50
FS3 Stephon Castle 2.00 5.00
FS4 Ron Holland II .60 1.50
FS5 Tidjane SalaÃ¼n .30 .75
FS6 Rob Dillingham .75 2.00
FS7 Zach Edey 1.00 2.50
FS8 Cody Williams .40 1.00
FS9 Nikola Topic 1.00 2.50
FS10 Devin Carter .40 1.00
FS11 Tristan da Silva .75 2.00
FS12 DaRon Holmes II .40 1.00
FS13 AJ Johnson .60 1.50
FS14 Terrence Shannon Jr. .60 1.50
FS15 Bronny James Jr. 1.00 2.50

2024-25 Topps Chrome Future Stars Autographs

*PINK BK REF/55: .6X TO 1.5X BASIC
FSAAJ AJ Johnson 10.00 25.00
FSAAR Antonio Reeves 5.00 12.00
FSAAS Alexandre Sarr 15.00 40.00
FSAAW Anton Watson 4.00 10.00
FSABJ Bronny James Jr. 40.00 100.00
FSACC Cam Christie 6.00 15.00
FSACS Cam Spencer 5.00 12.00
FSACW Cody Williams 6.00 15.00
FSADC Devin Carter 6.00 15.00
FSADJ Dillon Jones 5.00 12.00
FSAEF Enrique Freeman 4.00 10.00
FSAJF Johnny Furphy 8.00 20.00
FSAJM Jonathan Mogbo 8.00 20.00
FSAJS Jamal Shead 6.00 15.00
FSAKF Kyle Filipowski 10.00 25.00
FSANT Nikola Topic 40.00 100.00
FSAOI Oso Ighodaro 6.00 15.00
FSAPL Pelle Larsson 5.00 12.00
FSARD Rob Dillingham 12.00 30.00
FSARH Ron Holland II 10.00 25.00
FSASC Stephon Castle 75.00 200.00
FSATd Tristan da Silva 12.00 30.00
FSATK Tyler Kolek 8.00 20.00
FSATN Tristen Newton 5.00 12.00
FSATS Tidjane SalaÃ¼n 5.00 12.00
FSAUC Ulrich Chomche 4.00 10.00
FSAZE Zach Edey 15.00 40.00
FSAZR Zaccharie Risacher 15.00 40.00
FSATSM Tyler Smith 6.00 15.00

2024-25 Topps Chrome Helix

H1 Victor Wembanyama 75.00 200.00
H2 Kevin Durant 30.00 80.00
H3 Stephen Curry 80.00 200.00
H4 Jalen Brunson 20.00 50.00
H5 Joel Embiid 20.00 50.00
H6 Jayson Tatum 30.00 80.00
H7 LeBron James 80.00 200.00
H8 Anthony Edwards 50.00 125.00
H9 Giannis Antetokounmpo 40.00 100.00
H10 Damian Lillard 25.00 60.00
H11 Shaquille O'Neal 25.00 60.00
H12 Dirk Nowitzki 25.00 60.00
H13 Allen Iverson 25.00 60.00
H14 Larry Bird 30.00 80.00
H15 Magic Johnson 30.00 80.00
H16 Zaccharie Risacher 30.00 80.00
H17 Alexandre Sarr 30.00 80.00
H18 Stephon Castle 75.00 200.00
H19 Tidjane SalaÃ¼n 10.00 25.00
H20 Rob Dillingham 25.00 60.00

2024-25 Topps Chrome Instinct

*PRPL GEO REF: .75X TO 2X BASIC
*REFRACTOR: .75X TO 2X BASIC
*GREEN REF/99: 2X TO 5X BASIC
*GOLD GEO REF/50: 2.5X TO 6X BASIC
*GOLD REF/50: 2.5X TO 6X BASIC
*ORNG REF/25: 3X TO 8X BASIC
*ORNG GEO REF/25: 3X TO 8X BASIC
INS1 Donovan Mitchell .60 1.50
INS2 Nikola Jokic 1.50 4.00
INS3 Kawhi Leonard .60 1.50
INS4 Giannis Antetokounmpo 1.25 3.00
INS5 Trae Young .60 1.50
INS6 Joel Embiid .60 1.50
INS7 Anthony Edwards 1.50 4.00
INS8 Kevin Durant 1.00 2.50
INS9 Stephen Curry 2.50 6.00
INS10 LeBron James 2.50 6.00
INS11 Kyrie Irving .75 2.00
INS12 Jayson Tatum 1.00 2.50
INS13 Zach Lavine .50 1.25
INS14 Brandon Miller .50 1.25
INS15 Cade Cunningham .75 2.00
INS16 Tyrese Haliburton .60 1.50
INS17 Jalen Green .60 1.50
INS18 Jalen Brunson .60 1.50
INS19 Jimmy Butler .50 1.25
INS20 Jaylen Brown .50 1.25
INS21 Tyrese Maxey .60 1.50
INS22 De'Aaron Fox .60 1.50
INS23 Damian Lillard .75 2.00
INS24 Anthony Davis .75 2.00
INS25 Devin Booker .75 2.00
INS26 Zaccharie Risacher 1.00 2.50
INS27 Alexandre Sarr 1.00 2.50
INS28 Stephon Castle 2.00 5.00
INS29 Ron Holland II .60 1.50
INS30 Rob Dillingham .75 2.00

2024-25 Topps Chrome Let's Go!

LG1 Victor Wembanyama 75.00 200.00
LG2 Kevin Durant 20.00 50.00
LG3 Stephen Curry 50.00 125.00
LG4 Jalen Brunson 12.00 30.00
LG5 Joel Embiid 12.00 30.00
LG6 Nikola Jokic 30.00 80.00
LG7 LeBron James 50.00 125.00
LG8 Brandon Miller 10.00 25.00
LG9 Damian Lillard 15.00 40.00
LG10 Giannis Antetokounmpo 25.00 60.00
LG11 Zaccharie Risacher 20.00 50.00
LG12 Alexandre Sarr 20.00 50.00
LG13 Stephon Castle 40.00 100.00
LG14 Ron Holland II 12.00 30.00
LG15 Bronny James Jr. 20.00 50.00

2024-25 Topps Chrome Lock It Up

*PRPL GEO REF: .75X TO 2X BASIC
*REFRACTOR: .75X TO 2X BASIC
*GREEN REF/99: 2X TO 5X BASIC
*GOLD GEO REF/50: 2.5X TO 6X BASIC
*GOLD REF/50: 2.5X TO 6X BASIC
*ORNG REF/25: 3X TO 8X BASIC
*ORNG GEO REF/25: 3X TO 8X BASIC
LIU1 Jaylen Brown .50 1.25
LIU2 Nikola Jokic 1.50 4.00
LIU3 Kawhi Leonard .60 1.50
LIU4 Anthony Davis .75 2.00
LIU5 Giannis Antetokounmpo 1.25 3.00
LIU6 Karl-Anthony Towns .50 1.25
LIU7 Chet Holmgren .50 1.25
LIU8 Joel Embiid .60 1.50
LIU9 Victor Wembanyama 2.50 6.00
LIU10 Kevin Durant 1.00 2.50

2024-25 Topps Chrome Next Stop Signatures

*PRPL GEO REF: .5X TO 1.2X BASIC
*REFRACTOR: .5X TO 1.2X BASIC
*GOLD GEO REF/50: .6X TO 1.5X BASIC
*GOLD REF/50: .6X TO 1.5X BASIC
*ORNG GEO REF/25: .75X TO 2X BASIC
MSCC Cam Christie 6.00 15.00
NSSAB Adem Bona 6.00 15.00
NSSAJ AJ Johnson 10.00 25.00
NSSAM Ajay Mitchell 8.00 20.00
NSSAS Alexandre Sarr 15.00 40.00
NSSBJ Bronny James Jr. 40.00 100.00
NSSBS Baylor Scheierman 6.00 15.00
NSSCW Cody Williams 6.00 15.00
NSSDC Devin Carter 6.00 15.00
NSSDH DaRon Holmes II 6.00 15.00
NSSHI Harrison Ingram 5.00 12.00
NSSIC Isaiah Collier 10.00 25.00
NSSJT Jaylon Tyson 6.00 15.00
NSSJW Jaylen Wells 15.00 40.00
NSSKG Kyshawn George 8.00 20.00
NSSKM Kevin McCullar Jr. 5.00 12.00
NSSKS KJ Simpson Jr. 5.00 12.00
NSSKW Kel'el Ware 12.00 30.00
NSSNT Nikola Topic 40.00 100.00
NSSPD Pacome Dadiet 6.00 15.00
NSSPL Pelle Larsson 6.00 15.00
NSSRD Rob Dillingham 12.00 30.00
NSSRH Ron Holland II 10.00 25.00
NSSSC Stephon Castle 75.00 200.00
NSSTS Tidjane SalaÃ¼n 5.00 12.00
NSSYM Yves Missi 12.00 30.00
NSSZE Zach Edey 15.00 40.00
NSSZR Zaccharie Risacher 15.00 40.00
NSSRDU Ryan Dunn 6.00 15.00
NSSTSH Terrence Shannon Jr. 10.00 25.00

2024-25 Topps Chrome Radiating Rookies

RR1 Zaccharie Risacher 30.00 80.00
RR2 Alexandre Sarr 30.00 80.00
RR3 Stephon Castle 100.00 250.00
RR4 Ron Holland II 20.00 50.00
RR5 Tidjane SalaÃ¼n 12.00 30.00
RR6 Rob Dillingham 25.00 60.00
RR7 Zach Edey 30.00 80.00
RR8 Tristan da Silva 25.00 60.00
RR9 Ryan Dunn 12.00 30.00
RR10 Jonathan Mogbo 15.00 40.00

2024-25 Topps Chrome Rock Stars

RS1 Nikola Jokic 30.00 80.00
RS2 Giannis Antetokounmpo 25.00 60.00
RS3 Kawhi Leonard 12.00 30.00
RS4 Victor Wembanyama 50.00 125.00
RS5 LeBron James 50.00 125.00
RS6 Tyrese Haliburton 12.00 30.00
RS7 Joel Embiid 12.00 30.00
RS8 Jayson Tatum 20.00 50.00
RS9 Devin Booker 15.00 40.00
RS10 LaMelo Ball 12.00 30.00
RS11 Zaccharie Risacher 20.00 50.00
RS12 Alexandre Sarr 20.00 50.00
RS13 Stephon Castle 60.00 150.00
RS14 Zach Edey 20.00 50.00
RS15 Cody Williams 8.00 20.00
RS16 David Robinson 12.00 30.00
RS17 Hakeem Olajuwon 12.00 30.00
RS18 Shaquille O'Neal 15.00 40.00
RS19 Vince Carter 12.00 30.00
RS20 Allen Iverson 15.00 40.00

2024-25 Topps Chrome Show and Tell

*BLUE BK REF: .75X TO 2X BASIC
*PINK REF: .75X TO 2X BASIC
*REFRACTOR: .75X TO 2X BASIC
*TOPPS GRN REF: .75X TO 2X BASIC
ST1 Kevin Durant 1.00 2.50
ST2 Nikola Jokic 1.50 4.00
ST3 Giannis Antetokounmpo 1.25 3.00
ST4 Kawhi Leonard .60 1.50
ST5 Joel Embiid .60 1.50
ST6 LeBron James 2.50 6.00
ST7 Stephen Curry 2.50 6.00
ST8 LaMelo Ball .60 1.50
ST9 Victor Wembanyama 2.50 6.00
ST10 Jayson Tatum 1.00 2.50
ST11 Zaccharie Risacher 1.00 2.50
ST12 Alexandre Sarr 1.00 2.50
ST13 Stephon Castle 2.00 5.00
ST14 Ron Holland II .60 1.50
ST15 Rob Dillingham .75 2.00

2024-25 Topps Chrome Sky-Light Signatures

*PRPL GEO REF: .5X TO 1.2X BASIC
*REFRACTOR: .5X TO 1.2X BASIC
*GOLD GEO REF/50: .6X TO 1.5X BASIC
*GOLD REF/50: .6X TO 1.5X BASIC
*ORNG GEO REF/25: .75X TO 2X BASIC
SLSAE Alex English 6.00 15.00
SLSAH Anfernee Hardaway 20.00 50.00
SLSBM Brandon Miller 8.00 20.00
SLSBS Brice Sensabaugh 4.00 10.00
SLSDB Desmond Bane 5.00 12.00
SLSDM Donovan Mitchell 20.00 50.00
SLSDN Dirk Nowitzki 60.00 150.00
SLSDR David Robinson 20.00 50.00
SLSDS Domantas Sabonis 8.00 20.00
SLSDW Dominique Wilkins 8.00 20.00
SLSFW Franz Wagner 8.00 20.00
SLSGG George Gervin 8.00 20.00
SLSGW Grant Williams 3.00 8.00
SLSJC John Collins 4.00 10.00
SLSJG Jalen Green 10.00 25.00
SLSJH Jett Howard 5.00 12.00
SLSJJ Jaime Jaquez Jr. 5.00 12.00
SLSJK Jonathan Kuminga 6.00 15.00
SLSJP Jordan Poole 5.00 12.00
SLSJT Jayson Tatum 60.00 150.00
SLSKC Kentavious Caldwell-Pope 3.00 8.00
SLSKD Kevin Durant 60.00 150.00
SLSKG Kevin Garnett 20.00 50.00
SLSLB Larry Bird 60.00 150.00
SLSLD Luguentz Dort 4.00 10.00
SLSLM Lauri Markkanen 5.00 12.00
SLSMB Mikal Bridges 5.00 12.00
SLSMW Metta World Peace 5.00 12.00
SLSOO Onyeka Okongwu 5.00 12.00
SLSOT Obi Toppin 4.00 10.00
SLSSK Shawn Kemp 8.00 20.00
SLSSO Shaquille O'Neal 75.00 200.00
SLSTJ Trayce Jackson-Davis 5.00 12.00
SLSVC Vince Carter 20.00 50.00
SLSVW Victor Wembanyama 400.00 800.00
SLSARE Antonio Reeves 5.00 12.00
SLSAWA Anton Watson 4.00 10.00
SLSDMI Davion Mitchell 4.00 10.00
SLSDRO Dennis Rodman 20.00 50.00
SLSJED Justin Edwards 8.00 20.00
SLSJHD James Harden 60.00 150.00
SLSJJJ Jaren Jackson Jr. 8.00 20.00
SLSJLA Jock Landale 4.00 10.00
SLSJSH Jamal Shead 6.00 15.00
SLSJWE Jaylen Wells 15.00 40.00
SLSLBJ Lebron James 1,500.00 3,000.00
SLSPAC Precious Achiuwa 4.00 10.00
SLSTHA Tyrese Haliburton 40.00 100.00
SLSTHE Tyler Herro 8.00 20.00
SLSUCH Ulrich Chomche 4.00 10.00

2024-25 Topps Chrome Test Drive

*PRPL GEO REF: .75X TO 2X BASIC
*REFRACTOR: .75X TO 2X BASIC
*GREEN REF/99: 2X TO 5X BASIC
*GOLD GEO REF/50: 2.5X TO 6X BASIC
*GOLD REF/50: 2.5X TO 6X BASIC
*ORNG REF/25: 3X TO 8X BASIC
*ORNG GEO REF/25: 3X TO 8X BASIC
TD1 Trae Young .60 1.50
TD2 Jayson Tatum 1.00 2.50
TD3 Mikal Bridges .30 .75
TD4 Brandon Miller .50 1.25
TD5 Zach Lavine .50 1.25
TD6 Donovan Mitchell .60 1.50
TD7 Kyrie Irving .75 2.00
TD8 Jamal Murray .50 1.25
TD9 Cade Cunningham .75 2.00
TD10 Jalen Green .60 1.50
TD11 Tyrese Haliburton .60 1.50
TD12 LaMelo Ball .60 1.50
TD13 Paul George .50 1.25
TD14 LeBron James 2.50 6.00
TD15 Jalen Brunson .60 1.50
TD16 Damian Lillard .75 2.00
TD17 Tyrese Maxey .60 1.50
TD18 Devin Booker .75 2.00
TD19 De'Aaron Fox .60 1.50
TD20 Scoot Henderson .40 1.00

2024-25 Topps Chrome Ultra Violet All-Stars

UVAS1 Victor Wembanyama 150.00 400.00
UVAS2 Kevin Durant 60.00 150.00
UVAS3 Stephen Curry 150.00 400.00
UVAS4 Tyrese Haliburton 40.00 100.00
UVAS5 Jalen Brunson 40.00 100.00
UVAS6 Joel Embiid 40.00 100.00
UVAS7 Nikola Jokic 100.00 250.00
UVAS8 Jayson Tatum 60.00 150.00
UVAS9 LeBron James 150.00 400.00
UVAS10 Ja Morant 60.00 150.00
UVAS11 Anthony Edwards 100.00 250.00
UVAS12 Kawhi Leonard 40.00 100.00
UVAS13 De'Aaron Fox 40.00 100.00
UVAS14 Giannis Antetokounmpo 80.00 200.00
UVAS15 Kyrie Irving 50.00 125.00

2024-25 Topps Chrome Youthquake

*PRPL GEO REF: .75X TO 2X BASIC
*REFRACTOR: .75X TO 2X BASIC
*GREEN REF/99: 2X TO 5X BASIC
*GOLD GEO REF/50: 2.5X TO 6X BASIC
*GOLD REF/50: 2.5X TO 6X BASIC
*ORNG REF/25: 3X TO 8X BASIC
*ORNG GEO REF/25: 3X TO 8X BASIC
YQ1 Zaccharie Risacher 1.00 2.50
YQ2 Alexandre Sarr 1.00 2.50
YQ3 Stephon Castle 2.00 5.00
YQ4 Ron Holland II .60 1.50
YQ5 Tidjane SalaÃ¼n .30 .75
YQ6 Rob Dillingham .75 2.00
YQ7 Zach Edey 1.00 2.50
YQ8 Cody Williams .40 1.00
YQ9 Nikola Topic 1.00 2.50
YQ10 Devin Carter .40 1.00
YQ11 Kel'el Ware .75 2.00
YQ12 Tristan da Silva .75 2.00
YQ13 Jaylon Tyson .30 .75
YQ14 Bronny James Jr. 1.00 2.50
YQ15 DaRon Holmes II .40 1.00

2022 Topps Chrome McDonald's All American

COMMONS .30 .75
SEMISTARS .40 1.00
UNLISTED STARS .50 1.25
*REFRACTORS: .6X TO 1.5X BASIC
*RAYWAVE REF: .75X TO 2X BASIC
*PURPLE REF/299: 1.25X TO 3X BASIC
*LOGO REF: 1.5X TO 4X BASIC
*FUCHSIA REF/150: 2X TO 5X BASIC
*BLUE REF/99: 2.5X TO 6X BASIC
*BLUE MINI-DMD REF/99: 2.5X TO 6X BASIC
*GOLD REF/50: 4X TO 10X BASIC
*ORANGE REF/25: 6X TO 15X BASIC
*ORANGE REF/25: 8X TO 20X BASIC
1 Throwin' Down .60 1.50
2 Dereck Lively II 1.25 3.00
3 Chris Livingston 1.25 3.00
4 Brandon Miller 2.50 6.00
5 Dillon Mitchell .75 2.00
6 Julian Phillips 1.25 3.00
7 MJ Rice 1.00 2.50
8 JJ Starling 1.00 2.50
9 Ernest Udeh .75 2.00
10 Jarace Walker 1.25 3.00
11 Winning The Tip .60 1.50
12 Cam Whitmore 1.50 4.00
13 Amari Bailey 1.25 3.00
14 Anthony Black 1.25 3.00
15 Adem Bona .75 2.00
16 Gradey Dick 1.25 3.00
17 Rim Rockers .60 1.50
18 Mark Mitchell .75 2.00
19 Arterio Morris .75 2.00
20 Nick Smith Jr .60 1.50
21 Cason Wallace 1.25 3.00
22 Jordan Walsh .75 2.00
23 Kel'el Ware .75 2.00
24 Kijani Wright .60 1.50
25 Janiah Barker .60 1.50
26 Paris Clark .60 1.50
27 Talaysia Cooper .60 1.50
28 Chance Gray .60 1.50
29 Ta'Niya Latson .60 1.50
30 Indya Nivar .60 1.50
31 Kyla Oldacre .60 1.50
32 Ayanna Patterson .75 2.00
33 Justine Pissott .60 1.50
34 Kiki Rice .75 2.00
35 Grace VanSlooten .60 1.50
36 Ashlyn Watkins .75 2.00
37 Raegan Beers .60 1.50
38 Lauren Betts 1.25 3.00
39 Isuneh Brady .60 1.50
40 Kk Bransford .60 1.50
41 Timea Gardiner .60 1.50
42 Aaliyah Gayles .60 1.50
43 Ashlon Jackson .60 1.50
44 Gabriela Jaquez .75 2.00
45 Flau'jae Johnson 1.25 3.00
46 Bench Mob .60 1.50
47 Maya Nnaji .60 1.50
48 Ruby Whitehorn .60 1.50
49 Whole Squad Ready .60 1.50
50 Dereck Lively II 1.25 3.00
51 Chris Livingston 1.25 3.00
52 Brandon Miller 2.50 6.00
53 Dillon Mitchell .75 2.00
54 Julian Phillips 1.25 3.00
55 MJ Rice 1.00 2.50
56 JJ Starling 1.00 2.50
57 Ernest Udeh .75 2.00
58 Jarace Walker 1.25 3.00
59 High Flyer .75 2.00
60 Cam Whitmore 1.50 4.00
61 Amari Bailey 1.25 3.00
62 Anthony Black 1.25 3.00
63 Adem Bona .75 2.00
64 Gradey Dick 1.25 3.00
65 Arkansas Bound 1.25 3.00
66 Mark Mitchell .75 2.00
67 Arterio Morris .75 2.00
68 Nick Smith Jr .60 1.50
69 Cason Wallace 1.25 3.00
70 Jordan Walsh .75 2.00
71 Kel'el Ware .75 2.00
72 Kijani Wright .60 1.50
73 Janiah Barker .60 1.50
74 Paris Clark .60 1.50
75 Talaysia Cooper .60 1.50
76 Chance Gray .60 1.50
77 Ta'Niya Latson .60 1.50
78 Indya Nivar .60 1.50
79 Kyla Oldacre .60 1.50
80 Ayanna Patterson .75 2.00
81 Justine Pissott .60 1.50
82 Kiki Rice .75 2.00
83 Grace VanSlooten .60 1.50
84 Ashlyn Watkins .75 2.00
85 Raegan Beers .60 1.50
86 Lauren Betts 1.25 3.00
87 Isuneh Brady .60 1.50
88 Kk Bransford .60 1.50
89 Timea Gardiner .60 1.50
90 Aaliyah Gayles .60 1.50
91 Ashlon Jackson .60 1.50
92 Gabriela Jaquez .75 2.00
93 Flau'jae Johnson 1.25 3.00
94 Future Teammates 1.25 3.00
95 Maya Nnaji .60 1.50
96 Ruby Whitehorn .60 1.50
97 Powerade Jam Fest .60 1.50
98 McDonald's All-American Game .60 1.50
99 Kiki For MVP .60 1.50
100 Kiki Rice and Gabriela Jaquez .75 2.00

2022 Topps Chrome McDonald's All American '06 All American
COMMONS .30 .75
SEMISTARS .40 1.00
UNLISTED STARS .50 1.25
*GOLD REF/50: 4X TO 10X BASIC
*ORNG REF/25: 8X TO 20X BASIC
2K61 Amari Bailey 1.25 3.00
2K62 Dereck Lively II 1.25 3.00
2K63 MJ Rice 1.00 2.50
2K64 Nick Smith Jr .60 1.50
2K65 Cason Wallace 1.25 3.00
2K66 Brandon Miller 2.50 6.00
2K67 Anthony Black 1.25 3.00
2K68 Dillon Mitchell .75 2.00
2K69 Gradey Dick 1.25 3.00
2K610 Chris Livingston 1.25 3.00
2K611 Jordan Walsh .75 2.00
2K612 Jarace Walker 1.25 3.00
2K613 Julian Phillips 1.25 3.00
2K614 Janiah Barker .60 1.50
2K615 Lauren Betts 1.25 3.00
2K616 Isuneh Brady .60 1.50
2K617 Ayanna Patterson .75 2.00
2K618 Arterio Morris .75 2.00
2K619 Kiki Rice .75 2.00
2K620 JJ Starling 1.00 2.50
2K621 Cam Whitmore 1.50 4.00
2K622 Adem Bona .75 2.00
2K623 Kel'el Ware .75 2.00
2K624 Ashlon Jackson .60 1.50
2K625 Gabriela Jaquez .75 2.00

2022 Topps Chrome McDonald's All American Autographs
COMMONS 3.00 8.00
SEMISTARS 4.00 10.00
UNLISTED STARS 5.00 12.00
*AQUA REF/99: .5X TO 1.2X BASIC
*YELLOW REF/75: .6X TO 1.5X BASIC
*GOLD WAVE REF/50: .75X TO 2X BASIC
*ORANGE BK REF/25: 1X TO 2.5X BASIC
CAAB Amari Bailey 12.00 30.00
CAAG Aaliyah Gayles 6.00 15.00
CAAJ Ashlon Jackson 6.00 15.00
CAAM Arterio Morris 8.00 20.00
CAAP Ayanna Patterson 8.00 20.00
CAAW Ashlyn Watkins 8.00 20.00
CABM Brandon Miller 25.00 60.00
CACG Chance Gray 6.00 15.00
CACL Chris Livingston 12.00 30.00
CACW Cam Whitmore 15.00 40.00
CADL Dereck Lively II 12.00 30.00
CADM Dillon Mitchell 8.00 20.00
CAEU Ernest Udeh 8.00 20.00
CAFJ Flau'jae Johnson 40.00 100.00
CAGD Gradey Dick 12.00 30.00
CAGJ Gabriela Jaquez 8.00 20.00
CAGV Grace VanSlooten 6.00 15.00
CAIB Isuneh Brady 6.00 15.00
CAIN Indya Nivar 6.00 15.00
CAJP Julian Phillips 12.00 30.00
CAJS JJ Starling 10.00 25.00
CAJW Jarace Walker 12.00 30.00
CAKB Kiki Bransford 6.00 15.00
CAKO Kyla Oldacre 6.00 15.00
CAKR Kiki Rice 8.00 20.00
CAKW Kel'el Ware 8.00 20.00
CALB Lauren Betts 40.00 100.00
CAMM Mark Mitchell 8.00 20.00
CAMN Maya Nnaji 6.00 15.00
CAMR MJ Rice 10.00 25.00
CANS Nick Smith Jr 6.00 15.00
CAPC Paris Clark 6.00 15.00
CARB Raegan Beers 6.00 15.00
CARW Ruby Whitehorn 6.00 15.00
CATC Talaysia Cooper 6.00 15.00
CATG Timea Gardiner 6.00 15.00
CATL Ta'Niya Latson 6.00 15.00
CAABL Anthony Black 12.00 30.00
CAABO Adem Bona 8.00 20.00
CACWA Cason Wallace 12.00 30.00
CAJBA Janiah Barker 6.00 15.00
CAJPI Justine Pissott 6.00 15.00
CAJWA Jordan Walsh 8.00 20.00
CAKWR Kijani Wright 6.00 15.00

2022 Topps Chrome McDonald's All American Future Stars
COMMONS .50 1.25
SEMISTARS .60 1.50
UNLISTED STARS .75 2.00
*GOLD REF/50: 3X TO 8X BASIC
*ORNG REF/25: 6X TO 15X BASIC
FS1 Flau'jae Johnson 2.50 6.00
FS2 Adem Bona 1.50 4.00
FS3 Dillon Mitchell 1.50 4.00
FS4 Dereck Lively II 2.50 6.00
FS5 Anthony Black 2.50 6.00
FS6 Mark Mitchell 1.50 4.00
FS7 Kel'el Ware 1.50 4.00
FS8 Kijani Wright 1.25 3.00
FS9 Jordan Walsh 1.50 4.00
FS10 Timea Gardiner 1.25 3.00
FS11 Ashlyn Watkins 1.50 4.00
FS12 Maya Nnaji 1.25 3.00
FS13 Amari Bailey 2.50 6.00
FS14 Justine Pissott 1.25 3.00
FS15 Nick Smith Jr 1.25 3.00

2022 Topps Chrome McDonald's All American Gameday Autographs
COMMONS 5.00 12.00
SEMISTARS 6.00 15.00
UNLISTED STARS 8.00 20.00
PAAB Amari Bailey 20.00 50.00
PAAG Aaliyah Gayles 10.00 25.00
PAAJ Ashlon Jackson 10.00 25.00
PAAM Arterio Morris 12.00 30.00
PAAP Ayanna Patterson 12.00 30.00
PAAW Ashlyn Watkins 12.00 30.00
PABM Brandon Miller 100.00 250.00
PACG Chance Gray 10.00 25.00
PACL Chris Livingston 20.00 50.00
PACW Cam Whitmore 25.00 60.00
PADL Dereck Lively II 20.00 50.00
PADM Dillon Mitchell 12.00 30.00
PAEU Ernest Udeh 12.00 30.00
PAFJ Flau'jae Johnson 100.00 250.00
PAGD Gradey Dick 20.00 50.00
PAGJ Gabriela Jaquez 12.00 30.00
PAGV Grace VanSlooten 10.00 25.00
PAIB Isuneh Brady 10.00 25.00
PAIN Indya Nivar 10.00 25.00
PAJP Julian Phillips 20.00 50.00
PAJS JJ Starling 15.00 40.00
PAJW Jarace Walker 20.00 50.00
PAKB Kiki Bransford 10.00 25.00
PAKR Kiki Rice 12.00 30.00
PAKW Kel'el Ware 12.00 30.00
PALB Lauren Betts 50.00 120.00
PAMM Mark Mitchell 12.00 30.00
PAMN Maya Nnaji 10.00 25.00
PAMR MJ Rice 15.00 40.00
PANS Nick Smith Jr 10.00 25.00
PARB Raegan Beers 10.00 25.00
PATC Talaysia Cooper 10.00 25.00
PATG Timea Gardiner 10.00 25.00
PATL Ta'Niya Latson 10.00 25.00
PAABL Anthony Black 20.00 50.00
PAABO Adem Bona 12.00 30.00
PACWA Cason Wallace 20.00 50.00
PAJBA Janiah Barker 10.00 25.00
PAJPI Justine Pissott 10.00 25.00
PAJWA Jordan Walsh 12.00 30.00
PAKWR Kijani Wright 10.00 25.00

2022 Topps Chrome McDonald's All American Hoopers
*GOLD REF/50: 2.5X TO 6X BASIC
*ORNG REF/25: 4X TO 10X BASIC
HS1 Amari Bailey 2.00 5.00
HS2 Kiki Rice 1.25 3.00
HS3 Dereck Lively II 2.00 5.00
HS4 MJ Rice 1.50 4.00
HS5 Nick Smith Jr 1.00 2.50
HS6 Cason Wallace 2.00 5.00
HS7 JJ Starling 1.50 4.00
HS8 Brandon Miller 4.00 10.00
HS9 Anthony Black 2.00 5.00
HS10 Dillon Mitchell 1.25 3.00
HS11 Gradey Dick 2.00 5.00
HS12 Chris Livingston 2.00 5.00
HS13 Jordan Walsh 1.25 3.00
HS14 Jarace Walker 2.00 5.00
HS15 Julian Phillips 2.00 5.00
HS16 Janiah Barker 1.00 2.50
HS17 Lauren Betts 2.00 5.00
HS18 Isuneh Brady 1.00 2.50
HS19 Ayanna Patterson 1.25 3.00
HS20 Arterio Morris 1.25 3.00

2022 Topps Chrome McDonald's All American Image Variations
*GOLD REF/50: 2.5X TO 6X BASIC
*ORNG REF/25: 4X TO 10X BASIC
2 Dereck Lively II 2.50 6.00
4 Brandon Miller 5.00 12.00
6 Julian Phillips 2.50 6.00
7 MJ Rice 2.00 5.00
13 Amari Bailey 2.50 6.00
14 Anthony Black 2.50 6.00
16 Gradey Dick 2.50 6.00
19 Arterio Morris 1.50 4.00
20 Nick Smith Jr 1.25 3.00
21 Cason Wallace 2.50 6.00

2023 Topps Chrome McDonald's All American
*REFRACTORS: 1X TO 2.5X BASIC
*RAYWAVE REF: 1X TO 2.5X BASIC
*LAVA REF/299: 2X TO 5X BASIC
*LOGO REF: 2X TO 5X BASIC
*AQUA WAVE REF/199: 2.5X TO 6X BASIC
*FUCHSIA REF/150: 2.5X TO 6X BASIC
*FUCHSIA BLUE SWIRL REF/125: 3X TO 8X BASIC
*BLUE REF/99: 4X TO 10X BASIC
*BLUE MINI-DMD REF/99: 4X TO 10X BASIC
*YELLOW MINI DMD REF/75: 4X TO 10X BASIC
*GOLD REF/50: 6X TO 15X BASIC
*GOLD RAYWAVE REF/50: 6X TO 15X BASIC
*ORANGE REF/25: 8X TO 20X BASIC
*ORANGE BK REF/25: 8X TO 20X BASIC
1 Xavier Booker .60 1.50
2 Aaron Bradshaw 1.00 2.50
3 Matas Buzelis 1.25 3.00
4 Stephon Castle 1.50 4.00
5 Justin Edwards 1.00 2.50
6 Kwame Evans .60 1.50
7 Aden Holloway .60 1.50
8 Elmarko Jackson .60 1.50
9 Mackenzie Mgbako .60 1.50
10 Sean Stewart .60 1.50
11 DJ Wagner 1.25 3.00
12 Cody Williams 1.25 3.00
13 Omaha Biliew .60 1.50
14 Isaiah Collier 2.00 5.00
15 Mookie Cook .60 1.50
16 Baye Fall .60 1.50
17 Jeremy Fears Jr. .75 2.00
18 Brandon Garrison .60 1.50
19 Ron Holland II 1.25 3.00
20 Bronny James 4.00 10.00
21 Jared McCain 2.00 5.00
22 Reed Sheppard 3.00 8.00
23 Andrej Stojakovic .60 1.50
24 Ja'Kobe Walter .75 2.00
25 Zoe Brooks .50 1.25
26 Essence Cody .40 1.00
27 Aalyah DEL Rosario .40 1.00
28 Jadyn Donovan .40 1.00
29 Milaysia Fulwiley 1.25 3.00
30 Hannah Hidalgo 1.25 3.00
31 Riley Nelson .40 1.00
32 Courtney Ogden .40 1.00
33 Laila Reynolds .40 1.00
34 Emma Risch .50 1.25
35 Taliah Scott .50 1.25
36 Ashlynn Shade .50 1.25
37 KK Arnold .60 1.50
38 Sofia Bell .50 1.25
39 Madison Booker .40 1.00
40 Addy Brown .50 1.25
41 Breya Cunningham .40 1.00
42 Kymora Johnson .50 1.25
43 Tessa Johnson .50 1.25
44 Amanda Muse .50 1.25
45 Juju Watkins 2.50 6.00
46 Jada Williams .60 1.50
47 Mikaylah Williams .75 2.00
48 Sahara K Williams .50 1.25
49 Xavier Booker .60 1.50
50 Aaron Bradshaw 1.00 2.50
51 Matas Buzelis 1.25 3.00
52 Stephon Castle 1.50 4.00
53 Justin Edwards 1.00 2.50
54 Kwame Evans .60 1.50
55 Aden Holloway .60 1.50
56 Elmarko Jackson .60 1.50
57 Mackenzie Mgbako .60 1.50
58 Sean Stewart .60 1.50
59 DJ Wagner 1.25 3.00
60 Cody Williams 1.25 3.00
61 Omaha Biliew .60 1.50
62 Isaiah Collier 2.00 5.00
63 Mookie Cook .60 1.50
64 Baye Fall .60 1.50
65 Jeremy Fears Jr. .75 2.00
66 Brandon Garrison .60 1.50
67 Ron Holland II 1.25 3.00
68 Bronny James 4.00 10.00
69 Jared McCain 2.00 5.00
70 Reed Sheppard 3.00 8.00
71 Andrej Stojakovic .60 1.50
72 Ja'Kobe Walter .75 2.00
73 Zoe Brooks .50 1.25
74 Essence Cody .40 1.00
75 Aalyah DEL Rosario .40 1.00
76 Jadyn Donovan .40 1.00
77 Milaysia Fulwiley 1.25 3.00
78 Hannah Hidalgo 1.25 3.00
79 Riley Nelson .40 1.00
80 Courtney Ogden .40 1.00
81 Laila Reynolds .40 1.00
82 Emma Risch .50 1.25
83 Taliah Scott .50 1.25
84 Ashlynn Shade .50 1.25
85 KK Arnold .60 1.50
86 Sofia Bell .50 1.25
87 Madison Booker .40 1.00
88 Addy Brown .50 1.25
89 Breya Cunningham .40 1.00
90 Kymora Johnson .50 1.25
91 Tessa Johnson .50 1.25
92 Amanda Muse .50 1.25
93 Juju Watkins 2.50 6.00
94 Jada Williams .60 1.50
95 Mikaylah Williams .75 2.00
96 Sahara K Williams .50 1.25
97 Boys Group Shot .75 2.00
98 Girls Group Shot .40 1.00
99 Boys Co-MVPs 2.00 5.00
100 Girls Co-MVPs 2.50 6.00

2023 Topps Chrome McDonald's All American '07 All American
*GOLD REF/50: 4X TO 10X BASIC
*ORANGE BK REF/25: 6X TO 15X BASIC
2K71 Justin Edwards 1.50 4.00
2K72 Aaron Bradshaw 1.50 4.00
2K73 DJ Wagner 2.00 5.00
2K74 Cody Williams 2.00 5.00
2K75 Isaiah Collier 3.00 8.00
2K76 Ron Holland II 2.00 5.00
2K77 Bronny James 6.00 15.00
2K78 Mackenzie Mgbako 1.00 2.50
2K79 Matas Buzelis 2.00 5.00
2K710 Omaha Biliew 1.00 2.50
2K711 Stephon Castle 2.50 6.00
2K712 Sean Stewart 1.00 2.50
2K713 Xavier Booker 1.00 2.50
2K714 Kwame Evans 1.00 2.50
2K715 Aden Holloway 1.00 2.50
2K716 Jared McCain 3.00 8.00
2K717 Milaysia Fulwiley 2.00 5.00
2K718 Madison Booker .60 1.50
2K719 Juju Watkins 4.00 10.00
2K720 Mikaylah Williams 1.25 3.00
2K721 KK Arnold 1.00 2.50
2K722 Jadyn Donovan .60 1.50
2K723 Hannah Hidalgo 2.00 5.00
2K724 Aalyah Del Rosario .60 1.50
2K725 Zoe Brooks .75 2.00

2023 Topps Chrome McDonald's All American Autographs
*AQUA REF/99: .5X TO 1.2X BASIC
*YELLOW REF/75: .6X TO 1.5X BASIC
*GOLD RAYWAVE/50: .75X TO 2X BASIC
*GOLD WAVE/50: .75X TO 2X BASIC
*ORANGE BK REF/25: 1.25X TO 3X BASIC
CAAB Aaron Bradshaw 12.00 30.00
CAAD Aalyah Del Rosario 5.00 12.00
CAAH Aden Holloway 8.00 20.00
CAAM Amanda Muse 6.00 15.00
CAAS Andrej Stojakovic 8.00 20.00
CABC Breya Cunningham 5.00 12.00
CABF Baye Fall 8.00 20.00
CABG Brandon Garrison 8.00 20.00
CABJ Bronny James 150.00 400.00
CACO Courtney Ogden 5.00 12.00
CACW Cody Williams 15.00 40.00
CADW DJ Wagner 40.00 100.00
CAEC Essence Cody 5.00 12.00
CAEJ Elmarko Jackson 8.00 20.00
CAER Emma Risch 6.00 15.00
CAHH Hannah Hidalgo 15.00 40.00
CAIC Isaiah Collier 25.00 60.00
CAJD Jadyn Donovan 5.00 12.00
CAJE Justin Edwards 12.00 30.00
CAJF Jeremy Fears Jr. 10.00 25.00
CAJM Jared McCain 25.00 60.00
CAJW JA'Kobe Walter 10.00 25.00
CAKA KK Arnold 8.00 20.00
CAKE Kwame Evans 8.00 20.00
CAKJ Kymora Johnson 6.00 15.00
CALR Laila Reynolds 5.00 12.00
CAMB Matas Buzelis 15.00 40.00
CAMC Mookie Cook 8.00 20.00
CAMF Milaysia Fulwiley 15.00 40.00
CAMM Mackenzie Mgbako 8.00 20.00
CAMW Mikaylah Williams 10.00 25.00
CAOB Omaha Biliew 8.00 20.00
CARH Ron Holland II 15.00 40.00
CARN Riley Nelson 5.00 12.00
CARS Reed Sheppard 75.00 200.00
CASB Sofia Bell 6.00 15.00
CASC Stephon Castle 20.00 50.00
CASS Sean Stewart 8.00 20.00
CASW Sahara K Williams 6.00 15.00
CATJ Tessa Johnson 6.00 15.00
CATS Taliah Scott 6.00 15.00
CAXB Xavier Booker 8.00 20.00
CAZB Zoe Brooks 6.00 15.00
CAABR Addy Brown 6.00 15.00
CAASH Ashlynn Shade 6.00 15.00
CAJWA Juju Watkins 150.00 400.00
CAJWI Jada Williams 8.00 20.00
CAMBO Madison Booker 5.00 12.00

2023 Topps Chrome McDonald's All American Future Stars
*GOLD REF/50: 2.5X TO 6X BASIC
*ORANGE REF/25: 4X TO 10X BASIC
FS1 Aaron Bradshaw 2.00 5.00
FS2 Matas Buzelis 2.50 6.00
FS3 Justin Edwards 2.00 5.00
FS4 Mackenzie Mgbako 1.25 3.00
FS5 DJ Wagner 2.50 6.00
FS6 Cody Williams 2.50 6.00
FS7 Xavier Booker 1.25 3.00
FS8 Isaiah Collier 4.00 10.00
FS9 Ron Holland II 2.50 6.00
FS10 Bronny James 8.00 20.00
FS11 Juju Watkins 5.00 12.00
FS12 Mikaylah Williams 1.50 4.00
FS13 KK Arnold 1.25 3.00
FS14 Ashlynn Shade 1.00 2.50
FS15 Taliah Scott 1.00 2.50

2023 Topps Chrome McDonald's All American Image Variations
2 Aaron Bradshaw 6.00 15.00
5 Justin Edwards 6.00 15.00
6 Kwame Evans 4.00 10.00
11 DJ Wagner 8.00 20.00
12 Cody Williams 8.00 20.00
13 Omaha Biliew 4.00 10.00
14 Isaiah Collier 12.00 30.00
15 Mookie Cook 4.00 10.00
17 Jeremy Fears Jr. 5.00 12.00
19 Ron Holland II 8.00 20.00
20 Bronny James 40.00 100.00
21 Jared McCain 12.00 30.00
22 Reed Sheppard 20.00 50.00
23 Andrej Stojakovic 4.00 10.00
24 Ja'Kobe Walter 5.00 12.00
35 Taliah Scott 3.00 8.00
42 Kymora Johnson 3.00 8.00
45 Juju Watkins 15.00 40.00
97 Boys Group Shot 5.00 12.00
98 Girls Group Shot 2.50 6.00

2023 Topps Chrome McDonald's All American New Waves
*GOLD REF/50: 2.5X TO 6X BASIC
*ORANGE BK REF/25: 4X TO 10X BASIC
NW1 Xavier Booker 1.25 3.00
NW2 Aaron Bradshaw 2.00 5.00
NW3 Matas Buzelis 2.50 6.00
NW4 Justin Edwards 2.00 5.00
NW5 Mackenzie Mgbako 1.25 3.00
NW6 Sean Stewart 1.25 3.00
NW7 DJ Wagner 2.50 6.00
NW8 Cody Williams 2.50 6.00
NW9 Omaha Biliew 1.25 3.00
NW10 Isaiah Collier 4.00 10.00
NW11 Ron Holland II 2.50 6.00
NW12 Bronny James 8.00 20.00
NW13 Juju Watkins 5.00 12.00
NW14 Mikaylah Williams 1.50 4.00
NW15 Jadyn Donovan .75 2.00
NW16 Hannah Hidalgo 2.50 6.00
NW17 KK Arnold 1.25 3.00
NW18 Aalyah Del Rosario .75 2.00
NW19 Zoe Brooks 1.00 2.50
NW20 Courtney Ogden .75 2.00

2023 Topps Chrome McDonald's All American SuperFly
*GOLD REF/50: 1.25X TO 3X BASE HI
*ORANGE REF/25: 1.5X TO 4X BASE HI
SF1 Justin Edwards 10.00 25.00
SF2 Aaron Bradshaw 10.00 25.00
SF3 DJ Wagner 12.00 30.00
SF4 Cody Williams 12.00 30.00
SF5 Isaiah Collier 20.00 50.00
SF6 Ron Holland II 12.00 30.00
SF7 Bronny James 40.00 100.00
SF8 Mackenzie Mgbako 6.00 15.00
SF9 Matas Buzelis 12.00 30.00
SF10 Omaha Biliew 6.00 15.00
SF11 Juju Watkins 25.00 60.00
SF12 Mikaylah Williams 8.00 20.00
SF13 KK Arnold 6.00 15.00
SF14 Ashlynn Shade 5.00 12.00
SF15 Taliah Scott 5.00 12.00
SF16 Jadyn Donovan 4.00 10.00
SF17 Hannah Hidalgo 12.00 30.00
SF18 Aalyah Del Rosario 4.00 10.00
SF19 Zoe Brooks 5.00 12.00
SF20 Courtney Ogden 4.00 10.00

2024 Topps Chrome McDonald's All American
*REFRACTORS: .75X TO 2X BASIC
*RAYWAVE REF: .75X TO 2X BASIC
*BLUE RAYWAVE REF: 1.25X TO 3X BASIC
*MCFLURRY REF: 1.25X TO 3X BASIC
*LOGO REF: 1.5X TO 4X BASIC
*AQUA WAVE REF/199: 2X TO 5X BASIC
*PURPLE REF/150: 2.5X TO 6X BASIC
*RED LAVA REF/125: 3X TO 8X BASIC
*PURPLE LAVA REF/99: 3X TO 8X BASIC
*BLUE LAVA REF/75: 4X TO 10X BASIC
1 Mikayla Blakes .60 1.50
2 Kendall Dudley .50 1.25
3 Joyce Edwards .75 2.00
4 Kayleigh Heckel .40 1.00
5 Zam Jones .40 1.00
6 Kate Koval .40 1.00
7 Maddy McDaniel .40 1.00
8 Olivia Olson .60 1.50
9 Zania Socka-Nguemen .40 1.00
10 Sarah Strong 1.00 2.50
11 Syla Swords .75 2.00
12 Berry Wallace .40 1.00
13 Imari Berry .40 1.00
14 Jaloni Cambridge .50 1.25
15 Justice Carlton .40 1.00
16 Morgan Cheli .40 1.00
17 Avery Howell .50 1.25
18 Jordan Lee .40 1.00
19 Liv McGill .40 1.00
20 Me'Arah O'Neal .40 1.00
21 Mackenly Randolph .40 1.00
22 Arianna Roberson .40 1.00
23 Kennedy Smith .40 1.00
24 Allie Ziebell .40 1.00
25 Jalil Bethea .40 1.00
26 J. Bol .40 1.00
27 Isaiah Demonte Evans .50 1.25
28 Cooper Flagg 8.00 20.00
29 Boogie Fland .60 1.50
30 Liam McNeeley .60 1.50
31 Drake Powell .50 1.25
32 Derik Queen 1.00 2.50
33 Bryson Tucker .40 1.00
34 Ace Bailey 1.00 2.50
35 Flory Bidunga .40 1.00
36 Richard Jefferson .30 .75
37 Donavan Freeman .40 1.00
38 Dylan Harper 1.25 3.00
39 Karter Knox .75 2.00
40 Trent Perry .40 1.00
41 Derrion Reid .50 1.25
42 Aiden Sherrell .50 1.25
43 Carmelo Anthony .60 1.50
44 Grant Hill .60 1.50
45 Kevin Durant 1.25 3.00
46 Chris Paul .75 2.00
47 Jrue Holiday .50 1.25
48 Kevin Love .40 1.00
49 Zach Randolph .40 1.00
50 LeBron James 3.00 8.00
51 Mikayla Blakes .60 1.50
52 Kendall Dudley .50 1.25
53 Joyce Edwards .75 2.00
54 Kayleigh Heckel .40 1.00
55 Zam Jones .40 1.00
56 Kate Koval .40 1.00
57 Maddy McDaniel .40 1.00
58 Olivia Olson .60 1.50
59 Zania Socka-Nguemen .40 1.00
60 Sarah Strong 1.00 2.50
61 Syla Swords .75 2.00
62 Berry Wallace .40 1.00
63 Imari Berry .40 1.00
64 Jaloni Cambridge .50 1.25
65 Justice Carlton .40 1.00
66 Morgan Cheli .40 1.00
67 Avery Howell .50 1.25
68 Jordan Lee .40 1.00
69 Liv McGill .40 1.00
70 Me'Arah O'Neal .40 1.00
71 Mackenly Randolph .40 1.00
72 Arianna Roberson .40 1.00
73 Kennedy Smith .40 1.00
74 Allie Ziebell .40 1.00
75 Jalil Bethea .40 1.00
76 J. Bol .40 1.00
77 Isaiah Demonte Evans .50 1.25
78 Cooper Flagg 8.00 20.00
79 Boogie Fland .60 1.50
80 Liam McNeeley .60 1.50
81 Drake Powell .50 1.25
82 Derik Queen 1.00 2.50
83 Bryson Tucker .40 1.00
84 Ace Bailey 1.00 2.50
85 Flory Bidunga .40 1.00
86 Andrew Wiggins .50 1.25
87 Donavan Freeman .40 1.00
88 Dylan Harper 1.25 3.00
89 Karter Knox .75 2.00
90 Trent Perry .40 1.00
91 Derrion Reid .50 1.25
92 Aiden Sherrell .50 1.25
93 Michael Porter Jr. .50 1.25
94 Jaren Jackson Jr. .60 1.50
95 Collin Sexton .40 1.00
96 Malik Monk .40 1.00
97 Bradley Beal .50 1.25
98 Karl-Anthony Towns .60 1.50
99 Jalen Brunson .75 2.00
100 Aaron Gordon .40 1.00

2024 Topps Chrome McDonald's All American Gold RayWave Refractors
*GOLD RAYWAVE REF/50: 6X TO 15X BASIC
STATED PRINT RUN 50 SER.#'d SETS
28 Cooper Flagg 200.00 500.00
78 Cooper Flagg 200.00 500.00

2024 Topps Chrome McDonald's All American Gold Refractors
*GOLD REF: 6X TO 15X BASIC
STATED PRINT RUN 50 SER.#'d SETS
28 Cooper Flagg 200.00 500.00
78 Cooper Flagg 200.00 500.00

2024 Topps Chrome McDonald's All American Tie Dye RayWave Refractors
*TIE DYE RAYWAVE REF: 8X TO 20X BASIC
STATED PRINT RUN 25 SER.#'d SETS
28 Cooper Flagg 300.00 600.00
78 Cooper Flagg 300.00 600.00

2024 Topps Chrome McDonald's All American Tie Dye Refractors
*TIE DYE REF: 8X TO 20X BASIC
STATED PRINT RUN 25 SER.#'d SETS
28 Cooper Flagg 300.00 600.00
78 Cooper Flagg 300.00 600.00

2024 Topps Chrome McDonald's All American Action Shot Autographs
*BLUE RAYWAVE REF: .5X TO 1.25X BASIC
*LOGO REF: .6X TO 1.5X BASIC
*GOLD REF/50: .75X TO 2X BASIC
*TIE DYE REF/25: .75X TO 2X BASIC
1 Mikayla Blakes 12.00 30.00
2 Kendall Dudley 10.00 25.00
3 Joyce Edwards 15.00 40.00
4 Kayleigh Heckel 8.00 20.00
5 Zam Jones 8.00 20.00
6 Kate Koval 8.00 20.00
7 Maddy McDaniel 8.00 20.00
8 Olivia Olson 12.00 30.00
9 Zania Socka-Nguemen 8.00 20.00
10 Sarah Strong 20.00 50.00
11 Syla Swords 15.00 40.00
12 Berry Wallace 8.00 20.00
13 Imari Berry 8.00 20.00
14 Jaloni Cambridge 10.00 25.00
15 Justice Carlton 8.00 20.00
16 Morgan Cheli 8.00 20.00
17 Avery Howell 10.00 25.00
18 Jordan Lee 8.00 20.00
19 Liv McGill 8.00 20.00
20 Me'Arah O'Neal 8.00 20.00
21 Mackenly Randolph 8.00 20.00
22 Arianna Roberson 8.00 20.00
23 Kennedy Smith 8.00 20.00
24 Allie Ziebell 8.00 20.00
25 Jalil Bethea 8.00 20.00
26 J. Bol 8.00 20.00
27 Isaiah Demonte Evans 10.00 25.00
28 Cooper Flagg 500.00 1,000.00
29 Boogie Fland 12.00 30.00
30 Liam McNeeley 12.00 30.00
31 Drake Powell 10.00 25.00
32 Derik Queen 20.00 50.00
33 Bryson Tucker 8.00 20.00
34 Ace Bailey 40.00 100.00
35 Flory Bidunga 8.00 20.00
36 Richard Jefferson 6.00 15.00
37 Donavan Freeman 8.00 20.00
38 Dylan Harper 60.00 150.00
39 Karter Knox 15.00 40.00
40 Trent Perry 8.00 20.00
41 Derrion Reid 10.00 25.00
42 Aiden Sherrell 8.00 20.00
43 Carmelo Anthony 40.00 100.00
44 Grant Hill 12.00 30.00
45 Kevin Durant 75.00 200.00
46 Chris Paul 15.00 40.00
47 Jrue Holiday 10.00 25.00
48 Kevin Love 8.00 20.00
49 Zach Randolph 8.00 20.00
86 Andrew Wiggins 10.00 25.00
93 Michael Porter Jr. 10.00 25.00
94 Jaren Jackson Jr. 12.00 30.00
95 Collin Sexton 8.00 20.00
96 Malik Monk 8.00 20.00
97 Bradley Beal 10.00 25.00
98 Karl-Anthony Towns 12.00 30.00
99 Jalen Brunson 15.00 40.00
100 Aaron Gordon 8.00 20.00

2024 Topps Chrome McDonald's All American Autographs Refractors
*BLUE RAYWAVE REF: .5X TO 1.25X BASIC
*LOGO REF: .6X TO 1.5X BASIC
*GOLD REF/50: .75X TO 2X BASIC
*TIE DYE REF/25: .75X TO 2X BASIC
SMSAIR Ace Bailey 40.00 100.00
SMSALL Allie Ziebell 8.00 20.00
SMSCOO Cooper Flagg 500.00 1,000.00
SMSDER Derik Queen 20.00 50.00
SMSDRA Drake Powell 10.00 25.00
SMSDYL Dylan Harper 60.00 150.00
SMSFLO Flory Bidunga 8.00 20.00
SMSJAB Jalil Bethea 8.00 20.00
SMSJAL Jaloni Cambridge 10.00 25.00
SMSJOH Boogie Fland 12.00 30.00
SMSJOR Jordan Lee 8.00 20.00
SMSJOY Joyce Edwards 15.00 40.00
SMSJUS Justice Carlton 8.00 20.00
SMSKAR Karter Knox 15.00 40.00
SMSKAT Kate Koval 8.00 20.00
SMSKEN Kennedy Smith 8.00 20.00
SMSLIA Liam McNeeley 12.00 30.00
SMSMIK Mikayla Blakes 12.00 30.00
SMSSAR Sarah Strong 20.00 50.00
SMSSYL Syla Swords 15.00 40.00

2024 Topps Chrome McDonald's All American Combo Talents
*BLUE RAYWAVE REF: .75X TO 2X BASIC
*REF: .75X TO 2X BASIC
*GOLD REF/50: 6X TO 15X BASIC
*TIE DYE RAYWAVE REF/25: 8X TO 20X BASIC
*TIE DYE REF/25: 8X TO 20X BASIC
COTAIB Ace Bailey
Joyce Edwards 1.00 2.50
COTAIR Flory Bidunga
Ace Bailey 1.00 2.50
COTALI Liv McGill
Zam Jones .40 1.00
COTAVE Avery Howell
Zania Socka-Nguemen .50 1.25
COTBER Berry Wallace
Mackenly Randolph .40 1.00
COTBRY Derrion Reid
Bryson Tucker .50 1.25
COTCOF Ace Bailey
Cooper Flagg 3.00 8.00
COTCOO Cooper Flagg
Dylan Harper 3.00 8.00
COTCOP Sarah Strong
Cooper Flagg 3.00 8.00
COTDON J. Bol
Trent Perry .40 1.00
COTDYH Dylan Harper
Flory Bidunga 1.25 3.00
COTFRE Donavan Freeman
Dylan Harper 1.25 3.00
COTISE Aiden Sherrell
Isaiah Demonte Evans .50 1.25
COTJAB Drake Powell
Jalil Bethea .50 1.25
COTJAL Jaloni Cambridge
Allie Ziebell .50 1.25
COTJOF Boogie Fland
Liam McNeeley .60 1.50
COTJUS Justice Carlton
Jordan Lee .40 1.00
COTKAK Derik Queen
Karter Knox 1.00 2.50
COTKAT Kate Koval
Kennedy Smith .40 1.00
COTKAY Me'Arah O'Neal
Kayleigh Heckel .40 1.00
COTKEN Olivia Olson
Kendall Dudley .60 1.50
COTMAD Imari Berry
Maddy McDaniel .40 1.00
COTMIK Mikayla Blakes
Syla Swords .75 2.00
COTMOR Morgan Cheli
Arianna Roberson .40 1.00
COTSAR Sarah Strong
Joyce Edwards 1.00 2.50

2024 Topps Chrome McDonald's All American Drive Thru Service
*BLUE RAYWAVE REF: .75X TO 2X BASIC
*REF: .75X TO 2X BASIC
*GOLD REF/50: 6X TO 15X BASIC
*TIE DYE RAYWAVE REF/25: 8X TO 20X BASIC
*TIE DYE REF/25: 8X TO 20X BASIC
DTSAIB Ace Bailey 1.00 2.50
DTSAIS Aiden Sherrell .50 1.25
DTSALM Liv McGill .40 1.00
DTSALZ Allie Ziebell .40 1.00
DTSBRT Bryson Tucker .40 1.00
DTSCOF Cooper Flagg 8.00 20.00
DTSDEQ Derik Queen 1.00 2.50
DTSDER Derrion Reid .50 1.25
DTSDRP Drake Powell .50 1.25
DTSDYH Dylan Harper 1.25 3.00
DTSFLB Flory Bidunga .40 1.00
DTSIMB Imari Berry .40 1.00
DTSISE Isaiah Demonte Evans .50 1.25
DTSJAB Jalil Bethea .40 1.00
DTSJCA Jaloni Cambridge .50 1.25
DTSJOE Joyce Edwards .75 2.00
DTSJOF Boogie Fland .60 1.50
DTSJOL Jordan Lee .40 1.00
DTSJUC Justice Carlton .40 1.00
DTSKAK Kate Koval .40 1.00
DTSKED Kendall Dudley .50 1.25
DTSKES Kennedy Smith .40 1.00
DTSKKN Karter Knox .75 2.00
DTSLIM Liam McNeeley .60 1.50
DTSMAM Maddy McDaniel .40 1.00
DTSMIB Mikayla Blakes .60 1.50
DTSOLO Olivia Olson .60 1.50
DTSSST Sarah Strong 1.00 2.50
DTSSYS Syla Swords .75 2.00
DTSVAD Donavan Freeman .40 1.00

2024 Topps Chrome McDonald's All American Franchise Picks
*BLUE RAYWAVE REF: .75X TO 2X BASIC
*REF: .75X TO 2X BASIC
*GOLD REF/50: 6X TO 15X BASIC
*TIE DYE RAYWAVE REF/25: 8X TO 20X BASIC
*TIE DYE REF/25: 8X TO 20X BASIC
REAAGO Aaron Gordon .40 1.00
REAAWI Andrew Wiggins .50 1.25
REABRA Bradley Beal .50 1.25
REACAR Carmelo Anthony .60 1.50
REACPA Chris Paul .75 2.00
REAGRA Grant Hill .60 1.50
REAHOL Jrue Holiday .50 1.25
REAKCP Kentavious Caldwell-Pope .25 .60
REAKDT Kevin Durant 1.25 3.00
REAKLV Kevin Love .40 1.00
REALEB LeBron James 3.00 8.00
REAMCO Mike Conley .30 .75
REAMSM Marcus Smart .40 1.00
REARJE Richard Jefferson .30 .75
REAZAC Zach Randolph .40 1.00

2024 Topps Chrome McDonald's All American Golden Patch Autographs Tie Dye
STATED PRINT RUN 25 SER.#'d SETS
GPAAB Ace Bailey 100.00 250.00
GPAAH Avery Howell 50.00 125.00
GPAAR Arianna Roberson 40.00 100.00
GPAAS Aiden Sherrell 50.00 125.00
GPAAZ Allie Ziebell 40.00 100.00
GPABF Boogie Fland 60.00 150.00
GPABJ Bronny James 150.00 400.00
GPABM Brandon Miller 200.00 500.00
GPABT Bryson Tucker 40.00 100.00
GPABW Berry Wallace 40.00 100.00
GPACF Cooper Flagg 2,500.00 5,000.00
GPADF Donavan Freeman 40.00 100.00
GPADH Dylan Harper 125.00 300.00
GPADP Drake Powell 50.00 125.00
GPADQ Derik Queen 100.00 250.00
GPADR Derrion Reid 50.00 125.00
GPADW DJ Wagner 50.00 125.00
GPAFB Flory Bidunga 50.00 125.00
GPAGD Gradey Dick 80.00 200.00
GPAIB Imari Berry 40.00 100.00
GPAIC Isaiah Collier 50.00 125.00
GPAIE Isaiah Demonte Evans 50.00 125.00
GPAJB Jalil Bethea 40.00 100.00
GPAJC Jaloni Cambridge 50.00 125.00
GPAJE Joyce Edwards 80.00 200.00
GPAJL Jordan Lee 40.00 100.00
GPAKD Kendall Dudley 50.00 125.00
GPAKH Kayleigh Heckel 40.00 100.00
GPAKK Kate Koval 40.00 100.00
GPAKS Kennedy Smith 40.00 100.00
GPALM Liv McGill 40.00 100.00
GPAMB Mikayla Blakes 60.00 150.00
GPAMC Morgan Cheli 40.00 100.00
GPAMM Maddy McDaniel 40.00 100.00
GPAMO Me'Arah O'Neal 40.00 100.00
GPAMR Mackenly Randolph 40.00 100.00
GPAOO Olivia Olson 60.00 150.00
GPARH Ron Holland 60.00 150.00
GPASC Stephon Castle 150.00 400.00
GPASS Sarah Strong 100.00 250.00
GPATP Trent Perry 40.00 100.00
GPAZJ Zam Jones 40.00 100.00
GPAZS Zania Socka-Nguemen 40.00 100.00
GPAABL Anthony Black 100.00 250.00
GPAJBO J. Bol 40.00 100.00
GPAJCA Justice Carlton 40.00 100.00
GPAKKN Karter Knox 80.00 200.00
GPALMC Liam McNeeley 60.00 150.00
GPAMMI Mark Mitchell 40.00 100.00
GPASSW Syla Swords 80.00 200.00

2024 Topps Chrome McDonald's All American Half Court Offense Signatures

*BLUE RAYWAVE REF: .5X TO 1.25X BASIC
*LOGO REF: .6X TO 1.5X BASIC
*GOLD REF/50: .75X TO 2X BASIC
*TIE DYE REF/25: .75X TO 2X BASIC
IMLAID Aiden Sherrell 10.00 25.00
IMLAIR Ace Bailey 40.00 100.00
IMLALI Liv McGill 8.00 20.00
IMLALL Allie Ziebell 8.00 20.00
IMLARI Arianna Roberson 8.00 20.00
IMLAVE Avery Howell 10.00 25.00
IMLBER Berry Wallace 8.00 20.00
IMLBRY Bryson Tucker 8.00 20.00
IMLCOO Cooper Flagg 500.00 1,000.00
IMLDER Derik Queen 20.00 50.00
IMLDON Donavan Freeman 8.00 20.00
IMLDRA Drake Powell 10.00 25.00
IMLDRR Derrion Reid 10.00 25.00
IMLDYL Dylan Harper 60.00 150.00
IMLFLO Flory Bidunga 8.00 20.00
IMLIMA Imari Berry 8.00 20.00
IMLISA Isaiah Demonte Evans 10.00 25.00
IMLJAB Jalil Bethea 8.00 20.00
IMLJAL Jaloni Cambridge 10.00 25.00
IMLJOH Boogie Fland 12.00 30.00
IMLJOR Jordan Lee 8.00 20.00
IMLJOY Joyce Edwards 15.00 40.00
IMLJUS Justice Carlton 8.00 20.00
IMLKAR Karter Knox 15.00 40.00
IMLKAT Kate Koval 8.00 20.00
IMLKEN Kendall Dudley 10.00 25.00
IMLKES Kennedy Smith 8.00 20.00
IMLLIA Liam McNeeley 12.00 30.00
IMLMAC Mackenly Randolph 8.00 20.00
IMLMAD Maddy McDaniel 8.00 20.00
IMLMEA Me'Arah O'Neal 8.00 20.00
IMLMIK Mikayla Blakes 12.00 30.00
IMLMOR Morgan Cheli 8.00 20.00
IMLOOL Olivia Olson 12.00 30.00
IMLSAR Sarah Strong 20.00 50.00
IMLSYL Syla Swords 15.00 40.00
IMLTRE Trent Perry 8.00 20.00
IMLZAM Zam Jones 8.00 20.00
IMLZAN Zania Socka-Nguemen 8.00 20.00

2024 Topps Chrome McDonald's All American Head Shot Autographs

*BLUE RAYWAVE REF: .5X TO 1.25X BASIC
*LOGO REF: .6X TO 1.5X BASIC
*GOLD REF/50: .75X TO 2X BASIC
*TIE DYE REF/25: .75X TO 2X BASIC
51 Mikayla Blakes 12.00 30.00
52 Kendall Dudley 10.00 25.00
53 Joyce Edwards 15.00 40.00
54 Kayleigh Heckel 8.00 20.00
55 Zam Jones 8.00 20.00
56 Kate Koval 8.00 20.00
57 Maddy McDaniel 8.00 20.00
58 Olivia Olson 12.00 30.00
59 Zania Socka-Nguemen 8.00 20.00
60 Sarah Strong 20.00 50.00
61 Syla Swords 15.00 40.00
62 Berry Wallace 8.00 20.00
63 Imari Berry 8.00 20.00
64 Jaloni Cambridge 10.00 25.00
65 Justice Carlton 8.00 20.00
66 Morgan Cheli 8.00 20.00
67 Avery Howell 10.00 25.00
68 Jordan Lee 8.00 20.00
69 Liv McGill 8.00 20.00
70 Me'Arah O'Neal 8.00 20.00
71 Mackenly Randolph 8.00 20.00
72 Arianna Roberson 8.00 20.00
73 Kennedy Smith 8.00 20.00
74 Allie Ziebell 8.00 20.00
75 Jalil Bethea 8.00 20.00
76 J. Bol 8.00 20.00
77 Isaiah Demonte Evans 10.00 25.00
78 Cooper Flagg 500.00 1,000.00
79 Boogie Fland 12.00 30.00
80 Liam McNeeley 12.00 30.00
81 Drake Powell 10.00 25.00
82 Derik Queen 20.00 50.00
83 Bryson Tucker 8.00 20.00
84 Ace Bailey 40.00 100.00
85 Flory Bidunga 8.00 20.00
87 Donavan Freeman 8.00 20.00
88 Dylan Harper 60.00 150.00
89 Karter Knox 15.00 40.00
90 Trent Perry 8.00 20.00
91 Derrion Reid 10.00 25.00
92 Aiden Sherrell 10.00 25.00

2024 Topps Chrome McDonald's All American Major Star

*BLUE RAYWAVE REF: .75X TO 2X BASIC
*REF: .75X TO 2X BASIC
SESAIB Ace Bailey 1.00 2.50
SESALZ Allie Ziebell .40 1.00
SESARR Arianna Roberson .40 1.00
SESAVH Avery Howell .50 1.25
SESBEW Berry Wallace .40 1.00
SESCOF Cooper Flagg 8.00 20.00
SESDEQ Derik Queen 1.00 2.50
SESDFR Donavan Freeman .40 1.00
SESDRP Drake Powell .50 1.25
SESDYH Dylan Harper 1.25 3.00
SESFLB Flory Bidunga .40 1.00
SESJAB Jalil Bethea .40 1.00
SESJAC Jaloni Cambridge .50 1.25
SESJOB J. Bol .40 1.00
SESJOE Joyce Edwards .75 2.00
SESJOF Boogie Fland .60 1.50
SESJOL Jordan Lee .40 1.00
SESJUC Justice Carlton .40 1.00
SESKAH Kayleigh Heckel .40 1.00
SESKAK Kate Koval .40 1.00
SESKES Kennedy Smith .40 1.00
SESKKN Karter Knox .75 2.00
SESLIM Liam McNeeley .60 1.50
SESMAR Mackenly Randolph .40 1.00
SESMEO Me'Arah O'Neal .40 1.00
SESMOC Morgan Cheli .40 1.00
SESSAS Sarah Strong 1.00 2.50
SESTRP Trent Perry .40 1.00
SESZAJ Zam Jones .40 1.00
SESZAS Zania Socka-Nguemen .40 1.00

2024 Topps Chrome McDonald's All American Major Star Gold Refractors

*GOLD REF: 6X TO 15X BASIC
STATED PRINT RUN 50 SER.#'d SETS
SESCOF Cooper Flagg 200.00 500.00

2024 Topps Chrome McDonald's All American Major Star Tie Dye RayWave Refractors

*TIE DYE RAYWAVE REF: 8X TO 20X BASIC
STATED PRINT RUN 25 SER.#'d SETS
SESCOF Cooper Flagg 300.00 600.00

2024 Topps Chrome McDonald's All American Major Star Tie Dye Refractors

*TIE DYE REF: 8X TO 20X BASIC
STATED PRINT RUN 25 SER.#'d SETS
SESCOF Cooper Flagg 300.00 600.00

2024 Topps Chrome McDonald's All American New Hire Badge Autographs Refractors

*BLUE RAYWAVE REF: .5X TO 1.25X BASIC
*LOGO REF: .6X TO 1.5X BASIC
*GOLD REF/50: .75X TO 2X BASIC
*TIE DYE REF/25: .75X TO 2X BASIC
NHBIM Imari Berry 8.00 20.00
NHBAID Aiden Sherrell 10.00 25.00
NHBAIR Ace Bailey 40.00 100.00
NHBALI Liv McGill 8.00 20.00
NHBALL Allie Ziebell 8.00 20.00
NHBARI Arianna Roberson 8.00 20.00
NHBAVE Avery Howell 10.00 25.00
NHBBER Berry Wallace 8.00 20.00
NHBBRY Bryson Tucker 8.00 20.00
NHBCOO Cooper Flagg 500.00 1,000.00
NHBDER Derik Queen 20.00 50.00
NHBDON Donavan Freeman 8.00 20.00
NHBDRA Drake Powell 10.00 25.00
NHBDRE Derrion Reid 10.00 25.00
NHBDYL Dylan Harper 60.00 150.00
NHBFLO Flory Bidunga 8.00 20.00
NHBISA Isaiah Demonte Evans 10.00 25.00
NHBJAB Jalil Bethea 8.00 20.00
NHBJAL Jaloni Cambridge 10.00 25.00
NHBJOF Boogie Fland 12.00 30.00
NHBJOH J. Bol 8.00 20.00
NHBJOR Jordan Lee 8.00 20.00
NHBJOY Joyce Edwards 15.00 40.00
NHBJUS Justice Carlton 8.00 20.00
NHBKAR Karter Knox 15.00 40.00
NHBKAT Kate Koval 8.00 20.00
NHBKAY Kayleigh Heckel 8.00 20.00
NHBKEN Kendall Dudley 10.00 25.00
NHBKES Kennedy Smith 8.00 20.00
NHBLIA Liam McNeeley 12.00 30.00
NHBMAC Mackenly Randolph 8.00 20.00
NHBMAD Maddy McDaniel 8.00 20.00
NHBMIK Mikayla Blakes 12.00 30.00
NHBMOR Morgan Cheli 8.00 20.00
NHBOLI Olivia Olson 12.00 30.00
NHBSAR Sarah Strong 20.00 50.00
NHBSYL Syla Swords 15.00 40.00
NHBZAM Zam Jones 8.00 20.00
NHBZAN Zania Socka-Nguemen 8.00 20.00

2023-24 Topps Chrome NBL

*REFRACTOR: 1X TO 2.5X BASIC
*AQUA REF/199: 2.5X TO 6X BASIC
*GOLDEN WADDLE REF/149: 2.5X TO 6X BASIC
*GREEN REF/99: 3X TO 8X BASIC
*BLUE REF/75: 4X TO 10X BASIC
*GOLD REF/50: 5X TO 12X BASIC
*ORANGE REF/25: 6X TO 15X BASIC
1 Alex Starling .30 .75
2 Trentyn Flowers RC .60 1.50
3 Isaac Humphries .30 .75
4 Jacob Wiley .30 .75
5 Trey Kell III .30 .75
6 Kyrin Galloway .30 .75
7 Mitch McCarron .30 .75
8 DJ Vasiljevic .30 .75
9 Sunday Dech .30 .75
10 Jason Cadee .30 .75
11 Aron Baynes .30 .75
12 DJ Mitchell .30 .75
13 Isaac White .30 .75
14 Josh Bannan .30 .75
15 Mitch Norton .30 .75
16 Nathan Sobey .30 .75
17 Rocco Zikarsky RC 1.00 2.50
18 Sam McDaniel .30 .75
19 Shannon Scott .30 .75
20 Tyrell Harrison .30 .75
21 Josh Roberts .30 .75
22 Bobi Klintman RC .75 2.00
23 Bul Kuol .30 .75
24 Jonah Antonio .30 .75
25 Lat Mayen .30 .75
26 Patrick Miller .30 .75
27 Sam Mennenga RC .60 1.50
28 Sam Waardenburg .30 .75
29 Tahjere McCall .30 .75
30 Taran Armstrong RC .60 1.50
31 AJ Johnson RC 1.00 2.50
32 Dan Grida .30 .75
33 Gary Clark .30 .75
34 Justin Robinson .30 .75
35 Mason Peatling .30 .75
36 Sam Froling .30 .75
37 Todd Blanchfield .30 .75
38 Tyler Harvey .30 .75
39 Wani Swaka Lo Buluk .30 .75
40 Lachlan Olbrich RC .60 1.50
41 Ian Clark .30 .75
42 Ariel Hukporti .30 .75
43 Brad Newley .30 .75
44 Chris Goulding .30 .75
45 Flynn Cameron RC .60 1.50
46 Jo Lual Acuil .30 .75
47 Tanner Krebs .30 .75
48 Luke Travers .30 .75
49 Matthew Dellavedova .30 .75
50 Shea Ili .30 .75
51 Zylan Cheatham .30 .75
52 Finn Delany .30 .75
53 Cameron Gliddon .30 .75
54 Parker Jackson-Cartwright .30 .75
55 Justinian Jessup .30 .75
56 Izayah Le'Afa .30 .75
57 Mangok Mathiang .30 .75
58 Mantas Rubstavicius RC .60 1.50
59 Tom Abercrombie .30 .75
60 Will McDowell-White .30 .75
61 Alexandre Sarr RC 1.50 4.00
62 Ben Henshall .30 .75
63 Bryce Cotton .30 .75
64 Corey Webster .30 .75
65 Kristian Doolittle .30 .75
66 Hyrum Harris .30 .75
67 Jesse Wagstaff .30 .75
68 Keanu Pinder .30 .75
69 Jordan Usher .30 .75
70 Tai Webster .30 .75
71 Craig Moller .30 .75
72 Rhys Vague .30 .75
73 Alan Williams .30 .75
74 Ben Ayre .30 .75
75 Gorjok Gak .30 .75
76 Matt Kenyon .30 .75
77 Mitch Creek .30 .75
78 Owen Foxwell .30 .75
79 Reuben Te Rangi .30 .75
80 Gary Browne .30 .75
81 Jordan Hunter .30 .75
82 Alex Toohey RC .75 2.00
83 Angus Glover .30 .75
84 DJ Hogg .30 .75
85 Jaylin Galloway .30 .75
86 Jonah Bolden .30 .75
87 Denzel Valentine .30 .75
88 Kouat Noi .30 .75
89 Jaylen Adams .30 .75
90 Shaun Bruce .30 .75
91 Anthony Drmic .30 .75
92 Clint Steindl .30 .75
93 Fabijan Krslovic .30 .75
94 Jack McVeigh .30 .75
95 Majok Deng .30 .75
96 Jordon Crawford .30 .75
97 Junior Madut .30 .75
98 Marcus Lee .30 .75
99 Milton Doyle .30 .75
100 Will Magnay .30 .75

2023-24 Topps Chrome NBL '71 Topps

*REFRACTOR: 1X TO 2.5X BASIC
*GOLD REF/50: 5X TO 12X BASIC
*ORNG REF/25: 6X TO 15X BASIC
TB1 Tyler Harvey .50 1.25
TB2 Jacob Wiley .50 1.25
TB3 Mitch Creek .50 1.25
TB4 Aron Baynes .50 1.25
TB5 Matthew Dellavedova .50 1.25
TB6 Denzel Valentine .50 1.25
TB7 Nathan Sobey .50 1.25
TB8 Milton Doyle .50 1.25
TB9 Isaac Humphries .50 1.25
TB10 Gary Clark .50 1.25
TB11 Jo Lual Acuil .50 1.25
TB12 Tahjere McCall .50 1.25
TB13 Tom Abercrombie .50 1.25
TB14 Kristian Doolittle .50 1.25
TB15 Bobi Klintman .75 2.00
TB16 AJ Johnson 1.00 2.50
TB17 Jordan Usher .50 1.25
TB18 Alan Williams .50 1.25
TB19 Alexandre Sarr 1.50 4.00
TB20 Alex Toohey .75 2.00
TB21 Will McDowell-White .50 1.25
TB22 Jaylin Galloway .50 1.25
TB23 Jack McVeigh .50 1.25
TB24 Chris Goulding .50 1.25
TB25 Trentyn Flowers .60 1.50

2023-24 Topps Chrome NBL All-NBL Refractors

NBL1 Tyler Harvey 12.00 30.00
NBL2 Bryce Cotton 12.00 30.00
NBL3 Mitch Creek 12.00 30.00
NBL4 Aron Baynes 12.00 30.00
NBL5 Matthew Dellavedova 12.00 30.00
NBL6 Parker Jackson-Cartwright 12.00 30.00
NBL7 Jaylen Adams 12.00 30.00
NBL8 Milton Doyle 12.00 30.00
NBL9 DJ Hogg 12.00 30.00
NBL10 Tahjere McCall 12.00 30.00

2023-24 Topps Chrome NBL All-Time Greats Autographs

ATGAG Al Green 25.00 60.00
ATGBB Bruce Bolden 25.00 60.00
ATGBM Brett Maher 25.00 60.00
ATGCA Chris Anstey 25.00 60.00
ATGCB CJ Bruton 25.00 60.00
ATGCW Corey Williams 25.00 60.00
ATGDM Damian Martin 25.00 60.00
ATGDS Dave Simmons 25.00 60.00
ATGJR John Rillie 25.00 60.00
ATGJS Jason Smith 25.00 60.00
ATGKP Kirk Penney 25.00 60.00
ATGLC Lanard Copeland 25.00 60.00
ATGRB Ray Borner 25.00 60.00
ATGSM Sam Mackinnon 25.00 60.00

2023-24 Topps Chrome NBL Big City Ballers

*REFRACTOR: 1X TO 2.5X BASIC
*GOLD REF/50: 5X TO 12X BASIC
*ORNG REF/25: 6X TO 15X BASIC
BCB1 Mitch McCarron .50 1.25
BCB2 Jason Cadee .50 1.25
BCB3 Aron Baynes .50 1.25
BCB4 Chris Smith .50 1.25
BCB5 Rocco Zikarsky 1.00 2.50
BCB6 Patrick Miller .50 1.25
BCB7 Sam Waardenburg .50 1.25
BCB8 Justin Robinson .50 1.25
BCB9 Ian Clark .50 1.25
BCB10 Tyler Harvey .50 1.25
BCB11 Shea Ili .50 1.25
BCB12 Matthew Dellavedova .50 1.25
BCB13 Zylan Cheatham .50 1.25
BCB14 Finn Delany .50 1.25
BCB15 Will McDowell-White .50 1.25
BCB16 Alexandre Sarr 1.50 4.00
BCB17 Bryce Cotton .50 1.25
BCB18 Jordan Usher .50 1.25
BCB19 Alan Williams .50 1.25
BCB20 Mitch Creek .50 1.25
BCB21 Jaylen Adams .50 1.25
BCB22 DJ Hogg .50 1.25
BCB23 Marcus Lee .50 1.25
BCB24 Milton Doyle .50 1.25
BCB25 Jonah Bolden .50 1.25

2023-24 Topps Chrome NBL Coast to Coast

*REFRACTOR: 1X TO 2.5X BASIC
*GOLD REF/50: 5X TO 12X BASIC
*ORNG REF/25: 6X TO 15X BASIC
CC1 Mitch McCarron .50 1.25
CC2 Jacob Wiley .50 1.25
CC3 Bobi Klintman .75 2.00
CC4 Alex Toohey .75 2.00
CC5 DJ Mitchell .50 1.25
CC6 Ariel Hukporti .50 1.25
CC7 Alexandre Sarr 1.50 4.00
CC8 Shannon Scott .50 1.25
CC9 Nathan Sobey .50 1.25
CC10 Luke Travers .50 1.25
CC11 Taran Armstrong .60 1.50
CC12 Josh Roberts .50 1.25
CC13 Gary Clark .50 1.25
CC14 Hyunjung Lee .60 1.50
CC15 Justin Robinson .50 1.25
CC16 Ian Clark .50 1.25
CC17 Zylan Cheatham .50 1.25
CC18 Parker Jackson-Cartwright .50 1.25
CC19 Jordan Usher .50 1.25
CC20 Will McDowell-White .50 1.25
CC21 Bryce Cotton .50 1.25
CC22 Gary Browne .50 1.25
CC23 Mitch Creek .50 1.25
CC24 Ben Ayre .50 1.25
CC25 Jaylen Adams .50 1.25
CC26 Jaylin Galloway .50 1.25
CC27 Jordan Crawford .50 1.25
CC28 Trentyn Flowers .60 1.50
CC29 Milton Doyle .50 1.25
CC30 Anthony Drmic .50 1.25

2023-24 Topps Chrome NBL Highly Venomous

*REFRACTOR: 1X TO 2.5X BASIC
*GOLD REF/50: 5X TO 12X BASIC
*ORNG REF/25: 6X TO 15X BASIC
HV1 Trey Kell III .50 1.25
HV2 Jacob Wiley .50 1.25
HV3 Chris Smith .50 1.25
HV4 Nathan Sobey .50 1.25
HV5 Tahjere McCall .50 1.25
HV6 Patrick Miller .50 1.25
HV7 Justin Robinson .50 1.25
HV8 Jo Lual Acuil .50 1.25
HV9 Mitch Creek .50 1.25
HV10 Milton Doyle .50 1.25
HV11 Tyler Harvey .50 1.25
HV12 Zylan Cheatham .50 1.25
HV13 Parker Jackson-Cartwright .50 1.25
HV14 Bryce Cotton .50 1.25
HV15 Jordan Usher .50 1.25
HV16 Gary Browne .50 1.25
HV17 Matthew Dellavedova .50 1.25
HV18 Jaylen Adams .50 1.25
HV19 DJ Hogg .50 1.25
HV20 Jordon Crawford .50 1.25

2023-24 Topps Chrome NBL NBL Autographs

AAB Aron Baynes 12.00 30.00
AAH Ariel Hukporti 12.00 30.00
AAS Alexandre Sarr 40.00 100.00
AAT Alex Toohey 20.00 50.00
AAW Alan Williams 12.00 30.00
ABC Bryce Cotton 12.00 30.00
ABK Bobi Klintman 20.00 50.00
ACG Chris Goulding 12.00 30.00
ADZ Denzel Valentine 12.00 30.00
AGB Gary Browne 12.00 30.00
AIC Ian Clark 12.00 30.00
AJA Jaylen Adams 12.00 30.00
AJB Jonah Bolden 12.00 30.00
AJC Jordon Crawford 12.00 30.00
AJM Jack McVeigh 12.00 30.00
AKP Keanu Pinder 12.00 30.00
ALT Luke Travers 12.00 30.00
AMC Mitch Creek 12.00 30.00
AMM Mitch McCarron 12.00 30.00
AMR Mantas Rubstavicius 15.00 40.00
ANS Nathan Sobey 12.00 30.00
ARZ Rocco Zikarsky 25.00 60.00
ASF Sam Froling 12.00 30.00
ATF Trentyn Flowers 15.00 40.00
ATH Tyler Harvey 12.00 30.00
AZC Zylan Cheatham 12.00 30.00
AAJJ AJ Johnson 25.00 60.00
AJWI Jacob Wiley 12.00 30.00
AMDO Milton Doyle 12.00 30.00
ATAR Taran Armstrong 15.00 40.00
AWMW Will McDowell-White 12.00 30.00

2023-24 Topps Chrome NBL NBL Logo Refractor

LR1 NBL Logo 75.00 200.00

2023-24 Topps Chrome NBL Next Stars

NS1 Rocco Zikarsky 20.00 50.00
NS2 Bobi Klintman 15.00 40.00
NS3 AJ Johnson 20.00 50.00
NS4 Ariel Hukporti 10.00 25.00
NS5 Mantas Rubstavicius 12.00 30.00
NS6 Alexandre Sarr 30.00 80.00
NS7 Alex Toohey 15.00 40.00
NS8 Trentyn Flowers 12.00 30.00

2023-24 Topps Chrome NBL Relics

NRR1 Trentyn Flowers 8.00 20.00
NRR2 Trey Kell III 6.00 15.00
NRR3 Aron Baynes 6.00 15.00
NRR4 Bryce Cotton 6.00 15.00
NRR5 Rocco Zikarsky 12.00 30.00
NRR6 Bobi Klintman 10.00 25.00
NRR7 Sam Waardenburg 6.00 15.00
NRR8 Tahjere McCall 6.00 15.00
NRR9 AJ Johnson 12.00 30.00
NRR10 Taran Armstrong 8.00 20.00
NRR11 Ariel Hukporti 6.00 15.00
NRR12 Chris Goulding 6.00 15.00
NRR13 Luke Travers 6.00 15.00
NRR14 Finn Delany 6.00 15.00
NRR15 Mantas Rubstavicius 8.00 20.00
NRR16 Justin Robinson 6.00 15.00
NRR17 Parker Jackson-Cartwright 6.00 15.00
NRR18 Alexandre Sarr 20.00 50.00
NRR19 Bryce Cotton 6.00 15.00
NRR20 Keanu Pinder 6.00 15.00
NRR21 Alan Williams 6.00 15.00
NRR22 Mitch Creek 6.00 15.00
NRR23 Anthony Lamb 6.00 15.00
NRR24 Gary Browne 6.00 15.00
NRR25 Alex Toohey 10.00 25.00
NRR26 DJ Hogg 6.00 15.00
NRR27 Jordan Usher 6.00 15.00
NRR28 Ben Ayre 6.00 15.00
NRR29 Milton Doyle 6.00 15.00
NRR30 Mitch McCarron 6.00 15.00
NRR31 Gary Clark 6.00 15.00
NRR32 Jaylen Adams 6.00 15.00
NRR33 Denzel Valentine 6.00 15.00
NRR34 Jordon Crawford 6.00 15.00
NRR35 Marcus Lee 6.00 15.00
NRR36 Ian Clark 6.00 15.00

2021-22 Topps Chrome Overtime Elite

COMMON CARD .25 .60
SEMISTARS .30 .75
UNLISTED STARS .40 1.00
*REFRACTORS: 1X TO 2.5X BASIC
*OTE REF: 1.2X TO 3X BASIC
*PRPL REF/299: 1.2X TO 3X BASIC
*PRPL & PINK OTE REF/299: 1.5X TO 4X BASIC
*AQUA REF/199: 1.5X TO 4X BASIC
*BLUE REF/99: 2.5X TO 6X BASIC
*BLUE WAVE REF/99: 2.5X TO 6X BASIC
*GREEN RAYWAVE REF/75: 3X TO 8X BASIC
1 Ryan Bewley .50 1.25
2 Malik Bowman .50 1.25
3 De'Vontes Cobbs .50 1.25
4 Nathan Missia-Dio .50 1.25
5 Bryce Griggs .50 1.25
6 Ryan Bewley .50 1.25
7 Jazian Gortman .50 1.25
8 Emmanuel Maldonado .50 1.25
9 Emmanuel Maldonado .50 1.25
10 Jazian Gortman .50 1.25
11 Tyler Smith .50 1.25
12 Amen Thompson 2.50 6.00
13 Alexandre Sarr 1.50 4.00
14 Malik Bowman .50 1.25
15 Matt Bewley .50 1.25
16 Nathan Missia-Dio .50 1.25
17 De'Vontes Cobbs .50 1.25
18 Dominick Barlow .50 1.25
19 Izan Almansa .50 1.25
20 Malik Bowman .50 1.25
21 Lewis Duarte .50 1.25
22 Ausar Thompson 2.00 5.00
23 TJ Clark .50 1.25
24 Dominick Barlow .50 1.25
25 Jahzare Jackson 1.00 2.50
26 De'Vontes Cobbs .50 1.25
27 Malik Bowman .50 1.25
28 Lewis Duarte .50 1.25
29 Davion Mace .50 1.25
30 Amen Thompson 2.50 6.00
31 Tudor Somacescu .50 1.25
32 Kok Yat .50 1.25
33 Alexandre Sarr 1.50 4.00
34 Ausar Thompson 2.00 5.00
35 Davion Mace .50 1.25
36 Matt Bewley .50 1.25
37 Davion Mace .50 1.25
38 Emmanuel Maldonado .50 1.25
39 Tyler Smith .50 1.25
40 Ausar Thompson 2.00 5.00
41 TJ Clark .50 1.25
42 Nathan Missia-Dio .50 1.25
43 Jaylen Martin .50 1.25
44 Alexandre Sarr 1.50 4.00
45 Bryce Griggs .50 1.25
46 Bryce Griggs .50 1.25
47 Dominick Barlow .50 1.25
48 Jean Montero .60 1.50
49 Emmanuel Maldonado .50 1.25
50 Bryson Warren .50 1.25
51 Bryce Griggs .50 1.25
52 Jai Smith .50 1.25
53 Jalen Lewis .60 1.50
54 Tyler Smith .50 1.25
55 Matt Bewley .50 1.25
56 Jaylen Martin .50 1.25
57 Jalen Lewis .60 1.50
58 Bryson Warren .50 1.25
59 Jai Smith .50 1.25
60 Tudor Somacescu .50 1.25
61 Jalen Lewis .60 1.50
62 De'Vontes Cobbs .50 1.25
63 Kok Yat .50 1.25
64 Jazian Gortman .50 1.25
65 Ryan Bewley .50 1.25
66 TJ Clark .50 1.25
67 Jai Smith .50 1.25
68 Ausar Thompson 2.00 5.00
69 Jazian Gortman .50 1.25
70 Jalen Lewis .60 1.50
71 Tyler Smith .50 1.25
72 Jean Montero .60 1.50
73 Jaylen Martin .50 1.25
74 Johned Walker .50 1.25
75 Bryson Warren .50 1.25
76 Izan Almansa .50 1.25
77 Matt Bewley .50 1.25
78 Lewis Duarte .50 1.25
79 Jean Montero .60 1.50
80 Johned Walker .50 1.25
81 Amen Thompson 2.50 6.00
82 Izan Almansa .50 1.25
83 Jean Montero .60 1.50
84 Tudor Somacescu .50 1.25
85 TJ Clark .50 1.25
86 Jahzare Jackson 1.00 2.50
87 Bryson Warren .50 1.25
88 Izan Almansa .50 1.25
89 Jahzare Jackson 1.00 2.50
90 Ryan Bewley .50 1.25
91 Nathan Missia-Dio .50 1.25
92 Alexandre Sarr 1.50 4.00
93 Jaylen Martin .50 1.25
94 Amen Thompson 2.50 6.00
95 Dominick Barlow .50 1.25
96 Jai Smith .50 1.25
97 Lewis Duarte .50 1.25
98 Johned Walker .50 1.25
99 Davion Mace .50 1.25
100 Johned Walker .50 1.25

2021-22 Topps Chrome Overtime Elite Gold Refractors

*GOLD REF/50: 4X TO 10X BASIC
12 Amen Thompson 60.00 150.00
30 Amen Thompson 60.00 150.00
53 Jalen Lewis 30.00 80.00
57 Jalen Lewis 30.00 80.00
61 Jalen Lewis 30.00 80.00
70 Jalen Lewis 30.00 80.00
81 Amen Thompson 60.00 150.00
94 Amen Thompson 60.00 150.00

2021-22 Topps Chrome Overtime Elite Orange Basketball Refractors

*ORANGE BK REF/25: 5X TO 12X BASIC
12 Amen Thompson 75.00 200.00
30 Amen Thompson 75.00 200.00
53 Jalen Lewis 40.00 100.00
57 Jalen Lewis 40.00 100.00
61 Jalen Lewis 40.00 100.00
70 Jalen Lewis 40.00 100.00
81 Amen Thompson 75.00 200.00
94 Amen Thompson 75.00 200.00

2021-22 Topps Chrome Overtime Elite Orange Refractors

*ORANGE REF/25: 5X TO 12X BASIC
12 Amen Thompson 75.00 200.00
30 Amen Thompson 75.00 200.00
53 Jalen Lewis 40.00 100.00
57 Jalen Lewis 40.00 100.00
61 Jalen Lewis 40.00 100.00
70 Jalen Lewis 40.00 100.00
81 Amen Thompson 75.00 200.00
94 Amen Thompson 75.00 200.00

2021-22 Topps Chrome Overtime Elite '69 Topps

COMMON CARD .30 .75
SEMISTARS .40 1.00
UNLISTED STARS .50 1.25
*BLUE & PRPL REF/50: 4X TO 10X BASE HI
*ORANGE BK REF/25: 5X TO 12X BASE HI
69TB1 Izan Almansa .60 1.50
69TB2 Dominick Barlow .60 1.50
69TB3 Matt Bewley .60 1.50
69TB4 Ryan Bewley .60 1.50
69TB5 Malik Bowman .60 1.50
69TB6 TJ Clark .60 1.50
69TB7 De'Vontes Cobbs .60 1.50
69TB8 Jazian Gortman .60 1.50
69TB9 Bryce Griggs .60 1.50
69TB10 Jahzare Jackson 1.25 3.00
69TB11 Jalen Lewis 3.00 8.00
69TB12 Davion Mace .60 1.50
69TB13 Emmanuel Maldonado .60 1.50
69TB14 Jaylen Martin .60 1.50
69TB15 Nathan Missia-Dio .60 1.50
69TB16 Jean Montero .75 2.00
69TB17 Alexandre Sarr 2.00 5.00
69TB18 Jai Smith .60 1.50
69TB19 Tyler Smith .60 1.50
69TB20 Tudor Somacescu .60 1.50
69TB21 Amen Thompson 6.00 15.00
69TB22 Ausar Thompson 2.50 6.00
69TB23 Bryson Warren .60 1.50
69TB24 Kok Yat .60 1.50

2021-22 Topps Chrome Overtime Elite Autographs

COMMON CARD 3.00 8.00
SEMISTARS 4.00 10.00
UNLISTED STARS 5.00 12.00
*AQUA REF/99: .5X TO 1.2X BASE HI
*AQUA & RED OTE REF/99: .5X TO 1.2X BASE HI
*GREEN/75: .6X TO 1.5X BASE HI
*GOLD WAVE/50: .75X TO 2X BASE HI
*ORANGE BK REF/25: 1X TO 2.5X BASE HI
CADM Davion Mace 6.00 15.00
CAJW Johned Walker 6.00 15.00
CALD Lewis Duarte 6.00 15.00
CAAS1 Alexandre Sarr 20.00 50.00
CAAS2 Alexandre Sarr 20.00 50.00
CAAT1 Amen Thompson 40.00 100.00
CAAT2 Amen Thompson 40.00 100.00
CABG1 Bryce Griggs 6.00 15.00
CABG2 Bryce Griggs 6.00 15.00
CABW1 Bryson Warren 6.00 15.00
CABW2 Bryson Warren 6.00 15.00
CADB1 Dominick Barlow 6.00 15.00
CADB2 Dominick Barlow 6.00 15.00
CADC1 De'Vontes Cobbs 6.00 15.00
CADC2 De'Vontes Cobbs 6.00 15.00
CADM2 Davion Mace 6.00 15.00
CAEM1 Emmanuel Maldonado 6.00 15.00
CAEM2 Emmanuel Maldonado 6.00 15.00
CAIA1 Izan Almansa 6.00 15.00
CAIA2 Izan Almansa 6.00 15.00
CAJG1 Jazian Gortman 6.00 15.00
CAJG2 Jazian Gortman 6.00 15.00
CAJJ1 Jahzare Jackson 12.00 30.00
CAJJ2 Jahzare Jackson 12.00 30.00
CAJL1 Jalen Lewis 8.00 20.00
CAJL2 Jalen Lewis 8.00 20.00
CAJM1 Jaylen Martin 6.00 15.00
CAJM2 Jaylen Martin 6.00 15.00
CAJS1 Jai Smith 6.00 15.00
CAJS2 Jai Smith 6.00 15.00
CAKY1 Kok Yat 6.00 15.00
CAKY2 Kok Yat 6.00 15.00
CALD2 Lewis Duarte 6.00 15.00
CAMB1 Matt Bewley 6.00 15.00
CAMB2 Matt Bewley 6.00 15.00
CARB1 Ryan Bewley 6.00 15.00
CARB2 Ryan Bewley 6.00 15.00
CATC1 TJ Clark 6.00 15.00
CATC2 TJ Clark 6.00 15.00
CATS1 Tyler Smith 6.00 15.00
CATS2 Tyler Smith 6.00 15.00
CAATH1 Ausar Thompson 25.00 60.00
CAATH2 Ausar Thompson 25.00 60.00
CAJMO1 Jean Montero 8.00 20.00
CAJMO2 Jean Montero 8.00 20.00
CAMBO1 Malik Bowman 6.00 15.00
CAMBO2 Malik Bowman 6.00 15.00
CANMD1 Nathan Missia-Dio 6.00 15.00
CANMD2 Nathan Missia-Dio 6.00 15.00
CATSO1 Tudor Somacescu 6.00 15.00
CATSO2 Tudor Somacescu 6.00 15.00

2021-22 Topps Chrome Overtime Elite Future Problems

COMMON CARD .30 .75
SEMISTARS .40 1.00
UNLISTED STARS .50 1.25
*BLUE & PRPL REF/50: 4X TO 10X BASE HI
*ORANGE BK REF/25: 5X TO 12X BASE HI
FP1 Bryson Warren .60 1.50
FP2 Jean Montero .75 2.00
FP3 Jazian Gortman .60 1.50
FP4 Jalen Lewis 3.00 8.00
FP5 Matt Bewley .60 1.50
FP6 Ryan Bewley .60 1.50
FP7 Amen Thompson 6.00 15.00
FP8 Ausar Thompson 2.50 6.00
FP9 Malik Bowman .60 1.50
FP10 TJ Clark .60 1.50
FP11 Jai Smith .60 1.50
FP12 Tyler Smith .60 1.50
FP13 Jahzare Jackson 1.25 3.00

2021-22 Topps Chrome Overtime Elite Levitate

COMMON CARD .30 .75
SEMISTARS .40 1.00
UNLISTED STARS .50 1.25
*BLUE & PRPL REF/50: 4X TO 10X BASE HI
*ORANGE BK REF/25: 5X TO 12X BASE HI
LEV1 Dominick Barlow .60 1.50
LEV2 Matt Bewley .60 1.50
LEV3 Ryan Bewley .60 1.50
LEV4 Malik Bowman .60 1.50
LEV5 TJ Clark .60 1.50
LEV6 De'Vontes Cobbs .60 1.50
LEV7 Jazian Gortman .60 1.50
LEV8 Jalen Lewis 3.00 8.00
LEV9 Nathan Missia-Dio .60 1.50
LEV10 Alexandre Sarr 2.00 5.00
LEV11 Jai Smith .60 1.50
LEV12 Tyler Smith .60 1.50
LEV13 Amen Thompson 6.00 15.00
LEV14 Ausar Thompson 2.50 6.00
LEV15 Bryson Warren .60 1.50

2021-22 Topps Chrome Overtime Elite Super Fly

COMMON CARD 3.00 8.00
SEMISTARS 4.00 10.00
UNLISTED STARS 5.00 12.00
*BLUE & PRPL REF/50: 1.5X TO 4X BASE HI
*ORANGE BK REF/25: 2X TO 5X BASE HI
SF1 Izan Almansa 6.00 15.00
SF2 Dominick Barlow 6.00 15.00
SF3 Matt Bewley 6.00 15.00
SF4 Ryan Bewley 6.00 15.00
SF5 Malik Bowman 6.00 15.00
SF6 TJ Clark 6.00 15.00
SF7 De'Vontes Cobbs 6.00 15.00
SF8 Jazian Gortman 6.00 15.00
SF9 Bryce Griggs 6.00 15.00
SF10 Jahzare Jackson 12.00 30.00
SF11 Jalen Lewis 8.00 20.00
SF12 Lewis Duarte 6.00 15.00
SF13 Emmanuel Maldonado 6.00 15.00
SF14 Jaylen Martin 6.00 15.00
SF15 Nathan Missia-Dio 6.00 15.00
SF16 Jean Montero 8.00 20.00
SF17 Alexandre Sarr 20.00 50.00
SF18 Jai Smith 6.00 15.00
SF19 Tyler Smith 6.00 15.00
SF20 Tudor Somacescu 6.00 15.00
SF21 Amen Thompson 30.00 80.00
SF22 Ausar Thompson 25.00 60.00
SF23 Bryson Warren 6.00 15.00
SF24 Kok Yat 6.00 15.00

2022-23 Topps Chrome Overtime Elite

COMMON CARD .25 .60
SEMISTARS .30 .75
UNLISTED STARS .40 1.00
*REFRACTORS: .75X TO 2X BASIC
*OTE REF: 1.5X TO 4X BASIC
*MINI-DMD REF/399: 1.5X TO 4X BASIC
*PRPL REF/299: 2X TO 5X BASIC
*PRPL & PINK OTE REF/299: 2X TO 5X BASIC
*AQUA REF/199: 2.5X TO 6X BASIC
*AQUA GREEN REF/199: 2.5X TO 6X BASIC
*PINK PRISM REF/150: 2.5X TO 6X BASIC
*BLUE REF/99: 3X TO 8X BASIC
*BLUE WAVE REF/99: 3X TO 8X BASIC
*GREEN RAYWAVE REF/75: 3X TO 8X BASIC
*GOLD REF/50: 5X TO 12X BASIC
*ORANGE REF/25: 8X TO 20X BASIC
*ORANGE BK REF/25: 10X TO 25X BASIC
1 Amen Thompson 1.00 2.50
2 Jalen Lewis .40 1.00
3 Kanaan Carlyle .40 1.00
4 De'Vontes Cobbs .40 1.00
5 Naasir Cunningham .50 1.25
6 Ryan Bewley .40 1.00
7 Jazian Gortman .40 1.00
8 Jaylen Martin .40 1.00
9 Ausar Thompson 1.00 2.50
10 Trey Parker .50 1.25
11 Amen Thompson 1.00 2.50
12 Jalen Lewis .40 1.00
13 Jayden Williams .50 1.25
14 Somto Cyril .50 1.25
15 Rob Dillingham 1.25 3.00
16 Tyler Bey .40 1.00
17 Jahki Howard .50 1.25

18 Naassir Cunningham .50 1.25
19 ZZ Clark .40 1.00
20 Bryce Griggs .40 1.00
21 Jayden Williams .50 1.25
22 Bryce Griggs .40 1.00
23 Jahki Howard .50 1.25
24 ZZ Clark .40 1.00
25 Tyler Smith .50 1.25
26 Jalen Lewis .40 1.00
27 Tyler Bey .40 1.00
28 Izan Almansa .40 1.00
29 Jayden Williams .50 1.25
30 Eli Ellis .75 2.00
31 Rob Dillingham 1.25 3.00
32 Tudor Somacescu .40 1.00
33 Trey Parker .50 1.25
34 Kanaan Carlyle .40 1.00
35 Kok Yat .40 1.00
36 Malik Bowman .40 1.00
37 Johned Walker .40 1.00
38 Bryson Tiller .60 1.50
39 Jahki Howard .50 1.25
40 Kanaan Carlyle .40 1.00
41 TJ Clark .40 1.00
42 Trey Parker .50 1.25
43 Rob Dillingham 1.25 3.00
44 Matt Bewley .40 1.00
45 Nathan Missia-Dio .40 1.00
46 Jazian Gortman .40 1.00
47 Somto Cyril .50 1.25
48 Somto Cyril .50 1.25
49 TJ Clark .40 1.00
50 Naassir Cunningham .50 1.25
51 Ralph Martino Jr. .50 1.25
52 Alexandre Sarr 1.25 3.00
53 ZZ Clark .40 1.00
54 Jahzare Jackson .40 1.00
55 Johned Walker .40 1.00
56 Eli Ellis .75 2.00
57 Izan Almansa .40 1.00
58 Trey Parker .50 1.25
59 Alexandre Sarr 1.25 3.00
60 Ralph Martino Jr. .50 1.25
61 Bryson Tiller .60 1.50
62 Bryce Griggs .40 1.00
63 Eli Ellis .75 2.00
64 Izan Almansa .40 1.00
65 Ryan Bewley .40 1.00
66 Rob Dillingham 1.25 3.00
67 Bryson Tiller .60 1.50
68 Ryan Bewley .40 1.00
69 Jahzare Jackson .40 1.00
70 ZZ Clark .40 1.00
71 De'Vontes Cobbs .40 1.00
72 Eli Ellis .75 2.00
73 Tyler Bey .40 1.00
74 Tyler Smith .50 1.25
75 Matt Bewley .40 1.00
76 Somto Cyril .50 1.25
77 Kok Yat .40 1.00
78 Naassir Cunningham .50 1.25
79 Amen Thompson 1.00 2.50
80 Bryson Warren .40 1.00
81 Bryson Tiller .60 1.50
82 Ausar Thompson 1.00 2.50
83 Matt Bewley .40 1.00
84 Jayden Williams .50 1.25
85 Tyler Smith .50 1.25
86 Johned Walker .40 1.00
87 Malik Bowman .40 1.00
88 Jahki Howard .50 1.25
89 Malik Bowman .40 1.00
90 TJ Clark .40 1.00
91 Jaylen Martin .40 1.00
92 Bryson Warren .40 1.00
93 Jazian Gortman .40 1.00
94 Ralph Martino Jr. .50 1.25
95 Kanaan Carlyle .40 1.00
96 Nathan Missia-Dio .40 1.00
97 Kok Yat .40 1.00
98 Tudor Somacescu .40 1.00
99 Tyler Bey .40 1.00
100 Ausar Thompson 1.00 2.50

2022-23 Topps Chrome Overtime Elite '72 Topps

COMMON CARD .50 1.25
SEMISTARS .60 1.50
UNLISTED STARS .75 2.00
*BLUE REF/50: 2.5X TO 6X BASE HI
*ORANGE REF/25: 4X TO 10X BASE HI
TB721 Izan Almansa .75 2.00
TB722 Matt Bewley .75 2.00
TB723 Ryan Bewley .75 2.00
TB724 Malik Bowman .75 2.00
TB725 TJ Clark .75 2.00
TB726 De'Vontes Cobbs .75 2.00
TB727 Jazian Gortman .75 2.00
TB728 Bryce Griggs .75 2.00
TB729 Jahzare Jackson .75 2.00
TB7210 Jalen Lewis .75 2.00
TB7211 Rob Dillingham 2.50 6.00
TB7212 Jayden Williams 1.00 2.50
TB7213 Tyler Bey .75 2.00
TB7214 Tyler Smith 1.00 2.50
TB7215 ZZ Clark .75 2.00
TB7216 Amen Thompson 2.00 5.00
TB7217 Ausar Thompson 2.00 5.00
TB7218 Bryson Warren .75 2.00
TB7219 Eli Ellis 1.50 4.00
TB7220 Naassir Cunningham 1.00 2.50
TB7221 Trey Parker 1.00 2.50
TB7222 Kanaan Carlyle .75 2.00
TB7223 Bryson Tiller 1.25 3.00
TB7224 Jahki Howard 1.00 2.50
TB7225 Somto Cyril 1.00 2.50

2022-23 Topps Chrome Overtime Elite Autographs

COMMON CARD 4.00 10.00
SEMISTARS 5.00 12.00
UNLISTED STARS 6.00 15.00
*AQUA REF/99: .5X TO 1.2X BASE HI
*AQUA RED OTE REF/99: .5X TO 1.2X BASE HI
CARM Ralph Martino Jr. 8.00 20.00
CAAS1 Alexandre Sarr 20.00 50.00
CAAS2 Alexandre Sarr 20.00 50.00
CABG1 Bryce Griggs 6.00 15.00
CABG2 Bryce Griggs 6.00 15.00
CABT1 Bryson Tiller 10.00 25.00
CABT2 Bryson Tiller 10.00 25.00
CABT3 Bryson Tiller 10.00 25.00
CABW1 Bryson Warren 6.00 15.00
CABW2 Bryson Warren 6.00 15.00
CADC1 De'Vontes Cobbs 6.00 15.00
CADC2 De'Vontes Cobbs 6.00 15.00
CAEE1 Eli Ellis 12.00 30.00
CAEE3 Eli Ellis 12.00 30.00
CAIA1 Izan Almansa 6.00 15.00
CAIA2 Izan Almansa 6.00 15.00
CAJG1 Jazian Gortman 6.00 15.00
CAJG2 Jazian Gortman 6.00 15.00
CAJH1 Jahki Howard 8.00 20.00
CAJH2 Jahki Howard 8.00 20.00
CAJH3 Jahki Howard 8.00 20.00
CAJJ1 Jahzare Jackson 6.00 15.00
CAJJ2 Jahzare Jackson 6.00 15.00
CAJL1 Jalen Lewis 6.00 15.00
CAJL2 Jalen Lewis 6.00 15.00
CAJM1 Jaylen Martin 6.00 15.00
CAJM2 Jaylen Martin 6.00 15.00
CAJW1 Jayden Williams 8.00 20.00
CAJW2 Jayden Williams 8.00 20.00
CAJW3 Jayden Williams 8.00 20.00
CAKC1 Kanaan Carlyle 6.00 15.00
CAKC2 Kanaan Carlyle 6.00 15.00
CAKC3 Kanaan Carlyle 6.00 15.00
CAKY1 Kok Yat 6.00 15.00
CAKY2 Kok Yat 6.00 15.00
CAMB1 Malik Bowman 6.00 15.00
CAMB2 Malik Bowman 6.00 15.00
CANC1 Naassir Cunningham 8.00 20.00
CANC2 Naassir Cunningham 8.00 20.00
CANC3 Naassir Cunningham 8.00 20.00
CARB1 Ryan Bewley 6.00 15.00
CARB2 Ryan Bewley 6.00 15.00
CARD1 Rob Dillingham 20.00 50.00
CARD2 Rob Dillingham 20.00 50.00
CARD3 Rob Dillingham 20.00 50.00
CARMJ Ralph Martino Jr. 8.00 20.00
CASC1 Somto Cyril 8.00 20.00
CASC2 Somto Cyril 8.00 20.00
CASC3 Somto Cyril 8.00 20.00
CATB1 Tyler Bey 6.00 15.00
CATB2 Tyler Bey 6.00 15.00
CATB3 Tyler Bey 6.00 15.00
CATC1 TJ Clark 6.00 15.00
CATC2 TJ Clark 6.00 15.00
CATP1 Trey Parker 8.00 20.00
CATP2 Trey Parker 8.00 20.00
CATP3 Trey Parker 8.00 20.00
CATS1 Tudor Somacescu 6.00 15.00
CATS2 Tudor Somacescu 6.00 15.00
CAZC1 ZZ Clark 6.00 15.00
CAZC2 ZZ Clark 6.00 15.00
CAZC3 ZZ Clark 6.00 15.00
CAAMT1 Amen Thompson 15.00 40.00
CAAMT2 Amen Thompson 15.00 40.00
CAAUT1 Ausar Thompson 15.00 40.00
CAAUT2 Ausar Thompson 15.00 40.00
CAJWA1 Johned Walker 6.00 15.00
CAJWA2 Johned Walker 6.00 15.00
CAMBE1 Matt Bewley 6.00 15.00
CAMBE2 Matt Bewley 6.00 15.00
CANMD1 Nathan Missia-Dio 6.00 15.00
CANMD2 Nathan Missia-Dio 6.00 15.00
CATSM1 Tyler Smith 8.00 20.00
CATSM2 Tyler Smith 8.00 20.00

2022-23 Topps Chrome Overtime Elite Autographs Gold Wave Refractors

*GOLD WAVE REF: .75X TO 2X BASE HI
CAAMT1 Amen Thompson 75.00 200.00
CAAMT2 Amen Thompson 75.00 200.00
CAAUT1 Ausar Thompson 75.00 200.00
CAAUT2 Ausar Thompson 75.00 200.00

2022-23 Topps Chrome Overtime Elite Autographs Green Refractors

*GREEN REF: .5X TO 1.2X BASE HI
CAAMT1 Amen Thompson 50.00 120.00
CAAMT2 Amen Thompson 50.00 120.00
CAAUT1 Ausar Thompson 50.00 120.00
CAAUT2 Ausar Thompson 50.00 120.00

2022-23 Topps Chrome Overtime Elite Autographs Orange Basketball Refractors

*ORANGE BK REF: 1.25X TO 3X BASE HI
CAAMT1 Amen Thompson 125.00 300.00
CAAMT2 Amen Thompson 125.00 300.00
CAAUT1 Ausar Thompson 125.00 300.00
CAAUT2 Ausar Thompson 125.00 300.00

2022-23 Topps Chrome Overtime Elite Class Of

COMMON CARD .50 1.25
SEMISTARS .60 1.50
UNLISTED STARS .75 2.00
*BLUE REF/50: 2.5X TO 6X BASE HI
*ORANGE REF/25: 4X TO 10X BASE HI
CO1 Izan Almansa .75 2.00
CO2 Matt Bewley .75 2.00
CO3 Ryan Bewley .75 2.00
CO4 Malik Bowman .75 2.00
CO5 TJ Clark .75 2.00
CO6 De'Vontes Cobbs .75 2.00
CO7 Jazian Gortman .75 2.00
CO8 Bryce Griggs .75 2.00
CO9 Jahzare Jackson .75 2.00
CO10 Jalen Lewis .75 2.00
CO11 Jaylen Martin .75 2.00
CO12 Nathan Missia-Dio .75 2.00
CO13 Alexandre Sarr 2.50 6.00
CO14 Tyler Smith 1.00 2.50
CO15 Tudor Somacescu .75 2.00
CO16 Amen Thompson 2.00 5.00
CO17 Ausar Thompson 2.00 5.00
CO18 Bryson Warren .75 2.00
CO19 Kok Yat .75 2.00
CO20 Naassir Cunningham 1.00 2.50
CO21 Trey Parker 1.00 2.50
CO22 Kanaan Carlyle .75 2.00
CO23 Bryson Tiller 1.25 3.00
CO24 Jahki Howard 1.00 2.50
CO25 ZZ Clark .75 2.00
CO26 Tyler Bey .75 2.00
CO27 Jayden Williams 1.00 2.50
CO28 Eli Ellis 1.50 4.00
CO29 Somto Cyril 1.00 2.50
CO30 Rob Dillingham 2.50 6.00

2022-23 Topps Chrome Overtime Elite Hurricane

COMMON CARD .50 1.25
SEMISTARS .60 .15
UNLISTED STARS .75 2.00
*BLUE REF/50: 2.5X TO 6X BASE HI
*ORANGE REF/25: 4X TO 10X BASE HI
H1 Amen Thompson 2.00 5.00
H2 Ausar Thompson 2.00 5.00
H3 Naassir Cunningham 1.00 2.50
H4 Trey Parker 1.00 2.50
H5 Kanaan Carlyle .75 2.00
H6 Bryson Tiller 1.25 3.00
H7 Jahki Howard 1.00 2.50
H8 ZZ Clark .75 2.00
H9 Tyler Bey .75 2.00
H10 Jayden Williams 1.00 2.50
H11 Eli Ellis 1.50 4.00
H12 Matt Bewley .75 2.00
H13 Rob Dillingham 2.50 6.00
H14 Jazian Gortman .75 2.00
H15 Somto Cyril 1.00 2.50

2022-23 Topps Chrome Overtime Elite Superfly

COMMON CARD 3.00 8.00
SEMISTARS 4.00 10.00
UNLISTED STARS 5.00 12.00
*BLUE REF/50: 1.5X TO 4X BASE HI
*ORANGE REF/25: 2X TO 5X BASE HI
SF1 Amen Thompson 12.00 30.00
SF2 Ausar Thompson 12.00 30.00
SF3 Naassir Cunningham 6.00 15.00
SF4 Trey Parker 6.00 15.00
SF5 Kanaan Carlyle 5.00 12.00
SF6 Bryson Tiller 8.00 20.00
SF7 Jahki Howard 6.00 15.00
SF8 ZZ Clark 5.00 12.00
SF9 Tyler Bey 5.00 12.00
SF10 Jayden Williams 6.00 15.00
SF11 Eli Ellis 10.00 25.00
SF12 Matt Bewley 5.00 12.00
SF13 Rob Dillingham 15.00 40.00
SF14 Jazian Gortman 5.00 12.00
SF15 Somto Cyril 6.00 15.00

2003-04 Topps Collection

COMP.FACT.SET (265) 75.00 200.00
*SINGLES: .6X TO 1.5X BASE TOPPS HI
*RCs: .5X TO 1.25X BASE TOPPS HI
SOME PLAYERS HAVE PHOTO VARIATIONS
CARDS HAVE GOLD FOIL HIGHLIGHTS
173 Rodney Rogers .40 1.00

2003-04 Topps Contemporary Collection

21-30 AU RC PRINT RUN 499 SER.#'d SETS
131-140 AU RC PRINT RUN 499 SER.#'d SETS
1 LeBron James RC 600.00 1,200.00
2 Darko Milicic RC 2.00 5.00
3 Chris Bosh RC 8.00 20.00
4 Dwyane Wade RC 20.00 50.00
5 Chris Kaman RC 2.50 6.00
6 Kirk Hinrich RC 2.50 6.00
7 Jarvis Hayes RC 1.50 4.00
8 Mickael Pietrus RC 2.00 5.00
9 Luke Ridnour RC 2.50 6.00
10 David West RC 3.00 8.00
11 Aleksandar Pavlovic RC 2.00 5.00
12 Boris Diaw RC 2.50 6.00
13 Zoran Planinic RC 1.50 4.00
14 Francisco Elson RC 1.50 4.00
15 Leandro Barbosa RC 2.50 6.00
16 Josh Howard RC 2.50 6.00
17 Luke Walton RC 2.50 6.00
18 Willie Green RC 2.50 6.00
19 Maurice Williams RC 2.50 6.00
20 Udonis Haslem RC 3.00 8.00
21 Reece Gaines AU RC 3.00 8.00
22 Carmelo Anthony AU RC 25.00 60.00
23 Zarko Cabarkapa AU RC 3.00 8.00
24 Troy Bell AU RC 3.00 8.00
25 Travis Outlaw AU RC 4.00 10.00
26 Marcus Banks AU RC 3.00 8.00
27 Kendrick Perkins AU RC 4.00 10.00
28 Dahntay Jones AU RC 4.00 10.00
29 T.J. Ford AU RC 4.00 10.00
30 Mike Sweetney AU RC 3.00 8.00
31 Jason Terry .75 2.00
32 Theo Ratliff .60 1.50
33 Raef LaFrentz .60 1.50
34 Eddy Curry .60 1.50
35 Ricky Davis .75 2.00
36 Zydrunas Ilgauskas .75 2.00
37 Darius Miles .60 1.50
38 Dirk Nowitzki 2.50 6.00
39 Steve Nash 2.00 5.00
40 Antawn Jamison 1.00 2.50
41 Antoine Walker 1.00 2.50
42 Andre Miller .75 2.00
43 Nene .75 2.00
44 Richard Hamilton 1.25 3.00
45 Ben Wallace 1.25 3.00
46 Jason Richardson 1.00 2.50
47 Nick Van Exel 1.00 2.50
48 Troy Murphy .60 1.50
49 Yao Ming 2.50 6.00
50 Steve Francis 1.00 2.50
51 Ron Artest 1.00 2.50
52 Jermaine O'Neal 1.00 2.50
53 Al Harrington .75 2.00
54 Marko Jaric .60 1.50
55 Corey Maggette .75 2.00
56 Kobe Bryant 8.00 20.00
57 Shaquille O'Neal 4.00 10.00
58 Devean George .60 1.50
59 Gary Payton 1.50 4.00
60 Pau Gasol 1.50 4.00
61 Stromile Swift .60 1.50
62 Mike Miller .75 2.00
63 Lamar Odom .75 2.00
64 Caron Butler .75 2.00
65 Eddie Jones 1.00 2.50
66 Brian Grant .60 1.50
67 Desmond Mason .75 2.00
68 Tim Thomas .60 1.50
69 Michael Redd 1.00 2.50
70 Sam Cassell .75 2.00
71 Kevin Garnett 2.50 6.00
72 Latrell Sprewell 1.25 3.00
73 Michael Olowokandi .60 1.50
74 Wally Szczerbiak .75 2.00
75 Richard Jefferson .75 2.00
76 Kenyon Martin 1.00 2.50
77 Alonzo Mourning 1.25 3.00
78 Baron Davis 1.00 2.50
79 Jamal Mashburn .75 2.00
80 Allan Houston 1.00 2.50
81 Keith Van Horn .75 2.00
82 Kurt Thomas .60 1.50
83 Tracy McGrady 1.50 4.00
84 Juwan Howard .75 2.00
85 Drew Gooden .75 2.00
86 Allen Iverson 2.50 6.00
87 Glenn Robinson .75 2.00
88 Derrick Coleman 1.00 2.50
89 Stephon Marbury 1.25 3.00
90 Shawn Marion 1.00 2.50
91 Amare Stoudemire 1.25 3.00
92 Zach Randolph 1.25 3.00
93 Rasheed Wallace 1.25 3.00
94 Bonzi Wells .60 1.50
95 Mike Bibby 1.00 2.50
96 Chris Webber 1.25 3.00
97 Brad Miller .75 2.00
98 Tim Duncan 2.50 6.00
99 Rasho Nesterovic .60 1.50
100 Tony Parker 1.50 4.00
101 Manu Ginobili 2.00 5.00
102 Brent Barry .60 1.50
103 Rashard Lewis .75 2.00
104 Ray Allen 1.50 4.00
105 Vince Carter 2.00 5.00
106 Jerome Williams .60 1.50
107 Carlos Arroyo .75 2.00
108 Matt Harpring .60 1.50
109 Andrei Kirilenko .75 2.00
110 Gilbert Arenas 1.00 2.50
111 Kwame Brown .60 1.50
112 Jerry Stackhouse 1.25 3.00
113 Darrell Armstrong .60 1.50
114 Alvin Williams .60 1.50
115 Kelvin Cato .60 1.50
116 Stephen Jackson .75 2.00
117 Shareef Abdur-Rahim 1.00 2.50
118 Eric Williams .60 1.50
119 Tony Battie .60 1.50
120 Tyson Chandler .75 2.00
121 Scottie Pippen 2.50 6.00
122 Nikoloz Tskitishvili .60 1.50
123 Chauncey Billups 1.25 3.00
124 Quentin Richardson .60 1.50
125 Dikembe Mutombo 1.25 3.00
126 Joe Smith .75 2.00
127 Qyntel Woods .60 1.50
128 Dajuan Wagner .60 1.50
129 Robert Horry 1.00 2.50
130 Cuttino Mobley .60 1.50
131 Bobby Jackson AU 5.00 12.00
132 Elton Brand AU 6.00 15.00
133 Peja Stojakovic AU 6.00 15.00
134 Jamal Crawford AU 6.00 15.00
135 Jalen Rose AU 8.00 20.00
136 Paul Pierce AU 10.00 25.00
137 Jason Kidd AU 8.00 20.00
138 Tayshaun Prince AU 6.00 12.00
139 Morris Peterson AU 5.00 12.00
140 Speedy Claxton AU 5.00 12.00

2003-04 Topps Contemporary Collection Gold

*1-20 RCs GOLD: 1.25X TO 3X BASE HI
*31-130 STARS GOLD: 3X TO 8X BASE HI
GOLD PRINT RUN 25 SER.#'d SETS
1 LeBron James 1,000.00 2,000.00
56 Kobe Bryant 60.00 150.00

2003-04 Topps Contemporary Collection Red

*RED: .75X TO 2X BASE HI
1-20 PRINT RUN 225 SER.#'d SETS
21-30 AU PRINT RUN 50 SER.#'d SETS
31-130 PRINT RUN 225 SER.#'d SETS
131-140 AU PRINT RUN 50 SER.#'d SETS
56 Kobe Bryant 12.00 30.00

2003-04 Topps Contemporary Collection Caption Autographs

BJ1 B.Jackson Court Kings 8.00 20.00
BJ2 B.Jackson 6th Man 8.00 20.00
CA1 C.Anthony NCAA MVP 40.00 100.00
CA2 C.Anthony Mile High 40.00 80.00
DJ1 D.Jones Cameron 6.00 15.00
DJ2 D.Jones Grizzly Den 6.00 15.00
EB1 E.Brand ROY 99 10.00 25.00
EB2 E.Brand Hollywood 6.00 15.00
JC1 J.Crawford Go Blue 10.00 25.00
JC2 J.Crawford Windy City 15.00 40.00
JK1 J.Kidd ROY 94 20.00 50.00
JK2 J.Kidd Jersey Kidd 30.00 80.00
JR1 J.Rose FAB 5 15.00 30.00
JR2 J.Rose Hollywood North 10.00 25.00
KP1 K.Perkins Ozen Orig. 8.00 20.00
KP2 K.Perkins Celtic Pride 8.00 20.00
MB1 M.Banks Runnin Reb 8.00 20.00
MB2 M.Banks Celtic Pride 8.00 20.00
MP1 Mo Pete Rebel 6.00 15.00
MP2 Mo Pete Hollywood North 6.00 15.00
MS1 M.Sweetney HOYA 34 6.00 15.00
MS2 M.Sweetney Big Apple 6.00 15.00
PP1 P.Pierce The Truth 30.00 80.00
PP2 P.Pierce Celtic Pride 25.00 60.00
PS1 P.Stojakovic Court Kings 10.00 25.00
PS2 P.Stojakovic 3 Point King 8.00 20.00
RG1 R.Gaines Cardinals #1 6.00 15.00
RG2 R.Gaines Magic Tricks 6.00 15.00
SC1 S.Claxton Hofstra Pride 6.00 15.00
SC2 S.Claxton Oaktown 6.00 15.00
TB1 T.Bell BC Beast 6.00 15.00
TB2 T.Bell Grizzly Den 6.00 15.00
TO1 T.Outlaw Starkville's Son 6.00 15.00
TO2 T.Outlaw City of Roses 6.00 15.00
TP1 T.Prince UK Prince 15.00 40.00
TP2 T.Prince Motown Prince 15.00 40.00
ZC1 Cabarkapa Count of Mont. 6.00 15.00
ZC2 Cabarkapa Valley of Sun 6.00 15.00
TJF1 T.Ford Longhorn Legend 8.00 20.00
TJF2 T.Ford NCAA POY 03 12.50 30.00

2003-04 Topps Contemporary Collection Caption Autographs Dual

AF C.Anthony/T.Ford 100.00 200.00
BJ T.Bell/D.Jones 8.00 20.00
BP1 M.Banks/K.Perkins 10.00 25.00
BP2 M.Banks/MoPete 8.00 20.00
BS E.Brand/M.Sweetney 10.00 25.00
CR J.Crawford/J.Rose 30.00 80.00
GC R.Gaines/S.Claxton 8.00 20.00
OC T.Outlaw/Zarko 10.00 25.00
PC T.Prince/S.Claxton 10.00 25.00
PK P.Pierce/J.Kidd 100.00 200.00
PP P.Pierce/M.Peterson 40.00 100.00
SC Peja/Z.Cabarkapa 12.50 30.00
SJ P.Stojakovic/B.Jackson 12.50 30.00
SP M.Sweetney/T.Prince 12.00 30.00

2003-04 Topps Contemporary Collection Draft 03 Tribute

PRINT RUN 250 SER.#'d SETS
*RED SINGLES: .75X TO 2X BASE DRAFT HI
RED PRINT RUN 50 SER.#'d SETS
AP Aleksandar Pavlovic 2.00 5.00
BC Brian Cook 1.50 4.00
BD Boris Diaw 2.50 6.00
CA Carmelo Anthony 12.00 30.00
CB Chris Bosh 8.00 20.00
CK Chris Kaman 2.50 6.00
DJ Dahntay Jones 2.00 5.00
DW Dwyane Wade 20.00 50.00
JH Josh Howard 2.50 6.00
JK Jason Kapono 1.50 4.00
KH Kirk Hinrich 2.50 6.00
LB Leandro Barbosa 2.50 6.00
LR Luke Ridnour 2.50 6.00
LW Luke Walton 2.50 6.00
MB Marcus Banks 1.50 4.00
MP Mickael Pietrus 2.00 5.00
MW Maurice Williams 2.50 6.00
SB Steve Blake 2.00 5.00
TB Troy Bell 1.50 4.00
ZP Zoran Planinic 1.50 4.00
DWE David West 3.00 8.00
JHA Jarvis Hayes 1.50 4.00
TJF T.J. Ford 2.00 5.00

2003-04 Topps Contemporary Collection Lucky Draw

PRINT RUN 175 SER.#'d SETS
*50 SINGLES: .6X TO 1.5X BASE HI
*25 SINGLES: 1X TO 2.5X BASE HI
LD1 Carmelo Anthony 20.00 50.00
LD2 Marcus Banks 2.50 6.00
LD3 Chris Bosh 12.00 30.00
LD4 Dwyane Wade 30.00 80.00
LD5 Chris Kaman 4.00 10.00
LD6 Kirk Hinrich 4.00 10.00
LD7 Jarvis Hayes 2.50 6.00
LD8 Mickael Pietrus 3.00 8.00
LD9 Luke Ridnour 4.00 10.00
LD10 David West 5.00 12.00
LD11 Aleksandar Pavlovic 3.00 8.00
LD12 Boris Diaw 4.00 10.00
LD13 Zoran Planinic 2.50 6.00
LD14 Ndudi Ebi 2.50 6.00
LD15 Leandro Barbosa 4.00 10.00
LD16 Josh Howard 4.00 10.00
LD17 Luke Walton 4.00 10.00
LD18 Willie Green 4.00 10.00
LD19 Maurice Williams 4.00 10.00
LD20 Zarko Cabarkapa 2.50 6.00
LD21 Travis Outlaw 3.00 8.00
LD22 Dahntay Jones 3.00 8.00
LD23 Troy Bell 2.50 6.00
LD24 Reece Gaines 2.50 6.00
LD25 Mike Sweetney 2.50 6.00

2003-04 Topps Contemporary Collection Matching Marks Relics

PRINT RUN 250 SER.#'d SETS
*RED SINGLES: .5X TO 1.25X MATCH HI
RED PRINT RUN 50 SER.#'d SETS
AH R.Allen/A.Houston 6.00 15.00
GD K.Garnett/T.Duncan 10.00 25.00
IM A.Iverson/T.McGrady 8.00 20.00
KM J.Kidd/A.Miller 6.00 15.00
MM K.Malone/A.Mourning 8.00 20.00
OS Shaq/A.Stoudemire 10.00 25.00
WB C.Webber/E.Brand 6.00 15.00
WM B.Wallace/D.Mutombo 6.00 15.00
WR A.Walker/G.Robinson 6.00 15.00

2003-04 Topps Contemporary Collection Memorable Materials

PRINT RUN 250 SER.#'d SETS
*RED SINGLES: .75X TO 2X MEM.MAT.HI
RED PRINT RUN 50 SER.#'d SETS
AI Allen Iverson 8.00 20.00
JR Jason Richardson 3.00 8.00
KG Kevin Garnett 8.00 20.00
RH Robert Horry 3.00 8.00
RM Reggie Miller 6.00 15.00
SM Stephon Marbury 4.00 10.00
TD Tim Duncan 8.00 20.00

2003-04 Topps Contemporary Collection Milestone Materials

PRINT RUN 250 SER.#'d SETS
*RED SINGLES: .75X TO 2X MILE HI
RED PRINT RUN 50 SER.#'d SETS
DM Dikembe Mutombo 4.00 10.00
DN Dirk Nowitzki 8.00 20.00
GP Gary Payton 5.00 12.00
JS Jerry Stackhouse 4.00 10.00
KM Karl Malone 6.00 15.00
MB Mike Bibby 3.00 8.00
RA Ray Allen 5.00 12.00
SC Sam Cassell 2.50 6.00
SF Steve Francis 3.00 8.00
SO Shaquille O'Neal 12.00 30.00
TD Tim Duncan 8.00 20.00
NVE Nick Van Exel 3.00 8.00
RHA Richard Hamilton 4.00 10.00

2003-04 Topps Contemporary Collection Perennial All-Star Relics

PRINT RUN 175 TO 250 SER.#'d SETS
*RED SINGLES: .75X TO 2X ALL-STAR HI
RED PRINT RUN 50 SER.#'d SETS
AI Allen Iverson 8.00 20.00
AM Alonzo Mourning 5.00 12.00
CW Chris Webber/175 4.00 10.00
DN Dirk Nowitzki 8.00 20.00
GP Gary Payton 5.00 12.00
JK Jason Kidd 5.00 12.00
KG Kevin Garnett 8.00 20.00
KM Karl Malone 6.00 15.00
PP Paul Pierce 5.00 12.00
RA Ray Allen 5.00 12.00
RM Reggie Miller 6.00 15.00
SF Steve Francis 3.00 8.00
SN Steve Nash 6.00 15.00
SO Shaquille O'Neal 12.00 30.00
TD Tim Duncan 8.00 20.00
TM Tracy McGrady 5.00 12.00

2003-04 Topps Contemporary Collection Performance Tribute Doubles

PRINT RUN 250 SER.#'d SETS
*RED SINGLES: .6X TO 1.5X PERF. HI
RED PRINT RUN 50 SER.#'d SETS
AM R.Artest/K.Martin 5.00 12.00
BW E.Brand/C.Webber 5.00 12.00
ML T.Murphy/R.Lafrentz 5.00 12.00
MW D.Mutombo/B.Wallace 5.00 12.00
NK S.Nash/J.Kidd 6.00 15.00
NS Nene/A.Stoudemire 5.00 12.00
PB S.Pippen/S.Battier 8.00 20.00
RW G.Robinson/R.Wallace 5.00 12.00
WB Jer.Williams/Boozer 5.00 12.00

2003-04 Topps Contemporary Collection Performance Tribute Triples

PRINT RUN 200 TO 250 SER.#'d SETS
*RED SINGLES: .75X TO 2X PERF.TRIP HI
RED PRINT RUN 50 SER.#'d SETS
FDR Francis/B.Davis/J-Rich 6.00 15.00
HJP Rip/R.Jeff/MoPete/200 6.00 15.00
JAB Jaric/Arenas/Butler 6.00 15.00
MGM Yao/Garnett/Mourning 8.00 20.00
MIS T-Mac/Iverson/Shaq 12.00 30.00
OMR Odom/Miles/Rose/200 6.00 15.00
PWM Pierce/Walker/Marion 6.00 15.00
RWO Ratliff/Big Ben/J.O'Neal 6.00 15.00
TMW Terry/Marbury/Wagner/200 6.00 15.00

2003-04 Topps Contemporary Collection Team Tribute Doubles

PRINT RUN 250 SER.#'d SETS
*RED SINGLES: .6X TO 1.5X DOUBLE HI
RED PRINT RUN 50 SER.#'d SETS
AO R.Artest/J.O'Neal 5.00 12.00
GE K.Garnett/N.Ebi 6.00 15.00
HT R.Horry/H.Turkoglu 5.00 12.00
HV A.Houston/K.Van Horn 5.00 12.00
IR A.Iverson/G.Robinson 5.00 12.00
KP J.Kidd/Z.Planinic 5.00 12.00
MH R.Miller/A.Harrington 5.00 12.00
PB P.Pierce/M.Banks 5.00 12.00
PH T.Prince/R.Hamilton 6.00 15.00
SH J.Stack/J.Hayes 5.00 12.00
TS K.Thomas/M.Sweetney 5.00 12.00
WM C.Webber/B.Miller 5.00 12.00
PBO M.Peterson/C.Bosh 5.00 12.00

2003-04 Topps Contemporary Collection Team Tribute Triples

PRINT RUN 200 TO 250 SER.#'d SETS
*RED SINGLES: .6X TO 1.5X TRIB.TRIP.HI
RED PRINT RUN 50 SER.#'d SETS
BMR Brand/Maggette/Q-Rich 6.00 15.00
BOW Butler/Odom/Wade 8.00 20.00
BSJ Bibby/Peja/B.Jcksn/200 8.00 20.00
BSM Barbosa/Amare/Marion 6.00 15.00
DMW B.Davis/Mash/West 6.00 15.00
DNP Duncan/Rasho/Parker 8.00 20.00
FMR Ford/Mason/Redd 6.00 15.00
MAN A.Miller/Melo/Nene 8.00 20.00
MFM Yao/Francis/Mobley 8.00 20.00
MGG T-Mac/Gaines/Gooden 6.00 15.00
NNF Nash/Dirk/Finley 10.00 25.00
PCK Planinic/Clark/AK-47 6.00 15.00
PMO Payton/Malone/Shaq 12.50 30.00
SOC Spree/Olowok/Cassell 6.00 15.00
WMB Wagner/Miles/Boozer 6.00 15.00
WOW R.Wallace/Outlaw/Woods 6.00 15.00

2003-04 Topps Contemporary Collection Tribute to the Stars Relics

PRINT RUN 21 TO 50 SER.#'d SETS
N Nene/50 5.00 12.00
AK Andrei Kirilenko/50 5.00 12.00
AS Amare Stoudemire/50 8.00 20.00
BW Ben Wallace/50 8.00 20.00
CW Chris Webber/50 8.00 20.00
DM Desmond Mason/50 5.00 12.00
EB Elton Brand/50 5.00 12.00
EC Eddy Curry/50 4.00 10.00
JK Jason Kidd/50 10.00 25.00
JO Jermaine O'Neal/50 6.00 15.00
JR Jason Richardson/50 5.00 12.00
JT Jason Terry/50 5.00 12.00
KV Keith Van Horn/50 5.00 12.00
LO Lamar Odom/21 10.00 25.00
PG Pau Gasol/50 10.00 25.00
PP Paul Pierce/50 10.00 25.00
RW Rasheed Wallace/50 8.00 20.00
SM Stephon Marbury/50 8.00 20.00
TM Tracy McGrady/50 10.00 25.00
TP Tony Parker/50 10.00 25.00
YM Yao Ming/50 15.00 40.00

2007-08 Topps Co-Signers

COMP.SET w/o SP's (50) 20.00 40.00
ROOKIE PRINT RUN 499 SER.#'d SETS
1 Dwyane Wade .75 2.00
2 Chauncey Billups .50 1.25
3 Allen Iverson 1.00 2.50
4 Amare Stoudemire .40 1.00
5 Jason Kidd .60 1.50
6 Dirk Nowitzki 1.00 2.50
7 Jermaine O'Neal .40 1.00
8 Elton Brand .30 .75
9 Carlos Boozer .30 .75
10 Ray Allen .60 1.50
11 Yao Ming 1.00 2.50
12 Dwight Howard .50 1.25
13 Steve Nash .75 2.00
14 Chris Paul .75 2.00
15 Carmelo Anthony .60 1.50
16 Pau Gasol .60 1.50
17 Ben Gordon .30 .75
18 Andre Iguodala .40 1.00
19 Paul Pierce .60 1.50
20 Tracy McGrady .60 1.50
21 Tim Duncan 1.00 2.50
22 Josh Smith .25 .60
23 LeBron James 3.00 8.00
24 Kobe Bryant 3.00 8.00
25 Vince Carter .75 2.00
26 Shaquille O'Neal 1.50 4.00
27 Kevin Garnett 1.00 2.50
28 Chris Bosh .50 1.25
29 Baron Davis .30 .75
30 Gilbert Arenas .40 1.00
31 John Stockton 1.25 3.00
32 Magic Johnson 2.50 6.00
33 Larry Bird 2.50 6.00
34 Rick Barry .50 1.25
35 Isiah Thomas .60 1.50
36 Dominique Wilkins 1.00 2.50
37 Dennis Rodman 1.50 4.00
38 Wilt Chamberlain 2.00 5.00
39 Pete Maravich 1.50 4.00
40 Bill Russell 2.00 5.00
41 Byron Scott .50 1.25
42 Karl Malone .75 2.00
43 Chris Mullin .75 2.00
44 Kevin McHale .75 2.00
45 Clyde Drexler 1.00 2.50
46 James Worthy 1.00 2.50
47 Bill Walton .75 2.00
48 Earl Monroe .60 1.50
49 Elgin Baylor .60 1.50
50 David Robinson 1.25 3.00
51 Nick Young RC 2.00 5.00
52 Greg Oden RC 2.00 5.00
53 Morris Almond RC 1.25 3.00
54 Alando Tucker RC 1.25 3.00
55 Arron Afflalo RC 1.50 4.00
56 Derrick Byars RC 1.25 3.00
57 Adam Haluska RC 1.25 3.00
58 Corey Brewer RC 1.50 4.00
59 Ramon Sessions RC 1.50 4.00
60 Daequan Cook RC 1.50 4.00
61 Mike Conley Jr. RC 5.00 12.00
62 Javaris Crittenton RC 1.25 3.00
63 Jared Jordan RC 1.25 3.00
64 Aaron Brooks RC 1.50 4.00
65 Marco Belinelli RC 1.50 4.00
66 Sammy Mejia RC 1.25 3.00
67 Jared Dudley RC 1.50 4.00
68 Rodney Stuckey RC 1.25 3.00
69 JamesOn Curry RC 1.25 3.00
70 Gabe Pruitt RC 1.25 3.00
71 Acie Law RC 1.25 3.00
72 Dominic McGuire RC 1.25 3.00
73 Herbert Hill RC 1.25 3.00
74 Jeff Green RC 1.50 4.00
75 Wilson Chandler RC 1.50 4.00
76 Marcus Williams RC 1.25 3.00
77 Josh McRoberts RC 1.25 3.00
78 Thaddeus Young RC 2.00 5.00
79 Jared Newson RC 2.00 5.00
80 Stephane Lasme RC 1.25 3.00
81 Demetris Nichols RC 1.25 3.00
82 Julian Wright RC 1.25 3.00
83 Sean Williams RC 1.25 3.00
84 Chris Richard RC 1.25 3.00
85 Yi Jianlian RC 2.50 6.00
86 Al Thornton RC 1.25 3.00
87 Carl Landry RC 1.25 3.00
88 Kevin Durant RC 50.00 120.00
89 Brandan Wright RC 1.50 4.00
90 Nick Fazekas RC 1.25 3.00
91 Joakim Noah RC 2.00 5.00
92 Jermareo Davidson RC 1.25 3.00
93 D.J. Strawberry RC 1.25 3.00
94 Glen Davis RC 1.50 4.00
95 Al Horford RC 5.00 12.00
96 Spencer Hawes RC 1.25 3.00
97 Taurean Green RC 1.25 3.00
98 Jason Smith RC 1.25 3.00
99 Luis Scola RC 2.00 5.00
100 Aaron Gray RC 1.25 3.00

2007-08 Topps Co-Signers Gold Red

PRINT RUN 109 SER.#'d SETS
*GOLD BLUE: .5X TO 1.25X GOLD RED
GOLD BLUE PRINT RUN 89 SETS
*GOLD GREEN: .5X TO 1.25X GOLD RED
GOLD GREEN PRINT RUN 59 SETS
*G.GREEN FOIL: 1.5X TO 4X GOLD RED
GOLD GREEN FOIL PRINT RUN 19 SETS
*SILVER BLUE FOIL: 1.25X TO 3X GOLD RED
SILVER BLUE FOIL PRINT RUN 29 SETS
*SILVER GREEN FOIL: 1.5X TO 4X RED GOLD
SILVER GREEN FOIL PRINT RUN 19 SETS
*SILVER RED FOIL: 1.25X TO 3X BASE HI
SILVER RED FOIL PRINT RUN 39 SETS
1 D.Wade/S.O'Neal 1.50 4.00
1A D.Wade/A.Walker 1.25 3.00
2 C.Billups/R.Hamilton 1.25 3.00
2A C.Billups/T.Prince 1.25 3.00
3 A.Iverson/C.Anthony 1.25 3.00
3A A.Iverson/M.Camby 1.25 3.00
4 A.Stoudemire/S.Nash 1.25 3.00
4A A.Stoudemire/S.Marion 1.25 3.00
5 J.Kidd/V.Carter 1.25 3.00
5A J.Kidd/M.Williams 1.25 3.00
6 D.Nowitzki/J.Terry 1.25 3.00
6A D.Nowitzki/J.Howard 1.25 3.00
7 J.O'Neal/D.Granger 1.25 3.00
7A J.O'Neal/T.Murphy 1.25 3.00
8 E.Brand/C.Maggette 1.25 3.00
8A E.Brand/S.Livingston 1.25 3.00
9 C.Boozer/D.Williams 1.25 3.00
9A C.Boozer/A.Kirilenko 1.25 3.00

10 R.Allen/P.Pierce 1.25 3.00
10A R.Allen/K.Garnett 1.25 3.00
11 Y.Ming/T.McGrady 1.25 3.00
11A Y.Ming/S.Battier 1.25 3.00
12 D.Howard/R.Lewis 1.25 3.00
12A D.Howard/J.Nelson 1.25 3.00
13 S.Nash/S.Marion 1.25 3.00
13A S.Nash/A.Stoudemire 1.25 3.00
14 C.Paul/T.Chandler 1.25 3.00
14A C.Paul/D.West 1.25 3.00
15 C.Anthony/A.Iverson 1.25 3.00
15A C.Anthony/M.Camby 1.25 3.00
16 P.Gasol/M.Miller 1.25 3.00
16A P.Gasol/R.Gay 1.25 3.00
17 B.Gordon/L.Deng 1.25 3.00
17A B.Gordon/B.Wallace 1.25 3.00
18 A.Iguodala/K.Korver 1.25 3.00
18A A.Iguodala/A.Miller 1.25 3.00
19 P.Pierce/R.Allen 1.25 3.00
19A P.Pierce/K.Garnett 1.25 3.00
20 T.McGrady/Y.Ming 1.25 3.00
20A T.McGrady/S.Battier 1.25 3.00
21 T.Duncan/T.Parker 1.25 3.00
21A T.Duncan/M.Ginobili 1.25 3.00
22 J.Smith/M.Williams 1.25 3.00
22A J.Smith/J.Johnson 1.25 3.00
23 L.James/A.Varejao 2.50 6.00
23A L.James/D.Gibson 2.50 6.00
24 K.Bryant/A.Bynum 2.00 5.00
24A K.Bryant/L.Walton 1.50 4.00
25 V.Carter/J.Kidd 1.25 3.00
25A V.Carter/M.Williams 1.25 3.00
26 S.O'Neal/D.Wade 1.50 4.00
26A S.O'Neal/A.Walker 1.25 3.00
27 K.Garnett/P.Pierce 1.25 3.00
27A K.Garnett/R.Allen 1.25 3.00
28 C.Bosh/A.Bargnani 1.25 3.00
28A C.Bosh/T.Ford 1.25 3.00
29 B.Davis/A.Harrington 1.25 3.00
29A B.Davis/M.Ellis 1.25 3.00
30 G.Arenas/C.Butler 1.25 3.00
30A G.Arenas/A.Jamison 1.25 3.00
31 J.Stockton/D.Williams 1.25 3.00
31A J.Stockton/C.Boozer 1.25 3.00
32 M.Johnson/B.Scott 1.50 4.00
32A M.Johnson/K.Bryant 2.50 6.00
33 L.Bird/B.Russell 3.00 8.00
33A L.Bird/P.Pierce 2.50 6.00
34 R.Barry/B.Davis 1.25 3.00
34A R.Barry/C.Mullin 1.25 3.00
35 I.Thomas/C.Billups 1.25 3.00
35A I.Thomas/D.Rodman 1.50 4.00
36 D.Wilkins/J.Smith 1.25 3.00
36A D.Wilkins/J.Johnson 1.25 3.00
37 D.Rodman/B.Wallace 1.25 3.00
37A D.Rodman/L.Deng 1.25 3.00
38 W.Chamberlain/M.Malone 2.00 5.00
38A W.Chamberlain/M.Cheeks 2.00 5.00
39 P.Maravich/J.Stockton 4.00 10.00
39A P.Maravich/D.Williams 3.00 8.00
40 B.Russell/L.Bird 3.00 8.00
40A B.Russell/K.Garnett 3.00 8.00
41 B.Scott/M.Johnson 1.50 4.00
41A B.Scott/K.Bryant 2.00 5.00
42 K.Malone/J.Stockton 2.00 5.00
42A K.Malone/C.Boozer 1.25 3.00
43 C.Mullin/B.Davis 1.25 3.00
43A C.Mullin/R.Barry 1.25 3.00
44 K.McHale/L.Bird 1.50 4.00
44A K.McHale/J.Havlicek 1.50 4.00
45 C.Drexler/T.McGrady 1.25 3.00
45A C.Drexler/Y.Ming 1.25 3.00
46 J.Worthy/K.Bryant 1.25 3.00
46A J.Worthy/M.Johnson 2.00 5.00
47 B.Walton/G.Oden 1.25 3.00
47A B.Walton/B.Roy 1.25 3.00
48 E.Monroe/S.Marbury 1.25 3.00
48A E.Monroe/J.Crawford 1.25 3.00
49 E.Baylor/J.West 1.50 4.00
49A E.Baylor/K.Bryant 2.00 5.00
50 D.Robinson/T.Duncan 2.00 5.00
50A D.Robinson/T.Parker 1.50 4.00
51 N.Young/G.Arenas 1.25 3.00
51A N.Young/A.Jamison 1.25 3.00
52 G.Oden/B.Walton 2.50 6.00
52A G.Oden/B.Roy 2.50 6.00
53 M.Almond/C.Boozer 1.25 3.00
53A M.Almond/D.Williams 1.25 3.00
54 A.Tucker/S.Nash 1.25 3.00
54A A.Tucker/A.Stoudemire 1.25 3.00
55 A.Afflalo/C.Billups 1.25 3.00
55A A.Afflalo/R.Stuckey 1.50 4.00
56 D.Byars/A.Iguodala 1.25 3.00
56A D.Byars/J.Smith 1.25 3.00
57 A.Haluska/C.Paul 1.25 3.00
57A A.Haluska/T.Chandler 1.25 3.00
58 C.Brewer/A.Jefferson 1.50 4.00
58A C.Brewer/R.Foye 1.25 3.00
59 R.Sessions/M.Redd 1.25 3.00
59A R.Sessions/M.Williams 1.25 3.00
60 D.Cook/D.Wade 2.00 5.00
60A D.Cook/S.O'Neal 2.00 5.00
61 M.Conley/P.Gasol 1.25 3.00
61A M.Conley/R.Gay 1.25 3.00
62 J.Crittenton/K.Bryant 2.50 6.00
62A J.Crittenton/A.Bynum 1.25 3.00
63 J.Jordan/S.Marbury 1.25 3.00
63A J.Jordan/J.Crawford 1.25 3.00
64 A.Brooks/T.McGrady 1.50 4.00
64A A.Brooks/Y.Ming 2.00 5.00
65 M.Belinelli/B.Davis 1.25 3.00
65A M.Belinelli/A.Harrington 1.25 3.00
66 S.Mejia/A.Afflalo 1.25 3.00
66A S.Mejia/R.Stuckey 1.25 3.00
67 J.Dudley/E.Okafor 1.25 3.00
67A J.Dudley/R.Felton 1.25 3.00
68 R.Stuckey/A.Afflalo 1.25 3.00
68A R.Stuckey/C.Billups 1.25 3.00
69 J.Curry/B.Gordon 1.25 3.00
69A J.Curry/A.Gray 1.25 3.00
70 G.Pruitt/G.Davis 1.25 3.00
70A G.Pruitt/P.Pierce 1.25 3.00
71 A.Law/J.Smith 1.25 3.00
71A A.Law/J.Johnson 1.25 3.00
72 D.McGuire/G.Arenas 1.25 3.00
72A D.McGuire/N.Young 1.25 3.00
73 H.Hill/D.Byars 1.25 3.00
73A H.Hill/J.Smith 1.25 3.00
74 J.Green/K.Durant 60.00 150.00
74A J.Green/C.Wilcox 1.50 4.00
75 W.Chandler/S.Marbury 1.25 3.00
75A W.Chandler/J.Crawford 1.25 3.00
76 M.Williams/T.Duncan 1.50 4.00
76A M.Williams/T.Parker 1.25 3.00
77 J.McRoberts/G.Oden 2.00 5.00
77A J.McRoberts/T.Green 1.25 3.00
78 T.Young/A.Iguodala 1.25 3.00
78A T.Young/J.Smith 1.25 3.00
79 J.Newson/D.Nowitzki 1.25 3.00
79A J.Newson/J.Terry 1.25 3.00
80 S.Lasme/B.Wright 1.25 3.00
80A S.Lasme/B.Davis 1.25 3.00
81 D.Nichols/W.Chandler 1.25 3.00
81A D.Nichols/S.Marbury 1.25 3.00
82 J.Wright/C.Paul 1.50 4.00
82A J.Wright/D.West 1.25 3.00
83 S.Williams/J.Kidd 1.25 3.00
83A S.Williams/V.Carter 1.50 4.00
84 C.Richard/C.Brewer 1.25 3.00
84A C.Richard/A.Jefferson 1.25 3.00
85 Y.Jianlian/R.Sessions 2.00 5.00
85A Y.Jianlian/M.Redd 2.00 5.00
86 A.Thornton/E.Brand 1.25 3.00
86A A.Thornton/C.Maggette 1.25 3.00
87 C.Landry/Y.Ming 1.50 4.00
87A C.Landry/A.Brooks 1.50 4.00
88 K.Durant/J.Green 60.00 150.00
88A K.Durant/C.Wilcox 60.00 150.00
89 B.Wright/B.Davis 1.25 3.00
89A B.Wright/C.Mullin 1.25 3.00
90 N.Fazekas/D.Nowitzki 1.25 3.00
90A N.Fazekas/J.Newson 1.25 3.00
91 J.Noah/L.Deng 2.50 6.00
91A J.Noah/B.Wallace 1.50 4.00
92 J.Davidson/J.Dudley 1.25 3.00
92A J.Davidson/E.Okafor 1.25 3.00
93 D.Strawberry/S.Nash 1.25 3.00
93A D.Strawberry/A.Tucker 1.25 3.00
94 G.Davis/P.Pierce 1.50 4.00
94A G.Davis/G.Pruitt 1.25 3.00
95 A.Horford/J.Smith 2.00 5.00
95A A.Horford/A.Law 1.50 4.00
96 S.Hawes/M.Bibby 1.25 3.00
96A S.Hawes/B.Miller 1.25 3.00
97 T.Green/G.Oden 2.50 6.00
97A T.Green/J.McRoberts 1.25 3.00
98 J.Smith/D.Byars 1.25 3.00
98A J.Smith/H.Hill 1.25 3.00
99 L.Scola/T.McGrady 1.50 4.00
99A L.Scola/A.Brooks 1.50 4.00
100 A.Gray/B.Wallace 1.25 3.00
100A A.Gray/J.Noah 1.50 4.00

2007-08 Topps Co-Signers Dual Autographs

GROUP A ODDS 1:494, GROUP B 1:191
GROUP C ODDS 1:79, GROUP D 1:327
GROUP E ODDS 1:33, GROUP F 1:122
GROUP G ODDS 1:94
SILVER FOIL PRINT RUN FIVE SETS
EXCH EXPRE DATE 12/31/09
CS1 D.Wade/C.Anthony A 50.00 125.00
CS2 G.Oden/B.Walton A 40.00 100.00
CS3 D.Rodman/I.Thomas A 40.00 80.00
CS4 B.Russell/J.Havlicek A 600.00 1,200.00
CS5 R.Allen/P.Pierce B 35.00 75.00
CS7 S.O'Neal/D.Robinson A 50.00 100.00
CS8 E.Baylor/J.Havlicek B 20.00 50.00
CS9 R.Barry/B.Davis B 10.00 25.00
CS10 J.Stockton/D.Williams A 50.00 100.00
CS11 C.Bosh/A.Bargnani B 20.00 40.00
CS12 L.Walton/M.Williams E 6.00 15.00
CS13 D.Lee/T.Green E 6.00 15.00
CS14 D.McGuire/N.Fazekas E 6.00 15.00
CS15 D.Lee/W.Chandler E 8.00 20.00
CS16 H.Hill/D.Byars E 6.00 15.00
CS17 C.Hawkins/A.Tucker C 15.00 30.00
CS18 E.Okafor/J.Dudley D 6.00 15.00
CS19 M.Cheeks/M.Malone B 20.00 40.00
CS20 B.Love/K.Hinrich F 10.00 25.00
CS21 H.Turkoglu/J.Redick F 8.00 20.00
CS22 A.Bynum/J.Crittenton G 10.00 25.00
CS23 R.Tomjanovich/C.Landry G 8.00 20.00
CS24 M.Bol/J.Smith D 40.00 80.00
CS25 W.Chandler/S.Mejia E 6.00 15.00
CS26 S.Rodriguez/J.Jack E 6.00 15.00
CS27 R.Balkman/W.Chandler C 6.00 15.00
CS28 P.O'Bryant/S.Lasme F 6.00 15.00
CS29 D.Gibson/A.Law E 6.00 15.00
CS30 A.Iguodala/T.Young B 8.00 20.00
CS31 M.Williams/S.Williams C 6.00 15.00
CS32 D.Granger/I.Diogu G 6.00 15.00
CS33 G.Pruitt/G.Davis E 6.00 15.00
CS34 C.Maggette/A.Thornton C 6.00 15.00
CS35 A.Brooks/C.Landry E 8.00 20.00
CS37 B.Gordon/C.Duhon C 10.00 25.00
CS38 S.Dalembert/J.Smith C 6.00 15.00
CS39 R.Felton/J.Davidson C 6.00 15.00
CS40 L.Elmore/D.Strawberry G 6.00 15.00
CS41 R.Stuckey/A.Afflalo E 6.00 15.00
CS42 C.Boozer/M.Almond B 6.00 15.00
CS43 M.Belinelli/S.Lasme E 6.00 15.00
CS44 J.Smith/D.Cook C 6.00 15.00
CS45 T.Green/J.Jack E 6.00 15.00
CS46 S.Williams/J.Dudley C 6.00 15.00
CS47 G.Oden/J.Havlicek A 40.00 100.00
CS48 Y.Jianlian/M.Belinelli B 30.00 60.00
CS49 N.Young/G.Pruitt C 6.00 15.00
CS50 T.Young/J.Crittenton B 8.00 20.00

2007-08 Topps Co-Signers Rookie Autographs

GROUP A ODDS 1:112, GROUP B 1:1:16
*GOLD: .5X TO 1.25X BASE HI
GOLD PRINT RUN 25 SER.#'d SETS
51 Nick Young A 6.00 15.00
52 Greg Oden A 4.00 10.00
53 Morris Almond B 2.50 6.00
54 Alando Tucker A 2.50 6.00
55 Arron Afflalo B 3.00 8.00
56 Derrick Byars B 3.00 8.00
57 Adam Haluska B 2.50 6.00
62 Javaris Crittenton B 2.50 6.00
63 Jared Jordan B 2.50 6.00
64 Aaron Brooks B 3.00 8.00
68 Rodney Stuckey B 2.50 6.00
69 JamesOn Curry B 2.50 6.00
71 Acie Law A 2.50 6.00
72 Dominic McGuire B 2.50 6.00
73 Herbert Hill B 2.50 6.00
78 Thaddeus Young A 4.00 10.00
85 Yi Jianlian A 10.00 25.00
86 Al Thornton A 2.50 6.00
89 Brandan Wright A 3.00 8.00
90 Nick Fazekas B 2.50 6.00
92 Jermareo Davidson B 2.50 6.00
94 Glen Davis B 3.00 8.00
96 Spencer Hawes A 2.50 6.00
98 Jason Smith A 2.50 6.00
100 Aaron Gray B 2.50 6.00

2007-08 Topps Co-Signers Triple Autographs

STATED PRINT RUN 9 TO 19 SETS
UNLESS LISTED IN CHECKLIST
PRINT RUNS ANNOUNCED BY TOPPS
TS3 Wilkins/Smith/Law 30.00 60.00
TS4 Wallace/Okafor/Felton 30.00 60.00
TS7 Anthony/Bosh/Wade 100.00 200.00
TS8 Parker/Wade/Billups 60.00 120.00
TS9 Williams/Birdsong/Rich 25.00 50.00
TS10 Thomas/Johnson/Stktn 100.00 200.00

2008-09 Topps Co-Signers

ROOKIE PRINT RUN 2008 SER.#'d SETS
1 Tracy McGrady .75 2.00
2 Jason Kidd .75 2.00
3 Allen Iverson 1.00 2.50
4 Chris Bosh .60 1.50
5 Baron Davis .50 1.25
6 Chauncey Billups .60 1.50
7 Ben Gordon .40 1.00
8 Jermaine O'Neal .50 1.25
9 Jason Richardson .50 1.25
10 Gilbert Arenas .50 1.25
11 Jamal Crawford .50 1.25
12 Dwight Howard .60 1.50
13 Steve Nash 1.00 2.50
14 Vince Carter 1.00 2.50
15 Carmelo Anthony .60 1.50
16 Pau Gasol .60 1.50
17 Josh Smith .30 .75
18 Yi Jianlian .60 1.50
19 Andre Iguodala .40 1.00
20 Ray Allen .75 2.00
21 Tim Duncan 1.25 3.00
22 Tayshaun Prince .50 1.25
23 LeBron James 4.00 10.00
24 Kobe Bryant 4.00 10.00
25 Rudy Gay .50 1.25
26 Caron Butler .40 1.00
27 Al Jefferson .30 .75
28 Deron Williams .40 1.00
29 Luol Deng .40 1.00
30 Chris Paul 1.00 2.50
31 Brad Miller .40 1.00
32 Shaquille O'Neal 1.50 4.00
33 Dwyane Wade 1.00 2.50
34 Paul Pierce .75 2.00
35 Kevin Durant 2.00 5.00
36 Anderson Varejao .30 .75
37 Rashard Lewis .40 1.00
38 Jamario Moon .30 .75
39 Manu Ginobili 1.00 2.50
40 Mo Williams .40 1.00
41 Dirk Nowitzki 1.25 3.00
42 David Lee .30 .75
43 Stephen Jackson .40 1.00
44 Antawn Jamison .40 1.00
45 Mike Dunleavy .30 .75
46 Devin Harris .30 .75
47 Andrei Kirilenko .40 1.00
48 Gerald Wallace .40 1.00
49 Mike Miller .40 1.00
50 Corey Maggette .40 1.00
51 Yao Ming 1.25 3.00
52 Greg Oden .30 .75
53 Kevin Martin .40 1.00
54 Joe Johnson .50 1.25
55 Kevin Garnett 1.25 3.00
56 Ricky Davis .30 .75
57 Chris Wilcox .30 .75
58 Rashad McCants .30 .75
59 T.J. Ford .30 .75
60 David West .40 1.00
61 Amare Stoudemire .50 1.25
62 Al Thornton .30 .75
63 Kirk Hinrich .40 1.00
64 Samuel Dalembert .30 .75
65 Tony Parker .60 1.50
66 Ben Wallace .60 1.50
67 Shawn Marion .50 1.25
68 LaMarcus Aldridge .50 1.25
69 Eddy Curry .30 .75
70 Richard Hamilton .50 1.25
71 Danny Granger .40 1.00
72 Elton Brand .40 1.00
73 Raymond Felton .30 .75
74 Richard Jefferson .30 .75
75 Hedo Turkoglu .40 1.00
76 Peja Stojakovic .40 1.00
77 Brandon Roy .60 1.50
78 Ryan Gomes .30 .75
79 Jeff Green .30 .75
80 Michael Redd .40 1.00
81 Andre Miller .40 1.00
82 Carlos Boozer .40 1.00
83 Marcus Camby .30 .75
84 Hakim Warrick .30 .75
85 Mike Bibby .30 .75
86 Josh Howard .40 1.00
87 Andrew Bynum .40 1.00
88 Monta Ellis .40 1.00
89 Shane Battier .40 1.00
90 Ron Artest .40 1.00
91 Dennis Rodman 1.00 2.50
92 Dominique Wilkins .75 2.00
93 Larry Bird 1.50 4.00
94 John Stockton 1.00 2.50
95 Moses Malone .75 2.00
96 David Robinson 1.00 2.50
97 Jerry West 1.00 2.50
98 Bill Russell 1.50 4.00
99 George Gervin .75 2.00
100 Magic Johnson 1.50 4.00
101 Derrick Rose RC 4.00 10.00
102 Michael Beasley RC 1.00 2.50
103 O.J. Mayo RC .75 2.00
104 Russell Westbrook RC 5.00 12.00
105 Kevin Love RC 2.00 5.00
106 Danilo Gallinari RC 1.50 4.00
107 Eric Gordon RC 1.50 4.00
108 Joe Alexander RC .60 1.50
109 D.J. Augustin RC 1.00 2.50
110 Brook Lopez RC 1.25 3.00
111 Jerryd Bayless RC .75 2.00
112 Jason Thompson RC .60 1.50
113 Anthony Randolph RC .60 1.50
114 Robin Lopez RC .60 1.50
115 Marreese Speights RC .75 2.00
116 Roy Hibbert RC .75 2.00
117 JaVale McGee RC 1.00 2.50
118 J.J. Hickson RC .60 1.50
119 Alexis Ajinca RC .60 1.50
120 Ryan Anderson RC .75 2.00
121 Courtney Lee RC .75 2.00
122 Kosta Koufos RC .60 1.50
123 Donte Greene RC .60 1.50
124 George Hill RC 1.00 2.50
125 D.J. White RC .60 1.50
126 J.R. Giddens RC .60 1.50
127 Joey Dorsey RC .60 1.50
128 Mario Chalmers RC 1.00 2.50
129 DeAndre Jordan RC 1.25 3.00
130 Chris Douglas-Roberts RC .60 1.50
131 Malik Hairston RC .60 1.50
132 Sonny Weems RC .60 1.50
133 Kyle Weaver RC .60 1.50
134 Patrick Ewing Jr. RC .60 1.50
135 Mike Taylor RC .60 1.50
136 Walter Sharpe RC .60 1.50
137 Rudy Fernandez RC .75 2.00
138 Nicolas Batum RC 1.25 3.00
139 Brandon Rush RC .60 1.50
140 Darrell Arthur RC .75 2.00

2008-09 Topps Co-Signers Bronze

*1-100 BRONZE: 2X TO 5 BASE HI
*101-140 BRONZE: 1X TO 2.5 BASE HI
BRONZE PRINT RUN 299 SER.#'d SETS
23 LeBron James 40.00 100.00
24 Kobe Bryant 40.00 100.00

2008-09 Topps Co-Signers Gold

*1-100 GOLD: 3X TO 8X BASE HI
*101-140 GOLD: 1.5X TO 4X BASE HI
STATED PRINT RUN 99 SER.#'d SETS
23 LeBron James 60.00 150.00
24 Kobe Bryant 60.00 150.00

2008-09 Topps Co-Signers Hyper Bronze

*1-100 HYP.BRNZ: 4X TO 10X BASE
*101-140 HYP.BRNZ: 2X TO 5X BASE
STATED PRINT RUN 50 SER.#'d SETS
23 LeBron James 75.00 200.00
24 Kobe Bryant 75.00 200.00

2008-09 Topps Co-Signers Hyper Silver

*1-100 HYP.SILV: 5X TO 15X BASE
*101-140 HYP.SILV: 3X TO 8X BASE
STATED PRINT RUN 25 SER.#'d SETS
23 LeBron James 125.00 300.00
24 Kobe Bryant 125.00 300.00

2008-09 Topps Co-Signers Silver

*SILVER 1-100: 2.5X TO 6X BASE HI
*SILVER 101-140: 1.25X TO 3X BASE HI
STATED PRINT RUN 199 SER.#'d SETS
23 LeBron James 50.00 120.00
24 Kobe Bryant 50.00 120.00

2008-09 Topps Co-Signers Changing Faces

STATED PRINT RUN 899 SER.#'d SETS
*BRONZE: .5X TO 1.25X BASE HI
BRONZE PRINT RUN 399 SER.#'d SETS
*GOLD: .6X TO 1.5X BASE HI
GOLD PRINT RUN 199 SER.#'d SETS
*SILVER: .75X TO 2X BASE HI
SILVER PRINT RUN 99 SER.#'d SETS
CF1 Tracy McGrady 1.25 3.00
CF2 Chris Bosh 1.00 2.50
CF3 Chauncey Billups 1.00 2.50
CF4 Gilbert Arenas .75 2.00
CF5 Dwight Howard 1.00 2.50
CF6 LeBron James 6.00 15.00
CF7 Kobe Bryant 6.00 15.00
CF8 Chris Paul 1.50 4.00
CF9 Paul Pierce 1.25 3.00
CF10 Kevin Durant 3.00 8.00
CF11 Dirk Nowitzki 2.00 5.00
CF12 Greg Oden .50 1.25
CF13 Tony Parker 1.00 2.50
CF14 Elton Brand .60 1.50
CF15 Brandon Roy .60 1.50
CF16 Carlos Boozer .60 1.50
CF17 Allen Iverson 1.50 4.00
CF18 Steve Nash 1.50 4.00
CF19 Vince Carter 1.50 4.00
CF20 Carmelo Anthony 1.00 2.50
CF21 Andre Iguodala .60 1.50
CF22 Ray Allen 1.25 3.00
CF23 Tim Duncan 2.00 5.00
CF24 Shaquille O'Neal 2.50 6.00
CF25 Dwyane Wade 1.50 4.00
CF26 Manu Ginobili 1.50 4.00
CF27 Yao Ming 2.00 5.00
CF28 Kevin Garnett 2.00 5.00
CF29 Amare Stoudemire .75 2.00
CF30 Michael Redd .60 1.50
CF31 Jason Kidd 1.25 3.00
CF32 Deron Williams .75 2.00
CF33 Kevin Martin .60 1.50
CF34 Joe Johnson .75 2.00
CF35 Richard Hamilton .75 2.00
CF36 Magic Johnson 2.50 6.00
CF37 Dominique Wilkins 1.25 3.00
CF38 Larry Bird 2.50 6.00
CF39 Jerry West 1.50 4.00
CF40 Bill Russell 2.50 6.00
CF41 Derrick Rose 3.00 8.00
CF42 Michael Beasley .75 2.00
CF43 O.J. Mayo .60 1.50
CF44 Russell Westbrook 4.00 10.00
CF45 Kevin Love 1.50 4.00
CF46 Brook Lopez 1.00 2.50
CF47 Eric Gordon 1.25 3.00
CF48 Joe Alexander .50 1.25
CF49 D.J. Augustin .75 2.00
CF50 Jerryd Bayless .60 1.50

2008-09 Topps Co-Signers Dual Autographs

GROUP A PRINT RUN 7 SER.#'d SETS
GROUP B PRINT RUN 43 SER.#'d SETS
GROUP C PRINT RUN 240 SER.#'d SETS
CSAC D.Arthur/M.Chalmers C 8.00 20.00
CSBG A.Bargnani/D.Gallinari B 8.00 20.00
CSBJ C.Butler/A.Jamison C 12.00 30.00
CSBS E.Baylor/D.Schayes C 25.00 60.00
CSBT C.Billups/I.Thomas B 40.00 100.00
CSCB M.Chalmers/C.Boozer C 8.00 20.00
CSDG B.Davis/E.Gordon B 15.00 40.00
CSDM B.Davis/C.Maggette B 8.00 20.00
CSDRD C.Douglas-Roberts/J.Dorsey C 6.00 15.00
CSDT B.Davis/A.Thornton B 10.00 25.00
CSFA T.Ford/D.Augustin C 6.00 15.00
CSFG T.Ford/D.Granger B 8.00 20.00
CSFJ T.Ford/J.Jack C 6.00 15.00
CSGA B.Gordon/R.Allen B 20.00 50.00
CSGM R.Gay/J.Moon C 6.00 15.00
CSHB E.Hayes/R.Barry C 15.00 40.00
CSHC K.Hinrich/M.Chalmers B 8.00 20.00
CSHE R.Hibbert/P.Ewing Jr. C 6.00 15.00
CSHT S.Hawes/J.Thompson C 6.00 15.00
CSHW J.Havlicek/J.White B 75.00 200.00
CSHWI D.Harris/S.Williams B 6.00 15.00
CSHWS J.Hickson/J.Williams C 8.00 20.00
CSIY A.Iguodala/T.Young B 10.00 25.00
CSJC Y.Jianlian/V.Carter B 75.00 200.00
CSLC D.Lee/W.Chandler C 6.00 15.00
CSLD C.Landry/J.Dorsey C 6.00 15.00
CSLJ A.Law/D.Jordan C 10.00 25.00
CSLL B.Lopez/R.Lopez C 25.00 60.00
CSLLO S.Love/K.Love B 10.00 25.00
CSLS D.Lee/M.Speights C 6.00 15.00
CSLW K.Love/R.Westbrook B 100.00 250.00
CSMG O.Mayo/R.Gay B 8.00 20.00
CSML M.Miller/K.Love B 8.00 20.00
CSMM P.McGee/J.McGee C 12.00 30.00
CSMS M.Miller/M.Speights C 6.00 15.00
CSMY O.Mayo/N.Young B 6.00 15.00
CSPE R.Parish/M.Eaton C 15.00 40.00
CSPW M.Pietrus/G.Wallace C 6.00 15.00
CSRB D.Rose/M.Beasley B 75.00 200.00
CSRD D.Rose/L.Deng B 75.00 200.00
CSRH B.Rush/R.Hibbert C 6.00 15.00
CSSS D.Schayes/D.Schayes C 12.00 30.00
CSSY R.Stuckey/N.Young B 6.00 15.00
CSTG A.Thornton/E.Gordon B 8.00 20.00
CSTH J.Thompson/G.Hill C 8.00 20.00
CSWC D.Wilkins/V.Carter B 50.00 120.00
CSWL S.Webb/F.Lever C 12.00 30.00

2008-09 Topps Co-Signers Rookie Autographs

GROUP A PRINT RUN 50 SER.#'d SETS
GROUP B PRINT RUN 100 SER.#'d SETS
GROUP C PRINT RUN 350 SER.#'d SETS
*GOLD: .75X TO 2X BASE HI
GOLD PRINT RUN 5 TO 25 SETS
101 Derrick Rose A 125.00 250.00
102 Michael Beasley A 4.00 10.00
103 O.J. Mayo A 3.00 8.00
104 Russell Westbrook B 125.00 300.00
105 Kevin Love A 25.00 60.00
106 Danilo Gallinari B 6.00 15.00
107 Eric Gordon A 12.00 30.00
108 Joe Alexander B 2.50 6.00
109 D.J. Augustin C 4.00 10.00
110 Brook Lopez B 5.00 12.00
111 Jerryd Bayless B 3.00 8.00
112 Jason Thompson C 2.50 6.00
113 Anthony Randolph C 2.50 6.00
114 Robin Lopez C 3.00 8.00
115 Marreese Speights C 3.00 8.00
116 Roy Hibbert C 3.00 8.00
117 JaVale McGee C 4.00 10.00
118 J.J. Hickson C 2.50 6.00
120 Ryan Anderson C 3.00 8.00
121 Courtney Lee C 3.00 8.00
122 Kosta Koufos C 2.50 6.00
123 Donte Greene C 2.50 6.00
124 George Hill C 4.00 10.00
125 D.J. White C 2.50 6.00
126 J.R. Giddens C 2.50 6.00
127 Joey Dorsey C 2.50 6.00
128 Mario Chalmers C 4.00 10.00
130 Chris Douglas-Roberts C 2.50 6.00
139 Brandon Rush B 2.50 6.00
140 Darrell Arthur C 3.00 8.00

2008-09 Topps Co-Signers Rookie Photo Shoot Quad Autographs

ANNOUNCED PRINT RUN 25 SETS
RPQABRM Agstn/Byls/Rse/Myo 50.00 120.00
RPQBLGA Bsly/Lve/Lpz/Alxndr 30.00 80.00
RPQBLRM Bsly/Lve/Rose/Myo 100.00 250.00
RPQRARD Rsh/Arthr/Rse/Dgls-Rbt 50.00 120.00
RPQRMWG Rse/Myo/Wstbk/Grdn 200.00 400.00

2008-09 Topps Co-Signers Triple Autographs

STATED PRINT RUN 36 SER.#'d SETS
TSBLG Bsly/Love/Gallinari 50.00 100.00
TSGAB Gordon/Agstn/Bylss 20.00 50.00
TSGAR Gallinari/Alxndr/Rndlph 20.00 50.00
TSGGA Gallinari/Grdn/Alxndr 20.00 50.00
TSLTR Lpz/Thmpsn/Rndlph 20.00 50.00
TSMLB Mayo/Love/Bayless 40.00 100.00
TSRBM Rose/Beasley/Mayo 40.00 100.00
TSRGA Rose/Gordon/Agstn 100.00 250.00
TSRMB Rose/Mayo/Bayless 75.00 150.00
TSWLL Wstbrk/Love/Lopez 50.00 120.00

2023-24 Topps Cosmic Chrome

1 Trae Young .60 1.50
2 Dejounte Murray .40 1.00
3 Dominique Wilkins .50 1.25
4 Clint Capela .25 .60
5 Bogdan Bogdanovic .30 .75
6 Jayson Tatum 1.25 3.00
7 Jaylen Brown .60 1.50
8 Larry Bird 1.25 3.00
9 Jrue Holiday .40 1.00
10 Kristaps Porzingis .40 1.00
11 Mikal Bridges .40 1.00
12 Ben Simmons .30 .75
13 Richard Jefferson .25 .60
14 Cam Johnson .30 .75
15 Spencer Dinwiddie .25 .60
16 Brandon Ingram .40 1.00
17 LaMelo Ball .75 2.00
18 Larry Johnson .40 1.00
19 Mark Williams .30 .75
20 Zach Lavine .50 1.25
21 DeMar DeRozan .50 1.25
22 Dennis Rodman .75 2.00
23 Patrick Williams .25 .60
24 Ayo Dosunmu .30 .75
25 Donovan Mitchell .60 1.50
26 Evan Mobley .60 1.50
27 Giannis Antetokounmpo 1.50 4.00
28 Caris LeVert .30 .75
29 Shai Gilgeous-Alexander 1.50 4.00
30 Kyrie Irving .60 1.50
31 Grant Williams .25 .60
32 Dirk Nowitzki .75 2.00
33 Tim Hardaway Jr. .25 .60
34 Seth Curry .30 .75
35 Christian Braun .30 .75
36 Aaron Gordon .30 .75
37 Alex English .40 1.00
38 Kentavious Caldwell-Pope .25 .60
39 Michael Porter Jr. .40 1.00
40 Cade Cunningham .75 2.00
41 Damian Lillard .75 2.00
42 Rasheed Wallace .40 1.00
43 Ben Wallace .40 1.00
44 Isaiah Stewart .30 .75
45 Fred VanVleet .50 1.25
46 Jalen Green .50 1.25
47 Hakeem Olajuwon .60 1.50
48 Alperen Sengun .50 1.25
49 Jimmy Butler .50 1.25
50 Tyrese Haliburton .60 1.50
51 Myles Turner .30 .75
52 Metta World Peace .30 .75
53 Buddy Hield .30 .75
54 Obi Toppin .30 .75
55 Nikola Jokic 1.50 4.00
56 Austin Reaves .75 2.00
57 Magic Johnson 1.25 3.00
58 Jerry West .60 1.50
59 LeBron James 2.50 6.00
60 Paul George .50 1.25
61 Russell Westbrook .50 1.25
62 James Harden .60 1.50
63 Norman Powell .30 .75
64 Marcus Smart .40 1.00
65 Desmond Bane .40 1.00
66 Pau Gasol .50 1.25
67 Jaren Jackson Jr. .50 1.25
68 Jason Williams .50 1.25
69 Tyler Herro .50 1.25
70 Dwyane Wade .60 1.50
71 Shaquille O'Neal 1.00 2.50
72 Khris Middleton .30 .75
73 Ray Allen .50 1.25
74 Karl-Anthony Towns .50 1.25
75 Rudy Gobert .40 1.00
76 Kevin Garnett .75 2.00
77 Christian Laettner .30 .75
78 Naz Reid .30 .75
79 CJ McCollum .30 .75
80 Trey Murphy III .40 1.00
81 Jalen Brunson .60 1.50
82 Immanuel Quickley .30 .75
83 Carmelo Anthony .50 1.25
84 Donte DiVincenzo .30 .75
85 Julius Randle .40 1.00
86 Chet Holmgren .75 2.00
87 Jalen Williams .60 1.50
88 Shawn Kemp .40 1.00
89 Josh Giddey .40 1.00
90 Franz Wagner .50 1.25
91 Markelle Fultz .25 .60
92 Grant Hill .50 1.25
93 Cole Anthony .30 .75
94 Anfernee Hardaway .75 2.00
95 Joel Embiid .75 2.00
96 Tyrese Maxey .60 1.50
97 Maurice Cheeks .30 .75
98 Kelly Oubre .30 .75
99 Allen Iverson .75 2.00
100 Devin Booker .75 2.00
101 Kevin Durant 1.00 2.50
102 Bradley Beal .40 1.00
103 Shaedon Sharpe .60 1.50
104 Anfernee Simons .40 1.00
105 Bill Walton .50 1.25
106 Domantas Sabonis .60 1.50
107 De'Aaron Fox .60 1.50
108 Peja Stojakovic .30 .75
109 Kevin Huerter .25 .60
110 Malik Monk .40 1.00
111 Jeremy Sochan .40 1.00
112 David Robinson .60 1.50
113 Manu Ginobili .60 1.50
114 Tony Parker .50 1.25
115 George Gervin .50 1.25
116 Bam Adebayo .50 1.25
117 Zach Collins .25 .60
118 Stephen Curry 2.50 6.00
119 Klay Thompson .75 2.00
120 Draymond Green .40 1.00
121 Chris Paul .60 1.50
122 Jonathan Kuminga .75 2.00
123 Rick Barry .40 1.00
124 Andrew Wiggins .40 1.00
125 OG Anunoby .50 1.25
126 Pascal Siakam .50 1.25
127 Vince Carter .60 1.50
128 Jakob Poeltl .25 .60
129 Scottie Barnes .40 1.00
130 John Collins .30 .75
131 Lauri Markkanen .50 1.25
132 Bennedict Mathurin .50 1.25
133 Collin Sexton .40 1.00
134 Jordan Clarkson .30 .75
135 Deron Williams .25 .60
136 Daniel Gafford .30 .75
137 Kyle Kuzma .40 1.00
138 Corey Kispert .25 .60
139 Elvin Hayes .40 1.00
140 Robert Parish .40 1.00
141 Paul Pierce .50 1.25
142 Jalen Rose .30 .75
143 Jason Kidd .50 1.25
144 Zach Randolph .30 .75
145 Latrell Sprewell .40 1.00
146 Calvin Murphy .30 .75
147 John Stockton .60 1.50
148 Arvydas Sabonis .40 1.00
149 Juwan Howard .30 .75
150 Rip Hamilton .40 1.00
151 Victor Wembanyama RC 5.00 12.00
152 Brandon Miller RC 2.50 6.00
153 Scoot Henderson RC 2.00 5.00
154 Kawhi Leonard .75 2.00
155 Artis Gilmore .40 1.00
156 Anthony Black RC 1.25 3.00
157 Bilal Coulibaly RC 1.50 4.00
158 Jarace Walker RC 1.25 3.00
159 Taylor Hendricks RC .60 1.50
160 Jett Howard RC .75 2.00
161 Dereck Lively II RC 1.25 3.00
162 Gradey Dick RC 1.25 3.00
163 Jordan Hawkins RC 1.00 2.50
164 Kobe Bufkin RC .75 2.00
165 Jalen Hood-Schifino RC .60 1.50
166 Jaime Jaquez Jr. RC 1.00 2.50
167 Brandin Podziemski RC 2.00 5.00
168 Cam Whitmore RC 1.50 4.00
169 Noah Clowney RC .75 2.00
170 Kris Murray RC .60 1.50
171 Olivier-Maxence Prosper RC .60 1.50
172 Marcus Sasser RC 1.00 2.50
173 Ben Sheppard RC .60 1.50
174 Nick Smith Jr. RC .75 2.00
175 Brice Sensabaugh RC 1.00 2.50
176 Julian Strawther RC .75 2.00
177 Kobe Brown RC .60 1.50
178 James Nnaji RC .50 1.25
179 Jalen Pickett RC .50 1.25
180 Leonard Miller RC .60 1.50
181 Colby Jones RC .60 1.50
182 Julian Phillips RC .60 1.50
183 Andre Jackson Jr. RC 1.00 2.50
184 Jordan Walsh RC .60 1.50
185 Maxwell Lewis RC .50 1.25
186 Amari Bailey RC .60 1.50
187 Josh Hart .30 .75
188 Rayan Rupert RC .60 1.50
189 Sidy Cissoko RC .60 1.50
190 GG Jackson RC 1.25 3.00
191 Seth Lundy RC .50 1.25
192 Keyontae Johnson RC .60 1.50
193 Jalen Wilson RC .60 1.50
194 Jaylen Clark RC .60 1.50
195 Isaiah Wong RC .60 1.50
196 Trayce Jackson-Davis RC .75 2.00
197 Chris Livingston RC .60 1.50
198 Anthony Davis .75 2.00
199 Jamal Murray .60 1.50
200 Pete Nance RC .50 1.25

2023-24 Topps Cosmic Chrome Aqua Equinox Refractors

*AQUA EQUINOX REF: 2.5X TO 6X BASIC
STATED PRINT RUN 149 SER.#'d SETS
151 Victor Wembanyama 75.00 200.00

2023-24 Topps Cosmic Chrome Blue Moon Refractors

*BLUE MOON REF: 3X TO 8X BASIC
STATED PRINT RUN 99 SER.#'d SETS
151 Victor Wembanyama 125.00 300.00

2023-24 Topps Cosmic Chrome Gold Interstellar Refractors

*GOLD INTERSTELLAR REF: 5X TO 12X BASIC
STATED PRINT RUN 50 SER.#'d SETS
59 LeBron James 75.00 200.00
151 Victor Wembanyama 200.00 500.00

2023-24 Topps Cosmic Chrome Green Space Dust Refractors

*GRN SPACE DUST REF: 4X TO 10X BASIC
STATED PRINT RUN 75 SER.#'d SETS
151 Victor Wembanyama 150.00 400.00

2023-24 Topps Cosmic Chrome Nucleus Refractors

*NUCLEUS REF: .75X TO 2X BASIC
151 Victor Wembanyama 25.00 60.00

2023-24 Topps Cosmic Chrome Orange Galactic Refractors

*ORANGE GALACTIC REF: 6X TO 15X BASIC
STATED PRINT RUN 25 SER.#'d SETS
59 LeBron James 75.00 200.00
151 Victor Wembanyama 200.00 500.00

2023-24 Topps Cosmic Chrome Pink Galaxy Refractors

*PINK GALAXY REF: 1.25X TO 3X BASIC
151 Victor Wembanyama 40.00 100.00

2023-24 Topps Cosmic Chrome Refractors

*REF: .75X TO 2X BASIC
151 Victor Wembanyama 25.00 60.00

2023-24 Topps Cosmic Chrome White Hole Refractors

*WHITE HOLE REF: 5X TO 12X BASIC
59 LeBron James 60.00 150.00
151 Victor Wembanyama 150.00 400.00

2023-24 Topps Cosmic Chrome Autographs Refractors

STATED PRINT RUN 75 SER.#'d SETS
*GOLD INTST REF/50: .5X TO 1.2X BASIC
*ORNG GALACTIC REF/25: .6X TO 1.5X BASIC
CCAVAC Alex Caruso 8.00 20.00
CCAVAE Alex English 10.00 25.00
CCAVAG Artis Gilmore 10.00 25.00
CCAVAH Anfernee Hardaway 30.00 80.00
CCAVAS Anfernee Simons 10.00 25.00
CCAVBB Bogdan Bogdanovic 8.00 20.00
CCAVBC Brandon Clarke 6.00 15.00

CCAVBS Brice Sensabaugh 12.00 30.00
CCAVBW Ben Wallace 10.00 25.00
CCAVCB Christian Braun 8.00 20.00
CCAVCC Clint Capela 6.00 15.00
CCAVCJ Cameron Johnson 8.00 20.00
CCAVCK Corey Kispert 6.00 15.00
CCAVCL Christian Laettner 8.00 20.00
CCAVCM Calvin Murphy 8.00 20.00
CCAVCS Collin Sexton 10.00 25.00
CCAVDB Desmond Bane 10.00 25.00
CCAVDD Donte DiVincenzo 8.00 20.00
CCAVDF De'Aaron Fox 15.00 40.00
CCAVDG Daniel Gafford 8.00 20.00
CCAVDH Danuel House JR. 5.00 12.00
CCAVDI Dan Issel 10.00 25.00
CCAVDM Davion Mitchell 6.00 15.00
CCAVDN Dirk Nowitzki 50.00 120.00
CCAVDR David Robinson 40.00 100.00
CCAVDT David Thompson 10.00 25.00
CCAVDV Devin Vassell 10.00 25.00
CCAVDW Deron Williams 6.00 15.00
CCAVEF Evan Fournier 6.00 15.00
CCAVEH Elvin Hayes 10.00 25.00
CCAVFW Franz Wagner 12.00 30.00
CCAVGG George Gervin 12.00 30.00
CCAVGH Grant Hill 12.00 30.00
CCAVGJ GG Jackson 15.00 40.00
CCAVGT Gary Trent Jr. 8.00 20.00
CCAVHO Hakeem Olajuwon 40.00 100.00
CCAVIH Isaiah Hartenstein 8.00 20.00
CCAVIQ Immanuel Quickley 8.00 20.00
CCAVIS Isaiah Stewart 8.00 20.00
CCAVJA Jarrett Allen 8.00 20.00
CCAVJG Jeff Green 5.00 12.00
CCAVJH Juwan Howard 8.00 20.00
CCAVJK Jason Kidd 12.00 30.00
CCAVJL Jake LaRavia 6.00 15.00
CCAVJR Jalen Rose 8.00 20.00
CCAVJT Jae'Sean Tate 8.00 20.00
CCAVJV Jarred Vanderbilt 6.00 15.00
CCAVJW Jamaal Wilkes 8.00 20.00
CCAVKC Kentavious Caldwell-Pope 6.00 15.00
CCAVKG Kevin Garnett 50.00 120.00
CCAVKH Kevin Huerter 6.00 15.00
CCAVKT Karl-Anthony Towns 12.00 30.00
CCAVLB Larry Bird 50.00 120.00
CCAVLJ Larry Johnson 10.00 25.00
CCAVLW Lenny Wilkens 10.00 25.00
CCAVMB Mo Bamba 6.00 15.00
CCAVMC Maurice Cheeks 8.00 20.00
CCAVMF Markelle Fultz 6.00 15.00
CCAVMG Manu Ginobili 25.00 60.00
CCAVMJ Magic Johnson 50.00 120.00
CCAVMS Max Strus 8.00 20.00
CCAVMW Metta World Peace 8.00 20.00
CCAVNB Nicolas Batum 5.00 12.00
CCAVOB Oshae Brissett 6.00 15.00
CCAVPA Precious Achiuwa 6.00 15.00
CCAVPG Pau Gasol 12.00 30.00
CCAVPP Paul Pierce 12.00 30.00
CCAVPS Peja Stojakovic 8.00 20.00
CCAVPW Patrick Williams 6.00 15.00
CCAVQG Quentin Grimes 8.00 20.00
CCAVRA Ray Allen 25.00 60.00
CCAVRH Rip Hamilton 10.00 25.00
CCAVRP Robert Parish 10.00 25.00
CCAVRW Rasheed Wallace 10.00 25.00
CCAVSC Seth Curry 8.00 20.00
CCAVSD Spencer Dinwiddie 6.00 15.00
CCAVSK Shawn Kemp 12.00 30.00
CCAVSM Sandro Mamukelashvili 8.00 20.00
CCAVTM Terance Mann 6.00 15.00
CCAVTP Tony Parker 12.00 30.00
CCAVTS Terquavion Smith 8.00 20.00
CCAVVC Vince Carter 50.00 120.00
CCAVWK Walker Kessler 8.00 20.00
CCAVZC Zach Collins 6.00 15.00
CCAVZL Zach Lavine 12.00 30.00
CCAVZR Zach Randolph 8.00 20.00
CCAVAGO Aaron Gordon 8.00 20.00
CCAVAHO Al Horford 8.00 20.00
CCAVBWA Bill Walton 25.00 60.00
CCAVBWE Blake Wesley 5.00 12.00
CCAVDGR Devonte' Graham 6.00 15.00
CCAVDHU De'Andre Hunter 8.00 20.00
CCAVDMU Dejounte Murray 10.00 25.00
CCAVDWA Dwyane Wade 50.00 120.00
CCAVDWI Dominique Wilkins 12.00 30.00
CCAVJWE Jerry West 15.00 40.00
CCAVJWI Jason Williams 25.00 60.00
CCAVLWA Lonnie Walker IV 8.00 20.00
CCAVRHA Rui Hachimura 8.00 20.00
CCAVTMU Trey Murphy III 10.00 25.00

2023-24 Topps Cosmic Chrome Cosmic Dust

CD1 Shai Gilgeous-Alexander 80.00 200.00
CD2 Jayson Tatum 60.00 150.00
CD3 Kyrie Irving 30.00 80.00
CD4 Carmelo Anthony 25.00 60.00
CD5 Giannis Antetokounmpo 80.00 200.00
CD6 Shaquille O'Neal 50.00 120.00
CD7 Nikola Jokic 80.00 200.00
CD8 Kevin Durant 50.00 125.00
CD9 Chet Holmgren 40.00 100.00
CD10 Kevin Garnett 40.00 100.00
CD11 Jalen Brunson 30.00 80.00
CD12 Tyrese Maxey 30.00 80.00
CD13 De'Aaron Fox 30.00 80.00
CD14 Jaime Jaquez Jr. 25.00 60.00
CD15 Stephen Curry 200.00 500.00
CD16 Allen Iverson 40.00 100.00
CD17 Victor Wembanyama 400.00 800.00
CD18 Scoot Henderson 50.00 125.00
CD19 Brandon Miller 60.00 150.00
CD20 Dirk Nowitzki 40.00 100.00

2023-24 Topps Cosmic Chrome Cosmic Heroes

CH1 Anthony Davis 10.00 25.00
CH2 Larry Bird 15.00 40.00
CH3 Donovan Mitchell 8.00 20.00
CH4 Dirk Nowitzki 10.00 25.00
CH5 Allen Iverson 10.00 25.00
CH6 Shai Gilgeous-Alexander 20.00 50.00
CH7 Tyrese Haliburton 8.00 20.00
CH8 Magic Johnson 15.00 40.00
CH9 Jayson Tatum 15.00 40.00
CH10 Dwyane Wade 8.00 20.00
CH11 Joel Embiid 10.00 25.00
CH12 Devin Booker 10.00 25.00
CH13 Chet Holmgren 10.00 25.00
CH14 Giannis Antetokounmpo 20.00 50.00
CH15 Stephen Curry 30.00 80.00
CH16 Vince Carter 8.00 20.00
CH17 Shaquille O'Neal 12.00 30.00
CH18 Victor Wembanyama 75.00 200.00
CH19 Scoot Henderson 12.00 30.00
CH20 Brandon Miller 15.00 40.00

2023-24 Topps Cosmic Chrome Equinox Autographs Refractors

STATED PRINT RUN 75 SER.#'d SETS
*GOLD INTST REF/50: .5X TO 1.2X BASIC
*ORNG GALACTIC REF/25: .6X TO 1.5X BASIC
ERAAB Anthony Black 15.00 40.00
ERABB Bradley Beal 10.00 25.00
ERABC Bilal Coulibaly 20.00 50.00
ERABM Brandon Miller 30.00 80.00
ERACM CJ McCollum 8.00 20.00
ERACP Chris Paul 40.00 100.00
ERACW Cam Whitmore 20.00 50.00
ERADL Dereck Lively II 15.00 40.00
ERADM Donovan Mitchell 40.00 100.00
ERADR D'Angelo Russell 8.00 20.00
ERAFV Fred VanVleet 12.00 30.00
ERAGD Gradey Dick 15.00 40.00
ERAJH Jett Howard 10.00 25.00
ERAJJ Jaime Jaquez Jr. 12.00 30.00
ERAJK Jonathan Kuminga 20.00 50.00
ERAJS Jeremy Sochan 10.00 25.00
ERAJW Jalen Williams 15.00 40.00
ERAKB Kobe Bufkin 10.00 25.00
ERAKK Kyle Kuzma 10.00 25.00
ERALM Lauri Markkanen 12.00 30.00
ERAMB Mikal Bridges 10.00 25.00
ERAMP Michael Porter Jr. 10.00 25.00
ERAMT Myles Turner 8.00 20.00
ERANR Naz Reid 8.00 20.00
ERAOA OG Anunoby 10.00 25.00
ERASH Scoot Henderson 25.00 60.00
ERASS Shaedon Sharpe 15.00 40.00
ERATH Tyler Herro 12.00 30.00
ERATM Tyrese Maxey 40.00 100.00
ERAVW Victor Wembanyama 800.00 1,500.00
ERAJHA Jordan Hawkins 12.00 30.00
ERAJHS Jalen Hood-Schifino 8.00 20.00
ERAJWA Jarace Walker 15.00 40.00
ERATHA Tim Hardaway Jr. 6.00 15.00
ERATHE Taylor Hendricks 8.00 20.00

2023-24 Topps Cosmic Chrome Extraterrestrial Talent

ET1 Jalen Brunson 1.25 3.00
ET2 Jaylen Brown 1.25 3.00
ET3 Mikal Bridges .75 2.00
ET4 Donovan Mitchell 1.25 3.00
ET5 Jayson Tatum 2.50 6.00
ET6 Kyrie Irving 1.25 3.00
ET7 Karl-Anthony Towns 1.00 2.50
ET8 Giannis Antetokounmpo 3.00 8.00
ET9 Tyrese Haliburton 1.25 3.00
ET10 LaMelo Ball 1.50 4.00
ET11 Kevin Durant 2.00 5.00
ET12 De'Aaron Fox 1.25 3.00
ET13 Stephen Curry 5.00 12.00
ET14 Joel Embiid 1.50 4.00
ET15 Paul George 1.00 2.50
ET16 Victor Wembanyama 5.00 12.00
ET17 Scoot Henderson 2.00 5.00
ET18 Cam Whitmore 1.50 4.00
ET19 Brandon Miller 2.50 6.00
ET20 Shai Gilgeous-Alexander 3.00 8.00
ET21 Jordan Hawkins 1.00 2.50
ET22 Jaime Jaquez Jr. 1.00 2.50
ET23 Gradey Dick 1.25 3.00
ET24 Jimmy Butler 1.00 2.50
ET25 Nick Smith Jr. .75 2.00

2023-24 Topps Cosmic Chrome Extraterrestrial Talent Blue Moon Refractors

*BLUE MOON REF: 1.5X TO 4X BASIC
STATED PRINT RUN 99 SER.#'d SETS
ET16 Victor Wembanyama 100.00 250.00

2023-24 Topps Cosmic Chrome Extraterrestrial Talent Gold Interstellar Refractors

*GOLD INTST REF: 2.5X TO 6X BASIC
STATED PRINT RUN 50 SER.#'d SETS
ET16 Victor Wembanyama 150.00 400.00

2023-24 Topps Cosmic Chrome Extraterrestrial Talent Orange Galactic Refractors

*ORNG GALACTIC REF: 3X TO 8X BASIC
STATED PRINT RUN 25 SER.#'d SETS
ET16 Victor Wembanyama 200.00 500.00

2023-24 Topps Cosmic Chrome First Flight Signatures Refractors

STATED PRINT RUN 75 SER.#'d SETS
*GOLD INTST REF/50: .5X TO 1.2X BASIC
*ORNG GALACTIC REF/25: .6X TO 1.5X BASIC
FFSAB Anthony Black 15.00 40.00
FFSAR Austin Reaves 20.00 50.00
FFSAW Andrew Wiggins 10.00 25.00
FFSBC Bilal Coulibaly 20.00 50.00
FFSBM Brandon Miller 30.00 80.00
FFSBP Brandin Podziemski 25.00 60.00
FFSCW Cam Whitmore 20.00 50.00
FFSDA Deandre Ayton 8.00 20.00
FFSGD Gradey Dick 15.00 40.00
FFSGW Grant Williams 6.00 15.00
FFSJB Jalen Brunson 40.00 100.00
FFSJC John Collins 8.00 20.00
FFSJG Jalen Green 12.00 30.00
FFSJH Jordan Hawkins 12.00 30.00
FFSJJ Jaime Jaquez Jr. 12.00 30.00
FFSJS Julian Strawther 10.00 25.00
FFSJT Jayson Tatum 125.00 300.00
FFSJW Jarace Walker 15.00 40.00
FFSKD Kevin Durant 125.00 300.00
FFSMP Michael Porter Jr. 10.00 25.00
FFSNC Noah Clowney 10.00 25.00
FFSOP Olivier-Maxence Prosper 8.00 20.00
FFSPS Pascal Siakam 12.00 30.00
FFSSH Scoot Henderson 25.00 60.00
FFSTH Tyrese Haliburton 15.00 40.00
FFSVW Victor Wembanyama 800.00 1,500.00
FFSJHS Jalen Hood-Schifino 8.00 20.00
FFSJJJ Jaren Jackson Jr. 12.00 30.00

2023-24 Topps Cosmic Chrome Galaxy Greats

*BLUE MOON REF/99: 1.5X TO 4X BASIC
*GOLD INTST REF/50: 2.5X TO 6X BASIC
*ORNG GALACTIC REF/25: 3X TO 8X BASIC
GG1 Dominique Wilkins .60 1.50
GG2 Larry Bird 1.50 4.00
GG3 Larry Johnson .50 1.25
GG4 Dennis Rodman 1.00 2.50
GG5 Jason Kidd .60 1.50
GG6 Carmelo Anthony .60 1.50
GG7 Magic Johnson 1.50 4.00
GG8 Dwyane Wade .75 2.00
GG9 Shaquille O'Neal 1.25 3.00
GG10 Kevin Garnett 1.00 2.50
GG11 Anfernee Hardaway 1.00 2.50
GG12 Tony Parker .60 1.50
GG13 Vince Carter .75 2.00
GG14 Metta World Peace .40 1.00
GG15 Tracy McGrady .60 1.50
GG16 Bill Walton .60 1.50
GG17 Peja Stojakovic .40 1.00
GG18 Shawn Kemp .60 1.50
GG19 Hakeem Olajuwon .75 2.00
GG20 Ben Wallace .50 1.25
GG21 John Stockton .75 2.00
GG22 Jalen Rose .40 1.00
GG23 Alonzo Mourning .60 1.50
GG24 Alex English .50 1.25
GG25 Paul Pierce .60 1.50
GG26 Jerry West .75 2.00
GG27 Grant Hill .60 1.50
GG28 David Robinson .75 2.00
GG29 Dirk Nowitzki 1.00 2.50
GG30 Jamaal Wilkes .40 1.00
GG31 Zach Randolph .40 1.00
GG32 George Gervin .60 1.50
GG33 Manu Ginobili .75 2.00
GG34 Christian Laettner .40 1.00
GG35 Robert Parish .50 1.25

2023-24 Topps Cosmic Chrome Launched Into Orbit

LIO1 Victor Wembanyama 8.00 20.00
LIO2 Cam Whitmore 1.50 4.00
LIO3 Brandon Miller 2.50 6.00
LIO4 Scoot Henderson 2.00 5.00
LIO5 Jarace Walker 1.25 3.00
LIO6 Jaime Jaquez Jr. 1.00 2.50
LIO7 Bilal Coulibaly 1.50 4.00
LIO8 Jordan Hawkins 1.00 2.50
LIO9 Jalen Hood-Schifino .60 1.50
LIO10 Marcus Sasser 1.00 2.50
LIO11 Jayson Tatum 2.50 6.00
LIO12 Zach Lavine 1.00 2.50
LIO13 Jalen Brunson 1.25 3.00
LIO14 Anthony Edwards 3.00 8.00
LIO15 Giannis Antetokounmpo 3.00 8.00
LIO16 Tyrese Maxey 1.25 3.00
LIO17 Shai Gilgeous-Alexander 3.00 8.00
LIO18 Devin Booker 1.50 4.00
LIO19 Stephen Curry 5.00 12.00
LIO20 Allen Iverson 1.50 4.00
LIO21 Shaquille O'Neal 2.00 5.00
LIO22 Vince Carter 1.25 3.00
LIO23 Kevin Garnett 1.50 4.00
LIO24 Dwyane Wade 1.25 3.00
LIO25 Tracy McGrady 1.00 2.50

2023-24 Topps Cosmic Chrome Launched Into Orbit Blue Moon Refractors

*BLUE MOON REF: 1.5X TO 4X BASIC
STATED PRINT RUN 99 SER.#'d SETS
LIO1 Victor Wembanyama 75.00 200.00

2023-24 Topps Cosmic Chrome Launched Into Orbit Gold Interstellar Refractors

*GOLD INTST REF: 2.5X TO 6X BASIC
STATED PRINT RUN 50 SER.#'d SETS
LIO1 Victor Wembanyama 125.00 300.00

2023-24 Topps Cosmic Chrome Launched Into Orbit Orange Galactic Refractors

*ORNG GALACTIC REF: 3X TO 8X BASIC
STATED PRINT RUN 25 SER.#'d SETS
LIO1 Victor Wembanyama 150.00 400.00

2023-24 Topps Cosmic Chrome Milky Way Marks Refractors

STATED PRINT RUN 75 SER.#'d SETS
*GOLD INTST REF/50: .5X TO 1.2X BASIC
*ORNG GALACTIC REF/25: .6X TO 1.5X BASIC
MWMAB Anthony Black 15.00 40.00
MWMAR Austin Reaves 20.00 50.00
MWMBB Bradley Beal 10.00 25.00
MWMBC Bilal Coulibaly 20.00 50.00
MWMBM Brandon Miller 30.00 80.00
MWMBP Brandin Podziemski 25.00 60.00
MWMCC Clint Capela 6.00 15.00
MWMCW Cam Whitmore 20.00 50.00
MWMDA Deandre Ayton 8.00 20.00
MWMDL Dereck Lively II 15.00 40.00
MWMDM Donovan Mitchell 40.00 100.00
MWMDS Domantas Sabonis 12.00 30.00
MWMFV Fred VanVleet 12.00 30.00
MWMGD Gradey Dick 15.00 40.00
MWMGH Gordon Hayward 8.00 20.00
MWMGW Grant Williams 6.00 15.00
MWMJH Jrue Holiday 10.00 25.00
MWMJW Jarace Walker 15.00 40.00
MWMKB Kobe Bufkin 10.00 25.00
MWMMB Mikal Bridges 10.00 25.00
MWMMS Marcus Smart 10.00 25.00
MWMMT Myles Turner 8.00 20.00
MWMNV Nikola Vucevic 8.00 20.00
MWMOA OG Anunoby 10.00 25.00
MWMRG Rudy Gobert 10.00 25.00
MWMSC Stephen Curry 300.00 600.00
MWMSH Scoot Henderson 25.00 60.00
MWMTH Tyler Herro 12.00 30.00
MWMVW Victor Wembanyama 800.00 1,500.00
MWMJHA Jordan Hawkins 12.00 30.00
MWMJHO Jett Howard 10.00 25.00
MWMJHS Jalen Hood-Schifino 8.00 20.00
MWMNSJ Nick Smith Jr. 10.00 25.00
MWMTHE Taylor Hendricks 8.00 20.00

2023-24 Topps Cosmic Chrome Planetary Pursuit Earth

PPE1 Jayson Tatum 30.00 80.00
PPE2 Stephen Curry 60.00 150.00
PPE3 Giannis Antetokounmpo 40.00 100.00
PPE4 Donovan Mitchell 15.00 40.00
PPE5 Brandon Miller 30.00 80.00
PPE6 Joel Embiid 20.00 50.00
PPE7 Kevin Durant 25.00 60.00
PPE8 Chet Holmgren 25.00 60.00
PPE9 Victor Wembanyama 300.00 600.00
PPE10 Scoot Henderson 25.00 60.00

2023-24 Topps Cosmic Chrome Planetary Pursuit Jupiter

PPJ1 Jayson Tatum 50.00 125.00
PPJ2 Stephen Curry 100.00 250.00
PPJ3 Giannis Antetokounmpo 60.00 150.00
PPJ4 Donovan Mitchell 25.00 60.00
PPJ5 Brandon Miller 50.00 120.00
PPJ6 Joel Embiid 30.00 80.00
PPJ7 Kevin Durant 40.00 100.00
PPJ8 Chet Holmgren 30.00 80.00
PPJ9 Victor Wembanyama 500.00 1,000.00
PPJ10 Scoot Henderson 40.00 100.00

2023-24 Topps Cosmic Chrome Planetary Pursuit Mars

PPMA1 Jayson Tatum 40.00 100.00
PPMA2 Stephen Curry 80.00 200.00
PPMA3 Giannis Antetokounmpo 50.00 125.00
PPMA4 Donovan Mitchell 20.00 50.00
PPMA5 Brandon Miller 40.00 100.00
PPMA6 Joel Embiid 25.00 60.00
PPMA7 Kevin Durant 30.00 80.00
PPMA8 Chet Holmgren 25.00 60.00
PPMA9 Victor Wembanyama 400.00 800.00
PPMA10 Scoot Henderson 30.00 80.00

2023-24 Topps Cosmic Chrome Planetary Pursuit Mercury

PPM1 Jayson Tatum 15.00 40.00
PPM2 Stephen Curry 30.00 80.00
PPM3 Giannis Antetokounmpo 20.00 50.00
PPM4 Donovan Mitchell 8.00 20.00
PPM5 Brandon Miller 15.00 40.00
PPM6 Joel Embiid 10.00 25.00
PPM7 Kevin Durant 12.00 30.00
PPM8 Chet Holmgren 10.00 25.00
PPM9 Victor Wembanyama 125.00 300.00
PPM10 Scoot Henderson 12.00 30.00

2023-24 Topps Cosmic Chrome Planetary Pursuit Neptune

PPN1 Jayson Tatum 150.00 400.00
PPN2 Stephen Curry 300.00 800.00
PPN3 Giannis Antetokounmpo 200.00 500.00
PPN4 Donovan Mitchell 80.00 200.00
PPN5 Brandon Miller 150.00 400.00
PPN6 Joel Embiid 100.00 250.00
PPN7 Kevin Durant 125.00 300.00
PPN8 Chet Holmgren 100.00 250.00
PPN9 Victor Wembanyama 3,000.00 6,000.00
PPN10 Scoot Henderson 125.00 300.00

2023-24 Topps Cosmic Chrome Planetary Pursuit Pluto

PPP1 Jayson Tatum 200.00 500.00
PPP2 Stephen Curry 400.00 1,000.00
PPP3 Giannis Antetokounmpo 250.00 600.00
PPP4 Donovan Mitchell 100.00 250.00
PPP5 Brandon Miller 200.00 500.00
PPP6 Joel Embiid 125.00 300.00
PPP7 Kevin Durant 150.00 400.00
PPP8 Chet Holmgren 125.00 300.00
PPP9 Victor Wembanyama 4,000.00 8,000.00
PPP10 Scoot Henderson 150.00 400.00

2023-24 Topps Cosmic Chrome Planetary Pursuit Saturn

PPSA1 Jayson Tatum 80.00 200.00
PPSA2 Stephen Curry 150.00 400.00
PPSA3 Giannis Antetokounmpo 100.00 250.00
PPSA4 Donovan Mitchell 40.00 100.00
PPSA5 Brandon Miller 80.00 200.00
PPSA6 Joel Embiid 50.00 125.00
PPSA7 Kevin Durant 60.00 150.00
PPSA8 Chet Holmgren 50.00 125.00
PPSA9 Victor Wembanyama 1,500.00 3,000.00
PPSA10 Scoot Henderson 60.00 150.00

2023-24 Topps Cosmic Chrome Planetary Pursuit Sun

PPS1 Jayson Tatum 8.00 20.00
PPS2 Stephen Curry 15.00 40.00
PPS3 Giannis Antetokounmpo 10.00 25.00
PPS4 Donovan Mitchell 4.00 10.00
PPS5 Brandon Miller 8.00 20.00
PPS6 Joel Embiid 5.00 12.00
PPS7 Kevin Durant 6.00 15.00
PPS8 Chet Holmgren 5.00 12.00
PPS9 Victor Wembanyama 60.00 150.00
PPS10 Scoot Henderson 6.00 15.00

2023-24 Topps Cosmic Chrome Planetary Pursuit Uranus

PPU1 Jayson Tatum 125.00 300.00
PPU2 Stephen Curry 250.00 600.00
PPU3 Giannis Antetokounmpo 150.00 400.00
PPU4 Donovan Mitchell 60.00 150.00
PPU5 Brandon Miller 120.00 300.00
PPU6 Joel Embiid 80.00 200.00
PPU7 Kevin Durant 100.00 250.00
PPU8 Chet Holmgren 80.00 200.00
PPU9 Victor Wembanyama 2,500.00 5,000.00
PPU10 Scoot Henderson 100.00 250.00

2023-24 Topps Cosmic Chrome Planetary Pursuit Venus

PPV1 Jayson Tatum 25.00 60.00
PPV2 Stephen Curry 50.00 125.00
PPV3 Giannis Antetokounmpo 30.00 80.00
PPV4 Donovan Mitchell 12.00 30.00
PPV5 Brandon Miller 25.00 60.00
PPV6 Joel Embiid 15.00 40.00
PPV7 Kevin Durant 20.00 50.00
PPV8 Chet Holmgren 15.00 40.00
PPV9 Victor Wembanyama 200.00 500.00
PPV10 Scoot Henderson 20.00 50.00

2023-24 Topps Cosmic Chrome Star Clusters

*BLUE MOON REF/99: 1.5X TO 4X BASIC
*GOLD INTST REF/50: 2.5X TO 6X BASIC
*ORNG GALACTIC REF/25: 3X TO 8X BASIC
SC1 Dejounte Murray
Trae Young .75 2.00
SC2 Jrue Holiday
Kristaps Porzingis .50 1.25
SC3 Klay Thompson
Stephen Curry 3.00 8.00
SC4 Kevin Durant
Devin Booker 1.25 3.00
SC5 Jalen Williams
Shai Gilgeous-Alexander 2.00 5.00
SC6 Karl-Anthony Towns
Joel Embiid 1.00 2.50
SC7 De'Aaron Fox
Kyrie Irving .75 2.00
SC8 Jason Kidd
Dirk Nowitzki 1.00 2.50
SC9 Jayson Tatum
Jaylen Brown 1.50 4.00
SC10 Paul George
James Harden .75 2.00
SC11 Chet Holmgren
Jalen Green 1.00 2.50
SC12 Kevin Garnett
Shaquille O'Neal 1.25 3.00
SC13 Brandon Miller
Cam Whitmore 1.50 4.00
SC14 Jordan Hawkins
Gradey Dick .75 2.00
SC15 Scoot Henderson
Anthony Black 1.25 3.00

2008 Topps Draft Day Autographs

DDBL Brook Lopez/50 40.00 100.00
DDDR Derrick Rose/100 250.00 500.00
DDEG Eric Gordon/50 50.00 125.00
DDJB Jerryd Bayless/50 30.00 80.00
DDKL Kevin Love/50 75.00 200.00
DDMB Michael Beasley/100 40.00 100.00
DDOM O.J. Mayo/100 40.00 100.00

2007-08 Topps Echelon

55-62 RC PRINT RUN 399 SER.#'d SETS
63-72 RC PRINT RUN 199 SER.#'d SETS
73-85 RC PRINT RUN 199 SER.#'d SETS
1 Tracy McGrady 2.00 5.00
2 Chris Paul 2.50 6.00
3 Dwyane Wade 2.50 6.00
4 Elton Brand 1.00 2.50
5 Josh Smith .75 2.00
6 Brandon Roy 1.50 4.00
7 Andrea Bargnani .75 2.00
8 Deron Williams 1.00 2.50
9 Andre Iguodala 1.25 3.00
10 Mike Bibby 1.25 3.00
11 Yao Ming 3.00 8.00
12 Dwight Howard 1.50 4.00
13 Steve Nash 2.50 6.00
14 Randy Foye 1.00 2.50
15 Carmelo Anthony 2.00 5.00
16 Pau Gasol 2.00 5.00
17 Jermaine O'Neal 1.25 3.00
18 Ben Gordon 1.00 2.50
19 Vince Carter 2.50 6.00
20 Tim Duncan 3.00 8.00
21 Kevin Garnett 3.00 8.00
22 Michael Redd 1.00 2.50
23 LeBron James 15.00 40.00
24 Kobe Bryant 10.00 25.00
25 Chris Webber 1.50 4.00
26 Allen Iverson 2.50 6.00
27 Chauncey Billups 1.50 4.00
28 Paul Pierce 2.00 5.00
29 Amare Stoudemire 1.25 3.00
30 Emeka Okafor 1.00 2.50
31 Jason Kidd 2.00 5.00
32 Shaquille O'Neal 5.00 12.00
33 Grant Hill 2.00 5.00
34 Ray Allen 2.00 5.00
35 Adam Morrison .75 2.00
36 Gilbert Arenas 1.25 3.00
37 Baron Davis 1.00 2.50
38 Mike Miller 1.00 2.50
39 Chris Bosh 1.50 4.00
40 Dirk Nowitzki 3.00 8.00
41 Bob Pettit 1.50 4.00
42 Bill Russell 5.00 12.00
43 Rick Barry 1.25 3.00
44 Oscar Robertson 1.50 4.00
45 Jerry Lucas 1.50 4.00
46 Magic Johnson 6.00 15.00
47 Larry Bird 6.00 15.00
48 Wes Unseld 2.00 5.00
49 James Worthy 2.50 6.00
50 Bob McAdoo 1.25 3.00
51 Greg Oden RC 5.00 12.00
52 Yi Jianlian RC 6.00 15.00
53 Brandan Wright RC 4.00 10.00
54 Nick Young RC 5.00 12.00
55 Spencer Hawes RC 2.50 6.00
56 Acie Law RC 2.50 6.00
57 Rodney Stuckey RC 2.50 6.00
58 Al Thornton RC 2.50 6.00
59 Arron Afflalo RC 3.00 8.00
60 Marco Belinelli RC 3.00 8.00
61 Gabe Pruitt RC 2.50 6.00
62 Wilson Chandler RC 3.00 8.00
63 Jared Dudley RC 3.00 8.00
64 Marcus Williams RC 2.50 6.00
65 Aaron Brooks RC 3.00 8.00
66 Daequan Cook RC 3.00 8.00
67 Thaddeus Young RC 4.00 10.00
68 Josh McRoberts RC 2.50 6.00
69 Nick Fazekas RC 2.50 6.00
70 Javaris Crittenton RC 2.50 6.00
71 Alando Tucker RC 2.50 6.00
72 Carl Landry RC 2.50 6.00
73 Al Horford RC 8.00 20.00
74 Kevin Durant RC 60.00 150.00
75 Corey Brewer RC 2.50 6.00
76 Jeff Green RC 2.50 6.00
77 Mike Conley Jr. RC 8.00 20.00
78 Joakim Noah RC 3.00 8.00
79 Sean Williams RC 2.00 5.00
80 Julian Wright RC 2.00 5.00
81 Reyshawn Terry RC 2.00 5.00
82 Aaron Gray RC 2.00 5.00
83 Glen Davis RC 2.50 6.00
84 Jermareo Davidson RC 2.00 5.00
85 Taurean Green RC 2.00 5.00

2007-08 Topps Echelon Blue

*1-50 BLUE: 1.25X TO 3X BASE HI
1-50 BLUE PRINT RUN 25 SER.#'d SETS
51-85 BLUE PRINT RUN 10 SER.#'d SETS

2007-08 Topps Echelon Red

*1-40 RED: .75X TO 2X BASE HI
*41-50 RED: .6X TO 1.5X BASE HI
1-50 PRINT RUN 50 SER.#'d SETS
*51-85 RC RED: .75X TO 2X BASE HI
51-85 PRINT RUN 25 SER.#'d SETS
74 Kevin Durant 1,500.00 3,000.00

2007-08 Topps Echelon Autographs

PRINT RUN 99 SER.#'d SETS
*RELICS: .5X TO 1.25X BASE HI
RELIC PRINT RUN 99 TO 199 SETS
*RELICS GOLD: .6X TO 1.5X BASE HI
RELICS GOLD PRINT RUN 25 TO 50 SETS
AI Andre Iguodala/99 8.00 20.00
AM Adam Morrison/99 3.00 8.00
BD Baron Davis/99 8.00 20.00
BG Ben Gordon/99 4.00 10.00
BL Bob Love/99 12.00 30.00
BR Bill Russell/50 500.00 1,000.00
BW Bill Walton/99 12.00 30.00
CA Carmelo Anthony/99 30.00 80.00
CB Chris Bosh/50 12.00 30.00
CBI Chauncey Billups/50 12.00 30.00
CBO Carlos Boozer/99 4.00 10.00
CM Corey Maggette/99 4.00 10.00
DEW Deron Williams/99 4.00 10.00
DR Dennis Rodman/99 75.00 200.00
DRO David Robinson/99 40.00 100.00
DW Dwyane Wade/99 75.00 200.00
DWI Dominique Wilkins/99 20.00 50.00
EM Earl Monroe/50 20.00 50.00
EO Emeka Okafor/99 4.00 10.00
GW Gerald Wallace/99 4.00 10.00
IT Isiah Thomas/99 25.00 60.00
JF Jordan Farmar/99 3.00 8.00
JH Josh Howard/99 4.00 10.00
JJR J.J. Redick/99 6.00 15.00
JO Jermaine O'Neal/99 6.00 15.00
JS Josh Smith/99 3.00 8.00
JST John Stockton/99 40.00 100.00
KH Kirk Hinrich/99 5.00 12.00
LB Larry Bird/50 100.00 250.00
LE Len Elmore/99 10.00 25.00
MB Manute Bol/99 25.00 60.00
MJ Magic Johnson/50 100.00 250.00
RA Ray Allen/99 40.00 100.00
RB Rick Barry/99 12.00 30.00
RF Randy Foye/99 4.00 10.00
RT Rudy Tomjanovich/99 10.00 25.00
SO Shaquille O'Neal/50 125.00 300.00
TJF T.J. Ford/99 5.00 12.00
TP Tony Parker/99 20.00 50.00
VC Vince Carter/50 75.00 200.00

2007-08 Topps Echelon McDonald's All-American Autographs

PRINT RUN 100 SER.#'d SETS
BW Brandan Wright 10.00 25.00
DC Daequan Cook 10.00 25.00
GO Greg Oden 15.00 40.00
JC Javaris Crittenton 10.00 25.00
TY Thaddeus Young 10.00 25.00

2007-08 Topps Echelon McDonald's All-American Autographs Five-Piece Relics

PRINT RUN 75 SER.#'d SETS
GAME/NAME LETTER CARDS #'d ONE OF ONE
BW Brandan Wright 12.00 30.00
DC Daequan Cook 12.00 30.00
GO Greg Oden 12.00 30.00
JC Javaris Crittenton 12.00 30.00
SH Spencer Hawes 12.00 30.00
TY Thaddeus Young 12.00 30.00

2007-08 Topps Echelon McDonald's All-American Autographs Super Size Patches

PRINT RUN 25 SER.#'d SETS
BW Brandan Wright 30.00 80.00
DC Daequan Cook 30.00 80.00
JC Javaris Crittenton 30.00 80.00
SH Spencer Hawes 30.00 80.00
TY Thaddeus Young 30.00 80.00

2007-08 Topps Echelon Rookie Autographs

PRINT RUN 499 SER.#'d SETS
*GOLD: .5X TO 1.25X BASE HI
GOLD PRINT RUN 50 SER.#'d SETS
63 Jared Dudley 5.00 12.00
64 Marcus Williams 4.00 10.00
65 Aaron Brooks 5.00 12.00
66 Daequan Cook 5.00 12.00
67 Thaddeus Young 6.00 15.00
68 Josh McRoberts 4.00 10.00
69 Nick Fazekas 4.00 10.00
70 Javaris Crittenton 4.00 10.00
71 Alando Tucker 4.00 10.00
72 Carl Landry 4.00 10.00

2007-08 Topps Echelon Rookie Autographs Dual Relics

PRINT RUN 399 SER.#'d SETS
*GOLD: .6X TO 1.5X BASE HI
GOLD PRINT RUN 50 SER.#'d SETS
PATCHES: .75X TO 2X BASE HI
PATCH PRINT RUN 50 SER.#'d SETS
55 Spencer Hawes 4.00 10.00
56 Acie Law 4.00 10.00
57 Rodney Stuckey 4.00 10.00
58 Al Thornton 4.00 10.00
59 Arron Afflalo 4.00 10.00
60 Marco Belinelli 5.00 12.00
61 Gabe Pruitt 4.00 10.00
62 Wilson Chandler 5.00 12.00

2007-08 Topps Echelon Rookie Autographs Quad Relics

PRINT RUN 199 SER.#'d SETS
*GOLD: .5X TO 1.25X BASE HI
GOLD PRINT RUN 50 SER.#'d SETS
51 Greg Oden 12.00 30.00
52 Yi Jianlian 15.00 40.00
53 Brandan Wright 10.00 25.00
54 Nick Young 8.00 20.00

2007-08 Topps Echelon Rookie Autographs Quad Patches

PRINT RUN 25 SER.#'d SETS
51 Greg Oden 125.00 250.00
52 Yi Jianlian 50.00 120.00
53 Brandan Wright 30.00 80.00
54 Nick Young 40.00 100.00

2005-06 Topps First Row

RC PRINT RUN 549 SER.#'d SETS
CELEB.PRINT RUN 549 SER.#'d SETS
1 Shaquille O'Neal 1.50 4.00
2 Marcus Camby .40 1.00
3 Caron Butler .40 1.00
4 Carlos Boozer .40 1.00
5 Peja Stojakovic .40 1.00
6 Chris Webber .60 1.50
7 Vince Carter 1.00 2.50
8 Bobby Simmons .30 .75
9 Pau Gasol .75 2.00
10 Stromile Swift .30 .75
11 Carmelo Anthony .75 2.00
12 Drew Gooden .40 1.00
13 Al Harrington .40 1.00
14 Emeka Okafor .40 1.00
15 Gilbert Arenas .50 1.25
16 Tony Parker .75 2.00
17 Steve Nash 1.00 2.50
18 Jamal Crawford .50 1.25
19 Troy Hudson .30 .75
20 Kobe Bryant 4.00 10.00
21 Tracy McGrady .75 2.00
22 Chauncey Billups .60 1.50
23 Devin Harris .30 .75
24 Brevin Knight .30 .75
25 Joe Johnson .40 1.00
26 Nenad Krstic .30 .75
27 Primoz Brezec .30 .75
28 Mehmet Okur .30 .75
29 Shareef Abdur-Rahim .50 1.25
30 Amare Stoudemire .50 1.25
31 Quentin Richardson .30 .75
32 Kevin Garnett 1.25 3.00
33 Shane Battier .40 1.00
34 Elton Brand .40 1.00
35 Kenyon Martin .40 1.00
36 LeBron James 4.00 10.00
37 Al Jefferson .30 .75
38 Jermaine O'Neal .40 1.00
39 Ron Artest .40 1.00
40 Luke Ridnour .40 1.00
41 Sebastian Telfair .40 1.00
42 Steve Francis .50 1.25
43 Jason Kidd .75 2.00
44 Ben Wallace .60 1.50
45 Mike Miller .40 1.00
46 Jamaal Tinsley .30 .75
47 Richard Hamilton .60 1.50
48 Jerry Stackhouse .40 1.00
49 Kirk Hinrich .40 1.00
50 Josh Childress .30 .75
51 Jamaal Magloire .30 .75
52 Yao Ming 1.00 2.50
53 Tyson Chandler .40 1.00
54 Andrei Kirilenko .40 1.00
55 Rashard Lewis .40 1.00
56 Shawn Marion .40 1.00
57 Grant Hill .75 2.00
58 Wally Szczerbiak .40 1.00
59 Antoine Walker .40 1.00
60 Corey Maggette .40 1.00
61 Rasheed Wallace .50 1.25
62 Dirk Nowitzki 1.25 3.00
63 Paul Pierce .75 2.00
64 Tim Duncan 1.25 3.00
65 Desmond Mason .30 .75
66 Ray Allen .75 2.00
67 Mike Bibby .50 1.25
68 Andre Iguodala .50 1.25
69 J.R. Smith .50 1.25
70 Dwyane Wade 1.00 2.50
71 Shaun Livingston .40 1.00
72 Jason Richardson .50 1.25
73 Earl Boykins .30 .75
74 Ben Gordon .40 1.00
75 Stephen Jackson .40 1.00
76 Samuel Dalembert .30 .75
77 Kwame Brown .30 .75
78 Zydrunas Ilgauskas .40 1.00
79 Antawn Jamison .40 1.00
80 Chris Bosh .60 1.50
81 Zach Randolph .50 1.25
82 Dwight Howard .60 1.50
83 Richard Jefferson .40 1.00
84 Udonis Haslem .30 .75
85 Lamar Odom .40 1.00
86 Mike Dunleavy .30 .75
87 Josh Howard .40 1.00
88 Luol Deng .40 1.00
89 Josh Smith .40 1.00
90 Jalen Rose .40 1.00
91 Rafer Alston .40 1.00
92 Manu Ginobili 1.00 2.50
93 Allen Iverson 1.00 2.50
94 Stephon Marbury .60 1.50
95 Michael Redd .40 1.00
96 Sam Cassell .40 1.00
97 Baron Davis .50 1.25
98 Andre Miller .40 1.00
99 Larry Hughes .40 1.00
100 Ricky Davis .40 1.00
101 Nate Robinson RC 2.00 5.00
102 Danny Granger RC 2.00 5.00
103 Marvin Williams RC 2.00 5.00
104 Rashad McCants RC 1.50 4.00
105 Jarrett Jack RC 2.00 5.00
106 Andrew Bogut RC 2.50 6.00
107 Ike Diogu RC 1.25 3.00

108 Chris Paul RC 10.00 25.00
109 Julius Hodge RC 1.25 3.00
110 C.J. Miles RC 1.50 4.00
111 Francisco Garcia RC 1.25 3.00
112 Channing Frye RC 1.50 4.00
113 Deron Williams RC 3.00 8.00
114 Hakim Warrick RC 1.50 4.00
115 Salim Stoudamire RC 1.50 4.00
116 Raymond Felton RC 1.50 4.00
117 Joey Graham RC 1.50 4.00
118 Wayne Simien RC 1.25 3.00
119 David Lee RC 2.00 5.00
120 Luther Head RC 1.25 3.00
121 Andrew Bynum RC 1.50 4.00
122 Monta Ellis RC 2.50 6.00
123 Brandon Bass RC 1.50 4.00
124 Antoine Wright RC 1.50 4.00
125 Gerald Green RC 2.00 5.00
126 Charlie Villanueva RC 1.50 4.00
127 Chris Taft RC 1.25 3.00
128 Sarunas Jasikevicius RC 2.00 5.00
129 Sean May RC 1.25 3.00
130 Martell Webster RC 1.50 4.00
131 Yaroslav Korolev RC 1.25 3.00
132 Eddie Basden RC 1.25 3.00
133 Ersan Ilyasova RC 1.50 4.00
134 Martynas Andriuskevicius RC 1.25 3.00
135 Orien Greene RC 1.25 3.00
136 Johan Petro RC 1.25 3.00
137 Linas Kleiza RC 1.50 4.00
138 Daniel Ewing RC 1.50 4.00
139 Fabricio Oberto RC 1.50 4.00
140 Travis Diener RC 1.25 3.00
141 Ryan Gomes RC 1.50 4.00
142 Andray Blatche RC 1.25 3.00
143 Louis Williams RC 5.00 12.00
144 Jose Calderon RC 2.00 5.00
145 Robert Whaley RC 1.25 3.00
146 Jay-Z 4.00 10.00
147 Carmen Electra 4.00 10.00
148 Christie Brinkley 4.00 10.00
149 Shannon Elizabeth 4.00 10.00
150 Jenny McCarthy 4.00 10.00

2005-06 Topps First Row 325

*1-100: .6X TO 1.5X BASE HI
*101-150: .5X TO 1.25X BASE HI
PRINT RUN 325 SER.#'d SETS
36 LeBron James 8.00 20.00
146 Jay-Z 25.00 60.00

2005-06 Topps First Row 100

*ROW 100 VETS: 1.5X TO 4X BASE HI
*ROW 100 RCs: .75X TO 2X BASE HI
*ROW 100 CELEBS: .6X TO 1.5X BASE HI
ROW 100 PRINT RUN 100 SER.#'d SETS
20 Kobe Bryant 15.00 40.00
36 LeBron James 20.00 50.00
146 Jay-Z 40.00 100.00

2005-06 Topps First Row Black and White

*BLACK/WHITE: .6X TO 1.5X BASE HI
STATED PRINT RUN 225 SER.#'d SETS
36 LeBron James 8.00 20.00
146 Jay-Z 25.00 60.00

2005-06 Topps First Row Sepia

*SEPIA VETS: 5X TO 12X BASE HI
*SEPIA RCs: 1.5X TO 4X BASE HI
*SEPIA CELEB: 1.25X TO 3X BASE HI
STATED PRINT RUN 25 SER.'d SETS
146 Jay-Z 125.00 300.00

2005-06 Topps First Row Alley Oop Dual Relics

PRINT RUN 200 SER.#'d SETS
AB C.Anthony/E.Boykins 6.00 15.00
AJ G.Arenas/A.Jamison 5.00 12.00
FO R.Felton/E.Okafor 5.00 12.00
HC K.Hinrich/T.Chandler 5.00 12.00
NS S.Nash/A.Stoudemire 6.00 15.00
PS C.Paul/J.R. Smith 6.00 15.00

2005-06 Topps First Row Baseline

PRINT RUN 149 SER.#'d SETS
*BASELINE 99: .5X TO 1.25X BASE HI
*BASE.99 PRINT RUN 99 SER.#'d SETS
1 Baron Davis 1.25 3.00
2 Dwyane Wade 2.50 6.00
3 Allen Iverson 2.50 6.00
4 Ben Gordon 1.00 2.50
5 Andre Miller 1.00 2.50
6 Mike Bibby 1.25 3.00
7 Jason Kidd 2.00 5.00
8 Shaun Livingston 1.00 2.50
9 Steve Francis 1.25 3.00
10 Steve Nash 2.50 6.00
11 Luke Ridnour 1.00 2.50
12 T.J. Ford .75 2.00
13 Stephon Marbury 1.50 4.00
14 Brevin Knight .75 2.00
15 Jamaal Tinsley .75 2.00
16 Rafer Alston 1.00 2.50
17 Damon Jones .75 2.00
18 Chauncey Billups 1.50 4.00
19 Kirk Hinrich 1.00 2.50
20 Devin Harris .75 2.00
21 Tony Parker 2.00 5.00
22 Jason Williams 2.00 5.00
23 Troy Hudson .75 2.00
24 Deron Williams 2.00 5.00
25 Chris Paul 15.00 40.00
26 Tracy McGrady 2.00 5.00
27 Earl Boykins .75 2.00
28 Marcus Banks .75 2.00
29 Gilbert Arenas 1.25 3.00
30 Jamal Crawford 1.25 3.00
31 Larry Hughes 1.00 2.50
32 Jarrett Jack 1.25 3.00
33 Kobe Bryant 25.00 60.00
34 Damon Stoudamire 1.25 3.00
35 Jameer Nelson .75 2.00
36 Raymond Felton 1.00 2.50
37 Tyronn Lue .75 2.00
38 Manu Ginobili 2.50 6.00
39 Rashad McCants .75 2.00
40 Andre Iguodala 1.25 3.00
41 Carlos Arroyo .75 2.00
42 Jason Terry 1.00 2.50
43 Nate Robinson 1.25 3.00
44 Luther Head .75 2.00
45 Joe Johnson 1.00 2.50
46 Vince Carter 2.50 6.00
47 Monta Ellis 1.50 4.00
48 Sebastian Telfair 1.00 2.50
49 Cuttino Mobley .75 2.00
50 J.R. Smith 1.25 3.00

2005-06 Topps First Row Center Court

PRINT RUN 149 SER.#'d SETS
*CENTER 99: .5X TO 1.25X BASE HI
CENT.99 PRINT RUN 99 SER.#'d SETS
1 Jason Kidd 2.00 5.00
2 Richard Hamilton 1.50 4.00
3 Manu Ginobili 2.50 6.00
4 Elton Brand 1.00 2.50
5 Jason Richardson 1.25 3.00
6 Emeka Okafor 1.00 2.50
7 Shawn Marion 1.00 2.50
8 Ben Gordon 1.00 2.50
9 Gilbert Arenas 1.25 3.00
10 Jermaine O'Neal 1.00 2.50
11 Ben Wallace 1.50 4.00
12 LeBron James 25.00 60.00
13 Allen Iverson 2.50 6.00
14 Dirk Nowitzki 3.00 8.00
15 Tracy McGrady 2.00 5.00
16 Steve Nash 2.50 6.00
17 Vince Carter 2.50 6.00
18 Carmelo Anthony 2.00 5.00
19 Kobe Bryant 25.00 60.00
20 Kevin Garnett 3.00 8.00
21 Tim Duncan 3.00 8.00
22 Stephon Marbury 1.50 4.00
23 Kirk Hinrich 1.00 2.50
24 Amare Stoudemire 1.25 3.00
25 Steve Francis 1.00 2.50
26 Yao Ming 2.50 6.00
27 Jamal Crawford 1.25 3.00
28 Ray Allen 2.00 5.00
29 Paul Pierce 2.00 5.00
30 Dwyane Wade 2.50 6.00
31 Corey Maggette 1.00 2.50
32 Rashard Lewis 1.00 2.50
33 Chris Bosh 1.50 4.00
34 Mike Bibby 1.25 3.00
35 Antoine Walker 1.00 2.50
36 Tony Parker 2.00 5.00
37 Kenyon Martin 1.00 2.50
38 Michael Redd 1.00 2.50
39 Baron Davis 1.25 3.00
40 Al Harrington 1.00 2.50
41 Jalen Rose 1.00 2.50
42 Antawn Jamison 1.00 2.50
43 Andre Miller 1.00 2.50
44 Rafer Alston 1.00 2.50
45 Jason Terry 1.00 2.50
46 Pau Gasol 2.00 5.00
47 Andrei Kirilenko 1.00 2.50
48 Rasheed Wallace 1.25 3.00
49 Richard Jefferson 1.00 2.50
50 Shaquille O'Neal 4.00 10.00

2005-06 Topps First Row Charity Stripe

PRINT RUN 149 SER.#'d SETS
*STRIPE 99: .5X TO 1.25X BASE HI
STRIP.99 PRINT RUN 99 SER.#'d SETS
1 Earl Boykins .75 2.00
2 Peja Stojakovic 1.00 2.50
3 Damon Stoudamire 1.25 3.00
4 Chauncey Billups 1.50 4.00
5 Steve Nash 2.50 6.00
6 Ray Allen 2.00 5.00
7 Austin Croshere .75 2.00
8 Dirk Nowitzki 3.00 8.00
9 Sam Cassell 1.00 2.50
10 Ben Gordon 1.00 2.50
11 Caron Butler 1.00 2.50
12 Derek Fisher 1.25 3.00
13 David Wesley .75 2.00
14 Wally Szczerbiak 1.00 2.50
15 Michael Redd 1.00 2.50
16 Jalen Rose 1.00 2.50
17 Fred Jones .75 2.00
18 Brian Cardinal .75 2.00
19 Danny Fortson .75 2.00
20 Shareef Abdur-Rahim 1.25 3.00
21 Corey Maggette 1.00 2.50
22 Mehmet Okur .75 2.00
23 Josh Childress .75 2.00
24 Shawn Marion 1.00 2.50
25 Hedo Turkoglu 1.00 2.50
26 Jerry Stackhouse 1.00 2.50
27 Bobby Simmons .75 2.00
28 Jamal Crawford 1.25 3.00
29 Marvin Williams 1.25 3.00
30 Richard Hamilton 1.50 4.00
31 Luke Ridnour 1.00 2.50
32 Julius Hodge .75 2.00
33 Danny Granger 1.25 3.00
34 Gerald Green 1.25 3.00
35 Francisco Garcia .75 2.00
36 Daniel Ewing 1.00 2.50
37 Antoine Wright .75 2.00
38 Martell Webster 1.00 2.50
39 Morris Peterson .75 2.00
40 Andrew Bogut 1.50 4.00
41 Salim Stoudamire 1.00 2.50
42 Paul Pierce 2.00 5.00
43 Sean May .75 2.00
44 Kobe Bryant 40.00 100.00
45 Grant Hill 2.00 5.00
46 P.J. Brown .75 2.00
47 Dan Dickau .75 2.00
48 Richard Jefferson 1.00 2.50
49 Stephen Jackson 1.00 2.50
50 Dwyane Wade 2.50 6.00

2005-06 Topps First Row Direct Effect Relics

PRINT RUN 200 SER.#'d SETS
AI Allen Iverson 5.00 12.00
CP Chris Paul 12.00 30.00
DH Devin Harris 1.50 4.00
DW Dwyane Wade 10.00 25.00
EB Earl Boykins 2.00 5.00
ES Eric Snow 2.00 5.00
GA Gilbert Arenas 2.50 6.00
KH Kirk Hinrich 2.00 5.00
LR Luke Ridnour 2.00 5.00
MB Mike Bibby 2.50 6.00
RA Rafer Alston 2.00 5.00
RF Raymond Felton 2.00 5.00
SF Steve Francis 2.50 6.00
SL Shaun Livingston 2.00 5.00
SN Steve Nash 8.00 20.00
TM Tracy McGrady 8.00 20.00
DWI Deron Williams 4.00 10.00
TJF T.J. Ford 1.50 4.00

2005-06 Topps First Row In The Post

PRINT RUN 149 SER.#'d SETS
*POST 99: .5X TO 1.25X BASE HI
POST 99 PRINT RUN 99 SER.#'d SETS
1 Elton Brand 1.00 2.50
2 Emeka Okafor 1.00 2.50
3 Jermaine O'Neal 1.00 2.50
4 Ben Wallace 1.50 4.00
5 Dirk Nowitzki 3.00 8.00
6 Kevin Garnett 3.00 8.00
7 Tim Duncan 3.00 8.00
8 Amare Stoudemire 1.25 3.00
9 Yao Ming 2.50 6.00
10 Chris Bosh 1.50 4.00
11 Andrew Bogut 1.50 4.00
12 Zydrunas Ilgauskas 1.00 2.50
13 Pau Gasol 2.00 5.00
14 Shaquille O'Neal 4.00 10.00
15 Marcus Camby 1.00 2.50
16 Antawn Jamison 1.00 2.50
17 Charlie Villanueva 1.00 2.50
18 Carlos Boozer 1.00 2.50
19 Lamar Odom 1.00 2.50
20 Channing Frye 1.00 2.50
21 Zach Randolph 1.25 3.00
22 Carmelo Anthony 2.00 5.00
23 Ike Diogu .75 2.00
24 Chris Webber 1.50 4.00
25 Andrew Bynum 1.00 2.50
26 Sean May .75 2.00
27 Wayne Simien .75 2.00
28 Drew Gooden 1.00 2.50
29 Rasheed Wallace 1.25 3.00
30 Troy Murphy .75 2.00
31 Marvin Williams 1.25 3.00
32 Jason Kidd 2.00 5.00
33 Steve Francis 1.25 3.00
34 Tracy McGrady 2.00 5.00
35 Dwyane Wade 2.50 6.00
36 Quentin Richardson .75 2.00
37 Corey Maggette 1.00 2.50
38 Kobe Bryant 10.00 25.00
39 Paul Pierce 2.00 5.00
40 Jalen Rose 1.00 2.50
41 Danny Granger 1.25 3.00
42 Michael Finley 1.25 3.00
43 Tayshaun Prince 1.25 3.00
44 Kenyon Martin 1.00 2.50
45 Brad Miller 1.00 2.50
46 Joey Graham 1.00 2.50
47 Jason Maxiell 1.00 2.50
48 Primoz Brezec .75 2.00
49 Nenad Krstic .75 2.00
50 Ron Artest 1.00 2.50

2005-06 Topps First Row Pick n Roll Relics

PRINT RUN 200 SER.#'d SETS
AL R.Allen/R.Lewis 5.00 12.00
BL E.Brand/S.Livingston 5.00 12.00
BW C.Boozer/D.Williams 6.00 15.00
GD M.Ginobili/T.Duncan 6.00 15.00
MM T.McGrady/Y.Ming 6.00 15.00
OW S.O'Neal/D.Wade 12.50 30.00

2005-06 Topps First Row PTP Dual Relics

PRINT RUN 140 SER.#'d SETS
AW C.Anthony/H.Warrick 6.00 15.00
BO K.Bryant/S.O'Neal 75.00 200.00
DB T.Duncan/A.Bogut 6.00 15.00
IB A.Iverson/K.Bryant 75.00 200.00
IW A.Iverson/D.Wade 8.00 20.00
MG T.McGrady/G.Green 5.00 12.00
NW S.Nash/D.Williams 6.00 15.00
OI S.O'Neal/A.Iverson 10.00 25.00
OW S.O'Neal/D.Wade 15.00 40.00
PI C.Paul/A.Iverson 20.00 50.00
PM P.Pierce/R.McCants 6.00 15.00
WB D.Wade/K.Bryant 60.00 150.00
AB2 Andrew Bogut 4.00 10.00
AI2 Allen Iverson 6.00 15.00
BG2 Ben Gordon 2.50 6.00
CA2 Carmelo Anthony 5.00 12.00
CP2 Chris Paul 30.00 80.00
DN2 Dirk Nowitzki 10.00 25.00
DW1 Dwyane Wade 8.00 20.00
DW2 Deron Williams 5.00 12.00
EO2 Emeka Okafor 2.50 6.00
GA2 Gilbert Arenas 3.00 8.00
JT2 Jason Terry 2.50 6.00
KB2 Kobe Bryant 75.00 200.00
KM2 Kenyon Martin 2.50 6.00
RF2 Raymond Felton 2.50 6.00
SN2 Steve Nash 6.00 15.00
SO2 Shaquille O'Neal 10.00 25.00
TD2 Tim Duncan 10.00 25.00
TM2 Tracy McGrady 10.00 25.00
YM2 Yao Ming 10.00 25.00

2005-06 Topps First Row Range Relics

PRINT RUN 200 SER.#'d SETS
AW Antoine Wright 2.00 5.00
BG Ben Gordon 2.00 5.00
DN Dirk Nowitzki 6.00 15.00
DW Dwyane Wade 6.00 15.00
JC Jamal Crawford 2.50 6.00
JH Julius Hodge 1.50 4.00
KB Kobe Bryant 40.00 100.00
KK Kyle Korver 2.00 5.00
MG Manu Ginobili 5.00 12.00
MP Morris Peterson 1.50 4.00
PP Paul Pierce 4.00 10.00
PS Peja Stojakovic 2.00 5.00
RA Ray Allen 4.00 10.00
SJ Sarunas Jasikevicius 2.50 6.00
TP Tayshaun Prince 2.50 6.00

2005-06 Topps First Row Signature Dish

PRINT RUNS LISTED IN CHECKLIST
AB Andrew Bogut/190 5.00 12.00
AI Allen Iverson/150 50.00 120.00
AJ Amir Johnson/190 4.00 10.00
AW Antoine Wright/190 3.00 8.00
BW Bracey Wright/190 2.50 6.00
CA Carmelo Anthony/65 50.00 120.00
CV Charlie Villanueva/190 3.00 8.00
DB Dave Bing/67 30.00 80.00
DG Danny Granger/190 4.00 10.00
DL David Lee/190 4.00 10.00
DW Dwyane Wade/190 125.00 300.00
EM Earl Monroe/83 15.00 40.00
FG Francisco Garcia/190 2.50 6.00
GG Gerald Green/190 4.00 10.00
JH Julius Hodge/190 2.50 6.00
JJ Jarrett Jack/190 4.00 10.00
JK Jason Kidd/120 20.00 50.00
JN Jameer Nelson/157 2.50 6.00
JP Johan Petro/190 2.50 6.00
LH Luther Head/190 2.50 6.00
LO Lamar Odom/100 3.00 8.00
LW Louis Williams/190 10.00 25.00
ME Monta Ellis/190 5.00 12.00
MW Martell Webster/190 3.00 8.00
RF Raymond Felton/190 3.00 8.00
RG Ryan Gomes/190 3.00 8.00
RM Rashad McCants/190 2.50 6.00
RS Robert Swift/124 2.50 6.00
RW Robert Whaley/190 2.50 6.00
SJ Sarunas Jasikevicius/190 4.00 10.00
SL Shaun Livingston/190 4.00 10.00
SM Sean May/190 2.50 6.00
TD Travis Diener/110 2.50 6.00
DWI Deron Williams/190 6.00 15.00
JJW Jo Jo White/79 8.00 20.00
PJR Peter John Ramos/190 2.50 6.00

2005-06 Topps First Row Signature Dunk

PRINT RUNS LISTED IN CHECKLIST
AB Andrew Bogut/190 5.00 12.00
AI Allen Iverson/150 50.00 120.00
AW Antoine Wright/190 3.00 8.00
BB Brandon Bass/110 3.00 8.00
BW Bracey Wright/190 2.50 6.00
CA Carmelo Anthony/50 50.00 120.00
CT Chris Taft/190 2.50 6.00
CV Charlie Villanueva/190 3.00 8.00
DC Dave Cowens/83 10.00 25.00
DG Danny Granger/190 4.00 10.00
DL David Lee/190 4.00 10.00
DS Donta Smith/184 2.50 6.00
DW Dwyane Wade/190 125.00 300.00
EB Elgin Baylor/107 15.00 40.00
EO Emeka Okafor/190 3.00 8.00
FG Francisco Garcia/190 2.50 6.00
GG Gerald Green/190 4.00 10.00
ID Ike Diogu/190 2.50 6.00
JH Julius Hodge/190 2.50 6.00
JM Jason Maxiell/190 3.00 8.00
JP Johan Petro/190 2.50 6.00
LH Luther Head/190 2.50 6.00
LW Louis Williams/190 10.00 25.00
ME Mark Eaton/67 20.00 50.00
MM Moses Malone/78 25.00 60.00
MW Martell Webster/190 3.00 8.00
PP Pavel Podkolzin/190 2.50 6.00
RG Ryan Gomes/190 3.00 8.00
RM Rashad McCants/190 2.50 6.00
RW Robert Whaley/190 2.50 6.00
SJ Sarunas Jasikevicius/190 4.00 10.00
SM Sean May/190 2.50 6.00
SO Shaquille O'Neal/115 125.00 300.00
WS Wayne Simien/190 2.50 6.00
ABY Andrew Bynum/190 3.00 8.00
DWI Deron Williams/190 6.00 15.00
PJR Peter John Ramos/190 2.50 6.00

2005-06 Topps First Row Signature Swish

PRINT RUNS LISTED IN CHECKLIST
AI Allen Iverson/150 50.00 120.00
AJ Amir Johnson/190 4.00 10.00
AW Antoine Wright/190 3.00 8.00
BW Bill Walton/55 15.00 40.00
CA Carmelo Anthony/75 20.00 50.00
CB Christie Brinkley/50 50.00 120.00
CE Carmen Electra/50 60.00 120.00
CT Chris Taft/37 2.50 6.00
CV Charlie Villanueva/190 3.00 8.00
DE Daniel Ewing/85 3.00 8.00
DG Danny Granger/190 4.00 10.00
DL David Lee/190 4.00 10.00
DS Detlef Schrempf/91 12.00 30.00
DW Dwyane Wade/100 125.00 300.00
EO Emeka Okafor/190 3.00 8.00
FG Francisco Garcia/190 2.50 6.00
JG Joey Graham/190 2.50 6.00
JH Julius Hodge/190 2.50 6.00
JJ Jarrett Jack/190 4.00 10.00
JM Jenny McCarthy/50 60.00 120.00
JP Johan Petro/190 2.50 6.00
KM Kevin Martin/190 3.00 8.00
LH Luther Head/190 2.50 6.00
LO Lamar Odom/75 3.00 8.00
LW Louis Williams/190 10.00 25.00
MW Martell Webster/190 3.00 8.00
OG Orien Greene/190 3.00 8.00
RB Rick Barry/83 15.00 40.00
RG Ryan Gomes/190 3.00 8.00
RM Rashad McCants/190 2.50 6.00
RS Robert Swift/50 2.50 6.00
RW Robert Whaley/190 2.50 6.00
SE Shannon Elizabeth/50 50.00 120.00
SJ Sarunas Jasikevicius/190 4.00 10.00
SM Sean May/190 2.50 6.00
VW Von Wafer/190 2.50 6.00
BWR Bracey Wright/190 2.50 6.00
DWI Deron Williams/190 6.00 15.00
DWR Dorell Wright/190 2.50 6.00
PJR Peter John Ramos/190 2.50 6.00

2005-06 Topps First Row Spokesmen

PRINT RUNS LISTED IN CHECKLIST
SSRAI Allen Iverson JSY/200 5.00 12.00
SSRDW Dwyane Wade JSY/200 6.00 15.00
SSRJZ Jay-Z JSY/200 40.00 100.00

2005-06 Topps First Row Thunder Relics

PRINT RUN 200 SER.#'d SETS
AI Andre Iguodala 3.00 8.00
AJ Antawn Jamison 2.50 6.00
AS Amare Stoudemire 3.00 8.00
BW Ben Wallace 4.00 10.00
CA Carmelo Anthony 5.00 12.00
CB Chris Bosh 4.00 10.00
DG Drew Gooden 2.50 6.00
DW Dwyane Wade 8.00 20.00
GG Gerald Green 3.00 8.00
HW Hakim Warrick 2.50 6.00
JO Jermaine O'Neal 2.50 6.00
JS Josh Smith 2.50 6.00
KB Kobe Bryant 50.00 120.00
LD Luol Deng 2.50 6.00
PG Pau Gasol 5.00 12.00
RJ Richard Jefferson 2.50 6.00
RL Rashard Lewis 2.50 6.00
SO Shaquille O'Neal 10.00 25.00
TD Tim Duncan 8.00 20.00
VC Vince Carter 6.00 15.00
YM Yao Ming 6.00 15.00
JRS J.R. Smith 3.00 8.00

2006-07 Topps Full Court

COMP.SET w/o RC's (100) 12.50 30.00
101-150 RC PRINT RUN 999 SER.#'d SETS
1 Vince Carter 1.00 2.50
2 Josh Smith .30 .75
3 Dwyane Wade 1.00 2.50
4 Lamar Odom .40 1.00
5 Jermaine O'Neal .50 1.25
6 Andrei Kirilenko .40 1.00
7 Rasheed Wallace .60 1.50
8 Manu Ginobili 1.00 2.50
9 Richard Hamilton .50 1.25
10 Tim Duncan 1.25 3.00
11 Ricky Davis .40 1.00
12 Antoine Walker .50 1.25
13 Troy Murphy .30 .75
14 Ray Allen .75 2.00
15 Ben Wallace .60 1.50
16 Dwight Howard .60 1.50
17 Joe Johnson .50 1.25
18 Jason Kidd .75 2.00
19 Michael Redd .40 1.00
20 Kobe Bryant 4.00 10.00
21 Al Harrington .40 1.00
22 Mehmet Okur .30 .75
23 Danny Granger .30 .75
24 Caron Butler .40 1.00
25 Elton Brand .40 1.00
26 Gilbert Arenas .50 1.25
27 Sam Cassell .40 1.00
28 Antawn Jamison .40 1.00
29 Carmelo Anthony .75 2.00
30 Zach Randolph .50 1.25
31 Ben Gordon .40 1.00
32 Andre Iguodala .50 1.25
33 Paul Pierce .75 2.00
34 Peja Stojakovic .40 1.00
35 Andrew Bogut .40 1.00
36 Mike Miller .40 1.00
37 Mike James .30 .75
38 Shaquille O'Neal 2.00 5.00
39 Baron Davis .50 1.25
40 Jason Richardson .50 1.25
41 Rashard Lewis .40 1.00
42 Marcus Camby .40 1.00
43 Ron Artest .50 1.25
44 Larry Hughes .40 1.00
45 Allen Iverson 1.25 3.00
46 Al Jefferson .30 .75
47 Chris Paul 1.00 2.50
48 Tony Parker .75 2.00
49 Pau Gasol .75 2.00
50 Kevin Garnett 1.25 3.00
51 Richard Jefferson .40 1.00
52 Corey Maggette .40 1.00
53 Yao Ming 1.25 3.00
54 T.J. Ford .30 .75
55 Andre Miller .40 1.00
56 Mike Bibby .50 1.25
57 LeBron James 4.00 10.00
58 Chris Webber .60 1.50
59 Emeka Okafor .40 1.00
60 Tyson Chandler .40 1.00
61 Raymond Felton .30 .75
62 Channing Frye .30 .75
63 Gerald Wallace .40 1.00
64 Stephon Marbury .60 1.50
65 Kirk Hinrich .40 1.00
66 Jameer Nelson .30 .75
67 Charlie Villanueva .30 .75
68 Smush Parker .30 .75
69 Tracy McGrady .75 2.00
70 Chris Bosh .60 1.50
71 Chauncey Billups .60 1.50
72 Brad Miller .40 1.00
73 Drew Gooden .40 1.00
74 Amare Stoudemire .50 1.25
75 Dirk Nowitzki 1.25 3.00
76 Shawn Marion .50 1.25
77 Jason Terry .40 1.00
78 Steve Nash 1.00 2.50
79 Josh Howard .40 1.00
80 Darius Miles .30 .75
81 John Stockton 1.50 4.00
82 Wilt Chamberlain 3.00 8.00
83 Dennis Rodman 12.00 30.00
84 Karl Malone 1.25 3.00
85 Dominique Wilkins 1.50 4.00
86 Isiah Thomas 1.50 4.00
87 Earl Monroe 1.00 2.50
88 Hakeem Olajuwon 2.00 5.00
89 Clyde Drexler 1.25 3.00
90 George Gervin 1.50 4.00
91 Oscar Robertson 2.50 6.00
92 Rick Barry .75 2.00
93 Walt Frazier 1.25 3.00
94 Drazen Petrovic 1.25 3.00
95 Dan Majerle .75 2.00
96 Jerry West 1.50 4.00
97 Larry Bird 3.00 8.00
98 Moses Malone 1.50 4.00
99 Kareem Abdul-Jabbar 3.00 8.00
100 Bill Russell 3.00 8.00
101 Shelden Williams RC 1.00 2.50
102 Adam Morrison RC 1.25 3.00
103 Daniel Gibson RC 1.25 3.00
104 Mile Ilic RC 1.00 2.50
105 Jorge Garbajosa RC 1.25 3.00
106 David Noel RC 1.00 2.50
107 Hassan Adams RC 1.00 2.50
108 J.J. Redick RC 3.00 8.00
109 Brandon Roy RC 3.00 8.00
110 Damir Markota RC 1.00 2.50
111 Solomon Jones RC 1.00 2.50
112 Yakhouba Diawara RC 1.00 2.50
113 Maurice Ager RC 1.00 2.50
114 Steve Novak RC 1.25 3.00
115 Jordan Farmar RC 1.25 3.00
116 Randy Foye RC 1.25 3.00
117 Cedric Simmons RC 1.00 2.50
118 James Augustine RC 1.00 2.50
119 Sergio Rodriguez RC 1.25 3.00
120 P.J. Tucker RC 1.50 4.00
121 Rajon Rondo RC 5.00 12.00
122 Tyrus Thomas RC 1.25 3.00
123 Will Blalock RC 1.00 2.50
124 Shawne Williams RC 1.00 2.50
125 Rudy Gay RC 2.00 5.00
126 Craig Smith RC 1.25 3.00
127 Hilton Armstrong RC 1.00 2.50
128 Bobby Jones RC 1.00 2.50
129 Quincy Douby RC 1.00 2.50
130 Andrea Bargnani RC 1.25 3.00
131 Vassilis Spanoulis RC 1.25 3.00
132 Thabo Sefolosha RC 1.25 3.00
133 Pops Mensah-Bonsu RC 1.00 2.50
134 Paul Millsap RC 2.00 5.00
135 Kyle Lowry RC 5.00 12.00
136 Marcus Williams RC 1.00 2.50
137 Renaldo Balkman RC 1.25 3.00
138 Rodney Carney RC 1.00 2.50
139 Marcus Vinicius RC 1.00 2.50
140 Ronnie Brewer RC 1.50 4.00
141 Leon Powe RC 1.00 2.50
142 Shannon Brown RC 1.00 2.50
143 Patrick O'Bryant RC 1.00 2.50
144 Paul Davis RC 1.00 2.50
145 Alexander Johnson RC 1.00 2.50
146 Josh Boone RC 1.00 2.50
147 Mardy Collins RC 1.00 2.50
148 LaMarcus Aldridge RC 4.00 10.00
149 Saer Sene RC 1.00 2.50
150 Dee Brown RC 1.00 2.50

2006-07 Topps Full Court First Day Issue

*1-80 FIRST DAY: .75X TO 2X BASE HI
*81-100 FIRST DAY: .6X TO 1.5X BASE HI
PRINT RUN 429 SER.#'d SETS

2006-07 Topps Full Court Photographer's Proof

*1-80 PROOF: .6X TO 1.5X BASE HI
*81-100 PROOF: .5X TO 1.25X BASE HI
STATED PRINT RUN 1999 SER.#'d SETS

2006-07 Topps Full Court Photographer's Proof Gold

*1-80 PROOF GOLD: 1.25X TO 3X BASE HI
*81-100 PROOF GOLD: .75X TO 2X BASE HI
STATED PRINT RUN 199 SER.#'d SETS

2006-07 Topps Full Court Chrome Rookie Refractors

*REFRACTORS: .6X TO 1.5X BASE HI
PRINT RUN 199 SER.#'d SETS

2006-07 Topps Full Court Chrome Rookie Refractors Gold

*REF.GOLD: 1X TO 2.5X BASE HI
STATED PRINT RUN 50 SER.#'d SETS

2006-07 Topps Full Court Co-Signers

GROUP A ODDS 1:270, GROUP B 1:755
GROUP C ODDS 1:1100, GROUP D 1:375
GROUP E ODDS 1:470, GROUP F 1:218
GROUP G ODDS 1:82, GROUP H 1:36
CS1 A.Iverson/M.Cheeks 40.00 100.00
CS2 A.Morrison/L.Bird 40.00 100.00
CS3 D.Wade/S.O'Neal 150.00 400.00
CS4 B.Walton/J.Wooden 75.00 200.00
CS5 R.Felton/R.Williams 25.00 60.00
CS6 A.Morrison/J.Redick 15.00 40.00
CS7 V.Carter/D.Wilkins 60.00 150.00
CS8 B.Gordon/J.Calhoun 15.00 40.00
CS9 T.Parker/B.Diaw 12.00 30.00
CS10 C.Villanueva/E.Okafor 6.00 15.00
CS11 C.Anthony/J.Boeheim 60.00 150.00
CS12 J.O'Neal/L.Elmore 12.00 30.00
CS13 C.Bosh/C.Hawkins 20.00 50.00
CS14 T.Ford/S.Claxton 5.00 12.00
CS15 B.Lanier/S.O'Neal 50.00 120.00
CS16 A.Bargnani/A.Bogut 6.00 15.00
CS17 L.Deng/J.Redick 8.00 20.00
CS18 D.Ewing/C.Duhon 5.00 12.00
CS19 J.Farmer/B.Howland 6.00 15.00
CS20 B.Simmons/H.Turkoglu 8.00 20.00
CS21 J.Nelson/D.West 5.00 12.00
CS22 D.Brown/D.Williams 5.00 12.00
CS23 R.Bell/L.Barbosa 6.00 15.00
CS24 M.James/S.Parker 5.00 12.00
CS25 M.Bol/R.Barry 50.00 120.00
CS26 A.Ray/R.Foye 6.00 15.00
CS27 S.Brown/M.Ager 5.00 12.00
CS28 H.Armstrong/J.Boone 5.00 12.00
CS29 M.Williams/V.Carter 40.00 100.00
CS30 J.Farmar/R.Hollins 6.00 15.00
CS31 S.Williams/R.Carney 5.00 12.00
CS32 P.Tucker/D.Gibson 8.00 20.00
CS33 E.Monroe/I.Thomas 30.00 80.00
CS34 J.Redick/S.Williams 15.00 40.00
CS35 J.Howard/D.Harris 6.00 15.00
CS36 J.Howard/J.Smith 6.00 15.00
CS37 R.Rondo/Q.Douby 25.00 60.00
CS38 R.Balkman/M.Collins 6.00 15.00
CS39 P.O'Bryant/S.Sene 5.00 12.00
CS40 R.Allen/A.Iverson 75.00 200.00
CS41 R.Brewer/D.Brown 5.00 12.00
CS42 C.Smith/D.Noel 6.00 15.00
CS43 D.Wade/A.Morrison 25.00 60.00
CS44 B.Jones/S.Jones 5.00 12.00
CS45 A.Ray/K.Lowry 15.00 40.00
CS46 R.Carney/T.Sefolosha 6.00 15.00
CS47 R.Felton/B.Gordon 6.00 15.00
CS48 B.Walton/L.Walton 30.00 80.00
CS49 A.Iguodala/G.Wallace 8.00 20.00
CS50 M.Johnson/L.Bird 200.00 500.00

2006-07 Topps Full Court Court Records

COMPLETE SET (20) 10.00 25.00
PRINT RUN 1499 SER.#'d SETS
CR1 Larry Bird 2.00 5.00
CR2 Dwyane Wade 1.25 3.00
CR3 Adam Morrison .50 1.25
CR4 Allen Iverson 1.50 4.00
CR5 Shaquille O'Neal 2.50 6.00
CR6 Vince Carter 1.25 3.00
CR7 Chris Bosh .75 2.00
CR8 Ben Gordon .50 1.25
CR9 J.J. Redick 1.25 3.00
CR10 Dominique Wilkins 1.00 2.50
CR11 Isiah Thomas 1.00 2.50
CR12 Andre Iguodala .60 1.50
CR13 Earl Monroe .60 1.50
CR14 Shelden Williams .40 1.00
CR15 Dee Brown .40 1.00
CR16 Rodney Carney .40 1.00
CR17 Charlie Villanueva .40 1.00
CR18 Quincy Douby .40 1.00
CR19 Raymond Felton .40 1.00
CR20 Randy Foye .50 1.25

2006-07 Topps Full Court Court Records Relics

PRINT RUN 499 SER.#'d SETS
CR1 Larry Bird 8.00 20.00
CR2 Dwyane Wade 5.00 12.00
CR3 Adam Morrison 2.00 5.00
CR4 Allen Iverson 6.00 15.00
CR5 Shaquille O'Neal 10.00 25.00
CR6 Vince Carter 5.00 12.00
CR7 Chris Bosh 3.00 8.00
CR8 Ben Gordon 2.00 5.00
CR9 J.J. Redick 5.00 12.00
CR10 Dominique Wilkins 4.00 10.00
CR11 Isiah Thomas 4.00 10.00
CR12 Andre Iguodala 2.50 6.00
CR13 Earl Monroe 2.50 6.00
CR14 Shelden Williams 1.50 4.00
CR15 Dee Brown 1.50 4.00
CR16 Rodney Carney 1.50 4.00
CR17 Charlie Villanueva 1.50 4.00
CR18 Quincy Douby 1.50 4.00
CR19 Raymond Felton 1.50 4.00
CR20 Randy Foye 2.00 5.00

2006-07 Topps Full Court Court Records Relics Autographs

PRINT RUN 15 TO 50 SER.#'d SETS
CR1 Larry Bird/33 60.00 150.00
CR2 Dwyane Wade/50 30.00 80.00
CR3 Adam Morrison/50 10.00 25.00
CR4 Allen Iverson/50 40.00 100.00
CR5 Shaquille O'Neal/32 60.00 120.00
CR6 Vince Carter/50 20.00 50.00
CR7 Chris Bosh/50 15.00 40.00
CR8 Ben Gordon/50 12.50 30.00
CR9 J.J. Redick/50 12.50 30.00
CR10 Dominique Wilkins/21 25.00 60.00
CR11 Isiah Thomas/50 20.00 40.00
CR12 Andre Iguodala/50 10.00 25.00
CR13 Earl Monroe/15 30.00 60.00
CR14 Shelden Williams/50 10.00 25.00
CR15 Dee Brown/50 10.00 25.00
CR16 Rodney Carney/50 10.00 25.00
CR17 Charlie Villanueva/50 10.00 25.00
CR18 Quincy Douby/50 10.00 25.00

2006-07 Topps Full Court Full Court Press

COMPLETE SET (25) 12.50 30.00
PRINT RUN 1499 SER.#'d SETS
FCP1 Dwyane Wade 1.50 4.00
FCP2 Adam Morrison .60 1.50
FCP3 Joe Johnson .75 2.00
FCP4 Ben Gordon .60 1.50
FCP5 Jason Terry .60 1.50
FCP6 Baron Davis .75 2.00
FCP7 Jordan Farmar .60 1.50
FCP8 Randy Foye .60 1.50
FCP9 J.J. Redick 1.50 4.00
FCP10 Jason Kidd 1.25 3.00
FCP11 Allen Iverson 2.00 5.00
FCP12 Manu Ginobili 1.50 4.00
FCP13 Stephon Marbury 1.00 2.50
FCP14 Caron Butler .60 1.50
FCP15 T.J. Ford .50 1.25
FCP16 Ronnie Brewer .75 2.00
FCP17 Mike Bibby .75 2.00
FCP18 Rodney Carney .50 1.25
FCP19 Chauncey Billups 1.00 2.50
FCP20 Steve Nash 1.50 4.00
FCP21 Rudy Gay 1.00 2.50
FCP22 Rajon Rondo 2.50 6.00
FCP23 Raymond Felton .50 1.25
FCP24 Ron Artest .75 2.00
FCP25 Tony Parker 1.25 3.00

2006-07 Topps Full Court Full Court Press Relics

PRINT RUN 499 SER.#'d SETS
*DUAL: .5X TO 1.25X BASE HI
PRINT RUN 199 SER.#'d SETS
*TRIPLE: .6X TO 1.5X BASE HI
TRIPLE PRINT RUN 50 SER.#'d SETS
FCP1 Dwyane Wade 5.00 12.00
FCP3 Joe Johnson 2.50 6.00
FCP4 Ben Gordon 2.00 5.00
FCP5 Jason Terry 2.00 5.00
FCP6 Baron Davis 2.50 6.00
FCP7 Jordan Farmar 2.00 5.00
FCP8 Randy Foye 2.00 5.00
FCP9 J.J. Redick 5.00 12.00
FCP10 Jason Kidd 4.00 10.00

FCP11 Allen Iverson 6.00 15.00
FCP12 Manu Ginobili 5.00 12.00
FCP13 Stephon Marbury 3.00 8.00
FCP14 Caron Butler 2.00 5.00
FCP15 T.J. Ford 1.50 4.00
FCP16 Ronnie Brewer 2.50 6.00
FCP17 Mike Bibby 2.50 6.00
FCP18 Rodney Carney 1.50 4.00
FCP19 Chauncey Billups 3.00 8.00
FCP20 Steve Nash 5.00 12.00
FCP21 Rudy Gay 3.00 8.00
FCP22 Rajon Rondo 8.00 20.00
FCP23 Raymond Felton 1.50 4.00
FCP24 Ron Artest 2.50 6.00
FCP25 Tony Parker 4.00 10.00

2006-07 Topps Full Court Half Court Press

COMPLETE SET (25) 12.50 30.00
PRINT RUN 999 SER.#'d SETS
HCP1 Shaquille O'Neal 2.50 6.00
HCP2 Dirk Nowitzki 1.50 4.00
HCP3 Ben Wallace .75 2.00
HCP4 Carmelo Anthony 1.00 2.50
HCP5 Jermaine O'Neal .60 1.50
HCP6 Elton Brand .50 1.25
HCP7 J.J. Redick 1.25 3.00
HCP8 Andrew Bogut .50 1.25
HCP9 Chris Paul 1.25 3.00
HCP10 Dwyane Wade 1.25 3.00
HCP11 Kobe Bryant 10.00 25.00
HCP12 Dwight Howard .75 2.00
HCP13 Pau Gasol 1.00 2.50
HCP14 Tim Duncan 1.50 4.00
HCP15 LaMarcus Aldridge 1.50 4.00
HCP16 Ray Allen 1.00 2.50
HCP17 Yao Ming 1.50 4.00
HCP18 Allen Iverson 1.50 4.00
HCP19 Chris Bosh .75 2.00
HCP20 Adam Morrison .50 1.25
HCP21 Kevin Garnett 1.50 4.00
HCP22 Tracy McGrady 1.00 2.50
HCP23 Vince Carter 1.25 3.00
HCP24 Andrea Bargnani .50 1.25
HCP25 Gilbert Arenas .60 1.50

2006-07 Topps Full Court Half Court Press Relics

PRINT RUN 249 SER.#'d SETS
*DUAL: .5X TO 1.25X BASE HI
DUAL PRINT RUN 199 SER.#'d SETS
*TRIPLE: .75X TO 2X BASE HI
TRIPLE PRINT RUN 25 SER.#'d SETS
HCP1 Shaquille O'Neal 10.00 25.00
HCP2 Dirk Nowitzki 6.00 15.00
HCP3 Ben Wallace 3.00 8.00
HCP4 Carmelo Anthony 4.00 10.00
HCP5 Jermaine O'Neal 2.50 6.00
HCP6 Elton Brand 2.00 5.00
HCP7 J.J. Redick 5.00 12.00
HCP8 Andrew Bogut 2.00 5.00
HCP9 Chris Paul 5.00 12.00
HCP10 Dwyane Wade 5.00 12.00
HCP11 Kobe Bryant 40.00 100.00
HCP12 Dwight Howard 3.00 8.00
HCP13 Pau Gasol 4.00 10.00
HCP14 Tim Duncan 6.00 15.00
HCP15 LaMarcus Aldridge 6.00 15.00
HCP16 Ray Allen 4.00 10.00
HCP17 Yao Ming 6.00 15.00
HCP18 Allen Iverson 6.00 15.00
HCP19 Chris Bosh 3.00 8.00
HCP20 Adam Morrison 2.00 5.00
HCP21 Kevin Garnett 6.00 15.00
HCP22 Tracy McGrady 4.00 10.00
HCP23 Vince Carter 5.00 12.00
HCP24 Andrea Bargnani 2.00 5.00
HCP25 Gilbert Arenas 2.50 6.00

1995-96 Topps Gallery

COMPLETE SET (144) 15.00 30.00
1 Shaquille O'Neal 1.00 2.50
2 Shawn Kemp .40 1.00
3 Reggie Miller .50 1.25
4 Mitch Richmond .30 .75
5 Grant Hill .40 1.00
6 Magic Johnson .75 2.00
7 Vin Baker .20 .50
8 Charles Barkley .60 1.50
9 Hakeem Olajuwon .50 1.25
10 Michael Jordan 2.50 6.00
11 Patrick Ewing .40 1.00
12 David Robinson .50 1.25
13 Alonzo Mourning .40 1.00
14 Karl Malone .50 1.25
15 Chris Webber .30 .75
16 Dikembe Mutombo .40 1.00
17 Larry Johnson .30 .75
18 Jamal Mashburn .25 .60
19 Anfernee Hardaway .60 1.50
20 Bryant Stith .15 .40
21 Juwan Howard .25 .60
22 Jason Kidd .40 1.00
23 Sharone Wright .15 .40
24 Tom Gugliotta .15 .40
25 Eric Montross .15 .40
26 Allan Houston .20 .50
27 Antonio Davis .15 .40
28 Brian Grant .20 .50
29 Terrell Brandon .20 .50
30 Eddie Jones .25 .60
31 James Robinson .15 .40
32 Wesley Person .15 .40
33 Glenn Robinson .25 .60
34 Donyell Marshall .15 .40
35 Sam Cassell .25 .60
36 Lamond Murray .15 .40
37 Damon Stoudamire RC .60 1.50
38 Tyus Edney RC .25 .60
39 Jerry Stackhouse RC .75 2.00
40 Arvydas Sabonis RC .50 1.25
41 Kevin Garnett RC 2.00 5.00
42 Brent Barry RC .40 1.00
43 Alan Henderson RC .25 .60
44 Bryant Reeves RC .20 .50
45 Shawn Respert RC .20 .50
46 Michael Finley RC .60 1.50
47 Gary Trent RC .20 .50
48 Antonio McDyess RC .30 .75
49 George Zidek RC .20 .50
50 Joe Smith RC .30 .75
51 Ed O'Bannon RC .20 .50
52 Rasheed Wallace RC .75 2.00
53 Eric Williams RC .25 .60
54 Kurt Thomas RC .25 .60
55 Mookie Blaylock .25 .60
56 Robert Pack .15 .40
57 Dana Barros .20 .50
58 Eric Murdock .15 .40
59 Glen Rice .25 .60
60 John Stockton .50 1.25
61 Scottie Pippen .60 1.50
62 Oliver Miller .15 .40
63 Tyrone Hill .15 .40
64 Gary Payton .40 1.00
65 Jim Jackson .20 .50
66 Avery Johnson .20 .50
67 Mahmoud Abdul-Rauf .20 .50
68 Olden Polynice .15 .40
69 Joe Dumars .25 .60
70 Rod Strickland .15 .40
71 Chris Mullin .25 .60
72 Kevin Johnson .25 .60
73 Derrick Coleman .20 .50
74 Clyde Drexler .40 1.00
75 Dale Davis .15 .40
76 Horace Grant .20 .50
77 Loy Vaught .15 .40
78 Armon Gilliam .15 .40
79 Nick Van Exel .25 .60
80 Charles Oakley .20 .50
81 Kevin Willis .15 .40
82 Sherman Douglas .15 .40
83 Isaiah Rider .25 .60
84 Steve Smith .20 .50
85 Dee Brown .20 .50
86 Dell Curry .25 .60
87 Calbert Cheaney .15 .40
88 Greg Anthony .15 .40
89 Jeff Hornacek .20 .50
90 Dennis Rodman .50 1.25
91 Willie Anderson .15 .40
92 Chris Mills .15 .40
93 Hersey Hawkins .20 .50
94 Popeye Jones .15 .40
95 Chuck Person .20 .50
96 Reggie Williams .15 .40
97 A.C. Green .20 .50
98 Otis Thorpe .20 .50
99 Walt Williams .15 .40
100 Latrell Sprewell .20 .50
101 Buck Williams .15 .40
102 Robert Horry .25 .60
103 Clarence Weatherspoon .15 .40
104 Dennis Scott .15 .40
105 Rik Smits .20 .50
106 Jayson Williams .15 .40
107 Pooh Richardson .15 .40
108 Anthony Mason .15 .40
109 Cedric Ceballos .20 .50
110 Billy Owens .15 .40
111 Johnny Newman .15 .40
112 Christian Laettner .20 .50
113 Stacey Augmon .20 .50
114 Chris Morris .15 .40
115 Detlef Schrempf .25 .60
116 Dino Radja .15 .40
117 Sean Elliott .20 .50
118 Muggsy Bogues .25 .60
119 Toni Kukoc .30 .75
120 Clifford Robinson .25 .60
121 Bobby Hurley .15 .40
122 Lorenzo Williams .15 .40
123 Wayman Tisdale .15 .40
124 Bobby Phills .20 .50
125 Nick Anderson .20 .50
126 LaPhonso Ellis .20 .50
127 Scott Williams .15 .40
128 Mark West .15 .40
129 P.J. Brown .15 .40
130 Tim Hardaway .30 .75
131 Derek Harper .20 .50
132 Mario Elie .15 .40
133 Benoit Benjamin .15 .40
134 Terry Porter .15 .40
135 Derrick McKey .15 .40
136 Bimbo Coles .15 .40
137 John Salley .15 .40
138 Malik Sealy .15 .40
139 Byron Scott .25 .60
140 Vlade Divac .25 .60
141 Mark Price .25 .60
142 Rony Seikaly .15 .40
143 Mark Jackson .20 .50
144 John Starks .25 .60

1995-96 Topps Gallery Player's Private Issue

*STARS: 10X TO 25X BASE CARD HI
*RCs: 5X TO 12X BASE HI
STATED ODDS 1:12
1-18 INSERTED IN 96-97 STADIUM CLUB II
10 Michael Jordan 125.00 300.00
61 Scottie Pippen 12.00 30.00
100 Latrell Sprewell 8.00 20.00

1995-96 Topps Gallery Expressionists

COMPLETE SET (15) 30.00 80.00
STATED ODDS 1:24
EX1 Shawn Kemp 2.00 5.00
EX2 Michael Jordan 12.00 30.00
EX3 Reggie Miller 2.50 6.00
EX4 Kevin Willis .75 2.00
EX5 Jason Kidd 2.00 5.00
EX6 Larry Johnson 1.50 4.00
EX7 Patrick Ewing 2.00 5.00
EX8 Rasheed Wallace 4.00 10.00
EX9 Karl Malone 2.50 6.00
EX10 Shaquille O'Neal 5.00 12.00
EX11 Joe Smith 1.50 4.00
EX12 Jerry Stackhouse 4.00 10.00
EX13 Glen Rice 1.25 3.00
EX14 Clyde Drexler 2.00 5.00
EX15 Grant Hill 2.00 5.00

1995-96 Topps Gallery Photo Gallery

COMPLETE SET (17) 50.00 100.00
STATED ODDS 1:30
PG1 Vin Baker 2.50 6.00
PG2 Brian Grant 2.50 6.00
PG3 George Zidek 1.25 3.00
PG4 Hakeem Olajuwon 6.00 15.00
PG5 Stacey Augmon 2.50 6.00
PG6 Oliver Miller 2.00 5.00
PG7 Kenny Gattison 2.00 5.00
PG8 Dikembe Mutombo 5.00 12.00
PG9 Rony Seikaly 2.00 5.00
PG10 Tom Gugliotta 2.00 5.00
PG11 Scottie Pippen 8.00 20.00
PG12 David Robinson 6.00 15.00
PG13 Anfernee Hardaway 8.00 20.00
PG14 Dennis Rodman 6.00 15.00
PG15 Kevin Garnett 12.00 30.00
PG16 Damon Stoudamire 4.00 10.00
PG17 Charles Barkley 8.00 20.00

1999-00 Topps Gallery Promos

COMPLETE SET (6) 1.25 3.00
PP1 Jason Williams .30 .75
PP2 Eddie Jones .20 .50
PP3 Allan Houston .15 .40
PP4 Alonzo Mourning .30 .75
PP5 Shareef Abdur-Rahim .20 .50
PP6 Wally Szczerbiak .30 .75

1999-00 Topps Gallery

COMPLETE SET (150) 20.00 50.00
SUBSET CARDS SAME VALUE AS BASE
1 Gary Payton .50 1.25
2 Derek Anderson .20 .50
3 Jalen Rose .25 .60
4 Tim Hardaway .40 1.00
5 Jerry Stackhouse .30 .75
6 Antonio McDyess .25 .60
7 Paul Pierce .60 1.50
8 Reggie Miller .60 1.50
9 Maurice Taylor .20 .50
10 Stephon Marbury .40 1.00
11 Terrell Brandon .20 .50
12 Marcus Camby .25 .60
13 Michael Doleac .20 .50
14 Doug Christie .25 .60
15 Brent Barry .20 .50
16 John Stockton .50 1.25
17 Rod Strickland .25 .60
18 Shareef Abdur-Rahim .30 .75
19 Vin Baker .25 .60
20 Jason Kidd .50 1.25
21 Nick Anderson .20 .50
22 Brian Grant .20 .50
23 Chris Webber .40 1.00
24 Tariq Abdul-Wahad .20 .50
25 Jason Williams .50 1.25
26 Joe Smith .25 .60
27 Ray Allen .50 1.25
28 Glenn Robinson .25 .60
29 Alonzo Mourning .50 1.25
30 Scottie Pippen .75 2.00
31 Mookie Blaylock .20 .50
32 Christian Laettner .25 .60
33 Mark Jackson .25 .60
34 Shawn Kemp .50 1.25
35 Anfernee Hardaway .75 2.00
36 Chris Mullin .25 .60
37 Dennis Rodman .60 1.50
38 Lamond Murray .20 .50
39 Jim Jackson .20 .50
40 Shaquille O'Neal 1.25 3.00
41 Randy Brown .20 .50
42 Nick Van Exel .25 .60
43 Robert Traylor .20 .50
44 Vlade Divac .30 .75
45 Karl Malone .60 1.50
46 Avery Johnson .25 .60
47 Jayson Williams .20 .50
48 Darrell Armstrong .20 .50
49 Michael Olowokandi .20 .50
50 Kevin Garnett .75 2.00
51 Dirk Nowitzki 1.00 2.50
52 Antawn Jamison .30 .75
53 Latrell Sprewell .40 1.00
54 Ruben Patterson .20 .50
55 Vince Carter .75 2.00
56 Michael Dickerson .20 .50
57 Raef LaFrentz .20 .50
58 Keith Van Horn .25 .60
59 Tom Gugliotta .20 .50
60 Allen Iverson .75 2.00
61 Eric Snow .20 .50
62 Kerry Kittles .20 .50
63 Sam Cassell .25 .60
64 Rik Smits .25 .60
65 Isaiah Rider .25 .60
66 Anthony Mason .30 .75
67 Hersey Hawkins .20 .50
68 Cuttino Mobley .25 .60
69 Allan Houston .25 .60
70 Kobe Bryant 2.50 6.00
71 Damon Stoudamire .30 .75
72 Charles Oakley .30 .75
73 Mike Bibby .30 .75
74 David Robinson .60 1.50
75 Eddie Jones .30 .75
76 Juwan Howard .30 .75
77 Antoine Walker .30 .75
78 Michael Finley .30 .75
79 Larry Hughes .25 .60
80 Charles Barkley .75 2.00
81 Tracy McGrady .50 1.25
82 Dikembe Mutombo .50 1.25
83 Rasheed Wallace .40 1.00
84 Jeff Hornacek .25 .60
85 Patrick Ewing .40 1.00
86 P.J. Brown .20 .50
87 Brevin Knight .20 .50
88 Elden Campbell .20 .50
89 Kenny Anderson .25 .60
90 Grant Hill .50 1.25
91 Mitch Richmond .40 1.00
92 Steve Smith .25 .60
93 Jamal Mashburn .25 .60
94 Toni Kukoc .40 1.00
95 Hakeem Olajuwon .60 1.50
96 Ron Mercer .25 .60
97 John Starks .30 .75
98 Glen Rice .30 .75
99 Cedric Ceballos .20 .50
100 Tim Duncan .75 2.00
101 Karl Malone MAS .60 1.50
102 Alonzo Mourning MAS .50 1.25
103 Gary Payton MAS .50 1.25
104 Scottie Pippen MAS .75 2.00
105 Shaquille O'Neal MAS 1.25 3.00
106 Charles Barkley MAS .75 2.00
107 Grant Hill MAS .50 1.25
108 John Stockton MAS .50 1.25
109 Jason Kidd MAS .50 1.25
110 Reggie Miller MAS .60 1.50
111 Shawn Kemp MAS .50 1.25
112 Patrick Ewing MAS .40 1.00
113 Kevin Garnett ART .75 2.00
114 Vince Carter ART .75 2.00
115 Kobe Bryant ART 2.50 6.00
116 Chris Webber ART .40 1.00
117 Tracy McGrady ART .50 1.25
118 Shareef Abdur-Rahim ART .30 .75
119 Paul Pierce ART .60 1.50
120 Jason Williams ART .50 1.25
121 Tim Duncan ART .75 2.00
122 Eddie Jones ART .30 .75
123 Allen Iverson ART .75 2.00
124 Stephon Marbury ART .40 1.00
125 Elton Brand RC .75 2.00
126 Lamar Odom RC .75 2.00
127 Steve Francis RC .75 2.00
128 Adrian Griffin RC .30 .75
129 Wally Szczerbiak RC .60 1.50
130 Baron Davis RC 1.00 2.50
131 Richard Hamilton RC 1.00 2.50
132 Jonathan Bender RC .40 1.00
133 Andre Miller RC .75 2.00
134 Shawn Marion RC .75 2.00
135 Jason Terry RC .60 1.50
136 Trajan Langdon RC .30 .75
137 Corey Maggette RC .50 1.25
138 William Avery RC .25 .60
139 Ron Artest RC 1.00 2.50
140 Cal Bowdler RC .25 .60
141 James Posey RC .40 1.00
142 Quincy Lewis RC .25 .60
143 Kenny Thomas RC .40 1.00
144 Vonteego Cummings RC .25 .60
145 Todd MacCulloch RC .30 .75
146 Anthony Carter RC .30 .75
147 A.Radojevic RC .25 .60
148 Devean George RC .30 .75
149 Scott Padgett RC .30 .75
150 Jumaine Jones RC .25 .60

1999-00 Topps Gallery Player's Private Issue

*STARS: 6X TO 15X BASE CARD HI
*RCs: 3X TO 8X BASE HI
STATED PRINT RUN 250 SERIAL #'d SETS
STATED ODDS 1:17

1999-00 Topps Gallery Autographs

OVERALL STATED ODDS 1:375
GROUP B: STATED ODDS 1:2637
CM Corey Maggette A 6.00 15.00
EB Elton Brand B 6.00 15.00
TD Tim Duncan B 400.00 800.00
WS Wally Szczerbiak A 5.00 12.00

1999-00 Topps Gallery Exhibits

COMPLETE SET (30) 50.00 100.00
STATED ODDS 1:24
GE1 Shaquille O'Neal 6.00 15.00
GE2 Chris Webber 2.00 5.00
GE3 Karl Malone 3.00 8.00
GE4 Hakeem Olajuwon 3.00 8.00
GE5 Scottie Pippen 4.00 10.00
GE6 Patrick Ewing 2.00 5.00
GE7 John Stockton 2.50 6.00
GE8 Tim Duncan 4.00 10.00
GE9 Grant Hill 2.50 6.00
GE10 Dennis Rodman 3.00 8.00
GE11 Reggie Miller 3.00 8.00
GE12 Brian Grant 1.00 2.50
GE13 Antoine Walker 1.50 4.00
GE14 Damon Stoudamire 1.50 4.00
GE15 Tracy McGrady 2.50 6.00
GE16 Alonzo Mourning 2.50 6.00
GE17 Shawn Kemp 2.50 6.00
GE18 Isaiah Rider 1.25 3.00
GE19 Vince Carter 4.00 10.00
GE20 Antonio McDyess 1.25 3.00
GE21 Jason Kidd 2.50 6.00
GE22 Kobe Bryant 10.00 25.00
GE23 Kevin Garnett 4.00 10.00
GE24 Latrell Sprewell 2.00 5.00
GE25 Michael Finley 1.50 4.00
GE26 Nick Van Exel 1.25 3.00
GE27 Anfernee Hardaway 4.00 10.00
GE28 Elton Brand 2.00 5.00
GE29 Lamar Odom 2.00 5.00
GE30 Baron Davis 2.50 6.00

1999-00 Topps Gallery Gallery of Heroes

COMPLETE SET (10) 12.00 30.00
STATED ODDS 1:24
GH1 Kevin Garnett 2.50 6.00
GH2 Stephon Marbury 1.25 3.00
GH3 Kobe Bryant 10.00 25.00
GH4 Vince Carter 2.50 6.00
GH5 Tim Duncan 2.50 6.00
GH6 Gary Payton 1.50 4.00
GH7 Antoine Walker 1.00 2.50
GH8 Chris Webber 1.25 3.00
GH9 Alonzo Mourning 1.50 4.00
GH10 Karl Malone 2.00 5.00

1999-00 Topps Gallery Heritage

COMPLETE SET (10) 8.00 20.00
STATED ODDS 1:12
*PROOF: .75X TO 2X HI COLUMN
PROOF: STATED ODDS 1:36
TGH1 Tim Duncan 2.00 5.00
TGH2 Elton Brand 1.50 4.00
TGH3 Shaquille O'Neal 3.00 8.00
TGH4 Stephon Marbury 1.00 2.50
TGH5 Allen Iverson 2.00 5.00
TGH6 Grant Hill 1.25 3.00
TGH7 Charles Barkley 2.00 5.00
TGH8 Jason Williams 1.25 3.00
TGH9 Scottie Pippen 2.00 5.00
TGH10 Allan Houston .60 1.50

1999-00 Topps Gallery Originals

STATED ODDS 1:87
GO1 Elton Brand 3.00 8.00
GO2 Shawn Marion 3.00 8.00
GO3 Corey Maggette 2.00 5.00
GO4 Steve Francis 3.00 8.00
GO5 Wally Szczerbiak 2.50 6.00
GO6 Baron Davis 4.00 10.00
GO7 Jonathan Bender 1.50 4.00
GO8 Jason Terry 2.50 6.00
GO9 Richard Hamilton 4.00 10.00
GO10 Andre Miller 3.00 8.00

1999-00 Topps Gallery Photo Gallery

COMPLETE SET (10) 2.00 5.00
STATED ODDS 1:12
PG1 Tim Duncan .60 1.50
PG2 Allen Iverson .60 1.50
PG3 Gary Payton .40 1.00
PG4 Elton Brand .50 1.25
PG5 Steve Francis .50 1.25
PG6 Latrell Sprewell .30 .75
PG7 Jason Kidd .40 1.00
PG8 Shawn Marion .50 1.25
PG9 Shareef Abdur-Rahim .25 .60
PG10 Jason Williams .40 1.00

2000-01 Topps Gallery

COMP.SET w/o RC's 125) 15.00 40.00
126-150 STATED PRINT RUN 999 SER.#'d SETS
SUBSET CARDS SAME VALUE AS BASE
1 Allen Iverson .60 1.50
2 Terrell Brandon .20 .50
3 Tracy McGrady .50 1.25
4 Shawn Marion .25 .60
5 Steve Smith .25 .60
6 Avery Johnson .20 .50
7 Gary Payton .40 1.00
8 Mark Jackson .20 .50
9 Mike Bibby .25 .60
10 Karl Malone .50 1.25
11 Kevin Garnett .60 1.50
12 Tim Hardaway .30 .75
13 Isaiah Rider .20 .50
14 Corey Maggette .20 .50
15 Vince Carter .50 1.25
16 Vin Baker .20 .50
17 Paul Pierce .40 1.00
18 Matt Harpring .15 .40
19 Ron Artest .25 .60
20 Kenny Anderson .20 .50
21 Larry Hughes .25 .60
22 Antonio McDyess .25 .60
23 Shandon Anderson .15 .40
24 Joe Smith .20 .50
25 Jermaine O'Neal .20 .50
26 Horace Grant .25 .60
27 Ray Allen .40 1.00
28 Keith Van Horn .20 .50
29 Darrell Armstrong .15 .40
30 Shaquille O'Neal 1.00 2.50
31 Reggie Miller .50 1.25
32 Allan Houston .25 .60
33 Grant Hill .40 1.00
34 David Robinson .50 1.25
35 Clifford Robinson .25 .60
36 Theo Ratliff .15 .40
37 Rashard Lewis .20 .50
38 Peja Stojakovic .20 .50
39 Jason Kidd .40 1.00
40 Latrell Sprewell .30 .75
41 Stephon Marbury .30 .75
42 Sam Cassell .20 .50
43 Brian Grant .20 .50
44 Jalen Rose .20 .50
45 Antawn Jamison .25 .60
46 Raef LaFrentz .20 .50
47 Dirk Nowitzki .60 1.50
48 Lamond Murray .15 .40
49 Derrick Coleman .25 .60
50 Steve Francis .25 .60
51 Dikembe Mutombo .40 1.00
52 Elton Brand .25 .60
53 Christian Laettner .25 .60
54 Ben Wallace .30 .75
55 Jim Jackson .20 .50
56 Cuttino Mobley .20 .50
57 Jonathan Bender .15 .40
58 Anthony Mason .25 .60
59 Tim Thomas .15 .40
60 Lamar Odom .25 .60
61 Glenn Robinson .25 .60
62 Kendall Gill .25 .60
63 Glen Rice .25 .60
64 Anfernee Hardaway .40 1.00
65 Jason Williams .40 1.00
66 Shawn Kemp .40 1.00
67 Derek Anderson .20 .50
68 Patrick Ewing .40 1.00
69 Shareef Abdur-Rahim .25 .60
70 Tim Duncan .60 1.50
71 Rod Strickland .15 .40
72 Bryon Russell .15 .40
73 Antonio Davis .20 .50
74 Rasheed Wallace .30 .75
75 Wally Szczerbiak .20 .50
76 Eric Snow .15 .40
77 Toni Kukoc .30 .75
78 Michael Olowokandi .15 .40
79 Hakeem Olajuwon .50 1.25
80 Kobe Bryant 2.00 5.00
81 Mookie Blaylock .25 .60
82 Michael Finley .25 .60
83 Jerry Stackhouse .25 .60
84 Baron Davis .25 .60
85 Jason Terry .20 .50
86 Andre Miller .20 .50
87 Antoine Walker .25 .60
88 Jamal Mashburn .20 .50
89 Nick Van Exel .25 .60
90 Eddie Jones .25 .60
91 Marcus Camby .20 .50
92 Scottie Pippen .60 1.50
93 John Stockton .50 1.25
94 Richard Hamilton .30 .75
95 John Starks .25 .60
96 Juwan Howard .20 .50
97 Michael Dickerson .15 .40
98 Ron Mercer .20 .50
99 Chris Webber .30 .75
100 Magic Johnson .60 1.50
101 Shaquille O'Neal MAS 1.00 2.50
102 Tim Duncan MAS .60 1.50
103 Chris Webber MAS .30 .75
104 Grant Hill MAS .40 1.00
105 Kevin Garnett MAS .60 1.50
106 Vince Carter MAS .50 1.25
107 Gary Payton MAS .40 1.00
108 Jason Kidd MAS .40 1.00
109 Kobe Bryant MAS 2.00 5.00
110 Karl Malone MAS .50 1.25
111 Scottie Pippen MAS .60 1.50
112 Reggie Miller MAS .50 1.25
113 John Stockton MAS .50 1.25
114 Elton Brand ART .25 .60
115 Tracy McGrady ART .50 1.25
116 Steve Francis ART .25 .60
117 Lamar Odom ART .25 .60
118 Baron Davis ART .25 .60
119 Andre Miller ART .20 .50
120 Jonathan Bender ART .15 .40
121 Paul Pierce ART .40 1.00
122 Jason Williams ART .40 1.00
123 Rashard Lewis ART .20 .50
124 Larry Hughes ART .25 .60
125 Shawn Marion ART .25 .60
126 Kenyon Martin RC 2.50 6.00
127 Stromile Swift RC 1.00 2.50
128 Darius Miles RC 1.25 3.00
129 Marcus Fizer RC 1.00 2.50
130 Mike Miller RC 2.00 5.00
131 DerMarr Johnson RC .75 2.00
132 Chris Mihm RC .75 2.00
133 Jamal Crawford RC 3.00 8.00
134 Joel Przybilla RC 1.00 2.50
135 Keyon Dooling RC 1.00 2.50
136 Jerome Moiso RC .75 2.00
137 Etan Thomas RC 1.00 2.50
138 Courtney Alexander RC .75 2.00
139 Mateen Cleaves RC 1.00 2.50
140 Jason Collier RC 1.25 3.00
141 Hedo Turkoglu RC 2.00 5.00
142 Desmond Mason RC 1.50 4.00
143 Quentin Richardson RC 1.00 2.50
144 Jamaal Magloire RC 1.25 3.00
145 Speedy Claxton RC 1.25 3.00
146 Morris Peterson RC 1.25 3.00
147 Donnell Harvey RC 1.00 2.50
148 DeShawn Stevenson RC 1.25 3.00
149 Stephen Jackson RC 2.50 6.00
150 Marc Jackson RC 1.00 2.50

2000-01 Topps Gallery Charity Gallery

COMPLETE SET (10) 6.00 15.00
STATED ODDS 1:12
CG1 Eddie Jones 1.00 2.50
CG2 Ray Allen 1.50 4.00
CG3 Elton Brand 1.00 2.50
CG4 Jason Kidd 1.50 4.00
CG5 Derek Anderson .75 2.00
CG6 Karl Malone 2.00 5.00
CG7 Brian Grant .75 2.00
CG8 Shareef Abdur-Rahim 1.00 2.50
CG9 Rasheed Wallace 1.25 3.00
CG10 Marcus Camby .75 2.00

2000-01 Topps Gallery Extremes

COMPLETE SET (20) 20.00 50.00
STATED ODDS 1:18
E1 Shaquille O'Neal 5.00 12.00
E2 Vince Carter 2.50 6.00
E3 Allen Iverson 3.00 8.00
E4 Kevin Garnett 3.00 8.00
E5 Chris Webber 1.50 4.00
E6 Larry Hughes 1.25 3.00
E7 Jason Williams 2.00 5.00
E8 Steve Francis 1.25 3.00
E9 Antonio McDyess 1.00 2.50
E10 Tim Duncan 3.00 8.00
E11 Gary Payton 2.00 5.00
E12 Lamar Odom 1.25 3.00
E13 Elton Brand 1.25 3.00
E14 Michael Finley 1.25 3.00
E15 Latrell Sprewell 1.50 4.00
E16 Shareef Abdur-Rahim 1.25 3.00
E17 Jerry Stackhouse 1.25 3.00
E18 Rashard Lewis 1.00 2.50
E19 Shawn Marion 1.25 3.00
E20 Darius Miles 1.25 3.00

2000-01 Topps Gallery Gallery of Heroes

COMPLETE SET (10) 20.00 40.00
STATED ODDS 1:24
GH1 Allen Iverson 4.00 10.00
GH2 Tim Duncan 4.00 10.00
GH3 Kobe Bryant 10.00 25.00
GH4 Elton Brand 1.50 4.00
GH5 Ray Allen 2.50 6.00
GH6 Stephon Marbury 2.00 5.00
GH7 Eddie Jones 1.50 4.00
GH8 Gary Payton 2.50 6.00
GH9 Antonio McDyess 1.25 3.00
GH10 Shareef Abdur-Rahim 1.50 4.00

2000-01 Topps Gallery Heritage

COMPLETE SET (10) 8.00 20.00
STATED ODDS 1:10
*PROOFS: 1.5X TO 4X BASE CARD HI
PROOFS STATED ODDS 1:186
PROOFS PRINT RUN 250 SERIAL #'d SETS
H1 Tim Duncan 2.50 6.00
H2 Tracy McGrady 2.00 5.00
H3 Steve Francis 1.00 2.50
H4 Elton Brand 1.00 2.50
H5 Rashard Lewis .75 2.00
H6 Larry Hughes 1.00 2.50
H7 Shawn Marion 1.00 2.50
H8 Baron Davis 1.00 2.50
H9 Antawn Jamison 1.00 2.50
H10 Keyon Dooling .75 2.00

2000-01 Topps Gallery Originals

GROUP A ODDS 1:153; B ODDS 1:71
GROUP C ODDS 1:255; D ODDS 1:1148
ROOKIE STATED ODDS 1:48 OVERALL
VETERAN STATED ODDS 1:209 OVERALL
GO1 Kenyon Martin B 4.00 10.00
GO2 Stromile Swift B 1.50 4.00
GO3 Darius Miles B 2.00 5.00
GO4 Marcus Fizer B 1.50 4.00
GO5 Mike Miller B 3.00 8.00
GO6 DerMarr Johnson B 1.25 3.00
GO7 Chris Mihm B 1.25 3.00
GO8 Joel Przybilla B 1.50 4.00
GO9 Keyon Dooling B 1.50 4.00
GO10 Jerome Moiso B 1.25 3.00
GO11 Etan Thomas B 1.50 4.00
GO12 Courtney Alexander B 1.25 3.00
GO13 Mateen Cleaves B 1.50 4.00
GO14 Jason Collier A 2.00 5.00
GO15 Hedo Turkoglu A 3.00 8.00
GO16 Desmond Mason A 2.50 6.00
GO17 Quentin Richardson A 1.50 4.00
GO18 Jamaal Magloire A 2.00 5.00
GO19 Speedy Claxton A 2.00 5.00
GO20 Morris Peterson A 2.00 5.00
GO21 Donnell Harvey A 1.50 4.00
GO22 DeShawn Stevenson A 2.00 5.00
GO23 Mamadou N'Diaye A 1.25 3.00
GO24 Erick Barkley A 1.25 3.00
GO25 Mark Madsen A 2.00 5.00
GO26 Tracy McGrady C 4.00 10.00
GO27 Shaquille O'Neal D 8.00 20.00
GO28 Grant Hill C 3.00 8.00
GO29 Tim Duncan D 5.00 12.00
GO30 Antoine Walker C 2.00 5.00
GO31 Jason Kidd C 3.00 8.00

2000-01 Topps Gallery Photo Gallery

COMPLETE SET (10) 10.00 25.00
STATED ODDS 1:10
PG1 Kevin Garnett 2.00 5.00
PG2 Grant Hill 1.25 3.00
PG3 Kobe Bryant 6.00 15.00
PG4 Vince Carter 1.50 4.00
PG5 Lamar Odom .75 2.00
PG6 Stephon Marbury 1.00 2.50
PG7 Baron Davis .75 2.00
PG8 Chris Webber 1.00 2.50
PG9 Ray Allen 1.25 3.00
PG10 Kenyon Martin 1.50 4.00

2000-01 Topps Gallery Signatures

GROUP A ODDS 1:1836; B ODDS 1:765
GROUP C ODDS 1:574; D ODDS 1:918
GROUP E ODDS 1:612
STATED ODDS 1:158 OVERALL
GSEB Elton Brand C 6.00 15.00
GSEJ Eddie Jones A 10.00 25.00
GSGP Gary Payton E 12.50 30.00
GSJC Jamal Crawford B 6.00 15.00
GSMC Mateen Cleaves D 5.00 12.00
GSMJ Magic Johnson B 40.00 100.00

1999-00 Topps Gold Label Class 1

COMPLETE SET (100) 25.00 60.00
ONE TO ONE STATED ODDS 1:629
1 Tim Duncan 1.00 2.50
2 Steve Smith .30 .75
3 Jeff Hornacek .30 .75
4 Kevin Garnett 1.00 2.50
5 Paul Pierce .75 2.00
6 Doug Christie .30 .75
7 Charles Barkley 1.00 2.50
8 Nick Van Exel .30 .75
9 Shareef Abdur-Rahim .40 1.00
10 Rod Strickland .30 .75
11 Keith Van Horn .30 .75
12 Matt Harpring .25 .60
13 Randy Brown .25 .60
14 Vin Baker .30 .75
15 Mark Jackson .30 .75
16 Latrell Sprewell .50 1.25
17 Anthony Mason .40 1.00
18 Brian Grant .25 .60
19 Brevin Knight .25 .60
20 Elden Campbell .25 .60
21 Allen Iverson 1.00 2.50
22 Kobe Bryant 3.00 8.00
23 Antawn Jamison .40 1.00
24 Lindsey Hunter .25 .60
25 Eddie Jones .40 1.00
26 Michael Finley .40 1.00
27 Juwan Howard .30 .75
28 Antonio McDyess .30 .75
29 David Robinson .75 2.00
30 Karl Malone .75 2.00
31 Jason Kidd .60 1.50
32 Zydrunas Ilgauskas .30 .75
33 Vince Carter 1.00 2.50
34 Maurice Taylor .25 .60
35 Alonzo Mourning .60 1.50
36 Tim Thomas .30 .75
37 Dikembe Mutombo .60 1.50
38 Grant Hill .60 1.50
39 Jason Williams .60 1.50
40 Scottie Pippen 1.00 2.50
41 Stephon Marbury .50 1.25
42 Reggie Miller .75 2.00
43 Tyrone Nesby RC .25 .60
44 Ron Mercer .30 .75
45 Terrell Brandon .25 .60
46 Darrell Armstrong .25 .60
47 Larry Hughes .30 .75
48 Alan Henderson .25 .60
49 Ray Allen .60 1.50
50 Rasheed Wallace .50 1.25
51 Toni Kukoc .50 1.25
52 Patrick Ewing .50 1.25
53 Tom Gugliotta .30 .75
54 Chris Mills .25 .60
55 Gary Payton .60 1.50
56 Michael Olowokandi .25 .60
57 Chris Mullin .40 1.00
58 Shawn Kemp .60 1.50
59 Joe Smith .30 .75
60 Steve Nash .75 2.00

61 Gary Trent .25 .60
62 Shaquille O'Neal 1.50 4.00
63 Kerry Kittles .30 .75
64 Tim Hardaway .50 1.25
65 Glenn Robinson .30 .75
66 Damon Stoudamire .40 1.00
67 Anfernee Hardaway 1.00 2.50
68 Vlade Divac .40 1.00
69 John Starks .40 1.00
70 Allan Houston .30 .75
71 Jerry Stackhouse .40 1.00
72 Avery Johnson .30 .75
73 Glen Rice .40 1.00
74 Felipe Lopez .25 .60
75 Clifford Robinson .30 .75
76 Jamal Mashburn .30 .75
77 Hakeem Olajuwon .75 2.00
78 Matt Geiger .25 .60
79 John Stockton .60 1.50
80 Chauncey Billups .40 1.00
81 Chris Webber .50 1.25
82 Antoine Walker .40 1.00
83 Mike Bibby .40 1.00
84 Tracy McGrady .60 1.50
85 Mitch Richmond .50 1.25
86 Elton Brand RC .75 2.00
87 Steve Francis RC .75 2.00
88 Baron Davis RC 1.00 2.50
89 Lamar Odom RC .75 2.00
90 Jonathan Bender RC .40 1.00
91 Wally Szczerbiak RC .60 1.50
92 Richard Hamilton RC 1.00 2.50
93 Andre Miller RC .75 2.00
94 Shawn Marion RC .75 2.00
95 Jason Terry RC .60 1.50
96 Trajan Langdon RC .30 .75
97 A.Radojevic RC .25 .60
98 Corey Maggette RC .50 1.25
99 William Avery RC .25 .60
100 Cal Bowdler RC .25 .60

1999-00 Topps Gold Label Class 1 Black Label

*STARS: 1.5X TO 4X BASE HI
*RCs: 1.25X TO 3X BASE HI
STATED ODDS 1:8

1999-00 Topps Gold Label Class 1 Red Label

*STARS: 10X TO 25X BASE HI
*RCs: 6X TO 15X BASE HI
STATED PRINT RUN 100 SERIAL #'d SETS
5 Paul Pierce 15.00 40.00
67 Anfernee Hardaway 20.00 50.00
77 Hakeem Olajuwon 20.00 50.00
81 Chris Webber 30.00 80.00
84 Tracy McGrady 30.00 80.00

1999-00 Topps Gold Label Class 2

COMPLETE SET (100) 40.00 100.00
*STARS: .75X TO 2X CLASS 1 BASE
*RCs: .6X TO 1.5X CLASS 1 BASE
STATED ODDS 1:2

1999-00 Topps Gold Label Class 2 Black Label

*STARS: 3X TO 8X CLASS 1 BASE
*RCs: 2.5X TO 6X CLASS 1 BASE
STATED ODDS 1:16

1999-00 Topps Gold Label Class 2 Red Label

*STARS: 15X TO 40X CLASS 1 BASE
*RCs: 8X TO 20X CLASS 1 BASE
STATED PRINT RUN 50 SERIAL #'d SETS
5 Paul Pierce 25.00 60.00
67 Anfernee Hardaway 40.00 100.00
77 Hakeem Olajuwon 60.00 150.00
81 Chris Webber 50.00 120.00
84 Tracy McGrady 50.00 120.00

1999-00 Topps Gold Label Class 3

COMPLETE SET (100) 75.00 150.00
*STARS: 1.25X TO 3X CLASS 1 BASE
*RCs: 1X TO 2.5X CLASS 1 BASE
STATED ODDS 1:4

1999-00 Topps Gold Label Class 3 Black Label

*STARS: 5X TO 12X CLASS 1 BASE
*RCs: 4X TO 10X CLASS 1 BASE
STATED ODDS 1:32

1999-00 Topps Gold Label Class 3 Red Label

*STARS: 30X TO 80X CLASS 1 BASE
*RCs: 12X TO 30X CLASS 1 BASE
STATED PRINT RUN 25 SERIAL #'d SETS
30 Karl Malone 75.00 200.00
33 Vince Carter 100.00 250.00
39 Jason Williams 100.00 250.00
67 Anfernee Hardaway 50.00 125.00
77 Hakeem Olajuwon 125.00 300.00
81 Chris Webber 75.00 200.00
84 Tracy McGrady 75.00 200.00

1999-00 Topps Gold Label New Standard

COMPLETE SET (15) 15.00 40.00
STATED ODDS 1:12
*BLACK: 1X TO 2.5X HI COLUMN
BLACK: STATED ODDS 1:60
*RED STARS: 10X TO 25X HI
RED: STATED ODDS 1:1692
RED: PRINT RUN 25 SERIAL #'d SETS
NS1 Vince Carter 2.00 5.00
NS2 Kevin Garnett 2.00 5.00
NS3 Tim Duncan 2.00 5.00
NS4 Kobe Bryant 6.00 15.00
NS5 Allen Iverson 2.00 5.00
NS6 Jason Williams 1.25 3.00
NS7 Keith Van Horn .60 1.50
NS8 Elton Brand 1.25 3.00
NS9 Steve Francis 1.25 3.00
NS10 Baron Davis 1.50 4.00
NS11 Lamar Odom 1.25 3.00
NS12 Jonathan Bender .60 1.50
NS13 Wally Szczerbiak 1.00 2.50
NS14 Jason Terry 1.00 2.50
NS15 Corey Maggette .75 2.00

1999-00 Topps Gold Label Prime Gold

COMPLETE SET (11) 6.00 15.00
STATED ODDS 1:18
*BLACK: 1X TO 2.5X HI COLUMN
BLACK: STATED ODDS 1:90
*RED: 12X TO 30X HI
RED: STATED ODDS 1:2312
RED: PRINT RUN 25 SERIAL #'d SETS
PG1 John Stockton 1.25 3.00
PG2 Hakeem Olajuwon 1.50 4.00
PG3 Charles Barkley 2.00 5.00
PG4 Shaquille O'Neal 3.00 8.00
PG5 Alonzo Mourning 1.25 3.00
PG6 Scottie Pippen 2.00 5.00
PG7 Jason Kidd 1.25 3.00
PG8 David Robinson 1.50 4.00
PG9 Gary Payton 1.25 3.00
PG10 Karl Malone 1.50 4.00
PG11 Grant Hill 1.25 3.00

1999-00 Topps Gold Label Prime Gold Red Label

*RED: 30X TO 80X HI
PG2 Hakeem Olajuwon 200.00 500.00
PG11 Grant Hill 200.00 500.00

1999-00 Topps Gold Label Quest for the Gold

STATED ODDS 1:9
*BLACK: 1X TO 2.5X HI COLUMN
BLACK: STATED ODDS 1:45
*RED: 15X TO 40X HI
RED: STATED ODDS 1:2813
RED: PRINT RUN 25 SERIAL #'d SETS
Q1 Allan Houston .50 1.25
Q2 Kevin Garnett 1.50 4.00
Q3 Gary Payton 1.00 2.50
Q4 Steve Smith .50 1.25
Q5 Tim Hardaway .75 2.00
Q6 Tim Duncan 1.50 4.00
Q7 Jason Kidd 1.00 2.50
Q8 Tom Gugliotta .50 1.25
Q9 Vin Baker .50 1.25

2000-01 Topps Gold Label Class 1

COMPLETE SET w/o RC (80) 15.00 30.00
RCs: STATED ODDS 1:29
RCs: STATED PRINT RUN 1499 SERIAL #'d SETS
1 Steve Francis .40 1.00
2 Jalen Rose .40 1.00
3 Allen Iverson 1.00 2.50
4 Damon Stoudamire .40 1.00
5 David Robinson .75 2.00
6 Bryon Russell .25 .60
7 Toni Kukoc .60 1.50
8 Tracy McGrady .75 2.00
9 John Stockton .75 2.00
10 Tim Duncan 1.00 2.50
11 Hakeem Olajuwon .75 2.00
12 Antoine Walker .40 1.00
13 Dikembe Mutombo .60 1.50
14 Shawn Kemp .60 1.50
15 Ron Artest .40 1.00
16 Eddie Jones .40 1.00
17 Dirk Nowitzki 1.00 2.50
18 Nick Van Exel .40 1.00
19 Grant Hill .60 1.50
20 Antawn Jamison .60 1.50
21 Cuttino Mobley .30 .75
22 Jonathan Bender .25 .60
23 Maurice Taylor .25 .60
24 Kobe Bryant 3.00 8.00
25 Tim Hardaway .50 1.25
26 Tim Thomas .25 .60
27 Terrell Brandon .30 .75
28 Marcus Camby .30 .75
29 Keith Van Horn .30 .75
30 Shawn Marion .40 1.00
31 Rasheed Wallace .50 1.25
32 Corey Maggette .30 .75
33 Jason Kidd .60 1.50
34 Shaquille O'Neal 1.50 4.00
35 Rashard Lewis .30 .75
36 Karl Malone .75 2.00
37 Michael Dickerson .25 .60
38 Richard Hamilton .50 1.25
39 Darrell Armstrong .25 .60
40 Wally Szczerbiak .30 .75
41 Glen Rice .40 1.00
42 Glenn Robinson .40 1.00
43 Reggie Miller .75 2.00
44 Alonzo Mourning .60 1.50
45 Larry Hughes .40 1.00
46 Antonio McDyess .30 .75
47 Derrick Coleman .40 1.00
48 Brevin Knight .25 .60
49 Jason Terry .40 1.00
50 Elton Brand .40 1.00
51 Latrell Sprewell .50 1.25
52 Theo Ratliff .25 .60
53 Scottie Pippen 1.00 2.50
54 Jason Williams .60 1.50
55 Gary Payton .60 1.50
56 Mitch Richmond .50 1.25
57 Vin Baker .30 .75
58 Raef LaFrentz .30 .75
59 Anfernee Hardaway .60 1.50
60 Steve Smith .40 1.00
61 Stephon Marbury .50 1.25
62 Vlade Divac .40 1.00
63 Jamal Mashburn .30 .75
64 Jerome Williams .25 .60
65 Patrick Ewing .60 1.50
66 Lamar Odom .60 1.50
67 Jerry Stackhouse .60 1.50
68 Michael Finley .40 1.00
69 Vince Carter .75 2.00
70 Andre Miller .40 1.00
71 Paul Pierce .60 1.50
72 Baron Davis .40 1.00
73 Derek Anderson .30 .75
74 Chris Webber .50 1.25
75 Ray Allen .60 1.50
76 Kevin Garnett 1.00 2.50
77 Allan Houston .40 1.00
78 Mike Bibby .40 1.00
79 Shareef Abdur-Rahim .40 1.00
80 Juwan Howard .30 .75
81 Kenyon Martin RC 3.00 8.00
82 Stromile Swift RC 1.25 3.00
83 Darius Miles RC 1.50 4.00
84 Marcus Fizer RC 1.25 3.00
85 Mike Miller RC 2.50 6.00
86 DerMarr Johnson RC 1.00 2.50
87 Chris Mihm RC 1.00 2.50
88 Jamal Crawford RC 4.00 10.00
89 Joel Przybilla RC 1.25 3.00
90 Keyon Dooling RC 1.25 3.00
91 Jerome Moiso RC 1.00 2.50
92 Etan Thomas RC 1.25 3.00
93 Courtney Alexander RC 1.00 2.50
94 Mateen Cleaves RC 1.25 3.00
95 Jason Collier RC 1.50 4.00
96 Desmond Mason RC 2.00 5.00
97 Quentin Richardson RC 1.25 3.00
98 Jamaal Magloire RC 1.50 4.00
99 Speedy Claxton RC 1.50 4.00
100 Morris Peterson RC 1.50 4.00

2000-01 Topps Gold Label Class 2

*CLASS 2 VETS: .75X TO 2X CLASS 1 HI
*CLASS 2 RCs: .3X TO .8X CLASS 1 HI
CLASS 2 VETS: STATED ODDS 1:4
CLASS 2 RCs: PRINT RUN 999 SERIAL #'d SETS

2000-01 Topps Gold Label Class 3

*CLASS 3 VETS: 1.25X TO 3X CLASS 1 HI
*CLASS 3 RCs: .5X TO 1.25X CLASS 1 HI
CLASS 3 VETS: STATED ODDS 1:12
CLASS 3 RCs: PRINT RUN 499 SERIAL #'d SETS

2000-01 Topps Gold Label Premium

*STARS: 2.5X TO 6X BASE CARD HI
*RCs: .75X TO 2X BASE CARD HI
VETS: PRINT RUN 1000 SERIAL #'d SETS
RCs: PRINT RUN 100 SERIAL #'d SETS
RCs: STATED ODDS 1:430

2000-01 Topps Gold Label Autographs

STATED ODDS 1:1718
TTAJR Jalen Rose 10.00 25.00
TTASO Shaquille O'Neal 150.00 400.00

2000-01 Topps Gold Label Game Jerseys

OVERALL STATED ODDS 1:40
LAKERS (H) JERSEYS ARE YELLOW
LAKERS (A) JERSEYS ARE PURPLE
*LEATHER: 2X TO 5X BASE JSY HI
LEATHER STATED ODDS 1:1039
TT1A Shaquille O'Neal 12.00 30.00
TT1H Shaquille O'Neal 12.00 30.00
TT2A Glen Rice 10.00 25.00
TT2H Glen Rice 10.00 25.00
TT3A Robert Horry 6.00 15.00
TT3H Robert Horry 6.00 15.00
TT4A Rick Fox 5.00 12.00
TT4H Rick Fox 5.00 12.00
TT5A Brian Shaw 4.00 10.00
TT5H Brian Shaw 4.00 10.00
TT6A Ron Harper 6.00 15.00
TT6H Ron Harper 6.00 15.00
TT7A Derek Fisher 10.00 25.00
TT7H Derek Fisher 10.00 25.00
TT8A A.C. Green 5.00 12.00
TT8H A.C. Green 5.00 12.00
TT9A John Salley 4.00 10.00
TT9H John Salley 4.00 10.00
TT10A Travis Knight 4.00 10.00
TT10H Travis Knight 4.00 10.00
TT11A Devean George 4.00 10.00
TT11H Devean George 4.00 10.00
TT12 Reggie Miller 25.00 60.00
TT13 Jalen Rose 8.00 20.00
TT14 Dale Davis 5.00 12.00
TT15 Rik Smits 5.00 12.00
TT16 Mark Jackson 5.00 12.00
TT17 Travis Best 4.00 10.00
TT18 Austin Croshere 6.00 15.00
TT19 Derrick McKey 4.00 10.00
TT20 Sam Perkins 4.00 10.00
TT21 Chris Mullin 12.00 30.00
TT22 Jonathan Bender 4.00 10.00
TT23 Zan Tabak 4.00 10.00

2000-01 Topps Gold Label Great Expectations

COMPLETE SET (10) 7.50 15.00
STATED ODDS 1:32
GE1 Elton Brand 1.00 2.50
GE2 Shawn Marion 1.00 2.50
GE3 Jason Williams 1.50 4.00
GE4 Baron Davis 1.00 2.50
GE5 Andre Miller .75 2.00
GE6 Paul Pierce 1.50 4.00
GE7 Lamar Odom 1.50 4.00
GE8 Dirk Nowitzki 2.50 6.00
GE9 Kenyon Martin 2.00 5.00
GE10 Marcus Fizer .75 2.00

2000-01 Topps Gold Label Home Court Advantage

COMPLETE SET (15) 15.00 40.00
STATED ODDS 1:40
HCA1 Tim Duncan 4.00 10.00
HCA2 Antoine Walker 1.50 4.00
HCA3 Chris Webber 2.00 5.00
HCA4 Alonzo Mourning 2.50 6.00
HCA5 Karl Malone 3.00 8.00
HCA6 Allen Iverson 4.00 10.00
HCA7 Jason Kidd 2.50 6.00
HCA8 Rasheed Wallace 2.00 5.00
HCA9 Gary Payton 2.50 6.00
HCA10 Shareef Abdur-Rahim 1.50 4.00
HCA11 Eddie Jones 1.50 4.00
HCA12 Stephon Marbury 2.00 5.00
HCA13 Scottie Pippen 4.00 10.00
HCA14 Raef LaFrentz 1.25 3.00
HCA15 Elton Brand 1.50 4.00

2000-01 Topps Gold Label Jam Artists

COMPLETE SET (10) 4.00 10.00
STATED ODDS 1:8
JA1 Vince Carter .75 2.00
JA2 Tracy McGrady .75 2.00
JA3 Steve Francis .40 1.00
JA4 Jerry Stackhouse .40 1.00
JA5 Kevin Garnett 1.00 2.50
JA6 Michael Finley .40 1.00
JA7 Stromile Swift .30 .75
JA8 Kobe Bryant 3.00 8.00
JA9 Darius Miles .40 1.00
JA10 Larry Hughes .40 1.00

1998 Topps Golden Greats

COMPLETE SET (18) 25.00 60.00
1 Kareem Abdul-Jabbar 3.00 8.00
2 Elgin Baylor 2.00 5.00
3 Larry Bird 5.00 12.00
4 Wilt Chamberlain 4.00 10.00
5 Bob Cousy 3.00 8.00
6 Julius Erving 3.00 8.00
7 Walt Frazier 2.00 5.00
8 George Gervin 2.00 5.00
9 John Havlicek 2.50 6.00
10 Magic Johnson 5.00 12.00
11 Kevin McHale 2.50 6.00
12 Earl Monroe 2.00 5.00
13 Willis Reed 2.00 5.00
14 Oscar Robertson 2.50 6.00
15 Bill Russell 3.00 8.00
16 Bill Walton 2.00 5.00
17 Jerry West 3.00 8.00
18 Rick Barry 1.50 4.00

1998 Topps Golden Greats Laser Cuts

COMPLETE SET (18) 40.00 100.00
*LASER CUTS: .75X TO 2X BASE HI

2008-09 Topps Hardwood

COMP.SET w/o SPs (100) 20.00 40.00
RC PRINT RUN 2009 SER.#'d SETS
TWO VERSIONS EXIST FOR EACH RC
1 Paul Pierce .60 1.50
2 Andrew Bogut .30 .75
3 Greg Oden .25 .60
4 Monta Ellis .30 .75
5 Shaquille O'Neal 1.25 3.00
6 Al Horford .40 1.00
7 Al Thornton .25 .60
8 Anderson Varejao .25 .60
9 Andre Iguodala .30 .75
10 Carlos Boozer .30 .75
11 Chris Bosh .50 1.25
12 Corey Maggette .30 .75
13 Craig Smith .25 .60
14 Danny Granger .30 .75
15 David West .30 .75
16 Josh Howard .30 .75
17 Kevin Durant 1.50 4.00
18 Kevin Garnett 1.00 2.50
19 Luis Scola .30 .75
20 Luol Deng .30 .75
21 Yi Jianlian .50 1.25
22 Pau Gasol .50 1.25
23 Rasheed Wallace .50 1.25
24 Ben Gordon .30 .75
25 Dwyane Wade .75 2.00
26 Gilbert Arenas .40 1.00
27 Jamal Crawford .40 1.00
28 Gerald Wallace .30 .75
29 Jason Richardson .40 1.00
30 Kevin Martin .30 .75
31 Mike Conley Jr. .30 .75
32 Richard Hamilton .40 1.00
33 Tony Parker .50 1.25
34 Vince Carter .75 2.00
35 Brad Miller .30 .75
36 Al Jefferson .25 .60
37 Antawn Jamison .30 .75
38 Carmelo Anthony .50 1.25
39 David Lee .25 .60
40 Dirk Nowitzki 1.00 2.50
41 Elton Brand .30 .75
42 Jose Calderon .25 .60
43 Josh Smith .25 .60
44 LaMarcus Aldridge .40 1.00
45 LeBron James 3.00 8.00
46 Peja Stojakovic .30 .75
47 Rashard Lewis .30 .75
48 Richard Jefferson .30 .75
49 Devin Harris .25 .60
50 Joe Johnson .40 1.00
51 Shawn Marion .40 1.00
52 Stephen Jackson .30 .75
53 Tayshaun Prince .40 1.00
54 Baron Davis .40 1.00
55 Chris Paul .75 2.00
56 Mike Dunleavy .30 .75
57 Deron Williams .30 .75
58 Kobe Bryant 3.00 8.00
59 Jason Kidd .60 1.50
60 Ray Allen .60 1.50
61 Manu Ginobili .75 2.00
62 Michael Redd .30 .75
63 Rajon Rondo .50 1.25
64 Raymond Felton .25 .60
65 Steve Nash .75 2.00
66 T.J. Ford .25 .60
67 Tracy McGrady .60 1.50
68 Amare Stoudemire .40 1.00
69 Andrew Bynum .25 .60
70 Ben Wallace .50 1.25
71 Eddy Curry .25 .60
72 Marcus Camby .30 .75
73 Tyson Chandler .30 .75
74 Yao Ming 1.00 2.50
75 Andrei Kirilenko .30 .75
76 Andres Nocioni .25 .60
77 Caron Butler .30 .75
78 Hedo Turkoglu .30 .75
79 Jeff Green .30 .75
80 Mike Miller .30 .75
81 Ron Artest .40 1.00
82 Rudy Gay .40 1.00
83 Tim Duncan 1.00 2.50
84 Udonis Haslem .25 .60
85 Dwight Howard .50 1.25
86 Jermaine O'Neal .50 1.25
87 Allen Iverson .75 2.00
88 Andre Miller .30 .75
89 Brandon Roy .30 .75
90 Chauncey Billups .50 1.25
91 Dominique Wilkins .60 1.50
92 Isiah Thomas .60 1.50
93 John Stockton .75 2.00
94 Magic Johnson 1.25 3.00
95 George Gervin .60 1.50
96 Bill Russell 1.25 3.00
97 David Robinson .75 2.00
98 Larry Bird 1.25 3.00
99 Jerry West .75 2.00
100 Dennis Rodman .75 2.00
101 Derrick Rose 1 Ball RC 4.00 10.00
101B Derrick Rose 2 Balls RC 4.00 10.00
102 M.Beasley Shooting RC 1.00 2.50
102B M.Beasley Pointing RC 1.00 2.50
103 O.J. Mayo Shooting RC .75 2.00
103B O.J. Mayo Standing RC .75 2.00
104 R.Westbrook Shooting RC 20.00 50.00
104B R.Westbrook Standing RC 20.00 50.00
105 Kevin Love Shooting RC 2.00 5.00
105B Kevin Love Posing RC 2.00 5.00
106 D.Gallinari Dribbling RC 1.50 4.00
106B D.Gallinari Standing RC 1.50 4.00
107 Eric Gordon Shooting RC 1.50 4.00
107B Eric Gordon Standing RC 1.50 4.00
108 Joe Alexander Shooting RC .60 1.50
108B Joe Alexander Passing RC .60 1.50
109 D.J. Augustin Shooting RC 1.00 2.50
109B D.J. Augustin Posing RC 1.00 2.50
110 Brook Lopez Shooting RC 1.25 3.00
110B Brook Lopez Posing RC 1.25 3.00
111 Jerryd Bayless Passing RC .75 2.00
111B Jerryd Bayless Posing RC .75 2.00
112 J.Thompson Shooting RC .60 1.50
112B Jason Thompson Posing RC .60 1.50
113 Brandon Rush Action RC .60 1.50
113B Brandon Rush Posing RC .60 1.50
114 A.Randolph Finger RC .60 1.50
114B A.Randolph Posing RC .60 1.50
115 Robin Lopez Shooting RC .75 2.00
115B Robin Lopez Posing RC .75 2.00
116 M.Speights Action RC .75 2.00
116B M.Speights Posing RC .75 2.00
117 Roy Hibbert Shooting RC .75 2.00
117B Roy Hibbert Posing RC .75 2.00
118 J.J. Hickson Ball in Front RC .60 1.50
118B J.J. Hickson Ball on Side RC .60 1.50
119 Ryan Anderson Ball RC .75 2.00
119B Ryan Anderson Posing RC .75 2.00
120 Courtney Lee Face Right RC .75 2.00
120B Courtney Lee Face Left RC .75 2.00
121 Kosta Koufos Shooting RC .60 1.50
121B Kosta Koufos Posing RC .60 1.50
122 Darrell Arthur Forward RC .75 2.00
122B Darrell Arthur Face Left RC .75 2.00
123 Donte Greene Ball Up RC .60 1.50
123B Donte Greene Ball Down RC .60 1.50
124 Mario Chalmers 2 Balls RC 1.00 2.50
124B Mario Chalmers 1 Ball RC 1.00 2.50
125 Rudy Fernandez 2 Balls RC .75 2.00
125B Rudy Fernandez 1 Ball RC .75 2.00

2008-09 Topps Hardwood Hardwood

*WOOD: .6X TO 1.5X BASE HI
WOOD PRINT RUN 299 SER.#'d SETS
45 LeBron James 4.00 10.00
101 Derrick Rose 1 Ball 6.00 15.00
101B Derrick Rose 2 Balls 6.00 15.00
104 Russell Westbrook Shooting 40.00 100.00

2008-09 Topps Hardwood Mahogany

*1-100 MAHOGANY: 1.25X TO 3X HI
*101-125 MAHOG: 1X TO 2.5X HI
STATED PRINT RUN 75 SER.#'d SETS
45 LeBron James 12.00 30.00
101 Derrick Rose 1 Ball 10.00 25.00
101B Derrick Rose 2 Balls 10.00 25.00
104 Russell Westbrook Shooting 60.00 150.00

2008-09 Topps Hardwood Maple

*1-100 MAPLE: 1X TO 2.5X BASE HI
*101-125 MAPLE: .75X TO 2X HI
STATED PRINT RUN 175 SER.#'d SETS
45 LeBron James 6.00 15.00
104 Russell Westbrook Shooting 50.00 120.00

2008-09 Topps Hardwood Redwood

*1-100 RED: 6X TO 15X BASE HI
*101-125 RED: 2.5X TO 6X BASE HI
STATED PRINT RUN 15 SER.#'d SETS
45 LeBron James 60.00 150.00
101 Derrick Rose 1 Ball 25.00 60.00
101B Derrick Rose 2 Balls 25.00 60.00
104 Russell Westbrook Shooting 100.00 250.00

2008-09 Topps Hardwood Fabric Signature Patches

STATED PRINT RUN 50 SER.#'d SETS
*MAPLE: .5X TO 1.25X BASE HI
MAPLE PRINT RUN 25 SER.#'d SETS
HFSPBL Brook Lopez 12.00 30.00
HFSPBR Brandon Rush 6.00 15.00
HFSPCDR Chris Douglas-Roberts 6.00 15.00
HFSPDGR Donte Greene 6.00 15.00
HFSPEG Eric Gordon 15.00 40.00
HFSPGH George Hill 10.00 25.00
HFSPJH J.J. Hickson 6.00 15.00
HFSPKL Kevin Love 15.00 40.00
HFSPMS Marreese Speights 8.00 20.00
HFSPOJM O.J. Mayo 8.00 20.00
HFSPRA Ryan Anderson 8.00 20.00
HFSPRH Roy Hibbert 8.00 20.00

2008-09 Topps Hardwood Relics

STATED PRINT RUN 175 SER.#'d SETS
*MAHOGANY: .5X TO 1.25X BASE HI
MAHOG.PRINT RUN 75 SER.#'d SETS
*MAPLE: .6X TO 1.5X BASE HI
MAPLE PRINT RUN 50 SER.#'d SETS
*RED: 1.25X TO 3X BASE HI
RED PRINT RUN 25 SER.#'d SETS
HRAIG Andre Iguodala 2.00 5.00
HRAS Amare Stoudemire 2.50 6.00
HRBD Baron Davis 2.50 6.00
HRCA Carmelo Anthony 3.00 8.00
HRCB Chauncey Billups 3.00 8.00
HRCBH Chris Bosh 3.00 8.00
HRCBO Carlos Boozer 2.00 5.00
HRCM Corey Maggette 2.00 5.00
HRCP Chris Paul 5.00 12.00
HRDH Dwight Howard 3.00 8.00
HRDN Dirk Nowitzki 6.00 15.00
HRDR Derrick Rose 12.00 30.00
HRDW Dwyane Wade 5.00 12.00
HRDWI Deron Williams 2.00 5.00
HREB Elton Brand 2.00 5.00
HREG Eric Gordon 4.00 10.00
HRGA Gilbert Arenas 2.50 6.00
HRGO Greg Oden 1.50 4.00
HRJJ Joe Johnson 2.50 6.00
HRJO Jermaine O'Neal 2.50 6.00
HRJS Josh Smith 1.50 4.00
HRKB Kobe Bryant 40.00 100.00
HRKG Kevin Garnett 6.00 15.00
HRKL Kevin Love 5.00 12.00
HRKM Kevin Martin 2.00 5.00
HRMB Michael Beasley 2.50 6.00
HROJM O.J. Mayo 2.00 5.00
HRPP Paul Pierce 4.00 10.00
HRSN Steve Nash 5.00 12.00
HRSO Shaquille O'Neal 8.00 20.00
HRTD Tim Duncan 6.00 15.00
HRTM Tracy McGrady 4.00 10.00
HRTP Tony Parker 3.00 8.00
HRVC Vince Carter 5.00 12.00
HRYM Yao Ming 6.00 15.00

2008-09 Topps Hardwood Rookie Autographs

STATED PRINT RUN 69 SER.#'d SETS
MAHOGANY: .5X TO 1.25X BASE HI
MAHOGANY PRINT RUN 19 SER.#'d SETS
101 Derrick Rose 25.00 60.00
102 Michael Beasley 6.00 15.00
103 O.J. Mayo 5.00 12.00
104 Russell Westbrook 150.00 400.00
105 Kevin Love 12.00 30.00
106 Danilo Gallinari 10.00 25.00
107 Eric Gordon 10.00 25.00
108 Joe Alexander 4.00 10.00
109 D.J. Augustin 6.00 15.00
110 Brook Lopez 8.00 20.00
111 Jerryd Bayless 5.00 12.00
112 Jason Thompson 4.00 10.00
113 Brandon Rush 4.00 10.00
114 Anthony Randolph 4.00 10.00
115 Robin Lopez 5.00 12.00
116 Marreese Speights 5.00 12.00
117 Roy Hibbert 5.00 12.00
118 J.J. Hickson 4.00 10.00
119 Ryan Anderson 5.00 12.00
120 Courtney Lee 5.00 12.00
121 Kosta Koufos 4.00 10.00
122 Darrell Arthur 5.00 12.00
123 Donte Greene 4.00 10.00
124 Mario Chalmers 6.00 15.00
125 Rudy Fernandez 5.00 12.00

2008-09 Topps Hardwood Signatures

STATED PRINT RUN 39 SER.#'d SETS
*MAHOGANY: .5X TO 1.25X BASE HI
MAHOGANY PRINT RUN 19 SER.#'d SETS
HSAB Andrea Bargnani 4.00 10.00
HSABY Andrew Bynum 4.00 10.00
HSAJ Antawn Jamison 4.00 10.00
HSBG Ben Gordon 4.00 10.00
HSBR Brandon Roy 4.00 10.00
HSCA Carmelo Anthony 15.00 40.00
HSCB Chauncey Billups 4.00 10.00
HSCP Chris Paul 40.00 100.00
HSDG Danny Granger 4.00 10.00
HSDH Dwight Howard 12.00 30.00
HSDR David Robinson 25.00 60.00
HSDS Dolph Schayes 8.00 20.00
HSDW Dominique Wilkins 15.00 30.00
HSEH Elvin Hayes 5.00 12.00
HSGA Gilbert Arenas 4.00 10.00
HSGG George Gervin 12.00 30.00
HSGO Greg Oden 4.00 10.00
HSIT Isiah Thomas 12.00 30.00
HSJH John Havlicek 20.00 50.00
HSJW Jo Jo White 6.00 15.00
HSJS John Stockton 25.00 60.00
HSLB Larry Bird 30.00 80.00
HSLW Lenny Wilkens 6.00 15.00
HSMJ Magic Johnson 30.00 80.00
HSPP Paul Pierce 20.00 50.00
HSRB Rick Barry 8.00 20.00
HSRG Rudy Gay 4.00 10.00
HSRP Robert Parish 8.00 20.00
HSRT Reggie Theus 6.00 15.00
HSSH Spencer Haywood 8.00 20.00
HSSO Shaquille O'Neal 40.00 100.00
HSSP Sam Perkins 5.00 12.00
HSTJF T.J. Ford 4.00 10.00
HSTM Tracy McGrady 12.00 30.00
HSTY Thaddeus Young 6.00 15.00

2000-01 Topps Heritage

COMPLETE SET w/o RC (197) 20.00 50.00
RCs: STATED ODDS 1:9
RCs: STATED PRINT RUN 1972 SERIAL #'d SETS
1 Jason Kidd .60 1.50
2 Allen Iverson 1.00 2.50
3 Tracy McGrady .75 2.00
4 Tim Duncan 1.00 2.50
5 Michael Finley .40 1.00
6 Jason Williams .60 1.50
7 Kobe Bryant 6.00 15.00
8 Gary Payton .60 1.50
9 Latrell Sprewell .50 1.25
10 Antonio McDyess .30 .75
11 Antoine Walker .40 1.00
12 Steve Francis .40 1.00
13 Elton Brand .40 1.00
14 Larry Hughes .40 1.00
15 Shaquille O'Neal 1.50 4.00
16 Lamar Odom .60 1.50
17 Kevin Garnett 1.00 2.50
18 Vince Carter .75 2.00
19 Ray Allen .60 1.50
20 Grant Hill .60 1.50
21 Chris Webber .50 1.25
22 Paul Pierce .60 1.50
23 Shareef Abdur-Rahim .40 1.00
24 Eddie Jones .40 1.00
25 Kenyon Martin RC 3.00 8.00
26 Stromile Swift RC 1.25 3.00
27 Darius Miles RC 1.50 4.00
28 Marcus Fizer RC 1.25 3.00
29 Mike Miller RC 2.50 6.00
30 DerMarr Johnson RC 1.00 2.50
31 Chris Mihm RC 1.00 2.50
32 Jamal Crawford RC 4.00 10.00
33 Joel Przybilla RC 1.25 3.00
34 Keyon Dooling RC 1.25 3.00
35 Jerome Moiso RC 1.00 2.50
36 Etan Thomas RC 1.25 3.00
37 Courtney Alexander RC 1.00 2.50
38 Mateen Cleaves RC 1.25 3.00
39 Jason Collier RC 1.50 4.00
40 Hedo Turkoglu RC 2.50 6.00
41 Desmond Mason RC 2.00 5.00
42 Quentin Richardson RC 1.25 3.00
43 Jamaal Magloire RC 1.50 4.00
44 Speedy Claxton RC 1.50 4.00
45 Morris Peterson RC 1.50 4.00
46 Donnell Harvey RC 1.25 3.00
47 DeShawn Stevenson RC 1.50 4.00
48 Dalibor Bagaric RC 1.25 3.00
49 Iakovos Tsakalidis RC 1.00 2.50
50 Mamadou N'Diaye RC 1.00 2.50
51 Erick Barkley RC 1.00 2.50
52 Mark Madsen RC 1.50 4.00
53 Dan Langhi RC 1.00 2.50
54 A.J. Guyton RC 1.00 2.50
55 Jake Voskuhl RC 1.00 2.50
56 Khalid El-Amin RC 1.00 2.50
57 Lavor Postell RC 1.00 2.50
58 Eduardo Najera RC 1.50 4.00
59 Michael Redd RC 4.00 10.00
60 Stephen Jackson RC 3.00 8.00
61 Andrew DeClercq .25 .60
62 Darrell Armstrong .25 .60
63 Al Harrington .30 .75
64 Johnny Newman .25 .60
65 Baron Davis .40 1.00
66 Adrian Griffin .25 .60
67 Anthony Mason .40 1.00
68 Ron Harper .40 1.00
69 Michael Olowokandi .25 .60
70 Maurice Taylor .25 .60
71 Travis Best .25 .60
72 Chucky Atkins .25 .60
73 Bob Sura .25 .60
74 Jason Terry .40 1.00
75 Ervin Johnson .25 .60
76 Eric Snow .25 .60
77 Shawn Bradley .25 .60
78 Christian Laettner .40 1.00
79 Keith Van Horn .30 .75
80 Damon Stoudamire .40 1.00
81 Peja Stojakovic .30 .75
82 Clifford Robinson .40 1.00
83 Elden Campbell .25 .60
84 Kenny Anderson .30 .75
85 Patrick Ewing .60 1.50
86 Mookie Blaylock .40 1.00
87 Brian Skinner .25 .60
88 Rick Fox .30 .75
89 Tim Hardaway .50 1.25
90 Brian Grant .30 .75
91 Joe Smith .30 .75
92 Kerry Kittles .30 .75
93 Scottie Pippen 1.00 2.50
94 Steve Smith .40 1.00
95 Sean Elliott .30 .75
96 Rashard Lewis .30 .75
97 Michael Dickerson .25 .60
98 Rod Strickland .25 .60
99 Sam Cassell .30 .75
100 Lew Alcindor .60 1.50
101 John Amaechi .25 .60
102 Kendall Gill .40 1.00
103 Terrell Brandon .30 .75
104 Dan Majerle .40 1.00
105 Mark Jackson .30 .75
106 Hakeem Olajuwon .75 2.00
107 Antawn Jamison .40 1.00
108 Cedric Ceballos .25 .60
109 Shandon Anderson .25 .60
110 Gary Trent .25 .60
111 Wesley Person .25 .60
112 James Posey .25 .60
113 David Wesley .30 .75
114 Vitaly Potapenko .25 .60
115 P.J. Brown .25 .60
116 Alan Henderson .25 .60
117 Terry Porter .25 .60
118 Lindsey Hunter .25 .60
119 Chauncey Billups .50 1.25
120 Doug Christie .30 .75
121 Glen Rice .40 1.00
122 Jamie Feick .25 .60
123 Tom Gugliotta .30 .75
124 Arvydas Sabonis .40 1.00
125 Toni Kukoc .50 1.25
126 Shawn Marion .40 1.00
127 Dale Davis .30 .75
128 Corliss Williamson .25 .60
129 Brent Barry .30 .75
130 Shammond Williams .25 .60
131 Nick Anderson .30 .75
132 Charles Oakley .40 1.00
133 Shaquille O'Neal CHAMP .75 2.00
134 Ron Harper CHAMP .40 1.00
135 Kobe Bryant CHAMP 1.50 4.00
136 Shaquille O'Neal CHAMP .75 2.00
137 L.A. Lakers CHAMP .50 1.25
138 V.Carter/Iverson/J.Stack .50 1.25
139 Iverson/G.Hill/V.Carter .40 1.00
140 Mutombo/Mourning/D.Davis .40 1.00
141 R.Miller/D.Army/R.Allen .40 1.00
142 Mutombo/Brand/Je.Williams .40 1.00
143 S.Cassell/M.Jackson/E.Snow .40 1.00
144 Checklist .10 .30
145 Checklist .10 .30
146 Shaq/K.Malone/Payton .75 2.00
147 Shaq/K.Malone/Webber .60 1.50
148 Shaq/Patterson/R.Wallace .60 1.50
149 Horracek/Brandon/Stojakovic .25 .60
150 Shaq/Garnett/Duncan .60 1.50
151 Payton/Van Exel/Stockton .40 1.00
152 Chris Whitney .25 .60
153 Isaac Austin .25 .60
154 Kevin Willis .25 .60

2000-01 Topps Heritage

155 Vin Baker .30 .75
156 Avery Johnson .30 .75
157 Rodney Rogers .25 .60
158 Allan Houston .40 1.00
159 Austin Croshere .25 .60
160 George Lynch .25 .60
161 Howard Eisley .25 .60
162 Jerome Williams .25 .60
163 LaPhonso Ellis .25 .60
164 Ron Mercer .30 .75
165 Andre Miller .30 .75
166 Tariq Abdul-Wahad .25 .60
167 Donyell Marshall .30 .75
168 Quincy Lewis .25 .60
169 Mitch Richmond .50 1.25
170 Richard Hamilton .50 1.25
171 Bryant Reeves .25 .60
172 Jim Jackson .30 .75
173 David Robinson .75 2.00
174 Derrick Coleman .40 1.00
175 Anthony Peeler .25 .60
176 Theo Ratliff .25 .60
177 Roshown McLeod .25 .60
178 Ron Artest .40 1.00
179 Bryon Russell .25 .60
180 Othella Harrington .25 .60
181 Juwan Howard .30 .75
182 Antonio Davis .30 .75
183 Ruben Patterson .25 .60
184 Shawn Kemp .60 1.50
185 Larry Johnson .50 1.25
186 Marcus Camby .30 .75
187 Eric Piatkowski .25 .60
188 Reggie Miller .75 2.00
189 Anfernee Hardaway .60 1.50
190 Kelvin Cato .25 .60
191 Erick Dampier .25 .60
192 Keon Clark .25 .60
193 Dirk Nowitzki 1.00 2.50
194 Robert Traylor .25 .60
195 Lamond Murray .25 .60
196 John Wallace .25 .60
197 Robert Horry .40 1.00
198 Robert Pack .25 .60
199 Jamal Mashburn .30 .75
200 Corey Benjamin .25 .60
201 Matt Harpring .25 .60
202 Nick Van Exel .40 1.00
203 Vonteego Cummings .25 .60
204 Ben Wallace .50 1.25
205 Karl Malone .75 2.00
206 Jonathan Bender .25 .60
207 Cuttino Mobley .30 .75
208 Isaiah Rider .30 .75
209 Tyrone Nesby .25 .60
210 Jermaine O'Neal .30 .75
211 Corey Maggette .30 .75
212 Anthony Carter .25 .60
213 Horace Grant .40 1.00
214 Tim Thomas .25 .60
215 Wally Szczerbiak .30 .75
216 Stephon Marbury .50 1.25
217 Charlie Ward .30 .75
218 Bo Outlaw .25 .60
219 Matt Geiger .25 .60
220 Vlade Divac .40 1.00
221 Rasheed Wallace .50 1.25
222 Derek Anderson .30 .75
223 John Stockton .75 2.00
224 Dikembe Mutombo .60 1.50
225 John Starks .40 1.00
226 Mike Bibby .40 1.00
227 Jahidi White .25 .60
228 Jalen Rose .30 .75
229 Glenn Robinson .40 1.00
230 Brevin Knight .25 .60
231 Jerry Stackhouse .40 1.00
232 Raef LaFrentz .30 .75
233 Brad Miller .30 .75

2000-01 Topps Heritage Proofs

*PROOF VETS: 4X TO 10X BASE HI
*PROOF RCs: .6X TO 1.5X

2000-01 Topps Heritage Retrofractors

*STARS: 5X TO 12X BASE CARD HI
*RCs: 1.25X TO 3X BASE CARD HI
STARS: PRINT RUN 272 SERIAL #'d SETS
STARS: STATED ODDS 1:95
RCs: PRINT RUN 72 SERIAL #'d SETS
RCs: STATED ODDS 1:613
1 Jason Kidd 15.00 40.00
2 Allen Iverson 20.00 50.00
3 Tracy McGrady 20.00 50.00
4 Tim Duncan 20.00 50.00
6 Jason Williams 12.00 30.00
7 Kobe Bryant 125.00 300.00
15 Shaquille O'Neal 30.00 80.00
17 Kevin Garnett 20.00 50.00
18 Vince Carter 20.00 50.00
19 Ray Allen 12.00 30.00
20 Grant Hill 12.00 30.00
21 Chris Webber 12.00 30.00
22 Paul Pierce 12.00 30.00

2000-01 Topps Heritage Authentic Arena

STATED ODDS 1:87
AAR1 Shaquille O'Neal 15.00 40.00
AAR2 Gary Payton 6.00 15.00
AAR3 Anfernee Hardaway 6.00 15.00
AAR4 Hakeem Olajuwon 8.00 20.00
AAR5 Toni Kukoc 5.00 12.00
AAR6 Scottie Pippen 10.00 25.00
AAR7 Juwan Howard 3.00 8.00

2000-01 Topps Heritage Autographs

STATED ODDS 1:90
A-J PROOF: STATED ODDS 1:25,728
IVERSON WAS NEVER REDEEMED
HACA Courtney Alexander 4.00 10.00
HADM Desmond Mason 4.00 10.00
HAKD Keyon Dooling 4.00 10.00
HALH Larry Hughes 4.00 10.00
HASF Steve Francis 8.00 20.00
HASM Shawn Marion 8.00 20.00
HASO Shaquille O'Neal 100.00 250.00
HATM Tracy McGrady 75.00 200.00
NNO K.Abdul-Jabbar PROOF 200.00 500.00

2000-01 Topps Heritage Back to the Future Game Jerseys

STATED ODDS 1:113
BF1 Joel Przybilla 2.00 5.00
BF2 Jerome Moiso 1.50 4.00
BF3 Mateen Cleaves 2.00 5.00
BF4 Speedy Claxton 2.50 6.00
BF5 Mark Madsen 2.50 6.00
BF6 Jonathan Bender 1.50 4.00

2000-01 Topps Heritage Blast from the Past

COMPLETE SET (15) 6.00 15.00
STATED ODDS 1:8
BP1 Chris Webber .60 1.50
BP2 Kevin Garnett 1.25 3.00
BP3 Allen Iverson 1.25 3.00
BP4 Rasheed Wallace .60 1.50
BP5 Elton Brand .50 1.25
BP6 Grant Hill .75 2.00
BP7 Ray Allen .75 2.00
BP8 Allan Houston .50 1.25
BP9 Tim Duncan 1.25 3.00
BP10 Eddie Jones .50 1.25
BP11 Tracy McGrady 1.00 2.50
BP12 Lamar Odom .50 1.25
BP13 Steve Francis .50 1.25
BP14 Jason Williams .75 2.00
BP15 Vince Carter 1.00 2.50

2000-01 Topps Heritage Deja Vu

COMPLETE SET (10) 2.50 6.00
STATED ODDS 1:5
DV1 Larry Hughes .30 .75
DV2 Elton Brand .30 .75
DV3 Steve Francis .30 .75
DV4 Paul Pierce .50 1.25
DV5 Allen Iverson .75 2.00
DV6 Gary Payton .50 1.25
DV7 Rasheed Wallace .40 1.00
DV8 Jason Kidd .50 1.25
DV9 Kobe Bryant 2.50 6.00
DV10 Ray Allen .50 1.25

2000-01 Topps Heritage Dynamite Duds Game Jerseys

STATED ODDS 1:97
DD1 Dikembe Mutombo 4.00 10.00
DD2 Hanno Mottola 1.50 4.00
DD3 Stephon Marbury 3.00 8.00
DD4 Keith Van Horn 2.00 5.00
DD5 Anfernee Hardaway 4.00 10.00
DD6 Shawn Marion 2.50 6.00
DD7 Shareef Abdur-Rahim 2.50 6.00
DD8 Paul Pierce 4.00 10.00
DD9 Juwan Howard 2.00 5.00
DD10 DerMarr Johnson 1.50 4.00
DD11 Kenyon Martin 5.00 12.00
DD12 Mike Miller 4.00 10.00
DD13 Darius Miles 2.50 6.00
DD14 Keyon Dooling 2.00 5.00
DD15 Quentin Richardson 2.00 5.00
DD16 Iakovos Tsakalidis 1.50 4.00
DD17 Stromile Swift 2.00 5.00

2000-01 Topps Heritage Off the Hook

COMPLETE SET (15) 8.00 20.00
STATED ODDS 1:8
OH1 Kevin Garnett 1.25 3.00
OH2 Vince Carter 1.00 2.50
OH3 Tim Duncan 1.25 3.00
OH4 Allen Iverson 1.25 3.00
OH5 Elton Brand .50 1.25
OH6 Jason Kidd .75 2.00
OH7 Lamar Odom .50 1.25
OH8 Kobe Bryant 4.00 10.00
OH9 Tracy McGrady 1.00 2.50
OH10 Steve Francis .50 1.25
OH11 Chris Webber .60 1.50
OH12 Larry Hughes .50 1.25
OH13 Jason Williams .75 2.00
OH14 Shareef Abdur-Rahim .50 1.25
OH15 Darius Miles .50 1.25

2001-02 Topps Heritage

COMPLETE SET (264) 60.00 150.00
1 Shaquille O'Neal 1.50 4.00
2 Jalen Rose .30 .75
3 Kwame Brown RC .75 2.00
4 Bryon Russell .25 .60
5 Hakeem Olajuwon .75 2.00
6 Shammond Williams .25 .60
7 Aaron Mckie .25 .60
8 Anfernee Hardaway 1.00 2.50
9 Dale Davis .25 .60
10 Tracy McGrady .60 1.50
11 Speedy Claxton .25 .60
12 Kurt Thomas .25 .60
13 Keith Van Horn .30 .75
14 Tyson Chandler RC 1.25 3.00
15 Andre Miller .30 .75
16 Dirk Nowitzki 1.00 2.50
17 Raef Lafrentz .25 .60
18 Mateen Cleaves .25 .60
19 Danny Fortson .25 .60
20 Steve Francis .40 1.00
21 Al Harrington .30 .75
22 Keyon Dooling .25 .60
23 Rick Fox .30 .75
24 Michael Dickerson .25 .60
25 Alonzo Mourning .60 1.50
26 Glenn Robinson .40 1.00
27 Wally Szczerbiak .30 .75
28 Todd MacCulloch .25 .60
29 Shandon Anderson .25 .60
30 Kobe Bryant 3.00 8.00
31 Tyrone Hill .25 .60
32 Grant Hill .60 1.50
33 Shawn Marion .40 1.00
34 Derek Anderson .25 .60
35 Hedo Turkoglu .30 .75
36 David Robinson .75 2.00
37 Gary Payton .60 1.50
38 Alvin Williams .25 .60
39 Pau Gasol RC 3.00 8.00
40 Tim Duncan 1.00 2.50
41 Rashard Lewis .30 .75
42 Antonio Davis .30 .75
43 Donyell Marshall .30 .75
44 Jahidi White .25 .60
45 Shareef Abdur-Rahim .30 .75
46 Antoine Walker .30 .75
47 P.J. Brown .25 .60
48 Eddie Robinson .25 .60
49 Chris Mihm .25 .60
50 Kevin Garnett 1.00 2.50
51 Marcus Camby .30 .75
52 Mike Miller .30 .75
53 Tony Delk .30 .75
54 Mike Bibby .40 1.00
55 Dikembe Mutombo .60 1.50
56 Eddy Curry RC .75 2.00
57 Shawn Bradley .25 .60
58 James Posey .25 .60
59 Jason Richardson RC 1.25 3.00
60 Jason Kidd .60 1.50
61 Eddie Griffin RC .60 1.50
62 Larry Hughes .30 .75
63 Ben Wallace .50 1.25
64 Antonio McDyess .30 .75
65 Tim Hardaway .50 1.25
66 Shawn Kemp .40 1.00
67 Bobby Jackson .25 .60
68 Tom Gugliotta .25 .60
69 Antawn Jamison .30 .75
70 Lamar Odom .30 .75
71 Jamaal Tinsley RC .60 1.50
72 Moochie Norris .25 .60
73 Marc Jackson .25 .60
74 Andrei Kirilenko RC 1.25 3.00
75 Wang Zhizhi .40 1.00
76 Eric Snow .25 .60
77 Rasheed Wallace .50 1.25
78 Antonio Daniels .25 .60
79 Vladimir Radmanovic RC .60 1.50
80 Morris Peterson .25 .60
81 Terry/Terry/Mutombo/Terry .40 1.00
82 Pierce/Pilicio/Walkr/Walkr .25 .60
83 Mash/Hawkins/Brwn/Davis .25 .60
84 Brand/Hoiberg/Brand/Hoiberg .40 1.00
85 Millr/Lngdn/Mthrspoon/Millr .25 .60
86 Nowitz/Nash/Nowitz/Nash .40 1.00
87 McDys/McCld/McDys/VnEx .25 .60
88 Stack/Barros/Wllce/Stack .40 1.00
89 Jmisn/Jcksn/Jmisn/Blaylck .40 1.00
90 Frncis/Mobly/Frncis/Frncis .10 .30
91 Rose/Millr/O'Neal/Best .40 1.00
92 Odm/Piatkow/Odm/Mclnns .40 1.00
93 Shaq/Penbrthy/Shaq/Kobe .60 1.50
94 Rahim/Rahim/Rahim/Bibby .40 1.00
95 Jones/Jones/Masn/Hrdawy .25 .60
96 Robnsn/Allen/Jhnsn/Cassll .40 1.00
97 Grntt/Brandn/Grntt/Brandn .50 1.25
98 Mrbry/Newmn/Wllams/Mrbry .25 .60
99 Deshawn Stevenson .25 .60
100 Allen Iverson 1.00 2.50
101 Jeryl Sasser RC .50 1.25
102 Jason Terry .40 1.00
103 Vitaly Potapenko .25 .60
104 Elden Campbell .25 .60
105 Jamal Crawford .40 1.00
106 Michael Finley .40 1.00
107 Earl Watson RC .60 1.50
108 Clifford Robinson .25 .60
109 Chucky Atkins .25 .60
110 Glen Rice .40 1.00
111 Jermaine O'Neal .30 .75
112 Jonathan Bender .25 .60
113 Michael Olowokandi .25 .60
114 Derek Fisher .30 .75
115 Stromile Swift .25 .60
116 Toni Kukoc .50 1.25
117 Samuel Dalembert RC .75 2.00
118 Paul Pierce .60 1.50
119 Jamal Mashburn .30 .75
120 Ron Mercer .25 .60
121 Lamond Murray .25 .60
122 Steve Nash .75 2.00
123 Nick Van Exel .40 1.00
124 Desagana Diop RC .50 1.25
125 Ron Artest .30 .75
126 Marcus Fizer .25 .60
127 Jumaine Jones .25 .60
128 Corliss Williamson .25 .60
129 Rodney White RC .50 1.25
130 Cuttino Mobley .30 .75
131 Reggie Miller .75 2.00
132 Austin Croshere .25 .60
133 Jeff Mcinnis .25 .60
134 Joe Johnson RC 1.25 3.00
135 Kedrick Brown RC .50 1.25
136 Theo Ratliff .25 .60
137 Laphonso Ellis .30 .75
138 Ervin Johnson .25 .60
139 Terrell Brandon .30 .75
140 Chauncey Billups .50 1.25
141 Kenyon Martin .40 1.00
142 Richard Jefferson RC 1.00 2.50
143 Howard Eisley .25 .60
144 Stackhouse/Iverson/Shaq .50 1.25
145 Iverson/Stackhouse/Shaq .60 1.50
146 Shaq/Wells/Camby .40 1.00
147 Miller/Houston/Christie .25 .60
148 Mutombo/Wallace/Shaq .40 1.00
149 Kidd/Stockton/Van Exel .40 1.00
150 Vince Carter .75 2.00
151 Calvin Booth .25 .60
152 Chris Whitney .25 .60
153 John Amaechi .25 .60
154 Keon Clark .25 .60
155 Terry Porter .25 .60
156 Doug Christie .25 .60
157 Gerald Wallace RC 1.00 2.50
158 Zach Randolph RC 1.50 4.00
159 Iakovos Tsakalidis .25 .60
160 Damone Brown RC .50 1.25
161 Ivrsn/Miller/Grntt/Duncan .50 1.25
162 Allen/T-Mac/Shaq/Smith 1.00 2.50
163 Mornig/Dvis/Wbber/Hrdway .40 1.00
164 Houstn/Crtr/Nowitz/Malone .60 1.50
165 Christian Laettner .30 .75
166 John Starks .25 .60
167 Jerome Williams .25 .60
168 Brent Barry .25 .60
169 Malik Rose .25 .60
170 Vlade Divac .30 .75
171 Damon Stoudamire .40 1.00
172 Rodney Rogers .25 .60
173 Alvin Jones RC .50 1.25
174 Darrell Armstrong .25 .60
175 Mark Jackson .30 .75
176 Kerry Kittles ERR .25 .60
177 Radoslav Nesterovic .25 .60
178 Brandon Armstrong RC .50 1.25
179 Joe Smith .30 .75
180 Ray Allen .60 1.50
181 Anthony Mason .40 1.00
182 Bryant Reeves .25 .60
183 Jason Williams .60 1.50
184 Terence Morris RC .50 1.25
185 Travis Best .25 .60
186 Troy Murphy RC .60 1.50
187 Gilbert Arenas RC 2.00 5.00
188 Avery Johnson .30 .75
189 Juwan Howard .30 .75
190 Checklist .10 .30
191 Courtney Alexander .25 .60
192 John Stockton .75 2.00
193 Vin Baker .30 .75
194 Desmond Mason .30 .75
195 Steve Smith .30 .75
196 Steven Hunter RC .50 1.25
197 Stephon Marbury .50 1.25
198 Patrick Ewing .60 1.50
199 Allan Houston .40 1.00
200 Karl Malone .75 2.00
201 Peja Stojakovic .30 .75
202 Bonzi Wells .25 .60
203 Latrell Sprewell .50 1.25
204 Rafer Alston .25 .60
205 Tony Parker RC 3.00 8.00
206 Michael Bradley RC .50 1.25
207 Richard Hamilton .50 1.25
208 Zeljko Rebraca RC .75 2.00
209 Joel Przybilla .25 .60
210 Tim Thomas .25 .60
211 Eddie House .25 .60
212 Brian Grant .25 .60
213 Lindsey Hunter .25 .60
214 Corey Maggette .30 .75
215 Shane Battier RC 1.50 4.00
216 Will Solomon .30 .75
217 Mitch Richmond .50 1.25
218 Eddie Jones .40 1.00
219 Elton Brand .40 1.00
220 Quentin Richardson .25 .60
221 Hustn/Houstn/Cmby/Ward .25 .60
222 T-Mc/Armstrong/Outlw/Arm .40 1.00
223 Ivrsn/Ivrsn/Hill/McKie .60 1.50
224 Mrion/Kidd/Mrion/Kidd .40 1.00
225 Wllce/Smith/Davis/Stoudmr .25 .60
226 Wbbr/Christi/Wbbr/Wllams .40 1.00
227 Duncn/Andrsn/Duncn/Dnils .40 1.00
228 Pytn/Williams/Ewing/Pytn .25 .60
229 Cartr/Curry/Davis/Jackson .40 1.00
230 Malon/Stock/Malon/Stock .40 1.00
231 Hwrd/Whtny/White/Whtny .25 .60
232 Brendan Haywood RC .60 1.50
233 Scottie Pippen 1.00 2.50
234 Loren Woods RC .50 1.25
235 Sam Cassell .30 .75
236 Anthony Carter .25 .60
237 Raja Bell RC 1.00 2.50
238 Robert Horry .40 1.00
239 Maurice Taylor .25 .60
240 Zydrunas Ilgauskas .30 .75
241 Derrick Coleman .30 .75
242 Kenny Anderson .30 .75
243 Joseph Forte RC .50 1.25
244 Baron Davis .40 1.00
245 Nazr Mohammed .25 .60
246 Ivrsn/Cartr/Duncn/Bradly .50 1.25
247 Allen/Davis/Kobe/Divac .75 2.00
248 Mtmb/Robnsn/Robnsn/Lue .40 1.00
249 Shaq/Iverson .50 1.25
250 Darius Miles .25 .60
251 Samaki Walker .25 .60
252 Dermarr Johnson .25 .60
253 David Wesley .25 .60
254 Trenton Hassell RC .50 1.25
255 Jeff Trepagnier RC .50 1.25
256 Jacque Vaughn .25 .60
257 Kirk Haston RC .50 1.25
258 Jamaal Magloire .25 .60
259 Jason Collins RC .60 1.50
260 Chris Webber .50 1.25
261 Kenny Satterfield RC .50 1.25
262 Horace Grant .30 .75
263 Jerry Stackhouse .40 1.00
264 Michael Jordan 6.00 15.00

2001-02 Topps Heritage Air Alert

COMPLETE SET (10) 12.50 30.00
STATED ODDS 1:8
1 Shawn Marion .60 1.50
2 Vince Carter 1.25 3.00
3 Tracy McGrady 1.00 2.50
4 Steve Francis .60 1.50
5 Kobe Bryant 5.00 12.00
6 Darius Miles .40 1.00
7 Jerry Stackhouse .60 1.50
8 Baron Davis .60 1.50
9 Kevin Garnett 1.50 4.00
10 Michael Jordan 8.00 20.00
11 Kwame Brown .60 1.50
12 Jason Richardson 1.00 2.50

2001-02 Topps Heritage Articles of the Arena Relics

STATED ODDS 1:46
1 Shaquille O'Neal 15.00 40.00
2 Chris Webber 5.00 12.00
3 Jason Kidd 6.00 15.00
4 Latrell Sprewell 5.00 12.00
5 Jalen Rose 3.00 8.00
6 Grant Hill 6.00 15.00
7 Alonzo Mourning 6.00 15.00
8 Gary Payton 6.00 15.00
9 Anfernee Hardaway 10.00 25.00
10 Scottie Pippen 10.00 25.00
11 Tim Hardaway 5.00 12.00
12 Reggie Miller 8.00 20.00
13 Hakeem Olajuwon 8.00 20.00
14 Patrick Ewing 6.00 15.00
15 Karl Malone 8.00 20.00
16 John Stockton 8.00 20.00
17 Charles Oakley 3.00 8.00
18 Glenn Robinson 4.00 10.00
19 Dikembe Mutombo 6.00 15.00
20 Eddie Jones 4.00 10.00

2001-02 Topps Heritage Autographs

STATED ODDS 1:83
1 Antonio Daniels 4.00 10.00
2 Alvin Jones 4.00 10.00
3 Baron Davis 6.00 15.00
4 Damone Brown 4.00 10.00
5 Erick Barkley 4.00 10.00
6 Elton Brand 6.00 15.00
7 Joseph Forte 4.00 10.00
8 Mike Bibby 6.00 15.00
9 Peja Stojakovic 8.00 20.00
10 Richard Jefferson 4.00 10.00
11 Shane Battier 6.00 15.00
12 Shawn Marion 6.00 15.00
13 Vladimir Radmanovic 4.00 10.00

2001-02 Topps Heritage Ball Basics Relics

STATED ODDS 1:627
1 Courtney Alexander 3.00 8.00
2 Speedy Claxton 3.00 8.00
3 DerMarr Johnson 3.00 8.00
4 Darius Miles 3.00 8.00
5 Desmond Mason 4.00 10.00
6 Hedo Turkoglu 4.00 10.00
7 Kenyon Martin 5.00 12.00
8 Marcus Fizer 3.00 8.00
9 Mike Miller 4.00 10.00
10 Morris Peterson 3.00 8.00
11 Stromile Swift 3.00 8.00

2001-02 Topps Heritage Competitive Threads

STATED ODDS 1:61
1 Allan Houston 3.00 8.00
2 Allen Iverson 8.00 20.00
3 Andre Miller 2.50 6.00
4 Baron Davis 3.00 8.00
5 Chris Webber 4.00 10.00
6 Elton Brand 2.50 6.00
7 Jerry Stackhouse 3.00 8.00
8 Karl Malone 6.00 15.00
9 Latrell Sprewell 4.00 10.00
10 Michael Finley 3.00 8.00
11 Ray Allen 5.00 12.00
12 Rasheed Wallace 4.00 10.00
13 Tim Duncan 8.00 20.00
14 Tracy McGrady 5.00 12.00
15 Wally Szczerbiak 2.50 6.00

2001-02 Topps Heritage Competitive Threads Autographs

STATED ODDS 1:1862
1 Andre Miller 30.00 80.00
3 Elton Brand 30.00 80.00
4 Tim Duncan 600.00 1,200.00

2001-02 Topps Heritage Crossover

COMPLETE SET (12) 20.00 40.00
STATED ODDS 1:14
1 Jamaal Tinsley .75 2.00
2 Steve Francis 1.00 2.50
3 Vince Carter 2.00 5.00
4 Baron Davis 1.00 2.50
5 Tracy McGrady 1.50 4.00
6 Kobe Bryant 8.00 20.00
7 Jason Terry 1.00 2.50
8 Stephon Marbury 1.25 3.00
9 Jason Williams 1.50 4.00
10 Tim Hardaway 1.25 3.00
11 Jason Richardson 1.50 4.00
12 Michael Jordan 10.00 25.00

2001-02 Topps Heritage Out of Bounds

COMPLETE SET (10) 8.00 20.00
STATED ODDS 1:10
1 Dirk Nowitzki 2.00 5.00
2 Peja Stojakovic .60 1.50
3 Wang ZhiZhi .75 2.00
4 Dikembe Mutombo 1.25 3.00
5 Steve Nash 1.50 4.00
6 Hedo Turkoglu .60 1.50
7 Hakeem Olajuwon 1.50 4.00
8 Tony Parker 3.00 8.00
9 Vladimir Radmanovic .60 1.50
10 Pau Gasol 3.00 8.00

2001-02 Topps Heritage Unity

STATED ODDS 1:485
1 Baron Davis 10.00 25.00
2 Derrick Coleman 8.00 20.00
3 David Wesley 6.00 15.00
4 Elden Campbell 6.00 15.00
5 Eddie Robinson 6.00 15.00
6 Jamaal Magloire 6.00 15.00
7 Jamal Mashburn 8.00 20.00
8 P.J. Brown 6.00 15.00

2001-02 Topps High Topps

COMPLETE SET (164) 250.00 500.00
COMP.SET w/o SP's (105) 15.00 40.00
106-113 PRINT RUN 850 SER.#'d SETS
114-129 PRINT RUN 425 SER.#'d SETS
130-140 PRINT RUN 850 SER.#'d SETS
141-153 PRINT RUN 425 SER.#'d SETS
154-164 PRINT RUN 1500 SER.#'d SETS
1 Shaquille O'Neal 1.50 4.00
2 Reggie Miller .75 2.00
3 Steve Francis .40 1.00
4 Jerry Stackhouse .40 1.00
5 Nick Van Exel .40 1.00
6 Dirk Nowitzki 1.00 2.50
7 Dikembe Mutombo .60 1.50
8 Terrell Brandon .30 .75
9 Allan Houston .40 1.00
10 Kevin Garnett 1.00 2.50
11 Eric Snow .25 .60
12 Stephon Marbury .50 1.25
13 Jalen Rose .30 .75
14 Rick Fox .30 .75
15 Alonzo Mourning .60 1.50
16 Tim Thomas .25 .60
17 Keith Van Horn .30 .75
18 Glen Rice .40 1.00
19 Mike Miller .30 .75
20 Chris Webber .50 1.25
21 Larry Hughes .30 .75
22 Joe Smith .30 .75
23 Ron Mercer .25 .60
24 Jamal Mashburn .30 .75
25 Shareef Abdur-Rahim .30 .75
26 P.J. Brown .25 .60
27 Ben Wallace .50 1.25
28 Wang Zhizhi .40 1.00
29 Jermaine O'Neal .30 .75
30 Lamar Odom .30 .75
31 Stromile Swift .25 .60
32 Theo Ratliff .25 .60
33 Patrick Ewing .60 1.50
34 Antonio Davis .30 .75
35 John Stockton .75 2.00
36 Courtney Alexander .25 .60
37 Alvin Williams .25 .60
38 Rashard Lewis .30 .75
39 Mike Bibby .40 1.00
40 Scottie Pippen 1.00 2.50
41 Anfernee Hardaway 1.00 2.50
42 Marcus Camby .30 .75
43 Glenn Robinson .40 1.00
44 Jason Williams .60 1.50
45 Horace Grant .30 .75
46 Chris Mihm .25 .60
47 Paul Pierce .60 1.50
48 DerMarr Johnson .25 .60
49 Steve Nash .75 2.00
50 Vince Carter .75 2.00
51 Michael Jordan 5.00 12.00
52 Donyell Marshall .25 .60
53 Desmond Mason .30 .75
54 Tom Gugliotta .25 .60
55 Hedo Turkoglu .30 .75
56 Grant Hill .60 1.50
57 Kenyon Martin .40 1.00
58 Wally Szczerbiak .30 .75
59 Eddie Jones .40 1.00
60 Kobe Bryant 3.00 8.00
61 Cuttino Mobley .30 .75
62 Michael Dickerson .25 .60
63 Clifford Robinson .40 1.00
64 Raef LaFrentz .25 .60
65 Lamond Murray .25 .60
66 Kenny Anderson .30 .75
67 Antonio Daniels .25 .60
68 Hakeem Olajuwon .75 2.00
69 Eddie Robinson .25 .60
70 Karl Malone .75 2.00
71 Richard Hamilton .50 1.25
72 Derek Anderson .25 .60
73 Bonzi Wells .25 .60
74 Darrell Armstrong .25 .60
75 Gary Payton .60 1.50
76 Bryon Russell .25 .60
77 Steve Smith .30 .75
78 Sam Cassell .30 .75
79 Brian Grant .25 .60
80 Antoine Walker .30 .75
81 Marcus Fizer .25 .60
82 Tim Duncan AN 1.00 2.50
83 Chris Webber AN .50 1.25
84 Shaquille O'Neal AN 1.50 4.00
85 Allen Iverson AN 1.00 2.50
86 Jason Kidd AN .60 1.50
87 Kevin Garnett AN 1.00 2.50
88 Vince Carter AN .75 2.00
89 Dikembe Mutombo AN .60 1.50
90 Kobe Bryant AN 3.00 8.00
91 Tracy McGrady AN .60 1.50
92 Allen Iverson SL 1.00 2.50
93 Dikembe Mutombo SL .60 1.50
94 Jason Kidd SL .60 1.50
95 Allen Iverson SL 1.00 2.50
96 Theo Ratliff SL .25 .60
97 Shaquille O'Neal SL 1.50 4.00
98 Reggie Miller SL .75 2.00
99 Antoine Walker SL .30 .75
100 Michael Finley SL .40 1.00
101 Jason Kidd SL .60 1.50
102 Shaquille O'Neal RTC 1.50 4.00
103 Kobe Bryant RTC 10.00 25.00
104 Derek Fisher RTC .30 .75
105 Shaquille O'Neal RTC 1.50 4.00
106 Shawn Marion AU 6.00 15.00
107 Antawn Jamison AU 8.00 20.00
108 Peja Stojakovic AU 15.00 40.00
109 Jason Terry AU 5.00 12.00
110 Aaron McKie AU 5.00 12.00
111 Keyon Dooling AU 5.00 12.00
112 Al Harrington AU 5.00 12.00
113 Chauncey Billups AU 6.00 15.00
114 Tim Duncan JSY 12.00 30.00
115 Tracy McGrady JSY 8.00 20.00
116 Jason Kidd JSY 8.00 20.00
117 Latrell Sprewell JSY 6.00 15.00
118 David Robinson JSY 10.00 25.00
119 Baron Davis JSY 5.00 12.00
120 Allen Iverson JSY 12.00 30.00
121 Ray Allen JSY 8.00 20.00
122 Rasheed Wallace JSY 6.00 15.00
123 Morris Peterson JSY 3.00 8.00
124 Darius Miles JSY 3.00 8.00
125 Marc Jackson JSY 3.00 8.00
126 Michael Finley JSY 5.00 12.00
127 Elton Brand JSY 4.00 10.00
128 Antonio McDyess JSY 4.00 10.00
129 Andre Miller JSY 4.00 10.00
130 Kwame Brown AU RC 5.00 12.00
131 Eddy Curry AU RC 5.00 12.00
132 Loren Woods AU RC 3.00 8.00
133 Joe Johnson AU RC 10.00 25.00
134 Richard Jefferson AU RC 6.00 15.00
135 Zach Randolph AU RC 15.00 40.00
136 Brendan Haywood AU RC 4.00 10.00
137 Gilbert Arenas AU RC 12.00 30.00
138 Damone Brown AU RC 3.00 8.00
139 Kenny Satterfield AU RC 3.00 8.00
140 Vladimir Radmanovic AU RC 4.00 10.00
141 Eddie Griffin JSY RC 2.50 6.00
142 Shane Battier JSY RC 6.00 15.00
143 Michael Bradley JSY RC 2.00 5.00
144 Gerald Wallace JSY RC 4.00 10.00
145 Samuel Dalembert JSY RC 3.00 8.00
146 Tyson Chandler JSY RC 5.00 12.00
147 Pau Gasol JSY RC 12.00 30.00
148 Steven Hunter JSY RC 2.00 5.00
149 Rodney White JSY RC 2.00 5.00
150 Jeryl Sasser JSY RC 2.00 5.00
151 Brandon Armstrong JSY RC 2.00 5.00
152 Jamaal Tinsley JSY RC 2.50 6.00
153 DeSagana Diop JSY RC 2.00 5.00
154 Jason Richardson RC 2.00 5.00
155 Kirk Haston RC .75 2.00
156 Joseph Forte RC .75 2.00
157 Jason Collins RC 1.00 2.50
158 Kedrick Brown RC .75 2.00
159 Troy Murphy RC 1.00 2.50
160 Tony Parker RC 5.00 12.00
161 Raja Bell RC 1.50 4.00
162 Jeff Trepagnier RC .75 2.00
163 Terence Morris RC .75 2.00
164 Zeljko Rebraca RC 1.25 3.00

2001-02 Topps High Topps Above and Beyond

COMPLETE SET (7) 10.00 25.00
STATED ODDS 1:10
AB1 John Stockton 2.50 6.00
AB2 Shawn Marion 1.25 3.00
AB3 Jason Terry 1.25 3.00
AB4 Alonzo Mourning 2.00 5.00
AB5 Theo Ratliff .75 2.00
AB6 Michael Jordan 15.00 40.00
AB7 Marcus Camby 1.00 2.50

2001-02 Topps High Topps Dominant Figures

COMPLETE SET (8) 20.00 40.00
STATED ODDS 1:9
DF1 Alonzo Mourning 2.00 5.00
DF2 Shaquille O'Neal 5.00 12.00
DF3 Chris Webber 1.50 4.00
DF4 Michael Jordan 15.00 40.00
DF5 Kevin Garnett 3.00 8.00
DF6 Tracy McGrady 2.00 5.00
DF7 Vince Carter 2.50 6.00
DF8 Kobe Bryant 10.00 25.00

2001-02 Topps High Topps Giant Remains

STATED ODDS 1:16
GRAD Antonio Davis 3.00 8.00
GRAH Allan Houston 4.00 10.00
GRAKM Antonio McDyess 3.00 8.00
GRAM Anthony Mason 4.00 10.00
GRCM Cuttino Mobley 3.00 8.00
GRCW Chris Webber 5.00 12.00
GRGR Glenn Robinson 4.00 10.00
GRJS Jerry Stackhouse 4.00 10.00
GRJT Jason Terry 4.00 10.00
GRKLM Kenyon Martin 4.00 10.00
GRKM Karl Malone 8.00 20.00
GRMM Mike Miller 3.00 8.00
GRRH Richard Hamilton 5.00 12.00
GRSDM Shawn Marion 4.00 10.00
GRSF Steve Francis 4.00 10.00
GRSM Stephon Marbury 5.00 12.00
GRSO Shaquille O'Neal 15.00 40.00
GRTD Tim Duncan 10.00 25.00
GRVD Vlade Divac 3.00 8.00
GRWS Wally Szczerbiak 3.00 8.00

2001-02 Topps High Topps Lofty Lettering

STATED ODDS 1:38
LLBD Baron Davis 8.00 20.00
LLBJ Bobby Jackson 5.00 12.00
LLGW Gerald Wallace 6.00 15.00
LLHT Hedo Turkoglu 6.00 15.00
LLJF Joseph Forte 5.00 12.00
LLLP Lavor Postell 5.00 12.00
LLMB Mike Bibby 10.00 25.00
LLSB Shane Battier 6.00 15.00
LLTM Troy Murphy 6.00 15.00
LLTT Tim Thomas 5.00 12.00

2001-02 Topps High Topps Sky's The Limit

COMPLETE SET (13) 20.00 40.00
STATED ODDS 1:8
SL1 Darius Miles .75 2.00
SL2 Vince Carter 2.50 6.00
SL3 Tracy McGrady 2.00 5.00
SL4 Steve Francis 1.25 3.00
SL5 Baron Davis 1.25 3.00
SL6 Tim Duncan 3.00 8.00
SL7 Shawn Marion 1.25 3.00
SL8 Paul Pierce 2.00 5.00
SL9 Rashard Lewis 1.00 2.50
SL10 Lamar Odom 1.00 2.50
SL11 Antawn Jamison 1.00 2.50
SL12 Dirk Nowitzki 3.00 8.00
SL13 Michael Jordan 40.00 100.00

1983 Topps History's Greatest Olympians

COMPLETE SET (99) 12.00 30.00
9 Bill Bradley .50 1.25
17 Don Bragg .12 .30
63 Oscar Robertson .60 1.50
91 Jerry West .75 2.00

2021-22 Topps Inception Overtime Elite

COMMON CARD .30 .75
SEMISTARS .40 1.00
UNLISTED STARS .50 1.25
*BLUE/199: 1.2X TO 3X BASIC
*YELLOW/150: 1.2X TO 3X BASIC
*MAGENTA/99: 1.5X TO 4X BASIC
*RED/75: 1.5X TO 4X BASIC
*ORANGE/50: 2X TO 5X BASIC
*AQUA/25: 3X TO 8X BASIC
1 Ausar Thompson 2.50 6.00
2 TJ Clark .60 1.50
3 Jahzare Jackson 1.25 3.00
4 Tyler Smith .60 1.50
5 Bryson Warren .60 1.50
6 TJ Clark .60 1.50

7 Kok Yat .60 1.50
8 Kok Yat .60 1.50
9 Jahzare Jackson 1.25 3.00
10 Dominick Barlow .60 1.50
11 Jean Montero .75 2.00
12 Amen Thompson 3.00 8.00
13 De'Vontes Cobbs .60 1.50
14 Dominick Barlow .60 1.50
15 Malik Bowman .60 1.50
16 Matt Bewley .60 1.50
17 Matt Bewley .60 1.50
18 Bryson Warren .60 1.50
19 Tudor Somacescu .60 1.50
20 Dominick Barlow .60 1.50
21 Ausar Thompson 2.50 6.00
22 Emmanuel Maldonado .60 1.50
23 Amen Thompson 3.00 8.00
24 Ryan Bewley .60 1.50
25 Izan Almansa .60 1.50
26 Emmanuel Maldonado .60 1.50
27 De'Vontes Cobbs .60 1.50
28 Davion Mace .60 1.50
29 Tyler Smith .60 1.50
30 Jaylen Martin .60 1.50
31 Alexandre Sarr 2.00 5.00
32 Jahzare Jackson 1.25 3.00
33 Jalen Lewis .75 2.00
34 Nathan Missia-Dio .60 1.50
35 Malik Bowman .60 1.50
36 Malik Bowman .60 1.50
37 Alexandre Sarr 2.00 5.00
38 Jean Montero .75 2.00
39 Davion Mace .60 1.50
40 Jalen Lewis .75 2.00
41 Ryan Bewley .60 1.50
42 Matt Bewley .60 1.50
43 Johned Walker .60 1.50
44 Bryson Warren .60 1.50
45 Izan Almansa .60 1.50
46 Jahzare Jackson 1.25 3.00
47 Jaylen Martin .60 1.50
48 Ausar Thompson 2.50 6.00
49 Bryce Griggs .60 1.50
50 Lewis Duarte .60 1.50
51 Bryce Griggs .60 1.50
52 Kok Yat .60 1.50
53 Johned Walker .60 1.50
54 Emmanuel Maldonado .60 1.50
55 Alexandre Sarr 2.00 5.00
56 De'Vontes Cobbs .60 1.50
57 Ausar Thompson 2.50 6.00
58 Izan Almansa .60 1.50
59 Bryce Griggs .60 1.50
60 Jaylen Martin .60 1.50
61 De'Vontes Cobbs .60 1.50
62 Dominick Barlow .60 1.50
63 Amen Thompson 3.00 8.00
64 Nathan Missia-Dio .60 1.50
65 Matt Bewley .60 1.50
66 Johned Walker .60 1.50
67 Alexandre Sarr 2.00 5.00
68 Bryce Griggs .60 1.50
69 Nathan Missia-Dio .60 1.50
70 Nathan Missia-Dio .60 1.50
71 Izan Almansa .60 1.50
72 TJ Clark .60 1.50
73 Bryson Warren .60 1.50
74 Kok Yat .60 1.50
75 Amen Thompson 3.00 8.00
76 Lewis Duarte .60 1.50
77 Jalen Lewis .75 2.00
78 Emmanuel Maldonado .60 1.50
79 Lewis Duarte .60 1.50
80 Jai Smith .60 1.50
81 Davion Mace .60 1.50
82 Jazian Gortman .60 1.50
83 Malik Bowman .60 1.50
84 Jai Smith .60 1.50
85 Tyler Smith .60 1.50
86 Ryan Bewley .60 1.50
87 TJ Clark .60 1.50
88 Jalen Lewis .75 2.00
89 Jean Montero .75 2.00
90 Tudor Somacescu .60 1.50
91 Jai Smith .60 1.50
92 Jai Smith .60 1.50
93 Ryan Bewley .60 1.50
94 Jazian Gortman .60 1.50
95 Jaylen Martin .60 1.50
96 Jazian Gortman .60 1.50
97 Tudor Somacescu .60 1.50
98 Jazian Gortman .60 1.50
99 Jean Montero .75 2.00
100 Tyler Smith .60 1.50

2021-22 Topps Inception Overtime Elite Autographs

COMMON CARD 3.00 8.00
SEMISTARS 4.00 10.00
UNLISTED STARS 5.00 12.00
*MAGENTA/99: .5X TO 1.2X BASE HI
*RED/75: .5X TO 1.2X BASE HI
*ORANGE/50: .6X TO 1.5X BASE HI
IAAS Alexandre Sarr 15.00 40.00
IAAT Amen Thompson 25.00 60.00
IABG Bryce Griggs 5.00 12.00
IABW Bryson Warren 5.00 12.00
IADB Dominick Barlow 5.00 12.00
IADC De'Vontes Cobbs 5.00 12.00
IAIA Izan Almansa 5.00 12.00
IAJG Jazian Gortman 5.00 12.00
IAJJ Jahzare Jackson 10.00 25.00
IAJL Jalen Lewis 6.00 15.00
IAJM Jaylen Martin 5.00 12.00
IAJS Jai Smith 5.00 12.00
IAKY Kok Yat 5.00 12.00
IAMB Matt Bewley 5.00 12.00
IARB Ryan Bewley 5.00 12.00
IATC TJ Clark 5.00 12.00
IATS Tyler Smith 5.00 12.00
IAAS2 Alexandre Sarr 15.00 40.00
IAAT2 Amen Thompson 25.00 60.00
IAAT3 Amen Thompson 25.00 60.00
IAATH Ausar Thompson 20.00 50.00
IABG2 Bryce Griggs 5.00 12.00
IABG3 Bryce Griggs 5.00 12.00
IABW2 Bryson Warren 5.00 12.00
IABW3 Bryson Warren 5.00 12.00
IADB2 Dominick Barlow 5.00 12.00
IADB3 Dominick Barlow 5.00 12.00
IADC2 De'Vontes Cobbs 5.00 12.00
IADC3 De'Vontes Cobbs 5.00 12.00
IADM1 Davion Mace 5.00 12.00
IADM2 Davion Mace 5.00 12.00
IAIA2 Izan Almansa 5.00 12.00
IAIA3 Izan Almansa 5.00 12.00
IAJG2 Jazian Gortman 5.00 12.00
IAJG3 Jazian Gortman 5.00 12.00
IAJJ2 Jahzare Jackson 10.00 25.00
IAJJ3 Jahzare Jackson 10.00 25.00
IAJL2 Jalen Lewis 6.00 15.00
IAJL3 Jalen Lewis 6.00 15.00
IAJM2 Jaylen Martin 5.00 12.00
IAJM3 Jaylen Martin 5.00 12.00
IAJMO Jean Montero 6.00 15.00
IAJS2 Jai Smith 5.00 12.00
IAJW1 Johned Walker 5.00 12.00
IAJW2 Johned Walker 5.00 12.00
IAKY2 Kok Yat 5.00 12.00
IAKY3 Kok Yat 5.00 12.00
IALD1 Lewis Duarte 5.00 12.00
IALD2 Lewis Duarte 5.00 12.00
IAMB2 Matt Bewley 5.00 12.00
IAMB3 Matt Bewley 5.00 12.00
IAMBO Malik Bowman 5.00 12.00
IANMD Nathan Missia-Dio 5.00 12.00
IARB2 Ryan Bewley 5.00 12.00
IARB3 Ryan Bewley 5.00 12.00
IATC2 TJ Clark 5.00 12.00
IATC3 TJ Clark 5.00 12.00
IATS2 Tyler Smith 5.00 12.00
IATSO Tudor Somacescu 5.00 12.00
IAATH2 Ausar Thompson 20.00 50.00
IAATH3 Ausar Thompson 20.00 50.00
IAJMO2 Jean Montero 6.00 15.00
IAJMO3 Jean Montero 6.00 15.00
IAMBO2 Malik Bowman 5.00 12.00
IAMBO3 Malik Bowman 5.00 12.00
IANMD2 Nathan Missia-Dio 5.00 12.00
IANMD3 Nathan Missia-Dio 5.00 12.00
IATSO2 Tudor Somacescu 5.00 12.00

2021-22 Topps Inception Overtime Elite Autographs Blue

*BLUE/25: .75X TO 2X BASE HI
IAAT Amen Thompson 125.00 300.00
IAAT2 Amen Thompson 125.00 300.00
IAAT3 Amen Thompson 75.00 200.00

2021-22 Topps Inception Overtime Elite Game Ball Relic Autographs

AGBRAS Alexandre Sarr 40.00 100.00
AGBRAT Amen Thompson 60.00 150.00
AGBRBG Bryce Griggs 12.00 30.00
AGBRBW Bryson Warren 12.00 30.00
AGBRDB Dominick Barlow 12.00 30.00
AGBRDC De'Vontes Cobbs 12.00 30.00
AGBRIA Izan Almansa 12.00 30.00
AGBRJG Jazian Gortman 12.00 30.00
AGBRJJ Jahzare Jackson 25.00 60.00
AGBRJL Jalen Lewis 15.00 40.00
AGBRJM Jaylen Martin 12.00 30.00
AGBRJS Jai Smith 12.00 30.00
AGBRJW Johned Walker 12.00 30.00
AGBRKY Kok Yat 12.00 30.00
AGBRMB Malik Bowman 12.00 30.00
AGBRRB Ryan Bewley 12.00 30.00
AGBRTC TJ Clark 12.00 30.00
AGBRTS Tyler Smith 12.00 30.00
AGBRAUT Ausar Thompson 50.00 125.00
AGBRJMO Jean Montero 15.00 40.00
AGBRMBE Matt Bewley 12.00 30.00
AGBRNMD Nathan Missia-Dio 12.00 30.00
AGBRTSO Tudor Somacescu 12.00 30.00

2021-22 Topps Inception Overtime Elite Jumbo Patch Autographs

COMMON CARD 5.00 12.00
SEMISTARS 6.00 15.00
UNLISTED STARS 8.00 20.00
*ORANGE/25: .75X TO 2X BASE HI
IAJPCAS Alexandre Sarr 25.00 60.00
IAJPCAT Amen Thompson 40.00 100.00
IAJPCBG Bryce Griggs 8.00 20.00
IAJPCBW Bryson Warren 8.00 20.00
IAJPCDB Dominick Barlow 8.00 20.00
IAJPCDC De'Vontes Cobbs 8.00 20.00
IAJPCDM Davion Mace 8.00 20.00
IAJPCIA Izan Almansa 8.00 20.00
IAJPCJG Jazian Gortman 8.00 20.00
IAJPCJJ Jahzare Jackson 15.00 40.00
IAJPCJL Jalen Lewis 10.00 25.00
IAJPCJM Jaylen Martin 8.00 20.00
IAJPCJS Jai Smith 8.00 20.00
IAJPCKY Kok Yat 8.00 20.00
IAJPCMB Matt Bewley 8.00 20.00
IAJPCRB Ryan Bewley 8.00 20.00
IAJPCTC TJ Clark 8.00 20.00
IAJPCTS Tyler Smith 8.00 20.00
IAJPCAT2 Amen Thompson 40.00 100.00
IAJPCATH Ausar Thompson 30.00 80.00
IAJPCATH2 Ausar Thompson 30.00 80.00
IAJPCJL2 Jalen Lewis 10.00 25.00
IAJPCJMO Jean Montero 10.00 25.00
IAJPCMBO Malik Bowman 8.00 20.00
IAJPCNMD Nathan Missia-Dio 8.00 20.00
IAJPCTSO Tudor Somacescu 8.00 20.00

2021-22 Topps Inception Overtime Elite Patch Autographs

COMMON CARD 4.00 10.00
SEMISTARS 5.00 12.00
UNLISTED STARS 6.00 15.00
*MAGENTA/99: .5X TO 1.2X BASE HI
*RED/25: .75X TO 2X BASE HI
IAPCAS Alexandre Sarr 20.00 50.00
IAPCAT Amen Thompson 30.00 80.00
IAPCBG Bryce Griggs 6.00 15.00
IAPCBW Bryson Warren 6.00 15.00
IAPCDB Dominick Barlow 6.00 15.00
IAPCDC De'Vontes Cobbs 6.00 15.00
IAPCDM Davion Mace 6.00 15.00
IAPCIA Izan Almansa 6.00 15.00
IAPCJG Jazian Gortman 6.00 15.00
IAPCJJ Jahzare Jackson 12.00 30.00
IAPCJL Jalen Lewis 8.00 20.00
IAPCJM Jaylen Martin 6.00 15.00
IAPCJS Jai Smith 6.00 15.00
IAPCJW Johned Walker 6.00 15.00
IAPCKY Kok Yat 6.00 15.00
IAPCLD Lewis Duarte 6.00 15.00
IAPCMB Matt Bewley 6.00 15.00
IAPCMC Malik Bowman 6.00 15.00
IAPCRB Ryan Bewley 6.00 15.00
IAPCTC TJ Clark 6.00 15.00
IAPCTS Tyler Smith 6.00 15.00
IAPCAS2 Alexandre Sarr 20.00 50.00
IAPCAT2 Amen Thompson 30.00 80.00
IAPCATH Ausar Thompson 25.00 60.00
IAPCBG2 Bryce Griggs 6.00 15.00
IAPCBW2 Bryson Warren 6.00 15.00
IAPCDB2 Dominick Barlow 6.00 15.00
IAPCDC2 De'Vontes Cobbs 6.00 15.00
IAPCIA2 Izan Almansa 6.00 15.00
IAPCJG2 Jazian Gortman 6.00 15.00
IAPCJJ2 Jahzare Jackson 12.00 30.00
IAPCJL2 Jalen Lewis 8.00 20.00
IAPCJM2 Jaylen Martin 6.00 15.00
IAPCJMO Jean Montero 8.00 20.00
IAPCJS2 Jai Smith 6.00 15.00
IAPCKY2 Kok Yat 6.00 15.00
IAPCMB2 Matt Bewley 6.00 15.00
IAPCMBO Malik Bowman 6.00 15.00
IAPCNMD Nathan Missia-Dio 6.00 15.00
IAPCRB2 Ryan Bewley 6.00 15.00
IAPCTC2 TJ Clark 6.00 15.00
IAPCTS2 Tyler Smith 6.00 15.00
IAPCTSO Tudor Somacescu 6.00 15.00
IAPCATH2 Ausar Thompson 25.00 60.00
IAPCJMO2 Jean Montero 8.00 20.00
IAPCNMD2 Nathan Missia-Dio 6.00 15.00

2021-22 Topps Inception Overtime Elite Silver Signings

COMMON CARD 5.00 12.00
SEMISTARS 6.00 15.00
UNLISTED STARS 8.00 20.00
*GOLD INK/25: .75X TO 2X BASE
ISSAS Alexandre Sarr 25.00 60.00
ISSAT Amen Thompson 40.00 100.00
ISSBG Bryce Griggs 8.00 20.00
ISSBW Bryson Warren 8.00 20.00
ISSDB Dominick Barlow 8.00 20.00
ISSDC De'Vontes Cobbs 8.00 20.00
ISSIA Izan Almansa 8.00 20.00
ISSJG Jazian Gortman 8.00 20.00
ISSJJ Jahzare Jackson 15.00 40.00
ISSJL Jalen Lewis 10.00 25.00
ISSJM Jaylen Martin 8.00 20.00
ISSJS Jai Smith 8.00 20.00
ISSKY Kok Yat 8.00 20.00
ISSMB Matt Bewley 8.00 20.00
ISSRB Ryan Bewley 8.00 20.00
ISSTC TJ Clark 8.00 20.00
ISSTS Tyler Smith 8.00 20.00
ISSATH Ausar Thompson 30.00 80.00
ISSJMO Jean Montero 10.00 25.00
ISSMBO Malik Bowman 8.00 20.00
ISSNMD Nathan Missia-Dio 8.00 20.00
ISSTSO Tudor Somacescu 8.00 20.00

2002-03 Topps Jersey Edition

HOME JSY ON CARDS WITH H
ROAD JSY ON CARDS WITH R
ERR CARDS HAVE WRONG JSY SWATCH
STACKHOUSE REPLACE PAYTON ON EXCH
ASTERISKS PERCEIVED AS SP VERSION
JEAD Antonio Davis R UER 3.00 8.00
JEAI Allen Iverson R * 10.00 25.00
JEAJ Antawn Jamison R 3.00 8.00
JEAK Andrei Kirilenko R 3.00 8.00
JEAS Amare Stoudemire R RC 10.00 25.00
JEBD Baron Davis R 4.00 10.00
JEBG Brian Grant R 2.50 6.00
JEBW Ben Wallace R 5.00 12.00
JECA Courtney Alexander R UER 2.50 6.00
JECB Carlos Boozer R RC 4.00 10.00
JECJ Chris Jefferies H RC 2.50 6.00
JECM Cuttino Mobley R 2.50 6.00
JECW Chris Wilcox R UER RC 3.00 8.00
JEDD Dan Dickau R RC 2.50 6.00
JEDF Derek Fisher R 4.00 10.00
JEDN Dirk Nowitzki R 10.00 25.00
JEDW DaJuan Wagner R RC 3.00 8.00
JEEB Elton Brand R 3.00 8.00
JEEC Eddy Curry R 2.50 6.00
JEEG Eddie Griffin R UER 2.50 6.00
JEEJ Eddie Jones R 4.00 10.00
JEFJ Fred Jones R RC 3.00 8.00
JEGA Gilbert Arenas R UER 4.00 10.00
JEGG Gordan Giricek R RC 4.00 10.00
JEJH Juwan Howard R 3.00 8.00
JEJM Jamal Mashburn R 3.00 8.00
JEJO Jermaine O'Neal R 3.00 8.00
JEJR Jalen Rose R 3.00 8.00
JEJS Joe Smith R 3.00 8.00
JEJT Jamaal Tinsley R 2.50 6.00
JEKG Kevin Garnett R 10.00 25.00
JEKR Kareem Rush R RC 3.00 8.00
JEKS Kenny Satterfield R 2.50 6.00
JEKV Keith Van Horn R 3.00 8.00
JEMD Mike Dunleavy H RC 4.00 10.00
JEMF Michael Finley R 4.00 10.00
JEMO Mehmet Okur R RC 4.00 10.00
JEMP Morris Peterson R UER 3.00 8.00
JENT Nikoloz Tskitishvili R RC 2.50 6.00
JEPG Pau Gasol R 6.00 15.00
JEPP Paul Pierce R 6.00 15.00
JEQR Quentin Richardson R 2.50 6.00
JEQW Qyntel Woods R RC 2.50 6.00
JERA Ray Allen 6.00 15.00
JERB Rasual Butler R RC 3.00 8.00
JERM Reggie Miller R 8.00 20.00
JESA Shareef Abdur-Rahim R 4.00 10.00
JESM Stephon Marbury R 5.00 12.00
JESN Steve Nash R 8.00 20.00
JESO Shaquille O'Neal R 15.00 40.00
JETC Tyson Chandler R 4.00 10.00
JETH Troy Hudson R 2.50 6.00
JEWS Wally Szczerbiak R 3.00 8.00
JEYM Yao Ming R RC 20.00 50.00
JEAFM Aaron McKie R UER 2.50 6.00
JEAHO Allan Houston H 4.00 10.00
JEAIV Allen Iverson H 10.00 25.00
JEALM Andre Miller R 3.00 8.00
JEAMG Drew Gooden R RC 4.00 10.00
JEAMI Andre Miller H 3.00 8.00
JEAST Amare Stoudemire H RC 10.00 25.00
JEAWA Antoine Walker 3.00 8.00
JEBDA Baron Davis H 4.00 10.00
JEBWA Ben Wallace H 5.00 12.00
JECBU Caron Butler H RC 4.00 10.00
JEDAS Damon Stoudamire H 4.00 10.00
JEDDI Dan Dickau H UER RC 2.50 6.00
JEDGO Drew Gooden H RC 4.00 10.00
JEDJG Devean George R 2.50 6.00
JEDLM Darius Miles R 2.50 6.00
JEDMA Donyell Marshall R UER 2.50 6.00
JEDNO Dirk Nowitzki H 10.00 25.00
JEDWA DaJuan Wagner H RC 3.00 8.00
JEEBR Elton Brand H 3.00 8.00
JEECU Eddy Curry H 2.50 6.00
JEEJC Elden Campbell R UER 2.50 6.00
JEECW Chris Webber 5.00 12.00
JEEGI Manu Ginobili H RC 20.00 50.00
JEGDW Bonzi Wells R 2.50 6.00
JEGRO Glenn Robinson H 4.00 10.00
JEJAR Jason Richardson R 4.00 10.00
JEJAT Jason Terry R 3.00 8.00
JEJCB Caron Butler R RC 4.00 10.00
JEJDM Jamaal Magloire R UER 2.50 6.00
JEJHS John Stockton R 8.00 20.00
JEJKI Jason Kidd H 6.00 15.00
JEJMJ Joe Johnson R 3.00 8.00
JEJON Jermaine O'Neal H 3.00 8.00
JEJOS John Stockton H 8.00 20.00
JEJRI Jason Richardson H 4.00 10.00
JEJRO Jalen Rose H 3.00 8.00
JEJRS John Salmons R RC 4.00 10.00
JEJWL Jerome Williams H 2.50 6.00
JEKAM Karl Malone R 8.00 20.00
JEKGA Kevin Garnett H 10.00 25.00
JEKMA Karl Malone H 8.00 20.00
JEKRU Kareem Rush H RC 3.00 8.00
JEKVH Keith Van Horn H 3.00 8.00
JELSP Latrell Sprewell H 4.00 10.00
JEMAF Marcus Fizer R 2.50 6.00
JEMOK Mehmet Okur H RC 4.00 10.00
JENTS Nikoloz Tskitishvili H RC 2.50 6.00
JEPGA Pau Gasol H 6.00 15.00
JEQRI Quentin Richardson H 2.50 6.00
JEQWO Qyntel Woods H RC 2.50 6.00
JERAO Ron Artest R 3.00 8.00
JERAW Rasheed Wallace R 5.00 12.00
JERBU Rasual Butler H RC 3.00 8.00
JERCH Richard Hamilton R 5.00 12.00
JERHO Robert Horry R 4.00 10.00
JERIH Richard Hamilton H 5.00 12.00
JERWA Rasheed Wallace H 5.00 12.00
JESCB Shane Battier R 4.00 10.00
JESDM Shawn Marion R 4.00 10.00
JESFR Steve Francis R 4.00 10.00
JESMA Shawn Marion H 4.00 10.00
JESNA Steve Nash H * 8.00 20.00
JESON Shaquille O'Neal H 15.00 40.00
JETCH Tyson Chandler H 4.00 10.00
JETDU Tim Duncan H 10.00 25.00
JETDU Tim Duncan R 10.00 25.00
JETLM Tracy McGrady R 6.00 15.00
JETPA Tony Parker H 6.00 15.00
JETPR Tayshaun Prince R RC 8.00 20.00
JEWSZ Wally Szczerbiak H 3.00 8.00

2002-03 Topps Jersey Edition Black

*BLACK: .6X TO 1.5X BASE CARD HI
STATED PRINT RUN 99 SER.#'d SETS
JEYM Yao Ming R 30.00 80.00

2002-03 Topps Jersey Edition Copper

*COPPER: .5X TO 1.25X BASE CARD HI
STATED PRINT RUN 299 SER.#'d SETS

2003-04 Topps Jersey Edition

SS RC HAVE NBA DRAFT PATCH
SS RC STATED ODDS 1:9
AD Antonio Davis 2.00 5.00
AH Allan Houston 2.50 6.00
AI Allen Iverson 6.00 15.00
AJ Antawn Jamison 2.50 6.00
AK Andrei Kirilenko 2.50 6.00
AM Andre Miller 2.00 5.00
AP Aleksandar Pavlovic RC 2.00 5.00
AS Amare Stoudemire 3.00 8.00
BB Brent Barry 2.00 5.00
BC Brian Cook RC 2.00 5.00
BD Baron Davis 2.50 6.00
BH Brandon Hunter RC 2.00 5.00
BJ Bobby Jackson 2.00 5.00
BM Brad Miller 2.00 5.00
BW Ben Wallace 3.00 8.00
CA Carmelo Anthony SS RC 15.00 40.00
CB Caron Butler 2.00 5.00
CK Chris Kaman RC 3.00 8.00
CM Corey Maggette 2.00 5.00
CW Chris Webber 3.00 8.00
DC Derrick Coleman 2.50 6.00
DG Drew Gooden 2.00 5.00
DJ Dahntay Jones RC 2.50 6.00
DM Desmond Mason 2.00 5.00
DN Dirk Nowitzki 6.00 15.00
DW Dwyane Wade SS RC 200.00 500.00
EB Elton Brand AU 8.00 20.00
EC Eddy Curry 1.50 4.00
EG Manu Ginobili 5.00 12.00
GA Gilbert Arenas 2.50 6.00
GP Gary Payton 4.00 10.00
GR Glenn Robinson 2.00 5.00
HT Hedo Turkoglu 2.00 5.00
JB Jerome Beasley RC 2.00 5.00
JC Jamal Crawford 2.50 6.00
JH Juwan Howard 2.00 5.00
JJ James Jones RC 2.00 5.00
JK Jason Kidd 4.00 10.00
JM Jamal Mashburn 2.00 5.00
JO Jermaine O'Neal 2.50 6.00
JR Jalen Rose 2.00 5.00
JS Jerry Stackhouse 3.00 8.00
JT Jason Terry 2.50 6.00
JW Jason Williams 4.00 10.00
KB Kwame Brown 2.00 5.00
KC Keon Clark 2.00 5.00
KG Kevin Garnett 6.00 15.00
KH Kirk Hinrich AU RC 8.00 20.00
KM Karl Malone 5.00 12.00
KP Kendrick Perkins RC 2.50 6.00
KR Kareem Rush 2.00 5.00
KT Kurt Thomas 2.00 5.00
LB Leandro Barbosa SS RC 3.00 8.00
LJ LeBron James SS RC 1,000.00 2,500.00
LO Lamar Odom 2.00 5.00
LR Luke Ridnour AU RC 6.00 15.00
LS Latrell Sprewell 3.00 8.00
LW Luke Walton SS RC 3.00 8.00
MB Mike Bibby 2.50 6.00
MC Marcus Camby 2.00 5.00
MD Mike Dunleavy 2.00 5.00
MJ Marko Jaric 2.00 5.00
MM Mike Miller 2.00 5.00
MO Michael Olowokandi 2.00 5.00
MP Morris Peterson 1.50 4.00
MR Michael Redd 2.50 6.00
MS Mike Sweetney SS RC 2.00 5.00
MT Maurice Taylor 2.00 5.00
MW Maurice Williams RC 3.00 8.00
NE Ndudi Ebi RC 2.00 5.00
NH Nene 2.00 5.00
PG Pau Gasol 4.00 10.00
PP Paul Pierce 4.00 10.00
PS Peja Stojakovic 2.00 5.00
QR Quentin Richardson 1.50 4.00
QW Qyntel Woods 2.00 5.00
RA Ray Allen 4.00 10.00
RD Ricky Davis 2.00 5.00
RG Reece Gaines SS RC 2.00 5.00
RH Richard Hamilton 3.00 8.00
RJ Richard Jefferson 2.00 5.00
RL Rashard Lewis 2.00 5.00
RL Raef LaFrentz 2.00 5.00
RM Ron Mercer 2.00 5.00
RN Radoslav Nesterovic 2.00 5.00
RW Rasheed Wallace 3.00 8.00
SB Steve Blake RC 2.50 6.00
SC Sam Cassell 2.00 5.00
SF Steve Francis 2.50 6.00
SM Shawn Marion 2.50 6.00
SN Steve Nash 5.00 12.00
SO Shaquille O'Neal AU 30.00 80.00
SP Scottie Pippen 6.00 15.00
TB Troy Bell RC 3.00 8.00
TC Tyson Chandler 2.00 5.00
TD Tim Duncan 6.00 15.00
TM Tracy McGrady 4.00 10.00
TO Travis Outlaw RC 2.50 6.00
TP Tony Parker 4.00 10.00
TR Theo Ratliff 2.00 5.00
TS Theron Smith RC 2.00 5.00
TT Tim Thomas 2.00 5.00
WG Willie Green RC 3.00 8.00
YM Yao Ming 6.00 15.00
ZC Zarko Cabarkapa RC 2.00 5.00
ZI Zydrunas Ilgauskas 2.00 5.00
ZP Zoran Planinic RC 2.00 5.00
ZR Zach Randolph 2.50 6.00
AHA Al Harrington 2.00 5.00
BDR Boris Diaw RC 3.00 8.00
CBI Chauncey Billups 3.00 8.00
CBO Carlos Boozer 3.00 8.00
CBO Chris Bosh RC 10.00 25.00
CMO Cuttino Mobley 1.50 4.00
CWI Corliss Williamson 2.00 5.00
DAM Darko Milicic SS RC 2.50 6.00
DCH Doug Christie 2.00 5.00
DGE Devean George 2.00 5.00
DMI Darius Miles 2.00 5.00
DWA DaJuan Wagner 2.00 5.00
DWE David West SS RC 4.00 10.00
JHA Jarvis Hayes RC 2.00 5.00
JHO Josh Howard RC 3.00 8.00
JKA Jason Kapono SS RC 2.00 5.00
JMA Jamaal Magloire 2.00 5.00
JRI Jason Richardson 2.50 6.00
JSM Joe Smith 2.00 5.00
JWI Jerome Williams 2.00 5.00
KMA Kenyon Martin 2.50 6.00
KVH Keith Van Horn 2.00 5.00
MBA Marcus Banks RC 2.00 5.00
MJA Marc Jackson 2.00 5.00
MPI Mickael Pietrus RC 2.50 6.00
NVE Nick Van Exel 2.50 6.00
RAR Ron Artest 2.50 6.00
RHO Robert Horry 2.50 6.00
RLO Raul Lopez 2.50 6.00
RMI Reggie Miller 5.00 12.00
SAR Shareef Abdur-Rahim 2.50 6.00
SBA Shane Battier 2.50 6.00
SCL Speedy Claxton 2.00 5.00
SMA Stephon Marbury 3.00 8.00
TMU Troy Murphy 1.50 4.00
TPR Tayshaun Prince 2.50 6.00
ZPA Zaur Pachulia RC 3.00 8.00

2003-04 Topps Jersey Edition Black

*BLACK SINGLES: 1.25X TO 3X BASE HI
*BLACK AU: 1X TO 2.5X BASE HI
*BLACK RCs: 1X TO 2.5X BASE HI
*BLACK SS RCs: 1.5X TO 4X BASE HI
BLACK PRINT RUN 25 SER.#'d SETS
SP Scottie Pippen 25.00 60.00
TD Tim Duncan 15.00 40.00
RMI Reggie Miller 15.00 40.00

2003-04 Topps Jersey Edition Copper

*COPPER SINGLES: .6X TO 1.5X BASE HI
*COPPER AU: .5X TO 1.25X BASE HI
*COPPER RCs: .5X TO 1.25X BASE HI
*COPPER SS RCs: .75X TO 2X BASE HI
COPPER PRINT RUN 99 SER.#'d SETS

2003-04 Topps Jersey Edition Double Team

STATED ODDS 1:108
1 T.McGrady/R.Gaines 6.00 15.00
2 P.Pierce/M.Banks 6.00 15.00
3 S.Nash/D.Nowitzki 8.00 20.00
4 B.Wallace/R.Hamilton 6.00 15.00
5 J.Richardson/M.Pietrus 6.00 15.00
6 Y.Ming/S.Francis 10.00 25.00
8 J.Kidd/K.Martin 8.00 20.00
9 A.Stoudemire/S.Marbury 6.00 15.00
10 C.Webber/P.Stojakovic 6.00 15.00
11 T.Duncan/T.Parker 15.00 30.00
12 C.Anthony/Nene 10.00 25.00
14 A.Iverson/G.Robinson 6.00 15.00
15 K.Hinrich/T.Chandler 8.00 20.00

2003-04 Topps Jersey Edition Draft Day Hits

PRINT RUN 75 SER.#'d SETS
BC Brian Cook 2.00 5.00
CA Carmelo Anthony 15.00 40.00
CB Chris Bosh 10.00 25.00
CK Chris Kaman 3.00 8.00
DJ Dahntay Jones 2.50 6.00
DW Dwyane Wade 25.00 60.00
JH Jarvis Hayes 2.00 5.00
JK Jason Kapono 2.00 5.00
KH Kirk Hinrich 3.00 8.00
KP Kendrick Perkins 2.50 6.00
LB Leandro Barbosa 3.00 8.00
LR Luke Ridnour 3.00 8.00
LW Luke Walton 3.00 8.00
MB Marcus Banks 2.00 5.00
MP Mickael Pietrus 2.50 6.00
MS Mike Sweetney 2.00 5.00
NC Nick Collison 2.50 6.00
NE Ndudi Ebi 2.00 5.00
RG Reece Gaines 2.00 5.00
TB Troy Bell 2.00 5.00
TO Travis Outlaw 2.50 6.00
DWE David West 4.00 10.00
JHO Josh Howard 3.00 8.00
TJF T.J. Ford 2.50 6.00

2003-04 Topps Jersey Edition Patch Place

PRINT RUN 25 SER.#'d SETS
1 Paul Pierce 15.00 40.00
2 Baron Davis 10.00 25.00
3 Steve Nash 20.00 50.00
4 Dirk Nowitzki 25.00 60.00
5 Steve Francis 10.00 25.00
6 Yao Ming 25.00 60.00
7 Jason Richardson 10.00 25.00
8 Pau Gasol 15.00 40.00
9 Tracy McGrady 15.00 40.00
10 Ben Wallace 12.00 30.00
11 Zoran Planinic 6.00 15.00
12 Dajuan Wagner 6.00 15.00
13 Darius Miles 6.00 15.00
14 Jermaine O'Neal 10.00 25.00
15 Elton Brand 8.00 20.00
16 Shaquille O'Neal 30.00 80.00
17 Lamar Odom 8.00 20.00
18 Michael Redd 10.00 25.00
19 Kevin Garnett 25.00 60.00
20 Jason Kidd 15.00 40.00
21 Kenyon Martin 10.00 25.00
22 Allen Iverson 25.00 60.00
23 Amare Stoudemire 12.00 30.00
24 Tim Duncan 25.00 60.00
25 Ray Allen 15.00 40.00
26 Carmelo Anthony 50.00 120.00
27 Kirk Hinrich 10.00 25.00
28 T.J. Ford 8.00 20.00
29 Reece Gaines 6.00 15.00
30 Chris Bosh 30.00 80.00
31 Mickael Pietrus 8.00 20.00
32 Mike Sweetney 6.00 15.00
33 Jarvis Hayes 6.00 15.00

2003-04 Topps Jersey Edition Prime Pieces

STATED PRINT RUN ONE TO 43 SETS
11 Richard Hamilton/32 12.00 30.00
12 Allan Houston/20 10.00 25.00
15 Eddie Griffin/33 6.00 15.00
21 David West/30 12.00 30.00
24 Kendrick Perkins/43 8.00 20.00
31 Elton Brand/42 8.00 20.00
32 Shawn Marion/31 10.00 25.00

2003-04 Topps Jersey Edition Triple Threat

PRINT RUN 25 SER.#'d SETS
2 Pierce/McG/J-Rich 10.00 25.00
4 Carmelo/Wade/Gaines 60.00 150.00
10 Heinrich/Ford/Pietrus 10.00 25.00

1996 Topps Kellogg's Raptors

COMPLETE SET (5) 2.50 6.00
1 Willie Anderson .40 1.00
2 Damon Stoudamire 2.00 5.00
3 Alvin Robertson .40 1.00
4 Tony Massenburg .40 1.00
5 Tracy Murray .40 1.00

2007-08 Topps Letterman

PRINT RUN 599 SER.#'d SETS
1 Dwyane Wade 2.00 5.00
2 Kobe Bryant 8.00 20.00
3 Allen Iverson 2.50 6.00
4 Jason Kidd 1.50 4.00
5 Kevin Garnett 2.50 6.00
6 Tony Parker 1.50 4.00
7 Gilbert Arenas 1.00 2.50
8 Dwight Howard 1.25 3.00
9 Steve Nash 2.00 5.00
10 Carmelo Anthony 1.50 4.00
11 Tim Duncan 2.50 6.00
12 Chris Bosh 1.25 3.00
13 LeBron James 8.00 20.00
14 Tracy McGrady 1.50 4.00
15 Vince Carter 2.00 5.00
16 Amare Stoudemire 1.00 2.50
17 Shaquille O'Neal 4.00 10.00
18 Paul Pierce 1.50 4.00
19 Yao Ming 2.50 6.00
20 Dirk Nowitzki 2.50 6.00
21 Pau Gasol 1.50 4.00
22 Michael Redd .75 2.00
23 Carlos Boozer .75 2.00
24 Baron Davis .75 2.00
25 Caron Butler .75 2.00
26 Joe Johnson .75 2.00
27 Gerald Wallace .75 2.00
28 Al Jefferson .60 1.50
29 Chris Paul 2.00 5.00
30 Rudy Gay .75 2.00
31 Manu Ginobili 2.00 5.00
32 Corey Maggette .75 2.00
33 Ray Allen 1.50 4.00
34 Ben Gordon .75 2.00
35 Jamal Crawford 1.00 2.50
36 David West .75 2.00
37 Andre Iguodala 1.00 2.50
38 Deron Williams .75 2.00
39 Brandon Roy 1.25 3.00
40 Richard Hamilton 1.25 3.00
41 Larry Bird 5.00 12.00
42 John Stockton 2.50 6.00
43 Bill Russell 4.00 10.00
44 David Robinson 2.50 6.00
45 Isiah Thomas 1.25 3.00
46 Dennis Rodman 3.00 8.00
47 Jerry West 3.00 8.00
48 Moses Malone 2.00 5.00
49 Dominique Wilkins 2.00 5.00
50 Magic Johnson 5.00 12.00
51 Jamario Moon RC 1.50 4.00
52 Juan Carlos Navarro RC 1.50 4.00
53 Spencer Hawes RC 1.25 3.00
54 Glen Davis RC 1.50 4.00
55 Rodney Stuckey RC 1.25 3.00
56 Kevin Durant RC 100.00 250.00
57 Corey Brewer RC 1.50 4.00
58 Joakim Noah RC 2.00 5.00
59 Mike Conley Jr. RC 5.00 12.00
60 Al Horford RC 5.00 12.00
61 Julian Wright RC 1.25 3.00
62 Jeff Green RC 1.50 4.00
63 Luis Scola RC 2.00 5.00
64 Yi Jianlian RC 2.50 6.00
65 Sean Williams RC 1.25 3.00
66 Arron Afflalo RC 1.50 4.00
67 Al Thornton RC 1.25 3.00
68 Marco Belinelli RC 1.50 4.00
69 Javaris Crittenton RC 1.25 3.00
70 Thaddeus Young RC 2.00 5.00
71 Daequan Cook RC 1.50 4.00
72 Brandan Wright RC 1.50 4.00
73 Acie Law RC 1.25 3.00
74 Nick Young RC 2.00 5.00
75 Greg Oden RC 2.00 5.00
NNO Lottery Exchange 20.00 40.00

2007-08 Topps Letterman Refractors

*REFRACTORS: .75X TO 2X BASE HI
REFRACTOR PRINT RUN 99 SETS
2 Kobe Bryant 12.00 30.00
13 LeBron James 30.00 80.00
56 Kevin Durant 400.00 800.00

2007-08 Topps Letterman Xfractors

*1-50 XFRACTORS: 2X TO 5X BASE HI
*51-75 XFRACTORS: 1.5X TO 4X HI
XFRACTORS PRINT RUN 25 SETS
2 Kobe Bryant 40.00 100.00
13 LeBron James 100.00 250.00
56 Kevin Durant 1,500.00 3,000.00

2007-08 Topps Letterman Authentic Relics Quad Autographs

GROUP A PRINT RUN 9 SETS
GROUP B PRINT RUN 75 SETS
GRP B REF: .5X TO 1.25X BASE HI
GRP B REF.PRINT RUN 19 SETS
ABY Andrew Bynum B 10.00 25.00
AT Al Thornton B 6.00 15.00
ATU Alando Tucker B 6.00 15.00
CB Caron Butler B 8.00 20.00
DH Dwight Howard B 12.00 30.00
DM Darko Milicic B 6.00 15.00
DT David Thompson B 10.00 25.00
IT Isiah Thomas B 15.00 30.00
JJW Jo Jo White B 8.00 20.00
LD Luol Deng B 8.00 20.00
MW Maurice Williams B 6.00 15.00
RG Rudy Gay B 6.00 15.00
RR Rajon Rondo B 20.00 40.00
SM Shawn Marion B 10.00 25.00
YJ Yi Jianlian B 15.00 30.00
ZR Zach Randolph B 6.00 15.00

2007-08 Topps Letterman Booklet Autographs

PRINT RUN 19 SER.#'d SETS
AJ Antawn Jamison 20.00 50.00
AL4 Acie Law 20.00 50.00
BR Bill Russell 500.00 1,000.00
BWR Brandan Wright 20.00 50.00
CA Carmelo Anthony 40.00 100.00
CB Carlos Boozer 30.00 80.00
CBI Chauncey Billups 30.00 60.00
CBO Chris Bosh 50.00 120.00
CP Chris Paul 75.00 200.00
DR Dennis Rodman 75.00 150.00
DW Dwyane Wade 125.00 225.00
DWI Dominique Wilkins 50.00 120.00
GA Gilbert Arenas 40.00 80.00
GO Greg Oden 20.00 50.00
JW Jerry West 75.00 150.00
LB Larry Bird 125.00 250.00
MJ Magic Johnson 75.00 150.00
MM Mike Miller 20.00 50.00
NY Nick Young 25.00 60.00
PP Paul Pierce 100.00 200.00
RA Ray Allen 50.00 100.00
RB Rick Barry 30.00 60.00
RS Rodney Stuckey 40.00 100.00
TY Thaddeus Young 30.00 80.00
VC Vince Carter 20.00 50.00
YJ Yi Jianlian 30.00 80.00

2007-08 Topps Letterman Patches

STATED PRINT RUN NINE SETS
TOTAL PRINT RUNS 36-99
*REFRACTORS: .5X TO 1.25X BASE HI
REFRACTOR PRINT RUN FIVE SETS
FIVE CARDS FOR EACH LETTER
LPAA Arron Afflalo/63* 8.00 20.00
LPAH Al Horford/63* 6.00 15.00
LPAI Allen Iverson/63* 20.00 40.00
LPAL4 Acie Law/45* 6.00 15.00
LPAS Amare Stoudemire/90* 15.00 30.00

LPBD Baron Davis/45* 10.00 25.00
LPBG Ben Gordon/54* 6.00 15.00
LPBR Bill Russell/63* 15.00 40.00
LPBWR Brandan Wright/54* 6.00 15.00
LPCA Carmelo Anthony/63* 20.00 50.00
LPCB Corey Brewer/54* 6.00 15.00
LPCBO Carlos Boozer/54* 6.00 15.00
LPCP Chris Paul/36* 20.00 40.00
LPDN Dirk Nowitzki/72* 20.00 40.00
LPDR Dennis Rodman/54* 15.00 30.00
LPDW Dominique Wilkins/63* 8.00 20.00
LPDWA Dwyane Wade/36* 20.00 50.00
LPGA Gilbert Arenas/54* 15.00 30.00
LPGO Greg Oden/36* 20.00 40.00
LPJC Javaris Crittenton/90* 6.00 15.00
LPJG Jeff Green/45* 8.00 20.00
LPJW Julian Wright/54* 6.00 15.00
LPJWE Jerry West/36* 20.00 40.00
LPKB Kobe Bryant/54* 25.00 60.00
LPKD Kevin Durant/54* 25.00 60.00
LPKG Kevin Garnett/63* 15.00 40.00
LPLB Larry Bird/45* 20.00 50.00
LPLJ LeBron James/45* 30.00 80.00
LPMA Morris Almond/54* 6.00 15.00
LPMJ Magic Johnson/63* 20.00 40.00
LPMM Mike Miller/54* 6.00 15.00
LPNY Nick Young/45* 6.00 15.00
LPRS Rodney Stuckey/63* 6.00 15.00
LPSN Steve Nash/45* 15.00 30.00
LPSW Sean Williams/72* 6.00 15.00
LPTD Tim Duncan/54* 25.00 50.00
LPWC Wilt Chamberlain/99* 20.00 40.00
LPWCH Wilson Chandler/72* 8.00 20.00
LPYJ Yi Jianlian/72* 8.00 20.00
LPYM Yao Ming/27* 20.00 40.00

2007-08 Topps Letterman Patches Autographs

GROUP C PRINT RUN 33 SETS
GRP.C REF: .6X TO 1.5X BASE HI
GRP.C REF.PRINT RUN 15 SETS
AA Arron Afflalo C/231* 8.00 20.00
AL4 Acie Law C/165* 8.00 20.00
BD Baron Davis C/165* 10.00 25.00
BG Ben Gordon C/198* 8.00 20.00
DW Dominique Wilkins C/231* 15.00 40.00
JC Javaris Crittenton C/333* 8.00 20.00
MA Morris Almond C/198* 8.00 20.00
MM Mike Miller C/198* 10.00 25.00
NY Nick Young C/165* 10.00 25.00
RS Rodney Stuckey C/231* 12.00 30.00
SW Sean Williams C/264* 8.00 20.00
TY Thaddeus Young C/165* 8.00 20.00
WC Wilson Chandler C/264* 12.00 30.00

2007-08 Topps Letterman Patches Jersey Number Autographs

GROUP A PRINT RUN NINE SETS
GROUP B PRINT RUN 75 SETS
*REFRACTORS: .5X TO 1.25X BASE HI
GRP.A REF.PRINT RUN 19 SETS
AA Arron Afflalo B 6.00 15.00
AI Andre Iguodala B 8.00 20.00
AJ Antawn Jamison B 6.00 15.00
AL Acie Law B 6.00 15.00
CB Carlos Boozer B 6.00 15.00
CBI Chauncey Billups B 8.00 20.00
CBO Chris Bosh B 12.00 30.00
DC Daequan Cook B 6.00 15.00
DR Dennis Rodman B 25.00 60.00
MA Morris Almond B 6.00 15.00
NY Nick Young B 10.00 25.00
RB Rick Barry B 10.00 25.00
RF Raymond Felton B 6.00 15.00
RS Rodney Stuckey B 6.00 15.00
SW Sean Williams B 6.00 15.00
YJ Yi Jianlian B 15.00 30.00

2007-08 Topps Letterman Patches Team Logo Autographs

GROUP A PRINT RUN NINE SETS
GROUP B PRINT RUN 75 SETS
*REFRACTORS: .5X TO 1.25X BASE HI
GRP.A REF.PRINT RUN 19 SETS
AI Andre Iguodala B 6.00 15.00
AJ Antawn Jamison B 6.00 15.00
AL Acie Law B 6.00 15.00
BD Baron Davis B 10.00 25.00
CB Carlos Boozer B 6.00 15.00
DC Daequan Cook B 8.00 20.00
DW Dominique Wilkins B 15.00 30.00
MA Morris Almond B 6.00 15.00
NY Nick Young B 10.00 25.00
PP Paul Pierce B 20.00 50.00
RA Ray Allen B 20.00 40.00
RB Rick Barry B 10.00 25.00
RS Rodney Stuckey B 10.00 25.00
SH Spencer Hawes B 6.00 15.00
WC Wilson Chandler B 10.00 25.00

2007-08 Topps Letterman Redemptions

CARDS AVAILABLE VIA REDEMPTION
STATED PRINT RUN 25 SER.#'d SETS
BL Brook Lopez/125* 5.00 12.00
BR Brandon Rush/100* 3.00 8.00
DR Derrick Rose/100* 15.00 40.00
EG Eric Gordon/150* 8.00 20.00
JB Jerryd Bayless/175* 3.00 8.00
KL Kevin Love/100* 12.00 30.00
MB Michael Beasley/175* 4.00 10.00
RW Russell Westbrook/225* 25.00 60.00
DJA D.J. Augustin/200* 4.00 10.00
OJM O.J. Mayo/100* 4.00 10.00

2004-05 Topps Luxury Box

1 Andrei Kirilenko .40 1.00
2 Peja Stojakovic .40 1.00
3 Grant Hill .60 1.50
4 Baron Davis .50 1.25
5 Wally Szczerbiak .40 1.00
6 Ray Allen .75 2.00
7 Shawn Marion .50 1.25
8 Gilbert Arenas .50 1.25
9 Keith Van Horn .40 1.00
10 Eddie Jones .50 1.25
11 Lamar Odom .50 1.25
12 Stephen Jackson .40 1.00
13 Rasheed Wallace .60 1.50
14 Steve Smith .40 1.00
15 Gary Payton .75 2.00
16 Jason Terry .40 1.00
17 Eddy Curry .30 .75
18 Yao Ming 1.25 3.00
19 Kenyon Martin .50 1.25
20 Jason Richardson .50 1.25
21 Bonzi Wells .30 .75
22 Richard Jefferson .40 1.00
23 LeBron James 4.00 10.00
24 Marko Jaric .30 .75
25 Chauncey Billups .60 1.50
26 Jamal Crawford .50 1.25
27 Willie Green .50 1.25
28 Zach Randolph .50 1.25
29 Latrell Sprewell .60 1.50
30 Tim Duncan 1.25 3.00
31 Cuttino Mobley .40 1.00
32 Shaquille O'Neal 2.00 5.00
33 Carlos Arroyo .30 .75
34 Jamaal Tinsley .30 .75
35 Luke Ridnour .40 1.00
36 Kenny Anderson .40 1.00
37 Brad Miller .40 1.00
38 Caron Butler .40 1.00
39 Troy Murphy .30 .75
40 Vince Carter 1.00 2.50
41 Shane Battier .40 1.00
42 Joe Johnson .40 1.00
43 Jason Kapono .30 .75
44 Juwan Howard .40 1.00
45 Zydrunas Ilgauskas .40 1.00
46 Jerry Stackhouse .50 1.25
47 Jamaal Magloire .30 .75
48 Steve Francis .50 1.25
49 Kwame Brown .30 .75
50 Kevin Garnett 1.25 3.00
51 Shareef Abdur-Rahim .50 1.25
52 Tony Parker .75 2.00
53 Marcus Camby .40 1.00
54 Morris Peterson .30 .75
55 Antoine Walker .50 1.25
56 Elton Brand .40 1.00
57 Paul Pierce .75 2.00
58 Jason Kidd .75 2.00
59 Gerald Wallace .40 1.00
60 Jason Williams .40 1.00
61 Dwyane Wade 2.00 5.00
62 Amare Stoudemire .50 1.25
63 T.J. Ford .30 .75
64 Tyson Chandler .40 1.00
65 Alonzo Mourning .60 1.50
66 Dirk Nowitzki 1.25 3.00
67 Allan Houston .50 1.25
68 Andre Miller .40 1.00
69 Glenn Robinson .40 1.00
70 Richard Hamilton .60 1.50
71 Darius Miles .30 .75
72 Mike Dunleavy .30 .75
73 Mike Bibby .50 1.25
74 Tracy McGrady .75 2.00
75 Manu Ginobili 1.00 2.50
76 Jermaine O'Neal .40 1.00
77 Rashard Lewis .40 1.00
78 Corey Maggette .40 1.00
79 Chris Bosh .75 2.00
80 Pau Gasol .75 2.00
81 Carlos Boozer .40 1.00
82 Desmond Mason .40 1.00
83 Antawn Jamison .40 1.00
84 Sam Cassell .40 1.00
85 Al Harrington .40 1.00
86 Steve Nash 1.00 2.50
87 Ricky Davis .40 1.00
88 Chris Andersen .50 1.25
89 Kirk Hinrich .50 1.25
90 Carmelo Anthony 1.00 2.50
91 Ron Mercer .30 .75
92 Ben Wallace .60 1.50
93 Josh Howard .40 1.00
94 Reggie Miller 1.00 2.50
95 Chris Webber .60 1.50
96 Drew Gooden .30 .75
97 Michael Redd .40 1.00
98 Allen Iverson 1.25 3.00
99 Kobe Bryant 4.00 10.00
100 Stephon Marbury .60 1.50
101 Dwight Howard RC 3.00 8.00
102 Emeka Okafor RC .75 2.00
103 Ben Gordon RC 1.00 2.50
104 Shaun Livingston RC 1.00 2.50
105 Devin Harris RC .75 2.00
106 Josh Childress RC .60 1.50
107 Luol Deng RC 1.00 2.50
108 Rafael Araujo RC .60 1.50
109 Andre Iguodala RC 1.50 4.00
110 Luke Jackson RC .60 1.50
111 Andris Biedrins RC .60 1.50
112 Robert Swift RC .60 1.50
113 Sebastian Telfair RC .75 2.00
114 Kris Humphries RC .75 2.00
115 Al Jefferson RC 1.00 2.50
116 Kirk Snyder RC .60 1.50
117 Josh Smith RC 1.00 2.50
118 J.R. Smith RC 1.00 2.50
119 Dorell Wright RC .75 2.00
120 Jameer Nelson RC 1.00 2.50
121 Andres Nocioni RC 1.00 2.50
122 Kevin Martin RC 1.25 3.00
123 Tony Allen RC 1.00 2.50
124 Anderson Varejao RC .75 2.00
125 Nenad Krstic RC .75 2.00
126 Sasha Vujacic RC .75 2.00
127 David Harrison RC .60 1.50
128 Pavel Podkolzin RC .60 1.50
129 Trevor Ariza RC 1.00 2.50
130 Delonte West RC .75 2.00
131 Rick Barry .75 2.00
132 Elgin Baylor 1.00 2.50
133 Larry Bird 4.00 10.00
134 Bob Cousy 1.50 4.00
135 Bill Russell 1.50 4.00
136 Walt Frazier 1.25 3.00
137 George Gervin 1.00 2.50
138 John Havlicek 1.00 2.50
139 James Worthy 1.25 3.00
140 Wilt Chamberlain 2.00 5.00
141 Dave Cowens .75 2.00
142 Moses Malone 1.00 2.50
143 Kevin McHale 1.25 3.00
144 Earl Monroe 1.00 2.50
145 Pete Maravich 1.50 4.00
146 Willis Reed 1.50 4.00
147 Oscar Robertson 2.00 5.00
148 Isiah Thomas 1.50 4.00
149 Bill Walton 1.00 2.50
150 Kareem Abdul-Jabbar 1.50 4.00

2004-05 Topps Luxury Box Season Tickets

*SEASON TIX: .6X TO 1.5X BASE HI
*SEASON TIX RC's: .2X TO .5X BASE HI
ONE PER PACK w/o INSERT

2004-05 Topps Luxury Box 300

*BOX 300: .75X TO 2X BASE HI
*BOX 300 RC's: .5X TO 1.25X BASE HI
PRINT RUN 300 SER.#'d SETS
23 LeBron James 40.00 100.00
99 Kobe Bryant 15.00 40.00

2004-05 Topps Luxury Box 100

*BOX 100: 1.5X TO 4X BASE HI
*BOX 100 RC's: 1X TO 2X BASE HI
*BOX 100 RET: 1.5X TO 4X BASE HI
PRINT RUN 100 SER.#'d SETS
23 LeBron James 75.00 200.00
99 Kobe Bryant 30.00 80.00

2004-05 Topps Luxury Box 25

*BOX 25: 4X TO 10X BASE HI
*BOX 25 RCs: 2.5X TO 6X BASE HI
*BOX 25 RET: 2.5X TO 6X BASE HI
PRINT RUN 25 SER.#'d SETS
23 LeBron James 150.00 400.00
99 Kobe Bryant 60.00 150.00

2004-05 Topps Luxury Box and 1

PRINT RUN 450 SER.#'d SETS
*AND 1 200: .5X TO 1.25X BASE JSY HI
*AND 1 75: .6X TO 1.5X BASE JSY HI
*AND 1 30: .75X TO 2X BASE JSY HI
AMDB Melo/Yao/Baron/Brand 8.00 20.00
MIFK Marbury/Al/Francis/Kidd 8.00 20.00
OHIG Okafor/Howard/Iggy/Gordon 8.00 20.00
OWOO Shaq/BigBen/O'Neal/Okafor 8.00 20.00
PJPH Pierce/R-Jeff/Prince/Harring 8.00 20.00

2004-05 Topps Luxury Box Assist Dual Relics

PRINT RUN 350 SER.#'d SETS
*ASSIST 200: .5X TO 1.25X BASE JSY HI
*ASSIST 75: .6X TO 1.5X BASE JSY HI
*ASSIST 30: .75X TO 2X BASE JSY HI
ASAP R.Alston/M.Peterson 3.00 8.00
ASDS B.Davis/J.R.Smith 3.00 8.00
ASGD B.Gordon/L.Deng 8.00 20.00
ASID A.Iverson/S.Dalembert 4.00 10.00
ASJA A.Jamison/G.Arenas 3.00 8.00
ASKJ J.Kidd/R.Jefferson 4.00 10.00
ASLB S.Livingston/E.Brand 3.00 8.00
ASOJ J.O'Neal/F.Jones 3.00 8.00
ASPP G.Payton/P.Pierce 4.00 10.00
ASSN A.Stoudemire/S.Nash 6.00 15.00
ASTN J.Terry/D.Nowitzki 4.00 10.00
ASWW R.Wallace/B.Wallace 3.00 8.00

2004-05 Topps Luxury Box Champagne Toast Autographs

PRINT RUN 100 SER.#'d SETS
*AUTO 75: .5X TO 1.25X BASE AU HI
*AUTO 30: .6X TO 1.5X BASE AU HI
BW Ben Wallace 40.00 100.00
EO Emeka Okafor 12.00 30.00
RH Richard Hamilton 20.00 50.00
SO Shaquille O'Neal 75.00 200.00
TD Tim Duncan 600.00 1,200.00

2004-05 Topps Luxury Box Lay-Up Relics

PRINT RUN 500 SER.#'d SETS
*LAY UP 200: .4X TO 1X BASE JSY HI
*LAY UP 75: .5X TO 1.25X BASE JSY HI
*LAY UP 30: .6X TO 1.5X BASE JSY HI
AI Andre Iguodala 4.00 10.00
AJ Antawn Jamison 2.00 5.00
AK Andrei Kirilenko 2.00 5.00
AS Amare Stoudemire 2.50 6.00
AW Antoine Walker 2.50 6.00
BD Baron Davis 2.50 6.00
CA Carmelo Anthony 5.00 12.00
DH Dwight Howard 8.00 20.00
EB Elton Brand 2.00 5.00
EO Emeka Okafor 2.00 5.00
GP Gary Payton 4.00 10.00
JO Jermaine O'Neal 2.00 5.00
JS Jerry Stackhouse 2.50 6.00
KG Kevin Garnett 6.00 15.00
KM Kenyon Martin 2.50 6.00
NK Nenad Krstic 2.00 5.00
PG Pau Gasol 4.00 10.00
PP Paul Pierce 4.00 10.00
PS Peja Stojakovic 2.00 5.00
RH Richard Hamilton 3.00 8.00
SF Steve Francis 2.50 6.00
SL Shaun Livingston 2.50 6.00
SM Stephon Marbury 3.00 8.00
SO Shaquille O'Neal 10.00 25.00
ST Sebastian Telfair 2.00 5.00
TD Tim Duncan 6.00 15.00
TM Tracy McGrady 4.00 10.00
YM Yao Ming 6.00 15.00
AIV Allen Iverson 6.00 15.00
JRS J.R. Smith 2.50 6.00

2004-05 Topps Luxury Box Lay-Up Relics Autographs

PRINT RUN 15 SER.#'d SETS
SO Shaquille O'Neal 75.00 150.00
TD Tim Duncan 100.00 200.00
TM Tracy McGrady 40.00 100.00

2004-05 Topps Luxury Box Pre-Production

COMPLETE SET (6) 2.00 5.00
PP1 Emeka Okafor .40 1.00
PP2 Sebastian Telfair .40 1.00
PP3 Shaun Livingston .50 1.25
PP4 Shaquille O'Neal 2.00 5.00
PP5 Tracy McGrady .75 2.00
PP6 Carmelo Anthony 1.00 2.50

2004-05 Topps Luxury Box Red Carpet Autographs

PRINT RUN 135 SER.#'d SETS
*AUTO 75: .5X TO 1.2X BASE AU HI
*AUTO 30: .6X TO 1.5X BASE AU HI
AB Andris Biedrins 2.50 6.00
AV Anderson Varejao 3.00 8.00
BG Ben Gordon 4.00 10.00
BU Beno Udrih 3.00 8.00
CD Chris Duhon 3.00 8.00
EO Emeka Okafor 3.00 8.00
JC Josh Childress 2.50 6.00
JN Jameer Nelson 4.00 10.00
JR Justin Reed 2.50 6.00
JS Josh Smith 4.00 10.00
JV Jackson Vroman 2.50 6.00
KH Kris Humphries 3.00 8.00
KM Kevin Martin 5.00 12.00
LC Lionel Chalmers 3.00 8.00
LD Luol Deng 4.00 10.00
PP Pavel Podkolzin 2.50 6.00
RA Rafael Araujo 2.50 6.00
RS Romain Sato 2.50 6.00
SL Shaun Livingston 4.00 10.00
ST Sebastian Telfair 3.00 8.00
TA Tony Allen 4.00 10.00
DEH Devin Harris 3.00 8.00
DHA David Harrison 2.50 6.00
DWE Delonte West 3.00 8.00
DWR Dorell Wright 3.00 8.00
JRS J.R. Smith 4.00 10.00

2004-05 Topps Luxury Box Red Carpet Legends Autographs

PRINT RUN 30 SER.#'d SETS
BL Bob Lanier 15.00 40.00
BW Bill Walton 15.00 40.00
CD Clyde Drexler 40.00 80.00
DB Dave Bing 50.00 100.00
DS Detlef Schrempf 15.00 40.00
EB Elgin Baylor 20.00 50.00
GG George Gervin 15.00 40.00
GK George Karl 15.00 40.00
ME Mark Eaton 20.00 50.00
MM Moses Malone 20.00 50.00
RB Rick Barry 20.00 50.00
RP Robert Parish 30.00 80.00

2004-05 Topps Luxury Box Signs of Luxury

PRINT RUN 100 SER.#'d SETS
*SIGS 75: .6X TO 1.5X BASE AU HI
*SIGS 30: .75X TO 2X BASE AU HI
AS Amare Stoudemire 12.50 30.00
BD Baron Davis 6.00 15.00
CA Carmelo Anthony 15.00 40.00
FJ Fred Jones 6.00 15.00
JK Jason Kidd 12.50 30.00
JO Jermaine O'Neal 6.00 15.00
LO Lamar Odom 6.00 15.00
PS Peja Stojakovic 6.00 15.00
RA Rafer Alston 15.00 40.00
TM Tracy McGrady 15.00 40.00
STM Stephon Marbury 6.00 15.00

2004-05 Topps Luxury Box Three-Point Play Relics

PRINT RUN 450 SER.#'d SETS
*RELICS 200: .5X TO 1.25X BASE HI
*RELICS 75: .6X TO 1.5X BASE HI
*RELICS 30: .75X TO 2X BASE HI
AMM Carmelo/K-Mart/A.Miller 8.00 20.00
AWJ T.Allen/D.West/Big Al 4.00 10.00
DSM B.Davis/J.R.Smith/Magloire 4.00 10.00
GCS Garnett/Cassell/Spree 6.00 15.00
HFM D.Howard/Francis/Mobley 5.00 12.00
IID Iguodala/Iverson/Dalembert 5.00 12.00
KBA Kirilenko/Boozer/Arroyo 4.00 10.00
KMJ Kidd/Mourning/Jefferson 6.00 15.00
OBV Odom/Butler/Vujacic 4.00 10.00
OJW Shaq/E.Jones/D.Wright 8.00 20.00
RAT Randolph/Shareef/Telfair 4.00 10.00
WSC Walker/JoshSmith/Childress 6.00 15.00
WWH B.Wallace/R.Wallace/Rip 6.00 15.00

2004-05 Topps Luxury Box Triple Threat Relics

PRINT RUN 450 SER.#'d SETS
*RELICS 200: .5X TO 1.25X BASE HI
*RELICS 75: .6X TO 1.5X BASE HI
*RELICS 30: .75X TO 2X BASE HI
ALK Shareef/R.Lewis/Kirilenko 4.00 10.00
CJM Childress/E.Jones/Mobley 4.00 10.00
DJD Deng/L.Jackson/Delfino 4.00 10.00
HBF Hinrich/Billups/Ford 4.00 10.00
HES Harris/Emmett/J.R.Smith 4.00 10.00
JBS Big Al/Bosh/Sweetney 4.00 10.00
JIA Big Al/Igoudala/Araujo 5.00 12.00
KAG Kirilenko/Carmelo/Garnett 8.00 20.00
MCA A.Miller/Cassell/Arroyo 4.00 10.00
MND Yao/Dirk/Duncan 6.00 15.00
RMM J-Rich/Marion/Maggette 4.00 10.00
WJH Walker/Jamison/Hill 4.00 10.00

2005-06 Topps Luxury Box

COMP.SET w/o SP's (100) 20.00 50.00
101-145 RC PRINT RUN 999 SER.#'d SETS
1 Dwyane Wade .75 2.00
2 Joe Johnson .30 .75
3 Larry Hughes .30 .75
4 Michael Finley .40 1.00
5 Josh Howard .30 .75
6 Kenyon Martin .30 .75
7 Jermaine O'Neal .30 .75
8 Luke Ridnour .30 .75
9 Andre Iguodala .40 1.00
10 Wally Szczerbiak .30 .75
11 Yao Ming .75 2.00
12 Dwight Howard .50 1.25
13 Ricky Davis .30 .75
14 Baron Davis .40 1.00
15 Carmelo Anthony .60 1.50
16 Pau Gasol .60 1.50
17 Robert Horry .40 1.00
18 Andres Nocioni .25 .60
19 Sam Cassell .30 .75
20 Shareef Abdur-Rahim .40 1.00
21 Gerald Wallace .30 .75
22 Vince Carter .75 2.00
23 LeBron James 3.00 8.00
24 Richard Hamilton .50 1.25
25 Shawn Marion .30 .75
26 Stephon Marbury .50 1.25
27 Chris Bosh .50 1.25
28 Darius Miles .25 .60
29 Jamaal Magloire .25 .60
30 Kevin Garnett 1.00 2.50
31 Lamar Odom .30 .75
32 Shaquille O'Neal 1.25 3.00
33 Allen Iverson .75 2.00
34 Paul Pierce .60 1.50
35 Keith Van Horn .30 .75
36 Damon Stoudamire .40 1.00
37 Jason Richardson .40 1.00
38 Ben Gordon .30 .75
39 J.R. Smith .40 1.00
40 Brad Miller .30 .75
41 Dirk Nowitzki 1.00 2.50
42 Bonzi Wells .25 .60
43 Corey Maggette .30 .75
44 Tracy McGrady .60 1.50
45 T.J. Ford .25 .60
46 Steve Francis .40 1.00
47 Bobby Simmons .25 .60
48 Eddy Curry .25 .60
49 Antawn Jamison .30 .75
50 Emeka Okafor .30 .75
51 Tim Duncan 1.00 2.50
52 Chauncey Billups .50 1.25
53 Kwame Brown .25 .60
54 Ray Allen .60 1.50
55 Jason Kidd .60 1.50
56 Marcus Camby .30 .75
57 Stephen Jackson .30 .75
58 Rasheed Wallace .40 1.00
59 Rashard Lewis .30 .75
60 Sebastian Telfair .30 .75
61 Manu Ginobili .75 2.00
62 Kurt Thomas .25 .60
63 Jamal Crawford .40 1.00
64 Jamaal Tinsley .25 .60
65 Donyell Marshall .25 .60
66 Chris Webber .50 1.25
67 Peja Stojakovic .30 .75
68 P.J. Brown .25 .60
69 Nenad Krstic .25 .60
70 Ben Wallace .50 1.25
71 Grant Hill .60 1.50
72 Elton Brand .30 .75
73 Zach Randolph .40 1.00
74 Josh Smith .30 .75
75 Samuel Dalembert .25 .60
76 Andre Miller .30 .75
77 Al Jefferson .25 .60
78 Caron Butler .30 .75
79 Shaun Livingston .30 .75
80 Richard Jefferson .30 .75
81 Rafer Alston .30 .75
82 Antoine Walker .30 .75
83 Zydrunas Ilgauskas .30 .75
84 Morris Peterson .25 .60
85 Marko Jaric .25 .60
86 Steve Nash .75 2.00
87 Kirk Hinrich .30 .75
88 Kobe Bryant 3.00 8.00
89 Eddie Jones .30 .75
90 Luol Deng .30 .75
91 Ron Artest .30 .75
92 Desmond Mason .25 .60
93 Jason Terry .30 .75
94 Andrei Kirilenko .30 .75
95 Michael Redd .30 .75
96 Mehmet Okur .25 .60
97 Mike Dunleavy .25 .60
98 Mike Bibby .40 1.00
99 Amare Stoudemire .40 1.00
100 Gilbert Arenas .40 1.00
101 Daniel Ewing RC 1.00 2.50
102 Andray Blatche RC 1.25 3.00
103 Jose Calderon RC 1.25 3.00
104 Shavlik Randolph RC .75 2.00
105 Travis Diener RC .75 2.00
106 Brandon Bass RC 1.00 2.50
107 Fabricio Oberto RC 1.00 2.50
108 Ryan Gomes RC 1.00 2.50
109 Gerald Fitch RC .75 2.00
110 James Singleton RC .75 2.00
111 Deron Williams RC 2.00 5.00
112 Gerald Green RC 1.25 3.00
113 C.J. Miles RC 1.00 2.50
114 Chris Paul RC 6.00 15.00
115 Julius Hodge RC .75 2.00
116 Salim Stoudamire RC 1.00 2.50
117 Raymond Felton RC 1.00 2.50
118 Nate Robinson RC 1.25 3.00
119 Sarunas Jasikevicius RC 1.25 3.00
120 Monta Ellis RC 1.50 4.00
121 Jarrett Jack RC 1.25 3.00
122 Orien Greene RC 1.00 2.50
123 Rashad McCants RC .75 2.00
124 Francisco Garcia RC .75 2.00
125 Antoine Wright RC 1.00 2.50
126 Luther Head RC .75 2.00
127 Martell Webster RC 1.00 2.50
128 Eddie Basden RC .75 2.00
129 Marvin Williams RC 1.25 3.00
130 Danny Granger RC 1.25 3.00
131 Charlie Villanueva RC 1.00 2.50
132 Hakim Warrick RC 1.00 2.50
133 Ike Diogu RC .75 2.00
134 Wayne Simien RC .75 2.00
135 Yaroslav Korolev RC .75 2.00
136 David Lee RC 1.25 3.00
137 Sean May RC .75 2.00
138 Linas Kleiza RC 1.00 2.50
139 Joey Graham RC 1.00 2.50
140 Jason Maxiell RC 1.00 2.50
141 Andrew Bogut RC 1.50 4.00
142 Channing Frye RC 1.00 2.50
143 Andrew Bynum RC 1.00 2.50
144 Martynas Andriuskevicius RC .75 2.00
145 Johan Petro RC .75 2.00
146 Christie Brinkley 1.50 4.00
147 Jenny McCarthy 1.50 4.00
148 Shannon Elizabeth 1.50 4.00
149 Carmen Electra 1.50 4.00
150 Jay-Z 2.00 5.00

2005-06 Topps Luxury Box Season Ticket

*SEASON TICKET: .5X TO 1.25X BASE HI
STATED ODDS ONE PER PACK

2005-06 Topps Luxury Box 430

*BOX 430: .5X TO 1.25X BASE HI
150 Jay-Z 6.00 15.00

2005-06 Topps Luxury Box 350

*BOX 350: .6X TO 1.5X BASE HI
PRINT RUN 350 SER.#'d SETS
150 Jay-Z 6.00 15.00

2005-06 Topps Luxury Box 200

*BOX 200: .75X TO 2X BASE HI
PRINT RUN 200 SER.#'d SETS
150 Jay-Z 8.00 20.00

2005-06 Topps Luxury Box 100

*BOX 100 VETS: 1.5X TO 4X BASE HI
*BOX 100 RCs: .75X TO 2X BASE HI
PRINT RUN 100 SER.#'d SETS
150 Jay-Z 10.00 25.00

2005-06 Topps Luxury Box 25

*1-100 BOX 25: 3X TO 8X BASE HI
*101-145 BOX 25: 2X TO 5X BASE HI
*146-150 BOX 25: 4X TO 10X BASE HI
PRINT RUN 25 SER.#'d SETS
150 Jay-Z 25.00 60.00

2005-06 Topps Luxury Box 4 on 2 Break 8 Relics

PRINT RUN 90 SER.#'d SETS
*RELIC 25: .6X TO 1.5X BASE REL.HI
1 Jay-Z/NBA Stars 75.00 200.00
2 Jay-Z/NBA Guards 75.00 200.00
3 Jay-Z/NBA Stars 75.00 200.00
4 NBA Stars 25.00 60.00
5 Al/Wade/05 Draft Class 15.00 40.00
6 Al/Wade/J-Z/05 Draft Class 75.00 200.00
7 Jay-Z/NBA Guards 75.00 200.00
8 Jay-Z/NBA Guards 75.00 200.00
9 NBA Power Forwards 20.00 50.00
10 NBA Forwards 15.00 40.00

2005-06 Topps Luxury Box Box Out Quad Relics

PRINT RUN 193 SER.#'d SETS
*RELIC 25: .5X TO 1.25X BASE HI
1 Atlanta Hawks 5.00 12.00
2 Boston Celtics 8.00 20.00
3 Chicago Bulls 12.50 30.00
4 Cleveland Cavaliers 6.00 15.00
5 Dallas Mavericks 12.50 30.00
6 Denver Nuggets 6.00 15.00
7 Detroit Pistons 15.00 40.00
8 Golden State Warriors 5.00 12.00
9 Houston Rockets 8.00 20.00
10 Indiana Pacers 6.00 15.00
11 Los Angeles Clippers 6.00 15.00
12 Los Angeles Lakers 75.00 200.00
13 Memphis Grizzlies 6.00 15.00
14 Miami Heat 20.00 50.00
15 Milwaukee Bucks 5.00 12.00
16 Minnesota Timberwolves 8.00 20.00
17 New Jersey Nets 20.00 50.00
18 New York Knicks 6.00 15.00
19 New Orleans Hornets 6.00 15.00
20 Philadelphia 76ers 12.50 30.00
21 Phoenix Suns 10.00 25.00
22 Portland Trailblazers 5.00 12.00
23 Sacramento Kings 5.00 12.00
24 San Antonio Spurs 12.50 30.00
25 Seattle Supersonics 8.00 20.00
26 Toronto Raptors 6.00 15.00
27 Utah Jazz 5.00 12.00
28 Washington Wizards 6.00 15.00
29 Charlotte Bobcats 5.00 12.00
30 Orlando Magic 6.00 15.00
31 Celebrities 20.00 50.00
32 Jay-Z/Shaq/Ben/Yao 75.00 200.00
33 KG/Marion/Okafor/Ben 6.00 15.00
34 Bogut/Villan/Frye/Ike 5.00 12.00
35 Bynum/May/Warrk/Green 5.00 12.00
36 Jay-Z/Al/Wade/Melo 75.00 200.00
37 Duncan/Shaq/Al/Nash 12.50 30.00
38 Brand/Deng/Magg/Hill 6.00 15.00
39 Iggy/Frye/Arenas/R-Jeff 5.00 12.00
40 Okafor/Rip/Allen/Gordon 6.00 15.00

2005-06 Topps Luxury Box Box Seats Autographs

PRINT RUNS LISTED IN CHECKLIST
*PARALLEL 25: .6X TO 1.5X BASE HI
PARALLEL PRINT RUN 25 SETS
AB Andrew Bogut/124 10.00 25.00
AI Allen Iverson/224 40.00 100.00
CB Christie Brinkley/74 30.00 80.00
CE Carmen Electra/74 8.00 20.00
DE Daniel Ewing/624 5.00 12.00
DW Dwyane Wade/224 20.00 50.00
EO Emeka Okafor/224 6.00 15.00
JJ Jarrett Jack/44 5.00 12.00
OG Orien Greene/624 5.00 12.00
RF Raymond Felton/424 8.00 20.00
SE Shannon Elizabeth/74 30.00 80.00
SL Shaun Livingston/124 5.00 12.00
SO Shaquille O'Neal/74 30.00 80.00
VC Vince Carter/224 15.00 40.00

2005-06 Topps Luxury Box Divisions 6 Relics

PRINT RUN 192 SER.#'d SETS
*RELIC 25: .5X TO 1.25X BASE REL.HI
1 2005 NBA Draft Class 8.00 20.00
2 NBA Guards 75.00 200.00
3 NBA Centers 12.50 30.00
4 NBA Forwards 12.50 30.00
5 High School Draftees 75.00 200.00
6 NBA Guards 8.00 20.00
7 NBA Forwards 12.50 30.00
8 NBA Point Guards 12.50 30.00
9 NBA Power Forwards 10.00 25.00
10 Top NBA Shooters 8.00 20.00
11 NBA Point Guards 10.00 25.00
12 Foreign NBA Forwards 10.00 25.00
13 NBA Forward/Centers 6.00 15.00
14 ACC Players 10.00 25.00
15 NBA Forward/Centers 8.00 20.00
16 2005 NBA Draft Class 8.00 20.00
17 NBA Swing Men 8.00 20.00
18 NBA Point Guards 8.00 20.00
19 NBA Guards 15.00 40.00
20 NBA Power Forwards 10.00 25.00

2005-06 Topps Luxury Box Industry Anchors

COMMON IVERSON (1-9) 1.50 4.00
COMMON WADE (1-9) 2.50 6.00
COMMON JAY-Z (1-8) 2.50 6.00
AI/WADE PRINT RUN 599 SER.#'d SETS
JAY-Z PRINT RUN 100 SER.#'d SETS
*RELICS: 1X TO 2.5X BASE HI
RELIC PRINT RUN 279 SER.#'d SETS
JZ1 Jay-Z 75.00 200.00

2005-06 Topps Luxury Box Industry Anchors Relics Dual

PRINT RUN 99 SER.#'d SETS
IW A.Iverson/D.Wade 10.00 25.00
IZ A.Iverson/Jay-Z 75.00 200.00
WZ D.Wade/Jay-Z 100.00 250.00

2005-06 Topps Luxury Box Industry Anchors Relics Triple

IWZ A.Iverson/D.Wade/Jay-Z 125.00 300.00

2005-06 Topps Luxury Box One-on-One Autographs Dual

PRINT RUN 25 SER.#'d SETS
BO A.Bogut/S.O'Neal 75.00 150.00
WI D.Wade/A.Iverson 125.00 250.00
WW D.Williams/D.Wade 75.00 150.00

2005-06 Topps Luxury Box One Man Show Autographs

PRINT RUNS LISTED IN CHECKLIST
*PARALLEL 25: .6X TO 1.5X BASE HI
PARALLEL PRINT RUN 25 SETS
AI Allen Iverson/124 40.00 100.00
AJ Amir Johnson/449 4.00 10.00
AW Antoine Wright/426 4.00 10.00
BB Brandon Bass/724 5.00 12.00
DL David Lee/559 6.00 15.00
DW Dwyane Wade/124 20.00 50.00
FG Francisco Garcia/1121 4.00 10.00
FO Fabricio Oberto/724 4.00 10.00
ID Ike Diogu/67 5.00 12.00
JG Joey Graham/724 4.00 10.00
MW Martell Webster/124 4.00 10.00
RW Robert Whaley/167 4.00 10.00
SO Shaquille O'Neal/74 30.00 75.00
VC Vince Carter/124 15.00 40.00
DWI Deron Williams/124 10.00 25.00

2005-06 Topps Luxury Box One Man Show Relics

PRINT RUN 225 SER.#'d SETS
*RELIC 25: .75X TO 2X BASE HI
*RELIC 25 PRINT RUN 25 SETS
RELIC 1 NOT PRICED DUE TO SCARICTY
AI Allen Iverson 5.00 12.00
AK Andrei Kirilenko 2.00 5.00
AS Amare Stoudemire 2.50 6.00
AW Antoine Walker 2.00 5.00
BG Ben Gordon 2.00 5.00
CA Carmelo Anthony 4.00 10.00
CM Corey Maggette 2.00 5.00
CP Chris Paul 8.00 20.00
DM Desmond Mason 2.00 5.00
DN Dirk Nowitzki 6.00 15.00
DW Dwyane Wade 5.00 12.00
GA Gilbert Arenas 2.50 6.00
GG Gerald Green 2.50 6.00
HW Hakim Warrick 2.00 5.00
ID Ike Diogu 1.50 4.00
JC Josh Childress 1.50 4.00
JJ Joe Johnson 2.00 5.00
JS Jerry Stackhouse 2.00 5.00
JT Jamaal Tinsley 2.00 5.00
JZ Jay-Z 4.00 10.00
KB Kobe Bryant 40.00 100.00
KG Kevin Garnett 6.00 15.00
LJ Luke Jackson 2.00 5.00
LR Luke Ridnour 2.00 5.00
MG Manu Ginobili 5.00 12.00
MP Morris Peterson 1.50 4.00
MR Michael Redd 2.00 5.00
MW Martell Webster 2.00 5.00
PP Paul Pierce 4.00 10.00
PS Peja Stojakovic 2.00 5.00
RA Ray Allen 4.00 10.00
RF Raymond Felton 2.00 5.00
RH Robert Horry 3.00 8.00
RJ Richard Jefferson 2.00 5.00
RW Rasheed Wallace 2.50 6.00
SF Steve Francis 2.50 6.00
SL Shaun Livingston 2.00 5.00
SM Stephon Marbury 3.00 8.00
ST Sebastian Telfair 2.00 5.00
TM Tracy McGrady 4.00 10.00
TP Tony Parker 4.00 10.00
VC Vince Carter 5.00 12.00
AIG Andre Iguodala 2.50 6.00
DWI Deron Williams 4.00 10.00
JSM Josh Smith 2.00 5.00
JTE Jason Terry 2.00 5.00
SAR Shareef Abdur-Rahim 2.50 6.00
SMA Shawn Marion 2.00 5.00
J.R. Jason Richardson 2.50 6.00
J.R.S J.R. Smith 2.50 6.00

2005-06 Topps Luxury Box One on One Dual Relics

PRINT RUN 225 SER.#'d SET
*RELIC 25: .5X TO 1.25X BASE HI
AP C.Anthony/P.Pierce 5.00 12.00
AW R.Allen/B.Wells 4.00 10.00
BB K.Bryant/B.Bowen 40.00 100.00
BC E.Boykins/S.Cassell 4.00 10.00
BS K.Brown/S.Swift 4.00 10.00
CG M.Camby/P.Gasol 4.00 10.00
DG L.Deng/F.Garcia 4.00 10.00
DM T.Duncan/Y.Ming 5.00 12.00
FK C.Frye/N.Krstic 4.00 10.00
GB B.Gordon/C.Billups 5.00 12.00
HF J.Hodge/R.Felton 4.00 10.00
HM R.Hamilton/R.McCants 4.00 10.00
IF A.Iverson/S.Francis 6.00 15.00
JB A.Jamison/E.Brand 4.00 10.00
JP R.Jefferson/T.Prince 4.00 10.00
LW R.Lewis/R.Wallace 4.00 10.00

MG T.McGrady/M.Ginobili 5.00 12.00
MV J.Magloire/A.Varejao 4.00 10.00
NW A.Nocioni/A.Wright 4.00 10.00
OH E.Okafor/D.Howard 4.00 10.00
PC P.Pierce/V.Carter 5.00 12.00
PW C.Paul/D.Williams 6.00 15.00
RB Q.Richardson/C.Butler 4.00 10.00
SG A.Stoudemire/K.Garnett 6.00 15.00
TD J.Terry/B.Davis 4.00 10.00
TW K.Thomas/H.Warrick 4.00 10.00
WI D.Wade/A.Iguodala 5.00 12.00
WO B.Wallace/S.O'Neal 6.00 15.00
WT J.Williams/J.Tinsley 4.00 10.00
WW A.Walker/C.Webber 4.00 10.00

2005-06 Topps Luxury Box Stat Sheet 7 Relics

PRINT RUN 140 SER.#'d SETS
*RELIC 25: .5X TO 1.25X BASE REL.HI
1 Al/KG/Nash/Kirk+3 12.50 30.00
2 Kobe/Al/T-Mac/Wade+3 75.00 200.00
3 Dirk/Duncan/Al/Amare+3 12.50 30.00
4 Amare/Kobe/Al+4 75.00 200.00
5 T-Mac/Al/Steph+4 12.50 30.00
6 Shaq/T-Mac/Pierce+4 12.50 30.00
7 Vince/Shaq/Kobe+4 75.00 200.00
8 Wade/Brand/Pierce+4 12.50 30.00
9 Dirk/Wade/Yao/Manu+3 15.00 40.00
10 Hinrich/Wade/Dirk+4 15.00 40.00
11 Shaq/Brand/Melo+4 12.50 30.00
12 Al/Kobe/T-Mac/Vince+3 75.00 200.00
13 KG/Marion/Shaq+4 15.00 40.00
14 Nash/Kidd/Steph/Al+3 15.00 40.00
15 AK47/Duncan/Shaq+4 15.00 40.00
16 Al/Marion/T-Mac+4 12.50 30.00
17 Al/T-Mac/Kobe/Steph+3 75.00 200.00
18 Al/Wade/Pierce/Kobe+3 75.00 200.00
19 2005 NBA Draft Class 20.00 50.00
20 2005 NBA Draft Class 20.00 50.00

2005-06 Topps Luxury Box The Machine Autographs

PRINT RUNS LISTED IN CHECKLIST
PARALLEL 25: .6X TO 1.5X BASE HI
PARALLEL PRINT RUN 25 SETS
AB Andrew Bogut/224 8.00 20.00
AI Allen Iverson/224 50.00 120.00
AN Andres Nocioni/349 5.00 12.00
BW Bracey Wright/167 5.00 12.00
CA Carmelo Anthony/74 15.00 40.00
CV Charlie Villanueva/441 6.00 15.00
DW Dwyane Wade/224 30.00 60.00
EO Emeka Okafor/224 6.00 15.00
HW Hakim Warrick/1192 5.00 12.00
JH Julius Hodge/474 5.00 12.00
JM Jason Maxiell/474 5.00 12.00
JP Johan Petro/124 5.00 12.00
NK Nenad Krstic/388 5.00 12.00
SJ Sarunas Jasikevicius/224 5.00 12.00
SM Sean May/474 5.00 12.00
SO Shaquille O'Neal/74 35.00 75.00
VC Vince Carter/124 15.00 40.00
ABY Andrew Bynum/116 20.00 50.00

2005-06 Topps Luxury Box The Machine Relics

PRINT RUN 225 SER.#'d SETS
*RELIC 25: .75X TO 2X BASE REL.HI
RELIC 25 PRINT RUN 25 SETS
AB Andrew Bogut 3.00 8.00
AH Al Harrington 2.00 5.00
AJ Al Jefferson 1.50 4.00
AN Andres Nocioni 2.00 5.00
AV Anderson Varejao 1.50 4.00
AW Antoine Wright 2.00 5.00
BB Brandon Bass 2.00 5.00
BD Baron Davis 2.50 6.00
BW Ben Wallace 3.00 8.00
CB Carlos Boozer 2.00 5.00
CF Channing Frye 2.00 5.00
CV Charlie Villanueva 2.00 5.00
CW Chris Webber 3.00 8.00
DG Drew Gooden 2.00 5.00
DH Dwight Howard 3.00 8.00
EB Elton Brand 2.00 5.00
EO Emeka Okafor 2.00 5.00
JF Jeff Foster 2.00 5.00
JH Josh Howard 2.00 5.00
JJ Jarrett Jack 2.50 6.00
JK Jason Kidd 4.00 10.00
JM Jamaal Magloire 2.00 5.00
JO Jermaine O'Neal 2.00 5.00
KH Kirk Hinrich 2.00 5.00
KM Kenyon Martin 2.00 5.00
KT Kurt Thomas 2.00 5.00
LO Lamar Odom 2.00 5.00
MB Mike Bibby 2.50 6.00
MC Marcus Camby 2.00 5.00
NR Nate Robinson 2.50 6.00
PG Pau Gasol 4.00 10.00
RH Richard Hamilton 3.00 8.00
RL Rashard Lewis 2.00 5.00
RM Rashad McCants 1.50 4.00
SD Samuel Dalembert 2.00 5.00
SM Sean May 1.50 4.00
SN Steve Nash 5.00 12.00
SO Shaquille O'Neal 8.00 20.00
TD Tim Duncan 6.00 15.00
TR Theo Ratliff 2.00 5.00
YM Yao Ming 5.00 12.00
ABY Andrew Bynum 2.00 5.00
AJA Antawn Jamison 2.00 5.00
BBA Brent Barry 2.00 5.00
BBO Bruce Bowen 2.00 5.00
CBI Chauncey Billups 3.00 8.00
CBO Chris Bosh 3.00 8.00
CBU Caron Butler 2.00 5.00
CDU Chris Duhon 2.00 5.00
KVH Keith Van Horn 2.00 5.00

2005-06 Topps Luxury Box Trinity Triple Relics

PRINT RUN 250 SER.#'d SETS
*RELIC 25: .5X TO 1.25X BASE HI
RELIC 25 PRINT RUN 25 SETS
ABS Abdur-Rahim/Bibby/Stojakovic 5.00 12.00
BAM Boykins/Anthony/Martin 6.00 15.00
BBO Bynum/Bryant/Odom 40.00 100.00
BMI Bryant/McGrady/Iverson 60.00 150.00
BML Brand/Maggette/Livingston 5.00 12.00
BMR Bogut/Mason/Redd 5.00 12.00
CKJ Carter/Kidd/Jefferson 8.00 20.00
DDD Wade/Wade/Wade 15.00 40.00
DKI Dalembert/Korver/Iverson 6.00 15.00
DOI Duncan/O'Neal/Iverson 10.00 25.00
DRT Davis/Richardson/Taft 6.00 15.00
FMM Felton/May/McCants 5.00 12.00
FMR Frye/Marbury/Richardson 5.00 12.00
GJM Garnett/Jaric/McCants 5.00 12.00
GJP Green/Jefferson/Pierce 5.00 12.00
HBB Horry/Bowen/Barry 5.00 12.00
HFH Hill/Francis/Howard 6.00 15.00
HGN Hinrich/Gordon/Nocioni 8.00 20.00
HIG Hughes/Ilgauskas/Gooden 5.00 12.00
JBA Jamison/Butler/Arenas 5.00 12.00
KPI Kidd/Pierce/Iverson 8.00 20.00
MAI Marbury/Arenas/Iverson 6.00 15.00
MFO May/Felton/Okafor 5.00 12.00
MMS McGrady/Ming/Swift 6.00 15.00
NSM Nash/Stoudemire/Marion 8.00 20.00
OBM O'Neal/Bogut/Ming 6.00 15.00
OGA O'Neal/Granger/Artest 5.00 12.00
PBS Paul/Bass/Smith 6.00 15.00
PGD Parker/Ginobili/Duncan 10.00 25.00
RAL Ridnour/Allen/Lewis 5.00 12.00
RWT Ratliff/Webster/Telfair 5.00 12.00
SCJ Smith/Childress/Johnson 5.00 12.00
TND Terry/Nowitzki/Daniels 8.00 20.00
VGB Villanueva/Graham/Bosh 6.00 15.00
WAB Wade/Anthony/Bosh 10.00 25.00
WGA Wade/Gordon/Allen 6.00 15.00
WGJ Warrick/Gasol/Jones 5.00 12.00
WHD Wade/Hamilton/Davis 8.00 20.00
WHO Wade/O'Neal/Haslem 12.50 30.00
WHT Wade/Hinrich/Terry 8.00 20.00
WII Webber/Iguodala/Iverson 6.00 15.00
WKO Williams/Kirilenko/Okur 5.00 12.00
WMB Wade/McGrady/Bryant 60.00 150.00
WMK Wade/Marbury/Kidd 10.00 25.00
WPF Williams/Paul/Felton 8.00 20.00
WWF Wade/Wade/Felton 8.00 20.00
WWH Wallace/Wallace/Hamilton 10.00 25.00
WWP Williams/Walker/Posey 8.00 20.00
WWW Wade/Walker/Williams 12.50 30.00
WZI Wade/Jay-Z/Felton 60.00 150.00

2005-06 Topps Luxury Box Triple Double 5 Relics

PRINT RUN 193 SER.#'d SETS
*RELIC 25: .5X TO 1.25X BASE HI
RELIC 25 PRINT RUN 25 SETS
1 Toronto Raptors 6.00 15.00
2 Utah Jazz 6.00 15.00
3 Phoenix Suns 12.00 30.00
4 Atlanta Hawks 6.00 15.00
5 Chicago Bulls 10.00 25.00
6 Cleveland Cavaliers 6.00 15.00
7 Dallas Mavericks 10.00 25.00
8 Denver Nuggets 6.00 15.00
9 Detroit Pistons 15.00 40.00
10 Golden State Warriors 6.00 15.00
11 Indiana Pacers 6.00 15.00
12 Los Angeles Clippers 6.00 15.00
13 Miami Heat 15.00 40.00
14 Milwaukee Bucks 6.00 15.00
15 New Jersey Nets 10.00 25.00
16 New York Knicks 6.00 15.00
17 Portland Trailblazers 6.00 15.00
18 Sacramento Kings 6.00 15.00
19 San Antonio Spurs 10.00 25.00
20 Seattle Supersonics 6.00 15.00
21 Washington Wizards 6.00 15.00
22 Boston Celtics 8.00 20.00
23 Charlotte Bobcats 6.00 15.00
24 Houston Rockets 10.00 25.00
25 Los Angeles Lakers 75.00 200.00
26 Memphis Grizzlies 6.00 15.00
27 Minnesota Timberwolves 8.00 20.00
28 New Orleans Hornets 10.00 25.00
29 Orlando Magic 8.00 20.00
30 Philadelphia 76ers 10.00 25.00

2005-06 Topps Luxury Box Two's Company Dual Relics

PRINT RUN 193 SER.#'d SETS
*RELIC 25: .5X TO 1.25X BASE HI
RELIC 25 PRINT RUN 25 SETS
KW A.Kirilenko/D.Williams 5.00 12.00
AJ G.Arenas/A.Jamison 5.00 12.00
AW A.Iverson/C.Webber 10.00 25.00
BB K.Bryant/A.Bynum 40.00 100.00
BR A.Bogut/M.Redd 6.00 15.00
BV C.Bosh/C.Villanueva 5.00 12.00
CM S.Cassell/C.Mobley 5.00 12.00
DG T.Duncan/M.Ginobili 6.00 15.00
DR B.Davis/J.Richardson 5.00 12.00
HG K.Hinrich/B.Gordon 5.00 12.00
FM R.Felton/S.May 6.00 15.00
AM C.Anthony/K.Martin 5.00 12.00
GH D.Gooden/L.Hughes 5.00 12.00
GJ D.Granger/S.Jasikevicius 5.00 12.00
GM K.Garnett/R.McCants 6.00 15.00
GW P.Gasol/H.Warrick 5.00 12.00
HF D.Howard/S.Francis 6.00 15.00
JJ J.Smith/J.Johnson 5.00 12.00
KC J.Kidd/V.Carter 6.00 15.00
LP R.Lewis/J.Petro 5.00 12.00
MF S.Marbury/C.Frye 5.00 12.00
MM T.McGrady/Y.Ming 8.00 20.00
ND D.Nowitzki/M.Daniels 6.00 15.00
NS S.Nash/A.Stoudemire 6.00 15.00
PG P.Pierce/G.Green 5.00 12.00
PS C.Paul/J.R.Smith 6.00 15.00
SA P.Stojakovic/S.Abdur-Rahim 5.00 12.00
TW S.Telfair/M.Webster 5.00 12.00
WO D.Wade/S.O'Neal 12.50 30.00
WW B.Wallace/R.Wallace 8.00 20.00

2006-07 Topps Luxury Box

COMP.SET w/o SP's (50) 20.00 50.00
51-100 RC PRINT RUN 999 SER.#'d SETS
1 Chris Bosh .60 1.50
2 Dirk Nowitzki 1.25 3.00
3 Ben Wallace .60 1.50
4 Mike Bibby .50 1.25
5 Josh Howard .50 1.25
6 Vince Carter 1.00 2.50
7 Andrei Kirilenko .50 1.25
8 Richard Hamilton .50 1.25
9 Tony Parker .75 2.00
10 Dwyane Wade 1.00 2.50
11 Amare Stoudemire .50 1.25
12 Tim Duncan 1.25 3.00
13 Steve Nash 1.00 2.50
14 Dwight Howard .60 1.50
15 Carmelo Anthony .75 2.00
16 Pau Gasol .75 2.00
17 Zach Randolph .50 1.25
18 Kirk Hinrich .40 1.00
19 Stephon Marbury .60 1.50
20 Tracy McGrady .75 2.00
21 Kevin Garnett 1.25 3.00
22 Michael Redd .40 1.00
23 LeBron James 4.00 10.00
24 Kobe Bryant 4.00 10.00
25 Jason Kidd .75 2.00
26 Baron Davis .50 1.25
27 Jermaine O'Neal .50 1.25
28 Ray Allen .75 2.00
29 Joe Johnson .50 1.25
30 Elton Brand .40 1.00
31 Chris Paul 1.00 2.50
32 Shaquille O'Neal 2.00 5.00
33 Allen Iverson 1.25 3.00
34 Paul Pierce .75 2.00
35 Chauncey Billups .60 1.50
36 Gerald Wallace .40 1.00
37 Jason Richardson .50 1.25
38 Yao Ming 1.25 3.00
39 Andre Iguodala .50 1.25
40 Gilbert Arenas .50 1.25
41 Larry Bird 2.50 6.00
42 Isiah Thomas 1.25 3.00
43 Dominique Wilkins 1.25 3.00
44 Moses Malone 1.25 3.00
45 George Gervin 1.25 3.00
46 Chris Mullin .75 2.00
47 Karl Malone 1.00 2.50
48 Bob McAdoo .60 1.50
49 James Worthy .75 2.00
50 Walt Frazier 1.00 2.50
51 J.J. Redick RC 2.50 6.00
52 Tyrus Thomas RC 1.00 2.50
53 Rodney Carney RC .75 2.00
54 Jorge Garbajosa RC .75 2.00
55 Shawne Williams RC .75 2.00
56 Renaldo Balkman RC 1.00 2.50
57 Chris Quinn RC .75 2.00
58 Solomon Jones RC .75 2.00
59 Maurice Ager RC .75 2.00
60 Rudy Gay RC 1.50 4.00
61 Hassan Adams RC .75 2.00
62 Sergio Rodriguez RC 1.00 2.50
63 Dee Brown RC .75 2.00
64 Saer Sene RC .75 2.00
65 Allan Ray RC .75 2.00
66 Damir Markota RC .75 2.00
67 Bobby Jones RC .75 2.00
68 Kyle Lowry RC 4.00 10.00
69 Cedric Simmons RC .75 2.00
70 LaMarcus Aldridge RC 3.00 8.00
71 Mardy Collins RC .75 2.00
72 Daniel Gibson RC 1.00 2.50
73 Patrick O'Bryant RC .75 2.00
74 Josh Boone RC .75 2.00
75 Paul Davis RC .75 2.00
76 Craig Smith RC 1.00 2.50
77 Andrea Bargnani RC 1.00 2.50
78 Alexander Johnson RC .75 2.00
79 James Augustine RC .75 2.00
80 Jordan Farmar RC 1.00 2.50
81 Marcus Vinicius RC .75 2.00
82 Ryan Hollins RC .75 2.00
83 Marcus Williams RC .75 2.00
84 Will Blalock RC .75 2.00
85 Shannon Brown RC .75 2.00
86 Pops Mensah-Bonsu RC .75 2.00
87 P.J. Tucker RC 1.25 3.00
88 Steve Novak RC 1.00 2.50
89 Quincy Douby RC .75 2.00
90 Rajon Rondo RC 4.00 10.00
91 David Noel RC .75 2.00
92 Mile Ilic RC .75 2.00
93 Ronnie Brewer RC 1.25 3.00
94 James White RC .75 2.00
95 Hilton Armstrong RC .75 2.00
96 Randy Foye RC 1.00 2.50
97 Shelden Williams RC .75 2.00
98 Thabo Sefolosha RC 1.00 2.50
99 Brandon Roy RC 2.50 6.00
100 Adam Morrison RC 1.00 2.50

2006-07 Topps Luxury Box Blue

*BLUE: 2X TO 5X BASE HI
PRINT RUN 49 SER.#'d SETS

2006-07 Topps Luxury Box Green

*GREEN: .75X TO 2X BASE HI
PRINT RUN 329 SER.#'d SETS

2006-07 Topps Luxury Box Red

*RED: .6X TO 1.5X BASE HI
STATED PRINT RUN 499 SER.#'d SETS

2006-07 Topps Luxury Box Courtside Relics Dual

PRINT RUN 299 SER.#'d SETS
*BLUE: .5X TO 1.25X BASE HI
BLUE PRINT RUN 49 SER.#'d SETS
*BRONZE: .75X TO 2X BASE HI
BRONZE PRINT RUN 19 SER.#'d SETS
AM A.Miller/R.Carney 3.00 8.00
BB A.Bargnani/C.Bosh 5.00 12.00
BJ C.Butler/A.Jamison 3.00 8.00
BO K.Bryant/L.Odom 40.00 100.00
BO A.Biedrins/P.O'Bryant 4.00 10.00
BP C.Billups/T.Prince 4.00 10.00
DP T.Duncan/T.Parker 5.00 12.00
DS L.Deng/T.Sefolosha 5.00 12.00
GB D.Gooden/S.Brown 3.00 8.00
GJ K.Garnett/M.James 3.00 8.00
GM P.Gasol/M.Miller 3.00 8.00
HH D.Harris/J.Howard 3.00 8.00
HM D.Howard/D.Milicic 3.00 8.00
IA A.Iverson/C.Anthony 5.00 12.00
II A.Iguodala/A.Iverson 4.00 10.00
JK R.Jefferson/N.Krstic 3.00 8.00
KC J.Kidd/V.Carter 5.00 12.00
LA R.Lewis/R.Allen 3.00 8.00
LB S.Livingston/E.Brand 3.00 8.00
MAR B.Miller/R.Artest 3.00 8.00
MC C.Maggette/S.Cassell 4.00 10.00
MF S.Marbury/S.Francis 3.00 8.00
MO D.Miles/T.Outlaw 3.00 8.00
MY T.McGrady/Y.Ming 5.00 12.00
NT D.Nowitzki/J.Terry 4.00 10.00
OF E.Okafor/R.Felton 3.00 8.00
OG J.O'Neal/D.Granger 3.00 8.00
PF M.Peterson/T.Ford 3.00 8.00
PS C.Paul/P.Stojakovic 4.00 10.00
PT P.Pierce/S.Telfair 3.00 8.00
RD J.Richardson/B.Davis 3.00 8.00
SJ J.Smith/J.Johnson 3.00 8.00
SM A.Stoudemire/S.Marion 4.00 10.00
VR C.Villanueva/M.Redd 3.00 8.00
WB L.Walton/A.Bynum 4.00 10.00
WG B.Wallace/B.Gordon 3.00 8.00
WH R.Wallace/R.Hamilton 4.00 10.00
WK D.Williams/A.Kirilenko 3.00 8.00
WM G.Wallace/A.Morrison 5.00 12.00
WO D.Wade/S.O'Neal 6.00 15.00

2006-07 Topps Luxury Box Courtside Relics Triple

PRINT RUN 249 SER.#'d SETS
*BLUE: .5X TO 1.25X BASE HI
BLUE PRINT RUN 49 SER.#'d SETS
*BRONZE: 1.25X TO 3X BASE HI
BRONZE PRINT RUN 19 SER.#'d SETS
ABJ Arenas/Butler/Jamison 5.00 12.00
ACS Allen/Collison/Sene 4.00 10.00
AMB Artest/Martin/Bibby 5.00 12.00
ANI Anthony/Nene/Iverson 8.00 20.00
BDW Billups/Duncan/Wade 6.00 15.00
BGB Bosh/Garbajosa/Bargnani 6.00 15.00
BMM Brand/Maggette/Mobley 4.00 10.00
BOF Bryant/Odom/Farmar 40.00 100.00
BRV Bogut/Redd/Villanueva 4.00 10.00
CKJ Carter/Kidd/Jefferson 8.00 20.00
CWS Childress/Williams/Smith 5.00 12.00
DGN Duncan/Garnett/Nash 8.00 20.00
FOM Felton/Okafor/Morrison 6.00 15.00
GDP Ginobili/Duncan/Parker 8.00 20.00
GDW Gordon/Duhon/Wallace 4.00 10.00
GJF Garnett/Jaric/Foye 4.00 10.00
HHR Hill/Howard/Redick 8.00 20.00
IDM Iguodala/Dalembert/Miller 4.00 10.00
IVH Ilgauskas/Varejao/Hughes 5.00 12.00
JGM Jamison/Gordon/Miller 4.00 10.00
KOB Kirilenko/Okur/Brewer 4.00 10.00
MAW Mutombo/Artest/Wallace 5.00 12.00
MBH McDyess/Billups/Hamilton 6.00 15.00
MFR Marbury/Frye/Robinson 4.00 10.00
MIB McGrady/Iverson/Bryant 40.00 100.00
MJA Miles/Jack/Aldridge 4.00 10.00
MOW Mourning/O'Neal/Wade 10.00 25.00
MSD Marion/Stoudemire/Diaw 5.00 12.00
NHS Nowitzki/Howard/Stackhouse 5.00 12.00
OJT O'Neal/Granger/Tinsley 4.00 10.00
ORB O'Bryant/Richardson/Biedrins 5.00 12.00
PMA Paul/Mason/Armstrong 4.00 10.00
WGS Warrick/Gasol/Stoudamire 4.00 10.00
WJP West/Jefferson/Pierce 4.00 10.00
YMH Ming/McGrady/Head 6.00 15.00

2006-07 Topps Luxury Box Courtside Relics Autographs Dual

PRINT RUN 79 SER.#'d SETS
AG C.Anthony/B.Gordon 25.00 50.00
AR R.Allen/J.Redick 15.00 30.00
BC C.Bosh/V.Carter 30.00 60.00
BG A.Bargnani/J.Garbajosa 30.00 60.00
BJ L.Bird/M.Johnson 200.00 300.00
DW B.Diaw/H.Warrick 10.00 25.00
FB T.Ford/C.Billups 10.00 25.00
FD J.Farmar/Q.Douby 10.00 25.00
HB D.Harris/L.Barbosa 10.00 25.00
JL M.James/K.Lowry 10.00 25.00
KW A.Kirilenko/G.Wallace 10.00 25.00
MR A.Morrison/J.Redick 10.00 25.00
OI J.O'Neal/A.Iguodala 10.00 25.00
OM E.Okafor/A.Morrison 10.00 25.00
SD T.Sefolosha/C.Duhon 10.00 25.00
SW D.Wilkins/J.Smith 15.00 40.00
VB C.Villanueva/A.Bogut 10.00 25.00
WB D.Wade/C.Billups 40.00 80.00
WF L.Walton/C.Frye 12.50 30.00
WW D.Williams/M.Williams 15.00 40.00

2006-07 Topps Luxury Box Courtside Relics Autographs Triple

PRINT RUN 29 SER.#'d SETS
ABW Arenas/Bosh/Wade 100.00 225.00
BJW Billups/Johnson/Wade 50.00 120.00
IFW Iguodala/Frye/Walton 30.00 60.00
WOC Wade/O'Neal/Carter 75.00 150.00

2006-07 Topps Luxury Box Mezzanine Relics

PRINT RUN 349 SER.#'d SETS
*BLUE: .6X TO 1.5X BASE HI
BLUE PRINT RUN 49 SER.#'d SETS
*BRONZE: .75X TO 2X BASE HI
BRONZE PRINT RUN 19 SER.#'d SETS
AB Andrew Bogut 2.00 5.00
ABY Andrew Bynum 1.50 4.00
AJ Antawn Jamison 2.00 5.00
AK Andrei Kirilenko 2.00 5.00
AS Amare Stoudemire 2.50 6.00
BR Brandon Roy 5.00 12.00
BW Ben Wallace 3.00 8.00
CD Chris Duhon 2.00 5.00
CF Channing Frye 1.50 4.00
CP Chris Paul 5.00 12.00
CV Charlie Villanueva 1.50 4.00
CW Chris Webber 3.00 8.00
DH Devin Harris 1.50 4.00
DHO Dwight Howard 3.00 8.00
DM Darko Milicic 2.00 5.00
DN Dirk Nowitzki 6.00 15.00
DW Deron Williams 2.00 5.00
EB Elton Brand 2.00 5.00
EO Emeka Okafor 2.00 5.00
GA Gilbert Arenas 2.50 6.00
GH Grant Hill 4.00 10.00
JF Jordan Farmar 2.00 5.00
JG Jorge Garbajosa 2.00 5.00
JK Jason Kidd 4.00 10.00
JO Jermaine O'Neal 2.50 6.00
JR Jason Richardson 2.50 6.00
JS Josh Smith 1.50 4.00
JT Jason Terry 2.00 5.00
KB Kobe Bryant 40.00 100.00
KG Kevin Garnett 6.00 15.00
KL Kyle Lowry 8.00 20.00
LA LaMarcus Aldridge 6.00 15.00
LH Larry Hughes 2.00 5.00
LO Lamar Odom 2.00 5.00
LW Luke Walton 1.50 4.00
MA Maurice Ager 1.50 4.00
MB Mike Bibby 2.50 6.00
MG Manu Ginobili 5.00 12.00
MJ Mike James 2.00 5.00
MP Morris Peterson 1.50 4.00
MR Michael Redd 2.00 5.00
MW Marcus Williams 1.50 4.00
MWE Martell Webster 2.00 5.00
MWI Marvin Williams 1.50 4.00
PG Pau Gasol 4.00 10.00
PP Paul Pierce 4.00 10.00
PS Peja Stojakovic 2.00 5.00
RA Ron Artest 2.50 6.00
RC Rodney Carney 1.50 4.00
RG Rudy Gay 3.00 8.00
RH Richard Hamilton 2.50 6.00
RJ Richard Jefferson 2.00 5.00
RL Rashard Lewis 2.00 5.00
SM Shawn Marion 2.50 6.00
SMA Stephon Marbury 3.00 8.00
TD Tim Duncan 6.00 15.00
TJF T.J. Ford 1.50 4.00
TM Tracy McGrady 4.00 10.00
TS Thabo Sefolosha 2.00 5.00
YM Yao Ming 6.00 15.00

2006-07 Topps Luxury Box Mezzanine Relics Autographs

STATED PRINT RUN 139 SER.#'d SETS
AB Andrew Bogut 3.00 8.00
ABA Andrea Bargnani 3.00 8.00
ABY Andrew Bynum 2.50 6.00
AH Al Harrington 4.00 10.00
AIG Andre Iguodala 6.00 15.00
AK Andrei Kirilenko 3.00 8.00
AM Adam Morrison 3.00 8.00
BD Boris Diaw 3.00 8.00
BG Ben Gordon 3.00 8.00
CA Carmelo Anthony 15.00 40.00
CB Chauncey Billups 6.00 15.00
CD Chris Duhon 2.50 6.00
CF Channing Frye 2.50 6.00
CV Charlie Villanueva 2.50 6.00
DH Devin Harris 2.50 6.00
DW Dwyane Wade 20.00 50.00
DWI Deron Williams 3.00 8.00
EO Emeka Okafor 3.00 8.00
GW Gerald Wallace 3.00 8.00
HT Hedo Turkoglu 4.00 10.00
HW Hakim Warrick 2.50 6.00
JF Jordan Farmar 3.00 8.00
JG Jorge Garbajosa 3.00 8.00
JH Josh Howard 3.00 8.00
JJ Jarrett Jack 3.00 8.00
JJR J.J. Redick 8.00 20.00
JS Josh Smith 2.50 6.00
KL Kyle Lowry 12.00 30.00
LB Leandro Barbosa 3.00 8.00
LW Luke Walton 4.00 10.00
MA Maurice Ager 2.50 6.00
MJ Mike James 2.50 6.00
MW Marcus Williams 2.50 6.00
MWE Martell Webster 3.00 8.00
RA Ray Allen 15.00 40.00
RC Rodney Carney 2.50 6.00
SW Shelden Williams 2.50 6.00
TS Thabo Sefolosha 3.00 8.00
UH Udonis Haslem 2.50 6.00
VC Vince Carter 15.00 40.00

2006-07 Topps Luxury Box Relics Quad

PRINT RUN 199 SER.#'d SETS
*BLUE: .5X TO 1.25X BASE HI
BLUE PRINT RUN 49 SER.#'d SETS
*BRONZE: .6X TO 1.5X BASE HI
BRONZE PRINT RUN 19 SER.#'d SETS
1 Marion/Terry/Mourning/Billups 10.00 25.00
2 Amare/Brand/Duncan/Dirk 10.00 25.00
3 Wade/Carter/Hughes/Hamilton 10.00 25.00
4 Ginobili/Bibby/Nash/Bryant 60.00 150.00
5 Anthony/Maggette/Harris/Gasol 8.00 20.00
6 Wallace/Redd/O'Neal/Gordon 15.00 30.00
7 Kidd/O'Neal/Gooden/Jamison 8.00 20.00
8 O'Neal/Wade/Nowitzki/Terry 30.00 70.00
9 Bosh/Marbury/Okafor/Webster 8.00 20.00
10 Smith/Garnett/Pierce/Ming 8.00 20.00
11 Richardson/Allen/Hill/Paul 8.00 20.00
12 Stoudemire/Harris/Williams/Wallace 8.00 20.00
13 Marion/Livingston/Bowen/Howard 8.00 20.00
14 Walker/Jefferson/Varejao/McDyess 8.00 20.00
15 Parker/Artest/Nash/Odom 10.00 25.00
16 Miller/Cassell/Stackhouse/Miller 8.00 20.00
17 Billups/Bogut/O'Neal/Deng 15.00 30.00
18 Krstic/Granger/Gooden/Arenas 8.00 20.00
19 Bargnani/Francis/Felton/Miles 6.00 15.00
20 Williams/James/Kirilenko/Iverson 8.00 20.00

2006-07 Topps Luxury Box Relics Five

PRINT RUN 179 SER.#'d SETS
*BLUE: .5X TO 1.25X BASE HI
BLUE PRINT RUN 49 SER.#'d SETS
*BRONZE: .6X TO 1.5X BASE HI
BRONZE PRINT RUN 19 SER.#'d SETS
1 Telfair/Kidd/Iverson/Marbury/Ford 8.00 20.00
2 Billups/Hughes/Tinsley/Duhon/Redd 8.00 20.00
3 Redick/Arenas/Payton/Johnson/Felton 8.00 20.00
4 Parker/Harris/McGrady
Paul/Stoudamire 8.00 20.00
5 Williams/Boykins/James/Ridnour/Jack 8.00 20.00
6 Bryant/Nash/Cassell/Davis/Bibby 60.00 150.00
7 Jefferson/Jackson/Webber
Frye/Peterson 8.00 20.00
8 Prince/Gooden/Granger
Deng/Villanueva 8.00 20.00
9 Hwrd/Jmisn/Wlkr/Willi/Mrrsn 10.00 25.00
10 Duncan/Dirk/Battier/Peja/Gay 8.00 20.00
11 Kirilenko/Nene/Garnett/Lewis/Miles 8.00 20.00
12 Odom/Marion/Brand/Dunleavy/Artest 8.00 20.00
13 Krstic/Dalembert/Ilgauskas
O'Neal/Wallace 8.00 20.00
14 Bogut/O'Neal/Okafor/Dampier/Ming 8.00 20.00
15 Okur/Sene/Aldridge/Bynum/Miller 8.00 20.00

2006-07 Topps Luxury Box Relics Six

PRINT RUN 149 SER.#'d SETS
*BLUE: .5X TO 1.25X BASE HI
BLUE PRINT RUN 49 SER.#'d SETS
*BRONZE: .6X TO 1.5X BASE HI
BRONZE PRINT RUN 19 SER.#'d SETS
1 Felton/Wallace/Jamison
May/Noel/Stackhouse 8.00 20.00
2 Batt/Brnd/Deng/Hill/Magg/Rdck 10.00 25.00
3 Grdn/Rip/Allen/Villan/Okfr/Gay 8.00 20.00
4 Walton/Terry/Stoudamire
Bibby/Iguodala/Arenas 8.00 20.00
5 Stojakovic/Okur/Rodriguez/Diaw
Garbajosa/Ilgauskas 8.00 20.00
6 Dirk/Krst/Barg/Pau/AK47/Prkr 8.00 20.00
7 Baron/Roy/GP/Frmr/Nate/Walton 8.00 20.00
8 Wade/Wllms/Al/Dimb/Melo/Doby 10.00 25.00
9 TD/Steph/Cssll/Cedric/Noel/JJ 10.00 25.00
10 Pierce/Aldridge/Battie
Billups/Tinsley/Wright 8.00 20.00
11 Rndo/Wlkr/Shq/McD/Udn/Balk 10.00 25.00
12 Deron/Wbb/Mgic/Redd/Hrrs/Rse 10.00 25.00
13 Telfair/McGrady/Smith/Brown
Livingston/Garnett 8.00 20.00
14 Kobe/Shaq/Amare
Mses/Hwrd/BigAl 60.00 150.00
15 Redick/Bogut/Nelson
Ford/Battier/Brand 8.00 20.00

2006-07 Topps Luxury Box Relics Seven

PRINT RUN 99 SER.#'d SETS
*BLUE: .5X TO 1.25X BASE HI
BLUE PRINT RUN 49 SER.#'d SETS
*BRONZE: .6X TO 1.5X BASE HI
BRONZE PRINT RUN 19 SER.#'d SETS
1 CP/Will/Bog/Will/Frye/Grngr/Felt 12.00 30.00
2 Kobe/Nash/Dirk/SO/Bllps/Wade/TD 75.00 200.00
3 Bnd/Wllce/Ivsn/Arns/Mrn/Athny/Yao 12.50 30.00
4 Bowen/Wallace/Kirilenko
Artest/Bryant/Kidd/Duncan 60.00 150.00
5 Nash/CP/Daw/Bylr/Wllce/Mllr/Wade 20.00 40.00
6 Kobe/Al/Arns/Wade/Prce/Dirk/CA 75.00 200.00
7 KG/Hwrd/Mrn/Wllce/Dncn/Mrp/Bnd 12.50 30.00
8 Nash/Dvs/Blps/Kid/Mill/CP/Ivsn 12.50 30.00
9 Hamilton/Barbosa/James/Nash
Gordon/Billups/Bowen 10.00 25.00
10 Cam/Kir/Mou/Smi/Bra/Dal/Prz 12.50 30.00

2006-07 Topps Luxury Box Relics Eight

PRINT RUN 79 SER.#'d SETS
*BLUE: .5X TO 1.25X BASE HI
BLUE PRINT RUN 49 SER.#'d SETS
*BRONZE: .6X TO 1.5X BASE HI
BRONZE PRINT RUN 19 SER.#'d SETS
1 Bargnani/Aldridge/Morrison
Williams/Foye/Roy/Gay/Redick 15.00 30.00
2 Wade/Dirk/Wlkr/Jet/Shaq
JHo/JWill/Stack 15.00 30.00
3 Bargnani/Bogut/Howard/Ming/Brand
Duncan/Iverson/O'Neal 12.00 30.00
4 Kobe/KG/TMac/Hwrd/Amare/Shaq 75.00 200.00
5 Bird/Thms/Mgic/Nque/Stck/Glde 25.00 60.00

2006-07 Topps Luxury Box Rookie Relics Autographs

STATED PRINT RUN 249 SER.#'d SETS
AB Andrea Bargnani 10.00 25.00
AM Adam Morrison 3.00 8.00
AR Allan Ray 2.50 6.00
CS Cedric Simmons 2.50 6.00
CSM Craig Smith 3.00 8.00
DB Dee Brown 2.50 6.00
DM Damir Markota 2.50 6.00
DN David Noel 2.50 6.00
HA Hilton Armstrong 2.50 6.00
JB Josh Boone 2.50 6.00
JF Jordan Farmar 3.00 8.00
JG Jorge Garbajosa 3.00 8.00
JJR J.J. Redick 8.00 20.00
JW James White 2.50 6.00
KL Kyle Lowry 12.00 30.00
MA Maurice Ager 2.50 6.00
MC Mardy Collins 2.50 6.00
MW Marcus Williams 2.50 6.00
PD Paul Davis 2.50 6.00
PJT P.J. Tucker 4.00 10.00
PO Patrick O'Bryant 2.50 6.00
QD Quincy Douby 2.50 6.00
RB Renaldo Balkman 3.00 8.00
RBR Ronnie Brewer 4.00 10.00
RC Rodney Carney 2.50 6.00
RF Randy Foye 3.00 8.00
RR Rajon Rondo 12.00 30.00
SB Shannon Brown 2.50 6.00
SEW Shawne Williams 2.50 6.00
SJ Solomon Jones 2.50 6.00
SN Steve Novak 3.00 8.00
SNW Shelden Williams 2.50 6.00
SR Sergio Rodriguez 3.00 8.00
SS Saer Sene 2.50 6.00
TS Thabo Sefolosha 3.00 8.00

2007-08 Topps Luxury Box

COMP.SET w/o SP's (50) 15.00 40.00
51-100 RC PRINT RUN 699 SER.#'d SETS
1 Kevin Garnett 1.25 3.00
2 Kobe Bryant 4.00 10.00
3 Dwyane Wade 1.00 2.50
4 LeBron James 4.00 10.00
5 Baron Davis .40 1.00
6 Dirk Nowitzki 1.25 3.00
7 Jermaine O'Neal .50 1.25
8 Jason Richardson .50 1.25
9 Tony Parker .75 2.00
10 Chris Bosh .60 1.50
11 Yao Ming 1.25 3.00
12 Dwight Howard .60 1.50
13 Steve Nash 1.00 2.50
14 Luol Deng .40 1.00
15 Carmelo Anthony .75 2.00
16 Pau Gasol .75 2.00
17 Carlos Boozer .40 1.00
18 Vince Carter 1.00 2.50
19 Chauncey Billups .60 1.50
20 Ray Allen .75 2.00
21 Tim Duncan 1.25 3.00
22 Amare Stoudemire .50 1.25
23 Kevin Martin .40 1.00
24 Michael Redd .40 1.00
25 Corey Maggette .40 1.00
26 Al Jefferson .30 .75
27 Brandon Roy .60 1.50
28 Chris Paul 1.00 2.50
29 Andre Iguodala .50 1.25
30 Gilbert Arenas .50 1.25
31 Tracy McGrady .75 2.00
32 Shaquille O'Neal 2.00 5.00
33 Allen Iverson 1.25 3.00
34 Paul Pierce .75 2.00
35 Jason Kidd .75 2.00
36 John Stockton 1.50 4.00
37 Tim Hardaway .75 2.00
38 Dennis Rodman 2.00 5.00
39 Dominique Wilkins 1.25 3.00
40 David Thompson .60 1.50
41 Spencer Haywood .50 1.25
42 Larry Bird 3.00 8.00
43 Isiah Thomas .75 2.00
44 Magic Johnson 3.00 8.00
45 Bill Russell 2.50 6.00
46 Moses Malone 1.25 3.00
47 Sidney Moncrief .50 1.25
48 Bill Walton 1.00 2.50
49 David Robinson 1.50 4.00
50 Jerry West 2.00 5.00
51 Thaddeus Young RC 1.25 3.00
52 Javaris Crittenton RC .75 2.00
53 Sean Williams RC .75 2.00
54 Jared Dudley RC 1.00 2.50
55 Wilson Chandler RC 1.00 2.50
56 Mario West RC 1.00 2.50
57 Chris Richard RC .75 2.00
58 Al Horford RC 3.00 8.00
59 Taurean Green RC .75 2.00
60 Corey Brewer RC 1.00 2.50
61 Joakim Noah RC 1.25 3.00
62 Al Thornton RC .75 2.00
63 Nick Young RC 1.25 3.00
64 Arron Afflalo RC 1.00 2.50
65 Juan Carlos Navarro RC 1.00 2.50
66 Marco Belinelli RC 1.00 2.50
67 Yi Jianlian RC 1.50 4.00
68 Luis Scola RC 1.25 3.00
69 Jeff Green RC 1.00 2.50
70 Herbert Hill RC .75 2.00
71 Aaron Gray RC .75 2.00
72 Kosta Perovic RC .75 2.00
73 Spencer Hawes RC .75 2.00
74 Aaron Brooks RC 1.00 2.50
75 Kevin Durant RC 60.00 150.00
76 Alando Tucker RC .75 2.00
77 Julian Wright RC .75 2.00
78 Carl Landry RC .75 2.00
79 Acie Law RC .75 2.00
80 Morris Almond RC .75 2.00
81 Nick Fazekas RC .75 2.00
82 Glen Davis RC 1.00 2.50
83 Jermareo Davidson RC .75 2.00
84 Jamario Moon RC 1.00 2.50
85 Jason Smith RC .75 2.00
86 Cheikh Samb RC .75 2.00
87 Coby Karl RC .75 2.00
88 Dominic McGuire RC .75 2.00
89 Ramon Sessions RC 1.00 2.50
90 Rodney Stuckey RC .75 2.00
91 JamesOn Curry RC .75 2.00
92 Gabe Pruitt RC .75 2.00
93 Adam Haluska RC .75 2.00
94 Kyrylo Fesenko RC .75 2.00
95 Josh McRoberts RC .75 2.00
96 D.J. Strawberry RC .75 2.00
97 Brandan Wright RC 1.00 2.50
98 Mike Conley Jr. RC 3.00 8.00
99 Daequan Cook RC 1.00 2.50
100 Greg Oden RC 1.25 3.00

2007-08 Topps Luxury Box Bronze

*BRONZE 1-50: .75X TO 2X BASE HI
*BRONZE 51-100: .5X TO 1.25X BASE
BRONZE PRINT RUN 249 SER.#'d SETS

2007-08 Topps Luxury Box Silver

*SILVER 1-50: 1X TO 2.5X BASE HI
*SILVER 51-100: .6X TO 1.5X BASE HI
PRINT RUN 75 SER.#'d SETS
75 Kevin Durant 100.00 250.00

2007-08 Topps Luxury Box Courtside Dual Relics

PRINT RUN 179 SER.#'d SETS
*GOLD: .5X TO 1.25X BASE HI
GOLD PRINT RUN 75 SER.#'d SETS
AH R.Allen/R.Hamilton 4.00 10.00
AM C.Anthony/T.McGrady 4.00 10.00
AW G.Arenas/D.Wade 5.00 12.00
CR V.Carter/J.Richardson 5.00 12.00
DB L.Deng/C.Boozer 4.00 10.00
DM T.Duncan/Y.Ming 5.00 12.00
GJ K.Garnett/A.Jefferson 5.00 12.00
HB D.Howard/C.Bosh 5.00 12.00
HP K.Hinrich/P.Pierce 4.00 10.00
IM A.Iverson/S.Marbury 4.00 10.00
MD K.Martin/B.Davis 4.00 10.00
NG D.Nowitzki/P.Gasol 4.00 10.00
NP S.Nash/T.Parker 5.00 12.00
OB S.O'Neal/K.Bryant 40.00 100.00
OH J.O'Neal/A.Harrington 4.00 10.00
RM M.Redd/M.Miller 4.00 10.00
RP B.Roy/C.Paul 5.00 12.00
RS J.Richardson/J.Smith 4.00 10.00
SK A.Stoudemire/J.Kidd 5.00 12.00
WC B.Wallace/M.Camby 4.00 10.00

2007-08 Topps Luxury Box Courtside Triple Relics

PRINT RUN 149 SER.#'d SETS
*GOLD: .5X TO 1.25X BASE HI
GOLD PRINT RUN 49 SER.#'d SETS
AAW Anthony/Arenas/Wade 6.00 15.00
AWM Artest/Wallace/Marion 5.00 12.00

BGN Bryant/Garnett/Nash 50.00 120.00
BIW Butler/Iguodala/Wallace 5.00 12.00
FGT Foye/Gay/Thomas 5.00 12.00
HBC Howard/Boozer/Camby 5.00 12.00
HCG Horford/Cook/Green 5.00 12.00
IMJ Iguodala/McGrady/Johnson 5.00 12.00
MOR Ming/O'Neal/Robinson 8.00 20.00
NOB Noah/Oden/Brewer 8.00 20.00
OGT Okur/Ginobili/Turkoglu 5.00 12.00
OOS Okafor/O'Neal/Smith 5.00 12.00
RAI Redd/Allen/Iverson 5.00 12.00
RMB Roy/Morrison/Bargnani 5.00 12.00
SDB Stoudemire/Duncan/Bosh 5.00 12.00
TLD Ford/Aldridge/Gibson 5.00 12.00
VFG Villanueva/Frye/Gomes 5.00 12.00
WKP Williams/Kidd/Paul 6.00 15.00
YWC Young/Wright/Crittenton 5.00 12.00

2007-08 Topps Luxury Box Quad Relics

PRINT RUN 99 SER.#'d SETS
*GOLD: .5X TO 1.25X BASE HI
GOLD PRINT RUN 25 SER.#'d SETS
QR2 Horfrd/Green/Brwer/Noah 8.00 20.00
QR3 Duncn/Parker/Manu/DRob 12.50 30.00
QR4 Arenas/Butler/Jamisn/Young 6.00 15.00
QR5 Steph/Lee/ZBo/Chandler 6.00 15.00
QR7 Bird/Magic/DRob/Malone 20.00 40.00
QR8 BigAl/Green/Foye/Gomes 6.00 15.00
QR9 Billups/Rip/Afflalo/Stuckey 6.00 15.00
QR10 Davis/Harring/Ellis/Marco 6.00 15.00
QR11 Nash/Amare/Barbo/O'Neal 8.00 20.00
QR12 Harris/Dirk/Terry/Howard 8.00 20.00
QR13 Kidd/RJeff/Vince/Williams 6.00 15.00
QR14 KG/Pierce/Allen/Rondo 10.00 25.00
QR15 TMac/Yao/Brooks/Landry 8.00 20.00

2007-08 Topps Luxury Box Five Piece Relics

PRINT RUN 75 SER.#'d SETS
*GOLD: .5X TO 1.25X BASE HI
GOLD PRINT RUN 25 SER.#'d SETS
R1 Oden/YiWright/Young 10.00 25.00
R2 Noah/Brewer/Horford+2 15.00 30.00
R3 Dirk/Duncn/Amare/Kobe+1 50.00 120.00
R4 Bosh/Yao/TMac/KG+1 8.00 20.00
R5 Melo/Howard/Wade+2 8.00 20.00
R6 Camby/Kidd/Wallace+2 8.00 20.00
R7 Battier/Marion/Artest/Zo+1 8.00 20.00
R8 Dirk/Nash/KG/Duncan/Al 8.00 20.00
R9 Shaq/Howard/DRob+2 10.00 25.00
R10 Roy/Amare/Paul/Pau+1 8.00 20.00
R11 Vince/Al/Kidd/Brand+1 10.00 25.00
R13 Deke/Bird/Nique/Webb+2 20.00 50.00
R14 Kobe/Al/Shaq/KG/Duncan 75.00 200.00
R15 Oden/Bargs/Bogut/Yao+1 20.00 40.00

2007-08 Topps Luxury Box Six Piece Relics

PRINT RUN 75 SER.#'d SET
*GOLD: .5X TO 1.25X BASE HI
GOLD PRINT RUN 25 SER.#'d SETS
R1 Spurs and Suns 10.00 25.00
R2 Mavericks and Warriors 8.00 20.00
R3 Bulls and Heat 8.00 20.00
R4 Knicks and Nets 8.00 20.00
R5 Celtics and 76ers 10.00 25.00
R6 Trailblazers and Supersonics 8.00 20.00
R7 Magic and Hawks 8.00 20.00
R8 Nuggets and Jazz 8.00 20.00
R9 Rockets and Grizzlies 10.00 25.00
R10 Pistons and Wizards 8.00 20.00

2007-08 Topps Luxury Box Seven Piece Relics

PRINT RUN 50 SER.#'d SETS
R1 NBA Point Guards 6.00 15.00
R2 Vince/Bosh/Wade/KG+3 8.00 20.00
R3 NBA Centers 8.00 20.00
R5 RJeff/Bargs/Prince/ZBo+3 6.00 15.00
R7 Kobe/Melo/Dirk/Amare+3 75.00 200.00
R8 NBA Centers/Forwards 8.00 20.00
R9 Marion/Magg/How/Okur+3 6.00 15.00
R10 2007-08 Rookies 8.00 20.00

2007-08 Topps Luxury Box Eight Piece Relics

PRINT RUN 25 SER.#'d SETS
R1 Kidd/Wade/KG/Shaq+4 15.00 30.00
R2 Billups/Arenas/Howard+5 10.00 25.00
R4 Pierce/JRich/Allen/+5 15.00 30.00
R5 Kobe/Al/Dirk/Duncn+4 75.00 200.00
R6 Yao/Melo/Amare/CP3+4 20.00 50.00
R7 Manu/KMart/Marion+5 15.00 30.00
R8 Wade/Kobe/KG/Dirk/Yao+3 75.00 200.00
R10 2007-08 Rookies 20.00 50.00

2007-08 Topps Luxury Box Mezzanine Relics

PRINT RUN 199 SER.#'d SETS
*GOLD: .5X TO 1.25X BASE HI
GOLD PRINT RUN 99 SER.#'d SETS
AB Andrea Bargnani 1.50 4.00
AI Allen Iverson 6.00 15.00
AJ Al Jefferson 1.50 4.00
AJA Antawn Jamison 2.00 5.00
AS Amare Stoudemire 2.50 6.00
BG Ben Gordon 2.00 5.00
BR Brandon Roy 3.00 8.00
BW Buck Williams 1.50 4.00
CA Carmelo Anthony 4.00 10.00
CB Caron Butler 2.00 5.00
CBI Chauncey Billups 3.00 8.00
CBO Chris Bosh 3.00 8.00
CP Chris Paul 5.00 12.00
DL David Lee 1.50 4.00
DN Dirk Nowitzki 6.00 15.00
DW Dwyane Wade 5.00 12.00
EO Emeka Okafor 2.00 5.00
GA Gilbert Arenas 2.50 6.00
GG Gerald Green 2.00 5.00
JJ Joe Johnson 2.00 5.00
JJW Jo Jo White 2.00 5.00
JK Jason Kidd 4.00 10.00
JO Jermaine O'Neal 2.50 6.00
JR Jason Richardson 2.50 6.00
KB Kobe Bryant 75.00 200.00
KG Kevin Garnett 6.00 15.00
KM Kevin Martin 2.00 5.00
LA LaMarcus Aldridge 2.50 6.00
LB Leandro Barbosa 2.00 5.00
LD Luol Deng 2.00 5.00
LO Lamar Odom 2.00 5.00
MC Marcus Camby 2.00 5.00
MM Mike Miller 2.00 5.00
MO Mehmet Okur 2.00 5.00
MP Mickael Pietrus 2.00 5.00
MR Michael Redd 2.00 5.00
PG Pau Gasol 4.00 10.00
PP Paul Pierce 4.00 10.00
RA Ray Allen 4.00 10.00
RAR Ron Artest 2.50 6.00
RF Raymond Felton 2.00 5.00
RG Rudy Gay 2.00 5.00
RGO Ryan Gomes 2.00 5.00
RH Richard Hamilton 3.00 8.00
RJ Richard Jefferson 2.00 5.00
RL Rashard Lewis 2.00 5.00
RW Rasheed Wallace 3.00 8.00
SM Shawn Marion 2.50 6.00
SMA Stephon Marbury 3.00 8.00
SO Shaquille O'Neal 10.00 25.00
SW Spud Webb 2.00 5.00
TD Tim Duncan 6.00 15.00
TJF T.J. Ford 1.50 4.00
TM Tracy McGrady 4.00 10.00
TP Tony Parker 4.00 10.00
VC Vince Carter 5.00 12.00
YM Yao Ming 6.00 15.00
ZR Zach Randolph 2.50 6.00

2007-08 Topps Luxury Box Mezzanine Relics Autographs

PRINT RUN 39 SER.#'d SETS
*AUTO GOLD: .6X TO 1.5X BASE HI
GOLD PRINT RUN 25 SER.#'d SETS
AB Andrea Bargnani 5.00 12.00
AJ Al Jefferson 5.00 12.00
AJA Antawn Jamison 5.00 12.00
BG Ben Gordon 6.00 15.00
BW Buck Williams 6.00 15.00
CB Caron Butler 5.00 12.00
CBI Chauncey Billups 6.00 15.00
CBO Chris Bosh 12.00 30.00
DL David Lee 5.00 12.00
DW Dwyane Wade 25.00 60.00
GA Gilbert Arenas 8.00 20.00
JJW Jo Jo White 6.00 15.00
LB Leandro Barbosa 5.00 12.00
MP Mickael Pietrus 5.00 12.00
PP Paul Pierce 8.00 20.00
RA Ray Allen 15.00 40.00
RF Raymond Felton 5.00 12.00
RGO Ryan Gomes 5.00 12.00
SO Shaquille O'Neal 30.00 80.00
SW Spud Webb 15.00 30.00
TJF T.J. Ford 5.00 12.00
VC Vince Carter 20.00 40.00

2007-08 Topps Luxury Box Rookie Relics

PRINT RUN 499 SER.#'d SETS
*GOLD: .5X TO 1.25X BASE HI
GOLD PRINT RUN 149 SER.#'d SETS
AA Arron Afflalo 2.00 5.00
AB Aaron Brooks 2.00 5.00
AG Aaron Gray 1.50 4.00
AH Al Horford 6.00 15.00
AHA Adam Haluska 1.50 4.00
AL Acie Law 1.50 4.00
AT Al Thornton 1.50 4.00
ATU Alando Tucker 1.50 4.00
BW Brandan Wright 2.00 5.00
CB Corey Brewer 2.00 5.00
CL Carl Landry 1.50 4.00
CR Chris Richard 1.50 4.00
DC Daequan Cook 2.00 5.00
DJS D.J. Strawberry 1.50 4.00
DM Dominic McGuire 1.50 4.00
DN Demetris Nichols 1.50 4.00
GD Glen Davis 2.00 5.00
GO Greg Oden 2.50 6.00
GP Gabe Pruitt 1.50 4.00
HH Herbert Hill 1.50 4.00
JC Javaris Crittenton 1.50 4.00
JD Jared Dudley 2.00 5.00
JDA Jermareo Davidson 1.50 4.00
JG Jeff Green 2.00 5.00
JM Josh McRoberts 1.50 4.00
JN Joakim Noah 2.50 6.00
JS Jason Smith 1.50 4.00
JW Julian Wright 1.50 4.00
MA Morris Almond 1.50 4.00
MB Marco Belinelli 2.00 5.00
MC Mike Conley Jr. 6.00 15.00
NF Nick Fazekas 1.50 4.00
NY Nick Young 2.50 6.00
RS Rodney Stuckey 1.50 4.00
SH Spencer Hawes 1.50 4.00
SW Sean Williams 1.50 4.00
TG Taurean Green 1.50 4.00
TY Thaddeus Young 2.50 6.00
WC Wilson Chandler 2.00 5.00
YJ Yi Jianlian 3.00 8.00

2007-08 Topps Luxury Box Rookie Relics Autographs

PRINT RUN 99 TO 199 SER.#'d SETS
*GOLD: .5X TO 1.25X BASE HI
GOLD PRINT RUN 19 TO 39 SETS
AA Arron Afflalo 3.00 8.00
AB Aaron Brooks 3.00 8.00
AG Aaron Gray 2.50 6.00
AH Adam Haluska 2.50 6.00
AL Acie Law 2.50 6.00
AT Al Thornton 2.50 6.00
ATU Alando Tucker 2.50 6.00
BW Brandan Wright 3.00 8.00
CL Carl Landry 2.50 6.00
DC Daequan Cook 2.50 6.00
DJS D.J. Strawberry 2.50 6.00
DM Dominic McGuire 2.50 6.00
DN Demetris Nichols 2.50 6.00
GD Glen Davis 3.00 8.00
GO Greg Oden 25.00 60.00
GP Gabe Pruitt 2.50 6.00
HH Herbert Hill 2.50 6.00
JC Javaris Crittenton 2.50 6.00
JD Jared Dudley 3.00 8.00
JDA Jermareo Davidson 2.50 6.00
JM Josh McRoberts 2.50 6.00
JS Jason Smith 2.50 6.00
MA Morris Almond 2.50 6.00
MB Marco Belinelli 3.00 8.00
NF Nick Fazekas 2.50 6.00
NY Nick Young 4.00 10.00
RS Rodney Stuckey 2.50 6.00
SH Spencer Hawes 2.50 6.00
SW Sean Williams 2.50 6.00
TG Taurean Green 2.50 6.00
TY Thaddeus Young 4.00 10.00
WC Wilson Chandler 3.00 8.00
YJ Yi Jianlian 5.00 12.00

1983-84 Topps M&M's Olympic Heroes

COMPLETE SET (44) 8.00 20.00
3 Bill Bradley .50 1.25
33 Oscar Robertson .60 1.50
42 Jerry West .75 2.00

2006 Topps McDonald's All-American

COMPLETE SET (48) 15.00 40.00
B1 Earl Clark 1.00 2.50
B2 Mike Conley Jr. 1.50 4.00
B3 Jarvaris Crittenton .75 2.00
B4 Wayne Ellington .75 2.00
B5 Gerald Henderson 1.50 4.00
B6 Ty Lawson 1.50 4.00
B7 Vernon Macklin .75 2.00
B8 Greg Oden 2.00 5.00
B9 Scottie Reynolds .75 2.00
B10 Lance Thomas .75 2.00
B11 Brandan Wright .75 2.00
B12 Thaddeus Young 1.25 3.00
B13 Darrell Arthur .75 2.00
B14 D.J. Augustin 1.00 2.50
B15 Chase Budinger 1.00 2.50
B16 Edmond Carter .75 2.00
B17 Sherron Collins .75 2.00
B18 Daequan Cook 1.00 2.50
B19 Kevin Durant 8.00 20.00
B20 James Keefe .75 2.00
B21 Spencer Hawes 1.00 2.50
B22 Brook Lopez 2.00 5.00
B23 Robin Lopez 1.25 3.00
B24 Jon Scheyer 6.00 15.00
G1 Jessica Breland .75 2.00
G2 Tina Charles 3.00 8.00
G3 Joy Cheek .40 1.00
G4 Amber Harris .75 2.00
G5 Ashley Houts .40 1.00
G6 Kaili McLaren .40 1.00
G7 Bridgette Mitchell .40 1.00
G8 Porsha Phillips .40 1.00
G9 Epiphanny Prince .40 1.00
G10 Amber White .75 2.00
G11 Danielle Wilson .40 1.00
G12 Monica Wright .75 2.00
G13 Jayne Appel .40 1.00
G14 Jacki Gemelos .40 1.00
G15 Michelle Harrison .40 1.00
G16 Allison Hightower .40 1.00
G17 Dela Quese Jernigan .40 1.00
G18 Adrian McGowan .40 1.00
G19 Morghan Medlock .40 1.00
G20 Jordan Murphee .40 1.00
G21 Abi Olajuwon .75 2.00
G22 Brittainey Raven .40 1.00
G23 Dymond Simon .40 1.00
G24 Amanda Thompson .75 2.00

2007 Topps McDonald's All-American

COMPLETE SET (48) 20.00 50.00
AB Angie Bjorklund W .40 1.00
AC Ashley Cimino W .40 1.00
AF Austin Freeman .75 2.00
AJ Alison Jackson W .40 1.00
AJ2 Amy Jaeschke W .40 1.00
BG Blake Griffin 6.00 15.00
CA Cole Aldrich 1.25 3.00
CD Cetera DeGraffenrein W .40 1.00
CS Corey Stokes .75 2.00
CW Chris Wright .75 2.00
DG Donte Greene 1.25 3.00
DM Drey Mingo W .40 1.00
DP Devereaux Peters W .40 1.00
DR Derrick Rose 8.00 20.00
EG Eric Gordon 2.50 6.00
EM Erica Morrow W .40 1.00
GL Gani Lawal .75 2.00
IL Italee Lucas W .40 1.00
JA James Anderson 1.50 4.00
JB Jerryd Bayless 1.25 3.00
JF Jonny Flynn 2.00 5.00
JH James Harden 10.00 25.00
JJH J.J. Hickson 1.00 2.50
JL Jai Lucas .75 2.00
JL2 Jantel Lavender W .40 1.00
JP Jeanette Pohlen W .40 1.00
JT Jasmine Thomas W .40 1.00
KC Kelley Cain W .40 1.00
KK Kosta Koufos .75 2.00
KL Kevin Love 3.00 8.00
KP Kayla Pedersen W .50 1.25
KR Khadijah Rushdan W .40 1.00
KS Kyle Singler 1.00 2.50
KT Krystal Thomas W .40 1.00
LD Lorin Dixon W .40 1.00
LS Lenita Sanford W .40 1.00
MB Michael Beasley 4.00 10.00
MM Maya Moore W 2.00 5.00
MS Marah Strickland W .40 1.00
NC Nick Calathes .75 2.00
NS Nolan Smith 2.00 5.00
OM O.J. Mayo 3.00 8.00
PP Patrick Patterson 1.50 4.00
SG Stefanie Galbreath W .40 1.00
TK Tyler King .75 2.00
TP Ta'Shia Phillips W .40 1.00
TW Tyra White W .40 1.00
VB Victoria Baugh W .40 1.00

2008 Topps McDonald's All-American

COMPLETE SET (48) 25.00 60.00
AB Alyssia Brewer W .40 1.00
AC Ashley Corral W .40 1.00
AD Ayana Dunning W .40 1.00
AFA Al-Farouq Aminu 1.25 3.00
AG Ashley Gayle W .40 1.00
AG Amber Gray W .40 1.00
AM Alicia Manning W .40 1.00
AS April Sykes W .40 1.00
BG Briana Gilbreath W .40 1.00
BJ Brandon Jennings 4.00 10.00
BJM B.J. Mullens .75 2.00
BP Brooklyn Pope W .40 1.00
CL Chelsea Lee W .40 1.00
CS Chris Singleton 2.00 5.00
CS Chay Shegog W .40 1.00
DD DeMar DeRozan 2.00 5.00
DH Destiny Hughes W .40 1.00
ED Ed Davis 3.00 8.00
EDD Elena Delle Donna W .40 1.00
EW Elliot Williams 1.25 3.00
GJ Glory Johnson W .40 1.00
GM Greg Monroe 3.00 8.00
IS Iman Shumpert 2.50 6.00
JD Jasmine Dixon W .40 1.00
JG JaMychal Green 1.00 2.50
JH Jrue Holiday 3.00 8.00
KW Kemba Walker 6.00 15.00
LB Luke Babbitt 1.25 3.00
LD Larry Drew II 1.00 2.50
LK Lynetta Kizer W .40 1.00
LSB LaSondra Barrett W .40 1.00
MD Michael Dunigan .75 2.00
ML Malcolm Lee .75 2.00
MR Michael Rosario .75 2.00
NO Nnemkadi Ogwumike W .40 1.00
NS Nikki Speed W .40 1.00
SH Scotty Hopson 1.25 3.00
SJ Shenise Johnson W .40 1.00
SL Sylven Landesberg 1.25 3.00
SP Samantha Prahalis W .40 1.00
SS Samardo Samuels 1.25 3.00
SS Shekinna Stricklen W .40 1.00
SW She'la White W .40 1.00
TE Tyreke Evans 6.00 15.00
TH Tiffany Hayes W .40 1.00
TZ Tyler Zeller .75 2.00
WB William Buford .75 2.00
WW Willie Warren .75 2.00

2023-24 Topps Mercury Victor Wembanyama

COMMON WEMBY 30.00 80.00
*REF/99: 1X TO 2.5X BASIC
*BLUE REF/75: 1.25X TO 3X BASIC
*TX KALEIDO REF/75: 1.25X TO 3X BASIC
*GOLD REF/50: 2X TO 5X BASIC
*FRENCH/45: 2X TO 5X BASIC
*WHITE REF/35: 2X TO 5X BASIC
*ORANGE REF/25: 2.5X TO 6X BASIC
*SPECIMEN TANK/15: 3X TO 8X BASIC
*BLACK REF/10: 4X TO 10X BASIC
*TRACTOR BEAM REF/7: 5X TO 12X BASIC
*RED REF/5: 6X TO 15X BASIC
*ALIEN FACE REF/5: 8X TO 20X BASIC
*MOON ROCK REF/3: 8X TO 20X BASIC
1 Victor Wembanyama 25.00 60.00
2 Victor Wembanyama 25.00 60.00
3 Victor Wembanyama 25.00 60.00
4 Victor Wembanyama 25.00 60.00
5 Victor Wembanyama 25.00 60.00
6 Victor Wembanyama 25.00 60.00
7 Victor Wembanyama 25.00 60.00
8 Victor Wembanyama 25.00 60.00
9 Victor Wembanyama 25.00 60.00
10 Victor Wembanyama 25.00 60.00
11 Victor Wembanyama 25.00 60.00
12 Victor Wembanyama 25.00 60.00
13 Victor Wembanyama 25.00 60.00
14 Victor Wembanyama 25.00 60.00
15 Victor Wembanyama 25.00 60.00
16 Victor Wembanyama 25.00 60.00
17 Victor Wembanyama 25.00 60.00
18 Victor Wembanyama 25.00 60.00
19 Victor Wembanyama 25.00 60.00
20 Victor Wembanyama 25.00 60.00

2023-24 Topps Mercury Victor Wembanyama Autograph Relics

STATED PRINT RUN 99 SER.#'d SETS
*FRENCH/75: .5X TO 1.2X BASIC
*COSMIC/50: .6X TO 1.5X BASIC
*TEXAS/35: .6X TO 1.5X BASIC
*ORANGE/25: .75X TO 2X BASIC
*BLACK REF/10: 1.25X TO 3X BASIC
WAR1 Victor Wembanyama 1,250.00 2,500.00
WAR2 Victor Wembanyama 1,500.00 3,000.00
WAR3 Victor Wembanyama 1,500.00 3,000.00
WAR4 Victor Wembanyama 1,250.00 2,500.00
WAR5 Victor Wembanyama 1,250.00 2,500.00
WAR6 Victor Wembanyama 1,250.00 2,500.00
WAR7 Victor Wembanyama 1,250.00 2,500.00
WAR8 Victor Wembanyama 1,250.00 2,500.00
WAR9 Victor Wembanyama 1,250.00 2,500.00
WAR10 Victor Wembanyama 1,250.00 2,500.00

2023-24 Topps Mercury Victor Wembanyama Autographs

STATED PRINT RUN 99 SER.#'d SETS
*BLUE REF/75: .4X TO 1X BASIC
*GOLD REF/50: .5X TO 1.2X BASIC
*WHITE REF/35: .5X TO 1.2X BASIC
*ORANGE REF/25: .6X TO 1.5X BASIC
*BLACK REF/10: 1X TO 2.5X BASIC
*RED REF/5: 1X TO 2.5X BASIC
WA1 Victor Wembanyama 600.00 1,200.00
WA2 Victor Wembanyama 600.00 1,200.00
WA3 Victor Wembanyama 600.00 1,200.00
WA4 Victor Wembanyama 600.00 1,200.00
WA5 Victor Wembanyama 600.00 1,200.00
WA6 Victor Wembanyama 600.00 1,200.00
WA7 Victor Wembanyama 600.00 1,200.00
WA8 Victor Wembanyama 600.00 1,200.00
WA9 Victor Wembanyama 600.00 1,200.00
WA10 Victor Wembanyama 600.00 1,200.00

2023-24 Topps Mercury Victor Wembanyama Dual Autographs Black Refractors

VWDR Victor Wembanyama / David Robinson 3,500.00 7,000.00
VWJK Victor Wembanyama / Jason Kidd 3,500.00 7,000.00
VWSO Victor Wembanyama / Shaquille O'Neal 5,000.00 10,000.00
VWTP Victor Wembanyama / Tony Parker 3,500.00 7,000.00

2023-24 Topps Mercury Victor Wembanyama Inserts

STATED PRINT RUN 99 SER.#'d SETS
*BLUE REF/75: .5X TO 1.2X BASIC
*GOLD REF/50: .6X TO 1.5X BASIC
*WHITE REF/35: .6X TO 1.5X BASIC
*ORANGE REF/25: .75X TO 2X BASIC
VW1 Victor Wembanyama / Aptitude for Altitude 150.00 400.00
VW2 Victor Wembanyama / Sticky Fingers 150.00 400.00
VW3 Victor Wembanyama / Cote to Coast 150.00 400.00
VW4 Victor Wembanyama / Apparitions 150.00 400.00
VW5 Victor Wembanyama / Bound for Glory 150.00 400.00
VW6 Victor Wembanyama / '57-58 Topps 300.00 600.00
VW7 Victor Wembanyama / Embark 600.00 1,200.00
VW8 Victor Wembanyama / '71-72 Topps 300.00 600.00
VW9 Victor Wembanyama / Wingspan 600.00 1,200.00
VW10 Victor Wembanyama / To Ball or not to Ball? 150.00 400.00

2023-24 Topps Midnight

*ZODIAC: .5X TO 1.2X BASIC
*MORNING/149: 1.25X TO 3X BASIC
*TWILIGHT/99: 1.5X TO 4X BASIC
*DUSK/75: 1.5X TO 4X BASIC
*MOON BEAM: 2X TO 5X BASIC
*MOONRISE/25: 2.5X TO 6X BASIC
1 Kevin Durant 1.00 2.50
2 Dereck Lively II RC 1.00 2.50
3 Austin Reaves .75 2.00
4 Dejounte Murray .40 1.00
5 Jett Howard RC .60 1.50
6 Bradley Beal .40 1.00
7 Chet Holmgren .75 2.00
8 Markelle Fultz .25 .60
9 Jalen Hood-Schifino RC .50 1.25
10 Kentavious Caldwell-Pope .25 .60
11 Trae Young .60 1.50
12 Draymond Green .40 1.00
13 Tyler Herro .50 1.25
14 Myles Turner .30 .75
15 Brice Sensabaugh RC .75 2.00
16 Collin Sexton .40 1.00
17 Brandon Miller RC 2.00 5.00
18 Devin Vassell .40 1.00
19 Kobe Brown RC .50 1.25
20 Jordan Walsh RC .50 1.25
21 Joel Embiid .75 2.00
22 Jarrett Allen .30 .75
23 Kris Murray RC .50 1.25
24 Donte DiVincenzo .30 .75
25 Anthony Davis .75 2.00
26 Jrue Holiday .40 1.00
27 Mark Williams .30 .75
28 CJ McCollum .30 .75
29 Jaime Jaquez Jr. RC .75 2.00
30 Jalen Williams .60 1.50
31 LeBron James 2.50 6.00
32 Karl-Anthony Towns .50 1.25
33 Anthony Black RC 1.00 2.50
34 Ben Sheppard RC .50 1.25
35 Spencer Dinwiddie .25 .60
36 Colby Jones RC .50 1.25
37 Donovan Mitchell .60 1.50
38 Bilal Coulibaly RC 1.25 3.00
39 Rudy Gobert .40 1.00
40 Gradey Dick RC 1.00 2.50
41 Anfernee Simons .40 1.00
42 Lauri Markkanen .50 1.25
43 Pascal Siakam .50 1.25
44 Chris Paul .60 1.50
45 Domantas Sabonis .50 1.25
46 DeMar DeRozan .50 1.25
47 Tyrese Maxey .60 1.50
48 Shaedon Sharpe .60 1.50
49 Tyrese Haliburton .60 1.50
50 Victor Wembanyama RC 12.00 30.00
51 Olivier-Maxence Prosper RC .50 1.25
52 Daniel Gafford .30 .75
53 Russell Westbrook .50 1.25
54 James Harden .60 1.50
55 Jarace Walker RC 1.00 2.50
56 Naz Reid .30 .75
57 Kyrie Irving .60 1.50
58 Jeremy Sochan .40 1.00
59 Immanuel Quickley .30 .75
60 Giannis Antetokounmpo 1.50 4.00
61 Taylor Hendricks RC .50 1.25
62 Marcus Sasser RC .75 2.00
63 Jayson Tatum 1.25 3.00
64 Cade Cunningham .75 2.00
65 Fred VanVleet .50 1.25
66 Noah Clowney RC .60 1.50
67 Klay Thompson .60 1.50
68 Cam Whitmore RC 1.25 3.00
69 Maxwell Lewis RC .40 1.00
70 OG Anunoby .40 1.00
71 Kristaps Porzingis .40 1.00
72 Michael Porter Jr. .40 1.00
73 Zach LaVine .50 1.25
74 Nick Smith Jr. RC .60 1.50
75 Scoot Henderson RC 1.50 4.00
76 Julian Strawther RC .60 1.50
77 Josh Giddey .50 1.25
78 Paul George .50 1.25
79 Grant Williams .25 .60
80 Desmond Bane .40 1.00
81 Kobe Bufkin RC .60 1.50
82 Franz Wagner .50 1.25
83 Aaron Gordon .30 .75
84 Devin Booker .75 2.00
85 Mikal Bridges .40 1.00
86 Kyle Kuzma .40 1.00
87 Trey Murphy III .40 1.00
88 Jaren Jackson Jr. .50 1.25
89 Brandin Podziemski RC 1.50 4.00
90 Stephen Curry 2.50 6.00
91 Jaylen Brown .60 1.50
92 Shai Gilgeous-Alexander 1.50 4.00
93 Jalen Brunson .60 1.50
94 De'Aaron Fox .60 1.50
95 Jalen Green .50 1.25
96 Marcus Smart .40 1.00
97 GG Jackson RC 1.00 2.50
98 Jordan Hawkins RC .75 2.00
99 Rayan Rupert RC .50 1.25
100 Khris Middleton .30 .75

2023-24 Topps Midnight After Hours

AT1 Trae Young 10.00 25.00
AT2 Devin Booker 12.00 30.00
AT3 Kyrie Irving 10.00 25.00
AT4 Joel Embiid 12.00 30.00
AT5 Jaylen Brown 10.00 25.00
AT6 Kevin Durant 15.00 40.00
AT7 Stephen Curry 40.00 100.00
AT8 Jayson Tatum 20.00 50.00
AT9 Mikal Bridges 6.00 15.00
AT10 Chet Holmgren 12.00 30.00
AT11 Tyrese Haliburton 10.00 25.00
AT12 Giannis Antetokounmpo 25.00 60.00
AT13 Karl-Anthony Towns 8.00 20.00
AT14 Paul George 8.00 20.00
AT15 Jalen Brunson 10.00 25.00
AT16 Victor Wembanyama 40.00 100.00
AT17 Brandon Miller 20.00 50.00
AT18 Scoot Henderson 15.00 40.00
AT19 Jarace Walker 10.00 25.00
AT20 Jordan Hawkins 8.00 20.00
AT21 Anthony Black 10.00 25.00
AT22 Taylor Hendricks 5.00 12.00
AT23 Dereck Lively II 10.00 25.00
AT24 Bilal Coulibaly 12.00 30.00
AT25 Jaime Jaquez Jr. 8.00 20.00

2023-24 Topps Midnight Constellations

*TWILIGHT/99: 1.5X TO 4X BASIC
*DUSK/75: 1.5X TO 4X BASIC
*MOON BEAM: 2X TO 5X BASIC
*MOONRISE/25: 2.5X TO 6X BASIC
C1 Jayson Tatum / Jaylen Brown 1.50 4.00
C2 Brandon Miller / Nick Smith Jr. 1.50 4.00
C3 Olivier-Maxence Prosper / Dereck Lively II .75 2.00
C4 Alex English / Carmelo Anthony .60 1.50
C5 DeMar DeRozan / Zach LaVine .60 1.50
C6 Cam Whitmore / Jalen Green 1.00 2.50
C7 Paul George / Russell Westbrook .60 1.50
C8 Jerry West / Magic Johnson 1.50 4.00
C9 Jaren Jackson Jr. / Desmond Bane .60 1.50
C10 Dwyane Wade / Shaquille O'Neal 1.25 3.00
C11 Dejounte Murray Trae Young .50 1.25
C12 Jordan Hawkins / CJ McCollum .60 1.50
C13 Chet Holmgren / Jalen Williams 1.00 2.50
C14 Anthony Black / Jett Howard .75 2.00
C15 Joel Embiid / Tyrese Maxey 1.00 2.50
C16 Kevin Durant / Devin Booker 1.25 3.00
C17 Scoot Henderson / Kris Murray 1.25 3.00
C18 De'Aaron Fox / Domantas Sabonis .75 2.00
C19 Victor Wembanyama / David Robinson 10.00 25.00
C20 Klay Thompson / Stephen Curry 3.00 8.00
C21 Gradey Dick / Scottie Barnes .75 2.00
C22 Taylor Hendricks / Lauri Markkanen .60 1.50
C23 Kyle Kuzma / Bilal Coulibaly 1.00 2.50
C24 Damian Lillard / Giannis Antetokounmpo 2.00 5.00
C25 Jarace Walker / Tyrese Haliburton .75 2.00

2023-24 Topps Midnight Dream Chasers

DC1 Victor Wembanyama 40.00 100.00
DC2 Brandon Miller 10.00 25.00
DC3 Scoot Henderson 8.00 20.00
DC4 Olivier-Maxence Prosper 2.50 6.00
DC5 Jarace Walker 5.00 12.00
DC6 Ben Sheppard 2.50 6.00
DC7 Cam Whitmore 6.00 15.00
DC8 Anthony Black 5.00 12.00
DC9 Taylor Hendricks 2.50 6.00
DC10 Gradey Dick 5.00 12.00
DC11 Jordan Hawkins 4.00 10.00
DC12 Jett Howard 3.00 8.00
DC13 Dereck Lively II 5.00 12.00
DC14 Kobe Bufkin 3.00 8.00
DC15 Bilal Coulibaly 6.00 15.00
DC16 Noah Clowney 3.00 8.00
DC17 Marcus Sasser 4.00 10.00
DC18 Jaime Jaquez Jr. 4.00 10.00
DC19 Brandin Podziemski 8.00 20.00
DC20 Jalen Hood-Schifino 2.50 6.00
DC21 Julian Strawther 3.00 8.00
DC22 Nick Smith Jr. 3.00 8.00
DC23 Kris Murray 2.50 6.00
DC24 GG Jackson 5.00 12.00
DC25 Trayce Jackson-Davis 3.00 8.00

2023-24 Topps Midnight Horizon Signatures

*TWILIGHT/99: .5X TO 1.25X BASIC
*DUSK/75: .5X TO 1.25X BASIC
*MOON BEAM: .6X TO 1.5X BASIC
*MOONRISE/25: .75X TO 2X BASIC
HSAG Artis Gilmore 6.00 15.00
HSAH Al Horford 5.00 12.00
HSAN Aaron Nesmith 5.00 12.00
HSAR Austin Reaves 12.00 30.00
HSAS Alperen SengÃ¼n 8.00 20.00
HSBB Bogdan Bogdanovic 5.00 12.00
HSBC Brandon Clarke 4.00 10.00
HSBW Ben Wallace 6.00 15.00
HSCB Christian Braun 5.00 12.00
HSCC Clint Capela 4.00 10.00
HSCH Chet Holmgren 12.00 30.00
HSCL Christian Laettner 5.00 12.00
HSCM Calvin Murphy 5.00 12.00
HSDG Daniel Gafford 5.00 12.00
HSDH Danuel House Jr 3.00 8.00
HSDI Dan Issel 6.00 15.00
HSDM Dejounte Murray 6.00 15.00
HSDS Domantas Sabonis 8.00 20.00
HSDT David Thompson 6.00 15.00
HSDV Devin Vassell 6.00 15.00
HSEF Evan Fournier 4.00 10.00
HSFW Franz Wagner 8.00 20.00
HSGH Gordon Hayward 5.00 12.00
HSGW Grant Williams 4.00 10.00
HSIH Isaiah Hartenstein 5.00 12.00
HSIQ Immanuel Quickley 5.00 12.00
HSIS Isaiah Stewart 5.00 12.00
HSJC John Collins 5.00 12.00
HSJL Jake Laravia 4.00 10.00
HSJR Jalen Rose 5.00 12.00
HSJT Jae'Sean Tate 5.00 12.00
HSJV Jarred Vanderbilt 4.00 10.00
HSJW Jalen Williams 10.00 25.00
HSKK Kyle Kuzma 6.00 15.00
HSKP Kristaps Porzingis 6.00 15.00
HSMF Markelle Fultz 4.00 10.00
HSMM Malik Monk 6.00 15.00
HSMT Myles Turner 5.00 12.00
HSNV Nikola Vucevic 5.00 12.00
HSRG Rudy Gobert 6.00 15.00
HSSC Stephen Curry 300.00 600.00
HSSS Shaedon Sharpe 10.00 25.00
HSTM Tyrese Maxey 10.00 25.00
HSZC Zach Collins 4.00 10.00
HSZL Zach LaVine 8.00 20.00
HSAEN Alex English 6.00 15.00
HSANS Anfernee Simons 6.00 15.00
HSBWA Bill Walton 8.00 20.00
HSBWE Blake Wesley 3.00 8.00
HSDAM Davion Mitchell 4.00 10.00
HSDDI Donte DiVincenzo 5.00 12.00
HSDEB Desmond Bane 6.00 15.00
HSGTJ Gary Trent Jr. 5.00 12.00
HSJWI Jamaal Wilkes 5.00 12.00
HSTHJ Tim Hardaway Jr. 4.00 10.00
HSTRM Trey Murphy III 6.00 15.00

2023-24 Topps Midnight Lunar Tide

*TWILIGHT/99: 1.5X TO 4X BASIC
*DUSK/75: 1.5X TO 4X BASIC
*MOON BEAM: 2X TO 5X BASIC
*MOONRISE/25: 2.5X TO 6X BASIC
LT1 Trae Young .75 2.00
LT2 Jayson Tatum 1.50 4.00
LT3 Kyrie Irving .75 2.00
LT4 De'Aaron Fox .75 2.00
LT5 Stephen Curry 3.00 8.00
LT6 Giannis Antetokounmpo 2.00 5.00
LT7 Chet Holmgren 1.00 2.50
LT8 Tyrese Haliburton .75 2.00
LT9 Joel Embiid 1.00 2.50
LT10 Kevin Durant 1.25 3.00
LT11 Victor Wembanyama 12.00 30.00
LT12 Brandon Miller 1.50 4.00
LT13 Scoot Henderson 1.25 3.00
LT14 Jarace Walker .75 2.00
LT15 Jaime Jaquez Jr. .60 1.50

2023-24 Topps Midnight Nightball

*TWILIGHT/99: 1.5X TO 4X BASIC
*DUSK/75: 1.5X TO 4X BASIC
*MOON BEAM: 2X TO 5X BASIC
*MOONRISE/25: 2.5X TO 6X BASIC
NB1 Dejounte Murray .50 1.25
NB2 Jaylen Brown .75 2.00
NB3 Mikal Bridges .50 1.25
NB4 DeMar DeRozan .60 1.50
NB5 Shai Gilgeous-Alexander 2.00 5.00
NB6 Kyrie Irving .75 2.00
NB7 Carmelo Anthony .60 1.50
NB8 Giannis Antetokounmpo 2.00 5.00
NB9 Tyrese Haliburton .75 2.00
NB10 Paul George .60 1.50
NB11 Nikola Jokic 2.00 5.00
NB12 Jaren Jackson Jr. .60 1.50
NB13 Dwyane Wade .75 2.00
NB14 Kevin Garnett 1.00 2.50
NB15 Magic Johnson 1.50 4.00
NB16 Jalen Brunson .75 2.00
NB17 Larry Bird 1.50 4.00
NB18 Joel Embiid 1.00 2.50
NB19 Devin Booker 1.00 2.50
NB20 De'Aaron Fox .75 2.00
NB21 Victor Wembanyama 10.00 25.00
NB22 Brandon Miller 1.50 4.00
NB23 Scoot Henderson 1.25 3.00
NB24 Cam Whitmore 1.00 2.50
NB25 Bilal Coulibaly 1.00 2.50
NB26 Jaime Jaquez Jr. .60 1.50
NB27 GG Jackson .75 2.00
NB28 Jordan Hawkins .60 1.50
NB29 Jalen Hood-Schifino .40 1.00
NB30 Anthony Black .75 2.00

2023-24 Topps Midnight Rookie Horizon Signatures

*TWILIGHT/99: .5X TO 1.25X BASIC
*DUSK/75: .5X TO 1.25X BASIC
*MOON BEAM: .6X TO 1.5X BASIC
*MOONRISE/25: .75X TO 2X BASIC
RHSAB Anthony Black 10.00 25.00
RHSAJ Andre Jackson Jr. 8.00 20.00
RHSBC Bilal Coulibaly 12.00 30.00
RHSBM Brandon Miller 20.00 50.00
RHSBP Brandin Podziemski 15.00 40.00
RHSBS Brice Sensabaugh 8.00 20.00
RHSCJ Colby Jones 5.00 12.00

RHSCW Cam Whitmore 12.00 30.00
RHSGD Gradey Dick 10.00 25.00
RHSGG GG Jackson 10.00 25.00
RHSJC Jaylen Clark 5.00 12.00
RHSJH Jordan Hawkins 8.00 20.00
RHSJN James Nnaji 4.00 10.00
RHSJS Julian Strawther 6.00 15.00
RHSJW Jordan Walsh 5.00 12.00
RHSKB Kobe Bufkin 6.00 15.00
RHSKJ Keyontae Johnson 5.00 12.00
RHSKM Kris Murray 5.00 12.00
RHSLM Leonard Miller 5.00 12.00
RHSML Maxwell Lewis 4.00 10.00
RHSMS Marcus Sasser 8.00 20.00
RHSNC Noah Clowney 6.00 15.00
RHSRR Rayan Rupert 5.00 12.00
RHSSH Scoot Henderson 15.00 40.00
RHSTH Taylor Hendricks 5.00 12.00
RHSTV Tristan Vukcevic 5.00 12.00
RHSVW Victor Wembanyama 500.00 1,000.00
RHSAMB Amari Bailey 5.00 12.00
RHSBES Ben Sheppard 5.00 12.00
RHSJAW Jarace Walker 10.00 25.00
RHSJEH Jett Howard 6.00 15.00
RHSJHS Jalen Hood-Schifino 5.00 12.00
RHSJJJ Jaime Jaquez Jr. 8.00 20.00
RHSJUP Julian Phillips 5.00 12.00
RHSJWI Jalen Wilson 5.00 12.00
RHSKOB Kobe Brown 5.00 12.00
RHSNSJ Nick Smith Jr. 6.00 15.00
RHSOMP Olivier-Maxence Prosper 5.00 12.00
RHSTJD Trayce Jackson-Davis 6.00 15.00
RHSDLII Dereck Lively II 10.00 25.00

2023-24 Topps Midnight Rookie Jersey Autographs

*TWILIGHT/99: .5X TO 1.25X BASIC
*DUSK/75: .5X TO 1.25X BASIC
*MOON BEAM: .6X TO 1.5X BASIC
*MOONRISE/25: .75X TO 2X BASIC
RJAAB Amari Bailey 6.00 15.00
RJABC Bilal Coulibaly 15.00 40.00
RJABM Brandon Miller 25.00 60.00
RJACJ Colby Jones 6.00 15.00
RJAGD Gradey Dick 12.00 30.00
RJAIW Isaiah Wong 6.00 15.00
RJAJC Jaylen Clark 6.00 15.00
RJAJT Jacob Toppin 5.00 12.00
RJAJW Jalen Wilson 6.00 15.00
RJAKJ Keyontae Johnson 6.00 15.00
RJAKM Kris Murray 6.00 15.00
RJALM Leonard Miller 6.00 15.00
RJAMS Marcus Sasser 10.00 25.00
RJANC Noah Clowney 8.00 20.00
RJARR Rayan Rupert 6.00 15.00
RJASC Sidy Cissoko 6.00 15.00
RJASH Scoot Henderson 20.00 50.00
RJATS Terquavion Smith 6.00 15.00
RJAVW Victor Wembanyama 500.00 1,000.00
RJABES Ben Sheppard 6.00 15.00
RJAJAW Jarace Walker 12.00 30.00
RJAJJJ Jaime Jaquez Jr. 10.00 25.00
RJAJOH Jordan Hawkins 10.00 25.00
RJAJUP Julian Phillips 6.00 15.00
RJAKOB Kobe Brown 6.00 15.00
RJANSJ Nick Smith Jr. 8.00 20.00

2023-24 Topps Midnight Star Studded

*TWILIGHT/99: 1.5X TO 4X BASIC
*DUSK/75: 1.5X TO 4X BASIC
*MOON BEAM: 2X TO 5X BASIC
*MOONRISE/25: 2.5X TO 6X BASIC
SS1 Nikola Jokic 2.00 5.00
SS2 Zach LaVine .60 1.50
SS3 Donovan Mitchell .75 2.00
SS4 Jayson Tatum 1.50 4.00
SS5 Cade Cunningham 1.00 2.50
SS6 Stephen Curry 3.00 8.00
SS7 Klay Thompson 1.00 2.50
SS8 Kyrie Irving .75 2.00
SS9 Domantas Sabonis .60 1.50
SS10 Karl-Anthony Towns .60 1.50
SS11 Jalen Green .60 1.50
SS12 Josh Giddey .50 1.25
SS13 Jalen Brunson .75 2.00
SS14 Tyrese Maxey .75 2.00
SS15 Pascal Siakam .60 1.50
SS16 Kristaps Porzingis .50 1.25
SS17 Tyrese Haliburton .75 2.00
SS18 Giannis Antetokounmpo 2.00 5.00
SS19 Shai Gilgeous-Alexander 2.00 5.00
SS20 Bradley Beal .50 1.25
SS21 Victor Wembanyama 10.00 25.00
SS22 Brandon Miller 1.50 4.00
SS23 Scoot Henderson 1.25 3.00
SS24 Taylor Hendricks .40 1.00
SS25 Gradey Dick .75 2.00
SS26 Jordan Hawkins .60 1.50
SS27 Jaime Jaquez Jr. .60 1.50
SS28 Dereck Lively II .75 2.00
SS29 Cam Whitmore 1.00 2.50
SS30 Brandin Podziemski 1.25 3.00

2023-24 Topps Midnight Stroke of Midnight Autographs

*TWILIGHT/99: .5X TO 1.25X BASIC
*DUSK/75: .5X TO 1.25X BASIC
*MOON BEAM: .6X TO 1.5X BASIC
*MOONRISE/25: .75X TO 2X BASIC
SMAAB Anthony Black 10.00 25.00
SMAAC Alex Caruso 5.00 12.00
SMAAG Aaron Gordon 5.00 12.00
SMAAH Anfernee Hardaway 20.00 50.00
SMAAW Andrew Wiggins 6.00 15.00
SMABB Bradley Beal 6.00 15.00
SMABH Bones Hyland 4.00 10.00
SMABP Brandin Podziemski 15.00 40.00
SMACJ Cameron Johnson 5.00 12.00
SMACK Corey Kispert 4.00 10.00
SMACP Chris Paul 10.00 25.00
SMACS Collin Sexton 6.00 15.00
SMACW Cam Whitmore 12.00 30.00
SMADA Deandre Ayton 5.00 12.00
SMADF De'Aaron Fox 10.00 25.00
SMADH De'Andre Hunter 5.00 12.00
SMADL Dereck Lively II 10.00 25.00
SMADM Donovan Mitchell 10.00 25.00
SMADN Dirk Nowitzki 40.00 100.00
SMADR D'Angelo Russell 5.00 12.00
SMADW Dominique Wilkins 8.00 20.00
SMAGG George Gervin 8.00 20.00
SMAGH Grant Hill 8.00 20.00
SMAHO Hakeem Olajuwon 20.00 50.00
SMAJB Jalen Brunson 40.00 100.00
SMAJC Jordan Clarkson 5.00 12.00
SMAJG Jalen Green 8.00 20.00
SMAJH Josh Hart 5.00 12.00
SMAJJ Jaren Jackson Jr. 8.00 20.00
SMAJK Jason Kidd 8.00 20.00
SMAJT Jayson Tatum 40.00 100.00
SMAJV Jonas Valanciunas 4.00 10.00
SMAJW Jerry West 10.00 25.00
SMAKB Kobe Bufkin 6.00 15.00
SMAKD Kevin Durant 60.00 150.00
SMAKG Kevin Garnett 20.00 50.00
SMAKH Kevin Huerter 4.00 10.00
SMAKM Khris Middleton 5.00 12.00
SMALB Larry Bird 60.00 150.00
SMALJ Larry Johnson 6.00 15.00
SMALM Lauri Markkanen 8.00 20.00
SMAMG Manu Ginobili 10.00 25.00
SMAMJ Magic Johnson 40.00 100.00
SMAMP Michael Porter Jr. 6.00 15.00
SMAMS Marcus Smart 6.00 15.00
SMAPP Paul Pierce 8.00 20.00
SMARA Ray Allen 8.00 20.00
SMARH Rui Hachimura 5.00 12.00
SMARP Robert Parish 6.00 15.00
SMASD Spencer Dinwiddie 4.00 10.00
SMASK Shawn Kemp 8.00 20.00
SMATH Tyrese Haliburton 20.00 50.00
SMATP Tony Parker 8.00 20.00
SMAVC Vince Carter 20.00 50.00
SMAWK Walker Kessler 5.00 12.00
SMACJM CJ McCollum 5.00 12.00
SMADEG Devonte' Graham 4.00 10.00
SMADRO David Robinson 20.00 50.00
SMADWA Dwyane Wade 20.00 50.00
SMADWI Deron Williams 4.00 10.00
SMAFVV Fred VanVleet 8.00 20.00
SMAJES Jeremy Sochan 6.00 15.00
SMAJHO Jett Howard 6.00 15.00
SMAJHS Jalen Hood-Schifino 5.00 12.00
SMAJPO Jakob Poeltl 4.00 10.00
SMAJRH Jrue Holiday 6.00 15.00
SMAKAT Karl-Anthony Towns 8.00 20.00
SMAKCP Kentavious Caldwell-Pope 4.00 10.00
SMALBJ LeBron James 1,000.00 2,000.00
SMAOGA OG Anunoby 6.00 15.00
SMAOMP Olivier-Maxence Prosper 5.00 12.00
SMARHA Rip Hamilton 6.00 15.00
SMATHE Taylor Hendricks 5.00 12.00
SMATYH Tyler Herro 8.00 20.00

2023-24 Topps Motif

STATED PRINT RUN 99 SER.#'d SETS
JSY AU RC STATED PRINT RUN 49 SER.#'d SETS
*ULTRAMARINE BLUE/35-49: .5X TO 1.2X BASIC
*CADMIUM ORANGE/25: .6X TO 1.5X BASIC
1 LeBron James 15.00 40.00
2 Paul George 3.00 8.00
3 Giannis Antetokounmpo 10.00 25.00
4 De'Aaron Fox 4.00 10.00
5 Karl-Anthony Towns 3.00 8.00
6 Domantas Sabonis 3.00 8.00
7 Magic Johnson 8.00 20.00
8 Chet Holmgren 5.00 12.00
9 Rudy Gobert 2.50 6.00
10 Scottie Barnes 2.50 6.00
11 Bam Adebayo 3.00 8.00
12 Kevin Garnett 5.00 12.00
13 Markelle Fultz 1.50 4.00
14 Bennedict Mathurin 3.00 8.00
15 Deandre Ayton 2.00 5.00
16 Maxwell Lewis RC 1.50 4.00
17 Chris Paul 4.00 10.00
18 Brandin Podziemski RC 6.00 15.00
19 Tracy McGrady 3.00 8.00
20 Kobe Bufkin RC 2.50 6.00
21 Tyrese Haliburton 4.00 10.00
22 Evan Mobley 3.00 8.00
23 Bradley Beal 2.50 6.00
24 Trae Young 4.00 10.00
25 Joel Embiid 5.00 12.00
26 Nikola Vucevic 2.00 5.00
27 Cam Johnson 2.00 5.00
28 Dennis Rodman 5.00 12.00
29 Franz Wagner 3.00 8.00
30 Anfernee Simons 2.50 6.00
31 Ben Simmons 2.00 5.00
32 Josh Giddey 2.50 6.00
33 Larry Bird 8.00 20.00
34 Jaylen Brown 4.00 10.00
35 OG Anunoby 2.50 6.00
36 Myles Turner 2.00 5.00
37 Alonzo Mourning 3.00 8.00
38 Damian Lillard 5.00 12.00
39 Jalen Brunson 4.00 10.00
40 Shawn Kemp 3.00 8.00
41 Dirk Nowitzki 5.00 12.00
42 Collin Sexton 2.50 6.00
43 Jrue Holiday 2.50 6.00
44 Devin Booker 5.00 12.00
45 Jalen Green 3.00 8.00
46 Ben Wallace 2.50 6.00
47 Jordan Poole 3.00 8.00
48 Olivier-Maxence Prosper RC 2.00 5.00
49 Dejounte Murray 2.50 6.00
50 Julian Strawther RC 2.50 6.00
51 John Stockton 4.00 10.00
52 Anfernee Hardaway 5.00 12.00
53 Dereck Lively II RC 4.00 10.00
54 Brandon Clarke 1.50 4.00
55 Jimmy Butler 3.00 8.00
56 Marcus Smart 2.50 6.00
57 Julius Randle 2.50 6.00
58 Larry Johnson 2.50 6.00
59 Alperen Segun 3.00 8.00
60 Aaron Gordon 2.50 6.00
61 Zach LaVine 3.00 8.00
62 Jordan Walsh RC 2.00 5.00
63 Jeremy Sochan 2.50 6.00
64 Kyle Kuzma 2.50 6.00
65 Brice Sensabaugh RC 3.00 8.00
66 Kevin Durant 6.00 15.00
67 Jalen Williams 4.00 10.00
68 Tyler Herro 3.00 8.00
69 David Robinson 4.00 10.00
70 Carmelo Anthony 3.00 8.00
71 Kevin Love 2.00 5.00
72 Shaquille O'Neal 6.00 15.00
73 CJ McCollum 2.00 5.00
74 DeMar DeRozan 3.00 8.00
75 Manu Ginobili 4.00 10.00
76 Kyrie Irving 4.00 10.00
77 Jason Kidd 3.00 8.00
78 Austin Reaves 5.00 12.00
79 Desmond Bane 2.50 6.00
80 Mikal Bridges 2.50 6.00
81 Michael Porter Jr. 2.50 6.00
82 Pascal Siakam 3.00 8.00
83 Stephen Curry 15.00 40.00
84 Nikola Jokic 10.00 25.00
85 LaMelo Ball 5.00 12.00
86 Kawhi Leonard 5.00 12.00
87 Khris Middleton 2.00 5.00
88 Taylor Hendricks RC 2.00 5.00
89 Anthony Davis 5.00 12.00
90 Trayce Jackson-Davis RC 2.50 6.00
91 Cade Cunningham 5.00 12.00
92 Shaedon Sharpe 4.00 10.00
93 Tyrese Maxey 4.00 10.00
94 Jakob Poeltl 1.50 4.00
95 Donovan Mitchell 4.00 10.00
96 Dwyane Wade 4.00 10.00
97 Russell Westbrook 3.00 8.00
98 Brandon Ingram 2.50 6.00
99 Tony Parker 3.00 8.00
100 Jayson Tatum 8.00 20.00
101 Victor Wembanyama JSY AU RC 600.00 1,200.00
102 Brandon Miller JSY AU RC 40.00 100.00
103 Scoot Henderson JSY AU RC 30.00 80.00
104 Isaiah Wong JSY AU RC 10.00 25.00
105 Bilal Coulibaly JSY AU RC 25.00 60.00
106 Jarace Walker JSY AU RC 20.00 50.00
107 Amari Bailey JSY AU RC 10.00 25.00
109 Keyontae Johnson JSY AU RC 10.00 25.00
110 Gradey Dick JSY AU RC 20.00 50.00
111 Jordan Hawkins JSY AU RC 15.00 40.00
112 Jaylen Clark JSY AU RC 10.00 25.00
113 Julian Phillips JSY AU RC 10.00 25.00
114 Jaime Jaquez Jr. JSY AU RC 15.00 40.00
115 Rayan Rupert JSY AU RC 10.00 25.00
116 Colby Jones JSY AU RC 10.00 25.00
117 Noah Clowney JSY AU RC 12.00 30.00
118 Kris Murray JSY AU RC 10.00 25.00
119 Jalen Wilson JSY AU RC 10.00 25.00
120 Marcus Sasser JSY AU RC 15.00 40.00
121 Ben Sheppard JSY AU RC 10.00 25.00
122 Nick Smith Jr. JSY AU RC 12.00 30.00
123 Sidy Cissoko JSY AU RC 10.00 25.00
124 Terquavion Smith JSY AU RC 10.00 25.00
125 Kobe Brown JSY AU RC 10.00 25.00
126 Jacob Toppin JSY AU RC 8.00 20.00
127 Leonard Miller JSY AU RC 10.00 25.00

2023-24 Topps Motif Acrylic Drip Autographs

STATED PRINT RUN 99 SER.#'d SETS
*ULTRAMARINE BLUE/49: .5X TO 1.2X BASIC
*CADMIUM ORANGE/25: .6X TO 1.5X BASIC
ADAAS Alperen Sengun 10.00 25.00
ADAAW Andrew Wiggins 8.00 20.00
ADABC Brandon Clarke 5.00 12.00
ADABM Brandon Miller 25.00 60.00
ADABP Brandin Podziemski 20.00 50.00
ADABS Ben Sheppard 6.00 15.00
ADACA Carmelo Anthony 20.00 50.00
ADACJ Colby Jones 6.00 15.00
ADACL Chris Livingston 6.00 15.00
ADACW Cam Whitmore 15.00 40.00
ADADH De'Andre Hunter 6.00 15.00
ADADL Dereck Lively II 12.00 30.00
ADADM Donovan Mitchell 20.00 50.00
ADADN Dirk Nowitzki 50.00 120.00
ADADR D'Angelo Russell 6.00 15.00
ADADS Domantas Sabonis 10.00 25.00
ADADW Deron Williams 5.00 12.00
ADAEH Elvin Hayes 8.00 20.00
ADAHO Hakeem Olajuwon 20.00 50.00
ADAJH Jrue Holiday 8.00 20.00
ADAJK Jason Kidd 10.00 25.00
ADAJT Jayson Tatum 50.00 120.00
ADAJW Jalen Williams 12.00 30.00
ADAKB Kobe Bufkin 8.00 20.00
ADAKH Kevin Huerter 5.00 12.00
ADAKJ Keyontae Johnson 6.00 15.00
ADAKM Kris Murray 6.00 15.00
ADALM Leonard Miller 6.00 15.00
ADAMS Marcus Sasser 10.00 25.00
ADARH Rip Hamilton 8.00 20.00
ADARR Rayan Rupert 6.00 15.00
ADASD Spencer Dinwiddie 5.00 12.00
ADASL Seth Lundy 5.00 12.00
ADATH Tyrese Haliburton 25.00 60.00
ADATP Tony Parker 10.00 25.00
ADAVW Victor Wembanyama 500.00 1,000.00
ADAZR Zach Randolph 6.00 15.00
ADABSE Brice Sensabaugh 10.00 25.00
ADACJM CJ McCollum 5.00 12.00
ADAGGJ GG Jackson 12.00 30.00
ADAJHA Josh Hart 6.00 15.00
ADAJJJ Jaime Jaquez Jr. 10.00 25.00
ADAJOW Jordan Walsh 6.00 15.00
ADAJWA Jarace Walker 12.00 30.00
ADAJWI Jamaal Wilkes 6.00 15.00
ADAKBR Kobe Brown 6.00 15.00
ADALMA Lauri Markkanen 10.00 25.00
ADAOGA OG Anunoby 8.00 20.00

2023-24 Topps Motif Canvas Champions Autographs

STATED PRINT RUN 99 SER.#'d SETS
*ULTRAMARINE BLUE/49: .5X TO 1.2X BASIC
*CADMIUM ORANGE/25: .6X TO 1.5X BASIC
CCAAG Aaron Gordon 6.00 15.00
CCABW Bill Walton 10.00 25.00
CCADN Dirk Nowitzki 50.00 120.00
CCADR David Robinson 12.00 30.00
CCADW Dwyane Wade 12.00 30.00
CCAJH Jrue Holiday 8.00 20.00
CCAJK Jason Kidd 10.00 25.00
CCAJW Jerry West 12.00 30.00
CCAKD Kevin Durant 40.00 100.00
CCAKM Khris Middleton 6.00 15.00
CCAMJ Magic Johnson 25.00 60.00
CCAPG Pau Gasol 10.00 25.00
CCAPP Paul Pierce 10.00 25.00
CCARH Rip Hamilton 8.00 20.00
CCASC Stephen Curry 150.00 400.00
CCATP Tony Parker 10.00 25.00
CCADRO Dennis Rodman 20.00 50.00
CCAFVV Fred VanVleet 10.00 25.00
CCAMPJ Michael Porter Jr. 8.00 20.00
CCAOGA OG Anunoby 8.00 20.00

2023-24 Topps Motif Gallery Graphs

STATED PRINT RUN 99 SER.#'d SETS
*ULTRAMARINE BLUE/49: .5X TO 1.2X BASIC
*CADMIUM ORANGE/25: .6X TO 1.5X BASIC
GGAD Ayo Dosunmu 6.00 15.00
GGAE Alex English 8.00 20.00
GGAG Aaron Gordon 6.00 15.00
GGAH Al Horford 6.00 15.00
GGAS Anfernee Simons 8.00 20.00
GGBM Brandon Miller 25.00 60.00
GGBS Ben Sheppard 6.00 15.00
GGCL Christian Laettner 6.00 15.00
GGCP Chris Paul 12.00 30.00
GGCS Collin Sexton 8.00 20.00
GGCW Cam Whitmore 15.00 40.00
GGDL Dereck Lively II 12.00 30.00
GGDM Dejounte Murray 8.00 20.00
GGDR David Robinson 12.00 30.00
GGFW Franz Wagner 10.00 25.00
GGGH Gordon Hayward 6.00 15.00
GGJH Jrue Holiday 8.00 20.00
GGJP Jakob Poeltl 5.00 12.00
GGJR OG Anunoby 8.00 20.00
GGJS Julian Strawther 8.00 20.00
GGJV Jarred Vanderbilt 5.00 12.00
GGJW Jordan Walsh 6.00 15.00
GGKB Kobe Bufkin 8.00 20.00
GGKH Kevin Huerter 5.00 12.00
GGKJ Keyontae Johnson 6.00 15.00
GGKL Kevin Love 6.00 15.00
GGKM Kris Murray 6.00 15.00
GGLJ Larry Johnson 8.00 20.00
GGLM Leonard Miller 6.00 15.00
GGMG Manu Ginobili 12.00 30.00
GGMJ Magic Johnson 25.00 60.00
GGML Maxwell Lewis 5.00 12.00
GGMS Marcus Smart 6.00 15.00
GGNC Noah Clowney 8.00 20.00
GGPS Pascal Siakam 10.00 25.00
GGRW Rasheed Wallace 8.00 20.00
GGSC Stephen Curry 150.00 400.00
GGSD Spencer Dinwiddie 5.00 12.00
GGSK Shawn Kemp 10.00 25.00
GGTH Taylor Hendricks 6.00 15.00
GGVW Victor Wembanyama 500.00 1,000.00
GGBSE Brice Sensabaugh 10.00 25.00
GGCJM CJ McCollum 6.00 15.00
GGDMI Donovan Mitchell 12.00 30.00
GGFVV Fred VanVleet 10.00 25.00
GGJHA Jordan Hawkins 10.00 25.00
GGJPH Julian Phillips 6.00 15.00
GGKBR Kobe Brown 6.00 15.00
GGMSA Marcus Sasser 10.00 25.00
GGTJD Trayce Jackson-Davis 8.00 20.00

2023-24 Topps Motif Headline Signatures

STATED PRINT RUN 99 SER.#'d SETS
*ULTRAMARINE BLUE/49: .5X TO 1.2X BASIC
*CADMIUM ORANGE/25: .6X TO 1.5X BASIC
HSAB Anthony Black 12.00 30.00
HSAC Alex Caruso 6.00 15.00
HSAE Alex English 8.00 20.00
HSAG Aaron Gordon 6.00 15.00
HSAR Austin Reaves 15.00 40.00
HSAS Anfernee Simons 8.00 20.00
HSBB Bradley Beal 8.00 20.00
HSBC Bilal Coulibaly 15.00 40.00
HSBM Brandon Miller 25.00 60.00
HSBP Brandin Podziemski 20.00 50.00
HSBW Bill Walton 10.00 25.00
HSCH Chet Holmgren 15.00 40.00
HSCW Cam Whitmore 15.00 40.00
HSDL Dereck Lively II 12.00 30.00
HSDM Dejounte Murray 8.00 20.00
HSGD Gradey Dick 12.00 30.00
HSGH Grant Hill 10.00 25.00
HSHO Hakeem Olajuwon 12.00 30.00
HSIQ Immanuel Quickley 6.00 15.00
HSJH Jordan Hawkins 10.00 25.00
HSJJ Jaren Jackson Jr. 10.00 25.00
HSJR Jalen Rose 6.00 15.00
HSJS Jeremy Sochan 8.00 20.00
HSJW Jarace Walker 12.00 30.00
HSKB Kobe Bufkin 8.00 20.00
HSKM Kris Murray 6.00 15.00
HSKP Kristaps Porzingis 8.00 20.00
HSMJ Magic Johnson 25.00 60.00
HSMS Marcus Sasser 10.00 25.00
HSMT Myles Turner 6.00 15.00
HSNC Noah Clowney 8.00 20.00
HSPP Paul Pierce 10.00 25.00
HSRA Ray Allen 10.00 25.00
HSRB Rick Barry 8.00 20.00
HSSC Stephen Curry 150.00 400.00
HSSD Spencer Dinwiddie 5.00 12.00
HSSH Scoot Henderson 20.00 50.00
HSTH Taylor Hendricks 6.00 15.00
HSVC Vince Carter 12.00 30.00
HSVW Victor Wembanyama 500.00 1,000.00
HSCJM CJ McCollum 6.00 15.00
HSJHS Jalen Hood-Schifino 6.00 15.00
HSJJJ Jaime Jaquez Jr. 10.00 25.00
HSJWI Jalen Williams 12.00 30.00
HSKBR Kobe Brown 6.00 15.00
HSKMI Khris Middleton 6.00 15.00
HSMSM Marcus Smart 8.00 20.00
HSNSJ Nick Smith Jr. 8.00 20.00
HSOGA OG Anunoby 8.00 20.00

2023-24 Topps Motif Legends of the Court Dual Signatures

LDSAC Alex English
Carmelo Anthony 30.00 80.00
LDSAS Anfernee Hardaway
Shaquille O'Neal 125.00 300.00
LDSAV Allen Iverson
Vince Carter 75.00 200.00
LDSBA Artis Gilmore
Bill Walton 30.00 80.00
LDSCG Christian Laettner
Grant Hill 30.00 80.00
LDSDJ Jason Kidd
Dirk Nowitzki 75.00 200.00
LDSDS Dwyane Wade
Shaquille O'Neal 200.00 500.00
LDSGD David Robinson
George Gervin 40.00 100.00
LDSHC Hakeem Olajuwon
Calvin Murphy 40.00 100.00
LDSJJ John Stockton
Jason Kidd 40.00 100.00
LDSJM Magic Johnson
Jerry West 80.00 200.00
LDSJR Ray Allen
Jalen Rose 30.00 80.00
LDSJZ Jason Williams
Zach Randolph 30.00 80.00
LDSLW Larry Johnson
Shawn Kemp 30.00 80.00
LDSPK Kevin Garnett
Paul Pierce 75.00 200.00
LDSPP Peja Stojakovic
Pau Gasol 30.00 80.00
LDSRB Rip Hamilton
Ben Wallace 25.00 60.00
LDSRT Tim Hardaway
Rick Barry 25.00 60.00
LDSTM Tony Parker
Manu Ginobili 40.00 100.00
LDSDJA Dennis Rodman
Jalen Rose 50.00 125.00

2023-24 Topps Motif Legends of the Court Relics

STATED PRINT RUN 99 SER.#'d SETS
*ULTRAMARINE BLUE/35: .5X TO 1.2X BASIC
*CADMIUM ORANGE/25: .6X TO 1.5X BASIC
LCR1 Alex Caruso 2.50 6.00
LCR2 Anthony Davis 6.00 15.00
LCR3 Bogdan Bogdanovic 2.50 6.00
LCR4 Brandon Miller 10.00 25.00
LCR5 Cade Cunningham 6.00 15.00
LCR6 John Collins 2.50 6.00
LCR7 Cameron Johnson 2.50 6.00
LCR8 Clint Capela 2.00 5.00
LCR9 De'Aaron Fox 5.00 12.00
LCR10 Danuel House Jr. 1.50 4.00
LCR11 De'Andre Hunter 2.50 6.00
LCR12 Dejounte Murray 3.00 8.00
LCR13 Donte DiVincenzo 2.50 6.00
LCR14 Isaiah Hartenstein 2.50 6.00
LCR15 Isaiah Stewart 2.50 6.00
LCR16 Rudy Gobert 3.00 8.00
LCR17 Jaren Jackson Jr. 4.00 10.00
LCR18 Jaylen Brown 5.00 12.00
LCR19 Jayson Tatum 10.00 25.00
LCR20 Joel Embiid 6.00 15.00
LCR21 Josh Hart 2.50 6.00
LCR22 Jrue Holiday 3.00 8.00
LCR23 Julius Randle 3.00 8.00
LCR24 Karl-Anthony Towns 4.00 10.00
LCR25 Kawhi Leonard 6.00 15.00
LCR26 Kelly Oubre Jr. 2.50 6.00
LCR27 Tim Hardaway Jr. 2.00 5.00
LCR28 Michael Porter Jr. 3.00 8.00
LCR29 Mikal Bridges 3.00 8.00
LCR30 Zach Lavine 4.00 10.00
LCR32 Nic Claxton 2.50 6.00
LCR33 Nicolas Batum 1.50 4.00
LCR34 Onyeka Okongwu 2.00 5.00
LCR35 Oshae Brissett 2.00 5.00
LCR36 Jordan Poole 4.00 10.00
LCR37 Patty Mills 2.50 6.00
LCR38 Saddiq Bey 2.50 6.00
LCR39 Kevin Huerter 2.00 5.00
LCR40 Scoot Henderson 8.00 20.00
LCR41 Shaquille O'Neal 8.00 20.00
LCR42 Malik Monk 3.00 8.00
LCR43 Tobias Harris 2.50 6.00
LCR44 Trae Young 5.00 12.00
LCR45 Tyrese Maxey 5.00 12.00
LCR46 Donovan Mitchell 5.00 12.00

2023-24 Topps Motif Legends of the Court Signatures

STATED PRINT RUN 99 SER.#'d SETS
*ULTRAMARINE BLUE/49: .5X TO 1.2X BASIC
*CADMIUM ORANGE/25: .6X TO 1.5X BASIC
LCSAE Alex English 10.00 25.00
LCSAG Artis Gilmore 10.00 25.00
LCSAH Anfernee Hardaway 20.00 50.00
LCSAI Allen Iverson 40.00 100.00
LCSAM Alonzo Mourning 12.00 30.00
LCSAS Arvydas Sabonis 10.00 25.00
LCSBW Bill Walton 12.00 30.00
LCSCA Carmelo Anthony 20.00 50.00
LCSCL Christian Laettner 8.00 20.00
LCSCM Calvin Murphy 8.00 20.00
LCSDN Dirk Nowitzki 40.00 100.00
LCSDR David Robinson 15.00 40.00
LCSDW Dwyane Wade 15.00 40.00
LCSEH Elvin Hayes 10.00 25.00
LCSGG George Gervin 12.00 30.00
LCSGH Grant Hill 12.00 30.00
LCSHO Hakeem Olajuwon 15.00 40.00
LCSJK Jason Kidd 12.00 30.00
LCSJR Jalen Rose 8.00 20.00
LCSJS John Stockton 15.00 40.00
LCSJW Jerry West 15.00 40.00
LCSKG Kevin Garnett 20.00 50.00
LCSLB Larry Bird 40.00 100.00
LCSLJ Larry Johnson 10.00 25.00
LCSLS Latrell Sprewell 10.00 25.00
LCSLW Clyde Drexler 12.00 30.00
LCSMC Maurice Cheeks 8.00 20.00
LCSMG Manu Ginobili 15.00 40.00
LCSMJ Magic Johnson 30.00 80.00
LCSPG Pau Gasol 12.00 30.00
LCSPP Paul Pierce 12.00 30.00
LCSPS Peja Stojakovic 8.00 20.00
LCSRA Ray Allen 12.00 30.00
LCSRH Rip Hamilton 10.00 25.00
LCSRP Robert Parish 10.00 25.00
LCSRW Rasheed Wallace 10.00 25.00
LCSSK Shawn Kemp 12.00 30.00
LCSSO Shaquille O'Neal 40.00 100.00
LCSTM Tracy McGrady 12.00 30.00
LCSTP Tony Parker 12.00 30.00
LCSVC Vince Carter 15.00 40.00
LCSZR Zach Randolph 8.00 20.00
LCSBWA Ben Wallace 10.00 25.00
LCSDEW Deron Williams 6.00 15.00
LCSDOW Dominique Wilkins 12.00 30.00
LCSDRO Dennis Rodman 20.00 50.00
LCSJAW Jason Williams 12.00 30.00
LCSJST Jerry Stackhouse 8.00 20.00
LCSJWI Jamaal Wilkes 8.00 20.00
LCSMWP Metta World Peace 8.00 20.00

2023-24 Topps Motif Motif Endorsements Autographs

STATED PRINT RUN 99 SER.#'d SETS
*ULTRAMARINE BLUE/49: .5X TO 1.2X BASIC
*CADMIUM ORANGE/25: .6X TO 1.5X BASIC
MEAB Anthony Black 12.00 30.00
MEAN Aaron Nesmith 6.00 15.00
MEAS Alperen Sengun 10.00 25.00
MEAW Andrew Wiggins 8.00 20.00
MEBB Bradley Beal 8.00 20.00
MEBC Brandon Clarke 5.00 12.00
MEBP Brandin Podziemski 20.00 50.00
MEBW Bill Walton 10.00 25.00
MECA Cole Anthony 6.00 15.00
MECK Corey Kispert 5.00 12.00
MEDF De'Aaron Fox 12.00 30.00
MEDR D'Angelo Russell 6.00 15.00
MEDW Deron Williams 5.00 12.00
MEGD Gradey Dick 12.00 30.00
MEGW Grant Williams 5.00 12.00
MEJB Jalen Brunson 25.00 60.00
MEJK Jason Kidd 10.00 25.00
MEJR Jalen Rose 6.00 15.00
MEJT Jayson Tatum 40.00 100.00
MEJW Jalen Williams 12.00 30.00
MELJ Larry Johnson 8.00 20.00
MELW Lenny Wilkens 8.00 20.00
MEMB Mikal Bridges 8.00 20.00
MEMC Maurice Cheeks 6.00 15.00
MEMW Mark Williams 6.00 15.00
MEPG Pau Gasol 10.00 25.00
MEPP Paul Pierce 10.00 25.00
MERH Rip Hamilton 8.00 20.00
MESB Saddiq Bey 6.00 15.00
MESC Seth Curry 6.00 15.00
MESH Scoot Henderson 20.00 50.00
MESK Shawn Kemp 10.00 25.00
METP Tony Parker 10.00 25.00
MEWK Walker Kessler 6.00 15.00
MEZC Zach Collins 5.00 12.00
MEZR Zach Randolph 6.00 15.00
MEBCO Bilal Coulibaly 15.00 40.00
MECAN Carmelo Anthony 20.00 50.00
MECJM CJ McCollum 6.00 15.00
MEDWA Dwyane Wade 20.00 50.00
MEJHS Jalen Hood-Schifino 6.00 15.00
MEJJJ Jaime Jaquez Jr. 10.00 25.00
MEJWA Jarace Walker 12.00 30.00
MEKAT Karl-Anthony Towns 10.00 25.00
MEMPJ Michael Porter Jr. 8.00 20.00
MENSJ Nick Smith Jr. 8.00 20.00
MEOGA OG Anunoby 8.00 20.00
MEOMP Olivier-Maxence Prosper 6.00 15.00
METHE Tyler Herro 10.00 25.00

2023-24 Topps Motif Motif Rookie Relic Autographs Quad

STATED PRINT RUN 49 SER.#'d SETS
*ULTRAMARINE BLUE/35: .5X TO 1.2X BASIC
*CADMIUM ORANGE/25: .6X TO 1.5X BASIC
MQAAB Amari Bailey 8.00 20.00
MQABC Bilal Coulibaly 20.00 50.00
MQABM Brandon Miller 30.00 80.00
MQABS Ben Sheppard 8.00 20.00
MQAGD Gradey Dick 15.00 40.00
MQAJC Jaylen Clark 8.00 20.00
MQAJH Jordan Hawkins 12.00 30.00
MQAJJ Jaime Jaquez Jr. 12.00 30.00
MQAJP Julian Phillips 8.00 20.00
MQAJT Jacob Toppin 6.00 15.00
MQAJW Jarace Walker 15.00 40.00
MQAKB Kobe Brown 8.00 20.00
MQAKM Kris Murray 8.00 20.00
MQALM Leonard Miller 8.00 20.00
MQAMS Marcus Sasser 12.00 30.00
MQANC Noah Clowney 10.00 25.00
MQANS Nick Smith Jr. 10.00 25.00
MQASH Scoot Henderson 25.00 60.00
MQAVW Victor Wembanyama 600.00 1,200.00

2023-24 Topps Motif Motif Rookie Relics

STATED PRINT RUN 49 SER.#'d SETS
*ULTRAMARINE BLUE/35: .5X TO 1.2X BASIC
*CADMIUM ORANGE/25: .6X TO 1.5X BASIC
MRR1 Victor Wembanyama 40.00 100.00
MRR2 Brandon Miller 8.00 20.00
MRR3 Scoot Henderson 6.00 15.00
MRR4 Isaiah Wong 2.00 5.00
MRR5 Bilal Coulibaly 5.00 12.00
MRR6 Jarace Walker 4.00 10.00
MRR7 Jacob Toppin 1.50 4.00
MRR8 Jaylen Clark 2.00 5.00
MRR9 Terquavion Smith 2.00 5.00
MRR10 Gradey Dick 4.00 10.00
MRR11 Jordan Hawkins 3.00 8.00
MRR12 Jalen Wilson 2.00 5.00
MRR13 Keyontae Johnson 2.00 5.00
MRR14 Jaime Jaquez Jr. 3.00 8.00
MRR16 Sidy Cissoko 2.00 5.00
MRR17 Noah Clowney 2.50 6.00
MRR18 Kris Murray 2.00 5.00
MRR19 Rayan Rupert 2.00 5.00
MRR20 Marcus Sasser 3.00 8.00
MRR21 Ben Sheppard 2.00 5.00
MRR22 Nick Smith Jr. 2.50 6.00
MRR23 Amari Bailey 2.00 5.00
MRR24 Julian Phillips 2.00 5.00
MRR25 Kobe Brown 2.00 5.00
MRR27 Leonard Miller 2.00 5.00

2023-24 Topps Motif Motif Rookie Relics Dual

STATED PRINT RUN 49 SER.#'d SETS
*ULTRAMARINE BLUE/35: .5X TO 1.2X BASIC
*CADMIUM ORANGE/25: .6X TO 1.5X BASIC
MDR1 Victor Wembanyama 40.00 100.00
MDR2 Brandon Miller 8.00 20.00
MDR3 Scoot Henderson 6.00 15.00
MDR5 Bilal Coulibaly 5.00 12.00
MDR6 Jarace Walker 4.00 10.00
MDR7 Jacob Toppin 1.50 4.00
MDR8 Jalen Wilson 2.00 5.00
MDR9 Keyontae Johnson 2.00 5.00
MDR10 Gradey Dick 4.00 10.00
MDR11 Jordan Hawkins 3.00 8.00
MDR12 Terquavion Smith 2.00 5.00
MDR13 Isaiah Wong 2.00 5.00
MDR14 Jaime Jaquez Jr. 3.00 8.00
MDR15 Jaylen Clark 2.00 5.00
MDR16 Sidy Cissoko 2.00 5.00
MDR17 Noah Clowney 2.50 6.00
MDR18 Kris Murray 2.00 5.00
MDR19 Rayan Rupert 2.00 5.00
MDR20 Marcus Sasser 3.00 8.00
MDR21 Ben Sheppard 2.00 5.00
MDR22 Nick Smith Jr. 2.50 6.00
MDR23 Amari Bailey 2.00 5.00
MDR24 Julian Phillips 2.00 5.00
MDR25 Kobe Brown 2.00 5.00
MDR27 Leonard Miller 2.00 5.00

2023-24 Topps Motif Rookie Dual Relic Autographs

STATED PRINT RUN 49 SER.#'d SETS
*ULTRAMARINE BLUE/35: .5X TO 1.2X BASIC
*CADMIUM ORANGE/25: .6X TO 1.5X BASIC
101 Victor Wembanyama 600.00 1,200.00
102 Brandon Miller 30.00 80.00
103 Scoot Henderson 25.00 60.00
104 Isaiah Wong 8.00 20.00
105 Bilal Coulibaly 20.00 50.00
106 Jarace Walker 15.00 40.00
107 Amari Bailey 8.00 20.00
109 Keyontae Johnson 8.00 20.00
110 Gradey Dick 15.00 40.00
111 Jordan Hawkins 12.00 30.00
112 Jaylen Clark 8.00 20.00
113 Julian Phillips 8.00 20.00
114 Jaime Jaquez Jr. 12.00 30.00
115 Rayan Rupert 8.00 20.00
116 Colby Jones 8.00 20.00
117 Noah Clowney 10.00 25.00
118 Kris Murray 8.00 20.00
119 Jalen Wilson 8.00 20.00
120 Marcus Sasser 12.00 30.00
121 Ben Sheppard 8.00 20.00
122 Nick Smith Jr. 10.00 25.00
123 Sidy Cissoko 8.00 20.00
124 Terquavion Smith 8.00 20.00
125 Kobe Brown 8.00 20.00
126 Jacob Toppin 6.00 15.00
127 Leonard Miller 8.00 20.00

2023-24 Topps Motif Rookie Triple Relic Autographs

STATED PRINT RUN 49 SER.#'d SETS
*ULTRAMARINE BLUE/35: .5X TO 1.2X BASIC
*CADMIUM ORANGE/25: .6X TO 1.5X BASIC
101 Victor Wembanyama 600.00 1,200.00
102 Brandon Miller 30.00 80.00
103 Scoot Henderson 25.00 60.00
104 Isaiah Wong 8.00 20.00
105 Bilal Coulibaly 20.00 50.00
106 Jarace Walker 15.00 40.00
107 Amari Bailey 8.00 20.00
109 Keyontae Johnson 8.00 20.00
110 Gradey Dick 15.00 40.00
111 Jordan Hawkins 12.00 30.00
112 Jaylen Clark 8.00 20.00
113 Julian Phillips 8.00 20.00
114 Jaime Jaquez Jr. 12.00 30.00
115 Rayan Rupert 8.00 20.00
116 Colby Jones 8.00 20.00
117 Noah Clowney 10.00 25.00
118 Kris Murray 8.00 20.00
119 Jalen Wilson 8.00 20.00
120 Marcus Sasser 12.00 30.00
121 Ben Sheppard 8.00 20.00
122 Nick Smith Jr. 10.00 25.00
123 Sidy Cissoko 8.00 20.00
124 Terquavion Smith 8.00 20.00
125 Kobe Brown 8.00 20.00
126 Jacob Toppin 6.00 15.00
127 Leonard Miller 8.00 20.00

2005-06 Topps NBA Collector Chips

COMPLETE SET (111) 80.00 160.00
1 Al Harrington .60 1.50
2 Al Jefferson .50 1.25
3 Allen Iverson 1.50 4.00
4 Amare Stoudemire .75 2.00
5 Anderson Varejao .50 1.25
6 Andre Iguodala .75 2.00
7 Andre Miller .60 1.50
8 Andrei Kirilenko .60 1.50
9 Andrew Bogut 1.00 2.50
10 Antawn Jamison .60 1.50
11 Antoine Walker .60 1.50
12 Antoine Wright .60 1.50
13 Baron Davis .75 2.00
14 Ben Gordon .60 1.50
15 Ben Wallace 1.00 2.50
16 Bob Sura .50 1.25
17 Brad Miller .60 1.50
18 Brevin Knight .50 1.25
19 Carlos Boozer .60 1.50
20 Carmelo Anthony 1.25 3.00
21 Caron Butler .60 1.50
22 Channing Frye .60 1.50
23 Charlie Villanueva .60 1.50
24 Chris Bosh 1.00 2.50
25 Chris Paul 4.00 10.00
26 Chris Taft .50 1.25
27 Chris Webber 1.00 2.50
28 Corey Maggette .60 1.50
29 Dan Dickau .50 1.25
30 Danny Granger .75 2.00
31 Darius Miles .50 1.25

32 Deron Williams 1.25 3.00
33 Desmond Mason .50 1.25
34 Dirk Nowitzki 2.00 5.00
35 Drew Gooden .60 1.50
36 Dwight Howard 1.00 2.50
37 Dwyane Wade 1.50 4.00
38 Elton Brand .60 1.50
39 Emeka Okafor .60 1.50
40 Gerald Green .75 2.00
41 Gilbert Arenas .75 2.00
42 Grant Hill 1.25 3.00
43 Hakim Warrick .60 1.50
44 Ike Diogu .50 1.25
45 J.R. Smith .75 2.00
46 Jalen Rose .60 1.50
47 Jamaal Magloire .50 1.25
48 Jamal Crawford .75 2.00
49 Jason Kidd 1.25 3.00
50 Jason Richardson .75 2.00
51 Jermaine O'Neal .60 1.50
53 Joey Graham .60 1.50
54 Josh Childress .50 1.25
55 Josh Howard .60 1.50
56 Josh Smith .60 1.50
57 Julius Hodge .50 1.25
58 Kenyon Martin .60 1.50
59 Kevin Garnett 2.00 5.00
60 Kirk Hinrich .60 1.50
61 Kobe Bryant 6.00 15.00
62 Lamar Odom .60 1.50
63 Larry Hughes .60 1.50
64 Latrell Sprewell .75 2.00
65 LeBron James 6.00 15.00
66 Luke Ridnour .60 1.50
67 Luol Deng .60 1.50
68 Manu Ginobili 1.50 4.00
69 Martell Webster .60 1.50
70 Marvin Williams .75 2.00
71 Maurice Williams .60 1.50
72 Mehmet Okur .50 1.25
73 Michael Finley .75 2.00
74 Michael Redd .60 1.50
75 Mike Bibby .75 2.00
76 Mike Miller .60 1.50
77 Monta Ellis 1.00 2.50
78 Morris Peterson .50 1.25
79 Pau Gasol 1.25 3.00
80 Paul Pierce 1.25 3.00
81 Peja Stojakovic .60 1.50
82 Primoz Brezec .50 1.25
83 Rashad McCants .60 1.50
84 Rashard Lewis .60 1.50
85 Rasheed Wallace .75 2.00
86 Ray Allen 1.25 3.00
87 Raymond Felton .60 1.50
88 Richard Hamilton 1.00 2.50
89 Richard Jefferson .60 1.50
90 Ron Artest .60 1.50
91 Sean May .50 1.25
92 Sebastian Telfair .60 1.50
93 Shane Battier .60 1.50
94 Shaquille O'Neal 2.50 6.00
95 Shaun Livingston .60 1.50
96 Shawn Marion .60 1.50
97 Stephen Jackson .60 1.50
98 Stephon Marbury 1.00 2.50
99 Steve Francis .75 2.00
100 Steve Nash 1.50 4.00
101 Tim Duncan 2.00 5.00
102 Tony Parker 1.25 3.00
103 Tracy McGrady 1.25 3.00
104 Trevor Ariza .50 1.25
105 Troy Murphy .60 1.50
106 Udonis Haslem .50 1.25
107 Vince Carter 1.50 4.00
108 Wally Szczerbiak .60 1.50
109 Wayne Simien .50 1.25
110 Yao Ming 1.50 4.00
111 Zach Randolph .75 2.00

2005-06 Topps NBA Collector Chips 599

*1-110 BLUE FOIL: .6X TO 1.5X CHIP 599 HI
*1-10 GREEN FOIL: .75X TO 2X CHIP 599 HI
*1-50 RED FOIL: .5X TO 1.25X CHIP 599 HI
1 Al Jefferson .60 1.50
2 Allen Iverson 2.00 5.00
3 Amare Stoudemire 1.00 2.50
4 Andre Iguodala 1.00 2.50
5 Andrei Kirilenko .75 2.00
6 Andrew Bogut 1.25 3.00
7 Antawn Jamison .75 2.00
8 Antoine Walker .75 2.00
9 Antoine Wright .75 2.00
10 Baron Davis 1.00 2.50
11 Ben Wallace 1.25 3.00
12 Bill Walton 1.25 3.00
13 Bob Cousy 1.50 4.00
14 Bob Sura .60 1.50
15 Brad Miller .75 2.00
16 Carlos Boozer .75 2.00
17 Carmelo Anthony 1.50 4.00
18 Caron Butler .75 2.00
19 Channing Frye .75 2.00
20 Charlie Villanueva .75 2.00
21 Chris Bosh 1.25 3.00
22 Chris Paul 5.00 12.00
23 Chris Taft .60 1.50
24 Chris Webber 1.25 3.00
25 Dan Dickau .60 1.50
26 Danny Granger 1.00 2.50
27 Darius Miles .60 1.50
28 Dave Cowens .60 1.50
29 Deron Williams 1.50 4.00
30 Dirk Nowitzki 2.50 6.00
31 Drazen Petrovic 1.00 2.50
32 Drew Gooden .75 2.00
33 Dwight Howard 1.25 3.00
34 Dwyane Wade 2.00 5.00
35 Earl Monroe 1.25 3.00
36 Emeka Okafor .75 2.00
37 George Gervin 1.00 2.50
38 Gerald Green 1.00 2.50
39 Gilbert Arenas 1.00 2.50
40 Grant Hill 1.50 4.00
41 Hakim Warrick .75 2.00
42 Ike Diogu .60 1.50
43 Isiah Thomas 1.50 4.00
44 Jamaal Magloire .60 1.50
45 Jamal Crawford 1.00 2.50
46 Jason Richardson 1.00 2.50
47 Jermaine O'Neal .75 2.00
48 Jerry West 1.50 4.00
49 Joey Graham .75 2.00
50 John Havlicek 1.50 4.00
51 Josh Howard .75 2.00
52 Julius Erving 2.00 5.00
53 Julius Hodge .60 1.50
54 Kareem Abdul-Jabbar 1.50 4.00
55 Kevin Garnett 2.50 6.00
56 Kirk Hinrich .75 2.00
57 Kobe Bryant 8.00 20.00
58 Lamar Odom .75 2.00
59 Larry Bird 3.00 8.00
60 Larry Hughes .75 2.00
61 Latrell Sprewell 1.00 2.50
62 LeBron James 8.00 20.00
63 Luke Ridnour .75 2.00
64 Luol Deng .75 2.00
65 Manu Ginobili 2.00 5.00
66 Martell Webster .75 2.00
67 Marvin Williams 1.00 2.50
68 Maurice Williams .75 2.00
69 Michael Finley 1.00 2.50
70 Michael Redd .75 2.00
71 Monta Ellis 1.25 3.00
72 Morris Peterson .60 1.50
73 Moses Malone 1.00 2.50
74 Oscar Robertson 1.00 2.50
75 Pau Gasol 1.50 4.00
76 Paul Pierce 1.50 4.00
77 Peja Stojakovic .75 2.00
78 Pete Maravich 1.50 4.00
79 Primoz Brezec .60 1.50
80 Quentin Richardson .60 1.50
81 Rashad McCants .60 1.50
82 Rashard Lewis .75 2.00
83 Rasheed Wallace 1.00 2.50
84 Ray Allen 1.50 4.00
85 Raymond Felton .75 2.00
86 Richard Jefferson .75 2.00
87 Richard Hamilton 1.25 3.00
88 Rick Barry .75 2.00
89 Ron Artest .75 2.00
90 Sean May .60 1.50
91 Sebastian Telfair .75 2.00
92 Shane Battier .75 2.00
93 Shaquille O'Neal 3.00 8.00
94 Shaun Livingston .75 2.00
95 Shawn Marion .75 2.00
96 Steve Francis 1.00 2.50
97 Steve Nash 2.00 5.00
98 Tim Duncan 2.50 6.00
99 Tracy McGrady 1.50 4.00
100 Trevor Ariza .60 1.50
101 Troy Murphy .60 1.50
102 Quentin Richardson .60 1.50
103 Vince Carter 2.00 5.00
104 Walt Frazier 1.00 2.50
105 Wayne Simien .60 1.50
106 Willis Reed 1.50 4.00
107 Wilt Chamberlain 2.00 5.00
108 Yao Ming 2.00 5.00
109 Zach Randolph 1.00 2.50
110 Zydrunas Ilgauskas .75 2.00

2005-06 Topps NBA Collector Chips Autographs

PRINT RUN 100 SER.#'d SETS
1 Allen Iverson 60.00 120.00
2 Carmelo Anthony 30.00 60.00
3 Charlie Villanueva 10.00 25.00
4 Chris Taft 8.00 20.00
5 Emeka Okafor 15.00 40.00
6 Gerald Green 8.00 20.00
7 Hakim Warrick 10.00 25.00
8 Joey Graham 8.00 20.00
9 Rashad McCants 10.00 25.00
10 Raymond Felton 15.00 30.00
11 Wayne Simien 8.00 20.00

2005-06 Topps NBA Collector Chips Blue

1 LeBron James 8.00 20.00
2 Dirk Nowitzki 2.50 6.00
3 Carmelo Anthony 1.50 4.00
4 Ben Wallace 1.25 3.00
5 Tracy McGrady 1.50 4.00
6 Yao Ming 2.00 5.00
7 Jermaine O'Neal .75 2.00
8 Kobe Bryant 8.00 20.00
9 Dwyane Wade 2.00 5.00
10 Shaquille O'Neal 3.00 8.00
11 Kevin Garnett 2.50 6.00
12 Vince Carter 2.00 5.00
13 Jason Kidd 1.50 4.00
14 Stephon Marbury 1.25 3.00
15 Steve Francis 1.00 2.50
16 Allen Iverson 2.00 5.00
17 Amare Stoudemire 1.00 2.50
18 Steve Nash 2.00 5.00
19 Ben Gordon .75 2.00
20 Tim Duncan 2.50 6.00
21 Manu Ginobili 2.00 5.00
22 Ray Allen 1.50 4.00
23 Emeka Okafor .75 2.00
24 Paul Pierce 1.50 4.00
25 Andrew Bogut 1.25 3.00
26 Marvin Williams 1.00 2.50
27 Chris Paul 5.00 12.00
28 Deron Williams 1.50 4.00
29 Gerald Green 1.00 2.50
30 Raymond Felton .75 2.00

2005-06 Topps NBA Collector Chips Green

1 LeBron James 10.00 25.00
2 Tracy McGrady 2.00 5.00
3 Steve Nash 2.50 6.00
4 Shaquille O'Neal 4.00 10.00
5 Tim Duncan 3.00 8.00
6 Dwyane Wade 2.50 6.00
7 Allen Iverson 2.50 6.00
8 Andrew Bogut 1.50 4.00
9 Marvin Williams 1.25 3.00
10 Chris Paul 6.00 15.00

2005-06 Topps NBA Collector Chips Red

1 Bill Russell 3.00 8.00
2 Wilt Chamberlain 2.00 5.00
3 Bob Cousy 1.50 4.00
4 Dave Cowens .60 1.50
5 Walt Frazier 1.00 2.50
6 John Havlicek 1.50 4.00
7 Earl Monroe 1.25 3.00
8 Oscar Robertson 1.00 2.50
9 Jerry West 1.50 4.00
10 Kareem Abdul-Jabbar 1.50 4.00
11 Moses Malone 1.00 2.50
12 George Gervin 1.00 2.50
13 Julius Erving 2.00 5.00
14 Drazen Petrovic 1.00 2.50
15 Pete Maravich 1.50 4.00
16 Larry Bird 3.00 8.00
17 Isiah Thomas 1.50 4.00
18 Rick Barry .75 2.00
19 Willis Reed 1.50 4.00
20 Bill Walton 1.25 3.00
21 Gilbert Arenas 1.00 2.50
22 Grant Hill 1.50 4.00
23 Zydrunas Ilgauskas .75 2.00
24 Allen Iverson 2.00 5.00
25 Antawn Jamison .75 2.00
26 Jermaine O'Neal .75 2.00
27 Shaquille O'Neal 3.00 8.00
28 Paul Pierce 1.50 4.00
29 Dwyane Wade 2.00 5.00
30 Ben Wallace 1.25 3.00
31 Ray Allen 1.50 4.00
32 Tim Duncan 2.50 6.00
33 Kevin Garnett 2.50 6.00
34 Manu Ginobili 2.00 5.00
35 Rashard Lewis .75 2.00
36 Shawn Marion .75 2.00
37 Tracy McGrady 1.50 4.00
38 Yao Ming 2.00 5.00
39 Steve Nash 2.00 5.00
40 Dirk Nowitzki 2.50 6.00
41 Amare Stoudemire 1.00 2.50
42 LeBron James 8.00 20.00
43 Vince Carter 2.00 5.00
44 Kobe Bryant 8.00 20.00
45 Allen Iverson 2.00 5.00
46 Carmelo Anthony 1.50 4.00
47 Quentin Richardson .60 1.50
48 Steve Nash 2.00 5.00
49 Josh Smith .75 2.00
50 Shawn Marion .75 2.00

2023-24 Topps NBL

*OPAL: .75X TO 2X BASIC
*BLUE: 1X TO 2.5X BASIC
*GOLDEN WADDLE/175: 2.5X TO 6X BASIC
*AQUA/125: 2.5X TO 6X BASIC
*GREEN/99: 3X TO 8X BASIC
*FUCHSIA/75: 4X TO 10X BASIC
*GOLD/50: 5X TO 12X BASIC
*ORANGE/25: 6X TO 15X BASIC
1 Alex Starling .30 .75
2 Trentyn Flowers RC .60 1.50
3 Isaac Humphries .30 .75
4 Jacob Wiley .30 .75
5 Trey Kell III .30 .75
6 Kyrin Galloway .30 .75
7 Mitch McCarron .30 .75
8 Nick Marshall .30 .75
9 Sunday Dech .30 .75
10 Jason Cadee .30 .75
11 Aron Baynes .30 .75
12 DJ Mitchell .30 .75
13 Isaac White .30 .75
14 Josh Bannan .30 .75
15 Mitch Norton .30 .75
16 Nathan Sobey .30 .75
17 Rocco Zikarsky RC 1.00 2.50
18 Sam McDaniel .30 .75
19 Shannon Scott .30 .75
20 Tyrell Harrison .30 .75
21 Josh Roberts .30 .75
22 Bobi Klintman RC .75 2.00
23 Bul Kuol .30 .75
24 Jonah Antonio .30 .75
25 Lat Mayen .30 .75
26 Patrick Miller .30 .75
27 Sam Mennenga RC .60 1.50
28 Sam Waardenburg .30 .75
29 Tahjere McCall .30 .75
30 Taran Armstrong RC .60 1.50
31 AJ Johnson RC 1.00 2.50
32 Dan Grida .30 .75
33 Gary Clark .30 .75
34 Justin Robinson .30 .75
35 Mason Peatling .30 .75
36 Sam Froling .30 .75
37 Todd Blanchfield .30 .75
38 Tyler Harvey .30 .75
39 Wani Swaka Lo Buluk .30 .75
40 Lachlan Olbrich RC .60 1.50
41 Ian Clark .30 .75
42 Ariel Hukporti .30 .75
43 Brad Newley .30 .75
44 Chris Goulding .30 .75
45 Flynn Cameron RC .60 1.50
46 Jo Lual-Acuil JR .30 .75
47 Tanner Krebs .30 .75
48 Luke Travers .30 .75
49 Matthew Dellavedova .30 .75
50 Shea Ili .30 .75
51 Zylan Cheatham .30 .75
52 Finn Delany .30 .75
53 Cameron Gliddon .30 .75
54 Parker Jackson-Cartwright .30 .75
55 Justinian Jessup .30 .75
56 Izayah Le'Afa .30 .75
57 Mangok Mathiang .30 .75
58 Mantas Rubštavicius RC .60 1.50
59 Tom Abercrombie .30 .75
60 Will McDowell-White .30 .75
61 Alexandre Sarr RC 1.50 4.00
62 Ben Henshall .30 .75
63 Bryce Cotton .30 .75
64 Corey Webster .30 .75
65 Kristian Doolittle .30 .75
66 Hyrum Harris .30 .75
67 Jesse Wagstaff .30 .75
68 Keanu Pinder .30 .75
69 Jordan Usher .30 .75
70 Tai Webster .30 .75
71 Craig Moller .30 .75
72 Will Cummings .30 .75
73 Alan Williams .30 .75
74 Ben Ayre .30 .75
75 Gorjok Gak .30 .75
76 Matt Kenyon .30 .75
77 Mitch Creek .30 .75
78 Owen Foxwell .30 .75
79 Reuben Te Rangi .30 .75
80 Gary Browne .30 .75
81 Jordan Hunter .30 .75
82 Alex Toohey RC .75 2.00
83 Angus Glover .30 .75
84 DJ Hogg .30 .75
85 Jaylin Galloway .30 .75
86 Jonah Bolden .30 .75
87 Denzel Valentine .30 .75
88 Kouat Noi .30 .75
89 Jaylen Adams .30 .75
90 Shaun Bruce .30 .75
91 Anthony Drmic .30 .75
92 Clint Steindl .30 .75
93 Fabijan Krslovic .30 .75
94 Jack McVeigh .30 .75
95 Majok Deng .30 .75
96 Jordon Crawford .30 .75
97 Junior Madut .30 .75
98 Marcus Lee .30 .75
99 Milton Doyle .30 .75
100 Will Magnay .30 .75

2023-24 Topps NBL '71 Topps

*OPAL: .75X TO 2X BASIC
*GOLD/50: 5X TO 12X BASIC
*ORNG/25: 6X TO 15X BASIC
TB1 Tyler Harvey .50 1.25
TB2 Jacob Wiley .50 1.25
TB3 Mitch Creek .50 1.25
TB4 Aron Baynes .50 1.25
TB5 Matthew Dellavedova .50 1.25
TB6 Denzel Valentine .50 1.25
TB7 Nathan Sobey .50 1.25
TB8 Milton Doyle .50 1.25
TB9 Isaac Humphries .50 1.25
TB10 Gary Clark .50 1.25
TB11 Jo Lual Acuil .50 1.25
TB12 Tahjere McCall .50 1.25
TB13 Tom Abercrombie .50 1.25
TB14 Kristian Doolittle .50 1.25
TB15 Bobi Klintman .75 2.00
TB16 AJ Johnson 1.00 2.50
TB17 Jordan Usher .50 1.25
TB18 Will Cummings .50 1.25
TB19 Alexandre Sarr 1.50 4.00
TB20 Alex Toohey .75 2.00
TB21 Will McDowell-White .50 1.25
TB22 Jaylin Galloway .50 1.25
TB23 Jack McVeigh .50 1.25
TB24 Chris Goulding .50 1.25
TB25 Trentyn Flowers .60 1.50

2023-24 Topps NBL All-NBL

NBL1 Tyler Harvey 12.00 30.00
NBL2 Bryce Cotton 12.00 30.00
NBL3 Mitch Creek 12.00 30.00
NBL4 Aron Baynes 12.00 30.00
NBL5 Matthew Dellavedova 12.00 30.00
NBL6 Parker Jackson-Cartwright 12.00 30.00
NBL7 Jaylen Adams 12.00 30.00
NBL8 Milton Doyle 12.00 30.00
NBL9 DJ Hogg 12.00 30.00
NBL10 Keanu Pinder 12.00 30.00
NBL11 Alan Williams 12.00 30.00
NBL12 Tahjere McCall 12.00 30.00

2023-24 Topps NBL Autographs

AAB Aron Baynes 10.00 25.00
AAH Ariel Hukporti 10.00 25.00
AAS Alexandre Sarr 30.00 80.00
AAT Alex Toohey 15.00 40.00
AAW Alan Williams 10.00 25.00
ABC Bryce Cotton 10.00 25.00
ABK Bobi Klintman 15.00 40.00
ACG Chris Goulding 10.00 25.00
ADV Denzel Valentine 10.00 25.00
AGB Gary Browne 10.00 25.00
AIC Ian Clark 10.00 25.00
AJA Jaylen Adams 10.00 25.00
AJB Jonah Bolden 10.00 25.00
AJC Jordan Crawford 10.00 25.00
AJM Jack McVeigh 10.00 25.00
AKP Keanu Pinder 10.00 25.00
AMC Mitch Creek 10.00 25.00
AMD Luke Travers 10.00 25.00
AMM Mitch McCarron 10.00 25.00
AMR Mantas Rubštavicius 12.00 30.00
ANS Nathan Sobey 10.00 25.00
ARZ Rocco Zikarsky 20.00 50.00
ASF Sam Froling 10.00 25.00
ATA Will McDowell-White 10.00 25.00
ATF Trentyn Flowers 12.00 30.00
ATH Tyler Harvey 10.00 25.00
ATM Tahjere McCall 10.00 25.00
AZC Zylan Cheatham 10.00 25.00
AAJ AJ Johnson 20.00 50.00
AJWI Jacob Wiley 10.00 25.00
AMDO Milton Doyle 10.00 25.00
ATAR Taran Armstrong 12.00 30.00

2023-24 Topps NBL Big City Ballers

*OPAL: .75X TO 2X BASIC
*GOLD/50: 5X TO 12X BASIC
*ORNG/25: 6X TO 15X BASIC
BCB1 Mitch McCarron .50 1.25
BCB2 Jason Cadee .50 1.25
BCB3 Aron Baynes .50 1.25
BCB4 Chris Smith .50 1.25
BCB5 Rocco Zikarsky 1.00 2.50
BCB6 Patrick Miller .50 1.25
BCB7 Sam Waardenburg .50 1.25
BCB8 Justin Robinson .50 1.25
BCB9 Ian Clark .50 1.25
BCB10 Tyler Harvey .50 1.25
BCB11 Shea Ili .50 1.25
BCB12 Matthew Dellavedova .50 1.25
BCB13 Zylan Cheatham .50 1.25
BCB14 Finn Delany .50 1.25
BCB15 Will McDowell-White .50 1.25
BCB16 Alexandre Sarr 1.50 4.00
BCB17 Bryce Cotton .50 1.25
BCB18 Jordan Usher .50 1.25
BCB19 Alan Williams .50 1.25
BCB20 Mitch Creek .50 1.25
BCB21 Jaylen Adams .50 1.25
BCB22 DJ Hogg .50 1.25
BCB23 Marcus Lee .50 1.25
BCB24 Milton Doyle .50 1.25
BCB25 Jonah Bolden .50 1.25

2023-24 Topps NBL Coast to Coast

*OPAL: .75X TO 2X BASIC
*GOLD/50: 5X TO 12X BASIC
*ORNG/25: 6X TO 15X BASIC
CC1 Mitch McCarron .50 1.25
CC2 Jacob Wiley .50 1.25
CC3 Bobi Klintman .75 2.00
CC4 Alex Toohey .75 2.00
CC5 DJ Mitchell .50 1.25
CC6 Ariel Hukporti .50 1.25
CC7 Alexandre Sarr 1.50 4.00
CC8 Shannon Scott .50 1.25
CC9 Nathan Sobey .50 1.25
CC10 Luke Travers .50 1.25
CC11 Taran Armstrong .60 1.50
CC12 Josh Roberts .50 1.25
CC13 Gary Clark .50 1.25
CC14 Hyunjung Lee .60 1.50
CC15 Justin Robinson .50 1.25
CC16 Ian Clark .50 1.25
CC17 Zylan Cheatham .50 1.25
CC18 Parker Jackson-Cartwright .50 1.25
CC19 Jordan Usher .50 1.25
CC20 Will McDowell-White .50 1.25
CC21 Bryce Cotton .50 1.25
CC22 Gary Browne .50 1.25
CC23 Mitch Creek .50 1.25
CC24 Will Cummings .50 1.25
CC25 Jaylen Adams .50 1.25
CC26 Jaylin Galloway .50 1.25
CC27 Jordan Crawford .50 1.25
CC28 Trentyn Flowers .60 1.50
CC29 Milton Doyle .50 1.25
CC30 Anthony Drmic .50 1.25

2023-24 Topps NBL Down Under

*OPAL: .75X TO 2X BASIC
*GOLD/50: 5X TO 12X BASIC
*ORNG/25: 6X TO 15X BASIC
DU1 Nathan Sobey .50 1.25
DU2 Taran Armstrong .60 1.50
DU3 Sam Froling .50 1.25
DU4 Chris Goulding .50 1.25
DU5 Finn Delany .50 1.25
DU6 Ben Henshall .50 1.25
DU7 Alex Toohey .75 2.00
DU8 Isaac Humphries .50 1.25
DU9 Mitch Creek .50 1.25
DU10 Will Magnay .50 1.25
DU11 Lachlan Olbrich .60 1.50
DU12 Mitch McCarron .50 1.25
DU13 Ben Ayre .50 1.25
DU14 Keanu Pinder .50 1.25
DU15 Will McDowell-White .50 1.25
DU16 Aron Baynes .50 1.25
DU17 Matthew Dellavedova .50 1.25
DU18 Jaylin Galloway .50 1.25
DU19 Jack McVeigh .50 1.25
DU20 Sam Waardenburg .50 1.25

2023-24 Topps NBL Next Stars

NS1 Rocco Zikarsky 20.00 50.00
NS2 Bobi Klintman 15.00 40.00
NS3 AJ Johnson 20.00 50.00
NS4 Ariel Hukporti 10.00 25.00
NS5 Mantas Rubštavicius 12.00 30.00
NS6 Alexandre Sarr 30.00 80.00
NS7 Alex Toohey 15.00 40.00
NS8 Trentyn Flowers 12.00 30.00

1997-98 Topps O-Pee-Chee

COMPLETE SET (219) 900.00 1,700.00
COMPLETE SERIES 1 (110) 100.00 200.00
COMPLETE SERIES 2 (110) 800.00 1,500.00
*OPC: 10X TO 25X BASE TOPPS HI
115 Tim Duncan 200.00 500.00
123 Michael Jordan 400.00 800.00
125 Tracy McGrady 30.00 80.00
171 Kobe Bryant 400.00 800.00

1998-99 Topps O-Pee-Chee

COMPLETE SET (110) 800.00 1,500.00
*OPC STARS: 5X TO 12X BASE TOPPS HI
49 Tim Duncan 30.00 80.00
68 Kobe Bryant 150.00 400.00
77 Michael Jordan 400.00 800.00
109 Dennis Rodman 12.00 30.00

2001-02 Topps Pristine

COMPLETE SET (110) 150.00 300.00
COMP.SET w/o SP's (50) 30.00 80.00
1 Allen Iverson 2.50 6.00
2 Shawn Marion 1.00 2.50
3 Baron Davis 1.00 2.50
4 Peja Stojakovic .75 2.00
5 Dirk Nowitzki 2.50 6.00
6 Michael Jordan 8.00 20.00
7 Dikembe Mutombo 1.50 4.00
8 Antoine Walker .75 2.00
9 David Robinson 2.00 5.00
10 Tracy McGrady 1.50 4.00
11 Rasheed Wallace 1.25 3.00
12 Kenyon Martin 1.00 2.50
13 Glenn Robinson 1.00 2.50
14 Shareef Abdur-Rahim .75 2.00
15 Lamar Odom .75 2.00
16 Alonzo Mourning 1.50 4.00
17 Latrell Sprewell 1.25 3.00
18 Stephon Marbury 1.25 3.00
19 Chris Webber 1.25 3.00
20 Darius Miles .60 1.50
21 Tim Duncan 2.50 6.00
22 Antawn Jamison .75 2.00
23 Jason Kidd 1.50 4.00
24 John Stockton 2.00 5.00
25 Michael Finley 1.00 2.50
26 Eddie Jones 1.00 2.50
27 Jamal Mashburn .75 2.00
28 Paul Pierce 1.50 4.00
29 Jason Terry 1.00 2.50
30 Kobe Bryant 8.00 20.00
31 Reggie Miller 2.00 5.00
32 Elton Brand .75 2.00
33 Antonio McDyess .75 2.00
34 Ray Allen 1.50 4.00
35 Kevin Garnett 2.50 6.00
36 Allan Houston 1.00 2.50
37 Grant Hill 1.50 4.00
38 Jalen Rose .75 2.00
39 Gary Payton 1.50 4.00
40 Vince Carter 2.00 5.00
41 Jerry Stackhouse 1.00 2.50
42 Karl Malone 2.00 5.00
43 Wang Zhizhi 1.00 2.50
44 Marcus Fizer .60 1.50
45 Marcus Camby .75 2.00
46 Andre Miller .75 2.00
47 Jason Williams 1.50 4.00
48 Hakeem Olajuwon 2.00 5.00
49 Shaquille O'Neal 4.00 10.00
50 Steve Francis 1.00 2.50
51 Eddie Griffin C RC .60 1.50
52 Eddie Griffin U .75 2.00
53 Eddie Griffin R 1.25 3.00
54 Kwame Brown C RC .75 2.00
55 Kwame Brown U 1.00 2.50
56 Kwame Brown R 1.50 4.00
57 Shane Battier C RC 1.50 4.00
58 Shane Battier U 2.00 5.00
59 Shane Battier R 3.00 8.00
60 Eddy Curry C RC .75 2.00
61 Eddy Curry U 1.00 2.50
62 Eddy Curry R 1.50 4.00
63 Tyson Chandler C RC 1.25 3.00
64 Tyson Chandler U 1.50 4.00
65 Tyson Chandler R 2.50 6.00
66 Rodney White C RC .50 1.25
67 Rodney White U .60 1.50
68 Rodney White R 1.00 2.50
69 Jason Richardson C RC 1.25 3.00
70 Jason Richardson U 1.50 4.00
71 Jason Richardson R 2.50 6.00
72 Joe Johnson C RC 1.25 3.00
73 Joe Johnson U 1.50 4.00
74 Joe Johnson R 2.50 6.00
75 Pau Gasol C RC 3.00 8.00
76 Pau Gasol U 4.00 10.00
77 Pau Gasol R 6.00 15.00
78 Desagana Diop C RC .50 1.25
79 Desagana Diop U .60 1.50
80 Desagana Diop R 1.00 2.50
81 Vladimir Radmanovic C RC .60 1.50
82 Vladimir Radmanovic U .75 2.00
83 Vladimir Radmanovic R 1.25 3.00
84 Troy Murphy C RC .60 1.50
85 Troy Murphy U .75 2.00
86 Troy Murphy R 1.25 3.00
87 Zach Randolph C RC 1.50 4.00
88 Zach Randolph U 2.00 5.00
89 Zach Randolph R 3.00 8.00
90 Jamaal Tinsley C RC .60 1.50
91 Jamaal Tinsley U .75 2.00
92 Jamaal Tinsley R 1.25 3.00
93 Richard Jefferson C RC 1.00 2.50
94 Richard Jefferson U 1.25 3.00
95 Richard Jefferson R 2.00 5.00
96 Loren Woods C RC .50 1.25
97 Loren Woods U .60 1.50
98 Loren Woods R 1.00 2.50
99 Joseph Forte C RC .50 1.25
100 Joseph Forte U .60 1.50
101 Joseph Forte R 1.00 2.50
102 Gerald Wallace C RC 1.00 2.50
103 Gerald Wallace U 1.25 3.00
104 Gerald Wallace R 2.00 5.00
105 Andrei Kirilenko C RC 1.25 3.00
106 Andrei Kirilenko U 1.50 4.00
107 Andrei Kirilenko R 2.50 6.00
108 Tony Parker C RC 3.00 8.00
109 Tony Parker U 4.00 10.00
110 Tony Parker R 6.00 15.00

2001-02 Topps Pristine Refractors

*STARS: 6X TO 15X BASE CARD HI
1-50 PRINT RUN 50 SERIAL #'d SETS
*RCs: 1X TO 2.5X BASE CARD HI
*RC/750: 1.25X TO 3X BASE RC C VERSION
*RCs/250: 2X TO 5X BASE RC C VERSION
6 Michael Jordan 400.00 800.00
21 Tim Duncan 40.00 100.00
28 Paul Pierce 30.00 80.00
35 Kevin Garnett 50.00 120.00

2001-02 Topps Pristine Autographs

STATED ODDS 1:4
AAD Antonio Daniels 2.50 6.00
AAFM Aaron McKie 2.50 6.00
AAJ Antawn Jamison 3.00 8.00
AAM Andre Miller 3.00 8.00
ABD Baron Davis 4.00 10.00
ABH Brendan Haywood 3.00 8.00
ABJ Bobby Jackson 2.50 6.00
ACB Chauncey Billups 5.00 12.00
ADB Damone Brown 2.50 6.00
ADH Donnell Harvey 2.50 6.00
ADM Desmond Mason 3.00 8.00
AEB Elton Brand 3.00 8.00
AEC Eddy Curry 4.00 10.00
AGA Gilbert Arenas 10.00 25.00
AHT Hedo Turkoglu 6.00 15.00
AIT Iakovos Tsakalidis 2.50 6.00
AJB Jonathan Bender 2.50 6.00
AJF Joseph Forte 2.50 6.00
AJJ Joe Johnson 6.00 15.00
AJO Jermaine O'Neal 3.00 8.00
AJT Jason Terry 4.00 10.00
AJTR Jeff Trepagnier 2.50 6.00
AKAJ Kareem Abdul-Jabbar 50.00 120.00
AKB Kwame Brown 4.00 10.00
AKBR Kedrick Brown 2.50 6.00
AKS Kenny Satterfield 2.50 6.00
ALW Loren Woods 2.50 6.00
AMB Mike Bibby 4.00 10.00
AMJ Marc Jackson 2.50 6.00
APS Peja Stojakovic 3.00 8.00
ARH Richard Hamilton 8.00 20.00
ARJ Richard Jefferson 5.00 12.00
ARL Raef LaFrentz 2.50 6.00
ASB Shane Battier 6.00 15.00
ASM Shawn Marion 6.00 15.00
ASO Shaquille O'Neal 60.00 150.00
ATD Tim Duncan 300.00 600.00
ATMU Troy Murphy 3.00 8.00
AZR Zach Randolph 8.00 20.00

2001-02 Topps Pristine Oversized Relics

STATED ODDS 1 PER BOX
BLAH Allan Houston 5.00 12.00
BLAI Allen Iverson 12.00 30.00
BLAM Alonzo Mourning 8.00 20.00
BLCM Cuttino Mobley 4.00 10.00
BLDM Dikembe Mutombo 8.00 20.00
BLDN Dirk Nowitzki 12.00 30.00
BLDR David Robinson 8.00 20.00
BLDW David Wesley 3.00 8.00
BLGR Glenn Robinson 5.00 12.00
BLJK Jason Kidd 8.00 20.00
BLJS Jerry Stackhouse 5.00 12.00
BLJHS John Stockton 10.00 25.00
BLKM Karl Malone 10.00 25.00
BLLO Lamar Odom 4.00 10.00
BLLS Latrell Sprewell 6.00 15.00
BLRH Richard Hamilton 6.00 15.00
BLRW Rasheed Wallace 6.00 15.00
BLTD Tim Duncan 12.00 30.00

2001-02 Topps Pristine Partners

STATED ODDS 1:11
PAAH Allan Houston 3.00 8.00
PACM Cuttino Mobley 2.50 6.00
PADF Derek Fisher 2.50 6.00
PAGH Grant Hill 5.00 12.00
PAJW Jason Williams 5.00 12.00
PARH Richard Hamilton 4.00 10.00
PASF Steve Francis 3.00 8.00
PATL Trajan Langdon 2.00 5.00
PATM Tracy McGrady 5.00 12.00

2001-02 Topps Pristine Portions

STATED ODDS 1:3
PPAM Alonzo Mourning 4.00 10.00
PPDM Dikembe Mutombo 4.00 10.00
PPDN Dirk Nowitzki 6.00 15.00
PPEJ Eddie Jones 2.50 6.00
PPGP Gary Payton 4.00 10.00
PPJK Jason Kidd 4.00 10.00
PPJP James Posey 1.50 4.00
PPMB Mike Bibby 2.50 6.00
PPMC Mateen Cleaves 1.50 4.00
PPMD Michael Dickerson 1.50 4.00
PPMO Michael Olowokandi 1.50 4.00
PPRD Ricky Davis 2.00 5.00
PPRH Richard Hamilton 3.00 8.00
PPSJ Stephen Jackson 2.00 5.00
PPSO Shaquille O'Neal 10.00 25.00
PPTD Tim Duncan 6.00 15.00
PPTM Todd MacCulloch 1.50 4.00
PPTP Terry Porter 1.50 4.00

2001-02 Topps Pristine Premier

STATED ODDS 1:6
PRAD Antonio Davis 3.00 8.00
PRAH Allan Houston 4.00 10.00
PRAI Allen Iverson 10.00 25.00
PRAM Anthony Mason 4.00 10.00
PRAKM Antonio McDyess 3.00 8.00
PRDD Dale Davis 2.50 6.00
PRGR Glenn Robinson 4.00 10.00
PRJS Jerry Stackhouse 4.00 10.00
PRMF Michael Finley 4.00 10.00
PRRA Ray Allen 6.00 15.00
PRRW Rasheed Wallace 5.00 12.00
PRSM Stephon Marbury 5.00 12.00
PRTM Tracy McGrady 6.00 15.00
PRVD Vlade Divac 3.00 8.00

2001-02 Topps Pristine Slice of a Star

STATED ODDS 1:3
SAI Allen Iverson 8.00 20.00
SAM Alonzo Mourning 5.00 12.00
SBS Bob Sura 2.00 5.00
SCW Chris Webber 4.00 10.00
SDR David Robinson 6.00 15.00
SEJ Eddie Jones 3.00 8.00
SGH Grant Hill 5.00 12.00
SGP Gary Payton 5.00 12.00
SJDS Jerry Stackhouse 3.00 8.00
SJS John Stockton 6.00 15.00
SLH Larry Hughes 2.50 6.00
SLO Lamar Odom 2.50 6.00
SMF Michael Finley 3.00 8.00
SRA Ray Allen 5.00 12.00
SRM Reggie Miller 4.00 10.00
SSO Shaquille O'Neal 12.00 30.00
STD Tim Duncan 8.00 20.00
STP Terry Porter 2.00 5.00

2001-02 Topps Pristine Sweat and Tears

STATED ODDS 1:8
CHBD Baron Davis 6.00 15.00
CHDC Derrick Coleman 5.00 12.00
CHDW David Wesley 4.00 10.00
CHEC Elden Campbell 4.00 10.00
CHER Eddie Robinson 4.00 10.00
CHJM Jamal Mashburn 5.00 12.00
CHJDM Jamaal Magloire 4.00 10.00
CHPB P.J. Brown 4.00 10.00
DMCB Calvin Booth 4.00 10.00
DMDN Dirk Nowitzki 15.00 40.00
DMHE Howard Eisley 4.00 10.00
DMJH Juwan Howard 5.00 12.00
DMMF Michael Finley 6.00 15.00
DMSB Shawn Bradley 4.00 10.00
DMSN Steve Nash 12.00 30.00
DMWZ Wang Zhizhi 12.00 30.00
IPAC Austin Croshere 4.00 10.00
IPAH Al Harrington 5.00 12.00
IPJB Jonathan Bender 4.00 10.00
IPJO Jermaine O'Neal 5.00 12.00

IPJR Jalen Rose 5.00 12.00
IPRM Reggie Miller 12.00 30.00
IPTB Travis Best 4.00 10.00
MBEJ Ervin Johnson 4.00 10.00
MBGR Glenn Robinson 6.00 15.00
MBJP Joel Przybilla 4.00 10.00
MBRA Ray Allen 15.00 40.00
MBSC Sam Cassell 5.00 12.00
MBTT Tim Thomas 4.00 10.00
OMAD Andrew DeClercq 4.00 10.00
OMBO Bo Outlaw 4.00 10.00
OMDA Darrell Armstrong 4.00 10.00
OMMM Mike Miller 5.00 12.00
OMPG Pat Garrity 4.00 10.00
OMTM Tracy McGrady 10.00 25.00
PSCR Clifford Robinson 6.00 15.00
PSDS Daniel Santiago 4.00 10.00
PSIT Iakovos Tsakalidis 4.00 10.00
PSJK Jason Kidd 10.00 25.00
PSRR Rodney Rogers 4.00 10.00
PSSM Shawn Marion 6.00 15.00
PSTD Tony Delk 5.00 12.00
PSTG Tom Gugliotta 4.00 10.00
SSAD Antonio Daniels 4.00 10.00
SSAJ Avery Johnson 5.00 12.00
SSDA Derek Anderson 4.00 10.00
SSDR David Robinson 20.00 50.00
SSSE Sean Elliott 5.00 12.00
SSTD Tim Duncan 20.00 50.00
SSTP Terry Porter 4.00 10.00

2001-02 Topps Pristine Team Topps Captain Oversized

STATED ODDS: ONE PER CASE
CLSO Shaquille O'Neal 20.00 50.00
CLTD Tim Duncan 12.00 30.00

2002-03 Topps Pristine

COMP.SET w/o SP's (50) 20.00 50.00
UNCOMMON RC PRINT RUN 1499 SER.#'d SETS
RARE RC PRINT RUN 499 SER.#'d SETS
1 Shaquille O'Neal 2.50 6.00
2 Steve Nash 1.25 3.00
3 Vince Carter 1.25 3.00
4 Michael Jordan 15.00 40.00
5 Chris Webber .75 2.00
6 Tim Duncan 1.50 4.00
7 Vladimir Radmanovic .40 1.00
8 Kobe Bryant 12.00 30.00
9 Allan Houston .60 1.50
10 Tracy McGrady 1.00 2.50
11 Allen Iverson 1.50 4.00
12 Scottie Pippen 1.50 4.00
13 Steve Francis .60 1.50
14 Reggie Miller 1.25 3.00
15 Antoine Walker .50 1.25
16 Shawn Marion .60 1.50
17 Wally Szczerbiak .50 1.25
18 Elton Brand .60 1.50
19 Jerry Stackhouse .60 1.50
20 Andre Miller .50 1.25
21 Gary Payton 1.00 2.50
22 Richard Hamilton .75 2.00
23 Pau Gasol .60 1.50
24 Juwan Howard .50 1.25
25 Jalen Rose .50 1.25
26 Eddie Jones .60 1.50
27 Baron Davis .60 1.50
28 Darrell Armstrong .40 1.00
29 John Stockton 1.25 3.00
30 Mike Bibby .60 1.50
31 Eddy Curry .40 1.00
32 Kevin Garnett 1.50 4.00
33 Dikembe Mutombo .60 1.50
34 Jason Kidd 1.00 2.50
35 Clifford Robinson .60 1.50
36 Ray Allen 1.00 2.50
37 Paul Pierce 1.00 2.50
38 Shane Battier .60 1.50
39 Kenyon Martin .60 1.50
40 Rasheed Wallace .75 2.00
41 Latrell Sprewell .60 1.50
42 Cuttino Mobley .60 1.50
43 Karl Malone 1.25 3.00
44 Dirk Nowitzki 1.50 4.00
45 Antawn Jamison .50 1.25
46 Elden Campbell .40 1.00
47 Lamar Odom .60 1.50
48 Jason Richardson .60 1.50
49 Jermaine O'Neal .50 1.25
50 Shareef Abdur-Rahim .60 1.50
51 Yao Ming C RC 12.00 30.00
52 Yao Ming U 15.00 40.00
53 Yao Ming R 30.00 80.00
54 Jay Williams C RC 1.25 3.00
55 Jay Williams U 1.50 4.00
56 Jay Williams R 3.00 8.00
57 Mike Dunleavy C RC 1.50 4.00
58 Mike Dunleavy U 2.00 5.00
59 Mike Dunleavy R 4.00 10.00
60 Drew Gooden C RC 1.50 4.00
61 Drew Gooden U 2.00 5.00
62 Drew Gooden R 4.00 10.00
63 Nikoloz Tskitishvili C RC 1.00 2.50
64 Nikoloz Tskitishvili U 1.25 3.00
65 Nikoloz Tskitishvili R 2.50 6.00
66 DaJuan Wagner C RC 1.25 3.00
67 DaJuan Wagner U 1.50 4.00
68 DaJuan Wagner R 3.00 8.00
69 Nene Hilario C RC 1.50 4.00
70 Nene Hilario U 2.00 5.00
71 Nene Hilario R 4.00 10.00
72 Chris Wilcox C RC 1.25 3.00
73 Chris Wilcox U 1.50 4.00
74 Chris Wilcox R 3.00 8.00
75 Amare Stoudemire C RC 4.00 10.00
76 Amare Stoudemire U 5.00 12.00
77 Amare Stoudemire R 10.00 25.00
78 Caron Butler C RC 1.50 4.00
79 Caron Butler U 2.00 5.00
80 Caron Butler R 4.00 10.00
81 Jared Jeffries C RC 1.25 3.00
82 Jared Jeffries U 1.50 4.00
83 Jared Jeffries R 3.00 8.00
84 Melvin Ely C RC 1.25 3.00
85 Melvin Ely U 1.50 4.00
86 Melvin Ely R 3.00 8.00
87 Marcus Haislip C RC 1.00 2.50
88 Marcus Haislip U 1.25 3.00
89 Marcus Haislip R 2.50 6.00
90 Fred Jones C RC 1.25 3.00
91 Fred Jones U 1.50 4.00
92 Fred Jones R 3.00 8.00
93 Casey Jacobsen C RC 1.25 3.00
94 Casey Jacobsen U 1.50 4.00
95 Casey Jacobsen R 3.00 8.00
96 John Salmons C RC 1.50 4.00
97 John Salmons U 2.00 5.00
98 John Salmons R 4.00 10.00
99 Juan Dixon C RC 1.25 3.00
100 Juan Dixon U 1.50 4.00
101 Juan Dixon R 3.00 8.00
102 Chris Jefferies C RC 1.00 2.50
103 Chris Jefferies U 1.25 3.00
104 Chris Jefferies R 2.50 6.00
105 Ryan Humphrey C RC 1.25 3.00
106 Ryan Humphrey U 1.50 4.00
107 Ryan Humphrey R 3.00 8.00
108 Kareem Rush C RC 1.25 3.00
109 Kareem Rush U 1.50 4.00
110 Kareem Rush R 3.00 8.00
111 Qyntel Woods C RC 1.00 2.50
112 Qyntel Woods U 1.25 3.00
113 Qyntel Woods R 2.50 6.00
114 Frank Williams C RC 1.00 2.50
115 Frank Williams U 1.25 3.00
116 Frank Williams R 2.50 6.00
117 Tayshaun Prince C RC 3.00 8.00
118 Tayshaun Prince U 4.00 10.00
119 Tayshaun Prince R 8.00 20.00
120 Carlos Boozer C RC 1.50 4.00
121 Carlos Boozer U 2.00 5.00
122 Carlos Boozer R 4.00 10.00
123 Dan Dickau C RC 1.00 2.50
124 Dan Dickau U 1.25 3.00
125 Dan Dickau R 2.50 6.00

2002-03 Topps Pristine Refractors

*STARS: 10X TO 25X BASE CARD HI
1-50 PRINT RUN 50 SERIAL #'d SETS
*RC's/1899: 1X TO 2X BASE RC C VER. HI
*RC's/499: 1.25X TO 3X BASE RC C VER. HI
*RC's/99: 2.5X TO 6X BASE RC C VER. HI
4 Michael Jordan 400.00 800.00
8 Kobe Bryant 200.00 500.00

2002-03 Topps Pristine Refractors Gold

*STARS: 5X TO 12X BASE CARD HI
*C RCs: 2.5X TO 6X BASE CARD HI
*U RCs: 2X TO 5X BASE CARD HI
*R RCs: 1X TO 2.5X BASE CARD HI
PRINT RUN 99 SERIAL #'d SETS
GOLD REFRACTORS ARE DIE-CUTS
AVAIL. AS HOBBY EXCLUSIVE BOX LOADER
1 Shaquille O'Neal 25.00 60.00
3 Vince Carter 15.00 40.00
4 Michael Jordan 300.00 600.00
8 Kobe Bryant 150.00 400.00
14 Reggie Miller 25.00 60.00
51 Yao Ming C 30.00 80.00
52 Yao Ming U 30.00 80.00
53 Yao Ming R 30.00 80.00

2002-03 Topps Pristine Personal Endorsements

STATED ODDS ONE PER BOX
INSERTED INTO #3 PACKS
PEBJ Bobby Jackson 2.50 6.00
PEBN Bostjan Nachbar 3.00 8.00
PECJ Chris Jefferies 2.50 6.00
PECM Corey Maggette 3.00 8.00
PECW Chris Wilcox 3.00 8.00
PEDD Dan Dickau 2.50 6.00
PEDG Drew Gooden 4.00 10.00
PEDW DaJuan Wagner 3.00 8.00
PEFJ Fred Jones 3.00 8.00
PEFW Frank Williams 2.50 6.00
PEGA Gilbert Arenas 6.00 15.00
PEGW Gerald Wallace 3.00 8.00
PEJF Joseph Forte 2.50 6.00
PEJJ Joe Johnson 3.00 8.00
PEKB Kwame Brown 2.50 6.00
PEKD Keyon Dooling 2.50 6.00
PEKR Kareem Rush 3.00 8.00
PELP Lavor Postell 2.50 6.00
PELW Loren Woods 2.50 6.00
PEMD Mike Dunleavy 4.00 10.00
PEME Melvin Ely 3.00 8.00
PERJ Richard Jefferson 3.00 8.00
PESO Shaquille O'Neal 40.00 100.00
PETP Tayshaun Prince 8.00 20.00
PEYM Yao Ming 50.00 120.00

2002-03 Topps Pristine Popular Demand

*REF: 1.5X TO 4X HI
REFRACTOR PRINT RUN 25 SER.#'d SETS
PDAI Allen Iverson 8.00 20.00
PDBD Baron Davis 3.00 8.00
PDCW Chris Webber 4.00 10.00
PDDM Darius Miles 2.00 5.00
PDDN Dirk Nowitzki 8.00 20.00
PDDR David Robinson 6.00 15.00
PDJK Jason Kidd 5.00 12.00
PDJO Jermaine O'Neal 2.50 6.00
PDKA Kareem Abdul Jabbar 10.00 25.00
PDKG Kevin Garnett 8.00 20.00
PDKM Karl Malone 6.00 15.00
PDMB Mike Bibby 3.00 8.00
PDRA Ray Allen 5.00 12.00
PDSF Steve Francis 3.00 8.00
PDSM Shawn Marion 3.00 8.00
PDSO Shaquille O'Neal 12.00 30.00
PDTD Tim Duncan 8.00 20.00
PDTM Tracy McGrady 5.00 12.00

2002-03 Topps Pristine Patches

PPAI Allen Iverson 30.00 80.00
PPADM Darius Miles 8.00 20.00
PPAJO Jermaine O'Neal 10.00 25.00
PPAJR Jason Richardson 12.00 30.00
PPAKM Kenyon Martin 12.00 30.00
PPAMD Mike Dunleavy 12.00 30.00
PPAMM Mike Miller 10.00 25.00
PPAPG Pau Gasol 12.00 30.00
PPAPS Predrag Savovic 10.00 25.00
PPAPS Peja Stojakovic 20.00 50.00
PPAQR Quentin Richardson 8.00 20.00
PPARA Ray Allen 20.00 50.00
PPASB Shane Battier 12.00 30.00
PPASN Steve Nash 25.00 60.00
PPASO Shaquille O'Neal 50.00 125.00
PPASS Steve Smith 10.00 25.00
PPATD Tim Duncan 30.00 80.00

2002-03 Topps Pristine Performance

*REF: 1.5X TO 4X HI
REFRACTOR PRINT RUN 25 SER.#'d SETS
PPEAW Antoine Walker 2.50 6.00
PPEBD Baron Davis 3.00 8.00
PPEBH Brendan Haywood 2.00 5.00
PPECM Cuttino Mobley 2.00 5.00
PPEEN Eduardo Najera 2.00 5.00
PPEGA Gilbert Arenas 3.00 8.00
PPEJM Jamal Mashburn 2.50 6.00
PPEKM Kenyon Martin 3.00 8.00
PPELN Lee Nailon 2.00 5.00
PPENV Nick Van Exel 3.00 8.00
PPEQR Quentin Richardson 2.00 5.00
PPESM Stephon Marbury 4.00 10.00
PPESO Shaquille O'Neal 12.00 30.00
PPETD Tim Duncan 8.00 20.00

2002-03 Topps Pristine Portions

*REF: 1.5X TO 4X HI
REFRACTOR PRINT RUN 25 SER.#'d SETS
PPOAH Allan Houston 3.00 8.00
PPOCM Cuttino Mobley 2.00 5.00
PPOCW Chris Webber 4.00 10.00
PPODG Devean George 2.00 5.00
PPODJ DerMarr Johnson 2.00 5.00
PPOGR Glenn Robinson 3.00 8.00
PPOJO Jermaine O'Neal 2.50 6.00
PPOJT Jason Terry 2.50 6.00
PPOKM Kenyon Martin 3.00 8.00
PPOLO Lamar Odom 3.00 8.00
PPOMM Mike Miller 2.50 6.00
PPOMO Michael Olowokandi 2.00 5.00
PPOPS Peja Stojakovic 2.50 6.00
PPORL Raef LaFrentz 2.00 5.00
PPOSB Shawn Bradley 2.00 5.00
PPOSM Shawn Marion 3.00 8.00
PPOSS Steve Smith 2.50 6.00
PPOTD Tim Duncan 8.00 20.00
PPOTG Tom Gugliotta 2.00 5.00
PPOVD Vlade Divac 2.50 6.00
PPOAHA Anfernee Hardaway 8.00 20.00

2002-03 Topps Pristine Rookie Club

*REF: 1.25X TO 3X HI
REFRACTOR PRINT RUN 25 SER.#'d SETS
RCAS Amare Stoudemire 6.00 15.00
RCCB Caron Butler 2.50 6.00
RCCW Chris Wilcox 2.00 5.00
RCDG Drew Gooden 2.50 6.00
RCDW DaJuan Wagner 2.50 6.00
RCFJ Fred Jones 2.00 5.00
RCKR Kareem Rush 2.00 5.00
RCMD Mike Dunleavy 2.50 6.00
RCME Melvin Ely 2.00 5.00
RCPS Predrag Savovic 2.00 5.00
RCYM Yao Ming 12.00 30.00

2003-04 Topps Pristine

COMP.SET w/o RC's (100) 25.00 60.00
RARE RC PRINT RUN 499 SER.#'d SETS
FOUR (1-100) CARDS IN PACK #3
TWO (101-199) CARDS IN PACK #3
1 Tracy McGrady .75 2.00
2 DaJuan Wagner .30 .75
3 Allen Iverson 1.25 3.00
4 Chris Webber .60 1.50
5 Jason Kidd .75 2.00
6 Eddie Jones .50 1.25
7 Jermaine O'Neal .50 1.25
8 Kobe Bryant 4.00 10.00
9 Tony Parker .75 2.00
10 Wally Szczerbiak .40 1.00
11 Yao Ming 1.25 3.00
12 Amare Stoudemire .60 1.50
13 Steve Nash 1.00 2.50
14 Baron Davis .50 1.25
15 Vince Carter 1.00 2.50
16 Peja Stojakovic .40 1.00
17 Desmond Mason .40 1.00
18 Antoine Walker .50 1.25
19 Steve Francis .50 1.25
20 Gary Payton .75 2.00
21 Tim Duncan 1.25 3.00
22 Jalen Rose .40 1.00
23 Jason Richardson .50 1.25
24 Andre Miller .40 1.00
25 Allan Houston .50 1.25
26 Ron Artest .50 1.25
27 Andrei Kirilenko .50 1.25
28 Kenyon Martin .50 1.25
29 Kevin Garnett 1.25 3.00
30 Rasheed Wallace .60 1.50
31 Shawn Marion .50 1.25
32 Karl Malone 1.00 2.50
33 Antawn Jamison .60 1.50
34 Shaquille O'Neal 2.00 5.00
35 Paul Pierce .75 2.00
36 Nene .40 1.00
37 Ray Allen .75 2.00
38 Bonzi Wells .30 .75
39 Ben Wallace .60 1.50
40 Jerry Stackhouse .60 1.50
41 Dirk Nowitzki 1.25 3.00
42 Elton Brand .60 1.50
43 Pau Gasol .75 2.00
44 Richard Hamilton .60 1.50
45 Shareef Abdur-Rahim .50 1.25
46 Jason Terry .50 1.25
47 Jamal Mashburn .40 1.00
48 Latrell Sprewell .60 1.50
49 Keith Van Horn .50 1.25
50 Mike Miller .40 1.00
51 Theo Ratliff .30 .75
52 Scottie Pippen 1.25 3.00
53 Nick Van Exel .50 1.25
54 Chauncey Billups .60 1.50
55 Al Harrington .40 1.00
56 Corey Maggette .40 1.00
57 Shane Battier .40 1.00
58 Tim Thomas .30 .75
59 Darius Miles .30 .75
60 Alonzo Mourning .60 1.50
61 Jamaal Magloire .30 .75
62 Antonio McDyess .40 1.00
63 Juwan Howard .40 1.00
64 Eric Snow .30 .75
65 Anfernee Hardaway 1.25 3.00
66 Tayshaun Prince .50 1.25
67 Derek Anderson .30 .75
68 Mike Bibby .50 1.25
69 Deshawn Stevenson .30 .75
70 Kwame Brown .30 .75
71 Jerome Williams .30 .75
72 Radoslav Nesterovic .30 .75
73 Stephon Marbury .60 1.50
74 P.J. Brown .30 .75
75 Sam Cassell .40 1.00
76 Kenny Thomas .30 .75
77 Jason Williams .75 2.00
78 Jamaal Tinsley .30 .75
79 Nikoloz Tskitishvili .30 .75
80 Michael Finley .50 1.25
81 Jamal Crawford .50 1.25
82 Brent Barry .30 .75
83 Gilbert Arenas .50 1.25
84 Morris Peterson .30 .75
85 Manu Ginobili 1.00 2.50
86 Dale Davis .30 .75
87 Aaron McKie .30 .75
88 Richard Jefferson .40 1.00
89 Michael Redd .50 1.25
90 Reggie Miller 1.00 2.50
91 Cuttino Mobley .30 .75
92 Marcus Camby .40 1.00
93 Tony Delk .30 .75
94 Tyson Chandler .40 1.00
95 Caron Butler .40 1.00
96 Kurt Thomas .30 .75
97 Glenn Robinson .40 1.00
98 Brad Miller .40 1.00
99 Matt Harpring .30 .75
100 Alvin Williams .30 .75
101 LeBron James C RC 150.00 400.00
102 LeBron James U 200.00 500.00
103 LeBron James R 400.00 800.00
104 Darko Milicic C RC 1.50 4.00
105 Darko Milicic U 2.00 5.00
106 Darko Milicic R 2.50 6.00
107 Carmelo Anthony C RC 10.00 25.00
108 Carmelo Anthony U 12.00 30.00
109 Carmelo Anthony R 15.00 40.00
110 Chris Bosh C RC 6.00 15.00
111 Chris Bosh U 8.00 20.00
112 Chris Bosh R 10.00 25.00
113 Dwyane Wade C RC 15.00 40.00
114 Dwyane Wade U 20.00 50.00
115 Dwyane Wade R 25.00 60.00
116 Chris Kaman C RC 2.00 5.00
117 Chris Kaman U 2.50 6.00
118 Chris Kaman R 3.00 8.00
119 Kirk Hinrich C RC 2.00 5.00
120 Kirk Hinrich U 2.50 6.00
121 Kirk Hinrich R 3.00 8.00
122 T.J. Ford C RC 1.50 4.00
123 T.J. Ford U 2.00 5.00
124 T.J. Ford R 2.50 6.00
125 Mike Sweetney C RC 1.25 3.00
126 Mike Sweetney U 1.50 4.00
127 Mike Sweetney R 2.00 5.00
128 Jarvis Hayes C RC 1.25 3.00
129 Jarvis Hayes U 1.50 4.00
130 Jarvis Hayes R 2.00 5.00
131 Mickael Pietrus C RC 1.50 4.00
132 Mickael Pietrus U 2.00 5.00
133 Mickael Pietrus R 2.50 6.00
134 Nick Collison C RC 1.50 4.00
135 Nick Collison U 2.00 5.00
136 Nick Collison R 2.50 6.00
137 Marcus Banks C RC 1.25 3.00
138 Marcus Banks U 1.50 4.00
139 Marcus Banks R 2.00 5.00
140 Luke Ridnour C RC 2.00 5.00
141 Luke Ridnour U 2.50 6.00
142 Luke Ridnour R 3.00 8.00
143 Reece Gaines C RC 1.25 3.00
144 Reece Gaines U 1.50 4.00
145 Reece Gaines R 2.00 5.00
146 Troy Bell C RC 1.25 3.00
147 Troy Bell U 1.50 4.00
148 Troy Bell R 2.00 5.00
149 Zarko Cabarkapa C RC 1.25 3.00
150 Zarko Cabarkapa U 1.50 4.00
151 Zarko Cabarkapa R 2.00 5.00
152 David West C RC 2.50 6.00
153 David West U 3.00 8.00
154 David West R 4.00 10.00
155 Aleksandar Pavlovic C RC 1.50 4.00
156 Aleksandar Pavlovic U 2.00 5.00
157 Aleksandar Pavlovic R 2.50 6.00
158 Dahntay Jones C RC 1.50 4.00
159 Dahntay Jones U 2.00 5.00
160 Dahntay Jones R 2.50 6.00
161 Boris Diaw C RC 2.00 5.00
162 Boris Diaw U 2.50 6.00
163 Boris Diaw R 3.00 8.00
164 Zoran Planinic C RC 1.25 3.00
165 Zoran Planinic U 1.50 4.00
166 Zoran Planinic R 2.00 5.00
167 Travis Outlaw C RC 2.00 5.00
168 Travis Outlaw U 2.50 6.00
169 Travis Outlaw R 3.00 8.00
170 Brian Cook C RC 1.25 3.00
171 Brian Cook U 1.50 4.00
172 Brian Cook R 2.00 5.00
173 Travis Hansen C RC 1.25 3.00
174 Travis Hansen U 1.50 4.00
175 Travis Hansen R 2.00 5.00
176 Ndudi Ebi C RC 1.25 3.00
177 Ndudi Ebi U 1.50 4.00
178 Ndudi Ebi R 2.00 5.00
179 Kendrick Perkins C RC 1.50 4.00
180 Kendrick Perkins U 2.00 5.00
181 Kendrick Perkins R 2.50 6.00
182 Leandro Barbosa C RC 2.00 5.00
183 Leandro Barbosa U 2.50 6.00
184 Leandro Barbosa R 3.00 8.00
185 Josh Howard C RC 2.00 5.00
186 Josh Howard U 2.50 6.00
187 Josh Howard R 3.00 8.00
188 Maciej Lampe C RC 1.25 3.00
189 Maciej Lampe U 1.50 4.00
190 Maciej Lampe R 2.00 5.00
191 Jason Kapono C RC 1.25 3.00
192 Jason Kapono U 1.50 4.00
193 Jason Kapono R 2.00 5.00
194 Luke Walton C RC 2.00 5.00
195 Luke Walton U 2.50 6.00
196 Luke Walton R 3.00 8.00
197 Jerome Beasley C RC 1.25 3.00
198 Jerome Beasley U 1.50 4.00
199 Jerome Beasley R 2.00 5.00

2003-04 Topps Pristine Refractors

*1-100 STARS: 4X TO 10X BASE HI
1-100 PRINT RUN 149 SER.#'d SETS
*RC's/1999: .75X TO 2X BASE RC C VER.HI
*RC's/499: 1X TO 2.5X BASE RC U VER.HI
*RC's/149: 1X TO 2.5X BASE RC R VER.HI
ALL CARDS ARE ENCASED
8 Kobe Bryant 200.00 500.00
101 LeBron James C 800.00 1,500.00
102 LeBron James U 1,250.00 2,500.00
103 LeBron James R 2,000.00 4,000.00

2003-04 Topps Pristine Refractors Gold

*1-100 STARS: 5X TO 12X BASE HI
*RC C VER: 2X TO 5X RC C VER.BASE
*RC U VER: 1.5X TO 4X RC U VER.BASE
*RC R VER:1.25X TO 3X RC R VER.BASE
GOLD PRINT RUN 99 SER.#'d SETS
1 Tracy McGrady 25.00 60.00
3 Allen Iverson 40.00 100.00
5 Jason Kidd 25.00 60.00
8 Kobe Bryant 500.00 1,000.00
11 Yao Ming 40.00 100.00
13 Steve Nash 25.00 60.00
15 Vince Carter 30.00 80.00
20 Gary Payton 15.00 40.00
21 Tim Duncan 40.00 100.00
29 Kevin Garnett 40.00 100.00
32 Karl Malone 20.00 50.00
34 Shaquille O'Neal 40.00 100.00
35 Paul Pierce 20.00 50.00
41 Dirk Nowitzki 40.00 100.00
52 Scottie Pippen 40.00 100.00
65 Anfernee Hardaway 25.00 60.00
85 Manu Ginobili 25.00 60.00
90 Reggie Miller 20.00 50.00
101 LeBron James C 10,000.00 15,000.00
102 LeBron James U 10,000.00 15,000.00
103 LeBron James R 10,000.00 15,000.00
107 Carmelo Anthony C 100.00 250.00
108 Carmelo Anthony U 100.00 250.00
109 Carmelo Anthony R 100.00 250.00
113 Dwyane Wade C 150.00 400.00
114 Dwyane Wade U 150.00 400.00
115 Dwyane Wade R 150.00 400.00

2003-04 Topps Pristine Borders Relics

STATED ODDS: GROUP A 1:4433
GROUP B 1:41, NO ODDS FOR GROUP E
*REFRACTORS: 1.25X TO 3X BASE HI
REFRACTOR PRINT RUN 25 SER.#'d SETS
REFRACTORS INSERTED IN #1 PACKS
AK Andrei Kirilenko E 2.50 6.00
DN Dirk Nowitzki E 8.00 20.00
EG Manu Ginobili B 10.00 25.00
NH Nene E 2.50 6.00
PG Pau Gasol E 5.00 12.00
PS Peja Stojakovic 2.50 6.00
TD Tim Duncan E 8.00 20.00
TP Tony Parker E 5.00 12.00
YM Yao Ming B 25.00 60.00
ZI Zydrunas Ilgauskas E 2.50 6.00

2003-04 Topps Pristine Challenge Relics

STATED ODDS: GROUP C 1:51
NO ODDS GIVEN FOR GROUP E
*REFRACTORS: 1.25X TO 3X BASE HI
REFRACTOR PRINT RUN 25 SER.#'d SETS
REFRACTORS INSERTED IN #1 PACKS
AK Andrei Kirilenko E 2.50 6.00
AS Amare Stoudemire E 4.00 10.00
CB Carlos Boozer E 2.50 6.00
DG Drew Gooden E 2.50 6.00
DW Dajuan Wagner E 2.00 5.00
GA Gilbert Arenas E 3.00 8.00
JR Jason Richardson C 3.00 8.00
JT Jamaal Tinsley E 2.00 5.00
MJ Marko Jaric E 2.00 5.00
RJ Richard Jefferson E 2.50 6.00
TC Tyson Chandler E 2.50 6.00
TM Troy Murphy E 2.00 5.00
TP Tony Parker E 5.00 12.00
CBU Caron Butler E 2.50 6.00

2003-04 Topps Pristine Factor Relics

STATED ODDS: GROUP B 1:156
GROUP D 1:48, NO ODDS FOR GROUP E
*REFRACTORS: 1.25X TO 3X BASE HI
REFRACTOR PRINT RUN 25 SER.#'d SETS
REFRACTORS INSERTED IN #1 PACKS
AI Allen Iverson B 8.00 20.00
BD Baron Davis D 3.00 8.00
DA Darrell Armstrong E 2.00 5.00
DM Darius Miles E 2.00 5.00
EG Eddie Griffin E 2.00 5.00
JB J.R. Bremer 2.00 5.00
JK Jason Kidd D 5.00 12.00
JS Jerry Stackhouse E 4.00 10.00
KM Karl Malone E 6.00 15.00
LO Lamar Odom E 2.50 6.00
LS Latrell Sprewell E 4.00 10.00
MB Mike Bibby E 3.00 8.00
MP Morris Peterson E 2.00 5.00
PP Paul Pierce E 5.00 12.00
RL Rashard Lewis E 2.50 6.00
RW Rasheed Wallace B 4.00 10.00
SC Sam Cassell E 2.50 6.00
SF Steve Francis E 3.00 8.00
SM Stephon Marbury D 4.00 10.00
SO Shaquille O'Neal E 12.00 30.00
TM Tracy McGrady B 5.00 12.00
DMU Dikembe Mutombo E 4.00 10.00

2003-04 Topps Pristine Gems Relics

STATED ODDS GROUP B 1:41
GROUP C 1:51, NO ODDS FOR GROUP E
GROUP F 1:9, GROUP G 1:3
*REFRACTORS: 1.25X TO 3X BASE HI
REFRACTOR PRINT RUN 25 SER.#'d SETS
REFRACTORS INSERTED IN #1 PACKS
AH Allan Houston G 3.00 8.00
BW Ben Wallace E 4.00 10.00
CB Carlos Boozer C 2.50 6.00
CM Cuttino Mobley G 2.00 5.00
DD Dan Dickau G 2.00 5.00
DF Derek Fisher G 3.00 8.00
DG Drew Gooden F 2.50 6.00
DW David Wesley F 2.00 5.00
EG Eddie Griffin G 2.00 5.00
GH Grant Hill B 4.00 10.00
JJ Jared Jeffries G 2.00 5.00
JK Jason Kidd G 5.00 12.00
JO Jermaine O'Neal G 3.00 8.00
JR Jason Richardson F 3.00 8.00
MB Mike Bibby C 3.00 8.00
MD Mike Dunleavy C 2.50 6.00
MF Michael Finley E 3.00 8.00
MJ Marko Jaric G 2.00 5.00
PG Pat Garrity F 2.00 5.00
PS Peja Stojakovic E 2.50 6.00
RA Ray Allen F 5.00 12.00
RJ Richard Jefferson F 2.50 6.00
SC Sam Cassell G 2.50 6.00
SF Steve Francis F 3.00 8.00
SM Shawn Marion G 3.00 8.00
SN Steve Nash F 6.00 15.00
SO Shaquille O'Neal E 12.00 30.00
TC Tyson Chandler G 2.50 6.00
TD Tim Duncan F 8.00 20.00
TM Tracy McGrady G 5.00 12.00
TP Tayshaun Prince F 3.00 8.00
YM Yao Ming F 8.00 20.00
CBU Caron Butler G 2.50 6.00
PGA Pau Gasol F 3.00 8.00

2003-04 Topps Pristine Generals Relics

STATED ODDS GROUP B 1:41
GROUP C 1:28, NO ODDS FOR GROUP E
*REFRACTORS: 1.25X TO 3X BASE HI
REFRACTOR PRINT RUN 25 SER.#'d SETS
REFRACTORS INSERTED IN #1 PACKS
AH Anfernee Hardaway B 8.00 20.00
AI Allen Iverson B 8.00 20.00
AM Anthony Mason B 2.00 5.00
AW Antoine Walker E 3.00 8.00
BW Ben Wallace E 4.00 10.00
CM Cuttino Mobley E 2.00 5.00
CW Chris Webber 4.00 10.00
DD Dan Dickau E 2.00 5.00
EG Manu Ginobili B 6.00 15.00
GP Gary Payton E 5.00 12.00
JK Jason Kidd C 5.00 12.00
JM Jamal Mashburn E 2.50 6.00
KM Kenyon Martin E 3.00 8.00
MD Mike Dunleavy E 2.50 6.00
MF Michael Finley E 3.00 8.00
RA Ray Allen E 5.00 12.00
SO Shaquille O'Neal E 12.00 30.00
TD Tim Duncan E 8.00 20.00
VR Vladimir Radmanovic E 2.00 5.00
WS Wally Szczerbiak E 2.50 6.00

2003-04 Topps Pristine Minis

SHAQ AU INSERTED IN HOBBY ONLY
PM1 Paul Pierce 2.50 6.00
PM2 Dirk Nowitzki 4.00 10.00
PM3 Yao Ming 4.00 10.00
PM4 Steve Francis 1.50 4.00
PM5 Kobe Bryant 12.00 30.00
PM6 Shaquille O'Neal 6.00 15.00
PM7 Gary Payton 2.50 6.00
PM8 Kevin Garnett 4.00 10.00
PM9 Jason Kidd 2.50 6.00
PM10 Tracy Mcgrady 2.50 6.00
PM11 Allen Iverson 4.00 10.00
PM12 Chris Webber 2.00 5.00
PM13 Tim Duncan 4.00 10.00
PM14 Ray Allen 2.50 6.00
PM15 Vince Carter 3.00 8.00
PM16 Antoine Walker 1.50 4.00
PM17 Jermaine O'Neal 1.50 4.00
PM18 Elton Brand 1.25 3.00
PM19 Baron Davis 1.50 4.00
PM20 Shawn Marion 1.50 4.00
PM21 LeBron James 150.00 400.00
PM22 Darko Milicic 1.25 3.00
PM23 Carmelo Anthony 8.00 20.00
PM24 Chris Bosh 5.00 12.00
PM25 Dwyane Wade 12.00 30.00
PM26 Chris Kaman 1.50 4.00
PM27 Kirk Hinrich 1.50 4.00
PM28 T.J. Ford 1.25 3.00
PM29 Mike Sweetney 1.00 2.50
PM30 Jarvis Hayes 1.00 2.50
PM31 Mickael Pietrus 1.25 3.00
PM32 Nick Collison 1.25 3.00
PM33 Marcus Banks 1.00 2.50
PM34 Luke Ridnour 1.50 4.00
PM35 Reece Gaines 1.00 2.50
PM36 Troy Bell 1.00 2.50
PM37 Zarko Cabarkapa 1.00 2.50
PM38 David West 2.00 5.00
PM39 Aleksandar Pavlovic 1.25 3.00
PM40 Dahntay Jones 1.25 3.00
SO S.O'Neal AU/100 100.00 250.00

2003-04 Topps Pristine Personal Endorsements

STATED ODDS: GROUP A 1:36
GROUP B 1:156, GROUP C 1:28
GROUP D 1:48, GROUP E 1:9
*GOLD: 1.25X TO 3X BASE HI
GOLD PRINT RUN 25 SER.#'d SETS
ALL GOLD AU'S ENCASED
GOLDS INSERTED IN #1 PACKS
BB Bruce Bowen C 3.00 8.00
BC Brian Cook B 2.50 6.00
BW Boris Diaw A 4.00 10.00
CA Carmelo Anthony D 100.00 250.00
CB Chris Bosh C 20.00 50.00
DG Drew Gooden D 3.00 8.00
DJ Dahntay Jones D 3.00 8.00
EB Elton Brand C 3.00 8.00
JK Jason Kapono D 2.50 6.00
KB Keith Bogans A 2.50 6.00
KH Kirk Hinrich D 8.00 20.00
KJ Ken Johnson D 2.50 6.00
KP Kendrick Perkins A 3.00 8.00
LBO Leandro Barbosa A 4.00 10.00
LR Luke Ridnour C 4.00 10.00
LW Luke Walton D 4.00 10.00
ML Maciej Lampe A 2.50 6.00
MP Mickael Pietrus C 3.00 8.00
MR Malik Rose A 2.50 6.00
MS Mike Sweetney D 2.50 6.00
NC Nick Collison E 6.00 15.00
NE Ndudi Ebi A 2.50 6.00
RG Reece Gaines C 2.50 6.00
SB Steve Blake A 3.00 8.00
SO Shaquille O'Neal C 75.00 200.00
TB Troy Bell D 2.50 6.00
TF T.J. Ford B 3.00 8.00
TH Travis Hansen D 2.50 6.00
TO Travis Outlaw D 3.00 8.00
ZC Zarko Cabarkapa A 2.50 6.00
ZP Zaur Pachulia A 4.00 10.00
DWA Dwyane Wade C 125.00 300.00
DWE David West A 5.00 12.00
JHA Jarvis Hayes A 2.50 6.00
JHO Josh Howard E 4.00 10.00
MBA Marcus Banks E 2.50 6.00
ZPL Zoran Planinic D 2.50 6.00

2003-04 Topps Pristine Recruit Relics

STATED ODDS 1:3
*REFRACTORS: 1X TO 2.5X BASE HI
REFRACTOR PRINT RUN 25 SER.#'d SETS
REFRACTORS INSERTED IN #1 PACKS
BC Brian Cook 1.50 4.00
CA Carmelo Anthony 12.00 30.00
CB Chris Bosh 8.00 20.00
CK Chris Kaman 2.50 6.00
DJ Dahntay Jones 2.00 5.00
DW David West 3.00 8.00
JH Jarvis Hayes 1.50 4.00
KH Kirk Hinrich 2.50 6.00
KP Kendrick Perkins 2.00 5.00
LB Leandro Barbosa 2.50 6.00
LR Luke Ridnour 2.50 6.00
LW Luke Walton 2.50 6.00
MB Marcus Banks 1.50 4.00
MP Mickael Pietrus 2.00 5.00
MS Mike Sweetney 1.50 4.00
NC Nick Collison 2.00 5.00
NE Ndudi Ebi 1.50 4.00
RG Reece Gaines 1.50 4.00
SB Steve Blake 2.00 5.00
SV Slavko Vranes 1.50 4.00
TB Troy Bell 1.50 4.00
TF T.J. Ford 2.00 5.00
TH Travis Hansen 1.50 4.00
TO Travis Outlaw 2.00 5.00
DWY Dwyane Wade 20.00 50.00

2004-05 Topps Pristine

COMP.SET w/o SP's (100) 40.00 100.00
RARE RC PRINT RUN 239 SER.#'d SETS
ONE UNCIRCULATED CARD PER PACK #1
ONE RELIC CARD PER PACK #2
FOUR VETS AND TWO RC'S PER PACK #3
ONE PACK #4 INSERTED PER BOX
1 Ben Wallace .75 2.00
2 Michael Redd .50 1.25
3 Dwyane Wade 2.50 6.00
4 Chris Webber .75 2.00
5 Cuttino Mobley .50 1.25
6 Bonzi Wells .40 1.00
7 Rashard Lewis .50 1.25
8 Kobe Bryant 5.00 12.00
9 Gilbert Arenas .60 1.50
10 Jeff Foster .40 1.00
11 Yao Ming 12.00 30.00
12 Ricky Davis .50 1.25
13 Glenn Robinson .50 1.25
14 Chauncey Billups .75 2.00
15 Carmelo Anthony 1.25 3.00
16 Pau Gasol 1.00 2.50
17 Erick Dampier .40 1.00
18 Jason Terry .50 1.25
19 Corey Maggette .50 1.25
20 Zach Randolph .60 1.50
21 Kevin Garnett 1.50 4.00
22 Steve Nash 1.25 3.00
23 LeBron James 5.00 12.00
24 Andre Miller .50 1.25
25 Manu Ginobili 1.25 3.00
26 Gordan Giricek .40 1.00
27 Juwan Howard .50 1.25
28 Brad Miller .50 1.25
29 Al Harrington .50 1.25
30 Allen Iverson 1.50 4.00
31 Shawn Marion .60 1.50
32 Elton Brand .60 1.50
33 Steve Francis .60 1.50
34 Shaquille O'Neal 2.50 6.00
35 Marcus Camby .50 1.25
36 Tyson Chandler .50 1.25
37 Dirk Nowitzki 1.50 4.00
38 Damon Stoudamire .60 1.50
39 Richard Hamilton .75 2.00
40 Kurt Thomas .40 1.00
41 Paul Pierce 1.00 2.50
42 Jarvis Hayes .40 1.00
43 Ray Allen 1.00 2.50
44 Keith Van Horn .50 1.25
45 Kirk Hinrich .60 1.50
46 Caron Butler .50 1.25
47 Andrei Kirilenko .50 1.25
48 Jamaal Magloire .40 1.00
49 Chris Kaman .50 1.25
50 Stephon Marbury .75 2.00
51 Mike Miller .50 1.25
52 Eddy Curry .40 1.00

53 Sam Cassell .50 1.25
54 Vince Carter 1.25 3.00
55 Jason Kidd 1.00 2.50
56 Desmond Mason .50 1.25
57 Nene .50 1.25
58 Gerald Wallace .60 1.50
59 Baron Davis .60 1.50
60 Tim Duncan 1.50 4.00
61 Drew Gooden .40 1.00
62 Jason Williams .50 1.25
63 Eddie Jones .60 1.50
64 Michael Finley .60 1.50
65 Gary Payton 1.00 2.50
66 Kenyon Martin .60 1.50
67 Mike Bibby .60 1.50
68 Jason Kapono .40 1.00
69 Allan Houston .60 1.50
70 Ron Artest .60 1.50
71 Rasho Nesterovic .40 1.00
72 Kwame Brown .40 1.00
73 Wally Szczerbiak .50 1.25
74 Joe Johnson .50 1.25
75 Jamal Mashburn .50 1.25
76 Peja Stojakovic .50 1.25
77 Lamar Odom .60 1.50
78 Jalen Rose .50 1.25
79 Mike Dunleavy .40 1.00
80 Rasheed Wallace .75 2.00
81 Richard Jefferson .50 1.25
82 Luke Ridnour .50 1.25
83 Samuel Dalembert .40 1.00
84 Zydrunas Ilgauskas .50 1.25
85 Carlos Arroyo .40 1.00
86 Primoz Brezec .40 1.00
87 Chris Bosh 1.00 2.50
88 Antoine Walker .60 1.50
89 Boris Diaw .50 1.25
90 Tracy McGrady 1.00 2.50
91 Amare Stoudemire .60 1.50
92 Karl Malone 1.25 3.00
93 Jamal Crawford .60 1.50
94 Shareef Abdur-Rahim .60 1.50
95 Jason Richardson .60 1.50
96 Marcus Banks .40 1.00
97 Jermaine O'Neal .50 1.25
98 Latrell Sprewell .75 2.00
99 Tony Parker 1.00 2.50
100 Carlos Boozer .50 1.25
101 Dwight Howard C RC 5.00 12.00
102 Dwight Howard U 8.00 20.00
103 Dwight Howard R 10.00 25.00
104 Ben Gordon C RC 1.50 4.00
105 Ben Gordon U 2.50 6.00
106 Ben Gordon R 3.00 8.00
107 Devin Harris C RC 1.25 3.00
108 Devin Harris U 1.50 4.00
109 Devin Harris R 2.50 6.00
110 Rafael Araujo C RC 1.00 2.50
111 Rafael Araujo U 1.50 4.00
112 Rafael Araujo R 2.00 5.00
113 Luke Jackson C RC 1.00 2.50
114 Luke Jackson U 1.50 4.00
115 Luke Jackson R 2.00 5.00
116 Yuta Tabuse C RC 1.50 4.00
117 Yuta Tabuse U 2.50 6.00
118 Yuta Tabuse R 3.00 8.00
119 Kris Humphries C RC 1.25 3.00
120 Kris Humphries U 2.00 5.00
121 Kris Humphries R 2.50 6.00
122 Josh Smith C RC 1.50 4.00
123 Josh Smith U 2.50 6.00
124 Josh Smith R 3.00 8.00
125 Dorell Wright C RC 1.25 3.00
126 Dorell Wright U 2.00 5.00
127 Dorell Wright R 2.50 6.00
128 Jackson Vroman C RC 1.00 2.50
129 Jackson Vroman U 1.50 4.00
130 Jackson Vroman R 2.00 5.00
131 Sasha Vujacic C RC 1.25 3.00
132 Sasha Vujacic U 2.00 5.00
133 Sasha Vujacic R 2.50 6.00
134 David Harrison C RC 1.00 2.50
135 David Harrison U 1.50 4.00
136 David Harrison R 2.00 5.00
137 Blake Stepp C RC 1.50 4.00
138 Blake Stepp U 2.50 6.00
139 Blake Stepp R 3.00 8.00
140 Lionel Chalmers C RC 1.25 3.00
141 Lionel Chalmers U 2.00 5.00
142 Lionel Chalmers R 2.50 6.00
143 Delonte West C RC 1.25 3.00
144 Delonte West U 2.00 5.00
145 Delonte West R 2.50 6.00
146 Kevin Martin C RC 2.00 5.00
147 Kevin Martin U 3.00 8.00
148 Kevin Martin R 4.00 10.00
149 Robert Swift C RC 1.00 2.50
150 Robert Swift U 1.50 4.00
151 Robert Swift R 2.00 5.00
152 Trevor Ariza C RC 1.50 4.00
153 Trevor Ariza U 2.50 6.00
154 Trevor Ariza R 3.00 8.00
155 Peter John Ramos C RC 1.00 2.50
156 Peter John Ramos U 1.50 4.00
157 Peter John Ramos R 2.00 5.00
158 Anderson Varejao C RC 1.25 3.00
159 Anderson Varejao U 2.00 5.00
160 Anderson Varejao R 2.50 6.00
161 Andre Emmett C RC 1.00 2.50
162 Andre Emmett U 1.50 4.00
163 Andre Emmett R 2.00 5.00
164 Tony Allen C RC 1.50 4.00
165 Tony Allen U 2.50 6.00
166 Tony Allen R 3.00 8.00
167 Jameer Nelson C RC 1.50 4.00
168 Jameer Nelson U 2.50 6.00
169 Jameer Nelson R 3.00 8.00
170 J.R. Smith C RC 1.50 4.00
171 J.R. Smith U 2.50 6.00
172 J.R. Smith R 3.00 8.00
173 Kirk Snyder C RC 1.00 2.50
174 Kirk Snyder U 1.50 4.00
175 Kirk Snyder R 2.00 5.00
176 Al Jefferson C RC 1.50 4.00
177 Al Jefferson U 2.50 6.00
178 Al Jefferson R 3.00 8.00
179 Sebastian Telfair C RC 1.25 3.00
180 Sebastian Telfair U 2.00 5.00
181 Sebastian Telfair R 2.50 6.00
182 Andris Biedrins C RC 1.00 2.50
183 Andris Biedrins U 1.50 4.00
184 Andris Biedrins R 2.00 5.00
185 Andre Iguodala C RC 2.50 6.00
186 Andre Iguodala U 4.00 10.00
187 Andre Iguodala R 5.00 12.00
188 Luol Deng C RC 1.50 4.00
189 Luol Deng U 2.50 6.00
190 Luol Deng R 3.00 8.00
191 Josh Childress C RC 1.00 2.50
192 Josh Childress U 1.50 4.00
193 Josh Childress R 2.00 5.00
194 Shaun Livingston C RC 1.50 4.00
195 Shaun Livingston U 2.50 6.00
196 Shaun Livingston R 3.00 8.00
197 Emeka Okafor C RC 1.25 3.00
198 Emeka Okafor U 2.00 5.00
199 Emeka Okafor R 2.50 6.00

2004-05 Topps Pristine Refractors

*1-100: 5X TO 12X BASE HI
1-100 PRINT RUN 25 SER.#'d SETS
*COMMON RCs: .75X TO 2X BASE HI
COMMON RC PRINT RUN 599 SER.#'d SETS
*UNCOMMON RCs: .75X TO 2X BASE HI
UNCOMMON RC PRINT RUN 275 SER.#'d SETS
*RARE RCs: 1X TO 2.5X BASE HI
RARE RC PRINT RUN 49 SER.#'d SETS
23 LeBron James 300.00 600.00

2004-05 Topps Pristine Refractors Gold

*1-100: 6X TO 15X BASE HI
*COMMON RCs: 2.5X TO 6X BASE HI
*UNCOMMON RCs: 1.5X TO 4X BASE HI
*RARE RCs: 1.25X TO 3X BASE HI
PRINT RUN 27 SER.#'d SETS
3 Dwyane Wade 40.00 100.00
8 Kobe Bryant 200.00 500.00
22 Steve Nash 15.00 40.00
23 LeBron James 300.00 600.00
101 Dwight Howard C 40.00 100.00
102 Dwight Howard U 40.00 100.00
103 Dwight Howard R 40.00 100.00

2004-05 Topps Pristine Court Clash

STATED ODDS 1:47
AG C.Anthony/K.Garnett 8.00 20.00
AP R.Artest/P.Pierce 5.00 12.00
DM T.Duncan/K.Malone 10.00 25.00
MK S.Marbury/J.Kidd 6.00 15.00
NW D.Nowitzki/C.Webber 8.00 20.00
OM S.O'Neal/Y.Ming 8.00 20.00
PP G.Payton/T.Parker 6.00 15.00
WO B.Wallace/J.O'Neal 6.00 15.00

2004-05 Topps Pristine Fantasy Favorites

STATED ODDS 1:3
*REFRACTORS: .75X TO 2X BASE HI
REFRACTOR PRINT RUN 25 SER.#'d SETS
N Nene 2.00 5.00
AK Andrei Kirilenko 2.00 5.00
AS Amare Stoudemire 2.50 6.00
AW Antoine Walker 2.50 6.00
BM Brad Miller 2.00 5.00
CB Chauncey Billups 3.00 8.00
CK Chris Kaman 2.00 5.00
CW Chris Wilcox 2.00 5.00
DD Dan Dickau 2.00 5.00
DF Derek Fisher 2.00 5.00
DM Darko Milicic 2.00 5.00
DW Dajuan Wagner 2.00 5.00
EB Elton Brand 2.00 5.00
FW Frank Williams 2.00 5.00
GA Gilbert Arenas 2.50 6.00
JH Jarvis Hayes 2.00 5.00
JJ Jim Jackson 2.00 5.00
JK Jason Kidd 4.00 10.00
JM Jamaal Magloire 2.00 5.00
JO Jermaine O'Neal 2.00 5.00
JT Jason Terry 2.00 5.00
KG Kevin Garnett 6.00 15.00
KH Kirk Hinrich 2.50 6.00
KR Kareem Rush 2.00 5.00
LB Leandro Barbosa 2.00 5.00
LR Luke Ridnour 2.00 5.00
MB Marcus Banks 2.00 5.00
MD Mike Dunleavy 1.50 4.00
MJ Marko Jaric 2.00 5.00
MO Michael Olowokandi 2.00 5.00
MP Morris Peterson 1.50 4.00
NM Nazr Mohammed 2.00 5.00
PP Paul Pierce 4.00 10.00
PS Peja Stojakovic 2.00 5.00
RA Ron Artest 2.50 6.00
RL Rashard Lewis 2.00 5.00
RM Reggie Miller 5.00 12.00
SF Steve Francis 2.50 6.00
SO Shaquille O'Neal 10.00 25.00
TO Travis Outlaw 2.00 5.00
TP Tayshaun Prince 2.50 6.00
UH Udonis Haslem 1.50 4.00
VR Vladimir Radmanovic 2.00 5.00
WS Wally Szczerbiak 2.00 5.00
YM Yao Ming 6.00 15.00
ZR Zach Randolph 2.50 6.00
CBH Chris Bosh 4.00 10.00
CBO Carlos Boozer 2.00 5.00
CBU Caron Butler 2.00 5.00
DWE David Wesley 2.00 5.00
JAM Jamal Mashburn 2.00 5.00
JHO Josh Howard 2.00 5.00
MPI Mickael Pietrus 1.50 4.00
SAR Shareef Abdur-Rahim 2.50 6.00

2004-05 Topps Pristine Mini

STATED ODDS ONE PER BOX IN #4 PACKS
AI Andre Iguodala 2.00 5.00
AJ Antawn Jamison 1.00 2.50
AK Andrei Kirilenko 1.00 2.50
BD Baron Davis 1.25 3.00
BG Ben Gordon 1.25 3.00
BW Ben Wallace 1.50 4.00
CA Carmelo Anthony 2.50 6.00
DH Dwight Howard 4.00 10.00
DN Dirk Nowitzki 3.00 8.00
DW Dwyane Wade 5.00 12.00
EO Emeka Okafor 1.00 2.50
JC Josh Childress .75 2.00
JK Jason Kidd 2.00 5.00
JN Jameer Nelson 1.25 3.00
JO Jermaine O'Neal 1.50 4.00
JR Jason Richardson 1.25 3.00
KB Kobe Bryant 10.00 25.00
KG Kevin Garnett 3.00 8.00
KH Kris Humphries 1.50 4.00
LD Luol Deng 1.25 3.00
LJ Luke Jackson .75 2.00
LJ LeBron James 10.00 25.00
PG Pau Gasol 2.00 5.00
PP Paul Pierce 2.00 5.00
PS Peja Stojakovic 1.00 2.50
RA Rafael Araujo .75 2.00
SF Steve Francis 1.25 3.00
SL Shaun Livingston 1.25 3.00
SM Stephon Marbury 1.50 4.00
SO Shaquille O'Neal 5.00 12.00
ST Sebastian Telfair 1.00 2.50
TD Tim Duncan 3.00 8.00
TM Tracy McGrady 2.00 5.00
VC Vince Carter 2.50 6.00
YM Yao Ming 3.00 8.00
ALJ Al Jefferson 1.25 3.00
DHA Devin Harris 1.00 2.50
JRS J.R. Smith 1.25 3.00
RAL Ray Allen 2.00 5.00
SMA Shawn Marion 1.25 3.00

2004-05 Topps Pristine Mini Relics

STATED ODDS 1:47
AS Amare Stoudemire 2.50 6.00
BW Ben Wallace 3.00 8.00
CA Carmelo Anthony 5.00 12.00
KG Kevin Garnett 6.00 15.00
PS Peja Stojakovic 2.00 5.00
RA Ron Artest 2.50 6.00
SF Steve Francis 2.50 6.00
SM Stephon Marbury 3.00 8.00

2004-05 Topps Pristine Personal Endorsements

GROUP A STATED ODDS 1:47
GROUP B STATED ODDS 1:29
GROUP C STATED ODDS 1:7
AB Andris Biedrins C 3.00 8.00
AS Amare Stoudemire A 10.00 25.00
AV Anderson Varejao C 4.00 10.00
BD Baron Davis B 6.00 15.00
BG Ben Gordon C 5.00 12.00
BJ Bobby Jackson A 10.00 25.00
BW Ben Wallace A 12.00 30.00
CA Carmelo Anthony B 25.00 60.00
DH David Harrison C 3.00 8.00
DW Dorell Wright C 4.00 10.00
EB Elton Brand A 8.00 20.00
EO Emeka Okafor C 4.00 10.00
FJ Fred Jones B 3.00 8.00
JK Jason Kidd B 12.00 30.00
JO Jermaine O'Neal B 4.00 10.00
JR Jalen Rose A 6.00 15.00
JS Josh Smith C 5.00 12.00
KH Kris Humphries C 4.00 10.00
KS Kirk Snyder C 3.00 8.00
LD Luol Deng C 5.00 12.00
LJ Luke Jackson C 3.00 8.00
MP Morris Peterson A 3.00 8.00
PS Peja Stojakovic B 6.00 15.00
RA Rafael Araujo C 3.00 8.00
RH Richard Hamilton B 8.00 20.00
RS Robert Swift C 3.00 8.00
SC Speedy Claxton A 5.00 12.00
SL Shaun Livingston C 5.00 12.00
SM Shawn Marion A 6.00 15.00
SO Shaquille O'Neal A 50.00 120.00
ST Sebastian Telfair C 4.00 10.00
SV Sasha Vujacic C 4.00 10.00
TA Tony Allen C 5.00 12.00
TD Tim Duncan A 200.00 500.00
TM Tracy McGrady A 15.00 40.00
TP Tayshaun Prince A 6.00 15.00
DEH Devin Harris C 4.00 10.00
JOC Josh Childress C 3.00 8.00
JRS J.R. Smith C 5.00 12.00
PAP Pavel Podkolzin C 3.00 8.00
SMA Stephon Marbury C 8.00 20.00

2004-05 Topps Pristine Rookie Sign In

STATED ODDS 1:8
*REFRACTORS: 1X TO 2.5X BASE HI
REFRACTOR PRINT RUN 25 SER.#'d SETS
AI Andre Iguodala 4.00 10.00
AJ Al Jefferson 2.50 6.00
BG Ben Gordon 2.50 6.00
DH Dwight Howard 8.00 20.00
DW Dorell Wright 2.50 6.00
JC Josh Childress 1.50 4.00
JN Jameer Nelson 2.00 5.00
JS Josh Smith 2.50 6.00
LD Luol Deng 2.50 6.00
LJ Luke Jackson 1.50 4.00
RA Rafael Araujo 1.50 4.00
SL Shaun Livingston 2.50 6.00
ST Sebastian Telfair 2.00 5.00
TA Tony Allen 2.50 6.00
DHA Devin Harris 2.00 5.00

2004-05 Topps Pristine Two of a Kind Autographs

STATED ODDS 1:305
AO C.Anthony/E.Okafor 40.00 100.00
DO T.Duncan/E.Okafor 150.00 300.00

2004-05 Topps Pristine Verticality

GROUP A STATED ODDS 1:252
GROUP B STATED ODDS 1:11
*REFRACTORS: .75X TO 2X BASE HI
REFRACTOR PRINT RUN 25 SER.#'d SETS
AK Andrei Kirilenko B 2.00 5.00
AS Amare Stoudemire B 2.50 6.00
CA Chris Anderson B 2.50 6.00
DG Devean George B 2.00 5.00
DM Desmond Mason A 2.00 5.00
DW David West B 2.00 5.00
JR Jason Richardson B 2.50 6.00
RG Reece Gaines B 2.00 5.00
RJ Richard Jefferson B 2.00 5.00
SM Shawn Marion B 2.50 6.00
TC Tyson Chandler B 2.00 5.00
TM Tracy McGrady B 4.00 10.00

2004-05 Topps Pristine Winning Wardrobe

GROUP A STATED ODDS 1:252
GROUP B STATED ODDS 1:4
*REFRACTORS: 1X TO 2.5X BASE HI
REFRACTOR PRINT RUN 25 SER.#'d SETS
BD Baron Davis B 2.50 6.00
BW Ben Wallace B 3.00 8.00
CA Carmelo Anthony B 5.00 12.00
DF Derek Fisher B 2.00 5.00
DM Desmond Mason A 2.00 5.00
DN Dirk Nowitzki B 6.00 15.00
GP Gary Payton B 4.00 10.00
HT Hedo Turkoglu B 2.00 5.00
JK Jason Kidd B 4.00 10.00
JM Jamaal Magloire B 2.00 5.00
JO Jermaine O'Neal B 2.00 5.00
JT Jamaal Tinsley B 2.00 5.00
KH Kirk Hinrich B 2.50 6.00
KM Karl Malone B 5.00 12.00
MB Mike Bibby B 2.50 6.00
MJ Marko Jaric B 2.00 5.00
MR Michael Redd B 2.00 5.00
PG Pau Gasol B 4.00 10.00
PP Paul Pierce B 4.00 10.00
PS Peja Stojakovic B 2.00 5.00
RA Ray Allen B 4.00 10.00
RH Robert Horry B 2.00 5.00
RJ Richard Jefferson B 2.00 5.00
RM Reggie Miller B 5.00 12.00
RN Rasho Nesterovic B 2.00 5.00
SB Shane Battier B 2.00 5.00
SM Stephon Marbury B 3.00 8.00
SO Shaquille O'Neal B 10.00 25.00
TD Tim Duncan B 6.00 15.00
TM Tracy McGrady B 4.00 10.00
TP Tony Parker B 4.00 10.00
YM Yao Ming B 6.00 15.00
ZP Zoran Planinic B 2.00 5.00
TAP Tayshaun Prince B 2.50 6.00

2005-06 Topps Pristine

COMP.SET w/o SP's 25.00 60.00
RELIC PRINT RUN 500 SER.#'d SETS
AUTO PRINT RUN 60 TO 100 SETS
JSY AU PRINT RUN 50 SER.#'d SETS
1 Ray Allen .60 1.50
2 Cuttino Mobley .25 .60
3 Sebastian Telfair .30 .75
4 Dwight Howard .50 1.25
5 Udonis Haslem .25 .60
6 Luol Deng .30 .75
7 Lamar Odom .30 .75
8 Paul Pierce .60 1.50
9 Stephen Jackson .30 .75
10 Mike Dunleavy .25 .60
11 Andre Miller .30 .75
12 Ben Gordon .30 .75
13 Caron Butler .30 .75
14 Al Jefferson .25 .60
15 Jamaal Tinsley .25 .60
16 Josh Childress .25 .60
17 Larry Hughes .30 .75
18 Andrei Kirilenko .30 .75
19 Brad Miller .30 .75
20 Steve Nash .75 2.00
21 Grant Hill .60 1.50
22 Samuel Dalembert .25 .60
23 Quentin Richardson .25 .60
24 Wally Szczerbiak .30 .75
25 Desmond Mason .25 .60
26 Dwyane Wade .75 2.00
27 Richard Hamilton .50 1.25
28 Shane Battier .30 .75
29 Chauncey Billups .50 1.25
30 Shawn Marion .30 .75
31 Kenyon Martin .30 .75
32 Marquis Daniels .25 .60
33 Al Harrington .30 .75
34 Brendan Haywood .25 .60
35 Mehmet Okur .25 .60
36 Rafer Alston .30 .75
37 Luke Ridnour .30 .75
38 Tim Duncan 1.00 2.50
39 Mike Miller .30 .75
40 Allen Iverson .75 2.00
41 Jamal Crawford .40 1.00
42 J.R. Smith .40 1.00
43 Kevin Garnett 1.00 2.50
44 Baron Davis .40 1.00
45 Corey Maggette .30 .75
46 Jermaine O'Neal .30 .75
47 Yao Ming .75 2.00
48 Pau Gasol .60 1.50
49 Devin Harris .25 .60
50 Emeka Okafor .30 .75
51 Zydrunas Ilgauskas .30 .75
52 Vladimir Radmanovic .25 .60
53 Tracy McGrady .60 1.50
54 Steve Francis .40 1.00
55 Stephon Marbury .50 1.25
56 Shaun Livingston .30 .75
57 Sam Cassell .30 .75
58 Rasheed Wallace .40 1.00
59 Primoz Brezec .25 .60
60 Nenad Krstic .25 .60
61 Mike Bibby .40 1.00
62 Marcus Camby .30 .75
63 LeBron James 3.00 8.00
64 Kobe Bryant 3.00 8.00
65 Josh Smith .30 .75
66 Jason Richardson .40 1.00
67 Jamaal Magloire .25 .60
68 Gilbert Arenas .40 1.00
69 Zach Randolph .40 1.00
70 Vince Carter .75 2.00
71 Tony Parker .60 1.50
72 Shaquille O'Neal 1.25 3.00
73 Richard Jefferson .30 .75
74 Rashard Lewis .30 .75
75 Peja Stojakovic .30 .75
76 Mike Sweetney .25 .60
77 Elton Brand .30 .75
78 Drew Gooden .30 .75
79 Chris Webber .50 1.25
80 Carmelo Anthony .60 1.50
81 Bobby Simmons .25 .60
82 Bob Sura .25 .60
83 Antoine Walker .30 .75
84 Andre Iguodala .40 1.00
85 Michael Redd .30 .75
86 Manu Ginobili .75 2.00
87 Latrell Sprewell .40 1.00
88 Kirk Hinrich .30 .75
89 Josh Howard .30 .75
90 Jason Kidd .60 1.50
91 Jalen Rose .30 .75
92 Gerald Wallace .30 .75
93 Eddy Curry .25 .60
94 Dirk Nowitzki 1.00 2.50
95 Joe Johnson .30 .75
96 Chris Bosh .50 1.25
97 Carlos Boozer .30 .75
98 Ben Wallace .50 1.25
99 Antawn Jamison .30 .75
100 Amare Stoudemire .40 1.00
101 Andrew Bogut RC 2.50 6.00
102 Marvin Williams RC 2.00 5.00
103 Deron Williams RC 3.00 8.00
104 Chris Paul RC 20.00 50.00
105 Raymond Felton RC 1.50 4.00
106 Martell Webster RC 1.50 4.00
107 Charlie Villanueva RC 1.50 4.00
108 Channing Frye RC 1.50 4.00
109 Ike Diogu RC 1.25 3.00
110 Andrew Bynum RC 1.50 4.00
111 Monta Ellis RC 2.50 6.00
112 Yaroslav Korolev RC 1.25 3.00
113 Sean May RC 1.25 3.00
114 Rashad McCants RC 1.25 3.00
115 Antoine Wright RC 1.50 4.00
116 Joey Graham RC 1.50 4.00
117 Danny Granger RC 2.00 5.00
118 Gerald Green RC 2.00 5.00
119 Hakim Warrick RC 1.50 4.00
120 Julius Hodge RC 1.25 3.00
121 Nate Robinson RC 2.00 5.00
122 Jarrett Jack RC 2.00 5.00
123 Francisco Garcia RC 1.25 3.00
124 Luther Head RC 1.25 3.00
125 C.J. Miles RC 1.50 4.00
126 Salim Stoudamire RC 1.50 4.00
127 Sarunas Jasikevicius RC 2.00 5.00
128 Wayne Simien RC 1.25 3.00
129 David Lee RC 2.00 5.00
130 Jay-Z 1.50 4.00
131 Tim Duncan JSY 8.00 20.00
132 Ray Allen JSY 5.00 12.00
133 Grant Hill Warm 5.00 12.00
134 Dwyane Wade Shorts 6.00 15.00
135 Shawn Marion JSY 2.50 6.00
136 Jermaine O'Neal JSY 2.50 6.00
137 Emeka Okafor JSY 2.50 6.00
138 Tracy McGrady JSY 5.00 12.00
139 Chris Bosh Shorts 4.00 10.00
140 Dwight Howard JSY 4.00 10.00
141 Elton Brand JSY 2.50 6.00
142 Manu Ginobili JSY 6.00 15.00
143 Dirk Nowitzki JSY 8.00 20.00
144 Ben Wallace Warm 4.00 10.00
145 Steve Nash Warm 6.00 15.00
146 Allen Iverson Shirt 6.00 15.00
147 Kevin Garnett JSY 8.00 20.00
148 Corey Maggette JSY 2.50 6.00
149 Yao Ming JSY 6.00 15.00
150 Kobe Bryant Shorts 40.00 100.00
151 Rasheed Wallace JSY 3.00 8.00
152 Ben Gordon JSY 2.50 6.00
153 Gilbert Arenas Shirt 3.00 8.00
154 Shaquille O'Neal Warm 10.00 25.00
155 Peja Stojakovic JSY 2.50 6.00
156 Carmelo Anthony JSY 5.00 12.00
157 Kirk Hinrich JSY 2.50 6.00
158 Paul Pierce Shirt 5.00 12.00
159 Antawn Jamison JSY 2.50 6.00
160 Amare Stoudemire Shirt 3.00 8.00
161 Sarunas Jasikevicius Shorts 3.00 8.00
162 Wayne Simien JSY 2.00 5.00
163 Channing Frye JSY 2.50 6.00
164 Antoine Wright JSY 2.50 6.00
165 Sean May JSY 2.00 5.00
166 Rashad McCants JSY 2.00 5.00
167 Julius Hodge JSY 2.00 5.00
168 Nate Robinson JSY 3.00 8.00
169 Jarrett Jack JSY 3.00 8.00
170 Francisco Garcia JSY 2.00 5.00
171 Charlie Villanueva JSY 2.50 6.00
172 Andrew Bogut JSY 4.00 10.00
173 David Lee JSY 3.00 8.00
174 Deron Williams JSY 6.00 15.00
175 Chris Paul JSY 8.00 20.00
176 Raymond Felton JSY 2.50 6.00
177 Martell Webster JSY 2.50 6.00
178 Danny Granger JSY 3.00 8.00
179 Gerald Green JSY 3.00 8.00
180 Hakim Warrick JSY 2.50 6.00
181 Shaun Livingston AU 6.00 15.00
182 Danny Granger AU 6.00 15.00
183 Ryan Gomes AU RC 5.00 12.00
184 Jermaine O'Neal AU/75 10.00 25.00
185 George Gervin AU/60 6.00 15.00
186 Allen Iverson AU 50.00 100.00
187 Sean May AU 4.00 10.00
188 Andrew Bogut AU 8.00 20.00
189 Deron Williams AU 10.00 25.00
190 Stephon Marbury AU 10.00 25.00
191 Jason Kidd AU 12.50 30.00
192 Raymond Felton AU 5.00 12.00
193 Rashad McCants AU 4.00 10.00
194 Gerald Green AU 6.00 15.00
195 Andrew Bynum AU 5.00 12.00
196 Charlie Villanueva AU 5.00 12.00
197 Antoine Wright AU 5.00 12.00
198 Martell Webster AU 5.00 12.00
199 Francisco Garcia AU 4.00 10.00
200 Emeka Okafor AU 8.00 20.00
201 Hakim Warrick AU 5.00 12.00
202 Joey Graham AU 5.00 12.00
203 Julius Hodge AU 4.00 10.00
204 Ike Diogu AU 4.00 10.00
205 Johan Petro AU RC 4.00 10.00
206 Shaquille O'Neal JSY AU 40.00 80.00
208 Andrew Bogut JSY AU 15.00 40.00
209 Deron Williams JSY AU 40.00 80.00
210 Jay-Z Jeans AU 800.00 1,500.00

2005-06 Topps Pristine Die Cut

*1-100 VET DIE CUT: 3X TO 8X BASE HI
*101-130 DIE CUT: 1X TO 2.5X BASE HI
PRINT RUN 50 SER.#'d SETS
104 Chris Paul 125.00 300.00
130 Jay-Z 30.00 80.00

2005-06 Topps Pristine Uncirculated

*1-100 UNCIR: 1.5X TO 4X BASE HI
1-100 PRINT RUN 325 SER.#'d SETS
*101-130 UNCIR: .6X TO 1.5X BASE HI
*131-180 UNCIR: .5X TO 1.25X BASE HI
131-180 JSY PRINT RUN 100 SER.#'d SETS
*181-205 UNCIR: .6X TO 1.5X BASE HI
181-205 AU PRINT RUN 20 SER.#'d SETS
104 Chris Paul 40.00 100.00
130 Jay-Z 15.00 40.00
150 Kobe Bryant Shorts 50.00 120.00
185 George Gervin AU/60 12.50 30.00
189 Deron Williams AU 40.00 100.00
195 Andrew Bynum AU 40.00 100.00

2005-06 Topps Pristine Personal Endorsements

COMMON PRINT RUN 215 SER.#'d SETS
RARE PRINT RUN 50 SER.#'d SETS
UNCIR.COMMON PRINT RUN 7 SETS
UNCIR.UNCOMM.PRINT RUN 5 SETS
UNCIR.RARE PRINT RUN 3 SETS
UNCIR.SCARCE PRINT RUN ONE SET
CAI Allen Iverson/215 30.00 80.00
CBB Brandon Bass/215 3.00 8.00
CBW Bracey Wright/215 2.50 6.00
CCA Carmelo Anthony/215 15.00 30.00
CCT Chris Taft/215 2.50 6.00
CDE Daniel Ewing/215 3.00 8.00
CDG Danny Granger/215 4.00 10.00
CDL David Lee/215 4.00 10.00
CDW Dorell Wright/215 4.00 10.00
CEO Emeka Okafor/215 10.00 25.00
CJJ Jarrett Jack/215 4.00 10.00
CJM Jason Maxiell/215 3.00 8.00
CJN Jameer Nelson/215 4.00 10.00
CLD Luol Deng/215 5.00 12.00
CLH Luther Head/215 2.50 6.00
CLW Louis Williams/215 10.00 25.00
CME Monta Ellis/215 5.00 12.00
CRS Robert Swift/215 4.00 10.00
CRW Robert Whaley/215 4.00 10.00
CSL Shaun Livingston/215 4.00 10.00
CTD Travis Diener/215 2.50 6.00
CVW Von Wafer/215 2.50 6.00
CWS Wayne Simien/215 2.50 6.00
RAI Allen Iverson/50 50.00 125.00
RCB Christie Brinkley/50 40.00 100.00
RCE Carmen Electra/50 25.00 60.00
RJM Jenny McCarthy/50 40.00 100.00
RSE Shannon Elizabeth/50 25.00 60.00
RSN Steve Nash/50 40.00 80.00
RSO Shaquille O'Neal/50 40.00 80.00
UBD Baron Davis/125 5.00 12.00
UBU Beno Udrih/125 5.00 12.00
UBW Bill Walton/125 10.00 25.00
UCD Clyde Drexler/105 12.50 30.00
UHW Hakim Warrick/125 6.00 15.00
UJS Josh Smith/125 5.00 12.00
UKS Kirk Snyder/125 5.00 12.00
ULD Luol Deng/125 6.00 15.00
URF Raymond Felton/125 8.00 20.00
URP Robert Parish/109 15.00 30.00
USM Stephon Marbury/125 6.00 15.00
CDWA Dwyane Wade/215 25.00 60.00
USMA Sean May/125 5.00 12.00

2005-06 Topps Pristine Personal Pieces

COMMON PRINT RUN 350 SER.#'d SETS
RARE PRINT RUN 75 SER.#'d SETS
UNCIR.COMMON PRINT RUN 7 SETS
UNCIR.UNCOMM.PRINT RUN 5 SETS
UNCIR.RARE PRINT RUN 3 SETS
UNCIR.SCARCE PRINT RUN ONE SET
CAB Andrew Bogut Warm C 3.00 8.00
CAI Allen Iverson C 5.00 12.00
CAW Antoine Walker Shorts C 2.00 5.00
CBR Bernard Robinson C 2.00 5.00
CCA Carmelo Anthony C 4.00 10.00
CCB Chris Bosh C 3.00 8.00
CCE Carmen Electra Jeans C 8.00 20.00
CCF Channing Frye Warm C 2.00 5.00
CCK Chris Kaman C 2.00 5.00
CCP Chris Paul Warm C 8.00 20.00
CCV Charlie Villanueva Warm C 2.00 5.00
CDG Danny Granger Warm C 2.50 6.00
CDH David Harrison C 2.00 5.00
CDW Deron Williams Warm C 4.00 10.00
CEC Eddy Curry C 1.50 4.00
CEO Emeka Okafor C 2.00 5.00
CES Eric Snow C 2.00 5.00
CGA Gilbert Arenas C 2.50 6.00
CGG Gerald Green Warm C 2.50 6.00
CGP Gary Payton C 4.00 10.00
CHW Hakim Warrick Warm C 2.00 5.00
CJC Josh Childress C 1.50 4.00
CJH Julius Hodge Warm C 1.50 4.00
CJJ Jarrett Jack Warm C 2.50 6.00
CJM Jenny McCarthy Jeans C 8.00 20.00
CJS Josh Smith C 2.00 5.00
CJZ Jay-Z Jeans C 40.00 100.00
CKB Kobe Bryant Shorts C 40.00 100.00
CLR Luke Ridnour C 2.00 5.00
CMC Marcus Camby C 2.00 5.00
CMW Martell Webster Warm C 2.00 5.00
CPB Primoz Brezec C 2.00 5.00
CRF Raymond Felton Warm C 2.00 5.00
CRL Rashard Lewis C 2.00 5.00
CRW Rasheed Wallace C 2.50 6.00
CSD Samuel Dalembert C 2.00 5.00
CSE Shannon Elizabeth Jeans C 8.00 20.00
CSM Shawn Marion C 2.00 5.00
CSO S.O'Neal AS Shorts C 8.00 20.00
CSV Sasha Vujacic C 2.00 5.00
CTA Tony Allen C 2.00 5.00
CTD Tim Duncan AS Shorts C 6.00 15.00
CTM Troy Murphy C 1.50 4.00
CTP Tayshaun Prince C 2.50 6.00
CUH Udonis Haslem C 1.50 4.00
CWS Wally Szczerbiak C 2.00 5.00
CYM Yao Ming C 5.00 12.00
RAI Allen Iverson Shirt R 8.00 20.00
RCA Carmelo Anthony R 6.00 15.00
RDW Dwyane Wade Shorts R 8.00 20.00
REO Emeka Okafor R 3.00 8.00
RJZ Jay-Z Jeans R 60.00 150.00
RKB Kobe Bryant R 50.00 120.00
RMG Manu Ginobili Warm R 8.00 20.00
RSM Sean May R 2.50 6.00
RSO Shaquille O'Neal R 12.00 30.00
RYM Yao Ming R 8.00 20.00
SPP Paul Pierce S 4.00 10.00
UAB Andrew Bogut Shirt U 4.00 10.00
UAI Allen Iverson Shirt U 6.00 15.00
UBW Ben Wallace U 4.00 10.00
UCB Christie Brinkley Jeans U 10.00 25.00
UCE Carmen Electra Jeans U 10.00 25.00
UCP Chris Paul Shirt U 8.00 20.00
UDH Dwight Howard U 4.00 10.00
UDN Dirk Nowitzki U 8.00 20.00
UDW Deron Williams Shirt U 5.00 12.00
UGH Grant Hill U 5.00 12.00
UJM Jenny McCarthy Jeans U 10.00 25.00
UJZ Jay-Z Jeans U 50.00 120.00
UKB Kobe Bryant Warm U 40.00 100.00
UKG Kevin Garnett AS JSY U 8.00 20.00
UKH Kirk Hinrich U 2.50 6.00
UKM Kenyon Martin U 2.50 6.00
ULO Lamar Odom U 2.50 6.00
UMW Martell Webster Shirt U 2.50 6.00
URF Raymond Felton Shirt U 2.50 6.00
URM Rashad McCants Shirt U 2.00 5.00
USE Shannon Elizabeth Jeans U 10.00 25.00
USN Steve Nash Shorts U 6.00 15.00
UST Sebastian Telfair U 2.50 6.00
UTM Tracy McGrady U 5.00 12.00
CAIG Andre Iguodala C 2.50 6.00
CCBR Christie Brinkley Jeans C 8.00 20.00
CDWA Dwyane Wade C 5.00 12.00
UDWA Dwyane Wade Shorts U 6.00 15.00

2008 Topps Red Autographs

NNO Dwyane Wade 20.00 40.00
NNO Magic Johnson 40.00 80.00

2000-01 Topps Reserve

COMPLETE SET (134) 125.00 250.00
COMP.SET w/o SP's (100) 40.00 80.00
1 Tim Duncan 1.25 3.00
2 Clifford Robinson .50 1.25
3 Allen Iverson 1.25 3.00
4 Marcus Camby .40 1.00
5 Chauncey Billups .60 1.50
6 Anthony Mason .50 1.25
7 Toni Kukoc .60 1.50
8 Tim Thomas .30 .75
9 Corey Maggette .40 1.00
10 Steve Francis .50 1.25
11 Larry Hughes .50 1.25
12 Jerome Williams .30 .75
13 Reggie Miller 1.00 2.50
14 Chris Gatling .30 .75
15 Ron Artest .50 1.25
16 Derrick Coleman .50 1.25
17 Paul Pierce .75 2.00
18 Dikembe Mutombo .75 2.00
19 Andre Miller .40 1.00
20 Gary Payton .75 2.00
21 Kevin Garnett 1.25 3.00
22 Allan Houston .50 1.25
23 Rasheed Wallace .60 1.50
24 Derek Anderson .40 1.00
25 Vin Baker .40 1.00
26 John Stockton 1.00 2.50
27 Richard Hamilton .60 1.50
28 Mike Bibby .50 1.25
29 Dale Davis .40 1.00
30 Vince Carter 1.00 2.50
31 Shawn Marion .50 1.25
32 Karl Malone 1.00 2.50
33 Patrick Ewing .75 2.00
34 Shaquille O'Neal 2.00 5.00
35 Jermaine O'Neal .40 1.00
36 Danny Fortson .40 1.00
37 Steve Nash .75 2.00
38 Antoine Walker .50 1.25
39 Jason Terry .50 1.25
40 Vlade Divac .50 1.25
41 Avery Johnson .40 1.00
42 Elton Brand .50 1.25
43 Mitch Richmond .60 1.50
44 Antonio Davis .40 1.00
45 Shawn Kemp .75 2.00
46 Anfernee Hardaway .75 2.00
47 Kendall Gill .50 1.25
48 Glen Rice .50 1.25
49 Tim Hardaway .60 1.50
50 Tracy McGrady 1.00 2.50
51 Horace Grant .50 1.25
52 Hakeem Olajuwon 1.00 2.50
53 Antawn Jamison .50 1.25
54 Dirk Nowitzki 1.25 3.00
55 Antonio McDyess .40 1.00
56 Michael Dickerson .30 .75
57 Baron Davis .50 1.25
58 Nick Van Exel .50 1.25
59 Joe Smith .40 1.00
60 Kobe Bryant 4.00 10.00
61 Ray Allen .75 2.00
62 Keith Van Horn .40 1.00
63 Latrell Sprewell .60 1.50
64 Jason Kidd .75 2.00
65 Chris Webber .60 1.50
66 David Robinson 1.00 2.50
67 Mark Jackson .40 1.00
68 Bryon Russell .30 .75
69 Lamar Odom .50 1.25
70 Maurice Taylor .30 .75
71 Jonathan Bender .30 .75
72 Raef LaFrentz .40 1.00

73 Sam Cassell .40 1.00
74 Wally Szczerbiak .40 1.00
75 Grant Hill .75 2.00
76 Theo Ratliff .30 .75
77 Rashard Lewis .40 1.00
78 Darrell Armstrong .30 .75
79 Glenn Robinson .50 1.25
80 Stephon Marbury .60 1.50
81 Michael Olowokandi .30 .75
82 Isaiah Rider .40 1.00
83 Jalen Rose .40 1.00
84 Cuttino Mobley .40 1.00
85 Jerry Stackhouse .50 1.25
86 Jamal Mashburn .40 1.00
87 Kenny Anderson .40 1.00
88 Michael Finley .50 1.25
89 Lamond Murray .30 .75
90 Eddie Jones .50 1.25
91 Eric Snow .30 .75
92 Terrell Brandon .40 1.00
93 Jason Williams .75 2.00
94 Scottie Pippen 1.25 3.00
95 Rod Strickland .30 .75
96 Jim Jackson .40 1.00
97 Ron Mercer .40 1.00
98 Juwan Howard .40 1.00
99 Brian Grant .40 1.00
100 Shareef Abdur-Rahim .50 1.25
101 Kenyon Martin/499 RC 5.00 12.00
102 Stromile Swift/999 RC 1.50 4.00
103 Darius Miles/1499 RC 1.50 4.00
104 Marcus Fizer/499 RC 2.00 5.00
105 Mike Miller/999 RC 3.00 8.00
106 D.Johnson/1499 RC 1.00 2.50
107 Chris Mihm/499 RC 1.50 4.00
108 Jamal Crawford/999 RC 5.00 12.00
109 Joel Przybilla/1499 RC 1.25 3.00
110 Keyon Dooling/499 RC 2.00 5.00
111 Jerome Moiso/999 RC 1.25 3.00
112 Etan Thomas/1499 RC 1.25 3.00
113 C.Alexander/499 RC 1.50 4.00
114 Mateen Cleaves/999 RC 1.50 4.00
115 Jason Collier/1499 RC 1.50 4.00
116 Hedo Turkoglu/499 RC 4.00 10.00
117 Desmond Mason/999 RC 2.50 6.00
118 Q.Richardson/1499 RC 1.25 3.00
119 Jamaal Magloire/499 RC 2.50 6.00
120 Speedy Claxton/999 RC 2.00 5.00
121 Morris Peterson/1499 RC 1.50 4.00
122 Donnell Harvey/499 RC 2.00 5.00
123 D.Stevenson/999 RC 2.00 5.00
124 Dalibor Bagaric/1499 RC 1.25 3.00
125 I.Tsakalidis/499 RC 1.50 4.00
126 M.N'Diaye/999 RC 1.25 3.00
127 Erick Barkley/1499 RC 1.00 2.50
128 Mark Madsen/499 RC 2.50 6.00
129 A.J. Guyton/999 RC 1.25 3.00
130 Khalid El-Amin/1499 RC 1.00 2.50
131 Lavor Postell/499 RC 1.50 4.00
132 Marc Jackson/999 RC 1.50 4.00
133 S.Jackson/1499 RC 3.00 8.00
134 Wang Zhizhi/1499 RC 12.00 30.00

2000-01 Topps Reserve Canvas Autographs

OVERALL ODDS ONE PER HOBBY BOX
GROUP A STATED ODDS 1:68 BOXES
GROUP B STATED ODDS 1:34 BOXES
TRAJ Antawn Jamison E 6.00 15.00
TRAM Andre Miller F 6.00 15.00
TRBD Baron Davis E 6.00 15.00
TREB Elton Brand C 6.00 15.00
TRJO Jermaine O'Neal C 8.00 20.00
TRKD Keyon Dooling F 6.00 15.00
TRLH Larry Hughes D 6.00 15.00
TRMB Mike Bibby E 6.00 15.00
TRMJ Magic Johnson B 40.00 100.00
TRMT Maurice Taylor E 6.00 15.00
TRSM Shawn Marion E 8.00 20.00
TRSO Shaquille O'Neal A 50.00 120.00
TRWS Wally Szczerbiak E 6.00 15.00

2000-01 Topps Reserve Game Jerseys

OVERALL STATED ODDS ONE PER BOX
TAS1 Allen Iverson A 8.00 20.00
TAS2 Grant Hill A 5.00 12.00
TAS3 Alonzo Mourning A 5.00 12.00
TAS4 Eddie Jones A 3.00 8.00
TAS5 Allan Houston A 3.00 8.00
TAS6 Dale Davis A 2.50 6.00
TAS7 Reggie Miller A 6.00 15.00
TAS8 Dikembe Mutombo A 5.00 12.00
TAS9 Glenn Robinson A 3.00 8.00
TAS10 Ray Allen A 5.00 12.00
TAS11 Jerry Stackhouse A 3.00 8.00
TAS12 Tim Duncan A 8.00 20.00
TAS13 Shaquille O'Neal A 12.00 30.00
TAS14 Jason Kidd A 5.00 12.00
TAS15 Gary Payton A 5.00 12.00
TAS16 John Stockton A 6.00 15.00
TAS17 Karl Malone A 6.00 15.00
TAS18 David Robinson A 6.00 15.00
TAS19 Rasheed Wallace A 4.00 10.00
TAS20 Michael Finley A 3.00 8.00
TAS21 Chris Webber A 4.00 10.00
TAS22 Mike Bibby B 3.00 8.00
TAS23 Michael Dickerson B 2.00 5.00
TAS24 Cuttino Mobley B 2.50 6.00
TAS25 Raef LaFrentz B 2.50 6.00
TAS26 Dirk Nowitzki B 8.00 20.00
TAS27 Michael Olowokandi B 2.00 5.00
TAS28 Paul Pierce B 5.00 12.00
TAS29 Jason Williams B 2.50 6.00
TAS30 Elton Brand B 3.00 8.00
TAS31 Steve Francis B 3.00 8.00
TAS32 Adrian Griffin B 2.00 5.00
TAS33 Todd MacCulloch B 2.00 5.00
TAS34 Andre Miller B 2.50 6.00
TAS35 James Posey B 2.00 5.00
TAS36 Wally Szczerbiak B 2.50 6.00

2003-04 Topps Rookie Matrix Promos

COMPLETE SET (3) 10.00 25.00
PP1 Dwyane Wade
Carmelo Anthony
Chris Bosh 10.00 25.00
PP2 T.J. Ford
Kirk Hinrich
Marcus Banks 2.00 5.00
PP3 Elton Brand .40 1.00

2003-04 Topps Rookie Matrix

COMP.SET w/o RC's (110) 12.50 30.00
1 Allen Iverson .75 2.00
2 Anfernee Hardaway .75 2.00
3 Bonzi Wells .20 .50
4 Bobby Jackson .25 .60
5 Manu Ginobili .60 1.50
6 Andrei Kirilenko .25 .60
7 Ray Allen .50 1.25
8 Kwame Brown .20 .50
9 Jason Terry .25 .60
10 Paul Pierce .50 1.25
11 Tyson Chandler .25 .60
12 Darius Miles .20 .50
13 Antoine Walker .30 .75
14 Antawn Jamison .30 .75
15 Steve Nash .60 1.50
16 Marcus Camby .25 .60
17 Chauncey Billups .40 1.00
18 Jason Richardson .30 .75
19 Cuttino Mobley .20 .50
20 Yao Ming .75 2.00
21 Ron Artest .30 .75
22 Gary Payton .50 1.25
23 Jason Williams .50 1.25
24 Eddie Jones .30 .75
25 Kevin Garnett .75 2.00
26 Wally Szczerbiak .25 .60
27 Kenyon Martin .30 .75
28 Jamaal Magloire .20 .50
29 Keith Van Horn .25 .60
30 Tracy McGrady .50 1.25
31 Glenn Robinson .25 .60
32 Derek Anderson .25 .60
33 Chris Webber .40 1.00
34 Tony Parker .50 1.25
35 Morris Peterson .20 .50
36 Jerry Stackhouse .40 1.00
37 Theo Ratliff .20 .50
38 Jalen Rose .25 .60
39 Dajuan Wagner .20 .50
40 Dirk Nowitzki .75 2.00
41 Nikoloz Tskitishvili .20 .50
42 Ben Wallace .40 1.00
43 Tayshaun Prince .30 .75
44 Troy Murphy .30 .75
45 Jamaal Tinsley .20 .50
46 Corey Maggette .25 .60
47 Karl Malone .60 1.50
48 Mike Miller .25 .60
49 Lamar Odom .20 .50
50 Shaquille O'Neal 1.25 3.00
51 Michael Redd .30 .75
52 Sam Cassell .25 .60
53 Raef LaFrentz .20 .50
54 Baron Davis .30 .75
55 Allan Houston .30 .75
56 Drew Gooden .25 .60
57 Eric Snow .25 .60
58 Stephon Marbury .40 1.00
59 Zach Randolph .30 .75
60 Peja Stojakovic .25 .60
61 Brent Barry .20 .50
62 Radoslav Nesterovic .20 .50
63 Antonio Davis .25 .60
64 Gilbert Arenas .30 .75
65 Shareef Abdur-Rahim .30 .75
66 Scottie Pippen .75 2.00
67 Ronald Murray .20 .50
68 Zydrunas Ilgauskas .25 .60
69 Nene .25 .60
70 Steve Francis .30 .75
71 Mike Dunleavy .25 .60
72 Jermaine O'Neal .30 .75
73 Elton Brand .30 .75
74 Caron Butler .25 .60
75 Kobe Bryant 2.50 6.00
76 Kenny Thomas .20 .50
77 Joe Smith .20 .50
78 Jason Kidd .50 1.25
79 Antonio McDyess .25 .60
80 Shawn Marion .30 .75
81 Rasheed Wallace .40 1.00
82 Mike Bibby .30 .75
83 Tim Thomas .20 .50
84 Rashard Lewis .25 .60
85 Vince Carter .60 1.50
86 Matt Harpring .25 .60
87 Ricky Davis .25 .60
88 Michael Finley .30 .75
89 Andre Miller .25 .60
90 Pau Gasol .50 1.25
91 Dion Glover .20 .50
92 Jamal Crawford .25 .60
93 Richard Hamilton .40 1.00
94 Nick Van Exel .30 .75
95 Maurice Taylor .20 .50
96 Reggie Miller .60 1.50
97 Marko Jaric .20 .50
98 Brian Grant .20 .50
99 Desmond Mason .20 .50
100 Tim Duncan .75 2.00
101 Latrell Sprewell .40 1.00
102 Richard Jefferson .25 .60
103 David Wesley .20 .50
104 Kurt Thomas .25 .60
105 Juwan Howard .25 .60
106 Amare Stoudemire .40 1.00
107 Brad Miller .25 .60
108 Keon Clark .20 .50
109 Pat Garrity .20 .50
110 Jamal Mashburn .20 .50
AJF Carmelo/LeBron/Ford RC 25.00 60.00
AKM Carmelo/Kaman/Darko RC 2.00 5.00
AMB Carmelo/Darko/Bosh RC 3.00 8.00
AWB Carmelo/Wade/Bosh RC 5.00 12.00
BAH Bosh/Carmelo/Hinrich RC 2.50 6.00
BAJ Bosh/Carmelo/LeBron RC 25.00 60.00
BBG Barbosa/Bell/Gaines RC 1.25 3.00
BBR Banks/Bell/Ridnour RC 1.25 3.00
BCC Bell/Zarko/Collison RC 1.25 3.00
BCG Bell/Collison/Gaines RC 1.25 3.00
BCP Barbosa/Zarko/Pavlovic RC 1.25 3.00
BCP Banks/Collison/Pietrus RC 1.25 3.00
BHJ Bosh/Hinrich/LeBron RC 25.00 60.00
BJP Bell/Jones/Planinic RC 1.25 3.00
BKC Beasley/Kapono/Cook RC 1.25 3.00
BKS Banks/Kaman/Sweetney RC 1.25 3.00
BKW Bosh/Kaman/Wade RC 2.50 6.00
BPH Banks/Pietrus/Hayes RC 1.25 3.00
BPW Barbosa/Pavlovic/Williams RC 1.25 3.00
BRG Banks/Ridnour/Gaines RC 1.25 3.00
BWM Bosh/Wade/Darko RC 3.00 8.00
CEK Cook/Ebi/Kapono RC 1.25 3.00
CHB Collison/Hayes/Banks RC 1.25 3.00
CHC Cook/Howard/Zarko RC 1.25 3.00
CPD Zarko/Pietrus/Diaw RC 1.25 3.00
CPS Collison/Pietrus/Sweetney RC 1.25 3.00
CSH Collison/Sweetney/Hayes RC 1.25 3.00
CWC Cook/West/Collison RC 1.25 3.00
DPP Diaw/Pavlovic/Planinic RC 1.25 3.00
DPW Diaw/Pavlovic/West RC 1.25 3.00
EPW Ebi/Perkins/West RC 1.50 4.00
EWC Ebi/West/Cook RC 1.25 3.00
FAH Ford/Carmelo/Hinrich RC 2.00 5.00
FBH Ford/Banks/Hinrich RC 1.25 3.00
FBJ Ford/Bosh/LeBron RC 25.00 60.00
FBR Ford/Banks/Ridnour RC 1.25 3.00
FBW Ford/Bosh/Wade RC 2.50 6.00
FCH Ford/Collison/Hinrich RC 1.25 3.00
FGB Ford/Gaines/Banks RC 1.25 3.00
FKW Ford/Kaman/Wade RC 1.50 4.00
GBB Gaines/Banks/Bell RC 1.25 3.00
GBR Gaines/Bell/Ridnour RC 1.25 3.00
HAM Hinrich/Carmelo/Darko RC 2.50 6.00
HBM Hinrich/Bosh/Darko RC 1.50 4.00
HBS Hayes/Banks/Sweetney RC 1.25 3.00
HCJ Howard/Cook/Jones RC 1.25 3.00
HGP Hayes/Gaines/Pietrus RC 1.25 3.00
HJM Hinrich/LeBron/Darko RC 25.00 60.00
HKC Hayes/Kaman/Collison RC 1.25 3.00
HLC Howard/Lampe/Cook RC 1.25 3.00
HLK Howard/Lampe/Kapono RC 1.25 3.00
HPR Hayes/Pietrus/Ridnour RC 1.25 3.00
HSL Hayes/Sweetney/Lampe RC 1.25 3.00
HSP Hayes/Sweetney/Pietrus RC 1.25 3.00
HWS Hinrich/Wade/Sweetney RC 1.50 4.00
JAW LeBron/Carmelo/Wade RC 60.00 150.00
JBM LeBron/Bosh/Darko RC 25.00 60.00
JHA LeBron/Hinrich/Carmelo RC 25.00 60.00
JKA LeBron/Kaman/Carmelo RC 25.00 60.00
JMA LeBron/Darko/Carmelo RC 25.00 60.00
JMK LeBron/Darko/Kaman RC 25.00 60.00
JOB Jones/Outlaw/Barbosa RC 1.25 3.00
JWE Jones/Walton/Ebi RC 1.25 3.00
KCP Kaman/Zarko/Perkins RC 1.25 3.00
KEW Kapono/Ebi/Williams RC 1.25 3.00
KHW Kaman/Hinrich/Wade RC 1.50 4.00
KPH Kaman/Pietrus/Hayes RC 1.25 3.00
KSC Kaman/Sweetney/Collison RC 1.25 3.00
LBB Lampe/Barbosa/Beasley RC 1.25 3.00
LHC Lampe/Howard/Zarko RC 1.25 3.00
LSP Lampe/Sweetney/Planinic RC 1.25 3.00
MAF Darko/Carmelo/Ford RC 1.50 4.00
MBF Darko/Bosh/Ford RC 1.50 4.00
MFJ Darko/Ford/LeBron RC 25.00 60.00
MJW Darko/LeBron/Wade RC 40.00 100.00
OBD Outlaw/Barbosa/Diaw RC 1.25 3.00
OCB Outlaw/Cook/Beasley RC 1.25 3.00
OEJ Outlaw/Ebi/Jones RC 1.25 3.00
OPE Outlaw/Perkins/Ebi RC 1.25 3.00
PBE Perkins/Beasley/Ebi RC 1.25 3.00
PBG Perkins/Banks/Gaines RC 1.25 3.00
PBH Pietrus/Bell/Hayes RC 1.25 3.00
PCH Pietrus/Collison/Hayes RC 1.25 3.00
PCR Pietrus/Collison/Ridnour RC 1.25 3.00
PCW Perkins/Zarko/West RC 1.50 4.00
PDB Planinic/Diaw/Barbosa RC 1.25 3.00
PJD Pavlovic/Jones/Diaw RC 1.25 3.00
PLH Perkins/Lampe/Howard RC 1.25 3.00
POP Pavlovic/Outlaw/Planinic RC 1.25 3.00
PPC Pietrus/Pavlovic/Zarko RC 1.25 3.00
PSK Pietrus/Sweetney/Kaman RC 1.25 3.00
PWO Planinic/West/Outlaw RC 1.25 3.00
RFH Ridnour/Ford/Hinrich RC 1.25 3.00
RHC Ridnour/Hayes/Collison RC 1.25 3.00
SBC Sweetney/Banks/Collison RC 1.25 3.00
SHK Sweetney/Hayes/Kaman RC 1.25 3.00
SPB Sweetney/Pietrus/Banks RC 1.25 3.00
WBH Wade/Bosh/Hinrich RC 2.00 5.00
WBP Williams/Barbosa/Planinic RC 1.25 3.00
WDJ West/Diaw/Jones RC 1.25 3.00
WDP Williams/Diaw/Planinic RC 1.25 3.00
WFH Wade/Ford/Hinrich RC 2.00 5.00
WHL Walton/Howard/Lampe RC 1.25 3.00
WHO Walton/Outlaw/Howard RC 1.25 3.00
WJB Wade/LeBron/Bosh RC 150.00 400.00
WKP Walton/Kapono/Perkins RC 1.25 3.00
WKS Wade/Kaman/Sweetney RC 2.00 5.00
WMA Wade/Darko/Carmelo RC 5.00 12.00
WPJ West/Pavlovic/Jones RC 1.25 3.00
WWB Walton/Williams/Beasley RC 1.25 3.00

2003-04 Topps Rookie Matrix Minis

ONE PER PACK
*DOUBLE: .6X TO 1.5X MINI HI
DOUBLE STATED ODDS 1:13
*SWISH: 5X TO 12X MINI HI
SWISH STATED ODDS 1:1693
*TOPPS: .5X TO 1.25X MINI HI
TOPPS STATED ODDS 1:5
*TRIPLE: 1.25X TO 3X MINI HI
TRIPLE STATED ODDS 1:203
32 Derek Anderson .12 .30
49 Lamar Odom .12 .30
111 LeBron James 100.00 250.00
112 Darko Milicic .50 1.25
113 Carmelo Anthony 3.00 8.00
114 Chris Bosh 2.00 5.00
115 Dwyane Wade 5.00 12.00
116 Chris Kaman .60 1.50
117 Kirk Hinrich .60 1.50
118 T.J. Ford .50 1.25
119 Mike Sweetney .40 1.00
120 Jarvis Hayes .40 1.00
121 Mickael Pietrus .50 1.25
122 Nick Collison .50 1.25
123 Marcus Banks .40 1.00
124 Luke Ridnour .60 1.50
125 Reece Gaines .40 1.00
126 Troy Bell .40 1.00
127 Zarko Cabarkapa .40 1.00
128 David West .75 2.00
129 Aleksandar Pavlovic .50 1.25
130 Dahntay Jones .50 1.25
131 Boris Diaw .60 1.50
132 Zoran Planinic .40 1.00
133 Travis Outlaw .50 1.25
134 Brian Cook .40 1.00
135 Ndudi Ebi .40 1.00
136 Kendrick Perkins .50 1.25
137 Leandro Barbosa .60 1.50
138 Josh Howard .60 1.50
139 Maciej Lampe .40 1.00
140 Jason Kapono .40 1.00
141 Luke Walton .60 1.50
142 Jerome Beasley .40 1.00
143 Maurice Williams .60 1.50

2003-04 Topps Rookie Matrix Lottery Draw

THREE VERSIONS PER CARD VALUED SAME
STATED ODDS 1:371
LD1A LeBron James 400.00 800.00
LD2A Darko Milicic 3.00 8.00
LD3A Carmelo Anthony 20.00 50.00
LD4A Chris Bosh 12.00 30.00
LD5A Dwyane Wade 75.00 200.00
LD6A Chris Kaman 4.00 10.00
LD7A Kirk Hinrich 4.00 10.00
LD8A T.J. Ford 3.00 8.00
LD9A Mike Sweetney 2.50 6.00
LD10A Jarvis Hayes 2.50 6.00
LD11A Mickael Pietrus 3.00 8.00
LD12A Nick Collison 3.00 8.00
LD13A Marcus Banks 2.50 6.00

2003-04 Topps Rookie Matrix Mini Autographs

GROUP A ODDS 1:7164, B 1:3175, C 1:2039
GROUP D ODDS 1:412, E 1:913, F 1:148
GROUP G ODDS 1:49
AK Andrei Kirilenko F 5.00 12.00
BM Brad Miller F 5.00 12.00
CA Carmelo Anthony/100 A 30.00 60.00
DW Dwyane Wade D 30.00 80.00
GA Gilbert Arenas D 5.00 12.00
JC Jason Collins G 3.00 8.00
JK Jason Kidd E 8.00 20.00
LW Luke Walton G 5.00 12.00
MC Michael Curry G 5.00 12.00
MR Malik Rose B 5.00 12.00
PP Paul Pierce C 12.00 30.00
RG Reece Gaines F 3.00 8.00
RH Richard Hamilton D 5.00 12.00
TB Troy Bell G 3.00 8.00
TH Travis Hansen G 3.00 8.00
TP Tayshaun Prince G 5.00 12.00
ZC Zarko Cabarkapa G 3.00 8.00
ZP Zoran Planinic G 3.00 8.00
TPA Tony Parker F 8.00 20.00

2003-04 Topps Rookie Matrix Mini Relics

GROUP A ODDS 1:1259, B 1:372, C 1:473
GROUP D ODDS 1:792, E 1:219, F 1:148, G 1:49
AI Allen Iverson F 6.00 15.00
AJ Antawn Jamison/250 C 2.50 6.00
AM Andre Miller G 2.00 5.00
AS Amare Stoudemire G 3.00 8.00
BB Brent Barry/50 A 5.00 12.00
BW Ben Wallace G 3.00 8.00
CA Carmelo Anthony F 12.00 30.00
CB Caron Butler/250 C 2.00 5.00
CK Chris Kaman F 2.50 6.00
CM Corey Maggette A 2.00 5.00
CW Chris Webber/50 A 8.00 20.00
DG Drew Gooden E 2.00 5.00
DM Darius Miles G 2.00 5.00
DN Dirk Nowitzki G 6.00 15.00
DW Dajuan Wagner F 2.00 5.00
EB Elton Brand F 2.00 5.00
GR Glenn Robinson E 2.00 5.00
JH Jarvis Hayes F 1.50 4.00
JK Jason Kidd F 4.00 10.00
JO Jermaine O'Neal G 2.50 6.00
JR Jalen Rose F 2.50 6.00
JT Jason Terry/50 A 6.00 15.00
JW Jason Williams E 4.00 10.00
KB Kwame Brown/150 B 2.50 6.00
KG Kevin Garnett G 6.00 15.00
KH Kirk Hinrich F 2.50 6.00
KT Kurt Thomas/50 A 5.00 12.00
LO Lamar Odom F 2.00 5.00
LR Luke Ridnour F 2.50 6.00
LS Latrell Sprewell G 3.00 8.00
MB Marcus Banks F 1.50 4.00
MD Mike Dunleavy/50 A 5.00 12.00
MM Mike Miller F 2.00 5.00
MO Michael Olowokandi G 1.50 4.00
MP Mickael Pietrus/50 A 5.00 12.00
MS Mike Sweetney F 1.50 4.00
NH Nene G 2.00 5.00
PG Pau Gasol G 4.00 10.00
PP Paul Pierce G 4.00 10.00
QR Quentin Richardson/50 A 5.00 12.00
RA Ray Allen/150 B 4.00 10.00
RG Reece Gaines G 1.50 4.00
RH Richard Hamilton G 3.00 8.00
RJ Richard Jefferson D 2.00 5.00
RL Rashard Lewis/250 C 2.00 5.00
RM Reggie Miller D 5.00 12.00
RW Rasheed Wallace/50 A 6.00 15.00
SF Steve Francis F 2.50 6.00
SM Shawn Marion G 2.50 6.00
SN Steve Nash F 2.50 6.00
SO Shaquille O'Neal G 10.00 25.00
TB Troy Bell F 1.50 4.00
TD Tim Duncan F 6.00 15.00
TM Tracy McGrady G 4.00 10.00
TP Tayshaun Prince/150 B 2.50 6.00
YM Yao Ming F 6.00 15.00
ZC Zarko Cabarkapa/150 B 1.50 4.00
ZI Zydrunas Ilgauskas G 2.00 5.00
CBO Chris Bosh F 8.00 20.00
CMO Cuttino Mobley G 1.50 4.00
DWA Dwyane Wade F 20.00 50.00
JHO Juwan Howard E 2.00 5.00
JRI Jason Richardson/50 A 6.00 15.00
JWI Jerome Williams E 2.00 5.00
KMA Kenyon Martin/50 A 6.00 15.00
MBI Mike Bibby/150 B 2.50 6.00
MPE Morris Peterson F 1.50 4.00
RAR Ron Artest/150 B 2.50 6.00
SMA Stephon Marbury/150 B 3.00 8.00
TMU Troy Murphy E 1.50 4.00
TPA Tony Parker/250 C 4.00 10.00

2003-04 Topps Rookie Matrix Rookie Frames

STATED ODDS 1:13
*DOUBLE: .6X TO 1.5X BASE FRAME HI
DOUBLE STATED ODDS 1:125
*TOPPS: .5X TO 1.25X BASE FRAME
TOPPS STATED ODDS 1:51
*TRIPLE: 3X TO 8X BASE FRAME HI
TRIPLE STATED ODDS 1:2235
111 LeBron James 200.00 500.00
112 Darko Milicic 1.00 2.50
113 Carmelo Anthony 6.00 15.00
114 Chris Bosh 4.00 10.00
115 Dwyane Wade 10.00 25.00
116 Chris Kaman 1.25 3.00
117 Kirk Hinrich 1.25 3.00
118 T.J. Ford 1.00 2.50
119 Mike Sweetney .75 2.00
120 Jarvis Hayes .75 2.00
121 Mickael Pietrus 1.00 2.50
122 Nick Collison 1.00 2.50
123 Marcus Banks .75 2.00
124 Luke Ridnour 1.25 3.00
125 Reece Gaines .75 2.00
126 Troy Bell .75 2.00
127 Zarko Cabarkapa .75 2.00
128 David West 1.50 4.00
129 Aleksandar Pavlovic 1.00 2.50
130 Dahntay Jones 1.00 2.50
131 Boris Diaw 1.25 3.00
132 Zoran Planinic .75 2.00
133 Travis Outlaw 1.00 2.50
134 Brian Cook .75 2.00
135 Ndudi Ebi .75 2.00
136 Kendrick Perkins 1.00 2.50
137 Leandro Barbosa 1.25 3.00
138 Josh Howard 1.25 3.00
139 Maciej Lampe .75 2.00
140 Jason Kapono .75 2.00
141 Luke Walton 1.25 3.00
142 Jerome Beasley .75 2.00
143 Maurice Williams 1.25 3.00

2001 Topps Sean Elliott National Kidney Foundation

COMPLETE SET (2) .75 2.00
SE Sean Elliott .75 2.00
NNO Nation Kidney Foundation .05 .15

2008-09 Topps Signature

COMPLETE SET (85) 75.00 150.00
PRINT RUN 2325 SER.#'d SETS
TSAA Arron Afflalo .60 1.50
TSAT Al Thornton .60 1.50
TSBD Baron Davis 1.00 2.50
TSBR Brandon Roy .75 2.00
TSBW Brandon Wright .60 1.50
TSCL Courtney Lee RC 1.00 2.50
TSCP Chris Paul 2.00 5.00
TSDC Daequan Cook .60 1.50
TSDE Dale Ellis .60 1.50
TSDH Dwight Howard 1.25 3.00
TSDJ DeAndre Jordan RC 1.50 4.00
TSDR Derrick Rose RC 5.00 12.00
TSDS Dolph Schayes 1.00 2.50
TSEB Elgin Baylor 1.50 4.00
TSEG Eric Gordon RC 2.00 5.00
TSEH Elvin Hayes 1.00 2.50
TSFL Fat Lever .60 1.50
TSGA Gilbert Arenas 1.00 2.50
TSGG George Gervin 1.50 4.00
TSGH George Hill RC 1.25 3.00
TSGP Gabe Pruitt .60 1.50
TSGW Gerald Wallace .60 1.50
TSIT Isiah Thomas 1.50 4.00
TSJA Joe Alexander RC .75 2.00
TSJD Joey Dorsey RC .75 2.00
TSJH Josh Howard .75 2.00
TSJM JaVale McGee RC 1.25 3.00
TSJS John Stockton 2.00 5.00
TSJW Jerry West 2.00 5.00
TSKW Kyle Weaver RC .75 2.00
TSLB Larry Bird 3.00 8.00
TSLW Lenny Wilkens 1.00 2.50
TSMA Morris Almond .60 1.50
TSME Mark Eaton .60 1.50
TSMJ Magic Johnson 3.00 8.00
TSML Maurice Lucas .60 1.50
TSMP Mickael Pietrus .60 1.50
TSMW Marcus Williams .60 1.50
TSNY Nick Young .60 1.50
TSOB Otis Birdsong .75 2.00
TSPP Paul Pierce 1.50 4.00
TSRA Ryan Anderson RC 1.00 2.50
TSRF Raymond Felton .60 1.50
TSRG Rudy Gay 1.00 2.50
TSRP Robert Parish 1.00 2.50
TSRR Rajon Rondo 1.25 3.00
TSRS Rodney Stuckey .60 1.50
TSRT Reggie Theus .60 1.50
TSRW Russell Westbrook RC 6.00 15.00
TSSC Speedy Claxton .60 1.50
TSSD Samuel Dalembert .60 1.50
TSSH Spencer Hawes .60 1.50
TSSO Shaquille O'Neal 3.00 8.00
TSSP Sam Perkins .75 2.00
TSSS Sean Singletary RC .75 2.00
TSSW Sonny Weems RC .75 2.00
TSTY Thaddeus Young .75 2.00
TSVC Vince Carter 2.00 5.00
TSWS Walter Sharpe RC .75 2.00
TSYJ Yi Jianlian 1.25 3.00
TSZR Zach Randolph 1.00 2.50
TSABR Aaron Brooks .60 1.50
TSATU Alando Tucker .60 1.50
TSBRU Bill Russell 3.00 8.00
TSBWA Bill Walker RC .75 2.00
TSBWI Buck Williams .60 1.50
TSCBU Caron Butler .75 2.00
TSDGA Danilo Gallinari RC 2.00 5.00
TSDGI Daniel Gibson .60 1.50
TSDGR Donte Greene RC .75 2.00
TSDRO Dennis Rodman 2.00 5.00
TSDRO David Robinson 2.00 5.00
TSDSC Danny Schayes 1.00 2.50
TSDWA Dwyane Wade 2.00 5.00
TSJHA John Havlicek 1.00 2.50
TSJHI J.J. Hickson RC .75 2.00
TSJWO Jo Jo White 1.00 2.50
TSJRG J.R. Giddens RC .75 2.00
TSMRR Micheal Ray Richardson .75 2.00
TSOJM O.J. Mayo RC 1.00 2.50
TSRAL Ray Allen 1.50 4.00
TSRPI Ricky Pierce .60 1.50
TSSHA Spencer Haywood 1.00 2.50
TSSWE Spud Webb .75 2.00
TSJHRW John "Hot Rod" Williams .60 1.50

2008-09 Topps Signature Facsimile Black

*BLACK: .6X TO 1.5X BASE HI
STATED PRINT RUN 289 SER.#'d SETS
TSDR Derrick Rose 30.00 80.00
TSRW Russell Westbrook 40.00 100.00

2008-09 Topps Signature Facsimile Red

*RED: .5X TO 1.25X BASE HI
STATED PRINT RUN 869 SER.#'d SETS
TSDR Derrick Rose 15.00 40.00
TSRW Russell Westbrook 20.00 50.00

2008-09 Topps Signature Autographs

PRINT RUNS LISTED IN CHECKLIST
TSAAA Arron Afflalo/917 4.00 10.00
TSAAT Al Thornton/1799 4.00 10.00
TSABD Baron Davis/1079 10.00 25.00
TSABR Brandon Roy/649 10.00 25.00
TSABW Brandon Wright/3645 4.00 10.00
TSACL Courtney Lee/149 4.00 10.00
TSACP Chris Paul/649 40.00 100.00
TSADC Daequan Cook/1199 4.00 10.00
TSADE Dale Ellis/999 4.00 10.00
TSADH Dwight Howard/2499 25.00 60.00
TSADJ DeAndre Jordan/149 12.00 30.00
TSADR Derrick Rose/649 150.00 400.00
TSADS Dolph Schayes/425 8.00 20.00
TSAEB Elgin Baylor/1299 50.00 120.00
TSAEG Eric Gordon/275 5.00 12.00
TSAEH Elvin Hayes/625 10.00 25.00
TSAFL Fat Lever/750 4.00 10.00
TSAGA Gilbert Arenas/1199 8.00 20.00
TSAGG George Gervin/875 12.00 30.00
TSAGH George Hill/550 4.00 10.00
TSAGP Gabe Pruitt/1199 4.00 10.00
TSAGW Gerald Wallace/1499 4.00 10.00
TSAIT Isiah Thomas/999 25.00 60.00
TSAJA Joe Alexander/147 4.00 10.00
TSAJD Joey Dorsey/299 4.00 10.00
TSAJH Josh Howard/625 4.00 10.00
TSAJM JaVale McGee/275 6.00 15.00
TSAJS John Stockton/676 40.00 100.00
TSAJW Jerry West/649 30.00 80.00
TSAKW Kyle Weaver/699 4.00 10.00
TSALB Larry Bird/499 75.00 200.00
TSALW Lenny Wilkens/650 6.00 15.00
TSAMA Morris Almond/599 4.00 10.00
TSAME Mark Eaton/1029 10.00 25.00
TSAMJ Magic Johnson/499 75.00 200.00
TSAML Maurice Lucas/999 4.00 10.00
TSAMP Mickael Pietrus/1399 4.00 10.00
TSAMW Marcus Williams/1199 4.00 10.00
TSANY Nick Young/6225 8.00 20.00
TSAOB Otis Birdsong/1199 4.00 10.00
TSAPP Paul Pierce/1999 30.00 80.00
TSARA Ryan Anderson/499 4.00 10.00
TSARF Raymond Felton/1799 4.00 10.00
TSARG Rudy Gay/3640 4.00 10.00
TSARP Robert Parish/650 8.00 20.00
TSARR Rajon Rondo/1299 8.00 20.00
TSARS Rodney Stuckey/450 8.00 20.00
TSART Reggie Theus/940 4.00 10.00
TSARW R. Westbrook/184 150.00 300.00
TSASC Speedy Claxton/599 4.00 10.00
TSASD Samuel Dalembert/750 4.00 10.00
TSASH Spencer Hawes/999 4.00 10.00
TSASO Shaquille O'Neal/825 125.00 300.00
TSASP Sam Perkins/1199 4.00 10.00
TSASS Sean Singletary/1999 4.00 10.00
TSASW Sonny Weems/799 4.00 10.00
TSATY Thaddeus Young/5775 4.00 10.00
TSAVC Vince Carter/599 40.00 100.00
TSAWS Walter Sharpe/350 4.00 10.00
TSAYJ Yi Jianlian/6225 40.00 100.00
TSAZR Zach Randolph/1799 8.00 20.00
TSAABR Aaron Brooks/499 4.00 10.00
TSAATU Alando Tucker/2999 4.00 10.00
TSABRU Bill Russell/499 500.00 1,000.00
TSABWA Bill Walker/1999 4.00 10.00
TSABWI Buck Williams/1299 5.00 12.00
TSACBU Caron Butler/1309 4.00 10.00
TSADGA Danilo Gallinari/439 6.00 15.00
TSADGI Daniel Gibson/1799 4.00 10.00
TSADGR Donte Greene/1199 4.00 10.00
TSADRD Dennis Rodman/1299 40.00 100.00
TSADRO David Robinson/899 30.00 80.00
TSADSC Danny Schayes/750 4.00 10.00
TSADWA Dwyane Wade/649 60.00 150.00
TSAJHA John Havlicek/799 50.00 120.00
TSAJHI J.J. Hickson/125 4.00 10.00
TSAJWO Jo Jo White/989 8.00 20.00
TSAJRG J.R. Giddens/625 4.00 10.00
TSAMRR Micheal Ray Richardson/1199 4.00 10.00
TSAOJM O.J. Mayo/599 4.00 10.00
TSARAL Ray Allen/799 30.00 80.00
TSARPI Ricky Pierce/999 4.00 10.00
TSASHA Spencer Haywood/1179 10.00 25.00
TSASWE Spud Webb/1899 10.00 25.00
TSAJHRW Hot Rod Williams/750 5.00 12.00

2008-09 Topps Signature Autographs Dual

STATED PRINT RUN 49 SER.#'d SETS
TSDBA C.Billups/C.Anthony 40.00 100.00
TSDGM R.Gay/O.Mayo 8.00 20.00
TSDHW D.Howard/D.Wade 60.00 150.00
TSDIG A.Iguodala/D.Granger 8.00 20.00
TSDOR G.Oden/B.Roy 12.00 30.00
TSDPR C.Paul/D.Rose 125.00 300.00
TSDRG D.Robinson/G.Gervin 40.00 100.00
TSDSJ J.Stockton/M.Johnson 75.00 200.00
TSDWC D.Wilkins/V.Carter 50.00 120.00
TSDWR J.West/B.Russell 500.00 1,000.00

2008-09 Topps Signature Autographs Triple

PRINT RUNS B/WN 9-36 COPIES PER
TSTARM Arenas/Roy/Mayo 25.00 60.00
TSTHOR Howard/O'Neal/D.Rob 200.00 500.00
TSTJWB Magic/West/Baylor 125.00 300.00

2005 Topps Special Edition Authentic

AU ISSUED AS REPLACEMENT
EO1 Emeka Okafor/499 5.00 12.00
EO2 Emeka Okafor/99 8.00 20.00
EO3 Emeka Okafor/25 12.00 30.00

1996 Topps Stars

COMPLETE SET (150) 20.00 40.00
CL (NNO) .08 .25
1 Kareem Abdul-Jabbar .25 .60
2 Nate Archibald .12 .30
3 Paul Arizin .15 .40
4 Charles Barkley .25 .60
5 Rick Barry .12 .30
6 Elgin Baylor .15 .40
7 Dave Bing .15 .40
8 Larry Bird .40 1.00
9 Wilt Chamberlain .30 .75
10 Bob Cousy .25 .60
11 Dave Cowens .12 .30
12 Billy Cunningham .15 .40
13 Dave DeBusschere .15 .40
14 Clyde Drexler .20 .50
15 Julius Erving .25 .60
16 Patrick Ewing .20 .50
17 Walt Frazier .15 .40
18 George Gervin .15 .40
19 Hal Greer .12 .30
20 John Havlicek .20 .50
21 Elvin Hayes .15 .40
22 Magic Johnson .40 1.00
23 Sam Jones .20 .50
24 Michael Jordan 1.25 3.00
25 Jerry Lucas .15 .40
26 Karl Malone .20 .50
27 Moses Malone .15 .40
28 Pete Maravich .25 .60
29 Kevin McHale .20 .50
30 George Mikan .25 .60
31 Earl Monroe .15 .40
32 Shaquille O'Neal .40 1.00
33 Hakeem Olajuwon .20 .50
34 Robert Parish .15 .40
35 Bob Pettit .15 .40
36 Scottie Pippen .25 .60
37 Willis Reed .15 .40
38 Oscar Robertson .20 .50
39 David Robinson .25 .60
40 Bill Russell .25 .60
41 Dolph Schayes .15 .40
42 Bill Sharman .15 .40
43 John Stockton .20 .50
44 Isiah Thomas .15 .40
45 Nate Thurmond .12 .30
46 Wes Unseld .15 .40
47 Bill Walton .15 .40
48 Jerry West .25 .60
49 Lenny Wilkens .15 .40
50 James Worthy .20 .50
51 Kareem Abdul-Jabbar GS .25 .60
52 Nate Archibald GS .12 .30
53 Paul Arizin GS .15 .40
54 Charles Barkley GS .25 .60
55 Rick Barry GS .12 .30
56 Elgin Baylor GS .15 .40
57 Dave Bing GS .15 .40
58 Larry Bird GS .40 1.00
59 Wilt Chamberlain GS .30 .75
60 Bob Cousy GS .25 .60
61 Dave Cowens GS .12 .30
62 Billy Cunningham GS .15 .40
63 Dave DeBusschere GS .15 .40
64 Clyde Drexler GS .20 .50
65 Julius Erving GS .25 .60
66 Patrick Ewing GS .20 .50
67 Walt Frazier GS .15 .40
68 George Gervin GS .15 .40
69 Hal Greer GS .12 .30
70 John Havlicek GS .20 .50
71 Elvin Hayes GS .15 .40
72 Magic Johnson GS .40 1.00
73 Sam Jones GS .20 .50
74 Michael Jordan GS 1.25 3.00
75 Jerry Lucas GS .15 .40
76 Karl Malone GS .20 .50
77 Moses Malone GS .15 .40
78 Pete Maravich GS .25 .60
79 Kevin McHale GS .20 .50
80 George Mikan GS .25 .60
81 Earl Monroe GS .15 .40
82 Shaquille O'Neal GS .40 1.00
83 Hakeem Olajuwon GS .20 .50
84 Robert Parish GS .15 .40
85 Bob Pettit GS .15 .40
86 Scottie Pippen GS .25 .60
87 Willis Reed GS .15 .40
88 Oscar Robertson GS .20 .50
89 David Robinson GS .25 .60
90 Bill Russell GS .25 .60
91 Dolph Schayes GS .15 .40
92 Bill Sharman GS .15 .40
93 John Stockton GS .20 .50
94 Isiah Thomas GS .15 .40
95 Nate Thurmond GS .12 .30
96 Wes Unseld GS .15 .40
97 Bill Walton GS .15 .40
98 Jerry West GS .25 .60
99 Lenny Wilkens GS .15 .40
100 James Worthy GS .20 .50
101 Kareem Abdul-Jabbar .25 .60
102 Nate Archibald .12 .30
103 Paul Arizin .15 .40
104 Charles Barkley .25 .60
105 Rick Barry .12 .30
106 Elgin Baylor .15 .40
107 Dave Bing .15 .40
108 Larry Bird .40 1.00

109 Wilt Chamberlain .30 .75
110 Bob Cousy .25 .60
111 Dave Cowens .12 .30
112 Billy Cunningham .15 .40
113 Dave DeBusschere .15 .40
114 Clyde Drexler .20 .50
115 Julius Erving .25 .60
116 Patrick Ewing .20 .50
117 Walt Frazier .15 .40
118 George Gervin .15 .40
119 Hal Greer .12 .30
120 John Havlicek .20 .50
121 Elvin Hayes .15 .40
122 Magic Johnson .40 1.00
123 Sam Jones .20 .50
124 Michael Jordan 1.25 3.00
125 Jerry Lucas .15 .40
126 Karl Malone .20 .50
127 Moses Malone .15 .40
128 Pete Maravich .25 .60
129 Kevin McHale .20 .50
130 George Mikan .25 .60
131 Earl Monroe .15 .40
132 Shaquille O'Neal .40 1.00
133 Hakeem Olajuwon .20 .50
134 Robert Parish .15 .40
135 Bob Pettit .15 .40
136 Scottie Pippen .25 .60
137 Willis Reed .15 .40
138 Oscar Robertson .20 .50
139 David Robinson .25 .60
140 Bill Russell .25 .60
141 Dolph Schayes .15 .40
142 Bill Sharman .15 .40
143 John Stockton .20 .50
144 Isiah Thomas .15 .40
145 Nate Thurmond .12 .30
146 Wes Unseld .15 .40
147 Bill Walton .15 .40
148 Jerry West .25 .60
149 Lenny Wilkens .15 .40
150 James Worthy .20 .50

1996 Topps Stars Finest

COMPLETE SET (150) 150.00 300.00
*STARS: 2.5X TO 6X BASIC

1996 Topps Stars Finest Atomic Refractors

*ATOMIC: 25X TO 60X BASE HI

1996 Topps Stars Finest Refractors

*REFRACTORS: 8X TO 20X BASIC
24 Michael Jordan 60.00 150.00

1996 Topps Stars Imagine

COMPLETE SET (25) 65.00 125.00
I1 Shaquille O'Neal
Wilt Chamberlain 5.00 12.00
I2 David Robinson
Dave Cowens 2.00 5.00
I3 Kareem Abdul-Jabbar
Bill Russell 4.00 10.00
I4 Scottie Pippen
Julius Erving 4.00 10.00
I5 Hakeem Olajuwon
Elvin Hayes 2.00 5.00
I6 Michael Jordan
Oscar Robertson 8.00 20.00
I7 Clyde Drexler
Earl Monroe 1.50 4.00
I8 Magic Johnson
Jerry West 4.00 10.00
I9 Larry Bird
Rick Barry 3.00 8.00
I10 Kevin McHale
Dave DeBusschere 1.50 4.00
I11 Moses Malone
Jerry Lucas 1.25 3.00
I12 Robert Parish
Nate Thurmond 1.25 3.00
I13 Pete Maravich
Sam Jones 2.00 5.00
I14 John Stockton
Bob Cousy 3.00 8.00
I15 Isiah Thomas
Bill Sharman 1.25 3.00
I16 Karl Malone
Bob Pettit 3.00 8.00
I17 Bill Walton
George Mikan 2.50 6.00
I18 Patrick Ewing
Willis Reed 1.50 4.00
I19 Billy Cunningham
James Worthy 1.25 3.00
I20 George Gervin
Hal Greer 1.25 3.00
I21 Wes Unseld
Dolph Schayes 1.25 3.00
I22 Nate Archibald
Lenny Wilkens 1.25 3.00
I23 Walt Frazier
Paul Arizin 1.25 3.00
I24 Charles Barkley
Elgin Baylor 2.50 6.00
I25 Dave Bing
John Havlicek 2.50 6.00

1996 Topps Stars Reprints

COMPLETE SET (50) 150.00 250.00
1 Lew Alcindor 5.00 12.00
2 Nate Archibald 1.25 3.00
3 Paul Arizin .75 2.00
4 Charles Barkley 5.00 12.00
5 Rick Barry 1.00 2.50
6 Elgin Baylor .75 2.00
7 Dave Bing .75 2.00
8 Larry Bird
Julius Erving
Magic Johnson 12.00 30.00
9 Wilt Chamberlain 5.00 12.00
10 Bob Cousy 3.00 8.00
11 Dave Cowens .75 2.00
12 Billy Cunningham .75 2.00
13 Dave DeBusschere .75 2.00
14 Clyde Drexler 1.50 4.00
15 Julius Erving 5.00 12.00
16 Patrick Ewing 1.50 4.00
17 Walt Frazier 1.25 3.00
18 George Gervin 1.25 3.00
19 Hal Greer .75 2.00
20 John Havlicek 3.00 8.00
21 Elvin Hayes 1.25 3.00
22 Larry Bird
Julius Erving
Magic Johnson 10.00 25.00
23 Sam Jones .75 2.00
24 Michael Jordan 40.00 100.00
25 Jerry Lucas .75 2.00
26 Karl Malone 3.00 8.00
27 Moses Malone 1.50 4.00
28 Pete Maravich 3.00 8.00
29 Kevin McHale 1.25 3.00
30 George Mikan 3.00 8.00
31 Earl Monroe 1.25 3.00
32 Shaquille O'Neal 3.00 8.00
33 Hakeem Olajuwon 4.00 10.00
34 Robert Parish 1.25 3.00
35 Bob Pettit 1.00 2.50
36 Scottie Pippen 4.00 10.00
37 Willis Reed .75 2.00
38 Oscar Robertson 3.00 8.00
39 David Robinson 2.50 6.00
40 Bill Russell 5.00 12.00
41 Dolph Schayes 1.50 4.00
42 Bill Sharman .75 2.00
43 John Stockton 1.50 4.00
44 Isiah Thomas 1.50 4.00
45 Nate Thurmond .75 2.00
46 Wes Unseld .75 2.00
47 Bill Walton 1.25 3.00
48 Jerry West 4.00 10.00
49 Len Wilkens UER .75 2.00
50 James Worthy 1.50 4.00

1996 Topps Stars Reprint Autographs

COMPLETE SET (10) 150.00 300.00
2 Nate Archibald 10.00 25.00
5 Rick Barry 10.00 25.00
17 Walt Frazier 10.00 25.00
18 George Gervin 12.00 30.00
21 Elvin Hayes 12.00 30.00
23 Sam Jones 10.00 25.00
30 George Mikan 125.00 300.00
31 Earl Monroe 10.00 25.00
37 Willis Reed 50.00 120.00
47 Bill Walton 10.00 25.00

1996 Topps Stars Members Only Parallel

COMPLETE SET (150) 300.00 500.00
*MO: 5X TO 12X BASE TOPPS STARS HI

1996 Topps Stars Imagine Members Only Parallel

COMPLETE SET (25) 60.00 150.00
*MO: .6X TO 1.5X BASE IMAGINE HI

1996 Topps Stars Reprints Members Only Parallel

COMPLETE SET (50) 150.00 300.00
*MO: .6X TO 1.5X BASE REPRINT HI

1996 Topps Stars Uncut Sheets

COMPLETE SET (2) 20.00 50.00
1 Black Bordered Sheet 10.00 25.00
2 Gold Bordered Sheet 10.00 25.00

2000-01 Topps Stars Promos

COMPLETE SET (6) 2.00 5.00
PP1 Allen Iverson 1.25 3.00
PP2 Jason Williams .75 2.00
PP3 Antonio McDyess .40 1.00
PP4 Alonzo Mourning .75 2.00
PP5 Ray Allen .75 2.00
PP6 Larry Hughes .50 1.25

2000-01 Topps Stars

COMPLETE SET (150) 25.00 60.00
SUBSET CARDS SAME VALUE AS BASE
1 Elton Brand .40 1.00
2 Paul Pierce .60 1.50
3 Baron Davis .40 1.00
4 Corey Benjamin .25 .60
5 Jason Kidd .60 1.50
6 Stephon Marbury .50 1.25
7 Eric Snow .25 .60
8 Joe Smith .25 .60
9 Larry Hughes .40 1.00
10 Tim Duncan 1.00 2.50
11 Theo Ratliff .25 .60
12 Dikembe Mutombo .60 1.50
13 Tim Hardaway .50 1.25
14 Glenn Robinson .40 1.00
15 Grant Hill .60 1.50
16 Patrick Ewing .60 1.50
17 Ron Mercer .30 .75
18 Ron Artest .40 1.00
19 Tom Gugliotta .30 .75
20 Steve Smith .40 1.00
21 Vlade Divac .40 1.00
22 Rashard Lewis .30 .75
23 Tracy McGrady .75 2.00
24 Bryon Russell .25 .60
25 Michael Dickerson .25 .60
26 Juwan Howard .30 .75
27 Damon Stoudamire .40 1.00
28 Hakeem Olajuwon .75 2.00
29 Antonio McDyess .30 .75
30 Kobe Bryant 3.00 8.00
31 Lindsey Hunter .25 .60
32 Magic Johnson 1.00 2.50
33 Alonzo Mourning .60 1.50
34 Kenny Anderson .30 .75
35 Allan Houston .40 1.00
36 Keith Van Horn .30 .75
37 Shawn Marion .40 1.00
38 David Robinson .75 2.00
39 Mitch Richmond .50 1.25
40 Shaquille O'Neal 1.50 4.00
41 Gary Payton .60 1.50
42 Sean Elliott .30 .75
43 Sam Cassell .30 .75
44 Dale Davis .30 .75
45 Derek Anderson .30 .75
46 Jonathan Bender .25 .60
47 Shandon Anderson .25 .60
48 Raef LaFrentz .25 .60
49 Michael Finley .40 1.00
50 Toni Kukoc .50 1.25
51 Anthony Mason .40 1.00
52 Jim Jackson .30 .75
53 Glen Rice .40 1.00
54 Jalen Rose .30 .75
55 Keon Clark .25 .60
56 Anfernee Hardaway .60 1.50
57 Vin Baker .30 .75
58 Shawn Kemp .60 1.50
59 John Stockton .75 2.00
60 Shareef Abdur-Rahim .40 1.00
61 Doug Christie .30 .75
62 Lamond Murray .25 .60
63 Scottie Pippen 1.00 2.50
64 Darrell Armstrong .25 .60
65 Marcus Camby .30 .75
66 Wally Szczerbiak .30 .75
67 Jamal Mashburn .30 .75
68 Antonio Davis .30 .75
69 Kevin Garnett 1.00 2.50
70 Cuttino Mobley .30 .75
71 Jerry Stackhouse .40 1.00
72 Cedric Ceballos .30 .75
73 Nick Van Exel .40 1.00
74 Latrell Sprewell .50 1.25
75 Antoine Walker .40 1.00
76 Allen Iverson 1.00 2.50
77 Antawn Jamison .40 1.00
78 Derrick Coleman .40 1.00
79 Jason Terry .40 1.00
80 Steve Francis .40 1.00
81 Reggie Miller .75 2.00
82 Rasheed Wallace .50 1.25
83 Chris Webber .50 1.25
84 Donyell Marshall .30 .75
85 Ruben Patterson .25 .60
86 Terrell Brandon .30 .75
87 Mike Bibby .40 1.00
88 Richard Hamilton .50 1.25
89 Jason Williams .60 1.50
90 Corey Maggette .30 .75
91 Kerry Kittles .30 .75
92 Karl Malone .75 2.00
93 Rod Strickland .25 .60
94 Eddie Jones .40 1.00
95 Maurice Taylor .25 .60
96 Dirk Nowitzki 1.00 2.50
97 Andre Miller .30 .75
98 Lamar Odom .40 1.00
99 Ray Allen .60 1.50
100 Vince Carter .75 2.00
101 Chris Mihm RC .25 .60
102 Kenyon Martin RC .75 2.00
103 Stromile Swift RC .30 .75
104 Joel Przybilla RC .30 .75
105 Marcus Fizer RC .30 .75
106 Mike Miller RC .60 1.50
107 Darius Miles RC .50 1.25
108 Mark Madsen RC .40 1.00
109 Courtney Alexander RC .25 .60
110 DeShawn Stevenson RC .40 1.00
111 DerMarr Johnson RC .25 .60
112 Mamadou N'Diaye RC .25 .60
113 Mateen Cleaves RC .30 .75
114 Morris Peterson RC .40 1.00
115 Etan Thomas RC .30 .75
116 Erick Barkley RC .25 .60
117 Quentin Richardson RC .30 .75
118 Keyon Dooling RC .30 .75
119 Jerome Moiso RC .25 .60
120 Desmond Mason RC .50 1.25
121 Speedy Claxton RC .40 1.00
122 Jamaal Magloire RC .40 1.00
123 Donnell Harvey RC .30 .75
124 Jamal Crawford RC 1.00 2.50
125 Jason Collier RC .40 1.00
126 Tim Duncan SPOT 1.00 2.50
127 Shaquille O'Neal SPOT 1.50 4.00
128 Vince Carter SPOT .75 2.00
129 Allen Iverson SPOT 1.00 2.50
130 Jason Kidd SPOT .60 1.50
131 Kevin Garnett SPOT 1.00 2.50
132 Gary Payton SPOT .60 1.50
133 Tracy McGrady SPOT .75 2.00
134 Jason Williams SPOT .60 1.50
135 Kobe Bryant SPOT 3.00 8.00
136 Elton Brand SPOT .40 1.00
137 Ray Allen SPOT .60 1.50
138 Grant Hill SPOT .60 1.50
139 Chris Webber SPOT .50 1.25
140 Latrell Sprewell SPOT .50 1.25
141 Alonzo Mourning SPOT .60 1.50
142 Lamar Odom SPOT .40 1.00
143 Shareef Abdur-Rahim SPOT .40 1.00
144 Steve Francis SPOT .40 1.00
145 Magic Johnson SPOT 1.00 2.50
146 Darius Miles SPOT .40 1.00
147 Kenyon Martin SPOT .75 2.00
148 Marcus Fizer SPOT .30 .75
149 Mateen Cleaves SPOT .30 .75
150 Stromile Swift SPOT .30 .75

2000-01 Topps Stars Parallel

*BASE STARS: 4X TO 10X BASE CARD HI
*BASE RCs: 4X TO 10X BASE CARD HI
BASE: PRINT RUN 299 SERIAL #'d SETS
*SUB.STARS: 10X TO 25X SUBSET CARD HI
*SUB.RCs: 10X TO 25X SUBSET CARD HI
SUBSET: PRINT RUN 99 SERIAL #'d SETS
SUBSET: STATED ODDS 1:261
30 Kobe Bryant 125.00 300.00
135 Kobe Bryant SPOT 200.00 500.00

2000-01 Topps Stars All-Star Authority

COMPLETE SET (15) 7.50 15.00
STATED ODDS 1:12 HOB/RET
ASA1 John Stockton 1.25 3.00
ASA2 Shaquille O'Neal 2.50 6.00
ASA3 Patrick Ewing 1.00 2.50
ASA4 Hakeem Olajuwon 1.25 3.00
ASA5 Karl Malone 1.25 3.00
ASA6 Grant Hill 1.00 2.50
ASA7 Alonzo Mourning 1.00 2.50
ASA8 Jason Kidd 1.00 2.50
ASA9 Gary Payton 1.00 2.50
ASA10 Scottie Pippen 1.50 4.00
ASA11 Tim Duncan 1.50 4.00
ASA12 Kevin Garnett 1.50 4.00
ASA13 Reggie Miller 1.25 3.00
ASA14 David Robinson 1.25 3.00
ASA15 Dikembe Mutombo 1.00 2.50

2000-01 Topps Stars Autographs

GROUP A: STATED ODDS 1:359
GROUP B: STATED ODDS 1:2599
OVERALL STATED ODDS 1:316
TSAJ Antawn Jamison A 4.00 10.00
TSCA Courtney Alexander A 4.00 10.00
TSEB Elton Brand A 5.00 12.00
TSJC Jamal Crawford A 10.00 25.00
TSJR Jalen Rose A 5.00 12.00
TSMC Mateen Cleaves A 4.00 10.00
TSMJ Magic Johnson A 40.00 100.00
TSSF Steve Francis A 5.00 12.00
TSTD Tim Duncan B 300.00 600.00
TSTM Tracy McGrady A 20.00 50.00

2000-01 Topps Stars Game Jerseys

LAKERS HOME GJ: STATED ODDS 1:646
LAKERS AWAY GJ: STATED ODDS 1:117
PACERS HOME GJ: STATED ODDS 1:359
OVERALL STATED ODDS 1:71
LAKERS (H) JERSEYS ARE YELLOW
LAKERS (A) JERSEYS ARE PURPLE
TSR1A Shaquille O'Neal 12.00 30.00
TSR1H Shaquille O'Neal 12.00 30.00
TSR2A Glen Rice 8.00 20.00
TSR2H Glen Rice 8.00 20.00
TSR3A Robert Horry 8.00 20.00
TSR3H Robert Horry 8.00 20.00
TSR4A Rick Fox 6.00 15.00
TSR4H Rick Fox 6.00 15.00
TSR5A Brian Shaw 5.00 12.00
TSR5H Brian Shaw 5.00 12.00
TSR6A Ron Harper 8.00 20.00
TSR6H Ron Harper 8.00 20.00
TSR7A Derek Fisher 8.00 20.00
TSR7H Derek Fisher 8.00 20.00
TSR8A A.C. Green 10.00 25.00
TSR8H A.C. Green 10.00 25.00
TSR9A John Salley 5.00 12.00
TSR9H John Salley 5.00 12.00
TSR10A Travis Knight 5.00 12.00
TSR10H Travis Knight 5.00 12.00
TSR11A Devean George 5.00 12.00
TSR11H Devean George 5.00 12.00
TSR12 Reggie Miller 15.00 40.00
TSR13 Jalen Rose 6.00 15.00
TSR14 Dale Davis 6.00 15.00
TSR15 Rik Smits 5.00 12.00
TSR16 Mark Jackson 6.00 15.00
TSR17 Travis Best 5.00 12.00
TSR18 Austin Croshere 5.00 12.00
TSR19 Derrick McKey 5.00 12.00
TSR20 Sam Perkins 5.00 12.00
TSR21 Chris Mullin 15.00 40.00
TSR22 Jonathan Bender 5.00 12.00
TSR23 Zan Tabak 5.00 12.00
TSRMJ Magic Johnson 12.00 30.00

2000-01 Topps Stars On the Horizon

COMPLETE SET (10) 6.00 15.00
STATED ODDS 1:36 HOB/RET
H1 Steve Francis .75 2.00
H2 Elton Brand .75 2.00
H3 Tracy McGrady 1.50 4.00
H4 Stephon Marbury 1.00 2.50
H5 Lamar Odom .75 2.00
H6 Kenyon Martin 1.50 4.00
H7 Shareef Abdur-Rahim .75 2.00
H8 Marcus Fizer .60 1.50
H9 Larry Hughes .75 2.00
H10 Darius Miles .75 2.00

2000-01 Topps Stars Progression

COMPLETE SET (5) 5.00 12.00
STATED ODDS 1:24 HOB/RET
P1 Ewing/Zo/Mihm .75 2.00
P2 K.Malone/Brand/K.Martin 2.00 5.00
P3 Pippen/V.Carter/Miles 1.00 2.50
P4 Richmond/Kobe/C.Alex 1.50 4.00
P5 Magic/Stockton/Crawford 1.25 3.00

2000-01 Topps Stars Walk of Fame

COMPLETE SET (15) 12.00 30.00
STATED ODDS 1:8 HOB/RET
WF1 Grant Hill 1.00 2.50
WF2 Vince Carter 1.25 3.00
WF3 Kevin Garnett 1.50 4.00
WF4 Jason Kidd 1.00 2.50
WF5 Gary Payton 1.00 2.50
WF6 Tim Duncan 1.50 4.00
WF7 Allen Iverson 1.50 4.00
WF8 Kobe Bryant 5.00 12.00
WF9 Ray Allen 1.00 2.50
WF10 Shareef Abdur-Rahim .60 1.50
WF11 Chris Webber .75 2.00
WF12 Karl Malone 1.25 3.00
WF13 Reggie Miller 1.25 3.00
WF14 Jason Williams 1.00 2.50
WF15 Elton Brand .60 1.50

1997 Topps Stickers

COMPLETE SET (5) 3.00 8.00
1 Glen Rice
Dino Radja
Grant Hill
Clifford Robinson
Jerry Stackhouse
Horace Grant
Terrell Brandon
Lorenzen Wright
Sean Elliott
Stephon Marbury
Shaquille O'Neal
Ray Allen .75 2.00
2 Hakeem Olajuwon
Marcus Camby
Kobe Bryant
Chris Webber
Jayson Williams
Kenny Anderson
David Robinson
Joe Dumars
Michael Finley
Reggie Miller
Scottie Pippen
Latrell Sprewell .75 2.00
3 Alonzo Mourning
Bobby Phills
Christian Laettner
Dennis Rodman
Jason Kidd
Joe Smith
John Starks
Juwan Howard
Karl Malone
Kevin Garnett
Bryant Reeves
Mitch Richmond .75 2.00
4 Brent Barry
Anthony Mason
Antonio McDyess
Allen Iverson
Brian Grant
Charles Barkley
Dikembe Mutombo
John Stockton
Kerry Kittles
Rik Smits
Shawn Kemp
Tim Hardaway .75 2.00
5 Derek Harper
Patrick Ewing
Greg Anthony
Gary Payton
Kevin Johnson
Doug Christie
LaPhonso Ellis
Antoine Walker
Damon Stoudamire
Rony Seikaly
Vin Baker
Shareef Abdur-Rahim .75 2.00

2005-06 Topps Style

COMPLETE SET (135) 30.00 80.00
1 Ben Wallace .60 1.50
2 Joe Johnson .40 1.00
3 Luol Deng .40 1.00
4 Morris Peterson .30 .75
5 Jason Terry .40 1.00
6 Carmelo Anthony .75 2.00
7 Mickey Mantle 3.00 8.00
8 Ron Artest .40 1.00
9 Elton Brand .40 1.00
10 Chris Mihm .30 .75
11 Shane Battier .40 1.00
12 Speedy Claxton .30 .75
13 Baron Davis .50 1.25
14 Damon Stoudamire .50 1.25
15 Desmond Mason .30 .75
16 Marko Jaric .30 .75
17 Vince Carter 1.00 2.50
18 Sam Cassell .40 1.00
19 J.R. Smith .50 1.25
20 Trevor Ariza .30 .75
21 Quentin Richardson .30 .75
22 Jamal Crawford .50 1.25
23 Dwight Howard .60 1.50
24 Kyle Korver .40 1.00
25 Steve Nash 1.00 2.50
26 Amare Stoudemire .50 1.25
27 Zach Randolph .50 1.25
28 Brad Miller .40 1.00
29 Tim Duncan 1.25 3.00
30 Michael Finley .50 1.25
31 Ray Allen .75 2.00
32 Luke Ridnour .40 1.00
33 Andrei Kirilenko .40 1.00
34 Tony Allen .30 .75
35 Paul Pierce .75 2.00
36 Al Jefferson .30 .75
37 Emeka Okafor .40 1.00
38 Al Harrington .40 1.00
39 Ben Gordon .40 1.00
40 Andres Nocioni .30 .75
41 Zydrunas Ilgauskas .40 1.00
42 Anderson Varejao .30 .75
43 Keith Van Horn .30 .75
44 Richard Hamilton .60 1.50
45 Stromile Swift .30 .75
46 Dirk Nowitzki 1.25 3.00
47 Stephen Jackson .40 1.00
48 Pau Gasol .75 2.00
49 Lamar Odom .40 1.00
50 Kobe Bryant 4.00 10.00
51 Shaquille O'Neal 1.50 4.00
52 Jason Williams .75 2.00
53 Dwyane Wade 1.00 2.50
54 Michael Redd .40 1.00
55 Joe Smith .40 1.00
56 Troy Hudson .30 .75
57 Jameer Nelson .30 .75
58 Chris Webber .60 1.50
59 Darius Miles .30 .75
60 Chris Wilcox .30 .75
61 Rafer Alston .40 1.00
62 Kirk Hinrich .40 1.00
63 Jalen Rose .40 1.00
64 Matt Harpring .30 .75
65 Caron Butler .40 1.00
66 Shareef Abdur-Rahim .50 1.25
67 Josh Childress .30 .75
68 Delonte West .30 .75
69 Brevin Knight .30 .75
70 Larry Hughes .40 1.00
71 Dikembe Mutombo .60 1.50
72 Kenyon Martin .40 1.00
73 Earl Boykins .30 .75
74 Tayshaun Prince .50 1.25
75 Chauncey Billups .60 1.50
76 Josh Smith .40 1.00
77 Troy Murphy .30 .75
78 Jermaine O'Neal .40 1.00
79 Corey Maggette .40 1.00
80 Wally Szczerbiak .40 1.00
81 Richard Jefferson .40 1.00
82 Nenad Krstic .30 .75
83 Jason Kidd .75 2.00
84 Jamaal Magloire .30 .75
85 Stephon Marbury .60 1.50
86 Samuel Dalembert .30 .75
87 Andre Iguodala .50 1.25
88 Yao Ming 1.00 2.50
89 Kurt Thomas .30 .75
90 Brendan Haywood .30 .75
91 Peja Stojakovic .40 1.00
92 Mike Bibby .50 1.25
93 Tony Parker .75 2.00
94 Manu Ginobili 1.00 2.50
95 Rashard Lewis .40 1.00
96 Mehmet Okur .30 .75
97 Gilbert Arenas .50 1.25
98 Antawn Jamison .40 1.00
99 Ricky Davis .40 1.00
100 Shawn Marion .40 1.00
101 Melvin Ely .30 .75
102 Tyson Chandler .40 1.00
103 Jason Richardson .50 1.25
104 Drew Gooden .40 1.00
105 Josh Howard .40 1.00
106 Marcus Camby .40 1.00
107 Jerry Stackhouse .40 1.00
108 Andre Miller .40 1.00
109 Rasheed Wallace .50 1.25
110 Mike Dunleavy .30 .75
111 LeBron James 4.00 10.00
112 Allen Iverson 1.00 2.50
113 Tracy McGrady .75 2.00
114 Jamaal Tinsley .30 .75
115 Cuttino Mobley .30 .75
116 Kwame Brown .30 .75
117 Derek Anderson .30 .75
118 Eddie Jones .40 1.00
119 Antoine Walker .40 1.00
120 Alonzo Mourning .60 1.50
121 Bobby Simmons .30 .75
122 Kevin Garnett 1.25 3.00
123 P.J. Brown .30 .75
124 Steve Francis .50 1.25
125 Grant Hill .75 2.00
126 Primoz Brezec .30 .75
127 Mike Miller .40 1.00
128 Sebastian Telfair .40 1.00
129 Chris Bosh .60 1.50
130 Carlos Boozer .40 1.00
131 Andrew Bogut RC 1.00 2.50
132 Raymond Felton RC .60 1.50
133 Ike Diogu RC .50 1.25
134 Rashad McCants RC .50 1.25
135 Gerald Green RC .75 2.00
136 Jarrett Jack RC .75 2.00
137 Linas Kleiza RC .60 1.50
138 Brandon Bass RC .60 1.50
139 Marvin Williams RC .75 2.00
140 Martell Webster RC .60 1.50
141 Sarunas Jasikevicius RC .75 2.00
142 Antoine Wright RC .60 1.50
143 Hakim Warrick RC .60 1.50
144 Francisco Garcia RC .50 1.25
145 Wayne Simien RC .50 1.25
146 Monta Ellis RC 1.00 2.50
147 Deron Williams RC 1.25 3.00
148 Charlie Villanueva RC .60 1.50
149 Chris Taft RC .50 1.25
150 Joey Graham RC .60 1.50
151 Julius Hodge RC .50 1.25
152 Luther Head RC .50 1.25
153 David Lee RC .75 2.00
154 Chris Paul RC 4.00 10.00
155 Channing Frye RC .60 1.50
156 Sean May RC .50 1.25
157 Danny Granger RC .75 2.00
158 Nate Robinson RC .75 2.00
159 Jason Maxiell RC .60 1.50
160 Salim Stoudamire RC .60 1.50
161 Christie Brinkley 1.25 3.00
162 Carmen Electra 1.25 3.00
163 Shannon Elizabeth 1.25 3.00
164 Jenny McCarthy 1.25 3.00
165 Jay-Z 1.50 4.00

2005-06 Topps Style Chrome

*1-130 CHROME: 1.5X TO 4X BASE HI
*131-165 CHROME: 1X TO 2.5X BASE HI
CHROME PRINT RUN 499 SER.#'d SETS
50 Kobe Bryant 40.00 100.00
111 LeBron James 40.00 100.00
154 Chris Paul 20.00 50.00

2005-06 Topps Style Chrome Refractors

*1-130 REF: 6X TO 15X BASE HI
*131-165 REF: 4X TO 10X BASE HI
PRINT RUN 299 SER.#'d SETS
50 Kobe Bryant 150.00 400.00
111 LeBron James 150.00 400.00
154 Chris Paul 75.00 200.00

2005-06 Topps Style Chrome Refractors Blue

*1-130 REF.BLUE: 8X TO 20X BASE HI
*131-165 REF.BLUE: 5X TO 12X BASE HI
PRINT RUN 149 SER.#'d SETS
50 Kobe Bryant 200.00 500.00
111 LeBron James 200.00 500.00
154 Chris Paul 100.00 250.00

2005-06 Topps Style Chrome Refractors Gold

*1-130 GOLD: 50X TO 120X BASE HI
*131-160 GOLD: 30X TO 80X BASE HI
*161-165 GOLD: 30X TO 80X BASE HI
PRINT RUN 25 SER.#'d SETS
111 LeBron James 1,500.00 3,000.00
154 Chris Paul 800.00 1,500.00

2005-06 Topps Style Dwyane Wade Comics

COMPLETE SET (4) 4.00 10.00
COMMON CARD (1-4) 1.50 4.00
PRINT RUN 499 SER.#'d SETS
COMMON AUTO (1-4) 40.00 100.00
AUTO STATED ODDS 1:2991
COMMON ART.AU (1-4) 10.00 25.00
ART.AU PRINT RUN 75 SER.#'d SETS
AU DUAL STATED ODDS 1:7704
JSY AU STATED ODDS 1:14124
COMMON RELIC (1-4) 6.00 15.00
RELIC PRINT RUN 99 SER.#'d SETS

2005-06 Topps Style Fan Favorites Autographs

STATED ODDS 1:10
ASTERISK: ANNOUNCED PRINT RUNS
AA Al Attles/176* 20.00 50.00
AB Andrew Bogut/417* 8.00 20.00
AC Archie Clark/212* 12.00 30.00
AD Adrian Dantley/320* 8.00 20.00
AG A.C. Green/406* 10.00 25.00
AG Artis Gilmore/188* 10.00 25.00
AJ Aaron James/192* 6.00 15.00
AK Albert King/216* 6.00 15.00
BB Bill Bradley/223* 100.00 250.00
BC Billy Cunningham/214* 40.00 100.00
BH Bailey Howell/219* 15.00 40.00
BJ Bobby Jones/220* 15.00 40.00
BK Bernard King/420* 12.00 30.00
BL Bob Lanier/217* 20.00 50.00
BP Billy Paultz/220* 8.00 20.00
BS Bud Stallworth/196* 8.00 20.00
BT Brian Taylor/220* 8.00 20.00
BW Bill Walton/220* 20.00 50.00
CD Chris Dudley/210* 6.00 15.00
CE Craig Ehlo/318* 12.00 30.00
CH Clem Haskins/220* 8.00 20.00
CM Calvin Murphy/219* 10.00 25.00
CM Chris Morris/228* 6.00 15.00
CR Campy Russell/200* 6.00 15.00
CS Charles Smith/199* 8.00 20.00
CW Chuck Williams/220* 6.00 15.00
DA Dan Anderson/194* 6.00 15.00
DB Dee Brown/405* 8.00 20.00
DC Darwin Cook/217* 8.00 20.00
DD Darryl Dawkins/219* 15.00 40.00
DE Dale Ellis/212* 8.00 20.00
DG Danny Granger/410* 8.00 20.00
DI Dan Issel/220* 25.00 60.00
DK Don Kojis/215* 15.00 40.00
DL Dennis Layton/220* 6.00 15.00
DM Dan Majerle/220* 12.00 30.00
DR Dennis Rodman/218* 75.00 200.00
DS Danny Schayes/220* 8.00 20.00
DT David Thompson/220* 12.00 30.00
DW Deron Williams/419* 10.00 25.00
EB Elgin Baylor/417* 25.00 60.00
EJ Eddie Johnson/405* 6.00 15.00
EK Eugene Kennedy/205* 10.00 25.00
EM Eric Money/203* 6.00 15.00
EM Earl Monroe/85* 40.00 100.00
FB Frank Brickowski/213* 10.00 25.00
FC Fred Carter/220* 6.00 15.00
FE Franklin Edwards/219* 6.00 15.00
FL Fat Lever/219* 12.00 30.00
FR Flynn Robinson/209* 50.00 120.00
GG George Gervin/220* 20.00 50.00
GH Gar Heard/420* 8.00 20.00
GM Glenn McDonald/220* 6.00 15.00
GT George Tinsley/218* 12.00 30.00
GW Gerald Wilkens/415* 6.00 15.00
HC Harvey Catchings/219* 6.00 15.00
HG Harry Gallatin/220* 6.00 15.00
HH Hersey Hawkins/320* 6.00 15.00
HP Howard Porter/211* 10.00 25.00
HW Herb Williams/318* 8.00 20.00
JB Junior Bridgeman/220* 6.00 15.00
JE Johnny Egan/214* 10.00 25.00
JG Johnny Green/218* 12.00 30.00
JH Jeff Hornacek/420* 12.00 30.00
JJ J.J. Johnson/413* 6.00 15.00
JL John Lambert/217* 6.00 15.00
JM Jeff Mullins/220* 15.00 40.00
JN Johnny Newman/320* 6.00 15.00
JR Joe Roberts/409* 10.00 25.00
JS Jack Sikma/404* 12.00 30.00
JW Jim Washington/210* 6.00 15.00
KB Kent Benson/217* 6.00 15.00
KC Kenny Charles/215* 6.00 15.00
KE Keith Edmonson/218* 8.00 20.00
KH Keith Herron/220* 8.00 20.00
KT Kelly Tripucka/220* 8.00 20.00
KV Kiki Vandeweghe/420* 8.00 20.00
LC Len Chappell/219* 6.00 15.00
LE Len Elmore/215* 6.00 15.00
LG Lamar Green/199* 6.00 15.00
LH Lou Hudson/401* 10.00 25.00
LM Larue Martin/215* 10.00 25.00
LN Larry Nance/420* 8.00 20.00
LW Lenny Wilkens/405* 12.00 30.00
MB Muggsy Bogues/219* 20.00 50.00
MC Maurice Cheeks/218* 6.00 15.00
MD Mel Davis/215* 6.00 15.00
ME Mark Eaton/209* 10.00 25.00
MG Mike Gale/220* 6.00 15.00
MJ Magic Johnson/220* 100.00 250.00
ML Maurice Lucas/217* 8.00 20.00
MM Moses Malone/212* 40.00 100.00
MW Mark West/221* 6.00 15.00
NA Nate Archibald/220* 12.00 30.00
NN Norm Nixon/219* 8.00 20.00
OB Otis Birdsong/200* 6.00 15.00
OG Orien Greene/420* 6.00 15.00
OR Oscar Robertson/215* 75.00 200.00
OT Ollie Taylor/220* 6.00 15.00
PA Paul Arizin/219* 40.00 100.00
PW Paul Westphal/409* 12.00 30.00
RB Rick Barry/220* 15.00 40.00
RD Rick Darnell/217* 6.00 15.00
RF Raymond Felton/419* 8.00 20.00
RG Richie Guerin/219* 10.00 25.00
RH Roy Hinson/217* 10.00 25.00
RK Rich Kelley/220* 6.00 15.00
RM Rodney McCray/220* 6.00 15.00
RP Ricky Pierce/219* 6.00 15.00
RR Robert Reid/220* 6.00 15.00
RR Rich Rinaldi/190* 10.00 25.00
RS Rik Smits/384* 8.00 20.00
RT Reggie Theus/420* 10.00 25.00
SG Sidney Green/339* 6.00 15.00
SH Spencer Haywood Red/207* 6.00 15.00
SL Sam Lacey/220* 6.00 15.00
SM Sean May/417* 6.00 15.00
ST Sedric Toney/213* 6.00 15.00
SW Samuel Williams/220* 6.00 15.00
TC Terry Cummings/320* 8.00 20.00
TG Tate George/219* 8.00 20.00
TH Tom Hoover/219* 6.00 15.00
TR Tree Rollins/405* 6.00 15.00

TS Tom Sanders/220* 6.00 15.00
TT Thomas Thacker/219* 6.00 15.00
TW Reggie Williams/214* 6.00 15.00
WD Walter Davis/418* 8.00 20.00
WF Walt Frazier/217* 25.00 60.00
WH Walt Hazzard/218* 10.00 25.00
WJ Wali Jones/203* 6.00 15.00
WN Willie Norwood/205* 6.00 15.00
WT Wayman Tisdale/218* 20.00 50.00
WW Walt Wesley/220* 6.00 15.00
XM Xavier McDaniel/208* 8.00 20.00
ZA Zaid Abdul-Aziz/218* 6.00 15.00
AC2 Austin Carr/203* 8.00 20.00
AJ2 Alfonso Buck Johnson/215* 6.00 15.00
BB2 Bob Boozer/220* 12.00 30.00
BH2 Bobby Hansen/406* 10.00 25.00
BL2 Bob Love/208* 10.00 25.00
BS2 Byron Scott/420* 6.00 15.00
BW2 Buck Williams/211* 10.00 25.00
CD2 Clyde Drexler/419* 30.00 80.00
CH2 Cliff Hagan/189* 12.00 30.00
CH3 Connie Hawkins/420* 15.00 40.00
CM2 Cliff Meely/187* 8.00 20.00
DA2 Dennis Awtrey/219* 8.00 20.00
DA3 Don Adams/210* 10.00 25.00
DC2 Dave Cowens/220* 20.00 50.00
DC3 Duane Causwell/220* 6.00 15.00
DD2 Dwight Davis/219* 6.00 15.00
DM2 Dick McGuire/220* 10.00 25.00
DS2 Detlef Schrempf/420* 6.00 15.00
DS3 Dick Schnittker/220* 12.00 30.00
DS4 Dick Snyder/219* 10.00 25.00
DS5 Dolph Schayes/219* 12.00 30.00
DW2 Dominique Wilkins/213* 25.00 60.00
EB2 Em Bryant/217* 10.00 25.00
FB2 Fred Brown/216* 8.00 20.00
FC2 Fred Crawford/201* 12.00 30.00
GH2 Geoff Huston/205* 12.00 30.00
GM2 Greg Minor/210* 6.00 15.00
GW2 Gus Williams/218* 10.00 25.00
JJ2 Jimmy Jones/222* 8.00 20.00
JL2 John Lucas/218* 6.00 15.00
JM2 Jerrod Mustaf/209* 6.00 15.00
JS2 James Silas/206* 15.00 40.00
JS3 John Starks/196* 20.00 50.00
JW2 Jo Jo White/200* 12.00 30.00
KE2 Keith Erickson/218* 6.00 15.00
LG2 Leonard Gray/201* 8.00 20.00
LN2 Louie Nelson/194* 6.00 15.00
MD2 Mike Davis/180* 6.00 15.00
MJ2 Major Jones/204* 6.00 15.00
RB2 Rolando Blackman/218* 8.00 20.00
RB3 Ron Behagen/213* 8.00 20.00
RB4 Ron Boone/213* 8.00 20.00
RP2 Robert Parish/420* 10.00 25.00
RS2 Rory Sparrow/219* 6.00 15.00
SH2 Spencer Haywood/194* 12.00 30.00
SW2 Slick Watts/218* 15.00 30.00
TC2 Tom Chambers/405* 8.00 20.00
TC4 Tyrone Corbin/219* 12.00 30.00
TC3 Tony Campbell/218* 6.00 15.00
TH2 Tommy Hawkins/220* 8.00 20.00
TT2 Trent Tucker/421* 6.00 15.00
WF2 World B. Free/216* 15.00 40.00

2005-06 Topps Style Hardwood Classics

N Nene 2.00 5.00
AH Alan Henderson 1.50 4.00
AI Andre Iguodala 2.50 6.00
AJ Anthony Johnson 1.50 4.00
AM Aaron McKie 1.50 4.00
BC Brian Cook 1.50 4.00
BG Brian Grant 1.50 4.00
BR Bryon Russell 1.50 4.00
BW Ben Wallace 3.00 8.00
CA Carmelo Anthony 8.00 20.00
CB Caron Butler 2.00 5.00
CR Cliff Robinson 1.50 4.00
CW Corliss Williamson 1.50 4.00
DA Darrell Armstrong 1.50 4.00
DC Doug Christie 1.50 4.00
DD Dale Davis 1.50 4.00
DG Drew Gooden 2.00 5.00
DJ DerMarr Johnson 1.50 4.00
DW David Wesley 1.50 4.00
ED Erick Dampier 1.50 4.00
EN Eduardo Najera 1.50 4.00
ES Eric Snow 1.50 4.00
ET Etan Thomas 1.50 4.00
GA Gilbert Arenas 2.50 6.00
GO Greg Ostertag 1.50 4.00
HT Hedo Turkoglu 2.00 5.00
IN Ira Newble 1.50 4.00
JF Jeff Foster 1.50 4.00
JH Juwan Howard 2.00 5.00
JJ Jared Jeffries 1.50 4.00
JP Joel Przybilla 1.50 4.00
JS Jerry Stackhouse 2.00 5.00
JT Jamaal Tinsley 1.50 4.00
KB Kobe Bryant 60.00 150.00
KM Kenyon Martin 2.00 5.00
KO Kevin Ollie 1.50 4.00
KT Kurt Thomas 1.50 4.00
LH Lindsey Hunter 1.50 4.00
MB Michael Bradley 1.50 4.00
MD Mike Dunleavy 1.50 4.00
ME Maurice Evans 1.50 4.00
MJ Marc Jackson 1.50 4.00
MN Moochie Norris 1.50 4.00
MT Maurice Taylor 1.50 4.00
PG Pat Garrity 1.50 4.00
RB Ryan Bowen 1.50 4.00
RP Ruben Patterson 1.50 4.00
SA Stacey Augmon 2.00 5.00
SB Steve Blake 1.50 4.00
SJ Stephen Jackson 2.00 5.00
SM Stephon Marbury 3.00 8.00
SP Scott Padgett 1.50 4.00
TA Trevor Ariza 1.50 4.00
TB Tony Battie 1.50 4.00
TM Troy Murphy 1.50 4.00
TR Theo Ratliff 1.50 4.00
TT Tim Thomas 1.50 4.00
CAT Chucky Atkins 1.50 4.00
DAN Derek Anderson 1.50 4.00
DST Damon Stoudamire 2.50 6.00
JBA Jon Barry 1.50 4.00
JJO Jumaine Jones 1.50 4.00
JJS James Jones 1.50 4.00
JWI Jerome Williams 1.50 4.00
KBR Kwame Brown 1.50 4.00
KVH Keith Van Horn 2.00 5.00
MDA Marquis Daniels 1.50 4.00
NVE Nick Van Exel 2.50 6.00
SAR Shareef Abdur-Rahim 2.50 6.00
SBR Shawn Bradley 1.50 4.00
SME Slava Medvedenko 1.50 4.00

2008-09 Topps T51 Murad

COMPLETE SET (230) 100.00 200.00
SP STATED ODDS 1:3
1 Elton Brand .40 1.00
2 Ray Allen .75 2.00
3 Allen Iverson 1.00 2.50
4 Luis Scola .40 1.00
5 Jason Kidd .75 2.00
6 Lamar Odom .40 1.00
7 Yi Jianlian .60 1.50
8 Marcus Camby .40 1.00
9 Jamal Crawford .50 1.25
10 Steve Nash 1.00 2.50
11 Al Harrington .40 1.00
12 Carmelo Anthony .60 1.50
13 Peja Stojakovic .40 1.00
14 Mike Dunleavy .30 .75
15 Larry Hughes .40 1.00
16 Josh Smith .30 .75
17 Emeka Okafor .30 .75
18 Ron Artest .50 1.25
19 Vince Carter 1.00 2.50
20 Jamario Moon .30 .75
21 Mike Miller .40 1.00
22 Brendan Haywood .30 .75
23 Kirk Hinrich .40 1.00
24 Jason Terry .40 1.00
25 Brandan Wright .30 .75
26 Derek Fisher .40 1.00
27 Desmond Mason .30 .75
28 Tyson Chandler .40 1.00
29 Mickael Pietrus .30 .75
30 Ronnie Brewer .30 .75
31 Gerald Wallace .40 1.00
32 Daniel Gibson .30 .75
33 J.R. Smith .50 1.25
34 Monta Ellis .40 1.00
35 Kobe Bryant 4.00 10.00
36 Ramon Sessions .30 .75
37 Zach Randolph .50 1.25
38 Andre Miller .40 1.00
39 Tony Parker .60 1.50
40 Nick Young .30 .75
41 Kevin Garnett 1.25 3.00
42 Luol Deng .40 1.00
43 Josh Howard .40 1.00
44 Corey Maggette .40 1.00
45 Cuttino Mobley .30 .75
46 James Posey .30 .75
47 Hedo Turkoglu .40 1.00
48 Brad Miller .40 1.00
49 Andrei Kirilenko .40 1.00
50 Raymond Felton .30 .75
51 Zydrunas Ilgauskas .40 1.00
52 Jason Maxiell .30 .75
53 Yao Ming 1.25 3.00
54 Luke Walton .40 1.00
55 Mo Williams .40 1.00
56 David Lee .30 .75
57 Thaddeus Young .40 1.00
58 Raja Bell .40 1.00
59 Ime Udoka .50 1.25
60 Gilbert Arenas .50 1.25
61 Glen Davis .30 .75
62 Ben Wallace .60 1.50
63 Kenyon Martin .40 1.00
64 Stephen Jackson .40 1.00
65 Andrew Bynum .30 .75
66 Richard Jefferson .40 1.00
67 Chris Duhon .30 .75
68 John Salmons .30 .75
69 DeShawn Stevenson .40 1.00
70 Zaza Pachulia .30 .75
71 Jason Richardson .50 1.25
72 Anderson Varejao .30 .75
73 Rasheed Wallace .60 1.50
74 Rafer Alston .30 .75
75 Troy Murphy .30 .75
76 T.J. Ford .30 .75
77 Chris Kaman .30 .75
78 Hakim Warrick .30 .75
79 Daequan Cook .30 .75
80 Al Jefferson .30 .75
81 Sean Williams .30 .75
82 Eddy Curry .30 .75
83 Chris Wilcox .30 .75
84 Willie Green .30 .75
85 Martell Webster .40 1.00
86 Travis Outlaw .40 1.00
87 Bruce Bowen .40 1.00
88 Jermaine O'Neal .50 1.25
89 Ben Gordon .40 1.00
90 Antawn Jamison .40 1.00
91 Al Horford .50 1.25
92 Andres Nocioni .40 1.00
93 Rodney Stuckey .30 .75
94 Shane Battier .40 1.00
95 Jarrett Jack .40 1.00
96 Al Thornton .30 .75
97 Mike Conley Jr. .40 1.00
98 Udonis Haslem .30 .75
99 Rashad McCants .30 .75
100 Marcus Williams .30 .75
101 Jeff Green .30 .75
102 Jameer Nelson .30 .75
103 Shaquille O'Neal 1.50 4.00
104 LaMarcus Aldridge .50 1.25
105 Brandon Roy .40 1.00
106 Manu Ginobili 1.00 2.50
107 Jose Calderon .30 .75
108 Jason Kapono .30 .75
109 Mike Bibby .50 1.25
110 Andrea Bargnani .40 1.00
111 Jerry Stackhouse .50 1.25
112 Richard Hamilton .50 1.25
113 Brent Barry .30 .75
114 Baron Davis .50 1.25
115 Darko Milicic .30 .75
116 Ricky Davis .40 1.00
117 Corey Brewer .40 1.00
118 Nick Collison .30 .75
119 Rashard Lewis .40 1.00
120 Amare Stoudemire .50 1.25
121 Steve Blake .30 .75
122 Kevin Martin .40 1.00
123 Fabricio Oberto .30 .75
124 Mehmet Okur .30 .75
125 Wally Szczerbiak .40 1.00
126 Mark Aguirre .60 1.50
127 Danny Ainge .75 2.00
128 Rick Barry 1.00 2.50
129 Elgin Baylor 1.25 3.00
130 Dave Bing .75 2.00
131 Otis Birdsong .60 1.50
132 Gail Goodrich .60 1.50
133 Bill Bradley 1.00 2.50
134 Bill Cartwright .60 1.50
135 James Worthy .75 2.00
136 Tom Chambers .60 1.50
137 Maurice Cheeks .60 1.50
138 Archie Clark .75 2.00
139 Michael Cooper .60 1.50
140 Bob Cousy 1.25 3.00
141 Dave Cowens .60 1.50
142 Billy Cunningham .75 2.00
143 Adrian Dantley .60 1.50
144 Darryl Dawkins .50 1.25
145 Clyde Drexler 1.00 2.50
146 Joe Dumars .75 2.00
147 Mario Elie .50 1.25
148 Walt Frazier .75 2.00
149 George Gervin 1.25 3.00
150 Tim Hardaway 1.00 2.50
151 John Havlicek .75 2.00
152 Bill Russell 2.50 6.00
153 Bill Laimbeer .60 1.50
154 Karl Malone 1.00 2.50
155 Bob McAdoo .60 1.50
156 Larry Bird 2.50 6.00
157 Magic Johnson 2.50 6.00
158 Willis Reed 1.25 3.00
159 Wilt Chamberlain 2.50 6.00
160 Pete Maravich 2.00 5.00
161 George Mikan 1.50 4.00
162 Hakeem Olajuwon 1.50 4.00
163 Patrick Ewing 1.25 3.00
164 Oscar Robertson .75 2.00
165 Bill Sharman .75 2.00
166 Dennis Rodman 1.50 4.00
167 David Robinson 1.50 4.00
168 Dominique Wilkins 1.25 3.00
169 Isiah Thomas 1.25 3.00
170 Jerry West 1.50 4.00
171A Derrick Rose Dribbling RC 4.00 10.00
171B Derrick Rose Standing 5.00 12.00
172A Michael Beasley 1BK RC 1.00 2.50
172B Michael Beasley 2BK 1.25 3.00
173A O.J. Mayo Dribbling RC .75 2.00
173B O.J. Mayo Standing 1.00 2.50
174A Russell Westbrook Red RC 5.00 12.00
174B Russell Westbrook Blue 15.00 40.00
175A Kevin Love Shooting RC 2.00 5.00
175B Kevin Love Standing 2.50 6.00
176A Danilo Gallinari Standing RC 1.50 4.00
176B Danilo Gallinari Dribbling 2.00 5.00
177A Eric Gordon Dribbling RC 1.50 4.00
177B Eric Gordon Standing 2.00 5.00
178A Joe Alexander Dribbling RC .60 1.50
178B Joe Alexander Standing .75 2.00
179A D.J. Augustin Dribbling RC 1.00 2.50
179B D.J. Augustin Standing 1.25 3.00
180A Brook Lopez Blue RC 1.25 3.00
180B Brook Lopez Red 1.50 4.00
181A Jerryd Bayless Layup RC .75 2.00
181B Jerryd Bayless Standing 1.00 2.50
182 Jason Thompson RC .60 1.50
183A A.Randolph Crouching RC .60 1.50
183B A.Randolph Standing .75 2.00
184A Robin Lopez Standing RC .75 2.00
184B Robin Lopez Crouching 1.00 2.50
185 Marreese Speights RC .75 2.00
186 Roy Hibbert RC .75 2.00
187 JaVale McGee RC 1.00 2.50
188A J.J. Hickson Dribbling RC .60 1.50
188B J.J. Hickson Standing .75 2.00
189A Brandon Rush Dribbling RC .60 1.50
189B Brandon Rush Standing .75 2.00
190 Ryan Anderson RC .75 2.00
191A Courtney Lee Dribbling RC .75 2.00
191B Courtney Lee Standing 1.00 2.50
192A Kosta Koufos Dribbling RC .60 1.50
192B Kosta Koufos Standing .75 2.00
193 Rudy Fernandez RC .75 2.00
194 George Hill RC .75 2.00
195 D.J. White RC .60 1.50
196 J.R. Giddens RC .60 1.50
197A C.Douglas-Roberts Red RC .60 1.50
197B C.Douglas-Roberts Blue .75 2.00
198A Mario Chalmers Dribbling RC 1.00 2.50
198B Mario Chalmers Standing 1.25 3.00
199 DeAndre Jordan RC 1.25 3.00
200A Darrell Arthur Blue RC .75 2.00
200B Darrell Arthur Gold 1.00 2.50
201 Joe Johnson SP 1.00 2.50
202 Paul Pierce SP 1.50 4.00
203 LeBron James SP 8.00 20.00
204 Tayshaun Prince SP 1.00 2.50
205 Danny Granger SP .75 2.00
206 Pau Gasol SP 1.25 3.00
207 Shawn Marion SP 1.00 2.50
208 Michael Redd SP .75 2.00
209 Devin Harris SP .60 1.50
210 David West SP .75 2.00
211 Kevin Durant SP 4.00 10.00
212 Dwight Howard SP 1.25 3.00
213 Samuel Dalembert SP .60 1.50
214 Greg Oden SP .75 2.00
215 Tim Duncan SP 2.50 6.00
216 Carlos Boozer SP .75 2.00
217 Caron Butler SP .75 2.00
218 Chris Bosh SP 1.25 3.00
219 Leandro Barbosa SP .75 2.00
220 Tracy McGrady SP 1.50 4.00
221 Andrew Bogut SP .75 2.00
222 Rudy Gay SP 1.00 2.50
223 Andre Iguodala SP .75 2.00
224 Dirk Nowitzki SP 2.50 6.00
225 Deron Williams SP .75 2.00
226 Chauncey Billups SP 1.25 3.00
227 Rajon Rondo SP 1.25 3.00
228 Beno Udrih SP .75 2.00
229 Dwyane Wade SP 2.00 5.00
230 Chris Paul SP 2.00 5.00

2008-09 Topps T51 Murad Mini

*1-170 MINI: .75X TO 2X BASE HI
*171-200 RC MINI: .5X TO 1.25X BASE
*201-250 SP MINI: .6X TO 1.5X BASE
ONE MINI PER PACK
171-200 RC STATED ODDS 1:18
201-250 SP ODDS 1:12

2008-09 Topps T51 Murad Mini Black

*1-170 BLACK: 1X TO 2.5X BASE HI
*171-200 RC BLACK: .6X TO 1.5X BASE HI
*201-230 SP BLACK: .75X TO 2X BASE HI

2008-09 Topps T51 Murad Silk

*1-125 SILK: 10X TO 25X BASE HI
*126-170/201-230 SILK: 5X TO 12X BASE HI
*171-200 SILK: 4X TO 10X BASE HI
RC VARIATIONS: SAME VALUE
PRINT RUN 25 SER.#'d SETS
167 David Robinson 20.00 50.00

2008-09 Topps T51 Murad Autographs

*BLACK: .6X TO 1.5X BASE
BLACK PRINT RUN 25 SER.#'d SETS
T51AAB Andrea Bargnani 6.00 15.00
T51ABY Andrew Bynum 15.00 40.00
T51AIG Andre Iguodala 5.00 12.00
T51AAJ Antawn Jamison 4.00 10.00
T51AAR Anthony Randolph 2.50 6.00
T51ABD Baron Davis 6.00 15.00
T51ABL Brook Lopez 5.00 12.00
T51ABR Brandon Roy 10.00 25.00
T51ABRA Brandon Rush 2.50 6.00
T51ABRL Bill Russell 500.00 1,000.00
T51ACBI Chauncey Billups 6.00 15.00
T51ACBO Carlos Boozer 4.00 10.00
T51ACM Corey Maggette 4.00 10.00
T51ACP Chris Paul 30.00 80.00
T51ADA Darrell Arthur 3.00 8.00
T51ADG Danny Granger 5.00 12.00
T51ADGA Danilo Gallinari 10.00 25.00
T51ADH Devin Harris 8.00 20.00
T51ADHO Dwight Howard 15.00 40.00
T51ADJA D.J. Augustin 4.00 10.00
T51ADJW D.J. White 2.50 6.00
T51ADL David Lee 5.00 12.00
T51ADR Derrick Rose 30.00 80.00
T51AEG Eric Gordon 6.00 15.00
T51AGO Greg Oden 12.00 30.00
T51AGW Gerald Wallace 4.00 10.00
T51AJA Joe Alexander 2.50 6.00
T51AJB Jerryd Bayless 3.00 8.00
T51AJJ Jarrett Jack 4.00 10.00
T51AJJH J.J. Hickson 2.50 6.00
T51AJRG J.R. Giddens 2.50 6.00
T51AKH Kirk Hinrich 8.00 20.00
T51AKK Kosta Koufos 2.50 6.00
T51AKL Kevin Love 30.00 80.00
T51ALB Larry Bird 50.00 100.00
T51AMB Michael Beasley 12.00 30.00
T51AMC Mario Chalmers 4.00 10.00
T51AMJ Magic Johnson 40.00 80.00
T51AMM Mike Miller 4.00 10.00
T51AMP Mickael Pietrus 4.00 10.00
T51AOJM O.J. Mayo 12.00 30.00
T51APP Paul Pierce 10.00 25.00
T51ARG Rudy Gay 6.00 15.00
T51ARH Roy Hibbert 3.00 8.00
T51ARL Robin Lopez 3.00 8.00
T51ARM Rashad McCants 4.00 10.00
T51ARWE Russell Westbrook 125.00 300.00
T51ATJF T.J. Ford 4.00 10.00
T51ATM Tracy McGrady 10.00 25.00
T51AVC Vince Carter 20.00 40.00

2008-09 Topps T51 Murad Checklists

COMPLETE SET (30) 6.00 15.00
APPROXIMATE ODDS ONE PER PACK
CL1 Dwyane Wade 1.00 2.50
CL2 Travis Outlaw .40 1.00
CL3 Los Angeles Clippers .50 1.25
CL4 Michael Redd .40 1.00
CL5 E.Okafor/A.Jefferson .50 1.25
CL6 Tracy McGrady .75 2.00
CL7 Andre Iguodala .40 1.00
CL8 Brown/Brewer/Jefferson .50 1.25
CL9 Rudy Gay .50 1.25
CL10 J.Kidd/S.Nash 1.25 3.00
CL11 Shaquille O'Neal 1.50 4.00
CL12 Carmelo Anthony .60 1.50
CL13 Chris Bosh .60 1.50
CL14 Tony Parker .60 1.50
CL15 Gilbert Arenas .50 1.25
CL16 Sacramento Kings .54 1.25
CL17 Utah Jazz 1.00 2.50
CL18 A.Biedrins/M.Moore .75 1.25
CL19 Dwight Howard .60 1.50
CL20 Cleveland Cavaliers 1.25 3.00
CL21 Ray Allen .75 2.00
CL22 Detroit Pistons .50 1.25
CL23 Dallas Mavericks .75 2.00
CL24 Jamal Crawford .50 1.25
CL25 Danny Granger .40 1.00
CL26 Chauncey Billups .60 1.50
CL27 Atlanta Hawks .50 1.25
CL28 Kevin Garnett 1.25 3.00
CL29 Kobe Bryant 4.00 10.00
CL30 Larry Bird 1.50 4.00

2008-09 Topps T51 Murad Relics

APPROXIMATE ODDS 1:24 PACKS
*GOLD: .6X TO 1.5X BASE
GOLD PRINT RUN 51 SER.#'d SETS
T51RAI Allen Iverson 6.00 15.00
T51RAIG Andre Iguodala 2.50 6.00
T51RAS Amare Stoudemire 3.00 8.00
T51RBK Bernard King 2.50 6.00
T51RBL Bill Laimbeer 2.50 6.00
T51RBR Brandon Roy 2.50 6.00
T51RBW Bill Walton 4.00 10.00
T51RCA Carmelo Anthony 4.00 10.00
T51RCBI Chauncey Billups 4.00 10.00
T51RCBO Chris Bosh 4.00 10.00
T51RCBU Caron Butler 2.50 6.00
T51RCBZ Carlos Boozer 2.50 6.00
T51RCD Clyde Drexler 4.00 10.00
T51RCM Chris Mullin 3.00 8.00
T51RCP Chris Paul 6.00 15.00
T51RDH Dwight Howard 4.00 10.00
T51RDN Dirk Nowitzki 8.00 20.00
T51RDR Dennis Rodman 6.00 15.00
T51RDW Dwyane Wade 6.00 15.00
T51RDWI Deron Williams 2.50 6.00
T51REM Earl Monroe 3.00 8.00
T51RGA Gilbert Arenas 3.00 8.00
T51RGG George Gervin 5.00 12.00
T51RGO Greg Oden 2.00 5.00
T51RIT Isiah Thomas 5.00 12.00
T51RJJ Joe Johnson 3.00 8.00
T51RJK Jason Kidd 5.00 12.00
T51RJS Josh Smith 2.00 5.00
T51RKB Kobe Bryant 40.00 100.00
T51RKG Kevin Garnett 8.00 20.00
T51RKM Kevin Martin 2.50 6.00
T51RLB Larry Bird 10.00 25.00
T51RMC Michael Cooper 2.50 6.00
T51RMG Manu Ginobili 6.00 15.00
T51RMJ Magic Johnson 10.00 25.00
T51RMR Michael Redd 2.50 6.00
T51RMRI Mitch Richmond 3.00 8.00
T51RPG Pau Gasol 4.00 10.00
T51RPM Pete Maravich 30.00 80.00
T51RPP Paul Pierce 5.00 12.00
T51RRG Rudy Gay 3.00 8.00
T51RRR Rajon Rondo 4.00 10.00
T51RSN Steve Nash 6.00 15.00
T51RSO Shaquille O'Neal 10.00 25.00
T51RSP Scottie Pippen 10.00 25.00
T51RTD Tim Duncan 8.00 20.00
T51RTM Tracy McGrady 5.00 12.00
T51RTP Tony Parker 4.00 10.00
T51RVC Vince Carter 6.00 15.00
T51RYM Yao Ming 8.00 20.00

2008-09 Topps T51 Murad T6 Cabinets

ONE CABINET PER BOX
*BLACK: .75X TO 2X BASE HI
BLACK STATED PRINT RUN 51 SETS
T6BR Brandon Roy .75 2.00
T6CA Carmelo Anthony 1.25 3.00
T6CP Chris Paul 2.00 5.00
T6DH Dwight Howard 1.25 3.00
T6DR Derrick Rose 10.00 25.00
T6DW Dwyane Wade 2.00 5.00
T6GO Greg Oden .60 1.50
T6KB Kobe Bryant 8.00 20.00
T6KG Kevin Garnett 2.50 6.00
T6LB Larry Bird 3.00 8.00
T6LJ LeBron James 8.00 20.00
T6MB Michael Beasley 1.00 2.50
T6MJ Magic Johnson 3.00 8.00
T6OJM O.J. Mayo .75 2.00
T6PP Paul Pierce 1.50 4.00
T6YM Yao Ming 2.50 6.00

2001-02 Topps TCC

COMPLETE SET (150) 20.00 50.00
1 Shaquille O'Neal 1.00 2.50
2 Jason Williams .40 1.00
3 Eddie Jones .25 .60
4 Anthony Mason .25 .60
5 Joe Smith .25 .60
6 Kenyon Martin .25 .60
7 Tracy McGrady .40 1.00
8 Horace Grant .20 .50
9 Andre Miller .20 .50
10 Allen Iverson .60 1.50
11 Shawn Marion .25 .60
12 Derek Anderson .15 .40
13 Chris Webber .30 .75
14 Bruce Bowen .15 .40
15 Alvin Williams .15 .40
16 Brent Barry .15 .40
17 Donyell Marshall .15 .40
18 Richard Hamilton .30 .75
19 Vlade Divac .20 .50
20 Vince Carter .50 1.25
21 Kevin Garnett .60 1.50
22 Jason Terry .25 .60
23 Antoine Walker .20 .50
24 P.J. Brown .15 .40
25 Baron Davis .25 .60
26 Eddie Robinson .15 .40
27 Chris Mihm .15 .40
28 Michael Finley .25 .60
29 Nick Van Exel .25 .60
30 Steve Francis .25 .60
31 Chucky Atkins .15 .40
32 Raef LaFrentz .15 .40
33 Antawn Jamison .20 .50
34 Jalen Rose .25 .60
35 Lamar Odom .25 .60
36 Elton Brand .20 .50
37 Derek Fisher .20 .50
38 Alonzo Mourning .40 1.00
39 Ervin Johnson .15 .40
40 Tim Duncan .60 1.50
41 Kurt Thomas .15 .40
42 Latrell Sprewell .30 .75
43 Darrell Armstrong .15 .40
44 Tom Gugliotta .15 .40
45 Derrick Coleman .20 .50
46 Dale Davis .15 .40
47 David Robinson .20 .50
48 Scottie Pippen .60 1.50
49 Hakeem Olajuwon .50 1.25
50 Darius Miles .15 .40
51 Greg Ostertag .15 .40
52 Karl Malone .50 1.25
53 Morris Peterson .15 .40
54 Shareef Abdur-Rahim .25 .60
55 Dikembe Mutombo .40 1.00
56 Elden Campbell .15 .40
57 Ron Mercer .15 .40
58 Jumaine Jones .15 .40
59 Wang ZhiZhi .25 .60
60 Ray Allen .40 1.00
61 Marcus Camby .20 .50
62 Jermaine O'Neal .20 .50
63 Kenny Thomas .15 .40
64 Danny Fortson .15 .40
65 Ben Wallace .30 .75
66 DeShawn Stevenson .15 .40
67 Antonio Davis .20 .50
68 Doug Christie .15 .40
69 Rasheed Wallace .30 .75
70 Stephon Marbury .30 .75
71 Allan Houston .25 .60
72 Kerry Kittles .15 .40
73 Todd MacCulloch .15 .40
74 Sam Cassell .20 .50
75 Kobe Bryant 2.00 5.00
76 Aaron McKie .15 .40
77 Terrell Brandon .20 .50
78 Brian Grant .15 .40
79 Michael Dickerson .15 .40
80 Jerry Stackhouse .25 .60
81 Antonio McDyess .20 .50
82 Steve Nash .50 1.25
83 Paul Pierce .40 1.00
84 Jamal Mashburn .20 .50
85 Toni Kukoc .30 .75
86 James Posey .15 .40
87 Larry Hughes .20 .50
88 Cuttino Mobley .20 .50
89 Jeff Foster .15 .40
90 Jason Kidd .40 1.00
91 Keith Van Horn .20 .50
92 Mike Miller .20 .50
93 Anfernee Hardaway .60 1.50
94 Bonzi Wells .15 .40
95 Mike Bibby .25 .60
96 Steve Smith .20 .50
97 Gary Payton .40 1.00
98 John Stockton .50 1.25
99 Peja Stojakovic .30 .75
100 Michael Jordan 5.00 12.00
101 Iakovos Tsakalidis .15 .40
102 Mark Jackson .20 .50
103 Wally Szczerbiak .20 .50
104 Rod Strickland .15 .40
105 Rick Fox .20 .50
106 Glenn Robinson .25 .60
107 Michael Olowokandi .15 .40
108 Reggie Miller .50 1.25
109 Kelvin Cato .15 .40
110 Clifford Robinson .25 .60
111 Dirk Nowitzki .60 1.50
112 Brad Miller .25 .60
113 David Wesley .15 .40
114 Kenny Anderson .20 .50
115 Theo Ratliff .15 .40
116 Rashard Lewis .20 .50
117 Matt Harpring .15 .40
118 Eddie Griffin RC .30 .75
119 Brendan Haywood RC .30 .75
120 Steven Hunter RC .25 .60
121 Jamaal Tinsley RC .30 .75
122 Jason Richardson RC .60 1.50
123 Tony Parker RC 1.50 4.00
124 Pau Gasol RC 1.50 4.00
125 Shane Battier RC .75 2.00
126 Joe Johnson RC .60 1.50
127 Leon Smith RC .40 1.00
128 Mengke Bateer RC .60 1.50
129 Loren Woods RC .25 .60
130 Kwame Brown RC .40 1.00
131 Tyson Chandler RC .60 1.50
132 Eddy Curry RC .40 1.00
133 Kedrick Brown RC .25 .60
134 Joseph Forte RC .25 .60
135 Troy Murphy RC .30 .75
136 Richard Jefferson RC .50 1.25
137 DeSagana Diop RC .25 .60
138 Vladimir Radmanovic RC .25 .60
139 Zach Randolph RC .75 2.00
140 Gerald Wallace RC .50 1.25
141 Brandon Armstrong RC .25 .60
142 Jeryl Sasser RC .25 .60
143 Rodney White RC .25 .60
144 Samuel Dalembert RC .40 1.00
145 Jason Collins RC .30 .75
146 Michael Bradley RC .25 .60
147 Oscar Torres RC .40 1.00
148 Zeljko Rebraca RC .40 1.00
149 Andrei Kirilenko RC .60 1.50
150 Trenton Hassell RC .40 1.00

2001-02 Topps TCC Red

*STARS: 1.25X TO 3X BASE CARD HI
*RC's: .75X TO 2X BASE CARD HI
STATED ODDS 1:2

2001-02 Topps TCC Autographs

STATED ODDS 1:48
CCAAM Andre Miller 5.00 12.00
CCABJ Bobby Jackson 5.00 12.00
CCADB Damone Brown 2.50 6.00
CCADH Donnell Harvey 4.00 10.00
CCADM Desmond Mason 4.00 10.00
CCAGA Gilbert Arenas 6.00 15.00
CCAHT Hedo Turkoglu 5.00 12.00
CCAJF Joseph Forte 2.50 6.00
CCAJJ Joe Johnson 6.00 15.00
CCAJT Jason Terry 4.00 10.00
CCAKB Kedrick Brown 2.50 6.00
CCAKD Keyon Dooling 4.00 10.00
CCAKS Kenny Satterfield 2.50 6.00
CCALP Lavor Postell 4.00 10.00
CCALW Loren Woods 2.50 6.00
CCAMB Mike Bibby 6.00 15.00
CCAMD Michael Doleac 4.00 10.00
CCAPS Peja Stojakovic 8.00 20.00
CCARH Richard Hamilton 5.00 12.00
CCARL Raef LaFrentz 4.00 10.00
CCARM Roshown McLeod 4.00 10.00
CCASB Shane Battier 8.00 20.00
CCASM Shawn Marion 6.00 15.00
CCATM Troy Murphy 3.00 8.00
CCAAJO Alvin Jones 2.50 6.00
CCAJTR Jeff Trepagnier 2.50 6.00

2001-02 Topps TCC Challenging the Champ

STATED ODDS 1:32
CCAH Anfernee Hardaway 8.00 20.00
CCBD Baron Davis 3.00 8.00
CCDN Dirk Nowitzki 8.00 20.00
CCEB Elton Brand 2.50 6.00
CCJM Jamal Mashburn 2.50 6.00
CCJT Jason Terry 3.00 8.00
CCMF Michael Finley 3.00 8.00
CCSA Shareef Abdur-Rahim 2.50 6.00
CCSM Stephon Marbury 4.00 10.00
CCSN Steve Nash 6.00 15.00
CCSDM Shawn Marion 3.00 8.00
CCTD Tim Duncan 8.00 20.00
CCTG Tom Gugliotta 2.00 5.00
CCTK Toni Kukoc 4.00 10.00
CCTR Theo Ratliff 2.00 5.00
CCWZ Wang Zhizhi 10.00 25.00

2001-02 Topps TCC Crowning Moment

COMPLETE SET (10) 8.00 20.00
STATED ODDS 1:5
CM1 Karl Malone 1.00 2.50
CM2 Shaquille O'Neal 2.00 5.00
CM3 Tim Duncan 1.25 3.00
CM4 Michael Jordan 4.00 10.00
CM5 Kobe Bryant 4.00 10.00
CM6 Vince Carter 1.00 2.50
CM7 Dikembe Mutombo .75 2.00
CM8 Elton Brand .40 1.00
CM9 Jason Kidd .75 2.00
CM10 Steve Francis .50 1.25

2001-02 Topps TCC Finals Journey

STATED ODDS 1:22
FJAI Allen Iverson 10.00 25.00
FJAM Aaron McKie 2.00 5.00
FJBS Brian Shaw 2.00 5.00
FJDF Derek Fisher 2.50 6.00
FJDG Devean George 2.00 5.00
FJDM Dikembe Mutombo 5.00 12.00
FJES Eric Snow 2.00 5.00
FJGF Greg Foster 2.00 5.00
FJGL George Lynch 2.00 5.00
FJHG Horace Grant 2.50 6.00
FJJJ Jumaine Jones 2.00 5.00
FJKO Kevin Ollie 2.00 5.00
FJMG Matt Geiger 2.00 5.00
FJMM Mark Madsen 2.00 5.00
FJRB Raja Bell 4.00 10.00
FJRF Rick Fox 2.50 6.00
FJRH Robert Horry 3.00 8.00
FJRAB Rodney Buford 2.00 5.00
FJRKH Ron Harper 2.50 6.00
FJSO Shaquille O'Neal 10.00 25.00
FJTH Tyrone Hill 2.00 5.00
FJTL Tyronn Lue 3.00 8.00
FJTM Todd MacCulloch 2.00 5.00

2001-02 Topps TCC First Step Sneakers

STATED ODDS 1:222
FSAJ Antawn Jamison 4.00 10.00
FSBD Baron Davis 5.00 12.00
FSEB Elton Brand 4.00 10.00
FSEC Eddy Curry 5.00 12.00
FSJF Joseph Forte 3.00 8.00
FSJT Jason Terry 5.00 12.00
FSKB Kwame Brown 5.00 12.00
FSPS Peja Stojakovic 4.00 10.00
FSRH Richard Hamilton 6.00 15.00
FSSB Shane Battier 10.00 25.00
FSSM Shawn Marion 5.00 12.00
FSSO Shaquille O'Neal 20.00 50.00
FSTD Tim Duncan 12.00 30.00
FSVR Vladimir Radmanovic 4.00 10.00

2001-02 Topps TCC Heart of a Champion

COMPLETE SET (10) 25.00 60.00
STATED ODDS 1:19
HC1 Tim Duncan 2.50 6.00
HC2 Shaquille O'Neal 4.00 10.00
HC3 Michael Jordan 12.50 30.00
HC4 Karl Malone 2.00 5.00
HC5 Hakeem Olajuwon 2.00 5.00
HC6 David Robinson 2.00 5.00
HC7 Kobe Bryant 8.00 20.00
HC8 Scottie Pippen 2.50 6.00
HC9 Shane Battier 2.00 5.00
HC10 Jason Richardson 1.50 4.00

2001-02 Topps TCC Heroes Honor

COMPLETE SET (6) 3.00 8.00
STATED ODDS 1:5
HH1 Tim Duncan 1.50 4.00
HH2 Vince Carter 1.25 3.00
HH3 Tracy McGrady 1.00 2.50
HH4 Chris Webber .75 2.00
HH5 Baron Davis .60 1.50
HH6 Allan Houston .60 1.50

2001-02 Topps TCC Jump Ball

STATED ODDS 1:540
JBAI Allen Iverson 10.00 25.00
JBBD Baron Davis 4.00 10.00
JBCW Chris Webber 6.00 15.00
JBGR Glenn Robinson 4.00 10.00
JBPS Peja Stojakovic 3.00 8.00
JBRA Ray Allen 6.00 15.00
JBSC Sam Cassell 3.00 8.00
JBSM Shawn Marion 4.00 10.00
JBTM Tracy McGrady 6.00 15.00

2001-02 Topps TCC Setting the Stage

COMPLETE SET (10) 25.00 60.00
STATED ODDS 1:19
SS1 T.McGrady/R.Allen 3.00 8.00
SS2 K.Bryant/A.Iverson 4.00 10.00
SS3 S.O'Neal/D.Mutombo 2.50 6.00
SS4 S.O'Neal/T.Duncan 4.00 10.00
SS5 P.Ewing/A.Mourning 2.50 6.00
SS6 L.Sprewell/V.Carter 2.00 5.00
SS7 S.O'Neal/H.Olajuwon 3.00 8.00
SS8 M.Jordan/R.Miller 6.00 15.00
SS9 K.Malone/C.Webber 2.00 5.00
SS10 J.Stockton/G.Payton 2.00 5.00

2000 Topps Team USA
COMPLETE SET (96) 12.50 30.00
1 Tim Duncan ACH .40 1.00
2 Jason Kidd ACH .25 .60
3 Vin Baker ACH .15 .40
4 Steve Smith ACH .07 .20
5 Grant Hill ACH .25 .60
6 Gary Payton ACH .25 .60
7 Vince Carter ACH .50 1.25
8 Ray Allen ACH .25 .60
9 Kevin Garnett ACH .40 1.00
10 Tim Hardaway ACH .25 .60
11 Allan Houston ACH .25 .60
12 Alonzo Mourning ACH .25 .60
13 Lisa Leslie ACH .75 2.00
14 Dawn Staley ACH .40 1.00
15 Katie Smith ACH .40 1.00
16 Nikki McCray ACH UER numbered as 40 .40 1.00
17 Ruthie Bolton-Holifield ACH .40 1.00
18 Chamique Holdsclaw ACH 1.00 2.50
19 Yolanda Griffith ACH .50 1.25
20 Teresa Edwards ACH .30 .75
21 Natalie Williams ACH .50 1.25
22 Delisha Milton ACH .15 .40
23 Kara Wolters ACH .25 .60
24 Gary Payton ST .15 .40
25 Kevin Garnett ST .40 1.00
26 Tim Hardaway ST .15 .40
27 Steve Smith ST .07 .20
28 Ray Allen ST .15 .40
29 Alonzo Mourning ST .15 .40
30 Allan Houston ST .15 .40
31 Vince Carter ST .50 1.25
32 Grant Hill ST .15 .40
33 Tim Duncan ST .40 1.00
34 Jason Kidd ST .25 .60
35 Vin Baker ST .15 .40
36 Ruthie Bolton-Holifield ST .40 1.00
37 Natalie Williams ST .50 1.25
38 Lisa Leslie ST .75 2.00
39 Chamique Holdsclaw ST 1.00 2.50
40 Nikki McCray ST .40 1.00
41 Dawn Staley ST .40 1.00
42 Teresa Edwards ST .30 .75
43 Yolanda Griffith ST .50 1.25
44 Katie Smith ST .40 1.00
45 Delisha Milton ST .15 .40
46 Kara Wolters ST .25 .60
47 Vin Baker PAI .15 .40
48 Jason Kidd PAI .25 .60
49 Allan Houston PAI .15 .40
50 Ray Allen PAI .15 .40
51 Alonzo Mourning PAI .15 .40
52 Kevin Garnett PAI .40 1.00
53 Gary Payton PAI .15 .40
54 Steve Smith PAI .07 .20
55 Vince Carter PAI .50 1.25
56 Grant Hill PAI .15 .40
57 Tim Duncan PAI .40 1.00
58 Tim Hardaway PAI .15 .40
59 Chamique Holdsclaw PAI 1.00 2.50
60 Katie Smith PAI .40 1.00
61 Yolanda Griffith PAI .50 1.25
62 Nikki McCray PAI .40 1.00
63 Lisa Leslie PAI .75 2.00
64 Teresa Edwards PAI .30 .75
65 Dawn Staley PAI .40 1.00
66 Ruthie Bolton-Holifield PAI .40 1.00
67 Natalie Williams PAI .50 1.25
68 Delisha Milton PAI .15 .40
69 Kara Wolters PAI .25 .60
70 Allan Houston QU .15 .40
71 Kevin Garnett QU .40 1.00
72 Tim Duncan QU .40 1.00
73 Tim Hardaway QU .15 .40
74 Gary Payton QU .15 .40
75 Ray Allen QU .15 .40
76 Vince Carter QU .50 1.25
77 Grant Hill QU .15 .40
78 Vin Baker QU .15 .40
79 Alonzo Mourning QU .15 .40
80 Steve Smith QU .07 .20
81 Jason Kidd QU .25 .60
82 Chamique Holdsclaw QU 1.00 2.50
83 Lisa Leslie QU .75 2.00
84 Dawn Staley QU .40 1.00
85 Natalie Williams QU .50 1.25
86 Nikki McCray QU .40 1.00
87 Katie Smith QU .40 1.00
88 Teresa Edwards QU .30 .75
89 Yolanda Griffith QU .50 1.25
90 Ruthie Bolton-Holifield QU .40 1.00
91 Delisha Milton QU .15 .40
92 Kara Wolters QU .25 .60
93 Team USA Men's .40 1.00
94 Team USA Women's .40 1.00
95 Group Shot .60 1.50
96 Checklist .07 .20

2000 Topps Team USA Gold
*GOLD: 1.25X TO 3X BASE CARD HI

2000 Topps Team USA Autographs
CH Chamique Holdsclaw 100.00 200.00
DM Delisha Milton 10.00 25.00
DS Dawn Staley 20.00 50.00
KS Katie Smith 40.00 80.00
LL Lisa Leslie 40.00 100.00
NM Nikki McCray 40.00 80.00
NW Natalie Williams 10.00 25.00
RH Ruthie Bolton-Holifield 10.00 25.00
TE Teresa Edwards 40.00 80.00
YG Yolanda Griffith 40.00 80.00

2000 Topps Team USA National Spirit
COMPLETE SET (23) 20.00 40.00
NS1 Steve Smith .20 .50
NS2 Ray Allen .60 1.50
NS3 Grant Hill .60 1.50
NS4 Vince Carter 1.50 4.00
NS5 Tim Hardaway .40 1.00
NS6 Jason Kidd 1.00 2.50
NS7 Vin Baker .40 1.00
NS8 Alonzo Mourning .40 1.00
NS9 Tim Duncan 1.25 3.00
NS10 Gary Payton .60 1.50
NS11 Allan Houston .40 1.00
NS12 Kevin Garnett 1.25 3.00
NS13 Nikki McCray 1.25 3.00
NS14 Dawn Staley 1.25 3.00
NS15 Lisa Leslie 2.50 6.00
NS16 Teresa Edwards .75 2.00
NS17 Yolanda Griffith 1.50 4.00
NS18 Chamique Holdsclaw 3.00 8.00
NS19 Katie Smith 1.25 3.00
NS20 Ruthie Bolton-Holifield 1.25 3.00
NS21 Natalie Williams 1.50 4.00
NS22 Delisha Milton .50 1.25
NS23 Kara Wolters .75 2.00

2000 Topps Team USA Side by Side
COMPLETE SET (12) 12.00 30.00
RIGHT/LEFT VARIATIONS EQUAL VALUE
*DUAL REF: .75X TO 2X HI COLUMN
DUAL REF: STATED ODDS 1:36
SS1 Tim Duncan Lisa Leslie 2.50 6.00
SS2 Allan Houston Ruthie Bolton-Holifield 1.50 4.00
SS3 Kevin Garnett Chamique Holdsclaw 2.50 6.00
SS4 Jason Kidd Katie Smith 1.50 4.00
SS5 Vin Baker Natalie Williams 1.25 3.00
SS6 Gary Payton Dawn Staley 1.25 3.00
SS7 Vince Carter Theresa Edwards 1.25 3.00
SS8 Tim Hardaway Dawn Staley 1.00 2.50
SS9 Steve Smith Kara Wolters 1.00 2.50
SS10 Alonzo Mourning Yolanda Griffith 1.25 3.00
SS11 Ray Allen Delisha Milton 1.00 2.50
SS12 Grant Hill Nikki McCray 1.00 2.50

2000 Topps Team USA USArchival
USAR1 Tom Gugliotta 10.00 25.00
USAR2 Allan Houston 15.00 40.00
USAR3 Vin Baker 10.00 25.00
USAR4 Kevin Garnett 20.00 50.00
USAR5 Gary Payton 12.50 30.00
USAR6 Steve Smith 12.50 30.00
USAR7 Tim Duncan 30.00 80.00
USAR8 Jason Kidd 20.00 50.00
USAR9 Tim Hardaway 10.00 25.00

2002-03 Topps Ten
COMPLETE SET (150) 20.00 50.00
1 Allen Iverson .60 1.50
2 Shaquille O'Neal 1.00 2.50
3 Paul Pierce .40 1.00
4 Tracy McGrady .40 1.00
5 Tim Duncan .60 1.50
6 Kobe Bryant 2.00 5.00
7 Dirk Nowitzki .60 1.50
8 Karl Malone .50 1.25
9 Antoine Walker .20 .50
10 Gary Payton .40 1.00
11 Shaquille O'Neal 1.00 2.50
12 Allen Iverson .60 1.50
13 Tracy McGrady .40 1.00
14 Kobe Bryant 2.00 5.00
15 Michael Jordan 2.50 6.00
16 Paul Pierce .40 1.00
17 Chris Webber .30 .75
18 Tim Duncan .60 1.50
19 Corliss Williamson .15 .40
20 Dirk Nowitzki .60 1.50
21 Ben Wallace .30 .75
22 Tim Duncan .60 1.50
23 Kevin Garnett .60 1.50
24 Danny Fortson .15 .40
25 Elton Brand .20 .50
26 Dikembe Mutombo .20 .50
27 Jermaine O'Neal .20 .50
28 Dirk Nowitzki .60 1.50
29 Shawn Marion .25 .60
30 P.J. Brown .15 .40
31 Andre Miller .20 .50
32 Jason Kidd .40 1.00
33 Gary Payton .40 1.00
34 Baron Davis .25 .60
35 John Stockton .50 1.25
36 Stephon Marbury .30 .75
37 Jamaal Tinsley .15 .40
38 Jason Williams .15 .40
39 Steve Nash .50 1.25
40 Mark Jackson .20 .50
41 Ben Wallace .30 .75
42 Raef LaFrentz .15 .40
43 Alonzo Mourning .40 1.00
44 Tim Duncan .60 1.50
45 Dikembe Mutombo .40 1.00
46 Jermaine O'Neal .20 .50
47 Erick Dampier .15 .40
48 Adonal Foyle .15 .40
49 Pau Gasol .40 1.00
50 Shaquille O'Neal 1.00 2.50
51 Allen Iverson .60 1.50
52 Ron Artest .20 .50
53 Jason Kidd .40 1.00
54 Baron Davis .25 .60
55 Doug Christie .15 .40
56 Darrell Armstrong .15 .40
57 Karl Malone .50 1.25
58 Paul Pierce .40 1.00
59 Kenny Anderson .20 .50
60 John Stockton .50 1.25
61 Shaquille O'Neal 1.00 2.50
62 Elton Brand .20 .50
63 Donyell Marshall .15 .40
64 Pau Gasol .40 1.00
65 John Stockton .50 1.25
66 Alonzo Mourning .40 1.00
67 Ruben Patterson .15 .40
68 Corliss Williamson .15 .40
69 Tim Duncan .60 1.50
70 Brent Barry .15 .40
71 Steve Smith .20 .50
72 Jon Barry .15 .40
73 Eric Piatkowski .15 .40
74 Wally Szczerbiak .20 .50
75 Steve Nash .50 1.25
76 Hubert Davis .15 .40
77 Tyronn Lue .15 .40
78 Michael Redd .20 .50
79 Wesley Person .15 .40
80 Ray Allen .40 1.00
81 Reggie Miller .50 1.25
82 Richard Hamilton .30 .75
83 Darrell Armstrong .15 .40
84 Damon Stoudamire .25 .60
85 Steve Nash .50 1.25
86 Chauncey Billups .25 .60
87 Chris Whitney .15 .40
88 Steve Smith .20 .50
89 Peja Stojakovic .20 .50
90 Troy Hudson .15 .40
91 Allen Iverson .60 1.50
92 Cuttino Mobley .15 .40
93 Antoine Walker .20 .50
94 Steve Francis .25 .60
95 Latrell Sprewell .25 .60
96 Tim Duncan .60 1.50
97 Baron Davis .25 .60
98 Paul Pierce .40 1.00
99 Gary Payton .40 1.00
100 Michael Finley .25 .60
101 Tim Duncan .60 1.50
102 Kevin Garnett .60 1.50
103 Elton Brand .20 .50
104 Jason Kidd .40 1.00
105 Shawn Marion .25 .60
106 Andre Miller .20 .50
107 Shaquille O'Neal 1.00 2.50
108 Jermaine O'Neal .20 .50
109 Dirk Nowitzki .60 1.50
110 Pau Gasol .40 1.00
111 Pau Gasol .40 1.00
112 Shane Battier .25 .60
113 Jason Richardson .25 .60
114 Gilbert Arenas .25 .60
115 Andrei Kirilenko .20 .50
116 Richard Jefferson .20 .50
117 Jamaal Tinsley .15 .40
118 Tony Parker .40 1.00
119 Eddie Griffin .15 .40
120 Trenton Hassell .15 .40
121 Jay Williams RC .60 1.50
122 DaJuan Wagner RC .60 1.50
123 Fred Jones RC .60 1.50
124 Jiri Welsch RC .60 1.50
125 Juan Dixon RC .60 1.50
126 Kareem Rush RC .60 1.50
127 Casey Jacobsen RC .50 1.25
128 Frank Williams RC .50 1.25
129 John Salmons RC .75 2.00
130 Dan Dickau RC .50 1.25
131 Mike Dunleavy RC .75 2.00
132 Nikoloz Tskitishvili RC .50 1.25
133 Caron Butler RC .75 2.00
134 Jared Jeffries RC .60 1.50
135 Bostjan Nachbar RC .60 1.50
136 Ryan Humphrey RC .60 1.50
137 Qyntel Woods RC .50 1.25
138 Tayshaun Prince RC 1.50 4.00
139 Chris Jefferies RC .50 1.25
140 Vincent Yarbrough RC .50 1.25
141 Yao Ming RC 4.00 10.00
142 Drew Gooden RC .75 2.00
143 Nene Hilario RC .75 2.00
144 Chris Wilcox RC .60 1.50
145 Amare Stoudemire RC 2.00 5.00
146 Melvin Ely RC .60 1.50
147 Marcus Haislip RC .50 1.25
148 Curtis Borchardt RC .50 1.25
149 Robert Archibald RC .50 1.25
150 Dan Gadzuric RC .50 1.25

2002-03 Topps Ten Parallel
*STARS: 1X TO 2.5X BASE CARD HI
*RC's: .75X TO 2X BASE HI
ONE PARALLEL OR RELIC PER PACK

2002-03 Topps Ten Relic Parallel
ONE PARALLEL OR RELIC PER PACK
4 Tracy McGrady/1500 5.00 12.00
7 Dirk Nowitzki/1500 8.00 20.00
8 Karl Malone/1500 6.00 15.00
10 Gary Payton/300 5.00 12.00
11 Shaquille O'Neal/1500 12.00 30.00
17 Chris Webber/1500 4.00 10.00
22 Tim Duncan/1500 8.00 20.00
23 Kevin Garnett/1500 8.00 20.00
31 Andre Miller/300 2.50 6.00
34 Baron Davis/1500 3.00 8.00
51 Allen Iverson/1500 8.00 20.00
62 Elton Brand/750 2.50 6.00
66 Alonzo Mourning/300 5.00 12.00
75 Steve Nash/300 6.00 15.00
80 Ray Allen/1500 5.00 12.00
89 Peja Stojakovic/300 2.50 6.00
92 Cuttino Mobley/1500 2.50 6.00
93 Antoine Walker/1500 2.50 6.00
94 Steve Francis/750 3.00 8.00
95 Latrell Sprewell/300 3.00 8.00
108 Jermaine O'Neal/1500 2.50 6.00
111 Pau Gasol/400 5.00 12.00
114 Gilbert Arenas/750 3.00 8.00
115 Andrei Kirilenko/750 2.50 6.00
118 Tony Parker/300 5.00 12.00

2002-03 Topps Ten Autographs
STATED ODDS AS FOLLOWS:
GROUP A 1:335, GROUP B 1:679
GROUP C 1:220, GROUP D 1:283
GROUP E 1:184
TAAM Aaron McKie C 4.00 10.00
TABH Brendan Haywood B 5.00 12.00
TACB Chauncey Billups E 6.00 15.00
TAEC Eddy Curry B 4.00 10.00
TAGA Gilbert Arenas B 6.00 15.00
TAJJ Joe Johnson A 6.00 15.00
TAJO Jermaine O'Neal A 8.00 20.00
TAJT Jason Terry D 4.00 10.00
TAKS Kenny Satterfield E 4.00 10.00
TAMB Mike Bibby C 6.00 15.00
TAMD Mike Dunleavy A 6.00 15.00
TAPS Peja Stojakovic E 6.00 15.00
TARJ Richard Jefferson C 4.00 10.00
TARL Raef LaFrentz A 6.00 15.00
TASB Shane Battier D 5.00 12.00
TASM Shawn Marion A 6.00 15.00
TASO Shaquille O'Neal B 50.00 125.00
TATM Troy Murphy C 4.00 10.00
TAVR Vladimir Radmanovic C 4.00 10.00
TAYM Yao Ming 30.00 80.00

2002-03 Topps Ten Team Leader Relics
ONE PARALLEL OR RELIC PER PACK
TLAD Antonio Davis/1000 2.50 6.00
TLAH Allan Houston/1000 3.00 8.00
TLAM Antonio McDyess/290 2.50 6.00
TLAMI Andre Miller/400 2.50 6.00
TLBH Brendan Haywood/400 2.00 5.00
TLCM Cuttino Mobley/1000 2.00 5.00
TLDM Dikembe Mutombo/400 5.00 12.00
TLDMI Darius Miles/1500 2.00 5.00
TLGR Glenn Robinson/1500 3.00 8.00
TLJM Jamal Mashburn/1500 2.50 6.00
TLJS John Stockton/400 6.00 15.00
TLJSH Jerry Stackhouse/1000 3.00 8.00
TLKM Kenyon Martin/1500 3.00 8.00
TLMF Michael Finley/1000 3.00 8.00
TLPG Pat Garrity/400 2.00 5.00
TLPS Peja Stojakovic/1500 2.50 6.00
TLRA Ray Allen/1290 5.00 12.00
TLRH Richard Hamilton/1000 4.00 10.00
TLRM Reggie Miller/400 8.00 20.00
TLRW Rasheed Wallace/125 4.00 10.00
TLSA Shareef Abdur-Rahim/400 3.00 8.00
TLSF Steve Francis/1000 3.00 8.00
TLSM Shawn Marion/400 3.00 8.00
TLSO Shaquille O'Neal/1500 12.00 30.00
TLSS Steve Smith/1000 2.50 6.00
TLTD Tim Duncan/1500 8.00 20.00
TLTM Tracy McGrady/1500 5.00 12.00
TLWS Wally Szczerbiak/1500 2.50 6.00

2005-06 Topps The Finals Promos
COMPLETE SET (4) 2.50 6.00
SCDW Dwyane Wade 1.00 2.50
SCMJ Magic Johnson 1.25 3.00
NBAF1 Allen Iverson 1.00 2.50
NBAF2 Dwyane Wade 1.00 2.50

1999-00 Topps Tip-Off
COMPLETE SET (132) 12.50 30.00
1 Steve Smith .15 .40
2 Ron Harper .15 .40
3 Michael Dickerson .12 .30
4 LaPhonso Ellis .12 .30
5 Chris Webber .25 .60
6 Jason Caffey .12 .30
7 Bryon Russell .12 .30
8 Bison Dele .12 .30
9 Isaiah Rider .15 .40
10 Dean Garrett .12 .30
11 Eric Murdock .12 .30
12 Juwan Howard .15 .40
13 Latrell Sprewell .25 .60
14 Jalen Rose .15 .40
15 Larry Johnson .20 .50
16 Eric Williams .12 .30
17 Bryant Reeves .12 .30
18 Tony Battie .12 .30
19 Luc Longley .15 .40
20 Gary Payton .30 .75
21 Tariq Abdul-Wahad .12 .30
22 Armen Gilliam .12 .30
23 Shaquille O'Neal .75 2.00
24 Gary Trent .12 .30
25 John Stockton .30 .75
26 Mark Jackson .15 .40
27 Cherokee Parks .12 .30
28 Michael Olowokandi .12 .30
29 Raef LaFrentz .15 .40
30 Dell Curry .12 .30
31 Travis Best .12 .30
32 Shawn Kemp .30 .75
33 Voshon Lenard .12 .30
34 Brian Grant .12 .30
35 Alvin Williams .12 .30
36 Derek Fisher .15 .40
37 Allan Houston .15 .40
38 Arvydas Sabonis .15 .40
39 Terry Cummings .12 .30
40 Dale Ellis .12 .30
41 Maurice Taylor .12 .30
42 Grant Hill .30 .75
43 Anthony Mason .20 .50
44 John Wallace .12 .30
45 David Wesley .12 .30
46 Nick Van Exel .15 .40
47 Cuttino Mobley .15 .40
48 Anfernee Hardaway .50 1.25
49 Terry Porter .12 .30
50 Brent Barry .15 .40
51 Derek Harper .15 .40
52 Antoine Walker .20 .50
53 Karl Malone .40 1.00
54 Ben Wallace .15 .40
55 Vlade Divac .20 .50
56 Sam Mitchell .12 .30
57 Joe Smith .15 .40
58 Shawn Bradley .12 .30
59 Darrell Armstrong .12 .30
60 Kenny Anderson .15 .40
61 Jason Williams .30 .75
62 Alonzo Mourning .30 .75
63 Matt Harpring .12 .30
64 Antonio Davis .12 .30
65 Lindsey Hunter .12 .30
66 Allen Iverson .50 1.25
67 Mookie Blaylock .12 .30
68 Wesley Person .12 .30
69 Bobby Phills .12 .30
70 Theo Ratliff .15 .40
71 Antonio Daniels .12 .30
72 P.J. Brown .12 .30
73 David Robinson .40 1.00
74 Sean Elliott .15 .40
75 Zydrunas Ilgauskas .15 .40
76 Kerry Kittles .15 .40
77 Otis Thorpe .12 .30
78 John Starks .20 .50
79 Jaren Jackson .12 .30
80 Hersey Hawkins .12 .30
81 Glenn Robinson .15 .40
82 Tim Hardaway .40 1.00
83 Glen Rice .20 .50
84 Charlie Ward .12 .30
85 Dee Brown .12 .30
86 Danny Fortson .12 .30
87 Billy Owens .12 .30
88 Jason Kidd .30 .75
89 Brent Price .12 .30
90 Don Reid .12 .30
91 Mark Bryant .12 .30
92 Vinny Del Negro .12 .30
93 Stephon Marbury .25 .60
94 Donyell Marshall .15 .40
95 Jim Jackson .12 .30
96 Horace Grant .15 .40
97 Calbert Cheaney .12 .30
98 Vince Carter .50 1.25
99 Bobby Jackson .15 .40
100 Alan Henderson .12 .30
101 Mike Bibby .20 .50
102 Cedric Henderson .12 .30
103 Lamond Murray .12 .30
104 A.C. Green .15 .40
105 Hakeem Olajuwon .40 1.00
106 George Lynch .12 .30
107 Kendall Gill .20 .50
108 Rex Chapman .12 .30
109 Eddie Jones .20 .50
110 Kornel David RC .40 1.00
111 Jason Terry RC 1.00 2.50
112 Corey Maggette RC .75 2.00
113 Ron Artest RC 1.50 4.00
114 Richard Hamilton RC 1.50 4.00
115 Elton Brand RC 1.25 3.00
116 Baron Davis RC 1.50 4.00
117 Wally Szczerbiak RC 1.00 2.50
118 Steve Francis RC 1.25 3.00
119 James Posey RC .60 1.50
120 Shawn Marion RC 1.25 3.00
121 Tim Duncan .50 1.25
122 Danny Manning .15 .40
123 Chris Mullin .20 .50
124 Antawn Jamison .20 .50
125 Kobe Bryant 1.50 4.00
126 Matt Geiger .12 .30
127 Rod Strickland .15 .40
128 Howard Eisley .12 .30
129 Steve Nash .40 1.00
130 Felipe Lopez .12 .30
131 Ron Mercer .15 .40
132 Checklist .05 .15

1999-00 Topps Tip-Off Autographs
AG1 STATED ODDS 1:12,910
AG2 STATED ODDS 1:4,303
AG3 STATED ODDS 1:5,455
CARTER DID NOT SIGN EXCH.CARDS
AG1 Tim Duncan 300.00 600.00
AG3 Allen Iverson 200.00 500.00

2000-01 Topps Tip-Off
COMPLETE SET (160) 15.00 40.00
SUBSET CARDS SAME VALUE AS BASE
1 Elton Brand .20 .50
2 Marcus Camby .15 .40
3 Jalen Rose .15 .40
4 Jamie Feick .12 .30
5 Toni Kukoc .25 .60
6 Todd MacCulloch .12 .30
7 Mario Elie .12 .30
8 Doug Christie .15 .40
9 Sam Cassell .15 .40
10 Shaquille O'Neal .75 2.00
11 Larry Hughes .20 .50
12 Jerry Stackhouse .20 .50
13 Rick Fox .15 .40
14 Clifford Robinson .20 .50
15 Felipe Lopez .12 .30
16 Dirk Nowitzki .50 1.25
17 Cuttino Mobley .15 .40
18 Latrell Sprewell .25 .60
19 Nick Anderson .15 .40
20 Kevin Garnett .50 1.25
21 Rik Smits .12 .30
22 Jerome Williams .12 .30
23 Chris Webber .25 .60
24 Jason Terry .20 .50
25 Elden Campbell .12 .30
26 Kelvin Cato .12 .30
27 Tyrone Nesby .12 .30
28 Jonathan Bender .12 .30
29 Otis Thorpe .15 .40
30 Scottie Pippen .50 1.25
31 Radoslav Nesterovic .12 .30
32 P.J. Brown .12 .30
33 Reggie Miller .40 1.00
34 Andre Miller .15 .40
35 Tariq Abdul-Wahad .12 .30
36 Michael Doleac .12 .30
37 Rashard Lewis .15 .40
38 Jacque Vaughn .12 .30
39 Larry Johnson .25 .60
40 Steve Francis .20 .50
41 Arvydas Sabonis .15 .40
42 Jaren Jackson .12 .30
43 Howard Eisley .12 .30
44 Rod Strickland .12 .30
45 Tim Thomas .30 .75
46 Robert Horry .20 .50
47 Kenny Thomas .12 .30
48 Anthony Peeler .12 .30
49 Darrell Armstrong .12 .30
50 Vince Carter .40 1.00
51 Othella Harrington .12 .30
52 Derek Anderson .15 .40
53 Anthony Carter .15 .40
54 Scott Burrell .12 .30
55 Ray Allen .30 .75
56 Jason Kidd .30 .75
57 Sean Elliott .15 .40
58 Muggsy Bogues .20 .50
59 LaPhonso Ellis .15 .40
60 Tim Duncan .50 1.25
61 Adrian Griffin .12 .30
62 Wally Szczerbiak .15 .40
63 Austin Croshere .12 .30
64 Wesley Person .12 .30
65 James Posey .12 .30
66 Alan Henderson .12 .30
67 Ruben Patterson .12 .30
68 Jahidi White .12 .30
69 Shawn Marion .20 .50
70 Lamar Odom .20 .50
71 Lindsey Hunter .12 .30
72 Keon Clark .12 .30
73 Gary Trent .12 .30
74 Lamond Murray .12 .30
75 Paul Pierce .30 .75
76 Charlie Ward .15 .40
77 Matt Geiger .12 .30
78 Greg Anthony .12 .30
79 Horace Grant .20 .50
80 John Stockton .40 1.00
81 Peja Stojakovic .15 .40
82 William Avery .12 .30
83 Dan Majerle .20 .50
84 Christian Laettner .20 .50
85 Dana Barros .12 .30
86 Corey Benjamin .12 .30
87 Keith Van Horn .15 .40
88 Patrick Ewing .30 .75
89 Steve Smith .20 .50
90 Antonio Davis .15 .40
91 Samaki Walker .12 .30
92 Mitch Richmond .25 .60
93 Michael Olowokandi .12 .30
94 Baron Davis .20 .50
95 Dikembe Mutombo .30 .75
96 Andrew DeClercq .12 .30
97 Raef LaFrentz .15 .40
98 Trajan Langdon .12 .30
99 Ervin Johnson .12 .30
100 Alonzo Mourning .30 .75
101 Kendall Gill .20 .50
102 George Lynch .12 .30
103 Detlef Schrempf .12 .30
104 Donyell Marshall .15 .40
105 Bo Outlaw .12 .30
106 Kenny Anderson .15 .40
107 Eddie Robinson .12 .30
108 Jermaine O'Neal .15 .40
109 John Amaechi .12 .30
110 Glen Rice .20 .50
111 Vlade Divac .20 .50
112 Vin Baker .15 .40
113 Mike Bibby .20 .50
114 Richard Hamilton .25 .60
115 Mookie Blaylock .12 .30
116 Vitaly Potapenko .12 .30
117 Anthony Mason .20 .50
118 Robert Pack .12 .30
119 Vonteego Cummings .12 .30
120 Michael Finley .20 .50
121 Ron Artest .20 .50
122 Tyrone Hill .12 .30
123 Rodney Rogers .12 .30
124 Quincy Lewis .12 .30
125 Kenyon Martin RC .60 1.50
126 Stromile Swift RC .25 .60
127 Darius Miles RC .30 .75
128 Marcus Fizer RC .25 .60
129 Mike Miller RC .50 1.25
130 DerMarr Johnson RC .20 .50
131 Chris Mihm RC .20 .50
132 Jamal Crawford RC .75 2.00
133 Joel Przybilla RC .25 .60
134 Keyon Dooling RC .25 .60
135 Shaq/Iverson/G.Hill SL .15 .40
136 Kidd/Van Exel/Cassell SL .20 .50
137 Mutombo/Shaq/Duncan SL .25 .60
138 E.Jones/Pierce/Armstrong SL .10 .30
139 Mourning/Mutombo/Shaq SL .20 .50
140 Team Championship SL .30 .75
141 Kobe Bryant 1.50 4.00
142 Stephon Marbury .25 .60
143 Antoine Walker .25 .60
144 Jason Williams .30 .75
145 Shareef Abdur-Rahim .20 .50
146 Gary Payton .30 .75
147 Grant Hill .30 .75
148 Allen Iverson .50 1.25
149 Khalid El-Amin RC .20 .50
150 Chris Carrawell RC .20 .50
151 Shaquille O'Neal CS .75 2.00
152 Allen Iverson CS .50 1.25
153 Kevin Garnett CS .50 1.25
154 Vince Carter CS .40 1.00
155 Tim Duncan CS .50 1.25
156 Karl Malone CS .40 1.00
157 Chris Webber CS .25 .60
158 Latrell Sprewell CS .25 .60
159 Alonzo Mourning CS .30 .75
160 Checklist .12 .30

2000-01 Topps Tip-Off Autographs
GROUP A STATED ODDS 1:1,989
GROUP B STATED ODDS 1:4,773
OVERALL STATED ODDS 1:1,404
TOAEB Elton Brand B 10.00 25.00
TOAEJ Eddie Jones A 10.00 25.00
TOASF Steve Francis A 10.00 25.00
TOATM Tracy McGrady A 15.00 40.00

2008-09 Topps Tip-Off
COMPLETE SET (143) 15.00 30.00
1 Kobe Bryant 1.50 4.00
2 Kevin Garnett .50 1.25
3 Chris Paul .40 1.00
4 Chris Bosh .25 .60
5 Caron Butler .15 .40
6 Andrew Bogut .15 .40
7 Brandon Roy .15 .40
8 Richard Hamilton .20 .50
9 Tony Parker .25 .60
10 Yao Ming .50 1.25
11 Jamal Crawford .20 .50
12 Dwight Howard .25 .60
13 Steve Nash .40 1.00
14 Mike Miller .15 .40
15 Vince Carter .40 1.00
16 Pau Gasol .25 .60
17 Mike Dunleavy .12 .30
18 Josh Smith .12 .30
19 Kevin Martin .15 .40
20 Ray Allen .30 .75
21 Tim Duncan .50 1.25
22 Michael Redd .15 .40
23 LeBron James 1.50 4.00
24 Richard Jefferson .15 .40
25 Al Jefferson .12 .30
26 Corey Maggette .15 .40
27 Hedo Turkoglu .15 .40
28 Mo Williams .15 .40
29 Andre Iguodala .15 .40
30 David West .15 .40
31 Tracy McGrady .30 .75
32 Shaquille O'Neal .60 1.50
33 Dwyane Wade .40 1.00
34 Paul Pierce .30 .75
35 Kevin Durant .75 2.00
36 Tayshaun Prince .20 .50
37 Shawn Marion .20 .50
38 Anderson Varejao .12 .30
39 Stephen Jackson .15 .40
40 Marcus Camby .15 .40
41 Brad Miller .15 .40
42 David Lee .12 .30
43 Allen Iverson .40 1.00
44 Antawn Jamison .15 .40
45 Peja Stojakovic .15 .40
46 Rashad McCants .12 .30
47 Andrei Kirilenko .15 .40
48 Luol Deng .15 .40
49 Hakim Warrick .12 .30
50 Zach Randolph .20 .50
51 Danny Granger .15 .40
52 Greg Oden .12 .30
53 Jason Kidd .30 .75
54 Al Horford .20 .50
55 Carlos Boozer .15 .40
56 Jameer Nelson .12 .30
57 Andre Miller .15 .40
58 Ricky Davis .15 .40
59 Elton Brand .15 .40
60 Kirk Hinrich .15 .40
61 Amare Stoudemire .20 .50
62 Chris Wilcox .12 .30
63 Baron Davis .20 .50
64 Jason Richardson .20 .50
65 Jamario Moon .12 .30
66 LaMarcus Aldridge .20 .50
67 Jermaine O'Neal .20 .50
68 Joe Johnson .20 .50
69 Ben Wallace .25 .60
70 Carmelo Anthony .25 .60
71 T.J. Ford .12 .30
72 Dirk Nowitzki .50 1.25
73 Ryan Gomes .12 .30
74 Ben Gordon .15 .40
75 Gerald Wallace .15 .40
76 Rudy Gay .20 .50
77 Lamar Odom .15 .40
78 Jeff Green .15 .40
79 Devin Harris .12 .30
80 Monta Ellis .15 .40
81 Samuel Dalembert .12 .30
82 Raymond Felton .12 .30
83 Ron Artest .20 .50
84 Chauncey Billups .25 .60
85 Josh Howard .15 .40
86 Rafer Alston .12 .30
87 Chris Kaman .12 .30
88 Deron Williams .15 .40
89 Manu Ginobili .40 1.00
90 Gilbert Arenas .20 .50
91 Bill Russell .60 1.50
92 David Robinson .40 1.00
93 Bill Cartwright .15 .40
94 Dominique Wilkins .30 .75
95 Larry Bird .60 1.50
96 Dennis Rodman .40 1.00
97 Jerry West .40 1.00
98 George Gervin .30 .75
99 Rick Barry .25 .60
100 Bernard King .15 .40
101 Karl Malone .25 .60
102 Gail Goodrich .15 .40
103 Bill Bradley .25 .60
104 Adrian Dantley .15 .40
105 Joe Dumars .20 .50
106 Sam Jones .25 .60
107 John Stockton .40 1.00
108 Magic Johnson .60 1.50
109 Larry Nance .15 .40
110 Dave Bing .20 .50
111 Derrick Rose RC 1.50 4.00
112 Michael Beasley RC .40 1.00
113 O.J. Mayo RC .30 .75
114 Russell Westbrook RC 12.00 30.00
115 Kevin Love RC .75 2.00
116 Danilo Gallinari RC .60 1.50
117 Eric Gordon RC .60 1.50
118 Joe Alexander RC .25 .60
119 D.J. Augustin RC .40 1.00
120 Brook Lopez RC .50 1.25
121 Jerryd Bayless RC .30 .75
122 Jason Thompson RC .25 .60
123 Brandon Rush RC .25 .60
124 Anthony Randolph RC .25 .60
125 Robin Lopez RC .30 .75
126 Marreese Speights RC .30 .75
127 Roy Hibbert RC .30 .75
128 JaVale McGee RC .40 1.00
129 J.J. Hickson RC .25 .60
130 Alexis Ajinca RC .25 .60
131 Ryan Anderson RC .30 .75
132 Courtney Lee RC .30 .75
133 Kosta Koufos RC .25 .60
134 Darrell Arthur RC .30 .75
135 Donte Greene RC .25 .60
136 Nicolas Batum RC .50 1.25
137 George Hill RC .40 1.00
138 D.J. White RC .25 .60
139 J.R. Giddens RC .25 .60
140 Walter Sharpe RC .25 .60
141 Joey Dorsey RC .25 .60
142 Mario Chalmers RC .40 1.00
143 Chris Douglas-Roberts RC .25 .60

2008-09 Topps Tip-Off Gold
*1-110 GOLD: 2.5X TO 6X BASE HI
*111-143 GOLD RC: 2X TO 5X BASE
STATED PRINT RUN 99 SER.#'d SETS

2008-09 Topps Tip-Off Red
*1-110 RED: .75X TO 2X BASE HI
*111-143 RED RC: .6X TO 1.5X BASE
RED PRINT RUN 2008 SER.#'d SETS

2008-09 Topps Tip-Off Rookie Autographs
STATED PRINT RUN 20 SER.#'d SETS
111 Derrick Rose 150.00 300.00
112 Michael Beasley 25.00 50.00
113 O.J. Mayo 25.00 50.00
114 Russell Westbrook 200.00 500.00
116 Danilo Gallinari 15.00 40.00
117 Eric Gordon 15.00 40.00
118 Joe Alexander 6.00 15.00
120 Brook Lopez 12.00 30.00
123 Brandon Rush 6.00 15.00
124 Anthony Randolph 6.00 15.00
125 Robin Lopez 8.00 20.00
126 Marreese Speights 8.00 20.00
127 Roy Hibbert 8.00 20.00
131 Ryan Anderson 8.00 20.00
137 George Hill 10.00 25.00

2008-09 Topps Tip-Off Team Tattoos
COMPLETE SET (30) 6.00 15.00
1 Atlanta Hawks .40 1.00
2 Boston Celtics .75 2.00
3 Charlotte Bobcats .40 1.00
4 Chicago Bulls .75 2.00
5 Cleveland Cavaliers .40 1.00
6 Dallas Mavericks .40 1.00
7 Denver Nuggets .40 1.00
8 Detroit Pistons .40 1.00
9 Golden State Warriors .40 1.00
10 Houston Rockets .40 1.00
11 Indiana Pacers .40 1.00
12 Los Angeles Clippers .40 1.00
13 Los Angeles Lakers .75 2.00
14 Memphis Grizzlies .40 1.00
15 Miami Heat .40 1.00
16 Milwaukee Bucks .40 1.00
17 Minnesota Timberwolves .40 1.00
18 New Jersey Nets .40 1.00
19 New Orleans Hornets .40 1.00
20 New York Knicks .75 2.00
21 Oklahoma City Thunder .40 1.00
22 Orlando Magic .40 1.00
23 Philadelphia 76ers .40 1.00
24 Phoenix Suns .40 1.00
25 Portland Trail Blazers .40 1.00
26 Sacramento Kings .40 1.00
27 San Antonio Spurs .40 1.00
28 Toronto Raptors .40 1.00
29 Utah Jazz .40 1.00
30 Washington Wizards .40 1.00

2004-05 Topps Total
COMPLETE SET (440) 20.00 50.00
1 Antoine Walker .40 1.00
2 Paul Pierce .60 1.50
3 Tyson Chandler .30 .75
4 Lebron James 3.00 8.00
5 Dirk Nowitzki 1.00 2.50
6 Carmelo Anthony .75 2.00
7 Chauncey Billups .50 1.25
8 Juwan Howard .30 .75
9 Eddie Gill .25 .60
10 Elton Brand .30 .75
11 Chucky Atkins .25 .60
12 Shane Battier .30 .75
13 Shaquille O'Neal 1.50 4.00
14 T.J. Ford .25 .60
15 Sam Cassell .30 .75
16 Rodney Buford .25 .60
17 David West .30 .75
18 Stephon Marbury .50 1.25
19 Steve Francis .40 1.00
20 Samuel Dalembert .25 .60
21 Steve Nash .75 2.00
22 Shareef Abdur-Rahim .40 1.00
23 Mike Bibby .40 1.00
24 Tim Duncan 1.00 2.50
25 Ray Allen .60 1.50
26 Vince Carter .75 2.00
27 Carlos Arroyo .25 .60
28 Gilbert Arenas .40 1.00
29 Mark Blount .25 .60
30 Primoz Brezec .25 .60
31 Eddy Curry .25 .60
32 Lucious Harris .25 .60
33 Shawn Bradley .25 .60
34 Earl Boykins .25 .60
35 Elden Campbell .25 .60
36 Calbert Cheaney .25 .60
37 Jim Jackson .30 .75
38 Jonathan Bender .25 .60
39 Kobe Bryant 3.00 8.00
40 Malik Allen .25 .60
41 Dan Gadzuric .25 .60
42 Eddie Griffin .25 .60
43 Jason Collins .25 .60
44 Chris Andersen .40 1.00
45 Marc Jackson .25 .60
46 Leandro Barbosa .30 .75
47 Derek Anderson .30 .75
48 Doug Christie .30 .75
49 Brent Barry .25 .60
50 Nick Collison .25 .60
51 Carlos Boozer .30 .75
52 Steve Blake .25 .60
53 Al Harrington .30 .75
54 Melvin Ely .25 .60
55 Zydrunas Ilgauskas .30 .75
56 Erick Dampier .25 .60
57 Marcus Camby .30 .75
58 Derrick Coleman .30 .75
59 Speedy Claxton .25 .60
60 Tyronn Lue .25 .60
61 Austin Croshere .25 .60
62 Marko Jaric .25 .60
63 Caron Butler .30 .75
64 Pau Gasol .60 1.50
65 Christian Laettner .30 .75
66 Daniel Santiago .25 .60
67 Kevin Garnett 1.00 2.50
68 Richard Jefferson .30 .75
69 David Wesley .25 .60
70 Vin Baker .25 .60
71 Tony Battie .25 .60
72 Allen Iverson 1.00 2.50
73 Darius Miles .25 .60
74 Bobby Jackson .30 .75
75 Bruce Bowen .30 .75
76 Antonio Daniels .25 .60
77 Chris Bosh .60 1.50
78 Gordan Giricek .25 .60
79 Kwame Brown .25 .60
80 Raef Lafrentz .25 .60
81 Jason Hart .25 .60
82 Marquis Daniels .25 .60
83 Francisco Elson .25 .60
84 Carlos Delfino .25 .60
85 Dale Davis .25 .60
86 Tracy McGrady .60 1.50
87 Jeff Foster .25 .60
88 Chris Kaman .30 .75
89 Brian Cook .25 .60
90 Mike Miller .30 .75
91 Rasual Butler .25 .60
92 Mike James .25 .60
93 Trenton Hassell .25 .60
94 Jason Kidd .60 1.50
95 Lee Nailon .25 .60
96 Jerome Williams .25 .60
97 Stacey Augmon .30 .75
98 Willie Green .40 1.00
99 Amare Stoudemire .40 1.00
100 Ruben Patterson .25 .60
101 Chris Webber .50 1.25
102 Manu Ginobili .75 2.00
103 Danny Fortson .25 .60
104 Donyell Marshall .25 .60
105 Matt Harpring .25 .60
106 Juan Dixon .25 .60
107 Boris Diaw .30 .75
108 Ricky Davis .30 .75
109 Kareem Rush .25 .60
110 Kirk Hinrich .40 1.00
111 Jeff Mcinnis .25 .60
112 Michael Finley .40 1.00
113 Voshon Lenard .25 .60
114 Darvin Ham .30 .75
115 Mike Dunleavy .25 .60
116 Dikembe Mutombo .40 1.00
117 Kerry Kittles .25 .60
118 Vlade Divac .40 1.00
119 James Posey .30 .75
120 Michael Doleac .25 .60
121 Toni Kukoc .40 1.00
122 Troy Hudson .25 .60
123 Jamal Crawford .40 1.00
124 Grant Hill .50 1.25
125 Corliss Williamson .25 .60
126 Quentin Richardson .25 .60
127 Zach Randolph .40 1.00
128 Peja Stojakovic .30 .75
129 Robert Horry .30 .75
130 Jerome James .25 .60
131 Morris Peterson .25 .60
132 Jarvis Hayes .25 .60
133 Tony Delk .25 .60
134 Jason Kapono .25 .60
135 Adrian Griffin .25 .60
136 Aleksandar Pavlovic .25 .60
137 Kenyon Martin .40 1.00
138 Richard Hamilton .50 1.25
139 Derek Fisher .30 .75
140 Bob Sura .25 .60
141 Stephen Jackson .30 .75
142 Devean George .25 .60
143 Stromile Swift .25 .60
144 Keyon Dooling .25 .60
145 Desmond Mason .30 .75
146 Michael Olowokandi .25 .60
147 Ron Mercer .25 .60
148 P.J. Brown .25 .60
149 Tim Thomas .25 .60
150 Kelvin Cato .25 .60
151 Kenny Thomas .25 .60
152 Theo Ratliff .25 .60
153 Rasho Nesterovic .25 .60
154 Rashard Lewis .30 .75
155 Jalen Rose .30 .75
156 Brendan Haywood .25 .60
157 Kevin Willis .25 .60
158 Gary Payton .60 1.50
159 Brevin Knight .25 .60
160 Othella Harrington .25 .60
161 Eric Snow .25 .60
162 Josh Howard .30 .75
163 Andre Miller .30 .75
164 Lindsey Hunter .25 .60
165 Adonal Foyle .25 .60
166 Maurice Taylor .25 .60
167 Fred Jones .25 .60
168 Corey Maggette .30 .75
169 Brian Grant .30 .75
170 Bonzi Wells .30 .75
171 Michael Redd .30 .75
172 Latrell Sprewell .50 1.25
173 Steven Hunter .25 .60
174 Rodney Rogers .25 .60
175 Anfernee Hardaway 1.00 2.50
176 Pat Garrity .25 .60
177 Brian Skinner .25 .60
178 Zarko Cabarkapa .25 .60
179 Damon Stoudamire .40 1.00
180 Tony Parker .60 1.50
181 Ronald Murray .30 .75
182 Alvin Williams .30 .75
183 Raul Lopez .25 .60
184 Larry Hughes .30 .75
185 Predrag Drobnjak .25 .60
186 Jiri Welsch .25 .60
187 Robert Traylor .25 .60
188 Nene .30 .75
189 Antonio McDyess .30 .75
190 Troy Murphy .25 .60
191 Charlie Ward .25 .60
192 Reggie Miller .75 2.00
193 Bobby Simmons .25 .60
194 Stanislav Medvedenko .25 .60
195 Jason Williams .30 .75
196 Dwyane Wade 1.50 4.00
197 Joe Smith .30 .75
198 Wally Szczerbiak .30 .75
199 Zoran Planinic .25 .60
200 Baron Davis .40 1.00
201 Kurt Thomas .25 .60
202 Deshawn Stevenson .25 .60
203 John Salmons .30 .75
204 Maciej Lampe .25 .60
205 Greg Ostertag .25 .60
206 Malik Rose .25 .60
207 Matt Bonner .25 .60
208 Keith McLeod .25 .60
209 Antawn Jamison .30 .75
210 Marcus Banks .25 .60
211 Keith Bogans .25 .60
212 Antonio Davis .25 .60
213 Jerry Stackhouse .40 1.00
214 Nikoloz Tskitishvili .25 .60
215 Darko Milicic .25 .60
216 Eduardo Najera .25 .60
217 Yao Ming 1.00 2.50
218 Jermaine O'Neal .30 .75
219 Chris Wilcox .25 .60
220 Lamar Odom .40 1.00
221 Lorenzen Wright .25 .60
222 Damon Jones .25 .60
223 Keith Van Horn .30 .75
224 Fred Hoiberg .25 .60
225 Brian Scalabrine .25 .60
226 Jamaal Magloire .25 .60
227 Mike Sweetney .25 .60
228 Hedo Turkoglu .30 .75
229 Glenn Robinson .30 .75
230 Casey Jacobsen .25 .60
231 Nick Van Exel .40 1.00
232 Matt Barnes .25 .60
233 Luke Ridnour .30 .75
234 Loren Woods .25 .60
235 Raja Bell .30 .75
236 Walter McCarty .25 .60
237 Steve Smith .30 .75
238 Frank Williams .25 .60
239 Dajuan Wagner .25 .60
240 Jason Terry .30 .75
241 Rodney White .25 .60
242 Tayshaun Prince .40 1.00
243 Mickael Pietrus .25 .60
244 Reece Gaines .25 .60
245 Jamaal Tinsley .25 .60
246 Zeljko Rebraca .25 .60
247 Chris Mihm .25 .60
248 Eddie Jones .40 1.00
249 Zaza Pachulia .25 .60
250 Ervin Johnson .25 .60
251 Jabari Smith .25 .60
252 Nazr Mohammed .25 .60
253 Andrew Declercq .25 .60
254 Kyle Korver .30 .75
255 Jake Voskuhl .25 .60
256 Travis Outlaw .30 .75
257 Vladimir Radmanovic .25 .60
258 Lamond Murray .25 .60
259 Jarron Collins .25 .60
260 Jared Jeffries .25 .60
261 Jason Collier .25 .60
262 Tom Gugliotta .30 .75
263 Gerald Wallace .30 .75
264 Eric Piatkowski .25 .60
265 Desagana Diop .25 .60
266 Alan Henderson .25 .60
267 Greg Buckner .25 .60
268 Ben Wallace .50 1.25
269 Jason Richardson .40 1.00
270 Ryan Bowen .25 .60
271 Mikki Moore .25 .60
272 Brian Cardinal .25 .60
273 Maurice Williams .30 .75
274 Mark Madsen .25 .60
275 Jacque Vaughn .25 .60
276 George Lynch .25 .60
277 Allan Houston .40 1.00
278 Aaron McKie .30 .75
279 Joe Johnson .30 .75
280 Oyntel Woods .25 .60
281 Darius Songaila .25 .60
282 Devin Brown .25 .60
283 Mehmet Okur .30 .75
284 Kenny Anderson .30 .75
285 Jahidi White .25 .60
286 Jon Barry .25 .60
287 Drew Gooden .25 .60
288 Wesley Person .25 .60
289 Rasheed Wallace .50 1.25
290 Clifford Robinson .25 .60
291 Bostjan Nachbar .25 .60
292 Scot Pollard .25 .60
293 Quinton Ross .25 .60
294 Luke Walton .25 .60
295 Earl Watson .25 .60
296 Udonis Haslem .25 .60
297 Erick Strickland .25 .60
298 Eric Williams .25 .60
299 Junior Harrington .25 .60
300 Moochie Norris .25 .60
301 Cuttino Mobley .25 .60
302 Shawn Marion .40 1.00
303 Richie Frahm .25 .60
304 Brad Miller .30 .75
305 Michael Wilks .25 .60
306 Rafer Alston .25 .60
307 Andrei Kirilenko .30 .75
308 Etan Thomas .25 .60
309 Ndudi Ebi .25 .60
310 Anthony Peeler .25 .60
311 Pavel Podkolzin RC .25 .60
312 Lionel Chalmers RC .30 .75
313 Andre Emmett RC .25 .60
314 Trevor Ariza RC .40 1.00
315 Dwight Howard RC 1.25 3.00
316 Rafael Araujo RC .25 .60
317 Tony Allen RC .40 1.00
318 Luol Deng RC .40 1.00
319 Jackson Vroman RC .25 .60
320 Josh Smith RC .40 1.00
321 Ben Gordon RC .40 1.00
322 Luke Jackson RC .25 .60
323 David Harrison RC .25 .60
324 Nenad Krstic RC .30 .75
325 J.R. Smith RC .40 1.00
326 Kris Humphries RC .30 .75
327 Al Jefferson RC .40 1.00
328 Devin Harris RC .30 .75
329 Shaun Livingston RC .40 1.00
330 Kaniel Dickens RC .25 .60
331 Kevin Martin RC .50 1.25
332 Kirk Snyder RC .25 .60
333 Josh Childress RC .25 .60
334 Erik Daniels RC .30 .75
335 Bernard Robinson RC .25 .60
336 Andres Nocioni RC .40 1.00
337 D.J. Mbenga RC .25 .60
338 Sebastian Telfair RC .30 .75
339 Robert Swift RC .25 .60
340 Royal Ivey RC .25 .60
341 Anderson Varejao RC .30 .75
342 Romain Sato RC .25 .60
343 Peter John Ramos RC .25 .60
344 Chris Duhon RC .30 .75
345 Emeka Okafor RC .30 .75
346 Matt Freije RC .25 .60
347 Maurice Evans RC .40 1.00
348 Beno Udrih RC .30 .75
349 John Edwards RC .25 .60
350 Sasha Vujacic RC .30 .75
351 Dorell Wright RC .30 .75
352 Jameer Nelson RC .40 1.00
353 Damien Wilkins RC .30 .75
354 Pape Sow RC .25 .60
355 Andris Biedrins RC .25 .60
356 Delonte West RC .30 .75
357 Arthur Johnson RC .30 .75
358 Antonio Burks RC .25 .60
359 Andre Iguodala RC .60 1.50
360 Ibrahim Kutluay RC .40 1.00
361 Mike Woodson CO .20 .50
362 Larry Drew CO .20 .50
363 Doc Rivers CO .40 1.00
364 Tony Brown CO .20 .50
365 Bernie Bickerstaff CO .20 .50
366 Gary Brokaw CO .20 .50
367 Scott Skiles CO .40 1.00
368 Ron Adams CO .20 .50
369 Paul Silas CO .20 .50
370 Brendan Malone CO .20 .50
371 Don Nelson CO .40 1.00
372 Donnie Nelson CO RC .20 .50
373 Jeff Bzdelik CO .20 .50
374 Michael Cooper CO .40 1.00
375 Larry Brown CO .50 1.25
376 Dave Hanners CO .20 .50
377 Mike Montgomery CO .40 1.00
378 Terry Stotts CO .20 .50
379 Jeff Van Gundy CO .40 1.00
380 Tom Thibodeau CO .20 .50
381 Rick Carlisle CO .20 .50
382 Mike Brown CO .20 .50
383 Mike Dunleavy Sr. CO .40 1.00
384 Jim Eyen CO .20 .50
385 Rudy Tomjanovich CO .40 1.00
386 Frank Hamblen CO .20 .50
387 Mike Fratello CO .40 1.00
388 Eric Musselman CO .20 .50
389 Stan Van Gundy CO .40 1.00
390 Bob Mcadoo CO .40 1.00
391 Terry Porter CO .20 .50
392 Mike Schuler CO .20 .50
393 Flip Saunders CO .40 1.00
394 Jerry Sichting CO .20 .50
395 Lawrence Frank CO .40 1.00
396 Brian Hill CO .20 .50
397 Byron Scott CO .20 .50
398 Darrell Walker CO .20 .50
399 Lenny Wilkens CO .50 1.25
400 Mark Aguirre CO .20 .50
401 Johnny Davis CO .20 .50
402 Paul Westhead CO .20 .50
403 Jim O'Brien CO .40 1.00
404 Lester Conner CO .20 .50
405 Mike D'Antoni CO .40 1.00
406 Marc Iavaroni CO .20 .50
407 Maurice Cheeks CO .40 1.00
408 Jim Lynam CO .20 .50
409 Rick Adelman CO .40 1.00
410 Elston Turner CO .20 .50
411 Gregg Popovich CO 30.00 80.00
412 P.J. Carlesimo CO .40 1.00
413 Nate Mcmillan CO .20 .50
414 Dwane Casey CO .20 .50
415 Sam Mitchell CO .20 .50
416 Alex English CO .40 1.00
417 Jerry Sloan CO .40 1.00
418 Phil Johnson CO .20 .50
419 Eddie Jordan CO .20 .50
420 Mike O'Koren CO .20 .50
421 Harry The Hawk .75 2.00
422 Blaze .75 2.00
423 Benny Da Bull .75 2.00
424 Slamson .75 2.00
425 Champ .75 2.00
426 Rocky .75 2.00
427 Clutch .75 2.00
428 Squatch .75 2.00
429 Boomer .75 2.00
430 The Raptor .75 2.00
431 Super Grizz .75 2.00
432 G-Wiz .75 2.00
433 Crunch .75 2.00
434 Sly The Fox .75 2.00
435 Hip Hop .75 2.00
436 The Gorilla .75 2.00
437 Skyhawk .75 2.00
438 Turbo .75 2.00
439 Bowser .75 2.00
440 Da Bull .75 2.00

2004-05 Topps Total Silver
*PARALLEL: .75X TO 2X BASE HI
STATED ODDS ONE PER PACK

2004-05 Topps Total Domination
COMPLETE SET (20) 4.00 10.00
STATED ODDS 1:9
TD1 Shaquille O'Neal 1.25 3.00
TD2 Allen Iverson .75 2.00
TD3 Tim Duncan .75 2.00
TD4 Tracy McGrady .50 1.25
TD5 Emeka Okafor .25 .60
TD6 Vince Carter .60 1.50
TD7 Jermaine O'Neal .25 .60
TD8 Jason Kidd .50 1.25
TD9 Ben Wallace .40 1.00
TD10 Dirk Nowitzki .75 2.00
TD11 Peja Stojakovic .25 .60
TD12 Michael Redd .25 .60
TD13 Amare Stoudemire .30 .75
TD14 Yao Ming .75 2.00
TD15 Lamar Odom .30 .75
TD16 Steve Francis .30 .75
TD17 Sebastian Telfair .25 .60
TD18 Devin Harris .25 .60
TD19 Luol Deng .30 .75
TD20 Elton Brand .25 .60

2004-05 Topps Total Package
COMPLETE SET (20) 6.00 15.00
STATED ODDS 1:9
TP1 Kevin Garnett .75 2.00
TP2 Kobe Bryant 2.50 6.00
TP3 Lebron James 2.50 6.00
TP4 Dwyane Wade 1.25 3.00
TP5 Richard Jefferson .25 .60
TP6 Dwight Howard 1.00 2.50
TP7 Ben Gordon .30 .75
TP8 Shaun Livingston .30 .75
TP9 Carmelo Anthony .60 1.50
TP10 Paul Pierce .50 1.25
TP11 Baron Davis .30 .75
TP12 Chris Webber .40 1.00
TP13 Shawn Marion .30 .75
TP14 Andrei Kirilenko .25 .60
TP15 Ray Allen .50 1.25
TP16 Pau Gasol .50 1.25
TP17 Richard Hamilton .40 1.00
TP18 Stephon Marbury .40 1.00
TP19 Jason Richardson .40 1.00
TP20 Andre Iguodala .50 1.25

2004-05 Topps Total Signatures
GROUP C ODDS 1:537
CA Carmelo Anthony 20.00 50.00
DH Devin Harris 5.00 12.00
EO Emeka Okafor 5.00 12.00
JR Justin Reed 4.00 10.00
KH Kris Humphries 5.00 12.00
LC Lionel Chalmers 5.00 12.00
LD Luol Deng 6.00 15.00
RS Romain Sato 4.00 10.00
SO Shaquille O'Neal 50.00 100.00
YT Yuta Tabuse 6.00 15.00
RSW Robert Swift 4.00 10.00

2004-05 Topps Total Success
COMPLETE SET (10) 2.50 6.00
STATED ODDS 1:18
TS1 Carlos Boozer .40 1.00
TS2 Zach Randolph .50 1.25
TS3 Brad Miller .40 1.00
TS4 Ben Wallace .60 1.50
TS5 Cuttino Mobley .40 1.00
TS6 Rashard Lewis .40 1.00
TS7 Rafer Alston .30 .75
TS8 Carlos Arroyo .30 .75
TS9 Manu Ginobili 1.00 2.50
TS10 Sam Cassell .40 1.00

2004-05 Topps Total Team Checklists
COMPLETE SET (30) 10.00 25.00
STATED ODDS 1:4
1 Antoine Walker .40 1.00
2 Paul Pierce .60 1.50
3 Emeka Okafor .30 .75
4 Kirk Hinrich .40 1.00
5 Lebron James 3.00 8.00
6 Dirk Nowitzki 1.00 2.50
7 Carmelo Anthony .75 2.00
8 Ben Wallace .50 1.25
9 Mike Dunleavy .25 .60
10 Yao Ming 1.00 2.50
11 Jermaine O'Neal .30 .75
12 Elton Brand .30 .75
13 Kobe Bryant 3.00 8.00
14 Pau Gasol .60 1.50
15 Shaquille O'Neal 1.50 4.00
16 Michael Redd .30 .75
17 Kevin Garnett 1.00 2.50
18 Richard Jefferson .30 .75
19 Baron Davis .40 1.00
20 Stephon Marbury .50 1.25
21 Dwight Howard 1.25 3.00
22 Allen Iverson 1.00 2.50
23 Amare Stoudemire .40 1.00
24 Zach Randolph .40 1.00
25 Mike Bibby .40 1.00
26 Tim Duncan 1.00 2.50
27 Rashard Lewis .30 .75
28 Vince Carter .75 2.00
29 Andrei Kirilenko .30 .75
30 Antawn Jamison .30 .75

2005-06 Topps Total
COMPLETE SET (440) 20.00 50.00
*SILVER: .5X TO 1.2X BASE HI
1 Josh Childress .20 .50
2 Emeka Okafor .25 .60
3 Luol Deng .25 .60
4 Carmelo Anthony .50 1.25
5 Carlos Arroyo .20 .50
6 Shane Battier .25 .60
7 Vince Carter .60 1.50
8 Samuel Dalembert .20 .50
9 Leandro Barbosa .25 .60
10 Mike Bibby .30 .75
11 Brent Barry .25 .60
12 Ray Allen .50 1.25
13 Rafer Alston .25 .60
14 Gilbert Arenas .30 .75
15 Al Harrington .25 .60
16 Primoz Brezec .20 .50
17 Antonio Davis .20 .50
18 Earl Boykins .20 .50
19 Chauncey Billups .40 1.00
20 Antonio Burks .20 .50
21 Jason Collins .20 .50
22 P.J. Brown .20 .50
23 Andre Iguodala .30 .75
24 Bruce Bowen .25 .60
25 Nick Collison .20 .50
26 Rafael Araujo .20 .50
27 Josh Smith .25 .60
28 Melvin Ely .20 .50
29 Ben Gordon .25 .60
30 Zydrunas Ilgauskas .25 .60
31 Marcus Camby .25 .60
32 Carlos Delfino .20 .50
33 Mike James .20 .50
34 Brian Cardinal .20 .50
35 Udonis Haslem .20 .50
36 Toni Kukoc .30 .75
37 Kevin Garnett .75 2.00
38 Richard Jefferson .25 .60
39 Jamal Crawford .30 .75
40 Allen Iverson .60 1.50
41 Tim Duncan .75 2.00
42 Danny Fortson .20 .50
43 Chris Bosh .40 1.00
44 Ricky Davis .25 .60
45 LeBron James 2.50 6.00
46 Devin Harris .20 .50
47 Tracy McGrady .50 1.25
48 Chris Kaman .20 .50
49 Pau Gasol .50 1.25
50 Jamaal Magloire .20 .50
51 Trenton Hassell .20 .50
52 Jason Kidd .50 1.25
53 Speedy Claxton .20 .50
54 Kevin Martin .25 .60
55 Manu Ginobili .60 1.50
56 Rashard Lewis .25 .60
57 Matt Harpring .25 .60
58 Kenyon Martin .25 .60
59 Al Jefferson .25 .60
60 Josh Howard .25 .60
61 Bob Sura .20 .50
62 David Harrison .20 .50
63 Shaun Livingston .25 .60
64 Alonzo Mourning .40 1.00
65 Michael Redd .25 .60
66 Mark Madsen .20 .50
67 Brad Miller .25 .60
68 Robert Horry .30 .75
69 Luke Ridnour .20 .50
70 Paul Pierce .50 1.25
71 Anderson Varejao .20 .50
72 Dirk Nowitzki .75 2.00
73 Stephen Jackson .20 .50
74 Corey Maggette .20 .50
75 Shaquille O'Neal 1.00 2.50
76 Joe Smith .25 .60
77 Troy Hudson .20 .50
78 Steve Francis .30 .75
79 Shawn Marion .25 .60
80 Ruben Patterson .20 .50
81 Morris Peterson .20 .50
82 Jarvis Hayes .20 .50
83 Derek Fisher .30 .75
84 Fred Jones .20 .50
85 Chris Mihm .20 .50
86 Stephon Marbury .30 .75
87 Grant Hill .50 1.25
88 Steve Nash .60 1.50
89 Joel Przybilla .20 .50
90 Jalen Rose .25 .60
91 Brendan Haywood .20 .50
92 Jerry Stackhouse .25 .60
93 Adonal Foyle .20 .50
94 Lamar Odom .25 .60
95 Dwight Howard .40 1.00
96 Amare Stoudemire .50 1.25
97 Zach Randolph .30 .75
98 Peja Stojakovic .25 .60
99 Mehmet Okur .20 .50
100 Antawn Jamison .25 .60
101 Jason Terry .25 .60
102 Troy Murphy .25 .60
103 Sasha Vujacic .25 .60
104 Dwyane Wade .60 1.50
105 Jameer Nelson .20 .50
106 Jared Jeffries .20 .50
107 J.R. Smith .30 .75
108 Mike Sweetney .20 .50
109 DeShawn Stevenson .20 .50
110 Sebastian Telfair .25 .60
111 Eddie Griffin .20 .50
112 Tyronn Lue .20 .50
113 Jon Barry .20 .50
114 Eric Williams .20 .50
115 Rasho Nesterovic .20 .50
116 Keith Van Horn .25 .60
117 Kenny Thomas .20 .50
118 Chris Wilcox .20 .50
119 Chris Webber .40 1.00
120 Nene .25 .60
121 John Salmons .20 .50
122 Chris Andersen .30 .75
123 Lindsey Hunter .20 .50
124 Matt Bonner .20 .50
125 Darius Miles .25 .60
126 Orien Greene RC .25 .60
127 Jarron Collins .20 .50
128 Trevor Ariza .20 .50
129 Dan Gadzuric .20 .50
130 Loren Woods .20 .50
131 Jason Richardson .30 .75
132 Corliss Williamson .20 .50
133 Zeljko Rebraca .20 .50
134 Othella Harrington .20 .50
135 Theo Ratliff .20 .50
136 David Wesley .20 .50
137 Bostjan Nachbar .20 .50
138 Eric Snow .20 .50
139 Desmond Mason .20 .50
140 Dahntay Jones .20 .50
141 Andre Miller .25 .60
142 Travis Outlaw .25 .60
143 Jim Jackson .20 .50
144 Gordan Giricek .20 .50
145 Kelvin Cato .20 .50
146 Michael Doleac .20 .50
147 Lorenzen Wright .20 .50
148 Vladimir Radmanovic .20 .50
149 Maurice Evans .20 .50
150 Hedo Turkoglu .25 .60
151 Ryan Bowen .20 .50
152 Brevin Knight .20 .50
153 Jacque Vaughn .20 .50
154 Tayshaun Prince .30 .75
155 Clifford Robinson .20 .50
156 Delonte West .20 .50
157 Zoran Planinic .20 .50
158 Slava Medvedenko .20 .50
159 Andres Nocioni .20 .50
160 Kyle Korver .25 .60
161 Brian Cook .20 .50
162 Viktor Khryapa .20 .50
163 Malik Rose .20 .50
164 Elton Brand .25 .60
165 Gerald Wallace .25 .60
166 Michael Bradley .20 .50
167 DerMarr Johnson .20 .50
168 Reece Gaines .20 .50
169 Mickael Pietrus .20 .50
170 Donta Smith .20 .50
171 Wally Szczerbiak .25 .60
172 Aleksandar Pavlovic .20 .50
173 Michael Olowokandi .20 .50
174 Jose Calderon RC .30 .75
175 Jiri Welsch .20 .50
176 Antonio McDyess .25 .60
177 Andrei Kirilenko .25 .60
178 Nenad Krstic .20 .50
179 Richard Hamilton .40 1.00
180 Stacey Augmon .20 .50
181 Kobe Bryant 2.50 6.00
182 Erick Dampier .20 .50
183 Raef LaFrentz .20 .50
184 Jackie Butler RC .20 .50
185 Ira Newble .20 .50
186 Luke Walton .20 .50
187 Rasheed Wallace .30 .75
188 Alvin Williams .20 .50
189 Ben Wallace .40 1.00
190 Chris Duhon .20 .50
191 Maurice Williams .25 .60
192 Ronald Murray .20 .50
193 Yao Ming .60 1.50
194 Eduardo Najera .20 .50
195 Nazr Mohammed .20 .50
196 Devean George .20 .50
197 Kirk Hinrich .25 .60
198 Baron Davis .30 .75
199 Juwan Howard .20 .50
200 Drew Gooden .25 .60
201 Carlos Boozer .25 .60
202 Tony Delk .20 .50
203 David West .25 .60
204 Keith Bogans .20 .50
205 Quinton Ross .20 .50
206 Darrell Armstrong .20 .50
207 Damien Wilkins .20 .50
208 Voshon Lenard .20 .50
209 Vitaly Potapenko .20 .50
210 Mike Miller .25 .60
211 Beno Udrih .20 .50
212 Darko Milicic .20 .50
213 Tony Parker .50 1.25
214 Brian Skinner .20 .50
215 Mike Dunleavy .20 .50
216 Kris Humphries .20 .50
217 Mark Blount .20 .50
218 Marquis Daniels .20 .50
219 Tony Allen .20 .50
220 Tony Battie .20 .50
221 Luther Head RC .25 .60
222 Richie Frahm .20 .50
223 Arvydas Macijauskas RC .20 .50
224 Eddie Jones .25 .60
225 Dan Dickau .20 .50
226 Marko Jaric .20 .50
227 Daniel Ewing RC .25 .60
228 Keyon Dooling .20 .50
229 James Posey .20 .50
230 Earl Watson .20 .50
231 Juan Dixon .20 .50
232 Rasual Butler .20 .50
233 Bernard Robinson .20 .50
234 Joe Johnson .25 .60
235 Antoine Walker .25 .60
236 Andris Biedrins .20 .50
237 Gary Payton .50 1.25
238 Monta Ellis RC .40 1.00
239 Quentin Richardson .20 .50
240 Martynas Andriuskevicius RC .20 .50
241 Kwame Brown .20 .50
242 Travis Diener RC .20 .50
243 Stromile Swift .20 .50
244 Wayne Simien RC .20 .50
245 Zaza Pachulia .20 .50
246 Andrew Bogut RC .40 1.00
247 Marvin Williams RC .30 .75
248 David Lee RC .30 .75
249 Nate Robinson RC .30 .75
250 Jason Williams .50 1.25
251 Larry Hughes .25 .60
252 Ike Diogu RC .20 .50
253 Marc Jackson .20 .50
254 Luke Jackson .20 .50
255 Lee Nailon .20 .50

256 T.J. Ford .20 .50
257 Shavlik Randolph RC .20 .50
258 Eddie Basden RC .20 .50
259 Yaroslav Korolev RC .20 .50
260 James Jones .20 .50
261 Raja Bell .25 .60
262 Salim Stoudamire RC .25 .60
263 Cuttino Mobley .20 .50
264 Kurt Thomas .20 .50
265 D.J. Mbenga .20 .50
266 Zarko Cabarkapa .20 .50
267 Bobby Jackson .25 .60
268 Rashad McCants RC .20 .50
269 Antoine Wright RC .25 .60
270 Josh Powell RC .25 .60
271 Francisco Garcia RC .20 .50
272 Robert Swift .20 .50
273 Gerald Green RC .30 .75
274 Peter John Ramos .20 .50
275 Nick Van Exel .30 .75
276 Jarrett Jack RC .30 .75
277 Ronnie Price RC .25 .60
278 Jamaal Tinsley .20 .50
279 Jake Voskuhl .20 .50
280 Devin Brown .20 .50
281 James Singleton RC .20 .50
282 C.J. Miles RC .25 .60
283 Charlie Villanueva RC .25 .60
284 Jeff McInnis .20 .50
285 Eddie House .20 .50
286 Rawle Marshall RC .20 .50
287 Royal Ivey .20 .50
288 Dikembe Mutombo .40 1.00
289 Fabricio Oberto RC .25 .60
290 Damon Jones .20 .50
291 Jason Hart .20 .50
292 Jumaine Jones .20 .50
293 Greg Ostertag .20 .50
294 Ryan Gomes RC .25 .60
295 Derek Anderson .20 .50
296 Raymond Felton RC .25 .60
297 Johan Petro RC .20 .50
298 Bonzi Wells .20 .50
299 Tyson Chandler .25 .60
300 Sarunas Jasikevicius RC .30 .75
301 Joey Graham RC .25 .60
302 Alan Anderson RC .20 .50
303 Steve Blake .20 .50
304 Nikoloz Tskitishvili .20 .50
305 Shareef Abdur-Rahim .30 .75
306 Sean May RC .20 .50
307 Julius Hodge RC .20 .50
308 Deron Williams RC .50 1.25
309 Michael Ruffin .20 .50
310 Darius Songaila .20 .50
311 Donyell Marshall .20 .50
312 Jermaine O'Neal .25 .60
313 Bracey Wright RC .20 .50
314 Scot Pollard .20 .50
315 Linas Kleiza RC .25 .60
316 Jerome James .20 .50
317 Brian Scalabrine .20 .50
318 Tim Thomas .20 .50
319 Reggie Evans .20 .50
320 Jason Maxiell RC .25 .60
321 Jannero Pargo .20 .50
322 Michael Finley .30 .75
323 Ersan Ilyasova RC .20 .50
324 Robert Whaley RC .20 .50
325 Chris Taft RC .20 .50
326 Esteban Batista RC .20 .50
327 Louis Williams RC .75 2.00
328 Austin Croshere .20 .50
329 Martell Webster RC .25 .60
330 Etan Thomas .20 .50
331 Brandon Bass RC .25 .60
332 Ron Artest .20 .50
333 Gerald Fitch RC .20 .50
334 Chucky Atkins .20 .50
335 Jonathan Bender .20 .50
336 Boris Diaw .25 .60
337 Andray Blatche RC .30 .75
338 Jeff Foster .20 .50
339 Andrew Bynum RC .75 2.00
340 Caron Butler .25 .60
341 Danny Granger RC .30 .75
342 Channing Frye RC .25 .60
343 Antonio Daniels .20 .50
344 Brian Grant .20 .50
345 Steven Hunter .20 .50
346 Chris Paul RC 1.50 4.00
347 Lawrence Roberts RC .20 .50
348 Bobby Simmons .20 .50
349 Dijon Thompson RC .20 .50
350 Von Wafer RC .20 .50
351 Damon Stoudamire .30 .75
352 Kevin Ollie .20 .50
353 Kirk Snyder .20 .50
354 Hakim Warrick RC .25 .60
355 Eddy Curry .25 .60
356 Aaron McKie .20 .50
357 Sam Cassell .25 .60
358 Dorell Wright .20 .50
359 Scott Padgett .20 .50
360 Pat Garrity .20 .50
361 Mike Woodson .20 .50
362 Larry Drew .20 .50
363 Doc Rivers .20 .50
364 Tony Brown .20 .50
365 Bernie Bickerstaff .30 .75
366 Gary Brokaw .30 .75
367 Scott Skiles .25 .60
368 Ron Adams .30 .75
369 Mike Brown .20 .50
370 Kenny Natt .30 .75
371 Avery Johnson .25 .60
372 Del Harris .30 .75
373 George Karl .30 .75
374 Scott Brooks .20 .50
375 Flip Saunders .30 .75
376 Sid Lowe .30 .75
377 Mike Montgomery .30 .75
378 Mario Elie .20 .50
379 Jeff Van Gundy .30 .75
380 Tom Thibodeau .30 .75
381 Rick Carlisle .30 .75
382 Kevin O'Neill .30 .75
383 Mike Dunleavy Sr. .30 .75
384 Jim Eyen .30 .75
385 Phil Jackson .40 1.00
386 Frank Hamblen .30 .75
387 Mike Fratello .40 1.00
388 Eric Musselman .30 .75
389 Pat Riley .30 .75
390 Bob McAdoo .40 1.00
391 Terry Stotts .30 .75
392 Lester Conner .30 .75
393 Dwane Casey .30 .75
394 Johnny Davis .30 .75
395 Lawrence Frank .30 .75
396 Bill Cartwright .25 .60
397 Byron Scott .30 .75
398 Darrell Walker .30 .75
399 Larry Brown .30 .75
400 Herb Williams .20 .50
401 Brian Hill .30 .75
402 Randy Ayers .30 .75
403 Maurice Cheeks .25 .60
404 John Kuester .20 .50
405 Mike D'Antoni .30 .75
406 Marc Iavaroni .30 .75
407 Nate McMillan .20 .50
408 Dean Demopoulos .30 .75
409 Rick Adelman .30 .75
410 Elston Turner .30 .75
411 Gregg Popovich 10.00 25.00
412 P.J. Carlesimo .30 .75
413 Bob Weiss .30 .75
414 Jack Sikma .30 .75
415 Sam Mitchell .20 .50
416 Jim Todd .30 .75
417 Jerry Sloan .30 .75
418 Phil D. Johnson .30 .75
419 Eddie Jordan .30 .75
420 Mike O'Koren .30 .75
421 The Gorilla .30 .75
422 Rocky .30 .75
423 Slamson .30 .75
424 The Raptor .30 .75
425 Squatch .30 .75
426 Blaze .30 .75
427 Crunch .30 .75
428 Harry the Hawk .30 .75
429 Champ .30 .75
430 Hip Hop .30 .75
431 Sly the Silver Fox .30 .75
432 Benny the Bull .30 .75
433 G-Wiz .30 .75
434 Clutch .30 .75
435 Boomer .30 .75
436 Shannon Elizabeth .40 1.00
437 Christie Brinkley .40 1.00
438 Jenny McCarthy .40 1.00
439 Carmen Electra .40 1.00
440 Jay-Z 1.50 4.00

2005-06 Topps Total Silver

*SILVER: .5X TO 1.2X BASE HI
STATED ODDS ONE PER PACK

2005-06 Topps Total Competition

COMPLETE SET (10) 3.00 8.00
STATED ODDS 1:18
TC1 Jason Kidd 1.00 2.50
TC2 Richard Hamilton .75 2.00
TC3 Manu Ginobili 1.25 3.00
TC4 Elton Brand .50 1.25
TC5 Jason Richardson .60 1.50
TC6 Emeka Okafor .50 1.25
TC7 Allen Iverson 1.25 3.00
TC8 Shawn Marion .50 1.25
TC9 Ben Gordon .50 1.25
TC10 Dwyane Wade 1.25 3.00

2005-06 Topps Total Performance

COMPLETE SET (20) 8.00 20.00
STATED ODDS 1:9
TP1 Shaquille O'Neal 1.50 4.00
TP2 LeBron James 4.00 10.00
TP3 Allen Iverson 1.00 2.50
TP4 Dirk Nowitzki 1.25 3.00
TP5 Tracy McGrady .75 2.00
TP6 Steve Nash 1.00 2.50
TP7 Vince Carter 1.00 2.50
TP8 Carmelo Anthony .75 2.00
TP9 Kobe Bryant 4.00 10.00
TP10 Kevin Garnett 1.25 3.00
TP11 Tim Duncan 1.25 3.00
TP12 Stephon Marbury .60 1.50
TP13 Kirk Hinrich .40 1.00
TP14 Amare Stoudemire 1.25 3.00
TP15 Steve Francis .50 1.25
TP16 Yao Ming 1.00 2.50
TP17 Gilbert Arenas .50 1.25
TP18 Ray Allen .75 2.00
TP19 Paul Pierce .75 2.00
TP20 Dwyane Wade 1.00 2.50

2005-06 Topps Total Signatures

STATED ODDS 1:1634
TSAB Andrew Bogut 25.00 60.00
TSABY Andrew Bynum 15.00 40.00
TSDWA Dwyane Wade 50.00 120.00
TSJM Jenny McCarthy 50.00 125.00
TSJZ Jay-Z 500.00 1,000.00
TSSL Shaun Livingston 8.00 20.00
TSSO Shaquille O'Neal 40.00 100.00

2005-06 Topps Total Surprise

COMPLETE SET (10) 2.50 6.00
STATED ODDS 1:18
TS1 Chauncey Billups .75 2.00
TS2 Gilbert Arenas .60 1.50
TS3 Jermaine O'Neal .50 1.25
TS4 Marquis Daniels .40 1.00
TS5 Ben Wallace .75 2.00
TS6 Michael Redd .50 1.25
TS7 Earl Boykins .40 1.00
TS8 Shawn Marion .50 1.25
TS9 Rafer Alston .50 1.25
TS10 Manu Ginobili 1.25 3.00

2005-06 Topps Total Team Checklists

COMPLETE SET (30) 15.00 30.00
1 Josh Smith .50 1.25
2 Paul Pierce 1.00 2.50
3 Emeka Okafor .50 1.25
4 Kirk Hinrich .50 1.25
5 LeBron James 5.00 12.00
6 Dirk Nowitzki 1.50 4.00
7 Carmelo Anthony 1.00 2.50
8 Ben Wallace .75 2.00
9 Baron davis .60 1.50
10 Yao Ming 1.25 3.00
11 Jermaine O'Neal .50 1.25
12 Elton Brand .50 1.25
13 Kobe Bryant 5.00 12.00
14 Pau Gasol 1.00 2.50
15 Dwyane Wade 1.25 3.00
16 T.J. Ford .40 1.00
17 Kevin Garnett 1.50 4.00
18 Jason Kidd 1.00 2.50
19 J.R. Smith .60 1.50
20 Stephon Marbury .75 2.00
21 Dwight Howard .75 2.00
22 Allen Iverson 1.25 3.00
23 Steve Nash 1.25 3.00
24 Sebastian Telfair .50 1.25
25 Mike Bibby .60 1.50
26 Tim Duncan 1.50 4.00
27 Ray Allen 1.00 2.50
28 Chris Bosh .75 2.00
29 Andrei Kirilenko .50 1.25
30 Gilbert Arenas .60 1.50

2005-06 Topps Total Transfer

COMPLETE SET (10) 2.50 6.00
STATED ODDS 1:18
TT1 Michael Finley .60 1.50
TT2 Joe Johnson .50 1.25
TT3 Larry Hughes .50 1.25
TT4 Caron Butler .40 1.00
TT5 Quentin Richardson .40 1.00
TT6 Antoine Walker .50 1.25
TT7 Sam Cassell .50 1.25
TT8 Damon Stoudamire .60 1.50
TT9 Bobby Simmons .40 1.00
TT10 Shareef Abdur-Rahim .60 1.50

2006-07 Topps Trademark Moves

COMP.SET w/o SP's (100) 8.00 20.00
AU RC's SER.#'d TO 75 OR 149
1 Dwyane Wade .60 1.50
2 Richard Jefferson .25 .60
3 Raymond Felton .20 .50
4 Ray Allen .50 1.25
5 Peja Stojakovic .25 .60
6 Mike Miller .25 .60
7 Mike Bibby .30 .75
8 Marcus Camby .25 .60
9 LeBron James 2.50 6.00
10 Joe Johnson .30 .75
11 Corey Maggette .25 .60
12 Charlie Villanueva .20 .50
13 Caron Butler .25 .60
14 Amare Stoudemire .30 .75
15 Vince Carter .60 1.50
16 Tracy McGrady .50 1.25
17 Shawn Marion .30 .75
18 Ron Artest .30 .75
19 Pau Gasol .50 1.25
20 Smush Parker .20 .50
21 Josh Smith .20 .50
22 Gilbert Arenas .30 .75
23 Elton Brand .25 .60
24 Dwight Howard .40 1.00
25 Dirk Nowitzki .50 1.25
26 Chris Bosh .40 1.00
27 Chauncey Billups .40 1.00
28 Ben Gordon .25 .60
29 Yao Ming .75 2.00
30 Tyson Chandler .20 .50
31 T.J. Ford .20 .50
32 Steve Nash .60 1.50
33 Sam Cassell .25 .60
34 Speedy Claxton .20 .50
35 Manu Ginobili .60 1.50
36 Kevin Garnett .75 2.00
37 Jason Terry .25 .60
38 Jameer Nelson .20 .50
39 Ben Wallace .40 1.00
40 Antoine Walker .30 .75
41 Al Jefferson .20 .50
42 Tim Duncan .75 2.00
43 Richard Hamilton .30 .75
44 Paul Pierce .50 1.25
45 Mike James .20 .50
46 Martell Webster .25 .60
47 Kobe Bryant 2.50 6.00
48 Kirk Hinrich .25 .60
49 Josh Howard .25 .60
50 Bobby Simmons .20 .50
51 Channing Frye .20 .50
52 Andrei Kirilenko .25 .60
53 Allen Iverson .75 2.00
54 Al Harrington .20 .50
55 Zach Randolph .30 .75
56 Tony Parker .50 1.25
57 Stephon Marbury .40 1.00
58 Shaquille O'Neal 1.25 3.00
59 Ricky Davis .25 .60
60 Lamar Odom .25 .60
61 Emeka Okafor .25 .60
62 Raja Bell .25 .60
63 Deron Williams .25 .60
64 Danny Granger .25 .60
65 Baron Davis .25 .60
66 Andre Miller .25 .60
67 Andre Iguodala .30 .75
68 Michael Redd .25 .60
69 Rashard Lewis .25 .60
70 Larry Hughes .25 .60
71 Jermaine O'Neal .30 .75
72 Jason Richardson .30 .75
73 Jason Kidd .50 1.25
74 Gerald Wallace .25 .60
75 Leandro Barbosa .25 .60
76 Chris Paul .60 1.50
77 Carmelo Anthony .50 1.25
78 Brad Miller .25 .60
79 Antawn Jamison .25 .60
80 Andrew Bogut .25 .60
81 Dominique Wilkins .75 2.00
82 Larry Bird 1.50 4.00
83 Clyde Drexler .60 1.50
84 Dennis Rodman 1.00 2.50
85 Isiah Thomas .75 2.00
86 Rick Barry .40 1.00
87 Hakeem Olajuwon 1.00 2.50
88 George Gervin .75 2.00
89 Spud Webb .40 1.00
90 Kareem Abdul-Jabbar 1.50 4.00
91 Oscar Robertson 1.25 3.00
92 Earl Monroe .50 1.25
93 Walt Frazier .60 1.50
94 Moses Malone .75 2.00
95 Wilt Chamberlain 1.50 4.00
96 Karl Malone .60 1.50
97 Manute Bol .50 1.25
98 Bill Walton .60 1.50
99 Maurice Cheeks .40 1.00
100 Bob Lanier .40 1.00
101 Solomon Jones AU/149 RC 2.00 5.00
102 Kyle Lowry AU/149 RC 10.00 25.00
103 Maurice Ager AU/149 RC 2.00 5.00
104 Patrick O'Bryant AU/75 RC 2.50 6.00
105 Pops Mensah-Bonsu AU/149 RC 2.00 5.00
106 Marcus Vinicius AU/149 RC 2.00 5.00
107 Josh Boone AU/149 RC 2.00 5.00
108 Mardy Collins AU/149 RC 2.00 5.00
109 Rodney Carney AU/75 RC 2.50 6.00
110 P.J. Tucker AU/149 RC 3.00 8.00
111 Shelden Williams AU/75 RC 2.50 6.00
112 Ryan Hollins AU/149 RC 2.00 5.00
113 Sergio Rodriguez AU/149 RC 2.50 6.00
114 Steve Novak AU/149 RC 2.00 5.00
115 Paul Davis AU/149 RC 2.00 5.00
116 David Noel AU/149 RC 2.00 5.00
117 Marcus Williams AU/75 RC 2.50 6.00
118 Renaldo Balkman AU/75 RC 3.00 8.00
119 Quincy Douby AU/149 RC 2.00 5.00
120 Andrea Bargnani AU/75 RC 3.00 8.00
121 Chris Quinn AU/149 RC 2.00 5.00
122 Thabo Sefolosha AU/75 RC 3.00 8.00
123 Hassan Adams AU/149 RC 2.00 5.00
124 James White AU/149 RC 2.00 5.00
125 Jordan Farmar AU/75 RC 3.00 8.00
126 Damir Markota AU/149 RC 2.00 5.00
127 Mile Ilic AU/149 RC 2.00 5.00
128 James Augustine AU/149 RC 2.00 5.00
129 Paul Millsap AU/149 RC 4.00 10.00
130 Jorge Garbajosa AU/149 RC 2.50 6.00
131 Allan Ray AU/75 RC 2.50 6.00
132 Shannon Brown AU/149 RC 2.00 5.00
133 Will Blalock AU/149 RC 2.00 5.00
134 Vassilis Spanoulis AU/149 RC 2.00 5.00
135 Adam Morrison AU/75 RC 3.00 8.00
136 Craig Smith AU/149 RC 2.50 6.00
137 Cedric Simmons AU/149 RC 2.00 5.00
138 J.J. Redick AU/75 RC 8.00 20.00
140 Ronnie Brewer AU/75 RC 4.00 10.00
141 Rajon Rondo AU/149 RC 15.00 40.00
142 Daniel Gibson AU/149 RC 2.50 6.00
143 Mickael Gelabale AU/75 RC 2.50 6.00
144 Shawne Williams AU/75 RC 2.50 6.00
145 Alexander Johnson AU/149 RC 2.00 5.00
146 Randy Foye AU/75 RC 3.00 8.00
148 Bobby Jones AU/149 RC 2.00 5.00
149 Saer Sene AU/149 RC 2.00 5.00
150 Dee Brown AU/75 RC 2.50 6.00

2006-07 Topps Trademark Moves Foil

*1-100 FOIL: .75X TO 2X BASE HI
1-100 PRINT RUN 299 SER.#'d SETS
*101-150 AU/75 FOIL: .4X TO 1X BASE HI
*101-150 AU/35 FOIL: .5X TO 1.25X BASE HI

2006-07 Topps Trademark Moves Rainbow

*1-100 RAINBOW: 1X TO 2.5X BASE
1-100 RAINBOW PRINT RUN 149 SER.#'d SETS
*101-150 AU/35 RAINBOW: .6X TO 1.5X BASE
*101-150 AU/19 RAINBOW: .75X TO 2X BASE
47 Kobe Bryant 10.00 25.00

2006-07 Topps Trademark Moves Wood

*1-100 WOOD: 1.5X TO 4X BASE
1-100 WOOD PRINT RUN 75 SETS
*101-150 AU/19 WOOD: .75X TO 3X BASE
101-150 AU/10 WOOD NOT PRICED

2006-07 Topps Trademark Moves Wood Red

*1-80 WOOD RED: 4X TO 10X BASE
*81-100 WOOD RED: 3X TO 8X BASE
1-100 WOOD RED PRINT RUN 35 SETS
101-150 AU PRINT RUN 10 OR 3 SETS
RED WOOD AU NOT PRICED

2006-07 Topps Trademark Moves Autographs

PRINT RUNS 75 TO 149 SER.#'d SETS
*FOIL AU/75: SAME VALUE AS BASE
*FOIL AU/35: .5X TO 1.25X BASE HI
*RAINBOW AU/35: .5X TO 1.25X BASE
*RAINBOW AU/19: .6X TO 1.5X BASE
*WOOD AU/19: .75X TO 2X BASE
WOOD AU/10 NOT PRICED
1 Dwyane Wade/75 25.00 60.00
3 Raymond Felton/149 4.00 10.00
12 Charlie Villanueva/149 3.00 8.00
15 Vince Carter/75 8.00 20.00
20 Smush Parker/149 3.00 8.00
21 Josh Smith/149 4.00 10.00
26 Chris Bosh/149 10.00 25.00
28 Ben Gordon/149 6.00 15.00
31 T.J. Ford/149 3.00 8.00
34 Speedy Claxton/149 3.00 8.00
38 Jameer Nelson/149 3.00 8.00
45 Mike James/149 3.00 8.00
46 Martell Webster/149 3.00 8.00
50 Bobby Simmons/149 3.00 8.00
53 Allen Iverson/75 40.00 80.00
56 Tony Parker/149 6.00 15.00
58 Shaquille O'Neal/75 20.00 50.00
61 Emeka Okafor/149 3.00 8.00
62 Raja Bell/149 6.00 15.00
74 Gerald Wallace/149 3.00 8.00
75 Leandro Barbosa/149 3.00 8.00
80 Andrew Bogut/149 6.00 15.00
81 Dominique Wilkins/75 10.00 25.00
82 Larry Bird/75 40.00 80.00
85 Isiah Thomas/75 8.00 20.00
94 Moses Malone/149 8.00 20.00
98 Bill Walton/75 8.00 20.00
99 Maurice Cheeks/149 3.00 8.00
100 Bob Lanier/75 6.00 15.00

2006-07 Topps Trademark Moves Dish

COMPLETE SET (10) 4.00 10.00
*FOIL: .5X TO 1.25X BASE HI
FOIL PRINT RUN 299 SER.#'d SETS
*RAINBOW: .6X TO 1.5X BASE HI
RAINBOW PRINT RUN 149 SER.#'d SETS
*WOOD: 1X TO 2.5X BASE HI
WOOD PRINT RUN 75 SER.#'d SETS
*WOOD RED: 1.25X TO 3X BASE HI
WOOD RED PRINT RUN 35 SER.#'d SETS
TDI1 Allen Iverson 2.00 5.00
TDI2 Tony Parker 1.25 3.00
TDI3 Jarrett Jack .60 1.50
TDI4 Delonte West .50 1.25
TDI5 Chris Duhon .50 1.25
TDI6 Jameer Nelson .50 1.25
TDI7 Marcus Williams .50 1.25
TDI8 Dee Brown .50 1.25
TDI9 Luke Walton .50 1.25
TDI10 Jordan Farmar .60 1.50

2006-07 Topps Trademark Moves Dish Autographs

PRINT RUN 75 TO 149 SER.#'d SETS
*FOIL AU/75: .4X TO 1X BASE HI
*FOIL AU/35: .5X TO 1.25X BASE HI
*RAIN AU/35: .6X TO 1.5X BASE HI
*RAIN AU/19: .75X TO 2X BASE HI
*WOOD AU/19: 1.25X TO 3X BASE HI
WOOD AU/10 NOT PRICED
SDI1 Allen Iverson/75 40.00 80.00
SDI2 Tony Parker/75 6.00 15.00
SDI3 Jarrett Jack/149 3.00 8.00
SDI4 Delonte West/75 4.00 10.00
SDI5 Chris Duhon/149 3.00 8.00
SDI6 Jameer Nelson/75 4.00 10.00
SDI7 Marcus Williams/75 3.00 8.00
SDI8 Dee Brown/149 3.00 8.00
SDI9 Luke Walton/149 3.00 8.00
SDI10 Jordan Farmar/149 4.00 10.00

2006-07 Topps Trademark Moves Dunk

COMPLETE SET (20) 10.00 25.00
*FOIL: .5X TO 1.25X BASE HI
FOIL PRINT RUN 299 SER.#'d SETS
*RAINBOW: .6X TO 1.5X BASE HI
RAIN PRINT RUN 149 SER.#'d SETS
*WOOD: 1X TO 2.5X BASE HI
WOOD PRINT RUN 75 SER.#'d SETS
*WOOD RED: 1.25X TO 3X BASE HI
WOOD RED PRINT RUN 35 SER.#'d SETS
TDU1 Shaquille O'Neal 4.00 10.00
TDU2 Chris Bosh 1.25 3.00
TDU3 Dwyane Wade 2.00 5.00
TDU4 Hakim Warrick .60 1.50
TDU5 Josh Smith .60 1.50
TDU6 Andrew Bogut .75 2.00
TDU7 Ike Diogu .60 1.50
TDU8 J.R. Smith 1.00 2.50
TDU9 Josh Childress .60 1.50
TDU10 Emeka Okafor .75 2.00
TDU11 Shawne Williams .60 1.50
TDU12 Renaldo Balkman .75 2.00
TDU13 Gerald Wallace .75 2.00
TDU14 Craig Smith .75 2.00
TDU15 Andre Iguodala 1.00 2.50
TDU16 Shelden Williams .60 1.50
TDU17 Hilton Armstrong .60 1.50
TDU18 Vince Carter 2.00 5.00
TDU19 Connie Hawkins 1.00 2.50
TDU20 Dominique Wilkins 1.50 4.00

2006-07 Topps Trademark Moves Dunk Autographs

PRINT RUN 75 TO 149 SER.#'d SETS
*FOIL AU/75: .4X TO 1X BASE HI
*FOIL AU/35: .5X TO 1.25X BASE HI
*RAIN AU/35: .6X TO 1.5X BASE HI
*RAIN AU/19: .75X TO 2X BASE HI
*WOOD AU/19: 1.25X TO 3X BASE HI
WOOD AU/10 NOT PRICED
SDU1 Shaquille O'Neal/75 25.00 60.00
SDU2 Chris Bosh/75 10.00 25.00
SDU3 Dwyane Wade/75 25.00 60.00
SDU4 Hakim Warrick/149 3.00 8.00
SDU5 Josh Smith/75 5.00 12.00
SDU6 Andrew Bogut/75 5.00 12.00
SDU7 Ike Diogu/149 3.00 8.00
SDU8 J.R. Smith/149 3.00 8.00
SDU9 Josh Childress/75 4.00 10.00
SDU10 Emeka Okafor/75 4.00 10.00
SDU11 Shawne Williams/149 3.00 8.00
SDU12 Renaldo Balkman/149 3.00 8.00
SDU13 Gerald Wallace/149 3.00 8.00
SDU14 Craig Smith/149 3.00 8.00
SDU15 Andre Iguodala/149 3.00 8.00
SDU16 Shelden Williams/75 5.00 12.00
SDU17 Hilton Armstrong/149 3.00 8.00
SDU18 Vince Carter/75 12.50 30.00
SDU19 Connie Hawkins/149 8.00 20.00
SDU20 Dominique Wilkins/75 12.50 30.00

2006-07 Topps Trademark Moves Swish

COMPLETE SET (20) 10.00 25.00
*FOIL: .5X TO 1.25X BASE HI
FOIL PRINT RUN 299 SER.#'d SETS
*RAINBOW: .6X TO 1.5X BASE HI
RAIN PRINT RUN 149 SER.#'d SETS
*WOOD: 1X TO 2.5X BASE HI
WOOD PRINT RUN 75 SER.#'d SETS
*WOOD RED: 1.25X TO 3X BASE HI
WOOD RED PRINT RUN 35 SER.#'d SETS
TSW1 Adam Morrison .75 2.00
TSW2 Randy Foye .75 2.00
TSW3 Andrea Bargnani .75 2.00
TSW4 Thabo Sefolosha .75 2.00
TSW5 Maurice Ager .60 1.50
TSW6 Mike James .60 1.50
TSW7 J.J. Redick 2.00 5.00
TSW8 Quincy Douby .60 1.50
TSW9 Chauncey Billups 1.25 3.00
TSW10 Carmelo Anthony 1.50 4.00
TSW11 Ray Allen 1.50 4.00
TSW12 Rodney Carney .60 1.50
TSW13 Rick Barry .75 2.00
TSW14 Larry Bird 3.00 8.00
TSW15 Elgin Baylor 2.00 5.00
TSW16 Luol Deng .75 2.00
TSW17 Devin Harris .60 1.50
TSW18 Rashad McCants .60 1.50
TSW19 Martell Webster .75 2.00
TSW20 Ben Gordon .75 2.00

2006-07 Topps Trademark Moves Swish Autographs

PRINT RUN 75 TO 149 SER.#'d SETS
*FOIL AU/75: SAME VALUE AS BASE
*FOIL AU/35: .5X TO 1.25X BASE HI
*RAIN AU/35: .6X TO 1.5X BASE HI
*RAIN AU/19: .75X TO 2X BASE HI
*WOOD AU/19: 1.25X TO 3X BASE HI
WOOD AU/10 NOT PRICED
SSW1 Adam Morrison/75 5.00 12.00
SSW2 Randy Foye/149 5.00 12.00
SSW3 Andrea Bargnani/75 15.00 30.00
SSW4 Thabo Sefolosha/149 5.00 12.00
SSW5 Maurice Ager/149 3.00 8.00
SSW6 Mike James/149 3.00 8.00
SSW7 J.J. Redick/149 6.00 15.00
SSW8 Quincy Douby/149 3.00 8.00
SSW9 Chauncey Billups/75 4.00 10.00
SSW10 Carmelo Anthony/75 12.50 30.00
SSW11 Ray Allen/75 8.00 20.00
SSW12 Rodney Carney/149 3.00 8.00
SSW13 Rick Barry/75 8.00 20.00
SSW14 Larry Bird/75 40.00 100.00
SSW15 Elgin Baylor/75 15.00 40.00
SSW16 Luol Deng/75 8.00 20.00
SSW17 Devin Harris/149 3.00 8.00
SSW18 Rashad McCants/149 3.00 8.00
SSW19 Martell Webster/149 3.00 8.00
SSW20 Ben Gordon/75 10.00 25.00

2007-08 Topps Trademark Moves

COMP.SET w/o SP's (50) 15.00 30.00
RC PRINT RUN 1999 SER.#'d SETS
1 Amare Stoudemire .50 1.25
2 Elton Brand .40 1.00
3 Dwyane Wade 1.00 2.50
4 Dirk Nowitzki 1.25 3.00
5 Baron Davis .40 1.00
6 Brandon Roy .60 1.50
7 Ben Gordon .40 1.00
8 Richard Hamilton .40 1.00
9 Andre Iguodala .50 1.25
10 Tim Duncan 1.25 3.00
11 Yao Ming 1.25 3.00
12 Jason Kidd .75 2.00
13 Steve Nash 1.00 2.50
14 Chris Paul 1.00 2.50
15 Carmelo Anthony .75 2.00
16 Pau Gasol .75 2.00
17 Dwight Howard .60 1.50
18 Ray Allen .75 2.00
19 Deron Williams .40 1.00
20 Vince Carter 1.00 2.50
21 Kevin Garnett 1.25 3.00
22 Michael Redd .40 1.00
23 LeBron James 4.00 10.00
24 Kobe Bryant 4.00 10.00
25 Josh Smith .30 .75
26 Gilbert Arenas .50 1.25
27 Jermaine O'Neal .50 1.25
28 Kirk Hinrich .50 1.25
29 Eddy Curry .30 .75
30 Chauncey Billups .60 1.50
31 Shawn Marion .50 1.25
32 Shaquille O'Neal 2.00 5.00
33 Allen Iverson 1.25 3.00
34 Paul Pierce .75 2.00
35 Tony Parker .75 2.00
36 Gerald Wallace .40 1.00
37 Carlos Boozer .40 1.00
38 Chris Bosh .60 1.50
39 Mike Bibby .60 1.50
40 Tracy McGrady .75 2.00
41 Rick Barry .40 1.00
42 David Robinson 1.00 2.50
43 John Stockton 1.00 2.50
44 Bill Walton .60 1.50
45 Larry Bird 2.00 5.00
46 Isiah Thomas .50 1.25
47 Magic Johnson 2.00 5.00
48 Dennis Rodman 1.25 3.00
49 Dominique Wilkins .75 2.00
50 Bill Russell 1.50 4.00
51 Yi Jianlian RC 1.25 3.00
52 Greg Oden RC 1.00 2.50
53 Mike Conley Jr. RC 2.50 6.00
54 Jeff Green RC .75 2.00
55 Corey Brewer RC .75 2.00
56 Joakim Noah RC 1.00 2.50
57 Julian Wright RC .60 1.50
58 Ramon Sessions RC .75 2.00
59 Sammy Mejia RC .60 1.50
60 Dominic McGuire RC .60 1.50
61 Kevin Durant RC 40.00 100.00
62 Arron Afflalo RC .75 2.00
63 Acie Law RC .60 1.50
64 Alando Tucker RC .60 1.50
65 Gabe Pruitt RC .60 1.50
66 Marcus Williams RC .60 1.50
67 Spencer Hawes RC .60 1.50
68 Carl Landry RC .60 1.50
69 Thaddeus Young RC 1.00 2.50
70 Nick Fazekas RC .60 1.50
71 Al Thornton RC .60 1.50
72 Rodney Stuckey RC .60 1.50
73 Nick Young RC 1.00 2.50
74 Glen Davis RC .75 2.00
75 Jermareo Davidson RC .60 1.50
76 Luis Scola RC 1.00 2.50
77 Jason Smith RC .60 1.50
78 Daequan Cook RC .75 2.00
79 Jared Dudley RC .75 2.00
80 Derrick Byars RC .60 1.50
81 Josh McRoberts RC .60 1.50
82 Adam Haluska RC .60 1.50
83 Juan Carlos Navarro RC .75 2.00
84 Aaron Gray RC .60 1.50
85 Herbert Hill RC .60 1.50
86 Jared Jordan RC .60 1.50
87 Wilson Chandler RC .75 2.00
88 Morris Almond RC .60 1.50
89 Aaron Brooks RC .75 2.00
90 Chris Richard RC .60 1.50
91 JamesOn Curry RC .60 1.50
92 Al Horford RC 2.50 6.00
93 Stephane Lasme RC .60 1.50
94 D.J. Strawberry RC .60 1.50
95 Sean Williams RC .60 1.50
96 Marco Belinelli RC .75 2.00
97 Javaris Crittenton RC .60 1.50
98 Demetris Nichols RC .60 1.50
99 Taurean Green RC .60 1.50
100 Brandan Wright RC .75 2.00

2007-08 Topps Trademark Moves Blue

*BLUE 1-50: 3X TO 8X BASE HI
BLUE 1-50 PRINT RUN 25 SER.#'d SETS

2007-08 Topps Trademark Moves Orange

*1-50 ORANGE: .6X TO 1.5X BASE HI
1-50 ORANGE PRINT RUN 399 SETS
*RC ORANGE: 1.5X TO 4X BASE HI
RC ORANGE PRINT RUN 99 SETS

2007-08 Topps Trademark Moves Red

*1-50 RED: 1.25X TO 3X BASE HI
1-50 RED PRINT RUN 99 SER.#'d SETS
*RC RED: 2X TO 5X BASE HI
RC RED PRINT RUN 50 SER.#'d SETS

2007-08 Topps Trademark Moves Rookies Wood

*WOOD: .5X TO 1.25X BASE HI
PRINT RUN 199 SER.#'d SETS

2007-08 Topps Trademark Moves Ink

PRINT RUN 49 SER.#'d SETS
*ORANGE: .5X TO 1.25X BASE HI
ORANGE PRINT RUN 25 SER.#'d SETS
AB Andrew Bynum 4.00 10.00
AG Aaron Gray 4.00 10.00
AM Adam Morrison 5.00 12.00
AT Al Thornton 4.00 10.00
ATU Alando Tucker 4.00 10.00
BD Baron Davis 6.00 15.00
BR Bill Russell 400.00 800.00
BW Brandan Wright 4.00 10.00
CA Carmelo Anthony 15.00 40.00
DG Danny Granger 4.00 10.00
DH Devin Harris 4.00 10.00
DJS D.J. Strawberry 4.00 10.00
DL David Lee 4.00 10.00
DM Dominic McGuire 4.00 10.00
DR David Robinson 30.00 80.00
DRO Dennis Rodman 25.00 60.00
DW Dominique Wilkins 12.00 30.00
DWA Dwyane Wade 30.00 80.00
DWI Deron Williams 15.00 30.00
EM Earl Monroe 10.00 25.00
GD Glen Davis 6.00 15.00
GO Greg Oden 8.00 20.00
GW Gerald Wallace 6.00 15.00
HA Hilton Armstrong 4.00 10.00
HT Hedo Turkoglu 4.00 10.00
ID Ike Diogu 4.00 10.00
IT Isiah Thomas 15.00 30.00
JH John Havlicek 12.00 30.00
JS John Stockton 30.00 80.00
KH Kirk Hinrich 8.00 20.00
LB Larry Bird 50.00 100.00
MB Marco Belinelli 4.00 10.00
MJ Magic Johnson 40.00 100.00
MJA Mike James 4.00 10.00
MW Marcus Williams 4.00 10.00
MWE Martell Webster 4.00 10.00
NY Nick Young 6.00 15.00
RB Rick Barry 10.00 25.00
RF Randy Foye 4.00 10.00
RFE Raymond Felton 4.00 10.00
SC Speedy Claxton 4.00 10.00
SD Samuel Dalembert 4.00 10.00
TG Taurean Green 4.00 10.00
TJF T.J. Ford 4.00 10.00
TP Tony Parker 10.00 25.00
TY Thaddeus Young 8.00 20.00
UH Udonis Haslem 4.00 10.00
VC Vince Carter 20.00 40.00
YJ Yi Jianlian 10.00 25.00

2007-08 Topps Trademark Moves Relics

PRINT RUN 299 SER.#'d SETS
*ORANGE: SAME VALUE AS BASE
ORANGE PRINT RUN 199 SER.#'d SETS
*RED: .5X TO 1.25X BASE HI
RED PRINT RUN 50 SER.#'d SETS
AH Al Horford 6.00 15.00
AS Amare Stoudemire 2.50 6.00
CA Carmelo Anthony 4.00 10.00
CB Caron Butler 2.00 5.00
CBI Chauncey Billups 3.00 8.00
CBO Chris Bosh 3.00 8.00
CBR Corey Brewer 2.00 5.00
CBZ Carlos Boozer 2.00 5.00
DH Dwight Howard 3.00 8.00
DN Dirk Nowitzki 6.00 15.00

DW Dwyane Wade 5.00 12.00
GA Gilbert Arenas 2.50 6.00
GO Greg Oden 2.50 6.00
JG Jeff Green 2.00 5.00
JH Josh Howard 2.00 5.00
JJ Joe Johnson 2.00 5.00
JK Jason Kidd 4.00 10.00
JN Joakim Noah 2.50 6.00
JO Jermaine O'Neal 2.50 6.00
JW Julian Wright 1.50 4.00
KB Kobe Bryant 60.00 150.00
KG Kevin Garnett 6.00 15.00
MC Mike Conley Jr. 6.00 15.00
MO Mehmet Okur 2.00 5.00
RA Ray Allen 4.00 10.00
RH Richard Hamilton 3.00 8.00
SM Shawn Marion 2.50 6.00
SN Steve Nash 5.00 12.00
SO Shaquille O'Neal 10.00 25.00
TD Tim Duncan 6.00 15.00
TM Tracy McGrady 4.00 10.00
TP Tony Parker 4.00 10.00
VC Vince Carter 5.00 12.00
YJ Yi Jianlian 3.00 8.00
YM Yao Ming 6.00 15.00

2007-08 Topps Trademark Moves Rookie Relic Ink

PRINT RUN 149 OR 79 SER.#'d SETS
*ORANGE: .5X TO 1.25X BASE HI
ORANGE PRINT RUN 50 SER.#'d SETS
*RED: .6X TO 1.5X BASE HI
RED PRINT RUN 25 SER.#'d SETS
EXCH.EXPIRATION DATE 11/30/09
51 Yi Jianlian/79 12.00 30.00
52 Greg Oden/139 5.00 12.00
60 Dominic McGuire/139 3.00 8.00
62 Arron Afflalo/139 4.00 10.00
63 Acie Law/79 3.00 8.00
65 Gabe Pruitt/139 3.00 8.00
66 Marcus Williams/139 3.00 8.00
67 Spencer Hawes/79 3.00 8.00
68 Carl Landry/139 3.00 8.00
69 Thaddeus Young/79 5.00 12.00
70 Nick Fazekas/139 3.00 8.00
72 Rodney Stuckey/79 3.00 8.00
73 Nick Young/79 5.00 12.00
74 Glen Davis/139 4.00 10.00
75 Jermareo Davidson/139 3.00 8.00
77 Jason Smith/79 3.00 8.00
78 Daequan Cook/139 4.00 10.00
79 Jared Dudley/79 4.00 10.00
80 Derrick Byars/139 3.00 8.00
81 Josh McRoberts/139 3.00 8.00
82 Adam Haluska/139 3.00 8.00
84 Aaron Gray/139 3.00 8.00
87 Wilson Chandler/139 4.00 10.00
88 Morris Almond/79 3.00 8.00
89 Aaron Brooks/139 4.00 10.00
93 Stephane Lasme/139 3.00 8.00
97 Javaris Crittenton/79 3.00 8.00
99 Taurean Green/139 3.00 8.00
100 Brandan Wright/79 4.00 10.00

2007-08 Topps Trademark Moves Triple Ink

PRINT RUN 39 SER.#'d SETS
APD Allen/Pruitt/Davis 12.00 30.00
ASY Allen/Stuckey/Young 12.00 30.00
AYT Anthony/Young/Thornton 12.00 30.00
BBF Bosh/Bargnani/Ford 10.00 25.00
BLC Billups/Law/Crittenton 10.00 25.00
BSA Billups/Stuckey/Afflalo 10.00 25.00
BTS Barbosa/Tucker/Strawberry 10.00 25.00
BWA Boozer/Williams/Almond 10.00 25.00
BWB Barry/Wright/Belinelli 10.00 25.00
BYC Bosh/Young/Crittenton 10.00 25.00
CAA Cook/Almond/Afflalo 10.00 25.00
CAW Carter/Anthony/Wade 50.00 120.00
CFW Carter/Felton/Wright 12.00 30.00
CWW Carter/Williams/Williams 12.00 30.00
CYA Carter/Young/Almond 12.00 30.00
DPL Davis/Parker/Law 12.00 30.00
FBP Ford/Brooks/Pruitt 10.00 25.00
GGC Gordon/Gray/Curry 10.00 25.00
HFM Hawes/Fazekas/McRoberts 10.00 25.00
HSG Hawes/Smith/Gray 10.00 25.00
JBL James/Brooks/Landry 10.00 25.00
JBT Johnson/Bird/Thomas 75.00 200.00
JMG Jack/McRoberts/Green 10.00 25.00
LCB Law/Crittenton/Brooks 10.00 25.00
LCN Lee/Chandler/Nichols 10.00 25.00
MFD Morrison/Felton/Davidson 10.00 25.00
OMF Okafor/Morrison/Felton 10.00 25.00
OOY O'Neal/Okafor/Jianlian 12.00 30.00
OWD Okafor/Wallace/Dudley 10.00 25.00
OWY Oden/Wright/Young 10.00 25.00
PBF Parker/Billups/Ford 12.00 30.00
PBY Parker/Belinelli/Jianlian 15.00 40.00
RBH Russell/Baylor/Havlicek 1,000.00 2,000.00
ROO Robinson/O'Neal/Oden 75.00 200.00
RRO Russell/Robinson/O'Neal 1,500.00 3,000.00
RWD Rodman/Williams/Dudley 20.00 50.00
SBH Smith/Byars/Hill 10.00 25.00
SBW Stockton/Boozer/Williams 20.00 50.00
SYB Stuckey/Young/Belinelli 10.00 25.00
TCM Thornton/Crittenton/Maggette 10.00 25.00
TWS Tucker/Williams/Strawberry 10.00 25.00
WCB Williams/Chandler/Boone 10.00 25.00
WDA Walton/Davis/Afflalo 12.00 30.00
WGM Wallace/Granger/Maggette 10.00 25.00
WSR Wilkins/Stockton/Rodman 50.00 120.00
WTD Williams/Thornton/Dudley 10.00 25.00
WTY Wilkins/Thornton/Young 10.00 25.00
YBL Jianlian/Belinelli/Lasme 12.00 30.00
YSB Young/Smith/Byars 10.00 25.00
YTD Young/Thornton/Dudley 10.00 25.00

2007-08 Topps Trademark Moves Triple Relics

PRINT RUN 199 SER.#'d SETS
*BLUE: 1X TO 2.5X BASE HI
BLUE PRINT RUN 25 SER.#'d SETS
*ORANGE: .5X TO 1.25X BASE HI
ORANGE PRINT RUN 99 SER.#'d SETS
*RED: .6X TO 1.5X BASE HI
RED PRINT RUN 50 SER.#'d SETS
ABB Arenas/Butler/Bosh 4.00 10.00
AHM Anthony/Howard/McGrady 6.00 15.00
BEF Bogut/Ellis/Felton 4.00 10.00
BFF Bargnani/Farmar/Foye 4.00 10.00
BGH Bynum/Granger/Head 4.00 10.00
BGP Billups/Gordon/Parker 5.00 12.00
BSG Bryant/Stoudemire/Garnett 50.00 120.00
BSY Brewer/Stuckey/Young 4.00 10.00
CHW Carter/Howard/Wade 6.00 15.00
CLC Conley/Law/Crittenton 4.00 10.00
GDN Garnett/Duncan/Nowitzki 8.00 20.00
GGM Garbajosa/Gay/Millsap 4.00 10.00
GRH Green/Robinson/Howard 4.00 10.00
GYW Green/Young/Wright 4.00 10.00
HBB Hamilton/Billups/Bosh 4.00 10.00
HBN Horford/Brewer/Noah 6.00 15.00
HWW Horford/Wright/Williams 4.00 10.00
KAN Kapono/Arenas/Nowitzki 4.00 10.00
KNB Kidd/Nash/Boozer 6.00 15.00
LPW Lee/Paul/Williams 4.00 10.00
MJT Miller/Jones/Terry 4.00 10.00
MRW Morrison/Roy/Williams 4.00 10.00
NSM Nash/Stoudemire/Marion 5.00 12.00
OCC Oden/Conley/Cook 5.00 12.00
OGM Okur/Garnett/McGrady 4.00 10.00
OHA O'Neal/Howard/Arenas 5.00 12.00
OHS Oden/Hawes/Smith 4.00 10.00
PDA Parker/Duncan/Anthony 6.00 15.00
WBP Wade/Bryant/Paul 40.00 100.00
WOO Wade/O'Neal/O'Neal 6.00 15.00

2008-09 Topps Treasury

COMPLETE SET (120) 30.00 80.00
1 Kobe Bryant 4.00 10.00
2 Ray Allen .75 2.00
3 Chris Paul 1.00 2.50
4 Tim Duncan 1.25 3.00
5 Josh Smith .30 .75
6 Luis Scola .40 1.00
7 Rashad McCants .30 .75
8 Vince Carter 1.00 2.50
9 LeBron James 4.00 10.00
10 Mike Dunleavy .30 .75
11 Chauncey Billups .60 1.50
12 Dwight Howard .60 1.50
13 Steve Nash 1.00 2.50
14 Monta Ellis .40 1.00
15 Carmelo Anthony .60 1.50
16 Pau Gasol .60 1.50
17 Anderson Varejao .30 .75
18 Yi Jianlian .60 1.50
19 Deron Williams .40 1.00
20 Joe Johnson .50 1.25
21 Yao Ming 1.25 3.00
22 Rudy Gay .50 1.25
23 Jason Richardson .50 1.25
24 Andrew Bogut .40 1.00
25 Kevin Garnett 1.25 3.00
26 Chris Wilcox .30 .75
27 Zach Randolph .50 1.25
28 Kirk Hinrich .40 1.00
29 Tony Parker .60 1.50
30 Allen Iverson 1.00 2.50
31 David West .40 1.00
32 Shaquille O'Neal 1.50 4.00
33 Dwyane Wade 1.00 2.50
34 Paul Pierce .75 2.00
35 Mike Miller .40 1.00
36 Hedo Turkoglu .40 1.00
37 LaMarcus Aldridge .50 1.25
38 Kevin Martin .40 1.00
39 Jamal Crawford .50 1.25
40 Gilbert Arenas .50 1.25
41 Dirk Nowitzki 1.25 3.00
42 Amare Stoudemire .50 1.25
43 Danny Granger .40 1.00
44 Chris Bosh .60 1.50
45 Luol Deng .50 1.25
46 Al Thornton .30 .75
47 Andrei Kirilenko .40 1.00
48 Tayshaun Prince .50 1.25
49 Gerald Wallace .40 1.00
50 Corey Maggette .40 1.00
51 Andre Iguodala .40 1.00
52 Greg Oden .30 .75
53 Al Jefferson .30 .75
54 Devin Harris .30 .75
55 Baron Davis .50 1.25
56 Marcus Camby .40 1.00
57 Udonis Haslem .30 .75
58 Ron Artest .50 1.25
59 Jeff Green .40 1.00
60 Richard Hamilton .50 1.25
61 Samuel Dalembert .30 .75
62 Antawn Jamison .40 1.00
63 Mike Conley Jr. .30 .75
64 Raymond Felton .30 .75
65 Carlos Boozer .40 1.00
66 Ben Gordon .40 1.00
67 Jermaine O'Neal .50 1.25
68 Peja Stojakovic .40 1.00
69 Ryan Gomes .30 .75
70 Michael Redd .40 1.00
71 Manu Ginobili 1.00 2.50
72 Elton Brand .40 1.00
73 Josh Howard .40 1.00
74 Stephen Jackson .40 1.00
75 Richard Jefferson .40 1.00
76 Andrew Bynum .30 .75
77 Shawn Marion .50 1.25
78 David Lee .30 .75
79 Jamario Moon .30 .75
80 Caron Butler .40 1.00
81 Tracy McGrady .75 2.00
82 Al Horford .50 1.25
83 Brandon Roy .50 1.25
84 Ben Wallace .60 1.50
85 Andre Miller .40 1.00
86 Brad Miller .40 1.00
87 Jameer Nelson .30 .75
88 Andrea Bargnani .40 1.00
89 Kevin Durant 2.00 5.00
90 Jason Kidd .75 2.00
91 Dennis Rodman 1.00 2.50
92 Larry Bird 1.50 4.00
93 Moses Malone .75 2.00
94 Jerry West 1.00 2.50
95 Bill Russell 1.50 4.00
96 David Robinson 1.00 2.50
97 John Stockton 1.00 2.50
98 Magic Johnson 1.50 4.00
99 George Gervin .75 2.00
100 Dominique Wilkins .75 2.00
101 Derrick Rose RC 3.00 8.00
102 Michael Beasley RC .75 2.00
103 O.J. Mayo RC .60 1.50
104 Russell Westbrook RC 4.00 10.00
105 Kevin Love RC 1.50 4.00
106 Danilo Gallinari RC 1.25 3.00
107 Eric Gordon RC 1.25 3.00
108 Joe Alexander RC .50 1.25
109 D.J. Augustin RC .75 2.00
110 Brook Lopez RC 1.00 2.50
111 Jerryd Bayless RC .60 1.50
112 Brandon Rush RC .50 1.25
113 Anthony Randolph RC .50 1.25
114 Robin Lopez RC .60 1.50
115 Courtney Lee RC .60 1.50
116 Darrell Arthur RC .60 1.50
117 Joey Dorsey RC .50 1.25
118 Mario Chalmers RC .75 2.00
119 DeAndre Jordan RC 1.00 2.50
120 Kosta Koufos RC .50 1.25

2008-09 Topps Treasury Refractors Bronze

*BRONZE: 2X TO 5 BASE HI
*BRONZE 101-120: 1.25X TO 3X BASE HI
1-100 PRINT RUN 999 SER.#'d SETS
101-120 PRINT RUN 2008 SER.#'d SETS
1 Kobe Bryant 30.00 80.00
9 LeBron James 30.00 80.00
89 Kevin Durant 12.00 30.00

2008-09 Topps Treasury Refractors Gold

*GOLD 1-100: 8X TO 20X BASE HI
*GOLD 101-120: 5X TO 12X BASE HI
STATED PRINT RUN 50 SER.#'d SETS
1 Kobe Bryant 125.00 300.00
9 LeBron James 125.00 300.00
89 Kevin Durant 50.00 120.00

2008-09 Topps Treasury Refractors Silver

*SILVER 1-100: 4X TO 10X BASE HI
*SILVER 101-120: 2.5X TO 6X BASE HI
STATED PRINT RUN 199 SER.#'d SETS
1 Kobe Bryant 60.00 150.00
9 LeBron James 60.00 150.00
89 Kevin Durant 25.00 60.00

2008-09 Topps Treasury Bird's All Rookie Team Autographs Dual

STATED PRINT RUN 39 SER.#'d SETS
BA L.Bird/J.Alexander 75.00 200.00
BAU L.Bird/D.Augustin 75.00 200.00
BB L.Bird/M.Beasley 75.00 200.00
BBA L.Bird/J.Bayless 75.00 200.00
BG L.Bird/B.Rush 75.00 200.00
BGO L.Bird/E.Gordon 75.00 200.00
BL L.Bird/K.Love 100.00 250.00
BM L.Bird/O.Mayo 75.00 200.00
BR L.Bird/D.Rose 150.00 400.00
BW L.Bird/R.Westbrook 150.00 400.00

2008-09 Topps Treasury Magic's All Rookie Team Autographs Dual

STATED PRINT RUN 39 SER.#'d SETS
JA M.Johnson/J.Alexander 75.00 200.00
JAU M.Johnson/D.Augustin 75.00 200.00
JB M.Johnson/M.Beasley 75.00 200.00
JBA M.Johnson/J.Bayless 75.00 200.00
JG M.Johnson/E.Gordon 75.00 200.00
JL M.Johnson/K.Love 100.00 250.00
JLO M.Johnson/B.Lopez 75.00 200.00
JM M.Johnson/O.Mayo 75.00 200.00
JR M.Johnson/D.Rose 150.00 400.00
JW M.Johnson/R.Westbrook 150.00 400.00

2008-09 Topps Treasury Mini Exclusives

COMPLETE SET (50) 30.00 80.00
STATED PRINT RUN 278 SER.#'d SETS
ONE MINI CARD PER RIP CARD
*BRONZE: .75X TO 2X BASE HI
BRONZE PRINT RUN 99 SER.#'d SETS
*SILVER: 2X TO 5X BASE HI
SILVER PRINT RUN 25 SER.#'d SETS
MEAH Al Horford 1.00 2.50
MEAI Allen Iverson 2.00 5.00
MEAIG Andre Iguodala .75 2.00
MEAK Andrei Kirilenko .75 2.00
MEAS Amare Stoudemire 1.00 2.50
MEAT Al Thornton .60 1.50
MEBD Baron Davis 1.00 2.50
MEBG Ben Gordon .75 2.00
MEBR Bill Russell 3.00 8.00
MEBRO Brandon Roy 1.00 2.50
MECA Carmelo Anthony 1.25 3.00
MECB Chris Bosh 1.25 3.00
MECBO Carlos Boozer .75 2.00
MECBU Caron Butler .75 2.00
MECM Corey Maggette .75 2.00
MECP Chris Paul 2.00 5.00
MEDH Dwight Howard 1.25 3.00
MEDN Dirk Nowitzki 2.50 6.00
MEDR Dennis Rodman 2.00 5.00
MEDW Deron Williams .75 2.00
MEDWA Dwyane Wade 2.00 5.00
MEDWE David West .75 2.00
MEDWI Dominique Wilkins 1.50 4.00
MEGA Gilbert Arenas 1.00 2.50
MEGO Greg Oden .60 1.50
MEJJ Joe Johnson .75 2.00
MEJK Jason Kidd 1.50 4.00
MEJW Jerry West 2.00 5.00
MEKB Kobe Bryant 8.00 20.00
MEKD Kevin Durant 4.00 10.00
MEKG Kevin Garnett 2.50 6.00
MEKM Kevin Martin .75 2.00
MELA LaMarcus Aldridge 1.00 2.50
MELB Larry Bird 3.00 8.00
MELJ LeBron James 8.00 20.00
MEMG Manu Ginobili 2.00 5.00
MEMJ Magic Johnson 3.00 8.00
MEMM Mike Miller .75 2.00
MEMR Michael Redd .75 2.00
MEPG Pau Gasol 1.25 3.00
MEPP Paul Pierce 1.50 4.00
MERG Rudy Gay 1.00 2.50
MESN Steve Nash 2.00 5.00
MESO Shaquille O'Neal 3.00 8.00
METD Tim Duncan 2.50 6.00
METM Tracy McGrady 1.50 4.00
METP Tony Parker 1.25 3.00
MEVC Vince Carter 2.00 5.00
MEYJ Yi Jianlian 1.25 3.00
MEYM Yao Ming 2.50 6.00

2008-09 Topps Treasury Mini Exclusives Autographs

ONE MINI CARD PER RIP CARD
BD Baron Davis 10.00 25.00
BL Brook Lopez 10.00 25.00
BR Brandon Roy 6.00 15.00
CA Carmelo Anthony 30.00 80.00
CB Chris Bosh 12.00 30.00
CBO Carlos Boozer 8.00 20.00
CP Chris Paul 40.00 100.00
DJA D.J. Augustin 8.00 20.00
DR Derrick Rose 30.00 80.00
DW Dwyane Wade 30.00 60.00
EG Eric Gordon 12.00 30.00
GO Greg Oden 5.00 12.00
JB Jerryd Bayless 6.00 15.00
JJH J.J. Hickson 5.00 12.00
KL Kevin Love 15.00 40.00
MB Michael Beasley 8.00 20.00
MM Mike Miller 8.00 20.00
OJM O.J. Mayo 6.00 15.00
RL Robin Lopez 6.00 15.00
YJ Yi Jianlian 10.00 25.00

2008-09 Topps Treasury Relics

AB Andrea Bargnani 2.50 6.00
AH Al Horford 3.00 8.00
AT Al Thornton 2.00 5.00
CB Corey Brewer 2.50 6.00
CF Channing Frye 2.00 5.00
DW Dwyane Wade 6.00 15.00
GO Greg Oden 2.00 5.00
JC Javaris Crittenton 2.00 5.00
JG Jeff Green 2.50 6.00
JH Josh Howard 2.50 6.00
JJ Jarrett Jack 2.50 6.00
JO Jermaine O'Neal 3.00 8.00
JT Jason Terry 2.50 6.00
KB Kobe Bryant 40.00 100.00
PG Pau Gasol 4.00 10.00
RJ Richard Jefferson 2.50 6.00
SC Sam Cassell 2.50 6.00
SO Shaquille O'Neal 10.00 25.00
TY Thaddeus Young 2.50 6.00
DWI Deron Williams 2.50 6.00
JTI Jamaal Tinsley 2.00 5.00

2008-09 Topps Treasury Rip Cards

PRINT RUN 299 SER.#'d SETS
*BRONZE: .5X TO 1.25X BASE HI
BRONZE PRINT RUN 99 SER.#'d SETS
*SILVER: .6X TO 1.5X BASE HI
SILVER PRINT RUN 25 SETS
1 Kobe Bryant 20.00 50.00
2 Chris Paul 10.00 25.00
3 Tim Duncan 10.00 25.00
4 Vince Carter 8.00 20.00
5 LeBron James 20.00 50.00
6 Dwight Howard 10.00 25.00
7 Steve Nash 10.00 25.00
8 Carmelo Anthony 10.00 25.00
9 Pau Gasol 6.00 15.00
10 Yi Jianlian 8.00 20.00
11 Deron Williams 10.00 25.00
12 Joe Johnson 6.00 15.00
13 Yao Ming 10.00 25.00
14 Rudy Gay 6.00 15.00
15 Kevin Garnett 10.00 25.00
16 Tony Parker 8.00 20.00
17 Allen Iverson 8.00 20.00
18 David West 6.00 15.00
19 Shaquille O'Neal 12.00 30.00
20 Dwyane Wade 10.00 25.00
21 Paul Pierce 10.00 25.00
22 Mike Miller 6.00 15.00
23 Kevin Martin 10.00 25.00
24 Gilbert Arenas 10.00 25.00
25 Dirk Nowitzki 10.00 25.00
26 Amare Stoudemire 8.00 20.00
27 Chris Bosh 10.00 25.00
28 Corey Maggette 6.00 15.00
29 Andre Iguodala 6.00 15.00
30 Greg Oden 6.00 15.00
31 Baron Davis 6.00 15.00
32 Carlos Boozer 6.00 15.00
33 Ben Gordon 8.00 20.00
34 Michael Redd 8.00 20.00
35 Manu Ginobili 8.00 20.00
36 Caron Butler 6.00 15.00
37 Tracy McGrady 8.00 20.00
38 Al Horford 6.00 15.00
39 Brandon Roy 8.00 20.00
40 Kevin Durant 20.00 50.00
41 Jason Kidd 8.00 20.00
42 LaMarcus Aldridge 6.00 15.00
43 Al Thornton 6.00 15.00
44 Andrei Kirilenko 6.00 15.00
45 Jerry West 8.00 20.00
46 Bill Russell 8.00 20.00
47 Dennis Rodman 8.00 20.00
48 Dominique Wilkins 6.00 15.00
49 Larry Bird 15.00 40.00
50 Magic Johnson 12.00 30.00

2008-09 Topps Treasury Rookie Autographs

STATED ODDS 1:23 PACKS
*BRONZE: .5X TO 1.25X BASE HI
BRONZE PRINT RUN 50 SETS
*SILVER: .6X TO 1.5X BASE HI
SILVER PRINT RUN 25 SER.#'d SETS
121 Derrick Rose 150.00 400.00
122 Michael Beasley 5.00 12.00
123 O.J. Mayo 4.00 10.00
124 Russell Westbrook 150.00 400.00
125 Kevin Love 25.00 60.00
126 Danilo Gallinari 8.00 20.00
127 Eric Gordon 12.00 30.00
128 Joe Alexander 3.00 8.00
129 D.J. Augustin 5.00 12.00
130 Brook Lopez 6.00 15.00
131 Jerryd Bayless 4.00 10.00
132 Brandon Rush 3.00 8.00
133 Anthony Randolph 3.00 8.00
134 Robin Lopez 4.00 10.00
135 Courtney Lee 4.00 10.00
136 Darrell Arthur 4.00 10.00
137 Joey Dorsey 3.00 8.00
138 Mario Chalmers 5.00 12.00
139 DeAndre Jordan 6.00 15.00
140 Kosta Koufos 3.00 8.00

2008-09 Topps Treasury Rookie Medallions

STATED PRINT RUN 19 SER.#'d SETS
AR Anthony Randolph 12.00 30.00
BL Brook Lopez 25.00 60.00
BR Brandon Rush 12.00 30.00
DA Darrell Arthur 15.00 40.00
DG Danilo Gallinari 30.00 80.00
DJA D.J. Augustin 20.00 50.00
DR Derrick Rose 80.00 200.00
EG Eric Gordon 30.00 80.00
JA Joe Alexander 12.00 30.00
JB Jerryd Bayless 15.00 40.00
KL Kevin Love 40.00 100.00
MB Michael Beasley 20.00 50.00
OJM O.J. Mayo 15.00 40.00
RL Robin Lopez 15.00 40.00
RW Russell Westbrook 100.00 250.00

2008-09 Topps Treasury They're Money Rip Cards

STATED PRINT RUN 42 SER.#'d SETS
1 Kobe Bryant 200.00 500.00
2 LeBron James 300.00 600.00
3 Carmelo Anthony 60.00 120.00
4 Kevin Garnett 50.00 120.00
5 Allen Iverson 50.00 120.00
8 Dirk Nowitzki 40.00 100.00
10 Chris Paul 75.00 150.00

2006-07 Topps Triple Threads

1-100 PRINT RUN 899 SER.#'d SETS
JSY AU RC PRINT RUN 99 SER.#'d SETS
1 Amare Stoudemire 1.00 2.50
2 Dirk Nowitzki 2.50 6.00
3 Dwyane Wade 2.00 5.00
4 Allen Iverson 2.50 6.00
5 LeBron James 8.00 20.00
6 Tracy McGrady 1.50 4.00
7 Ben Wallace 1.25 3.00
8 Jason Richardson 1.00 2.50
9 Vince Carter 2.00 5.00
10 Joe Johnson 1.00 2.50
11 Paul Pierce 1.50 4.00
12 Gerald Wallace .75 2.00
13 Elton Brand .75 2.00
14 Gilbert Arenas 1.00 2.50
15 Marcus Camby .75 2.00
16 Andrew Bogut .75 2.00
17 Stephon Marbury 1.25 3.00
18 Kevin Garnett 2.50 6.00
19 Al Harrington .75 2.00
20 Tim Duncan 2.50 6.00
21 Pau Gasol 1.50 4.00
22 Kobe Bryant 8.00 20.00
23 Dwight Howard 1.25 3.00
24 Jarrett Jack .75 2.00
25 T.J. Ford .60 1.50
26 Ron Artest 1.00 2.50
27 Deron Williams .75 2.00
28 Rasheed Wallace 1.25 3.00
29 Shaquille O'Neal 4.00 10.00
30 Ray Allen 1.50 4.00
31 Peja Stojakovic .75 2.00
32 Jermaine O'Neal 1.00 2.50
33 Larry Hughes .75 2.00
34 Brad Miller .75 2.00
35 Caron Butler .75 2.00
36 Andre Miller .75 2.00
37 Kirk Hinrich .75 2.00
38 Andrei Kirilenko .75 2.00
39 Charlie Villanueva .60 1.50
40 Sebastian Telfair .60 1.50
41 Josh Howard .75 2.00
42 Emeka Okafor .75 2.00
43 Danny Granger .75 2.00
44 Tony Parker 1.50 4.00
45 Zach Randolph 1.25 3.00
46 Ricky Davis .75 2.00
47 Chris Webber 1.25 3.00
48 Mike Bibby 1.00 2.50
49 Troy Murphy .60 1.50
50 Josh Smith .60 1.50
51 Steve Nash 2.00 5.00
52 Chris Paul 2.00 5.00
53 Rashard Lewis .75 2.00
54 Ben Gordon .75 2.00
55 Mehmet Okur .60 1.50
56 Chris Bosh 1.25 3.00
57 Drew Gooden .75 2.00
58 Corey Maggette .75 2.00
59 Eddy Curry .75 2.00
60 Yao Ming 2.50 6.00
61 Al Jefferson .60 1.50
62 Smush Parker .60 1.50
63 Jason Kidd 1.50 4.00
64 Hakim Warrick .60 1.50
65 Richard Hamilton 1.00 2.50
66 Luke Ridnour .75 2.00
67 Raymond Felton .60 1.50
68 Andre Iguodala .75 2.00
69 Jason Terry .75 2.00
70 Richard Jefferson .75 2.00
71 Lamar Odom .75 2.00
72 Jameer Nelson .60 1.50
73 Mike James .60 1.50
74 Antawn Jamison .75 2.00
75 Shaun Livingston .75 2.00
76 Manu Ginobili 2.00 5.00
77 Antoine Walker 1.00 2.50
78 Desmond Mason .60 1.50
79 Channing Frye .60 1.50
80 Morris Peterson .60 1.50
81 Michael Redd .75 2.00
82 Shawn Marion 1.00 2.50
83 Bonzi Wells .60 1.50
84 Chauncey Billups 1.25 3.00
85 Baron Davis 1.00 2.50
86 Carmelo Anthony 1.50 4.00
87 Brandon Roy RC 3.00 8.00
88 Rudy Gay RC 2.00 5.00
89 Tyrus Thomas RC 1.25 3.00
90 LaMarcus Aldridge RC 4.00 10.00
91 Wilt Chamberlain 5.00 12.00
92 Larry Bird 5.00 12.00
93 Isiah Thomas 2.50 6.00
94 Bernard King 1.25 3.00
95 Elgin Baylor 3.00 8.00
96 Oscar Robertson 4.00 10.00
97 Walt Frazier 2.00 5.00
98 Chris Mullin 1.50 4.00
99 Bill Laimbeer 1.25 3.00
100 George Gervin 2.50 6.00
101 Dee Brown JSY AU RC 4.00 10.00
102 Renaldo Balkman JSY AU RC 5.00 12.00
103 Maurice Ager JSY AU RC 4.00 10.00
104 Shelden Williams JSY AU RC 4.00 10.00
105 Rodney Carney JSY AU RC 4.00 10.00
106 J.J. Redick JSY AU RC 12.00 30.00
107 Hilton Armstrong JSY AU RC 4.00 10.00
108 Craig Smith JSY AU RC 5.00 12.00
109 Kyle Lowry JSY AU RC 20.00 50.00
110 Josh Boone JSY AU RC 4.00 10.00
111 Saer Sene JSY AU RC 4.00 10.00
112 Jorge Garbajosa JSY AU RC 5.00 12.00
113 Paul Davis JSY AU RC 4.00 10.00
114 Thabo Sefolosha JSY AU RC 5.00 12.00
115 Shannon Brown JSY AU RC 4.00 10.00
116 Bobby Jones JSY AU RC 4.00 10.00
117 Jordan Farmar JSY AU RC 5.00 12.00
118 Allan Ray JSY AU RC 4.00 10.00
119 Randy Foye JSY AU RC 5.00 12.00
120 Marcus Williams JSY AU RC 4.00 10.00
121 Adam Morrison JSY AU RC 5.00 12.00
122 Cedric Simmons JSY AU RC 4.00 10.00
123 Rajon Rondo JSY AU RC 20.00 50.00
124 Patrick O'Bryant JSY AU RC 4.00 10.00
125 Shawne Williams JSY AU RC 4.00 10.00
126 Mardy Collins JSY AU RC 4.00 10.00
127 Steve Novak JSY AU RC 5.00 12.00
128 Ronnie Brewer JSY AU RC 6.00 15.00
129 Quincy Douby JSY AU RC 4.00 10.00
130 Andrea Bargnani JSY AU RC 5.00 12.00

2006-07 Topps Triple Threads Emerald

*EMERALD: .5X TO 1.25X BASE HI
1-100 EMERALD PRINT RUN 199 SER.#'d SETS
101-130 EMERALD PRINT RUN 50 SER.#'d SETS

2006-07 Topps Triple Threads Gold

*GOLD: .75X TO 2X BASE HI
1-100 PRINT RUN 99 SER.#'d SETS
101-130 PRINT RUN 25 SER.#'d SETS

2006-07 Topps Triple Threads Sapphire

*1-100 SAPPH: 1.25X TO 3X BASE HI
1-100 PRINT RUN 25 SER.#'d SETS
101-130 PRINT RUN 10 SER.#'d SETS

2006-07 Topps Triple Threads Sepia

SEPIA: 4X TO 1X BASE HI
STATED PRINT RUN 299 SER.#'d SETS

2006-07 Topps Triple Threads Relics

PRINT RUN 36 SER.#'d SETS
EACH PLAYER HAS THREE VERSIONS
ALL VERSIONS SAME VALUE
*EMERALD: .6X TO 1.5X BASE HI
EMERALD PRINT RUN 18 SER.#'d SETS
*SEPIA: .5X TO 1.25X BASE HI
SEPIA PRINT RUN 27 SER.#'d SETS
1 Adam Morrison NBA 4.00 10.00
4 Amare Stoudemire NBA 5.00 12.00
7 Andrea Bargnani NBA 4.00 10.00
10 Andrei Kirilenko AK47 4.00 10.00
13 Antawn Jamison NBA 4.00 10.00
16 Ben Wallace NBA 6.00 15.00
19 Brandon Roy NBA 10.00 25.00
22 Carmelo Anthony Nuggets 8.00 20.00
25 Charlie Villanueva NBA 3.00 8.00
28 Chauncey Billups NBA 6.00 15.00
31 Chris Paul NBA 10.00 25.00
34 Dirk Nowitzki Symbol 12.00 30.00
37 Dominique Wilkins HOF 8.00 20.00
40 Dwight Howard NBA 6.00 15.00
43 Dwyane Wade NBA 10.00 25.00
46 Isiah Thomas HOF 6.00 15.00
49 J.J. Redick NBA 10.00 25.00
52 Jason Kidd Symbol 8.00 20.00
55 Josh Smith NBA 3.00 8.00
58 Kevin Garnett KG 12.00 30.00
61 Kobe Bryant NBA 75.00 200.00
64 LaMarcus Aldridge Blazers 12.00 30.00
67 Larry Bird #33 20.00 50.00
70 Magic Johnson #32 15.00 40.00
73 Manu Ginobili Spurs 10.00 25.00
76 Pau Gasol #16 8.00 20.00
79 Paul Pierce #34 8.00 20.00
82 Rudy Gay NBA 6.00 15.00
85 Shaquille O'Neal MVP 20.00 50.00
88 Shawn Marion NBA 5.00 12.00
91 Steve Nash #13 10.00 25.00
94 Tim Duncan #21 12.00 30.00
97 Tracy McGrady NBA 8.00 20.00
100 Vince Carter NBA 10.00 25.00
103 Yao Ming Rockets 12.00 30.00

2006-07 Topps Triple Threads Relics Autographs

PRINT RUN 36 SER.#'d SETS
EACH PLAYER HAS THREE VERSIONS
ALL VERSIONS SAME VALUE
*EMERALD: .6X TO 1.5X BASE HI
EMERALD PRINT RUN 18 SER.#'d SETS
1 Adam Morrison #35 6.00 15.00
4 Chauncey Billups NBA 10.00 25.00
7 Andre Iguodala NBA 6.00 15.00
10 Andrea Bargnani Raptors 8.00 20.00
13 Andrew Bogut NBA 6.00 15.00
16 Ben Gordon Bulls 8.00 20.00
19 Bill Walton NBA 10.00 25.00
22 Bob Lanier NBA 8.00 20.00
25 Channing Frye NBA 6.00 15.00
28 Charlie Villanueva NBA 6.00 15.00
31 Chris Bosh Raptors 15.00 40.00
34 Chris Duhon NBA 6.00 15.00
37 Devin Harris NBA 6.00 15.00
40 Dominique Wilkins HOF 12.00 30.00
43 Dwyane Wade NBA 40.00 100.00
46 Earl Monroe #15 15.00 40.00
49 Emeka Okafor #50 6.00 15.00
52 Gerald Wallace NBA 6.00 15.00
55 Hakim Warrick NBA 6.00 15.00
58 John Stockton #12 40.00 100.00
61 Isiah Thomas HOF 15.00 40.00
64 J.J. Redick Magic 15.00 40.00
67 Jameer Nelson NBA 6.00 15.00
70 Jarrett Jack NBA 6.00 15.00
73 Josh Smith Dunking 6.00 15.00
76 Larry Bird Legend 75.00 200.00
77 Larry Bird BOS 75.00 200.00
78 Larry Bird #33 75.00 200.00
79 Luol Deng NBA 6.00 15.00
82 Magic Johnson #32 75.00 200.00
85 Dennis Rodman #91 30.00 80.00
88 Martell Webster Blazers 6.00 15.00
91 Randy Foye NBA 6.00 15.00
94 Ray Allen NBA 25.00 50.00
97 Luke Walton NBA 6.00 15.00
100 Ronnie Brewer NBA 6.00 15.00
103 Andrei Kirilenko AK47 6.00 15.00
106 Jermaine O'Neal NBA 6.00 15.00
109 Carmelo Anthony Nuggets 20.00 50.00
112 Shelden Williams #33 6.00 15.00
115 T.J. Ford NBA 6.00 15.00
118 Vince Carter NBA 40.00 100.00

2006-07 Topps Triple Threads Relics Combos

PRINT RUN 36 SER.#'d SETS
*EMERALD: .5X TO 1.25X BASE HI
EMERALD PRINT RUN 18 SER.#'d SETS
*SEPIA: .4X TO 1X BASE HI
SEPIA PRINT RUN 27 SER.#'d SETS
1 Morrison/Wade/Redick 12.00 30.00
2 Amare/Nash/Marion 15.00 40.00
3 Marion/Nash/Barbosa 10.00 25.00
4 Yao/T-Mac/Novak 12.50 30.00
5 Bargnani/Bogut/D.Howard 10.00 25.00
6 Wade/Shaq/Mourning 40.00 100.00
7 Wade/Bosh/Carmelo 15.00 40.00
8 T-Mac/Vince/Kobe 75.00 200.00
9 Kobe/Odom/Magic 75.00 200.00
10 Allen/Lewis/Ridnour 10.00 25.00
11 Duncan/Ginobili/Parker 15.00 40.00
12 Simmons/Redick/Sd.Williams 10.00 25.00
13 Gay/Morrison/Carney 10.00 25.00
14 Foye/Ray/Lowry 10.00 25.00
15 Allen/Gordon/Okafor 10.00 25.00
16 Barry/Allen/Bird 15.00 40.00
17 Bird/Magic/Isiah 30.00 80.00
18 Isiah/Hamilton/Billups 10.00 25.00
19 Garnett/Duncan/Amare 12.50 30.00
20 Morrison/Bird/Redick 15.00 50.00
21 Dirk/Bargnani/Kirilenko 10.00 25.00
22 D.Howard/Okafor/Gordon 10.00 25.00
23 D.Wilkins/J.Smith/Childress 12.50 30.00
24 Iggy/D.Wilkins/Vince 12.50 30.00
25 D.Howard/Nelson/Hill 10.00 25.00
26 Vince/Rasheed/Jamison 10.00 25.00
28 Morrison/Bogut/Okafor 10.00 25.00
29 Nash/Magic/Kidd 20.00 50.00
30 C.Paul/Okafor/Amare 10.00 25.00
31 Gasol/Brand/Vince 10.00 25.00
32 Duncan/Iverson/Kidd 15.00 40.00
33 Hill/Richmond/Shaq 15.00 30.00
34 Gay/Aldridge/Foye 10.00 25.00
35 Worthy/Shaq/Duncan 15.00 40.00
36 Bird/Magic/Isiah 30.00 80.00
37 Barry/M.Malone/D.Wade 12.50 30.00
38 Parker/Arenas/Billups 10.00 25.00
39 Redd/Ginobili/Arenas 10.00 25.00
40 Iverson/Kobe/T-Mac 75.00 200.00
41 Isiah/Magic/Bird 20.00 50.00
42 Garnett/Amare/Kobe 75.00 200.00
43 Duncan/Shaq/Garnett 15.00 40.00
44 Kobe/Iverson/K.Malone 75.00 200.00
45 D.Wilkins/Drexler/Erving 25.00 60.00
46 Duncan/Gervin/Parker 12.50 30.00
47 M.Malone/Iggy/Erving 15.00 40.00
48 J.West/Magic/Baylor 25.00 50.00
49 Marbury/E.Monroe/Frye 10.00 25.00
50 Magic/Kobe/Baylor 25.00 50.00
51 Lanier/Isiah/Rodman 15.00 40.00
52 Yao/Duncan/Iverson 15.00 40.00
53 Bird/Cowens/Walton 25.00 60.00
54 Bosh/Redick/Felton 10.00 25.00
55 Webber/Rose/Howard 20.00 50.00

2006-07 Topps Triple Threads Relics Combos Autographs

PRINT RUN 36 SER.#'d SETS
*EMERALD: .5X TO 1.25X BASE HI
EMERALD PRINT RUN 18 SER.#'d SETS
1 Wade/Morrison/Anthony 60.00 150.00
2 Bird/Magic/Barry 100.00 250.00
3 Nique/J.Smith/Vince 40.00 100.00
4 Elgin/Earl/Isiah 50.00 120.00
5 Bird/Morrison/Stockton 75.00 200.00
6 Walton/Magic/Bird 125.00 300.00
7 Lanier/Malone/Walton 50.00 120.00
8 Wade/Magic/Bird 150.00 400.00
9 Bird/Magic/Isiah 125.00 300.00
10 Bargnani/Morrison/Foye 20.00 50.00

2007-08 Topps Triple Threads

1-100 PRINT RUN 333 SER.#'d SETS
ROOKIE PRINT RUN 99 SER.#'d SETS
1 Yao Ming 4.00 10.00
2 Michael Redd 1.25 3.00
3 Dwyane Wade 3.00 8.00
4 Chris Bosh 2.00 5.00
5 Kevin Garnett 4.00 10.00
6 Sam Cassell 1.25 3.00
7 Ben Gordon 1.25 3.00
8 Deron Williams 1.25 3.00
9 Andre Iguodala 1.50 4.00
10 Mike Bibby 1.50 4.00
11 Chauncey Billups 2.00 5.00
12 Dwight Howard 2.00 5.00
13 Steve Nash 3.00 8.00
14 Raymond Felton 1.25 3.00
15 Carmelo Anthony 2.50 6.00
16 Pau Gasol 2.50 6.00
17 Brandon Roy 2.00 5.00
18 Chris Wilcox 1.00 2.50
19 Josh Howard 1.25 3.00
20 Ray Allen 2.50 6.00
21 Tim Duncan 4.00 10.00
22 Tayshaun Prince 1.50 4.00
23 LeBron James 12.00 30.00
24 Kobe Bryant 12.00 30.00
25 Al Jefferson 1.00 2.50
26 Stephon Marbury 2.00 5.00
27 Mike Miller 1.25 3.00
28 Jason Terry 1.25 3.00
29 Corey Maggette 1.25 3.00
30 Allen Iverson 4.00 10.00
31 Tracy McGrady 2.50 6.00
32 Shaquille O'Neal 6.00 15.00
33 Ben Wallace 2.00 5.00
34 Paul Pierce 2.50 6.00
35 Vince Carter 3.00 8.00
36 Chris Paul 3.00 8.00
37 Kyle Korver 1.50 4.00
38 LaMarcus Aldridge 1.50 4.00
39 Al Harrington 1.25 3.00
40 Gilbert Arenas 1.50 4.00
41 Dirk Nowitzki 4.00 10.00
42 David Lee 1.00 2.50
43 Gerald Wallace 1.25 3.00
44 Luke Walton 1.25 3.00
45 Manu Ginobili 3.00 8.00
46 Charlie Villanueva 1.00 2.50
47 Andrei Kirilenko 1.25 3.00
48 Richard Jefferson 1.25 3.00
49 Joe Johnson 1.25 3.00
50 Zach Randolph 1.50 4.00
51 Andrea Bargnani 1.00 2.50
52 Elton Brand 1.25 3.00
53 Anderson Varejao 1.00 2.50
54 Kirk Hinrich 1.50 4.00
55 Baron Davis 1.25 3.00
56 Shane Battier 1.25 3.00
57 Jameer Nelson 1.00 2.50
58 Antawn Jamison 1.25 3.00
59 Andrew Bynum 1.00 2.50
60 Kevin Martin 1.25 3.00
61 Amare Stoudemire 1.50 4.00
62 Randy Foye 1.25 3.00
63 Marcus Camby 1.25 3.00
64 Larry Hughes 1.25 3.00
65 Luol Deng 1.25 3.00
66 Danny Granger 1.00 2.50
67 Eddy Curry 1.00 2.50
68 David West 1.25 3.00
69 Tony Parker 2.50 6.00
70 Jason Kidd 2.50 6.00
71 Monta Ellis 1.25 3.00
72 Richard Hamilton 2.00 5.00
73 Udonis Haslem 1.00 2.50
74 Rudy Gay 1.25 3.00
75 Carlos Boozer 1.25 3.00
76 Luke Ridnour 1.25 3.00
77 Jermaine O'Neal 1.50 4.00
78 Ricky Davis 1.25 3.00
79 Desmond Mason 1.00 2.50
80 Lamar Odom 1.25 3.00
81 T.J. Ford 1.00 2.50
82 Jarrett Jack 1.00 2.50
83 Ron Artest 1.50 4.00
84 Sam Dalembert 1.00 2.50
85 Josh Smith 1.00 2.50
86 Tyson Chandler 1.50 4.00
87 Shawn Marion 1.50 4.00
88 Caron Butler 1.25 3.00
89 Jason Richardson 1.50 4.00
90 Rashard Lewis 1.25 3.00
91 Larry Bird 6.00 15.00
92 Isiah Thomas 1.50 4.00
93 Magic Johnson 6.00 15.00
94 John Stockton 3.00 8.00
95 Bill Russell 5.00 12.00
96 Dennis Rodman 4.00 10.00
97 Dominique Wilkins 2.50 6.00
98 David Robinson 3.00 8.00
99 Bill Walton 2.00 5.00
100 Jerry West 4.00 10.00
101 Greg Oden RC 2.50 6.00
102 Daequan Cook RC 2.00 5.00
103 Morris Almond RC 1.50 4.00
104 Sean Williams RC 1.50 4.00
105 Arron Afflalo RC 2.00 5.00
106 Coby Karl RC 1.50 4.00
107 Adam Haluska RC 1.50 4.00
108 Corey Brewer RC 2.00 5.00
109 Herbert Hill RC 1.50 4.00
110 Nick Young RC 2.50 6.00
111 Joakim Noah RC 2.50 6.00
112 Mike Conley Jr. RC 6.00 15.00
113 Kyrylo Fesenko RC 1.50 4.00
114 Aaron Brooks RC 2.00 5.00
115 Marco Belinelli RC 2.00 5.00
116 Juan Carlos Navarro RC 2.00 5.00
117 Jared Dudley RC 2.00 5.00
118 Rodney Stuckey RC 1.50 4.00
119 JamesOn Curry RC 1.50 4.00
120 Gabe Pruitt RC 1.50 4.00
121 Acie Law RC 1.50 4.00
122 Dominic McGuire RC 1.50 4.00
123 Ramon Sessions RC 2.00 5.00
124 Jeff Green RC 2.00 5.00
125 Wilson Chandler RC 2.00 5.00
126 Kosta Perovic RC 1.50 4.00
127 Josh McRoberts RC 1.50 4.00
128 Jason Smith RC 1.50 4.00
129 Cheik Samb RC 1.50 4.00
130 Stephane Lasme RC 1.50 4.00
131 Brandon Wallace RC 1.50 4.00
132 Alando Tucker RC 1.50 4.00
133 Javaris Crittenton RC 1.50 4.00
134 Chris Richard RC 1.50 4.00
135 Kevin Durant RC 100.00 250.00
136 Al Thornton RC 1.50 4.00
137 Carl Landry RC 1.50 4.00
138 Yi Jianlian RC 3.00 8.00
139 Brandan Wright RC 2.00 5.00
140 Nick Fazekas RC 1.50 4.00
141 Al Horford RC 6.00 15.00
142 Jermareo Davidson RC 1.50 4.00
143 D.J. Strawberry RC 1.50 4.00
144 Glen Davis RC 2.00 5.00
145 Julian Wright RC 1.50 4.00
146 Spencer Hawes RC 1.50 4.00
147 Taurean Green RC 1.50 4.00
148 Luis Scola RC 2.50 6.00
149 Aaron Gray RC 1.50 4.00
150 Thaddeus Young RC 2.50 6.00

2007-08 Topps Triple Threads Emerald

*1-100 EMERALD: 1X TO 2.5X BASE HI
*101-150 EMERALD RCs: .75X TO 2X BASE HI
1-100 EMERALD PRINT RUN 66 SER.#'d SETS
101-150 EMERALD RC PRINT RUN 33 SETS

2007-08 Topps Triple Threads Gold

*1-100 GOLD: 1.25X TO 3X BASE HI
1-100 PRINT RUN 33 SER.#'d SETS
101-150 PRINT RUN 3 SER.#'d SET

2007-08 Topps Triple Threads Sepia

*1-100 SEPIA: .75X TO 2X BASE HI
*101-150 SEPIA RCs: .6X TO 1.5X BASE HI
1-100 SEPIA PRINT RUN 99 SER.#'d SETS
101-150 SEPIA RC PRINT RUN 66 SETS
135 Kevin Durant 500.00 1,000.00

2007-08 Topps Triple Threads Relics

PRINT RUN 18 SER.#'d SETS
THREE VERSIONS OF EACH EXIST
ALL VERSIONS SAME VALUE
*SEPIA: .75X TO 2X BASE HI
SEPIA PRINT RUN NINE SETS
1 Kobe Bryant KB24 200.00 500.00
2 Kobe Bryant Ball 125.00 300.00
3 Kobe Bryant 81 Points 500.00 1,000.00
4 Allen Iverson Nuggets 25.00 60.00
5 Allen Iverson Answer 25.00 60.00
6 Allen Iverson MVP 25.00 60.00
7 Gilbert Arenas Ball 10.00 25.00
8 Gilbert Arenas Hibachi 10.00 25.00
9 Gilbert Arenas WAS 10.00 25.00
10 Kevin Garnett #5 25.00 60.00
11 Kevin Garnett Shamrock 25.00 60.00
12 Kevin Garnett Big Ticket 25.00 60.00
13 Dwight Howard 12.00 30.00
14 Dwight Howard Dunk 12.00 30.00
15 Dwight Howard Magic 12.00 30.00
16 Chris Paul ROY 20.00 50.00
17 Chris Paul Shoot 20.00 50.00
18 Chris Paul Hornets 20.00 50.00
19 Steve Nash APG 20.00 50.00
20 Steve Nash Floor General 20.00 50.00
21 Steve Nash Captain Canada 20.00 50.00
22 Tim Duncan Slam Duncan 25.00 60.00
23 Tim Duncan Spurs 25.00 60.00
24 Tim Duncan MVP 25.00 60.00
25 Jason Kidd JK5 15.00 40.00
26 Jason Kidd Trip.Double 15.00 40.00
27 Jason Kidd APG 15.00 40.00
28 Tracy McGrady Tmac 15.00 40.00
29 Tracy McGrady #1 15.00 40.00
30 Tracy McGrady Ball 15.00 40.00
31 Dirk Nowitzki MVP 25.00 60.00
32 Dirk Nowitzki All-Star 25.00 60.00
33 Dirk Nowitzki 3PT 25.00 60.00
34 Amare Stoudemire ROY 10.00 25.00
35 Amare Stoudemire Double 10.00 25.00
36 Amare Stoudemire Dunk 10.00 25.00
37 Joe Johnson NBA 8.00 20.00
38 Joe Johnson ATL 8.00 20.00
39 Joe Johnson Ball 8.00 20.00
40 Pau Gasol ROY 15.00 40.00
41 Pau Gasol Grizzlies 15.00 40.00
42 Pau Gasol Dunk 15.00 40.00
43 Baron Davis GSW 8.00 20.00
44 Baron Davis #5 8.00 20.00
45 Baron Davis Shoot 8.00 20.00
46 Richard Hamilton DET 12.00 30.00
47 Richard Hamilton RIP 12.00 30.00
48 Richard Hamilton Ball 12.00 30.00
49 Manu Ginobili Argentina 20.00 50.00
50 Manu Ginobili Ball 20.00 50.00
51 Manu Ginobili Manu 20.00 50.00
52 Lamar Odom LAL 8.00 20.00
53 Lamar Odom #7 8.00 20.00
54 Lamar Odom Shoot 8.00 20.00
55 Josh Smith #5 6.00 15.00
56 Josh Smith Jsmooth 6.00 15.00
57 Josh Smith Dunk 6.00 15.00
58 Yao Ming Chinese 25.00 60.00
59 Yao Ming #1 Pick 25.00 60.00
60 Yao Ming Ball 25.00 60.00
61 Jermaine O'Neal Pacers 10.00 25.00
62 Jermaine O'Neal #7 10.00 25.00
63 Jermaine O'Neal Double 10.00 25.00
64 Michael Redd PTS 8.00 20.00
65 Michael Redd 3PT 8.00 20.00
66 Michael Redd Ball 8.00 20.00
67 Shawn Marion Suns 10.00 25.00
68 Shawn Marion Dunk 10.00 25.00
69 Shawn Marion All-Star 10.00 25.00
70 Josh Howard DAL 8.00 20.00
71 Josh Howard #5 8.00 20.00
72 Josh Howard NBA 8.00 20.00
73 Ben Wallace Big Ben 12.00 30.00
74 Ben Wallace Bulls 12.00 30.00
75 Ben Wallace Defense 12.00 30.00
76 Kevin Martin #23 8.00 20.00
77 Kevin Martin SAC 8.00 20.00
78 Kevin Martin NBA 8.00 20.00
79 Carmelo Anthony Ball 15.00 40.00
80 Carmelo Anthony Melo 15.00 40.00
81 Carmelo Anthony PTS 15.00 40.00
82 Mike Conley Jr. MEM 25.00 60.00
83 Mike Conley Jr. #11 25.00 60.00
84 Mike Conley Jr. NBA 25.00 60.00
85 Al Horford ATL 25.00 60.00
86 Al Horford #15 25.00 60.00
87 Al Horford NBA 25.00 60.00
88 Corey Brewer MIN 8.00 20.00
89 Corey Brewer #22 8.00 20.00
90 Corey Brewer NBA 8.00 20.00
91 Joakim Noah CHI 10.00 25.00
92 Joakim Noah NBA 10.00 25.00
93 Joakim Noah #13 10.00 25.00
94 Greg Oden #52 10.00 25.00
95 Greg Oden #1 Pick 10.00 25.00
96 Greg Oden POR 10.00 25.00
97 Eddy Curry NYK 6.00 15.00
98 Eddy Curry #34 6.00 15.00
99 Eddy Curry NBA 6.00 15.00
100 Mike Miller #33 8.00 20.00
101 Mike Miller MEM 8.00 20.00
102 Mike Miller Ball 8.00 20.00
103 Dwyane Wade Heat 20.00 50.00
104 Dwyane Wade Flash 20.00 50.00
105 Dwyane Wade DW3 20.00 50.00

2007-08 Topps Triple Threads Relics Autographs

PRINT RUN NINE SETS
THREE VERSIONS OF EACH CARD EXIST
ALL VERSIONS SAME VALUE
1 Dwyane Wade Heat 75.00 200.00
2 Dwyane Wade Flash 75.00 200.00
3 Dwyane Wade DW3 75.00 200.00
7 Nick Young NY1 25.00 60.00
8 Nick Young WAS 25.00 60.00
9 Nick Young Ball 25.00 60.00
10 Brandan Wright #32 12.00 30.00
11 Brandan Wright GSW 12.00 30.00
12 Brandan Wright Ball 12.00 30.00
13 Yi Jianlian YI 50.00 120.00
14 Yi Jianlian MIL 50.00 120.00
15 Yi Jianlian Chinese 50.00 120.00
19 Paul Pierce #34 50.00 120.00
20 Paul Pierce Ball 50.00 120.00
21 Paul Pierce Shamrock 50.00 120.00
22 Vince Carter Nets 100.00 250.00
23 Vince Carter Dunk 100.00 250.00
24 Vince Carter Vinsanity 100.00 250.00
25 Andre Iguodala 73ers 20.00 50.00
26 Andre Iguodala Dunk 20.00 50.00
27 Andre Iguodala AI9 20.00 50.00
28 Corey Maggette LAC 12.00 30.00
29 Corey Maggette #50 12.00 30.00
30 Corey Maggette NBA 12.00 30.00
31 Mickael Pietrus MP2 12.00 30.00
32 Mickael Pietrus GSW 12.00 30.00
33 Mickael Pietrus Shoot 12.00 30.00
34 Raymond Felton CHA 12.00 30.00
35 Raymond Felton Floor Gen. 12.00 30.00
36 Raymond Felton #20 12.00 30.00
37 Rajon Rondo Bean Town 40.00 100.00
38 Rajon Rondo BOS 40.00 100.00
39 Rajon Rondo Ball 40.00 100.00
40 Jarrett Jack POR 12.00 30.00
41 Jarrett Jack NBA 12.00 30.00
42 Jarrett Jack Ball 12.00 30.00
43 Leandro Barbosa 6th Man 12.00 30.00
44 Leandro Barbosa PHO 12.00 30.00
45 Leandro Barbosa #10 12.00 30.00
46 Craig Smith MIN 12.00 30.00
47 Craig Smith Dunk 12.00 30.00
48 Craig Smith #5 12.00 30.00
49 Magic Johnson Ball 100.00 250.00
50 Magic Johnson MVP 100.00 250.00
51 Magic Johnson Champ 100.00 250.00
52 Larry Bird MVP 100.00 250.00
53 Larry Bird 3PT 100.00 250.00
54 Larry Bird All-Star 100.00 250.00
55 Rick Barry GSW 25.00 60.00
56 Rick Barry Under Hand 25.00 60.00
57 Rick Barry FT% 25.00 60.00
58 Dominique Wilkins HHFilm 25.00 60.00
59 Dominique Wilkins Dunk 25.00 60.00
60 Dominique Wilkins 23 FTs 25.00 60.00
61 David Robinson Admiral 75.00 200.00
62 David Robinson #50 75.00 200.00
63 David Robinson MVP 75.00 200.00
64 Mike Miller MEM 12.00 30.00
65 Mike Miller #33 12.00 30.00
66 Mike Miller Ball 12.00 30.00
67 John Stockton APG 75.00 200.00
68 John Stockton Double 75.00 200.00
69 John Stockton SPG 75.00 200.00
70 Dennis Rodman Worm 100.00 250.00
71 Dennis Rodman RPG 100.00 250.00
72 Dennis Rodman Defense 100.00 250.00
73 Isiah Thomas ZEKE 30.00 80.00
74 Isiah Thomas MVP 30.00 80.00
75 Isiah Thomas Shoot 30.00 80.00
76 Ray Allen #20 50.00 120.00
77 Ray Allen Bean Town 50.00 120.00
78 Ray Allen 3PT 50.00 120.00
79 Gilbert Arenas Ball 15.00 40.00
80 Gilbert Arenas Hibachi 15.00 40.00
81 Gilbert Arenas WAS 15.00 40.00
82 David Lee #42 12.00 30.00
83 David Lee NYK 12.00 30.00
84 David Lee Lee 12.00 30.00
85 Bill Walton Bean Town 40.00 100.00
86 Bill Walton Shamrock 40.00 100.00
87 Bill Walton Red Head 40.00 100.00
88 Chauncey Billups Big Shot 30.00 80.00
89 Chauncey Billups Pistons 30.00 80.00
90 Chauncey Billups MVP 30.00 80.00
91 Al Jefferson MIN 12.00 30.00
92 Al Jefferson #25 12.00 30.00
93 Al Jefferson Dunk 12.00 30.00
94 Luke Walton Shoot 12.00 30.00
95 Luke Walton #4 12.00 30.00
96 Luke Walton Walton 12.00 30.00
97 Ben Gordon #7 20.00 50.00
98 Ben Gordon 3PT 20.00 50.00
99 Ben Gordon 6th Man 20.00 50.00
100 Shaquille O'Neal Double 125.00 300.00
101 Shaquille O'Neal Dunk 125.00 300.00
102 Shaquille O'Neal MVP 125.00 300.00
103 Carmelo Anthony Ball 100.00 250.00
104 Carmelo Anthony Melo 100.00 250.00
105 Carmelo Anthony PTS 100.00 250.00
106 Chris Paul ROY 75.00 200.00
107 Chris Paul Shoot 75.00 200.00
108 Chris Paul Hornets 75.00 200.00
109 Deron Williams Jazz 20.00 50.00
110 Deron Williams UTA 20.00 50.00
111 Deron Williams Ball 20.00 50.00
112 Antawn Jamison WAS 15.00 40.00
113 Antawn Jamison 6th Man 15.00 50.00
114 Antawn Jamison PTS 15.00 50.00
115 Joe Johnson ATL 15.00 40.00
116 Joe Johnson Ball 15.00 40.00
117 Joe Johnson Hawks #2 15.00 40.00
118 Ryan Gomes Wolves #8 12.00 30.00
119 Ryan Gomes Shoot 12.00 30.00
120 Ryan Gomes MIN 12.00 30.00
121 David Thompson #33 20.00 50.00
122 David Thompson All-Star 20.00 50.00
123 David Thompson DEN 20.00 50.00
124 Moses Malone HOF 30.00 80.00
125 Moses Malone PTS 30.00 80.00
126 Moses Malone MVP 30.00 80.00
127 Dwight Howard Magic 12 30.00 80.00
128 Dwight Howard Dunk 30.00 80.00
129 Dwight Howard REB 30.00 80.00
130 Thaddeus Young PHI 12.00 30.00
131 Thaddeus Young #21 12.00 30.00
132 Thaddeus Young Shoot 12.00 30.00
133 Adam Morrison Cats 35 12.00 30.00
134 Adam Morrison Ball 12.00 30.00
135 Adam Morrison 3PT 12.00 30.00

2007-08 Topps Triple Threads Relics Autographs Sepia

PRINT RUN FIVE SETS
THREE VERSIONS OF EACH CARD
UNLISTED VERSIONS SAME VALUE
1 Dwyane Wade Heat 75.00 200.00
2 Dwyane Wade Flash 75.00 200.00
3 Dwyane Wade DW3 75.00 200.00
4 Greg Oden #52 20.00 50.00
5 Greg Oden #1Pick 20.00 50.00
6 Greg Oden POR 20.00 50.00
13 Yi Jianlian YI 50.00 120.00
14 Yi Jianlian MIL 50.00 120.00
15 Yi Jianlian Chinese 50.00 120.00
16 Chris Bosh CB4 25.00 60.00
17 Chris Bosh TOR 25.00 60.00
18 Chris Bosh All-Star 25.00 60.00
19 Paul Pierce #34 50.00 120.00
20 Paul Pierce Ball 50.00 120.00
21 Paul Pierce Shamrock 50.00 120.00
22 Vince Carter Nets 100.00 250.00
23 Vince Carter Dunk 100.00 250.00
24 Vince Carter Vinsanity 100.00 250.00
25 Andre Iguodala 73ers 20.00 50.00
26 Andre Iguodala Dunk 20.00 50.00
27 Andre Iguodala AI9 20.00 50.00
28 Corey Maggette LAC 12.00 30.00
29 Corey Maggette #50 12.00 30.00
30 Corey Maggette NBA 12.00 30.00
31 Mickael Pietrus MP2 12.00 30.00
32 Mickael Pietrus GSW 12.00 30.00
33 Mickael Pietrus Shoot 12.00 30.00
34 Raymond Felton CHA 12.00 30.00
35 Raymond Felton Floor Gen. 12.00 30.00
36 Raymond Felton #20 12.00 30.00
37 Rajon Rondo Bean Town 40.00 100.00
38 Rajon Rondo BOS 40.00 100.00
39 Rajon Rondo Ball 40.00 100.00
40 Jarrett Jack POR 12.00 30.00
41 Jarrett Jack NBA 12.00 30.00
42 Jarrett Jack Ball 12.00 30.00
46 Craig Smith MIN 12.00 30.00
47 Craig Smith Dunk 12.00 30.00
48 Craig Smith #5 12.00 30.00
49 Magic Johnson Ball 100.00 250.00
50 Magic Johnson MVP 100.00 250.00
51 Magic Johnson Champ 100.00 250.00
52 Larry Bird MVP 100.00 250.00
53 Larry Bird 3PT 100.00 250.00
54 Larry Bird All-Star 100.00 250.00
55 Rick Barry GSW 25.00 60.00
56 Rick Barry Under Hand 25.00 60.00
57 Rick Barry FT 25.00 60.00
58 Dominique Wilkins HHFilm 25.00 60.00
59 Dominique Wilkins Dunk 25.00 60.00
60 Dominique Wilkins 23 FTs 25.00 60.00
64 Mike Miller MEM 12.00 30.00
65 Mike Miller #33 12.00 30.00
66 Mike Miller Ball 12.00 30.00
67 John Stockton APG 75.00 200.00
68 John Stockton Double 75.00 200.00
69 John Stockton SPG 75.00 200.00
73 Isiah Thomas ZEKE 30.00 80.00
74 Isiah Thomas MVP 30.00 80.00
75 Isiah Thomas Shoot 30.00 80.00
76 Ray Allen #20 50.00 120.00
77 Ray Allen Bean Town 50.00 120.00
78 Ray Allen 3PT 50.00 120.00
79 Gilbert Arenas Ball 15.00 40.00
80 Gilbert Arenas Hibachi 15.00 40.00
81 Gilbert Arenas WAS 15.00 40.00
85 Bill Walton Bean Town 40.00 100.00
86 Bill Walton Shamrock 40.00 100.00
87 Bill Walton Red Head 40.00 100.00
88 Chauncey Billups Big Shot 30.00 80.00
89 Chauncey Billups Pistons 30.00 80.00
90 Chauncey Billups MVP 30.00 80.00
94 Luke Walton Shoot 12.00 30.00
95 Luke Walton #4 12.00 30.00
96 Luke Walton Walton 12.00 30.00
97 Ben Gordon #7 20.00 50.00
98 Ben Gordon 3PT 20.00 50.00
99 Ben Gordon 6th Man 20.00 50.00
100 Shaquille O'Neal Double 125.00 300.00
101 Shaquille O'Neal Dunk 125.00 300.00
102 Shaquille O'Neal MVP 125.00 300.00
103 Carmelo Anthony Ball 100.00 250.00
104 Carmelo Anthony Melo 100.00 250.00
105 Carmelo Anthony PTS 100.00 250.00
106 Chris Paul ROY 75.00 200.00
107 Chris Paul Shoot 75.00 200.00
108 Chris Paul Hornets 75.00 200.00
109 Deron Williams Jazz 20.00 50.00
110 Deron Williams UTA 20.00 50.00
111 Deron Williams Ball 20.00 50.00
112 Antawn Jamison WAS 15.00 50.00
113 Antawn Jamison 6th Man 15.00 50.00
114 Antawn Jamison PTS 15.00 50.00
115 Joe Johnson ATL 15.00 40.00
116 Joe Johnson Ball 15.00 40.00
117 Joe Johnson Hawks #2 15.00 40.00
118 Ryan Gomes Wolves #8 12.00 30.00
119 Ryan Gomes Shoot 12.00 30.00
120 Ryan Gomes MIN 12.00 30.00
121 David Thompson #33 20.00 50.00
122 David Thompson All-Star 20.00 50.00
123 David Thompson DEN 20.00 50.00
124 Moses Malone HOF 30.00 80.00
125 Moses Malone PTS 30.00 80.00
126 Moses Malone MVP 30.00 80.00
127 Dwight Howard Magic 12 30.00 80.00
128 Dwight Howard Dunk 30.00 80.00
129 Dwight Howard REB 30.00 80.00
130 Thaddeus Young PHI 12.00 30.00
131 Thaddeus Young #21 12.00 30.00
132 Thaddeus Young Shoot 12.00 30.00
133 Adam Morrison Cats 35 12.00 30.00
134 Adam Morrison Ball 12.00 30.00
135 Adam Morrison 3PT 12.00 30.00

2007-08 Topps Triple Threads Relics Combos

PRINT RUN 18 SER.#'d SETS
1 Pierce/Allen/Garnett 25.00 60.00
2 Iverson/Camby/Anthony 25.00 60.00
3 Oden/Roy/Aldridge 12.00 30.00
4 Wallace/Noah/Gordon 12.00 30.00
5 Conley/Gasol/Miller 25.00 60.00
6 Smith/Horford/Johnson 25.00 60.00
7 Jefferson/Brewer/Foye 8.00 20.00
8 Jianlian/Nowitzki/Ming 25.00 60.00
9 Nowitzki/Nash/Duncan 25.00 60.00
10 O'Neal/Malone/Robinson 40.00 100.00
11 Bird/Garnett/Walton 40.00 100.00
12 Wade/Thomas/Parker 20.00 50.00
13 Bryant/Arenas/Anthony 80.00 200.00
14 Redd/Allen/Iverson 25.00 60.00
15 Davis/Wright/Ellis 8.00 20.00
16 Jamison/Young/Butler 10.00 25.00
17 Young/Iguodala/Dalembert 10.00 25.00
18 Bird/Robinson/O'Neal 40.00 100.00
19 Roy/Paul/Carter 20.00 50.00
20 Stockton/Johnson/Thomas 40.00 100.00
21 Kidd/Marbury/Nash 20.00 50.00
22 Russell/Baylor/Rodman 30.00 80.00
23 O'Neal/Duncan/Wallace 40.00 100.00
24 Allen/Jones/Walker 15.00 40.00
25 Iverson/McGrady/Carter 25.00 60.00
26 Wilkins/Drexler/Johnson 40.00 100.00
27 Hardaway/Richmond/Mullin 12.00 30.00
28 Worthy/Johnson/Cooper 40.00 100.00
29 McGrady/Battier/Ming 25.00 60.00
30 Marion/Iguodala/Artest 10.00 25.00
31 Young/Wade/Young 20.00 50.00
32 Camby/Prince/Wallace 12.00 30.00
33 Barbosa/Miller/Gordon 8.00 20.00
34 Korver/Morrison/Kapono 10.00 25.00
35 Arenas/O'Neal/McGrady 15.00 40.00
36 Ming/Stoudemire/Boozer 25.00 60.00
37 Hinrich/Ford/Howard 10.00 25.00
38 Richardson/Felton/Wallace 10.00 25.00
39 Afflalo/Billups/Stuckey 12.00 30.00
40 Bryant/Duncan/Nash 80.00 200.00
41 Nowitzki/Stoudemire/Arenas 25.00 60.00
42 Bosh/McGrady/Anthony 15.00 40.00
43 Garnett/Howard/Wade 25.00 60.00
44 Ridnour/Green/West 8.00 20.00
45 Bibby/Hawes/Martin 10.00 25.00
46 Jefferson/Williams/Kidd 15.00 40.00
47 Horford/Brewer/Noah 25.00 60.00
48 Barry/Baylor/Bird 40.00 100.00
49 Johnson/O'Neal/Malone 40.00 100.00
50 Stockton/Walton/Thomas 20.00 50.00

2007-08 Topps Triple Threads Rookie Relics Autographs

SKIP-NUMBERED SET
PRINT RUN 50 SER.#'d SETS
*SEPIA: .5X TO 1.25X BASE HI
SEPIA PRINT RUN 23 SER.#'d SETS
101 Greg Oden 8.00 20.00
102 Daequan Cook 6.00 15.00
103 Morris Almond 5.00 12.00
104 Sean Williams 5.00 12.00
105 Arron Afflalo 6.00 15.00
107 Adam Haluska 5.00 12.00
109 Herbert Hill 5.00 12.00
110 Nick Young 8.00 20.00
113 Jared Jordan 5.00 12.00
114 Aaron Brooks 6.00 15.00
115 Marco Belinelli 6.00 15.00
117 Jared Dudley 6.00 15.00
118 Rodney Stuckey 5.00 12.00
120 Gabe Pruitt 5.00 12.00
121 Acie Law 5.00 12.00
122 Dominic McGuire 5.00 12.00
125 Wilson Chandler 6.00 15.00
126 Marcus Williams 5.00 12.00
127 Josh McRoberts 5.00 12.00
128 Jason Smith 5.00 12.00
130 Stephane Lasme 5.00 12.00
132 Alando Tucker 5.00 12.00
133 Javaris Crittenton 5.00 12.00
136 Al Thornton 5.00 12.00
137 Carl Landry 5.00 12.00
138 Yi Jianlian 10.00 25.00
139 Brandan Wright 6.00 15.00
140 Nick Fazekas 5.00 12.00
142 Jermareo Davidson 5.00 12.00
143 D.J. Strawberry 5.00 12.00
144 Glen Davis 6.00 15.00
146 Spencer Hawes 5.00 12.00
147 Taurean Green 5.00 12.00
149 Aaron Gray 5.00 12.00
150 Thaddeus Young 8.00 20.00

2006-07 Topps Turkey Red

COMPLETE SET (275) 60.00 120.00
COMP.SET w/o RC's (175) 15.00 40.00
1 Dwyane Wade SP 1.25 3.00
2 LeBron James 3.00 8.00
3 Allen Iverson SP 1.50 4.00
4 Sebastian Telfair .25 .60
5 Bonzi Wells .25 .60
6 Antawn Jamison .30 .75
7 Joe Johnson .40 1.00
8 DeSagana Diop .25 .60
9 Stromile Swift .25 .60
10 Shaun Livingston .30 .75
11 Baron Davis .40 1.00
12 Richard Hamilton .40 1.00
13 Andrei Kirilenko SP .50 1.25
14 Richard Jefferson .30 .75
15 T.J. Ford .25 .60
16 Luke Ridnour .30 .75
17 Carlos Boozer .30 .75
18 Al Jefferson .25 .60
19 Andrew Bogut SP .50 1.25
20 Kobe Bryant 6.00 15.00
21 Tim Duncan 1.00 2.50
22A Ben Gordon .30 .75
22B Ben Gordon Ad .50 1.25
23 Stephen Jackson .30 .75
24 Peja Stojakovic .30 .75
25 Mike Miller .30 .75
26 Ricky Davis SP .50 1.25
27 Boris Diaw SP .50 1.25
28 Shareef Abdur-Rahim .40 1.00
29 Caron Butler .30 .75
30 Al Harrington .30 .75
31 Ben Wallace SP .75 2.00
32 Jason Richardson .40 1.00
33 Channing Frye .25 .60
34 Paul Pierce .60 1.50
35A Andre Iguodala .40 1.00
35B Andre Iguodala Ad .60 1.50
36 Joey Graham .25 .60
37 Corey Maggette .30 .75
38 Sarunas Jasikevicius .30 .75
39 Lamar Odom .30 .75
40A Shaquille O'Neal 1.50 4.00
40B Shaquille O'Neal Ad 2.50 6.00
41 Larry Hughes SP .50 1.25
42 Darko Milicic SP .40 1.00
43 Jerry Stackhouse .30 .75
44 Raymond Felton .25 .60
45 Nenad Krstic SP .40 1.00
46 Michael Redd .30 .75
47 Shane Battier .30 .75
48 Kevin Garnett 1.00 2.50
49 Deron Williams .30 .75
50 Chris Paul SP 1.25 3.00
51 Rashard Lewis .30 .75
52 Kevin Martin SP .50 1.25
53 Zach Randolph .40 1.00
54 Jared Jeffries .25 .60
55 Donyell Marshall .25 .60
56 Josh Howard SP .50 1.25
57 Stephon Marbury .50 1.25
58 Raja Bell .30 .75
59 Tony Parker .60 1.50
60 Dwight Howard .50 1.25
61 Kirk Hinrich .30 .75
62 Emeka Okafor .30 .75
63 Zaza Pachulia .25 .60
64 Troy Murphy .25 .60
65A Chris Duhon .25 .60
65B Chris Duhon Ad .40 1.00
66 Earl Boykins SP .40 1.00
67 Tracy McGrady .60 1.50
68 Hakim Warrick .25 .60
69 Charlie Villanueva SP .40 1.00
70 Jason Kidd .60 1.50
71 Joel Przybilla SP .40 1.00
72 Antonio Daniels .25 .60
73 Wally Szczerbiak .30 .75
74 Drew Gooden .30 .75
75 Antonio McDyess .30 .75
76 Ray Allen SP 1.00 2.50
77 Rashad McCants .25 .60
78 Eddy Curry .30 .75
79 Chris Webber .50 1.25
80 Yao Ming SP 1.50 4.00
81 Tyson Chandler .30 .75
82 Bobby Simmons .25 .60
83 Jarrett Jack .30 .75
84 Jameer Nelson SP .40 1.00
85 Luol Deng .30 .75
86 Kurt Thomas .25 .60
87 Mickael Pietrus .30 .75
88 Chris Bosh SP .75 2.00
89 Devin Harris .25 .60
90 Jermaine O'Neal .40 1.00
91 Luther Head .25 .60
92 Elton Brand SP .50 1.25
93 Antoine Walker .40 1.00
94 Smush Parker .25 .60
95 Nate Robinson SP .50 1.25
96 Marvin Williams SP .40 1.00
97 Primoz Brezec .25 .60
98 Desmond Mason .25 .60
99 Ron Artest SP .60 1.50
100 Jason Terry .30 .75
101 Mehmet Okur .25 .60
102 Kenyon Martin .30 .75
103 Ike Diogu SP .40 1.00
104 Eddie Griffin .25 .60
105 Amare Stoudemire .40 1.00
106 Kwame Brown SP .40 1.00
107 Hedo Turkoglu .40 1.00
108A Chauncey Billups .50 1.25
108B Chauncey Billups Ad .75 2.00
109 Rafer Alston .30 .75
110 Dirk Nowitzki SP 1.50 4.00
111 Steve Francis .40 1.00
112 Mike Bibby .40 1.00
113 Kirk Snyder .25 .60
114A Luke Walton .25 .60
114B Luke Walton Ad .40 1.00
115 Maurice Williams .30 .75
116 Nick Collison .30 .75
117 Brendan Haywood .25 .60
118 Delonte West SP .40 1.00
119 Mike Dunleavy .25 .60
120A Vince Carter .75 2.00
120B Vince Carter Ad 1.25 3.00
121 Juwan Howard .30 .75
122 J.R. Smith .40 1.00
123 Gerald Wallace SP .50 1.25
124 Cuttino Mobley .30 .75
125 James Posey .25 .60
126 Tayshaun Prince SP .60 1.50
127 Anderson Varejao .25 .60
128 Trenton Hassell .25 .60
129 Matt Harpring .25 .60
130 Gilbert Arenas SP .60 1.50
131 Leandro Barbosa .30 .75
132 Bruce Bowen .30 .75
133 Morris Peterson .25 .60
134 David West SP .50 1.25
135 Joe Smith .30 .75
136 Rasheed Wallace .50 1.25
137 Nene .30 .75
138 Alonzo Mourning .60 1.50
139 Jamal Crawford .40 1.00
140 Carmelo Anthony SP 1.00 2.50
141 Brad Miller .30 .75
142 Tim Thomas .25 .60
143 Jose Calderon .25 .60
144 Sean May .25 .60
145 Andres Nocioni SP .40 1.00
146 Samuel Dalembert .25 .60
147 Chris Wilcox .25 .60
148 Jason Williams .50 1.25
149 DeShawn Stevenson .25 .60
150 Josh Smith SP .40 1.00
151 Andre Miller .30 .75
152 Michael Finley .40 1.00
153 Marquis Daniels .25 .60
154 Martell Webster .30 .75
155 Brevin Knight .25 .60
156 Steve Nash SP 1.25 3.00
157 Vladimir Radmanovic .25 .60
158A Speedy Claxton .25 .60
158B Speedy Claxton Ad .40 1.00
159 Darius Miles .25 .60
160 Pau Gasol SP 1.00 2.50
161 Sam Cassell .30 .75
162 Nazr Mohammed .25 .60
163 Shawn Marion .40 1.00
164 Francisco Garcia .25 .60
165 Kyle Korver .30 .75
166 Udonis Haslem .25 .60
167 Manu Ginobili SP 1.25 3.00
168 Zydrunas Ilgauskas .30 .75
169 Eddie Jones .40 1.00
170 Danny Granger SP .40 1.00
171 Mike James .25 .60
172 Ryan Gomes .25 .60
173 Josh Childress .25 .60
174 Marcus Camby .30 .75
175 Chris Kaman SP .40 1.00
176 Brandon Roy RC 2.00 5.00
177 Kyle Lowry RC 3.00 8.00
178 Tyrus Thomas RC .75 2.00
179 Hilton Armstrong RC .60 1.50
180 LaMarcus Aldridge RC 2.50 6.00
181 Ronnie Brewer RC 1.00 2.50
182 Rajon Rondo RC 3.00 8.00
183 Marcus Vinicius RC .60 1.50
184 Solomon Jones RC .60 1.50
185 Leon Powe RC .60 1.50
186 Shawne Williams RC .60 1.50
187A Craig Smith RC .75 2.00
187B Craig Smith Ad RC .75 2.00
188 Patrick O'Bryant RC .60 1.50
189 James Augustine RC .60 1.50
190 Maurice Ager RC .60 1.50
191 Quincy Douby RC .60 1.50
192 Rudy Gay RC 1.25 3.00
193 Thabo Sefolosha RC .75 2.00
194 Bobby Jones RC .60 1.50
195A Shelden Williams RC .60 1.50
195B Shelden Williams Ad RC .60 1.50
196 Mile Ilic RC .60 1.50
197 Jorge Garbajosa RC .75 2.00
198 Cedric Simmons RC .60 1.50
199 Josh Boone RC .60 1.50
200A Adam Morrison RC .75 2.00
200B Adam Morrison Ad RC .75 2.00
201A Marcus Williams RC .60 1.50
201B Marcus Williams Ad RC .60 1.50
202 Steve Novak RC .75 2.00
203 Vassilis Spanoulis RC .60 1.50
204 Allan Ray RC .60 1.50
205 David Noel RC .60 1.50
206 Alexander Johnson RC .60 1.50
207 Mardy Collins RC .60 1.50
208 Dee Brown RC .60 1.50
209 P.J. Tucker RC 1.00 2.50
210 Paul Millsap RC 1.25 3.00
211 Paul Davis RC .60 1.50
212A Rodney Carney RC .60 1.50
212B Rodney Carney Ad RC .60 1.50
213 Saer Sene RC .60 1.50
214 Renaldo Balkman RC .75 2.00
215 Ryan Hollins RC .60 1.50
216 Will Blalock RC .60 1.50
217 Mickael Gelabale RC .60 1.50
218 Daniel Gibson RC .75 2.00
219 Hassan Adams RC .60 1.50
220 J.J. Redick RC 2.00 5.00
221A Jordan Farmar RC .75 2.00
221B Jordan Farmar Ad RC .75 2.00
222 Randy Foye RC .75 2.00
223 Shannon Brown RC .60 1.50
224 Sergio Rodriguez RC .75 2.00
225A Andrea Bargnani RC .75 2.00
225B Andrea Bargnani Ad RC .75 2.00
226 Larry Bird 3.00 8.00
227 George Gervin 1.50 4.00
228 Earl Monroe 1.00 2.50
229 Kareem Abdul-Jabbar 3.00 8.00
230 Wilt Chamberlain 3.00 8.00
231 Bill Walton 1.25 3.00
232 Isiah Thomas 1.50 4.00

233 Oscar Robertson 2.50 6.00
234 Pete Maravich 6.00 15.00
235 Bill Russell 3.00 8.00
236 James Worthy 1.00 2.50
237 Rick Barry .75 2.00
238 Walt Frazier 1.25 3.00
239 Elgin Baylor 2.00 5.00
240 Karl Malone 1.25 3.00
241 Connie Hawkins 1.00 2.50
242 Dennis Rodman 2.00 5.00
243 John Stockton 1.50 4.00
244 Jerry West 1.50 4.00
245 Bob Cousy 1.50 4.00
246 Hakeem Olajuwon 2.00 5.00
247 John Havlicek 1.00 2.50
248 Spencer Haywood .60 1.50
249 Moses Malone 1.50 4.00
250 Willis Reed 1.50 4.00
251 LeBron James CL 2.00 5.00
252 Shaquille O'Neal CL 1.00 2.50
253 Dwyane Wade CL .50 1.25
254 Y.Ming/T.McGrady CL .60 1.50
255 Carmelo Anthony CL .40 1.00
256 K.Garnett/D.Howard CL .75 2.00
257 Nate Robinson CL .20 .50
258 Kobe Bryant/Team CL 1.00 2.50
259 Larry Bird CL 2.00 5.00
260 S.Nash/K.Thomas CL .60 1.50

2006-07 Topps Turkey Red Black
*1-175 BLACK: .75X TO 2X BASE HI
*176-225 BLACK RC: .4X TO 1X BASE HI
*226-260 BLACK: .75X TO 2X BASE HI
STATED ODDS 1:4

2006-07 Topps Turkey Red Red
*RED: .4X TO 1X BASE HI
STATED ODDS ONE PER PACK
20 Kobe Bryant 15.00 40.00
258 Kobe Bryant CL 8.00 20.00

2006-07 Topps Turkey Red White
*1-175 WHITE: .5X TO 1.25X BASE HI
*176-225 WHITE RC: .3X TO .75X BASE HI
*226-260 WHITE: .5X TO 1.25X BASE HI
STATED ODDS 1:4

2006-07 Topps Turkey Red Autographs
GROUP A ODDS 1:505, GROUP B ODDS 1:186
AB Andrea Bargnani A 4.00 10.00
ABO Andrew Bogut A 6.00 15.00
AI Allen Iverson A 75.00 200.00
AM Adam Morrison A 4.00 10.00
BG Ben Gordon A 4.00 10.00
CB Chris Bosh A 12.00 30.00
CD Chris Duhon B 4.00 10.00
CS Cedric Simmons B 4.00 10.00
CV Charlie Villanueva A 4.00 10.00
DH Devin Harris A 4.00 10.00
DW Dwyane Wade A 75.00 200.00
EO Emeka Okafor A 4.00 10.00
HA Hilton Armstrong B 4.00 10.00
HW Hakim Warrick B 4.00 10.00
JB Josh Boone B 4.00 10.00
JF Jordan Farmar B 4.00 10.00
JJR J.J. Redick A 12.50 30.00
JO Jermaine O'Neal A 5.00 12.00
KL Kyle Lowry B 10.00 25.00
LB Larry Bird A 75.00 200.00
LD Luol Deng A 4.00 10.00
LR Luke Ridnour B 4.00 10.00
MA Maurice Ager B 4.00 10.00
MC Mardy Collins B 4.00 10.00
MW Marcus Williams A 4.00 10.00
POB Patrick O'Bryant B 4.00 10.00
QD Quincy Douby B 4.00 10.00
RB Ronnie Brewer B 4.00 10.00
RBA Renaldo Balkman B 4.00 10.00
RC Rodney Carney B 4.00 10.00
RF Randy Foye B 4.00 10.00
RFE Raymond Felton A 4.00 10.00
RR Rajon Rondo B 20.00 50.00
SO Shaquille O'Neal A 75.00 200.00
ST Sebastian Telfair A 4.00 10.00
SW Shelden Williams A 4.00 10.00
SWI Shawne Williams B 4.00 10.00
TJF T.J. Ford B 4.00 10.00
TP Vince Carter A 75.00 200.00
TPA Tony Parker A 20.00 50.00

2006-07 Topps Turkey Red Autographs Red
PRINT RUN 25 TO 99 SER.#'d SETS
*WHITE: .5X TO 1.25X BASE HI
WHITE PRINT RUN 15 TO 50 SER.#'d SETS
AB Andrea Bargnani/25 6.00 15.00
AI Allen Iverson/25 100.00 250.00
AM Adam Morrison/25 6.00 15.00
BG Ben Gordon/25 6.00 15.00
CB Chris Bosh/25 15.00 40.00
CD Chris Duhon/99 5.00 12.00
CS Cedric Simmons/99 5.00 12.00
CV Charlie Villanueva/25 5.00 12.00
DH Devin Harris/25 6.00 15.00
DW Dwyane Wade/25 100.00 250.00
EO Emeka Okafor/25 6.00 15.00
HA Hilton Armstrong/99 5.00 12.00
HW Hakim Warrick/99 5.00 12.00
JB Josh Boone/99 5.00 12.00
JF Jordan Farmar/99 5.00 12.00
JO Jermaine O'Neal/25 6.00 15.00
KL Kyle Lowry/99 12.00 30.00
LB Larry Bird/25 100.00 250.00
LD Luol Deng/25 6.00 15.00
LR Luke Ridnour/99 5.00 12.00
MA Maurice Ager/99 5.00 12.00
MC Mardy Collins/99 5.00 12.00
MW Marcus Williams/25 5.00 12.00
QD Quincy Douby/99 5.00 12.00
RB Ronnie Brewer/99 6.00 15.00
RC Rodney Carney/99 5.00 12.00
RF Randy Foye/99 5.00 12.00
RR Rajon Rondo/99 25.00 60.00
SO Shaquille O'Neal/25 100.00 250.00
ST Sebastian Telfair/25 5.00 12.00
SW Shelden Williams/25 6.00 15.00
TP Vince Carter/25 100.00 250.00
ABO Andrew Bogut/25 8.00 20.00
JJR J.J. Redick/25 15.00 40.00
POB Patrick O'Bryant/99 5.00 12.00
RBA Renaldo Balkman/99 5.00 12.00
RFE Raymond Felton/25 6.00 15.00
SWI Shawne Williams/99 5.00 12.00
TJF T.J. Ford/99 5.00 12.00
TPA Tony Parker/25 25.00 60.00

2006-07 Topps Turkey Red Cabinet Jumbos
*GOLD: .5X TO 1.25X BASE HI
GOLD PRINT RUN 50 SER.#'d SET
ONE PER BOX AS TOPPER
1 Chris Paul 3.00 8.00
2 Gilbert Arenas 1.50 4.00
3 Dwyane Wade 3.00 8.00
4 Joe Johnson 1.50 4.00
5 Carmelo Anthony 2.50 6.00
6 Shane Battier 1.25 3.00
7 Bruce Bowen 1.25 3.00
8 LeBron James 12.00 30.00
9 Elton Brand 1.25 3.00
10 Antawn Jamison 1.25 3.00
11 Chris Bosh 2.00 5.00
12 Dwight Howard 2.00 5.00
13 Brad Miller 1.25 3.00
14 Kirk Hinrich 1.25 3.00
15 Amare Stoudemire 1.50 4.00
16 Andrea Bargnani 1.25 3.00
17 LaMarcus Aldridge 4.00 10.00
18 Adam Morrison 1.25 3.00
19 Tyrus Thomas 1.25 3.00
20 Shelden Williams 1.00 2.50
21 Brandon Roy 3.00 8.00
22 Randy Foye 1.25 3.00
23 Rudy Gay 2.00 5.00
24 Patrick O'Bryant 1.00 2.50
25 Saer Sene 1.00 2.50
26 J.J. Redick 3.00 8.00
27 Hilton Armstrong 1.00 2.50
28 Thabo Sefolosha 1.25 3.00
29 Ronnie Brewer 1.50 4.00
30 Cedric Simmons 1.00 2.50

2006-07 Topps Turkey Red Relics
GROUP A ODDS 1:88, GROUP B ODDS 1:23
*RED: .5X TO 1.25X BASE HI
RED PRINT RUN 99 SER.#'d SETS
*WHITE: .6X TO 1.5X BASE HI
WHITE PRINT RUN 50 SER.#'d SETS
AI Allen Iverson B 6.00 15.00
AM Adam Morrison A 2.00 5.00
BG Ben Gordon B 2.00 5.00
BR Brandon Roy A 5.00 12.00
CB Chris Bosh A 3.00 8.00
CP Chris Paul A 5.00 12.00
CS Cedric Simmons B 1.50 4.00
DH Dwight Howard B 3.00 8.00
DW Dwyane Wade B 5.00 12.00
GA Gilbert Arenas B 2.50 6.00
GW Gerald Wallace A 2.00 5.00
HA Hilton Armstrong B 1.50 4.00
JB Josh Boone B 1.50 4.00
JF Jordan Farmar B 2.00 5.00
JR Jason Richardson A 2.50 6.00
JT Jason Terry A 2.00 5.00
KB Kobe Bryant B 40.00 100.00
KG Kevin Garnett A 6.00 15.00
KL Kyle Lowry B 8.00 20.00
LA LaMarcus Aldridge B 6.00 15.00
MA Maurice Ager A 1.50 4.00
MW Marcus Williams A 1.50 4.00
PP Paul Pierce A 4.00 10.00
QD Quincy Douby B 1.50 4.00
RA Ray Allen B 4.00 10.00
RB Ronnie Brewer B 2.50 6.00
RC Rodney Carney B 1.50 4.00
RF Randy Foye B 2.00 5.00
RG Rudy Gay B 3.00 8.00
RR Rajon Rondo A 8.00 20.00
SM Shawn Marion B 2.50 6.00
SO Shaquille O'Neal B 10.00 25.00
SW Shelden Williams B 1.50 4.00
TD Tim Duncan B 6.00 15.00
TM Tracy McGrady A 4.00 10.00
VC Vince Carter A 5.00 12.00
AIG Andre Iguodala A 2.50 6.00
JJR J.J. Redick A 5.00 12.00
POB Patrick O'Bryant B 1.50 4.00
SWI Shawne Williams B 1.50 4.00

2012 Topps U.S. Olympic Team
COMPLETE SET (100) 10.00 25.00
20 Sue Bird .40 1.00
46 Candace Parker .25 .60
60 Maya Moore .50 1.25
91 Seimone Augustus .25 .60

2012 Topps U.S. Olympic Team Bronze
*BRONZE: .5X TO 1.2X BASIC CARDS
STATED ODDS 1:1
20 Sue Bird .50 1.25
46 Candace Parker .30 .75
60 Maya Moore .60 1.50
91 Seimone Augustus .30 .75

2012 Topps U.S. Olympic Team Gold
*GOLD: .8X TO 2X BASIC CARDS
STATED ODDS 1:3
20 Sue Bird .75 2.00
46 Candace Parker .50 1.25
60 Maya Moore 1.00 2.50
91 Seimone Augustus .50 1.25

2012 Topps U.S. Olympic Team Silver
*SILVER: .6X TO 1.5X BASIC CARDS
STATED ODDS 1:2
20 Sue Bird .60 1.50
46 Candace Parker .40 1.00
60 Maya Moore .75 2.00
91 Seimone Augustus .40 1.00

2012 Topps U.S. Olympic Team Autographs
STATED ODDS 1:23
20 Sue Bird 15.00 40.00
60 Maya Moore 25.00 50.00

2012 Topps U.S. Olympic Team Autographs Bronze
*BRONZE: SAME AS BASIC AUTO
STATED ODDS 1:202
STATED PRINT RUN 50 SER.#'d SETS
20 Sue Bird 15.00 40.00
60 Maya Moore 25.00 50.00

2012 Topps U.S. Olympic Team Autographs Gold
*GOLD: .6X TO 1.5X BASIC CARDS
STATED ODDS 1:577
STATED PRINT RUN 15 SER.#'d SETS
20 Sue Bird 25.00 60.00
60 Maya Moore 35.00 70.00

2012 Topps U.S. Olympic Team Autographs Silver
*SILVER: .5X TO 1.2X BASIC CARDS
STATED ODDS 1:286
STATED PRINT RUN 30 SER.#'d SETS
20 Sue Bird 20.00 50.00
60 Maya Moore 30.00 60.00

2012 Topps U.S. Olympic Team Event Pins
STATED ODDS 1:92
ELPCP Candace Parker 5.00 12.00
ELPMM Maya Moore 10.00 25.00
ELPSA Seimone Augustus 5.00 12.00
ELPSB Sue Bird 8.00 20.00

2012 Topps U.S. Olympic Team Games of the XXX Olympiad
COMPLETE SET (25) 12.00 30.00
STATED ODDS 1:4
OLY3 Maya Moore 2.00 5.00

2012 Topps U.S. Olympic Team Olympic Team Patch
STATED ODDS 1:131
ULPCP Candace Parker 5.00 12.00
ULPMM Maya Moore 10.00 25.00
ULPSA Seimone Augustus 5.00 12.00
ULPSB Sue Bird 8.00 20.00

2012 Topps U.S. Olympic Team Relics
STATED ODDS 1:31
ORMM Maya Moore 8.00 20.00
ORSB Sue Bird 8.00 20.00

2012 Topps U.S. Olympic Team Relics Bronze
*BRONZE: SAME PRICE AS BASIC CARDS
STATED ODDS 1:222
STATED PRINT RUN 75 SER.#'d SETS
ORMM Maya Moore 8.00 20.00
ORSB Sue Bird 8.00 20.00

2012 Topps U.S. Olympic Team Relics Gold
*GOLD: .6X TO 1.5X BASIC CARDS
STATED ODDS 1:666
STATED PRINT RUN 25 SER.#'d SETS
ORMM Maya Moore 12.00 30.00
ORSB Sue Bird 12.00 30.00

2012 Topps U.S. Olympic Team Relics Silver
*SILVER: .5X TO 1.2X BASIC CARDS
STATED ODDS 1:333
STATED PRINT RUN 50 SER.#'d SETS
ORMM Maya Moore 10.00 25.00
ORSB Sue Bird 10.00 25.00

2012 Topps U.S. Olympic Team U.S. Flag Patch
STATED ODDS 1:131
FLPCP Candace Parker 5.00 12.00
FLPMM Maya Moore 10.00 25.00
FLPSA Seimone Augustus 5.00 12.00
FLPSB Sue Bird 8.00 20.00

2012 Topps U.S. Olympic Team USOC Pins
STATED ODDS 1:92
PINCP Candace Parker 5.00 12.00
PINMM Maya Moore 10.00 25.00
PINSA Seimone Augustus 5.00 12.00
PINSB Sue Bird 8.00 20.00

1996 Topps USA Women's National Team
COMPLETE SET (24) 10.00 25.00
1 Jennifer Azzi 1.25 3.00
2 Ruthie Bolton 1.00 2.50
3 Teresa Edwards .75 2.00
4 Lisa Leslie 1.50 4.00
5 Rebecca Lobo 1.25 3.00
6 Katrina McClain .20 .50
7 Nikki McCray 1.25 3.00
8 Carla McGhee .20 .50
9 Dawn Staley 1.25 3.00
10 Katy Steding .20 .50
11 Sheryl Swoopes 2.00 5.00
12 Team Photo 1.25 3.00
13 Jennifer Azzi PRO .60 1.50
14 Ruthie Bolton PRO .50 1.25
15 Teresa Edwards PRO .40 1.00
16 Lisa Leslie PRO .75 2.00
17 Rebecca Lobo PRO .60 1.50
18 Katrina McClain PRO .08 .25
19 Nikki McCray PRO .60 1.50
20 Carla McGhee PRO .08 .25
21 Dawn Staley PRO .60 1.50
22 Katy Steding PRO .08 .25
23 Sheryl Swoopes PRO 1.00 2.50
24 Tara VanDerveer CO .20 .50

2001 Topps Wilkins Oversized
NNO Dominique Wilkins 2.00 5.00

2001-02 Topps Xpectations Promos
COMPLETE SET (6) .75 2.00
P1 Antawn Jamison .25 .60
P2 Paul Pierce .50 1.25
P3 Larry Hughes .25 .60
P4 Derek Anderson .20 .50
P5 Bonzi Wells .20 .50
P6 Wally Szczerbiak .25 .60

2001-02 Topps Xpectations
COMP.SET w/o SP's (145) 50.00 120.00
ROOKIES/250 STATED ODDS 1:191
1 Baron Davis .40 1.00
2 Jason Terry .40 1.00
3 Paul Pierce .60 1.50
4 Ron Mercer .25 .60
5 Dirk Nowitzki 1.00 2.50
6 Marc Jackson .25 .60
7 Cuttino Mobley .30 .75
8 Al Harrington .30 .75
9 Keyon Dooling .25 .60
10 Mark Madsen .25 .60
11 Jumaine Jones .25 .60
12 Shawn Marion .40 1.00
13 Mike Bibby .40 1.00
14 Antonio Daniels .25 .60
15 Vince Carter .75 2.00
16 Stromile Swift .25 .60
17 Courtney Alexander .25 .60
18 Desmond Mason .30 .75
19 Hedo Turkoglu .30 .75
20 Speedy Claxton .25 .60
21 Lavor Postell .25 .60
22 Chauncey Billups .50 1.25
23 Eddie House .25 .60
24 Maurice Taylor .25 .60
25 Lamar Odom .30 .75
26 Antawn Jamison .30 .75
27 Raef LaFrentz .25 .60
28 Marcus Fizer .25 .60
29 Chris Mihm .25 .60
30 Eddie Robinson .25 .60
31 Mark Blount .25 .60
32 DerMarr Johnson .25 .60
33 Wang Zhizhi .40 1.00
34 Danny Fortson .25 .60
35 Elton Brand .30 .75
36 Anthony Carter .25 .60
37 Wally Szczerbiak .30 .75
38 Mike Miller .30 .75
39 Bonzi Wells .30 .75
40 Tim Duncan 1.00 2.50
41 Ruben Patterson .25 .60
42 Keon Clark .25 .60
43 Jason Williams .60 1.50
44 Richard Hamilton .50 1.25
45 Scott Padgett .25 .60
46 Derek Anderson .25 .60
47 Keith Van Horn .30 .75
48 Tim Thomas .25 .60
49 Jonathan Bender .25 .60
50 Tracy McGrady .60 1.50
51 Tyronn Lue .40 1.00
52 Austin Croshere .25 .60
53 James Posey .25 .60
54 Mateen Cleaves .25 .60
55 Matt Harpring .25 .60
56 Calvin Booth .25 .60
57 Quentin Richardson .25 .60
58 Joel Przybilla .25 .60
59 Kenyon Martin .40 1.00
60 Iakovos Tsakalidis .25 .60
61 Peja Stojakovic .30 .75
62 Shammond Williams .25 .60
63 Alvin Williams .25 .60
64 Jahidi White .25 .60
65 Morris Peterson .25 .60
66 Larry Hughes .30 .75
67 Andre Miller .30 .75
68 Jamaal Magloire .25 .60
69 Steve Francis .40 1.00
70 Todd MacCulloch .25 .60
71 Rashard Lewis .30 .75
72 Michael Dickerson .25 .60
73 Nazr Mohammed .25 .60
74 Jamal Crawford .40 1.00
75 Darius Miles .25 .60
76 Allen Iverson 1.00 2.50
77 Shaquille O'Neal 1.50 4.00
78 Michael Finley .40 1.00
79 Antonio McDyess .30 .75
80 Jerry Stackhouse .40 1.00
81 Chris Webber .50 1.25
82 Eddie Jones .40 1.00
83 Reggie Miller .75 2.00
84 Antoine Walker .30 .75
85 Latrell Sprewell .50 1.25
86 Alonzo Mourning .60 1.50
87 Jalen Rose .30 .75
88 Ray Allen .60 1.50
89 Gary Payton .60 1.50
90 Jason Kidd .60 1.50
91 Stephon Marbury .50 1.25
92 Kobe Bryant 3.00 8.00
93 Grant Hill .60 1.50
94 Karl Malone .75 2.00
95 John Stockton .75 2.00
96 Anfernee Hardaway 1.00 2.50
97 Rasheed Wallace .50 1.25
98 Hakeem Olajuwon .75 2.00
99 Shareef Abdur-Rahim .30 .75
100 Kevin Garnett 1.00 2.50
101 Kwame Brown/250 RC 6.00 15.00
102 Tyson Chandler/250 RC 1.25 3.00
103 Pau Gasol RC 3.00 8.00
104 Eddy Curry RC .60 1.50
105 J.Richardson/250 RC 10.00 25.00
106 Shane Battier/250 RC 12.00 30.00
107 Eddie Griffin RC .60 1.50
108 DeSagana Diop RC .50 1.25
109 Rodney White RC .50 1.25
110 Joe Johnson/250 RC 10.00 25.00
111 Kedrick Brown RC .60 1.50
112 Vladimir Radmanovic RC .60 1.50
113 Richard Jefferson RC 1.00 2.50
114 Troy Murphy/250 RC 5.00 12.00
115 Steven Hunter RC .50 1.25
116 Kirk Haston RC .50 1.25
117 Michael Bradley RC .50 1.25
118 Jason Collins RC .50 1.25
119 Zach Randolph/250 RC 12.00 30.00
120 Brendan Haywood RC .60 1.50
121 Joseph Forte RC .50 1.25
122 Jeryl Sasser RC .50 1.25
123 Brandon Armstrong RC .50 1.25
124 Gerald Wallace RC 1.00 2.50
125 Samuel Dalembert RC .75 2.00
126 Jamaal Tinsley RC .60 1.50
127 Tony Parker RC 3.00 8.00
128 Trenton Hassell RC .50 1.25
129 Gilbert Arenas RC 2.00 5.00
130 Raja Bell RC 1.00 2.50
131 Will Solomon RC .60 1.50
132 Terence Morris RC .50 1.25
133 Brian Scalabrine RC .75 2.00
134 Jeff Trepagnier RC .50 1.25
135 Damone Brown RC .50 1.25
136 Carlos Arroyo RC 4.00 10.00
137 Earl Watson RC .60 1.50
138 Jamison Brewer RC .75 2.00
139 Bobby Simmons RC .75 2.00
140 Andrei Kirilenko RC 1.25 3.00
141 Zeljko Rebraca RC .75 2.00
142 Sean Lampley RC .75 2.00
143 Loren Woods RC .50 1.25
144 Alton Ford RC .75 2.00
145 Antonis Fotsis RC .50 1.25
146 Charlie Bell RC .75 2.00
147 R.Boumtje-Boumtje RC .60 1.50
148 Jarron Collins RC .75 2.00
149 Kenny Satterfield RC .50 1.25
150 Alvin Jones RC .50 1.25
151 Michael Jordan 5.00 12.00

2001-02 Topps Xpectations Autographs
STATED ODDS 1:13
TXAAD Antonio Daniels 4.00 10.00
TXAAJ Antawn Jamison 5.00 12.00
TXAAM Andre Miller 4.00 10.00
TXABD Baron Davis 6.00 15.00
TXABH Brendan Haywood 3.00 8.00
TXABJ Bobby Jackson 4.00 10.00
TXACA Courtney Alexander 3.00 8.00
TXACB Chauncey Billups 6.00 15.00
TXADB Damone Brown 3.00 8.00
TXADH Donnell Harvey 3.00 8.00
TXAEB Erick Barkley 3.00 8.00
TXAEC Eddy Curry 5.00 12.00
TXAGA Gilbert Arenas 12.00 30.00
TXAGW Gerald Wallace 6.00 15.00
TXAHT Hedo Turkoglu 4.00 10.00
TXAIT Iakovos Tsakalidis 3.00 8.00
TXAJB Jonathan Bender 3.00 8.00
TXAJF Joseph Forte 3.00 8.00
TXAJO Jermaine O'Neal 4.00 10.00
TXAJT Jason Terry 5.00 12.00
TXAKB Kwame Brown 5.00 12.00
TXAKD Keyon Dooling 3.00 8.00
TXALP Lavor Postell 3.00 8.00
TXALW Loren Woods 3.00 8.00
TXAMB Mike Bibby 5.00 12.00
TXAMD Michael Doleac 3.00 8.00
TXAMJ Marc Jackson 3.00 8.00
TXAPS Peja Stojakovic 4.00 10.00
TXARH Richard Hamilton 6.00 15.00
TXARL Raef LaFrentz 3.00 8.00
TXARM Roshown McLeod 3.00 8.00
TXASB Shane Battier 10.00 25.00
TXASM Shawn Marion 5.00 12.00
TXATT Tim Thomas 3.00 8.00
TXAVR Vladimir Radmanovic 4.00 10.00
TXAZR Zach Randolph 10.00 25.00
TXAAJO Alvin Jones 3.00 8.00
TXADTM Desmond Mason 4.00 10.00
TXAETB Elton Brand 4.00 10.00
TXAJTR Jeff Trepagnier 3.00 8.00
TXAKBR Kedrick Brown 3.00 8.00

2001-02 Topps Xpectations Bowman's Best
FF1 Magic Johnson JSY 40.00 100.00
FF2 Kareem Abdul-Jabbar JSY 40.00 100.00
FF3 Shaquille O'Neal JSY 40.00 100.00
FF4 Kareem/Magic JSY 50.00 120.00
FF5 Shaq/Kareem JSY 50.00 120.00
FF6 Shaq/Magic JSY 50.00 120.00
FF7 Kareem/Shaq/Magic JSY/50 60.00 150.00
FFA1 Magic Johnson JSY AU/50 75.00 200.00
FFA2 K.Abdul-Jabbar JSY AU/50 150.00 400.00
FFA3 S.O'Neal JSY AU/50 75.00 200.00
FFA4 Kareem/Magic JSY AU/25 300.00 600.00

2001-02 Topps Xpectations Changing of the Guard
COMPLETE SET (10) 8.00 20.00
STATED ODDS 1:10
CG1 Allen Iverson 2.00 5.00
CG2 Kobe Bryant 6.00 15.00
CG3 Vince Carter 1.50 4.00
CG4 Tracy McGrady 1.25 3.00
CG5 Jason Kidd 1.25 3.00
CG6 Steve Francis .75 2.00
CG7 Stephon Marbury 1.00 2.50
CG8 Gary Payton 1.25 3.00
CG9 Michael Finley .75 2.00
CG10 Baron Davis .75 2.00

2001-02 Topps Xpectations Class Challenge
STATED ODDS 1:9
CCAG Adrian Griffin 2.00 5.00
CCAM Andre Miller 2.50 6.00
CCBD Baron Davis 3.00 8.00
CCCM Cuttino Mobley 2.50 6.00
CCDM Darius Miles 2.00 5.00
CCDN Dirk Nowitzki 8.00 20.00
CCEB Elton Brand 2.50 6.00
CCJP James Posey 2.00 5.00
CCJT Jason Terry 3.00 8.00
CCJW Jason Williams 5.00 12.00
CCKM Kenyon Martin 3.00 8.00
CCLO Lamar Odom 2.50 6.00
CCMB Mike Bibby 3.00 8.00
CCMC Mateen Cleaves 2.00 5.00
CCMD Michael Dickerson 2.00 5.00
CCMJ Marc Jackson 2.00 5.00
CCMM Mike Miller 2.50 6.00
CCMO Michael Olowokandi 2.00 5.00
CCMP Morris Peterson 2.00 5.00
CCPP Paul Pierce 5.00 12.00
CCQR Quentin Richardson 2.00 5.00
CCRH Richard Hamilton 4.00 10.00
CCRL Raef LaFrentz 2.00 5.00
CCSF Steve Francis 3.00 8.00
CCSJ Stephen Jackson 2.50 6.00
CCSM Shawn Marion 3.00 8.00
CCTM Todd MacCulloch 2.00 5.00
CCWS Wally Szczerbiak 2.50 6.00

2001-02 Topps Xpectations Class Challenge Autographs
PRINT RUNS LISTED BELOW
CCAEB Elton Brand/43 25.00 60.00
CCAJT Jason Terry/31 25.00 60.00
CCARH Richard Hamilton/32 25.00 60.00
CCARL Raef LaFrentz/45 8.00 20.00
CCASM Shawn Marion/31 30.00 80.00

2001-02 Topps Xpectations First Shot
STATED ODDS 1:17
FS1 Kwame Brown 2.00 5.00
FS2 Tyson Chandler 3.00 8.00
FS3 Pau Gasol 8.00 20.00
FS4 Eddy Curry 2.00 5.00
FS5 Jason Richardson 3.00 8.00
FS6 Shane Battier 4.00 10.00
FS7 Eddie Griffin 1.50 4.00
FS8 DeSagana Diop 1.25 3.00
FS9 Rodney White 1.25 3.00
FS10 Joe Johnson 3.00 8.00
FS11 Kedrick Brown 1.25 3.00
FS12 Vladimir Radmanovic 1.50 4.00
FS13 Richard Jefferson 2.50 6.00
FS14 Troy Murphy 1.50 4.00
FS15 Steven Hunter 1.25 3.00
FS16 Kirk Haston 1.25 3.00
FS17 Michael Bradley 1.25 3.00
FS18 Zach Randolph 4.00 10.00
FS19 Brendan Haywood 1.50 4.00
FS20 Joseph Forte 1.25 3.00
FS21 Jeryl Sasser 1.25 3.00
FS22 Brandon Armstrong 1.25 3.00
FS23 Primoz Brezec 2.00 5.00
FS24 Jamaal Tinsley 1.50 4.00
FS25 Tony Parker 8.00 20.00

2001-02 Topps Xpectations Forward Thinking
COMPLETE SET (10) 8.00 20.00
STATED ODDS 1:10
FT1 Chris Webber 1.25 3.00
FT2 Kevin Garnett 2.50 6.00
FT3 Lamar Odom .75 2.00
FT4 Tim Duncan 2.50 6.00
FT5 Dirk Nowitzki 2.50 6.00
FT6 Karl Malone 2.00 5.00
FT7 Paul Pierce 1.50 4.00
FT8 Shawn Marion 1.00 2.50
FT9 Scottie Pippen 2.50 6.00
FT10 Darius Miles .60 1.50

2001-02 Topps Xpectations Future Features
STATED ODDS 1:31
FFAM Andre Miller 3.00 8.00
FFDM Darius Miles 2.50 6.00
FFDN Dirk Nowitzki 10.00 25.00
FFEB Elton Brand 3.00 8.00
FFJT Jason Terry 4.00 10.00
FFPP Paul Pierce 6.00 15.00
FFRH Richard Hamilton 5.00 12.00
FFRW Rasheed Wallace 5.00 12.00
FFSF Steve Francis 4.00 10.00
FFSM Shawn Marion 4.00 10.00

2001-02 Topps Xpectations Future Features Autographs
STATED ODDS 1:812
FFAEB Elton Brand/42 20.00 50.00
FFAJT Jason Terry/31 20.00 50.00
FFARH Richard Hamilton/32 20.00 50.00
FFASM Shawn Marion/31 30.00 80.00

2001-02 Topps Xpectations In The Center
COMPLETE SET (6) 4.00 10.00
STATED ODDS 1:17
IC1 Shaquille O'Neal 4.00 10.00
IC2 Alonzo Mourning 1.50 4.00
IC3 Jermaine O'Neal .75 2.00
IC4 Hakeem Olajuwon 2.00 5.00
IC5 David Robinson 2.00 5.00
IC6 Dikembe Mutombo 1.50 4.00

2002-03 Topps Xpectations
COMPLETE SET (178) 125.00 300.00
COMP.SET w/o SP's (100) 10.00 25.00
134-153 PRINT RUN 500 SER.#'d SETS
154-178 PRINT RUN 750 SER.#'d SETS
1 Darius Miles .15 .40
2 Jason Williams .30 .75
3 Speedy Claxton .15 .40
4 Eduardo Najera .15 .40
5 Chris Mihm .15 .40
6 Eddie Robinson .15 .40
7 Lee Nailon .15 .40
8 Joseph Forte .15 .40
9 Jason Terry .20 .50
10 Vince Carter .50 1.25
11 Matt Harpring .15 .40
12 Bonzi Wells .15 .40
13 Mike Bibby .25 .60
14 Jerome James .15 .40
15 Morris Peterson .20 .50
16 Jarron Collins .15 .40
17 Brendan Haywood .15 .40
18 Dermarr Johnson .15 .40
19 Kirk Haston .15 .40
20 Paul Pierce .40 1.00
21 Eddy Curry .15 .40
22 Ricky Davis .20 .50
23 James Posey .15 .40
24 Zeljko Rebraca .15 .40
25 Jason Richardson .25 .60
26 Ron Artest .20 .50
27 Jonathan Bender .15 .40
28 Elton Brand .20 .50
29 Stromile Swift .25 .60
30 Steve Francis .20 .50
31 Devean George .15 .40
32 Eddie House .15 .40
33 Loren Woods .15 .40
34 Richard Jefferson .20 .50
35 Mike Miller .20 .50
36 Joe Johnson .20 .50
37 Zach Randolph .20 .50
38 Peja Stojakovic .20 .50
39 Predrag Drobnjak .15 .40
40 Kwame Brown .15 .40
41 DeShawn Stevenson .15 .40
42 Desmond Mason .15 .40
43 Stephen Jackson .20 .50
44 Ruben Patterson .15 .40
45 Samuel Dalembert .15 .40
46 Pat Garrity .15 .40
47 Jason Collins .15 .40
48 Marc Jackson .15 .40
49 Rafer Alston .15 .40
50 Shawn Marion .25 .60
51 Joel Przybilla .15 .40
52 Shane Battier .25 .60
53 Quentin Richardson .15 .40
54 Jamaal Tinsley .15 .40
55 Cuttino Mobley .15 .40
56 Antawn Jamison .20 .50
57 Chucky Atkins .15 .40
58 Raef Lafrentz .15 .40
59 Jumaine Jones .15 .40
60 Dirk Nowitzki .60 1.50
61 Marcus Fizer .15 .40
62 Kedrick Brown .15 .40
63 Nazr Mohammed .15 .40
64 Jamaal Magloire .15 .40
65 Tyson Chandler .25 .60
66 Andre Miller .20 .50
67 Wang Zhizhi .25 .60
68 Mengke Bateer .25 .60
69 Gilbert Arenas .25 .60
70 Baron Davis .25 .60
71 Lamar Odom .25 .60
72 Mark Madsen .15 .40
73 Pau Gasol .40 1.00
74 Anthony Carter .15 .40
75 Wally Szczerbiak .20 .50
76 Todd MacCulloch .15 .40
77 Steven Hunter .15 .40
78 Iakovos Tsakalidis .15 .40
79 Ruben Boumtje-Boumtje .15 .40
80 Gerald Wallace .20 .50
81 Vladimir Radmanovic .15 .40
82 Keon Clark .15 .40
83 Andrei Kirilenko .20 .50
84 Richard Hamilton .30 .75
85 Trenton Hassell .15 .40
86 Donnell Harvey .15 .40
87 Rodney White .15 .40
88 Troy Murphy .20 .50
89 Terence Morris .15 .40
90 Al Harrington .20 .50
91 Michael Redd .20 .50
92 Kenyon Martin .25 .60
93 Lavor Postell .15 .40
94 Jeryl Sasser .15 .40
95 Hedo Turkoglu .20 .50
96 Tony Parker .40 1.00
97 Rashard Lewis .20 .50
98 Michael Bradley .15 .40
99 Courtney Alexander .15 .40
100 Eddie Griffin .15 .40
101 Yao Ming RC 4.00 10.00
102 Dan Gadzuric RC .60 1.50
103 Mike Dunleavy RC .75 2.00
104 Drew Gooden RC .75 2.00
105 Nikoloz Tskitishvili RC .50 1.25
106 Roger Mason RC .60 1.50
107 Nene Hilario RC .75 2.00
108 Chris Wilcox RC .60 1.50
109 Rod Grizzard RC .50 1.25
110 Chris Owens RC .50 1.25
111 Jared Jeffries RC .60 1.50
112 Efthimios Rentzias RC .50 1.25
113 Marcus Haislip RC .50 1.25
114 Fred Jones RC .60 1.50
115 Bostjan Nachbar RC .60 1.50
116 Jiri Welsch RC .60 1.50
117 Jannero Pargo RC .50 1.25
118 Curtis Borchardt RC .50 1.25
119 Ryan Humphrey RC .60 1.50
120 Raul Lopez RC .75 2.00
121 Cezary Trybanski RC .75 2.00
122 Predrag Savovic RC .60 1.50
123 Tayshaun Prince RC 1.50 4.00
124 Frank Williams RC .50 1.25
125 John Salmons RC .75 2.00
126 Chris Jefferies RC .50 1.25
127 Luke Recker RC .75 2.00
128 Tamar Slay RC .50 1.25
129 Matt Barnes RC 1.00 2.50
130 Rasual Butler RC .60 1.50
131 Vincent Yarbrough RC .50 1.25
132 Junior Harrington RC .50 1.25
133 Carlos Boozer RC 2.00 5.00
134 DaJuan Wagner/500 RC 2.00 5.00
135 Jay Williams/500 RC 2.00 5.00
136 Amare Stoudemire/500 RC 6.00 15.00
137 Caron Butler/500 RC 2.50 6.00
138 Melvin Ely/500 RC 2.00 5.00
139 Juan Dixon/500 RC 2.00 5.00
140 Kareem Rush/500 RC 2.00 5.00
141 Qyntel Woods/500 RC 1.50 4.00
142 Casey Jacobsen/500 RC 2.00 5.00
143 Robert Archibald/500 RC 1.50 4.00
144 Tito Maddox/500 RC 1.50 4.00
145 Ronald Murray/500 RC 2.50 6.00
146 Sam Clancy/500 RC 2.00 5.00
147 Dan Dickau/500 RC 1.50 4.00
148 Mehmet Okur/500 RC 2.50 6.00
149 Marko Jaric/500 2.50 6.00
150 Gordan Giricek 2.50 6.00
151 Manu Ginobili/500 RC 12.00 30.00
152 J.R. Bremer/500 RC 1.50 4.00
153 Corsley Edwards/500 RC 2.00 5.00
154 Michael Jordan XX 10.00 25.00
155 Allen Iverson XX 2.50 6.00
156 Shaquille O'Neal XX 4.00 10.00
157 Tim Duncan XX 2.50 6.00
158 Tracy McGrady XX 1.50 4.00
159 Kevin Garnett XX 2.50 6.00
160 Chris Webber XX 1.25 3.00
161 Alonzo Mourning XX 1.50 4.00
162 Antoine Walker XX .75 2.00
163 Latrell Sprewell XX 1.00 2.50

164 Eddie Jones XX 1.00 2.50
165 Kobe Bryant XX 8.00 20.00
166 Allan Houston XX 1.00 2.50
167 Ray Allen XX 1.50 4.00
168 Gary Payton XX 1.50 4.00
169 Antonio McDyess XX .75 2.00
170 Jason Kidd XX 1.50 4.00
171 Jerry Stackhouse XX 1.00 2.50
172 Stephon Marbury XX 1.25 3.00
173 Karl Malone XX 2.00 5.00
174 Reggie Miller XX 2.00 5.00
175 Shareef Abdur-Rahim XX 1.00 2.50
176 Rasheed Wallace XX 1.25 3.00
177 John Stockton XX 2.00 5.00
178 Grant Hill XX 1.50 4.00

2002-03 Topps Xpectations Parallel

*1-100 STARS: .6X TO 1.5X BASE CARD HI
*101-133 RCs: .6X TO 1.5X BASE CARD HI
*134-153 RCs: .2X TO .5X BASE CARD HI
*154-178 STARS: .15X TO .4X BASE CARD HI
STATED ODDS 1 PER PACK

2002-03 Topps Xpectations Parallel Xtra

*1-100 STARS: 6X TO 15X BASE CARD HI
*101-133 RCs: 2.5X TO 6X BASE CARD HI
*134-153 RCs: .75X TO 2X BASE CARD HI
*154-178 STARS: 1.5X TO 4X BASE CARD HI
PRINT RUN 99 SER.#'d SETS

2002-03 Topps Xpectations Autographs

GROUP A ODDS 1:117; B ODDS 1:312
GROUP C ODDS 1:42; D ODDS 1:412
GROUP E ODDS 1:332
XAAH Al Harrington C 4.00 10.00
XACM Corey Maggette E 3.00 8.00
XACBC Curtis Borchardt E 2.50 6.00
XACBO Carlos Boozer C 4.00 10.00
XADB Damone Brown A 4.00 10.00
XADG Drew Gooden A 4.00 10.00
XADH Donnell Harvey A 4.00 10.00
XADW DaJuan Wagner C 3.00 8.00
XAEC Eddy Curry C 4.00 10.00
XAFW Frank Williams B 2.50 6.00
XAHT Hedo Turkoglu E 3.00 8.00
XAJB Jonathan Bender B 4.00 10.00
XAJF Joseph Forte E 4.00 10.00
XAJJ Joe Johnson A 8.00 20.00
XAJT Iakovos Tsakalidis A 4.00 10.00
XAJJE Jared Jeffries C 3.00 8.00
XAJTR Jeff Trepagnier A 4.00 10.00
XAKBR Kedrick Brown C 2.50 6.00
XALW Loren Woods A 4.00 10.00
XAMD Mike Dunleavy C 4.00 10.00
XAMJ Marc Jackson A 4.00 10.00
XANT Nikoloz Tskitishvili C 2.50 6.00
XASB Shane Battier C 5.00 12.00
XASM Shawn Marion A 4.00 10.00
XATD Tim Duncan B 250.00 500.00
XATM Troy Murphy C 3.00 8.00
XATT Tim Thomas A 4.00 10.00
XAVY Vincent Yarbrough C 2.50 6.00
XAYM Yao Ming C 50.00 120.00
XAZR Zach Randolph D 6.00 15.00

2002-03 Topps Xpectations Class Challenge Relics

GROUP A ODDS: 1:298; B ODDS 1:30
CCAK Andrei Kirilenko D 2.50 6.00
CCBH Brendan Haywood D 2.00 5.00
CCCM Chris Mihm D 2.00 5.00
CCDM Darius Miles D 2.00 5.00
CCJR Jason Richardson D 3.00 8.00
CCKM Kenyon Martin D 3.00 8.00
CCLN Lee Nailon D 2.00 5.00
CCMF Marcus Fizer D 2.00 5.00
CCMM Mike Miller C 2.50 6.00
CCPG Pau Gasol C 5.00 12.00
CCQR Quentin Richardson C 2.00 5.00
CCSB Shane Battier A 3.00 8.00
CCTP Tony Parker B 5.00 12.00
CCZR Zeljko Rebraca D 2.00 5.00

2002-03 Topps Xpectations First Shot Relics

STATED ODDS 1:10
FSAS Amare Stoudemire 8.00 20.00
FSCB Caron Butler 3.00 8.00
FSCB Carlos Boozer 3.00 8.00
FSCW Chris Wilcox 2.50 6.00
FSCJA Casey Jacobsen 2.50 6.00
FSCJE Chris Jefferies 2.00 5.00
FSDW DaJuan Wagner 2.50 6.00
FSDGO Drew Gooden 3.00 8.00
FSFJ Fred Jones 2.50 6.00
FSJD Juan Dixon 2.50 6.00
FSJJ Jared Jeffries 2.50 6.00
FSJS John Salmons 3.00 8.00
FSKR Kareem Rush 2.50 6.00
FSMD Mike Dunleavy 3.00 8.00
FSME Melvin Ely 2.50 6.00
FSMH Marcus Haislip 2.00 5.00
FSNH Nene Hilario 3.00 8.00
FSNT Nikoloz Tskitishvili 2.00 5.00
FSPS Predrag Savovic 2.00 5.00
FSQW Qyntel Woods 2.00 5.00
FSRH Ryan Humphrey 2.50 6.00
FSSC Sam Clancy 2.50 6.00
FSSL Steve Logan 3.00 8.00
FSTP Tayshaun Prince 6.00 15.00
FSVY Vincent Yarbrough 2.00 5.00

2002-03 Topps Xpectations Future Features Relics

STATED ODDS 1:40
FFAM Andre Miller C 1.50 4.00
FFBH Brendan Haywood C 1.25 3.00
FFDN Dirk Nowitzki A 5.00 12.00
FFGW Gerald Wallace C 1.50 4.00
FFJJ Joe Johnson A 1.50 4.00
FFMM Mike Miller C 1.50 4.00
FFPP Paul Pierce C 3.00 8.00
FFPS Peja Stojakovic C 1.50 4.00
FFQR Quentin Richardson B 1.25 3.00
FFRL Raef LaFrentz A 1.25 3.00
FFSF Steve Francis A 2.00 5.00
FFSM Stephon Marbury C 2.50 6.00
FFSN Steve Nash A 4.00 10.00
FFSDM Shawn Marion C 2.00 5.00
FFWS Wally Szczerbiak C 1.50 4.00

2002-03 Topps Xpectations Future Features Relics Autographs

STATED ODDS 1:1259
FFAGW Gerald Wallace 10.00 25.00
FFAJJ Joe Johnson 10.00 25.00
FFAPS Peja Stojakovic 30.00 60.00

2002-03 Topps Xpectations Xtra Threads Relics

STATED ODDS 1:25
XTAH Anfernee Hardaway C 6.00 15.00
XTAI Allen Iverson C 6.00 15.00
XTAHO Allan Houston A 2.50 6.00
XTCW Chris Webber C 3.00 8.00
XTGR Glenn Robinson C 2.50 6.00
XTJK Jason Kidd C 4.00 10.00
XTJO Jermaine O'Neal C 2.00 5.00
XTMJ Michael Finley C 2.50 6.00
XTMO Michael Olowokandi C 1.50 4.00
XTNV Nick Van Exel C 2.50 6.00
XTRA Ray Allen C 4.00 10.00
XTSN Steve Nash C 5.00 12.00
XTSO Shaquille O'Neal C 10.00 25.00
XTTD Tim Duncan C 6.00 15.00
XTTG Tom Gugliotta C 1.50 4.00
XTTM Tracy McGrady B 4.00 10.00

2010-11 Totally Certified

COMP.SET w/o RCs (150) 40.00 100.00
1-150 PRINT RUN 1849 SER.#'d SETS
JSY AU RC PRINT RUN 575 TO 599 SETS
1 Andre Iguodala .75 2.00
2 Elton Brand .60 1.50
3 Jrue Holiday 1.00 2.50
4 Thaddeus Young .50 1.25
5 D.J. Augustin .50 1.25
6 Boris Diaw .60 1.50
7 Gerald Henderson .50 1.25
8 Stephen Jackson .60 1.50
9 Brandon Jennings .50 1.25
10 Andrew Bogut .60 1.50
11 John Salmons .50 1.25
12 Corey Maggette .60 1.50
13 Luc Mbah a Moute .50 1.25
14 Derrick Rose 1.50 4.00
15 Carlos Boozer .60 1.50
16 Luol Deng .60 1.50
17 Joakim Noah .75 2.00
18 Taj Gibson .50 1.25
19 Antawn Jamison .60 1.50
20 Daniel Gibson .50 1.25
21 Baron Davis .75 2.00
22 Anderson Varejao .50 1.25
23 Paul Pierce 1.25 3.00
24 Rajon Rondo 1.00 2.50
25 Kevin Garnett 2.00 5.00
26 Shaquille O'Neal 3.00 8.00
27 Ray Allen 1.25 3.00
28 Troy Murphy .50 1.25
29 Blake Griffin .75 2.00
30 DeAndre Jordan .60 1.50
31 Eric Gordon .60 1.50
32 Ryan Gomes .50 1.25
33 Chris Kaman .50 1.25
34 Shane Battier .60 1.50
35 Marc Gasol .75 2.00
36 Zach Randolph .75 2.00
37 Rudy Gay .75 2.00
38 O.J. Mayo .50 1.25
39 Joe Johnson .75 2.00
40 Josh Smith .50 1.25
41 Al Horford .75 2.00
42 Jamal Crawford .75 2.00
43 Kirk Hinrich .60 1.50
44 Dwyane Wade 1.50 4.00
45 LeBron James 10.00 25.00
46 Chris Bosh 1.00 2.50
47 Eddie House .50 1.25
48 Mike Bibby .75 2.00
49 Chris Paul 1.50 4.00
50 David West .60 1.50
51 Trevor Ariza .50 1.25
52 Emeka Okafor .60 1.50
53 Jarrett Jack .60 1.50
54 Al Jefferson .50 1.25
55 Devin Harris .60 1.50
56 Andrei Kirilenko .60 1.50
57 Paul Millsap .60 1.50
58 Mehmet Okur .50 1.25
59 Tyreke Evans .60 1.50
60 Omri Casspi .50 1.25
61 Samuel Dalembert .50 1.25
62 Marcus Thornton .50 1.25
63 Beno Udrih .50 1.25
64 Amare Stoudemire .75 2.00
65 Carmelo Anthony 1.25 3.00
66 Chauncey Billups 1.00 2.50
67 Toney Douglas .50 1.25
68 Ronny Turiaf .50 1.25
69 Kobe Bryant 10.00 25.00
70 Pau Gasol 1.25 3.00
71 Ron Artest .75 2.00
72 Lamar Odom .60 1.50
73 Derek Fisher .75 2.00
74 Matt Barnes .50 1.25
75 Dwight Howard 1.00 2.50
76 Jameer Nelson .50 1.25
77 Gilbert Arenas .60 1.50
78 J.J. Redick .75 2.00
79 Hedo Turkoglu .60 1.50
80 Dirk Nowitzki 2.00 5.00
81 Caron Butler .60 1.50
82 Shawn Marion .60 1.50
83 Jason Terry .60 1.50
84 Tyson Chandler .60 1.50
85 Jason Kidd 1.25 3.00
86 Deron Williams .60 1.50
87 Brook Lopez .60 1.50
88 Anthony Morrow .50 1.25
89 Sasha Vujacic .50 1.25
90 Travis Outlaw .50 1.25
91 Nene .60 1.50
92 Raymond Felton .50 1.25
93 Chris Andersen .75 2.00
94 Danilo Gallinari .60 1.50
95 Al Harrington .60 1.50
96 Danny Granger .50 1.25
97 Darren Collison .50 1.25
98 Mike Dunleavy .50 1.25
99 T.J. Ford .50 1.25
100 Jeff Foster .50 1.25
101 Ben Gordon .60 1.50
102 Richard Hamilton 1.00 2.50
103 Tracy McGrady 1.25 3.00
104 Tayshaun Prince .75 2.00
105 Rodney Stuckey .50 1.25
106 DeMar DeRozan 1.25 3.00
107 Jose Calderon .50 1.25
108 Andrea Bargnani .50 1.25
109 Leandro Barbosa .60 1.50
110 Linas Kleiza .50 1.25
111 Kevin Martin .60 1.50
112 Luis Scola .60 1.50
113 Goran Dragic 1.00 2.50
114 Chase Budinger .50 1.25
115 Kyle Lowry .75 2.00
116 Tim Duncan 2.00 5.00
117 Tony Parker 1.25 3.00
118 Manu Ginobili 1.50 4.00
119 Richard Jefferson .60 1.50
120 DeJuan Blair .60 1.50
121 Steve Nash 1.50 4.00
122 Grant Hill 1.25 3.00
123 Channing Frye .50 1.25
124 Aaron Brooks .50 1.25
125 Vince Carter 1.50 4.00
126 Kevin Durant 3.00 8.00
127 Russell Westbrook 1.25 3.00
128 Serge Ibaka .60 1.50
129 James Harden 2.00 5.00
130 Kendrick Perkins .50 1.25
131 Kevin Love .75 2.00
132 Michael Beasley .60 1.50
133 Jonny Flynn .50 1.25
134 Anthony Randolph .50 1.25
135 Darko Milicic .50 1.25
136 LaMarcus Aldridge .75 2.00
137 Brandon Roy 1.00 2.50
138 Andre Miller .60 1.50
139 Rudy Fernandez .60 1.50
140 Marcus Camby .50 1.25
141 Monta Ellis .60 1.50
142 Stephen Curry 20.00 50.00
143 David Lee .50 1.25
144 Al Thornton .50 1.25
145 Dorell Wright .50 1.25
146 Josh Howard .60 1.50
147 Nick Young .50 1.25
148 JaVale McGee .60 1.50
149 Rashard Lewis .60 1.50
150 Yi Jianlian .75 2.00
151 John Wall/599 JSY AU RC 20.00 50.00
152 D.Cousins/593 JSY AU RC 12.00 30.00
153 Quincy Pondexter/585 JSY AU RC 3.00 8.00
154 G.Hayward/579 JSY AU RC 12.00 30.00
155 Al-Farouq Aminu/596 JSY AU RC 4.00 10.00
156 Ed Davis/599 JSY AU RC 4.00 10.00
157 G.Vasquez/599 JSY AU RC 3.00 8.00
158 Ekpe Udoh/599 JSY AU RC 3.00 8.00
159 Damion James/599 JSY AU RC 3.00 8.00
160 Landry Fields/599 JSY AU RC 3.00 8.00
161 G.Monroe/599 JSY AU RC 4.00 10.00
162 Cole Aldrich/599 JSY AU RC 3.00 8.00
163 Evan Turner/599 JSY AU RC 4.00 10.00
164 Luke Babbitt/597 JSY AU RC 3.00 8.00
165 D.Favors/599 JSY AU RC 5.00 12.00
166 Xavier Henry/599 JSY AU RC 3.00 8.00
167 J.Crawford/595 JSY AU RC 3.00 8.00
168 Larry Sanders/583 JSY AU RC 3.00 8.00
169 Wesley Johnson/599 JSY AU RC 3.00 8.00
170 E.Bledsoe/599 JSY AU RC 6.00 15.00
171 A.Bradley/575 JSY AU RC 5.00 12.00
172 Daniel Orton/599 JSY AU RC 3.00 8.00
173 P.George/599 JSY AU RC 40.00 100.00
174 J.Anderson/599 JSY AU RC 3.00 8.00
175 Elliot Williams/599 JSY AU RC 3.00 8.00
176 Dominique Jones/599 JSY AU RC 3.00 8.00
177 Dexter Pittman/599 JSY AU RC 3.00 8.00
178 Lazar Hayward/599 JSY AU RC 3.00 8.00
179 Trevor Booker/599 JSY AU RC 3.00 8.00
180 Luke Harangody/599 JSY AU RC 3.00 8.00
181 P.Patterson/599 JSY AU RC 4.00 10.00
182 H. Whiteside/565 JSY AU RC 6.00 15.00
183 Willie Warren/599 JSY AU RC 3.00 8.00
184 Terrico White/599 JSY AU RC 3.00 8.00
185 Andy Rautins/599 JSY AU RC 3.00 8.00

2010-11 Totally Certified Blue

*BLUE: .75X TO 2X BASE HI
STATED PRINT RUN 299 SER.#'d SETS
122 Grant Hill 4.00 10.00

2010-11 Totally Certified Blue Autographs

*BLUE RC AUTOGRAPHS: .5X TO 1.25X BASE HI
STATED PRINT RUN 32 TO 49 SER.#'d SETS

2010-11 Totally Certified Blue Materials

*BLUE MATERIALS: 2X TO 5X BASE HI
STATED PRINT RUN 49 TO 99 SER.#'d SETS
45 LeBron James/99 12.00 30.00
69 Kobe Bryant/99 12.00 30.00
122 Grant Hill/99 10.00 25.00
126 Kevin Durant/99 10.00 25.00

2010-11 Totally Certified Gold

*GOLD: 6X TO 15X BASE HI
STATED PRINT RUN 25 SER.#'d SETS
14 Derrick Rose 50.00 125.00
26 Shaquille O'Neal 30.00 80.00
126 Kevin Durant 50.00 125.00

2010-11 Totally Certified Gold Autographs

*GOLD RC AUTOGRAPHS: 1.25X TO 3X BASE HI
STATED PRINT RUN 10 TO 25 SER.#'d SETS
1 Andre Iguodala/25 8.00 20.00
3 Jrue Holiday/25 10.00 25.00
5 D.J. Augustin/25 6.00 15.00
6 Boris Diaw/25 6.00 15.00
7 Gerald Henderson/25 6.00 15.00
8 Stephen Jackson/25 6.00 15.00
9 Brandon Jennings/25 12.00 30.00
10 Andrew Bogut/25 15.00 40.00
15 Carlos Boozer/25 12.00 30.00
17 Joakim Noah/25 15.00 40.00
18 Taj Gibson/25 10.00 25.00
19 Antawn Jamison/25 6.00 15.00
20 Daniel Gibson/25 6.00 15.00
21 Baron Davis/25 6.00 15.00
23 Paul Pierce/25 40.00 100.00
24 Rajon Rondo/25 10.00 25.00
27 Ray Allen/25 50.00 120.00
29 Blake Griffin/25 100.00 200.00
31 Eric Gordon/25 10.00 25.00
32 Ryan Gomes/25 6.00 15.00
34 Shane Battier/25 8.00 20.00
35 Marc Gasol/25 12.00 30.00
36 Zach Randolph/25 12.00 30.00
39 Joe Johnson/25 10.00 25.00
40 Josh Smith/25 8.00 20.00
41 Al Horford/25 6.00 15.00
46 Chris Bosh/25 25.00 60.00
48 Mike Bibby/25 10.00 25.00
51 Trevor Ariza/25 6.00 15.00
52 Emeka Okafor/25 6.00 15.00
54 Al Jefferson/25 6.00 15.00
55 Devin Harris/25 6.00 15.00
56 Andrei Kirilenko/25 6.00 15.00
59 Tyreke Evans/25 15.00 40.00
60 Omri Casspi/25 6.00 15.00
61 Samuel Dalembert/25 6.00 15.00
62 Marcus Thornton/25 6.00 15.00
63 Beno Udrih/25 6.00 15.00
66 Chauncey Billups/25 10.00 25.00
67 Toney Douglas/25 6.00 15.00
69 Kobe Bryant/25 1,500.00 3,000.00
72 Lamar Odom/25 12.00 30.00
73 Derek Fisher/25 20.00 50.00
78 J.J. Redick/25 10.00 25.00
79 Hedo Turkoglu/25 6.00 15.00
81 Caron Butler/25 8.00 20.00
85 Jason Kidd/25 30.00 80.00
86 Deron Williams/25 8.00 20.00
87 Brook Lopez/25 10.00 25.00
93 Chris Andersen/25 30.00 80.00
94 Danilo Gallinari/25 6.00 15.00
96 Danny Granger/25 8.00 20.00
97 Darren Collison/25 6.00 15.00
98 Mike Dunleavy/25 6.00 15.00
99 T.J. Ford/25 6.00 15.00
101 Ben Gordon/25 10.00 25.00
102 Richard Hamilton/25 12.00 30.00
106 DeMar DeRozan/25 30.00 80.00
108 Andrea Bargnani/25 8.00 20.00
113 Goran Dragic/25 30.00 80.00
114 Chase Budinger/25 6.00 15.00
117 Tony Parker/25 15.00 40.00
120 DeJuan Blair/25 6.00 15.00
122 Grant Hill/25 100.00 250.00
123 Channing Frye/25 6.00 15.00
124 Aaron Brooks/25 6.00 15.00
125 Vince Carter/25 25.00 60.00
127 Russell Westbrook/25 50.00 120.00
128 Serge Ibaka/25 15.00 40.00
129 James Harden/25 40.00 100.00
130 Kendrick Perkins/25 8.00 20.00
131 Kevin Love/25 15.00 40.00
132 Michael Beasley/25 10.00 25.00
133 Jonny Flynn/25 6.00 15.00
135 Darko Milicic/25 6.00 15.00
136 LaMarcus Aldridge/25 12.00 30.00
137 Brandon Roy/25 10.00 25.00
138 Andre Miller/25 8.00 20.00
139 Rudy Fernandez/25 8.00 20.00
140 Marcus Camby/25 10.00 25.00
141 Monta Ellis/25 6.00 15.00
142 Stephen Curry/25 800.00 1,500.00
143 David Lee/25 8.00 20.00
144 Al Thornton/25 6.00 15.00
146 Josh Howard/25 6.00 15.00
148 JaVale McGee/25 6.00 15.00

2010-11 Totally Certified Gold Materials Prime

*GOLD MATERIALS: 6X TO 15X BASE HI
STATED PRINT RUN 3 TO 25 SER.#'d SETS
46 Chris Bosh/25 20.00 50.00
49 Chris Paul/25 25.00 60.00
85 Jason Kidd/25 15.00 40.00
122 Grant Hill/25 50.00 125.00
126 Kevin Durant/25 40.00 100.00

2010-11 Totally Certified Red

*RED: .5X TO 1.25X BASE HI
STATED PRINT RUN 499 SER.#'d SETS

2010-11 Totally Certified Red Autographs

*RED RC AUTOGRAPHS: .4X TO 1X BASE HI
STATED PRINT RUN 3 TO 99 SER.#'d SETS
1 Andre Iguodala/25 6.00 15.00
3 Jrue Holiday/49 12.00 30.00
5 D.J. Augustin/49 4.00 10.00
6 Boris Diaw/49 4.00 10.00
7 Gerald Henderson/99 4.00 10.00
8 Stephen Jackson/49 4.00 10.00
9 Brandon Jennings/25 15.00 40.00
10 Andrew Bogut/49 10.00 25.00
15 Carlos Boozer/49 8.00 20.00
17 Joakim Noah/49 10.00 25.00
18 Taj Gibson/99 6.00 15.00
19 Antawn Jamison/49 4.00 10.00
20 Daniel Gibson/49 4.00 10.00
21 Baron Davis/25 8.00 20.00
24 Rajon Rondo/25 20.00 50.00
31 Eric Gordon/99 6.00 15.00
32 Ryan Gomes/99 4.00 10.00
33 Chris Kaman/25 6.00 15.00
34 Shane Battier/25 6.00 15.00
35 Marc Gasol/25 12.00 30.00
36 Zach Randolph/25 10.00 25.00
38 O.J. Mayo/20 10.00 25.00
39 Joe Johnson/25 10.00 25.00
40 Josh Smith/25 8.00 20.00
41 Al Horford/25 6.00 15.00
48 Mike Bibby/25 10.00 25.00
51 Trevor Ariza/25 6.00 15.00
52 Emeka Okafor/25 6.00 15.00
54 Al Jefferson/25 6.00 15.00
55 Devin Harris/25 6.00 15.00
56 Andrei Kirilenko/25 6.00 15.00
59 Tyreke Evans/49 12.00 30.00
60 Omri Casspi/99 4.00 10.00
61 Samuel Dalembert/49 4.00 10.00
62 Marcus Thornton/99 4.00 10.00
63 Beno Udrih/99 4.00 10.00
66 Chauncey Billups/25 10.00 25.00
67 Toney Douglas/49 4.00 10.00
69 Kobe Bryant/49 1,500.00 3,000.00
70 Pau Gasol/15 25.00 60.00
73 Derek Fisher/49 10.00 25.00
78 J.J. Redick/49 6.00 15.00
79 Hedo Turkoglu/49 4.00 10.00
81 Caron Butler/49 5.00 12.00
87 Brook Lopez/25 10.00 25.00
93 Chris Andersen/25 20.00 50.00
94 Danilo Gallinari/49 10.00 25.00
97 Darren Collison/49 4.00 10.00
98 Mike Dunleavy/49 4.00 10.00
99 T.J. Ford/99 4.00 10.00
101 Ben Gordon/25 10.00 25.00
102 Richard Hamilton/25 10.00 25.00
106 DeMar DeRozan/25 30.00 80.00
108 Andrea Bargnani/25 6.00 15.00
113 Goran Dragic/99 15.00 40.00
114 Chase Budinger/99 4.00 10.00
117 Tony Parker/25 12.00 30.00
120 DeJuan Blair/99 4.00 10.00
123 Channing Frye/49 4.00 10.00
124 Aaron Brooks/49 4.00 10.00
127 Russell Westbrook/25 50.00 120.00
128 Serge Ibaka/99 10.00 25.00
129 James Harden/25 15.00 40.00
130 Kendrick Perkins/49 6.00 15.00
131 Kevin Love/25 15.00 40.00
133 Jonny Flynn/99 4.00 10.00
134 Anthony Randolph/25 5.00 12.00
135 Darko Milicic/99 4.00 10.00
136 LaMarcus Aldridge/49 10.00 25.00
137 Brandon Roy/25 12.00 30.00
138 Andre Miller/49 4.00 10.00
139 Rudy Fernandez/99 4.00 10.00
140 Marcus Camby/25 10.00 25.00
141 Monta Ellis/25 15.00 40.00
142 Stephen Curry/99 500.00 1,000.00
143 David Lee/25 8.00 20.00
144 Al Thornton/99 4.00 10.00
146 Josh Howard/25 6.00 15.00
148 JaVale McGee/49 4.00 10.00
151 John Wall JSY AU/99 40.00 100.00
152 D.Cousins JSY AU/99 30.00 80.00
153 Quincy Pondexter JSY AU/99 3.00 8.00
154 Gordon Hayward JSY AU/99 20.00 50.00
155 Al-Farouq Aminu JSY AU/98 4.00 10.00
156 Ed Davis JSY AU/99 4.00 10.00
157 Greivis Vasquez JSY AU/99 3.00 8.00
158 Ekpe Udoh JSY AU/99 3.00 8.00
159 Damion James JSY AU/99 3.00 8.00
160 Landry Fields JSY AU/98 3.00 8.00
161 Greg Monroe JSY AU/99 4.00 10.00
162 Cole Aldrich JSY AU/99 3.00 8.00
163 Evan Turner JSY AU/99 4.00 10.00
164 Luke Babbitt JSY AU/99 3.00 8.00
169 Wesley Johnson JSY AU/99 3.00 8.00
170 Eric Bledsoe JSY AU/99 6.00 15.00
171 Avery Bradley JSY AU/99 5.00 12.00
172 Daniel Orton JSY AU/99 3.00 8.00
173 Paul George JSY AU/99 50.00 120.00
174 James Anderson JSY AU/99 3.00 8.00
175 Elliot Williams JSY AU/99 3.00 8.00
176 Dominique Jones JSY AU/99 3.00 8.00
177 Dexter Pittman JSY AU/99 3.00 8.00
178 Lazar Hayward JSY AU/99 3.00 8.00
179 Trevor Booker JSY AU/99 3.00 8.00
180 Luke Harangody JSY AU/99 3.00 8.00
181 Patrick Patterson JSY AU/99 4.00 10.00
183 Willie Warren JSY AU/99 3.00 8.00
184 Terrico White JSY AU/99 3.00 8.00
185 Andy Rautins JSY AU/99 3.00 8.00

2010-11 Totally Certified Red Materials

*RED MATERIALS: 1.5X TO 4X BASE HI
STATED PRINT RUN 199 TO 249 SER.#'d SETS
69 Kobe Bryant/249 8.00 20.00
122 Grant Hill/249 8.00 20.00
126 Kevin Durant/249 6.00 15.00

2010-11 Totally Certified Fabric of the Game Jumbo Jersey Number

STATED PRINT RUN ONE TO 299 SETS
1 Patrick Ewing/99 8.00 20.00
2 Dirk Nowitzki/299 8.00 20.00
3 Chris Andersen/299 3.00 8.00
4 Dwyane Wade/299 6.00 15.00
5 Chris Paul/299 6.00 15.00
6 Dwight Howard/299 4.00 10.00
7 Elton Brand/299 2.50 6.00
8 Grant Hill/299 5.00 12.00
9 Rudy Fernandez/299 2.00 5.00
10 LeBron James/299 40.00 100.00
11 Manu Ginobili/99 6.00 15.00
12 Karl Malone/299 6.00 15.00
13 Al Horford/299 3.00 8.00
14 Kevin McHale/99 5.00 12.00
15 Andres Nocioni/299 2.00 5.00
16 Larry Johnson/99 8.00 20.00
17 Scottie Pippen/299 8.00 20.00
18 Jason Terry/299 2.50 6.00
19 Tim Duncan/299 8.00 20.00
20 Dikembe Mutombo/99 5.00 12.00
21 Omri Casspi/299 2.00 5.00
22 Luis Scola/299 2.50 6.00
23 Chris Kaman/299 2.00 5.00
24 Ron Artest/299 3.00 8.00
25 O.J. Mayo/299 2.00 5.00
26 Andrew Bogut/299 2.50 6.00
27 Brook Lopez/299 2.50 6.00
28 Shawn Marion/299 3.00 8.00
30 Jonny Flynn/299 2.00 5.00
31 James Harden/299 8.00 20.00
32 Toni Kukoc/299 3.00 8.00
33 Udonis Haslem/299 2.00 5.00
34 LaMarcus Aldridge/299 3.00 8.00
35 Shawn Kemp/99 20.00 50.00
36 John Stockton/299 5.00 12.00
37 Josh Smith/299 2.00 5.00
38 Paul Pierce/299 5.00 12.00
39 Luol Deng/299 2.50 6.00
40 Ty Lawson/299 2.00 5.00
41 Joe Dumars/99 3.00 8.00
42 Nick Van Exel/99 4.00 10.00
43 Charles Oakley/99 6.00 15.00
44 Maurice Cheeks/99 2.50 6.00
45 David West/299 2.50 6.00
46 Andre Iguodala/299 3.00 8.00
47 Rasheed Wallace/299 3.00 8.00
48 Boris Diaw/299 2.50 6.00
49 Arron Afflalo/299 2.00 5.00
50 Andre Miller/299 2.50 6.00

2010-11 Totally Certified Fabric of the Game Jumbo Jersey Number Prime

*PRIME: 1X TO 2.5X BASE HI
STATED PRINT RUN ONE TO 25 SER.#'d SETS
1 Patrick Ewing/25 25.00 60.00
2 Dirk Nowitzki/25 15.00 40.00
4 Dwyane Wade/20 20.00 50.00
8 Grant Hill/25 20.00 50.00
10 LeBron James/25 125.00 300.00
11 Manu Ginobili/25 20.00 50.00
16 Larry Johnson/25 25.00 60.00
19 Tim Duncan/25 20.00 50.00
29 Hakeem Olajuwon/25 15.00 40.00
32 Toni Kukoc/25 10.00 25.00
42 Nick Van Exel/25 12.00 30.00
43 Charles Oakley/25 10.00 25.00

2010-11 Totally Certified Fabric of the Game Jumbo Team

STATED PRINT RUN 5 TO 299 SER.#'d SETS
2 Brook Lopez/99 2.50 6.00
3 Amare Stoudemire/49 3.00 8.00
4 Elton Brand/299 2.50 6.00
5 DeMar DeRozan/299 5.00 12.00
6 Derrick Rose/299 6.00 15.00
7 Antawn Jamison/299 2.50 6.00
8 Ben Gordon/299 2.50 6.00
9 Danny Granger/299 2.00 5.00
10 Brandon Jennings/299 2.00 5.00
11 Joe Johnson/299 3.00 8.00
12 Stephen Jackson/299 2.50 6.00
13 LeBron James/299 10.00 25.00
14 Dwight Howard/299 4.00 10.00
15 Jason Kidd/299 5.00 12.00
16 Luis Scola/299 2.50 6.00
17 Marc Gasol/299 3.00 8.00
18 Chris Paul/299 6.00 15.00
19 Tony Parker/25 6.00 15.00
20 Nene/99 2.50 6.00
21 Michael Beasley/299 2.00 5.00
22 Brandon Roy/299 4.00 10.00
23 Kevin Durant/299 8.00 20.00
24 Al Jefferson/49 2.00 5.00
25 Monta Ellis/299 2.50 6.00
26 Blake Griffin/49 3.00 8.00
27 Kobe Bryant/299 12.00 30.00
28 Steve Nash/299 6.00 15.00
29 Tyreke Evans/299 2.50 6.00
30 JaVale McGee/299 2.50 6.00
31 Shaquille O'Neal/299 12.00 30.00
32 Andre Iguodala/190 3.00 8.00
33 Andrea Bargnani/299 2.00 5.00
34 Carlos Boozer/299 2.50 6.00
35 Andrew Bogut/299 2.50 6.00
36 Dwyane Wade/299 6.00 15.00
37 Caron Butler/299 2.50 6.00
38 LaMarcus Aldridge/299 3.00 8.00
39 Stephen Curry/99 12.00 30.00
40 Eric Gordon/299 2.50 6.00
41 Pau Gasol/299 5.00 12.00
42 Tim Duncan/299 8.00 20.00
43 Kevin Love/299 3.00 8.00
44 Russell Westbrook/299 5.00 12.00
45 Joakim Noah/199 3.00 8.00
46 Chris Bosh/99 4.00 10.00
47 Chris Kaman/299 2.00 5.00
48 Manu Ginobili/99 6.00 15.00
49 Andrei Kirilenko/99 2.50 6.00
50 Tyson Chandler/299 2.50 6.00

2010-11 Totally Certified Fabric of the Game Jumbo Team Prime

*PRIME: 1X TO 2.5X BASE HI
STATED PRINT RUN ONE TO 25 SER.#'d SETS
1 Ray Allen/25 12.00 30.00
13 LeBron James/25 20.00 50.00
19 Tony Parker/25 12.00 30.00
23 Kevin Durant/25 30.00 80.00
28 Steve Nash/25 12.00 30.00
31 Shaquille O'Neal/25 25.00 60.00

2010-11 Totally Certified HRX Video Cards

STATED PRINT RUN 40 SER.#'d SETS
1 Kobe Bryant 200.00 500.00
2 Kevin Durant 125.00 250.00
3 Blake Griffin 60.00 150.00
4 John Wall 60.00 150.00

2010-11 Totally Certified Potential

STATED PRINT RUN 249 SER.#'d SETS
*BLUE: .75X TO 2X BASE HI
BLUE PRINT RUN 49 SER.#'d SETS
*GOLD: 2X TO 5X BASE HI
GOLD PRINT RUN 25 SER.#'d SETS
*RED: .6X TO 1.5X BASE HI
RED PRINT RUN 99 SER.#'d SETS
1 Blake Griffin 1.25 3.00
2 Derrick Rose 2.50 6.00
3 Stephen Curry 15.00 40.00
4 Tyreke Evans 1.00 2.50
5 DeJuan Blair .75 2.00
6 Eric Gordon 1.00 2.50
7 Brandon Jennings .75 2.00
8 Kevin Love 1.25 3.00
9 Michael Beasley .75 2.00
10 Wesley Matthews .75 2.00
11 Zach Randolph 1.25 3.00
12 Russell Westbrook 2.00 5.00
13 Taj Gibson .75 2.00
14 James Harden 3.00 8.00
15 JaVale McGee 1.00 2.50

2010-11 Totally Certified Potential Autographs Gold

STATED PRINT RUN 25 SER.#'d SETS
1 Blake Griffin 30.00 80.00
2 Derrick Rose 100.00 200.00
3 Stephen Curry 1,000.00 2,000.00
4 Tyreke Evans 15.00 40.00
5 DeJuan Blair 6.00 15.00
6 Eric Gordon 8.00 20.00
7 Brandon Jennings 15.00 40.00
8 Kevin Love 15.00 40.00
9 Michael Beasley 12.50 30.00
10 Wesley Matthews 15.00 40.00
11 Zach Randolph 10.00 25.00
12 Russell Westbrook 40.00 100.00
13 Taj Gibson 12.00 30.00
14 James Harden 15.00 40.00
15 JaVale McGee 6.00 15.00

2010-11 Totally Certified Potential Jerseys Prime Gold

*GOLD PRIME: 3X TO 8X BASE HI
STATED PRINT RUN 15 TO 25 SER.#'d SETS

2012-13 Totally Certified

COMPLETE SET (300) 125.00 250.00
1 Arron Afflalo .50 1.25
2 LaMarcus Aldridge .75 2.00
3 Drew Gooden .60 1.50
4 Tony Allen .50 1.25
5 Al-Farouq Aminu .50 1.25
6 Kenneth Faried RC .75 2.00
7 Carmelo Anthony 1.25 3.00
8 Trevor Ariza .50 1.25
9 Darrell Arthur .50 1.25
10 Thomas Robinson RC .60 1.50
11 Kawhi Leonard RC 10.00 25.00
12 Kyrie Irving RC 10.00 25.00
13 Brandon Bass .50 1.25
14 Matt Barnes .50 1.25
15 Shane Battier .60 1.50
16 Michael Kidd-Gilchrist RC .75 2.00
17 Jerryd Bayless .50 1.25
18 Iman Shumpert RC .75 2.00
19 Rodrigue Beaubois .50 1.25
20 Marco Belinelli .50 1.25
21 Andris Biedrins .50 1.25
22 Chauncey Billups 1.00 2.50
23 DeJuan Blair .50 1.25
24 Will Barton RC 1.25 3.00
25 Eric Bledsoe .60 1.50
26 Andrew Bogut .60 1.50
27 Matt Bonner .50 1.25
28 Trevor Booker .50 1.25
29 Anthony Davis RC 12.00 30.00
30 Chris Bosh 1.00 2.50
31 Avery Bradley .50 1.25
32 Elton Brand .60 1.50
33 Tobias Harris RC 2.00 5.00
34 Chase Budinger .50 1.25
35 Caron Butler .60 1.50
36 Andrew Bynum .60 1.50
37 Jose Calderon .50 1.25
38 Enes Kanter RC 1.00 2.50
39 Jordan Williams RC .75 2.00
40 Vince Carter 1.50 4.00
41 Omri Casspi .50 1.25
42 Mario Chalmers .60 1.50
43 Tyson Chandler .60 1.50
44 Darren Collison .50 1.25
45 Nick Collison .50 1.25
46 Nolan Smith RC .60 1.50
47 DeMarcus Cousins .75 2.00
48 Jamal Crawford .75 2.00
49 Stephen Curry 6.00 15.00
50 Malcolm Lee RC .60 1.50
51 JaJuan Johnson RC .60 1.50
52 Glen Davis .50 1.25
53 Carlos Delfino .50 1.25
54 Luol Deng .60 1.50
55 DeMar DeRozan 1.00 2.50
56 Goran Dragic .75 2.00
57 Josh Selby RC .60 1.50
58 Tim Duncan 2.00 5.00
59 Bradley Beal RC 5.00 12.00
60 Devin Ebanks .50 1.25
61 Monta Ellis .60 1.50
62 Tyreke Evans .60 1.50
63 Johan Petro .50 1.25
64 Raymond Felton .50 1.25
65 Wilson Chandler .60 1.50
66 Landry Fields .50 1.25
67 Dion Waiters RC .75 2.00
68 Jonny Flynn .50 1.25
69 Randy Foye .50 1.25
70 Damian Lillard RC 10.00 25.00
71 Danilo Gallinari .50 1.25
72 Kevin Garnett 2.00 5.00
73 Terrence Ross RC 1.50 4.00
74 Pau Gasol 1.25 3.00
75 Rudy Gay .75 2.00
76 Paul George 1.25 3.00
77 Harrison Barnes RC 1.25 3.00
78 Daniel Gibson .50 1.25
79 Taj Gibson .50 1.25
80 Manu Ginobili 1.50 4.00
81 Kobe Bryant 6.00 15.00
82 Kevin Durant 3.00 8.00
83 Amare Stoudemire .75 2.00
84 Marcin Gortat .50 1.25
85 Danny Granger .50 1.25
86 Andre Drummond RC 1.50 4.00
87 Blake Griffin .75 2.00
88 Richard Hamilton .75 2.00
89 Tyler Hansbrough .50 1.25
90 James Harden 1.50 4.00
91 Al Harrington .60 1.50
92 Devin Harris .50 1.25
93 Udonis Haslem .60 1.50
94 Austin Rivers RC 1.00 2.50
95 Gordon Hayward .75 2.00
96 Brendan Haywood .50 1.25
97 Gerald Henderson .50 1.25
98 Xavier Henry .50 1.25
99 Roy Hibbert .60 1.50

100 J.J. Hickson .50 1.25
101 George Hill .60 1.50
102 Jimmer Fredette RC 1.00 2.50
103 Kirk Hinrich .60 1.50
104 Jrue Holiday 1.00 2.50
105 Al Horford .75 2.00
106 Dwight Howard 1.00 2.50
107 Kris Humphries .50 1.25
108 Serge Ibaka .60 1.50
109 Andre Iguodala .75 2.00
110 Ersan Ilyasova .50 1.25
111 J.J. Barea .60 1.50
112 Stephen Jackson .60 1.50
113 LeBron James 6.00 15.00
114 Al Jefferson .50 1.25
115 Antawn Jamison .60 1.50
116 Brandon Jennings .50 1.25
117 James Johnson .50 1.25
118 Joe Johnson .60 1.50
119 Wesley Johnson .50 1.25
120 DeAndre Jordan .60 1.50
121 Chris Kaman .60 1.50
122 Jason Kidd 1.25 3.00
123 Linas Kleiza .50 1.25
124 Kyle Korver .60 1.50
125 Carl Landry .50 1.25
126 Norris Cole RC .60 1.50
127 Courtney Lee .50 1.25
128 David Lee .50 1.25
129 Jeremy Lin 1.25 3.00
130 Brook Lopez .60 1.50
131 Kevin Love .75 2.00
132 Kyle Lowry .75 2.00
133 John Lucas III .50 1.25
134 Corey Maggette .60 1.50
135 Ian Mahinmi .50 1.25
136 Shawn Marion .75 2.00
137 Cartier Martin RC 1.00 2.50
138 Kevin Martin .60 1.50
139 Wesley Matthews .60 1.50
140 Jordan Hamilton RC .60 1.50
141 Luc Mbah a Moute .50 1.25
142 JaVale McGee .60 1.50
143 DeShawn Stevenson .50 1.25
144 C.J. Miles .50 1.25
145 Andre Miller .60 1.50
146 Mike Miller .60 1.50
147 Paul Millsap .60 1.50
148 Greg Monroe .50 1.25
149 Timofey Mozgov .50 1.25
150 Marcus Morris RC 1.00 2.50
151 Steve Nash 1.50 4.00
152 Gary Neal .50 1.25
153 Jameer Nelson .50 1.25
154 Nene .60 1.50
155 Joakim Noah .60 1.50
156 Steve Novak .50 1.25
157 Dirk Nowitzki 2.00 5.00
158 Emeka Okafor .60 1.50
159 Daniel Orton .50 1.25
160 Tony Parker 1.25 3.00
161 Patrick Patterson .50 1.25
162 Chris Paul 1.50 4.00
163 Meyers Leonard RC .75 2.00
164 Paul Pierce 1.25 3.00
165 Tayshaun Prince .75 2.00
166 Anthony Randolph .60 1.50
167 Zach Randolph .75 2.00
168 J.J. Redick .75 2.00
169 Jason Richardson .75 2.00
170 Luke Ridnour .60 1.50
171 Nate Robinson .50 1.25
172 Derrick Rose 1.25 3.00
173 Rajon Rondo 1.00 2.50
174 Ricky Rubio .60 1.50
175 Brandon Rush .50 1.25
176 John Salmons .60 1.50
177 Alonzo Gee .50 1.25
178 Ramon Sessions .50 1.25
179 Jeremy Lamb RC 1.00 2.50
180 Josh Smith .50 1.25
181 Marreese Speights .50 1.25
182 Jerry Stackhouse .60 1.50
183 Eric Gordon .60 1.50
184 Rodney Stuckey .50 1.25
185 Jeff Teague .50 1.25
186 Jason Terry .60 1.50
187 Tyrus Thomas .50 1.25
188 Marcus Thornton .50 1.25
189 Hedo Turkoglu .60 1.50
190 Evan Turner .50 1.25
191 D.J. Augustin .50 1.25
192 Anderson Varejao .50 1.25
193 Greivis Vasquez .50 1.25
194 Dwyane Wade 1.50 4.00
195 John Wall 1.00 2.50
196 Hakim Warrick .50 1.25
197 Kendall Marshall RC .60 1.50
198 David West .60 1.50
199 Delonte West .50 1.25
200 Russell Westbrook 1.25 3.00
201 Deron Williams .60 1.50
202 Louis Williams .60 1.50
203 Mo Williams .60 1.50
204 Metta World Peace .60 1.50
205 Nick Young .50 1.25
206 Ryan Anderson .50 1.25
207 Jordan Crawford .50 1.25
208 Kendrick Perkins .50 1.25
209 Jason Smith .50 1.25
210 Marvin Williams .50 1.25
211 Jarrett Jack .60 1.50
212 Andrea Bargnani .50 1.25
213 Brandon Knight RC .75 2.00
214 MarShon Brooks RC .60 1.50
215 Klay Thompson RC 10.00 25.00
216 Kemba Walker RC 2.50 6.00
217 Isaiah Thomas RC 1.25 3.00
218 Michael Beasley .50 1.25
219 Chandler Parsons RC .75 2.00
220 Derrick Williams RC .60 1.50
221 Tristan Thompson RC 1.00 2.50
222 Grant Hill 1.25 3.00
223 Doron Lamb RC .60 1.50
224 Markieff Morris RC 1.00 2.50
225 Alec Burks RC 1.00 2.50
226 Ty Lawson .50 1.25
227 Ivan Johnson RC .60 1.50
228 Gustavo Ayon RC .60 1.50
229 Charles Jenkins RC .60 1.50
230 Nikola Vucevic RC 2.50 6.00
231 Donald Sloan RC .60 1.50
232 Bismack Biyombo RC .75 2.00
233 Ray Allen 1.25 3.00
234 Jeremy Tyler RC .60 1.50
235 Jon Leuer RC .60 1.50
236 Jan Vesely RC .60 1.50
237 Chris Singleton RC .60 1.50
238 Marcus Camby .75 2.00
239 DeMarre Carroll .50 1.25
240 O.J. Mayo .50 1.25
241 Kyle Singler RC .60 1.50
242 Andrew Goudelock RC .60 1.50
243 Lavoy Allen RC .60 1.50
244 Lance Thomas RC .60 1.50
245 Cory Higgins RC .60 1.50
246 Mike Conley .60 1.50
247 Elliot Williams .50 1.25
248 Terrel Harris RC .60 1.50
249 Shelvin Mack RC .75 2.00
250 Samuel Dalembert .50 1.25
251 Baron Davis .60 1.50
252 Reggie Jackson RC 1.00 2.50
253 Greg Stiemsma RC .60 1.50
254 Malik Wayns RC .75 2.00
255 Cory Joseph RC .75 2.00
256 Jimmy Butler RC 6.00 15.00
257 Jared Dudley .50 1.25
258 Julyan Stone RC .60 1.50
259 Jeremy Pargo RC .60 1.50
260 Byron Mullens .50 1.25
261 John Henson RC .75 2.00
262 Moe Harkless RC .75 2.00
263 Nikola Pekovic .50 1.25
264 Royce White RC .60 1.50
265 Tyler Zeller RC .60 1.50
266 Terrence Jones RC .60 1.50
267 Derek Fisher .60 1.50
268 Andrew Nicholson RC .60 1.50
269 Evan Fournier RC 1.00 2.50
270 Channing Frye .50 1.25
271 Jared Sullinger RC .60 1.50
272 Fab Melo RC .60 1.50
273 Marc Gasol .75 2.00
274 John Jenkins RC .60 1.50
275 Jared Cunningham RC .60 1.50
276 Tony Wroten RC .60 1.50
277 Luis Scola .60 1.50
278 Miles Plumlee RC .60 1.50
279 J.R. Smith .75 2.00
280 Arnett Moultrie RC .60 1.50
281 Perry Jones RC .60 1.50
282 Ben Gordon .60 1.50
283 Thabo Sefolosha .50 1.25
284 Festus Ezeli RC .60 1.50
285 Marquis Teague RC .60 1.50
286 Danny Green .60 1.50
287 Jeff Taylor RC .60 1.50
288 Bernard James RC .60 1.50
289 Nicolas Batum .60 1.50
290 Jae Crowder RC 1.25 3.00
291 Carlos Boozer .60 1.50
292 Draymond Green RC 4.00 10.00
293 Orlando Johnson RC .60 1.50
294 Spencer Hawes .50 1.25
295 Quincy Acy RC .60 1.50
296 Quincy Miller RC .60 1.50
297 C.J. Watson .50 1.25
298 Khris Middleton RC 3.00 8.00
299 Tyshawn Taylor RC .60 1.50
300 Ekpe Udoh .50 1.25

2012-13 Totally Certified Blue

*BLUE: .75X TO 2X BASE HI
STATED PRINT RUN 299 SER.#'d SETS
70 Damian Lillard 75.00 200.00

2012-13 Totally Certified Gold

*VETS: 4X TO 10X BASE HI
*ROOKIES: 3X TO 8X BASE HI
STATED PRINT RUN 25 SER.#'d SETS
7 Carmelo Anthony 12.00 30.00
10 Thomas Robinson 25.00 60.00
70 Damian Lillard 500.00 1,000.00
82 Kevin Durant 30.00 80.00
86 Andre Drummond 12.00 30.00
106 Dwight Howard 20.00 50.00
122 Jason Kidd 10.00 25.00
215 Klay Thompson 125.00 300.00
222 Grant Hill 15.00 40.00
233 Ray Allen 15.00 40.00

2012-13 Totally Certified Red

*RED: .5X TO 1.25X BASE HI
STATED PRINT RUN 499 SER.#'d SETS
70 Damian Lillard 40.00 100.00
113 LeBron James 5.00 12.00
129 Jeremy Lin 3.00 8.00

2012-13 Totally Certified Autographs

STATED PRINT RUN 25 TO 49 SER.#'d SETS
1 Brook Lopez/49 4.00 10.00
2 Danilo Gallinari/49 4.00 10.00
3 David Lee/49 6.00 15.00
4 Eric Gordon/49 6.00 15.00
5 Gordon Hayward/49 5.00 12.00
6 Kevin Durant/49 40.00 100.00
7 Chris Kaman/49 4.00 10.00
8 Jamal Crawford/44 10.00 25.00
9 Richard Hamilton/49 6.00 15.00
10 Ricky Rubio/49 10.00 25.00
11 Reggie Evans/49 4.00 10.00
12 Steve Nash/49 20.00 50.00
13 Ty Lawson/49 EXCH 6.00 15.00
14 Tyreke Evans/49 4.00 10.00
15 Wesley Matthews/49 4.00 10.00
16 Xavier Henry/49 4.00 10.00
18 Avery Bradley/49 EXCH 4.00 10.00
19 Ben Gordon/49 4.00 10.00
20 Channing Frye/49 4.00 10.00
21 DeJuan Blair/49 EXCH 4.00 10.00
22 DeMarcus Cousins/49 8.00 20.00
23 Derrick Favors/46 4.00 10.00
24 Jeff Teague/49 4.00 10.00
25 Jrue Holiday/49 6.00 15.00
26 Kobe Bryant/49 500.00 1,000.00
27 Jared Dudley/49 4.00 10.00
28 Omri Casspi/49 4.00 10.00
29 Zach Randolph/49 4.00 10.00
30 Kevin Love/49 8.00 20.00
31 Serge Ibaka/49 12.00 30.00
32 Tony Parker/49 8.00 20.00
33 Chris Bosh/49 6.00 15.00
34 DeAndre Jordan/49 5.00 12.00
35 Deron Williams/49 4.00 10.00
36 Stephen Curry/49 400.00 800.00
37 Mike Bibby/49 4.00 10.00
38 James Harden/49 25.00 60.00
39 Luol Deng/49 4.00 10.00
40 Brandon Jennings/49 EXCH 4.00 10.00
41 Blake Griffin/49 12.00 30.00
42 Jose Calderon/49 4.00 10.00
43 Chris Paul/49 30.00 80.00
44 Stephen Jackson/49 4.00 10.00
45 Andre Iguodala/49 8.00 20.00
46 David West/49 4.00 10.00
47 Andrew Bynum/49 4.00 10.00
49 Mike Conley/49 5.00 12.00
50 Darren Collison/49 4.00 10.00
51 JaVale McGee/49 4.00 10.00
52 Gary Neal/49 EXCH 4.00 10.00
53 Grant Hill/49 12.00 30.00
54 Jason Kidd/25 12.00 30.00
55 Kris Humphries/49 4.00 10.00
56 Tyson Chandler/49 6.00 15.00
57 Wesley Johnson/49 4.00 10.00
58 Delonte West/49 4.00 10.00
59 Joakim Noah/49 4.00 10.00
60 Greg Monroe/49 4.00 10.00
61 Monta Ellis/49 6.00 15.00
62 Roy Hibbert/49 4.00 10.00
63 Vince Carter/49 12.00 30.00
64 Derek Fisher/49 8.00 20.00
65 Raymond Felton/49 4.00 10.00
66 LaMarcus Aldridge/49 8.00 20.00
67 Josh Smith/49 4.00 10.00
68 Steve Novak/49 4.00 10.00
69 Marcin Gortat/49 4.00 10.00
70 Kyle Lowry/49 4.00 10.00
71 Pau Gasol/49 EXCH 10.00 25.00
72 Ersan Ilyasova/49 4.00 10.00
73 Nick Young/49 4.00 10.00
74 Al Horford/49 4.00 10.00
76 Adrian Dantley/49 4.00 10.00
77 Artis Gilmore/49 6.00 15.00
78 Magic Johnson/49 30.00 80.00
79 Mark Eaton/49 4.00 10.00
80 Ron Harper/34 10.00 25.00
81 Tim Hardaway/49 8.00 20.00
82 Bill Laimbeer/49 4.00 10.00
83 Dolph Schayes/49 4.00 10.00
84 Calvin Murphy/49 4.00 10.00
85 Rick Barry/49 6.00 15.00
86 Bill Russell/49 400.00 800.00
87 Chris Mullin/49 8.00 20.00
88 David Robinson/49 25.00 60.00
89 Bernard King/49 4.00 10.00
90 Detlef Schrempf/49 10.00 25.00
91 Cedric Ceballos/49 4.00 10.00
92 John Starks/49 6.00 15.00
93 Gail Goodrich/49 5.00 12.00
94 John Havlicek/49 6.00 15.00
95 James Worthy/49 15.00 40.00
96 Toni Kukoc/49 8.00 20.00
97 Larry Bird/49 40.00 100.00
98 Mark Jackson/49 6.00 15.00
99 Vlade Divac/49 6.00 15.00
100 Robert Horry/49 6.00 15.00

2012-13 Totally Certified Blue Autographs

*BLUE: .6X TO 1.5X BASE HI
STATED PRINT RUN 15 SER.#'d SETS
44 Stephen Jackson 10.00 25.00
54 Jason Kidd 15.00 40.00
79 Mark Eaton 12.00 30.00
88 David Robinson 40.00 100.00
97 Larry Bird 50.00 125.00
98 Mark Jackson 8.00 20.00
100 Robert Horry 15.00 40.00

2012-13 Totally Certified Red Autographs

*RED: .5X TO 1.25X BASE HI
STATED PRINT RUN 25 SER.#'d SETS
75 Dirk Nowitzki 40.00 100.00

2012-13 Totally Certified HRX Video Cards

STATED PRINT RUN 40 SER.#'d SETS
1 Kobe Bryant 175.00 350.00
2 Kevin Durant 125.00 250.00
3 Kyrie Irving 100.00 250.00
4 Anthony Davis 75.00 200.00

2012-13 Totally Certified Red Materials

1 Kobe Bryant 8.00 20.00
2 Kevin Durant 6.00 15.00
3 Chris Bosh 3.00 8.00
4 Brook Lopez 2.00 5.00
5 Al Jefferson 1.50 4.00
6 Amare Stoudemire 2.50 6.00
7 Andre Miller 2.00 5.00
8 Antawn Jamison 2.00 5.00
10 Carl Landry 1.50 4.00
11 Carmelo Anthony 4.00 10.00
13 Chris Paul 5.00 12.00
15 David West 2.00 5.00
17 Derrick Rose 4.00 10.00
19 Dwight Howard 3.00 8.00
21 Jalen Rose 2.00 5.00
22 Jason Richardson 2.50 6.00
23 Joakim Noah 2.00 5.00
24 Kirk Hinrich 2.00 5.00
25 Joe Johnson 2.00 5.00
26 John Salmons 2.00 5.00
27 John Stockton 5.00 12.00
28 Karl Malone 4.00 10.00
29 Kawhi Leonard 15.00 40.00
30 Kyrie Irving 12.00 30.00
32 Kevin Martin 2.00 5.00
34 LaMarcus Aldridge 2.50 6.00
35 Leandro Barbosa 2.00 5.00
36 LeBron James 10.00 25.00
37 Manu Ginobili 5.00 12.00
38 Landry Fields 1.50 4.00
39 MarShon Brooks 1.25 3.00
41 Patrick Ewing 4.00 10.00
42 Pau Gasol 4.00 10.00
43 Paul Pierce 4.00 10.00
44 Ray Allen 4.00 10.00
45 Raymond Felton 1.50 4.00
46 Shaquille O'Neal 8.00 20.00
47 Tayshaun Prince 2.50 6.00
48 Tim Duncan 6.00 15.00
50 Tony Parker 4.00 10.00
51 Tracy McGrady 4.00 10.00
52 Tristan Thompson 2.00 5.00
53 Tyrus Thomas 1.50 4.00
54 Vince Carter 5.00 12.00
55 Zach Randolph 2.50 6.00
56 Alonzo Mourning 4.00 10.00
57 Andre Iguodala 2.50 6.00
58 Blake Griffin 2.50 6.00
59 Carlos Boozer 2.00 5.00
60 Darren Collison 1.50 4.00
61 David Lee 1.50 4.00
62 Dennis Rodman 6.00 15.00
63 Derrick Favors 2.00 5.00
64 Dirk Nowitzki 6.00 15.00
65 Grant Hill 6.00 15.00
66 Hedo Turkoglu 2.00 5.00
67 J.J. Redick 2.50 6.00
68 Jameer Nelson 1.50 4.00
69 JaVale McGee 2.00 5.00
70 Josh Howard 2.00 5.00
72 Kemba Walker 5.00 12.00
73 Luol Deng 2.00 5.00
74 Markieff Morris 2.00 5.00
75 Michael Beasley 1.50 4.00
76 Metta World Peace 2.00 5.00
79 Ryan Gomes 1.50 4.00
80 Russell Westbrook 4.00 10.00
81 Steve Nash 5.00 12.00
82 Terrence Williams 1.50 4.00
83 Thaddeus Young 1.50 4.00
84 Ty Lawson 1.50 4.00
85 Alex English 3.00 8.00
86 Andrew Bynum 1.50 4.00
88 Derrick Williams 1.25 3.00
89 Wesley Matthews 1.50 4.00
90 Tyreke Evans 2.00 5.00
91 Jermaine O'Neal 2.00 5.00
92 Joe Dumars 3.00 8.00
93 Klay Thompson 12.00 30.00
94 Kenny Anderson 2.00 5.00
96 Josh Smith 1.50 4.00
97 Kevin Love 2.50 6.00
98 Marc Gasol 2.00 5.00
99 Mark Jackson 2.00 5.00
100 Raja Bell 2.00 5.00
101 Larry Bird 8.00 20.00
102 Taj Gibson 1.50 4.00
103 Steve Smith 2.00 5.00
104 Tyler Hansbrough 2.00 5.00
106 Jrue Holiday 3.00 8.00
107 Evan Turner 1.50 4.00
108 Emeka Okafor 2.00 5.00
109 Dikembe Mutombo 4.00 10.00
110 DeMar DeRozan 3.00 8.00
111 Marcus Morris 2.00 5.00
112 Chuck Person 2.00 5.00
113 Danny Granger 1.50 4.00
114 Chase Budinger 1.50 4.00
115 Channing Frye 1.50 4.00
116 Caron Butler 2.00 5.00
117 Bismack Biyombo 1.50 4.00
118 Ben Wallace 2.00 5.00
119 Al Horford 2.50 6.00
120 Dwyane Wade 5.00 12.00
121 Earl Monroe 3.00 8.00
122 Iman Shumpert 1.50 4.00
123 James Harden 5.00 12.00
124 Jimmer Fredette 2.00 5.00
126 Brandon Jennings 2.00 5.00
128 Mike Conley 2.00 5.00
129 Tiago Splitter 1.50 4.00
130 Andrea Bargnani 1.50 4.00
131 Wesley Johnson 1.50 4.00
132 Zydrunas Ilgauskas 2.00 5.00
133 Udonis Haslem 2.00 5.00
134 Spencer Hawes 1.50 4.00
136 Rudy Gay 2.50 6.00
137 Luke Ridnour 2.00 5.00
138 Jose Calderon 1.50 4.00
139 Carlos Delfino 1.50 4.00
141 Jason Williams 2.50 6.00
143 Joel Anthony 1.50 4.00
144 Larry Johnson 4.00 10.00
145 D.J. Augustin 1.50 4.00
146 Daniel Gibson 1.50 4.00
148 DeMarcus Cousins 2.50 6.00
149 Ed Davis 1.50 4.00
151 Enes Kanter 2.00 5.00
155 J.J. Barea 4.00 10.00
156 Jamaal Wilkes 2.50 6.00
157 Jamal Crawford 2.50 6.00
158 Jeff Foster 1.50 4.00
159 Jeff Teague 1.50 4.00
160 Jim Jackson 2.00 5.00
161 Kenneth Faried 1.50 4.00
162 Luis Scola 2.00 5.00
163 Mark Price 2.50 6.00
164 Marvin Williams 1.50 4.00
165 Maurice Cheeks 2.00 5.00
166 Nick Collison 1.50 4.00
168 Peja Stojakovic 2.00 5.00
169 Randy Foye 1.50 4.00
170 Bill Laimbeer 3.00 8.00
171 Richard Hamilton 2.50 6.00
172 Rodrigue Beaubois 1.50 4.00
174 Shawn Kemp 12.00 30.00
175 Stephen Curry 20.00 50.00
176 Trevor Booker 1.50 4.00
177 Vinnie Johnson 2.50 6.00
178 Allan Houston 2.00 5.00
179 Alvan Adams 1.50 4.00
180 Anderson Varejao 1.50 4.00
181 Toni Kukoc 2.50 6.00
182 Anthony Mason 2.00 5.00
183 Baron Davis 2.00 5.00
185 Bobby Jackson 1.50 4.00
186 Brendan Haywood 1.50 4.00
187 Charles Jenkins 1.25 3.00
188 Chauncey Billups 3.00 8.00
189 Eric Gordon 2.00 5.00
190 Goran Dragic 2.50 6.00
191 Gordon Hayward 2.50 6.00
192 Brandon Knight 1.50 4.00
193 Gary Neal 1.50 4.00
194 Chandler Parsons 1.50 4.00
195 Clyde Drexler 4.00 10.00
196 Tyson Chandler 2.00 5.00
197 David Robinson 4.00 10.00
198 Cedric Maxwell 1.50 4.00
199 Charles Oakley 2.50 6.00
200 Yao Ming 5.00 12.00

2012-13 Totally Certified Red Materials Prime

*RED PRIME: 1X TO 2.5X RED MAT HI
STATED PRINT RUN 49 SER.#'d SETS
2 Kevin Durant 20.00 50.00
27 John Stockton 12.00 30.00
36 LeBron James 50.00 120.00
41 Patrick Ewing 25.00 60.00
51 Tracy McGrady 15.00 40.00
56 Alonzo Mourning 12.00 30.00
81 Steve Nash 8.00 20.00
94 Kenny Anderson 8.00 20.00
109 Dikembe Mutombo 15.00 40.00
141 Jason Williams 10.00 25.00
144 Larry Johnson 25.00 60.00
153 Glen Rice 8.00 20.00
163 Mark Price 8.00 20.00
177 Vinnie Johnson 8.00 20.00
181 Toni Kukoc 8.00 20.00
195 Clyde Drexler 12.00 30.00
199 Charles Oakley 10.00 25.00

2012-13 Totally Certified Blue Materials

*BLUE: .5X TO 1.25X RED MAT HI
STATED PRINT RUN 5 TO 99 SER.#'d SETS
31 Kevin Garnett/35 8.00 20.00
36 LeBron James/99 10.00 25.00
41 Patrick Ewing/99 8.00 20.00
46 Shaquille O'Neal/99 12.00 30.00
56 Alonzo Mourning/99 6.00 15.00
65 Grant Hill/99 10.00 25.00
71 Julius Erving/99 8.00 20.00
76 Mo Williams/15 6.00 15.00
77 Rajon Rondo/99 5.00 12.00
81 Steve Nash/99 4.00 10.00
87 Dominique Wilkins/99 4.00 10.00
94 Kenny Anderson/99 6.00 15.00
109 Dikembe Mutombo/99 4.00 10.00
121 Earl Monroe/99 12.00 30.00
144 Larry Johnson/99 6.00 15.00
153 Glen Rice/99 5.00 12.00
173 Scottie Pippen/25 20.00 50.00
174 Shawn Kemp/99 20.00 50.00
181 Toni Kukoc/99 3.00 8.00

2012-13 Totally Certified Blue Materials Prime

*BLUE PRIME: 1.25X TO 3X RED MAT HI
STATED PRINT RUN 5 TO 25 SER.#'d SETS
2 Kevin Durant/25 30.00 80.00
36 LeBron James/25 30.00 60.00
41 Patrick Ewing/25 30.00 80.00
46 Shaquille O'Neal/25 30.00 80.00
56 Alonzo Mourning/25 15.00 40.00
58 Blake Griffin/25 25.00 60.00
62 Dennis Rodman/25 20.00 50.00
72 Kemba Walker/25 40.00 70.00
81 Steve Nash/25 12.00 30.00
109 Dikembe Mutombo/25 20.00 50.00
141 Jason Williams/25 10.00 25.00
144 Larry Johnson/25 25.00 60.00
152 Gary Payton/25 25.00 60.00
153 Glen Rice/25 15.00 40.00
155 J.J. Barea/25 20.00 50.00
163 Mark Price/25 15.00 40.00
195 Clyde Drexler/25 15.00 40.00

2012-13 Totally Certified Private Signings

1 Alvan Adams 6.00 15.00
2 Adrian Dantley 6.00 15.00
3 Al Attles 6.00 15.00
4 Kelly Tripucka 6.00 15.00
5 Larry Johnson 12.00 30.00
6 Al Horford 6.00 15.00
7 Roy Hibbert 3.00 8.00
8 Hedo Turkoglu 3.00 8.00
9 Darryl Dawkins 12.00 30.00
10 Campy Russell 6.00 15.00
11 Paul Millsap 6.00 15.00
12 Emeka Okafor 5.00 12.00
13 Ty Lawson 3.00 8.00
14 Glen Rice 12.00 30.00
15 Luke Ridnour 3.00 8.00
16 Juwan Howard 6.00 15.00
17 Jeff Teague 3.00 8.00
18 Michael Cooper 8.00 20.00
19 Josh Smith 3.00 8.00
20 Bernard King 8.00 20.00

2012-13 Totally Certified Rookie Roll Call Autographs

1 Kawhi Leonard 150.00 400.00
2 Iman Shumpert 3.00 8.00
3 Anthony Davis 100.00 250.00
4 Michael Kidd-Gilchrist 3.00 8.00
5 Chandler Parsons 3.00 8.00
6 Kyrie Irving 50.00 120.00
7 Thomas Robinson 2.50 6.00
8 Andre Drummond 6.00 15.00
9 Kenneth Faried 3.00 8.00
10 Isaiah Thomas 5.00 12.00
11 Harrison Barnes 6.00 15.00
12 Jeremy Lamb 4.00 10.00
13 Brandon Knight 3.00 8.00
14 MarShon Brooks 2.50 6.00
15 Bradley Beal 10.00 25.00
17 Klay Thompson 100.00 250.00
18 Jimmer Fredette 4.00 10.00
19 Austin Rivers 4.00 10.00
20 Lance Thomas 2.50 6.00
21 Kemba Walker 20.00 50.00
22 Bismack Biyombo 3.00 8.00
23 Tyler Zeller 2.50 6.00
24 Meyers Leonard 3.00 8.00
25 Derrick Williams 2.50 6.00
26 Enes Kanter 4.00 10.00
28 Kendall Marshall 2.50 6.00
29 Alec Burks 4.00 10.00
30 Jan Vesely 2.50 6.00
31 Jared Sullinger 2.50 6.00
32 John Henson 3.00 8.00
33 Markieff Morris 4.00 10.00
34 Norris Cole 2.50 6.00
35 Moe Harkless 3.00 8.00
36 Dion Waiters 3.00 8.00
37 Lavoy Allen 2.50 6.00
38 Tristan Thompson 4.00 10.00
39 Terrence Ross 6.00 15.00
41 Gustavo Ayon 2.50 6.00
42 Charles Jenkins 2.50 6.00
43 Terrence Jones 2.50 6.00
44 Andrew Nicholson 2.50 6.00
46 Jeremy Tyler 2.50 6.00
47 Julyan Stone 2.50 6.00
49 Jon Leuer 2.50 6.00
50 Kyle Singler 2.50 6.00
51 Fab Melo 2.50 6.00
52 John Jenkins 2.50 6.00
55 Jared Cunningham 2.50 6.00
56 Miles Plumlee 2.50 6.00
57 Nolan Smith 2.50 6.00
58 Travis Leslie 2.50 6.00
59 Tony Wroten 2.50 6.00
60 Marquis Teague 2.50 6.00
62 Courtney Fortson 2.50 6.00
63 Festus Ezeli 2.50 6.00
64 Jeff Taylor 2.50 6.00
65 Malcolm Lee 2.50 6.00
66 Reggie Jackson 4.00 10.00
67 Jonas Valanciunas 5.00 12.00
68 Bernard James 2.50 6.00
69 E'Twaun Moore 3.00 8.00
70 DeAndre Liggins 2.50 6.00
71 Quincy Acy 2.50 6.00
73 Jimmy Butler 15.00 40.00
74 Josh Selby 2.50 6.00
75 Jae Crowder 5.00 12.00
76 Draymond Green 15.00 40.00
77 Darius Morris 3.00 8.00
78 Trey Thompkins 2.50 6.00
79 Orlando Johnson 2.50 6.00
80 Khris Middleton 12.00 30.00
82 Tyler Honeycutt 2.50 6.00
83 Will Barton 5.00 12.00
85 Chris Singleton 2.50 6.00
88 Mike Scott 3.00 8.00
89 Jeremy Pargo 2.50 6.00
90 Kim English 2.50 6.00
91 Justin Hamilton 2.50 6.00
92 Darius Miller 3.00 8.00
93 Kevin Murphy 2.50 6.00
94 Nikola Vucevic 10.00 25.00
95 Kyle O'Quinn 3.00 8.00
97 Kris Joseph 2.50 6.00
98 Greg Stiemsma 2.50 6.00
100 Justin Harper 2.50 6.00

2012-13 Totally Certified Rookie Roll Call Autographs Blue

*BLUE: .6X TO 1.5X BASE HI
STATED PRINT RUN 49 TO 199 SER.#'d SETS

2012-13 Totally Certified Rookie Roll Call Autographs Gold

*GOLD: 1X TO 2.5X BASE HI
STATED PRINT RUN 15 TO 25 SER.#'d SETS
40 Royce White/25 EXCH 6.00 15.00
86 Tobias Harris/25 EXCH 20.00 50.00

2012-13 Totally Certified Rookie Roll Call Autographs Red

*RED: .5X TO 1.25X BASE HI
STATED PRINT RUN 68 TO 279 SER.#'d SETS
27 Perry Jones/199 EXCH 3.00 8.00

2013-14 Totally Certified

1 Kobe Bryant 6.00 15.00
2 Kevin Durant 2.50 6.00
3 Blake Griffin .75 2.00
4 Kyrie Irving 2.50 6.00
5 Dirk Nowitzki 2.00 5.00
6 LeBron James 6.00 15.00
7 Kevin Love .75 2.00
8 Damian Lillard 2.50 6.00
9 Carmelo Anthony 1.25 3.00
10 Paul Pierce 1.25 3.00
11 Roy Hibbert .50 1.25
12 James Harden 1.50 4.00
13 Russell Westbrook 1.25 3.00
14 Deron Williams .60 1.50
15 George Hill .60 1.50
16 Stephen Curry 6.00 15.00
17 Carlos Boozer .60 1.50
18 Kenneth Faried .60 1.50
19 Tim Duncan 2.00 5.00
20 DeMarcus Cousins .75 2.00
21 Ersan Ilyasova .50 1.25
22 Kendall Marshall .50 1.25
23 Ben Gordon .60 1.50
24 Jason Richardson .75 2.00
25 DeMar DeRozan 1.00 2.50
26 David Lee .50 1.25
27 Zach Randolph .60 1.50
28 Jeff Teague .50 1.25
29 Greivis Vasquez .50 1.25
30 Brandon Knight .60 1.50
31 Evan Turner .50 1.25
32 Amar'e Stoudemire .75 2.00
33 Tyreke Evans .60 1.50
34 Bradley Beal 1.25 3.00
35 Paul Millsap .60 1.50
36 Anderson Varejao .50 1.25
37 Klay Thompson 2.50 6.00
38 LaMarcus Aldridge .75 2.00
39 Dwyane Wade 1.50 4.00
40 Joe Johnson .60 1.50
41 Ricky Rubio .60 1.50
42 Pau Gasol 1.25 3.00
43 Luol Deng .60 1.50
44 Chris Paul 1.50 4.00
45 Kevin Garnett 2.00 5.00
46 Al Jefferson .50 1.25
47 Andre Iguodala .75 2.00
48 Vince Carter 1.50 4.00
49 Jimmer Fredette .75 2.00
50 Paul George 1.25 3.00
51 DeShawn Stevenson .50 1.25
52 Nick Young .50 1.25
53 Serge Ibaka .60 1.50
54 Glen Davis .50 1.25
55 Harrison Barnes .75 2.00
56 Michael Kidd-Gilchrist .50 1.25
57 Devin Harris .50 1.25
58 Marc Gasol .75 2.00
59 Jeremy Lin 1.25 3.00
60 Mike Conley .75 2.00
61 Jose Calderon .50 1.25
62 Isaiah Thomas .60 1.50
63 Tony Parker 1.25 3.00
64 Chris Bosh 1.00 2.50
65 Wesley Matthews .50 1.25
66 Brandon Jennings .50 1.25
67 Jimmy Butler 1.50 4.00
68 Anthony Davis 2.50 6.00
69 Shawn Marion .60 1.50
70 Tyson Chandler .60 1.50
71 Brook Lopez .75 2.00
72 Gordon Hayward .60 1.50
73 John Wall 1.00 2.50
74 Rajon Rondo 1.00 2.50
75 Ty Lawson .50 1.25
76 Andrea Bargnani .50 1.25
77 Marcin Gortat .50 1.25
78 Gary Neal .50 1.25
79 Thabo Sefolosha .60 1.50
80 Kemba Walker .75 2.00
81 Derrick Williams .50 1.25
82 Dwight Howard 1.00 2.50
83 Al Horford .75 2.00
84 JaVale McGee .60 1.50
85 Draymond Green 1.25 3.00
86 Lance Stephenson .60 1.50
87 Kawhi Leonard 2.50 6.00
88 Chandler Parsons .50 1.25
89 Martell Webster .50 1.25
90 Mario Chalmers .60 1.50
91 Metta World Peace .60 1.50
92 Gerald Wallace .60 1.50
93 Reggie Jackson .60 1.50
94 Austin Rivers .60 1.50
95 Jrue Holiday 1.00 2.50
96 Joakim Noah .75 2.00
97 Nene .60 1.50
98 Monta Ellis .60 1.50
99 Rudy Gay .60 1.50
100 Danilo Gallinari .60 1.50
101 J.J. Hickson .50 1.25
102 Ramon Sessions .50 1.25
103 Darrell Arthur .50 1.25
104 J.R. Smith .75 2.00
105 Jason Terry .60 1.50
106 Chase Budinger .50 1.25
107 Jameer Nelson .50 1.25
108 Danny Granger .50 1.25
109 Steve Nash 1.50 4.00
110 Tristan Thompson .50 1.25
111 Derrick Favors .50 1.25
112 Danny Green .60 1.50
113 J.J. Redick .75 2.00
114 DeAndre Jordan .60 1.50
115 Andre Drummond .75 2.00
116 Goran Dragic .60 1.50
117 Louis Williams .60 1.50
118 Chris Kaman .60 1.50
119 Kyle Lowry .75 2.00
120 Eric Gordon .60 1.50
121 Chris Andersen .60 1.50
122 Tayshaun Prince .75 2.00
123 Dion Waiters .50 1.25
124 Thomas Robinson .50 1.25
125 Thaddeus Young .50 1.25
126 Tyler Hansbrough .50 1.25
127 Rodney Stuckey .50 1.25
128 Derrick Rose 1.25 3.00
129 David West .60 1.50
130 Andrew Nicholson .50 1.25
131 Andrew Bogut .60 1.50
132 Arron Afflalo .50 1.25
133 Avery Bradley .50 1.25
134 Bismack Biyombo .50 1.25
135 Carl Landry .50 1.25
136 Carlos Delfino .50 1.25
137 Chris Copeland .50 1.25
138 Corey Brewer .50 1.25
139 Courtney Lee .50 1.25
140 Emeka Okafor .50 1.25
141 Eric Bledsoe .60 1.50
142 Evan Fournier .60 1.50
143 Jae Crowder .50 1.25
144 Jared Dudley .50 1.25
145 Jared Sullinger .50 1.25
146 Jarrett Jack .50 1.25
147 Jeff Green .50 1.25
148 Jeremy Lamb .50 1.25
149 Kevin Martin .60 1.50
150 Larry Sanders .50 1.25
151 Manu Ginobili 1.50 4.00
152 Matt Barnes .50 1.25
153 Maurice Harkless .50 1.25
154 Nikola Pekovic .50 1.25
155 Nikola Vucevic 1.00 2.50
156 Norris Cole .50 1.25
157 Richard Jefferson .60 1.50
158 Shane Battier .60 1.50
159 Shannon Brown .50 1.25
160 Tobias Harris .75 2.00
161 Trevor Ariza .50 1.25
162 Tyler Zeller .50 1.25
163 Udonis Haslem .60 1.50
164 Will Bynum .50 1.25
165 Zaza Pachulia .50 1.25
166 Tony Allen .50 1.25

167 Ryan Anderson .50 1.25
168 Steve Novak .50 1.25
169 Jonas Valanciunas .60 1.50
170 Kyle Korver .60 1.50
171 Mike Dunleavy .50 1.25
172 Darren Collison .50 1.25
173 Pablo Prigioni .50 1.25
174 Raymond Felton .50 1.25
175 Tiago Splitter .50 1.25
176 Andray Blatche .50 1.25
177 Gerald Henderson .50 1.25
178 Amir Johnson .50 1.25
179 Robin Lopez .50 1.25
180 Terrence Jones .50 1.25
181 Nicolas Batum .60 1.50
182 Brandon Rush .50 1.25
183 Iman Shumpert .50 1.25
184 Quincy Pondexter .50 1.25
185 Patrick Beverley .50 1.25
186 O.J. Mayo .50 1.25
187 Andre Miller .60 1.50
188 Victor Claver .50 1.25
189 Terrence Ross .60 1.50
190 Wilson Chandler .60 1.50
191 Eric Maynor .50 1.25
192 MarShon Brooks .50 1.25
193 Anthony Morrow .50 1.25
194 Lavoy Allen .50 1.25
195 Andrei Kirilenko .75 2.00
196 Luc Mbah a Moute .50 1.25
197 Jordan Farmar .50 1.25
198 Michael Beasley .50 1.25
199 Dorell Wright .50 1.25
200 Kosta Koufos .50 1.25
201 C.J. Leslie RC .60 1.50
202 Ricky Ledo RC .60 1.50
203 Jeff Withey RC .60 1.50
204 Archie Goodwin RC .60 1.50
205 Dwight Buycks RC .60 1.50
206 Gal Mekel RC .60 1.50
207 Elias Harris RC .60 1.50
208 Peyton Siva RC .60 1.50
209 Romero Osby RC 1.00 2.50
210 Luigi Datome RC .60 1.50
211 Erik Murphy RC .60 1.50
212 Ryan Kelly RC .60 1.50
213 Ian Clark RC .75 2.00
214 Jamaal Franklin RC .60 1.50
215 Grant Jerrett RC .60 1.50
216 Nate Wolters RC .60 1.50
217 Tony Mitchell RC .60 1.50
218 Ray McCallum RC .60 1.50
219 Glen Rice Jr. RC .60 1.50
220 Isaiah Canaan RC .60 1.50
221 Carrick Felix RC .60 1.50
222 Allen Crabbe RC .60 1.50
223 Phil Pressey RC .60 1.50
224 Rudy Gobert RC 2.50 6.00
225 Andre Roberson RC .75 2.00
226 Reggie Bullock RC .75 2.00
227 Tim Hardaway Jr. RC 1.25 3.00
228 Solomon Hill RC .75 2.00
229 Mason Plumlee RC .75 2.00
230 Gorgui Dieng RC .75 2.00
231 Tony Snell RC .75 2.00
232 Sergey Karasev RC .60 1.50
233 Shane Larkin RC .60 1.50
234 Dennis Schroder RC 2.00 5.00
235 Robert Covington RC 1.00 2.50
236 G.Antetokounmpo RC 30.00 80.00
237 Shabazz Muhammad RC .60 1.50
238 Kelly Olynyk RC .75 2.00
239 Steven Adams RC 1.50 4.00
240 M.Carter-Williams RC .75 2.00
241 C.J. McCollum RC 2.50 6.00
242 Trey Burke RC .75 2.00
243 Kentavious Caldwell-Pope RC 1.00 2.50
244 Ben McLemore RC .75 2.00
245 Nerlens Noel RC .75 2.00
246 Alex Len RC .75 2.00
247 Cody Zeller RC .75 2.00
248 Otto Porter RC 1.00 2.50
249 Victor Oladipo RC 1.50 4.00
250 Anthony Bennett RC .60 1.50
251 Grant Hill 1.50 4.00
252 Larry Bird 4.00 10.00
253 Jerry West 2.50 6.00
254 Rick Barry 1.25 3.00
255 John Stockton 2.00 5.00
256 Kevin McHale 1.50 4.00
257 Elgin Baylor 1.00 2.50
258 Jason Kidd 1.50 4.00
259 Magic Johnson 4.00 10.00
260 Walt Frazier 1.50 4.00
261 Gary Payton 1.50 4.00
262 Yao Ming 2.00 5.00
263 Allen Iverson 2.00 5.00
264 Kareem Abdul-Jabbar 3.00 8.00
265 Clyde Drexler 1.50 4.00
266 George Mikan 3.00 8.00
267 Pete Maravich 3.00 8.00
268 Hakeem Olajuwon 2.00 5.00
269 Shaquille O'Neal 4.00 10.00
270 Julius Erving 2.50 6.00
271 Scottie Pippen 2.50 6.00
272 Earl Monroe 1.50 4.00
273 Isiah Thomas 1.50 4.00
274 Bill Russell 3.00 8.00
275 Dominique Wilkins 1.50 4.00
276 Wilt Chamberlain 3.00 8.00
277 George Gervin 1.50 4.00
278 Oscar Robertson 1.50 4.00
279 Dennis Rodman 2.50 6.00
280 David Robinson 2.00 5.00
281 John Havlicek 2.50 6.00
282 Bill Laimbeer 1.00 2.50
283 Calvin Natt .60 1.50
284 Detlef Schrempf 1.00 2.50
285 Len Elmore .75 2.00
286 Gail Goodrich 1.00 2.50
287 Tim Hardaway 1.25 3.00
288 Moses Malone 1.50 4.00
289 Bill Walton 1.50 4.00
290 Norm Nixon .75 2.00
291 Jim Jackson .60 1.50
292 Phil Jackson 1.25 3.00
293 Rick Fox .75 2.00
294 Spencer Haywood 1.00 2.50
295 Tom Chambers 1.00 2.50
296 Toni Kukoc 1.25 3.00
297 Larry Johnson 1.25 3.00
298 Spud Webb 1.00 2.50
299 Shawn Kemp 1.50 4.00
300 Alonzo Mourning 1.50 4.00

2013-14 Totally Certified Blue

*BLUE: 1.5X TO 4X BASIC
*BLUE RC: 1.2X TO 3X BASIC RC
STATED PRINT RUN 49 SER.#'d SETS
236 Giannis Antetokounmpo 150.00 400.00

2013-14 Totally Certified Gold

*GOLD: 3X TO 8X BASIC
*GOLD RC: 2.5X TO 6X BASIC RC
STATED PRINT RUN 25 SER.#'d SETS
1 Kobe Bryant 40.00 100.00
2 Kevin Durant 30.00 80.00
6 LeBron James 40.00 100.00
236 Giannis Antetokounmpo 150.00 400.00
249 Victor Oladipo 20.00 50.00

2013-14 Totally Certified Red

*RED: 1.2X TO 3X BASIC
*RED RC: 1X TO 2.5X BASIC RC
STATED PRINT RUN 99 SER.#'d SETS

2013-14 Totally Certified Autographs

EXCHANGE DEADLINE 5/27/2015
3 Zydrunas Ilgauskas 3.00 8.00
10 Jim Jackson 2.50 6.00
16 Kenneth Faried 3.00 8.00
19 Sleepy Floyd 3.00 8.00
20 Iman Shumpert 2.50 6.00
21 Bruce Bowen 3.00 8.00
22 Kobe Bryant 400.00 800.00
23 Kevin Durant EXCH 60.00 120.00
24 Kyrie Irving 20.00 50.00
26 Kareem Abdul-Jabbar 25.00 60.00
27 Kawhi Leonard 25.00 60.00
30 Michael Cooper 4.00 10.00
32 David West 3.00 8.00
35 Jeff Malone 3.00 8.00
37 Scottie Pippen 60.00 150.00
40 Karl Malone 30.00 80.00
41 John Lucas 3.00 8.00
43 Bob Dandridge 3.00 8.00
47 Dan Majerle 3.00 8.00
49 A.C. Green 4.00 10.00
52 John Paxson 3.00 8.00
61 David Robinson 15.00 40.00
62 Horace Grant 10.00 25.00
63 Tom Chambers 4.00 10.00
65 Sidney Moncrief 4.00 10.00
69 Alonzo Mourning 15.00 40.00
70 Vernon Maxwell 3.00 8.00
72 Grant Hill 20.00 50.00
73 Corey Brewer 2.50 6.00
74 Sebastian Telfair 2.50 6.00
75 Anthony Mason 3.00 8.00
80 Chris Mullin 8.00 20.00
81 Scott Skiles 3.00 8.00
82 Jo Jo White 3.00 8.00
84 Ray Williams 2.50 6.00
88 Jarrett Jack 6.00 15.00
100 Danny Green 3.00 8.00
109 Antawn Jamison 3.00 8.00
123 Dwyane Wade 50.00 120.00
128 Timofey Mozgov 2.50 6.00
131 Landry Fields 2.50 6.00
133 Marcus Thornton 2.50 6.00
135 Andray Blatche 2.50 6.00
138 Anderson Varejao 2.50 6.00
144 Mike Conley 4.00 10.00
150 Kendall Marshall 2.50 6.00
151 Mel Davis 2.50 6.00
153 MarShon Brooks 2.50 6.00
154 Darryl Dawkins EXCH 3.00 8.00
156 Jack Sikma 4.00 10.00
163 Harrison Barnes 12.00 30.00
166 Spud Webb EXCH 4.00 10.00
169 Isaiah Thomas 10.00 25.00
172 Bradley Beal 8.00 20.00
175 Len Elmore 3.00 8.00
181 Ekpe Udoh 2.50 6.00
184 Larry Nance 3.00 8.00
185 Paul Westphal 4.00 10.00
188 Eric Maynor 2.50 6.00
190 Chase Budinger 2.50 6.00
193 Mitch Richmond 10.00 25.00
196 Reggie Jackson 3.00 8.00
197 Udonis Haslem 3.00 8.00
199 Kevin Willis 3.00 8.00
202 Micheal Ray Richardson 3.00 8.00
203 Rolando Blackman 3.00 8.00
205 Jerome Williams 2.50 6.00
206 John Lucas III 2.50 6.00
207 Otis Birdsong 3.00 8.00
208 Mark Aguirre 3.00 8.00
209 Dave Stallworth 4.00 10.00
210 Herb Williams 2.50 6.00
211 Kenny Anderson 3.00 8.00
212 Leonard "Truck" Robinson 2.50 6.00
213 John Salley 3.00 8.00
214 Campy Russell 3.00 8.00
215 Jason Smith 2.50 6.00
216 Norm Nixon 3.00 8.00
217 Bismack Biyombo 2.50 6.00
218 DeMarre Carroll 2.50 6.00
219 Roger Mason Jr. 2.50 6.00
220 Rod Strickland 3.00 8.00
221 Marvin Williams 2.50 6.00
222 Lance Thomas 2.50 6.00
223 Gus Williams 2.50 6.00
224 Reggie Theus 3.00 8.00
225 Bill Laimbeer 4.00 10.00
226 Darrell Armstrong 2.50 6.00
227 Buck Williams 3.00 8.00
228 Spencer Haywood 4.00 10.00
229 Luc Longley 4.00 10.00
230 Kenyon Martin 4.00 10.00
231 Mickael Pietrus 2.50 6.00
232 Jarvis Varnado 2.50 6.00
233 Justin Hamilton 2.50 6.00
234 Lance Stephenson 3.00 8.00
236 Keith Bogans 2.50 6.00
237 Jeremy Evans 2.50 6.00
239 Ronnie Brewer 2.50 6.00
241 Patrick Beverley 2.50 6.00
242 Maurice Harkless 2.50 6.00
243 Justin Holiday 2.50 6.00
244 Darrell Walker 3.00 8.00
246 Darrell Griffith 3.00 8.00
251 Xavier McDaniel 3.00 8.00
254 Robert Horry 4.00 10.00
255 Fat Lever 3.00 8.00
256 Harvey Grant 2.50 6.00
257 Tim Hardaway 5.00 12.00
258 Bobby Jones 5.00 12.00
259 O.J. Mayo 2.50 6.00
260 Bob McAdoo 15.00 40.00

2013-14 Totally Certified Autographs Blue

*BLUE p/r 49: .75X TO 2X BASIC
*BLUE p/r 25: 1X TO 2.5X BASIC
PRINT RUNS B/WN 5-49 COPIES PER
NO PRICING ON QTY 20 OR LESS
EXCHANGE DEADLINE 5/27/2015
33 Cedric Maxwell/49 EXCH 6.00 15.00
34 Chris Wilcox/49 12.00 30.00
129 Luc Mbah a Moute/49 EXCH 5.00 12.00
137 Jonas Jerebko/49 EXCH 5.00 12.00
146 Zaza Pachulia/49 5.00 12.00
157 Jordan Hamilton/49 5.00 12.00
162 Kim English/25 6.00 15.00
164 Jeff Taylor/49 5.00 12.00
204 Julyan Stone/49 5.00 12.00
235 DeSagana Diop/49 5.00 12.00
238 Jon Leuer/49 5.00 12.00

2013-14 Totally Certified Autographs Gold

*GOLD p/r 25: 1X TO 2.5X BASIC
PRINT RUNS B/WN 3-25 COPIES PER
NO PRICING ON QTY 20 OR LESS
EXCHANGE DEADLINE 5/27/2015
33 Cedric Maxwell/25 EXCH 8.00 20.00
34 Chris Wilcox/25 15.00 40.00
129 Luc Mbah a Moute/25 EXCH 6.00 15.00
137 Jonas Jerebko/25 EXCH 6.00 15.00
146 Zaza Pachulia/25 6.00 15.00
157 Jordan Hamilton/25 6.00 15.00
164 Jeff Taylor/25 6.00 15.00
204 Julyan Stone/25 6.00 15.00
235 DeSagana Diop/25 6.00 15.00
238 Jon Leuer/25 6.00 15.00

2013-14 Totally Certified Autographs Red

*RED p/r 99: .6X TO 1.5X BASIC
*RED p/r 49: .75X TO 2X BASIC
*RED p/r 25: 1X TO 2.5X BASIC
PRINT RUNS B/WN 8-99 COPIES PER
NO PRICING ON QTY 20 OR LESS
EXCHANGE DEADLINE 5/27/2015
33 Cedric Maxwell/99 EXCH 5.00 12.00
34 Chris Wilcox/99 10.00 25.00
129 Luc Mbah a Moute/99 EXCH 4.00 10.00
137 Jonas Jerebko/99 EXCH 4.00 10.00
146 Zaza Pachulia/99 4.00 10.00
157 Jordan Hamilton/99 4.00 10.00
162 Kim English/99 5.00 12.00
164 Jeff Taylor/99 4.00 10.00
204 Julyan Stone/99 4.00 10.00
235 DeSagana Diop/99 4.00 10.00
238 Jon Leuer/99 4.00 10.00
245 C.J. Miles/99 EXCH 4.00 10.00
247 Greg Ostertag/99 EXCH 4.00 10.00

2013-14 Totally Certified Ballot Busters Autographs

PRINT RUNS B/WN 10-99 COPIES PER
NO PRICING ON QTY 10
EXCHANGE DEADLINE 5/27/2015
BBAD Adrian Dantley/99 6.00 15.00
BBAE Alex English/99 8.00 20.00
BBAG Artis Gilmore/15 10.00 25.00
BBBH Bailey Howell/99 10.00 25.00
BBBL Bob Lanier/15 8.00 20.00
BBBW Bill Walton/25 8.00 20.00
BBCH Connie Hawkins/49 10.00 25.00
BBCM Chris Mullin/49 10.00 25.00
BBCM Calvin Murphy/25 10.00 25.00
BBDC Dave Cowens/25 6.00 15.00
BBDR Dennis Rodman/25 40.00 100.00
BBDR David Robinson/10 12.00 30.00
BBDT David Thompson/99 6.00 15.00
BBDW Dominique Wilkins/10 10.00 25.00
BBEH Elvin Hayes/25 12.00 30.00
BBGG Gail Goodrich/25 15.00 40.00
BBIT Isiah Thomas/15 10.00 25.00
BBJD Joe Dumars/25 10.00 25.00
BBJW Jamaal Wilkes/49 15.00 40.00
BBKM Karl Malone/10 12.00 30.00
BBMA Mark Aguirre/50 5.00 12.00
BBMJ Magic Johnson/10 25.00 60.00
BBRP Robert Parish/25 10.00 25.00
BBSS Satch Sanders/99 8.00 20.00

2013-14 Totally Certified Future Stars Autographs

PRINT RUNS B/WN 25-325 COPIES PER
EXCHANGE DEADLINE 5/27/2015
FSAB Anthony Bennett/25 4.00 10.00
FSAG Archie Goodwin/325 4.00 10.00
FSAL Alex Len/25 5.00 12.00
FSCM C.J. McCollum/25 60.00 120.00
FSCZ Cody Zeller/25 5.00 12.00
FSGD Gorgui Dieng/299 5.00 12.00
FSGJ Grant Jerrett/299 4.00 10.00
FSJF Jamaal Franklin/325 4.00 10.00
FSKC Kentavious Caldwell-Pope/25 6.00 15.00
FSKO Kelly Olynyk/199 5.00 12.00
FSMC M.Carter-Williams/25 12.00 30.00
FSNN Nerlens Noel/25 12.00 30.00
FSNW Nate Wolters/325 4.00 10.00
FSOP Otto Porter/25 12.00 30.00
FSPS Peyton Siva/325 4.00 10.00
FSRG Rudy Gobert/299 EXCH 8.00 20.00
FSRK Ryan Kelly/299 6.00 15.00
FSRM Ray McCallum/199 4.00 10.00
FSSH Solomon Hill/325 5.00 12.00
FSTB Trey Burke/25 75.00 150.00
FSTH Tim Hardaway Jr./299 12.00 30.00
FSTM Tony Mitchell/325 4.00 10.00

2013-14 Totally Certified Materials

COMMON CARD 1.50 4.00
SEMISTARS 2.00 5.00
UNLISTED STARS 2.50 6.00
1 Tim Duncan 6.00 15.00
2 Kevin Martin 2.00 5.00
3 Dee Brown 2.00 5.00
4 Nick Young 1.50 4.00
5 Carl Landry 1.50 4.00
6 Michael Beasley 1.50 4.00
7 Kevin Love 2.50 6.00
8 Louis Williams 2.00 5.00
9 Jason Terry 2.00 5.00
10 Mo Williams 2.00 5.00
11 Manu Ginobili 5.00 12.00
12 Steve Novak 1.50 4.00
13 Luc Mbah a Moute 1.50 4.00
14 Ersan Ilyasova 1.50 4.00
15 David Lee 1.50 4.00
16 Ray Allen 4.00 10.00
17 Brandon Jennings 1.50 4.00
18 Eddie Jones 2.00 5.00
19 Terrence Ross 2.00 5.00
20 Rasheed Wallace 2.50 6.00
21 Joakim Noah 2.50 6.00
22 J.R. Smith 2.50 6.00
23 Monta Ellis 2.00 5.00
24 Bobby Jackson 1.50 4.00
25 Klay Thompson 8.00 20.00
26 David West 2.00 5.00
27 Taj Gibson 1.50 4.00
28 Larry Nance 2.00 5.00
29 Ekpe Udoh 1.50 4.00
30 Deron Williams 2.00 5.00
31 Carlos Boozer 2.00 5.00
32 Karl Malone 5.00 12.00
33 Jrue Holiday 3.00 8.00
34 Spencer Hawes 1.50 4.00
35 Kyrie Irving 5.00 12.00
36 Orlando Johnson 1.50 4.00
37 Alan Anderson 1.50 4.00
38 Will Bynum 1.50 4.00
39 Brook Lopez 2.50 6.00
40 John Wall 3.00 8.00
41 Damian Lillard 8.00 20.00
42 Danny Manning 2.00 5.00
43 Evan Turner 1.50 4.00
44 Jeff Teague 1.50 4.00
45 Kyle Singler 1.50 4.00
46 Rajon Rondo 3.00 8.00
47 Roy Hibbert 1.50 4.00
48 Kobe Bryant 20.00 50.00
49 Jeff Green 1.50 4.00
50 Bradley Beal 4.00 10.00
52 Brent Barry 1.50 4.00
53 Carmelo Anthony 4.00 10.00
54 Zaza Pachulia 1.50 4.00
55 Andre Drummond 2.50 6.00
56 Dirk Nowitzki 6.00 15.00
57 DeMarcus Cousins 2.50 6.00
58 Steve Nash 5.00 12.00
59 Bill Laimbeer 2.50 6.00
60 Nene 2.00 5.00
61 Dwyane Wade 5.00 12.00
62 Bob Lanier 3.00 8.00
63 Paul Pierce 4.00 10.00
64 Devin Harris 1.50 4.00
65 Kent Bazemore 1.50 4.00
66 Brandon Bass 1.50 4.00
67 Jonas Jerebko 1.50 4.00
68 Jamal Crawford 2.50 6.00
69 Marcus Camby 2.00 5.00
70 Al Jefferson 1.50 4.00
71 Joel Anthony 1.50 4.00
72 Paul Westphal 2.50 6.00
73 Kevin Garnett 6.00 15.00
74 Pau Gasol 4.00 10.00
75 Chandler Parsons 1.50 4.00
76 Shaquille O'Neal 10.00 25.00
77 Spencer Haywood 2.50 6.00
78 Amar'e Stoudemire 2.50 6.00
79 Lucius Allen 2.50 6.00
80 Derrick Favors 1.50 4.00
81 Shane Battier 2.00 5.00
82 Larry Bird 10.00 25.00
83 Grant Hill 4.00 10.00
84 D.J. Augustin 1.50 4.00
85 LaMarcus Aldridge 2.50 6.00
86 John Lucas 2.00 5.00
89 John Henson 1.50 4.00
90 Gordon Hayward 2.00 5.00
91 Nate Robinson 1.50 4.00
92 Jayson Williams 1.50 4.00
93 Jason Richardson 2.50 6.00
94 Andrew Bogut 2.00 5.00
95 Kendall Marshall 1.50 4.00
96 Cazzie Russell 1.50 4.00
97 Marcin Gortat 1.50 4.00
98 Ryan Anderson 1.50 4.00
99 Draymond Green 4.00 10.00
101 Zydrunas Ilgauskas 2.00 5.00
102 JaVale McGee 2.00 5.00
103 Kemba Walker 2.50 6.00
104 Glen Davis 1.50 4.00
105 Kawhi Leonard 8.00 20.00
106 Rashard Lewis 2.00 5.00
107 Maurice Lucas 2.50 6.00
108 Avery Bradley 1.50 4.00
109 Moses Malone 4.00 10.00
110 Caron Butler 2.00 5.00
111 Shawn Marion 2.00 5.00
112 Jalen Rose 2.00 5.00
113 Gerald Henderson 1.50 4.00
114 Arron Afflalo 1.50 4.00
115 Tony Parker 4.00 10.00
116 Buck Williams 2.00 5.00
117 DeMar DeRozan 3.00 8.00
118 Tristan Thompson 1.50 4.00
119 Serge Ibaka 2.00 5.00
120 Blake Griffin 2.50 6.00
121 Evan Fournier 2.00 5.00
122 Alex English 3.00 8.00
123 Zach Randolph 2.00 5.00
124 J.J. Barea 2.00 5.00
125 Wesley Matthews 1.50 4.00
127 Jeff Hornacek 2.00 5.00
128 Derrick Rose 4.00 10.00
129 Cedric Maxwell 2.00 5.00
130 Tyson Chandler 2.00 5.00
131 Ty Lawson 1.50 4.00
132 Robert Parish 3.00 8.00
133 Vince Carter 5.00 12.00
134 Anderson Varejao 1.50 4.00
135 Nicolas Batum 2.00 5.00
136 Kevin Durant 8.00 20.00
137 Emeka Okafor 2.00 5.00
138 Marc Gasol 2.50 6.00
139 Danny Granger 1.50 4.00
140 Raymond Felton 1.50 4.00
141 Kenneth Faried 2.00 5.00
142 Michael Kidd-Gilchrist 1.50 4.00
143 Andrew Nicholson 1.50 4.00
144 Gerald Wallace 2.00 5.00
145 Dwight Howard 3.00 8.00
146 Jimmer Fredette 2.50 6.00
147 DeAndre Jordan 2.00 5.00
148 Chris Paul 5.00 12.00
149 Paul George 4.00 10.00
150 Dion Waiters 1.50 4.00
151 LeBron James 10.00 25.00
152 David West 2.00 5.00
153 Dwight Howard 3.00 8.00
154 Devin Harris 1.50 4.00
155 Rasheed Wallace 2.50 6.00
156 Rashard Lewis 2.00 5.00
157 Nick Young 1.50 4.00
158 Jeff Green 1.50 4.00
159 David Lee 1.50 4.00
160 Jalen Rose 2.00 5.00
161 Al Jefferson 1.50 4.00
162 Carmelo Anthony 4.00 10.00
163 Emeka Okafor 2.00 5.00
164 Marcus Camby 2.00 5.00
165 Steve Nash 5.00 12.00
166 Grant Hill 4.00 10.00
167 Nene 2.00 5.00
168 JaVale McGee 2.00 5.00
169 Chris Paul 5.00 12.00
170 Deron Williams 2.00 5.00
171 Amar'e Stoudemire 2.50 6.00
172 Caron Butler 2.00 5.00
173 Jason Richardson 2.50 6.00
174 Mo Williams 2.00 5.00
175 Vince Carter 5.00 12.00
176 Kevin Martin 2.00 5.00
177 Nate Robinson 1.50 4.00
178 Jason Terry 2.00 5.00
179 Michael Beasley 1.50 4.00
180 Raymond Felton 1.50 4.00
181 Giannis Antetokounmpo 40.00 100.00
182 Shane Larkin 1.50 4.00
183 Andre Roberson 2.00 5.00
184 Tim Hardaway Jr. 3.00 8.00
185 Anthony Bennett 1.50 4.00
186 Kelly Olynyk 2.00 5.00
187 Tony Snell 2.00 5.00
188 Cody Zeller 2.00 5.00
189 Victor Oladipo 4.00 10.00
190 Trey Burke 2.00 5.00
191 Steven Adams 4.00 10.00
192 Michael Carter-Williams 2.00 5.00
193 Nerlens Noel 2.00 5.00
194 Ryan Kelly 1.50 4.00
195 Shabazz Muhammad 1.50 4.00
196 C.J. McCollum 6.00 15.00
197 Ben McLemore 2.00 5.00
198 Otto Porter 2.50 6.00
199 Glen Rice Jr. 1.50 4.00
200 Jamaal Franklin 1.50 4.00

2013-14 Totally Certified Materials Blue

*BLUE p/r 75-99: .5X TO 1.2X BASIC
*BLUE p/r 49: .75X TO 2X BASIC
*BLUE p/r 15-25: 1.2X TO 3X BASIC
PRINT RUN B/WN 5-99 COPIES PER
NO PRICING ON QTY 10 OR LESS
51 LeBron James/99 25.00 60.00
87 George Mikan/15 25.00 60.00
88 Anthony Davis/99 10.00 25.00
100 Dominique Wilkins/25 12.00 30.00
126 Patrick Ewing/99 5.00 12.00

2013-14 Totally Certified Materials Blue Prime

*BLUE PRIME p/r 15-25: 1.2X TO 3X BASIC
PRINT RUN B/WN 2-25 COPIES PER
NO PRICING ON QTY 10 OR LESS
51 LeBron James/25 60.00 150.00
88 Anthony Davis/15 15.00 40.00
126 Patrick Ewing/15 12.00 30.00
151 LeBron James/25 60.00 150.00

2013-14 Totally Certified Materials Gold Prime

*GLD PRIME p/r 15-25: 1.2X TO 3X BASIC
PRINT RUN B/WN 2-25 COPIES PER
NO PRICING ON QTY 10 OR LESS
51 LeBron James/25 60.00 150.00
88 Anthony Davis/25 25.00 60.00

2013-14 Totally Certified Materials Red

*RED p/r 75-99: .5X TO 1.2X BASIC
*RED p/r 49: .75X TO 2X BASIC
*RED p/r 15-25: 1.2X TO 3X BASIC
PRINT RUN B/WN 5-199 COPIES PER
NO PRICING ON QTY 10 OR LESS
51 LeBron James/149 25.00 60.00
87 George Mikan/15 25.00 60.00
88 Anthony Davis/99 10.00 25.00
100 Dominique Wilkins/49 8.00 20.00
126 Patrick Ewing/49 8.00 20.00

2013-14 Totally Certified Materials Red Prime

*RED PREIM p/r 15-25: 1.2X TO 3X BASIC
PRINT RUN B/WN 2-25 COPIES PER
NO PRICING ON QTY 10 OR LESS
51 LeBron James/25 60.00 150.00
126 Patrick Ewing/15 12.00 30.00
151 LeBron James/25 60.00 150.00

2013-14 Totally Certified Present Potential Autographs

PRINT RUNS B/WN 25-299 COPIES PER
NO PRICING ON QTY 10
EXCHANGE DEADLINE 5/27/2015
PPAA Alan Anderson/199 4.00 10.00
PPCB Corey Brewer/125 4.00 10.00
PPDG Danny Green/99 10.00 25.00
PPDG Draymond Green/199 15.00 40.00
PPEC Earl Clark/99 4.00 10.00
PPEI Ersan Ilyasova/75 4.00 10.00
PPEM E'Twaun Moore/199 4.00 10.00
PPEU Ekpe Udoh/199 4.00 10.00
PPGV Greivis Vasquez/99 4.00 10.00
PPIS Iman Shumpert/99 4.00 10.00
PPJH Jrue Holiday/25 8.00 20.00
PPKL Kawhi Leonard/99 40.00 100.00
PPKL Kyle Lowry/49 6.00 15.00
PPLS Lance Stephenson/199 5.00 12.00
PPMC Mike Conley/25 6.00 15.00
PPME Monta Ellis/49 6.00 15.00
PPMH Maurice Harkless/299 4.00 10.00
PPMW Marvin Williams/199 4.00 10.00
PPNB Nicolas Batum/149 5.00 12.00
PPRB Ronnie Brewer/179 4.00 10.00
PPTB Trevor Booker/299 4.00 10.00
PPTH Tobias Harris/99 6.00 15.00

2013-14 Totally Certified Rookie Roll Call Autographs

EXCHANGE DEADLINE 5/27/2015
1 Anthony Bennett 3.00 8.00
2 Victor Oladipo 30.00 80.00
3 Archie Goodwin 3.00 8.00
4 Dennis Schroder 10.00 25.00
5 Glen Rice Jr. 3.00 8.00
6 Isaiah Canaan 3.00 8.00
7 Peyton Siva 3.00 8.00
8 Ryan Kelly 3.00 8.00
9 Phil Pressey 3.00 8.00
10 Shabazz Muhammad 3.00 8.00
11 Otto Porter 10.00 25.00
12 Trey Burke 4.00 10.00
13 Kelly Olynyk 4.00 10.00
14 Kentavious Caldwell-Pope 5.00 12.00
15 Carrick Felix 3.00 8.00
16 Cody Zeller 4.00 10.00
17 Ray McCallum 3.00 8.00
18 Ben McLemore 4.00 10.00
19 Giannis Antetokounmpo 200.00 500.00
20 Shane Larkin 3.00 8.00
21 Tim Hardaway Jr. 6.00 15.00
22 Andre Roberson 4.00 10.00
23 C.J. McCollum 20.00 50.00
24 Nerlens Noel 4.00 10.00
25 Alex Len 4.00 10.00
26 Michael Carter-Williams 4.00 10.00
27 Erik Murphy 3.00 8.00
28 Gorgui Dieng 4.00 10.00
29 Allen Crabbe 3.00 8.00
30 Reggie Bullock 4.00 10.00
31 Nate Wolters 3.00 8.00
32 Mason Plumlee 4.00 10.00
33 Ricky Ledo 3.00 8.00
34 Tony Mitchell 3.00 8.00
35 C.J. Leslie 3.00 8.00
36 Grant Jerrett 3.00 8.00
37 Solomon Hill 4.00 10.00
38 Tony Snell 4.00 10.00
39 Jamaal Franklin 3.00 8.00
40 Elias Harris 3.00 8.00

2013-14 Totally Certified Rookie Roll Call Autographs Blue

*BLUE p/r 49: .75X TO 2X BASIC
PRINT RUNS B/WN 15-49 COPIES PER
NO PRICING ON QTY 15
EXCHANGE DEADLINE 5/27/2015

2013-14 Totally Certified Rookie Roll Call Autographs Red

*RED p/r 35: .75X TO 2X BASIC
*RED p/r 99: .6X TO 1.5X BASIC
PRINT RUNS B/WN 20-99 COPIES PER
NO PRICING ON QTY 20 OR LESS
EXCHANGE DEADLINE 5/27/2015

2013-14 Totally Certified Select Few Autographs

PRINT RUNS B/WN 10-99 COPIES PER
NO PRICING ON QTY 10
EXCHANGE DEADLINE 5/27/2015
1 Kobe Bryant/99 1,500.00 3,000.00
2 Blake Griffin/49 12.00 30.00
3 Kyrie Irving/99 75.00 200.00
4 Kevin Durant/49 100.00 250.00
7 Larry Bird/25 125.00 300.00
8 Magic Johnson/25 125.00 300.00
9 Kareem Abdul-Jabbar/25 125.00 300.00
12 Gail Goodrich/25 10.00 25.00
14 George Gervin/25 25.00 60.00
24 Wes Unseld/25 20.00 50.00

2014-15 Totally Certified

1 LaMarcus Aldridge .60 1.50
2 Paul George 1.00 2.50
3 Kyle Lowry .75 2.00
4 Al Horford .60 1.50
5 Zach Randolph .60 1.50
6 Al Jefferson .40 1.00
7 Anthony Bennett .40 1.00
8 Stephen Curry 5.00 12.00
9 Nicolas Batum .50 1.25
10 Jeff Teague .40 1.00
11A LeBron James 5.00 12.00
11B LeBron James 5.00 12.00
12 Kemba Walker .60 1.50
13 Jrue Holiday .75 2.00
14 Dion Waiters .40 1.00
15 Tobias Harris .50 1.25
16 Andre Iguodala .60 1.50
17 C.J. McCollum .60 1.50
18 Blake Griffin .60 1.50
19 DeMar DeRozan .75 2.00
20 Paul Millsap .50 1.25
21 Dwyane Wade 1.25 3.00
22 Gerald Henderson .40 1.00
23 Ryan Anderson .40 1.00
24 Nikola Vucevic .50 1.25
25 Andrew Bogut .50 1.25
26 DeAndre Jordan .50 1.25
27 Terrence Ross .50 1.25
28 Chris Bosh .75 2.00
29 Shawn Marion .50 1.25
30 Arron Afflalo .40 1.00
31 Klay Thompson 1.50 4.00
32 Ben McLemore .40 1.00
33A Chris Paul 1.00 2.50
33B Chris Paul 1.00 2.50
34 Jonas Valanciunas .50 1.25
35 Jared Sullinger .40 1.00
36 Ray Allen 1.00 2.50
37 Anthony Davis 1.50 4.00
38 Dirk Nowitzki 1.50 4.00
39 Victor Oladipo .50 1.25
40 Harrison Barnes .50 1.25
41 Rudy Gay .60 1.50
42 J.J. Redick .60 1.50
43 Enes Kanter .50 1.25
44 Tim Hardaway Jr. .50 1.25
45 Vince Carter 1.25 3.00
46 Nerlens Noel .40 1.00
47A James Harden 1.25 3.00
47B James Harden 1.25 3.00
48 Trey Burke .40 1.00
49 Jeff Green .50 1.25
50 Brandon Knight .40 1.00
51 Jimmy Butler 1.00 2.50
52 Amar'e Stoudemire .60 1.50
53 Monta Ellis .50 1.25
54 Michael Carter-Williams .40 1.00
55 Jeremy Lin 1.25 3.00
56 Isaiah Thomas .50 1.25
57 Nick Young .40 1.00
58 Gordon Hayward .50 1.25
59 Rajon Rondo .75 2.00
60 O.J. Mayo .40 1.00
61 Derrick Rose 1.25 3.00
62A Carmelo Anthony 1.00 2.50
62B Carmelo Anthony 1.00 2.50
63 JaVale McGee .50 1.25
64 Thaddeus Young .40 1.00
65 DeMarcus Cousins .40 1.00
66A Kobe Bryant 5.00 12.00
66B Kobe Bryant 5.00 12.00
67 Derrick Favors .40 1.00
68 Avery Bradley .40 1.00
69 Giannis Antetokounmpo 4.00 10.00
70 Taj Gibson .40 1.00
71 Tyson Chandler .60 1.50
72 Kenneth Faried .40 1.00
73 Eric Bledsoe .50 1.25
74 Dwight Howard .75 2.00
75 Steve Nash 1.25 3.00
76 Nene .50 1.25
77 Ricky Rubio .50 1.25
78 Joakim Noah .60 1.50
79 Ty Lawson .40 1.00
80 Alex Len .40 1.00
81 Roy Hibbert .50 1.25
82 Tony Parker 1.00 2.50
83 Pau Gasol 1.00 2.50
84 Marcin Gortat .40 1.00
85 Deron Williams .50 1.25
86A Kyrie Irving 1.25 3.00
86B Kyrie Irving 1.25 3.00
87 Russell Westbrook 1.00 2.50
88 Josh Smith .40 1.00
89 Lance Stephenson .50 1.25
90A Kawhi Leonard 1.50 4.00
90B Kawhi Leonard 1.50 4.00
91 Marc Gasol .60 1.50
92 John Wall .75 2.00
93 Kevin Garnett 1.50 4.00
94 Nikola Pekovic .40 1.00
95 Luol Deng .50 1.25
96A Kevin Durant 2.00 5.00
96B Kevin Durant 2.00 5.00
97 Brandon Jennings .40 1.00
98 Goran Dragic .60 1.50
99 David West .50 1.25
100 Manu Ginobili 1.25 3.00
101 Tayshaun Prince .60 1.50
102 Bradley Beal 1.00 2.50
103 Paul Pierce 1.00 2.50
104A Kevin Love .60 1.50
104B Kevin Love .60 1.50
105 Anderson Varejao .40 1.00
106 Serge Ibaka .50 1.25
107 Andre Drummond .50 1.25
108 Channing Frye .40 1.00
109A Tim Duncan 1.50 4.00
109B Tim Duncan 1.50 4.00
110 Mike Conley .50 1.25
111 Joe Johnson .50 1.25
112 Kevin Martin .50 1.25
113 Steven Adams .75 2.00
114 Greg Monroe .40 1.00
115A Damian Lillard 1.50 4.00
115B Damian Lillard 1.50 4.00
116 Magic Johnson 2.50 6.00
117 Mitch Richmond .75 2.00
118A Scottie Pippen 1.50 4.00
118B Scottie Pippen 1.50 4.00
119 Bill Russell 2.00 5.00
120 Kareem Abdul-Jabbar 2.00 5.00
121A Shaquille O'Neal 2.50 6.00
121B Shaquille O'Neal 2.50 6.00
122 Larry Bird 2.50 6.00
123 Jason Kidd 1.00 2.50
124 Clyde Drexler 1.00 2.50
125 Alonzo Mourning 1.00 2.50
126A Karl Malone 1.25 3.00
126B Karl Malone 1.25 3.00
127 Patrick Ewing 1.00 2.50
128A Oscar Robertson 1.25 3.00
128B Oscar Robertson 1.25 3.00
129 John Stockton 1.25 3.00
130 Isiah Thomas 1.00 2.50
131 Anfernee Hardaway 1.50 4.00
132A Wilt Chamberlain 2.00 5.00
132B Wilt Chamberlain 2.00 5.00
133 Allen Iverson 1.50 4.00
134 Julius Erving 1.50 4.00
135 Shawn Kemp 1.00 2.50

136A Pete Maravich 2.00 5.00
136B Pete Maravich 2.00 5.00
137 Yao Ming 1.50 4.00
138 David Robinson 1.25 3.00
139 Jerry West 1.50 4.00
140 Elgin Baylor 1.25 3.00
141A Andrew Wiggins RC 2.50 6.00
141B Andrew Wiggins 2.50 6.00
142A J.Parker RC Grn uni .60 1.50
142B Jabari Parker
White uni .60 1.50
143 Joel Embiid RC 5.00 12.00
144 Aaron Gordon RC 2.50 6.00
145A Dante Exum RC .75 2.00
145B Dante Exum .75 2.00
146 Marcus Smart RC 2.00 5.00
147 Julius Randle RC 2.50 6.00
148 Nik Stauskas RC .50 1.25
149 Noah Vonleh RC .50 1.25
150 Elfrid Payton RC .75 2.00
151 Doug McDermott RC .75 2.00
152 Zach LaVine RC 3.00 8.00
153 T.J. Warren RC .75 2.00
154 Adreian Payne RC .50 1.25
155 James Young RC .50 1.25
156 Tyler Ennis RC .50 1.25
157 Gary Harris RC .75 2.00
158 Mitch McGary RC .50 1.25
159 Jordan Adams RC .50 1.25
160 Rodney Hood RC .60 1.50
161 Shabazz Napier RC .60 1.50
162 P.J. Hairston RC .50 1.25
163 C.J. Wilcox RC .50 1.25
164 Bruno Caboclo RC .60 1.50
165 Kyle Anderson RC .75 2.00
166 Nikola Mirotic RC .75 2.00
167 Joe Harris RC .60 1.50
168 Cleanthony Early RC .50 1.25
169 Jamell Stokes RC .50 1.25
170 Johnny O'Bryant RC .50 1.25
171 Erick Green RC .50 1.25
172 Spencer Dinwiddie RC .75 2.00
173 Glenn Robinson III RC .60 1.50
174 Nick Johnson RC .50 1.25
175 Damjan Rudez RC .50 1.25
176 Markel Brown RC .50 1.25
177 Cory Jefferson RC .50 1.25
178 Jusuf Nurkic RC 1.50 4.00
179 Damien Inglis RC .50 1.25
180 Russ Smith RC .50 1.25

2014-15 Totally Certified Platinum Blue

*VETS: .6X TO 1.5X BASE HI
*RC: .6X TO 1.5X BASE HI
STATED PRINT RUN 149 SER.#'d SETS

2014-15 Totally Certified Platinum Mirror Blue Die Cuts

*VETS: 1.2X TO 3X BASE HI
*RCs: 1.2X TO 3X BASE HI
STATED PRINT RUN 74 SER.#'d SETS
126A Karl Malone 8.00 20.00
141A Andrew Wiggins 25.00 60.00

2014-15 Totally Certified Platinum Mirror Purple Die Cuts

*VETS: 2.5X TO 6X BASE HI
*ROOKIES: 2.5X TO 6X BASE HI
STATED PRINT RUN 25 SER.#'d SETS
38 Dirk Nowitzki 12.00 30.00
113 Steven Adams 8.00 20.00

2014-15 Totally Certified Platinum Mirror Red Die Cuts

*VETS: 1X TO 2.5X BASE HI
*RCs: 1X TO 2.5X BASE HI
STATED PRINT RUN 135 SER.#'d SETS

2014-15 Totally Certified Platinum Purple

*VETS: 2X TO 5X BASE HI
*RCs: 2X TO 5X BASE HI
STATED PRINT RUN 49 SER.#'d SETS
141A Andrew Wiggins 30.00 80.00
152 Zach LaVine 12.00 30.00

2014-15 Totally Certified Platinum Red

*VETS: .5X TO 1.2X BASE HI
*RCs: .5X TO 1.2X BASE HI
STATED PRINT RUN 279 SER.#'d SETS

2014-15 Totally Certified Ballot Busters Signatures

PRINT RUNS B/WN 12-60 COPIES PER
NO PRICING ON QTY 12
EXCHANGE DEADLINE 5/19/2016
BBAE Alex English/60 8.00 20.00
BBAG Artis Gilmore/49 8.00 20.00
BBBH Bailey Howell/60 8.00 20.00
BBBK Bernard King/60 8.00 20.00
BBBW Bill Walton/60 10.00 25.00
BBCD Clyde Drexler/49 15.00 40.00
BBCL Clyde Lovellette/60 6.00 15.00
BBCM Calvin Murphy/49 5.00 12.00
BBDC Dave Cowens/25 8.00 20.00
BBDI Dan Issel/60 8.00 20.00
BBDN Don Nelson/60 6.00 15.00
BBDR Dennis Rodman/60 30.00 80.00
BBDT David Thompson/60 6.00 15.00
BBDW Dominique Wilkins/49 15.00 40.00
BBEB Elgin Baylor/35 15.00 40.00
BBEH Elvin Hayes/60 10.00 25.00
BBGG Gail Goodrich/60 6.00 15.00
BBGP Gary Payton/25 20.00 50.00
BBHG Harry Gallatin/60 6.00 15.00
BBJD Joe Dumars/60 10.00 25.00
BBJE Julius Erving/35 60.00 150.00
BBJH John Havlicek/25 12.00 30.00
BBJL Jerry Lucas/49 10.00 25.00
BBJW Jerry West/35 30.00 80.00
BBLB Larry Bird/25 100.00 250.00
BBLW Lenny Wilkens/49 6.00 15.00
BBMD Mel Daniels/60 10.00 25.00
BBMJ Magic Johnson/25 100.00 250.00
BBNA Nate Archibald/49 8.00 20.00
BBOR Oscar Robertson/25 60.00 150.00
BBRB Rick Barry/60 12.00 30.00
BBWF Walt Frazier/60 12.00 30.00
BBCHM Chris Mullin/60 12.00 30.00
BBDAR David Robinson/35 40.00 100.00
BBGEG George Gervin/60 12.00 30.00
BBJAW James Worthy/60 12.00 30.00
BBKAJ Kareem Abdul-Jabbar/35 100.00 250.00

2014-15 Totally Certified Clear Cloth Jerseys Red

PRINT RUNS B/WN 199-299 COPIES PER
*BLUE/99-199: .6X TO 1.5X BASE HI
1 Al Horford/199 2.00 5.00
2 LeBron James/299 15.00 40.00
3 Kevin Durant/299 5.00 12.00
4 Chris Paul/299 3.00 8.00
5 Damian Lillard/199 5.00 12.00
6 Deron Williams/199 1.50 4.00
7 Kyrie Irving/299 4.00 10.00
8 DeAndre Jordan/299 1.50 4.00
9 DeMarcus Cousins/299 1.50 4.00
10 Dirk Nowitzki/299 5.00 12.00
11 Eric Bledsoe/199 1.50 4.00
12 George Hill/199 1.50 4.00
13 Isaiah Thomas/299 1.50 4.00
14 J.R. Smith/299 2.00 5.00
15 Jamal Crawford/299 2.00 5.00
16 James Harden/299 4.00 10.00
17 Kemba Walker/299 2.00 5.00
18 Kevin Love/299 2.00 5.00
19 Kirk Hinrich/299 1.50 4.00
20 Klay Thompson/299 5.00 12.00
21 Kobe Bryant/299 15.00 40.00
22 LaMarcus Aldridge/299 2.00 5.00
23 Luis Scola/299 1.50 4.00
24 Manu Ginobili/299 4.00 10.00
25 Mike Conley/199 1.50 4.00
26 Nick Young/299 1.25 3.00
27 Dwight Howard/299 2.50 6.00
28 Kevin Garnett/299 5.00 12.00
29 Nikola Vucevic/299 1.50 4.00
30 Pau Gasol/299 3.00 8.00
31 Paul Pierce/299 3.00 8.00
32 Paul George/199 3.00 8.00
33 Paul Millsap/299 1.50 4.00
34 Rajon Rondo/299 2.50 6.00
35 Ray Allen/199 3.00 8.00
36 Russell Westbrook/299 3.00 8.00
37 Ryan Anderson/299 1.25 3.00
38 Serge Ibaka/299 1.50 4.00
39 Stephen Curry/299 15.00 40.00
40 Steve Nash/299 4.00 10.00
41 Terrence Ross/299 1.50 4.00
42 Tiago Splitter/299 1.25 3.00
43 Tim Duncan/299 5.00 12.00
44 Tony Allen/199 1.25 3.00
45 Tony Parker/299 3.00 8.00
46 Ty Lawson/199 1.25 3.00
47 Victor Oladipo/299 1.50 4.00
48 Vince Carter/299 4.00 10.00
49 Zach Randolph/299 2.00 5.00
50 Al Jefferson/299 1.25 3.00
51 Amar'e Stoudemire/299 2.00 5.00
52 Anderson Varejao/299 1.25 3.00
53 Andre Drummond/299 1.50 4.00
54 Andre Iguodala/199 2.00 5.00
55 Anthony Bennett/299 1.25 3.00
56 Carmelo Anthony/199 3.00 8.00
57 Chandler Parsons/299 1.25 3.00
58 Danny Green/299 1.50 4.00
59 David Lee/199 1.25 3.00
60 David West/299 1.50 4.00
61 Dion Waiters/299 1.25 3.00
62 Dwyane Wade/199 4.00 10.00
63 Greg Monroe/299 1.25 3.00
64 Harrison Barnes/299 1.50 4.00
65 Iman Shumpert/199 1.25 3.00
66 Derrick Favors/299 1.25 3.00
67 Goran Dragic/199 2.00 5.00
68 Gordon Hayward/199 1.50 4.00
69 Jeremy Lin/299 4.00 10.00
70 Jimmy Butler/299 3.00 8.00
71 Joe Johnson/299 1.50 4.00
72 John Wall/199 2.50 6.00
73 Jonas Valanciunas/299 1.50 4.00
74 Kawhi Leonard/299 5.00 12.00
75 Kenneth Faried/199 1.25 3.00
76 Kyle Lowry/299 2.50 6.00
77 Marc Gasol/299 2.00 5.00
78 Marco Belinelli/299 1.25 3.00
79 M.Carter-Williams/199 1.25 3.00
80 Michael Kidd-Gilchrist/199 1.25 3.00
81 Monta Ellis/299 1.50 4.00
82 Nene/299 1.25 3.00
83 Nick Collison/299 1.25 3.00
84 Nicolas Batum/299 1.50 4.00
85 Nikola Pekovic/299 1.25 3.00
86 Shawn Marion/299 1.50 4.00
87 Solomon Hill/299 1.25 3.00
88 Taj Gibson/299 1.25 3.00
89 Thaddeus Young/299 1.25 3.00
90 Tyreke Evans/299 1.50 4.00
91 Andrew Wiggins/299 6.00 15.00
92 Jabari Parker/299 1.50 4.00
93 Joel Embiid/299 12.00 30.00
94 Aaron Gordon/299 6.00 15.00
95 Dante Exum/299 2.00 5.00
96 Marcus Smart/299 3.00 8.00
97 Julius Randle/299 6.00 15.00
98 Nik Stauskas/299 1.25 3.00
99 Noah Vonleh/299 1.25 3.00
100 Elfrid Payton/299 2.00 5.00

2014-15 Totally Certified Competitor Autographs

PRINT RUNS B/WN 49-99 COPIES PER
EXCHANGE DEADLINE 5/19/2016
CAD Andre Drummond/49 5.00 12.00
CAD A.Davis/49 EXCH 30.00 80.00
CAH Anfernee Hardaway/49 15.00 40.00
CBL Bill Laimbeer/99 6.00 15.00
CBRL Brook Lopez/49 6.00 15.00
CBW Buck Williams/99 6.00 15.00
CCB Caron Butler/49 5.00 12.00
CCD Clyde Drexler/49 15.00 40.00
CCL Christian Laettner/49 6.00 15.00
CCP Chuck Person/99 5.00 12.00
CCR Cazzie Russell/99 6.00 15.00
CDC Doug Collins/99 6.00 15.00
CDG Danny Green/99 5.00 12.00
CDN Don Nelson/49 10.00 25.00
CGG Gail Goodrich/99 6.00 15.00
CGGH Gerald Henderson/99 4.00 10.00
CGH George Hill/99 5.00 12.00
CGK George Karl/99 6.00 15.00
CGMC George McGinnis/99 4.00 10.00
CGP Gary Payton/49 12.00 30.00
CGRH Grant Hill/49 15.00 40.00
CHB Harrison Barnes/49 5.00 12.00
CHO Hakeem Olajuwon/49 12.00 30.00
CJD Joe Dumars/49 8.00 20.00
CJET Jason Terry/99 5.00 12.00
CJH Jeff Hornacek/99 5.00 12.00
CJJ Jim Jackson/99 5.00 12.00
CJJT John Thompson/99 10.00 25.00
CJMC JaVale McGee/99 5.00 12.00
CJOS John Starks/99 6.00 15.00
CJS John Salley/99 5.00 12.00
CJW Jerry West/49 20.00 50.00
CJW Jo Jo White/99 6.00 15.00
CKB Kobe Bryant/99 75.00 150.00
CKD Kevin Durant/99 40.00 100.00
CKI Kyrie Irving/49 30.00 80.00
CKL Kevin Love/49 6.00 15.00
CKLJ Larry Johnson/99 5.00 12.00
CKM Karl Malone/49 25.00 60.00
CMAJ Mark Jackson/99 5.00 12.00
CMCH Maurice Cheeks/99 5.00 12.00
CMGO Marcin Gortat/99 4.00 10.00
CMJ Marques Johnson/99 5.00 12.00
CPB Patrick Beverley/99 4.00 10.00
CPC Phil Chenier/99 5.00 12.00
CRA Ryan Anderson/99 4.00 10.00
CRB Rolando Blackman/99 5.00 12.00
CRM Rick Mahorn/99 5.00 12.00
CSC Stephen Curry/99 400.00 800.00
CTL Ty Lawson/99 4.00 10.00
CTP Tayshaun Prince/99 6.00 15.00
CTS Thabo Sefolosha/99 4.00 10.00
CTV Tom Van Arsdale/99 5.00 12.00
CWM Wesley Matthews/99 4.00 10.00
CJOW John Wall/49 12.00 30.00

2014-15 Totally Certified Competitor Autographs Mirror

*MIRROR: .5X TO 1.2X BASE HI
STATED PRINT RUN 25 SER.#'d SETS
EXCHANGE DEADLINE 5/19/2016

2014-15 Totally Certified EPIX Play Memorabilia Red

STATED PRINT RUN 199 SER.#'d SETS
*BLUE/149: .5X TO 1.2X BASE HI
1 LeBron James 15.00 40.00
2 Kevin Durant 6.00 15.00
3 Kobe Bryant 15.00 40.00
4 Dwyane Wade 4.00 10.00
5 Blake Griffin 2.00 5.00
6 Carmelo Anthony 3.00 8.00
7 James Harden 4.00 10.00
8 Stephen Curry 15.00 40.00
9 Chris Paul 3.00 8.00
10 Damian Lillard 5.00 12.00
11 DeMar DeRozan 2.50 6.00
12 Dirk Nowitzki 5.00 12.00
13 Dwight Howard 2.50 6.00
14 Joakim Noah 2.00 5.00
15 Joe Johnson 1.50 4.00
16 John Wall 2.50 6.00
17 Kevin Garnett 5.00 12.00
18 Kevin Love 2.00 5.00
19 Kyrie Irving 4.00 10.00
20 LaMarcus Aldridge 2.00 5.00
21 Marc Gasol 2.00 5.00
22 Rajon Rondo 2.50 6.00
23 Paul George 3.00 8.00
24 Ricky Rubio 1.50 4.00
25 Russell Westbrook 3.00 8.00

2014-15 Totally Certified Excellence

STATED PRINT RUN 299 SER.#'d SETS
1 Kobe Bryant 8.00 20.00
2 Kevin Durant 3.00 8.00
3 Kevin Love 1.00 2.50
4 LeBron James 8.00 20.00
5 Tim Duncan 2.50 6.00
6 Chris Paul 1.50 4.00
7 Carmelo Anthony 1.50 4.00
8 James Harden 2.00 5.00
9 Paul George 1.50 4.00
10 Stephen Curry 8.00 20.00
11 Dirk Nowitzki 2.50 6.00
12 Tony Parker 1.50 4.00
13 Blake Griffin 1.00 2.50
14 Dwight Howard 1.25 3.00
15 Kyrie Irving 2.00 5.00
16 John Wall 1.25 3.00
17 Russell Westbrook 1.50 4.00
18 LaMarcus Aldridge 1.00 2.50
19 DeMar DeRozan 1.25 3.00
20 Joe Johnson .75 2.00
21 DeMarcus Cousins .75 2.00
22 Damian Lillard 2.50 6.00
23 Klay Thompson 2.50 6.00
24 Dwyane Wade 2.00 5.00
25 DeAndre Jordan .75 2.00
26 Anthony Davis 2.50 6.00
27 Zach Randolph 1.00 2.50
28 Kenneth Faried .60 1.50
29 Al Jefferson .60 1.50
30 Monta Ellis .75 2.00

2014-15 Totally Certified Excellence Mirror

*MIRROR: 2X TO 5X BASE HI
STATED PRINT RUN 25 SER.#'d SETS
4 LeBron James 40.00 80.00

2014-15 Totally Certified Future Stars Signatures

STATED PRINT RUN 99 SER.#'d SETS
EXCHANGE DEADLINE 5/19/2016
*MIRROR/25: .5X TO 1.2X BASE HI
FSABE Anthony Bennett 4.00 10.00
FSAC Allen Crabbe 4.00 10.00
FSAD Anthony Davis 25.00 60.00
FSAG Archie Goodwin 4.00 10.00
FSAM Arnett Moultrie 4.00 10.00
FSAP Adreian Payne 4.00 10.00
FSAS Alexey Shved 4.00 10.00
FSAV Anderson Varejao 4.00 10.00
FSBB Bradley Beal 8.00 20.00
FSBC Bruno Caboclo 5.00 12.00
FSCF Carrick Felix 4.00 10.00
FSCJ C.J. Wilcox 4.00 10.00
FSCJM C.J. Miles 4.00 10.00
FSCJW C.J. Watson 4.00 10.00
FSCZ Cody Zeller 4.00 10.00
FSDM Donatas Motiejunas 4.00 10.00
FSDS Dennis Schroder 6.00 15.00
FSEF Evan Fournier 4.00 10.00
FSEK Enes Kanter 5.00 12.00
FSFE Festus Ezeli 4.00 10.00
FSGA Giannis Antetokounmpo 75.00 200.00
FSGD Goran Dragic 6.00 15.00
FSGDI Gorgui Dieng 4.00 10.00
FSGH Gary Harris 6.00 15.00
FSGJ Grant Jerrett 4.00 10.00
FSGM Gal Mekel 4.00 10.00
FSGR Glen Rice Jr. 4.00 10.00
FSHS Henry Sims 4.00 10.00
FSIC Ian Clark 4.00 10.00
FSICA Isaiah Canaan 4.00 10.00
FSIS Iman Shumpert 4.00 10.00
FSIT Isaiah Thomas 5.00 12.00
FSJA Jordan Adams 4.00 10.00
FSJC Jared Cunningham 4.00 10.00
FSJH Justin Hamilton 4.00 10.00
FSJL Jon Leuer 4.00 10.00
FSJLIII John Lucas III 4.00 10.00
FSJM Jamaal Franklin 4.00 10.00
FSJSU Jared Sullinger 4.00 10.00
FSJV Jarvis Varnado 4.00 10.00
FSJVA Jonas Valanciunas 5.00 12.00
FSKJ K.J. McDaniels 4.00 10.00
FSKO Kelly Olynyk 4.00 10.00
FSKOQ Kyle O'Quinn 4.00 10.00
FSLA Lavoy Allen 4.00 10.00
FSLD Luigi Datome 4.00 10.00
FSMCW Michael Carter-Williams 4.00 10.00
FSMD Matthew Dellavedova 5.00 12.00
FSMM Mitch McGary 4.00 10.00
FSMP Mason Plumlee 4.00 10.00
FSMPL Miles Plumlee 4.00 10.00
FSPJ P.J. Hairston 4.00 10.00
FSRH Rodney Hood 5.00 12.00
FSRK Ryan Kelly 4.00 10.00
FSRMC Ray McCallum 4.00 10.00
FSSA Steven Adams 8.00 20.00
FSSN Shabazz Napier 4.00 10.00
FSTB Trey Burke 4.00 10.00
FSTJW T.J. Warren 6.00 15.00
FSTS Tony Snell 4.00 10.00

2014-15 Totally Certified Future Stars Signatures Mirror

*MIRROR: .5X TO 1.2X BASE HI
STATED PRINT RUN 25 SER.#'d SETS
EXCHANGE DEADLINE 5/19/2016
FSAD Anthony Davis 50.00 120.00
FSGA Giannis Antetokounmpo 100.00 250.00

2014-15 Totally Certified Great American Heroes

STATED PRINT RUN 299 SER.#'d SETS
1 Kobe Bryant 8.00 20.00
2 Kevin Durant 3.00 8.00
3 LeBron James 8.00 20.00
4 Chris Paul 1.50 4.00
5 Kevin Love 1.00 2.50
6 Paul George 1.50 4.00
7 Derrick Rose 2.00 5.00
8 Stephen Curry 6.00 15.00
9 Carmelo Anthony 1.50 4.00
10 James Harden 2.00 5.00
11 LaMarcus Aldridge 1.00 2.50
12 Russell Westbrook 1.50 4.00
13 Dwyane Wade 2.00 5.00
14 Dwight Howard 1.25 3.00
15 Kenneth Faried .60 1.50
16 Blake Griffin 1.00 2.50
17 Kyrie Irving 2.00 5.00
18 Anthony Davis 2.50 6.00
19 DeMar DeRozan 1.25 3.00
20 DeMarcus Cousins .75 2.00
21 Klay Thompson 2.50 6.00
22 Al Jefferson .60 1.50
23 Rudy Gay 1.00 2.50
24 Joe Johnson .75 2.00
25 Magic Johnson 4.00 10.00
26 Larry Bird 4.00 10.00
27 Pete Maravich 3.00 8.00
28 Jerry West 2.50 6.00
29 Oscar Robertson 2.00 5.00
30 Kareem Abdul-Jabbar 3.00 8.00
31 Bill Russell 3.00 8.00
32 Scottie Pippen 2.50 6.00
33 Shaquille O'Neal 4.00 10.00
34 Wilt Chamberlain 3.00 8.00
35 Allen Iverson 2.50 6.00
36 Clyde Drexler 1.50 4.00
37 David Robinson 2.00 5.00
38 Grant Hill 1.50 4.00
39 Isiah Thomas 1.50 4.00
40 John Havlicek 2.00 5.00
41 Julius Erving 2.50 6.00
42 Karl Malone 2.00 5.00
43 Bill Walton 1.50 4.00
44 Rick Barry 1.25 3.00
45 Tim Hardaway 1.25 3.00
46 Anfernee Hardaway 6.00 15.00
47 Bob Cousy 2.00 5.00
48 David Thompson 1.00 2.50
49 Bill Bradley 1.25 3.00
50 John Stockton 2.00 5.00

2014-15 Totally Certified Great American Heroes Mirror

*MIRROR: 2X TO 5X BASE HI
STATED PRINT RUN 25 SER.#'d SETS

2014-15 Totally Certified Jerseys Red

*BLUE/99-199: .4X TO 1X BASE HI
*BLUE/25: .4X TO 1X BASE HI
*PURPLE/25-99: .5X TO 1.2X BASE HI
PRINT RUNS B/WN 49-249 COPIES PER
1 Al Jefferson/249 1.25 3.00
2 Alex English/149 3.00 8.00
3 Allen Iverson/149 6.00 15.00
4 Amar'e Stoudemire/249 2.50 6.00
5 Anderson Varejao/249 1.50 4.00
6 Andre Drummond/149 2.00 5.00
7 Andre Iguodala/249 2.50 6.00
8 Andrew Bogut/249 2.00 5.00
9 Anfernee Hardaway/249 6.00 15.00
10 Anthony Davis/249 6.00 15.00
11 Blake Griffin/249 2.50 6.00
12 Bradley Beal/149 4.00 10.00
13 Carlos Boozer/249 2.00 5.00
14 Carmelo Anthony/249 4.00 10.00
15 Chandler Parsons/249 1.50 4.00
16 Chris Andersen/249 2.00 5.00
17 Chris Bosh/249 3.00 8.00
18 Chris Paul/249 4.00 10.00
19 Clyde Drexler/249 4.00 10.00
20 Damian Lillard/249 6.00 15.00
21 Dan Majerle/249 2.00 5.00
22 Danny Ainge/49 3.00 8.00
23 David Lee/249 1.50 4.00
24 David Robinson/249 5.00 12.00
25 David West/149 2.00 5.00
26 DeAndre Jordan/249 2.00 5.00
27 DeMar DeRozan/249 3.00 8.00
28 DeMarcus Cousins/249 2.00 5.00
29 Derek Fisher/249 2.00 5.00
30 Dikembe Mutombo/249 4.00 10.00
31 Dirk Nowitzki/249 6.00 15.00
32 Doc Rivers/149 2.50 6.00
33 Dominique Wilkins/149 4.00 10.00
34 Dwight Howard/249 3.00 8.00
35 Dwyane Wade/249 5.00 12.00
36 Gary Payton/149 4.00 10.00
37 Grant Hill/149 4.00 10.00
38 James Harden/249 5.00 12.00
39 Jason Kidd/149 4.00 10.00
40 Jeremy Lin/249 5.00 12.00
41 Jimmy Butler/149 4.00 10.00
42 Joe Dumars/149 3.00 8.00
43 Joe Johnson/249 2.00 5.00
44 John Wall/249 3.00 8.00
45 Julius Erving/149 6.00 15.00
46 Kawhi Leonard/249 6.00 15.00
47 Kenneth Faried/249 1.50 4.00
48 Kevin Durant/249 8.00 20.00
49 Kevin Garnett/249 6.00 15.00
50 Kevin Love/249 2.50 6.00
51 Klay Thompson/149 6.00 15.00
52 Kyrie Irving/249 5.00 12.00
53 LeBron James/249 20.00 50.00
54 Louie Dampier/99 2.50 6.00
55 Manu Ginobili/199 5.00 12.00
56 Marc Gasol/249 2.50 6.00
57 Patrick Ewing/249 4.00 10.00
58 Pau Gasol/249 4.00 10.00
59 Paul George/249 4.00 10.00
60 Paul Millsap/249 2.00 5.00
61 Paul Pierce/249 4.00 10.00
62 Rajon Rondo/249 3.00 8.00
63 Ray Allen/249 4.00 10.00
64 Ricky Rubio/149 2.00 5.00
65 Roy Hibbert/249 2.00 5.00
66 Scottie Pippen/249 6.00 15.00
67 Shaquille O'Neal/149 10.00 25.00
68 Steve Nash/249 5.00 12.00
69 Taj Gibson/249 1.50 4.00
70 Tim Duncan/249 6.00 15.00
71 Tom Chambers/149 2.50 6.00
72 Tracy McGrady/249 4.00 10.00
73 Xavier McDaniel/149 2.00 5.00
74 Yao Ming/149 6.00 15.00
75 Zach Randolph/149 2.50 6.00
76 Andrew Wiggins/249 8.00 20.00
77 Jabari Parker/249 2.00 5.00
78 Joel Embiid/249 15.00 40.00
79 Aaron Gordon/249 8.00 20.00
80 Dante Exum/249 2.50 6.00
81 Marcus Smart/249 6.00 15.00
82 Julius Randle/249 8.00 20.00
83 Nik Stauskas/249 1.50 4.00
84 Noah Vonleh/249 1.50 4.00
85 Elfrid Payton/249 2.50 6.00
86 Doug McDermott/249 2.50 6.00
87 Zach LaVine/249 10.00 25.00
88 T.J. Warren/249 2.50 6.00
89 Adreian Payne/249 1.50 4.00
90 Cory Jefferson/249 1.50 4.00
91 James Young/249 1.50 4.00
92 Tyler Ennis/249 1.50 4.00
93 Gary Harris/249 2.50 6.00
94 Bruno Caboclo/249 1.50 4.00
95 Mitch McGary/249 1.50 4.00
96 Jordan Adams/249 1.50 4.00
97 Rodney Hood/249 2.00 5.00
98 Shabazz Napier/249 2.00 5.00
99 Cleanthony Early/249 1.50 4.00
100 P.J. Hairston/249 1.50 4.00

2014-15 Totally Certified Present Potential Signatures

STATED PRINT RUN 99 SER.#'d SETS
EXCHANGE DEADLINE 5/19/2016
*MIRROR/25: .5X TO 1.2X BASE HI
PPSAB Anthony Bennett 4.00 10.00
PPSAD Anthony Davis 30.00 80.00
PPSCJ Cory Joseph 4.00 10.00
PPSDM Donatas Motiejunas 4.00 10.00
PPSGA Giannis Antetokounmpo 100.00 250.00
PPSGJ Grant Jerrett 4.00 10.00
PPSGR Glenn Robinson III 5.00 12.00
PPSIC Ian Clark 4.00 10.00
PPSIT Isaiah Thomas 5.00 12.00
PPSJC Jordan Clarkson 15.00 40.00
PPSJE James Ennis 4.00 10.00
PPSJH Jordan Hamilton 4.00 10.00
PPSJL Jon Leuer 4.00 10.00
PPSJP Jannero Pargo 5.00 12.00
PPSJS Jamell Stokes 4.00 10.00
PPSJW Jeff Withey 4.00 10.00
PPSKM Khris Middleton 8.00 20.00
PPSKS Kyle Singler 4.00 10.00
PPSLA Lavoy Allen 4.00 10.00
PPSMB Markel Brown 4.00 10.00
PPSMP Mason Plumlee 4.00 10.00
PPSMT Marquis Teague 4.00 10.00
PPSNC Norris Cole 4.00 10.00
PPSNN Nerlens Noel 4.00 10.00
PPSNS Nik Stauskas 4.00 10.00
PPSNV Nikola Vucevic 5.00 12.00
PPSNW Nate Wolters 5.00 12.00
PPSOP Otto Porter 5.00 12.00
PPSPA Pero Antic 4.00 10.00
PPSPP Phil Pressey 4.00 10.00
PPSPS Peyton Siva 5.00 12.00
PPSQA Quincy Acy 4.00 10.00
PPSRB Rasual Butler 4.00 10.00
PPSRG Rudy Gobert 10.00 25.00
PPSRJ Reggie Jackson 5.00 12.00
PPSRK Ryan Kelly 4.00 10.00
PPSRL Ricky Ledo 4.00 10.00
PPSRS Robert Sacre 4.00 10.00
PPSSA Steven Adams 8.00 20.00
PPSSD Spencer Dinwiddie 6.00 15.00
PPSSH Solomon Hill 4.00 10.00
PPSSM Shabazz Muhammad 6.00 15.00
PPSTB Trey Burke 4.00 10.00
PPSTS Tony Snell 4.00 10.00
PPSTT Tristan Thompson 4.00 10.00
PPSVO Victor Oladipo 8.00 20.00
PPSZL Zach LaVine 12.00 30.00
PPSCJE Cory Jefferson 4.00 10.00
PPSICA Isaiah Canaan 4.00 10.00
PPSJFR Jimmer Fredette 5.00 12.00
PPSJHA Joe Harris 8.00 20.00
PPSJSM Jason Smith 4.00 10.00
PPSJUH Justin Hamilton 4.00 10.00
PPSKCP Kentavious Caldwell-Pope 5.00 12.00
PPSMCW Michael Carter-Williams 4.00 10.00
PPSNEN Nemanja Nedovic 4.00 10.00
PPSREB Reggie Bullock 4.00 10.00
PPSRMC Ray McCallum 4.00 10.00
PPSRSM Russ Smith 5.00 12.00
PPSTMI Tony Mitchell 4.00 10.00

2014-15 Totally Certified Rookie Roll Call Autographs

PRINT RUN B/WN 249-299 COPIES PER
EXCHANGE DEADLINE 5/19/2016
RRCAG Aaron Gordon/249 20.00 50.00
RRCAP Adreian Payne/249 4.00 10.00
RRCAW Andrew Wiggins/249 20.00 50.00
RRCCE Cleanthony Early/249 4.00 10.00
RRCDE Dante Exum/249 6.00 15.00
RRCDP Dwight Powell/299 6.00 15.00
RRCEP Elfrid Payton/299 6.00 15.00
RRCGH Gary Harris/299 6.00 15.00
RRCGR Glenn Robinson III/299 5.00 12.00
RRCJA Jordan Adams/299 5.00 12.00
RRCJE Joel Embiid/249 50.00 120.00
RRCJG Jerami Grant/249 20.00 50.00
RRCJN Jusuf Nurkic/299 12.00 30.00
RRCJP Jabari Parker/249 5.00 12.00
RRCJR Julius Randle/249 20.00 50.00
RRCJY James Young/249 4.00 10.00
RRCKA Kyle Anderson/249 6.00 15.00
RRCMB Markel Brown/249 4.00 10.00
RRCMM Mitch McGary/249 4.00 10.00
RRCMS Marcus Smart/249 15.00 40.00
RRCNJ Nick Johnson/299 4.00 10.00
RRCNS Nik Stauskas/249 4.00 10.00
RRCNV Noah Vonleh/249 4.00 10.00
RRCRH Rodney Hood/249 5.00 12.00
RRCRS Russ Smith/299 4.00 10.00
RRCSD Spencer Dinwiddie/299 6.00 15.00
RRCSN Shabazz Napier/299 5.00 12.00
RRCTE Tyler Ennis/249 4.00 10.00
RRCZL Zach LaVine/249 12.00 30.00
RRCCJW C.J. Wilcox/299 4.00 10.00
RRCDMC Doug McDermott/249 6.00 15.00
RRCJH Joe Harris/249 6.00 15.00
RRCJOB Johnny O'Bryant/299 4.00 10.00
RRCJTS Jarnell Stokes/299 4.00 10.00
RRCKJM K.J. McDaniels/249 4.00 10.00
RRCPJH P.J. Hairston/249 4.00 10.00
RRCTJW T.J. Warren/249 6.00 15.00

2014-15 Totally Certified Rookie Roll Call Autographs Mirror

*MIRROR: .6X TO 1.5X BASE HI
STATED PRINT RUN 25 SER.#'d SETS
EXCHANGE DEADLINE 5/19/2016

2014-15 Totally Certified Select Few Signatures

PRINT RUNS B/WN 25-60 COPIES PER
EXCHANGE DEADLINE 5/19/2016
SFAG Artis Gilmore/60 8.00 20.00
SFAH Anfernee Hardaway/35 40.00 100.00
SFAS Arvydas Sabonis/60 10.00 25.00
SFBK Bernard King/60 8.00 20.00
SFBS Bill Sharman/49 15.00 40.00
SFCM Calvin Murphy/25 5.00 12.00
SFDS Dolph Schayes/60 6.00 15.00
SFIT Isiah Thomas/60 25.00 60.00
SFJD Joe Dumars/60 8.00 20.00
SFJE Julius Erving/25 75.00 200.00
SFJH John Havlicek/25 40.00 100.00
SFJMC Jon McGlocklin/60 5.00 12.00
SFJT John Thompson/49 10.00 25.00
SFKAJ Kareem Abdul-Jabbar/25 75.00 200.00
SFKM Karl Malone/25 25.00 60.00
SFKMC Kevin McHale/49 12.00 30.00
SFLB Larry Bird/25 75.00 200.00
SFMJ Magic Johnson/25 75.00 200.00
SFNN Norm Nixon/60 5.00 12.00
SFNT Nate Thurmond/49 6.00 15.00
SFPR Pat Riley/25 20.00 50.00
SFRB Rick Barry/60 10.00 25.00
SFRC Rick Carlisle/60 4.00 10.00
SFRS Ralph Sampson/49 6.00 15.00
SFSE Sean Elliott/60 6.00 15.00
SFSH Spencer Haywood/60 6.00 15.00
SFSJ Sam Jones/60 10.00 25.00
SFSK Steve Kerr/49 10.00 25.00
SFSO Shaquille O'Neal/25 75.00 200.00
SFSW Spud Webb/60 8.00 20.00
SFTH Tom Heinsohn/45 30.00 80.00
SFTK Toni Kukoc/49 12.00 30.00
SFTMC Tracy McGrady/49 40.00 100.00
SFWB Walt Bellamy/49 5.00 12.00
SFWF Walt Frazier/60 12.00 30.00
SFWR Willis Reed/60 40.00 100.00
SFWU Wes Unseld/60 8.00 20.00
SFXMC Xavier McDaniel/60 5.00 12.00
SFYM Yao Ming/25 200.00 500.00

2014-15 Totally Certified Select Few Signatures Mirror

*MIRROR p/r 25: .4X TO 1X BASIC p/r 25
*MIRROR p/r 25: .5X TO 1.2X BASIC p/r 40-75
STATED PRINT RUN 25 SER.#'d SETS
EXCHANGE DEADLINE 5/19/2016
SFBR Bill Russell 600.00 1,200.00

2014-15 Totally Certified Signatures

PRINT RUNS B/WN 25-75 COPIES PER
EXCHANGE DEADLINE 5/19/2016
*MIRROR/25: .5X TO 1.2X BASE HI
TCSAB Anthony Bennett/49 4.00 10.00
TCSAG Artis Gilmore/49 8.00 20.00
TCSAH Allan Houston/75 6.00 15.00
TCSBB Bismack Biyombo/49 4.00 10.00
TCSBBA Brent Barry/49 4.00 10.00
TCSBD Brad Daugherty/49 5.00 12.00
TCSBG Ben Gordon/49 5.00 12.00
TCSBGR Blake Griffin/49 15.00 40.00
TCSBJ Bobby Jones/49 5.00 12.00
TCSBK Bernard King/49 8.00 20.00
TCSBL Bob Lanier/49 8.00 20.00
TCSBRB Bradley Beal/75 10.00 25.00
TCSBRK Brandon Knight/49 4.00 10.00
TCSBS Bill Sharman/49 25.00 60.00
TCSBYS Byron Scott/75 6.00 15.00
TCSCAM Calvin Murphy/25 5.00 12.00
TCSCB Caron Butler/49 5.00 12.00
TCSCC Cedric Ceballos/75 5.00 12.00
TCSCF Chris Ford/49 6.00 15.00
TCSCH Chris Herren/49 6.00 15.00
TCSCHB Chris Bosh/49 8.00 20.00
TCSCJM C.J. McCollum/49 10.00 25.00
TCSCM Chris Mullin/49 8.00 20.00
TCSCW Chet Walker/75 5.00 12.00
TCSDV Dick Van Arsdale/75 6.00 15.00
TCSDW Dominique Wilkins/49 10.00 25.00
TCSDYW Dwyane Wade/49 20.00 50.00
TCSEH Elvin Hayes/49 10.00 25.00
TCSEM Earl Monroe/49 10.00 25.00
TCSFB Fred Brown/49 4.00 10.00
TCSFE Festus Ezeli/49 4.00 10.00
TCSGA G.Antetokounmpo/49 75.00 200.00
TCSGD Goran Dragic/49 6.00 15.00
TCSGG Gail Goodrich/49 6.00 15.00
TCSGH Gordon Hayward/49 5.00 12.00
TCSGK George Karl/49 6.00 15.00
TCSGL Glen Rice/49 6.00 15.00
TCSGM George McGinnis/49 4.00 10.00
TCSGP Gary Payton/49 10.00 25.00
TCSGRA Greg Anthony/49 4.00 10.00
TCSGW Gus Williams/49 4.00 10.00
TCSHB Henry Bibby/49 6.00 15.00
TCSHG Hal Greer/49 6.00 15.00
TCSHO Hakeem Olajuwon/49 15.00 40.00
TCSHOG Horace Grant/49 6.00 15.00
TCSHW Herb Williams/49 4.00 10.00
TCSIT Isiah Thomas/75 10.00 25.00
TCSJC Jose Calderon/49 4.00 10.00
TCSJD Jared Dudley/49 4.00 10.00
TCSJET Jason Terry/60 5.00 12.00
TCSJF Jimmer Fredette/75 5.00 12.00
TCSJG Jeff Green/75 5.00 12.00
TCSJH James Harden/49 25.00 60.00
TCSJJ Jim Jackson/75 5.00 12.00
TCSJK Jason Kidd/49 8.00 20.00
TCSJL Jerry Lucas/49 8.00 20.00
TCSJM Jodie Meeks/49 4.00 10.00
TCSJMC JaVale McGee/49 5.00 12.00
TCSJN Johnny Newman/49 4.00 10.00
TCSJOD Joe Dumars/49 8.00 20.00
TCSJOH Jordan Hill/49 4.00 10.00
TCSJOJ Joe Johnson/49 5.00 12.00
TCSJOS John Starks/75 6.00 15.00
TCSJP John Paxson/75 5.00 12.00
TCSJR Jalen Rose/49 5.00 12.00
TCSJS Jared Sullinger/49 4.00 10.00
TCSJT John Thompson/49 10.00 25.00
TCSJW James Worthy/49 10.00 25.00
TCSKB Kobe Bryant/49 125.00 300.00
TCSKD Kevin Durant/49 50.00 120.00
TCSKS Kenny Smith/49 5.00 12.00
TCSKW Kenny Walker/49 4.00 10.00
TCSLD Luol Deng/49 5.00 12.00
TCSLE Len Elmore/49 8.00 20.00
TCSMC Mike Conley/49 5.00 12.00
TCSME Monta Ellis/49 5.00 12.00
TCSMF Michael Finley/49 6.00 15.00
TCSMG Marcin Gortat/49 4.00 10.00
TCSMJ Marques Johnson/75 5.00 12.00
TCSMKG Michael Kidd-Gilchrist/49 4.00 10.00
TCSMT Marquis Teague/75 4.00 10.00
TCSNT Nate Thurmond/49 6.00 15.00
TCSNV Nick Van Exel/49 12.00 30.00
TCSRA Ray Allen/49 25.00 60.00
TCSRH Ron Harper/49 6.00 15.00
TCSRM Rick Mahorn/75 6.00 15.00
TCSRP Robert Parish/49 15.00 40.00
TCSSA Steven Adams/75 8.00 20.00
TCSSB Shane Battier/49 5.00 12.00
TCSSC Stephen Curry/49 400.00 800.00
TCSSE Sean Elliott/49 6.00 15.00
TCSSH Spencer Haywood/75 6.00 15.00
TCSSK Steve Kerr/49 6.00 15.00
TCSSW Scott Wedman/75 5.00 12.00
TCSSWE Spud Webb/75 6.00 15.00
TCSTA Tony Allen/49 4.00 10.00
TCSTB Trey Burke/75 4.00 10.00
TCSTMC Tracy McGrady/75 12.00 30.00
TCSVL Vlade Divac/75 6.00 15.00
TCSZI Zydrunas Ilgauskas/75 5.00 12.00

2014-15 Totally Certified Skills

STATED PRINT RUN 299 SER.#'d SETS
*MIRROR/25: 2X TO 5X BASE HI
1 Kevin Durant 3.00 8.00
2 Stephen Curry 8.00 20.00
3 DeAndre Jordan .75 2.00
4 James Harden 2.00 5.00
5 Kobe Bryant 8.00 20.00
6 LeBron James 8.00 20.00
7 Chris Paul 1.50 4.00

8 Tim Duncan 2.50 6.00
9 Dirk Nowitzki 2.50 6.00
10 Dwight Howard 1.25 3.00
11 Dwyane Wade 2.00 5.00
12 Jamal Crawford 1.00 2.50
13 Tony Allen .60 1.50
14 Joakim Noah 1.00 2.50
15 Paul George 1.50 4.00
16 Carmelo Anthony 1.50 4.00
17 DeMar DeRozan 1.25 3.00
18 John Wall 1.25 3.00
19 Damian Lillard 2.50 6.00
20 Chandler Parsons .60 1.50

2015-16 Totally Certified

1 Kevin Garnett 1.50 4.00
2 DeMar DeRozan .75 2.00
3 Marcin Gortat .40 1.00
4 Evan Turner .40 1.00
5 Noah Vonleh .40 1.00
6 Tobias Harris .50 1.25
7 Rudy Gay .60 1.50
8 Aaron Gordon .60 1.50
9 Jimmy Butler 1.25 3.00
10 Brandon Jennings .40 1.00
11 Kevin Love .60 1.50
12 DeMarcus Cousins .60 1.50
13 Marcus Smart .75 2.00
14 Gerald Henderson .40 1.00
15 O.J. Mayo .40 1.00
16 Tony Parker 1.00 2.50
17 Rudy Gobert .75 2.00
18 Al Horford .60 1.50
19 Joakim Noah .40 1.00
20 Brandon Knight .40 1.00
21 Kevin Martin .50 1.25
22 DeMarre Carroll .40 1.00
23 Mario Chalmers .50 1.25
24 Giannis Antetokounmpo 3.00 8.00
25 Omer Asik .40 1.00
26 Tony Wroten .40 1.00
27 Russell Westbrook 1.00 2.50
28 Al Jefferson .40 1.00
29 Jodie Meeks .40 1.00
30 Brook Lopez .60 1.50
31 Khris Middleton .75 2.00
32 Deron Williams .50 1.25
33 Goran Dragic .60 1.50
34 Gordon Hayward .60 1.50
35 P.J. Tucker .40 1.00
36 Trevor Ariza .40 1.00
37 Ryan Anderson .40 1.00
38 Al-Farouq Aminu .40 1.00
39 Joe Johnson .50 1.25
40 Carmelo Anthony 1.00 2.50
41 Klay Thompson 1.50 4.00
42 Derrick Favors .50 1.25
43 Markieff Morris .40 1.00
44 Greg Monroe .50 1.25
45 Patrick Beverley .40 1.00
46 Trey Burke .40 1.00
47 Serge Ibaka .50 1.25
48 Amir Johnson .40 1.00
49 John Wall .75 2.00
50 Chandler Parsons .40 1.00
51 Kobe Bryant 5.00 12.00
52 Derrick Rose 1.00 2.50
53 Mason Plumlee .40 1.00
54 Hassan Whiteside .50 1.25
55 Pau Gasol 1.00 2.50
56 Tristan Thompson .40 1.00
57 Solomon Hill .40 1.00
58 Andre Drummond .60 1.50
59 Jonas Valanciunas .40 1.00
60 Chase Budinger .40 1.00
61 Kyle Korver .50 1.25
62 Derrick Williams .40 1.00
63 Matt Barnes .40 1.00
64 Hollis Thompson .40 1.00
65 Paul George 1.00 2.50
66 Ty Lawson .40 1.00
67 Spencer Hawes .40 1.00
68 Andre Iguodala .60 1.50
69 Jordan Clarkson .60 1.50
70 Chris Andersen .50 1.25
71 Kyle Lowry .60 1.50
72 Dirk Nowitzki 1.50 4.00
73 Michael Carter-Williams .40 1.00
74 J.J. Barea .50 1.25
75 Paul Millsap .50 1.25
76 Tyreke Evans .50 1.25
77 Stephen Curry 5.00 12.00
78 Andre Roberson .40 1.00
79 Jordan Hill .40 1.00
80 Chris Bosh .75 2.00
81 Kyrie Irving 1.25 3.00
82 Donatas Motiejunas .40 1.00
83 Michael Kidd-Gilchrist .40 1.00
84 J.J. Redick .60 1.50
85 Paul Pierce 1.00 2.50
86 Tyson Chandler .50 1.25
87 Taj Gibson .40 1.00
88 Andrew Wiggins .75 2.00
89 Josh Smith .40 1.00
90 Chris Paul 1.25 3.00
91 LaMarcus Aldridge .60 1.50
92 Draymond Green .75 2.00
93 Mike Conley .60 1.50
94 J.R. Smith .60 1.50
95 Rajon Rondo .75 2.00
96 Victor Oladipo .50 1.25
97 Terrence Ross .50 1.25
98 Anthony Davis 1.50 4.00
99 Jrue Holiday .75 2.00
100 Damian Lillard 1.50 4.00
101 Lance Stephenson .50 1.25
102 Dwight Howard .75 2.00
103 Monta Ellis .50 1.25
104 Jabari Parker .50 1.25
105 Reggie Jackson .50 1.25
106 Vince Carter 1.25 3.00
107 Thomas Robinson .40 1.00
108 Arron Afflalo .40 1.00
109 Julius Randle .75 2.00
110 Danilo Gallinari .50 1.25
111 Langston Galloway .40 1.00
112 Dwyane Wade 1.25 3.00
113 Nene .50 1.25
114 James Harden 1.25 3.00
115 Ricky Rubio .50 1.25
116 Wesley Matthews .40 1.00
117 Tiago Splitter .40 1.00
118 Avery Bradley .50 1.25
119 Kawhi Leonard 2.00 5.00
120 Danny Green .50 1.25
121 LeBron James 5.00 12.00
122 Elfrid Payton .50 1.25
123 Nerlens Noel .40 1.00
124 Jared Sullinger .40 1.00
125 Robert Covington .50 1.25
126 Wilson Chandler .50 1.25
127 Tim Duncan 1.50 4.00
128 Ben McLemore .40 1.00
129 Kemba Walker .60 1.50
130 Dante Exum .50 1.25
131 Lou Williams .50 1.25
132 Eric Bledsoe .50 1.25
133 Nicolas Batum .40 1.00
134 Jarrett Jack .50 1.25
135 Robin Lopez .40 1.00
136 Zach LaVine 1.50 4.00
137 Tim Hardaway Jr. .50 1.25
138 Blake Griffin .60 1.50
139 Kenneth Faried .50 1.25
140 Darren Collison .40 1.00
141 Manu Ginobili 1.25 3.00
142 Eric Gordon .50 1.25
143 Nikola Mirotic .40 1.00
144 Jeff Teague .40 1.00
145 Rodney Stuckey .40 1.00
146 Zach Randolph .60 1.50
147 Timofey Mozgov .40 1.00
148 Bojan Bogdanovic .50 1.25
149 Kentavious Caldwell-Pope .50 1.25
150 David Lee .40 1.00
151 Marc Gasol .60 1.50
152 Ersan Ilyasova .40 1.00
153 Nikola Vucevic .50 1.25
154 Jeremy Lin 1.25 3.00
155 Roy Hibbert .50 1.25
156 Luol Deng .50 1.25
157 DeAndre Jordan .50 1.25
158 Bradley Beal .75 2.00
159 Kevin Durant 2.50 6.00
160 J.J. Hickson .40 1.00
161 Jarell Martin RC .40 1.00
162 Frank Kaminsky RC .50 1.25
163 Montrezl Harrell RC 1.25 3.00
164 Devin Booker RC 15.00 40.00
165 Richaun Holmes RC .60 1.50
166 Rashad Vaughn RC .40 1.00
167 Nikola Jokic RC 60.00 150.00
168 Karl-Anthony Towns RC 2.50 6.00
169 Justin Anderson RC .40 1.00
170 Mario Hezonja RC .50 1.25
171 Larry Nance Jr. RC .75 2.00
172 Justise Winslow RC .60 1.50
173 Jordan Mickey RC .40 1.00
174 Cameron Payne RC .60 1.50
175 Pat Connaughton RC .60 1.50
176 Sam Dekker RC .40 1.00
177 Raul Neto RC .40 1.00
178 D'Angelo Russell RC 1.50 4.00
179 Bobby Portis RC 1.00 2.50
180 Willie Cauley-Stein RC .50 1.25
181 R.J. Hunter RC .40 1.00
182 Myles Turner RC 1.50 4.00
183 Anthony Brown RC .40 1.00
184 Kelly Oubre Jr. RC 1.25 3.00
185 Pierre Jackson RC .40 1.00
186 Jerian Grant RC .40 1.00
187 Tyus Jones RC .50 1.25
188 Jahlil Okafor RC .50 1.25
189 Rondae Hollis-Jefferson RC .50 1.25
190 Emmanuel Mudiay RC .50 1.25
191 Chris McCullough RC .40 1.00
192 Trey Lyles RC .50 1.25
193 Rakeem Christmas RC .40 1.00
194 Terry Rozier RC 1.50 4.00
195 Nemanja Bjelica RC .60 1.50
196 Delon Wright RC .60 1.50
197 Kevon Looney RC 1.25 3.00
198 Kristaps Porzingis RC 2.50 6.00
199 Walter Tavares RC .40 1.00
200 Stanley Johnson RC .50 1.25

2015-16 Totally Certified Mirror Blue

*MIRROR BLUE: 1.25X TO 3X BASIC
STATED PRINT RUN 99 SER.#'d SETS

2015-16 Totally Certified Mirror Purple

*MIRROR PURPLE: 1X TO 2.5X BASIC
*MIRROR PURPLE RC: 1.2X TO 3X BASIC
STATED PRINT RUN 50 SER.#'d SETS
164 Devin Booker 75.00 200.00
168 Karl-Anthony Towns 12.00 30.00
198 Kristaps Porzingis 12.00 30.00

2015-16 Totally Certified Mirror Red

*MIRROR RED: 1X TO 2.5X BASIC
STATED PRINT RUN 149 SER.#'d SETS

2015-16 Totally Certified Champions

STATED PRINT RUN 199 SER.#'d SETS
*MIRROR/25: 1.5X TO 4X BASIC
1 Dirk Nowitzki 2.50 6.00
2 Scottie Pippen 2.50 6.00
3 Tony Parker 1.50 4.00
4 Shaquille O'Neal 3.00 8.00
5 Clyde Drexler 1.50 4.00
6 Larry Bird 4.00 10.00
7 Magic Johnson 4.00 10.00
8 LeBron James 8.00 20.00
9 Kobe Bryant 8.00 20.00
10 Dwyane Wade 2.00 5.00
11 Isiah Thomas 1.00 2.50
12 Tim Duncan 2.50 6.00
13 Bill Russell 3.00 8.00
14 Hakeem Olajuwon 2.00 5.00
15 Stephen Curry 8.00 20.00

2015-16 Totally Certified Competitor Autographs

PRINT RUNS B/WN 19-99 COPIES PER
*CAMO/25: .5X TO 1.2X BASIC p/r 99
*CAMO/25: .4X TO 1X BASIC p/r 25
CCAAD Anthony Davis/25 40.00 100.00
CCAAE Alex English/25 8.00 20.00
CCAAG Artis Gilmore/25 8.00 20.00
CCAAM Antonio McDyess/99 4.00 10.00
CCAAW Antoine Walker/99 4.00 10.00
CCABB Bradley Beal/25 8.00 20.00
CCABD Bob Dandridge/99 3.00 8.00
CCABL Bill Laimbeer/99 5.00 12.00
CCABM Bob McAdoo/25 15.00 40.00
CCACY Carmelo Anthony/25 10.00 25.00
CCADB Dee Brown/99 3.00 8.00
CCADC Dave Cowens/25 8.00 20.00
CCADI Dan Issel/25 8.00 20.00
CCADR Dino Radja/99 12.00 30.00
CCADS Damon Stoudamire/99 5.00 12.00
CCAEJ Eddie Jones/99 5.00 12.00
CCAEK Enes Kanter/25 4.00 10.00
CCAGP Gary Payton/25 8.00 20.00
CCAJD Joe Dumars/25 8.00 20.00
CCAJE Julius Erving/25 25.00 60.00
CCAJN Jusuf Nurkic/25 5.00 12.00
CCAJP Jabari Parker/25 15.00 40.00
CCAJR Julius Randle/25 8.00 20.00
CCAJW Jerome Williams/99 3.00 8.00
CCAJW John Wall/25 15.00 40.00
CCAJW Jo Jo White/99 5.00 12.00
CCAKA K. Abdul-Jabbar/25 25.00 60.00
CCAKB Kobe Bryant/25 500.00 1,000.00
CCAKD Kevin Durant/25 60.00 120.00
CCALB Larry Bird/25 30.00 80.00
CCAMA Mark Aguirre/25 5.00 12.00
CCAMC Michael Carter-Williams/25 4.00 10.00
CCAMG Marcin Gortat/25 10.00 25.00
CCAMJ Magic Johnson/25 25.00 60.00
CCANY Nick Young/25 4.00 10.00
CCARA Rafer Alston/99 3.00 8.00
CCARG Rudy Gobert/99 6.00 15.00
CCARL Raef LaFrentz/99 3.00 8.00
CCARP Robert Parish/25 8.00 20.00
CCARS Rony Seikaly/99 4.00 10.00
CCARS Rik Smits/99 4.00 10.00
CCASE Sean Elliott/99 4.00 10.00
CCASO Shaquille O'Neal/25 40.00 100.00
CCASS Steve Smith/99 4.00 10.00
CCATH Tim Hardaway/25 8.00 20.00
CCATY Thaddeus Young/99 3.00 8.00
CCAVD Vlade Divac/99 5.00 12.00
CCAZI Zydrunas Ilgauskas/99 4.00 10.00
CCAZR Zach Randolph/25 6.00 15.00

2015-16 Totally Certified EPIX Play Memorabilia

PRINT RUNS B/WN 49-99 COPIES PER
*PRIME/25: .75X TO 2X BASIC
*DUAL/49-99: .4X TO 1X BASIC
*TRIPLE/49-99: .4X TO 1X BASIC
*QUAD/49-99: .5X TO 1.2X BASIC
EPIXAD Anthony Davis/99 5.00 12.00
EPIXAM Alonzo Mourning/99 4.00 10.00
EPIXBD Baron Davis/99 2.00 5.00
EPIXCO Charles Oakley/99 2.00 5.00
EPIXCP Chandler Parsons/99 1.50 4.00
EPIXDJ DeAndre Jordan/99 2.00 5.00
EPIXDL Damian Lillard/99 6.00 15.00
EPIXDR Derrick Rose/99 4.00 10.00
EPIXDT David Thompson/49 3.00 8.00
EPIXGH Grant Hill/99 4.00 10.00
EPIXJD Joe Dumars/99 3.00 8.00
EPIXJH James Harden/99 5.00 12.00
EPIXJW John Wall/99 3.00 8.00
EPIXKB Kobe Bryant/99 8.00 20.00
EPIXKD Kevin Durant/99 5.00 12.00
EPIXKW Kemba Walker/99 2.50 6.00
EPIXMA Mark Aguirre/99 2.00 5.00
EPIXPE Patrick Ewing/99 4.00 10.00
EPIXRA Ray Allen/49 3.00 8.00
EPIXRL Reggie Lewis/99 2.50 6.00
EPIXSK Steve Kerr/99 2.50 6.00
EPIXTB Trey Burke/99 1.50 4.00
EPIXTD Tim Duncan/99 6.00 15.00
EPIXYM Yao Ming/49 6.00 15.00
EPIXZR Zach Randolph/99 2.50 6.00

2015-16 Totally Certified Fabric of the Game Materials Red

PRINT RUNS B/WN 99-199 COPIES PER
*BLUE/99: .4X TO 1X BASIC
*BLUE/49: .5X TO 1.2X BASIC
*CAMO/20-25: .75X TO 2X BASIC
FGAB Andrew Bogut/199 2.00 5.00
FGAD Andre Drummond/199 2.50 6.00
FGAD Anthony Davis/199 5.00 12.00
FGAE Alex English/199 3.00 8.00
FGAG Aaron Gordon/199 2.50 6.00
FGAH Anfernee Hardaway/199 6.00 15.00
FGAH Al Horford/199 2.50 6.00
FGAI Allen Iverson/199 5.00 12.00
FGAM Alonzo Mourning/199 4.00 10.00
FGBB Bradley Beal/199 3.00 8.00
FGBG Blake Griffin/199 2.50 6.00
FGBK Brandon Knight/199 1.50 4.00
FGBL Brook Lopez/199 2.50 6.00
FGBM Ben McLemore/199 1.50 4.00
FGCA Carmelo Anthony/99 4.00 10.00
FGCA Chris Andersen/199 2.00 5.00
FGCB Chris Bosh/199 3.00 8.00
FGCB Chris Paul/99 5.00 12.00
FGCD Clyde Drexler/99 4.00 10.00
FGDC DeMarcus Cousins/99 2.50 6.00
FGDG Danilo Gallinari/199 2.50 6.00
FGDH Dwight Howard/99 3.00 8.00
FGDJ DeAndre Jordan/99 2.00 5.00
FGDL Damian Lillard/99 6.00 15.00
FGDM Danny Manning/199 2.00 5.00
FGDM Dan Majerle/99 2.50 6.00
FGDM Doug McDermott/99 2.00 5.00
FGDN Dirk Nowitzki/199 6.00 15.00
FGDR David Robinson/99 5.00 12.00
FGDW David West/99 2.00 5.00
FGEP Elfrid Payton/99 2.00 5.00
FGGA Giannis Antetokounmpo/99 12.00 30.00
FGGD Goran Dragic/99 2.50 6.00
FGGH Grant Hill/99 4.00 10.00
FGHO Hakeem Olajuwon/99 5.00 12.00
FGIS Iman Shumpert/99 1.50 4.00
FGJB Jimmy Butler/99 5.00 12.00
FGJD Joe Dumars/99 3.00 8.00
FGJH James Harden/99 5.00 12.00
FGJH Jrue Holiday/99 3.00 8.00
FGJK Jason Kidd/199 4.00 10.00
FGJR J.J. Redick/99 2.50 6.00
FGJS John Starks/199 2.50 6.00
FGJS J.R. Smith/199 2.50 6.00
FGJT Jeff Teague/99 1.50 4.00
FGJV Jonas Valanciunas/99 2.00 5.00
FGJW John Wall/99 3.00 8.00
FGKD Kevin Duckworth/199 1.50 4.00
FGKG Kevin Garnett/99 6.00 15.00
FGKI Kyrie Irving/99 5.00 12.00
FGKK Kyle Korver/99 2.00 5.00
FGKL Kawhi Leonard/199 8.00 20.00
FGKL Kevin Love/199 2.50 6.00
FGKM Karl Malone/99 4.00 10.00
FGKT Klay Thompson/199 6.00 15.00
FGKW Kemba Walker/99 2.50 6.00
FGLA LaMarcus Aldridge/99 2.50 6.00
FGLD Luol Deng/99 2.00 5.00
FGLJ Larry Johnson/199 3.00 8.00
FGLJ LeBron James/199 6.00 15.00
FGLS Lance Stephenson/99 2.00 5.00
FGMA Mark Aguirre/199 2.00 5.00
FGMB Mike Bibby/199 2.00 5.00
FGMC Mike Conley/199 2.50 6.00
FGMC Mario Chalmers/199 2.00 5.00
FGMF Michael Finley/199 2.50 6.00
FGMG Manu Ginobili/99 5.00 12.00
FGMG Marc Gasol/199 2.50 6.00
FGMM Moses Malone/99 4.00 10.00
FGMR Michael Redd/199 2.00 5.00
FGMS Marcus Smart/99 3.00 8.00
FGNS Nik Stauskas/99 1.50 4.00
FGNV Nikola Vucevic/199 2.00 5.00
FGNY Nick Young/99 1.50 4.00
FGOP Otto Porter/99 2.00 5.00
FGPB Patrick Beverley/99 1.50 4.00
FGPP Paul Pierce/99 4.00 10.00
FGRH Roy Hibbert/99 2.00 5.00
FGRJ Reggie Jackson/99 2.00 5.00
FGRR Ricky Rubio/99 2.00 5.00
FGRR Rajon Rondo/199 3.00 8.00
FGRW Russell Westbrook/99 4.00 10.00
FGSC Stephen Curry/99 8.00 20.00
FGSM Shawn Marion/99 2.00 5.00
FGSN Shabazz Napier/199 1.50 4.00
FGSO Shaquille O'Neal/99 8.00 20.00
FGSP Scottie Pippen/199 6.00 15.00
FGTB Trey Burke/99 1.50 4.00
FGTC Tom Chambers/199 2.00 5.00
FGTC Tyson Chandler/99 2.00 5.00
FGTH Tim Hardaway Jr./99 2.00 5.00
FGTJ Terrence Jones/99 1.50 4.00
FGTL Ty Lawson/199 1.50 4.00
FGTM Tracy McGrady/199 4.00 10.00
FGTP Tony Parker/99 4.00 10.00
FGTS Tiago Splitter/199 1.50 4.00
FGTW T.J. Warren/99 2.50 6.00
FGVO Victor Oladipo/99 2.00 5.00
FGWD Walter Davis/199 1.50 4.00
FGZL Zach LaVine/99 6.00 15.00

2015-16 Totally Certified Hall Hopefuls

STATED PRINT RUN 199 SER.#'d SETS
*MIRROR/25: 1.5X TO 4X BASIC
1 Kobe Bryant 8.00 20.00
2 Tim Duncan 2.50 6.00
3 Kevin Garnett 2.50 6.00
4 LeBron James 8.00 20.00
5 Shaquille O'Neal 3.00 8.00
6 Dirk Nowitzki 2.50 6.00
7 Dwyane Wade 2.00 5.00
8 Allen Iverson 2.50 6.00
9 Jason Kidd 1.50 4.00
10 Steve Nash 1.50 4.00

2015-16 Totally Certified Hall Hopefuls Signatures

PRINT RUNS B/WN 5-49 COPIES PER
NO PRICING ON QTY 5
*CAMO/25: .5X TO 1.2X BASIC p/r 49
*CAMO/25: .4X TO 1X BASIC p/r 19-31
HHAI Allen Iverson/25 40.00 100.00
HHBD Bob Dandridge/49 3.00 8.00
HHCP Chris Paul/25 40.00 100.00
HHCW Chris Webber/25 100.00 200.00
HHGM George McGinnis/49 5.00 12.00
HHJK Jason Kidd/22 15.00 40.00
HHJS Jack Sikma/49 4.00 10.00
HHKB Kobe Bryant/25 500.00 1,000.00
HHLS Latrell Sprewell/49 12.00 30.00
HHMA Mark Aguirre/49 4.00 10.00
HHMC Maurice Cheeks/49 4.00 10.00
HHPW Paul Westphal/49 5.00 12.00
HHRA Ray Allen/25 20.00 50.00
HHRH Robert Horry/31 10.00 25.00
HHSN Steve Nash/25 40.00 100.00
HHTC Tom Chambers/49 4.00 10.00
HHVC Vince Carter/25 10.00 25.00

2015-16 Totally Certified Imports

STATED PRINT RUN 199 SER.#'d SETS
*MIRROR/25: 1.5X TO 4X BASIC
1 Pau Gasol 1.50 4.00
2 Hakeem Olajuwon 2.00 5.00
3 Manu Ginobili 2.00 5.00
4 Steve Nash 1.50 4.00
5 Yao Ming 2.50 6.00
6 Dirk Nowitzki 2.50 6.00
7 Drazen Petrovic 1.00 2.50
8 Tony Parker 1.50 4.00
9 Andrew Wiggins 1.25 3.00
10 Yuta Tabuse 1.00 2.50

2015-16 Totally Certified Materials Red

PRINT RUNS B/WN 99-199 COPIES PER
*BLUE/99: .4X TO 1X BASIC
*BLUE/49: .5X TO 1.2X BASIC
*CAMO/25: .75X TO 2X BASIC
TCMAD Adrian Dantley/99 2.50 6.00
TCMAI Andre Iguodala/199 2.50 6.00
TCMAJ Al Jefferson/199 1.50 4.00
TCMAL Alex Len/199 1.50 4.00
TCMAM Alonzo Mourning/99 4.00 10.00
TCMAW Andrew Wiggins/199 3.00 8.00
TCMBD Boris Diaw/199 2.00 5.00
TCMBK Bernard King/99 3.00 8.00
TCMBS Byron Scott/199 2.00 5.00
TCMCD Clyde Drexler/99 4.00 10.00
TCMCP Chandler Parsons/99 1.50 4.00
TCMCR Clifford Robinson/199 2.50 6.00
TCMDD DeMar DeRozan/99 3.00 8.00
TCMDE Dante Exum/199 2.00 5.00
TCMDG Danny Green/199 2.00 5.00
TCMDR Derrick Rose/199 4.00 10.00
TCMDW Dwyane Wade/199 5.00 12.00
TCMEB Eric Bledsoe/199 2.00 5.00
TCMGM Greg Monroe/199 2.00 5.00
TCMHB Harrison Barnes/199 2.00 5.00
TCMJC Jordan Clarkson/99 2.50 6.00
TCMJN Joakim Noah/199 1.50 4.00
TCMJR Jalen Rose/99 2.00 5.00
TCMJS Jared Sullinger/199 1.50 4.00
TCMKA Kareem Abdul-Jabbar/99 8.00 20.00
TCMKB Kobe Bryant/199 8.00 20.00
TCMKD Kevin Durant/199 5.00 12.00
TCMKF Kenneth Faried/99 2.00 5.00
TCMKL Kyle Lowry/99 2.50 6.00
TCMLB Larry Bird/99 10.00 25.00
TCMLJ Larry Johnson/199 3.00 8.00
TCMMB Manute Bol/99 4.00 10.00
TCMMC Michael Carter-Williams/199 1.50 4.00
TCMME Monta Ellis/199 2.00 5.00
TCMMG Marcin Gortat/199 1.50 4.00
TCMMK Michael Kidd-Gilchrist/99 1.50 4.00
TCMNB Nicolas Batum/99 1.50 4.00
TCMNM Nikola Mirotic/99 1.50 4.00
TCMNN Nerlens Noel/99 1.50 4.00
TCMOM O.J. Mayo/99 1.50 4.00
TCMPE Patrick Ewing/99 4.00 10.00
TCMPH P.J. Hairston/199 1.50 4.00
TCMRA Rafer Alston/199 1.50 4.00
TCMRA Ray Allen/199 3.00 8.00
TCMRG Rudy Gay/199 2.50 6.00
TCMRH Richard Hamilton/199 2.50 6.00
TCMRP Robert Parish/99 3.00 8.00
TCMSA Steven Adams/99 2.00 5.00
TCMSB Shane Battier/199 2.00 5.00
TCMSI Serge Ibaka/99 2.00 5.00
TCMSO Shaquille O'Neal/99 8.00 20.00
TCMSP Scottie Pippen/199 6.00 15.00
TCMTA Trevor Ariza/199 1.50 4.00
TCMTA Tony Allen/199 1.50 4.00
TCMTD Tim Duncan/199 6.00 15.00
TCMTE Tyreke Evans/199 2.00 5.00
TCMTG Taj Gibson/199 1.50 4.00
TCMTK Toni Kukoc/199 2.50 6.00
TCMTR Terrence Ross/99 2.00 5.00
TCMTT Tristan Thompson/199 1.50 4.00
TCMYM Yao Ming/99 6.00 15.00
TCMZR Zach Randolph/99 2.50 6.00

2015-16 Totally Certified Potential

STATED PRINT RUN 199 SER.#'d SETS
*MIRROR/25: 1.2X TO 3X BASIC
1 Mario Hezonja .75 2.00
2 Sam Dekker .60 1.50
3 Stanley Johnson .75 2.00
4 Justin Anderson .60 1.50
5 Myles Turner 2.50 6.00
6 Tyus Jones .75 2.00
7 Cameron Payne 1.00 2.50
8 Karl-Anthony Towns 4.00 10.00
9 Jahlil Okafor .75 2.00
10 Terry Rozier 2.50 6.00
11 Willie Cauley-Stein .75 2.00
12 Jerian Grant .60 1.50
13 Frank Kaminsky .75 2.00
14 Bobby Portis 1.50 4.00
15 Trey Lyles .75 2.00
16 Larry Nance Jr. 1.25 3.00
17 Kelly Oubre Jr. 2.00 5.00
18 D'Angelo Russell 2.50 6.00
19 Kristaps Porzingis 4.00 10.00
20 Rashad Vaughn .60 1.50
21 Emmanuel Mudiay .75 2.00
22 Delon Wright .75 2.00
23 Justise Winslow 1.00 2.50
24 Rondae Hollis-Jefferson .75 2.00
25 Devin Booker 8.00 20.00

2015-16 Totally Certified Rookie Fabric of the Game Jerseys Red

STATED PRINT RUN 199 SER.#'d SETS
*BLUE/99: .4X TO 1X BASIC
FRJAB Anthony Brown 1.50 4.00
FRJBP Bobby Portis 4.00 10.00
FRJCM Chris McCullough 1.50 4.00
FRJCP Cameron Payne 2.50 6.00
FRJDB Devin Booker 20.00 50.00
FRJDR D'Angelo Russell 6.00 15.00
FRJDW Delon Wright 2.00 5.00
FRJEM Emmanuel Mudiay 2.00 5.00
FRJFK Frank Kaminsky 2.00 5.00
FRJJA Justin Anderson 1.50 4.00
FRJJG Jerian Grant 1.50 4.00
FRJJH Josh Huestis 1.50 4.00
FRJJM Jordan Mickey 1.50 4.00
FRJJM Jarell Martin 1.50 4.00
FRJJO Jahlil Okafor 6.00 15.00
FRJJR Josh Richardson 2.50 6.00
FRJJW Justise Winslow 2.50 6.00
FRJJY Joe Young 1.50 4.00
FRJKL Kevon Looney 5.00 12.00
FRJKO Kelly Oubre Jr. 5.00 12.00
FRJKP Kristaps Porzingis 8.00 20.00
FRJKT Karl-Anthony Towns 10.00 25.00
FRJMH Mario Hezonja 2.00 5.00
FRJMH Montrezl Harrell 5.00 12.00
FRJMT Myles Turner 6.00 15.00
FRJPC Pat Connaughton 2.50 6.00
FRJRC Rakeem Christmas 1.50 4.00
FRJRH Rondae Hollis-Jefferson 2.00 5.00
FRJRH R.J. Hunter 1.50 4.00
FRJRH Richaun Holmes 2.50 6.00
FRJRV Rashad Vaughn 1.50 4.00
FRJSD Sam Dekker 1.50 4.00
FRJSJ Stanley Johnson 2.00 5.00
FRJTJ Tyus Jones 2.00 5.00
FRJTL Trey Lyles 2.00 5.00
FRJTR Terry Rozier 6.00 15.00
FRJWC Willie Cauley-Stein 2.00 5.00
FRJWT Walter Tavares 1.50 4.00

2015-16 Totally Certified Rookie Fabric of the Game Jerseys Camo

*CAMO: 1.2X TO 3X BASIC
STATED PRINT RUN 25 SER.#'d SETS
FRJKP Kristaps Porzingis 100.00 250.00
FRJKT Karl-Anthony Towns 100.00 250.00

2015-16 Totally Certified Rookie Fabric of the Game Signatures

STATED PRINT RUN 49 SER.#'d SETS
*PRIME/25: .75X TO 2X BASIC
RFGAB Anthony Brown 3.00 8.00
RFGBP Bobby Portis 3.00 8.00
RFGCM Chris McCullough 3.00 8.00
RFGCP Cameron Payne 10.00 25.00
RFGDB Devin Booker 150.00 400.00
RFGDR D'Angelo Russell 20.00 50.00
RFGDW Delon Wright 4.00 10.00
RFGEM Emmanuel Mudiay 8.00 20.00
RFGFK Frank Kaminsky 10.00 25.00
RFGJA Justin Anderson 3.00 8.00
RFGJG Jerian Grant 3.00 8.00
RFGJH Josh Huestis 3.00 8.00
RFGJM Jarell Martin 3.00 8.00
RFGJM Jordan Mickey 3.00 8.00
RFGJO Jahlil Okafor 15.00 40.00
RFGJR Josh Richardson 5.00 12.00
RFGJW Justise Winslow 15.00 40.00
RFGJY Joe Young 3.00 8.00
RFGKL Kevon Looney 10.00 25.00
RFGKO Kelly Oubre Jr. 10.00 25.00
RFGKP Kristaps Porzingis 125.00 250.00
RFGKT Karl-Anthony Towns 100.00 200.00
RFGMH Montrezl Harrell 10.00 25.00
RFGMH Mario Hezonja 15.00 40.00
RFGMT Myles Turner 10.00 25.00
RFGPC Pat Connaughton 5.00 12.00
RFGRC Rakeem Christmas 3.00 8.00
RFGRH R.J. Hunter 3.00 8.00
RFGRH Rondae Hollis-Jefferson 4.00 10.00
RFGRH Richaun Holmes 5.00 12.00
RFGRV Rashad Vaughn 3.00 8.00
RFGSD Sam Dekker 3.00 8.00
RFGSJ Stanley Johnson 12.00 30.00
RFGTJ Tyus Jones 4.00 10.00
RFGTL Trey Lyles 4.00 10.00
RFGTR Terry Rozier 12.00 30.00
RFGWC Willie Cauley-Stein 4.00 10.00
RFGWT Walter Tavares 3.00 8.00

2015-16 Totally Certified Rookie Roll Call Autographs

STATED PRINT RUN 99 SER.#'d SETS
*CAMO/25: .5X TO 1.2X BASIC p/r 49
RRCAB Anthony Brown 3.00 8.00
RRCBP Bobby Portis 8.00 20.00
RRCCM Chris McCullough 3.00 8.00
RRCCP Cameron Payne 5.00 12.00
RRCDB Devin Booker 150.00 400.00
RRCDR D'Angelo Russell 20.00 50.00
RRCDW Delon Wright 4.00 10.00
RRCEM Emmanuel Mudiay 6.00 15.00
RRCFK Frank Kaminsky 4.00 10.00
RRCJM Jarell Martin 3.00 8.00
RRCJM Jordan Mickey 3.00 8.00
RRCJO Jahlil Okafor 4.00 10.00
RRCJW Justise Winslow 5.00 12.00
RRCJY Joe Young 3.00 8.00
RRCKO Kelly Oubre Jr. 10.00 25.00
RRCKP Kristaps Porzingis 50.00 120.00
RRCKT Karl-Anthony Towns 75.00 200.00
RRCLN Larry Nance Jr. 6.00 15.00
RRCMH Mario Hezonja 4.00 10.00
RRCMT Myles Turner 12.00 30.00
RRCNB Nemanja Bjelica 5.00 12.00
RRCPC Pat Connaughton 5.00 12.00
RRCRC Rakeem Christmas 3.00 8.00
RRCRH Rondae Hollis-Jefferson 4.00 10.00
RRCRV Rashad Vaughn 3.00 8.00
RRCSD Sam Dekker 3.00 8.00
RRCTL Trey Lyles 4.00 10.00
RRCTR Terry Rozier 12.00 30.00
RRCWT Walter Tavares 3.00 8.00
RRRWC Willie Cauley-Stein 4.00 10.00

2015-16 Totally Certified Select Few Signatures

SFAD Adrian Dantley/49 8.00 20.00
SFAE Alex English/49 10.00 25.00
SFAG Artis Gilmore/25 10.00 25.00
SFAM Alonzo Mourning/19 12.00 30.00
SFAS Arvydas Sabonis/49 8.00 20.00
SFBK Bernard King/25 10.00 25.00
SFBM Bob McAdoo/49 10.00 25.00
SFBW Bill Walton/25 25.00 60.00
SFCD Clyde Drexler/25 12.00 30.00
SFCH Cliff Hagan/25 8.00 20.00
SFCM Chris Mullin/25 10.00 25.00
SFCM Calvin Murphy/25 6.00 15.00
SFDC Dave Cowens/25 10.00 25.00
SFDI Dan Issel/49 10.00 25.00
SFDM Dikembe Mutombo/49 12.00 30.00
SFDR Dennis Rodman/25 20.00 50.00
SFDS Dolph Schayes/25 8.00 20.00
SFDT David Thompson/29 10.00 25.00
SFDW Dominique Wilkins/25 12.00 30.00
SFEM Earl Monroe/25 10.00 25.00
SFGG Gail Goodrich/25 8.00 20.00
SFGG George Gervin/25 12.00 30.00
SFGP Gary Payton/25 12.00 30.00
SFHG Hal Greer/25 10.00 25.00
SFHO Hakeem Olajuwon/25 15.00 40.00
SFJD Joe Dumars/25 10.00 25.00
SFJL Jerry Lucas/25 10.00 25.00
SFJW James Worthy/25 12.00 30.00
SFJW Jamaal Wilkes/49 8.00 20.00
SFJW Jo Jo White/49 8.00 20.00
SFLB Larry Bird/25 50.00 120.00
SFMJ Magic Johnson/25 50.00 120.00
SFMR Mitch Richmond/49 10.00 25.00
SFNA Nate Archibald/25 10.00 25.00
SFRB Rick Barry/25 10.00 25.00
SFRP Robert Parish/25 10.00 25.00
SFRS Ralph Sampson/25 6.00 15.00
SFSH Spencer Haywood/49 8.00 20.00
SFSS Satch Sanders/49 8.00 20.00
SFWF Walt Frazier/25 12.00 30.00

2015-16 Totally Certified Signatures

PRINT RUNS B/WN 19-49 COPIES PER
*CAMO/25: .5X TO 1.2X BASIC p/r 49
*CAMO/25: .4X TO 1X BASIC p/r 19-25
TCAD Andre Drummond/25 10.00 25.00
TCAG Aaron Gordon/25 12.00 30.00
TCAG Artis Gilmore/25 8.00 20.00
TCAI Allen Iverson/25 40.00 100.00
TCAL Alex Len/49 3.00 8.00
TCAW Antoine Walker/49 4.00 10.00
TCAW Andrew Wiggins/25 10.00 25.00
TCBD Bob Dandridge/49 3.00 8.00
TCBK Bernard King/25 8.00 20.00
TCBL Bill Laimbeer/49 5.00 12.00
TCBM Ben McLemore/25 4.00 10.00
TCCB Cameron Bairstow/49 3.00 8.00
TCCC Cedric Ceballos/49 3.00 8.00
TCCD Clyde Drexler/25 15.00 40.00
TCCM Chris Mullin/25 8.00 20.00
TCCO Charles Oakley/49 6.00 15.00
TCCR Cazzie Russell/49 4.00 10.00
TCDB Dee Brown/49 3.00 8.00
TCDC DeMarre Carroll/49 3.00 8.00
TCDC Doug Collins/49 5.00 12.00
TCDE Dante Exum/25 5.00 12.00
TCDG Darrell Griffith/49 4.00 10.00
TCDM Dikembe Mutombo/25 12.00 30.00
TCDM Donatas Motiejunas/49 3.00 8.00
TCDR Dennis Rodman/25 20.00 50.00
TCDR Dino Radja/49 20.00 50.00
TCDS Damon Stoudamire/49 5.00 12.00
TCDV Dick Van Arsdale/49 4.00 10.00
TCDW Dominique Wilkins/25 10.00 25.00
TCEJ Eddie Jones/49 5.00 12.00
TCFE Festus Ezeli/49 3.00 8.00
TCFL Fat Lever/49 4.00 10.00
TCGA G. Antetokounmpo/25 75.00 200.00
TCGH Grant Hill/25 15.00 40.00
TCHB Harrison Barnes/25 5.00 12.00
TCJC Jordan Clarkson/49 5.00 12.00
TCJG Jerami Grant/49 5.00 12.00
TCJH Jrue Holiday/25 8.00 20.00
TCJR Julius Randle/25 8.00 20.00
TCJS Jared Sullinger/25 4.00 10.00
TCJS John Stockton/25 20.00 50.00
TCJS Josh Smith/25 4.00 10.00
TCJSL John Salley/49 3.00 8.00
TCJW James Worthy/25 10.00 25.00
TCJW Jo Jo White/49 5.00 12.00
TCJW Jerome Williams/49 3.00 8.00
TCKA Kenny Anderson/49 4.00 10.00
TCKG Kendall Gill/49 6.00 15.00
TCKV Keith Van Horn/49 4.00 10.00
TCKV Kiki Vandeweghe/49 4.00 10.00
TCLG Langston Galloway/49 3.00 8.00
TCLN Larry Nance/49 4.00 10.00
TCMA Mahmoud Abdul-Rauf/49 8.00 20.00
TCMB Muggsy Bogues/49 4.00 10.00
TCMC Michael Carter-Williams/25 4.00 10.00
TCMC Maurice Cheeks/49 4.00 10.00
TCMD Matthew Dellavedova/49 6.00 15.00
TCMG Manu Ginobili/25 15.00 40.00
TCMP Mason Plumlee/49 3.00 8.00
TCMP Mark Price/49 5.00 12.00
TCMR Mitch Richmond/25 10.00 25.00
TCMS Marcus Smart/25 8.00 20.00
TCNA Nate Archibald/25 15.00 40.00
TCNN Nerlens Noel/25 4.00 10.00
TCNV Nick Van Exel/25 15.00 40.00
TCOR Oscar Robertson/25 25.00 60.00
TCPG Pau Gasol/25 12.00 30.00
TCPS Peja Stojakovic/25 5.00 12.00
TCRA Ray Allen/25 12.00 30.00
TCRC Robert Covington/49 4.00 10.00
TCRG Rudy Gobert/49 10.00 25.00
TCRH Richard Hamilton/25 6.00 15.00
TCRM Ray McCallum/49 3.00 8.00
TCRR Ricky Rubio/25 5.00 12.00
TCRS Rik Smits/49 4.00 10.00
TCRS Rony Seikaly/49 4.00 10.00
TCRT Rudy Tomjanovich/49 4.00 10.00
TCSE Sean Elliott/49 4.00 10.00
TCSH Solomon Hill/49 3.00 8.00
TCSH Spencer Haywood/49 5.00 12.00
TCSM Sidney Moncrief/49 3.00 8.00
TCSS Scott Skiles/49 4.00 10.00
TCSW Sonny Weems/49 3.00 8.00
TCTE Tyreke Evans/25 5.00 12.00
TCTH Tim Hardaway/25 8.00 20.00
TCTH Tim Hardaway Jr./49 4.00 10.00
TCTM Tracy McGrady/25 12.00 30.00
TCTM Timofey Mozgov/49 3.00 8.00
TCTP Terry Porter/49 3.00 8.00
TCTT Tristan Thompson/19 4.00 10.00
TCVB Vin Baker/49 3.00 8.00
TCVD Vlade Divac/49 5.00 12.00
TCVO Victor Oladipo/25 5.00 12.00
TCWF Walt Frazier/25 10.00 25.00
TCWM Wesley Matthews/25 4.00 10.00
TCWU Wes Unseld/25 8.00 20.00

2015-16 Totally Certified Skills

STATED PRINT RUN 199 SER.#'d SETS
*MIRROR/25: 1.5X TO 4X BASIC
1 Klay Thompson 2.50 6.00
2 Joakim Noah .60 1.50
3 LaMarcus Aldridge 1.00 2.50
4 Andrew Wiggins 1.25 3.00
5 Pau Gasol 1.50 4.00
6 Carmelo Anthony 1.50 4.00
7 Tim Duncan 2.50 6.00
8 DeMarcus Cousins 1.00 2.50
9 Kenneth Faried .75 2.00
10 Dwyane Wade 2.00 5.00
11 Kobe Bryant 8.00 20.00
12 John Wall 1.25 3.00
13 LeBron James 8.00 20.00
14 Anthony Davis 2.50 6.00
15 Paul George 1.50 4.00
16 Chris Bosh 1.25 3.00
17 Tony Parker 1.50 4.00

18 Derrick Rose 1.50 4.00
19 Kevin Durant 4.00 10.00
20 Jabari Parker .60 1.50
21 Kyle Korver .75 2.00
22 Kawhi Leonard 3.00 8.00
23 Blake Griffin 1.00 2.50
24 Manu Ginobili 2.00 5.00
25 Russell Westbrook 1.50 4.00
26 Chris Paul 2.00 5.00
27 Victor Oladipo .75 2.00
28 Dirk Nowitzki 2.50 6.00
29 Kevin Garnett 2.50 6.00
30 James Harden 2.00 5.00
31 Kyrie Irving 2.00 5.00
32 Kemba Walker 1.00 2.50
33 DeAndre Jordan .75 2.00
34 Bradley Beal 1.25 3.00
35 Stephen Curry 8.00 20.00
36 Damian Lillard 2.50 6.00
37 Zach LaVine 2.50 6.00
38 Dwight Howard 1.25 3.00
39 Kevin Love 1.00 2.50
40 Jimmy Butler 2.00 5.00

2016-17 Totally Certified

COMP.SET w/o RCs (100) 15.00 40.00
1 Anthony Davis 1.25 3.00
2 James Harden .75 2.00
3 Chris Paul .60 1.50
4 Draymond Green .50 1.25
5 Dwyane Wade .75 2.00
6 Michael Kidd-Gilchrist .25 .60
7 Trevor Ariza .25 .60
8 Karl-Anthony Towns .75 2.00
9 Zach LaVine .75 2.00
10 Allen Crabbe .25 .60
11 Avery Bradley .25 .60
12 Markieff Morris .25 .60
13 Mason Plumlee .25 .60
14 Stephen Curry 3.00 8.00
15 Jimmy Butler .75 2.00
16 Kemba Walker .30 .75
17 Jeff Teague .25 .60
18 Andrew Wiggins .50 1.25
19 Jrue Holiday .50 1.25
20 Ben McLemore .25 .60
21 Nik Stauskas .25 .60
22 Marcin Gortat .25 .60
23 Damian Lillard 1.00 2.50
24 Klay Thompson 1.00 2.50
25 Nikola Mirotic .25 .60
26 Nicolas Batum .30 .75
27 Monta Ellis .25 .60
28 Khris Middleton .40 1.00
29 Carmelo Anthony .60 1.50
30 DeMarcus Cousins .30 .75
31 Bobby Portis .40 1.00
32 John Wall .50 1.25
33 C.J. McCollum .40 1.00
34 Kevin Durant 1.50 4.00
35 Chris Andersen .30 .75
36 Jeremy Lin .75 2.00
37 Paul George .60 1.50
38 Jabari Parker .25 .60
39 Derrick Rose .60 1.50
40 Rudy Gay .40 1.00
41 Mario Hezonja .25 .60
42 Rudy Gobert .50 1.25
43 Eric Bledsoe .30 .75
44 Tobias Harris .40 1.00
45 Kevin Love .40 1.00
46 Brook Lopez .30 .75
47 Blake Griffin .40 1.00
48 Giannis Antetokounmpo 2.00 5.00
49 Kristaps Porzingis .60 1.50
50 Kawhi Leonard 1.00 2.50
51 Willie Cauley-Stein .30 .75
52 Rodney Hood .30 .75
53 Devin Booker 1.50 4.00
54 Reggie Jackson .30 .75
55 Kyrie Irving .75 2.00
56 Jae Crowder .25 .60
57 Dennis Schroder .40 1.00
58 Tyler Johnson .25 .60
59 Russell Westbrook .60 1.50
60 Tony Parker .60 1.50
61 Tyreke Evans .30 .75
62 Gordon Hayward .40 1.00
63 Brandon Knight .30 .75
64 Andre Drummond .40 1.00
65 LeBron James 3.00 8.00
66 Isaiah Thomas .30 .75
67 DeAndre Jordan .30 .75
68 Hassan Whiteside .30 .75
69 Steven Adams .30 .75
70 LaMarcus Aldridge .40 1.00
71 Justise Winslow .30 .75
72 Dante Exum .30 .75
73 Joel Embiid 1.00 2.50
74 Nikola Jokic 2.00 5.00
75 Deron Williams .30 .75
76 Al Horford .40 1.00
77 D'Angelo Russell .50 1.25
78 Goran Dragic .40 1.00
79 Aaron Gordon .40 1.00
80 Manu Ginobili .75 2.00
81 Myles Turner .40 1.00
82 Kyle Lowry .40 1.00
83 Jahlil Okafor .25 .60
84 Jusuf Nurkic .30 .75
85 Dirk Nowitzki 1.00 2.50
86 Dwight Howard .50 1.25
87 Jordan Clarkson .40 1.00
88 Mike Conley .30 .75
89 DeMar DeRozan .50 1.25
90 Clint Capela .30 .75
91 Jonas Valanciunas .30 .75
92 Evan Fournier .30 .75
93 Emmanuel Mudiay .25 .60
94 Harrison Barnes .30 .75
95 Paul Millsap .30 .75
96 Julius Randle .50 1.25
97 Chandler Parsons .25 .60
98 Elfrid Payton .30 .75
99 DeMarre Carroll .25 .60
100 Bradley Beal .50 1.25
101 Brandon Ingram RC 2.00 5.00
102 Jaylen Brown RC 4.00 10.00
103 Dragan Bender RC .50 1.25
104 Kris Dunn RC .75 2.00
105 Buddy Hield RC 1.50 4.00
106 Jamal Murray RC 15.00 40.00
107 Marquese Chriss RC .60 1.50
108 Jakob Poeltl RC 1.00 2.50
109 Thon Maker RC .60 1.50
110 Taurean Prince RC .60 1.50
111 Denzel Valentine RC .50 1.25
112 Wade Baldwin IV RC .50 1.25
113 Henry Ellenson RC .50 1.25
114 Malik Beasley RC 1.00 2.50
115 DeAndre' Bembry RC .75 2.00
116 Malachi Richardson RC .50 1.25
117 T. Luwawu-Cabarrot RC .75 2.00
118 Brice Johnson RC .50 1.25
119 Pascal Siakam RC 3.00 8.00
120 Skal Labissiere RC .50 1.25
121 Damian Jones RC .50 1.25
122 Deyonta Davis RC .50 1.25
123 Cheick Diallo RC .50 1.25
124 Tyler Ulis RC .60 1.50
125 Patrick McCaw RC .50 1.25
126 Isaiah Whitehead RC .50 1.25
127 Demetrius Jackson RC .50 1.25
128 Ivica Zubac RC 1.25 3.00
129 Malcolm Brogdon RC 1.50 4.00
130 A.J. Hammons RC .50 1.25
131 Diamond Stone RC .50 1.25
132 Caris LeVert RC 1.25 3.00
133 Michael Gbinije RC .50 1.25
134 Jake Layman RC .60 1.50
135 Chinanu Onuaku RC .50 1.25
136 Stephen Zimmerman RC .50 1.25
137 Georges Niang RC .75 2.00
138 Dario Saric RC .75 2.00
139 Tomas Satoransky RC .75 2.00
140 Ben Simmons RC 8.00 20.00

2016-17 Totally Certified Blue

*BLUE VET: 1.2X TO 3X BASIC VET
*BLUE RC: .6X TO 1.5X BASIC RC
STATED PRINT RUN 99 SER.#'d SETS
65 LeBron James 8.00 20.00

2016-17 Totally Certified Camo

*CAMO VET: 4X TO 10X BASIC VET
*CAMO RC: 2X TO 5X BASIC RC
STATED PRINT RUN 25 SER.#'d SETS
65 LeBron James 25.00 60.00
106 Jamal Murray 125.00 300.00

2016-17 Totally Certified Orange

*ORANGE VET: 1.5X TO 4X BASIC VET
*ORANGE RC: .75X TO 2X BASIC RC
STATED PRINT RUN 60 SER.#'d SETS
65 LeBron James 10.00 25.00
106 Jamal Murray 40.00 100.00

2016-17 Totally Certified Red

*RED VET: 1X TO 2.5X BASIC VET
*RED RC: .5X TO 1.2X BASIC RC
STATED PRINT RUN 199 SER.#'d SETS
65 LeBron James 6.00 15.00

2016-17 Totally Certified Calling Cards

*MIRROR/25: 1.5X TO 4X BASIC
1 Damian Lillard 1.50 4.00
2 Dirk Nowitzki 1.50 4.00
3 Kyrie Irving 1.25 3.00
4 LeBron James 3.00 8.00
5 Hassan Whiteside .50 1.25
6 Stephen Curry 5.00 12.00
7 Andre Drummond .60 1.50
8 DeAndre Jordan .50 1.25
9 DeMarcus Cousins .50 1.25
10 James Harden 1.25 3.00
11 Russell Westbrook 1.00 2.50
12 Karl-Anthony Towns 1.25 3.00
13 John Wall .75 2.00
14 Wilt Chamberlain 2.00 5.00
15 Bill Russell 2.00 5.00
16 Dennis Rodman 1.25 3.00
17 Hakeem Olajuwon 1.25 3.00
18 Kevin Durant 2.50 6.00
19 Carmelo Anthony 1.00 2.50
20 Magic Johnson 2.50 6.00
21 John Stockton 1.00 2.50
22 Chris Paul 1.00 2.50
23 Allen Iverson 1.00 2.50
24 Kobe Bryant 5.00 12.00
25 Karl Malone 1.00 2.50
26 Shaquille O'Neal 2.00 5.00
27 Steve Nash 1.00 2.50
28 Larry Bird 2.50 6.00
29 J.J. Redick .60 1.50
30 Robert Parish .75 2.00
31 Anthony Davis 2.00 5.00
32 Ricky Rubio .50 1.25
33 Manute Bol .60 1.50
34 Kobe Bryant 5.00 12.00
35 Kendall Gill .60 1.50
36 Scott Skiles .50 1.25
37 Bill Russell 2.00 5.00
38 Charles Oakley .50 1.25
39 Stephen Curry 5.00 12.00
40 David Robinson 1.25 3.00
41 Wilt Chamberlain 2.00 5.00
42 Shaquille O'Neal 2.00 5.00
43 Scottie Pippen 1.25 3.00
44 George Mikan 1.25 3.00

2016-17 Totally Certified Energizers

*RED/199: .5X TO 1.2X BASIC
*BLUE/99: .6X TO 1.5X BASIC
*ORANGE/60: .75X TO 2X BASIC
*CAMO/25: 1.2X TO 3X BASIC
1 Elfrid Payton .60 1.50
2 John Wall 1.00 2.50
3 Chris Paul 1.25 3.00
4 Isaiah Thomas .60 1.50
5 Dennis Schroder .75 2.00
6 Damian Lillard 2.00 5.00
7 Leandro Barbosa .50 1.25
8 Stephen Curry 6.00 15.00
9 Nate Archibald .75 2.00
10 Allen Iverson 1.25 3.00
11 Isiah Thomas 1.25 3.00
12 Kenny Smith .60 1.50
13 Muggsy Bogues .60 1.50
14 Spud Webb .75 2.00
15 John Starks .75 2.00
16 Eddie Johnson .50 1.25

2016-17 Totally Certified Fabric of the Game Jerseys

*BLUE/99: .5X TO 1.2X BASIC
*CAMO/25: .75X TO 2X BASIC
1 Jeremy Lamb 1.50 4.00
2 Tim Duncan 3.00 8.00
3 Spencer Hawes 1.50 4.00
4 Chris Andersen 2.00 5.00
5 Hassan Whiteside 2.00 5.00
6 Andre Iguodala 2.50 6.00
7 Russell Westbrook 4.00 10.00
8 LeBron James 8.00 20.00
9 Justise Winslow 2.00 5.00
10 Goran Dragic 2.50 6.00
11 Robin Lopez 1.50 4.00
12 Carmelo Anthony 4.00 10.00
13 Andrew Wiggins 3.00 8.00
14 Serge Ibaka 2.00 5.00
15 Enes Kanter 1.50 4.00
16 Dwight Powell 1.50 4.00
17 Greg Monroe 1.50 4.00
18 Timofey Mozgov 1.50 4.00
19 Zach Randolph 2.50 6.00
20 R.J. Hunter 1.50 4.00
21 Kemba Walker 2.00 5.00
22 Jeff Green 1.50 4.00
23 Mike Conley 2.00 5.00
24 Noah Vonleh 1.50 4.00
25 Gerald Henderson 1.50 4.00
26 Vince Carter 4.00 10.00
27 Jrue Holiday 3.00 8.00
28 Tyreke Evans 2.00 5.00
29 Ryan Anderson 1.50 4.00
30 Chandler Parsons 1.50 4.00
31 Austin Rivers 2.00 5.00
32 Jimmy Butler 5.00 12.00
33 Nik Stauskas 1.50 4.00
34 Jahlil Okafor 1.50 4.00
35 Jeff Teague 1.50 4.00
36 Tim Hardaway Jr. 2.00 5.00
37 Tyus Jones 1.50 4.00
38 Kawhi Leonard 6.00 15.00
39 Manu Ginobili 5.00 12.00
40 Rodney Stuckey 1.50 4.00
41 Kelly Oubre Jr. 3.00 8.00
42 Tobias Harris 2.50 6.00
43 Kris Humphries 1.50 4.00
44 Nikola Mirotic 1.50 4.00
45 Brandon Knight 2.00 5.00
46 Cory Joseph 1.50 4.00
47 Mason Plumlee 1.50 4.00
48 Jerian Grant 1.50 4.00
49 Rudy Gobert 3.00 8.00
50 Derrick Favors 1.50 4.00

2016-17 Totally Certified Fabric of the Game Rookie Jerseys

*BLUE/99: .5X TO 1.2X BASIC
*CAMO/25: .75X TO 2X BASIC
1 Tyler Ulis 2.00 5.00
2 T. Luwawu-Cabarrot 2.50 6.00
3 Malachi Richardson 1.50 4.00
4 Brice Johnson 1.50 4.00
5 Brandon Ingram 4.00 10.00
6 Patrick McCaw 1.50 4.00
7 Marquese Chriss 2.00 5.00
8 DeAndre' Bembry 2.50 6.00
9 Pascal Siakam 10.00 25.00
10 Jaylen Brown 3.00 8.00
11 Isaiah Whitehead 1.50 4.00
12 Jakob Poeltl 3.00 8.00
13 Malik Beasley 3.00 8.00
14 Skal Labissiere 1.50 4.00
15 Dragan Bender 1.50 4.00
16 Demetrius Jackson 1.50 4.00
17 Thon Maker 3.00 8.00
18 Henry Ellenson 1.50 4.00
19 Damian Jones 1.50 4.00
20 Kris Dunn 2.50 6.00
21 Wade Baldwin IV 1.50 4.00
22 Deyonta Davis 1.50 4.00
23 Buddy Hield 3.00 8.00
24 Ivica Zubac 4.00 10.00
25 Taurean Prince 2.00 5.00
26 Denzel Valentine 3.00 8.00
27 Cheick Diallo 1.50 4.00
28 Jamal Murray 12.00 30.00
29 A.J. Hammons 1.50 4.00
30 Diamond Stone 1.50 4.00

2016-17 Totally Certified Franchise Foundations

1 Anthony Davis 2.50 6.00
2 James Harden 1.50 4.00
3 Chris Paul 1.25 3.00
4 Karl-Anthony Towns 1.50 4.00
5 Stephen Curry 6.00 15.00
6 Jimmy Butler 1.50 4.00
7 Kemba Walker .60 1.50
8 Damian Lillard 2.00 5.00
9 DeMarcus Cousins .60 1.50
10 John Wall 1.00 2.50
11 Paul George 1.25 3.00
12 Brook Lopez .60 1.50
13 Kristaps Porzingis 1.25 3.00
14 Kawhi Leonard 2.00 5.00
15 Devin Booker 3.00 8.00
16 Kyrie Irving 1.50 4.00
17 Dennis Schroder .75 2.00
18 Russell Westbrook 1.25 3.00
19 Gordon Hayward .75 2.00
20 Andre Drummond .75 2.00
21 Isaiah Thomas .60 1.50
22 Justise Winslow .60 1.50
23 Dirk Nowitzki 2.00 5.00
24 Mike Conley .60 1.50
25 DeMar DeRozan 1.00 2.50
26 Elfrid Payton .60 1.50
27 Kenneth Faried .50 1.25
28 Giannis Antetokounmpo 4.00 10.00
29 Brandon Ingram 2.00 5.00
30 Ben Simmons 1.50 4.00

2016-17 Totally Certified Franchise Foundations Blue

*BLUE: .6X TO 1.5X BASIC
STATED PRINT RUN 99 SER.#'d SETS

2016-17 Totally Certified Franchise Foundations Camo

*CAMO: 1.2X TO 3X BASIC
STATED PRINT RUN 25 SER.#'d SETS

2016-17 Totally Certified Franchise Foundations Orange

*ORANGE: .75X TO 2X BASIC
STATED PRINT RUN 60 SER.#'d SETS

2016-17 Totally Certified Franchise Foundations Red

*RED: .5X TO 1.2X BASIC
STATED PRINT RUN 199 SER.#'d SETS

2016-17 Totally Certified Materials

*BLUE/99: .5X TO 1.2X BASIC
*CAMO/25: .75X TO 2X BASIC
1 Carmelo Anthony 4.00 10.00
2 Kenneth Faried 2.00 5.00
3 Ricky Rubio 2.00 5.00
4 Richard Jefferson 2.00 5.00
5 Kevin Love 2.50 6.00
6 Karl-Anthony Towns 4.00 10.00
7 Cody Zeller 1.50 4.00
8 Rudy Gay 2.50 6.00
9 Paul Millsap 2.00 5.00
10 Stanley Johnson 1.50 4.00
11 Jusuf Nurkic 2.00 5.00
12 Eric Gordon 2.00 5.00
13 Tony Parker 4.00 10.00
14 Tim Duncan 3.00 8.00
15 Clint Capela 2.00 5.00
16 Monta Ellis 2.00 5.00
17 T.J. Warren 2.00 5.00
18 George Hill 2.00 5.00
19 Paul George 4.00 10.00
20 Andre Iguodala 2.50 6.00

2016-17 Totally Certified Representatives Autographs

PRINT RUN B/WN 14-100 COPIES PER
EXCHANGE DEADLINE 6/14/2018
*MIRROR/25: .6X TO 1.5X BASIC
1 Dikembe Mutombo/100 8.00 20.00
2 Larry Bird/30 30.00 80.00
3 Brook Lopez/25 3.00 8.00
4 Michael Kidd-Gilchrist/50 2.50 6.00
5 Scottie Pippen/50 40.00 100.00
6 Kyrie Irving/35 30.00 80.00
7 Dirk Nowitzki/50 40.00 100.00
8 Alex English/100 3.00 8.00
9 Reggie Jackson/100 3.00 8.00
10 Kevin Durant/35 40.00 100.00
11 Hakeem Olajuwon/35 10.00 25.00
12 Myles Turner/50 8.00 20.00
14 Kobe Bryant/50 400.00 800.00
15 Zach Randolph/65 4.00 10.00
16 Glen Rice/100 4.00 10.00
17 Michael Carter-Williams/75 2.50 6.00
18 Karl-Anthony Towns/50 30.00 80.00
19 Anthony Davis/35 25.00 60.00
20 Carmelo Anthony/50 20.00 50.00
21 Steven Adams/35 3.00 8.00
23 Allen Iverson/25 30.00 80.00
24 Dan Majerle/100 3.00 8.00
25 C.J. McCollum/75 4.00 10.00
26 Vlade Divac/100 4.00 10.00
27 David Robinson/50 12.00 30.00
28 Jonas Valanciunas/100 3.00 8.00
29 John Stockton/50 15.00 40.00
30 John Wall/35 EXCH 20.00 50.00

2016-17 Totally Certified Return to Sender

*RED/199: .5X TO 1.2X BASIC
*BLUE/99: .6X TO 1.5X BASIC
*ORANGE/60: .75X TO 2X BASIC
*CAMO/25: 1.2X TO 3X BASIC
1 DeAndre Jordan .60 1.50
2 Anthony Davis 2.50 6.00
3 Myles Turner .75 2.00
4 Jonas Valanciunas .60 1.50
5 Rudy Gobert 1.00 2.50
6 LeBron James 6.00 15.00
7 Hassan Whiteside .60 1.50
8 Willie Cauley-Stein .60 1.50
9 Hakeem Olajuwon 1.50 4.00
10 David Robinson 1.50 4.00
11 Manute Bol .75 2.00
12 Shawn Marion .60 1.50
13 Ben Wallace .60 1.50
14 Dikembe Mutombo 1.25 3.00

2016-17 Totally Certified Rookie Roll Call Autographs

EXCHANGE DEADLINE 6/14/2018
*BLUE/99: .5X TO 1.2X BASIC
*CAMO/25: .6X TO 1.5X BASIC
1 Brandon Ingram 30.00 80.00
2 Jaylen Brown 60.00 150.00
3 Dragan Bender 3.00 8.00
4 Kris Dunn 5.00 12.00
5 Buddy Hield 10.00 25.00
6 Jamal Murray 20.00 50.00
7 Marquese Chriss 4.00 10.00
8 Jakob Poeltl 6.00 15.00
9 Thon Maker 4.00 10.00
10 Domantas Sabonis 20.00 50.00
11 Taurean Prince 4.00 10.00
12 Denzel Valentine 3.00 8.00
13 Wade Baldwin IV 3.00 8.00
14 Henry Ellenson 3.00 8.00
15 Malik Beasley 6.00 15.00
16 DeAndre' Bembry 5.00 12.00
17 Malachi Richardson 3.00 8.00
18 T. Luwawu-Cabarrot 5.00 12.00
19 Brice Johnson 3.00 8.00
20 Pascal Siakam 12.00 30.00
21 Skal Labissiere 12.00 30.00
22 Damian Jones 3.00 8.00
23 Deyonta Davis 3.00 8.00
24 Cheick Diallo 3.00 8.00
25 Tyler Ulis 4.00 10.00
26 Patrick McCaw 3.00 8.00
27 Isaiah Whitehead 3.00 8.00
28 Demetrius Jackson 3.00 8.00
29 Kay Felder 3.00 8.00
30 Ivica Zubac 8.00 20.00
31 Malcolm Brogdon 12.00 30.00
32 A.J. Hammons 3.00 8.00
33 Diamond Stone 3.00 8.00
34 Gary Payton II 8.00 20.00
35 Caris LeVert 8.00 20.00
36 Michael Gbinije 3.00 8.00
37 Jake Layman 4.00 10.00
38 Ben Bentil 3.00 8.00
39 Chinanu Onuaku 3.00 8.00
40 Stephen Zimmerman 3.00 8.00
41 Georges Niang 5.00 12.00
42 Marcus Paige 3.00 8.00
43 Daniel Hamilton 3.00 8.00
44 Tyrone Wallace 3.00 8.00
45 Isaiah Cousins 3.00 8.00
47 Abdel Nader 3.00 8.00
48 Joel Bolomboy 3.00 8.00
49 Dario Saric 10.00 25.00
50 Tomas Satoransky 5.00 12.00

2016-17 Totally Certified Signed Sealed Delivered Autographs

PRINT RUNS B/WN 35-99 COPIES PER
EXCHANGE DEADLINE 6/14/2018
*MIRROR/25: .5X TO 1.5X BASIC
1 John Stockton/75 12.00 30.00
2 Kobe Bryant/75 400.00 800.00
3 Grant Hill/35 12.00 30.00
4 C.J. McCollum/75 5.00 12.00
5 Dikembe Mutombo/99 10.00 25.00
6 Spud Webb/99 4.00 10.00
7 Cody Zeller/75 2.50 6.00
8 Artis Gilmore/99 5.00 12.00
9 Jerry West/35 15.00 40.00
10 Pau Gasol/75 6.00 15.00
11 Oscar Robertson/75 20.00 50.00
12 Tristan Thompson/75 3.00 8.00
13 Dirk Nowitzki/75 40.00 100.00
14 Reggie Jackson/99 3.00 8.00
15 Draymond Green/35 12.00 30.00
16 Tim Hardaway/75 5.00 12.00
17 Hakeem Olajuwon/75 8.00 20.00
19 Patrick Ewing/75 60.00 150.00
20 Dwyane Wade/35 40.00 100.00

2016-17 Totally Certified The Mighty

1 Stephen Curry 20.00 50.00
2 LeBron James 30.00 80.00
3 Ben Simmons 8.00 20.00
4 Damian Lillard 10.00 25.00
5 Kawhi Leonard 10.00 25.00
6 James Harden 8.00 20.00

2017-18 Totally Certified

COMP.SET w/o RCs (100) 12.00 30.00
101-150 STATED PRINT RUN 299 SER.#'d SETS
1 Kevin Durant 1.50 4.00
2 Jimmy Butler .60 1.50
3 Kristaps Porzingis .50 1.25
4 John Wall .50 1.25
5 Kawhi Leonard 1.00 2.50
6 C.J. McCollum .40 1.00
7 Terrence Ross .30 .75
8 Goran Dragic .30 .75
9 Ivica Zubac .30 .75
10 Darren Collison .25 .60
11 Nikola Jokic 2.50 6.00
12 Kyrie Irving .75 2.00
13 Nicolas Batum .25 .60
14 Jaylen Brown 1.00 2.50
15 Dennis Schroder .30 .75
16 Klay Thompson 1.00 2.50
17 Gorgui Dieng .25 .60
18 Tim Hardaway Jr. .30 .75
19 Joe Johnson .30 .75
20 Skal Labissiere .25 .60
21 Damian Lillard 1.00 2.50
22 Ben Simmons .40 1.00
23 Hassan Whiteside .30 .75
24 Jordan Clarkson .40 1.00
25 Myles Turner .40 1.00
26 Paul Millsap .30 .75
27 LeBron James 3.00 8.00
28 Denzel Valentine .25 .60
29 Caris LeVert .40 1.00
30 Kent Bazemore .25 .60
31 Stephen Curry 3.00 8.00
32 Karl-Anthony Towns .60 1.50
33 Paul George .60 1.50
34 Rodney Hood .60 1.50
35 LaMarcus Aldridge .40 1.00
36 Jusuf Nurkic .30 .75
37 Giannis Antetokounmpo 2.00 5.00
38 Dario Saric .30 .75
39 Julius Randle .40 1.00
40 Thaddeus Young .25 .60
41 Andre Drummond .40 1.00
42 Dirk Nowitzki 1.00 2.50
43 Dwyane Wade .75 2.00
44 D'Angelo Russell .30 .75
45 Taurean Prince .30 .75
46 Chris Paul .60 1.50
47 Anthony Davis 1.00 2.50
48 Russell Westbrook .60 1.50
49 Rudy Gobert .60 1.50
50 Patty Mills .30 .75
51 Evan Turner .25 .60
52 Joel Embiid .75 2.00
53 Khris Middleton .50 1.25
54 Chandler Parsons .25 .60
55 Austin Rivers .30 .75
56 Reggie Jackson .30 .75
57 Harrison Barnes .30 .75
58 Robin Lopez .25 .60
59 Jeremy Lin .60 1.50
60 Al Horford .40 1.00
61 Eric Gordon .30 .75
62 DeMarcus Cousins .30 .75
63 Steven Adams .30 .75
64 Bradley Beal .50 1.25
65 Pau Gasol .60 1.50
66 Malcolm Brogdon .30 .75
67 Buddy Hield .40 1.00
68 Devin Booker 1.00 2.50
69 Marc Gasol .40 1.00
70 Blake Griffin .40 1.00
71 Tobias Harris .30 .75
72 Seth Curry .40 1.00
73 J.R. Smith .30 .75
74 Frank Kaminsky .25 .60
75 Gordon Hayward .30 .75
76 James Harden .75 2.00
77 Jrue Holiday .50 1.25
78 Aaron Gordon .40 1.00
79 Serge Ibaka .30 .75
80 DeMar DeRozan .50 1.25
81 George Hill .30 .75
82 Eric Bledsoe .30 .75
83 Matthew Dellavedova .30 .75
84 Mike Conley .30 .75
85 DeAndre Jordan .30 .75
86 Draymond Green .50 1.25
87 Jamal Murray .60 1.50
88 Kevin Love .30 .75
89 Kemba Walker .30 .75
90 Isaiah Thomas .30 .75
91 Trevor Ariza .25 .60
92 Carmelo Anthony .60 1.50
93 Elfrid Payton .25 .60
94 Otto Porter Jr. .30 .75
95 Kyle Lowry .40 1.00
96 Andrew Wiggins .50 1.25
97 Willie Cauley-Stein .25 .60
98 Marquese Chriss .25 .60
99 Dion Waiters .25 .60
100 Brandon Ingram .50 1.25
101 Markelle Fultz RC 2.00 5.00
102 Lonzo Ball RC 3.00 8.00
103 Jayson Tatum RC 10.00 25.00
104 Josh Jackson RC 1.00 2.50
105 De'Aaron Fox RC 6.00 15.00
106 Jonathan Isaac RC 2.00 5.00
107 Lauri Markkanen RC 5.00 12.00
108 Frank Ntilikina RC 1.00 2.50
109 Dennis Smith Jr. RC 1.00 2.50
110 Zach Collins RC 1.25 3.00
111 Malik Monk RC 3.00 8.00
112 Luke Kennard RC 1.50 4.00
113 Donovan Mitchell RC 8.00 20.00
114 Bam Adebayo RC 5.00 12.00
115 Justin Jackson RC .75 2.00
116 Justin Patton RC .75 2.00
117 D.J. Wilson RC .75 2.00
118 T.J. Leaf RC .75 2.00
119 John Collins RC 2.00 5.00
120 Harry Giles RC .75 2.00
121 Jarrett Allen RC 2.00 5.00
122 OG Anunoby RC 4.00 10.00
123 Tyler Lydon RC .75 2.00
124 Caleb Swanigan RC .75 2.00
125 Kyle Kuzma RC 3.00 8.00
126 Tony Bradley RC .75 2.00
127 Derrick White RC 3.00 8.00
128 Josh Hart RC .75 2.00
129 Frank Jackson RC .75 2.00
130 Frank Mason III RC .75 2.00
131 Jordan Bell RC .75 2.00
132 Jawun Evans RC .75 2.00
133 Dwayne Bacon RC .75 2.00
134 Milos Teodosic RC 1.00 2.50
135 Ike Anigbogu RC .75 2.00
136 Bogdan Bogdanovic RC 2.00 5.00
137 Wesley Iwundu RC .75 2.00
138 Sterling Brown RC .75 2.00
139 Ante Zizic RC 1.00 2.50
140 Terrance Ferguson RC 1.00 2.50
141 Cedi Osman RC 1.50 4.00
142 Semi Ojeleye RC 1.00 2.50
143 Davon Reed RC .75 2.00
144 Guerschon Yabusele RC .75 2.00
145 Ivan Rabb RC .75 2.00
146 Tyler Dorsey RC .75 2.00
147 Sindarius Thornwell RC .75 2.00
148 Damyean Dotson RC 1.00 2.50
149 Dillon Brooks RC 2.50 6.00
150 Daniel Theis RC 1.50 4.00

2017-18 Totally Certified Blue

*BLUE VET: 1.2X TO 3X BASIC VET
*BLUE RC: .75X TO 2X BASIC RC
STATED PRINT RUN 99 SER.#'d SETS

2017-18 Totally Certified Camo

*CAMO VET: 3X TO 8X BASIC VET
*CAMO RC: 2X TO 5X BASIC RC
STATED PRINT 25 SER.#'d SETS
27 LeBron James 25.00 60.00

2017-18 Totally Certified Purple

*PURPLE VET: .5X TO 1.2X BASIC VET
*PURPLE RC: .5X TO 1.2X BASIC RC
101-150 STATED PRINT RUN 199 SER.#'d SETS

2017-18 Totally Certified 2017

1 Markelle Fultz 1.50 4.00
2 Lonzo Ball 2.50 6.00
3 Jayson Tatum 8.00 20.00
4 Josh Jackson .75 2.00
5 De'Aaron Fox 5.00 12.00
6 Jonathan Isaac 1.50 4.00
7 Lauri Markkanen 4.00 10.00
8 Frank Ntilikina .75 2.00
9 Dennis Smith Jr. .75 2.00
10 Zach Collins 1.00 2.50
11 Malik Monk 2.50 6.00
12 Luke Kennard 1.25 3.00
13 Donovan Mitchell 6.00 15.00
14 Bam Adebayo 4.00 10.00
15 Justin Jackson .60 1.50
16 Justin Patton .60 1.50
17 D.J. Wilson .60 1.50
18 T.J. Leaf .60 1.50
19 John Collins 1.50 4.00
20 Harry Giles .60 1.50
21 Terrance Ferguson .60 1.50
22 Jarrett Allen 1.50 4.00
23 OG Anunoby 3.00 8.00
24 Tyler Lydon .60 1.50
25 Kyle Kuzma 2.50 6.00

2017-18 Totally Certified Autographs

PRINT RUNS B/WN 25-75 COPIES PER
EXCHANGE DEADLINE 6/13/2019
1 George Gervin/50 6.00 15.00
2 Tom Heinsohn/75 12.00 30.00
4 Dennis Rodman/25 20.00 50.00
5 Karl Malone/25 20.00 50.00
6 Calvin Murphy/75 4.00 10.00
7 Magic Johnson/25 20.00 50.00
8 Willis Reed/50 40.00 100.00
9 Kristaps Porzingis/50 20.00 50.00
10 Maurice Harkless/75 2.50 6.00
11 George Hill/75 3.00 8.00
12 LaMarcus Aldridge/50 8.00 20.00
13 Norman Powell/75 4.00 10.00
14 Ricky Rubio/25 10.00 25.00
15 Alan Williams/71 2.50 6.00
16 Mario Hezonja/75 2.50 6.00
17 Semaj Christon/75 2.50 6.00
18 E'Twaun Moore/75 2.50 6.00
19 Matthew Dellavedova/75 3.00 8.00
20 Julius Randle/50 4.00 10.00
21 Darren Collison/75 2.50 6.00
22 Clint Capela/75 3.00 8.00
23 Reggie Jackson/75 3.00 8.00
24 Kobe Bryant/75 500.00 1,000.00
25 Yogi Ferrell/75 2.50 6.00

2017-18 Totally Certified Certified Mail

1 Kawhi Leonard 1.50 4.00
2 Giannis Antetokounmpo 3.00 8.00
3 Anthony Davis 1.50 4.00
4 Isaiah Thomas .50 1.25
5 John Wall .75 2.00
6 Damian Lillard 1.50 4.00
7 Rudy Gobert .75 2.00
8 Marc Gasol .60 1.50
9 Nikola Jokic 4.00 10.00
10 Karl-Anthony Towns 1.00 2.50

2017-18 Totally Certified Choice Signatures

STATED PRINT RUN 35 SER.#'d SETS
EXCHANGE DEADLINE 6/13/2019
1 Karl-Anthony Towns 20.00 50.00
2 Scottie Pippen 40.00 100.00
3 Hakeem Olajuwon 12.00 30.00
4 James Harden 50.00 120.00
5 Kobe Bryant 500.00 1,000.00
6 Kyrie Irving 40.00 100.00
8 Giannis Antetokounmpo 50.00 120.00
9 Isaiah Thomas 6.00 15.00
10 Kevin Durant 50.00 120.00
11 Shaquille O'Neal 30.00 80.00
12 Allen Iverson 40.00 100.00
13 David Robinson 15.00 40.00
14 Karl Malone 20.00 50.00
15 Kareem Abdul-Jabbar 30.00 80.00
16 Magic Johnson 20.00 50.00
17 Alonzo Mourning 20.00 50.00
18 James Worthy 8.00 20.00
19 Reggie Miller 60.00 150.00
20 Lonzo Ball 60.00 150.00
21 Dennis Smith Jr. 3.00 8.00
22 Jayson Tatum 60.00 150.00
23 Josh Jackson 3.00 8.00
24 De'Aaron Fox 20.00 50.00
25 Markelle Fultz 40.00 100.00

2017-18 Totally Certified Energizers

1 Russell Westbrook 1.50 4.00
2 Stephen Curry 8.00 20.00
3 Isaiah Thomas .75 2.00
4 Kyle Lowry 1.00 2.50
5 Kyrie Irving 2.00 5.00
6 Kemba Walker .75 2.00
7 John Wall 1.25 3.00
8 Mike Conley .75 2.00
9 Damian Lillard 2.50 6.00
10 Goran Dragic .75 2.00

2017-18 Totally Certified Fabric of the Game

PRINT RUNS B/WN 25-199 COPIES PER
1 Jabari Parker/199 1.50 4.00
2 Wilson Chandler/199 2.00 5.00
3 Rodney Hood/199 1.50 4.00
4 Rudy Gobert/199 3.00 8.00
5 Blake Griffin/199 2.50 6.00
6 DeAndre Jordan/199 2.00 5.00
7 Michael Kidd-Gilchrist/199 1.50 4.00
8 Cody Zeller/199 1.50 4.00
9 Hassan Whiteside/99 2.00 5.00
10 Nikola Vucevic/199 2.00 5.00
11 Kevin Love/199 2.00 5.00
12 Tristan Thompson/199 1.50 4.00
13 Tyus Jones/199 1.50 4.00
14 Andrew Wiggins/199 3.00 8.00
15 Dragan Bender/99 1.50 4.00
16 Tyson Chandler/199 2.00 5.00
17 Russell Westbrook/25 4.00 10.00
18 Enes Kanter/99 2.00 5.00
19 Dirk Nowitzki/199 6.00 15.00
20 Andre Drummond/99 2.00 5.00
21 Al Horford/99 2.50 6.00
22 Paul Millsap/199 2.00 5.00
23 Elfrid Payton/199 1.50 4.00
24 Wade Baldwin IV/99 1.50 4.00
25 DeMar DeRozan/99 3.00 8.00
26 Kyle Lowry/199 2.50 6.00
27 Kristaps Porzingis/199 4.00 10.00
28 Kris Dunn/199 1.50 4.00
29 Harrison Barnes/199 1.50 4.00
30 Ryan Anderson/199 1.50 4.00
31 Otto Porter Jr./199 2.00 5.00
32 Kemba Walker/99 2.00 5.00
33 LaMarcus Aldridge/199 2.50 6.00
34 Kawhi Leonard/99 6.00 15.00
35 Victor Oladipo/99 2.00 5.00
36 Doug McDermott/99 1.50 4.00
37 Nikola Jokic/199 15.00 40.00
38 Jeff Teague/199 1.50 4.00
39 Giannis Antetokounmpo/25 12.00 30.00
40 Jae Crowder/45 1.50 4.00
41 Jeremy Lin/199 4.00 10.00
42 Timofey Mozgov/199 1.50 4.00
43 Justin Anderson/199 1.50 4.00
44 Avery Bradley/199 1.50 4.00
45 Courtney Lee/199 1.50 4.00

46 Bojan Bogdanovic/199 2.00 5.00
47 E'Twaun Moore/199 1.50 4.00
48 Al Jefferson/199 2.00 5.00
49 Damian Lillard/199 4.00 10.00
50 Gary Harris/199 2.00 5.00

2017-18 Totally Certified Fabric of the Game Rookies

PRINT RUNS B/WN 205-249 COPIES PER
1 Markelle Fultz/249 5.00 12.00
2 Lonzo Ball/249 8.00 20.00
3 Jayson Tatum/249 8.00 20.00
4 Josh Jackson/249 2.00 5.00
5 De'Aaron Fox/249 12.00 30.00
6 Jonathan Isaac/249 4.00 10.00
7 Frank Ntilikina/249 2.00 5.00
8 Dennis Smith Jr./249 2.00 5.00
9 Zach Collins/249 2.50 6.00
10 Malik Monk/249 6.00 15.00
11 Luke Kennard/249 3.00 8.00
12 Donovan Mitchell/249 8.00 20.00
13 Bam Adebayo/249 10.00 25.00
15 D.J. Wilson/249 1.50 4.00
16 T.J. Leaf/249 1.50 4.00
17 John Collins/249 4.00 10.00
18 Harry Giles/249 1.50 4.00
19 Jarrett Allen/249 4.00 10.00
20 OG Anunoby/249 8.00 20.00
21 Tyler Lydon/249 1.50 4.00
22 Caleb Swanigan/249 1.50 4.00
23 Kyle Kuzma/205 6.00 15.00
24 Tony Bradley/249 1.50 4.00
25 Derrick White/249 6.00 15.00
27 Frank Jackson/249 1.50 4.00
28 Jordan Bell/249 1.50 4.00
29 Jawun Evans/249 1.50 4.00
30 Dwayne Bacon/249 1.50 4.00
31 Wesley Iwundu/249 1.50 4.00
32 Sterling Brown/249 1.50 4.00
33 Ante Zizic/249 2.00 5.00
35 Terrance Ferguson/249 1.50 4.00
36 Sindarius Thornwell/249 1.50 4.00
37 Semi Ojeleye/249 2.00 5.00
38 Davon Reed/249 1.50 4.00
39 Ivan Rabb/249 1.50 4.00
40 Tyler Dorsey/249 1.50 4.00

2017-18 Totally Certified Materials

STATED PRINT RUN 199 SER.#'d SETS
1 Blake Griffin 2.50 6.00
2 Karl-Anthony Towns 4.00 10.00
3 Harrison Barnes 2.00 5.00
4 LeBron James 20.00 50.00
5 Carmelo Anthony 4.00 10.00
6 Marc Gasol 2.50 6.00
7 Zach LaVine 4.00 10.00
8 Goran Dragic 2.00 5.00
9 Andre Iguodala 2.50 6.00
10 James Harden 4.00 10.00

2017-18 Totally Certified Priority Mail

1 LeBron James 5.00 12.00
2 Kevin Durant 2.50 6.00
3 Russell Westbrook 1.00 2.50
4 James Harden 1.25 3.00
5 Stephen Curry 5.00 12.00

2017-18 Totally Certified Registered Mail

1 Paul Millsap .50 1.25
2 Mike Conley .50 1.25
3 Gordon Hayward .50 1.25
4 Klay Thompson 1.50 4.00
5 Bradley Beal .75 2.00
6 Blake Griffin .60 1.50
7 DeMarcus Cousins .50 1.25
8 Carmelo Anthony 1.00 2.50
9 C.J. McCollum .60 1.50
10 DeAndre Jordan .50 1.25
11 Goran Dragic .50 1.25
12 Kevin Love .60 1.50
13 Kyle Lowry .60 1.50
14 Hassan Whiteside .50 1.25
15 Kyrie Irving 1.25 3.00
16 Kemba Walker .50 1.25
17 Dwyane Wade 1.25 3.00
18 DeMar DeRozan .75 2.00
19 Kristaps Porzingis .75 2.00
20 Andrew Wiggins .75 2.00

2017-18 Totally Certified Return to Sender

1 Rudy Gobert .75 2.00
2 Anthony Davis 1.50 4.00
3 Myles Turner .60 1.50
4 Hassan Whiteside .50 1.25
5 Kristaps Porzingis .75 2.00
6 Giannis Antetokounmpo 3.00 8.00
7 DeAndre Jordan .50 1.25
8 Draymond Green .75 2.00
9 Kevin Durant 2.50 6.00
10 Serge Ibaka .50 1.25

2017-18 Totally Certified Rookie Duals Autographs Camo

STATED PRINT RUN 25 SER.#'d SETS
EXCHANGE DEADLINE 6/13/2019
1 Fox/Smith Jr. 75.00 200.00
2 Ball/Fultz 125.00 300.00
3 Jackson/Fultz 25.00 60.00
4 Mitchell/Kennard 60.00 150.00
5 Justin Jackson
Harry Giles 10.00 25.00
6 Hart/Kuzma 40.00 100.00
7 Monk/Ntilikina 40.00 100.00
8 Leaf/Ball 40.00 100.00
9 Mason/Jackson 12.00 30.00
10 Smith Jr/Mitchell 100.00 250.00

2017-18 Totally Certified Rookie Roll Call Autographs

EXCHANGE DEADLINE 6/13/2019
*CAMO/25: .75X TO 2X BASIC
1 Markelle Fultz 15.00 40.00
2 Lonzo Ball 20.00 50.00
3 Jayson Tatum 50.00 120.00
4 Josh Jackson 4.00 10.00
5 De'Aaron Fox 20.00 50.00
6 Jonathan Isaac 8.00 20.00
7 Lauri Markkanen 20.00 50.00
8 Frank Ntilikina 4.00 10.00
9 Dennis Smith Jr. 4.00 10.00
10 Zach Collins 5.00 12.00
11 Malik Monk 12.00 30.00
12 Luke Kennard 6.00 15.00
13 Donovan Mitchell 50.00 120.00
14 Bam Adebayo 20.00 50.00
15 Justin Jackson 3.00 8.00
16 Justin Patton 3.00 8.00
17 D.J. Wilson 3.00 8.00
18 T.J. Leaf 3.00 8.00
19 John Collins 8.00 20.00
20 Harry Giles 3.00 8.00
21 Jarrett Allen 8.00 20.00
22 OG Anunoby 15.00 40.00
23 Tyler Lydon 3.00 8.00
24 Caleb Swanigan 3.00 8.00
25 Kyle Kuzma 12.00 30.00
26 Tony Bradley 3.00 8.00
27 Derrick White 12.00 30.00
28 Josh Hart 8.00 20.00
29 Frank Jackson 3.00 8.00
30 Frank Mason III 3.00 8.00
31 Jordan Bell 3.00 8.00
32 Jawun Evans 3.00 8.00
33 Dwayne Bacon 3.00 8.00
34 Milos Teodosic 4.00 10.00
35 Ike Anigbogu 3.00 8.00
36 Bogdan Bogdanovic 8.00 20.00
37 Wesley Iwundu 3.00 8.00
38 Sterling Brown 3.00 8.00
39 Ante Zizic 4.00 10.00
40 Terrance Ferguson 3.00 8.00

2017-18 Totally Certified Signed Sealed and Delivered

PRINT RUNS B/WN 15-99 COPIES PER
NO PRICING ON QTY 15
EXCHANGE DEADLINE 6/13/2019
1 Jason Kidd/50 8.00 20.00
3 Gail Goodrich/21 4.00 10.00
4 Bill Walton/99 8.00 20.00
5 Cliff Hagan/99 5.00 12.00
7 Walter McCarty/99 2.50 6.00
8 Horace Grant/75 4.00 10.00
9 Zydrunas Ilgauskas/75 3.00 8.00
10 Jim Chones/99 2.50 6.00
11 Bill Laimbeer/99 4.00 10.00
12 Chris Ford/99 4.00 10.00
13 George McGinnis/75 2.50 6.00
14 Cazzie Russell/99 4.00 10.00
15 Eddie Jones/99 4.00 10.00
16 Cedric Ceballos/99 2.50 6.00
17 Rick Fox/99 3.00 8.00
18 Bob Dandridge/99 4.00 10.00
19 Sidney Moncrief/99 3.00 8.00
21 DeAndre' Bembry/99 2.50 6.00
22 Marcus Smart/99 4.00 10.00
23 Frank Kaminsky/75 2.50 6.00
24 Cody Zeller/99 2.50 6.00
25 Manu Ginobili/75 25.00 60.00
26 J.J. Barea/50 12.00 30.00
27 Juan Hernangomez/99 12.00 30.00
29 Darren Collison/75 2.50 6.00
30 Victor Oladipo/99 12.00 30.00
31 Larry Nance Jr./99 3.00 8.00
32 Deyonta Davis/99 2.50 6.00
33 Wade Baldwin IV/99 2.50 6.00
36 Clint Capela/99 3.00 8.00
37 Tarik Black/99 2.50 6.00
40 Kevin Durant/75 50.00 120.00
41 Trey Lyles/75 2.50 6.00
42 Henry Ellenson/99 2.50 6.00
43 Edmond Sumner/99 4.00 10.00
44 Abdel Nader/99 3.00 8.00
45 Semi Ojeleye/99 3.00 8.00
46 Davon Reed/99 2.50 6.00
47 Damyean Dotson/99 3.00 8.00
48 Wayne Selden Jr./99 2.50 6.00
49 Zhou Qi/99 20.00 50.00
50 Guerschon Yabusele/75 6.00 15.00

2017-18 Totally Certified The Mighty

1 Kevin Durant 4.00 10.00
2 LeBron James 8.00 20.00
3 Kawhi Leonard 2.50 6.00
4 Russell Westbrook 1.50 4.00
5 James Harden 2.00 5.00
6 Stephen Curry 8.00 20.00
7 Giannis Antetokounmpo 5.00 12.00
8 Isaiah Thomas .75 2.00
9 Anthony Davis 2.50 6.00
10 John Wall 1.25 3.00
11 Damian Lillard 2.50 6.00
12 Kristaps Porzingis 1.25 3.00
13 Kyrie Irving 2.00 5.00
14 DeMar DeRozan 1.25 3.00
15 Dirk Nowitzki 2.50 6.00
16 Markelle Fultz 1.50 4.00
17 Lonzo Ball 2.50 6.00
18 Jayson Tatum 8.00 20.00
19 De'Aaron Fox 5.00 12.00
20 Dennis Smith Jr. .75 2.00

2024-25 Totally Certified

*MIRROR: .5X TO 1.2X BASIC
*MIRROR BRONZE: .6X TO 1.5X BASIC
*MIRROR MAROON: .6X TO 1.5X BASIC
*MIRROR PURPLE: .6X TO 1.5X BASIC
*NEON ORNG MIRROR/299: .75X TO 2X BASIC
*MIRROR BLUE/199: 1.25X TO 3X BASIC
*MIRROR RED/149: 1.5X TO 4X BASIC
*MIRROR PINK/125: 2X TO 5X BASIC
*MIRROR PLATINUM PINK DC/125: 2X TO 5X BASIC
*MIRROR PLATINUM RED DC/125: 2X TO 5X BASIC
*MIRROR PLATINUM BLUE/99: 2.5X TO 6X BASIC
*MIRROR NEON GREEN/99: 2.5X TO 6X BASIC
*MIRROR PLATINUM ORANGE/75: 3X TO 8X BASIC
*MIRROR PLATINUM SILVER/75: 3X TO 8X BASIC
*MIRROR PLATINUM PURPLE DC/49: 4X TO 10X BASIC
*MIRROR PLATINUM BLUE CAMO/35: 5X TO 12X BASIC
*MIRROR PLATINUM CAMO/25: 6X TO 15X BASIC
*MIRROR PLATINUM WHITE/25: 6X TO 15X BASIC
1 Jayson Tatum 1.00 2.50
2 Bam Adebayo .40 1.00
3 Giannis Antetokounmpo 1.25 3.00
4 Mikal Bridges .30 .75
5 Scoot Henderson .40 1.00
6 Ben Simmons .30 .75
7 Devin Booker .75 2.00
8 Karl-Anthony Towns .50 1.25
9 De'Aaron Fox .60 1.50
10 Tyrese Haliburton .60 1.50
11 Alperen Sengun .50 1.25
12 Kawhi Leonard .60 1.50
13 Amen Thompson .75 2.00
14 Jaylen Brown .50 1.25
15 Domantas Sabonis .50 1.25
16 James Harden .60 1.50
17 Damian Lillard .75 2.00
18 Jalen Green .60 1.50
19 Nikola Jokic 1.50 4.00
20 Ja Morant 1.00 2.50
21 Immanuel Quickley .25 .60
22 Kyle Kuzma .25 .60
23 Jaren Jackson Jr. .50 1.25
24 Pascal Siakam .40 1.00
25 Zion Williamson .75 2.00
26 D'Angelo Russell .25 .60
27 Jalen Brunson .60 1.50
28 Kelly Oubre Jr. .25 .60
29 Kevin Durant 1.00 2.50
30 Rudy Gobert .30 .75
31 Jonas Valanciunas .25 .60
32 Brandon Miller .50 1.25
33 DeMar DeRozan .40 1.00
34 Trayce Jackson-Davis .30 .75
35 Kristaps Porzingis .40 1.00
36 Donte DiVincenzo .30 .75
37 Keyonte George .40 1.00
38 Andrew Nembhard .25 .60
39 Cade Cunningham .75 2.00
40 Bradley Beal .40 1.00
41 Quentin Grimes .30 .75
42 Cameron Thomas .30 .75
43 Naz Reid .30 .75
44 Jordan Poole .30 .75
45 Desmond Bane .30 .75
46 Ausar Thompson .50 1.25
47 Cam Whitmore .30 .75
48 Jimmy Butler .50 1.25
49 Jrue Holiday .40 1.00
50 Paul George .50 1.25
51 Marcus Smart .30 .75
52 Chet Holmgren .50 1.25
53 Shaedon Sharpe .40 1.00
54 Russell Westbrook .50 1.25
55 Terry Rozier III .25 .60
56 Jabari Smith Jr. .30 .75
57 Josh Hart .25 .60
58 Keegan Murray .25 .60
59 Jalen Suggs .30 .75
60 Fred VanVleet .30 .75
61 Bennedict Mathurin .40 1.00
62 GG Jackson II .30 .75
63 Jaden Ivey .40 1.00
64 Zach LaVine .50 1.25
65 Klay Thompson .75 2.00
66 Jaime Jaquez Jr. .30 .75
67 P.J. Washington Jr. .25 .60
68 Dereck Lively II .30 .75
69 Khris Middleton .30 .75
70 Miles Bridges .25 .60
71 Devin Vassell .40 1.00
72 Tyrese Maxey .60 1.50
73 Dejounte Murray .30 .75
74 Tyler Herro .50 1.25
75 Jusuf Nurkic .25 .60
76 Jamal Murray .50 1.25
77 Trae Young .60 1.50
78 Malik Monk .30 .75
79 Franz Wagner .50 1.25
80 Tobias Harris .25 .60
81 LeBron James 2.50 6.00
82 Evan Mobley .50 1.25
83 Draymond Green .40 1.00
84 Nikola Vucevic .25 .60
85 Josh Giddey .40 1.00
86 Derrick White .30 .75
87 Jose Alvarado .25 .60
88 Lauri Markkanen .40 1.00
89 Jeremy Sochan .30 .75
90 Gradey Dick .40 1.00
91 Julius Randle .30 .75
92 CJ McCollum .25 .60
93 Michael Porter Jr. .30 .75
94 Malcolm Brogdon .20 .50
95 Anfernee Simons .30 .75
96 Derrick Rose .75 2.00
97 Darius Garland .40 1.00
98 Victor Wembanyama 2.50 6.00
99 Dillon Brooks .25 .60
100 Anthony Black .40 1.00
101 Keldon Johnson .25 .60
102 Shai Gilgeous-Alexander 1.50 4.00
103 Myles Turner .25 .60
104 Scottie Barnes .40 1.00
105 Jonathan Kuminga .40 1.00
106 Jalen Williams .60 1.50
107 Anthony Davis .75 2.00
108 Jalen Johnson .40 1.00
109 Rui Hachimura .30 .75
110 Jalen Duren .30 .75
111 Stephen Curry 2.50 6.00
112 Brandon Ingram .30 .75
113 RJ Barrett .40 1.00
114 Luguentz Dort .25 .60
115 Austin Reaves .40 1.00
116 Brandin Podziemski .40 1.00
117 LaMelo Ball .60 1.50
118 Jordan Clarkson .30 .75
119 Aaron Gordon .30 .75
120 Jarrett Allen .25 .60
121 Luka Doncic 2.00 5.00
122 Donovan Mitchell .60 1.50
123 Cason Wallace .40 1.00
124 Bilal Coulibaly .40 1.00
125 Bogdan Bogdanovic .25 .60
126 Anthony Edwards 1.50 4.00
127 Collin Sexton .30 .75
128 Coby White .30 .75
129 Jaden McDaniels .30 .75
130 Paolo Banchero .75 2.00
131 Andrew Wiggins .40 1.00
132 Chris Paul .50 1.25
133 Kyrie Irving .75 2.00
134 Deandre Ayton .25 .60
135 Joel Embiid .50 1.25
136 Alexandre Sarr RC 2.00 5.00
137 Tidjane Salaun RC .60 1.50
138 Kel'el Ware RC 1.50 4.00
139 Yves Missi RC 1.50 4.00
140 Jared McCain RC 2.50 6.00
141 Devin Carter RC .75 2.00
142 Tristan da Silva RC 1.50 4.00
143 DaRon Holmes II RC .75 2.00
144 Zaccharie Risacher RC 2.00 5.00
145 Tyler Kolek RC 1.00 2.50
146 Bub Carrington RC 1.50 4.00
147 Donovan Clingan RC 1.50 4.00
148 Ja'Kobe Walter RC .75 2.00
149 AJ Johnson RC 1.25 3.00
150 Bronny James Jr. RC 2.00 5.00
151 Jaylon Tyson RC .60 1.50
152 Johnny Furphy RC 1.00 2.50
153 Kyshawn George RC 1.00 2.50
154 Dalton Knecht RC 2.00 5.00
155 Pacome Dadiet RC .75 2.00
156 Jamal Shead RC .75 2.00
157 Rob Dillingham RC 1.50 4.00
158 Cam Christie RC .75 2.00
159 Bobi Klintman RC .75 2.00
160 Dillon Jones RC .60 1.50
161 Ajay Mitchell RC 1.00 2.50
162 Reed Sheppard RC 2.00 5.00
163 Kyle Filipowski RC 1.50 4.00
164 Zach Edey RC 2.00 5.00
165 Tyler Smith RC .75 2.00
166 Terrence Shannon Jr. RC 1.25 3.00
167 Stephon Castle RC 4.00 10.00
168 Cody Williams RC .75 2.00
169 Ryan Dunn RC .75 2.00
170 Ron Holland II RC 1.25 3.00
171 Isaiah Collier RC 1.25 3.00
172 Baylor Scheierman RC .75 2.00
173 Jonathan Mogbo RC 1.00 2.50
174 Matas Buzelis RC 3.00 8.00
175 Nikola Topic RC 2.00 5.00
176 Tim Duncan LGD 2.00 5.00
177 Yao Ming LGD .60 1.50
178 Allen Iverson LGD 1.25 3.00
179 Dirk Nowitzki LGD .75 2.00
180 Magic Johnson LGD 1.00 2.50
181 Shaquille O'Neal LGD .75 2.00
182 Isiah Thomas LGD .50 1.25
183 Charles Barkley LGD .75 2.00
184 Julius Erving LGD .75 2.00
185 Carmelo Anthony LGD .50 1.25
186 Karl Malone LGD .60 1.50
187 Paul Pierce LGD .50 1.25
188 Dwyane Wade LGD .60 1.50
189 Kevin Garnett LGD .75 2.00
190 Gary Payton LGD .50 1.25
191 Dennis Rodman LGD .75 2.00
192 John Stockton LGD .60 1.50
193 Patrick Ewing LGD .50 1.25
194 Kareem Abdul-Jabbar LGD 1.00 2.50
195 Dominique Wilkins LGD .50 1.25
196 Ray Allen LGD .50 1.25
197 Larry Bird LGD 1.00 2.50
198 Hakeem Olajuwon LGD .60 1.50
199 Steve Nash LGD .60 1.50
200 David Robinson LGD .60 1.50

2024-25 Totally Certified '24

*MIRROR RED/99: 2.5X TO 6X BASIC
*MIRROR BLUE/49: 4X TO 10X BASIC
*MIRROR PLATINUM CAMO/25: 6X TO 15X BASIC
1 Alexandre Sarr 2.00 5.00
2 Ja'Kobe Walter .75 2.00
3 Cody Williams .75 2.00
4 Rob Dillingham 1.50 4.00
5 Jaylen Wells .75 2.00
6 Kel'el Ware 1.50 4.00
7 Nikola Topic 2.00 5.00
8 Ron Holland II 1.25 3.00
9 Tidjane Salaun .60 1.50
10 Jaylon Tyson .60 1.50
11 Tyler Kolek 1.00 2.50
12 Tristan da Silva 1.50 4.00
13 Devin Carter .75 2.00
14 Dalton Knecht 2.00 5.00
15 Jared McCain 2.50 6.00
16 Zaccharie Risacher 2.00 5.00
17 Stephon Castle 4.00 10.00
18 Yves Missi 1.50 4.00
19 Donovan Clingan 1.50 4.00
20 Zach Edey 2.00 5.00
21 Bub Carrington 1.50 4.00
22 Matas Buzelis 3.00 8.00
23 Johnny Furphy 1.00 2.50
24 Bronny James Jr. 2.00 5.00
25 Reed Sheppard 2.00 5.00

2024-25 Totally Certified Action Packed

1 Shai Gilgeous-Alexander 30.00 80.00
2 Anthony Davis 15.00 40.00
3 Alexandre Sarr 20.00 50.00
4 Jaylen Brown 10.00 25.00
5 Zaccharie Risacher 20.00 50.00
6 Luka Doncic 40.00 100.00
7 Giannis Antetokounmpo 25.00 60.00
8 Ja Morant 20.00 50.00
9 Damian Lillard 15.00 40.00
10 Nikola Jokic 30.00 80.00
11 Kyrie Irving 15.00 40.00
12 James Harden 12.00 30.00
13 Bub Carrington 15.00 40.00
14 LeBron James 50.00 125.00
15 Reed Sheppard 20.00 50.00
16 Jayson Tatum 20.00 50.00
17 Tyrese Haliburton 12.00 30.00
18 Stephon Castle 40.00 100.00
19 Paolo Banchero 15.00 40.00
20 Kevin Durant 20.00 50.00
21 Donovan Clingan 15.00 40.00
22 Victor Wembanyama 50.00 120.00
23 Stephen Curry 50.00 120.00
24 Anthony Edwards 30.00 80.00
25 Matas Buzelis 30.00 80.00

2024-25 Totally Certified Baller Materials

STATED PRINT RUN 99-125 SER.#'d SETS
*MIRROR PURPLE/99: .4X TO 1X BASIC
*MIRROR RED/75: .5X TO 1.2X BASIC
*MIRROR BLUE/49: .6X TO 1.5X BASIC
*MIRROR PLATINUM CAMO/25: .75X TO 2X BASIC
1 Dejounte Murray/99 4.00 10.00
2 Tyrese Maxey/99 8.00 20.00
3 Anthony Edwards/99 20.00 50.00
4 Victor Wembanyama/125 30.00 80.00
5 LeBron James/125 30.00 80.00
6 Scoot Henderson/99 5.00 12.00
7 Cade Cunningham/99 10.00 25.00
8 Dalton Knecht/125 12.00 30.00
9 Zaccharie Risacher/125 12.00 30.00
10 Jayson Tatum/125 12.00 30.00
11 De'Aaron Fox/99 8.00 20.00
12 Matas Buzelis/125 20.00 50.00
13 Stephon Castle/125 25.00 60.00
14 Donovan Clingan/125 10.00 25.00
15 Ron Holland II/125 8.00 20.00
16 Tyler Kolek/125 6.00 15.00
17 Reed Sheppard/125 12.00 30.00
18 Paolo Banchero/99 10.00 25.00
19 Kevin Durant/125 12.00 30.00
20 Jalen Brunson/99 8.00 20.00
21 Damian Lillard/125 10.00 25.00
22 Alexandre Sarr/125 12.00 30.00
23 Kawhi Leonard/99 8.00 20.00
24 Nikola Jokic/99 20.00 50.00
25 Luka Doncic/99 25.00 60.00

2024-25 Totally Certified Certified Bucket

*MIRROR RED/99: 2.5X TO 6X BASIC
*MIRROR BLUE/49: 4X TO 10X BASIC
*MIRROR PLATINUM CAMO/25: 6X TO 15X BASIC
1 Ja Morant 2.00 5.00
2 Stephen Curry 5.00 12.00
3 Nikola Jokic 3.00 8.00
4 Matas Buzelis 3.00 8.00
5 LeBron James 5.00 12.00
6 Paolo Banchero 1.50 4.00
7 Dalton Knecht 2.00 5.00
8 Jalen Brunson 1.25 3.00
9 Trae Young 1.25 3.00
10 Rob Dillingham 1.50 4.00
11 Jayson Tatum 2.00 5.00
12 Giannis Antetokounmpo 2.50 6.00
13 Victor Wembanyama 5.00 12.00
14 Reed Sheppard 2.00 5.00
15 Anthony Edwards 3.00 8.00
16 Shai Gilgeous-Alexander 3.00 8.00
17 Kyrie Irving 1.50 4.00
18 Bronny James Jr. 2.00 5.00
19 Zaccharie Risacher 2.00 5.00
20 Stephon Castle 4.00 10.00
21 Kevin Durant 2.00 5.00
22 James Harden 1.25 3.00
23 Damian Lillard 1.50 4.00
24 Luka Doncic 4.00 10.00
25 Tyrese Maxey 1.25 3.00

2024-25 Totally Certified Certified Competitor Autographs Mirror Red

PRINT RUNS B/WN 49-75 COPIES PER
*MIRROR PURPLE/49: .5X TO 1.2X BASIC
*MIRROR BLUE/35: .6X TO 1.5X BASIC
*MIRROR PLATINUM CAMO/25: .6X TO 1.5X BASIC
1 Dejounte Murray/75 8.00 20.00
2 Jaden Hardy/75 8.00 20.00
3 Ben Simmons/75 8.00 20.00
4 Cason Wallace/75 10.00 25.00
5 Shaedon Sharpe/75 10.00 25.00
6 Ausar Thompson/75 12.00 30.00
7 Jalen Suggs/75 8.00 20.00
8 Jalen Duren/75 8.00 20.00
9 Amen Thompson/75 40.00 100.00
10 Jaden Ivey/75 10.00 25.00
12 Rudy Gobert/75 8.00 20.00
13 Jalen Green/75 15.00 40.00
14 Julius Randle/75 8.00 20.00
15 Tyler Herro/75 12.00 30.00
16 Bennedict Mathurin/75 10.00 25.00
17 Kristaps Porzingis/75 10.00 25.00
18 Anfernee Simons/75 8.00 20.00
19 Tayshaun Prince/49 12.00 30.00
20 Jeremy Lin/49 50.00 120.00
21 Grant Hill/75 12.00 30.00
22 Carlos Boozer/49 8.00 20.00
23 Jermaine O'Neal/75 6.00 15.00
24 Lance Stephenson/75 6.00 15.00
25 Shawn Kemp/75 12.00 30.00

2024-25 Totally Certified Certified Gamers Materials

*MIRROR PLAT BLUE CAMO/35: 1X TO 2.5X BASIC
1 Jayson Tatum 12.00 30.00
2 Tyler Herro 6.00 15.00
3 Khris Middleton 4.00 10.00
4 Luka Doncic 25.00 60.00
5 Bam Adebayo 5.00 12.00
6 Karl-Anthony Towns 6.00 15.00
7 Kevin Durant 12.00 30.00
8 Kawhi Leonard 8.00 20.00
9 Jimmy Butler 6.00 15.00
10 Darius Garland 5.00 12.00
11 LeBron James 30.00 80.00
12 Scottie Barnes 5.00 12.00
13 Joel Embiid 6.00 15.00
14 Jaylen Brown 6.00 15.00
15 Zach LaVine 6.00 15.00
16 Devin Booker 10.00 25.00
17 Julius Randle 4.00 10.00
18 Dejounte Murray 4.00 10.00
19 Pascal Siakam 5.00 12.00
20 Cameron Johnson 3.00 8.00
21 Klay Thompson 10.00 25.00
22 Jaren Jackson Jr. 6.00 15.00
23 Austin Reaves 6.00 15.00
24 Damian Lillard 10.00 25.00
25 Keldon Johnson 3.00 8.00
26 LaMelo Ball 8.00 20.00
27 Domantas Sabonis 6.00 15.00
28 Paul George 6.00 15.00
29 Tyrese Haliburton 8.00 20.00
30 James Harden 8.00 20.00
31 Trae Young 8.00 20.00
32 Mikal Bridges 4.00 10.00
33 Victor Wembanyama 30.00 80.00
34 Scoot Henderson 5.00 12.00
35 Jaime Jaquez Jr. 4.00 10.00

2024-25 Totally Certified Fabric of the Game

STATED PRINT RUN 99-125 SER.#'d SETS
*MIRROR PURPLE/99: .4X TO 1X BASIC
*MIRROR RED/75: .5X TO 1.2X BASIC
*MIRROR BLUE/49: .6X TO 1.5X BASIC
*MIRROR PLATINUM CAMO/25: .75X TO 2X BASIC
1 #VALUE! 5.00 12.00
2 #VALUE! 30.00 80.00
3 #VALUE! 4.00 10.00
4 #VALUE! 10.00 25.00
5 #VALUE! 5.00 12.00
6 #VALUE! 8.00 20.00
7 #VALUE! 30.00 80.00
8 #VALUE! 6.00 15.00
9 #VALUE! 5.00 12.00
10 #VALUE! 4.00 10.00
11 #VALUE! 12.00 30.00
12 #VALUE! 10.00 25.00
13 #VALUE! 4.00 10.00
14 #VALUE! 8.00 20.00
15 #VALUE! 6.00 15.00
16 #VALUE! 6.00 15.00
17 #VALUE! 20.00 50.00
18 #VALUE! 6.00 15.00
19 #VALUE! 5.00 12.00
20 #VALUE! 10.00 25.00
21 #VALUE! 30.00 80.00
22 #VALUE! 8.00 20.00
23 #VALUE! 5.00 12.00
24 #VALUE! 6.00 15.00
25 #VALUE! 4.00 10.00

2024-25 Totally Certified Fabric of the Game Rookies

STATED PRINT RUN 125 SER.#'d SETS
*MIRROR PURPLE/99: .4X TO 1X BASIC
*MIRROR RED/75: .5X TO 1.2X BASIC
*MIRROR BLUE/49: .6X TO 1.5X BASIC
*MIRROR PLATINUM CAMO/25: .75X TO 2X BASIC
1 Alexandre Sarr 8.00 20.00
2 Tristan da Silva 6.00 15.00
3 Bronny James Jr. 8.00 20.00
4 Nikola Topic 8.00 20.00
5 Matas Buzelis 12.00 30.00
6 Reed Sheppard 8.00 20.00
7 Zach Edey 8.00 20.00
8 Ron Holland II 5.00 12.00
9 AJ Johnson 5.00 12.00
10 Cody Williams 3.00 8.00
11 Rob Dillingham 6.00 15.00
12 Zaccharie Risacher 8.00 20.00
13 Devin Carter 3.00 8.00
14 Kyle Filipowski 6.00 15.00
15 Jaylon Tyson 2.50 6.00
16 Ja'Kobe Walter 3.00 8.00
17 Dalton Knecht 8.00 20.00
18 Bub Carrington 6.00 15.00
19 Tidjane Salaun 2.50 6.00
20 Kyshawn George 4.00 10.00
21 Kel'el Ware 6.00 15.00
22 Yves Missi 6.00 15.00
23 Jared McCain 10.00 25.00
24 Stephon Castle 15.00 40.00
25 Donovan Clingan 6.00 15.00

2024-25 Totally Certified Franchise Foundations

*MIRROR: .5X TO 1.2X BASIC
*MIRROR BLUE/265: .75X TO 2X BASIC
*MIRROR NEON ORNG/249: .75X TO 2X BASIC
*MIRROR PINK/199: 1.25X TO 3X BASIC
*MIRROR PLATINUM SILVER/75: 3X TO 8X BASIC
*MIRROR PLATINUM BLUE CAMO/35: 5X TO 12X BASIC
*MIRROR PLATINUM WHITE/25: 6X TO 15X BASIC
1 Jayson Tatum 2.00 5.00
2 Alperen Sengun 1.00 2.50
3 Zion Williamson 1.50 4.00
4 Anthony Edwards 3.00 8.00
5 Paolo Banchero 1.50 4.00
6 Shai Gilgeous-Alexander 3.00 8.00
7 Trae Young 1.25 3.00
8 Jimmy Butler 1.00 2.50
9 Nikola Jokic 3.00 8.00
10 Ja Morant 2.00 5.00
11 Tyrese Maxey 1.25 3.00
12 Donovan Mitchell 1.25 3.00
13 Scottie Barnes .75 2.00
14 Giannis Antetokounmpo 2.50 6.00
15 Kevin Durant 2.00 5.00
16 Jalen Brunson 1.25 3.00
17 De'Aaron Fox 1.25 3.00
18 Stephen Curry 5.00 12.00
19 Lauri Markkanen .60 1.50
20 LeBron James 5.00 12.00
21 Tyrese Haliburton 1.25 3.00
22 Victor Wembanyama 5.00 12.00
23 Matas Buzelis 3.00 8.00
24 Kawhi Leonard 1.25 3.00
25 Luka Doncic 4.00 10.00

2024-25 Totally Certified Freshman Fabric Signatures Mirror Red

PRINT RUN 75 COPIES PER
*MIRROR PURPLE/49: .5X TO 1.2X BASIC
*MIRROR BLUE/35: .6X TO 1.5X BASIC
*MIRROR PLATINUM CAMO/25: .6X TO 1.5X BASIC
*MIRROR PLATINUM WHITE/25: .6X TO 1.5X BASIC
1 Reed Sheppard 30.00 80.00
2 Jared McCain 40.00 100.00
3 Dalton Knecht 30.00 80.00
4 Matas Buzelis 50.00 120.00
5 Zach Edey 30.00 80.00
6 Tidjane Salaun 10.00 25.00
7 Donovan Clingan 25.00 60.00
8 Devin Carter 12.00 30.00
10 Bub Carrington 25.00 60.00
11 Tristan da Silva 25.00 60.00
12 Jaylon Tyson 10.00 25.00
13 Ja'Kobe Walter 12.00 30.00
14 Yves Missi 25.00 60.00
15 Kyshawn George 15.00 40.00
16 Pacome Dadiet 12.00 30.00
17 Dillon Jones 10.00 25.00
18 Terrence Shannon Jr. 20.00 50.00
19 Baylor Scheierman 12.00 30.00
20 AJ Johnson 20.00 50.00
21 Johnny Furphy 15.00 40.00
22 Oso Ighodaro 12.00 30.00
23 Adem Bona 12.00 30.00
24 KJ Simpson Jr. 10.00 25.00
25 Jamal Shead 12.00 30.00
26 Cam Christie 12.00 30.00
27 Bobi Klintman 12.00 30.00
28 Ajay Mitchell 15.00 40.00
29 Jaylen Wells 30.00 80.00
30 Tyler Kolek 15.00 40.00

2024-25 Totally Certified Gold Team

*MIRROR RED/99: 2.5X TO 6X BASIC
*MIRROR BLUE/49: 4X TO 10X BASIC
*MIRROR PLATINUM CAMO/25: 6X TO 15X BASIC
1 Jared McCain 2.50 6.00
2 Ron Holland II 1.25 3.00
3 Kevin Durant 2.00 5.00
4 Jayson Tatum 2.00 5.00
5 Nikola Jokic 3.00 8.00
6 Jrue Holiday .75 2.00
7 Giannis Antetokounmpo 2.50 6.00
8 Ja Morant 2.00 5.00
9 Bub Carrington 1.50 4.00
10 Joel Embiid 1.00 2.50
11 Stephen Curry 5.00 12.00
12 Tyrese Haliburton 1.25 3.00
13 Anthony Edwards 3.00 8.00
14 Anthony Davis 1.50 4.00
15 Kawhi Leonard 1.25 3.00
16 Cody Williams .75 2.00
17 Victor Wembanyama 5.00 12.00
18 LeBron James 5.00 12.00
19 Alexandre Sarr 2.00 5.00
20 Shai Gilgeous-Alexander 3.00 8.00
21 Reed Sheppard 2.00 5.00
22 Devin Booker 1.50 4.00
23 Luka Doncic 4.00 10.00
24 Zaccharie Risacher 2.00 5.00
25 Bam Adebayo .75 2.00

2024-25 Totally Certified New Generation Jerseys

*MIRROR PLAT BLUE CAMO/35: 1X TO 2.5X BASIC
1 Zaccharie Risacher 8.00 20.00
2 Alexandre Sarr 8.00 20.00
3 Reed Sheppard 8.00 20.00
4 Stephon Castle 15.00 40.00
5 Ron Holland II 5.00 12.00
6 Tidjane Salaun 2.50 6.00
7 Donovan Clingan 6.00 15.00
8 Rob Dillingham 6.00 15.00
9 Zach Edey 8.00 20.00
10 Cody Williams 3.00 8.00
11 Matas Buzelis 12.00 30.00
12 Nikola Topic 8.00 20.00
13 Devin Carter 3.00 8.00
14 Bub Carrington 6.00 15.00
15 Kel'el Ware 6.00 15.00
16 Jared McCain 10.00 25.00
17 Dalton Knecht 8.00 20.00
18 Tristan da Silva 6.00 15.00
19 Ja'Kobe Walter 3.00 8.00
20 Bronny James Jr. 8.00 20.00
21 AJ Johnson 5.00 12.00
22 Isaiah Collier 5.00 12.00
23 Yuki Kawamura 20.00 50.00
24 Yves Missi 6.00 15.00
25 Jaylen Wells 8.00 20.00

2024-25 Totally Certified On Target

*MIRROR: .5X TO 1.2X BASIC
*MIRROR BLUE/265: .75X TO 2X BASIC
*MIRROR NEON ORNG/249: .75X TO 2X BASIC
*MIRROR PINK/199: 1.25X TO 3X BASIC
*MIRROR PLATINUM SILVER/75: 3X TO 8X BASIC
*MIRROR PLATINUM BLUE CAMO/35: 5X TO 12X BASIC
*MIRROR PLATINUM WHITE/25: 6X TO 15X BASIC
1 Rob Dillingham 1.50 4.00
2 Trae Young 1.25 3.00
3 Tyrese Maxey 1.25 3.00
4 Alexandre Sarr 2.00 5.00
5 Damian Lillard 1.50 4.00
6 Jared McCain 2.50 6.00
7 Tyrese Haliburton 1.25 3.00
8 De'Aaron Fox 1.25 3.00
9 Stephen Curry 5.00 12.00
10 LeBron James 5.00 12.00
11 Bub Carrington 1.50 4.00
12 Devin Booker 1.50 4.00
13 Zaccharie Risacher 2.00 5.00
14 Shai Gilgeous-Alexander 3.00 8.00
15 Jalen Brunson 1.25 3.00
16 Kevin Durant 2.00 5.00
17 Nikola Jokic 3.00 8.00
18 Jayson Tatum 2.00 5.00
19 Anthony Edwards 3.00 8.00
20 Dalton Knecht 2.00 5.00
21 Ja Morant 2.00 5.00
22 Victor Wembanyama 5.00 12.00
23 Luka Doncic 4.00 10.00
24 Stephon Castle 4.00 10.00
25 Reed Sheppard 2.00 5.00

2024-25 Totally Certified Piece of the Game Materials

*MIRROR PLAT BLUE CAMO/35: 1X TO 2.5X BASIC
1 Stephen Curry 20.00 50.00
2 LeBron James 20.00 50.00
3 Jaylen Brown 4.00 10.00
4 Darius Garland 3.00 8.00
5 Jabari Smith Jr. 2.50 6.00
6 Devin Booker 6.00 15.00
7 Kawhi Leonard 5.00 12.00
8 Jimmy Butler 4.00 10.00

9 Giannis Antetokounmpo 10.00 25.00
10 Zion Williamson 6.00 15.00
11 De'Aaron Fox 5.00 12.00
12 Jamal Murray 4.00 10.00
13 DeMar DeRozan 3.00 8.00
14 Russell Westbrook 4.00 10.00
15 Kyrie Irving 6.00 15.00
16 Tyrese Maxey 5.00 12.00
17 Victor Wembanyama 20.00 50.00
18 Kyle Kuzma 2.00 5.00
19 Zaccharie Risacher 8.00 20.00
20 Alexandre Sarr 8.00 20.00
21 Reed Sheppard 8.00 20.00
22 Stephon Castle 15.00 40.00
23 Ron Holland II 5.00 12.00
24 Rob Dillingham 6.00 15.00
25 Cody Williams 3.00 8.00
26 Donovan Clingan 6.00 15.00
27 Matas Buzelis 12.00 30.00
28 Dalton Knecht 8.00 20.00
29 Bub Carrington 6.00 15.00
30 Bronny James Jr. 8.00 20.00

2024-25 Totally Certified Portraits
*MIRROR: .5X TO 1.2X BASIC
*MIRROR BLUE/265: .75X TO 2X BASIC
*MIRROR NEON ORNG/249: .75X TO 2X BASIC
*MIRROR PINK/199: 1.25X TO 3X BASIC
*MIRROR PLATINUM SILVER/75: 3X TO 8X BASIC
*MIRROR PLATINUM BLUE CAMO/35: 5X TO 12X BASIC
*MIRROR PLATINUM WHITE/25: 6X TO 15X BASIC
1 Nikola Jokic 3.00 8.00
2 Kevin Durant 2.00 5.00
3 Matas Buzelis 3.00 8.00
4 Donovan Clingan 1.50 4.00
5 Shai Gilgeous-Alexander 3.00 8.00
6 Giannis Antetokounmpo 2.50 6.00
7 Victor Wembanyama 5.00 12.00
8 Anthony Edwards 3.00 8.00
9 LeBron James 5.00 12.00
10 Luka Doncic 4.00 10.00
11 Bronny James Jr. 2.00 5.00
12 Tidjane Salaun .60 1.50
13 Cody Williams .75 2.00
14 Jayson Tatum 2.00 5.00
15 Alexandre Sarr 2.00 5.00
16 Stephen Curry 5.00 12.00
17 Rob Dillingham 1.50 4.00
18 Stephon Castle 4.00 10.00
19 Dalton Knecht 2.00 5.00
20 Reed Sheppard 2.00 5.00
21 Bub Carrington 1.50 4.00
22 Zach Edey 2.00 5.00
23 Ron Holland II 1.25 3.00
24 Zaccharie Risacher 2.00 5.00
25 Ja Morant 2.00 5.00

2024-25 Totally Certified Rock the Rim
*MIRROR: .5X TO 1.2X BASIC
*MIRROR BLUE/265: .75X TO 2X BASIC
*MIRROR NEON ORNG/249: .75X TO 2X BASIC
*MIRROR PINK/199: 1.25X TO 3X BASIC
*MIRROR PLATINUM SILVER/75: 3X TO 8X BASIC
*MIRROR PLATINUM BLUE CAMO/35: 5X TO 12X BASIC
*MIRROR PLATINUM WHITE/25: 6X TO 15X BASIC
1 Zach Edey 2.00 5.00
2 Donovan Mitchell 1.25 3.00
3 Jaylen Brown 1.00 2.50
4 Jayson Tatum 2.00 5.00
5 Ja Morant 2.00 5.00
6 Paolo Banchero 1.50 4.00
7 Chet Holmgren 1.00 2.50
8 Joel Embiid 1.00 2.50
9 Anthony Davis 1.50 4.00
10 Anthony Edwards 3.00 8.00
11 Donovan Clingan 1.50 4.00
12 Zaccharie Risacher 2.00 5.00
13 Kawhi Leonard 1.25 3.00
14 Matas Buzelis 3.00 8.00
15 Alexandre Sarr 2.00 5.00
16 LeBron James 5.00 12.00
17 Kel'el Ware 1.50 4.00
18 Ron Holland II 1.25 3.00
19 Zion Williamson 1.50 4.00
20 Giannis Antetokounmpo 2.50 6.00
21 Nikola Jokic 3.00 8.00
22 Tidjane Salaun .60 1.50
23 Bub Carrington 1.50 4.00
24 Kevin Durant 2.00 5.00
25 Victor Wembanyama 5.00 12.00

2024-25 Totally Certified Rookie Dual Swatches
*MIRROR PLAT BLUE CAMO/35: 1X TO 2.5X BASIC
1 Reed Sheppard
Rob Dillingham 8.00 20.00
2 Donovan Clingan
Stephon Castle 15.00 40.00
3 Cody Williams
Tristan da Silva 6.00 15.00
4 Ja'Kobe Walter
Yves Missi 6.00 15.00
5 Alexandre Sarr
Zaccharie Risacher 8.00 20.00
6 Matas Buzelis
Ron Holland II 12.00 30.00
7 Nikola Topic
Tidjane Salaun 8.00 20.00
8 Jared McCain
Zach Edey 10.00 25.00
9 Bronny James Jr.
Dalton Knecht 8.00 20.00
10 Bub Carrington
Kyshawn George 6.00 15.00

2024-25 Totally Certified Rookie Roll Call Autographs Mirror Red
PRINT RUN 75 COPIES PER
*MIRROR PURPLE/49: .5X TO 1.2X BASIC
*MIRROR BLUE/35: .5X TO 1.5X BASIC
*MIRROR PLATINUM CAMO/25: .6X TO 1.5X BASIC
*MIRROR PLATINUM WHITE/25: .6X TO 1.5X BASIC
1 Bub Carrington 20.00 50.00
2 Zach Edey 25.00 60.00
3 Reed Sheppard 25.00 60.00
4 Matas Buzelis 40.00 100.00
5 Jared McCain 30.00 80.00
6 Dalton Knecht 25.00 60.00
7 Tidjane Salaun 8.00 20.00
8 Donovan Clingan 20.00 50.00
9 Tristan da Silva 20.00 50.00
10 Devin Carter 10.00 25.00
11 Ja'Kobe Walter 10.00 25.00
12 Jaylon Tyson 8.00 20.00
13 Kyshawn George 12.00 30.00
14 Baylor Scheierman 10.00 25.00
15 Pacome Dadiet 10.00 25.00
17 AJ Johnson 15.00 40.00
18 Dillon Jones 8.00 20.00
19 Terrence Shannon Jr. 15.00 40.00
20 Yves Missi 20.00 50.00

2024-25 Totally Certified Rookie Yearbook Autographs
*MIRROR PLAT BLUE CAMO/35: .75X TO 2X BASIC
1 Dalton Knecht 20.00 50.00
2 Donovan Clingan 15.00 40.00
3 Bub Carrington 15.00 40.00
4 Reed Sheppard 20.00 50.00
5 Zach Edey 20.00 50.00
6 Tidjane Salaun 6.00 15.00
7 Matas Buzelis 30.00 80.00
8 Devin Carter 8.00 20.00
9 Jared McCain 25.00 60.00
10 Ja'Kobe Walter 8.00 20.00
11 Tristan da Silva 15.00 40.00
12 Yves Missi 15.00 40.00
14 Jaylon Tyson 6.00 15.00
15 Kyshawn George 10.00 25.00
16 Baylor Scheierman 8.00 20.00
17 Tyler Kolek 10.00 25.00
18 Johnny Furphy 10.00 25.00
19 Bobi Klintman 8.00 20.00
20 Pacome Dadiet 8.00 20.00
21 Ajay Mitchell 10.00 25.00
22 Dillon Jones 6.00 15.00
25 AJ Johnson 12.00 30.00

2024-25 Totally Certified Signed Sealed and Delivered
*MIRROR PLAT BLUE CAMO/35: .75X TO 2X BASIC
1 Jaden Hardy 6.00 15.00
2 Paolo Banchero 40.00 100.00
3 Jalen Duren 6.00 15.00
4 Zeke Nnaji 4.00 10.00
5 Adam Flagler 6.00 15.00
6 Cade Cunningham 40.00 100.00
7 David Duke Jr. 4.00 10.00
8 Maxwell Lewis 5.00 12.00
9 Blake Wesley 4.00 10.00
10 Amen Thompson 30.00 80.00
11 Ausar Thompson 10.00 25.00
14 Keshad Johnson 5.00 12.00
15 Jacky Cui 12.00 30.00
16 PJ Hall 5.00 12.00
17 Trey Alexander 5.00 12.00
19 Ariel Hukporti 5.00 12.00
21 Kevin McCullar Jr. 6.00 15.00
22 Anton Watson 5.00 12.00
23 Cam Spencer 6.00 15.00
24 Quinten Post 12.00 30.00

2024-25 Totally Certified The Mighty
*MIRROR RED/99: 2.5X TO 6X BASIC
*MIRROR BLUE/49: 4X TO 10X BASIC
*MIRROR PLATINUM CAMO/25: 6X TO 15X BASIC
1 Kawhi Leonard .75 2.00
2 LeBron James 3.00 8.00
3 Kel'el Ware 1.00 2.50
4 Jaylen Brown .60 1.50
5 Jimmy Butler .60 1.50
6 Chet Holmgren .60 1.50
7 Stephen Curry 3.00 8.00
8 Giannis Antetokounmpo 1.50 4.00
9 Zaccharie Risacher 1.25 3.00
10 Luka Doncic 2.50 6.00
11 Zach Edey 1.25 3.00
12 Jayson Tatum 1.25 3.00
13 Zion Williamson 1.00 2.50
14 De'Aaron Fox .75 2.00
15 Nikola Jokic 2.00 5.00
16 Paul George .60 1.50
17 Alexandre Sarr 1.25 3.00
18 Anthony Edwards 2.00 5.00
19 Victor Wembanyama 3.00 8.00
20 Tidjane Salaun .40 1.00
21 Trae Young .75 2.00
22 Shai Gilgeous-Alexander 2.00 5.00
23 Ja Morant 1.25 3.00
24 Donovan Mitchell .75 2.00
25 Donovan Clingan 1.00 2.50

2024-25 Totally Certified Totally Certified Materials
STATED PRINT RUN 99-125 SER.#'d SETS
*MIRROR PURPLE/99: .4X TO 1X BASIC
*MIRROR RED/75: .5X TO 1.2X BASIC
*MIRROR BLUE/49: .6X TO 1.5X BASIC
*MIRROR PLATINUM CAMO/25: .75X TO 2X BASIC
1 Trae Young/125 8.00 20.00
2 Devin Booker/99 10.00 25.00
3 Brandon Miller/99 6.00 15.00
4 Bronny James Jr./125 12.00 30.00
5 Bub Carrington/125 10.00 25.00
6 Joel Embiid/99 6.00 15.00
7 Alexandre Sarr/125 12.00 30.00
8 Tidjane Salaun/125 4.00 10.00
9 Anthony Davis/99 10.00 25.00
10 Johnny Furphy/125 6.00 15.00
11 Giannis Antetokounmpo/99 15.00 40.00
12 Kristaps Porzingis/125 5.00 12.00
13 Ja Morant/99 12.00 30.00
14 Jaylen Brown/99 6.00 15.00
15 Stephon Castle/125 25.00 60.00
16 Rob Dillingham/125 10.00 25.00
17 Klay Thompson/99 10.00 25.00
18 Reed Sheppard/125 12.00 30.00
19 Donovan Mitchell/99 8.00 20.00
20 Brandon Ingram/125 4.00 10.00
21 Alperen Sengun/99 6.00 15.00
22 Zaccharie Risacher/125 12.00 30.00
23 Stephen Curry/125 30.00 80.00
24 Jimmy Butler/99 6.00 15.00
25 Paul George/125 6.00 15.00

2024-25 Totally Certified Totally Certified Signatures
1 Jay Huff 4.00 10.00
2 Cason Wallace 6.00 15.00
3 Cole Swider 4.00 10.00
5 Jabari Smith Jr. 5.00 12.00
6 Jabari Walker 3.00 8.00
7 E.J. Liddell 4.00 10.00
8 Usman Garuba 3.00 8.00
9 Sam Merrill 4.00 10.00
10 Johnny Juzang 4.00 10.00
11 Pete Nance 3.00 8.00
12 Tosan Evbuomwan 3.00 8.00
13 Johnny Davis 4.00 10.00
14 David Roddy 4.00 10.00
15 Keon Ellis 4.00 10.00
16 Perry Dozier Jr 3.00 8.00
17 Josh Minott 3.00 8.00
18 AJ Lawson 3.00 8.00
20 Keita Bates-Diop 3.00 8.00
21 Bryce McGowens 4.00 10.00
22 Mark Williams 4.00 10.00
23 Justin Champagnie 5.00 12.00
24 Ricky Council IV 3.00 8.00
25 Kevin Porter Jr. 5.00 12.00
26 Collin Gillespie 4.00 10.00
27 Nick Anderson 4.00 10.00
28 Gerald Wilkins 3.00 8.00
29 Charlie Scott 6.00 15.00
30 Alton Lister 3.00 8.00
31 Mark Aguirre 4.00 10.00
32 Brad Daugherty 4.00 10.00
33 Craig Hodges 4.00 10.00
34 Antoine Carr 4.00 10.00
35 James Donaldson 3.00 8.00
36 Cedric Ceballos 4.00 10.00
37 Melvin Ajinca 4.00 10.00
40 KJ Simpson Jr. 5.00 12.00
41 Adem Bona 6.00 15.00
42 Oso Ighodaro 6.00 15.00
43 Jaylen Wells 15.00 40.00
45 Pelle Larsson 6.00 15.00
46 Nikola Durisic 6.00 15.00
47 Harrison Ingram 5.00 12.00
48 Antonio Reeves 5.00 12.00
50 Tristen Newton 5.00 12.00

2024-25 Totally Certified Z Team Mirror
1 Ron Holland II 12.00 30.00
2 Victor Wembanyama 50.00 120.00
3 Dalton Knecht 20.00 50.00
4 Bronny James Jr. 20.00 50.00
5 Zaccharie Risacher 20.00 50.00
6 Luka Doncic 40.00 100.00
7 Zion Williamson 15.00 40.00
8 Chet Holmgren 10.00 25.00
9 Jalen Brunson 12.00 30.00
10 LeBron James 50.00 125.00
11 Trae Young 12.00 30.00
12 Devin Booker 15.00 40.00
13 Anthony Edwards 30.00 80.00
14 Alexandre Sarr 20.00 50.00
15 Kevin Durant 20.00 50.00
16 Reed Sheppard 20.00 50.00
17 Tyrese Maxey 12.00 30.00
18 Jayson Tatum 20.00 50.00
19 Giannis Antetokounmpo 25.00 60.00
20 Donovan Mitchell 12.00 30.00
21 Rob Dillingham 15.00 40.00
22 Ja Morant 20.00 50.00
23 Nikola Jokic 30.00 80.00
24 Shai Gilgeous-Alexander 30.00 80.00
25 Stephen Curry 50.00 120.00

1984-85 Trail Blazers Ball Boy
1 Kiki Vandeweghe 4.00 10.00

1990-91 Trail Blazers British Petroleum
COMPLETE SET (6) 6.00 15.00
1 Danny Ainge 1.50 4.00
2 Clyde Drexler 3.00 8.00
3 Kevin Duckworth .75 2.00
4 Jerome Kersey .75 2.00
5 Terry Porter .75 2.00
6 Buck Williams .75 2.00

1991-92 Trail Blazers Dairy Queen Glasses
COMPLETE SET (6) 6.00 15.00
1 Clyde Drexler 2.00 5.00
2 Kevin Duckworth .75 2.00
3 Jerome Kersey .75 2.00
4 Terry Porter .75 2.00
5 Clifford Robinson 1.25 3.00
6 Buck Williams .75 2.00

1992-93 Trail Blazers Dairy Queen Glasses
COMPLETE SET (6) 6.00 15.00
1 Clyde Drexler 2.00 5.00
2 Kevin Duckworth .75 2.00
3 Jerome Kersey .75 2.00
4 Terry Porter .75 2.00
5 Clifford Robinson 1.25 3.00
6 Buck Williams .75 2.00

1984-85 Trail Blazers Franz/Star
COMPLETE SET (13) 50.00 120.00
1 Jack Ramsay CO 1.50 4.00
2 Sam Bowie 2.50 6.00
3 Kenny Carr .75 2.00
4 Steve Colter .75 2.00
5 Clyde Drexler 40.00 100.00
6 Jerome Kersey 2.50 6.00
7 Audie Norris .75 2.00
8 Jim Paxson 1.25 3.00
9 Tom Scheffler 1.00 2.50
10 Bernard Thompson .75 2.00
11 Mychal Thompson 1.25 3.00
12 Darnell Valentine 1.00 2.50
13 Kiki Vandeweghe 1.25 3.00

1985-86 Trail Blazers Franz/Star
COMPLETE SET (13) 20.00 50.00
1 Jack Ramsay CO 1.50 4.00
2 Sam Bowie 1.50 4.00
3 Kenny Carr .75 2.00
4 Steve Colter .75 2.00
5 Clyde Drexler 12.00 30.00
6 Ken Johnson .75 2.00
7 Caldwell Jones .75 2.00
8 Jerome Kersey 1.25 3.00
9 Jim Paxson 1.25 3.00
10 Terry Porter 4.00 10.00
11 Mychal Thompson 1.25 3.00
12 Darnell Valentine .75 2.00
13 Kiki Vandeweghe 1.25 3.00

1986-87 Trail Blazers Franz
COMPLETE SET (13) 40.00 80.00
1 Walter Berry 1.50 4.00
2 Sam Bowie 2.50 6.00
3 Kenny Carr 1.50 4.00
4 Clyde Drexler 15.00 40.00
5 Michael Holton 1.50 4.00
6 Steve Johnson 1.50 4.00
7 Caldwell Jones 1.50 4.00
8 Jerome Kersey 2.00 5.00
9 Fernando Martin 1.50 4.00
10 Jim Paxson 2.00 5.00
11 Terry Porter 3.00 8.00
12 Kiki Vandeweghe 3.00 8.00
13 Mike Schuler CO 1.50 4.00

1987-88 Trail Blazers Franz
COMPLETE SET (13) 50.00 100.00
1 Clyde Drexler 20.00 50.00
2 Kevin Duckworth 2.50 6.00
3 Michael Holton 2.00 5.00
4 Steve Johnson 1.50 4.00
5 Caldwell Jones 2.00 5.00
6 Jerome Kersey 3.00 8.00
7 Maurice Lucas 4.00 10.00
8 Jim Paxson 2.50 6.00
9 Terry Porter 4.00 10.00
10 Mike Schuler CO 1.50 4.00
11 Kiki Vandeweghe 3.00 8.00
12 Steve Johnson 1.50 4.00
13 Kiki Vandeweghe 4.00 10.00

1988-89 Trail Blazers Franz
COMPLETE SET (13) 30.00 60.00
1 Richard Anderson 1.50 4.00
2 Sam Bowie 2.00 5.00
3 Mark Bryant 1.50 4.00
4 Clyde Drexler 15.00 40.00
5 Kevin Duckworth 1.50 4.00
6 Rolando Ferreira 1.00 2.50
7 Steve Johnson 1.00 2.50
8 Caldwell Jones 1.50 4.00
9 Jerome Kersey 1.50 4.00
10 Terry Porter 2.50 6.00
11 Mike Schuler CO 1.00 2.50
12 Jerry Sichting 1.50 4.00
13 Kiki Vandeweghe 2.50 6.00

1989-90 Trail Blazers Franz
COMPLETE SET (20) 20.00 50.00
1 Rick Adelman CO 1.00 2.50
2 Mark Bryant .75 2.00
3 Wayne Cooper .75 2.00
4 Kevin Duckworth .75 2.00
5 Clyde Drexler 8.00 20.00
6 Byron Irvin .75 2.00
7 Jerome Kersey 1.00 2.50
8 Drazen Petrovic 8.00 20.00
9 Terry Porter 1.25 3.00
10 Cliff Robinson 4.00 10.00
11 Buck Williams 2.00 5.00
12 Lionel Hollins 1.00 2.50
13 Maurice Lucas 1.00 2.50
14 Calvin Natt .75 2.00
15 Lloyd Neal .75 2.00
16 Jim Paxson 1.00 2.50
17 Geoff Petrie 1.00 2.50
18 Larry Steele .75 2.00
19 Mychal Thompson 1.00 2.50
20 Bill Walton 4.00 10.00

1990-91 Trail Blazers Franz
COMPLETE SET (20) 15.00 40.00
1 Team Card .75 2.00
2 1989-90 Playoffs .30 .75
3 1989-90 Playoffs .30 .75
4 1989-90 Playoffs .30 .75
5 1989-90 Playoffs
Clyde Drexler 2.50 6.00
6 Bill Walton 2.00 5.00
7 Rick Adelman CO .40 1.00
8 John Schalow ACO and
John Wetzel ACO .30 .75
9 Alaa Abdelnaby .30 .75
10 Danny Ainge 1.25 3.00
11 Mark Bryant .30 .75
12 Wayne Cooper .30 .75
13 Clyde Drexler 5.00 12.00
14 Kevin Duckworth .40 1.00
15 Jerome Kersey .40 1.00
16 Drazen Petrovic 3.00 8.00
17 Terry Porter 1.25 3.00
18 Cliff Robinson 8.00 20.00
19 Buck Williams 1.25 3.00
20 Danny Young .30 .75

1991-92 Trail Blazers Franz
COMPLETE SET (17) 10.00 25.00
1 Team Photo .75 2.00
2 Blazers All-Star Weekend .40 1.00
3 Buck Williams .75 2.00
4 Rick Adelman CO .60 1.50
5 Alaa Abdelnaby .30 .75
6 Danny Ainge 1.25 3.00
7 Mark Bryant .30 .75
8 Wayne Cooper .30 .75
9 Walter Davis 1.25 3.00
10 Clyde Drexler 5.00 12.00
11 Kevin Duckworth .40 1.00
12 Jerome Kersey .60 1.50
13 Terry Porter .75 2.00
14 Cliff Robinson 1.50 4.00
15 Buck Williams .75 2.00
16 Danny Young .30 .75
17 Robert Pack 1.25 3.00

1992-93 Trail Blazers Franz
COMPLETE SET (20) 10.00 25.00
1 Team Photo .75 2.00
2 Buck Williams
1991-92 NBA Playoffs .75 2.00
3 Clifford Robinson
1991-92 NBA Playoffs .75 2.00
4 Terry Porter
1991-92 NBA Playoffs .40 1.00
5 Jerome Kersey
Clyde Drexler
1991-92 NBA Playoffs 1.25 3.00
6 Clyde Drexler AS 1.50 4.00
7 Rick Adelman CO .40 1.00
8 Mark Bryant .20 .50
9 Clyde Drexler 3.00 8.00
10 Kevin Duckworth .30 .75
11 Jerome Kersey UER
(Card back has bio and
stats for Tracy Murray) .40 1.00
12 Terry Porter .60 1.50
13 Cliff Robinson .75 2.00
14 Rod Strickland .60 1.50
15 Buck Williams .75 2.00
16 Mario Elie .40 1.00
17 Lamont Strothers .20 .50
18 Dave Johnson .20 .50
19 Tracy Murray .60 1.50
20 Reggie Smith .20 .50

1993-94 Trail Blazers Franz
COMPLETE SET (20) 10.00 25.00
1 Team Photo .75 2.00
2 Jack Schalow ACO
Rick Adelman CO
John Wetzel ACO .40 1.00
3 Harry Glickman
Trail Blazers Walk of
Fame Charter Member .40 1.00
4 Mark Bryant .20 .50
5 Clyde Drexler 4.00 10.00
6 Maurice Lucas
Trail Blazers Walk of
Fame Charter Member .75 2.00
7 Chris Dudley .20 .50
8 Harvey Grant .20 .50
9 Geoff Petrie
Trail Blazers Walk of
Fame Charter Member .40 1.00
10 Reggie Smith .20 .50
11 Jerome Kersey UER
(Bio& stats& and career
summary are Murray's) .40 1.00
12 Jack Ramsay CO
Trail Blazers Walk of
Fame Charter Member .60 1.50
13 Tracy Murray .40 1.00
14 Terry Porter .60 1.50
15 Bill Walton
Trail Blazers Walk of
Fame Charter Member 2.00 5.00
16 Cliff Robinson 1.25 3.00
17 James Robinson .40 1.00
18 Larry Weinberg
Trail Blazers Walk of
Fame Charter Member .40 1.00
19 Rod Strickland .60 1.50
20 Buck Williams .75 2.00

1994-95 Trail Blazers Franz
COMPLETE SET (20) 10.00 25.00
1 Team Photo .75 2.00
2 P.J. Carlesimo CO .75 2.00
3 Bill Walton
Glickman's All-Time Team 1.50 4.00
4 Mark Bryant .20 .50
5 Clyde Drexler 2.50 6.00
6 Chris Dudley .20 .50
7 Buck Williams
Glickman's All-Time Team .75 2.00
8 James Edwards .20 .50
9 Harvey Grant .30 .75
10 Jerome Kersey .30 .75
11 Clyde Drexler
Glickman's All-Time Team 1.50 4.00
12 Aaron McKie .50 1.25
13 Tracy Murray .20 .50
14 Terry Porter .40 1.00
15 Geoff Petrie
Glickman's All-Time Team .40 1.00
16 Clifford Robinson .75 2.00
17 James Robinson .20 .50
18 Rod Strickland .50 1.25
19 Maurice Lucas
Glickman's All-Time Team .60 1.50
20 Buck Williams .75 2.00

1995-96 Trail Blazers Franz
COMPLETE SET (13) 4.00 10.00
1 Clifford Robinson .60 1.50
2 Randolph Childress .20 .50
3 Chris Dudley .20 .50
4 Aaron McKie .40 1.00
5 Harvey Grant .30 .75
6 Gary Trent .60 1.50
7 P.J. Carlesimo CO .20 .50
8 Dontonio Wingfield .20 .50
9 Arvydas Sabonis 1.50 4.00
10 James Robinson .20 .50
11 Rod Strickland .40 1.00
12 Bill Curley .20 .50
13 Buck Williams .60 1.50

1996-97 Trail Blazers Franz
COMPLETE SET (7) 6.00 15.00
1 Jermaine O'Neal 3.00 8.00
2 Clifford Robinson .40 1.00
3 Gary Trent .20 .50
4 Kenny Anderson .20 .50
5 Arvydas Sabonis .75 2.00
6 Isaiah Rider .50 1.25
7 Rasheed Wallace 2.00 5.00
NNO Arvydas Sabonis Tatoo
In Black Uniform 2.00 5.00
NNO Arvydas Sabonis Tatoo
Passing behind back 2.00 5.00

1975-76 Trail Blazers Iron Ons
COMPLETE SET (7) 20.00 40.00
1 Dan Anderson 1.25 3.00
2 Barry Clemens 1.25 3.00
3 Bob Gross 1.50 4.00
4 LaRue Martin 1.25 3.00
5 Larry Steele 1.50 4.00
6 Bill Walton 12.50 25.00
7 Sidney Wicks 3.00 8.00

1984 Trail Blazers Mr. Z's/Star 5x7
COMPLETE SET (5) 100.00 200.00
1 Kenny Carr 8.00 20.00
2 Clyde Drexler 60.00 120.00
3 Audie Norris 20.00 40.00
4 Mychal Thompson 8.00 20.00
5 Darnell Valentine 8.00 20.00

1981-82 Trail Blazers Playoff Tickets
COMPLETE SET 40.00 100.00
1A Billy Ray Bates
White 1.50 4.00
1B Billy Ray Bates
Blue 1.50 4.00
2A Bob Gross
Orange 2.00 5.00
2B Bob Gross
Yellow 2.00 5.00
3A Michael Harper
Orange 1.50 4.00
3B Michael Harper
Yellow 1.50 4.00
4A Kevin Kunnert
Yellow 1.50 4.00
4B Kevin Kunnert
Orange 1.50 4.00
4C Kevin Kunnert
Pink 1.50 4.00
5A Calvin Natt
Yellow 1.50 4.00
5B Calvin Natt
Blue 1.50 4.00
6A Jim Paxson
Orange 2.00 5.00
6B Jim Paxson
Yellow 2.00 5.00
7A Kelvin Ransey
Blue 1.50 4.00
7B Kelvin Ransey
Pink 1.50 4.00
8A Larry Steele
Pink 1.50 4.00
8B Larry Steele
Yellow 1.50 4.00
9 Mychal Thompson
Yellow 2.00 5.00
10 Dave Twardzik 1.50 4.00
11A Marvin Webster
Yellow 1.50 4.00
11B Marvin Webster
White 1.50 4.00
12 George Gervin 3.00 8.00
13 Julius Erving 6.00 15.00
14 Moses Malone 3.00 8.00

1982-83 Trail Blazers Playoff Tickets
COMPLETE SET (10) 30.00 75.00
1 Wayne Cooper
Blue 1.50 4.00
1 Wayne Cooper
White 1.50 4.00
2 Jeff Judkins
White 1.50 4.00
2 Jeff Judkins
Blue 1.50 4.00
3 Jeff Lamp
Blue 1.50 4.00
3 Jeff Lamp
White 1.50 4.00
4 Lafayette Lever
White 2.00 5.00
4 Lafayette Lever
Blue 2.00 5.00
5 Audie Norris
White 1.50 4.00
5 Audie Norris
Blue 1.50 4.00
6 Larry Steele
Blue 1.50 4.00
6 Larry Steele
White 1.50 4.00
7 Linton Townes
Blue 1.50 4.00
7 Linton Townes
White 1.50 4.00
8 Dave Twardzik
White UER
Spelled Twarzik 1.50 4.00
8 Dave Twardzik
Blue UER
Spelled Twarzik 1.50 4.00
9 Darnell Valentine
White 1.50 4.00
9 Darnell Valentine
Blue 1.50 4.00
10 Pete Verhoeven
White 1.50 4.00
10 Pete Verhoeven
Blue 1.50 4.00

1983-84 Trail Blazers Playoff Tickets
COMPLETE SET (2) 4.00 10.00
1 Jim Paxson
Blue 2.00 5.00
2 Mychal Thompson
White 2.00 5.00

1984-85 Trail Blazers Playoff Tickets
COMPLETE SET (7) 15.00 30.00
1 Rick Adelman ACO 2.00 5.00
2 Bucky Buckwalter ACO 1.50 4.00
3 Audie Norris 1.50 4.00
4 Jim Paxson 1.50 4.00
5 Jack Ramsay CO 3.00 8.00
6 Tom Scheffler 1.50 4.00
7 Kiki Vandeweghe 3.00 8.00

1977-78 Trail Blazers Police
COMPLETE SET (14) 25.00 50.00
10 Corky Calhoun 1.25 3.00
13 Dave Twardzik 2.00 5.00
14 Lionel Hollins 2.00 5.00
15 Larry Steele 2.00 5.00
16 Johnny Davis 1.50 4.00
20 Maurice Lucas 3.00 8.00
23 T.R. Dunn 1.50 4.00
25 Tom Owens 1.25 3.00
30 Bob Gross 1.50 4.00
32 Bill Walton 10.00 20.00
36 Lloyd Neal 1.25 3.00
NNO Jack Ramsay CO 2.50 6.00
NNO Jack McKinney ACO 2.00 5.00
NNO Ron Culp TR 1.25 3.00

1979-80 Trail Blazers Police
COMPLETE SET (16) 4.00 10.00
4 Jim Paxson .75 2.00
9 Lionel Hollins .60 1.50
10 Ron Brewer .30 .75
11 Abdul Jeelani .30 .75
13 Dave Twardzik .60 1.50
15 Larry Steele .50 1.25
20 Maurice Lucas .75 2.00
23 T.R. Dunn .40 1.00
25 Tom Owens .30 .75
30 Bob Gross .40 1.00
42 Kermit Washington .50 1.25
43 Mychal Thompson .75 2.00
44 Kevin Kunnert .30 .75
xx Jack Ramsay CO .60 1.50
xx Bucky Buckwalter ACO .30 .75
xx Bill Schonely ANN .30 .75

1981-82 Trail Blazers Police
COMPLETE SET (16) 4.00 10.00
3 Jeff Lamp .75 2.00
4 Jim Paxson .60 1.50
10 Darnell Valentine .40 1.00
12 Billy Ray Bates .40 1.00
14 Kelvin Ransey .30 .75
30 Bob Gross .40 1.00
31 Peter Verhoeven .40 1.00
32 Mike Harper .30 .75
33 Calvin Natt .40 1.00
40 Petur Gudmundsson .40 1.00
42 Kermit Washington .40 1.00
43 Mychal Thompson .60 1.50
44 Kevin Kunnert .40 1.00
NNO Jack Ramsay CO .60 1.50
NNO Bucky Buckwalter ACO .30 .75
NNO Jimmy Lynam ACO .40 1.00

1982-83 Trail Blazers Police
COMPLETE SET (16) 4.00 10.00
2 Linton Townes .30 .75
3 Jeff Lamp .40 1.00
4 Jim Paxson .40 1.00
12 Lafayette Lever .75 2.00
14 Darnell Valentine .40 1.00
22 Jeff Judkins .30 .75
24 Audie Norris .30 .75
31 Peter Verhoeven .30 .75
33 Calvin Natt .40 1.00
34 Kenny Carr .40 1.00
42 Wayne Cooper .40 1.00
43 Mychal Thompson .60 1.50
NNO Jack Ramsay CO .75 2.00
NNO Bucky Buckwalter ACO .30 .75
NNO Jim Lynam ACO .40 1.00

1983-84 Trail Blazers Police
COMPLETE SET (15) 10.00 25.00
3 Jeff Lamp .40 1.00
4 Jim Paxson .40 1.00
12 Lafayette Lever .40 1.00
14 Darnell Valentine .40 1.00
22 Clyde Drexler 6.00 15.00
24 Audie Norris .30 .75
31 Peter Verhoeven .30 .75
33 Calvin Natt .40 1.00
34 Kenny Carr .30 .75
42 Wayne Cooper .30 .75
43 Mychal Thompson .60 1.50
54 Tom Piotrowski .30 .75
NNO Jack Ramsay CO .60 1.50
NNO Morris Buckwalter ACO
Rick Adelman ACO .50 1.25
NNO Ron Culp TR .30 .75
NNO Dave Twardzik ANN
and Bill Schonely ANN .30 .75

1984-85 Trail Blazers Police
COMPLETE SET (16) 6.00 15.00
1 Portland Team .75 2.00
2 Jim Paxson .40 1.00
3 Bernard Thompson .30 .75
4 Darnell Valentine .30 .75
5 Jack Ramsay CO
Rick Adelman ACO
Bucky Buckwalter ACO .75 2.00
6 Steve Colter .30 .75
7 Clyde Drexler 3.00 8.00
8 Audie Norris .30 .75
9 Jerome Kersey 1.25 3.00
10 Sam Bowie 1.25 3.00
11 Kenny Carr .30 .75
12 Lloyd Neal .30 .75
13 Mychal Thompson .40 1.00
14 Geoff Petrie .40 1.00
15 Tom Scheffler .30 .75
16 Kiki Vandeweghe .75 2.00

1978-79 Trail Blazers Portfolio
COMPLETE SET (10) 20.00 40.00
1 Kim Anderson and
Clemon Johnson 1.25 3.00
2 T.R. Dunn 1.50 4.00
3 Bob Gross 1.50 4.00
4 Lionel Hollins 2.50 6.00
5 Maurice Lucas 3.00 8.00
6 Lloyd Neal 1.25 3.00
7 Tom Owens 1.25 3.00
8 Willie Smith and
Ron Brewer 1.25 3.00
9 Larry Steele 2.50 6.00
10 Dave Twardzik 2.50 6.00

1991-92 Trail Blazers Posters
COMPLETE SET (5) 8.00 20.00
1 Clyde Drexler 6.00 15.00
2 Kevin Duckworth 1.25 3.00

3 Jerome Kersey 1.25 3.00
4 Terry Porter 1.50 4.00
5 Buck Williams 1.50 4.00

1977-78 Trail Blazers RC Glasses
COMPLETE SET (8) 50.00 100.00
1 Johnny Davis 5.00 10.00
2 Bob Gross 5.00 10.00
3 Lionel Hollins 5.00 10.00
4 Maurice Lucas 7.50 15.00
5 Lloyd Neal 5.00 10.00
6 Larry Steele 5.00 10.00
7 Dave Twardzik 5.00 10.00
8 Bill Walton 20.00 40.00

1972-73 Trail Blazers Team Issue
COMPLETE SET (25) 65.00 125.00
1 Rick Adelman 3.00 8.00
2 Rick Adelman IA 2.50 6.00
3 Bob Davis 2.00 5.00
4 Bob Davis IA 2.00 5.00
5 Bobby Fields 2.00 5.00
6 Bobby Fields IA 2.00 5.00
7 Stu Inman VP 2.00 5.00
8 Neil Johnston ACO 3.00 8.00
9 Ollie Johnson 2.00 5.00
10 Ollie Johnson IA 2.00 5.00
11 LaRue Martin 2.00 5.00
12 LaRue Martin IA 2.00 5.00
13 Leo Marty TR 2.00 5.00
14 Jack McCloskey CO 2.00 5.00
15 Stan McKenzie 2.00 5.00
16 Stan McKenzie IA 2.00 5.00
17 Lloyd Neal 2.00 5.00
18 Lloyd Neal IA 2.00 5.00
19 Geoffrey Petrie 5.00 10.00
20 Geoffrey Petrie IA 3.00 8.00
21 Dale Schlueter 2.00 5.00
22 Dale Schlueter IA 2.00 5.00
23 Larry Steele 3.00 8.00
24 Larry Steele IA 2.50 6.00
25 Sidney Wicks IA 7.50 15.00

1976-77 Trail Blazers Team Issue
COMPLETE SET (15) 20.00 40.00
1 Dan Anderson 1.25 3.00
2 Barry Clemens 1.25 3.00
3 Bob Gross 1.25 3.00
4 Steve Hawes 1.25 3.00
5 Lionel Hollins 1.50 4.00
6 Maurice Lucas 2.50 6.00
7 Lloyd Neal 1.25 3.00
8 Larry Steele 1.25 3.00
9 Dave Twardzik 1.25 3.00
10 Wally Walker 1.25 3.00
11 Stu Inman VP 1.25 3.00
12 Ron Culp TR 1.25 3.00
13 Jack McKinney CO 1.25 3.00
14 Harry Glickman EVP 1.25 3.00
15 Larry Weinberg PRES 1.25 3.00

1977-78 Trail Blazers Team Issue
COMPLETE SET (13) 17.50 35.00
1 Corky Calhoun .75 2.00
2 Johnny Davis .75 2.00
3 T.R. Dunn .75 2.00
4 Bob Gross .75 2.00
5 Lionel Hollins .75 2.00
6 Maurice Lucas 1.50 4.00
7 Lloyd Neal .75 2.00
8 Tom Owens .75 2.00
9 Jack Ramsey CO 1.50 4.00
10 Larry Steele .75 2.00
11 Dave Twardzik .75 2.00
12 Bill Walton 3.00 8.00
13 Portland Trail Blazers Team Composite 1.50 4.00

1971-72 Trail Blazers Texaco
COMPLETE SET (12) 30.00 60.00
1 Rick Adelman 5.00 12.00
2 Gary Gregor 3.00 8.00
3 Ron Knight 3.00 8.00
4 Jim Marsh 3.00 8.00
5 Willie McCarter 3.00 8.00
6 Stan McKenzie 3.00 8.00
7 Geoff Petrie 5.00 12.00
8 Dale Schlueter 3.00 8.00
9 Bill Smith 3.00 8.00
10 Larry Steele 3.00 8.00
11 Sidney Wicks 6.00 15.00
12 Charles Yelverton 3.00 8.00

1996-97 UD3
COMPLETE SET (60) 40.00 100.00
1 Kerry Kittles RC .40 1.00
2 Stephon Marbury RC 1.25 3.00
3 Jermaine O'Neal RC .60 1.50
4 Shareef Abdur-Rahim RC .60 1.50
5 Ray Allen RC 2.00 5.00
6 Antoine Walker RC .60 1.50
7 Erick Dampier RC .40 1.00
8 Walter McCarty RC .40 1.00
9 Todd Fuller RC .25 .60
10 Tony Delk RC .40 1.00
11 Marcus Camby RC .60 1.50
12 John Wallace RC .30 .75
13 Vitaly Potapenko RC .30 .75
14 Allen Iverson RC 3.00 8.00
15 Steve Nash RC 2.50 6.00
16 Derek Fisher RC .50 1.25
17 Samaki Walker RC .30 .75
18 Roy Rogers RC .30 .75
19 Kobe Bryant RC 20.00 50.00
20 Lorenzen Wright RC .30 .75
21 Kevin Garnett 1.25 3.00
22 Hakeem Olajuwon .75 2.00
23 Michael Jordan 4.00 10.00
24 John Stockton .75 2.00
25 Terrell Brandon .30 .75
26 Damon Stoudamire .40 1.00
27 Charles Barkley 1.00 2.50
28 Dikembe Mutombo .60 1.50
29 Gary Payton .60 1.50
30 Patrick Ewing .60 1.50
31 Dennis Rodman 1.00 2.50
32 Joe Smith .30 .75
33 Grant Hill .60 1.50
34 Shaquille O'Neal 1.50 4.00
35 Kevin Johnson .40 1.00
36 David Robinson .75 2.00
37 Juwan Howard .40 1.00
38 Mitch Richmond .50 1.25
39 Alonzo Mourning .60 1.50
40 Reggie Miller .75 2.00
41 Shawn Kemp .60 1.50
42 Scottie Pippen 1.00 2.50
43 Kobe Bryant 12.00 30.00
44 Anfernee Hardaway 1.00 2.50
45 Brent Barry .30 .75
46 Glenn Robinson .40 1.00
47 Karl Malone .75 2.00
48 Chris Webber .50 1.25
49 Danny Manning .30 .75
50 Antonio McDyess .40 1.00
51 Dominique Wilkins .60 1.50
52 Vin Baker .30 .75
53 Isaiah Rider .30 .75
54 Eddie Jones .40 1.00
55 Glen Rice .40 1.00
56 Larry Johnson .50 1.25
57 Latrell Sprewell .40 1.00
58 Sean Elliott .40 1.00
59 Clyde Drexler .60 1.50
60 Jerry Stackhouse .50 1.25

1996-97 UD3 Court Commemorative Autographs
STATED ODDS 1:1500
C1 Michael Jordan 2,000.00 4,000.00
C2 Damon Stoudamire 20.00 50.00
C3 Anfernee Hardaway 125.00 250.00
C4 Shawn Kemp 125.00 250.00

1996-97 UD3 Superstar Spotlight
COMPLETE SET (10) 125.00 300.00
STATED ODDS 1:144
S1 Shaquille O'Neal 8.00 20.00
S2 Alonzo Mourning 6.00 15.00
S3 Anfernee Hardaway 8.00 20.00
S4 Karl Malone 8.00 20.00
S5 Michael Jordan 125.00 300.00
S6 Hakeem Olajuwon 8.00 20.00
S7 Shawn Kemp 6.00 15.00
S8 Allen Iverson 30.00 80.00
S9 Dennis Rodman 10.00 25.00
S10 Charles Barkley 10.00 25.00

1996-97 UD3 The Winning Edge
COMPLETE SET (20) 12.00 30.00
STATED ODDS 1:11
W1 Michael Jordan 8.00 20.00
W2 Charles Barkley 2.00 5.00
W3 Reggie Miller 1.50 4.00
W4 Grant Hill 1.25 3.00
W5 Larry Johnson 1.00 2.50
W6 Hakeem Olajuwon 1.50 4.00
W7 Anfernee Hardaway 2.00 5.00
W8 Shaquille O'Neal 3.00 8.00
W9 Vin Baker .60 1.50
W10 Kevin Garnett 2.50 6.00
W11 Juwan Howard .75 2.00
W12 John Stockton 1.50 4.00
W13 Mookie Blaylock .75 2.00
W14 Shawn Kemp 1.25 3.00
W15 David Robinson 1.50 4.00
W16 Kevin Johnson .75 2.00
W17 Joe Dumars 1.00 2.50
W18 Marcus Camby 1.25 3.00
W19 Clyde Drexler 1.25 3.00
W20 Chris Webber 1.00 2.50

1997-98 UD3
COMPLETE SET (60) 15.00 40.00
1 Anfernee Hardaway JM 1.00 2.50
2 Alonzo Mourning JM .60 1.50
3 Grant Hill JM .60 1.50
4 Kerry Kittles JM .30 .75
5 Latrell Sprewell JM .50 1.25
6 Rasheed Wallace JM .50 1.25
7 Jerry Stackhouse JM .40 1.00
8 Glen Rice JM .40 1.00
9 Marcus Camby JM .40 1.00
10 Scottie Pippen JM 1.00 2.50
11 Patrick Ewing JM .60 1.50
12 Michael Finley JM .40 1.00
13 Karl Malone JM .75 2.00
14 Antonio McDyess JM .40 1.00
15 Michael Jordan JM 4.00 10.00
16 Clyde Drexler JM .60 1.50
17 Brent Barry JM .30 .75
18 Glenn Robinson JM .40 1.00
19 Kobe Bryant JM 4.00 10.00
20 Reggie Miller JM .75 2.00
21 John Stockton AS .75 2.00
22 Gary Payton AS .60 1.50
23 Michael Jordan AS 4.00 10.00
24 Vin Baker AS .30 .75
25 Karl Malone AS .75 2.00
26 Juwan Howard AS .30 .75
27 Charles Barkley AS 1.00 2.50
28 Jason Kidd AS .60 1.50
29 Joe Dumars AS .50 1.25
30 Anfernee Hardaway AS 1.00 2.50
31 Mitch Richmond AS .50 1.25
32 Alonzo Mourning AS .60 1.50
33 Grant Hill AS .60 1.50
34 Shaquille O'Neal AS 1.25 3.00
35 Scottie Pippen AS 1.00 2.50
36 Reggie Miller AS .75 2.00
37 Hakeem Olajuwon AS .75 2.00
38 Tim Hardaway AS .50 1.25
39 David Robinson AS .75 2.00
40 Shawn Kemp AS .60 1.50
41 Allen Iverson BP 1.25 3.00
42 Stephon Marbury BP .50 1.25
43 Dennis Rodman BP 1.00 2.50
44 Terrell Brandon BP .30 .75
45 Michael Jordan BP 4.00 10.00
46 Kerry Kittles BP .30 .75
47 Hakeem Olajuwon BP .75 2.00
48 Loy Vaught BP .30 .75
49 Antoine Walker BP .40 1.00
50 Gary Payton BP .60 1.50
51 Kevin Johnson BP .40 1.00
52 Kevin Garnett BP 1.00 2.50
53 Shareef Abdur-Rahim BP .40 1.00
54 Larry Johnson BP .50 1.25
55 Dikembe Mutombo BP .60 1.50
56 Chris Webber BP .50 1.25
57 Joe Smith BP .30 .75
58 Kendall Gill BP .30 .75
59 Kenny Anderson BP .30 .75
60 Damon Stoudamire BP .40 1.00
NNO Michael Jordan PROMO 4.00 10.00

1997-98 UD3 Awesome Action
COMPLETE SET (20) 50.00 120.00
STATED ODDS 1:11
A1 Michael Jordan 20.00 50.00
A2 Nick Van Exel 2.00 5.00
A3 Jerry Stackhouse 2.00 5.00
A4 Shawn Kemp 3.00 8.00
A5 Hakeem Olajuwon 4.00 10.00
A6 Grant Hill 3.00 8.00
A7 Scottie Pippen 5.00 12.00
A8 Alonzo Mourning 6.00 15.00
A9 Damon Stoudamire 2.00 5.00
A10 Kevin Garnett 5.00 12.00
A11 Anfernee Hardaway 5.00 12.00
A12 Shareef Abdur-Rahim 2.00 5.00
A13 Allen Iverson 6.00 15.00
A14 Dennis Rodman 5.00 12.00
A15 Shaquille O'Neal 6.00 15.00
A16 Jason Kidd 3.00 8.00
A17 Gary Payton 3.00 8.00
A18 Dikembe Mutombo 3.00 8.00
A19 Karl Malone 4.00 10.00
A20 Stephon Marbury 2.50 6.00

1997-98 UD3 MJ3
MJ3-1 STATED ODDS 1:45
MJ3-2 STATED ODDS 1:119
MJ3-3 STATED ODDS 1:167
MJ31 Michael Jordan 50.00 120.00
MJ32 Michael Jordan 75.00 200.00
MJ33 Michael Jordan 150.00 400.00

1997-98 UD3 Rookie Portfolio
COMPLETE SET (10) 25.00 60.00
STATED ODDS 1:144
R1 Tim Duncan 25.00 60.00
R2 Keith Van Horn 2.50 6.00
R3 Chauncey Billups 5.00 12.00
R4 Antonio Daniels 1.50 4.00
R5 Tony Battie 1.50 4.00
R6 Ron Mercer 2.00 5.00
R7 Tim Thomas 2.00 5.00
R8 Adonal Foyle 1.25 3.00
R9 Tracy McGrady 8.00 20.00
R10 Danny Fortson 1.50 4.00

1997-98 UD3 Season Ticket Autographs
STATED ODDS 1:1,800
AH Anfernee Hardaway 500.00 1,000.00
JH Juwan Howard 75.00 200.00
MJ Michael Jordan 60,000.00 100,000.00
TH Tim Hardaway 200.00 500.00

1997-98 UD3 Season Ticket Trade
AHT Anfernee Hardaway 500.00 1,000.00
AMT Alonzo Mourning 125.00 300.00
EJT Eddie Jones 75.00 200.00
GPT Gary Payton 300.00 600.00
JHT Juwan Howard 50.00 120.00
KBT Kobe Bryant 2,000.00 4,000.00
LST Latrell Sprewell 75.00 200.00
MJT Michael Jordan 4,000.00 8,000.00
TDT Tim Duncan 1,000.00 2,000.00
THT Tim Hardaway 125.00 300.00

2000 UDA The Jordan Experience Printer's Proofs
COMMON CARD (1-12) 40.00 100.00

2002-03 UD Authentics
COMPLETE SET (132) 150.00 300.00
COMP.SET w/o SP's (90) 15.00 40.00
91-123 PRINT RUN 799 SER.#'d SETS
124-132 PRINT RUN 499 SER.#'d SETS
1 Shareef Abdur-Rahim .30 .75
2 Jason Terry .25 .60
3 Glenn Robinson .30 .75
4 Paul Pierce .50 1.25
5 Antoine Walker .25 .60
6 Eric Williams .20 .50
7 Kedrick Brown .20 .50
8 Jalen Rose .25 .60
9 Tyson Chandler .30 .75
10 Eddy Curry .20 .50
11 Darius Miles .20 .50
12 Lamond Murray .20 .50
13 Chris Mihm .20 .50
14 Dirk Nowitzki .75 2.00
15 Steve Nash .60 1.50
16 Michael Finley .30 .75
17 Raef LaFrentz .20 .50
18 James Posey .20 .50
19 Juwan Howard .25 .60
20 Jerry Stackhouse .30 .75
21 Ben Wallace .40 1.00
22 Clifford Robinson .30 .75
23 Jason Richardson .30 .75
24 Antawn Jamison .25 .60
25 Gilbert Arenas .30 .75
26 Steve Francis .30 .75
27 Eddie Griffin .20 .50
28 Cuttino Mobley .20 .50
29 Reggie Miller .60 1.50
30 Jamaal Tinsley .30 .75
31 Jermaine O'Neal .25 .60
32 Elton Brand .25 .60
33 Lamar Odom .30 .75
34 Andre Miller .25 .60
35 Kobe Bryant 2.50 6.00
36 Shaquille O'Neal 1.25 3.00
37 Derek Fisher .30 .75
38 Devean George .20 .50
39 Pau Gasol .50 1.25
40 Shane Battier .30 .75
41 Alonzo Mourning .50 1.25
42 Brian Grant .20 .50
43 Eddie Jones .30 .75
44 Ray Allen .50 1.25
45 Tim Thomas .20 .50
46 Kevin Garnett .75 2.00
47 Wally Szczerbiak .25 .60
48 Terrell Brandon .25 .60
49 Jason Kidd .50 1.25
50 Dikembe Mutombo .50 1.25
51 Richard Jefferson .25 .60
52 Baron Davis .30 .75
53 Jamal Mashburn .25 .60
54 David Wesley .20 .50
55 P.J. Brown .20 .50
56 Latrell Sprewell .30 .75
57 Allan Houston .30 .75
58 Antonio McDyess .25 .60
59 Tracy McGrady .50 1.25
60 Mike Miller .25 .60
61 Darrell Armstrong .20 .50
62 Allen Iverson .75 2.00
63 Keith Van Horn .25 .60
64 Stephon Marbury .40 1.00
65 Shawn Marion .30 .75
66 Anfernee Hardaway .75 2.00
67 Rasheed Wallace .40 1.00
68 Bonzi Wells .20 .50
69 Scottie Pippen .75 2.00
70 Chris Webber .40 1.00
71 Peja Stojakovic .25 .60
72 Mike Bibby .30 .75
73 Hedo Turkoglu .25 .60
74 Tim Duncan .75 2.00
75 David Robinson .60 1.50
76 Tony Parker .50 1.25
77 Malik Rose .20 .50
78 Gary Payton .50 1.25
79 Rashard Lewis .25 .60
80 Desmond Mason .25 .60
81 Brent Barry .20 .50
82 Vince Carter .60 1.50
83 Morris Peterson .25 .60
84 Antonio Davis .25 .60
85 Karl Malone .60 1.50
86 John Stockton .60 1.50
87 Andrei Kirilenko .25 .60
88 Michael Jordan 3.00 8.00
89 Richard Hamilton .40 1.00
90 Kwame Brown .20 .50
91 Efthimios Rentzias RC 1.25 3.00
92 Darius Songaila RC 2.00 5.00
93 Matt Barnes RC 2.50 6.00
94 Sam Clancy RC 1.50 4.00
95 Lonny Baxter RC 1.25 3.00
96 Manu Ginobili RC 15.00 40.00
97 Rod Grizzard RC 1.25 3.00
98 Tito Maddox RC 1.25 3.00
99 Predrag Savovic RC 1.50 4.00
100 Carlos Boozer RC 2.00 5.00
101 Dan Gadzuric RC 1.50 4.00
102 Vincent Yarbrough RC 1.25 3.00
103 Robert Archibald RC 1.25 3.00
104 Roger Mason RC 1.50 4.00
105 Steve Logan RC 2.00 5.00
106 Dan Dickau RC 1.25 3.00
107 Chris Jefferies RC 1.25 3.00
108 John Salmons RC 2.00 5.00
109 Frank Williams RC 1.25 3.00
110 Tayshaun Prince RC 4.00 10.00
111 Casey Jacobsen RC 1.50 4.00
112 Qyntel Woods RC 1.50 4.00
113 Kareem Rush RC 1.50 4.00
114 Ryan Humphrey RC 1.50 4.00
115 Curtis Borchardt RC 1.25 3.00
116 Juan Dixon RC 1.50 4.00
117 Jiri Welsch RC 1.50 4.00
118 Bostjan Nachbar RC 1.50 4.00
119 Fred Jones RC 1.50 4.00
120 Marcus Haislip RC 1.25 3.00
121 Melvin Ely RC 1.50 4.00
122 Jared Jeffries RC 1.50 4.00
123 Caron Butler RC 2.00 5.00
124 Amare Stoudemire RC 6.00 15.00
125 Chris Wilcox RC 2.00 5.00
126 Nene Hilario RC 2.50 6.00
127 DaJuan Wagner RC 2.00 5.00
128 Nikoloz Tskitishvili RC 1.50 4.00
129 Drew Gooden RC 2.50 6.00
130 Mike Dunleavy RC 2.50 6.00
131 Jay Williams RC 2.00 5.00
132 Yao Ming RC 15.00 40.00

2002-03 UD Authentics Gold
*1-90 STARS: 4X TO 10X BASE CARD HI
1-90 PRINT RUN 250 SER.#'d SETS
*91-123 RCs: 1.25X TO 3X BASE RC HI
*124-132 RCs: 1X TO 2.5X BASE HI
91-132 PRINT RUN 100 SER.#'d SETS
88 Michael Jordan 30.00 80.00

2002-03 UD Authentics Rainbow
*STARS: 8X TO 20X BASE CARD HI
1-90 PRINT RUN 50 SER.#'d SETS
*RCs 91-123: 2.5X TO 6X HI
*RCs 124-132: 2X TO 5X HI
91-132 PRINT RUN 25 SER.#'d SETS
88 Michael Jordan 100.00 250.00

2002-03 UD Authentics 100% Amazing
PRINT RUN 100 SER.#'d SETS
AI Allen Iverson 12.00 30.00
AM Alonzo Mourning 8.00 20.00
CW Chris Webber 6.00 15.00
JK Jason Kidd 8.00 20.00
KB Kobe Bryant 75.00 200.00
KG Kevin Garnett 12.00 30.00
MJ Michael Jordan 75.00 150.00
TM Tracy McGrady 8.00 20.00

2002-03 UD Authentics Awesome Authentics
PRINT RUN 250 SER.#'d SETS
AWA Antoine Walker 2.50 6.00
CWA Chris Webber 4.00 10.00
DMA Darius Miles 2.00 5.00
DNA Dirk Nowitzki 8.00 20.00
EBA Elton Brand 2.50 6.00
JMA Jamal Mashburn 2.50 6.00
KBA Kobe Bryant 60.00 150.00
KGA Kevin Garnett 8.00 20.00
MJA Michael Jordan 40.00 100.00
MPA Morris Peterson 2.50 6.00
QRA Quentin Richardson 2.00 5.00
RWA Rasheed Wallace 4.00 10.00
SFA Steve Francis 3.00 8.00
SMA Stephon Marbury 4.00 10.00
SSA Stromile Swift 2.00 5.00
WSA Wally Szczerbiak 2.50 6.00

2002-03 UD Authentics Court Quality
PRINT RUN 350 SER.#'d SETS
AMQ Alonzo Mourning 5.00 12.00
CMQ Chris Mihm 2.00 5.00
DJQ DerMarr Johnson 2.00 5.00
DMQ Darius Miles 2.00 5.00
DWQ David Wesley 2.00 5.00
ECQ Eddy Curry 2.00 5.00
GHQ Grant Hill 5.00 12.00
GRQ Glenn Robinson 3.00 8.00
KBQ Kobe Bryant 75.00 200.00
KGQ Kevin Garnett 8.00 20.00
KMQ Kenyon Martin 3.00 8.00
KVQ Keith Van Horn 2.50 6.00
PEQ Patrick Ewing 4.00 10.00
TBQ Terrell Brandon 2.00 5.00
TCQ Tyson Chandler 3.00 8.00

2002-03 UD Authentics Kevin Garnett Heroes of Basketball
COMPLETE SET (10) 15.00 40.00
COMMON CARD (KG1-KG10) 2.50 6.00
PRINT RUN 1989 SER.#'d SETS

2002-03 UD Authentics Kobe Bryant Heroes of Basketball
COMPLETE SET (10) 25.00 60.00
COMMON CARD (KB1-KB10) 5.00 12.00
PRINT RUN 989 SER.#'d SETS

2002-03 UD Authentics Michael Jordan Heroes of Basketball
COMPLETE SET (10) 175.00 350.00
COMMON CARD (1-10) 20.00 50.00
PRINT RUN 198 SER.#'d SETS

2002-03 UD Authentics Signatures
STATED ODDS 1:10E
BA Brandon Armstrong 4.00 10.00
BR Brian Scalabrine 4.00 10.00
CM Corey Maggette 4.00 10.00
EC Eddy Curry 5.00 12.00
EG Eddie Griffin 4.00 10.00
EW Earl Watson 4.00 10.00
JA Jarron Collins 4.00 10.00
JC Jason Collins 4.00 10.00
JR Jason Richardson 6.00 15.00
JS Jeryl Sasser 4.00 10.00
KE Kedrick Brown 4.00 10.00
KH Kirk Haston 4.00 10.00
KS Kenny Satterfield 4.00 10.00
KW Kwame Brown 5.00 12.00
MB Michael Bradley 4.00 10.00
RB Ruben Boumtje-Boumtje 4.00 10.00
RJ Richard Jefferson 5.00 12.00
RW Rodney White 4.00 10.00
SD Samuel Dalembert 4.00 10.00
SH Steven Hunter 4.00 10.00
TC Tyson Chandler 6.00 15.00
TM Troy Murphy 4.00 10.00
ZR Zeljko Rebraca 4.00 10.00

2002-03 UD Authentics Stat Patterns
PRINT RUN 500 SER.#'d SETS
AIS Allen Iverson 8.00 20.00
AMS Andre Miller 2.50 6.00
CMS Corey Maggette 2.50 6.00
CWS Chris Webber 4.00 10.00
DMS Dikembe Mutombo 5.00 12.00
EBS Elton Brand 2.50 6.00
ESS Eric Snow 2.00 5.00
GPS Gary Payton 5.00 12.00
JOS Jermaine O'Neal 2.50 6.00
KAS Kenny Anderson 2.50 6.00
KBS Kobe Bryant 75.00 200.00
KGS Kevin Garnett 8.00 20.00
MOS Michael Olowokandi 2.00 5.00
PSS Peja Stojakovic 2.50 6.00
RLS Rashard Lewis 2.50 6.00
SMS Joe Smith 2.50 6.00
TMS Tracy McGrady 5.00 12.00
WSS Wally Szczerbiak 2.50 6.00

2002-03 UD Authentics Uniform Greatness
STATED ODDS 1:1C
AHU Anfernee Hardaway 8.00 20.00
ALU Allan Houston 3.00 8.00
BRU Bryon Russell 2.00 5.00
DFU Derek Fisher 3.00 8.00
DGU Devean George 2.00 5.00
DMU Desmond Mason 2.50 6.00
JSU Joe Smith 2.50 6.00
JTU Jason Terry 2.50 6.00
KBU Kobe Bryant 40.00 100.00
KGU Kevin Garnett 8.00 20.00
LSU Latrell Sprewell 3.00 8.00
MAU Marcus Fizer 2.00 5.00
MJU Michael Jordan 30.00 80.00
RHU Robert Horry 3.00 8.00
SHU Shawn Marion 3.00 8.00
SMU Stephon Marbury 4.00 10.00
SNU Steve Nash 6.00 15.00
SSU Stromile Swift 2.00 5.00
TBU Terrell Brandon 2.00 5.00
TGU Tom Gugliotta 2.00 5.00
WSU Wally Szczerbiak 2.50 6.00

2006-07 UD Black
STATED PRINT RUN 99 SER.#'d SETS
1 Moses Malone 12.00 30.00
2 Jerry West 12.00 30.00
3 Michael Jordan 60.00 150.00
4 Kevin McHale 10.00 25.00
5 Ben Wallace 10.00 25.00
6 Antawn Jamison 6.00 15.00
7 Andrei Kirilenko 6.00 15.00
8 Ray Allen 12.00 30.00
9 Tony Parker 12.00 30.00
10 Manu Ginobili 15.00 40.00
11 Shawn Marion 8.00 20.00
12 Chris Webber 10.00 25.00
13 Grant Hill 12.00 30.00
14 Stephon Marbury 10.00 25.00
15 Antoine Walker 8.00 20.00
16 Gary Payton 10.00 25.00
17 Jason Terry 6.00 15.00
18 Luol Deng 6.00 15.00
19 Josh Smith 5.00 12.00
20 Peja Stojakovic 6.00 15.00

2006-07 UD Black 25
*BLACK: .75X TO 2X BASE HI
STATED PRINT RUN 25 SER.#'d SETS

2006-07 UD Black Autographs Dual
STATED PRINT RUN 25 SER.#'d SETS
BA S.Brown/M.Ager 8.00 20.00
BB Dee Brown/Dee Brown 8.00 20.00
BF C.Bosh/T.J.Ford 10.00 25.00
BP T.Prince/C.Billups 10.00 25.00
BW J.Boone/Marc.Williams 8.00 20.00
CI R.Carney/A.Iguodala 10.00 25.00
GP P.Gasol/R.Gay 10.00 25.00
JH L.James/D.Howard 1,500.00 3,000.00
JJ B.Jones/B.Jones 8.00 20.00
JR M.Jordan/D.Rodman 1,500.00 3,000.00
KA B.J.Armstrong/S.Kerr 25.00 60.00
NW P.Westphal/S.Nash 25.00 60.00
OF R.Felton/E.Okafor 8.00 20.00
PS C.Paul/C.Simmons 15.00 40.00
RF W.Frazier/N.Robinson 25.00 60.00
RR B.Roy/A.Ray 8.00 20.00
WJ Sd.Williams/Sol.Jones 8.00 20.00

2006-07 UD Black Autographs Flags
STATED PRINT RUN 25 SER.#'d SETS
AB Andrea Bargnani 8.00 20.00
AI Andre Iguodala 15.00 40.00
DB Denham Brown 8.00 20.00
DE Dee Brown 8.00 20.00
EH Elvin Hayes 10.00 25.00
JM Jamaal Magloire 8.00 20.00
LA LaMarcus Aldridge 20.00 50.00
RG Rudy Gay 10.00 25.00
RO Brandon Roy 10.00 25.00
SS Saer Sene 8.00 20.00
TS Thabo Sefolosha 8.00 20.00
TT Tyrus Thomas 8.00 20.00
WF World Free 10.00 25.00
YK Yaroslav Korolev 8.00 20.00
YM Yao Ming 50.00 120.00

2006-07 UD Black Autographs Legends
STATED PRINT RUN 25 SER.#'d SETS
AD Adrian Dantley 10.00 25.00
BD Brad Daugherty 10.00 25.00
BK Bernard King 10.00 25.00
BL Bill Laimbeer 10.00 25.00
BM Bob McAdoo 12.00 30.00
BR Bill Russell 800.00 1,500.00
BW Bill Walton 10.00 25.00
CM Cedric Maxwell 10.00 25.00
DR David Robinson 50.00 120.00
GG George Gervin 15.00 40.00
JE Julius Erving 60.00 150.00
JS John Stockton 50.00 120.00
LB Larry Bird 60.00 150.00
MA Magic Johnson 60.00 150.00
NA Nate Archibald 10.00 25.00
NT Nate Thurmond 10.00 25.00
PW Paul Westphal 10.00 25.00
RP Robert Parish 12.00 30.00
WF Walt Frazier 10.00 25.00

2006-07 UD Black Autographs Nameplates
STATED PRINT RUN 50 SER.#'d SETS
AB Andrea Bargnani 8.00 20.00
AR Allan Ray 6.00 15.00
BO Chris Bosh 12.00 30.00
BR Brandon Roy 20.00 50.00
CB Chauncey Billups 12.00 30.00
FE Raymond Felton 6.00 15.00
GG George Gervin 20.00 50.00
HA Hassan Adams 6.00 15.00
JB Josh Boone 6.00 15.00
JF Jordan Farmar 8.00 20.00
KL Kyle Lowry 30.00 80.00
LA LaMarcus Aldridge 25.00 60.00
LJ LeBron James 1,500.00 3,000.00
PO Patrick O'Bryant 6.00 15.00
QD Quincy Douby 6.00 15.00
RB Ronnie Brewer 10.00 25.00
RC Rodney Carney 6.00 15.00
RF Randy Foye 8.00 20.00
RG Rudy Gay 12.00 30.00
RR Rajon Rondo 25.00 60.00
SB Shannon Brown 6.00 15.00
SN Steve Novak 8.00 20.00
SW Shawne Williams 6.00 15.00
TT Tyrus Thomas 8.00 20.00
WF World B. Free 8.00 20.00

2006-07 UD Black Autographs Rookie Materials
STATED PRINT RUN 50 SER.#'d SETS
AB Andrea Bargnani 8.00 20.00
AR Allan Ray 6.00 15.00
BR Brandon Roy 20.00 50.00
CS Cedric Simmons 6.00 15.00
DB Denham Brown 6.00 15.00
HA Hilton Armstrong 6.00 15.00
JB Josh Boone 6.00 15.00
JF Jordan Farmar 8.00 20.00
KL Kyle Lowry 30.00 80.00
KP Kevin Pittsnogle 8.00 20.00
LA LaMarcus Aldridge 25.00 60.00
MC Mardy Collins 6.00 15.00
PD Paul Davis 6.00 15.00
PO Patrick O'Bryant 6.00 15.00
PT P.J. Tucker 10.00 25.00
QD Quincy Douby 6.00 15.00
RB Renaldo Balkman 8.00 20.00
RC Rodney Carney 6.00 15.00
RF Randy Foye 8.00 20.00
RG Rudy Gay 12.00 30.00
RO Ronnie Brewer 10.00 25.00
RR Rajon Rondo 25.00 60.00
SB Shannon Brown 6.00 15.00
SJ Solomon Jones 6.00 15.00
SN Steve Novak 8.00 20.00
SS Saer Sene 6.00 15.00
SW Shelden Williams 6.00 15.00
TS Thabo Sefolosha 8.00 20.00
TT Tyrus Thomas 8.00 20.00
WI Shawne Williams 6.00 15.00

2006-07 UD Black Autographs Rookies
STATED PRINT RUN 99 SER.#'d SETS
AB Andrea Bargnani 6.00 15.00
BA Renaldo Balkman 6.00 15.00
BR Brandon Roy 15.00 40.00
CS Cedric Simmons 5.00 12.00
HA Hilton Armstrong 5.00 12.00
JB Josh Boone 5.00 12.00
JF Jordan Farmar 6.00 15.00
KL Kyle Lowry 25.00 60.00
MC Mardy Collins 5.00 12.00
MW Marcus Williams 5.00 12.00
PO Patrick O'Bryant 5.00 12.00
QD Quincy Douby 5.00 12.00
RB Ronnie Brewer 8.00 20.00
RC Rodney Carney 5.00 12.00
RR Rajon Rondo 25.00 60.00
SB Shannon Brown 5.00 12.00
SS Saer Sene 5.00 12.00
SW Shelden Williams 5.00 12.00
TS Thabo Sefolosha 6.00 15.00
WI Shawne Williams 5.00 12.00

2006-07 UD Black Autographs Tickets
STATED PRINT RUN 50 SER.#'d SETS
AB Andrea Bargnani 6.00 15.00
BJ Bobby Jones 5.00 12.00
BR Brandon Roy 15.00 40.00
CS Cedric Simmons 5.00 12.00
DH Dwight Howard 10.00 25.00
DN David Noel 5.00 12.00
FO Randy Foye 6.00 15.00
HA Hassan Adams 5.00 12.00
JF Jordan Farmar 6.00 15.00
JS J.R. Smith 8.00 20.00
LA LaMarcus Aldridge 20.00 50.00
LB Leandro Barbosa 6.00 15.00
LJ LeBron James 1,250.00 2,500.00
MA Maurice Ager 5.00 12.00
NR Nate Robinson 6.00 15.00
PD Paul Davis 5.00 12.00
PO Patrick O'Bryant 5.00 12.00
PT P.J. Tucker 8.00 20.00
QD Quincy Douby 5.00 12.00
RB Ronnie Brewer 8.00 20.00
RF Raymond Felton 5.00 12.00
RG Rudy Gay 10.00 25.00
RR Rajon Rondo 20.00 50.00
SC Craig Smith 6.00 15.00
SN Steve Novak 6.00 15.00
SS Saer Sene 5.00 12.00
SW Shelden Williams 5.00 12.00
TT Tyrus Thomas 6.00 15.00
WB Will Blalock 5.00 12.00
WI Shawne Williams 5.00 12.00

2006-07 UD Black Autographs Veteran Materials
STATED PRINT RUN 25 SER.#'d SETS
AI Andre Iguodala 12.00 30.00
AJ Antawn Jamison 10.00 25.00
BD Baron Davis 12.00 30.00
BG Ben Gordon 10.00 25.00
CB Chris Bosh 12.00 30.00
CF Channing Frye 10.00 25.00
CM Corey Maggette 10.00 25.00
CP Chris Paul 40.00 100.00
DH Dwight Howard 20.00 50.00
DW Deron Williams 10.00 25.00
EB Elton Brand 10.00 25.00
HW Hakim Warrick 10.00 25.00
JH Julius Hodge 10.00 25.00
KH Kirk Hinrich 10.00 25.00
KK Kyle Korver 10.00 25.00
LB Leandro Barbosa 10.00 25.00
LH Luther Head 10.00 25.00
LJ LeBron James 1,500.00 3,000.00
NR Nate Robinson 10.00 25.00
PP Paul Pierce 30.00 80.00
PS Peja Stojakovic 20.00 50.00
RF Raymond Felton 10.00 25.00
RJ Richard Jefferson 10.00 25.00
RM Rashad McCants 10.00 25.00
TP Tayshaun Prince 10.00 25.00
VC Vince Carter 20.00 50.00

2006-07 UD Black Autographs Veterans
AB Andrew Bogut 8.00 20.00
CF Channing Frye 8.00 20.00
CV Charlie Villanueva 8.00 20.00
GG Gerald Green 8.00 20.00
MW Marvin Williams 8.00 20.00
NR Nate Robinson 8.00 20.00
RM Rashad McCants/99 8.00 20.00
RT Ronny Turiaf/99 8.00 20.00
TF T.J. Ford/89 8.00 20.00
TP Tayshaun Prince 8.00 20.00

2006-07 UD Black Dual Materials
STATED PRINT RUN 99 SER.#'d SETS
*DUAL 25: .5X TO 1.25X BASE HI
DUAL PRINT RUN 25 SER.#'d SETS
AB Andrea Bargnani 3.00 8.00
AI Allen Iverson 10.00 25.00
AK Andrei Kirilenko 3.00 8.00
AS Amare Stoudemire 4.00 10.00
BW Ben Wallace 5.00 12.00
CA Carmelo Anthony 6.00 15.00
CD Clyde Drexler 5.00 12.00
CM Corey Maggette 3.00 8.00
CP Chris Paul 8.00 20.00
DG Drew Gooden 3.00 8.00
DH Devin Harris 3.00 8.00
DR David Robinson 6.00 15.00
JE Julius Erving 8.00 20.00
JH Josh Howard 3.00 8.00
JO Jermaine O'Neal 4.00 10.00
JR Jason Richardson 4.00 10.00
JS John Stockton 6.00 15.00
KK Kyle Korver 3.00 8.00

LA LaMarcus Aldridge 10.00 25.00
LD Luol Deng 3.00 8.00
LJ LeBron James 30.00 80.00
MG Manu Ginobili 8.00 20.00
MJ Michael Jordan 100.00 250.00
RA Ray Allen 6.00 15.00
RE J.J. Redick 8.00 20.00
RF Randy Foye 3.00 8.00
RG Rudy Gay 5.00 12.00
RH Richard Hamilton 4.00 10.00
RJ Richard Jefferson 3.00 8.00
RO Brandon Roy 8.00 20.00
RW Rasheed Wallace 5.00 12.00
SM Shawn Marion 4.00 10.00
SN Steve Nash 8.00 20.00
SW Shelden Williams 2.50 6.00
TD Tim Duncan 10.00 25.00
TM Tracy McGrady 6.00 15.00
TP Tony Parker 6.00 15.00
TT Tyrus Thomas 3.00 8.00
WC Wilt Chamberlain 60.00 150.00
WF Walt Frazier 5.00 12.00
YM Yao Ming 10.00 25.00
ZI Zydrunas Ilgauskas 3.00 8.00

2006-07 UD Black Dual Materials Autographs

STATED PRINT RUN 25 SER.#'d SETS
BR Brandon Roy 25.00 60.00
CD Clyde Drexler 15.00 40.00
CP Chris Paul 40.00 100.00
EB Elton Brand 8.00 20.00
LA LaMarcus Aldridge 30.00 80.00
LJ LeBron James 1,500.00 3,000.00
NR Nate Robinson 15.00 40.00
PP Paul Pierce 15.00 40.00
PS Peja Stojakovic 20.00 50.00
RB Renaldo Balkman 8.00 20.00
RF Raymond Felton 10.00 25.00
RG Rudy Gay 25.00 60.00
RR Rajon Rondo 75.00 150.00

2006-07 UD Black Jerseys Autographs

STATED PRINT RUN 50 SER.#'d SETS
AI Andre Iguodala 6.00 15.00
BM Brad Miller 6.00 15.00
CB Chris Bosh 8.00 20.00
DG Danny Granger 6.00 15.00
DH Dwight Howard 10.00 25.00
DR Dennis Rodman 40.00 100.00
DW Deron Williams 6.00 15.00
EB Elton Brand 6.00 15.00
EO Emeka Okafor 6.00 15.00
FO Randy Foye 6.00 15.00
HW Hakim Warrick 6.00 15.00
JF Jordan Farmar 6.00 15.00
KK Kyle Korver 6.00 15.00
LA LaMarcus Aldridge 20.00 50.00
LO Lamar Odom 8.00 20.00
PG Pau Gasol 10.00 25.00
RF Raymond Felton 6.00 15.00
RG Rudy Gay 6.00 15.00
TC Tyson Chandler 6.00 15.00
TT Tyrus Thomas 6.00 15.00

2006-07 UD Black Jerseys Dual

STATED PRINT RUN 50 SER.#'d SETS
AH M.Ager/J.Howard 6.00 15.00
BD M.Bibby/Q.Douby 6.00 15.00
BJ K.Bryant/M.Johnson 75.00 200.00
BM L.Bird/K.McHale 15.00 40.00
BT I.Thomas/C.Billups 10.00 25.00
CA T.Chandler/H.Armstrong 6.00 15.00
DA C.Drexler/L.Aldridge 8.00 20.00
DM P.Davis/C.Maggette 6.00 15.00
FM S.Marbury/S.Francis 6.00 15.00
GJ K.Garnett/M.James 10.00 25.00
GL P.Gasol/K.Lowry 10.00 25.00
HR J.J.Redick/D.Howard 8.00 20.00
IC A.Iguodala/R.Carney 6.00 15.00
JB L.James/S.Brown 20.00 50.00
KW J.Kidd/Marc.Williams 10.00 25.00
OF E.Okafor/R.Felton 6.00 15.00
OM Y.Ming/H.Olajuwon 12.00 30.00
OW S.O'Neal/A.Walker 12.00 30.00
RT Ty.Thomas/D.Rodman 10.00 25.00
SW J.Stockton/D.Williams 10.00 25.00

2006-07 UD Black Jerseys Dual Autographs

STATED PRINT RUN 25 SER.#'d SETS
AM S.Abdur-Rahim/T.McGrady 30.00 80.00
CJ L.James/V.Carter 2,000.00 4,000.00
EC M.Eaton/T.Chambers 10.00 25.00
KB C.Billups/J.Kidd 20.00 50.00
KD J.Kidd/B.Davis 40.00 100.00
LT B.Laimbeer/R.Theus 10.00 25.00
MY B.Miller/Y.Ming 50.00 125.00

2006-07 UD Black Legends Materials Autographs

STATED PRINT RUN 25 SER.#'d SETS
BW Bill Walton 12.50 30.00
MJ Michael Jordan 1,500.00 3,000.00

2006-07 UD Black Patches

STATED PRINT RUN 50 SER.#'d SETS
*PATCH 25: .5X TO 1.25X BASE HI
PATCH 25 PRINT RUN 25 SETS
AI Allen Iverson 60.00 150.00
AM Alonzo Mourning 40.00 100.00
AS Amare Stoudemire 10.00 25.00
DH Devin Harris 8.00 20.00
JN Jameer Nelson 8.00 20.00
JO Jermaine O'Neal 8.00 20.00
JR Jason Richardson 8.00 20.00
KB Kobe Bryant 100.00 250.00
KG Kevin Garnett 25.00 60.00
KM Kevin McHale 20.00 50.00
LJ LeBron James 150.00 400.00
MK Karl Malone 25.00 60.00
MM Moses Malone 20.00 50.00
MR Michael Redd 8.00 20.00
MW Marvin Williams 8.00 20.00
RL Rashard Lewis 8.00 20.00
RW Rasheed Wallace 10.00 25.00
SO Shaquille O'Neal 25.00 60.00
TD Tim Duncan 25.00 60.00
ZI Zydrunas Ilgauskas 8.00 20.00

2006-07 UD Black Patches Autographs

STATED PRINT RUN 25 SER.#'d SETS
AR Allan Ray 5.00 12.00
BJ Bobby Jones 5.00 12.00
CR Craig Smith 6.00 15.00
CS Cedric Simmons 5.00 12.00
DE Dee Brown 5.00 12.00
DN David Noel 5.00 12.00
HI Hilton Armstrong 5.00 12.00
JB Josh Boone 5.00 12.00
MA Maurice Ager 5.00 12.00
PD Paul Davis 5.00 12.00
PT P.J. Tucker 8.00 20.00
QD Quincy Douby 5.00 12.00
RB Renaldo Balkman 6.00 15.00
RC Rodney Carney 5.00 12.00
RF Randy Foye 6.00 15.00
RR Rajon Rondo 50.00 120.00
SB Shannon Brown 5.00 12.00
SN Steve Novak 6.00 15.00
SS Saer Sene 5.00 12.00
SW Shawne Williams 5.00 12.00

2006-07 UD Black Patches Dual

STATED PRINT RUN 25 SER.#'d SETS
BD E.Brand/P.Davis 8.00 20.00
CW R.Carney/Sw.Williams 8.00 20.00
DD L.Deng/C.Duhon 8.00 20.00
JM A.Jamison/S.May 8.00 20.00
JR L.Ridnour/F.Jones 8.00 20.00
MI A.Iverson/A.Mourning 50.00 120.00
OA E.Okafor/R.Allen 15.00 40.00
OT S.O'Neal/Ty.Thomas 20.00 50.00
PH P.Pierce/K.Hinrich 12.00 30.00
WH L.Head/D.Williams 8.00 20.00

2006-07 UD Black Patches Numbers

STATED PRINT RUN 25 SER.#'d SETS
BD Baron Davis 12.00 30.00
BW Ben Wallace 15.00 40.00
CM Corey Maggette 8.00 20.00
JK Jason Kidd 15.00 40.00
JR Jason Richardson 12.00 30.00
KB Kobe Bryant 125.00 300.00
KM Kenyon Martin 8.00 20.00
QR Quentin Richardson 8.00 20.00
SF Steve Francis 8.00 20.00
TP Tayshaun Prince 8.00 20.00

2007-08 UD Black

1-84 JSY PRINT RUN 25 SER.#'d SETS
85-126 PRINT RUN 99 SER.#'d SETS
1 Clyde Drexler JSY 15.00 40.00
2 Al Jefferson JSY 6.00 15.00
3 Allen Iverson JSY 40.00 100.00
4 Alonzo Mourning JSY 25.00 60.00
5 Amare Stoudemire JSY 15.00 40.00
6 Andre Iguodala JSY 10.00 25.00
7 Andrea Bargnani JSY 6.00 15.00
8 Andrew Bogut JSY 8.00 20.00
9 Antawn Jamison JSY 8.00 20.00
10 Baron Davis JSY 8.00 20.00
11 Ben Gordon JSY 8.00 20.00
12 Bernard King JSY 8.00 20.00
13 Bill Laimbeer JSY 8.00 20.00
14 Bill Russell JSY 40.00 100.00
15 Dwyane Wade JSY 20.00 50.00
16 Brandon Roy JSY 15.00 40.00
17 Carlos Arroyo JSY 10.00 25.00
18 Carlos Boozer JSY 8.00 20.00
19 Carmelo Anthony JSY 20.00 50.00
20 Chris Bosh JSY 12.00 30.00
21 Chris Mullin JSY 20.00 40.00
22 Chris Paul JSY 25.00 60.00
23 Corey Maggette JSY 10.00 25.00
24 Adrian Dantley JSY 8.00 20.00
25 Dennis Rodman JSY 25.00 60.00
26 Deron Williams JSY 12.00 30.00
27 Dirk Nowitzki JSY 20.00 50.00
28 Dominique Wilkins JSY 15.00 40.00
29 Dwight Howard JSY 20.00 50.00
30 Eddy Curry JSY 10.00 25.00
31 Elton Brand JSY 8.00 20.00
32 Emeka Okafor JSY 8.00 20.00
33 George Gervin JSY 12.50 30.00
34 Gilbert Arenas JSY 12.50 30.00
35 Hakeem Olajuwon JSY 20.00 40.00
36 Jamaal Tinsley JSY 10.00 25.00
37 James Worthy JSY 20.00 50.00
38 Jason Kidd JSY 15.00 40.00
39 Jason Richardson JSY 10.00 25.00
40 Jermaine O'Neal JSY 10.00 25.00
41 Jerry West JSY 30.00 80.00
42 Joe Dumars JSY 15.00 40.00
43 John Stockton JSY 20.00 40.00
44 Josh Howard JSY 10.00 25.00
45 Julius Erving JSY 25.00 60.00
46 Kareem Abdul-Jabbar JSY 30.00 80.00
47 Karl Malone JSY 20.00 50.00
48 Kevin Garnett JSY 40.00 100.00
49 Kevin McHale JSY 12.00 30.00
50 Kirk Hinrich JSY 8.00 20.00
51 Kobe Bryant JSY 125.00 300.00
52 Kyle Korver JSY 10.00 25.00
53 Lamar Odom JSY 8.00 20.00
54 LaMarcus Aldridge JSY 20.00 50.00
55 Larry Bird JSY 40.00 100.00
56 Larry Hughes JSY 10.00 25.00
57 LeBron James JSY 150.00 400.00
58 Magic Johnson JSY 40.00 75.00
59 Marvin Williams JSY 10.00 25.00
60 Michael Jordan JSY 300.00 600.00
61 Michael Redd JSY 8.00 20.00
62 Mike Bibby JSY 10.00 25.00
63 Oscar Robertson JSY 35.00 70.00
64 Pau Gasol JSY 15.00 40.00
65 Paul Pierce JSY 15.00 40.00
66 Pete Maravich JSY 60.00 120.00
67 Randy Foye JSY 8.00 20.00
68 Rashard Lewis JSY 10.00 25.00
69 Rasheed Wallace JSY 12.50 30.00
70 Ray Allen JSY 15.00 40.00
71 Ron Artest JSY 10.00 25.00
72 Rudy Gay JSY 8.00 20.00
73 Shaquille O'Neal JSY 40.00 100.00
74 Shelden Williams JSY 10.00 25.00
75 Stephon Marbury JSY 10.00 25.00
76 Steve Nash JSY 20.00 40.00
77 Tayshaun Prince JSY 10.00 25.00
78 Tim Duncan JSY 30.00 60.00
79 Tony Parker JSY 15.00 40.00
80 Tracy McGrady JSY 15.00 40.00
81 Vince Carter JSY 25.00 50.00
82 Walt Frazier JSY 15.00 40.00
83 Wilt Chamberlain JSY 50.00 120.00
84 Yao Ming JSY 20.00 50.00
85 Carl Landry JSY AU RC 6.00 15.00
86 Gabe Pruitt JSY AU RC 6.00 15.00
87 Marcus Williams JSY AU RC 6.00 15.00
88 Nick Fazekas JSY AU RC 6.00 15.00
89 Glen Davis JSY AU RC 8.00 20.00
90 Jermareo Davidson JSY AU RC 6.00 15.00
91 Josh McRoberts JSY AU RC 6.00 15.00
92 Chris Richard JSY AU RC 6.00 15.00
93 Derrick Byars JSY AU RC 6.00 15.00
94 Adam Haluska JSY AU RC 6.00 15.00
95 Reyshawn Terry JSY AU RC 6.00 15.00
96 Jared Jordan JSY AU RC 6.00 15.00
97 Stephane Lasme JSY AU RC 6.00 15.00
98 Dominic McGuire JSY AU RC 6.00 15.00
99 Al Horford JSY AU RC 25.00 60.00
100 Mike Conley Jr. JSY AU RC 25.00 60.00
101 Jeff Green JSY AU RC 8.00 20.00
102 Corey Brewer JSY AU RC 8.00 20.00
103 Joakim Noah JSY AU RC 10.00 25.00
104 Spencer Hawes JSY AU RC 6.00 15.00
105 Acie Law JSY AU RC 6.00 15.00
106 Kevin Durant JSY AU RC 2,500.00 5,000.00
107 Julian Wright JSY AU RC 6.00 15.00
108 Al Thornton JSY AU RC 6.00 15.00
109 Rodney Stuckey JSY AU RC 6.00 15.00
110 Sean Williams JSY AU RC 6.00 15.00
111 Marco Belinelli JSY AU RC 8.00 20.00
112 Javaris Crittenton JSY AU RC 8.00 20.00
113 Jason Smith JSY AU RC 6.00 15.00
114 Daequan Cook JSY AU RC 8.00 20.00
115 Aaron Brooks JSY AU RC 8.00 20.00
116 Arron Afflalo JSY AU RC 8.00 20.00
117 Alando Tucker JSY AU RC 6.00 15.00
118 Jared Dudley JSY AU RC 8.00 20.00
119 Wilson Chandler JSY AU RC 8.00 20.00
120 Morris Almond JSY AU RC 8.00 20.00
121 Greg Oden RC 8.00 20.00
122 Nick Young RC 8.00 20.00
123 Yi Jianlian RC 10.00 25.00
124 Brandan Wright RC 6.00 15.00
125 Sun Yue RC 8.00 20.00
126 Thaddeus Young RC 8.00 20.00

2007-08 UD Black 50th Anniversary Autographs

PRINT RUN 50 SER.#'d SETS
BR Bill Russell 2,000.00 4,000.00
BS Bill Sharman 60.00 150.00
BW Bill Walton 30.00 80.00
CD Clyde Drexler 125.00 225.00
DC Dave Cowens 25.00 60.00
DR David Robinson 75.00 200.00
DS Dolph Schayes 25.00 60.00
EB Elgin Baylor 60.00 150.00
HG Hal Greer 25.00 60.00
HO Hakeem Olajuwon 75.00 200.00
JE Julius Erving 100.00 250.00
JH John Havlicek 75.00 200.00
JL Jerry Lucas 30.00 80.00
JO Michael Jordan 5,000.00 8,000.00
JS John Stockton 75.00 200.00
JW Jerry West 100.00 250.00
KA Kareem Abdul-Jabbar 100.00 250.00
LB Larry Bird 125.00 300.00
LW Lenny Wilkens 30.00 80.00
MJ Magic Johnson 125.00 300.00
NA Nate Tiny Archibald 25.00 60.00
NT Nate Thurmond 25.00 60.00
RB Rick Barry 30.00 80.00
RP Robert Parish 25.00 60.00
SJ Sam Jones 75.00 200.00
WF Walt Frazier 40.00 100.00
WO James Worthy 75.00 200.00
WU Wes Unseld 30.00 80.00

2007-08 UD Black All-Star Autographs

PRINT RUN 25 SER.#'d SETS
*GOLD: .5X TO 1.25X BASE HI
GOLD PRINT RUN 15 SER.#'d SETS
UAJ Antawn Jamison 30.00 80.00
UBD Brad Daugherty 20.00 50.00
UCD Clyde Drexler 50.00 125.00
UDR David Robinson 100.00 250.00
UDT David Thompson 20.00 50.00
UDW Dominique Wilkins 50.00 120.00
UGR Glen Rice 30.00 80.00
UHG Horace Grant 20.00 50.00
UJE Julius Erving 100.00 250.00
UJK Jason Kidd 75.00 200.00
UJS John Stockton 100.00 250.00
UKB Kobe Bryant 1,500.00 3,000.00
UKG Kevin Garnett 150.00 400.00
ULJ LeBron James 3,000.00 6,000.00
UMJ Michael Jordan 4,000.00 8,000.00
UMR Mitch Richmond 30.00 80.00
UNA Nate Archibald 25.00 60.00
UPP Paul Pierce 75.00 200.00
URB Rick Barry 30.00 80.00

2007-08 UD Black Autographs

PRINT RUN 25 OR 50 SER.#'d SETS
*GOLD/25: .5X TO 1.25X BASE HI
AUAB Andrea Bargnani/50 10.00 25.00
AUAD Adrian Dantley/50 10.00 25.00
AUAE Alex English/50 10.00 25.00
AUAH Al Horford/25 10.00 25.00
AUAJ Antawn Jamison/50 10.00 25.00
AUAL Acie Law/50 10.00 25.00
AUAM Alonzo Mourning/25 25.00 60.00
AUAT Al Thornton/50 10.00 25.00
AUBA Leandro Barbosa/50 10.00 25.00
AUBE Marco Belinelli/50 10.00 25.00
AUBG Ben Gordon/50 10.00 25.00
AUBL Bill Laimbeer/50 10.00 25.00
AUBR Brandon Roy/50 10.00 25.00
AUBW Bill Walton/25 10.00 25.00
AUCA Carmelo Anthony/25 30.00 80.00
AUCB Chris Bosh/25 10.00 25.00
AUCD Chuck Daly/50 20.00 50.00
AUCH Connie Hawkins/25 10.00 25.00
AUCR Javaris Crittenton/50 10.00 25.00
AUCY Corey Brewer/25 10.00 25.00
AUDC Daequan Cook/50 10.00 25.00
AUDH Dwight Howard/25 20.00 50.00
AUDT David Thompson/50 10.00 25.00
AUDW Dominique Wilkins/25 20.00 50.00
AUHO Hakeem Olajuwon/25 20.00 50.00
AUJA James Worthy/25 15.00 40.00
AUJG Jeff Green/50 10.00 25.00
AUJK Jason Kidd/25 30.00 80.00
AUJM Josh McRoberts/50 10.00 25.00
AUJN Joakim Noah/25 10.00 25.00
AUJO Michael Jordan/25 1,000.00 3,000.00
AUJS Jason Smith/50 10.00 25.00
AUJS John Stockton/25 40.00 100.00
AUJW Julian Wright/25 10.00 25.00
AUKH Kirk Hinrich/25 10.00 25.00
AULA LaMarcus Aldridge/25 10.00 25.00
AULJ LeBron James/25 1,500.00 3,000.00
AUMB Mike Bibby/25 10.00 25.00
AUMC Mike Conley Jr./25 15.00 40.00
AUMJ Magic Johnson/25 50.00 120.00
AUPP Paul Pierce/25 30.00 80.00
AUPP Pat Riley/50 12.00 30.00
AUPR Pat Riley/25 15.00 40.00
AURB Rick Barry/25 10.00 25.00
AURG Rudy Gay/50 12.00 30.00
AURR Rajon Rondo/50 20.00 50.00
AURS Rodney Stuckey/50 10.00 25.00
AUSH Spencer Hawes/50 10.00 25.00
AUSP Sam Perkins/50 10.00 25.00
AUSW Sean Williams/25 10.00 25.00
AUTP Tayshaun Prince/25 10.00 25.00
AUTT Tyrus Thomas/25 10.00 25.00
AUWF Walt Frazier/50 15.00 40.00
AUWI Deron Williams/50 10.00 25.00
AUWU Wes Unseld/50 10.00 25.00
AUYM Yao Ming/25 50.00 120.00

2007-08 UD Black Autographs Dual

PRINT RUN 25 SER.#'d SETS
*GOLD: .5X TO 1.25X BASE HI
GOLD PRINT RUN 15 SER.#'d SETS
BB C.Bosh/A.Bargnani 15.00 40.00
BC J.Crittenton/C.Bosh 15.00 40.00
BL E.Banks/A.Law 15.00 40.00
BW K.Bryant/J.West 300.00 600.00
CB M.Conley/C.Brewer 15.00 40.00
CC M.Conley Jr./M.Conley Sr. 15.00 40.00
CM V.Carter/T.McGrady 60.00 150.00
DA K.Durant/L.Aldridge 125.00 300.00
DC D.Cook/M.Conley 15.00 40.00
GB C.Brewer/T.Green 15.00 40.00
GN B.Gordon/J.Noah 15.00 40.00
GT J.Green/J.Thompson III 15.00 40.00
HH A.Horford/A.Horford 15.00 40.00
HR S.Hawes/B.Roy 15.00 40.00
JA C.Anthony/L.James 1,500.00 3,000.00
JB M.Johnson/L.Bird 150.00 400.00
JJ L.James/M.Jordan 4,000.00 8,000.00
JR M.Jordan/D.Rodman 1,000.00 3,000.00
KA B.Armstrong/S.Kerr 20.00 50.00
LD B.Laimbeer/A.Dantley 15.00 40.00
NK S.Nash/J.Kidd 60.00 150.00
OD H.Olajuwon/C.Drexler 30.00 80.00
OG E.Okafor/B.Gordon 15.00 40.00
PM P.Riley/M.Johnson 60.00 150.00
RH B.Russell/T.Heinsohn 1,000.00 2,000.00
RJ S.Jones/B.Russell 1,000.00 2,000.00
WS D.Williams/J.Stockton 50.00 120.00
WW D.Wilkins/S.Webb 25.00 60.00
YD K.Durant/V.Young 125.00 300.00

2007-08 UD Black Autographs Triple

PRINT RUN 15 SER.#'d SETS
ECW Erving/Wilkins/Carter 150.00 400.00
GBM Garnett/Bryant/Malone 300.00 600.00
HBN Horford/Brewer/Noah 40.00 100.00
JBJ Bryant/James/Jordan 6,000.00 12,000.00
NKS Stockton/Nash/Kidd 200.00 500.00
OSM Samp/Olajuwon/Ming 100.00 250.00
PRB Russell/Bird/Pierce 3,000.00 6,000.00
WJA Kareem/Johnson/Worthy 300.00 600.00

2007-08 UD Black Flags Autographs

PRINT RUN 25 SER.#'d SETS
FAAB Andrea Bargnani 12.00 30.00
FAAH Al Horford 15.00 40.00
FABE Raja Bell 12.00 30.00
FABG Ben Gordon 12.00 30.00
FACB Corey Brewer 12.00 30.00
FADW Dominique Wilkins 25.00 60.00
FAGR Jeff Green 12.00 30.00
FAHO Hakeem Olajuwon 40.00 80.00
FAJG Jorge Garbajosa 12.00 30.00
FAJN Joakim Noah 12.00 30.00
FAJW Julian Wright 12.00 30.00
FAKB Kobe Bryant 300.00 600.00
FAKD Kevin Durant 400.00 800.00
FALB Leandro Barbosa 12.00 30.00
FARB Rolando Blackman 15.00 40.00
FASK Steve Kerr 25.00 60.00
FASN Steve Nash 60.00 150.00
FATP Tony Parker 40.00 100.00

2007-08 UD Black Framed Autographs

PRINT RUN 25 SER.#'d SETS
AB Andrea Bargnani 10.00 25.00
AD Adrian Dantley 10.00 25.00
AH Al Horford 12.00 30.00
AL Acie Law 10.00 25.00
AT Al Thornton 10.00 25.00
BG Ben Gordon 10.00 25.00
BO Chris Bosh 10.00 25.00
BR Brandon Roy 10.00 25.00
CB Corey Brewer 10.00 25.00
CM Corey Maggette 10.00 25.00
CP Chris Paul 100.00 250.00
DG Darrell Griffith 10.00 25.00
DW Dominique Wilkins 15.00 40.00
GA Jorge Garbajosa 10.00 25.00
JG Jeff Green 10.00 25.00
JL Jerry Lucas 10.00 25.00
JN Joakim Noah 10.00 25.00
JO Magic Johnson 40.00 100.00
JS John Stockton 40.00 100.00
JW Julian Wright 10.00 25.00
LA LaMarcus Aldridge 15.00 40.00
MC Mike Conley Jr. 12.00 30.00
MP Morris Peterson 10.00 25.00
PP Paul Pierce 15.00 40.00
RF Randy Foye 10.00 25.00
RG Rudy Gay 12.00 30.00
RR Rajon Rondo 20.00 50.00
SN Steve Nash 40.00 100.00
TT Tyrus Thomas 10.00 25.00
VC Vince Carter 25.00 60.00
WI Deron Williams 10.00 25.00
WO James Worthy 20.00 50.00

2007-08 UD Black Letters Autographs

PRINT RUN 25 SER.#'d SETS
LAAD Adrian Dantley 20.00 50.00
LAAE Alex English 20.00 50.00
LAAG Artis Gilmore 20.00 50.00
LAAI Andre Iguodala 20.00 50.00
LAAJ Antawn Jamison 20.00 50.00
LAAM Alonzo Mourning 50.00 120.00
LAAR Arnie Risen 20.00 50.00
LABG Ben Gordon 20.00 50.00
LABL Bill Laimbeer 20.00 50.00
LABS Bill Sharman 25.00 60.00
LABW Bill Walton 20.00 50.00
LADH Dwight Howard 20.00 50.00
LADM Danny Manning 20.00 50.00
LADR David Robinson 50.00 120.00
LADS Dolph Schayes 20.00 50.00
LADW Deron Williams 20.00 50.00
LAGM George McGinnis 20.00 50.00
LAJE Julius Erving 100.00 250.00
LAJK Jason Kidd 50.00 120.00
LAJS John Stockton 40.00 100.00
LAKB Kobe Bryant 1,500.00 3,000.00
LAKH Kirk Hinrich 20.00 50.00
LANN Norm Nixon 20.00 50.00
LAPP Paul Pierce 40.00 100.00
LARO Dennis Rodman 50.00 120.00
LASN Steve Nash 60.00 150.00
LASP Sam Perkins 20.00 50.00
LATP Tony Parker 30.00 80.00
LAWE Jerry West 75.00 200.00

2007-08 UD Black Numbers Autographs

PRINT RUNS LISTED IN CHECKLIST
NAAA Al Attles/16 20.00 50.00
NAAJ Al Jefferson/25 10.00 25.00
NABL Bob Lanier/16 20.00 50.00
NABW Bill Walton/32 10.00 25.00
NACD Clyde Drexler/22 40.00 100.00
NACH Connie Hawkins/42 15.00 40.00
NADC Dave Cowens/18 10.00 25.00
NADH Dwight Howard/12 50.00 120.00
NADN Don Nelson/19 20.00 50.00
NAEB Elgin Baylor/22 25.00 60.00
NAEO Emeka Okafor/50 10.00 25.00
NAHG Hal Greer/15 20.00 50.00
NAHO Hakeem Olajuwon/34 30.00 80.00
NAJS Jack Sikma/43 10.00 25.00
NAKB Kobe Bryant/24 1,500.00 3,000.00
NAKD Kevin Durant/35 150.00 400.00
NAKV Kiki Vandeweghe/55 10.00 25.00
NALA LaMarcus Aldridge/12 25.00 60.00
NALB Larry Bird/33 100.00 250.00
NANT Nate Thurmond/42 15.00 40.00
NARB Rolando Blackman/22 10.00 25.00
NARG Rudy Gay/22 20.00 50.00
NART Rudy Tomjanovich/45 20.00 50.00
NASN Steve Nash/13 75.00 200.00
NATH Tom Heinsohn/15 40.00 100.00
NAVC Vince Carter/15 40.00 100.00
NAWU Wes Unseld/41 20.00 50.00

2007-08 UD Black Patch Material Autographs

PRINT RUN 25 OR 50 SER.#'d SETS
AA Al Attles/50 10.00 25.00
AB Andrea Bargnani/25 10.00 25.00
AC Al Cervi/50 10.00 25.00
AE Alex English/50 10.00 25.00
AH Al Horford/25 12.00 30.00
AM Alonzo Mourning/25 40.00 100.00
AR Arnie Risen/50 10.00 25.00
AT Al Thornton/50 10.00 25.00
BD Baron Davis/50 12.00 30.00
BG Ben Gordon/50 10.00 25.00
BL Bill Laimbeer/50 10.00 25.00
BR Brandon Roy/50 10.00 25.00
CB Chris Bosh/25 12.00 30.00
CD Clyde Drexler/50 25.00 60.00
CL Walt Frazier/50 10.00 25.00
CO Corey Brewer/25 10.00 25.00
CP Chris Paul/25 100.00 250.00
DC Daequan Cook/50 10.00 25.00
DL David Lee/50 10.00 25.00
DO Dominique Wilkins/25 12.00 30.00
DR Dennis Rodman/25 40.00 100.00
DW Deron Williams/50 10.00 25.00
EB Elgin Baylor/50 12.00 30.00
EO Emeka Okafor/25 10.00 25.00
GG Gail Goodrich/50 15.00 40.00
GR Jeff Green/25 10.00 25.00
HG Hal Greer/25 20.00 40.00
JC Javaris Crittenton/50 10.00 25.00
JE Julius Erving/25 75.00 200.00
JG Jorge Garbajosa/50 10.00 25.00
JL Jerry Lucas/25 30.00 80.00
JN Joakim Noah/25 10.00 25.00
JO Magic Johnson/25 75.00 200.00
JS John Stockton/25 60.00 150.00
JW Julian Wright/25 10.00 25.00
KB Kobe Bryant/25 1,500.00 3,000.00
KD Kevin Durant/50 1,500.00 3,000.00
KH Kirk Hinrich/25 10.00 25.00
LA LaMarcus Aldridge/50 10.00 25.00
LB Larry Bird/25 75.00 200.00
LJ LeBron James/25 1,500.00 3,000.00
MC Dick McGuire/50 10.00 25.00
MI Mike Conley Jr./25 15.00 40.00
MJ Michael Jordan/25 1,000.00 3,000.00
PP Paul Pierce/50 30.00 80.00
RB Renaldo Balkman/50 10.00 25.00
RG Rudy Gay/50 10.00 25.00
RI Rick Barry/25 10.00 25.00
RO David Robinson/25 60.00 150.00
RP Robert Parish/50 15.00 40.00
SH Spencer Hawes/50 10.00 25.00
SN Steve Nash/25 40.00 100.00
TG Taurean Green/50 10.00 25.00
TH Tom Heinsohn/50 10.00 25.00
TY Acie Law/50 10.00 25.00
VC Vince Carter/25 30.00 80.00
WO James Worthy/25 30.00 80.00

2007-08 UD Black Patch Material Autographs Dual

PRINT RUN 15 SER.#'d SETS
AE C.Anthony/A.English 30.00 80.00
AR L.Aldridge/B.Roy 25.00 60.00
BG E.Baylor/G.Goodrich 25.00 60.00
BN K.Bryant/S.Nash 1,500.00 3,000.00
CR A.Risen/A.Cervi 25.00 60.00
DA B.Davis/A.Attles 25.00 60.00
EW J.Erving/D.Wilkins 100.00 200.00
FD W.Frazier/C.Drexler 60.00 120.00
JB M.Jordan/L.Bird 500.00 800.00
JD K.Durant/L.James 2,000.00 4,000.00
LC A.Law/J.Crittenton 25.00 60.00
LM J.Lucas/D.McGuire 25.00 60.00
LR B.Laimbeer/D.Rodman 50.00 100.00
MR A.Mourning/D.Robinson 100.00 200.00
NG J.Noah/T.Greeg 40.00 80.00
OG R.Gay/E.Okafor 25.00 60.00
WJ M.Johnson/J.Worthy 200.00 300.00
WS J.Stockton/D.Williams 75.00 150.00

2007-08 UD Black Patches Dual

PRINT RUN 15 SER.#'d SETS
DPAJ G.Arenas/A.Jamison 12.00 30.00
DPAR L.Aldridge/B.Roy 12.00 30.00
DPBB C.Bosh/A.Bargnani 12.00 30.00
DPBM E.Brand/C.Maggette 12.00 30.00
DPBO K.Bryant/L.Odom 75.00 200.00
DPBP C.Billups/T.Prince 12.00 30.00
DPBW C.Boozer/D.Williams 12.00 30.00
DPDG K.Durant/J.Green 30.00 80.00
DPDR T.Duncan/D.Robinson 25.00 60.00
DPGG P.Gasol/R.Gay 12.00 30.00
DPHD A.Harrington/B.Davis 12.00 30.00
DPHR D.Howard/J.Redick 12.00 30.00
DPIA A.Iverson/C.Anthony 20.00 50.00
DPJF A.Jefferson/R.Foye 12.00 30.00
DPJR M.Jordan/D.Rodman 125.00 300.00
DPKC V.Carter/J.Kidd 20.00 50.00
DPMB L.Bird/K.McHale 25.00 60.00
DPML S.Marbury/D.Lee 12.00 30.00
DPMM Y.Ming/T.McGrady 12.00 30.00
DPMS K.Malone/J.Stockton 25.00 60.00
DPNS S.Nash/A.Stoudemire 15.00 40.00
DPOD H.Olajuwon/C.Drexler 20.00 50.00
DPOM A.Morrison/E.Okafor 12.00 30.00
DPPG M.Ginobili/T.Parker 20.00 50.00
DPPR P.Pierce/R.Rondo 15.00 40.00
DPRF W.Frazier/W.Reed 25.00 60.00
DPSP C.Paul/P.Stojakovic 12.00 30.00
DPTO J.O'Neal/J.Tinsley 12.00 30.00

2007-08 UD Black Ticket Autographs

PRINT RUN 50 SER.#'d SETS
*GOLD: .5X TO 1.25X BASE HI
GOLD PRINT RUN 15 SER.#'d SETS
TAAB Aaron Brooks 8.00 20.00
TAAH Al Horford 8.00 20.00
TAAI Andre Iguodala 8.00 20.00
TAAJ Antawn Jamison 8.00 20.00
TAAL Acie Law 8.00 20.00
TAAM Alonzo Mourning 20.00 50.00
TAAT Al Thornton 8.00 20.00
TABA Andrea Bargnani 8.00 20.00
TABD Baron Davis 10.00 25.00
TABG Ben Gordon 8.00 20.00
TABI Mike Bibby 8.00 20.00
TABR Brandon Roy 8.00 20.00
TACA Carmelo Anthony 25.00 60.00
TACB Corey Brewer 8.00 20.00
TACH Chris Mihm 8.00 20.00
TACL Carl Landry 8.00 20.00
TACM Corey Maggette 8.00 20.00
TACP Chris Paul 60.00 150.00
TADB Derrick Byars 8.00 20.00
TADC Daequan Cook 8.00 20.00
TADG Danny Granger 8.00 20.00
TADH Dwight Howard 15.00 40.00
TADL David Lee 8.00 20.00
TADW Deron Williams 8.00 20.00
TAEO Emeka Okafor 8.00 20.00
TAGD Glen Davis 8.00 20.00
TAGP Gabe Pruitt 8.00 20.00
TAJC Javaris Crittenton 8.00 20.00
TAJD Jared Dudley 8.00 20.00
TAJG Jeff Green 8.00 20.00
TAJM Josh McRoberts 8.00 20.00
TAJN Joakim Noah 8.00 20.00
TAJS Jason Smith 8.00 20.00
TAJW Julian Wright 8.00 20.00
TAKB Kobe Bryant 200.00 500.00
TAKD Kevin Durant 150.00 400.00
TAKG Kevin Garnett 125.00 300.00
TALA LaMarcus Aldridge 10.00 25.00
TALJ LeBron James 1,000.00 2,000.00
TAMA Morris Almond 8.00 20.00
TAMB Marco Belinelli 8.00 20.00
TAMC Mike Conley Jr. 10.00 25.00
TAMW Marcus Williams 8.00 20.00
TANF Nick Fazekas 8.00 20.00
TAPP Paul Pierce 25.00 60.00
TAPR Tayshaun Prince 8.00 20.00
TARF Randy Foye 8.00 20.00
TARG Rudy Gay 10.00 25.00
TARS Rodney Stuckey 8.00 20.00
TASE Shawne Williams 8.00 20.00
TASH Spencer Hawes 8.00 20.00
TASN Steve Nash 25.00 60.00
TASW Sean Williams 8.00 20.00
TATP Tony Parker 10.00 25.00
TATU Alando Tucker 8.00 20.00
TAVC Vince Carter 25.00 60.00
TAWC Wilson Chandler 8.00 20.00
TAWI Maurice Williams 8.00 20.00
TAWS Shelden Williams 8.00 20.00
TAYM Yao Ming 25.00 60.00

2007-08 UD Black Ticket Autographs Dual

PRINT RUN 15 SER.#'d SETS
AD K.Durant/C.Anthony 400.00 800.00
BH M.Bibby/S.Hawes 20.00 40.00
BM Y.Ming/K.Bryant 400.00 800.00
BP M.Bibby/C.Paul 75.00 200.00
DG K.Durant/J.Green 300.00 600.00
DW D.Williams/B.Davis 30.00 60.00
FB C.Brewer/R.Foye 25.00 50.00
GC M.Conley/R.Gay 20.00 50.00
GN B.Gordon/J.Noah 30.00 60.00
HL A.Law/A.Horford 20.00 40.00
HW S.Hawes/J.Wright 20.00 40.00
JG A.Jamison/D.Granger 20.00 40.00
MP T.Prince/A.Mourning 25.00 60.00
MT A.Thornton/C.Maggette 20.00 40.00
NT S.Nash/A.Tucker 40.00 80.00
NW J.Noah/S.Williams 25.00 50.00
OD E.Okafor/J.Dudley 20.00 40.00
PD G.Davis/G.Pruitt 20.00 50.00
PG P.Pierce/K.Garnett 200.00 300.00
PR B.Roy/T.Parker 30.00 60.00
PW C.Paul/J.Wright 40.00 100.00
RM B.Roy/J.McRoberts 20.00 50.00
SC R.Stuckey/D.Cook 25.00 50.00

2007-08 UD Black Trophy Autographs

PRINT RUN 25 SER.#'d SETS
BL Bill Laimbeer 25.00 60.00
BR Bill Russell 800.00 1,500.00
BW Bill Walton 40.00 100.00
DR Dennis Rodman 125.00 300.00
GR Hal Greer 25.00 60.00
HO Hakeem Olajuwon 75.00 200.00
JO Michael Jordan 2,000.00 5,000.00
JS Jack Sikma 25.00 60.00
JW James Worthy 60.00 150.00
KA Kareem Abdul-Jabbar 100.00 250.00
KB Kobe Bryant 1,500.00 3,000.00
LB Larry Bird 150.00 400.00
MJ Magic Johnson 150.00 400.00
RP Robert Parish 30.00 80.00
TH Tom Heinsohn 30.00 80.00
TP Tony Parker 125.00 300.00
VM Vern Mikkelsen 30.00 80.00
WF Walt Frazier 30.00 80.00

2008-09 UD Black

1-42 PRINT RUN 25 SER.#'d SETS
JSY AU RC PRINT RUN 99 SER.#'d SETS
1 Al Horford 12.00 30.00
2 Allen Iverson 25.00 60.00
3 Amare Stoudemire 12.00 30.00
4 Baron Davis 12.00 30.00
5 Kirk Hinrich 10.00 25.00
6 Brandon Roy 10.00 25.00
7 Carmelo Anthony 30.00 80.00
8 Chauncey Billups 15.00 40.00
9 Chris Bosh 15.00 40.00
10 Peja Stojakovic 10.00 25.00
11 Corey Maggette 10.00 25.00
12 Danny Granger 10.00 25.00
13 Andrei Kirilenko 10.00 25.00
14 Dirk Nowitzki 20.00 50.00
15 Dwight Howard 15.00 40.00
16 Elton Brand 10.00 25.00
17 Gerald Wallace 10.00 25.00
18 Gilbert Arenas 12.00 30.00
19 Jason Kidd 15.00 40.00
20 Kevin Durant 40.00 100.00
21 Kevin Garnett 40.00 100.00
22 Kevin Martin 10.00 25.00
23 Kobe Bryant 75.00 200.00
24 LeBron James 100.00 250.00
25 Michael Redd 10.00 25.00
26 Mike Miller 10.00 25.00
27 Pau Gasol 15.00 40.00
28 Paul Pierce 15.00 40.00
29 Rudy Gay 12.00 30.00
30 Shawn Marion 12.00 30.00
31 Steve Nash 25.00 60.00
32 Tim Duncan 25.00 60.00
33 Tracy McGrady 20.00 50.00
34 Vince Carter 25.00 60.00
35 Yao Ming 20.00 50.00
36 Zach Randolph 12.00 30.00
37 Julius Erving 30.00 80.00
38 Larry Bird 40.00 100.00
39 Magic Johnson 40.00 100.00
40 Michael Jordan 300.00 600.00
41 Oscar Robertson 25.00 60.00
42 Patrick Ewing 30.00 80.00
43 Derrick Rose JSY AU RC 75.00 200.00
44 M.Beasley JSY AU RC 8.00 20.00
45 O.J. Mayo JSY AU RC 6.00 15.00
46 R.Westbrook JSY AU RC 300.00 600.00
47 Kevin Love JSY AU RC 40.00 100.00
48 Eric Gordon JSY AU RC 15.00 40.00
49 Joe Alexander JSY AU RC 5.00 12.00
50 D.J. Augustin JSY AU RC 8.00 20.00
51 Brook Lopez JSY AU RC 10.00 25.00
52 Jerryd Bayless JSY AU RC 6.00 15.00
53 Jason Thompson JSY AU RC 5.00 12.00
54 Brandon Rush JSY AU RC 5.00 12.00
55 A.Randolph JSY AU RC 5.00 12.00
56 Robin Lopez JSY AU RC 6.00 15.00
57 Marreese Speights JSY AU RC 6.00 15.00
58 Roy Hibbert JSY AU RC 6.00 15.00
59 Javale McGee JSY AU RC 15.00 40.00
60 J.J. Hickson JSY AU RC 5.00 12.00
61 Ryan Anderson JSY AU RC 6.00 15.00
62 Kosta Koufos JSY AU RC 5.00 12.00
63 George Hill JSY AU RC 8.00 20.00
64 Darrell Arthur JSY AU RC 6.00 15.00
65 Donte Greene JSY AU RC 5.00 12.00
66 J.R. Giddens JSY AU RC 5.00 12.00
67 Walter Sharpe JSY AU RC 5.00 12.00
68 Joey Dorsey JSY AU RC 5.00 12.00
69 M.Chalmers JSY AU RC 8.00 20.00
70 Sonny Weems JSY AU RC 5.00 12.00

71 R.Fernandez JSY AU RC 6.00 15.00
72 Patrick Ewing Jr. JSY AU RC 5.00 12.00

2008-09 UD Black Gold
*GOLD 1-42: .5X TO 1.25X BASE HI
STATED PRINT RUN 15 SER.#'d SETS
*GOLD 43-72: .6X TO 1.5X BASE HI
STATED PRINT RUN 30 SER.#'d SETS
28 Paul Pierce 25.00 60.00
44 Michael Beasley JSY AU 30.00 80.00

2008-09 UD Black 50 Greatest Autographs
PRINT RUN 50 SER.#'d SETS
*GOLD: .5X TO 1.25X BASE HI
GOLD PRINT RUN 15 SER.#'d SETS
50AUBP Bob Pettit 30.00 60.00
50AUBR Bill Russell 800.00 1,500.00
50AUBS Bill Sharman 20.00 50.00
50AUBW Bill Walton 25.00 60.00
50AUCD Clyde Drexler 30.00 80.00
50AUDC Dave Cowens 20.00 50.00
50AUDR David Robinson 40.00 80.00
50AUDS Dolph Schayes 20.00 50.00
50AUHO Hakeem Olajuwon 30.00 80.00
50AUJE Julius Erving 50.00 125.00
50AUJH John Havlicek 25.00 60.00
50AUJO Michael Jordan 600.00 1,200.00
50AUJS John Stockton 50.00 120.00
50AUJW Jerry West 50.00 120.00
50AUKA Kareem Abdul-Jabbar 50.00 120.00
50AULB Larry Bird 60.00 150.00
50AULW Lenny Wilkens 20.00 50.00
50AUMJ Magic Johnson 50.00 120.00
50AUNT Nate Thurmond 20.00 50.00
50AUOR Oscar Robertson 50.00 100.00
50AURB Rick Barry 20.00 50.00
50AURP Robert Parish 20.00 50.00
50AUWF Walt Frazier 20.00 50.00
50AUWO James Worthy 30.00 60.00

2008-09 UD Black ABA Autographs
STATED PRINT RUN 25 SER.#'d SETS
*GOLD: .5X TO 1.25X BASE HI
GOLD PRINT RUN 10 SER.#'d SETS
ABAAG Artis Gilmore 8.00 20.00
ABACS Charlie Scott 10.00 25.00
ABADB Don Buse 8.00 20.00
ABAFL Freddie Lewis 8.00 20.00
ABAJE Julius Erving 60.00 120.00
ABALD Louie Dampier 8.00 20.00

2008-09 UD Black ABA/NBA 30th Anniversary Autographs
PRINT RUN 20 TO 30 SER.#'d SETS
30DB Don Buse/30 8.00 20.00
30DT David Thompson/30 8.00 20.00
30FL Freddie Lewis/30 8.00 20.00
30GK George Karl/29 12.00 30.00
30GM George McGinnis/20 8.00 20.00
30JE Julius Erving/30 60.00 120.00
30JS James Silas/30 8.00 20.00
30RB Rick Barry/30 15.00 30.00

2008-09 UD Black All-Star Autographs
STATED PRINT RUN 24 TO 25 SER.#'d SETS
ASAJ Antawn Jamison/25 15.00 40.00
ASAS Amare Stoudemire/25 15.00 40.00
ASBM Brad Miller/25 8.00 20.00
ASCP Chris Paul/25 60.00 150.00
ASDW David West/25 8.00 20.00
ASJK Jason Kidd/24 50.00 120.00
ASKB Kobe Bryant/25 800.00 1,500.00
ASKG Kevin Garnett/25 125.00 300.00
ASLJ LeBron James/25 2,000.00 4,000.00
ASPP Paul Pierce/25 30.00 80.00
ASRA Ray Allen/25 40.00 100.00
ASTM Tracy McGrady/24 40.00 100.00
ASYM Yao Ming/25 75.00 200.00

2008-09 UD Black Autographs
STATED PRINT RUN 23 TO 50 SER.#'d SETS
A1AJ Antawn Jamison/35 10.00 25.00
A1AM Alonzo Mourning/35 30.00 80.00
A1BL Bob Lanier/35 8.00 20.00
A1BR Brandon Roy/35 12.00 30.00
A1BW Bill Walton/35 25.00 60.00
A1CP Chris Paul/35 60.00 150.00
A1HO Hakeem Olajuwon/35 25.00 60.00
A1JE Julius Erving/32 60.00 120.00
A1JO Magic Johnson/32 40.00 100.00
A1JS J.R. Smith/35 10.00 25.00
A1KA Kareem Abdul-Jabbar/33 50.00 100.00
A1KD Kevin Durant/35 75.00 150.00
A1KG Kevin Garnett/35 50.00 100.00
A1LB Larry Bird/33 40.00 80.00
A1LJ LeBron James/23 2,000.00 4,000.00
A1MJ Michael Jordan/23 400.00 700.00
A1MP Mark Price/35 25.00 60.00
A1PP Paul Pierce/35 30.00 80.00
A1RA Ray Allen/35 30.00 80.00
A1ST John Stockton/35 30.00 80.00
A1TM Tracy McGrady/35 15.00 40.00
A2AB Andrew Bynum/50 25.00 50.00
A2AE Alex English/50 8.00 20.00
A2AJ Al Jefferson/50 8.00 20.00
A2AT Al Thornton/50 8.00 20.00
A2BB Bruce Bowen/50 8.00 20.00
A2BD Brad Daugherty/50 10.00 25.00
A2BS Bill Sharman/50 8.00 20.00
A2CL Carl Landry/50 8.00 20.00
A2FL Freddie Lewis/50 8.00 20.00
A2RR Rajon Rondo/50 25.00 60.00

2008-09 UD Black Autographs Jerseys Quad
STATED PRINT RUN 10 SER.#'d SETS
QAJ08RK 2008-09 Rookies 125.00 300.00
QAJBSTN Boston Celtics 150.00 400.00
QAJBULL Chicago Bulls 125.00 300.00
QAJCAVS Cleveland Cavaliers 800.00 1,500.00
QAJEVSW Celtics/Lakers 2,000.00 4,000.00
QAJHAWK Atlanta Hawks 50.00 120.00
QAJLAKR Los Angeles Lakers 1,500.00 3,000.00
QAJROCK Houston Rockets 50.00 120.00
QAJROOK 2008-09 Rookies 2 50.00 120.00
QAJUDEX LeBron/Kobe/MJ/KG 6,000.00 12,000.00

2008-09 UD Black Commemorative Logo Autographs
STATED PRINT RUN 19 TO 25 SER.#'d SETS
*GOLD: .6X TO 1.5X BASE HI
GOLD PRINT RUN 10 SER.#'d SETS
CBB Bruce Bowen/25 8.00 20.00
CBG Ben Gordon/25 15.00 40.00
CBR Bill Russell/20 1,000.00 2,000.00
CBS Bill Sharman/25 10.00 25.00
CCH Chuck Daly/25 30.00 60.00
CDH Dwight Howard/23 50.00 100.00
CHO Hakeem Olajuwon/25 20.00 50.00
CJO M.Jordan Finals/19 800.00 1,200.00
CJW Jerry West/25 30.00 60.00
CKB Kobe Bryant/24 800.00 1,500.00
CKG Kevin Garnett/25 60.00 120.00
CKV Kiki Vandeweghe/25 8.00 20.00
CLO Lamar Odom/25 20.00 50.00
CMI Michael Jordan/23 350.00 700.00
CMJ Magic Johnson/25 40.00 100.00
CPP Paul Pierce/25 40.00 80.00
CPR Tayshaun Prince/25 8.00 20.00
CRA Ray Allen/25 40.00 100.00
CRR Rajon Rondo/24 25.00 60.00
CRS Rodney Stuckey/25 12.00 30.00
CSK Steve Kerr/25 20.00 50.00
CST John Stockton/25 40.00 100.00
CTP Tony Parker/25 15.00 30.00
CYM Yao Ming/24 20.00 50.00

2008-09 UD Black Dual Autographs
STATED PRINT RUN 15 SER.#'d SETS
DAAS M.Almond/D.Strawberry 25.00 60.00
DABG K.Bryant/K.Garnett 500.00 1,000.00
DABL S.Battier/C.Landry 25.00 60.00
DABW C.Boozer/D.Williams 25.00 60.00
DACW V.Carter/D.Wilkins 60.00 150.00
DADH K.Durant/A.Horford 75.00 200.00
DAEJ J.Erving/L.James 1,000.00 2,000.00
DAGT B.Gordon/T.Thomas 25.00 60.00
DAJA Kareem/Magic 100.00 200.00
DAJB K.Bryant/M.Jordan 3,000.00 6,000.00
DAJS R.Jefferson/R.Sessions 25.00 60.00
DALT B.Laimbeer/I.Thomas 40.00 100.00
DAMS Y.Ming/L.Scola 30.00 80.00
DANK S.Nash/J.Kidd 100.00 250.00
DAPG Garnett/Pierce 150.00 400.00
DAPR C.Paul/R.Rondo 200.00 500.00
DAPS T.Prince/R.Stuckey 25.00 60.00
DARA Kareem/Robertson 125.00 300.00
DARC Q.Richardson/E.Curry 25.00 60.00
DARJ B.Russell/S.Jones 1,000.00 2,000.00
DAVF J.Farmar/S.Vujacic 25.00 60.00
DAWP C.Paul/D.West 125.00 300.00
DAWW L.Walton/B.Walton 25.00 60.00

2008-09 UD Black Dual Inscriptions
STATED PRINT RUN 10 SER.#'d SETS
DIDG K.Durant/J.Green 125.00 225.00
DIMB S.Battier/T.McGrady 75.00 150.00
DIPG P.Pierce/K.Garnett 60.00 150.00
DIRA Abdul-Jabbar/D.Robinson 250.00 350.00
DIWR J.Wilkes/D.Rodman 100.00 200.00

2008-09 UD Black Dual Patch Autographs
STATED PRINT RUN 15 SER.#'d SETS
DPAAF R.Fernandez/L.Aldridge 40.00 80.00
DPABC D.Cook/M.Beasley 25.00 60.00
DPABF J.Farmar/A.Bynum 25.00 60.00
DPABH M.Bibby/A.Horford 25.00 60.00
DPABJ K.Bryant/L.James 3,000.00 6,000.00
DPADG K.Durant/J.Green 125.00 250.00
DPAGC Mike Conley/Rudy Gay 25.00 60.00
DPAJB A.Bogut/R.Jefferson 25.00 60.00
DPAJJ M.Jordan/L.James 5,000.00 8,000.00
DPALB C.Brewer/K.Love 30.00 80.00
DPAMB T.McGrady/S.Battier 40.00 100.00
DPAMH A.Harrington/C.Maggette 25.00 60.00
DPAMS Y.Ming/A.Stoudemire 40.00 100.00
DPANK J.Kidd/S.Nash 50.00 100.00
DPAOF E.Okafor/R.Felton 25.00 60.00
DPAPG P.Pierce/K.Garnett 200.00 500.00
DPAPS T.Prince/R.Stuckey 25.00 60.00
DPATN T.Thomas/J.Noah 25.00 60.00

2008-09 UD Black Dual Rookie Autographs
STATED PRINT RUN 10 SER.#'d SETS
DRAAB D.Augustin/J.Bayless 25.00 50.00
DRABR D.Rose/Beasley 100.00 200.00
DRAFG Gallinari/Fernandez 40.00 80.00
DRAGL C.Lee/E.Gordon 25.00 60.00
DRAHS J.Hickson/M.Speights 25.00 60.00
DRALG K.Love/M.Gasol 40.00 80.00
DRALL R.Lopez/B.Lopez 25.00 60.00
DRAMW Westbrook/Mayo 60.00 150.00
DRART A.Randolph/J.Thompson 25.00 60.00

2008-09 UD Black Dual Rookie Jersey Autographs
STATED PRINT RUN 25 SER.#'d SETS
*GOLD: .75X TO 2X BASE HI
GOLD PRINT RUN 10 SER.#'d SETS
DRBR M.Beasley/D.Rose 40.00 100.00
DRDE P.Ewing Jr./J.Dorsey 8.00 20.00
DRGL E.Gordon/K.Love 20.00 50.00
DRGS W.Sharpe/J.Giddens 8.00 20.00
DRHM J.McGee/R.Hibbert 8.00 20.00
DRHS J.Hickson/M.Speights 12.50 30.00
DRLL R.Lopez/B.Lopez 20.00 50.00
DRMW R.Westbrook/O.Mayo 75.00 200.00
DRRB B.Rush/J.Bayless 15.00 30.00
DRRT Thompson/Randolph 20.00 40.00

2008-09 UD Black Flag Autographs
STATED PRINT RUN 23 TO 50 SER.#'d SETS
*GOLD: .5X TO 1.25X BASE HI
GOLD PRINT RUN 10 TO 25 SER.#'d SETS
USAA Arron Afflalo/50 10.00 25.00
USAG Artis Gilmore/50 15.00 40.00
USAJ Al Jefferson/50 10.00 25.00
USAM Alonzo Mourning/50 30.00 80.00
USAT Al Thornton/50 10.00 25.00
USAU D.J. Augustin/50 10.00 25.00
USBL Bill Laimbeer/50 20.00 50.00
USBM Brad Miller/50 10.00 25.00
USBR Brandon Roy/50 60.00 150.00
USBW Bill Walton/50 15.00 40.00
USCB Corey Brewer/50 10.00 25.00
USCH Tom Chambers/50 10.00 25.00
USCL Carl Landry/50 10.00 25.00
USCP Chris Paul/50 100.00 250.00
USDT David Thompson/50 10.00 25.00
USDW David West/50 10.00 25.00
USGI Daniel Gibson/50 10.00 25.00
USGR Donte Greene/50 10.00 25.00
USJB Jerryd Bayless/50 10.00 25.00
USJF Jordan Farmar/50 10.00 25.00
USJG Joey Graham/50 10.00 25.00
USJJ Jarrett Jack/50 10.00 25.00
USJK Jason Kidd/50 50.00 120.00
USKB Kobe Bryant/24 1,500.00 3,000.00
USKD Kevin Durant/50 125.00 300.00
USKG Kevin Garnett/25 125.00 300.00
USLB Larry Bird/33 150.00 400.00
USLJ LeBron James/23 2,500.00 5,000.00
USMJ Michael Jordan/23 4,000.00 8,000.00
USMP Mark Price/50 15.00 40.00
USRP Robert Parish/50 15.00 40.00
USSB Shane Battier/50 15.00 40.00
USTC Tyson Chandler/50 10.00 25.00

2008-09 UD Black Flag Autographs Dual
STATED PRINT RUN 10 SER.#'d SETS
DUSBR A.Bynum/D.Rodman 75.00 200.00
DUSDD A.Dantley/K.Durant 150.00 400.00
DUSGE K.Garnett/A.English 150.00 400.00
DUSGJ M.Johnson/G.Gervin 100.00 200.00
DUSHF W.Frazier/D.Howard 75.00 200.00
DUSJE J.Erving/M.Jordan 500.00 800.00
DUSRH O.Robertson/B.Howell 75.00 200.00
DUSRP R.Parish/B.Russell 500.00 1,000.00
DUSSR D.Robinson/A.Stoudemire 100.00 250.00
DUSTP C.Paul/D.Thompson 100.00 250.00
DUSWW J.West/D.Williams 100.00 250.00

2008-09 UD Black HOF Letters Autographs
TOTAL PRINT RUNS LISTED IN CHECKLIST
HOFAD Adrian Dantley/84* 15.00 40.00
HOFAE Alex English/98* 15.00 40.00
HOFAR Arnie Risen/98* 15.00 40.00
HOFBH Bailey Howell/98* 15.00 40.00
HOFBI Larry Bird/56* 75.00 150.00
HOFBL Bob Lanier/70* 15.00 40.00
HOFBR Bill Russell/56* 1,000.00 2,000.00
HOFBS Bill Sharman/70* 15.00 40.00
HOFBW Bill Walton/84* 15.00 40.00
HOFCD Clyde Drexler/70* 40.00 80.00
HOFDC Dave Cowens/70* 20.00 50.00
HOFDT David Thompson/84* 15.00 40.00
HOFDW D.Wilkins/70* 30.00 80.00
HOFEB Elgin Baylor/70* 20.00 50.00
HOFGO Gail Goodrich/70* 15.00 40.00
HOFHG Hal Greer/70* 15.00 40.00
HOFHO Hakeem Olajuwon/70* 30.00 80.00
HOFJH John Havlicek/70* 40.00 100.00
HOFJW James Worthy/70* 25.00 60.00
HOFKA K.Abdul-Jabbar/70* 40.00 100.00
HOFLW Lenny Wilkens/84* 15.00 40.00
HOFMJ Magic Johnson/56* 60.00 150.00
HOFOR Oscar Robertson/70* 30.00 80.00
HOFPR Pat Riley/70* 40.00 70.00
HOFRB Rick Barry/70* 15.00 40.00
HOFRP Robert Parish/98* 15.00 40.00
HOFWE Jerry West/70* 40.00 80.00
HOFWF Walt Frazier/84* 15.00 40.00

2008-09 UD Black Inscriptions Autographs
STATED PRINT RUN 25 SER.#'d SETS
*GOLD: .6X TO 1.5X BASE HI
GOLD PRINT RUN 10 SER.#'d SETS
AIJO L.Johnson Grandmama 50.00 120.00
AICB3 Corey Brewer C-Brew 8.00 20.00
AIDH1 D.Howard Manchild 75.00 150.00
AIDR1 Dennis Rodman Worm 400.00 800.00
AIDW1 Deron Williams Slick 50.00 100.00
AIKD1 Kevin Durant 100.00 250.00
AIKG1 Kevin Garnett None 75.00 150.00
AILJ1 LeBron James None 1,000.00 2,000.00
AIPP1 P.Pierce Go Jayhawks 75.00 150.00

2008-09 UD Black Legend Signed Jersey Pieces
STATED PRINT RUN 23 TO 25 SER.#'d SETS
SPLBK Bernard King 10.00 25.00
SPLDR David Robinson 40.00 100.00
SPLJO Magic Johnson 50.00 120.00
SPLJS John Stockton 50.00 120.00
SPLLB Larry Bird 50.00 120.00
SPLMJ Michael Jordan 500.00 700.00
SPLRO Dennis Rodman 60.00 120.00
SPLSA Stacey Augmon 10.00 25.00
SPLSK Steve Kerr 25.00 50.00

2008-09 UD Black Legend Signed Jersey Pieces Dual
STATED PRINT RUN 10 SER.#'d SETS
DJLEG J.Erving/G.Gervin 60.00 120.00
DJLJB M.Johnson/L.Bird 200.00 400.00
DJLJJ M.Johnson/M.Jordan 600.00 1,000.00
DJLKR S.Kerr/D.Rodman 80.00 160.00
DJLOR H.Olajuwon/D.Robinson 60.00 120.00
DJLSK J.Stockton/S.Kerr 60.00 120.00

2008-09 UD Black Michael Jordan Signed Floor
STATED PRINT RUN 23 SER.#'d SETS
MJ Michael Jordan/23 600.00 1,200.00

2008-09 UD Black MJ Induction
MJHOF Michael Jordan 25.00 60.00
MJHOFG Michael Jordan Gold/23 75.00 200.00

2008-09 UD Black Quad Autographs
STATED PRINT RUN 10 SER.#'d SETS
QA2007 Thornton/Horford/Green/Scola 40.00 100.00
QA2008 Myo/Rse/Bsly/Wstbrk 300.00 600.00
QADUNK Hwrd/Spud/VC/Nique 100.00 250.00
QAPGDS Stktn/Isiah/Deron/Paul 125.00 300.00
QAROOK Love/Alxndr/Grdn/Glinri 60.00 150.00
QASTUD LeBron/KG/Kobe/MJ 6,000.00 12,000.00

2008-09 UD Black Rookie Signed Jersey Pieces
STATED PRINT RUN 50 SER.#'d SETS
*GOLD: .75X TO 2X BASIC HI
GOLD PRINT RUN 15 SER.#'d SETS
SJRAR Anthony Randolph 5.00 12.00
SJRBL Brook Lopez 10.00 25.00
SJRBR Brandon Rush 5.00 12.00
SJRCD Chris Douglas-Roberts 5.00 12.00
SJRCL Courtney Lee 6.00 15.00
SJRDA D.J. Augustin 8.00 20.00
SJRDG Donte Greene 5.00 12.00
SJRDR Derrick Rose 75.00 200.00
SJRDW D.J. White 5.00 12.00
SJREG Eric Gordon 12.00 30.00
SJRGH George Hill 8.00 20.00
SJRJA Joe Alexander 5.00 12.00
SJRJB Jerryd Bayless 6.00 15.00
SJRJD Joey Dorsey 5.00 12.00
SJRJG J.R. Giddens 5.00 12.00
SJRJH J.J. Hickson 5.00 12.00
SJRJM Javale McGee 8.00 20.00
SJRJT Jason Thompson 5.00 12.00
SJRKK Kosta Koufos 5.00 12.00
SJRKL Kevin Love 20.00 50.00
SJRMB Michael Beasley 8.00 20.00
SJRMC Mario Chalmers 8.00 20.00
SJRMS Marreese Speights 6.00 15.00
SJROM O.J. Mayo 6.00 15.00
SJRRA Ryan Anderson 6.00 15.00
SJRRF Rudy Fernandez 6.00 15.00
SJRRH Roy Hibbert 6.00 15.00
SJRRL Robin Lopez 6.00 15.00
SJRRW Russell Westbrook 100.00 250.00
SJRSW Sonny Weems 5.00 12.00
SJRWS Walter Sharpe 5.00 12.00

2008-09 UD Black Rookie Signed Jersey Pieces Dual
STATED PRINT RUN 10 SER.#'d SETS
DJRAL R.Anderson/B.Lopez 20.00 50.00
DJRAM D.Arthur/O.Mayo 25.00 50.00
DJRAR B.Rush/D.Augustin 10.00 25.00
DJRBC M.Chalmers/M.Beasley 30.00 80.00
DJRBR M.Beasley/D.Rose 250.00 500.00
DJRDD C.-Roberts/J.Dorsey 10.00 25.00
DJRDH G.Hill/C.D-Roberts 20.00 40.00
DJRGB E.Gordon/J.Bayless 10.00 25.00
DJRGJ Jordan/Gordon 15.00 40.00
DJRGS J.Giddens/W.Sharpe 10.00 25.00
DJRGW S.Weems/J.Giddens 10.00 25.00
DJRHB R.Hibbert/B.Rush 12.00 30.00
DJRHS J.Hickson/W.Sharpe 10.00 25.00
DJRLA J.Alexander/K.Love 25.00 60.00
DJRLL R.Lopez/B.Lopez 15.00 40.00
DJRML R.Lopez/J.McGee 12.00 30.00
DJRRA Randolph/Alexander 20.00 40.00
DJRRH Randolph/Hickson 10.00 25.00
DJRSK K.Koufos/M.Speights 10.00 25.00
DJRTL K.Love/J.Thompson 25.00 60.00
DJRTS Thompson/Speights 10.00 25.00
DJRWG S.Weems/D.Greene 10.00 25.00
DJRWW R.Westbrook/D.White 30.00 80.00

2008-09 UD Black Team Logo Autographs
STATED PRINT RUN 21 TO 49 SER.#'d SETS
*GOLD: .6X TO 1.5X BASE HI
GOLD PRINT RUN 9 TO 20 SETS
TLAH Al Horford/25 6.00 15.00
TLAJ Antawn Jamison/24 6.00 15.00
TLAT Al Thornton/21 6.00 15.00
TLBG Ben Gordon/25 10.00 25.00
TLBR Brandon Roy/25 25.00 60.00
TLCB Corey Brewer/25 6.00 15.00
TLCP Chris Paul/25 100.00 250.00
TLDC Daequan Cook/49 8.00 20.00
TLDH Dwight Howard/25 30.00 80.00
TLDL David Lee/25 6.00 15.00
TLJC Javaris Crittenton/24 6.00 15.00
TLJD Jared Dudley/25 6.00 15.00
TLJK Jason Kidd/25 25.00 60.00
TLJS Jason Smith/25 6.00 15.00
TLKG Kevin Garnett/25 50.00 120.00
TLLJ LeBron James/25 2,000.00 4,000.00
TLRA Ramon Sessions/25 6.00 15.00
TLRJ Richard Jefferson/25 6.00 15.00
TLRS Rodney Stuckey/25 10.00 25.00
TLSM J.R. Smith/25 10.00 25.00

2008-09 UD Black Trophy Patch Autographs
STATED PRINT RUN 5 TO 25 SER.#'d SETS
TPDR David Robinson/25 200.00 500.00
TPJO Michael Jordan/25 3,000.00 5,000.00
TPKG Kevin Garnett/25 150.00 400.00
TPLB Larry Bird/25 600.00 1,200.00
TPMJ Magic Johnson/25 400.00 800.00
TPOR Oscar Robertson/25 150.00 400.00

2008-09 UD Black Veteran Signed Jersey Pieces
STATED PRINT RUN 5 TO 50 SER.#'d SETS
SPVAB Andrew Bynum/50 8.00 20.00
SPVAH Al Horford/50 8.00 20.00
SPVAM Alonzo Mourning/50 25.00 50.00
SPVAS Amare Stoudemire/50 12.00 30.00
SPVBE Marco Belinelli/50 8.00 20.00
SPVDH Dwight Howard/50 25.00 60.00
SPVGI Daniel Gibson/50 10.00 25.00
SPVJF Jordan Farmar/50 8.00 20.00
SPVJJ Jarrett Jack/50 8.00 20.00
SPVKB Kobe Bryant/50 1,000.00 2,000.00
SPVKD Kevin Durant/50 125.00 300.00
SPVKG Kevin Garnett/50 125.00 300.00
SPVLJ LeBron James/50 800.00 1,500.00
SPVMB Mike Bibby/50 10.00 25.00
SPVMC Mike Conley Jr./50 8.00 20.00
SPVPP Paul Pierce/50 40.00 100.00
SPVRF Randy Foye/50 8.00 20.00
SPVRJ Richard Jefferson/50 8.00 20.00
SPVSN Steve Nash/50 75.00 200.00
SPVTC Tyson Chandler/50 8.00 20.00
SPVYM Yao Ming/50 15.00 40.00

2008-09 UD Black Veteran Signed Jersey Pieces Dual
STATED PRINT RUN 10 SER.#'d SETS
DJVAP R.Allen/P.Pierce/5 125.00 300.00
DJVBG K.Garnett/K.Bryant 800.00 1,500.00
DJVBJ M.Bibby/J.Jack 25.00 50.00
DJVBP M.Bibby/C.Paul 50.00 120.00
DJVGJ R.Jefferson/R.Gay 15.00 40.00
DJVGS D.Gibson/R.Stuckey 15.00 40.00
DJVHC D.Howard/T.Chandler 30.00 60.00
DJVJD L.James/K.Durant 1,000.00 2,000.00
DJVNS A.Stoudemire/S.Nash 75.00 150.00
DJVPJ L.James/P.Pierce 1,000.00 2,000.00

2008-09 UD Black Veteran Signed Patch Pieces
STATED PRINT RUN 15 SER.#'d SETS
AB Andrew Bynum 12.50 30.00
DC Daequan Cook 12.50 30.00
DG Danny Granger 20.00 50.00
JF Jordan Farmar 15.00 40.00
KD Kevin Durant 100.00 200.00
KG Kevin Garnett 75.00 200.00
LJ LeBron James 1,250.00 2,500.00
MB Mike Bibby 15.00 40.00
PP Paul Pierce 40.00 80.00
RF Randy Foye 12.50 30.00
RJ Richard Jefferson 12.50 30.00
SN Steve Nash 50.00 120.00
TC Tyson Chandler 12.50 30.00
YM Yao Ming 50.00 120.00
AH2 Al Harrington 12.50 30.00

2013-14 UD Black
1-45 PRINT RUN 175 SER.#'d SETS
46-67 PRINT RUNS 199 SER.#'d SETS
68-72 PRINT RUN 99 SER.#'d SETS
EXCHANGE DEADLINE 2/24/2016
1 Michael Jordan/175 6.00 15.00
2 LeBron James/175 6.00 15.00
3 Clyde Drexler/175 3.00 8.00
4 Julius Erving/175 5.00 12.00
5 Joe Smith/175 1.50 4.00
6 Antoine Walker/175 1.50 4.00
7 Jerry Lucas/175 2.00 5.00
8 Elvin Hayes/175 2.50 6.00
9 Tony Gwynn/175 2.00 5.00
10 Magic Johnson/175 8.00 20.00
11 Allan Houston/175 2.00 5.00
12 Dave Cowens/175 2.00 5.00
13 David Thompson/175 2.00 5.00
14 Jamal Mashburn/175 1.50 4.00
15 Danny Manning/175 1.50 4.00
16 John Havlicek/175 5.00 12.00
17 Larry Bird/175 8.00 20.00
18 Toni Kukoc/175 2.50 6.00
19 Tim Hardaway Sr/175 2.50 6.00
20 Anfernee Hardaway/175 5.00 12.00
21 Alonzo Mourning/175 3.00 8.00
22 Larry Johnson/175 2.50 6.00
23 David Robinson/175 4.00 10.00
24 Sam Perkins/175 1.50 4.00
25 Reggie Miller/175 3.00 8.00
26 Dennis Rodman/175 5.00 12.00
27 Isiah Thomas/175 3.00 8.00
28 Hakeem Olajuwon/175 4.00 10.00
29 Grant Hill/175 3.00 8.00
30 Allen Iverson/175 4.00 10.00
31 Bill Walton/175 3.00 8.00
32 Karl Malone/175 4.00 10.00
33 Dominique Wilkins/175 3.00 8.00
34 Cheryl Miller/175 2.00 5.00
35 Corliss Williamson/175 1.25 3.00
36 Kenny Anderson/175 1.50 4.00
37 Donyell Marshall/175 1.25 3.00
38 Glenn Robinson/175 1.50 4.00
39 Jason Kidd/175 3.00 8.00
40 Jay Williams/175 1.25 3.00
41 Glen Rice/175 1.50 4.00
42 Paul George/175 3.00 8.00
43 Keith Smart/175 2.00 5.00
44 Rajon Rondo/175 2.50 6.00
45 Chris Paul/175 4.00 10.00
46 Grant Jerrett AU/199 4.00 10.00
47 Sergey Karasev AU/199 EXCH 4.00 10.00
48 Allen Crabbe AU/199 4.00 10.00
49 Nemanja Nedovic AU/199 4.00 10.00
50 Peyton Siva AU/199 4.00 10.00
51 Andre Roberson AU/199 5.00 12.00
52 Isaiah Canaan AU/199 4.00 10.00
53 Lorenzo Brown AU/199 4.00 10.00
54 Erick Green AU/199 5.00 12.00
55 Jamaal Franklin AU/199 4.00 10.00
56 Tony Snell AU/199 5.00 12.00
57 Deshaun Thomas AU/199 4.00 10.00
58 Reggie Bullock AU/199 5.00 12.00
59 Pierre Jackson AU/199 4.00 10.00
60 Ryan Kelly AU/199 4.00 10.00
61 R.Gobert AU/199 EXCH 10.00 25.00
62 Archie Goodwin AU/199 4.00 10.00
63 G.Antetokounmpo AU/199 150.00 400.00
64 Livio Jean-Charles AU/199 4.00 10.00
65 Mike Muscala AU/199 6.00 15.00
67 Solomon Hill AU/199 5.00 12.00
68 Shane Larkin AU/99 6.00 15.00
69 Lucas Nogueira AU/99 6.00 15.00
70 Skylar Diggins AU/99 10.00 25.00
71 Tim Hardaway Jr. AU/99 12.00 30.00
72 Mason Plumlee AU/99 8.00 20.00
73 D.Schroeder AU/99 EXCH 12.00 30.00

2013-14 UD Black Gold Spectrum
1-44 PRINT RUN 1 SER.#'d SET
*GOLD 46-67: .75X TO 2X BASIC
*GOLD 68-73: .75X TO 2X BASIC
46-73 PRINT RUN 25 SER.#'d SETS
EXCHANGE DEADLINE 2/24/2016
50 Peyton Siva/25 10.00 25.00

2013-14 UD Black Arena Art
PRINT RUNS B/WN 23-65 COPIES PER
EXCHANGE DEADLINE 2/24/2016
AAC A.C. Green/65 6.00 15.00
AAE Alex English/65 8.00 20.00
AAH Allan Houston/65 6.00 15.00
ABD Brad Daugherty/65 8.00 20.00
ABL Bill Laimbeer/65 12.00 30.00
ABM Bob McAdoo/65 8.00 20.00
ABR Bryant Reeves/65 6.00 15.00
ABW Bill Walton/65 10.00 25.00
ACL Christian Laettner/65 12.00 30.00
ADM Danny Manning/65 12.00 30.00
ADS Detlef Schrempf/65 10.00 25.00
ADW D.Wilkins/65 EXCH 10.00 25.00
AGH Grant Hill/65 25.00 60.00
AHI Grant Hill/65 25.00 60.00
AHO Hakeem Olajuwon/65 20.00 50.00
AIT Isiah Thomas/65 10.00 25.00
AJH Jeff Hornacek/65 5.00 12.00
AJO Michael Jordan/23 400.00 800.00
AJW Jay Williams/65 12.00 30.00
AKA Kenny Anderson/65 10.00 25.00
AKG Kendall Gill/65 10.00 25.00
AKM Karl Malone/30 50.00 100.00
AKS Keith Smart/65 10.00 25.00
ALA Larry Johnson/65 12.00 30.00
ALB Larry Bird/30 60.00 150.00
ALS Lonnie Shelton/65 4.00 10.00
AMI Michael Jordan/23 400.00 800.00
AMJ Michael Jordan/23 400.00 800.00
AMR M.Ray Richardson/65 10.00 25.00
ANV Nick Van Exel/65 10.00 25.00
APG Paul George/65 20.00 50.00
ARH Robert Horry/65 10.00 25.00
ASB Shawn Bradley/65 4.00 10.00
ASE Sean Elliott/65 20.00 50.00
ASN Swen Nater/65 10.00 25.00

2013-14 UD Black Chalk Signatures
PRINT RUNS B/WN 23-40 COPIES PER
EXCHANGE DEADLINE 2/24/2016
CSAH Anfernee Hardaway/40 20.00 50.00
CSAW Antoine Walker/40 12.00 30.00
CSCM Cheryl Miller/40 6.00 15.00
CSDM Danny Manning/40 10.00 25.00
CSDR David Robinson/25 20.00 50.00
CSDT David Thompson/40 10.00 25.00
CSGH Grant Hill/40 12.00 30.00
CSHO Hakeem Olajuwon/40 20.00 50.00
CSJO Magic Johnson/25 EXCH 25.00 60.00
CSJW Jay Williams/40 4.00 10.00
CSKA Kenny Anderson/40 5.00 12.00
CSKM Karl Malone/40 25.00 60.00
CSLB Larry Bird/25 50.00 100.00
CSLJ LeBron James/40 EXCH 1,500.00 3,000.00
CSMJ Michael Jordan/23 350.00 450.00

2013-14 UD Black Jordan Brand Classic Dual Autographs
PRINT RUNS B/WN 10-99 COPIES PER
NO PRICING ON QTY 13 OR LESS
EXCHANGE DEADLINE 2/24/2016
JBC21 J.Sullinger/A.Bradley/40 4.00 10.00
JBC24 R.Sidney/R.White/40 8.00 20.00
JBC25 D.Lamb/R.Sidney/40 8.00 20.00
JBC27 P.Jones/Q.Miller/40 6.00 15.00
JBC28 K.Irving/A.Rivers/40 25.00 60.00
JBC29 B.Knight/T.Jones/35 15.00 40.00
JBC210 J.Holiday/M.Teague/45 8.00 20.00
JBC212 H.Barnes/E.Davis/35 15.00 40.00
JBC213 H.Barnes/J.Sullinger/40 20.00 50.00
JBC215 P.Jones/T.Jones/40 10.00 25.00
JBC216 R.Sidney/T.Wroten/99 8.00 20.00
JBC219 B.Knight/J.Holiday/40 10.00 25.00
JBC220 M.Gilchrist/Q.Miller/30 10.00 25.00
JBC221 B.Beal/X.Henry/40 12.00 30.00
JBC222 D.Waiters/A.Bradley/40 4.00 10.00

2013-14 UD Black Jordan Brand Classic Triple Autographs
PRINT RUNS B/WN 10-99 COPIES PER
NO PRICING ON QTY 15 OR LESS
EXCHANGE DEADLINE 2/24/2016
JBC35 Bradley/White/Griffin/90 4.00 10.00
JBC36 Holiday/White/Griffin/50 8.00 20.00
JBC39 Noel/Bennett/Muhammad/99 5.00 12.00

2013-14 UD Black Legendary Lustrous Signatures
STATED PRINT RUN 25 SER.#'d SETS
EXCHANGE DEADLINE 2/24/2016
LLAH Anfernee Hardaway 30.00 60.00
LLAM Alonzo Mourning 20.00 50.00
LLDR David Robinson 20.00 50.00
LLGH Grant Hill 20.00 50.00
LLJE Julius Erving 30.00 60.00
LLJO Magic Johnson EXCH 40.00 100.00
LLKM Karl Malone 25.00 60.00
LLLB Larry Bird 25.00 60.00
LLMI Michael Jordan 250.00 400.00
LLMJ Michael Jordan 250.00 400.00
LLTG Tony Gwynn 30.00 80.00

2013-14 UD Black Logo Signatures
STATED PRINT RUN 40 SER.#'d SETS
EXCHANGE DEADLINE 2/24/2016
LSAE Alex English 10.00 25.00
LSAG A.C. Green 10.00 25.00
LSAH Anfernee Hardaway 30.00 60.00
LSAL Allan Houston 8.00 20.00
LSAM Alonzo Mourning 12.00 30.00
LSAW Antoine Walker 10.00 25.00
LSBD Brad Daugherty 10.00 25.00
LSBR Bryant Reeves 10.00 25.00
LSBU Buck Williams 10.00 25.00
LSBW Bill Walton 10.00 25.00
LSCL Christian Laettner 12.00 30.00
LSCM Cheryl Miller 8.00 20.00
LSCO Dave Cowens 8.00 20.00
LSCW Corliss Williamson 10.00 25.00
LSDA Danny Manning 12.00 30.00
LSDM Donyell Marshall 5.00 12.00
LSDS Detlef Schrempf 12.00 30.00
LSDT David Thompson 12.00 30.00
LSDW Dominique Wilkins EXCH 20.00 50.00
LSGH Grant Hill 40.00 100.00
LSGL Glenn Robinson EXCH 12.00 30.00
LSGR Glen Rice 12.00 30.00
LSHM Harold Miner 5.00 12.00
LSHO Hakeem Olajuwon 10.00 25.00
LSIT Isiah Thomas 12.00 30.00
LSJA Mark A. Jackson 6.00 15.00
LSJE Julius Erving 40.00 80.00
LSJH Jeff Hornacek 15.00 40.00
LSJL Jerry Lucas 15.00 40.00
LSJM Jamal Mashburn 10.00 25.00
LSJO Larry Johnson 12.00 30.00
LSJW Jay Williams 10.00 25.00
LSKA Kenny Anderson 6.00 15.00
LSKK Kerry Kittles 10.00 25.00
LSKM Karl Malone 20.00 50.00
LSKS Keith Smart 8.00 20.00
LSLB Larry Bird 60.00 120.00
LSLJ LeBron James EXCH 1,500.00 3,000.00
LSLS Lonnie Shelton 5.00 12.00
LSMB Muggsy Bogues 8.00 20.00
LSMC Michael Cooper 8.00 20.00
LSMJ Michael Jordan 300.00 600.00
LSPG Paul George 20.00 50.00
LSRO David Robinson 20.00 50.00
LSRR Rajon Rondo 15.00 40.00
LSRS Rod Strickland 6.00 15.00
LSRT Reggie Theus 6.00 15.00
LSRU Bill Russell 500.00 1,000.00
LSSB Shawn Bradley 5.00 12.00
LSSE Sean Elliott 15.00 40.00
LSTB Terrell Brandon 5.00 12.00
LSTG Tony Gwynn 25.00 60.00
LSTH Tim Hardaway 10.00 25.00
LSVN Vinny Del Negro 5.00 12.00

2013-14 UD Black Old School Signatures
PRINT RUNS B/WN 23-75 COPIES PER
EXCHANGE DEADLINE 2/24/2016
OSAE Alex English/75 8.00 20.00
OSAG A.C. Green/75 6.00 15.00
OSAM Alonzo Mourning/75 10.00 25.00
OSCC Calbert Cheaney/75 10.00 25.00
OSCW Corliss Williamson/75 4.00 10.00
OSDM Danny Manning/75 5.00 12.00
OSDT David Thompson/75 8.00 20.00
OSEH Elvin Hayes/75 10.00 25.00
OSHA Anfernee Hardaway/75 20.00 50.00
OSHO Hakeem Olajuwon/75 15.00 40.00
OSJE Julius Erving/25 40.00 80.00
OSJL Jerry Lucas/75 6.00 15.00
OSJO Magic Johnson/25 EXCH 40.00 80.00
OSKK Kerry Kittles/75 4.00 10.00
OSKS Keith Smart/75 6.00 15.00
OSLB Larry Bird/25 40.00 80.00
OSLJ LeBron James/75 EXCH 1,000.00 2,000.00
OSRI Glen Rice/75 5.00 12.00
OSRU Bill Russell/25 1,000.00 2,000.00
OSTG Tony Gwynn/75 25.00 60.00

2013-14 UD Black Scenes Booklet Signatures
PRINT RUNS B/WN 23-35 COPIES PER
EXCHANGE DEADLINE 2/24/2016
SCAH Anfernee Hardaway/35 20.00 50.00
SCAM Alonzo Mourning/35 20.00 50.00
SCAW Antoine Walker/35 20.00 50.00
SCCC Calbert Cheaney/35 25.00 60.00
SCGH Grant Hill/35 25.00 60.00
SCGR Glenn Robinson/35 EXCH 15.00 40.00
SCHA Hakeem Olajuwon/35 25.00 60.00
SCIT Isiah Thomas/35 20.00 50.00
SCJO Michael Jordan/35 350.00 500.00
SCKG Kendall Gill/35 20.00 50.00
SCLJ LeBron James/35 EXCH 1,500.00 3,000.00
SCMA Magic Johnson/35 EXCH 40.00 100.00
SCMI Michael Jordan/23 350.00 500.00
SCMJ Michael Jordan/23 350.00 500.00
SCRR Rajon Rondo/35 20.00 50.00
SCTH Tim Hardaway/35 10.00 25.00

2013-14 UD Black Signatures
PRINT RUNS B/WN 23-75 COPIES PER
EXCHANGE DEADLINE 2/24/2016
SAE Alex English/75 8.00 20.00
SAG A.C. Green/75 10.00 25.00
SAH Allan Houston/75 8.00 20.00
SAI Allen Iverson/25 60.00 120.00
SAW Antoine Walker/75 8.00 20.00
SBR Bill Russell/25 1,000.00 2,000.00
SBW Bill Walton/75 10.00 25.00
SCC Calbert Cheaney/75 8.00 20.00
SCW Corliss Williamson/75 15.00 40.00
SDR David Robinson/75 20.00 50.00
SEH Elvin Hayes/75 8.00 20.00
SGH Grant Hill/75 20.00 50.00
SGR Glenn Robinson/75 EXCH 10.00 25.00
SHA Anfernee Hardaway/75 20.00 50.00
SJA LeBron James/75 EXCH 1,000.00 2,000.00
SJE Julius Erving/75 30.00 80.00
SJL Jerry Lucas/75 10.00 25.00
SJM Jamal Mashburn/75 10.00 25.00
SJO Michael Jordan/23 350.00 600.00
SJW Jay Williams/75 4.00 10.00
SKA Kenny Anderson/75 5.00 12.00
SKK Kerry Kittles/75 4.00 10.00
SKM Karl Malone/75 20.00 50.00
SKS Keith Smart/75 6.00 15.00
SLB Larry Bird/25 50.00 100.00
SLJ Larry Johnson/75 8.00 20.00
SMA Mark A. Jackson/75 5.00 12.00
SMJ Magic Johnson/75 EXCH 40.00 80.00
SOB Otis Birdsong/75 5.00 12.00
SPG Paul George/75 25.00 60.00
SRR Rajon Rondo/75 12.00 30.00
STC Toni Kukoc/75 8.00 20.00
STG Tony Gwynn/75 25.00 60.00

2014 UD Black Autographs
STATED PRINT RUN 10-65
27 Michael Jordan/25 1,000.00 2,000.00

2014 UD Black Pride of a Nation Patches Autographs
STATED PRINT RUN 10-35

1998-99 UD Choice Preview
COMPLETE SET (55) 3.00 8.00
1 Dikembe Mutombo .15 .40
3 Mookie Blaylock .07 .20
7 Ron Mercer .07 .20
9 Walter McCarty .05 .15
13 Anthony Mason .07 .20
14 Glen Rice .10 .25
18 Toni Kukoc .10 .25
23 Michael Jordan 1.00 2.50
26 Zydrunas Ilgauskas .10 .25
27 Cedric Henderson .05 .15
29 Michael Finley .10 .25
32 Hubert Davis .05 .15
34 Bobby Jackson .07 .20
37 Danny Fortson .05 .15
41 Grant Hill .15 .40
43 Jerome Williams .05 .15

45 Erick Dampier .05 .15
48 Donyell Marshall .05 .15
50 Charles Barkley .25 .60
51 Hakeem Olajuwon .20 .50
56 Reggie Miller .20 .50
60 Chris Mullin .12 .30
64 Eric Piatkowski .05 .15
65 Maurice Taylor .05 .15
68 Shaquille O'Neal .40 1.00
69 Kobe Bryant .75 2.00
74 Alonzo Mourning .15 .40
75 Tim Hardaway .12 .30
79 Ray Allen .15 .40
80 Terrell Brandon .07 .20
84 Stephon Marbury .12 .30
85 Kevin Garnett .25 .60
89 Keith Van Horn .10 .25
90 Sam Cassell .07 .20
95 Patrick Ewing .15 .40
97 John Starks .10 .25
100 Anfernee Hardaway .25 .60
101 Nick Anderson .05 .15
105 Allen Iverson .25 .60
110 Jason Kidd .15 .40
117 Isaiah Rider .07 .20
118 Rasheed Wallace .12 .30
121 Corliss Williamson .05 .15
123 Billy Owens .07 .20
126 Tim Duncan .25 .60
127 Sean Elliott .10 .25
131 Vin Baker .07 .20
135 Gary Payton .15 .40
137 Chauncey Billups .12 .30
142 John Stockton .20 .50
143 Karl Malone .20 .50
148 Bryant Reeves .05 .15
149 Shareef Abdur-Rahim .10 .25
152 Harvey Grant .05 .15
153 Juwan Howard .07 .20

1998-99 UD Choice Preview Michael Jordan NBA Finals Shots

COMMON CARD (1-10) 2.00 5.00

1998-99 UD Choice

COMPLETE SET (200) 8.00 20.00
1 Dikembe Mutombo .20 .50
2 Alan Henderson .07 .20
3 Mookie Blaylock .10 .25
4 Ed Gray .07 .20
5 Eldridge Recasner .07 .20
6 Kenny Anderson .10 .25
7 Ron Mercer .12 .30
8 Dana Barros .07 .20
9 Walter McCarty .07 .20
10 Travis Knight .07 .20
11 Andrew DeClercq .07 .20
12 David Wesley .07 .20
13 Anthony Mason .10 .25
14 Glen Rice .12 .30
15 J.R. Reid .07 .20
16 Bobby Phills .07 .20
17 Dell Curry .07 .20
18 Toni Kukoc .12 .30
19 Randy Brown .07 .20
20 Ron Harper .12 .30
21 Keith Booth .07 .20
22 Scott Burrell .07 .20
23 Michael Jordan 1.25 3.00
24 Derek Anderson .10 .25
25 Brevin Knight .07 .20
26 Zydrunas Ilgauskas .12 .30
27 Cedric Henderson .07 .20
28 Vitaly Potapenko .07 .20
29 Michael Finley .12 .30
30 Erick Strickland .07 .20
31 Shawn Bradley .07 .20
32 Hubert Davis .07 .20
33 Khalid Reeves .07 .20
34 Bobby Jackson .10 .25
35 Tony Battie .07 .20
36 Bryant Stith .07 .20
37 Danny Fortson .07 .20
38 Dean Garrett .07 .20
39 Eric Williams .07 .20
40 Brian Williams .07 .20
41 Grant Hill .20 .50
42 Lindsey Hunter .07 .20
43 Jerome Williams .07 .20
44 Eric Montross .07 .20
45 Erick Dampier .07 .20
46 Muggsy Bogues .10 .25
47 Tony Delk .07 .20
48 Donyell Marshall .07 .20
49 Bimbo Coles .07 .20
50 Charles Barkley .30 .75
51 Hakeem Olajuwon .25 .60
52 Brent Price .07 .20
53 Mario Elie .07 .20
54 Rodrick Rhodes .07 .20
55 Kevin Willis .07 .20
56 Reggie Miller .25 .60
57 Jalen Rose .10 .25
58 Mark Jackson .10 .25
59 Dale Davis .07 .20
60 Chris Mullin .15 .40
61 Derrick McKey .07 .20
62 Lorenzen Wright .07 .20
63 Rodney Rogers .07 .20
64 Eric Piatkowski .07 .20
65 Maurice Taylor .07 .20
66 Isaac Austin .07 .20
67 Corie Blount .07 .20
68 Shaquille O'Neal .50 1.25
69 Kobe Bryant 1.00 2.50
70 Robert Horry .10 .25
71 Sean Rooks .07 .20
72 Derek Fisher .10 .25
73 P.J. Brown .07 .20
74 Alonzo Mourning .20 .50
75 Tim Hardaway .15 .40
76 Voshon Lenard .07 .20
77 Dan Majerle .12 .30
78 Ervin Johnson .07 .20
79 Ray Allen .20 .50
80 Terrell Brandon .10 .25
81 Tyrone Hill .07 .20
82 Elliot Perry .07 .20
83 Anthony Peeler .07 .20
84 Stephon Marbury .15 .40
85 Kevin Garnett .30 .75
86 Paul Grant .07 .20
87 Chris Carr .07 .20
88 Micheal Williams UER .07 .20
89 Keith Van Horn .12 .30
90 Sam Cassell .10 .25
91 Kendall Gill .10 .25
92 Chris Gatling .07 .20
93 Kerry Kittles .10 .25
94 Allan Houston .12 .30
95 Patrick Ewing UER .20 .50
96 Charles Oakley .10 .25
97 John Starks .12 .30
98 Charlie Ward .07 .20
99 Chris Mills .07 .20
100 Anfernee Hardaway .30 .75
101 Nick Anderson .07 .20
102 Mark Price .12 .30
103 Horace Grant .12 .30
104 David Benoit .07 .20
105 Allen Iverson .30 .75
106 Joe Smith .10 .25
107 Tim Thomas .10 .25
108 Brian Shaw .07 .20
109 Aaron McKie .07 .20
110 Jason Kidd .20 .50
111 Danny Manning .10 .25
112 Steve Nash .25 .60
113 Rex Chapman .10 .25
114 Dennis Scott .07 .20
115 Antonio McDyess .10 .25
116 Damon Stoudamire .12 .30
117 Isaiah Rider .07 .20
118 Rasheed Wallace .15 .40
119 Kelvin Cato .07 .20
120 Jermaine O'Neal .12 .30
121 Corliss Williamson .07 .20
122 Olden Polynice .07 .20
123 Billy Owens .10 .25
124 Lawrence Funderburke .07 .20
125 Anthony Johnson .07 .20
126 Tim Duncan .30 .75
127 Sean Elliott .12 .30
128 Avery Johnson .10 .25
129 Vinny Del Negro .07 .20
130 Monty Williams .10 .25
131 Vin Baker .10 .25
132 Hersey Hawkins .10 .25
133 Nate McMillan .12 .30
134 Detlef Schrempf .12 .30
135 Gary Payton .20 .50
136 Jim McIlvaine .07 .20
137 Chauncey Billups .15 .40
138 Doug Christie .10 .25
139 John Wallace .07 .20
140 Tracy McGrady .20 .50
141 Dee Brown .07 .20
142 John Stockton .25 .60
143 Karl Malone .25 .60
144 Shandon Anderson .07 .20
145 Jacque Vaughn .07 .20
146 Bryon Russell .07 .20
147 Lee Mayberry .07 .20
148 Bryant Reeves .07 .20
149 Shareef Abdur-Rahim .12 .30
150 Michael Smith .07 .20
151 Pete Chilcutt .07 .20
152 Harvey Grant .10 .25
153 Juwan Howard .10 .25
154 Calbert Cheaney .07 .20
155 Tracy Murray .07 .20
156 Dikembe Mutombo FS .20 .50
157 Antoine Walker FS .12 .30
158 Glen Rice FS .12 .30
159 Michael Jordan FS 1.25 3.00
160 Wesley Person FS .07 .20
161 Shawn Bradley FS .07 .20
162 Dean Garrett FS .07 .20
163 Jerry Stackhouse FS .12 .30
164 Donyell Marshall FS .07 .20
165 Hakeem Olajuwon FS .25 .60
166 Chris Mullin FS .15 .40
167 Isaac Austin FS .07 .20
168 Shaquille O'Neal FS .50 1.25
169 Tim Hardaway FS .15 .40
170 Glenn Robinson FS .12 .30
171 Kevin Garnett FS .30 .75
172 Keith Van Horn FS .12 .30
173 Larry Johnson FS .20 .50
174 Horace Grant FS .10 .25
175 Derrick Coleman FS .10 .25
176 Steve Nash FS .25 .60
177 Arvydas Sabonis FS UER .12 .30
178 Corliss Williamson FS .07 .20
179 David Robinson FS .25 .60
180 Vin Baker FS .10 .25
181 Marcus Camby FS .12 .30
182 John Stockton FS .25 .60
183 Antonio Daniels FS .07 .20
184 Rod Strickland FS .10 .25
185 Michael Jordan FS 1.25 3.00
186 Kobe Bryant YIR 1.00 2.50
187 Clyde Drexler YIR .15 .40
188 Gary Payton YIR .20 .50
189 Michael Jordan YIR 1.25 3.00
190 D.Robinson/T.Duncan YIR .30 .75
191 Attendance Record YIR .07 .20
192 Karl Malone YIR .25 .60
193 Dikembe Mutombo YIR .07 .20
194 New Jersey Nets YIR .12 .30
195 Ray Allen YIR .20 .50
196 Michael Jordan YIR 1.25 3.00
197 Los Angeles Lakers YIR 1.00 2.50
198 Michael Jordan YIR 1.25 3.00
199 Michael Jordan CL .40 1.00
200 Michael Jordan CL .40 1.00

1998-99 UD Choice Reserve

*STARS: 3X TO 8X BASE CARD HI
STATED ODDS 1:6 HOB/RET

1998-99 UD Choice Premium Choice Reserve

*STARS: 40X TO 100X BASE CARD HI
STATED PRINT RUN 100 SERIAL #'d SETS
23 Michael Jordan 250.00 350.00
69 Kobe Bryant 75.00 200.00

1998-99 UD Choice Mini Bobbing Heads

COMPLETE SET (30) 4.00 10.00
STATED ODDS 1:4 HOB/RET
1 Dikembe Mutombo .25 .60
2 Antoine Walker .15 .40
3 Anthony Mason .12 .30
4 Toni Kukoc .15 .40
5 Shawn Kemp .25 .60
6 Shawn Bradley .12 .30
7 Danny Fortson .10 .25
8 Brian Williams .10 .25
9 Muggsy Bogues .12 .30
10 Charles Barkley .40 1.00
11 Mark Jackson .12 .30
12 Rodney Rogers .10 .25
13 Kobe Bryant 1.25 3.00
14 Tim Hardaway .20 .50
15 Ray Allen .25 .60
16 Kevin Garnett .40 1.00
17 Sam Cassell .12 .30
18 John Starks .15 .40
19 Anfernee Hardaway .40 1.00
20 Allen Iverson .40 1.00
21 Danny Manning .12 .30
22 Rasheed Wallace .20 .50
23 Chris Webber .20 .50
24 David Robinson .30 .75
25 Gary Payton .25 .60
26 Marcus Camby .12 .30
27 John Stockton .30 .75
28 Bryant Reeves .10 .25
29 Juwan Howard .12 .30
30 Michael Jordan 1.50 4.00

1998-99 UD Choice StarQuest Blue

STATED ODDS 1:1 HOB/RET
*GREEN STARS: 1.25X TO 3X HI COLUMN
GREEN: STATED ODDS 1:8 H/R
*RED STARS: 3X TO 8X HI COLUMN
RED: STATED ODDS 1:23 H/R
SQ1 Steve Smith .15 .40
SQ2 Kenny Anderson .15 .40
SQ3 Glen Rice .20 .50
SQ4 Toni Kukoc .20 .50
SQ5 Shawn Kemp .30 .75
SQ6 Michael Finley .20 .50
SQ7 Bobby Jackson .15 .40
SQ8 Grant Hill .30 .75
SQ9 Donyell Marshall .12 .30
SQ10 Hakeem Olajuwon .40 1.00
SQ11 Reggie Miller .40 1.00
SQ12 Maurice Taylor .12 .30
SQ13 Kobe Bryant 1.50 4.00
SQ14 Alonzo Mourning .30 .75
SQ15 Terrell Brandon .15 .40
SQ16 Stephon Marbury .25 .60
SQ17 Keith Van Horn .20 .50
SQ18 Patrick Ewing .30 .75
SQ19 Anfernee Hardaway .50 1.25
SQ20 Allen Iverson .50 1.25
SQ21 Jason Kidd .30 .75
SQ22 Damon Stoudamire .20 .50
SQ23 Corliss Williamson .12 .30
SQ24 Tim Duncan .50 1.25
SQ25 Gary Payton .30 .75
SQ26 Chauncey Billups .25 .60
SQ27 Karl Malone .40 1.00
SQ28 Shareef Abdur-Rahim .20 .50
SQ29 Juwan Howard .20 .50
SQ30 Michael Jordan 2.00 5.00

1998-99 UD Choice StarQuest Gold

*STARS: 125X TO 300X BASE INSERT
STATED PRINT RUN 100 SERIAL #'d SETS
SQ8 Grant Hill 400.00 800.00
SQ13 Kobe Bryant 10,000.00 15,000.00
SQ19 Anfernee Hardaway 400.00 800.00
SQ24 Tim Duncan 400.00 800.00
SQ30 Michael Jordan 15,000.00 30,000.00

2002-03 UD Glass

COMP.SET w/o SP's (90) 15.00 40.00
91-110 CW STATED ODDS 1:15
111-120 PRINT RUN 250 SERIAL #'d SETS
121-130 PRINT RUN 500 SERIAL #'d SETS
131-150 PRINT RUN 900 SERIAL #'d SETS
**91-150 PRINTED ON GLASS
1 Shareef Abdur-Rahim .40 1.00
2 Glenn Robinson .40 1.00
3 Jason Terry .30 .75
4 Paul Pierce .60 1.50
5 Antoine Walker .30 .75
6 Vin Baker .30 .75
7 Jalen Rose .30 .75
8 Eddy Curry .25 .60
9 Tyson Chandler .40 1.00
10 Darius Miles .25 .60
11 Ricky Davis .30 .75
12 Zydrunas Ilgauskas .30 .75
13 Dirk Nowitzki 1.00 2.50
14 Michael Finley .40 1.00
15 Steve Nash .75 2.00
16 Raef LaFrentz .25 .60
17 Rodney White .25 .60
18 Marcus Camby .25 .60
19 Juwan Howard .30 .75
20 Richard Hamilton .50 1.25
21 Ben Wallace .50 1.25
22 Chauncey Billups .40 1.00
23 Jason Richardson .40 1.00
24 Antawn Jamison .30 .75
25 Steve Francis .40 1.00
26 Cuttino Mobley .25 .60
27 Eddie Griffin .25 .60
28 Jermaine O'Neal .30 .75
29 Reggie Miller .75 2.00
30 Jamaal Tinsley .25 .60
31 Andre Miller .30 .75
32 Elton Brand .30 .75
33 Quentin Richardson .25 .60
34 Kobe Bryant 3.00 8.00
35 Shaquille O'Neal 1.50 4.00
36 Robert Horry .40 1.00
37 Pau Gasol .60 1.50
38 Shane Battier .40 1.00
39 Jason Williams .50 1.25
40 Eddie Jones .40 1.00
41 Brian Grant .25 .60
42 Malik Allen .25 .60
43 Ray Allen .60 1.50
44 Tim Thomas .25 .60
45 Sam Cassell .30 .75
46 Kevin Garnett 1.00 2.50
47 Wally Szczerbiak .30 .75
48 Troy Hudson .25 .60
49 Loren Woods .25 .60
50 Jason Kidd .60 1.50
51 Richard Jefferson .30 .75
52 Kenyon Martin .40 1.00
53 Baron Davis .40 1.00
54 Jamal Mashburn .30 .75
55 David Wesley .25 .60
56 P.J. Brown .25 .60
57 Allan Houston .40 1.00
58 Kurt Thomas .25 .60
59 Latrell Sprewell .40 1.00
60 Tracy McGrady .60 1.50
61 Mike Miller .30 .75
62 Grant Hill .40 1.00
63 Allen Iverson 1.00 2.50
64 Keith Van Horn .30 .75
65 Aaron McKie .25 .60
66 Stephon Marbury .50 1.25
67 Shawn Marion .40 1.00
68 Anfernee Hardaway 1.00 2.50
69 Rasheed Wallace .50 1.25
70 Damon Stoudamire .25 .60
71 Bonzi Wells .25 .60
72 Chris Webber .50 1.25
73 Mike Bibby .40 1.00
74 Peja Stojakovic .30 .75
75 Hedo Turkoglu .30 .75
76 Tim Duncan 1.00 2.50
77 David Robinson .75 2.00
78 Tony Parker .60 1.50
79 Gary Payton .60 1.50
80 Rashard Lewis .30 .75
81 Desmond Mason .30 .75
82 Vince Carter .75 2.00
83 Antonio Davis .30 .75
84 Morris Peterson .30 .75
85 John Stockton .75 2.00
86 Karl Malone .75 2.00
87 Andrei Kirilenko .30 .75
88 Jerry Stackhouse .40 1.00
89 Larry Hughes .30 .75
90 Michael Jordan 4.00 10.00
91 Kobe Bryant CW 20.00 50.00
92 Paul Pierce CW 4.00 10.00
93 Chris Webber CW 3.00 8.00
94 Vince Carter CW 5.00 12.00
95 Tracy McGrady CW 4.00 10.00
96 Allen Iverson CW 6.00 15.00
97 Pau Gasol CW 4.00 10.00
98 Steve Francis CW 2.50 6.00
99 Jason Kidd CW 4.00 10.00
100 Dirk Nowitzki CW 6.00 15.00
101 Antoine Walker CW 2.00 5.00
102 Jason Richardson CW 2.50 6.00
103 Baron Davis CW 2.50 6.00
104 Elton Brand CW 2.00 5.00
105 Stephon Marbury CW 3.00 8.00
106 Ray Allen CW 4.00 10.00
107 Shaquille O'Neal CW 10.00 25.00
108 Kevin Garnett CW 6.00 15.00
109 Tim Duncan CW 6.00 15.00
110 Mike Bibby CW 2.50 6.00
111 Jay Williams RC 5.00 12.00
112 Yao Ming RC 30.00 80.00
113 Mike Dunleavy RC 6.00 15.00
114 Drew Gooden RC 6.00 15.00
115 Nikoloz Tskitishvili RC 4.00 10.00
116 DaJuan Wagner RC 5.00 12.00
117 Nene Hilario RC 6.00 15.00
118 Amare Stoudemire RC 15.00 40.00
119 Caron Butler RC 6.00 15.00
120 Manu Ginobili RC 30.00 80.00
121 Juaquin Hawkins RC 2.50 6.00
122 Kareem Rush RC 3.00 8.00
123 Jiri Welsch RC 3.00 8.00
124 Chris Wilcox RC 3.00 8.00
125 Tayshaun Prince RC 8.00 20.00
126 Qyntel Woods RC 2.50 6.00
127 Jared Jeffries RC 3.00 8.00
128 Gordan Giricek RC 4.00 10.00
129 Ryan Humphrey RC 3.00 8.00
130 Marko Jaric 4.00 10.00
131 Casey Jacobsen RC 2.00 5.00
132 Dan Dickau RC 1.50 4.00
133 Juan Dixon RC 4.00 10.00
134 Melvin Ely RC 2.00 5.00
135 Fred Jones RC 2.00 5.00
136 John Salmons RC 2.50 6.00
137 Marcus Haislip RC 1.50 4.00
138 Carlos Boozer RC 2.50 6.00
139 Chris Jefferies RC 1.50 4.00
140 Smush Parker RC 2.50 6.00
141 Vincent Yarbrough RC 1.50 4.00
142 Pat Burke RC 1.50 4.00
143 Lonny Baxter RC 1.50 4.00
144 Bostjan Nachbar RC 2.00 5.00
145 Rasual Butler RC 2.00 5.00
146 Ronald Murray RC 2.50 6.00
147 J.R. Bremer RC 1.50 4.00
148 Reggie Evans RC 2.00 5.00
149 Sam Clancy RC 2.00 5.00
150 Tamar Slay RC 1.50 4.00
NNO Kobe Bryant AF PROMO 4.00 10.00

2002-03 UD Glass UD Promos

*PROMOS: .6X TO 1.5X BASIC

2002-03 UD Glass Auto Focus

STATED ODDS 1:72
AW Antoine Walker 6.00 15.00
CB Chauncey Billups 8.00 20.00
DS DeShawn Stevenson 4.00 10.00
DW Dominique Wilkins 12.00 30.00
ET Etan Thomas 4.00 10.00
GW Gerald Wallace 4.00 10.00
JK Jason Kidd 20.00 50.00
JM Jamaal Magloire 4.00 10.00
JO Jermaine O'Neal 4.00 10.00
JR Jason Richardson 4.00 10.00
JW Jay Williams 4.00 10.00
KA Kareem Abdul-Jabbar/20 75.00 200.00
KB Kobe Bryant/50 200.00 500.00
KG Kevin Garnett/50 75.00 200.00
MB Mike Bibby 4.00 10.00
MJ Michael Jordan/23 2,000.00 4,000.00
MM Mike Miller 4.00 10.00
PP Paul Pierce 20.00 50.00
TC Tyson Chandler 4.00 10.00
YM Yao Ming 30.00 80.00

2002-03 UD Glass One Two Combo Jerseys

PRINT RUN 125 SERIAL #'d SETS
ASCJ A.Stoudemire/C.Jacobsen 6.00 15.00
CWME C.Wilcox/M.Ely 6.00 15.00
DWCB D.Wagner/C.Boozer 6.00 15.00
JJDC J.Jeffries/J.Dixon 6.00 15.00
JOFJ J.O'Neal/F.Jones 6.00 15.00
JWJR J.Williams/J.Richardson 6.00 15.00
JWTC J.Williams/T.Chandler 6.00 15.00
KBKR K.Bryant/K.Rush 40.00 100.00
MJKB M.Jordan/K.Bryant 150.00 400.00
MMRH M.Miller/R.Humphrey 6.00 15.00
MPCJ M.Peterson/C.Jefferies 6.00 15.00
NHNT N.Hilario/N.Tskitishvili 6.00 15.00
SMAS S.Marion/A.Stoudemire 8.00 20.00

2002-03 UD Glass One Two Combo Jerseys Autographs

PRINT RUN 25 SERIAL #'d SETS
ASCJ Stoudemire/Jacobsen 15.00 40.00
CWME C.Wilcox/M.Ely 15.00 40.00
DWCB D.Wagner/C.Boozer 15.00 40.00
JJJD J.Jeffries/J.Dixon 15.00 40.00
JOFJ J.O'Neal/F.Jones 15.00 40.00
JWJR J.Williams/Richardson 15.00 40.00
JWTC J.Williams/Chandler 15.00 40.00
KBKR K.Bryant/K.Rush 200.00 500.00
MBGW M.Bibby/G.Wallace 15.00 40.00
MJKB M.Jordan/K.Bryant 6,000.00 10,000.00
MMRH M.Miller/Humphrey 15.00 40.00
MPCJ M.Peterson/Jefferies 15.00 40.00
NHNT N.Hilario/Tskitishvili 15.00 40.00
SMAS Marion/Stoudemire 20.00 50.00

2002-03 UD Glass 2 Exciting Dual Jersey

PRINT RUN 50 SERIAL #'d SETS
JKKM J.Kidd/K.Martin 15.00 40.00
KBJK K.Bryant/J.Kidd 50.00 120.00
KBKG K.Bryant/K.Garnett 40.00 100.00
MJKB M.Jordan/K.Bryant 200.00 500.00
PPAW P.Pierce/A.Walker 15.00 40.00
SMAS S.Marion/A.Stoudemire 12.00 30.00
YMJW Y.Ming/J.Williams 15.00 40.00

2002-03 UD Glass Game Gear

STATED ODDS 1:24
DMGG Darius Miles 2.00 5.00
DNGG Dirk Nowitzki 8.00 20.00
DWGG David Wesley 2.00 5.00
EBGG Elton Brand 2.50 6.00
JMGG Jamaal Mashburn 2.50 6.00
JTGG Jamaal Tinsley 2.00 5.00
LSGG Latrell Sprewell 3.00 8.00
RAGG Ray Allen 5.00 12.00
RLGG Rashard Lewis 2.50 6.00
RWGG Rasheed Wallace 4.00 10.00
SAGG Shareef Abdur-Rahim 3.00 8.00
SBGG Shane Battier 3.00 8.00
SMGG Shawn Marion 3.00 8.00
WZGG Wang Zhizhi 3.00 8.00

2002-03 UD Glass Get Real Jersey

STATED ODDS 1:48
JKR Jason Kidd 6.00 15.00
KBR Kobe Bryant SP 40.00 100.00
KGR Kevin Garnett 10.00 25.00
MBR Mike Bibby 4.00 10.00
PPR Paul Pierce 6.00 15.00
SPR Scottie Pippen 10.00 25.00

2002-03 UD Glass Magnifying Glass

ONE PER BOX TOPPER
AIM Allen Iverson 5.00 12.00
BDM Baron Davis 2.00 5.00
CWM Chris Webber 2.50 6.00
DGM Drew Gooden 2.00 5.00
DMM Darius Miles 1.25 3.00
JRM Jason Richardson 2.00 5.00
JSM Jerry Stackhouse 2.00 5.00
JWM Jay Williams 1.50 4.00
KBM Kobe Bryant 15.00 40.00
KMM Karl Malone 4.00 10.00
MJM Michael Jordan 20.00 50.00
PSM Peja Stojakovic 1.50 4.00
RAM Ray Allen 3.00 8.00
RLM Rashard Lewis 1.50 4.00
SAM Shareef Abdur-Rahim 2.00 5.00
SBM Shane Battier 2.00 5.00
SFM Steve Francis 2.00 5.00
SHM Shawn Marion 2.00 5.00
SMM Stephon Marbury 2.50 6.00
YMM Yao Ming 10.00 25.00

2002-03 UD Glass Magnifying Glass Autographs

STATED ODDS 1:6 BOX TOPPER
AWA Antoine Walker/84 12.50 30.00
CBA Chauncey Billups 8.00 20.00
DSA DeShawn Stevenson 5.00 12.00
ETA Etan Thomas 5.00 12.00
GWA Gerald Wallace 10.00 25.00
JKA Jason Kidd 25.00 60.00
JMA Jamaal Magloire 5.00 12.00
JOA Jermaine O'Neal 12.50 30.00
JRA Jason Richardson 10.00 25.00
JWA Jay Williams 8.00 20.00
KBA Kobe Bryant/50 300.00 600.00
KGA Kevin Garnett/21 75.00 150.00
KMA Kenyon Martin 6.00 15.00
MBA Mike Bibby 8.00 20.00
MFA Marcus Fizer 5.00 12.00
MJA Michael Jordan/23 2,000.00 4,000.00
MMA Mike Miller 10.00 25.00
PPA Paul Pierce 15.00 40.00
TCA Tyson Chandler 10.00 25.00
YMA Yao Ming 25.00 60.00

2002-03 UD Glass Premiere Issues Jersey

STATED ODDS 1:48
CBP Carlos Boozer 3.00 8.00
CJP Chris Jefferies 2.00 5.00
JDP Juan Dixon 2.50 6.00
JWP Jay Williams SP 2.50 6.00
SCP Sam Clancy 2.50 6.00
VYP Vincent Yarbrough 2.00 5.00

2002-03 UD Glass Superlative Swatch

STATED ODDS 1:36
AMS Andre Miller 2.50 6.00
AWS Antoine Walker 2.50 6.00
BDS Baron Davis 3.00 8.00
CWS Chris Webber 4.00 10.00
DMS Darius Miles 2.00 5.00
KBS Kobe Bryant SP 40.00 100.00
KMS Karl Malone 6.00 15.00
MFS Michael Finley 3.00 8.00
PGS Pau Gasol 5.00 12.00
SMS Stephon Marbury 4.00 10.00

2002-03 UD Glass VIP Access Jersey

STATED ODDS 1:72
AI Allen Iverson 10.00 25.00
JW Jay Williams 3.00 8.00
KB Kobe Bryant SP 40.00 100.00
MJ Michael Jordan SP 40.00 100.00
SF Steve Francis 4.00 10.00
TM Tracy McGrady 6.00 15.00

2003-04 UD Glass

COMP.SET w/o SP's (60) 17.50 35.00
61-80 RC 3 PRINT RUN 1100 SER.#'d SETS
81-90 RC 2 PRINT RUN 750 SER.#'d SETS
91-100 RC 1 PRINT RUN 250 SER.#'d SETS
1 Shareef Abdur-Rahim .50 1.25
2 Jason Terry .40 1.00
3 Paul Pierce .75 2.00
4 Antoine Walker .50 1.25
5 Scottie Pippen 1.25 3.00
6 Jalen Rose .40 1.00
7 Darius Miles .30 .75
8 Dajuan Wagner .30 .75
9 Dirk Nowitzki 1.25 3.00
10 Steve Nash 1.00 2.50
11 Michael Finley .50 1.25
12 Andre Miller .40 1.00
13 Nene .40 1.00
14 Richard Hamilton .60 1.50
15 Ben Wallace .60 1.50
16 Jason Richardson .50 1.25
17 Nick Van Exel .50 1.25
18 Steve Francis .50 1.25
19 Yao Ming 1.25 3.00
20 Jermaine O'Neal .50 1.25
21 Reggie Miller 1.00 2.50
22 Elton Brand .40 1.00
23 Corey Maggette .40 1.00
24 Kobe Bryant 4.00 10.00
25 Shaquille O'Neal 2.00 5.00
26 Gary Payton .75 2.00
27 Pau Gasol .75 2.00
28 Shane Battier .40 1.00
29 Caron Butler .40 1.00
30 Eddie Jones .50 1.25
31 Desmond Mason .40 1.00
32 Michael Redd .50 1.25
33 Kevin Garnett 1.25 3.00
34 Latrell Sprewell .60 1.50
35 Jason Kidd .75 2.00
36 Richard Jefferson .40 1.00
37 Baron Davis .50 1.25
38 Jamal Mashburn .50 1.25
39 Allan Houston .50 1.25
40 Keith Van Horn .40 1.00
41 Tracy McGrady .75 2.00
42 Juwan Howard .40 1.00
43 Allen Iverson 1.25 3.00
44 Glenn Robinson .40 1.00
45 Amare Stoudemire .60 1.50
46 Stephon Marbury .60 1.50
47 Rasheed Wallace .60 1.50
48 Bonzi Wells .30 .75
49 Chris Webber .60 1.50
50 Mike Bibby .50 1.25
51 Tim Duncan 1.25 3.00
52 Tony Parker .75 2.00
53 Ray Allen .75 2.00
54 Rashard Lewis .40 1.00
55 Vince Carter 1.00 2.50
56 Antonio Davis .40 1.00
57 Andrei Kirilenko .40 1.00
58 Jarron Collins .30 .75
59 Gilbert Arenas .60 1.50
60 Jerry Stackhouse .60 1.50
61 Kyle Korver RC 2.50 6.00
62 Travis Hansen RC 1.25 3.00
63 Willie Green RC 1.25 3.00
64 Keith Bogans RC 1.25 3.00
65 Theron Smith RC 1.25 3.00
66 Zaur Pachulia RC 2.00 5.00
67 Derrick Zimmerman RC 2.00 5.00
68 Jason Kapono RC 1.25 3.00
69 Steve Blake RC 1.50 4.00
70 Slavko Vranes RC 1.25 3.00
71 Jerome Beasley RC 1.25 3.00
72 Aleksandar Pavlovic RC 1.50 4.00
73 Boris Diaw RC 2.00 5.00
74 Kendrick Perkins RC 1.50 4.00
75 Leandro Barbosa RC 2.50 6.00
76 Josh Howard RC 2.00 5.00
77 Luke Walton RC 2.00 5.00
78 Maciej Lampe RC 1.25 3.00
79 Brian Cook RC 1.25 3.00
80 Zarko Cabarkapa RC 1.25 3.00
81 Travis Outlaw RC 2.50 6.00
82 Ndudi Ebi RC 2.00 5.00
83 David West RC 4.00 10.00
84 Reece Gaines RC 2.00 5.00
85 Dahntay Jones RC 2.50 6.00
86 Marcus Banks RC 2.00 5.00
87 Troy Bell RC 2.00 5.00
88 Luke Ridnour RC 3.00 8.00
89 Mickael Pietrus RC 2.50 6.00
90 Chris Kaman RC 3.00 8.00
91 Nick Collison RC 6.00 15.00
92 Mike Sweetney RC 5.00 12.00
93 Jarvis Hayes RC 5.00 12.00
94 T.J. Ford RC 6.00 15.00
95 Kirk Hinrich RC 8.00 20.00
96 Chris Bosh RC 12.00 30.00
97 Dwyane Wade RC 20.00 50.00
98 Carmelo Anthony RC 40.00 100.00
99 Darko Milicic RC 6.00 15.00
100 LeBron James RC 1,500.00 3,000.00

2003-04 UD Glass Crystal

*1-60 SINGLES: 4X TO 10X BASE HI
*61-80 RCs: 2X TO 5X BASE HI
*81-90 RCs: 1.25X TO 3X BASE HI
*91-100 RCs: .5X TO 1.25X BASE HI
1-60 PRINT RUN 100 SER.#'d SETS
61-100 PRINT RUN 25 SER.#'d SETS
CRYSTAL PRINTED ON PLEXI-GLASS
96 Chris Bosh 20.00 50.00
97 Dwyane Wade 150.00 300.00
98 Carmelo Anthony 75.00 150.00
100 LeBron James 6,000.00 12,000.00

2003-04 UD Glass Gold

*1-60 SINGLES: 2.5X TO 6X BASE HI
PRINT RUN 100 SER.#'d SETS
24 Kobe Bryant 25.00 60.00

2003-04 UD Glass Plexi-Glass

*GLASS SINGLES: 1.5X TO 4X BASE HI
STATED ODDS 1:20

2003-04 UD Glass Auto Focus

STATED ODDS 1:48
BC Brian Cook 3.00 8.00
CA Carmelo Anthony 25.00 60.00
CB Caron Butler 5.00 12.00
CK Chris Kaman 5.00 12.00
DA Darius Miles 5.00 12.00
DJ DerMarr Johnson 5.00 12.00
DM Darko Milicic 4.00 10.00
GA Gilbert Arenas 6.00 15.00
GG Gordan Giricek 5.00 12.00
GP Gary Payton 12.50 30.00
KB Kobe Bryant SP 125.00 300.00
LJ LeBron James/100 5,000.00 10,000.00
MC Antonio McDyess 5.00 12.00
MJ Michael Jordan SP 2,000.00 4,000.00
PI Mickael Pietrus 4.00 10.00
PS Peja Stojakovic 6.00 15.00
RG Reece Gaines 3.00 8.00
SB Shane Battier 5.00 12.00
TB Troy Bell 3.00 8.00
TM Tracy McGrady 15.00 40.00
YM Yao Ming 30.00 80.00

2003-04 UD Glass Auto Focus Crystal

*CRYSTAL: 1X TO 2.5X BASE HI
PRINT RUN 25 SER.#'d SETS

2003-04 UD Glass Clear Cut Winners Jerseys

PRINT RUN 350 SER.#'d SETS
CWAH Allan Houston 2.50 6.00
CWAJ Antawn Jamison 2.50 6.00
CWDN Dirk Nowitzki 6.00 15.00
CWDR David Robinson 6.00 15.00
CWJK Jason Kidd 4.00 10.00
CWKB Kobe Bryant 20.00 50.00
CWKG Kevin Garnett 6.00 15.00
CWKM Kenyon Martin 2.50 6.00
CWLJ LeBron James 300.00 600.00
CWMJ Michael Jordan 30.00 80.00
CWSF Steve Francis 2.50 6.00
CWSM Stephon Marbury 3.00 8.00
CWSO Shaquille O'Neal 10.00 25.00
CWTD Tim Duncan 6.00 15.00

2003-04 UD Glass Cutting Edge Jerseys

PRINT RUN 100 SER.#'d SETS
CEAS Amare Stoudemire 5.00 12.00
CEDR David Robinson 10.00 25.00
CEDW Dajuan Wagner 2.50 6.00
CEGH Grant Hill 5.00 12.00
CEJK Jason Kidd 6.00 15.00
CEKB Kobe Bryant 25.00 60.00
CEKG Kevin Garnett 10.00 25.00
CELJ LeBron James 500.00 1,000.00
CELS Latrell Sprewell 5.00 12.00
CEMJ Michael Jordan 60.00 150.00
CERW Rasheed Wallace 5.00 12.00
CESF Steve Francis 4.00 10.00
CESN Steve Nash 8.00 20.00
CESO Shaquille O'Neal 15.00 40.00

2003-04 UD Glass Game Gear

STATED ODDS 1:24
GGAI Allen Iverson 6.00 15.00
GGAM Alonzo Mourning 4.00 10.00
GGAN Andre Miller 2.00 5.00
GGAS Amare Stoudemire 3.00 8.00
GGAW Antoine Walker 2.50 6.00
GGCB Caron Butler SP 2.00 5.00
GGCW Chris Webber 3.00 8.00
GGDM Darius Miles 2.00 5.00
GGDN Dirk Nowitzki 6.00 15.00
GGDW Dajuan Wagner 1.50 4.00
GGEB Elton Brand 2.00 5.00
GGEG Manu Ginobili 5.00 12.00
GGGH Grant Hill 4.00 10.00
GGKB Kobe Bryant SP 10.00 25.00
GGKG Kevin Garnett 6.00 15.00
GGLJ LeBron James SP 500.00 1,000.00
GGLO Lamar Odom 2.00 5.00
GGLS Latrell Sprewell 3.00 8.00
GGMB Mike Bibby 2.50 6.00
GGMJ Michael Jordan SP 60.00 150.00
GGPP Paul Pierce 4.00 10.00
GGSA Shareef Abdur-Rahim 2.50 6.00
GGSF Steve Francis 2.50 6.00
GGSM Stephon Marbury SP 3.00 8.00
GGSN Steve Nash 5.00 12.00
GGTD Tim Duncan 6.00 15.00
GGTM Tracy McGrady 4.00 10.00
GGTP Tony Parker 4.00 10.00
GGWS Wally Szczerbiak 2.00 5.00
GGYM Yao Ming 6.00 15.00

2003-04 UD Glass Monumental Marks
STATED ODDS 1:144
AMJ Andre Miller 6.00 15.00
DAJ Darius Miles 6.00 15.00
DMJ Darko Milicic 5.00 12.00
JKJ Jason Kidd 20.00 50.00
JRJ Jason Richardson 6.00 15.00
KBJ Kobe Bryant/100 150.00 400.00
LJJ LeBron James/100 5,000.00 10,000.00
LOJ Lamar Odom 10.00 25.00
LRJ Luke Ridnour 6.00 15.00
MBJ Mike Bibby 6.00 15.00
MJJ Michael Jordan/50 2,000.00 4,000.00
MPJ Morris Peterson 6.00 15.00
MSJ Mike Sweetney 4.00 10.00
PIJ Mickael Pietrus 5.00 12.00
PPJ Paul Pierce 30.00 80.00
PSJ Peja Stojakovic 10.00 25.00
RHJ Richard Hamilton 8.00 20.00
RJJ Richard Jefferson 8.00 20.00
RMJ Reggie Miller 60.00 150.00
SFJ Steve Francis 8.00 20.00

2003-04 UD Glass Premier Issue Jerseys
STATED ODDS 1:96
PIBC Brian Cook 1.50 4.00
PICA Carmelo Anthony 12.00 30.00
PICB Chris Bosh 8.00 20.00
PICK Chris Kaman 2.50 6.00
PIDE David West 3.00 8.00
PIDJ Dahntay Jones 2.00 5.00
PIDM Darko Milicic 2.00 5.00
PIDY Dwyane Wade 10.00 25.00
PIHO Josh Howard 2.50 6.00
PIJH Jarvis Hayes 1.50 4.00
PILJ LeBron James SP 200.00 500.00
PILR Luke Ridnour 2.50 6.00
PILW Luke Walton 2.50 6.00
PIMB Marcus Banks 1.50 4.00
PIMP Mickael Pietrus 2.00 5.00
PIMS Mike Sweetney 1.50 4.00
PIRG Reece Gaines 1.50 4.00
PISB Steve Blake 2.00 5.00
PITB Troy Bell 1.50 4.00
PITO Travis Outlaw 2.00 5.00
PIZC Zarko Cabarkapa 1.50 4.00

2003-04 UD Glass Superlative Swatches
STATED ODDS 1:24
SSAH Allan Houston 2.50 6.00
SSAI Allen Iverson 6.00 15.00
SSCB Caron Butler 2.00 5.00
SSCW Charlie Ward 2.00 5.00
SSDN Dirk Nowitzki 6.00 15.00
SSEC Eddy Curry 1.50 4.00
SSGA Gilbert Arenas 2.50 6.00
SSJJ Joe Johnson 2.00 5.00
SSJK Jason Kidd 4.00 10.00
SSJR Jason Richardson 2.50 6.00
SSKB Kobe Bryant SP 10.00 25.00
SSLO Lamar Odom 2.00 5.00
SSMJ Michael Jordan SP 40.00 100.00
SSMM Mark Madsen 2.00 5.00
SSRS Radoslav Nesterovic 2.00 5.00
SSTB Terrell Brandon 2.00 5.00
SSTC Tyson Chandler 2.00 5.00
SSTD Tim Duncan 6.00 15.00
SSTM Tracy McGrady 4.00 10.00
SSWS Wally Szczerbiak 2.00 5.00
SSYM Yao Ming 6.00 15.00

2003-04 UD Glass Swatch of Class
STATED ODDS 1:96
SCAJ Antawn Jamison 2.50 6.00
SCEB Elton Brand 2.00 5.00
SCJO Jermaine O'Neal 2.50 6.00
SCJS Jerry Stackhouse 3.00 8.00
SCKB Kobe Bryant SP 20.00 50.00
SCKE Kenyon Martin 2.50 6.00
SCKM Karl Malone 5.00 12.00
SCLJ LeBron James SP 200.00 500.00
SCLO Lamar Odom 2.00 5.00
SCMC Marcus Camby 2.00 5.00
SCMF Michael Finley 2.50 6.00
SCMJ Michael Jordan SP 75.00 150.00
SCPG Pau Gasol 4.00 10.00
SCPP Paul Pierce 4.00 10.00
SCPS Peja Stojakovic 2.00 5.00
SCRA Ray Allen 4.00 10.00
SCRL Rashard Lewis 2.00 5.00
SCRM Reggie Miller 5.00 12.00
SCSH Shawn Marion 2.50 6.00
SCSM Stephon Marbury 3.00 8.00
SCTP Tony Parker 4.00 10.00

2003-04 UD Glass VIP Access Jerseys
PRINT RUN 25 SER.#'d SETS
AI Allen Iverson 25.00 60.00
BW Ben Wallace 12.00 30.00
CA Carmelo Anthony 50.00 120.00
CW Chris Webber 12.00 30.00
DM Darko Milicic 8.00 20.00
DW Dajuan Wagner 6.00 15.00
JO Jermaine O'Neal 10.00 25.00
KB Kobe Bryant 80.00 200.00
LJ LeBron James 1,000.00 2,000.00
MJ Michael Jordan 100.00 250.00
PP Paul Pierce 15.00 40.00
SO Shaquille O'Neal 40.00 100.00
TM Tracy McGrady 15.00 40.00
YM Yao Ming 25.00 60.00

2002-03 UD Glass Beckett.com Samples
*SINGLES: .75X TO 2X BASE UD GLASS HI

1998-99 UD Ionix
COMPLETE SET (80) 25.00 60.00
COMPLETE SET w/o RC (60) 10.00 25.00
ELECTRIX RC SUBSET STATED ODDS 1:4
1 Michael Jordan 3.00 8.00
2 Michael Jordan 3.00 8.00
3 Michael Jordan 3.00 8.00
4 Michael Jordan 3.00 8.00
5 Michael Jordan 3.00 8.00
6 Michael Jordan 3.00 8.00
7 Steve Smith .25 .60
8 Dikembe Mutombo .50 1.25
9 Ron Mercer .25 .60
10 Antoine Walker .30 .75
11 Derrick Coleman .25 .60
12 Glen Rice .30 .75
13 Michael Jordan 3.00 8.00
14 Toni Kukoc .30 .75
15 Derek Anderson .25 .60
16 Shawn Kemp .50 1.25
17 Michael Finley .30 .75
18 Steve Nash .60 1.50
19 Antonio McDyess .30 .75
20 Nick Van Exel .30 .75
21 Grant Hill .50 1.25
22 Jerry Stackhouse .30 .75
23 Donyell Marshall .20 .50
24 John Starks .30 .75
25 Charles Barkley .75 2.00
26 Hakeem Olajuwon .60 1.50
27 Scottie Pippen .75 2.00
28 Reggie Miller .60 1.50
29 Rik Smits .25 .60
30 Maurice Taylor .20 .50
31 Kobe Bryant 2.50 6.00
32 Shaquille O'Neal 1.25 3.00
33 Tim Hardaway .40 1.00
34 Alonzo Mourning .50 1.25
35 Ray Allen .50 1.25
36 Glenn Robinson .30 .75
37 Stephon Marbury .40 1.00
38 Kevin Garnett .75 2.00
39 Jayson Williams .20 .50
40 Keith Van Horn .30 .75
41 Patrick Ewing .50 1.25
42 Allan Houston .30 .75
43 Anfernee Hardaway .75 2.00
44 Isaac Austin .20 .50
45 Tim Thomas .25 .60
46 Allen Iverson .75 2.00
47 Tom Gugliotta .25 .60
48 Jason Kidd .50 1.25
49 Damon Stoudamire .30 .75
50 Chris Webber .40 1.00
51 Tim Duncan .75 2.00
52 David Robinson .50 1.25
53 Gary Payton .50 1.25
54 Vin Baker .25 .60
55 Tracy McGrady .50 1.25
56 John Stockton .60 1.50
57 Karl Malone .60 1.50
58 Shareef Abdur-Rahim .30 .75
59 Juwan Howard .25 .60
60 Mitch Richmond .40 1.00
61 Michael Olowokandi RC .75 2.00
62 Mike Bibby RC 1.25 3.00
63 Raef LaFrentz RC .75 2.00
64 Antawn Jamison RC 1.00 2.50
65 Vince Carter RC 3.00 8.00
66 Robert Traylor RC .60 1.50
67 Jason Williams RC 2.00 5.00
68 Larry Hughes RC 1.00 2.50
69 Dirk Nowitzki RC 4.00 10.00
70 Paul Pierce RC 2.50 6.00
71 Cuttino Mobley RC 2.00 5.00
72 Corey Benjamin RC .40 1.00
73 Peja Stojakovic RC 1.25 3.00
74 Michael Dickerson RC .60 1.50
75 Matt Harpring RC .60 1.50
76 Rashard Lewis RC 2.00 5.00
77 Pat Garrity RC .50 1.25
78 Roshown McLeod RC .40 1.00
79 Ricky Davis RC 1.00 2.50
80 Felipe Lopez RC .40 1.00
J1A Michael Jordan AU/23 2,500.00 5,000.00

1998-99 UD Ionix Reciprocal
COMMON MJ (R1-R6/13) 50.00 120.00
*STARS: 4X TO 10X BASE CARD HI
*RCs: 6X TO 15X BASE HI
STARS: PRINT RUN 750 SERIAL #'d SETS
RCs: PRINT RUN 100 SERIAL #'d SETS
R65 Vince Carter 200.00 500.00
R69 Dirk Nowitzki 300.00 600.00

1998-99 UD Ionix Area 23
COMPLETE SET (10) 20.00 50.00
COMMON CARD (A1-A10) 4.00 10.00
STATED ODDS 1:18

1998-99 UD Ionix Kinetix
COMPLETE SET (20) 12.00 30.00
STATED ODDS 1:9
K1 Michael Jordan 8.00 20.00
K2 Michael Olowokandi .60 1.50
K3 Keith Van Horn .75 2.00
K4 Grant Hill 1.25 3.00
K5 Stephon Marbury 1.00 2.50
K6 Larry Hughes .75 2.00
K7 Vince Carter 2.50 6.00
K8 Jason Kidd 1.25 3.00
K9 Robert Traylor .50 1.25
K10 Ron Mercer .60 1.50
K11 Dirk Nowitzki 3.00 8.00
K12 Antawn Jamison .75 2.00
K13 Kobe Bryant 6.00 15.00
K14 Jason Williams 1.50 4.00
K15 Raef LaFrentz .60 1.50
K16 Gary Payton 1.25 3.00
K17 Tim Duncan 2.00 5.00
K18 Paul Pierce 2.00 5.00
K19 Mike Bibby .75 2.00
K20 Scottie Pippen 2.00 5.00

1998-99 UD Ionix MJ HoloGrFX
COMMON CARD (MJ1-10) 200.00 500.00
STATED ODDS 1:1500

1998-99 UD Ionix Skyonix
COMPLETE SET (25) 100.00 200.00
STATED ODDS 1:53
S1 Michael Jordan 125.00 300.00
S2 Scottie Pippen 8.00 20.00
S3 Derek Anderson 2.50 6.00
S4 Jason Kidd 5.00 12.00
S5 Damon Stoudamire 3.00 8.00
S6 Antoine Walker 3.00 8.00
S7 Shaquille O'Neal 12.00 30.00
S8 Tim Thomas 2.50 6.00
S9 Reggie Miller 6.00 15.00
S10 Allen Iverson 8.00 20.00
S11 Antonio McDyess 2.50 6.00
S12 Michael Finley 3.00 8.00
S13 Charles Barkley 8.00 20.00
S14 Shareef Abdur-Rahim 3.00 8.00
S15 Gary Payton 5.00 12.00
S16 David Robinson 6.00 15.00
S17 Anfernee Hardaway 8.00 20.00
S18 Ray Allen 5.00 12.00
S19 Ron Mercer 2.50 6.00
S20 Tim Hardaway 4.00 10.00
S21 Chris Webber 4.00 10.00
S22 Kevin Garnett 8.00 20.00
S23 Juwan Howard 2.50 6.00
S24 Karl Malone 6.00 15.00
S25 Keith Van Horn 3.00 8.00

1998-99 UD Ionix UD Authentics
STATED PRINT RUN 475 SETS
CB Corey Benjamin 2.50 6.00
DO Michael Doleac 3.00 8.00
JW Jason Williams 12.00 30.00
RL Raef LaFrentz 5.00 12.00
RM Roshown McLeod 2.50 6.00

1998-99 UD Ionix Warp Zone
COMPLETE SET (15) 200.00 400.00
Z1 Michael Jordan 400.00 800.00
Z2 Tim Duncan 20.00 60.00
Z3 Robert Traylor 6.00 15.00
Z4 Michael Olowokandi 6.00 15.00
Z5 Vince Carter 60.00 150.00
Z6 Dirk Nowitzki 75.00 200.00
Z7 Antawn Jamison 8.00 20.00
Z8 Jason Williams 15.00 40.00
Z9 Larry Hughes 8.00 20.00
Z10 Raef LaFrentz 6.00 15.00
Z11 Allen Iverson 20.00 50.00
Z12 Kobe Bryant 100.00 250.00
Z13 Grant Hill 20.00 50.00
Z14 Mike Bibby 8.00 20.00
Z15 Paul Pierce 15.00 40.00

1999-00 UD Ionix
COMPLETE SET (90) 30.00 80.00
COMPLETE SET w/o SP (60) 10.00 25.00
61-90 PRINT RUN 3500 SERIAL #'d SETS
MJ FINAL FLOOR LISTED UNDER 99-00 UD
1 Dikembe Mutombo .50 1.25
2 Isaiah Rider .25 .60
3 Antoine Walker .30 .75
4 Paul Pierce .60 1.50
5 Eddie Jones .30 .75
6 Anthony Mason .30 .75
7 Toni Kukoc .40 1.00
8 Hersey Hawkins .20 .50
9 Shawn Kemp .50 1.25
10 Lamond Murray .20 .50
11 Michael Finley .30 .75
12 Cedric Ceballos .20 .50
13 Antonio McDyess .25 .60
14 Ron Mercer .25 .60
15 Grant Hill .50 1.25
16 Jerry Stackhouse .30 .75
17 Antawn Jamison .30 .75
18 Mookie Blaylock .20 .50
19 Charles Barkley .75 2.00
20 Hakeem Olajuwon .60 1.50
21 Reggie Miller .60 1.50
22 Rik Smits .25 .60
23 Maurice Taylor .20 .50
24 Derek Anderson .20 .50
25 Kobe Bryant 2.50 6.00
26 Shaquille O'Neal 1.25 3.00
27 Tim Hardaway .40 1.00
28 Alonzo Mourning .50 1.25
29 Ray Allen .50 1.25
30 Glenn Robinson .25 .60
31 Kevin Garnett .75 2.00
32 Terrell Brandon .20 .50
33 Stephon Marbury .40 1.00
34 Keith Van Horn .30 .75
35 Allan Houston .30 .75
36 Latrell Sprewell .40 1.00
37 Darrell Armstrong .20 .50
38 Tariq Abdul-Wahad .20 .50
39 Allen Iverson .75 2.00
40 Larry Hughes .25 .60
41 Anfernee Hardaway .75 2.00
42 Jason Kidd .50 1.25
43 Tom Gugliotta .25 .60
44 Scottie Pippen .75 2.00
45 Damon Stoudamire .30 .75
46 Rasheed Wallace .40 1.00
47 Jason Williams .50 1.25
48 Chris Webber .40 1.00
49 Tim Duncan .75 2.00
50 David Robinson .60 1.50
51 Gary Payton .50 1.25
52 Vin Baker .25 .60
53 Vince Carter .75 2.00
54 Tracy McGrady .50 1.25
55 Karl Malone .60 1.50
56 John Stockton .50 1.25
57 Mike Bibby .50 1.25
58 Shareef Abdur-Rahim .30 .75
59 Mitch Richmond .30 .75
60 Juwan Howard .25 .60
61 Elton Brand RC 1.50 4.00
62 Steve Francis RC 1.50 4.00
63 Baron Davis RC 2.00 5.00
64 Lamar Odom RC 1.50 4.00
65 Jonathan Bender RC .75 2.00
66 Wally Szczerbiak RC 1.25 3.00
67 Richard Hamilton RC 2.00 5.00
68 Andre Miller RC 1.50 4.00
69 Shawn Marion RC 1.50 4.00
70 Jason Terry RC 1.25 3.00
71 Trajan Langdon RC .60 1.50
72 A.Radojevic RC .50 1.25
73 Corey Maggette RC 1.00 2.50
74 William Avery RC .50 1.25
75 Ron Artest RC 2.00 5.00
76 Cal Bowdler RC .50 1.25
77 James Posey RC .75 2.00
78 Quincy Lewis RC .50 1.25
79 Dion Glover RC .50 1.25
80 Jeff Foster RC .75 2.00
81 Kenny Thomas RC .75 2.00
82 Devean George RC .60 1.50
83 Tim James RC .50 1.25
84 Vonteego Cummings RC .50 1.25
85 Jumaine Jones RC .50 1.25
86 Scott Padgett RC .60 1.50
87 Chucky Atkins RC .60 1.50
88 Adrian Griffin RC .60 1.50
89 Todd MacCulloch RC .60 1.50
90 Anthony Carter RC .60 1.50

1999-00 UD Ionix Reciprocal
*STARS: 1.5X TO 4X BASE CARD HI
*RCs: 1.25X TO 3X BASE HI
STARS: STATED ODDS 1:4
RCs: PRINT RUN 100 SERIAL #'d SETS

1999-00 UD Ionix Awesome Powers
COMPLETE SET (15) 6.00 15.00
STATED ODDS 1:23
AP1 Elton Brand .75 2.00
AP2 Corey Maggette .50 1.25
AP3 Wally Szczerbiak .60 1.50
AP4 Charles Barkley 2.00 5.00
AP5 Shawn Marion .75 2.00
AP6 Jason Terry .60 1.50
AP7 Keith Van Horn .60 1.50
AP8 Steve Francis .75 2.00
AP9 Trajan Langdon .30 .75
AP10 Reggie Miller 1.50 4.00
AP11 Richard Hamilton 1.00 2.50
AP12 Jonathan Bender .40 1.00
AP13 Baron Davis 1.00 2.50
AP14 Paul Pierce 1.50 4.00
AP15 Andre Miller .75 2.00

1999-00 UD Ionix BIOrhythm
COMPLETE SET (15) 5.00 12.00
STATED ODDS 1:7
B1 Grant Hill 1.00 2.50
B2 Antawn Jamison .60 1.50
B3 Shaquille O'Neal 2.50 6.00
B4 Stephon Marbury .75 2.00
B5 Michael Finley .60 1.50
B6 Hakeem Olajuwon 1.25 3.00
B7 Ron Mercer .50 1.25
B8 Tim Hardaway .75 2.00
B9 Jason Kidd 1.00 2.50
B10 Allan Houston .50 1.25
B11 Ray Allen 1.00 2.50
B12 Shawn Kemp 1.00 2.50
B13 Alonzo Mourning 1.00 2.50
B14 Tim Duncan 1.50 4.00
B15 Eddie Jones .60 1.50

1999-00 UD Ionix Pyrotechnics
COMPLETE SET (15) 40.00 80.00
STATED ODDS 1:72
P1 Kevin Garnett 6.00 15.00
P2 Shareef Abdur-Rahim 2.50 6.00
P3 Jason Kidd 4.00 10.00
P4 Antonio McDyess 2.00 5.00
P5 Karl Malone 5.00 12.00
P6 Eddie Jones 2.50 6.00
P7 Antoine Walker 2.50 6.00
P8 Kobe Bryant 20.00 50.00
P9 Anfernee Hardaway 6.00 15.00
P10 Antawn Jamison 2.50 6.00
P11 Keith Van Horn 2.00 5.00
P12 Grant Hill 4.00 10.00
P13 Gary Payton 4.00 10.00
P14 Allen Iverson 6.00 15.00
P15 Vince Carter 6.00 15.00

1999-00 UD Ionix UD Authentics
STATED ODDS 1:144
AH Anfernee Hardaway 100.00 250.00
AJ Antawn Jamison 3.00 8.00
AM Andre Miller 5.00 12.00
BD Baron Davis 8.00 20.00
BG Brian Grant 2.00 5.00
CM Corey Maggette 4.00 10.00
JB Jonathan Bender 3.00 8.00
JP James Posey 3.00 8.00
JT Jason Terry 5.00 12.00
KB Kobe Bryant 150.00 400.00
KG Kevin Garnett 100.00 250.00
MJ Michael Jordan/23 8,000.00 12,000.00
MT Maurice Taylor 2.00 5.00
RA Ron Artest 8.00 20.00
RH Richard Hamilton 8.00 20.00
RT Robert Traylor 3.00 8.00
SF Steve Francis 6.00 15.00
SM Shawn Marion 6.00 15.00
TG Tom Gugliotta 3.00 8.00
TL Trajan Langdon 2.50 6.00
WA William Avery 2.00 5.00
WS Wally Szczerbiak 4.00 10.00

1999-00 UD Ionix Warp Zone
COMPLETE SET (15) 150.00 300.00
STATED ODDS 1:144
WZ1 Kobe Bryant 40.00 100.00
WZ2 Kevin Garnett 12.00 30.00
WZ3 Tim Duncan 12.00 30.00
WZ4 Elton Brand 10.00 25.00
WZ5 Wally Szczerbiak 8.00 20.00
WZ6 Stephon Marbury 6.00 15.00
WZ7 Allen Iverson 12.00 30.00
WZ8 Anfernee Hardaway 12.00 30.00
WZ9 Shaquille O'Neal 20.00 50.00
WZ10 Baron Davis 12.00 30.00
WZ11 Scottie Pippen 12.00 30.00
WZ12 Jason Williams 8.00 20.00
WZ13 Steve Francis 10.00 25.00
WZ14 Vince Carter 12.00 30.00
WZ15 Lamar Odom 10.00 25.00

2005-06 UD Portraits
COMP.SET w/o SP's (100) 50.00 125.00
137-142 RC PRINT RUN 99 SER.#'d SETS
1 Al Harrington .60 1.50
2 Al Jefferson .50 1.25
3 Allen Iverson 1.50 4.00
4 Amare Stoudemire .75 2.00
5 Andre Iguodala .75 2.00
6 Andre Miller .60 1.50
7 Andrei Kirilenko .60 1.50
8 Antawn Jamison .60 1.50
9 Antoine Walker .60 1.50
10 Baron Davis .75 2.00
11 Ben Gordon .60 1.50
12 Ben Wallace 1.00 2.50
13 Bob Sura .50 1.25
14 Brevin Knight .50 1.25
15 Carlos Boozer .60 1.50
16 Carmelo Anthony 1.25 3.00
17 Caron Butler .60 1.50
18 Chauncey Billups 1.00 2.50
19 Chris Bosh 1.00 2.50
20 Chris Webber 1.00 2.50
21 Corey Maggette .60 1.50
22 Cuttino Mobley .50 1.25
23 Damon Jones .50 1.25
24 Dan Dickau .50 1.25
25 Desmond Mason .50 1.25
26 Dirk Nowitzki 2.00 5.00
27 Donyell Marshall .50 1.25
28 Drew Gooden .60 1.50
29 Dwight Howard 1.00 2.50
30 Dwyane Wade 1.50 4.00
31 Elton Brand .60 1.50
32 Emeka Okafor .60 1.50
33 Gary Payton 1.25 3.00
34 Gerald Wallace .60 1.50
35 Gilbert Arenas .75 2.00
36 Grant Hill 1.25 3.00
37 J.R. Smith .75 2.00
38 Jalen Rose .60 1.50
39 Jamaal Magloire .50 1.25
40 Jamaal Tinsley .60 1.50
41 Jamal Crawford .75 2.00
42 Jameer Nelson .50 1.25
43 Jason Kidd 1.25 3.00
44 Jason Richardson .75 2.00
45 Jason Terry .60 1.50
46 Jason Williams 1.25 3.00
47 Jermaine O'Neal .60 1.50
48 Joe Johnson .60 1.50
49 Josh Childress .50 1.25
50 Josh Howard .60 1.50
51 Josh Smith .60 1.50
52 Kenyon Martin .60 1.50
53 Kevin Garnett 2.00 5.00
54 Kirk Hinrich .60 1.50
55 Kobe Bryant 6.00 15.00
56 Kurt Thomas .50 1.25
57 Kyle Korver .60 1.50
58 Lamar Odom .60 1.50
59 Larry Hughes .60 1.50
60 Eddie Griffin .50 1.25
61 LeBron James 6.00 15.00
62 Luke Ridnour .60 1.50
63 Luol Deng .60 1.50
64 Manu Ginobili 1.50 4.00
65 Marcus Camby .50 1.25
66 Maurice Williams .50 1.25
67 Michael Finley .75 2.00
68 Michael Jordan 6.00 15.00
69 Michael Redd .60 1.50
70 Mike Bibby .75 2.00
71 Pau Gasol 1.25 3.00
72 Paul Pierce 1.25 3.00
73 Peja Stojakovic .60 1.50
74 Raja Bell .60 1.50
75 Rashard Lewis .60 1.50
76 Rasheed Wallace .75 2.00
77 Ray Allen 1.25 3.00
78 Richard Hamilton 1.00 2.50
79 Richard Jefferson .60 1.50
80 Ron Artest .60 1.50
81 Sam Cassell .60 1.50
82 Sebastian Telfair .60 1.50
83 Shaquille O'Neal 2.50 6.00
84 Shareef Abdur-Rahim .75 2.00
85 Shaun Livingston .60 1.50
86 Shawn Marion .60 1.50
87 Stephon Marbury 1.00 2.50
88 Steve Francis .75 2.00
89 Steve Nash 1.50 4.00
90 Stromile Swift .50 1.25
91 Tim Duncan 2.00 5.00
92 Tony Parker 1.25 3.00
93 Tracy McGrady 1.25 3.00
94 Troy Murphy .50 1.25
95 Tyronn Lue .50 1.25
96 Vince Carter 1.50 4.00
97 Vladimir Radmanovic .50 1.25
98 Yao Ming 1.50 4.00
99 Zach Randolph .75 2.00
100 Zydrunas Ilgauskas .60 1.50
101 Andray Blatche RC 2.00 5.00
102 Andrew Bynum RC 1.50 4.00
103 Antoine Wright RC 1.50 4.00
104 Brandon Bass RC 1.50 4.00
105 C.J. Miles RC 1.50 4.00
106 Channing Frye RC 1.50 4.00
107 Charlie Villanueva RC 1.50 4.00
108 Chris Taft RC 1.25 3.00
109 Daniel Ewing RC 1.25 3.00
110 Danny Granger RC 2.00 5.00
111 David Lee RC 2.00 5.00
112 Dijon Thompson RC 1.25 3.00
113 Ersan Ilyasova RC 1.50 4.00
114 Sarunas Jasikevicius RC 2.00 5.00
115 Francisco Garcia RC 1.25 3.00
116 Gerald Green RC 1.50 4.00
117 Hakim Warrick RC 1.50 4.00
118 Jose Calderon RC 2.00 5.00
119 Ike Diogu RC 1.25 3.00
120 Jarrett Jack RC 2.00 5.00
121 Jason Maxiell RC 1.50 4.00
122 Joey Graham RC 1.50 4.00
123 Julius Hodge RC 1.25 3.00
124 Linas Kleiza RC 1.25 3.00
125 Louis Williams RC 5.00 12.00
126 Luther Head RC 1.50 4.00
127 Martell Webster RC 1.50 4.00
128 Monta Ellis RC 2.50 6.00
129 Nate Robinson RC 2.00 5.00
130 Rashad McCants RC 1.25 3.00
131 James Singleton RC 1.25 3.00
132 Ryan Gomes RC 1.50 4.00
133 Salim Stoudamire RC 1.50 4.00
134 Travis Diener RC 1.25 3.00
135 Wayne Simien RC 1.25 3.00
136 Yaroslav Korolev RC 1.25 3.00
137 Andrew Bogut RC 4.00 10.00
138 Chris Paul RC 15.00 40.00
139 Deron Williams RC 5.00 12.00
140 Raymond Felton RC 2.50 6.00
141 Marvin Williams RC 3.00 8.00
142 Sean May RC 2.00 5.00

2005-06 UD Portraits 75
*1-100 PORT.75: .75X TO 2X BASE HI
*101-136 PORT.75: .6X TO 1.5X BASE HI
*137-142 PORT.75: .4X TO 1X BASE HI
PORT.75 PRINT RUN 75 SER.#'d SETS
68 Michael Jordan 15.00 40.00

2005-06 UD Portraits 30
*1-100 PORT.30: 1.5X TO 4X BASE HI
*101-136 PORT.30: 1X TO 2.5X BASE HI
*137-142 PORT.30: .6X TO 1.5X BASE HI
PORT.30 PRINT RUN 30 SER.#'d SETS
68 Michael Jordan 30.00 80.00

2005-06 UD Portraits Material Moments
STATED ODDS ONE PER PACK
AB Andrew Bogut 3.00 8.00
AM Aaron McKie 2.00 5.00
AS Amare Stoudemire 2.50 6.00
AW Antoine Wright 2.00 5.00
CB Caron Butler 2.00 5.00
CF Channing Frye 2.00 5.00
CM C.J. Miles 2.00 5.00
CP Chris Paul 8.00 20.00
CW Chris Webber 3.00 8.00
DA David Wesley 2.00 5.00
DE Deron Williams 4.00 10.00
DF Derek Fisher 2.50 6.00
DG Danny Granger 2.50 6.00
DH Dwight Howard 3.00 8.00
DN Dirk Nowitzki 6.00 15.00
EB Elton Brand 2.00 5.00
ES Eric Snow 2.00 5.00
GG Gerald Green 2.50 6.00
HW Hakim Warrick 2.00 5.00
JA Jason Terry 2.00 5.00
JK Jason Kidd 4.00 10.00
JM Jamaal Magloire 2.00 5.00
JO Jermaine O'Neal 2.00 5.00
JR Jason Richardson 2.50 6.00
JT Jamaal Tinsley 2.00 5.00
KB Kobe Bryant 40.00 100.00
KD Keyon Dooling 2.00 5.00
KG Kevin Garnett 6.00 15.00
KM Kenyon Martin 2.00 5.00
LJ LeBron James 12.50 30.00
LW Luke Walton 2.00 5.00
MA Marvin Williams 2.50 6.00
MJ Michael Jordan SP 40.00 80.00
MW Martell Webster 2.00 5.00
QR Quentin Richardson 1.50 4.00
RF Raymond Felton 2.00 5.00
RW Rasheed Wallace 2.50 6.00
SH Shawn Marion 2.00 5.00
SM Sean May 1.50 4.00
SO Shaquille O'Neal 8.00 20.00
TD Tim Duncan 6.00 15.00
YM Yao Ming 5.00 12.00

2005-06 UD Portraits Scrapbook Signatures
PRINT RUN 25 SER.#'d SETS
AB Andrew Bogut 10.00 25.00
AN Andrew Bynum 6.00 15.00
BB Brandon Bass 6.00 15.00
CA Carmelo Anthony 30.00 80.00
CJ C.J. Miles 6.00 15.00
CP Chris Paul 80.00 200.00
DE Daniel Ewing 6.00 15.00
DG Danny Granger 8.00 20.00
DH Dwight Howard 25.00 60.00
DL David Lee 8.00 20.00
DT Dijon Thompson 5.00 12.00
DW Deron Williams 12.00 30.00
EI Ersan Ilyasova 6.00 15.00
FG Francisco Garcia 5.00 12.00
GA Gilbert Arenas 12.00 30.00
GG Gerald Green 8.00 20.00
ID Ike Diogu 5.00 12.00
JG Joey Graham 6.00 15.00
JH Julius Hodge 5.00 12.00
JJ Jarrett Jack 8.00 20.00
JM Jason Maxiell 6.00 15.00
JP Johan Petro 5.00 12.00
LH Luther Head 5.00 12.00
LJ LeBron James 1,250.00 2,500.00
LW Louis Williams 20.00 50.00
MA Marvin Williams 8.00 20.00
MB Mike Bibby 8.00 20.00
MJ Michael Jordan 2,000.00 4,000.00
MW Martell Webster 6.00 15.00
PP Paul Pierce 20.00 50.00
RF Raymond Felton 6.00 15.00
RJ Richard Jefferson 6.00 15.00
RM Rashad McCants 5.00 12.00
SM Sean May 5.00 12.00
SN Steve Nash 30.00 80.00
ST Stephon Marbury 12.00 30.00
WS Wayne Simien 5.00 12.00

2005-06 UD Portraits Scrapbook Swatches
STATED ODDS ONE PER PACK
AB Andrew Bogut 3.00 8.00
AI Andre Iguodala 2.50 6.00
AW Antoine Wright 2.00 5.00
BG Ben Gordon 2.00 5.00
CA Carmelo Anthony 4.00 10.00
CF Channing Frye 2.00 5.00
CM Corey Maggette 2.00 5.00
CP Chris Paul 8.00 20.00
CT Chris Taft 1.50 4.00
CV Charlie Villanueva 2.00 5.00
DE Daniel Ewing 2.00 5.00
DG Danny Granger 2.50 6.00
DH Dwight Howard 3.00 8.00
DW Deron Williams 4.00 10.00
FG Francisco Garcia 1.50 4.00
GA Gilbert Arenas 2.50 6.00
GG Gerald Green 2.50 6.00
GP Gary Payton 4.00 10.00
HK Hakim Warrick 2.00 5.00
JA Jason Maxiell 2.00 5.00
JC Josh Childress 1.50 4.00
JG Joey Graham 2.00 5.00
JH Julius Hodge 1.50 4.00
JJ Jarrett Jack 2.50 6.00
JK Jason Kidd 4.00 10.00
JM Jamaal Magloire 2.00 5.00
JR J.R. Smith 2.50 6.00
LJ LeBron James 15.00 40.00
LW Louis Williams 6.00 15.00
MA Marvin Williams 2.50 6.00
ME Monta Ellis 3.00 8.00
MJ Michael Jordan SP 50.00 120.00
MW Martell Webster 2.00 5.00
QR Quentin Richardson 1.50 4.00
RF Raymond Felton 2.00 5.00
RM Rashad McCants 1.50 4.00
SH Shawn Marion 2.00 5.00
SM Sean May 1.50 4.00
TM Tracy McGrady 4.00 10.00
UH Udonis Haslem 1.50 4.00
WS Wayne Simien 1.50 4.00
YM Yao Ming 5.00 12.00

2005-06 UD Portraits Scrapbook Swatches Autographs
PRINT RUN 10 TO 49 SER.#'d SETS
CM Corey Maggette/49 6.00 15.00
DE Daniel Ewing/40 6.00 15.00
DG Danny Granger/40 8.00 20.00
FG Francisco Garcia/40 5.00 12.00
GA Gilbert Arenas/40 12.00 30.00
GG Gerald Green/40 8.00 20.00
GP Gary Payton/40 12.00 30.00
JA Jason Maxiell/40 6.00 15.00
JG Joey Graham/40 6.00 15.00
JH Julius Hodge/40 5.00 12.00
JJ Jarrett Jack/40 8.00 20.00
JR J.R. Smith/40 8.00 20.00
LW Louis Williams/40 20.00 50.00
MW Martell Webster/40 6.00 15.00
QR Quentin Richardson/40 5.00 12.00
RF Raymond Felton/40 6.00 15.00
RM Rashad McCants/40 5.00 12.00
SH Shawn Marion/40 12.00 30.00
WS Wayne Simien/40 5.00 12.00

2005-06 UD Portraits Signature Portraits 8x10
STATED ODDS ONE PER BOX
*BLACK/WHITE: .5X TO 1.25X BASE HI
AB Andrew Bogut 8.00 20.00
AI Andre Iguodala 12.50 30.00
AN Andrew Bynum 5.00 12.00
BK Bernard King 8.00 20.00
CA Carmelo Anthony SP 25.00 50.00
CB Chauncey Billups 12.50 30.00
CP Chris Paul 40.00 100.00
DE Dennis Rodman SP 40.00 100.00
DG Danny Granger 6.00 15.00
DH Dwight Howard 15.00 40.00
DR David Robinson SP 40.00 80.00
DW Deron Williams 10.00 25.00
EH Elvin Hayes 10.00 25.00
HO Hakeem Olajuwon SP 20.00 50.00
ID Ike Diogu 4.00 10.00
IT Isiah Thomas SP 20.00 50.00
JC Josh Childress 6.00 15.00
JG Joey Graham 5.00 12.00
JH Julius Hodge 4.00 10.00
JJ Jarrett Jack 6.00 15.00
JK Jason Kidd SP 20.00 50.00
JN Jameer Nelson 8.00 20.00
JS John Stockton SP 75.00 150.00
JW John Wooden SP 50.00 120.00
KA Kareem Abdul-Jabbar 40.00 100.00
KN Bob Knight SP 60.00 150.00
LJ1 LeBron James 1,000.00 2,000.00
LJ2 LeBron James 1,000.00 2,000.00
MJ1 Michael Jordan SP 1,500.00 3,000.00
MJ2 Michael Jordan SP 1,500.00 3,000.00
MW Martell Webster 5.00 12.00
PP Paul Pierce 15.00 40.00
RF Raymond Felton 5.00 12.00
RH Richard Hamilton 8.00 20.00
RJ Richard Jefferson 6.00 15.00
RM Rashad McCants 4.00 10.00
SE Sebastian Telfair 6.00 15.00
SH Shawn Marion 15.00 40.00
SM Sean May 4.00 10.00
SN Steve Nash SP 40.00 100.00
SP Scottie Pippen SP 80.00 200.00
ST Stephon Marbury SP 15.00 40.00
WF Walt Frazier 10.00 25.00
WI Marvin Williams SP 6.00 15.00
WR Willis Reed 60.00 150.00
YM Yao Ming SP 15.00 40.00

2005-06 UD Portraits Signature Portraits 8x10 Dual
PRINT RUN 40 SER.#'d SETS
DSP1 M.Jordan/L.James 3,000.00 6,000.00
DSP2 L.James/D.Howard 1,000.00 2,000.00
DSP3 M.Jordan/L.Bird 1,500.00 3,000.00
DSP4 Mv.Williams/C.Paul 50.00 100.00
DSP5 D.Howard/A.Bogut 25.00 60.00
DSP6 T.McGrady/G.Green 25.00 60.00
DSP7 R.Felton/R.McCants 20.00 50.00
DSP8 C.Frye/I.Diogu 20.00 50.00
DSP9 Magic/J.Stockton 125.00 300.00
DSP10 C.Anthony/H.Warrick 30.00 80.00
DSP11 S.May/A.Jamison 20.00 50.00
DSP12 W.Frazier/W.Reed 60.00 150.00
DSP14 K.Hinrich/W.Simien 20.00 50.00
DSP16 Y.Ming/A.Bogut 40.00 100.00
DSP17 B.Knight/J.Wooden 100.00 250.00
DSP19 J.Jack/M.Webster 20.00 50.00
DSP20 E.Hayes/G.Arenas 20.00 50.00
DSP21 H.Olajuwon/Y.Ming 75.00 200.00
DSP22 J.R.Smith/M.Webster 20.00 50.00
DSP23 D.Williams/L.Head 20.00 50.00
DSP24 M.Bibby/S.Stoudamire 20.00 50.00
DSP26 S.Pippen/D.Rodman 150.00 400.00

2005-06 UD Portraits Signature Portraits 8x10 Triple
PRINT RUN 20 SER.#'d SETS
TSP2 LeBron/Carmelo/Bosh 1,000.00 2,000.00

TSP3 Bogut/MvWilliams/Paul 60.00 150.00
TSP4 May/Felton/McCants 30.00 80.00
TSP6 Pierce/A.Jefferson/Green 30.00 80.00
TSP7 Nash/Marion/D.Thompson 50.00 120.00
TSP8 Arenas/Bibby/Salim 30.00 80.00

2000-01 UD Reserve

COMP.SET w/o SP's (90) 8.00 20.00
91-120 STATED ODDS 1:2
1 Dikembe Mutombo .50 1.25
2 Jason Terry .30 .75
3 Alan Henderson .20 .50
4 Paul Pierce .50 1.25
5 Antoine Walker .30 .75
6 Kenny Anderson .25 .60
7 Derrick Coleman .30 .75
8 Baron Davis .30 .75
9 Jamal Mashburn .25 .60
10 Elton Brand .30 .75
11 Ron Mercer .25 .60
12 Ron Artest .30 .75
13 Lamond Murray .20 .50
14 Andre Miller .25 .60
15 Matt Harpring .20 .50
16 Michael Finley .30 .75
17 Dirk Nowitzki .75 2.00
18 Steve Nash .50 1.25
19 Antonio McDyess .25 .60
20 James Posey .20 .50
21 Nick Van Exel .30 .75
22 Jerry Stackhouse .30 .75
23 Jerome Williams .20 .50
24 Chucky Atkins .20 .50
25 Antawn Jamison .30 .75
26 Larry Hughes .30 .75
27 Chris Mills .20 .50
28 Steve Francis .30 .75
29 Hakeem Olajuwon .60 1.50
30 Cuttino Mobley .25 .60
31 Reggie Miller .60 1.50
32 Jalen Rose .25 .60
33 Austin Croshere .20 .50
34 Lamar Odom .30 .75
35 Jeff McInnis .20 .50
36 Corey Maggette .25 .60
37 Shaquille O'Neal 1.25 3.00
38 Kobe Bryant 2.50 6.00
39 Isaiah Rider .25 .60
40 Horace Grant .30 .75
41 Eddie Jones .30 .75
42 Tim Hardaway .40 1.00
43 Brian Grant .25 .60
44 Ray Allen .50 1.25
45 Tim Thomas .20 .50
46 Glenn Robinson .30 .75
47 Sam Cassell .25 .60
48 Kevin Garnett .75 2.00
49 Wally Szczerbiak .25 .60
50 Terrell Brandon .25 .60
51 Chauncey Billups .40 1.00
52 Stephon Marbury .40 1.00
53 Keith Van Horn .25 .60
54 Kendall Gill .30 .75
55 Latrell Sprewell .40 1.00
56 Marcus Camby .25 .60
57 Allan Houston .30 .75
58 Grant Hill .50 1.25
59 Tracy McGrady .60 1.50
60 Darrell Armstrong .20 .50
61 Allen Iverson .75 2.00
62 Theo Ratliff .20 .50
63 Toni Kukoc .40 1.00
64 Jason Kidd .50 1.25
65 Clifford Robinson .30 .75
66 Shawn Marion .30 .75
67 Rasheed Wallace .40 1.00
68 Scottie Pippen .75 2.00
69 Damon Stoudamire .30 .75
70 Chris Webber .40 1.00
71 Jason Williams .50 1.25
72 Vlade Divac .30 .75
73 Tim Duncan .75 2.00
74 David Robinson .60 1.50
75 Derek Anderson .25 .60
76 Gary Payton .50 1.25
77 Patrick Ewing .50 1.25
78 Rashard Lewis .25 .60
79 Vince Carter .60 1.50
80 Mark Jackson .25 .60
81 Antonio Davis .25 .60
82 Karl Malone .60 1.50
83 John Stockton .60 1.50
84 John Starks .30 .75
85 Shareef Abdur-Rahim .30 .75
86 Mike Bibby .30 .75
87 Michael Dickerson .20 .50
88 Mitch Richmond .40 1.00
89 Richard Hamilton .40 1.00
90 Juwan Howard .25 .60
91 Kenyon Martin RC .75 2.00
92 Stromile Swift RC .30 .75
93 Darius Miles RC .40 1.00
94 Marcus Fizer RC .30 .75
95 Mike Miller RC .60 1.50
96 DerMarr Johnson RC .25 .60
97 Chris Mihm RC .25 .60
98 Jamal Crawford RC 1.00 2.50
99 Joel Przybilla RC .30 .75
100 Keyon Dooling RC .30 .75
101 Jerome Moiso RC .25 .60
102 Etan Thomas RC .30 .75
103 Courtney Alexander RC .25 .60
104 Mateen Cleaves RC .30 .75
105 Hedo Turkoglu RC .60 1.50
106 Desmond Mason RC .50 1.25
107 Quentin Richardson RC .30 .75
108 Jamaal Magloire RC .40 1.00
109 Speedy Claxton RC .40 1.00
110 Morris Peterson RC .40 1.00
111 Donnell Harvey RC .30 .75
112 DeShawn Stevenson RC .40 1.00
113 Mamadou N'Diaye RC .25 .60
114 Erick Barkley RC .25 .60
115 Mark Madsen RC .40 1.00
116 Eduardo Najera RC .40 1.00
117 Lavor Postell RC .25 .60
118 Hanno Mottola RC .25 .60
119 Stephen Jackson RC .75 2.00
120 Marc Jackson RC .30 .75

2000-01 UD Reserve Bank Shots

COMPLETE SET (10) 4.00 10.00
STATED ODDS 1:14
BK1 Kevin Garnett 1.25 3.00
BK2 Lamar Odom .50 1.25
BK3 Grant Hill .75 2.00
BK4 Rashard Lewis .40 1.00
BK5 Reggie Miller 1.00 2.50
BK6 Ray Allen .75 2.00
BK7 Eddie Jones .50 1.25
BK8 Kobe Bryant 4.00 10.00
BK9 Michael Finley .50 1.25
BK10 Jerry Stackhouse .50 1.25

2000-01 UD Reserve BuyBacks

STATED ODDS 1:239
1 C.Alexander 00-1P&PPM/98 10.00 25.00
6 S.Claxton 00-1UD/190 10.00 25.00
7 M.Cleaves 00-1UD/74 10.00 25.00
8 M.Cleaves 00-1P&PSF/25 12.50 30.00
9 J.Crawford 00-1UD/120 15.00 40.00
10 K.El-Amin 00-1UD/95 10.00 25.00
11 M.Fizer 00-1UD/50 10.00 25.00
12 M.Fizer 00-1P&PPM/48 10.00 25.00
13 M.Fizer 00-1P&PSF/100 10.00 25.00
15 K.Garnett 95-96UD/21 100.00 200.00
16 D.Harvey 00-1UD/98 10.00 25.00
17 D.Johnson 00-1P&PPM/48 10.00 25.00
18 D.Johnson 00-1P&PSF/95 10.00 25.00
22 M.Madsen 00-1UD/95 10.00 25.00
23 J.Magloire 00-1UD/98 10.00 25.00
24 K.Martin P&PPM/50 20.00 40.00
25 C.Mihm 00-1UD/95 10.00 25.00
26 D.Miles 00-1UD/50 15.00 40.00
27 D.Miles 00-1P&PM/48 15.00 40.00
28 D.Miles 00-1P&PSF/48 15.00 40.00
29 M.Miller 00-1P&PPM/24 10.00 25.00
30 M.Miller 00-1P&PSF/23 10.00 25.00
31 M.Miller 99-0UD/48 20.00 50.00
32 J.Moiso 00-1UD/95 10.00 25.00
33 H.Mottola 00-1UD/95 10.00 25.00
34 M.N'diaye 00-1UD/95 10.00 25.00
35 M.Peterson 00-1UD/95 12.50 30.00
36 J.Przybilla 00-1UD/238 10.00 25.00
37 Q.Richardson 00-1UD/95 20.00 50.00
38 D.Stevenson 00-1UD/95 12.50 30.00
39 S.Swift 00-1UD/50 10.00 25.00
40 S.Swift 00-1P&PPM/50 10.00 25.00
41 S.Swift 00-1P&PSF/50 10.00 25.00

2000-01 UD Reserve Fast Company

COMPLETE SET (10) 4.00 10.00
STATED ODDS 1:14
FC1 Steve Francis .50 1.25
FC2 Kobe Bryant 4.00 10.00
FC3 Allen Iverson 1.25 3.00
FC4 Jason Kidd .75 2.00
FC5 Larry Hughes .50 1.25
FC6 Stephon Marbury .60 1.50
FC7 Jason Williams .50 1.25
FC8 Andre Miller .40 1.00
FC9 Gary Payton .75 2.00
FC10 Paul Pierce .75 2.00

2000-01 UD Reserve NBA Start-Ups

STATED ODDS 1:120
DA Darius Miles 2.50 6.00
DJ DerMarr Johnson 1.50 4.00
JC Jamal Crawford 6.00 15.00
KB Kobe Bryant 50.00 120.00
KG Kevin Garnett 6.00 15.00
KM Kenyon Martin 5.00 12.00
MC Mateen Cleaves 2.00 5.00
MF Marcus Fizer 2.00 5.00
QR Quentin Richardson 2.00 5.00

2000-01 UD Reserve NBA Start-Ups Autographs

STATED ODDS 1:479
DAA Darius Miles 3.00 8.00
DJA DerMarr Johnson 2.00 5.00
JCA Jamal Crawford 12.00 30.00
KGA Kevin Garnett/21 75.00 150.00
KMA Kenyon Martin 6.00 15.00
MFA Marcus Fizer 2.50 6.00
QRA Quentin Richardson 2.50 6.00

2000-01 UD Reserve Power Portfolios

COMPLETE SET (6) 3.00 8.00
STATED ODDS 1:23
PW1 Tim Duncan 1.25 3.00
PW2 Chris Webber .60 1.50
PW3 Grant Hill .75 2.00
PW4 Elton Brand .50 1.25
PW5 Kevin Garnett 1.25 3.00
PW6 Kobe Bryant 4.00 10.00

2000-01 UD Reserve Principal Powers

COMPLETE SET (10) 6.00 15.00
STATED ODDS 1:14
PP1 Shaquille O'Neal 2.00 5.00
PP2 Tim Duncan 1.25 3.00
PP3 Vince Carter 1.00 2.50
PP4 Elton Brand .50 1.25
PP5 Kevin Garnett 1.25 3.00
PP6 Tracy McGrady 1.00 2.50
PP7 Karl Malone 1.00 2.50
PP8 Kobe Bryant 4.00 10.00
PP9 Shareef Abdur-Rahim .50 1.25
PP10 Antonio McDyess .40 1.00

2000-01 UD Reserve Setting the Standard

COMPLETE SET (6) 4.00 10.00
STATED ODDS 1:23
SS1 Steve Francis .50 1.25
SS2 Vince Carter 1.00 2.50
SS3 Kobe Bryant 4.00 10.00
SS4 Kevin Garnett 1.25 3.00
SS5 Allen Iverson 1.25 3.00
SS6 Shaquille O'Neal 2.00 5.00

2006-07 UD Reserve

COMP.SET w/o SP's (200) 30.00 60.00
RC APPROXIMATE ODDS 1:4
1 Josh Childress .40 1.00
2 Al Harrington .50 1.25
3 Joe Johnson .60 1.50
4 Josh Smith .40 1.00
5 Salim Stoudamire .40 1.00
6 Marvin Williams .40 1.00
7 Tony Allen .40 1.00
8 Dan Dickau .40 1.00
9 Al Jefferson .40 1.00
10 Raef LaFrentz .40 1.00
11 Michael Olowokandi .40 1.00
12 Paul Pierce 1.00 2.50
13 Wally Szczerbiak .50 1.25
14 Brevin Knight .40 1.00
15 Raymond Felton .40 1.00
16 Othella Harrington .40 1.00
17 Sean May .40 1.00
18 Emeka Okafor .50 1.25
19 Primoz Brezec .40 1.00
20 Gerald Wallace .50 1.25
21 Tyson Chandler .50 1.25
22 Michael Jordan 5.00 12.00
23 Luol Deng .50 1.25
24 Chris Duhon .40 1.00
25 Ben Gordon .50 1.25
26 Kirk Hinrich .50 1.25
27 Mike Sweetney .40 1.00
28 Drew Gooden .50 1.25
29 Larry Hughes .50 1.25
30 Zydrunas Ilgauskas .50 1.25
31 LeBron James 5.00 12.00
32 Damon Jones .40 1.00
33 Donyell Marshall .40 1.00
34 Anderson Varejao .40 1.00
35 Erick Dampier .40 1.00
36 Marquis Daniels .40 1.00
37 Devin Harris .40 1.00
38 Josh Howard .50 1.25
39 Dirk Nowitzki 1.50 4.00
40 Jerry Stackhouse .50 1.25
41 Jason Terry .50 1.25
42 Carmelo Anthony 1.00 2.50
43 Earl Boykins .40 1.00
44 Marcus Camby .50 1.25
45 Kenyon Martin .50 1.25
46 Andre Miller .50 1.25
47 Eduardo Najera .40 1.00
48 Nene .50 1.25
49 Chauncey Billups .75 2.00
50 Richard Hamilton .50 1.25
51 Lindsey Hunter .40 1.00
52 Antonio McDyess .50 1.25
53 Tayshaun Prince .60 1.50
54 Ben Wallace .75 2.00
55 Rasheed Wallace .75 2.00
56 Baron Davis .60 1.50
57 Ike Diogu .40 1.00
58 Mike Dunleavy .40 1.00
59 Derek Fisher .60 1.50
60 Troy Murphy .40 1.00
61 Mickael Pietrus .40 1.00
62 Jason Richardson .60 1.50
63 Rafer Alston .50 1.25
64 Luther Head .40 1.00
65 Juwan Howard .50 1.25
66 Tracy McGrady 1.00 2.50
67 Dikembe Mutombo .60 1.50
68 Stromile Swift .40 1.00
69 Yao Ming 1.50 4.00
70 Austin Croshere .40 1.00
71 Stephen Jackson .40 1.00
72 Sarunas Jasikevicius .50 1.25
73 Jermaine O'Neal .60 1.50
74 Peja Stojakovic .60 1.50
75 Jamaal Tinsley .40 1.00
76 Elton Brand .50 1.25
77 Sam Cassell .50 1.25
78 Chris Kaman .40 1.00
79 Shaun Livingston .50 1.25
80 Corey Maggette .50 1.25
81 Cuttino Mobley .50 1.25
82 Vladimir Radmanovic .40 1.00
83 Kwame Brown .40 1.00
84 Kobe Bryant 5.00 12.00
85 Devean George .40 1.00
86 Lamar Odom .50 1.25
87 Ronny Turiaf .50 1.25
88 Sasha Vujacic .40 1.00
89 Luke Walton .40 1.00
90 Shane Battier .50 1.25
91 Pau Gasol 1.00 2.50
92 Bobby Jackson .40 1.00
93 Eddie Jones .60 1.50
94 Mike Miller .50 1.25
95 Damon Stoudamire .50 1.25
96 Hakim Warrick .40 1.00
97 Alonzo Mourning 1.00 2.50
98 Shaquille O'Neal 2.50 6.00
99 Gary Payton .75 2.00
100 Wayne Simien .40 1.00
101 Dwyane Wade 1.25 3.00
102 Antoine Walker .60 1.50
103 Jason Williams .75 2.00
104 Andrew Bogut .50 1.25
105 T.J. Ford .50 1.25
106 Jamaal Magloire .40 1.00
107 Michael Redd .50 1.25
108 Bobby Simmons .40 1.00
109 Maurice Williams .40 1.00
110 Ricky Davis .50 1.25
111 Kevin Garnett 1.50 4.00
112 Kelenna Azubuike .75 2.00
113 Trenton Hassell .40 1.00
114 Troy Hudson .40 1.00
115 Rashad McCants .40 1.00
116 Vince Carter 1.25 3.00
117 Jason Collins .40 1.00
118 Richard Jefferson .50 1.25
119 Jason Kidd 1.00 2.50
120 Nenad Krstic .40 1.00
121 Jeff McInnis .40 1.00
122 Antoine Wright .40 1.00
123 P.J. Brown .40 1.00
124 Speedy Claxton .40 1.00
125 Desmond Mason .40 1.00
126 Chris Paul 1.25 3.00
127 J.R. Smith .60 1.50
128 Kirk Snyder .40 1.00
129 David West .50 1.25
130 Jamal Crawford .60 1.50
131 Eddy Curry .50 1.25
132 Channing Frye .40 1.00
133 Stephon Marbury .75 2.00
134 Quentin Richardson .40 1.00
135 Nate Robinson .50 1.25
136 David Lee .40 1.00
137 Carlos Arroyo .40 1.00
138 Tony Battie .40 1.00
139 Keyon Dooling .40 1.00
140 Grant Hill 1.00 2.50
141 Dwight Howard .75 2.00
142 Darko Milicic .40 1.00
143 Jameer Nelson .40 1.00
144 Samuel Dalembert .40 1.00
145 Steven Hunter .40 1.00
146 Andre Iguodala .60 1.50
147 Allen Iverson 1.50 4.00
148 Kyle Korver .50 1.25
149 Shavlik Randolph .40 1.00
150 Chris Webber .75 2.00
151 Raja Bell .50 1.25
152 Boris Diaw .50 1.25
153 Shawn Marion .60 1.50
154 Steve Nash 1.25 3.00
155 Amare Stoudemire .60 1.50
156 Kurt Thomas .40 1.00
157 Tim Thomas .40 1.00
158 Steve Blake .40 1.00
159 Juan Dixon .40 1.00
160 Zach Randolph .60 1.50
161 Joel Przybilla .40 1.00
162 Sebastian Telfair .40 1.00
163 Martell Webster .40 1.00
164 Shareef Abdur-Rahim .60 1.50
165 Ron Artest .60 1.50
166 Mike Bibby .60 1.50
167 Brad Miller .50 1.25
168 Kenny Thomas .40 1.00
169 Bonzi Wells .40 1.00
170 Bruce Bowen .50 1.25
171 Tim Duncan 1.50 4.00
172 Michael Finley .60 1.50
173 Manu Ginobili 1.25 3.00
174 Nazr Mohammed .40 1.00
175 Tony Parker 1.00 2.50
176 Ray Allen 1.00 2.50
177 Danny Fortson .40 1.00
178 Rashard Lewis .50 1.25
179 Luke Ridnour .50 1.25
180 Earl Watson .40 1.00
181 Chris Wilcox .40 1.00
182 Rafael Araujo .40 1.00
183 Chris Bosh .75 2.00
184 Joey Graham .40 1.00
185 Mike James .40 1.00
186 Morris Peterson .40 1.00
187 Charlie Villanueva .40 1.00
188 Carlos Boozer .50 1.25
189 Matt Harpring .40 1.00
190 Kris Humphries .40 1.00
191 Andrei Kirilenko .50 1.25
192 C.J. Miles .40 1.00
193 Paul Millsap .75 2.00
194 Deron Williams .75 2.00
195 Gilbert Arenas .60 1.50
196 Andray Blatche .50 1.25
197 Caron Butler .50 1.25
198 Antonio Daniels .40 1.00
199 Brendan Haywood .40 1.00
200 Antawn Jamison .50 1.25
201 Andrea Bargnani RC 1.00 2.50
202 LaMarcus Aldridge RC 3.00 8.00
203 Adam Morrison RC 1.00 2.50
204 Tyrus Thomas RC 1.00 2.50
205 Shelden Williams RC .60 1.50
206 Brandon Roy RC 2.50 6.00
207 Randy Foye RC 1.00 2.50
208 Rudy Gay RC 1.50 4.00
209 Patrick O'Bryant RC .75 2.00
210 Saer Sene RC .75 2.00
211 J.J. Redick RC 2.50 6.00
212 Hilton Armstrong RC .75 2.00
213 Thabo Sefolosha RC .75 2.00
214 Ronnie Brewer RC 1.25 3.00
215 Cedric Simmons RC .75 2.00
216 Rodney Carney RC .75 2.00
217 Shawne Williams RC .75 2.00
218 Quincy Douby RC .75 2.00
219 Renaldo Balkman RC 1.00 2.50
220 Rajon Rondo RC 4.00 10.00
221 Marcus Williams RC .75 2.00
222 Josh Boone RC .75 2.00
223 Kyle Lowry RC 4.00 10.00
224 Shannon Brown RC .75 2.00
225 Jordan Farmar RC .75 2.00
226 Maurice Ager RC .75 2.00
227 Mardy Collins RC .75 2.00
228 Jorge Garbajosa RC 1.00 2.50
229 James White RC .75 2.00
230 Steve Novak RC 1.00 2.50
231 Solomon Jones RC .75 2.00
232 Paul Davis RC .75 2.00
233 P.J. Tucker RC 1.25 3.00
234 Craig Smith RC .75 2.00
235 Bobby Jones RC .75 2.00
236 David Noel RC .75 2.00
237 Vassilis Spanoulis RC .75 2.00
238 James Augustine RC .75 2.00
239 Daniel Gibson RC 1.00 2.50
240 Alexander Johnson RC .75 2.00

2006-07 UD Reserve Gold

GOLD: 1.25X TO 3X BASE HI
APPROXIMATE ODDS ONE PER BOX

2006-07 UD Reserve Flight Team

COMPLETE SET (30) 15.00 40.00
APPROXIMATE ODDS 1:4
*GOLD: 1X TO 2.5X BASE HI
APPROXIMATE GOLD ODDS 1:20
AI Andre Iguodala .75 2.00
AS Amare Stoudemire .75 2.00
BB Brent Barry .50 1.25
BD Boris Diaw .60 1.50
CA Carmelo Anthony 1.25 3.00
CB Chris Bosh 1.00 2.50
CM Corey Maggette .60 1.50
DH Dwight Howard 1.00 2.50
DM Desmond Mason .50 1.25
DW Dwyane Wade 1.50 4.00
EJ Eddie Jones .75 2.00
FJ Fred Jones .50 1.25
GA Gilbert Arenas .75 2.00
JR Jason Richardson .75 2.00
JS J.R. Smith .60 1.50
KB Kobe Bryant 6.00 15.00
KM Kenyon Martin .60 1.50
LJ LeBron James 6.00 15.00
MA Shawn Marion .75 2.00
MG Manu Ginobili 1.50 4.00
MI Darius Miles .50 1.25
MJ Michael Jordan 6.00 15.00
NR Nate Robinson .60 1.50
RD Ricky Davis .60 1.50
RJ Richard Jefferson .60 1.50
SM Josh Smith .50 1.25
SS Stromile Swift .50 1.25
TM Tracy McGrady 1.25 3.00
TP Tayshaun Prince .75 2.00
VC Vince Carter 1.50 4.00

2006-07 UD Reserve Game Jerseys

APPROXIMATE ODDS ONE PER BOX
*PATCHES: .75X TO 2X BASE HI
APPROXIMATE ODDS 1:12
AB Andrew Bogut 2.50 6.00
AC Carlos Arroyo 2.00 5.00
AI Allen Iverson 8.00 20.00
AJ Al Jefferson 2.00 5.00
AK Andrei Kirilenko 2.50 6.00
AL Rafer Alston 2.50 6.00
AN Antawn Jamison 2.50 6.00
AR Ron Artest 3.00 8.00
AS Amare Stoudemire 3.00 8.00
AW Antoine Walker 3.00 8.00
BB Bruce Bowen 2.50 6.00
BD Baron Davis 3.00 8.00
BG Ben Gordon 2.50 6.00
BM Brad Miller 2.50 6.00
BW Ben Wallace 4.00 10.00
CB Chauncey Billups 4.00 10.00
CF Channing Frye 2.00 5.00
CM Corey Maggette 2.50 6.00
CP Chris Paul 6.00 15.00
CW Chris Webber 4.00 10.00
DG Drew Gooden 2.50 6.00
DH Devin Harris 2.00 5.00
DM Donyell Marshall 2.00 5.00
DN Dirk Nowitzki 8.00 20.00
DW Deron Williams 2.50 6.00
EO Emeka Okafor 2.50 6.00
GA Gilbert Arenas 3.00 8.00
GE Devean George 2.00 5.00
GH Grant Hill 6.00 15.00
HE Luther Head 2.00 5.00
HO Dwight Howard 4.00 10.00
ID Ike Diogu 2.00 5.00
IG Andre Iguodala 3.00 8.00
JC Jamal Crawford 3.00 8.00
JD Juan Dixon 2.00 5.00
JH Josh Howard 2.50 6.00
JJ Joe Johnson 3.00 8.00
JK Jason Kidd 5.00 12.00
JN Jameer Nelson 2.00 5.00
JO Jermaine O'Neal 3.00 8.00
JR Jason Richardson 3.00 8.00
JS J.R. Smith 3.00 8.00
JT Jason Terry 2.50 6.00
JW Jason Williams 4.00 10.00
KB Kwame Brown 2.00 5.00
KG Kevin Garnett 8.00 20.00
KH Kirk Hinrich 2.50 6.00
KK Kyle Korver 2.50 6.00
KM Kenyon Martin 2.50 6.00
LB Leandro Barbosa 2.50 6.00
LD Luol Deng 2.50 6.00
LH Larry Hughes 2.50 6.00
LJ LeBron James 20.00 50.00
LO Lamar Odom 2.50 6.00
LW Luke Walton 2.50 6.00
MA Stephon Marbury 4.00 10.00
MB Mike Bibby 3.00 8.00
MD Marquis Daniels 2.00 5.00
MG Manu Ginobili 5.00 12.00
MJ Michael Jordan 60.00 150.00
MR Michael Redd 2.50 6.00
MW Marvin Williams 2.00 5.00
NR Nate Robinson 2.00 5.00
PA Tony Parker 5.00 12.00
PG Pau Gasol 5.00 12.00
PS Peja Stojakovic 2.50 6.00
QR Quentin Richardson 2.00 5.00
RA Ray Allen 5.00 12.00
RF Raymond Felton 2.00 5.00
RH Richard Hamilton 3.00 8.00
RL Rashard Lewis 2.50 6.00
RM Rashad McCants 2.00 5.00
RW Rasheed Wallace 4.00 10.00
SD Samuel Dalembert 2.00 5.00
SF Steve Francis 3.00 8.00
SH Shawn Marion 3.00 8.00
SJ Sarunas Jasikevicius 2.50 6.00
SL Shaun Livingston 2.50 6.00
SM Sean May 2.00 5.00
SO Shaquille O'Neal 12.00 30.00
ST Sebastian Telfair 2.00 5.00
TC Tyson Chandler 2.50 6.00
TF T.J. Ford 2.50 6.00
TP Tayshaun Prince 3.00 8.00
VC Vince Carter 6.00 15.00
WE Martell Webster 2.50 6.00
WS Wally Szczerbiak 2.50 6.00
ZI Zydrunas Ilgauskas 2.50 6.00

2006-07 UD Reserve Legendary Signatures

APPROXIMATE ODDS ONE PER BOX
BK Bernard King 6.00 15.00
BM Bob McAdoo 6.00 15.00
CD Clyde Drexler 12.50 30.00
CH Connie Hawkins 6.00 15.00
CM Cedric Maxwell 6.00 15.00
DD Darryl Dawkins 8.00 20.00
DR David Robinson 40.00 80.00
HO Hakeem Olajuwon 15.00 40.00
JE Julius Erving 40.00 80.00
JO Michael Jordan 1,500.00 3,000.00
JS John Stockton 60.00 120.00
KV Kiki Vandeweghe 6.00 15.00
LB Larry Bird 75.00 150.00
MC Maurice Cheeks 6.00 15.00
MJ Magic Johnson 60.00 120.00
ML Maurice Lucas 6.00 15.00
NA Nate Archibald 6.00 15.00
RO Dennis Rodman 40.00 75.00
SP Sam Perkins 6.00 15.00
SW Spud Webb 8.00 20.00

2006-07 UD Reserve Materials

STATED PRINT RUN 100 SER.#'d SETS
*PATCHES: .75X TO 2X BASE HI
PRINT RUN 35 SER.#'d SETS
AB Andray Blatche 2.00 5.00
AI Allen Iverson 10.00 25.00
AJ Antawn Jamison 3.00 8.00
AK Andrei Kirilenko 3.00 8.00
BD Baron Davis 4.00 10.00
BG Ben Gordon 3.00 8.00
BM Brad Miller 3.00 8.00
BO Chris Bosh 5.00 12.00
BW Ben Wallace 5.00 12.00
CA Carmelo Anthony 6.00 15.00
CB Carlos Boozer 3.00 8.00
CM Corey Maggette 3.00 8.00
CP Chris Paul 8.00 20.00
DG Danny Granger 2.50 6.00
DH Dwight Howard 5.00 12.00
DN Dirk Nowitzki 10.00 25.00
DW David West 3.00 8.00
EB Elton Brand 3.00 8.00
EO Emeka Okafor 3.00 8.00
GH Grant Hill 8.00 20.00
HW Hakim Warrick 2.50 6.00
JC Josh Childress 2.50 6.00
JG Joey Graham 2.50 6.00
JK Jason Kidd 6.00 15.00
JN Jameer Nelson 2.50 6.00
JO Jermaine O'Neal 4.00 10.00
JS Josh Smith 2.50 6.00
KB Kobe Bryant 50.00 120.00
KG Kevin Garnett 10.00 25.00
LH Luther Head 2.50 6.00
LJ LeBron James 30.00 80.00
LW Luke Walton 2.50 6.00
MB Mike Bibby 4.00 10.00
MG Manu Ginobili 8.00 20.00
MJ Michael Jordan 30.00 80.00
MR Michael Redd 3.00 8.00
MW Marvin Williams 2.50 6.00
NE Nene 3.00 8.00
PP Paul Pierce 6.00 15.00
PS Peja Stojakovic 3.00 8.00
RA Ray Allen 6.00 15.00
RB Raja Bell 3.00 8.00
RF Raymond Felton 2.50 6.00
RH Richard Hamilton 4.00 10.00
RJ Richard Jefferson 3.00 8.00
RM Rashad McCants 2.50 6.00
RW Rasheed Wallace 5.00 12.00
SM Stephon Marbury 5.00 12.00
SN Steve Nash 8.00 20.00
TD Tim Duncan 10.00 25.00
TP Tony Parker 6.00 15.00
WI Deron Williams 3.00 8.00
WS Wally Szczerbiak 3.00 8.00
YM Yao Ming 10.00 25.00
ZI Zydrunas Ilgauskas 3.00 8.00

2006-07 UD Reserve Materials Dual

PRINT RUN 50 SER.#'d SETS
*PATCHES: .75X TO 2X BASE HI
PATCH PRINT RUN 15 SER.#'d SETS
AR L.Aldridge/B.Roy 10.00 25.00
BG C.Bosh/J.Graham 6.00 15.00
BM E.Brand/C.Maggette 5.00 12.00
BO K.Brown/L.Odom 5.00 12.00
CJ J.Childress/J.Johnson 5.00 12.00
FM R.Foye/R.McCants 5.00 12.00
GW P.Gasol/H.Warrick 5.00 12.00
HB R.Hamilton/C.Billups 8.00 20.00
HH D.Harris/J.Howard 5.00 12.00
HN G.Hill/J.Nelson 6.00 15.00
JB A.Jamison/A.Blatche 5.00 12.00
JJ L.James/M.Jordan 60.00 150.00
KB A.Kirilenko/C.Boozer 5.00 12.00
MB B.Miller/M.Bibby 5.00 12.00
MF C.Frye/S.Marbury 5.00 12.00
MM Y.Ming/T.McGrady 10.00 25.00
MO Y.Ming/S.O'Neal 20.00 40.00
OG J.O'Neal/D.Granger 5.00 12.00
PD T.Parker/T.Duncan 10.00 25.00
PJ P.Pierce/A.Jefferson 5.00 12.00
PW C.Paul/D.West 6.00 15.00
RD J.Richardson/B.Davis 5.00 12.00
VR C.Villanueva/M.Redd 5.00 12.00
WB M.Williams/J.Boone 5.00 12.00
PAN C.Anthony/Nene 6.00 15.00

2006-07 UD Reserve Materials Triple

PRINT RUN 25 SER.#'d SETS
ARW Aldridge/Roy/Webster 20.00 40.00
BSS Bargnani/Sene/Sefolosha 10.00 25.00
CWS Childress/Williams/Smith 8.00 20.00
GST Gordon/Sefolosha/Thomas 8.00 20.00
GWB Gay/Williams/Boone 8.00 20.00
GWG Gasol/Warrick/Gay 8.00 20.00
ICK Iguodala/Carney/Korver 8.00 20.00
KCJ Kidd/Carter/Jefferson 20.00 40.00
SNM Stoudemire/Nash/Marion 20.00 40.00
SRR Szczerbiak/Rondo/Ray 8.00 20.00

2006-07 UD Reserve MVP Watch

COMPLETE SET (15) 15.00 40.00
APPROXIMATE ODDS 1:6
*GOLD: .75X TO 2X BASE HI
APPROXIMATE GOLD ODDS 1:24
AI Allen Iverson 2.50 6.00
BW Ben Wallace 1.25 3.00
CB Chauncey Billups 1.25 3.00
DN Dirk Nowitzki 2.50 6.00
DW Dwyane Wade 2.00 5.00
EB Elton Brand .75 2.00
GA Gilbert Arenas 1.00 2.50
KB Kobe Bryant 8.00 20.00
KG Kevin Garnett 2.50 6.00
LJ LeBron James 8.00 20.00
PP Paul Pierce 1.50 4.00
SN Steve Nash 2.00 5.00
SO Shaquille O'Neal 4.00 10.00
TD Tim Duncan 2.50 6.00
TM Tracy McGrady 1.50 4.00

2006-07 UD Reserve Signatures

APPROXIMATE ODDS ONE PER BOX
AI Andre Iguodala 5.00 12.00
AJ Al Jefferson 3.00 8.00
AN Antawn Jamison 4.00 10.00
AR Hilton Armstrong 3.00 8.00
BA Andrea Bargnani 4.00 10.00
BB Brent Barry 6.00 15.00
BD Baron Davis 5.00 12.00
BE Raja Bell 4.00 10.00
BG Ben Gordon 4.00 10.00
BJ Bobby Jackson 3.00 8.00
BO Bruce Bowen 4.00 10.00
BS Bobby Simmons 3.00 8.00
CA Carmelo Anthony 15.00 40.00
CB Chauncey Billups 8.00 20.00
CD Chris Duhon 3.00 8.00
CH Charlie Bell 3.00 8.00
CM Corey Maggette 4.00 10.00
CS Cedric Simmons 3.00 8.00
DB Dee Brown 3.00 8.00
DE Daniel Ewing 3.00 8.00
DG Danny Granger 3.00 8.00
DI Boris Diaw 4.00 10.00
DM Damir Markota 3.00 8.00
DN David Noel 3.00 8.00
DW Deron Williams 4.00 10.00
EC Eddy Curry 4.00 10.00
EO Emeka Okafor 4.00 10.00
FE Raymond Felton 3.00 8.00
GG Gerald Green 4.00 10.00
GI Daniel Gibson 4.00 10.00
GR Joey Graham 3.00 8.00
HA Hassan Adams 3.00 8.00
HW Hakim Warrick 3.00 8.00
IU Ime Udoka 10.00 25.00
JA James Augustine 3.00 8.00
JB Josh Boone 3.00 8.00
JC Josh Childress 3.00 8.00
JF Jordan Farmar 4.00 10.00
JG Jorge Garbajosa 4.00 10.00
JJ Jarrett Jack 4.00 10.00
JO Bobby Jones 3.00 8.00
JS J.R. Smith 5.00 12.00
KD Keyon Dooling 3.00 8.00
KH Kirk Hinrich 4.00 10.00
KK Kyle Korver 4.00 10.00
KL Kyle Lowry 6.00 15.00
LA LaMarcus Aldridge 15.00 40.00
LB Leandro Barbosa 4.00 10.00
LH Larry Hughes 4.00 10.00
LJ LeBron James 1,000.00 2,000.00
LR Luke Ridnour 4.00 10.00
MA Maurice Ager 3.00 8.00
MC Mardy Collins 3.00 8.00
MI Mile Ilic 3.00 8.00
MM Chris Mihm 3.00 8.00
MO Cuttino Mobley 4.00 10.00
MW Marvin Williams 3.00 8.00
NO Steve Novak 4.00 10.00
PD Paul Davis 3.00 8.00
PM Paul Millsap 5.00 12.00
PO Patrick O'Bryant 3.00 8.00
PP Paul Pierce 8.00 20.00
PS Peja Stojakovic 4.00 10.00
PT P.J. Tucker 5.00 12.00
QD Quincy Douby 3.00 8.00
QR Quentin Richardson 3.00 8.00
RB Ronnie Brewer 5.00 12.00
RC Rodney Carney 3.00 8.00
RE Renaldo Balkman 4.00 10.00
RF Randy Foye 4.00 10.00
RG Rudy Gay 6.00 15.00
RH Ryan Hollins 3.00 8.00
RM Rashad McCants 3.00 8.00
RO Brandon Roy 10.00 25.00
RR Rajon Rondo 15.00 40.00
SA Shareef Abdur-Rahim 5.00 12.00
SB Shannon Brown 3.00 8.00
SH Shawne Williams 3.00 8.00
SJ Solomon Jones 3.00 8.00
SM Craig Smith 4.00 10.00
SN Steve Nash 15.00 40.00
SR Sergio Rodriguez 4.00 10.00
SS Saer Sene 3.00 8.00
ST Sebastian Telfair 3.00 8.00
SW Shelden Williams 3.00 8.00
TA Tony Allen 5.00 12.00
TF T.J. Ford 3.00 8.00
TM Tracy McGrady 12.00 30.00
TS Thabo Sefolosha 4.00 10.00
TT Tyrus Thomas 4.00 10.00
VC Vince Carter 30.00 60.00
VS Vassilis Spanoulis 3.00 8.00
WB Will Blalock 3.00 8.00
WE Martell Webster 4.00 10.00
WH James White 3.00 8.00
WM Marcus Williams 3.00 8.00
YM Yao Ming 15.00 40.00

2006-07 UD Reserve Signatures Dual

PRINT RUN 50 SER.#'d SETS
AB H.Armstrong/J.Boone 6.00 15.00
AM C.Anthony/T.McGrady 25.00 60.00
AP M.Ager/S.Perkins 6.00 15.00
AR L.Aldridge/B.Roy 20.00 50.00
AW J.Augustine/D.Williams 15.00 40.00
BB C.Billups/W.Blalock 8.00 20.00
BG S.Brown/D.Gibson 8.00 20.00
CB R.Balkman/M.Collins 6.00 15.00
CW R.Carney/S.Williams 6.00 15.00
DA Q.Douby/S.Abdur-Rahim 6.00 15.00

DO B.Davis/P.O'Bryant 8.00 20.00
FS R.Foye/C.Smith 8.00 20.00
GF T.Ford/J.Graham 6.00 15.00
HD K.Hinrich/C.Duhon 12.50 30.00
HF R.Felton/R.Hollins 6.00 15.00
IK A.Iguodala/K.Korver 8.00 20.00
JD J.Augustine/D.Brown 6.00 15.00
JJ L.James/M.Jordan 4,000.00 8,000.00
LR D.Lee/Q.Richardson 6.00 15.00
MD C.Maggette/P.Davis 6.00 15.00
OF E.Okafor/R.Felton 15.00 30.00
OM H.Olajuwon/Y.Ming 40.00 80.00
RB D.Robinson/B.Barry 40.00 80.00
RD R.Brewer/D.Brown 6.00 15.00
RF A.Ray/R.Foye 10.00 25.00
SM S.Williams/M.Williams 6.00 15.00
TJ S.Telfair/A.Jefferson 6.00 15.00
TR T.Allen/R.Rondo 15.00 40.00
TS T.Thomas/T.Sefolosha 15.00 40.00
VS K.Vandeweghe/J.Smith 6.00 15.00
WC J.Childress/S.Webb 6.00 15.00
WG S.Williams/D.Granger 6.00 15.00
WS D.Wilkins/S.Sene 6.00 15.00
WW J.White/B.Barry 6.00 15.00

2006-07 UD Reserve Signatures Triple

PRINT RUN 25 SER.#'d SETS
AWB Adams/Williams/Boone 12.00 30.00
BAT Bargnani/Aldridge/Thomas 25.00 60.00
BCR Balkman/Collins/Richardson 12.00 30.00
FSM Foye/Smith/McCants 12.00 30.00
GBH Gibson/Brown/Hughes 12.00 30.00
RGR Rondo/Green/Ray 25.00 60.00
RWS Ridnour/Wilkins/Sene 12.00 30.00
SSA Stojakovic/Simmons/Armstrong 12.00 30.00
WLG Warrick/Lowry/Gay 25.00 50.00

2006-07 UD Reserve The LeBrons

COMPLETE SET (15) 20.00 50.00
APPROXIMATE ODDS 1:12
COMMON GOLD 15.00 30.00
COMMON MEMORABILIA 10.00 25.00
COMMON DUAL/TRIP.MEM. 15.00 40.00

1996 UDA 22kt Gold Michael Jordan Slam Dunk Champion

NNO Michael Jordan 75.00 200.00

2003 UDA LeBron James

NNO LeBron James
First Game/2323 50.00 120.00
NNO LeBron James
Youngest to 1000/5000 50.00 120.00

1995-98 UDA Michael Jordan Commemorative Cards

NNO 1981-84 A Higher Education 8.00 20.00
NNO 1995 He's Back
55 points vs Knicks 8.00 20.00
NNO 1995 He's Back
Conclusion of the 94-95 season 8.00 20.00
NNO 1995 He's Back
Jersey #45 8.00 20.00
NNO 1995 UNC 1st
Champ.blue foil/5000 10.00 25.00
NNO 1995 UNC 1st
Champ.gold foil/5000 10.00 25.00
NNO 1996 10-Time All-Star/5000 10.00 25.00
NNO 1996 25,000 Points (no serial #) 8.00 20.00
NNO 1996 4-Time Finals MVP/2500 12.50 30.00
NNO 1996 8-Time Scoring Champ/5000 10.00 25.00
NNO 1996 All-Star First Team/2500 12.50 30.00
NNO 1996 Magic Memories MTS 8.00 20.00
NNO 1996 National Hero/5000 10.00 25.00
NNO 1996 Reg.season MVP/2500 12.50 30.00
NNO 1996 Space Jam w/ball/5000 10.00 25.00
NNO 1996 Space Jam w/Bugs/5000 10.00 25.00
NNO 1996 Space Jam w/Porky/5000 10.00 25.00
NNO 1997 11-Time All-Star/5000 10.00 25.00
NNO 1997 25,000 Career
Point 22kt/10000 8.00 20.00
NNO 1997 5-Time NBA
Finals MVP/5000 10.00 25.00
NNO 1997 9-Time Scoring Champ/5000 10.00 25.00
NNO Celebration of Excellence 8.00 20.00
NNO Olympic Gold '84 and '92 8.00 20.00

2000 UDA Michael Jordan Final Shot

1A Michael Jordan
Floor AU/100 2,000.00 4,000.00
1B Michael Jordan
Floor/900 150.00 400.00

1996 UDA SPx Record Breaker Michael Jordan

R1 Michael Jordan AU/250 6,000.00 10,000.00

2000-01 Ultimate Collection

RCs STATED PRINT RUN 750 SERIAL #'d SETS
1 Dikembe Mutombo 4.00 10.00
2 Hanno Mottola RC 2.00 5.00
3 Paul Pierce 4.00 10.00
4 Antoine Walker 2.50 6.00
5 Derrick Coleman 2.50 6.00
6 Baron Davis 2.50 6.00
7 Elton Brand 2.50 6.00
8 Michael Jordan 150.00 400.00
9 Andre Miller 2.00 5.00
10 Chris Mihm RC 2.00 5.00
11 Michael Finley 2.50 6.00
12 Donnell Harvey RC 2.50 6.00
13 Antonio McDyess 2.00 5.00
14 Nick Van Exel 2.50 6.00
15 Jerry Stackhouse 2.50 6.00
16 Jerome Williams 1.50 4.00
17 Larry Hughes 2.50 6.00
18 Antawn Jamison 2.50 6.00
19 Steve Francis 2.50 6.00
20 Hakeem Olajuwon 5.00 12.00
21 Reggie Miller 5.00 12.00
22 Jalen Rose 2.50 6.00
23 Lamar Odom 2.50 6.00
24 Michael Olowokandi 1.50 4.00
25 Shaquille O'Neal 10.00 25.00
26 Kobe Bryant 10.00 25.00
27 Ron Harper 2.50 6.00
28 Alonzo Mourning 4.00 10.00
29 Eddie House RC 2.50 6.00
30 Glenn Robinson 2.50 6.00
31 Ray Allen 4.00 10.00
32 Kevin Garnett 6.00 15.00
33 Wally Szczerbiak 2.00 5.00
34 Terrell Brandon 2.00 5.00
35 Stephon Marbury 3.00 8.00
36 Keith Van Horn 2.00 5.00
37 Allan Houston 2.50 6.00
38 Latrell Sprewell 3.00 8.00
39 Grant Hill 4.00 10.00
40 Tracy McGrady 5.00 12.00
41 Allen Iverson 6.00 15.00
42 Toni Kukoc 3.00 8.00
43 Jason Kidd 4.00 10.00
44 Anfernee Hardaway 4.00 10.00
45 Scottie Pippen 6.00 15.00
46 Rasheed Wallace 3.00 8.00
47 Chris Webber 3.00 8.00
48 Jason Williams 4.00 10.00
49 Tim Duncan 6.00 15.00
50 David Robinson 5.00 12.00
51 Gary Payton 4.00 10.00
52 Rashard Lewis 2.00 5.00
53 Vince Carter 5.00 12.00
54 Morris Peterson RC 3.00 8.00
55 Karl Malone 5.00 12.00
56 John Stockton 5.00 12.00
57 Shareef Abdur-Rahim 2.50 6.00
58 Mike Bibby 2.50 6.00
59 Mike Smith RC 2.00 5.00
60 Richard Hamilton 3.00 8.00
P1 Kenyon Martin SAMPLE 1.00 2.50

2000-01 Ultimate Collection Rookies

STATED PRINT RUN 250 SERIAL #'d SETS
61 Mamadou N'Diaye RC 4.00 10.00
62 Erick Barkley RC 4.00 10.00
63 Desmond Mason RC 8.00 20.00
64 Speedy Claxton RC 6.00 15.00
65 Jamaal Magloire RC 6.00 15.00
66 DeShawn Stevenson RC 6.00 15.00
67 Etan Thomas RC 5.00 12.00
68 Jamal Crawford RC 15.00 40.00
69 Joel Przybilla RC 5.00 12.00
70 Keyon Dooling RC 5.00 12.00
71 Jerome Moiso RC 4.00 10.00
72 Quentin Richardson RC 6.00 15.00
73 Courtney Alexander RC 4.00 10.00
74 Mateen Cleaves RC 6.00 15.00
75 Mike Miller AU RC 10.00 25.00
76 DerMarr Johnson AU RC 4.00 10.00
77 Darius Miles AU RC 6.00 15.00
78 Marcus Fizer AU RC 5.00 12.00
79 Kenyon Martin AU RC 12.00 30.00
80 Stromile Swift AU RC 5.00 12.00

2000-01 Ultimate Collection Game Jerseys Bronze

STATED ODDS 1:3
*GOLD: .6X TO 1.5X BRONZE HI
GOLD STATED ODDS 1:17
*SILVER: .5X TO 1.25X BRONZE HI
SILVER STATED ODDS 1:6
DSJ Damon Stoudamire 5.00 12.00
JKJ Jason Kidd 8.00 20.00
JSJ John Stockton 8.00 20.00
KBJ Kobe Bryant 75.00 200.00
KGJ Kevin Garnett 12.00 30.00
KMJ Kenyon Martin 8.00 20.00
MFJ Marcus Fizer 4.00 10.00
MJJ Michael Jordan 50.00 120.00
WSJ Wally Szczerbiak 4.00 10.00

2000-01 Ultimate Collection Game Jerseys Patches

STATED ODDS 1:11
STATED PRINT RUN 8 TO 100 SETS
AHP Anfernee Hardaway/75 75.00 150.00
AIP Allen Iverson/75 80.00 200.00
AMP Alonzo Mourning/100 30.00 80.00
DRP David Robinson/100 40.00 100.00
DSP Damon Stoudamire/75 20.00 50.00
GPP Gary Payton/100 30.00 60.00
JKP Jason Kidd/75 50.00 120.00
JSP John Stockton/100 50.00 120.00
JWP Jason Williams/25 50.00 100.00
KGA Kevin Garnett AU/21 150.00 300.00
KGP Kevin Garnett/21 75.00 150.00
KMP Karl Malone/100 40.00 100.00
KVP Keith Van Horn/100 20.00 50.00
MFP Michael Finley/75 25.00 60.00
MJA Michael Jordan AU/23 2,500.00 5,000.00
PPP Paul Pierce/50 40.00 100.00
RAP Ray Allen/100 40.00 100.00
RMP Reggie Miller/100 50.00 120.00
SAP Shareef Abdur-Rahim/100 20.00 50.00
SHP Shawn Marion/25 40.00 100.00
SMP Stephon Marbury/75 20.00 50.00
SOP Shaquille O'Neal/75 60.00 150.00
WSP Wally Szczerbiak/100 20.00 50.00

2000-01 Ultimate Collection Signatures Bronze

STATED PRINT RUN 200 SERIAL #'d SETS
AHB Anfernee Hardaway 75.00 200.00
AJB Antawn Jamison 6.00 15.00
AMB Andre Miller 6.00 15.00
CAB Courtney Alexander 6.00 15.00
DJB DerMarr Johnson 6.00 15.00
JMB Jerome Moiso 6.00 15.00
JRB Jalen Rose 6.00 15.00
KBB Kobe Bryant 2,000.00 4,000.00
KGB Kevin Garnett 200.00 500.00
LHB Larry Hughes 6.00 15.00
MFB Marcus Fizer 6.00 15.00
QRB Quentin Richardson 6.00 15.00
SAB Shareef Abdur-Rahim 6.00 15.00
SMB Shawn Marion 6.00 15.00
TMB Tracy McGrady 75.00 200.00

2000-01 Ultimate Collection Signatures Gold

STATED PRINT RUN 25 SERIAL #'d SETS
AHG Anfernee Hardaway 300.00 600.00
BRG Bill Russell 3,000.00 6,000.00
DMG Darius Miles 15.00 40.00
GPG Gary Payton 75.00 200.00
JRG Jalen Rose 15.00 40.00
KBG Kobe Bryant 15,000.00 30,000.00
KGG Kevin Garnett 1,500.00 3,000.00
KMG Kenyon Martin 30.00 80.00
LHG Larry Hughes 15.00 40.00
MJG Michael Jordan 20,000.00 40,000.00
SAG Shareef Abdur-Rahim 15.00 40.00
SFG Steve Francis 15.00 40.00
SSG Stromile Swift 15.00 40.00
TMG Tracy McGrady 150.00 400.00

2000-01 Ultimate Collection Signatures Silver

STATED PRINT RUN 75 SERIAL #'d SETS
AHSI Anfernee Hardaway 100.00 250.00
AMSI Antonio McDyess 10.00 25.00
DSSI DeShawn Stevenson 8.00 20.00
GPSI Gary Payton 20.00 50.00
JCSI Jamal Crawford 10.00 25.00
KBSI Kobe Bryant 5,000.00 10,000.00
KGSI Kevin Garnett 500.00 1,000.00
MCSI Mateen Cleaves 8.00 20.00
MMSI Mike Miller 15.00 40.00
MPSI Morris Peterson 8.00 20.00
PPSI Paul Pierce 20.00 50.00
SFSI Steve Francis 8.00 20.00
SMSI Shawn Marion 8.00 20.00
THSI Tim Hardaway 100.00 250.00

2001-02 Ultimate Collection

COMP.SET w/o SP's (60) 60.00 120.00
1-70 PRINT RUN 750 SER.#'d SETS
71-84 PRINT RUN 250 SER.#'d SETS
85-90 PRINT RUN 250 SER.#'d SETS
1 Jason Terry 2.50 6.00
2 Shareef Abdur-Rahim 2.00 5.00
3 Paul Pierce 4.00 10.00
4 Antoine Walker 2.00 5.00
5 Baron Davis 2.50 6.00
6 Jamal Mashburn 2.00 5.00
7 Ron Mercer 1.50 4.00
8 Marcus Fizer 1.50 4.00
9 Andre Miller 2.00 5.00
10 Lamond Murray 1.50 4.00
11 Dirk Nowitzki 6.00 15.00
12 Michael Finley 2.50 6.00
13 Antonio McDyess 2.00 5.00
14 Nick Van Exel 2.50 6.00
15 Jerry Stackhouse 2.50 6.00
16 Zeljko Rebraca RC 3.00 8.00
17 Antawn Jamison 2.00 5.00
18 Larry Hughes 2.00 5.00
19 Steve Francis 2.50 6.00
20 Cuttino Mobley 2.00 5.00
21 Reggie Miller 5.00 12.00
22 Jalen Rose 2.00 5.00
23 Darius Miles 1.50 4.00
24 Quentin Richardson 1.50 4.00
25 Kobe Bryant 20.00 50.00
26 Shaquille O'Neal 10.00 25.00
27 Mitch Richmond 3.00 8.00
28 Stromile Swift 1.50 4.00
29 Jason Williams 4.00 10.00
30 Alonzo Mourning 4.00 10.00
31 Eddie Jones 2.50 6.00
32 Ray Allen 4.00 10.00
33 Glenn Robinson 2.50 6.00
34 Kevin Garnett 6.00 15.00
35 Terrell Brandon 2.00 5.00
36 Wally Szczerbiak 2.00 5.00
37 Jason Kidd 4.00 10.00
38 Kenyon Martin 2.50 6.00
39 Latrell Sprewell 3.00 8.00
40 Allan Houston 2.50 6.00
41 Tracy McGrady 4.00 10.00
42 Grant Hill 4.00 10.00
43 Allen Iverson 6.00 15.00
44 Dikembe Mutombo 4.00 10.00
45 Stephon Marbury 3.00 8.00
46 Anfernee Hardaway 6.00 15.00
47 Rasheed Wallace 3.00 8.00
48 Derek Anderson 1.50 4.00
49 Chris Webber 3.00 8.00
50 Peja Stojakovic 2.00 5.00
51 Tim Duncan 6.00 15.00
52 David Robinson 5.00 12.00
53 Rashard Lewis 2.00 5.00
54 Desmond Mason 2.00 5.00
55 Vince Carter 5.00 12.00
56 Morris Peterson 1.50 4.00
57 Karl Malone 5.00 12.00
58 John Stockton 5.00 12.00
59 Richard Hamilton 3.00 8.00
60 Michael Jordan 40.00 100.00
61 Andrei Kirilenko RC 5.00 12.00
62 Gilbert Arenas RC 8.00 20.00
63 Trenton Hassell RC 2.00 5.00
64 Tony Parker RC 20.00 50.00
65 Jamaal Tinsley RC 2.50 6.00
66 Samuel Dalembert RC 3.00 8.00
67 Gerald Wallace RC 4.00 10.00
68 Brandon Armstrong RC 2.00 5.00
69 Jeryl Sasser RC 2.00 5.00
70 Joseph Forte RC 2.00 5.00
71 Pau Gasol RC 40.00 100.00
72 Brendan Haywood RC 5.00 12.00
73 Zach Randolph RC 12.00 30.00
74 Jason Collins RC 5.00 12.00
75 Michael Bradley RC 4.00 10.00
76 Kirk Haston RC 4.00 10.00
77 Steven Hunter RC 4.00 10.00
78 Troy Murphy RC 5.00 12.00
79 Richard Jefferson RC 8.00 20.00
80 Vladimir Radmanovic RC 5.00 12.00
81 Kedrick Brown RC 4.00 10.00
82 Joe Johnson RC 10.00 25.00
83 DeSagana Diop RC 4.00 10.00
84 Shane Battier RC 12.00 30.00
85 Rodney White AU RC 4.00 10.00
86 Eddie Griffin AU RC 5.00 12.00
87 Jason Richardson AU RC 10.00 25.00
88 Eddy Curry AU RC 6.00 15.00
89 Tyson Chandler AU RC 10.00 25.00
90 Kwame Brown AU RC 6.00 15.00

2001-02 Ultimate Collection Platinum

*STARS: 3X TO 8X BASE CARD HI
*ROOKIES 16/61-70: 4X TO 10X HI
*ROOKIES 71-84: 2X TO 5X HI
*ROOKIES 85-90: 2X TO 5X HI
PRINT RUN 25 SERIAL #'d SETS
60 Michael Jordan 600.00 1,000.00
71 Pau Gasol JSY 120.00 300.00

2001-02 Ultimate Collection BuyBacks

STATED ODDS 1:16
4 A.Walker 98-9SPA/18 25.00 60.00
7 A.Walker 00-1BlaDia/26 10.00 25.00
12 C.Alexandr 00-1SPGamF/30 10.00 25.00
35 J.Kidd 00-1UltColJsyBrnz/31 75.00 150.00
45 K.Bryant 00-1BlaDiaDia/40 2,500.00 5,000.00
47 K.Bryant 00-1SPA/31 2,500.00 5,000.00
52 K.Bryant 00-1SPGameFlr/24 2,500.00 5,000.00
56 K.Bryant 00-1UltColJsyBrz/27 3,000.00 6,000.00
59 K.Bryant 00-1UltVic/15 2,500.00 5,000.00
75 K.Grntt 00-1SPxWM#KG1/32 125.00 300.00
81 K.Garnett 00-1UltColJsyBz/21 125.00 300.00
84 K.Martin 00-1SPGFlrAFlr/39 40.00 100.00
86 K.Martin 00-1UppDeck/97 10.00 25.00
90 K.Martin 00-1UltColJsyBrz/19 75.00 150.00
108 L.Odom 99-0UD/37 40.00 80.00
110 L.Odom 99-0UDOvat/48 30.00 80.00
120 M.Jordan 98-9SPA#7/25 2,500.00 5,000.00
138 M.Jordan 00-1UltColJsyB/20 2,500.00 5,000.00
156 W.Sztz 00-1UltColJsySilv/22 25.00 60.00

2001-02 Ultimate Collection BuyBacks Unsigned

4 S.O'Neal 92-3UD#1B/38 40.00 100.00

2001-02 Ultimate Collection Jerseys

PRINT RUN 250 SERIAL #'d SETS
*GOLD: 1X TO 2.5X BASE HI
GOLD PRINT RUN 50 SER.#'d SETS
*SILVER: .6X TO 1.5X BASE HI
SILVER PRINT RUN 125 SER.#'d SETS
AI Allen Iverson 12.00 30.00
BR Kedrick Brown 3.00 8.00
CW Chris Webber 6.00 15.00
DM Darius Miles 3.00 8.00
EC Eddy Curry 5.00 12.00
EG Eddie Griffin 4.00 10.00
JJ Joe Johnson 8.00 20.00
JR Jason Richardson 8.00 20.00
JS John Stockton 10.00 25.00
JT Jamaal Tinsley 4.00 10.00
KB Kobe Bryant 100.00 250.00
KB2 Kobe Bryant 100.00 250.00
KE Kenyon Martin 5.00 12.00
KG Kevin Garnett 12.00 30.00
KG2 Kevin Garnett 12.00 30.00
KM Karl Malone 10.00 25.00
KW Kwame Brown 5.00 12.00
MF Michael Finley 5.00 12.00
MJ Michael Jordan 125.00 300.00
MJ2 Michael Jordan 125.00 300.00
MM Mike Miller 4.00 10.00
NO Dirk Nowitzki 12.00 30.00
PP Paul Pierce 8.00 20.00
RA Ray Allen 8.00 20.00
RJ Richard Jefferson 6.00 15.00
RW Rodney White 3.00 8.00
SF Steve Francis 5.00 12.00
TC Tyson Chandler 8.00 20.00
TM Tracy McGrady 8.00 20.00
TP Tony Parker 20.00 50.00

2001-02 Ultimate Collection Jerseys Patches

PRINT RUN 100 SERIAL #'d SETS
*SILVER: .75X TO 2X HI
SILVER PRINT RUN 25 SETS
KB2P Kobe Bryant 400.00 800.00
KG2P Kevin Garnett 20.00 50.00
MJ2P Michael Jordan 250.00 500.00
AIP Allen Iverson 40.00 100.00
BDP Baron Davis 10.00 25.00
BRP Kedrick Brown 8.00 20.00
CWP Chris Webber 20.00 50.00
DMP Darius Miles 10.00 25.00
ECP Eddy Curry 20.00 50.00
EGP Eddie Griffin 10.00 25.00
JJP Joe Johnson 10.00 25.00
JRP Jason Richardson 10.00 25.00
JSP John Stockton 25.00 60.00
JTP Jamaal Tinsley 15.00 40.00
JTP Jason Terry 15.00 40.00
KBP Kobe Bryant 100.00 250.00
KEP Kenyon Martin 15.00 40.00
KGP Kevin Garnett 25.00 60.00
KMP Karl Malone 15.00 40.00
KWP Kwame Brown 12.00 30.00
MFP Michael Finley 15.00 40.00
MJP Michael Jordan 250.00 500.00
MMP Mike Miller 12.00 30.00
NOP Dirk Nowitzki 40.00 100.00
PPP Paul Pierce 10.00 25.00
RWP Rodney White 8.00 20.00
SFP Steve Francis 15.00 40.00
TCP Tyson Chandler 10.00 25.00
TMP Tracy McGrady 25.00 60.00
TPP Tony Parker 20.00 50.00

2001-02 Ultimate Collection Signatures

STATED ODDS 1:4
DMA Darius Miles 6.00 15.00
DRA Julius Erving 50.00 120.00
ECA Eddy Curry 6.00 15.00
EGA Eddie Griffin 6.00 15.00
JJA Joe Johnson 6.00 15.00
JKA Jason Kidd 20.00 50.00
JRA Jason Richardson 10.00 25.00
KBA Kobe Bryant 200.00 500.00
KGA Kevin Garnett 50.00 120.00
KWA Kwame Brown 6.00 15.00
LBA Larry Bird 60.00 150.00
MGA Magic Johnson 60.00 150.00
MJA Michael Jordan 1,500.00 3,000.00
RWA Rodney White 6.00 15.00
TCA Tyson Chandler 6.00 15.00

2001-02 Ultimate Collection Signatures Gold

STATED PRINT RUN 2 TO 33 SER.#'d SETS
DMA Darius Miles/21 25.00 60.00
EGA Eddie Griffin/33 15.00 40.00
JJA Joe Johnson/31 20.00 50.00
JRA Jason Richardson/23 40.00 100.00
KGA Kevin Garnett/21 150.00 400.00
LBA Larry Bird/33 150.00 300.00
MGA Magic Johnson/32 75.00 150.00
MJA Michael Jordan/23 2,000.00 4,000.00

2002-03 Ultimate Collection

COMP.SET w/o SP's (67) 150.00 300.00
1-67 PRINT RUN 750 SER.#'d SETS
68-79 PRINT RUN 250 SER.#'d SETS
80-103 PRINT RUN 250 SER.#'d SETS
104-120 PRINT RUN 750 SER.#'d SETS
1 Shareef Abdur-Rahim 2.00 5.00
2 Glenn Robinson 2.00 5.00
3 Jason Terry 1.50 4.00
4 Paul Pierce 3.00 8.00
5 Antoine Walker 1.50 4.00
6 Vin Baker 1.50 4.00
7 Jalen Rose 1.50 4.00
8 Darius Miles 1.25 3.00
9 Dirk Nowitzki 5.00 12.00
10 Michael Finley 2.00 5.00
11 Steve Nash 4.00 10.00
12 Raef LaFrentz 1.25 3.00
13 Juwan Howard 1.50 4.00
14 Richard Hamilton 2.50 6.00
15 Chauncey Billups 2.00 5.00
16 Ben Wallace 2.50 6.00
17 Jason Richardson 2.00 5.00
18 Gilbert Arenas 2.00 5.00
19 Antawn Jamison 1.50 4.00
20 Steve Francis 2.00 5.00
21 Reggie Miller 4.00 10.00
22 Jamaal Tinsley 1.25 3.00
23 Jermaine O'Neal 1.50 4.00
24 Elton Brand 1.50 4.00
25 Andre Miller 1.50 4.00
26 Kobe Bryant 15.00 40.00
27 Shaquille O'Neal 8.00 20.00
28 Pau Gasol 3.00 8.00
29 Shane Battier 2.00 5.00
30 Eddie Jones 2.00 5.00
31 Brian Grant 1.25 3.00
32 Ray Allen 3.00 8.00
33 Kevin Garnett 5.00 12.00
34 Wally Szczerbiak 1.50 4.00
35 Troy Hudson 1.25 3.00
36 Jason Kidd 3.00 8.00
37 Richard Jefferson 1.50 4.00
38 Kenyon Martin 2.00 5.00
39 Baron Davis 2.00 5.00
40 Jamal Mashburn 1.50 4.00
41 David Wesley 1.25 3.00
42 P.J. Brown 1.25 3.00
43 Allan Houston 2.00 5.00
44 Latrell Sprewell 2.50 6.00
45 Kurt Thomas 1.25 3.00
46 Tracy McGrady 3.00 8.00
47 Grant Hill 3.00 8.00
48 Allen Iverson 5.00 12.00
49 Stephon Marbury 2.50 6.00
50 Shawn Marion 2.00 5.00
51 Rasheed Wallace 2.50 6.00
52 Derek Anderson 1.25 3.00
53 Bonzi Wells 1.25 3.00
54 Chris Webber 2.50 6.00
55 Mike Bibby 2.00 5.00
56 Peja Stojakovic 2.00 5.00
57 Tim Duncan 5.00 12.00
58 David Robinson 4.00 10.00
59 Tony Parker 3.00 8.00
60 Gary Payton 3.00 8.00
61 Rashard Lewis 1.50 4.00
62 Desmond Mason 1.50 4.00
63 Vince Carter 4.00 10.00
64 Morris Peterson 1.50 4.00
65 Karl Malone 4.00 10.00
66 John Stockton 4.00 10.00
67 Michael Jordan 12.00 30.00
68 Chris Wilcox AU RC 5.00 12.00
69 Drew Gooden AU RC 6.00 15.00
70 Marcus Haislip AU RC 4.00 10.00
71 Melvin Ely AU RC 4.00 10.00
72 Jared Jeffries AU RC 5.00 12.00
73 Caron Butler AU RC 6.00 15.00
74 Amare Stoudemire AU RC 15.00 40.00
75 Nene Hilario AU RC 6.00 15.00
76 DaJuan Wagner AU RC 5.00 12.00
77 Nikoloz Tskitishvili AU RC 4.00 10.00
78 Jay Williams AU RC 5.00 12.00
79 Yao Ming AU RC 500.00 1,000.00
80 Predrag Savovic RC 4.00 10.00
81 Igor Rakocevic RC 3.00 8.00
82 Sam Clancy RC 3.00 8.00
83 Ronald Murray RC 5.00 12.00
84 Tito Maddox RC 3.00 8.00
85 Carlos Boozer RC 5.00 12.00
86 Dan Gadzuric RC 4.00 10.00
87 Vincent Yarbrough RC 3.00 8.00
88 Robert Archibald RC 3.00 8.00
89 Roger Mason RC 4.00 10.00
90 Juaquin Hawkins RC 4.00 10.00
91 Chris Jefferies RC 3.00 8.00
92 John Salmons RC 5.00 12.00
93 Manu Ginobili RC 25.00 60.00
94 Tayshaun Prince RC 10.00 25.00
95 Casey Jacobsen RC 4.00 10.00
96 Qyntel Woods RC 3.00 8.00
97 Kareem Rush RC 4.00 10.00
98 Ryan Humphrey RC 4.00 10.00
99 Juan Dixon RC 5.00 12.00
100 Fred Jones RC 4.00 10.00
101 Jiri Welsch RC 3.00 8.00
102 Bostjan Nachbar RC 4.00 10.00
103 Marko Jaric 5.00 12.00
104 Gordan Giricek RC 3.00 8.00
105 Frank Williams RC 2.00 5.00
106 Pat Burke RC 2.00 5.00
107 Junior Harrington RC 2.00 5.00
108 Rasual Butler RC 2.50 6.00
109 Raul Lopez RC 3.00 8.00
110 Cezary Trybanski RC 3.00 8.00
111 Dan Dickau RC 3.00 8.00
112 Efthimios Rentzias RC 2.00 5.00
113 Mehmet Okur RC 3.00 8.00
114 Curtis Borchardt RC 2.00 5.00
115 J.R. Bremer RC 2.00 5.00
116 Lonny Baxter RC 2.00 5.00
117 Jamal Sampson RC 2.00 5.00
118 Tamar Slay RC 2.00 5.00
119 Jannero Pargo RC 2.00 5.00
120 Smush Parker RC 3.00 8.00

2002-03 Ultimate Collection Ultimate Parallel

*STARS: 3X TO 8X BASE CARD HI
*RCs 68-79: 1.5X TO 4X HI
*RCs 80-103: 1.5X TO 4X HI
*RCs 104-120: 2X TO 5X HI
68-79 FEATURE PATCH AND AUTO
PRINT RUN 25 SER.#'d SETS
68 Chris Wilcox JSY AU 30.00 80.00
74 Amare Stoudemire JSY AU 300.00 600.00
75 Nene Hilario JSY AU 40.00 100.00
79 Yao Ming JSY AU 400.00 800.00

2002-03 Ultimate Collection Buybacks

17 K.Bryant 01-2SPAuth/38 150.00 400.00
18 K.Bryant 01-2SPx/32 150.00 400.00
21 K.Bryant 01-2UDFlightTm/24 150.00 400.00
27 K.Garnett 95-6SPAuth/23 50.00 120.00
32 K.Garnett 01-2SPAuth/23 50.00 120.00
34 K.Garnett 01-2SPx/46 50.00 120.00
35 Garnt 00-1SPGFAF#KG2/18 50.00 120.00
36 Garnett 01-2UDFlightTm/18 50.00 120.00
42 MJ 00-1UDMJMater#MJ1/24 2,500.00 5,000.00
47 J.Kidd 01-2 UDLegLFloor/22 25.00 60.00
54 K.Martin 00-1UD/97 15.00 40.00
70 T.Parker 01-2UD#185/155 20.00 50.00
72 P.Pierce 01-2UDGJPatch/20 75.00 150.00
78 P.Stojakovic 01-2SPAuth/23 20.00 50.00
79 P.Stojakovic 01-2SPx/17 20.00 50.00
80 P.Stojak 01-2UDInspir/26 20.00 50.00
84 A.Walk 00-1UDHardGF/54 20.00 50.00
87 A.Walk 01-2UDOvSSWU/26 20.00 50.00
94 J.Kidd 94-5SP/33 25.00 60.00

2002-03 Ultimate Collection Jerseys

STATED PRINT RUN 250 SER.#'d SETS
AI Allen Iverson 10.00 25.00
AM Andre Miller 3.00 8.00
AW Antoine Walker 3.00 8.00
BD Baron Davis 4.00 10.00
CB Caron Butler 4.00 10.00
CW Chris Webber 5.00 12.00
DG Drew Gooden 4.00 10.00
DM Darius Miles 2.50 6.00
DN Dirk Nowitzki 10.00 25.00
DW DaJuan Wagner 3.00 8.00
JK Jason Kidd 6.00 15.00
JR Jason Richardson 4.00 10.00
JW Jay Williams 3.00 8.00
KB Kobe Bryant 75.00 200.00
KG Kevin Garnett 10.00 25.00
KR Kareem Rush 3.00 8.00
MB Mike Bibby 4.00 10.00
MJ Michael Jordan 40.00 100.00
NH Nene Hilario 4.00 10.00
PG Pau Gasol 6.00 15.00
PP Paul Pierce 6.00 15.00
PS Peja Stojakovic 3.00 8.00
RJ Richard Jefferson 3.00 8.00
RL Rashard Lewis 3.00 8.00
SB Shane Battier 4.00 10.00
SF Steve Francis 4.00 10.00
SM Stephon Marbury 5.00 12.00
TM Tracy McGrady 6.00 15.00
WI Chris Wilcox 3.00 8.00
YM Yao Ming 20.00 50.00

2002-03 Ultimate Collection Jerseys Gold

STATED PRINT RUN 50 SER.#'d SETS
AI Allen Iverson 40.00 100.00
BD Baron Davis 8.00 20.00
CW Chris Webber 30.00 80.00
DN Dirk Nowitzki 20.00 50.00
DW DaJuan Wagner 6.00 15.00
JK Jason Kidd 12.00 30.00
JR Jason Richardson 8.00 20.00
JW Jay Williams 6.00 15.00
KB Kobe Bryant 75.00 200.00
KG Kevin Garnett 20.00 50.00
MJ Michael Jordan 75.00 200.00
PP Paul Pierce 12.00 30.00
SF Steve Francis 8.00 20.00
TM Tracy McGrady 12.00 30.00
YM Yao Ming 60.00 150.00

2002-03 Ultimate Collection Jerseys Silver

STATED PRINT RUN 125 SER.#'d SETS
AM Andre Miller 4.00 10.00
AW Antoine Walker 4.00 10.00
CB Caron Butler 5.00 12.00
DG Drew Gooden 5.00 12.00
DM Darius Miles 3.00 8.00
KR Kareem Rush 4.00 10.00
MB Mike Bibby 5.00 12.00
NH Nene Hilario 5.00 12.00
PG Pau Gasol 8.00 20.00
PS Peja Stojakovic 4.00 10.00
RJ Richard Jefferson 4.00 10.00
RL Rashard Lewis 4.00 10.00
SB Shane Battier 5.00 12.00
SM Stephon Marbury 6.00 15.00
WI Chris Wilcox 4.00 10.00

2002-03 Ultimate Collection Jerseys Dual

STATED PRINT RUN 125 SER.#'d SETS
*SILVER: .75X TO 2X BASE HI
SILVER PRINT RUN 25 SER.#'d SETS
AISF A.Iverson/S.Francis 12.50 30.00
AMEB A.Miller/E.Brand 10.00 25.00
CWMB C.Webber/M.Bibby 10.00 25.00
DNSN D.Nowitzki/S.Nash 10.00 25.00
JKBD J.Kidd/B.Davis 10.00 25.00
KBJW K.Bryant/J.Williams 40.00 100.00
MJKB M.Jordan/K.Bryant 200.00 500.00
PPAW P.Pierce/A.Walker 10.00 25.00
SBPG S.Battier/P.Gasol 10.00 25.00
SMSM S.Marbury/S.Marion 10.00 25.00
TMKG T.McGrady/K.Garnett 12.50 30.00
YMJW Y.Ming/J.Williams 20.00 50.00

2002-03 Ultimate Collection Jerseys Patches

STATED PRINT RUN 50 SER.#'d SETS
ASP Amare Stoudemire 60.00 120.00
AWP Antoine Walker 10.00 25.00
BZP Carlos Boozer 12.00 30.00
CAP Casey Jacobsen 10.00 25.00
CBP Caron Butler 12.00 30.00
CJP Chris Jefferies 8.00 20.00
CWP Chris Wilcox 10.00 25.00
DGP Drew Gooden 12.00 30.00
FJP Fred Jones 10.00 25.00
GAP Dan Gadzuric 10.00 25.00
JJP Jared Jeffries 10.00 25.00
JRP Jason Richardson 12.00 30.00
JSP John Salmons 12.00 30.00
JWP Jay Williams 10.00 25.00
KBP Kobe Bryant 100.00 250.00
KMP Karl Malone 25.00 60.00
KRP Kareem Rush 10.00 25.00
MEP Melvin Ely 10.00 25.00
MHP Marcus Haislip 8.00 20.00
NHP Nene Hilario 12.00 30.00
NTP Nikoloz Tskitishvili 8.00 20.00
PPP Paul Pierce 20.00 50.00
QWP Qyntel Woods 8.00 20.00
RHP Ryan Humphrey 10.00 25.00
RLP Rashard Lewis 12.00 30.00
RMP Roger Mason 10.00 25.00
SHP Shareef Abdur-Rahim 12.00 30.00
TPP Tayshaun Prince 12.00 30.00
VYP Vincent Yarbrough 8.00 20.00
YMP Yao Ming 60.00 120.00

2002-03 Ultimate Collection Jerseys Patches Dual

STATED PRINT RUN 25 SER.#'d SETS
BDJMP B.Davis/J.Mashburn 25.00 60.00
CWMBP C.Webber/M.Bibby 50.00 120.00
DMDWP D.Miles/D.Wagner 25.00 60.00
DNSNP D.Nowitzki/S.Nash 60.00 150.00
KBAIP K.Bryant/A.Iverson 150.00 400.00
KBJWP K.Bryant/J.Williams 125.00 300.00
MJKBP M.Jordan/K.Bryant 500.00 1,000.00
PGDGP P.Gasol/D.Gooden 25.00 60.00
SFJDP S.Francis/J.Dixon 25.00 60.00
SMSMP S.Marbury/S.Marion 40.00 100.00
TMJKP T.McGrady/J.Kidd 60.00 150.00
YMJWP Y.Ming/J.Williams 150.00 300.00

2002-03 Ultimate Collection Signatures

ASS Amare Stoudemire 15.00 40.00
BRS Bill Russell 1,000.00 2,000.00
CBS Caron Butler 12.00 30.00
DRS Julius Erving 75.00 200.00
DWS DaJuan Wagner 6.00 15.00
JKS Jason Kidd 40.00 100.00
JWS Jay Williams 15.00 40.00
KAS Kareem Abdul-Jabbar 125.00 300.00
KBS Kobe Bryant 1,500.00 3,000.00
KGS Kevin Garnett 150.00 400.00
KRS Kareem Rush 6.00 15.00
LBS Larry Bird 125.00 300.00
MJS Michael Jordan 2,000.00 4,000.00
NTS Nikoloz Tskitishvili 6.00 15.00
YMS Yao Ming 300.00 600.00

2002-03 Ultimate Collection Signatures Gold

ASS Amare Stoudemire/32 75.00 200.00
JWS Jay Williams/22 30.00 80.00
KAS Kareem Abdul-Jabbar/33 150.00 400.00
KGS Kevin Garnett/21 300.00 600.00
KRS Kareem Rush/21 20.00 50.00
LBS Larry Bird/33 150.00 400.00
MJS Michael Jordan/23 4,000.00 8,000.00
NTS Nikoloz Tskitishvili/22 20.00 50.00

2003-04 Ultimate Collection

1-116 PRINT RUN 750 SER.#'d SETS
165-190 PRINT RUN 500 SER.#'d SETS
1 Dominique Wilkins 2.50 6.00
2 Jason Terry 1.50 4.00
3 Dion Glover 1.25 3.00
4 Stephen Jackson 1.50 4.00
5 Bill Russell 3.00 8.00
6 Paul Pierce 3.00 8.00
7 Larry Bird 5.00 12.00
8 Ricky Davis 1.50 4.00
9 Antonio Davis 1.50 4.00
10 Michael Jordan 75.00 200.00
11 Scottie Pippen 5.00 12.00
12 Tyson Chandler 1.50 4.00
13 Jeff McInnis 1.25 3.00
14 Dajuan Wagner 1.25 3.00
15 Carlos Boozer 1.50 4.00
16 Zydrunas Ilgauskas 1.50 4.00
17 Dirk Nowitzki 5.00 12.00
18 Steve Nash 4.00 10.00
19 Antoine Walker 2.00 5.00
20 Michael Finley 2.00 5.00
21 Andre Miller 1.50 4.00
22 Nene 1.50 4.00
23 Nikoloz Tskitishvili 1.25 3.00
24 Marcus Camby 1.50 4.00
25 Richard Hamilton 2.50 6.00
26 Ben Wallace 2.50 6.00
27 Chauncey Billups 2.50 6.00
28 Rasheed Wallace 2.50 6.00
29 Jason Richardson 2.00 5.00
30 Nick Van Exel 2.00 5.00
31 Speedy Claxton 1.25 3.00
32 Mike Dunleavy 1.50 4.00
33 Yao Ming 5.00 12.00
34 Steve Francis 2.00 5.00
35 Cuttino Mobley 1.25 3.00
36 Jim Jackson 1.25 3.00
37 Reggie Miller 4.00 10.00
38 Jermaine O'Neal 2.00 5.00
39 Ron Artest 2.00 5.00
40 Al Harrington 1.50 4.00
41 Elton Brand 1.50 4.00
42 Corey Maggette 1.50 4.00
43 Quentin Richardson 1.25 3.00

44 Chris Wilcox 1.25 3.00
45 Kobe Bryant 15.00 40.00
46 Shaquille O'Neal 8.00 20.00
47 Gary Payton 3.00 8.00
48 Karl Malone 4.00 10.00
49 Pau Gasol 3.00 8.00
50 Bonzi Wells 1.25 3.00
51 Mike Miller 1.50 4.00
52 Jason Williams 3.00 8.00
53 Caron Butler 1.50 4.00
54 Lamar Odom 1.50 4.00
55 Eddie Jones 2.00 5.00
56 Brian Grant 1.25 3.00
57 Desmond Mason 1.50 4.00
58 Oscar Robertson 2.00 5.00
59 Michael Redd 2.00 5.00
60 Toni Kukoc 2.00 5.00
61 Latrell Sprewell 2.50 6.00
62 Kevin Garnett 5.00 12.00
63 Wally Szczerbiak 1.50 4.00
64 Sam Cassell 1.50 4.00
65 Kenyon Martin 2.00 5.00
66 Jason Kidd 3.00 8.00
67 Richard Jefferson 1.50 4.00
68 Alonzo Mourning 2.50 6.00
69 Jamal Mashburn 1.50 4.00
70 David Wesley 1.25 3.00
71 Baron Davis 2.00 5.00
72 Jamaal Magloire 1.25 3.00
73 Allan Houston 2.00 5.00
74 Patrick Ewing 2.50 6.00
75 Stephon Marbury 2.50 6.00
76 Dikembe Mutombo 2.50 6.00
77 Tracy McGrady 3.00 8.00
78 Drew Gooden 1.50 4.00
79 Juwan Howard 1.50 4.00
80 DeShawn Stevenson 1.25 3.00
81 Julius Erving 3.00 8.00
82 Allen Iverson 5.00 12.00
83 Glenn Robinson 1.50 4.00
84 Eric Snow 1.25 3.00
85 Amare Stoudemire 2.50 6.00
86 Shawn Marion 2.00 5.00
87 Antonio McDyess 1.50 4.00
88 Joe Johnson 1.50 4.00
89 Shareef Abdur-Rahim 2.00 5.00
90 Derek Anderson 1.50 4.00
91 Damon Stoudamire 1.50 4.00
92 Zach Randolph 2.00 5.00
93 Mike Bibby 2.00 5.00
94 Chris Webber 2.50 6.00
95 Peja Stojakovic 1.50 4.00
96 Bobby Jackson 1.50 4.00
97 Manu Ginobili 4.00 10.00
98 Tim Duncan 5.00 12.00
99 Tony Parker 3.00 8.00
100 Radoslav Nesterovic 1.25 3.00
101 Rashard Lewis 1.50 4.00
102 Ray Allen 3.00 8.00
103 Vladimir Radmanovic 1.25 3.00
104 Brent Barry 1.25 3.00
105 Vince Carter 4.00 10.00
106 Morris Peterson 1.25 3.00
107 Jalen Rose 1.50 4.00
108 Donyell Marshall 1.25 3.00
109 John Stockton 4.00 10.00
110 Andrei Kirilenko 2.50 6.00
111 Matt Harpring 1.50 4.00
112 Carlos Arroyo 1.50 4.00
113 Gilbert Arenas 2.00 5.00
114 Jerry Stackhouse 2.50 6.00
115 Kwame Brown 1.25 3.00
116 Larry Hughes 1.50 4.00
117 T.J. Ford RC 3.00 8.00
118 Kirk Hinrich RC 4.00 10.00
119 Nick Collison RC 3.00 8.00
120 James Jones RC 2.50 6.00
121 Travis Hansen RC 2.50 6.00
122 Alex Garcia RC 2.50 6.00
123 Theron Smith RC 2.50 6.00
124 Francisco Elson RC 2.50 6.00
125 Jon Stefansson RC 2.50 6.00
126 Ronald Dupree RC 2.50 6.00
127 L.James AU RC 30,000.00 60,000.00
128 Darko Milicic AU RC 5.00 12.00
129 Carmelo Anthony AU RC 60.00 150.00
130 Chris Bosh AU RC 30.00 80.00
131 Dwyane Wade AU RC 150.00 400.00
132 Chris Kaman AU RC 6.00 15.00
133 Jarvis Hayes AU RC 4.00 10.00
134 Mickael Pietrus AU RC 5.00 12.00
135 Dahntay Jones AU RC 5.00 12.00
136 Marcus Banks AU RC 4.00 10.00
137 Luke Ridnour AU RC 6.00 15.00
138 Reece Gaines AU RC 4.00 10.00
139 Troy Bell AU RC 4.00 10.00
140 Mike Sweetney AU RC 4.00 10.00
141 David West AU RC 8.00 20.00
142 Aleksandar Pavlovic AU RC 5.00 12.00
143 Steve Blake AU RC 5.00 12.00
144 Boris Diaw AU RC 6.00 15.00
145 Zoran Planinic AU RC 4.00 10.00
146 Travis Outlaw AU RC 5.00 12.00
147 Brian Cook AU RC 4.00 10.00
148 Jerome Beasley AU RC 4.00 10.00
149 Ndudi Ebi AU RC 4.00 10.00
150 Kendrick Perkins AU RC 5.00 12.00
151 Leandro Barbosa AU RC 6.00 15.00
152 Josh Howard AU RC 6.00 15.00
153 Maciej Lampe AU RC 4.00 10.00
154 Jason Kapono AU RC 4.00 10.00
155 Luke Walton AU RC 5.00 12.00
156 Kyle Korver AU RC 8.00 20.00
157 Zarko Cabarkapa AU RC 4.00 10.00
158 Zaur Pachulia AU RC 6.00 15.00
159 Maurice Williams AU RC 6.00 15.00
160 Brandon Hunter AU RC 4.00 10.00
161 Keith Bogans AU RC 4.00 10.00
162 Marquis Daniels AU RC 5.00 12.00
163 Willie Green AU RC 6.00 15.00
164 Udonis Haslem AU RC 8.00 20.00
165 Larry Bird US 6.00 15.00
166 Bill Russell US 4.00 10.00
167 Michael Jordan US 12.00 30.00
168 Steve Nash US 5.00 12.00
169 Michael Finley US 2.50 6.00
170 Ben Wallace US 3.00 8.00
171 Jason Richardson US 2.50 6.00
172 Yao Ming US 6.00 15.00
173 Reggie Miller US 5.00 12.00
174 Kobe Bryant US 20.00 50.00
175 Shaquille O'Neal US 10.00 25.00
176 Gary Payton US 4.00 10.00
177 Magic Johnson US 6.00 15.00
178 Pau Gasol US 3.00 8.00
179 Lamar Odom US 2.00 5.00
180 Oscar Robertson US 2.50 6.00
181 Kenyon Martin US 2.50 6.00
182 Baron Davis US 2.50 6.00
183 Julius Erving US 4.00 10.00
184 Amare Stoudemire US 3.00 8.00
185 Mike Bibby US 2.50 6.00
186 Tony Parker US 4.00 10.00
187 Rashard Lewis US 2.00 5.00
188 Vince Carter US 5.00 12.00
189 Andrei Kirilenko US 2.00 5.00
190 Gilbert Arenas US 2.50 6.00

2003-04 Ultimate Collection Limited

*SINGLES 1-116: 2X TO 5X BASE HI
*RCs 117-126: .75X TO 2X BASE HI
*AUTO RCs: 2X TO 5X BASE HI
*US 165-190: 1.5X TO 4X BASE HI
PRINT RUN 25 SER.#'d SETS
127-158 HAVE BOTH JERSEY AND AUTO
11 Scottie Pippen 25.00 60.00
127 LeBron James JSY AU 150,000.00 300,000.00
129 Carmelo Anthony JSY AU 600.00 1,200.00

2003-04 Ultimate Collection BuyBacks

5 S.Battier02-3UDSwtSht/33 12.50 30.00
6 M.Bibby02-3SPGameUse/19 20.00 50.00
9 M.Bibby02-3MVPMatShirt/17 20.00 50.00
10 M.Bibby02-3UDSwtSht/35 20.00 50.00
12 C.Billups02-3UDSwtSht/27 12.50 30.00
21 Kobe02-3UDSwtShtGlass/15 125.00 300.00
23 Ewing01-2UD15000Jsy/18 150.00 300.00
25 Garnett02-3SPxWinMat/33 50.00 120.00
29 Garnett02-3UDSwtSht/22 50.00 120.00
30 Garnett02-3UDSwtShtJsy/21 50.00 120.00
33 Hamilton02-3SPxWinMat/32 15.00 40.00
34 Hamilton02-3UDSeaPrmJsy/19 20.00 50.00
35 Hamilton02-3UDSwtSht/39 15.00 40.00
36 Hamilton02-3UDSwtShtJsy/18 20.00 50.00
37 Jamison02-3UDAll-AccJsy/18 20.00 50.00
38 Jamison02-3UDSwtSht/28 12.50 30.00
39 Jamison02-3UDSwtShtJsy/16 15.00 40.00
40 Jefferson02-3SPxWinMat/17 15.00 40.00
41 Jefferson02-3UDSwtSht/31 12.50 30.00
43 Jordan03-4UDSEDieCut/24 2,500.00 5,000.00
44 Jordan03-4UDHardcourt/21 2,500.00 5,000.00
45 Kidd02-3SPGU#60 SP/16 30.00 80.00
46 KiddSPxWinMat/16 30.00 80.00
48 Kidd02-3UDSwtSht/40 20.00 50.00
49 Kidd02-3UDSwtShtGlass/15 30.00 80.00
50 Maggette02-3UDAll-AccJsy/16 12.50 30.00
51 Marion02-3SPx/31 20.00 50.00
52 Marion02-3SPxWinMat/21 20.00 50.00
55 Marion02-3UDSweetShot/36 15.00 40.00
56 Marion02-3UDSwtShtSwSw/20 20.00 50.00
57 McDyess02-3SPxWinMat/19 20.00 50.00
58 McDyess02-3MVPMatWarm/15 20.00 50.00
62 McGrady02-3UDGenRTJsy/19 60.00 150.00
63 McGrady02-3SwtSht/26 50.00 120.00
64 McGrady02-3SwtShtSwSw/20 60.00 150.00
65 Miles02-3SPGU/21 15.00 40.00
66 Miles02-3UDAirAppJsy/17 15.00 40.00
67 Miles02-3UDSwtSht/34 12.50 30.00
68 Miles02-3UDSwtShtSwSw/19 15.00 40.00
70 A.Miller02-3SPGU/19 12.50 30.00
71 A.Miller02-3UDSwtSht/38 12.50 30.00
72 A.Miller02-3UDSwtShtSSw/20 12.50 30.00
75 Mobley02-3UDSwtSht/30 12.50 30.00
77 Odom02-3MVPMatComb/17 15.00 40.00
78 Odom02-3UDAirAppJsy/19 15.00 40.00
79 Odom02-3UDSwtShot/20 15.00 40.00
80 Odom02-3UDSwtShtSSw/32 12.50 30.00
81 Parker02-3SPGU/18 40.00 100.00
82 Parker02-3UDAll-SAShort/19 40.00 100.00
84 Parker02-3UDSwtSht/22 40.00 100.00
85 Payton02-3SPGUA-Sapp/19 50.00 120.00
86 Pierce02-3SPxWinMat/27 40.00 80.00
90 Pierce02-3UDSwtSht/37 20.00 50.00
91 Pierce02-3UDSwtShtGlass/16 40.00 80.00
92 Robinson02-3SPxWinMat/16 100.00 200.00
93 Robinson02-3UDSwtSht/24 75.00 150.00
94 Rose02-3UDSwtSht/20 20.00 50.00
95 Stack02-3UDAll-AuthJsy/16 20.00 50.00
96 Stack02-3UDGmJsy2/14 20.00 50.00
97 Stack02-3UDSwtSht/37 15.00 40.00
100 Stockton02-3UDSwtSht/32 125.00 250.00
102 Peja02-3UDAll-StAuth/16 40.00 100.00
103 Peja02-3UDInspirations/26 20.00 50.00
104 Peja02-3UDSwtSht/37 20.00 50.00

2003-04 Ultimate Collection Jerseys

PRINT RUN 200 SER.#'d SETS
*DUAL: .6X TO 1.5X BASE JSY HI
DUAL PRINT RUN 100 SER.#'d SETS
*TRIPLE: 1.25X TO 3X BASE HI
TRIPLE PRINT RUN 25 SER.#'d SETS
AI Allen Iverson 10.00 25.00
AS Amare Stoudemire 5.00 12.00
AW Antoine Walker 4.00 10.00
BR Bill Russell 20.00 50.00
BW Ben Wallace 5.00 12.00
CA Carmelo Anthony 20.00 50.00
CB Caron Butler 3.00 8.00
CH Chris Bosh 12.00 30.00
CW Chris Webber 6.00 15.00
DM Darko Milicic 3.00 8.00
DN Dirk Nowitzki 10.00 25.00
DR David Robinson 8.00 20.00
DW Dajuan Wagner 2.50 6.00
DY Dwyane Wade 30.00 80.00
EB Elton Brand 3.00 8.00
EG Manu Ginobili 8.00 20.00
GP Gary Payton 6.00 15.00
JE Julius Erving 8.00 20.00
JK Jason Kidd 6.00 15.00
JO Jermaine O'Neal 4.00 10.00
JR Jason Richardson 4.00 10.00
JS John Stockton 8.00 20.00
KB Kobe Bryant 25.00 60.00
KG Kevin Garnett 10.00 25.00
KM Karl Malone 8.00 20.00
LB Larry Bird 10.00 25.00
LJ LeBron James 1,000.00 2,000.00
MA Magic Johnson 10.00 25.00
MJ Michael Jordan 60.00 150.00
OR Oscar Robertson 20.00 50.00
PE Patrick Ewing 8.00 20.00
PP Paul Pierce 6.00 15.00
RA Ray Allen 6.00 15.00
RJ Richard Jefferson 3.00 8.00
SF Steve Francis 4.00 10.00
SH Shawn Marion 4.00 10.00
SM Stephon Marbury 5.00 12.00
SN Steve Nash 8.00 20.00
SO Shaquille O'Neal 15.00 40.00
TD Tim Duncan 10.00 25.00
TM Tracy McGrady 6.00 15.00
YM Yao Ming 10.00 25.00

2003-04 Ultimate Collection Patches

AH Allan Houston 8.00 20.00
AI Allen Iverson 20.00 50.00
AJ Antawn Jamison 8.00 20.00
AK Andrei Kirilenko 6.00 15.00
AL Alonzo Mourning 15.00 40.00
AM Andre Miller 6.00 15.00
AP Aleksandar Pavlovic 6.00 15.00
AS Amare Stoudemire 5.00 12.00
BD Baron Davis 8.00 20.00
BG Keith Bogans 5.00 12.00
BO Boris Diaw 8.00 20.00
CA Carmelo Anthony 40.00 80.00
CH Chris Bosh 25.00 60.00
CK Chris Kaman 8.00 20.00
CM Corey Maggette 6.00 15.00
CW Chris Webber 10.00 25.00
DA Darius Miles 5.00 12.00
DE Desmond Mason 6.00 15.00
DJ Dahntay Jones 6.00 15.00
DM Darko Milicic 6.00 15.00
DN Dirk Nowitzki 20.00 50.00
DR David Robinson 25.00 60.00
DW David West 10.00 25.00
DY Dwyane Wade 50.00 120.00
EB Elton Brand 6.00 15.00
GA Gilbert Arenas 8.00 20.00
GH Grant Hill 15.00 40.00
GP Gary Payton 12.00 30.00
JA Jalen Rose 6.00 15.00
JD Josh Howard 8.00 20.00
JE Jerry Stackhouse 10.00 25.00
JH Jarvis Hayes 5.00 12.00
JK Jason Kidd 12.00 30.00
JM Jamal Mashburn 6.00 15.00
JO Jermaine O'Neal 8.00 20.00
JR Jason Richardson 8.00 20.00
JS John Stockton 15.00 40.00
JT Jason Terry 6.00 15.00
KE Kenyon Martin 8.00 20.00
KG Kevin Garnett 20.00 50.00
KM Karl Malone 12.00 30.00
LJ LeBron James 2,000.00 4,000.00
LO Lamar Odom 6.00 15.00
LR Luke Ridnour 8.00 20.00
LS Latrell Sprewell 8.00 20.00
MB Mike Bibby 8.00 20.00
MF Michael Finley 8.00 20.00
MO Morris Peterson 5.00 12.00
MP Mickael Pietrus 6.00 15.00
MR Marcus Banks 5.00 12.00
MS Mike Sweetney 5.00 12.00
PG Pau Gasol 12.00 30.00
PP Paul Pierce 12.00 30.00
PS Peja Stojakovic 6.00 15.00
QR Quentin Richardson 5.00 12.00
RA Ray Allen 15.00 40.00
RG Reece Gaines 5.00 12.00
RJ Richard Jefferson 6.00 15.00
RM Reggie Miller 30.00 80.00
SA Shareef Abdur-Rahim 8.00 20.00
SB Steve Blake 6.00 15.00
SF Steve Francis 8.00 20.00
SH Shawn Marion 8.00 20.00
SM Stephon Marbury 10.00 25.00
SN Steve Nash 15.00 40.00
SO Shaquille O'Neal 30.00 80.00
SP Scottie Pippen 40.00 100.00
TB Troy Bell 5.00 12.00
TD Tim Duncan 20.00 50.00
TM Tracy McGrady 25.00 60.00
TP Tony Parker 12.00 30.00
YM Yao Ming 25.00 60.00

2003-04 Ultimate Collection Patches Dual

*DUAL: .6X TO 1.5X BASE PATCH HI
PRINT RUN 50 SER.#'d SETS
AW Antoine Walker 12.00 30.00
JS John Stockton 40.00 100.00
KB Kobe Bryant 150.00 300.00
MJ Michael Jordan 400.00 800.00
PE Patrick Ewing 75.00 200.00

2003-04 Ultimate Collection Patches Triple

TRIPLE PRINT RUN 15 SER.#'d SETS
AI3 Allen Iverson 125.00 250.00
CA3 Carmelo Anthony 150.00 300.00
DM3 Darko Milicic 25.00 60.00
DU3 Dajuan Wagner 20.00 50.00
DY3 Dwyane Wade 200.00 400.00
KB3 Kobe Bryant 250.00 500.00
LB3 Larry Bird 80.00 200.00
LJ3 LeBron James 3,000.00 6,000.00
MA3 Magic Johnson 200.00 400.00
MJ3 Michael Jordan 1,000.00 2,000.00
TD3 Tim Duncan 80.00 200.00

2003-04 Ultimate Collection Signatures

AUTOGRAPH ODDS 1:4
AS Amare Stoudemire 6.00 15.00
CA Carmelo Anthony 25.00 60.00
DM Darko Milicic 5.00 12.00
DY Dwyane Wade 200.00 500.00
GP Gary Payton 25.00 60.00
JE Julius Erving 75.00 200.00
JH Jarvis Hayes 4.00 10.00
JK Jason Kidd 15.00 40.00
JS John Stockton 60.00 150.00
KB Kobe Bryant 1,500.00 3,000.00
KG Kevin Garnett SP 150.00 400.00
LB Larry Bird SP 150.00 400.00
LJ LeBron James 10,000.00 15,000.00
MA Magic Johnson SP 150.00 400.00
MJ Michael Jordan 2,500.00 5,000.00
MS Mike Sweetney 4.00 10.00
PE Patrick Ewing 150.00 400.00
RM Reggie Miller 125.00 300.00
RO Dennis Rodman 75.00 200.00
TM Tracy McGrady 75.00 200.00
YM Yao Ming 125.00 300.00

2003-04 Ultimate Collection Signatures Gold

PRINT RUNS LISTED BELOW
AS Amare Stoudemire/32 30.00 80.00
CA Carmelo Anthony/15 150.00 400.00
DM Darko Milicic/31 15.00 40.00
GP Gary Payton/20 60.00 150.00
JH Jarvis Hayes/24 15.00 40.00
KG Kevin Garnett/21 400.00 800.00
LB Larry Bird/33 400.00 800.00
LJ LeBron James/23 20,000.00 40,000.00
MA Magic Johnson/32 400.00 800.00
MJ Michael Jordan/23 5,000.00 10,000.00
MS Mike Sweetney/50 15.00 40.00
PE Patrick Ewing/33 300.00 600.00
RM Reggie Miller/31 200.00 500.00
RO Dennis Rodman/91 150.00 400.00

2004-05 Ultimate Collection

1-116 PRINT RUN 750 SER.#'d SETS
127-168 PRINT RUN 250 SER.#'d SETS
1 Tyronn Lue 1.00 2.50
2 Tony Delk 1.00 2.50
3 Al Harrington 1.25 3.00
4 Paul Pierce 2.50 6.00
5 Antoine Walker 1.50 4.00
6 Bill Russell 2.50 6.00
7 Larry Bird 6.00 15.00
8 Gerald Wallace 1.25 3.00
9 Jason Kapono 1.00 2.50
10 Primoz Brezec 1.00 2.50
11 Kirk Hinrich 1.50 4.00
12 Eddy Curry 1.00 2.50
13 Tyson Chandler 1.25 3.00
14 Michael Jordan 60.00 150.00
15 LeBron James 40.00 100.00
16 Drew Gooden 1.00 2.50
17 Jeff McInnis 1.00 2.50
18 Zydrunas Ilgauskas 1.25 3.00
19 Dirk Nowitzki 4.00 10.00
20 Michael Finley 1.50 4.00
21 Josh Howard 1.25 3.00
22 Marquis Daniels 1.00 2.50
23 Carmelo Anthony 3.00 8.00
24 Kenyon Martin 1.50 4.00
25 Andre Miller 1.25 3.00
26 Nene 1.25 3.00
27 Ben Wallace 2.00 5.00
28 Richard Hamilton 2.00 5.00
29 Isiah Thomas 2.50 6.00
30 Chauncey Billups 2.00 5.00
31 Jason Richardson 1.50 4.00
32 Baron Davis 1.50 4.00
33 Derek Fisher 1.25 3.00
34 Tracy McGrady 2.50 6.00
35 Yao Ming 4.00 10.00
36 Hakeem Olajuwon 3.00 8.00
37 Jermaine O'Neal 1.50 4.00
38 Reggie Miller 3.00 8.00
39 Ron Artest 1.50 4.00
40 Stephen Jackson 1.25 3.00
41 Elton Brand 1.25 3.00
42 Chris Kaman 1.25 3.00
43 Corey Maggette 1.25 3.00
44 Bobby Simmons 1.00 2.50
45 Kobe Bryant 40.00 100.00
46 Magic Johnson 6.00 15.00
47 Wilt Chamberlain 3.00 8.00
48 Lamar Odom 1.50 4.00
49 Pau Gasol 2.50 6.00
50 Bonzi Wells 1.00 2.50
51 Jason Williams 1.25 3.00
52 Mike Miller 1.25 3.00
53 Shaquille O'Neal 6.00 15.00
54 Dwyane Wade 6.00 15.00
55 Eddie Jones 1.50 4.00
56 Udonis Haslem 1.00 2.50
57 Oscar Robertson 1.25 3.00
58 Michael Redd 1.25 3.00
59 Desmond Mason 1.00 2.50
60 T.J. Ford 1.00 2.50
61 Kevin Garnett 4.00 10.00
62 Latrell Sprewell 2.00 5.00
63 Sam Cassell 1.25 3.00
64 Michael Olowokandi 1.00 2.50
65 Jason Kidd 2.50 6.00
66 Richard Jefferson 1.25 3.00
67 Vince Carter 3.00 8.00
68 Ron Mercer 1.00 2.50
69 Dan Dickau 1.00 2.50
70 Jamaal Magloire 1.00 2.50
71 P.J. Brown 1.00 2.50
72 Lee Nailon 1.00 2.50
73 Stephon Marbury 2.00 5.00
74 Allan Houston 1.50 4.00
75 Jamal Crawford 1.50 4.00
76 Bernard King 2.00 5.00
77 Steve Francis 1.50 4.00
78 Doug Christie 1.25 3.00
79 Grant Hill 2.00 5.00
80 Hedo Turkoglu 1.25 3.00
81 Allen Iverson 4.00 10.00
82 Julius Erving 4.00 10.00
83 Chris Webber 2.00 5.00
84 Kyle Korver 1.25 3.00
85 Amare Stoudemire 1.50 4.00
86 Steve Nash 2.00 5.00
87 Shawn Marion 1.50 4.00
88 Quentin Richardson 1.00 2.50
89 Shareef Abdur-Rahim 1.50 4.00
90 Darius Miles 1.00 2.50
91 Zach Randolph 1.50 4.00
92 Damon Stoudamire 1.50 4.00
93 Peja Stojakovic 1.25 3.00
94 Mike Bibby 1.50 4.00
95 Cuttino Mobley 1.25 3.00
96 Brad Miller 1.25 3.00
97 Tim Duncan 4.00 10.00
98 Manu Ginobili 3.00 8.00
99 Tony Parker 2.50 6.00
100 David Robinson 3.00 8.00
101 Ray Allen 2.50 6.00
102 Rashard Lewis 1.25 3.00
103 Ronald Murray 1.00 2.50
104 Luke Ridnour 1.25 3.00
105 Rafer Alston 1.00 2.50
106 Jalen Rose 1.25 3.00
107 Chris Bosh 2.50 6.00
108 Morris Peterson 1.00 2.50
109 Andrei Kirilenko 1.25 3.00
110 Carlos Boozer 1.25 3.00
111 John Stockton 3.00 8.00
112 Matt Harpring 1.00 2.50
113 Gilbert Arenas 1.50 4.00
114 Antawn Jamison 1.25 3.00
115 Jarvis Hayes 1.00 2.50
116 Larry Hughes 1.25 3.00
117 D.J. Mbenga RC 2.00 5.00
118 Damien Wilkins RC 2.50 6.00
119 Billy Thomas RC 2.00 5.00
120 Andre Barrett RC 2.00 5.00
121 Erik Daniels RC 2.50 6.00
122 Justin Reed RC 2.00 5.00
123 Viktor Khryapa RC 2.00 5.00
124 Mario Kasun RC 2.50 6.00
125 Luis Flores RC 2.50 6.00
126 Emeka Okafor RC 2.50 6.00
127 Dwight Howard AU RC 25.00 60.00
128 Ben Gordon AU RC 6.00 15.00
129 Shaun Livingston AU RC 6.00 15.00
130 Devin Harris AU RC 5.00 12.00
131 Josh Childress AU RC 4.00 10.00
132 Luol Deng AU RC 6.00 15.00
133 Rafael Araujo AU RC 4.00 10.00
134 Andre Iguodala AU RC 10.00 25.00
135 Luke Jackson AU RC 4.00 10.00
136 Andris Biedrins AU RC 4.00 10.00
137 Robert Swift AU RC 4.00 10.00
138 Sebastian Telfair AU RC 5.00 12.00
139 Kris Humphries AU RC 5.00 12.00
140 Al Jefferson AU RC 6.00 15.00
141 Kirk Snyder AU RC 4.00 10.00
142 Josh Smith AU RC 6.00 15.00
143 J.R. Smith AU RC 6.00 15.00
144 Dorell Wright AU RC 5.00 12.00
145 Jameer Nelson AU RC 6.00 15.00
146 Pavel Podkolzin AU RC 4.00 10.00
147 Delonte West AU RC 5.00 12.00
148 Tony Allen AU RC 6.00 15.00
149 Kevin Martin AU RC 8.00 20.00
150 Sasha Vujacic AU RC 5.00 12.00
151 Beno Udrih AU RC 5.00 12.00
152 David Harrison AU RC 4.00 10.00
153 Anderson Varejao AU RC 5.00 12.00
154 Jackson Vroman AU RC 4.00 10.00
155 Peter John Ramos AU RC 4.00 10.00
156 Lionel Chalmers AU RC 4.00 10.00
157 Donta Smith AU RC 4.00 10.00
158 Andre Emmett AU RC 4.00 10.00
159 Antonio Burks AU RC 4.00 10.00
160 Royal Ivey AU RC 4.00 10.00
161 Chris Duhon AU RC 5.00 12.00
162 Nenad Krstic AU RC 5.00 12.00
163 Trevor Ariza AU RC 6.00 15.00
164 Matt Freije AU RC 4.00 10.00
165 Bernard Robinson AU RC 4.00 10.00
166 Andres Nocioni AU RC 5.00 12.00
167 Pape Sow AU RC 4.00 10.00
168 Ha Seung-Jin AU RC 8.00 20.00

2004-05 Ultimate Collection Limited

*1-116: 1.5X TO 4X BASE HI
*117-126: 1X TO 2.5X BASE HI
*127-168: 1.25X TO 3X BASE HI
STATED PRINT RUN 25 SER.#'d SETS
127-168 HAVE JSY's AND AU's
14 Michael Jordan 300.00 600.00
15 LeBron James 150.00 400.00
45 Kobe Bryant 150.00 400.00
81 Allen Iverson 15.00 40.00
127 Dwight Howard JSY AU 200.00 400.00
134 Andre Iguodala JSY AU 100.00 200.00
143 J.R. Smith JSY AU 40.00 100.00

2004-05 Ultimate Collection Achievements Signatures

STATED PRINT RUN 24 TO 71 SER.#'d SETS
BK Bernard King/60 20.00 50.00
CA Carmelo Anthony/41 75.00 200.00
CD Clyde Drexler/50 75.00 200.00
DR David Robinson/71 125.00 300.00
HO Hakeem Olajuwon/52 125.00 300.00
JS John Stockton/28 125.00 300.00
KB Kobe Bryant/56 4,000.00 8,000.00
KG Kevin Garnett/40 400.00 800.00
LB Larry Bird/60 200.00 500.00
LJ LeBron James/43 5,000.00 10,000.00
MA Magic Johnson/24 200.00 500.00
MJ Michael Jordan/69 6,000.00 12,000.00
TM Tracy McGrady/62 150.00 400.00

2004-05 Ultimate Collection Buybacks

1 Abdur-R 03-4SPGUFab/18 20.00 50.00
2 Ray Allen EXCH 100.00 250.00
3 Melo 03-4FnlElmJsy/16 125.00 300.00
6 Gilbert Arenas SwtShJsy/18 20.00 50.00
7 Bibby 02-3OvatShtSht/14 25.00 60.00
8 Bibby 02-3OvatWrmUp/21 25.00 60.00
10 Bibby 03-4GlasGamGr/15 25.00 60.00
13 Billups 04-5ASLUWkTh/28 40.00 100.00
14 Billups03-4SPGUAFab/17 40.00 100.00
15 Kobe 02-3HardCrtGmFlr/14 2,000.00 4,000.00
16 Kobe 02-3HrdCrtGmFlrFm/17 2,000.00 4,000.00
22 B.Davis 03-4SwtShtJsy/20 20.00 50.00
23 B.Davis 01-2FltTmPtrn/34 20.00 50.00
24 B.Davis 01-2UDAirApp/17 20.00 50.00
25 B.Davis 02-3FinteEleJsy/20 20.00 50.00
26 B.Davis 02-3OvatAthUni/20 20.00 50.00
27 B.Davis 02-3SPxWinMat/19 20.00 50.00
28 B.Davis 02-3SwtShtSS/19 20.00 50.00
29 B.Davis 02-3UDGamPlnJsy/19 20.00 50.00
30 B.Davis 03-4SPGUAuthFab/19 20.00 50.00
31 B.Davis 03-4SPxWinMat/22 20.00 50.00
32 Drexler 02-3GenATAth/18 60.00 150.00
33 Dr.J 02-3GenAllTmAth/15 125.00 300.00
35 Garnett 02-3OvatAthWU/15 150.00 400.00
36 Garnett 03-4SPxWinMat/18 150.00 400.00
37 Garnett 03-4SwtShtJsy/20 150.00 400.00
39 Gasol 02-3ChpDrvPropJsy/14 75.00 200.00
41 Gasol 03-4SPxWinMat/22 75.00 200.00
42 Gasol 03-4UDAllStWkAth/18 75.00 200.00
45 Hamilton 03-4UDSPGUAthFb/18 40.00 100.00
46 Harmgtn 01-2UDAirApp/26 10.00 25.00
47 D.Harris 04-5SwtShtJsy/16 40.00 100.00
48 Hinrich 03-4UpperDeck/28 40.00 80.00
49 D.Howard 04-5SwtShtJsy/18 50.00 120.00
50 LeBron 03-4FinElemJsy/19 15,000.00 30,000.00
53 Jamison 02-3UDPracIJsy/24 15.00 40.00
55 Jamison 03-4SPxWinMat/23 15.00 40.00
57 Jefferson 03-4SPxWinMat/15 10.00 25.00
58 Magic 02-3GenATAWht/16 150.00 400.00
59 Magic 02-3GenATAYel/19 150.00 400.00
60 Kidd 02-3HardFlr/15 60.00 150.00
61 Kidd 02-3HardFlrFilm/14 60.00 150.00
62 Kidd 02-3OvatWarUp/16 60.00 150.00
64 Kidd 03-4SPxWinMat/21 60.00 150.00
65 Kidd 03-4SwtShtJsy/19 60.00 150.00
66 Kidd 03-4UDGlsSupSw/20 60.00 150.00
67 AK-47 02-3UDASAuth/21 40.00 100.00
68 AK-47 03-4UDASWkAth/18 40.00 100.00
69 AK-47 04-5HardMat/21 40.00 100.00
70 AK-47 04-5HardMatCom/21 40.00 100.00
71 AK-47 04-5SwtShtSwt/14 40.00 100.00
72 AK-47 04-5UDASWkAth/17 40.00 100.00
73 C.Magg 01-2FltTmPatrn/28 10.00 25.00
74 C.Magg 02-3UDGamPln/19 10.00 25.00
76 C.Magg 04-5SPGUAthFab/19 10.00 25.00
77 C.Magg 04-5SwShtSw/17 10.00 25.00
78 Marbury 01-2FltTmJmJsy/22 30.00 80.00
81 Marbury 02-3SPxWinMat/17 30.00 80.00
82 Marbury 03-4FinEleWU/20 30.00 80.00
83 Marion 02-3SwtShot/36 15.00 40.00
84 Marion 02-3UDPractice/16 15.00 40.00
86 Marion 03-4SwtShtJsy/18 15.00 40.00
89 Mason 02-3UDAllStrAuth/15 10.00 25.00
95 T-Mac 03-4SPxWinMat/23 100.00 250.00
96 T-Mac
Amare 03-4SPxWMC/18 100.00 250.00
98 A.Miller 02-3SwtSht/38 10.00 25.00
99 A.Miller 03-4SPxWinMat/22 10.00 25.00
100 A.Miller 04-5SPGUAuthFab/20 10.00 25.00
103 Ming 03-4FiniteElemJsy/15 200.00 500.00
104 Ming 03-4GlasSupSw/18 200.00 500.00
109 Zo 03-4GlasGamGr/17 100.00 200.00
110 Zo 03-4SPGUAuthFab/15 100.00 200.00
111 Nash 03-4SPGUAthFab/20 100.00 250.00
112 Nash 03-4SPxWinMat/20 100.00 250.00
113 Nash 03-4SwtShtJsy/15 100.00 250.00
114 Nash 04-5HardMat/19 100.00 250.00
115 Nash 04-5HardMatCom/21 100.00 250.00
116 Odom 02-3MVPMatComb/17 15.00 40.00
117 Odom 03-4GlasGamGr/19 15.00 40.00
118 Odom 04-5HrdMatCom/21 15.00 40.00
120 Odom 04-5SPGUAthFab/23 15.00 40.00
123 Parker 03-4SPxWinMat/21 60.00 150.00
124 Parker 04-5HardMat/19 60.00 150.00
125 Parker 04-5HardMatCom/21 60.00 150.00
126 Parker 04-5SwShtSwt/14 60.00 150.00
127 Payton 02-3GenATAth/19 60.00 150.00
128 Payton 03-4HardFloor/14 60.00 150.00
129 Payton 03-4SPxWinMat/21 60.00 150.00
130 Payton 04-5SwtShtSwt/18 60.00 150.00
131 Paul Pierce Jsy/17 60.00 150.00
132 Scottie Pippen Jsy/19 150.00 400.00
135 J-Rich 03-4SwtShtSwt/17 20.00 50.00
138 D-Rob 03-4SPGUAthFab/18 100.00 250.00
139 D-Rob 03-4SPxWinMat/17 100.00 250.00
141 Stockton 02-3OvatAthShrt/14 100.00 250.00
142 Stockton 03-4SwtShtSwt/20 100.00 250.00
145 Peja 03-4BlkDiamJsy/14 20.00 50.00
147 Peja 03-4SPGUAuthFab/16 20.00 50.00
148 Peja 03-4UDAllStWkAth/14 20.00 50.00
149 Amare 03-4GlasGamGr/17 25.00 60.00
150 Amare 03-4SPxWinMat/20 25.00 60.00
151 Amare 03-4SwtShtJsy/20 25.00 60.00
152 Amare 03-4SwtShtSwt/17 25.00 60.00
153 Amare 04-5HardMatCom/21 25.00 60.00
154 Amare 04-5HardMater/20 25.00 60.00
155 Amare 04-5SPGUAuthFab/16 25.00 60.00
156 Amare 04-5SwtShtSwt/16 25.00 60.00
159 B.Wallace 03-4BlaDiaJsy/14 40.00 100.00
160 B.Wallace 03-4SPGUFab/20 40.00 100.00
161 B.Wallace 03-4UDASWAth/21 40.00 100.00
163 Kidd
Jeff 03-4SPxWinMat/18 60.00 150.00

2004-05 Ultimate Collection Debuts

PRINT RUN 350 SER.#'d SETS
UD1 Dwight Howard 8.00 20.00
UD2 Emeka Okafor 2.00 5.00
UD3 Ben Gordon 2.50 6.00
UD4 Shaun Livingston 2.50 6.00
UD5 Devin Harris 2.00 5.00
UD6 Josh Childress 1.50 4.00
UD7 Luol Deng 2.50 6.00
UD8 Rafael Araujo 1.50 4.00
UD9 Andre Iguodala 4.00 10.00
UD10 Luke Jackson 1.50 4.00
UD11 Andris Biedrins 1.50 4.00
UD12 Robert Swift 1.50 4.00
UD13 Sebastian Telfair 2.00 5.00
UD14 Kris Humphries 2.00 5.00
UD15 Al Jefferson 2.50 6.00
UD16 Kirk Snyder 1.50 4.00
UD17 Josh Smith 2.50 6.00
UD18 J.R. Smith 2.50 6.00
UD19 Dorell Wright 2.00 5.00
UD20 Jameer Nelson 2.50 6.00
UD21 Nenad Krstic 2.00 5.00
UD22 Anderson Varejao 2.00 5.00
UD23 Jackson Vroman 1.50 4.00
UD24 Delonte West 2.00 5.00
UD25 Tony Allen 2.50 6.00
UD26 Kevin Martin 3.00 8.00
UD27 Sasha Vujacic 2.00 5.00
UD28 Beno Udrih 2.00 5.00
UD29 Ha Seung-Jin 2.50 6.00
UD30 Andres Nocioni 2.50 6.00

2004-05 Ultimate Collection Game Jerseys

PRINT RUN 175 SER.#'d SETS
*EXTRA: 1X TO 2.5X BASE HI
EXTRA PRINT RUN 25 SER.#'d SETS
*LIMITED: .5X TO 1.25X BASE JSY HI
LIMITED PRINT RUN 75 SER.#'d SETS
AI Allen Iverson 15.00 40.00
AK Andrei Kirilenko 3.00 8.00
AS Amare Stoudemire 4.00 10.00
BD Baron Davis 4.00 10.00
BG Ben Gordon 4.00 10.00
BK Bernard King 5.00 12.00
BW Ben Wallace 5.00 12.00
CA Carmelo Anthony 8.00 20.00
CD Clyde Drexler 6.00 15.00
DE Dennis Rodman 15.00 40.00
DH Dwight Howard 12.00 30.00
DN Dirk Nowitzki 15.00 40.00
DR David Robinson 8.00 20.00
EG Manu Ginobili 8.00 20.00
HO Hakeem Olajuwon 8.00 20.00
IT Isiah Thomas 6.00 15.00
JE Julius Erving 15.00 40.00
JK Jason Kidd 6.00 15.00
JO Jermaine O'Neal 3.00 8.00
JR Jason Richardson 4.00 10.00
JS John Stockton 8.00 20.00
KB Kobe Bryant 125.00 300.00
KG Kevin Garnett 15.00 40.00
LB Larry Bird 20.00 50.00
LD Luol Deng 4.00 10.00
LJ LeBron James 125.00 300.00
MA Magic Johnson 20.00 50.00
MB Mike Bibby 4.00 10.00
MJ Michael Jordan 150.00 400.00
OR Oscar Robertson 15.00 40.00
PG Pau Gasol 6.00 15.00
PP Paul Pierce 6.00 15.00
PS Peja Stojakovic 3.00 8.00
RM Reggie Miller 8.00 20.00
SF Steve Francis 4.00 10.00
SM Stephon Marbury 5.00 12.00
SN Steve Nash 8.00 20.00
SO Shaquille O'Neal 20.00 50.00
TD Tim Duncan 15.00 40.00
TM Tracy McGrady 6.00 15.00
WC Wilt Chamberlain 75.00 200.00
YM Yao Ming 10.00 25.00

2004-05 Ultimate Collection Game Patches

PRINT RUN 50 TO 100 SER.#'d SETS
*LIMITED: .5X TO 1.25X BASE JSY HI
LIMITED PRINT RUN 25 SER.#'d SETS
AI Allen Iverson/100 60.00 150.00
AK Andrei Kirilenko/100 6.00 15.00
AS Amare Stoudemire/100 8.00 20.00
BD Baron Davis/100 8.00 20.00
BG Ben Gordon/100 8.00 20.00
BK Bernard King/100 10.00 25.00
BW Ben Wallace/100 10.00 25.00
CA Carmelo Anthony/100 15.00 40.00
CD Clyde Drexler/100 15.00 40.00
DE Dennis Rodman/100 40.00 100.00
DH Dwight Howard/100 20.00 50.00
DN Dirk Nowitzki/100 40.00 100.00
DR David Robinson/100 15.00 40.00
EG Manu Ginobili/100 40.00 100.00
HO Hakeem Olajuwon/100 15.00 40.00
IT Isiah Thomas/100 15.00 40.00
JE Julius Erving/100 20.00 50.00
JK Jason Kidd/100 12.00 30.00
JO Jermaine O'Neal/100 6.00 15.00
JR Jason Richardson/100 8.00 20.00
JS John Stockton/100 15.00 40.00
KB Kobe Bryant/100 200.00 500.00
KG Kevin Garnett/100 40.00 100.00
LB Larry Bird/50 40.00 100.00
LD Luol Deng/100 8.00 20.00
LJ LeBron James/100 125.00 300.00
MA Magic Johnson/100 30.00 80.00
MB Mike Bibby/100 8.00 20.00
MJ Michael Jordan/100 300.00 600.00
OR Oscar Robertson/50 125.00 300.00
PG Pau Gasol/100 15.00 40.00
PP Paul Pierce/100 30.00 80.00
PS Peja Stojakovic/100 6.00 15.00
RM Reggie Miller/100 40.00 100.00
SF Steve Francis/100 8.00 20.00
SM Stephon Marbury/100 10.00 25.00
SN Steve Nash/100 15.00 40.00
SO Shaquille O'Neal/100 30.00 80.00
TD Tim Duncan/100 15.00 40.00
TM Tracy McGrady/100 12.00 30.00
WC Wilt Chamberlain/100 125.00 300.00
YM Yao Ming/100 40.00 100.00

2004-05 Ultimate Collection MVP Autographs

STATED PRINT RUN 3 TO 94 SER.#'d SETS
HO Hakeem Olajuwon/94 100.00 250.00
JE Julius Erving/81 125.00 300.00

2004-05 Ultimate Collection Premium Patches

PRINT RUN 25 TO 75 SER.#'d SETS
AI Allen Iverson/75 300.00 600.00
AK Andrei Kirilenko/75 20.00 50.00
AS Amare Stoudemire/50 25.00 60.00
BD Baron Davis/75 25.00 60.00
BG Ben Gordon/75 25.00 60.00
BW Ben Wallace/75 25.00 60.00
CA Carmelo Anthony/75 150.00 400.00
CW Chris Webber/75 150.00 400.00
DE Devin Harris/75 20.00 50.00
DH Dwight Howard/50 100.00 250.00
DN Dirk Nowitzki/75 200.00 500.00
EB Elton Brand/75 20.00 50.00
JC Josh Childress/75 20.00 50.00

JK Jason Kidd/75 100.00 250.00
JN Jameer Nelson/75 25.00 60.00
JO Jermaine O'Neal/75 20.00 50.00
JR Jason Richardson/75 25.00 60.00
KB Kobe Bryant/75 500.00 1,000.00
KG Kevin Garnett/75 300.00 600.00
LD Luol Deng/75 25.00 60.00
LJ LeBron James/50 500.00 1,000.00
LO Lamar Odom/50 25.00 60.00
MJ Michael Jordan/25 1,000.00 2,000.00
PG Pau Gasol/75 75.00 200.00
PP Paul Pierce/75 75.00 200.00
PS Peja Stojakovic/50 20.00 50.00
RA Ray Allen/75 100.00 250.00
RH Richard Hamilton/75 40.00 100.00
RJ Richard Jefferson/75 20.00 50.00
RM Reggie Miller/75 125.00 300.00
SA Shareef Abdur-Rahim/75 25.00 60.00
SF Steve Francis/75 25.00 60.00
SH Shawn Marion/75 25.00 60.00
SL Shaun Livingston/75 25.00 60.00
SM Stephon Marbury/50 75.00 200.00
SN Steve Nash/75 125.00 300.00
SO Shaquille O'Neal/75 300.00 600.00
ST Sebastian Telfair/75 20.00 50.00
TD Tim Duncan/75 200.00 500.00
TM Tracy McGrady/50 125.00 300.00
TP Tony Parker/75 100.00 250.00
YM Yao Ming/75 150.00 400.00

2004-05 Ultimate Collection Rookie Jerseys

PRINT RUN 275 SER.#'d SETS
*PARALLEL: .5X TO 1.25X BASE HI
PARALLEL PRINT RUN 75 SER.#'d SETS
AB Andris Biedrins 2.00 5.00
AE Andre Emmett 2.00 5.00
AI Andre Iguodala 5.00 12.00
AJ Al Jefferson 3.00 8.00
AV Anderson Varejao 2.50 6.00
BG Ben Gordon 3.00 8.00
DA David Harrison 2.00 5.00
DE Devin Harris 2.50 6.00
DH Dwight Howard 10.00 25.00
DW Dorell Wright 2.50 6.00
HS Ha Seung-Jin 3.00 8.00
JC Josh Childress 2.00 5.00
JN Jameer Nelson 3.00 8.00
JR J.R. Smith 3.00 8.00
JS Josh Smith 3.00 8.00
JV Jackson Vroman 2.00 5.00
KH Kris Humphries 2.50 6.00
KM Kevin Martin 4.00 10.00
KS Kirk Snyder 2.00 5.00
LC Lionel Chalmers 2.50 6.00
LD Luol Deng 3.00 8.00
LU Luke Jackson 2.00 5.00
PR Peter John Ramos 2.00 5.00
RA Rafael Araujo 2.00 5.00
SL Shaun Livingston 3.00 8.00
ST Sebastian Telfair 2.50 6.00
SV Sasha Vujacic 2.50 6.00
TA Tony Allen 3.00 8.00
WE Delonte West 2.50 6.00

2004-05 Ultimate Collection Signature Patches

PRINT RUN 25 SER.#'d SETS
AI Andre Iguodala 50.00 120.00
AS Amare Stoudemire 40.00 100.00
BG Ben Gordon 30.00 80.00
BK Bernard King 40.00 100.00
BW Ben Wallace 50.00 120.00
CA Carmelo Anthony 100.00 250.00
CD Clyde Drexler 150.00 300.00
DE Dennis Rodman 150.00 300.00
DH Dwight Howard 125.00 300.00
DR David Robinson 100.00 250.00
IT Isiah Thomas 40.00 100.00
JC Josh Childress 20.00 50.00
JE Julius Erving 100.00 250.00
JK Jason Kidd 75.00 200.00
JS John Stockton 150.00 300.00
KB Kobe Bryant 2,000.00 4,000.00
KG Kevin Garnett 500.00 1,000.00
LB Larry Bird 150.00 300.00
LD Luol Deng 20.00 50.00
LJ LeBron James 6,000.00 12,000.00
MA Magic Johnson 125.00 250.00
MJ Michael Jordan 3,000.00 6,000.00
PG Pau Gasol 25.00 60.00
PP Paul Pierce 150.00 400.00
PS Peja Stojakovic 50.00 100.00
TM Tracy McGrady 100.00 250.00
YM Yao Ming 150.00 400.00

2004-05 Ultimate Collection Signatures

AM Alonzo Mourning 40.00 100.00
AS Amare Stoudemire 20.00 50.00
BG Ben Gordon 20.00 50.00
BK Bernard King 20.00 50.00
BR Bill Russell 1,500.00 3,000.00
BW Ben Wallace 75.00 200.00
CA Carmelo Anthony 100.00 250.00
CD Clyde Drexler 40.00 100.00
DE Devin Harris 10.00 25.00
DH Dwight Howard 40.00 100.00
DR David Robinson 60.00 150.00
HO Hakeem Olajuwon 60.00 150.00
IT Isiah Thomas 40.00 100.00
JE Julius Erving 125.00 300.00
JK Jason Kidd 40.00 100.00
JS John Stockton 60.00 150.00
KB Kobe Bryant SP 2,000.00 4,000.00
KG Kevin Garnett SP 150.00 400.00
KH Kirk Hinrich 20.00 50.00
LB Larry Bird 125.00 300.00
LD Luol Deng 6.00 15.00
LJ LeBron James 3,000.00 6,000.00
MA Magic Johnson 125.00 300.00
MJ Michael Jordan 2,500.00 5,000.00
PS Peja Stojakovic 10.00 25.00
RA Ray Allen 60.00 150.00
RO Dennis Rodman 200.00 500.00
SL Shaun Livingston 6.00 15.00
SM Stephon Marbury 40.00 100.00
TM Tracy McGrady 100.00 250.00
YM Yao Ming 150.00 400.00

2004-05 Ultimate Collection Signatures Gold

STATED PRINT RUN ONE TO 91 SETS
AM Alonzo Mourning/33 60.00 150.00
AS Amare Stoudemire/32 30.00 80.00
BK Bernard King/30 30.00 80.00
CA Carmelo Anthony/15 200.00 500.00
CD Clyde Drexler/22 60.00 150.00
DE Devin Harris/34 15.00 40.00
DR David Robinson/50 100.00 250.00
HO Hakeem Olajuwon/34 100.00 250.00
KG Kevin Garnett/21 300.00 600.00
KH Kirk Hinrich/31 30.00 80.00
LB Larry Bird/33 200.00 500.00
LJ LeBron James/23 6,000.00 12,000.00
MA Magic Johnson/32 200.00 500.00
MJ Michael Jordan/23 3,000.00 6,000.00
RA Ray Allen/34 100.00 250.00
RO Dennis Rodman/91 400.00 800.00

2005-06 Ultimate Collection

1-130 PRINT RUN 750 SER.#'d SETS
143-183 AU RC PRINT RUN 250 SER.#'d SETS
1 Josh Smith .75 2.00
2 Josh Childress .60 1.50
3 Joe Johnson .75 2.00
4 Al Harrington .75 2.00
5 Tony Allen .60 1.50
6 Ricky Davis .75 2.00
7 Al Jefferson .60 1.50
8 Paul Pierce 1.50 4.00
9 Delonte West .60 1.50
10 Brevin Knight .60 1.50
11 Emeka Okafor .75 2.00
12 Kareem Rush .60 1.50
13 Gerald Wallace .75 2.00
14 Tyson Chandler .75 2.00
15 Luol Deng .75 2.00
16 Michael Jordan 100.00 250.00
17 Ben Gordon .75 2.00
18 Kirk Hinrich .75 2.00
19 LeBron James 75.00 200.00
20 Drew Gooden .75 2.00
21 Larry Hughes .75 2.00
22 Donyell Marshall .60 1.50
23 Zydrunas Ilgauskas .75 2.00
24 Marquis Daniels .60 1.50
25 Josh Howard .75 2.00
26 Dirk Nowitzki 2.50 6.00
27 Jason Terry .75 2.00
28 Devin Harris .60 1.50
29 Carmelo Anthony 1.50 4.00
30 Marcus Camby .75 2.00
31 Nene .75 2.00
32 Kenyon Martin .75 2.00
33 Andre Miller .75 2.00
34 Ben Wallace 1.25 3.00
35 Richard Hamilton 1.25 3.00
36 Tayshaun Prince 1.00 2.50
37 Chauncey Billups 1.25 3.00
38 Rasheed Wallace 1.25 3.00
39 Baron Davis 1.25 3.00
40 Mike Dunleavy .60 1.50
41 Troy Murphy .60 1.50
42 Jason Richardson 1.00 2.50
43 Tracy McGrady 1.50 4.00
44 Yao Ming 2.00 5.00
45 Stromile Swift .60 1.50
46 Juwan Howard .75 2.00
47 Bob Sura .60 1.50
48 Ron Artest .75 2.00
49 Stephen Jackson .75 2.00
50 Jermaine O'Neal .75 2.00
51 Jamaal Tinsley .60 1.50
52 Elton Brand .75 2.00
53 Corey Maggette .75 2.00
54 Sam Cassell .75 2.00
55 Shaun Livingston .75 2.00
56 Cuttino Mobley .60 1.50
57 Kobe Bryant 8.00 20.00
58 Kwame Brown .60 1.50
59 Lamar Odom .75 2.00
60 Devean George .60 1.50
61 Pau Gasol 1.50 4.00
62 Damon Stoudamire 1.00 2.50
63 Eddie Jones .75 2.00
64 Bobby Jackson .75 2.00
65 Shaquille O'Neal 3.00 8.00
66 Gary Payton 1.50 4.00
67 Antoine Walker .75 2.00
68 Dwyane Wade 2.00 5.00
69 Jason Williams 1.50 4.00
70 Jamaal Magloire .60 1.50
71 Michael Redd .75 2.00
72 Bobby Simmons .60 1.50
73 Maurice Williams .75 2.00
74 Kevin Garnett 2.50 6.00
75 Marko Jaric .60 1.50
76 Wally Szczerbiak .75 2.00
77 Michael Olowokandi .60 1.50
78 Vince Carter 2.00 5.00
79 Richard Jefferson .75 2.00
80 Jason Kidd 1.50 4.00
81 Jeff McInnis .60 1.50
82 J.R. Smith 1.00 2.50
83 Desmond Mason .60 1.50
84 Speedy Claxton .60 1.50
85 David West .75 2.00
86 Stephon Marbury 1.25 3.00
87 Jamal Crawford 1.00 2.50
88 Quentin Richardson .60 1.50
89 Eddy Curry .60 1.50
90 Steve Francis 1.00 2.50
91 Grant Hill 1.00 2.50
92 Dwight Howard 1.25 3.00
93 Jameer Nelson .60 1.50
94 Hedo Turkoglu .75 2.00
95 Allen Iverson 2.00 5.00
96 Andre Iguodala 1.00 2.50
97 Kyle Korver .75 2.00
98 Chris Webber 1.25 3.00
99 Steve Nash 2.00 5.00
100 Shawn Marion .75 2.00
101 Amare Stoudemire 1.00 2.50
102 Kurt Thomas .60 1.50
103 Juan Dixon .60 1.50
104 Darius Miles .60 1.50
105 Zach Randolph 1.00 2.50
106 Sebastian Telfair .75 2.00
107 Shareef Abdur-Rahim 1.00 2.50
108 Mike Bibby 1.00 2.50
109 Brad Miller .75 2.00
110 Peja Stojakovic .75 2.00
111 Tim Duncan 2.50 6.00
112 Manu Ginobili 2.00 5.00
113 Tony Parker 1.50 4.00
114 Michael Finley 1.00 2.50
115 Ray Allen 1.50 4.00
116 Rashard Lewis .75 2.00
117 Vladimir Radmanovic .60 1.50
118 Luke Ridnour .75 2.00
119 Chris Bosh 1.25 3.00
120 Morris Peterson .60 1.50
121 Jalen Rose .75 2.00
122 Alvin Williams .60 1.50
123 Carlos Boozer .75 2.00
124 Matt Harpring .60 1.50
125 Andrei Kirilenko .75 2.00
126 Mehmet Okur .60 1.50
127 Gilbert Arenas 1.00 2.50
128 Caron Butler .75 2.00
129 Antawn Jamison .75 2.00
130 Brendan Haywood .60 1.50
131 Von Wafer RC 1.50 4.00
132 Bracey Wright RC 1.50 4.00
133 Ryan Gomes RC 2.00 5.00
134 Robert Whaley RC 1.50 4.00
135 Orien Greene RC 2.00 5.00
136 Dijon Thompson RC 1.50 4.00
137 Lawrence Roberts RC 1.50 4.00
138 Amir Johnson RC 2.50 6.00
139 John Lucas III RC 2.00 5.00
140 Chuck Hayes RC 2.50 6.00
141 Alex Acker RC 1.50 4.00
142 Fabricio Oberto RC 2.00 5.00
143 Andrew Bogut AU RC 6.00 15.00
144 Marvin Williams AU RC 5.00 12.00
145 Deron Williams AU RC 8.00 20.00
146 Chris Paul AU RC 400.00 800.00
147 Raymond Felton AU RC 4.00 10.00
148 Martell Webster AU RC 4.00 10.00
149 Charlie Villanueva AU RC 4.00 10.00
150 Channing Frye AU RC 4.00 10.00
151 Ike Diogu AU RC 3.00 8.00
152 Andrew Bynum AU RC 4.00 10.00
153 Yaroslav Korolev AU RC 4.00 10.00
154 Sean May AU RC 3.00 8.00
155 Rashad McCants AU RC 3.00 8.00
156 Antoine Wright AU RC 4.00 10.00
157 Joey Graham AU RC 4.00 10.00
158 Danny Granger AU RC 5.00 12.00
159 Gerald Green AU RC 5.00 12.00
160 Hakim Warrick AU RC 4.00 10.00
161 Julius Hodge AU RC 3.00 8.00
162 Nate Robinson AU RC 5.00 12.00
163 Jarrett Jack AU RC 5.00 12.00
164 Francisco Garcia AU RC 3.00 8.00
165 Luther Head AU RC 3.00 8.00
166 Johan Petro AU RC 3.00 8.00
167 Jason Maxiell AU RC 4.00 10.00
168 Linas Kleiza AU RC 4.00 10.00
169 Wayne Simien AU RC 3.00 8.00
170 David Lee AU RC 5.00 12.00
171 Salim Stoudamire AU RC 4.00 10.00
172 Daniel Ewing AU RC 4.00 10.00
173 Brandon Bass AU RC 4.00 10.00
174 C.J. Miles AU RC 4.00 10.00
175 Ersan Ilyasova AU RC 4.00 10.00
176 Travis Diener AU RC 3.00 8.00
177 Chris Taft AU RC 3.00 8.00
178 M.Andriuskevicius AU RC 3.00 8.00
179 Louis Williams AU RC 12.00 30.00
180 Monta Ellis AU RC 6.00 15.00
181 Andray Blatche AU RC 8.00 20.00
182 Sarunas Jasikevicius AU RC 5.00 12.00
183 James Singleton AU RC 5.00 12.00

2005-06 Ultimate Collection Blue

*1-130 BLUE: .75X TO 2X BASE HI
*131-142 RC BLUE: .6X TO 1.5X BASE HI
PRINT RUN 125 SER.#'d SETS
57 Kobe Bryant 12.00 30.00

2005-06 Ultimate Collection Red

*1-130 RED: 1.25X TO 3X BASE HI
*131-142 RC RED: .75X TO 2X BASE HI
RED PRINT RUN 50 SER.#'d SETS

2005-06 Ultimate Collection Silver

*1-130 SILV: 2.5X TO 6X BASE HI
*131-142 SILV.RC: 1X TO 2.5X BASE HI
SILVER PRINT RUN 25 SER.#'d SETS
68 Dwyane Wade 20.00 50.00

2005-06 Ultimate Collection Achievements Signatures

PRINT RUNS LISTED IN CHECKLIST
UABG Ben Gordon/35 10.00 25.00
UABK Bernard King/85 20.00 50.00
UADH Dwight Howard/20 60.00 150.00
UADR Dennis Rodman/34 125.00 300.00
UAEB Elton Brand/44 25.00 60.00
UAHO Hakeem Olajuwon/89 125.00 300.00
UAJK Jason Kidd/25 125.00 300.00
UAKA K.Abdul-Jabbar/76 200.00 500.00
UAKG Kevin Garnett/47 125.00 300.00
UALB Larry Bird/84 125.00 300.00
UALJ LeBron James/56 2,500.00 5,000.00
UAMA Magic Johnson/46 125.00 300.00
UAMJ Michael Jordan/63 6,000.00 12,000.00
UAPG Pau Gasol/37 40.00 100.00
UAPP Paul Pierce/48 125.00 300.00
UASM Stephon Marbury/50 40.00 100.00
UASN Steve Nash/19 125.00 300.00
UATM Tracy McGrady/17 125.00 300.00
UAVC Vince Carter/51 125.00 300.00
UAYM Yao Ming/41 500.00 1,000.00

2005-06 Ultimate Collection All-Stars Signatures

PRINT RUNS LISTED IN CHECKLIST
ASBR Bill Russell/12 1,500.00 3,000.00
ASGG George Gervin/12 50.00 100.00
ASHO Hakeem Olajuwon/12 50.00 100.00
ASKA K.Abdul-Jabbar/19 60.00 120.00
ASLB Larry Bird/12 150.00 250.00
ASMJ Michael Jordan/14 450.00 650.00

2005-06 Ultimate Collection Honors Signatures

PRINT RUNS LISTED IN CHECKLIST
HSHO Hakeem Olajuwon/93 25.00 60.00
HSJK Jason Kidd/95 20.00 50.00
HSPP Paul Pierce/99 30.00 80.00
HSWF Walt Frazier/68 15.00 40.00

2005-06 Ultimate Collection Jerseys

PRINT RUN 99 SER.#'d SETS
*GOLD: .75X TO 2X BASE JSY HI
GOLD PRINT RUN 25 SER.#'d SETS
UJAB Andrew Bogut 4.00 10.00
UJAN Andrew Bynum 2.50 6.00
UJAS Amare Stoudemire 3.00 8.00
UJAW Antoine Wright 2.50 6.00
UJBG Ben Gordon 2.50 6.00
UJBK Bernard King 4.00 10.00
UJCA Carmelo Anthony 5.00 12.00
UJCB Chauncey Billups 4.00 10.00
UJCD Clyde Drexler 5.00 12.00
UJCF Channing Frye 2.50 6.00
UJCP Chris Paul 40.00 100.00
UJCV Charlie Villanueva 2.50 6.00
UJDA David Robinson 6.00 15.00
UJDG Danny Granger 3.00 8.00
UJDH Dwight Howard 4.00 10.00
UJDN Dirk Nowitzki 8.00 20.00
UJDR Dennis Rodman 6.00 15.00
UJDW Deron Williams 5.00 12.00
UJEO Emeka Okafor 2.50 6.00
UJFG Francisco Garcia 2.00 5.00
UJGG Gerald Green 3.00 8.00
UJHO Hakeem Olajuwon 6.00 15.00
UJHW Hakim Warrick 2.50 6.00
UJID Ike Diogu 2.00 5.00
UJIT Isiah Thomas 5.00 12.00
UJJA Jason Richardson 3.00 8.00
UJJG Joey Graham 2.50 6.00
UJJH Julius Hodge 2.00 5.00
UJJJ Jarrett Jack 3.00 8.00
UJJR J.R. Smith 3.00 8.00
UJJS John Stockton 6.00 15.00
UJJW James Worthy 4.00 10.00
UJKB Kobe Bryant 150.00 400.00
UJKE Kevin McHale 4.00 10.00
UJKG Kevin Garnett 8.00 20.00
UJKM Karl Malone 5.00 12.00
UJLB Larry Bird 10.00 25.00
UJLJ LeBron James 25.00 60.00
UJMA Magic Johnson 8.00 20.00
UJMG Manu Ginobili 6.00 15.00
UJMJ Michael Jordan 40.00 100.00
UJMR Martell Webster 2.50 6.00
UJMW Marvin Williams 3.00 8.00
UJNR Nate Robinson 3.00 8.00
UJOR Oscar Robertson/35 20.00 50.00
UJPP Paul Pierce 5.00 12.00
UJRA Ray Allen 5.00 12.00
UJRF Raymond Felton 2.50 6.00
UJRM Rashad McCants 2.00 5.00
UJSE Sean May 2.00 5.00
UJSF Steve Francis 3.00 8.00
UJSM Shawn Marion 2.50 6.00
UJSN Steve Nash 6.00 15.00
UJSO Shaquille O'Neal 8.00 20.00
UJST Stephon Marbury 4.00 10.00
UJTD Tim Duncan 8.00 20.00
UJTM Tracy McGrady 5.00 12.00
UJTP Tony Parker 5.00 12.00
UJVC Vince Carter 6.00 15.00
UJYM Yao Ming 6.00 15.00

2005-06 Ultimate Collection Jerseys Dual

PRINT RUN 50 SER.#'d SETS
DJAO R.Artest/J.O'Neal 3.00 8.00
DJAS A.Stoudemire/S.Marion 4.00 10.00
DJBA C.Bosh/C.Anthony 6.00 15.00
DJBS M.Bibby/P.Stojakovic 4.00 10.00
DJBW A.Bogut/M.Williams 5.00 12.00
DJCL C.Anthony/L.James 30.00 80.00
DJDG T.Duncan/M.Ginobili 10.00 25.00
DJDL D.Williams/L.Head 6.00 15.00
DJFB C.Frye/A.Bynum 3.00 8.00
DJGV J.Graham/C.Villanueva 3.00 8.00
DJGW G.Green/M.Webster 4.00 10.00
DJHF D.Howard/S.Francis 5.00 12.00
DJJB M.Johnson/L.Bird 50.00 120.00
DJJJ M.Jordan/L.James 200.00 500.00
DJKJ A.Kirilenko/A.Jamison 3.00 8.00
DJLK L.James/K.Bryant 300.00 600.00
DJMF R.McCants/R.Felton 3.00 8.00
DJMG T.McGrady/K.Garnett 10.00 25.00
DJMK S.Marbury/J.Kidd 6.00 15.00
DJMM M.Jordan/M.Johnson 125.00 300.00
DJNH D.Nowitzki/J.Howard 10.00 25.00
DJNK S.Nash/J.Kidd 8.00 20.00
DJOG E.Okafor/B.Gordon 3.00 8.00
DJOM S.O'Neal/Y.Ming 15.00 40.00
DJPG T.Parker/M.Ginobili 10.00 25.00
DJPW C.Paul/D.Williams 20.00 50.00
DJRA M.Redd/R.Allen 6.00 15.00
DJRD J.Richardson/B.Davis 4.00 10.00
DJRJ N.Robinson/J.Jack 4.00 10.00
DJRO D.Robinson/H.Olajuwon 8.00 20.00
DJSM J.Stockton/K.Malone 8.00 20.00
DJSR S.May/R.Felton 3.00 8.00
DJSS J.Smith/J.Smith 4.00 10.00
DJTL S.Telfair/S.Livingston 3.00 8.00
DJTS I.Thomas/J.Stockton 8.00 20.00
DJVJ V.Carter/R.Jefferson 8.00 20.00
DJWD H.Warrick/I.Diogu 3.00 8.00
DJWH B.Wallace/R.Hamilton 5.00 12.00
DJWS M.Williams/S.Stoudamire 4.00 10.00
DJWW M.Webster/A.Wright 3.00 8.00

2005-06 Ultimate Collection Loyalty Signatures

PRINT RUNS LISTED IN CHECKLIST

2005-06 Ultimate Collection Patches

PRINT RUN 75 SER.#'d SETS
GOLD: .75X TO 2X BASE PAT.HI
GOLD PRINT RUN 20 SER.#'d SETS
UJPAB Andrew Bogut 8.00 20.00
UJPAN Andrew Bynum 5.00 12.00
UJPAS Amare Stoudemire 6.00 15.00
UJPAW Antoine Wright 5.00 12.00
UJPBG Ben Gordon 5.00 12.00
UJPBK Bernard King 8.00 20.00
UJPCA Carmelo Anthony 10.00 25.00
UJPCB Chauncey Billups 8.00 20.00
UJPCD Clyde Drexler 10.00 25.00
UJPCF Channing Frye 5.00 12.00
UJPCP Chris Paul 75.00 200.00
UJPCV Charlie Villanueva 5.00 12.00
UJPDA David Robinson 12.00 30.00
UJPDG Danny Granger 6.00 15.00
UJPDH Dwight Howard 8.00 20.00
UJPDN Dirk Nowitzki 15.00 40.00
UJPDR Dennis Rodman 15.00 40.00
UJPDW Deron Williams 10.00 25.00
UJPEO Emeka Okafor 5.00 12.00
UJPFG Francisco Garcia 4.00 10.00
UJPGG Gerald Green 6.00 15.00
UJPHO Hakeem Olajuwon 12.00 30.00
UJPHW Hakim Warrick 5.00 12.00
UJPID Ike Diogu 4.00 10.00
UJPIT Isiah Thomas 10.00 25.00
UJPJA Jason Richardson 6.00 15.00
UJPJG Joey Graham 5.00 12.00
UJPJH Julius Hodge 4.00 10.00
UJPJJ Jarrett Jack 6.00 15.00
UJPJR J.R. Smith 6.00 15.00
UJPJS John Stockton 12.00 30.00
UJPJW James Worthy 12.00 30.00
UJPKB Kobe Bryant 400.00 800.00
UJPKE Kevin McHale 8.00 20.00
UJPKG Kevin Garnett 15.00 40.00
UJPKM Karl Malone 12.00 30.00
UJPLB Larry Bird 20.00 50.00
UJPLJ LeBron James 75.00 200.00
UJPMA Magic Johnson 15.00 40.00
UJPMG Manu Ginobili 12.00 30.00
UJPMJ Michael Jordan 300.00 600.00
UJPMR Martell Webster 5.00 12.00
UJPMW Marvin Williams 6.00 15.00
UJPNR Nate Robinson 6.00 15.00
UJPOR Oscar Robertson/20 25.00 60.00
UJPPP Paul Pierce 10.00 25.00
UJPRA Ray Allen 10.00 25.00
UJPRF Raymond Felton 5.00 12.00
UJPRM Rashad McCants 4.00 10.00
UJPSE Sean May 4.00 10.00
UJPSF Steve Francis 6.00 15.00
UJPSM Shawn Marion 5.00 12.00
UJPSO Shaquille O'Neal 20.00 50.00
UJPST Stephon Marbury 8.00 20.00
UJPTD Tim Duncan 15.00 40.00
UJPTM Tracy McGrady 12.00 30.00
UJPTP Tony Parker 8.00 20.00
UJPVC Vince Carter 12.00 30.00
UJPYM Yao Ming 20.00 50.00

2005-06 Ultimate Collection Patches Dual

PRINT RUN 40 SER.#'d SETS
DPAO R.Artest/J.O'Neal 10.00 25.00
DPAS A.Stoudemire/S.Marion 12.00 30.00
DPBA C.Bosh/C.Anthony 15.00 40.00
DPBS M.Bibby/P.Stojakovic 12.00 30.00
DPBW A.Bogut/M.Williams 12.00 30.00
DPCL C.Anthony/L.James 75.00 200.00
DPDG T.Duncan/M.Ginobili 30.00 80.00
DPDL D.Williams/L.Head 12.00 30.00
DPFB C.Frye/A.Bynum 10.00 25.00
DPGV J.Graham/C.Villanueva 10.00 25.00
DPGW G.Green/M.Webster 12.00 30.00
DPHF D.Howard/S.Francis 12.00 30.00
DPJB M.Johnson/L.Bird 60.00 150.00
DPJJ M.Jordan/L.James 300.00 600.00
DPKJ A.Kirilenko/A.Jamison 10.00 25.00
DPLK L.James/K.Bryant 1,000.00 2,000.00
DPMF R.McCants/R.Felton 10.00 25.00
DPMG T.McGrady/K.Garnett 25.00 60.00
DPMK S.Marbury/J.Kidd 25.00 60.00
DPMM M.Jordan/M.Johnson 150.00 400.00
DPNH D.Nowitzki/J.Howard 12.00 30.00
DPOG E.Okafor/B.Gordon 10.00 25.00
DPOM S.O'Neal/Y.Ming 40.00 100.00
DPPG T.Parker/M.Ginobili 20.00 50.00
DPPW C.Paul/D.Williams 25.00 60.00
DPRA M.Redd/R.Allen 12.00 30.00
DPRD J.Richardon/B.Davis 12.00 30.00
DPRJ N.Robinson/J.Jack 12.00 30.00
DPRO D.Robinson/H.Olajuwon 20.00 50.00
DPSM J.Stockton/K.Malone 60.00 150.00
DPSR S.May/R.Felton 10.00 25.00
DPSS J.R. Smith/Josh Smith 12.00 30.00
DPTL S.Telfair/S.Livingston 10.00 25.00
DPTS I.Thomas/J.Stockton 15.00 40.00
DPVJ V.Carter/R.Jefferson 15.00 40.00
DPWD H.Warrick/I.Diogu 10.00 25.00
DPWH B.Wallace/R.Hamilton 20.00 50.00
DPWS M.Williams/S.Stoudamire 12.00 30.00
DPWW M.Webster/A.Wright 10.00 25.00

2005-06 Ultimate Collection Premium Patches

PRINT RUN 25 TO 50 SER.#'d SETS
PPAB Andrew Bogut/50 12.00 30.00
PPAK Andrei Kirilenko/50 8.00 20.00
PPAS Amare Stoudemire/50 10.00 25.00
PPBD Baron Davis/50 10.00 25.00
PPBG Ben Gordon/50 8.00 20.00
PPCB Chris Bosh/50 12.00 30.00
PPCF Channing Frye/50 8.00 20.00
PPCM Corey Maggette/50 8.00 20.00
PPCP Chris Paul/50 50.00 120.00
PPCV Charlie Villanueva/50 8.00 20.00
PPDH Dwight Howard/25 12.00 30.00
PPDN Dirk Nowitzki/25 30.00 80.00
PPDW Deron Williams/50 15.00 40.00
PPEB Elton Brand/50 8.00 20.00
PPEO Emeka Okafor/50 8.00 20.00
PPID Ike Diogu/50 6.00 15.00
PPJK Jason Kidd/50 15.00 40.00
PPJR Jason Richardson/50 10.00 25.00
PPJS J.R. Smith/50 10.00 25.00
PPKB Kobe Bryant/25 600.00 1,200.00
PPKG Kevin Garnett/25 30.00 80.00
PPLJ LeBron James/25 125.00 300.00
PPMA Marvin Williams/50 10.00 25.00
PPMB Mike Bibby/50 10.00 25.00
PPMJ Michael Jordan/25 350.00 700.00
PPMR Michael Redd/50 8.00 20.00
PPMW Martell Webster/50 8.00 20.00
PPPP Paul Pierce/50 15.00 40.00
PPPP Peja Stojakovic/50 8.00 20.00
PPRF Raymond Felton/50 8.00 20.00
PPRM Rashad McCants/50 6.00 15.00
PPSE Sean May/50 6.00 15.00
PPSF Steve Francis/50 10.00 25.00
PPSH Shawn Marion/50 8.00 20.00
PPSM Stephon Marbury/50 12.00 30.00
PPSN Steve Nash/25 30.00 80.00
PPSO Shaquille O'Neal/25 30.00 80.00
PPTD Tim Duncan/25 30.00 80.00
PPTM Tracy McGrady/25 25.00 60.00
PPTP Tony Parker/50 15.00 40.00
PPVC Vince Carter/25 40.00 100.00
PPYM Yao Ming/25 25.00 60.00

2005-06 Ultimate Collection Premium Swatches

PRINT RUN 100 SER.#'d SETS
PSAB Andrew Bogut 5.00 12.00
PSAK Andrei Kirilenko 3.00 8.00
PSAS Amare Stoudemire 4.00 10.00
PSBD Baron Davis 4.00 10.00
PSBG Ben Gordon 3.00 8.00
PSCB Chris Bosh 5.00 12.00
PSCF Channing Frye 3.00 8.00
PSCM Corey Maggette 3.00 8.00
PSCP Chris Paul 20.00 50.00
PSCV Charlie Villanueva 3.00 8.00
PSDH Dwight Howard 5.00 12.00
PSDN Dirk Nowitzki 10.00 25.00
PSDW Deron Williams 6.00 15.00
PSEB Elton Brand 3.00 8.00
PSEO Emeka Okafor 3.00 8.00
PSID Ike Diogu 2.50 6.00
PSJK Jason Kidd 6.00 15.00
PSJR Jason Richardson 4.00 10.00
PSJS J.R. Smith 4.00 10.00
PSKB Kobe Bryant 200.00 500.00
PSKG Kevin Garnett 10.00 25.00
PSLJ LeBron James 25.00 60.00
PSMA Marvin Williams 4.00 10.00
PSMB Mike Bibby 4.00 10.00
PSMJ Michael Jordan 100.00 200.00
PSMR Michael Redd 3.00 8.00
PSMW Martell Webster 3.00 8.00
PSPP Paul Pierce 6.00 15.00
PSPS Peja Stojakovic 3.00 8.00
PSRF Raymond Felton 3.00 8.00
PSRM Rashad McCants 2.50 6.00
PSSE Sean May 2.50 6.00
PSSF Steve Francis 4.00 10.00
PSSH Shawn Marion 3.00 8.00
PSSM Stephon Marbury 5.00 12.00
PSSO Shaquille O'Neal 12.00 30.00
PSTD Tim Duncan 10.00 25.00
PSTM Tracy McGrady 6.00 15.00
PSTP Tony Parker 6.00 15.00
PSVC Vince Carter 8.00 20.00
PSYM Yao Ming 8.00 20.00

2005-06 Ultimate Collection Rookie Autographs Gold

PRINT RUN 25 SER.#'d SETS
143 Andrew Bogut 40.00 100.00
144 Marvin Williams 15.00 40.00
145 Deron Williams 100.00 200.00
146 Chris Paul 300.00 600.00
147 Raymond Felton 12.00 30.00
148 Martell Webster 12.00 30.00
149 Charlie Villanueva 12.00 30.00
150 Channing Frye 12.00 30.00
151 Ike Diogu 10.00 25.00
152 Andrew Bynum 60.00 150.00
153 Yaroslav Korolev 10.00 25.00
154 Sean May 10.00 25.00
155 Rashad McCants 10.00 25.00
156 Antoine Wright 12.00 30.00
157 Joey Graham 12.00 30.00
158 Danny Granger 15.00 40.00
159 Gerald Green 15.00 40.00
160 Hakim Warrick 12.00 30.00
161 Julius Hodge 10.00 25.00
162 Nate Robinson 15.00 40.00
163 Jarrett Jack 15.00 40.00
164 Francisco Garcia 10.00 25.00
165 Luther Head 10.00 25.00
166 Johan Petro 10.00 25.00
167 Jason Maxiell 12.00 30.00
168 Linas Kleiza 12.00 30.00
169 Wayne Simien 10.00 25.00
170 David Lee 15.00 40.00
171 Salim Stoudamire 12.00 30.00
172 Daniel Ewing 12.00 30.00
173 Brandon Bass 12.00 30.00
174 C.J. Miles 12.00 30.00
175 Ersan Ilyasova 12.00 30.00
176 Travis Diener 10.00 25.00
177 Chris Taft 10.00 25.00
178 Martynas Andriuskevicius 10.00 25.00
179 Louis Williams 40.00 100.00
180 Monta Ellis 50.00 100.00
181 Andray Blatche 15.00 40.00
182 Sarunas Jasikevicius 15.00 40.00
183 James Singleton 10.00 25.00

2005-06 Ultimate Collection Rookie Autographs Patches

PRINT RUN 25 SER.#'d SETS
RPAB Andrew Bogut 100.00 200.00
RPAN Andrew Bynum 75.00 150.00
RPAW Antoine Wright 15.00 40.00
RPBB Brandon Bass 15.00 40.00
RPBL Andray Blatche 20.00 50.00
RPCF Channing Frye 15.00 40.00
RPCJ C.J. Miles 15.00 40.00
RPCP Chris Paul 500.00 1,000.00
RPCT Chris Taft 12.00 30.00
RPCV Charlie Villanueva 15.00 40.00
RPDE Daniel Ewing 15.00 40.00
RPDG Danny Granger 20.00 50.00
RPDL David Lee 20.00 50.00
RPDW Deron Williams 125.00 250.00
RPEI Ersan Ilyasova 15.00 40.00
RPFG Francisco Garcia 12.00 30.00
RPGG Gerald Green 20.00 50.00
RPHW Hakim Warrick 15.00 40.00
RPID Ike Diogu 12.00 30.00
RPJG Joey Graham 15.00 40.00
RPJH Julius Hodge 12.00 30.00
RPJJ Jarrett Jack 20.00 50.00
RPJM Jason Maxiell 15.00 40.00
RPJP Johan Petro 12.00 30.00
RPLH Luther Head 12.00 30.00
RPLK Linas Kleiza 15.00 40.00
RPLW Louis Williams 50.00 120.00
RPMA Martynas Andriuskevicius 12.00 30.00
RPME Monta Ellis 100.00 200.00
RPMW Marvin Williams 20.00 50.00
RPNR Nate Robinson 15.00 40.00
RPRF Raymond Felton 15.00 40.00
RPRG Ryan Gomes 15.00 40.00
RPRM Rashad McCants 12.00 30.00
RPSJ Sarunas Jasikevicius 20.00 50.00
RPSM Sean May 12.00 30.00
RPSS Salim Stoudamire 15.00 40.00
RPTD Travis Diener 12.00 30.00
RPWE Martell Webster 15.00 40.00
RPWS Wayne Simien 12.00 30.00

2005-06 Ultimate Collection Signatures

USAB Andrew Bogut 6.00 15.00
USAN Andrew Bynum 4.00 10.00
USBD Baron Davis 5.00 12.00
USBK Bernard King 5.00 12.00
USBR Bill Russell SP 1,500.00 3,000.00
USCA Carmelo Anthony SP 40.00 100.00
USCF Channing Frye 4.00 10.00
USCP Chris Paul 200.00 500.00
USCV Charlie Villanueva 4.00 10.00
USDE Dennis Rodman 30.00 80.00
USDG Danny Granger 5.00 12.00
USDH Dwight Howard 10.00 25.00
USDR David Robinson 25.00 60.00
USDW Deron Williams 8.00 20.00
USEB Elton Brand 6.00 15.00
USEO Emeka Okafor 6.00 15.00
USGG Gerald Green 5.00 12.00
USHO Hakeem Olajuwon 25.00 60.00
USHW Hakim Warrick 4.00 10.00
USID Ike Diogu 3.00 8.00
USJE Julius Erving SP 50.00 120.00
USJK Jason Kidd 10.00 25.00
USKA Kareem Abdul-Jabbar SP 40.00 80.00
USKG Kevin Garnett 60.00 150.00
USLB Larry Bird SP 60.00 150.00
USLH Larry Hughes 5.00 12.00
USLJ LeBron James 2,000.00 4,000.00
USLR Luke Ridnour 5.00 12.00
USMA Magic Johnson SP 50.00 100.00
USMJ Michael Jordan SP 3,000.00 6,000.00
USMR Martell Webster 4.00 10.00
USMW Marvin Williams 5.00 12.00
USRF Raymond Felton 4.00 10.00
USRM Rashad McCants 3.00 8.00
USSM Sean May 3.00 8.00
USSN Steve Nash 75.00 200.00
USSP Scottie Pippen 100.00 250.00
USST Stephon Marbury 8.00 20.00
USTM Tracy McGrady 15.00 40.00
USTP Tayshaun Prince 5.00 12.00
USVC Vince Carter 60.00 150.00
USYM Yao Ming 60.00 150.00

2005-06 Ultimate Collection Signatures Dual

PRINT RUN 25 SER.#'d SETS
DSAR R.Artest/D.Rodman 75.00 200.00
DSAW C.Anthony/H.Warrick 30.00 80.00
DSBF A.Bogut/C.Frye 25.00 60.00
DSBJ L.Bird/M.Johnson 200.00 500.00
DSBR A.Bogut/M.Redd 25.00 60.00
DSCK V.Carter/J.Kidd 100.00 250.00
DSDD B.Davis/I.Diogu 20.00 50.00
DSFO R.Felton/E.Okafor 20.00 50.00
DSGM K.Garnett/R.McCants 75.00 200.00
DSGV J.Graham/C.Villanueva 20.00 50.00
DSHB R.Hamilton/C.Billups 75.00 200.00
DSHM D.Howard/T.McGrady 60.00 150.00
DSHO D.Howard/E.Okafor 40.00 80.00
DSJA Magic/Abdul-Jabbar 200.00 350.00
DSJG Al Jefferson/G.Green 20.00 50.00
DSJH L.James/D.Howard 1,500.00 3,000.00
DSJJ L.James/M.Jordan 20,000.00 40,000.00
DSJP M.Jordan/S.Pippen 3,000.00 6,000.00
DSLB L.Bird/B.Russell 2,000.00 4,000.00
DSMF S.Marbury/C.Frye 20.00 50.00
DSMH Y.Ming/D.Howard 75.00 200.00
DSMM S.May/R.McCants 20.00 50.00
DSMS T.McGrady/S.Swift 30.00 80.00
DSPS Chris Paul/J.R. Smith 75.00 200.00
DSWF M.Williams/R.Felton 20.00 50.00
DSWJ M.Williams/J.Johnson 20.00 50.00
DSWM D.Williams/C.J.Miles 20.00 50.00
DSWP D.Williams/C.Paul 100.00 250.00
DSWT M.Webster/S.Telfair 20.00 50.00

2006-07 Ultimate Collection

1-140 PRINT RUN 450 SER.#'d SETS
AU RC PRINT RUN 350 SER.#'d SETS
225-243 RC PRINT RUN 499 SER.#'d SETS
1 Josh Childress 1.00 2.50
2 Joe Johnson 1.50 4.00
3 Salim Stoudamire 1.00 2.50
4 Marvin Williams 1.00 2.50
5 Tony Allen 1.00 2.50
6 Al Jefferson 1.00 2.50
7 Paul Pierce 2.50 6.00
8 Wally Szczerbiak 1.25 3.00
9 Sebastian Telfair 1.00 2.50
10 Raymond Felton 1.00 2.50
11 Sean May 1.00 2.50
12 Emeka Okafor 1.25 3.00
13 Gerald Wallace 1.25 3.00

14 Luol Deng 1.25 3.00
15 Chris Duhon 1.00 2.50
16 Ben Gordon 1.25 3.00
17 Kirk Hinrich 1.25 3.00
18 Ben Wallace 2.00 5.00
19 Drew Gooden 1.25 3.00
20 Larry Hughes 1.25 3.00
21 Zydrunas Ilgauskas 1.25 3.00
22 LeBron James 20.00 50.00
23 Donyell Marshall 1.00 2.50
24 Devin Harris 1.00 2.50
25 Josh Howard 1.25 3.00
26 Dirk Nowitzki 4.00 10.00
27 Jerry Stackhouse 1.25 3.00
28 Jason Terry 1.25 3.00
29 Carmelo Anthony 2.50 6.00
30 Marcus Camby 1.25 3.00
31 Kenyon Martin 1.25 3.00
32 Andre Miller 1.25 3.00
33 J.R. Smith 1.50 4.00
34 Chauncey Billups 2.00 5.00
35 Richard Hamilton 1.50 4.00
36 Antonio McDyess 1.25 3.00
37 Tayshaun Prince 1.50 4.00
38 Rasheed Wallace 2.00 5.00
39 Baron Davis 1.50 4.00
40 Mike Dunleavy 1.00 2.50
41 Troy Murphy 1.00 2.50
42 Jason Richardson 1.50 4.00
43 Rafer Alston 1.25 3.00
44 Shane Battier 1.25 3.00
45 Tracy McGrady 2.50 6.00
46 Bonzi Wells 1.00 2.50
47 Yao Ming 4.00 10.00
48 Marquis Daniels 1.00 2.50
49 Al Harrington 1.25 3.00
50 Sarunas Jasikevicius 1.25 3.00
51 Jermaine O'Neal 1.50 4.00
52 Elton Brand 1.25 3.00
53 Sam Cassell 1.25 3.00
54 Chris Kaman 1.00 2.50
55 Shaun Livingston 1.25 3.00
56 Corey Maggette 1.25 3.00
57 Kobe Bryant 12.00 30.00
58 Andrew Bynum 1.25 3.00
59 Lamar Odom 1.25 3.00
60 Vladimir Radmanovic 1.00 2.50
61 Kwame Brown 1.00 2.50
62 Eddie Jones 1.50 4.00
63 Mike Miller 1.25 3.00
64 Hakim Warrick 1.00 2.50
65 Pau Gasol 2.50 6.00
66 Stromile Swift 1.00 2.50
67 Alonzo Mourning 2.50 6.00
68 Shaquille O'Neal 6.00 15.00
69 Gary Payton 2.00 5.00
70 Dwyane Wade 3.00 8.00
71 Jason Williams 2.00 5.00
72 Andrew Bogut 1.25 3.00
73 Michael Redd 1.25 3.00
74 Charlie Villanueva 1.00 2.50
75 Bobby Simmons 1.00 2.50
76 Ricky Davis 1.25 3.00
77 Kevin Garnett 4.00 10.00
78 Troy Hudson 1.00 2.50
79 Mike James 1.00 2.50
80 Rashad McCants 1.00 2.50
81 Vince Carter 3.00 8.00
82 Richard Jefferson 1.00 2.50
83 Jason Kidd 2.50 6.00
84 Nenad Krstic 1.00 2.50
85 Tyson Chandler 1.25 3.00
86 Bobby Jackson 1.00 2.50
87 Desmond Mason 1.00 2.50
88 Chris Paul 3.00 8.00
89 Peja Stojakovic 1.25 3.00
90 Steve Francis 1.50 4.00
91 Channing Frye 1.00 2.50
92 Stephon Marbury 2.00 5.00
93 Quentin Richardson 1.00 2.50
94 Nate Robinson 1.25 3.00
95 Carlos Arroyo 1.00 2.50
96 Grant Hill 2.50 6.00
97 Dwight Howard 2.00 5.00
98 Darko Milicic 1.00 2.50
99 Jameer Nelson 1.00 2.50
100 Samuel Dalembert 1.00 2.50
101 Andre Iguodala 1.50 4.00
102 Allen Iverson 4.00 10.00
103 Kyle Korver 1.25 3.00
104 Chris Webber 2.00 5.00
105 Leandro Barbosa 1.25 3.00
106 Boris Diaw 1.25 3.00
107 Shawn Marion 1.50 4.00
108 Steve Nash 3.00 8.00
109 Amare Stoudemire 1.50 4.00
110 Juan Dixon 1.00 2.50
111 Jarrett Jack 1.25 3.00
112 Jamaal Magloire 1.00 2.50
113 Zach Randolph 1.50 4.00
114 Martell Webster 1.25 3.00
115 Shareef Abdur-Rahim 1.50 4.00
116 Ron Artest 1.50 4.00
117 Brad Miller 1.25 3.00
118 Mike Bibby 1.50 4.00
119 Tim Duncan 4.00 10.00
120 Michael Finley 1.50 4.00
121 Manu Ginobili 3.00 8.00
122 Robert Horry 1.50 4.00
123 Tony Parker 2.50 6.00
124 Ray Allen 2.50 6.00
125 Rashard Lewis 1.25 3.00
126 Luke Ridnour 1.25 3.00
127 Chris Wilcox 1.00 2.50
128 Chris Bosh 2.00 5.00
129 T.J. Ford 1.00 2.50
130 Joey Graham 1.00 2.50
131 Morris Peterson 1.00 2.50
132 Carlos Boozer 1.25 3.00
133 Andrei Kirilenko 1.25 3.00
134 C.J. Miles 1.00 2.50
135 Mehmet Okur 1.00 2.50
136 Deron Williams 2.00 5.00
137 Gilbert Arenas 1.50 4.00
138 Caron Butler 1.25 3.00
139 Antonio Daniels 1.00 2.50
140 Antawn Jamison 1.25 3.00
141 David Robinson 6.00 15.00
142 Hakeem Olajuwon 8.00 20.00
143 Bill Russell 12.00 30.00
144 Walt Frazier 5.00 12.00
145 Nate Archibald 3.00 8.00
146 Spud Webb 3.00 8.00
147 Larry Bird 12.00 30.00
148 Michael Jordan 40.00 100.00
149 Magic Johnson 12.00 30.00
150 Julius Erving 8.00 20.00
151 Alvin Robertson 2.50 6.00
152 Bill Laimbeer 3.00 8.00
153 Bill Walton 5.00 12.00
154 Bob McAdoo 3.00 8.00
155 Clyde Drexler 5.00 12.00
156 Connie Hawkins 4.00 10.00
157 Dennis Rodman 8.00 20.00
158 Earl Monroe 4.00 10.00
159 Elvin Hayes 4.00 10.00
160 George Gervin 6.00 15.00
161 Kareem Abdul-Jabbar 12.00 30.00
162 Elgin Baylor 8.00 20.00
163 Rolando Blackman 3.00 8.00
164 Maurice Cheeks 3.00 8.00
165 Adrian Dantley 3.00 8.00
166 Joe Dumars 4.00 10.00
167 World B. Free 3.00 8.00
168 Robert Parish 5.00 12.00
169 Kevin McHale 5.00 12.00
170 Kevin Johnson 4.00 10.00
171 Bernard King 3.00 8.00
172 Moses Malone 6.00 15.00
173 Chris Mullin 4.00 10.00
174 Calvin Murphy 3.00 8.00
175 Oscar Robertson 10.00 25.00
176 Isiah Thomas 6.00 15.00
177 Reggie Theus 3.00 8.00
178 Rudy Tomjanovich 3.00 8.00
179 Wes Unseld 4.00 10.00
180 John Starks 3.00 8.00
181 Allan Ray AU RC 3.00 8.00
182 Andrea Bargnani AU RC 4.00 10.00
183 Bobby Jones AU RC 3.00 8.00
184 Brandon Roy AU RC 10.00 25.00
185 Cedric Simmons AU RC 3.00 8.00
186 Craig Smith AU RC 4.00 10.00
187 Damir Markota AU RC 3.00 8.00
188 Daniel Gibson AU RC 4.00 10.00
189 David Noel AU RC 3.00 8.00
190 Dee Brown AU RC 3.00 8.00
191 Hassan Adams AU RC 3.00 8.00
192 Hilton Armstrong AU RC 3.00 8.00
193 James Augustine AU RC 3.00 8.00
194 James White AU RC 3.00 8.00
195 Jordan Farmar AU RC 4.00 10.00
196 Jorge Garbajosa AU RC 3.00 8.00
197 Josh Boone AU RC 3.00 8.00
198 Kyle Lowry AU RC 15.00 40.00
199 LaMarcus Aldridge AU RC 12.00 30.00
200 Marcus Williams AU RC 3.00 8.00
201 Mardy Collins AU RC 3.00 8.00
202 Maurice Ager AU RC 3.00 8.00
203 Patrick O'Bryant AU RC 3.00 8.00
204 Paul Davis AU RC 3.00 8.00
205 Paul Millsap AU RC 6.00 15.00
206 P.J. Tucker AU RC 5.00 12.00
207 Pops Mensah-Bonsu AU RC 3.00 8.00
208 Quincy Douby AU RC 3.00 8.00
209 Rajon Rondo AU RC 15.00 40.00
210 Randy Foye AU RC 4.00 10.00
211 Renaldo Balkman AU RC 3.00 8.00
212 Rodney Carney AU RC 3.00 8.00
213 Ronnie Brewer AU RC 5.00 12.00
214 Rudy Gay AU RC 6.00 15.00
215 Yakhouba Diawara AU 3.00 8.00
216 Saer Sene AU RC 3.00 8.00
217 Sergio Rodriguez AU RC 4.00 10.00
218 Shannon Brown AU RC 3.00 8.00
219 Shawne Williams AU RC 3.00 8.00
220 Shelden Williams AU RC 3.00 8.00
221 Solomon Jones AU RC 3.00 8.00
222 Steve Novak AU RC 4.00 10.00
223 Thabo Sefolosha AU RC 4.00 10.00
224 Tyrus Thomas AU RC 4.00 10.00
225 Will Blalock AU RC 3.00 8.00
226 Robert Hite AU RC 3.00 8.00
227 Vassilis Spanoulis AU RC 3.00 8.00
228 Leon Powe AU RC 3.00 8.00
236 Adam Morrison RC 2.50 6.00
237 Alexander Johnson RC 2.00 5.00
238 J.J. Redick RC 6.00 15.00
239 Kelenna Azubuike RC 4.00 10.00
240 Chris Quinn RC 2.00 5.00
241 Tarence Kinsey RC 2.00 5.00
242 Vassilis Spanoulis RC 2.00 5.00
243 Yakhouba Diawara RC 2.00 5.00
244 Mike Hall RC 2.00 5.00
245 Randolph Morris RC 2.50 6.00
246 Walter Herrmann RC 2.00 5.00
247 Mickael Gelabale RC 2.00 5.00
248 Andre Brown RC 2.00 5.00
249 Justin Williams RC 2.00 5.00
250 Lynn Greer RC 2.00 5.00

2006-07 Ultimate Collection Achievements Signatures

STATED PRINT RUN ONE TO 51 SER.#'d SETS
UAAI Andre Iguodala/27 12.00 30.00
UAAJ Antawn Jamison/51 10.00 25.00
UABG Ben Gordon/39 6.00 15.00
UABJ Bobby Jackson/31 10.00 25.00
UABL Bill Laimbeer/14 100.00 200.00
UABM Bob McAdoo/14 100.00 200.00
UABO Chris Bosh/22 15.00 40.00
UABS Byron Scott/14 50.00 100.00
UACK Chris Kaman/23 10.00 25.00
UACM Corey Maggette/13 20.00 40.00
UACS Cedric Simmons/15 10.00 25.00
UADM Desmond Mason/17 10.00 25.00
UADO Dennis Rodman/34 50.00 125.00
UADU Chris Duhon/38 10.00 25.00
UAGG George Gervin/33 30.00 60.00
UAHO Hakeem Olajuwon/18 40.00 70.00
UAHW Hakim Warrick/19 12.00 30.00
UAJJ Jarrett Jack/22 10.00 25.00
UAJS J.R. Smith/33 10.00 25.00
UALE Leandro Barbosa/28 10.00 25.00
UAMA Magic Johnson/13 80.00 160.00
UAMO Cuttino Mobley/41 10.00 25.00
UAPS Peja Stojakovic/41 10.00 25.00
UARP Robert Parish/21 20.00 40.00
UASE Sean Elliott/12 75.00 150.00
UASK Steve Kerr/15 30.00 60.00
UASN Steve Nash/22 100.00 175.00
UASW Spud Webb/12 10.00 25.00
UATE Sebastian Telfair/13 10.00 25.00

2006-07 Ultimate Collection Autographs Jerseys

PRINT RUN 75 SER.#'d SETS
AUAH Al Harrington 6.00 15.00
AUAI Andre Iguodala 8.00 20.00
AUAJ Al Jefferson 6.00 15.00
AUAM Andre Miller 6.00 15.00
AUBD Baron Davis 8.00 20.00
AUBG Ben Gordon 8.00 20.00
AUBJ Bobby Jackson 6.00 15.00
AUBM Brad Miller 6.00 15.00
AUBO Chris Bosh 12.00 30.00
AUCA Carmelo Anthony 15.00 40.00
AUCB Chauncey Billups 10.00 25.00
AUCD Chris Duhon 6.00 15.00
AUCF Channing Frye 6.00 15.00
AUCM Corey Maggette 6.00 15.00
AUCP Chris Paul 400.00 800.00
AUDM Donyell Marshall 6.00 15.00
AUDR Clyde Drexler 30.00 60.00
AUDW Deron Williams 20.00 50.00
AUEO Emeka Okafor 6.00 15.00
AUHO Hakeem Olajuwon 30.00 80.00
AUID Ike Diogu 6.00 15.00
AUJA Antawn Jamison 6.00 15.00
AUJC Josh Childress 6.00 15.00
AUJG Joey Graham 6.00 15.00
AUJJ Jarrett Jack 6.00 15.00
AUJM Jamaal Magloire 6.00 15.00
AUJO Jermaine O'Neal 10.00 25.00
AUJS J.R. Smith 6.00 15.00
AUKB Kobe Bryant 4,000.00 8,000.00
AUKH Kirk Hinrich 6.00 15.00
AUKK Kyle Korver 8.00 20.00
AULB Larry Bird 50.00 120.00
AULH Larry Hughes 8.00 20.00
AULJ LeBron James 5,000.00 10,000.00
AULR Luke Ridnour 6.00 15.00
AUMA Magic Johnson 60.00 120.00
AUMB Mike Bibby 6.00 15.00
AUMD Marquis Daniels 6.00 15.00
AUMJ Michael Jordan 800.00 1,200.00
AUMO Alonzo Mourning 25.00 60.00
AUMR Michael Ray Richardson 8.00 20.00
AUMW Marvin Williams 6.00 15.00
AUPP Paul Pierce 12.00 30.00
AUQR Quentin Richardson 6.00 15.00
AURF Raymond Felton 8.00 20.00
AURJ Richard Jefferson 6.00 15.00
AURM Rashad McCants 6.00 15.00
AURO David Robinson 30.00 80.00
AUSK Steve Kerr 10.00 25.00
AUSL Shaun Livingston 6.00 15.00
AUSS Stromile Swift 6.00 15.00
AUST Sebastian Telfair 6.00 15.00
AUTC Tyson Chandler 8.00 20.00
AUTM Tracy McGrady 15.00 40.00
AUTP Tony Parker 20.00 50.00
AUVC Vince Carter 20.00 50.00
AUWF Walt Frazier 15.00 40.00
AUYM Yao Ming 40.00 100.00

2006-07 Ultimate Collection Autographs Patches

*PATCHES: .75X TO 2X BASE HI
PRINT RUN 15 SER.#'d SETS
AULB Larry Bird 100.00 250.00
AULJ LeBron James 10,000.00 15,000.00
AUMA Magic Johnson 100.00 200.00
AUMJ Michael Jordan 3,000.00 4,000.00

2006-07 Ultimate Collection Combos Jerseys Dual

PRINT RUN 75 SER.#'d SETS
*PATCHES: .75X TO 2X BASE HI
PATCH PRINT RUN 25 SER.#'d SETS
AB S.Brown/M.Ager 4.00 10.00
AN J.Nelson/C.Arroyo 4.00 10.00
AR L.Aldridge/B.Roy 8.00 20.00
BB L.Barbosa/R.Bell 4.00 10.00
BD M.Bibby/Q.Douby 4.00 10.00
BV C.Villanueva/A.Bogut 5.00 12.00
CB R.Balkman/M.Collins 4.00 10.00
CS T.Chandler/C.Simmons 4.00 10.00
CW S.Williams/R.Carney 4.00 10.00
DO I.Diogu/J.O'Neal 4.00 10.00
DR B.Davis/J.Richardson 4.00 10.00
GH B.Gordon/K.Hinrich 4.00 10.00
GW P.Gasol/H.Warrick 4.00 10.00
HB C.Billups/R.Hamilton 5.00 12.00
HG D.Gooden/L.Hughes 4.00 10.00
IK Z.Ilgauskas/C.Kaman 4.00 10.00
JC R.Carney/B.Jones 4.00 10.00
JJ M.Jordan/L.James 50.00 100.00
JL A.Johnson/K.Lowry 4.00 10.00
JR A.Jefferson/A.Ray 4.00 10.00
JW S.Jones/M.Williams 4.00 10.00
MJ D.Mason/B.Jackson 4.00 10.00
ML S.Livingston/C.Maggette 4.00 10.00
MO S.O'Neal/A.Mourning 20.00 50.00
MS R.McCants/C.Smith 4.00 10.00
OH E.Okafor/D.Howard 6.00 15.00
OS P.O'Bryant/S.Sene 4.00 10.00
PA P.Pierce/C.Anthony 8.00 20.00
PW G.Payton/J.Williams 8.00 20.00
RM J.Magloire/Z.Randolph 4.00 10.00
RN M.Redd/D.Noel 4.00 10.00
SN P.Stojakovic/S.Novak 5.00 12.00
TG P.Tucker/J.Garbajosa 4.00 10.00
TH D.Harris/J.Terry 4.00 10.00
TR A.Ray/S.Telfair 4.00 10.00
TS T.Thomas/T.Sefolosha 5.00 12.00
WB M.Williams/J.Boone 4.00 10.00
WI C.Webber/A.Iverson 10.00 25.00
WP R.Wallace/T.Prince 4.00 10.00
WR J.Redick/S.Williams 4.00 10.00

2006-07 Ultimate Collection Combos Jerseys Triple

PRINT RUN 25 SER.#'d SETS
ADB Brown/Ager/Davis 8.00 20.00
AKS Allen/Stojakovic/Korver 12.00 30.00
BBB Brand/Boozer/Battier 8.00 20.00
BBS Bosh/Boozer/Stoudemire 12.00 30.00
DPG Duncan/Ginobili/Parker 25.00 50.00
FMR Marbury/Francis/Robinson 12.00 30.00
FRF Richardson/Frye/Francis 8.00 20.00
GDF Garnett/Foye/Davis 25.00 50.00
LRS Lewis/Ridnour/Sene 8.00 20.00
NKB Kirilenko/Bargnani/Nowitzki 15.00 30.00
WBB Williams/Brewer/Brown 8.00 20.00

2006-07 Ultimate Collection Debut Jerseys

PRINT RUN 50 SER.#'d SETS
*PATCHES: .75X TO 2X BASE HI
PATCH PRINT RUN 25 SER.#'d SETS
UDAB Andrea Bargnani 2.50 6.00
UDAR Allan Ray 2.00 5.00
UDBA Renaldo Balkman 2.50 6.00
UDBJ Bobby Jones 2.00 5.00
UDBR Brandon Roy 6.00 15.00
UDCS Cedric Simmons 2.00 5.00
UDDB Dee Brown 2.00 5.00
UDDG Daniel Gibson 2.50 6.00
UDDN David Noel 2.00 5.00
UDHA Hilton Armstrong 2.00 5.00
UDJB Josh Boone 2.00 5.00
UDJF Jordan Farmar 2.50 6.00
UDJG Jorge Garbajosa 2.50 6.00
UDJR J.J. Redick 6.00 15.00
UDJW James White 2.00 5.00
UDKL Kyle Lowry 10.00 25.00
UDLA LaMarcus Aldridge 8.00 20.00
UDMA Maurice Ager 2.00 5.00
UDMC Mardy Collins 2.00 5.00
UDMW Marcus Williams 2.00 5.00
UDPD Paul Davis 2.00 5.00
UDPO Patrick O'Bryant 2.00 5.00
UDPT P.J. Tucker 3.00 8.00
UDQD Quincy Douby 2.00 5.00
UDRB Ronnie Brewer 3.00 8.00
UDRC Rodney Carney 2.00 5.00
UDRF Randy Foye 2.50 6.00
UDRG Rudy Gay 4.00 10.00
UDRR Rajon Rondo 10.00 25.00
UDSB Shannon Brown 2.00 5.00
UDSJ Solomon Jones 2.00 5.00
UDSM Craig Smith 2.50 6.00
UDSN Steve Novak 2.00 5.00
UDSS Saer Sene 2.00 5.00
UDSW Shelden Williams 2.00 5.00
UDTS Thabo Sefolosha 2.50 6.00
UDTT Tyrus Thomas 2.50 6.00
UDWB Will Blalock 2.00 5.00
UDWI Shawne Williams 2.00 5.00

2006-07 Ultimate Collection Debut Jerseys Autographs

PRINT RUN 35 SER.#'d SETS
UDAB Andrea Bargnani 12.00 30.00
UDAR Allan Ray 5.00 12.00
UDBA Renaldo Balkman 6.00 15.00
UDBJ Bobby Jones 5.00 12.00
UDBR Brandon Roy 15.00 40.00
UDCS Cedric Simmons 5.00 12.00
UDDB Dee Brown 5.00 12.00
UDDN David Noel 5.00 12.00
UDHA Hilton Armstrong 5.00 12.00
UDJB Josh Boone 5.00 12.00
UDJF Jordan Farmar 6.00 15.00
UDJG Jorge Garbajosa 6.00 15.00
UDJW James White 5.00 12.00
UDKL Kyle Lowry 25.00 60.00
UDLA LaMarcus Aldridge 20.00 50.00
UDMA Maurice Ager 5.00 12.00
UDMC Mardy Collins 5.00 12.00
UDMW Marcus Williams 5.00 12.00
UDPO Patrick O'Bryant 5.00 12.00
UDPT P.J. Tucker 8.00 20.00
UDQD Quincy Douby 5.00 12.00
UDRB Ronnie Brewer 8.00 20.00
UDRF Randy Foye 6.00 15.00
UDRG Rudy Gay 10.00 25.00
UDRR Rajon Rondo 25.00 60.00
UDSB Shannon Brown 5.00 12.00
UDSJ Solomon Jones 5.00 12.00
UDSM Craig Smith 6.00 15.00
UDSN Steve Novak 6.00 15.00
UDSS Saer Sene 5.00 12.00
UDSW Shelden Williams 5.00 12.00
UDTS Thabo Sefolosha 6.00 15.00
UDTT Tyrus Thomas 6.00 15.00
UDWB Will Blalock 5.00 12.00
UDWI Shawne Williams 5.00 12.00

2006-07 Ultimate Collection Jerseys Dual

PRINT RUN 25 SER.#'d SETS
*PATCH DUAL: 1X TO 2.5X BASE HI
PATCH DUAL PRINT RUN 25 SER.#'d SETS
UJAB Andrea Bargnani 4.00 10.00
UJAI Andre Iguodala 5.00 12.00
UJAS Amare Stoudemire 5.00 12.00
UJBC Carlos Boozer 4.00 10.00
UJBD Baron Davis 5.00 12.00
UJBJ Bobby Jones 3.00 8.00
UJBO Chris Bosh 6.00 15.00
UJBW Ben Wallace 6.00 15.00
UJCA Carmelo Anthony 8.00 20.00
UJCB Chauncey Billups 6.00 15.00
UJCP Chris Paul 10.00 25.00
UJCW Chris Webber 6.00 15.00
UJDB Dee Brown 3.00 8.00
UJDG Drew Gooden 4.00 10.00
UJDH Dwight Howard 6.00 15.00
UJDN Dirk Nowitzki 12.00 30.00
UJDW Deron Williams 4.00 10.00
UJEB Elton Brand 4.00 10.00
UJEO Emeka Okafor 4.00 10.00
UJFE Raymond Felton 3.00 8.00
UJHA Hilton Armstrong 3.00 8.00
UJJF Jordan Farmar 4.00 10.00
UJJK Jason Kidd 8.00 20.00
UJJO Jermaine O'Neal 5.00 12.00
UJJR J.J. Redick 10.00 25.00
UJKB Kobe Bryant 600.00 1,200.00
UJKG Kevin Garnett 12.00 30.00
UJKH Kirk Hinrich 4.00 10.00
UJKL Kyle Lowry 15.00 40.00
UJLA LaMarcus Aldridge 12.00 30.00
UJLD Luol Deng 4.00 10.00
UJLJ LeBron James 30.00 80.00
UJLO Lamar Odom 4.00 10.00
UJMA Shawn Marion 5.00 12.00
UJMJ Michael Jordan 100.00 200.00
UJMR Michael Redd 4.00 10.00
UJMW Marvin Williams 3.00 8.00
UJNA Steve Nash 10.00 25.00
UJPG Pau Gasol 8.00 20.00
UJPO Patrick O'Bryant 3.00 8.00
UJPP Paul Pierce 8.00 20.00
UJRB Ronnie Brewer 5.00 12.00
UJRC Rodney Carney 3.00 8.00
UJRF Randy Foye 4.00 10.00
UJRG Rudy Gay 6.00 15.00
UJRH Richard Hamilton 5.00 12.00
UJRO Brandon Roy 10.00 25.00
UJSJ Solomon Jones 3.00 8.00
UJSM Stephon Marbury 6.00 15.00
UJSN Steve Novak 4.00 10.00
UJSO Shaquille O'Neal 20.00 50.00
UJSW Shelden Williams 3.00 8.00
UJTD Tim Duncan 12.00 30.00
UJTM Tracy McGrady 8.00 20.00
UJTP Tony Parker 8.00 20.00
UJTT Tyrus Thomas 4.00 10.00
UJVC Vince Carter 8.00 20.00
UJWI Shawne Williams 3.00 8.00
UJYM Yao Ming 12.00 30.00
UJZI Zydrunas Ilgauskas 4.00 10.00

2006-07 Ultimate Collection Numbers

STATED PRINT RUN ONE TO 40 SER.#'d SETS
UNBL Bill Laimbeer/40 10.00 25.00
UNCA Carmelo Anthony/15 50.00 120.00
UNCD Clyde Drexler/22 50.00 120.00
UNDM Desmond Mason/24 10.00 25.00
UNGO Sebastian Telfair/30 10.00 25.00
UNMW Marvin Williams/24 12.00 30.00
UNPP Paul Pierce/34 40.00 100.00
UNPS Peja Stojakovic/16 15.00 40.00
UNRJ Richard Jefferson/24 10.00 25.00
UNST John Stockton/12 100.00 250.00
UNVC Vince Carter/15 60.00 120.00
UNWI Maurice Williams/25 10.00 25.00
UNYM Yao Ming/11 50.00 100.00

2006-07 Ultimate Collection Premium Swatches

PRINT RUN 75 SER.#'d SETS
PRAB Andrea Bargnani 3.00 8.00
PRAI Allen Iverson 15.00 40.00
PRAJ Antawn Jamison 5.00 12.00
PRBA Renaldo Balkman 3.00 8.00
PRBD Baron Davis 6.00 15.00
PRBG Ben Gordon 5.00 12.00
PRBJ Bobby Jones 2.50 6.00
PRBR Brandon Roy 8.00 20.00
PRCA Carlos Arroyo 4.00 10.00
PRCP Chris Paul 12.00 30.00
PRCS Cedric Simmons 2.50 6.00
PRDB Dee Brown 2.50 6.00
PRDG Drew Gooden 5.00 12.00
PRDH Dwight Howard 8.00 20.00
PRDN Dirk Nowitzki 15.00 40.00
PRDW Deron Williams 5.00 12.00
PREB Elton Brand 5.00 12.00
PRHA Hilton Armstrong 2.50 6.00
PRJB Josh Boone 2.50 6.00
PRJF Jordan Farmar 3.00 8.00
PRJK Jason Kidd 10.00 25.00
PRJN Jameer Nelson 4.00 10.00
PRKB Kobe Bryant 400.00 800.00
PRKG Kevin Garnett 15.00 40.00
PRKL Kyle Lowry 12.00 30.00
PRLA LaMarcus Aldridge 10.00 25.00
PRLB Leandro Barbosa 5.00 12.00
PRLJ LeBron James 30.00 80.00
PRMA Maurice Ager 2.50 6.00
PRMB Mike Bibby 6.00 15.00
PRMC Mardy Collins 2.50 6.00
PRMG Manu Ginobili 12.00 30.00
PRMR Michael Redd 5.00 12.00
PRMW Marcus Williams 2.50 6.00
PRNA Steve Nash 12.00 30.00
PRPD Paul Davis 2.50 6.00
PRPG Pau Gasol 10.00 25.00
PRPO Patrick O'Bryant 2.50 6.00
PRPP Paul Pierce 10.00 25.00
PRPT P.J. Tucker 4.00 10.00
PRQD Quincy Douby 2.50 6.00
PRRA Rafer Alston 5.00 12.00
PRRB Ronnie Brewer 4.00 10.00
PRRF Randy Foye 3.00 8.00
PRRG Rudy Gay 5.00 12.00
PRRR Rajon Rondo 10.00 25.00
PRSB Shannon Brown 2.50 6.00
PRSJ Solomon Jones 2.50 6.00
PRSM Craig Smith 3.00 8.00
PRSN Steve Novak 3.00 8.00
PRSO Shaquille O'Neal 25.00 60.00
PRSS Saer Sene 2.50 6.00
PRST Stephon Marbury 8.00 20.00
PRSW Shelden Williams 2.50 6.00
PRTM Tracy McGrady 10.00 25.00
PRTP Tayshaun Prince 6.00 15.00
PRTT Tyrus Thomas 3.00 8.00
PRVC Vince Carter 12.00 30.00
PRWI Shawne Williams 2.50 6.00
PRZI Zydrunas Ilgauskas 5.00 12.00

2006-07 Ultimate Collection Premium Swatches Patch

PRINT RUN 50 SER.#'d SETS
PRAB Andrea Bargnani 12.00 30.00
PRAI Allen Iverson 50.00 120.00
PRAJ Antawn Jamison 12.00 30.00
PRBA Renaldo Balkman 12.00 30.00
PRBD Baron Davis 15.00 40.00
PRBG Ben Gordon 12.00 30.00
PRBJ Bobby Jones 10.00 25.00
PRBR Brandon Roy 12.00 30.00
PRCA Carlos Arroyo 15.00 40.00
PRCP Chris Paul 30.00 80.00
PRCS Cedric Simmons 10.00 25.00
PRDB Dee Brown 10.00 25.00
PRDG Drew Gooden 12.00 30.00
PRDH Dwight Howard 25.00 60.00
PRDN Dirk Nowitzki 75.00 200.00
PRDW Deron Williams 12.00 30.00
PREB Elton Brand 12.00 30.00
PRHA Hilton Armstrong 10.00 25.00
PRJB Josh Boone 10.00 25.00
PRJF Jordan Farmar 12.00 30.00
PRJK Jason Kidd 35.00 75.00
PRJN Jameer Nelson 10.00 25.00
PRKB Kobe Bryant 500.00 1,000.00
PRKG Kevin Garnett 60.00 150.00
PRKL Kyle Lowry 50.00 120.00
PRLA LaMarcus Aldridge 15.00 40.00
PRLB Leandro Barbosa 12.00 30.00
PRLJ LeBron James 200.00 500.00
PRMA Maurice Ager 10.00 25.00
PRMB Mike Bibby 15.00 40.00
PRMC Mardy Collins 10.00 25.00
PRMG Manu Ginobili 30.00 80.00
PRMR Michael Redd 12.00 30.00
PRMW Marcus Williams 10.00 25.00
PRPD Paul Davis 10.00 25.00
PRPG Pau Gasol 25.00 60.00
PRPO Patrick O'Bryant 10.00 25.00
PRPT P.J. Tucker 15.00 40.00
PRQD Quincy Douby 10.00 25.00
PRRA Rafer Alston 12.00 30.00
PRRB Ronnie Brewer 15.00 40.00
PRRF Randy Foye 12.00 30.00
PRRG Rudy Gay 20.00 50.00
PRRR Rajon Rondo 40.00 100.00
PRSB Shannon Brown 10.00 25.00
PRSJ Solomon Jones 10.00 25.00
PRSM Craig Smith 12.00 30.00
PRSN Steve Novak 12.00 30.00
PRSO Shaquille O'Neal 40.00 100.00
PRSS Saer Sene 10.00 25.00
PRST Stephon Marbury 12.00 30.00
PRSW Shelden Williams 10.00 25.00
PRTM Tracy McGrady 25.00 60.00
PRTP Tayshaun Prince 15.00 40.00
PRTT Tyrus Thomas 12.00 30.00
PRVC Vince Carter 50.00 120.00
PRWI Shawne Williams 10.00 25.00
PRZI Zydrunas Ilgauskas 12.00 30.00

2006-07 Ultimate Collection Rookie Patches Autographs

PRINT RUN 25 SER.#'d SETS
AB Andrea Bargnani 12.00 30.00
AR Allan Ray 10.00 25.00
BJ Bobby Jones 10.00 25.00
BR Brandon Roy 75.00 200.00
CS Cedric Simmons 10.00 25.00
DB Dee Brown 10.00 25.00
DN David Noel 10.00 25.00
HA Hilton Armstrong 10.00 25.00
JB Josh Boone 10.00 25.00
JF Jordan Farmar 12.00 30.00
JG Jorge Garbajosa 12.00 30.00
JW James White 10.00 25.00
KL Kyle Lowry 50.00 120.00
LA LaMarcus Aldridge 100.00 250.00
MA Maurice Ager 10.00 25.00
MC Mardy Collins 10.00 25.00
MW Marcus Williams 10.00 25.00
PT P.J. Tucker 15.00 40.00
QD Quincy Douby 10.00 25.00
RB Renaldo Balkman 12.00 30.00
RC Rodney Carney 10.00 25.00
RF Randy Foye 12.00 30.00
RG Rudy Gay 75.00 150.00
RO Ronnie Brewer 15.00 40.00
RR Rajon Rondo 125.00 300.00
SB Shannon Brown 10.00 25.00
SJ Solomon Jones 10.00 25.00
SM Craig Smith 12.00 30.00
SN Steve Novak 12.00 30.00
SW Shawne Williams 10.00 25.00
TS Thabo Sefolosha 12.00 30.00
TT Tyrus Thomas 12.00 30.00
WB Will Blalock 10.00 25.00
WI Shelden Williams 10.00 25.00

2006-07 Ultimate Collection Signatures

APPROXIMATE ODDS ONE PER BOX
USAB Andrea Bargnani 5.00 12.00
USBL Bill Laimbeer 5.00 12.00
USBO Chris Bosh 5.00 12.00
USBR Brandon Roy 5.00 12.00
USCA Carmelo Anthony 15.00 40.00
USCP Chris Paul 125.00 300.00
USDW Deron Williams 5.00 12.00
USHO Hakeem Olajuwon 15.00 40.00
USHW Hakim Warrick 5.00 12.00
USJE Julius Erving 50.00 120.00
USJF Jordan Farmar 5.00 12.00
USJK Jason Kidd 12.00 30.00
USJO Jermaine O'Neal 5.00 12.00
USJS J.R. Smith 5.00 12.00
USKB Kobe Bryant 500.00 1,000.00
USLJ LeBron James 3,000.00 6,000.00
USMB Mike Bibby 5.00 12.00
USMG Magic Johnson 40.00 100.00
USMJ Michael Jordan 2,000.00 4,000.00
USNA Steve Nash 30.00 80.00
USRG Rudy Gay 5.00 12.00
USRO Dennis Rodman 30.00 80.00
USRU Bill Russell 1,000.00 2,000.00
USSW Shelden Williams 5.00 12.00

2007-08 Ultimate Collection

1-100 PRINT RUN 199 SER.#'d SETS
145-150 RC PRINT RUN 50 SER.#'d SETS
1 LaMarcus Aldridge 1.25 3.00
2 Ray Allen 2.00 5.00
3 Carmelo Anthony 2.00 5.00
4 Gilbert Arenas 1.25 3.00
5 Ron Artest 1.25 3.00
6 Andrea Bargnani .75 2.00
7 Mike Bibby 1.25 3.00
8 Chauncey Billups 1.50 4.00
9 Andrew Bogut 1.00 2.50
10 Carlos Boozer 1.00 2.50
11 Chris Bosh 1.50 4.00
12 Elton Brand 1.00 2.50
13 Kobe Bryant 10.00 25.00
14 Caron Butler 1.00 2.50
15 Jorge Garbajosa 1.00 2.50
16 Marcus Camby 1.00 2.50
17 Rodney Carney .75 2.00
18 Vince Carter 2.50 6.00
19 Tyson Chandler 1.25 3.00
20 Damien Wilkins .75 2.00
21 Eddy Curry .75 2.00
22 Baron Davis 1.00 2.50
23 Ricky Davis 1.00 2.50
24 Luol Deng 1.00 2.50
25 Tim Duncan 3.00 8.00
26 Shawne Williams .75 2.00
27 Monta Ellis 1.00 2.50
28 Jordan Farmar .75 2.00
29 T.J. Ford .75 2.00
30 Randy Foye 1.00 2.50
31 Channing Frye .75 2.00
32 Al Jefferson .75 2.00
33 Pau Gasol 2.00 5.00
34 Rudy Gay 1.00 2.50
35 Manu Ginobili 2.50 6.00
36 Ben Gordon 1.00 2.50
37 Richard Hamilton 1.50 4.00
38 Luther Head .75 2.00
39 Grant Hill 2.00 5.00
40 Kirk Hinrich 1.25 3.00
41 Dwight Howard 1.50 4.00
42 Josh Howard 1.00 2.50
43 Larry Hughes 1.00 2.50
44 Andre Iguodala 1.25 3.00
45 Daniel Gibson .75 2.00
46 Allen Iverson 3.00 8.00
47 Morris Peterson .75 2.00
48 Stephen Jackson 1.00 2.50
49 LeBron James 20.00 50.00
50 Antawn Jamison 1.00 2.50
51 Kevin Garnett 3.00 8.00
52 Richard Jefferson 1.00 2.50
53 Joe Johnson 1.00 2.50
54 Jason Kidd 2.00 5.00
55 Andrei Kirilenko 1.00 2.50
56 David Lee .75 2.00
57 Rashard Lewis 1.00 2.50
58 Corey Maggette 1.00 2.50
59 Stephon Marbury 1.50 4.00
60 Shawn Marion 1.25 3.00
61 Kevin Martin 1.00 2.50
62 Tracy McGrady 2.00 5.00
63 Al Harrington 1.00 2.50
64 Andre Miller 1.00 2.50
65 Francisco Garcia .75 2.00
66 Yao Ming 3.00 8.00
67 Cuttino Mobley 1.00 2.50
68 Alonzo Mourning 2.00 5.00
69 Steve Nash 2.50 6.00
70 Dirk Nowitzki 3.00 8.00
71 Jermaine O`Neal 1.25 3.00
72 Shaquille O`Neal 5.00 12.00
73 Lamar Odom 1.00 2.50
74 Adam Morrison .75 2.00
75 Mehmet Okur .75 2.00
76 Tony Parker 2.00 5.00
77 Chris Paul 2.50 6.00
78 Johan Petro .75 2.00
79 Paul Pierce 2.00 5.00
80 Tayshaun Prince 1.25 3.00
81 Zach Randolph 1.25 3.00
82 Michael Redd 1.00 2.50
83 Jason Richardson 1.25 3.00
84 Brandon Roy 1.50 4.00
85 Josh Smith .75 2.00
86 Amare Stoudemire 1.25 3.00
87 Jason Terry 1.00 2.50
88 Jamaal Tinsley .75 2.00
89 Hedo Turkoglu 1.00 2.50
90 Desmond Mason .75 2.00
91 Dwyane Wade 2.50 6.00
92 Ben Wallace 1.50 4.00
93 Gerald Wallace 1.00 2.50
94 Rasheed Wallace 1.50 4.00
95 Mike Miller 1.00 2.50
96 David West 1.00 2.50
97 Delonte West .75 2.00
98 Deron Williams 1.00 2.50
99 Marvin Williams .75 2.00
100 Raymond Felton 1.00 2.50
101 Arron Afflalo AU/99 RC 5.00 12.00
102 Morris Almond AU/99 RC 4.00 10.00
103 Marco Belinelli AU/99 RC 5.00 12.00
104 Corey Brewer AU/150 RC 5.00 12.00
105 Aaron Brooks AU/99 RC 5.00 12.00
106 Julian Wright AU/150 RC 4.00 10.00
107 Wilson Chandler AU/99 RC 5.00 12.00
108 Mike Conley Jr. AU/150 RC 15.00 40.00
109 Daequan Cook AU/99 RC 5.00 12.00
110 Javaris Crittenton AU/150 RC 4.00 10.00
111 JamesOn Curry AU/99 RC 4.00 10.00
112 Jermareo Davidson AU/99 RC 4.00 10.00
113 Glen Davis AU/150 RC 5.00 12.00
114 Jared Dudley AU/99 RC 5.00 12.00
115 Kevin Durant AU/150 RC 2,000.00 4,000.00
116 Nick Fazekas AU/99 RC 4.00 10.00
117 Aaron Gray AU/99 RC 4.00 10.00
118 Jeff Green AU/150 RC 5.00 12.00
119 Taurean Green AU/99 RC 4.00 10.00
120 Adam Haluska AU/99 RC 4.00 10.00
121 Spencer Hawes AU/99 RC 4.00 10.00
122 Herbert Hill AU/99 RC 4.00 10.00
123 Al Horford AU/150 RC 15.00 40.00
124 Louis Amundson AU/99 RC 4.00 10.00
125 Carl Landry AU/99 RC 4.00 10.00
126 Jamario Moon AU/150 RC 5.00 12.00
127 Acie Law AU/150 RC 4.00 10.00
128 Dominic McGuire AU/99 RC 4.00 10.00
129 Josh McRoberts AU/99 RC 4.00 10.00
130 Oleksiy Pecherov AU/99 RC 6.00 15.00
131 Coby Karl AU/99 RC 4.00 10.00
132 Joakim Noah AU/150 RC 6.00 15.00
133 Gabe Pruitt AU/99 RC 4.00 10.00

134 Chris Richard AU/99 RC 4.00 10.00
135 Juan Navarro AU/150 RC 5.00 12.00
136 Ramon Sessions AU/99 RC 5.00 12.00
137 Jason Smith AU/99 RC 4.00 10.00
138 D.J. Strawberry AU/99 RC 4.00 10.00
139 Rodney Stuckey AU/150 RC 4.00 10.00
140 Luis Scola AU/150 RC 6.00 15.00
141 Al Thornton AU/150 RC 4.00 10.00
142 Alando Tucker AU/99 RC 4.00 10.00
143 Sean Williams AU/99 RC 4.00 10.00
144 Cheikh Samb AU/99 RC 4.00 10.00
145 Yi Jianlian RC 5.00 12.00
146 Thaddeus Young RC 4.00 10.00
147 Nick Young RC 4.00 10.00
148 Kyrylo Fesenko RC 2.50 6.00
149 Greg Oden RC 4.00 10.00
150 Brandan Wright RC 3.00 8.00

2007-08 Ultimate Collection Foil

*1-100 FOIL: 2.5X TO 6X BASE HI
PRINT RUN 10 SER.#'d SETS

2007-08 Ultimate Collection Rookies Gold

*GOLD: 4X TO 1X BASE HI
PRINT RUN 50 SER.#'d SETS
115 Kevin Durant AU 3,000.00 6,000.00

2007-08 Ultimate Collection Rookies Signature Patches

PRINT RUN 25 SER.#'d SETS
AL Acie Law 12.00 30.00
AT Al Thornton 12.00 30.00
CB Corey Brewer 15.00 40.00
DC Daequan Cook 15.00 40.00
DS D.J. Strawberry 12.00 30.00
GD Glen Davis 15.00 40.00
HO Al Horford 20.00 50.00
JC Javaris Crittenton 12.00 30.00
JG Jeff Green 15.00 40.00
JN Joakim Noah 20.00 50.00
JS Jason Smith 12.00 30.00
JW Julian Wright 12.00 30.00
KD Kevin Durant 2,000.00 4,000.00
MC Mike Conley Jr. 50.00 120.00
RS Rodney Stuckey 12.00 30.00
SW Sean Williams 12.00 30.00

2007-08 Ultimate Collection Archetypal Autographs

PRINT RUN 25 SER.#'d SETS
AD Adrian Dantley 10.00 25.00
BL Bill Laimbeer 15.00 30.00
DH Dwight Howard 35.00 75.00
HO Hakeem Olajuwon 20.00 40.00
JW Jerry West 30.00 60.00
LB Larry Bird 75.00 150.00
RB Rick Barry 10.00 25.00
RP Robert Parish 10.00 25.00
TC Tom Chambers 8.00 20.00
TY Tyson Chandler 8.00 20.00
WF Walt Frazier 15.00 30.00
XM Xavier McDaniel 8.00 20.00

2007-08 Ultimate Collection Commitment

PRINT RUN 25 SER.#'d SETS
CA Carmelo Anthony 50.00 120.00
CD Clyde Drexler 25.00 60.00
CH Chris Mullin 25.00 60.00
DH Dwight Howard 30.00 60.00
DR David Robinson 40.00 80.00
DW Deron Williams 20.00 40.00
JE Julius Erving 60.00 120.00
JS John Stockton 50.00 100.00
KB Kobe Bryant 1,500.00 3,000.00
LJ LeBron James 6,000.00 12,000.00
MJ Michael Jordan 1,000.00 2,000.00
SN Steve Nash 30.00 60.00
VC Vince Carter 25.00 50.00
YM Yao Ming 25.00 50.00

2007-08 Ultimate Collection Leadership

PRINT RUN 99 SER.#'d SETS
*GOLD: .5X TO 1.25X BASE HI
GOLD PRINT RUN 50 SER.#'d SETS
AB Andrea Bargnani 3.00 8.00
AI Andre Iguodala 5.00 12.00
AM Alonzo Mourning 8.00 20.00
BD Baron Davis 4.00 10.00
BG Ben Gordon 4.00 10.00
BO Chris Bosh 6.00 15.00
BR Brandon Roy 6.00 15.00
CA Carmelo Anthony 8.00 20.00
CB Chauncey Billups 6.00 15.00
CP Chris Paul 10.00 25.00
DH Dwight Howard 6.00 15.00
DR David Robinson 10.00 25.00
DW Deron Williams 4.00 10.00
EO Emeka Okafor 4.00 10.00
JE Julius Erving 12.00 30.00
JK Jason Kidd 8.00 20.00
JO Michael Jordan 125.00 300.00
JS John Stockton 10.00 25.00
KA Kareem Abdul-Jabbar 15.00 40.00
UL-KB Kobe Bryant 100.00 250.00
KG Kevin Garnett 12.00 30.00
KH Kirk Hinrich 5.00 12.00
LA LaMarcus Aldridge 5.00 12.00
LB Larry Bird 20.00 50.00
LJ LeBron James 50.00 120.00
MB Mike Bibby 5.00 12.00
MJ Magic Johnson 20.00 50.00
PP Paul Pierce 8.00 20.00
RO Dennis Rodman 15.00 40.00
SN Steve Nash 10.00 25.00
TA Tayshaun Prince 5.00 12.00
TM Tracy McGrady 8.00 20.00
TP Tony Parker 8.00 20.00
VC Vince Carter 10.00 25.00
WI Dominique Wilkins 8.00 20.00

2007-08 Ultimate Collection Leadership Patches

*PRIME: .75X TO 2X HI COLUMN
PRINT RUN 25 SER.#'d SETS

2007-08 Ultimate Collection Leadership Autographs

PRINT RUN 25 SER.#'d SETS
BR Brandon Roy 20.00 50.00
CA Carmelo Anthony 25.00 60.00
CP Chris Paul 75.00 200.00
DR David Robinson 50.00 120.00
JE Julius Erving 100.00 250.00
JK Jason Kidd 30.00 80.00
JO Michael Jordan 2,000.00 4,000.00
JS John Stockton 30.00 80.00
KA Kareem Abdul-Jabbar 40.00 100.00
KB Kobe Bryant 1,500.00 3,000.00
KG Kevin Garnett 100.00 250.00
KH Kirk Hinrich 20.00 50.00
LA LaMarcus Aldridge 25.00 60.00
LB Larry Bird 75.00 200.00
LJ LeBron James 6,000.00 12,000.00
MJ Magic Johnson 75.00 200.00
PP Paul Pierce 40.00 100.00
RO Dennis Rodman 75.00 200.00
VC Vince Carter 40.00 100.00
WI Dominique Wilkins 25.00 60.00

2007-08 Ultimate Collection Matchups

PRINT RUN 99 SER.#'d SETS
*GOLD: .5X TO 1.25X BASE HI
GOLD PRINT RUN 50 SER.#'d SETS
BG K.Bryant/G.Gervin 200.00 500.00
CB R.Carney/R.Brewer 5.00 12.00
CJ V.Carter/A.Jamison 6.00 15.00
CM V.Carter/T.McGrady 10.00 25.00
DA L.Aldridge/K.Durant 60.00 150.00
DR D.Marshall/R.Brewer 5.00 12.00
EA J.Erving/C.Anthony 10.00 25.00
FF R.Felton/R.Foye 5.00 12.00
GH H.Grant/D.Howard 5.00 12.00
GI B.Gordon/A.Iguodala 5.00 12.00
GR K.Garnett/D.Rodman 12.00 30.00
HC L.Hughes/M.Collins 5.00 12.00
HG K.Hinrich/D.Gibson 5.00 12.00
JB M.Johnson/L.Bird 20.00 50.00
JJ M.Jordan/L.James 75.00 200.00
JP P.Pierce/R.Jefferson 6.00 15.00
MB S.Marion/S.Brown 5.00 12.00
MC T.Chandler/S.May 5.00 12.00
MF B.Miller/C.Frye 5.00 12.00
MR Y.Ming/D.Robinson 6.00 15.00
OM H.Olajuwon/A.Mourning 8.00 20.00
PJ T.Prince/A.Jefferson 5.00 12.00
PR C.Paul/B.Roy 6.00 15.00
PW T.Parker/D.Williams 5.00 12.00
RD D.Marshall/R.Carney 5.00 12.00
TB T.Thomas/A.Bargnani 5.00 12.00
TO E.Okafor/T.Thomas 5.00 12.00
WS M.Williams/C.Simmons 5.00 12.00

2007-08 Ultimate Collection Matchups Patches

PRINT RUN 25 SER.#'d SETS
BG K.Bryant/G.Gervin 500.00 1,000.00
CM V.Carter/T.McGrady 60.00 150.00
DA L.Aldridge/K.Durant 75.00 200.00
EA J.Erving/C.Anthony 30.00 80.00
GH H.Grant/D.Howard 25.00 50.00
GR K.Garnett/D.Rodman 50.00 120.00
JB M.Johnson/L.Bird 60.00 150.00
JJ M.Jordan/L.James 150.00 400.00
MR Y.Ming/D.Robinson 40.00 100.00
OM H.Olajuwon/A.Mourning 30.00 80.00
PR C.Paul/B.Roy 20.00 50.00
PW T.Parker/D.Williams 15.00 40.00

2007-08 Ultimate Collection Matchups Autographs

PRINT RUN 25 SER.#'d SETS
BG K.Bryant/G.Gervin 1,500.00 3,000.00
CM V.Carter/T.McGrady 150.00 400.00
DA L.Aldridge/K.Durant 400.00 800.00
EA J.Erving/C.Anthony 60.00 120.00
GR K.Garnett/D.Rodman 125.00 300.00
JB M.Johnson/L.Bird 150.00 400.00
JJ M.Jordan/L.James 20,000.00 40,000.00
MR Y.Ming/D.Robinson 125.00 300.00
OM H.Olajuwon/A.Mourning 75.00 200.00
PR C.Paul/B.Roy 75.00 200.00
PW T.Parker/D.Williams 30.00 80.00

2007-08 Ultimate Collection Materials

*GOLD: .5X TO 1.25X BASE HI
GOLD PRINT RUN 50 SER.#'d SETS
AB Andrea Bargnani 1.50 4.00
AD Adrian Dantley 2.00 5.00
AG Maurice Ager 1.50 4.00
AH Al Harrington 2.00 5.00
AI Andre Iguodala 2.50 6.00
AJ Antawn Jamison 2.00 5.00
AL Al Jefferson 1.50 4.00
AM Alonzo Mourning 4.00 10.00
AZ Kelenna Azubuike 1.50 4.00
BD Baron Davis 2.00 5.00
BG Ben Gordon 2.00 5.00
BM Brad Miller 2.00 5.00
BR Brandon Roy 3.00 8.00
CA Carmelo Anthony 4.00 10.00
CB Carlos Boozer 2.00 5.00
CD Chris Duhon 1.50 4.00
CF Channing Frye 1.50 4.00
CP Chris Paul 5.00 12.00
CS Cedric Simmons 1.50 4.00
DG Daniel Gibson 1.50 4.00
DL David Lee 2.00 5.00
DM Donyell Marshall 1.50 4.00
DN David Noel 1.50 4.00
DR David Robinson 5.00 12.00
DW Deron Williams 2.00 5.00
EO Emeka Okafor 2.00 5.00
FE Raymond Felton 2.00 5.00
FG Francisco Garcia 1.50 4.00
GG George Gervin 3.00 8.00
GR Gerald Green 2.00 5.00
HA Hilton Armstrong 1.50 4.00
HE Luther Head 1.50 4.00
HG Horace Grant 2.50 6.00
HO Hakeem Olajuwon 5.00 12.00
JA James Augustine 1.50 4.00
JB Josh Boone 1.50 4.00
JE Julius Erving 6.00 15.00
JG Jorge Garbajosa 2.00 5.00
JK Jason Kidd 4.00 10.00
JS J.R. Smith 2.50 6.00
JW Julian Wright 1.50 4.00
KA Kareem Abdul-Jabbar 8.00 20.00
KB Kobe Bryant 50.00 120.00
KD Keyon Dooling 1.50 4.00
KG Kevin Garnett 6.00 15.00
KH Kirk Hinrich 2.50 6.00
KL Kyle Lowry 2.50 6.00
LA LaMarcus Aldridge 2.50 6.00
LB Larry Bird 10.00 25.00
LD Luol Deng 2.00 5.00
LE LeBron James 25.00 60.00
LH Larry Hughes 2.00 5.00
LJ LeBron James 25.00 60.00
MA Corey Maggette 2.00 5.00
MB Mike Bibby 2.50 6.00
MC Mardy Collins 1.50 4.00
MI Andre Miller 2.00 5.00
MJ Magic Johnson 10.00 25.00
MW Marvin Williams 1.50 4.00
PA Tony Parker 4.00 10.00
PG Pau Gasol 4.00 10.00
PM Paul Millsap 2.00 5.00
PO Patrick O'Bryant 1.50 4.00
PP Paul Pierce 4.00 10.00
QR Quentin Richardson 1.50 4.00
RB Ronnie Brewer 1.50 4.00
RC Rodney Carney 1.50 4.00
RF Randy Foye 2.00 5.00
RG Rudy Gay 2.00 5.00
RH Richard Hamilton 3.00 8.00
RJ Richard Jefferson 2.00 5.00
RO Dennis Rodman 6.00 15.00
RR Rajon Rondo 3.00 8.00
RY Ryan Hollins 1.50 4.00
SB Shannon Brown 1.50 4.00
SE Sean May 1.50 4.00
SL Shaun Livingston 2.00 5.00
SM Craig Smith 1.50 4.00
SN Steve Nash 5.00 12.00
SR Sergio Rodriguez 1.50 4.00
SS Stromile Swift 1.50 4.00
ST John Stockton 5.00 12.00
TC Tyson Chandler 2.50 6.00
TM Tracy McGrady 4.00 10.00
TP Tayshaun Prince 2.50 6.00
TS Thabo Sefolosha 1.50 4.00
TT Tyrus Thomas 1.50 4.00
VC Vince Carter 5.00 12.00
WF Walt Frazier 4.00 10.00
WI Shelden Williams 1.50 4.00
YM Yao Ming 6.00 15.00

2007-08 Ultimate Collection Materials Autographs

AL Al Jefferson 8.00 20.00
BD Baron Davis 8.00 20.00
BG Ben Gordon 8.00 20.00
BR Brandon Roy 8.00 20.00
CA Carmelo Anthony 15.00 40.00
CP Chris Paul 40.00 100.00
DR David Robinson 25.00 60.00
DW Deron Williams 8.00 20.00
GG George Gervin 12.00 30.00
HG Horace Grant 25.00 60.00
HO Hakeem Olajuwon 25.00 60.00
JE Julius Erving 40.00 100.00
JK Jason Kidd 25.00 60.00
JW Julian Wright 8.00 20.00
KA Kareem Abdul-Jabbar 40.00 100.00
KB Kobe Bryant 1,500.00 3,000.00
KH Kirk Hinrich 8.00 20.00
LA LaMarcus Aldridge 10.00 25.00
LJ LeBron James 2,000.00 4,000.00
PA Tony Parker 12.00 30.00
PP Paul Pierce 25.00 60.00
RG Rudy Gay 8.00 20.00
RH Richard Hamilton 8.00 20.00
RJ Richard Jefferson 8.00 20.00
RO Dennis Rodman 75.00 200.00
RR Rajon Rondo 20.00 50.00
SN Steve Nash 30.00 80.00
ST John Stockton 30.00 80.00
TM Tracy McGrady 10.00 25.00
TT Tyrus Thomas 8.00 20.00
VC Vince Carter 15.00 40.00
WF Walt Frazier 15.00 40.00

2007-08 Ultimate Collection Materials Patches

PRINT RUN 25 SER.#'d SETS
AL Al Jefferson 6.00 15.00
BG Ben Gordon 6.00 15.00
BR Brandon Roy 6.00 15.00
CA Carmelo Anthony 10.00 25.00
CP Chris Paul 12.00 30.00
DR David Robinson 15.00 40.00
DW Deron Williams 6.00 15.00
GG George Gervin 8.00 20.00
HO Hakeem Olajuwon 8.00 20.00
JE Julius Erving 10.00 25.00
JK Jason Kidd 6.00 15.00
JW Julian Wright 5.00 12.00
KA Kareem Abdul-Jabbar 20.00 50.00
KB Kobe Bryant 200.00 500.00
KG Kevin Garnett 20.00 50.00
KH Kirk Hinrich 8.00 20.00
LA LaMarcus Aldridge 6.00 15.00
LB Larry Bird 20.00 50.00
LD Luol Deng 6.00 15.00
LJ LeBron James 75.00 200.00
MJ Magic Johnson 15.00 40.00
MW Marvin Williams 6.00 15.00
PA Tony Parker 8.00 20.00
PG Pau Gasol 6.00 15.00
PP Paul Pierce 8.00 20.00
RG Rudy Gay 8.00 20.00
RH Richard Hamilton 6.00 15.00
RJ Richard Jefferson 6.00 15.00
RO Dennis Rodman 10.00 25.00
SN Steve Nash 10.00 25.00
ST John Stockton 12.00 30.00
TM Tracy McGrady 8.00 20.00
TT Tyrus Thomas 6.00 15.00
VC Vince Carter 12.00 30.00
WF Walt Frazier 10.00 25.00
YM Yao Ming 10.00 25.00

2007-08 Ultimate Collection Materials Dual

PRINT RUN 99 SER.#'d SETS
DAB R.Artest/C.Butler 5.00 12.00
DAG R.Allen/K.Garnett 8.00 20.00
DBD M.Bibby/Q.Douby 5.00 12.00
DBG E.Brand/K.Garnett 6.00 15.00
DBH B.Haywood/C.Butler 5.00 12.00
DBJ K.Bryant/L.James 500.00 1,000.00
DBO E.Brand/S.O'Neal 6.00 15.00
DDP T.Duncan/T.Parker 6.00 15.00
DDS T.Duncan/A.Stoudemire 6.00 15.00
DDT L.Deng/T.Thomas 5.00 12.00
DFH S.Francis/L.Head 5.00 12.00
DGB K.Bryant/K.Garnett 200.00 500.00
DGI B.Gordon/A.Iguodala 5.00 12.00
DGJ K.Garnett/L.James 20.00 50.00
DGM P.Gasol/D.Milicic 5.00 12.00
DHB R.Hamilton/C.Billups 5.00 12.00
DIA A.Iverson/C.Anthony 6.00 15.00
DJC V.Carter/R.Jefferson 6.00 15.00
DJW L.James/D.Wade 20.00 50.00
DKW A.Kirilenko/D.Williams 5.00 12.00
DLR R.Lewis/J.Redick 5.00 12.00
DMB D.Mason/A.Bogut 5.00 12.00
DMC C.Maggette/S.Cassell 5.00 12.00
DMD T.Duncan/Y.Ming 6.00 15.00
DMM T.McGrady/Y.Ming 6.00 15.00
DNA J.Nelson/T.Ariza 5.00 12.00
DNH D.Nowitzki/J.Howard 6.00 15.00
DNS S.Nash/A.Stoudemire 6.00 15.00
DOH L.Odom/G.Hill 6.00 15.00
DOM E.Okafor/S.May 5.00 12.00
DPH P.Pierce/K.Hinrich 6.00 15.00
DPP M.Peterson/C.Paul 6.00 15.00
DRR Z.Randolph/J.Richardson 5.00 12.00
DSH A.Stoudemire/D.Howard 6.00 15.00
DTW J.Terry/J.Williams 6.00 15.00
DWD B.Wallace/L.Deng 5.00 12.00
DWS C.Wilcox/S.Sene 5.00 12.00
DWW R.Wallace/B.Wallace 6.00 15.00

2007-08 Ultimate Collection Materials Dual Patches

PRINT RUN 25 SER.#'d SETS
DBJ K.Bryant/L.James 1,000.00 2,000.00
DDP T.Duncan/T.Parker 12.00 30.00
DDS T.Duncan/A.Stoudemire 12.00 30.00
DGB K.Bryant/K.Garnett 500.00 1,000.00
DGJ K.Garnett/L.James 100.00 250.00
DHB R.Hamilton/C.Billups 8.00 20.00
DIA A.Iverson/C.Anthony 20.00 40.00
DJC V.Carter/R.Jefferson 10.00 25.00
DJW L.James/D.Wade 100.00 250.00
DKW A.Kirilenko/D.Williams 8.00 20.00
DMD T.Duncan/Y.Ming 15.00 40.00
DMM T.McGrady/Y.Ming 15.00 40.00
DNH D.Nowitzki/J.Howard 12.00 30.00
DNS S.Nash/A.Stoudemire 12.00 30.00
DSH A.Stoudemire/D.Howard 10.00 25.00

2007-08 Ultimate Collection Materials Triple

PRINT RUN 50 SER.#'d SETS
TCCM Milicic/Crittenton/Conley 4.00 10.00
TDGT Deng/Gordon/Thomas 4.00 10.00
TDPG Duncan/Parker/Ginobili 5.00 12.00
TDRG Ridnour/Durant/Green 8.00 20.00
THSB Stevenson/Haywood/Butler 4.00 10.00
THWP Hamilton/Wallace/Prince 5.00 12.00
TJMF Jefferson/McCants/Foye 5.00 12.00
TLHN Lewis/Howard/Nelson 4.00 10.00
TMBM McGrady/Battier/Ming 4.00 10.00
TMRB Mason/Redd/Bogut 4.00 10.00
TMRR Marbury/Richardson/Randolph 4.00 10.00
TPAG Pierce/Allen/Garnett 20.00 40.00
TPWP Peterson/West/Paul 8.00 20.00
TWRM Marion/Davis/Wade 5.00 12.00

2007-08 Ultimate Collection Materials Quad

PRINT RUN 25 SER.#'d SETS
ABWK Artest/Bowen/Wallace/AK47 10.00 25.00
BBPW Butler/Prince/Battier/Wallace 10.00 25.00
BGJW Kobe/KG/LJ/Wade 1,000.00 2,000.00
BPPW Bibby/Parker/Paul/Will 15.00 30.00
BRJA Kobe/Redd/LJ/Anthony 1,000.00 2,000.00
CGBH Camby/KG/Bzer/Hwrd 15.00 30.00
DPGR Dncn/Prkr/Manu/D-Rob 25.00 50.00
DSHJ Dncn/Amare/Hwrd/Jffrsn 10.00 25.00
GMMW KG/McG/Marion/Wllce 10.00 25.00
HRSG Hamilton/Redd/Peja/Gibson 10.00 25.00
HWBP Hamilton/Wallace/Billups/Prince 10.00 25.00
JDGT MJ/Deng/Gordon/Thomas 60.00 120.00
JEJB MJ/Erving/Johnson/Bird 100.00 200.00
JIPG James/Iggy/Paul/Green 30.00 60.00
JWHR LJ/Wade/Howard/Roy 25.00 50.00
NKPW Nash/Kidd/Paul/Williams 15.00 30.00
OMMO Olaj/Zo/Yao/Shaq 30.00 60.00
PAGB Pierce/Allen/KG/Bird 40.00 80.00

2007-08 Ultimate Collection Materials Rookies

*GOLD: .5X TO 1.25X BASE HI
GOLD PRINT RUN 99 SER.#'d SETS
*PATCH: .75X TO 2X BASE HI
PATCH PRINT RUN 25 SER.#'d SETS
AA Arron Afflalo 1.50 4.00
AB Aaron Brooks 1.50 4.00
AG Aaron Gray 1.25 3.00
AH Al Horford 5.00 12.00
AL Acie Law 1.25 3.00
AT Al Thornton 1.25 3.00
CB Corey Brewer 1.50 4.00
CL Carl Landry 1.25 3.00
DA Jermareo Davidson 1.25 3.00
DC Daequan Cook 1.50 4.00
DM Dominic McGuire 1.25 3.00
GD Glen Davis 1.50 4.00
GP Gabe Pruitt 1.25 3.00
HA Adam Haluska 1.25 3.00
HH Herbert Hill 1.25 3.00
JC Javaris Crittenton 1.25 3.00
JD Jared Dudley 1.50 4.00
JG Jeff Green 1.50 4.00
JN Joakim Noah 2.00 5.00
JS Jason Smith 1.25 3.00
JW Julian Wright 1.25 3.00
KD Kevin Durant 40.00 100.00
MA Morris Almond 1.25 3.00
MC Mike Conley Jr. 5.00 12.00
NF Nick Fazekas 1.25 3.00
RS Rodney Stuckey 1.25 3.00
SH Spencer Hawes 1.25 3.00
SW Sean Williams 1.25 3.00
TU Alando Tucker 1.25 3.00
WC Wilson Chandler 1.50 4.00

2007-08 Ultimate Collection Materials Rookies Autographs

AA Arron Afflalo 3.00 8.00
AB Aaron Brooks 3.00 8.00
AH Al Horford 10.00 25.00
AL Acie Law 2.50 6.00
AT Al Thornton 2.50 6.00
CB Corey Brewer 3.00 8.00
CL Carl Landry 2.50 6.00
DC Daequan Cook 3.00 8.00
GD Glen Davis 3.00 8.00
JC Javaris Crittenton 2.50 6.00
JD Jared Dudley 3.00 8.00
JG Jeff Green 3.00 8.00
JN Joakim Noah 4.00 10.00
JS Jason Smith 2.50 6.00
JW Julian Wright 2.50 6.00
KD Kevin Durant 1,000.00 2,000.00
MC Mike Conley Jr. 25.00 60.00
RS Rodney Stuckey 2.50 6.00
SH Spencer Hawes 2.50 6.00
SW Sean Williams 2.50 6.00

2007-08 Ultimate Collection Rookie Matchups

PRINT RUN 99 SER.#'d SETS
*GOLD: .5X TO 1.25X HI COLUMN
GOLD PRINT RUN 50 SER.#'d SETS
AB M.Almond/A.Brooks 3.00 8.00
AP A.Afflalo/G.Pruitt 3.00 8.00
BC C.Brewer/M.Conley 3.00 8.00
CD G.Davis/W.Chandler 3.00 8.00
CT J.Crittenton/A.Tucker 3.00 8.00
DC J.Dudley/W.Chandler 3.00 8.00
DD D.Cook/J.Dudley 3.00 8.00
DH K.Durant/A.Horford 50.00 120.00
DW K.Durant/J.Wright 20.00 50.00
FB N.Fazekas/A.Brooks 3.00 8.00
FD N.Fazekas/J.Davidson 3.00 8.00
GA A.Gray/A.Afflalo 3.00 8.00
GH A.Gray/H.Hill 3.00 8.00
GS T.Green/D.Strawberry 3.00 8.00
GW J.Green/J.Wright 3.00 8.00
HD G.Davis/S.Hawes 3.00 8.00
HM A.Haluska/D.McGuire 3.00 8.00
HN J.Noah/A.Horford 3.00 8.00
LA M.Almond/A.Law 3.00 8.00
LG T.Green/C.Landry 3.00 8.00
LP G.Pruitt/A.Law 3.00 8.00
MH J.McRoberts/A.Haluska 3.00 8.00
MR J.McRoberts/C.Richard 3.00 8.00
SC R.Stuckey/D.Cook 3.00 8.00
ST A.Tucker/D.Strawberry 3.00 8.00
SW J.Smith/S.Williams 3.00 8.00
TC A.Thornton/J.Crittenton 3.00 8.00
TH A.Thornton/H.Hill 3.00 8.00
TL A.Tucker/C.Landry 3.00 8.00
WD J.Davidson/S.Williams 3.00 8.00

2007-08 Ultimate Collection Rookie Matchups Patches

PRINT RUN 25 SER.#'d SETS
BC C.Brewer/M.Conley 8.00 20.00
CD G.Davis/W.Chandler 8.00 20.00
DH K.Durant/A.Horford 75.00 200.00
DW K.Durant/J.Wright 40.00 100.00
GS T.Green/D.Strawberry 8.00 20.00
GW J.Green/J.Wright 8.00 20.00
HN J.Noah/A.Horford 8.00 20.00
LA M.Almond/A.Law 8.00 20.00
SC R.Stuckey/D.Cook 8.00 20.00
TC A.Thornton/J.Crittenton 8.00 20.00

2007-08 Ultimate Collection Rookie Matchups Autographs

PRINT RUN 25 SER.#'d SETS
BC C.Brewer/M.Conley 12.00 30.00
CD G.Davis/W.Chandler 12.00 30.00
DH K.Durant/A.Horford 400.00 800.00
DW K.Durant/J.Wright 300.00 600.00
GS T.Green/D.Strawberry 12.00 30.00
GW J.Green/J.Wright 12.00 30.00
HN J.Noah/A.Horford 12.00 30.00
LA M.Almond/A.Law 12.00 30.00
SC R.Stuckey/D.Cook 12.00 30.00
TC A.Thornton/J.Crittenton 12.00 30.00

2007-08 Ultimate Collection Signatures

STATED PRINT RUN 20 TO 75 SER.#'d SETS
AD Adrian Dantley/50 6.00 15.00
AM Alonzo Mourning/50 30.00 80.00
BA B.J. Armstrong/75 10.00 25.00
BD Baron Davis/25 8.00 20.00
BR Brandon Roy/50 8.00 20.00
BW Bill Walton/25 15.00 30.00
CA Carmelo Anthony/20 30.00 80.00
CM Corey Maggette/75 6.00 15.00
CO Corey Brewer/50 6.00 15.00
DA Brad Daugherty/75 6.00 15.00
DF Derek Fisher/50 8.00 20.00
DG Daniel Gibson/75 6.00 15.00
DH Dwight Howard/50 15.00 40.00
DM Donyell Marshall/75 6.00 15.00
DO Dominique Wilkins/50 15.00 40.00
DR David Robinson/20 50.00 100.00
DY Danny Manning/25 15.00 30.00
EC Eddy Curry/25 8.00 20.00
GG George Gervin/50 10.00 25.00
GH Horace Grant/25 20.00 40.00
HA Hilton Armstrong/75 6.00 15.00
HE Luther Head/75 6.00 15.00
HO Hakeem Olajuwon/20 30.00 60.00
JE Al Jefferson/50 6.00 15.00
JJ Jarrett Jack/75 6.00 15.00
JK Jason Kidd/20 20.00 40.00
JW James Worthy/20 25.00 60.00
KG Kevin Garnett/20 300.00 600.00
KH Kirk Hinrich/50 6.00 15.00
KV Kiki Vandeweghe/75 6.00 15.00
LA LaMarcus Aldridge/25 10.00 25.00
LJ LeBron James/20 6,000.00 12,000.00
MJ Magic Johnson/20 50.00 120.00
PA Tony Parker/25 20.00 50.00
PR Pat Riley/25 15.00 30.00
RA Randolph Morris/75 6.00 15.00
RF Randy Foye/50 6.00 15.00
RG Rudy Gay/50 6.00 15.00
RO Dennis Rodman/25 30.00 80.00
SJ Solomon Jones/75 6.00 15.00
SM Craig Smith/75 6.00 15.00
SP Sam Perkins/50 6.00 15.00
TC Terry Cummings/75 6.00 15.00
TM Tracy McGrady/20 20.00 50.00
TO Tom Chambers/50 10.00 25.00
TT Tyrus Thomas/25 6.00 15.00
TY Tyson Chandler/75 6.00 15.00
VC Vince Carter/20 25.00 60.00
WE Jerry West/20 30.00 80.00
WF Walt Frazier/50 12.00 30.00
WI Deron Williams/50 10.00 25.00

2007-08 Ultimate Collection Signatures Dual

PRINT RUN 25 SER.#'d SETS
AM H.Armstrong/P.Millsap 10.00 25.00
AS A.Afflalo/R.Stuckey 10.00 25.00
AW L.Aldridge/S.Williams 10.00 25.00
BD B.Davis/M.Belinelli 12.00 30.00
BH C.Bosh/D.Howard 30.00 80.00
BJ R.Jefferson/B.Bowen 25.00 60.00
CJ V.Carter/A.Jamison 25.00 60.00
CL K.Lowry/M.Conley 15.00 40.00
CM V.Carter/T.McGrady 25.00 60.00
CP T.Chandler/T.Prince 15.00 40.00
CS R.Carney/C.Smith 10.00 25.00
CW T.Chandler/J.Wright 10.00 25.00
DB B.Diaw/L.Barbosa 10.00 25.00
DL K.Dooling/K.Lowry 10.00 25.00
FR R.Foye/R.Rondo 12.00 30.00
FS D.Fisher/J.Stockton 30.00 80.00
GA B.Gordon/M.Ager 10.00 25.00
GB D.Gibson/S.Brown 10.00 25.00
GD K.Garnett/K.Durant 2,000.00 4,000.00
GH H.Grant/D.Howard 25.00 60.00
GP A.Gilmore/R.Parish 15.00 40.00
HP A.Harrington/L.Powe 10.00 25.00
HW A.Harrington/M.Williams 10.00 25.00
JG A.Jefferson/R.Gay 10.00 25.00
JM C.Maggette/R.Jefferson 10.00 25.00
JP R.Jefferson/T.Prince 10.00 25.00
KA S.Kerr/B.Armstrong 20.00 50.00
LC D.Lee/R.Carney 10.00 25.00
LG D.Lee/R.Gay 10.00 25.00
MB R.Barry/C.Mullin 20.00 50.00
MJ P.Millsap/S.Jones 10.00 25.00
MW Y.Ming/B.Walton 25.00 60.00
OM P.O'Bryant/P.Millsap 10.00 25.00
OR H.Olajuwon/D.Robinson 50.00 120.00
OT J.O'Neal/T.Thomas 10.00 25.00
PD P.Pierce/A.Dantley 20.00 50.00
PW C.Paul/D.Williams 75.00 200.00
RF R.Foye/B.Roy 10.00 25.00
RG Q.Richardson/G.Green 10.00 25.00
RP R.Rondo/G.Pruitt 12.00 30.00
RS Q.Richardson/D.Stevenson 10.00 25.00
MA C.Simmons/H.Armstrong 10.00 25.00
WH D.Wilkins/A.Horford 25.00 60.00

2007-08 Ultimate Collection Signatures Triple

PRINT RUN 15 SER.#'d SETS
BMG Bibby/Miller/Garcia 25.00 50.00
CPW Chandler/Paul/Wright 60.00 150.00
DAE Davis/Anthony/English 25.00 50.00
DAR Drexler/Aldridge/Roy 60.00 120.00
DHB Davis/Harrington/Belinelli 20.00 40.00
FSB Foye/Smith/Brewer 15.00 30.00
GLC Gay/Lowry/Conley 15.00 30.00
GTN Gordon/Thomas/Noah 40.00 80.00
KCJ Kidd/Carter/Jefferson 40.00 100.00
LPR Laimbeer/Prince/Rodman 60.00 120.00
MLT Maggette/Livingston/Thornton 15.00 30.00
OMM Olajuwon/McGrady/Ming 75.00 200.00
PRB Bowen/Parker/Robinson 50.00 100.00
WDG Wilkins/Durant/Green 100.00 200.00
WHL Wilkins/Horford/Law 12.00 30.00

2007-08 Ultimate Collection Virtuoso

PRINT RUN 25 SER.#'d SETS
AM Alonzo Mourning 40.00 100.00
BG Ben Gordon 10.00 25.00
BR Brandon Roy 10.00 25.00
CB Carlos Boozer 10.00 25.00
CM Chris Mullin 20.00 50.00
CP Chris Paul 75.00 200.00
DH Dwight Howard 25.00 60.00
GG George Gervin 12.00 30.00
KB Kobe Bryant 1,500.00 3,000.00
KH Kirk Hinrich 10.00 25.00
LA LaMarcus Aldridge 15.00 40.00
600 LeBron James 6,000.00 12,000.00
YM Yao Ming 25.00 50.00

2007-08 Ultimate Collection Write of Passage Autographs Dual

PRINT RUN 25 SER.#'d SETS
AS A.Afflalo/R.Stuckey 12.00 30.00
CC D.Cook/M.Conley 12.00 30.00
DG K.Durant/J.Green 300.00 600.00
DH K.Durant/A.Horford 400.00 800.00
GN A.Gray/J.Noah 12.00 30.00
HL A.Horford/A.Law 15.00 40.00
LB C.Landry/A.Brooks 12.00 30.00
PD G.Pruitt/G.Davis 12.00 30.00
SC J.Crittenton/L.Scola 12.00 30.00

2008-09 Ultimate Collection

1-80 PRINT RUN 499 SER.#'d SETS
81-100 PRINT RUN 499 SER.#'d SETS
101-120 PRINT RUN 499 SER.#'d SETS
121-141 PRINT RUN 150 SER.#'d SETS
1 LaMarcus Aldridge 2.00 5.00
2 Ray Allen 3.00 8.00
3 Carmelo Anthony 2.50 6.00
4 Gilbert Arenas 2.00 5.00
5 Ron Artest 2.00 5.00
6 Chauncey Billups 2.50 6.00
7 Carlos Boozer 1.50 4.00
8 Chris Bosh 2.50 6.00
9 Elton Brand 1.50 4.00
10 Kobe Bryant 15.00 40.00
11 Caron Butler 1.50 4.00
12 Andrew Bynum 1.25 3.00
13 Jose Calderon 1.25 3.00
14 Vince Carter 4.00 10.00
15 Tyson Chandler 1.50 4.00
16 Mike Conley Jr. 1.50 4.00
17 Jamal Crawford 1.50 4.00
18 Baron Davis 2.00 5.00
19 Luol Deng 1.50 4.00
20 Chris Duhon 1.25 3.00
21 Tim Duncan 5.00 12.00
22 Kevin Durant 8.00 20.00
23 Raymond Felton 1.25 3.00
24 T.J. Ford 1.25 3.00
25 Kevin Garnett 5.00 12.00
26 Pau Gasol 2.50 6.00
27 Rudy Gay 2.00 5.00
28 Manu Ginobili 4.00 10.00
29 Ben Gordon 1.50 4.00
30 Danny Granger 1.50 4.00
31 Jeff Green 1.50 4.00
32 Al Harrington 1.50 4.00
33 Devin Harris 1.25 3.00
34 Kirk Hinrich 1.50 4.00
35 Al Horford 2.00 5.00
36 Dwight Howard 2.50 6.00
37 Josh Howard 1.50 4.00
38 Andre Iguodala 1.50 4.00
39 Allen Iverson 4.00 10.00
40 Stephen Jackson 1.50 4.00
41 LeBron James 20.00 50.00
42 Antawn Jamison 1.50 4.00
43 Al Jefferson 1.25 3.00
44 Richard Jefferson 1.50 4.00
45 Yi Jianlian 2.50 6.00
46 Joe Johnson 2.00 5.00
47 Jason Kidd 3.00 8.00
48 David Lee 1.25 3.00
49 Rashard Lewis 1.50 4.00
50 Corey Maggette 1.50 4.00
51 Shawn Marion 2.00 5.00
52 Kevin Martin 1.50 4.00
53 Tracy McGrady 3.00 8.00
54 Andre Miller 1.50 4.00
55 Mike Miller 1.50 4.00
56 Paul Millsap 1.50 4.00
57 Yao Ming 5.00 12.00
58 Steve Nash 4.00 10.00
59 Jameer Nelson 1.25 3.00
60 Dirk Nowitzki 5.00 12.00
61 Greg Oden 1.25 3.00
62 Tony Parker 2.50 6.00
63 Chris Paul 4.00 10.00
64 Paul Pierce 3.00 8.00
65 Tayshaun Prince 1.25 3.00
66 Zach Randolph 2.00 5.00
67 Michael Redd 1.50 4.00
68 Jason Richardson 2.00 5.00
69 Brandon Roy 1.50 4.00
70 John Salmons 1.50 4.00
71 Josh Smith 1.25 3.00
72 Amare Stoudemire 2.00 5.00
73 Rodney Stuckey 1.25 3.00
74 Al Thornton 1.25 3.00
75 Dwyane Wade 4.00 10.00
76 Gerald Wallace 1.50 4.00
77 David West 1.50 4.00
78 Deron Williams 1.50 4.00
79 Mo Williams 1.50 4.00
80 Thaddeus Young 1.50 4.00
81 Sean Singletary RC 1.50 4.00
82 Luc Mbah A Moute RC 2.00 5.00
83 Darrell Jackson/491 RC 1.50 4.00
84 Nathan Jawai RC 2.50 6.00
85 Jawad Williams RC 2.50 6.00
86 Joey Dorsey RC 1.50 4.00
87 Alexis Ajinca RC 1.50 4.00
88 DeAndre Jordan/491 RC 3.00 8.00
89 Javale McGee RC 2.50 6.00
90 Hamed Haddadi RC 2.50 6.00
91 Roko Ukic RC 1.50 4.00
92 Kosta Koufos RC 1.50 4.00
93 Nicolas Batum RC 3.00 8.00
94 Ryan Anderson/491 RC 2.00 5.00
95 Joe Alexander RC 1.50 4.00
96 Chris Douglas-Roberts RC 1.50 4.00
97 Anthony Morrow RC 6.00 15.00
98 Darrell Arthur RC 2.00 5.00
99 Danilo Gallinari RC 4.00 10.00
100 Marc Gasol RC 5.00 12.00
101 Michael Jordan 30.00 80.00
102 Larry Bird 6.00 15.00
103 Magic Johnson 6.00 15.00
104 Oscar Robertson 2.00 5.00
105 John Stockton 4.00 10.00
106 Julius Erving 5.00 12.00
107 Manute Bol 2.00 5.00
108 Dee Brown 1.25 3.00
109 Joe Dumars 2.00 5.00
110 James Edwards 2.00 5.00
111 A.C. Green 2.00 5.00
112 Tim Hardaway 2.50 6.00
113 Kevin Johnson 2.00 5.00
114 Karl Malone 2.50 6.00
115 Danny Ainge 2.00 5.00
116 Kurt Rambis 1.25 3.00
117 Willis Reed 2.00 5.00
118 Scottie Pippen 3.00 8.00
119 Wilt Chamberlain 6.00 15.00
120 Drazen Petrovic 3.00 8.00
121 Kevin Love JSY AU RC 15.00 40.00
122 Michael Beasley JSY AU RC 8.00 20.00
123 Rudy Fernandez JSY AU RC 6.00 15.00
124 O.J. Mayo JSY AU RC 6.00 15.00
125 Derrick Rose JSY AU RC 75.00 200.00
126 Brook Lopez JSY AU RC 10.00 25.00
127 R.Westbrook JSY AU RC 200.00 500.00

128 Courtney Lee JSY AU RC 6.00 15.00
129 Jerryd Bayless JSY AU RC 6.00 15.00
130 Marreese Speights JSY AU RC 6.00 15.00
131 Donte Greene JSY AU RC 5.00 12.00
132 J.J. Hickson JSY AU RC 5.00 12.00
133 D.J. Augustin JSY AU RC 8.00 20.00
134 J.Thompson JSY AU RC 5.00 12.00
135 Robin Lopez JSY AU RC 6.00 15.00
136 A.Randolph JSY AU RC 5.00 12.00
137 Eric Gordon JSY AU RC 12.00 30.00
138 Brandon Rush JSY AU RC 5.00 12.00
139 Roy Hibbert JSY AU RC 6.00 15.00
140 Mario Chalmers JSY AU RC 8.00 20.00
141 George Hill JSY AU RC 8.00 20.00

2008-09 Ultimate Collection Rookies Patches

STATED PRINT RUN 10 SER.#'d SETS
121 Kevin Love JSY AU 60.00 150.00
122 Michael Beasley JSY AU 30.00 80.00
123 Rudy Fernandez JSY AU 25.00 60.00
124 O.J. Mayo JSY AU 25.00 60.00
125 Derrick Rose JSY AU 300.00 600.00
126 Brook Lopez JSY AU 40.00 100.00
127 Russell Westbrook JSY AU 1,000.00 2,000.00
128 Courtney Lee JSY AU 25.00 60.00
129 Jerryd Bayless JSY AU 25.00 60.00
130 Marreese Speights JSY AU 25.00 60.00
131 Donte Greene JSY AU 20.00 50.00
132 J.J. Hickson JSY AU 20.00 50.00
133 D.J. Augustin JSY AU 30.00 80.00
134 Jason Thompson JSY AU 20.00 50.00
135 Robin Lopez JSY AU 25.00 60.00
136 Anthony Randolph JSY AU 20.00 50.00
137 Eric Gordon JSY AU 75.00 200.00
138 Brandon Rush JSY AU 20.00 50.00
139 Roy Hibbert JSY AU 25.00 60.00
140 Mario Chalmers JSY AU 30.00 80.00
141 George Hill JSY AU 30.00 80.00

2008-09 Ultimate Collection Rookies Silver

*SILVER: .5X TO 1.25X BASE HI
SILVER PRINT RUN 60 SER.#'d SETS

2008-09 Ultimate Collection Century Legends Epic Signature Update

COMBINED AUTO ODDS 1:3
CLAA Adrian Dantley 8.00 20.00
CLAG Artis Gilmore 8.00 20.00
CLAH Al Horford 8.00 20.00
CLAM Alonzo Mourning 25.00 60.00
CLBK Bernard King 8.00 20.00
CLBL Bill Laimbeer 8.00 20.00
CLBM Bob McAdoo 12.00 30.00
CLBR Brandon Roy 8.00 20.00
CLBS Bill Sharman 12.00 30.00
CLCP Chris Paul SP 200.00 500.00
CLDE Derrick Rose 100.00 250.00
CLDF Derek Fisher 10.00 25.00
CLDG Darrell Griffith 8.00 20.00
CLDH Dwight Howard 20.00 50.00
CLDR David Robinson 50.00 120.00
CLDW Deron Williams 12.00 30.00
CLHG Horace Grant 25.00 60.00
CLJK Jason Kidd 30.00 80.00
CLJS John Stockton 50.00 125.00
CLKB Kobe Bryant 500.00 1,000.00
CLKD Kevin Durant 150.00 400.00
CLLJ LeBron James 3,000.00 6,000.00
CLLW Lenny Wilkens 12.00 30.00
CLMB Michael Beasley 10.00 25.00
CLMJ Magic Johnson 100.00 250.00
CLOJ O.J. Mayo 8.00 20.00
CLPP Paul Pierce 60.00 150.00
CLRB Rick Barry 15.00 40.00
CLRO Dennis Rodman 50.00 120.00
CLRP Robert Parish 15.00 40.00
CLRS Ralph Sampson 8.00 20.00
CLSJ Sam Jones 15.00 40.00
CLSN Steve Nash 60.00 150.00
CLSW Spud Webb 8.00 20.00
CLTM Tracy McGrady 30.00 80.00
CLVC Vince Carter 30.00 80.00

2008-09 Ultimate Collection Entry

STATED PRINT RUN 10 SER.#'d SETS
UEAD Adrian Dantley 12.00 30.00
UEAE Alex English 12.00 30.00
UEBD Brad Daugherty 12.00 30.00
UEBL Bob Lanier 12.00 30.00
UEBS Bill Sharman 15.00 40.00
UEBW Bill Walton 20.00 50.00
UECL Clyde Lovellette 12.00 30.00
UEDC Dave Cowens 20.00 50.00
UEDW Dominique Wilkins 25.00 60.00
UEGE George Gervin 20.00 50.00
UEGG Gail Goodrich 15.00 40.00
UEHG Hal Greer 15.00 40.00
UEJH John Havlicek 40.00 100.00
UEJK Jason Kidd 40.00 100.00
UEJS Jack Sikma 12.00 30.00
UEKG Kevin Garnett 75.00 200.00
UELW Lenny Wilkens 12.00 30.00
UEMJ Michael Jordan 1,000.00 3,000.00
UENT Nate Thurmond 15.00 40.00
UERB Rick Barry 15.00 40.00
UERP Robert Parish 20.00 50.00
UESJ Sam Jones 30.00 80.00
UEVC Vince Carter 60.00 150.00

2008-09 Ultimate Collection Initiation Writes

STATED PRINT RUN 25 SER.#'d SETS
IWAA Alexis Ajinca 4.00 10.00
IWAR Anthony Randolph 4.00 10.00
IWBL Brook Lopez 8.00 20.00
IWBR Brandon Rush 4.00 10.00
IWCL Courtney Lee 5.00 12.00
IWDA D.J. Augustin 6.00 15.00
IWDG Danilo Gallinari 10.00 25.00
IWDR Derrick Rose 125.00 300.00
IWDW D.J. White 4.00 10.00
IWEG Eric Gordon 10.00 25.00
IWGH George Hill 6.00 15.00
IWGR Donte Greene 4.00 10.00
IWJA Joe Alexander 4.00 10.00
IWJB Jerryd Bayless 5.00 12.00
IWJG J.R. Giddens 4.00 10.00
IWJH J.J. Hickson 4.00 10.00
IWJM Javale McGee 6.00 15.00
IWJT Jason Thompson 4.00 10.00
IWKK Kosta Koufos 4.00 10.00
IWKL Kevin Love 12.00 30.00
IWMB Michael Beasley 6.00 15.00
IWMG Marc Gasol 12.00 30.00
IWMS Marreese Speights 5.00 12.00
IWNB Nicolas Batum 8.00 20.00
IWOM O.J. Mayo 5.00 12.00
IWRA Ryan Anderson 5.00 12.00
IWRF Rudy Fernandez 5.00 12.00
IWRH Roy Hibbert 5.00 12.00
IWRL Robin Lopez 5.00 12.00
IWRW Russell Westbrook 200.00 500.00

2008-09 Ultimate Collection Jerseys Eight

STATED PRINT RUN 25 SER.#'d SETS
76ERS Philadelphia 76ers 25.00 60.00
BULLS Chicago Bulls 40.00 100.00
HAWKS Atlanta Hawks 15.00 40.00
KNICK New York Knicks 40.00 100.00
SPURS San Antonio Spurs 50.00 120.00
CELTIC Boston Celtics 60.00 150.00
LACLIP Los Angeles Clippers 15.00 40.00
LAKERS LA Lakers 100.00 250.00
PISTON Detroit Pistons 40.00 100.00
ROCKET Houston Rockets 20.00 50.00
UTAHJZ Utah Jazz 20.00 50.00
ROOKIE08 08-09 Rookies 20.00 50.00

2008-09 Ultimate Collection Jerseys Foursome Combos

STATED PRINT RUN 35 SER.#'d SETS
*PATCHES: .75X TO 2X BASE HI
PATCH PRINT RUN 10 SER.#'d SETS
UFCOKC Oklahom.City Thndr 12.00 30.00
UFC3PTS ThreePoint Shooters 12.00 30.00
UFC76ER Philadelphia 76ers 10.00 25.00
UFCBLAZ Portland Trail Blzrs 10.00 25.00
UFCBSTN Boston Celtics 20.00 50.00
UFCBULL Chicago Bulls 25.00 60.00
UFCCHMP Point Guards 12.00 30.00
UFCCLIP LA Clippers 8.00 20.00
UFCDETP Detroit Pistons 10.00 25.00
UFCEVSW Mgic/Kobe/KG/Bird 60.00 150.00
UFCGRDS Point Guards 15.00 40.00
UFCGRIZ Memphis Grizzlies 8.00 20.00
UFCHAWK Atlanta Hawks 8.00 20.00
UFCHEAT Miami Heat 10.00 25.00
UFCJAZG Utah Jazz 10.00 25.00
UFCJAZZ Utah Jazz 10.00 25.00
UFCKNIC New York Knicks 8.00 20.00
UFCLAKR Los Angeles Lakers 60.00 150.00
UFCLEGS Prsh/Rssll/Reed/Karm 40.00 100.00
UFCLGND Riley/Dntly/Olaj/Ewing 12.00 30.00
UFCNETS New Jersey Nets 8.00 20.00
UFCNICK New York Knicks 20.00 50.00
UFCPSTN Detroit Pistons 10.00 25.00
UFCROCK Houston Rockets 10.00 25.00
UFCSCOR Kareem/Kobe/Wilt/Ice 60.00 150.00
UFCSGRD Kobe/Pearl/AI/Pistol 60.00 150.00
UFCTWLV Minnesota Tmbrwlvs 8.00 20.00
UFCUDEX LBJ/Kobe/KG/Jordan 200.00 500.00
UFCWARS Golden State Warriors 8.00 20.00

2008-09 Ultimate Collection Jerseys Foursome Legends

STATED PRINT RUN 25 SER.#'d SETS
*PATCHES: 1X TO 2.5X BASE HI
PATCH PRINT RUN 10 SER.#'d SETS
UFL76ER Philadelphia 76ers 30.00 80.00
UFLBBOY Detroit Pistons 20.00 50.00
UFLBIGS Reed/Olaj/Rssll/DR 75.00 200.00
UFLBULL Chicago Bulls 100.00 250.00
UFLCELT Boston Celtics 40.00 100.00
UFLCLSC Prsh/Wilt/JoJo/PM 75.00 200.00
UFLDUNK Grffth/DW/MM/Grvn 20.00 50.00
UFLEGRD Mo/Spud/Strk/Isah 10.00 25.00
UFLGRDS Coop/JW/Agmn/AD 12.00 30.00
UFLGSTB JoJo/Mulln/Drxl/Pip 25.00 60.00
UFLHRSA Olaj/Drx/DR/Gevn 25.00 60.00
UFLJAZZ Horn/Mail/Etn/Stck 20.00 50.00
UFLLABC McH/Brd/Mgic/KAJ 30.00 80.00
UFLLAKR Wilt/Rdmn/Mail/MJ 50.00 120.00
UFLLGND Magic/Bird/Rssll/MJ 75.00 200.00
UFLMBBC McH/Prsh/Oscr/KAJ 25.00 60.00
UFLNYKK Reed/Pearl/King/Fraz 40.00 100.00
UFLNYJJ Ewing/Strk/Stck/Mail 20.00 50.00
UFLUJCB Mail/Stock/MJ/Pip 75.00 200.00
UFLWRGD Kerr/Mgic/Stck/Drex 20.00 50.00

2008-09 Ultimate Collection Jerseys Foursome Rookies

STATED PRINT RUN 50 SER.#'d SETS
*PATCHES: 1X TO 2.5X BASE HI
PATCH PRINT RUN 15 SER.#'d SETS
UFR1234 Rse/Bsly/Myo/Wstbrk 12.00 30.00
UFRBGEA McG/Grn/Alxndr/Hbbrt 6.00 15.00
UFRCNTR Hbbrt/Lpz/Thmpsn/Lpz 6.00 15.00
UFRCUSA Rbrts/Drsy/Shrp/Rose 10.00 25.00
UFREACE Shrp/Hbbrt/Alxndr/Hick 6.00 15.00
UFREASE Mario/Lee/McG/D.J. 6.00 15.00
UFRLASK Grdn/Jrdn/Thmpsn/Grn 6.00 15.00
UFRMGOC Wstbrk/White/O.J./Arthr 8.00 20.00
UFRMHIP Rush/Hibrt/Mario/Bsly 6.00 15.00
UFRNCAA Mario/Rose/Rbrts/Arthur 8.00 20.00
UFRPC10 Jerryd/Wvr/Andrsn/Lpz 6.00 15.00
UFRPFWD Love/Hcksn/Spghts/Bsly 6.00 15.00
UFRPGRD Rose/Wstbrk/D.J./Jerryd 15.00 40.00
UFRROOK Frnndz/Alxndr/Love/Grdn 8.00 20.00
UFRSGRD Grdn/Lee/Frnndz/O.J. 6.00 15.00
UFRWEAT Gddns/Spghts/Rbrts/Lpz 6.00 15.00
UFRWENW Kls/Wems/Jerryd/Wvr 6.00 15.00
UFRWEPA Grn/Rndlph/Jrdn/Lpz 6.00 15.00
UFRWESW Drsy/Hill/O.J./Arthur 6.00 15.00

2008-09 Ultimate Collection Jerseys Foursome Veterans

PRINT RUN 50 SER.#'d SETS
UFV05AS Centers/PF 10.00 25.00
UFV06AS Pau/Rip/Sheed/Arns 10.00 25.00
UFV07AS Two Guards 10.00 25.00
UFV76ER Philadelphia 76ers 6.00 15.00
UFVA06S Prkr/Pierce/Allen/LBJ 15.00 40.00
UFVA07S Three Point Shooters 15.00 40.00
UFVAS03 Al/Duncan/Prce/Kidd 15.00 40.00
UFVAS05 Kobe/Nash/LBJ/TMac 125.00 300.00
UFVAS06 Centers/PF2 10.00 25.00
UFVAS07 Melo/Jrmain/Okr/Booz 8.00 20.00
UFVBUCK Milwaukee Bucks 6.00 15.00
UFVBULL Chicago Bulls 6.00 15.00
UFVCAVS Cleveland Cavaliers 15.00 40.00
UFVCBOB Charlotte Bobcats 6.00 15.00
UFVCELT Boston Celtics 15.00 40.00
UFVDETP Detroit Pistons 10.00 25.00
UFVDNUG Denver Nuggets 8.00 20.00
UFVHAWK Atlanta Hawks 6.00 15.00
UFVKING Sacramento Kings 6.00 15.00
UFVLACP Los Angeles Clippers 6.00 15.00
UFVMAVS Dallas Mavericks 8.00 20.00
UFVNOHO New Orleans Hornets 8.00 20.00
UFVNYKK New York Knicks 6.00 15.00
UFVOMAG Orlando Magic 8.00 20.00
UFVRG03 Pau/Parker/Jeff/Tinsley 6.00 15.00
UFVRG04 Dnlvy/Hayes/Nene/Hslm 6.00 15.00
UFVRG05 Dng/Smth/J-Ho/Hrris 6.00 15.00
UFVSPUR San Antonio Spurs 10.00 25.00
UFVSUNS Phoenix Suns 10.00 25.00
UFVUDEX LJ/Kobe/KG/Drnt 125.00 300.00

2008-09 Ultimate Collection Jerseys Six

STATED PRINT RUN 35 SER.#'d SETS
US05AS Rckts/Spurs/Heat/Magic 12.00 30.00
US06AS Celt/Sun/Cav/Pistn/Wiz 15.00 40.00
US76ER Philadelphia 76ers 10.00 25.00
USBLAZ Portland Trail Blazers 12.00 30.00
USBULL Chicago Bulls 30.00 80.00
USCAVS Cleveland Cavaliers 40.00 100.00
USCELT Boston Celtics 40.00 100.00
USCLIP Los Angeles Clippers 10.00 25.00
USDNUG Denver Nuggets 10.00 25.00
USGSWR Goldein State Warriors 10.00 25.00
USHAWK Atlanta Hawks 10.00 25.00
USHEAT Miami Heat 10.00 25.00
USJAZZ Utah Jazz 15.00 40.00
USLSHO Los Angeles Lakers 125.00 300.00
USNETS New Jersey Nets 10.00 25.00
USNICK New York Knicks 12.00 30.00
USPSTN Detroit Pistons 12.00 30.00
USROCK Houston Rockets 15.00 40.00
USSPUR San Antonio Spurs 20.00 50.00
USSUNS Phoenix Suns 15.00 40.00

2008-09 Ultimate Collection Jerseys Ten

STATED PRINT RUN 15 SER.#'d SETS
UTAH Utah Jazz 25.00 60.00
PHILY Philadelphia 76ers 30.00 80.00
SPURS San Antonio Spurs 75.00 200.00
08ROOKIE 2008-09 Rookies 25.00 60.00
BOSTON Boston Celtics 75.00 200.00
LAKERS Los Angeles Lakers 125.00 300.00
CHICAGO Chicago Bulls 50.00 120.00
DETROIT Detroit Pistons 40.00 100.00
NEW YORK New York Knicks 40.00 100.00
ROOKIE08 2008-09 Rookies 2 40.00 100.00

2008-09 Ultimate Collection Legendary Signatures

STATED PRINT RUN 10 SER.#'d SETS

2008-09 Ultimate Collection Memories

STATED PRINT RUN 50 SER.#'d SETS
UMDF Derek Fisher Draft 125.00 300.00
UMDH Dwight Howard 50.00 120.00
UMDW D.Wilkins GM7 75.00 200.00
UMIT Isiah Thomas 50.00 120.00
UMJP John Paxson 40.00 100.00
UMJS John Stockton 60.00 150.00
UMJW Jerry West Gold Med 150.00 400.00
UMKG Kevin Garnett 150.00 400.00
UMMJ M.Johnson AS MVP 150.00 400.00

2008-09 Ultimate Collection Patches Foursome Veterans

*PATCHES: 1X TO 2.5X BASE HI
PATCH PRINT RUN 20 SER.#'d SETS
UFVAS05 Kobe/Nash/LBJ/T-Mac 300.00 600.00

2008-09 Ultimate Collection Patches Six

STATED PRINT RUN 10 SER.#'d SETS
US05AS Mm/Mnu/Dunc/Stat/Yao 60.00 150.00
US76ER Philadelphia 76ers 50.00 120.00
USBLAZ Portland Trail Blazers 40.00 100.00
USBULL Chicago Bulls 60.00 150.00
USCAVS Cleveland Cavaliers 75.00 200.00
USCELT Boston Celtics 100.00 250.00
USCLIP Los Angeles Clippers 20.00 50.00
USDNUG Denver Nuggets 25.00 60.00
USGSWR Golden State Warriors 20.00 50.00
USHAWK Atlanta Hawks 30.00 80.00
USHEAT Miami Heat 25.00 60.00
USJAZZ Utah Jazz 50.00 120.00
USLSHO Los Angeles Lakers 300.00 600.00
USNETS New Jersey Nets 25.00 60.00
USNICK New York Knicks 30.00 80.00
USPSTN Detroit Pistons 30.00 80.00
USROCK Houston Rockets 50.00 120.00
USSPUR San Antonio Spurs 75.00 200.00
USSUNS Phoenix Suns 50.00 120.00

2008-09 Ultimate Collection Prototypical Portraits

STATED PRINT RUN 25 SER.#'d SETS
PPBL Bill Laimbeer 12.00 30.00
PPBM Bob McAdoo 20.00 50.00
PPCD Chris Douglas-Roberts 10.00 25.00
PPCK Chris Kaman 10.00 25.00
PPCM Corey Maggette 10.00 25.00
PPDF Derek Fisher 12.00 30.00
PPDJ DeAndre Jordan 30.00 80.00
PPDR Dennis Rodman 50.00 120.00
PPFE Rudy Fernandez 10.00 25.00
PPHO Hakeem Olajuwon 20.00 50.00
PPJD Joey Dorsey 10.00 25.00
PPJK Jason Kidd 20.00 50.00
PPJS Jack Sikma 10.00 25.00
PPLJ LeBron James 5,000.00 10,000.00
PPMJ Michael Jordan 2,000.00 5,000.00
PPRF Raymond Felton 10.00 25.00
PPRS Ramon Sessions 10.00 25.00
PPSA Ralph Sampson 12.00 30.00
PPTC Tom Chambers 10.00 25.00

2008-09 Ultimate Collection Signature Materials Combos

STATED PRINT RUN 10 SER.#'d SETS
UMCBJ L.James/K.Bryant 15,000.00 30,000.00
UMCBR M.Beasley/D.Rose 125.00 300.00
UMCFM O.Mayo/R.Fernandez 30.00 80.00
UMCGL K.Love/K.Garnett 100.00 250.00
UMCGR D.Granger/B.Rush 30.00 80.00
UMCHH A.Horford/D.Howard 30.00 80.00

2008-09 Ultimate Collection Signature Materials Legends

STATED PRINT RUN 10 SER.#'d SETS
UMLBK Bernard King 30.00 80.00
UMLDR David Robinson 125.00 300.00
UMLGG George Gervin 75.00 200.00
UMLIT Isiah Thomas 60.00 150.00
UMLJS John Stockton 125.00 300.00
UMLLB Larry Bird 150.00 400.00
UMLMJ Michael Jordan 2,000.00 5,000.00
UMLSK Steve Kerr 60.00 150.00

2008-09 Ultimate Collection Signature Materials Rookies

STATED PRINT RUN 25 SER.#'d SETS
UMRCD Chris Douglas-Roberts 5.00 12.00
UMRDA Darrell Arthur 6.00 15.00
UMRDJ DeAndre Jordan 20.00 50.00
UMRDR Derrick Rose 200.00 500.00
UMRGH George Hill 20.00 50.00
UMRJA Joe Alexander 5.00 12.00
UMRJB Jerryd Bayless 6.00 15.00
UMRJD Joey Dorsey 5.00 12.00
UMRJG J.R. Giddens 5.00 12.00
UMRJM Javale McGee 8.00 20.00
UMRKK Kosta Koufos 5.00 12.00
UMRKL Kevin Love 25.00 60.00
UMRMB Michael Beasley 8.00 20.00
UMROM O.J. Mayo 6.00 15.00
UMRRA Ryan Anderson 6.00 15.00
UMRRF Rudy Fernandez 6.00 15.00
UMRWS Walter Sharpe 5.00 12.00

2008-09 Ultimate Collection Signature Materials Veterans

STATED PRINT RUN 10 SER.#'d SETS
UMVAH Al Horford 12.00 30.00
UMVAM Alonzo Mourning 75.00 200.00
UMVAS Amare Stoudemire 20.00 50.00
UMVBD Baron Davis 15.00 40.00
UMVCM Corey Maggette 12.00 30.00
UMVJJ Jarrett Jack 12.00 30.00
UMVJO Jermaine O'Neal 12.00 30.00
UMVKB Kobe Bryant 2,000.00 4,000.00
UMVKG Kevin Garnett 300.00 600.00
UMVMB Mike Bibby 15.00 40.00
UMVYM Yao Ming 200.00 500.00

2008-09 Ultimate Collection Signatures

STATED PRINT RUN 23 TO 25 SER.#'d SETS
UAB Aaron Brooks/25 6.00 15.00
UAT Al Thornton/25 6.00 15.00
UBB Bobby Brown/25 6.00 15.00
UBO Josh Boone/25 6.00 15.00
UBR Brandon Roy/25 12.00 30.00
UCB Corey Brewer/25 6.00 15.00
UCL Carl Landry/25 6.00 15.00
UDC Daequan Cook/25 6.00 15.00
UDF Derek Fisher/25 12.00 30.00
UDW Deron Williams/25 10.00 25.00
UEC Eddy Curry/25 6.00 15.00
UGD Glen Davis/25 6.00 15.00
UJB Jose Barea/25 25.00 60.00
UJF Jordan Farmar/25 6.00 15.00
UJG Jeff Green/25 6.00 15.00
UJN Joakim Noah/25 12.00 30.00
UJW Julian Wright/25 6.00 15.00
UKG Kevin Garnett/25 100.00 250.00
ULJ LeBron James/23 10,000.00 15,000.00
ULO Lamar Odom/25 20.00 50.00
UMC Mike Conley Jr./25 8.00 20.00
URR Rajon Rondo/25 12.00 30.00
URS Rodney Stuckey/25 6.00 15.00

2008-09 Ultimate Collection Signatures Dual

STATED PRINT RUN 25 SER.#'d SETS
SD76 A.Iguodala/A.Miller 10.00 25.00
SDAH M.Bibby/A.Horford 12.00 30.00
SDBC P.Pierce/K.Garnett 200.00 500.00
SDCB R.Pierce/S.Singletary 10.00 25.00
SDCC L.James/M.Williams 1,000.00 2,000.00
SDCH J.Noah/T.Thomas 10.00 25.00
SDDM J.Barea/J.Kidd 30.00 80.00
SDDN C.Anthony/J.Smith 15.00 40.00
SDDP R.Stuckey/T.Prince 10.00 25.00
SDGS M.Belinelli/C.Maggette 10.00 25.00
SDHR J.Dorsey/C.Landry 10.00 25.00
SDIP T.Ford/D.Granger 10.00 25.00
SDLA D.Fisher/J.Farmar 10.00 25.00
SDLC A.Thornton/D.Jordan 10.00 25.00
SDMB R.Sessions/R.Jefferson 10.00 25.00
SDMG M.Conley/R.Gay 10.00 25.00
SDMH D.Cook/S.Livingston 10.00 25.00
SDMT R.Foye/C.Brewer 10.00 25.00
SDNJ J.Boone/R.Anderson 10.00 25.00
SDNO D.West/J.Wright 10.00 25.00
SDNY W.Chandler/Richardson 10.00 25.00
SDOC J.Green/K.Durant 100.00 250.00
SDOM C.Lee/D.Howard 15.00 40.00
SDPS J.Dudley/R.Lopez 10.00 25.00
SDSA B.Bowen/T.Parker 20.00 50.00
SDTB L.Aldridge/B.Roy 15.00 40.00
SDUJ D.Williams/C.Boozer 10.00 25.00

2008-09 Ultimate Collection Signatures Rookie

STATED PRINT RUN 25 SER.#'d SETS
URAR Anthony Randolph 5.00 12.00
URBR Brandon Rush 5.00 12.00
URCD Chris Douglas-Roberts 5.00 12.00
URDA D.J. Augustin 8.00 20.00
URDG Danilo Gallinari 10.00 25.00
URDR Derrick Rose 100.00 250.00
UREG Eric Gordon 20.00 50.00
URGH George Hill 15.00 40.00
URGR Donte Greene 5.00 12.00
URJA Joe Alexander 5.00 12.00
URJB Jerryd Bayless 6.00 15.00
URJJ J.J. Hickson 5.00 12.00
URKL Kevin Love 15.00 40.00
URMB Michael Beasley 8.00 20.00
URMC Mario Chalmers 8.00 20.00
URMS Marreese Speights 6.00 15.00
UROM O.J. Mayo 6.00 15.00
URRF Rudy Fernandez 6.00 15.00
URRW Russell Westbrook 500.00 1,000.00

2008-09 Ultimate Collection Signatures Triple

STATED PRINT RUN 10 SER.#'d SETS
ST76R Iggy/Dwkns/Speights 20.00 50.00
STBOS Giddens/Allen/Rondo 25.00 60.00
STCAV Daughty/LeBron/Hcksn 600.00 1,200.00
STCHI Rose/Grdn/Armstrng 75.00 200.00
STCLP Davis/Gordon/Walton 30.00 80.00
STDEN Smith/Weems/English 15.00 40.00
STDET Prince/Sharpe/Laimbeer 25.00 60.00
STHOU Lndry/Drsy/Bttr 15.00 40.00
STLAL Frmr/Odm/Coopr 15.00 40.00
STMIA Cook/Beasley/Zo 25.00 60.00
STMIL Jeffersn/J.Alex/Mncrf 15.00 40.00
STMIN Love/BigAl/Brwr 20.00 50.00
STNJN CarterWilliams/Lopez 30.00 80.00
STNYK Q-Rich/Gallinari/Rich 15.00 40.00
STPTB Roy/Drexler/Bylss 20.00 50.00
STSAC Miller/Thmpsn/Williams 15.00 40.00
STSAS Hill/Prkr/Grvin 40.00 100.00
STSUN Amare/Lopez/Chmbers 15.00 40.00
STUTA Dantley/Boozer/Koufos 15.00 40.00

2008-09 Ultimate Collection Validation

STATED PRINT RUN 25 SER.#'d SETS
VAI Andre Iguodala 10.00 25.00
VAM Alonzo Mourning 50.00 100.00
VBK Bernard King 10.00 25.00
VCB Carlos Boozer 6.00 15.00
VCD Chris Duhon 6.00 15.00
VCL Carl Landry 6.00 15.00
VGW Gerald Wallace 6.00 15.00
VMR Micheal Ray Richardson 6.00 15.00
VMW Mo Williams 6.00 15.00
VPW Paul Westphal 6.00 15.00
VRR Rajon Rondo 12.00 30.00
VRS Ramon Sessions 6.00 15.00
VSK Steve Kerr 10.00 25.00
VSV Sasha Vujacic 6.00 15.00
VSW Spud Webb 10.00 25.00

2010-11 Ultimate Collection

COMP.SET w/o AUs (60) 20.00 50.00
AU PRINT RUN 99 SER.#'d SETS
1 Michael Jordan 8.00 20.00
2 James Harden 2.50 6.00
3 Bill Russell 3.00 8.00
4 Larry Bird 4.00 10.00
5 Magic Johnson 4.00 10.00
6 Jerry West 2.00 5.00
7 Hakeem Olajuwon 2.00 5.00
8 David Robinson 2.00 5.00
9 Dennis Rodman 2.00 5.00
10 Rick Fox .75 2.00
11 LeBron James 8.00 20.00
12 Julius Erving 2.00 5.00
13 Roy Williams 1.00 2.50
14 Clyde Drexler 1.50 4.00
15 George Gervin 1.50 4.00
16 Dominique Wilkins 1.50 4.00
17 Tracy McGrady 1.50 4.00
18 Hal Greer .75 2.00
19 Cazzie Russell .75 2.00
20 George Lynch 1.00 2.50
21 Alonzo Mourning 1.50 4.00
22 Adrian Dantley 1.00 2.50
23 John Stockton 1.50 4.00
24 Tim Hardaway 1.25 3.00
25 James Worthy 1.25 3.00
26 Rudy Tomjanovich .75 2.00
27 Gail Goodrich 1.00 2.50
28 Jack Sikma .75 2.00
29 Hubert Davis .60 1.50
30 David Thompson 1.00 2.50
31 Bill Walton 1.50 4.00
32 Sam Cassell 1.25 3.00
33 Walter Davis .60 1.50
34 Jerry Sloan 1.00 2.50
35 Yao Ming 2.00 5.00
36 Bill Laimbeer .75 2.00
37 Glen Rice .75 2.00
38 Anfernee Hardaway 2.50 6.00
39 B.J. Armstrong 1.00 2.50
40 Robert Horry 1.00 2.50
41 Mike Krzyzewski 1.25 3.00
42 Michael Cooper 1.00 2.50
43 Elgin Baylor 2.00 5.00
44 Tom Izzo 1.00 2.50
45 Brandon Roy 1.25 3.00
46 Christian Laettner 1.00 2.50
47 Larry Johnson 1.25 3.00
48 Mark Jackson .75 2.00
49 Ricky Rubio .75 2.00
50 Darrell Griffith .60 1.50
51 John Calipari 1.00 2.50
52 Sam Perkins .60 1.50
53 Bobby Hurley .75 2.00
54 Mateen Cleaves .75 2.00
55 Derrick Rose 2.00 5.00
56 Steve Alford .75 2.00
57 Kenny Smith .75 2.00
58 Avery Johnson .75 2.00
59 Danny Manning .75 2.00
60 Calbert Cheaney .60 1.50
61 Paul George AU 100.00 250.00
62 Deon Thompson AU 6.00 15.00
63 Derrick Favors AU 6.00 15.00
64 DeMarcus Cousins AU 15.00 40.00
65 Jordan Crawford AU 4.00 10.00
66 Cole Aldrich AU 4.00 10.00
67 Ed Davis AU 5.00 12.00
68 Al-Farouq Aminu AU 5.00 12.00
69 Greg Monroe AU 6.00 15.00
70 Ekpe Udoh AU 4.00 10.00
71 Daniel Orton AU 4.00 10.00
72 Gani Lawal AU 4.00 10.00
73 Hassan Whiteside AU 8.00 20.00
74 Xavier Henry AU 4.00 10.00
75 James Anderson AU 4.00 10.00
76 Eric Bledsoe AU 8.00 20.00
77 Damion James AU 4.00 10.00
78 Solomon Alabi AU 4.00 10.00
79 Gordon Hayward AU 15.00 40.00
80 Quincy Pondexter AU 4.00 10.00
81 Patrick Patterson AU 5.00 12.00

2010-11 Ultimate Collection 1997 Legends Autographs

AL1 Michael Jordan 1,000.00 2,000.00
AL2 LeBron James 1,000.00 2,000.00
AL3 Magic Johnson 60.00 150.00
AL4 Larry Bird 60.00 150.00
AL5 Julius Erving 50.00 120.00
AL6 Yao Ming 75.00 200.00
AL7 Brandon Roy 5.00 12.00
AL8 Derrick Rose 20.00 50.00
AL9 Tracy McGrady 40.00 100.00
AL11 Gail Goodrich 8.00 20.00
AL12 Dominique Wilkins 15.00 40.00
AL13 George Gervin 12.00 30.00
AL15 David Robinson 40.00 100.00
AL16 Alonzo Mourning 25.00 60.00
AL17 Bill Walton 20.00 50.00
AL18 Mark Jackson 5.00 12.00
AL19 Bobby Hurley 5.00 12.00
AL20 Jerry West 30.00 80.00
AL21 Christian Laettner 6.00 15.00

2010-11 Ultimate Collection All-Time Draft Signatures Gold

STATED PRINT RUN 25 TO 75 SER.#'d SETS
1 Michael Jordan/25 2,000.00 4,000.00
2 LeBron James/25 1,000.00 2,000.00
3 Bill Russell/25 500.00 1,000.00
4 Julius Erving/25 60.00 150.00
5 Magic Johnson/25 60.00 150.00
6 Jerry West/25 25.00 60.00
7 Larry Bird/25 60.00 150.00
8 Chris Mullin/25 15.00 40.00
9 Bill Walton/75 15.00 40.00
10 Bob Lanier/25 10.00 25.00
11 David Robinson/25 40.00 100.00
12 Elgin Baylor/25 12.00 30.00
13 George Gervin/25 12.00 30.00
14 Hakeem Olajuwon/25 40.00 100.00
15 Moses Malone/75 15.00 40.00
16 Yao Ming/75 75.00 200.00
17 Alonzo Mourning/25 30.00 80.00
18 Bobby Hurley/75 6.00 15.00
19 Bill Sharman/75 6.00 15.00
20 Calbert Cheaney/75 6.00 15.00
21 Christian Laettner/75 10.00 25.00
22 Cazzie Russell/75 6.00 15.00
23 Derrick Rose/75 30.00 80.00
24 Danny Ferry/75 6.00 15.00
25 Darrell Griffith/75 6.00 15.00
26 Danny Manning/75 8.00 20.00
27 David Thompson/75 6.00 15.00
28 Gail Goodrich/75 6.00 15.00
29 Hal Greer/75 6.00 15.00
30 Lennie Rosenbluth/75 12.00 30.00
31 Mateen Cleaves/75 6.00 15.00
32 Phil Ford/75 8.00 20.00
33 Brandon Roy/75 8.00 20.00
35 Steve Alford/75 8.00 20.00
36 Tim Hardaway/75 6.00 15.00
37 Tracy McGrady/75 15.00 40.00
38 Adrian Dantley/75 8.00 20.00

2010-11 Ultimate Collection All-Time Team Signatures Gold

STATED PRINT RUN 23 TO 25 SER.#'d SETS
ATAH Anfernee Hardaway/25 25.00 60.00
ATAM Alonzo Mourning/25 30.00 80.00
ATBR Brandon Roy/25 8.00 20.00
ATBW Bill Walton/25 25.00 60.00
ATCC Calbert Cheaney/25 10.00 25.00
ATCL Christian Laettner/25 25.00 60.00
ATDF Danny Ferry/25 8.00 20.00
ATDR Derrick Rose/25 30.00 80.00
ATHO Hakeem Olajuwon/25 20.00 50.00
ATKS Kenny Smith/25 12.00 30.00
ATLB Larry Bird/25 50.00 120.00
ATLJ Larry Johnson/25 30.00 80.00
ATMC Mateen Cleaves/25 8.00 20.00
ATMJ Michael Jordan/23 1,500.00 3,000.00
ATRO David Robinson/25 50.00 100.00
ATRU Bill Russell/25 50.00 100.00
ATSA Steve Alford/25 8.00 20.00

2010-11 Ultimate Collection Base Autographs

STATED PRINT RUN 25 TO 99 SER.#'d SETS
1 Michael Jordan/25 2,000.00 4,000.00
2 James Harden/99 100.00 250.00
3 Bill Russell/25 500.00 1,000.00
4 Larry Bird/25 60.00 150.00
5 Magic Johnson/25 60.00 150.00
6 Jerry West/25 30.00 80.00
7 Hakeem Olajuwon/75 40.00 100.00
8 David Robinson/75 40.00 100.00
9 Dennis Rodman/75 20.00 50.00
10 Rick Fox/99 10.00 25.00
11 LeBron James/25 1,000.00 2,000.00
12 Julius Erving/25 50.00 120.00
14 Clyde Drexler/25 20.00 50.00
15 George Gervin/99 8.00 20.00
16 Dominique Wilkins/25 8.00 20.00
17 Tracy McGrady/25 20.00 50.00
18 Hal Greer/75 8.00 20.00
19 Cazzie Russell/75 6.00 15.00
20 George Lynch/75 6.00 15.00
21 Alonzo Mourning/25 30.00 80.00
22 Adrian Dantley/99 6.00 15.00
24 Tim Hardaway/99 6.00 15.00
25 James Worthy/75 15.00 40.00
26 Rudy Tomjanovich/99 6.00 15.00
27 Gail Goodrich/75 4.00 10.00
28 Jack Sikma/75 4.00 10.00
29 Hubert Davis/75 6.00 15.00
30 David Thompson/99 5.00 12.00
31 Bill Walton/99 12.00 30.00
32 Sam Cassell/99 6.00 15.00
33 Walter Davis/75 8.00 20.00
34 Jerry Sloan/99 15.00 40.00
35 Yao Ming/75 75.00 200.00
36 Bill Laimbeer/75 6.00 15.00
37 Glen Rice/75 6.00 15.00
38 Anfernee Hardaway/99 30.00 80.00
39 B.J. Armstrong/99 4.00 10.00
40 Robert Horry/75 6.00 15.00
42 Michael Cooper/75 4.00 10.00
43 Elgin Baylor/75 6.00 15.00
45 Brandon Roy/99 8.00 20.00
46 Christian Laettner/75 10.00 25.00
47 Larry Johnson/25 30.00 80.00
48 Mark Jackson/99 4.00 10.00
49 Ricky Rubio/75 20.00 50.00
50 Darrell Griffith/99 4.00 10.00
52 Sam Perkins/75 6.00 15.00
53 Bobby Hurley/75 6.00 15.00
54 Mateen Cleaves/99 4.00 10.00
55 Derrick Rose/99 20.00 50.00
56 Steve Alford/99 4.00 10.00
57 Kenny Smith/99 6.00 15.00
58 Avery Johnson/99 6.00 15.00
59 Danny Manning/75 6.00 15.00
60 Calbert Cheaney/75 6.00 15.00

2010-11 Ultimate Collection Big Game Signatures Gold

STATED PRINT RUN 23 TO 75 SER.#'d SETS
BGAJ Avery Johnson/75 4.00 10.00
BGAL Al-Farouq Aminu/75 6.00 15.00
BGAW Al Wood/75 10.00 25.00
BGBH Bobby Hurley/75 6.00 15.00
BGBR Bill Russell/25 500.00 1,000.00
BGBW Bill Walton/75 15.00 40.00
BGCL Christian Laettner/75 20.00 50.00
BGCS Charlie Scott/75 10.00 25.00
BGDF Derrick Favors/75 12.00 30.00
BGDG Darrell Griffith/75 4.00 10.00
BGDM Danny Manning/75 8.00 20.00
BGDR Derrick Rose/75 30.00 80.00
BGDT David Thompson/75 4.00 10.00
BGEB Elgin Baylor/75 8.00 20.00
BGGR Glen Rice/75 6.00 15.00
BGHO Hakeem Olajuwon/75 15.00 40.00
BGJE Julius Erving/25 30.00 80.00
BGJH James Harden/25 60.00 150.00
BGJO Magic Johnson/25 40.00 100.00
BGJW James Worthy/75 40.00 100.00
BGLB Larry Bird/25 50.00 100.00
BGMC Mateen Cleaves/75 6.00 15.00
BGMJ Michael Jordan/23 400.00 700.00
BGRO Brandon Roy/75 8.00 20.00
BGSA Steve Alford/75 8.00 20.00
BGWD Walter Davis/75 6.00 15.00
BGWE Jerry West/75 25.00 60.00
BGYM Yao Ming/75 12.00 30.00

2010-11 Ultimate Collection College Shout Out Signatures

STATED PRINT RUN 25 TO 35 SER.#'d SETS
SOBA B.J. Armstrong/35 12.00 30.00
SOBL Bill Laimbeer/35 6.00 15.00
SOBR Brandon Roy/35 10.00 25.00
SOBW Bill Walton/35 20.00 50.00
SOCL Christian Laettner/35 12.00 30.00
SOCP Candace Parker/35 30.00 80.00
SODM Danny Manning/35 25.00 60.00
SODR Derrick Rose/35 50.00 120.00
SOJE Julius Erving/35 50.00 120.00
SOJR J.R. Reid/35 15.00 40.00
SOJW James Worthy/35 25.00 60.00
SOLB Larry Bird/35 50.00 120.00
SOLJ Larry Johnson/35 12.00 30.00
SOMC Mateen Cleaves/35 6.00 15.00
SOMJ Michael Jordan/35 2,000.00 4,000.00
SOPW Paul Westphal/35 10.00 25.00
SORF Rick Fox/35 12.00 30.00
SOTM Tracy McGrady/35 20.00 50.00

2010-11 Ultimate Collection Personal Touch Hero Autographs

STATED PRINT RUN 25 SER.#'d SETS
HAH Anfernee Hardaway 75.00 200.00
HAM Alonzo Mourning 40.00 100.00
HBR Brandon Roy 10.00 25.00
HCD Clyde Drexler 40.00 100.00
HCL Christian Laettner 25.00 60.00
HDR David Robinson 75.00 200.00
HDW Dominique Wilkins 40.00 100.00
HFA Derrick Favors 8.00 20.00
HHO Hakeem Olajuwon/25 75.00 200.00
HJE Julius Erving 125.00 300.00
HJR J.R. Reid 5.00 12.00
HLB Larry Brown 20.00 50.00
HLJ LeBron James 2,000.00 4,000.00
HMA Mark Jackson 6.00 15.00
HMJ Magic Johnson 125.00 300.00
HPP Patrick Patterson 6.00 15.00
HPR Pat Riley 40.00 100.00
HPW Paul Westphal 15.00 40.00
HRF Rick Fox 6.00 15.00
HRH Robert Horry 10.00 25.00
HRR Ricky Rubio 30.00 80.00
HRT Rudy Tomjanovich 8.00 20.00
HSL Jerry Sloan 40.00 100.00
HTM Tracy McGrady 75.00 200.00
HYM Yao Ming 200.00 500.00

2010-11 Ultimate Collection Personal Touch Movie Autographs

STATED PRINT RUN 25 SER.#'d SETS
MAF Al-Farouq Aminu 6.00 15.00
MAH Anfernee Hardaway 75.00 200.00
MAM Alonzo Mourning 40.00 100.00
MBR Brandon Roy 10.00 25.00
MBW Bill Walton 20.00 50.00
MCL Christian Laettner 30.00 60.00
MDO Donald Williams 5.00 12.00
MDR Derrick Rose 40.00 100.00
MDW Dominique Wilkins 20.00 50.00
MED Ed Davis 6.00 15.00
MFA Derrick Favors 8.00 20.00
MGL George Lynch 8.00 20.00
MJC Jordan Crawford 5.00 12.00
MJE Julius Erving 125.00 300.00
MJR J.R. Reid 5.00 12.00
MKS Kenny Smith 15.00 40.00
MLJ LeBron James 2,000.00 4,000.00
MMJ Magic Johnson 125.00 300.00
MRH Robert Horry 8.00 20.00
MRO David Robinson 75.00 200.00

MRR Ricky Rubio 30.00 80.00
MRT Rudy Tomjanovich 10.00 25.00
MTM Tracy McGrady 75.00 200.00
MYM Yao Ming 200.00 500.00

2010-11 Ultimate Collection Rivalries Signatures

STATED PRINT RUN 25 SER.#'d SETS
RAS S.Alford/K.Smith 10.00 25.00
RBJ M.Johnson/L.Bird 200.00 500.00
RCR C.Cheaney/G.Rice 15.00 40.00
RFA D.Favors/A.Aminu 10.00 25.00
RFJ W.Frazier/L.James 1,000.00 2,000.00
RHH A.Hardaway/T.Hard 50.00 120.00
RHW B.Hurley/D.Williams 10.00 25.00
RJB M.Jordan/L.Bird 2,000.00 4,000.00
RJE M.Jordan/J.Erving 2,000.00 4,000.00
RJG M.Jackson/D.Griffith 10.00 25.00
RJR M.Jordan/Russell 6,000.00 12,000.00
RJU D.James/E.Udoh 10.00 25.00
RLD C.Laettner/E.Davis 15.00 40.00
RLJ C.Laettner/L.Johnson 30.00 80.00
RMJ L.James/T.McGrady 1,000.00 2,000.00
RRC M.Cleaves/G.Rice 15.00 40.00
RRM D.Manning/D.Rose 30.00 80.00
RRR B.Roy/D.Rose 30.00 80.00
RTW D.Thompson/B.Walton 25.00 60.00
RWG P.Westphal/G.Goodrich 20.00 50.00

2010-11 Ultimate Collection Signatures

STATED PRINT RUN 23 TO 99 SER.#'d SETS
SAF Al-Farouq Aminu/99 5.00 12.00
SAH Anfernee Hardaway/99 12.00 30.00
SAM Alonzo Mourning/99 12.00 30.00
SBL Bob Lanier/99 6.00 15.00
SBR Brandon Roy/99 8.00 20.00
SCL Christian Laettner/99 10.00 25.00
SDC DeMarcus Cousins/99 15.00 40.00
SDF Derrick Favors/99 6.00 15.00
SDR Derrick Rose/99 15.00 40.00
SDW Dominique Wilkins/99 10.00 25.00
SFL Freddie Lewis/99 5.00 12.00
SGL George Lynch/99 6.00 15.00
SGO Gail Goodrich/99 5.00 12.00
SHW Hassan Whiteside/99 15.00 40.00
SJA James Anderson/99 4.00 10.00
SJC Jordan Crawford/99 4.00 10.00
SJE Julius Erving/25 40.00 80.00
SLA Larry Johnson/99 10.00 25.00
SLB Larry Bird/25 50.00 100.00
SLJ LeBron James/23 1,000.00 2,000.00
SMA Mark Jackson/99 5.00 12.00
SMJ Michael Jordan/23 2,000.00 4,000.00
SMM Moses Malone/99 10.00 25.00
SRF Rick Fox/25 15.00 40.00
SRR Ricky Rubio/99 15.00 40.00
STH Tim Hardaway/99 6.00 15.00
STM Tracy McGrady/99 10.00 25.00
SXH Xavier Henry/99 4.00 10.00
SYM Yao Ming/99 60.00 150.00

2010-11 Ultimate Collection Signatures Dual

STATED PRINT RUN 10 TO 50 SER.#'d SETS
DBJ M.Jordan/L.Bird/25 2,000.00 4,000.00
DBM L.Bird/C.Mullin/25 75.00 200.00
DEM J.Erving/T.McGrady/50 60.00 150.00
DHH A.Hardaway/T.Hard/50 30.00 80.00
DJB M.Johnson/L.Bird/25 200.00 500.00
DJR Jordan/Russell/25 6,000.00 12,000.00
DKD B.Knight/B.Donovan/50 150.00 400.00
DKJ S.Kemp/L.Johnson/50 50.00 120.00
DLD L.James/Rose/23 1,250.00 2,500.00
DMH T.Hard/A.Mourning/50 25.00 60.00
DMJ L.Johnson/Mourning/50 25.00 60.00
DML F.Lewis/C.Mullin/50 10.00 25.00
DOB D.Orton/E.Bledsoe/50 12.00 30.00
DOM Olajuwon/Ming/50 75.00 200.00
DOR D.Rob/Olajuwon/50 75.00 200.00
DPP D.Cousins/Patterson/50 25.00 60.00
DRJ L.James/R.Rubio/25 800.00 1,500.00
DRR B.Roy/D.Rose/50 20.00 50.00

2010-11 Ultimate Collection Signatures Quad

STATED PRINT RUN 15 SER.#'d SETS
UNC Perk/Ford/Lynch/Mont 40.00 100.00
1987 Rbnsn/Smith/Jksn/Dnvn 75.00 150.00
1993 Lynch/Hard/Cassell/Chny 50.00 120.00
2010 Davis/Hay/Fav/Cousins 40.00 100.00
9192 Laettner/Mourning/LJ/Davis 50.00 120.00
09HOF Jordan/Rob/Stock/Sloan 1,000.00 2,000.00
JHRR James/Hard/Rubio/Rose 1,000.00 2,000.00
JJJB Erving/James/Johnson/Bird 1,500.00 3,000.00
JREA Jordan/Russell/Erving/Bird 6,000.00 12,000.00
ROCK Ming/Olaj/McG/Smith 75.00 150.00
RRBE Roy/Rose/Bird/Erving 175.00 350.00
RRRM Rose/Rubio/McG/Roy 150.00 300.00
TSRS Tomj/Sloan/Riley/Shrmn 50.00 120.00

2010-11 Ultimate Collection Signatures Triple

STATED PRINT RUN 25 SER.#'d SETS
TDET Laimbeer/Dantley/Rod 25.00 60.00
TEML Lewis/Erving/Malone 50.00 100.00
THOU Drex/Smith/Olajuwon 50.00 120.00
TJBE Bird/Erving/Johnson 200.00 500.00
TJJJ Jordan/Erving/Johnson 2,000.00 4,000.00
TJRB Jordan/Russell/James 5,000.00 10,000.00
TJRR Rose/James/Roy 1,000.00 2,000.00
TLAL Good/Johnson/West 75.00 200.00
TLCH Cheaney/Hurley/Lynch 15.00 40.00
TMHL Lynch/Hardaway/McG 40.00 100.00
TNYK Frazier/Jack/Johnson 60.00 150.00
TSAS Johnson/Rob/Wilkins 40.00 100.00
TUOM Rice/Tomj/Russell 20.00 50.00

2010-11 Ultimate Collection Ultimate Inscriptions

STATED PRINT RUN 25 SER.#'d SETS
NAH Anfernee Hardaway 100.00 250.00
NBR Brandon Roy 15.00 40.00
NBW Bill Walton 25.00 60.00
NCD Clyde Drexler 40.00 100.00
NDR Derrick Rose 75.00 200.00
NDT David Thompson 10.00 25.00
NHO Hakeem Olajuwon 75.00 200.00
NJA LeBron James 1,000.00 2,000.00
NJE Julius Erving 75.00 200.00
NJS Jerry Sloan 40.00 100.00
NLJ Larry Johnson 20.00 50.00
NMA Mark Jackson 5.00 12.00
NSP Sam Perkins 20.00 40.00
NYM Yao Ming 200.00 500.00

2013-14 Ultimate Collection Ultimate Legendary Booklets Signatures

OVERALL ULTIMATE ODDS 1:96 HOBBY
PRINT RUNS B/WN 10-60 COPIES PER
NO PRICING ON QTY 10
ISSUED IN 13-14 SP AUTHENTIC
EXCHANGE DEADLINE 3/13/2016
USCW Corliss Williamson/60 6.00 15.00
USDM Donyell Marshall/60 4.00 10.00
USEJ Eddie Jones/60 EXCH 10.00 25.00
USGR Glenn Robinson/60 10.00 25.00
USJL Jerry Lucas/60 6.00 15.00
USJS Joe Smith/60 15.00 40.00
USJW Jay Williams/60 4.00 10.00
USKA Kenny Anderson/60 6.00 15.00
USKK Kerry Kittles/60 4.00 10.00
USKS Keith Smart/60 10.00 25.00
USLJ LeBron James/60 1,500.00 3,000.00
USRI Glen Rice/60 6.00 15.00
USSP Sam Perkins/60 6.00 15.00

2013-14 Ultimate Collection Ultimate Rookie Booklets Signatures

OVERALL ULTIMATE ODDS 1:96 HOBBY
PRINT RUNS B/WN 150-250 COPIES PER
ISSUED IN 13-14 SP AUTHENTIC
EXCHANGE DEADLINE 3/13/2016
URS1 G.Antetokounmpo/250 150.00 400.00
URS2 Lucas Nogueira/250 3.00 8.00
URS3 Dennis Schroeder/250 EXCH 10.00 25.00
URS4 Tony Snell/250 4.00 10.00
URS5 Mason Plumlee/250 4.00 10.00
URS6 Solomon Hill/250 4.00 10.00
URS7 Reggie Bullock/250 4.00 10.00
URS8 Andre Roberson/250 4.00 10.00
URS9 Archie Goodwin/250 3.00 8.00
URS10 Skylar Diggins/150 10.00 25.00
URS11 Shane Larkin/150 3.00 8.00
URS12 Tim Hardaway Jr./150 6.00 15.00

1992-93 Ultimate USBL Promo Sheet

NNO USBL Promo Sheet
Norris Coleman
Dallas Comegys
Kermit Holmes
Anthony Mason
Anthony Pullard
Lloyd Daniels
Michael Anderson
Darrell Armstrong
Roy Tarpley 2.00 5.00

1999-00 Ultimate Victory

COMPLETE SET (150) 50.00 120.00
COMP. SET w/o RC (120) 20.00 50.00
MJ HITS SUBSET STATED ODDS 1:2
121-150 SUBSET STATED ODDS 1:4
1 Dikembe Mutombo .60 1.50
2 Alan Henderson .25 .60
3 LaPhonso Ellis .25 .60
4 Kenny Anderson .30 .75
5 Antoine Walker .40 1.00
6 Paul Pierce .75 2.00
7 Elden Campbell .25 .60
8 Eddie Jones .40 1.00
9 David Wesley .25 .60
10 Michael Jordan 4.00 10.00
11 Kornell David RC .25 .60
12 Toni Kukoc .50 1.25
13 Shawn Kemp .60 1.50
14 Brevin Knight .25 .60
15 Zydrunas Ilgauskas .30 .75
16 Michael Finley .40 1.00
17 Shawn Bradley .25 .60
18 Dirk Nowitzki 1.25 3.00
19 Antonio McDyess .30 .75
20 Nick Van Exel .30 .75
21 Ron Mercer .30 .75
22 Grant Hill .60 1.50
23 Lindsey Hunter .25 .60
24 Jerry Stackhouse .40 1.00
25 John Starks .40 1.00
26 Antawn Jamison .40 1.00
27 Mookie Blaylock .25 .60
28 Hakeem Olajuwon .75 2.00
29 Cuttino Mobley .25 .60
30 Charles Barkley 1.00 2.50
31 Reggie Miller .75 2.00
32 Rik Smits .30 .75
33 Jalen Rose .30 .75
34 Maurice Taylor .25 .60
35 Tyrone Nesby RC .25 .60
36 Michael Olowokandi .25 .60
37 Kobe Bryant 3.00 8.00
38 Shaquille O'Neal 1.50 4.00
39 Glen Rice .40 1.00
40 Robert Horry .30 .75
41 Tim Hardaway .50 1.25
42 Alonzo Mourning .60 1.50
43 Jamal Mashburn .30 .75
44 Ray Allen .60 1.50
45 Glenn Robinson .30 .75
46 Robert Traylor .25 .60
47 Kevin Garnett 1.00 2.50
48 Joe Smith .30 .75
49 Bobby Jackson .30 .75
50 Keith Van Horn .30 .75
51 Stephon Marbury .50 1.25
52 Jayson Williams .25 .60
53 Patrick Ewing .50 1.25
54 Allan Houston .40 1.00
55 Latrell Sprewell .50 1.25
56 Marcus Camby .40 1.00
57 Darrell Armstrong .25 .60
58 Matt Harpring .25 .60
59 Bo Outlaw .25 .60
60 Allen Iverson 1.00 2.50
61 Theo Ratliff .30 .75
62 Larry Hughes .30 .75
63 Jason Kidd .60 1.50
64 Tom Gugliotta .30 .75
65 Anfernee Hardaway 1.00 2.50
66 Scottie Pippen 1.00 2.50
67 Damon Stoudamire .40 1.00
68 Brian Grant .25 .60
69 Jason Williams .60 1.50
70 Vlade Divac .40 1.00
71 Chris Webber .50 1.25
72 Tim Duncan 1.00 2.50
73 Sean Elliott .30 .75
74 David Robinson .75 2.00
75 Avery Johnson .30 .75
76 Gary Payton .60 1.50
77 Vin Baker .30 .75
78 Brent Barry .30 .75
79 Vince Carter 1.00 2.50
80 Doug Christie .30 .75
81 Tracy McGrady .60 1.50
82 Karl Malone .75 2.00
83 John Stockton .60 1.50
84 Bryon Russell .25 .60
85 Shareef Abdur-Rahim .40 1.00
86 Mike Bibby .40 1.00
87 Felipe Lopez .25 .60
88 Juwan Howard .30 .75
89 Rod Strickland .30 .75
90 Mitch Richmond .50 1.25
121 Elton Brand RC 1.25 3.00
122 Steve Francis RC 1.25 3.00
123 Baron Davis RC 1.50 4.00
124 Lamar Odom RC 1.25 3.00
125 Jonathan Bender RC .60 1.50
126 Wally Szczerbiak RC 1.00 2.50
127 Richard Hamilton RC 1.50 4.00
128 Andre Miller RC 1.25 3.00
129 Shawn Marion RC 1.25 3.00
130 Jason Terry RC 1.00 2.50
131 Trajan Langdon RC .50 1.25
132 A.Radojevic RC .40 1.00
133 Corey Maggette RC .75 2.00
134 William Avery RC .40 1.00
135 Ron Artest RC 1.50 4.00
136 Cal Bowdler RC .40 1.00
137 James Posey RC .60 1.50
138 Quincy Lewis RC .40 1.00
139 Dion Glover RC .40 1.00
140 Jeff Foster RC .60 1.50
141 Kenny Thomas RC .60 1.50
142 Devean George RC .50 1.25
143 Tim James RC .40 1.00
144 Vonteego Cummings RC .40 1.00
145 Jumaine Jones RC .40 1.00
146 Scott Padgett RC .50 1.25
147 John Celestand RC .40 1.00
148 Adrian Griffin RC .50 1.25
149 Chris Herren RC .50 1.25
150 Anthony Carter RC .50 1.25

1999-00 Ultimate Victory Victory Collection

COMMON MJ GH (91-120) 25.00 60.00
*STARS: 1.25X TO 3X BASE CARD HI
*RCs: .75X TO 2X BASE HI
STARS: STATED ODDS 1:12
RCs: STATED ODDS 1:24

1999-00 Ultimate Victory Parallel 100

COMMON MJ GH (91-120) 50.00 120.00
*STARS: 12X TO 30X BASE CARD HI
*RCs: 6X TO 15X BASE HI
STATED PRINT RUN 100 SERIAL #'d SETS
10 Michael Jordan 200.00 500.00
37 Kobe Bryant 100.00 250.00

1999-00 Ultimate Victory Court Impact

COMPLETE SET (10) 50.00 120.00
STATED ODDS 1:24
C1 Michael Jordan 40.00 100.00
C2 Vince Carter 3.00 8.00
C3 Kobe Bryant 15.00 40.00
C4 Kevin Garnett 3.00 8.00
C5 Tim Duncan 3.00 8.00
C6 Jason Williams 2.00 5.00
C7 Grant Hill 2.00 5.00
C8 Keith Van Horn 1.00 2.50
C9 Allen Iverson 3.00 8.00
C10 Karl Malone 2.50 6.00

1999-00 Ultimate Victory Dr. J Glory Days

COMPLETE SET (8) 15.00 40.00
COMMON CARD (DR1-DR8) 2.50 6.00
STATED ODDS 1:24

1999-00 Ultimate Victory Got Skills?

COMPLETE SET (8) 4.00 10.00
STATED ODDS 1:24
GS1 Kevin Garnett 2.00 5.00
GS2 Tim Hardaway 1.00 2.50
GS3 Mike Bibby .75 2.00
GS4 Stephon Marbury 1.00 2.50
GS5 Reggie Miller 1.50 4.00
GS6 Jason Williams 1.25 3.00
GS7 Antoine Walker .75 2.00
GS8 Jason Kidd 1.25 3.00

1999-00 Ultimate Victory MJ's World Famous

COMPLETE SET (12) 75.00 200.00
COMMON CARD (MJ1-MJ12) 10.00 25.00
STATED ODDS 1:24

1999-00 Ultimate Victory Scorin' Legion

COMPLETE SET (10) 6.00 15.00
STATED ODDS 1:12
SL1 Tim Duncan 2.00 5.00
SL2 Karl Malone 1.50 4.00
SL3 Stephon Marbury 1.00 2.50
SL4 Shaquille O'Neal 3.00 8.00
SL5 Antonio McDyess .60 1.50
SL6 Gary Payton 1.25 3.00
SL7 Allen Iverson 2.00 5.00
SL8 Keith Van Horn .60 1.50
SL9 Shareef Abdur-Rahim .75 2.00
SL10 Grant Hill 1.25 3.00

1999-00 Ultimate Victory Surface to Air

COMPLETE SET (12) 10.00 25.00
STATED ODDS 1:6
SA1 Vince Carter 2.00 5.00
SA2 Antawn Jamison .75 2.00
SA3 Eddie Jones .75 2.00
SA4 Anfernee Hardaway 2.00 5.00
SA5 Latrell Sprewell 1.00 2.50
SA6 Antonio McDyess .60 1.50
SA7 Michael Finley .75 2.00
SA8 Kobe Bryant 8.00 20.00
SA9 Chris Webber 1.00 2.50
SA10 Shawn Kemp 1.25 3.00
SA11 Ray Allen 1.25 3.00
SA12 Shaquille O'Neal 3.00 8.00

1999-00 Ultimate Victory Ultimate Fabrics

PRINT RUNS LISTED BELOW
UF1 Julius Erving/300 15.00 40.00
UF2 Wilt Chamberlain/100 200.00 500.00
UF3 J.Erving/K.Bryant/25 400.00 800.00

2000-01 Ultimate Victory

COMP.SET w/o SP (60) 12.00 30.00
FLY2K: STATED ODDS 1:6
RCs: STATED PRINT RUN 1500 SERIAL #'d SETS
1 Dikembe Mutombo .60 1.50
2 Jim Jackson .30 .75
3 Paul Pierce .60 1.50
4 Antoine Walker .40 1.00
5 Jamal Mashburn .30 .75
6 Baron Davis .40 1.00
7 Elton Brand .40 1.00
8 Ron Artest .40 1.00
9 Lamond Murray .25 .60
10 Andre Miller .30 .75
11 Michael Finley .40 1.00
12 Dirk Nowitzki 1.00 2.50
13 Antonio McDyess .30 .75
14 Nick Van Exel .40 1.00
15 Jerry Stackhouse .40 1.00
16 Chucky Atkins .25 .60
17 Antawn Jamison .40 1.00
18 Larry Hughes .40 1.00
19 Steve Francis .40 1.00
20 Hakeem Olajuwon .75 2.00
21 Reggie Miller .75 2.00
22 Jalen Rose .30 .75
23 Lamar Odom .40 1.00
24 Corey Maggette .30 .75
25 Shaquille O'Neal 1.50 4.00
26 Kobe Bryant 3.00 8.00
27 Ron Harper .40 1.00
28 Tim Hardaway .50 1.25
29 Eddie Jones .40 1.00
30 Ray Allen .60 1.50
31 Tim Thomas .25 .60
32 Kevin Garnett 1.00 2.50
33 Wally Szczerbiak .30 .75
34 Terrell Brandon .30 .75
35 Stephon Marbury .50 1.25
36 Keith Van Horn .30 .75
37 Allan Houston .40 1.00
38 Latrell Sprewell .50 1.25
39 Grant Hill .60 1.50
40 Tracy McGrady .75 2.00
41 Allen Iverson 1.00 2.50
42 Toni Kukoc .50 1.25
43 Jason Kidd .60 1.50
44 Anfernee Hardaway .60 1.50
45 Scottie Pippen 1.00 2.50
46 Rasheed Wallace .50 1.25
47 Jason Williams .60 1.50
48 Chris Webber .50 1.25
49 Tim Duncan 1.00 2.50
50 David Robinson .75 2.00
51 Gary Payton .60 1.50
52 Rashard Lewis .30 .75
53 Vince Carter .75 2.00
54 Mark Jackson .30 .75
55 Karl Malone .75 2.00
56 John Stockton .75 2.00
57 Shareef Abdur-Rahim .40 1.00
58 Mike Bibby .40 1.00
59 Mitch Richmond .50 1.25
60 Richard Hamilton .50 1.25
61 Kobe Bryant FLY 3.00 8.00
62 Kobe Bryant FLY 3.00 8.00
63 Kobe Bryant FLY 3.00 8.00
64 Kobe Bryant FLY 3.00 8.00
65 Kobe Bryant FLY 3.00 8.00
66 Kobe Bryant FLY 3.00 8.00
67 Kobe Bryant FLY 3.00 8.00
68 Kobe Bryant FLY 3.00 8.00
69 Kobe Bryant FLY 3.00 8.00
70 Kobe Bryant FLY 3.00 8.00
71 Kobe Bryant FLY 3.00 8.00
72 Kobe Bryant FLY 3.00 8.00
73 Kobe Bryant FLY 3.00 8.00
74 Kobe Bryant FLY 3.00 8.00
75 Kobe Bryant FLY 3.00 8.00
76 Kevin Garnett FLY 1.00 2.50
77 Kevin Garnett FLY 1.00 2.50
78 Kevin Garnett FLY 1.00 2.50
79 Kevin Garnett FLY 1.00 2.50
80 Kevin Garnett FLY 1.00 2.50
81 Kevin Garnett FLY 1.00 2.50
82 Kevin Garnett FLY 1.00 2.50
83 Kevin Garnett FLY 1.00 2.50
84 Kevin Garnett FLY 1.00 2.50
85 Kevin Garnett FLY 1.00 2.50
86 Kevin Garnett FLY 1.00 2.50
87 Kevin Garnett FLY 1.00 2.50
88 Kevin Garnett FLY 1.00 2.50
89 Kevin Garnett FLY 1.00 2.50
90 Kevin Garnett FLY 1.00 2.50
91 Kenyon Martin RC 3.00 8.00
92 Stromile Swift RC 1.25 3.00
93 Darius Miles RC 1.50 4.00
94 Marcus Fizer RC 1.25 3.00
95 Mike Miller RC 2.50 6.00
96 DerMarr Johnson RC 1.00 2.50
97 Chris Mihm RC 1.00 2.50
98 Jamal Crawford RC 4.00 10.00
99 Joel Przybilla RC 1.25 3.00
100 Keyon Dooling RC 1.25 3.00
101 Jerome Moiso RC 1.00 2.50
102 Etan Thomas RC 1.25 3.00
103 Courtney Alexander RC 1.00 2.50
104 Mateen Cleaves RC 1.25 3.00
105 Jason Collier RC 1.50 4.00
106 Hedo Turkoglu RC 2.50 6.00
107 Desmond Mason RC 2.00 5.00
108 Quentin Richardson RC 1.25 3.00
109 Jamaal Magloire RC 1.50 4.00
110 Speedy Claxton RC 1.50 4.00
111 Morris Peterson RC 1.50 4.00
112 Donnell Harvey RC 1.25 3.00
113 DeShawn Stevenson RC 1.50 4.00
114 Mamadou N'Diaye RC 1.00 2.50
115 Erick Barkley RC 1.00 2.50
116 Mike Smith RC 1.00 2.50
117 Eddie House RC 1.25 3.00
118 Eduardo Najera RC 1.50 4.00
119 Jason Hart RC 1.50 4.00
120 Chris Porter RC 1.00 2.50

2000-01 Ultimate Victory Victory Collection

COMMON KOBE (61-75) 6.00 15.00
COMMON KG (76-90) 4.00 10.00
*STARS: 4X TO 10X BASE CARD HI
*RCs: .75X TO 2X BASE CARD HI
STATED PRINT RUN 350 SERIAL #'d SETS

2000-01 Ultimate Victory Ultimate Collection

COMMON KOBE (61-75) 100.00 250.00
COMMON KG (76-90) 30.00 80.00
*STARS: 12X TO 30X BASE CARD HI
*RCs: 1.25X TO 3X BASE CARD HI
STATED PRINT RUN 100 SERIAL #'d SETS

2000-01 Ultimate Victory Ultimate Victory

COMMON KOBE (61-75) 200.00 500.00
COMMON KG (76-90) 60.00 150.00
*STARS: 25X TO 60X BASE CARD HI
*RCs: 3X TO 8X BASE HI
STATED PRINT RUN 25 SERIAL #'d SETS

2000-01 Ultimate Victory Championship Fabrics

STATED ODDS 1:480
CF1 Kobe Bryant 150.00 400.00
CF2 Shaquille O'Neal 40.00 100.00
CF3 Michael Jordan 300.00 600.00
CF4 Julius Erving 20.00 50.00
CF5 Larry Bird 40.00 100.00
CF6 Isiah Thomas 12.00 30.00
CFC1 K.Bryant/L.Bird/25 400.00 800.00

2000-01 Ultimate Victory Starstruck

COMPLETE SET (10) 6.00 15.00
STATED ODDS 1:11
S1 Kobe Bryant 5.00 12.00
S2 Gary Payton 1.00 2.50
S3 Chris Webber .75 2.00
S4 Kevin Garnett 1.50 4.00
S5 Stephon Marbury .75 2.00
S6 Shareef Abdur-Rahim .60 1.50
S7 Steve Francis .60 1.50
S8 Tim Duncan 1.50 4.00
S9 Anfernee Hardaway 1.00 2.50
S10 Vince Carter 1.25 3.00

2000-01 Ultimate Victory The Reel World

COMPLETE SET (10) 6.00 15.00
STATED ODDS 1:11
RW1 Kobe Bryant 5.00 12.00
RW2 Vince Carter 1.25 3.00
RW3 Tim Duncan 1.50 4.00
RW4 Allen Iverson 1.50 4.00
RW5 Elton Brand .60 1.50
RW6 Jason Kidd 1.00 2.50
RW7 Kevin Garnett 1.50 4.00
RW8 Lamar Odom .60 1.50
RW9 Scottie Pippen 1.50 4.00
RW10 Karl Malone 1.25 3.00

2000-01 Ultimate Victory Ultimate Fabrics

STATED ODDS 1:240
AU: PRINT RUN 25 SERIAL #'d SETS
UFC1 K.Martin/S.Swift 5.00 12.00
UFC2 K.Martin/D.Miles 5.00 12.00
UFC3 K.Martin/D.Johnson 5.00 12.00
UFC4 K.Martin/M.Fizer 5.00 12.00
UFCA1 K.Martin/S.Swift AU 15.00 40.00

2000-01 Ultimate Victory Ultimate Powers

COMPLETE SET (10) 12.50 25.00
STATED ODDS 1:23
U1 Shaquille O'Neal 3.00 8.00
U2 Grant Hill 1.25 3.00
U3 Vince Carter 1.50 4.00
U4 Allen Iverson 2.00 5.00
U5 Kevin Garnett 2.00 5.00
U6 Tim Duncan 2.00 5.00
U7 Gary Payton 1.25 3.00
U8 Kobe Bryant 6.00 15.00
U9 Steve Francis .75 2.00
U10 Elton Brand .75 2.00

1992-93 Ultra Promo Sheet

NNO Ultra Panel 3.00 8.00

1992-93 Ultra

COMPLETE SET (375) 15.00 40.00
COMPLETE SERIES 1 (200) 8.00 20.00
COMPLETE SERIES 2 (175) 8.00 20.00
1 Stacey Augmon .30 .75
2 Duane Ferrell .20 .50
3 Paul Graham .20 .50
4 Blair Rasmussen .20 .50
5 Rumeal Robinson .20 .50
6 Dominique Wilkins .50 1.25
7 Kevin Willis .25 .60
8 John Bagley .20 .50
9 Dee Brown .25 .60
10 Rick Fox .30 .75
11 Kevin Gamble .20 .50
12 Joe Kleine .20 .50
13 Reggie Lewis .30 .75
14 Kevin McHale .50 1.25
15 Robert Parish .40 1.00
16 Ed Pinckney .20 .50
17 Muggsy Bogues .30 .75
18 Dell Curry .25 .60
19 Kenny Gattison .20 .50
20 Kendall Gill .25 .60
21 Larry Johnson .40 1.00
22 Johnny Newman .20 .50
23 J.R. Reid .25 .60
24 B.J. Armstrong .30 .75
25 Bill Cartwright .25 .60
26 Horace Grant .30 .75
27 Michael Jordan 2.50 6.00
28 Stacey King .20 .50
29 John Paxson .25 .60
30 Will Perdue .20 .50
31 Scottie Pippen .75 2.00
32 Scott Williams .20 .50
33 John Battle .25 .60
34 Terrell Brandon .25 .60
35 Brad Daugherty .25 .60
36 Craig Ehlo .25 .60
37 Larry Nance .25 .60
38 Mark Price .30 .75
39 Mike Sanders .20 .50
40 John Williams .25 .60
41 Terry Davis .20 .50
42 Derek Harper .25 .60
43 Donald Hodge .20 .50
44 Mike Iuzzolino .20 .50
45 Fat Lever .25 .60
46 Doug Smith .20 .50
47 Randy White .20 .50
48 Winston Garland .20 .50
49 Chris Jackson .25 .60
50 Marcus Liberty .20 .50
51 Todd Lichti .20 .50
52 Mark Macon .20 .50
53 Dikembe Mutombo .50 1.25
54 Reggie Williams .20 .50
55 Mark Aguirre .25 .60
56 Joe Dumars .40 1.00
57 Bill Laimbeer .30 .75
58 Dennis Rodman .75 2.00
59 Isiah Thomas .50 1.25
60 Darrell Walker .20 .50
61 Orlando Woolridge .30 .75
62 Victor Alexander .20 .50
63 Chris Gatling .20 .50
64 Tim Hardaway .40 1.00
65 Tyrone Hill .20 .50
66 Sarunas Marciulionis .30 .75
67 Chris Mullin .40 1.00
68 Billy Owens .25 .60
69 Sleepy Floyd .25 .60
70 Avery Johnson .25 .60
71 Vernon Maxwell .25 .60
72 Hakeem Olajuwon .60 1.50
73 Kenny Smith .25 .60
74 Otis Thorpe .25 .60
75 Dale Davis .20 .50
76 Vern Fleming .25 .60
77 George McCloud .20 .50
78 Reggie Miller .60 1.50
79 Detlef Schrempf .30 .75
80 Rik Smits .25 .60
81 LaSalle Thompson .20 .50
82 Gary Grant .20 .50
83 Ron Harper .30 .75
84 Mark Jackson .30 .75
85 Danny Manning .25 .60
86 Ken Norman .20 .50
87 Stanley Roberts .20 .50
88 Loy Vaught .20 .50
89 Elden Campbell .20 .50
90 Vlade Divac .30 .75
91 A.C. Green .25 .60
92 Sam Perkins .25 .60
93 Byron Scott .30 .75
94 Tony Smith .20 .50
95 Sedale Threatt .20 .50
96 James Worthy .50 1.25
97 Willie Burton .20 .50
98 Bimbo Coles .20 .50
99 Kevin Edwards .20 .50
100 Grant Long .20 .50
101 Glen Rice .30 .75
102 Rony Seikaly .25 .60
103 Brian Shaw .20 .50
104 Steve Smith .30 .75
105 Frank Brickowski .20 .50
106 Moses Malone .30 .75
107 Fred Roberts .20 .50
108 Alvin Robertson .25 .60
109 Thurl Bailey .25 .60
110 Gerald Glass .20 .50
111 Luc Longley .30 .75
112 Felton Spencer .20 .50
113 Doug West .25 .60
114 Kenny Anderson .25 .60
115 Mookie Blaylock .30 .75
116 Sam Bowie .25 .60
117 Derrick Coleman .30 .75
118 Chris Dudley .20 .50
119 Chris Morris .25 .60
120 Drazen Petrovic .40 1.00
121 Greg Anthony .25 .60
122 Patrick Ewing .50 1.25
123 Anthony Mason .25 .60
124 Charles Oakley .30 .75
125 Doc Rivers .30 .75
126 Charles Smith .25 .60
127 John Starks .30 .75
128 Nick Anderson .25 .60
129 Anthony Bowie .20 .50
130 Terry Catledge .20 .50
131 Jerry Reynolds .20 .50
132 Dennis Scott .25 .60
133 Scott Skiles .25 .60
134 Brian Williams .25 .60
135 Ron Anderson .20 .50
136 Manute Bol .30 .75
137 Johnny Dawkins .25 .60
138 Armon Gilliam .20 .50
139 Hersey Hawkins .25 .60
140 Jeff Ruland .25 .60
141 Charles Shackleford .20 .50
142 Cedric Ceballos .25 .60
143 Tom Chambers .30 .75
144 Kevin Johnson .30 .75
145 Negele Knight .20 .50
146 Dan Majerle .30 .75
147 Mark West .25 .60
148 Mark Bryant .20 .50
149 Clyde Drexler .50 1.25
150 Kevin Duckworth .25 .60
151 Jerome Kersey .25 .60
152 Robert Pack .20 .50
153 Terry Porter .25 .60
154 Clifford Robinson .25 .60
155 Buck Williams .25 .60
156 Anthony Bonner .20 .50
157 Duane Causwell .20 .50
158 Mitch Richmond .40 1.00
159 Lionel Simmons .20 .50
160 Wayman Tisdale .30 .75
161 Spud Webb .30 .75
162 Willie Anderson .25 .60
163 Antoine Carr .25 .60
164 Terry Cummings .25 .60
165 Sean Elliott .30 .75
166 Sidney Green .20 .50
167 David Robinson .60 1.50
168 Dana Barros .20 .50
169 Benoit Benjamin .20 .50
170 Michael Cage .25 .60
171 Eddie Johnson .25 .60
172 Shawn Kemp .50 1.25
173 Derrick McKey .25 .60
174 Nate McMillan .25 .60
175 Gary Payton .50 1.25
176 Ricky Pierce .25 .60
177 David Benoit .20 .50
178 Mike Brown .20 .50
179 Tyrone Corbin .25 .60
180 Mark Eaton .30 .75
181 Jeff Malone .25 .60
182 Karl Malone .60 1.50
183 John Stockton .60 1.50
184 Michael Adams .25 .60
185 Ledell Eackles .20 .50
186 Pervis Ellison .20 .50
187 A.J. English .20 .50
188 Harvey Grant .25 .60
189 Buck Johnson .20 .50
190 LaBradford Smith .20 .50
191 Larry Stewart .20 .50
192 David Wingate .20 .50
193 Alonzo Mourning RC 1.50 4.00
194 Adam Keefe RC .20 .50
195 Robert Horry RC .75 2.00
196 Anthony Peeler RC .25 .60
197 Tracy Murray RC .25 .60
198 Dave Johnson RC .20 .50
199 Checklist 1-104 .40 1.00
200 Checklist 105-200 .40 1.00
201 David Robinson JS .60 1.50
202 Dikembe Mutombo JS .50 1.25
203 Otis Thorpe JS .25 .60
204 Hakeem Olajuwon JS .60 1.50
205 Shawn Kemp JS 1.25 3.00
206 Charles Barkley JS .75 2.00
207 Pervis Ellison JS .20 .50
208 Chris Morris JS .25 .60
209 Brad Daugherty JS .25 .60
210 Derrick Coleman JS .30 .75
211 Tim Perry JS .20 .50
212 Duane Causwell JS .20 .50
213 Scottie Pippen JS .75 2.00
214 Robert Parish JS .40 1.00
215 Stacey Augmon JS .30 .75
216 Michael Jordan JS 2.50 6.00
217 Karl Malone JS .60 1.50
218 John Williams JS .25 .60
219 Horace Grant JS .30 .75
220 Orlando Woolridge JS .30 .75
221 Mookie Blaylock .30 .75
222 Greg Foster .20 .50
223 Steve Henson .20 .50
224 Adam Keefe .20 .50
225 Jon Koncak .20 .50
226 Travis Mays .20 .50
227 Alaa Abdelnaby .20 .50
228 Sherman Douglas .25 .60
229 Xavier McDaniel .25 .60
230 Marcus Webb RC .20 .50
231 Tony Bennett RC .20 .50
232 Mike Gminski .20 .50
233 Kevin Lynch .20 .50
234 Alonzo Mourning 1.50 4.00
235 David Wingate .20 .50
236 Rodney McCray .20 .50
237 Trent Tucker .20 .50
238 Corey Williams RC .20 .50
239 Danny Ferry .25 .60
240 Jay Guidinger RC .20 .50
241 Jerome Lane .20 .50
242 Bobby Phills RC .25 .60
243 Gerald Wilkins .25 .60
244 Walter Bond RC .20 .50
245 Dexter Cambridge RC .20 .50
246 Radisav Curcic UER RC .20 .50
247 Brian Howard RC .20 .50
248 Tracy Moore RC .20 .50
249 Sean Rooks RC .20 .50
250 Kevin Brooks .20 .50
251 LaPhonso Ellis RC .30 .75
252 Scott Hastings .20 .50
253 Robert Pack .20 .50
254 Gary Plummer RC .20 .50
255 Bryant Stith RC .25 .60
256 Robert Werdann RC .20 .50
257 Gerald Glass .20 .50
258 Terry Mills .20 .50
259 Olden Polynice .20 .50
260 Danny Young .20 .50
261 Jud Buechler .25 .60
262 Jeff Grayer .20 .50
263 Byron Houston RC .20 .50
264 Keith Jennings RC .20 .50
265 Ed Nealy .20 .50
266 Latrell Sprewell RC 1.00 2.50

267 Scott Brooks .25 .60
268 Matt Bullard .20 .50
269 Winston Garland .20 .50
270 Carl Herrera .20 .50
271 Robert Horry .75 2.00
272 Tree Rollins .25 .60
273 Greg Dreiling .20 .50
274 Sean Green .20 .50
275 Sam Mitchell .20 .50
276 Pooh Richardson .20 .50
277 Malik Sealy RC .25 .60
278 Kenny Williams .20 .50
279 Mark Jackson .30 .75
280 Stanley Roberts .20 .50
281 Elmore Spencer RC .20 .50
282 Kiki Vandeweghe .25 .60
283 John S. Williams .25 .60
284 Randy Woods RC .20 .50
285 Alex Blackwell RC .20 .50
286 Duane Cooper RC .20 .50
287 James Edwards .20 .50
288 Jack Haley .20 .50
289 Anthony Peeler .25 .60
290 Keith Askins .20 .50
291 Matt Geiger RC .20 .50
292 Alec Kessler .20 .50
293 Harold Miner w/M.Jordan RC .40 1.00
294 John Salley .25 .60
295 Anthony Avent RC .20 .50
296 Jon Barry RC .20 .50
297 Todd Day RC .20 .50
298 Blue Edwards .20 .50
299 Brad Lohaus .20 .50
300 Lee Mayberry RC .20 .50
301 Eric Murdock .20 .50
302 Danny Schayes .20 .50
303 Lance Blanks .20 .50
304 Christian Laettner RC 1.00 2.50
305 Marlon Maxey RC .20 .50
306 Bob McCann RC .20 .50
307 Chuck Person .25 .60
308 Brad Sellers .25 .60
309 Chris Smith RC .20 .50
310 Gundars Vetra RC .20 .50
311 Micheal Williams .20 .50
312 Rafael Addison .20 .50
313 Chucky Brown .20 .50
314 Maurice Cheeks .25 .60
315 Tate George .20 .50
316 Rick Mahorn .25 .60
317 Rumeal Robinson .20 .50
318 Eric Anderson RC .20 .50
319 Rolando Blackman .25 .60
320 Tony Campbell .20 .50
321 Hubert Davis RC .25 .60
322 Doc Rivers .30 .75
323 Charles Smith .25 .60
324 Herb Williams .25 .60
325 Litterial Green RC .20 .50
326 Steve Kerr .25 .60
327 Greg Kite .20 .50
328 Shaquille O'Neal RC 3.00 8.00
329 Tom Tolbert .25 .60
330 Jeff Turner .20 .50
331 Greg Grant .20 .50
332 Jeff Hornacek .25 .60
333 Andrew Lang .20 .50
334 Tim Perry .20 .50
335 C.Weatherspoon RC .30 .75
336 Danny Ainge .30 .75
337 Charles Barkley .75 2.00
338 Richard Dumas RC .25 .60
339 Frank Johnson .25 .60
340 Tim Kempton .20 .50
341 Oliver Miller RC .25 .60
342 Jerrod Mustaf .20 .50
343 Mario Elie .25 .60
344 Dave Johnson .20 .50
345 Tracy Murray .25 .60
346 Rod Strickland .25 .60
347 Randy Brown .20 .50
348 Pete Chilcutt .20 .50
349 Marty Conlon .20 .50
350 Jim Les .20 .50
351 Kurt Rambis .25 .60
352 Walt Williams RC .30 .75
353 Lloyd Daniels RC .20 .50
354 Vinny Del Negro .25 .60
355 Dale Ellis .25 .60
356 Avery Johnson .25 .60
357 Sam Mack RC .20 .50
358 J.R. Reid .25 .60
359 David Wood .20 .50
360 Vincent Askew .20 .50
361 Isaac Austin RC .20 .50
362 John Crotty RC .20 .50
363 Stephen Howard RC .20 .50
364 Jay Humphries .20 .50
365 Larry Krystkowiak .25 .60
366 Rex Chapman .25 .60
367 Tom Gugliotta RC .30 .75
368 Buck Johnson .20 .50
369 Charles Jones .20 .50
370 Don MacLean RC .25 .60
371 Doug Overton .20 .50
372 Brent Price RC .20 .50
373 Checklist 201-266 .40 1.00
374 Checklist 267-330 .40 1.00
375 Checklist 331-375 .40 1.00
JS207 Pervis Ellison AU 12.00 30.00
JS212 Duane Causwell AU 8.00 20.00
JS215 Stacey Augmon AU 15.00 40.00
NNO Jam Session Rank 1-10 1.25 3.00
NNO Jam Session Rank 11-20 1.50 4.00

1992-93 Ultra All-NBA

COMPLETE SET (15) 12.00 30.00
SER.1 STATED ODDS 1:14
1 Karl Malone 1.25 3.00
2 Chris Mullin .75 2.00
3 David Robinson 1.25 3.00
4 Michael Jordan 10.00 25.00
5 Clyde Drexler 1.00 2.50
6 Scottie Pippen 1.50 4.00
7 Charles Barkley 1.50 4.00
8 Patrick Ewing 1.00 2.50
9 Tim Hardaway .75 2.00
10 John Stockton 1.25 3.00
11 Dennis Rodman 1.50 4.00
12 Kevin Willis .50 1.25
13 Brad Daugherty .50 1.25
14 Mark Price .60 1.50
15 Kevin Johnson .60 1.50

1992-93 Ultra All-Rookies

COMPLETE SET (10) 12.00 30.00
SER.2 STATED ODDS 1:13
1 LaPhonso Ellis 1.00 2.50
2 Tom Gugliotta 1.00 2.50
3 Robert Horry 2.50 6.00
4 Christian Laettner 3.00 8.00
5 Harold Miner 1.25 3.00
6 Alonzo Mourning 5.00 12.00
7 Shaquille O'Neal 8.00 20.00
8 Latrell Sprewell 3.00 8.00
9 Clarence Weatherspoon 1.00 2.50
10 Walt Williams 1.00 2.50

1992-93 Ultra Award Winners

COMPLETE SET (5) 8.00 20.00
SER.1 STATED ODDS 1:42
1 Michael Jordan 6.00 15.00
2 David Robinson 1.25 3.00
3 Larry Johnson .75 2.00
4 Detlef Schrempf .60 1.50
5 Pervis Ellison .40 1.00

1992-93 Ultra Scottie Pippen

COMPLETE SET (10) 8.00 20.00
COMMON PIPPEN (1-10) .75 2.00
SER.1 STATED ODDS 1:21
CERTIFIED AUTOGRAPH (AU) 30.00 80.00
PIPPEN AU: SER.1 STATED ODDS 1:9,000
COMMON SEND-OFF (11-12) .75 2.00
TWO CARDS PER 10 SER.1 WRAPPERS

1992-93 Ultra Playmakers

COMPLETE SET (10) 4.00 10.00
SER.2 STATED ODDS 1:13
1 Kenny Anderson .50 1.25
2 Muggsy Bogues .40 1.00
3 Tim Hardaway .75 2.00
4 Mark Jackson .60 1.50
5 Kevin Johnson .60 1.50
6 Mark Price .60 1.50
7 Terry Porter .50 1.25
8 Scott Skiles .50 1.25
9 John Stockton 1.25 3.00
10 Isiah Thomas 1.00 2.50

1992-93 Ultra Rejectors

SER.2 STATED ODDS 1:26
1 Alonzo Mourning 3.00 8.00
2 Dikembe Mutombo 1.00 2.50
3 Hakeem Olajuwon 1.25 3.00
4 Shaquille O'Neal 5.00 12.00
5 David Robinson 1.25 3.00

1993-94 Ultra

COMPLETE SET (375) 15.00 40.00
COMPLETE SERIES 1 (200) 8.00 20.00
COMPLETE SERIES 2 (175) 8.00 20.00
SUBSET CARDS SAME VALUE AS BASE CARDS
1 Stacey Augmon .30 .75
2 Mookie Blaylock .40 1.00
3 Doug Edwards RC .40 1.00
4 Duane Ferrell .25 .60
5 Paul Graham .25 .60
6 Adam Keefe .25 .60
7 Dominique Wilkins .60 1.50
8 Kevin Willis .30 .75
9 Alaa Abdelnaby .25 .60
10 Dee Brown .30 .75
11 Sherman Douglas .25 .60
12 Rick Fox .30 .75
13 Kevin Gamble .25 .60
14 Xavier McDaniel .40 1.00
15 Robert Parish .50 1.25
16 Muggsy Bogues .40 1.00
17 Scott Burrell RC .40 1.00
18 Dell Curry .40 1.00
19 Kenny Gattison .25 .60
20 Hersey Hawkins .30 .75
21 Eddie Johnson .25 .60
22 Larry Johnson .50 1.25
23 Alonzo Mourning .60 1.50
24 Johnny Newman .25 .60
25 David Wingate .25 .60
26 B.J. Armstrong .40 1.00
27 Corie Blount RC .40 1.00
28 Bill Cartwright .30 .75
29 Horace Grant .40 1.00
30 Michael Jordan 4.00 10.00
31 Stacey King .25 .60
32 John Paxson .40 1.00
33 Will Perdue .25 .60
34 Scottie Pippen 1.00 2.50
35 Terrell Brandon .30 .75
36 Brad Daugherty .30 .75
37 Danny Ferry .25 .60
38 Chris Mills RC .40 1.00
39 Larry Nance .30 .75
40 Mark Price .40 1.00
41 Gerald Wilkins .30 .75
42 John Williams .25 .60
43 Terry Davis .25 .60
44 Derek Harper .30 .75
45 Donald Hodge .25 .60
46 Jim Jackson .30 .75
47 Sean Rooks .25 .60
48 Doug Smith .25 .60
49 Mahmoud Abdul-Rauf .25 .60
50 LaPhonso Ellis .25 .60
51 Mark Macon .25 .60
52 Dikembe Mutombo .60 1.50
53 Bryant Stith .25 .60
54 Reggie Williams .25 .60
55 Mark Aguirre .25 .60
56 Joe Dumars .50 1.25
57 Bill Laimbeer .40 1.00
58 Terry Mills .25 .60
59 Olden Polynice .25 .60
60 Alvin Robertson .30 .75
61 Sean Elliott .40 1.00
62 Isiah Thomas .60 1.50
63 Victor Alexander .25 .60
64 Chris Gatling .25 .60
65 Tim Hardaway .50 1.25
66 Byron Houston .25 .60
67 Sarunas Marciulionis .40 1.00
68 Chris Mullin .50 1.25
69 Billy Owens .30 .75
70 Latrell Sprewell .60 1.50
71 Matt Bullard .25 .60
72 Sam Cassell RC .75 2.00
73 Carl Herrera .25 .60
74 Robert Horry .40 1.00
75 Vernon Maxwell .30 .75
76 Hakeem Olajuwon .75 2.00
77 Kenny Smith .25 .60
78 Otis Thorpe .40 1.00
79 Dale Davis .30 .75
80 Vern Fleming .25 .60
81 Reggie Miller .75 2.00
82 Sam Mitchell .25 .60
83 Pooh Richardson .30 .75
84 Detlef Schrempf .40 1.00
85 Rik Smits .30 .75
86 Ron Harper .40 1.00
87 Mark Jackson .30 .75
88 Danny Manning .30 .75
89 Stanley Roberts .25 .60
90 Loy Vaught .25 .60
91 John Williams .25 .60
92 Sam Bowie .30 .75
93 Doug Christie .30 .75
94 Vlade Divac .40 1.00
95 George Lynch RC .40 1.00
96 Anthony Peeler .25 .60
97 James Worthy .50 1.25
98 Bimbo Coles .25 .60
99 Grant Long .25 .60
100 Harold Miner .30 .75
101 Glen Rice .40 1.00
102 Rony Seikaly .30 .75
103 Brian Shaw .25 .60
104 Steve Smith .30 .75
105 Anthony Avent .25 .60
106 Vin Baker RC .60 1.50
107 Frank Brickowski .25 .60
108 Todd Day .25 .60
109 Blue Edwards .25 .60
110 Lee Mayberry .25 .60
111 Eric Murdock .25 .60
112 Orlando Woolridge .25 .60
113 Thurl Bailey .25 .60
114 Christian Laettner .40 1.00
115 Chuck Person .25 .60
116 Doug West .25 .60
117 Micheal Williams .25 .60
118 Kenny Anderson .30 .75
119 Derrick Coleman .40 1.00
120 Rick Mahorn .30 .75
121 Chris Morris .25 .60
122 Rumeal Robinson .25 .60
123 Rex Walters RC .30 .75
124 Greg Anthony .25 .60
125 Rolando Blackman .30 .75
126 Hubert Davis .25 .60
127 Patrick Ewing .60 1.50
128 Anthony Mason .30 .75
129 Charles Oakley .40 1.00
130 Doc Rivers .30 .75
131 Charles Smith .25 .60
132 John Starks .40 1.00
133 Nick Anderson .30 .75
134 Anthony Bowie .25 .60
135 Shaquille O'Neal 2.00 5.00
136 Dennis Scott .30 .75
137 Scott Skiles .25 .60
138 Jeff Turner .25 .60
139 Shawn Bradley RC .40 1.00
140 Johnny Dawkins .30 .75
141 Jeff Hornacek .30 .75
142 Tim Perry .25 .60
143 Clarence Weatherspoon .25 .60
144 Danny Ainge .40 1.00
145 Charles Barkley 1.00 2.50
146 Cedric Ceballos .30 .75
147 Kevin Johnson .40 1.00
148 Negele Knight .25 .60
149 Malcolm Mackey RC .25 .60
150 Dan Majerle .40 1.00
151 Oliver Miller .25 .60
152 Mark West .25 .60
153 Mark Bryant .25 .60
154 Clyde Drexler .60 1.50
155 Jerome Kersey .25 .60
156 Terry Porter .30 .75
157 Clifford Robinson .40 1.00
158 Rod Strickland .30 .75
159 Buck Williams .30 .75
160 Duane Causwell .25 .60
161 Bobby Hurley RC .40 1.00
162 Mitch Richmond .50 1.25
163 Lionel Simmons .25 .60
164 Wayman Tisdale .30 .75
165 Spud Webb .30 .75
166 Walt Williams .40 1.00
167 Willie Anderson .25 .60
168 Antoine Carr .25 .60
169 Lloyd Daniels .25 .60
170 Dennis Rodman 1.00 2.50
171 Dale Ellis .25 .60
172 Avery Johnson .25 .60
173 J.R. Reid .30 .75
174 David Robinson .75 2.00
175 Michael Cage .30 .75
176 Kendall Gill .30 .75
177 Ervin Johnson RC .40 1.00
178 Shawn Kemp .60 1.50
179 Derrick McKey .30 .75
180 Nate McMillan .30 .75
181 Gary Payton .50 1.25
182 Sam Perkins .30 .75
183 Ricky Pierce .30 .75
184 David Benoit .25 .60
185 Tyrone Corbin .25 .60
186 Mark Eaton .40 1.00
187 Jay Humphries .25 .60
188 Jeff Malone .25 .60
189 Karl Malone .75 2.00
190 John Stockton .75 2.00
191 Luther Wright RC .25 .60
192 Michael Adams .30 .75
193 Calbert Cheaney RC .40 1.00
194 Pervis Ellison .25 .60
195 Tom Gugliotta .30 .75
196 Buck Johnson .25 .60
197 LaBradford Smith .25 .60
198 Larry Stewart .25 .60
199 Checklist .40 1.00
200 Checklist .40 1.00
201 Doug Edwards .40 1.00
202 Craig Ehlo .25 .60
203 Jon Koncak .25 .60
204 Andrew Lang .25 .60
205 Ennis Whatley .25 .60
206 Chris Corchiani .25 .60
207 Acie Earl RC .40 1.00
208 Jimmy Oliver .25 .60
209 Ed Pinckney .25 .60
210 Dino Radja RC .40 1.00
211 Matt Wenstrom RC .25 .60
212 Tony Bennett .25 .60
213 Scott Burrell .40 1.00
214 LeRon Ellis .25 .60
215 Hersey Hawkins .30 .75
216 Eddie Johnson .25 .60
217 Rumeal Robinson .25 .60
218 Corie Blount .40 1.00
219 Dave Johnson .25 .60
220 Steve Kerr .30 .75
221 Toni Kukoc RC 1.00 2.50
222 Pete Myers .25 .60
223 Bill Wennington .25 .60
224 Scott Williams .25 .60
225 John Battle .25 .60
226 Tyrone Hill .25 .60
227 Gerald Madkins RC .40 1.00
228 Chris Mills .40 1.00
229 Bobby Phills .25 .60
230 Greg Dreiling .25 .60
231 Lucious Harris RC .40 1.00
232 Popeye Jones RC .40 1.00
233 Tim Legler RC .40 1.00
234 Fat Lever .30 .75
235 Jamal Mashburn RC .75 2.00
236 Tom Hammonds .25 .60
237 Darnell Mee RC .25 .60
238 Robert Pack .25 .60
239 Rodney Rogers RC .40 1.00
240 Brian Williams .25 .60
241 Greg Anderson .25 .60
242 Sean Elliott .40 1.00
243 Allan Houston RC .75 2.00
244 Lindsey Hunter RC .40 1.00
245 Mark Macon .25 .60
246 David Wood .25 .60
247 Jud Buechler .25 .60
248 Josh Grant RC .30 .75
249 Jeff Grayer .25 .60
250 Keith Jennings .25 .60
251 Avery Johnson .25 .60
252 Chris Webber RC 2.00 5.00
253 Scott Brooks .25 .60
254 Sam Cassell .75 2.00
255 Mario Elie .30 .75
256 Richard Petruska RC .40 1.00
257 Eric Riley RC .40 1.00
258 Antonio Davis RC .50 1.25
259 Scott Haskin RC .25 .60
260 Derrick McKey .30 .75
261 Byron Scott .40 1.00
262 Malik Sealy .25 .60
263 Kenny Williams .25 .60
264 Haywoode Workman .25 .60
265 Mark Aguirre .30 .75
266 Terry Dehere RC .25 .60
267 Harold Ellis RC .40 1.00
268 Gary Grant .25 .60
269 Bob Martin RC .40 1.00
270 Elmore Spencer .25 .60
271 Tom Tolbert .25 .60
272 Sam Bowie .30 .75
273 Elden Campbell .25 .60
274 Antonio Harvey RC .40 1.00
275 George Lynch .40 1.00
276 Tony Smith .25 .60
277 Sedale Threatt .25 .60
278 Nick Van Exel RC 1.00 2.50
279 Willie Burton .25 .60
280 Matt Geiger .25 .60
281 John Salley .30 .75
282 Vin Baker .60 1.50
283 Jon Barry .25 .60
284 Brad Lohaus .25 .60
285 Ken Norman .25 .60
286 Derek Strong RC .30 .75
287 Mike Brown .25 .60
288 Brian Davis RC .40 1.00
289 Tellis Frank .25 .60
290 Luc Longley .30 .75
291 Marlon Maxey .25 .60
292 Isaiah Rider RC .60 1.50
293 Chris Smith .25 .60
294 P.J. Brown RC .40 1.00
295 Kevin Edwards .25 .60
296 Armon Gilliam .25 .60
297 Johnny Newman .25 .60
298 Rex Walters .30 .75
299 David Wesley RC .40 1.00
300 Jayson Williams .25 .60
301 Anthony Bonner .25 .60
302 Derek Harper .30 .75
303 Herb Williams .25 .60
304 Litterial Green .25 .60
305 Anfernee Hardaway RC 2.00 5.00
306 Greg Kite .25 .60
307 Larry Krystkowiak .25 .60
308 Keith Tower RC .40 1.00
309 Dana Barros .25 .60
310 Shawn Bradley .40 1.00
311 Greg Graham RC .25 .60
312 Sean Green .25 .60
313 Warren Kidd RC .25 .60
314 Eric Leckner .25 .60
315 Moses Malone .60 1.50
316 Orlando Woolridge .25 .60
317 Duane Cooper .25 .60
318 Joe Courtney RC .40 1.00
319 A.C. Green .30 .75
320 Frank Johnson .25 .60
321 Joe Kleine .25 .60
322 Chris Dudley .25 .60
323 Harvey Grant .30 .75
324 Jaren Jackson .25 .60
325 Tracy Murray .25 .60
326 James Robinson RC .40 1.00
327 Reggie Smith .25 .60
328 Kevin Thompson RC .25 .60
329 Randy Brown .25 .60
330 Evers Burns RC .40 1.00
331 Pete Chilcutt .25 .60
332 Bobby Hurley .40 1.00
333 Mike Peplowski RC .40 1.00
334 LaBradford Smith .25 .60
335 Trevor Wilson .25 .60
336 Terry Cummings .30 .75
337 Vinny Del Negro .25 .60
338 Sleepy Floyd .30 .75
339 Negele Knight .25 .60
340 Dennis Rodman 1.00 2.50
341 Chris Whitney RC .30 .75
342 Vincent Askew .30 .75
343 Kendall Gill .30 .75
344 Ervin Johnson .40 1.00
345 Chris King RC .40 1.00
346 Detlef Schrempf .40 1.00
347 Walter Bond .25 .60
348 Tom Chambers .40 1.00
349 John Crotty .25 .60
350 Bryon Russell RC .40 1.00
351 Felton Spencer .25 .60
352 Mitchell Butler RC .40 1.00
353 Rex Chapman .25 .60
354 Calbert Cheaney .40 1.00
355 Kevin Duckworth .30 .75
356 Don MacLean .25 .60
357 Gheorghe Muresan RC .40 1.00
358 Doug Overton .25 .60
359 Brent Price .25 .60
360 Kenny Walker .25 .60
361 Derrick Coleman USA .40 1.00
362 Joe Dumars USA .50 1.25
363 Tim Hardaway USA .50 1.25
364 Larry Johnson USA .50 1.25
365 Shawn Kemp USA .60 1.50
366 Dan Majerle USA .40 1.00
367 Alonzo Mourning USA .60 1.50
368 Mark Price USA .40 1.00
369 Steve Smith USA .30 .75
370 Isiah Thomas USA .60 1.50
371 Dominique Wilkins USA .60 1.50
372 Don Nelson
Don Chaney .40 1.00
373 Jamal Mashburn CL .75 2.00
374 Checklist .40 1.00
375 Checklist .40 1.00
M1 Reggie Miller USA 1.00 2.50
M2 Shaquille O'Neal USA 2.50 6.00
M3 Team Checklist USA .75 2.00

1993-94 Ultra All-Defensive

COMPLETE SET (10) 75.00 200.00
SER.1 STATED ODDS 1:24 JUMBO
1 Joe Dumars 6.00 15.00
2 Michael Jordan 75.00 200.00
3 Hakeem Olajuwon 10.00 25.00
4 Scottie Pippen 10.00 25.00
5 Dennis Rodman 10.00 25.00
6 Horace Grant 6.00 15.00
7 Dan Majerle 4.00 10.00
8 Larry Nance 3.00 8.00
9 David Robinson 10.00 25.00
10 John Starks 6.00 15.00

1993-94 Ultra All-NBA

COMPLETE SET (14) 12.00 30.00
SER.1 STATED ODDS 1:16
1 Charles Barkley 2.50 6.00
2 Michael Jordan 10.00 25.00
3 Karl Malone 2.00 5.00
4 Hakeem Olajuwon 2.00 5.00
5 Mark Price 1.00 2.50
6 Joe Dumars 1.25 3.00
7 Patrick Ewing 1.50 4.00
8 Larry Johnson 1.25 3.00
9 John Stockton 2.00 5.00
10 Dominique Wilkins 1.50 4.00
11 Derrick Coleman 1.00 2.50
12 Tim Hardaway 1.25 3.00
13 Scottie Pippen 2.50 6.00
14 David Robinson 2.00 5.00

1993-94 Ultra All-Rookie Series

COMPLETE SET (15) 8.00 20.00
SER.2 STATED ODDS 1:7
1 Vin Baker .75 2.00
2 Shawn Bradley .50 1.25
3 Calbert Cheaney .50 1.25
4 Anfernee Hardaway 2.50 6.00
5 Lindsey Hunter .50 1.25
6 Bobby Hurley .50 1.25
7 Popeye Jones .50 1.25
8 Toni Kukoc 1.25 3.00
9 Jamal Mashburn 1.00 2.50
10 Chris Mills .50 1.25
11 Dino Radja .50 1.25
12 Isaiah Rider .75 2.00
13 Rodney Rogers .50 1.25
14 Nick Van Exel 1.25 3.00
15 Chris Webber 2.50 6.00

1993-94 Ultra All-Rookie Team

COMPLETE SET (5) 2.50 6.00
SER.1 STATED ODDS 1:24
1 LaPhonso Ellis .40 1.00
2 Tom Gugliotta w/Jordan 2.00 5.00
3 Christian Laettner .50 1.25
4 Alonzo Mourning .75 2.00
5 Shaquille O'Neal 4.00 10.00

1993-94 Ultra Award Winners

COMPLETE SET (5) 10.00 25.00
SER.1 STATED ODDS 1:36 JUMBO
1 Mahmoud Abdul-Rauf 1.25 3.00
2 Charles Barkley 4.00 10.00
3 Hakeem Olajuwon 3.00 8.00
4 Shaquille O'Neal 8.00 20.00
5 Clifford Robinson 1.50 4.00

1993-94 Ultra Famous Nicknames

COMPLETE SET (15) 20.00 50.00
SER.2 STATED ODDS 1:5
1 Charles Barkley 2.50 6.00
2 Muggsy Bogues 1.00 2.50
3 Derrick Coleman 1.00 2.50
4 Clyde Drexler 1.50 4.00
5 Anfernee Hardaway 5.00 12.00
6 Larry Johnson 1.25 3.00
7 Michael Jordan 25.00 60.00
8 Toni Kukoc 2.50 6.00
9 Karl Malone 2.00 5.00
10 Harold Miner .75 2.00
11 Alonzo Mourning 1.50 4.00
12 Hakeem Olajuwon 2.00 5.00
13 Shaquille O'Neal 5.00 12.00
14 David Robinson 2.00 5.00
15 Dominique Wilkins 1.50 4.00

1993-94 Ultra Inside/Outside

COMPLETE SET (10) 6.00 15.00
1 Patrick Ewing 1.00 2.50
2 Jim Jackson .50 1.25
3 Larry Johnson .75 2.00
4 Michael Jordan 10.00 25.00
5 Dan Majerle .60 1.50
6 Hakeem Olajuwon 1.25 3.00
7 Scottie Pippen 1.50 4.00
8 Latrell Sprewell 1.00 2.50
9 John Starks .60 1.50
10 Walt Williams .60 1.50

1993-94 Ultra Jam City

COMPLETE SET (9) 40.00 100.00
SER.2 STATED ODDS 1:37 JUMBO
1 Charles Barkley 10.00 25.00
2 Derrick Coleman 4.00 10.00
3 Clyde Drexler 6.00 15.00
4 Patrick Ewing 6.00 15.00
5 Shawn Kemp 6.00 15.00
6 Harold Miner 3.00 8.00
7 Shaquille O'Neal 20.00 50.00
8 David Robinson 8.00 20.00
9 Dominique Wilkins 6.00 15.00

1993-94 Ultra Karl Malone

COMPLETE SET (10) 6.00 15.00
COMMON MALONE (1-10) .75 2.00
SER.1 STATED ODDS 1:16
CERTIFIED AUTOGRAPH (AU) 40.00 100.00
COMMON SEND-OFF (11-12) .75 2.00
TWO CARDS PER 10 SER.1 WRAPPERS

1993-94 Ultra Power In The Key

COMPLETE SET (9) 100.00 250.00
SER.2 STATED ODDS 1:37 HOBBY
1 Larry Johnson 6.00 15.00
2 Michael Jordan 75.00 200.00
3 Karl Malone 8.00 20.00
4 Oliver Miller 5.00 12.00
5 Alonzo Mourning 6.00 15.00
6 Hakeem Olajuwon 10.00 25.00
7 Shaquille O'Neal 12.00 30.00
8 Otis Thorpe 5.00 12.00
9 Chris Webber 8.00 20.00

1993-94 Ultra Rebound Kings

COMPLETE SET (10) 5.00 12.00
SER.2 STATED ODDS 1:4
1 Charles Barkley 1.50 4.00
2 Derrick Coleman .60 1.50
3 Shawn Kemp 1.00 2.50
4 Karl Malone 1.25 3.00
5 Alonzo Mourning 1.00 2.50
6 Dikembe Mutombo 1.00 2.50
7 Charles Oakley .60 1.50
8 Hakeem Olajuwon 1.25 3.00
9 Shaquille O'Neal 3.00 8.00
10 Dennis Rodman 1.50 4.00

1993-94 Ultra Scoring Kings

COMPLETE SET (10) 300.00 600.00
SER.1 STATED ODDS 1:36 HOBBY
1 Charles Barkley 20.00 50.00
2 Joe Dumars 15.00 40.00
3 Patrick Ewing 20.00 50.00
4 Larry Johnson 20.00 50.00
5 Michael Jordan 300.00 600.00
6 Karl Malone 20.00 50.00
7 Alonzo Mourning 20.00 50.00
8 Shaquille O'Neal 40.00 100.00
9 David Robinson 20.00 50.00
10 Dominique Wilkins 20.00 50.00

1994-95 Ultra

COMPLETE SET (350) 20.00 50.00
COMPLETE SERIES 1 (200) 12.00 30.00
COMPLETE SERIES 2 (150) 8.00 20.00
1 Stacey Augmon .30 .75
2 Mookie Blaylock .40 1.00
3 Craig Ehlo .25 .60
4 Adam Keefe .25 .60
5 Andrew Lang .25 .60
6 Ken Norman .25 .60
7 Kevin Willis .30 .75
8 Dee Brown .30 .75
9 Sherman Douglas .25 .60
10 Acie Earl .25 .60
11 Pervis Ellison .25 .60
12 Rick Fox .25 .60
13 Xavier McDaniel .25 .60
14 Eric Montross RC .30 .75
15 Dino Radja .25 .60
16 Dominique Wilkins .60 1.50
17 Michael Adams .25 .60
18 Muggsy Bogues .30 .75
19 Dell Curry .25 .60
20 Kenny Gattison .25 .60
21 Hersey Hawkins .25 .60
22 Larry Johnson .50 1.25
23 Alonzo Mourning .60 1.50
24 Robert Parish .40 1.00
25 B.J. Armstrong .40 1.00
26 Steve Kerr .30 .75
27 Toni Kukoc .50 1.25
28 Luc Longley .30 .75
29 Pete Myers .25 .60
30 Will Perdue .25 .60
31 Scottie Pippen 1.00 2.50
32 Terrell Brandon .25 .60
33 Brad Daugherty .30 .75
34 Tyrone Hill .25 .60
35 Chris Mills .30 .75
36 Bobby Phills .25 .60
37 Mark Price .40 1.00
38 Gerald Wilkins .30 .75
39 John Williams .25 .60
40 Terry Davis .25 .60
41 Jim Jackson .30 .75
42 Popeye Jones .25 .60
43 Jason Kidd RC 2.00 5.00
44 Jamal Mashburn .40 1.00
45 Sean Rooks .25 .60
46 Doug Smith .25 .60
47 Mahmoud Abdul-Rauf .25 .60
48 LaPhonso Ellis .25 .60
49 Dikembe Mutombo .60 1.50
50 Robert Pack .30 .75
51 Rodney Rogers .25 .60
52 Bryant Stith .25 .60
53 Brian Williams .25 .60
54 Reggie Williams .25 .60
55 Greg Anderson .25 .60
56 Joe Dumars .40 1.00
57 Allan Houston .40 1.00
58 Lindsey Hunter .25 .60
59 Terry Mills .25 .60
60 Tim Hardaway .50 1.25
61 Chris Mullin .50 1.25
62 Billy Owens .25 .60
63 Latrell Sprewell .50 1.25
64 Chris Webber .75 2.00
65 Sam Cassell .40 1.00
66 Carl Herrera .25 .60
67 Robert Horry .40 1.00
68 Vernon Maxwell .25 .60
69 Hakeem Olajuwon .75 2.00
70 Kenny Smith .30 .75
71 Otis Thorpe .30 .75
72 Antonio Davis .30 .75
73 Dale Davis .25 .60
74 Mark Jackson .30 .75
75 Derrick McKey .25 .60
76 Reggie Miller .75 2.00
77 Byron Scott .30 .75
78 Rik Smits .30 .75
79 Haywoode Workman .25 .60
80 Gary Grant .25 .60
81 Ron Harper .30 .75
82 Elmore Spencer .25 .60
83 Loy Vaught .25 .60
84 Elden Campbell .25 .60
85 Doug Christie .30 .75
86 Vlade Divac .40 1.00
87 Eddie Jones RC 1.25 3.00
88 George Lynch .25 .60
89 Anthony Peeler .25 .60
90 Sedale Threatt .25 .60
91 Nick Van Exel .40 1.00
92 James Worthy .50 1.25
93 Bimbo Coles .25 .60
94 Matt Geiger .25 .60
95 Grant Long .25 .60
96 Harold Miner .25 .60
97 Glen Rice .40 1.00
98 John Salley .25 .60
99 Rony Seikaly .25 .60
100 Brian Shaw .25 .60
101 Steve Smith .30 .75
102 Vin Baker .40 1.00
103 Jon Barry .25 .60
104 Todd Day .25 .60
105 Lee Mayberry .25 .60
106 Eric Murdock .25 .60
107 Thurl Bailey .25 .60
108 Stacey King .25 .60
109 Christian Laettner .30 .75
110 Isaiah Rider .40 1.00
111 Chris Smith .25 .60
112 Doug West .25 .60
113 Micheal Williams .25 .60
114 Kenny Anderson .30 .75
115 Benoit Benjamin .25 .60
116 P.J. Brown .25 .60
117 Derrick Coleman .40 1.00
118 Yinka Dare RC .25 .60
119 Kevin Edwards .25 .60
120 Armon Gilliam .25 .60
121 Chris Morris .25 .60
122 Greg Anthony .25 .60
123 Anthony Bonner .25 .60
124 Hubert Davis .25 .60
125 Patrick Ewing .60 1.50
126 Derek Harper .30 .75
127 Anthony Mason .30 .75
128 Charles Oakley .40 1.00
129 Doc Rivers .30 .75
130 John Starks .40 1.00
131 Nick Anderson .25 .60
132 Anthony Avent .25 .60
133 Anthony Bowie .25 .60
134 Anfernee Hardaway .75 2.00
135 Shaquille O'Neal 1.50 4.00
136 Dennis Scott .30 .75
137 Jeff Turner .25 .60
138 Dana Barros .25 .60
139 Shawn Bradley .25 .60
140 Greg Graham .25 .60
141 Jeff Malone .25 .60
142 Tim Perry .25 .60
143 Clarence Weatherspoon .25 .60
144 Scott Williams .25 .60
145 Danny Ainge .40 1.00
146 Charles Barkley 1.00 2.50
147 Cedric Ceballos .30 .75
148 A.C. Green .30 .75
149 Frank Johnson .25 .60
150 Kevin Johnson .40 1.00
151 Dan Majerle .40 1.00
152 Oliver Miller .25 .60
153 Wesley Person RC .40 1.00
154 Mark Bryant .25 .60
155 Clyde Drexler .60 1.50
156 Harvey Grant .25 .60
157 Jerome Kersey .25 .60

158 Tracy Murray .25 .60
159 Terry Porter .25 .60
160 Clifford Robinson .30 .75
161 James Robinson .25 .60
162 Rod Strickland .25 .60
163 Buck Williams .25 .60
164 Duane Causwell .25 .60
165 Olden Polynice .25 .60
166 Mitch Richmond .50 1.25
167 Lionel Simmons .25 .60
168 Walt Williams .25 .60
169 Willie Anderson .25 .60
170 Terry Cummings .30 .75
171 Sean Elliott .30 .75
172 Avery Johnson .30 .75
173 J.R. Reid .25 .60
174 David Robinson .75 2.00
175 Dennis Rodman 1.00 2.50
176 Kendall Gill .25 .60
177 Shawn Kemp .60 1.50
178 Nate McMillan .30 .75
179 Gary Payton .60 1.50
180 Sam Perkins .25 .60
181 Detlef Schrempf .40 1.00
182 David Benoit .25 .60
183 Tyrone Corbin .25 .60
184 Jeff Hornacek .30 .75
185 Jay Humphries .25 .60
186 Karl Malone .75 2.00
187 Bryon Russell .25 .60
188 Felton Spencer .25 .60
189 John Stockton .75 2.00
190 Mitchell Butler .25 .60
191 Rex Chapman .25 .60
192 Calbert Cheaney .30 .75
193 Kevin Duckworth .25 .60
194 Tom Gugliotta .25 .60
195 Don MacLean .25 .60
196 Gheorghe Muresan .25 .60
197 Scott Skiles .25 .60
198 Checklist .12 .30
199 Checklist .12 .30
200 Checklist .12 .30
201 Tyrone Corbin .25 .60
202 Doug Edwards .25 .60
203 Jim Les .25 .60
204 Grant Long .25 .60
205 Ken Norman .25 .60
206 Steve Smith .30 .75
207 Blue Edwards .25 .60
208 Greg Minor RC .40 1.00
209 Eric Montross .30 .75
210 Derek Strong .25 .60
211 David Wesley .25 .60
212 Tony Bennett .25 .60
213 Scott Burrell .25 .60
214 Darrin Hancock .30 .75
215 Greg Sutton .25 .60
216 Corie Blount .25 .60
217 Jud Buechler .25 .60
218 Ron Harper .30 .75
219 Larry Krystkowiak .25 .60
220 Dickey Simpkins RC .30 .75
221 Bill Wennington .25 .60
222 Michael Cage .25 .60
223 Tony Campbell .25 .60
224 Steve Colter .25 .60
225 Greg Dreiling .25 .60
226 Danny Ferry .25 .60
227 Tony Dumas RC .30 .75
228 Lucious Harris .25 .60
229 Donald Hodge .25 .60
230 Jason Kidd 2.00 5.00
231 Lorenzo Williams .25 .60
232 Dale Ellis .25 .60
233 Tom Hammonds .25 .60
234 Jalen Rose RC 1.00 2.50
235 Reggie Slater .25 .60
236 Rafael Addison .25 .60
237 Bill Curley RC .25 .60
238 Johnny Dawkins .25 .60
239 Grant Hill RC 2.00 5.00
240 Eric Leckner .25 .60
241 Mark Macon .25 .60
242 Oliver Miller .25 .60
243 Mark West .25 .60
244 Victor Alexander .25 .60
245 Chris Gatling .25 .60
246 Tom Gugliotta .25 .60
247 Keith Jennings .25 .60
248 Ricky Pierce .25 .60
249 Carlos Rogers RC .30 .75
250 Clifford Rozier RC .25 .60
251 Rony Seikaly .25 .60
252 David Wood .25 .60
253 Tim Breaux .25 .60
254 Scott Brooks .25 .60
255 Zan Tabak .25 .60
256 Duane Ferrell .25 .60
257 Mark Jackson .30 .75
258 Sam Mitchell .25 .60
259 John Williams .25 .60
260 Terry Dehere .25 .60
261 Harold Ellis .25 .60
262 Matt Fish .25 .60
263 Tony Massenburg .25 .60
264 Lamond Murray RC .40 1.00
265 Bo Outlaw RC .40 1.00
266 Eric Piatkowski RC .40 1.00
267 Pooh Richardson .25 .60
268 Malik Sealy .25 .60
269 Randy Woods .25 .60
270 Sam Bowie .25 .60
271 Cedric Ceballos .30 .75
272 Antonio Harvey .25 .60
273 Eddie Jones 1.25 3.00
274 Anthony Miller RC .40 1.00
275 Tony Smith .25 .60
276 Ledell Eackles .25 .60
277 Kevin Gamble .25 .60
278 Brad Lohaus .25 .60
279 Billy Owens .25 .60
280 Khalid Reeves RC .30 .75
281 Kevin Willis .30 .75
282 Marty Conlon .25 .60
283 Alton Lister .25 .60
284 Eric Mobley RC .25 .60
285 Johnny Newman .25 .60
286 Ed Pinckney .25 .60
287 Glenn Robinson RC .75 2.00
288 Howard Eisley .40 1.00
289 Winston Garland .25 .60
290 Andres Guibert .25 .60
291 Donyell Marshall RC .40 1.00
292 Sean Rooks .25 .60
293 Yinka Dare .25 .60
294 Sleepy Floyd .25 .60
295 Sean Higgins .25 .60
296 Rex Walters .25 .60
297 Jayson Williams .25 .60
298 Charles Smith .25 .60
299 Charlie Ward RC .40 1.00
300 Herb Williams .25 .60
301 Monty Williams RC .50 1.25
302 Horace Grant .40 1.00
303 Geert Hammink .25 .60
304 Tree Rollins .25 .60
305 Donald Royal .25 .60
306 Brian Shaw .25 .60
307 Brooks Thompson RC .30 .75
308 Derrick Alston RC .25 .60
309 Willie Burton .25 .60
310 Jaren Jackson .25 .60
311 B.J. Tyler RC .25 .60
312 Scott Williams .25 .60
313 Sharone Wright RC .30 .75
314 Joe Kleine .25 .60
315 Danny Manning .30 .75
316 Elliot Perry .25 .60
317 Wesley Person .40 1.00
318 Trevor Ruffin RC .25 .60
319 Danny Schayes .25 .60
320 Wayman Tisdale .25 .60
321 Chris Dudley .25 .60
322 James Edwards .25 .60
323 Alaa Abdelnaby .25 .60
324 Randy Brown .25 .60
325 Brian Grant RC .60 1.50
326 Bobby Hurley .25 .60
327 Michael Smith RC .25 .60
328 Henry Turner .25 .60
329 Trevor Wilson .25 .60
330 Vinny Del Negro .25 .60
331 Moses Malone .40 1.00
332 Julius Nwosu .25 .60
333 Chuck Person .30 .75
334 Chris Whitney .25 .60
335 Vincent Askew .25 .60
336 Bill Cartwright .30 .75
337 Ervin Johnson .25 .60
338 Sarunas Marciulionis .25 .60
339 Antoine Carr .25 .60
340 Tom Chambers .30 .75
341 John Crotty .25 .60
342 Jamie Watson RC .25 .60
343 Juwan Howard RC .60 1.50
344 Jim McIlvaine RC .30 .75
345 Doug Overton .25 .60
346 Scott Skiles .25 .60
347 Anthony Tucker RC .25 .60
348 Chris Webber .75 2.00
349 Checklist .20 .50
350 Checklist .20 .50

1994-95 Ultra All-NBA

COMPLETE SET (15) 4.00 10.00
SER.1 STATED ODDS 1:3 HOBBY/RETAIL
1 Karl Malone 1.00 2.50
2 Hakeem Olajuwon 1.00 2.50
3 Scottie Pippen 1.25 3.00
4 Latrell Sprewell .60 1.50
5 John Stockton 1.00 2.50
6 Charles Barkley 1.25 3.00
7 Kevin Johnson .50 1.25
8 Shawn Kemp .75 2.00
9 Mitch Richmond .60 1.50
10 David Robinson 1.00 2.50
11 Derrick Coleman .50 1.25
12 Shaquille O'Neal 2.00 5.00
13 Gary Payton .75 2.00
14 Mark Price .50 1.25
15 Dominique Wilkins .75 2.00

1994-95 Ultra All-Rookie Team

COMPLETE SET (10) 20.00 50.00
SER.1 STATED ODDS 1:36 JUMBO
1 Vin Baker 3.00 8.00
2 Anfernee Hardaway 8.00 20.00
3 Jamal Mashburn 3.00 8.00
4 Isaiah Rider 3.00 8.00
5 Chris Webber 8.00 20.00
6 Shawn Bradley 2.00 5.00
7 Lindsey Hunter 2.00 5.00
8 Toni Kukoc 4.00 10.00
9 Dino Radja 2.00 5.00
10 Nick Van Exel 3.00 8.00

1994-95 Ultra All-Rookies

COMPLETE SET (15) 6.00 15.00
SER.2 STATED ODDS 1:5 HOBBY/RETAIL
1 Brian Grant .60 1.50
2 Grant Hill 2.00 5.00
3 Juwan Howard .60 1.50
4 Eddie Jones 1.25 3.00
5 Jason Kidd 2.00 5.00
6 Donyell Marshall .40 1.00
7 Eric Montross .30 .75
8 Lamond Murray .40 1.00
9 Wesley Person .40 1.00
10 Khalid Reeves .30 .75
11 Glenn Robinson .75 2.00
12 Carlos Rogers .30 .75
13 Jalen Rose 1.00 2.50
14 B.J. Tyler .25 .60
15 Sharone Wright .30 .75

1994-95 Ultra Award Winners

COMPLETE SET (4) 2.50 6.00
SER.1 STATED ODDS 1:4 HOBBY/RETAIL
1 Dell Curry .30 .75
2 Don MacLean .30 .75
3 Hakeem Olajuwon 1.00 2.50
4 Chris Webber 1.00 2.50

1994-95 Ultra Defensive Gems

COMPLETE SET (6) 6.00 15.00
SER.2 STATED ODDS 1:37 HOBBY/RETAIL
1 Mookie Blaylock 1.50 4.00
2 Hakeem Olajuwon 3.00 8.00
3 Gary Payton 2.50 6.00
4 Scottie Pippen 4.00 10.00
5 David Robinson 3.00 8.00
6 Latrell Sprewell 2.00 5.00

1994-95 Ultra Double Trouble

COMPLETE SET (10) 5.00 12.00
SER.1 STATED ODDS 1:5 HOBBY/RETAIL
1 Derrick Coleman .50 1.25
2 Patrick Ewing .75 2.00
3 Anfernee Hardaway 1.00 2.50
4 Jamal Mashburn .50 1.25
5 Reggie Miller 1.00 2.50
6 Alonzo Mourning .75 2.00
7 Scottie Pippen 1.25 3.00
8 David Robinson 1.00 2.50
9 Latrell Sprewell .60 1.50
10 John Stockton 1.00 2.50

1994-95 Ultra Inside/Outside

COMPLETE SET (10) 4.00 10.00
SER.2 STATED ODDS 1:7 HOBBY
1 Sam Cassell .50 1.25
2 Cedric Ceballos .40 1.00
3 Calbert Cheaney .40 1.00
4 Anfernee Hardaway 1.00 2.50
5 Jim Jackson .40 1.00
6 Dan Majerle .50 1.25
7 Robert Pack .40 1.00
8 Scottie Pippen 1.25 3.00
9 Mitch Richmond .60 1.50
10 Latrell Sprewell .60 1.50

1994-95 Ultra Jam City

COMPLETE SET (10) 10.00 25.00
SER.2 STATED ODDS 1:7 JUMBO
1 Vin Baker .75 2.00
2 Grant Hill 4.00 10.00
3 Robert Horry .75 2.00
4 Shawn Kemp 1.25 3.00
5 Jamal Mashburn .75 2.00
6 Alonzo Mourning 1.25 3.00
7 Dikembe Mutombo 1.25 3.00
8 Shaquille O'Neal 8.00 20.00
9 Glenn Robinson 1.50 4.00
10 Dominique Wilkins 1.25 3.00

1994-95 Ultra Power

COMPLETE SET (10) 5.00 12.00
SER.1 STATED ODDS 1:3 HOBBY/RETAIL
1 Charles Barkley 1.25 3.00
2 Derrick Coleman .50 1.25
3 Larry Johnson .60 1.50
4 Shawn Kemp .75 2.00
5 Karl Malone 1.00 2.50
6 Dikembe Mutombo .75 2.00
7 Charles Oakley .50 1.25
8 Shaquille O'Neal 2.00 5.00
9 Dennis Rodman 1.25 3.00
10 Chris Webber 1.00 2.50

1994-95 Ultra Power In The Key

COMPLETE SET (10) 10.00 25.00
SER.2 STATED ODDS 1:7 RETAIL
1 Charles Barkley 2.50 6.00
2 Patrick Ewing 1.50 4.00
3 Horace Grant 1.00 2.50
4 Larry Johnson 1.25 3.00
5 Karl Malone 2.00 5.00
6 Hakeem Olajuwon 2.00 5.00
7 Shaquille O'Neal 4.00 10.00
8 David Robinson 2.00 5.00
9 Chris Webber 2.00 5.00
10 Kevin Willis .75 2.00

1994-95 Ultra Rebound Kings

COMPLETE SET (10) 6.00 15.00
SER.2 STATED ODDS 1:2 HOBBY/RETAIL
1 Derrick Coleman .60 1.50
2 A.C. Green .50 1.25
3 Alonzo Mourning 1.00 2.50
4 Dikembe Mutombo 1.00 2.50
5 Charles Oakley .60 1.50
6 Hakeem Olajuwon 1.25 3.00
7 Shaquille O'Neal 2.50 6.00
8 David Robinson 1.25 3.00
9 Chris Webber 1.25 3.00
10 Kevin Willis .50 1.25

1994-95 Ultra Scoring Kings

COMPLETE SET (10) 10.00 25.00
SER.1 STATED ODDS 1:37 HOBBY
1 Charles Barkley 5.00 12.00
2 Patrick Ewing 3.00 8.00
3 Karl Malone 4.00 10.00
4 Hakeem Olajuwon 4.00 10.00
5 Shaquille O'Neal 8.00 20.00
6 Scottie Pippen 5.00 12.00
7 Mitch Richmond 2.50 6.00
8 David Robinson 4.00 10.00
9 Latrell Sprewell 2.50 6.00
10 Dominique Wilkins 3.00 8.00

1995-96 Ultra Promo Sheet

COMPLETE SET (6) 2.00 5.00
4 Antonio McDyess 1.25 3.00
8 Damon Stoudamire 2.50 6.00
202 Mookie Blaylock .25 .60
219 Hakeem Olajuwon .50 1.25
344 Nick Van Exel .25 .60
S3 Jerry Stackhouse 1.25 3.00

1995-96 Ultra

COMPLETE SET (350) 20.00 50.00
COMPLETE SERIES 1 (200) 10.00 25.00
COMPLETE SERIES 2 (150) 10.00 25.00
1 Stacey Augmon .40 1.00
2 Mookie Blaylock .50 1.25
3 Craig Ehlo .30 .75
4 Andrew Lang .30 .75
5 Grant Long .30 .75
6 Ken Norman .30 .75
7 Steve Smith .40 1.00
8 Spud Webb .50 1.25
9 Dee Brown .40 1.00
10 Sherman Douglas .30 .75
11 Pervis Ellison .30 .75
12 Rick Fox .30 .75
13 Eric Montross .30 .75
14 Dino Radja .30 .75
15 David Wesley .30 .75
16 Dominique Wilkins .75 2.00
17 Muggsy Bogues .50 1.25
18 Scott Burrell .30 .75
19 Dell Curry .50 1.25
20 Kendall Gill .30 .75
21 Larry Johnson .60 1.50
22 Alonzo Mourning .75 2.00
23 Robert Parish .60 1.50
24 Ron Harper .40 1.00
25 Michael Jordan 5.00 12.00
26 Toni Kukoc .60 1.50
27 Will Perdue .40 1.00
28 Scottie Pippen 1.25 3.00
29 Terrell Brandon .40 1.00
30 Michael Cage .30 .75
31 Tyrone Hill .30 .75
32 Chris Mills .30 .75
33 Bobby Phills .40 1.00
34 Mark Price .50 1.25
35 John Williams .30 .75
36 Lucious Harris .30 .75
37 Jim Jackson .40 1.00
38 Popeye Jones .30 .75
39 Jason Kidd .75 2.00
40 Jamal Mashburn .50 1.25
41 George McCloud .30 .75
42 Roy Tarpley .40 1.00
43 Lorenzo Williams .30 .75
44 Mahmoud Abdul-Rauf .40 1.00
45 Dikembe Mutombo .75 2.00
46 Robert Pack .30 .75
47 Jalen Rose .60 1.50
48 Bryant Stith .30 .75
49 Brian Williams .30 .75
50 Reggie Williams .30 .75
51 Joe Dumars .50 1.25
52 Grant Hill .75 2.00
53 Allan Houston .40 1.00
54 Lindsey Hunter .30 .75
55 Terry Mills .30 .75
56 Mark West .30 .75
57 Chris Gatling .30 .75
58 Tim Hardaway .60 1.50
59 Donyell Marshall .30 .75
60 Chris Mullin .50 1.25
61 Carlos Rogers .30 .75
62 Clifford Rozier .30 .75
63 Rony Seikaly .30 .75
64 Latrell Sprewell .50 1.25
65 Sam Cassell .50 1.25
66 Clyde Drexler .75 2.00
67 Mario Elie .30 .75
68 Carl Herrera .30 .75
69 Robert Horry .50 1.25
70 Hakeem Olajuwon 1.00 2.50
71 Kenny Smith .40 1.00
72 Antonio Davis .30 .75
73 Dale Davis .30 .75
74 Mark Jackson .40 1.00
75 Derrick McKey .30 .75
76 Reggie Miller 1.00 2.50
77 Rik Smits .40 1.00
78 Terry Dehere .30 .75
79 Lamond Murray .30 .75
80 Bo Outlaw .30 .75
81 Pooh Richardson .30 .75
82 Rodney Rogers .40 1.00
83 Malik Sealy .30 .75
84 Loy Vaught .30 .75
85 Sam Bowie .30 .75
86 Elden Campbell .30 .75
87 Cedric Ceballos .40 1.00
88 Vlade Divac .50 1.25
89 Eddie Jones .50 1.25
90 Anthony Peeler .30 .75
91 Sedale Threatt .30 .75
92 Nick Van Exel .50 1.25
93 Rex Chapman .30 .75
94 Bimbo Coles .30 .75
95 Matt Geiger .30 .75
96 Billy Owens .30 .75
97 Khalid Reeves .30 .75
98 Glen Rice .50 1.25
99 Kevin Willis .40 1.00
100 Vin Baker .40 1.00
101 Marty Conlon .30 .75
102 Todd Day .30 .75
103 Eric Murdock .30 .75
104 Glenn Robinson .50 1.25
105 Winston Garland .30 .75
106 Tom Gugliotta .30 .75
107 Christian Laettner .40 1.00
108 Isaiah Rider .50 1.25
109 Sean Rooks .30 .75
110 Doug West .30 .75
111 Kenny Anderson .40 1.00
112 P.J. Brown .30 .75
113 Derrick Coleman .40 1.00
114 Armon Gilliam .30 .75
115 Chris Morris .30 .75
116 Anthony Bonner .30 .75
117 Patrick Ewing .75 2.00
118 Derek Harper .40 1.00
119 Anthony Mason .40 1.00
120 Charles Oakley .40 1.00
121 Charles Smith .30 .75
122 John Starks .50 1.25
123 Nick Anderson .40 1.00
124 Horace Grant .40 1.00
125 Anfernee Hardaway 1.25 3.00
126 Shaquille O'Neal 2.00 5.00
127 Donald Royal .30 .75
128 Dennis Scott .30 .75
129 Brian Shaw .30 .75
130 Derrick Alston .30 .75
131 Dana Barros .40 1.00
132 Shawn Bradley .30 .75
133 Willie Burton .40 1.00
134 Jeff Malone .30 .75
135 Clarence Weatherspoon .30 .75
136 Scott Williams .30 .75
137 Sharone Wright .30 .75
138 Danny Ainge .50 1.25
139 Charles Barkley 1.25 3.00
140 A.C. Green .40 1.00
141 Kevin Johnson .50 1.25
142 Dan Majerle .50 1.25
143 Danny Manning .40 1.00
144 Elliot Perry .30 .75
145 Wesley Person .30 .75
146 Wayman Tisdale .30 .75
147 Chris Dudley .30 .75
148 Harvey Grant .30 .75
149 Aaron McKie .30 .75
150 Terry Porter .30 .75
151 Clifford Robinson .50 1.25
152 Rod Strickland .30 .75
153 Otis Thorpe .40 1.00
154 Buck Williams .30 .75
155 Brian Grant .40 1.00
156 Bobby Hurley .30 .75
157 Olden Polynice .30 .75
158 Mitch Richmond .60 1.50
159 Michael Smith .30 .75
160 Walt Williams .30 .75
161 Vinny Del Negro .30 .75
162 Sean Elliott .40 1.00
163 Avery Johnson .40 1.00
164 Chuck Person .40 1.00
165 J.R. Reid .30 .75
166 Doc Rivers .40 1.00
167 David Robinson 1.00 2.50
168 Dennis Rodman 1.00 2.50
169 Vincent Askew .30 .75
170 Hersey Hawkins .40 1.00
171 Shawn Kemp .75 2.00
172 Sarunas Marciulionis .50 1.25
173 Nate McMillan .30 .75
174 Gary Payton .75 2.00
175 Sam Perkins .30 .75
176 Detlef Schrempf .50 1.25
177 B.J. Armstrong .50 1.25
178 Jerome Kersey .30 .75
179 Tony Massenburg .30 .75
180 Oliver Miller .30 .75
181 John Salley .30 .75
182 David Benoit .30 .75
183 Antoine Carr .30 .75
184 Jeff Hornacek .40 1.00
185 Karl Malone 1.00 2.50
186 Felton Spencer .30 .75
187 John Stockton 1.00 2.50
188 Greg Anthony .30 .75
189 Benoit Benjamin .30 .75
190 Byron Scott .50 1.25
191 Calbert Cheaney .30 .75
192 Juwan Howard .50 1.25
193 Don MacLean .30 .75
194 Gheorghe Muresan .30 .75
195 Doug Overton .30 .75
196 Scott Skiles .30 .75
197 Chris Webber .60 1.50
198 Checklist (1-94) .40 1.00
199 Checklist (95-190) .40 1.00
200 Checklist (191-200) .40 1.00
201 Stacey Augmon .40 1.00
202 Mookie Blaylock .50 1.25
203 Grant Long .30 .75
204 Steve Smith .40 1.00
205 Dana Barros .40 1.00
206 Kendall Gill .30 .75
207 Khalid Reeves .30 .75
208 Glen Rice .50 1.25
209 Luc Longley .40 1.00
210 Dennis Rodman 1.00 2.50
211 Dan Majerle .50 1.25
212 Tony Dumas .30 .75
213 Elmore Spencer .30 .75
214 Otis Thorpe .40 1.00
215 B.J. Armstrong .50 1.25
216 Sam Cassell .50 1.25
217 Clyde Drexler .75 2.00
218 Robert Horry .50 1.25
219 Hakeem Olajuwon 1.00 2.50
220 Eddie Johnson .30 .75
221 Ricky Pierce .30 .75
222 Eric Piatkowski .30 .75
223 Rodney Rogers .40 1.00
224 Brian Williams .30 .75
225 George Lynch .30 .75
226 Alonzo Mourning .75 2.00
227 Benoit Benjamin .30 .75
228 Terry Porter .30 .75
229 Shawn Bradley .30 .75
230 Kevin Edwards .30 .75
231 Jayson Williams .30 .75
232 Charlie Ward .40 1.00
233 Jon Koncak .30 .75
234 Derrick Coleman .40 1.00
235 Richard Dumas .30 .75
236 Vernon Maxwell .30 .75
237 John Williams .30 .75
238 Dontonio Wingfield .30 .75
239 Tyrone Corbin .30 .75
240 Will Perdue .40 1.00
241 Shawn Kemp .75 2.00
242 Gary Payton .75 2.00
243 Sam Perkins .30 .75
244 Detlef Schrempf .50 1.25
245 Chris Morris .30 .75
246 Robert Pack .30 .75
247 Willie Anderson EXP .40 1.00
248 Oliver Miller EXP .30 .75
249 Tracy Murray EXP .30 .75
250 Alvin Robertson EXP .40 1.00
251 Carlos Rogers EXP .30 .75
252 John Salley EXP .30 .75
253 Damon Stoudamire EXP 1.25 3.00
254 Zan Tabak EXP .30 .75
255 Greg Anthony EXP .30 .75
256 Blue Edwards EXP .30 .75
257 Kenny Gattison EXP .30 .75
258 Chris King EXP .30 .75
259 Lawrence Moten EXP .50 1.25
260 Eric Murdock EXP .30 .75
261 Bryant Reeves EXP .40 1.00
262 Byron Scott EXP .50 1.25
263 Cory Alexander RC .50 1.25
264 Brent Barry RC .75 2.00
265 Mario Bennett RC .40 1.00
266 Travis Best RC .50 1.25
267 Junior Burrough RC .50 1.25
268 Jason Caffey RC .50 1.25
269 Randolph Childress RC .40 1.00
270 Sasha Danilovic RC .50 1.25
271 Tyus Edney RC .50 1.25
272 Michael Finley RC 1.25 3.00
273 Sherrell Ford RC .40 1.00
274 Kevin Garnett RC 4.00 10.00
275 Alan Henderson RC .50 1.25
276 Donny Marshall RC .50 1.25
277 Antonio McDyess RC .60 1.50
278 Loren Meyer RC .30 .75
279 Lawrence Moten RC .50 1.25
280 Ed O'Bannon RC .40 1.00
281 Greg Ostertag RC .50 1.25
282 Cherokee Parks RC .40 1.00
283 Theo Ratliff RC .75 2.00
284 Bryant Reeves RC .40 1.00
285 Shawn Respert RC .40 1.00
286 Lou Roe RC .50 1.25
287 Arvydas Sabonis RC 1.00 2.50
288 Joe Smith RC .60 1.50
289 Jerry Stackhouse RC 1.50 4.00
290 Damon Stoudamire RC 1.25 3.00
291 Bob Sura RC .40 1.00
292 Kurt Thomas RC .50 1.25
293 Gary Trent RC .40 1.00
294 David Vaughn RC .50 1.25
295 Rasheed Wallace RC 1.50 4.00
296 Eric Williams RC .50 1.25
297 Corliss Williamson RC .50 1.25
298 George Zidek RC .40 1.00
299 Mahmoud Abdul-Rauf ENC .40 1.00
300 Kenny Anderson ENC .40 1.00
301 Vin Baker ENC .40 1.00
302 Charles Barkley ENC 1.25 3.00
303 Mookie Blaylock ENC .50 1.25
304 Cedric Ceballos ENC .40 1.00
305 Vlade Divac ENC .50 1.25
306 Clyde Drexler ENC .75 2.00
307 Joe Dumars ENC .50 1.25
308 Sean Elliott ENC .40 1.00
309 Patrick Ewing ENC .75 2.00
310 Anfernee Hardaway ENC 1.25 3.00
311 Tim Hardaway ENC .60 1.50
312 Grant Hill ENC .75 2.00
313 Tyrone Hill ENC .30 .75
314 Robert Horry ENC .50 1.25
315 Juwan Howard ENC .50 1.25
316 Jim Jackson ENC .40 1.00
317 Kevin Johnson ENC .50 1.25
318 Larry Johnson ENC .60 1.50
319 Eddie Jones ENC .50 1.25
320 Shawn Kemp ENC .75 2.00
321 Jason Kidd ENC .75 2.00
322 Christian Laettner ENC .40 1.00
323 Karl Malone ENC 1.00 2.50
324 Jamal Mashburn ENC .50 1.25
325 Reggie Miller ENC 1.00 2.50
326 Alonzo Mourning ENC .75 2.00
327 Dikembe Mutombo ENC .75 2.00
328 Hakeem Olajuwon ENC 1.00 2.50
329 Gary Payton ENC .75 2.00
330 Scottie Pippen ENC 1.25 3.00
331 Dino Radja ENC .30 .75
332 Glen Rice ENC .50 1.25
333 Mitch Richmond ENC .60 1.50
334 Clifford Robinson ENC .50 1.25
335 David Robinson ENC 1.00 2.50
336 Glenn Robinson ENC .50 1.25
337 Dennis Rodman ENC 1.00 2.50
338 Carlos Rogers ENC .30 .75
339 Detlef Schrempf ENC .50 1.25
340 Byron Scott ENC .50 1.25
341 Rik Smits ENC .40 1.00
342 Latrell Sprewell ENC .50 1.25
343 John Stockton ENC 1.00 2.50
344 Nick Van Exel ENC .50 1.25
345 Loy Vaught ENC .30 .75
346 Clarence Weatherspoon ENC .30 .75
347 Chris Webber ENC .60 1.50
348 Kevin Willis ENC .30 .75
349 Checklist (201-298) .40 1.00
350 Checklist (299-350/inserts) .40 1.00

1995-96 Ultra Gold Medallion

COMPLETE SET (200) 60.00 150.00
*STARS: 1.5X TO 4X BASE CARD HI
ONE PER SERIES 1 PACK
25 Michael Jordan 125.00 300.00

1995-96 Ultra All-NBA

COMPLETE SET (15) 6.00 15.00
SER.1 STATED ODDS 1:5 HOBBY/RETAIL
*GOLD MEDALLION: 1.25X TO 3X HI COLUMN
GOLD: SER.1 STATED ODDS 1:50 HOB/RET
1 Anfernee Hardaway 1.50 4.00
2 Karl Malone 1.25 3.00
3 Scottie Pippen 1.50 4.00
4 David Robinson 1.25 3.00
5 John Stockton 1.25 3.00
6 Charles Barkley 1.50 4.00
7 Shawn Kemp 1.00 2.50
8 Shaquille O'Neal 2.50 6.00
9 Gary Payton 1.00 2.50
10 Mitch Richmond .75 2.00
11 Clyde Drexler 1.00 2.50
12 Reggie Miller 1.25 3.00
13 Hakeem Olajuwon 1.25 3.00
14 Dennis Rodman 1.25 3.00
15 Detlef Schrempf .60 1.50

1995-96 Ultra All-Rookie Team

COMPLETE SET (10) 12.00 30.00
SER.1 STATED ODDS 1:7 RETAIL
*GOLD MEDALLION: 1.5X TO 4X HI COLUMN
GOLD: SER.1 STATED ODDS 1:70 RETAIL
1 Brian Grant 1.50 4.00
2 Grant Hill 3.00 8.00
3 Eddie Jones 2.00 5.00
4 Jason Kidd 3.00 8.00
5 Glenn Robinson 2.00 5.00
6 Juwan Howard 2.00 5.00
7 D.Marshall/S.Wright 1.25 3.00
8 Eric Montross 1.25 3.00
9 Wesley Person 1.25 3.00
10 Jalen Rose 2.50 6.00

1995-96 Ultra All-Rookies

COMPLETE SET (10) 12.00 30.00
SER.2 STATED ODDS 1:30 HOBBY/RETAIL
1 Tyus Edney .75 2.00
2 Michael Finley 2.00 5.00
3 Kevin Garnett 6.00 15.00
4 Antonio McDyess DP 1.00 2.50
5 Ed O'Bannon .60 1.50
6 Joe Smith 1.00 2.50
7 Jerry Stackhouse 2.50 6.00
8 Damon Stoudamire DP 2.00 5.00
9 Rasheed Wallace 2.50 6.00
10 Eric Williams .75 2.00

1995-96 Ultra Double Trouble

COMPLETE SET (10) 12.00 30.00
SER.1 STATED ODDS 1:5 HOBBY/RETAIL
GOLD: SER.1 STATED ODDS 1:50 HOB/RET
1 Charles Barkley 2.00 5.00
2 Anfernee Hardaway 2.00 5.00
3 Michael Jordan 8.00 20.00
4 Alonzo Mourning 1.25 3.00
5 Hakeem Olajuwon 1.50 4.00
6 Shaquille O'Neal 3.00 8.00
7 Gary Payton 1.25 3.00
8 Scottie Pippen 2.00 5.00
9 David Robinson 1.50 4.00
10 John Stockton 1.50 4.00

1995-96 Ultra Double Trouble Gold Medallion

COMPLETE SET (10) 60.00 150.00
*GOLD MEDALLION: 1.25X TO 3X BASIC
STATED ODDS 1:50
3 Michael Jordan 40.00 100.00

1995-96 Ultra Fabulous Fifties

COMPLETE SET (7) 8.00 20.00
SER.1 STATED ODDS 1:12 HOBBY
*GOLD MEDALLION: 1.25X TO 3X HI COLUMN
GOLD: SER.1 STATED ODDS 1:120 HOBBY
1 Dana Barros .60 1.50
2 Willie Burton .60 1.50
3 Cedric Ceballos .60 1.50
4 Jim Jackson .60 1.50
5 Michael Jordan 8.00 20.00
6 Jamal Mashburn .75 2.00
7 Glen Rice .75 2.00

1995-96 Ultra Jam City

COMPLETE SET (12) 15.00 40.00
SER.2 STATED ODDS 1:12 RETAIL
HP: SER.2 STATED ODDS 1:72 RETAIL
1 Grant Hill 2.00 5.00
2 Robert Horry 1.25 3.00
3 Michael Jordan 20.00 50.00
4 Shawn Kemp 2.00 5.00
5 Jamal Mashburn 1.25 3.00
6 Antonio McDyess 1.50 4.00
7 Alonzo Mourning 2.00 5.00
8 Hakeem Olajuwon 2.50 6.00
9 Shaquille O'Neal 5.00 12.00
10 David Robinson 2.50 6.00
11 Joe Smith 1.50 4.00
12 Jerry Stackhouse 4.00 10.00

1995-96 Ultra Power

COMPLETE SET (10) 2.00 5.00
SER.1 STATED ODDS 1:4 HOBBY/RETAIL
*GOLD MEDALLION: 1.5X TO 4X HI COLUMN
GOLD: SER.1 STATED ODDS 1:40 HOB/RET
1 Charles Barkley .75 2.00
2 Patrick Ewing .50 1.25
3 Larry Johnson .40 1.00
4 Shawn Kemp .50 1.25
5 Karl Malone .60 1.50
6 Alonzo Mourning .50 1.25
7 Dikembe Mutombo .50 1.25
8 Hakeem Olajuwon .60 1.50
9 Shaquille O'Neal 1.25 3.00
10 David Robinson .60 1.50

1995-96 Ultra Rising Stars

COMPLETE SET (9) 12.00 30.00
SER.1 STATED ODDS 1:37 HOBBY/RETAIL
*GOLD MEDALLION: 1.5X TO 4X HI COLUMN
GOLD: SER.1 STATED ODDS 1:370 HOB/RET
1 Vin Baker 1.25 3.00
2 Anfernee Hardaway 4.00 10.00
3 Grant Hill 2.50 6.00
4 Jason Kidd 2.50 6.00
5 Jamal Mashburn 1.50 4.00
6 Shaquille O'Neal 6.00 15.00
7 Glenn Robinson 1.50 4.00
8 Nick Van Exel 1.50 4.00
9 Chris Webber 2.00 5.00

1995-96 Ultra Scoring Kings

COMPLETE SET (12) 40.00 100.00
SER.2 STATED ODDS 1:24 HOBBY
1 Patrick Ewing 2.00 5.00
2 Grant Hill 2.00 5.00
3 Jim Jackson 1.00 2.50
4 Michael Jordan 40.00 100.00
5 Karl Malone 2.50 6.00
6 Reggie Miller 2.50 6.00
7 Hakeem Olajuwon 2.50 6.00
8 Shaquille O'Neal 8.00 20.00
9 Scottie Pippen 3.00 8.00
10 David Robinson 2.50 6.00
11 Glenn Robinson 1.25 3.00
12 Jerry Stackhouse 4.00 10.00

1995-96 Ultra Scoring Kings Hot Pack

COMPLETE SET (12) 40.00 100.00
*HOT PACK CARDS: .4X TO 1X HI COLUMN
STATED ODDS 1:72 HOBBY

1995-96 Ultra Stackhouse's Scrapbook

COMPLETE SET (2) 1.50 4.00
COMMON CARD (S3-S4) 1.00 2.50
STATED ODDS 1:24

1995-96 Ultra USA Basketball

COMPLETE SET (10) 25.00 60.00
SER.2 STATED ODDS 1:54 HOBBY/RETAIL
1 Anfernee Hardaway 6.00 15.00
2 Grant Hill 4.00 10.00
3 Karl Malone 5.00 12.00

4 Reggie Miller 5.00 12.00
5 Hakeem Olajuwon 5.00 12.00
6 Shaquille O'Neal 10.00 25.00
7 Scottie Pippen 6.00 15.00
8 David Robinson 5.00 12.00
9 Glenn Robinson 2.50 6.00
10 John Stockton 5.00 12.00

1996-97 Ultra

COMPLETE SET (300) 40.00 100.00
COMPLETE SERIES 1 (150) 25.00 60.00
COMPLETE SERIES 2 (150) 15.00 40.00
1 Mookie Blaylock .40 1.00
2 Alan Henderson .25 .60
3 Christian Laettner .40 1.00
4 Dikembe Mutombo .60 1.50
5 Steve Smith .30 .75
6 Dana Barros .25 .60
7 Rick Fox .25 .60
8 Dino Radja .25 .60
9 Antoine Walker RC .60 1.50
10 Eric Williams .25 .60
11 Dell Curry .40 1.00
12 Tony Delk RC .40 1.00
13 Matt Geiger .25 .60
14 Glen Rice .40 1.00
15 Ron Harper .30 .75
16 Michael Jordan 4.00 10.00
17 Toni Kukoc .40 1.00
18 Scottie Pippen 1.00 2.50
19 Dennis Rodman 1.00 2.50
20 Terrell Brandon .30 .75
21 Chris Mills .25 .60
22 Bobby Phills .25 .60
23 Bob Sura .25 .60
24 Jim Jackson .25 .60
25 Jason Kidd .60 1.50
26 Jamal Mashburn .40 1.00
27 George McCloud .25 .60
28 Samaki Walker RC .30 .75
29 LaPhonso Ellis .25 .60
30 Antonio McDyess .40 1.00
31 Bryant Stith .25 .60
32 Joe Dumars .50 1.25
33 Grant Hill .60 1.50
34 Theo Ratliff .25 .60
35 Otis Thorpe .30 .75
36 Chris Mullin .50 1.25
37 Joe Smith .30 .75
38 Latrell Sprewell .40 1.00
39 Charles Barkley 1.00 2.50
40 Clyde Drexler .60 1.50
41 Mario Elie .25 .60
42 Hakeem Olajuwon .75 2.00
43 Erick Dampier RC .40 1.00
44 Dale Davis .25 .60
45 Derrick McKey .25 .60
46 Reggie Miller .75 2.00
47 Rik Smits .30 .75
48 Brent Barry .30 .75
49 Malik Sealy .25 .60
50 Loy Vaught .25 .60
51 Lorenzen Wright RC .40 1.00
52 Kobe Bryant RC 30.00 80.00
53 Cedric Ceballos .30 .75
54 Eddie Jones .40 1.00
55 Shaquille O'Neal 1.50 4.00
56 Nick Van Exel .40 1.00
57 Tim Hardaway .50 1.25
58 Alonzo Mourning .60 1.50
59 Kurt Thomas .25 .60
60 Ray Allen RC 2.00 5.00
61 Vin Baker .30 .75
62 Sherman Douglas .25 .60
63 Glenn Robinson .40 1.00
64 Kevin Garnett 1.25 3.00
65 Tom Gugliotta .25 .60
66 Stephon Marbury RC 1.25 3.00
67 Doug West .25 .60
68 Shawn Bradley .25 .60
69 Kendall Gill .40 1.00
70 Kerry Kittles RC .40 1.00
71 Ed O'Bannon .25 .60
72 Patrick Ewing .60 1.50
73 Larry Johnson .50 1.25
74 Charles Oakley .40 1.00
75 John Starks .40 1.00
76 John Wallace RC .30 .75
77 Nick Anderson .30 .75
78 Horace Grant .40 1.00
79 Anfernee Hardaway 1.00 2.50
80 Dennis Scott .30 .75
81 Derrick Coleman .30 .75
82 Allen Iverson RC 3.00 8.00
83 Jerry Stackhouse .50 1.25
84 Clarence Weatherspoon .25 .60
85 Michael Finley .40 1.00
86 Kevin Johnson .40 1.00
87 Steve Nash RC 2.50 6.00
88 Wesley Person .25 .60
89 Jermaine O'Neal RC .60 1.50
90 Clifford Robinson .40 1.00
91 Arvydas Sabonis .40 1.00
92 Gary Trent .25 .60
93 Tyus Edney .25 .60
94 Brian Grant .30 .75
95 Olden Polynice .25 .60
96 Mitch Richmond .50 1.25
97 Corliss Williamson .25 .60
98 Vinny Del Negro .25 .60
99 Sean Elliott .40 1.00
100 Avery Johnson .30 .75
101 David Robinson .75 2.00
102 Hersey Hawkins .25 .60
103 Shawn Kemp .60 1.50
104 Gary Payton .60 1.50
105 Sam Perkins .30 .75
106 Detlef Schrempf .40 1.00
107 Marcus Camby RC .60 1.50
108 Doug Christie .25 .60
109 Damon Stoudamire .40 1.00
110 Sharone Wright .25 .60
111 Jeff Hornacek .30 .75
112 Karl Malone .75 2.00
113 Chris Morris .25 .60
114 Bryon Russell .25 .60
115 John Stockton .75 2.00
116 Shareef Abdur-Rahim RC .60 1.50
117 Greg Anthony .25 .60
118 Blue Edwards .25 .60
119 Bryant Reeves .25 .60
120 Calbert Cheaney .25 .60
121 Juwan Howard .40 1.00
122 Gheorghe Muresan .25 .60
123 Chris Webber .50 1.25
124 Vin Baker OTB .30 .75
125 Charles Barkley OTB 1.00 2.50
126 Kevin Garnett OTB 1.25 3.00
127 Juwan Howard OTB .40 1.00
128 Larry Johnson OTB .50 1.25
129 Shawn Kemp OTB .60 1.50
130 Karl Malone OTB .75 2.00
131 Anthony Mason OTB .30 .75
132 Antonio McDyess OTB .40 1.00
133 Alonzo Mourning OTB .60 1.50
134 Hakeem Olajuwon OTB .75 2.00
135 Shaquille O'Neal OTB 1.50 4.00
136 David Robinson OTB .75 2.00
137 Dennis Rodman OTB 1.00 2.50
138 Joe Smith OTB .30 .75
139 Mookie Blaylock UE .40 1.00
140 Terrell Brandon UE .30 .75
141 Anfernee Hardaway UE 1.00 2.50
142 Grant Hill UE .60 1.50
143 Michael Jordan UE 4.00 10.00
144 Jason Kidd UE .60 1.50
145 Gary Payton UE .60 1.50
146 Jerry Stackhouse UE .50 1.25
147 Damon Stoudamire UE .40 1.00
148 H.Olajuwon/D.Robinson ME .75 2.00
149 Checklist .40 1.00
150 Checklist .40 1.00
151 Tyrone Corbin .25 .60
152 Priest Lauderdale RC .25 .60
153 Dikembe Mutombo .60 1.50
154 Eldridge Recasner RC .40 1.00
155 Todd Day .25 .60
156 Greg Minor .25 .60
157 David Wesley .25 .60
158 Vlade Divac .40 1.00
159 Anthony Mason .30 .75
160 Malik Rose RC .50 1.25
161 Jason Caffey .25 .60
162 Steve Kerr .30 .75
163 Luc Longley .25 .60
164 Danny Ferry .25 .60
165 Tyrone Hill .25 .60
166 Vitaly Potapenko RC .30 .75
167 Sam Cassell .30 .75
168 Michael Finley .40 1.00
169 Chris Gatling .25 .60
170 A.C. Green .30 .75
171 Oliver Miller .25 .60
172 Eric Montross .25 .60
173 Dale Ellis .30 .75
174 Mark Jackson .30 .75
175 Ervin Johnson .25 .60
176 Sarunas Marciulionis .25 .60
177 Stacey Augmon .30 .75
178 Joe Dumars .50 1.25
179 Grant Hill .60 1.50
180 Lindsey Hunter .25 .60
181 Grant Long .25 .60
182 Terry Mills .25 .60
183 Otis Thorpe .30 .75
184 Jerome Williams RC .30 .75
185 Todd Fuller RC .25 .60
186 Ray Owes RC .25 .60
187 Mark Price .40 1.00
188 Felton Spencer .25 .60
189 Charles Barkley 1.00 2.50
190 Emanual Davis RC .30 .75
191 Othella Harrington RC .30 .75
192 Matt Maloney RC .30 .75
193 Brent Price .25 .60
194 Kevin Willis .30 .75
195 Travis Best .25 .60
196 Antonio Davis .25 .60
197 Jalen Rose .30 .75
198 Pooh Richardson .25 .60
199 Stanley Roberts .25 .60
200 Rodney Rogers .25 .60
201 Elden Campbell .25 .60
202 Derek Fisher RC .50 1.25
203 Travis Knight RC .30 .75
204 Shaquille O'Neal 1.50 4.00
205 Byron Scott .40 1.00
206 Sasha Danilovic .25 .60
207 Dan Majerle .40 1.00
208 Martin Muursepp RC .25 .60
209 Armon Gilliam .25 .60
210 Andrew Lang .25 .60
211 Johnny Newman .25 .60
212 Kevin Garnett 1.25 3.00
213 Tom Gugliotta .25 .60
214 Shane Heal RC .40 1.00
215 Stojko Vrankovic .25 .60
216 Robert Pack .25 .60
217 Khalid Reeves .25 .60
218 Jayson Williams .25 .60
219 Chris Childs .25 .60
220 Allan Houston .40 1.00
221 Larry Johnson .50 1.25
222 Walter McCarty RC .40 1.00
223 Charlie Ward .25 .60
224 Brian Evans RC .25 .60
225 Amal McCaskill RC .40 1.00
226 Rony Seikaly .30 .75
227 Gerald Wilkins .30 .75
228 Mark Davis .25 .60
229 Lucious Harris .25 .60
230 Don MacLean .25 .60
231 Cedric Ceballos .30 .75
232 Rex Chapman .25 .60
233 Jason Kidd .60 1.50
234 Danny Manning .30 .75
235 Kenny Anderson .30 .75
236 Aaron McKie .25 .60
237 Isaiah Rider .30 .75
238 Rasheed Wallace .50 1.25
239 Mahmoud Abdul-Rauf .30 .75
240 Billy Owens .25 .60
241 Michael Smith .25 .60
242 Vernon Maxwell .25 .60
243 Charles Smith .25 .60
244 Dominique Wilkins .60 1.50
245 Craig Ehlo .25 .60
246 Jim McIlvaine .25 .60
247 Nate McMillan .25 .60
248 Hubert Davis .25 .60
249 Carlos Rogers .25 .60
250 Zan Tabak .25 .60
251 Walt Williams .25 .60
252 Jeff Hornacek .30 .75
253 Karl Malone .75 2.00
254 Greg Ostertag .25 .60
255 Bryon Russell .25 .60
256 John Stockton .75 2.00
257 George Lynch .25 .60
258 Lawrence Moten .25 .60
259 Anthony Peeler .25 .60
260 Roy Rogers RC .30 .75
261 Tracy Murray .25 .60
262 Rod Strickland .40 1.00
263 Ben Wallace RC 2.50 6.00
264 Shareef Abdur-Rahim RE .60 1.50
265 Ray Allen RE 2.00 5.00
266 Kobe Bryant RE 20.00 50.00
267 Marcus Camby RE .60 1.50
268 Erick Dampier RE .40 1.00
269 Tony Delk RE .40 1.00
270 Allen Iverson RE 3.00 8.00
271 Kerry Kittles RE .40 1.00
272 Stephon Marbury RE 1.25 3.00
273 Steve Nash RE 2.50 6.00
274 Jermaine O'Neal RE .60 1.50
275 Antoine Walker RE .60 1.50
276 Samaki Walker RE .30 .75
277 John Wallace RE .30 .75
278 Lorenzen Wright RE .30 .75
279 Anfernee Hardaway SU 1.00 2.50
280 Michael Jordan SU 4.00 10.00
281 Jason Kidd SU .60 1.50
282 Hakeem Olajuwon SU .75 2.00
283 Gary Payton SU .60 1.50
284 Mitch Richmond SU .50 1.25
285 David Robinson SU .75 2.00
286 John Stockton SU .75 2.00
287 Damon Stoudamire SU .40 1.00
288 Chris Webber SU .50 1.25
289 Clyde Drexler PG .60 1.50
290 Kevin Garnett PG 1.25 3.00
291 Grant Hill PG .60 1.50
292 Shawn Kemp PG .60 1.50
293 Karl Malone PG .75 2.00
294 Antonio McDyess PG .40 1.00
295 Alonzo Mourning PG .60 1.50
296 Shaquille O'Neal PG 1.50 4.00
297 Scottie Pippen PG 1.00 2.50
298 Jerry Stackhouse PG .50 1.25
299 Checklist (151-263) .40 1.00
300 Checklist (264-300/inserts) .40 1.00
NNO Jerry Stackhouse Promo 1.25 3.00

1996-97 Ultra Gold Medallion

*SER.1 STARS: 2X TO 5X BASE CARD HI
*SER.1 RCs: 1.5X TO 4X BASE HI
*SER.2 STARS: .6X TO 1.5X BASE HI
*SER.2 RCs: .6X TO 1.5X BASE HI
*SER.2 SUBSET: .6X TO 1.5X BASE HI
SER.1 STATED ODDS 1:12 H/R
SER.2 STATED ODDS ONE PER PACK
SER.1 SUB.CARDS HAVE NO "G" PREFIX
G16 Michael Jordan 125.00 300.00
G280 Michael Jordan SU 20.00 50.00

1996-97 Ultra Platinum Medallion

*STARS: 25X TO 60X BASE CARD HI
*RCs: 25X TO 60X BASE HI
SER.1 STATED ODDS 1:180 HOB/RET
SER.2 STATED ODDS 1:100 HOB/RET
STATED PRINT RUN LESS THAN 250 SETS
SER.1 PLAT.SUB.CARDS HAVE NO "P" PREFIX
P16 Michael Jordan 1,500.00 3,000.00
P52 Kobe Bryant 2,500.00 5,000.00
P82 Allen Iverson 1,000.00 2,000.00
P204 Shaquille O'Neal 100.00 250.00
P263 Ben Wallace 150.00 400.00
P266 Kobe Bryant RE 600.00 1,200.00
P280 Michael Jordan SU 600.00 1,200.00

1996-97 Ultra All-Rookies

COMPLETE SET (15) 12.00 30.00
SER.2 STATED ODDS 1:4 HOBBY/RETAIL
1 Shareef Abdur-Rahim 1.00 2.50
2 Ray Allen 3.00 8.00
3 Kobe Bryant 25.00 60.00
4 Marcus Camby 1.00 2.50
5 Tony Delk .60 1.50
6 Derek Fisher .75 2.00
7 Allen Iverson 5.00 12.00
8 Kerry Kittles .60 1.50
9 Matt Maloney .50 1.25
10 Stephon Marbury 2.00 5.00
11 Vitaly Potapenko .50 1.25
12 Roy Rogers .50 1.25
13 Antoine Walker 1.00 2.50
14 Samaki Walker .50 1.25
15 John Wallace .50 1.25

1996-97 Ultra Board Game

COMPLETE SET (20) 15.00 40.00
SER.2 STATED ODDS 1:9 HOBBY/RETAIL
1 Vin Baker .75 2.00
2 Charles Barkley 2.50 6.00
3 Dale Davis .60 1.50
4 Clyde Drexler 1.50 4.00
5 Patrick Ewing 1.50 4.00
6 Grant Hill 1.50 4.00
7 Michael Jordan 10.00 25.00
8 Shawn Kemp 1.50 4.00
9 Jason Kidd 1.50 4.00
10 Karl Malone 2.00 5.00
11 Alonzo Mourning 1.50 4.00
12 Dikembe Mutombo 1.50 4.00
13 Hakeem Olajuwon 2.00 5.00
14 Shaquille O'Neal 4.00 10.00
15 Scottie Pippen 2.50 6.00
16 David Robinson 2.00 5.00
17 Dennis Rodman 2.50 6.00
18 Loy Vaught .60 1.50
19 Chris Webber 1.25 3.00
20 Jayson Williams .60 1.50

1996-97 Ultra Court Masters

COMPLETE SET (15) 400.00 800.00
SER.1 STATED ODDS 1:180 RETAIL
1 Anfernee Hardaway 75.00 200.00
2 Michael Jordan 800.00 1,500.00
3 Karl Malone 75.00 200.00
4 Scottie Pippen 100.00 250.00
5 David Robinson 75.00 200.00
6 Grant Hill 40.00 100.00
7 Shawn Kemp 60.00 150.00
8 Hakeem Olajuwon 75.00 200.00
9 Gary Payton 40.00 100.00
10 John Stockton 60.00 150.00
11 Charles Barkley 60.00 150.00
12 Juwan Howard 20.00 50.00
13 Reggie Miller 75.00 200.00
14 Shaquille O'Neal 100.00 250.00
15 Mitch Richmond 30.00 80.00

1996-97 Ultra Decade of Excellence

COMPLETE SET (20) 25.00 60.00
COMPLETE SERIES 1 (10) 15.00 40.00
COMPLETE SERIES 2 (10) 12.50 25.00
SER.1/2 STATED ODDS 1:100 HOBBY/RETAIL
U1 Clyde Drexler 3.00 8.00
U2 Joe Dumars 2.50 6.00
U3 Derek Harper 1.50 4.00
U4 Michael Jordan 15.00 40.00
U5 Karl Malone 4.00 10.00
U6 Chris Mullin 2.50 6.00
U7 Charles Oakley 2.00 5.00
U8 Sam Perkins 1.50 4.00
U9 Ricky Pierce 1.50 4.00
U10 Buck Williams 2.00 5.00
U11 Charles Barkley 5.00 12.00
U12 Patrick Ewing 3.00 8.00
U13 Eddie Johnson 1.25 3.00
U14 Hakeem Olajuwon 4.00 10.00
U15 Robert Parish 2.50 6.00
U16 Byron Scott 2.00 5.00
U17 Wayman Tisdale 1.50 4.00
U18 Gerald Wilkins 1.50 4.00
U19 Herb Williams 1.25 3.00
U20 Kevin Willis 1.50 4.00

1996-97 Ultra Fresh Faces

COMPLETE SET (9) 40.00 80.00
SER.1 STATED ODDS 1:72 HOBBY/RETAIL
1 Shareef Abdur-Rahim 2.50 6.00
2 Ray Allen 8.00 20.00
3 Kobe Bryant 125.00 300.00
4 Marcus Camby 2.50 6.00
5 Allen Iverson 20.00 50.00
6 Kerry Kittles 1.50 4.00
7 Stephon Marbury 5.00 12.00
8 Steve Nash 10.00 25.00
9 Antoine Walker 2.50 6.00

1996-97 Ultra Full Court Trap

COMPLETE SET (10) 60.00 150.00
SER.1 STATED ODDS 1:15 HOBBY/RETAIL
*GOLD: 2.5X TO 6X HI COLUMN
GOLD: SER.1 STATED ODDS 1:180 HOB/RET
1 Michael Jordan 50.00 120.00
2 Gary Payton 1.25 3.00
3 Scottie Pippen 2.00 5.00
4 David Robinson 1.50 4.00
5 Dennis Rodman 2.00 5.00
6 Mookie Blaylock .75 2.00
7 Horace Grant .75 2.00
8 Derrick McKey .50 1.25
9 Hakeem Olajuwon 1.50 4.00
10 Bobby Phills .50 1.25

1996-97 Ultra Give and Take

COMPLETE SET (10) 15.00 40.00
SER.2 STATED ODDS 1:18 RETAIL
1 Mookie Blaylock 1.25 3.00
2 Anfernee Hardaway 3.00 8.00
3 Tim Hardaway 1.50 4.00
4 Allen Iverson 10.00 25.00
5 Michael Jordan 12.00 30.00
6 Jason Kidd 2.00 5.00
7 Gary Payton 2.00 5.00
8 Scottie Pippen 3.00 8.00
9 John Stockton 2.50 6.00
10 Damon Stoudamire 1.25 3.00

1996-97 Ultra Rising Stars

COMPLETE SET (10) 50.00 120.00
SER.1 STATED ODDS 1:180 HOBBY
1 Shareef Abdur-Rahim 2.50 6.00
2 Kobe Bryant 500.00 1,000.00
3 Anfernee Hardaway 12.00 30.00
4 Grant Hill 8.00 20.00
5 Juwan Howard 5.00 12.00
6 Allen Iverson 60.00 150.00
7 Jason Kidd 8.00 20.00
8 Stephon Marbury 5.00 12.00
9 Joe Smith 4.00 10.00
10 Damon Stoudamire 5.00 12.00

1996-97 Ultra Rookie Flashback

COMPLETE SET (11) 20.00 40.00
SER.1 STATED ODDS 1:45 HOBBY/RETAIL
1 Michael Finley 2.50 6.00
2 Antonio McDyess 2.50 6.00
3 Arvydas Sabonis 2.50 6.00
4 Joe Smith 2.00 5.00
5 Jerry Stackhouse 3.00 8.00
6 Damon Stoudamire 2.50 6.00
7 Brent Barry 2.00 5.00
8 Tyus Edney 1.50 4.00
9 Kevin Garnett 8.00 20.00
10 Bryant Reeves 1.50 4.00
11 Rasheed Wallace 3.00 8.00

1996-97 Ultra Scoring Kings

COMPLETE SET (29) 400.00 800.00
SER.2 STATED ODDS 1:24 HOBBY
*PLUS STARS: 1.25X TO 3X HI COLUMN
PLUS: SER.2 STATED ODDS 1:96 HOBBY
1 Steve Smith 2.50 6.00
2 Dino Radja 2.00 5.00
3 Glen Rice 3.00 8.00
4 Michael Jordan 400.00 800.00
5 Terrell Brandon 2.50 6.00
6 Jim Jackson 2.00 5.00
7 Antonio McDyess 3.00 8.00
8 Grant Hill 5.00 12.00
9 Latrell Sprewell 3.00 8.00
10 Hakeem Olajuwon 6.00 15.00
11 Reggie Miller 6.00 15.00
12 Loy Vaught 2.00 5.00
13 Shaquille O'Neal 12.00 30.00
14 Alonzo Mourning 5.00 12.00
15 Vin Baker 2.50 6.00
16 Tom Gugliotta 2.00 5.00
17 Kendall Gill 3.00 8.00
18 Patrick Ewing 5.00 12.00
19 Anfernee Hardaway 8.00 20.00
20 Allen Iverson 20.00 50.00
21 Danny Manning 2.50 6.00
22 Kenny Anderson 2.50 6.00
23 Mitch Richmond 4.00 10.00
24 David Robinson 6.00 15.00
25 Shawn Kemp 5.00 12.00
26 Damon Stoudamire 3.00 8.00
27 Karl Malone 6.00 15.00
28 Shareef Abdur-Rahim 5.00 12.00
29 Chris Webber 4.00 10.00

1996-97 Ultra Starring Role

COMPLETE SET (10) 800.00 1,500.00
SER.2 STATED ODDS 1:288 HOBBY/RETAIL
1 Kevin Garnett 40.00 100.00
2 Anfernee Hardaway 50.00 120.00
3 Grant Hill 20.00 50.00
4 Michael Jordan 500.00 1,000.00
5 Shawn Kemp 25.00 60.00
6 Karl Malone 40.00 100.00
7 Hakeem Olajuwon 25.00 60.00
8 Shaquille O'Neal 75.00 200.00
9 David Robinson 20.00 50.00
10 Damon Stoudamire 20.00 50.00

1997-98 Ultra

COMPLETE SET (275) 40.00 100.00
COMPLETE SERIES 1 (150) 20.00 50.00
COMPLETE SERIES 2 (125) 20.00 50.00
SER.1 ROOKIE SUBSET ODDS 1:4 H/R
GREATS SUBSET ODDS 1:4 H/R
1 Kobe Bryant 4.00 10.00
2 Charles Barkley 1.00 2.50
3 Joe Dumars .50 1.25
4 Wesley Person .30 .75
5 Walt Williams .30 .75
6 Vlade Divac .40 1.00
7 Mookie Blaylock .40 1.00
8 Jason Kidd .60 1.50
9 Ron Harper .40 1.00
10 Sherman Douglas .25 .60
11 Cedric Ceballos .30 .75
12 Karl Malone .75 2.00
13 Antonio McDyess .40 1.00
14 Steve Kerr .50 1.25
15 Matt Maloney .25 .60
16 Glenn Robinson .40 1.00
17 Rony Seikaly .30 .75
18 Derrick Coleman .40 1.00
19 Jermaine O'Neal .30 .75
20 Scott Burrell .25 .60
21 Glen Rice .40 1.00
22 Dale Ellis .30 .75
23 Michael Jordan 4.00 10.00
24 Anfernee Hardaway 1.00 2.50
25 Bryon Russell .25 .60
26 Toni Kukoc .50 1.25
27 Theo Ratliff .30 .75
28 Tom Gugliotta .30 .75
29 Dennis Rodman 1.00 2.50
30 John Stockton .75 2.00
31 Priest Lauderdale .25 .60
32 Luc Longley .40 1.00
33 Grant Hill .60 1.50
34 Antonio Davis .30 .75
35 Eddie Jones .40 1.00
36 Nick Anderson .30 .75
37 Shareef Abdur-Rahim .40 1.00
38 Stephon Marbury .50 1.25
39 Todd Day .25 .60
40 Tim Hardaway .50 1.25
41 Larry Johnson .50 1.25
42 Sam Perkins .30 .75
43 Dikembe Mutombo .60 1.50
44 Bo Outlaw .25 .60
45 Mitch Richmond .50 1.25
46 Bryant Reeves .25 .60
47 P.J. Brown .25 .60
48 Steve Smith .30 .75
49 Martin Muursepp .25 .60
50 Jamal Mashburn .30 .75
51 Kendall Gill .30 .75
52 Vinny Del Negro .25 .60
53 Roy Rogers .25 .60
54 Khalid Reeves .25 .60
55 Scottie Pippen 1.00 2.50
56 Joe Smith .30 .75
57 Mark Jackson .30 .75
58 Voshon Lenard .25 .60
59 Dan Majerle .40 1.00
60 Alonzo Mourning .60 1.50
61 Kerry Kittles .30 .75
62 Chris Childs .25 .60
63 Patrick Ewing .60 1.50
64 Allan Houston .40 1.00
65 Marcus Camby .40 1.00
66 Christian Laettner .40 1.00
67 Loy Vaught .25 .60
68 Jayson Williams .25 .60
69 Avery Johnson .30 .75
70 Damon Stoudamire .40 1.00
71 Kevin Johnson .40 1.00
72 Gheorghe Muresan .25 .60
73 Reggie Miller .75 2.00
74 John Wallace .30 .75
75 Terrell Brandon .30 .75
76 Dale Davis .30 .75
77 Latrell Sprewell .50 1.25
78 Lorenzen Wright .25 .60
79 Rod Strickland .30 .75
80 Kenny Anderson .30 .75
81 Anthony Mason .30 .75
82 Hakeem Olajuwon .75 2.00
83 Kevin Garnett 1.00 2.50
84 Isaiah Rider .30 .75
85 Mark Price .40 1.00
86 Shawn Bradley .25 .60
87 Vin Baker .30 .75
88 Steve Nash 1.00 2.50
89 Jeff Hornacek .40 1.00
90 Tony Delk .30 .75
91 Horace Grant .40 1.00
92 Othella Harrington .25 .60
93 Arvydas Sabonis .50 1.25
94 Antoine Walker .40 1.00
95 Todd Fuller .25 .60
96 John Starks .40 1.00
97 Olden Polynice .25 .60
98 Sean Elliott .30 .75
99 Travis Best .25 .60
100 Chris Gatling .25 .60
101 Derek Harper .30 .75
102 LaPhonso Ellis .25 .60
103 Dean Garrett .25 .60
104 Hersey Hawkins .30 .75
105 Jerry Stackhouse .40 1.00
106 Ray Allen .75 2.00
107 Allen Iverson 1.25 3.00
108 Chris Webber .50 1.25
109 Robert Pack .25 .60
110 Gary Payton .60 1.50
111 Mario Elie .25 .60
112 Dell Curry .30 .75
113 Lindsey Hunter .25 .60
114 Robert Horry .40 1.00
115 David Robinson .75 2.00
116 Kevin Willis .30 .75
117 Tyrone Hill .30 .75
118 Vitaly Potapenko .25 .60
119 Clyde Drexler .60 1.50
120 Derek Fisher .40 1.00
121 Detlef Schrempf .40 1.00
122 Gary Trent .25 .60
123 Danny Ferry .25 .60
124 Derek Anderson RC .75 2.00
125 Chris Anstey RC .50 1.25
126 Tony Battie RC .75 2.00
127 Chauncey Billups RC 2.50 6.00
128 Kelvin Cato RC .60 1.50
129 Austin Croshere RC .60 1.50
130 Antonio Daniels RC .75 2.00
131 Tim Duncan RC 5.00 12.00
132 Danny Fortson RC .75 2.00
133 Adonal Foyle RC .60 1.50
134 Paul Grant RC .50 1.25
135 Ed Gray RC .75 2.00
136 Bobby Jackson RC 1.00 2.50
137 Brevin Knight RC .75 2.00
138 Tracy McGrady RC 4.00 10.00
139 Ron Mercer RC 1.00 2.50
140 Anthony Parker RC .75 2.00
141 Scot Pollard RC .60 1.50
142 Rodrick Rhodes RC .60 1.50
143 Olivier Saint-Jean RC .60 1.50
144 Maurice Taylor RC .60 1.50
145 Johnny Taylor RC .50 1.25
146 Tim Thomas RC 1.00 2.50
147 Keith Van Horn RC 1.25 3.00
148 Jacque Vaughn RC .60 1.50
149 Checklist .40 1.00
150 Checklist .40 1.00
151 Scott Burrell .25 .60
152 Brian Williams .30 .75
153 Terry Mills .25 .60
154 Jim Jackson .25 .60
155 Michael Finley .40 1.00
156 Jeff Nordgaard RC .25 .60
157 Carl Herrera .25 .60
158 Otis Thorpe .30 .75
159 Wesley Person .30 .75
160 Tyrone Hill .30 .75
161 Charles O'Bannon RC .30 .75
162 Greg Anthony .30 .75
163 Rusty LaRue RC .30 .75
164 David Wesley .30 .75
165 Chris Garner RC .30 .75
166 George McCloud .25 .60
167 Mark Price .40 1.00
168 God Shammgod RC .40 1.00
169 Isaac Austin .25 .60
170 Alan Henderson .25 .60
171 Eric Washington RC .40 1.00
172 Darrell Armstrong .25 .60
173 Calbert Cheaney .30 .75
174 Cedric Henderson RC .30 .75
175 Bryant Stith .25 .60
176 Sean Rooks .25 .60
177 Chris Mills .25 .60
178 Eldridge Recasner .25 .60
179 Priest Lauderdale .25 .60
180 Rick Fox .30 .75
181 Keith Closs RC .40 1.00
182 Chris Dudley .30 .75
183 Lawrence Funderburke RC .30 .75
184 Michael Stewart RC .40 1.00
185 Alvin Williams RC .40 1.00
186 Adam Keefe .25 .60
187 Chauncey Billups 1.25 3.00
188 Jon Barry .25 .60
189 Bobby Jackson .50 1.25
190 Sam Cassell .30 .75
191 Dee Brown .30 .75
192 Travis Knight .30 .75
193 Dean Garrett .25 .60
194 David Benoit .25 .60
195 Chris Morris .25 .60
196 Bubba Wells RC .25 .60
197 James Robinson .25 .60
198 Anthony Johnson RC .40 1.00
199 Dennis Scott .30 .75
200 DeJuan Wheat RC .40 1.00
201 Rodney Rogers .30 .75
202 Tariq Abdul-Wahad .30 .75
203 Cherokee Parks .25 .60
204 Jacque Vaughn .25 .60
205 Cory Alexander .25 .60
206 Kevin Ollie RC .40 1.00
207 George Lynch .25 .60
208 Lamond Murray .25 .60
209 Jud Buechler .25 .60
210 Erick Dampier .30 .75
211 Malcolm Huckaby RC .40 1.00
212 Chris Webber .50 1.25
213 Chris Crawford RC .40 1.00
214 J.R. Reid .30 .75
215 Eddie Johnson .30 .75
216 Nick Van Exel .40 1.00
217 Antonio McDyess .40 1.00
218 David Wingate .25 .60
219 Malik Sealy .30 .75
220 Bo Outlaw .25 .60
221 Serge Zwikker RC .30 .75
222 Bobby Phills .30 .75
223 Shea Seals RC .30 .75
224 Clifford Robinson .30 .75
225 Zydrunas Ilgauskas .40 1.00
226 John Thomas RC .25 .60
227 Rik Smits .30 .75
228 Rasheed Wallace .50 1.25
229 John Wallace .25 .60
230 Bob Sura .25 .60
231 Ervin Johnson .25 .60
232 Keith Booth RC .30 .75
233 Chuck Person .30 .75
234 Brian Shaw .30 .75
235 Todd Day .25 .60
236 Clarence Weatherspoon .25 .60
237 Charlie Ward .30 .75
238 Rod Strickland .30 .75
239 Shawn Kemp .60 1.50
240 Terrell Brandon .30 .75
241 Corey Beck RC .40 1.00
242 Vin Baker .30 .75
243 Fred Hoiberg .30 .75
244 Chris Mullin .50 1.25
245 Brian Grant .30 .75
246 Derek Anderson .40 1.00
247 Zan Tabak .25 .60
248 Charles Smith RC .30 .75
249 Shareef Abdur-Rahim GRE .50 1.25
250 Ray Allen GRE 1.00 2.50
251 Charles Barkley GRE 1.25 3.00
252 Kobe Bryant GRE 5.00 12.00
253 Marcus Camby GRE .50 1.25
254 Kevin Garnett GRE 1.25 3.00
255 Anfernee Hardaway GRE 1.25 3.00
256 Grant Hill GRE .75 2.00
257 Juwan Howard GRE .40 1.00
258 Allen Iverson GRE 1.50 4.00
259 Michael Jordan GRE 5.00 12.00
260 Shawn Kemp GRE .75 2.00
261 Kerry Kittles GRE .40 1.00
262 Karl Malone GRE 1.00 2.50
263 Stephon Marbury GRE .60 1.50
264 Hakeem Olajuwon GRE 1.00 2.50
265 Shaquille O'Neal GRE 1.50 4.00
266 Gary Payton GRE .75 2.00
267 Scottie Pippen GRE 1.25 3.00
268 David Robinson GRE 1.00 2.50
269 Dennis Rodman GRE 1.25 3.00
270 Joe Smith GRE .40 1.00
271 Jerry Stackhouse GRE .50 1.25
272 Damon Stoudamire GRE .50 1.25
273 Antoine Walker GRE .50 1.25
274 Checklist .40 1.00
275 Checklist .40 1.00
NNO Jerry Stackhouse PROMO .75 2.00

1997-98 Ultra Gold Medallion

*SER.1 STARS: .75X TO 2X BASE CARD HI
*SER.1 RCs: .75X TO 2X BASE HI
*SER.2 STARS/RCs: .75X TO 2X BASE HI
*SER.2 98 GREATS: .75X TO 2X BASE HI
ONE PER SER.1/2 HOBBY PACK
SUBSETS ARE NOT SP's
1 Kobe Bryant 40.00 100.00
23G Michael Jordan 50.00 120.00
252G Kobe Bryant GRE 20.00 50.00
259G Michael Jordan GRE 25.00 60.00

1997-98 Ultra Platinum Medallion

*STARS: 60X TO 150X BASE CARD HI
*RCs: 30X TO 80X BASE HI
*GREATS: 50X TO 120X BASE HI
*SER.2 RCs: 60X TO 150X BASE HI
STATED PRINT RUN 100 SERIAL #'d SETS
LAST 10 SETS AVAILABLE VIA RED.CARDS
1P Kobe Bryant 4,000.00 8,000.00
23P Michael Jordan 6,000.00 12,000.00
127P Chauncey Billups 300.00 600.00
131P Tim Duncan 2,500.00 5,000.00
138P Tracy McGrady 1,000.00 2,000.00
252P Kobe Bryant GRE 1,500.00 3,000.00
259P Michael Jordan GRE 2,500.00 5,000.00

1997-98 Ultra All-Rookies

COMPLETE SET (15) 8.00 20.00
SER.2 STATED ODDS 1:4 HOB/RET
AR1 Tim Duncan 5.00 12.00
AR2 Tony Battie .75 2.00
AR3 Keith Van Horn 1.25 3.00
AR4 Antonio Daniels .75 2.00
AR5 Chauncey Billups 2.50 6.00
AR6 Ron Mercer 1.00 2.50
AR7 Tracy McGrady 4.00 10.00
AR8 Danny Fortson .75 2.00
AR9 Brevin Knight .75 2.00
AR10 Derek Anderson .75 2.00
AR11 Cedric Henderson .60 1.50
AR12 Jacque Vaughn .60 1.50
AR13 Tim Thomas 1.00 2.50
AR14 Austin Croshere .60 1.50
AR15 Kelvin Cato .60 1.50

1997-98 Ultra Big Shots

COMPLETE SET (15) 12.00 30.00
SER.1 STATED ODDS 1:4 HOB/RET
1 Michael Jordan 12.00 30.00
2 Allen Iverson 2.00 5.00
3 Shaquille O'Neal 2.00 5.00
4 Anfernee Hardaway 1.50 4.00
5 Dennis Rodman 1.50 4.00
6 Grant Hill 1.00 2.50
7 Juwan Howard .50 1.25
8 David Robinson 1.25 3.00
9 Gary Payton 1.00 2.50
10 Joe Smith .50 1.25
11 Charles Barkley 1.50 4.00
12 Terrell Brandon .50 1.25
13 John Stockton 1.25 3.00
14 Mitch Richmond .75 2.00
15 Vin Baker .50 1.25

1997-98 Ultra Court Masters
COMPLETE SET (20) 1,250.00 2,500.00
SER.2 STATED ODDS 1:144 HOB/RET
CM1 Michael Jordan 1,000.00 2,000.00
CM2 Allen Iverson 75.00 200.00
CM3 Kobe Bryant 300.00 600.00
CM4 Shaquille O'Neal 100.00 250.00
CM5 Stephon Marbury 25.00 60.00
CM6 Shawn Kemp 30.00 80.00
CM7 Anfernee Hardaway 100.00 250.00
CM8 Kevin Garnett 75.00 200.00
CM9 Shareef Abdur-Rahim 25.00 60.00
CM10 Dennis Rodman 100.00 250.00
CM11 Grant Hill 60.00 150.00
CM12 Kerry Kittles 20.00 50.00
CM13 Antoine Walker 20.00 50.00
CM14 Scottie Pippen 75.00 200.00
CM15 Damon Stoudamire 20.00 50.00
CM16 Marcus Camby 20.00 50.00
CM17 Hakeem Olajuwon 40.00 100.00
CM18 Tim Duncan 125.00 300.00
CM19 Keith Van Horn 20.00 50.00
CM20 Chauncey Billups 25.00 60.00

1997-98 Ultra Heir to the Throne
COMPLETE SET (15) 12.00 30.00
SER.1 STATED ODDS 1:18 HOB/RET
1 Derek Anderson .75 2.00
2 Tony Battie .75 2.00
3 Chauncey Billups 2.50 6.00
4 Kelvin Cato .60 1.50
5 Austin Croshere .60 1.50
6 Antonio Daniels .75 2.00
7 Tim Duncan 5.00 12.00
8 Danny Fortson .75 2.00
9 Jacque Vaughn .60 1.50
10 Tracy McGrady 4.00 10.00
11 Ron Mercer 1.00 2.50
12 Olivier Saint-Jean .60 1.50
13 Maurice Taylor .60 1.50
14 Tim Thomas 1.00 2.50
15 Keith Van Horn 1.25 3.00

1997-98 Ultra Inside/Outside
COMPLETE SET (15) 3.00 8.00
SER.1 STATED ODDS 1:6 HOB/RET
1 Shareef Abdur-Rahim .60 1.50
2 Juwan Howard .50 1.25
3 David Robinson 1.25 3.00
4 Joe Smith .50 1.25
5 Charles Barkley 1.50 4.00
6 Tom Gugliotta .50 1.25
7 Glenn Robinson .60 1.50
8 Patrick Ewing 1.00 2.50
9 Chris Webber .75 2.00
10 Glen Rice .60 1.50
11 Shawn Kemp 1.00 2.50
12 Antonio McDyess .60 1.50
13 Clyde Drexler 1.00 2.50
14 Eddie Jones .60 1.50
15 Jason Kidd 1.00 2.50

1997-98 Ultra Jam City
COMPLETE SET (18) 25.00 60.00
SER.1 STATED ODDS 1:8 HOB/RET
1 Kevin Garnett 2.50 6.00
2 Antoine Walker 1.00 2.50
3 Scottie Pippen 2.50 6.00
4 Shawn Kemp 1.50 4.00
5 Hakeem Olajuwon 2.00 5.00
6 Jerry Stackhouse 1.00 2.50
7 Karl Malone 2.00 5.00
8 Shaquille O'Neal 3.00 8.00
9 John Wallace .60 1.50
10 Marcus Camby 1.00 2.50
11 Juwan Howard .75 2.00
12 David Robinson 2.00 5.00
13 Gary Payton 1.50 4.00
14 Dennis Rodman 2.50 6.00
15 Joe Smith .75 2.00
16 Charles Barkley 2.50 6.00
17 Terrell Brandon .75 2.00
18 Kobe Bryant 25.00 60.00

1997-98 Ultra Neat Feats
COMPLETE SET (18) 5.00 12.00
SER.2 STATED ODDS 1:8 HOB/RET
NF1 Michael Finley .60 1.50
NF2 Jason Kidd 1.00 2.50
NF3 Rasheed Wallace .75 2.00
NF4 Shaquille O'Neal 2.00 5.00
NF5 Tom Gugliotta .50 1.25
NF6 Marcus Camby .60 1.50
NF7 Jerry Stackhouse .60 1.50
NF8 John Wallace .40 1.00
NF9 Juwan Howard .50 1.25
NF10 David Robinson 1.25 3.00
NF11 Gary Payton 1.00 2.50
NF12 Joe Smith .50 1.25
NF13 Charles Barkley 1.50 4.00
NF14 Terrell Brandon .50 1.25
NF15 John Stockton 1.25 3.00
NF16 Vin Baker .50 1.25
NF17 Antonio McDyess .60 1.50
NF18 Antonio Daniels .60 1.50

1997-98 Ultra Quick Picks
COMPLETE SET (12) 4.00 10.00
SER.1 STATED ODDS 1:8 HOB/RET
1 Stephon Marbury .75 2.00
2 Ray Allen 1.25 3.00
3 Damon Stoudamire .60 1.50
4 Kerry Kittles .50 1.25
5 Gary Payton 1.00 2.50
6 Terrell Brandon .50 1.25
7 John Stockton 1.25 3.00
8 Mookie Blaylock .60 1.50
9 Eddie Jones .60 1.50
10 Nick Van Exel .60 1.50
11 Kenny Anderson .50 1.25
12 Tim Hardaway .75 2.00

1997-98 Ultra Rim Rocker
COMPLETE SET (12) 4.00 10.00
SER.2 STATED ODDS 1:8 HOB/RET
RR1 Ron Mercer .75 2.00
RR2 Juwan Howard .50 1.25
RR3 David Robinson 1.25 3.00
RR4 Gary Payton 1.00 2.50
RR5 Joe Smith .50 1.25
RR6 Charles Barkley 1.50 4.00
RR7 Terrell Brandon .50 1.25
RR8 John Stockton 1.25 3.00
RR9 Adonal Foyle .50 1.25
RR10 Tim Thomas .75 2.00
RR11 Tony Battie .60 1.50
RR12 Antonio McDyess .60 1.50

1997-98 Ultra Star Power
COMPLETE SET (20) 12.00 30.00
SER.2 STATED ODDS 1:4 HOB/RET
*PLUS: 2X TO 5X BASE STAR POWER
PLUS: SER.2 STATED ODDS 1:36 H/R
SP1 Michael Jordan 50.00 120.00
SP2 Allen Iverson 1.50 4.00
SP3 Kobe Bryant 5.00 12.00
SP4 Shaquille O'Neal 1.50 4.00
SP5 Stephon Marbury .60 1.50
SP6 Shawn Kemp .75 2.00
SP7 Anfernee Hardaway 1.25 3.00
SP8 Kevin Garnett 1.25 3.00
SP9 Shareef Abdur-Rahim .50 1.25
SP10 Dennis Rodman 1.25 3.00
SP11 Grant Hill .75 2.00
SP12 Gary Payton .75 2.00
SP13 Antoine Walker .50 1.25
SP14 Scottie Pippen 1.25 3.00
SP15 Damon Stoudamire .50 1.25
SP16 Marcus Camby .50 1.25
SP17 Hakeem Olajuwon 1.00 2.50
SP18 Tim Duncan 1.50 4.00
SP19 Keith Van Horn .40 1.00
SP20 Jerry Stackhouse .50 1.25

1997-98 Ultra Star Power Supreme
*SUPREME: 15X TO 40X VALUE
SPS1 Michael Jordan 2,000.00 4,000.00
SPS2 Allen Iverson 200.00 500.00
SPS3 Kobe Bryant 1,500.00 3,000.00
SPS6 Shawn Kemp 30.00 80.00
SPS7 Anfernee Hardaway 200.00 500.00
SPS10 Dennis Rodman 200.00 500.00
SPS14 Scottie Pippen 200.00 500.00
SPS17 Hakeem Olajuwon 75.00 200.00
SPS18 Tim Duncan 200.00 500.00
SPS19 Keith Van Horn 25.00 60.00

1997-98 Ultra Stars
SER.1 STATED ODDS 1:144 HOB/RET
1 Michael Jordan 1,500.00 3,000.00
2 Allen Iverson 125.00 300.00
3 Kobe Bryant 1,000.00 2,000.00
4 Shaquille O'Neal 75.00 200.00
5 Stephon Marbury 25.00 60.00
6 Marcus Camby 20.00 50.00
7 Anfernee Hardaway 60.00 150.00
8 Kevin Garnett 60.00 150.00
9 Shareef Abdur-Rahim 20.00 50.00
10 Dennis Rodman 50.00 120.00
11 Ray Allen 40.00 100.00
12 Grant Hill 30.00 80.00
13 Kerry Kittles 15.00 40.00
14 Antoine Walker 20.00 50.00
15 Scottie Pippen 75.00 200.00
16 Damon Stoudamire 20.00 50.00
17 Shawn Kemp 40.00 100.00
18 Hakeem Olajuwon 50.00 120.00
19 Jerry Stackhouse 20.00 50.00
20 John Wallace 12.00 30.00

1997-98 Ultra Stars Gold
*GOLD: 2.5X TO 6X HI COLUMN
FIRST TEN PERCENT OF PRINT RUN IN GOLD
1 Michael Jordan 15,000.00 30,000.00
2 Allen Iverson 1,000.00 2,000.00
3 Kobe Bryant 10,000.00 20,000.00
4 Shaquille O'Neal 1,000.00 2,000.00
5 Stephon Marbury 150.00 400.00
7 Anfernee Hardaway 500.00 1,000.00
8 Kevin Garnett 500.00 1,000.00
9 Shareef Abdur-Rahim 150.00 400.00
10 Dennis Rodman 500.00 1,000.00
11 Ray Allen 500.00 1,000.00
12 Grant Hill 400.00 800.00
15 Scottie Pippen 1,000.00 2,000.00
16 Damon Stoudamire 300.00 600.00
17 Shawn Kemp 400.00 800.00
18 Hakeem Olajuwon 500.00 1,000.00
19 Jerry Stackhouse 125.00 300.00

1997-98 Ultra Sweet Deal
COMPLETE SET (12) 2.50 6.00
SER.2 STATED ODDS 1:6 HOB/RET
SD1 Ray Allen .75 2.00
SD2 Chauncey Billups 1.25 3.00
SD3 Ron Mercer .50 1.25
SD4 Hakeem Olajuwon .75 2.00
SD5 Jerry Stackhouse .50 1.25
SD6 John Wallace .25 .60
SD7 Juwan Howard .30 .75
SD8 David Robinson .75 2.00
SD9 Bobby Jackson .50 1.25
SD10 Joe Smith .30 .75
SD11 Charles Barkley 1.00 2.50
SD12 Terrell Brandon .30 .75

1997-98 Ultra Ultrabilities
COMPLETE SET (20) 12.00 30.00
SER.1 STATED ODDS 1:4 HOB/RET
*ALL-STAR: 2X TO 5X BASE ULTRABIL.
ALL-STAR: SER.1 STATED ODDS 1:36 H/R
1 Michael Jordan 5.00 12.00
2 Allen Iverson 1.50 4.00
3 Kobe Bryant 5.00 12.00
4 Shaquille O'Neal 1.50 4.00
5 Stephon Marbury .60 1.50
6 Gary Payton .75 2.00
7 Anfernee Hardaway 1.25 3.00
8 Kevin Garnett 1.25 3.00
9 Scottie Pippen 1.25 3.00
10 Grant Hill .75 2.00
11 Marcus Camby .50 1.25
12 Ray Allen 1.00 2.50
13 Kerry Kittles .40 1.00
14 Antoine Walker .50 1.25
15 Shareef Abdur-Rahim .50 1.25
16 Damon Stoudamire .50 1.25
17 Shawn Kemp .75 2.00
18 Hakeem Olajuwon 1.00 2.50
19 Jerry Stackhouse .50 1.25
20 Juwan Howard .40 1.00

1997-98 Ultra Ultrabilities Superstar
*SUPERSTAR: 6X TO 15X VALUE
SER.1 STATED ODDS 1:288 HOBBY/RETAIL
1 Michael Jordan 500.00 1,000.00
2 Allen Iverson 25.00 60.00
3 Kobe Bryant 100.00 250.00
4 Shaquille O'Neal 30.00 80.00
6 Gary Payton 12.00 30.00
7 Anfernee Hardaway 40.00 100.00
8 Kevin Garnett 25.00 60.00
9 Scottie Pippen 25.00 60.00
10 Grant Hill 20.00 50.00
12 Ray Allen 15.00 40.00
17 Shawn Kemp 15.00 40.00

1997-98 Ultra View to a Thrill
COMPLETE SET (15) 20.00 50.00
SER.2 STATED ODDS 1:18 HOB/RET
VT1 Michael Jordan 12.00 30.00
VT2 Allen Iverson 3.00 8.00
VT3 Kobe Bryant 8.00 20.00
VT4 Tracy McGrady 2.50 6.00
VT5 Stephon Marbury 1.25 3.00
VT6 Shawn Kemp 1.50 4.00
VT7 Anfernee Hardaway 2.50 6.00
VT8 Kevin Garnett 2.50 6.00
VT9 Shareef Abdur-Rahim 1.00 2.50
VT10 Dennis Rodman 2.50 6.00
VT11 Grant Hill 1.50 4.00
VT12 Kerry Kittles .75 2.00
VT13 Antoine Walker 1.00 2.50
VT14 Scottie Pippen 2.50 6.00
VT15 Damon Stoudamire 1.00 2.50

1998-99 Ultra
COMPLETE SET (125) 60.00 150.00
COMPLETE SET w/o SP (100) 20.00 50.00
ROOKIE SUBSET ODDS 1:4 H/R
1 Keith Van Horn .40 1.00
1B Keith Van Horn PROMO .40 1.00
2 Antonio Daniels .25 .60
3 Patrick Ewing .60 1.50
4 Alonzo Mourning .60 1.50
5 Isaac Austin .25 .60
6 Bryant Reeves .25 .60
7 Dennis Scott .25 .60
8 Damon Stoudamire .40 1.00
9 Kenny Anderson .40 1.00
10 Mookie Blaylock .25 .60
11 Mitch Richmond .50 1.25
12 Jalen Rose .30 .75
13 Vin Baker .30 .75
14 Donyell Marshall .25 .60
15 Bryon Russell .25 .60
16 Rasheed Wallace .50 1.25
17 Allan Houston .40 1.00
18 Shawn Kemp .60 1.50
19 Nick Van Exel .40 1.00
20 Theo Ratliff .30 .75
21 Jayson Williams .30 .75
22 Chauncey Billups .50 1.25
23 Brent Barry .30 .75
24 David Wesley .25 .60
25 Joe Dumars .40 1.00
26 Marcus Camby .40 1.00
27 Juwan Howard .30 .75
28 Brevin Knight .25 .60
29 Reggie Miller .75 2.00
30 Ray Allen .60 1.50
31 Michael Finley .40 1.00
32 Tom Gugliotta .30 .75
33 Allen Iverson 1.00 2.50
34 Toni Kukoc .40 1.00
35 Tim Thomas .30 .75
36 Jeff Hornacek .30 .75
37 Bobby Jackson .30 .75
38 Bo Outlaw .25 .60
39 Steve Smith .30 .75
40 Terrell Brandon .30 .75
41 Glen Rice .40 1.00
42 Rik Smits .30 .75
43 Calbert Cheaney .25 .60
44 Stephon Marbury .50 1.25
45 Glenn Robinson .40 1.00
46 Corliss Williamson .25 .60
47 Larry Johnson .60 1.50
48 Antonio McDyess .30 .75
49 Detlef Schrempf .40 1.00
50 Jerry Stackhouse .40 1.00
51 Doug Christie .30 .75
52 Eddie Jones .40 1.00
53 Karl Malone .75 2.00
54 Anthony Mason .30 .75
55 Tim Duncan 1.00 2.50
56 Christian Laettner .30 .75
57 Isaiah Rider .30 .75
58 Shawn Bradley .25 .60
59 Jim Jackson .25 .60
60 Mark Jackson .25 .60
61 Kobe Bryant 3.00 8.00
62 Zydrunas Ilgauskas .40 1.00
63 Ron Mercer .25 .60
64 Hersey Hawkins .25 .60
65 John Wallace .25 .60
66 Avery Johnson .30 .75
67 Dikembe Mutombo .60 1.50
68 Hakeem Olajuwon .75 2.00
69 Tony Battie .25 .60
70 Jason Kidd .60 1.50
71 Latrell Sprewell .60 1.50
72 Kevin Garnett 1.00 2.50
73 Voshon Lenard .25 .60
74 Gary Payton .60 1.50
75 Cherokee Parks .25 .60
76 Antoine Walker .40 1.00
77 Anthony Johnson .25 .60
78 Danny Fortson .25 .60
79 Grant Hill .60 1.50
80 Dennis Rodman 1.00 2.50
81 Arvydas Sabonis .40 1.00
82 Tracy McGrady .60 1.50
83 David Robinson .75 2.00
84 Tariq Abdul-Wahad .25 .60
85 Michael Jordan 4.00 10.00
86 Kerry Kittles .30 .75
87 Maurice Taylor .25 .60
88 Cedric Ceballos .30 .75
89 Anfernee Hardaway 1.00 2.50
90 John Stockton .75 2.00
91 Shareef Abdur-Rahim .40 1.00
92 Tim Hardaway .50 1.25
93 Shaquille O'Neal 1.50 4.00
94 Rodney Rogers .25 .60
95 Derek Anderson .30 .75
96 Kendall Gill .30 .75
97 Rod Strickland .30 .75
98 Charles Barkley 1.00 2.50
99 Chris Webber .50 1.25
100 Scottie Pippen 1.00 2.50
101 Raef LaFrentz RC 1.00 2.50
102 Ricky Davis RC 1.25 3.00
103 Robert Traylor RC .75 2.00
104 Roshown McLeod RC .50 1.25
105 Tyronn Lue RC 1.00 2.50
106 Vince Carter RC 4.00 10.00
107 Miles Simon RC .75 2.00
108 Paul Pierce RC 3.00 8.00
109 Pat Garrity RC .60 1.50
110 Nazr Mohammed RC .75 2.00
111 Mike Bibby RC 1.50 4.00
112 Michael Dickerson RC .75 2.00
113 Michael Doleac RC .60 1.50
114 Matt Harpring RC .75 2.00
115 Larry Hughes RC 1.25 3.00
116 Keon Clark RC .75 2.00
117 Felipe Lopez RC .50 1.25
118 Dirk Nowitzki RC 8.00 20.00
119 Corey Benjamin RC .50 1.25
120 Bryce Drew RC .50 1.25
121 Brian Skinner RC .60 1.50
122 Bonzi Wells RC .75 2.00
123 Antawn Jamison RC 1.25 3.00
124 Al Harrington RC 1.00 2.50
125 Michael Olowokandi RC 1.00 2.50

1998-99 Ultra Gold Medallion
*STARS: 1.25X TO 3X BASE CARD HI
*RCs: .1.25X TO 3X BASE HI
RCs: STATED ODDS 1:35 HOBBY
61G Kobe Bryant 40.00 100.00
85G Michael Jordan 50.00 120.00
106G Vince Carter 30.00 80.00
118G Dirk Nowitzki 50.00 120.00

1998-99 Ultra Platinum Medallion
*STARS: 30X TO 80X BASE CARD HI
*RCs: 12X TO 30X HI
STARS: PRINT RUN 99 SERIAL #'d SETS
RCs: STATED PRINT RUN 66 SERIAL #'d SETS
3 Patrick Ewing 100.00 250.00
4 Alonzo Mourning 100.00 250.00
16 Rasheed Wallace 75.00 200.00
18 Shawn Kemp 125.00 300.00
29 Reggie Miller 150.00 400.00
30 Ray Allen 100.00 250.00
33 Allen Iverson 200.00 500.00
47 Larry Johnson 125.00 300.00
53 Karl Malone 100.00 250.00
55 Tim Duncan 200.00 500.00
61 Kobe Bryant 1,500.00 3,000.00
67 Dikembe Mutombo 125.00 300.00
68 Hakeem Olajuwon 125.00 300.00
72 Kevin Garnett 150.00 400.00
74 Gary Payton 150.00 400.00
79 Grant Hill 125.00 300.00
80 Dennis Rodman 400.00 800.00
82 Tracy McGrady 150.00 400.00
83 David Robinson 125.00 300.00
85 Michael Jordan 2,500.00 5,000.00
89 Anfernee Hardaway 150.00 400.00
93 Shaquille O'Neal 200.00 500.00
98 Charles Barkley 150.00 400.00
99 Chris Webber 150.00 400.00
100 Scottie Pippen 150.00 400.00
106 Vince Carter 600.00 1,200.00
108 Paul Pierce 200.00 500.00
118 Dirk Nowitzki 1,000.00 2,000.00

1998-99 Ultra Exclamation Points
COMPLETE SET (15) 700.00 1,000.00
STATED ODDS 1:288 HOB/RET
1 Vince Carter 75.00 200.00
2 Tim Duncan 75.00 200.00
3 Shawn Kemp 75.00 200.00
4 Shaquille O'Neal 75.00 200.00
5 Mike Bibby 40.00 100.00
6 Michael Jordan 1,000.00 2,000.00
7 Michael Olowokandi 25.00 60.00
8 Larry Hughes 40.00 100.00
9 Kobe Bryant 150.00 400.00
10 Kevin Garnett 30.00 80.00
11 Keith Van Horn 25.00 60.00
12 Grant Hill 60.00 150.00
13 Gary Payton 60.00 150.00
14 Antoine Walker 40.00 100.00
15 Antawn Jamison 25.00 60.00

1998-99 Ultra Give and Take
COMPLETE SET (10) 6.00 15.00
STATED ODDS 1:18 RETAIL
1 Gary Payton 1.50 4.00
2 Shawn Kemp 1.50 4.00
3 Kerry Kittles .75 2.00
4 Ron Mercer .75 2.00
5 Scottie Pippen 2.50 6.00
6 Ray Allen 1.50 4.00
7 Anfernee Hardaway 2.50 6.00
8 Maurice Taylor .60 1.50
9 Brevin Knight .60 1.50
10 Karl Malone 2.00 5.00

1998-99 Ultra Leading Performers
COMPLETE SET (15) 40.00 100.00
STATED ODDS 1:72 HOB/RET
1 Allen Iverson 10.00 25.00
2 Anfernee Hardaway 10.00 25.00
3 Kobe Bryant 15.00 40.00
4 Michael Jordan 60.00 150.00
5 Ron Mercer 1.50 4.00
6 Stephon Marbury 2.50 6.00
7 Tim Duncan 10.00 25.00
8 Shareef Abdur-Rahim 2.00 5.00
9 Kevin Garnett 10.00 25.00
10 Grant Hill 3.00 8.00
11 Damon Stoudamire 2.00 5.00
12 Dennis Rodman 10.00 25.00
13 Keith Van Horn 2.00 5.00
14 Scottie Pippen 10.00 25.00
15 Shaquille O'Neal 10.00 25.00

1998-99 Ultra NBAttitude
COMPLETE SET (20) 5.00 12.00
STATED ODDS 1:6 HOB/RET
1 Allen Iverson 1.50 4.00
2 Chauncey Billups .75 2.00
3 Keith Van Horn .60 1.50
4 Ray Allen 1.00 2.50
5 Shareef Abdur-Rahim .60 1.50
6 Stephon Marbury .75 2.00
7 Kerry Kittles .50 1.25
8 Tim Thomas .50 1.25
9 Damon Stoudamire .60 1.50
10 Antoine Walker .60 1.50
11 Brevin Knight .40 1.00
12 Maurice Taylor .40 1.00
13 Ron Mercer .50 1.25
14 Tim Duncan 1.50 4.00
15 Zydrunas Ilgauskas .60 1.50
16 Michael Finley .60 1.50
17 Bobby Jackson .50 1.25
18 Tim Hardaway .75 2.00
19 David Robinson 1.25 3.00
20 Vin Baker .50 1.25

1998-99 Ultra Unstoppable
COMPLETE SET (15) 25.00 60.00
STATED ODDS 1:36 HOB/RET
1 Michael Jordan 15.00 40.00
2 Scottie Pippen 3.00 8.00
3 Grant Hill 2.00 5.00
4 Dennis Rodman 3.00 8.00
5 Stephon Marbury 1.50 4.00
6 Antoine Walker 1.25 3.00
7 Shareef Abdur-Rahim 1.25 3.00
8 Shaquille O'Neal 5.00 12.00
9 Damon Stoudamire 1.25 3.00
10 Kerry Kittles 1.00 2.50
11 Maurice Taylor .75 2.00
12 Kobe Bryant 10.00 25.00
13 Kevin Garnett 3.00 8.00
14 Anfernee Hardaway 3.00 8.00
15 Allen Iverson 3.00 8.00

1998-99 Ultra World Premiere
COMPLETE SET (15) 12.00 30.00
STATED ODDS 1:20 HOB/RET
1 Robert Traylor .75 2.00
2 Paul Pierce 3.00 8.00
3 Michael Olowokandi 1.00 2.50
4 Felipe Lopez .50 1.25
5 Raef LaFrentz 1.00 2.50
6 Antawn Jamison 1.25 3.00
7 Larry Hughes 1.25 3.00
8 Al Harrington 1.00 2.50
9 Pat Garrity .60 1.50
10 Bryce Drew .50 1.25
11 Michael Doleac .60 1.50
12 Michael Dickerson .75 2.00
13 Keon Clark .75 2.00
14 Vince Carter 4.00 10.00
15 Mike Bibby 1.50 4.00

1999-00 Ultra
COMPLETE SET (150) 30.00 80.00
COMPLETE SET w/o RC (125) 12.00 30.00
126-150 SUBSET ODDS 1:4 HOB/RET
1 Vince Carter 1.00 2.50
2 Randell Jackson .25 .60
3 Ray Allen .60 1.50
4 Corliss Williamson .25 .60
5 Darrell Armstrong .25 .60
6 Charles Oakley .40 1.00
7 Tyrone Nesby RC .25 .60
8 Eddie Jones .40 1.00
9 Kerry Kittles .30 .75
10 Jason Williams .60 1.50
11 Elden Campbell .25 .60
12 Mookie Blaylock .25 .60
13 Brent Barry .30 .75
14 Mark Jackson .30 .75
15 Tim Hardaway .50 1.25
16 Kendall Gill .40 1.00
17 Larry Johnson .40 1.00
18 Eric Snow .25 .60
19 Raef LaFrentz .30 .75
20 Allen Iverson 1.00 2.50
21 Kenny Anderson .30 .75
22 John Starks .40 1.00
23 Isaiah Rider .30 .75
24 Tariq Abdul-Wahad .25 .60
25 Vitaly Potapenko .25 .60
26 Patrick Ewing .50 1.25
27 Mitch Richmond .50 1.25
28 Steve Nash .75 2.00
29 Dickey Simpkins .25 .60
30 Grant Hill .60 1.50
31 Matt Geiger .25 .60
32 John Stockton .60 1.50
33 Jayson Williams .25 .60
34 Reggie Miller .75 2.00
35 Eric Piatkowski .25 .60
36 Jason Kidd .60 1.50
37 Allan Houston .30 .75
38 Christian Laettner .30 .75
39 Marcus Camby .30 .75
40 Shaquille O'Neal 1.50 4.00
41 Derek Anderson .25 .60
42 Gary Trent .25 .60
43 Vin Baker .30 .75
44 Alonzo Mourning .60 1.50
45 Latrell Sprewell .50 1.25
46 Rod Strickland .30 .75
47 Bobby Jackson .30 .75
48 Karl Malone .75 2.00
49 Mario Elie .25 .60
50 Kobe Bryant 3.00 8.00
51 Clifford Robinson .30 .75
52 Jamal Mashburn .30 .75
53 Dirk Nowitzki 1.25 3.00
54 Rik Smits .30 .75
55 Doug Christie .30 .75
56 Ricky Davis .40 1.00
57 Jalen Rose .30 .75
58 Michael Olowokandi .25 .60
59 Cedric Ceballos .25 .60
60 Ron Mercer .25 .60
61 Brevin Knight .25 .60
62 Rashard Lewis .30 .75
63 Detlef Schrempf .30 .75
64 Keith Van Horn .30 .75
64B Keith Van Horn PROMO .30 .75
65 Nick Anderson .25 .60
66 Larry Hughes .30 .75
67 Antonio McDyess .30 .75
68 Terrell Brandon .25 .60
69 Felipe Lopez .25 .60
70 Scottie Pippen 1.00 2.50
71 Erick Dampier .25 .60
72 Arvydas Sabonis .30 .75
73 Brian Grant .25 .60
74 Nick Van Exel .30 .75
75 Bryon Russell .25 .60
76 Danny Fortson .25 .60
77 Avery Johnson .30 .75
78 Jerry Stackhouse .40 1.00
79 Robert Traylor .25 .60
80 Tim Duncan 1.00 2.50
81 Lindsey Hunter .25 .60
82 Tyronn Lue .25 .60
83 Michael Finley .40 1.00
84 Dikembe Mutombo .60 1.50
85 Zydrunas Ilgauskas .30 .75
86 Pat Garrity .25 .60
87 Damon Stoudamire .40 1.00
88 Shareef Abdur-Rahim .40 1.00
89 Matt Harpring .25 .60
90 Michael Dickerson .25 .60
91 Steve Smith .30 .75
92 Bison Dele .25 .60
93 Glenn Robinson .30 .75
94 Antawn Jamison .40 1.00
95 Glen Rice .40 1.00
96 Vlade Divac .40 1.00
97 Vladimir Stepania .25 .60
98 Kornell David RC .25 .60
99 Shawn Kemp .60 1.50
100 Kevin Garnett 1.00 2.50
101 Tim Thomas .30 .75
102 Mike Bibby .40 1.00
103 Maurice Taylor .25 .60
104 Gary Payton .60 1.50
105 Voshon Lenard .25 .60
106 Theo Ratliff .30 .75
107 Hakeem Olajuwon .75 2.00
108 Joe Smith .30 .75
109 Toni Kukoc .50 1.25
110 Stephon Marbury .50 1.25
111 Anthony Mason .40 1.00
112 Anfernee Hardaway 1.00 2.50
113 Juwan Howard .30 .75
114 Charles Barkley 1.00 2.50
115 Antoine Walker .40 1.00
116 Donyell Marshall .30 .75
117 Tom Gugliotta .30 .75
118 Rasheed Wallace .50 1.25
119 Tracy McGrady .60 1.50
120 Paul Pierce .75 2.00
121 Sean Elliott .30 .75
122 Bryant Reeves .25 .60
123 Michael Doleac .25 .60
124 Chris Webber .50 1.25
125 David Robinson .75 2.00
126 Steve Francis RC 1.25 3.00
127 Elton Brand RC 1.25 3.00
128 Wally Szczerbiak RC 1.00 2.50
129 Richard Hamilton RC 1.50 4.00
130 Shawn Marion RC 1.25 3.00
131 Trajan Langdon RC .50 1.25
132 Corey Maggette RC .75 2.00
133 Dion Glover RC .40 1.00
134 James Posey RC .60 1.50
135 Lamar Odom RC 1.25 3.00
136 A.Radojevic RC .40 1.00
137 Cal Bowdler RC .40 1.00
138 Scott Padgett RC .50 1.25
139 Jumaine Jones RC .40 1.00
140 Jonathan Bender RC .60 1.50
141 Tim James RC .40 1.00
142 Jason Terry RC 1.00 2.50
143 Quincy Lewis RC .40 1.00
144 William Avery RC .40 1.00
145 Galen Young RC .60 1.50
146 Ron Artest RC 1.50 4.00
147 Kenny Thomas RC .60 1.50
148 Devean George RC .50 1.25
149 Andre Miller RC 1.25 3.00
150 Baron Davis RC 1.50 4.00

1999-00 Ultra Gold Medallion
*STARS: 1.25X TO 3X BASE CARD HI
*RCs: .75X TO 2X BASE HI
RCs: STATED ODDS 1:35 HOBBY

1999-00 Ultra Platinum Medallion
*STARS: 30X TO 80X BASE CARD HI
*RCs: 12X TO 30X BASE HI
STARS: PRINT RUN 50 SERIAL #'d SETS
RCs: PRINT RUN 25 SERIAL #'d SETS
1 Vince Carter 150.00 400.00
3 Ray Allen 100.00 250.00
10 Jason Williams 100.00 250.00
17 Larry Johnson 100.00 250.00
20 Allen Iverson 150.00 400.00
26 Patrick Ewing 100.00 250.00
28 Steve Nash 125.00 300.00
30 Grant Hill 100.00 250.00
32 John Stockton 125.00 300.00
34 Reggie Miller 150.00 400.00
36 Jason Kidd 125.00 300.00
40 Shaquille O'Neal 150.00 400.00
44 Alonzo Mourning 100.00 250.00
45 Latrell Sprewell 75.00 200.00
48 Karl Malone 125.00 300.00
50 Kobe Bryant 1,500.00 3,000.00
53 Dirk Nowitzki 150.00 400.00
70 Scottie Pippen 150.00 400.00
80 Tim Duncan 150.00 400.00
90 Michael Dickerson 100.00 250.00
99 Shawn Kemp 125.00 300.00
100 Kevin Garnett 150.00 400.00
104 Gary Payton 125.00 300.00
107 Hakeem Olajuwon 125.00 300.00
109 Toni Kukoc 75.00 200.00
110 Stephon Marbury 75.00 200.00
112 Anfernee Hardaway 150.00 400.00
114 Charles Barkley 125.00 300.00
118 Rasheed Wallace 75.00 200.00
119 Tracy McGrady 125.00 300.00
120 Paul Pierce 125.00 300.00
124 Chris Webber 125.00 300.00
125 David Robinson 125.00 300.00

1999-00 Ultra Feel the Game
1 Steve Francis 3.00 8.00
2 Richard Hamilton 4.00 10.00
3 Jonathan Bender 1.50 4.00
4 Baron Davis 4.00 10.00
5 Wally Szczerbiak 2.50 6.00
6 Lamar Odom 3.00 8.00
7 Andre Miller 3.00 8.00
8 Jason Terry 2.50 6.00
9 Trajan Langdon 1.25 3.00
10 Corey Maggette 2.00 5.00
11 Cal Bowdler 1.00 2.50
12 James Posey 1.50 4.00
13 Tim James 1.00 2.50
14 Scott Padgett 1.25 3.00
15 Jumaine Jones 1.00 2.50

1999-00 Ultra Fresh Ink
PRINT RUNS LISTED BELOW
1 Ray Allen/300 30.00 80.00
2 Ron Artest/1000 12.00 30.00
3 William Avery/1000 3.00 8.00
4 Jonathan Bender/500 5.00 12.00
5 Mike Bibby/550 5.00 12.00
6 Calvin Booth/975 3.00 8.00
7 Cal Bowdler/1000 3.00 8.00
8 Bruce Bowen/1000 5.00 12.00
9 Marcus Camby/750 4.00 10.00
10 John Celestand/1000 3.00 8.00
11 Baron Davis/475 12.00 30.00
12 Michael Dickerson/975 3.00 8.00
13 Michael Doleac/1000 3.00 8.00
14 Bryce Drew/1000 3.00 8.00
15 Evan Eschmeyer/1000 4.00 10.00
16 Steve Francis/500 10.00 25.00
17 Pat Garrity/500 3.00 8.00
18 Devean George/1000 4.00 10.00
19 Dion Glover/875 3.00 8.00
20 Brian Grant/500 3.00 8.00
21 Richard Hamilton/750 12.00 30.00
22 Juwan Howard/225 4.00 10.00
23 Larry Hughes/750 4.00 10.00
24 Jumaine Jones/1000 3.00 8.00
25 Eddie Jones/250 5.00 12.00
26 Raef LaFrentz/500 4.00 10.00
27 Quincy Lewis/1000 3.00 8.00
28 Felipe Lopez/1000 3.00 8.00
29 Corey Maggette/250 6.00 15.00
30 Stephon Marbury/400 15.00 40.00
31 Shawn Marion/1000 10.00 25.00
32 Lamar Odom/350 10.00 25.00
33 Shaquille O'Neal/200 200.00 500.00
34 Scottie Pippen/130 150.00 400.00
35 James Posey/1000 5.00 12.00
36 A.Radojevic/1000 3.00 8.00
37 David Robinson/155 125.00 300.00
38 Jalen Rose/500 4.00 10.00
39 Wally Szczerbiak/500 8.00 20.00
40 Jerry Stackhouse/650 5.00 12.00
41 Maurice Taylor/400 5.00 12.00
42 Jason Terry/1000 8.00 20.00
43 Robert Traylor/1000 3.00 8.00
44 Keith Van Horn/500 4.00 10.00
45 Antoine Walker/245 5.00 12.00
46 Chris Webber/200 300.00 600.00

1999-00 Ultra Good Looks
COMPLETE SET (15) 8.00 20.00
STATED ODDS 1:6 HOB/RET
1 Grant Hill 1.00 2.50
2 Kevin Garnett 1.50 4.00
3 Richard Hamilton 1.50 4.00
4 Larry Hughes .50 1.25
5 Shaquille O'Neal 2.50 6.00
6 Kobe Bryant 5.00 12.00
7 Antoine Walker .60 1.50
8 Lamar Odom 1.25 3.00
9 Allen Iverson 1.50 4.00
10 Scottie Pippen 1.50 4.00
11 Ron Mercer .50 1.25
12 Anfernee Hardaway 1.50 4.00
13 Chris Webber .75 2.00
14 Jason Williams 1.00 2.50
15 Baron Davis 1.50 4.00

1999-00 Ultra Heir to the Throne
COMPLETE SET (10) 6.00 15.00
STATED ODDS 1:24 HOB/RET
1 Allen Iverson 2.00 5.00
2 Keith Van Horn .60 1.50
3 Paul Pierce 1.50 4.00
4 Stephon Marbury 1.00 2.50
5 Vince Carter 2.00 5.00
6 Tim Duncan 2.00 5.00
7 Ron Mercer .60 1.50
8 Antawn Jamison .75 2.00
9 Shaquille O'Neal 3.00 8.00
10 Grant Hill 1.25 3.00

1999-00 Ultra Millennium Men
PRINT RUN 100 SERIAL #'d SETS
1 Allen Iverson 300.00 600.00
2 Paul Pierce 150.00 400.00
3 Steve Francis 100.00 250.00
4 Kobe Bryant 1,000.00 2,000.00
5 Vince Carter 200.00 500.00
6 Ron Mercer 60.00 150.00
7 Jason Williams 400.00 800.00
8 Elton Brand 75.00 200.00
9 Grant Hill 200.00 500.00
10 Tim Duncan 300.00 600.00
11 Stephon Marbury 75.00 200.00
12 Keith Van Horn 75.00 200.00
13 Kevin Garnett 400.00 800.00
14 Antawn Jamison 75.00 200.00
15 Antoine Walker 100.00 250.00

1999-00 Ultra Parquet Players
COMPLETE SET (15) 50.00 100.00
STATED ODDS 1:72 HOB/RET
1 Kobe Bryant 20.00 50.00
2 Keith Van Horn 2.00 5.00
3 Tim Duncan 6.00 15.00
4 Shaquille O'Neal 10.00 25.00
5 Kevin Garnett 6.00 15.00
6 Jason Williams 4.00 10.00
7 Vince Carter 6.00 15.00
8 Stephon Marbury 3.00 8.00
9 Paul Pierce 5.00 12.00
10 Scottie Pippen 6.00 15.00
11 Baron Davis 4.00 10.00
12 Antoine Walker 2.50 6.00
13 Larry Hughes 2.00 5.00
14 Antawn Jamison 2.50 6.00
15 Elton Brand 3.00 8.00

1999-00 Ultra World Premiere
COMPLETE SET (10) 6.00 15.00
STATED ODDS 1:12 HOB/RET
1 Elton Brand 1.25 3.00
2 Andre Miller 1.25 3.00
3 Baron Davis 1.50 4.00
4 Steve Francis 1.25 3.00
5 Richard Hamilton 1.50 4.00
6 Jason Terry 1.00 2.50
7 Jonathan Bender .60 1.50
8 Trajan Langdon .50 1.25
9 Wally Szczerbiak 1.00 2.50
10 Lamar Odom 1.25 3.00

2000-01 Ultra
COMPLETE SET w/o RC (200) 15.00 40.00
RCs: STATED PRINT RUN 2999 SERIAL #'d SETS
1 Vince Carter .75 2.00
2 Antawn Jamison .40 1.00
3 Shaquille O'Neal 1.50 4.00
4 Paul Pierce .60 1.50
5 Antonio McDyess .30 .75
6 Scott Burrell .25 .60
7 Elton Brand .40 1.00
8 Lamar Odom .40 1.00
9 Nick Van Exel .40 1.00
10 Kobe Bryant 3.00 8.00
11 Reggie Miller .75 2.00
12 Sam Cassell .30 .75
13 Darrell Armstrong .25 .60
14 Rasheed Wallace .50 1.25
15 Charles Oakley .40 1.00
16 David Wesley .30 .75
17 Al Harrington .30 .75
18 Latrell Sprewell .50 1.25
19 Rick Brunson .25 .60
20 Steve Smith .40 1.00
21 Antonio Davis .30 .75
22 Michael Finley .40 1.00
23 Shandon Anderson .25 .60
24 Danny Fortson .30 .75
25 Kerry Kittles .30 .75
26 Anfernee Hardaway .60 1.50
27 Vin Baker .30 .75
28 Calvin Booth .25 .60
29 Haywoode Workman .25 .60
30 Dickey Simpkins .25 .60
31 Jerome Williams .25 .60
32 Ron Artest .40 1.00
33 Dennis Scott .30 .75
34 Ron Mercer .30 .75
35 Chris Webber .50 1.25
36 Bryon Russell .25 .60
37 Dale Davis .30 .75
38 Dirk Nowitzki 1.00 2.50
39 Steve Francis .40 1.00
40 Glen Rice .40 1.00
41 Stephon Marbury .50 1.25
42 Jason Kidd .60 1.50
43 Brent Barry .30 .75
44 Richard Hamilton .50 1.25
45 Antoine Walker .40 1.00
46 Gary Trent .25 .60
47 Cuttino Mobley .30 .75
48 P.J. Brown .25 .60
49 Elliot Perry .25 .60
50 Shawn Marion .40 1.00
51 Horace Grant .40 1.00
52 Juwan Howard .30 .75
53 Elden Campbell .25 .60
54 Erick Strickland .25 .60
55 Hakeem Olajuwon .75 2.00
56 Anthony Carter .25 .60
57 Keith Van Horn .30 .75
58 Clifford Robinson .40 1.00
59 Ruben Patterson .40 1.00
60 Mitch Richmond .50 1.25
61 Jason Terry .40 1.00
62 Andre Miller .30 .75
63 Vonteego Cummings .25 .60
64 Joe Smith .30 .75
65 Toni Kukoc .50 1.25
66 Sean Elliott .30 .75
67 Michael Dickerson .25 .60
68 Derrick Coleman .40 1.00
69 Shawn Bradley .25 .60
70 Kenny Thomas .25 .60
71 Tim Hardaway .50 1.25
72 Rex Chapman .30 .75
73 Gary Payton .60 1.50
74 Jahidi White .25 .60
75 Baron Davis .40 1.00
76 Chauncey Billups .50 1.25
77 Moochie Norris .25 .60
78 Dan Majerle .40 1.00
79 Marcus Camby .30 .75
80 Rodney Rogers .25 .60
81 Rashard Lewis .30 .75
82 Laron Profit .25 .60
83 Ricky Davis .30 .75
84 Keon Clark .25 .60
85 Anthony Miller .25 .60
86 Jamal Mashburn .30 .75
87 Chris Childs .25 .60
88 Brian Grant .30 .75
89 Muggsy Bogues .40 1.00
90 Randy Brown .25 .60
91 Tariq Abdul-Wahad .25 .60
92 Lindsey Hunter .25 .60
93 Rik Smits .25 .60
94 Glenn Robinson .40 1.00
95 Michael Doleac .25 .60
96 Quincy Lewis .25 .60
97 Grant Hill .60 1.50
98 Jalen Rose .30 .75
99 Ervin Johnson .25 .60
100 Chucky Atkins .25 .60
101 Jermaine O'Neal .30 .75
102 Howard Eisley .25 .60
103 Kenny Anderson .30 .75
104 Lamond Murray .25 .60
105 Adonal Foyle .25 .60
106 Derek Fisher .40 1.00
107 Wally Szczerbiak .30 .75
108 Todd MacCulloch .25 .60
109 Avery Johnson .30 .75
110 Othella Harrington .25 .60
111 Tony Battie .25 .60
112 Bob Sura .25 .60
113 Larry Hughes .40 1.00
114 Rick Fox .30 .75
115 Travis Best .25 .60
116 Theo Ratliff .25 .60
117 David Robinson .75 2.00
118 Felipe Lopez .25 .60
119 John Amaechi .25 .60
120 George Lynch .25 .60
121 Christian Laettner .40 1.00
122 Derek Anderson .30 .75
123 Tim Thomas .25 .60
124 Matt Harpring .25 .60
125 Nick Anderson .30 .75
126 Karl Malone .75 2.00
127 Dion Glover .25 .60
128 Wesley Person .25 .60
129 Mikki Moore RC .40 1.00
130 Michael Olowokandi .25 .60
131 William Avery .25 .60
132 Bo Outlaw .25 .60
133 Jason Williams .60 1.50
134 John Stockton .75 2.00
135 Adrian Griffin .25 .60
136 Hubert Davis .25 .60
137 Donyell Marshall .30 .75
138 Travis Knight .25 .60
139 Kendall Gill .40 1.00
140 Tom Gugliotta .30 .75
141 Malik Rose .25 .60
142 Isaac Austin .25 .60
143 Alan Henderson .25 .60
144 Shawn Kemp .60 1.50
145 Terry Mills .25 .60
146 Maurice Taylor .25 .60
147 Terrell Brandon .30 .75
148 Matt Geiger .25 .60
149 Corliss Williamson .25 .60
150 Jacque Vaughn .25 .60
151 Dikembe Mutombo .60 1.50
152 Trajan Langdon .25 .60
153 Jason Caffey .25 .60
154 Tyrone Nesby .25 .60
155 Bobby Jackson .30 .75
156 Allen Iverson 1.00 2.50
157 Mario Elie .25 .60
158 Mike Bibby .40 1.00
159 Robert Horry .40 1.00
160 James Posey .30 .75
161 Mark Jackson .30 .75
162 Ray Allen .60 1.50
163 Charlie Ward .30 .75
164 Damon Stoudamire .40 1.00
165 Tracy McGrady .75 2.00
166 Bimbo Coles .25 .60
167 Chucky Brown .25 .60
168 Jerry Stackhouse .40 1.00
169 Greg Ostertag .25 .60
170 Radoslav Nesterovic .25 .60
171 Corey Maggette .30 .75
172 Vlade Divac .40 1.00
173 Scott Padgett .25 .60
174 Anthony Mason .40 1.00
175 Raef LaFrentz .30 .75
176 Austin Croshere .25 .60
177 Mark Strickland .25 .60
178 Allan Houston .40 1.00
179 Arvydas Sabonis .40 1.00
180 Doug Christie .30 .75
181 Jim Jackson .30 .75
182 Brevin Knight .25 .60
183 Mookie Blaylock .40 1.00
184 Chris Herren .25 .60
185 Kevin Garnett 1.00 2.50
186 Tyrone Hill .25 .60
187 Tim Duncan 1.00 2.50
188 Shareef Abdur-Rahim .40 1.00
189 Eddie Jones .40 1.00
190 Jonathan Bender .25 .60
191 Alonzo Mourning .60 1.50
192 Patrick Ewing .60 1.50
193 Scottie Pippen 1.00 2.50
194 Scot Pollard .25 .60
195 Cedric Ceballos .30 .75
196 Clarence Weatherspoon .25 .60
197 Jamie Feick .25 .60
198 Eric Snow .25 .60
199 Ron Harper .40 1.00
200 Bryant Reeves .25 .60
201 Chris Mihm RC .50 1.25
202 Joel Przybilla RC .60 1.50
203 Kenyon Martin RC 1.50 4.00
204 Stromile Swift RC .60 1.50
205 Etan Thomas RC .60 1.50
206 Jason Collier RC .75 2.00
207 Marcus Fizer RC .60 1.50
208 Mateen Cleaves RC .60 1.50
209 Dan Langhi RC .50 1.25
210 Mike Miller RC 1.25 3.00
211 Jabari Smith RC .50 1.25
212 Hanno Mottola RC .50 1.25
213 Chris Porter RC .50 1.25
214 Desmond Mason RC 1.00 2.50
215 Erick Barkley RC .50 1.25
216 Donnell Harvey RC .60 1.50
217 DerMarr Johnson RC .50 1.25
218 Jerome Moiso RC .50 1.25
219 Quentin Richardson RC .60 1.50
220 Courtney Alexander RC .50 1.25
221 Michael Redd RC 2.00 5.00
222 Morris Peterson RC .75 2.00
223 Darius Miles RC .75 2.00
224 Jamal Crawford RC 2.00 5.00
225 Keyon Dooling RC .60 1.50

2000-01 Ultra Gold Medallion
STARS: ONE PER PACK
RCs: STATED ODDS 1:24
10 Kobe Bryant 40.00 100.00

2000-01 Ultra Platinum Medallion
*STARS: 30X TO 80X BASE CARD HI
STARS: PRINT RUN 50 SERIAL #'d SETS
RCs: PRINT RUN 25 SERIAL #'d SETS
1 Vince Carter 125.00 300.00
3 Shaquille O'Neal 150.00 400.00
4 Paul Pierce 100.00 250.00
10 Kobe Bryant 1,500.00 3,000.00
11 Reggie Miller 150.00 400.00
14 Rasheed Wallace 75.00 200.00
18 Latrell Sprewell 75.00 200.00
26 Anfernee Hardaway 150.00 400.00
35 Chris Webber 125.00 300.00
38 Dirk Nowitzki 150.00 400.00
41 Stephon Marbury 75.00 200.00
42 Jason Kidd 100.00 250.00
55 Hakeem Olajuwon 125.00 300.00
65 Toni Kukoc 75.00 200.00
73 Gary Payton 125.00 300.00
97 Grant Hill 125.00 300.00
117 David Robinson 125.00 300.00
126 Karl Malone 125.00 300.00
133 Jason Williams 75.00 200.00
134 John Stockton 125.00 300.00
144 Shawn Kemp 100.00 250.00
151 Dikembe Mutombo 100.00 250.00
156 Allen Iverson 150.00 400.00
162 Ray Allen 100.00 250.00
165 Tracy McGrady 125.00 300.00
185 Kevin Garnett 150.00 400.00
187 Tim Duncan 150.00 400.00
191 Alonzo Mourning 100.00 250.00
192 Patrick Ewing 100.00 250.00
193 Scottie Pippen 150.00 400.00

2000-01 Ultra Air Club for Men
COMPLETE SET (15) 10.00 25.00
STATED ODDS 1:6
*PLATINUM: 40X TO 100X AIR CLUB HI
PLATINUM: PRINT RUN 100 SERIAL #'d SETS
AC1 Kobe Bryant 5.00 12.00
AC2 Lamar Odom .60 1.50
AC3 Vince Carter 1.25 3.00
AC4 Tim Duncan 1.50 4.00
AC5 Grant Hill 1.00 2.50
AC6 Tracy McGrady 1.25 3.00
AC7 Kevin Garnett 1.50 4.00
AC8 Steve Francis .60 1.50
AC9 Allen Iverson 1.50 4.00
AC10 Jason Williams 1.00 2.50
AC11 Shaquille O'Neal 2.50 6.00
AC12 Jason Kidd 1.00 2.50
AC13 Elton Brand .60 1.50
AC14 Eddie Jones .60 1.50
AC15 Stephon Marbury .75 2.00

2000-01 Ultra Air Club for Men Platinum
*PLATINUM: 40X TO 100X AIR CLUB HI

2000-01 Ultra Vince Carter Rookie Remnants
NNO Vince Carter FLR/100 12.50 30.00
NNO Vince Carter FLR JSY/15 30.00 80.00

2000-01 Ultra Slam Show
COMPLETE SET (10) 12.00 30.00
STATED ODDS 1:24
*PLATINUM: 4X TO 10X SLAM SHOW HI
PLATINUM: PRINT RUN 100 SERIAL #'d SETS
SS1 Steve Francis 1.00 2.50
SS2 Tracy McGrady 2.00 5.00
SS3 Jerry Stackhouse 1.00 2.50
SS4 Larry Hughes 1.00 2.50
SS5 Ricky Davis .75 2.00
SS6 Vince Carter 5.00 12.00
SS7 Vince Carter 5.00 12.00
SS8 Vince Carter 5.00 12.00
SS9 Vince Carter 5.00 12.00
SS10 Vince Carter 5.00 12.00

2000-01 Ultra Thrillinium
COMPLETE SET (10) 25.00 50.00
STATED ODDS 1:48
*PLATINUM: 4X TO 10X THRILLINIUM HI
PLATINUM: PRINT RUN 100 SERIAL #'d SETS
T1 Vince Carter 3.00 8.00
T2 Kobe Bryant 10.00 25.00
T3 Tim Duncan 4.00 10.00
T4 Kevin Garnett 3.00 8.00
T5 Allen Iverson 4.00 10.00
T6 Jason Williams 2.50 6.00
T7 Shaquille O'Neal 6.00 15.00
T8 Lamar Odom 1.50 4.00
T9 Eddie Jones 1.50 4.00
T10 Stephon Marbury 2.00 5.00

2000-01 Ultra Two Ball
COMPLETE SET (15) 2.00 5.00
STATED ODDS 1:3
*PLATINUM: 8X TO 20X TWO BALL HI
PLATINUM: PRINT RUN 100 SERIAL #'d SETS
TB1 Lamar Odom .30 .75
TB2 Elton Brand .30 .75
TB3 Steve Francis .30 .75
TB4 Adrian Griffin .20 .50
TB5 Todd MacCulloch .20 .50
TB6 Andre Miller .25 .60
TB7 James Posey .25 .60
TB8 Wally Szczerbiak .25 .60
TB9 Ron Artest .30 .75
TB10 Corey Maggette .25 .60
TB11 Shawn Marion .25 .60
TB12 Chucky Atkins .20 .50
TB13 Vonteego Cummings .20 .50
TB14 Kenny Thomas .20 .50
TB15 Richard Hamilton .40 1.00

2000-01 Ultra Year 3
COMPLETE SET (10) 2.50 6.00
STATED ODDS 1:12
*PLATINUM: 6X TO 15X YEAR 3 HI
PLATINUM: PRINT RUN 100 SERIAL #'d SETS
YT1 Mike Bibby .50 1.25
YT2 Michael Dickerson .30 .75
YT3 Larry Hughes .50 1.25
YT4 Raef LaFrentz .40 1.00
YT5 Dirk Nowitzki 1.25 3.00
YT6 Michael Olowokandi .30 .75
YT7 Paul Pierce .75 2.00
YT8 Jason Williams .75 2.00
YT9 Vince Carter 1.00 2.50
YT10 Antawn Jamison .50 1.25

2001-02 Ultra
COMP.SET w/o SP's (150) 10.00 25.00
COMP.UPDATE SET (6) 8.00 20.00
151-181 PRINT RUN 2222 SERIAL #'d SETS
1 Vince Carter .60 1.50
2 Allen Iverson .75 2.00
3 Jerry Stackhouse .30 .75
4 Travis Best .20 .50
5 Eddie Jones .30 .75
6 Felipe Lopez .20 .50
7 Antonio Daniels .20 .50
8 A.J. Guyton .20 .50
9 Quentin Richardson .20 .50
10 Charlie Ward .20 .50
11 Ron Mercer .20 .50
12 Shandon Anderson .20 .50
13 Antawn Jamison .25 .60
14 Darius Miles .20 .50
15 Anthony Mason .30 .75
16 Latrell Sprewell .40 1.00
17 Scottie Pippen .75 2.00
18 Shammond Williams .20 .50
19 P.J. Brown .20 .50
20 Dirk Nowitzki .75 2.00
21 Mateen Cleaves .20 .50
22 Tim Hardaway .40 1.00
23 Christian Laettner .25 .60
24 Toni Kukoc .40 1.00
25 Bob Sura .20 .50
26 Kobe Bryant 2.50 6.00
27 Wally Szczerbiak .25 .60
28 Darrell Armstrong .20 .50
29 Chris Webber .40 1.00
30 David Wesley .20 .50
31 Michael Finley .30 .75
32 Jermaine O'Neal .25 .60
33 Jason Kidd .50 1.25
34 Tony Delk .20 .50
35 Avery Johnson .25 .60
36 Elden Campbell .20 .50
37 Lamond Murray .20 .50
38 Ben Wallace .40 1.00
39 Jalen Rose .30 .75
40 Michael Dickerson .20 .50
41 Shawn Marion .30 .75
42 Jahidi White .20 .50
43 Jamal Mashburn .25 .60
44 Trajan Langdon .20 .50
45 Reggie Miller .60 1.50
46 Stromile Swift .20 .50
47 Keith Van Horn .20 .50
48 Tom Gugliotta .20 .50
49 Brent Barry .20 .50
50 Courtney Alexander .20 .50
51 Antonio McDyess .25 .60
52 Robert Horry .30 .75
53 Ervin Johnson .20 .50
54 Speedy Claxton .20 .50
55 Bryon Russell .20 .50
56 Baron Davis .30 .75
57 Robert Traylor .20 .50
58 Chucky Atkins .20 .50
59 Stephon Marbury .40 1.00
60 Desmond Mason .25 .60
61 Tyrone Nesby .20 .50
62 Brevin Knight .20 .50
63 Kenyon Martin .30 .75
64 Jumaine Jones .25 .60
65 Rashard Lewis .25 .60
66 Kenny Anderson .25 .60
67 Andre Miller .25 .60
68 Joe Smith .25 .60
69 Kelvin Cato .20 .50
70 Jason Williams .50 1.25
71 Marcus Camby .25 .60
72 Eric Snow .20 .50
73 Gary Payton .50 1.25
74 Robert Pack .20 .50
75 Brian Cardinal .20 .50
76 Sam Cassell .25 .60
77 Allan Houston .30 .75
78 Anfernee Hardaway .75 2.00
79 Morris Peterson .20 .50
80 Chris Mihm .20 .50
81 Elton Brand .25 .60
82 Glenn Robinson .30 .75
83 Damon Stoudamire .30 .75
84 Alvin Williams .20 .50
85 Paul Pierce .50 1.25
86 James Posey .25 .60
87 Cuttino Mobley .25 .60
88 Tim Thomas .20 .50
89 Dikembe Mutombo .50 1.25
90 Tim Duncan .75 2.00
91 John Starks .20 .50
92 Antoine Walker .25 .60
93 Moochie Norris .20 .50
94 Dalibor Bagaric .20 .50
95 Ray Allen .50 1.25
96 David Robinson .60 1.50
97 Shareef Abdur-Rahim .25 .60
98 Wang Zhizhi .30 .75
99 Chris Porter .20 .50
100 Chauncey Billups .40 1.00
101 Tracy McGrady .50 1.25
102 Michael Jordan 2.50 6.00
103 Jerome Williams .20 .50
104 Jason Terry .20 .50
105 Calvin Booth .20 .50
106 Shaquille O'Neal 1.25 3.00
107 Kevin Garnett .75 2.00
108 Doug Christie .20 .50
109 Karl Malone .60 1.50
110 Steve Nash .60 1.50
111 Austin Croshere .20 .50
112 Alonzo Mourning .50 1.25
113 Dan Majerle .30 .75
114 Malik Rose .20 .50
115 Richard Hamilton .40 1.00
116 DerMarr Johnson .20 .50
117 Raef LaFrentz .20 .50
118 Derek Fisher .25 .60
119 Vlade Divac .25 .60
120 John Stockton .60 1.50
121 Dion Glover .20 .50
122 Voshon Lenard .20 .50
123 Steve Francis .30 .75
124 Darvin Ham .25 .60
125 Aaron McKie .20 .50
126 Peja Stojakovic .25 .60
127 Ron Artest .25 .60
128 Keyon Dooling .20 .50
129 Anthony Carter .20 .50
130 Kurt Thomas .20 .50
131 Rasheed Wallace .40 1.00
132 Theo Ratliff .20 .50
133 Eric Piatkowski .20 .50
134 Terrell Brandon .25 .60
135 Mike Miller .25 .60
136 Mike Bibby .30 .75
137 Antonio Davis .25 .60
138 Lamar Odom .25 .60
139 Eddie House .20 .50
140 Nick Van Exel .30 .75
141 Rick Fox .25 .60
142 Juwan Howard .25 .60
143 Hedo Turkoglu .25 .60
144 Donyell Marshall .20 .50
145 Marcus Fizer .20 .50
146 Larry Hughes .25 .60
147 Steve Smith .25 .60
148 Brian Grant .20 .50
149 Grant Hill .50 1.25
150 Derek Anderson .20 .50
151 Kwame Brown RC 1.25 3.00
152 Eddie Griffin RC 1.00 2.50
153 Eddy Curry RC 1.25 3.00
154 Jamaal Tinsley RC 1.00 2.50
155 Jason Richardson RC 2.00 5.00
156 Shane Battier RC 2.50 6.00
157 Troy Murphy RC 1.00 2.50
158 Richard Jefferson RC 1.50 4.00
159 DeSagana Diop RC .75 2.00
160 Tyson Chandler RC 2.00 5.00
161 Joe Johnson RC 2.00 5.00
162 Zach Randolph RC 2.50 6.00
163 Andrei Kirilenko RC 2.00 5.00
164 Loren Woods RC .75 2.00
165 Jason Collins RC 1.00 2.50
166 Rodney White RC .75 2.00
167 Jeryl Sasser RC .75 2.00
168 Kirk Haston RC .75 2.00
169 Pau Gasol RC 5.00 12.00
170 Kedrick Brown RC .75 2.00
171 Steven Hunter RC .75 2.00
172 Michael Bradley RC .75 2.00
173 Joseph Forte RC .75 2.00
174 Brandon Armstrong RC .75 2.00
175 Primoz Brezec RC 1.25 3.00
176U Gerald Wallace RC 1.50 4.00
177U Tony Parker RC 5.00 12.00
178U Vladimir Radmanovic RC 1.00 2.50
179U Trenton Hassell RC .75 2.00
180U Zeljko Rebraca RC 1.25 3.00
181U Oscar Torres RC .75 2.00

2001-02 Ultra Gold Medallion
*GOLD STARS: .6X TO 1.5X BASE CARD HI
*GOLD RC's: 1.5X TO 4X BASE CARD HI

2001-02 Ultra 02 Good
COMPLETE SET (20) 10.00 20.00
STATED ODDS 1:20
1 Vince Carter 1.50 4.00
1A Vince Carter AU 25.00 50.00
2 Allen Iverson 2.00 5.00
3 Shawn Marion .75 2.00
4 Jalen Rose .60 1.50
5 Steve Francis .75 2.00
6 Kenyon Martin .75 2.00
7 Sam Cassell .60 1.50
8 Darius Miles .50 1.25
9 Mike Miller .60 1.50
10 Jason Terry .75 2.00
11 Baron Davis .75 2.00
12 Lamar Odom .60 1.50
13 Latrell Sprewell 1.00 2.50
14 Morris Peterson .50 1.25
15 Antonio Davis .60 1.50
16 Ray Allen 1.25 3.00
17 Rashard Lewis .60 1.50
18 Desmond Mason .60 1.50
19 Antonio McDyess .60 1.50
20 Keith Van Horn .60 1.50

2001-02 Ultra 02 Good Game Worn
STATED ODDS 1:157
1 Vince Carter 8.00 20.00
2 Allen Iverson 12.00 30.00
3 Shawn Marion 4.00 10.00
4 Jalen Rose 3.00 8.00
5 Steve Francis 4.00 10.00
6 Kenyon Martin 4.00 10.00
7 Sam Cassell 3.00 8.00
8 Darius Miles 2.50 6.00
9 Mike Miller 3.00 8.00
10 Jason Terry 4.00 10.00
11 Baron Davis 4.00 10.00
12 Lamar Odom 3.00 8.00
13 Latrell Sprewell 5.00 12.00
14 Morris Peterson 2.50 6.00
15 Antonio Davis 3.00 8.00
16 Ray Allen 6.00 15.00
17 Rashard Lewis 3.00 8.00
18 Desmond Mason 3.00 8.00
19 Antonio McDyess 3.00 8.00
20 Keith Van Horn 3.00 8.00

2001-02 Ultra League Leaders
COMPLETE SET (20) 10.00 20.00
STATED ODDS 1:20
*PLATINUM: 12X TO 30X HI
PLATINUM PRINT RUN 25 SER.#'d SETS
1 Vince Carter 1.50 4.00
2 Allen Iverson 2.00 5.00
3 Ray Allen 1.25 3.00
4 Reggie Miller 1.50 4.00
5 Karl Malone 1.50 4.00
6 Jalen Rose .60 1.50
7 Baron Davis .75 2.00
8 Tracy McGrady 1.25 3.00
9 Chris Webber 1.00 2.50
10 John Stockton 1.50 4.00
11 Dikembe Mutombo 1.25 3.00
12 Steve Francis .75 2.00
13 Andre Miller .60 1.50
14 Kenyon Martin .75 2.00
15 Mike Miller .60 1.50
16 Antonio Davis .60 1.50
17 Darius Miles .50 1.25
18 Latrell Sprewell 1.00 2.50
19 Cuttino Mobley .60 1.50
20 Lamar Odom .60 1.50

2001-02 Ultra League Leaders Game Worn
PRINT RUN 450 SERIAL #'d SETS
1 Vince Carter 8.00 20.00
2 Allen Iverson 10.00 25.00
3 Ray Allen 6.00 15.00
4 Reggie Miller 8.00 20.00
5 Karl Malone 8.00 20.00
6 Jalen Rose 3.00 8.00
7 Baron Davis 4.00 10.00
8 Tracy McGrady 6.00 15.00
9 Chris Webber 5.00 12.00
10 John Stockton 8.00 20.00
11 Dikembe Mutombo 6.00 15.00
12 Steve Francis 4.00 10.00
13 Andre Miller 3.00 8.00
14 Kenyon Martin 4.00 10.00
15 Mike Miller 3.00 8.00
16 Antonio Davis 3.00 8.00
17 Darius Miles 2.50 6.00
18 Latrell Sprewell 5.00 12.00
19 Cuttino Mobley 3.00 8.00
20 Lamar Odom 3.00 8.00

2001-02 Ultra On the Road Game Worn
STATED ODDS 1:156
*PLATINUM: 2.5X TO 6X HI
PLATINUM PRINT RUN 25 SER.#'d SETS
1 Vince Carter 8.00 20.00
2 Morris Peterson 2.50 6.00
3 Rashard Lewis 3.00 8.00
4 Keith Van Horn 3.00 8.00
5 Cuttino Mobley 3.00 8.00
6 Tracy McGrady 6.00 15.00
7 Tom Gugliotta 2.50 6.00
8 Dikembe Mutombo 6.00 15.00
9 Stromile Swift 2.50 6.00
10 Mike Miller 3.00 8.00

2001-02 Ultra Triple Double Trouble
COMPLETE SET (15) 25.00 60.00
STATED ODDS 1:72
*PLATINUM: 4X TO 10X HI
PLATINUM PRINT RUN 25 SER.#'d SETS
1 Vince Carter 5.00 12.00
2 Steve Francis 2.50 6.00
3 Ray Allen 4.00 10.00
4 Chris Webber 3.00 8.00
5 Kobe Bryant 20.00 50.00
6 Kenyon Martin 2.50 6.00
7 Shaquille O'Neal 10.00 25.00
8 Kevin Garnett 6.00 15.00
9 Tracy McGrady 4.00 10.00
10 Baron Davis 2.50 6.00
11 Lamar Odom 2.00 5.00
12 Allen Iverson 6.00 15.00
13 Antoine Walker 2.00 5.00
14 Reggie Miller 5.00 12.00
15 Terrell Brandon 2.00 5.00

2001-02 Ultra Triple Double Trouble Game Worn
STATED ODDS 1:156
1 Vince Carter 10.00 25.00
2 Steve Francis 5.00 12.00
3 Ray Allen 8.00 20.00
4 Chris Webber 6.00 15.00
6 Kenyon Martin 5.00 12.00
9 Tracy McGrady 8.00 20.00
10 Baron Davis 5.00 12.00
11 Lamar Odom 4.00 10.00
12 Allen Iverson 12.00 30.00
13 Antoine Walker 4.00 10.00
14 Reggie Miller 10.00 25.00
15 Terrell Brandon 4.00 10.00

2002-03 Ultra
COMPLETE SET (210) 75.00 150.00
COMP.SET w/o RC's (180) 20.00 50.00
1 Vince Carter .60 1.50
2 Ben Wallace .40 1.00
3 Tim Thomas .20 .50
4 Eric Snow .20 .50
5 Peja Stojakovic .25 .60
6 Andrei Kirilenko .25 .60
7 Dion Glover .20 .50
8 James Posey .20 .50
9 Kenny Thomas .20 .50
10 Michael Dickerson .20 .50
11 Charlie Ward .20 .50
12 Gary Payton .50 1.25
13 Eddy Curry .30 .75
14 Rick Fox .20 .50
15 Joel Przybilla .20 .50
16 Aaron McKie .20 .50
17 Hedo Turkoglu .25 .60
18 Jarron Collins .20 .50
19 Jason Collins .20 .50
20 Nick Van Exel .30 .75
21 Reggie Miller .60 1.50
22 Devean George .20 .50
23 Michael Jordan 3.00 8.00
24 Tony Parker .50 1.25
25 Robert Horry .30 .75
26 Wally Szczerbiak .25 .60
27 Dikembe Mutombo .50 1.25
28 Scot Pollard .20 .50
29 Darrell Armstrong .20 .50
30 Jalen Rose .25 .60
31 Antawn Jamison .25 .60
32 Anfernee Hardaway .75 2.00
33 Paul Pierce .50 1.25
34 Juwan Howard .25 .60
35 Eddie Griffin .20 .50
36 Shane Battier .30 .75
37 Shandon Anderson .20 .50
38 Vladimir Radmanovic .20 .50
39 DerMarr Johnson .20 .50
40 Antonio McDyess .25 .60
41 Cuttino Mobley .20 .50
42 Stromile Swift .20 .50
43 Tracy McGrady .50 1.25
44 Charles Smith .20 .50
45 Shawn Marion .30 .75
46 P.J. Brown .20 .50
47 Wang Zhizhi .30 .75
48 Austin Croshere .20 .50
49 Ervin Johnson .20 .50
50 Jason Kidd .50 1.25
51 Tom Gugliotta .20 .50
52 Jamal Crawford .30 .75
53 Toni Kukoc .30 .75
54 Mengke Bateer .30 .75
55 Moochie Norris .20 .50
56 Jason Williams .40 1.00
57 Mike Miller .25 .60
58 Steve Smith .25 .60
59 Shareef Abdur-Rahim .30 .75
60 Michael Finley .30 .75
61 Jermaine O'Neal .25 .60
62 Mark Madsen .20 .50
63 Troy Hudson .20 .50
64 David Robinson .60 1.50
65 Corliss Williamson .20 .50
66 Rodney Rogers .20 .50
67 Derek Fisher .30 .75
68 Anthony Carter .20 .50
69 Allan Houston .30 .75
70 Desmond Mason .25 .60
71 Brendan Haywood .20 .50
72 Tony Delk .20 .50
73 Ryan Bowen .20 .50
74 Danny Fortson .20 .50
75 Alonzo Mourning .50 1.25
76 Latrell Sprewell .30 .75
77 Rashard Lewis .25 .60
78 Courtney Alexander .25 .60
79 Marcus Fizer .20 .50
80 Jason Richardson .30 .75
81 Terrell Brandon .20 .50
82 Allen Iverson .75 2.00
83 Vlade Divac .20 .50
84 Jahidi White .20 .50
85 Eric Piatkowski .20 .50
86 Marc Jackson .20 .50
87 Pat Garrity .20 .50
88 Tim Duncan .75 2.00
89 Kwame Brown .20 .50
90 Andre Miller .25 .60
91 Troy Murphy .25 .60
92 John Stockton .60 1.50
93 Kenny Anderson .25 .60
94 Chris Mihm .20 .50
95 Larry Hughes .20 .50
96 Lamar Odom .30 .75
97 Brian Grant .20 .50
98 Marcus Camby .25 .60
99 Mike Bibby .30 .75
100 Joseph Forte .20 .50
101 Lamond Murray .20 .50
102 Darius Miles .20 .50
103 Eddie Jones .30 .75
104 Aaron Williams .20 .50
105 Derek Anderson .20 .50
106 Karl Malone .60 1.50
107 Jon Barry .20 .50
108 Tony Battie .20 .50
109 Jumaine Jones .20 .50
110 Corey Maggette .25 .60
111 Eddie House .20 .50
112 Theo Ratliff .20 .50
113 Scottie Pippen .75 2.00
114 Hakeem Olajuwon .40 1.00
115 Antoine Walker .25 .60
116 Tim Hardaway .30 .75
117 Steve Francis .30 .75
118 Lorenzen Wright .20 .50
119 Howard Eisley .20 .50
120 Brent Barry .20 .50
121 Baron Davis .30 .75
122 Michael Doleac .20 .50
123 Quentin Richardson .20 .50
124 LaPhonso Ellis .20 .50
125 Richard Jefferson .25 .60
126 Damon Stoudamire .30 .75
127 Alvin Williams .20 .50
128 Chucky Atkins .20 .50
129 Jamal Mashburn .25 .60
130 Wesley Person .20 .50
131 Elton Brand .25 .60
132 Ray Allen .50 1.25
133 Kerry Kittles .20 .50
134 Rasheed Wallace .40 1.00
135 Antonio Davis .25 .60
136 David Wesley .20 .50
137 Dirk Nowitzki .75 2.00
138 Rodney White .20 .50
139 Jamaal Tinsley .20 .50
140 Sam Cassell .20 .50
141 Keith Van Horn .25 .60
142 Ruben Patterson .20 .50
143 Jerome Williams .20 .50
144 Jason Terry .25 .60
145 Eduardo Najera .20 .50
146 Maurice Taylor .20 .50
147 Pau Gasol .50 1.25
148 Grant Hill .50 1.25

149 Antonio Daniels .20 .50
150 George Lynch .20 .50
151 Steve Nash .60 1.50
152 Al Harrington .25 .60
153 Anthony Mason .25 .60
154 Kenyon Martin .30 .75
155 Bonzi Wells .20 .50
156 Morris Peterson .25 .60
157 Eddie Robinson .20 .50
158 Kevin Garnett .75 2.00
159 Chris Webber .40 1.00
160 John Amaechi .20 .50
161 Kobe Bryant 2.50 6.00
162 Joe Smith .25 .60
163 Speedy Claxton .20 .50
164 Doug Christie .20 .50
165 Richard Hamilton .40 1.00
166 Tyson Chandler .30 .75
167 Gilbert Arenas .30 .75
168 Stephon Marbury .40 1.00
169 Jamaal Magloire .20 .50
170 Raef LaFrentz .20 .50
171 Ron Mercer .20 .50
172 Glenn Robinson .30 .75
173 Chauncey Billups .30 .75
174 Iakovos Tsakalidis .20 .50
175 Vin Baker .25 .60
176 Joe Johnson .25 .60
177 Jerry Stackhouse .30 .75
178 Shaquille O'Neal 1.25 3.00
179 Derrick Coleman .25 .60
180 Bryon Russell .20 .50
181 Yao Ming RC 8.00 20.00
182 Jay Williams RC 1.00 2.50
183 Drew Gooden RC 1.25 3.00
184 DaJuan Wagner RC 1.00 2.50
185 Qyntel Woods RC .75 2.00
186 Chris Wilcox RC 1.00 2.50
187 Curtis Borchardt RC .75 2.00
188 Nikoloz Tskitishvili RC .75 2.00
189 Caron Butler RC 1.25 3.00
190 Nene Hilario RC 1.25 3.00
191 Jared Jeffries RC 1.00 2.50
192 Mike Dunleavy RC 1.25 3.00
193 Kareem Rush RC 1.00 2.50
194 Amare Stoudemire RC 3.00 8.00
195 Melvin Ely RC 1.00 2.50
196 Marcus Haislip RC .75 2.00
197 Jiri Welsch RC 1.00 2.50
198 Frank Williams RC .75 2.00
199 John Salmons RC 1.25 3.00
200 Gordan Giricek RC 1.25 3.00
201 Ryan Humphrey RC 1.00 2.50
202 Casey Jacobsen RC 1.00 2.50
203 Carlos Boozer RC 1.25 3.00
204 Manu Ginobili RC 8.00 20.00
205 Bostjan Nachbar RC 1.00 2.50
206 Fred Jones RC 1.00 2.50
207 Dan Dickau RC .75 2.00
208 Tayshaun Prince RC 2.50 6.00
209 Memo Okur RC 1.25 3.00
210 Juan Dixon RC 1.00 2.50

2002-03 Ultra Gold Medallion
*GOLD STARS: .6X TO 1.5X BASE CARD HI
*GOLD RCs: 1.25X TO 3X BASE CARD HI
1-180 STATED ODDS 1:1
181-210 PRINT RUN 100 SER.#'d SETS

2002-03 Ultra Back 2 Back
COMPLETE SET (18) 20.00 50.00
STATED PRINT RUN 1000 SERIAL #'D SETS
1 Vince Carter 3.00 8.00
2 Tracy McGrady 2.50 6.00
3 Allen Iverson 4.00 10.00
4 Baron Davis 1.50 4.00
5 Chris Webber 2.00 5.00
6 Michael Finley 1.50 4.00
7 Steve Francis 1.50 4.00
8 Elton Brand 1.50 4.00
9 Mike Miller 1.25 3.00
10 Morris Peterson 1.25 3.00
11 Dikembe Mutombo 2.50 6.00
12 Alonzo Mourning 2.50 6.00
13 Darius Miles 1.00 2.50
14 Quentin Richardson 1.00 2.50
15 John Stockton 3.00 8.00
16 Karl Malone 3.00 8.00
17 Stephon Marbury 2.00 5.00
18 Jerry Stackhouse 1.50 4.00

2002-03 Ultra Back 2 Back Game Used
STATED PRINT RUN 500 SERIAL #'D SETS
*GOLD: 1X TO 2.5X BASE HI
GOLD PRINT RUN 50 SER.#'d SETS
1 Vince Carter 8.00 20.00
2 Tracy McGrady 6.00 15.00
3 Allen Iverson 10.00 25.00
4 Baron Davis 4.00 10.00
5 Chris Webber 5.00 12.00
6 Michael Finley 4.00 10.00
7 Steve Francis 4.00 10.00
8 Elton Brand 3.00 8.00
9 Mike Miller 3.00 8.00
10 Morris Peterson 3.00 8.00
11 Dikembe Mutombo 6.00 15.00
12 Alonzo Mourning 8.00 20.00
13 Darius Miles 2.50 6.00
14 Quentin Richardson 2.50 6.00
15 John Stockton 8.00 20.00
16 Karl Malone 8.00 20.00
17 Stephon Marbury 5.00 12.00
18 Jerry Stackhouse 4.00 10.00

2002-03 Ultra O!
COMPLETE SET (20) 8.00 20.00
STATED ODDS 1:12
1 Vince Carter 1.25 3.00
2 Shareef Abdur-Rahim .60 1.50
3 Baron Davis .60 1.50
4 Quentin Richardson .40 1.00
5 John Stockton 1.25 3.00
6 Morris Peterson .50 1.25
7 Elton Brand .50 1.25
8 Glenn Robinson .60 1.50
9 Latrell Sprewell .60 1.50
10 Darius Miles .40 1.00
11 Jason Terry .50 1.25
12 Keith Van Horn .50 1.25
13 Karl Malone 1.25 3.00
14 Antoine Walker .50 1.25
15 Jason Williams .75 2.00
16 Rasheed Wallace .75 2.00
17 Gary Payton 1.00 2.50
18 Lamar Odom .60 1.50
19 Cuttino Mobley .40 1.00
20 Desmond Mason .50 1.25

2002-03 Ultra O! Game Used
STATED ODDS 1:30
1 Vince Carter 6.00 15.00
2 Shareef Abdur-Rahim 3.00 8.00
3 Baron Davis 3.00 8.00
4 Quentin Richardson 2.00 5.00
5 John Stockton 6.00 15.00
6 Morris Peterson 2.50 6.00
7 Elton Brand 2.50 6.00
8 Glenn Robinson 3.00 8.00
9 Latrell Sprewell 3.00 8.00
10 Darius Miles 2.00 5.00
11 Jason Terry 2.50 6.00
12 Keith Van Horn 2.50 6.00
13 Karl Malone 6.00 15.00
14 Antoine Walker 2.50 6.00
15 Jason Williams 4.00 10.00
16 Rasheed Wallace 4.00 10.00
17 Gary Payton 5.00 12.00
18 Lamar Odom 3.00 8.00
19 Cuttino Mobley 2.00 5.00

2002-03 Ultra One on One
COMPLETE SET (10) 10.00 25.00
STATED ODDS 1:8
1 V.Carter/T.McGrady 3.00 8.00
2 A.Iverson/B.Davis 1.25 3.00
3 C.Webber/M.Finley 1.25 3.00
4 S.Francis/E.Brand 1.25 3.00
5 M.Miller/M.Peterson 1.25 3.00
6 D.Mutombo/A.Mourning 1.25 3.00
7 D.Miles/Q.Richardson 1.25 3.00
8 J.Stockton/K.Malone 1.25 3.00
9 S.Marbury/J.Kidd 1.25 3.00
10 V.Carter/J.Stackhouse 1.50 4.00

2002-03 Ultra One on One Game Used
PRINT RUN 100 SER.#'d SETS
1 V.Carter/T.McGrady 30.00 80.00
2 A.Iverson/B.Davis 20.00 50.00
3 C.Webber/M.Finley 12.00 30.00
4 S.Francis/E.Brand 12.00 30.00
5 M.Miller/M.Peterson 12.00 30.00
6 D.Mutombo/A.Mourning 12.00 30.00
7 D.Miles/Q.Richardson 12.00 30.00
8 J.Stockton/K.Malone 12.00 30.00
9 S.Marbury/J.Kidd 20.00 50.00
10 V.Carter/J.Stackhouse 25.00 60.00

2002-03 Ultra Photo Effex
COMPLETE SET (20) 12.50 30.00
STATED ODDS 1:12
*MASTERPIECE: 8X TO 20X BASE HI
MASTERPIECE PRINT RUN 25 SETS
1 Vince Carter 1.25 3.00
2 Kobe Bryant 6.00 15.00
3 Michael Jordan 10.00 25.00
4 Peja Stojakovic .50 1.25
5 Allen Iverson 1.50 4.00
6 Shaquille O'Neal 2.50 6.00
7 Tracy McGrady 1.00 2.50
8 Mike Bibby .60 1.50
9 Dirk Nowitzki 1.50 4.00
10 Pau Gasol 1.00 2.50
11 Jason Kidd 1.00 2.50
12 Ben Wallace .75 2.00
13 Andrei Kirilenko .50 1.25
14 Paul Pierce 1.00 2.50
15 Antoine Walker .50 1.25
16 Kevin Garnett 1.50 4.00
17 Tony Parker 1.00 2.50
18 Ray Allen 1.00 2.50
19 Kenyon Martin .60 1.50
20 Tim Duncan 1.50 4.00

2003-04 Ultra
COMP. SET w/o SP's 12.50 30.00
171-183 PRINT RUN 500 SER.#'d SETS
184-195 STATED ODDS 1:4
1 Yao Ming 1.00 2.50
2 DeShawn Stevenson .25 .60
3 Malik Rose .25 .60
4 DaJuan Wagner .25 .60
5 Troy Murphy .25 .60
6 Caron Butler .30 .75
7 Radoslav Nesterovic .25 .60
8 Joe Johnson .30 .75
9 Al Harrington .30 .75
10 Carlos Boozer .30 .75
11 Morris Peterson .25 .60
12 Malik Allen .25 .60
13 Kurt Thomas .25 .60
14 Derek Anderson .30 .75
15 Zydrunas Ilgauskas .30 .75
16 Jason Richardson .40 1.00
17 Brian Grant .25 .60
18 Allan Houston .40 1.00
19 Bonzi Wells .25 .60
20 Stephen Jackson .30 .75
21 Eddy Curry .25 .60
22 Tayshaun Prince .40 1.00
23 Brad Miller .30 .75
24 Stromile Swift .25 .60
25 Kendall Gill .40 1.00
26 Vladimir Radmanovic .25 .60
27 Theo Ratliff .25 .60
28 Nick Van Exel .40 1.00
29 Marko Jaric .25 .60
30 Jason Collins .25 .60
31 Darrell Armstrong .25 .60
32 Vlade Divac .40 1.00
33 Juan Dixon .25 .60
34 Calbert Cheaney .25 .60
35 Tyson Chandler .30 .75
36 Chauncey Billups .50 1.25
37 Reggie Miller .75 2.00
38 Mike Miller .30 .75
39 Marc Jackson .25 .60
40 Casey Jacobsen .25 .60
41 Ray Allen .60 1.50
42 Mehmet Okur .30 .75
43 Jermaine O'Neal .40 1.00
44 Lorenzen Wright .25 .60
45 Wally Szczerbiak .30 .75
46 Anfernee Hardaway 1.00 2.50
47 Matt Harpring .25 .60
48 Jay Williams .25 .60
49 Corliss Williamson .25 .60
50 Jamaal Tinsley .25 .60
51 Shane Battier .30 .75
52 Kevin Garnett 1.00 2.50
53 Shawn Marion .40 1.00
54 Alvin Williams .25 .60
55 Juwan Howard .30 .75
56 Shaquille O'Neal 1.50 4.00
57 Jamal Mashburn .25 .60
58 Kenny Thomas .25 .60
59 Tim Duncan 1.00 2.50
60 Predrag Drobnjak .25 .60
61 Jalen Rose .30 .75
62 Ben Wallace .50 1.25
63 James Posey .25 .60
64 Pau Gasol .60 1.50
65 Michael Redd .40 1.00
66 Amare Stoudemire .50 1.25
67 Karl Malone .75 2.00
68 Richard Hamilton .50 1.25
69 Eddie Griffin .25 .60
70 Robert Horry .40 1.00
71 Tim Thomas .25 .60
72 Eric Snow .25 .60
73 Brent Barry .25 .60
74 Jamal Crawford .40 1.00
75 Nikoloz Tskitishvili .25 .60
76 Bostjan Nachbar .25 .60
77 Devean George .25 .60
78 Dan Gadzuric .25 .60
79 Brian Skinner .25 .60
80 Cuttino Mobley .25 .60
81 Desmond Mason .30 .75
82 Othella Harrington .25 .60
83 Chris Webber .50 1.25
84 Dirk Nowitzki 1.00 2.50
85 Steve Francis .40 1.00
86 Gary Payton .60 1.50
87 Howard Eisley .25 .60
88 Zach Randolph .40 1.00
89 Sam Cassell .30 .75
90 Tony Battie .25 .60
91 Shammond Williams .25 .60
92 Rick Fox .30 .75
93 David Wesley .25 .60
94 Frank Williams .25 .60
95 Tony Delk .30 .75
96 Troy Hudson .25 .60
97 Donnell Harvey .25 .60
98 Derek Fisher .40 1.00
99 Jamaal Magloire .25 .60
100 Keith Van Horn .30 .75
101 Tony Parker .60 1.50
102 Rashard Lewis .30 .75
103 Shareef Abdur-Rahim .40 1.00
104 Michael Finley .40 1.00
105 Jason Kidd .60 1.50
106 Drew Gooden .30 .75
107 Mike Bibby .40 1.00
108 Jerry Stackhouse .50 1.25
109 Chris Jefferies .25 .60
110 Glenn Robinson .30 .75
111 Shawn Bradley .25 .60
112 Corey Maggette .30 .75
113 Richard Jefferson .30 .75
114 Gordan Giricek .25 .60
115 Bobby Jackson .30 .75
116 Larry Hughes .30 .75
117 Scott Padgett .25 .60
118 Gilbert Arenas .40 1.00
119 Ron Artest .40 1.00
120 Jason Williams .60 1.50
121 Eric Williams .25 .60
122 Stephon Marbury .50 1.25
123 Vince Carter .75 2.00
124 Jason Terry .30 .75
125 Raef LaFrentz .25 .60
126 Michael Olowokandi .25 .60
127 Kerry Kittles .30 .75
128 Pat Garrity .25 .60
129 Peja Stojakovic .30 .75
130 Jared Jeffries .25 .60
131 Antonio Davis .30 .75
132 Rodney White .25 .60
133 Kobe Bryant 3.00 8.00
134 Baron Davis .40 1.00
135 Derrick Coleman .40 1.00
136 Walter McCarty .25 .60
137 Bruce Bowen .30 .75
138 Mike Dunleavy .30 .75
139 Rasual Butler .25 .60
140 Latrell Sprewell .50 1.25
141 Rasheed Wallace .50 1.25
142 Andrei Kirilenko .30 .75
143 Dan Dickau .25 .60
144 Steve Nash .75 2.00
145 Elton Brand .25 .60
146 Kenyon Martin .40 1.00
147 Jeryl Sasser .25 .60
148 Doug Christie .30 .75
149 Kwame Brown .30 .75
150 Ricky Davis .30 .75
151 Antawn Jamison .40 1.00
152 Travis Best .25 .60
153 Courtney Alexander .25 .60
154 Scottie Pippen 1.00 2.50
155 Jerome Williams .25 .60
156 Quentin Richardson .25 .60
157 Lucious Harris .25 .60
158 Allen Iverson 1.00 2.50
159 Manu Ginobili .75 2.00
160 Bryon Russell .25 .60
161 Paul Pierce .60 1.50
162 Nene .30 .75
163 Darius Miles .25 .60
164 Earl Boykins .25 .60
165 Eddie Jones .40 1.00
166 P.J. Brown .25 .60
167 Qyntel Woods .25 .60
168 Andre Miller .30 .75
169 Tracy McGrady .60 1.50
170 Antoine Walker .40 1.00
171 LeBron James L13 RC 400.00 800.00
172 Darko Milicic L13 RC 2.50 6.00
173 Carmelo Anthony L13 RC 30.00 80.00
174 Chris Bosh L13 RC 10.00 25.00
175 Dwyane Wade L13 RC 40.00 100.00
176 Chris Kaman L13 RC 3.00 8.00
177 Kirk Hinrich L13 RC 3.00 8.00
178 T.J. Ford L13 RC 2.50 6.00
179 Mike Sweetney L13 RC 2.00 5.00
180 Jarvis Hayes L13 RC 2.00 5.00
181 Mickael Pietrus L13 RC 2.50 6.00
182 Nick Collison L13 RC 2.50 6.00
183 Marcus Banks L13 RC 2.00 5.00
184 Luke Ridnour RC 1.25 3.00
185 Troy Bell RC .75 2.00
186 Zarko Cabarkapa RC .75 2.00
187 David West RC 1.50 4.00
188 Sofoklis Schortsanitis RC .75 2.00
189 Travis Outlaw RC 1.00 2.50
190 Leandro Barbosa RC 1.25 3.00
191 Josh Howard RC 1.25 3.00
192 Maciej Lampe RC .75 2.00
193 Luke Walton RC 1.25 3.00
194 Travis Hansen RC .75 2.00
195 Rick Rickert RC .75 2.00

2003-04 Ultra Gold Medallion
*STARS: .75X TO 2X BASE CARD HI
*171-182 L13s: .25X TO .6X BASE CARD HI
*183-195 RCs: .6X TO 1.5X BASE CARD HI
STATED ODDS 1:1
171-195 ROOKIE STATED ODDS 1:8
171 LeBron James L13 100.00 250.00

2003-04 Ultra Platinum Medallion
*1-170 STARS: 10X TO 25X BASE CARD HI
*171-182 L13s: 1X TO 2.5X BASE CARD HI
*183-195 RCs: 2.5X TO 6X BASE CARD HI
PRINT RUN 100 SER.#'d SETS
1 Yao Ming 75.00 200.00
37 Reggie Miller 40.00 100.00
41 Ray Allen 40.00 100.00
46 Anfernee Hardaway 75.00 200.00
52 Kevin Garnett 75.00 200.00
56 Shaquille O'Neal 75.00 200.00
67 Karl Malone 40.00 100.00
83 Chris Webber 40.00 100.00
84 Dirk Nowitzki 75.00 200.00
86 Gary Payton 40.00 100.00
101 Tony Parker 40.00 100.00
105 Jason Kidd 40.00 100.00
120 Jason Williams 40.00 100.00
123 Vince Carter 75.00 200.00
133 Kobe Bryant 200.00 500.00
144 Steve Nash 40.00 100.00
154 Scottie Pippen 75.00 200.00
158 Allen Iverson 75.00 200.00
159 Manu Ginobili 40.00 100.00
161 Paul Pierce 40.00 100.00
169 Tracy McGrady 40.00 100.00
171 LeBron James L13 2,000.00 4,000.00

2003-04 Ultra Leaps and Bounds
COMPLETE SET (15) 25.00 60.00
PRINT RUN 500 SER.#'d SETS
1 Ben Wallace 2.50 6.00
2 Amare Stoudemire 2.50 6.00
3 Tracy McGrady 3.00 8.00
4 Dirk Nowitzki 5.00 12.00
5 Vince Carter 4.00 10.00
6 Ricky Davis 1.50 4.00
7 Shawn Marion 2.00 5.00
8 Steve Francis 2.00 5.00
9 Jason Richardson 2.00 5.00
10 Nene 1.50 4.00
11 Richard Jefferson 1.50 4.00
12 Yao Ming 5.00 12.00
13 Tim Duncan 5.00 12.00
14 Kobe Bryant 15.00 40.00
15 Kevin Garnett 5.00 12.00

2003-04 Ultra Leaps and Bounds Game Used
STATED ODDS 1:36
LBN Nene 2.00 5.00
LBAS Amare Stoudemire 3.00 8.00
LBBW Ben Wallace 3.00 8.00
LBDN Dirk Nowitzki 6.00 15.00
LBJR Jason Richardson 2.50 6.00
LBKG Kevin Garnett 6.00 15.00
LBRJ Richard Jefferson 2.00 5.00
LBSF Steve Francis 2.50 6.00
LBSM Shawn Marion 2.50 6.00
LBTM Tracy McGrady 4.00 10.00
LBVC Vince Carter 5.00 12.00
LBYM Yao Ming 6.00 15.00

2003-04 Ultra Leaps and Bounds Ultra Swatch
SERIAL #'d TO PLAYER JERSEY NUMBER
LBN Nene/31 8.00 20.00
LBAS Amare Stoudemire/32 12.00 30.00
LBDN Dirk Nowitzki/41 25.00 60.00
LBJR Jason Richardson/23 10.00 25.00
LBKG Kevin Garnett/21 25.00 60.00
LBSM Shawn Marion/31 10.00 25.00

2003-04 Ultra Roundball Discs
COMPLETE SET (36) 25.00 50.00
STATED ODDS 1:8
1 Vince Carter 1.25 3.00
2 Tracy McGrady 1.00 2.50
3 Allen Iverson 1.50 4.00
4 Yao Ming 1.50 4.00
5 Dirk Nowitzki 1.50 4.00
6 Ben Wallace .75 2.00
7 Paul Pierce 1.00 2.50
8 Jason Kidd 1.00 2.50
9 Baron Davis .60 1.50
10 Gilbert Arenas .60 1.50
11 DaJuan Wagner .40 1.00
12 Pau Gasol 1.00 2.50
13 Chris Webber .75 2.00
14 Jermaine O'Neal .60 1.50
15 Steve Francis .60 1.50
16 Ray Allen 1.00 2.50
17 Steve Nash 1.25 3.00
18 Gary Payton 1.00 2.50
19 Caron Butler .50 1.25
20 Karl Malone 1.25 3.00
21 Mike Bibby .60 1.50
22 Allan Houston .60 1.50
23 Amare Stoudemire .75 2.00
24 Scottie Pippen 1.50 4.00
25 Kevin Garnett 1.50 4.00
26 Michael Finley .60 1.50
27 Richard Hamilton .75 2.00
28 Shaquille O'Neal 2.50 6.00
29 Tim Duncan 1.50 4.00
30 Kobe Bryant 5.00 12.00
31 LeBron James 40.00 100.00
32 Mike Sweetney .40 1.00
33 Carmelo Anthony 3.00 8.00
34 Chris Bosh 2.00 5.00
35 Dwyane Wade 5.00 12.00
36 Chris Kaman .60 1.50

2003-04 Ultra Roundball Discs Game Used
STATED ODDS 1:24
RDAH Allan Houston 2.50 6.00
RDAI Allen Iverson 6.00 15.00
RDAS Amare Stoudemire 3.00 8.00
RDBD Baron Davis 2.50 6.00
RDBW Ben Wallace 3.00 8.00
RDCB Caron Butler 2.00 5.00
RDCW Chris Webber 3.00 8.00
RDDN Dirk Nowitzki 6.00 15.00
RDDWO DaJuan Wagner 1.50 4.00
RDGP Gary Payton 4.00 10.00
RDJK Jason Kidd 4.00 10.00
RDJO Jermaine O'Neal 2.50 6.00
RDKG Kevin Garnett 6.00 15.00
RDKM Karl Malone 5.00 12.00
RDMB Mike Bibby 2.50 6.00
RDMF Michael Finley 2.50 6.00
RDPG Pau Gasol 4.00 10.00
RDPP Paul Pierce 4.00 10.00
RDRA Ray Allen 4.00 10.00
RDRH Richard Hamilton 3.00 8.00
RDSF Steve Francis 2.50 6.00
RDSN Steve Nash 5.00 12.00
RDSP Scottie Pippen 6.00 15.00
RDTM Tracy McGrady 4.00 10.00
RDVC Vince Carter 5.00 12.00
RDYM Yao Ming 6.00 15.00

2003-04 Ultra Roundball Discs Ultra Swatch
SERIAL #'d TO PLAYER JERSEY NUMBER
RDAH Allan Houston/20 12.00 30.00
RDAS Amare Stoudemire/32 15.00 40.00
RDDN Dirk Nowitzki/41 30.00 80.00
RDKG Karl Malone/32 25.00 60.00
RDKG Kevin Garnett/21 30.00 80.00
RDPG Pau Gasol/16 12.00 30.00
RDPP Paul Pierce/34 20.00 50.00
RDRA Ray Allen/34 15.00 40.00
RDRH Richard Hamilton/32 15.00 40.00
RDSP Scottie Pippen/33 40.00 100.00

2003-04 Ultra Scoring Kings
COMPLETE SET (10) 8.00 20.00
STATED ODDS 1:24
1 Vince Carter 2.00 5.00
2 Allen Iverson 2.50 6.00
3 Tracy McGrady 1.50 4.00
4 Dirk Nowitzki 2.50 6.00
5 Kevin Garnett 2.50 6.00
6 Steve Francis 1.00 2.50
7 Chris Webber 1.25 3.00
8 Ray Allen 1.50 4.00
9 Paul Pierce 1.50 4.00
10 Yao Ming 2.50 6.00

2003-04 Ultra Scoring Kings Game Used
STATED ODDS 1:100
1 Vince Carter 6.00 15.00
2 Allen Iverson 8.00 20.00
3 Tracy McGrady 5.00 12.00
4 Dirk Nowitzki 8.00 20.00
5 Kevin Garnett 8.00 20.00
6 Steve Francis 3.00 8.00
7 Chris Webber 4.00 10.00
8 Ray Allen 5.00 12.00
9 Paul Pierce 5.00 12.00
10 Yao Ming 8.00 20.00

2003-04 Ultra Scoring Kings PPG
PRINT RUNS LISTED BELOW
AI Allen Iverson/27 25.00 60.00
DN Dirk Nowitzki/25 25.00 60.00
KG Kevin Garnett/25 25.00 60.00
RA Ray Allen/22 15.00 40.00
SF Steve Francis/21 10.00 25.00
TM Tracy McGrady/32 15.00 40.00

2003-04 Ultra Scoring Kings Ultra Swatch
SERIAL #'d TO PLAYER JERSEY NUMBER
4 Dirk Nowitzki/41 25.00 60.00
5 Kevin Garnett/21 25.00 60.00
8 Ray Allen/34 15.00 40.00

2003-04 Ultra Signatures
PRINT RUN 350 SER.#'d SETS
1 Carmelo Anthony 60.00 150.00
2 Leandro Barbosa 4.00 10.00
3 Mike Bibby 12.00 30.00
4 Chris Bosh 12.00 30.00
5 Earl Boykins 8.00 20.00
6 Vince Carter 60.00 150.00
7 Manu Ginobili 40.00 100.00
8 Richard Jefferson 4.00 10.00
9 Mike Sweetney 2.50 6.00
11 Jermaine O'Neal 8.00 20.00
12 Tracy McGrady 60.00 150.00
13 Tayshaun Prince 10.00 25.00
14 Luke Ridnour 4.00 10.00
15 Amare Stoudemire 15.00 40.00
16A Dwyane Wade 100.00 250.00
16B Dwyane Wade/250 125.00 300.00
17 DaJuan Wagner 4.00 10.00
18 Ben Wallace 40.00 100.00
19 Luke Walton 4.00 10.00
20 David West 5.00 12.00

2004-05 Ultra
COMP.SET w/o RC's (175) 15.00 40.00
176-188 PRINT RUN 500 SER.#'d SETS
189-199 STATED ODDS 1:4
UPDATE INSERTED IN TWO PER TRADITION BOX
1 Ben Wallace .50 1.25
2 Chris Kaman .30 .75
3 Steve Nash .75 2.00
4 Al Harrington .30 .75
5 T.J. Ford .30 .75
6 Jason Collins .25 .60
7 Theo Ratliff .25 .60
8 Kobe Bryant 3.00 8.00
9 Kirk Hinrich .40 1.00
10 Darko Milicic .25 .60
11 Karl Malone .75 2.00
12 Michael Olowokandi .25 .60
13 Frank Williams .25 .60
14 Vlade Divac .40 1.00
15 Vince Carter .75 2.00
16 Eddy Curry .25 .60
17 Keith Van Horn .30 .75
18 Chris Wilcox .25 .60
19 Tim Thomas .25 .60
20 Shareef Abdur-Rahim .40 1.00
21 Carlos Arroyo .25 .60
22 Jason Collier .25 .60
23 Voshon Lenard .25 .60
24 Reggie Miller .75 2.00
25 Dan Gadzuric .25 .60
26 David Wesley .25 .60
27 Vladimir Radmanovic .25 .60
28 Derek Anderson .30 .75
29 Zydrunas Ilgauskas .30 .75
30 Nick Van Exel .40 1.00
31 Stromile Swift .25 .60
32 Kerry Kittles .30 .75
33 Zaza Pachulia .25 .60
34 Brad Miller .30 .75
35 Jerry Stackhouse .40 1.00
36 Jason Terry .30 .75
37 Earl Boykins .30 .75
38 Jermaine O'Neal .30 .75
39 Joe Smith .30 .75
40 Jamaal Magloire .25 .60
41 Zarko Cabarkapa .25 .60
42 Ronald Murray .25 .60
43 Bob Sura .25 .60
44 Andre Miller .30 .75
45 Jamaal Tinsley .25 .60
46 Michael Redd .30 .75
47 Baron Davis .40 1.00
48 Amare Stoudemire .40 1.00
49 Rashard Lewis .30 .75
50 Jiri Welsch .25 .60
51 Marcus Camby .30 .75
52 Ron Artest .40 1.00
53 Eddie Jones .40 1.00
54 Darrell Armstrong .25 .60
55 Shawn Marion .40 1.00
56 Brent Barry .25 .60
57 Michael Finley .40 1.00
58 Jim Jackson .30 .75
59 Jason Williams .30 .75
60 Kenyon Martin .40 1.00
61 Kyle Korver .30 .75
62 Marquis Daniels .30 .75
63 Chucky Atkins .25 .60
64 Nene .30 .75
65 Marko Jaric .25 .60
66 Dwyane Wade 1.50 4.00
67 P.J. Brown .25 .60
68 Casey Jacobsen .25 .60
69 Morris Peterson .25 .60
70 Ricky Davis .30 .75
71 Tayshaun Prince .40 1.00
72 Corey Maggette .30 .75
73 Udonis Haslem .25 .60
74 Kurt Thomas .25 .60
75 Leandro Barbosa .30 .75
76 Alvin Williams .25 .60
77 Mark Blount .25 .60
78 Chauncey Billups .50 1.25
79 Boris Diaw .30 .75
80 Brian Grant .30 .75
81 Allan Houston .40 1.00
82 Joe Johnson .30 .75
83 Donyell Marshall .30 .75
84 Jamal Crawford .40 1.00
85 Jason Richardson .40 1.00
86 Gary Payton .60 1.50
87 Nazr Mohammed .25 .60
88 Mike Bibby .40 1.00
89 Jalen Rose .30 .75
90 Scottie Pippen 1.00 2.50
91 Speedy Claxton .25 .60
92 Devean George .25 .60
93 Sam Cassell .30 .75
94 Mike Sweetney .25 .60
95 Chris Webber .50 1.25
96 Chris Bosh .60 1.50
97 Antoine Walker .40 1.00
98 Cuttino Mobley .30 .75
99 Caron Butler .30 .75
100 John Salmons .30 .75
101 Bruce Bowen .30 .75
102 Josh Howard .30 .75
103 Steve Francis .40 1.00
104 Lamar Odom .40 1.00
105 Troy Hudson .25 .60
106 Allen Iverson 1.00 2.50
107 Dajuan Wagner .25 .60
108 Erick Dampier .25 .60
109 Luke Walton .30 .75
110 Aaron Williams .25 .60
111 Juwan Howard .30 .75
112 Bobby Jackson .30 .75
113 Andrei Kirilenko .30 .75
114 LeBron James 10.00 25.00
115 Brian Cardinal .25 .60
116 Mike Miller .30 .75
117 Tracy McGrady .60 1.50
118 Doug Christie .30 .75
119 Larry Hughes .30 .75
120 Stephen Jackson .30 .75
121 Carmelo Anthony .75 2.00
122 Fred Jones .25 .60
123 Desmond Mason .30 .75
124 Jamal Mashburn .30 .75
125 Ray Allen .60 1.50
126 Jeff McInnis .25 .60
127 Yao Ming 1.00 2.50
128 Bonzi Wells .25 .60
129 Richard Jefferson .30 .75
130 Kenny Thomas .25 .60
131 Hedo Turkoglu .30 .75
132 Kwame Brown .25 .60
133 Dirk Nowitzki 1.00 2.50
134 Maurice Taylor .25 .60
135 Pau Gasol .60 1.50
136 Jason Kidd .60 1.50
137 Samuel Dalembert .25 .60
138 Tim Duncan 1.00 2.50
139 Gilbert Arenas .40 1.00
140 Tony Parker .60 1.50
141 Tyson Chandler .30 .75
142 Richard Hamilton .50 1.25
143 Shaquille O'Neal 1.50 4.00
144 Stephon Marbury .50 1.25
145 Damon Stoudamire .40 1.00
146 Gordan Giricek .25 .60
147 Latrell Sprewell .50 1.25
148 Carlos Boozer .30 .75
149 Mike Dunleavy .25 .60
150 Luke Ridnour .30 .75
151 Reece Gaines .25 .60
152 Peja Stojakovic .30 .75
153 Juan Dixon .25 .60
154 Marcus Banks .25 .60
155 Rasheed Wallace .50 1.25
156 Quentin Richardson .25 .60
157 Wally Szczerbiak .30 .75
158 Keith Bogans .25 .60
159 Darius Miles .25 .60
160 Matt Harpring .25 .60
161 Antawn Jamison .30 .75
162 Kelvin Cato .25 .60
163 James Posey .30 .75
164 Willie Green .40 1.00
165 Rasho Nesterovic .25 .60
166 Jarvis Hayes .25 .60
167 Paul Pierce .60 1.50
168 Mehmet Okur .30 .75
169 Elton Brand .30 .75
170 Kevin Garnett 1.00 2.50
171 Drew Gooden .25 .60
172 Zach Randolph .40 1.00
173 Raul Lopez .25 .60
174 Manu Ginobili .75 2.00
175 Raja Bell .30 .75
176 Dwight Howard L13 RC 10.00 25.00
177 Emeka Okafor L13 RC 2.50 6.00
178 Ben Gordon L13 RC 3.00 8.00
179 Shaun Livingston L13 RC 3.00 8.00
180 Devin Harris L13 RC 2.50 6.00
181 Josh Childress L13 RC 2.00 5.00
182 Luol Deng L13 RC 3.00 8.00
183 Rafael Araujo L13 RC 2.00 5.00
184 Andre Iguodala L13 RC 5.00 12.00
185 Luke Jackson L13 RC 2.00 5.00
186 Andris Biedrins L13 RC 2.00 5.00
187 Robert Swift L13 RC 2.00 5.00
188 Sebastian Telfair L13 RC 2.50 6.00
189 Kris Humphries RC 1.25 3.00
190 Al Jefferson RC 1.50 4.00
191 Kirk Snyder RC 1.00 2.50
192 Josh Smith RC 1.50 4.00
193 J.R. Smith RC 1.50 4.00
194 Dorell Wright RC 1.25 3.00
195 Jameer Nelson RC 1.50 4.00
196 Pavel Podkolzin RC 1.00 2.50
197 Ha Seung-Jin RC 1.50 4.00
198 Sasha Vujacic RC 1.25 3.00
199 Anderson Varejao RC 1.25 3.00
200U Bernard Robinson RC 1.25 3.00
201U Andres Nocioni RC 2.00 5.00
202U Delonte West RC 1.50 4.00
203U Tony Allen RC 2.00 5.00
204U Kevin Martin RC 2.50 6.00
205U Beno Udrih RC 1.50 4.00
206U David Harrison RC 1.25 3.00
207U Jackson Vroman RC 1.25 3.00
208U Peter John Ramos RC 1.25 3.00
209U Lionel Chalmers RC 1.50 4.00
210U Donta Smith RC 1.25 3.00
211U Andre Emmett RC 1.25 3.00
212U Antonio Burks RC 1.25 3.00
213U Royal Ivey RC 1.25 3.00
214U Chris Duhon RC 1.50 4.00
215U Damien Wilkins RC 1.50 4.00
216U Justin Reed RC 1.25 3.00
217U Trevor Ariza RC 2.00 5.00
218U Tim Pickett RC 1.50 4.00
219U Yuta Tabuse RC 2.00 5.00

2004-05 Ultra Gold Medallion
*1-175 GOLD: 1.25X TO 3X BASE HI
1-175 STATED ODDS ONE PER PACK
*176-188 GOLD: .25X TO .6X BASE HI
*189-199 GOLD: .5X TO 1.25X BASE HI
176-199 STATED ODDS 1:8
114 LeBron James 30.00 80.00

2004-05 Ultra Platinum Medallion
*1-175 SINGLES: 12X TO 30X BASE HI
*189-199 SINGLES: 2X TO 5X BASE HI
1-175 PRINT RUN 100 SER.#'d SETS
189-199 PRINT RUN 100 SER.#'d SETS
3 Steve Nash 40.00 100.00
8 Kobe Bryant 200.00 500.00
15 Vince Carter 75.00 200.00
59 Jason Williams 40.00 100.00
66 Dwyane Wade 75.00 200.00
90 Scottie Pippen 75.00 200.00
95 Chris Webber 50.00 120.00
106 Allen Iverson 75.00 200.00
114 LeBron James 400.00 800.00
117 Tracy McGrady 75.00 200.00
121 Carmelo Anthony 75.00 200.00
125 Ray Allen 75.00 200.00
127 Yao Ming 75.00 200.00
133 Dirk Nowitzki 75.00 200.00
135 Pau Gasol 40.00 100.00
136 Jason Kidd 40.00 100.00

138 Tim Duncan 75.00 200.00
140 Tony Parker 25.00 60.00
143 Shaquille O'Neal 125.00 300.00
167 Paul Pierce 75.00 200.00
170 Kevin Garnett 75.00 200.00
174 Manu Ginobili 50.00 120.00

2004-05 Ultra Hoop Nation

COMPLETE SET (15) 10.00 25.00
THREE PER EXCEL/MVP RETAIL BOX
1 LeBron James 5.00 12.00
2 Kobe Bryant 5.00 12.00
3 Tim Duncan 1.50 4.00
4 Vince Carter 1.25 3.00
5 Allen Iverson 1.50 4.00
6 Shaquille O'Neal 2.50 6.00
7 Tracy McGrady 1.00 2.50
8 Carmelo Anthony 1.25 3.00
9 Yao Ming 1.50 4.00
10 Dwyane Wade 2.50 6.00
11 Dirk Nowitzki 1.50 4.00
12 Jason Kidd 1.00 2.50
13 Kevin Garnett 1.50 4.00
14 Jermaine O'Neal .50 1.25
15 Paul Pierce 1.00 2.50

2004-05 Ultra Point Gods

COMPLETE SET (15) 10.00 25.00
STATED ODDS 1:36
1 Jason Kidd 1.25 3.00
2 Stephon Marbury 1.00 2.50
3 Allen Iverson 2.00 5.00
4 Chauncey Billups 1.00 2.50
5 Vince Carter 1.50 4.00
6 Steve Nash 1.50 4.00
7 Michael Redd .60 1.50
8 Baron Davis .75 2.00
9 Mike Bibby .75 2.00
10 Reggie Miller 1.50 4.00
11 LeBron James 10.00 25.00
12 Tracy McGrady 1.25 3.00
13 Kirk Hinrich .75 2.00
14 Kobe Bryant 10.00 25.00
15 Dwyane Wade 3.00 8.00

2004-05 Ultra Point Gods Game Used

PRINT RUN 250 SER.#'d SETS
*ULTRA SWATCH: 1.5X TO 4X BASE HI
AI Allen Iverson 8.00 20.00
BD Baron Davis 3.00 8.00
CB Chauncey Billups 4.00 10.00
DW Dwyane Wade 12.00 30.00
JK Jason Kidd 5.00 12.00
MB Mike Bibby 3.00 8.00
SM Stephon Marbury 4.00 10.00
TM Tracy McGrady 5.00 12.00
VC Vince Carter 6.00 15.00

2004-05 Ultra Scoring Kings

COMPLETE SET (25) 20.00 50.00
STATED ODDS 1:6
1 Vince Carter 2.00 5.00
2 Tracy McGrady 1.50 4.00
3 Peja Stojakovic .75 2.00
4 Kevin Garnett 2.50 6.00
5 Paul Pierce 1.50 4.00
6 Baron Davis 1.00 2.50
7 Tim Duncan 2.50 6.00
8 Dirk Nowitzki 2.50 6.00
9 Michael Redd .75 2.00
10 Shaquille O'Neal 4.00 10.00
11 Carmelo Anthony 2.00 5.00
12 Stephon Marbury 1.25 3.00
13 Corey Maggette .75 2.00
14 Zach Randolph 1.00 2.50
15 Jermaine O'Neal .75 2.00
16 Yao Ming 2.50 6.00
17 Andrei Kirilenko .75 2.00
18 Rashard Lewis .75 2.00
19 Latrell Sprewell 1.25 3.00
20 Pau Gasol 1.50 4.00
21 Kobe Bryant 10.00 25.00
22 LeBron James 10.00 25.00
23 Michael Finley 1.00 2.50
24 Jason Richardson 1.00 2.50
25 Richard Hamilton 1.25 3.00

2004-05 Ultra Scoring Kings Game Used

STATED ODDS 1:72
*ULTRA SWATCH: 1.25X TO 3X BASE HI
AK Andrei Kirilenko 2.50 6.00
BD Baron Davis 3.00 8.00
CA Carmelo Anthony 6.00 15.00
CM Corey Maggette 2.50 6.00
JO Jermaine O'Neal 2.50 6.00
JR Jason Richardson 3.00 8.00
KG Kevin Garnett 8.00 20.00
LS Latrell Sprewell 4.00 10.00
MR Michael Redd 2.50 6.00
PG Pau Gasol 5.00 12.00
PP Paul Pierce 5.00 12.00
PS Peja Stojakovic 2.50 6.00
RH Richard Hamilton 4.00 10.00
SM Stephon Marbury 4.00 10.00
SO Shaquille O'Neal 12.00 30.00
TD Tim Duncan 8.00 20.00
TM Tracy McGrady 5.00 12.00
VC Vince Carter 6.00 15.00
YM Yao Ming 8.00 20.00
ZR Zach Randolph 3.00 8.00

2004-05 Ultra Season Crowns Autographs

STATED ODDS 1:75
N Nene 6.00 15.00
AK Andrei Kirilenko/74 12.00 30.00
AS Amare Stoudemire/238 8.00 20.00
AW Antoine Walker 6.00 15.00
BG Ben Gordon 6.00 15.00
DM Darius Miles/386 5.00 12.00
DW Dwyane Wade 60.00 150.00
EC Eddy Curry/86 5.00 12.00
FJ Fred Jones/46 5.00 12.00
GA Gilbert Arenas/86 8.00 20.00
JJ Joe Johnson/222 6.00 15.00
JN Jameer Nelson 5.00 12.00
JS J.R. Smith 8.00 20.00
KB Kwame Brown/86 5.00 12.00
KK Kyle Korver 12.00 30.00
KM Kenyon Martin/50 10.00 25.00
MS Mike Sweetney/86 5.00 12.00
PP Paul Pierce 30.00 80.00
PS Peja Stojakovic/390 6.00 15.00
RG Reece Gaines/386 5.00 12.00
RM Ronald Murray/286 6.00 15.00
SM Shawn Marion/86 8.00 20.00
ST Sebastian Telfair/182 6.00 15.00
TM Tracy McGrady/278 50.00 120.00
VC Vince Carter/286 50.00 120.00

2004-05 Ultra Season Crowns Autographs Gold

PRINT RUN 15 SER.#'d SETS
N Nene 12.00 30.00
AS Amare Stoudemire 20.00 50.00
DW Dwyane Wade 100.00 250.00
EC Eddy Curry 12.00 30.00
JN Jameer Nelson 12.00 30.00
KM Kenyon Martin 12.00 30.00
RM Ronald Murray 12.00 30.00
ST Sebastian Telfair 12.00 30.00
TM Tracy McGrady 75.00 200.00

2004-05 Ultra Season Crowns Autographs Silver

PRINT RUN 99 SER.#'d SETS
N Nene 8.00 20.00
AK Andrei Kirilenko 10.00 25.00
AS Amare Stoudemire 10.00 25.00
AW Antoine Walker 8.00 20.00
BG Ben Gordon 8.00 20.00
DM Darius Miles 6.00 15.00
DW Dwyane Wade 75.00 200.00
EC Eddy Curry 6.00 15.00
GA Gilbert Arenas 8.00 20.00
JJ Joe Johnson 8.00 20.00
JS J.R. Smith 10.00 25.00
JW Jason Williams 15.00 40.00
KB Kwame Brown 6.00 15.00
KK Kyle Korver 15.00 40.00
KM Kenyon Martin 8.00 20.00
MS Mike Sweetney 6.00 15.00
PP Paul Pierce 40.00 100.00
PS Peja Stojakovic 10.00 25.00
RG Reece Gaines 6.00 15.00
RM Ronald Murray 8.00 20.00
SM Shawn Marion 8.00 20.00
ST Sebastian Telfair 8.00 20.00
TM Tracy McGrady 60.00 150.00
VC Vince Carter 60.00 150.00

2004-05 Ultra Season Crowns Game Used

PRINT RUN 349 SER.#'d SETS
*149 JSY SINGLES: .5X TO 1.25X BASE JSY HI
*99 JSY SINGLES: .6X TO 1.5X BASE JSY HI
*29 JSY SINGLES: 1.25X TO 3X BASE JSY HI
N Nene 2.00 5.00
AI Allen Iverson 6.00 15.00
AK Andrei Kirilenko 2.00 5.00
AS Amare Stoudemire 2.50 6.00
BD Boris Diaw 2.00 5.00
BW Ben Wallace 3.00 8.00
CA Carmelo Anthony 5.00 12.00
CB Chris Bosh 4.00 10.00
CB Carlos Boozer 2.00 5.00
CK Chris Kaman 2.00 5.00
CM Corey Maggette 2.00 5.00
DM Darius Miles 2.00 5.00
DW Dwyane Wade 10.00 25.00
EB Elton Brand 2.00 5.00
EC Eddy Curry 1.50 4.00
GP Gary Payton 4.00 10.00
JC Jamal Crawford 2.50 6.00
JJ Joe Johnson 2.00 5.00
JK Jason Kidd 4.00 10.00
JO Jermaine O'Neal 2.00 5.00
JW Jason Williams 2.00 5.00
KM Kenyon Martin 2.50 6.00
LO Lamar Odom 2.50 6.00
MG Manu Ginobili 5.00 12.00
MS Mike Sweetney 2.00 5.00
RA Ray Allen 4.00 10.00
RA Ron Artest 2.50 6.00
RJ Richard Jefferson 2.00 5.00
RL Rashard Lewis 2.00 5.00
RM Reggie Miller 5.00 12.00
SM Shawn Marion 2.50 6.00
SM Stephon Marbury 2.50 6.00
SN Steve Nash 5.00 12.00
SP Scottie Pippen 6.00 15.00
TD Tim Duncan 6.00 15.00
TM Tracy McGrady 4.00 10.00
TP Tayshaun Prince 2.50 6.00
TP Tony Parker 4.00 10.00
VC Vince Carter 5.00 12.00
YM Yao Ming 6.00 15.00

2004-05 Ultra Ten for Ten

COMPLETE SET (10) 15.00 35.00
STATED ODDS 1:100
1 Kevin Garnett 3.00 8.00
2 Vince Carter 2.50 6.00
3 Shaquille O'Neal 5.00 12.00
4 Tim Duncan 3.00 8.00
5 Dirk Nowitzki 3.00 8.00
6 Yao Ming 3.00 8.00
7 Carmelo Anthony 2.50 6.00
8 Allen Iverson 3.00 8.00
9 Tracy McGrady 2.00 5.00
10 Ben Wallace 1.50 4.00

2004-05 Ultra Ten for Ten Game Used

PRINT RUN 100 SER.#'d SETS
AI Allen Iverson 10.00 25.00
BW Ben Wallace 5.00 12.00
DA Carmelo Anthony 8.00 20.00
DN Dirk Nowitzki 10.00 25.00
KG Kevin Garnett 10.00 25.00
SO Shaquille O'Neal 15.00 40.00
TD Tim Duncan 10.00 25.00
TM Tracy McGrady 8.00 20.00
VC Vince Carter 8.00 20.00
YM Yao Ming 10.00 25.00

2006-07 Ultra

COMP.SET w/o SP's (170) 20.00 50.00
L14 RC PRINT RUN 500 SER.#'d SETS
1 Josh Childress .20 .50
2 Al Harrington .25 .60
3 Joe Johnson .30 .75
4 Tyronn Lue .20 .50
5 Josh Smith .20 .50
6 Tony Allen .20 .50
7 Dan Dickau .20 .50
8 Al Jefferson .20 .50
9 Paul Pierce .50 1.25
10 Wally Szczerbiak .25 .60
11 Raef LaFrentz .20 .50
12 Primoz Brezec .20 .50
13 Brevin Knight .20 .50
14 Emeka Okafor .25 .60
15 Kareem Rush .20 .50
16 Gerald Wallace .25 .60
17 Bernard Robinson .20 .50
18 Tyson Chandler .25 .60
19 Luol Deng .25 .60
20 Chris Duhon .20 .50
21 Ben Gordon .25 .60
22 Kirk Hinrich .25 .60
23 Drew Gooden .25 .60
24 Larry Hughes .25 .60
25 Zydrunas Ilgauskas .25 .60
26 LeBron James 2.50 6.00
27 Luke Jackson .20 .50
28 Anderson Varejao .20 .50
29 Erick Dampier .20 .50
30 Marquis Daniels .20 .50
31 Devin Harris .20 .50
32 Josh Howard .25 .60
33 Dirk Nowitzki .75 2.00
34 Jason Terry .25 .60
35 Carmelo Anthony .50 1.25
36 Earl Boykins .20 .50
37 Marcus Camby .25 .60
38 Kenyon Martin .25 .60
39 Andre Miller .25 .60
40 Eduardo Najera .20 .50
41 Chauncey Billups .40 1.00
42 Richard Hamilton .30 .75
43 Antonio McDyess .25 .60
44 Tayshaun Prince .30 .75
45 Ben Wallace .40 1.00
46 Rasheed Wallace .40 1.00
47 Baron Davis .30 .75
48 Mike Dunleavy .20 .50
49 Derek Fisher .30 .75
50 Troy Murphy .20 .50
51 Jason Richardson .30 .75
52 Rafer Alston .25 .60
53 Juwan Howard .25 .60
54 Tracy McGrady .50 1.25
55 Stromile Swift .20 .50
56 David Wesley .20 .50
57 Yao Ming .75 2.00
58 Austin Croshere .20 .50
59 Stephen Jackson .20 .50
60 Jermaine O'Neal .30 .75
61 Peja Stojakovic .25 .60
62 Jamaal Tinsley .25 .60
63 Elton Brand .25 .60
64 Sam Cassell .25 .60
65 Chris Kaman .25 .60
66 Shaun Livingston .25 .60
67 Corey Maggette .25 .60
68 Cuttino Mobley .25 .60
69 Kwame Brown .25 .60
70 Kobe Bryant 2.50 6.00
71 Devean George .25 .60
72 Lamar Odom .20 .50
73 Smush Parker .20 .50
74 Luke Walton .20 .50
75 Shane Battier .25 .60
76 Pau Gasol .50 1.25
77 Bobby Jackson .20 .50
78 Mike Miller .25 .60
79 Damon Stoudamire .25 .60
80 Alonzo Mourning .50 1.25
81 Shaquille O'Neal 1.25 3.00
82 Gary Payton .40 1.00
83 Dwyane Wade .60 1.50
84 Antoine Walker .30 .75
85 Jason Williams .40 1.00
86 T.J. Ford .20 .50
87 Jamaal Magloire .20 .50
88 Michael Redd .25 .60
89 Bobby Simmons .20 .50
90 Maurice Williams .20 .50
91 Mark Blount .20 .50
92 Ricky Davis .25 .60
93 Kevin Garnett .75 2.00
94 Eddie Griffin .20 .50
95 Trenton Hassell .20 .50
96 Troy Hudson .20 .50
97 Vince Carter .60 1.50
98 Jason Collins .20 .50
99 Richard Jefferson .20 .50
100 Jason Kidd .50 1.25
101 Jeff McInnis .20 .50
102 Antoine Wright .20 .50
103 P.J. Brown .20 .50
104 Speedy Claxton .20 .50
105 Marc Jackson .20 .50
106 Desmond Mason .20 .50
107 J.R. Smith .25 .60
108 Eddy Curry .25 .60
109 Steve Francis .30 .75
110 Stephon Marbury .40 1.00
111 Quentin Richardson .20 .50
112 Jalen Rose .25 .60
113 Maurice Taylor .20 .50
114 Carlos Arroyo .20 .50
115 Grant Hill .50 1.25
116 Dwight Howard .40 1.00
117 Darko Milicic .20 .50
118 Jameer Nelson .20 .50
119 DeShawn Stevenson .20 .50
120 Samuel Dalembert .20 .50
121 Steven Hunter .20 .50
122 Andre Iguodala .30 .75
123 Allen Iverson .75 2.00
124 Kyle Korver .25 .60
125 Chris Webber .40 1.00
126 Raja Bell .25 .60
127 Boris Diaw .25 .60
128 Shawn Marion .30 .75
129 Steve Nash .60 1.50
130 Amare Stoudemire .30 .75
131 Kurt Thomas .20 .50
132 Darius Miles .20 .50
133 Joel Przybilla .20 .50
134 Zach Randolph .30 .75
135 Ha Seung-Jin .20 .50
136 Sebastian Telfair .20 .50
137 Shareef Abdur-Rahim .30 .75
138 Ron Artest .30 .75
139 Mike Bibby .30 .75
140 Brad Miller .25 .60
141 Vitaly Potapenko .20 .50
142 Bruce Bowen .25 .60
143 Tim Duncan .75 2.00
144 Michael Finley .30 .75
145 Manu Ginobili .60 1.50
146 Robert Horry .30 .75
147 Tony Parker .50 1.25
148 Ray Allen .50 1.25
149 Rashard Lewis .25 .60
150 Luke Ridnour .25 .60
151 Robert Swift .20 .50
152 Earl Watson .20 .50
153 Chris Wilcox .20 .50
154 Rafael Araujo .20 .50
155 Chris Bosh .40 1.00
156 Jose Calderon .20 .50
157 Mike James .20 .50
158 Morris Peterson .20 .50
159 Pape Sow .20 .50
160 Carlos Boozer .25 .60
161 Gordan Giricek .20 .50
162 Kris Humphries .20 .50
163 Andrei Kirilenko .25 .60
164 Mehmet Okur .20 .50
165 Greg Ostertag .20 .50
166 Gilbert Arenas .30 .75
167 Calvin Booth .20 .50
168 Caron Butler .25 .60
169 Antonio Daniels .20 .50
170 Antawn Jamison .25 .60
171 Andrew Bogut L14 Ret 1.00 2.50
172 Marvin Williams L14 Ret .75 2.00
173 Deron Williams L14 Ret 1.00 2.50
174 Chris Paul L14 Ret 2.50 6.00
175 Raymond Felton L14 Ret .75 2.00
176 Martell Webster L14 Ret 1.00 2.50
177 Charlie Villanueva L14 Ret .75 2.00
178 Channing Frye L14 Ret .75 2.00
179 Ike Diogu L14 Ret .75 2.00
180 Andrew Bynum L14 Ret .75 2.00
181 Yaroslav Korolev L14 Ret .75 2.00
182 Sean May L14 Ret .75 2.00
183 Rashad McCants L14 Ret .75 2.00
184 Antoine Wright L14 Ret .75 2.00
185 Nate Robinson WP Ret 1.00 2.50
186 Luther Head WP Ret .75 2.00
187 Joey Graham WP Ret .75 2.00
188 Johan Petro WP Ret .75 2.00
189 Wayne Simien WP Ret .75 2.00
190 David Lee WP Ret .75 2.00
191 Salim Stoudamire WP Ret .75 2.00
192 Travis Diener WP Ret .75 2.00
193 Monta Ellis WP Ret 1.00 2.50
194 Martynas Andriuskevicius WP Ret .75 2.00
195 Chuck Hayes WP Ret .75 2.00
196 Danny Granger WP Ret .75 2.00
197 Sarunas Jasikevicius WP Ret 1.00 2.50
198 Francisco Garcia WP Ret .75 2.00
199 Jarrett Jack WP Ret 1.00 2.50
200 Jose Calderon WP Ret .75 2.00
201 Andrea Bargnani L14/500 RC 3.00 8.00
202 LaMarcus Aldridge L14/500 RC 10.00 25.00
203 Adam Morrison L14/500 RC 3.00 8.00
204 Tyrus Thomas L14/500 RC 3.00 8.00
205 Shelden Williams L14/500 RC 2.50 6.00
206 Brandon Roy L14/500 RC 8.00 20.00
207 Randy Foye L14/500 RC 3.00 8.00
208 Rudy Gay L14/500 RC 5.00 12.00
209 Patrick O'Bryant L14/500 RC 2.50 6.00
210 Saer Sene L14/500 RC 2.50 6.00
211 J.J. Redick L14/500 RC 8.00 20.00
212 Hilton Armstrong L14/500 RC 2.50 6.00
213 Thabo Sefolosha L14/500 RC 3.00 8.00
214 Ronnie Brewer L14/500 RC 4.00 10.00
215 Allan Ray WP RC .60 1.50
216 Leon Powe WP RC .60 1.50
217 Joel Freeland WP RC .60 1.50
218 Shawne Williams WP RC .60 1.50
219 Kevin Pittsnogle WP RC .75 2.00
220 Shannon Brown WP RC .60 1.50
221 Kyle Lowry WP RC 3.00 8.00
222 Mardy Collins WP RC .60 1.50
223 Rodney Carney WP RC .60 1.50
224 Maurice Ager WP RC .60 1.50
225 Quincy Douby WP RC .60 1.50
226 Rajon Rondo WP RC 3.00 8.00
227 Jordan Farmar WP RC .75 2.00
228 Marcus Williams WP RC .60 1.50
229 Josh Boone WP RC .60 1.50
230 Solomon Jones WP RC .60 1.50
231 Denham Brown WP RC .60 1.50
232 Renaldo Balkman WP RC .75 2.00
233 Will Blalock WP RC .60 1.50
234 Bobby Jones WP RC .60 1.50
235 Steve Novak WP RC .75 2.00
236 James Augustine WP RC .60 1.50
237 Dee Brown WP RC .60 1.50
238 Hassan Adams WP RC .60 1.50
239 Alexander Johnson WP RC .60 1.50
240 Cedric Simmons WP RC .60 1.50
241 James White WP RC .60 1.50
242 Paul Davis WP RC .60 1.50
243 P.J. Tucker WP RC 1.00 2.50
244 Ryan Hollins WP RC .60 1.50

2006-07 Ultra Gold Medallion

*1-200 GOLD: .75X TO 2X BASE HI
*201-214 GOLD: HALF VALUE OF BASE
*215-244 GOLD: .75X TO 2X BASE HI
ONE PER PACK
26 LeBron James 10.00 25.00

2006-07 Ultra Platinum Medallion

*1-170 PLATINUM: 5X TO 12X BASE HI
*171-200 PLATINUM: 1X TO 2.5X BASE HI
1-200 PLAT.PRINT RUN 100 SER.#'d SETS
201-214 PRINT RUN 14 SER.#'d SETS
*215-244 PLAT.PRINT: 4X TO 10X BASE HI
215-244 PLAT.PRINT RUN 25 SER.#'d SETS
26 LeBron James 125.00 300.00
70 Kobe Bryant 100.00 250.00
80 Alonzo Mourning 6.00 15.00

2006-07 Ultra Red

*201-214 RED: 3X TO .75X BASE HI
*215-244 RED: 1.25X TO 3X BASE HI
RED APPROXIMATELY ONE PER BOX

2006-07 Ultra Fresh Ink

FIBB Brent Barry 6.00 15.00
FIDH Dwight Howard 8.00 20.00
FIHW Hakim Warrick 6.00 15.00
FIKM Kevin Martin 5.00 12.00
FILJ LeBron James SP 1,500.00 3,000.00
FIRF Raymond Felton 6.00 15.00
FIRT Ronny Turiaf 6.00 15.00

2006-07 Ultra Kings of the Court

APPROXIMATE ODDS 1:24
KKAI Andre Iguodala 3.00 8.00
KKAJ Antawn Jamison 2.50 6.00
KKAL Al Jefferson 2.00 5.00
KKBD Baron Davis 3.00 8.00
KKBH Brendan Haywood 2.00 5.00
KKBW Ben Wallace 4.00 10.00
KKCM Corey Maggette 2.50 6.00
KKDG Drew Gooden 2.50 6.00
KKDN Dirk Nowitzki 8.00 20.00
KKJM Jeff McInnis 2.00 5.00
KKJO Jermaine O'Neal 3.00 8.00
KKJR Jason Richardson 3.00 8.00
KKKB Kobe Bryant 8.00 20.00
KKKG Kevin Garnett 8.00 20.00
KKLD Luol Deng 2.50 6.00
KKLJ LeBron James 8.00 20.00
KKMG Manu Ginobili 6.00 15.00
KKPS Peja Stojakovic 2.50 6.00
KKSM Stephon Marbury 4.00 10.00
KKYM Yao Ming 8.00 20.00

2006-07 Ultra One on One

PRINT RUN 100 SER.#'d SETS
OOBN C.Billups/S.Nash 6.00 15.00
OOFM S.Francis/S.Marbury 5.00 12.00
OOHD R.Hamilton/R.Davis 5.00 12.00
OOMB S.Marion/C.Bosh 6.00 15.00
OOMO Y.Ming/S.O'Neal 10.00 25.00
OOMP K.Martin/T.Prince 5.00 12.00
OOSH A.Stoudemire/D.Howard 6.00 15.00

2006-07 Ultra Scoring Kings

COMPLETE SET 10.00 25.00
APPROXIMATE ODDS 1:6
SKAI Allen Iverson 1.50 4.00
SKCA Carmelo Anthony 1.00 2.50
SKDN Dirk Nowitzki 1.50 4.00
SKDW Dwyane Wade 1.25 3.00
SKEB Elton Brand .50 1.25
SKGA Gilbert Arenas .60 1.50
SKJR Jason Richardson .60 1.50
SKKB Kobe Bryant 5.00 12.00
SKKG Kevin Garnett 1.50 4.00
SKLJ LeBron James 5.00 12.00
SKPP Paul Pierce 1.00 2.50
SKRA Ray Allen 1.00 2.50
SKRH Richard Hamilton .60 1.50
SKRJ Richard Jefferson .50 1.25
SKSM Shawn Marion .60 1.50
SKSN Steve Nash 1.25 3.00
SKTD Tim Duncan 1.50 4.00
SKTM Tracy McGrady 1.50 4.00
SKTP Tony Parker 1.00 2.50
SKVC Vince Carter 1.25 3.00

2006-07 Ultra Season Crowns

COMPLETE SET 8.00 20.00
APPROXIMATE ODDS 1:12
SCAI Allen Iverson 2.00 5.00
SCAS Amare Stoudemire .75 2.00
SCCP Chris Paul 1.50 4.00
SCGA Gilbert Arenas .75 2.00
SCJK Jason Kidd 1.25 3.00
SCKG Kevin Garnett 2.00 5.00
SCSO Shaquille O'Neal 3.00 8.00
SCTD Tim Duncan 2.00 5.00
SCTP Tony Parker 1.25 3.00
SCVC Vince Carter 1.50 4.00

2006-07 Ultra Three Kings

PRINT RUN 50 SER.#'d SETS
TKBMJ Kobe/McGrady/LeBron 150.00 400.00
TKDMO Duncan/Yao/Shaq 15.00 40.00
TKJHB LeBron/Howard/Bogut 15.00 40.00
TKJWD Jamison/Wallace/Deng 6.00 15.00
TKKMN Kidd/Marbury/Nash 12.50 30.00
TKPFV Paul/Frye/Villanueva 12.00 30.00

2007-08 Ultra SE

COMP.SET w/o SP's (200) 20.00 50.00
1 Joe Johnson .30 .75
2 Josh Smith .25 .60
3 Josh Childress .25 .60
4 Marvin Williams .25 .60
5 Anthony Johnson .25 .60
6 Shelden Williams .25 .60
7 Tyronn Lue .25 .60
8 Al Jefferson .25 .60
9 Paul Pierce .60 1.50
10 Wally Szczerbiak .30 .75
11 Sebastian Telfair .25 .60
12 Gerald Green .25 .60
13 Rajon Rondo .50 1.25
14 Delonte West .25 .60
15 Adam Morrison .30 .75
16 Emeka Okafor .30 .75
17 Gerald Wallace .30 .75
18 Raymond Felton .30 .75
19 Sean May .25 .60
20 Matt Carroll .25 .60
21 Ben Wallace .50 1.25
22 Ben Gordon .30 .75
23 Tyrus Thomas .25 .60
24 Luol Deng .30 .75
25 Kirk Hinrich .40 1.00
26 Andres Nocioni .25 .60
27 Thabo Sefolosha .25 .60
28 LeBron James 3.00 8.00
29 Larry Hughes .30 .75
30 Zydrunas Ilgauskas .30 .75
31 Drew Gooden .25 .60
32 Daniel Gibson .25 .60
33 Shannon Brown .25 .60
34 Dirk Nowitzki 1.00 2.50
35 Josh Howard .30 .75
36 Jason Terry .30 .75
37 Jerry Stackhouse .40 1.00
38 Devin Harris .25 .60
39 Erick Dampier .25 .60
40 Jose Barea .60 1.50
41 Carmelo Anthony .60 1.50
42 Allen Iverson 1.00 2.50
43 J.R. Smith .40 1.00
44 Yakhouba Diawara .25 .60
45 Marcus Camby .30 .75
46 Eduardo Najera .25 .60
47 Chauncey Billups .50 1.25
48 Richard Hamilton .50 1.25
49 Tayshaun Prince .40 1.00
50 Chris Webber .50 1.25
51 Rasheed Wallace .50 1.25
52 Will Blalock .25 .60
53 Nazr Mohammed .25 .60
54 Baron Davis .30 .75
55 Al Harrington .25 .60
56 Stephen Jackson .30 .75
57 Jason Richardson .40 1.00
58 Monta Ellis .40 1.00
59 Mickael Pietrus .25 .60
60 Kelenna Azubuike .25 .60
61 Yao Ming 1.00 2.50
62 Tracy McGrady .60 1.50
63 Rafer Alston .40 1.00
64 Luther Head .25 .60
65 Shane Battier .30 .75
66 Juwan Howard .40 1.00
67 Bonzi Wells .25 .60
68 Jermaine O'Neal .40 1.00
69 Danny Granger .25 .60
70 Jamaal Tinsley .25 .60
71 Mike Dunleavy .25 .60
72 Troy Murphy .25 .60
73 Shawne Williams .25 .60
74 Elton Brand .25 .60
75 Corey Maggette .30 .75
76 Sam Cassell .30 .75
77 Cuttino Mobley .30 .75
78 Tim Thomas .25 .60
79 Chris Kaman .30 .75
80 Kobe Bryant 3.00 8.00
81 Jordan Farmar .25 .60
82 Lamar Odom .30 .75
83 Andrew Bynum .25 .60
84 Smush Parker .25 .60
85 Luke Walton .30 .75
86 Maurice Evans .25 .60
87 Rudy Gay .30 .75
88 Pau Gasol .60 1.50
89 Mike Miller .30 .75
90 Hakim Warrick .25 .60
91 Kyle Lowry .40 1.00
92 Damon Stoudamire .25 .60
93 Shaquille O'Neal 1.50 4.00
94 Dwyane Wade .75 2.00
95 Jason Williams .60 1.50
96 Jason Kapono .25 .60
97 Alonzo Mourning .60 1.50
98 Udonis Haslem .25 .60
99 Gary Payton .60 1.50
100 Michael Redd .30 .75
101 Maurice Williams .30 .75
102 Andrew Bogut .30 .75
103 Charlie Villanueva .25 .60
104 Ruben Patterson .25 .60
105 Charlie Bell .25 .60
106 Kevin Garnett 1.00 2.50
107 Rashad McCants .25 .60
108 Ricky Davis .30 .75
109 Randy Foye .30 .75
110 Craig Smith .25 .60
111 Mike James .25 .60
112 Jason Kidd .60 1.50
113 Vince Carter .75 2.00
114 Richard Jefferson .30 .75
115 Nenad Krstic .25 .60
116 Bernard Robinson .25 .60
117 Marcus Williams .25 .60
118 Josh Boone .25 .60
119 Chris Paul .75 2.00
120 Peja Stojakovic .30 .75
121 David West .30 .75
122 Desmond Mason .25 .60
123 Cedric Simmons .25 .60
124 Hilton Armstrong .25 .60
125 Devin Brown .25 .60
126 Nate Robinson .40 1.00
127 Eddy Curry .25 .60
128 Jamal Crawford .25 .60
129 Stephon Marbury .50 1.25
130 Quentin Richardson .25 .60
131 David Lee .25 .60
132 Channing Frye .25 .60
133 Dwight Howard .50 1.25
134 J.J. Redick .40 1.00
135 Grant Hill .60 1.50
136 Jameer Nelson .25 .60
137 Hedo Turkoglu .30 .75
138 Tony Battie .25 .60
139 Darko Milicic .25 .60
140 Carlos Arroyo .25 .60
141 Andre Iguodala .40 1.00
142 Kyle Korver .40 1.00
143 Samuel Dalembert .25 .60
144 Rodney Carney .25 .60
145 Willie Green .25 .60
146 Andre Miller .30 .75
147 Bobby Jones .40 1.00
148 Steve Nash .75 2.00
149 Amare Stoudemire .40 1.00
150 Shawn Marion .40 1.00
151 Leandro Barbosa .30 .75
152 Raja Bell .30 .75
153 Boris Diaw .30 .75
154 LaMarcus Aldridge .40 1.00
155 Zach Randolph .40 1.00
156 Brandon Roy .50 1.25
157 Jarrett Jack .30 .75
158 Ime Udoka .40 1.00
159 Martell Webster .30 .75
160 Sergio Rodriguez .25 .60
161 Fred Jones .25 .60
162 Kevin Martin .30 .75
163 Ron Artest .40 1.00
164 Mike Bibby .40 1.00
165 Brad Miller .30 .75
166 Quincy Douby .25 .60
167 Shareef Abdur-Rahim .40 1.00
168 Radoslav Nesterovic .25 .60
169 Tony Parker .60 1.50
170 Tim Duncan 1.00 2.50
171 Manu Ginobili .75 2.00
172 Michael Finley .40 1.00
173 Brent Barry .25 .60
174 Bruce Bowen .25 .60
175 Ray Allen .60 1.50
176 Rashard Lewis .30 .75
177 Chris Wilcox .25 .60
178 Luke Ridnour .30 .75
179 Nick Collison .25 .60
180 Earl Watson .25 .60
181 Mickael Gelabale .25 .60
182 Chris Bosh .50 1.25
183 Andrea Bargnani .25 .60
184 T.J. Ford .25 .60
185 Anthony Parker .25 .60
186 Jorge Garbajosa .30 .75
187 Morris Peterson .25 .60
188 Jose Calderon .25 .60
189 Carlos Boozer .30 .75
190 Mehmet Okur .25 .60
191 Deron Williams .30 .75
192 Paul Millsap .30 .75
193 Ronnie Brewer .25 .60
194 Andrei Kirilenko .30 .75
195 Gilbert Arenas .40 1.00
196 Caron Butler .30 .75
197 Antawn Jamison .30 .75
198 DeShawn Stevenson .25 .60
199 Brendan Haywood .25 .60
200 Etan Thomas .25 .60
201 Al Thornton RC 1.25 3.00
201B Al Thornton BB 1.25 3.00
202 Rodney Stuckey RC 1.25 3.00
203 Nick Young RC 2.00 5.00
204 Sean Williams RC 1.25 3.00
205 Marco Belinelli RC 1.50 4.00
206 Javaris Crittenton RC 1.25 3.00
206B Javaris Crittenton BB 1.25 3.00
207 Jason Smith RC 1.25 3.00
208 Daequan Cook RC 1.50 4.00
209 Jared Dudley RC 1.50 4.00
210 Wilson Chandler RC 1.50 4.00
211 Morris Almond RC 1.25 3.00
212 Aaron Brooks RC 1.50 4.00
213 Arron Afflalo RC 1.50 4.00
214 Alando Tucker RC 1.25 3.00
215 Petteri Koponen RC 1.50 4.00
216 Carl Landry RC 1.25 3.00
217 Gabe Pruitt RC 1.25 3.00
217B Gabe Pruitt BB 1.25 3.00
218 Marcus Williams RC 1.25 3.00
219 Nick Fazekas RC 1.25 3.00
220 Glen Davis RC 1.50 4.00
220B Glen Davis BB 1.50 4.00
221 Jermareo Davidson RC 1.25 3.00
222 Josh McRoberts RC 1.25 3.00
223 Kyrylo Fesenko RC 1.25 3.00
224 Stanko Barac RC 2.00 5.00
225 Sun Yue RC 2.00 5.00
225B Sun Yue BB 2.00 5.00
226 Chris Richard RC 1.25 3.00
227 Derrick Byars RC 1.25 3.00
227B Derrick Byars BB 1.25 3.00
228 Adam Haluska RC 1.25 3.00
229 Reyshawn Terry RC 1.25 3.00
230 Taurean Green RC 1.25 3.00
231 Greg Oden L13 RC 2.50 6.00
231B Greg Oden BB 2.50 6.00
232 Kevin Durant L13 RC 25.00 60.00
233 Al Horford L13 RC 6.00 15.00
233B Al Horford BB 6.00 15.00
234 Mike Conley Jr. L13 RC 6.00 15.00
235 Jeff Green L13 RC 2.00 5.00
236 Yi Jianlian L13 RC 3.00 8.00
236B Yi Jianlian BB 3.00 8.00
237 Corey Brewer L13 RC 2.00 5.00
238 Brandan Wright L13 RC 2.00 5.00
239 Joakim Noah L13 RC 2.50 6.00
239B Joakim Noah BB 2.50 6.00
240 Spencer Hawes L13 RC 1.50 4.00
241 Acie Law L13 RC 1.50 4.00
242 Thaddeus Young L13 RC 2.50 6.00
242B Thaddeus Young BB 2.50 6.00
243 Julian Wright L13 RC 1.50 4.00
243B Julian Wright BB 1.50 4.00
244 Michael Jordan L13 15.00 40.00
244B Michael Jordan BB 15.00 40.00
245 Larry Bird L13 6.00 15.00
246 Magic Johnson L13 6.00 15.00
246B Magic Johnson BB 6.00 15.00
247 Bill Russell L13 5.00 12.00
248 Dennis Rodman L13 4.00 10.00
248B Dennis Rodman BB 4.00 10.00
249 Kareem Abdul-Jabbar L13 5.00 12.00
249B Kareem Abdul-Jabbar BB 5.00 12.00
250 Clyde Drexler L13 2.50 6.00
251 Hakeem Olajuwon L13 3.00 8.00
252 John Havlicek L13 3.00 8.00
253 David Robinson L13 3.00 8.00
254 John Stockton L13 3.00 8.00
254B John Stockton BB 3.00 8.00
255 Jerry West L13 4.00 10.00
256 Julius Erving L13 4.00 10.00

2007-08 Ultra SE Gold Medallion

*1-200 GOLD: 1.5X TO 4X BASE HI
*201-230 GOLD: .6X TO 1.5X BASE HI

*231-243 GOLD: .5X TO 1.25X BASE HI
*243-256 GOLD: .6X TO 1.5X BASE
GOLD ODDS ONE PER PACK
28 LeBron James 20.00 50.00
232 Kevin Durant L13 40.00 100.00

2007-08 Ultra SE Platinum Medallion

*1-200 PLAT: 6X TO 15X BASE HI
*201-230 PLAT: 2X TO 5X BASE
*231-243 PLAT: 1.5X TO 4X BASE
*244-256 PLAT: 2X TO 5X BASE HI
PRINT RUN 25 SER.#'d SETS
28 LeBron James 300.00 600.00
80 Kobe Bryant 150.00 400.00
232 Kevin Durant L13 300.00 600.00
244 Michael Jordan L13 300.00 600.00

2007-08 Ultra SE Autographics Black

ONE AUTO CARD PER HOBBY BOX
CARDS WITH (F) INSERTED IN FLEER
AUAB Andrea Bargnani 4.00 10.00
AUAH Al Harrington 5.00 12.00
AUAI Andre Iguodala 6.00 15.00
AUAJ Antawn Jamison 5.00 12.00
AUAR Allan Ray 4.00 10.00
AUAU James Augustine 4.00 10.00
AUBB Bruce Bowen Ultra, F 4.00 10.00
AUBD Boris Diaw F 5.00 12.00
AUBG Ben Gordon 5.00 12.00
AUBJ Bobby Jackson 4.00 10.00
AUBJ2 Bobby Jones 6.00 15.00
AUBM Brad Miller F 5.00 12.00
AUBR Ronnie Brewer 4.00 10.00
AUCB Charlie Bell 4.00 10.00
AUCM Chris Mihm 4.00 10.00
AUCS Cedric Simmons 4.00 10.00
AUDB Dee Brown 4.00 10.00
AUDE Daniel Ewing 4.00 10.00
AUDL David Lee F 4.00 10.00
AUDM Donyell Marshall 4.00 10.00
AUDN David Noel 4.00 10.00
AUDW Damien Wilkens F 4.00 10.00
AUFE Raymond Felton Ultra, F 5.00 12.00
AUGK George Karl 6.00 15.00
AUHW Hakim Warrick 4.00 10.00
AUJB Josh Boone 4.00 10.00
AUJJ Jarrett Jack 5.00 12.00
AUJK Jason Kapono 4.00 10.00
AUJS J.R. Smith 6.00 15.00
AUJW James White 4.00 10.00
AUKO Keyon Dooling 4.00 10.00
AUKH Kirk Hinrich 6.00 15.00
AUKK Kyle Korver 6.00 15.00
AULA Larry Hughes 5.00 12.00
AULP Leon Powe 4.00 10.00
AUMA Mardy Collins 4.00 10.00
AUMD Marquis Daniels Ultra, F 4.00 10.00
AUMG Corey Maggette 5.00 12.00
AUMI Andre Miller 5.00 12.00
AUMP Morris Peterson 4.00 10.00
AUPD Paul Davis 4.00 10.00
AUPM Paul Millsap 5.00 12.00
AUQR Quentin Richardson 4.00 10.00
AURB Raja Bell F 5.00 12.00
AURC Rodney Carney Ultra, F 4.00 10.00
AURF Randy Foye 5.00 12.00
AURH Ryan Hollins Ultra, F 4.00 10.00
AURM Rashad McCants 4.00 10.00
AURR Rajon Rondo 8.00 20.00
AURT Ronny Turiaf F 5.00 12.00
AUSA Shareef Abdur-Rahim F 6.00 15.00
AUSB Shannon Brown Ultra, F 4.00 10.00
AUSE Sean May F 4.00 10.00
AUSI James Singleton 4.00 10.00
AUSJ Solomon Jones 4.00 10.00
AUSM Craig Smith 4.00 10.00
AUSN Steve Novak 4.00 10.00
AUST DeShawn Stevenson 4.00 10.00
AUTA Tony Allen 4.00 10.00
AUTC Tyson Chandler 6.00 15.00
AUTF T.J. Ford 4.00 10.00
AUWB Will Blalock 4.00 10.00
AUWI Deron Williams F 5.00 12.00

2007-08 Ultra SE Autographics Blue

ONE AUTO CARD PER HOBBY BOX
CARDS WITH (F) INSERTED IN FLEER
AUAB Andrea Bargnani 4.00 10.00
AUAH Al Harrington 5.00 12.00
AUAI Andre Iguodala 6.00 15.00
AUAJ Antawn Jamison 5.00 12.00
AUAM Alonzo Mourning 40.00 100.00
AUAR Allan Ray 4.00 10.00
AUAU James Augustine 4.00 10.00
AUBB Bruce Bowen Ultra, F 4.00 10.00
AUBG Ben Gordon 5.00 12.00
AUBJ Bobby Jackson 4.00 10.00
AUBR Ronnie Brewer 4.00 10.00
AUCA Carmelo Anthony Ultra, F 75.00 200.00
AUCB Charlie Bell 4.00 10.00
AUCM Chris Mihm 4.00 10.00
AUCP Chris Paul 60.00 150.00
AUCS Cedric Simmons 4.00 10.00
AUDB Dee Brown 4.00 10.00
AUDE Daniel Ewing 4.00 10.00
AUDM Donyell Marshall 4.00 10.00
AUDN David Noel 4.00 10.00
AUDS Dean Smith 100.00 250.00
AUEO Emeka Okafor 5.00 12.00
AUFE Raymond Felton 5.00 12.00
AUHW Hakim Warrick 4.00 10.00
AUJB Josh Boone 4.00 10.00
AUJE Julius Erving Ultra, F 75.00 200.00
AUJG Joey Graham 4.00 10.00
AUJJ Jarrett Jack 5.00 12.00
AUJK Jason Kapono 4.00 10.00
AUJO Bobby Jones 6.00 15.00
AUJW James White 4.00 10.00
AUKB Kobe Bryant 1,000.00 2,000.00
AUKH Kirk Hinrich 6.00 15.00
AUKI Jason Kidd 30.00 80.00
AUKK Kyle Korver 6.00 15.00
AULA LaMarcus Aldridge Ultra, F 12.00 30.00
AULB Larry Bird 125.00 300.00
AULH Larry Hughes 5.00 12.00
AULJ LeBron James 1,000.00 2,000.00
AULP Leon Powe 4.00 10.00
AUMA Magic Johnson 100.00 250.00
AUMC Mardy Collins 4.00 10.00
AUMD Marquis Daniels Ultra, F 4.00 10.00
AUMG Corey Maggette 5.00 12.00
AUMI Andre Miller 5.00 12.00
AUMJ Michael Jordan 1,500.00 3,000.00
AUMP Morris Peterson 4.00 10.00
AUNO Steve Novak 4.00 10.00
AUON Jermaine O'Neal 6.00 15.00
AUPD Paul Davis 4.00 10.00
AUPM Paul Millsap 5.00 12.00
AUPP Paul Pierce 30.00 80.00
AUPR Pat Riley 25.00 60.00
AUQR Quentin Richardson 4.00 10.00
AURB Raja Bell F 5.00 12.00
AURF Randy Foye 5.00 12.00
AURH Ryan Hollins 4.00 10.00
AURM Rashad McCants 4.00 10.00
AURR Rajon Rondo 8.00 20.00
AURT Ronny Turiaf Ultra, F 5.00 12.00
AUSB Shannon Brown 4.00 10.00
AUSI James Singleton 4.00 10.00
AUSJ Solomon Jones Ultra, F 4.00 10.00
AUSM Craig Smith 4.00 10.00
AUSN Steve Nash 50.00 120.00
AUST DeShawn Stevenson 4.00 10.00
AUTA Tony Allen 4.00 10.00
AUTC Tyson Chandler 6.00 15.00
AUTF T.J. Ford 4.00 10.00
AUTM Tracy McGrady 100.00 250.00
AUTP Tony Parker F 30.00 80.00
AUTT Tyrus Thomas 4.00 10.00
AUWB Will Blalock 4.00 10.00
AUWI Deron Williams 5.00 12.00
AUYM Yao Ming 125.00 300.00

2007-08 Ultra SE Award Winners Jersey

PRINT RUN 199 SER.#'d SETS
*PATCH: 1.25X TO 3X BASE HI
PATCH PRINT RUN 25 SER.#'d SETS
AWAI Allen Iverson 8.00 20.00
AWAJ Antawn Jamison 2.50 6.00
AWAM Alonzo Mourning 5.00 12.00
AWAS Amare Stoudemire 3.00 8.00
AWBD Boris Diaw 2.50 6.00
AWBR Brandon Roy 4.00 10.00
AWBW Ben Wallace 4.00 10.00
AWCB Chauncey Billups 4.00 10.00
AWCW Chris Webber 4.00 10.00
AWDM Dikembe Mutombo 5.00 12.00
AWDN Dirk Nowitzki 8.00 20.00
AWDS Damon Stoudamire 3.00 8.00
AWEB Elton Brand 2.50 6.00
AWEO Emeka Okafor 2.50 6.00
AWGA Gilbert Arenas 3.00 8.00
AWGH Grant Hill 5.00 12.00
AWGP Gary Payton 5.00 12.00
AWJK Jason Kidd 5.00 12.00
AWJN Jameer Nelson 2.00 5.00
AWJO Jermaine O'Neal 3.00 8.00
AWKB Kobe Bryant 50.00 120.00
AWKG Kevin Garnett 8.00 20.00
AWLJ LeBron James 50.00 120.00
AWMC Marcus Camby 2.50 6.00
AWNR Nate Robinson 3.00 8.00
AWPG Pau Gasol 5.00 12.00
AWRA Ron Artest 3.00 8.00
AWSN Steve Nash 6.00 15.00
AWTD Tim Duncan 8.00 20.00
AWVC Vince Carter 6.00 15.00

2007-08 Ultra SE Call to the Hall

COMPLETE SET (10) 15.00 40.00
CH1 Kobe Bryant 6.00 15.00
CH2 LeBron James 6.00 15.00
CH3 Paul Pierce 1.25 3.00
CH4 Shaquille O'Neal 3.00 8.00
CH5 Kevin Garnett 2.00 5.00
CH6 Yao Ming 2.00 5.00
CH7 Michael Jordan 8.00 20.00
CH8 Gary Payton 1.25 3.00
CH9 Tim Duncan 2.00 5.00
CH10 Allen Iverson 2.00 5.00

2007-08 Ultra SE Call to the Hall Memorabilia

CHAI Allen Iverson 6.00 15.00
CHGP Gary Payton 4.00 10.00
CHKB Kobe Bryant 40.00 100.00
CHKG Kevin Garnett 6.00 15.00
CHLJ LeBron James 40.00 100.00
CHMJ Michael Jordan 100.00 250.00
CHPP Paul Pierce 4.00 10.00
CHSO Shaquille O'Neal 10.00 25.00
CHTD Tim Duncan 6.00 15.00
CHYM Yao Ming 6.00 15.00

2007-08 Ultra SE Court Masters

COMPLETE SET (15) 10.00 25.00
CM1 Steve Nash 2.00 5.00
CM2 Jason Williams 1.50 4.00
CM3 John Stockton 2.00 5.00
CM4 Gary Payton 1.50 4.00
CM5 Stephon Marbury 1.25 3.00
CM6 Damon Stoudamire 1.00 2.50
CM7 Jason Kidd 1.50 4.00
CM8 Deron Williams .75 2.00
CM9 Chris Paul 2.00 5.00
CM10 Baron Davis .75 2.00
CM11 Kevin Garnett 2.50 6.00
CM12 Chauncey Billups 1.25 3.00
CM13 Jamaal Tinsley .60 1.50
CM14 Grant Hill 1.50 4.00
CM15 Jarrett Jack .75 2.00

2007-08 Ultra SE Court Masters Memorabilia

CMBD Baron Davis 2.00 5.00
CMCB Chauncey Billups 3.00 8.00
CMCP Chris Paul 5.00 12.00
CMDS Damon Stoudamire 2.50 6.00
CMDW Deron Williams 2.00 5.00
CMGH Grant Hill 4.00 10.00
CMGP Gary Payton 4.00 10.00
CMJJ Jarrett Jack 2.00 5.00
CMJK Jason Kidd 4.00 10.00
CMJS John Stockton 5.00 12.00
CMJT Jamaal Tinsley 1.50 4.00
CMJW Jason Williams 4.00 10.00
CMKG Kevin Garnett 6.00 15.00
CMSM Stephon Marbury 3.00 8.00
CMSN Steve Nash 5.00 12.00

2007-08 Ultra SE Heir to the Throne Jersey

PRINT RUN 199 SER.#'d SETS
*PATCHES: 1.25X TO 3X BASE HI
PATCH PRINT RUN 25 SER.#'d SETS
HTAB Andrea Bargnani 2.00 5.00
HTAI Andre Iguodala 3.00 8.00
HTAJ Al Jefferson 2.00 5.00
HTAS Amare Stoudemire 3.00 8.00
HTBL Andray Blatche 2.00 5.00
HTBO Andrew Bogut 2.50 6.00
HTBR Brandon Roy 4.00 10.00
HTCA Carmelo Anthony 5.00 12.00
HTCB Caron Butler 2.50 6.00
HTCP Chris Paul 6.00 15.00
HTDH Dwight Howard 4.00 10.00
HTDW David West 2.50 6.00
HTEO Emeka Okafor 2.50 6.00
HTFE Raymond Felton 2.50 6.00
HTGW Gerald Wallace 2.50 6.00
HTHW Hakim Warrick 2.00 5.00
HTJC Josh Childress 2.00 5.00
HTJF Jordan Farmar 2.00 5.00
HTJH Josh Howard 2.50 6.00
HTJR J.J. Redick 3.00 8.00
HTJS J.R. Smith 3.00 8.00
HTKH Kirk Hinrich 3.00 8.00
HTLA LaMarcus Aldridge 3.00 8.00
HTLD Luol Deng 2.50 6.00
HTLH Luther Head 2.00 5.00
HTLJ LeBron James 8.00 20.00
HTMW Marvin Williams 2.00 5.00
HTPA Tony Parker 5.00 12.00
HTPD Paul Davis 2.00 5.00
HTQD Quincy Douby 2.00 5.00
HTRF Randy Foye 2.50 6.00
HTRG Rudy Gay 2.50 6.00
HTRJ Richard Jefferson 2.50 6.00
HTRM Rashad McCants 2.00 5.00
HTSB Shannon Brown 2.00 5.00
HTSJ Josh Smith 2.00 5.00
HTSM Sean May 2.00 5.00
HTTP Tayshaun Prince 3.00 8.00
HTTS Thabo Sefolosha 2.00 5.00
HTWI Deron Williams 2.50 6.00

2007-08 Ultra SE Jam City

JC1 Baron Davis .75 2.00
JC2 Clyde Drexler 1.50 4.00
JC3 Dee Brown .60 1.50
JC4 Dwight Howard 1.25 3.00
JC5 Desmond Mason .60 1.50
JC6 DeShawn Stevenson .60 1.50
JC7 Fred Jones .60 1.50
JC8 Gerald Green .75 2.00
JC9 Julius Erving 2.50 6.00
JC10 Michael Jordan 25.00 60.00
JC11 Jason Richardson 1.00 2.50
JC12 Josh Smith .60 1.50
JC13 Kobe Bryant 8.00 20.00
JC14 Larry Nance .75 2.00
JC15 Michael Finley 1.00 2.50
JC16 Michael Jordan 25.00 60.00
JC17 Nate Robinson 1.00 2.50
JC18 Tom Chambers 1.00 2.50
JC19 Tyrus Thomas .60 1.50
JC20 Vince Carter 2.00 5.00

2007-08 Ultra SE Jersey

PRINT RUN 50 SER.#'d SETS
UJAB Andrew Bogut 3.00 8.00
UJAJ Al Jefferson 2.50 6.00
UJAR Allan Ray 2.50 6.00
UJBJ Bobby Jones 4.00 10.00
UJCF Channing Frye 2.50 6.00
UJCM Corey Maggette 3.00 8.00
UJCP Chris Paul 8.00 20.00
UJCS Cedric Simmons 2.50 6.00
UJDS DeShawn Stevenson 2.50 6.00
UJGW Gerald Wallace 3.00 8.00
UJHA Hilton Armstrong 2.50 6.00
UJJC Jose Calderon 2.50 6.00
UJJO Jermaine O'Neal 4.00 10.00
UJJT Jamaal Tinsley 2.50 6.00
UJKB Kwame Brown 2.50 6.00
UJKM Kenyon Martin 3.00 8.00
UJLA LaMarcus Aldridge 4.00 10.00
UJLH Larry Hughes 3.00 8.00
UJLJ LeBron James 12.00 30.00
UJLW Luke Walton 3.00 8.00
UJMA Maurice Ager 2.50 6.00
UJMB Mike Bibby 4.00 10.00
UJMD Mike Dunleavy 2.50 6.00
UJMP Morris Peterson 2.50 6.00
UJQR Quentin Richardson 2.50 6.00
UJRA Ray Allen 6.00 15.00
UJRD Ricky Davis 2.50 6.00
UJRH Richard Hamilton 5.00 12.00
UJRW Rasheed Wallace 5.00 12.00
UJSD Samuel Dalembert 2.50 6.00
UJSF Steve Francis 3.00 8.00
UJSN Steve Novak 2.50 6.00
UJTP Tayshaun Prince 4.00 10.00
UJUH Udonis Haslem 2.50 6.00
UJWB Will Blalock 2.50 6.00
UJWS Wally Szczerbiak 3.00 8.00
UJZI Zydrunas Ilgauskas 3.00 8.00

2007-08 Ultra SE Mini Jerseys

1 LeBron James 60.00 150.00
2 Kobe Bryant 25.00 60.00
3 Allen Iverson 15.00 40.00
4 Shaquille O'Neal 12.00 30.00
5 Paul Pierce 8.00 20.00
6 Dirk Nowitzki 12.00 30.00
7 Tim Duncan 12.00 30.00
8 Kevin Garnett 12.00 30.00
9 Dwight Howard 8.00 20.00
10 Yao Ming 10.00 25.00
11 Steve Nash 8.00 20.00
12 Chris Bosh 6.00 15.00
13 Michael Jordan 75.00 200.00

2007-08 Ultra SE Mini Jerseys Autographs

13 Michael Jordan 1,500.00 3,000.00

2007-08 Ultra SE One on One Jersey

PRINT RUN 99 SER.#'d SETS
OOAH R.Allen/R.Hamilton 6.00 15.00
OOBA M.Bibby/G.Arenas 4.00 10.00
OOBB C.Boozer/S.Battier 3.00 8.00
OOBH E.Brand/G.Hill 6.00 15.00
OOBJ K.Bryant/L.James 200.00 500.00
OOCB C.Butler/C.Bosh 5.00 12.00
OOCC J.Collins/J.Collins 2.50 6.00
OOCM A.Jamison/S.May 3.00 8.00
OOGO B.Gordon/E.Okafor 3.00 8.00
OOGS P.Gasol/W.Szczerbiak 6.00 15.00
OOHC L.Head/B.Cook 2.50 6.00
OOHP K.Hinrich/P.Pierce 6.00 15.00
OOHW J.Howard/C.Webber 5.00 12.00
OOIW A.Iguodala/L.Walton 4.00 10.00
OOJC B.Jones/M.Collins 4.00 10.00
OOJJ M.Jordan/L.James 400.00 800.00
OOJR F.Jones/L.Ridnour 3.00 8.00
OOJW J.Magloire/A.Walker 4.00 10.00
OOKF J.Kapono/J.Farmar 2.50 6.00
OOMB Y.Ming/A.Bargnani 10.00 25.00
OOMD C.Maggette/L.Deng 3.00 8.00
OOMK D.Milicic/N.Krstic 2.50 6.00
OOML L.Bird/M.Johnson 15.00 40.00
OOMW J.Nelson/J.McInnis 2.50 6.00
OOOL L.Odom/S.Livingston 3.00 8.00
OOOM S.O'Neal/D.Mutombo 15.00 40.00
OORR Z.Randolph/J.Richardson 4.00 10.00
OOSR J.Smith/N.Robinson 4.00 10.00
OOWT J.Williams/J.Terry 6.00 15.00
OOWW B.Wallace/R.Wallace 5.00 12.00

2007-08 Ultra SE Rising Stars

COMPLETE SET (19) 15.00 40.00
RS1 Kevin Durant 12.00 30.00
RS2 Al Horford 2.50 6.00
RS3 Mike Conley Jr. 2.50 6.00
RS4 Jeff Green .75 2.00
RS5 Corey Brewer .75 2.00
RS6 Greg Oden 1.00 2.50
RS8 Brandan Wright .75 2.00
RS9 Joakim Noah 1.00 2.50
RS10 Spencer Hawes .60 1.50
RS11 Acie Law .60 1.50
RS12 Thaddeus Young 1.00 2.50
RS13 Julian Wright .60 1.50
RS14 Al Thornton .60 1.50
RS15 Rodney Stuckey .60 1.50
RS16 Nick Young 1.00 2.50
RS17 Sean Williams .60 1.50
RS18 Marco Belinelli .75 2.00
RS19 Javaris Crittenton .60 1.50
RS20 Jason Smith .60 1.50

2007-08 Ultra SE Scoring Kings

COMPLETE SET (20) 8.00 20.00
SK1 Carmelo Anthony 1.00 2.50
SK2 Gilbert Arenas .60 1.50
SK3 LeBron James 5.00 12.00
SK4 Mehmet Okur .40 1.00
SK5 Michael Redd .50 1.25
SK6 Joe Johnson .50 1.25
SK7 Ray Allen 1.00 2.50
SK8 Vince Carter 1.25 3.00
SK9 Tracy McGrady 1.00 2.50
SK10 Carlos Boozer .50 1.25
SK11 Kevin Martin .50 1.25
SK12 Ben Gordon .50 1.25
SK13 Elton Brand .50 1.25
SK14 Jermaine O'Neal .60 1.50
SK15 Josh Howard .50 1.25
SK16 Zach Randolph .60 1.50
SK17 Luol Deng .50 1.25
SK18 Ron Artest .60 1.50
SK19 Shawn Marion .60 1.50
SK20 Peja Stojakovic .50 1.25

2007-08 Ultra SE Scoring Kings Memorabilia

SKAR Ron Artest 2.50 6.00
SKBG Ben Gordon 2.00 5.00
SKCA Carmelo Anthony 4.00 10.00
SKCB Carlos Boozer 2.00 5.00
SKEB Elton Brand 2.00 5.00
SKGA Gilbert Arenas 2.50 6.00
SKJH Josh Howard 2.00 5.00
SKJJ Joe Johnson 2.00 5.00
SKJO Jermaine O'Neal 2.50 6.00
SKKM Kevin Martin 2.00 5.00
SKLD Luol Deng 2.00 5.00
SKLJ LeBron James 10.00 25.00
SKME Mehmet Okur 1.50 4.00
SKMR Michael Redd 2.00 5.00
SKPS Peja Stojakovic 2.00 5.00
SKRA Ray Allen 4.00 10.00
SKSM Shawn Marion 2.50 6.00
SKTM Tracy McGrady 4.00 10.00
SKVC Vince Carter 5.00 12.00
SKZR Zach Randolph 2.50 6.00

2007-08 Ultra SE Season Crowns

COMPLETE SET (25) 20.00 40.00
SC1 Tim Duncan 1.50 4.00
SC2 Michael Jordan 6.00 15.00
SC3 Chauncey Billups .75 2.00
SC4 Shaquille O'Neal 2.50 6.00
SC5 Kareem Abdul-Jabbar 2.00 5.00
SC6 Hakeem Olajuwon 1.25 3.00
SC7 Alonzo Mourning 1.00 2.50
SC8 Horace Grant .60 1.50
SC9 Tony Parker 1.00 2.50
SC10 Manu Ginobili 1.25 3.00
SC11 David Robinson 1.25 3.00
SC12 Richard Hamilton .75 2.00
SC13 Tayshaun Prince .60 1.50
SC14 Clyde Drexler 1.00 2.50
SC15 Dennis Rodman 1.50 4.00
SC16 Larry Bird 2.50 6.00
SC17 Julius Erving 1.50 4.00
SC18 Magic Johnson 2.50 6.00
SC19 Sean Elliott .50 1.25
SC20 Jason Williams 1.00 2.50
SC21 Ben Wallace .75 2.00
SC22 Michael Jordan 6.00 15.00
SC23 Bruce Bowen .40 1.00
SC24 Devean George .40 1.00
SC25 Bill Laimbeer .50 1.25

2007-08 Ultra SE Season Crowns Memorabilia

SC1 Tim Duncan 6.00 15.00
SC2 Michael Jordan 60.00 150.00
SC3 Chauncey Billups 3.00 8.00
SC4 Shaquille O'Neal 10.00 25.00
SC5 Kareem Abdul-Jabbar 8.00 20.00
SC6 Hakeem Olajuwon 5.00 12.00
SC7 Alonzo Mourning 4.00 10.00
SC8 Horace Grant 2.50 6.00
SC9 Tony Parker 4.00 10.00
SC10 Manu Ginobili 5.00 12.00
SC11 David Robinson 5.00 12.00
SC12 Richard Hamilton 3.00 8.00
SC13 Tayshaun Prince 2.50 6.00
SC14 Clyde Drexler 4.00 10.00
SC15 Dennis Rodman 6.00 15.00
SC16 Larry Bird 10.00 25.00
SC17 Julius Erving 6.00 15.00
SC18 Magic Johnson 10.00 25.00
SC19 Sean Elliott 2.00 5.00
SC20 Jason Williams 4.00 10.00
SC21 Ben Wallace 3.00 8.00
SC22 Michael Jordan 60.00 150.00
SC23 Bruce Bowen 1.50 4.00
SC24 Devean George 1.50 4.00
SC25 Bill Laimbeer 2.00 5.00

2007-08 Ultra SE Signature Class

PRINT RUN 50 SER.#'d SETS
SCAA Arron Afflalo 5.00 12.00
SCAB Aaron Brooks 5.00 12.00
SCAG Aaron Gray 4.00 10.00
SCAH Al Horford 15.00 40.00
SCAL Acie Law 4.00 10.00
SCAT Al Thornton 4.00 10.00
SCCB Corey Brewer 5.00 12.00
SCCL Carl Landry 4.00 10.00
SCDA Jermareo Davidson 4.00 10.00
SCDB Derrick Byars 4.00 10.00
SCDC Daequan Cook 5.00 12.00
SCDJ D.J. Strawberry 4.00 10.00
SCDN Demetris Nichols 4.00 10.00
SCGD Glen Davis 5.00 12.00
SCGP Gabe Pruitt 4.00 10.00
SCHH Herbert Hill 4.00 10.00
SCJC Javaris Crittenton 4.00 10.00
SCJD Jared Dudley 5.00 12.00
SCJG Jeff Green 5.00 12.00
SCJJ Jared Jordan 4.00 10.00
SCJM Josh McRoberts 4.00 10.00
SCJN Joakim Noah 6.00 15.00
SCJO JamesOn Curry 4.00 10.00
SCJS Jason Smith 4.00 10.00
SCJW Julian Wright 4.00 10.00
SCKD Kevin Durant 200.00 500.00
SCMB Marco Belinelli 5.00 12.00
SCMC Mike Conley Jr. 15.00 40.00
SCMW Marcus Williams 4.00 10.00
SCNF Nick Fazekas 4.00 10.00
SCPK Petteri Koponen 5.00 12.00
SCRS Rodney Stuckey 4.00 10.00
SCRT Reyshawn Terry 4.00 10.00
SCSB Stanko Barac 6.00 15.00
SCSH Spencer Hawes 4.00 10.00
SCSL Stephane Lasme 4.00 10.00
SCSM Sammy Mejia 4.00 10.00
SCSW Sean Williams 4.00 10.00
SCTG Taurean Green 4.00 10.00
SCTU Alando Tucker 4.00 10.00
SCWC Wilson Chandler 5.00 12.00

2007-08 Ultra SE Snap Shots

COMPLETE SET (40) 30.00 60.00
SS1 Marvin Williams .50 1.25
SS2 Larry Bird 3.00 8.00
SS3 John Havlicek 1.50 4.00
SS4 Bill Russell 2.50 6.00
SS5 Adam Morrison .50 1.25
SS6 Raymond Felton .60 1.50
SS7 Michael Jordan 8.00 20.00
SS8 Ben Gordon .60 1.50
SS9 Dennis Rodman 2.00 5.00
SS10 LeBron James 6.00 15.00
SS11 Dirk Nowitzki 2.00 5.00
SS12 Carmelo Anthony 1.25 3.00
SS13 Allen Iverson 2.00 5.00
SS14 Tracy McGrady 1.25 3.00
SS15 Stephon Marbury 1.00 2.50
SS16 Clyde Drexler 1.25 3.00
SS17 Hakeem Olajuwon 1.50 4.00
SS18 Kobe Bryant 6.00 15.00
SS19 Magic Johnson 3.00 8.00
SS20 Kareem Abdul-Jabbar 2.50 6.00
SS21 Shaquille O'Neal 3.00 8.00
SS22 Dwyane Wade 1.50 4.00
SS23 Andrew Bogut .60 1.50
SS24 Kevin Garnett 2.00 5.00
SS25 Peja Stojakovic .60 1.50
SS26 Jason Kidd 1.25 3.00
SS27 Chris Paul 1.50 4.00
SS28 Dwight Howard 1.00 2.50
SS29 J.J. Redick .75 2.00
SS30 Julius Erving 2.00 5.00
SS31 Andre Iguodala .75 2.00
SS32 Steve Nash 1.50 4.00
SS33 LaMarcus Aldridge .75 2.00
SS34 Brandon Roy 1.00 2.50
SS35 Paul Pierce 1.25 3.00
SS36 David Robinson 1.50 4.00
SS37 Lenny Wilkens .75 2.00
SS38 Kevin Martin .60 1.50
SS39 Lamar Odom .60 1.50
SS40 John Stockton 1.50 4.00

2007-08 Ultra SE Stars

COMPLETE SET (30) 10.00 25.00
US1 LeBron James 4.00 10.00
US2 Kevin Martin .40 1.00
US3 Kobe Bryant 4.00 10.00
US4 Jason Richardson .50 1.25
US5 Alonzo Mourning .75 2.00
US6 Brad Miller .40 1.00
US7 Carlos Boozer .40 1.00
US8 Amare Stoudemire .50 1.25
US9 Andrei Kirilenko .40 1.00
US10 Baron Davis .40 1.00
US11 Corey Maggette .40 1.00
US12 Brandon Roy .60 1.50
US13 Lamar Odom .40 1.00
US14 Larry Hughes .40 1.00
US15 Chris Bosh .60 1.50
US16 Tracy McGrady .75 2.00
US17 Yao Ming 1.25 3.00
US18 Richard Jefferson .40 1.00
US19 Andrea Bargnani .30 .75
US20 Jordan Farmar .30 .75
US21 Raymond Felton .40 1.00
US22 Drew Gooden .40 1.00
US23 Dirk Nowitzki 1.25 3.00
US24 Pau Gasol .75 2.00
US25 Mike Bibby .50 1.25
US26 Zach Randolph .50 1.25
US27 Michael Redd .40 1.00
US28 Marvin Williams .30 .75
US29 Deron Williams .40 1.00
US30 Antoine Walker .50 1.25

2007-08 Ultra SE Stars Memorabilia

USAB Andrea Bargnani 1.50 4.00
USAK Andrei Kirilenko 2.00 5.00
USAM Alonzo Mourning 4.00 10.00
USAS Amare Stoudemire 2.50 6.00
USAW Antoine Walker 2.50 6.00
USBD Baron Davis 2.00 5.00
USBM Brad Miller 2.00 5.00
USBO Chris Bosh 3.00 8.00
USBR Brandon Roy 3.00 8.00
USCB Carlos Boozer 2.00 5.00
USCM Corey Maggette 2.00 5.00
USDG Drew Gooden 2.00 5.00
USDN Dirk Nowitzki 6.00 15.00
USDW Deron Williams 2.00 5.00
USJF Jordan Farmar 1.50 4.00
USJR Jason Richardson 2.50 6.00
USKB Kobe Bryant 40.00 100.00
USKM Kevin Martin 2.00 5.00
USLH Larry Hughes 2.00 5.00
USLJ LeBron James 12.00 30.00
USLO Lamar Odom 2.00 5.00
USMB Mike Bibby 2.50 6.00
USMR Michael Redd 2.00 5.00
USMW Marvin Williams 1.50 4.00
USPG Pau Gasol 4.00 10.00
USRF Raymond Felton 2.00 5.00
USRJ Richard Jefferson 2.00 5.00
USTM Tracy McGrady 4.00 10.00
USYM Yao Ming 6.00 15.00
USZR Zach Randolph 2.50 6.00

1992-93 Ultra Jam Session Cassette Insert

1 David Robinson
Dikembe Mutombo
Otis Thorpe
Hakeem Olajuwon
Shawn Kemp 1.25 3.00

1999 Ultra WNBA

COMPLETE SET (125) 40.00 100.00
COMPLETE SET w/o SP (100) 10.00 25.00
CARDS 101-125: STATED ODDS 1:2 H/R
SUBSET CARDS SAME VALUE OF BASE CARDS
1 Sheryl Swoopes 1.50 4.00
2 Christy Smith .25 .60
3 Nikki McCray .75 2.00
4 Coquese Washington RC .50 1.25
5 Vickie Johnson .40 1.00
6 Toni Foster .40 1.00
7 Allison Feaster RC .60 1.50
8 Penny Toler .40 1.00
9 Brandy Reed RC .75 2.00
10 Yolanda Moore .25 .60
11 Lisa Leslie 1.25 3.00
12 Kisha Ford .25 .60
13 Merlakia Jones .40 1.00
14 Umeki Webb .25 .60
15 Tora Suber .40 1.00
16 Octavia Blue RC .25 .60
17 Bridget Pettis .25 .60
18 LaTonya Johnson RC .40 1.00
19 A.Santos de Oliveria RC .40 1.00
20 Tia Paschal RC .25 .60
21 Jennifer Gillom .60 1.50
22 Wanda Guyton .25 .60
23 Franthea Price RC .25 .60
24 Andrea Kuklova .25 .60
25 Vicky Bullett .40 1.00
26 Dena Head .25 .60
27 Isabelle Fijalkowski .25 .60
28 Michelle Edwards .50 1.25
29 Pamela McGee .40 1.00
30 Elisabeth Cebrian RC .25 .60
31 Olympia Scott-Richardson .25 .60
32 Murriel Page .40 1.00
33 Korie Hlede RC .75 2.00
34 Andrea Stinson .50 1.25
35 Kristie Harrower RC .40 1.00
36 Kym Hampton .40 1.00
37 Gergana Branzova RC .25 .60
38 Teresa Weatherspoon 1.00 2.50
39 Rebecca Lobo .75 2.00
40 Michele Timms .75 2.00
41 Tamecka Dixon .40 1.00
42 Tina Thompson 1.00 2.50
43 Janice Braxton .25 .60
44 Elena Baranova .60 1.50
45 Adrienne Johnson RC .75 2.00
46 Adia Barnes RC .40 1.00
47 Elaine Powell RC .40 1.00
48 Lady Hardmon .25 .60
49 Kim Perrot .75 2.00
50 Marlies Askamp RC .40 1.00
51 Deborah Carter .25 .60
52 Sandy Brondello RC 1.00 2.50
53 Heidi Burge .25 .60
54 Janeth Arcain .25 .60
55 Rushia Brown .25 .60
56 Suzie McConnell-Serio .60 1.50
57 Penny Moore .40 1.00
58 Margo Dydek RC 1.00 2.50
59 Angie Potthoff RC .25 .60
60 Monica Lamb RC .40 1.00
61 Jamila Wideman .40 1.00
62 Ticha Penicheiro RC 1.25 3.00
63 Andrea Congreaves .25 .60
64 Rachael Sporn RC .40 1.00
65 Chantel Tremitiere .25 .60
66 Carla McGhee RC .40 1.00
67 Kim Williams .25 .60
68 Tangela Smith .25 .60
69 Quacy Barnes .25 .60
70 Sue Wicks .40 1.00
71 Tracy Reid RC .50 1.25
72 Linda Burgess .25 .60
73 Razija Brcaninovic RC .40 1.00
74 Sharon Manning .25 .60
75 Tammy Jackson .25 .60
76 Rita Williams .30 .75
77 Carla Porter RC .40 1.00
78 Michelle Griffiths RC .50 1.25
79 Eva Nemcova .40 1.00
80 Sophia Witherspoon .40 1.00
81 Sonja Tate RC .40 1.00
82 Cynthia Cooper 1.50 4.00
83 Wendy Palmer .60 1.50
84 Ruthie Bolton-Holifield .75 2.00
85 Tammi Reiss .40 1.00
86 Katrina Colleton RC .25 .60
87 Cindy Brown .50 1.25
88 Latasha Byears .40 1.00
89 Mwadi Mabika .25 .60
90 Rhonda Mapp .30 .75
91 Tina Thompson AW 1.00 2.50
92 Sheryl Swoopes AW 1.50 4.00
93 Jennifer Gillom AW .60 1.50
94 Cynthia Cooper AW 1.50 4.00
95 Suzie McConnell Serio AW .60 1.50
96 Cindy Brown AW .50 1.25
97 Eva Nemcova AW .40 1.00
98 Lisa Leslie AW 1.25 3.00
99 Andrea Stinson AW .50 1.25
100 Teresa Weatherspoon AW 1.00 2.50
101 Dawn Staley RC 8.00 20.00
102 Chamique Holdsclaw RC 4.00 10.00
103 Kristin Folkl RC 1.50 4.00
104 Nykesha Sales RC 2.00 5.00
105 Natalie Williams RC 2.00 5.00
106 Yolanda Griffith RC 4.00 10.00
107 Crystal Robinson RC 1.25 3.00
108 Edna Campbell RC 1.50 4.00
109 Tari Phillips RC 1.25 3.00
110 Tonya Edwards RC 1.00 2.50
111 Debbie Black RC 1.50 4.00
112 Kate Starbird RC 1.50 4.00
113 Adrienne Goodson RC 1.25 3.00
114 Sheri Sam RC 1.00 2.50
115 DeLisha Milton RC 1.00 2.50
116 Shannon Johnson RC 1.00 2.50
117 Katie Smith RC 2.50 6.00
118 Kara Wolters RC 1.50 4.00
119 Jennifer Azzi RC 2.50 6.00
120 Michele VanGorp RC 1.25 3.00
121 Stephanie White-McCarty RC 1.50 4.00
122 Ukari Figgs RC 1.25 3.00
123 Val Whiting RC 1.00 2.50
124 Mery Andrade RC 1.00 2.50
125 Charlotte Smith RC 1.00 2.50

1999 Ultra WNBA Gold Medallion

COMPLETE SET (125) 75.00 200.00
*GOLD 1-100: 1.25X TO 3X BASE HI
ONE PER HOBBY PACK

1999 Ultra WNBA Platinum Medallion

*PLATINUM 1-100: 15X TO 40X HI COL.
*PLATINUM 101-125: 6X TO 15X HI COL.
1-100: PRINT RUN 99 SERIAL #'d SETS
101-125: PRINT RUN 66 SERIAL #'d SETS
SUBSET CARDS SAME VALUE

1999 Ultra WNBA Fresh Ink

COMPLETE SET (13) 175.00 350.00
STATED PRINT RUN 400 SERIAL #'d SETS
1 Elena Baranova 12.00 30.00
2 Cynthia Cooper 30.00 80.00
3 Kristin Folkl 10.00 25.00
4 Lisa Leslie 25.00 60.00
5 Suzie McConnell-Serio 12.00 30.00
6 Nikki McCray 15.00 40.00
7 Nykesha Sales 12.00 30.00
8 Dawn Staley 30.00 80.00
9 Andrea Stinson 10.00 25.00
10 Sheryl Swoopes 30.00 80.00
11 Michele Timms 15.00 40.00
12 Penny Toler 8.00 20.00
13 Teresa Weatherspoon 20.00 50.00

1999 Ultra WNBA Rock Talk

COMPLETE SET (10) 15.00 40.00
1 Eva Nemcova 1.25 3.00
2 Cynthia Cooper 5.00 12.00
3 Ruthie Bolton-Holifield 2.50 6.00
4 Michele Timms 2.50 6.00
5 Jennifer Gillom 2.00 5.00
6 Cindy Brown 1.50 4.00
7 Lisa Leslie 4.00 10.00
8 Andrea Stinson 1.50 4.00
9 Teresa Weatherspoon 3.00 8.00
10 Rebecca Lobo 2.50 6.00

1999 Ultra WNBA WNBAttitude

COMPLETE SET (10) 6.00 15.00
1 Lisa Leslie 1.50 4.00
2 Cynthia Cooper 2.00 5.00
3 Ruthie Bolton-Holifield 1.00 2.50
4 Rebecca Lobo 1.00 2.50
5 Sheryl Swoopes 2.00 5.00
6 Nikki McCray 1.00 2.50
7 Cindy Brown .60 1.50
8 Jennifer Gillom .75 2.00
9 Wendy Palmer .75 2.00
10 Michele Timms 1.00 2.50

1999 Ultra WNBA World Premiere

COMPLETE SET (10) 8.00 20.00
1 Chamique Holdsclaw 2.50 6.00
2 Dawn Staley 2.50 6.00
3 Nykesha Sales 1.25 3.00
4 Kristin Folkl 1.00 2.50

5 Natalie Williams 1.25 3.00
6 Yolanda Griffith 2.50 6.00
7 Crystal Robinson .75 2.00
8 Edna Campbell 1.00 2.50
9 DeLisha Milton .60 1.50
10 Debbie Black 1.00 2.50

2000 Ultra WNBA Promo

1 Cynthia Cooper 1.50 4.00

2000 Ultra WNBA

COMPLETE SET (150) 35.00 70.00
COMPLETE SET w/o SP (125) 15.00 40.00
RC SUBSET: STATED ODDS 1:2
1 Cynthia Cooper 1.50 4.00
2 Chamique Holdsclaw 1.50 4.00
3 Lisa Leslie 1.25 3.00
4 Anna DeForge RC .25 .60
5 Stephanie McCarty .50 1.25
6 Katrina Colleton .25 .60
7 Clarisse Machanguana RC .25 .60
8 Adrienne Goodson .25 .60
9 Charlotte Smith .25 .60
10 DeLisha Milton .25 .60
11 Janeth Arcain .25 .60
12 Donna Harrington RC .25 .60
13 Michele Timms .75 2.00
14 Charmin Smith RC .60 1.50
15 Tricia Bader RC .25 .60
16 Vickie Johnson .40 1.00
17 Monica Lamb .25 .60
18 Dawn Staley .60 1.50
19 Ruthie Bolton-Holifield .75 2.00
20 Jennifer Azzi .75 2.00
21 Becky Hammon RC 12.00 30.00
22 Latasha Byears .40 1.00
23 Lisa Harrison RC .60 1.50
24 Jennifer Rizzotti RC 1.25 3.00
25 Yolanda Griffith .75 2.00
26 Tracy Henderson RC .25 .60
27 Sophia Witherspoon .40 1.00
28 Sheryl Swoopes 1.50 4.00
29 Korie Hlede .40 1.00
30 Shannon Johnson .25 .60
31 Chasity Melvin RC .25 .60
32 Tamika Whitmore RC .40 1.00
33 Tina Thompson .75 2.00
34 Kedra Holland-Corn RC .40 1.00
35 Markita Aldridge RC .25 .60
36 Dalma Ivanyi RC .25 .60
37 Ticha Penicheiro .60 1.50
38 Quacy Barnes .25 .60
39 Ukari Figgs .25 .60
40 Andrea Lloyd Curry RC .40 1.00
41 Tammy Jackson .25 .60
42 Nikki McCray .60 1.50
43 Kate Starbird .40 1.00
44 Andrea Nagy RC .60 1.50
45 Bridget Pettis .25 .60
46 Eva Nemcova .40 1.00
47 Tangela Smith .25 .60
48 Astou Ndiaye-Diatta RC .75 2.00
49 Tamecka Dixon .40 1.00
50 Taj McWilliams RC .40 1.00
51 Kristin Folkl .40 1.00
52 Amanda Wilson RC .75 2.00
53 Chantel Tremitiere .25 .60
54 Dominique Canty RC .75 2.00
55 Allison Feaster .30 .75
56 Angie Potthoff .25 .60
57 Nykesha Sales .40 1.00
58 Rhonda Mapp .30 .75
59 Murriel Page .30 .75
60 Maria Stepanova .25 .60
61 Katie Smith .75 2.00
62 Michelle Edwards .50 1.25
63 Venus Lacy RC .25 .60
64 Adrienne Johnson .40 1.00
65 Rita Williams .30 .75
66 Andrea Stinson .50 1.25
67 La'Keshia Frett RC .40 1.00
68 Jennifer Gillom .60 1.50
69 LaTonya Johnson .25 .60
70 Joy Holmes-Harris RC .25 .60
71 Rushia Brown .25 .60
72 Michelle Campbell RC .25 .60
73 Angie Braziel RC .50 1.25
74 Crystal Robinson .25 .60
75 Alicia Thompson .25 .60
76 Suzie McConnell-Serio .50 1.25
77 Tanja Kostic RC .25 .60
78 Amaya Valdemoro RC .40 1.00
79 Sue Wicks .40 1.00
80 Sonja Tate .25 .60
81 Natalie Williams .50 1.25
82 Mery Andrade .25 .60
83 Tracy Reid .40 1.00
84 Olympia Scott-Richardson .25 .60
85 Rebecca Lobo .75 2.00
86 Margo Dydek .50 1.25
87 Sonja Henning RC .40 1.00
88 Vicky Bullett .40 1.00
89 Mwadi Mabika .25 .60
90 Linda Burgess .25 .60
91 Merlakia Jones .40 1.00
92 Umeki Webb .25 .60
93 Niesa Johnson RC .25 .60
94 Texlan Quinney RC .25 .60
95 Teresa Weatherspoon 1.00 2.50
96 Wendy Palmer .60 1.50
97 Brandy Reed .40 1.00
98 Oksana Zakaluzhnaya RC .25 .60
99 Sharon Manning .25 .60
100 Kara Wolters .30 .75
101 Keisha Anderson RC .40 1.00
102 Edna Campbell .30 .75
103 DeMya Walker RC .25 .60
104 Michele VanGorp .30 .75
105 Coquese Washington .25 .60
106 Marlies Askamp .25 .60
107 Michelle Marciniak RC .60 1.50
108 Angela Aycock RC .40 1.00
109 Tari Phillips .25 .60
110 Sylvia Crawley RC .40 1.00
111 Tonya Edwards .25 .60
112 Monica Maxwell RC .25 .60
113 Beth Cunningham RC .25 .60
114 Debbie Black .40 1.00
115 Shalonda Enis RC .25 .60
116 Naomi Mulitauaopele RC .40 1.00
117 Jamila Wideman .40 1.00
118 Shanele Stires RC .40 1.00
119 Alisa Burras RC .40 1.00
120 Gordana Grubin RC .25 .60
121 Elaine Powell .25 .60
122 Tausha Mills RC .40 1.00
123 Katy Steding RC .25 .60
124 Jannon Roland RC .25 .60
125 Jessie Hicks .25 .60
126 Ann Wauters RC 1.00 2.50
127 Edwina Brown RC 1.00 2.50
128 Grace Daley RC 1.00 2.50
129 Helen Darling RC 1.00 2.50
130 Summer Erb RC 1.00 2.50
131 Kamila Vodichkova RC 1.00 2.50
132 Tamicha Jackson RC 1.00 2.50
133 Betty Lennox RC 4.00 10.00
134 Maylana Martin RC 1.00 2.50
135 Lynn Pride RC 1.00 2.50
136 Paige Sauer RC 1.00 2.50
137 Madinah Slaise RC 1.00 2.50
138 Stacey Thomas RC 1.00 2.50
139 Cintia Dos Santos RC 1.00 2.50
140 Milena Flores RC 1.00 2.50
141 Rhonda Banchero RC 1.00 2.50
142 Jameka Jones RC 1.00 2.50
143 Jessica Bibby RC 1.00 2.50
144 Adrain Williams RC 1.00 2.50
145 Olga Firsova RC 1.00 2.50
146 Usha Gilmore RC 1.00 2.50
147 Shantia Owens RC 1.00 2.50
148 Jurgita Streimikyte RC 1.00 2.50
149 Katrina Hibbert RC 1.00 2.50
150 Tonya Washington RC 1.00 2.50

2000 Ultra WNBA Gold Medallion

COMPLETE SET (150) 80.00 200.00
*GOLD 1-125: .75X TO 2X BASE CARD HI
*GOLD 126-150: 1.25X TO 3X BASE HI
GOLD 126-150: STATED ODDS 1:24

2000 Ultra WNBA Platinum Medallion

*PLAT 1-125: 12X TO 30X BASE CARD HI
*PLAT 126-150: 8X TO 20X HI COL.
1-125: PRINT RUN 50 SERIAL #'d SETS
126-150: PRINT RUN 25 SERIAL #'d SETS
21 Becky Hammon 500.00 1,000.00

2000 Ultra WNBA Feel the Game

STATED ODDS 1:144
1 Debbie Black 10.00 25.00
2 Ruthie Bolton-Holifield 20.00 50.00
3 Cynthia Cooper 15.00 40.00
3A C.Cooper AU/14 400.00 600.00
4 Tonya Edwards 6.00 15.00
5 Jennifer Gillom 15.00 40.00
6 Yolanda Griffith 20.00 50.00
7 Kedra Holland-Corn 10.00 25.00
8 Lisa Leslie 30.00 80.00
9 Suzie McConnell-Serio 12.00 30.00
10 Taj McWilliams 10.00 25.00
11 DeLisha Milton 6.00 15.00
12 Ticha Penicheiro 15.00 40.00
13 Dawn Staley 15.00 40.00
14 Kate Starbird 12.00 30.00
15 Sheryl Swoopes 40.00 100.00
15A S.Swoopes AU/22 300.00 500.00
16 Natalie Williams 12.00 30.00

2000 Ultra WNBA Feminine Adrenaline

COMPLETE SET (10) 6.00 15.00
1 Nikki McCray 1.00 2.50
2 Ticha Penicheiro 1.00 2.50
3 Teresa Weatherspoon 1.50 4.00
4 Jennifer Azzi 1.25 3.00
5 Lisa Leslie 2.00 5.00
6 Sheryl Swoopes 2.50 6.00
7 Tina Thompson 1.25 3.00
8 Jennifer Gillom 1.00 2.50
9 Suzie McConnell-Serio .75 2.00
10 Dawn Staley 1.00 2.50

2000 Ultra WNBA Fresh Ink

COMPLETE SET (18) 75.00 150.00
STATED ODDS 1:72
NNO CARDS LISTED BELOW ALPHABETICALLY
*GOLD: 1.25X TO 3X BASE HI
GOLD PRINT RUN 50 SER.#'d SETS
1 Debbie Black 4.00 10.00
2 Ruthie Bolton-Holifield 8.00 20.00
3 Cynthia Cooper 15.00 40.00
4 Tonya Edwards 2.50 6.00
5 Jennifer Gillom 6.00 15.00
6 Yolanda Griffith 8.00 20.00
7 Vickie Johnson 4.00 10.00
8 Carolyn Jones-Young 4.00 10.00
9 Lisa Leslie 12.00 30.00
10 Suzie McConnell-Serio 5.00 12.00
11 DeLisha Milton 2.50 6.00
12 Eva Nemcova 4.00 10.00
13 Ticha Penicheiro 6.00 15.00
14 Nykesha Sales 4.00 10.00
15 Dawn Staley 20.00 50.00
16 Sheryl Swoopes 15.00 40.00
17 T.Weatherspoon/500 10.00 25.00
18 Natalie Williams 5.00 12.00

2000 Ultra WNBA Trophy Case

COMPLETE SET (10) 15.00 40.00
1 Sheryl Swoopes 4.00 10.00
2 Natalie Williams 1.25 3.00
3 Yolanda Griffith 2.00 5.00
4 Cynthia Cooper 4.00 10.00
5 Ticha Penicheiro 1.50 4.00
6 Chamique Holdsclaw 4.00 10.00
7 Tina Thompson 2.00 5.00
8 Lisa Leslie 3.00 8.00
9 Teresa Weatherspoon 2.50 6.00
10 Shannon Johnson .60 1.50

2000 Ultra WNBA WNBAttitude

COMPLETE SET (10) 8.00 20.00
1 Andrea Stinson 1.00 2.50
2 Eva Nemcova .75 2.00
3 Wendy Palmer 1.25 3.00
4 Shannon Johnson .50 1.25
5 Jennifer Gillom 1.25 3.00
6 Yolanda Griffith 1.50 4.00
7 Natalie Williams 1.00 2.50
8 Chamique Holdsclaw 3.00 8.00
9 Cynthia Cooper 3.00 8.00
10 Vickie Johnson .75 2.00

2001 Ultra WNBA

COMPLETE SET (150) 100.00 250.00
RC SUBSET STATED ODDS 1:2
1 Betty Lennox 1.00 2.50
2 Ukari Figgs .30 .75
3 Tangela Smith .30 .75
4 Sue Wicks .50 1.25
5 Marla Brumfield RC .30 .75
6 Maria Stepanova .30 .75
7 Murriel Page .40 1.00
8 Michele Timms 1.00 2.50
9 Janeth Arcain .30 .75
10 Lisa Harrison .50 1.25
11 Tausha Mills .30 .75
12 Sheri Sam .30 .75
13 Sonja Henning .30 .75
14 Adrienne Johnson .50 1.25
15 Mwadi Mabika .30 .75
16 Chasity Melvin .30 .75
17 Allison Feaster .40 1.00
18 Monica Maxwell .30 .75
19 Katie Smith 1.00 2.50
20 Stacey Thomas .30 .75
21 Robin Threatt-Elliott RC .30 .75
22 Jennifer Azzi 1.00 2.50
23 Shannon Johnson .30 .75
24 Rhonda Mapp .40 1.00
25 Eva Nemcova .50 1.25
26 Edwina Brown .40 1.00
27 Margo Dydek .50 1.25
28 Ann Wauters .40 1.00
29 Nicky McCrimmon RC .30 .75
30 Dominique Canty .50 1.25
31 Adrienne Goodson .30 .75
32 Taj McWilliams-Franklin .30 .75
33 DeLisha Milton .30 .75
34 Mery Andrade .30 .75
35 Yolanda Griffith 1.00 2.50
36 Tari Phillips .30 .75
37 Rita Williams .40 1.00
38 Marlies Askamp .30 .75
39 Korie Hlede .50 1.25
40 Tamicha Jackson .30 .75
41 Elaine Powell .30 .75
42 Elena Baranova .75 2.00
43 Astou Ndiaye-Diatta .50 1.25
44 Nykesha Sales .50 1.25
45 Natalie Williams .60 1.50
46 Debbie Black .50 1.25
47 Vicky Bullett .50 1.25
48 Michelle Cleary RC .30 .75
49 Wendy Palmer .75 2.00
50 Tully Bevilaqua RC .40 1.00
51 Helen Darling .40 1.00
52 Katy Steding .30 .75
53 Sheryl Swoopes 2.00 5.00
54 Kristin Folkl .50 1.25
55 Lady Hardmon .30 .75
56 Jennifer Rizzotti .75 2.00
57 Adrain Williams .30 .75
58 Tricia Bader Binford .30 .75
59 Kedra Holland-Corn .30 .75
60 Crystal Robinson .30 .75
61 Kara Wolters .30 .75
62 Rushia Brown .30 .75
63 Tamecka Dixon .50 1.25
64 Ticha Penicheiro .75 2.00
65 Teresa Weatherspoon 1.25 3.00
66 Edna Campbell .40 1.00
67 Sylvia Crawley .30 .75
68 Shalonda Enis .30 .75
69 Andrea Lloyd-Curry .30 .75
70 Tina Thompson 1.00 2.50
71 Michelle Edwards .60 1.50
72 Stephanie McCarty .60 1.50
73 Shantia Owens .30 .75
74 Shanele Stires .30 .75
75 DeMya Walker .30 .75
76 Quacy Barnes .30 .75
77 Cintia Dos Santos .30 .75
78 Merlakia Jones .50 1.25
79 Lisa Leslie 1.50 4.00
80 Grace Daley .30 .75
81 Jamie Redd RC .30 .75
82 Charlotte Smith .30 .75
83 Jurgita Streimikyte .30 .75
84 Sophia Witherspoon .50 1.25
85 Ruthie Bolton-Holifield 1.00 2.50
86 Vickie Johnson .50 1.25
87 Andrea Stinson .60 1.50
88 Texlan Quinney .30 .75
89 Tammy Jackson .30 .75
90 Andrea Nagy .50 1.25
91 Brandy Reed .50 1.25
92 Umeki Webb .30 .75
93 Andrea Garner RC .30 .75
94 Maylana Martin .40 1.00
95 Vanessa Nygaard RC .30 .75
96 Kamila Vodichkova .30 .75
97 Coquese Washington .30 .75
98 Jennifer Gillom .75 2.00
99 Nikki McCray .75 2.00
100 Tracy Reid .50 1.25
101 Elena Tornikidou RC .30 .75
102 Becky Hammon 6.00 15.00
103 Dawn Staley .75 2.00
104 Alicia Thompson .30 .75
105 Tiffany Travis RC .50 1.25
106 Sandy Brondello .75 2.00
107 Tonya Edwards .30 .75
108 Chamique Holdsclaw 2.00 5.00
109 Olympia Scott-Richardson .30 .75
110 Anne Donovan CO .75 2.00
111 Brian Agler CO .75 2.00
112 Lin Dunn CO .75 2.00
113 Van Chancellor CO .75 2.00
114 Nell Fortner CO .75 2.00
115 Michael Cooper CO .75 2.00
116 Ron Rothstein CO .75 2.00
117 Richie Adubato CO .75 2.00
118 Cynthia Cooper CO 1.50 4.00
119 Linda Hargrove CO .75 2.00
120 Fred Williams CO .75 2.00
121 Dan Hughes CO .75 2.00
122 Carolyn Peck CO .75 2.00
123 Sonny Allen CO .75 2.00
124 Brooke Wyckoff RC 6.00 15.00
125 Jackie Stiles RC 40.00 100.00
126 Svetlana Abrosimova RC 2.50 6.00
127 Tamika Catchings RC 40.00 100.00
128 Katie Douglas RC 4.00 10.00
129 Lauren Jackson RC 40.00 100.00
130 Shea Ralph RC 2.50 6.00
131 Ruth Riley RC 3.00 8.00
132 Kelly Miller RC 2.50 6.00
133 Marie Ferdinand RC 2.50 6.00
134 Tammy Sutton-Brown RC 2.50 6.00
135 Camille Cooper RC 2.50 6.00
136 Janell Burse RC 2.50 6.00
137 LaQuanda Barksdale RC 2.50 6.00
138 Niele Ivey RC 2.50 6.00
139 Coco Miller RC 2.50 6.00
140 Deanna Nolan RC 2.50 6.00
141 Penny Taylor RC 8.00 20.00
142 Kristen Veal RC 2.50 6.00
143 Kelly Schumacher RC 2.50 6.00
144 Amanda Lassiter RC 2.50 6.00
145 Semeka Randall RC 2.50 6.00
146 Jenny Mowe RC 2.50 6.00
147 Georgia Schweitzer RC 2.50 6.00
148 Jae Kingi RC 2.50 6.00
149 Erin Buescher RC 2.50 6.00
150 Michaela Pavlickova RC 2.50 6.00
NNO Cynthia Cooper AU/350 60.00 150.00

2001 Ultra WNBA Autographics

1 Cynthia Cooper 40.00 100.00
2 Ticha Penicheiro 8.00 20.00

2001 Ultra WNBA Feel the Game

COMPLETE SET (6) 20.00 50.00
STATED ODDS 1:6
1 Jennifer Azzi 6.00 15.00
2 Cynthia Cooper 8.00 20.00
3 Yolanda Griffith 3.00 8.00
4 Chamique Holdsclaw 6.00 15.00
5 Lisa Leslie 8.00 20.00
6 Natalie Williams 2.00 5.00

2002 Ultra WNBA

COMPLETE SET (120) 200.00 500.00
COMP.SET w/o SP's (100) 15.00 40.00
RC STATED ODDS 1:4
1 Jackie Stiles 1.25 3.00
2 Sheryl Swoopes 2.00 5.00
3 Katie Smith 1.00 2.50
4 Sophia Witherspoon .50 1.25
5 Natalie Williams .60 1.50
6 Trisha Stafford-Odom .30 .75
7 Lynn Pride .30 .75
8 Ruthie Bolton-Holifield 1.00 2.50
9 Coquese Washington .30 .75
10 Erin Buescher .30 .75
11 Tully Bevilaqua .30 .75
12 Deanna Nolan .30 .75
13 Kristen Rasmussen .30 .75
14 Bridget Pettis .30 .75
15 Marie Ferdinand .30 .75
16 Andrea Stinson .60 1.50
17 Olympia Scott-Richardson .30 .75
18 Teresa Weatherspoon 1.25 3.00
19 Edna Campbell .40 1.00
20 Elena Tornikidou .30 .75
21 Elena Baranova .75 2.00
22 Kristen Veal .30 .75
23 Margo Dydek .50 1.25
24 Wendy Palmer .75 2.00
25 Sandy Brondello .75 2.00
26 Lisa Harrison .50 1.25
27 Korie Hlede .50 1.25
28 Astou Ndiaye-Diatta .50 1.25
29 Sheri Sam .30 .75
30 Trisha Fallon RC .30 .75
31 Chamique Holdsclaw 2.00 5.00
32 Chasity Melvin .30 .75
33 Mwadi Mabika .30 .75
34 Shannon Johnson .30 .75
35 Kamila Vodichkova .30 .75
36 Edwina Brown .40 1.00
37 Ruth Riley .50 1.25
38 Maria Stepanova .30 .75
39 Coco Miller .30 .75
40 Eva Nemcova .50 1.25
41 DeLisha Milton .30 .75
42 Jennifer Gillom .75 2.00
43 Vicky Bullett .50 1.25
44 Penny Taylor .50 1.25
45 Rhonda Mapp .40 1.00
46 Tawona Alehaleem .30 .75
47 Murriel Page .40 1.00
48 Tamika Catchings .75 2.00
49 Sue Wicks .50 1.25
50 Ticha Penicheiro .75 2.00
51 Tammy Jackson .30 .75
52 Rebecca Lobo 1.00 2.50
53 Yolanda Griffith 1.00 2.50
54 Ann Wauters .40 1.00
55 Latasha Byears .50 1.25
56 Katie Douglas .50 1.25
57 Sonja Henning .30 .75
58 Rushia Brown .30 .75
59 Ukari Figgs .30 .75
60 Elaine Powell .30 .75
61 Jennifer Azzi 1.00 2.50
62 Allison Feaster .40 1.00
63 Rita Williams .40 1.00
64 Tangela Smith .30 .75
65 Tari Phillips .30 .75
66 Shalonda Enis .30 .75
67 Alicia Thompson .30 .75
68 Crystal Robinson .30 .75
69 Lauren Jackson 1.50 4.00
70 Jae Kingi .30 .75
71 Marla Brumfield .30 .75
72 Dawn Staley .75 2.00
73 Adrienne Goodson .30 .75
74 Clarisse Machanguana .30 .75
75 Nikki McCray .75 2.00
76 Becky Hammon 2.00 5.00
77 Semeka Randall .30 .75
78 Merlakia Jones .50 1.25
79 Tamecka Dixon .50 1.25
80 Taj McWilliams-Franklin .30 .75
81 Jamie Redd .30 .75
82 Amanda Lassiter .30 .75
83 Maylana Martin .40 1.00
84 Tamicha Jackson .30 .75
85 Tammy Sutton-Brown .30 .75
86 Jurgita Streimikyte .30 .75
87 Vickie Johnson .50 1.25
88 Kedra Holland-Corn .30 .75
89 Janeth Arcain .30 .75
90 Betty Lennox .75 2.00
91 Kristin Folkl .50 1.25
92 Helen Luz .30 .75
93 Kelly Miller .30 .75
94 Lisa Leslie 1.50 4.00
95 Nykesha Sales .50 1.25
96 Simone Edwards RC .30 .75
97 Tina Thompson 1.00 2.50
98 Svetlana Abrosimova .30 .75
99 Sylvia Crawley .30 .75
100 Annie Burgess RC .30 .75
101 Sue Bird RC 200.00 500.00
102 Swin Cash RC 25.00 60.00
103 Stacey Dales-Schuman RC 3.00 8.00
104 Asjha Jones RC 3.00 8.00
105 Nikki Teasley RC 2.00 5.00
106 Tamika Williams RC 3.00 8.00
107 Shiela Lambert RC 2.00 5.00
108 Lindsay Yamasaki RC 2.00 5.00
109 Shaunzinski Gortman RC 2.00 5.00
110 Michelle Snow RC 4.00 10.00
111 Danielle Crockrom RC 2.50 6.00
112 Hamchetou Maiga RC 2.00 5.00
113 Towana McDonald RC 2.00 5.00
114 Laneisha Caufield RC 2.00 5.00
115 Tamara Moore RC 2.00 5.00
116 Rosalind Ross RC 2.00 5.00
117 Zuzi Klimesova RC 2.00 5.00
118 Lanae Williams RC 2.00 5.00
119 Iziane Castro-Marques RC 2.00 5.00
120 Ayana Walker RC 2.50 6.00

2002 Ultra WNBA Gold Medallion

*STARS: .6X TO 1.5X BASE CARD HI
STATED ODDS 1:1
101-120 PRINT RUN 25 SER.#'d SETS

2002 Ultra WNBA House of Stiles

COMPLETE SET (5) 6.00 15.00
COMMON CARD (HS1-HS5) 2.50 6.00
STATED ODDS 1:24
NNO J.Stiles JSY AU/50 125.00 300.00
NNO Jackie Stiles JSY/110 40.00 100.00

2002 Ultra WNBA Summer Love

COMPLETE SET (18) 15.00 40.00
SL1 Sheryl Swoopes 3.00 8.00
SL2 Ruthie Bolton-Holifield 1.50 4.00
SL3 Natalie Williams 1.00 2.50
SL4 Jennifer Gillom 1.25 3.00
SL5 Becky Hammon 3.00 8.00
SL6 Dawn Staley 1.25 3.00
SL7 Nikki McCray 1.25 3.00
SL8 Eva Nemcova .75 2.00
SL9 Nykesha Sales .75 2.00
SL10 Jennifer Azzi 1.50 4.00
SL11 Chamique Holdsclaw 3.00 8.00
SL12 Yolanda Griffith 1.50 4.00
SL13 Lisa Leslie 2.50 6.00
SL14 Jackie Stiles 2.00 5.00
SL15 Lauren Jackson 2.50 6.00
SL16 Katie Smith 1.50 4.00
SL17 Deanna Nolan .50 1.25
SL18 Ruth Riley .75 2.00

2002 Ultra WNBA Summer Love Memorabilia

STATED ODDS 1:12
SL1 Sheryl Swoopes 8.00 20.00
SL2 Ruthie Bolton-Holifield 4.00 10.00
SL3 Natalie Williams 2.50 6.00
SL4 Jennifer Gillom 3.00 8.00
SL5 Becky Hammon 8.00 20.00
SL6 Dawn Staley 3.00 8.00
SL7 Nikki McCray 3.00 8.00
SL8 Eva Nemcova 2.00 5.00
SL9 Nykesha Sales 2.00 5.00
SL10 Jennifer Azzi 4.00 10.00
SL11 Chamique Holdsclaw 8.00 20.00
SL12 Yolanda Griffith 4.00 10.00
SL13 Lisa Leslie 6.00 15.00
SL14 Jackie Stiles 5.00 12.00

2003 Ultra WNBA

COMP.SET w/o SP's (105) 30.00 80.00
106-120 STATED ODDS 1:3
1 Sue Bird 25.00 60.00
2 Kelly Schumacher .30 .75
3 Tamika Williams .40 1.00
4 Rebecca Lobo 1.00 2.50
5 Stacey Thomas .30 .75
6 Lisa Leslie 1.50 4.00
7 Adrain Williams .30 .75
8 Helen Luz .30 .75
9 Rushia Brown .30 .75
10 Bridget Pettis .30 .75
11 Annie Burgess .30 .75
12 Allison Feaster .40 1.00
13 Sylvia Crawley .30 .75
14 Svetlana Abrosimova .30 .75
15 Jessie Hicks .30 .75
16 Dominique Canty .50 1.25
17 Michele VanGorp .30 .75
18 Yolanda Griffith 1.00 2.50
19 Dawn Staley .75 2.00
20 Shalonda Enis .30 .75
21 Katie Smith 1.00 2.50
22 Brooke Wyckoff .50 1.25
23 Adrienne Goodson .30 .75
24 Erin Buescher .30 .75
25 Sonja Henning .30 .75
26 Betty Lennox .60 1.50
27 Wendy Palmer .75 2.00
28 Semeka Randall .30 .75
29 Charlotte Smith-Taylor .30 .75
30 Tully Bevilaqua .30 .75
31 DeLisha Milton .30 .75
32 Katie Douglas .50 1.25
33 Natalie Williams .60 1.50
34 Kayte Christensen RC .50 1.25
35 Janeth Arcain .30 .75
36 Vickie Johnson .50 1.25
37 Kamila Vodichkova .30 .75
38 Kelly Miller .30 .75
39 Grace Daley .30 .75
40 Nicky McCrimmon .30 .75
41 Taj McWilliams-Franklin .30 .75
42 LaTonya Johnson .30 .75
43 Jackie Stiles 1.25 3.00
44 Rita Williams .40 1.00
45 Tamecka Dixon .50 1.25
46 Nykesha Sales .50 1.25
47 Murriel Page .40 1.00
48 Marie Ferdinand .30 .75
49 Penny Taylor .50 1.25
50 Tina Thompson 1.00 2.50
51 Anna DeForge .30 .75
52 Ruth Riley .50 1.25
53 Stacey Dales-Schuman .50 1.25
54 Merlakia Jones .50 1.25
55 Nikki Teasley .30 .75
56 Ticha Penicheiro .75 2.00
57 Lindsey Yamasaki .30 .75
58 Chasity Melvin .30 .75
59 Mwadi Mabika .30 .75
60 Alisa Burras .30 .75
61 Tonya Washington .30 .75
62 Michelle Snow .40 1.00
63 Tari Phillips .30 .75
64 Simone Edwards .30 .75
65 Sheryl Swoopes 2.00 5.00
66 Crystal Robinson .30 .75
67 Adia Barnes .30 .75
68 DeMya Walker .30 .75
69 Lynn Pride .30 .75
70 Ruthie Bolton-Holifield 1.00 2.50
71 Sandy Brondello .75 2.00
72 Debbie Black .50 1.25
73 Sheri Sam .30 .75
74 Kedra Holland-Corn .30 .75
75 Andrea Stinson .60 1.50
76 Tamika Catchings .50 1.25
77 Georgia Schweitzer .30 .75
78 Shannon Johnson .30 .75
79 Jennifer Azzi 1.00 2.50
80 Deanna Nolan .30 .75
81 Teresa Weatherspoon 1.25 3.00
82 Tangela Smith .30 .75
83 Ukari Figgs .30 .75
84 Becky Hammon 4.00 10.00
85 Lauren Jackson 1.50 4.00
86 LaQuanda Quick RC .30 .75
87 Jennifer Rizzotti .75 2.00
88 Tamicha Jackson .30 .75
89 Asjha Jones .40 1.00
90 Margo Dydek .50 1.25
91 Swintayla Cash .50 1.25
92 Kristi Harrower .30 .75
93 Edna Campbell .40 1.00
94 Deanna Jackson RC .30 .75
95 Nikki McCray .75 2.00
96 Cynthia Cooper 2.00 5.00
97 Jennifer Gillom .75 2.00
98 Coco Miller .30 .75
99 Ayana Walker .30 .75
100 Tamika Whitmore .30 .75
101 Tammy Sutton-Brown .30 .75
102 Edwina Brown .30 .75
103 Coquese Washington .30 .75
104 Lisa Harrison .50 1.25
105 Chamique Holdsclaw 2.00 5.00
106 LaToya Thomas RC 2.00 5.00
107 Plenette Pierson RC 4.00 10.00
108 Coretta Brown RC 2.00 5.00
109 Sun-Min Jung RC 2.00 5.00
110 Kara Lawson RC 6.00 15.00
111 Gwen Jackson RC 2.00 5.00
112 Cheryl Ford RC 5.00 12.00
113 Courtney Coleman RC 2.00 5.00
114 Chantelle Anderson RC 2.00 5.00
115 Shaquala Williams RC 2.50 6.00
116 Tamara Bowie RC 2.00 5.00
117 Teresa Edwards RC 6.00 15.00
118 Aiysha Smith RC 2.50 6.00
119 Petra Ujhelyi RC 2.00 5.00
120 Allison Curtin RC 2.50 6.00

2003 Ultra WNBA Gold Medallion

*1-105: .6X TO 1.5X BASE CARD HI
*106-120: 5X TO 12X BASE HI
1-105 STATED ODDS ONE PER PACK
106-120 PRINT RUN 25 SER.#'d SETS

2003 Ultra WNBA All-Star Review

COMPLETE SET (20) 12.00 30.00
1 Tamecka Dixon .60 1.50
2 Katie Smith 1.25 3.00
3 Ticha Penicheiro 1.00 2.50
4 Tari Phillips .40 1.00
5 Teresa Weatherspoon 1.50 4.00
6 Andrea Stinson .75 2.00
7 Lauren Jackson 2.00 5.00
8 Nykesha Sales .60 1.50
9 Tina Thompson 1.25 3.00
10 Lisa Leslie 2.00 5.00
11 Yolanda Griffith 1.25 3.00
12 Janeth Arcain .40 1.00
13 Vickie Johnson .60 1.50
14 Mwadi Mabika .40 1.00
15 Chamique Holdsclaw 2.50 6.00
16 Tamika Catchings .60 1.50
17 Sheryl Swoopes 2.50 6.00
18 Penny Taylor .60 1.50
19 Stacey Dales-Schuman .60 1.50
20 Sue Bird 2.50 6.00

2003 Ultra WNBA All-Star Review Material

COMMON CARD 2.00 5.00
STATED ODDS 1:18
*PATCHES: 1.5X TO 4X BASE HI
PATCH PRINT RUN 100 SER.#'d SETS
1 Tamecka Dixon 2.00 5.00
2 Katie Smith 4.00 10.00
3 Ticha Penicheiro 3.00 8.00
4 Tari Phillips 2.00 5.00
5 Teresa Weatherspoon 5.00 12.00
6 Andrea Stinson 2.50 6.00
7 Lauren Jackson 6.00 15.00
8 Nykesha Sales 2.00 5.00
9 Tina Thompson 4.00 10.00
10 Lisa Leslie 6.00 15.00
11 Yolanda Griffith 4.00 10.00
12 Janeth Arcain 2.00 5.00
13 Vickie Johnson 2.00 5.00
14 Mwadi Mabika 2.00 5.00
15 Chamique Holdsclaw 6.00 15.00
16 Tamika Catchings 2.00 5.00
17 Sheryl Swoopes 6.00 15.00
18 Penny Taylor 2.00 5.00
19 Stacey Dales-Schuman 2.00 5.00
20 Sue Bird 8.00 20.00

2003 Ultra WNBA Nameplates

PRINT RUN 50 SERIAL #'d SETS
1 Tamecka Dixon 30.00 80.00
3 Ticha Penicheiro 50.00 125.00
4 Tari Phillips 30.00 80.00
5 Teresa Weatherspoon 80.00 200.00
7 Lauren Jackson 100.00 250.00
8 Nykesha Sales 30.00 80.00
9 Tina Thompson 60.00 150.00
10 Lisa Leslie 100.00 250.00
13 Vickie Johnson 30.00 80.00
14 Mwadi Mabika 30.00 80.00
15 Chamique Holdsclaw 100.00 250.00
16 Tamika Catchings 30.00 80.00
17 Sheryl Swoopes 75.00 200.00
18 Penny Taylor 30.00 80.00
19 Stacey Dales-Schuman 30.00 80.00
20 Sue Bird 200.00 500.00

2003 Ultra WNBA Who I AM

COMPLETE SET (14) 8.00 20.00
1 Chamique Holdsclaw 1.50 4.00
2 Tamika Catchings .40 1.00
3 Tina Thompson .75 2.00
4 Dawn Staley .60 1.50
5 Nykesha Sales .40 1.00
6 Teresa Weatherspoon 1.00 2.50
7 Lisa Leslie 1.25 3.00
8 Sheryl Swoopes 1.50 4.00
9 Swintayla Cash .40 1.00
10 Tamika Williams .30 .75
11 Jennifer Azzi .75 2.00
12 Ticha Penicheiro .60 1.50
13 Sue Bird 8.00 20.00
14 Lisa Harrison .40 1.00

2003 Ultra WNBA Who I AM Game Used

STATED ODDS 1:9
1 Chamique Holdsclaw 6.00 15.00
2 Tamika Catchings 2.00 5.00
3 Tina Thompson 4.00 10.00
4 Dawn Staley 3.00 8.00
5 Nykesha Sales 2.00 5.00
6 Teresa Weatherspoon 5.00 12.00
7 Lisa Leslie 6.00 15.00
8 Sheryl Swoopes 6.00 15.00
9 Ticha Penicheiro 3.00 8.00
10 Sue Bird 15.00 40.00

2004 Ultra WNBA

COMPLETE SET (110) 30.00 80.00
COMP.SET w/o SP's (90) 12.00 30.00
91-110 STATED ODDS 1:4
1 Tamika Catchings .50 1.25
2 Sheri Sam .30 .75
3 Ruthie Bolton 1.00 2.50
4 Chamique Holdsclaw 2.00 5.00
5 Michelle Snow .40 1.00
6 Crystal Robinson .30 .75
7 Betty Lennox .60 1.50
8 Dominique Canty .50 1.25
9 Vickie Johnson .50 1.25
10 Margo Dydek .50 1.25
11 Charlotte Smith-Taylor .30 .75
12 Katie Smith 1.00 2.50
13 Shannon Johnson .30 .75
14 Teresa Weatherspoon 1.25 3.00
15 Natalie Williams .60 1.50
16 Yolanda Griffith 1.00 2.50
17 Adia Barnes .30 .75
18 Andrea Stinson .60 1.50
19 Michele VanGorp .30 .75
20 Kara Lawson .75 2.00
21 Tammy Sutton-Brown .30 .75
22 Svetlana Abrosimova .30 .75
23 Chantelle Anderson .30 .75
24 Tynesha Lewis .30 .75
25 Tamika Williams .40 1.00
26 LaToya Thomas .30 .75
27 Edna Campbell .40 1.00
28 Lisa Leslie 1.50 4.00
29 Kayte Christensen .30 .75
30 Stacey Dales-Schuman .50 1.25
31 Wendy Palmer .75 2.00
32 Swin Cash .75 2.00
33 Jessie Hicks .30 .75
34 Katie Douglas .50 1.25
35 Mwadi Mabika .30 .75
36 Adrienne Goodson .30 .75
37 Taj McWilliams-Franklin .30 .75
38 Slobodanka Tuvic RC .50 1.25
39 Semeka Randall .30 .75
40 Kelly Miller .30 .75
41 Tamika Whitmore .30 .75
42 Tully Bevilaqua .30 .75
43 Sheryl Swoopes 2.00 5.00
44 Becky Hammon 2.00 5.00
45 Sue Bird 12.00 30.00
46 Debbie Black .50 1.25
47 DeLisha Milton-Jones .30 .75
48 Adrain Williams .30 .75
49 Asjha Jones .40 1.00
50 Janell Burse .30 .75
51 Tamecka Dixon .50 1.25
52 Penny Taylor .50 1.25
53 Coco Miller .30 .75
54 Cheryl Ford .60 1.50
55 Deanna Jackson .30 .75
56 DeMya Walker .30 .75
57 Kamila Vodichkova .30 .75

58 Deanna Nolan .30 .75
59 Allison Feaster .40 1.00
60 Plenette Pierson .50 1.25
61 Lauren Jackson 1.50 4.00
62 Dawn Staley 1.00 2.50
63 Nykesha Sales .50 1.25
64 Tangela Smith .30 .75
65 Aiysha Smith .30 .75
66 Ruth Riley .50 1.25
67 Nikki McCray .75 2.00
68 Nikki Teasley .30 .75
69 Chasity Melvin .30 .75
70 Merlakia Jones .50 1.25
71 Coretta Brown .30 .75
72 Anna DeForge .30 .75
73 Murriel Page .40 1.00
74 Tina Thompson 1.00 2.50
75 Tari Phillips .30 .75
76 Gwen Jackson .30 .75
77 Ayana Walker .30 .75
78 Kelly Schumacher .30 .75
79 Ticha Penicheiro .75 2.00
80 Simone Edwards .30 .75
81 Kedra Holland-Corn .30 .75
82 K.B. Sharp RC .50 1.25
83 LaQuanda Quick .30 .75
84 Barbara Farris RC .50 1.25
85 Stephanie White .60 1.50
86 Tamicha Jackson .30 .75
87 Elena Baranova .75 2.00
88 Elaine Powell .30 .75
89 Teresa Edwards .75 2.00
90 Marie Ferdinand .30 .75
91 Diana Taurasi RC 200.00 500.00
92 Alana Beard RC 2.00 5.00
93 Nicole Powell RC 2.50 6.00
94 Lindsay Whalen RC 4.00 10.00
95 Shameka Christon RC 2.00 5.00
96 Nicole Ohlde RC 2.00 5.00
97 Vanessa Hayden RC 2.00 5.00
98 Chandi Jones RC 1.50 4.00
99 Ebony Hoffman RC 2.50 6.00
100 Rebekkah Brunson RC 1.50 4.00
101 Iciss Tillis RC 1.50 4.00
102 Christi Thomas RC 1.50 4.00
103 Shereka Wright RC 1.50 4.00
104 Ashley Robinson RC 1.50 4.00
105 Kaayla Chones RC 1.50 4.00
106 Jessica Brungo RC 1.50 4.00
107 Kelly Mazzante RC 2.50 6.00
108 Catrina Frierson RC 1.50 4.00
109 Bethany Donaphin RC 1.50 4.00
110 Agnieszka Bibrzycka RC 1.50 4.00

2004 Ultra WNBA Gold Medallion

*1-90 GOLD SINGLES: .6X TO 1.5X BASE HI
1-90 STATED ODDS 1:1
*91-110 GOLD RC: 1.5X TO 4X BASE HI
91-110 PRINT RUN 100 SER.#'d SETS

2004 Ultra WNBA Platinum Medallion

*PLATINUM 1-90: 8X TO 20X HI
*PLATINUM 91-110: 4X TO 10X HI
STATED PRINT RUN 25 SER.#'d SETS
44 Becky Hammon 150.00 400.00
59 Allison Feaster 25.00 60.00
91 Diana Taurasi 2,500.00 5,000.00
102 Christi Thomas 25.00 60.00
103 Shereka Wright 25.00 60.00
104 Ashley Robinson 30.00 80.00

2004 Ultra WNBA All-Star Review

COMPLETE SET (20) 12.00 30.00
1 Lauren Jackson 2.00 5.00
2 Chamique Holdsclaw 2.50 6.00
3 Tamika Catchings .60 1.50
4 Lisa Leslie 2.00 5.00
5 Katie Smith 1.25 3.00
6 Nikki Teasley .40 1.00
7 Swin Cash 1.00 2.50
8 Tari Phillips .40 1.00
9 Sheryl Swoopes 2.50 6.00
10 Marie Ferdinand .40 1.00
11 Yolanda Griffith 1.25 3.00
12 Tamecka Dixon .60 1.50
13 Natalie Williams .75 2.00
14 Deanna Nolan .40 1.00
15 Sue Bird 2.50 6.00
16 Dawn Staley 1.25 3.00
17 Cheryl Ford .75 2.00
18 Margo Dydek .60 1.50
19 Adrain Williams .40 1.00
20 Teresa Weatherspoon 1.50 4.00

2004 Ultra WNBA All-Star Review Jerseys

STATED ODDS 1:24
*PATCHES: 1.25X TO 3X BASE JSY HI
PATCH PRINT RUN 100 SER.#'d SETS
1 Lauren Jackson 8.00 20.00
2 Chamique Holdsclaw 10.00 25.00
3 Tamika Catchings 2.50 6.00
4 Lisa Leslie 8.00 20.00
5 Katie Smith 5.00 12.00
6 Nikki Teasley 1.50 4.00
7 Swin Cash 4.00 10.00
8 Tari Phillips 1.50 4.00
9 Sheryl Swoopes 10.00 25.00
10 Marie Ferdinand 1.50 4.00
11 Yolanda Griffith 5.00 12.00
12 Tamecka Dixon 2.50 6.00
13 Natalie Williams 3.00 8.00
14 Deanna Nolan 1.50 4.00
15 Sue Bird 10.00 25.00
16 Dawn Staley 5.00 12.00
17 Cheryl Ford 3.00 8.00
18 Margo Dydek 2.50 6.00
19 Adrain Williams 1.50 4.00
20 Teresa Weatherspoon 6.00 15.00

2004 Ultra WNBA Scoring Stars

COMPLETE SET (15) 8.00 20.00
1 Lauren Jackson 1.50 4.00
2 Chamique Holdsclaw 2.00 5.00
3 Tamika Catchings .50 1.25
4 Lisa Leslie 1.50 4.00
5 Katie Smith 1.00 2.50
6 Tina Thompson 1.00 2.50
7 Swin Cash .75 2.00
8 Cheryl Ford .60 1.50
9 Sheryl Swoopes 2.00 5.00
10 Marie Ferdinand .30 .75
11 Yolanda Griffith 1.00 2.50
12 Tamecka Dixon .50 1.25
13 Natalie Williams .60 1.50
14 Deanna Nolan .30 .75
15 Sue Bird 12.00 30.00

2004 Ultra WNBA Scoring Stars Jerseys

STATED ODDS 1:24
1 Lauren Jackson 5.00 12.00
2 Chamique Holdsclaw 6.00 15.00
3 Tamika Catchings 1.50 4.00
4 Lisa Leslie 5.00 12.00
5 Katie Smith 3.00 8.00
6 Tina Thompson 3.00 8.00
7 Swin Cash 2.50 6.00
8 Cheryl Ford 2.00 5.00
9 Sheryl Swoopes 6.00 15.00
10 Marie Ferdinand 1.50 4.00
11 Yolanda Griffith 3.00 8.00
12 Tamecka Dixon 1.50 4.00
13 Natalie Williams 2.00 5.00
14 Deanna Nolan 1.50 4.00
15 Sue Bird 20.00 50.00

2004 Ultra WNBA Season Crowns Autographs

STATED PRINT RUN 100 SER.#'d SETS
1 Tamika Catchings 75.00 200.00
2 Chamique Holdsclaw 20.00 50.00
3 Swin Cash 12.00 30.00
4 Alana Beard 10.00 25.00
5 Becky Hammon 75.00 200.00
6 Cheryl Ford 10.00 25.00
7 Tangela Smith 5.00 12.00
8 Delisha Milton-Jones 5.00 12.00
9 Deanna Nolan 5.00 12.00
10 Elaine Powell 5.00 12.00
11 Taj McWilliams-Franklin 5.00 12.00
12 Vanessa Hayden 10.00 25.00
13 Ruth Riley 12.00 30.00

2004 Ultra WNBA Season Crowns Rookie Jerseys

PRINT RUN 500 SER.#'d SETS
1 Alana Beard 5.00 12.00
2 Diana Taurasi 200.00 500.00

1961 Union Oil Chiefs

COMPLETE SET (10) 125.00 250.00
1 Frank Burgess 12.50 25.00
2 Jeff Cohen 12.50 25.00
3 Lee Harman 12.50 25.00
4 Rick Herrscher 15.00 40.00
5 Lowery Kirk 12.50 25.00
6 Dave Mills 12.50 25.00
7 Max Perry 12.50 25.00
8 George Price 12.50 25.00
9 Fred Sawyer 12.50 25.00
10 Dale Wise 12.50 25.00

1990-91 Upper Deck Prototypes

COMPLETE SET (2) 700.00 1,000.00
32 Magic Johnson 250.00 500.00
33 Larry Bird 300.00 600.00

1991-92 Upper Deck Promos

COMPLETE SET (2) 8.00 20.00
1 Michael Jordan 8.00 20.00
400 David Robinson 2.00 5.00

1991-92 Upper Deck

COMPLETE SET (500) 12.00 30.00
COMPLETE FACT.SET (500) 20.00 50.00
COMPLETE SERIES 1 (400) 8.00 20.00
COMPLETE SERIES 2 (100) 4.00 10.00
1 S.Augmon/R.Monroe CL .20 .50
2 Larry Johnson UER RC 1.00 2.50
3 Dikembe Mutombo RC 1.25 3.00
4 Steve Smith RC .50 1.25
5 Stacey Augmon RC .30 .75
6 Terrell Brandon RC .25 .60
7 Greg Anthony RC .25 .60
8 Rich King RC .20 .50
9 Chris Gatling RC .25 .60
10 Victor Alexander RC .20 .50
11 John Turner RC .20 .50
12 Eric Murdock RC .20 .50
13 Mark Randall RC .20 .50
14 Rodney Monroe RC .20 .50
15 Myron Brown RC .20 .50
16 Mike Iuzzolino RC .20 .50
17 Chris Corchiani RC .20 .50
18 Elliot Perry RC .20 .50
19 Jimmy Oliver RC .20 .50
20 Doug Overton RC .25 .60
21 Steve Hood UER RC .20 .50
22 Michael Jordan SCHOOL .60 1.50
23 Kevin Johnson SCHOOL .30 .75
24 Kurk Lee .20 .50
25 Sean Higgins RC .20 .50
26 Morlon Wiley .20 .50
27 Derek Smith .20 .50
28 Kenny Payne .20 .50
29 Magic Johnson SPEC 1.00 2.50
30 L.Bird/C.Person CC 1.00 2.50
31 K.Malone/C.Barkley CC .60 1.50
32 K.Johnson/Stockton CC .60 1.50
33 H.Olajuwon/P.Ewing CC .60 1.50
34 M.Johnson/M.Jordan CC 2.00 5.00
35 Derrick Coleman ART .30 .75
36 Lionel Simmons ART .20 .50
37 Dee Brown ART .25 .60
38 Dennis Scott ART .25 .60
39 Kendall Gill ART .30 .75
40 Winston Garland .20 .50
41 Danny Young .20 .50
42 Rick Mahorn .25 .60
43 Michael Adams .25 .60
44 Michael Jordan 1.25 3.00
45 Magic Johnson .40 1.00
46 Doc Rivers .30 .75
47 Moses Malone .50 1.25
48 Michael Jordan AS CL 1.00 25.00
49 James Worthy AS .40 1.00
50 Tim Hardaway AS .40 1.00
51 Karl Malone AS .60 1.50
52 John Stockton AS .60 1.50
53 Clyde Drexler AS .50 1.25
54 Terry Porter AS .25 .60
55 Kevin Duckworth AS .25 .60
56 Tom Chambers AS .30 .75
57 Magic Johnson AS 1.00 2.50
58 David Robinson AS .60 1.50
59 Kevin Johnson AS .30 .75
60 Chris Mullin AS .40 1.00
61 Joe Dumars AS .40 1.00
62 Kevin McHale AS .50 1.25
63 Brad Daugherty AS .30 .75
64 Alvin Robertson AS .25 .60
65 Bernard King AS .40 1.00
66 Dominique Wilkins AS .50 1.25
67 Ricky Pierce AS .25 .60
68 Patrick Ewing AS .50 1.25
69 Michael Jordan AS 2.00 5.00
70 Charles Barkley AS .60 1.50
71 Hersey Hawkins AS .25 .60
72 Robert Parish AS .40 1.00
73 Alvin Robertson TC .25 .60
74 Bernard King TC .40 1.00
75 Michael Jordan TC .75 2.00
76 Brad Daugherty TC .30 .75
77 Larry Bird TC 1.00 2.50
78 Ron Harper TC .30 .75
79 Dominique Wilkins TC .50 1.25
80 Rony Seikaly TC .25 .60
81 Rex Chapman TC .25 .60
82 Mark Eaton TC .30 .75
83 Lionel Simmons TC .20 .50
84 Gerald Wilkins TC .25 .60
85 James Worthy TC .40 1.00
86 Scott Skiles TC .25 .60
87 Rolando Blackman TC .25 .60
88 Derrick Coleman TC .30 .75
89 Chris Jackson TC .25 .60
90 Reggie Miller TC .50 1.25
91 Isiah Thomas TC .50 1.25
92 Hakeem Olajuwon TC .60 1.50
93 Hersey Hawkins TC .25 .60
94 David Robinson TC .60 1.50
95 Tom Chambers TC .30 .75
96 Shawn Kemp TC .50 1.25
97 Pooh Richardson TC .25 .60
98 Clyde Drexler TC .50 1.25
99 Chris Mullin TC .40 1.00
100 Checklist 1-100 .20 5.00
101 John Shasky .20 .50
102 Dana Barros .25 .60
103 Stojko Vrankovic .20 .50
104 Larry Drew .20 .50
105 Randy White .20 .50
106 Dave Corzine .20 .50
107 Joe Kleine .20 .50
108 Lance Blanks .20 .50
109 Rodney McCray .25 .60
110 Sedale Threatt .20 .50
111 Ken Norman .25 .60
112 Rickey Green .25 .60
113 Andy Toolson .20 .50
114 Bo Kimble .25 .60
115 Mark West .25 .60
116 Mark Eaton .30 .75
117 John Paxson .25 .60
118 Mike Brown .25 .60
119 Brian Oliver .20 .50
120 Will Perdue .25 .60
121 Michael Smith .20 .50
122 Sherman Douglas .25 .60
123 Reggie Lewis .30 .75
124 James Donaldson .25 .60
125 Scottie Pippen .75 2.00
126 Elden Campbell .25 .60
127 Michael Cage .25 .60
128 Tony Smith .20 .50
129 Ed Pinckney .25 .60
130 Keith Askins RC .20 .50
131 Darrell Griffith .30 .75
132 Vinnie Johnson .30 .75
133 Ron Harper .30 .75
134 Andre Turner .20 .50
135 Jeff Hornacek .25 .60
136 John Stockton .60 1.50
137 Derek Harper .25 .60
138 Loy Vaught .25 .60
139 Thurl Bailey .25 .60
140 Olden Polynice .20 .50
141 Kevin Edwards .20 .50
142 Byron Scott .30 .75
143 Dee Brown .25 .60
144 Sam Perkins .25 .60
145 Rony Seikaly .25 .60
146 James Worthy .40 1.00
147 Glen Rice .30 .75
148 Craig Hodges .25 .60
149 Bimbo Coles .25 .60
150 Mychal Thompson .25 .60
151 Xavier McDaniel .25 .60
152 Roy Tarpley .25 .60
153 Gary Payton .50 1.25
154 Rolando Blackman .25 .60
155 Hersey Hawkins .25 .60
156 Ricky Pierce .25 .60
157 Fat Lever .25 .60
158 Andrew Lang .20 .50
159 Benoit Benjamin .20 .50
160 Cedric Ceballos .25 .60
161 Charles Smith .25 .60
162 Jeff Martin .20 .50
163 Robert Parish .40 1.00
164 Danny Manning .25 .60
165 Mark Aguirre .25 .60
166 Jeff Malone .25 .60
167 Bill Laimbeer .30 .75
168 Willie Burton .20 .50
169 Dennis Hopson .20 .50
170 Kevin Gamble .20 .50
171 Terry Teagle .25 .60
172 Dan Majerle .30 .75
173 Shawn Kemp .50 1.25
174 Tom Chambers .30 .75
175 Vlade Divac .25 .60
176 Johnny Dawkins .25 .60
177 A.C. Green .25 .60
178 Manute Bol .30 .75
179 Terry Davis .20 .50
180 Ron Anderson .20 .50
181 Horace Grant .30 .75
182 Stacey King .25 .60
183 William Bedford .20 .50
184 B.J. Armstrong .30 .75
185 Dennis Rodman .60 1.50
186 Nate McMillan .25 .60
187 Cliff Levingston .25 .60
188 Quintin Dailey .20 .50
189 Bill Cartwright .25 .60
190 John Salley .25 .60
191 Jayson Williams .20 .50
192 Grant Long .20 .50
193 Negele Knight .20 .50
194 Alec Kessler .20 .50
195 Gary Grant .20 .50
196 Billy Thompson .20 .50
197 Delaney Rudd .20 .50
198 Alan Ogg .20 .50
199 Blue Edwards .20 .50
200 Checklist 101-200 .20 5.00
201 Mark Acres .20 .50
202 Craig Ehlo .25 .60
203 Anthony Cook .20 .50
204 Eric Leckner .20 .50
205 Terry Catledge .20 .50
206 Reggie Williams .25 .60
207 Greg Kite .20 .50
208 Steve Kerr .40 1.00
209 Kenny Battle .20 .50
210 John Morton .20 .50
211 Kenny Williams .20 .50
212 Mark Jackson .25 .60
213 Alaa Abdelnaby .20 .50
214 Rod Strickland .25 .60
215 Micheal Williams .20 .50
216 Kevin Duckworth .25 .60
217 David Wingate .25 .60
218 LaSalle Thompson .20 .50
219 John Starks RC 1.00 2.50
220 Clifford Robinson .25 .60
221 Jeff Grayer .20 .50
222 Marcus Liberty .20 .50
223 Larry Nance .30 .75
224 Michael Ansley .20 .50
225 Kevin McHale .50 1.25
226 Scott Skiles .25 .60
227 Darnell Valentine .20 .50
228 Nick Anderson .25 .60
229 Brad Davis .20 .50
230 Gerald Paddio .20 .50
231 Sam Bowie .25 .60
232 Sam Vincent .20 .50
233 George McCloud .20 .50
234 Gerald Wilkins .25 .60
235 Mookie Blaylock .30 .75
236 Jon Koncak .20 .50
237 Danny Ferry .20 .50
238 Vern Fleming .25 .60
239 Mark Price .30 .75
240 Sidney Moncrief .30 .75
241 Jay Humphries .25 .60
242 Muggsy Bogues .30 .75
243 Tim Hardaway .40 1.00
244 Alvin Robertson .25 .60
245 Chris Mullin .40 1.00
246 Pooh Richardson .25 .60
247 Winston Bennett .20 .50
248 Kelvin Upshaw .20 .50
249 John Williams .20 .50
250 Steve Alford .25 .60
251 Spud Webb .30 .75
252 Sleepy Floyd .25 .60
253 Chuck Person .25 .60
254 Hakeem Olajuwon .60 1.50
255 Dominique Wilkins .50 1.25
256 Reggie Miller .50 1.25
257 Dennis Scott .25 .60
258 Charles Oakley .25 .60
259 Sidney Green .20 .50
260 Detlef Schrempf .25 .60
261 Rod Higgins .20 .50
262 J.R. Reid .20 .50
263 Tyrone Hill .25 .60
264 Reggie Theus .25 .60
265 Mitch Richmond .40 1.00
266 Dale Ellis .25 .60
267 Terry Cummings .30 .75
268 Johnny Newman .20 .50
269 Doug West .20 .50
270 Jim Petersen .20 .50
271 Otis Thorpe .25 .60
272 John Williams .20 .50
273 Kennard Winchester RC .20 .50
274 Duane Ferrell .20 .50
275 Vernon Maxwell .25 .60
276 Kenny Smith .25 .60
277 Jerome Kersey .25 .60
278 Kevin Willis .25 .60
279 Danny Ainge .25 .60
280 Larry Smith .20 .50
281 Maurice Cheeks .25 .60
282 Willie Anderson .25 .60
283 Tom Tolbert .20 .50
284 Jerrod Mustaf .20 .50
285 Randolph Keys .20 .50
286 Jerry Reynolds .20 .50
287 Sean Elliott .25 .60
288 Otis Smith .20 .50
289 Terry Mills RC .20 .50
290 Kelly Tripucka .25 .60
291 Jon Sundvold .20 .50
292 Rumeal Robinson .20 .50
293 Fred Roberts .20 .50
294 Rik Smits .25 .60
295 Jerome Lane .20 .50
296 Dave Jamerson .20 .50
297 Joe Wolf .20 .50
298 David Wood RC .20 .50
299 Todd Lichti .20 .50
300 Checklist 201-300 .20 .50
301 Randy Breuer .20 .50
302 Buck Johnson .20 .50
303 Scott Brooks .20 .50
304 Jeff Turner .20 .50
305 Felton Spencer .20 .50
306 Greg Dreiling .20 .50
307 Gerald Glass .20 .50
308 Tony Brown .20 .50
309 Sam Mitchell .20 .50
310 Adrian Caldwell .20 .50
311 Chris Dudley .20 .50
312 Blair Rasmussen .20 .50
313 Antoine Carr .25 .60
314 Greg Anderson .20 .50
315 Drazen Petrovic .40 1.00
316 Alton Lister .20 .50
317 Jack Haley .20 .50
318 Bobby Hansen .20 .50
319 Chris Jackson .25 .60
320 Herb Williams .25 .60
321 Kendall Gill .30 .75
322 Tyrone Corbin .20 .50
323 Kiki Vandeweghe .25 .60
324 David Robinson .60 1.50
325 Rex Chapman .25 .60
326 Tony Campbell .20 .50
327 Dell Curry .25 .60
328 Charles Jones .20 .50
329 Kenny Gattison .20 .50
330 Haywoode Workman RC .20 .50
331 Travis Mays .20 .50
332 Derrick Coleman .30 .75
333 Isiah Thomas .50 1.25
334 Jud Buechler .25 .60
335 Joe Dumars .40 1.00
336 Tate George .20 .50
337 Mike Sanders .20 .50
338 James Edwards .25 .60
339 Chris Morris .20 .50
340 Scott Hastings .20 .50
341 Trent Tucker .25 .60
342 Harvey Grant .25 .60
343 Patrick Ewing .50 1.25
344 Larry Bird 1.00 2.50
345 Charles Barkley .60 1.50
346 Brian Shaw .25 .60
347 Kenny Walker .20 .50
348 Danny Schayes .20 .50
349 Tom Hammonds .20 .50
350 Frank Brickowski .20 .50
351 Terry Porter .25 .60
352 Orlando Woolridge .25 .60
353 Buck Williams .25 .60
354 Sarunas Marciulionis .30 .75
355 Karl Malone .60 1.50
356 Kevin Johnson .30 .75
357 Clyde Drexler .50 1.25
358 Duane Causwell .20 .50
359 Paul Pressey .25 .60
360 Jim Les RC .20 .50
361 Derrick McKey .20 .50
362 Scott Williams RC .30 .75
363 Mark Alarie .20 .50
364 Brad Daugherty .30 .75
365 Bernard King .40 1.00
366 Steve Henson .20 .50
367 Darrell Walker .20 .50
368 Larry Krystkowiak .20 .50
369 Henry James UER .20 .50
370 Jack Sikma .30 .75
371 Eddie Johnson .20 .50
372 Wayman Tisdale .25 .60
373 Joe Barry Carroll .20 .50
374 David Greenwood .20 .50
375 Lionel Simmons .20 .50
376 Dwayne Schintzius .20 .50
377 Tod Murphy .20 .50
378 Wayne Cooper .20 .50
379 Anthony Bonner .20 .50
380 Walter Davis .25 .60
381 Lester Conner .20 .50
382 Ledell Eackles .20 .50
383 Brad Lohaus .20 .50
384 Derrick Gervin .20 .50
385 Pervis Ellison .20 .50
386 Tim McCormick .20 .50
387 A.J. English .20 .50
388 John Battle .20 .50
389 Roy Hinson .20 .50
390 Armon Gilliam .20 .50
391 Kurt Rambis .25 .60
392 Mark Bryant .20 .50
393 Chucky Brown .20 .50
394 Avery Johnson .25 .60
395 Rory Sparrow .20 .50
396 Mario Elie RC .20 .50
397 Ralph Sampson .25 .60
398 Mike Gminski .20 .50
399 Bill Wennington .25 .60
400 Checklist 301-400 .20 .50
401 David Wingate .25 .60
402 Moses Malone .50 1.25
403 Darrell Walker .20 .50
404 Antoine Carr .25 .60
405 Charles Shackleford .20 .50
406 Orlando Woolridge .25 .60
407 Robert Pack RC .25 .60
408 Bobby Hansen .20 .50
409 Dale Davis RC .30 .75
410 Vincent Askew RC .20 .50
411 Alexander Volkov .20 .50
412 Dwayne Schintzius .20 .50
413 Tim Perry .20 .50
414 Tyrone Corbin .20 .50
415 Pete Chilcutt RC .20 .50
416 James Edwards .25 .60
417 Jerrod Mustaf .20 .50
418 Thurl Bailey .25 .60
419 Spud Webb .30 .75
420 Doc Rivers .30 .75
421 Sean Green RC .20 .50
422 Walter Davis .25 .60
423 Terry Davis .20 .50
424 John Battle .20 .50
425 Vinnie Johnson .30 .75
426 Sherman Douglas .25 .60
427 Kevin Brooks RC .20 .50
428 Greg Sutton RC .20 .50
429 Rafael Addison RC .20 .50
430 Anthony Mason RC .40 1.00
431 Paul Graham RC .20 .50
432 Anthony Frederick RC .20 .50
433 Dennis Hopson .20 .50
434 Rory Sparrow .20 .50
435 Michael Adams .25 .60
436 Kevin Lynch RC .20 .50
437 Randy Brown RC .30 .75
438 L.Johnson/B.Owens TP CL 1.00 2.50
439 Stacey Augmon TP .30 .75
440 Larry Stewart TP RC .20 .50
441 Terrell Brandon TP .25 .60
442 Billy Owens TP RC .30 .75
443 Rick Fox TP RC .30 .75
444 Kenny Anderson TP RC .30 .75
445 Larry Johnson TP 1.00 2.50
446 Dikembe Mutombo TP 1.25 3.00
447 Steve Smith TP .50 1.25
448 Greg Anthony TP .25 .60
449 East All-Star CL 2.50 6.00
450 West All-Star CL .20 .50
451 Isiah Thomas AS w/Magic 1.00 2.50
452 Michael Jordan AS 2.00 5.00
453 Scottie Pippen AS .75 2.00
454 Charles Barkley AS .60 1.50
455 Patrick Ewing AS .50 1.25
456 Michael Adams AS .25 .60
457 Dennis Rodman AS .60 1.50
458 Reggie Lewis AS .30 .75
459 Joe Dumars AS .40 1.00
460 Mark Price AS .30 .75
461 Brad Daugherty AS .30 .75
462 Kevin Willis AS .25 .60
463 Clyde Drexler AS .50 1.25
464 Magic Johnson AS 1.00 2.50
465 Chris Mullin AS .40 1.00
466 Karl Malone AS .60 1.50
467 David Robinson AS .60 1.50
468 Tim Hardaway AS .40 1.00
469 Jeff Hornacek AS .25 .60
470 John Stockton AS .60 1.50
471 Dikembe Mutombo AS UER 1.25 3.00
472 Hakeem Olajuwon AS .60 1.50
473 James Worthy AS .40 1.00
474 Otis Thorpe AS .25 .60
475 Dan Majerle AS .30 .75
476 Cedric Ceballos SD CL .25 .60
477 Nick Anderson SD .25 .60
478 Stacey Augmon SD .30 .75
479 Cedric Ceballos SD .25 .60
480 Larry Johnson SD 1.00 2.50
481 Shawn Kemp SD .50 1.25
482 John Starks SD 1.00 2.50
483 Doug West SD .20 .50
484 Craig Hodges LD .25 .60
485 LaBradford Smith RC .30 .75
486 Winston Garland .20 .50
487 David Benoit RC .30 .75
488 John Bagley .20 .50
489 Mark Macon RC .30 .75
490 Mitch Richmond .40 1.00
491 Luc Longley RC .50 1.25
492 Sedale Threatt .20 .50
493 Doug Smith RC .20 .50
494 Travis Mays .20 .50
495 Xavier McDaniel .25 .60
496 Brian Shaw .25 .60
497 Stanley Roberts RC .25 .60
498 Blair Rasmussen .20 .50
499 Brian Williams RC .30 .75
500 Checklist Card .20 .50

1991-92 Upper Deck Award Winner Holograms

COMPLETE SET (9) 5.00 12.00
AW1 Michael Jordan 4.00 10.00
AW2 Alvin Robertson .40 1.00
AW3 John Stockton 1.00 2.50
AW4 Michael Jordan 4.00 10.00
AW5 Detlef Schrempf .50 1.25
AW6 David Robinson 1.25 3.00
AW7 Derrick Coleman .50 1.25
AW8 Hakeem Olajuwon 1.25 3.00
AW9 Dennis Rodman 1.25 3.00

1991-92 Upper Deck Rookie Standouts

COMPLETE SET (40) 10.00 25.00
COMPLETE SERIES 1 (20) 3.00 8.00
COMPLETE SERIES 2 (20) 6.00 15.00
R1 Gary Payton .60 1.50
R2 Dennis Scott .30 .75
R3 Kendall Gill .40 1.00
R4 Felton Spencer .25 .60
R5 Bo Kimble .30 .75
R6 Willie Burton .25 .60
R7 Tyrone Hill .30 .75
R8 Loy Vaught .30 .75
R9 Travis Mays .25 .60
R10 Derrick Coleman .40 1.00
R11 Duane Causwell .25 .60
R12 Dee Brown .30 .75
R13 Gerald Glass .25 .60
R14 Jayson Williams .25 .60
R15 Elden Campbell .30 .75
R16 Negele Knight .25 .60
R17 Chris Jackson .30 .75
R18 Danny Ferry .25 .60
R19 Tony Smith .25 .60
R20 Cedric Ceballos .30 .75
R21 Victor Alexander .25 .60
R22 Terrell Brandon .30 .75
R23 Rick Fox .40 1.00
R24 Stacey Augmon .40 1.00
R25 Mark Macon .40 1.00
R26 Larry Johnson 1.25 3.00
R27 Paul Graham .25 .60
R28 Stanley Roberts UER .30 .75
R29 Dikembe Mutombo 1.50 4.00
R30 Robert Pack .30 .75
R31 Doug Smith .25 .60
R32 Steve Smith .60 1.50
R33 Billy Owens .40 1.00
R34 David Benoit .40 1.00
R35 Brian Williams .40 1.00
R36 Kenny Anderson .40 1.00
R37 Greg Anthony .30 .75
R38 Dale Davis .40 1.00
R39 Larry Stewart .25 .60
R40 Mike Iuzzolino .25 .60

1991-92 Upper Deck Jerry West Heroes

COMMON WEST (1-9) 1.00 2.50
AU Jerry West AU/2500 100.00 250.00
NNO Jerry West Cover 1.00 2.50

1991-92 Upper Deck Jerry West Box Bottoms

COMPLETE SET (8) 2.00 5.00
COMMON CARD (1-8) .30 .75

1992-93 Upper Deck

COMPLETE SET (514) 40.00 100.00
COMPLETE LO SERIES (311) 20.00 50.00
COMPLETE HI SERIES (203) 20.00 50.00
SP1: SER.1 STATED ODDS 1:72
SP2: SER.2 STATED ODDS 1:72
1 Shaquille O'Neal SP RC 12.00 30.00
1A Draft Trade Card .10 .30
1B Shaquille O'Neal TRADE 10.00 25.00
1AX Draft Trade Redeemed .10 .30
2 Alonzo Mourning RC .75 2.00
3 Christian Laettner RC .25 .60
4 LaPhonso Ellis RC .10 .30
5 Clarence Weatherspoon RC .10 .30
6 Adam Keefe RC .02 .10
7 Robert Horry RC .15 .40
8 Harold Miner RC .10 .30
9 Bryant Stith RC .05 .15
10 Malik Sealy RC .05 .15
11 Anthony Peeler RC .05 .15
12 Randy Woods RC .02 .10
13 Tracy Murray RC .05 .15
14 Tom Gugliotta RC .40 1.00
15 Hubert Davis RC .05 .15
16 Don MacLean RC .02 .10
17 Lee Mayberry RC .02 .10
18 Corey Williams RC .02 .10
19 Sean Rooks RC .02 .10
20 Todd Day RC .05 .15
21 B.Stith/L.Ellis CL .10 .30
22 Jeff Hornacek .05 .15
23 Michael Jordan 1.50 4.00
24 John Salley .02 .10
25 Andre Turner .02 .10
26 Charles Barkley .20 .50
27 Anthony Frederick .02 .10
28 Mario Elie .05 .15
29 Olden Polynice .02 .10
30 Rodney Monroe .02 .10
31 Tim Perry .02 .10
32 Doug Christie SP RC .40 1.00
32A Magic Johnson SP .75 2.00
33 Jim Jackson SP RC 1.00 2.50
33A Larry Bird SP 1.00 2.50
34 Randy White .02 .10
35 Frank Brickowski TC .02 .10
36 Michael Adams TC .02 .10
37 Scottie Pippen TC .20 .50
38 Mark Price TC .02 .10
39 Robert Parish TC .02 .10
40 Danny Manning TC .02 .10
41 Kevin Willis TC .02 .10
42 Glen Rice TC .05 .15
43 Kendall Gill TC .02 .10
44 Karl Malone TC .10 .30
45 Mitch Richmond TC .10 .30
46 Patrick Ewing TC .10 .30
47 Sam Perkins TC .02 .10
48 Dennis Scott TC .02 .10
49 Derek Harper TC .02 .10
50 Drazen Petrovic TC .02 .10
51 Reggie Williams TC .02 .10
52 Rik Smits TC .02 .10
53 Joe Dumars TC .05 .15
54 Otis Thorpe TC .02 .10
55 Johnny Dawkins TC .02 .10
56 Sean Elliott TC .02 .10
57 Kevin Johnson TC .05 .15
58 Ricky Pierce TC .02 .10
59 Doug West TC .02 .10
60 Terry Porter TC .02 .10
61 Tim Hardaway TC .10 .30
62 M.Jordan/S.Pippen ST 1.00 2.50
63 K.Gill/L.Johnson ST .10 .30
64 T.Chambers/K.Johnson ST .05 .15
65 T.Hardaway/C.Mullin ST .05 .15
66 K.Malone/J.Stockton ST .10 .30
67 Michael Jordan MVP .75 2.00
68 Stacey Augmon 6 MIL .02 .10
69 Bob Lanier .05 .15
70 Alaa Abdelnaby .02 .10
71 Andrew Lang .02 .10
72 Larry Krystkowiak .02 .10
73 Gerald Wilkins .02 .10
74 Rod Strickland .10 .30
75 Danny Ainge .05 .15
76 Chris Corchiani .02 .10
77 Jeff Grayer .02 .10
78 Eric Murdock .02 .10
79 Rex Chapman .02 .10
80 LaBradford Smith .02 .10
81 Jay Humphries .02 .10
82 David Robinson .20 .50
83 William Bedford .02 .10
84 James Edwards .02 .10
85 Danny Schayes .02 .10
86 Lloyd Daniels RC .02 .10
87 Blue Edwards .02 .10
88 Dale Ellis .02 .10
89 Rolando Blackman .02 .10
90 Michael Jordan CL .10 .30
91 Rik Smits .05 .15
92 Terry Davis .02 .10
93 Bill Cartwright .02 .10
94 Avery Johnson .02 .10
95 Micheal Williams .02 .10
96 Spud Webb .05 .15
97 Benoit Benjamin .02 .10
98 Derek Harper .05 .15
99 Matt Bullard .02 .10
100A Tyrone Corbin ERR Heat .40 1.00
100B Tyrone Corbin COR Jazz .02 .10
101 Doc Rivers .05 .15
102 Tony Smith .02 .10

103 Doug West .02 .10
104 Kevin Duckworth .02 .10
105 Luc Longley .05 .15
106 Antoine Carr .02 .10
107 Clifford Robinson .05 .15
108 Grant Long .02 .10
109 Terry Porter .02 .10
110A Steve Smith ERR Jazz 4.00 10.00
110B Steve Smith COR .15 .40
111 Brian Williams .02 .10
112 Karl Malone .20 .50
113 Reggie Williams .02 .10
114 Tom Chambers .02 .10
115 Winston Garland .02 .10
116 John Stockton .10 .30
117 Chris Jackson .02 .10
118 Mike Brown .02 .10
119 Kevin Johnson .10 .30
120 Reggie Lewis .05 .15
121 Bimbo Coles .02 .10
122 Drazen Petrovic .02 .10
123 Reggie Miller .10 .30
124 Derrick Coleman .05 .15
125 Chuck Person .02 .10
126 Glen Rice .10 .30
127 Kenny Anderson .10 .30
128 Willie Burton .02 .10
129 Chris Morris .02 .10
130 Patrick Ewing .10 .30
131 Sean Elliott .05 .15
132 Clyde Drexler .10 .30
133 Scottie Pippen .40 1.00
134 Pooh Richardson .02 .10
135 Horace Grant .05 .15
136 Hakeem Olajuwon .20 .50
137 John Paxson .02 .10
138 Kendall Gill .05 .15
139 Michael Adams .02 .10
140 Otis Thorpe .05 .15
141 Dennis Scott .05 .15
142 Stacey Augmon .05 .15
143 Robert Pack .02 .10
144 Kevin Willis .02 .10
145 Jerome Kersey .02 .10
146 Paul Graham .02 .10
147 Stanley Roberts .02 .10
148 Dominique Wilkins .10 .30
149 Scott Skiles .02 .10
150 Rumeal Robinson .02 .10
151 Mookie Blaylock .05 .15
152 Elden Campbell .05 .15
153 Chris Dudley .02 .10
154 Sedale Threatt .02 .10
155 Tate George .02 .10
156 James Worthy .10 .30
157 B.J. Armstrong .02 .10
158 Gary Payton .25 .60
159 Ledell Eackles .02 .10
160 Sam Perkins .05 .15
161 Nick Anderson .05 .15
162 Mitch Richmond .10 .30
163 Buck Williams .05 .15
164 Blair Rasmussen .02 .10
165 Vern Fleming .02 .10
166 Duane Ferrell .02 .10
167 George McCloud .02 .10
168 Terry Cummings .05 .15
169 Detlef Schrempf .05 .15
170 Willie Anderson .02 .10
171 Scott Williams .02 .10
172 Vernon Maxwell .02 .10
173 Todd Lichti .02 .10
174 David Benoit .02 .10
175 Marcus Liberty .02 .10
176 Kenny Smith .02 .10
177 Dan Majerle .05 .15
178 Jeff Malone .02 .10
179 Robert Parish .05 .15
180 Mark Eaton .02 .10
181 Rony Seikaly .02 .10
182 Tony Campbell .02 .10
183 Kevin McHale .10 .30
184 Thurl Bailey .02 .10
185 Kevin Edwards .02 .10
186 Gerald Glass .02 .10
187 Hersey Hawkins .05 .15
188 Sam Mitchell .02 .10
189 Brian Shaw .02 .10
190 Felton Spencer .02 .10
191 Mark Macon .02 .10
192 Jerry Reynolds .02 .10
193 Dale Davis .02 .10
194 Sleepy Floyd .02 .10
195 A.C. Green .05 .15
196 Terry Catledge .02 .10
197 Byron Scott .05 .15
198 Sam Bowie .02 .10
199 Vlade Divac .05 .15
200 Michael Jordan CL .10 .30
201 Brad Lohaus .02 .10
202 Johnny Newman .02 .10
203 Gary Grant .02 .10
204 Sidney Green .02 .10
205 Frank Brickowski .02 .10
206 Anthony Bowie .02 .10
207 Duane Causwell .02 .10
208 A.J. English .02 .10
209 Mark Aguirre .02 .10
210 Jon Koncak .02 .10
211 Kevin Gamble .02 .10
212 Craig Ehlo .02 .10
213 Herb Williams .05 .15
214 Cedric Ceballos .05 .15
215 Mark Jackson .05 .15
216 John Bagley .02 .10
217 Ron Anderson .02 .10
218 John Battle .02 .10
219 Kevin Lynch .02 .10
220 Donald Hodge .02 .10
221 Chris Gatling .02 .10
222 Muggsy Bogues .05 .15
223 Bill Laimbeer .05 .15
224 Anthony Bonner .02 .10
225 Fred Roberts .02 .10
226 Larry Stewart .02 .10
227 Darrell Walker .02 .10
228 Larry Smith .02 .10
229 Billy Owens .05 .15
230 Vinnie Johnson .02 .10
231 Johnny Dawkins .02 .10
232 Rick Fox .05 .15
233 Travis Mays .02 .10
234 Mark Price .02 .10
235 Derrick McKey .02 .10
236 Greg Anthony .02 .10
237 Doug Smith .02 .10
238 Alec Kessler .02 .10
239 Anthony Mason .10 .30
240 Shawn Kemp .25 .60
241 Jim Les .02 .10
242 Dennis Rodman .25 .60
243 Lionel Simmons .02 .10
244 Pervis Ellison .02 .10
245 Terrell Brandon .10 .30
246 Mark Bryant .02 .10
247 Brad Daugherty .02 .10
248 Scott Brooks .02 .10
249 Sarunas Marciulionis .02 .10
250 Danny Ferry .02 .10
251 Loy Vaught .02 .10
252 Dee Brown .02 .10
253 Alvin Robertson .02 .10
254 Charles Smith .02 .10
255 Dikembe Mutombo .15 .40
256 Greg Kite .02 .10
257 Ed Pinckney .02 .10
258 Ron Harper .05 .15
259 Elliot Perry .02 .10
260 Rafael Addison .02 .10
261 Tim Hardaway .15 .40
262 Randy Brown .02 .10
263 Isiah Thomas .10 .30
264 Victor Alexander .02 .10
265 Wayman Tisdale .02 .10
266 Harvey Grant .02 .10
267 Mike Iuzzolino .02 .10
268 J.Dumars/M.Jordan .10 .30
269 Xavier McDaniel .02 .10
270 Jeff Sanders .02 .10
271 Danny Manning .05 .15
272 Jayson Williams .05 .15
273 Ricky Pierce .02 .10
274 Will Perdue .02 .10
275 Dana Barros .02 .10
276 Randy Breuer .02 .10
277 Manute Bol .02 .10
278 Negele Knight .02 .10
279 Rodney McCray .02 .10
280 Greg Sutton .02 .10
281 L.Nance/M.Jordan .10 .30
282 John Starks .05 .15
283 Pete Chilcutt .02 .10
284 Kenny Gattison .02 .10
285 S.King/M.Jordan .10 .30
286 Bernard King .02 .10
287 Larry Johnson .15 .40
288 John Williams .02 .10
289 Dell Curry .02 .10
290 Orlando Woolridge .02 .10
291 Nate McMillan .02 .10
292 Terry Mills .02 .10
293 Sherman Douglas .02 .10
294 Charles Shackleford .02 .10
295 Ken Norman .02 .10
296 LaSalle Thompson .02 .10
297 Chris Mullin .10 .30
298 Eddie Johnson .02 .10
299 Armon Gilliam .02 .10
300 Michael Cage .02 .10
301 Moses Malone .10 .30
302 Charles Oakley .05 .15
303 David Wingate .02 .10
304 Steve Kerr .05 .15
305 Tyrone Hill .05 .15
306 Mark West .02 .10
307 Fat Lever .02 .10
308 J.R. Reid .02 .10
309 Ed Nealy .02 .10
310 Michael Jordan CL .10 .30
311 Alaa Abdelnaby .02 .10
312 Stacey Augmon .05 .15
313 Anthony Avent RC .02 .10
314 Walter Bond RC .02 .10
315 Byron Houston RC .02 .10
316 Rick Mahorn .02 .10
317 Sam Mitchell .02 .10
318 Mookie Blaylock .05 .15
319 Lance Blanks .02 .10
320 John Williams .02 .10
321 Rolando Blackman .02 .10
322 Danny Ainge .05 .15
323 Gerald Glass .02 .10
324 Robert Pack .02 .10
325 Oliver Miller RC .05 .15
326 Charles Smith .02 .10
327 Duane Ferrell .02 .10
328 Pooh Richardson .02 .10
329 Scott Brooks .02 .10
330 Walt Williams RC .10 .30
331 Andrew Lang .02 .10
332 Eric Murdock .02 .10
333 Vinny Del Negro .02 .10
334 Charles Barkley .20 .50
335 James Edwards .02 .10
336 Xavier McDaniel .02 .10
337 Paul Graham .02 .10
338 David Wingate .02 .10
339 Richard Dumas RC .02 .10
340 Jay Humphries .02 .10
341 Mark Jackson .05 .15
342 John Salley .02 .10
343 Jon Koncak .02 .10
344 Rodney McCray .02 .10
345 Chuck Person .02 .10
346 Mario Elie .02 .10
347 Frank Johnson .02 .10
348 Rumeal Robinson .02 .10
349 Terry Mills .02 .10
350 Kevin Willis TFC .02 .10
351 Dee Brown TFC .02 .10
352 Muggsy Bogues TFC .02 .10
353 B.J. Armstrong TFC .02 .10
354 Larry Nance TFC .02 .10
355 Doug Smith TFC .02 .10
356 Robert Pack TFC .02 .10
357 Joe Dumars TFC .05 .15
358 Sarunas Marciulionis TFC .02 .10
359 Kenny Smith TFC .02 .10
360 Pooh Richardson TFC .02 .10
361 Mark Jackson TFC .02 .10
362 Sedale Threatt TFC .02 .10
363 Grant Long TFC .02 .10
364 Eric Murdock TFC .02 .10
365 Doug West TFC .02 .10
366 Kenny Anderson TFC .05 .15
367 Anthony Mason TFC .05 .15
368 Nick Anderson TFC .02 .10
369 Jeff Hornacek TFC .02 .10
370 Dan Majerle TFC .02 .10
371 Clifford Robinson TFC .02 .10
372 Lionel Simmons TFC .02 .10
373 Dale Ellis TFC .02 .10
374 Gary Payton TFC .10 .30
375 David Benoit TFC .02 .10
376 Harvey Grant TFC .02 .10
377 Buck Johnson .02 .10
378 Brian Howard RC .02 .10
379 Travis Mays .02 .10
380 Jud Buechler .02 .10
381 Matt Geiger RC .02 .10
382 Bob McCann RC .02 .10
383 Cedric Ceballos .05 .15
384 Rod Strickland .10 .30
385 Kiki Vandeweghe .02 .10
386 Latrell Sprewell RC 1.00 2.50
387 Larry Krystkowiak .02 .10
388 Dale Ellis .02 .10
389 Trent Tucker .02 .10
390 Negele Knight .02 .10
391 Stanley Roberts .02 .10
392 Tony Campbell .02 .10
393 Tim Perry .02 .10
394 Doug Overton .02 .10
395 Dan Majerle .05 .15
396 Duane Cooper RC .02 .10
397 Kevin Willis .02 .10
398 Micheal Williams .02 .10
399 Avery Johnson .02 .10
400 Dominique Wilkins .10 .30
401 Chris Smith RC .02 .10
402 Blair Rasmussen .02 .10
403 Jeff Hornacek .05 .15
404 Blue Edwards .02 .10
405 Olden Polynice .02 .10
406 Jeff Grayer .02 .10
407 Tony Bennett RC .02 .10
408 Don MacLean .02 .10
409 Tom Chambers .02 .10
410 Keith Jennings RC .02 .10
411 Gerald Wilkins .02 .10
412 Kennard Winchester .02 .10
413 Doc Rivers .05 .15
414 Brent Price RC .02 .10
415 Mark West .02 .10
416 J.R. Reid .02 .10
417 Jon Barry RC .05 .15
418 Kevin Johnson .10 .30
419 Michael Jordan CL .10 .30
420 Michael Jordan CL .10 .30
421 Daugh/Price/Nance AS CL .02 .10
422 Scottie Pippen AS .20 .50
423 Larry Johnson AS .10 .30
424 Shaquille O'Neal AS 1.00 2.50
425 Michael Jordan AS .75 2.00
426 Isiah Thomas AS .05 .15
427 Brad Daugherty AS .02 .10
428 Joe Dumars AS .05 .15
429 Patrick Ewing AS .05 .15
430 Larry Nance AS .02 .10
431 Mark Price AS .02 .10
432 Detlef Schrempf AS .02 .10
433 Dominique Wilkins AS .05 .15
434 Karl Malone AS .10 .30
435 Charles Barkley AS .10 .30
436 David Robinson AS .10 .30
437 John Stockton AS .05 .15
438 Clyde Drexler AS .05 .15
439 Sean Elliott AS .02 .10
440 Tim Hardaway AS .10 .30
441 Shawn Kemp AS .10 .30
442 Dan Majerle AS .02 .10
443 Danny Manning AS .02 .10
444 Hakeem Olajuwon AS .10 .30
445 Terry Porter AS .02 .10
446 Harold Miner FACE .05 .15
447 David Benoit FACE .02 .10
448 Cedric Ceballos FACE .02 .10
449 Chris Jackson FACE .02 .10
450 Tim Perry FACE .02 .10
451 Kenny Smith FACE .02 .10
452 Clar.Weatherspoon FACE .10 .30
453A M.Jordan FACE 85 ERR 10.00 25.00
453B M.Jordan FACE 87 COR .75 2.00
454A D.Wilkins FACE 87 ERR 1.00 2.50
454B D.Wilkins FACE 85 COR .10 .30
455 D.Cooper/A.Peeler TP CL .02 .10
456 Adam Keefe TP .02 .10
457 Alonzo Mourning TP .20 .50
458 Jim Jackson TP .10 .30
459 Sean Rooks TP .02 .10
460 LaPhonso Ellis TP .05 .15
461 Bryant Stith TP .02 .10
462 Byron Houston TP .02 .10
463 Latrell Sprewell TP .10 .30
464 Robert Horry TP .05 .15
465 Malik Sealy TP .02 .10
466 Doug Christie TP .02 .10
467 Duane Cooper TP .02 .10
468 Anthony Peeler TP .02 .10
469 Harold Miner TP .02 .10
470 Todd Day TP .02 .10
471 Lee Mayberry TP .02 .10
472 Christian Laettner TP .10 .30
473 Hubert Davis TP .02 .10
474 Shaquille O'Neal TP 1.00 2.50
475 Clarence Weatherspoon TP .10 .30
476 Richard Dumas TP .02 .10
477 Oliver Miller TP .02 .10
478 Tracy Murray TP .02 .10
479 Walt Williams TP .05 .15
480 Lloyd Daniels TP .02 .10
481 Tom Gugliotta TP .10 .30
482 Brent Price TP .02 .10
483 Mark Aguirre GF .02 .10
484 Frank Brickowski GF .02 .10
485 Derrick Coleman GF .02 .10
486 Clyde Drexler GF .05 .15
487 Harvey Grant GF .02 .10
488 Michael Jordan GF .75 2.00
489 Karl Malone GF .10 .30
490 Xavier McDaniel GF .02 .10
491 Drazen Petrovic GF .02 .10
492 John Starks GF .02 .10
493 Robert Parish GF .02 .10
494 Christian Laettner GF .10 .30
495 Ron Harper GF .02 .10
496 David Robinson GF .10 .30
497 John Salley GF .02 .10
498 B.Daugherty/M.Price ST .02 .10
499 D.Mutombo/C.Jackson ST .10 .30
500 I.Thomas/J.Dumars ST .10 .30
501 H.Olajuwon/Thorpe ST .10 .30
502 D.Coleman/D.Petrovic ST .05 .15
503 T.Porter/C.Drexler ST .10 .30
504 L.Simmons/M.Richmond ST .05 .15
505 D.Robinson/S.Elliott ST .10 .30
506 Michael Jordan FAN 12.00 30.00
507 Larry Bird FAN 2.00 5.00
508 Karl Malone FAN .75 2.00
509 Dikembe Mutombo FAN .40 1.00
510 L.Bird/M.Jordan FAN 8.00 20.00
SP1 L.Bird/M.Johnson Retire 1.25 3.00
SP2 D.Wilkins/M.Jordan 20K 2.50 6.00

1992-93 Upper Deck All-Division

COMPLETE SET (20) 6.00 15.00
ONE PER HI SERIES JUMBO PACK
AD1 Shaquille O'Neal 3.00 8.00
AD2 Derrick Coleman .15 .40
AD3 Glen Rice .30 .75
AD4 Reggie Lewis .15 .40
AD5 Kenny Anderson .30 .75
AD6 Brad Daugherty .08 .20
AD7 Dominique Wilkins .30 .75
AD8 Larry Johnson .40 1.00
AD9 Michael Jordan 4.00 10.00
AD10 Mark Price .08 .20
AD11 David Robinson .50 1.25
AD12 Karl Malone .50 1.25
AD13 Sean Elliott .15 .40
AD14 John Stockton .30 .75
AD15 Derek Harper .15 .40
AD16 Kevin Duckworth .08 .20
AD17 Chris Mullin .30 .75
AD18 Charles Barkley .50 1.25
AD19 Tim Hardaway .40 1.00
AD20 Clyde Drexler .30 .75

1992-93 Upper Deck All-NBA

COMPLETE SET (10) 6.00 15.00
ONE PER LO SERIES LOCKER PACK
AN1 Michael Jordan ! 4.00 10.00
AN2 Clyde Drexler .75 2.00
AN3 David Robinson 1.25 3.00
AN4 Karl Malone 1.25 3.00
AN5 Chris Mullin .75 2.00
AN6 John Stockton .75 2.00
AN7 Tim Hardaway 1.00 2.50
AN8 Patrick Ewing .75 2.00
AN9 Scottie Pippen 2.50 6.00
AN10 Charles Barkley 1.25 3.00

1992-93 Upper Deck All-Rookies

COMPLETE SET (10) 5.00 10.00
LO SERIES STATED ODDS 1:12 RETAIL
AR1 Larry Johnson 1.00 2.50
AR2 Dikembe Mutombo 1.00 2.50
AR3 Billy Owens .40 1.00
AR4 Steve Smith 1.00 2.50
AR5 Stacey Augmon .40 1.00
AR6 Rick Fox .40 1.00
AR7 Terrell Brandon .75 2.00
AR8 Larry Stewart .10 .30
AR9 Stanley Roberts .10 .30
AR10 Mark Macon .10 .30

1992-93 Upper Deck Award Winner Holograms

COMPLETE SET (9) 8.00 20.00
COMPLETE LO SERIES (6) 5.00 12.00
COMPLETE HI SERIES (3) 3.00 8.00
LO/HI SERIES STATED ODDS 1:18 HOB/RET
AW1 Michael Jordan 6.00 15.00
AW2 John Stockton 1.00 2.50
AW3 Dennis Rodman 1.50 4.00
AW4 Detlef Schrempf .60 1.50
AW5 Larry Johnson .75 2.00
AW6 David Robinson 1.00 2.50
AW7 David Robinson 1.00 2.50
AW8 John Stockton 1.00 2.50
AW9 Michael Jordan 6.00 15.00

1992-93 Upper Deck Larry Bird Heroes

COMMON BIRD (19-27) .30 .75
HI SERIES STATED ODDS 1:9
NNO Larry Bird .75 2.00

1992-93 Upper Deck Wilt Chamberlain Heroes

COMMON CHAMBER. (10-18) .30 .75
LO SERIES STATED ODDS 1:9
NNO Wilt Chamberlain .50 1.25

1992-93 Upper Deck Wilt Chamberlain Box Bottom

NNO Wilt Chamberlain .30 .75

1992-93 Upper Deck 15000 Point Club

COMPLETE SET (20) 15.00 40.00
HI SERIES STATED ODDS 1:9 HOBBY
PC1 Dominique Wilkins 1.00 2.50
PC2 Kevin McHale 1.00 2.50
PC3 Robert Parish .50 1.25
PC4 Michael Jordan 10.00 25.00
PC5 Isiah Thomas 1.00 2.50
PC6 Mark Aguirre .30 .75
PC7 Kiki Vandeweghe .30 .75
PC8 James Worthy 1.00 2.50
PC9 Rolando Blackman .30 .75
PC10 Moses Malone 1.00 2.50
PC11 Charles Barkley 1.50 4.00
PC12 Tom Chambers .30 .75
PC13 Clyde Drexler 1.00 2.50
PC14 Terry Cummings .50 1.25
PC15 Eddie Johnson .30 .75
PC16 Karl Malone 1.50 4.00
PC17 Bernard King .30 .75
PC18 Larry Nance .30 .75
PC19 Jeff Malone .30 .75
PC20 Hakeem Olajuwon 1.50 4.00

1992-93 Upper Deck Foreign Exchange

COMPLETE SET (10) 7.50 15.00
ONE PER HI SERIES LOCKER PACK
FE1 Manute Bol .25 .60
FE2 Vlade Divac .75 2.00
FE3 Patrick Ewing 1.50 4.00
FE4 Sarunas Marciulionis .25 .60
FE5 Dikembe Mutombo 2.00 5.00
FE6 Hakeem Olajuwon 2.50 6.00
FE7 Drazen Petrovic .75 2.00
FE8 Detlef Schrempf .75 2.00
FE9 Rik Smits .75 2.00
FE10 Dominique Wilkins 1.50 4.00

1992-93 Upper Deck Rookie Standouts

COMPLETE SET (20) 10.00 25.00
HI SERIES STATED ODDS 1:9 RET/JUM
RS1 Adam Keefe .20 .50
RS2 Alonzo Mourning 2.00 5.00
RS3 Sean Rooks .20 .50
RS4 LaPhonso Ellis .40 1.00
RS5 Latrell Sprewell 1.25 3.00
RS6 Robert Horry .75 2.00
RS7 Malik Sealy .20 .50
RS8 Anthony Peeler .20 .50
RS9 Harold Miner .60 1.50
RS10 Anthony Avent .20 .50
RS11 Todd Day .40 1.00
RS12 Lee Mayberry .20 .50
RS13 Christian Laettner .75 2.00
RS14 Hubert Davis .40 1.00
RS15 Shaquille O'Neal 6.00 15.00
RS16 Clarence Weatherspoon .40 1.00
RS17 Richard Dumas .40 1.00
RS18 Walt Williams .40 1.00
RS19 Lloyd Daniels .40 1.00
RS20 Tom Gugliotta 1.00 2.50

1992-93 Upper Deck Team MVPs

COMPLETE SET (28) 15.00 40.00
ONE PER LO SERIES JUMBO PACK
TM1 Michael Jordan CL 8.00 20.00
TM2 Dominique Wilkins .75 2.00
TM3 Reggie Lewis .40 1.00
TM4 Kendall Gill .40 1.00
TM5 Michael Jordan 8.00 20.00
TM6 Brad Daugherty .10 .30
TM7 Derek Harper .40 1.00
TM8 Dikembe Mutombo 1.00 2.50
TM9 Isiah Thomas .75 2.00
TM10 Chris Mullin .75 2.00
TM11 Hakeem Olajuwon 1.25 3.00
TM12 Reggie Miller .75 2.00
TM13 Ron Harper .40 1.00
TM14 James Worthy .75 2.00
TM15 Rony Seikaly .10 .30
TM16 Alvin Robertson .10 .30
TM17 Pooh Richardson .10 .30
TM18 Derrick Coleman .40 1.00
TM19 Patrick Ewing .75 2.00
TM20 Scott Skiles .10 .30
TM21 Hersey Hawkins .40 1.00
TM22 Kevin Johnson .75 2.00
TM23 Clyde Drexler .75 2.00
TM24 Mitch Richmond .75 2.00
TM25 David Robinson 1.25 3.00
TM26 Ricky Pierce .10 .30
TM27 John Stockton .75 2.00
TM28 Pervis Ellison .10 .30

1992-93 Upper Deck Jerry West Selects

COMPLETE SET (20) 15.00 40.00
LO SERIES STATED ODDS 1:9 HOBBY
JW1 Michael Jordan 4.00 10.00
JW2 Dennis Rodman 1.50 4.00
JW3 David Robinson 1.25 3.00
JW4 Michael Jordan 4.00 10.00
JW5 Magic Johnson 2.50 6.00
JW6 Detlef Schrempf .40 1.00
JW7 Magic Johnson 4.00 10.00
JW8A Michael Jordan 4.00 10.00
JW8B Michael Jordan
Best All-Around Player
Jumbo/5000 4.00 10.00
JW9 Michael Jordan 4.00 10.00
JW10 Magic Johnson 4.00 10.00
JW11 Glen Rice .75 2.00
JW12 Dikembe Mutombo 1.00 2.50
JW13 Dikembe Mutombo 1.00 2.50
JW14 Stacey Augmon .40 1.00
JW15 Tim Hardaway 1.00 2.50
JW16 Shawn Kemp 1.50 4.00
JW17 Danny Manning .40 1.00
JW18 Larry Johnson 1.00 2.50
JW19 Reggie Lewis .40 1.00
JW20 Tim Hardaway 1.00 2.50

1993-94 Upper Deck

COMPLETE SET (510) 15.00 30.00
COMPLETE SERIES 1 (255) 7.50 15.00
COMPLETE SERIES 2 (255) 7.50 15.00
SP3: SER.1 STATED ODDS 1:72
SP4: SER.2 STATED ODDS 1:72
1 Muggsy Bogues .40 1.00
2 Kenny Anderson .30 .75
3 Dell Curry .40 1.00
4 Charles Smith .25 .60
5 Chuck Person .30 .75
6 Chucky Brown .25 .60
7 Kevin Johnson .40 1.00
8 Winston Garland .25 .60
9 John Salley .30 .75
10 Dale Ellis .25 .60
11 Otis Thorpe .40 1.00
12 John Stockton .75 2.00
13 Kendall Gill .30 .75
14 Randy White .25 .60
15 Mark Jackson .30 .75
16 Vlade Divac .40 1.00
17 Scott Skiles .25 .60
18 Xavier McDaniel .40 1.00
19 Jeff Hornacek .30 .75
20 Stanley Roberts .25 .60
21 Harold Miner .30 .75
22 Terrell Brandon .30 .75
23B M.Jordan Black 4.00 10.00
23A Michael Jordan 4.00 10.00
24 Jim Jackson .30 .75
25 Keith Askins .25 .60
26 Corey Williams .25 .60
27 David Benoit .25 .60
28 Charles Oakley .40 1.00
29 Michael Adams .30 .75
30 Clarence Weatherspoon .25 .60
31 Jon Koncak .25 .60
32 Gerald Wilkins .30 .75
33 Anthony Bowie .25 .60
34 Willie Burton .25 .60
35 Stacey Augmon .30 .75
36 Doc Rivers .30 .75
37 Luc Longley .30 .75
38 Dee Brown .30 .75
39 Litterial Green .25 .60
40 Dan Majerle .40 1.00
41 Doug West .25 .60
42 Joe Dumars .50 1.25
43 Dennis Scott .30 .75
44 Mahmoud Abdul-Rauf .30 .75
45 Mark Eaton .40 1.00
46 Danny Ferry .25 .60
47 Kenny Smith .30 .75
48 Ron Harper .40 1.00
49 Adam Keefe .25 .60
50 David Robinson .75 2.00
51 John Starks .40 1.00
52 Jeff Malone .30 .75
53 Vern Fleming .30 .75
54 Olden Polynice .25 .60
55 Dikembe Mutombo .60 1.50
56 Chris Morris .25 .60
57 Paul Graham .25 .60
58 Richard Dumas .25 .60
59 J.R. Reid .30 .75
60 Brad Daugherty .30 .75
61 Blue Edwards .25 .60
62 Mark Macon .25 .60
63 Latrell Sprewell .60 1.50
64 Mitch Richmond .50 1.25
65 David Wingate .25 .60
66 LaSalle Thompson .25 .60
67 Sedale Threatt .25 .60
68 Larry Krystkowiak .25 .60
69 John Paxson .40 1.00
70 Frank Brickowski .25 .60
71 Duane Causwell .25 .60
72 Fred Roberts .25 .60
73 Rod Strickland .30 .75
74 Willie Anderson .25 .60
75 Thurl Bailey .25 .60
76 Ricky Pierce .30 .75
77 Todd Day .25 .60
78 Hot Rod Williams .25 .60
79 Danny Ainge .40 1.00
80 Mark West .25 .60
81 Marcus Liberty .25 .60
82 Keith Jennings .25 .60
83 Derrick Coleman .40 1.00
84 Larry Stewart .25 .60
85 Tracy Murray .25 .60
86 Robert Horry .40 1.00
87 Derek Harper .30 .75
88 Scott Hastings .25 .60
89 Sam Perkins .30 .75
90 Clyde Drexler .60 1.50
91 Brent Price .25 .60
92 Chris Mullin .50 1.25
93 Rafael Addison .25 .60
94 Tyrone Corbin .25 .60
95 Sarunas Marciulionis .40 1.00
96 Antoine Carr .25 .60
97 Tony Bennett .25 .60
98 Sam Mitchell .25 .60
99 Lionel Simmons .25 .60
100 Tim Perry .25 .60
101 Horace Grant .40 1.00
102 Tom Hammonds .25 .60
103 Walter Bond .25 .60
104 Detlef Schrempf .40 1.00
105 Terry Porter .30 .75
106 Danny Schayes .25 .60
107 Rumeal Robinson .25 .60
109 Mike Gminski .25 .60
110 Terry Mills .25 .60
111 Loy Vaught .25 .60
112 Jim Les .25 .60
113 Byron Houston .25 .60
114 Randy Brown .25 .60
115 Anthony Avent .25 .60
116 Donald Hodge .25 .60
117 Kevin Willis .30 .75
118 Robert Pack .25 .60
119 Dale Davis .30 .75
120 Grant Long .25 .60
121 Anthony Bonner .25 .60
122 Chris Smith .25 .60
123 Elden Campbell .25 .60
124 Clifford Robinson .40 1.00
125 Sherman Douglas .25 .60
126 Alvin Robertson .30 .75
127 Rolando Blackman .30 .75
128 Malik Sealy .25 .60
129 Ed Pinckney .25 .60
130 Anthony Peeler .25 .60
131 Scott Brooks .25 .60
132 Rik Smits .30 .75
133 Derrick McKey .30 .75
134 Alaa Abdelnaby .25 .60
135 Rex Chapman .25 .60
136 Tony Campbell .25 .60
137 John Williams .25 .60
138 Vincent Askew .25 .60
139 LaBradford Smith .25 .60
140 Vinny Del Negro .25 .60
141 Darrell Walker .25 .60
142 James Worthy .50 1.25
143 Jeff Turner .25 .60
144 Duane Ferrell .25 .60
145 Larry Smith .25 .60
146 Eddie Johnson .25 .60
147 Chris Gatling .25 .60
148 Buck Williams .30 .75
149 Donald Royal .25 .60
150 Dino Radja RC .40 1.00
151 Johnny Dawkins .30 .75
152 Tim Legler RC .40 1.00
153 Bill Laimbeer .40 1.00
154 Glen Rice .40 1.00
155 Bill Cartwright .30 .75
156 Luther Wright RC .25 .60
157 Rex Walters RC .30 .75
158 Doug Edwards RC .40 1.00
159 George Lynch RC .40 1.00
160 Chris Mills RC .40 1.00
161 Sam Cassell RC .75 2.00
162 Nick Van Exel RC 1.00 2.50
163 Shawn Bradley RC .40 1.00
164 Calbert Cheaney RC .40 1.00
165 Corie Blount RC .40 1.00
166 Michael Jordan SL 4.00 10.00
167 Dennis Rodman SL 1.00 2.50
168 John Stockton SL .75 2.00
169 B.J. Armstrong SL .40 1.00
170 Hakeem Olajuwon SL .75 2.00
171 Michael Jordan SL 4.00 10.00
172 Cedric Ceballos SL .30 .75
173 Mark Price SL .40 1.00
174 Charles Barkley SL 1.00 2.50
175 Clifford Robinson SL .40 1.00
176 Hakeem Olajuwon SL .75 2.00
177 Shaquille O'Neal SL 2.00 5.00
178 R.Miller/C.Oakley PO .75 2.00
179 R.Fox/K.Gattison PO .30 .75
180 M.Jordan/S.Augmon PO 4.00 10.00
181 Brad Daugherty PO .30 .75
182 O.Miller/B.Scott PO .40 1.00
183 D.Robinson/S.Elliott PO .75 2.00
184 K.Smith/M.Jackson PO .30 .75
185 Eddie Johnson PO .25 .60
186 A.Mason/P.Ewing/Zo PO .60 1.50
187 M.Jordan/G.Wilkins PO 4.00 10.00
188 Oliver Miller PO .25 .60
189 S.Perkins/H.Olajuwon PO .75 2.00
190 Bill Cartwright PO .30 .75
191 Kevin Johnson PO .40 1.00
192 Dan Majerle PO .40 1.00
193 Michael Jordan PO 4.00 10.00
194 L.Johnson/Bogues PO .50 1.25
195 Reggie Miller PO .75 2.00
196 J.Starks/S.Pippen PO 1.00 2.50
197 Charles Barkley PO 1.00 2.50
198 Michael Jordan FIN 4.00 10.00
199 Scottie Pippen FIN 1.00 2.50
200 Kevin Johnson FIN .40 1.00
201 Michael Jordan FIN 4.00 10.00
202 Richard Dumas FIN .25 .60
203 Horace Grant FIN .40 1.00
204 Michael Jordan FIN 4.00 10.00
205 S.Pippen/C.Barkley FIN 1.00 2.50
206 John Paxson FIN .40 1.00
207 B.J. Armstrong FIN .40 1.00
208 1992-93 Bulls FIN .40 1.00
209 1992-93 Suns FIN .20 .50
210 K.Willis SKED .20 .50
211 B.Shaw SKED .20 .50
212 Charlotte Hornets SKED .20 .50
213 M.Jordan/Group SKED 4.00 10.00
214 M.Price SKED .40 1.00
215 J.Jackson/S.Rooks SKED .30 .75
216 D.Mutombo SKED .60 1.50
217 Detroit Pistons SKED .60 1.50
219 H.Olajuwon SKED .75 2.00
220 Indiana Pacers SKED .40 1.00
221 L.A. Clippers SKED .40 1.00
222 L.A. Lakers SKED .20 .50
223 Miami Heat SKED .30 .75
224 Milwaukee Bucks SKED .20 .50
225 Minnesota Timberwolves SKED .20 .50
226 New Jersey Nets SKED .30 .75
227 New York Knicks SKED .30 .75
228 S.O'Neal/Group SKED 2.00 5.00
229 Philadelphia 76ers SKED .30 .75
230 C.Barkley/Group SKED 1.00 2.50
231 Portland Trail Blazers SKED .30 .75
232 Sacramento Kings SKED .20 .50
233 D.Robinson/Group SKED .75 2.00
234 S.Kemp/G.Payton SKED .60 1.50
235 Utah Jazz SKED .20 .50
236 Gugliotta/Adams SKED .30 .75
237 Michael Jordan SM 4.00 10.00
238 Clyde Drexler SM .60 1.50
239 Tim Hardaway SM .50 1.25
240 Dominique Wilkins SM .60 1.50
241 Brad Daugherty SM .30 .75
242 Chris Mullin SM .50 1.25
243 Kenny Anderson SM .30 .75
244 Patrick Ewing SM .60 1.50
245 Isiah Thomas SM .60 1.50
246 Dikembe Mutombo SM .60 1.50
247 Danny Manning SM .30 .75
248 David Robinson SM .75 2.00
249 Karl Malone SM .75 2.00
250 James Worthy SM .50 1.25
251 Shawn Kemp SM .60 1.50
252 Checklist 1-64 .20 .50
253 Checklist 65-128 .20 .50
254 Checklist 129-192 .20 .50
255 Checklist 193-255 .20 .50
256 Patrick Ewing .60 1.50
257 B.J. Armstrong .40 1.00
258 Oliver Miller .25 .60
259 Jud Buechler .25 .60
260 Pooh Richardson .30 .75
261 Victor Alexander .25 .60
262 Kevin Gamble .25 .60
263 Doug Smith .25 .60

264 Isiah Thomas .60 1.50
265 Doug Christie .30 .75
266 Mark Bryant .25 .60
267 Lloyd Daniels .25 .60
268 Micheal Williams .25 .60
269 Nick Anderson .30 .75
270 Tom Gugliotta .30 .75
271 Kenny Gattison .25 .60
272 Vernon Maxwell .25 .60
273 Terry Cummings .30 .75
274 Karl Malone .75 2.00
275 Rick Fox .30 .75
276 Matt Bullard .25 .60
277 Johnny Newman .25 .60
278 Mark Price .40 1.00
279 Mookie Blaylock .40 1.00
280 Charles Barkley 1.00 2.50
281 Larry Nance .30 .75
282 Walt Williams .40 1.00
283 Brian Shaw .25 .60
284 Robert Parish .50 1.25
285 Pervis Ellison .25 .60
286 Spud Webb .30 .75
287 Hakeem Olajuwon .75 2.00
288 Jerome Kersey .25 .60
289 Carl Herrera .25 .60
290 Dominique Wilkins .60 1.50
291 Billy Owens .25 .60
292 Greg Anthony .25 .60
293 Nate McMillan .30 .75
294 Christian Laettner .40 1.00
295 Gary Payton .50 1.25
296 Steve Smith .30 .75
297 Anthony Mason .30 .75
298 Sean Rooks .25 .60
299 Toni Kukoc RC 1.00 2.50
300 Shaquille O'Neal 2.00 5.00
301 Jay Humphries .30 .75
302 Sleepy Floyd .30 .75
303 Bimbo Coles .25 .60
304 John Battle .25 .60
305 Shawn Kemp .60 1.50
306 Scott Williams .25 .60
307 Wayman Tisdale .30 .75
308 Rony Seikaly .30 .75
309 Reggie Miller .75 2.00
310 Scottie Pippen 1.00 2.50
311 Chris Webber RC 2.00 5.00
312 Trevor Wilson .25 .60
313 Derek Strong RC .30 .75
314 Bobby Hurley RC .40 1.00
315 Herb Williams .25 .60
316 Rex Walters .30 .75
317 Doug Edwards .40 1.00
318 Ken Williams .25 .60
319 Jon Barry .25 .60
320 Joe Courtney RC .40 1.00
321 Ervin Johnson RC .40 1.00
322 Sam Cassell .75 2.00
323 Tim Hardaway .50 1.25
324 Steve Kerr .30 .75
325 Pete Chilcutt .25 .60
326 Doug Overton .25 .60
327 Reggie Williams .25 .60
328 Avery Johnson .30 .75
329 Stacey King .25 .60
330 Vin Baker RC .60 1.50
331 Greg Kite .25 .60
332 Michael Cage .30 .75
333 Alonzo Mourning .60 1.50
334 Acie Earl RC .40 1.00
335 Terry Dehere RC .40 1.00
336 Negele Knight .25 .60
337 Gerald Madkins RC .40 1.00
338 Lindsey Hunter RC .40 1.00
339 Luther Wright .25 .60
340 Mike Peplowski RC .25 .60
341 Dino Radja .25 .60
342 Danny Manning .30 .75
343 Chris Mills .40 1.00
344 Hubert Davis .30 .75
345 Shawn Bradley .40 1.00
346 Evers Burns RC .40 1.00
347 Rodney Rogers RC .40 1.00
348 Cedric Ceballos .30 .75
349 Warren Kidd RC .25 .60
350 Darnell Mee RC .25 .60
351 Matt Geiger .25 .60
352 Jamal Mashburn RC .75 2.00
353 Antonio Davis RC .50 1.25
354 Calbert Cheaney .40 1.00
355 George Lynch .40 1.00
356 Derrick McKey .30 .75
357 Jerry Reynolds .25 .60
358 Don MacLean .25 .60
359 Scott Haskin RC .25 .60
360 Malcolm Mackey RC .25 .60
361 Isaiah Rider RC .60 1.50
362 Detlef Schrempf .40 1.00
363 Josh Grant RC .30 .75
364 Kurt Rambis .30 .75
365 Larry Johnson .50 1.25
366 Richard Petruska RC .40 1.00
367 Ken Norman .25 .60
369 James Robinson RC .40 1.00
370 Kevin Duckworth .25 .60
371 Chris Whitney RC .30 .75
372 Moses Malone .60 1.50
373 Nick Van Exel 1.00 2.50
374 Scott Burrell RC .40 1.00
375 Harvey Grant .30 .75
376 Benoit Benjamin .25 .60
377 Henry James .25 .60
378 Pete Myers .25 .60
379 Dwayne Schintzius .25 .60
380 Sean Green .25 .60
381 Eric Murdock .25 .60
382 Anfernee Hardaway RC 2.00 5.00
383 Gheorghe Muresan RC .40 1.00
384 Kendall Gill .30 .75
385 David Wood .25 .60
386 Mario Elie .30 .75
387 Chris Corchiani .25 .60
388 Greg Graham RC .25 .60
389 Hersey Hawkins .30 .75
390 Mark Aguirre .30 .75
391 LaPhonso Ellis .30 .75
392 Anthony Bonner .25 .60
393 Lucious Harris RC .40 1.00
394 Andrew Lang .25 .60
395 Chris Dudley .25 .60
396 Dennis Rodman 1.00 2.50
397 Larry Krystkowiak .25 .60
398 A.C. Green .30 .75
399 Eddie Johnson .25 .60
400 Kevin Edwards .25 .60
401 Tyrone Hill .25 .60
402 Greg Anderson .25 .60
403 P.J. Brown RC .40 1.00
404 Dana Barros .25 .60
405 Allan Houston RC .75 2.00
406 Mike Brown .25 .60
407 Lee Mayberry .25 .60
408 Fat Lever .30 .75
409 Tony Smith .25 .60
410 Tom Chambers .40 1.00
411 Manute Bol .25 .60
412 Joe Kleine .25 .60
413 Bryant Stith .25 .60
415 Jo Jo English RC .40 1.00
416 Sean Elliott .30 .75
417 Sam Bowie .30 .75
418 Armon Gilliam .25 .60
419 Brian Williams .25 .60
420 Popeye Jones RC .40 1.00
421 Dennis Rodman EB 1.00 2.50
422 Karl Malone EB .75 2.00
423 Tom Gugliotta EB .30 .75
424 Kevin Willis EB .30 .75
425 Hakeem Olajuwon EB .75 2.00
426 Charles Oakley EB .40 1.00
427 Clarence Weatherspoon EB .25 .60
428 Derrick Coleman EB .40 1.00
429 Buck Williams EB .30 .75
430 Christian Laettner EB .40 1.00
431 Dikembe Mutombo EB .60 1.50
432 Rony Seikaly EB .30 .75
433 Brad Daugherty EB .30 .75
434 Horace Grant EB .40 1.00
435 Larry Johnson EB .50 1.25
436 Dee Brown BT .30 .75
437 Muggsy Bogues BT .40 1.00
438 Michael Jordan BT 4.00 10.00
439 Tim Hardaway BT .50 1.25
440 Micheal Williams BT .25 .60
441 Gary Payton BT .50 1.25
442 Mookie Blaylock BT .40 1.00
443 Doc Rivers BT .30 .75
444 Kenny Smith BT .30 .75
445 John Stockton BT .75 2.00
446 Alvin Robertson BT .30 .75
447 Mark Jackson BT .30 .75
448 Kenny Anderson BT .30 .75
449 Scottie Pippen BT 1.00 2.50
450 Isiah Thomas BT .60 1.50
451 Mark Price BT .40 1.00
452 Latrell Sprewell BT .60 1.50
453 Sedale Threatt BT .25 .60
454 Nick Anderson BT .30 .75
455 Rod Strickland BT .30 .75
456 Oliver Miller GI .25 .60
457 J.Worthy/V.Divac GI .50 1.25
458 Robert Horry GI .40 1.00
459 Rockets Shoot-Around GI .20 .50
460 Rooks/Jackson/Legler GI .20 .50
461 Mitch Richmond GI .50 1.25
462 Chris Morris GI .25 .60
463 M.Jackson/G.Grant GI .30 .75
464 David Robinson GI .75 2.00
465 Danny Ainge GI .40 1.00
466 Michael Jordan SKL 4.00 10.00
467 Dominique Wilkins SKL .60 1.50
468 Alonzo Mourning SKL .60 1.50
469 Shaquille O'Neal SKL 2.00 5.00
470 Tim Hardaway SL .50 1.25
471 Patrick Ewing SKL .60 1.50
472 Kevin Johnson SL .40 1.00
473 Clyde Drexler SKL .60 1.50
474 David Robinson SKL .75 2.00
475 Shawn Kemp SKL .60 1.50
476 Dee Brown SL .30 .75
477 Jim Jackson SKL .30 .75
478 John Stockton SKL .75 2.00
479 Robert Horry SL .40 1.00
480 Glen Rice SL .40 1.00
481 Micheal Williams SIS .25 .60
482 G.Lynch/T.Dehere CL .40 1.00
483 Chris Webber TP 2.00 5.00
484 Anfernee Hardaway TP 2.00 5.00
485 Shawn Bradley TP .40 1.00
486 Jamal Mashburn TP .75 2.00
487 Calbert Cheaney TP .40 1.00
488 Isaiah Rider TP .60 1.50
489 Bobby Hurley TP .40 1.00
490 Vin Baker TP .60 1.50
491 Rodney Rogers TP .40 1.00
492 Lindsey Hunter TP .40 1.00
493 Allan Houston TP .75 2.00
494 Terry Dehere TP .40 1.00
495 George Lynch TP .40 1.00
496 Toni Kukoc TP 1.00 2.50
497 Nick Van Exel TP 1.00 2.50
498 Charles Barkley MO 1.00 2.50
499 A.C. Green MO .30 .75
500 Dan Majerle MO .40 1.00
501 Jerrod Mustaf MO .25 .60
502 Kevin Johnson MO .40 1.00
503 Joe Kleine MO .25 .60
504 Danny Ainge MO .40 1.00
505 Oliver Miller MO .25 .60
506 Joe Courtney MO .40 1.00
507 Checklist .20 .50
508 Checklist .20 .50
509 Checklist .20 .50
510 Checklist .20 .50
SP3 M.Jordan/W.Chamberlain 4.00 10.00
SP4 Bulls 3rd Champ 4.00 10.00

1993-94 Upper Deck All-NBA

COMPLETE SET (15) 6.00 12.00
ONE PER SER.1 RETAIL/GREEN JUMBO PACK
AN1 Charles Barkley 1.00 2.50
AN2 Karl Malone .75 2.00
AN3 Hakeem Olajuwon .75 2.00
AN4 Michael Jordan 4.00 10.00
AN5 Mark Price .40 1.00
AN6 Dominique Wilkins .60 1.50
AN7 Larry Johnson .50 1.25
AN8 Patrick Ewing .60 1.50
AN9 John Stockton .75 2.00
AN10 Joe Dumars .50 1.25
AN11 Scottie Pippen 1.00 2.50
AN12 Derrick Coleman .40 1.00
AN13 David Robinson .75 2.00
AN14 Tim Hardaway .50 1.25
AN15 Michael Jordan CL 4.00 10.00

1993-94 Upper Deck All-Rookies

COMPLETE SET (10) 7.50 15.00
SER.1 STATED ODDS 1:30 RETAIL
AR1 Shaquille O'Neal 4.00 10.00
AR2 Alonzo Mourning 1.25 3.00
AR3 Christian Laettner .40 1.00
AR4 Tom Gugliotta .75 2.00
AR5 LaPhonso Ellis .10 .30
AR6 Walt Williams .10 .30
AR7 Robert Horry .40 1.00
AR8 Latrell Sprewell 2.00 5.00
AR9 Clarence Weatherspoon .10 .30
AR10 Richard Dumas .10 .30

1993-94 Upper Deck Box Bottoms

COMPLETE SET (2) .75 2.00
1 Bobby Hurley .08 .25
2 Michael Jordan .75 2.00

1993-94 Upper Deck Flight Team

COMPLETE SET (20) 30.00 80.00
SER.1 STATED ODDS 1:30 HOBBY
FT1 Stacey Augmon .40 1.00
FT2 Charles Barkley 4.00 10.00
FT3 David Benoit .40 1.00
FT4 Dee Brown .40 1.00
FT5 Cedric Ceballos 1.25 3.00
FT6 Derrick Coleman 1.25 3.00
FT7 Clyde Drexler 2.50 6.00
FT8 Sean Elliott 1.25 3.00
FT9 LaPhonso Ellis .40 1.00
FT10 Kendall Gill 1.25 3.00
FT11 Larry Johnson 2.50 6.00
FT12 Shawn Kemp 4.00 10.00
FT13 Karl Malone 4.00 10.00
FT14 Harold Miner .40 1.00
FT15 Alonzo Mourning 4.00 10.00
FT16 Shaquille O'Neal 8.00 20.00
FT17 Scottie Pippen 8.00 20.00
FT18 Clarence Weatherspoon .40 1.00
FT19 Spud Webb 1.25 3.00
FT20 Dominique Wilkins 2.50 6.00

1993-94 Upper Deck Future Heroes

COMPLETE SET (10) 10.00 25.00
ONE PER SER.1 LOCKER PACK
28 Derrick Coleman .50 1.25
29 LaPhonso Ellis .15 .40
30 Jim Jackson .50 1.25
31 Larry Johnson 1.00 2.50
32 Shawn Kemp 1.50 4.00
33 Christian Laettner .50 1.25
34 Alonzo Mourning 1.50 4.00
35 Shaquille O'Neal 4.00 10.00
36 Walt Williams .15 .40
NNO L.Ellis/C.Laettner CL .50 1.25

1993-94 Upper Deck Locker Talk

COMPLETE SET (15) 10.00 25.00
ONE PER SER.2 LOCKER PACK
LT1 Michael Jordan 8.00 20.00
LT2 Stacey Augmon .60 1.50
LT3 Shaquille O'Neal 4.00 10.00
LT4 Alonzo Mourning 1.25 3.00
LT5 Harold Miner .60 1.50
LT6 Clarence Weatherspoon .50 1.25
LT7 Derrick Coleman .75 2.00
LT8 Charles Barkley 2.00 5.00
LT9 David Robinson 1.50 4.00
LT10 Chuck Person .60 1.50
LT11 Karl Malone 1.50 4.00
LT12 Muggsy Bogues .75 2.00
LT13 Latrell Sprewell 1.25 3.00
LT14 John Starks .75 2.00
LT15 Jim Jackson .60 1.50

1993-94 Upper Deck Mr. June

COMPLETE SET (10) 15.00 40.00
COMMON JORDAN (1-10) 2.50 6.00
SER.2 STATED ODDS 1:30 HOBBY

1993-94 Upper Deck Rookie Exchange

COMPLETE SILVER SET (10) 4.00 8.00
*GOLD CARDS: 1X TO 2X HI COLUMN
SIL.EXCH: SER.1 STATED ODDS 1:72
GOLD EXCH: SER.1 STATED ODDS 1:288
RE1 Chris Webber 1.25 3.00
RE2 Shawn Bradley .10 .30
RE3 Anfernee Hardaway 1.00 2.50
RE4 Jamal Mashburn .30 .75
RE5 Isaiah Rider .25 .60
RE6 Calbert Cheaney .05 .15
RE7 Bobby Hurley .05 .15
RE8 Vin Baker .30 .75
RE9 Rodney Rogers .10 .30
RE10 Lindsey Hunter .10 .30
TC2 Expired Silver Trade .08 .25
TC2 Redeemed Silver Trade .02 .10

1993-94 Upper Deck Rookie Standouts

COMPLETE SET (20) 12.00 30.00
SER.2 STATED ODDS 1:30 RETAIL
RS1 Chris Webber 5.00 12.00
RS2 Bobby Hurley .25 .60
RS3 Isaiah Rider 1.00 2.50
RS4 Terry Dehere .07 .20
RS5 Toni Kukoc 2.00 5.00
RS6 Shawn Bradley .50 1.25
RS7 Allan Houston 2.00 5.00
RS8 Chris Mills .50 1.25
RS9 Jamal Mashburn 1.25 3.00
RS10 Acie Earl .07 .20
RS11 George Lynch .07 .20
RS12 Scott Burrell .50 1.25
RS13 Calbert Cheaney .25 .60
RS14 Lindsey Hunter .50 1.25
RS15 Nick Van Exel 1.50 4.00
RS16 Rex Walters .07 .20
RS17 Anfernee Hardaway 4.00 10.00
RS18 Sam Cassell 2.00 5.00
RS19 Vin Baker 1.25 3.00
RS20 Rodney Rogers .50 1.25

1993-94 Upper Deck Team MVPs

COMPLETE SET (27) 6.00 12.00
ONE PER SER.2 RETAIL/PURPLE JUM.PACK
TM1 Dominique Wilkins .30 .75
TM2 Robert Parish .15 .40
TM3 Larry Johnson .30 .75
TM4 Scottie Pippen 1.00 2.50
TM5 Mark Price .05 .15
TM6 Jim Jackson .15 .40
TM7 Mahmoud Abdul-Rauf .05 .15
TM8 Joe Dumars .30 .75
TM9 Chris Mullin .30 .75
TM10 Hakeem Olajuwon .50 1.25
TM11 Reggie Miller .30 .75
TM12 Danny Manning .15 .40
TM13 James Worthy .30 .75
TM14 Glen Rice .15 .40
TM15 Blue Edwards .05 .15
TM16 Christian Laettner .15 .40
TM17 Derrick Coleman .15 .40
TM18 Patrick Ewing .30 .75
TM19 Shaquille O'Neal 1.50 4.00
TM20 Clarence Weatherspoon .05 .15
TM21 Charles Barkley .50 1.25
TM22 Clyde Drexler .30 .75
TM23 Mitch Richmond .30 .75
TM24 David Robinson .50 1.25
TM25 Shawn Kemp .50 1.25
TM26 John Stockton .30 .75
TM27 Tom Gugliotta .30 .75

1993-94 Upper Deck Triple Double

COMPLETE SET (10) 10.00 20.00
SER.1 STATED ODDS 1:20
TD1 Charles Barkley .75 2.00
TD2 Michael Jordan 6.00 15.00
TD3 Scottie Pippen 1.50 4.00
TD4 Detlef Schrempf .25 .60
TD5 Mark Jackson .25 .60
TD6 Kenny Anderson .25 .60
TD7 Larry Johnson .50 1.25
TD8 Dikembe Mutombo .50 1.25
TD9 Rumeal Robinson .07 .20
TD10 Micheal Williams .07 .20

1994-95 Upper Deck

COMPLETE SET (360) 15.00 40.00
COMPLETE SERIES 1 (180) 8.00 20.00
COMPLETE SERIES 2 (180) 8.00 20.00
1 Chris Webber ART .60 1.50
2 Anfernee Hardaway ART .60 1.50
3 Vin Baker ART .30 .75
4 Jamal Mashburn ART .30 .75
5 Isaiah Rider ART .20 .50
6 Dino Radja ART .20 .50
7 Nick Van Exel ART .30 .75
8 Shawn Bradley ART .30 .75
9 Toni Kukoc ART .40 1.00
10 Lindsey Hunter ART .20 .50
11 Scottie Pippen AN .75 2.00
12 Karl Malone AN .60 1.50
13 Hakeem Olajuwon AN .60 1.50
14 John Stockton AN .60 1.50
15 Latrell Sprewell AN .40 1.00
16 Shawn Kemp AN .50 1.25
17 Charles Barkley AN .75 2.00
18 David Robinson AN .60 1.50
19 Mitch Richmond AN .40 1.00
20 Kevin Johnson AN .30 .75
21 Derrick Coleman AN .30 .75
22 Dominique Wilkins AN .50 1.25
23 Shaquille O'Neal AN 1.25 3.00
24 Mark Price AN .30 .75
25 Gary Payton AN .50 1.25
26 Dan Majerle .20 .50
27 Vernon Maxwell .20 .50
28 Matt Geiger .20 .50
29 Jeff Turner .20 .50
30 Vinny Del Negro .20 .50
31 B.J. Armstrong .30 .75
32 Chris Gatling .20 .50
33 Tony Smith .20 .50
34 Doug West .20 .50
35 Clyde Drexler .50 1.25
36 Keith Jennings .20 .50
37 Steve Smith .25 .60
38 Kendall Gill .25 .60
39 Bob Martin .20 .50
40 Calbert Cheaney .25 .60
41 Terrell Brandon .20 .50
42 Pete Chilcutt .20 .50
43 Avery Johnson .25 .60
44 Tom Gugliotta .20 .50
45 LaBradford Smith .20 .50
46 Sedale Threatt .20 .50
47 Chris Smith .20 .50
48 Kevin Edwards .20 .50
49 Lucious Harris .20 .50
50 Tim Perry .20 .50
51 Lloyd Daniels .20 .50
52 Dee Brown .25 .60
53 Sean Elliott .25 .60
54 Tim Hardaway .40 1.00
55 Christian Laettner .25 .60
56 Bo Outlaw RC .30 .75
57 Henry James .30 .75
58 Duane Ferrell .20 .50
59 Jo Jo English .20 .50
60 Stanley Roberts .20 .50
61 Kevin Willis .25 .60
62 Dana Barros .20 .50
63 Gheorghe Muresan .20 .50
64 Vern Fleming .20 .50
65 Anthony Peeler .20 .50
66 Negele Knight .20 .50
67 Harold Ellis .20 .50
68 Vincent Askew .20 .50
69 Ennis Whatley .20 .50
70 Elden Campbell .20 .50
71 Sherman Douglas .20 .50
72 Luc Longley .25 .60
73 Lorenzo Williams .20 .50
74 Jay Humphries .20 .50
75 Chris King .20 .50
76 Tyrone Corbin .20 .50
77 Bobby Hurley .20 .50
78 Dell Curry .20 .50
79 Dino Radja .20 .50
80 A.C. Green .25 .60
81 Craig Ehlo .20 .50
82 Gary Payton .50 1.25
83 Sleepy Floyd .20 .50
84 Rodney Rogers .20 .50
85 Brian Shaw .20 .50
86 Kevin Gamble .20 .50
87 John Stockton .60 1.50
88 Hersey Hawkins .20 .50
89 Johnny Newman .20 .50
90 Larry Johnson .40 1.00
91 Robert Pack .25 .60
92 Willie Burton .20 .50
93 Bobby Phills .20 .50
94 David Benoit .20 .50
95 Harold Miner .20 .50
96 David Robinson .60 1.50
97 Nate McMillan .25 .60
98 Chris Mills .25 .60
99 Hubert Davis .20 .50
100 Shaquille O'Neal 1.25 3.00
101 Loy Vaught .20 .50
102 Kenny Smith .25 .60
103 Terry Dehere .20 .50
104 Carl Herrera .20 .50
105 LaPhonso Ellis .20 .50
106 Armon Gilliam .20 .50
107 Greg Graham .20 .50
108 Eric Murdock .20 .50
109 Ron Harper .25 .60
110 Andrew Lang .20 .50
111 Johnny Dawkins .20 .50
112 David Wingate .20 .50
113 Tom Hammonds .20 .50
114 Brad Daugherty .25 .60
115 Charles Smith .20 .50
116 Dale Ellis .20 .50
117 Bryant Stith .20 .50
118 Lindsey Hunter .20 .50
119 Patrick Ewing .50 1.25
120 Kenny Anderson .25 .60
121 Charles Barkley .75 2.00
122 Harvey Grant .20 .50
123 Anthony Bowie .20 .50
124 Shawn Kemp .50 1.25
125 Lee Mayberry .20 .50
126 Reggie Miller .60 1.50
127 Scottie Pippen .75 2.00
128 Spud Webb .25 .60
129 Antonio Davis .25 .60
130 Greg Anderson .20 .50
131 Jim Jackson .25 .60
132 Dikembe Mutombo .50 1.25
133 Terry Porter .20 .50
134 Mario Elie .20 .50
135 Vlade Divac .30 .75
136 Robert Horry .30 .75
137 Popeye Jones .20 .50
138 Brad Lohaus .20 .50
139 Anthony Bonner .20 .50
140 Doug Christie .25 .60
141 Rony Seikaly .20 .50
142 Allan Houston .30 .75
143 Tyrone Hill .20 .50
144 Latrell Sprewell .40 1.00
145 Andres Guibert .20 .50
146 Dominique Wilkins .50 1.25
147 Jon Barry .20 .50
148 Tracy Murray .20 .50
149 Mike Peplowski .20 .50
150 Mike Brown .20 .50
151 Cedric Ceballos .25 .60
152 Stacey King .20 .50
153 Trevor Wilson .20 .50
154 Anthony Avent .20 .50
155 Horace Grant .30 .75
156 Bill Curley RC .20 .50
157 Grant Hill RC 1.50 4.00
158 Charlie Ward RC .30 .75
159 Jalen Rose RC .75 2.00
160 Jason Kidd RC 1.50 4.00
161 Yinka Dare RC .20 .50
162 Eric Montross RC .20 .50
163 Donyell Marshall RC .30 .75
164 Tony Dumas RC .25 .60
165 Wesley Person RC .30 .75
166 Eddie Jones RC 1.00 2.50
167 Tim Hardaway USA .40 1.00
168 Isiah Thomas USA .30 .75
169 Joe Dumars USA .30 .75
170 Mark Price USA .30 .75
171 Derrick Coleman USA .30 .75
172 Shawn Kemp USA .30 .75
173 Steve Smith USA .25 .60
174 Dan Majerle USA .30 .75
175 Reggie Miller USA .60 1.50
176 Kevin Johnson USA .30 .75
177 Dominique Wilkins USA .50 1.25
178 Shaquille O'Neal USA 1.25 3.00
179 Alonzo Mourning USA .50 1.25
180 Larry Johnson USA .40 1.00
181 Brian Grant DA .50 1.25
182 Darrin Hancock DA .25 .60
183 Grant Hill DA 1.50 4.00
184 Jalen Rose DA .75 2.00
185 Lamond Murray DA .30 .75
186 Jason Kidd DA 1.50 4.00
187 Donyell Marshall DA .30 .75
188 Eddie Jones DA 1.00 2.50
189 Eric Montross DA .25 .60
190 Khalid Reeves DA .25 .60
191 Sharone Wright DA .25 .60
192 Wesley Person DA .30 .75
193 Glenn Robinson DA .60 1.50
194 Carlos Rogers DA .25 .60
195 Aaron McKie DA .30 .75
196 Juwan Howard DA .50 1.25
197 Charlie Ward DA .30 .75
198 Brooks Thompson DA .25 .60
199 Tony Massenburg .20 .50
200 James Robinson .20 .50
201 Dickey Simpkins RC .25 .60
202 Johnny Dawkins .20 .50
203 Joe Kleine .20 .50
204 Bill Wennington .20 .50
205 Sean Higgins .20 .50
206 Larry Krystkowiak .20 .50
207 Winston Garland .20 .50
208 Muggsy Bogues .25 .60
209 Charles Oakley .25 .60
210 Vin Baker .30 .75
211 Malik Sealy .20 .50
212 Willie Anderson .20 .50
213 Dale Davis .20 .50
214 Grant Long .20 .50
215 Danny Ainge .30 .75
216 Toni Kukoc .40 1.00
217 Doug Smith .20 .50
218 Danny Manning .25 .60
219 Otis Thorpe .25 .60
220 Mark Price .30 .75
221 Victor Alexander .20 .50
222 Brent Price .20 .50
223 Howard Eisley RC .30 .75
224 Chris Mullin .40 1.00
225 Nick Van Exel .50 1.25
226 Xavier McDaniel .20 .50
227 Khalid Reeves RC .25 .60
228 Anfernee Hardaway .60 1.50
229 B.J. Tyler RC .20 .50
230 Elmore Spencer .20 .50
231 Rick Fox .20 .50
232 Alonzo Mourning .50 1.25
233 Hakeem Olajuwon .60 1.50
234 Blue Edwards .20 .50
235 P.J. Brown .20 .50
236 Ron Harper .25 .60
237 Isaiah Rider .30 .75
238 Eric Mobley RC .20 .50
239 Brian Williams .20 .50
240 Eric Piatkowski RC .30 .75
241 Karl Malone .60 1.50
242 Wayman Tisdale .20 .50
243 Sarunas Marciulionis .20 .50
244 Sean Rooks .20 .50
245 Ricky Pierce .20 .50
246 Don MacLean .20 .50
247 Aaron McKie RC .30 .75
248 Kenny Gattison .20 .50
249 Derek Harper .25 .60
250 Michael Smith RC .20 .50
251 John Williams .20 .50
252 Pooh Richardson .20 .50
253 Sergei Bazarevich RC .20 .50
254 Brian Grant RC .50 1.25
255 Ed Pinckney .20 .50
256 Ken Norman .20 .50
257 Marty Conlon .20 .50
258 Matt Fish .20 .50
259 Darrin Hancock RC .25 .60
260 Mahmoud Abdul-Rauf .20 .50
261 Roy Tarpley .20 .50
262 Chris Morris .20 .50
263 Sharone Wright RC .25 .60
264 Jamal Mashburn .30 .75
265 John Starks .30 .75
266 Rod Strickland .30 .75
267 Adam Keefe .20 .50
268 Scott Burrell .20 .50
269 Eric Riley .20 .50
270 Sam Perkins .20 .50
271 Stacey Augmon .25 .60
272 Kevin Willis .25 .60
273 Lamond Murray RC .30 .75
274 Derrick Coleman .30 .75
275 Scott Skiles .20 .50
276 Buck Williams .20 .50
277 Sam Cassell .30 .75
278 Rik Smits .25 .60
279 Dennis Rodman .75 2.00
280 Olden Polynice .20 .50
281 Glenn Robinson RC .60 1.50
282 Clarence Weatherspoon .20 .50
283 Monty Williams RC .40 1.00
284 Terry Mills .20 .50
285 Oliver Miller .20 .50
286 Dennis Scott .25 .60
287 Micheal Williams .20 .50
288 Moses Malone .25 .60
289 Donald Royal .20 .50
290 Mark Jackson .25 .60
291 Walt Williams .20 .50
292 Bimbo Coles .20 .50
293 Derrick Alston RC .20 .50
294 Scott Williams .20 .50
295 Acie Earl .20 .50
296 Jeff Hornacek .25 .60
297 Kevin Duckworth .20 .50
298 Dontonio Wingfield RC .30 .75
299 Danny Ferry .20 .50
300 Mark West .20 .50
301 Jayson Williams .25 .60
302 David Wesley .20 .50
303 Jim McIlvaine RC .20 .50
304 Michael Adams .20 .50
305 Greg Minor RC .20 .50
306 Jeff Malone .20 .50
307 Pervis Ellison .20 .50
308 Clifford Rozier RC .20 .50
309 Billy Owens .20 .50
310 Duane Causwell .20 .50
311 Rex Chapman .20 .50
312 Detlef Schrempf .30 .75
313 Mitch Richmond .40 1.00
314 Carlos Rogers RC .25 .60
315 Byron Scott .25 .60
316 Dwayne Morton .20 .50
317 Bill Cartwright .20 .50
318 J.R. Reid .20 .50
319 Derrick McKey .20 .50
320 Jamie Watson RC .20 .50
321 Mookie Blaylock .25 .60
322 Chris Webber .60 1.50
323 Joe Dumars .30 .75
324 Shawn Bradley .20 .50
325 Chuck Person .25 .60
326 Haywoode Workman .20 .50
327 Benoit Benjamin .20 .50
328 Will Perdue .20 .50
329 Sam Mitchell .20 .50
330 George Lynch .20 .50
331 Juwan Howard RC .50 1.25
332 Robert Parish .30 .75
333 Glen Rice .30 .75
334 Michael Cage .20 .50
335 Brooks Thompson RC .25 .60
336 Rony Seikaly .20 .50
337 Steve Kerr .25 .60
338 Anthony Miller RC .30 .75
339 Nick Anderson .20 .50
340 Clifford Robinson .25 .60
341 Todd Day .20 .50
342 Jon Koncak .20 .50
343 Felton Spencer .20 .50
344 Willie Burton .20 .50
345 Ledell Eackles .20 .50
346 Anthony Mason .25 .60
347 Derek Strong .20 .50
348 Reggie Williams .20 .50
349 Johnny Newman .20 .50
350 Terry Cummings .25 .60
351 Anthony Tucker RC .25 .60
352 Junior Bridgeman TN .20 .50
353 Jerry West TN .50 1.25
354 Harvey Catchings TN .30 .75
355 John Lucas TN .25 .60
356 Bill Bradley TN .40 1.00
357 Bill Walton TN .30 .75
358 Don Nelson TN .30 .75
359 Michael Jordan TN 2.50 6.00
360 Tom (Satch) Sanders TN .30 .75

1994-95 Upper Deck Draft Trade

COMPLETE SET (10) 5.00 12.00
TRADE: SER.1 STATED ODDS 1:240
D1 Glenn Robinson .75 2.00
D2 Jason Kidd 2.00 5.00
D3 Grant Hill 2.00 5.00
D4 Donyell Marshall .40 1.00
D5 Juwan Howard .60 1.50
D6 Sharone Wright .30 .75
D7 Lamond Murray .40 1.00
D8 Brian Grant .60 1.50
D9 Eric Montross .30 .75
D10 Eddie Jones 1.25 3.00
NNO Expired Exchange Card .07 .20

1994-95 Upper Deck Jordan He's Back Reprints

COMPLETE SET (10) 12.00 30.00
COMMON CARD (1-10) 3.00 8.00
COMPLETE JUMBO SET (3) 12.00 30.00
COMMON JUMBO (1-3) 3.00 8.00

1994-95 Upper Deck Jordan Heroes

COMPLETE SET (10) 15.00 40.00
COMMON JORDAN 4.00 10.00
SER.1 STATED ODDS 1:30 HOB/RET

1994-95 Upper Deck Predictor Award Winners

COMPLETE SET (40) 25.00 60.00
COMPLETE SERIES 1 (20) 12.00 30.00
COMPLETE SERIES 2 (20) 12.00 30.00
SER.1 STATED ODDS 1:25 HOBBY
SER.2 STATED ODDS 1:30 HOBBY
*RED.CARDS: .2X TO .5X HI COLUMN
TWO RED.SETS PER W1 CARD BY MAIL
ONE RED.SET PER W2 CARD BY MAIL
H1 Charles Barkley 2.00 5.00
H2 Hakeem Olajuwon 1.50 4.00
H3 Shaquille O'Neal 3.00 8.00
H4 Scottie Pippen 2.00 5.00
H5 David Robinson 1.50 4.00
H6 Shawn Kemp W2 1.25 3.00
H7 Alonzo Mourning 1.25 3.00
H8 Larry Johnson 1.00 2.50
H9 Patrick Ewing 1.25 3.00
H10 AS-MVP Wild Card W1 .50 1.25
H11 Hakeem Olajuwon 1.50 4.00
H12 Dikembe Mutombo W1 1.25 3.00
H13 Nate McMillan .60 1.50
H14 Dennis Rodman 2.00 5.00
H15 Alonzo Mourning 1.25 3.00
H16 Patrick Ewing 1.25 3.00
H17 Charles Barkley 2.00 5.00
H18 David Robinson 1.50 4.00
H19 John Stockton 1.50 4.00
H20 DEF-POY Wild Card W2 .50 1.25
H21 Shaquille O'Neal W2 3.00 8.00
H22 Hakeem Olajuwon 1.50 4.00
H23 David Robinson W1 1.50 4.00
H24 Scottie Pippen 2.00 5.00
H25 Alonzo Mourning 1.25 3.00
H26 Shawn Kemp 1.25 3.00
H27 Charles Barkley 2.00 5.00
H28 Patrick Ewing 1.25 3.00
H29 Larry Johnson 1.00 2.50
H30 MVP Wild Card .50 1.25
H31 Jason Kidd W1 2.50 6.00
H32 Grant Hill W1 2.50 6.00
H33 Glenn Robinson 1.00 2.50
H34 Eddie Jones 1.50 4.00
H35 Donyell Marshall .50 1.25
H36 Eric Montross .40 1.00
H37 Sharone Wright .40 1.00
H38 Juwan Howard .75 2.00
H39 Carlos Rogers .40 1.00
H40 ROY Wild Card W1 .50 1.25

1994-95 Upper Deck Predictor League Leaders

COMPLETE SET (40) 20.00 50.00
COMPLETE SERIES 1 (20) 10.00 25.00
COMPLETE SERIES 2 (20) 10.00 25.00
SER.1 STATED ODDS 1:25 RETAIL
SER.2 STATED ODDS 1:30 RETAIL
*RED.CARDS: .2X TO .5X HI COLUMN
TWO RED.SETS PER W1 CARD BY MAIL
ONE EXCH.SET PER W2 CARD BY MAIL
R1 David Robinson 1.50 4.00

R2 Shaquille O'Neal W1 3.00 8.00
R3 Hakeem Olajuwon W2 1.50 4.00
R4 Scottie Pippen 2.00 5.00
R5 Chris Webber 1.50 4.00
R6 Karl Malone 1.50 4.00
R7 Patrick Ewing 1.25 3.00
R8 Mitch Richmond 1.00 2.50
R9 Charles Barkley 2.00 5.00
R10 Scorers Wild Card .50 1.25
R11 John Stockton W1 1.50 4.00
R12 Mookie Blaylock .75 2.00
R13 Kenny Anderson W2 .60 1.50
R14 Kevin Johnson .75 2.00
R15 Muggsy Bogues .60 1.50
R16 Tim Hardaway 1.00 2.50
R17 Anfernee Hardaway 1.50 4.00
R18 Rod Strickland .50 1.25
R19 Sherman Douglas .50 1.25
R20 Assists Wild Card .50 1.25
R21 Shaquille O'Neal 3.00 8.00
R22 Hakeem Olajuwon 1.50 4.00
R23 Dennis Rodman W1 2.00 5.00
R24 Dikembe Mutombo W2 1.25 3.00
R25 Karl Malone 1.50 4.00
R26 Kevin Willis .60 1.50
R27 Chris Webber 1.50 4.00
R28 Alonzo Mourning 1.25 3.00
R29 Derrick Coleman .75 2.00
R30 Rebounds Wild Card .50 1.25
R31 Dikembe Mutombo W1 1.25 3.00
R32 Hakeem Olajuwon W2 1.50 4.00
R33 David Robinson 1.50 4.00
R34 Shawn Bradley .50 1.25
R35 Shaquille O'Neal 3.00 8.00
R36 Patrick Ewing 1.25 3.00
R37 Alonzo Mourning 1.25 3.00
R38 Shawn Kemp 1.25 3.00
R39 Derrick Coleman .75 2.00
R40 Blocks Wild Card .50 1.25

1994-95 Upper Deck Rookie Standouts

COMPLETE SET (20) 10.00 25.00
SER.2 STATED ODDS 1:30 HOBBY/RETAIL
RS1 Glenn Robinson 1.25 3.00
RS2 Jason Kidd 3.00 8.00
RS3 Grant Hill 3.00 8.00
RS4 Donyell Marshall .60 1.50
RS5 Juwan Howard 1.00 2.50
RS6 Sharone Wright .50 1.25
RS7 Lamond Murray .60 1.50
RS8 Brian Grant 1.00 2.50
RS9 Eric Montross .50 1.25
RS10 Eddie Jones 2.00 5.00
RS11 Carlos Rogers .50 1.25
RS12 Khalid Reeves .50 1.25
RS13 Jalen Rose 1.50 4.00
RS14 Michael Smith .40 1.00
RS15 Eric Piatkowski .60 1.50
RS16 Clifford Rozier .40 1.00
RS17 Aaron McKie .60 1.50
RS18 Eric Mobley .40 1.00
RS19 Bill Curley .40 1.00
RS20 Wesley Person .60 1.50

1994-95 Upper Deck Slam Dunk Stars

COMPLETE SET (20) 25.00 60.00
SER.2 STATED ODDS 1:30 HOBBY/RETAIL
S1 Vin Baker 2.00 5.00
S2 Charles Barkley 5.00 12.00
S3 Derrick Coleman 2.00 5.00
S4 Clyde Drexler 3.00 8.00
S5 LaPhonso Ellis 1.25 3.00
S6 Larry Johnson 2.50 6.00
S7 Shawn Kemp 3.00 8.00
S8 Donyell Marshall 2.00 5.00
S9 Jamal Mashburn 2.00 5.00
S10 Gheorghe Muresan 1.25 3.00
S11 Alonzo Mourning 3.00 8.00
S12 Shaquille O'Neal 8.00 20.00
S13 Hakeem Olajuwon 4.00 10.00
S14 Scottie Pippen 5.00 12.00
S15 Isaiah Rider 2.00 5.00
S16 David Robinson 4.00 10.00
S17 Clarence Weatherspoon 1.25 3.00
S18 Chris Webber 4.00 10.00
S19 Dominique Wilkins 3.00 8.00
S20 Rik Smits 1.50 4.00

1994-95 Upper Deck Special Edition

COMPLETE SET (180) 20.00 40.00
COMPLETE SERIES 1 (90) 7.50 15.00
COMPLETE SERIES 2 (90) 15.00 30.00
ONE PER PACK
1 Stacey Augmon .50 1.25
2 Kevin Willis .50 1.25
3 Mookie Blaylock .60 1.50
4 Rick Fox .40 1.00
5 Xavier McDaniel .40 1.00
6 Dee Brown .50 1.25
7 Muggsy Bogues .50 1.25
8 Kenny Gattison .40 1.00
9 Alonzo Mourning 1.00 2.50
10 B.J. Armstrong .60 1.50
11 Bill Cartwright .50 1.25
12 Toni Kukoc .75 2.00
13 Mark Price .60 1.50
14 Gerald Wilkins .50 1.25
15 John Williams .40 1.00
16 Jamal Mashburn .60 1.50
17 Sean Rooks .40 1.00
18 Doug Smith .40 1.00
19 Jim Jackson .50 1.25
20 Mahmoud Abdul-Rauf .40 1.00
21 Rodney Rogers .40 1.00
22 Reggie Williams .40 1.00
23 LaPhonso Ellis .40 1.00
24 Allan Houston .60 1.50
25 Terry Mills .40 1.00
26 Joe Dumars .60 1.50
27 Chris Mullin .75 2.00
28 Billy Owens .40 1.00
29 Latrell Sprewell .75 2.00
30 Chris Webber 1.25 3.00
31 Sam Cassell .60 1.50
32 Vernon Maxwell .40 1.00
33 Hakeem Olajuwon 1.25 3.00
34 Otis Thorpe .40 1.00
35 Rik Smits .50 1.25
36 Derrick McKey .40 1.00
37 Haywoode Workman .40 1.00
38 Bo Outlaw .60 1.50
39 Elmore Spencer .40 1.00
40 Loy Vaught .40 1.00
41 George Lynch .40 1.00
42 Nick Van Exel .60 1.50
43 James Worthy .75 2.00
44 Elden Campbell .40 1.00
45 Grant Long .40 1.00
46 Harold Miner .40 1.00
47 Glen Rice .60 1.50
48 Steve Smith .50 1.25
49 Todd Day .40 1.00
50 Eric Murdock .40 1.00
51 Vin Baker .60 1.50
52 Christian Laettner .50 1.25
53 Isaiah Rider .60 1.50
54 Micheal Williams .40 1.00
55 Benoit Benjamin .40 1.00
56 Derrick Coleman .60 1.50
57 Chris Morris .40 1.00
58 Charles Smith .40 1.00
59 Greg Anthony .40 1.00
60 Doc Rivers .50 1.25
61 Derek Harper .50 1.25
62 John Starks .60 1.50
63 Anfernee Hardaway 1.25 3.00
64 Dennis Scott .50 1.25
65 Nick Anderson .40 1.00
66 Shawn Bradley .40 1.00
67 Clarence Weatherspoon .40 1.00
68 Jeff Malone .40 1.00
69 Cedric Ceballos .50 1.25
70 Kevin Johnson .60 1.50
71 Oliver Miller .40 1.00
72 Clifford Robinson .50 1.25
73 Rod Strickland .40 1.00
74 Buck Williams .40 1.00
75 Mitch Richmond .75 2.00
76 Walt Williams .40 1.00
77 Lionel Simmons .40 1.00
78 Willie Anderson .40 1.00
79 Terry Cummings .50 1.25
80 J.R. Reid .40 1.00
81 Dennis Rodman 1.50 4.00
82 Kendall Gill .40 1.00
83 Sam Perkins .40 1.00
84 Detlef Schrempf .60 1.50
85 Jeff Hornacek .50 1.25
86 Karl Malone 1.25 3.00
87 Felton Spencer .40 1.00
88 Calbert Cheaney .50 1.25
89 Don MacLean .40 1.00
90 Brent Price .40 1.00
91 Tyrone Corbin .40 1.00
92 Rex Chapman .40 1.00
93 Ken Norman .40 1.00
94 Steve Smith .50 1.25
95 Eric Montross .50 1.25
96 Dino Radja .40 1.00
97 Dominique Wilkins 1.00 2.50
98 Scott Burrell .40 1.00
99 Hersey Hawkins .40 1.00
100 Larry Johnson .75 2.00
101 Ron Harper .50 1.25
102 Scottie Pippen 1.50 4.00
103 Dickey Simpkins .50 1.25
104 Tyrone Hill .40 1.00
105 Chris Mills .50 1.25
106 Bobby Phills .40 1.00
107 Lorenzo Williams .40 1.00
108 Popeye Jones .40 1.00
109 Jason Kidd 3.00 8.00
110 Dikembe Mutombo 1.00 2.50
111 Robert Pack .50 1.25
112 Jalen Rose 1.50 4.00
113 Bill Curley .40 1.00
114 Grant Hill 3.00 8.00
115 Lindsey Hunter .40 1.00
116 Roy Tarpley .40 1.00
117 Tim Hardaway .75 2.00
118 Ricky Pierce .40 1.00
119 Carlos Rogers .50 1.25
120 Clifford Rozier .40 1.00
121 Rony Seikaly .40 1.00
122 Mario Elie .40 1.00
123 Robert Horry .60 1.50
124 Kenny Smith .50 1.25
125 Antonio Davis .50 1.25
126 Dale Davis .40 1.00
127 Reggie Miller 1.25 3.00
128 Lamond Murray .60 1.50
129 Eric Piatkowski .60 1.50
130 Pooh Richardson .40 1.00
131 Cedric Ceballos .50 1.25
132 Vlade Divac .60 1.50
133 Eddie Jones 2.00 5.00
134 Mark Jackson .50 1.25
135 Matt Geiger .40 1.00
136 Khalid Reeves .50 1.25
137 Kevin Willis .50 1.25
138 Lee Mayberry .40 1.00
139 Eric Mobley .40 1.00
140 Glenn Robinson 1.25 3.00
141 Doug West .40 1.00
142 Donyell Marshall .60 1.50
143 Chris Smith .40 1.00
144 Kenny Anderson .50 1.25
145 Chris Morris .40 1.00
146 Armon Gilliam .40 1.00
147 Dana Barros .40 1.00
148 Patrick Ewing 1.00 2.50
149 Charles Oakley .60 1.50
150 Charlie Ward .60 1.50
151 Horace Grant .60 1.50
152 Shaquille O'Neal 2.50 6.00
153 Brian Shaw .40 1.00
154 Brooks Thompson .50 1.25
155 B.J. Tyler .40 1.00
156 Scott Williams .40 1.00
157 Sharone Wright .50 1.25
158 Charles Barkley 1.50 4.00
159 Dan Majerle .60 1.50
160 Danny Manning .50 1.25
161 Wesley Person .60 1.50
162 Clyde Drexler 1.00 2.50
163 Harvey Grant .40 1.00
164 Terry Porter .40 1.00
165 Brian Grant 1.00 2.50
166 Bobby Hurley .40 1.00
167 Olden Polynice .40 1.00
168 Sean Elliott .50 1.25
169 Chuck Person .50 1.25
170 David Robinson 1.25 3.00
171 Shawn Kemp 1.00 2.50
172 Nate McMillan .50 1.25
173 Gary Payton 1.00 2.50
174 Michael Smith .40 1.00
175 David Benoit .40 1.00
176 Jay Humphries .40 1.00
177 John Stockton 1.25 3.00
178 Juwan Howard 1.00 2.50
179 Chris Webber 1.25 3.00
180 Scott Skiles .40 1.00

1994-95 Upper Deck Special Edition Gold

*STARS: 3X TO 8X HI COLUMN
*RCs: 3X TO 8X HI
SER.1/2 STATED ODDS 1:35 HOB/RET

1994-95 Upper Deck Special Edition Jumbos

COMPLETE SET (27) 15.00 40.00
1 Steve Smith .60 1.50
2 Dominique Wilkins 1.25 3.00
3 Larry Johnson 1.00 2.50
4 Scottie Pippen 2.00 5.00
5 Chris Mills .60 1.50
6 Jason Kidd 4.00 10.00
7 Jalen Rose 2.00 5.00
8 Lindsey Hunter .50 1.25
9 Tim Hardaway 1.00 2.50
10 Kenny Smith .60 1.50
11 Mark Jackson .60 1.50
12 Lamond Murray .75 2.00
13 Cedric Ceballos .60 1.50
14 Kevin Willis .60 1.50
15 Glenn Robinson 1.50 4.00
16 Doug West .50 1.25
17 Kenny Anderson .60 1.50
18 Patrick Ewing 1.25 3.00
19 Horace Grant .75 2.00
20 Sharone Wright .60 1.50
21 Charles Barkley 2.00 5.00
22 Clyde Drexler 1.25 3.00
23 Brian Grant 1.25 3.00
24 Sean Elliott .60 1.50
25 Shawn Kemp 1.25 3.00
26 John Stockton 1.50 4.00
27 Juwan Howard 1.25 3.00

1995 Upper Deck

COMPLETE SET (300) 12.50 30.00
COMP.SERIES 1 SET (150) 8.00 20.00
COMP.SERIES 2 SET (150) 6.00 15.00
WAX BOX HOBBY SER.1 20.00 50.00
WAX BOX HOBBY SER.2 20.00 50.00
133 Michael Jordan CPC 2.50 6.00

1995-96 Upper Deck

COMPLETE SET (360) 25.00 60.00
COMPLETE SERIES 1 (180) 12.00 30.00
COMPLETE SERIES 2 (180) 12.00 30.00
1 Eddie Jones .40 1.00
2 Hubert Davis .25 .60
3 Latrell Sprewell .40 1.00
4 Stacey Augmon .30 .75
5 Mario Elie .25 .60
6 Tyrone Hill .25 .60
7 Dikembe Mutombo .60 1.50
8 Antonio Davis .25 .60
9 Horace Grant .30 .75
10 Ken Norman .25 .60
11 Aaron McKie .30 .75
12 Vinny Del Negro .25 .60
13 Glenn Robinson .40 1.00
14 Allan Houston .30 .75
15 Bryon Russell .25 .60
16 Tony Dumas .25 .60
17 Gary Payton .60 1.50
18 Rik Smits .30 .75
19 Dino Radja .25 .60
20 Robert Pack .25 .60
21 Calbert Cheaney .25 .60
22 Clarence Weatherspoon .25 .60
23 Michael Jordan 4.00 10.00
24 Felton Spencer .25 .60
25 J.R. Reid .25 .60
26 Cedric Ceballos .30 .75
27 Dan Majerle .40 1.00
28 Donald Hodge .25 .60
29 Nate McMillan .25 .60
30 Bimbo Coles .25 .60
31 Mitch Richmond .50 1.25
32 Scott Brooks .25 .60
33 Patrick Ewing .60 1.50
34 Carl Herrera .25 .60
35 Rick Fox .25 .60
36 James Robinson .25 .60
37 Donald Royal .25 .60
38 Joe Dumars .40 1.00
39 Rony Seikaly .25 .60
40 Dennis Rodman .75 2.00
41 Muggsy Bogues .40 1.00
42 Gheorghe Muresan .25 .60
43 Ervin Johnson .25 .60
44 Todd Day .25 .60
45 Rex Walters .25 .60
46 Terrell Brandon .30 .75
47 Wesley Person .25 .60
48 Terry Dehere .25 .60
49 Steve Smith .30 .75
50 Brian Grant .30 .75
51 Eric Piatkowski .25 .60
52 Lindsey Hunter .25 .60
53 Chris Webber .50 1.25
54 Antoine Carr .25 .60
55 Chris Dudley .25 .60
56 Clyde Drexler .60 1.50
57 P.J. Brown .25 .60
58 Kevin Willis .25 .60
59 Jeff Turner .25 .60
60 Sean Elliott .30 .75
61 Kevin Johnson .30 .75
62 Scott Skiles .25 .60
63 Charles Smith .25 .60
64 Derrick McKey .25 .60
65 Danny Ferry .25 .60
66 Detlef Schrempf .40 1.00
67 Shawn Bradley .25 .60
68 Isaiah Rider .25 .60
69 Karl Malone .75 2.00
70 Will Perdue .30 .75
71 Terry Mills .25 .60
72 Glen Rice .40 1.00
73 Tim Breaux .25 .60
74 Malik Sealy .25 .60
75 Walt Williams .25 .60
76 Bobby Phills .30 .75
77 Anthony Avent .25 .60
78 Jamal Mashburn UER .40 1.00
79 Vlade Divac .40 1.00
80 Reggie Williams .25 .60
81 Xavier McDaniel .25 .60
82 Avery Johnson .30 .75
83 Derek Harper .30 .75
84 Don MacLean .25 .60
85 Tom Gugliotta .25 .60
86 Craig Ehlo .25 .60
87 Robert Horry .40 1.00
88 Kevin Edwards .25 .60
89 Chuck Person .30 .75
90 Sharone Wright .25 .60
91 Steve Kerr .40 1.00
92 Marty Conlon .25 .60
93 Jalen Rose .50 1.25
94 Bryant Reeves RC .30 .75
95 Shaquille O'Neal 1.50 4.00
96 David Wesley .25 .60
97 Chris Mills .25 .60
98 Rod Strickland .25 .60
99 Pooh Richardson .25 .60
100 Sam Perkins .25 .60
101 Dell Curry .25 .60
102 David Benoit .25 .60
103 Christian Laettner .30 .75
104 Duane Causwell .25 .60
105 Jason Kidd .60 1.50
106 Mark West .25 .60
107 Lee Mayberry .25 .60
108 Adam Keefe .25 .60
109 Jeff Malone .25 .60
110 George Zidek RC .30 .75
111 Kenny Smith .30 .75
112 George Lynch .25 .60
113 Toni Kukoc .50 1.25
114 A.C. Green .30 .75
115 Kenny Anderson .30 .75
116 Robert Parish .50 1.25
117 Chris Mullin .40 1.00
118 Loy Vaught .25 .60
119 Olden Polynice .25 .60
120 Clifford Robinson .40 1.00
121 Eric Mobley .25 .60
122 Doug West .25 .60
123 Sam Cassell .40 1.00
124 Nick Anderson .30 .75
125 Matt Geiger .25 .60
126 Elden Campbell .25 .60
127 Alonzo Mourning .60 1.50
128 Bryant Stith .25 .60
129 Mark Jackson .30 .75
130 Cherokee Parks RC .30 .75
131 Shawn Respert RC .30 .75
132 Alan Henderson RC .40 1.00
133 Jerry Stackhouse RC 1.25 3.00
134 Rasheed Wallace RC 1.25 3.00
135 Antonio McDyess RC .50 1.25
136 Charles Barkley ROO 1.00 2.50
137 Michael Jordan ROO 4.00 10.00
138 Hakeem Olajuwon ROO .75 2.00
139 Joe Dumars ROO .40 1.00
140 Patrick Ewing ROO .60 1.50
141 A.C. Green ROO .30 .75
142 Karl Malone ROO .75 2.00
143 Detlef Schrempf ROO .40 1.00
144 Chuck Person ROO .30 .75
145 Muggsy Bogues ROO .30 .75
146 Horace Grant ROO .30 .75
147 Mark Jackson ROO .30 .75
148 Kevin Johnson ROO .30 .75
149 Mitch Richmond ROO .50 1.25
150 Rik Smits ROO .30 .75
151 Nick Anderson ROO .30 .75
152 Tim Hardaway ROO .50 1.25
153 Shawn Kemp ROO .60 1.50
154 David Robinson ROO .75 2.00
155 Jason Kidd ART .60 1.50
156 Grant Hill ART .60 1.50
157 Glenn Robinson ART .40 1.00
158 Eddie Jones ART .40 1.00
159 Brian Grant ART .30 .75
160 Juwan Howard ART .40 1.00
161 Eric Montross ART .25 .60
162 Wesley Person ART .25 .60
163 Jalen Rose ART .50 1.25
164 Donyell Marshall ART .25 .60
165 Sharone Wright ART .25 .60
166 Karl Malone AN .75 2.00
167 Scottie Pippen AN 1.00 2.50
168 David Robinson AN .75 2.00
169 John Stockton AN .75 2.00
170 Anfernee Hardaway AN 1.00 2.50
171 Charles Barkley AN 1.00 2.50
172 Shawn Kemp AN .60 1.50
173 Shaquille O'Neal AN 1.50 4.00
174 Gary Payton AN .60 1.50
175 Mitch Richmond AN .50 1.25
176 Dennis Rodman AN .75 2.00
177 Detlef Schrempf AN .40 1.00
178 Hakeem Olajuwon AN .75 2.00
179 Reggie Miller AN .75 2.00
180 Clyde Drexler AN .60 1.50
181 Hakeem Olajuwon .75 2.00
182 Vin Baker .30 .75
183 Jeff Hornacek .30 .75
184 Popeye Jones .25 .60
185 Sedale Threatt .25 .60
186 Scottie Pippen 1.00 2.50
187 Terry Porter .25 .60
188 Dan Majerle .40 1.00
189 Clifford Rozier .25 .60
190 Greg Minor .25 .60
191 Dennis Scott .25 .60
192 Hersey Hawkins .30 .75
193 Chris Gatling .25 .60
194 Charles Oakley .30 .75
195 Dale Davis .25 .60
196 Robert Pack .30 .75
197 Lamond Murray .25 .60
198 Mookie Blaylock .40 1.00
199 Dickey Simpkins .25 .60
200 Kevin Gamble .25 .60
201 Lorenzo Williams .25 .60
202 Scott Burrell .25 .60
203 Armon Gilliam .25 .60
204 Doc Rivers .30 .75
205 Blue Edwards .25 .60
206 Billy Owens .25 .60
207 Juwan Howard .40 1.00
208 Harvey Grant .25 .60
209 Richard Dumas .25 .60
210 Anthony Peeler .25 .60
211 Matt Geiger .25 .60
212 Lucious Harris .25 .60
213 Grant Long .25 .60
214 Sasha Danilovic RC .40 1.00
215 Chris Morris .25 .60
216 Donyell Marshall .25 .60
217 Alonzo Mourning .60 1.50
218 John Stockton .75 2.00
219 Jayson Williams .30 .75
220 Mahmoud Abdul-Rauf .30 .75
221 Sean Rooks .25 .60
222 Shawn Kemp .60 1.50
223 John Williams .25 .60
224 Dee Brown .30 .75
225 Jim Jackson .30 .75
226 Harold Miner .25 .60
227 B.J. Armstrong .25 .60
228 Elliot Perry .25 .60
229 Anthony Miller .25 .60
230 Donny Marshall RC .40 1.00
231 Tyrone Corbin .25 .60
232 Anthony Mason .25 .60
233 Grant Hill .60 1.50
234 Buck Williams .25 .60
235 Brian Shaw .25 .60
236 Dale Ellis .30 .75
237 Magic Johnson 1.25 3.00
238 Eric Montross .25 .60
239 Rex Chapman .25 .60
240 Otis Thorpe .30 .75
241 Tracy Murray .30 .75
242 Sarunas Marciulionis .40 1.00
243 Luc Longley .30 .75
244 Elmore Spencer .25 .60
245 Terry Cummings .30 .75
246 Sam Mitchell .25 .60
247 Terrence Rencher RC .40 1.00
248 Byron Houston .25 .60
249 Pervis Ellison .25 .60
250 Carlos Rogers .25 .60
251 Kendall Gill .25 .60
252 Sherrell Ford RC .30 .75
253 Michael Finley RC 1.00 2.50
254 Kurt Thomas RC .40 1.00
255 Joe Smith RC .50 1.25
256 Bobby Hurley .25 .60
257 Greg Anthony .25 .60
258 Willie Anderson .25 .60
259 Theo Ratliff RC .60 1.50
260 Duane Ferrell .25 .60
261 Antonio Harvey .25 .60
262 Gary Grant .25 .60
263 Brian Williams .25 .60
264 Danny Manning .30 .75
265 Micheal Williams .25 .60
266 Dennis Rodman .75 2.00
267 Arvydas Sabonis RC .75 2.00
268 Don MacLean .25 .60
269 Keith Askins .25 .60
270 Reggie Miller .75 2.00
271 Ed Pinckney .25 .60
272 Bob Sura RC .30 .75
273 Kevin Garnett RC 3.00 8.00
274 Byron Scott .40 1.00
275 Mario Bennett RC .30 .75
276 Junior Burrough RC .40 1.00
277 Anfernee Hardaway 1.00 2.50
278 George McCloud .25 .60
279 Loren Meyer RC .25 .60
280 Ed O'Bannon RC .30 .75
281 Lawrence Moten RC .40 1.00
282 Dana Barros .30 .75
283 Damon Stoudamire RC 1.00 2.50
284 Eric Williams RC .40 1.00
285 Wayman Tisdale .25 .60
286 Rodney Rogers .25 .60
287 Sherman Douglas .25 .60
288 Greg Ostertag RC .40 1.00
289 Alvin Robertson .25 .60
290 Tim Legler .25 .60
291 Zan Tabak .25 .60
292 Gary Trent RC .30 .75
293 Haywoode Workman .25 .60
294 Charles Barkley 1.00 2.50
295 Derrick Coleman .30 .75
296 Ricky Pierce .25 .60
297 Benoit Benjamin .25 .60
298 Larry Johnson .50 1.25
299 Travis Best RC .40 1.00
300 Jason Caffey RC .40 1.00
301 Cory Alexander RC .40 1.00
302 Nick Van Exel .40 1.00
303 Corliss Williamson RC .40 1.00
304 Eric Murdock .25 .60
305 Tyus Edney RC .40 1.00
306 Lou Roe RC .40 1.00
307 John Salley .25 .60
308 Spud Webb .40 1.00
309 Brent Barry RC .60 1.50
310 David Robinson .75 2.00
311 Glen Rice .40 1.00
312 Chris King .25 .60
313 David Vaughn RC .40 1.00
314 Kenny Gattison .25 .60
315 Randolph Childress RC .30 .75
316 Anfernee Hardaway USA 1.00 2.50
317 Grant Hill USA .60 1.50
318 Karl Malone USA .75 2.00
319 Reggie Miller USA .75 2.00
320 Hakeem Olajuwon USA .75 2.00
321 Shaquille O'Neal USA 1.50 4.00
322 Scottie Pippen USA 1.00 2.50
323 David Robinson USA .75 2.00
324 Glenn Robinson USA .40 1.00
325 John Stockton USA .75 2.00
326 Cedric Ceballos I95 .30 .75
327 Shaquille O'Neal I95 1.50 4.00
328 Glenn Robinson I95 .40 1.00
329 Shawn Kemp I95 .60 1.50
330 Nick Anderson I95 .30 .75
331 Shawn Bradley I95 .25 .60
332 H.Grant/B.Thomp I95 .30 .75
333 Robert Horry I95 .40 1.00
334 NBA Expansion I95 .20 .50
335 Michael Jordan I95 4.00 10.00
336 N.Van Exel/D.Cannon MA .40 1.00
337 M.Jordan/D.Hanson MA 4.00 10.00
338 S.Pippen/J.Von Oy MA 1.00 2.50
339 M.Jordan/C.Sheen MA 4.00 10.00
340 J.Kidd/C.Reid MA .60 1.50
341 M.Jordan/Q.Latifah MA 4.00 10.00
342 C.Barkley/D.Johnson MA 1.00 2.50
343 Olajuwon/C.Bernsen MA .75 2.00
344 Ahmad Rashad MA .40 1.00
345 Willow Bay MA .40 1.00
346 G.Payton/M.Curry MA .60 1.50
347 Horace Grant SJ .30 .75
348 Juwan Howard SJ .40 1.00
349 David Robinson SJ .75 2.00
350 Reggie Miller SJ .75 2.00
351 Brian Grant SJ .30 .75
352 Michael Jordan SJ 4.00 10.00
353 Cedric Ceballos SJ .30 .75
354 Blue Edwards SJ .25 .60
355 Acie Earl SJ .25 .60
356 Dennis Rodman SJ .75 2.00
357 Shawn Kemp SJ .60 1.50
358 Jerry Stackhouse SJ 1.25 3.00
359 Jamal Mashburn SJ .40 1.00
360 Antonio McDyess SJ .50 1.25

1995-96 Upper Deck Electric Court

COMPLETE SET (360) 50.00 100.00
COMPLETE SERIES 1 (180) 25.00 50.00
COMPLETE SERIES 2 (180) 25.00 50.00
*STARS: 1X TO 2.5X BASE CARD HI
*SUBSETS/RCs: .75X TO 2X BASE HI
ONE PER RETAIL PACK

1995-96 Upper Deck Electric Court Gold

*STARS: 10X TO 25X BASE CARD HI
*SUBSETS/RCs: 5X TO 12X BASE HI
SER.1/2 STATED ODDS 1:35 RETAIL
23 Michael Jordan 150.00 400.00
137 Michael Jordan ROO 60.00 150.00
237 Magic Johnson 40.00 100.00
273 Kevin Garnett 50.00 120.00
277 Anfernee Hardaway 30.00 80.00
335 Michael Jordan I95 60.00 150.00
337 M.Jordan/D.Hanson MA 60.00 150.00
339 M.Jordan/C.Sheen MA 60.00 150.00
341 M.Jordan/Q.Latifah MA 60.00 150.00
352 Michael Jordan SJ 60.00 150.00

1995-96 Upper Deck All Star Class

COMPLETE SET (25) 60.00 120.00
SER.1 STATED ODDS 1:17 HOBBY/RETAIL
AS1 Anfernee Hardaway 6.00 15.00
AS2 Reggie Miller 5.00 12.00
AS3 Grant Hill 4.00 10.00
AS4 Scottie Pippen 6.00 15.00
AS5 Shaquille O'Neal 10.00 25.00
AS6 Larry Johnson 3.00 8.00
AS7 Dana Barros 2.50 6.00
AS8 Vin Baker 2.00 5.00
AS9 Alonzo Mourning 4.00 10.00
AS10 Joe Dumars 2.50 6.00
AS11 Patrick Ewing 4.00 10.00
AS12 Tyrone Hill 1.50 4.00
AS13 Latrell Sprewell 2.50 6.00
AS14 Dan Majerle 2.50 6.00
AS15 Shawn Kemp 4.00 10.00
AS16 Karl Malone 5.00 12.00
AS17 Hakeem Olajuwon 5.00 12.00
AS18 Gary Payton 4.00 10.00
AS19 Mitch Richmond 3.00 8.00
AS20 David Robinson 5.00 12.00
AS21 Detlef Schrempf 2.50 6.00
AS22 Cedric Ceballos 2.00 5.00
AS23 John Stockton 5.00 12.00
AS24 Dikembe Mutombo 4.00 10.00
AS25 Charles Barkley 6.00 15.00

1995-96 Upper Deck Jordan Collection

COMPLETE SER.1 (4) 10.00 25.00
COMPLETE SER.2 (4) 10.00 25.00
COMMON UD 1 (JC5-JC8) 3.00 8.00
COMMON UD 2 (JC13-JC16) 3.00 8.00
SER.1/2 UD STATED ODDS 1:29 HOB/RET

1995-96 Upper Deck Jordan Collection Jumbos

COMPLETE SET (25) 12.00 30.00
COMMON CARD 2.00 5.00

1995-96 Upper Deck Predictor MVP

COMPLETE SET (10) 10.00 25.00
SER.2 STATED ODDS 1:30 RETAIL
*RED.CARDS: .20X TO .50X HI COLUMN
ONE RED.SET PER "W" CARD BY MAIL
R1 Michael Jordan 3.00 8.00
R2 Michael Jordan 3.00 8.00
R3 Michael Jordan 3.00 8.00
R4 Michael Jordan 3.00 8.00
R5 Michael Jordan 3.00 8.00
R6 Hakeem Olajuwon 1.50 4.00
R7 Charles Barkley 2.00 5.00
R8 Karl Malone 1.50 4.00
R9 Anfernee Hardaway 2.00 5.00
R10 Long Shot Card .75 2.00

1995-96 Upper Deck Predictor Player of the Month

COMPLETE SET (10) 10.00 25.00
SER.1 STATED ODDS 1:30 RETAIL
*RED.CARDS: .20X TO .50X HI COLUMN
ONE RED.SET PER "W" CARD BY MAIL
R1 Michael Jordan 3.00 8.00
R2 Michael Jordan 3.00 8.00
R3 Michael Jordan 3.00 8.00
R4 Michael Jordan 3.00 8.00
R5 Michael Jordan 3.00 8.00
R6 Jamal Mashburn .75 2.00
R7 David Robinson 1.50 4.00
R8 Latrell Sprewell .75 2.00
R9 Chris Webber 1.00 2.50
R10 Long Shot Card .75 2.00

1995-96 Upper Deck Predictor Player of the Week

SER.1 STATED ODDS 1:30 HOBBY
*RED.CARDS: .20X TO .50X HI COLUMN
ONE RED.SET PER "W" CARD BY MAIL
H1 Michael Jordan 3.00 8.00
H2 Michael Jordan 3.00 8.00
H3 Michael Jordan 3.00 8.00
H4 Michael Jordan 3.00 8.00
H5 Michael Jordan 3.00 8.00
H6 Anfernee Hardaway 2.00 5.00
H7 Hakeem Olajuwon 1.50 4.00
H8 Scottie Pippen 2.00 5.00
H9 Glenn Robinson .75 2.00
H10 Long Shot Card .75 2.00

1995-96 Upper Deck Predictor Scoring

SER.2 STATED ODDS 1:30 HOBBY
*RED.CARDS: .20X TO .50X HI COLUMN
ONE RED.SET PER "W" CARD BY MAIL
H1 Michael Jordan 3.00 8.00
H2 Michael Jordan 3.00 8.00
H3 Michael Jordan 3.00 8.00
H4 Michael Jordan 3.00 8.00
H5 Michael Jordan 3.00 8.00
H6 David Robinson 1.50 4.00
H7 Scottie Pippen 2.00 5.00
H8 Jerry Stackhouse 1.25 3.00
H9 Glenn Robinson .75 2.00
H10 Long Shot Card .75 2.00

1995-96 Upper Deck Special Edition

COMPLETE SET (180) 40.00 80.00
COMPLETE SERIES 1 (90) 15.00 30.00
COMPLETE SERIES 2 (90) 20.00 50.00
ONE PER BOTH SERIES HOBBY PACK
1 Mookie Blaylock .60 1.50
2 Tyrone Corbin .40 1.00
3 Grant Long .40 1.00
4 Dee Brown .50 1.25
5 Sherman Douglas .40 1.00
6 Eric Montross .40 1.00
7 Scott Burrell .40 1.00
8 Dell Curry .60 1.50
9 Larry Johnson .75 2.00
10 Will Perdue .50 1.25
11 Scottie Pippen 1.50 4.00
12 Dickey Simpkins .40 1.00
13 Michael Cage .40 1.00
14 Mark Price .60 1.50
15 John Williams .40 1.00
16 Lucious Harris .40 1.00
17 Jim Jackson .50 1.25
18 Popeye Jones .40 1.00
19 Mahmoud Abdul-Rauf .50 1.25
20 LaPhonso Ellis .50 1.25
21 Robert Pack .40 1.00
22 Bill Curley .40 1.00
23 Grant Hill 1.00 2.50
24 Allan Houston .60 1.50
25 Chris Gatling .40 1.00
26 Tim Hardaway .75 2.00
27 Donyell Marshall .40 1.00
28 Clifford Rozier .40 1.00
29 Mario Elie .40 1.00
30 Robert Horry .60 1.50
31 Hakeem Olajuwon 1.25 3.00
32 Kenny Smith .50 1.25
33 Dale Davis .40 1.00
34 Duane Ferrell .40 1.00
35 Derrick McKey .40 1.00
36 Reggie Miller 1.25 3.00
37 Lamond Murray .40 1.00
38 Bo Outlaw .40 1.00
39 Eric Piatkowski .40 1.00
40 Anthony Peeler .40 1.00
41 Sedale Threatt .40 1.00
42 Nick Van Exel .60 1.50
43 Kevin Gamble .40 1.00
44 Matt Geiger .40 1.00
45 Billy Owens .40 1.00
46 Khalid Reeves .40 1.00
47 Vin Baker .50 1.25
48 Eric Murdock .40 1.00
49 Lee Mayberry .40 1.00
50 Christian Laettner .50 1.25
51 Sean Rooks .40 1.00
52 Doug West .40 1.00
53 P.J. Brown .40 1.00
54 Derrick Coleman .50 1.25
55 Armon Gilliam .40 1.00
56 Hubert Davis .40 1.00
57 Charles Oakley .50 1.25
58 John Starks .60 1.50
59 Monty Williams .40 1.00
60 Anfernee Hardaway 1.50 4.00
61 Donald Royal .40 1.00
62 Dennis Scott .40 1.00
63 Jeff Turner .40 1.00
64 Clarence Weatherspoon .40 1.00
65 Jeff Malone .40 1.00
66 Scott Williams .40 1.00
67 A.C. Green .50 1.25

1995-96 Upper Deck Special Edition

68 Kevin Johnson .60 1.50
69 Elliot Perry .40 1.00
70 Wesley Person .40 1.00
71 Harvey Grant .40 1.00
72 Aaron McKie .40 1.00
73 Rod Strickland .40 1.00
74 Buck Williams .40 1.00
75 Randy Brown .40 1.00
76 Bobby Hurley .40 1.00
77 Lionel Simmons .40 1.00
78 Terry Cummings .50 1.25
79 Vinny Del Negro .40 1.00
80 Avery Johnson .50 1.25
81 David Robinson 1.25 3.00
82 Vincent Askew .40 1.00
83 Shawn Kemp 1.00 2.50
84 Nate McMillan .40 1.00
85 David Benoit .40 1.00
86 Jeff Hornacek .50 1.25
87 John Stockton 1.25 3.00
88 Juwan Howard .60 1.50
89 Gheorghe Muresan .40 1.00
90 Doug Overton .40 1.00
91 Stacey Augmon .50 1.25
92 Alan Henderson .60 1.50
93 Steve Smith .50 1.25
94 Rick Fox .40 1.00
95 Dino Radja .40 1.00
96 Eric Williams .60 1.50
97 Muggsy Bogues .60 1.50
98 Kendall Gill .40 1.00
99 Glen Rice .60 1.50
100 Michael Jordan 15.00 40.00
101 Toni Kukoc .75 2.00
102 Dennis Rodman 1.25 3.00
103 Terrell Brandon .50 1.25
104 Tyrone Hill .40 1.00
105 Dan Majerle .60 1.50
106 Jason Kidd 1.00 2.50
107 Jamal Mashburn .60 1.50
108 Cherokee Parks .50 1.25
109 Antonio McDyess .75 2.00
110 Dikembe Mutombo 1.00 2.50
111 Reggie Williams .40 1.00
112 Joe Dumars .60 1.50
113 Lindsey Hunter .40 1.00
114 Otis Thorpe .50 1.25
115 Chris Mullin .60 1.50
116 Joe Smith .75 2.00
117 Latrell Sprewell .60 1.50
118 Chucky Brown .40 1.00
119 Sam Cassell .60 1.50
120 Clyde Drexler 1.00 2.50
121 Travis Best .60 1.50
122 Mark Jackson .50 1.25
123 Rik Smits .50 1.25
124 Brent Barry 1.00 2.50
125 Rodney Rogers .50 1.25
126 Loy Vaught .40 1.00
127 Cedric Ceballos .50 1.25
128 Magic Johnson 2.00 5.00
129 Eddie Jones .60 1.50
130 Alonzo Mourning 1.00 2.50
131 Kurt Thomas .60 1.50
132 Kevin Willis .40 1.00
133 Sherman Douglas .40 1.00
134 Shawn Respert .50 1.25
135 Glenn Robinson .60 1.50
136 Kevin Garnett 5.00 12.00
137 Tom Gugliotta .40 1.00
138 Isaiah Rider .60 1.50
139 Kenny Anderson .50 1.25
140 Ed O'Bannon .50 1.25
141 Jayson Williams .40 1.00
142 Patrick Ewing 1.00 2.50
143 Derek Harper .50 1.25
144 Charles Smith .40 1.00
145 Nick Anderson .50 1.25
146 Horace Grant .50 1.25
147 Shaquille O'Neal 2.50 6.00
148 Vernon Maxwell .40 1.00
149 Jerry Stackhouse 2.00 5.00
150 Sharone Wright .40 1.00
151 Charles Barkley 1.50 4.00
152 Michael Finley 1.50 4.00
153 Danny Manning .50 1.25
154 John Williams .40 1.00
155 Clifford Robinson .60 1.50
156 Arvydas Sabonis 1.25 3.00
157 Gary Trent .50 1.25
158 Brian Grant .50 1.25
159 Mitch Richmond .75 2.00
160 Corliss Williamson .60 1.50
161 Sean Elliott .50 1.25
162 Will Perdue .50 1.25
163 Doc Rivers .50 1.25
164 Gary Payton 1.00 2.50
165 Sam Perkins .40 1.00
166 Detlef Schrempf .60 1.50
167 Tracy Murray .40 1.00
168 Ed Pinckney .40 1.00
169 Carlos Rogers .40 1.00
170 Damon Stoudamire 1.50 4.00
171 Karl Malone 1.25 3.00
172 Chris Morris .40 1.00
173 Greg Ostertag .60 1.50
174 Greg Anthony .40 1.00
175 Lawrence Moten .60 1.50
176 Bryant Reeves .50 1.25
177 Byron Scott .60 1.50
178 Calbert Cheaney .40 1.00
179 Rasheed Wallace 2.00 5.00
180 Chris Webber .75 2.00

1995-96 Upper Deck Special Edition Gold

*STARS: 2.5X TO 6X HI COLUMN
*RCs: 1.5X TO 4X HI
SER.1/2 STATED ODDS 1:35 HOBBY
100 Michael Jordan 100.00 250.00

1996-97 Upper Deck

COMPLETE SET (360) 30.00 80.00
COMPLETE SERIES 1 (180) 25.00 60.00
COMPLETE SERIES 2 (180) 10.00 20.00
1 Mookie Blaylock .40 1.00
2 Alan Henderson .25 .60
3 Christian Laettner .40 1.00
4 Ken Norman .25 .60
5 Dee Brown .25 .60
6 Todd Day .25 .60
7 Rick Fox .25 .60
8 Dino Radja .25 .60
9 Dana Barros .25 .60
10 Eric Williams .25 .60
11 Scott Burrell .25 .60
12 Dell Curry .40 1.00
13 Matt Geiger .25 .60
14 Glen Rice .40 1.00
15 Ron Harper .30 .75
16 Michael Jordan 4.00 10.00
17 Luc Longley .30 .75
18 Toni Kukoc .40 1.00
19 Dennis Rodman 1.00 2.50
20 Danny Ferry .25 .60
21 Tyrone Hill .25 .60
22 Bobby Phills .25 .60
23 Bob Sura .25 .60
24 Tony Dumas .25 .60
25 George McCloud .25 .60
26 Jim Jackson .25 .60
27 Jamal Mashburn .40 1.00
28 Loren Meyer .25 .60
29 Dale Ellis .30 .75
30 LaPhonso Ellis .25 .60
31 Tom Hammonds .25 .60
32 Antonio McDyess .40 1.00
33 Joe Dumars .50 1.25
34 Grant Hill .60 1.50
35 Lindsey Hunter .25 .60
36 Terry Mills .25 .60
37 Theo Ratliff .25 .60
38 B.J. Armstrong .30 .75
39 Donyell Marshall .25 .60
40 Chris Mullin .50 1.25
41 Rony Seikaly .30 .75
42 Joe Smith .30 .75
43 Sam Cassell .30 .75
44 Clyde Drexler .60 1.50
45 Mario Elie .25 .60
46 Robert Horry .40 1.00
47 Travis Best .25 .60
48 Antonio Davis .25 .60
49 Dale Davis .25 .60
50 Eddie Johnson .25 .60
51 Derrick McKey .25 .60
52 Reggie Miller .75 2.00
53 Brent Barry .30 .75
54 Lamond Murray .25 .60
55 Eric Piatkowski .25 .60
56 Rodney Rogers .25 .60
57 Loy Vaught .25 .60
58 Kobe Bryant RC 25.00 60.00
59 Eddie Jones .40 1.00
60 Elden Campbell .25 .60
61 Shaquille O'Neal 1.50 4.00
62 Nick Van Exel .40 1.00
63 Keith Askins .25 .60
64 Rex Chapman .25 .60
65 Sasha Danilovic .25 .60
66 Alonzo Mourning .60 1.50
67 Kurt Thomas .25 .60
68 Tim Hardaway .50 1.25
69 Ray Allen RC 2.00 5.00
70 Johnny Newman .25 .60
71 Shawn Respert .25 .60
72 Glenn Robinson .40 1.00
73 Tom Gugliotta .25 .60
74 Stephon Marbury RC 1.25 3.00
75 Terry Porter .25 .60
76 Doug West .25 .60
77 Shawn Bradley .25 .60
78 Kevin Edwards .25 .60
79 Vern Fleming .25 .60
80 Ed O'Bannon .25 .60
81 Jayson Williams .25 .60
82 John Starks .40 1.00
83 Patrick Ewing .60 1.50
84 Charlie Ward .25 .60
85 Nick Anderson .25 .60
86 Anfernee Hardaway 1.00 2.50
87 Jon Koncak .25 .60
88 Donald Royal .25 .60
89 Brian Shaw .25 .60
90 Derrick Coleman .30 .75
91 Allen Iverson RC 3.00 8.00
92 Jerry Stackhouse .50 1.25
93 Clarence Weatherspoon .25 .60
94 Charles Barkley 1.00 2.50
95 Kevin Johnson .40 1.00
96 Danny Manning .30 .75
97 Elliot Perry .25 .60
98 Wayman Tisdale .30 .75
99 Randolph Childress .25 .60
100 Aaron McKie .25 .60
101 Arvydas Sabonis .40 1.00
102 Gary Trent .25 .60
103 Chris Dudley .25 .60
104 Tyus Edney .25 .60
105 Brian Grant .30 .75
106 Bobby Hurley .25 .60
107 Olden Polynice .25 .60
108 Corliss Williamson .25 .60
109 Vinny Del Negro .25 .60
110 Avery Johnson .30 .75
111 Will Perdue .25 .60
112 David Robinson .75 2.00
113 Hersey Hawkins .25 .60
114 Shawn Kemp .60 1.50
115 Nate McMillan .25 .60
116 Detlef Schrempf .40 1.00
117 Gary Payton .60 1.50
118 Marcus Camby RC .60 1.50
119 Zan Tabak .25 .60
120 Damon Stoudamire .40 1.00
121 Carlos Rogers .25 .60
122 Sharone Wright .25 .60
123 Antoine Carr .25 .60
124 Jeff Hornacek .30 .75
125 Adam Keefe .25 .60
126 Chris Morris .25 .60
127 John Stockton .75 2.00
128 Blue Edwards .25 .60
129 Shareef Abdur-Rahim RC .60 1.50
130 Bryant Reeves .25 .60
131 Roy Rogers RC .30 .75
132 Calbert Cheaney .25 .60
133 Tim Legler .25 .60
134 Gheorghe Muresan .25 .60
135 Chris Webber .50 1.25
136 Mutombo/Blaylock/Smith BW .60 1.50
137 Barros/Radja/Williams BW .25 .60
138 Rice/Geiger/Divac BW .40 1.00
139 Jordan/Pip/Rodman BW 1.00 2.50
140 Brandon/Ferry/Hill BW .30 .75
141 Kidd/Mash/Jackson BW .60 1.50
142 L.Ellis/McDyess/Jackson BW .40 1.00
143 Dumars/Hill/Augmon BW .60 1.50
144 Smith/Sprewell/Mullin BW .50 1.25
145 Olaj/Drexler/Barkley BW 1.00 2.50
146 R.Miller/Best/Smits BW .75 2.00
147 B.Barry/Murray/Rogers BW .30 .75
148 O'Neal/Jones/Bryant BW 4.00 10.00
149 Zo/Hardaway/Danilovic BW .60 1.50
150 Baker/Robinson/Douglas BW .40 1.00
151 Garnett/Gug/Parks BW 1.25 3.00
152 Bradley/Gill/O'Bannon BW .40 1.00
153 Ewing/Houston/L.Johnson BW .60 1.50
154 Hardaway/Scott/Grant BW 1.00 2.50
155 Stack/W'spoon/Cole BW .50 1.25
156 K.Johnson/Manning/Finley BW .40 1.00
157 Robinson/Rider/Sabonis BW .40 1.00
158 Richmond/Grant/Owens BW .50 1.25
159 D.Rob/Elliott/Johnson BW .75 2.00
160 Kemp/Payton/Schrem BW .60 1.50
161 Stoud/Tabak/Wright BW .40 1.00
162 Stockton/Malone/Hornacek BW .75 2.00
163 Reeves/Rahim/Edwards BW .60 1.50
164 Howard/Muresan/Web BW .50 1.25
165 Michael Jordan GP 4.00 10.00
166 Corliss Williamson GP .25 .60
167 Dell Curry GP .40 1.00
168 John Starks GP .40 1.00
169 Dennis Rodman GP 1.00 2.50
170 C.Webber/L.Sprewell GP .50 1.25
171 Cedric Ceballos GP .30 .75
172 Theo Ratliff GP .30 .75
173 Anfernee Hardaway GP 1.00 2.50
174 Grant Hill GP .60 1.50
175 Alonzo Mourning GP .60 1.50
176 Shawn Kemp GP .60 1.50
177 Jason Kidd GP .60 1.50
178 Avery Johnson GP .30 .75
179 Gary Payton GP .60 1.50
180 Michael Jordan CL 1.00 2.50
181 Priest Lauderdale RC .25 .60
182 Dikembe Mutombo .60 1.50
183 Eldridge Recasner RC .40 1.00
184 Steve Smith .30 .75
185 Pervis Ellison .25 .60
186 Greg Minor .25 .60
187 Antoine Walker RC .60 1.50
188 David Wesley .25 .60
189 Muggsy Bogues .40 1.00
190 Tony Delk RC .40 1.00
191 Vlade Divac .40 1.00
192 Anthony Mason .30 .75
193 George Zidek .25 .60
194 Jason Caffey .25 .60
195 Steve Kerr .30 .75
196 Robert Parish .50 1.25
197 Scottie Pippen 1.00 2.50
198 Terrell Brandon .30 .75
199 Tony Dumas .25 .60
200 Chris Mills .25 .60
201 Vitaly Potapenko RC .30 .75
202 Mark West .25 .60
203 Chris Gatling .25 .60
204 Derek Harper .30 .75
205 Sam Cassell .30 .75
206 Eric Montross .25 .60
207 Samaki Walker RC .30 .75
208 Mark Jackson .30 .75
209 Ervin Johnson .25 .60
210 Sarunas Marciulionis .25 .60
211 Ricky Pierce .30 .75
212 Bryant Stith .25 .60
213 Stacey Augmon .25 .60
214 Grant Long .25 .60
215 Rick Mahorn .25 .60
216 Otis Thorpe .30 .75
217 Jerome Williams RC .30 .75
218 Bimbo Coles .25 .60
219 Todd Fuller RC .25 .60
220 Mark Price .40 1.00
221 Felton Spencer .25 .60
222 Latrell Sprewell .40 1.00
223 Charles Barkley 1.00 2.50
224 Othella Harrington RC .30 .75
225 Hakeem Olajuwon .75 2.00
226 Matt Maloney RC .30 .75
227 Kevin Willis .40 1.00
228 Erick Dampier RC .40 1.00
229 Duane Ferrell .25 .60
230 Jalen Rose .25 .60
231 Rik Smits .30 .75
232 Terry Dehere .25 .60
233 Bo Outlaw .25 .60
234 Pooh Richardson .25 .60
235 Malik Sealy .25 .60
236 Lorenzen Wright RC .25 .60
237 Cedric Ceballos .25 .60
238 Derek Fisher RC .50 1.25
239 Travis Knight RC .30 .75
240 Sean Rooks .25 .60
241 Byron Scott .40 1.00
242 P.J. Brown .25 .60
243 Voshon Lenard RC .40 1.00
244 Dan Majerle .40 1.00
245 Martin Muursepp RC .25 .60
246 Gary Grant .25 .60
247 Vin Baker .30 .75
248 Armon Gilliam .25 .60
249 Andrew Lang .25 .60
250 Elliot Perry .25 .60
251 Kevin Garnett 1.25 3.00
252 Shane Heal RC .40 1.00
253 Cherokee Parks .25 .60
254 Stojko Vrankovic .25 .60
255 Kendall Gill .40 1.00
256 Kerry Kittles RC .40 1.00
257 Xavier McDaniel .25 .60
258 Robert Pack .25 .60
259 Chris Childs .25 .60
260 Allan Houston .40 1.00
261 Larry Johnson .50 1.25
262 Dontae' Jones RC .30 .75
263 Walter McCarty RC .40 1.00
264 Charles Oakley .40 1.00
265 John Wallace RC .30 .75
266 Buck Williams .40 1.00
267 Brian Evans RC .25 .60
268 Horace Grant .40 1.00
269 Dennis Scott .30 .75
270 Rony Seikaly .30 .75
271 David Vaughn .25 .60
272 Michael Cage .25 .60
273 Lucious Harris .25 .60
274 Don MacLean .25 .60
275 Mark Davis .25 .60
276 Jason Kidd .60 1.50
277 Michael Finley .40 1.00
278 A.C. Green .30 .75
279 Robert Horry .40 1.00
280 Steve Nash RC 2.00 5.00
281 Wesley Person .25 .60
282 Kenny Anderson .30 .75
283 Aleksandar Djordjevic RC .40 1.00
284 Jermaine O'Neal RC .60 1.50
285 Isaiah Rider .30 .75
286 Clifford Robinson .40 1.00
287 Rasheed Wallace .50 1.25
288 Mahmoud Abdul-Rauf .30 .75
289 Billy Owens .25 .60
290 Mitch Richmond .50 1.25
291 Michael Smith .25 .60
292 Cory Alexander .25 .60
293 Sean Elliott .40 1.00
294 Vernon Maxwell .25 .60
295 Dominique Wilkins .60 1.50
296 Craig Ehlo .25 .60
297 Jim McIlvaine .25 .60
298 Sam Perkins .30 .75
299 Steve Scheffler .40 1.00
300 Hubert Davis .25 .60
301 Popeye Jones .25 .60
302 Donald Whiteside RC .40 1.00
303 Walt Williams .25 .60
304 Karl Malone .75 2.00
305 Greg Ostertag .25 .60
306 Bryon Russell .25 .60
307 Jamie Watson .25 .60
308 Greg Anthony .25 .60
309 George Lynch .25 .60
310 Lawrence Moten .25 .60
311 Anthony Peeler .25 .60
312 Juwan Howard .40 1.00
313 Tracy Murray .25 .60
314 Rod Strickland .40 1.00
315 Harvey Grant .25 .60
316 Charles Barkley DN 1.00 2.50
317 Clyde Drexler DN .60 1.50
318 Dikembe Mutombo DN .60 1.50
319 Larry Johnson DN .50 1.25
320 Shaquille O'Neal DN 1.50 4.00
321 Mookie Blaylock DN .40 1.00
322 Tim Hardaway DN .50 1.25
323 Dennis Rodman DN 1.00 2.50
324 Dan Majerle DN .40 1.00
325 Stacey Augmon DN .30 .75
326 Anthony Mason DN .30 .75
327 Kenny Anderson DN .30 .75
328 Mahmoud Abdul-Rauf DN .30 .75
329 Chris Webber DN .50 1.25
330 Dominique Wilkins DN .60 1.50
331 Dikembe Mutombo WD .60 1.50
332 Dana Barros WD .25 .60
333 Glen Rice WD .40 1.00
334 Dennis Rodman WD 1.00 2.50
335 Terrell Brandon WD .30 .75
336 Jason Kidd WD .60 1.50
337 Antonio McDyess WD .40 1.00
338 Grant Hill WD .60 1.50
339 Joe Smith WD .30 .75
340 Charles Barkley WD 1.00 2.50
341 Reggie Miller WD .75 2.00
342 Brent Barry WD .30 .75
343 Shaquille O'Neal WD 1.50 4.00
344 Alonzo Mourning WD .60 1.50
345 Glenn Robinson WD .40 1.00
346 Stephon Marbury WD 1.25 3.00
347 Kerry Kittles WD .40 1.00
348 Patrick Ewing WD .60 1.50
349 Anfernee Hardaway WD 1.00 2.50
350 Allen Iverson WD 3.00 8.00
351 Danny Manning WD .30 .75
352 Arvydas Sabonis WD .40 1.00
353 Mitch Richmond WD .50 1.25
354 David Robinson WD .75 2.00
355 Shawn Kemp WD .60 1.50
356 Marcus Camby WD .60 1.50
357 Karl Malone WD .75 2.00
358 Shareef Abdur-Rahim WD .60 1.50
359 Gheorghe Muresan WD .25 .60
360 Michael Jordan CL 1.00 2.50

1996-97 Upper Deck Autographs

HAND NUMBERED TO 500
A1 Anfernee Hardaway 75.00 200.00
A2 Shawn Kemp 40.00 100.00
A3 Antonio McDyess 20.00 50.00
A4 Damon Stoudamire 20.00 50.00

1996-97 Upper Deck Fast Break Connections

COMPLETE SET (30) 15.00 40.00
SER.1 STATED ODDS 1:8
FB1 Jim Jackson .40 1.00
FB2 Jason Kidd 1.00 2.50
FB3 Jamal Mashburn .60 1.50
FB4 Mario Elie .40 1.00
FB5 Hakeem Olajuwon 1.25 3.00
FB6 Clyde Drexler 1.00 2.50
FB7 Cedric Ceballos .50 1.25
FB8 Nick Van Exel .60 1.50
FB9 Eddie Jones .60 1.50
FB10 Danny Manning .50 1.25
FB11 Michael Finley .60 1.50
FB12 Kevin Johnson .60 1.50
FB13 Tyus Edney .40 1.00
FB14 Brian Grant .50 1.25
FB15 Mitch Richmond .75 2.00
FB16 Sean Elliott .60 1.50
FB17 David Robinson 1.25 3.00
FB18 Avery Johnson .50 1.25
FB19 Shawn Kemp 1.00 2.50
FB20 Gary Payton 1.00 2.50
FB21 Detlef Schrempf .60 1.50
FB22 Scottie Pippen 1.50 4.00
FB23 Michael Jordan 12.00 30.00
FB24 Toni Kukoc .60 1.50
FB25 Sherman Douglas .40 1.00
FB26 Glenn Robinson .60 1.50
FB27 Vin Baker .50 1.25
FB28 Jeff Hornacek .50 1.25
FB29 John Stockton 1.25 3.00
FB30 Karl Malone 1.25 3.00

1996-97 Upper Deck Generation Excitement

COMPLETE SET (20) 30.00 80.00
SER.1 STATED ODDS 1:33
G1 Steve Smith 2.00 5.00
G2 Eric Williams 1.50 4.00
G3 Jason Kidd 4.00 10.00
G4 Antonio McDyess 2.50 6.00
G5 Grant Hill 4.00 10.00
G6 Joe Smith 2.00 5.00
G7 Brent Barry 2.00 5.00
G8 Eddie Jones 2.50 6.00
G9 Vin Baker 2.00 5.00
G10 Kevin Garnett 8.00 20.00
G11 Ed O'Bannon 1.50 4.00
G12 Anfernee Hardaway 6.00 15.00
G13 Jerry Stackhouse 3.00 8.00
G14 Michael Finley 2.50 6.00
G15 Gary Trent 1.50 4.00
G16 Tyus Edney 1.50 4.00
G17 Sean Elliott 2.50 6.00
G18 Shawn Kemp 4.00 10.00
G19 Damon Stoudamire 2.50 6.00
G20 Gheorghe Muresan 1.50 4.00

1996-97 Upper Deck Jordan Greater Heights

COMPLETE SET (10) 20.00 50.00
COMMON JORDAN (1-10) 6.00 15.00
SER.1 STATED ODDS 1:66 HOB/RET

1996-97 Upper Deck Jordan Greater Heights Jumbos

COMPLETE SET (10) 10.00 25.00
COMMON CARD (GH1-GH10) 1.25 3.00

1996-97 Upper Deck Jordan's Viewpoints

COMPLETE SET (10) 25.00 60.00
COMMON JORDAN (1-10) 5.00 12.00
SER.2 STATED ODDS 1:34 HOB/RET

1996-97 Upper Deck Michael's Viewpoints Jumbos

COMPLETE SET (10) 10.00 25.00
COMMON CARD (VP1-VP10) 1.25 3.00

1996-97 Upper Deck Predictor Scoring 1

COMPLETE SET (20) 20.00 50.00
SER.1 STATED ODDS 1:23
PREDICTOR EXPIRATION: 5/1/97
*TV CEL RED.CARDS: .3X TO 1.5X HI COL.
P1 Mookie Blaylock 1.00 2.50
P2 Dino Radja .60 1.50
P3 Michael Jordan 15.00 40.00
P4 Terrell Brandon .75 2.00
P5 Jason Kidd 1.50 4.00
P6 Joe Dumars 1.25 3.00
P7 Joe Smith .75 2.00
P8 Hakeem Olajuwon 2.00 5.00
P9 Rik Smits .75 2.00
P10 Brent Barry .75 2.00
P11 Kurt Thomas .60 1.50
P12 Anfernee Hardaway 2.50 6.00
P13 Clarence Weatherspoon .60 1.50
P14 Clifford Robinson 1.00 2.50
P15 Mitch Richmond 1.25 3.00
P16 David Robinson 2.00 5.00
P17 Shawn Kemp 1.50 4.00
P18 Damon Stoudamire 1.00 2.50
P19 Karl Malone 2.00 5.00
P20 Bryant Reeves .60 1.50

1996-97 Upper Deck Predictor Scoring 2

COMPLETE SET (20) 20.00 50.00
SER.2 STATED ODDS 1:23
*TV CEL RED.CARDS: .6X TO 1.5X HI COL.
P1 Glen Rice 1.00 2.50
P2 Michael Jordan 15.00 40.00
P3 Jamal Mashburn 1.00 2.50
P4 Antonio McDyess 1.00 2.50
P5 Charles Barkley 2.50 6.00
P6 Reggie Miller 2.00 5.00
P7 Shaquille O'Neal 4.00 10.00
P8 Alonzo Mourning 1.50 4.00
P9 Vin Baker .75 2.00
P10 Kevin Garnett 3.00 8.00
P11 Kerry Kittles .60 1.50
P12 Patrick Ewing 1.50 4.00
P13 Anfernee Hardaway 2.50 6.00
P14 Allen Iverson 4.00 10.00
P15 Robert Horry 1.00 2.50
P16 Shawn Kemp 1.50 4.00
P17 Marcus Camby 1.00 2.50
P18 John Stockton 2.00 5.00
P19 Shareef Abdur-Rahim 1.00 2.50
P20 Juwan Howard 1.00 2.50

1996-97 Upper Deck Rookie Exclusives

COMPLETE SET (20) 15.00 40.00
SER.2 STATED ODDS 1:4 HOB/RET, 1:2 JUM
R1 Allen Iverson 4.00 10.00
R2 John Wallace .40 1.00
R3 Kerry Kittles .50 1.25
R4 Roy Rogers .40 1.00
R5 Marcus Camby .75 2.00
R6 Antoine Walker .75 2.00
R7 Ray Allen 2.50 6.00
R8 Samaki Walker .40 1.00
R9 Walter McCarty .50 1.25
R10 Kobe Bryant 40.00 100.00
R11 Shareef Abdur-Rahim .75 2.00
R12 Dontae' Jones .40 1.00
R13 Todd Fuller .30 .75
R14 Lorenzen Wright .40 1.00
R15 Stephon Marbury 1.50 4.00
R16 Vitaly Potapenko .40 1.00
R17 Tony Delk .50 1.25
R18 Steve Nash 3.00 8.00
R19 Jermaine O'Neal .75 2.00
R20 Erick Dampier .50 1.25
R1P Allen Iverson PROMO 1.00 2.50
R10P Kobe Bryant PROMO 40.00 100.00

1996-97 Upper Deck Rookie of the Year Collection

COMPLETE SET (14) 75.00 150.00
SER.2 STATED ODDS 1:138
RC1 Damon Stoudamire 4.00 10.00
RC2 Grant Hill 6.00 15.00
RC3 Jason Kidd 5.00 12.00
RC4 Chris Webber 5.00 12.00
RC5 Shaquille O'Neal 15.00 40.00
RC6 Larry Johnson 5.00 12.00
RC7 Derrick Coleman 3.00 8.00
RC8 David Robinson 8.00 20.00
RC9 Mitch Richmond 5.00 12.00
RC10 Mark Jackson 3.00 8.00
RC11 Chuck Person 3.00 8.00
RC12 Patrick Ewing 6.00 15.00
RC13 Michael Jordan 30.00 80.00
RC14 Buck Williams 4.00 10.00

1996-97 Upper Deck Smooth Grooves

COMPLETE SET (15) 50.00 120.00
SER.2 STATED ODDS 1:72
SG1 Dennis Rodman 5.00 12.00
SG2 Jason Kidd 3.00 8.00
SG3 Grant Hill 3.00 8.00
SG4 Damon Stoudamire 2.00 5.00
SG5 Shaquille O'Neal 8.00 20.00
SG6 Clyde Drexler 3.00 8.00
SG7 Shareef Abdur-Rahim 3.00 8.00
SG8 Michael Jordan 125.00 300.00
SG9 Alonzo Mourning 3.00 8.00
SG10 Allen Iverson 15.00 40.00
SG11 Vin Baker 1.50 4.00
SG12 Kevin Garnett 6.00 15.00
SG13 Anfernee Hardaway 5.00 12.00
SG14 Jerry Stackhouse 2.50 6.00
SG15 Shawn Kemp 3.00 8.00

1997-98 Upper Deck

COMPLETE SET (360) 25.00 50.00
COMPLETE SERIES 1 (180) 12.50 25.00
COMPLETE SERIES 2 (180) 12.50 25.00
BLACK POWER AUDIO 1:23 HOBBY
RED POWER AUDIO 1:72 HOBBY
1 Steve Smith .20 .50
2 Christian Laettner .25 .60
3 Alan Henderson .15 .40
4 Dikembe Mutombo .40 1.00
5 Dana Barros .15 .40
6 Antoine Walker .25 .60
7 Dee Brown .20 .50
8 Eric Williams .15 .40
9 Muggsy Bogues .20 .50
10 Dell Curry .20 .50
11 Vlade Divac .25 .60
12 Anthony Mason .20 .50
13 Glen Rice .25 .60
14 Jason Caffey .15 .40
15 Steve Kerr .30 .75
16 Toni Kukoc .30 .75
17 Luc Longley .20 .50
18 Michael Jordan 2.50 6.00
19 Terrell Brandon .20 .50
20 Danny Ferry .15 .40
21 Tyrone Hill .15 .40
22 Derek Anderson RC .25 .60
23 Bob Sura .15 .40
24 Shawn Bradley .15 .40
25 Michael Finley .25 .60
26 Ed O'Bannon .15 .40
27 Robert Pack .15 .40
28 Samaki Walker .15 .40
29 LaPhonso Ellis .15 .40
30 Tony Battie RC .25 .60
31 Antonio McDyess .25 .60
32 Bryant Stith .15 .40
33 Randolph Childress .15 .40
34 Grant Hill .40 1.00
35 Lindsey Hunter .15 .40
36 Grant Long .15 .40
37 Theo Ratliff .20 .50
38 B.J. Armstrong .15 .40
39 Adonal Foyle RC .25 .60
40 Mark Price .25 .60
41 Felton Spencer .15 .40
42 Latrell Sprewell .30 .75
43 Clyde Drexler .40 1.00
44 Mario Elie .15 .40
45 Hakeem Olajuwon .50 1.25
46 Brent Price .15 .40
47 Kevin Willis .20 .50
48 Erick Dampier .20 .50
49 Antonio Davis .20 .50
50 Dale Davis .20 .50
51 Mark Jackson .20 .50
52 Rik Smits .20 .50
53 Brent Barry .20 .50
54 Lamond Murray .15 .40
55 Eric Piatkowski .15 .40
56 Loy Vaught .20 .50
57 Lorenzen Wright .15 .40
58 Kobe Bryant 2.50 6.00
59 Elden Campbell .15 .40
60 Derek Fisher .25 .60
61 Eddie Jones .25 .60
62 Nick Van Exel .25 .60
63 Keith Askins .15 .40
64 Isaac Austin .15 .40
65 P.J. Brown .15 .40
66 Tim Hardaway .30 .75
67 Alonzo Mourning .40 1.00
68 Ray Allen .50 1.25
69 Vin Baker .20 .50
70 Sherman Douglas .15 .40
71 Armon Gilliam .15 .40
72 Elliot Perry .15 .40
73 Chris Carr .15 .40
74 Tom Gugliotta .20 .50
75 Kevin Garnett .60 1.50
76 Doug West .15 .40
77 Keith Van Horn RC .40 1.00
78 Chris Gatling .15 .40
79 Kendall Gill .20 .50
80 Kerry Kittles .20 .50
81 Jayson Williams .20 .50
82 Chris Childs .15 .40
83 Allan Houston .25 .60
84 Larry Johnson .30 .75
85 Charles Oakley .25 .60
86 John Starks .25 .60
87 Horace Grant .25 .60
88 Anfernee Hardaway .60 1.50
89 Dennis Scott .20 .50
90 Rony Seikaly .20 .50
91 Brian Shaw .20 .50
92 Derrick Coleman .20 .50
93 Allen Iverson .75 2.00
94 Tim Thomas RC .30 .75
95 Scott Williams .15 .40
96 Cedric Ceballos .20 .50
97 Kevin Johnson .25 .60
98 Loren Meyer .20 .50
99 Steve Nash .60 1.50
100 Wesley Person .20 .50
101 Kenny Anderson .20 .50
102 Jermaine O'Neal .20 .50
103 Isaiah Rider .20 .50
104 Arvydas Sabonis .30 .75
105 Gary Trent .15 .40
106 Mahmoud Abdul-Rauf .15 .40
107 Billy Owens .15 .40
108 Olden Polynice .15 .40
109 Mitch Richmond .30 .75
110 Michael Smith .15 .40
111 Cory Alexander .15 .40
112 Vinny Del Negro .20 .50
113 Carl Herrera .15 .40
114 Tim Duncan RC 1.50 4.00
115 Hersey Hawkins .20 .50
116 Shawn Kemp .40 1.00
117 Nate McMillan .15 .40
118 Sam Perkins .20 .50
119 Detlef Schrempf .25 .60
120 Doug Christie .15 .40
121 Popeye Jones .15 .40
122 Carlos Rogers .15 .40
123 Damon Stoudamire .25 .60
124 Adam Keefe .15 .40
125 Chris Morris .15 .40
126 Greg Ostertag .15 .40
127 John Stockton .50 1.25
128 Shareef Abdur-Rahim .25 .60
129 George Lynch .15 .40
130 Lee Mayberry .15 .40
131 Anthony Peeler .15 .40
132 Calbert Cheaney .20 .50
133 Tracy Murray .15 .40
134 Rod Strickland .20 .50
135 Chris Webber .30 .75
136 Christian Laettner JAM .25 .60
137 Eric Williams JAM .15 .40
138 Vlade Divac JAM .25 .60
139 Michael Jordan JAM 2.50 6.00
140 Tyrone Hill JAM .20 .50
141 Michael Finley JAM .25 .60
142 Tom Hammonds JAM .15 .40
143 Theo Ratliff JAM .20 .50
144 Latrell Sprewell JAM .30 .75
145 Hakeem Olajuwon JAM .50 1.25
146 Reggie Miller JAM .50 1.25
147 Rodney Rogers JAM .20 .50
148 Eddie Jones JAM .25 .60
149 Jamal Mashburn JAM .25 .60
150 Glenn Robinson JAM .25 .60
151 Chris Carr JAM .15 .40
152 Kendall Gill JAM .20 .50
153 John Starks JAM .25 .60
154 Anfernee Hardaway JAM .60 1.50
155 Derrick Coleman JAM .25 .60
156 Cedric Ceballos JAM .20 .50
157 Rasheed Wallace JAM .30 .75
158 Corliss Williamson JAM .15 .40
159 Sean Elliott JAM .20 .50
160 Shawn Kemp JAM .40 1.00
161 Doug Christie JAM .15 .40
162 Karl Malone JAM .50 1.25
163 Bryant Reeves JAM .15 .40
164 Gheorghe Muresan JAM .15 .40
165 Michael Jordan CP 2.50 6.00
166 Dikembe Mutombo CP .40 1.00
167 Glen Rice CP .25 .60
168 Mitch Richmond CP .30 .75
169 Juwan Howard CP .20 .50
170 Clyde Drexler CP .40 1.00
171 Terrell Brandon CP .20 .50
172 Jerry Stackhouse CP .25 .60
173 Damon Stoudamire CP .25 .60
174 Jayson Williams CP .20 .50
175 P.J. Brown CP .15 .40
176 Anfernee Hardaway CP .60 1.50
177 Vin Baker CP .20 .50
178 LaPhonso Ellis CP .20 .50
179 Shawn Kemp CP .40 1.00
180 Checklist .15 .40
181 Mookie Blaylock .15 .40
182 Tyrone Corbin .15 .40
183 Chucky Brown .15 .40
184 Ed Gray RC .25 .60
185 Chauncey Billups RC .75 2.00
186 Tyus Edney .15 .40
187 Travis Knight .15 .40
188 Ron Mercer RC .30 .75
189 Walter McCarty .15 .40
190 B.J. Armstrong .15 .40
191 Matt Geiger .15 .40
192 Bobby Phills .20 .50
193 David Wesley .20 .50

194 Keith Booth RC .20 .50
195 Randy Brown .15 .40
196 Ron Harper .25 .60
197 Scottie Pippen .60 1.50
198 Dennis Rodman .60 1.50
199 Zydrunas Ilgauskas .25 .60
200 Brevin Knight RC .25 .60
201 Shawn Kemp .40 1.00
202 Vitaly Potapenko .15 .40
203 Wesley Person .20 .50
204 Erick Strickland RC .15 .40
205 A.C. Green .20 .50
206 Khalid Reeves .15 .40
207 Hubert Davis .15 .40
208 Dennis Scott .20 .50
209 Danny Fortson RC .25 .60
210 Bobby Jackson RC .30 .75
211 Eric Washington .15 .40
212 Dean Garrett .15 .40
213 Priest Lauderdale .15 .40
214 Joe Dumars .30 .75
215 Aaron McKie .15 .40
216 Scot Pollard RC .20 .50
217 Brian Williams .20 .50
218 Malik Sealy .20 .50
219 Duane Ferrell .15 .40
220 Erick Dampier .20 .50
221 Todd Fuller .15 .40
222 Donyell Marshall .15 .40
223 Joe Smith .20 .50
224 Charles Barkley .60 1.50
225 Matt Bullard .15 .40
226 Othella Harrington .15 .40
227 Rodrick Rhodes RC .20 .50
228 Eddie Johnson .15 .40
229 Matt Maloney .15 .40
230 Travis Best .15 .40
231 Reggie Miller .50 1.25
232 Chris Mullin .30 .75
233 Fred Hoiberg .20 .50
234 Austin Croshere RC .20 .50
235 Keith Closs RC .25 .60
236 Darrick Martin .15 .40
237 Pooh Richardson .15 .40
238 Rodney Rogers .20 .50
239 Maurice Taylor RC .20 .50
240 Robert Horry .25 .60
241 Rick Fox .20 .50
242 Shaquille O'Neal .75 2.00
243 Corie Blount .15 .40
244 Charles Smith RC .20 .50
245 Voshon Lenard .15 .40
246 Eric Murdock .15 .40
247 Dan Majerle .25 .60
248 Terry Mills .15 .40
249 Terrell Brandon .20 .50
250 Tyrone Hill .20 .50
251 Ervin Johnson .15 .40
252 Glenn Robinson .25 .60
253 Terry Porter .15 .40
254 Paul Grant RC .15 .40
255 Stephon Marbury .30 .75
256 Sam Mitchell .15 .40
257 Cherokee Parks .15 .40
258 Sam Cassell .20 .50
259 David Benoit .15 .40
260 Kevin Edwards .15 .40
261 Don MacLean .15 .40
262 Patrick Ewing .40 1.00
263 Herb Williams .15 .40
264 John Starks .25 .60
265 Chris Mills .15 .40
266 Chris Dudley .15 .40
267 Darrell Armstrong .15 .40
268 Nick Anderson .20 .50
269 Derek Harper .20 .50
270 Johnny Taylor RC .15 .40
271 Mark Price .25 .60
272 Clarence Weatherspoon .15 .40
273 Jerry Stackhouse .25 .60
274 Eric Montross .15 .40
275 Anthony Parker RC .25 .60
276 Antonio McDyess .25 .60
277 Clifford Robinson .20 .50
278 Jason Kidd .40 1.00
279 Danny Manning .20 .50
280 Rex Chapman .15 .40
281 Stacey Augmon .15 .40
282 Kelvin Cato RC .20 .50
283 Brian Grant .20 .50
284 Rasheed Wallace .30 .75
285 Lawrence Funderburke RC .20 .50
286 Anthony Johnson .25 .60
287 Tariq Abdul-Wahad RC .20 .50
288 Corliss Williamson .15 .40
289 Sean Elliott .20 .50
290 Avery Johnson .20 .50
291 David Robinson .50 1.25
292 Will Perdue .15 .40
293 Greg Anthony .20 .50
294 Jim McIlvaine .15 .40
295 Dale Ellis .20 .50
296 Gary Payton .40 1.00
297 Aaron Williams .15 .40
298 Marcus Camby .25 .60
299 John Wallace .15 .40
300 Tracy McGrady RC 1.25 3.00
301 Walt Williams .20 .50
302 Shandon Anderson .15 .40
303 Antoine Carr .15 .40
304 Jeff Hornacek .25 .60
305 Karl Malone .50 1.25
306 Bryon Russell .15 .40
307 Jacque Vaughn RC .20 .50
308 Antonio Daniels RC .25 .60
309 Blue Edwards .15 .40
310 Bryant Reeves .15 .40
311 Otis Thorpe .20 .50
312 Harvey Grant .15 .40
313 Terry Davis .15 .40
314 Juwan Howard .20 .50
315 Gheorghe Muresan .15 .40
316 Michael Jordan OT 2.50 6.00
317 Allen Iverson OT .75 2.00
318 Karl Malone OT .50 1.25
319 Glen Rice OT .25 .60
320 Dikembe Mutombo OT .40 1.00
321 Grant Hill OT .40 1.00
322 Hakeem Olajuwon OT .50 1.25
323 Stephon Marbury OT .30 .75
324 Anfernee Hardaway OT .60 1.50
325 Eddie Jones OT .25 .60
326 Mitch Richmond OT .30 .75
327 Kevin Johnson OT .25 .60
328 Kevin Garnett OT .60 1.50
329 Shareef Abdur-Rahim OT .25 .60
330 Damon Stoudamire OT .25 .60
331 Atlanta Hawks DM .20 .50
332 Boston Celtics DM .20 .50
333 Charlotte Hornets DM .20 .50
334 Chicago Bulls DM .40 1.00
335 Cleveland Cavaliers DM .20 .50
336 Dallas Mavericks DM .20 .50
337 Denver Nuggets DM .25 .60
338 Detroit Pistons DM .25 .60
339 Golden State Warriors DM .25 .60
340 Houston Rockets DM .30 .75
341 Indiana Pacers DM .20 .50
342 Los Angeles Clippers DM .20 .50
343 Los Angeles Lakers DM .40 1.00
344 Miami Heat DM .25 .60
345 Milwaukee Bucks DM .20 .50
346 Minnesota Timberwolves DM .20 .50
347 New Jersey Nets DM .20 .50
348 New York Knicks DM .20 .50
349 Orlando Magic DM .25 .60
350 Philadelphia 76ers DM .20 .50
351 Phoenix Suns DM .20 .50
352 Portland Trail Blazers DM .20 .50
353 Sacramento Kings DM .20 .50
354 San Antonio Spurs DM .40 1.00
355 Seattle Sonics DM .25 .60
356 Toronto Raptors DM .40 1.00
357 Utah Jazz DM .25 .60
358 Vancouver Grizzlies DM .20 .50
359 Washington Wizards DM .20 .50
360 Checklist .15 .40
NNO Michael Jordan Red Audio 10.00 25.00
NNO Michael Jordan Black Audio 4.00 10.00

1997-98 Upper Deck Game Dated Memorable Moments

*STARS: 12X TO 30X BASE CARD HI
SER.1 STATED ODDS 1:1500
18 Michael Jordan 1,000.00 2,000.00
34 Grant Hill 20.00 50.00

1997-98 Upper Deck AIRlines

COMPLETE SET (12) 250.00 500.00
COMMON JORDAN (AL1-12) 25.00 60.00
SER.2 STATED ODDS 1:230 HOB/RET

1997-98 Upper Deck Game Jerseys

SER.1/2 STATED ODDS 1:2500
GJ1 Charles Barkley 1,000.00 2,000.00
GJ2 Clyde Drexler 200.00 500.00
GJ3 Kevin Garnett 1,500.00 3,000.00
GJ4 Anfernee Hardaway HOME 2,000.00 4,000.00
GJ5 Grant Hill HOME 1,000.00 2,000.00
GJ6 Allen Iverson 2,000.00 4,000.00
GJ7 Kerry Kittles 125.00 300.00
GJ8 Toni Kukoc 150.00 400.00
GJ9 Reggie Miller 1,000.00 2,000.00
GJ10 Hakeem Olajuwon 500.00 1,000.00
GJ11 Glen Rice 150.00 400.00
GJ12 David Robinson 600.00 1,200.00
GJ13 Michael Jordan 60,000.00 100,000.00
GJ14 Alonzo Mourning 200.00 500.00
GJ15 Tim Hardaway 200.00 500.00
GJ16 Marcus Camby 125.00 300.00
GJ17 Antoine Walker 125.00 300.00
GJ18 Kevin Johnson 200.00 500.00
GJ19 Glenn Robinson 200.00 500.00
GJ20 Patrick Ewing 350.00 700.00
GJ21 Anfernee Hardaway AWAY 2,000.00 4,000.00
GJ22 Grant Hill AWAY 1,000.00 2,000.00

1997-98 Upper Deck Great Eight

STATED PRINT RUN 800 SERIAL #'d SETS
G1 Charles Barkley 15.00 40.00
G2 Clyde Drexler 10.00 25.00
G3 Joe Dumars 8.00 20.00
G4 Patrick Ewing 10.00 25.00
G5 Michael Jordan 100.00 250.00
G6 Karl Malone 12.00 30.00
G7 Hakeem Olajuwon 12.00 30.00
G8 John Stockton 12.00 30.00

1997-98 Upper Deck High Dimensions

STATED PRINT RUN 2000 SERIAL #'d SETS
D1 Anfernee Hardaway 12.00 30.00
D2 Gary Payton 8.00 20.00
D3 Marcus Camby 5.00 12.00
D4 Charles Barkley 12.00 30.00
D5 Jason Kidd 8.00 20.00
D6 Alonzo Mourning 8.00 20.00
D7 Kenny Anderson 4.00 10.00
D8 Kobe Bryant 50.00 125.00
D9 Dennis Rodman 12.00 30.00
D10 Kerry Kittles 4.00 10.00
D11 Dikembe Mutombo 8.00 20.00
D12 Shaquille O'Neal 15.00 40.00
D13 Glenn Robinson 5.00 12.00
D14 Tony Delk 4.00 10.00
D15 Larry Johnson 6.00 15.00
D16 Brent Barry 4.00 10.00
D17 Scottie Pippen 12.00 30.00
D18 Shareef Abdur-Rahim 5.00 12.00
D19 Sean Elliott 4.00 10.00
D20 Damon Stoudamire 5.00 12.00
D21 Kevin Garnett 12.00 30.00
D22 Bob Sura 3.00 8.00
D23 Michael Jordan 60.00 150.00
D24 Latrell Sprewell 6.00 15.00
D25 Karl Malone 10.00 25.00
D26 Antonio McDyess 5.00 12.00
D27 Allen Iverson 15.00 40.00
D28 Dale Davis 4.00 10.00
D29 Antoine Walker 5.00 12.00
D30 Chris Webber 6.00 15.00

1997-98 Upper Deck Diamond Dimensions

*STARS: 5X TO 12X HIGH DIMEN. HI
STATED PRINT RUN 100 SERIAL #'d SETS
D1 Anfernee Hardaway 300.00 600.00
D4 Charles Barkley 200.00 300.00
D6 Alonzo Mourning 75.00 200.00
D9 Dennis Rodman 175.00 350.00
D12 Shaquille O'Neal 200.00 500.00
D17 Scottie Pippen 200.00 500.00
D21 Kevin Garnett 150.00 400.00
D23 Michael Jordan 1,000.00 3,000.00
D24 Latrell Sprewell 60.00 150.00
D25 Karl Malone 75.00 200.00
D27 Allen Iverson 500.00 1,000.00
D30 Chris Webber 200.00 500.00

1997-98 Upper Deck Jordan Air Time

COMPLETE SET (10) 25.00 60.00
COMMON JORDAN (AT1-9) 2.50 6.00
COMMON JORDAN (AT10) 15.00 40.00
SER.1 STATED ODDS 1:12

1997-98 Upper Deck Records Collection

COMPLETE SET (30) 200.00 500.00
SER.2 STATED ODDS 1:23
RC1 Dikembe Mutombo 5.00 12.00
RC2 Dana Barros 2.00 5.00
RC3 Glen Rice 3.00 8.00
RC4 Dennis Rodman 12.00 30.00
RC5 Shawn Kemp 5.00 12.00
RC6 A.C. Green 2.50 6.00
RC7 LaPhonso Ellis 2.50 6.00
RC8 Grant Hill 12.00 30.00
RC9 Joe Smith 2.50 6.00
RC10 Charles Barkley 12.00 30.00
RC11 Reggie Miller 12.00 30.00
RC12 Loy Vaught 2.50 6.00
RC13 Shaquille O'Neal 15.00 40.00
RC14 Tim Hardaway 4.00 10.00
RC15 Glenn Robinson 3.00 8.00
RC16 Stephon Marbury 4.00 10.00
RC17 Sam Cassell 2.50 6.00
RC18 Patrick Ewing 8.00 20.00
RC19 Anfernee Hardaway 12.00 30.00
RC20 Allen Iverson 20.00 50.00
RC21 Kevin Johnson 3.00 8.00
RC22 Kenny Anderson 2.50 6.00
RC23 Mitch Richmond 4.00 10.00
RC24 David Robinson 12.00 30.00
RC25 Gary Payton 5.00 12.00
RC26 Damon Stoudamire 3.00 8.00
RC27 John Stockton 6.00 15.00
RC28 Bryant Reeves 2.00 5.00
RC29 Chris Webber 4.00 10.00
RC30 Michael Jordan 150.00 400.00

1997-98 Upper Deck Rookie Discovery 1

COMPLETE SET (15) 6.00 15.00
SER.2 STATED ODDS 1:4
*RD2: 2.5X TO 6X HI COLUMN
RD2: SER.2 STATED ODDS 1:108
R1 Tim Duncan 2.00 5.00
R2 Keith Van Horn .50 1.25
R3 Chauncey Billups 1.00 2.50
R4 Antonio Daniels .30 .75
R5 Tony Battie .30 .75
R6 Ron Mercer .30 .75
R7 Tim Thomas .40 1.00
R8 Adonal Foyle .25 .60
R9 Tracy McGrady 1.50 4.00
R10 Danny Fortson .30 .75
R11 Tariq Abdul-Wahad .25 .60
R12 Austin Croshere .25 .60
R13 Derek Anderson .30 .75
R14 Maurice Taylor .25 .60
R15 Kelvin Cato .25 .60

1997-98 Upper Deck Teammates

COMPLETE SET (60) 20.00 50.00
SER.1 STATED ODDS 1:4
T1 Mookie Blaylock .60 1.50
T2 Steve Smith .50 1.25
T3 Antoine Walker .60 1.50
T4 Dana Barros .40 1.00
T5 Anthony Mason .50 1.25
T6 Glen Rice .60 1.50
T7 Michael Jordan 10.00 25.00
T8 Scottie Pippen 1.50 4.00
T9 Terrell Brandon .50 1.25
T10 Tyrone Hill .40 1.00
T11 Shawn Bradley .40 1.00
T12 Robert Pack .40 1.00
T13 LaPhonso Ellis .50 1.25
T14 Antonio McDyess .60 1.50
T15 Grant Hill 1.00 2.50
T16 Lindsey Hunter .40 1.00
T17 Latrell Sprewell .75 2.00
T18 Joe Smith .50 1.25
T19 Hakeem Olajuwon 1.25 3.00
T20 Charles Barkley 1.50 4.00
T21 Mark Jackson .50 1.25
T22 Reggie Miller 1.25 3.00
T23 Brent Barry .50 1.25
T24 Loy Vaught .50 1.25
T25 Shaquille O'Neal 2.00 5.00
T26 Nick Van Exel .60 1.50
T27 Tim Hardaway .75 2.00
T28 Alonzo Mourning 1.00 2.50
T29 Vin Baker .60 1.50
T30 Glenn Robinson .60 1.50
T31 Kevin Garnett 1.50 4.00
T32 Stephon Marbury .75 2.00
T33 Kendall Gill .50 1.25
T34 Kerry Kittles .50 1.25
T35 Patrick Ewing 1.00 2.50
T36 John Starks .60 1.50
T37 Horace Grant .60 1.50
T38 Anfernee Hardaway 1.50 4.00
T39 Allen Iverson 2.00 5.00
T40 Jerry Stackhouse .60 1.50
T41 Jason Kidd 1.00 2.50
T42 Kevin Johnson .60 1.50
T43 Kenny Anderson .50 1.25
T44 Isaiah Rider .50 1.25
T45 Billy Owens .40 1.00
T46 Mitch Richmond .75 2.00
T47 Sean Elliott .50 1.25
T48 David Robinson 1.25 3.00
T49 Gary Payton 1.00 2.50
T50 Shawn Kemp 1.00 2.50
T51 Marcus Camby .60 1.50
T52 Damon Stoudamire .60 1.50
T53 John Stockton 1.25 3.00
T54 Karl Malone 1.25 3.00
T55 Shareef Abdur-Rahim .60 1.50
T56 Bryant Reeves .40 1.00
T57 Juwan Howard .50 1.25
T58 Chris Webber .75 2.00
T59 Michael Jordan 10.00 25.00
T60 Anfernee Hardaway 1.50 4.00

1997-98 Upper Deck Ultimates

COMPLETE SET (30) 15.00 40.00
SER.1 STATED ODDS 1:23
U1 Michael Jordan 10.00 25.00
U2 Grant Hill 1.50 4.00
U3 Charles Barkley 2.50 6.00
U4 Tom Gugliotta .75 2.00
U5 Dennis Rodman 2.50 6.00
U6 Reggie Miller 2.00 5.00
U7 Jason Kidd 2.00 5.00
U8 Loy Vaught .75 2.00
U9 Mookie Blaylock 1.00 2.50
U10 Tim Hardaway 1.25 3.00
U11 Juwan Howard .75 2.00
U12 Shawn Kemp 1.50 4.00
U13 Mitch Richmond 1.25 3.00
U14 Patrick Ewing 1.50 4.00
U15 Marcus Camby 1.00 2.50
U16 Bryant Stith .60 1.50
U17 Bryant Reeves .60 1.50
U18 Joe Smith .75 2.00
U19 Jerry Stackhouse 1.00 2.50
U20 Arvydas Sabonis 1.25 3.00
U21 John Stockton 2.00 5.00
U22 Eddie Jones 1.00 2.50
U23 Anfernee Hardaway 2.50 6.00
U24 Ray Allen 2.00 5.00
U25 Terrell Brandon .75 2.00
U26 David Robinson 2.00 5.00
U27 Anthony Mason .75 2.00
U28 Robert Pack .60 1.50
U29 Shareef Abdur-Rahim .60 1.50
U30 Kendall Gill .75 2.00

1998-99 Upper Deck

COMPLETE SET (355) 60.00 150.00
COMPLETE SERIES 1 (175) 30.00 75.00
COMPLETE SERIES 2 (180) 30.00 75.00
HS SUBSET STATED ODDS 1:4 HOB, 1:2 RET
TN SUBSET STATED ODDS 1:9 H/R
JORDAN SUBSET STATED ODDS 1:4 H/R
ROOKIE SUBSET STATED ODDS 1:4 H/R
1 Mookie Blaylock .20 .50
2 Ed Gray .15 .40
3 Dikembe Mutombo .40 1.00
4 Steve Smith .20 .50
5 D.Mutombo/S.Smith HS .60 1.50
6 Kenny Anderson .20 .50
7 Dana Barros .15 .40
8 Travis Knight .15 .40
9 Walter McCarty .15 .40
10 Ron Mercer .20 .50
11 Greg Minor .15 .40
12 A.Walker/R.Mercer HS .40 1.00
13 B.J. Armstrong .15 .40
14 David Wesley .15 .40
15 Anthony Mason .20 .50
16 Glen Rice .25 .60
17 J.R. Reid .15 .40
18 Bobby Phills .15 .40
19 G.Rice/A.Mason HS .40 1.00
20 Ron Harper .20 .50
21 Toni Kukoc .25 .60
22 Scottie Pippen .60 1.50
23 Michael Jordan 2.50 6.00
24 Dennis Rodman .60 1.50
25 M.Jordan/S.Pippen HS 4.00 10.00
26 M.Jordan/M.Jordan HS 4.00 10.00
27 Shawn Kemp .40 1.00
28 Zydrunas Ilgauskas .25 .60
29 Cedric Henderson .15 .40
30 Vitaly Potapenko .15 .40
31 Derek Anderson .25 .60
32 S.Kemp/Z.Ilgauskas HS .60 1.50
33 Shawn Bradley .15 .40
34 Khalid Reeves .15 .40
35 Robert Pack .15 .40
36 Michael Finley .25 .60
37 Erick Strickland .15 .40
38 M.Finley/S.Bradley HS .40 1.00
39 Bryant Stith .15 .40
40 Dean Garrett .15 .40
41 Eric Williams .15 .40
42 Bobby Jackson .20 .50
43 Danny Fortson .15 .40
44 L.Ellis/B.Stith HS .25 .60
45 Grant Hill .40 1.00
46 Lindsey Hunter .15 .40
47 Brian Williams .15 .40
48 Scot Pollard .15 .40
49 G.Hill/B.Williams HS .60 1.50
50 Donyell Marshall .15 .40
51 Tony Delk .15 .40
52 Erick Dampier .15 .40
53 Felton Spencer .15 .40
54 Bimbo Coles .15 .40
55 Muggsy Bogues .20 .50
56 D.Marshall/M.Bogues HS .30 .75
57 Charles Barkley .60 1.50
58 Brent Price .15 .40
59 Hakeem Olajuwon .50 1.25
60 Rodrick Rhodes .15 .40
61 C.Barkley/H.Olajuwon HS 1.00 2.50
62 Dale Davis .15 .40
63 Antonio Davis .15 .40
64 Chris Mullin .30 .75
65 Jalen Rose .25 .60
66 Reggie Miller .50 1.25
67 Mark Jackson .20 .50
68 R.Miller/M.Jackson HS .75 2.00
69 Rodney Rogers .15 .40
70 Lamond Murray .15 .40
71 Eric Piatkowski .15 .40
72 Lorenzen Wright .15 .40
73 Maurice Taylor .15 .40
74 M.Taylor/L.Murray HS .25 .60
75 Kobe Bryant 2.00 5.00
76 Shaquille O'Neal 1.00 2.50
77 Derek Fisher .20 .50
78 Elden Campbell .15 .40
79 Corie Blount .15 .40
80 S.O'Neal/K.Bryant HS 3.00 8.00
81 Jamal Mashburn .25 .60
82 Alonzo Mourning .40 1.00
83 Tim Hardaway .30 .75
84 Voshon Lenard .15 .40
85 A.Mourning/T.Hardaway HS .60 1.50
86 Ray Allen .40 1.00
87 Terrell Brandon .20 .50
88 Elliot Perry .15 .40
89 Ervin Johnson .15 .40
90 R.Allen/G.Robinson HS .60 1.50
91 Micheal Williams .15 .40
92 Anthony Peeler .15 .40
93 Chris Carr .15 .40
94 Kevin Garnett .60 1.50
95 K.Garnett/S.Marbury HS 1.00 2.50
96 Keith Van Horn .25 .60
97 Kerry Kittles .20 .50
98 Kendall Gill .20 .50
99 Sam Cassell .20 .50
100 Chris Gatling .15 .40
101 K.Van Horn/Cassell HS .40 1.00
102 Patrick Ewing .40 1.00
103 John Starks .25 .60
104 Allan Houston .25 .60
105 Chris Mills .15 .40
106 Chris Childs .15 .40
107 Charlie Ward .15 .40
108 P.Ewing/J.Starks HS .60 1.50
109 Anfernee Hardaway .60 1.50
110 Horace Grant .25 .60
111 Nick Anderson .15 .40
112 Johnny Taylor .15 .40
113 A.Hardaway/H.Grant HS 1.00 2.50
114 Allen Iverson .60 1.50
115 Scott Williams .15 .40
116 Tim Thomas .20 .50
117 Brian Shaw .15 .40
118 Anthony Parker .15 .40
119 A.Iverson/T.Thomas HS 1.00 2.50
120 Jason Kidd .40 1.00
121 Rex Chapman .20 .50
122 Danny Manning .20 .50
123 J.Kidd/D.Manning HS .60 1.50
124 Rasheed Wallace .30 .75
125 Walt Williams .15 .40
126 Kelvin Cato .15 .40
127 Arvydas Sabonis .25 .60
128 Brian Grant .15 .40
129 R.Wallace/I.Rider HS .50 1.25
130 Tariq Abdul-Wahad .15 .40
131 Corliss Williamson .15 .40
132 Olden Polynice .15 .40
133 Chris Robinson .15 .40
134 T.Abdul-Wahad/O.Polynice HS .25 .60
135 Tim Duncan .60 1.50
136 Avery Johnson .15 .40
137 David Robinson .50 1.25
138 Monty Williams .15 .40
139 T.Duncan/D.Rob HS 1.00 2.50
140 Vin Baker .20 .50
141 Hersey Hawkins .15 .40
142 Detlef Schrempf .25 .60
143 Jim McIlvaine .15 .40
144 G.Payton/V.Baker HS .60 1.50
145 Chauncey Billups .30 .75
146 Tracy McGrady .40 1.00
147 John Wallace .15 .40
148 Doug Christie .20 .50
149 Dee Brown .15 .40
150 T.McGrady/C.Billups HS .60 1.50
151 Karl Malone .60 1.50
152 John Stockton .50 1.25
153 Adam Keefe .15 .40
154 Howard Eisley .15 .40
155 K.Malone/J.Stockton HS .75 2.00
156 Bryant Reeves .15 .40
157 Lee Mayberry .15 .40
158 Michael Smith .15 .40
159 Abdur-Rahim/Reeves HS .40 1.00
160 Juwan Howard .20 .50
161 Calbert Cheaney .15 .40
162 Tracy Murray .15 .40
163 J.Howard/C.Cheaney HS .30 .75
164 Shaquille O'Neal TN 2.00 5.00
165 Maurice Taylor TN .30 .75
166 Stephon Marbury TN .60 1.50
167 Tracy McGrady TN .75 2.00
168 Antoine Walker TN .50 1.25
169 Michael Jordan TN 5.00 12.00
170 Keith Van Horn TN .50 1.25
171 S.Abdur-Rahim TN .50 1.25
172 Kobe Bryant TN 4.00 10.00
173 Gary Payton TN .75 2.00
174 Michael Jordan CL .40 1.00
175 Michael Jordan CL .40 1.00
176 Kevin Johnson .25 .60
177 Glenn Robinson .25 .60
178 Antoine Walker .25 .60
179 Jerry Stackhouse .25 .60
180 Mark Price .25 .60
181 Stephon Marbury .30 .75
182 Shareef Abdur-Rahim .25 .60
183 Wesley Person .15 .40
184 Keith Booth .15 .40
185 Sean Elliott .25 .60
186 Allan Henderson .15 .40
187 Bryon Russell .15 .40
188 Jermaine O'Neal .40 1.00
189 Steve Nash .50 1.25
190 Eldridge Recasner .15 .40
191 Damon Stoudamire .25 .60
192 Dell Curry .15 .40
193 Michael Stewart .15 .40
194 Bruce Bowen RC .30 .75
195 Steve Kerr .20 .50
196 Dale Ellis .15 .40
197 Shandon Anderson .15 .40
198 Larry Johnson .40 1.00
199 Chris Webber .30 .75
200 Matt Geiger .15 .40
201 Chris Ansley .15 .40
202 Loy Vaught .15 .40
203 Aaron McKie .15 .40
204 A.C. Green .15 .40
205 Bo Outlaw .15 .40
206 Antonio McDyess .20 .50
207 Priest Lauderdale .15 .40
208 Greg Ostertag .15 .40
209 Dan Majerle .25 .60
210 Johnny Newman .15 .40
211 Tyrone Corbin .15 .40
212 Pervis Ellison .15 .40
213 Shawnelle Scott .15 .40
214 Travis Best .15 .40
215 Stacey Augmon .20 .50
216 Brevin Knight .15 .40
217 Jerome Williams .15 .40
218 Terry Mills .15 .40
219 Matt Maloney .15 .40
220 Dennis Scott .15 .40
221 John Thomas .15 .40
222 Nick Van Exel .25 .60
223 Duane Ferrell .15 .40
224 Chris Whitney .15 .40
225 Luc Longley .20 .50
226 Robert Horry .20 .50
227 Clifford Robinson .15 .40
228 Samaki Walker .15 .40
229 Derrick McKey .15 .40
230A Michael Jordan 1.50 4.00
230B Michael Jordan 1.50 4.00
230C Michael Jordan 1.50 4.00
230D Michael Jordan 1.50 4.00
230E Michael Jordan 1.50 4.00
230F Michael Jordan 1.50 4.00
230G Michael Jordan 1.50 4.00
230H Michael Jordan 1.50 4.00
230I Michael Jordan 1.50 4.00
230J Michael Jordan 1.50 4.00
230K Michael Jordan 1.50 4.00
230L Michael Jordan 1.50 4.00
230M Michael Jordan 1.50 4.00
230N Michael Jordan 1.50 4.00
230O Michael Jordan 1.50 4.00
230P Michael Jordan 1.50 4.00
230Q Michael Jordan 1.50 4.00
230R Michael Jordan 1.50 4.00
230S Michael Jordan 1.50 4.00
230T Michael Jordan 1.50 4.00
230U Michael Jordan 1.50 4.00
230V Michael Jordan 1.50 4.00
230W Michael Jordan 1.50 4.00
231 Armon Gilliam .15 .40
232 Andrew DeClercq .15 .40
233 Stojko Vrankovic .15 .40
234 Jayson Williams .15 .40
235 Vinny Del Negro .15 .40
236 Theo Ratliff .20 .50
237 Othella Harrington .15 .40
238 Mitch Richmond .30 .75
239 Vlade Divac .25 .60
240 Duane Causwell .15 .40
241 Todd Fuller .15 .40
242 Tom Gugliotta .20 .50
243 LaPhonso Ellis .15 .40
244 Brian Evans .15 .40
245 Jason Caffey .15 .40
246 Pooh Richardson .15 .40
247 George Lynch .15 .40
248 Bill Wennington .15 .40
249 Rik Smits .20 .50
250 Kevin Willis .15 .40
251 Mario Elie .15 .40
252 Austin Croshere .15 .40
253 Sharone Wright .15 .40
254 Danny Ferry .15 .40
255 Jacque Vaughn .15 .40
256 Adonal Foyle .15 .40
257 Billy Owens .20 .50
258 Randy Brown .15 .40
259 Joe Smith .20 .50
260 Joe Dumars .25 .60
261 Sean Rooks .15 .40
262 Eric Montross .15 .40
263 Hubert Davis .15 .40
264 Gary Payton .40 1.00
265 Tyrone Hill .15 .40
266 John Crotty .15 .40
267 P.J. Brown .15 .40
268 Michael Cage .15 .40
269 Scott Burrell .15 .40
270 Marcus Camby .20 .50
271 Rod Strickland .20 .50
272 Jim Jackson .15 .40
273 Corey Beck .15 .40
274 James Robinson .15 .40
275 Cedric Ceballos .20 .50
276 Charles Oakley .20 .50
277 Anthony Johnson .15 .40
278 Bob Sura .15 .40
279 Isaiah Rider .20 .50
280 Jeff Hornacek .20 .50
281 Rony Seikaly .15 .40
282 Charles Smith .15 .40
283 Eddie Jones .25 .60
284 Lucious Harris .15 .40
285 Andrew Lang .15 .40
286 Terry Cummings .20 .50
287 Keith Closs .15 .40
288 Chris Anstey .15 .40
289 Clarence Weatherspoon .15 .40
290 Michael Jordan H99 2.50 6.00
291 Shawn Kemp H99 .40 1.00
292 Tracy McGrady H99 .60 1.50
293 Glen Rice H99 .25 .60
294 David Robinson H99 .50 1.25
295 Antonio McDyess H99 .25 .60
296 Vin Baker H99 .20 .50
297 Juwan Howard H99 .20 .50
298 Ron Mercer H99 .20 .50
299 Michael Finley H99 .20 .50
300 Scottie Pippen H99 .60 1.50
301 Tim Thomas H99 .20 .50
302 Rasheed Wallace H99 .30 .75
303 Alonzo Mourning H99 .40 1.00
304 Dikembe Mutombo H99 .40 1.00
305 Derek Anderson H99 .20 .50
306 Ray Allen H99 .40 1.00
307 Patrick Ewing H99 .40 1.00
308 Sean Elliott H99 .25 .60
309 Shaquille O'Neal H99 1.00 2.50
310 Michael Jordan CL .40 1.00
311 Michael Jordan CL .40 1.00
312 Michael Olowokandi RC 1.00 2.50
313 Mike Bibby RC 1.50 4.00
314 Raef LaFrentz RC 1.00 2.50
315 Antawn Jamison RC 1.25 3.00
316 Vince Carter RC 4.00 10.00
317 Robert Traylor RC .75 2.00
318 Jason Williams RC 2.50 6.00
319 Larry Hughes RC 1.25 3.00
320 Dirk Nowitzki RC 6.00 15.00
321 Paul Pierce RC 3.00 8.00
322 Bonzi Wells RC .75 2.00
323 Michael Doleac RC .60 1.50
324 Keon Clark RC .75 2.00
325 Michael Dickerson RC .75 2.00
326 Matt Harpring RC .75 2.00
327 Bryce Drew RC .50 1.25
328 Pat Garrity RC .60 1.50
329 Roshown McLeod RC .50 1.25
330 Ricky Davis RC 1.25 3.00
331 Peja Stojakovic RC 1.50 4.00
332 Felipe Lopez RC .50 1.25
333 Al Harrington RC 1.00 2.50
UDX M.Jordan Retires 1.00 2.50
P123 Michael Jordan PROMO 2.00 5.00

1998-99 Upper Deck Bronze

COMMON MJ (230A-230W) 25.00 60.00
*STARS: 15X TO 40X BASE CARD HI
*HS SUBSET: 10X TO 25X BASE HI
*TN SUBSET: 8X TO 20X BASE HI
*RCs: 3X TO 8X BASE HI
STATED PRINT RUN 100 SERIAL #'d SETS
NUMBER 230 HAS 23 DIFFERENT CARDS
24 Dennis Rodman 30.00 80.00
26 M.Jordan/M.Jordan HS 125.00 300.00
174 Michael Jordan CL 30.00 80.00
175 Michael Jordan CL 30.00 80.00
310 Michael Jordan CL 30.00 80.00
311 Michael Jordan CL 30.00 80.00
316 Vince Carter 75.00 200.00
320 Dirk Nowitzki 125.00 300.00

1998-99 Upper Deck AeroDynamics

COMPLETE SET (30) 15.00 40.00
SER.1 STATED ODDS 1:7 HOB/RET
*BRONZE: 1.25X TO 3X HI COLUMN
STATED PRINT RUN 2000 SERIAL #'d SETS
*SILVER: 10X TO 25X HI
STATED PRINT RUN 100 SERIAL #'d SETS
A1 Michael Jordan 8.00 20.00
A2 Shawn Kemp 1.00 2.50
A3 Anfernee Hardaway 1.50 4.00
A4 Tracy McGrady 1.00 2.50
A5 Glen Rice .60 1.50
A6 Maurice Taylor .40 1.00
A7 Kevin Garnett 1.50 4.00
A8 Jason Kidd 1.00 2.50
A9 Grant Hill 1.00 2.50
A10 Kendall Gill .50 1.25
A11 Hakeem Olajuwon 1.25 3.00
A12 Mookie Blaylock .50 1.25
A13 Toni Kukoc .60 1.50
A14 Kobe Bryant 5.00 12.00
A15 Corliss Williamson .40 1.00
A16 Ray Allen 1.00 2.50
A17 Vin Baker .50 1.25
A18 Reggie Miller 1.25 3.00
A19 Allan Houston .60 1.50
A20 Shareef Abdur-Rahim .60 1.50
A21 Tim Duncan 1.50 4.00
A22 Michael Finley .60 1.50
A23 Damon Stoudamire .60 1.50
A24 Juwan Howard .50 1.25
A25 Antoine Walker .60 1.50
A26 Donyell Marshall .40 1.00
A27 Allen Iverson 1.50 4.00
A28 Karl Malone 1.25 3.00
A29 Bobby Jackson .50 1.25
A30 Tim Hardaway .75 2.00

1998-99 Upper Deck AeroDynamics Gold

*STARS: 30X TO 80X BASE INSERT
STATED PRINT RUN 25 SERIAL #'d SETS
A1 Michael Jordan 2,500.00 5,000.00
A14 Kobe Bryant 1,000.00 2,000.00

1998-99 UD Choice Draw Your Own Trading Card

COMPLETE SET (1)
NNO Michael Jordan EXCH 2.00 5.00

1998-99 Upper Deck Forces

COMPLETE SET (30) 30.00 80.00
SER.1 STATED ODDS 1:23 HOB/RET
*BRONZE: 1X TO 2.5X HI COLUMN
STATED PRINT RUN 1000 SERIAL #'d SETS
*GOLD: 15X TO 40X HI
STATED PRINT RUN 25 SER.#'d SETS
*SILVER: 6X TO 15X HI
STATED PRINT RUN 50 SERIAL #'d SETS
F1 Michael Jordan 12.00 30.00
F2 Shareef Abdur-Rahim 1.25 3.00
F3 Shaquille O'Neal 5.00 12.00
F4 Gary Payton 2.00 5.00
F5 Allen Iverson 3.00 8.00
F6 Allan Houston 1.25 3.00
F7 LaPhonso Ellis .75 2.00
F8 Kevin Garnett 3.00 8.00
F9 Chauncey Billups 1.50 4.00
F10 Tim Hardaway 1.50 4.00
F11 Reggie Miller 2.50 6.00
F12 Glen Rice 1.25 3.00
F13 Damon Stoudamire 1.25 3.00
F14 Lamond Murray .75 2.00
F15 Shawn Kemp 2.00 5.00
F16 Steve Smith 1.00 2.50
F17 Tim Duncan 3.00 8.00

F18 Hakeem Olajuwon 2.50 6.00
F19 Karl Malone 2.50 6.00
F20 Donyell Marshall .75 2.00
F21 Anfernee Hardaway 3.00 8.00
F22 Grant Hill 2.00 5.00
F23 Antoine Walker 1.25 3.00
F24 Toni Kukoc 1.25 3.00
F25 Corliss Williamson .75 2.00
F26 Glenn Robinson 1.25 3.00
F27 Keith Van Horn 1.25 3.00
F28 Jason Kidd 2.00 5.00
F29 Juwan Howard 1.00 2.50
F30 Michael Finley 1.25 3.00

1998-99 Upper Deck Forces Bronze

*BRONZE: 1X TO 2.5X VALUE
F1 Michael Jordan 30.00 80.00

1998-99 Upper Deck Game Jerseys

1-10/21-30/41-50: STATED ODDS 1:2500
11-20/31-40: STATED ODDS 1:288 HOBBY
GJ1 Glen Rice 50.00 120.00
GJ2 Shawn Kemp 125.00 300.00
GJ3 Reggie Miller 125.00 300.00
GJ4 Shaquille O'Neal 300.00 600.00
GJ5 Ray Allen 150.00 400.00
GJ6 Keith Van Horn 10.00 25.00
GJ7 Allen Iverson 200.00 500.00
GJ8 David Robinson 100.00 250.00
GJ9 Karl Malone 100.00 250.00
GJ10 Shareef Abdur-Rahim 15.00 40.00
GJ11 Grant Hill 200.00 500.00
GJ12 Hakeem Olajuwon 200.00 500.00
GJ13 Kevin Garnett 200.00 500.00
GJ14 Jayson Williams 25.00 60.00
GJ15 Tim Duncan 300.00 600.00
GJ16 Gary Payton 40.00 100.00
GJ17 John Stockton 100.00 250.00
GJ18 Bryant Reeves 30.00 80.00
GJ19 Kobe Bryant 4,000.00 8,000.00
GJ20 Michael Jordan 10,000.00 20,000.00
GJ21 Kobe Bryant 4,000.00 8,000.00
GJ22 Grant Hill 100.00 250.00
GJ23 Anfernee Hardaway 500.00 1,000.00
GJ24 Tim Thomas 20.00 50.00
GJ25 Hakeem Olajuwon 150.00 400.00
GJ26 Damon Stoudamire 30.00 80.00
GJ27 Gary Payton 60.00 150.00
GJ28 Jason Kidd 60.00 150.00
GJ29 Reggie Miller 125.00 300.00
GJ30 Kevin Garnett 200.00 500.00
GJ31 Tim Duncan 200.00 500.00
GJ32 Keith Van Horn 40.00 100.00
GJ33 Stephon Marbury 75.00 200.00
GJ34 Shaquille O'Neal 200.00 500.00
GJ35 Allen Iverson 200.00 500.00
GJ36 Antoine Walker 15.00 40.00
GJ37 Karl Malone 125.00 300.00
GJ39 Shareef Abdur-Rahim 20.00 50.00
GJ40 David Robinson 125.00 300.00
GJ41 Corey Benjamin 10.00 25.00
GJ42 Mike Bibby 125.00 300.00
GJ43 Vince Carter 500.00 1,000.00
GJ44 Michael Doleac 10.00 25.00
GJ45 Larry Hughes 40.00 100.00
GJ46 Antawn Jamison 40.00 100.00
GJ47 Raef LaFrentz 40.00 100.00
GJ48 Robert Traylor 30.00 80.00
GJ49 Bonzi Wells 15.00 40.00
GJ50 Jason Williams 300.00 600.00

1998-99 Upper Deck Intensity

COMPLETE SET (30) 15.00 40.00
SER.1 STATED ODDS 1:12 HOB/RET
*BRONZE: 1X TO 2.5X HI COLUMN
STATED PRINT RUN 1500 SERIAL #'d SETS
*GOLD: 20X TO 50X HI
STATED PRINT RUN 25 SER.#'d SETS
*SILVER: 6X TO 15X HI
STATED PRINT RUN 75 SERIAL #'d SETS
I1 Michael Jordan 10.00 25.00
I2 Tracy Murray .60 1.50
I3 Ron Mercer .75 2.00
I4 Terrell Brandon .75 2.00
I5 Brevin Knight .60 1.50
I6 Rasheed Wallace 1.25 3.00
I7 Sam Cassell .75 2.00
I8 Erick Dampier .60 1.50
I9 LaPhonso Ellis .60 1.50
I10 Tim Thomas .75 2.00
I11 Anfernee Hardaway 2.50 6.00
I12 Tariq Abdul-Wahad .60 1.50
I13 Lorenzen Wright .60 1.50
I14 Bryant Reeves .60 1.50
I15 Charles Barkley 2.50 6.00
I16 Chauncey Billups 1.25 3.00
I17 John Starks 1.00 2.50
I18 Jerry Stackhouse 1.00 2.50
I19 Vlade Divac 1.00 2.50
I20 Detlef Schrempf 1.00 2.50
I21 John Stockton 2.00 5.00
I22 Nick Anderson .60 1.50
I23 Alonzo Mourning 1.50 4.00
I24 Dikembe Mutombo 1.50 4.00
I25 Jalen Rose .75 2.00
I26 Robert Pack .60 1.50
I27 Antonio McDyess .75 2.00
I28 Eddie Jones 1.00 2.50
I29 Stephon Marbury 1.25 3.00
I30 David Robinson 2.00 5.00

1998-99 Upper Deck MJ23

COMMON CARD (M1-M30) 4.00 10.00
SER.2 STATED ODDS 1:23 HOB/RET
*BRONZE: .6X TO 1.5X HI COLUMN
BRONZE PRINT RUN 2300 SETS
*SILVER: 12X TO 30X HI COLUMN
SILVER PRINT RUN 23 SETS

1998-99 Upper Deck Michael Jordan Game Jersey Autographs

COMMON CARD 15,000.00 20,000.00

1998-99 Upper Deck Next Wave

SER.2 STATED ODDS 1:11 HOB/RET
*BRONZE: 1X TO 2.5X HI COLUMN
STATED PRINT RUN 1500 SERIAL #'d SETS
*GOLD: 6X TO 15X HI
STATED PRINT RUN 75 SERIAL #'d SETS
*SILVER: 4X TO 10X HI
STATED PRINT RUN 200 SERIAL #'d SETS
NW1 Kobe Bryant 6.00 15.00
NW2 John Wallace .60 1.50
NW3 Kerry Kittles .75 2.00
NW4 Tim Thomas .75 2.00
NW5 Maurice Taylor .60 1.50
NW6 Antonio McDyess .75 2.00
NW7 Jermaine O'Neal 1.00 2.50
NW8 Zydrunas Ilgauskas 1.00 2.50
NW9 Danny Fortson .60 1.50
NW10 Tim Duncan 2.50 6.00
NW11 Derek Anderson .75 2.00
NW12 Ron Mercer .75 2.00
NW13 Joe Smith .75 2.00
NW14 Eddie Jones 1.00 2.50
NW15 Rodrick Rhodes .60 1.50
NW16 Kevin Garnett 2.50 6.00
NW17 Ed Gray .60 1.50
NW18 Bobby Jackson .75 2.00
NW19 Allan Houston 1.00 2.50
NW20 Chauncey Billups 1.25 3.00
NW21 Keith Booth .60 1.50
NW22 Brevin Knight .60 1.50
NW23 Othella Harrington .60 1.50
NW24 Keith Van Horn 1.00 2.50
NW25 Michael Finley 1.00 2.50
NW26 Tracy McGrady 1.50 4.00
NW27 Derek Fisher .75 2.00
NW28 Ray Allen 1.50 4.00
NW29 Anthony Johnson .60 1.50
NW30 Vin Baker .75 2.00

1998-99 Upper Deck Super Powers

COMPLETE SET (30) 15.00 40.00
SER.2 STATED ODDS 1:5 HOB/RET
*BRONZE: 2X TO 5X HI COLUMN
STATED PRINT RUN 1000 SERIAL #'d SETS
*GOLD: 15X TO 40X HI
STATED PRINT RUN 50 SERIAL #'d SETS
*SILVER: 10X TO 25X HI
STATED PRINT RUN 100 SERIAL #'d SETS
S1 Dikembe Mutombo 1.00 2.50
S2 Ron Mercer .50 1.25
S3 Glen Rice .60 1.50
S4 Scottie Pippen 1.50 4.00
S5 Shawn Kemp 1.00 2.50
S6 Michael Finley .60 1.50
S7 Bobby Jackson .50 1.25
S8 Grant Hill 1.00 2.50
S9 Jim Jackson .40 1.00
S10 Hakeem Olajuwon 1.25 3.00
S11 Reggie Miller 1.25 3.00
S12 Maurice Taylor .40 1.00
S13 Kobe Bryant 5.00 12.00
S14 Tim Hardaway .75 2.00
S15 Ray Allen 1.00 2.50
S16 Stephon Marbury .75 2.00
S17 Keith Van Horn .60 1.50
S18 Allan Houston .60 1.50
S19 Anfernee Hardaway 1.50 4.00
S20 Allen Iverson 1.50 4.00
S21 Jason Kidd 1.00 2.50
S22 Damon Stoudamire .60 1.50
S23 Corliss Williamson .40 1.00
S24 Tim Duncan 1.50 4.00
S25 Gary Payton 1.00 2.50
S26 Tracy McGrady 1.00 2.50
S27 Karl Malone 1.25 3.00
S28 Shareef Abdur-Rahim .60 1.50
S29 Juwan Howard .50 1.25
S30 Michael Jordan 8.00 20.00

1999-00 Upper Deck

COMPLETE SET (360) 60.00 150.00
COMPLETE SERIES 1 (180) 40.00 100.00
COMPLETE SERIES 2 (180) 20.00 50.00
COMP.SERIES 1 w/o RC (155) 15.00 40.00
COMP.SERIES 2 w/o SP (133) 4.00 10.00
ROOKIE SUBSET STATED ODDS 1:4 H/R
MJ SUBSET STATED ODDS 1:4 H/R
1 Roshown McLeod .20 .50
2 Dikembe Mutombo .50 1.25
3 Alan Henderson .20 .50
4 LaPhonso Ellis .20 .50
5 Chris Crawford .20 .50
6 Kenny Anderson .25 .60
7 Antoine Walker .30 .75
8 Paul Pierce .60 1.50
9 Vitaly Potapenko .20 .50
10 Dana Barros .20 .50
11 Eldren Campbell .20 .50
12 Eddie Jones .30 .75
13 David Wesley .20 .50
14 Derrick Coleman .25 .60
15 Ricky Davis .30 .75
16 Corey Benjamin .20 .50
17 Randy Brown .20 .50
18 Kornel David RC .20 .50
19 Toni Kukoc .40 1.00
20 Keith Booth .20 .50
21 Shawn Kemp .50 1.25
22 Wesley Person .20 .50
23 Brevin Knight .20 .50
24 Bob Sura .20 .50
25 Zydrunas Ilgauskas .25 .60
26 Michael Finley .30 .75
27 Shawn Bradley .30 .75
28 Dirk Nowitzki 1.00 2.50
29 Steve Nash .60 1.50
30 Antonio McDyess .25 .60
31 Nick Van Exel .25 .60
32 Chauncey Billups .30 .75
33 Bryant Stith .20 .50
34 Raef LaFrentz .25 .60
35 Grant Hill .50 1.25
36 Lindsey Hunter .20 .50
37 Bison Dele .20 .50
38 Jerry Stackhouse .30 .75
39 John Starks .30 .75
40 Antawn Jamison .30 .75
41 Erick Dampier .20 .50
42 Jason Caffey .20 .50
43 Hakeem Olajuwon .60 1.50
44 Scottie Pippen .75 2.00
45 Cuttino Mobley .20 .50
46 Charles Barkley .75 2.00
47 Bryce Drew .20 .50
48 Reggie Miller .60 1.50
49 Jalen Rose .20 .50
50 Mark Jackson .25 .60
51 Dale Davis .20 .50
52 Chris Mullin .30 .75
53 Maurice Taylor .20 .50
54 Tyrone Nesby RC .20 .50
55 Michael Olowokandi .20 .50
56 Eric Piatkowski .20 .50
57 Troy Hudson RC .30 .75
58 Kobe Bryant 2.50 6.00
59 Shaquille O'Neal 1.25 3.00
60 Glen Rice .30 .75
61 Robert Horry .25 .60
62 Tim Hardaway .40 1.00
63 Alonzo Mourning .50 1.25
64 P.J. Brown .20 .50
65 Dan Majerle .30 .75
66 Ray Allen .50 1.25
67 Glenn Robinson .30 .75
68 Sam Cassell .25 .60
69 Robert Traylor .20 .50
70 Kevin Garnett .75 2.00
71 Sam Mitchell .20 .50
72 Dean Garrett .20 .50
73 Bobby Jackson .25 .60
74 Radoslav Nesterovic RC .30 .75
75 Keith Van Horn .25 .60
76 Stephon Marbury .40 1.00
77 Kendall Gill .30 .75
78 Scott Burrell .20 .50
79 Patrick Ewing .40 1.00
80 Allan Houston .25 .60
81 Latrell Sprewell .40 1.00
82 Larry Johnson .30 .75
83 Marcus Camby .25 .60
84 Darrell Armstrong .20 .50
85 Derek Strong .20 .50
86 Matt Harpring .20 .50
87 Michael Doleac .20 .50
88 Bo Outlaw .20 .50
89 Allen Iverson .75 2.00
90 Theo Ratliff .25 .60
91 Larry Hughes .25 .60
92 Eric Snow .20 .50
93 Jason Kidd .50 1.25
94 Clifford Robinson .25 .60
95 Tom Gugliotta .25 .60
96 Luc Longley .25 .60
97 Rasheed Wallace .40 1.00
98 Arvydas Sabonis .25 .60
99 Damon Stoudamire .30 .75
100 Brian Grant .20 .50
101 Jason Williams .50 1.25
102 Vlade Divac .30 .75
103 Peja Stojakovic .30 .75
104 Lawrence Funderburke .20 .50
105 Tim Duncan .75 2.00
106 Sean Elliott .25 .60
107 David Robinson .60 1.50
108 Mario Elie .20 .50
109 Avery Johnson .25 .60
110 Gary Payton .50 1.25
111 Vin Baker .25 .60
112 Rashard Lewis .25 .60
113 Jelani McCoy .20 .50
114 Vladimir Stepania .20 .50
115 Vince Carter .75 2.00
116 Doug Christie .25 .60
117 Kevin Willis .20 .50
118 Dee Brown .20 .50
119 John Thomas .20 .50
120 Karl Malone .60 1.50
121 John Stockton .50 1.25
122 Howard Eisley .20 .50
123 Bryon Russell .20 .50
124 Greg Ostertag .20 .50
125 Shareef Abdur-Rahim .30 .75
126 Mike Bibby .30 .75
127 Felipe Lopez .20 .50
128 Cherokee Parks .20 .50
129 Juwan Howard .25 .60
130 Rod Strickland .25 .60
131 Chris Whitney .20 .50
132 Tracy Murray .20 .50
133 Jahidi White .20 .50
134 Michael Jordan AIR 1.50 4.00
135 Michael Jordan AIR 1.50 4.00
136 Michael Jordan AIR 1.50 4.00
137 Michael Jordan AIR 1.50 4.00
138 Michael Jordan AIR 1.50 4.00
139 Michael Jordan AIR 1.50 4.00
140 Michael Jordan AIR 1.50 4.00
141 Michael Jordan AIR 1.50 4.00
142 Michael Jordan AIR 1.50 4.00
143 Michael Jordan AIR 1.50 4.00
144 Michael Jordan AIR 1.50 4.00
145 Michael Jordan AIR 1.50 4.00
146 Michael Jordan AIR 1.50 4.00
147 Michael Jordan AIR 1.50 4.00
148 Michael Jordan AIR 1.50 4.00
149 Michael Jordan AIR 1.50 4.00
150 Michael Jordan AIR 1.50 4.00
151 Michael Jordan AIR 1.50 4.00
152 Michael Jordan AIR 1.50 4.00
153 Michael Jordan AIR 1.50 4.00
154 Michael Jordan CL 1.00 2.50
155 Michael Jordan CL 1.00 2.50
156 Elton Brand RC 1.25 3.00
157 Steve Francis RC 1.25 3.00
158 Baron Davis RC 1.50 4.00
159 Lamar Odom RC 1.25 3.00
160 Jonathan Bender RC .60 1.50
161 Wally Szczerbiak RC 1.25 3.00
162 Richard Hamilton RC 1.50 4.00
163 Andre Miller RC 1.25 3.00
164 Shawn Marion RC 1.25 3.00
165 Jason Terry RC 1.00 2.50
166 Trajan Langdon RC .50 1.25
167 Kenny Thomas RC .60 1.50
168 Corey Maggette RC .75 2.00
169 William Avery RC .40 1.00
170 Jumaine Jones RC .40 1.00
171 Ron Artest RC 1.50 4.00
172 Cal Bowdler RC .40 1.00
173 James Posey RC .60 1.50
174 Quincy Lewis RC .40 1.00
175 Vonteego Cummings RC .40 1.00
176 Jeff Foster RC .60 1.50
177 Dion Glover RC .40 1.00
178 Devean George RC .50 1.25
179 Evan Eschmeyer RC .50 1.25
180 Tim James RC .40 1.00
181 Jim Jackson .20 .50
182 Isaiah Rider .25 .60
183 Lorenzen Wright .20 .50
184 Bimbo Coles .20 .50
185 Anthony Johnson .20 .50
186 Calbert Cheaney .20 .50
187 Pervis Ellison .20 .50
188 Walter McCarty .20 .50
189 Eric Williams .20 .50
190 Tony Battie .20 .50
191 Anthony Mason .30 .75
192 Bobby Phills .20 .50
193 Todd Fuller .20 .50
194 Brad Miller .25 .60
195 Eldridge Recasner .20 .50
196 Chris Anstey .20 .50
197 Fred Hoiberg .20 .50
198 Hersey Hawkins .20 .50
199 Will Perdue .20 .50
200 Mark Bryant .20 .50
201 Lamond Murray .20 .50
202 Cedric Henderson .20 .50
203 Andrew DeClercq .20 .50
204 Danny Ferry .20 .50
205 Erick Strickland .20 .50
206 Cedric Ceballos .20 .50
207 Hubert Davis .20 .50
208 Robert Pack .20 .50
209 Gary Trent .20 .50
210 Ron Mercer .25 .60
211 George McCloud .20 .50
212 Roy Rogers .20 .50
213 Keon Clark .20 .50
214 Terry Mills .20 .50
215 Michael Curry .20 .50
216 Christian Laettner .25 .60
217 Jerome Williams .20 .50
218 Loy Vaught .20 .50
219 Jud Buechler .20 .50
220 Mookie Blaylock .20 .50
221 Terry Cummings .20 .50
222 Donyell Marshall .25 .60
223 Chris Mills .20 .50
224 Adonal Foyle .20 .50
225 Shandon Anderson .20 .50
226 Kelvin Cato .20 .50
227 Walt Williams .20 .50
228 Al Harrington .30 .75
229 Rik Smits .25 .60
230 Derrick McKey .20 .50
231 Sam Perkins .20 .50
232 Austin Croshere .20 .50
233 Derek Anderson .25 .60
234 Keith Closs .20 .50
235 Eric Murdock .20 .50
236 Brian Skinner .20 .50
237 Charles Jones RC .20 .50
238 Ron Harper .25 .60
239 Derek Fisher .25 .60
240 Rick Fox .25 .60
241 A.C. Green .25 .60
242 Jamal Mashburn .25 .60
243 Mark Strickland .20 .50
244 Rex Walters .20 .50
245 Clarence Weatherspoon .20 .50
246 Tim Thomas .25 .60
247 J.R. Reid .20 .50
248 Dale Ellis .20 .50
249 Danny Manning .25 .60
250 Tim Thomas .25 .60
251 Terrell Brandon .25 .60
252 Malik Sealy .20 .50
253 Joe Smith .25 .60
254 Anthony Peeler .20 .50
255 Jayson Williams .20 .50
256 Jamie Feick RC .20 .50
257 Kerry Kittles .25 .60
258 Johnny Newman .20 .50
259 Chris Childs .20 .50
260 Kurt Thomas .25 .60
261 Charlie Ward .25 .60
262 Chris Dudley .20 .50
263 John Wallace .20 .50
264 Tariq Abdul-Wahad .20 .50
265 John Amaechi RC .30 .75
266 Chris Gatling .20 .50
267 Monty Williams .20 .50
268 Ben Wallace .25 .60
269 George Lynch .20 .50
270 Tyrone Hill .20 .50
271 Billy Owens .20 .50
272 Anfernee Hardaway .75 2.00
273 Rex Chapman .20 .50
274 Oliver Miller .20 .50
275 Rodney Rogers .20 .50
276 Randy Livingston .20 .50
277 Scottie Pippen .75 2.00
278 Detlef Schrempf .25 .60
279 Steve Smith .25 .60
280 Jermaine O'Neal .25 .60
281 Bonzi Wells .20 .50
282 Chris Webber .40 1.00
283 Nick Anderson .20 .50
284 Darrick Martin .20 .50
285 Corliss Williamson .20 .50
286 Samaki Walker .20 .50
287 Terry Porter .20 .50
288 Malik Rose .20 .50
289 Jaren Jackson .20 .50
290 Antonio Daniels .20 .50
291 Steve Kerr .25 .60
292 Brent Barry .25 .60
293 Horace Grant .25 .60
294 Vernon Maxwell .20 .50
295 Ruben Patterson .20 .50
296 Shammond Williams .20 .50
297 Antonio Davis .20 .50
298 Tracy McGrady .50 1.25
299 Dell Curry .20 .50
300 Charles Oakley .30 .75
301 Muggsy Bogues .25 .60
302 Jeff Hornacek .25 .60
303 Adam Keefe .20 .50
304 Olden Polynice .20 .50
305 Doug West .20 .50
306 Michael Dickerson .20 .50
307 Othella Harrington .20 .50
308 Bryant Reeves .20 .50
309 Brent Price .20 .50
310 Mitch Richmond .40 1.00
311 Aaron Williams .20 .50
312 Isaac Austin .20 .50
313 Michael Smith .20 .50
314 Michael Jordan CL 1.00 2.50
315 Kevin Garnett CL .25 .60
316 Elton Brand .60 1.50
317 Steve Francis .60 1.50
318 Baron Davis .75 2.00
319 Lamar Odom .60 1.50
320 Jonathan Bender .30 .75
321 Wally Szczerbiak .50 1.25
322 Richard Hamilton .75 2.00
323 Andre Miller .60 1.50
324 Shawn Marion .60 1.50
325 Jason Terry .50 1.25
326 Trajan Langdon .25 .60
327 A.Radojevic RC .40 1.00
328 Corey Maggette .40 1.00
329 William Avery .20 .50
330 Ron Artest .75 2.00
331 Cal Bowdler .20 .50
332 James Posey .30 .75
333 Quincy Lewis .20 .50
334 Dion Glover .20 .50
335 Jeff Foster .30 .75
336 Kenny Thomas .30 .75
337 Devean George .25 .60
338 Tim James .20 .50
339 Vonteego Cummings .20 .50
340 Jumaine Jones .20 .50
341 Scott Padgett RC .50 1.25
342 John Celestand RC .40 1.00
343 Adrian Griffin RC .50 1.25
344 Michael Ruffin RC .40 1.00
345 Chris Herren RC .50 1.25
346 Evan Eschmeyer .50 1.25
347 Eddie Robinson RC .60 1.50
348 Obinna Ekezie RC .40 1.00
349 Laron Profit RC .40 1.00
350 Jermaine Jackson RC .60 1.50
351 Lazaro Borrell RC .60 1.50
352 Chucky Atkins RC .50 1.25
353 Ryan Robertson RC .40 1.00
354 Todd MacCulloch RC .50 1.25
355 Rafer Alston RC .75 2.00
356 Mirsad Turkcan RC .60 1.50
357 Anthony Carter RC .50 1.25
358 Ryan Bowen RC .50 1.25
359 Rodney Buford RC .60 1.50
360 Tim Young RC .40 1.00

1999-00 Upper Deck Bronze

COMMON MJ (134-153) 40.00 100.00
*STARS: 12.5X TO 30X BASE CARD HI
*RCs: 2.5X TO 6X BASE HI
*SER.2 DRAFT PICKS: 5X TO 12X BASE HI
STATED PRINT RUN 100 SERIAL #'d SETS

1999-00 Upper Deck BioGraphics

COMPLETE SET (30) 10.00 25.00
SER.2 STATED ODDS 1:4 HOB/RET
*LEVEL 1: 6X TO 15X VALUE
LEVEL 1: PRINT RUN 100 SERIAL #'d SETS
*LEVEL 2: 15X TO 40X VALUE
LEVEL 2: PRINT RUN 25 SERIAL #'d SETS
B1 Antawn Jamison .60 1.50
B2 Mike Bibby .60 1.50
B3 Antoine Walker .60 1.50
B4 Ray Allen 1.00 2.50
B5 Anfernee Hardaway 1.50 4.00
B6 Hakeem Olajuwon 1.25 3.00
B7 Jason Williams 1.00 2.50
B8 Keith Van Horn .50 1.25
B9 Jason Kidd 1.00 2.50
B10 Reggie Miller 1.25 3.00
B11 Eddie Jones .60 1.50
B12 Jim Jackson .40 1.00
B13 Jerry Stackhouse .60 1.50
B14 Tim Duncan 1.50 4.00
B15 Kevin Garnett 1.50 4.00
B16 Mitch Richmond .75 2.00
B17 Steve Smith .50 1.25
B18 Charles Barkley 1.50 4.00
B19 Glen Rice .60 1.50
B20 Paul Pierce 1.25 3.00
B21 Alonzo Mourning 1.00 2.50
B22 Karl Malone 1.25 3.00
B23 Stephon Marbury .75 2.00
B24 Chris Webber .75 2.00
B25 Michael Finley .60 1.50
B26 Shawn Kemp 1.00 2.50
B27 John Stockton 1.00 2.50
B28 Ron Mercer .50 1.25
B29 Tim Hardaway .75 2.00
B30 Allan Houston .50 1.25

1999-00 Upper Deck Cool Air

COMPLETE SET (8) 30.00 80.00
COMMON CARD (MJ1-MJ8) 5.00 12.00
SER.2 STATED ODDS 1:72 HOB/RET
*LEVEL 1: 2.5X TO 6X HI
LEVEL 1: PRINT RUN 100 SERIAL #'d SETS

1999-00 Upper Deck Julius Erving Heroes

COMMON CARD (H46-H55) 2.00 5.00
SER.1 STATED ODDS 1:23
*LEVEL 1: 2X TO 5X HI COLUMN
LEVEL 1: PRINT RUN 100 SERIAL #'d SETS

1999-00 Upper Deck Future Charge

COMPLETE SET (15) 4.00 10.00
SER.1 STATED ODDS 1:8 HOB/RET
*LEVEL 1: 6X TO 15X HI COLUMN
LEVEL 1: PRINT RUN 100 SERIAL #'d SETS
*LEVEL 2: 15X TO 40X HI
LEVEL 2: PRINT RUN 25 SERIAL #'d SETS
FC1 Antawn Jamison .50 1.25
FC2 Mike Bibby .50 1.25
FC3 Antoine Walker .50 1.25
FC4 Baron Davis .75 2.00
FC5 Jason Terry .50 1.25
FC6 Andre Miller .60 1.50
FC7 Ray Allen .75 2.00
FC8 Wally Szczerbiak .50 1.25
FC9 Raef LaFrentz .40 1.00
FC10 William Avery .20 .50
FC11 Jason Williams .75 2.00
FC12 Michael Olowokandi .30 .75
FC13 Stephon Marbury .60 1.50
FC14 Quincy Lewis .20 .50
FC15 Shawn Marion .60 1.50

1999-00 Upper Deck Game Jerseys

GJ1-GJ10 STATED ODDS 1:2500 HOB/RET
GJ21-GJ42 STATED ODDS 1:288 H/1:2500 R
GJ11-GJ20 STATED ODDS 1:287 HOBBY
GJ43-GJ64 STATED ODDS 1:288 HOBBY
*CENT.CLUB: .6X TO 1.5X HI COLUMN
CENT.CLUB: PRINT RUN 100 SERIAL #'d SETS
GJ1 Jason Kidd 35.00 70.00
GJ2 Shaquille O'Neal 20.00 50.00
GJ3 Tim Duncan 40.00 100.00
GJ4 Charles Barkley 75.00 150.00
GJ5 Kevin Garnett 25.00 60.00
GJ5A Kevin Garnett AU/21 100.00 200.00
GJ6 John Stockton 25.00 60.00
GJ7 Keith Van Horn 10.00 25.00
GJ8 Hakeem Olajuwon 15.00 40.00
GJ9 Paul Pierce 20.00 40.00
GJ10 Michael Jordan 300.00 600.00
GJ10A Michael Jordan AU/23 2,500.00 5,000.00
GJ11 Kobe Bryant 125.00 300.00
GJ12 Scottie Pippen 25.00 60.00
GJ13 Grant Hill 25.00 60.00
GJ14 Gary Payton 15.00 40.00
GJ15 Vince Carter 60.00 150.00
GJ16 Reggie Miller 40.00 100.00
GJ17 Allen Iverson 60.00 150.00
GJ18 David Robinson 40.00 100.00
GJ19 Antoine Walker 8.00 20.00
GJ20 Karl Malone 25.00 60.00
GJ20A Karl Malone AU/32 500.00 1,000.00
GJ21 Kobe Bryant 125.00 300.00
GJ22 Wally Szczerbiak 8.00 20.00
GJ23 Richard Hamilton 8.00 20.00
GJ24 Shawn Marion 10.00 25.00
GJ25 Trajan Langdon 8.00 20.00
GJ26 Aleksandar Radojevic 8.00 20.00
GJ27 Corey Maggette 8.00 20.00
GJ28 William Avery 8.00 20.00
GJ29 Quincy Lewis 8.00 20.00
GJ30 Dion Glover 8.00 20.00
GJ31 Jeff Foster 8.00 20.00
GJ32 Devean George 8.00 20.00
GJ33 Shareef Abdur-Rahim 12.50 30.00
GJ34 John Stockton 25.00 60.00
GJ35 Allen Iverson 30.00 80.00
GJ36 Kevin Garnett 25.00 60.00
GJ36A Kevin Garnett AU/21 600.00 900.00
GJ37 Grant Hill 25.00 60.00
GJ38 Vin Baker 8.00 20.00
GJ39 Keith Van Horn 10.00 25.00
GJ40 Reggie Miller 40.00 100.00
GJ41 Tim Hardaway 10.00 25.00
GJ42 Hakeem Olajuwon 10.00 25.00
GJ43 Steve Francis 20.00 50.00
GJ44 Jonathan Bender 8.00 20.00
GJ45 Andre Miller 10.00 25.00
GJ46 Jason Terry 8.00 20.00
GJ47 Alonzo Mourning 15.00 40.00
GJ48 Cal Bowdler 8.00 20.00
GJ49 James Posey 8.00 20.00
GJ50 Kenny Thomas 8.00 20.00
GJ51 Tim James 8.00 20.00
GJ52 Vonteego Cummings 8.00 20.00
GJ53 Jumaine Jones 8.00 20.00
GJ54 Scott Padgett 8.00 20.00
GJ55 Baron Davis 15.00 40.00
GJ56 Karl Malone 15.00 40.00
GJ56A Karl Malone AU/32 500.00 1,000.00
GJ57 Gary Payton 20.00 50.00
GJ58 Michael Finley 12.00 30.00
GJ59 Bryon Russell 10.00 25.00
GJ60 Antoine Walker 8.00 20.00
GJ61 Shaquille O'Neal 40.00 100.00
GJ62 Jason Kidd 40.00 100.00
GJ63 Jason Williams 50.00 120.00
GJ64 Antonio McDyess 12.00 30.00

1999-00 Upper Deck Game Jerseys Patch

SER.1/2 STATED ODDS 1:7500 HOB/RET
GJP1 Jason Kidd 150.00 400.00
GJP2 Shaquille O'Neal 200.00 500.00
GJP3 Tim Duncan 400.00 800.00
GJP4 Charles Barkley 200.00 500.00
GJP5 Kevin Garnett 400.00 800.00
GJP6 John Stockton 150.00 400.00
GJP7 Keith Van Horn 75.00 200.00
GJP8 Hakeem Olajuwon 150.00 400.00
GJP9 Paul Pierce 150.00 400.00
GJP10 Michael Jordan 1,000.00 3,000.00
GJP11 Kobe Bryant 300.00 600.00
GJP12 Scottie Pippen 150.00 400.00
GJP13 Grant Hill 150.00 400.00
GJP14 Gary Payton 150.00 400.00
GJP15 Vince Carter 300.00 600.00
GJP16 Reggie Miller 200.00 500.00
GJP17 Allen Iverson 200.00 500.00
GJP18 David Robinson 150.00 400.00
GJP19 Antoine Walker 100.00 250.00
GJP20 Karl Malone 150.00 400.00
GJP21 Baron Davis 150.00 400.00
GJP22 Shaquille O'Neal 200.00 500.00
GJP23 Grant Hill 150.00 400.00
GJP24 Allen Iverson 200.00 500.00
GJP25 Steve Francis 100.00 250.00
GJP26 Jonathan Bender 75.00 200.00
GJP27 Kobe Bryant 400.00 800.00
GJP28 Kevin Garnett 200.00 500.00
GJP29 Jason Williams 500.00 1,000.00
GJP30 Jason Kidd 150.00 400.00

1999-00 Upper Deck Game Jerseys Patch Super

STATED PRINT RUN 25 SERIAL #'d SETS
AI Allen Iverson 1 400.00 800.00
AI Allen Iverson 2 400.00 800.00
AW Antoine Walker 125.00 300.00
BD Baron Davis 150.00 400.00
GH Grant Hill 1 400.00 800.00
GH Grant Hill 2 400.00 800.00
JB Jonathan Bender 125.00 300.00
JK Jason Kidd 300.00 600.00
JW Jason Williams 600.00 1,200.00
KB Kobe Bryant 1 1,000.00 2,000.00
KB Kobe Bryant 2 1,000.00 2,000.00
KG Kevin Garnett 1 1,000.00 2,000.00
KG Kevin Garnett 2 1,000.00 2,000.00
KV Keith Van Horn 125.00 300.00
MJ Michael Jordan 3,000.00 6,000.00
SF Steve Francis 125.00 300.00
SO Shaquille O'Neal 1 400.00 800.00
SO Shaquille O'Neal 2 400.00 800.00
TD Tim Duncan 1,000.00 2,000.00
VC Vince Carter 400.00 800.00

1999-00 Upper Deck High Definition

COMPLETE SET (20) 12.00 30.00
SER.2 STATED ODDS 1:11 HOB/RET
*LEVEL 1: 4X TO 10X HI COLUMN
LEVEL 1: PRINT RUN 100 SERIAL #'d SETS
*LEVEL 2: 10X TO 25X HI
LEVEL 2: PRINT RUN 25 SERIAL #'d SETS
HD1 Antonio McDyess .75 2.00
HD2 Kevin Garnett 2.50 6.00
HD3 Vince Carter 2.50 6.00
HD4 Shareef Abdur-Rahim 1.00 2.50
HD5 Patrick Ewing 1.25 3.00
HD6 Gary Payton 1.50 4.00
HD7 Glenn Robinson .75 2.00
HD8 Kobe Bryant 8.00 20.00
HD9 Antawn Jamison 1.00 2.50
HD10 Chris Webber 1.25 3.00
HD11 Corey Maggette 1.25 3.00
HD12 Shawn Kemp 1.50 4.00
HD13 Derek Anderson .60 1.50
HD14 Michael Finley 1.00 2.50
HD15 Allan Houston .75 2.00
HD16 Anfernee Hardaway 2.50 6.00
HD17 Grant Hill 1.50 4.00
HD18 Shaquille O'Neal 4.00 10.00
HD19 Paul Pierce 2.00 5.00
HD20 Scottie Pippen 2.50 6.00

1999-00 Upper Deck History Class

COMPLETE SET (20) 15.00 40.00
SER.1 STATED ODDS 1:11 HOB/RET
*LEVEL 1: 5X TO 12X HI COLUMN
LEVEL 1: PRINT RUN 100 SER.#'d SETS
*LEVEL 2: 10X TO 25X HI COLUMN
LEVEL 2: PRINT RUN 25 SER.#'d SETS
HC1 Michael Jordan 25.00 60.00
HC2 Julius Erving 2.50 6.00
HC3 Jamaal Wilkes .75 2.00
HC4 John Havlicek 1.25 3.00
HC5 Moses Malone 1.00 2.50
HC6 Nate Archibald .75 2.00
HC7 Jerry West 1.50 4.00
HC8 Dave DeBusschere 1.00 2.50
HC9 Bob Cousy 1.50 4.00
HC10 Kevin McHale 1.25 3.00
HC11 Dave Bing 1.00 2.50
HC12 Walt Frazier 1.00 2.50
HC13 Bob Lanier .75 2.00
HC14 George Gervin 1.00 2.50
HC15 Hal Greer .75 2.00
HC16 Earl Monroe 1.00 2.50
HC17 David Thompson .75 2.00
HC18 Wes Unseld 1.00 2.50
HC19 Bill Walton 1.00 2.50
HC20 Larry Bird 2.50 6.00

1999-00 Upper Deck Jamboree

COMPLETE SET (15) 8.00 20.00
SER.1 STATED ODDS 1:11 HOB/RET
*LEVEL 1: 6X TO 15X HI COLUMN
LEVEL 1: PRINT RUN 100 SERIAL #'d SETS
*LEVEL 2: 15X TO 40X VALUE
LEVEL 2: PRINT RUN 25 SERIAL #'d SETS
J1 Michael Jordan 6.00 15.00
J2 Karl Malone 1.25 3.00
J3 Kevin Garnett 1.50 4.00
J4 Antonio McDyess .50 1.25
J5 Shareef Abdur-Rahim .60 1.50
J6 David Robinson 1.25 3.00
J7 Marcus Camby .50 1.25
J8 Kobe Bryant 5.00 12.00
J9 Jason Kidd 1.00 2.50
J10 Scottie Pippen 1.50 4.00
J11 Keith Van Horn .50 1.25
J12 Glenn Robinson .50 1.25
J13 Grant Hill 1.00 2.50
J14 Michael Finley .60 1.50
J15 Alonzo Mourning 1.00 2.50

1999-00 Upper Deck MJ - A Higher Power

COMPLETE SET (12) 50.00 120.00
COMMON CARD (MJ1-MJ12) 5.00 12.00
SER.1 STATED ODDS 1:23 HOB/RET
LEVEL 1: PRINT RUN 100 SERIAL #'d SETS

1999-00 Upper Deck MJ Final Floor

COMMON CARD (FF1-FF12) 40.00 100.00
COMMON AU (FF1A-FF12A) 600.00 1,200.00
STATED ODDS 1:2500 IN EACH RELEASE
AU PRINT RUN 23 SERIAL #'d SETS

1999-00 Upper Deck Now Showing

COMPLETE SET (30) 12.50 30.00
SER.1 STATED ODDS 1:4 HOB/RET
*LEVEL 1: 6X TO 15X HI COLUMN
LEVEL 1: PRINT RUN 100 SERIAL #'d SETS
*LEVEL 2: 15X TO 40X VALUE
LEVEL 2: PRINT RUN 25 SERIAL #'d SETS
NS1 Dikembe Mutombo 1.00 2.50
NS2 Antoine Walker .60 1.50
NS3 Eddie Jones .60 1.50

NS4 Toni Kukoc .75 2.00
NS5 Shawn Kemp 1.00 2.50
NS6 Michael Finley .60 1.50
NS7 Antonio McDyess .50 1.25
NS8 Grant Hill 1.00 2.50
NS9 Antawn Jamison .60 1.50
NS10 Scottie Pippen 1.50 4.00
NS11 Reggie Miller 1.25 3.00
NS12 Maurice Taylor .40 1.00
NS13 Shaquille O'Neal 2.50 6.00
NS14 Tim Hardaway .75 2.00
NS15 Ray Allen 1.00 2.50
NS16 Kevin Garnett 1.50 4.00
NS17 Stephon Marbury .75 2.00
NS18 Marcus Camby .50 1.25
NS19 Darrell Armstrong .40 1.00
NS20 Allen Iverson 1.50 4.00
NS21 Jason Kidd 1.00 2.50
NS22 Damon Stoudamire .60 1.50
NS23 Jason Williams 1.00 2.50
NS24 Tim Duncan 1.50 4.00
NS25 Gary Payton 1.00 2.50
NS26 Vince Carter 1.50 4.00
NS27 Karl Malone 1.25 3.00
NS28 Shareef Abdur-Rahim .60 1.50
NS29 Juwan Howard .50 1.25
NS30 Michael Jordan 6.00 15.00

1999-00 Upper Deck Now Showing Level 1

*LEVEL 1: 6X TO 15X HI COLUMN
NS5 Shawn Kemp 20.00 50.00
NS11 Reggie Miller 25.00 60.00
NS20 Allen Iverson 50.00 120.00

1999-00 Upper Deck Now Showing Level 2

*LEVEL 2: 20X TO 50X VALUE
NS5 Shawn Kemp 60.00 150.00
NS11 Reggie Miller 75.00 200.00
NS20 Allen Iverson 150.00 400.00

1999-00 Upper Deck PowerDeck

SER.1 STATED ODDS 1:23 HOBBY
SER.2 STATED ODDS 1:72 HOBBY
MJPD1/2: SER.1 STATED ODDS 1:288 HOB
PDX1/2: SER.2 STATED ODDS 1:2500 HOB
PD1 Michael Jordan 10.00 25.00
PD2 Kobe Bryant 8.00 20.00
PD3 Tim Duncan 2.50 6.00
PD4 Allen Iverson 2.50 6.00
PD5 Vince Carter 2.50 6.00
PD6 Jason Kidd 1.50 4.00
PD7 Scottie Pippen 2.50 6.00
PD8 Elton Brand 2.00 5.00
PD9 Steve Francis 2.00 5.00
PD10 Baron Davis 2.50 6.00
PD11 Lamar Odom 2.00 5.00
PD12 Wally Szczerbiak 1.50 4.00
PD13 Richard Hamilton 2.50 6.00
PD14 Shawn Marion 2.00 5.00
PDX1 Michael Jordan 40.00 100.00
PDX2 Kevin Garnett 8.00 20.00
MJPD1 Michael Jordan 10.00 25.00
MJPD2 Michael Jordan 10.00 25.00

1999-00 Upper Deck Rookies Illustrated

COMPLETE SET (10) 4.00 10.00
SER.2 STATED ODDS 1:11 HOB/RET
*LEVEL 1: 6X TO 15X HI COLUMN
LEVEL 1: PRINT RUN 100 SERIAL #'d SETS
*LEVEL 2: 15X TO 40X HI
LEVEL 2: PRINT RUN 25 SERIAL #'d SETS
RI1 Elton Brand .60 1.50
RI2 Shawn Marion .60 1.50
RI3 Trajan Langdon .25 .60
RI4 Adrian Griffin .25 .60
RI5 Baron Davis .75 2.00
RI6 Richard Hamilton .75 2.00
RI7 Lamar Odom .60 1.50
RI8 Corey Maggette .40 1.00
RI9 Steve Francis .60 1.50
RI10 Wally Szczerbiak .50 1.25

1999-00 Upper Deck Star Surge

COMPLETE SET (15) 15.00 40.00
SER.2 STATED ODDS 1:23 HOB/RET
*LEVEL 1: 3X TO 8X HI COLUMN
LEVEL 1: PRINT RUN 100 SERIAL #'d SETS
*LEVEL 2: 8X TO 20X HI
LEVEL 2: PRINT RUN 25 SERIAL #'d SETS
S1 Michael Jordan 15.00 40.00
S2 Kevin Garnett 3.00 8.00
S3 Allen Iverson 3.00 8.00
S4 Vince Carter 3.00 8.00
S5 Karl Malone 2.50 6.00
S6 Tim Duncan 3.00 8.00
S7 Grant Hill 2.00 5.00
S8 Scottie Pippen 3.00 8.00
S9 Shaquille O'Neal 5.00 12.00
S10 Antoine Walker 1.25 3.00
S11 Shareef Abdur-Rahim 1.25 3.00
S12 Keith Van Horn 1.00 2.50
S13 Gary Payton 2.00 5.00
S14 John Stockton 2.00 5.00
S15 Stephon Marbury 1.50 4.00

1999-00 Upper Deck Wild!

COMPLETE SET (19) 20.00 50.00
SER.2 STATED ODDS 1:23 HOB/RET
*LEVEL 1: 3X TO 8X HI COLUMN
LEVEL 1: PRINT RUN 100 SERIAL #'d SETS
*LEVEL 2: 8X TO 20X HI
LEVEL 2: PRINT RUN 25 SERIAL #'d SETS
W1 Kobe Bryant 10.00 25.00
W2 Kevin Garnett 3.00 8.00
W3 Shareef Abdur-Rahim 1.25 3.00
W4 Tim Hardaway 1.50 4.00
W5 Jason Williams 2.00 5.00
W6 Grant Hill 2.00 5.00
W7 Vince Carter 3.00 8.00
W8 Ron Mercer 1.00 2.50
W9 Charles Barkley 3.00 8.00
W10 Eddie Jones 1.25 3.00
W11 Tim Duncan 3.00 8.00
W12 Antonio McDyess 1.00 2.50
W13 Allen Iverson 3.00 8.00
W14 Anfernee Hardaway 3.00 8.00
W15 Michael Jordan 12.00 30.00
W16 Stephon Marbury 1.50 4.00
W17 Paul Pierce 2.50 6.00
W18 Elton Brand 1.50 4.00
W19 Jason Terry 1.25 3.00

2000-01 Upper Deck

COMPLETE SET (445) 100.00 200.00
COMPLETE SERIES 1 (245) 60.00 120.00
COMPLETE SER.1 w/o RC (200) 20.00 40.00
COMPLETE SERIES 2 (200) 40.00 80.00
COMMON MARTIN (196-200) .60 1.50
RC: SER.1 STATED ODDS 1:4 H/R
SER.2 CARDS SAY GAME JSY EDITION
SUBSET CARDS SAME VALUE AS BASE
1 Dikembe Mutombo .50 1.25
2 Jim Jackson .25 .60
3 Alan Henderson .20 .50
4 Jason Terry .30 .75
5 Roshown McLeod .20 .50
6 Lorenzen Wright .20 .50
7 Paul Pierce .50 1.25
8 Antoine Walker .30 .75
9 Vitaly Potapenko .20 .50
10 Kenny Anderson .25 .60
11 Tony Battie .20 .50
12 Adrian Griffin .20 .50
13 Eric Williams .20 .50
14 Derrick Coleman .20 .50
15 David Wesley .25 .60
16 Baron Davis .30 .75
17 Elden Campbell .20 .50
18 Jamal Mashburn .25 .60
19 Eddie Robinson .20 .50
20 Elton Brand .30 .75
21 Chris Carr .20 .50
22 Ron Artest .30 .75
23 Michael Ruffin .20 .50
24 Fred Hoiberg .20 .50
25 Corey Benjamin .20 .50
26 Shawn Kemp .50 1.25
27 Lamond Murray .20 .50
28 Andre Miller .25 .60
29 Cedric Henderson .20 .50
30 Wesley Person .20 .50
31 Brevin Knight .20 .50
32 Mark Bryant .20 .50
33 Michael Finley .30 .75
34 Cedric Ceballos .25 .60
35 Dirk Nowitzki .75 2.00
36 Hubert Davis .20 .50
37 Steve Nash .50 1.25
38 Gary Trent .20 .50
39 Antonio McDyess .25 .60
40 James Posey .20 .50
41 Nick Van Exel .30 .75
42 Raef LaFrentz .25 .60
43 George McCloud .20 .50
44 Keon Clark .20 .50
45 Jerry Stackhouse .30 .75
46 Christian Laettner .20 .50
47 Loy Vaught .20 .50
48 Jerome Williams .20 .50
49 Michael Curry .20 .50
50 Lindsey Hunter .20 .50
51 Antawn Jamison .30 .75
52 Larry Hughes .30 .75
53 Chris Mills .20 .50
54 Donyell Marshall .25 .60
55 Mookie Blaylock .20 .50
56 Vonteego Cummings .20 .50
57 Erick Dampier .20 .50
58 Steve Francis .30 .75
59 Shandon Anderson .20 .50
60 Hakeem Olajuwon .60 1.50
61 Walt Williams .20 .50
62 Kenny Thomas .20 .50
63 Kelvin Cato .20 .50
64 Cuttino Mobley .25 .60
65 Reggie Miller .60 1.50
66 Jalen Rose .25 .60
67 Austin Croshere .20 .50
68 Dale Davis .25 .60
69 Travis Best .20 .50
70 Jonathan Bender .20 .50
71 Al Harrington .25 .60
72 Lamar Odom .30 .75
73 Tyrone Nesby .20 .50
74 Michael Olowokandi .20 .50
75 Brian Skinner .20 .50
76 Eric Piatkowski .20 .50
77 Keith Closs .20 .50
78 Shaquille O'Neal 1.25 3.00
79 Ron Harper .20 .50
80 Kobe Bryant 2.50 6.00
81 Rick Fox .25 .60
82 Robert Horry .30 .75
83 Derek Fisher .30 .75
84 Devean George .20 .50
85 Alonzo Mourning .50 1.25
86 Eddie Jones .30 .75
87 Anthony Carter .20 .50
88 Bruce Bowen .20 .50
89 Clarence Weatherspoon .20 .50
90 Tim Hardaway .40 1.00
91 Ray Allen .50 1.25
92 Tim Thomas .20 .50
93 Glenn Robinson .30 .75
94 Scott Williams .20 .50
95 Sam Cassell .25 .60
96 Ervin Johnson .20 .50
97 Darvin Ham .25 .60
98 Kevin Garnett .75 2.00
99 Wally Szczerbiak .25 .60
100 Terrell Brandon .25 .60
101 Joe Smith .25 .60
102 Radoslav Nesterovic .20 .50
103 William Avery .20 .50
104 Stephon Marbury .40 1.00
105 Kerry Kittles .25 .60
106 Keith Van Horn .25 .60
107 Lucious Harris .20 .50
108 Jamie Feick .20 .50
109 Johnny Newman .20 .50
110 Patrick Ewing .50 1.25
111 Latrell Sprewell .40 1.00
112 Marcus Camby .25 .60
113 Larry Johnson .40 1.00
114 Charlie Ward .25 .60
115 Allan Houston .30 .75
116 Chris Childs .20 .50
117 Grant Hill .50 1.25
118 John Amaechi .20 .50
119 Tracy McGrady .60 1.50
120 Michael Doleac .20 .50
121 Darrell Armstrong .20 .50
122 Bo Outlaw .20 .50
123 Allen Iverson .75 2.00
124 Theo Ratliff .20 .50
125 Matt Geiger .20 .50
126 Tyrone Hill .20 .50
127 George Lynch .20 .50
128 Toni Kukoc .40 1.00
129 Jason Kidd .50 1.25
130 Rodney Rogers .20 .50
131 Anfernee Hardaway .50 1.25
132 Clifford Robinson .20 .50
133 Tom Gugliotta .25 .60
134 Shawn Marion .30 .75
135 Luc Longley .25 .60
136 Rasheed Wallace .40 1.00
137 Scottie Pippen .75 2.00
138 Arvydas Sabonis .30 .75
139 Steve Smith .30 .75
140 Damon Stoudamire .30 .75
141 Bonzi Wells .20 .50
142 Jermaine O'Neal .25 .60
143 Chris Webber .40 1.00
144 Jason Williams .50 1.25
145 Nick Anderson .25 .60
146 Vlade Divac .30 .75
147 Peja Stojakovic .25 .60
148 Jon Barry .20 .50
149 Corliss Williamson .20 .50
150 Tim Duncan .75 2.00
151 David Robinson .60 1.50
152 Terry Porter .20 .50
153 Malik Rose .20 .50
154 Steve Kerr .20 .50
155 Avery Johnson .25 .60
156 Gary Payton .50 1.25
157 Brent Barry .25 .60
158 Vin Baker .25 .60
159 Rashard Lewis .25 .60
160 Ruben Patterson .20 .50
161 Shammond Williams .20 .50
162 Vince Carter .60 1.50
163 Dell Curry .20 .50
164 Doug Christie .25 .60
165 Antonio Davis .20 .50
166 Kevin Willis .20 .50
167 Charles Oakley .30 .75
168 Karl Malone .60 1.50
169 John Stockton .60 1.50
170 Bryon Russell .20 .50
171 Olden Polynice .20 .50
172 Quincy Lewis .20 .50
173 Scott Padgett .20 .50
174 Shareef Abdur-Rahim .30 .75
175 Mike Bibby .30 .75
176 Michael Dickerson .20 .50
177 Bryant Reeves .20 .50
178 Othella Harrington .20 .50
179 Grant Long .20 .50
180 Mitch Richmond .40 1.00
181 Richard Hamilton .40 1.00
182 Juwan Howard .25 .60
183 Rod Strickland .20 .50
184 Tracy Murray .20 .50
185 Chris Whitney .20 .50
186 Kobe Bryant Y3K 2.50 6.00
187 Kobe Bryant Y3K 2.50 6.00
188 Kobe Bryant Y3K 2.50 6.00
189 Kobe Bryant Y3K 2.50 6.00
190 Kobe Bryant Y3K 2.50 6.00
191 Kevin Garnett Y3K .75 2.00
192 Kevin Garnett Y3K .75 2.00
193 Kevin Garnett Y3K .75 2.00
194 Kevin Garnett Y3K .75 2.00
195 Kevin Garnett Y3K .75 2.00
196 Kenyon Martin Y3K .60 1.50
197 Kenyon Martin Y3K .60 1.50
198 Kenyon Martin Y3K .60 1.50
199 Kenyon Martin Y3K .60 1.50
200 Kenyon Martin Y3K .60 1.50
201 Kenyon Martin RC .75 2.00
202 Stromile Swift RC .30 .75
203 Chris Mihm RC .25 .60
204 Marcus Fizer RC .30 .75
205 Darius Miles RC .40 1.00
206 Joel Przybilla RC .30 .75
207 Mike Miller RC .60 1.50
208 Courtney Alexander RC .25 .60
209 DerMarr Johnson RC .25 .60
210 Iakovos Tsakalidis RC .20 .50
211 Jerome Moiso RC .20 .50
212 Keyon Dooling RC .25 .60
213 Erick Barkley RC .20 .50
214 Jason Collier RC .40 1.00
215 Jamaal Magloire RC .40 1.00
216 DeShawn Stevenson RC .40 1.00
217 Hedo Turkoglu RC .60 1.50
218 Morris Peterson RC .40 1.00
219 Jamal Crawford RC 1.00 2.50
220 Etan Thomas RC .30 .75
221 Quentin Richardson RC .30 .75
222 Mateen Cleaves RC .30 .75
223 Chris Carrawell RC .25 .60
224 Corey Hightower RC .20 .50
225 Donnell Harvey RC .30 .75
226 Mark Madsen RC .40 1.00
227 Jake Voskuhl RC .25 .60
228 Soumaila Samake RC .25 .60
229 Mamadou N'Diaye RC .40 1.00
230 Dan Langhi RC .25 .60
231 Hanno Mottola RC .25 .60
232 Olumide Oyedeji RC .25 .60
233 Jason Hart RC .40 1.00
234 Mike Smith RC .25 .60
235 Chris Porter RC .25 .60
236 Jabari Smith RC .25 .60
237 Desmond Mason RC .50 1.25
238 Eddie House RC .30 .75
239 A.J. Guyton RC .25 .60
240 Speedy Claxton RC .40 1.00
241 Lavor Postell RC .25 .60
242 Khalid El-Amin RC .25 .60
243 Pepe Sanchez RC .30 .75
244 Eduardo Najera RC .40 1.00
245 Michael Redd RC 1.00 2.50
246 DerMarr Johnson .20 .50
247 Hanno Mottola .20 .50
248 Dion Glover .20 .50
249 Matt Maloney .20 .50
250 Jason Terry .30 .75
251 Jerome Moiso .20 .50
252 Bryant Stith .20 .50
253 Randy Brown .20 .50
254 Mark Blount .25 .60
255 Chris Herren .20 .50
256 Jamal Mashburn .25 .60
257 P.J. Brown .20 .50
258 Lee Nailon .20 .50
259 Jamaal Magloire .30 .75
260 Otis Thorpe .20 .50
261 Ron Mercer .25 .60
262 Marcus Fizer .25 .60
263 Jamal Crawford .75 2.00
264 A.J. Guyton .20 .50
265 Dalibor Bagaric RC .30 .75
266 Chris Mihm .20 .50
267 Robert Traylor .20 .50
268 Matt Harpring .20 .50
269 Clarence Weatherspoon .20 .50
270 Bimbo Coles .20 .50
271 Etan Thomas .25 .60
272 Courtney Alexander .25 .60
273 Donnell Harvey .25 .60
274 Eduardo Najera .30 .75
275 Christian Laettner .30 .75
276 Mamadou N'Diaye .20 .50
277 Tariq Abdul-Wahad .20 .50
278 Voshon Lenard .20 .50
279 Robert Pack .20 .50
280 Tracy Murray .20 .50
281 Mateen Cleaves .25 .60
282 Ben Wallace .40 1.00
283 Chucky Atkins .25 .60
284 Billy Owens .20 .50
285 Brian Cardinal RC .25 .60
286 Chris Porter .25 .60
287 Bob Sura .20 .50
288 Vinny Del Negro .20 .50
289 Marc Jackson RC .30 .75
290 Danny Fortson .25 .60
291 Jason Collier .30 .75
292 Maurice Taylor .20 .50
293 Dan Langhi .20 .50
294 Carlos Rogers .20 .50
295 Moochie Norris .20 .50
296 Jermaine O'Neal .30 .75
297 Derrick McKey .20 .50
298 Sam Perkins .20 .50
299 Zan Tabak .20 .50
300 Jeff Foster .20 .50
301 Corey Maggette .30 .75
302 Darius Miles .30 .75
303 Keyon Dooling .25 .60
304 Quentin Richardson .30 .75
305 Jeff McInnis .20 .50
306 Isaiah Rider .25 .60
307 Mark Madsen .25 .60
308 Mike Penberthy RC .40 1.00
309 Brian Shaw .20 .50
310 Horace Grant .30 .75
311 Eddie Jones .30 .75
312 Brian Grant .25 .60
313 Anthony Mason .25 .60
314 Duane Causwell .20 .50
315 Eddie House .25 .60
316 Lindsey Hunter .20 .50
317 Jason Caffey .20 .50
318 Joel Przybilla .20 .50
319 Michael Redd .75 2.00
320 Rafer Alston .20 .50
321 Chauncey Billups .40 1.00
322 LaPhonso Ellis .20 .50
323 Sam Mitchell .20 .50
324 Dean Garrett .20 .50
325 Tom Hammonds .20 .50
326 Kenyon Martin .60 1.50
327 Soumaila Samake .20 .50
328 Aaron Williams .20 .50
329 Kendall Gill .20 .50
330 Stephen Jackson RC .75 2.00
331 Lavor Postell .20 .50
332 Pete Mickeal RC .30 .75
333 Kurt Thomas .25 .60
334 Erick Strickland .20 .50
335 Glen Rice .25 .60
336 Grant Hill .50 1.25
337 Tracy McGrady .60 1.50
338 Pat Garrity .20 .50
339 Troy Hudson .20 .50
340 Mike Miller .50 1.25
341 Speedy Claxton .30 .75
342 Eric Snow .25 .60
343 Pepe Sanchez .20 .50
344 Aaron McKie .20 .50
345 Nazr Mohammed .20 .50
346 Ruben Garces RC .40 1.00
347 Daniel Santiago RC .40 1.00
348 Tony Delk .20 .50
349 Paul McPherson RC .25 .60
350 Iakovos Tsakalidis .20 .50
351 Dale Davis .25 .60
352 Shawn Kemp .50 1.25
353 Erick Barkley .20 .50
354 Greg Anthony .20 .50
355 Stacey Augmon .20 .50
356 Bobby Jackson .25 .60
357 Hedo Turkoglu .50 1.25
358 Jabari Smith .20 .50
359 Doug Christie .25 .60
360 Darrick Martin .20 .50
361 Sean Elliott .25 .60
362 Jaren Jackson .20 .50
363 Samaki Walker .20 .50
364 Derek Anderson .25 .60
365 Antonio Daniels .20 .50
366 Patrick Ewing .50 1.25
367 Desmond Mason .40 1.00
368 Jelani McCoy .20 .50
369 Ruben Wolkowyski RC .25 .60
370 Emanual Davis .20 .50
371 Mark Jackson .25 .60
372 Morris Peterson .30 .75
373 Muggsy Bogues .30 .75
374 Alvin Williams .20 .50
375 Corliss Williamson .20 .50
376 John Starks .30 .75
377 Danny Manning .20 .50
378 DeShawn Stevenson .20 .50
379 Donyell Marshall .25 .60
380 David Benoit .20 .50
381 Isaac Austin .20 .50
382 Mahmoud Abdul-Rauf .20 .50
383 Stromile Swift .25 .60
384 Kevin Edwards .20 .50
385 Brent Price .20 .50
386 Popeye Jones .20 .50
387 Mike Smith .20 .50
388 Jahidi White .20 .50
389 Laron Profit .20 .50
390 Felipe Lopez .20 .50
391 Dikembe Mutombo MVP .50 1.25
392 Paul Pierce MVP .50 1.25
393 Derrick Coleman MVP .20 .50
394 Elton Brand MVP .30 .75
395 Andre Miller MVP .25 .60
396 Michael Finley MVP .30 .75
397 Antonio McDyess MVP .25 .60
398 Jerry Stackhouse MVP .30 .75
399 Larry Hughes MVP .30 .75
400 Steve Francis MVP .30 .75
401 Reggie Miller MVP .60 1.50
402 Lamar Odom MVP .30 .75
403 Shaquille O'Neal MVP 1.25 3.00
404 Tim Hardaway MVP .40 1.00
405 Ray Allen MVP .50 1.25
406 Kevin Garnett MVP .75 2.00
407 Stephon Marbury MVP .40 1.00
408 Allan Houston MVP .30 .75
409 Grant Hill MVP .50 1.25
410 Allen Iverson MVP .75 2.00
411 Jason Kidd MVP .50 1.25
412 Rasheed Wallace MVP .40 1.00
413 Chris Webber MVP .40 1.00
414 Tim Duncan MVP .75 2.00
415 Gary Payton MVP .50 1.25
416 Vince Carter MVP .60 1.50
417 Karl Malone MVP .60 1.50
418 Shareef Abdur-Rahim MVP .30 .75
419 Mitch Richmond MVP .40 1.00
420 Kobe Bryant MVP 2.50 6.00
421 Mateen Cleaves ROC .25 .60
422 Speedy Claxton ROC .25 .60
423 Courtney Alexander ROC .20 .50
424 Desmond Mason ROC .20 .50
425 Mike Miller ROC .50 1.25
426 DerMarr Johnson ROC .20 .50
427 Chris Mihm ROC .20 .50
428 Jamal Crawford ROC .75 2.00
429 Joel Przybilla ROC .25 .60
430 Keyon Dooling ROC .25 .60
431 Kobe Bryant PR 2.50 6.00
432 Kobe Bryant PR 2.50 6.00
433 Kobe Bryant PR 2.50 6.00
434 Kobe Bryant PR 2.50 6.00
435 Kobe Bryant PR 2.50 6.00
436 Kobe Bryant PR 2.50 6.00
437 Kobe Bryant PR 2.50 6.00
438 Kobe Bryant PR 2.50 6.00
439 Kobe Bryant PR 2.50 6.00
440 Kobe Bryant PR 2.50 6.00
441 Kobe Bryant PR 2.50 6.00
442 Kobe Bryant PR 2.50 6.00
443 Kobe Bryant PR 2.50 6.00
444 Kobe Bryant PR 2.50 6.00
445 Kobe Bryant PR 2.50 6.00
CL1 Checklist .08 .25
CL1 Checklist .08 .25
CL2 Checklist .08 .25
CL2 Checklist .08 .25
CL3 Checklist .08 .25
CL3 Checklist .08 .25

2000-01 Upper Deck Gold

*SER.1 STARS: 6X TO 15X BASE CARD HI
*SER.2 STARS: 12X TO 30X BASE CARD HI
*RCs: 10X TO 25X BASE CARD HI
*SER.2 DP: 12X TO 30X BASE CARD HI
SER.1 STARS: PRINT RUN 100 SERIAL #'d SETS
SER.2 STARS: PRINT RUN 25 SERIAL #'d SETS
RCs: PRINT RUN 25 SERIAL #'d SETS

2000-01 Upper Deck Silver

*SER.1 STARS: 2.5X TO 6X BASE CARD HI
*SER.2 STARS: 8X TO 20X BASE CARD HI
*RCs: 2X TO 5X BASE CARD HI
*SER.2 DP: 6X TO 15X BASE CARD HI
SER.1 STARS: PRINT RUN 500 SERIAL #'d SETS
SER.2 STARS: PRINT RUN 100 SERIAL #'d SETS
RCs: PRINT RUN 100 SERIAL #'d SETS

2000-01 Upper Deck All Star Class

COMPLETE SET (10) 12.00 30.00
SER.2 STATED ODDS 1:23
AS1 Tim Duncan 2.50 6.00
AS2 Shaquille O'Neal 4.00 10.00
AS3 Chris Webber 1.25 3.00
AS4 Allan Houston 1.00 2.50
AS5 Kobe Bryant 8.00 20.00
AS6 Ray Allen 1.50 4.00
AS7 Karl Malone 2.00 5.00
AS8 Rasheed Wallace 1.25 3.00
AS9 Kevin Garnett 2.50 6.00
AS10 Vince Carter 2.00 5.00

2000-01 Upper Deck Combo Materials

SER.2 STATED ODDS 1:144
AMCM Andre Miller 3.00 8.00
DMCM Darius Miles 4.00 10.00
JKCM Jason Kidd 6.00 15.00
JSCM Jerry Stackhouse 4.00 10.00
MCCM Mateen Cleaves 3.00 8.00
QRCM Quentin Richardson 3.00 8.00
SMCM Shawn Marion 4.00 10.00

2000-01 Upper Deck e-Card 1

COMPLETE SET (6) 4.00 10.00
SER.1 STATED ODDS 1:12 HOB/RET
EC1 Kobe Bryant 5.00 12.00
EC1A Kobe Bryant JSY AU/50 2,000.00 4,000.00
EC1J Kobe Bryant JSY/300 100.00 250.00
EC1S Kobe Bryant AU/200 1,500.00 3,000.00
EC2 Kevin Garnett 1.50 4.00
EC2A Kevin Garnett JSY AU/50 150.00 400.00
EC2J Kevin Garnett JSY/300 15.00 40.00
EC2S Kevin Garnett AU/200 125.00 300.00
EC3 Anfernee Hardaway 1.00 2.50
EC3A A.Hardaway JSY AU/50 125.00 300.00
EC3J A.Hardaway JSY/300 15.00 40.00
EC3S A.Hardaway AU/200 100.00 250.00
EC4 Shareef Abdur-Rahim .60 1.50
EC4A S.Abdur-Rahim JSY AU/50 25.00 60.00
EC4J S.Abdur-Rahim JSY/300 8.00 20.00
EC4S S.Abdur-Rahim AU/200 20.00 50.00
EC5 Reggie Miller 1.25 3.00
EC5A Reggie Miller JSY AU/50 150.00 400.00
EC5J Reggie Miller JSY/300 15.00 40.00
EC5S Reggie Miller AU/200 125.00 300.00
EC6 Karl Malone 1.25 3.00
EC6A Karl Malone JSY AU/50 75.00 200.00
EC6J Karl Malone JSY/300 12.00 30.00
EC6S Karl Malone AU/200 60.00 150.00

2000-01 Upper Deck e-Card 2

COMPLETE SET (6) 5.00 12.00
SER.2 STATED ODDS 1:12 HOB/RET
EC1 Kobe Bryant 5.00 12.00
EC1A Kobe Bryant JSY AU/50 2,000.00 4,000.00
EC1J Kobe Bryant JSY/300 100.00 250.00
EC1S Kobe Bryant AU/200 1,500.00 3,000.00
EC2 Kevin Garnett 1.50 4.00
EC2A Kevin Garnett JSY AU/50 150.00 400.00
EC2J Kevin Garnett JSY/300 15.00 40.00
EC2S Kevin Garnett AU/200 125.00 300.00
EC3 Kenyon Martin 1.25 3.00
EC3A Kenyon Martin JSY AU/50 15.00 40.00
EC3J Kenyon Martin JSY/300 8.00 20.00
EC3S Kenyon Martin AU/200 10.00 25.00
EC4 Stromile Swift .50 1.25
EC4J Stromile Swift JSY/300 5.00 12.00
EC4S Stromile Swift AU/200 8.00 20.00
EC5 Darius Miles .60 1.50
EC5J Darius Miles JSY/300 5.00 12.00
EC5S Darius Miles AU/200 8.00 20.00
EC6 Marcus Fizer .50 1.25
EC6J Marcus Fizer JSY/300 5.00 12.00
EC6S Marcus Fizer AU/200 8.00 20.00

2000-01 Upper Deck Game Jerseys 1

SER.1 GJ: STATED ODDS 1:287
SER.1 AU GJ: STATED ODDS 1:287 H/R
AGH Adrian Griffin AU 5.00 12.00
AHH Anfernee Hardaway AU 30.00 80.00
AIC Allen Iverson 10.00 25.00
AMC Alonzo Mourning 8.00 20.00
AWC Antoine Walker 4.00 10.00
BDH Baron Davis AU 12.00 30.00
DRC David Robinson 10.00 25.00
EJH Eddie Jones AU 6.00 15.00
GPC Gary Payton 6.00 15.00
GRH Glenn Robinson AU 8.00 20.00
JKC Jason Kidd 6.00 15.00
JSC Joe Smith 3.00 8.00
KBC Kobe Bryant 75.00 200.00
KBH Kobe Bryant AU 1,500.00 3,000.00
KGA Kevin Garnett AU/21 300.00 600.00
KGC Kevin Garnett 10.00 25.00
KGH Kevin Garnett AU 50.00 120.00
KVC Keith Van Horn 3.00 8.00
MBH Mike Bibby AU 6.00 15.00
PPH Paul Pierce AU 40.00 100.00
RMA Reggie Miller AU/31 300.00 600.00
RMC Reggie Miller 8.00 20.00
SAC Shareef Abdur-Rahim 4.00 10.00
SMC Stephon Marbury 5.00 12.00
SOC Shaquille O'Neal 6.00 15.00
STC John Stockton 8.00 20.00
TBH Terrell Brandon AU 8.00 20.00
VBA Vin Baker AU/42 8.00 20.00
VBC Vin Baker 3.00 8.00
WAH William Avery AU 5.00 12.00
WSH Wally Szczerbiak AU 5.00 12.00

2000-01 Upper Deck Game Jerseys 2

SER.2 GJ HOB: STATED ODDS 1:72 H
SER.2 AU GJ: STATED ODDS 1:287 HOB
AAG Adrian Griffin AU 5.00 12.00
AAH Anfernee Hardaway AU 30.00 80.00
ACM Chris Mihm AU 5.00 12.00
ADM Darius Miles AU 6.00 15.00
AJC Jamal Crawford AU 8.00 20.00
AJM Jamaal Magloire AU 5.00 12.00
AKB Kobe Bryant AU 200.00 500.00
AKG Kevin Garnett AU 50.00 120.00
ASS Stromile Swift AU 3.00 8.00
AHC Allan Houston 4.00 10.00
AHH Anfernee Hardaway 8.00 20.00
AMC Andre Miller 3.00 8.00
CMH Chris Mihm 2.50 6.00
DAH Darrell Armstrong 2.50 6.00
DBC Dalibor Bagaric 3.00 8.00
DMH Darius Miles 4.00 10.00
GHH Grant Hill 8.00 20.00
JCH Jamal Crawford 10.00 25.00
JKC Jason Kidd 6.00 15.00
JKH Jason Kidd 6.00 15.00
JMH Jamaal Magloire 4.00 10.00
JSC Jerry Stackhouse 4.00 10.00
KBC Kobe Bryant 75.00 200.00
KBH Kobe Bryant 75.00 200.00
KDC Keyon Dooling 3.00 8.00
KDH Keyon Dooling 3.00 8.00
KGA Kevin Garnett AU/21 300.00 600.00
KGC Kevin Garnett 10.00 25.00
KGH Kevin Garnett 10.00 25.00
KMC Kenyon Martin 8.00 20.00
LSC Latrell Sprewell 5.00 12.00
LSH Latrell Sprewell 5.00 12.00
MAH Marcus Camby 3.00 8.00
MCC Mateen Cleaves 3.00 8.00
MFC Marcus Fizer 3.00 8.00
QRC Quentin Richardson 3.00 8.00
SMC Shawn Marion 4.00 10.00
SMH Shawn Marion 4.00 10.00
SSH Stromile Swift 3.00 8.00
TGC Tom Gugliotta 3.00 8.00
TMH Tracy McGrady 8.00 20.00

2000-01 Upper Deck Game Jerseys Combo 1

STATED PRINT RUN 50 SERIAL #'d SETS
DRLB J.Erving/L.Bird 75.00 200.00
JKAH J.Kidd/A.Hardaway 75.00 200.00
KBDR K.Bryant/J.Erving 125.00 300.00
KBKG K.Bryant/K.Garnett 125.00 300.00
KBSO K.Bryant/S.O'Neal 150.00 400.00
KMJS K.Malone/J.Stockton 40.00 100.00
MJLB M.Johnson/L.Bird 100.00 250.00
WCBR W.Chamb/B.Russell 200.00 500.00

2000-01 Upper Deck Game Jerseys Combo 2

STATED PRINT RUN 50 SERIAL #'d SETS
AHLS A.Houston/L.Sprewell 25.00 60.00
KBDM K.Bryant/D.Miles 40.00 100.00
KBKG K.Bryant/K.Garnett 125.00 300.00
KBKM K.Bryant/K.Martin 40.00 100.00
KBSO K.Bryant/S.O'Neal 150.00 400.00
MJKB M.Jordan/K.Bryant 150.00 400.00
SASS S.A-Rahim/S.Swift 25.00 60.00

2000-01 Upper Deck Game Jerseys Patch 1

SER.1 STATED ODDS 1:7500
AHP Anfernee Hardaway 50.00 120.00
AIP Allen Iverson 60.00 150.00
GPP Gary Payton 40.00 100.00
GPPA Gary Payton AU/20 350.00 700.00
JKP Jason Kidd 40.00 100.00
KBP Kobe Bryant 200.00 500.00
KGP Kevin Garnett 60.00 150.00
KGPA Kevin Garnett AU/21 800.00 1,200.00
MJP Michael Jordan 300.00 600.00
MJPA Michael Jordan AU/23 10,000.00 15,000.00
RMP Reggie Miller 75.00 150.00
SAP Shareef Abdur-Rahim 25.00 60.00
SMP Stephon Marbury 30.00 80.00
SOP Shaquille O'Neal 100.00 250.00
STP John Stockton 30.00 80.00

2000-01 Upper Deck Game Jerseys Patch 2

SER.2 STATED ODDS 1:5000
AIP Allen Iverson 60.00 150.00
DJP DerMarr Johnson 8.00 20.00
DMP Darius Miles 12.00 30.00
DMPA Darius Miles AU/21 75.00 150.00
JCP Jamal Crawford 30.00 80.00
KBP Kobe Bryant 200.00 500.00
KDP Keyon Dooling 10.00 25.00
KGP Kevin Garnett 60.00 150.00
KGPA Kevin Garnett AU/21 800.00 1,500.00
KMP Kenyon Martin 25.00 60.00
MFP Marcus Fizer 10.00 25.00
MJP Michael Jordan 500.00 1,000.00
MJPA Michael Jordan AU/23 10,000.00 15,000.00
MMP Mike Miller 15.00 40.00
SOP Shaquille O'Neal 100.00 250.00
SSP Stromile Swift 10.00 25.00

2000-01 Upper Deck Game Jerseys Patch Gold 1

*GOLD: .75X TO 2X BASE HI
STATED PRINT RUN 25 SERIAL #'d SETS
AIG Allen Iverson 200.00 400.00
GHG Grant Hill 200.00 400.00
KBG Kobe Bryant 300.00 600.00
KGG Kevin Garnett 100.00 200.00

2000-01 Upper Deck Game Jerseys Patch Gold 2

*GOLD: .75X TO 2X BASE HI
STATED PRINT RUN 25 SERIAL #'d SETS
AIG Allen Iverson 200.00 400.00
KBG Kobe Bryant 300.00 600.00
MJG Michael Jordan 300.00 600.00
SOG Shaquille O'Neal 150.00 300.00

2000-01 Upper Deck Graphic Jam

COMPLETE SET (12) 6.00 15.00
SER.1 STATED ODDS 1:14 HOB/RET
G1 Kobe Bryant 5.00 12.00
G2 Kevin Garnett 1.50 4.00
G3 Chris Webber .75 2.00
G4 Larry Hughes .60 1.50
G5 Tim Duncan 1.50 4.00
G6 Latrell Sprewell .75 2.00
G7 Vince Carter 1.25 3.00
G8 Shareef Abdur-Rahim .60 1.50
G9 Elton Brand .60 1.50
G10 Antonio McDyess .50 1.25
G11 Lamar Odom .60 1.50
G12 Rasheed Wallace .75 2.00

2000-01 Upper Deck Highlight Zone

COMPLETE SET (10) 8.00 20.00
SER.2 STATED ODDS 1:23 HOB/RET
HZ1 Kobe Bryant 6.00 15.00
HZ2 Eddie Jones .75 2.00
HZ3 Lamar Odom .75 2.00
HZ4 Steve Francis .75 2.00
HZ5 Stephon Marbury 1.00 2.50
HZ6 Scottie Pippen 2.00 5.00
HZ7 Kevin Garnett 2.00 5.00
HZ8 Chris Webber 1.00 2.50
HZ9 Anfernee Hardaway 1.25 3.00
HZ10 Shareef Abdur-Rahim .75 2.00

2000-01 Upper Deck Lightning Strikes

COMPLETE SET (15) 7.50 15.00
SER.1 STATED ODDS 1:12 HOB/RET
LS1 Allen Iverson 1.25 3.00
LS2 Stephon Marbury .60 1.50
LS3 Ray Allen .75 2.00
LS4 Allan Houston .50 1.25
LS5 Kevin Garnett 1.25 3.00
LS6 Gary Payton .75 2.00
LS7 Shawn Marion .50 1.25
LS8 Kobe Bryant 4.00 10.00

LS9 Tim Duncan 1.25 3.00
LS10 Scottie Pippen 1.25 3.00
LS11 Andre Miller .40 1.00
LS12 Steve Francis .50 1.25
LS13 Jalen Rose .40 1.00
LS14 Jason Williams .75 2.00
LS15 Larry Hughes .50 1.25

2000-01 Upper Deck Live Action

COMPLETE SET (8) 2.50 6.00
SER.2 STATED ODDS 1:12 HOB/RET
LA1 Kevin Garnett 1.00 2.50
LA2 Lamar Odom .40 1.00
LA3 Jalen Rose .30 .75
LA4 Larry Hughes .40 1.00
LA5 Tim Thomas .25 .60
LA6 Kobe Bryant 3.00 8.00
LA7 Wally Szczerbiak .30 .75
LA8 Anfernee Hardaway .60 1.50

2000-01 Upper Deck Masters of Arts

COMPLETE SET (10) 2.00 5.00
SER.1 STATED ODDS 1:6 HOB/RET
MA1 Vince Carter .50 1.25
MA2 Ray Allen .40 1.00
MA3 Larry Hughes .25 .60
MA4 Kevin Garnett .60 1.50
MA5 Antonio McDyess .20 .50
MA6 Steve Francis .25 .60
MA7 Stephon Marbury .30 .75
MA8 Kobe Bryant 2.00 5.00
MA9 Paul Pierce .40 1.00
MA10 Reggie Miller .25 .60

2000-01 Upper Deck MJ Materials

STATED ODDS ONE PER CASE
MJ1 M.Jordan Suit 60.00 150.00
MJ2 M.Jordan Jersey 350.00 750.00
MJ3 M.Jordan Shoe 350.00 750.00
MJ4 M.Jordan/Suit-Jsy/25 400.00 800.00
MJ5 M.Jordan/Shrt-Shoe/100 400.00 800.00
MJ6 M.Jordan/Jsy-Shrt/100 400.00 800.00
MJ7 M.Jordan/S-J-S-P/23 1,500.00 3,000.00

2000-01 Upper Deck Pure Basketball

COMPLETE SET (8) 2.50 6.00
SER.2 STATED ODDS 1:12 HOB/RET
PB1 Elton Brand .40 1.00
PB2 Andre Miller .30 .75
PB3 Mitch Richmond .50 1.25
PB4 Kobe Bryant 3.00 8.00
PB5 John Stockton .75 2.00
PB6 Antawn Jamison .40 1.00
PB7 Kevin Garnett 1.00 2.50
PB8 Reggie Miller .75 2.00

2000-01 Upper Deck Rookie Focus

COMPLETE SET (9) 2.00 5.00
SER.2 STATED ODDS 1:10 HOB/RET
RF1 Kenyon Martin .60 1.50
RF2 Jamal Crawford .75 2.00
RF3 Keyon Dooling .25 .60
RF4 Mike Miller .50 1.25
RF5 Morris Peterson .30 .75
RF6 DerMarr Johnson .20 .50
RF7 Marcus Fizer .25 .60
RF8 DeShawn Stevenson .30 .75
RF9 Chris Mihm .20 .50

2000-01 Upper Deck Super Powers

COMPLETE SET (10) 20.00 50.00
SER.2 STATED ODDS 1:72 HOB/RET
SP1 Kobe Bryant 12.00 30.00
SP2 Vince Carter 3.00 8.00
SP3 Tim Duncan 4.00 10.00
SP4 Steve Francis 1.50 4.00
SP5 Gary Payton 2.50 6.00
SP6 Chris Webber 2.00 5.00
SP7 Kevin Garnett 4.00 10.00
SP8 Allen Iverson 4.00 10.00
SP9 Jason Kidd 2.50 6.00
SP10 Elton Brand 1.50 4.00

2000-01 Upper Deck Total Dominance

COMPLETE SET (15) 10.00 25.00
SER.1 STATED ODDS 1:12 HOB/RET
TD1 Shaquille O'Neal 2.50 6.00
TD2 Gary Payton 1.00 2.50
TD3 Kevin Garnett 1.50 4.00
TD4 Elton Brand .60 1.50
TD5 Jalen Rose .50 1.25
TD6 Allen Iverson 1.50 4.00
TD7 Vince Carter 1.25 3.00
TD8 Kobe Bryant 5.00 12.00
TD9 Lamar Odom .60 1.50
TD10 Jason Kidd 1.00 2.50
TD11 Rasheed Wallace .75 2.00
TD12 Chris Webber .75 2.00
TD13 Ray Allen 1.00 2.50
TD14 Alonzo Mourning 1.00 2.50
TD15 Tim Duncan 1.50 4.00

2000-01 Upper Deck Touch the Sky

COMPLETE SET (9) 10.00 25.00
SER.2 STATED ODDS 1:10 HOB/RET
T1 Kobe Bryant 8.00 20.00
T2 Kevin Garnett 2.50 6.00
T3 Michael Finley 1.00 2.50
T4 Anfernee Hardaway 1.50 4.00
T5 Scottie Pippen 2.50 6.00
T6 Antonio McDyess .75 2.00
T7 Larry Hughes 1.00 2.50
T8 Latrell Sprewell 1.25 3.00
T9 Rashard Lewis .75 2.00

2000-01 Upper Deck True Talents

COMPLETE SET (20) 6.00 15.00
SER.1 STATED ODDS 1:3 HOB/RET
TT1 Kobe Bryant 4.00 10.00
TT2 Jalen Rose .40 1.00
TT3 Chris Webber .60 1.50
TT4 Alonzo Mourning .75 2.00
TT5 Paul Pierce .75 2.00
TT6 Allan Houston .50 1.25
TT7 Keith Van Horn .40 1.00
TT8 Andre Miller .40 1.00
TT9 Dirk Nowitzki 1.25 3.00
TT10 Richard Hamilton .60 1.50
TT11 Jason Williams .75 2.00
TT12 Antonio McDyess .40 1.00
TT13 Antoine Walker .50 1.25
TT14 Antawn Jamison .50 1.25
TT15 Glenn Robinson .50 1.25
TT16 Lamar Odom .50 1.25
TT17 Scottie Pippen 1.25 3.00
TT18 Mike Bibby .50 1.25
TT19 Elton Brand .50 1.25
TT20 Kevin Garnett 1.25 3.00

2000-01 Upper Deck Unleashed

COMPLETE SET (8) 25.00 60.00
SER.2 STATED ODDS 1:12 HOB/RET
U1 Vince Carter 2.00 5.00
U2 Lamar Odom 1.00 2.50
U3 Jason Williams 1.50 4.00
U4 Kevin Garnett 2.50 6.00
U5 Paul Pierce 1.50 4.00
U6 Shareef Abdur-Rahim 1.00 2.50
U7 Elton Brand 1.00 2.50
U8 Kobe Bryant 20.00 50.00

2001-02 Upper Deck

COMP.SET w/o SP's (360) 45.00 90.00
COMPLETE SER.1 (225) 75.00 150.00
COMP.SER.1 w/o SP's (180) 12.00 30.00
COMPLETE SER.2 (225) 75.00 150.00
COMP.SER.2 w/o SP's (180) 30.00 60.00
TWO VERSIONS FOR 406-450 SAME VALUE
406B-450B NOT INCLUDED IN SET PRICES
*SER.2 RCs HALF VALUE SER.1
151-225 STATED ODDS 1:4
MJ BUYBACK EXCH 100 TOTAL CARDS
1 Jason Terry .30 .75
2 Toni Kukoc .40 1.00
3 Alan Henderson .20 .50
4 Theo Ratliff .20 .50
5 Shareef Abdur-Rahim .25 .60
6 DerMarr Johnson .20 .50
7 Paul Pierce .50 1.25
8 Antoine Walker .25 .60
9 Kenny Anderson .25 .60
10 Vitaly Potapenko .20 .50
11 Eric Williams .20 .50
12 Jamal Mashburn .25 .60
13 Baron Davis .30 .75
14 David Wesley .20 .50
15 P.J. Brown .20 .50
16 Elden Campbell .20 .50
17 Jamaal Magloire .20 .50
18 Lee Nailon .20 .50
19 A.J. Guyton .20 .50
20 Ron Mercer .20 .50
21 Jamal Crawford .30 .75
22 Fred Hoiberg .20 .50
23 Marcus Fizer .20 .50
24 Ron Artest .25 .60
25 Lamond Murray .20 .50
26 Andre Miller .25 .60
27 Jim Jackson .20 .50
28 Chris Mihm .20 .50
29 Trajan Langdon .20 .50
30 Chris Gatling .20 .50
31 Michael Finley .30 .75
32 Dirk Nowitzki .75 2.00
33 Steve Nash .60 1.50
34 Juwan Howard .25 .60
35 Wang Zhizhi .30 .75
36 Eduardo Najera .25 .60
37 Shawn Bradley .20 .50
38 Antonio McDyess .20 .50
39 Nick Van Exel .30 .75
40 Raef LaFrentz .25 .60
41 James Posey .25 .60
42 Voshon Lenard .20 .50
43 Ben Wallace .40 1.00
44 Jerry Stackhouse .25 .60
45 Corliss Williamson .20 .50
46 Chucky Atkins .20 .50
47 Michael Curry .20 .50
48 Dana Barros .20 .50
49 Antawn Jamison .25 .60
50 Larry Hughes .25 .60
51 Bob Sura .20 .50
52 Marc Jackson .20 .50
53 Chris Porter .20 .50
54 Vonteego Cummings .20 .50
55 Steve Francis .30 .75
56 Cuttino Mobley .25 .60
57 Maurice Taylor .20 .50
58 Kenny Thomas .20 .50
59 Moochie Norris .20 .50
60 Walt Williams .20 .50
61 Reggie Miller .60 1.50
62 Jalen Rose .25 .60
63 Jermaine O'Neal .25 .60
64 Austin Croshere .20 .50
65 Travis Best .20 .50
66 Jonathan Bender .20 .50
67 Eric Piatkowski .20 .50
68 Darius Miles .25 .60
69 Lamar Odom .25 .60
70 Quentin Richardson .20 .50
71 Corey Maggette .25 .60
72 Elton Brand .25 .60
73 Jeff McInnis .20 .50
74 Kobe Bryant 2.50 6.00
75 Shaquille O'Neal 1.25 3.00
76 Derek Fisher .25 .60
77 Rick Fox .25 .60
78 Mitch Richmond .40 1.00
79 Ron Harper .25 .60
80 Brian Shaw .20 .50
81 Stromile Swift .20 .50
82 Michael Dickerson .20 .50
83 Jason Williams .50 1.25
84 Grant Long .20 .50
85 Bryant Reeves .20 .50
86 Alonzo Mourning .50 1.25
87 Eddie Jones .30 .75
88 Brian Grant .20 .50
89 Anthony Mason .30 .75
90 LaPhonso Ellis .25 .60
91 Anthony Carter .20 .50
92 Jason Caffey .20 .50
93 Ray Allen .50 1.25
94 Glenn Robinson .30 .75
95 Sam Cassell .25 .60
96 Tim Thomas .20 .50
97 Ervin Johnson .20 .50
98 Joel Przybilla .20 .50
99 Kevin Garnett .75 2.00
100 Terrell Brandon .25 .60
101 Wally Szczerbiak .25 .60
102 Felipe Lopez .20 .50
103 Chauncey Billups .40 1.00
104 Anthony Peeler .20 .50
105 Kenyon Martin .30 .75
106 Keith Van Horn .25 .60
107 Jamie Feick .20 .50
108 Aaron Williams .20 .50
109 Lucious Harris .20 .50
110 Jason Kidd .50 1.25
111 Latrell Sprewell .40 1.00
112 Allan Houston .30 .75
113 Marcus Camby .25 .60
114 Mark Jackson .25 .60
115 Othella Harrington .20 .50
116 Kurt Thomas .20 .50
117 Tracy McGrady .50 1.25
118 Mike Miller .25 .60
119 Darrell Armstrong .20 .50
120 Grant Hill .50 1.25
121 Pat Garrity .20 .50
122 Bo Outlaw .20 .50
123 Allen Iverson .75 2.00
124 Dikembe Mutombo .50 1.25
125 Aaron McKie .20 .50
126 Matt Geiger .20 .50
127 Eric Snow .20 .50
128 George Lynch .20 .50
129 Raja Bell RC .75 2.00
130 Shawn Marion .30 .75
131 Tom Gugliotta .20 .50
132 Rodney Rogers .20 .50
133 Anfernee Hardaway .75 2.00
134 Tony Delk .25 .60
135 Stephon Marbury .40 1.00
136 Rasheed Wallace .40 1.00
137 Damon Stoudamire .30 .75
138 Rod Strickland .20 .50
139 Dale Davis .20 .50
140 Scottie Pippen .75 2.00
141 Bonzi Wells .20 .50
142 Peja Stojakovic .25 .60
143 Chris Webber .40 1.00
144 Doug Christie .20 .50
145 Mike Bibby .30 .75
146 Hedo Turkoglu .25 .60
147 Scot Pollard .20 .50
148 Vlade Divac .25 .60
149 Tim Duncan .75 2.00
150 David Robinson .60 1.50
151 Antonio Daniels .20 .50
152 Danny Ferry .20 .50
153 Malik Rose .20 .50
154 Terry Porter .20 .50
155 Rashard Lewis .25 .60
156 Gary Payton .50 1.25
157 Brent Barry .20 .50
158 Vin Baker .25 .60
159 Desmond Mason .25 .60
160 Shammond Williams .20 .50
161 Vince Carter .60 1.50
162 Antonio Davis .25 .60
163 Morris Peterson .20 .50
164 Keon Clark .20 .50
165 Chris Childs .20 .50
166 Alvin Williams .20 .50
167 Karl Malone .60 1.50
168 John Stockton .60 1.50
169 Donyell Marshall .20 .50
170 John Starks .20 .50
171 Bryon Russell .20 .50
172 David Benoit .20 .50
173 DeShawn Stevenson .20 .50
174 Richard Hamilton .40 1.00
175 Jahidi White .20 .50
176 Courtney Alexander .20 .50
177 Chris Whitney .20 .50
178 Michael Jordan 4.00 10.00
179 Kobe Bryant CL 1.25 3.00
180 Kevin Garnett CL .40 1.00
181 Sean Lampley RC 1.00 2.50
182 Andrei Kirilenko RC 1.50 4.00
183 Brandon Armstrong RC .60 1.50
184 Gerald Wallace RC 1.25 3.00
185 Tony Parker RC 4.00 10.00
186 Jeryl Sasser RC .60 1.50
187 Alton Ford RC 1.00 2.50
188 Kenny Satterfield RC .60 1.50
189 Will Solomon RC .75 2.00
190 Earl Watson RC .75 2.00
191 Michael Wright RC 1.00 2.50
192 Samuel Dalembert RC 1.00 2.50
193 Ousmane Cisse RC .60 1.50
194 Ruben Boumtje-Boumtje RC .75 2.00
195 Damone Brown RC .60 1.50
196 Jarron Collins RC 1.00 2.50
197 Terence Morris RC .60 1.50
198 Pau Gasol RC 4.00 10.00
199 Trenton Hassell RC .60 1.50
200 Kirk Haston RC .60 1.50
201 Brian Scalabrine RC 1.00 2.50
202 Gilbert Arenas RC 2.50 6.00
203 Jeff Trepagnier RC .60 1.50
204 Joseph Forte RC .60 1.50
205 Steven Hunter RC .60 1.50
206 Omar Cook RC 1.00 2.50
207 Jason Collins RC .75 2.00
208 Kedrick Brown RC .60 1.50
209 Michael Bradley RC .60 1.50
210 Zach Randolph RC 2.00 5.00
211 Richard Jefferson RC 1.25 3.00
212 Jamaal Tinsley RC .75 2.00
213 Vladimir Radmanovic RC .75 2.00
214 Brendan Haywood RC .75 2.00
215 Troy Murphy RC .75 2.00
216 DeSagana Diop RC .60 1.50
217 Jason Richardson RC 1.50 4.00
218 Joe Johnson RC 1.50 4.00
219 Rodney White RC .60 1.50
220 Loren Woods RC .60 1.50
221 Tyson Chandler RC 1.50 4.00
222 Eddy Curry RC 1.00 2.50
223 Shane Battier RC 2.00 5.00
224 Eddie Griffin RC .75 2.00
225 Kwame Brown RC 1.00 2.50
226 Shareef Abdur-Rahim .25 .60
227 Nazr Mohammed .20 .50
228 Hanno Mottola .20 .50
229 Emanual Davis .20 .50
230 Dion Glover .20 .50
231 Chris Crawford .20 .50
232 Mark Blount .20 .50
233 Joe Johnson .75 2.00
234 Milt Palacio .20 .50
235 Kedrick Brown .30 .75
236 Tony Battie .20 .50
237 Erick Strickland .20 .50
238 Kirk Haston .30 .75
239 Stacey Augmon .20 .50
240 Matt Bullard .20 .50
241 Bryce Drew .20 .50
242 Jerome Moiso .20 .50
243 Robert Traylor .20 .50
244 Tyson Chandler .75 2.00
245 Eddy Curry .50 1.25
246 Charles Oakley .25 .60
247 Brad Miller .30 .75
248 Kevin Ollie .20 .50
249 Trenton Hassell .30 .75
250 Ricky Davis .25 .60
251 Jumaine Jones .20 .50
252 DeSagana Diop .30 .75
253 Bryant Stith .20 .50
254 Jeff Trepagnier .30 .75
255 Michael Doleac .20 .50
256 Tim Hardaway .40 1.00
257 Danny Manning .25 .60
258 Johnny Newman .20 .50
259 Adrian Griffin .20 .50
260 Greg Buckner .20 .50
261 Donnell Harvey .20 .50
262 Evan Eschmeyer .20 .50
263 Avery Johnson .25 .60
264 Kenny Satterfield .30 .75
265 Scott Williams .20 .50
266 Tariq Abdul-Wahad .20 .50
267 George McCloud .20 .50
268 Clifford Robinson .30 .75
269 Jon Barry .20 .50
270 Brian Cardinal .20 .50
271 Rodney White .30 .75
272 Mikki Moore .20 .50
273 Victor Alexander .20 .50
274 Jason Richardson .75 2.00
275 Adonal Foyle .20 .50
276 Troy Murphy .40 1.00
277 Chris Mills .20 .50
278 Gilbert Arenas 1.25 3.00
279 Erick Dampier .20 .50
280 Glen Rice .30 .75
281 Eddie Griffin .40 1.00
282 Kevin Willis .20 .50
283 Terence Morris .30 .75
284 Kelvin Cato .20 .50
285 Dan Langhi .20 .50
286 Jason Collier .20 .50
287 Jamaal Tinsley .40 1.00
288 Carlos Rogers .20 .50
289 Jeff Foster .20 .50
290 Al Harrington .25 .60
291 Bruno Sundov .20 .50
292 Elton Brand .25 .60
293 Keyon Dooling .20 .50
294 Michael Olowokandi .20 .50
295 Obinna Ekezie .20 .50
296 Earl Boykins .25 .60
297 Harold Jamison .20 .50
298 Sean Rooks .20 .50
299 Lindsey Hunter .20 .50
300 Samaki Walker .20 .50
301 Mitch Richmond .40 1.00
302 Stanislav Medvedenko .20 .50
303 Devean George .20 .50
304 Robert Horry .30 .75
305 Jelani McCoy .20 .50
306 Pau Gasol 2.00 5.00
307 Shane Battier 1.00 2.50
308 Jason Williams .50 1.25
309 Isaac Austin .20 .50
310 Will Solomon .40 1.00
311 Lorenzen Wright .20 .50
312 Kendall Gill .20 .50
313 LaPhonso Ellis .25 .60
314 Sean Marks .20 .50
315 Rod Strickland .20 .50
316 Jim Jackson .20 .50
317 Eddie House .20 .50
318 Jason Caffey .20 .50
319 Rafer Alston .20 .50
320 Anthony Mason .30 .75
321 Mark Pope .20 .50
322 Michael Redd .30 .75
323 Darvin Ham .25 .60
324 Joe Smith .25 .60
325 William Avery .20 .50
326 Sam Mitchell .20 .50
327 Loren Woods .30 .75
328 Dean Garrett .20 .50
329 Gary Trent .20 .50
330 Jason Kidd .50 1.25
331 Todd MacCulloch .20 .50
332 Richard Jefferson .60 1.50
333 Brandon Armstrong .30 .75
334 Jason Collins .40 1.00
335 Kerry Kittles .20 .50
336 Shandon Anderson .20 .50
337 Howard Eisley .20 .50
338 Charlie Ward .20 .50
339 Lavor Postell .20 .50
340 Clarence Weatherspoon .20 .50
341 Travis Knight .20 .50
342 Horace Grant .25 .60
343 Steven Hunter .30 .75
344 Patrick Ewing .50 1.25
345 Jeryl Sasser .30 .75
346 Don Reid .20 .50
347 Troy Hudson .20 .50
348 Speedy Claxton .20 .50
349 Derrick Coleman .25 .60
350 Damone Brown .30 .75
351 Samuel Dalembert .50 1.25
352 Vonteego Cummings .20 .50
353 Matt Harpring .20 .50
354 Corie Blount .20 .50
355 Stephon Marbury .40 1.00
356 Dan Majerle .30 .75
357 Jake Voskuhl .20 .50
358 Alton Ford .50 1.25
359 Iakovos Tsakalidis .20 .50
360 John Wallace .20 .50
361 Derek Anderson .20 .50
362 Erick Barkley .20 .50
363 Ruben Boumtje-Boumtje .40 1.00
364 Zach Randolph 1.00 2.50
365 Steve Kerr .20 .50
366 Shawn Kemp .30 .75
367 Mateen Cleaves .20 .50
368 Bobby Jackson .20 .50
369 Mike Bibby .30 .75
370 Gerald Wallace .60 1.50
371 Jabari Smith .20 .50
372 Lawrence Funderburke .20 .50
373 Brent Price .20 .50
374 Bruce Bowen .20 .50
375 Stephen Jackson .25 .60
376 Tony Parker 2.00 5.00
377 Steve Smith .25 .60
378 Cherokee Parks .20 .50
379 Mark Bryant .20 .50
380 Jerome James .20 .50
381 Earl Watson .25 .60
382 Vladimir Radmanovic .40 1.00
383 Art Long .20 .50
384 Calvin Booth .20 .50
385 Olumide Oyedeji .20 .50
386 Jerome Williams .20 .50
387 Hakeem Olajuwon .60 1.50
388 Dell Curry .20 .50
389 Michael Bradley .30 .75
390 Tracy Murray .20 .50
391 Eric Montross .20 .50
392 John Amaechi .20 .50
393 John Crotty .20 .50
394 Scott Padgett .20 .50
395 Andrei Kirilenko .75 2.00
396 Jarron Collins .50 1.25
397 Quincy Lewis .20 .50
398 Kwame Brown .50 1.25
399 Christian Laettner .25 .60
400 Tyrone Nesby .20 .50
401 Brendan Haywood .40 1.00
402 Tyronn Lue .30 .75
403 Michael Jordan 5.00 12.00
404 Kobe Bryant CL 1.25 3.00
405 Michael Jordan CL 2.00 5.00
406A Zeljko Rebraca RC 1.00 2.50
406B Zeljko Rebraca RC 1.00 2.50
407A Jamison Brewer RC 1.00 2.50
407B Jamison Brewer RC 1.00 2.50
408A Shawn Marion .60 1.50
408B Shawn Marion .60 1.50
409A Primoz Brezec RC 1.00 2.50
409B Primoz Brezec RC 1.00 2.50
410A Antonis Fotsis RC .60 1.50
410B Antonis Fotsis RC .60 1.50
411A Bobby Simmons RC 1.00 2.50
411B Bobby Simmons RC 1.00 2.50
412A Malik Allen RC 1.00 2.50
412B Malik Allen RC 1.00 2.50
413A Ratko Varda RC 1.00 2.50
413B Ratko Varda RC 1.00 2.50
414A Tierre Brown RC 1.00 2.50
414B Tierre Brown RC 1.00 2.50
415A Norm Richardson RC 1.00 2.50
415B Norm Richardson RC 1.00 2.50
416A Oscar Torres RC 1.00 2.50
416B Oscar Torres RC 1.00 2.50
417A Chris Andersen RC 5.00 12.00
417B Chris Andersen RC 5.00 12.00
418A Predrag Drobnjak RC 1.00 2.50
418B Predrag Drobnjak RC 1.00 2.50
419A Dirk Nowitzki 1.50 4.00
419B Dirk Nowitzki 1.50 4.00
420A Shareef Abdur-Rahim .50 1.25
420B Shareef Abdur-Rahim .50 1.25
421A Kenny Anderson .50 1.25
421B Kenny Anderson .50 1.25
422A Jamal Mashburn .50 1.25
422B Jamal Mashburn .50 1.25
423A Charles Oakley .50 1.25
423B Charles Oakley .50 1.25
424A Andre Miller .50 1.25
424B Andre Miller .50 1.25
425A Michael Finley .60 1.50
425B Michael Finley .60 1.50
426A Tim Hardaway .75 2.00
426B Tim Hardaway .75 2.00
427A Nick Van Exel .60 1.50
427B Nick Van Exel .60 1.50
428A Jerry Stackhouse .60 1.50
428B Jerry Stackhouse .60 1.50
429A Mookie Blaylock .40 1.00
429B Mookie Blaylock .40 1.00
430A Glen Rice .60 1.50
430B Glen Rice .60 1.50
431A Reggie Miller 1.25 3.00
431B Reggie Miller 1.25 3.00
432A Elton Brand .50 1.25
432B Elton Brand .50 1.25
433A Kobe Bryant
Driving 5.00 12.00
433B Kobe Bryant
Looking to pass 5.00 12.00
434A Jason Williams 1.00 2.50
434B Jason Williams 1.00 2.50
435A Eddie Jones .60 1.50
435B Eddie Jones .60 1.50
436A Alonzo Mourning 1.00 2.50
436B Alonzo Mourning 1.00 2.50
437A Glenn Robinson .60 1.50
437B Glenn Robinson .60 1.50
438A Kevin Garnett 1.50 4.00
438B Kevin Garnett 1.50 4.00
439A Jason Kidd 1.00 2.50
439B Jason Kidd 1.00 2.50
440A Latrell Sprewell .75 2.00
440B Latrell Sprewell .75 2.00
441A Grant Hill 1.00 2.50
441B Grant Hill 1.00 2.50
442A Dikembe Mutombo 1.00 2.50
442B Dikembe Mutombo 1.00 2.50
443A Anfernee Hardaway 1.50 4.00
443B Anfernee Hardaway 1.50 4.00
444A Scottie Pippen 1.50 4.00
444B Scottie Pippen 1.50 4.00
445A Mike Bibby .60 1.50
445B Mike Bibby .60 1.50
446A David Robinson 1.25 3.00
446B David Robinson 1.25 3.00
447A Gary Payton 1.00 2.50
447B Gary Payton 1.00 2.50
448A Vince Carter 1.25 3.00
448B Vince Carter 1.25 3.00
449A John Stockton 1.25 3.00
449B John Stockton 1.25 3.00
450A Jordan Shooting 6.00 15.00
450B Jordan Dribbling 6.00 15.00

2001-02 Upper Deck UDX

*UDX STARS: 6X TO 15X BASE CARD HI
*UDX RCs: 3X TO 8X BASE CARD HI
*UDX CLs: 12X TO 30X BASE CARD HI
STARS STATED PRINT RUN 100 SETS
RC STATED PRINT RUN 50 SETS
301 Mitch Richmond 10.00 25.00

2001-02 Upper Deck 10th Power Game Jerseys

STATED ODDS 1:144 SER.1
AWX Antoine Walker 3.00 8.00
DRX David Robinson 8.00 20.00
KBX Kobe Bryant 125.00 300.00
KGX Kevin Garnett 10.00 25.00
KVX Keith Van Horn 3.00 8.00
MJX Michael Jordan 200.00 500.00
MTX Dikembe Mutombo 6.00 15.00
NVX Nick Van Exel 4.00 10.00
RAX Ray Allen 6.00 15.00
RHH Richard Hamilton 5.00 12.00
WSX Wally Szczerbiak 3.00 8.00

2001-02 Upper Deck 15000 Point Club Jerseys

STATED ODDS 1:120 SER.2
GR15K Glen Rice 4.00 10.00
IT15K Isiah Thomas 8.00 20.00
JH15K John Havlicek 12.00 30.00
JW15K Jerry West 12.00 30.00
KM15K Karl Malone 10.00 25.00
LB15K Larry Bird 25.00 60.00
MJ15K Michael Jordan 200.00 500.00
MM15K Moses Malone 10.00 25.00
PE15K Patrick Ewing 10.00 25.00

2001-02 Upper Deck Breakout Performers

COMPLETE SET (15) 12.00 30.00
STATED ODDS 1:12 SER.2
BP1 Kenyon Martin .75 2.00
BP2 Steve Francis .75 2.00
BP3 Stromile Swift .50 1.25
BP4 Baron Davis .75 2.00
BP5 Rashard Lewis .60 1.50
BP6 Vince Carter 1.50 4.00
BP7 Richard Hamilton 1.00 2.50
BP8 Kobe Bryant 15.00 40.00
BP9 DerMarr Johnson .50 1.25
BP10 Andre Miller .60 1.50
BP11 Kevin Garnett 2.00 5.00
BP12 Morris Peterson .50 1.25
BP13 Dirk Nowitzki 2.00 5.00
BP14 Mike Miller .60 1.50
BP15 Shawn Marion .75 2.00

2001-02 Upper Deck BuyBacks

PRINT RUNS LISTED BELOW
2 K.Bryant 00-1UD#80/88 1,000.00 2,000.00
3 M.Jordan 01-2UD#178/23 3,000.00 6,000.00
12 J.Stackhouse 00-1 SPA/21 25.00 60.00

2001-02 Upper Deck Class

COMPLETE SET (7) 8.00 20.00
STATED ODDS 1:24 SER.1
C1 Michael Jordan 8.00 20.00
C2 Shaquille O'Neal 3.00 8.00
C3 Alonzo Mourning 1.25 3.00
C4 Steve Francis .75 2.00
C5 Kobe Bryant 6.00 15.00
C6 Tim Duncan 2.00 5.00
C7 Kevin Garnett 2.00 5.00

2001-02 Upper Deck Classic Duals Jerseys

STATED ODDS 1:240 SER.2
JS/GP J.Stockton/G.Payton 10.00 25.00
JT/TP J.Tinsley/T.Parker 10.00 25.00
KB/AI K.Bryant/A.Iverson 100.00 250.00
KB/DM K.Bryant/D.Miles 40.00 100.00
KB/TM K.Bryant/T.McGrady 100.00 250.00
KM/KG K.Malone/K.Garnett 12.00 30.00
MJ/KB M.Jordan/K.Bryant 800.00 1,500.00

2001-02 Upper Deck Cool Cats Jerseys

STATED ODDS 1:288 SER.2
AWC Antoine Walker 4.00 10.00
BRC Michael Bradley 3.00 8.00
DJC DerMarr Johnson 3.00 8.00
JMC Jamal Mashburn 4.00 10.00
KMC Kenyon Martin 5.00 12.00
RJC Richard Jefferson 6.00 15.00
RMC Ron Mercer 3.00 8.00
TDC Tony Delk 4.00 10.00

2001-02 Upper Deck Game Jerseys

STATED ODDS 1:144 SER.1
BR Bryon Russell 1.50 4.00
CM Cuttino Mobley 2.00 5.00
GP Gary Payton 4.00 10.00
JS Joe Smith 2.00 5.00
JT Jason Terry 2.50 6.00
KB Kobe Bryant 100.00 250.00
KG Kevin Garnett 6.00 15.00
KM Karl Malone 5.00 12.00
MC Marc Jackson 1.50 4.00
RA Ron Artest 2.00 5.00

2001-02 Upper Deck Game Jerseys Autographs 1

PRINT RUN 100 SERIAL #'d SETS
CHA Chris Mihm 6.00 15.00
CMA Corey Maggette 6.00 15.00
DJA DerMarr Johnson 6.00 15.00
KBA Kobe Bryant 1,500.00 4,000.00
KGA Kevin Garnett 75.00 200.00
KMA Kenyon Martin 25.00 60.00
LHA Larry Hughes 15.00 40.00
MAA Marcus Fizer 6.00 15.00
MMA Mike Miller 8.00 20.00
MPA Morris Peterson 6.00 15.00
WZA Wang Zhizhi 500.00 1,200.00

2001-02 Upper Deck Game Jerseys Autographs 2

PRINT RUN 100 SER.#'d SETS
DJA DerMarr Johnson 6.00 15.00
DMA Desmond Mason 12.00 30.00
EGA Eddie Griffin 12.00 30.00
JRA Jason Richardson 15.00 40.00
KBA Kobe Bryant 1,500.00 4,000.00
KGA Kevin Garnett 75.00 200.00
PPA Paul Pierce 40.00 100.00
RMA Ron Mercer 12.00 30.00
RWA Rodney White 12.00 30.00

2001-02 Upper Deck Game Jerseys Combos

STATED ODDS 1:144 SER.1
AJLH A.Jamison/L.Hughes 6.00 15.00
AMLM A.Miller/L.Murray 6.00 15.00
DMCM D.Miles/C.Maggette 6.00 15.00
DMQR D.Miles/Q.Richardson 6.00 15.00
JCRM J.Crawford/R.Mercer 6.00 15.00
JMBD J.Mashburn/B.Davis 6.00 15.00
JTTK J.Terry/T.Kukoc 6.00 15.00
KBKG K.Bryant/K.Garnett 60.00 150.00
KMJS K.Malone/J.Stockton 15.00 40.00
MFDN M.Finley/D.Nowitzki 10.00 25.00

2001-02 Upper Deck Game Jerseys Logos

STATED ODDS 1:5000 SER.2
AHPL Allan Houston 25.00 60.00
KBPL Kobe Bryant 200.00 500.00
MMPL Mike Miller 20.00 50.00

2001-02 Upper Deck Game Jerseys Names

STATED ODDS 1:7500 SER.2
MJ2PN Michael Jordan 500.00 1,000.00
KGPN Kevin Garnett 60.00 150.00

2001-02 Upper Deck Game Jerseys Numbers

STATED ODDS 1:2500 SER.2
AMP Antonio McDyess 15.00 40.00
JMP Jamal Mashburn 15.00 40.00
KBP Kobe Bryant 150.00 400.00
KMP Karl Malone 40.00 100.00
MFP Michael Finley 20.00 50.00

2001-02 Upper Deck Game Jerseys Patches

STATED ODDS 1:2500 SER.1
AIP Allen Iverson 50.00 125.00
AMP Andre Miller 15.00 40.00
JMP Jamal Mashburn 15.00 40.00
JTP Jason Terry 20.00 50.00
KBP Kobe Bryant 150.00 400.00
KGP Kevin Garnett 50.00 125.00
KMP Kenyon Martin 20.00 50.00
MAP Marc Jackson 12.00 30.00
MFP Michael Finley 20.00 50.00
MMP Mike Miller 15.00 40.00
QRP Quentin Richardson 12.00 30.00
RAP Ray Allen 30.00 80.00
RWP Rasheed Wallace 25.00 60.00
SMP Shawn Marion 20.00 50.00

2001-02 Upper Deck Higher Ground

COMPLETE SET (10) 7.50 15.00
STATED ODDS 1:18 SER.1
HG1 Vince Carter 1.50 4.00
HG2 Kevin Garnett 2.00 5.00
HG3 Paul Pierce 1.25 3.00
HG4 Mike Miller .60 1.50
HG5 Jamal Mashburn .60 1.50
HG6 Steve Francis .75 2.00
HG7 Jerry Stackhouse .75 2.00
HG8 Kobe Bryant 6.00 15.00
HG9 Eddie Jones .75 2.00
HG10 Shawn Marion .75 2.00

2001-02 Upper Deck MJ Jersey Collection

COMMON CARD 400.00 800.00
MJC1-MJC10 SER.1/MJC11-MJC19 SER.2
PRINT RUN 50 SERIAL #'d SETS

2001-02 Upper Deck MJ's Back

COMMON CARD (MJ1-MJ90) 3.00 8.00
ONE PACK INSERTED IN THE FOLLOWING BRANDS: HARDCOURT, UD 1, UD 2, OVATION, AND SWEET SHOT

2001-02 Upper Deck MJ's Back 23 Karat Gold

COMMON CARD 40.00 100.00
STATED PRINT RUN 23 SER.#'d SETS

2001-02 Upper Deck MJ's Back Jerseys

COMMON CARD (CC1-CC5) 150.00 400.00
STATED PRINT RUN 100 SER.#'d SETS
DUAL PRINT RUN 50 SER.#'d SETS

2001-02 Upper Deck MJ's Back Jerseys Autographs

COMMON CARD (1-5) 6,000.00 12,000.00
PRINT RUN 23 SER.#'d SETS

2001-02 Upper Deck MJ's Back Jerseys Dual

COMMON CARD (CCD1-CCD5) 200.00 400.00

2001-02 Upper Deck MJ's Back Jerseys Dual Autographs
COMMON CARD (1-5) 6,000.00 12,000.00
STATED PRINT RUN 23 SER.#'d SETS

2001-02 Upper Deck MJ's Back Jerseys Triple
STATED PRINT RUN 25 SER.#'d SETS
CCT1 M.Jordan UNC/Bulls/Wiz 400.00 800.00

2001-02 Upper Deck MJ's Back Jerseys Quad
STATED PRINT RUN 23 SER.#'d SETS
CCQ1 Jordan NC/Bull/Bull/Wiz 500.00 1,000.00

2001-02 Upper Deck MJ Tributes MJ Milestones
COMMON CARD (M1-M7) 3,000.00 6,000.00
PRINT RUN 30 SER.#'d SETS
CARDS ISSUED AS EXCHANGES

2001-02 Upper Deck MJ Tributes Portrait of a Champion
COMMON CARD 4,000.00 8,000.00
PRINT RUN 23 SER.#'d SETS
CARDS ISSUED AS EXCHANGES

2001-02 Upper Deck Motion Pictures
COMPLETE SET (10) 12.00 30.00
STATED ODDS 1:18 SER.2
MP1 Kobe Bryant 6.00 15.00
MP2 Tim Duncan 2.00 5.00
MP3 Michael Jordan 8.00 20.00
MP4 Elton Brand .60 1.50
MP5 Vince Carter 1.50 4.00
MP6 Eddie Jones .75 2.00
MP7 Kevin Garnett 2.00 5.00
MP8 Michael Finley .75 2.00
MP9 Paul Pierce 1.25 3.00
MP10 Shaquille O'Neal 3.00 8.00

2001-02 Upper Deck NBA All-Star Authentics
STATED ODDS 1:96 SER.1
BDAS Baron Davis 5.00 12.00
DMAS Desmond Mason 4.00 10.00
PSAS Peja Stojakovic 4.00 10.00
RLAS Rashard Lewis 4.00 10.00
SSAS Stromile Swift 3.00 8.00

2001-02 Upper Deck NBA Finals Fabrics
STATED ODDS 1:120 SER.2
AIF Allen Iverson 15.00 40.00
AMF Aaron McKie 4.00 10.00
BSF Brian Shaw 4.00 10.00
DFF Derek Fisher 5.00 12.00
DGF Devean George 4.00 10.00
DMF Dikembe Mutombo 10.00 25.00
ESF Eric Snow 4.00 10.00
GFF Greg Foster 4.00 10.00
HGF Horace Grant 5.00 12.00
JJF Jumaine Jones 4.00 10.00
KBF Kobe Bryant 75.00 200.00
KOF Kevin Ollie 4.00 10.00
MMF Mark Madsen 4.00 10.00
RBF Rodney Buford 4.00 10.00
RFF Rick Fox 5.00 12.00
RJF Raja Bell 8.00 20.00
ROF Robert Horry 8.00 20.00
THF Tyrone Hill 4.00 10.00
TLF Tyronn Lue 6.00 15.00
TMF Todd MacCulloch 4.00 10.00

2001-02 Upper Deck Rookie Threads
STATED ODDS 1:144 SER.2 HOBBY
ECT Eddy Curry 2.50 6.00
EGT Eddie Griffin 2.00 5.00
GWT Gerald Wallace 3.00 8.00
JJT Joe Johnson 4.00 10.00
JRT Jason Richardson 4.00 10.00
KET Kedrick Brown 1.50 4.00
KWT Kwame Brown 2.50 6.00
RJT Richard Jefferson 3.00 8.00
RWT Rodney White 1.50 4.00
TCT Tyson Chandler 4.00 10.00

2001-02 Upper Deck Sky High
COMPLETE SET (7) 15.00 40.00
STATED ODDS 1:24 SER.2
SH1 Kobe Bryant 12.00 30.00
SH2 Kevin Garnett 2.00 5.00
SH3 Darius Miles .50 1.25
SH4 Tracy McGrady 1.25 3.00
SH5 Kwame Brown .75 2.00
SH6 Eddy Curry .75 2.00
SH7 Tyson Chandler 1.25 3.00

2001-02 Upper Deck SlamCenter
STATED ODDS 1:12 SER.1
SC1 Kobe Bryant 6.00 15.00
SC2 Desmond Mason .60 1.50
SC3 Vince Carter 1.50 4.00
SC4 Antonio McDyess .60 1.50
SC5 Lamar Odom .60 1.50
SC6 Rashard Lewis .60 1.50
SC7 Chris Webber 1.00 2.50
SC8 Latrell Sprewell 1.00 2.50
SC9 Antoine Walker .60 1.50
SC10 Stromile Swift .50 1.25
SC11 Glenn Robinson .75 2.00
SC12 Kevin Garnett 2.00 5.00
SC13 Antawn Jamison .60 1.50
SC14 Jerry Stackhouse .75 2.00
SC15 Shaquille O'Neal 3.00 8.00

2001-02 Upper Deck Superstar Summit
COMPLETE SET (10) 12.50 25.00
STATED ODDS 1:18 SER.2
SS1 Kobe Bryant 6.00 15.00
SS2 Vince Carter 1.50 4.00
SS3 Kevin Garnett 2.00 5.00
SS4 Chris Webber 1.00 2.50
SS5 Shaquille O'Neal 3.00 8.00
SS6 Tim Duncan 2.00 5.00
SS7 Allen Iverson 2.00 5.00
SS8 Ray Allen 1.25 3.00
SS9 Steve Francis .75 2.00
SS10 Michael Jordan 6.00 15.00

2001-02 Upper Deck Triple Jump Jerseys
STATED PRINT RUN 25 SER.#'d SETS
DMBDJB Mason/B.Davis/Bender 20.00 50.00
JTJRTP Tinsley/J.Rich/Parker 25.00 60.00
KBKGKM Bryant/Garnett/Martin 125.00 300.00
KBTMCW Bryant/T-Mac/Webber 150.00 400.00
KWTCEC Brown/Chandler/Curry 20.00 50.00
MJDRKB Jordan/J.Erving/Kobe 500.00 1,000.00
MJKBKG Jordan/Kobe/Garnett 500.00 1,000.00
MJMJMJ Jordan/Jordan/Jordan 400.00 800.00
RJJCBA Jefferson/Collins/Armstrng 20.00 50.00

2001-02 Upper Deck UD Originals Jerseys
STATED ODDS 1:120 SER.2
BDO Baron Davis 5.00 12.00
CWO Chris Webber 6.00 15.00
DMO Darius Miles 3.00 8.00
KBO Kobe Bryant 40.00 100.00
KGO Kevin Garnett 12.00 30.00
MMO Mike Miller 4.00 10.00
RAO Ray Allen 8.00 20.00
SHO Shawn Marion 5.00 12.00
SMO Stephon Marbury 6.00 15.00
SSO Stromile Swift 3.00 8.00

2001-02 Upper Deck Upper Decade Team
COMPLETE SET (10) 12.50 30.00
STATED ODDS 1:18 SER.1
UD1 Michael Jordan 6.00 15.00
UD2 Kobe Bryant 6.00 15.00
UD3 Vince Carter 1.50 4.00
UD4 Kevin Garnett 2.00 5.00
UD5 Shaquille O'Neal 3.00 8.00
UD6 Tim Hardaway 1.00 2.50
UD7 Gary Payton 1.25 3.00
UD8 Scottie Pippen 2.00 5.00
UD9 Tim Duncan 2.00 5.00
UD10 David Robinson 1.50 4.00

2001-02 Upper Deck Winning Touch Game Jerseys
STATED ODDS 1:144 SER.1
AIWT Allen Iverson 10.00 25.00
DRWT David Robinson 8.00 20.00
JSWT John Stockton 8.00 20.00
KMWT Karl Malone 8.00 20.00
PEWT Patrick Ewing 6.00 15.00
RFWT Rick Fox 3.00 8.00
RPWT Robert Parish 5.00 12.00
SEWT Sean Elliott 3.00 8.00
SKWT Steve Kerr 5.00 12.00

2001-02 Upper Deck World Piece Game Jerseys
STATED ODDS 1:288 SER.1 HOBBY
DBWP Dalibor Bagaric 2.50 6.00
DNWP Dirk Nowitzki 10.00 25.00
FLWP Felipe Lopez 2.50 6.00
HMWP Hanno Mottola 2.50 6.00
MOWP Michael Olowokandi 2.50 6.00
MTWP Dikembe Mutombo 6.00 15.00
SNWP Steve Nash 8.00 20.00
TKWP Toni Kukoc 5.00 12.00
VLWP Vlade Divac 3.00 8.00
ZWWP Wang Zhizhi 4.00 10.00

2002-03 Upper Deck
COMPLETE SER.1 (210) 80.00 160.00
COMPLETE SER.2 (210) 20.00 40.00
COMP.SER.1 w/o SP's (180) 15.00 40.00
RC STATED ODDS 1:4
1 Shareef Abdur-Rahim .30 .75
2 Jason Terry .25 .60
3 Glenn Robinson .30 .75
4 Nazr Mohammed .20 .50
5 DerMarr Johnson .20 .50
6 Dion Glover .20 .50
7 Paul Pierce .50 1.25
8 Antoine Walker .25 .60
9 Vin Baker .25 .60
10 Eric Williams .20 .50
11 Tony Delk .20 .50
12 Kedrick Brown .20 .50
13 Jalen Rose .25 .60
14 Eddy Curry .30 .75
15 Tyson Chandler .30 .75
16 Jamal Crawford .30 .75
17 Marcus Fizer .20 .50
18 Trenton Hassell .20 .50
19 Zydrunas Ilgauskas .25 .60
20 Tyrone Hill .20 .50
21 Darius Miles .30 .75
22 Chris Mihm .20 .50
23 Ricky Davis .25 .60
24 Jumaine Jones .20 .50
25 Dirk Nowitzki .75 2.00
26 Michael Finley .30 .75
27 Steve Nash .60 1.50
28 Raef LaFrentz .20 .50
29 Nick Van Exel .30 .75
30 Adrian Griffin .20 .50
31 Wang Zhizhi .30 .75
32 Marcus Camby .25 .60
33 Juwan Howard .25 .60
34 James Posey .20 .50
35 Donnell Harvey .20 .50
36 Ryan Bowen .20 .50
37 Zeljko Rebraca .20 .50
38 Ben Wallace .40 1.00
39 Clifford Robinson .30 .75
40 Corliss Williamson .30 .75
41 Chucky Atkins .20 .50
42 Michael Curry .20 .50
43 Jason Richardson .30 .75
44 Antawn Jamison .25 .60
45 Troy Murphy .25 .60
46 Gilbert Arenas .30 .75
47 Danny Fortson .20 .50
48 Steve Francis .30 .75
49 Eddie Griffin .20 .50
50 Cuttino Mobley .20 .50
51 Kenny Thomas .20 .50
52 Moochie Norris .20 .50
53 Kelvin Cato .20 .50
54 Reggie Miller .60 1.50
55 Jermaine O'Neal .25 .60
56 Ron Mercer .20 .50
57 Austin Croshere .20 .50
58 Ron Artest .25 .60
59 Jamaal Tinsley .20 .50
60 Elton Brand .25 .60
61 Andre Miller .25 .60
62 Lamar Odom .30 .75
63 Michael Olowokandi .20 .50
64 Quentin Richardson .20 .50
65 Corey Maggette .25 .60
66 Kobe Bryant 2.50 6.00
67 Shaquille O'Neal 1.25 3.00
68 Rick Fox .20 .50
69 Robert Horry .30 .75
70 Devean George .20 .50
71 Samaki Walker .20 .50
72 Brian Shaw .20 .50
73 Pau Gasol .50 1.25
74 Jason Williams .40 1.00
75 Shane Battier .30 .75
76 Stromile Swift .20 .50
77 Lorenzen Wright .20 .50
78 LaPhonso Ellis .25 .60
79 Eddie Jones .30 .75
80 Brian Grant .20 .50
81 Vladimir Stepania .20 .50
82 Eddie House .20 .50
83 Anthony Carter .20 .50
84 Ray Allen .50 1.25
85 Sam Cassell .25 .60
86 Tim Thomas .20 .50
87 Toni Kukoc .30 .75
88 Jason Caffey .20 .50
89 Anthony Mason .25 .60
90 Joel Przybilla .20 .50
91 Kevin Garnett .75 2.00
92 Wally Szczerbiak .25 .60
93 Terrell Brandon .20 .50
94 Joe Smith .25 .60
95 Felipe Lopez .20 .50
96 Anthony Peeler .20 .50
97 Radoslav Nesterovic .20 .50
98 Jason Kidd .50 1.25
99 Kenyon Martin .30 .75
100 Dikembe Mutombo .50 1.25
101 Richard Jefferson .25 .60
102 Kerry Kittles .20 .50
103 Lucious Harris .20 .50
104 Jason Collins .20 .50
105 Baron Davis .30 .75
106 Jamal Mashburn .25 .60
107 Elden Campbell .20 .50
108 David Wesley .20 .50
109 P.J. Brown .20 .50
110 Lee Nailon .20 .50
111 Latrell Sprewell .30 .75
112 Allan Houston .30 .75
113 Kurt Thomas .20 .50
114 Antonio McDyess .25 .60
115 Othella Harrington .20 .50
116 Clarence Weatherspoon .20 .50
117 Tracy McGrady .50 1.25
118 Mike Miller .25 .60
119 Darrell Armstrong .20 .50
120 Grant Hill .50 1.25
121 Pat Garrity .20 .50
122 Steven Hunter .20 .50
123 Allen Iverson .75 2.00
124 Keith Van Horn .25 .60
125 Aaron McKie .20 .50
126 Eric Snow .20 .50
127 Derrick Coleman .25 .60
128 Samuel Dalembert .20 .50
129 Stephon Marbury .40 1.00
130 Shawn Marion .30 .75
131 Joe Johnson .25 .60
132 Tom Gugliotta .20 .50
133 Anfernee Hardaway .75 2.00
134 Iakovos Tsakalidis .20 .50
135 Rasheed Wallace .40 1.00
136 Bonzi Wells .20 .50
137 Damon Stoudamire .30 .75
138 Scottie Pippen .75 2.00
139 Derek Anderson .20 .50
140 Ruben Patterson .20 .50
141 Dale Davis .20 .50
142 Mike Bibby .30 .75
143 Chris Webber .40 1.00
144 Peja Stojakovic .25 .60
145 Doug Christie .20 .50
146 Hedo Turkoglu .25 .60
147 Vlade Divac .25 .60
148 Scot Pollard .20 .50
149 Tim Duncan .75 2.00
150 David Robinson .60 1.50
151 Tony Parker .50 1.25
152 Malik Rose .20 .50
153 Steve Smith .25 .60
154 Bruce Bowen .20 .50
155 Danny Ferry .20 .50
156 Gary Payton .50 1.25
157 Rashard Lewis .25 .60
158 Brent Barry .25 .60
159 Kenny Anderson .20 .50
160 Desmond Mason .25 .60
161 Predrag Drobnjak .20 .50
162 Vince Carter .60 1.50
163 Morris Peterson .25 .60
164 Antonio Davis .25 .60
165 Alvin Williams .20 .50
166 Jerome Williams .20 .50
167 Michael Bradley .20 .50
168 Karl Malone .60 1.50
169 John Stockton .60 1.50
170 John Amaechi .20 .50
171 Andrei Kirilenko .25 .60
172 Greg Ostertag .20 .50
173 Jarron Collins .20 .50
174 DeShawn Stevenson .20 .50
175 Christian Laettner .25 .60
176 Brendan Haywood .20 .50
177 Chris Whitney .20 .50
178 Tyronn Lue .20 .50
179 Kwame Brown .25 .60
180 Michael Jordan 3.00 8.00
181 Jay Williams RC 1.00 2.50
182 Juan Dixon RC 1.00 2.50
183 Vincent Yarbrough RC .75 2.00
184 Casey Jacobsen RC 1.00 2.50
185 Chris Wilcox RC 1.00 2.50
186 John Salmons RC 1.25 3.00
187 Marcus Haislip RC .75 2.00
188 Robert Archibald RC .75 2.00
189 Jared Jeffries RC 1.00 2.50
190 Nikoloz Tskitishvili RC .75 2.00
191 Kareem Rush RC 1.00 2.50
192 Fred Jones RC 1.00 2.50
193 Caron Butler RC 1.25 3.00
194 Chris Jefferies RC .75 2.00
195 Ryan Humphrey RC 1.00 2.50
196 Frank Williams RC .75 2.00
197 DaJuan Wagner RC 1.00 2.50
198 Bostjan Nachbar RC 1.00 2.50
199 Mike Dunleavy RC 1.25 3.00
200 Roger Mason RC 1.00 2.50
201 Nene Hilario RC 1.25 3.00
202 Melvin Ely RC 1.00 2.50
203 Tayshaun Prince RC 2.50 6.00
204 Jiri Welsch RC 1.00 2.50
205 Dan Dickau RC .75 2.00
206 Qyntel Woods RC .75 2.00
207 Curtis Borchardt RC .75 2.00
208 Amare Stoudemire RC 3.00 8.00
209 Drew Gooden RC 1.25 3.00
210 Yao Ming RC 8.00 20.00
211 Glenn Robinson .30 .75
212 Theo Ratliff .20 .50
213 Emanual Davis .20 .50
214 Dan Dickau .40 1.00
215 Alan Henderson .20 .50
216 Chris Crawford .20 .50
217 Darvin Ham .25 .60
218 Ira Newble .20 .50
219 Vin Baker .25 .60
220 Shammond Williams .20 .50
221 Tony Battie .20 .50
222 Walter McCarty .20 .50
223 Bruno Sundov .20 .50
224 Ruben Wolkowyski .20 .50
225 Eddie Robinson .20 .50
226 Jay Williams .50 1.25
227 Fred Hoiberg .20 .50
228 Donyell Marshall .20 .50
229 Roger Mason .50 1.25
230 Darius Miles .20 .50
231 Michael Stewart .20 .50
232 Tyrone Hill .20 .50
233 DaJuan Wagner .50 1.25
234 DeSagana Diop .20 .50
235 Bimbo Coles .20 .50
236 Milt Palacio .20 .50
237 Avery Johnson .25 .60
238 Evan Eschmeyer .20 .50
239 Raja Bell .25 .60
240 Shawn Bradley .20 .50
241 Walt Williams .20 .50
242 Eduardo Najera .20 .50
243 Marcus Camby .25 .60
244 Chris Whitney .20 .50
245 Nikoloz Tskitishvili .40 1.00
246 Kenny Satterfield .20 .50
247 Nene Hilario .60 1.50
248 Mark Blount .20 .50
249 Richard Hamilton .40 1.00
250 Chauncey Billups .30 .75
251 Tayshaun Prince 1.25 3.00
252 Don Reid .20 .50
253 Jon Barry .20 .50
254 Hubert Davis .20 .50
255 Pepe Sanchez .20 .50
256 Chris Mills .20 .50
257 Bob Sura .20 .50
258 Mike Dunleavy .60 1.50
259 Jiri Welsch .50 1.25
260 Adonal Foyle .20 .50
261 Erick Dampier .20 .50
262 Maurice Taylor .20 .50
263 Glen Rice .25 .60
264 Yao Ming 3.00 8.00
265 Bostjan Nachbar .50 1.25
266 Jason Collier .20 .50
267 Terence Morris .20 .50
268 Jonathan Bender .20 .50
269 Jeff Foster .20 .50
270 Fred Jones .50 1.25
271 Al Harrington .20 .50
272 Brad Miller .25 .60
273 Jamison Brewer .20 .50
274 Erick Strickland .20 .50
275 Andre Miller .25 .60
276 Melvin Ely .50 1.25
277 Keyon Dooling .20 .50
278 Chris Wilcox .50 1.25
279 Eric Piatkowski .20 .50
280 Sean Rooks .20 .50
281 Wang Zhi Zhi .30 .75
282 Mark Madsen .20 .50
283 Kareem Rush .50 1.25
284 Stanislav Medvedenko .20 .50
285 Derek Fisher .30 .75
286 Tracy Murray .20 .50
287 Michael Dickerson .20 .50
288 Wesley Person .20 .50
289 Drew Gooden .60 1.50
290 Robert Archibald .40 1.00
291 Brevin Knight .20 .50
292 Mike James .20 .50
293 LaPhonso Ellis .25 .60
294 Caron Butler .60 1.50
295 Malik Allen .20 .50
296 Travis Best .20 .50
297 Alonzo Mourning .50 1.25
298 Toni Kukoc .30 .75
299 Michael Redd .30 .75
300 Marcus Haislip .40 1.00
301 Ervin Johnson .20 .50
302 Kevin Ollie .20 .50
303 Troy Hudson .20 .50
304 Marc Jackson .20 .50
305 Gary Trent .20 .50
306 Kendall Gill .20 .50
307 Loren Woods .20 .50
308 Dikembe Mutombo .50 1.25
309 Anthony Johnson .20 .50
310 Rodney Rogers .20 .50
311 Brandon Armstrong .20 .50
312 Brian Scalabrine .20 .50
313 Aaron Williams .20 .50
314 Courtney Alexander .20 .50
315 Kirk Haston .20 .50
316 George Lynch .20 .50
317 Stacey Augmon .20 .50
318 Robert Traylor .20 .50
319 Jamaal Magloire .20 .50
320 Lee Nailon .20 .50
321 Frank Williams .40 1.00
322 Michael Doleac .20 .50
323 Shandon Anderson .20 .50
324 Howard Eisley .20 .50
325 Travis Knight .20 .50
326 Lavor Postell .20 .50
327 Charlie Ward .20 .50
328 Mark Pope .20 .50
329 Olumide Oyedeji .20 .50
330 Shawn Kemp .30 .75
331 Jacque Vaughn .20 .50
332 Ryan Humphrey .50 1.25
333 Andrew DeClercq .20 .50
334 Jeryl Sasser .20 .50
335 Keith Van Horn .25 .60
336 Todd MacCulloch .20 .50
337 Monty Williams .20 .50
338 John Salmons .60 1.50
339 Brian Skinner .20 .50
340 Mark Bryant .20 .50
341 Greg Buckner .20 .50
342 Bo Outlaw .20 .50
343 Amare Stoudemire 1.50 4.00
344 Casey Jacobsen .50 1.25
345 Alton Ford .20 .50
346 Scott Williams .20 .50
347 Dan Langhi .20 .50
348 Arvydas Sabonis .25 .60
349 Antonio Daniels .20 .50
350 Jeff McInnis .20 .50
351 Qyntel Woods .40 1.00
352 Zach Randolph .25 .60
353 Ruben Boumtje-Boumtje .20 .50
354 Chris Dudley .20 .50
355 Charles Smith .20 .50
356 Keon Clark .20 .50
357 Bobby Jackson .20 .50
358 Mateen Cleaves .20 .50
359 Gerald Wallace .25 .60
360 Lawrence Funderburke .20 .50
361 Speedy Claxton .20 .50
362 Stephen Jackson .25 .60
363 Kevin Willis .20 .50
364 Steve Kerr .25 .60
365 Mengke Bateer .30 .75
366 Kenny Anderson .25 .60
367 Vladimir Radmanovic .20 .50
368 Joseph Forte .20 .50
369 Jerome James .20 .50
370 Vitaly Potapenko .20 .50
371 Calvin Booth .20 .50
372 Ansu Sesay .20 .50
373 Voshon Lenard .20 .50
374 Lindsey Hunter .20 .50
375 Mamadou N'Diaye .20 .50
376 Chris Jefferies .40 1.00
377 Jelani McCoy .20 .50
378 Lamond Murray .20 .50
379 Eric Montross .20 .50
380 Matt Harpring .20 .50
381 Calbert Cheaney .20 .50
382 Curtis Borchardt .40 1.00
383 Mark Jackson .25 .60
384 Scott Padgett .20 .50
385 Jerry Stackhouse .30 .75
386 Jared Jeffries .50 1.25
387 Larry Hughes .25 .60
388 Juan Dixon .50 1.25
389 Bryon Russell .20 .50
390 Etan Thomas .20 .50
391 Efthimios Rentzias RC .75 2.00
392 Manu Ginobili RC 8.00 20.00
393 Juaquin Hawkins RC .75 2.00
394 Rasual Butler RC 1.00 2.50
395 Ronald Murray RC 1.25 3.00
396 Igor Rakocevic RC .75 2.00
397 Tito Maddox RC .75 2.00
398 Mike Batiste RC .75 2.00
399 Sam Clancy RC 1.00 2.50
400 Tamar Slay RC .75 2.00
401 Lonny Baxter RC .75 2.00
402 Marko Jaric 1.25 3.00
403 Dan Gadzuric RC 1.00 2.50
404 Jannero Pargo RC .75 2.00
405 Pat Burke RC .75 2.00
406 Smush Parker RC 1.25 3.00
407 Reggie Evans RC 1.00 2.50
408 Gordan Giricek RC 1.25 3.00
409 Mehmet Okur RC 1.25 3.00
410 Jamal Sampson RC .75 2.00
411 Raul Lopez RC .75 2.00
412 Predrag Savovic RC 1.00 2.50
413 Carlos Boozer RC 1.25 3.00
414 Ken Johnson 1.00 2.50
415 Cezary Trybanski RC 1.25 3.00
416 Mike Wilks RC 1.25 3.00
417 J.R. Bremer RC .75 2.00
418 Junior Harrington RC .75 2.00
419 Nate Huffman RC .75 2.00
420 Michael Jordan 6.00 15.00

2002-03 Upper Deck Exclusives
*STARS: 5X TO 12X BASE CARD HI
STARS PRINT RUN 100 SER.#'d SETS
*RCs: 2.5X TO 6X BASE CARD HI
RC PRINT RUN 50 SER.#'d SETS
*NON RC ROOKIES: 4X TO 10X BASE CARD HI
NON RC ROOKIES PRINT RUN 100 SETS

2002-03 Upper Deck Air Apparel
STATED ODDS 1:72 SER.1
BDAA Baron Davis 3.00 8.00
DJAA DerMarr Johnson 2.00 5.00
DMAA Darius Miles 2.00 5.00
JMAA Jamal Mashburn 2.50 6.00
JPAA James Posey 2.00 5.00
KMAA Kenyon Martin 3.00 8.00
KWAA Kwame Brown 2.00 5.00
LOAA Lamar Odom 3.00 8.00
LSAA Latrell Sprewell 3.00 8.00
RHAA Richard Hamilton 4.00 10.00
SAAA Shareef Abdur-Rahim SP 3.00 8.00
TCAA Tyson Chandler 3.00 8.00

2002-03 Upper Deck All-ACCess Jerseys
STATED ODDS 1:96 SER.2
AAJ Antawn Jamison 2.50 6.00
ABH Brendan Haywood 2.00 5.00
ACM Corey Maggette 2.50 6.00
AEB Elton Brand 2.50 6.00
AJS Joe Smith 2.50 6.00
AMJ Michael Jordan SP 75.00 150.00
ARF Rick Fox 2.00 5.00
ARM Roger Mason 2.50 6.00
ASB Shane Battier 3.00 8.00
ASF Steve Francis SP 3.00 8.00
ASM Stephon Marbury 4.00 10.00
AST Jerry Stackhouse 3.00 8.00

2002-03 Upper Deck All-Star Authentics Jerseys
STATED ODDS 1:288 SER 1
AIAJ Allen Iverson 12.00 30.00
AMAJ Alonzo Mourning SP 8.00 20.00
BHAJ Brendan Haywood SP 3.00 8.00
CWAJ Chris Webber 6.00 15.00
GAAJ Gilbert Arenas SP 5.00 12.00
KMAJ Kenyon Martin/61* 6.00 15.00
MFAJ Marcus Fizer SP 3.00 8.00
PGAJ Pau Gasol/80* 8.00 20.00
PPAJ Paul Pierce 8.00 20.00
PSAJ Peja Stojakovic 4.00 10.00

2002-03 Upper Deck All-Star Authentics Jerseys Autographs
PRINT RUN 25 SER.#'d SETS
KGAAA Kevin Garnett 40.00 100.00
KMAAA Kenyon Martin 12.50 30.00
MJAAA Michael Jordan 1,500.00 3,000.00
PPAAJ Paul Pierce 20.00 50.00

2002-03 Upper Deck All-Star Authentics Shorts
STATED ODDS 1:96 SER.1
AKAS Andrei Kirilenko 2.50 6.00
BHAS Brendan Haywood 2.00 5.00
CMAS Chris Mihm 2.00 5.00
DMAS Desmond Mason 2.50 6.00
DNAS Dirk Nowitzki 8.00 20.00
KBAS Kobe Bryant 40.00 100.00
LNAS Lee Nailon 2.00 5.00
MJAS Michael Jordan SP 60.00 150.00
QRAS Quentin Richardson 2.00 5.00
SNAS Steve Nash 6.00 15.00
SSAS Steve Smith 2.50 6.00
TPAS Tony Parker 5.00 12.00
WSAS Wally Szczerbiak SP 2.50 6.00
ZRAS Zeljko Rebraca 2.00 5.00

2002-03 Upper Deck All-Star Authentics Warm-Ups
STATED ODDS 1:48 SER 1
AKAW Andrei Kirilenko 2.00 5.00
AMAW Alonzo Mourning 4.00 10.00
CMAW Chris Mihm 2.00 5.00
DFAW Derek Fisher 2.50 6.00
DMAW Desmond Mason 2.00 5.00
KBAW Kobe Bryant 40.00 100.00
KGAW Kevin Garnett 6.00 15.00
MFAW Marcus Fizer 2.00 5.00
MJAW Michael Jordan SP 30.00 80.00
RAAW Ray Allen 4.00 10.00
SBAW Shane Battier 2.50 6.00
TMAW Tracy McGrady 4.00 10.00
WPAW Wesley Person 2.00 5.00
ZRAW Zeljko Rebraca 2.00 5.00

2002-03 Upper Deck BuyBacks
2 M.Bibby 01-2UD#369/29 30.00 80.00
13 T.Chandler 01-2UD#244/54 25.00 60.00
14 M.Fizer 00-1UDEncWup/28 20.00 50.00
18 K.Garnett 01-2UDBrPerf/25 100.00 200.00
22 J.Kidd 00-1UD#129/32 20.00 50.00
29 K.Martin 01-2UDHnRoll/50 40.00 100.00
31 M.Miller 01-2UD#207/95 10.00 25.00
33 M.Miller 01-2UDHRoll/26 40.00 100.00
36 J.Moiso 01-2UD#242/113 8.00 20.00
38 T.Parker 01-2UD#376/155 25.00 60.00
39 Parker 01-2UDHRollFFR/46 30.00 80.00
41 J-Rich 01-2UDHRFFR/41 60.00 120.00
42 D.Stvnson 00-1SPGFAFr/35 25.00 60.00
45 E.Thomas 00-1UD#220/84 8.00 20.00
46 G.Wallace 01-2UD#370/63 20.00 50.00

2002-03 Upper Deck Combo All-Star Authentics
PRINT RUN 300 SER.#'d SETS
DNSN D.Nowitzki/S.Nash 10.00 25.00
EBQR E.Brand/Q.Richardson 6.00 15.00
JRGA J.Richardson/G.Arenas 6.00 15.00
JTMF J.Tinsley/M.Fizer 6.00 15.00
KBKG K.Garnett/K.Bryant 60.00 150.00
KGWS Garnett/Szczerbiak 10.00 25.00
MJKB M.Jordan/K.Bryant 200.00 500.00
RATM T.McGrady/R.Allen 10.00 25.00
SAJK Abdur-Rahim/J.Kidd 10.00 25.00
WPSB W.Person/S.Battier 6.00 15.00

2002-03 Upper Deck Double Team Dual Jerseys
STATED ODDS 1:960 SER.2 RET.
CWMBD C.Webber/M.Bibby 15.00 40.00
JWJRD J.Williams/J.Rose 6.00 15.00
PGDGD P.Gasol/D.Gooden 6.00 15.00
PPAWD P.Pierce/A.Walker 15.00 40.00
TMRHD T.McGrady/R.Humphrey 12.50 30.00

2002-03 Upper Deck Dual Shooting Shirts
STATED ODDS 1:288 SER.2
BDDWS B.Davis/D.Wesley 2.00 5.00
CWPJS C.Webber/P.Stojakovic 2.50 6.00
DRTPS D.Robinson/T.Parker 4.00 10.00
ECJCS E.Curry/J.Crawford 2.00 5.00
JPJHS J.Posey/J.Howard 1.50 4.00
KBJWS K.Bryant/J.Williams 40.00 100.00
MJKBS M.Jordan/K.Bryant SP 150.00 400.00
SBDGS S.Battier/D.Gooden 2.00 5.00
SMSMS S.Marbury/S.Marion 2.50 6.00

2002-03 Upper Deck Dunkvision
COMPLETE SET (7) 10.00 25.00
STATED ODDS 1:24 SER 1
DV1 Michael Jordan 8.00 20.00
DV2 Kobe Bryant 6.00 15.00
DV3 Tim Duncan 2.00 5.00
DV4 Vince Carter 1.50 4.00
DV5 Shaquille O'Neal 3.00 8.00
DV6 Jason Richardson .75 2.00
DV7 Steve Francis .75 2.00

2002-03 Upper Deck Electric Company
COMPLETE SET (7) 6.00 15.00
STATED ODDS 1:24 SER.2
EC1 Jay Williams .60 1.50
EC2 Paul Pierce 1.25 3.00
EC3 Tracy McGrady 1.25 3.00
EC4 Nene Hilario .75 2.00
EC5 Caron Butler .75 2.00
EC6 Kareem Rush .60 1.50
EC7 Kobe Bryant 6.00 15.00

2002-03 Upper Deck Electric Company Jerseys
STATED ODDS 1:480 SER.2 RET.
ECCB Caron Butler 4.00 10.00
ECJW Jay Williams 3.00 8.00
ECKR Kareem Rush 3.00 8.00
ECNH Nene Hilario 4.00 10.00
ECPP Paul Pierce 6.00 15.00
ECTM Tracy McGrady 6.00 15.00

2002-03 Upper Deck Game Night
COMPLETE SET (14) 10.00 25.00
STATED ODDS 1:12 SER.2
GN1 Kobe Bryant 5.00 12.00
GN2 Ray Allen 1.00 2.50
GN3 Michael Finley .60 1.50
GN4 Karl Malone 1.25 3.00
GN5 Kevin Garnett 1.50 4.00
GN6 Jason Richardson .60 1.50
GN7 Shawn Marion .60 1.50
GN8 Mike Miller .50 1.25
GN9 Jamaal Tinsley .40 1.00
GN10 Jay Williams .50 1.25
GN11 Rashard Lewis .50 1.25
GN12 Michael Jordan 6.00 15.00
GN13 Tim Duncan 1.50 4.00
GN14 Vince Carter 1.25 3.00

2002-03 Upper Deck Game Night Jerseys
STATED ODDS 1:72 SER.2 H
GNJR Jason Richardson 3.00 8.00
GNJT Jamaal Tinsley 2.00 5.00
GNKB Kobe Bryant SP 40.00 100.00
GNKG Kevin Garnett 8.00 20.00
GNKM Karl Malone 6.00 15.00
GNMF Michael Finley 3.00 8.00
GNMM Mike Miller 2.50 6.00
GNRA Ray Allen 5.00 12.00
GNSM Shawn Marion 3.00 8.00

2002-03 Upper Deck Game Plan Jerseys
STATED ODDS 1:144 SER 1
BDGP Baron Davis 3.00 8.00
CMGP Corey Maggette 2.50 6.00
EBGP Elton Brand 2.50 6.00
ECGP Eddy Curry 2.00 5.00
GHGP Grant Hill 5.00 12.00
KMGP Karl Malone 6.00 15.00
SAGP Shareef Abdur-Rahim 3.00 8.00

2002-03 Upper Deck I Love L.A.
COMPLETE SET (14) 15.00 40.00
STATED ODDS 1:12 SER 1
LA1 Kobe Bryant 3.00 8.00
LA2 Shaquille O'Neal 2.00 5.00
LA3 Rick Fox 1.25 3.00
LA4 Robert Horry 1.25 3.00
LA5 Brian Shaw 1.25 3.00
LA6 Derek Fisher 1.25 3.00
LA7 Devean George 1.25 3.00
LA8 Stanislav Medvedenko 1.25 3.00
LA9 Mark Madsen 1.25 3.00
LA10 Samaki Walker 1.25 3.00
LA11 Shaquille O'Neal 2.00 5.00
LA12 Mitch Richmond 1.25 3.00
LA13 Kobe Bryant 3.00 8.00
LA14 Kobe Bryant 3.00 8.00

2002-03 Upper Deck MJ The Comeback
COMPLETE SET (7) 20.00 50.00
COMMON CARD (J1-J7) 4.00 10.00
STATED ODDS 1:24 SER 1

2002-03 Upper Deck New Wave
COMPLETE SET (14) 6.00 15.00
STATED ODDS 1:12 SER 1
NW1 Dirk Nowitzki 2.00 5.00
NW2 Wally Szczerbiak .60 1.50
NW3 Richard Jefferson .60 1.50
NW4 Mike Miller .60 1.50
NW5 Shawn Marion .75 2.00
NW6 Tyson Chandler .75 2.00
NW7 Baron Davis .75 2.00
NW8 Jamaal Tinsley .50 1.25
NW9 Rashard Lewis .60 1.50
NW10 Eddy Curry .50 1.25
NW11 Vince Carter 1.50 4.00
NW12 Shane Battier .75 2.00
NW13 Tony Parker 1.25 3.00
NW14 Eddie Griffin .50 1.25

2002-03 Upper Deck Practice Session Jerseys
STATED ODDS 1:72 SER 1
AJPS Antawn Jamison 2.50 6.00
AWPS Antoine Walker 2.50 6.00
CAPS Courtney Alexander 2.00 5.00
DAPS Darrell Armstrong 2.00 5.00
JTPS Jason Terry 2.50 6.00
KWPS Kwame Brown 2.00 5.00
SMPS Shawn Marion 3.00 8.00

2002-03 Upper Deck Rated PG
COMPLETE SET (7) 5.00 12.00
STATED ODDS 1:24 SER.2
PG1 Jay Williams .60 1.50
PG2 Tony Parker 1.25 3.00
PG3 Jason Kidd 1.25 3.00
PG4 Baron Davis .75 2.00
PG5 DaJuan Wagner .60 1.50
PG6 Steve Francis .75 2.00
PG7 Allen Iverson 2.00 5.00

2002-03 Upper Deck Rated PG Jerseys
STATED ODDS 1:960 SER.2 RET.
PGBD Baron Davis 4.00 10.00
PGDW DaJuan Wagner 3.00 8.00
PGJK Jason Kidd 6.00 15.00
PGJW Jay Williams 3.00 8.00
PGSM Stephon Marbury 5.00 12.00
PGTP Tony Parker 6.00 15.00

2002-03 Upper Deck Rookie Portfolio Jerseys
STATED ODDS 1:72 SER.2
RPAS Amare Stoudemire 8.00 20.00
RPCA Carlos Boozer 3.00 8.00
RPCB Caron Butler SP 3.00 8.00
RPCW Chris Wilcox 2.50 6.00
RPDG Drew Gooden 3.00 8.00
RPDW DaJuan Wagner 2.50 6.00
RPJD Juan Dixon 2.50 6.00
RPJJ Jared Jeffries 2.50 6.00
RPKR Kareem Rush 2.50 6.00
RPMH Marcus Haislip 2.00 5.00
RPNH Nene Hilario 3.00 8.00
RPNT Nikoloz Tskitishvili 2.00 5.00
RPPS Peja Stojakovic 2.50 6.00
RPQW Qyntel Woods 2.00 5.00
RPRH Ryan Humphrey 2.50 6.00
RPYM Yao Ming SP 15.00 40.00

2002-03 Upper Deck Scoring Threads
STATED ODDS 1:288
CARDS WITH "H" HOBBY, "R" RETAIL
AHST Allan Houston H 3.00 8.00
AWST Antoine Walker H 2.50 6.00
CWST Chris Webber H 4.00 10.00
SCAM Andre Miller R SP 2.50 6.00
SCJM Jamal Mashburn R 2.50 6.00
SCKB Kobe Bryant R SP 40.00 100.00
SCPP Paul Pierce R SP 5.00 12.00
SCRM Ron Mercer R 2.00 5.00
SCSM Shawn Marion R 3.00 8.00
SCTP Tony Parker R 5.00 12.00
SMST Stephon Marbury H 4.00 10.00

2002-03 Upper Deck Season Premier Jerseys
STATED ODDS 1:144 SER.2
CAP Caron Butler 3.00 8.00
CJP Casey Jacobsen 2.50 6.00
JEP Chris Jefferies 2.00 5.00
MTP Dikembe Mutombo 5.00 12.00
NTP Nikoloz Tskitishvili 2.00 5.00
RHP Richard Hamilton 4.00 10.00
TPP Tayshaun Prince 6.00 15.00

2002-03 Upper Deck Star Imports
COMPLETE SET (14) 10.00 25.00
STATED ODDS 1:12 SER.2
SI1 Yao Ming 4.00 10.00
SI2 Dirk Nowitzki 2.00 5.00
SI3 Pau Gasol 1.25 3.00
SI4 Peja Stojakovic .60 1.50
SI5 Nene Hilario .75 2.00
SI6 Tony Parker 1.25 3.00
SI7 Hedo Turkoglu .60 1.50
SI8 Nikoloz Tskitishvili .50 1.25
SI9 Andrei Kirilenko .60 1.50
SI10 Manu Ginobili 4.00 10.00
SI11 Steve Nash 1.50 4.00
SI12 Dikembe Mutombo 1.25 3.00
SI13 Marko Jaric .75 2.00
SI14 Tim Duncan 2.00 5.00

2002-03 Upper Deck Star Imports Jerseys
STATED ODDS 1:72 SER.2 HOB.
AKSI Andrei Kirilenko 2.50 6.00
DNSI Dirk Nowitzki 8.00 20.00
NHSI Nene Hilario 3.00 8.00
NTSI Nikoloz Tskitishvili 2.00 5.00
PGSI Pau Gasol 5.00 12.00
RFSI Rick Fox 2.00 5.00
TPSI Tony Parker SP 5.00 12.00
VDSI Vlade Divac 2.50 6.00
YMSI Yao Ming SP 15.00 40.00

2002-03 Upper Deck Super Swatches Jerseys
PRINT RUN 200 SERIAL #'d SETS
AIS Allen Iverson 12.00 30.00
ASS Amare Stoudemire 15.00 40.00
AWS Antoine Walker 5.00 12.00
CJS Casey Jacobsen 5.00 12.00
DWS DaJuan Wagner 5.00 12.00
FJS Fred Jones 5.00 12.00
JJS Jared Jeffries 5.00 12.00
JWS Jay Williams 5.00 12.00
KBS Kobe Bryant 50.00 125.00
KGS Kevin Garnett 15.00 40.00
MES Melvin Ely 5.00 12.00
MHS Marcus Haislip 4.00 10.00
QWS Qyntel Woods 4.00 10.00
RHS Ryan Humphrey 5.00 12.00
TMS Tracy McGrady 10.00 25.00
TPS Tayshaun Prince 12.00 30.00

2002-03 Upper Deck Triple Shooting Shirts
PRINT RUN 25 SERIAL #'d SETS
1 K.Bryant/M.Jordan/J.Williams 150.00 400.00
4 D.Wesley/B.Davis/J.Mashburn 20.00 50.00

2002-03 Upper Deck UD Game Jerseys 1
CARDS WITH "H" HOBBY, "R" RETAIL
AH Allan Houston H 3.00 8.00
KB Kobe Bryant H SP 40.00 100.00
MB Mike Bibby H 3.00 8.00
MC Antonio McDyess H 2.50 6.00
PG Pau Gasol H 5.00 12.00
RA Ron Artest H 2.50 6.00
AMRJ Aaron McKie R 2.00 5.00
JSRJ Joe Smith R 2.50 6.00
KBRJ Kobe Bryant R SP 75.00 200.00
MJRJ Michael Jordan R SP 100.00 200.00
RFRJ Rick Fox R 2.00 5.00
TBRJ Terrell Brandon R 2.00 5.00

2002-03 Upper Deck UD Game Jerseys 2
STATED ODDS 1:144 SER.2
GJAW Antoine Walker 2.50 6.00
GJCW Chris Wilcox 2.50 6.00
GJJR Jason Richardson 3.00 8.00
GJJS Jerry Stackhouse 3.00 8.00
GJJW Jay Williams SP 2.50 6.00
GJKB Kobe Bryant SP 40.00 100.00
GJWS Wally Szczerbiak 2.50 6.00

2002-03 Upper Deck UD Game Jerseys Autographs 1
PRINT RUN 275 SER.#'d SETS
AUCB Chauncey Billups 8.00 20.00
AUDS DeShawn Stevenson 6.00 15.00
AUJR Jason Richardson 8.00 20.00
AUKM Kenyon Martin 6.00 15.00
AUMB Mike Bibby 10.00 25.00
AUMB2 Mike Bibby 10.00 25.00
AUMM Mike Miller 12.00 30.00
AUPP Paul Pierce 15.00 40.00
AUQR Quentin Richardson 6.00 15.00
AURM Ron Mercer 6.00 15.00
AUTB Terrell Brandon 8.00 20.00
AUTC Tyson Chandler 12.00 30.00

2002-03 Upper Deck UD Game Jerseys Autographs 2
PRINT RUN 100 SERIAL #'d SETS
AUAW Antoine Walker 8.00 20.00
AUDG Drew Gooden 12.00 30.00
AUDS DeShawn Stevenson 8.00 20.00
AUDW DaJuan Wagner 8.00 20.00
AUET Etan Thomas 8.00 20.00
AUJK Jason Kidd 30.00 80.00
AUJM Jerome Moiso 8.00 20.00
AUJW Jay Williams 12.50 30.00
AUKB Kobe Bryant 125.00 300.00
AUKG Kevin Garnett 40.00 100.00
AUKM Kenyon Martin 12.00 30.00
AUMB Mike Bibby 12.50 30.00
AUMF Marcus Fizer 10.00 25.00
AUMM Mike Miller 10.00 25.00
AUPP Paul Pierce 25.00 60.00
AUTC Tyson Chandler 12.00 30.00

2002-03 Upper Deck UD Game Jerseys Combos 2
STATED ODDS 1:72 SER.2 HOB.
AIJR A.Iverson/J.Rose 8.00 20.00
BDJM B.Davis/J.Mashburn 5.00 12.00
DNSN D.Nowitzki/S.Nash 8.00 20.00
JWTC J.Williams/T.Chandler 5.00 12.00
KBJW K.Bryant/J.Williams 40.00 100.00
MBPS M.Bibby/P.Stojakovic 6.00 15.00
PGSB P.Gasol/S.Battier 5.00 12.00
PPAW P.Pierce/A.Walker 6.00 15.00
SMSM S.Marbury/S.Marion 5.00 12.00

2002-03 Upper Deck UD Game Jerseys Patch Logos 1
STATED ODDS 1:5000
AIPL Allen Iverson 50.00 120.00
JKPL Jason Kidd 40.00 100.00
JRPL Jason Richardson 25.00 60.00
KBPL Kobe Bryant 100.00 200.00
KGPL Kevin Garnett 50.00 120.00
MMPL Mike Miller 25.00 60.00
PSPL Peja Stojakovic 25.00 60.00
TMPL Tracy McGrady 50.00 120.00

2002-03 Upper Deck UD Game Jerseys Patch Logos 2
STATED ODDS 1:5000
AIPL Allen Iverson 50.00 120.00
JKPL Jason Kidd 40.00 100.00
KBPL Kobe Bryant 75.00 150.00
KGPL Kevin Garnett 50.00 120.00
TMPL Tracy McGrady 50.00 120.00

2002-03 Upper Deck UD Game Jerseys Patch Names 1
STATED ODDS 1:7500
AIPN Allen Iverson 60.00 150.00
JKPN Jason Kidd 40.00 100.00
KBPN Kobe Bryant 125.00 300.00
KGPN Kevin Garnett 50.00 120.00
MMPN Mike Miller 30.00 80.00
SFPN Steve Francis 30.00 80.00
TMPN Tracy McGrady 50.00 120.00

2002-03 Upper Deck UD Game Jerseys Patch Names 2
STATED ODDS 1:7500
AIPN Allen Iverson 60.00 150.00
CWPN Chris Webber 50.00 120.00
DNPN Dirk Nowitzki 75.00 150.00
KBPN Kobe Bryant 125.00 300.00
MJPN Michael Jordan 300.00 500.00
SFPN Steve Francis 40.00 100.00

2002-03 Upper Deck UD Game Jerseys Patch Numbers 1
STATED ODDS 1:2500
AIP Allen Iverson 40.00 100.00
JKP Jason Kidd 40.00 100.00
JRP Jason Richardson 20.00 50.00
KBP Kobe Bryant 75.00 150.00
KGP Kevin Garnett 40.00 100.00
MJP Michael Jordan 150.00 300.00
MMP Mike Miller 20.00 50.00
PSP Peja Stojakovic 20.00 50.00
SFP Steve Francis 20.00 50.00
TMP Tracy McGrady 20.00 50.00

2002-03 Upper Deck UD Game Jerseys Patch Numbers 2
STATED ODDS 1:2500 SER.2
AIP Allen Iverson 40.00 100.00
CWP Chris Webber 40.00 80.00
DNP Dirk Nowitzki 50.00 120.00
JKP Jason Kidd 40.00 100.00
JWP Jay Williams 20.00 50.00
KBP Kobe Bryant SP 75.00 150.00
KGP Kevin Garnett 40.00 100.00
SFP Steve Francis 20.00 50.00
TMP Tracy McGrady 40.00 100.00

2002-03 Upper Deck UD Playbook Jerseys
PRINT RUN 100 TOTAL SETS
JWH Jay Williams Gold 10.00 25.00
JWR Jay Williams Silver 10.00 25.00
KBH Kobe Bryant Gold 40.00 100.00
KBR Kobe Bryant Silver 50.00 120.00
MJH Michael Jordan Gold 125.00 250.00
MJR Michael Jordan Silver 125.00 250.00

2002-03 Upper Deck UD Playbook Jerseys Combos
KBJWH K.Bryant/J. Williams 40.00 100.00
MJJWH M.Jordan/J.Williams 100.00 250.00
MJKBH M.Jordan/K.Bryant 200.00 500.00

2002-03 Upper Deck Beckett UD Promos
*SINGLES: .75X TO 2X BASE UD HI
*NON RC ROOKIES: .4X TO 1X BASE UD HI

2003-04 Upper Deck
COMP.SET w/o SP's (300) 25.00 50.00
301-342 STATED ODDS 1:4
1 Shareef Abdur-Rahim .30 .75
2 Alan Henderson .20 .50
3 Dan Dickau .20 .50
4 Theo Ratliff .20 .50
5 Terrell Brandon .20 .50
6 Darvin Ham .25 .60
7 Nazr Mohammed .20 .50
8 Jason Terry .25 .60
9 Dion Glover .20 .50
10 Chris Crawford .20 .50
11 Paul Pierce .50 1.25
12 Antoine Walker .30 .75
13 Eric Williams .20 .50
14 Kedrick Brown .20 .50
15 Tony Battie .20 .50
16 Vin Baker .20 .50
17 Mark Blount .20 .50
18 Tony Delk .25 .60
19 Walter McCarty .20 .50
20 Jumaine Jones .20 .50
21 Jalen Rose .25 .60
22 Marcus Fizer .20 .50
23 Jamal Crawford .30 .75
24 Donyell Marshall .20 .50
25 Eddy Curry .20 .50
26 Trenton Hassell .20 .50
27 Michael Jordan 3.00 8.00
28 Tyson Chandler .25 .60
29 Jay Williams .20 .50
30 Scottie Pippen .75 2.00
31 Eddie Robinson .20 .50
32 Lonny Baxter .20 .50
33 Darius Miles .20 .50
34 DeSagana Diop .20 .50
35 Ricky Davis .25 .60
36 Chris Mihm .20 .50
37 Carlos Boozer .20 .50
38 Michael Stewart .20 .50
39 Zydrunas Ilgauskas .25 .60
40 Dajuan Wagner .20 .50
41 J.R. Bremer .20 .50
42 Kevin Ollie .20 .50
43 Dirk Nowitzki .75 2.00
44 Antawn Jamison .30 .75
45 Shawn Bradley .20 .50
46 Raef LaFrentz .20 .50
47 Eduardo Najera .20 .50
48 Travis Best .20 .50
49 Danny Fortson .20 .50
50 Michael Finley .30 .75
51 Jiri Welsch .20 .50
52 Steve Nash .60 1.50
53 Marcus Camby .25 .60
54 Chris Anderson .40 1.00
55 Rodney White .20 .50
56 Vincent Yarbrough .20 .50
57 Nikoloz Tskitishvili .20 .50
58 Nene .25 .60
59 Andre Miller .25 .60
60 Earl Boykins .25 .60
61 Ryan Bowen .20 .50
62 Ben Wallace .40 1.00
63 Tayshaun Prince .30 .75
64 Richard Hamilton .40 1.00
65 Mehmet Okur .25 .60
66 Bob Sura .20 .50
67 Chucky Atkins .20 .50
68 Chauncey Billups .40 1.00
69 Elden Campbell .20 .50
70 Corliss Williamson .20 .50
71 Zeljko Rebraca .20 .50
72 Jason Richardson .30 .75
73 Popeye Jones .20 .50
74 Clifford Robinson .20 .50
75 Mike Dunleavy .25 .60
76 Troy Murphy .30 .75
77 Speedy Claxton .20 .50
78 Erick Dampier .20 .50
79 Nick Van Exel .30 .75
80 Avery Johnson .25 .60
81 Adonal Foyle .20 .50
82 Pepe Sanchez .20 .50
83 Steve Francis .30 .75
84 Glen Rice .20 .50
85 Eddie Griffin .20 .50
86 Moochie Norris .20 .50
87 Maurice Taylor .20 .50
88 Kelvin Cato .20 .50
89 Jason Collier .20 .50
90 Cuttino Mobley .25 .60
91 Yao Ming .75 2.00
92 Eric Piatkowski .20 .50
93 Bostjan Nachbar .20 .50
94 Adrian Griffin .20 .50
95 Reggie Miller .60 1.50
96 Fred Jones .20 .50
97 Scot Pollard .20 .50
98 Jamaal Tinsley .20 .50
99 Al Harrington .25 .60
100 Jonathan Bender .20 .50
101 Primoz Brezec .20 .50
102 Ron Artest .30 .75
103 Jermaine O'Neal .30 .75
104 Kenny Anderson .25 .60
105 Jeff Foster .20 .50
106 Austin Croshere .20 .50
107 Elton Brand .25 .60
108 Tremaine Fowlkes .20 .50
109 Quentin Richardson .20 .50
110 Melvin Ely .20 .50
111 Marko Jaric .20 .50
112 Chris Wilcox .20 .50
113 Wang Zhizhi .30 .75
114 Corey Maggette .25 .60
115 Keyon Dooling .20 .50
116 Kobe Bryant 2.50 6.00
117 Shaquille O'Neal 1.25 3.00
118 Slava Medvedenko .20 .50
119 Gary Payton .50 1.25
120 Jannero Pargo .20 .50
121 Kareem Rush .20 .50
122 Karl Malone .60 1.50
123 Derek Fisher .30 .75
124 Rick Fox .25 .60
125 Devean George .20 .50
126 Pau Gasol .50 1.25
127 Jason Williams .50 1.25
128 Stromile Swift .20 .50
129 Wesley Person .20 .50
130 Michael Dickerson .20 .50
131 Lorenzen Wright .20 .50
132 Earl Watson .20 .50
133 Mike Miller .25 .60
134 Shane Battier .25 .60
135 Eddie Jones .30 .75
136 Rasual Butler .20 .50
137 Caron Butler .25 .60
138 Brian Grant .20 .50
139 Lamar Odom .25 .60
140 Malik Allen .20 .50
141 Ken Johnson .20 .50
142 Samaki Walker .20 .50
143 Sean Lampley .20 .50
144 Vladimir Stepania .20 .50
145 Erick Strickland .20 .50
146 Toni Kukoc .30 .75
147 Joel Przybilla .20 .50
148 Tim Thomas .20 .50
149 Dan Gadzuric .20 .50
150 Joe Smith .25 .60
151 Michael Redd .30 .75
152 Desmond Mason .25 .60
153 Brian Skinner .20 .50
154 Kevin Garnett .75 2.00
155 Michael Olowokandi .20 .50
156 Troy Hudson .20 .50
157 Latrell Sprewell .40 1.00
158 Wally Szczerbiak .20 .50
159 Sam Cassell .25 .60
160 Fred Hoiberg .20 .50
161 Ervin Johnson .20 .50
162 Mark Madsen .20 .50
163 Gary Trent .20 .50
164 Jason Kidd .50 1.25
165 Dikembe Mutombo .40 1.00
166 Lucious Harris .20 .50
167 Kerry Kittles .25 .60
168 Brandon Armstrong .20 .50
169 Jason Collins .20 .50
170 Alonzo Mourning .40 1.00
171 Kenyon Martin .30 .75
172 Richard Jefferson .25 .60
173 Rodney Rogers .20 .50
174 Aaron Williams .20 .50
175 Jamal Mashburn .25 .60
176 David Wesley .20 .50
177 Kirk Haston .30 .75
178 Courtney Alexander .20 .50
179 Darrell Armstrong .20 .50
180 Robert Traylor .20 .50
181 George Lynch .20 .50
182 Jamaal Magloire .20 .50
183 Baron Davis .20 .50
184 P.J. Brown .20 .50
185 Sean Rooks .20 .50
186 Stacey Augmon .20 .50
187 Allan Houston .30 .75
188 Antonio McDyess .25 .60
189 Clarence Weatherspoon .20 .50
190 Kurt Thomas .20 .50
191 Shandon Anderson .20 .50
192 Keith Van Horn .25 .60
193 Michael Doleac .20 .50
194 Othella Harrington .20 .50
195 Charlie Ward .20 .50
196 Lee Nailon .20 .50
197 Tracy McGrady .50 1.25
198 Pat Garrity .20 .50
199 Grant Hill .40 1.00
200 Gordan Giricek .20 .50
201 Steven Hunter .20 .50
202 Jeryl Sasser .20 .50
203 Andrew DeClercq .20 .50
204 Juwan Howard .20 .50
205 Tyronn Lue .20 .50
206 Drew Gooden .25 .60
207 Marc Jackson .20 .50
208 Aaron McKie .20 .50
209 Derrick Coleman .30 .75
210 Eric Snow .20 .50
211 Glenn Robinson .25 .60
212 Greg Buckner .20 .50
213 Allen Iverson .75 2.00
214 Kenny Thomas .20 .50
215 Sam Clancy .20 .50
216 Monty Williams .20 .50
217 Stephon Marbury .40 1.00
218 Shawn Marion .20 .50
219 Joe Johnson .25 .60
220 Bo Outlaw .20 .50
221 Amare Stoudemire .40 1.00
222 Casey Jacobsen .20 .50
223 Tom Gugliotta .20 .50
224 Scott Williams .20 .50
225 Jake Tsakalidis .20 .50
226 Damon Stoudamire .25 .60
227 Arvydas Sabonis .25 .60
228 Zach Randolph .30 .75
229 Ruben Patterson .20 .50
230 Derek Anderson .25 .60
231 Dale Davis .20 .50
232 Bonzi Wells .20 .50
233 Rasheed Wallace .40 1.00
234 Jeff McInnis .20 .50
235 Qyntel Woods .20 .50
236 Chris Webber .40 1.00
237 Doug Christie .25 .60
238 Vlade Divac .30 .75
239 Bobby Jackson .25 .60
240 Lawrence Funderburke .20 .50
241 Peja Stojakovic .25 .60
242 Gerald Wallace .25 .60
243 Brad Miller .25 .60
244 Mike Bibby .30 .75
245 Anthony Peeler .20 .50
246 Jim Jackson .20 .50
247 David Robinson .60 1.50
248 Ron Mercer .20 .50
249 Tony Parker .50 1.25
250 Malik Rose .20 .50
251 Kevin Willis .20 .50
252 Manu Ginobili .60 1.50
253 Bruce Bowen .25 .60
254 Hedo Turkoglu .25 .60
255 Tim Duncan .75 2.00
256 Robert Horry .30 .75
257 Radoslav Nesterovic .20 .50
258 Ray Allen .50 1.25
259 Rashard Lewis .25 .60
260 Reggie Evans .20 .50
261 Brent Barry .20 .50
262 Ronald Murray .20 .50
263 Vladimir Radmanovic .20 .50
264 Predrag Drobnjak .20 .50
265 Antonio Daniels .20 .50
266 Vitaly Potapenko .20 .50
267 Calvin Booth .20 .50
268 Vince Carter .60 1.50
269 Chris Jefferies .20 .50
270 Mengke Bateer .30 .75
271 Alvin Williams .20 .50
272 Jerome Williams .30 .75
273 Michael Bradley .20 .50
274 Lamond Murray .20 .50
275 Antonio Davis .25 .60
276 Morris Peterson .25 .60
277 Jerome Moiso .20 .50
278 Carlos Arroyo .25 .60
279 Matt Harpring .20 .50
280 Andrei Kirilenko .25 .60
281 Jarron Collins .20 .50
282 Greg Ostertag .20 .50
283 Curtis Borchardt .20 .50
284 DeShawn Stevenson .25 .60
285 Keon Clark .25 .60
286 John Amaechi .20 .50
287 Raul Lopez .20 .50
288 Jerry Stackhouse .40 1.00
289 Kwame Brown .20 .50
290 Larry Hughes .25 .60
291 Brendan Haywood .20 .50
292 Juan Dixon .20 .50
293 Bryon Russell .20 .50
294 Christian Laettner .25 .60
295 Jahidi White .20 .50
296 Jared Jeffries .20 .50
297 Gilbert Arenas .30 .75
298 Kobe Bryant CL 1.25 3.00
299 Michael Jordan CL 1.50 4.00
300 Michael Jordan CL 1.50 4.00
301 LeBron James RC 75.00 200.00
302 Darko Milicic RC 1.00 2.50
303 Carmelo Anthony RC 6.00 15.00
304 Chris Bosh RC 4.00 10.00
305 Dwyane Wade RC 10.00 25.00
306 Chris Kaman RC 1.25 3.00
307 Kirk Hinrich RC 1.25 3.00
308 T.J. Ford RC 1.00 2.50
309 Mike Sweetney RC .75 2.00
310 Jarvis Hayes RC .75 2.00
311 Mickael Pietrus RC 1.00 2.50
312 Nick Collison RC 1.00 2.50
313 Marcus Banks RC .75 2.00
314 Luke Ridnour RC 1.25 3.00
315 Reece Gaines RC .75 2.00
316 Troy Bell RC .75 2.00
317 Zarko Cabarkapa RC .75 2.00
318 David West RC 1.50 4.00
319 Aleksandar Pavlovic RC 1.00 2.50
320 Dahntay Jones RC 1.00 2.50
321 Boris Diaw RC 1.25 3.00
322 Zoran Planinic RC .75 2.00
323 Travis Outlaw RC 1.00 2.50
324 Brian Cook RC .75 2.00
325 Kirk Penney RC 1.00 2.50
326 Ndudi Ebi RC .75 2.00
327 Kendrick Perkins RC 1.00 2.50
328 Leandro Barbosa RC 1.25 3.00
329 Josh Howard RC 1.25 3.00
330 Maciej Lampe RC .75 2.00
331 Jason Kapono RC .75 2.00
332 Luke Walton RC 1.25 3.00
333 Jerome Beasley RC .75 2.00
334 Brandon Hunter RC .75 2.00
335 Kyle Korver RC 1.50 4.00
336 Travis Hansen RC .75 2.00
337 Steve Blake RC 1.00 2.50
338 Slavko Vranes RC .75 2.00
339 Zaur Pachulia RC 1.25 3.00
340 Keith Bogans RC .75 2.00
341 Willie Green RC 1.25 3.00
342 Maurice Williams RC 1.25 3.00

2003-04 Upper Deck Gold
*1-297 GOLD SINGLES: 5X TO 12X BASE HI
*298-300 GOLD CL: 10X TO 25X BASE HI
*301-342 GOLD RCs: 2X TO 5X BASE HI
GOLD PRINT RUN 100 SER.#'d SETS
301 LeBron James 2,500.00 5,000.00
305 Dwyane Wade 500.00 1,000.00

2003-04 Upper Deck Rainbow
*1-297 RAINBOW: 8X TO 20X BASE HI
*298-300 RAINBOW: 15X TO 40X BASE HI
*301-342 RAINBOW: 3X TO 8X BASE CARD HI
RAINBOW PRINT RUN 25 SER.#'d SETS
27 Michael Jordan 75.00 150.00
301 LeBron James 5,000.00 10,000.00
305 Dwyane Wade 1,500.00 3,000.00

2003-04 Upper Deck Air Academy
COMPLETE SET (42) 50.00 120.00
STATED ODDS 1:4 H/R SER.1
AA1 Michael Jordan 12.00 30.00
AA2 Kobe Bryant 3.00 8.00
AA3 LeBron James 25.00 60.00
AA4 Vince Carter .75 2.00
AA5 Shaquille O'Neal 1.50 4.00
AA6 Richard Jefferson .30 .75
AA7 Jason Richardson .40 1.00
AA8 Paul Pierce .60 1.50
AA9 Michael Finley .40 1.00
AA10 Steve Francis .40 1.00
AA11 Shareef Abdur-Rahim .40 1.00
AA12 Desmond Mason .30 .75
AA13 Latrell Sprewell .50 1.25
AA14 Baron Davis .40 1.00
AA15 Glenn Robinson .30 .75
AA16 Joe Johnson .30 .75
AA17 Rasheed Wallace .50 1.25
AA18 Gerald Wallace .30 .75
AA19 Rashard Lewis .30 .75
AA20 Jamaal Tinsley .25 .60
AA21 Karl Malone .75 2.00
AA22 Jerry Stackhouse .50 1.25
AA23 Gilbert Arenas .40 1.00
AA24 Boris Diaw .40 1.00
AA25 Josh Howard .40 1.00
AA26 Antoine Walker .40 1.00
AA27 Darius Miles .25 .60
AA28 Darko Milicic .30 .75
AA29 Carmelo Anthony 2.00 5.00
AA30 Chris Bosh 1.25 3.00
AA31 Dwyane Wade 3.00 8.00
AA32 Mike Sweetney .25 .60
AA33 Jarvis Hayes .25 .60
AA34 Mickael Pietrus .30 .75
AA35 Nick Collison .30 .75
AA36 Elton Brand .30 .75
AA37 David West .50 1.25
AA38 Aleksandar Pavlovic .30 .75
AA39 Zarko Cabarkapa .25 .60
AA40 Travis Outlaw .30 .75
AA41 Brian Cook .25 .60
AA42 Ndudi Ebi .25 .60

2003-04 Upper Deck All-Star Weekend Authentics
STATED ODDS 1:144 H/R SER.1
ASAK Andrei Kirilenko 2.00 5.00
ASBM Brad Miller 2.00 5.00
ASBW Ben Wallace 3.00 8.00
ASCB Carlos Boozer 2.00 5.00
ASCB Caron Butler 2.00 5.00
ASDG Drew Gooden 2.00 5.00
ASDN Dirk Nowitzki 6.00 15.00
ASGG Gordan Giricek 2.00 5.00
ASGP Gary Payton 4.00 10.00
ASJA Marko Jaric 2.00 5.00
ASJK Jason Kidd 4.00 10.00
ASJM Jamal Mashburn 2.00 5.00
ASJO Jermaine O'Neal 2.50 6.00
ASJT Jamaal Tinsley 2.00 5.00
ASJW Jay Williams 2.00 5.00
ASKB Kobe Bryant 10.00 25.00
ASKG Kevin Garnett 6.00 15.00
ASNH Nene 2.00 5.00
ASPG Pau Gasol 4.00 10.00
ASPS Peja Stojakovic 2.00 5.00
ASSF Steve Francis 2.50 6.00
ASSM Stephon Marbury 4.00 10.00
ASSN Steve Nash 5.00 12.00
ASTC Tyson Chandler 2.00 5.00
ASTD Tim Duncan 6.00 15.00
ASTM Tracy McGrady 4.00 10.00
ASTP Tony Parker 4.00 10.00
ASYM Yao Ming 6.00 15.00
ASZI Zydrunas Ilgauskas 2.00 5.00

2003-04 Upper Deck All-Star Weekend Authentics Dual
STATED ODDS 1:144 H/R SER.1
BMBW B.Miller/B.Wallace 4.00 10.00
CBDW C.Boozer/D.Wagner 4.00 10.00
DGGG D.Gooden/G.Giricek 4.00 10.00
DMJR D.Mason/J.Richardson 4.00 10.00
JWTC J.Williams/T.Chandler 4.00 10.00
KBKG K.Bryant/K.Garnett 10.00 25.00
KBMJ K.Bryant/M.Jordan 30.00 80.00
NHAK Nene/A.Kirilenko 4.00 10.00
PPAW P.Pierce/A.Walker 4.00 10.00
SFYM S.Francis/Y.Ming 5.00 12.00
SMSM S.Marion/S.Marbury 4.00 10.00
TMJO T.McGrady/J.O'Neal 5.00 12.00

2003-04 Upper Deck Black Diamond Rookies F/X
STATED ODDS 1:288 H/R SER.1
BD1 LeBron James 600.00 1,200.00
BD2 Darko Milicic 5.00 12.00
BD3 Carmelo Anthony 30.00 80.00
BD4 Chris Bosh 20.00 50.00
BD5 Dwyane Wade 60.00 150.00
BD6 Chris Kaman 6.00 15.00
BD7 Kirk Hinrich 6.00 15.00
BD8 T.J. Ford 5.00 12.00
BD9 Mike Sweetney 4.00 10.00
BD10 Jarvis Hayes 4.00 10.00
BD11 Mickael Pietrus 5.00 12.00
BD12 Nick Collison 5.00 12.00
BD13 Marcus Banks 4.00 10.00
BD14 Luke Ridnour 6.00 15.00
BD15 Reece Gaines 4.00 10.00
BD16 Troy Bell 4.00 10.00
BD17 Zarko Cabarkapa 4.00 10.00
BD18 David West 8.00 20.00
BD19 Aleksandar Pavlovic 5.00 12.00
BD20 Dahntay Jones 5.00 12.00
BD21 Boris Diaw 6.00 15.00
BD22 Zoran Planinic 4.00 10.00
BD23 Travis Outlaw 5.00 12.00
BD24 Brian Cook 4.00 10.00
BD25 Kirk Penney 5.00 12.00
BD26 Ndudi Ebi 4.00 10.00
BD27 Kendrick Perkins 5.00 12.00
BD28 Leandro Barbosa 6.00 15.00
BD29 Josh Howard 6.00 15.00
BD30 Maciej Lampe 4.00 10.00
BD31 Jason Kapono 4.00 10.00
BD32 Luke Walton 6.00 15.00
BD33 Jerome Beasley 4.00 10.00
BD34 Brandon Hunter 4.00 10.00
BD35 Kyle Korver 8.00 20.00
BD36 Travis Hansen 4.00 10.00
BD37 Steve Blake 5.00 12.00
BD38 Slavko Vranes 4.00 10.00
BD39 Zaur Pachulia 6.00 15.00
BD40 Keith Bogans 4.00 10.00
BD41 Willie Green 6.00 15.00
BD42 Maurice Williams 6.00 15.00

2003-04 Upper Deck East Coast/West Coast Jerseys
STATED ODDS 1:36 H SER.1
BATB M.Banks/T.Bell 4.00 10.00
BLAJ S.Blake/A.Jamison 4.00 10.00
DEMF D.Mason/M.Finley 4.00 10.00
JOMC J.O'Neal/M.Olowokandi 4.00 10.00
JTMB J.Terry/M.Bibby 4.00 10.00
KPNE K.Perkins/N.Ebi 4.00 10.00
KVLW K.Van Horn/L.Walton 4.00 10.00
KWHT Kw.Brown/H.Turkoglu 4.00 10.00
MJKB M.Jordan/K.Bryant 50.00 120.00
MPJR M.Peterson/J.Richardson 4.00 10.00
RGCO R.Gaines/B.Cook 4.00 10.00
RHDJ R.Hamilton/D.Jones 4.00 10.00
SAPG S.Abdur-Rahim/P.Gasol 4.00 10.00
TISB J.Tinsely/S.Battier 4.00 10.00

2003-04 Upper Deck LeBron's Diary
COMPLETE SET (15) 60.00 150.00
COMMON LEBRON (1-15) 8.00 20.00
ONE PER SER.1 RETAIL

2003-04 Upper Deck Rookie Review Jerseys
STATED ODDS 1:96 H SER.1
RRAS Amare Stoudemire 3.00 8.00
RRCB Caron Butler 2.00 5.00
RRCJ Casey Jacobsen 2.00 5.00
RRCW Chris Wilcox 2.00 5.00
RRDG Dan Gadzuric 2.00 5.00
RRDG Drew Gooden 2.00 5.00
RRDW DaJuan Wagner 2.00 5.00
RRJD Juan Dixon 2.00 5.00
RRJJ Jared Jeffries 2.00 5.00
RRJS John Salmons 2.00 5.00
RRKR Kareem Rush 2.00 5.00
RRQW Qyntel Woods 2.00 5.00
RRRA Robert Archibald 2.00 5.00
RRYM Yao Ming 6.00 15.00

2003-04 Upper Deck SE Die Cut All-Stars
COMPLETE SET (15) 2,000.00 3,500.00
STATED ODDS 1:288 H SER.1
*BLACK: .75X TO 2X BASE HI
BLACK PRINT RUN 25 SER.#'d SETS
SE1 Michael Jordan 1,200.00 2,500.00
SE2 Kobe Bryant 150.00 400.00
SE3 Shaquille O'Neal 75.00 200.00
SE4 Vince Carter 50.00 120.00
SE5 Ray Allen 30.00 80.00
SE6 Kevin Garnett 60.00 150.00
SE7 Jason Kidd 30.00 80.00
SE8 Paul Pierce 25.00 60.00
SE9 Dirk Nowitzki 75.00 200.00
SE10 Ben Wallace 20.00 50.00
SE11 Tracy McGrady 30.00 80.00
SE12 Allen Iverson 125.00 300.00
SE13 Gary Payton 30.00 80.00
SE14 Elton Brand 15.00 40.00
SE15 Tim Duncan 75.00 200.00

2003-04 Upper Deck SE Die Cut Future All-Stars
COMPLETE SET (15) 200.00 500.00
STATED ODDS 1:24 H SER.1
*BLACK: 1X TO 2.5X BASE HI
BLACK PRINT RUN 25 SER.#'d SETS
E1 Nick Collison 2.50 6.00
E2 Dahntay Jones 2.50 6.00
E3 Zarko Cabarkapa 2.00 5.00
E4 Marcus Banks 2.00 5.00
E5 Mickael Pietrus 2.50 6.00
E6 Jarvis Hayes 2.00 5.00
E7 Mike Sweetney 2.00 5.00
E8 T.J. Ford 2.50 6.00
E9 Kirk Hinrich 3.00 8.00
E10 Chris Kaman 3.00 8.00
E11 Dwyane Wade 75.00 200.00
E12 Chris Bosh 10.00 25.00
E13 Carmelo Anthony 15.00 40.00
E14 Darko Milicic 2.50 6.00
E15 LeBron James 400.00 800.00

2003-04 Upper Deck SE Die Cut Future All-Stars Black
E11 Dwyane Wade 300.00 600.00
E15 LeBron James 10,000.00 20,000.00

2003-04 Upper Deck Shooting Stars Jerseys
STATED ODDS 1:96 H/R SER.1
SSDW David Wesley 2.00 5.00
SSGG Gordan Giricek 2.00 5.00
SSJA Jamaal Magloire 2.00 5.00
SSJT Jason Terry 2.00 5.00
SSKV Keith Van Horn 2.00 5.00
SSMM Mike Miller 2.00 5.00
SSPS Peja Stojakovic 2.00 5.00
SSRH Richard Hamilton 3.00 8.00
SSRM Reggie Miller 5.00 12.00
SSSS Steve Smith 2.00 5.00
SSTB Terrell Brandon 2.00 5.00
SSTK Toni Kukoc 2.50 6.00
SSWP Wesley Person 2.00 5.00
SSWS Wally Szczerbiak 2.00 5.00

2003-04 Upper Deck Super Swatches
PRINT RUN 250 SER.#'d SETS
AISS Allen Iverson 15.00 40.00

AMSS Antonio McDyess 5.00 12.00
ASSS Amare Stoudemire 8.00 20.00
BDSS Baron Davis 6.00 15.00
CMSS Corey Maggette 5.00 12.00
DMSS Darius Miles 4.00 10.00
DWSS Dajuan Wagner 4.00 10.00
EBSS Elton Brand 5.00 12.00
ECSS Eddy Curry 4.00 10.00
GHSS Grant Hill 8.00 20.00
JMSS Jamal Mashburn 5.00 12.00
JOSS Joe Smith 5.00 12.00
JPSS James Posey 4.00 10.00
KBSS Kobe Bryant 20.00 50.00
LOSS Lamar Odom 5.00 12.00
MJSS Michael Jordan 50.00 120.00
SPSS Scottie Pippen 15.00 40.00
TESS Jason Terry 5.00 12.00

2003-04 Upper Deck UD Game Jerseys

STATED ODDS 1:288 H/R SER.1
GJ1 Caron Butler 2.00 5.00
GJ2 Gilbert Arenas 2.50 6.00
GJ3 Mike Bibby 2.50 6.00
GJ4 Tony Parker 4.00 10.00
GJ5 Manu Ginobili 5.00 12.00
GJ6 Darius Miles 1.50 4.00
GJ7 David Robinson 5.00 12.00
GJ8 Allen Iverson 6.00 15.00
GJ9 Kenyon Martin 2.50 6.00
GJ10 Eddie Jones 2.50 6.00
GJ11 Eddy Curry 1.50 4.00
GJ12 Jalen Rose 2.00 5.00
GJ13 Antawn Jamison 2.50 6.00
GJ14 Lamar Odom 2.00 5.00
GJ15 Karl Malone 5.00 12.00
GJ16 Jamal Mashburn 2.00 5.00
GJ17 Richard Jefferson 2.00 5.00
GJ18 Shaquille O'Neal 10.00 25.00
GJ19 LeBron James 150.00 400.00
GJ20 Kobe Bryant 100.00 250.00
GJ21 Michael Jordan 150.00 400.00
GJ22 Speedy Claxton 1.50 4.00

2003-04 Upper Deck UD Game Jerseys Autographs

PRINT RUN 100 SER.#'d SETS
1 Kobe Bryant 1,500.00 3,000.00
2 Paul Pierce 40.00 100.00
3 Jason Kidd 40.00 100.00
4 Etan Thomas 8.00 20.00
5 Jerome Moiso 8.00 20.00
6 Shawn Marion 12.00 30.00
7 Mike Bibby 12.00 30.00
8 Peja Stojakovic 10.00 25.00
9 Chauncey Billups 15.00 40.00
10 Richard Hamilton 15.00 40.00
11 Richard Jefferson 10.00 25.00
12 Jason Richardson 12.00 30.00
13 Tony Parker 40.00 100.00
14 David Robinson 40.00 100.00
15 Jalen Rose 10.00 25.00
16 Corey Maggette 10.00 25.00
17 Jamaal Tinsley 8.00 20.00
18 Yao Ming 25.00 60.00
19 Drew Gooden 10.00 25.00
20 Caron Butler 10.00 25.00
21 Manu Ginobili 150.00 400.00
22 Marko Jaric 8.00 20.00
23 Wang Zhizhi 100.00 250.00
24 Tracy McGrady 150.00 400.00
25 Morris Peterson 8.00 20.00
27 Amare Stoudemire 15.00 40.00
28 Dajuan Wagner 8.00 20.00
30 Steve Francis 12.00 30.00
31 Andre Miller 10.00 25.00
32 Shane Battier 10.00 25.00
34 Dan Dickau 8.00 20.00
35 Earl Boykins 10.00 25.00
36 Jerry Stackhouse 15.00 40.00
37 Gilbert Arenas 12.00 30.00
38 Lamar Odom 10.00 25.00
40 Antawn Jamison 12.00 30.00
41 Kevin Garnett 100.00 250.00
26 Carlos Boozer 10.00 25.00
29 Eddie Griffin 8.00 20.00
33 Cuttino Mobley 8.00 20.00
42 DerMarr Johnson 8.00 20.00

2003-04 Upper Deck UD Game Jerseys Patches Logo

STATED ODDS 1:5000 H/R SER.1
ASPL Amare Stoudemire 15.00 40.00
CWPL Chris Webber 15.00 40.00
GHPL Grant Hill 20.00 50.00
KVPL Keith Van Horn 10.00 25.00
TDPL Tim Duncan 30.00 80.00

2003-04 Upper Deck UD Game Jerseys Patches Name

STATED ODDS 1:7500 H/R SER.1
AJPN Antawn Jamison 15.00 40.00
DRPN David Robinson 30.00 80.00
KBPN Kobe Bryant 125.00 300.00
KVPN Keith Van Horn 12.00 30.00
MJPN Michael Jordan 250.00 500.00

2003-04 Upper Deck UD Game Jerseys Patches Numbers

STATED ODDS 1:2500 H/R SER.1
AWPN Antoine Walker 10.00 25.00
DRPN David Robinson 20.00 50.00
KBPN Kobe Bryant 80.00 200.00
KMPN Kenyon Martin 10.00 25.00
KVPN Keith Van Horn 8.00 20.00
MJPN Michael Jordan 200.00 350.00
SNPN Steve Nash 20.00 50.00
TDPN Tim Duncan 25.00 60.00

2004-05 Upper Deck

COMPLETE SET (230) 60.00 120.00
COMP.SET w/o SP's (200) 20.00 40.00
201-220 RC STATED ODDS 1:4
221-230 RC STATED ODDS 1:20
1 Antoine Walker .30 .75
2 Boris Diaw .25 .60
3 Al Harrington .25 .60
4 Tony Delk .20 .50
5 Jason Collier .20 .50
6 Chris Crawford .20 .50
7 Ricky Davis .25 .60
8 Paul Pierce .50 1.25
9 Jiri Welsch .20 .50
10 Gary Payton .50 1.25
11 Rick Fox .20 .50
12 Mark Blount .20 .50
13 Adrian Griffin .20 .50
14 Tyson Chandler .25 .60
15 Eddy Curry .25 .60
16 Kirk Hinrich .30 .75
17 Scottie Pippen .75 2.00
18 Jannero Pargo .20 .50
19 Antonio Davis .20 .50
20 Gerald Wallace .25 .60
21 Eddie House .20 .50
22 Steve Smith .25 .60
23 Brandon Hunter .20 .50
24 Theron Smith .20 .50
25 Jahidi White .20 .50
26 LeBron James 2.50 6.00
27 DeSagana Diop .20 .50
28 Zydrunas Ilgauskas .25 .60
29 Dajuan Wagner .25 .60
30 Jeff McInnis .20 .50
31 Eric Snow .20 .50
32 Dirk Nowitzki .75 2.00
33 Jason Terry .25 .60
34 Michael Finley .30 .75
35 Jerry Stackhouse .30 .75
36 Erick Dampier .20 .50
37 Josh Howard .25 .60
38 Marquis Daniels .20 .50
39 Carmelo Anthony .60 1.50
40 Nene .25 .60
41 Andre Miller .25 .60
42 Earl Boykins .25 .60
43 Marcus Camby .25 .60
44 Voshon Lenard .20 .50
45 Kenyon Martin .30 .75
46 Richard Hamilton .40 1.00
47 Chauncey Billups .40 1.00
48 Rasheed Wallace .40 1.00
49 Tayshaun Prince .30 .75
50 Ben Wallace .40 1.00
51 Antonio McDyess .25 .60
52 Carlos Delfino .20 .50
53 Jason Richardson .30 .75
54 Dale Davis .20 .50
55 Adonal Foyle .20 .50
56 Mickael Pietrus .20 .50
57 Mike Dunleavy .20 .50
58 Speedy Claxton .20 .50
59 Derek Fisher .25 .60
60 Yao Ming .75 2.00
61 Jim Jackson .25 .60
62 Tracy McGrady .50 1.25
63 Maurice Taylor .20 .50
64 Juwan Howard .20 .50
65 Tyronn Lue .20 .50
66 Dikembe Mutombo .30 .75
67 Reggie Miller .60 1.50
68 Stephen Jackson .20 .50
69 Jermaine O'Neal .25 .60
70 Jamaal Tinsley .25 .60
71 Ron Artest .30 .75
72 Fred Jones .30 .75
73 Jonathan Bender .20 .50
74 Kerry Kittles .25 .60
75 Chris Kaman .25 .60
76 Elton Brand .25 .60
77 Marko Jaric .20 .50
78 Corey Maggette .25 .60
79 Bobby Simmons .20 .50
80 Chris Wilcox .20 .50
81 Lamar Odom .25 .60
82 Karl Malone .60 1.50
83 Kobe Bryant 2.50 6.00
84 Kareem Rush .20 .50
85 Caron Butler .25 .60
86 Devean George .20 .50
87 Vlade Divac .20 .50
88 Pau Gasol .50 1.25
89 Bonzi Wells .25 .60
90 Mike Miller .25 .60
91 Jason Williams .20 .50
92 Shane Battier .25 .60
93 James Posey .25 .60
94 Stromile Swift .20 .50
95 Shaquille O'Neal 1.25 3.00
96 Dwyane Wade 1.25 3.00
97 Eddie Jones .30 .75
98 Wang Zhizhi .30 .75
99 Rasual Butler .20 .50
100 Malik Allen .20 .50
101 Udonis Haslem .20 .50
102 Michael Redd .25 .60
103 T.J. Ford .20 .50
104 Keith Van Horn .25 .60
105 Toni Kukoc .30 .75
106 Desmond Mason .25 .60
107 Mike James .20 .50
108 Joe Smith .25 .60
109 Kevin Garnett .75 2.00
110 Michael Olowokandi .20 .50
111 Sam Cassell .25 .60
112 Troy Hudson .20 .50
113 Latrell Sprewell .40 1.00
114 Fred Hoiberg .20 .50
115 Wally Szczerbiak .25 .60
116 Richard Jefferson .25 .60
117 Alonzo Mourning .40 1.00
118 Jason Kidd .50 1.25
119 Jacque Vaughn .20 .50
120 Jason Collins .20 .50
121 Aaron Williams .20 .50
122 Zoran Planinic .20 .50
123 Jamaal Magloire .20 .50
124 P.J. Brown .20 .50
125 Baron Davis .30 .75
126 Darrell Armstrong .20 .50
127 Jamal Mashburn .25 .60
128 Rodney Rogers .20 .50
129 David Wesley .20 .50
130 Allan Houston .30 .75
131 Jamal Crawford .30 .75
132 Stephon Marbury .40 1.00
133 Tim Thomas .20 .50
134 Anfernee Hardaway .75 2.00
135 Kurt Thomas .20 .50
136 Mike Sweetney .20 .50
137 Tony Battie .20 .50
138 DeShawn Stevenson .20 .50
139 Steve Francis .30 .75
140 Cuttino Mobley .25 .60
141 Hedo Turkoglu .25 .60
142 Keith Bogans .20 .50
143 Samuel Dalembert .20 .50
144 Kenny Thomas .20 .50
145 Allen Iverson .75 2.00
146 Aaron McKie .20 .50
147 Glenn Robinson .25 .60
148 Willie Green .30 .75
149 Corliss Williamson .20 .50
150 Shawn Marion .30 .75
151 Leandro Barbosa .25 .60
152 Amare Stoudemire .30 .75
153 Quentin Richardson .25 .60
154 Joe Johnson .25 .60
155 Steve Nash .60 1.50
156 Damon Stoudamire .30 .75
157 Theo Ratliff .20 .50
158 Shareef Abdur-Rahim .30 .75
159 Derek Anderson .25 .60
160 Zach Randolph .30 .75
161 Nick Van Exel .30 .75
162 Darius Miles .20 .50
163 Mike Bibby .30 .75
164 Brad Miller .25 .60
165 Peja Stojakovic .25 .60
166 Bobby Jackson .25 .60
167 Chris Webber .40 1.00
168 Darius Songaila .20 .50
169 Doug Christie .25 .60
170 Manu Ginobili .60 1.50
171 Brent Barry .20 .50
172 Tony Parker .50 1.25
173 Malik Rose .20 .50
174 Tim Duncan .75 2.00
175 Radoslav Nesterovic .20 .50
176 Bruce Bowen .25 .60
177 Rashard Lewis .25 .60
178 Vladimir Radmanovic .20 .50
179 Ray Allen .50 1.25
180 Antonio Daniels .20 .50
181 Ronald Murray .20 .50
182 Luke Ridnour .25 .60
183 Vince Carter .60 1.50
184 Donyell Marshall .20 .50
185 Chris Bosh .50 1.25
186 Morris Peterson .20 .50
187 Jalen Rose .20 .50
188 Rafer Alston .20 .50
189 Carlos Arroyo .20 .50
190 Matt Harpring .20 .50
191 Andrei Kirilenko .25 .60
192 Carlos Boozer .25 .60
193 Gordan Giricek .20 .50
194 Mehmet Okur .25 .60
195 Antawn Jamison .25 .60
196 Larry Hughes .25 .60
197 Gilbert Arenas .30 .75
198 Kwame Brown .20 .50
199 Jarvis Hayes .20 .50
200 Juan Dixon .20 .50
201 Rafael Araujo RC .75 2.00
202 Luke Jackson RC .75 2.00
203 Andris Biedrins RC .75 2.00
204 Robert Swift RC .75 2.00
205 Kris Humphries RC 1.00 2.50
206 Al Jefferson RC 1.25 3.00
207 Kirk Snyder RC .75 2.00
208 J.R. Smith RC 1.25 3.00
209 Dorell Wright RC 1.00 2.50
210 Jameer Nelson RC 1.25 3.00
211 Pavel Podkolzin RC .75 2.00
212 Viktor Khryapa RC .75 2.00
213 Sergei Monia RC .75 2.00
214 Delonte West RC 1.00 2.50
215 Tony Allen RC 1.25 3.00
216 Kevin Martin RC 1.50 4.00
217 Sasha Vujacic RC 1.00 2.50
218 Beno Udrih RC 1.00 2.50
219 David Harrison RC .75 2.00
220 Chris Duhon RC 1.00 2.50
221 Josh Smith SP RC 1.50 4.00
222 Sebastian Telfair SP RC 1.25 3.00
223 Andre Iguodala SP RC 2.50 6.00
224 Dwight Howard SP RC 5.00 12.00
225 Emeka Okafor SP RC 1.25 3.00
226 Ben Gordon SP RC 1.50 4.00
227 Shaun Livingston SP RC 1.50 4.00
228 Devin Harris SP RC 1.25 3.00
229 Josh Childress SP RC 1.00 2.50
230 Luol Deng SP RC 1.50 4.00

2004-05 Upper Deck UD Promos

*PROMOS: .75X TO 2X BASIC

2004-05 Upper Deck Exclusives

*1-200: 4X TO 10X BASE HI
*201-220: 1.25X TO 3X BASE HI
*221-230: 1X TO 2.5X BASE HI
PRINT RUN 100 SER.#'d SETS
26 LeBron James 40.00 100.00

2004-05 Upper Deck Exclusives Spectrum

*1-200: 10X TO 25X BASE HI
*201-220: 2.5X TO 6X BASE HI
*221-230: 2X TO 5X BASE HI
PRINT RUN 25 SER.#'d SETS
26 LeBron James 100.00 250.00

2004-05 Upper Deck All-Star Weekend Authentics

STATED ODDS 1:48
AK Andrei Kirilenko 2.00 5.00
AL Ray Allen 4.00 10.00
AS Amare Stoudemire 2.50 6.00
BD Baron Davis 2.50 6.00
BM Brad Miller 2.00 5.00
BW Ben Wallace 3.00 8.00
CA Carlos Boozer 2.00 5.00
CB Chauncey Billups SP 4.00 10.00
CH Chris Bosh SP 5.00 12.00
CK Chris Kaman 2.00 5.00
CM Cuttino Mobley 2.00 5.00
DF Derek Fisher 2.00 5.00
EB Earl Boykins 2.00 5.00
EG Manu Ginobili 5.00 12.00
FJ Fred Jones 2.00 5.00
JH Jarvis Hayes 2.00 5.00
JM Jamaal Magloire 2.00 5.00
JO Josh Howard 2.00 5.00
JR Jason Richardson 2.50 6.00
KB Kobe Bryant 40.00 100.00
KK Kyle Korver 2.00 5.00
KM Kenyon Martin 2.50 6.00
LJ LeBron James SP 25.00 60.00
MD Mike Dunleavy 1.50 4.00
MJ Marko Jaric SP 2.00 5.00
NH Nene 2.00 5.00
PP Paul Pierce 4.00 10.00
PS Peja Stojakovic 2.00 5.00
RA Ron Artest 2.50 6.00
RL Rashard Lewis 2.00 5.00
RM Ronald Murray 2.00 5.00
SC Sam Cassell 2.00 5.00
SF Steve Francis 2.50 6.00
SM Stephon Marbury 3.00 8.00
TD Tim Duncan 6.00 15.00
UH Udonis Haslem 1.50 4.00
VL Voshon Lenard 2.00 5.00
YM Yao Ming 6.00 15.00

2004-05 Upper Deck All-Star Weekend Authentics Dual

STATED ODDS 1:288 HOBBY
AC R.Allen/S.Cassell 6.00 15.00
FB D.Fisher/C.Billups 5.00 12.00
GN M.Ginobili/Nene 5.00 12.00
HH U.Haslem/J.Howard 5.00 12.00
JB L.James/C.Boozer SP 15.00 40.00
JR F.Jones/J.Richardson 5.00 12.00
KH K.Korver/J.Hayes 5.00 12.00
LB V.Lenard/E.Boykins 5.00 12.00
ML R.Murray/R.Lewis 5.00 12.00
NL Nene/V.Lenard 5.00 12.00

2004-05 Upper Deck All-Star Weekend Authentics Triple

STATED ODDS 1:288 HOBBY
AI Allen Iverson 12.00 30.00
DN Dirk Nowitzki 12.00 30.00
JK Jason Kidd 8.00 20.00
KB Kobe Bryant 75.00 200.00
KG Kevin Garnett 12.00 30.00
KK Kyle Korver 4.00 10.00
LJ LeBron James SP 20.00 50.00
MD Mike Dunleavy 3.00 8.00
RL Rashard Lewis 4.00 10.00
SO Shaquille O'Neal SP 20.00 50.00
TM Tracy McGrady 3.00 8.00

2004-05 Upper Deck East Coast West Coast

STATED ODDS 1:288 HOBBY
BN C.Billups/S.Nash 6.00 15.00
CR E.Curry/Z.Randolph 5.00 12.00
JB L.James/K.Bryant SP 125.00 300.00
JM R.Jefferson/C.Maggette 5.00 12.00
MB R.Miller/M.Bibby 6.00 15.00
MG D.Mason/M.Ginobili 5.00 12.00
MR K.Martin/Q.Richardson 5.00 12.00
PB P.Pierce/E.Brand 6.00 15.00
WA R.Wallace/S.Abdur-Rahim 5.00 12.00

2004-05 Upper Deck Flight Team

COMPLETE SET (50) 15.00 40.00
STATED ODDS 1:4
*RAINBOW: 12X TO 30X BASE HI
RAINBOW STATED ODDS 1:1000 PACKS
FT1 Scottie Pippen 1.00 2.50
FT2 Lamar Odom .40 1.00
FT3 Andrei Kirilenko .30 .75
FT4 Dirk Nowitzki .60 1.50
FT5 Michael Redd .30 .75
FT6 Kobe Bryant 3.00 8.00
FT7 Jermaine O'Neal .30 .75
FT8 Shawn Marion .40 1.00
FT9 Antawn Jamison .30 .75
FT10 Kevin Garnett 1.00 2.50
FT11 Michael Finley .40 1.00
FT12 Latrell Sprewell .50 1.25
FT13 Richard Hamilton .50 1.25
FT14 Al Harrington .30 .75
FT15 Dwyane Wade 1.50 4.00
FT16 Shaquille O'Neal 1.50 4.00
FT17 Chris Webber .50 1.25
FT18 Rasheed Wallace .50 1.25
FT19 Kenyon Martin .40 1.00
FT20 Ben Wallace .50 1.25
FT21 Baron Davis .40 1.00
FT22 Mickael Pietrus .25 .60
FT23 Stephon Marbury .50 1.25
FT24 Ricky Davis .30 .75
FT25 Pau Gasol .60 1.50
FT26 Tim Duncan 1.00 2.50
FT27 Gilbert Arenas .40 1.00
FT28 Bonzi Wells .30 .75
FT29 Chris Bosh .60 1.50
FT30 Carmelo Anthony .75 2.00
FT31 Yao Ming 1.00 2.50
FT32 Tracy McGrady .60 1.50
FT33 Michael Jordan 3.00 8.00
FT34 Fred Jones .25 .60
FT35 Amare Stoudemire .40 1.00
FT36 Dajuan Wagner .25 .60
FT37 Desmond Mason .30 .75
FT38 Jerry Stackhouse .40 1.00
FT39 Caron Butler .30 .75
FT40 Quentin Richardson .25 .60
FT41 Shareef Abdur-Rahim .40 1.00
FT42 Vince Carter .75 2.00
FT43 Corey Maggette .30 .75
FT44 Peja Stojakovic .30 .75
FT45 LeBron James 3.00 8.00
FT46 Steve Francis .40 1.00
FT47 Allen Iverson 1.00 2.50
FT48 Ray Allen .60 1.50
FT49 Elton Brand .30 .75
FT50 Darius Miles .25 .60

2004-05 Upper Deck Flight Team Onyx

CARDS #'d TO PLAYER JERSEY
FT1 Scottie Pippen/33 25.00 60.00
FT3 Andrei Kirilenko/47 8.00 20.00
FT4 Dirk Nowitzki/41 25.00 60.00
FT5 Michael Redd/22 8.00 20.00
FT26 Tim Duncan/21 50.00 120.00
FT38 Jerry Stackhouse/42 10.00 25.00
FT44 Peja Stojakovic/16 8.00 20.00
FT45 LeBron James/23 400.00 800.00
FT48 Ray Allen/34 15.00 40.00

2004-05 Upper Deck Majestic Materials

STATED ODDS 1:288 HOBBY
AH Al Harrington 5.00 12.00
AL Allan Houston 6.00 15.00
AN Anfernee Hardaway 15.00 40.00
BM Brad Miller 5.00 12.00
BW Bonzi Wells 4.00 10.00
CB Caron Butler 5.00 12.00
CM Corey Maggette 5.00 12.00
CU Cuttino Mobley 5.00 12.00
DA Darko Milicic 4.00 10.00
DM Darius Miles 4.00 10.00
DW Dajuan Wagner 4.00 10.00
ES Eric Snow 4.00 10.00
GA Gilbert Arenas 6.00 15.00
GG Gordan Giricek 4.00 10.00
JC Jamal Crawford 6.00 15.00
JH Juwan Howard 5.00 12.00
JJ Joe Johnson 5.00 12.00
JM Jamaal Magloire 4.00 10.00
JP James Posey 5.00 12.00
JS Joe Smith 5.00 12.00
JT Jason Terry 5.00 12.00
KK Kerry Kittles 5.00 12.00
KV Keith Van Horn 5.00 12.00
KW Kwame Brown 4.00 10.00
LJ LeBron James SP 20.00 50.00
LO Lamar Odom 6.00 15.00
LS Latrell Sprewell 6.00 15.00
MO Michael Olowokandi 4.00 10.00
MP Morris Peterson 4.00 10.00
QR Quentin Richardson 4.00 10.00
RH Richard Hamilton 8.00 20.00
SB Shane Battier 5.00 12.00
SD Samuel Dalembert 4.00 10.00
SF Steve Francis 6.00 15.00
SM Shawn Marion 6.00 15.00
TC Tyson Chandler 5.00 12.00
TT Tim Thomas 4.00 10.00
WS Wally Szczerbiak 5.00 12.00
ZI Zydrunas Ilgauskas 5.00 12.00
ZR Zach Randolph 6.00 15.00

2004-05 Upper Deck March Memories

STATED ODDS 1:72 HOBBY
AW Antoine Walker 3.00 8.00
BG Ben Gordon 3.00 8.00
CB Carlos Boozer 2.50 6.00
CW Chris Wilcox 2.00 5.00
GH Grant Hill 4.00 10.00
JD Juan Dixon 2.00 5.00
JM Jamaal Magloire 2.00 5.00
JR Jason Richardson 3.00 8.00
JT Jason Terry 2.50 6.00
MA Magic Johnson SP 40.00 100.00
MB Mike Bibby 3.00 8.00
MD Mike Dunleavy 2.00 5.00
MP Morris Peterson 2.00 5.00
RH Richard Hamilton 4.00 10.00
SB Shane Battier 2.50 6.00

2004-05 Upper Deck Rookie Academy

COMPLETE SET (30) 25.00 60.00
STATED ODDS 1:24
RA1 Rafael Araujo .60 1.50
RA2 Luke Jackson .60 1.50
RA3 Andris Biedrins .60 1.50
RA4 Robert Swift .60 1.50
RA5 Kris Humphries .75 2.00
RA6 Al Jefferson 1.00 2.50
RA7 Kirk Snyder .60 1.50
RA8 J.R. Smith 1.00 2.50
RA9 Dorell Wright .75 2.00
RA10 Jameer Nelson 1.00 2.50
RA11 Pavel Podkolzin .60 1.50
RA12 Viktor Khryapa .60 1.50
RA13 Nenad Krstic .75 2.00
RA14 Delonte West .75 2.00
RA15 Tony Allen 1.00 2.50
RA16 Kevin Martin 1.25 3.00
RA17 Sasha Vujacic .75 2.00
RA18 Beno Udrih .75 2.00
RA19 David Harrison .60 1.50
RA20 Andre Emmett .60 1.50
RA21 Josh Smith 1.00 2.50
RA22 Sebastian Telfair .75 2.00
RA23 Andre Iguodala 1.50 4.00
RA24 Dwight Howard 3.00 8.00
RA25 Emeka Okafor 1.00 2.50
RA26 Ben Gordon 1.00 2.50
RA27 Shaun Livingston 1.00 2.50
RA28 Devin Harris .75 2.00
RA29 Josh Childress .60 1.50
RA30 Luol Deng 1.00 2.50

2004-05 Upper Deck Rookie Academy Onyx

CARDS #'d TO PLAYER JERSEY
RA3 Andris Biedrins/15 3.00 8.00
RA16 Kevin Martin/23 6.00 15.00
RA27 Shaun Livingston/14 5.00 12.00

2004-05 Upper Deck Rookie Review

STATED ODDS 1:48
BD Boris Diaw 2.00 5.00
CA Carmelo Anthony SP 8.00 20.00
CB Chris Bosh 4.00 10.00
CK Chris Kaman 2.00 5.00
DA David West 2.00 5.00
DJ Dahntay Jones 2.00 5.00
DM Darko Milicic 2.00 5.00
JH Jarvis Hayes 2.00 5.00
JO Josh Howard 2.00 5.00
KB Keith Bogans 2.00 5.00
LB Leandro Barbosa SP 2.00 5.00
LJ LeBron James SP 15.00 40.00
LR Luke Ridnour 2.00 5.00
LW Luke Walton 2.00 5.00
MB Marcus Banks 2.00 5.00
MP Mickael Pietrus 1.50 4.00
MS Mike Sweetney 2.00 5.00
NE Ndudi Ebi 2.00 5.00
RG Reece Gaines 2.00 5.00
SB Steve Blake 2.00 5.00

2004-05 Upper Deck Rookie Scrapbook

COMPLETE SET (30) 6.00 15.00
STATED ODDS ONE PER RETAIL PACK
RS1 Rafael Araujo .20 .50
RS2 Luke Jackson .20 .50
RS3 Andris Biedrins .20 .50
RS4 Robert Swift .20 .50
RS5 Kris Humphries .25 .60
RS6 Al Jefferson .30 .75
RS7 Kirk Snyder .20 .50
RS8 J.R. Smith .30 .75
RS9 Dorell Wright .25 .60
RS10 Jameer Nelson .30 .75
RS11 Pavel Podkolzin .20 .50
RS12 Viktor Khryapa .20 .50
RS13 Nenad Krstic .25 .60
RS14 Delonte West .25 .60
RS15 Tony Allen .30 .75
RS16 Kevin Martin .40 1.00
RS17 Sasha Vujacic .25 .60
RS18 Beno Udrih .25 .60
RS19 David Harrison .20 .50
RS20 Andre Emmett .20 .50
RS21 Josh Smith .30 .75
RS22 Sebastian Telfair .25 .60
RS23 Andre Iguodala .50 1.25
RS24 Dwight Howard 1.00 2.50
RS25 Emeka Okafor .25 .60
RS26 Ben Gordon .30 .75
RS27 Shaun Livingston .30 .75
RS28 Devin Harris .25 .60
RS29 Josh Childress .20 .50
RS30 Luol Deng .30 .75

2004-05 Upper Deck UD Game Jerseys

STATED ODDS 1:72 HOBBY
AH Allan Houston 3.00 8.00
AJ Antawn Jamison 2.50 6.00
AK Andrei Kirilenko 2.50 6.00
AM Andre Miller 2.50 6.00
BA Marcus Banks 2.00 5.00
BD Baron Davis 3.00 8.00
BW Ben Wallace 4.00 10.00
CB Caron Butler 2.50 6.00
CW Chris Webber 4.00 10.00
DA Darko Milicic 2.00 5.00
DE Desmond Mason 2.50 6.00
DM Darius Miles 2.00 5.00
DS Damon Stoudamire 3.00 8.00
DW Dajuan Wagner 2.00 5.00
EB Elton Brand 2.50 6.00
GA Gilbert Arenas 3.00 8.00
GP Gary Payton 5.00 12.00
JO Jermaine O'Neal 2.50 6.00
JS Jerry Stackhouse 3.00 8.00
JT Jason Terry 2.50 6.00
KM Karl Malone 6.00 15.00
LJ LeBron James SP 25.00 60.00
LO Lamar Odom 3.00 8.00
LS Latrell Sprewell 4.00 10.00
MB Mike Bibby 3.00 8.00
MF Michael Finley 3.00 8.00
MJ Michael Jordan SP 75.00 200.00
MR Michael Redd 2.50 6.00
PG Pau Gasol 5.00 12.00
PS Peja Stojakovic 2.50 6.00
RJ Richard Jefferson 2.50 6.00
RM Reggie Miller 6.00 15.00
RW Rasheed Wallace 4.00 10.00
SA Shareef Abdur-Rahim 3.00 8.00
SM Shawn Marion 3.00 8.00
SN Steve Nash 6.00 15.00
SP Scottie Pippen 8.00 20.00
TP Tony Parker 5.00 12.00
VD Vlade Divac 3.00 8.00
YM Yao Ming 8.00 20.00

2004-05 Upper Deck UD Game Jerseys Autographs

PRINT RUN 25 TO 100 SER.#'d SETS
AJ Antawn Jamison/100 10.00 25.00
AK Andrei Kirilenko/100 15.00 40.00
BD Baron Davis/100 10.00 25.00
BM Brad Miller/100 8.00 20.00
CB Carlos Boozer/100 10.00 25.00
DF Derek Fisher/100 15.00 40.00
DM Darko Milicic/100 8.00 20.00
JS Jerry Stackhouse/100 12.00 30.00
LJ LeBron James/25 5,000.00 10,000.00
MB Mike Bibby/100 8.00 20.00
MJ Michael Jordan/25 10,000.00 15,000.00
MR Michael Redd/100 10.00 25.00
PPO Paul Pierce/25 125.00 300.00
RM Reggie Miller/100 200.00 500.00
SC Sam Cassell/100 10.00 25.00
SM Stephon Marbury/25 15.00 40.00
TM Tracy McGrady/25 40.00 100.00
ZR Zach Randolph/100 10.00 25.00

2004-05 Upper Deck UD Game Jerseys Patches Logos

STATED ODDS 1:5000
CA Carmelo Anthony 25.00 60.00
DN Dirk Nowitzki 30.00 80.00
JK Jason Kidd 20.00 50.00
KB Kobe Bryant 75.00 200.00
KG Kevin Garnett 30.00 80.00
SO Shaquille O'Neal 40.00 100.00

2004-05 Upper Deck UD Game Jerseys Patches Names

STATED ODDS 1:7500
CA Carmelo Anthony 30.00 80.00
JK Jason Kidd 25.00 60.00
MJ Michael Jordan 250.00 400.00
PP Paul Pierce 25.00 60.00
TD Tim Duncan 40.00 100.00
TM Tracy McGrady 25.00 60.00

2004-05 Upper Deck UD Game Jerseys Patches Numbers

STATED ODDS 1:2500
AI Allen Iverson 25.00 60.00
JK Jason Kidd 15.00 40.00
KB Kobe Bryant 150.00 400.00
KG Kevin Garnett 25.00 60.00
MJ Michael Jordan SP 150.00 400.00
SO Shaquille O'Neal 40.00 100.00
TD Tim Duncan 25.00 60.00

2005-06 Upper Deck

COMP.SET w/o SP's (200) 20.00 40.00
210-220 RC STATED ODDS 1:4
221-230 RC STATED ODDS 1:20
1 Josh Childress .20 .50
2 Josh Smith .25 .60
3 Al Harrington .25 .60
4 Tyronn Lue .20 .50
5 Boris Diaw .25 .60
6 Tony Delk .20 .50
7 Paul Pierce .50 1.25
8 Antoine Walker .25 .60
9 Gary Payton .50 1.25
10 Al Jefferson .20 .50
11 Tony Allen .20 .50
12 Ricky Davis .25 .60
13 Delonte West .20 .50
14 Emeka Okafor .25 .60
15 Primoz Brezec .20 .50
16 Kareem Rush .20 .50
17 Gerald Wallace .25 .60
18 Brevin Knight .20 .50
19 Jason Kapono .20 .50
20 Kirk Hinrich .25 .60
21 Ben Gordon .25 .60
22 Eddy Curry .20 .50
23 Michael Jordan 2.50 6.00
24 Andres Nocioni .20 .50
25 Chris Duhon .20 .50
26 Luol Deng .25 .60
27 LeBron James 2.50 6.00
28 Zydrunas Ilgauskas .25 .60
29 Drew Gooden .20 .50
30 Jeff McInnis .20 .50
31 Dajuan Wagner .20 .50
32 Larry Hughes .25 .60
33 Robert Traylor .20 .50
34 Dirk Nowitzki .75 2.00
35 Michael Finley .30 .75
36 Jerry Stackhouse .25 .60
37 Josh Howard .25 .60
38 Marquis Daniels .20 .50
39 Devin Harris .20 .50
40 Jason Terry .25 .60
41 Carmelo Anthony .50 1.25
42 Kenyon Martin .25 .60
43 Andre Miller .25 .60
44 Earl Boykins .25 .60
45 Nene .25 .60
46 Marcus Camby .25 .60
47 Ben Wallace .40 1.00
48 Richard Hamilton .40 1.00
49 Chauncey Billups .40 1.00
50 Rasheed Wallace .30 .75
51 Tayshaun Prince .30 .75
52 Carlos Arroyo .25 .60
53 Antonio McDyess .25 .60
54 Jason Richardson .30 .75
55 Baron Davis .30 .75
56 Troy Murphy .20 .50
57 Mickael Pietrus .20 .50
58 Derek Fisher .30 .75
59 Mike Dunleavy .20 .50
60 Yao Ming .60 1.50
61 Tracy McGrady .50 1.25
62 David Wesley .20 .50
63 Bob Sura .20 .50
64 Mike James .20 .50
65 Jon Barry .20 .50
66 Jermaine O'Neal .25 .60
67 Ron Artest .25 .60
68 Stephen Jackson .25 .60
69 Jamaal Tinsley .25 .60
70 Dale Davis .20 .50
71 Anthony Johnson .20 .50
72 Elton Brand .25 .60
73 Corey Maggette .25 .60
74 Bobby Simmons .25 .60
75 Marko Jaric .20 .50
76 Shaun Livingston .25 .60
77 Chris Kaman .25 .60
78 Chris Wilcox .20 .50
79 Kobe Bryant 2.50 6.00
80 Caron Butler .25 .60
81 Lamar Odom .25 .60
82 Chucky Atkins .20 .50
83 Brian Cook .20 .50
84 Devean George .20 .50
85 Sasha Vujacic .25 .60
86 Pau Gasol .50 1.25
87 Mike Miller .25 .60
88 Jason Williams .50 1.25
89 Shane Battier .25 .60
90 Bonzi Wells .20 .50
91 James Posey .20 .50
92 Stromile Swift .20 .50
93 Shaquille O'Neal 1.00 2.50
94 Dwyane Wade .60 1.50
95 Eddie Jones .25 .60
96 Udonis Haslem .20 .50
97 Damon Jones .20 .50
98 Alonzo Mourning .40 1.00
99 Keyon Dooling .20 .50
100 Michael Redd .25 .60
101 Desmond Mason .20 .50
102 Maurice Williams .25 .60
103 Joe Smith .25 .60
104 Toni Kukoc .30 .75
105 Dan Gadzuric .20 .50
106 T.J. Ford .20 .50
107 Kevin Garnett .75 2.00
108 Sam Cassell .25 .60

109 Latrell Sprewell .30 .75
110 Wally Szczerbiak .25 .60
111 Troy Hudson .20 .50
112 Eddie Griffin .20 .50
113 Jason Kidd .50 1.25
114 Richard Jefferson .25 .60
115 Vince Carter .60 1.50
116 Nenad Krstic .20 .50
117 Scott Padgett .20 .50
118 Jason Collins .20 .50
119 Jamaal Magloire .20 .50
120 J.R. Smith .30 .75
121 Speedy Claxton .20 .50
122 Lee Nailon .20 .50
123 P.J. Brown .20 .50
124 Chris Andersen .30 .75
125 Stephon Marbury .40 1.00
126 Jamal Crawford .30 .75
127 Allan Houston .25 .60
128 Trevor Ariza .20 .50
129 Quentin Richardson .20 .50
130 Tim Thomas .20 .50
131 Michael Sweetney .20 .50
132 Dwight Howard .40 1.00
133 Steve Francis .30 .75
134 Grant Hill .50 1.25
135 Jameer Nelson .20 .50
136 Hedo Turkoglu .25 .60
137 Doug Christie .20 .50
138 DeShawn Stevenson .20 .50
139 Allen Iverson .60 1.50
140 Chris Webber .40 1.00
141 Andre Iguodala .30 .75
142 Samuel Dalembert .20 .50
143 Kyle Korver .25 .60
144 Willie Green .20 .50
145 Marc Jackson .20 .50
146 Steve Nash .60 1.50
147 Amare Stoudemire .30 .75
148 Joe Johnson .25 .60
149 Shawn Marion .25 .60
150 Kurt Thomas .20 .50
151 Jim Jackson .20 .50
152 Leandro Barbosa .25 .60
153 Damon Stoudamire .30 .75
154 Shareef Abdur-Rahim .30 .75
155 Zach Randolph .30 .75
156 Darius Miles .20 .50
157 Sebastian Telfair .25 .60
158 Theo Ratliff .20 .50
159 Nick Van Exel .30 .75
160 Peja Stojakovic .25 .60
161 Mike Bibby .30 .75
162 Brad Miller .25 .60
163 Cuttino Mobley .20 .50
164 Bobby Jackson .25 .60
165 Kenny Thomas .20 .50
166 Corliss Williamson .20 .50
167 Tim Duncan .75 2.00
168 Tony Parker .50 1.25
169 Manu Ginobili .60 1.50
170 Robert Horry .30 .75
171 Beno Udrih .20 .50
172 Nazr Mohammed .20 .50
173 Brent Barry .25 .60
174 Ray Allen .50 1.25
175 Rashard Lewis .25 .60
176 Ronald Murray .20 .50
177 Luke Ridnour .25 .60
178 Vladimir Radmanovic .20 .50
179 Antonio Daniels .20 .50
180 Danny Fortson .20 .50
181 Chris Bosh .40 1.00
182 Donyell Marshall .20 .50
183 Jalen Rose .25 .60
184 Morris Peterson .20 .50
185 Rafer Alston .25 .60
186 Matt Bonner .20 .50
187 Aaron Williams .20 .50
188 Andrei Kirilenko .25 .60
189 Carlos Boozer .25 .60
190 Matt Harpring .20 .50
191 Keith McLeod .20 .50
192 Raja Bell .25 .60
193 Raul Lopez .20 .50
194 Gordan Giricek .20 .50
195 Gilbert Arenas .30 .75
196 Antawn Jamison .25 .60
197 Jarvis Hayes .20 .50
198 Brendan Haywood .20 .50
199 Juan Dixon .20 .50
200 Etan Thomas .20 .50
201 Daniel Ewing RC 1.00 2.50
202 Nate Robinson RC 1.25 3.00
203 C.J. Miles RC 1.00 2.50
204 Salim Stoudamire RC 1.00 2.50
205 Francisco Garcia RC .75 2.00
206 Julius Hodge RC .75 2.00
207 Andrew Bynum RC 1.00 2.50
208 Joey Graham RC 1.00 2.50
209 Johan Petro RC .75 2.00
210 Luther Head RC .75 2.00
211 Channing Frye RC 1.00 2.50
212 Sean May RC .75 2.00
213 Wayne Simien RC .75 2.00
214 Antoine Wright RC 1.00 2.50
215 Ike Diogu RC .75 2.00
216 Jarrett Jack RC 1.25 3.00
217 Jason Maxiell RC 1.00 2.50
218 David Lee RC 1.25 3.00
219 Travis Diener RC .75 2.00
220 Danny Granger RC 1.25 3.00
221 Charlie Villanueva SP RC 1.50 4.00
222 Hakim Warrick SP RC 1.50 4.00
223 Rashad McCants SP RC 1.25 3.00
224 Raymond Felton SP RC 1.50 4.00
225 Martell Webster SP RC 1.50 4.00
226 Gerald Green SP RC 2.00 5.00
227 Deron Williams SP RC 3.00 8.00
228 Andrew Bogut SP RC 2.50 6.00
229 Marvin Williams SP RC 2.00 5.00
230 Chris Paul SP RC 10.00 25.00

2005-06 Upper Deck Gold

*1-200 GOLD: 4X TO 10X BASE HI
201-220 RC GOLD: 1.25X TO 3X BASE HI
221-230 RC GOLD: .75X TO 2X BASE HI
GOLD PRINT RUN 50 SER.#'d SETS

2005-06 Upper Deck Silver

*1-200 SILVER: 2.5X TO 6X BASE HI
201-220 RC SILVER: .75X TO 2X BASE HI
221-230 RC SILVER: .5X TO 1.25X BASE HI
SILVER PRINT RUN 100 SER.#'d SETS

2005-06 Upper Deck All-Star Weekend Authentics

APPROXIMATELY ONE PER BOX
AJ Antawn Jamison 2.50 6.00
AL Al Jefferson 2.00 5.00
AM Andre Miller 2.50 6.00
AN Andre Iguodala 3.00 8.00
AS Amare Stoudemire 3.00 8.00
BG Ben Gordon 2.50 6.00
BU Beno Udrih 2.00 5.00
BW Ben Wallace 4.00 10.00
CA Carmelo Anthony 5.00 12.00
CB Chris Bosh 4.00 10.00
DE Devin Harris 2.00 5.00
DN Dirk Nowitzki 8.00 20.00
GA Gilbert Arenas 3.00 8.00
GH Grant Hill 5.00 12.00
JH Josh Howard 2.50 6.00
JJ Joe Johnson 2.50 6.00
JO Jermaine O'Neal 2.50 6.00
JR J.R. Smith 3.00 8.00
JS Josh Smith 2.50 6.00
KB Kobe Bryant 40.00 100.00
KG Kevin Garnett 8.00 20.00
KH Kirk Hinrich 2.50 6.00
KK Kyle Korver 2.50 6.00
LD Luol Deng 2.50 6.00
LJ LeBron James 12.50 30.00
LR Luke Ridnour 2.50 6.00
MG Manu Ginobili 6.00 15.00
PP Paul Pierce 5.00 12.00
QR Quentin Richardson 2.00 5.00
RA Ray Allen 5.00 12.00
RL Rashard Lewis 2.50 6.00
SM Shawn Marion 2.50 6.00
SN Steve Nash 6.00 15.00
SO Shaquille O'Neal 10.00 25.00
TA Tony Allen 2.00 5.00
TD Tim Duncan 8.00 20.00
TM Tracy McGrady 5.00 12.00
UH Udonis Haslem 2.00 5.00
YM Yao Ming 6.00 15.00
ZI Zydrunas Ilgauskas 2.50 6.00

2005-06 Upper Deck Game Jerseys

APPROXIMATELY ONE PER BOX
AD Antonio Davis 1.50 4.00
AH Allan Houston 2.00 5.00
AJ Antawn Jamison 2.00 5.00
AK Andrei Kirilenko 2.00 5.00
AM Andre Miller 2.00 5.00
AN Antoine Walker 2.00 5.00
AS Amare Stoudemire 2.50 6.00
AW Aaron Williams 1.50 4.00
BB Bruce Bowen 2.00 5.00
BD Baron Davis 2.50 6.00
BG Ben Gordon 2.50 6.00
BH Brendan Haywood 1.50 4.00
BN Bostjan Nachbar 1.50 4.00
BO Boris Diaw 2.00 5.00
BR Bryon Russell 1.50 4.00
BW Ben Wallace 3.00 8.00
BZ Carlos Boozer 2.00 5.00
CA Carmelo Anthony 4.00 10.00
CA Chris Anderson 2.50 6.00
CB Caron Butler 2.00 5.00
CH Chauncey Billups 3.00 8.00
CJ Andris Biedrins 1.50 4.00
CM Chris Mihm 1.50 4.00
CO Corey Maggette 2.00 5.00
CU Cuttino Mobley 1.50 4.00
CW Charlie Ward 1.50 4.00
DA David Wesley 1.50 4.00
DF Derek Fisher 2.50 6.00
DG Drew Gooden 2.00 5.00
DH Dwight Howard 3.00 8.00
DM Darius Miles 1.50 4.00
DN Dirk Nowitzki 6.00 15.00
DO Donyell Marshall 1.50 4.00
DS DeShawn Stevenson 1.50 4.00
DW Dajuan Wagner 1.50 4.00
EB Elton Brand 2.00 5.00
ES Eric Snow 1.50 4.00
GA Gilbert Arenas 2.50 6.00
GE Devean George 1.50 4.00
GH Grant Hill 4.00 10.00
GP Gary Payton 4.00 10.00
HA Devin Harris 1.50 4.00
JA Jamal Crawford 2.50 6.00
JC Jason Collins 1.50 4.00
JK Jason Kidd 4.00 10.00
JL Jalen Rose 2.00 5.00
JM Jeff McInnis 1.50 4.00
JO Jermaine O'Neal 2.00 5.00
JR Jason Richardson 2.50 6.00
JT Jason Terry 2.00 5.00
KB Kobe Bryant 50.00 120.00
KD Keyon Dooling 1.50 4.00
KG Kevin Garnett 6.00 15.00
KH Kirk Hinrich 2.00 5.00
KK Kerry Kittles 1.50 4.00
KM Kenyon Martin 2.00 5.00
KP Kendrick Perkins 2.00 5.00
KR Kareem Rush 1.50 4.00
KT Kurt Thomas 1.50 4.00
LD Luol Deng 2.00 5.00
LF Luis Flores 1.50 4.00
LJ LeBron James 15.00 40.00
LO Lamar Odom 2.00 5.00
LU Luke Jackson 1.50 4.00
LW Luke Walton 1.50 4.00
LZ Raul Lopez 1.50 4.00
MA Mark Blount 1.50 4.00
MB Mike Bibby 2.50 6.00
MG Manu Ginobili 5.00 12.00
MI Michael Finley 2.50 6.00
MJ Michael Jordan 60.00 150.00
MP Michael Pietrus 1.50 4.00
MU Troy Murphy 1.50 4.00
NH Nene 2.00 5.00
PG Pau Gasol 4.00 10.00
PP Paul Pierce 4.00 10.00
PS Peja Stojakovic 2.00 5.00
QR Quentin Richardson 1.50 4.00
RA Ray Allen 4.00 10.00
RB Ryan Bowen 1.50 4.00
RH Richard Hamilton 3.00 8.00
RJ Richard Jefferson 2.00 5.00
RL Rashard Lewis 2.00 5.00
RO Ron Artest 2.00 5.00
RW Rasheed Wallace 2.50 6.00
SA Shareef Abdur-Rahim 2.50 6.00
SC Sam Cassell 2.00 5.00
SF Steve Francis 2.50 6.00
SM Shawn Marion 2.00 5.00
SN Steve Nash 5.00 12.00
SO Shaquille O'Neal 8.00 20.00
ST Stephon Marbury 3.00 8.00
TD Tim Duncan 6.00 15.00
TM Tracy McGrady 4.00 10.00
TP Tony Parker 4.00 10.00
TR Theo Ratliff 1.50 4.00
TT Tim Thomas 1.50 4.00
VB Vin Baker 1.50 4.00
WE Chris Webber 3.00 8.00
WI Chris Wilcox 1.50 4.00
YM Yao Ming 5.00 12.00
ZI Zydrunas Ilgauskas 2.00 5.00

2005-06 Upper Deck Game Jerseys Patches

*PATCHES: 1.25X TO 3X BASE HI
PRINT RUN 25 SER.#'d SETS
JO Jermaine O'Neal 6.00 15.00
KB Kobe Bryant 125.00 300.00
RW Rasheed Wallace 8.00 20.00
WE Chris Webber 12.00 30.00

2005-06 Upper Deck LeBron James

COMPLETE SET (45) 15.00 40.00
COMMON CARD (LJ1-LJ45) 1.25 3.00

2005-06 Upper Deck LeBron James Gold

*GOLD: 6X TO 15X BASE
STATED PRINT RUN 23 SER.#'d SETS

2005-06 Upper Deck Michael Jordan

COMPLETE SET (45) 25.00 60.00
COMMON CARD (MJ1-MJ45) 1.50 4.00

2005-06 Upper Deck Michael Jordan Gold

PRINT RUN FIVE SER.#'d SETS
PRINT RUN 23 SER.#'d SETS
MJ1 Michael Jordan 25.00 60.00
MJ2 Michael Jordan 25.00 60.00
MJ3 Michael Jordan 25.00 60.00
MJ4 Michael Jordan 25.00 60.00
MJ5 Michael Jordan 25.00 60.00
MJ6 Michael Jordan 25.00 60.00
MJ7 Michael Jordan 25.00 60.00
MJ8 Michael Jordan 25.00 60.00
MJ9 Michael Jordan 25.00 60.00
MJ10 Michael Jordan 25.00 60.00
MJ11 Michael Jordan 25.00 60.00
MJ12 Michael Jordan 25.00 60.00
MJ13 Michael Jordan 25.00 60.00
MJ14 Michael Jordan 25.00 60.00
MJ15 Michael Jordan 25.00 60.00
MJ16 Michael Jordan 25.00 60.00
MJ17 Michael Jordan 25.00 60.00
MJ18 Michael Jordan 25.00 60.00
MJ19 Michael Jordan 25.00 60.00
MJ20 Michael Jordan 25.00 60.00
MJ21 Michael Jordan 25.00 60.00
MJ22 Michael Jordan 25.00 60.00
MJ23 Michael Jordan 25.00 60.00
MJ24 Michael Jordan 25.00 60.00
MJ25 Michael Jordan 25.00 60.00
MJ26 Michael Jordan 25.00 60.00
MJ27 Michael Jordan 25.00 60.00
MJ28 Michael Jordan 25.00 60.00
MJ29 Michael Jordan 25.00 60.00
MJ30 Michael Jordan 25.00 60.00
MJ31 Michael Jordan 25.00 60.00
MJ32 Michael Jordan 25.00 60.00
MJ33 Michael Jordan 25.00 60.00
MJ34 Michael Jordan 25.00 60.00
MJ35 Michael Jordan 25.00 60.00
MJ36 Michael Jordan 25.00 60.00
MJ37 Michael Jordan 25.00 60.00
MJ38 Michael Jordan 25.00 60.00
MJ39 Michael Jordan 25.00 60.00
MJ40 Michael Jordan 25.00 60.00
MJ41 Michael Jordan 25.00 60.00
MJ42 Michael Jordan 25.00 60.00
MJ43 Michael Jordan 25.00 60.00
MJ44 Michael Jordan 25.00 60.00
MJ45 Michael Jordan 25.00 60.00

2005-06 Upper Deck Michael Jordan/LeBron James

COMPLETE SET (10) 15.00 40.00
COMMON CARD 3.00 8.00

2005-06 Upper Deck Michael Jordan/LeBron James Silver

*SILVER: 3X TO 6X BASE MJ/LJ HI

2005-06 Upper Deck Performance Clause Jerseys

STATED PRINT RUN 250 SER.#'d SETS
AK Andrei Kirilenko 2.00 5.00
AN Andre Iguodala 2.50 6.00
BG Ben Gordon 2.00 5.00
BO Carlos Boozer 2.00 5.00
CA Carmelo Anthony 4.00 10.00
CF Channing Frye 2.00 5.00
CP Chris Paul 12.00 30.00
CT Chris Taft 1.50 4.00
CV Charlie Villanueva 2.00 5.00
DG Danny Granger 2.50 6.00
DH Dwight Howard 3.00 8.00
DN Dirk Nowitzki 6.00 15.00
DW Deron Williams 4.00 10.00
FG Francisco Garcia 1.50 4.00
GA Gilbert Arenas 2.50 6.00
JJ Jarrett Jack 2.50 6.00
JO Josh Childress 1.50 4.00
JR J.R. Smith 2.50 6.00
KB Kobe Bryant 50.00 120.00
KG Kevin Garnett 3.00 8.00
KK Kyle Korver 2.00 5.00
LH Luther Head 1.50 4.00
LJ LeBron James 10.00 25.00
LO Lamar Odom 2.00 5.00
MA Marvin Williams 2.50 6.00
MB Mike Bibby 2.50 6.00
MR Michael Redd 2.00 5.00
PG Pau Gasol 4.00 10.00
RF Raymond Felton 2.00 5.00
RG Ryan Gomes 2.00 5.00
RM Rashad McCants 1.50 4.00
SB Shane Battier 2.00 5.00
SF Steve Francis 2.50 6.00
SL Shaun Livingston 2.00 5.00
SM Sean May 1.50 4.00
SO Shaquille O'Neal 8.00 20.00
SS Salim Stoudamire 2.00 5.00
TD Tim Duncan 6.00 15.00
TR Trevor Ariza 2.00 5.00
VC Vince Carter 5.00 12.00
WE Delonte West 1.50 4.00
YM Yao Ming 5.00 12.00

2005-06 Upper Deck Performance Clause Jerseys Autographs

STATED PRINT RUN 50 SER.#'d SETS
CP Chris Paul 25.00 60.00
KB Kobe Bryant 1,000.00 2,000.00

2005-06 Upper Deck Rookie Review Materials

APPROXIMATELY ONE PER BOX
AB Andris Biedrins 1.50 4.00
AE Andre Emmett 2.00 5.00
AI Andre Iguodala 2.50 6.00
AJ Al Jefferson 1.50 4.00
AV Anderson Varejao 1.50 4.00
BU Beno Udrih 2.00 5.00
CD Chris Duhon 1.50 4.00
DE Devin Harris 1.50 4.00
DH Dwight Howard 3.00 8.00
DO Dorell Wright 2.00 5.00
DW Delonte West 1.50 4.00
HA David Harrison 2.00 5.00
HS Ha Seung-Jin 2.00 5.00
JC Josh Childress 1.50 4.00
JN Jameer Nelson 1.50 4.00
JR J.R. Smith 2.50 6.00
JS Josh Smith 2.00 5.00
JV Jackson Vroman 2.00 5.00
KH Kris Humphries 2.00 5.00
KM Kevin Martin 2.00 5.00
KS Kirk Snyder 2.00 5.00
LC Lionel Chalmers 2.00 5.00
LD Luol Deng 2.00 5.00
NK Nenad Krstic 2.00 5.00
RA Rafael Araujo 2.00 5.00
SL Shaun Livingston 2.00 5.00
ST Sebastian Telfair 2.00 5.00
SV Sasha Vujacic 2.00 5.00
TA Tony Allen 2.00 5.00
TR Trevor Ariza 2.00 5.00

2005-06 Upper Deck Rookie Scrapbook

COMPLETE SET (30) 12.50 30.00
STATED ODDS ONE PER RETAIL PACK
1 Andrew Bogut .60 1.50
2 Andrew Bynum .40 1.00
3 Antoine Wright .40 1.00
4 Channing Frye .40 1.00
5 Charlie Villanueva .40 1.00
6 Chris Paul 2.50 6.00
7 Daniel Ewing .40 1.00
8 Danny Granger .50 1.25
9 David Lee .50 1.25
10 Deron Williams .75 2.00
11 Travis Diener .30 .75
12 Francisco Garcia .30 .75
13 Gerald Green .50 1.25
14 Hakim Warrick .40 1.00
15 Ike Diogu .30 .75
16 Jarrett Jack .50 1.25
17 Jason Maxiell .40 1.00
18 Joey Graham .40 1.00
19 Julius Hodge .30 .75
20 Luther Head .30 .75
21 Martell Webster .40 1.00
22 Marvin Williams .50 1.25
23 Monta Ellis .60 1.50
24 Nate Robinson .50 1.25
25 Rashad McCants .30 .75
26 Raymond Felton .40 1.00
27 C.J. Miles .40 1.00
28 Salim Stoudamire .40 1.00
29 Sean May .30 .75
30 Wayne Simien .30 .75

2005-06 Upper Deck Signature Sensations

PRINT RUN 25 SER.#'d SETS
AE Andre Emmett 5.00 12.00
AH Al Harrington 6.00 15.00
AI Andre Iguodala 8.00 20.00
AJ Antawn Jamison 6.00 15.00
AL Al Jefferson 5.00 12.00
AN Antonio Burks 5.00 12.00
AW Antoine Wright 6.00 15.00
BG Ben Gordon 6.00 15.00
BI Andris Biedrins 5.00 12.00
BM Brad Miller 6.00 15.00
BU Beno Udrih 5.00 12.00
BW Ben Wallace 12.00 30.00
BY Andrew Bynum 6.00 15.00
CA Carmelo Anthony 25.00 60.00
CB Chris Bosh 10.00 25.00
CF Channing Frye 6.00 15.00
CJ C.J. Miles 6.00 15.00
CM Corey Maggette 6.00 15.00
CP Chris Paul 40.00 100.00
CT Chris Taft 5.00 12.00
CV Charlie Villanueva 6.00 15.00
CW Chris Wilcox 5.00 12.00
DE Devin Harris 5.00 12.00
DF Derek Fisher 12.00 30.00
DG Danny Granger 8.00 20.00
DH Dwight Howard 10.00 25.00
DL David Lee 8.00 20.00
DM Desmond Mason 5.00 12.00
DT Dijon Thompson 5.00 12.00
EI Ersan Ilyasova 6.00 15.00
EW Daniel Ewing 6.00 15.00
FG Francisco Garcia 5.00 12.00
GA Gilbert Arenas 8.00 20.00
GG Gerald Green 8.00 20.00
GW Gerald Wallace 6.00 15.00
HW Hakim Warrick 6.00 15.00
ID Ike Diogu 5.00 12.00
JA Jalen Rose 6.00 15.00
JC Josh Childress 5.00 12.00
JG Joey Graham 6.00 15.00
JH Julius Hodge 5.00 12.00
JJ Jarrett Jack 8.00 20.00
JK Jason Kidd 12.00 30.00
JN Jameer Nelson 5.00 12.00
JP Johan Petro 5.00 12.00
JR J.R. Smith 8.00 20.00
JW Jason Williams 75.00 200.00
KR Kris Humphries 5.00 12.00
LH Luther Head 5.00 12.00
LJ LeBron James 1,000.00 2,000.00
LU Luke Jackson 5.00 12.00
LW Louis Williams 20.00 50.00
MA Marvin Williams 8.00 20.00
MD Marquis Daniels 5.00 12.00
ME Monta Ellis 10.00 25.00
MJ Michael Jordan 2,500.00 5,000.00
ML Martell Webster 6.00 15.00
MP Morris Peterson 5.00 12.00
MR Michael Redd 6.00 15.00
MW Maurice Williams 6.00 15.00
PB Primoz Brezec 5.00 12.00
PG Pau Gasol 60.00 150.00
PP Paul Pierce 30.00 80.00
QR Quentin Richardson 5.00 12.00
RA Rashad McCants 5.00 12.00
RF Raymond Felton 6.00 15.00
RG Ryan Gomes 6.00 15.00
RH Richard Hamilton 10.00 25.00
RI Royal Ivey 5.00 12.00
RJ Richard Jefferson 6.00 15.00
RM Ronald Murray 5.00 12.00
SB Shane Battier 6.00 15.00
SE Sean May 6.00 15.00
SL Shaun Livingston 6.00 15.00
SM Stephon Marbury 15.00 40.00
SS Salim Stoudamire 6.00 15.00
ST Sebastian Telfair 6.00 15.00
TA Tony Allen 5.00 12.00
TM Tracy McGrady 20.00 50.00
TR Trevor Ariza 5.00 12.00
UH Udonis Haslem 5.00 12.00
WI Deron Williams 12.00 30.00
WS Wayne Simien 5.00 12.00
YM Yao Ming 30.00 80.00
ZP Zoran Planinic 5.00 12.00

2005-06 Upper Deck UD Materials

APPROXIMATELY ONE PER BOX
AK Andrei Kirilenko 2.00 5.00
AW Antoine Walker 2.00 5.00
BD Baron Davis 2.50 6.00
BO Carlos Boozer 2.00 5.00
CB Caron Butler 2.00 5.00
CH Chris Anderson 2.50 6.00
CM Corey Maggette 2.00 5.00
CW Chris Webber 3.00 8.00
DA David Wesley 1.50 4.00
DW Dajuan Wagner 1.50 4.00
EB Earl Boykins 2.00 5.00
EC Eddy Curry 1.50 4.00
GP Gary Payton 4.00 10.00
JJ Joe Johnson 2.00 5.00
JK Jason Kidd 4.00 10.00
JM Jamaal Magloire 2.00 5.00
JO Jermaine O'Neal 2.00 5.00
JT Jason Terry 2.00 5.00
KB Kobe Bryant 40.00 100.00
KM Kenyon Martin 2.00 5.00
LJ LeBron James 15.00 40.00
MJ Michael Jordan 25.00 60.00
RD Ronald Dupree 2.00 5.00
RJ Richard Jefferson 2.00 5.00
SD Samuel Dalember 1.50 4.00
SF Steve Francis 2.50 6.00
TP Tony Parker 4.00 10.00
UH Udonis Haslem 1.50 4.00
VL Voshon Lenard 1.50 4.00
VR Vladimir Radmanovic 1.50 4.00

2006-07 Upper Deck

COMP.SET w/o SP's (200) 15.00 40.00
ROOKIE ODDS 1:3
1 Josh Childress .20 .50
2 Al Harrington .25 .60
3 Joe Johnson .30 .75
4 Josh Smith .20 .50
5 Salim Stoudamire .20 .50
6 Marvin Williams .20 .50
7 Tony Allen .20 .50
8 Dan Dickau .20 .50
9 Al Jefferson .20 .50
10 Raef LaFrentz .20 .50
11 Michael Olowokandi .20 .50
12 Paul Pierce .50 1.25
13 Wally Szczerbiak .25 .60
14 Alan Anderson .20 .50
15 Raymond Felton .20 .50
16 Othella Harrington .20 .50
17 Sean May .20 .50
18 Emeka Okafor .25 .60
19 Primoz Brezec .20 .50
20 Gerald Wallace .25 .60
21 Tyson Chandler .25 .60
22 Michael Jordan 2.50 6.00
23 Luol Deng .25 .60
24 Chris Duhon .20 .50
25 Ben Gordon .25 .60
26 Kirk Hinrich .25 .60
27 Mike Sweetney .20 .50
28 Drew Gooden .25 .60
29 Larry Hughes .25 .60
30 Zydrunas Ilgauskas .25 .60
31 LeBron James 2.50 6.00
32 Damon Jones .20 .50
33 Donyell Marshall .20 .50
34 Anderson Varejao .20 .50
35 Erick Dampier .20 .50
36 Marquis Daniels .20 .50
37 Devin Harris .20 .50
38 Josh Howard .25 .60
39 Dirk Nowitzki .75 2.00
40 Jerry Stackhouse .25 .60
41 Jason Terry .25 .60
42 Carmelo Anthony .50 1.25
43 Earl Boykins .20 .50
44 Marcus Camby .25 .60
45 Kenyon Martin .25 .60
46 Andre Miller .25 .60
47 Eduardo Najera .20 .50
48 Nene .20 .50
49 Chauncey Billups .40 1.00
50 Richard Hamilton .30 .75
51 Lindsey Hunter .20 .50
52 Antonio McDyess .25 .60
53 Tayshaun Prince .30 .75
54 Ben Wallace .40 1.00
55 Rasheed Wallace .40 1.00
56 Baron Davis .30 .75
57 Ike Diogu .20 .50
58 Mike Dunleavy .20 .50
59 Derek Fisher .30 .75
60 Troy Murphy .30 .75
61 Mickael Pietrus .25 .60
62 Jason Richardson .30 .75
63 Rafer Alston .25 .60
64 Luther Head .20 .50
65 Juwan Howard .25 .60
66 Tracy McGrady .50 1.25
67 Dikembe Mutombo .30 .75
68 Stromile Swift .20 .50
69 Yao Ming .75 2.00
70 Austin Croshere .20 .50
71 Stephen Jackson .20 .50
72 Sarunas Jasikevicius .25 .60
73 Jermaine O'Neal .30 .75
74 Peja Stojakovic .25 .60
75 Jamaal Tinsley .25 .60
76 Elton Brand .25 .60
77 Sam Cassell .25 .60
78 Chris Kaman .25 .60
79 Shaun Livingston .25 .60
80 Corey Maggette .25 .60
81 Cuttino Mobley .25 .60
82 Vladimir Radmanovic .20 .50
83 Kwame Brown .20 .50
84 Kobe Bryant 2.50 6.00
85 Devean George .20 .50
86 Lamar Odom .25 .60
87 Ronny Turiaf .20 .50
88 Sasha Vujacic .20 .50
89 Luke Walton .20 .50
90 Shane Battier .25 .60
91 Pau Gasol .50 1.25
92 Bobby Jackson .20 .50
93 Eddie Jones .30 .75
94 Mike Miller .25 .60
95 Damon Stoudamire .25 .60
96 Hakim Warrick .20 .50
97 Alonzo Mourning .50 1.25
98 Shaquille O'Neal 1.25 3.00
99 Gary Payton .40 1.00
100 Wayne Simien .20 .50
101 Dwyane Wade .60 1.50
102 Antoine Walker .30 .75
103 Jason Williams .40 1.00
104 Andrew Bogut .25 .60
105 T.J. Ford .20 .50
106 Jamaal Magloire .20 .50
107 Michael Redd .25 .60
108 Bobby Simmons .20 .50
109 Maurice Williams .25 .60
110 Ricky Davis .25 .60
111 Kevin Garnett .75 2.00
112 Eddie Griffin .20 .50
113 Trenton Hassell .20 .50
114 Troy Hudson .20 .50
115 Rashad McCants .20 .50
116 Vince Carter .60 1.50
117 Jason Collins .20 .50
118 Richard Jefferson .25 .60
119 Jason Kidd .50 1.25
120 Nenad Krstic .20 .50
121 Jeff McInnis .20 .50
122 Antoine Wright .20 .50
123 P.J. Brown .20 .50
124 Speedy Claxton .20 .50
125 Desmond Mason .20 .50
126 Chris Paul .60 1.50
127 J.R. Smith .30 .75
128 Kirk Snyder .25 .60
129 David West .25 .60
130 Jamal Crawford .30 .75
131 Steve Francis .30 .75
132 Channing Frye .20 .50
133 Stephon Marbury .40 1.00
134 Quentin Richardson .25 .60
135 Nate Robinson .25 .60
136 Maurice Taylor .20 .50
137 Carlos Arroyo .20 .50
138 Tony Battie .20 .50
139 Keyon Dooling .20 .50
140 Grant Hill .50 1.25
141 Dwight Howard .40 1.00
142 Darko Milicic .20 .50
143 Jameer Nelson .20 .50
144 Samuel Dalembert .20 .50
145 Steven Hunter .20 .50
146 Andre Iguodala .30 .75
147 Allen Iverson .75 2.00
148 Kyle Korver .25 .60
149 Shavlik Randolph .20 .50
150 Chris Webber .40 1.00
151 Raja Bell .25 .60
152 Boris Diaw .25 .60
153 Shawn Marion .30 .75
154 Steve Nash .60 1.50
155 Amare Stoudemire .30 .75
156 Kurt Thomas .20 .50
157 Tim Thomas .20 .50
158 Steve Blake .20 .50
159 Juan Dixon .20 .50
160 Zach Randolph .30 .75
161 Ha Seung-Jin .20 .50
162 Sebastian Telfair .20 .50
163 Martell Webster .25 .60
164 Shareef Abdur-Rahim .30 .75
165 Ron Artest .30 .75
166 Mike Bibby .30 .75
167 Brad Miller .25 .60
168 Kenny Thomas .20 .50
169 Bonzi Wells .20 .50
170 Bruce Bowen .25 .60
171 Tim Duncan .75 2.00
172 Michael Finley .30 .75
173 Manu Ginobili .60 1.50
174 Nazr Mohammed .20 .50
175 Tony Parker .50 1.25
176 Ray Allen .50 1.25
177 Danny Fortson .20 .50
178 Rashard Lewis .25 .60
179 Luke Ridnour .25 .60
180 Earl Watson .20 .50
181 Chris Wilcox .20 .50
182 Rafael Araujo .20 .50
183 Chris Bosh .40 1.00
184 Joey Graham .20 .50
185 Mike James .20 .50
186 Morris Peterson .20 .50
187 Charlie Villanueva .20 .50
188 Carlos Boozer .25 .60
189 Matt Harpring .20 .50
190 Kris Humphries .20 .50
191 Andrei Kirilenko .25 .60
192 C.J. Miles .20 .50
193 Chris Taft .20 .50
194 Deron Williams .20 .50
195 Gilbert Arenas .30 .75
196 Andray Blatche .20 .50
197 Caron Butler .25 .60
198 Antonio Daniels .20 .50
199 Brendan Haywood .20 .50
200 Antawn Jamison .25 .60
201 Andrea Bargnani RC .75 2.00
202 LaMarcus Aldridge RC 2.50 6.00
203 Adam Morrison RC .75 2.00
204 Tyrus Thomas RC .75 2.00
205 Shelden Williams RC .60 1.50
206 Brandon Roy RC 2.00 5.00
207 Randy Foye RC .75 2.00
208 Rudy Gay RC 1.25 3.00
209 Patrick O'Bryant RC .60 1.50
210 Saer Sene RC .60 1.50
211 J.J. Redick RC 2.00 5.00
212 Hilton Armstrong RC .60 1.50
213 Thabo Sefolosha RC .75 2.00
214 Ronnie Brewer RC 1.00 2.50
215 Cedric Simmons RC .60 1.50
216 Rodney Carney RC .60 1.50
217 Shawne Williams RC .60 1.50
218 Quincy Douby RC .60 1.50
219 Renaldo Balkman RC .75 2.00
220 Rajon Rondo RC 3.00 8.00
221 Marcus Williams RC .60 1.50
222 Josh Boone RC .60 1.50
223 Kyle Lowry RC 3.00 8.00
224 Shannon Brown RC .60 1.50
225 Jordan Farmar RC .75 2.00
226 Maurice Ager RC .60 1.50
227 Mardy Collins RC .60 1.50
228 Jorge Garbajosa RC .75 2.00
229 James White RC .60 1.50
230 Steve Novak RC .75 2.00
231 Solomon Jones RC .60 1.50
232 Paul Davis RC .60 1.50
233 P.J. Tucker RC 1.00 2.50
234 Craig Smith RC .75 2.00
235 Bobby Jones RC .75 2.00
236 David Noel RC .60 1.50
237 Denham Brown RC .60 1.50
238 James Augustine RC .60 1.50
239 Daniel Gibson RC .75 2.00
240 Alexander Johnson RC .60 1.50

2006-07 Upper Deck Star Rookies Hot Pack

*HOT PACK: .5X TO 1.25X BASE HI
ONE HOT PACK PER BOX

2006-07 Upper Deck Flight Team

COMPLETE SET (30) 12.50 30.00
*HOT PACK SILVER: .5X TO 1.25X BASE HI
ONE HOT PACK PER BOX
APPROXIMATE ODDS 1:12
AI Andre Iguodala .75 2.00
AS Amare Stoudemire .75 2.00
BB Brent Barry .50 1.25
CA Carmelo Anthony 1.25 3.00
CB Chris Bosh 1.00 2.50
CM Corey Maggette .60 1.50
DH Dwight Howard 1.00 2.50
DM Desmond Mason .50 1.25
DW Dwyane Wade 1.50 4.00
FJ Fred Jones .50 1.25
GA Gilbert Arenas .75 2.00
JR Jason Richardson .75 2.00
JS J.R. Smith .75 2.00
KB Kobe Bryant 6.00 15.00
KG Kevin Garnett 2.00 5.00
KM Kenyon Martin .60 1.50
LJ LeBron James 6.00 15.00
MA Shawn Marion .75 2.00
MG Manu Ginobili 1.50 4.00
MI Darius Miles .50 1.25
MJ Michael Jordan 6.00 15.00
NR Nate Robinson .60 1.50
RJ Richard Jefferson .60 1.50
SF Steve Francis .75 2.00
SM Josh Smith .50 1.25
SO Shaquille O'Neal 3.00 8.00
SS Stromile Swift .50 1.25
TM Tracy McGrady 1.25 3.00
TP Tayshaun Prince .75 2.00
VC Vince Carter 1.50 4.00

2006-07 Upper Deck MVP Watch
COMPLETE SET (15) 8.00 20.00
APPROXIMATE ODDS 1:12
*HOT PACK: .5X TO 1.25X BASE HI
ONE HOT PACK PER BOX
AI Allen Iverson 1.50 4.00
CB Chauncey Billups .75 2.00
DN Dirk Nowitzki 1.50 4.00
DW Dwyane Wade 1.25 3.00
EB Elton Brand .50 1.25
GA Gilbert Arenas .60 1.50
KB Kobe Bryant 5.00 12.00
KG Kevin Garnett 1.50 4.00
LJ LeBron James 5.00 12.00
PP Paul Pierce 1.00 2.50
SM Shawn Marion .60 1.50
SN Steve Nash 1.25 3.00
SO Shaquille O'Neal 2.50 6.00
TD Tim Duncan 1.50 4.00
TM Tracy McGrady 1.00 2.50

2006-07 Upper Deck Signature Sensations
PRINT RUN 25 SER.#'d SETS
AB Andrew Bogut 8.00 20.00
AI Andre Iguodala 10.00 25.00
BB Bruce Bowen 6.00 15.00
BD Dee Brown 6.00 15.00
BR Brandon Roy 10.00 25.00
CA Carmelo Anthony 30.00 80.00
CP Chris Paul 125.00 300.00
CS Craig Smith 6.00 15.00
DB Denham Brown 6.00 15.00
DM Donyell Marshall 6.00 15.00
DN David Noel 6.00 15.00
HA Hassan Adams 6.00 15.00
ID Ike Diogu 6.00 15.00
JK Jason Kapono 6.00 15.00
KB Kwame Brown 6.00 15.00
KK Kyle Korver 8.00 20.00
LA LaMarcus Aldridge 20.00 50.00
NR Nate Robinson 12.00 30.00
RH Ryan Hollins 6.00 15.00
RT Ronny Turiaf 8.00 20.00
VW Von Wafer 6.00 15.00
WM Maurice Williams 6.00 15.00
YK Yaroslav Korolev 6.00 15.00

2006-07 Upper Deck Signature Sensations Dual
BB B.Barry/B.Bowen 10.00 25.00
GG J.Graham/S.Graham 10.00 25.00
LP S.Livingston/C.Paul 25.00 60.00
PC P.Pierce/V.Carter 20.00 50.00

2006-07 Upper Deck The LeBrons
COMPLETE SET (15) 10.00 25.00
COMMON LEBRON (1-12) 2.50 6.00
*HOT PACK: .5X TO 1.25X BASE HI
ONE HOT PACK PER BOX
APPROXIMATE ODDS 1:3
COMMON MEMORABILIA 12.00 30.00
COMMON DUAL MEM. 40.00 100.00
13 LeBron James Dual 3.00 8.00
14 LeBron James Dual 3.00 8.00
15 LeBron James Triple 3.00 8.00

2006-07 Upper Deck UD Game Jersey
APPROXIMATE ODDS ONE PER BOX
AB Andrew Bogut 2.00 5.00
AI Allen Iverson 6.00 15.00
AJ Al Jefferson 1.50 4.00
AK Andrei Kirilenko 2.00 5.00
AL Ray Allen 4.00 10.00
AS Amare Stoudemire 2.50 6.00
AW Antoine Walker 2.50 6.00
BB Bruce Bowen 2.00 5.00
BD Baron Davis 2.50 6.00
BG Ben Gordon 2.00 5.00
BK Kwame Brown 1.50 4.00
BM Brad Miller 2.00 5.00
BW Ben Wallace 3.00 8.00
CA Carmelo Anthony 4.00 10.00
CB Chauncey Billups 3.00 8.00
CF Channing Frye 1.50 4.00
CM Corey Maggette 2.00 5.00
CP Chris Paul 5.00 12.00
CW Chris Webber 3.00 8.00
DG Drew Gooden 2.00 5.00
DH Devin Harris 1.50 4.00
DM Donyell Marshall 1.50 4.00
DN Dirk Nowitzki 6.00 15.00
EB Elton Brand 2.00 5.00
EO Emeka Okafor 2.00 5.00
GA Gilbert Arenas 2.50 6.00
GE Devean George 1.50 4.00
GH Grant Hill 4.00 10.00
HD Dwight Howard 3.00 8.00
HU Larry Hughes 2.00 5.00
IA Andre Iguodala 2.50 6.00
ID Ike Diogu 1.50 4.00
JC Jamal Crawford 2.50 6.00
JD Juan Dixon 1.50 4.00
JH Josh Howard 2.00 5.00
JJ Joe Johnson 2.50 6.00
JK Jason Kidd 4.00 10.00
JM Jeff McInnis 1.50 4.00
JO Jermaine O'Neal 2.50 6.00
JR Jason Richardson 2.50 6.00
JS J.R. Smith 2.50 6.00
JT Jason Terry 2.00 5.00
KB Kobe Bryant 40.00 100.00
KG Kevin Garnett 6.00 15.00
KH Kirk Hinrich 2.00 5.00
KK Kyle Korver 2.00 5.00
LD Luol Deng 2.00 5.00
LH Luther Head 1.50 4.00
LJ LeBron James 10.00 25.00
LO Lamar Odom 2.00 5.00
LW Luke Walton 1.50 4.00
MA Sean May 1.50 4.00
MB Mike Bibby 2.50 6.00
MD Marquis Daniels 1.50 4.00
MG Manu Ginobili 5.00 12.00
MJ Michael Jordan SP 30.00 80.00
MS Stephon Marbury 3.00 8.00
MW Marvin Williams 1.50 4.00
NR Nate Robinson 2.00 5.00
PG Pau Gasol 4.00 10.00
PP Paul Pierce 4.00 10.00
PS Peja Stojakovic 2.00 5.00
PT Tayshaun Prince 2.50 6.00
QR Quentin Richardson 1.50 4.00
RA Ron Artest 2.50 6.00
RF Raymond Felton 1.50 4.00
RH Richard Hamilton 2.50 6.00
RJ Richard Jefferson 2.00 5.00
RL Rashard Lewis 2.00 5.00
RM Rashad McCants 1.50 4.00
RW Rasheed Wallace 3.00 8.00
SD Samuel Dalembert 1.50 4.00
SJ Sarunas Jasikevicius 2.00 5.00
SL Shaun Livingston 2.00 5.00
SM Shawn Marion 2.50 6.00
SN Steve Nash 5.00 12.00
SO Shaquille O'Neal 10.00 25.00
ST Sebastian Telfair 1.50 4.00
TC Tyson Chandler 2.00 5.00
TD Tim Duncan 6.00 15.00
TF T.J. Ford 1.50 4.00
TM Tracy McGrady 4.00 10.00
TP Tony Parker 4.00 10.00
VC Vince Carter 5.00 12.00
WM Martell Webster 2.00 5.00
WS Wally Szczerbiak 2.00 5.00
YM Yao Ming 6.00 15.00
ZI Zydrunas Ilgauskas 2.00 5.00

2006-07 Upper Deck UD Game Patch
*PATCH: .75X TO 2X BASE HI
PRINT RUN 25 SER.#'d SETS
KB Kobe Bryant 100.00 250.00
LJ LeBron James 25.00 60.00

2007-08 Upper Deck
COMPLETE SET (242) 75.00 150.00
COMP.SET w/o SP's (200) 15.00 30.00
APPROXIMATE ODDS 1:2
1 Austin Croshere .20 .50
2 Devean George .20 .50
3 Devin Harris .20 .50
4 Josh Howard .25 .60
5 Jerry Stackhouse .30 .75
6 Jason Terry .25 .60
7 Rafer Alston .30 .75
8 Shane Battier .25 .60
9 Luther Head .20 .50
10 Juwan Howard .30 .75
11 Tracy McGrady .50 1.25
12 Steve Novak .20 .50
13 Rudy Gay .25 .60
14 Eddie Jones .30 .75
15 Kyle Lowry .30 .75
16 Mike Miller .25 .60
17 Damon Stoudamire .30 .75
18 Hakim Warrick .20 .50
19 Brandon Bass .20 .50
20 Tyson Chandler .30 .75
21 Bobby Jackson .20 .50
22 Desmond Mason .20 .50
23 Cedric Simmons .20 .50
24 Peja Stojakovic .25 .60
25 Bruce Bowen .20 .50
26 Michael Finley .30 .75
27 Manu Ginobili .60 1.50
28 Tony Parker .50 1.25
29 Beno Udrih .20 .50
30 Monta Ellis .25 .60
31 Al Harrington .25 .60
32 Sarunas Jasikevicius .20 .50
33 Stephen Jackson .20 .50
34 Jason Richardson .30 .75
35 Sam Cassell .25 .60
36 Chris Kaman .25 .60
37 Shaun Livingston .20 .50
38 Corey Maggette .25 .60
39 Cuttino Mobley .25 .60
40 Tim Thomas .20 .50
41 Kwame Brown .20 .50
42 Andrew Bynum .20 .50
43 Jordan Farmar .20 .50
44 Lamar Odom .25 .60
45 Ronny Turiaf .20 .50
46 Luke Walton .25 .60
47 Leandro Barbosa .25 .60
48 Raja Bell .25 .60
49 Boris Diaw .25 .60
50 Shawn Marion .25 .60
51 Amare Stoudemire .30 .75
52 Shareef Abdur-Rahim .30 .75
53 Ron Artest .25 .60
54 Quincy Douby .20 .50
55 Kevin Martin .25 .60
56 Brad Miller .25 .60
57 Allen Iverson .75 2.00
58 Kenyon Martin .25 .60
59 Eduardo Najera .20 .50
60 Nene .25 .60
61 J.R. Smith .30 .75
62 Ricky Davis .25 .60
63 Randy Foye .25 .60
64 Troy Hudson .25 .60
65 Mike James .20 .50
66 Rashad McCants .25 .60
67 Craig Smith .25 .60
68 LaMarcus Aldridge .25 .60
69 Jarrett Jack .20 .50
70 Jamaal Magloire .20 .50
71 Sergio Rodriguez .20 .50
72 Brandon Roy .40 1.00
73 Martell Webster .25 .60
74 Rashard Lewis .25 .60
75 Luke Ridnour .25 .60
76 Danny Fortson .20 .50
77 Chris Wilcox .20 .50
78 Damien Wilkins .20 .50
79 Ronnie Brewer .20 .50
80 Derek Fisher .30 .75
81 Matt Harpring .20 .50
82 Andrei Kirilenko .25 .60
83 Paul Millsap .25 .60
84 Deron Williams .25 .60
85 Tony Allen .20 .50
86 Gerald Green .25 .60
87 Al Jefferson .20 .50
88 Wally Szczerbiak .25 .60
89 Allan Ray .20 .50
90 Delonte West .20 .50
91 Hassan Adams .20 .50
92 Richard Jefferson .25 .60
93 Jason Kidd .50 1.25
94 Nenad Krstic .20 .50
95 Marcus Williams .20 .50
96 Renaldo Balkman .20 .50
97 Jamal Crawford .30 .75
98 Eddy Curry .20 .50
99 Channing Frye .20 .50
100 Quentin Richardson .20 .50
101 Nate Robinson .30 .75
102 Rodney Carney .20 .50
103 Samuel Dalembert .20 .50
104 Steven Hunter .20 .50
105 Kyle Korver .30 .75
106 Andre Miller .25 .60
107 Shavlik Randolph .20 .50
108 Andrea Bargnani .20 .50
109 Jose Calderon .20 .50
110 T.J. Ford .20 .50
111 Jorge Garbajosa .25 .60
112 Joey Graham .20 .50
113 Morris Peterson .20 .50
114 Luol Deng .25 .60
115 Ben Gordon .20 .50
116 Kirk Hinrich .30 .75
117 Thabo Sefolosha .20 .50
118 Tyrus Thomas .20 .50
119 Ben Wallace .40 1.00
120 Shannon Brown .20 .50
121 Drew Gooden .25 .60
122 Larry Hughes .25 .60
123 Zydrunas Ilgauskas .25 .60
124 Donyell Marshall .20 .50
125 Richard Hamilton .40 1.00
126 Amir Johnson .20 .50
127 Antonio McDyess .25 .60
128 Tayshaun Prince .30 .75
129 Rasheed Wallace .40 1.00
130 Chris Webber .40 1.00
131 Marquis Daniels .20 .50
132 Ike Diogu .20 .50
133 Mike Dunleavy .20 .50
134 Jeff Foster .20 .50
135 Troy Murphy .20 .50
136 Jamaal Tinsley .20 .50
137 Charlie Bell .20 .50
138 Andrew Bogut .25 .60
139 Earl Boykins .20 .50
140 Bobby Simmons .20 .50
141 Charlie Villanueva .20 .50
142 Maurice Williams .25 .60
143 Speedy Claxton .20 .50
144 Solomon Jones .20 .50
145 Tyronn Lue .20 .50
146 Marvin Williams .20 .50
147 Shelden Williams .20 .50
148 Raymond Felton .25 .60
149 Othella Harrington .20 .50
150 Sean May .20 .50
151 Adam Morrison .20 .50
152 Gerald Wallace .25 .60
153 Udonis Haslem .20 .50
154 Alonzo Mourning .50 1.25
155 Shaquille O'Neal 1.25 3.00
156 Gary Payton .50 1.25
157 Antoine Walker .30 .75
158 Jason Williams .50 1.25
159 Carlos Arroyo .20 .50
160 Travis Diener .20 .50
161 Grant Hill .50 1.25
162 Darko Milicic .20 .50
163 Jameer Nelson .20 .50
164 J.J. Redick .30 .75
165 Andray Blatche .20 .50
166 Caron Butler .25 .60
167 Antonio Daniels .20 .50
168 Brendan Haywood .20 .50
169 Antawn Jamison .25 .60
170 DeShawn Stevenson .20 .50
171 Dirk Nowitzki .75 2.00
172 Yao Ming .75 2.00
173 Pau Gasol .50 1.25
174 Chris Paul .60 1.50
175 Tim Duncan .75 2.00
176 Baron Davis .25 .60
177 Elton Brand .25 .60
178 Kobe Bryant 2.50 6.00
179 Steve Nash .50 1.25
180 Mike Bibby .30 .75
181 Carmelo Anthony .50 1.25
182 Kevin Garnett .75 2.00
183 Zach Randolph .30 .75
184 Ray Allen .50 1.25
185 Carlos Boozer .25 .60
186 Paul Pierce .50 1.25
187 Vince Carter .60 1.50
188 Stephon Marbury .30 .75
189 Andre Iguodala .30 .75
190 Chris Bosh .25 .60
191 Michael Jordan 3.00 8.00
192 LeBron James 2.50 6.00
193 Chauncey Billups .25 .60
194 Jermaine O'Neal .30 .75
195 Michael Redd .25 .60
196 Joe Johnson .25 .60
197 Emeka Okafor .20 .50
198 Dwyane Wade .60 1.50
199 Dwight Howard .40 1.00
200 Gilbert Arenas .20 .50
201 Acie Law RC .60 1.50
202 Thaddeus Young RC 1.00 2.50
203 Julian Wright RC .60 1.50
204 Al Thornton RC .60 1.50
205 Rodney Stuckey RC .60 1.50
206 Nick Young RC 1.00 2.50
207 Sean Williams RC .60 1.50
208 Marco Belinelli RC .75 2.00
209 Javaris Crittenton RC .60 1.50
210 Jason Smith RC .60 1.50
211 Daequan Cook RC .75 2.00
212 Jared Dudley RC .75 2.00
213 Wilson Chandler RC .75 2.00
214 Morris Almond RC .60 1.50
215 Aaron Brooks RC .75 2.00
216 Arron Afflalo RC .75 2.00
217 Alando Tucker RC .60 1.50
218 Petteri Koponen RC .75 2.00
219 Carl Landry RC .60 1.50
220 Gabe Pruitt RC .60 1.50
221 Marcus Williams RC .60 1.50
222 Nick Fazekas RC .60 1.50
223 Glen Davis RC .75 2.00
224 Jermareo Davidson RC .60 1.50
225 Josh McRoberts RC .60 1.50
226 Chris Richard RC .60 1.50
227 Derrick Byars RC .60 1.50
228 Adam Haluska RC .60 1.50
229 Reyshawn Terry RC .60 1.50
230 Jared Jordan RC .60 1.50
231 Stephane Lasme RC .60 1.50
232 Dominic McGuire RC .60 1.50
233 Greg Oden SP RC 1.25 3.00
234 Kevin Durant SP RC 25.00 60.00
235 Al Horford SP RC 3.00 8.00
236 Mike Conley Jr. SP RC 3.00 8.00
237 Jeff Green SP RC 1.00 2.50
238 Taurean Green SP RC .75 2.00
239 Corey Brewer SP RC 1.00 2.50
240 Brandan Wright SP RC 1.00 2.50
241 Joakim Noah SP RC 1.25 3.00
242 Spencer Hawes SP RC .75 2.00

2007-08 Upper Deck Championship Court Stamp
*COURT STAMP: 4X TO 10X BASE HI

2007-08 Upper Deck Electric Court Gold
*1-200 GOLD: 1.25X TO 3X BASE HI
*200-242 GOLD RC: .5X TO 1.25X HI
APPROXIMATE ODDS 1:4

2007-08 Upper Deck All-NBA
COMPLETE SET (15) 8.00 20.00
1 Dirk Nowitzki 1.50 4.00
2 Tim Duncan 1.50 4.00
3 Amare Stoudemire .60 1.50
4 Steve Nash 1.25 3.00
5 Kobe Bryant 5.00 12.00
6 LeBron James 5.00 12.00
7 Chris Bosh .75 2.00
8 Yao Ming 1.50 4.00
9 Gilbert Arenas .60 1.50
10 Tracy McGrady 1.00 2.50
11 Kevin Garnett 1.50 4.00
12 Carmelo Anthony 1.50 4.00
13 Dwight Howard .75 2.00
14 Dwyane Wade 1.25 3.00
15 Chauncey Billups .75 2.00

2007-08 Upper Deck All-Star Die Cuts
AS1 Antawn Jamison 8.00 20.00
AS2 Ben Wallace 12.00 30.00
AS3 Bill Russell 25.00 60.00
AS4 Chauncey Billups 12.00 30.00
AS5 Jason Kidd 20.00 50.00
AS6 Jermaine O'Neal 10.00 25.00
AS7 John Havlicek 20.00 50.00
AS8 Larry Bird 40.00 100.00
AS9 LeBron James 150.00 400.00
AS10 Michael Jordan 500.00 1,000.00
AS11 Michael Redd 8.00 20.00
AS12 Paul Pierce 30.00 80.00
AS13 Richard Hamilton 12.00 30.00
AS14 Robert Parish 10.00 25.00
AS15 Walt Frazier 15.00 40.00
AS16 Amare Stoudemire 10.00 25.00
AS17 Bill Walton 12.00 30.00
AS18 Carmelo Anthony 15.00 40.00
AS19 David Robinson 30.00 80.00
AS20 Elton Brand 8.00 20.00
AS21 Hakeem Olajuwon 20.00 50.00
AS22 James Worthy 20.00 50.00
AS23 Jerry West 60.00 150.00
AS24 John Stockton 30.00 80.00
AS25 Josh Howard 8.00 20.00
AS26 Magic Johnson 40.00 100.00
AS27 Manu Ginobili 20.00 50.00
AS28 Yao Ming 15.00 40.00
AS29 Rick Barry 12.00 30.00
AS30 Tony Parker 15.00 40.00

2007-08 Upper Deck Behind the Glass
COMPLETE SET (25) 20.00 40.00
AI Allen Iverson 2.00 5.00
AS Amare Stoudemire .75 2.00
BO Carlos Boozer .60 1.50
BW Ben Wallace 1.00 2.50
CA Carmelo Anthony 1.25 3.00
CB Chris Bosh 1.00 2.50
CP Chris Paul 1.50 4.00
DH Dwight Howard 1.00 2.50
DN Dirk Nowitzki 2.00 5.00
DW Dwyane Wade 1.50 4.00
GA Gilbert Arenas .75 2.00
JR Jason Richardson .75 2.00
KB Kobe Bryant 6.00 15.00
KG Kevin Garnett 2.00 5.00
LJ LeBron James 6.00 15.00
MA Shawn Marion .75 2.00
MG Manu Ginobili 1.50 4.00
MJ Michael Jordan 10.00 25.00
PP Paul Pierce 1.25 3.00
SM Stephon Marbury 1.00 2.50
SN Steve Nash 1.50 4.00
SO Shaquille O'Neal 3.00 8.00
TD Tim Duncan 2.00 5.00
TM Tracy McGrady 1.25 3.00
YM Yao Ming 2.00 5.00

2007-08 Upper Deck Champions of the Court
COMPLETE SET (25) 15.00 40.00
BR Bill Russell 2.50 6.00
BW Bill Walton 1.00 2.50
CB Chauncey Billups 1.00 2.50
DR Dennis Rodman 2.00 5.00
DW Dwyane Wade 1.50 4.00
GM George Mikan 1.50 4.00
HO Hakeem Olajuwon 1.50 4.00
JD Joe Dumars .75 2.00
JE Julius Erving 2.00 5.00
JH John Havlicek 1.50 4.00
JO Magic Johnson 3.00 8.00
JW James Worthy 1.25 3.00
KA Kareem Abdul-Jabbar 2.50 6.00
KB Kobe Bryant 6.00 15.00
LB Larry Bird 3.00 8.00
MG Manu Ginobili 1.50 4.00
MJ Michael Jordan 8.00 20.00
MM Moses Malone 1.25 3.00
RH Robert Horry .75 2.00
RO David Robinson 1.50 4.00
SK Steve Kerr 1.00 2.50
SO Shaquille O'Neal 3.00 8.00
TD Tim Duncan 2.00 5.00
TP Tony Parker 1.25 3.00
WC Wilt Chamberlain 2.50 6.00

2007-08 Upper Deck Championship Predictor
CP1 Atlanta Hawks 2.00 5.00
CP2 Boston Celtics 4.00 10.00
CP3 Charlotte Bobcats 2.00 5.00
CP4 Chicago Bulls 2.00 5.00
CP5 Cleveland Cavaliers 4.00 10.00
CP6 Dallas Mavericks 2.00 5.00
CP7 Denver Nuggets 2.00 5.00
CP8 Detroit Pistons 2.00 5.00
CP9 Golden State Warriors 2.00 5.00
CP10 Houston Rockets 2.00 5.00
CP11 Indiana Pacers 2.00 5.00
CP12 Los Angeles Clippers 2.00 5.00
CP13 Los Angeles Lakers 4.00 10.00
CP14 Memphis Grizzlies 2.00 5.00
CP15 Miami Heat 2.00 5.00
CP16 Milwaukee Bucks 2.00 5.00
CP17 Minnesota Timberwolves 2.00 5.00
CP18 New Jersey Nets 2.00 5.00
CP19 New Orleans Hornets 2.00 5.00
CP20 New York Knicks 2.00 5.00
CP21 Orlando Magic 2.00 5.00
CP22 Philadelphia 76ers 2.00 5.00
CP23 Phoenix Suns 2.00 5.00
CP24 Portland Trail Blazers 2.00 5.00
CP25 Sacramento Kings 2.00 5.00
CP26 San Antonio Spurs 2.00 5.00
CP27 Seattle Supersonics 2.00 5.00
CP28 Toronto Raptors 2.00 5.00
CP29 Utah Jazz 2.00 5.00
CP30 Washington Wizards 2.00 5.00

2007-08 Upper Deck Draft Notices
COMPLETE SET (25) 10.00 25.00
DN1 Greg Oden .60 1.50
DN2 Kevin Durant 6.00 15.00
DN3 Al Horford 1.50 4.00
DN4 Mike Conley Jr. 1.50 4.00
DN5 Jeff Green .50 1.25
DN6 Alando Tucker .40 1.00
DN7 Corey Brewer .50 1.25
DN8 Brandan Wright .50 1.25
DN9 Joakim Noah .60 1.50
DN10 Spencer Hawes .40 1.00
DN11 Acie Law .40 1.00
DN12 Thaddeus Young .60 1.50
DN13 Julian Wright .40 1.00
DN14 Al Thornton .40 1.00
DN15 Rodney Stuckey .40 1.00
DN16 Nick Young .60 1.50
DN17 Sean Williams .40 1.00
DN18 Javaris Crittenton .40 1.00
DN19 Jason Smith .40 1.00
DN20 Daequan Cook .50 1.25
DN21 Jared Dudley .50 1.25
DN22 Wilson Chandler .50 1.25
DN23 Morris Almond .40 1.00
DN24 Aaron Brooks .50 1.25
DN25 Arron Afflalo .50 1.25

2007-08 Upper Deck Jordan Chronicles
COMPLETE SET (20) 40.00 80.00
COMMON JORDAN 4.00 10.00

2007-08 Upper Deck Legendary All-Stars
COMPLETE SET (20) 15.00 40.00
LA1 Michael Jordan 12.00 30.00
LA2 Bill Laimbeer 1.00 2.50
LA3 Isiah Thomas 1.25 3.00
LA4 Larry Bird 5.00 12.00
LA5 Magic Johnson 5.00 12.00
LA6 Bill Russell 4.00 10.00
LA7 Kareem Abdul-Jabbar 4.00 10.00
LA8 David Robinson 2.50 6.00
LA9 Hakeem Olajuwon 2.50 6.00
LA10 James Worthy 2.00 5.00
LA11 Robert Parish 1.25 3.00
LA12 Jerry West 3.00 8.00
LA13 Bill Walton 1.50 4.00
LA14 John Havlicek 2.50 6.00
LA15 Rick Barry 1.00 2.50
LA16 Walt Frazier 2.00 5.00
LA17 Bernard King 1.00 2.50
LA18 Clyde Drexler 2.00 5.00
LA19 Elgin Baylor 1.25 3.00
LA20 Maurice Cheeks 1.00 2.50

2007-08 Upper Deck Mini Jersey
1 LeBron James 12.00 30.00
2 Kobe Bryant 25.00 60.00
3 Allen Iverson 2.50 6.00
4 Shaquille O'Neal 3.00 8.00
5 Paul Pierce 2.50 6.00
6 Dirk Nowitzki 2.50 6.00
7 Tim Duncan 2.50 6.00
8 Kevin Garnett 3.00 8.00
9 Dwight Howard 2.50 6.00
10 Yao Ming 3.00 8.00
11 Steve Nash 3.00 8.00
12 Chris Bosh 2.50 6.00
13 Michael Jordan 25.00 60.00

2007-08 Upper Deck MVP Predictor
1 Allen Iverson 2.00 5.00
2 Amare Stoudemire .75 2.00
3 Andre Iguodala .75 2.00
4 Baron Davis .60 1.50
5 Ben Gordon .60 1.50
6 Carlos Boozer .60 1.50
7 Carmelo Anthony 1.25 3.00
8 Chauncey Billups 1.00 2.50
9 Chris Bosh 1.00 2.50
10 Chris Paul 1.50 4.00
11 Dirk Nowitzki 2.00 5.00
12 Dwight Howard 1.00 2.50
13 Dwyane Wade 1.50 4.00
14 Eddy Curry .50 1.25
15 Elton Brand .60 1.50
16 Emeka Okafor .60 1.50
17 Gilbert Arenas .75 2.00
18 Jason Kidd 1.25 3.00
19 Jermaine O'Neal .75 2.00
20 Joe Johnson .60 1.50
21 Kevin Garnett 2.00 5.00
22 Kobe Bryant 6.00 15.00
23 LeBron James 6.00 15.00
24 Michael Redd .60 1.50
25 Mike Bibby .75 2.00
26 Pau Gasol 1.25 3.00
27 Paul Pierce 1.25 3.00
28 Ray Allen 1.25 3.00
29 Tim Duncan 2.00 5.00
30 Tony Parker 1.25 3.00
31 Tracy McGrady 1.25 3.00
32 Vince Carter 1.50 4.00
33 Yao Ming 2.00 5.00
34 Zach Randolph .75 2.00
35 Wild Card .60 1.50

2007-08 Upper Deck NBA Heroes
COMMON DURANT 2.50 6.00
COMMON LEBRON 3.00 8.00
COMMON JORDAN 3.00 8.00
APPROXIMATELY TWO PER BOX

2007-08 Upper Deck Rookie Debut Signatures
AA Arron Afflalo 6.00 15.00
AB Aaron Brooks 6.00 15.00
AG Aaron Gray 5.00 12.00
AH Al Horford 20.00 50.00
AL Acie Law 5.00 12.00
AT Al Thornton 5.00 12.00
CB Corey Brewer 6.00 15.00
CL Carl Landry 5.00 12.00
CR Chris Richard 5.00 12.00
DB Derrick Byars 5.00 12.00
DC Daequan Cook 6.00 15.00
DM Dominic McGuire 5.00 12.00
DN Demetris Nichols 5.00 12.00
DS D.J. Strawberry 5.00 12.00
DU Jared Dudley 6.00 15.00
GD Glen Davis 6.00 15.00
GP Gabe Pruitt 5.00 12.00
HA Adam Haluska 5.00 12.00
JC Javaris Crittenton 5.00 12.00
JD Jermareo Davidson 5.00 12.00
JJ Jared Jordan 5.00 12.00
JM Josh McRoberts 5.00 12.00
JN Joakim Noah 8.00 20.00
JS Jason Smith 5.00 12.00
JW Julian Wright 5.00 12.00
KD Kevin Durant 400.00 800.00
MA Morris Almond 5.00 12.00
MC Mike Conley Jr. 20.00 50.00
MW Marcus Williams 5.00 12.00
NF Nick Fazekas 5.00 12.00
RS Rodney Stuckey 5.00 12.00
RT Reyshawn Terry 5.00 12.00
SH Spencer Hawes 5.00 12.00
SL Stephane Lasme 5.00 12.00
SW Sean Williams 5.00 12.00
TG Taurean Green 5.00 12.00
TU Alando Tucker 5.00 12.00
TY Thaddeus Young 8.00 20.00
WC Wilson Chandler 6.00 15.00

2007-08 Upper Deck ROY Predictor
1 Greg Oden 2.00 5.00
2 Kevin Durant 25.00 60.00
3 Al Horford 5.00 12.00
4 Mike Conley Jr. 5.00 12.00
5 Jeff Green 1.50 4.00
6 Derrick Byars 1.25 3.00
7 Corey Brewer 1.50 4.00
8 Brandan Wright 1.50 4.00
9 Joakim Noah 2.00 5.00
10 Spencer Hawes 1.25 3.00
11 Acie Law 1.25 3.00
12 Thaddeus Young 2.00 5.00
13 Julian Wright 1.25 3.00
14 Al Thornton 1.25 3.00
15 Rodney Stuckey 1.25 3.00
16 Nick Young 2.00 5.00
17 Sean Williams 1.25 3.00
18 Marco Belinelli 1.50 4.00
19 Javaris Crittenton 1.25 3.00
20 Jason Smith 1.25 3.00
21 Daequan Cook 1.50 4.00
22 Jared Dudley 1.50 4.00
23 Wilson Chandler 1.50 4.00
24 Morris Almond 1.25 3.00
25 Aaron Brooks 1.50 4.00
26 Arron Afflalo 1.50 4.00
27 Alando Tucker 1.25 3.00
28 Reyshawn Terry 1.25 3.00
29 Carl Landry 1.25 3.00
30 Gabe Pruitt 1.25 3.00
31 Marcus Williams 1.25 3.00
32 Nick Fazekas 1.25 3.00
33 Glen Davis 1.50 4.00
34 Jermareo Davidson 1.25 3.00
35 Josh McRoberts 1.25 3.00

2007-08 Upper Deck Santa Hat Rookies
*HAT RCs: .5X TO 1.25X BASE HI
*HAT SP RCs: .4X TO 1X BASE HI

2007-08 Upper Deck Star Signings
APPROXIMATELY ONE PER BOX
AB Andrea Bargnani 4.00 10.00
AG Aaron Gray 4.00 10.00
AH Al Harrington 4.00 10.00
AI Andre Iguodala 4.00 10.00
AJ Antawn Jamison 4.00 10.00
AM Alonzo Mourning 25.00 60.00
BA Leandro Barbosa 4.00 10.00
BB Bruce Bowen 4.00 10.00
BG Ben Gordon 4.00 10.00
BJ Bobby Jackson 4.00 10.00
BM Brad Miller 4.00 10.00
BR Brandon Roy 4.00 10.00
BW Bill Walton 10.00 25.00
CA Carmelo Anthony 40.00 100.00
CD Chris Duhon 4.00 10.00
CL Carl Landry 4.00 10.00
CM Corey Maggette 4.00 10.00
CP Chris Paul 60.00 150.00
CS Cedric Simmons 4.00 10.00
DG Daniel Gibson 4.00 10.00
DI Boris Diaw 4.00 10.00
DL David Lee 4.00 10.00
DM Damir Markota 4.00 10.00
DO Keyon Dooling 4.00 10.00
DR Dennis Rodman 60.00 150.00
DS DeShawn Stevenson 4.00 10.00
DW Deron Williams 4.00 10.00
EC Eddy Curry 4.00 10.00
FE Raymond Felton 4.00 10.00
FG Francisco Garcia 4.00 10.00
GA Jorge Garbajosa 4.00 10.00
GG George Gervin 12.00 30.00
HO Al Horford 8.00 20.00
HW Hakim Warrick 4.00 10.00
IL Mile Ilic 4.00 10.00
IU Ime Udoka 4.00 10.00
JA James Augustine 4.00 10.00
JG Joey Graham 4.00 10.00
JJ Jarrett Jack 4.00 10.00
JK Jason Kidd 15.00 40.00
JM Jamaal Magloire 4.00 10.00
JO Jermaine O'Neal 4.00 10.00
JS J.R. Smith 8.00 20.00
JW Julian Wright 4.00 10.00
KB Kobe Bryant 1,000.00 2,000.00
KD Kevin Durant 300.00 600.00
KK Kyle Korver 4.00 10.00
LA LaMarcus Aldridge 8.00 20.00
LB Larry Bird 100.00 250.00
LH Larry Hughes 4.00 10.00
LJ LeBron James 1,000.00 2,000.00
LL Donyell Marshall 4.00 10.00
MA Magic Johnson 100.00 250.00
MB Mike Bibby 8.00 20.00
MC Mardy Collins 4.00 10.00
MI Mike James 4.00 10.00
MJ Michael Jordan 2,000.00 4,000.00
MW Marcus Williams 4.00 10.00
NO Steve Novak 4.00 10.00
OL Hakeem Olajuwon 60.00 150.00
PA Tony Parker 15.00 40.00
PM Paul Millsap 4.00 10.00
PO Patrick O'Bryant 4.00 10.00
PS Peja Stojakovic 4.00 10.00
RF Randy Foye 4.00 10.00
RG Rudy Gay 4.00 10.00
RH Richard Hamilton 8.00 20.00
RJ Richard Jefferson 4.00 10.00
RM Rashad McCants 4.00 10.00
RR Rajon Rondo 10.00 25.00
SA Shareef Abdur-Rahim 4.00 10.00
SB Shannon Brown 4.00 10.00
SJ Solomon Jones 4.00 10.00
SN Steve Nash 40.00 100.00
SS Stromile Swift 4.00 10.00
SW Shawne Williams 4.00 10.00
TA Tony Allen 4.00 10.00
TC Tyson Chandler 4.00 10.00
TF T.J. Ford 4.00 10.00
TM Tracy McGrady 60.00 150.00
TP Tayshaun Prince 4.00 10.00
TS Thabo Sefolosha 4.00 10.00
TT Tyrus Thomas 4.00 10.00
VC Vince Carter 75.00 200.00
WI Shelden Williams 4.00 10.00
WS Wayne Simien 4.00 10.00
YM Yao Ming 150.00 400.00

2007-08 Upper Deck UD Game Jersey
APPROXIMATELY TWO PER BOX
*PATCHES: 1.25X TO 3X BASE HI
AB Andrew Bogut 2.00 5.00
AI Allen Iverson 6.00 15.00
AJ Al Jefferson 1.50 4.00
AK Andrei Kirilenko 2.00 5.00
AM Alonzo Mourning 4.00 10.00
AW Antoine Walker 2.50 6.00
BC Brian Cook 1.50 4.00
BG Ben Gordon 2.00 5.00
BH Brendan Haywood 1.50 4.00
BO Chris Bosh 3.00 8.00
BR Brandon Roy 3.00 8.00
BW Ben Wallace 3.00 8.00
BY Andrew Bynum 1.50 4.00
CA Carmelo Anthony 4.00 10.00
CB Caron Butler 2.00 5.00
CM Corey Maggette 2.00 5.00
CV Charlie Villanueva 1.50 4.00
DG Danny Granger 1.50 4.00
DH Devin Harris 1.50 4.00
DM Darko Milicic 1.50 4.00
DN Dirk Nowitzki 10.00 25.00
DR Dennis Rodman 15.00 40.00
EB Elton Brand 2.00 5.00
EO Emeka Okafor 2.00 5.00
FG Francisco Garcia 1.50 4.00
GA Gilbert Arenas 2.50 6.00
GH Grant Hill 4.00 10.00
GO Drew Gooden 2.00 5.00
GP Gary Payton 4.00 10.00
HE Luther Head 1.50 4.00
HO Dwight Howard 3.00 8.00
IG Andre Iguodala 2.50 6.00
JA Antawn Jamison 2.00 5.00
JC Josh Childress 1.50 4.00
JE Julius Erving 6.00 15.00
JH Josh Howard 2.00 5.00
JK Jason Kidd 4.00 10.00
JM Michael Jordan 150.00 400.00
JN Jameer Nelson 1.50 4.00
JO Jermaine O'Neal 2.50 6.00

JP Johan Petro 1.50 4.00
JR J.J. Redick 2.50 6.00
JS John Stockton 5.00 12.00
JU Juwan Howard 2.50 6.00
JW Jason Williams 4.00 10.00
KB Kobe Bryant 50.00 120.00
KG Kevin Garnett 6.00 15.00
KH Kirk Hinrich 2.50 6.00
KM Kenyon Martin 2.00 5.00
KT Kevin Garnett 6.00 15.00
KW Kwame Brown 1.50 4.00
LB Larry Bird 20.00 50.00
LD Luol Deng 2.00 5.00
LH Larry Hughes 2.00 5.00
LJ LeBron James 50.00 120.00
LK Linas Kleiza 1.50 4.00
LO Lamar Odom 2.00 5.00
MA Donyell Marshall 1.50 4.00
MB Mike Bibby 2.50 6.00
MD Mike Dunleavy 1.50 4.00
MG Manu Ginobili 5.00 12.00
MI Andre Miller 2.00 5.00
MJ Magic Johnson 20.00 50.00
MO Mehmet Okur 1.50 4.00
MR Michael Redd 2.00 5.00
MW Martell Webster 2.00 5.00
NH Nene 2.00 5.00
PG Pau Gasol 4.00 10.00
PP Paul Pierce 4.00 10.00
RA Ray Allen 4.00 10.00
RI Jason Richardson 2.50 6.00
RJ Richard Jefferson 2.00 5.00
RL Rashard Lewis 2.00 5.00
RO David Robinson 5.00 12.00
RP Robert Parish 2.50 6.00
RW Rasheed Wallace 3.00 8.00
SB Shannon Brown 1.50 4.00
SD Samuel Dalembert 1.50 4.00
SH Shawn Marion 2.50 6.00
SJ Josh Smith 1.50 4.00
SM Sean May 1.50 4.00
SN Steve Nash 5.00 12.00
SO Shaquille O'Neal 20.00 50.00
TD Tim Duncan 10.00 25.00
TM Tracy McGrady 4.00 10.00
TP Tony Parker 4.00 10.00
VC Vince Carter 5.00 12.00
WI Marvin Williams 1.50 4.00
YM Yao Ming 6.00 15.00
ZR Zach Randolph 2.50 6.00

2007-08 Upper Deck UD Top 30

COMPLETE SET (30) 12.00 30.00
UT1 Al Jefferson .50 1.25
UT2 Baron Davis .60 1.50
UT3 Ben Gordon .60 1.50
UT4 Brandon Roy 1.00 2.50
UT5 Carlos Boozer .60 1.50
UT6 Chris Paul 1.50 4.00
UT7 Corey Maggette .60 1.50
UT8 Deron Williams .60 1.50
UT9 Dwyane Wade 1.50 4.00
UT10 Eddy Curry .50 1.25
UT11 Emeka Okafor .60 1.50
UT12 Gerald Wallace .60 1.50
UT13 Grant Hill 1.25 3.00
UT14 Jason Richardson .75 2.00
UT15 Jason Terry .60 1.50
UT16 Joe Johnson .60 1.50
UT17 Josh Howard .60 1.50
UT18 Kirk Hinrich .75 2.00
UT19 LeBron James 6.00 15.00
UT20 Luol Deng .60 1.50
UT21 Mike Bibby .75 2.00
UT22 Rashard Lewis .60 1.50
UT23 Raymond Felton .60 1.50
UT24 Richard Hamilton 1.00 2.50
UT25 Richard Jefferson .60 1.50
UT26 Shaquille O'Neal 3.00 8.00
UT27 Shawn Marion .75 2.00
UT28 Stephon Marbury 1.00 2.50
UT29 Steve Nash 1.50 4.00
UT30 Tayshaun Prince .75 2.00

2008-09 Upper Deck

COMP.SET w/o SPs (200) 10.00 25.00
LEGEND ODDS 1:2
ROOKIE ODDS 1:4.5
1 Mike Bibby .40 1.00
2 Al Horford .40 1.00
3 Joe Johnson .40 1.00
4 Josh Childress .25 .60
5 Josh Smith .25 .60
6 Marvin Williams .25 .60
7 Eddie House .25 .60
8 Glen Davis .25 .60
9 Sam Cassell .30 .75
10 Kevin Garnett 1.00 2.50
11 Rajon Rondo .50 1.25
12 Ray Allen .60 1.50
13 Paul Pierce .60 1.50
14 Adam Morrison .25 .60
15 Emeka Okafor .25 .60
16 Gerald Wallace .30 .75
17 Jared Dudley .30 .75
18 Jason Richardson .40 1.00
19 Nazr Mohammed .25 .60
20 Raymond Felton .25 .60
21 Andres Nocioni .25 .60
22 Ben Gordon .30 .75
23 Larry Hughes .30 .75
24 Joakim Noah .25 .60
25 Kirk Hinrich .30 .75
26 Luol Deng .30 .75
27 Tyrus Thomas .30 .75
28 Aleksandar Pavlovic .25 .60
29 Anderson Varejao .25 .60
30 Daniel Gibson .25 .60
31 Wally Szczerbiak .30 .75
32 Ben Wallace .50 1.25
33 LeBron James 3.00 8.00
34 Zydrunas Ilgauskas .30 .75
35 Jason Kidd .60 1.50
36 Dirk Nowitzki 1.00 2.50
37 Jason Terry .30 .75
38 Jerry Stackhouse .40 1.00
39 Jose Barea .50 1.25
40 Josh Howard .30 .75
41 Allen Iverson .75 2.00
42 Carmelo Anthony .50 1.25
43 J.R. Smith .40 1.00
44 Kenyon Martin .30 .75
45 Linas Kleiza .25 .60
46 Marcus Camby .30 .75
47 Antonio McDyess .30 .75
48 Chauncey Billups .50 1.25
49 Jason Maxiell .25 .60
50 Rasheed Wallace .50 1.25
51 Richard Hamilton .40 1.00
52 Rodney Stuckey .25 .60
53 Tayshaun Prince .40 1.00
54 Al Harrington .30 .75
55 Baron Davis .40 1.00
56 Kelenna Azubuike .25 .60
57 Matt Barnes .25 .60
58 Monta Ellis .30 .75
59 Stephen Jackson .30 .75
60 Luis Scola .30 .75
61 Luther Head .25 .60
62 Rafer Alston .25 .60
63 Shane Battier .30 .75
64 Tracy McGrady .60 1.50
65 Yao Ming 1.00 2.50
66 Andre Owens .25 .60
67 Danny Granger .30 .75
68 Jamaal Tinsley .25 .60
69 Jermaine O'Neal .40 1.00
70 Kareem Rush .25 .60
71 Mike Dunleavy .25 .60
72 Troy Murphy .25 .60
73 Al Thornton .25 .60
74 Chris Kaman .25 .60
75 Corey Maggette .30 .75
76 Cuttino Mobley .25 .60
77 Elton Brand .30 .75
78 Tim Thomas .25 .60
79 Andrew Bynum .25 .60
80 Derek Fisher .30 .75
81 Jordan Farmar .25 .60
82 Kobe Bryant 3.00 8.00
83 Pau Gasol .50 1.25
84 Lamar Odom .30 .75
85 Luke Walton .30 .75
86 Darko Milicic .25 .60
87 Javaris Crittenton .25 .60
88 Kyle Lowry .40 1.00
89 Mike Conley Jr. .30 .75
90 Mike Miller .30 .75
91 Kwame Brown .25 .60
92 Rudy Gay .40 1.00
93 Daequan Cook .25 .60
94 Dorell Wright .25 .60
95 Dwyane Wade .75 2.00
96 Jason Williams .30 .75
97 Ricky Davis .30 .75
98 Shawn Marion .40 1.00
99 Udonis Haslem .25 .60
100 Andrew Bogut .30 .75
101 Charlie Villanueva .25 .60
102 Desmond Mason .25 .60
103 Michael Redd .30 .75
104 Mo Williams .30 .75
105 Yi Jianlian .50 1.25
106 Al Jefferson .25 .60
107 Corey Brewer .30 .75
108 Craig Smith .25 .60
109 Randy Foye .40 1.00
110 Rashad McCants .25 .60
111 Ryan Gomes .25 .60
112 Sebastian Telfair .25 .60
113 Bostjan Nachbar .25 .60
114 Devin Harris .30 .75
115 Josh Boone .25 .60
116 Nenad Krstic .25 .60
117 Richard Jefferson .30 .75
118 Sean Williams .25 .60
119 Vince Carter .75 2.00
120 David Lee .30 .75
121 Eddy Curry .25 .60
122 Jamal Crawford .40 1.00
123 Nate Robinson .25 .60
124 Quentin Richardson .25 .60
125 Stephon Marbury .40 1.00
126 Zach Randolph .40 1.00
127 Chris Paul .75 2.00
128 David West .30 .75
129 Julian Wright .30 .75
130 Morris Peterson .25 .60
131 Peja Stojakovic .30 .75
132 Tyson Chandler .25 .60
133 Carlos Arroyo .25 .60
134 Dwight Howard .50 1.25
135 Hedo Turkoglu .30 .75
136 J.J. Redick .40 1.00
137 Jameer Nelson .25 .60
138 Maurice Evans .25 .60
139 Rashard Lewis .30 .75
140 Andre Iguodala .30 .75
141 Andre Miller .30 .75
142 Jason Smith .30 .75
143 Louis Williams .30 .75
144 Samuel Dalembert .30 .75
145 Thaddeus Young .30 .75
146 Willie Green .25 .60
147 Amare Stoudemire .40 1.00
148 Boris Diaw .30 .75
149 Grant Hill .60 1.50
150 Leandro Barbosa .30 .75
151 Raja Bell .30 .75
152 Shaquille O'Neal 1.25 3.00
153 Steve Nash .75 2.00
154 Brandon Roy .30 .75
155 Channing Frye .25 .60
156 Greg Oden .25 .60
157 LaMarcus Aldridge .40 1.00
158 Martell Webster .25 .60
159 Steve Blake .25 .60
160 Beno Udrih .25 .60
161 Brad Miller .30 .75
162 Francisco Garcia .25 .60
163 John Salmons .30 .75
164 Kevin Martin .30 .75
165 Mikki Moore .25 .60
166 Ron Artest .40 1.00
167 Brent Barry .25 .60
168 Bruce Bowen .30 .75
169 Manu Ginobili .75 2.00
170 Michael Finley .40 1.00
171 Robert Horry .30 .75
172 Tim Duncan 1.00 2.50
173 Tony Parker .50 1.25
174 Chris Wilcox .25 .60
175 Damien Wilkins .25 .60
176 Jeff Green .30 .75
177 Kevin Durant 1.50 4.00
178 Nick Collison .25 .60
179 Earl Watson .25 .60
180 Andrea Bargnani .30 .75
181 Anthony Parker .25 .60
182 Carlos Delfino .25 .60
183 Chris Bosh .50 1.25
184 Jamario Moon .25 .60
185 Jose Calderon .25 .60
186 T.J. Ford .25 .60
187 Andrei Kirilenko .30 .75
188 Carlos Boozer .30 .75
189 Deron Williams .30 .75
190 Kyle Korver .30 .75
191 Mehmet Okur .25 .60
192 Paul Millsap .30 .75
193 Ronnie Brewer .25 .60
194 Antawn Jamison .30 .75
195 Antonio Daniels .25 .60
196 Brendan Haywood .25 .60
197 Caron Butler .30 .75
198 DeShawn Stevenson .30 .75
199 Gilbert Arenas .40 1.00
200 Nick Young .25 .60
201 Spud Webb .40 1.00
202 Bob Cousy .75 2.00
203 Kevin McHale .60 1.50
204 Larry Bird 1.50 4.00
205 Dennis Rodman 1.00 2.50
206 Michael Jordan 4.00 10.00
207 Isiah Thomas .75 2.00
208 Joe Dumars .50 1.25
209 Nate Thurmond .40 1.00
210 Hakeem Olajuwon 1.00 2.50
211 Calvin Murphy .40 1.00
212 Kareem Abdul-Jabbar .75 2.00
213 Magic Johnson 1.50 4.00
214 Oscar Robertson .50 1.25
215 Bill Bradley .60 1.50
216 Earl Monroe .50 1.25
217 Willis Reed .75 2.00
218 Julius Erving 1.25 3.00
219 Clyde Drexler .60 1.50
220 Bill Walton .75 2.00
221 Maurice Lucas .50 1.25
222 David Robinson 1.00 2.50
223 John Stockton 1.00 2.50
224 Karl Malone .60 1.50
225 D.J. Augustin RC 1.00 2.50
226 Brook Lopez RC 1.25 3.00
227 Jerryd Bayless RC .75 2.00
228 Jason Thompson RC .60 1.50
229 Brandon Rush RC .60 1.50
230 Anthony Randolph RC .75 2.00
231 Robin Lopez RC .75 2.00
232 Marreese Speights RC .75 2.00
233 Roy Hibbert RC .75 2.00
234 Courtney Lee RC .75 2.00
235 J.J. Hickson RC .60 1.50
236 Ryan Anderson RC .75 2.00
237 Kosta Koufos RC .60 1.50
238 James Gist RC .60 1.50
239 Darrell Arthur RC .75 2.00
240 Donte Greene RC .60 1.50
241 D.J. White RC .60 1.50
242 J.R. Giddens RC .60 1.50
243 Deron Washington RC .60 1.50
244 Joey Dorsey RC .60 1.50
245 Mario Chalmers RC 1.00 2.50
246 DeAndre Jordan RC 1.25 3.00
247 Luc Richard Mbah A Moute RC .75 2.00
248 Kyle Weaver RC .60 1.50
249 Sonny Weems RC .60 1.50
250 Chris Douglas-Roberts RC .60 1.50
251 Sean Singletary RC .60 1.50
252 Patrick Ewing Jr. RC .60 1.50
253 Shan Foster RC .60 1.50
254 Bill Walker RC .60 1.50
255 Malik Hairston RC .60 1.50
256 Richard Hendrix RC .60 1.50
257 DeVon Hardin RC .60 1.50
258 Darnell Jackson RC .60 1.50
259 Derrick Rose RC 4.00 10.00
260 Michael Beasley RC 1.00 2.50
261 O.J. Mayo RC .75 2.00
262 Russell Westbrook RC 8.00 20.00
263 Kevin Love RC 2.00 5.00
264 Danilo Gallinari RC 1.50 4.00
265 Eric Gordon RC 1.50 4.00
266 Joe Alexander RC .60 1.50

2008-09 Upper Deck Electric Court Gold

*GOLD: .6X TO 1.5X BASE HI
GOLD STATED ODDS 1:5
206 Michael Jordan 25.00 60.00
262 Russell Westbrook 25.00 60.00

2008-09 Upper Deck All Star Class

COMPLETE SET (30) 30.00 60.00
ASAI Allen Iverson 2.00 5.00
ASBL Bill Laimbeer .75 2.00
ASBO Chris Bosh 1.25 3.00
ASCB Chauncey Billups 1.25 3.00
ASDN Dirk Nowitzki 2.50 6.00
ASDR David Robinson 2.00 5.00
ASDW Dominique Wilkins 1.50 4.00
ASGG George Gervin 1.50 4.00
ASJE Julius Erving 2.50 6.00
ASJK Jason Kidd 1.50 4.00
ASJO Magic Johnson 3.00 8.00
ASKA Kareem Abdul-Jabbar 1.50 4.00
ASKB Kobe Bryant 8.00 20.00
ASKG Kevin Garnett 2.50 6.00
ASKM Karl Malone 1.25 3.00
ASLJ LeBron James 8.00 20.00
ASMJ Michael Jordan 8.00 20.00
ASNA Nate Archibald .75 2.00
ASRA Ray Allen 1.50 4.00
ASRB Rick Barry 1.25 3.00
ASSM Shawn Marion 1.00 2.50
ASSN Steve Nash 2.00 5.00
ASSO Shaquille O'Neal 3.00 8.00
ASTD Tim Duncan 2.50 6.00
ASTM Tracy McGrady 1.50 4.00
ASTP Tony Parker 1.25 3.00
ASVC Vince Carter 2.00 5.00
ASWA Dwyane Wade 2.00 5.00
ASWF Walt Frazier 1.00 2.50
ASYM Yao Ming 2.50 6.00

2008-09 Upper Deck Bulls Dynasty

COMPLETE SET (30) 25.00 50.00
STATED ODDS 1:8
CHI1 Dennis Rodman 1.50 4.00
CHI2 Horace Grant .75 2.00
CHI3 Toni Kukoc .75 2.00
CHI4 Horace Grant .75 2.00
CHI5 Toni Kukoc .75 2.00
CHI6 Steve Kerr .75 2.00
CHI7 John Paxson .60 1.50
CHI8 Michael Jordan 6.00 15.00
CHI9 Michael Jordan 6.00 15.00
CHI10 Michael Jordan 6.00 15.00
CHI11 Michael Jordan 6.00 15.00
CHI12 Michael Jordan 6.00 15.00
CHI13 Michael Jordan 6.00 15.00
CHI14 Michael Jordan 6.00 15.00
CHI15 Michael Jordan 6.00 15.00
CHI16 Dennis Rodman 1.50 4.00
CHI17 Bill Wennington .75 2.00
CHI18 Bill Cartwright .60 1.50
CHI19 Bill Cartwright .60 1.50
CHI20 Will Perdue .50 1.25
CHI21 Will Perdue .50 1.25
CHI22 Dennis Rodman 1.50 4.00
CHI23 B.J. Armstrong .75 2.00
CHI24 Ron Harper .75 2.00
CHI25 Ron Harper .75 2.00
CHI26 Scottie Pippen 1.25 3.00
CHI27 B.J. Armstrong .75 2.00
CHI28 John Paxson .60 1.50
CHI29 Steve Kerr .75 2.00
CHI30 Scottie Pippen 1.25 3.00

2008-09 Upper Deck Celtics Dynasty

COMPLETE SET (30) 10.00 25.00
STATED ODDS 1:8
BOS1 John Havlicek .75 2.00
BOS2 John Havlicek .75 2.00
BOS3 John Havlicek .75 2.00
BOS4 Sam Jones 1.00 2.50
BOS5 Sam Jones 1.00 2.50
BOS6 Sam Jones 1.00 2.50
BOS7 Bob Cousy 1.25 3.00
BOS8 Don Nelson .75 2.00
BOS9 Don Nelson .75 2.00
BOS10 Tom Sanders .75 2.00
BOS11 Tom Sanders .75 2.00
BOS12 Tom Sanders .75 2.00
BOS13 Gene Conley .75 2.00
BOS14 Bill Russell 2.50 6.00
BOS15 Bill Russell 2.50 6.00
BOS16 Tom Heinsohn .75 2.00
BOS17 Tom Heinsohn .75 2.00
BOS18 Tom Heinsohn .75 2.00
BOS19 Bill Sharman .75 2.00
BOS20 Bill Sharman .75 2.00
BOS21 Bill Sharman .75 2.00
BOS22 Em Bryant .75 2.00
BOS23 Bailey Howell .75 2.00
BOS24 K.C. Jones .75 2.00
BOS25 Clyde Lovellette .75 2.00
BOS26 Bob Cousy 1.25 3.00
BOS27 Wayne Embry .50 1.25
BOS28 Jim Loscutoff .75 2.00
BOS29 Frank Ramsey .75 2.00
BOS30 K.C. Jones .75 2.00

2008-09 Upper Deck Emulation Memorabilia Dual

STATED ODDS 1:32
*PATCHES: .4X TO 1.2X BASE HI
PATCH STATED ODDS 1:600
EAB R.Allen/L.Bird 12.00 30.00
EBW K.Bryant/D.Wilkins 60.00 150.00
EDR T.Duncan/D.Robinson 10.00 25.00
EEJ J.Erving/L.James 30.00 80.00
EGB K.Garnett/A.Bynum 10.00 25.00
EGM G.Gervin/T.McGrady 6.00 15.00
EHO D.Howard/S.O'Neal 12.00 30.00
EIP C.Paul/A.Iverson 8.00 20.00
EKJ J.Kidd/M.Johnson 12.00 30.00
EWR B.Wallace/D.Rodman 8.00 20.00

2008-09 Upper Deck Game Jerseys

STATED ODDS 1:7
*PATCHES: 1.25X TO 3X BASE HI
PATCH STATED ODDS 1:250
GAAB Andrea Bargnani 2.00 5.00
GAAI Allen Iverson 5.00 12.00
GAAJ Al Jefferson 1.50 4.00
GAAK Andrei Kirilenko 2.00 5.00
GAAS Amare Stoudemire 2.50 6.00
GABG Ben Gordon 2.00 5.00
GABI Chauncey Billups 3.00 8.00
GABO Chris Bosh 3.00 8.00
GABU Caron Butler 2.00 5.00
GABW Ben Wallace 3.00 8.00
GACA Carmelo Anthony 3.00 8.00
GACB Carlos Boozer 2.00 5.00
GACP Chris Paul 5.00 12.00
GADG Danny Granger 2.00 5.00
GADH Dwight Howard 3.00 8.00
GADN Dirk Nowitzki 6.00 15.00
GADW Deron Williams 2.00 5.00
GAEB Elton Brand 2.00 5.00
GAEO Emeka Okafor 1.50 4.00
GAIG Andre Iguodala 2.00 5.00
GAJA Antawn Jamison 2.00 5.00
GAJH Josh Howard 2.00 5.00
GAJJ Joe Johnson 2.50 6.00
GAJK Jason Kidd 4.00 10.00
GAJO Jermaine O'Neal 2.50 6.00
GAJR Jason Richardson 2.50 6.00
GAJS Josh Smith 2.50 6.00
GAKB Kobe Bryant 40.00 100.00
GAKG Kevin Garnett 6.00 15.00
GAKH Kirk Hinrich 2.00 5.00
GALJ LeBron James 12.00 30.00
GAMB Mike Bibby 2.50 6.00
GAMG Manu Ginobili 5.00 12.00
GAMR Michael Redd 2.00 5.00
GAMW Marvin Williams 1.50 4.00
GAPA Tony Parker 3.00 8.00
GAPG Pau Gasol 3.00 8.00
GAPP Paul Pierce 4.00 10.00
GARH Richard Hamilton 2.50 6.00
GARJ Richard Jefferson 2.00 5.00
GARL Rashard Lewis 2.00 5.00
GARW Rasheed Wallace 3.00 8.00
GASM Shawn Marion 2.50 6.00
GASO Shaquille O'Neal 8.00 20.00
GATD Tim Duncan 6.00 15.00
GATM Tracy McGrady 4.00 10.00
GATP Tayshaun Prince 2.50 6.00
GAVC Vince Carter 5.00 12.00
GAYM Yao Ming 6.00 15.00
GAZR Zach Randolph 2.50 6.00

2008-09 Upper Deck Kobe Bryant Heroes

COMPLETE SET (10) 15.00 40.00
COMMON CARD (KB1-KB10) 2.50 6.00
STATED ODDS 1:25

2008-09 Upper Deck Lakers Dynasty

COMPLETE SET (30) 15.00 30.00
STATED ODDS 1:8
LAL1 Kobe Bryant 6.00 15.00
LAL2 Kobe Bryant 6.00 15.00
LAL3 Kobe Bryant 6.00 15.00
LAL4 Derek Fisher .60 1.50
LAL5 Derek Fisher .60 1.50
LAL6 Horace Grant .75 2.00
LAL7 Horace Grant .75 2.00
LAL8 A.C. Green .75 2.00
LAL9 A.C. Green .75 2.00
LAL10 Byron Scott .60 1.50
LAL11 James Worthy .75 2.00
LAL12 James Worthy .75 2.00
LAL13 Magic Johnson 2.50 6.00
LAL14 Magic Johnson 2.50 6.00
LAL15 Magic Johnson 2.50 6.00
LAL16 Kareem Abdul-Jabbar 1.25 3.00
LAL17 Kareem Abdul-Jabbar 1.25 3.00
LAL18 Kareem Abdul-Jabbar 1.25 3.00
LAL19 Michael Cooper .60 1.50
LAL20 Michael Cooper .60 1.50
LAL21 Jamaal Wilkes .60 1.50
LAL22 Jamaal Wilkes .60 1.50
LAL23 Norm Nixon .50 1.25
LAL24 Slater Martin .75 2.00
LAL25 Mitch Richmond .75 2.00
LAL26 Ron Harper .75 2.00
LAL27 George Mikan 1.50 4.00
LAL28 Clyde Lovellette .75 2.00
LAL29 Mitch Kupchak .75 2.00
LAL30 Kurt Rambis .50 1.25

2008-09 Upper Deck Same Day Signatures

RPSBR Brandon Rush 6.00 15.00
RPSCD Chris Douglas-Roberts 6.00 15.00
RPSCL Courtney Lee 8.00 20.00
RPSDJ DeAndre Jordan 10.00 25.00
RPSDW D.J. White 6.00 15.00
RPSEG Eric Gordon 15.00 40.00
RPSGH George Hill 10.00 25.00
RPSGR Donte Greene 6.00 15.00
RPSHE Patrick Ewing Jr. 6.00 15.00
RPSJB Jerryd Bayless 8.00 20.00
RPSJG J.R. Giddens 6.00 15.00
RPSJH J.J. Hickson 6.00 15.00
RPSJT Jason Thompson 6.00 15.00
RPSKK Kosta Koufos 6.00 15.00
RPSKL Kevin Love 20.00 50.00
RPSKW Kyle Weaver 6.00 15.00
RPSMC Mario Chalmers 10.00 25.00
RPSMS Marreese Speights 8.00 20.00
RPSOM O.J. Mayo 8.00 20.00
RPSRA Ryan Anderson 8.00 20.00
RPSRH Roy Hibbert 8.00 20.00
RPSSW Sonny Weems 6.00 15.00
RPSWS Walter Sharpe 6.00 15.00

2008-09 Upper Deck Star Signings

STATED ODDS 1:2[illegible]
GOLD: .6X TO 1.5X BASE HI
GOLD PRINT RUN 25 SER.#'d SETS
SSAH Al Harrington 3.00 8.00
SSAI Andre Iguodala 5.00 12.00
SSAJ Antawn Jamison 3.00 8.00
SSBB Bruce Bowen 3.00 8.00
SSBD Baron Davis 4.00 10.00
SSBG Ben Gordon 5.00 12.00
SSBK Coby Karl 3.00 8.00
SSBM Brad Miller 3.00 8.00
SSBR Brandon Roy 10.00 25.00
SSCA Carmelo Anthony 20.00 40.00
SSCB Corey Brewer 3.00 8.00
SSCM Corey Maggette 3.00 8.00
SSCP Chris Paul 50.00 120.00
SSCS Cedric Simmons 3.00 8.00
SSDA Danny Granger 5.00 12.00
SSDC Daequan Cook 3.00 8.00
SSDG Daniel Gibson 3.00 8.00
SSDM Donyell Marshall 3.00 8.00
SSDO Keyon Dooling 3.00 8.00
SSDS DeShawn Stevenson 3.00 8.00
SSDW Deron Williams 10.00 25.00
SSGD Glen Davis 3.00 8.00
SSGR Jeff Green 4.00 10.00
SSHO Al Horford 5.00 12.00
SSID Ike Diogu 3.00 8.00
SSJB Josh Boone 3.00 8.00
SSJG Joey Graham 3.00 8.00
SSJK Jason Kidd 6.00 15.00
SSJM Jamario Moon 3.00 8.00
SSJO Joakim Noah 10.00 25.00
SSKA Kelenna Azubuike 4.00 10.00
SSKD Kevin Durant 75.00 150.00
SSLA LaMarcus Aldridge 20.00 50.00
SSLH Larry Hughes 4.00 10.00
SSLJ LeBron James 1,000.00 2,000.00
SSLP Leon Powe 3.00 8.00
SSLS Luis Scola 3.00 8.00
SSMB Mike Bibby 3.00 8.00
SSMC Mike Conley Jr. 4.00 10.00
SSMW Mo Williams 3.00 8.00
SSNO Steve Novak 3.00 8.00
SSOP Oleksiy Pecherov 3.00 8.00
SSRB Renaldo Balkman 3.00 8.00
SSRF Randy Foye 3.00 8.00
SSRG Rudy Gay 6.00 15.00
SSRJ Richard Jefferson 3.00 8.00
SSSM Craig Smith 3.00 8.00
SSTC Tyson Chandler 3.00 8.00
SSTF T.J. Ford 3.00 8.00
SSTM Tracy McGrady 20.00 40.00
SSTP Tayshaun Prince 3.00 8.00
SSTT Tyrus Thomas 3.00 8.00
SSVC Vince Carter 12.00 30.00
SSWI Marvin Williams 3.00 8.00

2008-09 Upper Deck Starquest

COMPLETE SET (30) 20.00 50.00
APPROXIMATE ODDS 1:8
*BLACK: 1.5X TO 4X BASE HI
BLACK STATED ODDS 1:16
*BLUE: 1X TO 2.5X BASE HI
*COPPER: .6X TO 1.5X BASE HI
*CYAN: 1X TO 2.5X BASE HI
*GOLD: 1X TO 2.5X BASE HI
SQ1 Carmelo Anthony .75 2.00
SQ2 Chauncey Billups .75 2.00
SQ3 Larry Bird 2.00 5.00
SQ4 Chris Bosh .75 2.00
SQ5 Kobe Bryant 5.00 12.00
SQ6 Vince Carter 1.25 3.00
SQ7 Baron Davis .60 1.50
SQ8 Tim Duncan 1.50 4.00
SQ9 Kevin Durant 2.50 6.00
SQ10 Julius Erving 1.50 4.00
SQ11 Walt Frazier .60 1.50
SQ12 Kevin Garnett 1.50 4.00
SQ13 Rudy Gay .60 1.50
SQ14 Artis Gilmore .50 1.25
SQ15 Dwight Howard .75 2.00
SQ16 Allen Iverson 1.25 3.00
SQ17 LeBron James 5.00 12.00
SQ18 Al Jefferson .40 1.00
SQ19 Magic Johnson 2.00 5.00
SQ20 Michael Jordan 8.00 20.00
SQ21 Shawn Marion .60 1.50
SQ22 Tracy McGrady 1.00 2.50
SQ23 Yao Ming 1.50 4.00
SQ24 Dirk Nowitzki 1.50 4.00
SQ25 Shaquille O'Neal 2.00 5.00
SQ26 Greg Oden .40 1.00
SQ27 Chris Paul 1.25 3.00
SQ28 Brandon Roy .50 1.25
SQ29 Dwyane Wade 1.25 3.00
SQ30 Deron Williams .50 1.25

2008-09 Upper Deck Team MVPs

COMPLETE SET (30) 10.00 25.00
THREE PER RACK PACK
MVP1 Josh Smith .40 1.00
MVP2 Kevin Garnett 1.50 4.00
MVP3 Gerald Wallace .50 1.25
MVP4 Luol Deng .50 1.25
MVP5 LeBron James 5.00 12.00
MVP6 Dirk Nowitzki 1.50 4.00
MVP7 Carmelo Anthony .75 2.00
MVP8 Chauncey Billups .75 2.00
MVP9 Baron Davis .60 1.50
MVP10 Yao Ming 1.50 4.00
MVP11 Jermaine O'Neal .60 1.50
MVP12 Chris Kaman .60 1.50
MVP13 Kobe Bryant 5.00 12.00
MVP14 Rudy Gay .60 1.50
MVP15 Dwyane Wade 1.25 3.00
MVP16 Michael Redd .50 1.25
MVP17 Al Jefferson .40 1.00
MVP18 Jason Kidd 1.00 2.50
MVP19 Chris Paul 1.25 3.00
MVP20 Zach Randolph .60 1.50
MVP21 Dwight Howard .75 2.00
MVP22 Andre Iguodala .50 1.25
MVP23 Steve Nash 1.25 3.00
MVP24 Brandon Roy .50 1.25
MVP25 Kevin Martin .50 1.25
MVP26 Tony Parker .75 2.00
MVP27 Kevin Durant 2.50 6.00
MVP28 Chris Bosh .75 2.00
MVP29 Deron Williams .50 1.25
MVP30 Caron Butler .50 1.25

2008-09 Upper Deck True Talents

COMPLETE SET (30) 8.00 20.00
TWO PER RETAIL VALUE PACK
TT1 Thaddeus Young .50 1.25
TT2 Julian Wright .40 1.00
TT3 Sean Williams .40 1.00
TT4 David West .50 1.25
TT5 Luke Walton .50 1.25
TT6 Al Thornton .40 1.00
TT7 Rodney Stuckey .40 1.00
TT8 J.R. Smith .60 1.50
TT9 Luis Scola .50 1.25
TT10 Greg Oden .40 1.00
TT11 Joakim Noah .40 1.00
TT12 Mike Conley Jr. .50 1.25
TT13 Jamario Moon .40 1.00
TT14 Jason Maxiell .40 1.00
TT15 Chris Kaman .40 1.00
TT16 Yi Jianlian .75 2.00
TT17 Al Horford .60 1.50
TT18 Jeff Green .50 1.25
TT19 Daniel Gibson .40 1.00
TT20 Rudy Gay .60 1.50
TT21 Francisco Garcia .40 1.00
TT22 Jordan Farmar .40 1.00
TT23 Monta Ellis .50 1.25
TT24 Kevin Durant 2.50 6.00
TT25 Luol Deng .50 1.25
TT26 Daequan Cook .40 1.00
TT27 Andrew Bynum .40 1.00
TT28 Ronnie Brewer .40 1.00
TT29 Corey Brewer .50 1.25
TT30 Jose Barea .75 2.00

2008-09 Upper Deck Ultimates

COMPLETE SET (30) 25.00 50.00
U1 Danny Ainge 1.00 2.50
U2 Dave Bing 1.00 2.50
U3 Larry Bird 3.00 8.00
U4 Muggsy Bogues .75 2.00
U5 Manute Bol 1.00 2.50
U6 Bill Bradley 1.25 3.00
U7 Wilt Chamberlain 3.00 8.00
U8 Vlade Divac 1.00 2.50
U9 Clyde Drexler 1.25 3.00
U10 Joe Dumars 1.00 2.50
U11 Julius Erving 2.50 6.00
U12 Patrick Ewing 1.50 4.00
U13 Kevin Johnson 1.00 2.50
U14 Larry Johnson 1.00 2.50
U15 Magic Johnson 3.00 8.00
U16 Michael Jordan 8.00 20.00
U17 Karl Malone 1.25 3.00
U18 Pete Maravich 2.50 6.00
U19 Gheorghe Muresan 1.00 2.50
U20 Hakeem Olajuwon 2.00 5.00
U21 Scottie Pippen 1.50 4.00
U22 Oscar Robertson 1.00 2.50
U23 David Robinson 2.00 5.00
U24 Bill Russell 3.00 8.00
U25 John Salley .60 1.50
U26 Kenny Smith .75 2.00
U27 John Stockton 2.00 5.00
U28 Isiah Thomas 1.50 4.00
U29 Jerry West 2.00 5.00
U30 Dominique Wilkins 1.50 4.00

2009-10 Upper Deck

COMPLETE SET (295) 150.00 400.00
COMP.SET w/o RCs (200) 20.00 50.00
1 Josh Smith .25 .60
2 Al Horford .40 1.00
3 Mike Bibby .40 1.00
4 Joe Johnson .40 1.00
5 Marvin Williams .25 .60
6 Maurice Evans .25 .60
7 Kevin Garnett 1.00 2.50
8 Paul Pierce .60 1.50
9 Ray Allen .60 1.50
10 Rajon Rondo .50 1.25
11 Kendrick Perkins .25 .60
12 Bill Walker .25 .60
13 Leon Powe .25 .60
14 Raymond Felton .25 .60
15 Raja Bell .30 .75
16 D.J. Augustin .25 .60
17 Gerald Wallace .30 .75
18 Boris Diaw .30 .75
19 Emeka Okafor .30 .75
20 Vladimir Radmanovic .25 .60
21 Derrick Rose .60 1.50
22 Luol Deng .30 .75
23 Michael Jordan 3.00 8.00
24 John Salmons .30 .75
25 Joakim Noah .25 .60
26 Tyrus Thomas .25 .60
27 Ben Gordon .30 .75
28 LeBron James 3.00 8.00
29 Mo Williams .30 .75
30 Ben Wallace .50 1.25
31 Delonte West .25 .60
32 Zydrunas Ilgauskas .30 .75
33 Daniel Gibson .25 .60
34 Wally Szczerbiak .30 .75
35 Josh Howard .30 .75
36 Dirk Nowitzki 1.00 2.50
37 Jason Kidd .60 1.50
38 Antoine Wright .25 .60
39 Erick Dampier .25 .60
40 Jason Terry .30 .75
41 Chauncey Billups .50 1.25
42 Carmelo Anthony .60 1.50
43 Kenyon Martin .25 .60
44 Dahntay Jones .25 .60
45 Nene .30 .75
46 J.R. Smith .40 1.00
47 Allen Iverson .75 2.00
48 Richard Hamilton .40 1.00
49 Tayshaun Prince .40 1.00
50 Rodney Stuckey .25 .60
51 Amir Johnson .25 .60
52 Rasheed Wallace .50 1.25
53 Monta Ellis .30 .75
54 Stephen Jackson .30 .75
55 Jamal Crawford .40 1.00
56 Kelenna Azubuike .25 .60
57 Andris Biedrins .25 .60
58 Anthony Morrow .25 .60
59 Corey Maggette .30 .75
60 Luis Scola .30 .75
61 Tracy McGrady .75 2.00
62 Yao Ming 1.00 2.50
63 Ron Artest .40 1.00
64 Aaron Brooks .25 .60
65 Shane Battier .40 1.00
66 Von Wafer .25 .60
67 T.J. Ford .25 .60
68 Danny Granger .25 .60
69 Mike Dunleavy .25 .60
70 Troy Murphy .25 .60
71 Jeff Foster .25 .60
72 Jarrett Jack .30 .75
73 Eric Gordon .30 .75
74 Baron Davis .30 .75
75 Al Thornton .25 .60
76 Zach Randolph .40 1.00
77 Chris Kaman .30 .75
78 Mardy Collins .25 .60
79 Kobe Bryant 3.00 8.00
80 Pau Gasol .60 1.50
81 Lamar Odom .30 .75
82 Derek Fisher .40 1.00
83 Adam Morrison .25 .60
84 Andrew Bynum .25 .60
85 Sasha Vujacic .25 .60
86 Trevor Ariza .25 .60
87 O.J. Mayo .25 .60

88 Marc Gasol .40 1.00
89 Rudy Gay .40 1.00
90 Darrell Arthur .25 .60
91 Marko Jaric .25 .60
92 Mike Conley Jr. .30 .75
93 Michael Beasley .25 .60
94 Mario Chalmers .30 .75
95 Dwyane Wade .75 2.00
96 Jermaine O'Neal .40 1.00
97 Udonis Haslem .25 .60
98 Chris Quinn .25 .60
99 Daequan Cook .25 .60
100 Luke Ridnour .30 .75
101 Michael Redd .30 .75
102 Richard Jefferson .30 .75
103 Charlie Villanueva .25 .60
104 Andrew Bogut .30 .75
105 Ramon Sessions .25 .60
106 Joe Alexander .25 .60
107 Kevin Love .40 1.00
108 Sebastian Telfair .25 .60
109 Al Jefferson .25 .60
110 Randy Foye .25 .60
111 Ryan Gomes .25 .60
112 Craig Smith .25 .60
113 Mike Miller .30 .75
114 Devin Harris .25 .60
115 Vince Carter .75 2.00
116 Yi Jianlian .50 1.25
117 Bobby Simmons .25 .60
118 Brook Lopez .40 1.00
119 Chris Douglas-Roberts .25 .60
120 Eduardo Najera .25 .60
121 Chris Paul .75 2.00
122 Peja Stojakovic .30 .75
123 David West .30 .75
124 Tyson Chandler .30 .75
125 Rasual Butler .25 .60
126 James Posey .25 .60
127 Al Harrington .30 .75
128 Chris Duhon .30 .75
129 Quentin Richardson .25 .60
130 David Lee .25 .60
131 Jared Jeffries .25 .60
132 Wilson Chandler .30 .75
133 Danilo Gallinari .30 .75
134 Russell Westbrook .75 2.00
135 Kevin Durant 1.50 4.00
136 Jeff Green .30 .75
137 Desmond Mason .25 .60
138 Nick Collison .25 .60
139 Earl Watson .25 .60
140 Dwight Howard .50 1.25
141 Courtney Lee .25 .60
142 Hedo Turkoglu .30 .75
143 Jameer Nelson .25 .60
144 Rashard Lewis .30 .75
145 Mickael Pietrus .25 .60
146 Elton Brand .30 .75
147 Andre Miller .40 1.00
148 Andre Iguodala .40 1.00
149 Thaddeus Young .30 .75
150 Willie Green .25 .60
151 Samuel Dalembert .25 .60
152 Jason Richardson .40 1.00
153 Shaquille O'Neal 1.25 3.00
154 Steve Nash .75 2.00
155 Grant Hill .60 1.50
156 Amare Stoudemire .50 1.25
157 Leandro Barbosa .30 .75
158 Robin Lopez .30 .75
159 Brandon Roy .50 1.25
160 LaMarcus Aldridge .40 1.00
161 Jerryd Bayless .25 .60
162 Rudy Fernandez .25 .60
163 Steve Blake .25 .60
164 Martell Webster .25 .60
165 Greg Oden .25 .60
166 Spencer Hawes .25 .60
167 Kevin Martin .30 .75
168 Beno Udrih .25 .60
169 Andres Nocioni .25 .60
170 Jason Thompson .25 .60
171 Rashad McCants .25 .60
172 Francisco Garcia .25 .60
173 Tim Duncan 1.00 2.50
174 Tony Parker .60 1.50
175 Manu Ginobili .75 2.00
176 Roger Mason .25 .60
177 Michael Finley .40 1.00
178 Matt Bonner .25 .60
179 George Hill .30 .75
180 Chris Bosh .50 1.25
181 Jose Calderon .25 .60
182 Andrea Bargnani .25 .60
183 Shawn Marion .40 1.00
184 Anthony Parker .25 .60
185 Jason Kapono .25 .60
186 Roko Leni Ukic .25 .60
187 Deron Williams .30 .75
188 Carlos Boozer .30 .75
189 Ronnie Brewer .25 .60
190 C.J. Miles .25 .60
191 Mehmet Okur .25 .60
192 Kyle Korver .30 .75
193 Andrei Kirilenko .30 .75
194 Gilbert Arenas .30 .75
195 Antawn Jamison .30 .75
196 DeShawn Stevenson .25 .60
197 Caron Butler .30 .75
198 Brendan Haywood .25 .60
199 Nick Young .25 .60
200 Dominic McGuire .25 .60
201 Toney Douglas RC .50 1.25
202 Taylor Griffin RC .50 1.25
203 DeJuan Blair RC .60 1.50
204 Darren Collison RC .75 2.00
205 Patrick Mills RC 1.25 3.00
206 DaJuan Summers RC .50 1.25
207 Austin Daye RC .50 1.25
208 Eric Maynor RC .50 1.25
209 DeMarre Carroll RC .60 1.50
210 Taj Gibson RC .60 1.50
211 Patrick Beverley RC .75 2.00
212 Dante Cunningham RC .75 2.00
213 Sam Young RC .50 1.25
214 Terrence Williams RC .50 1.25
215 Omri Casspi RC .50 1.25
216 Jeff Pendergraph RC .50 1.25
217 Jrue Holiday RC 2.50 6.00
218 Jeff Teague RC .60 1.50
219 James Johnson RC .60 1.50
220 B.J. Mullens RC .50 1.25
221 Nick Calathes RC .50 1.25
222 A.J. Price RC .50 1.25
223 Danny Green RC .75 2.00
224 Marcus Thornton RC .60 1.50
225 Chase Budinger RC .50 1.25
226 Blake Griffin SP RC 4.00 10.00
227 James Harden SP RC 6.00 15.00
228 Tyler Hansbrough SP RC .75 2.00
229 Gerald Henderson SP RC .60 1.50
230 Jordan Hill SP RC .60 1.50
231 Hasheem Thabeet SP RC .60 1.50
232 Earl Clark SP RC .60 1.50
233 Brandon Jennings SP RC 1.00 2.50
234 Stephen Curry SP RC 75.00 200.00
235 Ty Lawson SP RC .75 2.00
236 Wayne Ellington SP RC .75 2.00
237 Ricky Rubio SP RC 1.25 3.00
238 DeMar DeRozan SP RC 4.00 10.00
239 Jonny Flynn SP RC .60 1.50
240 Tyreke Evans SP RC .75 2.00
241 Michael Jordan 8.00 20.00
242 Larry Bird 3.00 8.00
243 Horace Grant .75 2.00
244 Kiki Vandeweghe .60 1.50
245 Michael Cooper .75 2.00
246 Magic Johnson 3.00 8.00
247 Kareem Abdul-Jabbar 2.50 6.00
248 Julius Erving 2.00 5.00
249 Oscar Robertson 1.00 2.50
250 Isiah Thomas .75 2.00
251 Patrick Ewing 1.25 3.00
252 A.C. Green .75 2.00
253 Adrian Dantley .60 1.50
254 Alex English 1.00 2.50
255 Jerry West 1.25 3.00
256 Bernard King 1.00 2.50
257 Bill Laimbeer .75 2.00
258 Bob McAdoo 1.00 2.50
259 Byron Scott .60 1.50
260 Calvin Murphy .60 1.50
261 Clyde Drexler 1.25 3.00
262 David Robinson 1.50 4.00
263 Dominique Wilkins 1.25 3.00
264 Glen Rice .60 1.50
265 Hakeem Olajuwon 1.00 2.50
266 John Stockton 1.25 3.00
267 Robert Parish 1.00 2.50
268 Scottie Pippen 2.00 5.00
269 Sean Elliott .60 1.50
270 Bill Walton 1.25 3.00
271 Chris Mullin 1.00 2.50
272 Dee Brown .50 1.25
273 Dennis Rodman 1.50 4.00
274 Joe Dumars 1.00 2.50
275 John Paxson .60 1.50
276 Mark Price .75 2.00
277 Maurice Cheeks .60 1.50
278 Moses Malone 1.25 3.00
279 Spud Webb .60 1.50
280 Terry Porter .50 1.25
281 Darryl Dawkins .75 2.00
282 Dino Radja .50 1.25
283 Jamaal Wilkes .60 1.50
284 John Salley .60 1.50
285 Larry Johnson .75 2.00
286 Larry Nance .60 1.50
287 Pooh Richardson .50 1.25
288 Reggie Theus .60 1.50
289 Rick Mahorn .50 1.25
290 Rick Barry .60 1.50
291 Ron Harper .75 2.00
292 Steve Kerr .75 2.00
293 Tom Chambers .75 2.00
294 Spencer Haywood .50 1.25
295 Walt Frazier 1.25 3.00

2009-10 Upper Deck Star Rookies Gold

COMPLETE SET (25) 7.50 15.00
GOLD FOIL RETAIL BLASTER INSERT
201 Toney Douglas .40 1.00
202 Taylor Griffin .40 1.00
203 DeJuan Blair .50 1.25
204 Darren Collison .60 1.50
205 Patrick Mills 1.00 2.50
206 DaJuan Summers .40 1.00
207 Austin Daye .40 1.00
208 Eric Maynor .40 1.00
209 DeMarre Carroll .50 1.25
210 Taj Gibson .50 1.25
211 Patrick Beverley .60 1.50
212 Dante Cunningham .60 1.50
213 Sam Young .40 1.00
214 Terrence Williams .40 1.00
215 Omri Casspi .40 1.00
216 Jeff Pendergraph .40 1.00
217 Jrue Holiday 2.00 5.00
218 Jeff Teague .50 1.25
219 James Johnson .50 1.25
220 B.J. Mullens .40 1.00
221 Nick Calathes .40 1.00
222 A.J. Price .40 1.00
223 Danny Green .60 1.50
224 Marcus Thornton .50 1.25
225 Chase Budinger .40 1.00

2009-10 Upper Deck 3D NBA Stars

COMPLETE SET (50) 60.00 120.00
STATED ODDS 1:8
3DAI Allen Iverson 2.50 6.00
3DAR B.Roy/L.Aldridge 1.50 4.00
3DAS D.Stevenson/G.Arenas 1.00 2.50
3DAT R.Alston/S.Telfair .75 2.00
3DBA C.Anthony/C.Billups 2.00 5.00
3DBD Baron Davis 1.00 2.50
3DBJ K.Bryant/L.James 75.00 200.00
3DBR D.Rose/M.Beasley 2.00 5.00
3DBW C.Boozer/D.Williams 1.00 2.50
3DCA Carmelo Anthony 2.00 5.00
3DCH D.Harris/V.Carter 2.50 6.00
3DCP C.Paul/T.Chandler 2.50 6.00
3DDE Deron Williams 1.00 2.50
3DDG B.Davis/E.Gordon 1.00 2.50
3DDH Dwight Howard 1.50 4.00
3DDK D.Howard/K.Garnett 3.00 8.00
3DDP T.Duncan/T.Parker 6.00 15.00
3DDR D.Rose/L.Deng 2.00 5.00
3DDW K.Durant/R.Westbrook 8.00 20.00
3DGA Gilbert Arenas 1.00 2.50
3DGG M.Gasol/P.Gasol 2.00 5.00
3DHN D.Howard/J.Nelson 1.50 4.00
3DIB A.Iverson/C.Billups 2.50 6.00
3DIS A.Iverson/R.Stuckey 2.50 6.00
3DJB K.Bryant/M.Jordan 150.00 400.00
3DJJ L.James/M.Jordan 75.00 200.00
3DJR M.Redd/R.Jefferson 1.00 2.50
3DJS J.Johnson/J.Smith 1.25 3.00
3DJW L.James/M.Williams 20.00 50.00
3DKB Kobe Bryant 75.00 200.00
3DKD Kevin Durant 8.00 20.00
3DKN D.Nowitzki/J.Kidd 3.00 8.00
3DLJ LeBron James 60.00 150.00
3DMI A.Iguodala/A.Miller 1.25 3.00
3DMJ Michael Jordan 75.00 200.00
3DMM T.McGrady/Y.Ming 3.00 8.00
3DNK J.Kidd/S.Nash 2.50 6.00
3DNR Nate Robinson 1.00 2.50
3DNS A.Stoudemire/S.Nash 2.50 6.00
3DPA Chris Paul 2.50 6.00
3DPG K.Garnett/P.Pierce 3.00 8.00
3DPW C.Paul/D.Williams 2.50 6.00
3DRF Rudy Fernandez .75 2.00
3DRO Brandon Roy 1.50 4.00
3DSM Josh Smith .75 2.00
3DSN Steve Nash 2.50 6.00
3DTP Tayshaun Prince 1.25 3.00
3DVC Vince Carter 2.50 6.00
3DWA Dwyane Wade 2.50 6.00
3DWC D.Wade/M.Chalmers 2.50 6.00

2009-10 Upper Deck Game Materials

COMBINED MEM ODDS 3:16
*GOLD: .5X TO 1.25X BASE HI
GOLD PRINT RUN 150 SER.#'d SETS
GJAA Arron Afflalo/550 2.00 5.00
GJAB Andray Blatche/545 2.00 5.00
GJAH Al Harrington/550 2.50 6.00
GJAI Andre Iguodala/550 3.00 8.00
GJAJ Antawn Jamison/550 2.50 6.00
GJAL Acie Law/550 2.00 5.00
GJAM Alonzo Mourning/400 5.00 12.00
GJAW Antoine Wright/305 2.00 5.00
GJBA Andrea Bargnani/550 2.00 5.00
GJBD Baron Davis/550 2.50 6.00
GJBG Ben Gordon/400 2.50 6.00
GJBH Brendan Haywood/550 2.00 5.00
GJBI Chauncey Billups/550 4.00 10.00
GJBO Andrew Bogut/550 2.50 6.00
GJBR Brandon Roy/400 4.00 10.00
GJBU Beno Udrih/487 2.00 5.00
GJBW Ben Wallace/550 4.00 10.00
GJCA Carmelo Anthony/550 5.00 12.00
GJCB Carlos Boozer/550 2.50 6.00
GJCF Channing Frye/550 2.00 5.00
GJCH Chris Bosh/400 4.00 10.00
GJCK Chris Kaman/550 2.50 6.00
GJCM Chris Mullin/550 4.00 10.00
GJCP Chris Paul/400 6.00 15.00
GJCS Craig Smith/550 2.00 5.00
GJCV Charlie Villanueva/550 2.00 5.00
GJDA Dan Majerle/550 2.50 6.00
GJDG Daniel Gibson/600 2.00 5.00
GJDH Dwight Howard/545 4.00 10.00
GJDI Boris Diaw/545 2.50 6.00
GJDL David Lee/550 2.00 5.00
GJDM Desmond Mason/550 2.00 5.00
GJDN Dirk Nowitzki/400 8.00 20.00
GJDR David Robinson/400 6.00 15.00
GJDS DeShawn Stevenson/550 2.00 5.00
GJDW Dorell Wright/550 2.00 5.00
GJEB Elton Brand/400 2.50 6.00
GJEH Eddie House/400 2.00 5.00
GJEO Emeka Okafor/550 2.50 6.00
GJFE Raymond Felton/550 2.50 6.00
GJGW Gerald Wallace/400 2.50 6.00
GJHE Luther Head 2.00 5.00
GJHO Juwan Howard/550 2.50 6.00
GJJC Jarron Collins/550 2.00 5.00
GJJF Jordan Farmar/400 2.00 5.00
GJJH Josh Howard/550 2.50 6.00
GJJK Jason Kapono/550 2.00 5.00
GJJN Joakim Noah/238 2.50 6.00
GJJO Jermaine O'Neal/545 3.00 8.00
GJJS J.R. Smith/481 3.00 8.00
GJJU Julian Wright/550 2.00 5.00
GJKA Kelenna Azubuike/550 2.00 5.00
GJKB Keith Bogans/400 2.00 5.00
GJKG Kevin Garnett/550 8.00 20.00
GJKO Kobe Bryant/550 8.00 20.00
GJLA LaMarcus Aldridge/550 3.00 8.00
GJLD Luol Deng/550 2.50 6.00
GJLH Larry Hughes/508 2.50 6.00
GJLJ LeBron James/545 8.00 20.00
GJLO Lamar Odom/550 2.50 6.00
GJLS Luis Scola/550 2.50 6.00
GJLU Luke Walton/550 2.50 6.00
GJLW Lorenzen Wright/400 2.00 5.00
GJMA Maurice Ager/550 2.00 5.00
GJMC Mike Conley Jr./397 2.50 6.00
GJMD Marquis Daniels/479 2.00 5.00
GJMJ Mike James/400 2.00 5.00
GJMM Mikki Moore/550 2.00 5.00
GJMO Mehmet Okur/400 2.00 5.00
GJPE Patrick Ewing/400 5.00 12.00
GJPG Pau Gasol/400 5.00 12.00
GJPP Paul Pierce/508 5.00 12.00
GJQD Quincy Douby/550 2.00 5.00
GJRA Ron Artest/550 3.00 8.00
GJRF Randy Foye/545 2.00 5.00
GJRG Rudy Gay/545 3.00 8.00
GJRS Robert Swift/550 2.00 5.00
GJRW Rasheed Wallace/550 4.00 10.00
GJSB Shannon Brown/550 2.00 5.00
GJSI James Singleton/400 2.00 5.00
GJSM Sean May/550 2.00 5.00
GJSN Steve Novak/545 2.00 5.00
GJSO Shaquille O'Neal/550 10.00 25.00
GJSR Sergio Rodriguez/250 2.00 5.00
GJST Stephon Marbury/545 4.00 10.00
GJSW Shawne Williams/550 2.00 5.00
GJTC Tyson Chandler/400 2.50 6.00
GJTF T.J. Ford/550 2.00 5.00
GJTM Tracy McGrady/550 6.00 15.00
GJTP Tayshaun Prince/550 3.00 8.00
GJTT Tyrus Thomas/550 2.00 5.00
GJUH Udonis Haslem/563 2.00 5.00
GJVC Vince Carter/550 6.00 15.00
GJWA Dwyane Wade/550 6.00 15.00
GJWC Wilson Chandler/545 2.50 6.00
GJWE Martell Webster/550 2.00 5.00
GJWI Shelden Williams/563 2.00 5.00
GJWR Brandan Wright/550 2.00 5.00
GJYM Yao Ming/550 8.00 20.00
GJZR Zach Randolph/400 3.00 8.00

2009-10 Upper Deck Game Materials Dual

COMBINED MEM ODDS 3:16
*GOLD: .5X TO 1.25X BASE HI
GOLD PRINT RUN 150 SER.#'d SETS
DGAB L.Bird/R.Allen 15.00 40.00
DGAD G.Davis/R.Allen 6.00 15.00
DGAG A.Iguodala/G.Arenas 4.00 10.00
DGAJ G.Arenas/L.James 30.00 80.00
DGAP M.Price/N.Archibald 5.00 12.00
DGAT C.Anthony/T.McGrady 8.00 20.00
DGBB A.Bargnani/C.Bosh 5.00 12.00
DGBF C.Billups/T.Ford 5.00 12.00
DGBH A.Bynum/D.Howard 5.00 12.00
DGBI A.Iguodala/E.Brand 4.00 10.00
DGBJ C.Billups/J.Johnson 5.00 12.00
DGBO C.Boozer/M.Okur 3.00 8.00
DGBP L.Bird/R.Parish 15.00 40.00
DGBR B.Roy/C.Billups 5.00 12.00
DGCB C.Bosh/V.Carter 8.00 20.00
DGCK C.Bosh/K.Garnett 10.00 25.00
DGCM S.May/V.Carter 8.00 20.00
DGCN D.Nowitzki/V.Carter 10.00 25.00
DGCT C.Drexler/T.McGrady 8.00 20.00
DGDA C.Anthony/T.Duncan 10.00 25.00
DGDL B.Laimbeer/J.Dumars 5.00 12.00
DGDO S.O'Neal/T.Duncan 12.00 30.00
DGDS D.Gibson/S.Brown 2.50 6.00
DGEM J.Erving/M.Malone 10.00 25.00
DGGH D.Gibson/K.Hinrich 3.00 8.00
DGFB R.Foye/S.Brown 2.50 6.00
DGFC M.Conley/R.Felton 3.00 8.00
DGFD C.Drexler/R.Felton 6.00 15.00
DGFF J.Farmar/T.Ford 2.50 6.00
DGFG D.Gibson/J.Farmar 2.50 6.00
DGFJ A.Jefferson/R.Foye 2.50 6.00
DGGA C.Anthony/G.Gervin 6.00 15.00
DGGD B.Davis/B.Gordon 3.00 8.00
DGGG K.Garnett/P.Gasol 10.00 25.00
DGGJ K.Garnett/L.James 25.00 60.00
DGGM K.Garnett/T.McGrady 10.00 25.00
DGGN D.Nowitzki/K.Garnett 10.00 25.00
DGGO J.O'Neal/K.Garnett 10.00 25.00
DGGS A.Stoudemire/K.Garnett 10.00 25.00
DGHB J.Howard/S.Brown 3.00 8.00
DGHC R.Hamilton/V.Carter 8.00 20.00
DGHG B.Gordon/R.Hamilton 4.00 10.00
DGHH J.Howard/L.Hughes 3.00 8.00
DGHT L.Hughes/T.Thomas 3.00 8.00
DGIB A.Iverson/C.Billups 8.00 20.00
DGIP A.Iverson/C.Paul 8.00 20.00
DGJA C.Anthony/L.James 40.00 100.00
DGJD C.Drexler/L.James 30.00 80.00
DGJE J.Erving/M.Jordan 100.00 250.00
DGJG B.Gordon/J.Johnson 4.00 10.00
DGJH A.Horford/J.Johnson 4.00 10.00
DGJJ L.James/M.Johnson 50.00 120.00
DGJP C.Paul/M.Johnson 15.00 40.00
DGJR B.Roy/J.Johnson 5.00 12.00
DGJW D.Wade/L.James 40.00 100.00
DGKL K.Durant/L.Aldridge 15.00 40.00
DGKM Abdul-Jabbar/M.Jordan 125.00 300.00
DGLG K.Garnett/L.Bird 15.00 40.00
DGLK K.Garnett/L.James 40.00 100.00
DGLR B.Laimbeer/D.Rodman 8.00 20.00
DGMA C.Anthony/S.Marion 6.00 15.00
DGMB C.Bosh/C.Maggette 5.00 12.00
DGMD C.Drexler/T.McGrady 8.00 20.00
DGMK K.Abdul-Jabbar/M.Johnson 15.00 40.00
DGML L.James/M.Jordan 400.00 800.00
DGMM A.Mourning/M.Malone 6.00 15.00
DGMN C.Maggette/D.Nowitzki 10.00 25.00
DGMP T.Prince/T.McGrady 8.00 20.00
DGMS A.Stoudemire/S.Marion 4.00 10.00
DGMW C.Maggette/S.Williams 3.00 8.00
DGNB D.Nowitzki/L.Bird 15.00 40.00
DGNH D.Nowitzki/J.Howard 10.00 25.00
DGNK C.Anthony/M.Jordan 30.00 80.00
DGNP C.Paul/S.Nash 8.00 20.00
DGNS A.Stoudemire/D.Nowitzki 10.00 25.00
DGOD C.Drexler/H.Olajuwon 6.00 15.00
DGOM E.Okafor/S.May 3.00 8.00
DGON J.O'Neal/L.Odom 4.00 10.00
DGOO H.Olajuwon/S.O'Neal 12.00 30.00
DGOR D.Robinson/H.Olajuwon 8.00 20.00
DGPS C.Paul/J.Stockton 8.00 20.00
DGRF W.Frazier/W.Reed 6.00 15.00
DGRG D.Robinson/M.Ginobili 8.00 20.00
DGRT D.Rodman/T.Thomas 8.00 20.00
DGRW D.Rodman/S.Williams 8.00 20.00
DGSB A.Stoudemire/C.Bosh 5.00 12.00
DGSM S.Marion/T.McGrady 8.00 20.00
DGST S.Williams/T.McGrady 8.00 20.00
DGSW D.Williams/J.Stockton 6.00 15.00
DGTB B.Roy/T.Parker 6.00 15.00
DGTD D.Robinson/T.Parker 8.00 20.00
DGVT T.McGrady/V.Carter 12.00 30.00
DGWA J.West/K.Abdul-Jabbar 20.00 50.00
DGWB M.Williams/M.Bibby 4.00 10.00
DGWJ J.Worthy/M.Johnson 15.00 40.00
DGWO E.Okafor/R.Wallace 5.00 12.00
DGWS A.Stoudemire/R.Wallace 5.00 12.00
DGYH H.Olajuwon/Y.Ming 12.00 30.00
DGYM M.Malone/Y.Ming 12.00 30.00
DGYS L.Scola/Y.Ming 10.00 25.00

2009-10 Upper Deck Jordan Brand Classic

JCBJ Brandon Jennings 3.00 8.00
JCBM B.J. Mullens 2.00 5.00
JCBR Brandon Jennings 3.00 8.00
JCBS B.J. Mullens 2.00 5.00
JCDD DeMar DeRozan 15.00 40.00
JCDM DeMar DeRozan 15.00 40.00
JCDZ DeMar DeRozan 15.00 40.00
JCEV Tyreke Evans 2.50 6.00
JCJE Brandon Jennings 3.00 8.00
JCJH Jrue Holiday 10.00 25.00
JCJR Jrue Holiday 10.00 25.00
JCMU B.J. Mullens 2.00 5.00
JCTE Tyreke Evans 2.50 6.00

2009-10 Upper Deck Masterpieces

COMPLETE SET (35) 25.00 60.00
STATED ODDS 1:8
MAAR Anthony Randolph .75 2.00
MABL Brook Lopez 1.25 3.00
MABR Brandon Rush .75 2.00
MACL Courtney Lee .75 2.00
MACP Chris Paul 2.50 6.00
MADE Deron Williams 1.00 2.50
MADG Danilo Gallinari 1.00 2.50
MADH Dwight Howard 1.50 4.00
MADR Derrick Rose 2.00 5.00
MADW Dwyane Wade 2.50 6.00
MAGR Donte Greene .75 2.00
MAHI J.J. Hickson .75 2.00
MAJB Jerryd Bayless .75 2.00
MAJE Julius Erving 3.00 8.00
MAJG J.R. Gidders .75 2.00
MAJH John Havlicek 3.00 8.00
MAJO Michael Jordan 10.00 25.00
MAKA Kareem Abdul-Jabbar 4.00 10.00
MAKB Kobe Bryant 10.00 25.00
MAKG Kevin Garnett 3.00 8.00
MAKL Kevin Love 1.25 3.00
MALB Larry Bird 5.00 12.00
MALJ LeBron James 10.00 25.00
MAMB Michael Beasley .75 2.00
MAMJ Michael Jordan 10.00 25.00
MAMS Marreese Speights 1.00 2.50
MAOM O.J. Mayo .75 2.00
MAPP Paul Pierce 2.00 5.00
MARA Ryan Anderson .75 2.00
MARH Roy Hibbert 1.00 2.50
MARL Robin Lopez .75 2.00
MASN Steve Nash 2.50 6.00
MATP Tony Parker 2.00 5.00
MAWI Dominique Wilkins 2.00 5.00

2009-10 Upper Deck Now Appearing

COMPLETE SET (20) 40.00 100.00
STATED ODDS 1:8
NA1 Derrick Rose 1.25 3.00
NA2 Michael Beasley .50 1.25
NA3 O.J. Mayo .50 1.25
NA4 Russell Westbrook 1.50 4.00
NA5 Kevin Love .75 2.00
NA6 Michael Jordan 40.00 100.00
NA7 Kevin Durant 3.00 8.00
NA8 LeBron James 6.00 15.00
NA9 Kobe Bryant 6.00 15.00
NA10 Kevin Garnett 2.00 5.00
NA11 Rasheed Wallace 1.00 2.50
NA12 Tim Duncan 2.00 5.00
NA13 Shaquille O'Neal 2.50 6.00
NA14 Dwight Howard 1.00 2.50
NA15 Tracy McGrady 1.50 4.00
NA16 Chris Paul 1.50 4.00
NA17 Dwyane Wade 2.00 5.00
NA18 Dirk Nowitzki 2.00 5.00
NA19 Paul Pierce 1.25 3.00
NA20 Baron Davis .60 1.50

2009-10 Upper Deck Signature Collection

COMBINED AUTO ODDS 1:19
1 Alexis Ajinca 4.00 10.00
2 Joe Alexander 4.00 10.00
3 Steve Nash 60.00 150.00
4 Clyde Drexler 40.00 100.00
5 Ryan Anderson 4.00 10.00
6 T.J. Ford SP 8.00 20.00
7 D.J. Augustin 4.00 10.00
8 Rajon Rondo 12.00 30.00
9 Chris Paul 40.00 100.00
10 Jerryd Bayless 4.00 10.00
12 Michael Beasley 4.00 10.00
13 Von Wafer 4.00 10.00
14 Stephen Graham 4.00 10.00
15 Josh Boone 4.00 10.00
16 David Robinson 40.00 100.00
17 Bruce Bowen 5.00 12.00
18 Corey Brewer 4.00 10.00
19 Kirk Hinrich 5.00 12.00
20 Bobby Brown 4.00 10.00
21 Hilton Armstrong 4.00 10.00
22 Andrew Bynum 4.00 10.00
23 Louie Dampier 8.00 20.00
25 Mike Conley Jr. 5.00 12.00
26 DaJuan Summers 4.00 10.00
27 Ricky Rubio 50.00 120.00
28 Javaris Crittenton 4.00 10.00
29 Keyon Dooling 4.00 10.00
30 Joey Dorsey 4.00 10.00
31 Jared Dudley 4.00 10.00
32 Hakeem Olajuwon 60.00 150.00
34 Oscar Robertson 50.00 125.00
35 Danilo Gallinari 5.00 12.00
36 Spud Webb 8.00 20.00
37 Kevin Garnett 75.00 200.00
38 Emeka Okafor 5.00 12.00
39 Eric Gordon 5.00 12.00
40 Aaron Gray 4.00 10.00
41 Jeff Green 5.00 12.00
42 Spencer Hawes 4.00 10.00
43 Richard Hendrix 4.00 10.00
44 J.J. Hickson 4.00 10.00
45 Dwight Howard 20.00 50.00
46 Darnell Jackson 4.00 10.00
47 Antawn Jamison 5.00 12.00
48 Al Jefferson 4.00 10.00
49 Bobby Jackson 4.00 10.00
50 DeAndre Jordan 5.00 12.00
51 Kosta Koufos 4.00 10.00
52 Andre Iguodala 6.00 15.00
53 Glen Davis 4.00 10.00
54 Courtney Lee 4.00 10.00
55 Brook Lopez 6.00 15.00
56 Kyle Korver 8.00 20.00
57 Robin Lopez 4.00 10.00
58 Kevin Love 12.00 30.00
59 Walter Herrmann 4.00 10.00
60 Moses Malone 40.00 100.00
61 O.J. Mayo 4.00 10.00
62 Luc Mbah A Moute 4.00 10.00
63 Rashad McCants 4.00 10.00
64 Javale McGee 5.00 12.00
65 Josh McRoberts 4.00 10.00
66 Jerry West 30.00 80.00
67 Larry Hughes 5.00 12.00
68 Yao Ming 100.00 250.00
69 Shannon Brown 4.00 10.00
70 Joakim Noah 4.00 10.00
71 Donte Greene 4.00 10.00
73 Tony Parker 20.00 50.00
75 Darren Collison 6.00 15.00
76 Tayshaun Prince 6.00 15.00
77 Quentin Richardson 4.00 10.00
78 Derrick Rose 75.00 200.00
79 Brandon Rush 4.00 10.00
80 James Worthy SP 20.00 50.00
81 Walter Sharpe 4.00 10.00
82 Sean Singletary 4.00 10.00
83 Jason Smith 4.00 10.00
84 J.R. Giddens 4.00 10.00
85 Marreese Speights 5.00 12.00
86 A.J. Price 4.00 10.00
87 Rodney Stuckey 4.00 10.00
88 Mike Taylor 4.00 10.00
89 Jason Thompson 4.00 10.00
90 Al Thornton 4.00 10.00
91 Alando Tucker 4.00 10.00
92 Ike Diogu 4.00 10.00
94 Kyle Weaver 4.00 10.00
95 Russell Westbrook 75.00 200.00
97 Deron Williams 5.00 12.00
98 Mo Williams 5.00 12.00
99 Sean Williams 4.00 10.00
100 Shelden Williams 4.00 10.00
101 Kareem Abdul-Jabbar 125.00 300.00
102 Arron Afflalo 4.00 10.00
103 Shane Battier 6.00 15.00
104 LaMarcus Aldridge 12.00 30.00
105 Andre Miller 6.00 15.00
106 Chase Budinger 4.00 10.00
107 James Harden 125.00 300.00
108 Al Harrington 5.00 12.00
109 Alonzo Mourning 60.00 150.00
110 Jack Sikma 5.00 12.00
111 Anthony Randolph 4.00 10.00
112 Patrick Beverley 6.00 15.00
114 Brad Daugherty 6.00 15.00
115 Bailey Howell SP 25.00 60.00
116 Patrick O'Bryant 4.00 10.00
117 James Johnson 5.00 12.00
118 Earl Clark 4.00 10.00
119 Brandon Roy 8.00 20.00
120 Bill Sharman 30.00 80.00
121 Bill Walton 12.00 30.00
122 Jeff Adrien 4.00 10.00
123 Gerald Henderson 4.00 10.00
125 Corey Maggette 5.00 12.00
126 Dominic McGuire 4.00 10.00
127 Wayne Ellington 5.00 12.00
128 B.J. Mullens 4.00 10.00
129 Danny Green 6.00 15.00
130 Jonny Flynn 4.00 10.00
131 Joe Crawford 4.00 10.00
132 David Lee 5.00 12.00
133 Donyell Marshall 4.00 10.00
134 Chris Douglas-Roberts 4.00 10.00
135 Damon Stoudamire 20.00 50.00
136 David West 5.00 12.00
137 Eddy Curry 4.00 10.00
138 D.J. White 4.00 10.00
139 Francisco Garcia 4.00 10.00
140 Gail Goodrich 10.00 25.00
141 George Hill 5.00 12.00
142 George Karl 20.00 50.00
143 Gabe Pruitt 4.00 10.00
144 Will Bynum 4.00 10.00
145 Derek Fisher 10.00 25.00
146 Hal Greer 12.00 30.00
147 Horace Grant 15.00 40.00
148 Isiah Thomas 40.00 100.00
149A LeBron James SVSM 1,250.00 2,500.00
149B LeBron James Cavs 1,500.00 3,000.00
150 Julius Erving SP 75.00 200.00
151 Magic Johnson 75.00 200.00
152 Jason Kidd 60.00 150.00
153 Sonny Weems 4.00 10.00
154 Jeff Pendergraph 4.00 10.00
155 J.R. Smith 6.00 15.00
156 Taj Gibson 5.00 12.00
157 Maurice Ager 4.00 10.00
158 Mike Bibby 6.00 15.00
159 Ronnie Brewer 4.00 10.00
160 Larry Bird SP 150.00 400.00
161 Larry Johnson 25.00 60.00
162 Carmelo Anthony 50.00 120.00
163 Desmond Mason SP 25.00 60.00
164 Mario Chalmers 5.00 12.00
165 Michael Jordan 3,000.00 6,000.00
166 Randy Foye 4.00 10.00
168 Cedric Simmons SP 10.00 25.00
169 Mario West SP 40.00 100.00
170 Marvin Williams 4.00 10.00
171 Nicolas Batum 5.00 12.00
172 Jrue Holiday 20.00 50.00
173 Jermaine O'Neal 6.00 15.00
174 Pat Riley 20.00 50.00
175 Stephen Curry 1,000.00 2,000.00
176 Ben Gordon 5.00 12.00
177 Joey Graham 4.00 10.00
178 Dionte Christmas 4.00 10.00
179 Raymond Felton 4.00 10.00
180 Rudy Gay 6.00 15.00
181 Roy Hibbert 5.00 12.00
182 George Gervin 12.00 30.00
183 Dennis Rodman SP 60.00 150.00
184 Aaron Brooks 4.00 10.00
185 Robert Parish 10.00 25.00
187 David Noel 4.00 10.00
188 Jamario Moon 5.00 12.00
189 John Stockton SP 100.00 250.00
190 Solomon Jones 4.00 10.00
191 Jermaine Taylor 4.00 10.00
192 Carlos Boozer 5.00 12.00
193 Tracy McGrady 100.00 250.00
194 Tyrus Thomas 4.00 10.00
195 Vince Carter 75.00 200.00
196 Paul Pierce 40.00 100.00
198 Ty Lawson 5.00 12.00
199 Luis Scola 5.00 12.00
200 Julian Wright 4.00 10.00

2009-10 Upper Deck Sophomore Sensations

COMPLETE SET (30) 10.00 25.00
SSAA Alexis Ajinca .60 1.50
SSAR Darrell Arthur .60 1.50
SSBB Bobby Brown .60 1.50
SSBL Brook Lopez 1.00 2.50
SSBR Brandon Rush .60 1.50
SSBW Bill Walker .60 1.50
SSCL Courtney Lee .60 1.50
SSDA D.J. Augustin .60 1.50
SSDG Danilo Gallinari .75 2.00
SSDJ Darnell Jackson .60 1.50
SSDR Derrick Rose 1.50 4.00
SSEG Eric Gordon .75 2.00
SSJB Jerryd Bayless .60 1.50
SSJM Javale McGee .75 2.00
SSJO DeAndre Jordan .75 2.00
SSJT Jason Thompson .60 1.50
SSKK Kosta Koufos .60 1.50
SSKL Kevin Love 1.00 2.50
SSLM Luc Mbah A Moute .60 1.50
SSMB Michael Beasley .60 1.50
SSMS Marreese Speights .75 2.00
SSMT Mike Taylor .60 1.50
SSOM O.J. Mayo .60 1.50
SSRA Ryan Anderson .60 1.50
SSRF Rudy Fernandez .60 1.50
SSRH Richard Hendrix .60 1.50
SSRL Robin Lopez .60 1.50
SSRW Russell Westbrook 2.00 5.00
SSSS Sean Singletary .60 1.50
SSWS Walter Sharpe .60 1.50

2009-10 Upper Deck Sophomore Sensations Autographs

COMBINED AUTO ODDS 1:16
STATED PRINT RUN 199 SER.#'d SETS
SSAA Alexis Ajinca 5.00 12.00
SSBB Bobby Brown 5.00 12.00
SSBL Brook Lopez 5.00 12.00
SSBR Brandon Rush 5.00 12.00
SSBW Bill Walker 5.00 12.00
SSCL Courtney Lee 5.00 12.00
SSDA D.J. Augustin 5.00 12.00
SSDG Danilo Gallinari 6.00 15.00
SSDJ Darnell Jackson 5.00 12.00
SSDR Derrick Rose 30.00 80.00
SSEG Eric Gordon 6.00 15.00
SSJB Jerryd Bayless 5.00 12.00
SSJM Javale McGee 5.00 12.00
SSJO DeAndre Jordan 10.00 25.00
SSJT Jason Thompson 5.00 12.00
SSKK Kosta Koufos 5.00 12.00
SSKL Kevin Love 8.00 20.00
SSLM Luc Mbah A Moute 5.00 12.00
SSMB Michael Beasley 5.00 12.00
SSMS Marreese Speights 5.00 12.00
SSMT Mike Taylor 5.00 12.00
SSOM O.J. Mayo 5.00 12.00
SSRA Ryan Anderson 5.00 12.00
SSRH Richard Hendrix 5.00 12.00
SSRL Robin Lopez 5.00 12.00
SSRW Russell Westbrook 60.00 150.00
SSSS Sean Singletary 5.00 12.00
SSWS Walter Sharpe 5.00 12.00

2009-10 Upper Deck UD Select Spokesman Signatures

SSAH Al Horford 5.00 12.00
SSKG Kevin Garnett 150.00 400.00
SSLJ LeBron James 1,500.00 3,000.00
SSMJ Michael Jordan SP 600.00 1,200.00

2009-10 Upper Deck VS Dual Materials

COMBINED MEM ODDS 3:16
STATED PRINT RUN 400 TO 795 SETS
*BRONZE: .5X TO 1.25X BASE HI
BRONZE PRINT RUN 150 SER.#'d SETS
VSAA C.Anthony/R.Artest 5.00 12.00
VSAB C.Billups/R.Allen 6.00 15.00
VSAC A.Stoudemire/C.Bosh 4.00 10.00
VSAM C.Maggette/R.Allen 5.00 12.00
VSAO A.Bargnani/S.O'Neal 6.00 15.00
VSAR N.Robinson/R.Alston 4.00 10.00
VSAS C.Anthony/T.Sefolosha 5.00 12.00
VSAW A.Horford/M.Williams 4.00 10.00
VSBA K.Bryant/R.Artest 30.00 80.00
VSBB K.Bryant/R.Bell 30.00 80.00
VSBJ K.Bryant/L.James 125.00 300.00
VSBK B.King/B.Walton 4.00 10.00
VSBL C.Landry/K.Brown 4.00 10.00
VSBM E.Brand/Y.Ming 6.00 15.00
VSBN K.Bryant/S.Nash 50.00 120.00
VSBR M.Redd/M.Bibby 4.00 10.00
VSBS C.Boozer/L.Scola 4.00 10.00
VSBT A.Tucker/S.Brown/570 4.00 10.00
VSCA C.Anthony/V.Carter 6.00 15.00
VSCD E.Curry/S.Dalembert 4.00 10.00
VSCF J.Farmar/J.Calderon 4.00 10.00
VSCK A.Kirilenko/M.Camby 4.00 10.00
VSCM S.Marion/V.Carter 5.00 12.00
VSCO E.Curry/J.O'Neal 4.00 10.00
VSCS J.Smith/V.Carter 5.00 12.00
VSCW M.Williams/V.Carter 5.00 12.00
VSDB C.Duhon/C.Brewer 4.00 10.00
VSDC G.Davis/W.Chandler 4.00 10.00
VSDF C.Frye/D.Milicic 4.00 10.00
VSDJ D.Williams/J.Kidd 5.00 12.00

VSDL K.Lowry/M.Daniels 4.00 10.00
VSDS B.Davis/D.Stevenson 4.00 10.00
VSEB J.Erving/L.Bird 12.00 30.00
VSEC C.Bosh/E.Brand 4.00 10.00
VSEE M.Eaton/P.Ewing/400 5.00 12.00
VSER D.Robinson/M.Eaton/570 5.00 12.00
VSFG D.Gibson/R.Felton 4.00 10.00
VSFM M.Finley/T.McGrady/570 6.00 15.00
VSFW B.Wright/C.Frye/570 4.00 10.00
VSGA G.Arenas/K.Garnett/570 6.00 15.00
VSGL K.Garnett/R.Lewis 6.00 15.00
VSGN D.Nowitzki/K.Garnett/570 10.00 25.00
VSGO K.Garnett/S.O'Neal/570 10.00 25.00
VSGR D.Robinson/K.Garnett/570 8.00 20.00
VSGW C.Webber/K.Garnett/570 8.00 20.00
VSHB C.Brewer/L.Hughes/795 4.00 10.00
VSHI A.Iguodala/J.Howard/570 4.00 10.00
VSHW A.Horford/J.Wright/570 4.00 10.00
VSIB A.Bogut/Z.Ilgauskas 4.00 10.00
VSIH D.Howard/Z.Ilgauskas 4.00 10.00
VSJS J.Farmar/S.Marbury/776 4.00 10.00
VSJW A.Jefferson/S.Williams/570 4.00 10.00
VSKA A.Jamison/K.Bryant 30.00 80.00
VSKD J.Kidd/K.Durant 8.00 20.00
VSKH J.Kidd/K.Hinrich 4.00 10.00
VSKT K.Martin/T.Ariza 4.00 10.00
VSKU B.Udrih/J.Kidd 4.00 10.00
VSKW C.Kaman/S.Williams 4.00 10.00
VSLA C.Anthony/R.Lewis 4.00 10.00
VSLL A.Law/K.Lowry 4.00 10.00
VSMA C.Anthony/S.Marion/776 5.00 12.00
VSMB C.Bosh/Y.Ming 8.00 20.00
VSMF D.Mason/R.Foye 4.00 10.00
VSMK B.King/K.McHale/551 5.00 12.00
VSMM B.Miller/S.May/570 4.00 10.00
VSMO S.O'Neal/Y.Ming/570 12.00 30.00
VSMP K.Malone/S.Pippen/570 8.00 20.00
VSMR C.Maggette/J.Redick 4.00 10.00
VSMT C.Maggette/T.Thomas/570 4.00 10.00
VSMW D.Marshall/L.Walton 4.00 10.00
VSNB C.Billups/S.Nash 5.00 12.00
VSNK A.Kirilenko/D.Nowitzki/570 6.00 15.00
VSNR D.Robinson/D.Nowitzki/570 8.00 20.00
VSOB A.Bogut/E.Okafor/570 4.00 10.00
VSOD E.Okafor/L.Diogu 4.00 10.00
VSOE H.Olajuwon/P.Ewing/570 8.00 20.00
VSOO H.Olajuwon/S.O'Neal 12.00 30.00
VSOP L.Odom/T.Prince/551 4.00 10.00
VSOW E.Okafor/H.Warrick/570 4.00 10.00
VSPA P.Pierce/T.Ariza/570 4.00 10.00
VSPG D.Granger/T.Prince 4.00 10.00
VSPH M.Peterson/U.Haslem 4.00 10.00
VSPJ L.James/T.Prince 25.00 60.00
VSPK G.Payton/S.Kerr 8.00 20.00
VSRS J.Smith/L.Ridnour 4.00 10.00
VSSB C.Simmons/S.Brown 4.00 10.00
VSSJ J.Starks/M.Johnson 8.00 20.00
VSST R.Sessions/S.Telfair 4.00 10.00
VSTC C.Paul/T.McGrady 10.00 25.00
VSTG D.Gibson/S.Telfair 4.00 10.00
VSTM M.Webster/T.Sefolosha 4.00 10.00
VSVA A.Jamison/V.Carter 4.00 10.00
VSVJ J.Jack/S.Vujacic/570 4.00 10.00
VSVW C.Villanueva/M.Williams 4.00 10.00
VSWH B.Wallace/D.Howard 6.00 15.00
VSWN M.Williams/N. 4.00 10.00
VSWS C.Simmons/H.Warrick 4.00 10.00
VSWY M.Williams/T.Young 4.00 10.00
VSYA A.Bargnani/Y.Ming 6.00 15.00
VSYD D.Mutombo/Y.Ming 8.00 20.00

1996 Upper Deck 22K Gold Michael Jordan

NNO Michael Jordan ROY/1985 30.00 80.00
NNO Michael Jordan 4-Time MVP 20.00 50.00
NNO Michael Jordan First Championship 20.00 50.00
NNO Michael Jordan He's Back 20.00 50.00

1998 Upper Deck 22K Gold Michael Jordan

COMMON CARD 10.00 25.00

1999 Upper Deck 22K Gold Michael Jordan

COMMON CARD 20.00 50.00

2000 Upper Deck 22K Gold Michael Jordan

1 Michael Jordan 100.00 200.00

1996 Upper Deck 23 Nights Jordan Experience

COMPLETE SET w/CD (23) 12.00 30.00
COMPLETE SET (23) 10.00 25.00
COMMON CARD (1-23) .60 1.50
NNO Cardboard Disk (Michael Jordan) .40 1.00
NNO Compact Disc The Jordan Interview 2.00 5.00

2002 Upper Deck All-Star Game Jordan

COMPLETE SET (3) 8.00 20.00
COMMON CARD 3.00 8.00

2003 Upper Deck All-Star Game

COMPLETE SET (4) 10.00 25.00
DW1 Dominique Wilkins/1985 1.50 4.00
KB1 Kobe Bryant/1997 4.00 10.00
MJ1 Michael Jordan/1987 6.00 15.00
MJ2 Michael Jordan/1988 6.00 15.00

2004 Upper Deck All-Star Game

COMPLETE SET (10) 75.00 150.00
BO Chris Bosh 3.00 8.00
LJ1 LeBron James 12.50 30.00
LJ2 LeBron James 12.50 30.00
LJ3 LeBron James 12.50 30.00
LJ4 LeBron James 12.50 30.00
LJ5 LeBron James 12.50 30.00
CA Carmelo Anthony 4.00 10.00
GP Gary Payton 3.00 8.00
KB Kobe Bryant 5.00 12.00
MJ Michael Jordan 6.00 15.00
SZMJ Michael Jordan Star Zone SAMPLE 6.00 15.00

2005 Upper Deck All-Star Game

COMPLETE SET 8.00 20.00
LJ LeBron James 3.00 8.00
MJ Michael Jordan 5.00 12.00
KB Kobe Bryant 3.00 8.00

2006-07 Upper Deck All-Star Game

COMPLETE SET (13) 8.00 20.00
AS1 Yao Ming 1.25 3.00
AS2 Julius Erving 1.00 2.50
AS3 Larry Bird 1.50 4.00
AS4 Magic Johnson 1.50 4.00
AS5 Steve Nash 1.00 2.50
AS6 LaMarcus Aldridge 1.25 3.00
AS7 Rudy Gay .60 1.50
AS8 Brandon Roy 1.00 2.50
AS9 Tyrus Thomas .40 1.00
AS10 Jerry Tarkanian .50 1.25
AS11 LeBron James 4.00 10.00
AS12 Michael Jordan 4.00 10.00
AS13 Kobe Bryant 4.00 10.00

2008-09 Upper Deck All-Star Game

AS1 Amar'e Stoudemire 1.00 2.50
AS2 Michael Beasley 1.00 2.50
AS3 Derrick Rose 4.00 10.00
AS4 Kobe Bryant 8.00 20.00
AS5 Kevin Garnett 2.50 6.00
AS6 LeBron James 8.00 20.00
AS7 Michael Jordan 8.00 20.00
AS8 O.J. Mayo .75 2.00
AS9 Steve Nash 2.00 5.00
AS10 Rudy Fernandez .75 2.00

2004-05 Upper Deck All-Star Lineup

COMP.SET w/o SP's (90) 12.00 30.00
91-132 STATED ODDS 1:6
1 Jason Terry .25 .60
2 Al Harrington .25 .60
3 Boris Diaw .25 .60
4 Paul Pierce .50 1.25
5 Ricky Davis .25 .60
6 Jiri Welsch .20 .50
7 Marcus Fizer .20 .50
8 Gerald Wallace .25 .60
9 Jahidi White .20 .50
10 Eddy Curry .20 .50
11 Kirk Hinrich .30 .75
12 Jamal Crawford .20 .50
13 LeBron James 2.50 6.00
14 Dajuan Wagner .20 .50
15 Jeff McInnis .20 .50
16 Dirk Nowitzki .75 2.00
17 Antoine Walker .30 .75
18 Michael Finley .30 .75
19 Carmelo Anthony .60 1.50
20 Andre Miller .25 .60
21 Kenyon Martin .30 .75
22 Chauncey Billups .40 1.00
23 Rasheed Wallace .40 1.00
24 Ben Wallace .40 1.00
25 Erick Dampier .20 .50
26 Jason Richardson .30 .75
27 Mike Dunleavy .30 .75
28 Yao Ming .75 2.00
29 Tracy McGrady .50 1.25
30 Juwan Howard .25 .60
31 Jermaine O'Neal .25 .60
32 Reggie Miller .60 1.50
33 Ron Artest .30 .75
34 Elton Brand .25 .60
35 Corey Maggette .25 .60
36 Quentin Richardson .20 .50
37 Kobe Bryant 2.50 6.00
38 Gary Payton .50 1.25
39 Lamar Odom .30 .75
40 Pau Gasol .50 1.25
41 Jason Williams .25 .60
42 Bonzi Wells .25 .60
43 Shaquille O'Neal 1.25 3.00
44 Dwyane Wade 1.25 3.00
45 Eddie Jones .30 .75
46 Michael Redd .25 .60
47 Desmond Mason .25 .60
48 T.J. Ford .20 .50
49 Latrell Sprewell .40 1.00
50 Kevin Garnett .75 2.00
51 Sam Cassell .25 .60
52 Richard Jefferson .25 .60
53 Kerry Kittles .25 .60
54 Jason Kidd .50 1.25
55 Jamal Mashburn .25 .60
56 Baron Davis .30 .75
57 Jamaal Magloire .20 .50
58 Allan Houston .30 .75
59 Kurt Thomas .20 .50
60 Stephon Marbury .40 1.00
61 Cuttino Mobley .25 .60
62 Drew Gooden .25 .60
63 Steve Francis .30 .75
64 Glenn Robinson .25 .60
65 Allen Iverson .75 2.00
66 Samuel Dalembert .20 .50
67 Amare Stoudemire .30 .75
68 Steve Nash .60 1.50
69 Shawn Marion .30 .75
70 Shareef Abdur-Rahim .30 .75
71 Damon Stoudamire .30 .75
72 Zach Randolph .30 .75
73 Peja Stojakovic .25 .60
74 Chris Webber .40 1.00
75 Mike Bibby .30 .75
76 Tony Parker .50 1.25
77 Tim Duncan .75 2.00
78 Manu Ginobili .60 1.50
79 Ronald Murray .20 .50
80 Ray Allen .50 1.25
81 Rashard Lewis .25 .60
82 Chris Bosh .50 1.25
83 Vince Carter .60 1.50
84 Jalen Rose .25 .60
85 Andrei Kirilenko .25 .60
86 Carlos Boozer .25 .60
87 Carlos Arroyo .20 .50
88 Gilbert Arenas .30 .75
89 Jarvis Hayes .20 .50
90 Antawn Jamison .25 .60
91 Emeka Okafor RC .60 1.50
92 Dwight Howard RC 2.50 6.00
93 Shaun Livingston RC .75 2.00
94 Luol Deng RC .75 2.00
95 Ben Gordon RC .75 2.00
96 Devin Harris RC .60 1.50
97 Andre Iguodala RC 1.25 3.00
98 Andris Biedrins RC .50 1.25
99 Josh Childress RC .50 1.25
100 Josh Smith RC .75 2.00
101 Jameer Nelson RC .75 2.00
102 J.R. Smith RC .75 2.00
103 Sergei Monia RC .50 1.25
104 Sebastian Telfair RC .60 1.50
105 Pavel Podkolzin RC .50 1.25
106 Luke Jackson RC .50 1.25
107 Dorell Wright RC .60 1.50
108 Robert Swift RC .50 1.25
109 Anderson Varejao RC .60 1.50
110 Sasha Vujacic RC .60 1.50
111 Rafael Araujo RC .50 1.25
112 Al Jefferson RC .75 2.00
113 Kris Humphries RC .60 1.50
114 Kirk Snyder RC .50 1.25
115 Darius Rice RC .75 2.00
116 Beno Udrih RC .60 1.50
117 Viktor Khryapa RC .50 1.25
118 David Harrison RC .50 1.25
119 Trevor Ariza RC .75 2.00
120 Ha Seung-Jin RC .75 2.00
121 Kevin Martin RC 1.00 2.50
122 Delonte West RC .60 1.50
123 Rickey Paulding RC .50 1.25
124 Chris Duhon RC .60 1.50
125 Tony Allen RC .75 2.00
126 Donta Smith RC .50 1.25
127 Andre Emmett RC .50 1.25
128 Royal Ivey RC .50 1.25
129 Matt Freije RC .50 1.25
130 Romain Sato RC .50 1.25
131 Antonio Burks RC .50 1.25
132 Lionel Chalmers RC .60 1.50

2004-05 Upper Deck All-Star Lineup Gold

*1-90 GOLD: 3X TO 8X BASE HI
1-90 PRINT RUN 100 SER.#'d SETS
*91-132 GOLD RCs: 2X TO 5X BASE HI
91-132 PRINT RUN 25 SER.#'d SETS

2004-05 Upper Deck All-Star Lineup All-Star Staples

COMPLETE SET (14) 6.00 15.00
STATED ODDS 1:3
AI Allen Iverson 1.25 3.00
BW Ben Wallace .60 1.50
DN Dirk Nowitzki 1.25 3.00
JK Jason Kidd .75 2.00
JO Jermaine O'Neal .40 1.00
KB Kobe Bryant 4.00 10.00
KG Kevin Garnett 1.25 3.00
KM Kenyon Martin .50 1.25
PP Paul Pierce .75 2.00
SF Steve Francis .50 1.25
SO Shaquille O'Neal 2.00 5.00
TD Tim Duncan 1.25 3.00
TM Tracy McGrady .75 2.00
YM Yao Ming 1.25 3.00

2004-05 Upper Deck All-Star Lineup All-Star Staples Threads

STATED ODDS 1:12
AI Allen Iverson 6.00 15.00
BW Ben Wallace 3.00 8.00
DN Dirk Nowitzki 6.00 15.00
JK Jason Kidd 4.00 10.00
JO Jermaine O'Neal 2.00 5.00
KB Kobe Bryant 40.00 100.00
KG Kevin Garnett 6.00 15.00
KM Kenyon Martin 2.50 6.00
PP Paul Pierce 4.00 10.00
SF Steve Francis 2.50 6.00
SO Shaquille O'Neal 10.00 25.00
TD Tim Duncan 6.00 15.00
TM Tracy McGrady 4.00 10.00
YM Yao Ming 6.00 15.00

2004-05 Upper Deck All-Star Lineup Prominent Futures

COMPLETE SET (15) 6.00 15.00
STATED ODDS 1:3
*PARALLEL: 1.5X TO 4X BASE HI
PARALLEL PRINT RUN 50 SER.#'d SETS
BD C.Boozer/M.Dunleavy .60 1.50
HH J.Howard/J.Hayes .60 1.50
HK U.Haslem/C.Kaman .60 1.50
JA L.James/C.Anthony 2.00 5.00
JB M.Jaric/C.Bosh .60 1.50
JS L.James/A.Stoudemire 1.50 4.00
KD C.Kaman/M.Dunleavy .60 1.50
MH R.Murray/J.Hayes .60 1.50
MN Y.Ming/Nene 1.00 2.50
NH Nene/U.Haslem .60 1.50
PH T.Prince/J.Howard .60 1.50
PM T.Prince/R.Murray .60 1.50
SG A.Stoudemire/M.Ginobili 1.00 2.50
WG D.Wade/M.Ginobili 1.25 3.00

2004-05 Upper Deck All-Star Lineup Prominent Futures Threads

STATED ODDS 1:12
BD C.Boozer/M.Dunleavy 4.00 10.00
HH J.Howard/J.Hayes 4.00 10.00
HK U.Haslem/C.Kaman 4.00 10.00
JA L.James/C.Anthony SP 20.00 50.00
JB M.Jaric/C.Bosh 4.00 10.00
JS L.James/A.Stoudemire 12.00 30.00
KD C.Kaman/M.Dunleavy 4.00 10.00
MH R.Murray/J.Hayes 4.00 10.00
MN Y.Ming/Nene 5.00 12.00
NH Nene/U.Haslem 4.00 10.00
PH T.Prince/J.Howard 4.00 10.00
PM T.Prince/R.Murray 4.00 10.00
SG A.Stoudemire/M.Ginobili 5.00 12.00
WG D.Wade/M.Ginobili 8.00 20.00

2004-05 Upper Deck All-Star Lineup Promos/eCards

eCARD STATED ODDS 1:6
eCARD PRICES FOR UNSCRACHED CARDS
PROMO STATED ODDS 2:1
AS1 Kobe Bryant EC 4.00 10.00
AS2 LeBron James EC 4.00 10.00
AS3 Kevin Garnett EC 1.25 3.00
AS4 Tracy McGrady EC .75 2.00
AS5 Shaquille O'Neal EC 2.00 5.00
AS6 Allen Iverson EC 1.25 3.00
AS7 Tim Duncan EC 1.25 3.00
AS8 Jason Kidd EC .75 2.00
AS9 Paul Pierce .50 1.25
AS10 Carmelo Anthony .60 1.50
AS11 Ben Wallace .40 1.00
AS12 Yao Ming .75 2.00
AS13 Jermaine O'Neal .25 .60
AS14 Dirk Nowitzki .75 2.00
AS15 Dwyane Wade 1.25 3.00
AS16 Brad Miller .25 .60
AS17 Kenyon Martin .30 .75
AS18 Jason Richardson .30 .75
AS19 Stephon Marbury .40 1.00
AS20 Amare Stoudemire .30 .75
AS21 Baron Davis .30 .75
AS22 Ray Allen .50 1.25
AS23 Vince Carter .60 1.50
AS24 Andrei Kirilenko .25 .60
AS25 Jamal Mashburn .25 .60
AS26 Chris Webber .40 1.00
AS27 Chris Bosh .50 1.25
AS28 Shareef Abdur-Rahim .30 .75
AS29 Michael Redd .25 .60
AS30 Zach Randolph .30 .75
AS31 Rasheed Wallace .40 1.00
AS32 Peja Stojakovic .25 .60
AS33 Pau Gasol .50 1.25
AS34 Shawn Marion .30 .75
AS35 Jamaal Magloire .20 .50
AS36 Tony Parker .50 1.25
AS37 Ron Artest .30 .75
AS38 Elton Brand .25 .60
AS39 Wild Card EC .40 1.00

2004-05 Upper Deck All-Star Lineup Rookie Review

COMPLETE SET (30) 15.00 40.00
STATED ODDS ONE PER BOX TOPPER
RR1 LeBron James 1.50 4.00
RR2 LeBron James 1.50 4.00
RR3 LeBron James 1.50 4.00
RR4 LeBron James 1.50 4.00
RR5 LeBron James 1.50 4.00
RR6 LeBron James 1.50 4.00
RR7 LeBron James 1.50 4.00
RR8 LeBron James 1.50 4.00
RR9 LeBron James 1.50 4.00
RR10 LeBron James 1.50 4.00
RR11 LeBron James 1.50 4.00
RR12 LeBron James 1.50 4.00
RR13 LeBron James 1.50 4.00
RR14 LeBron James 1.50 4.00
RR15 LeBron James 1.50 4.00
RR16 LeBron James 1.50 4.00
RR17 LeBron James 1.50 4.00
RR18 LeBron James 1.50 4.00
RR19 LeBron James 1.50 4.00
RR20 LeBron James 1.50 4.00
RR21 LeBron James 1.50 4.00
RR22 Udonis Haslem .30 .75
RR23 T.J. Ford .30 .75
RR24 Marquis Daniels .30 .75
RR25 Josh Howard .40 1.00
RR26 Kirk Hinrich .50 1.25
RR27 Jarvis Hayes .30 .75
RR28 Carmelo Anthony 1.00 2.50
RR29 Chris Bosh .75 2.00
RR30 Dwyane Wade 2.00 5.00

2004-05 Upper Deck All-Star Lineup Signature Class

COMMON CARD 8.00 20.00
STATED ODDS 1:240
AK Andrei Kirilenko 8.00 20.00
BD Boris Diaw 8.00 20.00
CW Chris Wilcox 8.00 20.00
FE Francisco Elson 8.00 20.00
GR Glenn Robinson 8.00 20.00
GW Gerald Wallace 8.00 20.00
JD Juan Dixon 8.00 20.00
KB Kobe Bryant 125.00 300.00
KG Kevin Garnett 75.00 200.00
LJ LeBron James 800.00 1,500.00
MA Marcus Banks 8.00 20.00
MB Mike Bibby 8.00 20.00
MD Marquis Daniels 8.00 20.00
MP Mickael Pietrus 8.00 20.00
RM Reggie Miller 75.00 200.00
SA Shareef Abdur-Rahim 8.00 20.00
SC Sam Cassell 8.00 20.00
SM Shawn Marion 8.00 20.00
ZR Zach Randolph 8.00 20.00

2004-05 Upper Deck All-Star Lineup Weekend Highlights

COMPLETE SET (14) 3.00 8.00
STATED ODDS 1:3
*L1 PARALLEL: 2.5X TO 6X BASE HI
L1 PAR.PRINT RUN 100 SER.#'d SETS
*L2 PARALLEL: 1.5X TO 4X BASE HI
L2 PAR.PRINT RUN 250 SER.#'d SETS
AN Chris Anderson L1 .50 1.25
BD Baron Davis L2 .50 1.25
CB Chauncey Billups L2 .60 1.50
CM Cuttino Mobley L2 .40 1.00
DF Derek Fisher L1 .40 1.00
EB Earl Boykins L1 .30 .75
FJ Fred Jones L1 .30 .75
JA Marko Jaric L1 .30 .75
JR Jason Richardson L2 .50 1.25
KK Kyle Korver L1 .40 1.00
PS Peja Stojakovic L2 .40 1.00
RD Ricky Davis L2 .40 1.00
SM Stephon Marbury L2 .60 1.50
VL Voshon Lenard L1 .30 .75

2004-05 Upper Deck All-Star Lineup Weekend Highlights Threads

STATED ODDS 1:12
AN Chris Anderson 2.50 6.00
BD Baron Davis 2.50 6.00
CB Chauncey Billups 3.00 8.00
CM Cuttino Mobley 2.00 5.00
DF Derek Fisher 2.00 5.00
EB Earl Boykins 2.00 5.00
FJ Fred Jones 2.00 5.00
JA Marko Jaric 2.00 5.00
JR Jason Richardson 2.50 6.00
KK Kyle Korver 2.00 5.00
PS Peja Stojakovic SP 2.00 5.00
RD Ricky Davis 2.00 5.00
SM Stephon Marbury 3.00 8.00
VL Voshon Lenard 2.00 5.00

1992-93 Upper Deck All-Star Weekend

COMP. FACT SET (40) 5.00 12.00
*GOLD: 1.5X TO 4X BASE HI
1 Nate Archibald .08 .25
2 Elgin Baylor .15 .40
3 Wilt Chamberlain .40 1.00
4 Dave Cowens .08 .25
5 Walt Frazier .08 .25
6 George Gervin .15 .40
7 John Havlicek .25 .60
8 Elvin Hayes .10 .30
9 Oscar Robertson .25 .60
10 Jerry West .30 .75
11 Charles Barkley .25 .60
12 Brad Daugherty .08 .25
13 Clyde Drexler .20 .50
14 Patrick Ewing .20 .50
15 Michael Jordan 1.25 3.00
16 Karl Malone .20 .50
17 Moses Malone .08 .25
18 Chris Mullin .08 .25
19 Hakeem Olajuwon .20 .50
20 Robert Parish .08 .25
21 David Robinson .20 .50
22 John Stockton .20 .50
23 Isiah Thomas .08 .25
24 Dominique Wilkins .08 .25
25 James Worthy .10 .30
26 Kenny Anderson .08 .25
27 Stacey Augmon .08 .25
28 Derrick Coleman .08 .25
29 Larry Johnson .10 .30
30 Christian Laettner .25 .60
31 Harold Miner .08 .25
32 Alonzo Mourning .50 1.25
33 Dikembe Mutombo .08 .25
34 Shaquille O'Neal 1.25 3.00
35 Steve Smith .08 .25
36 Larry Nance .08 .25
37 Larry Bird .40 1.00
38 Tom Chambers MVP .08 .25
39 Karl Malone John Stockton .15 .40
40 Charles Barkley MVP .25 .60

2011 Upper Deck All Time Greats

STATED PRINT RUN 50 TO 80 SER.#'d SETS
ONLY FIRST CARD LISTED PER PLAYER
1 Michael Jordan 1-23/80 20.00 50.00
2 Michael Jordan/80 20.00 50.00
3 Michael Jordan/80 20.00 50.00
4 Michael Jordan/80 20.00 50.00
5 Michael Jordan/80 20.00 50.00
6 Michael Jordan/80 20.00 50.00
7 Michael Jordan/80 20.00 50.00
8 Michael Jordan/80 20.00 50.00
9 Michael Jordan/80 20.00 50.00
10 Michael Jordan/80 20.00 50.00
11 Michael Jordan/80 20.00 50.00
12 Michael Jordan/80 20.00 50.00
13 Michael Jordan/80 20.00 50.00
14 Michael Jordan/80 20.00 50.00
15 Michael Jordan/80 20.00 50.00
16 Michael Jordan/80 20.00 50.00
17 Michael Jordan/80 20.00 50.00
18 Michael Jordan/80 20.00 50.00
19 Michael Jordan/80 20.00 50.00
20 Michael Jordan/80 20.00 50.00
21 Michael Jordan/80 20.00 50.00
22 Michael Jordan/80 20.00 50.00
23 Michael Jordan/80 20.00 50.00
24 Michael Jordan/80 20.00 50.00
25 LeBron James 25-44/50 15.00 40.00
26 LeBron James/50 15.00 40.00
27 LeBron James/50 15.00 40.00
28 LeBron James/50 15.00 40.00
29 LeBron James/50 15.00 40.00
30 LeBron James/50 15.00 40.00
31 LeBron James/50 15.00 40.00
32 LeBron James/50 15.00 40.00
33 LeBron James/50 15.00 40.00
34 LeBron James/50 15.00 40.00
35 LeBron James/50 15.00 40.00
36 LeBron James/50 15.00 40.00
37 LeBron James/50 15.00 40.00
38 LeBron James/50 15.00 40.00
39 LeBron James/50 15.00 40.00
40 LeBron James/50 15.00 40.00
41 LeBron James/50 15.00 40.00
42 LeBron James/50 15.00 40.00
43 LeBron James/50 15.00 40.00
44 LeBron James/50 15.00 40.00
45 Steve Nash 45-48/50 5.00 12.00
46 Steve Nash/50 5.00 12.00
47 Steve Nash/50 5.00 12.00
48 Steve Nash/50 5.00 12.00
49 James Worthy 49-58/50 4.00 10.00
50 James Worthy/50 4.00 10.00
51 James Worthy/50 4.00 10.00
52 James Worthy/50 4.00 10.00
53 James Worthy/50 4.00 10.00
54 James Worthy/50 4.00 10.00
55 James Worthy/50 4.00 10.00
56 James Worthy/50 4.00 10.00
57 James Worthy/50 4.00 10.00
58 James Worthy/50 4.00 10.00
59 John Havlicek 59-61/50 4.00 10.00
60 John Havlicek/50 4.00 10.00
61 John Havlicek/50 4.00 10.00
62 D.Robinson 62-71/50 5.00 12.00
63 David Robinson/50 5.00 12.00
64 David Robinson/50 5.00 12.00
65 David Robinson/50 5.00 12.00
66 David Robinson/50 5.00 12.00
67 David Robinson/50 5.00 12.00
68 David Robinson/50 5.00 12.00
69 David Robinson/50 5.00 12.00
70 David Robinson/50 5.00 12.00
71 David Robinson/50 5.00 12.00
72 Bill Russell 72-76/50 6.00 15.00
73 Bill Russell/50 6.00 15.00
74 Bill Russell/50 6.00 15.00
75 Bill Russell/50 6.00 15.00
76 Bill Russell/50 6.00 15.00
77 A.Mourning 77-91/50 5.00 12.00
78 Alonzo Mourning/50 5.00 12.00
79 Alonzo Mourning/50 5.00 12.00
80 Alonzo Mourning/50 5.00 12.00
81 Alonzo Mourning/50 5.00 12.00
82 Alonzo Mourning/50 5.00 12.00
83 Alonzo Mourning/50 5.00 12.00
84 Alonzo Mourning/50 5.00 12.00
85 Alonzo Mourning/50 5.00 12.00
86 Alonzo Mourning/50 5.00 12.00
87 Alonzo Mourning/50 5.00 12.00
88 Alonzo Mourning/50 5.00 12.00
89 Alonzo Mourning/50 5.00 12.00
90 Alonzo Mourning/50 5.00 12.00
91 Alonzo Mourning/50 5.00 12.00
92 H.Olajuwon 92-98/50 5.00 12.00
93 Hakeem Olajuwon/50 5.00 12.00
94 Hakeem Olajuwon/50 5.00 12.00
95 Hakeem Olajuwon/50 5.00 12.00
96 Hakeem Olajuwon/50 5.00 12.00
97 Hakeem Olajuwon/50 5.00 12.00
98 Hakeem Olajuwon/50 5.00 12.00
99 Walt Frazier 99-103/50 3.00 8.00
100 Walt Frazier/50 3.00 8.00
101 Walt Frazier/50 3.00 8.00
102 Walt Frazier/50 3.00 8.00
103 Walt Frazier/50 3.00 8.00
104 Julius Erving 104-108/50 5.00 12.00
105 Julius Erving/50 5.00 12.00
106 Julius Erving/50 5.00 12.00
107 Julius Erving/50 5.00 12.00
108 Julius Erving/50 5.00 12.00
109 Larry Bird 109-123/50 6.00 15.00
110 Larry Bird/50 6.00 15.00
111 Larry Bird/50 6.00 15.00
112 Larry Bird/50 6.00 15.00
113 Larry Bird/50 6.00 15.00
114 Larry Bird/50 6.00 15.00
115 Larry Bird/50 6.00 15.00
116 Larry Bird/50 6.00 15.00
117 Larry Bird/50 6.00 15.00
118 Larry Bird/50 6.00 15.00
119 Larry Bird/50 6.00 15.00
120 Larry Bird/50 6.00 15.00
121 Larry Bird/50 6.00 15.00
122 Larry Bird/50 6.00 15.00
123 Larry Bird/50 6.00 15.00
124 Derrick Rose 124-128/50 6.00 15.00
125 Derrick Rose/50 6.00 15.00
126 Derrick Rose/50 6.00 15.00
127 Derrick Rose/50 6.00 15.00
128 Derrick Rose/50 6.00 15.00
129 Clyde Drexler 129-136/50 5.00 12.00
130 Clyde Drexler/50 5.00 12.00
131 Clyde Drexler/50 5.00 12.00
132 Clyde Drexler/50 5.00 12.00
133 Clyde Drexler/50 5.00 12.00
134 Clyde Drexler/50 5.00 12.00
135 Clyde Drexler/50 5.00 12.00
136 Clyde Drexler/50 5.00 12.00
137 M.Johnson 137-151/50 6.00 15.00
138 Magic Johnson/50 6.00 15.00
139 Magic Johnson/50 6.00 15.00
140 Magic Johnson/50 6.00 15.00
141 Magic Johnson/50 6.00 15.00
142 Magic Johnson/50 6.00 15.00
143 Magic Johnson/50 6.00 15.00
144 Magic Johnson/50 6.00 15.00
145 Magic Johnson/50 6.00 15.00
146 Magic Johnson/50 6.00 15.00
147 Magic Johnson/50 6.00 15.00
148 Magic Johnson/50 6.00 15.00
149 Magic Johnson/50 6.00 15.00
150 Magic Johnson/50 6.00 15.00
151 Magic Johnson/50 6.00 15.00
152 Larry Johnson 152-161/50 4.00 10.00
153 Larry Johnson/50 4.00 10.00
154 Larry Johnson/50 4.00 10.00
155 Larry Johnson/50 4.00 10.00
156 Larry Johnson/50 4.00 10.00
157 Larry Johnson/50 4.00 10.00
158 Larry Johnson/50 4.00 10.00
159 Larry Johnson/50 4.00 10.00
160 Larry Johnson/50 4.00 10.00
161 Larry Johnson/50 4.00 10.00
162 Grant Hill 162-171/50 5.00 12.00
163 Grant Hill/50 5.00 12.00
164 Grant Hill/50 5.00 12.00
165 Grant Hill/50 5.00 12.00
166 Grant Hill/50 5.00 12.00
167 Grant Hill/50 5.00 12.00
168 Grant Hill/50 5.00 12.00
169 Grant Hill/50 5.00 12.00
170 Grant Hill/50 5.00 12.00
171 Grant Hill/50 5.00 12.00
172 Chris Paul 172-186/50 4.00 10.00
173 Chris Paul/50 4.00 10.00
174 Chris Paul/50 4.00 10.00
175 Chris Paul/50 4.00 10.00
176 Chris Paul/50 4.00 10.00
177 Chris Paul/50 4.00 10.00
178 Chris Paul/50 4.00 10.00
179 Chris Paul/50 4.00 10.00
180 Chris Paul/50 4.00 10.00
181 Chris Paul/50 4.00 10.00
182 Chris Paul/50 4.00 10.00
183 Chris Paul/50 4.00 10.00
184 Chris Paul/50 4.00 10.00
185 Chris Paul/50 4.00 10.00
186 Chris Paul/50 4.00 10.00
187 Jerry West 187-189/50 5.00 12.00
188 Jerry West/50 5.00 12.00
189 Jerry West/50 5.00 12.00
190 A.Hardaway 190-200/50 5.00 12.00
191 Anfernee Hardaway/50 5.00 12.00
192 Anfernee Hardaway/50 5.00 12.00
193 Anfernee Hardaway/50 5.00 12.00
194 Anfernee Hardaway/50 5.00 12.00
195 Anfernee Hardaway/50 5.00 12.00
196 Anfernee Hardaway/50 5.00 12.00
197 Anfernee Hardaway/50 5.00 12.00
198 Anfernee Hardaway/50 5.00 12.00
199 Anfernee Hardaway/50 5.00 12.00
200 Anfernee Hardaway/50 5.00 12.00

2011 Upper Deck All Time Greats Career Book Card Autographs

STATED PRINT RUN ONE TO 15 SER.#'d SETS
SCCP1 Chris Paul/15 60.00 150.00
SCCP2 Chris Paul/15 60.00 150.00
SCMJ1 Michael Jordan/15 1,000.00 2,000.00
SCMJ2 Michael Jordan/15 1,000.00 2,000.00
SCMJ3 Michael Jordan/15 1,000.00 2,000.00
SCRO1 Derrick Rose/15 60.00 150.00

2011 Upper Deck All Time Greats Illustrious Signatures

COMMON CARD
STATED PRINT RUN 3 TO 15 SER.#'d SETS
ONLY FIRST CARD LISTED PER PLAYER
ISAM1 A.Mourning 1-4/15 40.00 100.00
ISAM2 Alonzo Mourning/15 40.00 100.00
ISAM3 Alonzo Mourning/15 40.00 100.00
ISAM4 Alonzo Mourning/15 40.00 100.00
ISCD1 Clyde Drexler 1-6/10 50.00 120.00
ISCD2 Clyde Drexler/10 50.00 120.00
ISCD3 Clyde Drexler/10 50.00 120.00
ISCD4 Clyde Drexler/10 50.00 120.00
ISCD5 Clyde Drexler/10 50.00 120.00
ISCD6 Clyde Drexler/10 50.00 120.00
ISCP1 Chris Paul 1-7/10 50.00 120.00
ISCP2 Chris Paul/10 50.00 120.00
ISCP3 Chris Paul/10 50.00 120.00
ISCP4 Chris Paul/10 50.00 120.00
ISCP5 Chris Paul/10 50.00 120.00
ISCP6 Chris Paul/10 50.00 120.00
ISCP7 Chris Paul/10 50.00 120.00
ISDR1 D.Robinson 1-6/10 50.00 120.00
ISDR2 David Robinson/10 50.00 120.00
ISDR3 David Robinson/10 50.00 120.00
ISDR4 David Robinson/10 50.00 120.00
ISDR5 David Robinson/10 50.00 120.00
ISDR6 David Robinson/10 50.00 120.00
ISGH1 Grant Hill 1-5/10 50.00 120.00
ISGH2 Grant Hill/10 50.00 120.00
ISGH3 Grant Hill/10 50.00 120.00
ISGH4 Grant Hill/10 50.00 120.00
ISGH5 Grant Hill/10 50.00 120.00
ISJA1 LeBron James 1-8/15 600.00 1,200.00
ISJA2 LeBron James/15 600.00 1,200.00
ISJA3 LeBron James/15 600.00 1,200.00
ISJA4 LeBron James/15 600.00 1,200.00
ISJA5 LeBron James/15 600.00 1,200.00
ISJA6 LeBron James/15 600.00 1,200.00
ISJA7 LeBron James/15 600.00 1,200.00
ISJA8 LeBron James/15 600.00 1,200.00
ISJO1 Magic Johnson 1-5/15 60.00 150.00
ISJO2 Magic Johnson/15 60.00 150.00
ISJO3 Magic Johnson/15 60.00 150.00
ISJO4 Magic Johnson/15 60.00 150.00
ISJO5 Magic Johnson/15 60.00 150.00
ISJW1 James Worthy 1-6/10 30.00 80.00
ISJW2 James Worthy/10 30.00 80.00
ISJW3 James Worthy/10 30.00 80.00
ISJW4 James Worthy/10 30.00 80.00
ISJW5 James Worthy/10 30.00 80.00
ISJW6 James Worthy/10 30.00 80.00
ISLB1 Larry Bird 1-6/15 60.00 150.00
ISLB2 Larry Bird/15 60.00 150.00
ISLB3 Larry Bird/15 60.00 150.00
ISLB4 Larry Bird/15 60.00 150.00
ISLB5 Larry Bird/15 60.00 150.00
ISLB6 Larry Bird/15 60.00 150.00
ISLJ1 Larry Johnson 1-5/10 30.00 80.00
ISLJ2 Larry Johnson/10 30.00 80.00
ISLJ3 Larry Johnson/10 30.00 80.00
ISLJ4 Larry Johnson/10 30.00 80.00
ISLJ5 Larry Johnson/10 30.00 80.00
ISMJ1 M.Jordan 1-10/15 1,000.00 2,000.00
ISMJ2 Michael Jordan/15 1,000.00 2,000.00
ISMJ3 Michael Jordan/15 1,000.00 2,000.00
ISMJ4 Michael Jordan/15 1,000.00 2,000.00
ISMJ5 Michael Jordan/15 1,000.00 2,000.00
ISMJ6 Michael Jordan/15 1,000.00 2,000.00
ISMJ7 Michael Jordan/15 1,000.00 2,000.00
ISMJ8 Michael Jordan/15 1,000.00 2,000.00
ISMJ9 Michael Jordan/15 1,000.00 2,000.00
ISMJ10 Michael Jordan/15 1,000.00 2,000.00

2011 Upper Deck All Time Greats Lettermen Autographs

STATED PRINT RUN 12 TO 80 SER.#'d SETS
PRINT RUNS BASED ON LAST NAME
TOTAL PRINT RUN LISTED WITH ASTERISK
LAH Anfernee Hardaway/80* 125.00 300.00
LAM Alonzo Mourning/80* 60.00 150.00
LBR Bill Russell/21* 400.00 800.00
LCD Clyde Drexler/21* 75.00 150.00
LCP Chris Paul/20* 75.00 150.00
LDR David Robinson/24* 75.00 200.00
LGH Grant Hill/12* 75.00 200.00
LHO Hakeem Olajuwon/32* 75.00 200.00
LJA LeBron James/25* 600.00 1,200.00
LJE Julius Erving/18* 125.00 300.00
LJH John Havlicek/24* 100.00 250.00
LJO Magic Johnson/21* 150.00 400.00
LJW James Worthy/24* 50.00 125.00
LLB Larry Bird/40* 150.00 400.00
LLJ Larry Johnson/35* 50.00 100.00
LMJ Michael Jordan/30* 1,000.00 2,000.00
LRO Derrick Rose/20* 100.00 250.00
LSN Steve Nash/20* 100.00 250.00
LWE Jerry West/12* 100.00 250.00
LWF Walt Frazier/21* 60.00 150.00

2011 Upper Deck All Time Greats Signatures
STATED PRINT RUN 5 TO 25 SER.#'d SETS
ONLY FIRST CARD LISTED PER PLAYER
AGSAH1 A.Hardaway 1-4/15 100.00 250.00
AGSAH2 Anfernee Hardaway/15 100.00 250.00
AGSAH3 Anfernee Hardaway/15 100.00 250.00
AGSAH4 Anfernee Hardaway/15 100.00 250.00
AGSAM1 A.Mourning 1-6/10 40.00 100.00
AGSAM2 Alonzo Mourning/10 40.00 100.00
AGSAM3 Alonzo Mourning/10 40.00 100.00
AGSAM4 Alonzo Mourning/10 40.00 100.00
AGSAM5 Alonzo Mourning/10 40.00 100.00
AGSAM6 Alonzo Mourning/10 40.00 100.00
AGSCP1 Chris Paul 1-7/10 75.00 200.00
AGSCP2 Chris Paul/10 75.00 200.00
AGSCP3 Chris Paul/10 75.00 200.00
AGSCP4 Chris Paul/10 75.00 200.00
AGSCP5 Chris Paul/10 75.00 200.00
AGSCP6 Chris Paul/10 75.00 200.00
AGSCP7 Chris Paul/10 75.00 200.00
AGSDR1 D.Robinson 1-4/15 75.00 200.00
AGSDR2 David Robinson/15 75.00 200.00
AGSDR3 David Robinson/15 75.00 200.00
AGSDR4 David Robinson/15 75.00 200.00
AGSGH1 Grant Hill 1-5/10 75.00 200.00
AGSGH2 Grant Hill/10 75.00 200.00
AGSGH3 Grant Hill/10 75.00 200.00
AGSGH4 Grant Hill/10 75.00 200.00
AGSGH5 Grant Hill/10 75.00 200.00
AGSHO1 H.Olajuwon 1-4/10 75.00 200.00
AGSHO2 Hakeem Olajuwon/10 75.00 200.00
AGSHO3 Hakeem Olajuwon/10 75.00 200.00
AGSHO4 Hakeem Olajuwon/10 75.00 200.00
AGSJA1 L.James 1-10/15 600.00 1,200.00
AGSJA2 LeBron James/15 600.00 1,200.00
AGSJA3 LeBron James/15 600.00 1,200.00
AGSJA4 LeBron James/15 600.00 1,200.00
AGSJA5 LeBron James/15 600.00 1,200.00
AGSJA6 LeBron James/15 600.00 1,200.00
AGSJA7 LeBron James/15 600.00 1,200.00
AGSJA8 LeBron James/15 600.00 1,200.00
AGSJA9 LeBron James/15 600.00 1,200.00
AGSJO1 M.Johnson 1-7/15 125.00 300.00
AGSJO2 Magic Johnson/15 125.00 300.00
AGSJO3 Magic Johnson/15 125.00 300.00
AGSJO4 Magic Johnson/15 125.00 300.00
AGSJO5 Magic Johnson/15 125.00 300.00
AGSJO6 Magic Johnson/15 125.00 300.00
AGSJO7 Magic Johnson/15 125.00 300.00
AGSJW1 James Worthy 1-4/10 30.00 80.00
AGSJW2 James Worthy/10 30.00 80.00
AGSJW3 James Worthy/10 30.00 80.00
AGSJW4 James Worthy/10 30.00 80.00
AGSLB1 Larry Bird 1-5/15 125.00 300.00
AGSLB2 Larry Bird/15 125.00 300.00
AGSLB3 Larry Bird/15 125.00 300.00
AGSLB4 Larry Bird/15 125.00 300.00
AGSLB5 Larry Bird/15 125.00 300.00
AGSLJ1 L.Johnson 1-4/10 40.00 100.00
AGSLJ2 Larry Johnson/10 40.00 100.00
AGSLJ3 Larry Johnson/10 40.00 100.00
AGSLJ4 Larry Johnson/10 40.00 100.00
AGSMJ1 M.Jordan 1-12/25 1,000.00 2,000.00
AGSMJ2 Michael Jordan/25 1,000.00 2,000.00
AGSMJ3 Michael Jordan/25 1,000.00 2,000.00
AGSMJ4 Michael Jordan/25 1,000.00 2,000.00
AGSMJ5 Michael Jordan/25 1,000.00 2,000.00
AGSMJ6 Michael Jordan/25 1,000.00 2,000.00
AGSMJ7 Michael Jordan/25 1,000.00 2,000.00
AGSMJ8 Michael Jordan/25 1,000.00 2,000.00
AGSMJ9 Michael Jordan/25 1,000.00 2,000.00
AGSJA10 LeBron James/15 600.00 1,200.00
AGSMJ10 Michael Jordan/25 1,000.00 2,000.00
AGSMJ11 Michael Jordan/25 1,000.00 2,000.00
AGSMJ12 Michael Jordan/25 1,000.00 2,000.00

2013 Upper Deck All-Time Greats
STATED PRINT RUN 150 SER.#'d SETS
ALL VERSIONS PRICED EQUALLY
1 Allen Iverson 4.00 10.00
2 Allen Iverson 4.00 10.00
3 Allen Iverson 4.00 10.00
4 Allen Iverson 4.00 10.00
5 Allen Iverson 4.00 10.00
6 Allen Iverson 4.00 10.00
7 Bill Russell 6.00 15.00
8 Bill Russell 6.00 15.00
9 Bill Russell 6.00 15.00
10 David Robinson 3.00 8.00
11 David Robinson 3.00 8.00
12 David Robinson 3.00 8.00
13 David Robinson 3.00 8.00
14 David Robinson 3.00 8.00
15 Dennis Rodman 4.00 10.00
16 Dennis Rodman 4.00 10.00
17 Dennis Rodman 4.00 10.00
18 Grant Hill 2.50 6.00
19 Grant Hill 2.50 6.00
20 Grant Hill 2.50 6.00
21 Grant Hill 2.50 6.00
22 Grant Hill 2.50 6.00
23 Grant Hill 2.50 6.00
24 Grant Hill 2.50 6.00
25 Hakeem Olajuwon 2.50 6.00
26 Hakeem Olajuwon 2.50 6.00
27 Hakeem Olajuwon 2.50 6.00
28 Hakeem Olajuwon 2.50 6.00
29 Isiah Thomas 2.50 6.00
30 Isiah Thomas 2.50 6.00
31 Isiah Thomas 2.50 6.00
32 Isiah Thomas 2.50 6.00
33 Isiah Thomas 2.50 6.00
34 Isiah Thomas 2.50 6.00
35 Jason Kidd 2.50 6.00
36 Jason Kidd 2.50 6.00
37 Jason Kidd 2.50 6.00
38 Jason Kidd 2.50 6.00
39 Jason Kidd 2.50 6.00
40 Jason Kidd 2.50 6.00
41 Julius Erving 3.00 8.00
42 Julius Erving 3.00 8.00
43 Julius Erving 3.00 8.00
44 Karl Malone 2.50 6.00
45 Karl Malone 2.50 6.00
46 Karl Malone 2.50 6.00
47 Karl Malone 2.50 6.00
48 Karl Malone 2.50 6.00
49 Larry Bird 5.00 12.00
50 Larry Bird 5.00 12.00
51 Larry Bird 5.00 12.00
52 Larry Bird 5.00 12.00
53 LeBron James 8.00 20.00
54 LeBron James 8.00 20.00
55 LeBron James 8.00 20.00
56 LeBron James 8.00 20.00
57 LeBron James 8.00 20.00
58 Magic Johnson 5.00 12.00
59 Magic Johnson 5.00 12.00
60 Magic Johnson 5.00 12.00
61 Magic Johnson 5.00 12.00
62 Magic Johnson 5.00 12.00
63 Magic Johnson 5.00 12.00
64 Magic Johnson 5.00 12.00
65 Michael Jordan 25.00 60.00
66 Michael Jordan 25.00 60.00
67 Michael Jordan 25.00 60.00
68 Michael Jordan 25.00 60.00
69 Michael Jordan 25.00 60.00
70 Michael Jordan 25.00 60.00
71 Michael Jordan 25.00 60.00
72 Michael Jordan 25.00 60.00
73 Michael Jordan 25.00 60.00
74 Michael Jordan 25.00 60.00
75 Michael Jordan 25.00 60.00
76 Michael Jordan 25.00 60.00
77 Michael Jordan 25.00 60.00
78 Michael Jordan 25.00 60.00
79 Michael Jordan 25.00 60.00
80 Gary Payton 2.50 6.00
81 Gary Payton 2.50 6.00
82 Gary Payton 2.50 6.00
83 Gary Payton 2.50 6.00
84 Gary Payton 2.50 6.00
85 Paul Pierce 2.50 6.00
86 Paul Pierce 2.50 6.00
87 Paul Pierce 2.50 6.00
88 Paul Pierce 2.50 6.00
89 Paul Pierce 2.50 6.00
90 Ray Allen 2.50 6.00
91 Ray Allen 2.50 6.00
92 Ray Allen 2.50 6.00
93 Ray Allen 2.50 6.00
94 Ray Allen 2.50 6.00
95 Reggie Miller 3.00 8.00
96 Reggie Miller 3.00 8.00
97 Reggie Miller 3.00 8.00
98 Reggie Miller 3.00 8.00
99 Reggie Miller 3.00 8.00
100 Reggie Miller 3.00 8.00

2013 Upper Deck All-Time Greats Silver 10
*SILVER: 1.25X TO 3X BASIC
STATED PRINT RUN 10 SER.#'d SETS
ALL VERSIONS PRICED EQUALLY

2013 Upper Deck All-Time Greats Gold
*GOLD: .6X TO 1.5X BASIC
STATED PRINT RUN 50 SER.#'d SETS
ALL VERSIONS PRICED EQUALLY

2013 Upper Deck All-Time Greats All-Time Forces
STATED PRINT RUN 35 SER.#'d SETS
ATFAI Allen Iverson 100.00 250.00
ATFBR Bill Russell 350.00 700.00
ATFDR Dennis Rodman 75.00 200.00
ATFGH Grant Hill 40.00 100.00
ATFGP Gary Payton 40.00 100.00
ATFHO Hakeem Olajuwon 100.00 250.00
ATFIT Isiah Thomas 40.00 100.00
ATFJE Julius Erving 75.00 200.00
ATFJK Jason Kidd 40.00 100.00
ATFJO Magic Johnson 125.00 300.00
ATFKM Karl Malone 50.00 120.00
ATFLB Larry Bird 125.00 300.00
ATFLJ LeBron James 2,000.00 4,000.00
ATFMA Karl Malone 50.00 120.00
ATFMI Reggie Miller 100.00 250.00
ATFMJ Michael Jordan 2,000.00 4,000.00
ATFOL Hakeem Olajuwon 100.00 250.00
ATFPP Paul Pierce 40.00 100.00
ATFRA Ray Allen 60.00 150.00
ATFRM Reggie Miller 100.00 250.00
ATFRO David Robinson 75.00 200.00

2013 Upper Deck All-Time Greats Banner Season
STATED PRINT RUN 25 SER.#'d SETS
BSAI Allen Iverson 100.00 250.00
BSBR Bill Russell 200.00 500.00
BSDR David Robinson 75.00 200.00
BSGH Grant Hill 60.00 150.00
BSGP Gary Payton 60.00 150.00
BSHO Hakeem Olajuwon 75.00 200.00
BSIT Isiah Thomas 60.00 150.00
BSJE Julius Erving 125.00 300.00
BSJK Jason Kidd 60.00 150.00
BSJO Michael Jordan 2,000.00 4,000.00
BSKM Karl Malone 75.00 200.00
BSLB Larry Bird 125.00 300.00
BSLJ LeBron James 1,500.00 3,000.00
BSMJ Magic Johnson 125.00 300.00
BSPP Paul Pierce 60.00 150.00
BSRA Ray Allen 60.00 150.00
BSRM Reggie Miller 100.00 250.00
BSRO Dennis Rodman 75.00 200.00

2013 Upper Deck All-Time Greats Jordan Vs.
STATED PRINT RUN 23 SER.#'d SETS
ALL VERSIONS PRICED EQUALLY
JV1 Michael Jordan 50.00 125.00
JV2 Michael Jordan 50.00 125.00
JV3 Michael Jordan 50.00 125.00
JV4 Michael Jordan 50.00 125.00
JV5 Michael Jordan 50.00 125.00
JV6 Michael Jordan 50.00 125.00
JV7 Michael Jordan 50.00 125.00
JV8 Michael Jordan 50.00 125.00
JV9 Michael Jordan 50.00 125.00
JV10 Michael Jordan 50.00 125.00
JV11 Allen Iverson 40.00 100.00
JV12 David Robinson 20.00 50.00
JV13 Julius Erving 20.00 50.00
JV14 Karl Malone 20.00 50.00
JV15 Larry Bird 40.00 100.00
JV16 LeBron James 50.00 120.00
JV17 Magic Johnson 40.00 100.00
JV18 Michael Jordan 50.00 125.00
JV19 Isiah Thomas 20.00 50.00
JV20 Reggie Miller 40.00 100.00

2013 Upper Deck All-Time Greats Jordan Vs. Signatures
STATED PRINT RUN 23 SER.#'d SETS
JVSAI A.Iverson/M.Jordan 2,500.00 5,000.00
JVSDR M.Jordan/D.Robinson 2,000.00 4,000.00
JVSJE M.Jordan/J.Erving 2,000.00 4,000.00
JVSJO M.Jordan/M.Jordan 3,000.00 6,000.00
JVSJT M.Jordan/I.Thomas 1,500.00 3,000.00
JVSKM M.Jordan/K.Malone 1,500.00 3,000.00
JVSLB M.Jordan/L.Bird 2,500.00 5,000.00
JVSLJ L.James/M.Jordan 3,000.00 6,000.00
JVSMJ M.Jordan/M.Johnson 2,500.00 5,000.00
JVSRM M.Jordan/R.Miller 2,000.00 4,000.00

2013 Upper Deck All-Time Greats Program of Excellence
PRINT RUNS B/WN 10-23 COPIES PER
PEDR David Robinson/15 75.00 200.00
PEGH Grant Hill/15 75.00 200.00
PEHA Hakeem Olajuwon/15 125.00 300.00
PEHI Grant Hill/15 60.00 150.00
PEHO Hakeem Olajuwon/15 125.00 300.00
PEIT Isiah Thomas/15 60.00 150.00
PEJO Michael Jordan/23 2,000.00 4,000.00
PEMI Michael Jordan/23 2,000.00 4,000.00
PEMJ Magic Johnson/15 150.00 400.00
PEOL Hakeem Olajuwon/15 125.00 300.00
PERO David Robinson/15 75.00 200.00

2013 Upper Deck All-Time Greats Signatures
PRINT RUNS B/WN 25-55 COPIES PER
ALL VERSIONS PRICED EQUALLY
ATGAI1 Allen Iverson/35 100.00 250.00
ATGAI2 Allen Iverson/35 100.00 250.00
ATGAI3 Allen Iverson/35 100.00 250.00
ATGAI4 Allen Iverson/35 100.00 250.00
ATGAI5 Allen Iverson/35 100.00 250.00
ATGAI6 Allen Iverson/35 100.00 250.00
ATGAI7 Allen Iverson/35 100.00 250.00
ATGBR1 Bill Russell/50 400.00 800.00
ATGBR2 Bill Russell/55 400.00 800.00
ATGDR1 David Robinson/30 60.00 150.00
ATGDR2 David Robinson/30 60.00 150.00
ATGDR3 David Robinson/30 60.00 150.00
ATGDR4 David Robinson/30 60.00 150.00
ATGDR5 David Robinson/30 60.00 150.00
ATGDR6 David Robinson/30 60.00 150.00
ATGGH1 Grant Hill/35 60.00 150.00
ATGGH2 Grant Hill/35 60.00 150.00
ATGGH3 Grant Hill/35 60.00 150.00
ATGGH4 Grant Hill/35 60.00 150.00
ATGGH5 Grant Hill/35 60.00 150.00
ATGGH6 Grant Hill/35 60.00 150.00
ATGGH7 Grant Hill/35 60.00 150.00
ATGGH8 Grant Hill/35 60.00 150.00
ATGGP1 Gary Payton/30 40.00 100.00
ATGGP2 Gary Payton/30 40.00 100.00
ATGGP3 Gary Payton/30 40.00 100.00
ATGGP4 Gary Payton/30 40.00 100.00
ATGGP5 Gary Payton/30 40.00 100.00
ATGHO1 Hakeem Olajuwon/35 100.00 250.00
ATGHO2 Hakeem Olajuwon/35 100.00 250.00
ATGHO3 Hakeem Olajuwon/35 100.00 250.00
ATGIT1 Isiah Thomas/45 40.00 100.00
ATGIT2 Isiah Thomas/45 40.00 100.00
ATGIT3 Isiah Thomas/45 40.00 100.00
ATGIT4 Isiah Thomas/45 40.00 100.00
ATGIT5 Isiah Thomas/45 40.00 100.00
ATGJE1 Julius Erving/55 60.00 150.00
ATGJE2 Julius Erving/55 60.00 150.00
ATGJK1 Jason Kidd/35 40.00 100.00
ATGJK2 Jason Kidd/35 40.00 100.00
ATGJK3 Jason Kidd/35 40.00 100.00
ATGJK4 Jason Kidd/35 40.00 100.00
ATGJK5 Jason Kidd/35 40.00 100.00
ATGJK6 Jason Kidd/35 40.00 100.00
ATGJK7 Jason Kidd/35 40.00 50.00
ATGJO1 Magic Johnson/50 125.00 300.00
ATGJO2 Magic Johnson/50 125.00 300.00
ATGJO3 Magic Johnson/50 125.00 300.00
ATGJO4 Magic Johnson/50 125.00 300.00
ATGJO5 Magic Johnson/50 125.00 300.00
ATGJO6 Magic Johnson/50 125.00 300.00
ATGJO7 Magic Johnson/50 125.00 300.00
ATGKM1 Karl Malone/35 60.00 150.00
ATGKM2 Karl Malone/35 60.00 150.00
ATGKM3 Karl Malone/35 60.00 150.00
ATGKM4 Karl Malone/35 60.00 150.00
ATGKM5 Karl Malone/35 60.00 150.00
ATGLB1 Larry Bird/33 125.00 300.00
ATGLB2 Larry Bird/33 125.00 300.00
ATGLB3 Larry Bird/33 125.00 300.00
ATGLB4 Larry Bird/33 125.00 300.00
ATGLB5 Larry Bird/33 125.00 300.00
ATGLJ1 LeBron James/30 1,000.00 2,000.00
ATGLJ2 LeBron James/30 1,000.00 2,000.00
ATGLJ3 LeBron James/30 1,000.00 2,000.00
ATGLJ4 LeBron James/30 1,000.00 2,000.00
ATGLJ5 LeBron James/30 1,000.00 2,000.00
ATGMJ1 Michael Jordan/45 1,500.00 3,000.00
ATGMJ2 Michael Jordan/45 1,500.00 3,000.00
ATGMJ3 Michael Jordan/45 1,500.00 3,000.00
ATGMJ4 Michael Jordan/45 1,500.00 3,000.00
ATGMJ5 Michael Jordan/45 1,500.00 3,000.00
ATGMJ6 Michael Jordan/45 1,500.00 3,000.00
ATGMJ7 Michael Jordan/45 1,500.00 3,000.00
ATGMJ8 Michael Jordan/45 1,500.00 3,000.00
ATGMJ9 Michael Jordan/45 1,500.00 3,000.00
ATGPP1 Paul Pierce/50 40.00 100.00
ATGPP2 Paul Pierce/50 40.00 100.00
ATGPP3 Paul Pierce/50 40.00 100.00
ATGPP4 Paul Pierce/50 40.00 100.00
ATGRA1 Ray Allen/40 20.00 50.00
ATGRA2 Ray Allen/40 20.00 50.00
ATGRA3 Ray Allen/40 20.00 50.00
ATGRA4 Ray Allen/40 20.00 50.00
ATGRA5 Ray Allen/40 20.00 50.00
ATGRM1 Reggie Miller/30 100.00 250.00
ATGRM2 Reggie Miller/30 100.00 250.00
ATGRM3 Reggie Miller/25 100.00 250.00
ATGRM4 Reggie Miller/25 100.00 250.00
ATGRM5 Reggie Miller/25 100.00 250.00
ATGRO1 Dennis Rodman/55 20.00 50.00
ATGRO2 Dennis Rodman/55 20.00 50.00
ATGMJ10 Michael Jordan/45 1,500.00 3,000.00
ATGMJ11 Michael Jordan/45 1,500.00 3,000.00
ATGMJ12 Michael Jordan/45 1,500.00 3,000.00
ATGMJ13 Michael Jordan/45 1,500.00 3,000.00
ATGMJ14 Michael Jordan/50 1,500.00 3,000.00
ATGMJ15 Michael Jordan/45 1,500.00 3,000.00
ATGMJ16 Michael Jordan/45 1,500.00 3,000.00
ATGMJ17 Michael Jordan/45 1,500.00 3,000.00

1996 Upper Deck Authenticated Space Jam Celcards
COMPLETE SET 1 (4) 30.00 80.00
COMPLETE SET 2 (2) 15.00 40.00
NNO Michael Jordan Bugs Bunny 8.00 20.00
NNO Michael Jordan Bugs Bunny #2 8.00 20.00
NNO Michael Jordan Monstar 8.00 20.00
NNO Michael Jordan The Tune Squad 8.00 20.00
NNO Michael Jordan Bugs Bunny 8.00 20.00
NNO Michael Jordan Porky Pig 8.00 20.00

1995-96 Upper Deck Ball Park Jordan
COMPLETE SET (5) 15.00 40.00
COMMON CARD (1-5) 4.00 10.00

1995-96 Upper Deck Ball Park Jordan Gold
COMPLETE SET (5) 25.00 60.00
COMMON CARD (1-5) 6.00 15.00

1996-97 Upper Deck Ball Park Jordan
COMPLETE SET (5) 10.00 25.00
COMMON CARD (1-5) 2.50 6.00

1996-97 Upper Deck Ball Park Jordan Gold
COMPLETE SET (5) 12.00 30.00
COMMON CARD (1-5) 3.00 8.00

1999 Upper Deck Century Legends
COMPLETE SET (89) 20.00 40.00
1 Michael Jordan 2.00 5.00
2 Bill Russell .40 1.00
3 Wilt Chamberlain .50 1.25
4 George Mikan .40 1.00
5 Oscar Robertson .30 .75
7 Larry Bird .60 1.50
8 Karl Malone .30 .75
9 Elgin Baylor .25 .60
10 Kareem Abdul-Jabbar .40 1.00
11 Jerry West .40 1.00
12 Bob Cousy .40 1.00
13 Julius Erving .40 1.00
14 Hakeem Olajuwon .30 .75
15 John Havlicek .30 .75
16 John Stockton .30 .75
17 Rick Barry .20 .50
18 Moses Malone .25 .60
19 Nate Thurmond .25 .60
20 Bob Pettit .25 .60
21 Pete Maravich .40 1.00
22 Willis Reed .25 .60
23 Isiah Thomas .25 .60
24 Dolph Schayes .25 .60
25 Walt Frazier .25 .60
26 Wes Unseld .25 .60
27 Bill Sharman .25 .60
28 George Gervin .25 .60
29 Hal Greer .20 .50
30 Dave DeBusschere .25 .60
31 Earl Monroe .25 .60
32 Kevin McHale .30 .75
33 Charles Barkley .30 .75
34 Elvin Hayes .25 .60
35 Scottie Pippen .40 1.00
36 Jerry Lucas .25 .60
37 Dave Bing .25 .60
38 Lenny Wilkens .25 .60
39 Paul Arizin .25 .60
40 Nate Archibald .20 .50
41 James Worthy .25 .60
42 Patrick Ewing .30 .75
43 Billy Cunningham .25 .60
44 Sam Jones .30 .75
45 Dave Cowens .15 .40
46 Robert Parish .25 .60
47 Bill Walton .25 .60
48 Shaquille O'Neal .60 1.50
49 David Robinson .40 1.00
50 Dominique Wilkins .30 .75
51 Kobe Bryant 1.25 3.00
52 Vince Carter .50 1.25
53 Paul Pierce .40 1.00
54 Allen Iverson .50 1.25
55 Stephon Marbury .25 .60
56 Mike Bibby .25 .60
57 Jason Williams .30 .75
58 Kevin Garnett .50 1.25
59 Tim Duncan .50 1.25
60 Antawn Jamison .25 .60
61 Antoine Walker .25 .60
62 Shareef Abdur-Rahim .20 .50
63 Michael Olowokandi .15 .40
64 Robert Traylor .15 .40
65 Keith Van Horn .20 .50
66 Shaquille O'Neal .60 1.50
67 Ray Allen .25 .60
68 Gary Payton .25 .60
69 Raef LaFrentz .15 .40
70 Grant Hill .30 .75
71 Anfernee Hardaway .40 1.00
72 Maurice Taylor .15 .40
73 Ron Mercer .20 .50
74 Michael Finley .25 .60
75 Jason Kidd .40 1.00
76 Allan Houston .20 .50
77 Damon Stoudamire .20 .50
78 Antonio McDyess .20 .50
79 Eddie Jones .20 .50
80 Michael Dickerson .15 .40
81 Michael Jordan 1.25 3.00
82 Michael Jordan 1.25 3.00
83 Michael Jordan 1.25 3.00
84 Michael Jordan 1.25 3.00
85 Michael Jordan 1.25 3.00
86 Michael Jordan 1.25 3.00
87 Michael Jordan 1.25 3.00
88 Michael Jordan 1.25 3.00
89 Michael Jordan 1.25 3.00
90 Michael Jordan 1.25 3.00
S1 Michael Jordan PROMO 2.00 5.00

1999 Upper Deck Century Legends Century Collection
COMMON MJ (81-90) 100.00 250.00
*STARS: 20X TO 50X BASE CARD HI
STATED PRINT RUN 100 SERIAL #'d SETS
CARD NUMBER 6 DOES NOT EXIST
1 Michael Jordan 200.00 400.00
51 Kobe Bryant 200.00 400.00
54 Allen Iverson 30.00 80.00
70 Grant Hill 20.00 50.00
71 Anfernee Hardaway 30.00 80.00

1999 Upper Deck Century Legends All-Century Team
COMPLETE SET (12) 20.00 40.00
STATED ODDS 1:11
A1 Michael Jordan 8.00 20.00
A2 Oscar Robertson 1.25 3.00
A3 Wilt Chamberlain 2.00 5.00
A4 Larry Bird 2.50 6.00
A5 Julius Erving 1.50 4.00
A6 Jerry West 1.50 4.00
A7 Charles Barkley 1.25 3.00
A8 John Stockton 1.25 3.00
A9 Hakeem Olajuwon 1.25 3.00
A10 Karl Malone 1.25 3.00
A11 Scottie Pippen 1.50 4.00
A12 David Robinson 1.50 4.00

1999 Upper Deck Century Legends Epic Milestones
COMPLETE SET (12) 20.00 40.00
STATED ODDS 1:11
EM1 Michael Jordan 8.00 20.00
EM2 Jerry West 1.50 4.00
EM3 John Stockton 1.25 3.00
EM4 Wilt Chamberlain 2.00 5.00
EM5 Julius Erving 1.50 4.00
EM6 Reggie Miller 1.25 3.00
EM7 Hakeem Olajuwon 1.25 3.00
EM8 Robert Parish 1.00 2.50
EM9 Kobe Bryant 5.00 12.00
EM10 Rick Barry .75 2.00
EM11 Patrick Ewing 1.25 3.00
EM12 Charles Barkley 1.25 3.00

1999 Upper Deck Century Legends Epic Signatures
STATED ODDS 1:23
AE Alex English 15.00 40.00
AI Allen Iverson 500.00 1,000.00
BC Bob Cousy 125.00 300.00
BL Bob Lanier 12.00 30.00
BP Bob Pettit 75.00 200.00
BR Bill Russell 2,000.00 4,000.00
BS Bill Sharman 40.00 100.00
BW Bill Walton 20.00 50.00
CD Clyde Drexler 50.00 120.00
DC Dave Cowens 15.00 40.00
DR Julius Erving 200.00 400.00
DT David Thompson 15.00 40.00
EB Elgin Baylor 30.00 80.00
EH Elvin Hayes 15.00 40.00
EM Earl Monroe 20.00 50.00
GG George Gervin 25.00 60.00
JL Jerry Lucas 15.00 40.00
JW Jerry West 100.00 250.00
KA Kareem Abdul-Jabbar 800.00 1,500.00
LB Larry Bird 800.00 1,500.00
MB Mike Bibby 12.00 30.00
MM Moses Malone 75.00 200.00
MO Michael Olowokandi 8.00 20.00
NA Nate Archibald 25.00 60.00
OR Oscar Robertson 60.00 150.00
TH Tim Hardaway 20.00 50.00
WC Wilt Chamberlain 6,000.00 12,000.00
WF Walt Frazier 40.00 100.00
WR Willis Reed 50.00 120.00
WU Wes Unseld 20.00 50.00
JH John Havlicek 100.00 250.00

1999 Upper Deck Century Legends Epic Signatures Century
*CENTURY: 1.25X TO 3X HI COLUMN
STATED PRINT RUN 100 SERIAL #'d SETS
EXCEPTIONS NOTED BELOW
OLAJUWON DID NOT SIGN TRADE CARDS
IVERSON AU REPLACES OLAJUWON
AE Alex English/100 75.00 200.00
AI Allen Iverson/100 2,000.00 4,000.00
BC Bob Cousy/100 500.00 1,000.00
BW Bill Walton/100 125.00 300.00
GG George Gervin/100 150.00 400.00
JW Jerry West/100 500.00 1,000.00
LB Larry Bird/33 3,000.00 6,000.00
MJ Michael Jordan/23 25,000.00 50,000.00
OR Oscar Robertson/100 500.00 1,000.00
WC Wilt Chamberlain/100 15,000.00 30,000.00
WR Willis Reed/100 150.00 400.00
WU Wes Unseld/100 100.00 250.00
JH John Havlicek/100 500.00 1,000.00

1999 Upper Deck Century Legends Generations
COMPLETE SET (12) 12.50 30.00
STATED ODDS 1:4
G1 M.Jordan/J.Erving 5.00 12.00
G2 K.Bryant/M.Jordan 5.00 12.00
G3 S.O'Neal/W.Chamberlain 1.50 4.00
G4 J.Williams/P.Maravich 1.00 2.50
G5 S.Marbury/N.Archibald .50 1.25
G6 A.Walker/K.Malone .75 2.00
G7 G.Hill/G.Gervin .75 2.00
G8 G.Payton/I.Thomas .60 1.50
G9 K.Garnett/D.Wilkins 1.25 3.00
G10 H.Olajuwon/M.Malone .75 2.00
G11 K.Van Horn/L.Bird 1.50 4.00
G12 V.Carter/O.Robertson 1.25 3.00

1999 Upper Deck Century Legends Jerseys of the Century
STATED ODDS 1:475
CD Clyde Drexler 20.00 50.00
DR Julius Erving 30.00 80.00
JS John Stockton 15.00 40.00
KA Kareem Abdul-Jabbar 40.00 80.00
KM Karl Malone 15.00 40.00
LB Larry Bird 20.00 50.00
MJ Michael Jordan 350.00 700.00
SO Shaquille O'Neal 30.00 80.00
KAA K.Abdul-Jabbar AU/33 150.00 300.00

1999 Upper Deck Century Legends MJ's Most Memorable Shots
COMPLETE SET (6) 20.00 50.00
COMMON CARD (MJ1-MJ6) 4.00 10.00
STATED ODDS 1:23

2000 Upper Deck Century Legends
COMPLETE SET (90) 20.00 50.00
1 Michael Jordan 3.00 8.00
2 Magic Johnson 1.25 3.00
3 Larry Bird 1.25 3.00
4 Bob Cousy 1.00 2.50
5 Bill Russell 1.25 3.00
6 Julius Erving 1.00 2.50
7 Nate Archibald .50 1.25
8 Oscar Robertson .75 2.00
9 Elgin Baylor .75 2.00
10 Jo Jo White .40 1.00
11 Hal Greer .50 1.25
12 Clyde Drexler .60 1.50
13 Wilt Chamberlain 1.25 3.00
14 Walt Bellamy .40 1.00
15 Walt Frazier .60 1.50
16 Earl Monroe .60 1.50
17 John Havlicek 1.00 2.50
18 George Mikan 1.25 3.00
19 George Karl .40 1.00
20 Tom Heinsohn .60 1.50
21 Kareem Abdul-Jabbar 1.25 3.00
22 Bill Sharman .50 1.25
23 Elvin Hayes .50 1.25
24 Rick Barry .50 1.25
25 Paul Silas .40 1.00
26 Mitch Kupchak .40 1.00
27 Dave Cowens .50 1.25
28 Nate Thurmond .50 1.25
29 Dave DeBusschere .50 1.25
30 Jerry Lucas .50 1.25
31 Bill Walton .50 1.25
32 Jerry West 1.00 2.50
33 David Thompson .40 1.00
34 Spencer Haywood .40 1.00
35 Moses Malone .60 1.50
36 Alex English .50 1.25
37 Willis Reed .60 1.50
38 George Gervin .60 1.50
39 Dolph Schayes .50 1.25
40 Wes Unseld .50 1.25
41 Bob Lanier .60 1.50
42 James Worthy .60 1.50
43 Maurice Lucas .40 1.00
44 Pete Maravich 1.00 2.50
45 Isiah Thomas .60 1.50
46 Robert Parish .50 1.25
47 Dominique Wilkins .60 1.50
48 Walter Davis .40 1.00
49 Bob Pettit .60 1.50
50 Kevin McHale .60 1.50
51 Julius Erving HD 1.00 2.50
52 Dominique Wilkins HD .60 1.50
53 George Gervin HD .60 1.50
54 Kareem Abdul-Jabbar HD 1.25 3.00
55 Clyde Drexler HD .60 1.50
56 David Thompson HD .40 1.00
57 Walter Davis HD .40 1.00
58 James Worthy HD .60 1.50
59 Moses Malone HD .60 1.50
60 Bob Lanier HD .60 1.50
61 Robert Parish HD .50 1.25
62 Maurice Lucas HD .40 1.00
63 Wes Unseld HD .50 1.25
64 Ron Boone HD .40 1.00
65 Larry Nance HD .40 1.00
66 Michael Jordan HD 3.00 8.00
67 Michael Jordan HD 3.00 8.00
68 Michael Jordan HD 3.00 8.00
69 Michael Jordan HD 3.00 8.00
70 Michael Jordan HD 3.00 8.00
71 Michael Jordan UDT 3.00 8.00
72 Wilt Chamberlain UDT 1.25 3.00
73 Magic Johnson UDT 1.25 3.00
74 Julius Erving UDT 1.00 2.50
75 Larry Bird UDT 1.25 3.00
76 Bill Russell UDT 1.25 3.00
77 Jerry West UDT 1.00 2.50
78 Oscar Robertson UDT .75 2.00
79 John Havlicek UDT 1.00 2.50
80 Elgin Baylor UDT .75 2.00
81 Michael Jordan TB 3.00 8.00
82 Michael Jordan TB 3.00 8.00
83 Michael Jordan TB 3.00 8.00
84 Michael Jordan TB 3.00 8.00
85 Michael Jordan TB 3.00 8.00
86 Michael Jordan TB 3.00 8.00
87 Michael Jordan TB 3.00 8.00
88 Michael Jordan TB 3.00 8.00
89 Michael Jordan TB 3.00 8.00
90 Michael Jordan TB 3.00 8.00

2000 Upper Deck Century Legends Commemorative Collection
*STARS: 12.5X TO 30X BASE CARD HI
*SUBSETS: 25X TO 60X BASE HI
STATED PRINT RUN 50 SERIAL #'d SETS

2000 Upper Deck Century Legends History's Heroes
COMPLETE SET (9) 6.00 15.00
STATED ODDS 1:12
HH1 Michael Jordan 5.00 12.00
HH2 Julius Erving 1.50 4.00
HH3 Larry Bird 2.00 5.00
HH4 Clyde Drexler 1.00 2.50
HH5 Elgin Baylor 1.25 3.00
HH6 George Gervin 1.00 2.50
HH7 Oscar Robertson 1.25 3.00
HH8 Jerry West 1.50 4.00
HH9 Alex English .75 2.00

2000 Upper Deck Century Legends Legendary Jerseys
STATED ODDS 1:288
*GOLD: 1.5X TO 4X HI
GOLD PRINT RUN 25 SER.#'d SETS
BCJ Bob Cousy 20.00 50.00
CDJ Clyde Drexler 12.00 30.00
DRJ Julius Erving 20.00 50.00
DWJ Dominique Wilkins 12.00 30.00
ITJ Isiah Thomas 12.00 30.00
KAJ Kareem Abdul-Jabbar 25.00 60.00
LBA Larry Bird AU/33 500.00 1,000.00
LBJ Larry Bird 25.00 60.00
MJA Michael Jordan AU/23 4,000.00 8,000.00
MJJ Michael Jordan 200.00 500.00
MMJ Moses Malone 12.00 30.00
WCJ Wilt Chamberlain 75.00 200.00

2000 Upper Deck Century Legends Legendary Signatures
STATED ODDS 1:24
AE Alex English 12.00 30.00
BC Bob Cousy 125.00 300.00
BL Bob Lanier 15.00 40.00
BP Bob Pettit 40.00 100.00
BR Bill Russell 500.00 1,000.00
BS Bill Sharman 12.00 30.00
BW Bill Walton 12.00 30.00
CD Clyde Drexler 40.00 100.00
DC Dave Cowens 12.00 30.00
DD Dave DeBusschere 12.00 30.00
DR Julius Erving 100.00 250.00
DS Dolph Schayes 12.00 30.00
DT David Thompson 10.00 25.00
DW Dominique Wilkins 15.00 40.00
EB Elgin Baylor 40.00 100.00
EH Elvin Hayes 12.00 30.00
EM Earl Monroe 25.00 60.00
GA Gail Goodrich 12.00 30.00
GG George Gervin 15.00 40.00
HG Hal Greer 12.00 30.00
IT Isiah Thomas 40.00 100.00
JA Jamaal Wilkes 10.00 25.00
JH John Havlicek 125.00 300.00
JJ Jo Jo White 10.00 25.00
JL Jerry Lucas 12.00 30.00
JW Jerry West 25.00 60.00
KA Kareem Abdul-Jabbar 125.00 300.00
LB Larry Bird 125.00 300.00
MG Magic Johnson 125.00 300.00
MM Moses Malone 50.00 120.00
NA Nate Archibald 12.00 30.00
NT Nate Thurmond 12.00 30.00
OR Oscar Robertson 60.00 150.00
PA Paul Arizin 12.00 30.00
PS Paul Silas 10.00 25.00
RB Rick Barry 12.00 30.00
SH Spencer Haywood 10.00 25.00
WB Walt Bellamy 10.00 25.00
WF Walt Frazier 15.00 40.00
WR Willis Reed 50.00 120.00
WU Wes Unseld 12.00 30.00

2000 Upper Deck Century Legends Legendary Signatures Gold
*GOLD: 1.25X TO 3X HI COLUMN
STATED PRINT RUN 25 SERIAL #'d SETS
BL Bob Lanier 50.00 125.00
BR Bill Russell 1,500.00 3,000.00
MJ Michael Jordan 4,000.00 8,000.00

2000 Upper Deck Century Legends MJ Final Floor Jumbos
COMPLETE SET (12) 500.00 1,000.00
COMMON CARD (FF1-FF12) 40.00 100.00
ONE PER BOX

2000 Upper Deck Century Legends NBA Originals
COMPLETE SET (6) 6.00 15.00
STATED ODDS 1:12
O1 Magic Johnson 2.00 5.00
O2 Julius Erving 1.50 4.00
O3 Michael Jordan 5.00 12.00
O4 David Thompson .60 1.50
O5 Kareem Abdul-Jabbar 2.00 5.00
O6 Clyde Drexler 1.00 2.50

2000 Upper Deck Century Legends Players of the Century
COMPLETE SET (20) 10.00 25.00
STATED ODDS 1:4
P1 Michael Jordan 5.00 12.00
P2 Wilt Chamberlain 2.00 5.00
P3 Magic Johnson 2.00 5.00
P4 Larry Bird 2.00 5.00
P5 Bill Russell 2.00 5.00
P6 Jerry West 1.50 4.00
P7 Oscar Robertson 1.25 3.00
P8 John Havlicek 1.50 4.00
P9 Kareem Abdul-Jabbar 2.00 5.00
P10 Pete Maravich 1.50 4.00
P11 Willis Reed 1.00 2.50
P12 Bob Lanier 1.00 2.50
P13 George Gervin 1.00 2.50
P14 Bill Walton .75 2.00
P15 Elvin Hayes .75 2.00
P16 Julius Erving 1.50 4.00
P17 Rick Barry .75 2.00
P18 Walt Frazier 1.00 2.50
P19 Nate Thurmond .75 2.00
P20 Moses Malone 1.00 2.50

2000 Upper Deck Century Legends Recollections

COMPLETE SET (7) 8.00 20.00
STATED ODDS 1:24
R1 Michael Jordan 6.00 15.00
R2 Isiah Thomas 1.25 3.00
R3 Julius Erving 2.00 5.00
R4 Wilt Chamberlain 2.50 6.00
R5 Clyde Drexler 1.25 3.00
R6 Bill Walton 1.00 2.50
R7 Dominique Wilkins 1.25 3.00

2002-03 Upper Deck Championship Drive

COMP.SET w/o SP's (100) 15.00 40.00
101-130 PRINT RUN 400 SER.#'d SETS
131-155 PRINT RUN 500 SER.#'d SETS
1 Shareef Abdur-Rahim .40 1.00
2 Glenn Robinson .40 1.00
3 Jason Terry .30 .75
4 Dion Glover .25 .60
5 Antoine Walker .30 .75
6 Paul Pierce .60 1.50
7 Vin Baker .30 .75
8 Kedrick Brown .25 .60
9 Jalen Rose .30 .75
10 Tyson Chandler .40 1.00
11 Eddy Curry .25 .60
12 Darius Miles .25 .60
13 Ricky Davis .30 .75
14 Zydrunas Ilgauskas .30 .75
15 Dirk Nowitzki 1.00 2.50
16 Michael Finley .40 1.00
17 Steve Nash .75 2.00
18 Raef LaFrentz .25 .60
19 Nick Van Exel .40 1.00
20 James Posey .25 .60
21 Juwan Howard .30 .75
22 Chauncey Billups .40 1.00
23 Ben Wallace .50 1.25
24 Richard Hamilton .50 1.25
25 Jason Richardson .40 1.00
26 Antawn Jamison .30 .75
27 Gilbert Arenas .40 1.00
28 Steve Francis .40 1.00
29 Cuttino Mobley .25 .60
30 Eddie Griffin .25 .60
31 Reggie Miller .75 2.00
32 Jermaine O'Neal .30 .75
33 Jamaal Tinsley .25 .60
34 Ron Mercer .25 .60
35 Elton Brand .30 .75
36 Andre Miller .30 .75
37 Kobe Bryant 3.00 8.00
38 Shaquille O'Neal 1.50 4.00
39 Rick Fox .25 .60
40 Devean George .25 .60
41 Pau Gasol .60 1.50
42 Shane Battier .40 1.00
43 Jason Williams .50 1.25
44 Eddie Jones .40 1.00
45 Brian Grant .25 .60
46 Anthony Carter .25 .60
47 Ray Allen .60 1.50
48 Tim Thomas .25 .60
49 Kevin Garnett 1.00 2.50
50 Terrell Brandon .25 .60
51 Wally Szczerbiak .25 .60
52 Joe Smith .30 .75
53 Jason Kidd .60 1.50
54 Richard Jefferson .30 .75
55 Dikembe Mutombo .60 1.50
56 Kenyon Martin .40 1.00
57 Baron Davis .40 1.00
58 Jamal Mashburn .30 .75
59 David Wesley .25 .60
60 P.J. Brown .25 .60
61 Courtney Alexander .25 .60
62 Latrell Sprewell .40 1.00
63 Allan Houston .40 1.00
64 Kurt Thomas .25 .60
65 Antonio McDyess .30 .75
66 Tracy McGrady .60 1.50
67 Mike Miller .30 .75
68 Grant Hill .60 1.50
69 Allen Iverson 1.00 2.50
70 Keith Van Horn .30 .75
71 Shawn Marion .40 1.00
72 Stephon Marbury .50 1.25
73 Anfernee Hardaway 1.00 2.50
74 Rasheed Wallace .50 1.25
75 Bonzi Wells .25 .60
76 Scottie Pippen 1.00 2.50
77 Mike Bibby .40 1.00
78 Peja Stojakovic .30 .75
79 Chris Webber .50 1.25
80 Hedo Turkoglu .30 .75
81 Vlade Divac .30 .75
82 Tim Duncan 1.00 2.50
83 David Robinson .75 2.00
84 Tony Parker .60 1.50
85 Malik Rose .25 .60
86 Gary Payton .60 1.50
87 Rashard Lewis .30 .75
88 Brent Barry .25 .60
89 Desmond Mason .30 .75
90 Vladimir Radmanovic .25 .60
91 Vince Carter .75 2.00
92 Morris Peterson .30 .75
93 Antonio Davis .30 .75
94 Karl Malone .75 2.00
95 John Stockton .75 2.00
96 Andrei Kirilenko .30 .75
97 Matt Harpring .25 .60
98 Jerry Stackhouse .40 1.00
99 Larry Hughes .30 .75
100 Michael Jordan 4.00 10.00
101 Juan Dixon JSY RC 3.00 8.00
102 Carlos Boozer JSY RC 4.00 10.00
103 Dan Gadzuric JSY RC 3.00 8.00
104 Vincent Yarbrough JSY RC 2.50 6.00
105 Robert Archibald JSY RC 2.50 6.00
106 Roger Mason JSY RC 3.00 8.00
107 Ronald Murray JSY RC 4.00 10.00
108 Chris Jefferies JSY RC 2.50 6.00
109 John Salmons JSY RC 4.00 10.00
110 Predrag Savovic JSY RC 3.00 8.00
111 Tayshaun Prince JSY RC 8.00 20.00
112 Casey Jacobsen JSY RC 3.00 8.00
113 Qyntel Woods JSY RC 2.50 6.00
114 Kareem Rush JSY RC 3.00 8.00
115 Ryan Humphrey JSY RC 3.00 8.00
116 Sam Clancy JSY RC 3.00 8.00
117 Lonny Baxter JSY RC 2.50 6.00
118 Fred Jones JSY RC 3.00 8.00
119 Marcus Haislip JSY RC 2.50 6.00
120 Melvin Ely JSY RC 3.00 8.00
121 Jared Jeffries JSY RC 3.00 8.00
122 Caron Butler JSY RC 4.00 10.00
123 Amare Stoudemire JSY RC 10.00 25.00
124 Chris Wilcox JSY RC 3.00 8.00
125 Nene Hilario JSY RC 4.00 10.00
126 DaJuan Wagner JSY RC 3.00 8.00
127 Nikoloz Tskitishvili JSY RC 2.50 6.00
128 Drew Gooden JSY RC 4.00 10.00
129 Jay Williams JSY RC 3.00 8.00
130 Yao Ming JSY RC 12.00 30.00
131 Manu Ginobili RC 15.00 40.00
132 Efthimios Rentzias RC 1.25 3.00
133 Juaquin Hawkins RC 1.25 3.00
134 Marko Jaric 2.00 5.00
135 Dan Dickau RC 1.25 3.00
136 Frank Williams RC 1.25 3.00
137 Curtis Borchardt RC 1.25 3.00
138 Mike Dunleavy RC 2.00 5.00
139 Smush Parker RC 2.00 5.00
140 Tito Maddox RC 1.25 3.00
141 Jannero Pargo RC 1.25 3.00
142 Jiri Welsch RC 1.50 4.00
143 Bostjan Nachbar RC 1.50 4.00
144 Rasual Butler RC 1.50 4.00
145 Gordan Giricek RC 2.00 5.00
146 Igor Rakocevic RC 1.25 3.00
147 Tamar Slay RC 1.25 3.00
148 Junior Harrington RC 1.25 3.00
149 Nate Huffman RC 1.25 3.00
150 Jamal Sampson RC 1.25 3.00
151 Reggie Evans RC 1.50 4.00
152 Cezary Trybanski RC 2.00 5.00
153 Pat Burke RC 1.25 3.00
154 J.R. Bremer RC 1.25 3.00
155 Mehmet Okur RC 2.00 5.00

2002-03 Upper Deck Championship Drive Parallel

*STARS: 3X TO 8X BASE CARD HI
1-100 PRINT RUN 125 SER.#'d SETS
*RCs 101-130: 1.5X TO 4X HI
*RCs 131-155: 2.5X TO 6X HI
101-155 RC PRINT RUN 25 SER.#'d SETS

2002-03 Upper Deck Championship Drive 2 Amazing Jerseys

STATED ODDS 1:144
AIJKJ A.Iverson/J.Kidd 10.00 25.00
CWMBJ C.Webber/M.Bibby 8.00 20.00
KBJRJ K.Bryant/J.Richardson 40.00 100.00
KGWSJ K.Garnett/W.Szczerbiak 10.00 25.00
MJKBM M.Jordan/K.Bryant SP 150.00 400.00
PPAWJ P.Pierce/A.Walker 8.00 20.00
SMSFJ S.Marbury/S.Francis 8.00 20.00
TMGHJ T.McGrady/G.Hill 10.00 25.00

2002-03 Upper Deck Championship Drive Best of Seven Jersey

PRINT RUN 50 SER.#'d SETS
AIB Allen Iverson 25.00 60.00
JKB Jason Kidd 15.00 40.00
JWB Jay Williams 8.00 20.00
KBB Kobe Bryant 75.00 200.00
MJB Michael Jordan 150.00 300.00
PPB Paul Pierce 15.00 40.00
YMB Yao Ming 50.00 120.00

2002-03 Upper Deck Championship Drive Key Pieces Jersey

STATED ODDS 1:96
BDKP Baron Davis 3.00 8.00
DNKP Dirk Nowitzki 8.00 20.00
JSKP Jerry Stackhouse 3.00 8.00
KBKP Kobe Bryant SP 40.00 100.00
KGKP Kevin Garnett 8.00 20.00
KMKP Karl Malone 6.00 15.00
MBKP Michael Jordan SP 60.00 150.00
MBKP Mike Bibby 3.00 8.00
PPKP Paul Pierce 5.00 12.00
RAKP Ray Allen 5.00 12.00
SBKP Shane Battier 3.00 8.00
SMKP Stephon Marbury 4.00 10.00

2002-03 Upper Deck Championship Drive Prized Properties Jersey

STATED ODDS 1:36
AHPP Allan Houston 3.00 8.00
AWPP Antoine Walker 2.50 6.00
BDPP Baron Davis 3.00 8.00
CWPP Chris Webber 4.00 10.00
EBPP Elton Brand 2.50 6.00
JRPP Jason Richardson 3.00 8.00
KBPP Kobe Bryant 40.00 100.00
KMPP Karl Malone 6.00 15.00
MJPP Michael Jordan 60.00 150.00
PGPP Pau Gasol 5.00 12.00
SAPP Shareef Abdur-Rahim 3.00 8.00
TMPP Tracy McGrady 5.00 12.00

2002-03 Upper Deck Championship Drive Signs of Success Dual Jersey

PRINT RUN 25 SER.#'d SETS
CBDG C.Butler/D.Gooden 25.00 60.00
CWME C.Wilcox/M.Ely 25.00 60.00
KBKG K.Bryant/K.Garnett 300.00 600.00
MJKB M.Jordan/K.Bryant 6,000.00 10,000.00
PPAW P.Pierce/A.Walker 40.00 100.00
YMJW Y.Ming/J.Williams 100.00 200.00

2002-03 Upper Deck Championship Drive Signs of Success Jersey

PRINT RUN 225 SER.#'d SETS
AWA Antoine Walker 8.00 20.00
JKA Jason Kidd 25.00 60.00
JWA Jay Williams 12.50 30.00
KMA Kenyon Martin 8.00 20.00
MFA Marcus Fizer 12.50 30.00
YMA Yao Ming 40.00 100.00

2002-03 Upper Deck Championship Drive Superstar Material Jersey

PRINT RUN 100 SER.#'d SETS
AIM Allen Iverson 10.00 25.00
AWM Antoine Walker 3.00 8.00
BDM Baron Davis 4.00 10.00
CWM Chris Webber 5.00 12.00
DNM Dirk Nowitzki 10.00 25.00
JRM Jason Richardson 4.00 10.00
JWM Jay Williams 3.00 8.00
KGM Kevin Garnett 10.00 25.00
KMB Kobe Bryant 40.00 100.00
MJM Michael Jordan 60.00 150.00
PGM Pau Gasol 6.00 15.00
RAM Ray Allen 6.00 15.00
SFM Steve Francis 4.00 10.00
YMM Yao Ming 20.00 50.00

2002-03 Upper Deck Championship Drive Then and Now Jersey

STATED ODDS 1:108
TNAM Andre Miller 4.00 10.00
TNJH Juwan Howard 4.00 10.00
TNJK Jason Kidd 8.00 20.00
TNJM Jamal Mashburn 4.00 10.00
TNMB Mike Bibby 5.00 12.00
TNMJ Michael Jordan SP 125.00 250.00
TNSA Shareef Abdur-Rahim 5.00 12.00
TNSM Stephon Marbury 6.00 15.00
TNTM Tracy McGrady 8.00 20.00

2005 Upper Deck Chicago National

COMPLETE SET (6) 10.00 25.00
NBA1 Dwight Howard 6.00 15.00
NBA2 Luol Deng 2.50 6.00
NBA3 Ben Gordon 2.50 6.00
NBA4 Chris Duhon 2.00 5.00
NBA5 Josh Smith 3.00 8.00
NBA6 Andre Iguodala 3.00 8.00

1995-96 Upper Deck Chinese Basketball Alliance

COMPLETE SET (125) 12.00 30.00
1 Chu Chung-Chi .08 .25
2 Lin Chien-Ping .08 .25
3 Roderick James Hannibal .20 .50
4 Tau Song .08 .25
5 Tsi-Fu-Tsi .08 .25
6 Chen Hung-Zung .08 .25
7 Chen Cheng-Sbiun .08 .25
8 Kuo Tien-Lung .08 .25
9 Tungfang Chieh-Teh .08 .25
10 Li Yung-Kung .08 .25
11 Hsu Tung-Ching .08 .25
12 Chang Hsien-Ming .08 .25
13 Mark Clark .20 .50
14 Brenton Lloyd Moore .20 .50
15 Arlando F. Bennett .20 .50
16 Christopher Edward Knight .20 .50
17 Tsou Jiunn-San .08 .25
18 Li Chung-Shi .08 .25
19 Liu I-Shang .08 .25
20 Chio Teh-Chih .08 .25
21 Michael Lee Johnson .20 .50
22 Jeng Jyh-Long .08 .25
23 Lo Hsing-Liang .08 .25
24 Huang Chun-Hsiung .08 .25
25 Chang Ya-Tang .08 .25
26 Chu Hao-Ren .08 .25
27 Jye Song .08 .25
28 Stacey Cornilius .20 .50
29 Keith Smith .20 .50
30 Rex Harrison Manu .20 .50
31 Daryl Scott .20 .50
32 Joseph Nathenial Temple .20 .50
33 Laurent Crawford .20 .50
34 David Lewayne Cooke .20 .50
35 Tsou Hai-Zunkg .08 .25
36 Wang Li-Bin .08 .25
37 Bai Ming-Li .08 .25
38 Kofi Kyei .20 .50
39 Lin Chai-Hung .08 .25
40 Chen Chung-Chian .08 .25
41 Li Chi-Chian .08 .25
42 Sun Mao-Shen .08 .25
43 Tzeng Tzeng-Cho .08 .25
44 Cheyenne Durell Gibson .20 .50
45 Chen Jiunn-Chie .08 .25
46 Kelvin Cornell Allen .20 .50
47 Chamg Bing-Hsiang .08 .25
48 Kennard Robison .20 .50
49 David Edward Davies .20 .50
50 Todd Alan Rowe .20 .50
51 Mike Sterner .20 .50
52 Robert John Fife .20 .50
53 Carroll Boudreaux .20 .50
54 Chen Cheng-Kwei .08 .25
55 Hung Chang-Ching .08 .25
56 Yen Chao-Chyun .08 .25
57 Lai Kwo-Hong .08 .25
58 Ko Yiing-Yan .08 .25
59 Gerard Arcement .20 .50
60 Jerry Lew .20 .50
61 Tien Su-Chung .08 .25
62 Chris Collier .20 .50
63 Tzeng Yih-Chin .08 .25
64 Dwight Myvett .20 .50
65 Anthony Robert Block .20 .50
66 Lan Chih-Ming .08 .25
67 Lin Shin-Hwa .08 .25
68 Derrell Cunegin .20 .50
69 Harold Boudreaux .20 .50
70 Wu Jye-Wei .08 .25
71 Jerry Lew .20 .50
72 Tsou Jiunn-San .08 .25
73 Derrell Cunegin .20 .50
74 Huang Chun-Hsiung .08 .25
75 Christopher Edward Knight .20 .50
76 Huang Chun-Hsiung .08 .25
77 Joseph Nathenial Temple .20 .50
78 Lo Hsing-Liang .08 .25
79 Hung Chang-Ching .08 .25
80 Tsou Jiunn-San .08 .25
81 Christopher Edward Knight .20 .50
82 David Edward Davies .20 .50
83 Christopher Edward Knight .20 .50
84 Harold Boudreaux .20 .50
85 Arlando F. Bennett .20 .50
86 Arlando F. Bennett .20 .50
87 Tungfang Chieh-Teh .08 .25
88 Arlando F. Bennett .20 .50
89 Christopher Edward Knight .20 .50
90 Tungfang Chieh-Teh .08 .25
91 Li Yung-Kung .08 .25
92 Tsi Fu Tsi .08 .25
93 Tsou Jiunn-San .08 .25
94 Jeng Jyh-Long .08 .25
95 Lo Hsing-Liang .08 .25
96 Rex Harrison Manu .20 .50
97 Stacey Cornilius .20 .50
98 Wang Li-Bin .08 .25
99 Chen Chung-Chian .08 .25
100 Tzeng Tzeng-Cho .08 .25
101 Todd Alan Rowe .20 .50
102 Kennard Robison .20 .50
103 Tzeng Yih-Chin .08 .25
104 Jerry Lew .20 .50
105 Chen Cheng-Kwei .08 .25
106 Dwight Myvett .20 .50
107 Harold Boudreaux .20 .50
108 Dwight Myvett .20 .50
109 Harold Boudreaux .20 .50
110 Todd Alan Rowe .20 .50
111 Jeng Jyh-Long .08 .25
112 Li Chi-Chian .08 .25
113 Harold Boudreaux .20 .50
114 Dwight Myvett .20 .50
115 Tsou Jiunn-San .08 .25
116 Christopher Edward Knight .20 .50
117 Anthony Robert Block .20 .50
118 Rex Harrison Manu .20 .50
119 Rex Harrison Manu .20 .50
120 Yue Lon .08 .25
121 Hung Kuo .08 .25
122 Tera .08 .25
123 Luckipar .08 .25
124 Checklist #1 .08 .25
125 Checklist #2 .08 .25

1995-96 Upper Deck Chinese Alliance MVP's

COMPLETE SET (9) 4.00 10.00
M1 Jeng Jyh-Long .40 1.00
M2 Tsou Jiunn-San .40 1.00
M3 Todd Alan Rowe .75 2.00
M4 Tungfang Chieh-Teh .40 1.00
M5 Arlando F. Bennett .75 2.00
M6 Roderick Nathenial Temple .75 2.00
M7 Joseph Nathenial Temple .40 1.00
M8 Tungfang Chieh-Teh .40 1.00
M9 CBA President .40 1.00

2003 Upper Deck City Heights LeBron James

NNO LeBron James 15.00 40.00

2004 Upper Deck Collectibles All-Star Game LeBron James

LJAS LeBron James 2.00 5.00

2002 Upper Deck Collector's Club

COMPLETE SET (21) 10.00 25.00
NBA1 Kobe Bryant 1.25 3.00
NBA2 Allen Iverson .60 1.50
NBA3 Vince Carter 1.00 2.50
NBA4 Jason Kidd .40 1.00
NBA5 Tracy McGrady .50 1.25
NBA6 Pau Gasol .30 .75
NBA7 Kevin Garnett .60 1.50
NBA8 Steve Francis .40 1.00
NBA9 Chris Webber .40 1.00
NBA10 Ray Allen .25 .60
NBA11 Kwame Brown .25 .60
NBA12 Paul Pierce .25 .60
NBA13 Stephon Marbury .25 .60
NBA14 Tim Duncan .50 1.25
NBA15 Shaquille O'Neal .60 1.50
NBA16 Jerry Stackhouse .25 .60
NBA17 Rashard Lewis .15 .40
NBA18 Darius Miles .40 1.00
NBA19 Jamaal Tinsley .40 1.00
NBA20 Michael Jordan 2.00 5.00
KGU Kevin Garnett JSY 6.00 15.00

2008 Upper Deck Diamond Club Autographs

DC3 LeBron James 300.00 600.00
DC5 Derrick Rose 300.00 600.00
DC6 Michael Beasley 100.00 200.00

2014 Upper Deck Diamond Club Trade Card Autograph

SAUTO Shaquille O'Neal 125.00 300.00

1997-98 Upper Deck Diamond Vision

COMPLETE SET (29) 40.00 100.00
1 Dikembe Mutombo 2.00 5.00
2 Dana Barros .75 2.00
3 Glen Rice 1.25 3.00
4 Michael Jordan 12.00 30.00
5 Terrell Brandon 1.00 2.50
6 Michael Finley 1.25 3.00
7 Antonio McDyess 1.25 3.00
8 Grant Hill 2.00 5.00
9 Latrell Sprewell 1.50 4.00
10 Hakeem Olajuwon 2.50 6.00
11 Reggie Miller 2.50 6.00
12 Loy Vaught 1.00 2.50
13 Shaquille O'Neal 4.00 10.00
14 Alonzo Mourning 2.00 5.00
15 Vin Baker 1.00 2.50
16 Kevin Garnett 3.00 8.00
17 Kerry Kittles 1.00 2.50
18 Patrick Ewing 2.00 5.00
19 Anfernee Hardaway 3.00 8.00
20 Allen Iverson 4.00 10.00
21 Jason Kidd 2.00 5.00
22 Isaiah Rider 1.00 2.50
23 Mitch Richmond 1.50 4.00
24 David Robinson 2.50 6.00
25 Gary Payton 2.00 5.00
26 Damon Stoudamire 1.25 3.00
27 Karl Malone 2.50 6.00
28 Shareef Abdur-Rahim 1.25 3.00
29 Chris Webber 1.50 4.00

1997-98 Upper Deck Diamond Vision Signature Moves

*STARS: .75X TO 2X BASE CARD HI

1997-98 Upper Deck Diamond Vision Dunk Vision

COMPLETE SET (6) 30.00 80.00
D1 Michael Jordan 50.00 120.00
D2 Anfernee Hardaway 8.00 20.00
D3 Shaquille O'Neal 10.00 25.00
D4 Grant Hill 5.00 12.00
D5 Kevin Garnett 8.00 20.00
D6 Hakeem Olajuwon 6.00 15.00

1997-98 Upper Deck Diamond Vision Jordan Highlight Reels

COMPLETE SET (5) 12.00 30.00
COMMON CARD (1-5) 5.00 12.00

1997-98 Upper Deck Diamond Vision Reel Time

RT1 Michael Jordan 40.00 100.00

2007-08 Upper Deck Dodge Charger

DC6 Kevin Durant 10.00 25.00

1992 Upper Deck Draft Party Sheets

COMPLETE SET (20) 30.00 80.00
COMMON SHEET 2.00 5.00

1993 Upper Deck Draft Party Sheets

COMPLETE SET (27) 60.00 150.00
COMMON SHEET 4.00 10.00

1993-94 Upper Deck Draft Preview Promos

COMPLETE SET (3) 6.00 15.00
DP1 Shawn Bradley 3.00 8.00
DP2 Calbert Cheaney 3.00 8.00
DP3 Bobby Hurley 1.50 4.00

2007-08 Upper Deck Kevin Durant Promo

KDRC1 Kevin Durant/999 4.00 10.00
KDRC2 Kevin Durant/499 6.00 15.00

1999 Upper Deck Employee Game Jersey

NNO Michael Jordan 1,000.00 1,500.00

2000 Upper Deck Employee Game Jersey

KB2000 Kobe Bryant AU/300 500.00 1,000.00

2003 Upper Deck Employee LeBron James

LBEC LJames JSY/450 600.00 1,200.00
LBNPL03 LeBron James 30.00 80.00

2007 Upper Deck Employee Quad Jerseys

MJKBLJKD Jordan/
Bryant/James/Durant 1,500.00 3,000.00

1998-99 Upper Deck Encore

COMPLETE SET (150) 60.00 120.00
MJ SUBSET STATED ODDS 1:4
ROOKIE SUBSET STATED ODDS 1:4
BONUS SUBSET STATED ODDS 1:8
1 Mookie Blaylock .20 .50
2 Dikembe Mutombo .40 1.00
3 Steve Smith .20 .50
4 Kenny Anderson .20 .50
5 Antoine Walker .25 .60
6 Ron Mercer .20 .50
7 David Wesley .15 .40
8 Elden Campbell .15 .40
9 Eddie Jones .25 .60
10 Ron Harper .25 .60
11 Toni Kukoc .25 .60
12 Brent Barry .20 .50
13 Shawn Kemp .40 1.00
14 Brevin Knight .15 .40
15 Derek Anderson .20 .50
16 Shawn Bradley .15 .40
17 Robert Pack .15 .40
18 Michael Finley .25 .60
19 Antonio McDyess .25 .60
20 Nick Van Exel .25 .60
21 Danny Fortson .15 .40
22 Grant Hill .40 1.00
23 Jerry Stackhouse .25 .60
24 Bison Dele .15 .40
25 Donyell Marshall .15 .40
26 Tony Delk .15 .40
27 Erick Dampier .15 .40
28 John Starks .25 .60
29 Charles Barkley .60 1.50
30 Hakeem Olajuwon .50 1.25
31 Othella Harrington .15 .40
32 Scottie Pippen .60 1.50
33 Rik Smits .20 .50
34 Reggie Miller .50 1.25
35 Mark Jackson .20 .50
36 Rodney Rogers .15 .40
37 Lamond Murray .15 .40
38 Maurice Taylor .15 .40
39 Kobe Bryant 2.00 5.00
40 Shaquille O'Neal 1.00 2.50
41 Derek Fisher .25 .60
42 Glen Rice .25 .60
43 Jamal Mashburn .25 .60
44 Alonzo Mourning .40 1.00
45 Tim Hardaway .30 .75
46 Ray Allen .40 1.00
47 Vinny Del Negro .15 .40
48 Glenn Robinson .25 .60
49 Joe Smith .20 .50
50 Terrell Brandon .20 .50
51 Kevin Garnett .60 1.50
52 Keith Van Horn .30 .75
53 Stephon Marbury .30 .75
54 Jayson Williams .15 .40
55 Patrick Ewing .40 1.00
56 Allan Houston .25 .60
57 Latrell Sprewell .30 .75
58 Anfernee Hardaway .60 1.50
59 Horace Grant .25 .60
60 Nick Anderson .15 .40
61 Allen Iverson .60 1.50
62 Matt Geiger .15 .40
63 Theo Ratliff .15 .40
64 Jason Kidd .40 1.00
65 Rex Chapman .20 .50
66 Tom Gugliotta .20 .50
67 Rasheed Wallace .30 .75
68 Arvydas Sabonis .25 .60
69 Damon Stoudamire .25 .60
70 Vlade Divac .25 .60
71 Corliss Williamson .15 .40
72 Chris Webber .30 .75
73 Tim Duncan .60 1.50
74 Sean Elliott .25 .60
75 David Robinson .50 1.25
76 Vin Baker .20 .50
77 Gary Payton .40 1.00
78 Detlef Schrempf .25 .60
79 Tracy McGrady .40 1.00
80 John Wallace .15 .40
81 Doug Christie .20 .50
82 Karl Malone .50 1.25
83 John Stockton .50 1.25
84 Jeff Hornacek .20 .50
85 Bryant Reeves .15 .40
86 Michael Smith .15 .40
87 Shareef Abdur-Rahim .25 .60
88 Juwan Howard .20 .50
89 Rod Strickland .20 .50
90 Mitch Richmond .30 .75
91 Michael Jordan 1.50 4.00
92 Michael Jordan 1.50 4.00
93 Michael Jordan 1.50 4.00
94 Michael Jordan 1.50 4.00
95 Michael Jordan 1.50 4.00
96 Michael Jordan 1.50 4.00
97 Michael Jordan 1.50 4.00
98 Michael Jordan 1.50 4.00
99 Michael Jordan 1.50 4.00
100 Michael Jordan 1.50 4.00
101 Michael Jordan 1.50 4.00
102 Michael Jordan 1.50 4.00
103 Michael Jordan 1.50 4.00
104 Michael Jordan 1.50 4.00
105 Michael Jordan 1.50 4.00
106 Michael Jordan 1.50 4.00
107 Michael Jordan 1.50 4.00
108 Michael Jordan 1.50 4.00
109 Michael Jordan 1.50 4.00
110 Michael Jordan 1.50 4.00
111 Michael Jordan 1.50 4.00
112 Michael Jordan 1.50 4.00
113 Michael Jordan 1.50 4.00
114 Michael Olowokandi RC 1.00 2.50
115 Mike Bibby RC 4.00 10.00
116 Raef LaFrentz RC 1.00 2.50
117 Antawn Jamison RC 1.25 3.00
118 Vince Carter RC 4.00 10.00
119 Robert Traylor RC .75 2.00
120 Jason Williams RC 2.50 6.00
121 Larry Hughes RC 1.25 3.00
122 Dirk Nowitzki RC 5.00 12.00
123 Paul Pierce RC 3.00 8.00
124 Michael Doleac RC .60 1.50
125 Keon Clark RC .75 2.00
126 Michael Dickerson RC .75 2.00
127 Matt Harpring RC .75 2.00
128 Bryce Drew RC .50 1.25
129 Pat Garrity RC .60 1.50
130 Roshown McLeod RC .50 1.25
131 Ricky Davis RC 1.25 3.00
132 Peja Stojakovic RC 1.50 4.00
133 Felipe Lopez RC .50 1.25
134 Al Harrington RC 1.00 2.50
135 Ruben Patterson RC .75 2.00
136 Cuttino Mobley RC 1.25 3.00
137 Tyronn Lue RC 1.00 2.50
138 Brian Skinner RC .60 1.50
139 Nazr Mohammed RC .75 2.00
140 Toby Bailey RC .60 1.50
141 Casey Shaw RC .75 2.00
142 Corey Benjamin RC .50 1.25
143 Rashard Lewis RC 1.25 3.00
144 Jason Williams BON 1.50 4.00
145 Paul Pierce BON 2.00 5.00
146 Vince Carter BON 2.50 6.00
147 Antawn Jamison BON .75 2.00
148 Raef LaFrentz BON .60 1.50
149 Mike Bibby BON 1.00 2.50
150 Michael Olowokandi BON .60 1.50
MJ Michael Jordan AU/50 4,000.00 8,000.00

1998-99 Upper Deck Encore F/X

COMMON MJ (91-113) 40.00 100.00
*STARS: 12X TO 30X BASE CARD HI
*RCs: 2X TO 5X BASE HI
*BONUS: 3X TO 8X BASE HI
STATED PRINT RUN 125 SERIAL #'d SETS
122 Dirk Nowitzki 30.00 80.00
123 Paul Pierce 25.00 60.00

1998-99 Upper Deck Encore Driving Forces

COMPLETE SET (15) 20.00 50.00
STATED ODDS 1:23
*FX CARDS: 1.5X TO 4X HI COLUMN
FX: STATED PRINT RUN 500 SERIAL #'d SETS
F1 Michael Jordan 15.00 40.00
F2 Kobe Bryant 10.00 25.00
F3 Keith Van Horn 1.25 3.00
F4 Kevin Garnett 3.00 8.00
F5 Tim Duncan 3.00 8.00
F6 Gary Payton 2.00 5.00
F7 Antoine Walker 1.25 3.00
F8 Grant Hill 2.00 5.00
F9 Scottie Pippen 3.00 8.00
F10 Tim Hardaway 1.50 4.00
F11 Reggie Miller 2.50 6.00
F12 Shareef Abdur-Rahim 1.25 3.00
F13 Anfernee Hardaway 3.00 8.00
F14 Allen Iverson 3.00 8.00
F15 Ray Allen 2.00 5.00

1998-99 Upper Deck Encore Intensity

COMPLETE SET (30) 15.00 40.00
STATED ODDS 1:11
I1 Michael Jordan 8.00 20.00
I2 Mitch Richmond 1.00 2.50
I3 Ron Mercer .60 1.50
I4 Terrell Brandon .60 1.50
I5 Brevin Knight .50 1.25
I6 Rasheed Wallace 1.00 2.50
I7 Keith Van Horn .75 2.00
I8 Antawn Jamison 1.25 3.00
I9 Antonio McDyess .60 1.50
I10 Allen Iverson 2.00 5.00
I11 Anfernee Hardaway 2.00 5.00
I12 Chris Webber 1.00 2.50
I13 Lorenzen Wright .50 1.25
I14 Bryant Reeves .50 1.25
I15 Charles Barkley 2.00 5.00
I16 Tracy McGrady 1.25 3.00
I17 Larry Johnson 1.25 3.00
I18 Jerry Stackhouse .75 2.00
I19 Derrick Coleman .60 1.50
I20 Detlef Schrempf .75 2.00
I21 John Stockton 1.50 4.00
I22 Kobe Bryant 6.00 15.00
I23 Alonzo Mourning 1.25 3.00
I24 Dikembe Mutombo 1.25 3.00
I25 Jalen Rose .60 1.50
I26 Robert Pack .50 1.25
I27 Tom Gugliotta .60 1.50
I28 Shaquille O'Neal 3.00 8.00
I29 Stephon Marbury 1.00 2.50
I30 David Robinson 1.50 4.00

1998-99 Upper Deck Encore MJ23

COMPLETE SET (20) 60.00 120.00
COMMON CARD (M1-M20) 4.00 10.00
STATED ODDS 1:23
*FX: 10X TO 25X BASE HI
FX: STATED PRINT RUN 23 SERIAL #'d SETS

1998-99 Upper Deck Encore PowerDeck

STATED ODDS 1:47
1 Charles Barkley 5.00 12.00
2 Kobe Bryant 8.00 20.00
3 Vince Carter 6.00 15.00
4 Julius Erving 4.00 10.00
5 Kevin Garnett 4.00 10.00
6 Michael Jordan 15.00 40.00
7 Shaquille O'Neal 4.00 10.00
8 Paul Pierce 4.00 10.00
9 Jason Williams 4.00 10.00

1998-99 Upper Deck Encore Rookie Encore

COMPLETE SET (10) 15.00 40.00
STATED ODDS 1:23
*FX: .75X TO 2X HI COLUMN
FX: STATED PRINT RUN 1000 SERIAL #'d SETS
RE1 Jason Williams 2.50 6.00
RE2 Michael Olowokandi 1.00 2.50
RE3 Paul Pierce 3.00 8.00
RE4 Robert Traylor .75 2.00
RE5 Raef LaFrentz 1.00 2.50
RE6 Mike Bibby 1.50 4.00
RE7 Dirk Nowitzki 5.00 12.00
RE8 Antawn Jamison 1.25 3.00
RE9 Larry Hughes 1.25 3.00
RE10 Vince Carter 4.00 10.00

1998-99 Upper Deck Encore Rookie Encore F/X

*FX: .75X TO 2X BASE CARD HI
RE7 Dirk Nowitzki 15.00 40.00

1999-00 Upper Deck Encore

COMPLETE SET (120) 40.00 100.00
COMPLETE SET w/o RC (90) 10.00 25.00
91-120 PRINT RUN 1999 SERIAL #'d SETS
1 Dikembe Mutombo .60 1.50
2 Alan Henderson .25 .60
3 Isaiah Rider .30 .75
4 Kenny Anderson .30 .75
5 Antoine Walker .40 1.00
6 Paul Pierce .75 2.00
7 Elden Campbell .25 .60
8 Eddie Jones .40 1.00
9 David Wesley .25 .60
10 Hersey Hawkins .25 .60
11 Randy Brown .25 .60
12 Toni Kukoc .50 1.25
13 Shawn Kemp .60 1.50
14 Bob Sura .25 .60
15 Michael Finley .40 1.00
16 Dirk Nowitzki 1.25 3.00
17 Gary Trent .25 .60
18 Antonio McDyess .30 .75
19 Nick Van Exel .30 .75
20 Raef LaFrentz .30 .75
21 Christian Laettner .30 .75
22 Grant Hill .60 1.50
23 Lindsey Hunter .25 .60
24 Jerry Stackhouse .40 1.00
25 John Starks .40 1.00
26 Antawn Jamison .40 1.00
27 Tony Farmer .25 .60
28 Hakeem Olajuwon .75 2.00
29 Cuttino Mobley .25 .60
30 Charles Barkley 1.00 2.50
31 Reggie Miller .75 2.00
32 Jalen Rose .30 .75
33 Mark Jackson .30 .75
34 Maurice Taylor .25 .60
35 Derek Anderson .25 .60
36 Michael Olowokandi .25 .60
37 Kobe Bryant 3.00 8.00
38 Shaquille O'Neal 1.50 4.00
39 Glen Rice .40 1.00
40 Tim Hardaway .50 1.25
41 Alonzo Mourning .60 1.50
42 Ray Allen .60 1.50
43 Glenn Robinson .30 .75
44 Sam Cassell .30 .75
45 Tim Thomas .30 .75
46 Kevin Garnett 1.00 2.50
47 Terrell Brandon .25 .60
48 Keith Van Horn .30 .75
49 Stephon Marbury .50 1.25
50 Kendall Gill .40 1.00
51 Patrick Ewing .50 1.25
52 Allan Houston .30 .75
53 Latrell Sprewell .50 1.25

54 Darrell Armstrong .25 .60
55 John Amaechi RC .40 1.00
56 Michael Doleac .25 .60
57 Allen Iverson 1.00 2.50
58 Theo Ratliff .30 .75
59 Larry Hughes .30 .75
60 Jason Kidd .60 1.50
61 Tom Gugliotta .30 .75
62 Anfernee Hardaway 1.00 2.50
63 Rasheed Wallace .50 1.25
64 Steve Smith .30 .75
65 Damon Stoudamire .40 1.00
66 Scottie Pippen 1.00 2.50
67 Corliss Williamson .25 .60
68 Jason Williams .60 1.50
69 Vlade Divac .40 1.00
70 Chris Webber .50 1.25
71 Tim Duncan 1.00 2.50
72 David Robinson .75 2.00
73 Avery Johnson .30 .75
74 Mario Elie .25 .60
75 Gary Payton .60 1.50
76 Vin Baker .30 .75
77 Ruben Patterson .25 .60
78 Brent Barry .30 .75
79 Vince Carter 1.00 2.50
80 Antonio Davis .25 .60
81 Tracy McGrady .60 1.50
82 Karl Malone .75 2.00
83 John Stockton .60 1.50
84 Bryon Russell .25 .60
85 Shareef Abdur-Rahim .40 1.00
86 Mike Bibby .40 1.00
87 Othella Harrington .25 .60
88 Juwan Howard .30 .75
89 Rod Strickland .30 .75
90 Mitch Richmond .50 1.25
91 Elton Brand RC 2.00 5.00
92 Steve Francis RC 2.00 5.00
93 Baron Davis RC 2.50 6.00
94 Lamar Odom RC 2.00 5.00
95 Jonathan Bender RC 1.00 2.50
96 Wally Szczerbiak RC 1.50 4.00
97 Richard Hamilton RC 2.50 6.00
98 Andre Miller RC 2.00 5.00
99 Shawn Marion RC 2.00 5.00
100 Jason Terry RC 1.50 4.00
101 Trajan Langdon RC .75 2.00
102 Kenny Thomas RC 1.00 2.50
103 Corey Maggette RC 1.25 3.00
104 William Avery RC .60 1.50
105 Ron Artest RC 2.50 6.00
106 A.Radojevic RC .60 1.50
107 James Posey RC 1.00 2.50
108 Quincy Lewis RC .60 1.50
109 Vonteego Cummings RC .60 1.50
110 Jeff Foster RC 1.00 2.50
111 Dion Glover RC .60 1.50
112 Devean George RC .75 2.00
113 Evan Eschmeyer RC .75 2.00
114 Tim James RC .60 1.50
115 Adrian Griffin RC .75 2.00
116 Anthony Carter RC .75 2.00
117 Obinna Ekezie RC .60 1.50
118 Todd MacCulloch RC .75 2.00
119 Chucky Atkins RC .75 2.00
120 Lazaro Borrell RC .60 1.50

1999-00 Upper Deck Encore Electric Currents

COMPLETE SET (20) 5.00 12.00
STATED ODDS 1:3
*F/X: 5X TO 12X BASE HI
F/X: PRINT RUN 150 SERIAL #'d SETS
EC1 Kevin Garnett 1.00 2.50
EC2 Anfernee Hardaway 1.00 2.50
EC3 Shareef Abdur-Rahim .40 1.00
EC4 Allan Houston .30 .75
EC5 Michael Finley .40 1.00
EC6 Tim Duncan 1.00 2.50
EC7 Gary Payton .60 1.50
EC8 Kobe Bryant 3.00 8.00
EC9 Derek Anderson .25 .60
EC10 Reggie Miller .75 2.00
EC11 Keith Van Horn .30 .75
EC12 Jason Kidd .60 1.50
EC13 Ray Allen .60 1.50
EC14 Tim Hardaway .50 1.25
EC15 Darrell Armstrong .25 .60
EC16 Antonio McDyess .30 .75
EC17 Eddie Jones .40 1.00
EC18 Paul Pierce .75 2.00
EC19 Stephon Marbury .50 1.25
EC20 Chris Webber .50 1.25

1999-00 Upper Deck Encore Electric Currents F/X

*F/X: 5X TO 12X VALUE
EC8 Kobe Bryant 60.00 150.00

1999-00 Upper Deck Encore Future Charge

COMPLETE SET (15) 4.00 10.00
STATED ODDS 1:6
FC1 Antawn Jamison .50 1.25
FC2 Mike Bibby .50 1.25
FC3 Antoine Walker .50 1.25
FC4 Baron Davis .75 2.00
FC5 Jason Terry .50 1.25
FC6 Andre Miller .60 1.50
FC7 Ray Allen .75 2.00
FC8 Wally Szczerbiak .50 1.25
FC9 Raef LaFrentz .40 1.00
FC10 William Avery .20 .50
FC11 Jason Williams .75 2.00
FC12 Michael Olowokandi .30 .75
FC13 Stephon Marbury .60 1.50
FC14 Quincy Lewis .20 .50
FC15 Shawn Marion .60 1.50

1999-00 Upper Deck Encore Game Jerseys

STATED ODDS 1:300
MJ Michael Jordan AU/23 2,500.00 5,000.00
AIJ Allen Iverson 60.00 150.00
AMJ Andre Miller 8.00 20.00
BDJ Baron Davis 12.00 30.00
GHJ Grant Hill 25.00 60.00
JBJ Jonathan Bender 8.00 20.00
JKJ Jason Kidd 20.00 50.00
JTJ Jason Terry 8.00 20.00
JWJ Jason Williams 60.00 150.00
KBJ Kobe Bryant 125.00 300.00
KGA Kevin Garnett AU/21 300.00 600.00
KGJ Kevin Garnett 30.00 80.00
MCJ Antonio McDyess 8.00 20.00
RHJ Richard Hamilton 8.00 20.00
SFJ Steve Francis 15.00 40.00
SMJ Shawn Marion 10.00 25.00
SOJ Shaquille O'Neal 30.00 80.00
TLJ Trajan Langdon 8.00 20.00
WSJ Wally Szczerbiak 8.00 20.00

1999-00 Upper Deck Encore High Definition

COMPLETE SET (20) 15.00 40.00
STATED ODDS 1:15
HD1 Antonio McDyess .75 2.00
HD2 Kevin Garnett 2.50 6.00
HD3 Vince Carter 2.50 6.00
HD4 Shareef Abdur-Rahim 1.00 2.50
HD5 Stephon Marbury 1.25 3.00
HD6 Gary Payton 1.50 4.00
HD7 Glenn Robinson .75 2.00
HD8 Kobe Bryant 8.00 20.00
HD9 Antawn Jamison 1.00 2.50
HD10 Chris Webber 1.25 3.00
HD11 Corey Maggette 1.25 3.00
HD12 Shawn Kemp 1.50 4.00
HD13 Derek Anderson .60 1.50
HD14 Michael Finley 1.00 2.50
HD15 Allan Houston .75 2.00
HD16 Anfernee Hardaway 2.50 6.00
HD17 Grant Hill 1.50 4.00
HD18 Shaquille O'Neal 4.00 10.00
HD19 Paul Pierce 2.00 5.00
HD20 Scottie Pippen 2.50 6.00

1999-00 Upper Deck Encore Jamboree

COMPLETE SET (15) 8.00 20.00
STATED ODDS 1:6
J1 Michael Jordan 6.00 15.00
J2 Karl Malone 1.25 3.00
J3 Kevin Garnett 1.50 4.00
J4 Antonio McDyess .50 1.25
J5 Shareef Abdur-Rahim .60 1.50
J6 David Robinson 1.25 3.00
J7 Marcus Camby .50 1.25
J8 Kobe Bryant 5.00 12.00
J9 Jason Kidd 1.00 2.50
J10 Tim Duncan 1.50 4.00
J11 Keith Van Horn .50 1.25
J12 Glenn Robinson .50 1.25
J13 Grant Hill 1.00 2.50
J14 Michael Finley .60 1.50
J15 Vince Carter 1.50 4.00

1999-00 Upper Deck Encore MJ - A Higher Power

COMPLETE SET (10) 125.00 300.00
COMMON CARD (MJ1-MJ10) 12.00 30.00
STATED ODDS 1:90

1999-00 Upper Deck Encore Upper Realm

COMPLETE SET (10) 4.00 10.00
STATED ODDS 1:6
*F/X: 6X TO 15X HI COLUMN
F/X: PRINT RUN 150 SERIAL #'d SETS
UR1 Kevin Garnett 1.00 2.50
UR2 Kobe Bryant 3.00 8.00
UR3 Tim Duncan 1.00 2.50
UR4 Vince Carter 1.00 2.50
UR5 Gary Payton .60 1.50
UR6 Allen Iverson 1.00 2.50
UR7 Karl Malone .75 2.00
UR8 Jason Williams .60 1.50
UR9 Scottie Pippen 1.00 2.50
UR10 Shaquille O'Neal 1.50 4.00

2000-01 Upper Deck Encore

COMPLETE SET w/o RC's 10.00 25.00
136-165 PRINT RUN 1600 SERIAL #'d SETS
1 Brevin Knight .25 .60
2 Lorenzen Wright .25 .60
3 Alan Henderson .25 .60
4 Jason Terry .40 1.00
5 Paul Pierce .60 1.50
6 Antoine Walker .40 1.00
7 Kenny Anderson .30 .75
8 Tony Battie .25 .60
9 Adrian Griffin .25 .60
10 Derrick Coleman .40 1.00
11 David Wesley .30 .75
12 Baron Davis .40 1.00
13 Elden Campbell .25 .60
14 Jamal Mashburn .30 .75
15 Elton Brand .40 1.00
16 Ron Mercer .30 .75
17 Ron Artest .40 1.00
18 Michael Ruffin .25 .60
19 Lamond Murray .25 .60
20 Andre Miller .30 .75
21 Matt Harpring .25 .60
22 Jim Jackson .30 .75
23 Michael Finley .40 1.00
24 Dirk Nowitzki 1.00 2.50
25 Steve Nash .60 1.50
26 Howard Eisley .25 .60
27 Antonio McDyess .30 .75
28 James Posey .25 .60
29 Nick Van Exel .40 1.00
30 Raef LaFrentz .30 .75
31 Voshon Lenard .25 .60
32 Jerry Stackhouse .40 1.00
33 Ben Wallace .50 1.25
34 Michael Curry .25 .60
35 Joe Smith .30 .75
36 Chucky Atkins .25 .60
37 Antawn Jamison .40 1.00
38 Larry Hughes .30 .75
39 Chris Mills .25 .60
40 Mookie Blaylock .40 1.00
41 Vonteego Cummings .25 .60
42 Steve Francis .40 1.00
43 Maurice Taylor .25 .60
44 Hakeem Olajuwon .75 2.00
45 Walt Williams .25 .60
46 Cuttino Mobley .30 .75
47 Reggie Miller .75 2.00
48 Jalen Rose .30 .75
49 Austin Croshere .25 .60
50 Travis Best .25 .60
51 Jermaine O'Neal .30 .75
52 Lamar Odom .40 1.00
53 Jeff McInnis .25 .60
54 Michael Olowokandi .25 .60
55 Brian Skinner .25 .60
56 Corey Maggette .30 .75
57 Shaquille O'Neal 1.50 4.00
58 Ron Harper .40 1.00
59 Kobe Bryant 3.00 8.00
60 Robert Horry .40 1.00
61 Isaiah Rider .30 .75
62 Eddie Jones .40 1.00
63 Anthony Carter .25 .60
64 Tim Hardaway .50 1.25
65 Brian Grant .30 .75
66 Anthony Mason .40 1.00
67 Ray Allen .60 1.50
68 Tim Thomas .25 .60
69 Glenn Robinson .40 1.00
70 Sam Cassell .40 1.00
71 Lindsey Hunter .25 .60
72 Kevin Garnett 1.00 2.50
73 Wally Szczerbiak .30 .75
74 Terrell Brandon .30 .75
75 Chauncey Billups .50 1.25
76 Stephon Marbury .50 1.25
77 Keith Van Horn .40 1.00
78 Lucious Harris .25 .60
79 Kendall Gill .40 1.00
80 Latrell Sprewell .50 1.25
81 Marcus Camby .30 .75
82 Larry Johnson .50 1.25
83 Allan Houston .40 1.00
84 Glen Rice .40 1.00
85 Grant Hill .60 1.50
86 Tracy McGrady .75 2.00
87 John Amaechi .25 .60
88 Darrell Armstrong .25 .60
89 Allen Iverson 1.00 2.50
90 Dikembe Mutombo .60 1.50
91 George Lynch .25 .60
92 Aaron McKie .25 .60
93 Eric Snow .25 .60
94 Jason Kidd .60 1.50
95 Tony Delk .25 .60
96 Clifford Robinson .40 1.00
97 Tom Gugliotta .30 .75
98 Shawn Marion .40 1.00
99 Rasheed Wallace .50 1.25
100 Scottie Pippen 1.00 2.50
101 Steve Smith .40 1.00
102 Damon Stoudamire .40 1.00
103 Bonzi Wells .25 .60
104 Chris Webber .50 1.25
105 Jason Williams .60 1.50
106 Peja Stojakovic .30 .75
107 Vlade Divac .40 1.00
108 Doug Christie .30 .75
109 Tim Duncan 1.00 2.50
110 David Robinson .75 2.00
111 Derek Anderson .30 .75
112 Antonio Daniels .25 .60
113 Sean Elliott .30 .75
114 Gary Payton .60 1.50
115 Patrick Ewing .60 1.50
116 Vin Baker .30 .75
117 Rashard Lewis .30 .75
118 Vince Carter .75 2.00
119 Alvin Williams .25 .60
120 Antonio Davis .30 .75
121 Charles Oakley .40 1.00
122 Karl Malone .75 2.00
123 John Stockton .60 1.50
124 Bryon Russell .25 .60
125 John Starks .40 1.00
126 Shareef Abdur-Rahim .40 1.00
127 Mike Bibby .40 1.00
128 Michael Dickerson .25 .60
129 Grant Long .25 .60
130 Mitch Richmond .50 1.25
131 Richard Hamilton .50 1.25
132 Chris Whitney .25 .60
133 Jahidi White .25 .60
134 Checklist 1 .40 1.00
135 Checklist 2 .40 1.00
136 Kenyon Martin RC 2.50 6.00
137 Stromile Swift RC .75 2.00
138 Chris Mihm RC .75 2.00
139 Marcus Fizer RC 1.00 2.50
140 Darius Miles RC 1.25 3.00
141 Joel Przybilla RC 1.00 2.50
142 Mike Miller RC 2.00 5.00
143 Courtney Alexander RC .75 2.00
144 DerMarr Johnson RC .75 2.00
145 Stephen Jackson RC 2.50 6.00
146 Jerome Moiso RC .75 2.00
147 Keyon Dooling RC 1.00 2.50
148 Erick Barkley RC .75 2.00
149 Jason Collier RC 1.25 3.00
150 Jamaal Magloire RC 1.25 3.00
151 DeShawn Stevenson RC 1.25 3.00
152 Hedo Turkoglu RC 2.00 5.00
153 Morris Peterson RC 1.25 3.00
154 Jamal Crawford RC 3.00 8.00
155 Etan Thomas RC 1.00 2.50
156 Quentin Richardson RC 1.00 2.50
157 Mateen Cleaves RC 1.00 2.50
158 Donnell Harvey RC 1.00 2.50
159 Mark Madsen RC 1.25 3.00
160 Desmond Mason RC 1.50 4.00
161 Speedy Claxton RC 1.25 3.00
162 Hanno Mottola RC .75 2.00
163 Mamadou N'Diaye RC .75 2.00
164 Eduardo Najera RC 1.25 3.00
165 Khalid El-Amin RC .75 2.00

2000-01 Upper Deck Encore High Definition

COMPLETE SET (6) 15.00 40.00
STATED ODDS 1:16
HD1 Stephon Marbury 1.25 3.00
HD2 Steve Francis 1.00 2.50
HD3 Shaquille O'Neal 4.00 10.00
HD4 Kevin Garnett 2.50 6.00
HD5 Kobe Bryant 15.00 40.00
HD6 Tracy McGrady 2.00 5.00

2000-01 Upper Deck Encore NBA Warm-Ups

STATED ODDS 1:8
AMW Andre Miller 2.00 5.00
BDW Baron Davis 2.50 6.00
CAW Courtney Alexander 1.50 4.00
CMW Chris Mihm 1.50 4.00
DJW DerMarr Johnson 1.50 4.00
DMW Darius Miles 2.50 6.00
DSW DeShawn Stevenson 2.50 6.00
HMW Hanno Mottola 1.50 4.00
JCW Jamal Crawford 6.00 15.00
JMW Jerome Moiso 1.50 4.00
JSW Jerry Stackhouse 2.50 6.00
KBW Kobe Bryant 40.00 100.00
KDW Keyon Dooling 2.00 5.00
KEW Khalid El-Amin 1.50 4.00
KGW Kevin Garnett 6.00 15.00
KMW Kenyon Martin 5.00 12.00
MAW Corey Maggette 2.00 5.00
MFW Marcus Fizer 2.00 5.00
MMW Mike Miller 4.00 10.00
TMW Tracy McGrady 5.00 12.00
WSW Wally Szczerbiak 2.00 5.00

2000-01 Upper Deck Encore NBA Warm-Ups Autographs

STATED PRINT RUN 8 TO 50 SETS
CMA Chris Mihm/50 5.00 12.00
DJA DerMarr Johnson/50 5.00 12.00
DMA Darius Miles/50 8.00 20.00
DSA DeShawn Stevenson/50 8.00 20.00
JCA Jamal Crawford/50 20.00 50.00
JSA Jerry Stackhouse/50 8.00 20.00
KEA Khalid El-Amin/50 5.00 12.00
KGA Kevin Garnett/21 150.00 400.00
KMA Kenyon Martin/50 15.00 40.00
MFA Marcus Fizer/50 6.00 15.00
MMA Mike Miller/50 12.00 30.00
TMA Tracy McGrady/50 75.00 200.00

2000-01 Upper Deck Encore Performers

COMPLETE SET (12) 10.00 25.00
STATED ODDS 1:8
EP1 Jason Kidd 1.50 4.00
EP2 Stephon Marbury 1.25 3.00
EP3 Gary Payton 1.50 4.00
EP4 Kevin Garnett 2.50 6.00
EP5 Antonio McDyess .75 2.00
EP6 Shareef Abdur-Rahim 1.00 2.50
EP7 Tim Duncan 2.50 6.00
EP8 Allan Houston 1.00 2.50
EP9 Kobe Bryant 8.00 20.00
EP10 Andre Miller .75 2.00
EP11 Vince Carter 2.00 5.00
EP12 Ray Allen 1.50 4.00

2000-01 Upper Deck Encore Powerful Stuff

COMPLETE SET (12) 15.00 40.00
STATED ODDS 1:8
PS1 Kobe Bryant 12.00 30.00
PS2 Tim Duncan 2.50 6.00
PS3 Allen Iverson 2.50 6.00
PS4 Karl Malone 2.00 5.00
PS5 Tracy McGrady 2.00 5.00
PS6 Shaquille O'Neal 4.00 10.00
PS7 Vince Carter 2.00 5.00
PS8 Chris Webber 1.25 3.00
PS9 Eddie Jones 1.00 2.50
PS10 Kevin Garnett 2.50 6.00
PS11 Elton Brand 1.00 2.50
PS12 Paul Pierce 1.50 4.00

2000-01 Upper Deck Encore Star Signatures

STATED ODDS 1:48
CA Courtney Alexander 3.00 8.00
CM Chris Mihm 3.00 8.00
CO Corey Maggette 4.00 10.00
CR Jamal Crawford 12.00 30.00
DH Donnell Harvey 4.00 10.00
DJ DerMarr Johnson 3.00 8.00
DM Darius Miles 5.00 12.00
DS DeShawn Stevenson 5.00 12.00
EB Erick Barkley 3.00 8.00
EJ Eddie Jones 12.00 30.00
ET Etan Thomas 4.00 10.00
GP Gary Payton 20.00 50.00
HM Hanno Mottola 3.00 8.00
JA Jamaal Magloire 4.00 10.00
JM Jerome Moiso 3.00 8.00
JO Jermaine O'Neal 6.00 15.00
JP Joel Przybilla 4.00 10.00
JS Jerry Stackhouse 8.00 20.00
KB Kobe Bryant 1,000.00 2,000.00
KE Khalid El-Amin 3.00 8.00
KM Kenyon Martin 8.00 20.00
LH Larry Hughes 4.00 10.00
MC Mateen Cleaves 4.00 10.00
MK Mark Madsen 5.00 12.00
MM Mike Miller 8.00 20.00
MN Mamadou N'Diaye 3.00 8.00
MP Morris Peterson 5.00 12.00
RH Richard Hamilton 6.00 15.00
RM Reggie Miller 75.00 200.00
SC Speedy Claxton 5.00 12.00
SF Steve Francis 5.00 12.00
SM Shawn Marion 5.00 12.00
SS Stromile Swift 4.00 10.00
TH Tim Hardaway 6.00 15.00
WS Wally Szczerbiak 4.00 10.00

2000-01 Upper Deck Encore Upper Realm

COMPLETE SET (6) 15.00 40.00
STATED ODDS 1:16
UR1 Shaquille O'Neal 4.00 10.00
UR2 Allen Iverson 2.50 6.00
UR3 Tim Duncan 2.50 6.00
UR4 Kobe Bryant 12.00 30.00
UR5 Chris Webber 1.25 3.00
UR6 Kevin Garnett 2.50 6.00

2000-01 Upper Deck Encore Vertical Forces

COMPLETE SET (6) 15.00 40.00
STATED ODDS 1:16
VF1 Kobe Bryant 12.00 30.00
VF2 Vince Carter 2.00 5.00
VF3 Rashard Lewis .75 2.00
VF4 Chris Webber 1.25 3.00
VF5 Steve Francis 1.00 2.50
VF6 Kevin Garnett 2.50 6.00

2005-06 Upper Deck ESPN

COMPLETE SET (132) 15.00 40.00
COMP.SET w/o SP's (90) 6.00 15.00
91-132 RC STATED ODDS 1:4
1 Josh Childress .12 .30
2 Josh Smith .15 .40
3 Al Harrington .15 .40
4 Antoine Walker .15 .40
5 Ricky Davis .15 .40
6 Paul Pierce .30 .75
7 Kareem Rush .12 .30
8 Emeka Okafor .15 .40
9 Gerald Wallace .15 .40
10 Eddy Curry .12 .30
11 Kirk Hinrich .15 .40
12 Ben Gordon .15 .40
13 Drew Gooden .15 .40
14 LeBron James 1.50 4.00
15 Zydrunas Ilgauskas .15 .40
16 Dirk Nowitzki .50 1.25
17 Jason Terry .15 .40
18 Josh Howard .15 .40
19 Carmelo Anthony .30 .75
20 Kenyon Martin .15 .40
21 Andre Miller .15 .40
22 Ben Wallace .25 .60
23 Chauncey Billups .25 .60
24 Richard Hamilton .25 .60
25 Troy Murphy .12 .30
26 Jason Richardson .20 .50
27 Baron Davis .20 .50
28 Tracy McGrady .30 .75
29 Yao Ming .40 1.00
30 Juwan Howard .15 .40
31 Jermaine O'Neal .15 .40
32 Reggie Miller .30 .75
33 Ron Artest .15 .40
34 Corey Maggette .15 .40
35 Elton Brand .15 .40
36 Bobby Simmons .12 .30
37 Caron Butler .15 .40
38 Kobe Bryant 1.50 4.00
39 Lamar Odom .15 .40
40 Mike Miller .15 .40
41 Jason Williams .30 .75
42 Pau Gasol .30 .75
43 Dwyane Wade .40 1.00
44 Eddie Jones .15 .40
45 Shaquille O'Neal .60 1.50
46 Desmond Mason .12 .30
47 Maurice Williams .15 .40
48 Michael Redd .15 .40
49 Kevin Garnett .50 1.25
50 Latrell Sprewell .20 .50
51 Sam Cassell .15 .40
52 Vince Carter .40 1.00
53 Jason Kidd .30 .75
54 Richard Jefferson .15 .40
55 Dan Dickau .12 .30
56 Jamaal Magloire .12 .30
57 J.R. Smith .20 .50
58 Jamal Crawford .15 .40
59 Stephon Marbury .25 .60
60 Allan Houston .15 .40
61 Dwight Howard .25 .60
62 Grant Hill .30 .75
63 Steve Francis .20 .50
64 Allen Iverson .40 1.00
65 Andre Iguodala .20 .50
66 Chris Webber .25 .60
67 Amare Stoudemire .20 .50
68 Shawn Marion .15 .40
69 Steve Nash .40 1.00
70 Damon Stoudamire .15 .40
71 Shareef Abdur-Rahim .15 .40
72 Zach Randolph .20 .50
73 Brad Miller .15 .40
74 Mike Bibby .20 .50
75 Peja Stojakovic .15 .40
76 Manu Ginobili .40 1.00
77 Tim Duncan .50 1.25
78 Tony Parker .30 .75
79 Rashard Lewis .15 .40
80 Ray Allen .30 .75
81 Luke Ridnour .15 .40
82 Rafer Alston .15 .40
83 Jalen Rose .15 .40
84 Chris Bosh .25 .60
85 Andrei Kirilenko .15 .40
86 Carlos Boozer .15 .40
87 Matt Harpring .12 .30
88 Antawn Jamison .15 .40
89 Gilbert Arenas .20 .50
90 Larry Hughes .15 .40
91 Chris Taft RC .50 1.25
92 Marvin Williams RC .75 2.00
93 Chris Paul RC 4.00 10.00
94 Andrew Bogut RC 1.00 2.50
95 Martynas Andriuskevicius RC .50 1.25
96 Louis Williams RC 2.00 5.00
97 C.J. Miles RC .60 1.50
98 Gerald Green RC .75 2.00
99 Rashad McCants RC .60 1.50
100 Sarunas Jasikevicius RC .75 2.00
101 Andrew Bynum RC .60 1.50
102 Raymond Felton RC .60 1.50
103 Hakim Warrick RC .60 1.50
104 Deron Williams RC 1.25 3.00
105 Daniel Ewing RC .60 1.50
106 Martell Webster RC .60 1.50
107 Johan Petro RC .50 1.25
108 Travis Diener RC .50 1.25
109 Joey Graham RC .60 1.50
110 Antoine Wright RC .60 1.50
111 Ersan Ilyasova RC .60 1.50
112 Jason Maxiell RC .60 1.50
113 Linas Kleiza RC .60 1.50
114 Jarrett Jack RC .75 2.00
115 Danny Granger RC .75 2.00
116 Monta Ellis RC 1.00 2.50
117 Francisco Garcia RC .50 1.25
118 Ryan Gomes RC .60 1.50
119 Wayne Simien RC .50 1.25
120 Von Wafer RC .50 1.25
121 Dijon Thompson RC .50 1.25
122 Nate Robinson RC .75 2.00
123 Bracey Wright RC .50 1.25
124 Andray Blatche RC .75 2.00
125 Channing Frye RC .60 1.50
126 Salim Stoudamire RC .60 1.50
127 Luther Head RC .50 1.25
128 Julius Hodge RC .50 1.25
129 David Lee RC .75 2.00
130 Ike Diogu RC .50 1.25
131 Sean May RC .50 1.25
132 Brandon Bass RC .60 1.50

2005-06 Upper Deck ESPN 25th Anniversary

*1-90 25th: 12X TO 30X BASE HI
*91-132 RC 25th: 3X TO 8X BASE HI
PRINT RUN 25 SER.#'d SETS
41 Jason Williams 30.00 80.00

2005-06 Upper Deck ESPN ESPY Award Winners

COMPLETE SET (20) 15.00 40.00
STATED ODDS 1:1 WITH OTHER INSERTS
*25th ANNIV: 6X TO 15X BASE HI
25th ANNIVERSARY PRINT RUN 25 SETS
AJ Antawn Jamison .30 .75
CA Carmelo Anthony .60 1.50
EB Elton Brand .30 .75
GH Grant Hill .60 1.50
KG Kevin Garnett 1.00 2.50
KV Keith Van Horn .30 .75
LJ LeBron James 3.00 8.00
MF Michael Finley .40 1.00
MJ1 Michael Jordan 2.50 6.00
MJ2 Michael Jordan 2.50 6.00
MJ3 Michael Jordan 2.50 6.00
MJ4 Michael Jordan 2.50 6.00
MJ5 Michael Jordan 2.50 6.00
MJ6 Michael Jordan 2.50 6.00
MJ7 Michael Jordan 2.50 6.00
MJ8 Michael Jordan 2.50 6.00
MJ9 Michael Jordan 2.50 6.00
MJ10 Michael Jordan 2.50 6.00
SO Shaquille O'Neal 1.25 3.00
TD Tim Duncan 1.00 2.50

2005-06 Upper Deck ESPN Highlight Reel

COMPLETE SET (20) 10.00 25.00
STATED ODDS 1:1 WITH OTHER INSERTS
*25th ANNIV: 6X TO 15X BASE HI
25th ANNIVERSARY PRINT RUN 25 SETS
HR1 Paul Pierce .60 1.50
HR2 Michael Jordan 3.00 8.00
HR3 LeBron James 3.00 8.00
HR4 Dirk Nowitzki 1.00 2.50
HR5 Ben Wallace .50 1.25
HR6 Jason Richardson .40 1.00
HR7 Yao Ming .75 2.00
HR8 Jermaine O'Neal .30 .75
HR9 Kobe Bryant 3.00 8.00
HR10 Dwyane Wade .75 2.00
HR11 Vince Carter .75 2.00
HR12 Richard Jefferson .30 .75
HR13 Baron Davis .40 1.00
HR14 Stephon Marbury .50 1.25
HR15 Allen Iverson .75 2.00
HR16 Amare Stoudemire .40 1.00
HR17 Steve Nash .75 2.00
HR18 Tim Duncan 1.00 2.50
HR19 Ray Allen .60 1.50
HR20 Chris Bosh .50 1.25

2005-06 Upper Deck ESPN Ink

COMBINED AUTO ODDS 1:480
SP INFO PROVIDED BY UPPER DECK
AJ Antawn Jamison SP 8.00 20.00
AM Antonio McDyess 4.00 10.00
CD Chris Duhon 4.00 10.00
DH Dwight Howard 10.00 25.00
ED Erik Daniels 4.00 10.00
GW Gerald Wallace 4.00 10.00
JM Jamaal Magloire SP 4.00 10.00
JN Jameer Nelson SP 4.00 10.00
KD Keyon Dooling 4.00 10.00
LC Linda Cohn 8.00 20.00
LF Luis Flores 4.00 10.00
LJ LeBron James 1,000.00 2,000.00
MD Marquis Daniels 4.00 10.00
MW Maurice Williams 4.00 10.00
TA Trevor Ariza 4.00 10.00

2005-06 Upper Deck ESPN NBA Fast Break

COMPLETE SET (20) 8.00 20.00
STATED ODDS 1:1 WITH OTHER INSERTS
*25th ANNIV: 6X TO 15X BASE HI
25th ANNIVERSARY PRINT RUN 25 SETS
FB1 Antoine Walker .30 .75
FB2 Gary Payton .60 1.50
FB3 Michael Jordan 3.00 8.00
FB4 LeBron James 3.00 8.00
FB5 Carmelo Anthony .60 1.50
FB6 Chauncey Billups .50 1.25
FB7 Richard Hamilton .50 1.25
FB8 Jason Richardson .40 1.00
FB9 Yao Ming .75 2.00
FB10 Kobe Bryant 3.00 8.00
FB11 Dwyane Wade .75 2.00
FB12 Jason Kidd .60 1.50
FB13 Stephon Marbury .50 1.25
FB14 Steve Francis .40 1.00
FB15 Steve Nash .75 2.00
FB16 Mike Bibby .40 1.00
FB17 Tony Parker .60 1.50
FB18 Rashard Lewis .30 .75
FB19 Andrei Kirilenko .30 .75
FB20 Gilbert Arenas .40 1.00

2005-06 Upper Deck ESPN Plays of the Day

COMPLETE SET (20) 6.00 15.00
STATED ODDS 1:1 WITH OTHER INSERTS,
*25th ANNIV: 6X TO 15X BASE HI
25th ANNIVERSARY PRINT RUN 25 SETS
PD1 Paul Pierce .60 1.50
PD2 Michael Jordan 3.00 8.00
PD3 LeBron James 3.00 8.00
PD4 Tracy McGrady .60 1.50
PD5 Kobe Bryant 3.00 8.00
PD6 Corey Maggette .30 .75
PD7 Pau Gasol .60 1.50
PD8 Dwyane Wade .75 2.00
PD9 Michael Redd .30 .75
PD10 Jason Kidd .60 1.50
PD11 Dwight Howard .50 1.25
PD12 Amare Stoudemire .40 1.00
PD13 Shawn Marion .30 .75
PD14 Damon Stoudamire .40 1.00
PD15 Peja Stojakovic .30 .75
PD16 Manu Ginobili .75 2.00
PD17 Ray Allen .60 1.50
PD18 Andrei Kirilenko .30 .75
PD19 Carlos Boozer .30 .75
PD20 Gilbert Arenas .40 1.00

2005-06 Upper Deck ESPN Sports Center Swatches

STATED ODDS 1:12
AM Andre Miller 2.50 6.00
AN Andre Iguodala 3.00 8.00
AS Amare Stoudemire 3.00 8.00
AW Antoine Walker 2.50 6.00
BD Baron Davis 3.00 8.00
BW Ben Wallace 4.00 10.00
CA Carmelo Anthony 5.00 12.00
CB Caron Butler 2.50 6.00
CH Chauncey Billups 4.00 10.00
CM Corey Maggette 2.50 6.00
CW Chris Webber 4.00 10.00
DH Devin Harris 2.00 5.00
DM Desmond Mason 2.00 5.00
DN Dirk Nowitzki 8.00 20.00
EC Eddy Curry 2.00 5.00
ES Eric Snow 2.00 5.00
GA Gilbert Arenas 3.00 8.00
GP Gary Payton 5.00 12.00
JC Josh Childress 2.00 5.00
JH Josh Howard 2.50 6.00
JK Jason Kidd 5.00 12.00
JO Jermaine O'Neal 2.50 6.00
JR Jalen Rose 2.50 6.00
KB Kobe Bryant 40.00 100.00
KG Kevin Garnett 8.00 20.00
KM Kenyon Martin 2.50 6.00
KR Kareem Rush 2.00 5.00
LJ LeBron James 20.00 50.00
LO Lamar Odom 2.50 6.00
LS Latrell Sprewell 3.00 8.00
MJ Michael Jordan 30.00 80.00
PG Pau Gasol 5.00 12.00
PP Paul Pierce 5.00 12.00
RA Ray Allen 5.00 12.00
RM Reggie Miller 5.00 12.00
SF Steve Francis 3.00 8.00
SN Steve Nash 6.00 15.00
SO Shaquille O'Neal 10.00 25.00
ST Sebastian Telfair 2.50 6.00
TD Tim Duncan 8.00 20.00
TM Tracy McGrady 5.00 12.00
YM Yao Ming 6.00 15.00

2005-06 Upper Deck ESPN the Magazine Covers

COMPLETE SET (7) 6.00 15.00
STATED ODDS 1:1 WITH OTHER INSERTS
*25th ANNIV: 6X TO 15X MAG COV. HI
25th ANNIVERSARY PRINT RUN 25 SETS
BW Ben Wallace .50 1.25
CP Chris Paul 2.00 5.00
DH Dwight Howard .50 1.25
LJ1 LeBron James 3.00 8.00
LJ2 LeBron James 3.00 8.00
MJ1 Michael Jordan 3.00 8.00
MJ2 Michael Jordan 3.00 8.00

2006 Upper Deck Finals

LJ1 LeBron James 2.00 5.00
MJ1 Michael Jordan 4.00 10.00

2007 Upper Deck Finals

FLJ1 LeBron James 2.50 6.00
FMJ1 Michael Jordan 4.00 10.00

2002-03 Upper Deck Finite

COMP.SET w/o SP's (100) 15.00 40.00
1-100 PRINT RUN 1999 SER.#'d SETS
101-150 MF PRINT RUN 500 SER.#'d SETS
151-180 PP PRINT RUN 250 SER.#'d SETS
181-200 FC PRINT RUN 25 SER.#'d SETS
201-221 PRINT RUN 900 SER.#'d SETS
222-233 PRINT RUN 600 SER.#'d SETS
234-242 PRINT RUN 200 SER.#'d SETS
1 Shareef Abdur-Rahim .60 1.50
2 Theo Ratliff .40 1.00
3 Glenn Robinson .60 1.50
4 Jason Terry .50 1.25
5 Vin Baker .50 1.25
6 Kedrick Brown .40 1.00
7 Paul Pierce 1.00 2.50
8 Antoine Walker .50 1.25
9 Tyson Chandler .60 1.50
10 Eddy Curry .40 1.00
11 Jalen Rose .50 1.25
12 Chris Mihm .40 1.00
13 Darius Miles .40 1.00
14 Ricky Davis .50 1.25
15 Michael Finley .50 1.25
16 Raef LaFrentz .40 1.00
17 Steve Nash 1.25 3.00
18 Dirk Nowitzki 1.50 4.00
19 Nick Van Exel .60 1.50
20 Marcus Camby .50 1.25
21 Juwan Howard .50 1.25
22 James Posey .50 1.25
23 Chauncey Billups .60 1.50
24 Richard Hamilton .75 2.00
25 Ben Wallace .75 2.00

26 Clifford Robinson	.60	1.50
27 Gilbert Arenas	.60	1.50
28 Antawn Jamison	.50	1.25
29 Jason Richardson	.60	1.50
30 Eddie Griffin	.40	1.00
31 Steve Francis	.60	1.50
32 Cuttino Mobley	.40	1.00
33 Reggie Miller	1.25	3.00
34 Jermaine O'Neal	.50	1.25
35 Jamaal Tinsley	.40	1.00
36 Ron Mercer	.40	1.00
37 Elton Brand	.50	1.25
38 Andre Miller	.50	1.25
39 Lamar Odom	.60	1.50
40 Kobe Bryant	5.00	12.00
41 Rick Fox	.40	1.00
42 Devean George	.40	1.00
43 Shaquille O'Neal	2.50	6.00
44 Shane Battier	.60	1.50
45 Pau Gasol	1.00	2.50
46 Jason Williams	.75	2.00
47 LaPhonso Ellis	.50	1.25
48 Eddie Jones	.60	1.50
49 Brian Grant	.40	1.00
50 Ray Allen	1.00	2.50
51 Tim Thomas	.40	1.00
52 Sam Cassell	.50	1.25
53 Terrell Brandon	.40	1.00
54 Kevin Garnett	1.50	4.00
55 Wally Szczerbiak	.50	1.25
56 Marc Jackson	.40	1.00
57 Richard Jefferson	.50	1.25
58 Jason Kidd	1.00	2.50
59 Kenyon Martin	.60	1.50
60 Kerry Kittles	.40	1.00
61 Baron Davis	.60	1.50
62 Jamal Mashburn	.50	1.25
63 David Wesley	.40	1.00
64 P.J. Brown	.40	1.00
65 Latrell Sprewell	.60	1.50
66 Antonio McDyess	.50	1.25
67 Allan Houston	.60	1.50
68 Tracy McGrady	1.00	2.50
69 Mike Miller	.50	1.25
70 Darrell Armstrong	.40	1.00
71 Allen Iverson	1.50	4.00
72 Aaron McKie	.40	1.00
73 Keith Van Horn	.60	1.50
74 Stephon Marbury	.75	2.00
75 Shawn Marion	.60	1.50
76 Anfernee Hardaway	1.50	4.00
77 Rasheed Wallace	.75	2.00
78 Bonzi Wells	.40	1.00
79 Scottie Pippen	1.50	4.00
80 Mike Bibby	.60	1.50
81 Peja Stojakovic	.50	1.25
82 Chris Webber	.75	2.00
83 Hedo Turkoglu	.50	1.25
84 Tim Duncan	1.50	4.00
85 David Robinson	1.25	3.00
86 Tony Parker	1.00	2.50
87 Malik Rose	.40	1.00
88 Gary Payton	1.00	2.50
89 Rashard Lewis	.50	1.25
90 Brent Barry	.40	1.00
91 Desmond Mason	.50	1.25
92 Vince Carter	1.25	3.00
93 Morris Peterson	.50	1.25
94 Antonio Davis	.50	1.25
95 Karl Malone	1.25	3.00
96 John Stockton	1.25	3.00
97 Andrei Kirilenko	.50	1.25
98 Kwame Brown	.40	1.00
99 Jerry Stackhouse	.60	1.50
100 Michael Jordan	6.00	15.00
101 Kobe Bryant MF	10.00	25.00
102 Eddie Griffin MF	.75	2.00
103 Shawn Marion MF	1.25	3.00
104 Richard Jefferson MF	1.00	2.50
105 Jermaine O'Neal MF	1.00	2.50
106 Allan Houston MF	1.25	3.00
107 Shane Battier MF	1.25	3.00
108 Hedo Turkoglu MF	1.00	2.50
109 Michael Finley MF	1.25	3.00
110 Jamal Mashburn MF	1.00	2.50
111 Rashard Lewis MF	1.00	2.50
112 Tyson Chandler MF	1.25	3.00
113 Terrell Brandon MF	.75	2.00
114 Antonio Davis MF	1.00	2.50
115 Jamaal Tinsley MF	.75	2.00
116 Tony Parker MF	2.00	5.00
117 Ray Allen MF	2.00	5.00
118 Rasheed Wallace MF	1.50	4.00
119 Cuttino Mobley MF	.75	2.00
120 Jason Terry MF	1.00	2.50
121 Mike Miller MF	1.00	2.50
122 Jalen Rose MF	1.00	2.50
123 Morris Peterson MF	1.00	2.50
124 Ricky Davis MF	1.00	2.50
125 Peja Stojakovic MF	1.00	2.50
126 Gary Payton MF	2.00	5.00
127 Andrei Kirilenko MF	1.00	2.50
128 Tim Duncan MF	3.00	8.00
129 Anfernee Hardaway MF	3.00	8.00
130 Shaquille O'Neal MF	5.00	12.00
131 Latrell Sprewell MF	1.25	3.00
132 Shareef Abdur-Rahim MF	1.25	3.00
133 Steve Nash MF	2.50	6.00
134 Lamar Odom MF	1.25	3.00
135 Antawn Jamison MF	1.00	2.50
136 Reggie Miller MF	2.50	6.00
137 Tim Thomas MF	.75	2.00
138 Eddy Curry MF	.75	2.00
139 Jason Williams MF	1.50	4.00
140 John Stockton MF	2.50	6.00
141 Ben Wallace MF	1.50	4.00
142 Bonzi Wells MF	.75	2.00
143 David Robinson MF	2.50	6.00
144 Stephon Marbury MF	1.50	4.00
145 Vince Carter MF	2.50	6.00
146 James Posey MF	.75	2.00
147 Wally Szczerbiak MF	1.00	2.50
148 Eddie Jones MF	1.25	3.00
149 Scottie Pippen MF	3.00	8.00
150 Michael Jordan MF	15.00	40.00
151 Kobe Bryant PP	20.00	50.00
152 Pau Gasol PP	4.00	10.00
153 Tim Duncan PP	6.00	15.00
154 Karl Malone PP	5.00	12.00
155 Allan Houston PP	2.50	6.00
156 Steve Nash PP	5.00	12.00
157 Shawn Marion PP	2.50	6.00
158 Jamal Mashburn PP	2.00	5.00
159 Shaquille O'Neal PP	10.00	25.00
160 Reggie Miller PP	5.00	12.00
161 Latrell Sprewell PP	2.50	6.00
162 Peja Stojakovic PP	2.00	5.00
163 Jalen Rose PP	2.00	5.00
164 Kenyon Martin PP	2.50	6.00
165 Baron Davis PP	2.50	6.00
166 Ray Allen PP	4.00	10.00
167 Vince Carter PP	5.00	12.00
168 Rashard Lewis PP	2.00	5.00
169 Steve Francis PP	2.50	6.00
170 Jermaine O'Neal PP	2.00	5.00
171 Shane Battier PP	2.50	6.00
172 Shareef Abdur-Rahim PP	2.50	6.00
173 Michael Finley PP	2.50	6.00
174 John Stockton PP	5.00	12.00
175 Jamaal Tinsley PP	1.50	4.00
176 Wally Szczerbiak PP	2.00	5.00
177 Antawn Jamison PP	2.00	5.00
178 Richard Jefferson PP	2.00	5.00
179 Rasheed Wallace PP	3.00	8.00
180 Michael Jordan PP	25.00	60.00
181 Kobe Bryant FC	120.00	300.00
182 Paul Pierce FC	25.00	60.00
183 Nikoloz Tskitishvili FC	10.00	25.00
184 Kareem Rush FC	12.00	30.00
185 Jason Kidd FC	25.00	60.00
186 Dominique Wilkins FC	20.00	50.00
187 Kevin Garnett FC	40.00	100.00
188 Antoine Walker FC	12.00	30.00
189 Jay Williams FC	12.00	30.00
190 DaJuan Wagner FC	12.00	30.00
191 Caron Butler FC	15.00	40.00
192 Mike Bibby FC	15.00	40.00
193 Mike Miller FC	12.00	30.00
194 Tyson Chandler FC	15.00	40.00
195 Drew Gooden FC	15.00	40.00
196 Kenyon Martin FC	15.00	40.00
197 Marcus Fizer FC	10.00	25.00
198 Nene Hilario FC	15.00	40.00
199 Yao Ming FC	80.00	200.00
200 Michael Jordan FC	150.00	400.00
201 Marko Jaric	1.50	4.00
202 Dan Dickau RC	1.00	2.50
203 Tito Maddox RC	1.00	2.50
204 Predrag Savovic RC	1.25	3.00
205 Robert Archibald RC	1.00	2.50
206 Frank Williams RC	1.00	2.50
207 Ronald Murray RC	1.50	4.00
208 Lonny Baxter RC	1.00	2.50
209 Efthimios Rentzias RC	1.00	2.50
210 Vincent Yarbrough RC	1.00	2.50
211 Gordan Giricek RC	1.50	4.00
212 Carlos Boozer RC	1.50	4.00
213 John Salmons RC	1.50	4.00
214 Manu Ginobili RC	6.00	15.00
215 Roger Mason Jr. RC	1.25	3.00
216 Chris Jefferies RC	1.00	2.50
217 Sam Clancy RC	1.25	3.00
218 Rasual Butler RC	1.25	3.00
219 Dan Gadzuric RC	1.25	3.00
220 Tayshaun Prince RC	3.00	8.00
221 Casey Jacobsen RC	1.25	3.00
222 Qyntel Woods RC	1.25	3.00
223 Jiri Welsch RC	1.50	4.00
224 Curtis Borchardt RC	1.25	3.00
225 Marcus Haislip RC	1.25	3.00
226 Kareem Rush RC	1.50	4.00
227 Fred Jones RC	1.50	4.00
228 Caron Butler RC	2.00	5.00
229 Juan Dixon RC	1.50	4.00
230 Ryan Humphrey RC	1.50	4.00
231 Melvin Ely RC	1.50	4.00
232 Bostjan Nachbar RC	1.50	4.00
233 Jared Jeffries RC	1.50	4.00
234 Jay Williams RC	4.00	10.00
235 Nikoloz Tskitishvili RC	3.00	8.00
236 Chris Wilcox RC	4.00	10.00
237 Drew Gooden RC	5.00	12.00
238 Amare Stoudemire RC	12.00	30.00
239 DaJuan Wagner RC	4.00	10.00
240 Nene Hilario RC	5.00	12.00
241 Mike Dunleavy RC	5.00	12.00
242 Yao Ming RC	25.00	60.00

2002-03 Upper Deck Finite Elements Dual Uniforms

STATED ODDS 1:20

AIJKU A.Iverson/J.Kidd	6.00	15.00
JSSFU J.Smith/S.Francis	5.00	12.00
KBJRU K.Bryant/J.Richardson	40.00	100.00
KGTBU K.Garnett/T.Brandon	6.00	15.00
LSCWU L.Sprewell/C.Ward	5.00	12.00
MJKBU M.Jordan/K.Bryant	150.00	400.00
PPAWU P.Pierce/A.Walker	8.00	20.00
TMMMU T.McGrady/M.Miller	6.00	15.00

2002-03 Upper Deck Finite Elements Dual Warm-Ups

STATED ODDS 1:4

AHJJ A.Hardaway/J.Johnson	4.00	10.00
AIJK A.Iverson/J.Kidd	4.00	10.00
BDJM B.Davis/J.Mashburn	3.00	8.00
DNSN D.Nowitzki/S.Nash	6.00	15.00
ECTC E.Curry/T.Chandler	3.00	8.00
HTMB H.Turkoglu/M.Bibby	3.00	8.00
JRAJ J.Richardson/A.Jamison	3.00	8.00
KBAI K.Bryant/A.Iverson	40.00	100.00
KBTM K.Bryant/T.McGrady	40.00	100.00
KGWS K.Garnett/W.Szczerbiak	5.00	12.00
KMJS K.Malone/J.Stockton	5.00	12.00
KWBH K.Brown/B.Haywood	3.00	8.00
MFRL M.Finley/R.LaFrentz	3.00	8.00
MJKB M.Jordan/K.Bryant	150.00	400.00
MOCM M.Olowokandi/C.Maggette	3.00	8.00
PPAW P.Pierce/A.Walker	5.00	12.00
QREB Q.Richardson/E.Brand	3.00	8.00
RHKW R.Hamilton/K.Brown	3.00	8.00
SADJ S.Rahim/D.Johnson	3.00	8.00
SMSM S.Marbury/S.Marion	4.00	10.00

2002-03 Upper Deck Finite Elements Jerseys

STATED ODDS 1:10

AHJ Allan Houston	3.00	8.00
BDJ Baron Davis	3.00	8.00
DNJ Dirk Nowitzki	8.00	20.00
EBJ Elton Brand	2.50	6.00
JJJ Joe Johnson	2.50	6.00
JRJ Jason Richardson	3.00	8.00
JWJ Jay Williams	2.50	6.00
KBJ Kobe Bryant	40.00	100.00
KMJ Karl Malone	6.00	15.00
MJJ Michael Jordan	50.00	120.00
MOJ Michael Olowokandi	2.00	5.00
RLJ Raef LaFrentz	2.00	5.00
RMJ Ron Mercer	2.00	5.00
SMJ Stephon Marbury	4.00	10.00

2002-03 Upper Deck Finite Signatures

PRINT RUNS LISTED BELOW

ASA Amare Stoudemire/80	8.00	20.00
AWA Antoine Walker/50	15.00	40.00
CBA Caron Butler/80	5.00	12.00
CWA Chris Wilcox/80	5.00	12.00
DGA Drew Gooden/80	5.00	12.00
DSA DeShawn Stevenson/100	5.00	12.00
DWA DaJuan Wagner/80	5.00	12.00
ETA Etan Thomas/146	5.00	12.00
JJA Jared Jeffries/80	5.00	12.00
JKA Jason Kidd/128	20.00	50.00
JMA Jamaal Magloire/100	5.00	12.00
JTA Jeff Trepagnier/112	5.00	12.00
JWA Jay Williams/80	5.00	12.00
KBA Kobe Bryant	200.00	500.00
KGA Kevin Garnett/25	60.00	150.00
KMA Kenyon Martin/104	10.00	25.00
KRA Kareem Rush/80	5.00	12.00
MBA Mike Bibby/80	6.00	15.00
MEA Melvin Ely/80	5.00	12.00
MFA Marcus Fizer/104	5.00	12.00
MJA Michael Jordan/23	2,000.00	4,000.00
MMA Mike Miller/80	5.00	12.00
MOA Jerome Moiso/146	5.00	12.00
NHA Nene Hilario/80	5.00	12.00
PPA Paul Pierce/104	15.00	40.00
TCA Tyson Chandler/80	10.00	25.00
YMA Yao Ming/80	60.00	150.00

2003-04 Upper Deck Finite

1-200 ODD PRINT RUN 2999 SER.#'d SETS
201-228 PRINT RUN 1500 SER.#'d SETS
201-236 PRINT RUN 750 SER.#'d SETS
237-242 PRINT RUN 200 SER.#'d SETS
MAJ.FACT.PRINT RUN 1000 SER.#'d SETS
PROM.POW.PRINT RUN 500 SER.#'d SETS
FIRST CLASS PRINT RUN 50 SER.#'d SETS

1 Shareef Abdur-Rahim	.50	1.25
2 Dominique Wilkins	1.00	2.50
3 Theo Ratliff	.30	.75
4 Dan Dickau	.50	1.25
5 Jason Terry	.40	1.00
6 Dion Glover	.50	1.25
7 Alan Henderson	.30	.75
8 Paul Pierce	1.25	3.00
9 Larry Bird	1.25	3.00
10 Raef LaFrentz	.50	1.25
11 Robert Parish	.60	1.50
12 Jiri Welsch	.50	1.25
13 John Havlicek	.50	1.25
14 Vin Baker	.50	1.25
15 Jamal Crawford	.50	1.25
16 Michael Jordan	8.00	20.00
17 Scottie Pippen	1.25	3.00
18 Reggie Theus	.60	1.50
19 Jalen Rose	.40	1.00
20 Tyson Chandler	.60	1.50
21 Eddy Curry	.30	.75
22 Dajuan Wagner	.50	1.25
23 Lenny Wilkens	.50	1.25
24 Carlos Boozer	.60	1.50
25 World B. Free	.40	1.00
26 Darius Miles	.50	1.25
27 Craig Ehlo	.30	.75
28 Ricky Davis	.60	1.50
29 Dirk Nowitzki	1.25	3.00
30 Rolando Blackman	.60	1.50
31 Steve Nash	1.00	2.50
32 Tony Delk	.60	1.50
33 Antawn Jamison	.50	1.25
34 Antoine Walker	.75	2.00
35 Michael Finley	.50	1.25
36 Andre Miller	.60	1.50
37 David Thompson	.40	1.00
38 Nene	.60	1.50
39 Dan Issel	.40	1.00
40 Nikoloz Tskitishvili	.50	1.25
41 Alex English	.40	1.00
42 Earl Boykins	.50	1.25
43 Richard Hamilton	.60	1.50
44 Mehmet Okur	.60	1.50
45 Ben Wallace	.60	1.50
46 Bob Lanier	.60	1.50
47 Chauncey Billups	.60	1.50
48 Dave Bing	.75	2.00
49 Tayshaun Prince	.50	1.25
50 Nick Van Exel	.75	2.00
51 Erick Dampier	.30	.75
52 Jason Richardson	.75	2.00
53 Joe Barry Carroll	.30	.75
54 Mike Dunleavy	.60	1.50
55 Wilt Chamberlain	1.00	2.50
56 Troy Murphy	.50	1.25
57 Steve Francis	.50	1.25
58 Maurice Taylor	.50	1.25
59 Yao Ming	1.25	3.00
60 Robert Reid	.75	2.00
61 Cuttino Mobley	.30	.75
62 Moses Malone	.75	2.00
63 Eddie Griffin	.30	.75
64 Jermaine O'Neal	.75	2.00
65 George McGinnis	.30	.75
66 Reggie Miller	1.50	4.00
67 Clark Kellogg	.50	1.25
68 Jamaal Tinsley	.50	1.25
69 Al Harrington	.40	1.00
70 Ron Artest	.75	2.00
71 Elton Brand	.40	1.00
72 Corey Maggette	.60	1.50
73 Chris Wilcox	.30	.75
74 Quentin Richardson	.50	1.25
75 Bill Walton	.75	2.00
76 Marko Jaric	.50	1.25
77 Kobe Bryant	4.00	10.00
78 Kareem Abdul-Jabbar	1.25	3.00
79 Shaquille O'Neal	2.00	5.00
80 Michael Cooper	.60	1.50
81 Gary Payton	.75	2.00
82 James Worthy	1.00	2.50
83 Karl Malone	1.00	2.50
84 Pau Gasol	1.25	3.00
85 Michael Dickerson	.30	.75
86 Mike Miller	.60	1.50
87 Brevin Knight	.30	.75
88 Shane Battier	.60	1.50
89 Stromile Swift	.30	.75
90 Jason Williams	1.25	3.00
91 Caron Butler	.40	1.00
92 Samaki Walker	.50	1.25
93 Eddie Jones	.50	1.25
94 Rasual Butler	.50	1.25
95 Brian Grant	.30	.75
96 Loren Woods	.50	1.25
97 Lamar Odom	.40	1.00
98 Desmond Mason	.60	1.50
99 Sidney Moncrief	.30	.75
100 Toni Kukoc	.75	2.00
101 Oscar Robertson	.50	1.25
102 Michael Redd	.75	2.00
103 Terry Cummings	.40	1.00
104 Tim Thomas	.50	1.25
105 Kevin Garnett	1.25	3.00
106 Troy Hudson	.50	1.25
107 Sam Cassell	.40	1.00
108 Latrell Sprewell	1.00	2.50
109 Michael Olowokandi	.30	.75
110 Wally Szczerbiak	.60	1.50
111 Jason Kidd	.75	2.00
112 Otis Birdsong	.60	1.50
113 Kenyon Martin	.50	1.25
114 Albert King	.50	1.25
115 Richard Jefferson	.40	1.00
116 Kerry Kittles	.60	1.50
117 Alonzo Mourning	.60	1.50
118 Baron Davis	.75	2.00
119 Darrell Armstrong	.30	.75
120 Jamal Mashburn	.60	1.50
121 P.J. Brown	.30	.75
122 David Wesley	.50	1.25
123 Courtney Alexander	.30	.75
124 Jamaal Magloire	.50	1.25
125 Allan Houston	.50	1.25
126 Willis Reed	1.25	3.00
127 Keith Van Horn	.40	1.00
128 Walt Frazier	.75	2.00
129 Antonio McDyess	.40	1.00
130 Earl Monroe	.75	2.00
131 Kurt Thomas	.30	.75
132 Tracy McGrady	1.25	3.00
133 Pat Garrity	.30	.75
134 Grant Hill	1.00	2.50
135 Tyronn Lue	.30	.75
136 Drew Gooden	.60	1.50
137 Juwan Howard	.40	1.00
138 Gordan Giricek	.50	1.25
139 Allen Iverson	1.25	3.00
140 Julius Erving	1.25	3.00
141 Glenn Robinson	.40	1.00
142 Maurice Cheeks	.60	1.50
143 Aaron McKie	.30	.75
144 Billy Cunningham	.75	2.00
145 Eric Snow	.30	.75
146 Stephon Marbury	1.00	2.50
147 Kevin Johnson	.50	1.25
148 Amare Stoudemire	1.00	2.50
149 Larry Nance	.40	1.00
150 Shawn Marion	.75	2.00
151 Walter Davis	.50	1.25
152 Anfernee Hardaway	2.00	5.00
153 Rasheed Wallace	.60	1.50
154 Zach Randolph	.75	2.00
155 Derek Anderson	.40	1.00
156 Dale Davis	.50	1.25
157 Bonzi Wells	.30	.75
158 Jim Paxson	.75	2.00
159 Damon Stoudamire	.40	1.00
160 Chris Webber	1.00	2.50
161 Vlade Divac	.50	1.25
162 Mike Bibby	.75	2.00
163 Bobby Jackson	.40	1.00
164 Peja Stojakovic	.60	1.50
165 Doug Christie	.40	1.00
166 Brad Miller	.60	1.50
167 Tim Duncan	1.25	3.00
168 Radoslav Nesterovic	.50	1.25
169 Tony Parker	.75	2.00
170 George Gervin	1.25	3.00
171 Manu Ginobili	1.00	2.50
172 Artis Gilmore	.60	1.50
173 Ron Mercer	.30	.75
174 Ray Allen	1.25	3.00
175 Spencer Haywood	.30	.75
176 Rashard Lewis	.60	1.50
177 Fred Brown	.30	.75
178 Vladimir Radmanovic	.50	1.25
179 Jack Sikma	.40	1.00
180 Brent Barry	.50	1.25
181 Vince Carter	1.00	2.50
182 Antonio Davis	.60	1.50
183 Morris Peterson	.30	.75
184 Alvin Williams	.50	1.25
185 Chris Jefferies	.30	.75
186 Jerome Williams	.50	1.25
187 Andrei Kirilenko	.40	1.00
188 Pete Maravich	1.50	4.00
189 Matt Harpring	.30	.75
190 Mark Eaton	.50	1.25
191 Jarron Collins	.30	.75
192 Greg Ostertag	.50	1.25
193 Carlos Arroyo	.40	1.00
194 Jerry Stackhouse	1.00	2.50
195 Wes Unseld	.50	1.25
196 Gilbert Arenas	.75	2.00
197 Larry Hughes	.40	1.00
198 Kwame Brown	.50	1.25
199 Jeff Malone	.30	.75
200 Jared Jeffries	.50	1.25
201 Aleksandar Pavlovic RC	1.50	4.00
202 James Lang RC	1.25	3.00
203 Jason Kapono RC	1.25	3.00
204 Luke Walton RC	2.00	5.00
205 Jerome Beasley RC	1.25	3.00
206 Willie Green RC	2.00	5.00
207 Steve Blake RC	1.50	4.00
208 Slavko Vranes RC	1.25	3.00
209 Zaur Pachulia RC	2.00	5.00
210 Travis Hansen RC	1.25	3.00
211 Keith Bogans RC	1.25	3.00
212 Kyle Korver RC	2.50	6.00
213 Brandon Hunter RC	1.25	3.00
214 James Jones RC	1.25	3.00
215 Josh Howard RC	2.00	5.00
216 Leandro Barbosa RC	2.00	5.00
217 Kendrick Perkins RC	1.50	4.00
218 Ndudi Ebi RC	1.25	3.00
219 Brian Cook RC	1.25	3.00
220 Travis Outlaw RC	1.50	4.00
221 Zoran Planinic RC	1.25	3.00
222 Dahntay Jones RC	1.50	4.00
223 Boris Diaw RC	2.00	5.00
224 Zarko Cabarkapa RC	1.25	3.00
225 Troy Bell RC	1.25	3.00
226 Reece Gaines RC	1.25	3.00
227 Luke Ridnour RC	2.00	5.00
228 Chris Kaman RC	2.00	5.00
229 Marcus Banks RC	1.50	4.00
230 Maciej Lampe RC	1.50	4.00
231 David West RC	3.00	8.00
232 Mickael Pietrus RC	2.00	5.00
233 Jarvis Hayes RC	1.50	4.00
234 Mike Sweetney RC	1.50	4.00
235 Kirk Hinrich RC	2.50	6.00
236 Chris Bosh RC	8.00	20.00
237 Nick Collison RC	6.00	15.00
238 T.J. Ford RC	6.00	15.00
239 Dwyane Wade RC	15.00	40.00
240 Carmelo Anthony RC	15.00	40.00
241 Darko Milicic RC	6.00	15.00
242 LeBron James RC	1,500.00	3,000.00
243 Michael Jordan MF	8.00	20.00
244 Kobe Bryant MF	6.00	15.00
245 Michael Finley MF	.75	2.00
246 Andrei Kirilenko MF	.60	1.50
247 Desmond Mason MF	.60	1.50
248 Kenyon Martin MF	.75	2.00
249 Shaquille O'Neal MF	3.00	8.00
250 Jamal Mashburn MF	.60	1.50
251 Jason Terry MF	.60	1.50
252 Andre Miller MF	.60	1.50
253 Keith Van Horn MF	.60	1.50
254 Derek Anderson MF	.60	1.50
255 Stephon Marbury MF	1.00	2.50
256 Glenn Robinson MF	.60	1.50
257 Richard Hamilton MF	1.00	2.50
258 Lamar Odom MF	.60	1.50
259 Bonzi Wells MF	.50	1.25
260 Wally Szczerbiak MF	.60	1.50
261 Alonzo Mourning MF	1.00	2.50
262 Gilbert Arenas MF	.75	2.00
263 Mike Bibby MF	.75	2.00
264 Antawn Jamison MF	.75	2.00
265 Tony Parker MF	1.25	3.00
266 Reggie Miller MF	1.50	4.00
267 Vince Carter MF	1.50	4.00
268 Richard Jefferson MF	.60	1.50
269 Nene MF	.60	1.50
270 Grant Hill MF	1.00	2.50
271 Rashard Lewis MF	.60	1.50
272 Shawn Marion MF	.75	2.00
273 Morris Peterson MF	.50	1.25
274 Chauncey Billups MF	1.00	2.50
275 Eddie Jones MF	.75	2.00
276 Raef LaFrentz MF	.50	1.25
277 Jerry Stackhouse MF	1.00	2.50
278 Pau Gasol MF	1.25	3.00
279 Darius Miles MF	.50	1.25
280 Nick Van Exel MF	.75	2.00
281 Gary Payton MF	1.25	3.00
282 Peja Stojakovic MF	.60	1.50
283 Karl Malone MF	1.50	4.00
284 Mike Miller MF	.60	1.50
285 Caron Butler MF	.60	1.50
286 Cuttino Mobley MF	.50	1.25
287 Zach Randolph MF	.75	2.00
288 Scottie Pippen MF	2.00	5.00
289 Gordan Giricek MF	.50	1.25
290 Ben Wallace MF	1.00	2.50
291 Manu Ginobili MF	1.50	4.00
292 Vladimir Radmanovic MF	.50	1.25
293 Michael Jordan PP	15.00	40.00
294 Kobe Bryant PP	12.00	30.00
295 Vince Carter PP	3.00	8.00
296 Steve Nash PP	3.00	8.00
297 Shaquille O'Neal PP	6.00	15.00
298 Amare Stoudemire PP	2.00	5.00
299 Tracy McGrady PP	2.50	6.00
300 Gary Payton PP	2.50	6.00
301 Chris Bosh PP	5.00	12.00
302 Michael Finley PP	1.50	4.00
303 Caron Butler PP	1.25	3.00
304 Jarvis Hayes PP	1.00	2.50
305 Ben Wallace PP	2.00	5.00
306 Allan Houston PP	1.50	4.00
307 Mike Bibby PP	1.50	4.00
308 Antoine Walker PP	1.50	4.00
309 Dajuan Wagner PP	1.00	2.50
310 Kevin Garnett PP	4.00	10.00
311 Mickael Pietrus PP	1.25	3.00
312 Baron Davis PP	1.50	4.00
313 Paul Pierce PP	2.50	6.00
314 Rasheed Wallace PP	2.00	5.00
315 Chris Webber PP	2.00	5.00
316 Jermaine O'Neal PP	1.50	4.00
317 Shareef Abdur-Rahim PP	1.50	4.00
318 Ray Allen PP	2.50	6.00
319 Peja Stojakovic PP	1.25	3.00
320 Tim Duncan PP	4.00	10.00
321 Gilbert Arenas PP	1.50	4.00
322 Jason Richardson PP	1.50	4.00
323 Dwyane Wade FC	125.00	300.00
324 Gary Payton FC	10.00	25.00
325 Karl Malone FC	12.00	30.00
326 Jason Kidd FC	10.00	25.00
327 Darko Milicic FC	5.00	12.00
328 Steve Francis FC	6.00	15.00
329 Vince Carter FC	12.00	30.00
330 Elton Brand FC	5.00	12.00
331 Amare Stoudemire FC	8.00	20.00
332 Shaquille O'Neal FC	25.00	60.00
333 Carmelo Anthony FC	30.00	80.00
334 Tracy McGrady FC	10.00	25.00
335 Tim Duncan FC	15.00	40.00
336 Chris Webber FC	8.00	20.00
337 Allen Iverson FC	15.00	40.00
338 Dirk Nowitzki FC	15.00	40.00
339 Kevin Garnett FC	15.00	40.00
340 Kobe Bryant FC	50.00	120.00
341 LeBron James FC	1,500.00	3,000.00
342 Michael Jordan FC	60.00	150.00

2003-04 Upper Deck Finite Gold

*1-200 EVEN SINGLES: 2X TO 5X BASE HI
1-200 EVEN PRINT RUN 100 SER.#'d SETS
*1-200 ODD SINGLES: 2X TO 5X BASE HI
*201-228 RC SINGLES: 1.25X TO 3X BASE HI
201-228 PRINT RUN 100 SER.#'d SETS
*229-236 RC SINGLES: 1X TO 2.5X BASE HI
229-236 PRINT RUN 100 SER.#'d SETS
*237-242 RC SINGLES: .6X TO 1.5X BASE HI
237-242 PRINT RUN 25 SER.#'d SETS
*243-292 SINGLES: 3X TO 8X BASE HI
243-292 PRINT RUN 50 SER.#'d SETS
*293-322 SINGLES: 2X TO 5X BASE HI
293-322 PRINT RUN 25 SER.#'d SETS

16 Michael Jordan	50.00	120.00
239 Dwyane Wade	100.00	250.00
242 LeBron James	15,000.00	30,000.00

2003-04 Upper Deck Finite Elements Warmups

STATED ODDS 1:4

FE1 M.Jordan/K.Bryant SP	50.00	120.00
FE2 A.Walker/P.Pierce	4.00	10.00
FE3 V.Divac/G.Wallace	4.00	10.00
FE4 A.Houston/L.Sprewell	4.00	10.00
FE5 Y.Ming/S.Francis	5.00	12.00
FE6 A.Harrington/J.Bender	4.00	10.00
FE7 R.Jefferson/K.Martin	4.00	10.00
FE8 B.Davis/J.Mashburn	4.00	10.00
FE9 J.Richardson/G.Arenas	4.00	10.00
FE10 T.McGrady/K.Garnett	6.00	15.00
FE11 W.Szczerbiak/J.Smith	4.00	10.00
FE12 J.Rose/E.Curry	4.00	10.00
FE13 S.Marion/S.Marbury	4.00	10.00
FE14 M.Sweetney/K.Van Horn	4.00	10.00
FE15 A.Stoudemire/A.Hardaway	5.00	12.00
FE16 T.Ratliff/S.Abdur-Rahim	4.00	10.00
FE17 J.Howard/S.Nash	4.00	10.00
FE18 Magic/Julius Erving SP	15.00	40.00
FE19 J.Stockton/A.Kirilenko	5.00	12.00
FE20 D.Miles/Q.Richardson	4.00	10.00
FE21 L.Odom/E.Brand	4.00	10.00
FE22 J.Tinsley/R.Miller	4.00	10.00
FE23 B.Wallace/R.Hamilton	4.00	10.00
FE24 C.Mihm/D.Wagner	4.00	10.00
FE25 D.Robinson/S.Claxton	5.00	12.00
FE26 T.Chandler/M.Fizer	4.00	10.00
FE27 A.Miller/C.Maggette	4.00	10.00
FE28 S.Battier/P.Gasol	4.00	10.00
FE29 M.Miller/S.Swift	4.00	10.00
FE30 D.Fisher/K.Bryant	10.00	25.00
FE31 Magloire/B.Davis/Wesley	8.00	20.00
FE32 Ratliff/Shareef/Terry	8.00	20.00
FE33 Hard/Marbury/J.Johnson	25.00	60.00
FE34 Chandler/Fizer/Curry	8.00	20.00
FE35 Ming/Mobley/Posey	15.00	40.00
FE36 Iverson/McKie/Snow	12.00	30.00
FE37 Brand/Maggette/Q-Rich	8.00	20.00
FE38 Rose/Webber/Howard	25.00	60.00
FE39 B.Miller/J.O'Neal/Tinisley	8.00	20.00
FE40 Bosh/Sweetney/Hayes	10.00	25.00
FE41 Pietrus/Darko/Wade	12.00	30.00
FE42 Kobe/Jordan/Kidd	100.00	250.00

2003-04 Upper Deck Finite Elements Jerseys

STATED ODDS 1:10
DUAL STATED ODDS 1:20

FJ1 Michael Jordan SP	50.00	120.00
FJ2 Kobe Bryant SP	12.00	30.00
FJ3 Latrell Sprewell	4.00	10.00
FJ4 Dirk Nowitzki	8.00	20.00
FJ5 Paul Pierce	5.00	12.00
FJ6 John Stockton	6.00	15.00
FJ7 Karl Malone	6.00	15.00
FJ8 Grant Hill	4.00	10.00
FJ9 Shawn Marion	3.00	8.00
FJ10 Ray Allen	5.00	12.00
FJ11 Steve Francis	3.00	8.00
FJ12 Steve Nash	6.00	15.00
FJ13 Antoine Walker	3.00	8.00
FJ14 David Robinson	6.00	15.00
FJ15 Yao Ming	8.00	20.00
FJ16 Allen Iverson	6.00	15.00
FJ17 Carmelo Anthony	15.00	40.00
FJ18 LeBron James	150.00	400.00
FJ19 Darko Milicic	2.50	6.00
FJ20 Chris Bosh	10.00	25.00
FJ21 Mike Sweetney	2.00	5.00
FS1 M.Jordan/K.Bryant SP	100.00	250.00
FS2 A.Houston/C.Ward	5.00	12.00
FS3 L.Sprewell/K.Thomas	5.00	12.00
FS4 D.Stoudamire/R.Wallace	5.00	12.00
FS5 J.Williams/M.Fizer	5.00	12.00
FS6 Nesterovic/Szczerbiak	5.00	12.00
FS7 J.Kidd/T.Parker	6.00	15.00
FS8 R.Miller/J.Bender	5.00	12.00
FS9 A.Jamison/J.Richardson	5.00	12.00
FS10 L.Odom/C.Maggette	5.00	12.00
FS11 J.Rose/E.Curry	5.00	12.00
FS12 J.O'Neal/J.Tinsley	5.00	12.00
FS13 D.Robinson/T.Duncan	10.00	25.00
FS14 D.Miles/D.Wagner	5.00	12.00
FS15 M.Miller/P.Gasol	5.00	12.00
FS16 C.Ward/K.Thomas	5.00	12.00
FS17 K.Martin/R.Jefferson	5.00	12.00
FS18 R.Allen/R.Lewis	5.00	12.00
FS19 M.Ginobili/T.Parker	6.00	15.00
FS20 M.Finley/D.Nowitzki	5.00	12.00
FS21 M.Fizer/T.Chandler	5.00	12.00

2003-04 Upper Deck Finite Signatures

STATED ODDS 1:30

AJ Antawn Jamison	5.00	12.00
AM Andre Miller	5.00	12.00
BI Chauncey Billups	6.00	15.00
BO Chris Bosh	20.00	50.00
CA Carmelo Anthony	40.00	100.00
CB Caron Butler	5.00	12.00
CK Chris Kaman	6.00	15.00
DA Darius Miles	5.00	12.00
DJ DerMarr Johnson	5.00	12.00
DM Darko Milicic	6.00	15.00
DW Dwyane Wade	200.00	500.00
GA Gilbert Arenas	8.00	20.00
GP Gary Payton	12.00	30.00
JH Jarvis Hayes	5.00	12.00
JM Jerome Moiso	5.00	12.00
JR Jason Richardson	5.00	12.00
JS Jerry Stackhouse	6.00	15.00
KB Kobe Bryant/100	600.00	1,200.00
LJ LeBron James/150	4,000.00	8,000.00
MB Mike Bibby	6.00	15.00
MJ Michael Jordan/23	2,500.00	5,000.00
PP Paul Pierce	15.00	40.00
PS Peja Stojakovic	8.00	20.00
RJ Richard Jefferson	5.00	12.00
SA Shareef Abdur-Rahim	5.00	12.00
SB Shane Battier	5.00	12.00
SF Steve Francis	6.00	15.00
TM Tracy McGrady/100	20.00	50.00
YM Yao Ming	30.00	80.00

2004-05 Upper Deck Finite Dual Signatures Gold

STATED PRINT RUN 25 SER.#'d SETS
NO PRICING DUE TO LACK OF MARKET INFO

2004-05 Upper Deck Finite Signatures

FSJC Jamal Crawford	8.00	20.00
FSJR J.R. Smith	3.00	8.00
FSLU Luke Jackson	3.00	8.00
FSMJ Michael Jordan	500.00	800.00
FSTM Tracy McGrady	10.00	25.00

2007-08 Upper Deck First Edition

COMP.SET w/o RC's (200)	10.00	25.00
ROOKIE ODDS ONE PER PACK		
1 Austin Croshere	.20	.50
2 Devean George	.20	.50
3 Devin Harris	.20	.50
4 Josh Howard	.25	.60
5 Jerry Stackhouse	.30	.75
6 Jason Terry	.25	.60
7 Rafer Alston	.30	.75
8 Shane Battier	.25	.60
9 Luther Head	.20	.50
10 Juwan Howard	.30	.75
11 Tracy McGrady	.50	1.25
12 Steve Novak	.20	.50
13 Rudy Gay	.25	.60
14 Eddie Jones	.30	.75
15 Kyle Lowry	.30	.75
16 Mike Miller	.25	.60
17 Damon Stoudamire	.30	.75
18 Hakim Warrick	.20	.50
19 Brandon Bass	.20	.50
20 Tyson Chandler	.30	.75
21 Bobby Jackson	.20	.50
22 Desmond Mason	.20	.50
23 Cedric Simmons	.20	.50
24 Peja Stojakovic	.25	.60
25 Bruce Bowen	.20	.50
26 Michael Finley	.30	.75
27 Manu Ginobili	.60	1.50
28 Tony Parker	.50	1.25
29 Beno Udrih	.20	.50
30 Monta Ellis	.25	.60
31 Al Harrington	.25	.60
32 Sarunas Jasikevicius	.20	.50
33 Stephen Jackson	.25	.60
34 Jason Richardson	.30	.75
35 Sam Cassell	.25	.60
36 Chris Kaman	.25	.60
37 Shaun Livingston	.25	.60
38 Corey Maggette	.25	.60
39 Cuttino Mobley	.25	.60
40 Tim Thomas	.20	.50
41 Kwame Brown	.20	.50
42 Andrew Bynum	.20	.50
43 Jordan Farmar	.20	.50
44 Lamar Odom	.25	.60
45 Ronny Turiaf	.25	.60
46 Luke Walton	.25	.60
47 Leandro Barbosa	.25	.60
48 Raja Bell	.25	.60
49 Boris Diaw	.25	.60
50 Shawn Marion	.30	.75
51 Amare Stoudemire	.30	.75
52 Shareef Abdur-Rahim	.30	.75
53 Ron Artest	.30	.75
54 Quincy Douby	.20	.50
55 Kevin Martin	.25	.60
56 Brad Miller	.25	.60
57 Allen Iverson	.75	2.00
58 Kenyon Martin	.25	.60
59 Eduardo Najera	.20	.50
60 Nene	.25	.60
61 J.R. Smith	.30	.75
62 Ricky Davis	.25	.60
63 Randy Foye	.25	.60
64 Troy Hudson	.20	.50
65 Mike James	.20	.50
66 Rashad McCants	.20	.50
67 Craig Smith	.20	.50
68 LaMarcus Aldridge	.30	.75
69 Jarrett Jack	.25	.60
70 Jamaal Magloire	.20	.50
71 Sergio Rodriguez	.20	.50
72 Brandon Roy	.40	1.00
73 Martell Webster	.25	.60
74 Rashard Lewis	.25	.60
75 Luke Ridnour	.25	.60
76 Danny Fortson	.20	.50

77 Chris Wilcox .20 .50
78 Damien Wilkins .20 .50
79 Ronnie Brewer .20 .50
80 Derek Fisher .30 .75
81 Matt Harpring .20 .50
82 Andrei Kirilenko .25 .60
83 Paul Millsap .25 .60
84 Deron Williams .25 .60
85 Tony Allen .20 .50
86 Gerald Green .25 .60
87 Al Jefferson .20 .50
88 Wally Szczerbiak .25 .60
89 Allan Ray .20 .50
90 Delonte West .20 .50
91 Hassan Adams .20 .50
92 Richard Jefferson .25 .60
93 Jason Kidd .50 1.25
94 Nenad Krstic .20 .50
95 Marcus Williams .20 .50
96 Renaldo Balkman .20 .50
97 Jamal Crawford .30 .75
98 Eddy Curry .20 .50
99 Channing Frye .20 .50
100 Quentin Richardson .20 .50
101 Nate Robinson .30 .75
102 Rodney Carney .20 .50
103 Samuel Dalembert .20 .50
104 Steven Hunter .20 .50
105 Kyle Korver .30 .75
106 Andre Miller .25 .60
107 Shavlik Randolph .20 .50
108 Andrea Bargnani .20 .50
109 Jose Calderon .20 .50
110 T.J. Ford .20 .50
111 Jorge Garbajosa .25 .60
112 Joey Graham .20 .50
113 Morris Peterson .20 .50
114 Luol Deng .25 .60
115 Ben Gordon .25 .60
116 Kirk Hinrich .30 .75
117 Thabo Sefolosha .20 .50
118 Tyrus Thomas .20 .50
119 Ben Wallace .40 1.00
120 Shannon Brown .20 .50
121 Drew Gooden .25 .60
122 Larry Hughes .25 .60
123 Zydrunas Ilgauskas .25 .60
124 Donyell Marshall .20 .50
125 Richard Hamilton .40 1.00
126 Amir Johnson .20 .50
127 Antonio McDyess .25 .60
128 Tayshaun Prince .30 .75
129 Rasheed Wallace .40 1.00
130 Chris Webber .40 1.00
131 Marquis Daniels .20 .50
132 Ike Diogu .20 .50
133 Mike Dunleavy .20 .50
134 Jeff Foster .20 .50
135 Troy Murphy .20 .50
136 Jamaal Tinsley .20 .50
137 Charlie Bell .20 .50
138 Andrew Bogut .25 .60
139 Earl Boykins .20 .50
140 Bobby Simmons .20 .50
141 Charlie Villanueva .20 .50
142 Maurice Williams .25 .60
143 Speedy Claxton .20 .50
144 Solomon Jones .20 .50
145 Tyronn Lue .20 .50
146 Marvin Williams .25 .60
147 Shelden Williams .20 .50
148 Raymond Felton .25 .60
149 Othella Harrington .20 .50
150 Sean May .20 .50
151 Adam Morrison .20 .50
152 Gerald Wallace .25 .60
153 Udonis Haslem .20 .50
154 Alonzo Mourning .50 1.25
155 Shaquille O'Neal 1.25 3.00
156 Gary Payton .50 1.25
157 Antoine Walker .30 .75
158 Jason Williams .50 1.25
159 Carlos Arroyo .20 .50
160 Travis Diener .20 .50
161 Grant Hill .50 1.25
162 Darko Milicic .20 .50
163 Jameer Nelson .20 .50
164 J.J. Redick .30 .75
165 Andray Blatche .20 .50
166 Caron Butler .25 .60
167 Antonio Daniels .20 .50
168 Brendan Haywood .20 .50
169 Antawn Jamison .25 .60
170 DeShawn Stevenson .20 .50
171 Dirk Nowitzki .75 2.00
172 Yao Ming .75 2.00
173 Pau Gasol .50 1.25
174 Chris Paul .60 1.50
175 Tim Duncan .75 2.00
176 Baron Davis .25 .60
177 Elton Brand .25 .60
178 Kobe Bryant 2.50 6.00
179 Steve Nash .60 1.50
180 Mike Bibby .30 .75
181 Carmelo Anthony .50 1.25
182 Kevin Garnett .75 2.00
183 Zach Randolph .30 .75
184 Ray Allen .50 1.25
185 Carlos Boozer .25 .60
186 Paul Pierce .50 1.25
187 Vince Carter .60 1.50
188 Stephon Marbury .40 1.00
189 Andre Iguodala .30 .75
190 Chris Bosh .40 1.00
191 Michael Jordan 3.00 8.00
192 LeBron James 2.50 6.00
193 Chauncey Billups .40 1.00
194 Jermaine O'Neal .30 .75
195 Michael Redd .30 .75
196 Joe Johnson .25 .60
197 Emeka Okafor .25 .60
198 Dwyane Wade .60 1.50
199 Dwight Howard .40 1.00
200 Gilbert Arenas .30 .75
201 Greg Oden RC .50 1.25
202 Kevin Durant RC 25.00 60.00
203 Al Horford RC 1.25 3.00
204 Mike Conley Jr. RC 1.25 3.00
205 Jeff Green RC .40 1.00
206 Marcus Williams RC .30 .75
207 Corey Brewer RC .40 1.00
208 Brandan Wright RC .40 1.00
209 Joakim Noah RC .50 1.25
210 Spencer Hawes RC .30 .75
211 Acie Law RC .30 .75
212 Thaddeus Young RC .50 1.25
213 Julian Wright RC .30 .75
214 Al Thornton RC .30 .75
215 Rodney Stuckey RC .30 .75
216 Nick Young RC .50 1.25
217 Sean Williams RC .30 .75
218 Marco Belinelli RC .40 1.00
219 Javaris Crittenton RC .30 .75
220 Jason Smith RC .30 .75
221 Daequan Cook RC .40 1.00
222 Jared Dudley RC .40 1.00
223 Wilson Chandler RC .40 1.00
224 Morris Almond RC .30 .75
225 Aaron Brooks RC .40 1.00
226 Arron Afflalo RC .40 1.00
227 Alando Tucker RC .30 .75
228 Petteri Koponen RC .40 1.00
229 Carl Landry RC .50 1.25
230 Gabe Pruitt RC .30 .75

2007-08 Upper Deck First Edition Gold

*GOLD: .6X TO 1.5X BASE HI
APPROXIMATE ODDS 1:6

2007-08 Upper Deck First Edition All-NBA

COMPLETE SET (15) 6.00 15.00
APPROXIMATE ODDS 1:8
NBA1 Dirk Nowitzki 1.50 4.00
NBA2 Tim Duncan 1.50 4.00
NBA3 Amare Stoudemire .60 1.50
NBA4 Steve Nash 1.25 3.00
NBA5 Kobe Bryant 5.00 12.00
NBA6 LeBron James 5.00 12.00
NBA7 Chris Bosh .75 2.00
NBA8 Yao Ming 1.50 4.00
NBA9 Gilbert Arenas .60 1.50
NBA10 Tracy McGrady 1.00 2.50
NBA11 Kevin Garnett 1.50 4.00
NBA12 Carmelo Anthony 1.00 2.50
NBA13 Dwight Howard .75 2.00
NBA14 Dwyane Wade 1.25 3.00
NBA15 Chauncey Billups .75 2.00

2007-08 Upper Deck First Edition Behind the Glass

COMPLETE SET (25) 8.00 20.00
APPROXIMATE ODDS 1:5
BGAI Allen Iverson .75 2.00
BGAS Amare Stoudemire .30 .75
BGBO Carlos Boozer .25 .60
BGBW Ben Wallace .40 1.00
BGCA Carmelo Anthony .50 1.25
BGCB Chris Bosh .40 1.00
BGCP Chris Paul .60 1.50
BGDH Dwight Howard .40 1.00
BGDN Dirk Nowitzki .75 2.00
BGDW Dwyane Wade .60 1.50
BGGA Gilbert Arenas .30 .75
BGJR Jason Richardson .30 .75
BGKB Kobe Bryant 2.50 6.00
BGKG Kevin Garnett .75 2.00
BGLJ LeBron James 2.50 6.00
BGMA Shawn Marion .30 .75
BGMG Manu Ginobili .60 1.50
BGMJ Michael Jordan 3.00 8.00
BGPP Paul Pierce .50 1.25
BGSM Stephon Marbury .40 1.00
BGSN Steve Nash .60 1.50
BGSO Shaquille O'Neal 1.25 3.00
BGTD Tim Duncan .75 2.00
BGTM Tracy McGrady .50 1.25
BGYM Yao Ming .75 2.00

2007-08 Upper Deck First Edition Champions of the Court

COMPLETE SET (25) 8.00 20.00
APPROXIMATE ODDS 1:5
CCBR Bill Russell 1.25 3.00
CCBW Bill Walton .50 1.25
CCCB Chauncey Billups .50 1.25
CCDR Dennis Rodman 1.00 2.50
CCDW Dwyane Wade .75 2.00
CCGM George Mikan .75 2.00
CCHO Hakeem Olajuwon .75 2.00
CCJD Joe Dumars .40 1.00
CCJE Julius Erving 1.00 2.50
CCJH John Havlicek .75 2.00
CCJO Magic Johnson 1.50 4.00
CCJW James Worthy .60 1.50
CCKA Kareem Abdul-Jabbar 1.25 3.00
CCKB Kobe Bryant 3.00 8.00
CCLB Larry Bird 1.50 4.00
CCMG Manu Ginobili .75 2.00
CCMJ Michael Jordan 4.00 10.00
CCMM Moses Malone .60 1.50
CCRH Robert Horry .40 1.00
CCRO David Robinson .75 2.00
CCSK Steve Kerr .50 1.25
CCSO Shaquille O'Neal 1.50 4.00
CCTD Tim Duncan 1.00 2.50
CCTP Tony Parker .60 1.50
CCWC Wilt Chamberlain 1.25 3.00

2007-08 Upper Deck First Edition Draft Notices

COMPLETE SET (25) 8.00 20.00
APPROXIMATE ODDS 1:5
DN1 Greg Oden .40 1.00
DN2 Kevin Durant 4.00 10.00
DN3 Al Horford 1.00 2.50
DN4 Mike Conley Jr. 1.00 2.50
DN5 Jeff Green .30 .75
DN6 Alando Tucker .25 .60
DN7 Corey Brewer .30 .75
DN8 Brandan Wright .30 .75
DN9 Joakim Noah .40 1.00
DN10 Spencer Hawes .25 .60
DN11 Acie Law .25 .60
DN12 Thaddeus Young .40 1.00
DN13 Julian Wright .25 .60
DN14 Al Thornton .25 .60
DN15 Rodney Stuckey .25 .60
DN16 Nick Young .40 1.00
DN17 Sean Williams .25 .60
DN18 Javaris Crittenton .25 .60
DN19 Jason Smith .25 .60
DN20 Daequan Cook .30 .75
DN21 Jared Dudley .30 .75
DN22 Wilson Chandler .30 .75
DN23 Morris Almond .25 .60
DN24 Aaron Brooks .30 .75
DN25 Arron Afflalo .30 .75

2007-08 Upper Deck First Edition Kevin Durant Exclusive

COMPLETE SET (6) 6.00 15.00
COMMON CARD (KD1-KD6) 1.50 4.00

2008-09 Upper Deck First Edition

COMPLETE SET (266) 15.00 40.00
1 Mike Bibby .40 1.00
2 Al Horford .40 1.00
3 Joe Johnson .40 1.00
4 Josh Childress .25 .60
5 Josh Smith .25 .60
6 Marvin Williams .25 .60
7 Eddie House .25 .60
8 Glen Davis .25 .60
9 Sam Cassell .30 .75
10 Kevin Garnett 1.00 2.50
11 Rajon Rondo .50 1.25
12 Ray Allen .60 1.50
13 Paul Pierce .60 1.50
14 Adam Morrison .25 .60
15 Emeka Okafor .25 .60
16 Gerald Wallace .30 .75
17 Jared Dudley .30 .75
18 Jason Richardson .40 1.00
19 Nazr Mohammed .25 .60
20 Raymond Felton .25 .60
21 Andres Nocioni .25 .60
22 Ben Gordon .30 .75
23 Larry Hughes .30 .75
24 Joakim Noah .30 .75
25 Kirk Hinrich .30 .75
26 Luol Deng .30 .75
27 Tyrus Thomas .25 .60
28 Aleksandar Pavlovic .25 .60
29 Anderson Varejao .25 .60
30 Daniel Gibson .25 .60
31 Wally Szczerbiak .25 .60
32 Ben Wallace .50 1.25
33 LeBron James 3.00 8.00
34 Zydrunas Ilgauskas .30 .75
35 Jason Kidd .60 1.50
36 Dirk Nowitzki 1.00 2.50
37 Jason Terry .30 .75
38 Jerry Stackhouse .40 1.00
39 Jose Barea .50 1.25
40 Josh Howard .30 .75
41 Allen Iverson .75 2.00
42 Carmelo Anthony .50 1.25
43 J.R. Smith .40 1.00
44 Kenyon Martin .30 .75
45 Linas Kleiza .25 .60
46 Marcus Camby .30 .75
47 Antonio McDyess .30 .75
48 Chauncey Billups .50 1.25
49 Jason Maxiell .25 .60
50 Rasheed Wallace .50 1.25
51 Richard Hamilton .40 1.00
52 Rodney Stuckey .25 .60
53 Tayshaun Prince .40 1.00
54 Al Harrington .30 .75
55 Baron Davis .40 1.00
56 Kelenna Azubuike .25 .60
57 Matt Barnes .25 .60
58 Monta Ellis .30 .75
59 Stephen Jackson .30 .75
60 Luis Scola .30 .75
61 Luther Head .25 .60
62 Rafer Alston .25 .60
63 Shane Battier .30 .75
64 Tracy McGrady .60 1.50
65 Yao Ming 1.00 2.50
66 Andre Owens .25 .60
67 Danny Granger .30 .75
68 Jamaal Tinsley .25 .60
69 Jermaine O'Neal .40 1.00
70 Kareem Rush .25 .60
71 Mike Dunleavy .25 .60
72 Troy Murphy .25 .60
73 Al Thornton .25 .60
74 Chris Kaman .25 .60
75 Corey Maggette .25 .60
76 Cuttino Mobley .25 .60
77 Elton Brand .30 .75
78 Tim Thomas .25 .60
79 Andrew Bynum .30 .75
80 Derek Fisher .30 .75
81 Jordan Farmar .25 .60
82 Kobe Bryant 3.00 8.00
83 Pau Gasol .50 1.25
84 Lamar Odom .30 .75
85 Luke Walton .30 .75
86 Darko Milicic .25 .60
87 Javaris Crittenton .25 .60
88 Kyle Lowry .40 1.00
89 Mike Conley Jr. .30 .75
90 Mike Miller .30 .75
91 Kwame Brown .25 .60
92 Rudy Gay .40 1.00
93 Daequan Cook .25 .60
94 Dorell Wright .25 .60
95 Dwyane Wade .75 2.00
96 Jason Williams .30 .75
97 Ricky Davis .30 .75
98 Shawn Marion .40 1.00
99 Udonis Haslem .30 .75
100 Andrew Bogut .30 .75
101 Charlie Villanueva .25 .60
102 Desmond Mason .25 .60
103 Michael Redd .30 .75
104 Mo Williams .30 .75
105 Yi Jianlian .50 1.25
106 Al Jefferson .25 .60
107 Corey Brewer .30 .75
108 Craig Smith .25 .60
109 Randy Foye .40 1.00
110 Rashad McCants .25 .60
111 Ryan Gomes .25 .60
112 Sebastian Telfair .25 .60
113 Bostjan Nachbar .25 .60
114 Devin Harris .25 .60
115 Josh Boone .25 .60
116 Nenad Krstic .25 .60
117 Richard Jefferson .30 .75
118 Sean Williams .25 .60
119 Vince Carter .75 2.00
120 David Lee .25 .60
121 Eddy Curry .25 .60
122 Jamal Crawford .40 1.00
123 Nate Robinson .25 .60
124 Quentin Richardson .25 .60
125 Stephon Marbury .40 1.00
126 Zach Randolph .40 1.00
127 Chris Paul .75 2.00
128 David West .30 .75
129 Julian Wright .25 .60
130 Morris Peterson .25 .60
131 Peja Stojakovic .30 .75
132 Tyson Chandler .30 .75
133 Carlos Arroyo .25 .60
134 Dwight Howard .50 1.25
135 Hedo Turkoglu .30 .75
136 J.J. Redick .40 1.00
137 Jameer Nelson .25 .60
138 Maurice Evans .25 .60
139 Rashard Lewis .30 .75
140 Andre Iguodala .30 .75
141 Andre Miller .25 .60
142 Jason Smith .25 .60
143 Louis Williams .30 .75
144 Samuel Dalembert .25 .60
145 Thaddeus Young .30 .75
146 Willie Green .25 .60
147 Amare Stoudemire .40 1.00
148 Boris Diaw .30 .75
149 Grant Hill .60 1.50
150 Leandro Barbosa .30 .75
151 Raja Bell .30 .75
152 Shaquille O'Neal 1.25 3.00
153 Steve Nash .75 2.00
154 Brandon Roy .25 .60
155 Channing Frye .25 .60
156 Greg Oden .25 .60
157 LaMarcus Aldridge .40 1.00
158 Martell Webster .25 .60
159 Steve Blake .25 .60
160 Beno Udrih .25 .60
161 Brad Miller .25 .60
162 Francisco Garcia .25 .60
163 John Salmons .25 .60
164 Kevin Martin .30 .75
165 Mikki Moore .25 .60
166 Ron Artest .40 1.00
167 Brent Barry .25 .60
168 Bruce Bowen .30 .75
169 Manu Ginobili .75 2.00
170 Michael Finley .40 1.00
171 Robert Horry .30 .75
172 Tim Duncan 1.00 2.50
173 Tony Parker .50 1.25
174 Chris Wilcox .25 .60
175 Damien Wilkins .25 .60
176 Jeff Green .30 .75
177 Kevin Durant 1.50 4.00
178 Nick Collison .25 .60
179 Earl Watson .25 .60
180 Andrea Bargnani .30 .75
181 Anthony Parker .25 .60
182 Carlos Delfino .25 .60
183 Chris Bosh .50 1.25
184 Jamario Moon .25 .60
185 Jose Calderon .25 .60
186 T.J. Ford .25 .60
187 Andrei Kirilenko .30 .75
188 Carlos Boozer .25 .60
189 Deron Williams .30 .75
190 Kyle Korver .30 .75
191 Mehmet Okur .25 .60
192 Paul Millsap .25 .60
193 Ronnie Brewer .25 .60
194 Antawn Jamison .30 .75
195 Antonio Daniels .25 .60
196 Brendan Haywood .25 .60
197 Caron Butler .30 .75
198 DeShawn Stevenson .25 .60
199 Gilbert Arenas .40 1.00
200 Nick Young .30 .75
201 Spud Webb .30 .75
202 Bob Cousy .60 1.50
203 Kevin McHale .50 1.25
204 Larry Bird 1.25 3.00
205 Dennis Rodman .75 2.00
206 Michael Jordan 3.00 8.00
207 Isiah Thomas .60 1.50
208 Joe Dumars .40 1.00
209 Nate Thurmond .30 .75
210 Hakeem Olajuwon .75 2.00
211 Calvin Murphy .30 .75
212 Kareem Abdul-Jabbar .60 1.50
213 Magic Johnson 1.25 3.00
214 Oscar Robertson .40 1.00
215 Bill Bradley .50 1.25
216 Earl Monroe .40 1.00
217 Willis Reed .60 1.50
218 Julius Erving 1.00 2.50
219 Clyde Drexler .50 1.25
220 Bill Walton .60 1.50
221 Maurice Lucas .40 1.00
222 David Robinson .75 2.00
223 John Stockton .75 2.00
224 Karl Malone .50 1.25
225 D.J. Augustin .60 1.50
226 Brook Lopez .75 2.00
227 Jerryd Bayless .50 1.25
228 Jason Thompson .40 1.00
229 Brandon Rush .40 1.00
230 Anthony Randolph .40 1.00
231 Robin Lopez .50 1.25
232 Marreese Speights .50 1.25
233 Roy Hibbert .50 1.25
234 Courtney Lee .50 1.25
235 J.J. Hickson .40 1.00
236 Ryan Anderson .50 1.25
237 Kosta Koufos .40 1.00
238 James Gist .40 1.00
239 Darrell Arthur .50 1.25
240 Donte Greene .40 1.00
241 D.J. White .40 1.00
242 J.R. Giddens .40 1.00
243 Deron Washington .40 1.00
244 Joey Dorsey .40 1.00
245 Mario Chalmers .60 1.50
246 DeAndre Jordan .75 2.00
247 Luc Richard Mbah A Moute .50 1.25
248 Kyle Weaver .40 1.00
249 Sonny Weems .40 1.00
250 Chris Douglas-Roberts .40 1.00
251 Sean Singletary .40 1.00
252 Patrick Ewing Jr. .40 1.00
253 Shan Foster .40 1.00
254 Bill Walker .40 1.00
255 Malik Hairston .40 1.00
256 Richard Hendrix .40 1.00
257 DeVon Hardin .40 1.00
258 Darnell Jackson .40 1.00
259 Derrick Rose 2.50 6.00
260 Michael Beasley .60 1.50
261 O.J. Mayo .50 1.25
262 Russell Westbrook 8.00 20.00
263 Kevin Love 1.25 3.00
264 Danilo Gallinari 1.00 2.50
265 Eric Gordon 1.00 2.50
266 Joe Alexander .40 1.00

2008-09 Upper Deck First Edition Gold

*GOLD: .5X TO 1.25X BASE HI
ONE PER PACK
33 LeBron James 12.00 30.00
82 Kobe Bryant 12.00 30.00
177 Kevin Durant 12.00 30.00
262 Russell Westbrook 15.00 40.00

2008-09 Upper Deck First Edition Chalk Talk

COMPLETE SET (30) 4.00 10.00
APPROXIMATE ODDS 1:2 PACKS
CT1 Joe Johnson .30 .75
CT2 Paul Pierce .50 1.25
CT3 Gerald Wallace .25 .60
CT4 Ben Gordon .25 .60
CT5 LeBron James 2.50 6.00
CT6 Josh Howard .25 .60
CT7 Allen Iverson .60 1.50
CT8 Richard Hamilton .30 .75
CT9 Stephen Jackson .25 .60
CT10 Tracy McGrady .50 1.25
CT11 Danny Granger .25 .60
CT12 Corey Maggette .25 .60
CT13 Kobe Bryant 2.50 6.00
CT14 Pau Gasol .40 1.00
CT15 Dwyane Wade .60 1.50
CT16 Yi Jianlian .40 1.00
CT17 Al Jefferson .20 .50
CT18 Richard Jefferson .25 .60
CT19 Chris Paul .60 1.50
CT20 Jamal Crawford .30 .75
CT21 Dwight Howard .40 1.00
CT22 Andre Iguodala .25 .60
CT23 Amare Stoudemire .30 .75
CT24 LaMarcus Aldridge .30 .75
CT25 Mike Bibby .30 .75
CT26 Tony Parker .40 1.00
CT27 Kevin Durant 1.25 3.00
CT28 T.J. Ford .25 .60
CT29 Deron Williams .25 .60
CT30 Antawn Jamison .25 .60

2008-09 Upper Deck First Edition Rookie Standouts

COMPLETE SET (30) 30.00 60.00
RSAR Anthony Randolph .60 1.50
RSBL Brook Lopez 1.25 3.00
RSBR Brandon Rush .60 1.50
RSBW Bill Walker .60 1.50
RSCD Chris Douglas-Roberts .60 1.50
RSCL Courtney Lee .75 2.00
RSDA D.J. Augustin 1.00 2.50
RSDG Danilo Gallinari 1.50 4.00
RSDR Derrick Rose 4.00 10.00
RSDW D.J. White .60 1.50
RSEG Eric Gordon 1.50 4.00
RSJA Joe Alexander .60 1.50
RSJB Jerryd Bayless .75 2.00
RSJD Joey Dorsey .60 1.50
RSJG James Gist .60 1.50
RSJH J.J. Hickson .60 1.50
RSJT Jason Thompson .60 1.50
RSKK Kosta Koufos .60 1.50
RSKL Kevin Love 2.00 5.00
RSLM Luc Richard Mbah A Moute .75 2.00
RSMB Michael Beasley 1.00 2.50
RSMC Mario Chalmers 1.00 2.50
RSMS Marreese Speights .75 2.00
RSOM O.J. Mayo .75 2.00
RSPE Patrick Ewing Jr. .60 1.50
RSRA Ryan Anderson .75 2.00
RSRH Roy Hibbert .75 2.00
RSRL Robin Lopez .75 2.00
RSRW Russell Westbrook 5.00 12.00
RSSW Sonny Weems .60 1.50

2008-09 Upper Deck First Edition Starquest Green

COMPLETE SET (30) 15.00 40.00
ONE PER PACK
SQ1 Carmelo Anthony .50 1.25
SQ2 Chauncey Billups .50 1.25
SQ3 Larry Bird 1.25 3.00
SQ4 Chris Bosh .50 1.25
SQ5 Kobe Bryant 4.00 10.00
SQ6 Vince Carter .75 2.00
SQ7 Baron Davis .40 1.00
SQ8 Tim Duncan 1.00 2.50
SQ9 Kevin Durant 4.00 10.00
SQ10 Julius Erving 1.00 2.50
SQ11 Walt Frazier .40 1.00
SQ12 Kevin Garnett 1.00 2.50
SQ13 Rudy Gay .40 1.00
SQ14 Artis Gilmore .30 .75
SQ15 Dwight Howard .50 1.25
SQ16 Allen Iverson .75 2.00
SQ17 LeBron James 4.00 10.00
SQ18 Al Jefferson .25 .60
SQ19 Magic Johnson 1.25 3.00
SQ20 Michael Jordan 5.00 12.00
SQ21 Shawn Marion .40 1.00
SQ22 Tracy McGrady .60 1.50
SQ23 Yao Ming 1.00 2.50
SQ24 Dirk Nowitzki 1.00 2.50
SQ25 Shaquille O'Neal 1.25 3.00
SQ26 Greg Oden .25 .60
SQ27 Chris Paul .75 2.00
SQ28 Brandon Roy .30 .75
SQ29 Dwyane Wade .75 2.00
SQ30 Deron Williams .30 .75

2009-10 Upper Deck First Edition

COMPLETE SET (200) 20.00 50.00
1 Josh Smith .25 .60
2 Al Horford .40 1.00
3 Mike Bibby .40 1.00
4 Joe Johnson .40 1.00
5 Marvin Williams .25 .60
6 Kevin Garnett 1.00 2.50
7 Paul Pierce .60 1.50
8 Ray Allen .60 1.50
9 Rajon Rondo .50 1.25
10 Kendrick Perkins .25 .60
11 Raymond Felton .25 .60
12 Raja Bell .30 .75
13 D.J. Augustin .25 .60
14 Gerald Wallace .30 .75
15 Boris Diaw .30 .75
16 Emeka Okafor .30 .75
17 Derrick Rose .60 1.50
18 Luol Deng .30 .75
19 Ben Gordon .30 .75
20 John Salmons .30 .75
21 Joakim Noah .25 .60
22 Tyrus Thomas .25 .60
23 Michael Jordan 3.00 8.00
24 LeBron James 3.00 8.00
25 Mo Williams .30 .75
26 Ben Wallace .50 1.25
27 Delonte West .25 .60
28 Zydrunas Ilgauskas .30 .75
29 Wally Szczerbiak .30 .75
30 Josh Howard .30 .75
31 Dirk Nowitzki 1.00 2.50
32 Jason Kidd .60 1.50
33 Erick Dampier .25 .60
34 Jason Terry .30 .75
35 Chauncey Billups .50 1.25
36 Carmelo Anthony .60 1.50
37 Kenyon Martin .30 .75
38 Nene .30 .75
39 J.R. Smith .40 1.00
40 Allen Iverson .75 2.00
41 Richard Hamilton .40 1.00
42 Tayshaun Prince .40 1.00
43 Rodney Stuckey .25 .60
44 Amir Johnson .25 .60
45 Rasheed Wallace .50 1.25
46 Monta Ellis .30 .75
47 Stephen Jackson .30 .75
48 Jamal Crawford .40 1.00
49 Kelenna Azubuike .25 .60
50 Andris Biedrins .25 .60
51 Corey Maggette .30 .75
52 Luis Scola .30 .75
53 Tracy McGrady .75 2.00
54 Yao Ming 1.00 2.50
55 Ron Artest .40 1.00
56 Shane Battier .40 1.00
57 Von Wafer .25 .60
58 T.J. Ford .25 .60
59 Danny Granger .25 .60
60 Mike Dunleavy .25 .60
61 Troy Murphy .25 .60
62 Jeff Foster .25 .60
63 Jarrett Jack .30 .75
64 Eric Gordon .30 .75
65 Baron Davis .30 .75
66 Al Thornton .25 .60
67 Zach Randolph .40 1.00
68 Chris Kaman .30 .75
69 Kobe Bryant 3.00 8.00
70 Pau Gasol .60 1.50
71 Lamar Odom .40 1.00
72 Derek Fisher .40 1.00
73 Andrew Bynum .25 .60
74 Sasha Vujacic .25 .60
75 Trevor Ariza .25 .60
76 O.J. Mayo .25 .60
77 Marc Gasol .40 1.00
78 Rudy Gay .40 1.00
79 Darrell Arthur .25 .60
80 Marko Jaric .25 .60
81 Mike Conley Jr. .30 .75
82 Michael Beasley .25 .60
83 Mario Chalmers .30 .75
84 Dwyane Wade .75 2.00
85 Chris Quinn .25 .60
86 Udonis Haslem .25 .60
87 Daequan Cook .25 .60
88 Jermaine O'Neal .40 1.00
89 Luke Ridnour .25 .60
90 Michael Redd .30 .75
91 Richard Jefferson .30 .75
92 Charlie Villanueva .25 .60
93 Andrew Bogut .30 .75
94 Ramon Sessions .25 .60
95 Kevin Love .40 1.00
96 Sebastian Telfair .25 .60
97 Al Jefferson .25 .60
98 Randy Foye .25 .60
99 Mike Miller .30 .75
100 Devin Harris .25 .60
101 Vince Carter .75 2.00
102 Yi Jianlian .50 1.25
103 Brook Lopez .40 1.00
104 Chris Douglas-Roberts .25 .60
105 Eduardo Najera .25 .60
106 Chris Paul .75 2.00
107 Peja Stojakovic .30 .75
108 David West .30 .75
109 Tyson Chandler .30 .75
110 James Posey .25 .60
111 Al Harrington .30 .75
112 Chris Duhon .25 .60
113 Quentin Richardson .25 .60
114 David Lee .25 .60
115 Jared Jeffries .25 .60
116 Wilson Chandler .30 .75
117 Danilo Gallinari .30 .75
118 Russell Westbrook .75 2.00
119 Kevin Durant 1.50 4.00
120 Jeff Green .30 .75
121 Desmond Mason .25 .60
122 Nick Collison .25 .60
123 Earl Watson .25 .60
124 Dwight Howard .50 1.25
125 Courtney Lee .25 .60
126 Hedo Turkoglu .30 .75
127 Jameer Nelson .25 .60
128 Rashard Lewis .30 .75
129 Mickael Pietrus .25 .60
130 Elton Brand .30 .75
131 Andre Miller .40 1.00
132 Andre Iguodala .40 1.00
133 Thaddeus Young .25 .60
134 Willie Green .25 .60
135 Samuel Dalembert .25 .60
136 Jason Richardson .40 1.00
137 Shaquille O'Neal 1.25 3.00
138 Steve Nash .75 2.00
139 Grant Hill .60 1.50
140 Amare Stoudemire .30 .75
141 Leandro Barbosa .30 .75
142 Robin Lopez .25 .60
143 Brandon Roy .50 1.25
144 LaMarcus Aldridge .40 1.00
145 Jerryd Bayless .25 .60
146 Rudy Fernandez .25 .60
147 Steve Blake .25 .60
148 Martell Webster .25 .60
149 Greg Oden .25 .60
150 Kevin Martin .30 .75
151 Beno Udrih .25 .60
152 Francisco Garcia .25 .60
153 Tim Duncan 1.00 2.50
154 Tony Parker .60 1.50
155 Manu Ginobili .75 2.00
156 Roger Mason .25 .60
157 Michael Finley .40 1.00
158 George Hill .30 .75
159 Chris Bosh .50 1.25
160 Jose Calderon .25 .60
161 Andrea Bargnani .25 .60
162 Anthony Parker .25 .60
163 Deron Williams .30 .75
164 Carlos Boozer .25 .60
165 Ronnie Brewer .25 .60
166 C.J. Miles .25 .60
167 Mehmet Okur .25 .60
168 Kyle Korver .30 .75
169 Andrei Kirilenko .30 .75
170 Gilbert Arenas .30 .75
171 Antawn Jamison .30 .75
172 DeShawn Stevenson .25 .60
173 Caron Butler .30 .75
174 Brendan Haywood .25 .60
175 Nick Young .25 .60
176 B.J. Mullens RC .40 1.00
177 Blake Griffin RC 2.50 6.00
178 Brandon Jennings RC .60 1.50
179 Chase Budinger RC .40 1.00
180 DaJuan Summers RC .40 1.00
181 Darren Collison RC .60 1.50
182 DeJuan Blair RC .50 1.25
183 Earl Clark RC .40 1.00
184 Eric Maynor RC .40 1.00
185 Gerald Henderson RC .40 1.00
186 Taj Gibson RC .50 1.25
187 Hasheem Thabeet RC .40 1.00
188 James Harden RC 4.00 10.00
189 Jeff Teague RC .50 1.25
190 Jonny Flynn RC .40 1.00
191 Jordan Hill RC .40 1.00
192 Jrue Holiday RC 2.00 5.00
193 Omri Casspi RC .40 1.00
194 Austin Daye RC .40 1.00
195 Sam Young RC .40 1.00
196 Stephen Curry RC 75.00 200.00
197 Terrence Williams RC .40 1.00
198 Ty Lawson RC .50 1.25
199 Tyler Hansbrough RC .50 1.25
200 Tyreke Evans RC .50 1.25

2009-10 Upper Deck First Edition Gold

*1-175 GOLD: .75X TO 2X BASE HI
*176-200 GOLD: .5X TO 1.25X BASE HI
GOLD CARDS ONE PER PACK
23 Michael Jordan 4.00 10.00

2009-10 Upper Deck First Edition Behind the Arc

COMPLETE SET (25) 5.00 12.00
INSERT ODDS TWO PER PACK
BA1 Rashard Lewis .40 1.00
BA2 Danny Granger .30 .75
BA3 Ray Allen .75 2.00
BA4 Mike Bibby .50 1.25
BA5 Ben Gordon .40 1.00
BA6 Roger Mason .30 .75
BA7 Peja Stojakovic .40 1.00
BA8 Daequan Cook .30 .75
BA9 Al Harrington .40 1.00
BA10 Rudy Fernandez .30 .75
BA11 Troy Murphy .30 .75
BA12 Chauncey Billups .60 1.50
BA13 Mo Williams .40 1.00
BA14 Jason Terry .40 1.00
BA15 O.J. Mayo .30 .75
BA16 Hedo Turkoglu .40 1.00
BA17 Joe Johnson .50 1.25
BA18 Jamal Crawford .50 1.25
BA19 J.R. Smith .50 1.25
BA20 Ron Artest .50 1.25
BA21 Vince Carter 1.00 2.50

BA22 Eddie House .30 .75
BA23 Quentin Richardson .30 .75
BA24 Chris Duhon .30 .75
BA25 Rasual Butler .30 .75

2009-10 Upper Deck First Edition Rejected!

COMPLETE SET (25) 6.00 15.00
INSERT ODDS TWO PER PACK
R1 Dwight Howard .60 1.50
R2 Ronny Turiaf .30 .75
R3 Lamar Odom .40 1.00
R4 Marcus Camby .40 1.00
R5 Tim Duncan 1.25 3.00
R6 Emeka Okafor .40 1.00
R7 Samuel Dalembert .30 .75
R8 Tyrus Thomas .30 .75
R9 Chris Andersen .50 1.25
R10 Yao Ming 1.25 3.00
R11 Kendrick Perkins .30 .75
R12 Jermaine O'Neal .50 1.25
R13 Andrew Bynum .30 .75
R14 Al Jefferson .30 .75
R15 Danny Granger .30 .75
R16 Andris Biedrins .30 .75
R17 Dwyane Wade 1.00 2.50
R18 Joakim Noah .30 .75
R19 Spencer Hawes .30 .75
R20 Nene .40 1.00
R21 Erick Dampier .30 .75
R22 Ben Wallace .60 1.50
R23 Shaquille O'Neal 1.50 4.00
R24 Rasheed Wallace .60 1.50
R25 Josh Smith .30 .75

2009-10 Upper Deck First Edition Slam Dunk

COMPLETE SET 15.00 30.00
INSERT ODDS TWO PER PACK
SD1 Josh Smith .40 1.00
SD2 Dwight Howard .75 2.00
SD3 Nate Robinson .50 1.25
SD4 Gerald Green .50 1.25
SD5 LeBron James 5.00 12.00
SD6 Kobe Bryant 5.00 12.00
SD7 Amare Stoudemire .50 1.25
SD8 Shawn Marion .60 1.50
SD9 Carmelo Anthony 1.00 2.50
SD10 Dwyane Wade 1.25 3.00
SD11 Pau Gasol 1.00 2.50
SD12 Andre Iguodala .60 1.50
SD13 Ben Wallace .75 2.00
SD14 Richard Jefferson .50 1.25
SD15 Vince Carter 1.25 3.00
SD16 Kenyon Martin .50 1.25
SD17 Kevin Garnett 1.50 4.00
SD18 Chris Bosh .75 2.00
SD19 Jason Richardson .60 1.50
SD20 Tim Duncan 1.50 4.00
SD21 Yao Ming 1.50 4.00
SD22 Shaquille O'Neal 2.00 5.00
SD23 Gerald Wallace .50 1.25
SD24 Tyson Chandler .50 1.25
SD25 Andrew Bynum .40 1.00

2009-10 Upper Deck First Edition Star Attractions

COMPLETE SET (25) 15.00 30.00
INSERT ODDS TWO PER PACK
SA1 Kobe Bryant 5.00 12.00
SA2 LeBron James 5.00 12.00
SA3 Carmelo Anthony 1.00 2.50
SA4 Kevin Durant 2.50 6.00
SA5 Tim Duncan 1.50 4.00
SA6 Deron Williams .50 1.25
SA7 Steve Nash 1.25 3.00
SA8 Allen Iverson 1.25 3.00
SA9 Chauncey Billups .75 2.00
SA10 Kevin Garnett 1.50 4.00
SA11 Paul Pierce 1.00 2.50
SA12 Jason Kidd 1.00 2.50
SA13 Dirk Nowitzki 1.50 4.00
SA14 Chris Bosh .75 2.00
SA15 Vince Carter 1.25 3.00
SA16 Michael Redd .50 1.25
SA17 Brandon Roy .75 2.00
SA18 Tracy McGrady 1.25 3.00
SA19 Chris Paul 1.25 3.00
SA20 Dwight Howard .75 2.00
SA21 Danny Granger .40 1.00
SA22 Kevin Martin .50 1.25
SA23 Devin Harris .40 1.00
SA24 Gilbert Arenas .50 1.25
SA25 Joe Johnson .60 1.50

2001-02 Upper Deck Flight Team

COMPLETE SET (240) 60.00 120.00
COMP.SET w/o SP's (90) 10.00 25.00
91-120 PRINT RUN 1500 PER PLAYER
91-120 THREE VERSIONS SER.#'d TO 500
121-134 PRINT RUN 1125 PER PLAYER
121-134 THREE VERSIONS SER.#'d TO 375
135-140 PRINT RUN 750 PER PLAYER
135-140 THREE VERSIONS SER.#'d TO 250
1 Michael Jordan 3.00 8.00
2 Dirk Nowitzki 1.00 2.50
3 Antawn Jamison .30 .75
4 Latrell Sprewell .50 1.25
5 Peja Stojakovic .30 .75
6 Dikembe Mutombo .60 1.50
7 Jason Williams .60 1.50
8 Kobe Bryant 3.00 8.00
9 Baron Davis .40 1.00
10 Wally Szczerbiak .30 .75
11 Reggie Miller .75 2.00
12 Marcus Fizer .25 .60
13 Desmond Mason .30 .75
14 Glenn Robinson .40 1.00
15 Vince Carter .75 2.00
16 James Posey .25 .60
17 Darius Miles .25 .60
18 Jason Kidd .60 1.50
19 Anfernee Hardaway 1.00 2.50
20 Karl Malone .75 2.00
21 Kevin Garnett 1.00 2.50
22 Shareef Abdur-Rahim .30 .75
23 Steve Francis .40 1.00
24 Paul Pierce .60 1.50
25 Mike Miller .30 .75
26 Tim Duncan 1.00 2.50
27 Derek Anderson .25 .60
28 Eddie Jones .40 1.00
29 Keith Van Horn .30 .75
30 Chris Mihm .25 .60
31 Clifford Robinson .40 1.00
32 Gary Payton .60 1.50
33 Courtney Alexander .25 .60
34 Shaquille O'Neal 1.50 4.00
35 Tim Thomas .25 .60
36 Raef LaFrentz .25 .60
37 Stromile Swift .25 .60
38 Stephon Marbury .50 1.25
39 Morris Peterson .25 .60
40 Donyell Marshall .25 .60
41 Kenny Thomas .25 .60
42 Juwan Howard .30 .75
43 Tracy McGrady .60 1.50
44 Kenny Anderson .30 .75
45 Larry Hughes .30 .75
46 Allan Houston .40 1.00
47 Chris Webber .50 1.25
48 Andre Miller .30 .75
49 Corey Maggette .30 .75
50 Sam Cassell .30 .75
51 Steve Smith .30 .75
52 Jamal Mashburn .30 .75
53 Al Harrington .30 .75
54 Brian Grant .25 .60
55 Rasheed Wallace .50 1.25
56 Rick Fox .30 .75
57 Jason Terry .40 1.00
58 Rashard Lewis .30 .75
59 Joe Smith .30 .75
60 Michael Dickerson .25 .60
61 Michael Finley .40 1.00
62 Danny Fortson .25 .60
63 Allen Iverson 1.00 2.50
64 Richard Hamilton .50 1.25
65 Antonio McDyess .30 .75
66 David Wesley .25 .60
67 Ben Wallace .50 1.25
68 Mike Bibby .40 1.00
69 Antonio Davis .30 .75
70 Cuttino Mobley .30 .75
71 Lamond Murray .25 .60
72 Antoine Walker .30 .75
73 Jermaine O'Neal .30 .75
74 Alonzo Mourning .60 1.50
75 Shawn Marion .40 1.00
76 John Stockton .75 2.00
77 Marcus Camby .30 .75
78 Derek Fisher .30 .75
79 DerMarr Johnson .25 .60
80 Aaron McKie .25 .60
81 David Robinson .75 2.00
82 Steve Nash .75 2.00
83 Ray Allen .60 1.50
84 Elton Brand .30 .75
85 Kenyon Martin .40 1.00
86 Bonzi Wells .25 .60
87 Grant Hill .60 1.50
88 Terrell Brandon .30 .75
89 Toni Kukoc .50 1.25
90 Jerry Stackhouse .40 1.00
91A Tierre Brown RC .75 2.00
91B Tierre Brown RC .75 2.00
91C Tierre Brown RC .75 2.00
92A Jamison Brewer RC .75 2.00
92B Jamison Brewer RC .75 2.00
92C Jamison Brewer RC .75 2.00
93A Antonis Fotsis RC .50 1.25
93B Antonis Fotsis RC .50 1.25
93C Antonis Fotsis RC .50 1.25
94A Mike James RC .75 2.00
94B Mike James RC .75 2.00
94C Mike James RC .75 2.00
95A Primoz Brezec RC .75 2.00
95B Primoz Brezec RC .75 2.00
95C Primoz Brezec RC .75 2.00
96A Jeryl Sasser RC .50 1.25
96B Jeryl Sasser RC .50 1.25
96C Jeryl Sasser RC .50 1.25
97A DeSagana Diop RC .50 1.25
97B DeSagana Diop RC .50 1.25
97C DeSagana Diop RC .50 1.25
98A Mengke Bateer RC 1.25 3.00
98B Mengke Bateer RC 1.25 3.00
98C Mengke Bateer RC 1.25 3.00
99A Gerald Wallace RC 1.00 2.50
99B Gerald Wallace RC 1.00 2.50
99C Gerald Wallace RC 1.00 2.50
100A Kenny Satterfield RC .50 1.25
100B Kenny Satterfield RC .50 1.25
100C Kenny Satterfield RC .50 1.25
101A Ruben Boumtje-Boumtje RC .60 1.50
101B Ruben Boumtje-Boumtje RC .60 1.50
101C Ruben Boumtje-Boumtje RC .60 1.50
102A Brian Scalabrine RC .75 2.00
102B Brian Scalabrine RC .75 2.00
102C Brian Scalabrine RC .75 2.00
103A Oscar Torres RC .75 2.00
103B Oscar Torres RC .75 2.00
103C Oscar Torres RC .75 2.00
104A Jarron Collins RC .75 2.00
104B Jarron Collins RC .75 2.00
104C Jarron Collins RC .75 2.00
105A Jeff Trepagnier RC .50 1.25
105B Jeff Trepagnier RC .50 1.25
105C Jeff Trepagnier RC .50 1.25
106A Brendan Haywood RC .60 1.50
106B Brendan Haywood RC .60 1.50
106C Brendan Haywood RC .60 1.50
107A Vladimir Radmanovic RC .60 1.50
107B Vladimir Radmanovic RC .60 1.50
107C Vladimir Radmanovic RC .60 1.50
108A Loren Woods RC .50 1.25
108B Loren Woods RC .50 1.25
108C Loren Woods RC .50 1.25
109A Terence Morris RC .50 1.25
109B Terence Morris RC .50 1.25
109C Terence Morris RC .50 1.25
110A Kirk Haston RC .50 1.25
110B Kirk Haston RC .50 1.25
110C Kirk Haston RC .50 1.25
111A Earl Watson RC .60 1.50
111B Earl Watson RC .60 1.50
111C Earl Watson RC .60 1.50
112A Brandon Armstrong RC .50 1.25
112B Brandon Armstrong RC .50 1.25
112C Brandon Armstrong RC .50 1.25
113A Zach Randolph RC 1.50 4.00
113B Zach Randolph RC 1.50 4.00
113C Zach Randolph RC 1.50 4.00
114A Bobby Simmons RC .75 2.00
114B Bobby Simmons RC .75 2.00
114C Bobby Simmons RC .75 2.00
115A Alton Ford RC .75 2.00
115B Alton Ford RC .75 2.00
115C Alton Ford RC .75 2.00
116A Predrag Drobnjak RC .75 2.00
116B Predrag Drobnjak RC .75 2.00
116C Predrag Drobnjak RC .75 2.00
117A Michael Bradley RC .50 1.25
117B Michael Bradley RC .50 1.25
117C Michael Bradley RC .50 1.25
118A Samuel Dalembert RC .75 2.00
118B Samuel Dalembert RC .75 2.00
118C Samuel Dalembert RC .75 2.00
119A Gilbert Arenas RC 2.00 5.00
119B Gilbert Arenas RC 2.00 5.00
119C Gilbert Arenas RC 2.00 5.00
120A Kedrick Brown RC .50 1.25
120B Kedrick Brown RC .50 1.25
120C Kedrick Brown RC .50 1.25
121A Trenton Hassell RC .60 1.50
121B Trenton Hassell RC .60 1.50
121C Trenton Hassell RC .60 1.50
122A Zeljko Rebraca RC 1.00 2.50
122B Zeljko Rebraca RC 1.00 2.50
122C Zeljko Rebraca RC 1.00 2.50
123A Jason Collins RC .75 2.00
123B Jason Collins RC .75 2.00
123C Jason Collins RC .75 2.00
124A Will Solomon RC .75 2.00
124B Will Solomon RC .75 2.00
124C Will Solomon RC .75 2.00
125A Joseph Forte RC .60 1.50
125B Joseph Forte RC .60 1.50
125C Joseph Forte RC .60 1.50
126A Steven Hunter RC .60 1.50
126B Steven Hunter RC .60 1.50
126C Steven Hunter RC .60 1.50
127A Eddy Curry RC 1.00 2.50
127B Eddy Curry RC 1.00 2.50
127C Eddy Curry RC 1.00 2.50
128A Troy Murphy RC .75 2.00
128B Troy Murphy RC .75 2.00
128C Troy Murphy RC .75 2.00
129A Shane Battier RC 2.00 5.00
129B Shane Battier RC 2.00 5.00
129C Shane Battier RC 2.00 5.00
130A Tyson Chandler RC 1.50 4.00
130B Tyson Chandler RC 1.50 4.00
130C Tyson Chandler RC 1.50 4.00
131A Joe Johnson RC 1.50 4.00
131B Joe Johnson RC 1.50 4.00
131C Joe Johnson RC 1.50 4.00
132A Richard Jefferson RC 1.25 3.00
132B Richard Jefferson RC 1.25 3.00
132C Richard Jefferson RC 1.25 3.00
133A Eddie Griffin RC .75 2.00
133B Eddie Griffin RC .75 2.00
133C Eddie Griffin RC .75 2.00
134A Rodney White RC .60 1.50
134B Rodney White RC .60 1.50
134C Rodney White RC .60 1.50
135A Andrei Kirilenko RC 2.00 5.00
135B Andrei Kirilenko RC 2.00 5.00
135C Andrei Kirilenko RC 2.00 5.00
136A Tony Parker RC 5.00 12.00
136B Tony Parker RC 5.00 12.00
136C Tony Parker RC 5.00 12.00
137A Jamaal Tinsley RC 1.00 2.50
137B Jamaal Tinsley RC 1.00 2.50
137C Jamaal Tinsley RC 1.00 2.50
138A Pau Gasol RC 5.00 12.00
138B Pau Gasol RC 5.00 12.00
138C Pau Gasol RC 5.00 12.00
139A Jason Richardson RC 2.00 5.00
139B Jason Richardson RC 2.00 5.00
139C Jason Richardson RC 2.00 5.00
140A Kwame Brown RC 1.25 3.00
140B Kwame Brown RC 1.25 3.00
140C Kwame Brown RC 1.25 3.00

2001-02 Upper Deck Flight Team Copper

*COPPER STARS: 5X TO 12X BASE CARD HI
*COPPER RC/500: 2X TO 5X BASE CARD HI
*COPPER RC/375: 1.5X TO 4X BASE CARD HI
*COPPER RC/250: 1.25X TO 3X BASE CARD HI
COPPER PRINT RUN 125 SER.#'d SETS
1 Michael Jordan 150.00 400.00
8 Kobe Bryant 75.00 200.00

2001-02 Upper Deck Flight Team Gold

*GOLD STARS: 10X TO 25X BASE CARD HI
*GOLD RC/500: 4X TO 10X BASE CARD HI
*GOLD RC/350: 3X TO 8X BASE CARD HI
*GOLD RC/250: 2.5X TO 6X BASE CARD HI
GOLD PRINT RUN 50 SER.#'d SETS
1 Michael Jordan 400.00 800.00
8 Kobe Bryant 150.00 400.00

2001-02 Upper Deck Flight Team 2 the Air

PRINT RUN 100 SER.#'d SETS
2AI Allen Iverson 20.00 50.00
2CW Chris Webber 10.00 25.00
2KB Kobe Bryant 125.00 300.00
2KG Kevin Garnett 20.00 50.00
2MC Tracy McGrady 12.00 30.00
2MJ Michael Jordan 300.00 600.00

2001-02 Upper Deck Flight Team Flight Patterns

STATED ODDS 1:14
*GOLD: .75X TO 2X FLT.PAT HI
GOLD PRINT RUN 125 SER.#'d SETS
AH Anfernee Hardaway 10.00 25.00
AJ Antawn Jamison 3.00 8.00
AL Al Harrington 3.00 8.00
AM Andre Miller 3.00 8.00
BD Baron Davis 4.00 10.00
BR Bryon Russell 2.50 6.00
CM Corey Maggette 3.00 8.00
DG Devean George 2.50 6.00
DM Desmond Mason 3.00 8.00
DS DeShawn Stevenson 2.50 6.00
GH Grant Hill 6.00 15.00
JK Jason Kidd 6.00 15.00
JM Jamal Mashburn 3.00 8.00
JS Jerry Stackhouse 4.00 10.00
JT Jason Terry 4.00 10.00
KE Kedrick Brown 2.50 6.00
KV Keith Van Horn 3.00 8.00
KW Kwame Brown 4.00 10.00
LO Lamar Odom 3.00 8.00
MF Marcus Fizer 2.50 6.00
MP Morris Peterson 2.50 6.00
QR Quentin Richardson 2.50 6.00
SH Shawn Marion 4.00 10.00
WS Wally Szczerbiak 3.00 8.00

2001-02 Upper Deck Flight Team Key Signatures

PRINT RUN 23 TO 100 SER.#'d SETS
BAS Brandon Armstrong/100 5.00 12.00
CWS Kenyon Martin/100 15.00 40.00
ECS Eddy Curry/100 8.00 20.00
JKS Jason Kidd/100 60.00 150.00
JRS Jason Richardson/100 12.00 30.00
JTS Jamaal Tinsley/100 6.00 15.00
KBS Kobe Bryant/100 3,000.00 6,000.00
KGS Kevin Garnett/100 150.00 400.00
KWS Kwame Brown/100 8.00 20.00
MJS Michael Jordan/23 6,000.00 12,000.00
RJS Richard Jefferson/100 10.00 25.00
SDS Samuel Dalembert/100 8.00 20.00
TCS Tyson Chandler/100 12.00 30.00
TMS Troy Murphy/100 6.00 15.00
TPS Tony Parker/100 100.00 250.00

2001-02 Upper Deck Flight Team Superstar Flight Patterns

PRINT RUN 100 SER.#'d SETS
*GOLD: 1.25X TO 3X HI
GOLD PRINT RUN 25 SER.#'d SETS
AI Allen Iverson 20.00 50.00
CW Chris Webber 12.00 30.00
KB Kobe Bryant 125.00 300.00
KG Kevin Garnett 15.00 40.00
MC Tracy McGrady 15.00 40.00
MJ Michael Jordan 200.00 500.00

2001-02 Upper Deck Flight Team UD Jersey Jams

STATED ODDS 1:19
*GOLD: 1.25X TO 3X JSY JAM HI
GOLD PRINT RUN 50 SER.#'d SETS
AWJ Antoine Walker 3.00 8.00
BDJ Baron Davis 4.00 10.00
DMJ Darius Miles 2.50 6.00
ECJ Eddy Curry 4.00 10.00
EGJ Eddie Griffin 3.00 8.00
GRJ Glenn Robinson 4.00 10.00
JKJ Jason Kidd 6.00 15.00
JRJ Jason Richardson 6.00 15.00
JSJ Jeryl Sasser 2.50 6.00
KBJ Kobe Bryant 75.00 200.00
KGJ Kevin Garnett 10.00 25.00
KMJ Karl Malone 8.00 20.00
LOJ Lamar Odom 3.00 8.00
MJJ Michael Jordan 125.00 300.00
PPJ Paul Pierce 6.00 15.00
RJJ Richard Jefferson 5.00 12.00
RLJ Rashard Lewis 3.00 8.00
SAJ Shareef Abdur-Rahim 3.00 8.00
SFJ Steve Francis 4.00 10.00
SHJ Steven Hunter 2.50 6.00
SMJ Stephon Marbury 5.00 12.00
TCJ Tyson Chandler 6.00 15.00
TMJ Troy Murphy 3.00 8.00
WSJ Wally Szczerbiak 3.00 8.00

1993 Upper Deck French McDonald's

COMPLETE SET (40) 15.00 40.00
1 Charles Barkley 2.00 5.00
2 Muggsy Bogues .60 1.50
3 Derrick Coleman .30 .75
4 Brad Daugherty .20 .50
5 Vlade Divac .40 1.00
6 Clyde Drexler 1.50 4.00
7 Joe Dumars .75 2.00
8 Pervis Ellison .20 .50
9 Patrick Ewing .75 2.00
10 Horace Grant .40 1.00
11 Tim Hardaway .50 1.25
12 Derek Harper .30 .75
13 Hersey Hawkins .30 .75
14 Larry Johnson .40 1.00
15 Michael Jordan 4.00 10.00
16 Shawn Kemp .60 1.50
17 Reggie Lewis .30 .75
18 Karl Malone 2.00 5.00
19 Moses Malone .40 1.00
20 Danny Manning .40 1.00
21 Sarunas Marciulionis .40 1.00
22 Reggie Miller 1.00 2.50
23 Chris Mullin .60 1.50
24 Dikembe Mutombo .75 2.00
25 Hakeem Olajuwon .75 2.00
26 Robert Parish .60 1.50
27 Scottie Pippen 1.50 4.00
28 Mark Price .60 1.50
29 Glen Rice .60 1.50
30 Mitch Richmond .75 2.00
31 David Robinson 2.00 5.00
32 Detlef Schrempf .60 1.50
33 Rony Seikaly .40 1.00
34 Scott Skiles .40 1.00
35 Rik Smits .40 1.00
36 John Stockton 2.50 6.00
37 Isiah Thomas 1.25 3.00
38 Doug West .40 1.00
39 Dominique Wilkins 2.50 6.00
40 James Worthy 1.50 4.00

1994 Upper Deck French McDonald's Team

COMPLETE SET (33) 60.00 150.00
COMP.TEAM CARD SET (27) 6.00 15.00
COMP.HOLOGRAM SET (6) 50.00 125.00
1 Atlanta Hawks
Group .20 .50
2 Boston Celtics
Group .20 .50
3 Charlotte Hornets
Group .20 .50
4 Chicago Bulls
Michael Jordan 2.50 6.00
5 Cleveland Cavs
Mark Price .30 .75
6 Dallas Mavericks
Jim Jackson .20 .50
7 Denver Nuggets
Group .20 .50
8 Detroit Pistons
Isiah Thomas .50 1.25
9 Golden State Warriors
Group .20 .50
10 Houston Rockets
Hakeem Olajuwon .40 1.00
11 Indiana Pacers
Rik Smits .25 .60
12 Los Angeles Clippers
Group .20 .50
13 Los Angeles Lakers
Group .20 .50
14 Miami Heat
Group .20 .50
15 Milwaukee Bucks
Group .20 .50
16 Minnesota Timberwolves
Group .20 .50
17 New Jersey Nets
Kenny Anderson .25 .60
18 New York Knicks
Group .20 .50
19 Orlando Magic
Shaquille O'Neal 1.00 2.50
20 Philadelphia 76ers
Hersey Hawkins .20 .50
21 Phoenix Suns
Charles Barkley
Cedric Ceballos .50 1.25
22 Portland Trail Blazers
Group .20 .50
23 Sacramento Kings
Mitch Richmond .30 .75
24 San Antonio Spurs
David Robinson
Sean Elliott .50 1.25
25 Seattle Supersonics
Gary Payton
Shawn Kemp .40 1.00
26 Utah Jazz
Group .20 .50
27 Washington Bullets
Group .20 .50
28H Hakeem Olajuwon
Hologram 6.00 15.00
29H Michael Jordan
Hologram 40.00 100.00
30H Charles Barkley
Hologram 8.00 20.00
31H Shawn Kemp
Hologram 6.00 15.00
32H Patrick Ewing
Hologram 6.00 15.00
33H Ron Harper
Hologram 4.00 10.00

1998-99 Upper Deck Game Call

COMMON CARD 4.00 10.00

1999 Upper Deck Kevin Garnett Santa Game Jersey

HH2 Kevin Garnett 20.00 50.00

2002-03 Upper Deck Generations

COMP.SET w/o SP's (130) 25.00 60.00
51-92 PRINT RUN 999 SER.#'d SETS
1-92 INSERTED IN NEW SCHOOL PACKS
193-234 PRINT RUN 999 SER.#'d SETS
93-192 INSERTED IN NEW SCHOOL PACKS
1 Shareef Abdur-Rahim .30 .75
2 Paul Pierce .50 1.25
3 Antoine Walker .25 .60
4 Jalen Rose .25 .60
5 Tyson Chandler .30 .75
6 Darius Miles .25 .60
7 Dirk Nowitzki .75 2.00
8 Steve Nash .60 1.50
9 James Posey .20 .50
10 Richard Hamilton .40 1.00
11 Ben Wallace .40 1.00
12 Antawn Jamison .25 .60
13 Jason Richardson .30 .75
14 Steve Francis .30 .75
15 Eddie Griffin .20 .50
16 Reggie Miller .60 1.50
17 Jamaal Tinsley .20 .50
18 Elton Brand .25 .60
19 Andre Miller .25 .60
20 Kobe Bryant 2.50 6.00
21 Shaquille O'Neal 1.25 3.00
22 Pau Gasol .50 1.25
23 Shane Battier .30 .75
24 Alonzo Mourning .50 1.25
25 Ray Allen .50 1.25
26 Kevin Garnett .75 2.00
27 Wally Szczerbiak .25 .60
28 Jason Kidd .50 1.25
29 Kenyon Martin .30 .75
30 Jamal Mashburn .25 .60
31 Baron Davis .30 .75
32 Latrell Sprewell .30 .75
33 Tracy McGrady .50 1.25
34 Allen Iverson .75 2.00
35 Stephon Marbury .40 1.00
36 Shawn Marion .30 .75
37 Rasheed Wallace .40 1.00
38 Bonzi Wells .20 .50
39 Chris Webber .40 1.00
40 Mike Bibby .30 .75
41 Tim Duncan .75 2.00
42 Tony Parker .50 1.25
43 Gary Payton .50 1.25
44 Rashard Lewis .25 .60
45 Vince Carter .60 1.50
46 Morris Peterson .25 .60
47 Karl Malone .60 1.50
48 John Stockton .60 1.50
49 Michael Jordan 3.00 8.00
50 Jerry Stackhouse .30 .75
51 Yao Ming RC 8.00 20.00
52 Jay Williams RC 1.25 3.00
53 Mike Dunleavy RC 1.50 4.00
54 Drew Gooden RC 1.50 4.00
55 Nikoloz Tskitishvili RC 1.00 2.50
56 DaJuan Wagner RC 1.25 3.00
57 Nene Hilario RC 1.50 4.00
58 Chris Wilcox RC 1.25 3.00
59 Amare Stoudemire RC 4.00 10.00
60 Caron Butler RC 1.50 4.00
61 Jared Jeffries RC 1.25 3.00
62 Melvin Ely RC 1.25 3.00
63 Marcus Haislip RC 1.00 2.50
64 Fred Jones RC 1.25 3.00
65 Bostjan Nachbar RC 1.25 3.00
66 Jiri Welsch RC 1.25 3.00
67 Juan Dixon RC 1.50 4.00
68 Curtis Borchardt RC 1.00 2.50
69 Ryan Humphrey RC 1.25 3.00
70 Kareem Rush RC 1.25 3.00
71 Qyntel Woods RC 1.00 2.50
72 Casey Jacobsen RC 1.25 3.00
73 Tayshaun Prince RC 3.00 8.00
74 Predrag Savovic RC 1.25 3.00
75 Frank Williams RC 1.00 2.50
76 John Salmons RC 1.50 4.00
77 Chris Jefferies RC 1.00 2.50
78 Dan Dickau RC 1.00 2.50
79 Marcus Taylor RC 1.50 4.00
80 Roger Mason RC 1.25 3.00
81 Robert Archibald RC 1.00 2.50
82 Vincent Yarbrough RC 1.00 2.50
83 Dan Gadzuric RC 1.25 3.00
84 Carlos Boozer RC 1.50 4.00
85 Tito Maddox RC 1.00 2.50
86 Rod Grizzard RC 1.00 2.50
87 Ronald Murray RC 1.50 4.00
88 Marko Jaric 1.50 4.00
89 Lonny Baxter RC 1.00 2.50
90 Sam Clancy RC 1.25 3.00
91 Matt Barnes RC 2.00 5.00
92 Jamal Sampson RC 1.00 2.50
93 Oscar Robertson .60 1.50
94 Moses Malone .30 .75
95 Earl Monroe .30 .75
96 Pete Maravich .75 2.00
97 Artis Gilmore .25 .60
98 Julius Erving .50 1.25
99 Nate Archibald .25 .60
100 Wes Unseld .25 .60
101 Willis Reed .50 1.25
102 Jo Jo White .25 .60
103 Isiah Thomas .50 1.25
104 Bill Sharman .25 .60
105 Wilt Chamberlain .60 1.50
106 Bob Cousy .50 1.25
107 Tom Heinsohn .30 .75
108 Terry Cummings .25 .60
109 John Havlicek .40 1.00
110 Bob Pettit .30 .75
111 Drazen Petrovic .30 .75
112 Dan Roundfield .30 .75
113 David Thompson .25 .60
114 Bobby Jones .25 .60
115 Clyde Lovellette .30 .75
116 Rick Barry .25 .60
117 K.C. Jones .30 .75
118 Lionel Hollins .20 .50
119 Bob Lanier .30 .75
120 Al Attles .25 .60
121 Jack Sikma .20 .50
122 George McGinnis .20 .50
123 Quinn Buckner .20 .50
124 Magic Johnson .75 2.00
125 Larry Bird .75 2.00
126 Cliff Hagan .25 .60
127 Jerry Lucas .30 .75
128 Ricky Pierce .20 .50
129 Walter Davis .30 .75
130 Danny Ainge .30 .75
131 Reggie Theus .25 .60
132 Darryl Dawkins .20 .50
133 Tom Chambers .25 .60
134 M.L. Carr .25 .60
135 Kelly Tripucka .30 .75
136 George Gervin .40 1.00
137 Robert Parish .40 1.00
138 Mitch Kupchak .30 .75
139 Lou Hudson .20 .50
140 Bill Cartwright .25 .60
141 Lafayette Lever .25 .60
142 Kevin Loughery .30 .75
143 Hal Greer .20 .50
144 Jamaal Wilkes .20 .50
145 Alvan Adams .25 .60
146 Thomas Sanders .30 .75
147 Cazzie Russell .25 .60
148 Austin Carr .30 .75
149 Gail Goodrich .25 .60
150 Billy Knight .30 .75
151 Dave Bing .30 .75
152 Bill Walton .30 .75
153 Sam Jones .30 .75
154 Swen Nater .30 .75
155 Bobby Dandridge .20 .50
156 Junior Bridgeman .20 .50
157 Paul Silas .30 .75
158 John Kerr .30 .75
159 Phil Chenier .30 .75
160 Alex English .25 .60
161 Geoff Petrie .30 .75
162 Walt Bellamy .25 .60
163 Don Nelson .30 .75
164 Byron Scott .25 .60
165 Harvey Catchings .30 .75
166 Ed Macauley .30 .75
167 John Drew .30 .75
168 Detlef Schrempf .30 .75
169 Rolando Blackman .25 .60
170 Dave DeBusschere .30 .75
171 Marvin Barnes .30 .75
172 Elgin Baylor .30 .75
173 Cedric Maxwell .20 .50
174 Vern Mikkelsen .30 .75
175 Larry Brown .30 .75
176 Rick Mahorn .20 .50
177 Dolph Schayes .30 .75
178 Kevin McHale .40 1.00
179 Clark Kellogg .30 .75
180 Otis Birdsong .25 .60
181 Michael Cooper .25 .60
182 Mike Dunleavy .30 .75
183 Spencer Haywood .20 .50
184 Larry Nance .25 .60
185 Maurice Lucas .30 .75
186 Fred Brown .20 .50
187 Jerry West .50 1.25
188 Joe Barry Carroll .30 .75
189 Dave Cowens .25 .60
190 Sidney Moncrief .20 .50
191 Kiki Vandeweghe .25 .60
192 Walt Frazier .30 .75
193 Y.Ming/W.Chamberlain 4.00 10.00
194 J.Williams/J.Erving 2.50 6.00
195 M.Dunleavy/M.Dunleavy 2.50 6.00
196 D.Gooden/J.Havlicek 3.00 8.00
197 N.Tskitishvili/K.McHale 1.50 4.00
198 D.Wagner/O.Robertson 1.50 4.00
199 N.Hilario/K.Vandeweghe 2.50 6.00
200 Chris Wilcox 1.25 3.00
201 A.Stoudamire/G.McGinnis 5.00 12.00
202 C.Butler/W.Reed 2.50 6.00
203 J.Jeffries/L.Bird 2.00 5.00
204 M.Ely/E.Baylor 1.50 4.00
205 M.Haislip/K.Abdul-Jabbar 1.50 4.00
206 F.Jones/K.C.Jones 1.50 4.00
207 Bostjan Nachbar 1.25 3.00
208 Jiri Welsch 1.25 3.00
209 Juan Dixon 1.25 3.00
210 Curtis Borchardt 1.00 2.50
211 R.Humphrey/B.Lanier 1.50 4.00
212 K.Rush/W.Frazier 1.50 4.00
213 Q.Woods/J.Wilkes 1.50 4.00
214 C.Jacobsen/T.Chambers 1.50 4.00
215 T.Prince/B.Scott 2.00 5.00
216 P.Savovic/D.Petrovic 1.50 4.00
217 Frank Williams 1.00 2.50
218 J.Salmons/E.Baylor 1.50 4.00
219 C.Jefferies/W.Davis 1.50 4.00
220 Dan Dickau 1.00 2.50
221 M.Taylor/O.Robertson 1.50 4.00
222 R.Mason/J.White 1.50 4.00
223 R.Archibald/S.Moncrief 1.50 4.00
224 V.Yarbrough/E.Monroe 1.50 4.00
225 D.Gadzuric/B.Walton 1.50 4.00
226 C.Boozer/R.Parish 3.00 8.00
227 Tito Maddox 1.00 2.50
228 R.Grizzard/G.Gervin 1.50 4.00
229 R.Murray/L.Lever 1.50 4.00
230 Marko Jaric 1.50 4.00
231 Lonny Baxter 1.00 2.50
232 S.Clancy/W.Unseld 1.50 4.00
233 Matt Barnes 2.00 5.00
234 Jamal Sampson 1.00 2.50

2002-03 Upper Deck Generations All-Time Authentics

STATED ODDS 1:18 OLD SCHOOL
AMA Alonzo Mourning 6.00 15.00
BCA Bob Cousy 12.00 30.00
BWA Bill Walton 6.00 15.00
CDA Clyde Drexler 5.00 12.00
DRA David Robinson 8.00 20.00
GPA Gary Payton 6.00 15.00
JEA Julius Erving Blue 15.00 30.00
JE2A Julius Erving White 15.00 30.00
JKA Jason Kidd 6.00 15.00
JSA John Stockton 8.00 20.00
KAA Kareem Abdul-Jabbar 8.00 20.00
KBA Kobe Bryant 40.00 100.00
KMA Karl Malone 8.00 20.00
LBA Larry Bird 10.00 25.00
MCA Kevin McHale 5.00 12.00
MGA Magic Johnson Yellow 8.00 20.00
MG2A Magic Johnson White 8.00 20.00
MJA Michael Jordan Warm 30.00 80.00
MJ2A Michael Jordan Shirt 60.00 150.00
MRA Mitch Richmond 4.00 10.00
ORA Oscar Robertson 10.00 25.00
RBA Rick Barry 5.00 12.00
RMA Reggie Miller 8.00 20.00
SPA Scottie Pippen 10.00 25.00
TAA Nate Archibald Green 3.00 8.00
TA2A Nate Archibald White 3.00 8.00
WCA Wilt Chamberlain 40.00 100.00

2002-03 Upper Deck Generations All-Time Dual Autographs

PRINT RUN 25 SER.#'d SETS
DT/GG D.Thompson/G.Gervin 25.00 60.00
DW/JR Wilkins/J.Richardson 60.00 120.00
EB/KM E.Baylor/K.Martin 25.00 60.00
KA/TC Abdul-Jabbar/Chandler 100.00 200.00
LB/MM L.Bird/M.Miller 125.00 250.00
MG/JK M.Johnson/J.Kidd 150.00 300.00
MJ/KB M.Jordan/K.Bryant 5,000.00 10,000.00
WF/DJ W.Frazier/D.Johnson 25.00 60.00

2002-03 Upper Deck Generations All-Time Dual Jerseys

PRINT RUN 100 SER.#'d SETS
JEAIJ J.Erving/A.Iverson 30.00 60.00
JELBJ J.Erving/L.Bird 60.00 150.00
MGLBJ M.Johnson/L.Bird 40.00 100.00
MJJEJ M.Jordan/J.Erving 50.00 100.00
MJKBJ M.Jordan/K.Bryant 200.00 500.00
MJMGJ M.Jordan/M.Johnson 60.00 150.00
WCBRJ Chamberlain/Russell 75.00 150.00

2002-03 Upper Deck Generations Reel Time Jersey

STATED ODDS 1:18 NEW SCHOOL
AIJ Allen Iverson 8.00 20.00
AWJ Antoine Walker 2.50 6.00
BDJ Baron Davis 3.00 8.00
CWJ Chris Webber 4.00 10.00
DNJ Dirk Nowitzki 8.00 20.00
EBJ Elton Brand 2.50 6.00

JKJ Jason Kidd 5.00 12.00
JOJ Jermaine O'Neal 2.50 6.00
JSJ Jerry Stackhouse 3.00 8.00
KBJ Kobe Bryant 40.00 100.00
KGJ Kevin Garnett 8.00 20.00
KMJ Kenyon Martin 3.00 8.00
MBJ Mike Bibby 3.00 8.00
MCJ Antonio McDyess 2.50 6.00
MJJ Michael Jordan 30.00 60.00
PPJ Paul Pierce 5.00 12.00
SFJ Steve Francis 3.00 8.00
SMJ Stephon Marbury 4.00 10.00
TCJ Tyson Chandler 3.00 8.00
TMJ Tracy McGrady 5.00 12.00

2002-03 Upper Deck Generations Signature Classics

STATED ODDS 1:54 OLD SCHOOL
AES Alex English 8.00 20.00
BCS Bob Cousy 40.00 100.00
BWS Bill Walton 8.00 20.00
BYS Byron Scott 8.00 20.00
CDS Clyde Drexler 12.00 30.00
DTS David Thompson 8.00 20.00
DWS Dominique Wilkins 12.00 30.00
EBS Elgin Baylor 15.00 40.00
ETS Etan Thomas 4.00 10.00
GGS George Gervin 10.00 25.00
JES Julius Erving 40.00 100.00
JHS John Havlicek 25.00 60.00
JMS Jerome Moiso 4.00 10.00
KAS Kareem Abdul-Jabbar 30.00 80.00
LBS Larry Bird 60.00 150.00
MGS Magic Johnson 50.00 120.00
MJS Michael Jordan 1,500.00 3,000.00
MMS Mike Miller 4.00 10.00
NAS Nate Archibald 8.00 20.00
QRS Quentin Richardson 4.00 10.00
RBS Rick Barry 10.00 25.00
RMS Ron Mercer 4.00 10.00
SAS Shareef Abdur-Rahim 6.00 15.00
TBS Terrell Brandon 4.00 10.00
WFS Walt Frazier 8.00 20.00

1996 Upper Deck German Kellogg's

COMPLETE SET (40) 40.00 100.00
CHECKLIST (NNO) .75 2.00
1 Jerry Stackhouse 3.00 8.00
2 Clifford Robinson 2.50 6.00
3 Glenn Robinson 2.50 6.00
4 Chris Webber 3.00 8.00
5 Dennis Rodman 5.00 12.00
6 Scottie Pippen 4.00 10.00
7 Toni Kukoc 2.50 6.00
8 Dan Majerle 2.50 6.00
9 Dino Radja 1.50 4.00
10 Loy Vaught 1.50 4.00
11 Bryant Reeves 1.50 4.00
12 Stacey Augmon 2.00 5.00
13 Kevin Willis 1.50 4.00
14 Muggsy Bogues 2.00 5.00
15 John Stockton 3.00 8.00
16 Karl Malone 3.00 8.00
17 Mitch Richmond 2.50 6.00
18 Charles Oakley 2.00 5.00
19 Nick Van Exel 2.50 6.00
20 Anfernee Hardaway 4.00 10.00
21 Horace Grant 2.00 5.00
22 Jason Kidd 4.00 10.00
23 Ed O'Bannon 1.50 4.00
24 Dikembe Mutombo 2.50 6.00
25 Dale Davis 1.50 4.00
26 Derrick McKey 1.50 4.00
27 Mark Jackson 2.50 6.00
28 Rik Smits 2.00 5.00
29 Grant Hill 4.00 10.00
30 Damon Stoudamire 2.00 5.00
31 Clyde Drexler 3.00 8.00
32 Hakeem Olajuwon 3.00 8.00
33 Detlef Schrempf 2.50 6.00
34 Gary Payton 2.50 6.00
35 Hersey Hawkins 1.50 4.00
36 Sam Perkins 1.50 4.00
37 David Robinson 4.00 10.00
38 Charles Barkley 4.00 10.00
39 Christian Laettner 2.00 5.00
40 B.J. Armstrong 1.50 4.00

1999-00 Upper Deck Gold Reserve

COMPLETE SET (270) 60.00 120.00
COMPLETE SET w/o RC (240) 15.00 40.00
241-270 PRINT RUN 3500 SERIAL #'d SETS
MAXWELL CARD #294 SHOULD BE #204
1 Roshown McLeod .20 .50
2 Dikembe Mutombo .50 1.25
3 Alan Henderson .20 .50
4 Chris Crawford .20 .50
5 Jim Jackson .20 .50
6 Isaiah Rider .25 .60
7 Lorenzen Wright .20 .50
8 Bimbo Coles .20 .50
9 Kenny Anderson .25 .60
10 Antoine Walker .30 .75
11 Paul Pierce .60 1.50
12 Vitaly Potapenko .20 .50
13 Dana Barros .20 .50
14 Calbert Cheaney .20 .50
15 Pervis Ellison .20 .50
16 Eric Williams .20 .50
17 Tony Battie .20 .50
18 Elden Campbell .20 .50
19 Eddie Jones .30 .75
20 David Wesley .20 .50
21 Derrick Coleman .25 .60
22 Ricky Davis .30 .75
23 Anthony Mason .30 .75
24 Todd Fuller .20 .50
25 Brad Miller .25 .60
26 Corey Benjamin .20 .50
27 Randy Brown .20 .50
28 Dickey Simpkins .20 .50
29 Toni Kukoc .40 1.00
30 Fred Hoiberg .20 .50
31 Hersey Hawkins .20 .50
32 Will Perdue .20 .50
33 Chris Anstey .20 .50
34 Shawn Kemp .50 1.25
35 Wesley Person .20 .50
36 Brevin Knight .20 .50
37 Bob Sura .20 .50
38 Danny Ferry .20 .50
39 Lamond Murray .20 .50
40 Cedric Henderson .20 .50
41 Andrew DeClercq .20 .50
42 Michael Finley .30 .75
43 Shawn Bradley .20 .50
44 Dirk Nowitzki 1.00 2.50
45 Erick Strickland .20 .50
46 Cedric Ceballos .20 .50
47 Hubert Davis .20 .50
48 Robert Pack .20 .50
49 Gary Trent .20 .50
50 Antonio McDyess .25 .60
51 Nick Van Exel .25 .60
52 Chauncey Billups .30 .75
53 Bryant Stith .20 .50
54 Raef LaFrentz .25 .60
55 Ron Mercer .20 .50
56 George McCloud .20 .50
57 Roy Rogers .20 .50
58 Keon Clark .20 .50
59 Grant Hill .50 1.25
60 Lindsey Hunter .20 .50
61 Jerry Stackhouse .30 .75
62 Terry Mills .20 .50
63 Michael Curry .20 .50
64 Christian Laettner .25 .60
65 Jerome Williams .20 .50
66 Loy Vaught .20 .50
67 John Starks .30 .75
68 Antawn Jamison .30 .75
69 Erick Dampier .25 .60
70 Jason Caffey .20 .50
71 Terry Cummings .25 .60
72 Donyell Marshall .25 .60
73 Chris Mills .20 .50
74 Tony Farmer .20 .50
75 Adonal Foyle .20 .50
76 Hakeem Olajuwon .60 1.50
77 Cuttino Mobley .25 .60
78 Charles Barkley .75 2.00
79 Bryce Drew .20 .50
80 Shandon Anderson .20 .50
81 Kelvin Cato .20 .50
82 Walt Williams .20 .50
83 Carlos Rogers .20 .50
84 Reggie Miller .60 1.50
85 Jalen Rose .25 .60
86 Mark Jackson .25 .60
87 Dale Davis .20 .50
88 Chris Mullin .30 .75
89 Al Harrington .30 .75
90 Rik Smits .25 .60
91 Sam Perkins .20 .50
92 Austin Croshere .20 .50
93 Maurice Taylor .20 .50
94 Tyrone Nesby RC .20 .50
95 Michael Olowokandi .20 .50
96 Eric Piatkowski .20 .50
97 Troy Hudson .30 .75
98 Derek Anderson .20 .50
99 Eric Murdock .20 .50
100 Brian Skinner .20 .50
101 Kobe Bryant 2.50 6.00
102 Shaquille O'Neal 1.25 3.00
103 Glen Rice .25 .60
104 Robert Horry .25 .60
105 Ron Harper .25 .60
106 Derek Fisher .25 .60
107 Rick Fox .25 .60
108 A.C. Green .25 .60
109 Tim Hardaway .40 1.00
110 Alonzo Mourning .50 1.25
111 P.J. Brown .20 .50
112 Dan Majerle .30 .75
113 Jamal Mashburn .25 .60
114 Voshon Lenard .20 .50
115 Clarence Weatherspoon .20 .50
116 Rex Walters .20 .50
117 Ray Allen .50 1.25
118 Glenn Robinson .25 .60
119 Sam Cassell .25 .60
120 Robert Taylor .20 .50
121 J.R. Reid .20 .50
122 Ervin Johnson .20 .50
123 Danny Manning .20 .50
124 Tim Thomas .25 .60
125 Kevin Garnett .75 2.00
126 Sam Mitchell .20 .50
127 Dean Garrett .20 .50
128 Bobby Jackson .20 .50
129 Radoslav Nesterovic .30 .75
130 Terrell Brandon .20 .50
131 Joe Smith .25 .60
132 Anthony Peeler .20 .50
133 Keith Van Horn .20 .50
134 Stephon Marbury .40 1.00
135 Kendall Gill .30 .75
136 Scott Burrell .20 .50
137 Jayson Williams .20 .50
138 Jamie Feick RC .20 .50
139 Kerry Kittles .20 .50
140 Johnny Newman .20 .50
141 Patrick Ewing .40 1.00
142 Allan Houston .25 .60
143 Latrell Sprewell .40 1.00
144 Larry Johnson .30 .75
145 Marcus Camby .25 .60
146 Chris Childs .20 .50
147 Kurt Thomas .20 .50
148 Charlie Ward .20 .50
149 Darrell Armstrong .20 .50
150 Matt Harpring .20 .50
151 Michael Doleac .20 .50
152 Bo Outlaw .20 .50
153 Tariq Abdul-Wahad .20 .50
154 John Amaechi RC .30 .75
155 Ben Wallace .25 .60
156 Monty Williams .25 .60
157 Allen Iverson .75 2.00
158 Theo Ratliff .25 .60
159 Larry Hughes .25 .60
160 Eric Snow .20 .50
161 George Lynch .20 .50
162 Tyrone Hill .20 .50
163 Billy Owens .20 .50
164 Aaron McKie .20 .50
165 Jason Kidd .50 1.25
166 Clifford Robinson .25 .60
167 Tom Gugliotta .25 .60
168 Luc Longley .25 .60
169 Anfernee Hardaway .75 2.00
170 Rex Chapman .20 .50
171 Oliver Miller .20 .50
172 Rodney Rogers .20 .50
173 Rasheed Wallace .40 1.00
174 Arvydas Sabonis .25 .60
175 Damon Stoudamire .30 .75
176 Brian Grant .20 .50
177 Scottie Pippen .75 2.00
178 Detlef Schrempf .25 .60
179 Steve Smith .25 .60
180 Jermaine O'Neal .25 .60
181 Bonzi Wells .20 .50
182 Jason Williams .50 1.25
183 Vlade Divac .30 .75
184 Peja Stojakovic .30 .75
185 Lawrence Funderburke .20 .50
186 Chris Webber .40 1.00
187 Nick Anderson .20 .50
188 Darrick Martin .20 .50
189 Corliss Williamson .20 .50
190 Tim Duncan .75 2.00
191 Sean Elliott .25 .60
192 David Robinson .60 1.50
193 Mario Elie .25 .60
194 Avery Johnson .25 .60
195 Terry Porter .25 .60
196 Malik Rose .20 .50
197 Jaren Jackson .20 .50
198 Gary Payton .50 1.25
199 Vin Baker .25 .60
200 Rashard Lewis .25 .60
201 Jelani McCoy .20 .50
202 Brent Barry .25 .60
203 Horace Grant .25 .60
204 Vernon Maxwell UER .20 .50
205 Ruben Patterson .20 .50
206 Vince Carter .75 2.00
207 Doug Christie .25 .60
208 Kevin Willis .20 .50
209 Dee Brown .20 .50
210 Antonio Davis .20 .50
211 Tracy McGrady .50 1.25
212 Dell Curry .20 .50
213 Charles Oakley .30 .75
214 Karl Malone .60 1.50
215 John Stockton .60 1.50
216 Howard Eisley .20 .50
217 Bryon Russell .20 .50
218 Greg Ostertag .20 .50
219 Jeff Hornacek .25 .60
220 Olden Polynice .20 .50
221 Adam Keefe .20 .50
222 Shareef Abdur-Rahim .30 .75
223 Mike Bibby .30 .75
224 Felipe Lopez .20 .50
225 Cherokee Parks .20 .50
226 Michael Dickerson .20 .50
227 Othella Harrington .20 .50
228 Bryant Reeves .20 .50
229 Brent Price .20 .50
230 Michael Smith .20 .50
231 Juwan Howard .25 .60
232 Rod Strickland .25 .60
233 Chris Whitney .20 .50
234 Tracy Murray .20 .50
235 Mitch Richmond .40 1.00
236 Aaron Williams .20 .50
237 Isaac Austin .20 .50
238 Kobe Bryant CL 2.50 6.00
239 Michael Jordan CL 3.00 8.00
240 Kevin Garnett CL .75 2.00
241 Elton Brand RC 1.50 4.00
242 Steve Francis RC 1.50 4.00
243 Baron Davis RC 2.00 5.00
244 Lamar Odom RC 1.50 4.00
245 Jonathan Bender RC 1.25 3.00
246 Wally Szczerbiak RC 1.25 3.00
247 Richard Hamilton RC 2.00 5.00
248 Andre Miller RC 1.50 4.00
249 Shawn Marion RC 1.50 4.00
250 Jason Terry RC 1.25 3.00
251 Trajan Langdon RC .60 1.50
252 A.Radojevic RC .50 1.25
253 Corey Maggette RC 1.00 2.50
254 William Avery RC .50 1.25
255 Ron Artest RC 2.00 5.00
256 Cal Bowdler RC .50 1.25
257 James Posey RC .75 2.00
258 Quincy Lewis RC .50 1.25
259 Dion Glover RC .50 1.25
260 Jeff Foster RC .75 2.00
261 Kenny Thomas RC .75 2.00
262 Devean George RC .60 1.50
263 Tim James RC .50 1.25
264 Vonteego Cummings RC .50 1.25
265 Jumaine Jones RC .50 1.25
266 Scott Padgett RC .50 1.25
267 Rodney Buford RC .75 2.00
268 Adrian Griffin RC .60 1.50
269 Anthony Carter RC .60 1.50
270 Eddie Robinson RC .75 2.00

1999-00 Upper Deck Gold Reserve Gold Mine

COMPLETE SET (15) 10.00 25.00
STATED ODDS 1:11
R1 Kobe Bryant 5.00 12.00
R2 Vince Carter 1.50 4.00
R3 Steve Francis 1.25 3.00
R4 Kevin Garnett 1.50 4.00
R5 Elton Brand 1.25 3.00
R6 Gary Payton 1.00 2.50
R7 Lamar Odom 1.25 3.00
R8 Grant Hill 1.00 2.50
R9 Jason Williams 1.00 2.50
R10 Shareef Abdur-Rahim .60 1.50
R11 Tim Duncan 1.50 4.00
R12 Keith Van Horn .50 1.25
R13 Tim Hardaway .75 2.00
R14 Karl Malone 1.25 3.00
R15 Shaquille O'Neal 2.50 6.00

1999-00 Upper Deck Gold Reserve Gold Strike

COMPLETE SET (15) 6.00 15.00
STATED ODDS 1:4
GS1 Kevin Garnett 1.00 2.50
GS2 Kobe Bryant 3.00 8.00
GS3 Tim Duncan 1.00 2.50
GS4 Adrian Griffin .30 .75
GS5 Lamar Odom .75 2.00
GS6 Jason Kidd .60 1.50
GS7 Wally Szczerbiak .60 1.50
GS8 Stephon Marbury .50 1.25
GS9 Shaquille O'Neal 1.50 4.00
GS10 Elton Brand .75 2.00
GS11 Allen Iverson 1.00 2.50
GS12 Shawn Marion .75 2.00
GS13 Jason Williams .60 1.50
GS14 Antonio McDyess .30 .75
GS15 Vince Carter 1.00 2.50

1999-00 Upper Deck Gold Reserve UD Authentics

STATED ODDS 1:480
AH Anfernee Hardaway 50.00 120.00
AW Antoine Walker 4.00 10.00
BD Baron Davis 8.00 20.00
JB Jonathan Bender 3.00 8.00
JT Jason Terry 5.00 12.00
KB Kobe Bryant 150.00 400.00
KG Kevin Garnett 100.00 200.00
RH Richard Hamilton 8.00 20.00
SF Steve Francis 6.00 15.00
WS Wally Szczerbiak 5.00 12.00

1993-94 Upper Deck Golden Grahams French

1 Charles Barkley 6.00 15.00
2 Alonzo Mourning 4.00 10.00
3 Billy Owens 2.00 5.00
4 Patrick Ewing 4.00 10.00
5 Toni Kukoc 6.00 15.00
6 Hakeem Olajuwon 5.00 12.00
7 Dan Majerle 2.50 6.00
8 Larry Johnson 3.00 8.00
9 John Stockton 5.00 12.00
10 Christian Laettner 2.50 6.00
11 Dominique Wilkins 4.00 10.00
12 Detlef Schrempf 2.50 6.00
13 Shawn Kemp 4.00 10.00
14 Derrick Coleman 2.50 6.00
15 Shaquille O'Neal 12.00 30.00
16 Clyde Drexler 4.00 10.00
17 David Robinson 4.00 10.00
18 Tom Gugliotta 2.50 6.00
19 Mark Price 2.50 6.00
20 Sean Elliott 2.50 6.00
21 Reggie Miller 5.00 12.00
22 Todd Day 1.50 4.00
23 Mitch Richmond 3.00 8.00
24 Jim Jackson 2.00 5.00
25 Mahmoud Abdul-Rauf 2.00 5.00
26 Danny Manning 2.00 5.00
27 Doug Christie 2.00 5.00
28 Chris Webber 12.00 30.00
29 Anfernee Hardaway 12.00 30.00
30 Karl Malone 5.00 12.00
31 Jamal Mashburn 5.00 12.00
32 Shawn Bradley 2.50 6.00
33 Dino Radja 2.50 6.00
34 Ken Norman 1.50 4.00
35 Harold Miner 2.00 5.00
36 John Starks 2.50 6.00
37 Dale Ellis 1.50 4.00
38 Glen Rice 2.50 6.00
39 Clarence Weatherspoon 1.50 4.00
40 Dee Brown 2.00 5.00

1993-94 Upper Deck Golden Grahams German

1 Charles Barkley 12.00 30.00
2 Alonzo Mourning 8.00 20.00
3 Billy Owens 4.00 10.00
4 Patrick Ewing 8.00 20.00
5 Toni Kukoc 12.00 30.00
6 Hakeem Olajuwon 10.00 25.00
7 Dan Majerle 5.00 12.00
8 Larry Johnson 6.00 15.00
9 John Stockton 10.00 25.00
10 Christian Laettner 5.00 12.00
11 Dominique Wilkins 8.00 20.00
12 Detlef Schrempf 5.00 12.00
13 Shawn Kemp 8.00 20.00
14 Derrick Coleman 5.00 12.00
15 Shaquille O'Neal 25.00 60.00
16 Clyde Drexler 8.00 20.00
17 David Robinson 10.00 25.00
18 Tom Gugliotta 4.00 10.00
19 Mark Price 5.00 12.00
20 Sean Elliott 5.00 12.00
21 Reggie Miller 10.00 25.00
22 Todd Day 3.00 8.00
23 Mitch Richmond 6.00 15.00
24 Jim Jackson 4.00 10.00
25 Mahmoud Abdul-Rauf 4.00 10.00
26 Danny Manning 4.00 10.00
27 Doug Christie 4.00 10.00
28 Chris Webber 25.00 60.00
29 Anfernee Hardaway 25.00 60.00
30 Karl Malone 10.00 25.00
31 Jamal Mashburn 10.00 25.00
32 Shawn Bradley 5.00 12.00
33 Dino Radja 5.00 12.00
34 Ken Norman 3.00 8.00
35 Harold Miner 4.00 10.00
36 John Starks 5.00 12.00
37 Dale Ellis 3.00 8.00
38 Glen Rice 5.00 12.00
39 Clarence Weatherspoon 3.00 8.00
40 Dee Brown 4.00 10.00

1993-94 Upper Deck Golden Grahams Italian

1 Charles Barkley 12.00 30.00
2 Alonzo Mourning 8.00 20.00
3 Billy Owens 4.00 10.00
4 Patrick Ewing 8.00 20.00
5 Toni Kukoc 12.00 30.00
6 Hakeem Olajuwon 10.00 25.00
7 Dan Majerle 5.00 12.00
8 Larry Johnson 6.00 15.00
9 John Stockton 10.00 25.00
10 Christian Laettner 5.00 12.00
11 Dominique Wilkins 8.00 20.00
12 Detlef Schrempf 5.00 12.00
13 Shawn Kemp 8.00 20.00
14 Derrick Coleman 5.00 12.00
15 Shaquille O'Neal 25.00 60.00
16 Clyde Drexler 8.00 20.00
17 David Robinson 10.00 25.00
18 Tom Gugliotta 4.00 10.00
19 Mark Price 5.00 12.00
20 Sean Elliott 5.00 12.00
21 Reggie Miller 10.00 25.00
22 Todd Day 3.00 8.00
23 Mitch Richmond 6.00 15.00
24 Jim Jackson 4.00 10.00
25 Mahmoud Abdul-Rauf 4.00 10.00
26 Danny Manning 4.00 10.00
27 Doug Christie 4.00 10.00
28 Chris Webber 25.00 60.00
29 Anfernee Hardaway 25.00 60.00
30 Karl Malone 10.00 25.00
31 Jamal Mashburn 10.00 25.00
32 Shawn Bradley 5.00 12.00
33 Dino Radja 5.00 12.00
34 Ken Norman 3.00 8.00
35 Harold Miner 4.00 10.00
36 John Starks 5.00 12.00
37 Dale Ellis 3.00 8.00
38 Glen Rice 5.00 12.00
39 Clarence Weatherspoon 3.00 8.00
40 Dee Brown 4.00 10.00

1993-94 Upper Deck Golden Grahams Portuguese

1 Charles Barkley 15.00 40.00
2 Alonzo Mourning 10.00 25.00
3 Billy Owens 5.00 12.00
4 Patrick Ewing 10.00 25.00
5 Toni Kukoc 15.00 40.00
6 Hakeem Olajuwon 12.00 30.00
7 Dan Majerle 6.00 15.00
8 Larry Johnson 8.00 20.00
9 John Stockton 12.00 30.00
10 Christian Laettner 6.00 15.00
11 Dominique Wilkins 10.00 25.00
12 Detlef Schrempf 6.00 15.00
13 Shawn Kemp 10.00 25.00
14 Derrick Coleman 6.00 15.00
15 Shaquille O'Neal 30.00 80.00
16 Clyde Drexler 10.00 25.00
17 David Robinson 12.00 30.00
18 Tom Gugliotta 5.00 12.00
19 Mark Price 6.00 15.00
20 Sean Elliott 6.00 15.00
21 Reggie Miller 12.00 30.00
22 Todd Day 4.00 10.00
23 Mitch Richmond 8.00 20.00
24 Jim Jackson 5.00 12.00
25 Mahmoud Abdul-Rauf 5.00 12.00
26 Danny Manning 5.00 12.00
27 Doug Christie 5.00 12.00
28 Chris Webber 30.00 80.00
29 Anfernee Hardaway 30.00 80.00
30 Karl Malone 12.00 30.00
31 Jamal Mashburn 12.00 30.00
32 Shawn Bradley 6.00 15.00
33 Dino Radja 6.00 15.00
34 Ken Norman 4.00 10.00
35 Harold Miner 5.00 12.00
36 John Starks 6.00 15.00
37 Dale Ellis 4.00 10.00
38 Glen Rice 6.00 15.00
39 Clarence Weatherspoon 4.00 10.00
40 Dee Brown 5.00 12.00

2009 Upper Deck Goodwin Champions Preview

GCP8 Michael Jordan 6.00 15.00

2014 Upper Deck Goodwin Champions Sport Royalty Autographs

GROUP A ODDS 1:17,130 HOBBY
GROUP B ODDS 1:4670 HOBBY
GROUP C ODDS 1:2855 HOBBY
GROUP D ODDS 1:1070 HOBBY
'16 GROUP A ODDS 1:21,760 HOBBY
'16 GROUP B ODDS 1:5440 HOBBY

2015 Upper Deck Goodwin Champions Goudey Sport Royalty Autographs

GROUP A ODDS 1:1:24,960 PACKS
GROUP B ODDS 1:9985 PACKS
GROUP C ODDS 1:3995 PACKS
OVERALL GOUDEY ODDS 1:2560 PACKS
'16 STATED ODDS 1:32,640 HOBBY
EXCHANGE DEADLINE 6/10/2017

2016 Upper Deck Goodwin Champions Variations

STATED ODDS 1:1080 HOBBY
SP1 Michael Jordan 25.00 60.00
SP2 LeBron James 30.00 80.00

2016 Upper Deck Goodwin Champions Black and White Autographs

GROUP A STATED ODDS 1:24,235 PACKS
GROUP B STATED ODDS 1:17,310 PACKS
GROUP C STATED ODDS 1:9694 PACKS
GROUP D STATED ODDS 1:1727 PACKS
EXCHANGE DEADLINE 6/21/2018
BAJH John Havlicek C 25.00 60.00
BALJ LeBron James B 175.00 350.00

2016 Upper Deck Goodwin Champions Black and White Memorabilia

GROUP A STATED ODDS 1:1740 PACKS
GROUP B STATED ODDS 1:1269 PACKS
GROUP C STATED ODDS 1:508 PACKS
BWMLJ LeBron James A 15.00 40.00

2016 Upper Deck Goodwin Champions Black and White Memorabilia Premium

PRINT RUNS B/WN 6-50 COPIES PER
NO PRICING ON QTY 15 OR LESS
BWMLJ LeBron James/25 25.00 60.00
BWMMJ Michael Jordan/25 60.00 150.00

2016 Upper Deck Goodwin Champions Goudey Memorabilia Premium

GMMJ Michael Jordan C 30.00 80.00

2016 Upper Deck Goodwin Champions Goudey Sport Royalty Autographs

GROUP A STATED ODDS 1:200,192 PACKS
GROUP B STATED ODDS 1:52,682 PACKS
GROUP C STATED ODDS 1:19,627 PACKS
GROUP D STATED ODDS 1:3168 PACKS
EXCHANGE DEADLINE 6/21/2018
SRBS Ben Simmons D 1,200.00 2,200.00
SRJH John Havlicek D 20.00 50.00

2016 Upper Deck Goodwin Champions Goudey Sport Royalty Memorabilia

GROUP A STATED ODDS 1:7200 PACKS
GROUP B STATED ODDS 1:4800 PACKS
GROUP C STATED ODDS 1:3600 PACKS
GROUP D STATED ODDS 1:2400 PACKS
SRMLJ LeBron James A 20.00 50.00

2016 Upper Deck Goodwin Champions Goudey Sport Royalty Memorabilia Dual Swatch

GROUP A STATED ODDS 1:8320 PACKS
GROUP B STATED ODDS 1:2496 PACKS
SRM2LJ LeBron James A 20.00 50.00

2016 Upper Deck Goodwin Champions Goudey Sport Royalty Memorabilia Premium

STATED PRINT RUN 15 SER.#'d SETS
SRMLJ LeBron James 25.00 60.00

2016 Upper Deck Goodwin Champions Memorabilia Premium

GROUP A STATED ODDS 1:129,280 PACKS
GROUP B STATED ODDS 1:5621 PACKS
GROUP C STATED ODDS 1:6804 PACKS
GROUP D STATED ODDS 1:6529 PACKS
GROUP E STATED ODDS 1:260 PACKS
MMJ Michael Jordan D 25.00 60.00

2017 Upper Deck Goodwin Champions Goudey Sport Royalty Autographs

GROUP A 1:155,520 HOBBY
GROUP B 1:55,543 HOBBY
GROUP C 1:31,104 HOBBY
GROUP D 1:3908 HOBBY

2017 Upper Deck Goodwin Champions Goudey Sport Royalty Dual Autographs

STATED ODDS 1:16,000 HOBBY

2017 Upper Deck Goodwin Champions Goudey Sport Royalty Memorabilia

STATED GROUP A ODDS 1:3733 HOBBY
STATED GROUP B ODDS 1:2800 HOBBY
*PREMIUM/25: 1X TO 2.5X BASIC
SRMBS Ben Simmons A 15.00 40.00

2017 Upper Deck Goodwin Champions Goudey Sport Royalty Memorabilia Dual Swatch

STATED GROUP A ODDS 1:22,400 HOBBY
STATED GROUP B ODDS 1:3733 HOBBY
SRM2BS Ben Simmons B 20.00 50.00

2018 Upper Deck Goodwin Champions Goudey Sport Royalty Autographs

GROUP A ODDS 1:116,880 HOBBY
GROUP B ODDS 1:8588 HOBBY

2018 Upper Deck Goodwin Champions Goudey Sport Royalty Dual Swatches

SRM2BS Ben Simmons B 12.00 30.00

2018 Upper Deck Goodwin Champions Goudey Sport Royalty Dual Swatches Premium

*PREMIUM/25: 1.5X TO 4X BASIC
PRINT RUNS BW/N 10-25 COPIES PER
NO PRICING ON QTY 10
SRM2MJ Michael Jordan/23 150.00 400.00

2018 Upper Deck Goodwin Champions Goudey Sport Royalty Memorabilia

STATED ODDS 1:1520 HOBBY
SRMBS Ben Simmons 10.00 25.00

2018 Upper Deck Goodwin Champions Goudey Sport Royalty Memorabilia Premium

*PREMIUM/25: 1X TO 2.5X BASIC
PRINT RUNS BW/N 10-25 COPIES PER
NO PRICING ON QTY 10
SRMLJ LeBron James/25 60.00 150.00
SRMMJ Michael Jordan/23 50.00 120.00

2009 Upper Deck Goudey Sport Royalty Autographs

OVERALL AUTO ODDS 1:18 HOBBY
EXCHANGE DEADLINE 4/1/2011
BS Bill Sharman 15.00 40.00
JH John Havlicek 125.00 250.00
JO Michael Jordan 1,000.00 2,000.00
JW Jerry West 75.00 150.00
LB Larry Bird 30.00 60.00

2009 Upper Deck Griffey-Jordan

KGMJ K.Griffey Jr./M.Jordan 20.00 50.00

1998 Upper Deck Hardcourt

COMPLETE SET (90) 40.00 75.00
JORDAN SPEC. INSERTED EVERY TWO BOXES
ONE JORDAN JUMBO PER BOX
1 Kobe Bryant 3.00 8.00
2 Donyell Marshall .40 1.00
3 Bryant Reeves .40 1.00
4 Keith Van Horn .60 1.50
5 David Robinson 1.00 2.50
6 Nick Anderson .40 1.00
7 Nick Van Exel .50 1.25
8 David Wesley .40 1.00
9 Alonzo Mourning .75 2.00
10 Shawn Kemp .60 1.50
11 Maurice Taylor .40 1.00
12 Kenny Anderson .50 1.25
13 Jason Kidd 1.00 2.50
14 Marcus Camby .50 1.25
15 Tim Hardaway .60 1.50
16 Damon Stoudamire .60 1.50
17 Detlef Schrempf .60 1.50
18 Dikembe Mutombo .60 1.50
19 Charles Barkley 1.00 2.50
20 Ray Allen .75 2.00
21 Ron Mercer .50 1.25
22 Shawn Bradley .40 1.00
23 Michael Jordan 5.00 12.00
23A Michael Jordan Special 8.00 20.00
24 Antonio McDyess .50 1.25
25 Stephon Marbury .75 2.00
26 Rik Smits .50 1.25
27 Michael Stewart .40 1.00
28 Steve Smith .50 1.25
29 Glenn Robinson .50 1.25
30 Chris Webber .60 1.50
31 Antoine Walker .60 1.50
32 Eddie Jones .50 1.25
33 Mitch Richmond .60 1.50
34 Kevin Garnett 1.00 2.50
35 Grant Hill 1.00 2.50
36 John Stockton .75 2.00
37 Allan Houston .50 1.25
38 Bobby Jackson .40 1.00
39 Sam Cassell .50 1.25
40 Allen Iverson 1.25 3.00
41 LaPhonso Ellis .40 1.00
42 Lorenzen Wright .40 1.00
43 Gary Payton .60 1.50
44 Patrick Ewing .75 2.00
45 Scottie Pippen 1.00 2.50
46 Hakeem Olajuwon .75 2.00
47 Glen Rice .60 1.50
48 Antonio Daniels .40 1.00
49 Jayson Williams .40 1.00
50 Juwan Howard .50 1.25
51 Reggie Miller .75 2.00
52 Joe Smith .50 1.25
53 Shaquille O'Neal 1.50 4.00
54 Dennis Rodman 1.25 3.00
55 Vin Baker .50 1.25
56 Rod Strickland .40 1.00
57 Anfernee Hardaway 1.00 2.50
58 Zydrunas Ilgauskas .60 1.50
59 Chris Mullin .60 1.50
60 Rasheed Wallace .60 1.50
61 Shareef Abdur-Rahim .60 1.50
62 Tom Gugliotta .40 1.00
63 Tim Duncan 1.25 3.00
64 Michael Finley .60 1.50
65 Jim Jackson .40 1.00
66 Chauncey Billups .75 2.00
67 Jerry Stackhouse .60 1.50
68 Jeff Hornacek .50 1.25
69 Clyde Drexler .75 2.00
70 Karl Malone .75 2.00
71 Tim Duncan RE 1.25 3.00
72 Keith Van Horn RE .60 1.50
73 Chauncey Billups RE .75 2.00
74 Antonio Daniels RE .40 1.00
75 Tony Battie RE .50 1.25
76 Ron Mercer RE .50 1.25
77 Tim Thomas RE .50 1.25
78 Tracy McGrady RE 1.00 2.50
79 Danny Fortson RE .40 1.00
80 Derek Anderson RE .40 1.00
81 Maurice Taylor RE .40 1.00
82 Kelvin Cato RE .40 1.00
83 Brevin Knight RE .40 1.00
84 Bobby Jackson RE .40 1.00
85 Rodrick Rhodes RE .40 1.00
86 Anthony Johnson RE .40 1.00
87 Cedric Henderson RE .40 1.00
88 Chris Anstey RE .40 1.00
89 Michael Stewart RE .40 1.00
90 Zydrunas Ilgauskas RE .60 1.50
NNO Michael Jordan Jumbo 4.00 10.00

1998 Upper Deck Hardcourt Home Court Advantage

*STARS: .75X TO 2X BASE CARD HI
STATED ODDS 1:4

1998 Upper Deck Hardcourt Home Court Advantage Plus

*STARS: 4X TO 10X BASE CARD HI
STATED PRINT RUN 500 SERIAL #'d SETS
23 Michael Jordan 75.00 200.00

1998 Upper Deck Hardcourt High Court

STATED PRINT RUN 1300 SERIAL #'d SETS
H1 Dikembe Mutombo 2.00 5.00
H2 Ron Mercer 1.50 4.00
H3 Glen Rice 2.00 5.00
H4 Scottie Pippen 3.00 8.00
H5 Shawn Kemp 2.00 5.00
H6 Michael Finley 2.00 5.00
H7 LaPhonso Ellis 1.25 3.00
H8 Grant Hill 3.00 8.00
H9 Erick Dampier 1.25 3.00
H10 Hakeem Olajuwon 2.50 6.00
H11 Chris Mullin 2.00 5.00
H12 Lamond Murray 1.25 3.00
H13 Kobe Bryant 10.00 25.00
H14 Tim Hardaway 2.00 5.00
H15 Ray Allen 2.50 6.00
H16 Stephon Marbury 2.50 6.00
H17 Keith Van Horn 2.00 5.00
H18 Allan Houston 1.50 4.00
H19 Anfernee Hardaway 3.00 8.00
H20 Allen Iverson 4.00 10.00
H21 Antonio McDyess 1.50 4.00
H22 Rasheed Wallace 2.00 5.00
H23 Mitch Richmond 2.00 5.00
H24 Tim Duncan 4.00 10.00
H25 Gary Payton 2.00 5.00

H26 Chauncey Billups 2.50 6.00
H27 John Stockton 2.50 6.00
H28 Shareef Abdur-Rahim 2.00 5.00
H29 Juwan Howard 1.50 4.00
H30 Michael Jordan 25.00 60.00

1998 Upper Deck Hardcourt Jordan Holding Court Red

STATED ODDS 2300 SERIAL #'d SETS
*BRONZE: 1.5X TO 4X HI COLUMN
BRONZE: PRINT RUN 230 SERIAL #'d SETS
J1 S.Smith/M.Jordan 2.50 6.00
J2 A.Walker/M.Jordan 3.00 8.00
J3 G.Rice/M.Jordan 3.00 8.00
J4 S.Pippen/M.Jordan 8.00 20.00
J5 S.Kemp/M.Jordan 4.00 10.00
J6 M.Finley/M.Jordan 4.00 10.00
J7 B.Jackson/M.Jordan 2.50 6.00
J8 G.Hill/M.Jordan 6.00 15.00
J9 J.Jackson/M.Jordan 2.00 5.00
J10 C.Barkley/M.Jordan 5.00 12.00
J11 R.Miller/M.Jordan 4.00 10.00
J12 L.Wright/M.Jordan 2.00 5.00
J13 K.Bryant/M.Jordan 15.00 40.00
J14 T.Hardaway/M.Jordan 3.00 8.00
J15 G.Robinson/M.Jordan 2.50 6.00
J16 K.Garnett/M.Jordan 6.00 15.00
J17 K.Van Horn/M.Jordan 3.00 8.00
J18 P.Ewing/M.Jordan 4.00 10.00
J19 A.Hardaway/M.Jordan 6.00 15.00
J20 A.Iverson/M.Jordan 8.00 20.00
J21 J.Kidd/M.Jordan 6.00 15.00
J22 D.Stoudamire/M.Jordan 3.00 8.00
J23 M.Richmond/M.Jordan 3.00 8.00
J24 T.Duncan/M.Jordan 8.00 20.00
J25 G.Payton/M.Jordan 3.00 8.00
J26 C.Billups/M.Jordan 4.00 10.00
J27 K.Malone/M.Jordan 4.00 10.00
J28 S.Abdur-Rahim/M.Jordan 3.00 8.00
J29 C.Webber/M.Jordan 6.00 15.00
J30 M.Jordan/M.Jordan 20.00 50.00

1998 Upper Deck Hardcourt Jordan Holding Court Silver

*SILVER: 5X TO 12X BASE HI
STATED PRINT RUN 23 SETS
J13 K.Bryant/M.Jordan 600.00 1,100.00
J20 A.Iverson/M.Jordan 125.00 300.00
J30 M.Jordan/M.Jordan 600.00 1,000.00

1999-00 Upper Deck Hardcourt

COMPLETE SET (90) 30.00 80.00
COMPLETE SET w/o RC (60) 10.00 25.00
61-90 STATED ODDS 1:4
1 Dikembe Mutombo .60 1.50
2 Alan Henderson .25 .60
3 Antoine Walker .40 1.00
4 Paul Pierce .75 2.00
5 Eddie Jones .40 1.00
6 Elden Campbell .25 .60
7 Toni Kukoc .50 1.25
8 Randy Brown .25 .60
9 Shawn Kemp .60 1.50
10 Brevin Knight .25 .60
11 Michael Finley .40 1.00
12 Dirk Nowitzki 1.25 3.00
13 Antonio McDyess .30 .75
14 Nick Van Exel .30 .75
15 Grant Hill .60 1.50
16 Jerry Stackhouse .40 1.00
17 Antawn Jamison .40 1.00
18 John Starks .40 1.00
19 Hakeem Olajuwon .75 2.00
20 Scottie Pippen 1.00 2.50
21 Reggie Miller .75 2.00
22 Jalen Rose .30 .75
23 Maurice Taylor .25 .60
24 Michael Olowokandi .25 .60
25 Shaquille O'Neal 1.50 4.00
26 Kobe Bryant 3.00 8.00
27 Tim Hardaway .50 1.25
28 Alonzo Mourning .60 1.50
29 Glenn Robinson .30 .75
30 Ray Allen .60 1.50
31 Kevin Garnett 1.00 2.50
32 Terrell Brandon .25 .60
33 Stephon Marbury .50 1.25
34 Keith Van Horn .30 .75
35 Latrell Sprewell .50 1.25
36 Allan Houston .30 .75
37 Patrick Ewing .50 1.25
38 Darrell Armstrong .25 .60
39 Bo Outlaw .25 .60
40 Allen Iverson 1.00 2.50
41 Larry Hughes .30 .75
42 Jason Kidd .60 1.50
43 Tom Gugliotta .30 .75
44 Brian Grant .25 .60
45 Damon Stoudamire .40 1.00
46 Jason Williams .60 1.50
47 Vlade Divac .40 1.00
48 Tim Duncan 1.00 2.50
49 David Robinson .75 2.00
50 Avery Johnson .30 .75
51 Gary Payton .60 1.50
52 Vin Baker .30 .75
53 Vince Carter 1.00 2.50
54 Tracy McGrady .60 1.50
55 Karl Malone .75 2.00
56 John Stockton .60 1.50
57 Shareef Abdur-Rahim .40 1.00
58 Mike Bibby .40 1.00
59 Juwan Howard .30 .75
60 Mitch Richmond .50 1.25
61 Elton Brand RC 1.25 3.00
62 Jason Terry RC 1.00 2.50
63 Kenny Thomas RC .60 1.50
64 Jonathan Bender RC .60 1.50
65 A.Radojevic RC .40 1.00
66 Galen Young RC .60 1.50
67 Baron Davis RC 1.50 4.00
68 Corey Maggette RC .75 2.00
69 Dion Glover RC .40 1.00
70 Scott Padgett RC .50 1.25
71 Steve Francis RC 1.25 3.00
72 Richard Hamilton RC 1.50 4.00
73 James Posey RC .60 1.50
74 Jumaine Jones RC .40 1.00
75 Chris Herren RC .50 1.25
76 Andre Miller RC 1.25 3.00
77 Lamar Odom RC 1.25 3.00
78 Wally Szczerbiak RC 1.00 2.50
79 William Avery RC .40 1.00
80 Devean George RC .50 1.25
81 Trajan Langdon RC .50 1.25
82 Cal Bowdler RC .40 1.00
83 Kris Clack RC .40 1.00
84 Tim James RC .40 1.00
85 Shawn Marion RC 1.25 3.00
86 Ryan Robertson RC .40 1.00
87 Quincy Lewis RC .40 1.00
88 Vonteego Cummings RC .40 1.00
89 Obinna Ekezie RC .40 1.00
90 Jeff Foster RC .60 1.50
GF1 M.Jordan Floor/50 250.00 500.00
GF6 W.Chamberlain Flr/100 100.00 200.00

1999-00 Upper Deck Hardcourt Baseline Grooves Rainbow

*STARS: 2.5X TO 6X BASE CARD HI
*RCs: .75X TO 2X BASE HI
STATED PRINT RUN 500 SERIAL #'d SETS

1999-00 Upper Deck Hardcourt Baseline Grooves Silver

*STARS: 15X TO 40X BASE CARD HI
*RCs: 5X TO 12X BASE HI
STATED PRINT RUN 50 SERIAL #'d SETS
26 Kobe Bryant 150.00 300.00
48 Tim Duncan 75.00 200.00

1999-00 Upper Deck Hardcourt Court Authority

COMPLETE SET (10) 40.00 80.00
STATED ODDS 1:99
A1 Tim Duncan 8.00 20.00
A2 Vince Carter 8.00 20.00
A3 Allen Iverson 8.00 20.00
A4 Jason Williams 5.00 12.00
A5 Kevin Garnett 8.00 20.00
A6 Keith Van Horn 2.50 6.00
A7 Jason Kidd 5.00 12.00
A8 Grant Hill 5.00 12.00
A9 Antoine Walker 3.00 8.00
A10 Michael Jordan 10.00 25.00

1999-00 Upper Deck Hardcourt Court Forces

COMPLETE SET (10) 3.00 8.00
STATED ODDS 1:8
CF1 Shareef Abdur-Rahim .50 1.25
CF2 Scottie Pippen 1.25 3.00
CF3 Latrell Sprewell .60 1.50
CF4 Tim Hardaway .60 1.50
CF5 Shaquille O'Neal 2.00 5.00
CF6 Mike Bibby .50 1.25
CF7 Allen Iverson 1.25 3.00
CF8 John Stockton .75 2.00
CF9 Michael Finley .50 1.25
CF10 Reggie Miller 1.00 2.50

1999-00 Upper Deck Hardcourt Legends of the Hardcourt

COMPLETE SET (10) 12.50 30.00
STATED ODDS 1:19
L1 Michael Jordan 12.00 30.00
L2 Elgin Baylor 1.25 3.00
L3 Kevin McHale 1.50 4.00
L4 Julius Erving 3.00 8.00
L5 Larry Bird 3.00 8.00
L6 George Gervin 1.25 3.00
L7 Bob Cousy 2.00 5.00
L8 John Havlicek 1.50 4.00
L9 Jerry West 2.00 5.00
L10 Walt Frazier 1.25 3.00

1999-00 Upper Deck Hardcourt MJ Records Almanac

COMPLETE SET (10) 30.00 80.00
COMMON CARD (J1-J10) 4.00 10.00
STATED ODDS 1:19

1999-00 Upper Deck Hardcourt New Court Order

COMPLETE SET (20) 5.00 12.00
STATED ODDS 1:3
NC1 Vince Carter 1.00 2.50
NC2 Allan Houston .30 .75
NC3 Paul Pierce .75 2.00
NC4 Eddie Jones .40 1.00
NC5 Antawn Jamison .40 1.00
NC6 Mike Bibby .40 1.00
NC7 Tim Duncan 1.00 2.50
NC8 Kobe Bryant 3.00 8.00
NC9 Maurice Taylor .25 .60
NC10 Darrell Armstrong .25 .60
NC11 Stephon Marbury .50 1.25
NC12 Gary Payton .60 1.50
NC13 Brian Grant .25 .60
NC14 Jason Williams .60 1.50
NC15 Shareef Abdur-Rahim .40 1.00
NC16 Damon Stoudamire .40 1.00
NC17 Keith Van Horn .30 .75
NC18 Tom Gugliotta .30 .75
NC19 Antonio McDyess .30 .75
NC20 Ray Allen .60 1.50

1999-00 Upper Deck Hardcourt Power in the Paint

COMPLETE SET (12) 3.00 8.00
STATED ODDS 1:6
P1 Antoine Walker .50 1.25
P2 Karl Malone 1.00 2.50
P3 Hakeem Olajuwon 1.00 2.50
P4 David Robinson 1.00 2.50
P5 Antonio McDyess .40 1.00
P6 Shawn Kemp .75 2.00
P7 Glenn Robinson .40 1.00
P8 Juwan Howard .40 1.00
P9 Patrick Ewing .60 1.50
P10 Alonzo Mourning .75 2.00
P11 Antawn Jamison .50 1.25
P12 Dikembe Mutombo .75 2.00

2000-01 Upper Deck Hardcourt

COMPLETE SET w/o RC (60) 10.00 25.00
RCs: PRINT RUN 900 SERIAL #'d SETS
1 Dikembe Mutombo .50 1.25
2 Jason Terry .30 .75
3 Antoine Walker .30 .75
4 Paul Pierce .50 1.25
5 Eddie Jones .30 .75
6 Baron Davis .30 .75
7 Elton Brand .30 .75
8 Ron Artest .30 .75
9 Andre Miller .25 .60
10 Shawn Kemp .50 1.25
11 Dirk Nowitzki .75 2.00
12 Michael Finley .30 .75
13 Antonio McDyess .25 .60
14 Nick Van Exel .30 .75
15 Grant Hill .50 1.25
16 Jerry Stackhouse .30 .75
17 Antawn Jamison .30 .75
18 Larry Hughes .30 .75
19 Steve Francis .30 .75
20 Hakeem Olajuwon .60 1.50
21 Reggie Miller .60 1.50
22 Jalen Rose .25 .60
23 Lamar Odom .30 .75
24 Eric Piatkowski .20 .50
25 Shaquille O'Neal 1.25 3.00
26 Kobe Bryant 2.50 6.00
27 Alonzo Mourning .50 1.25
28 Jamal Mashburn .25 .60
29 Ray Allen .50 1.25
30 Glenn Robinson .30 .75
31 Kevin Garnett .75 2.00
32 Wally Szczerbiak .25 .60
33 Keith Van Horn .25 .60
34 Stephon Marbury .40 1.00
35 Allan Houston .30 .75
36 Latrell Sprewell .40 1.00
37 Darrell Armstrong .20 .50
38 Ron Mercer .25 .60
39 Allen Iverson .75 2.00
40 Toni Kukoc .40 1.00
41 Jason Kidd .50 1.25
42 Anfernee Hardaway .50 1.25
43 Shawn Marion .40 1.00
44 Scottie Pippen .75 2.00
45 Damon Stoudamire .40 1.00
46 Chris Webber .40 1.00
47 Jason Williams .50 1.25
48 Tim Duncan .75 2.00
49 David Robinson .60 1.50
50 Gary Payton .50 1.25
51 Vin Baker .25 .60
52 Rashard Lewis .25 .60
53 Tracy McGrady .60 1.50
54 Vince Carter .60 1.50
55 Karl Malone .60 1.50
56 John Stockton .60 1.50
57 Shareef Abdur-Rahim .30 .75
58 Mike Bibby .30 .75
59 Mitch Richmond .40 1.00
60 Richard Hamilton .40 1.00
61 Kenyon Martin RC 3.00 8.00
62 Marcus Fizer RC 1.25 3.00
63 Chris Mihm RC 1.00 2.50
64 Chris Porter RC 1.00 2.50
65 Stromile Swift RC 1.25 3.00
66 Morris Peterson RC 1.50 4.00
67 Quentin Richardson RC 1.25 3.00
68 Courtney Alexander RC 1.00 2.50
69 Scoonie Penn RC 1.50 4.00
70 Mateen Cleaves RC 1.25 3.00
71 Erick Barkley RC 1.00 2.50
72 A.J. Guyton RC 1.00 2.50
73 Darius Miles RC 1.50 4.00
74 DerMarr Johnson RC 1.00 2.50
75 Hedo Turkoglu RC 2.50 6.00
76 Hanno Mottola RC 1.00 2.50
77 Mike Miller RC 2.50 6.00
78 Desmond Mason RC 2.00 5.00
79 Mark Madsen RC 1.50 4.00
80 Eduardo Najera RC 1.50 4.00
81 Speedy Claxton RC 1.50 4.00
82 Joel Przybilla RC 1.25 3.00
83 Brian Cardinal RC 1.00 2.50
84 Khalid El-Amin RC 1.00 2.50
85 Etan Thomas RC 1.25 3.00
86 Corey Hightower RC 1.50 4.00
87 Dan Langhi RC 1.00 2.50
88 Michael Redd RC 4.00 10.00
89 Pete Mickeal RC 1.25 3.00
90 Mamadou N'Diaye RC 1.00 2.50
91 Jerome Moiso RC 1.00 2.50
92 Chris Carrawell RC 1.00 2.50
93 Jason Collier RC 1.50 4.00
94 Keyon Dooling RC 1.25 3.00
95 Mark Karcher RC 1.00 2.50
96 Jamaal Magloire RC 1.50 4.00
97 Jason Hart RC 1.50 4.00
98 Jabari Smith RC 1.00 2.50
99 Donnell Harvey RC 1.25 3.00
100 Lavor Postell RC 1.00 2.50
101 Eddie House RC 1.25 3.00
102 Dan McClintock RC 1.50 4.00

2000-01 Upper Deck Hardcourt Court Authority

COMPLETE SET (15) 15.00 40.00
STATED ODDS 1:15
CA1 Kobe Bryant 8.00 20.00
CA2 Allen Iverson 2.50 6.00
CA3 Gary Payton 1.50 4.00
CA4 Tim Duncan 2.50 6.00
CA5 Kevin Garnett 2.50 6.00
CA6 Steve Francis 1.00 2.50
CA7 Vince Carter 2.00 5.00
CA8 Shaquille O'Neal 4.00 10.00
CA9 Jason Kidd 1.50 4.00
CA10 Karl Malone 2.00 5.00
CA11 Shareef Abdur-Rahim 1.00 2.50
CA12 Grant Hill 1.00 2.50
CA13 Reggie Miller 2.00 5.00
CA14 Keith Van Horn .75 2.00
CA15 John Stockton 2.00 5.00

2000-01 Upper Deck Hardcourt Court Forces

COMPLETE SET (11) 12.00 30.00
STATED ODDS 1:12
C1 Elton Brand 1.00 2.50
C2 Steve Francis 1.00 2.50
C3 Allan Houston 1.00 2.50
C4 Lamar Odom 1.00 2.50
C5 Andre Miller .75 2.00
C6 Jason Williams 1.50 4.00
C7 Ron Mercer .75 2.00
C8 Kobe Bryant 8.00 20.00
C9 Kevin Garnett 2.50 6.00
C10 Jerry Stackhouse 1.00 2.50
C11 Latrell Sprewell 1.25 3.00

2000-01 Upper Deck Hardcourt Floor Leaders

COMPLETE SET (20) 15.00 40.00
STATED ODDS 1:7
FL1 Kobe Bryant 8.00 20.00
FL2 Eddie Jones 1.00 2.50
FL3 Kevin Garnett 2.50 6.00
FL4 Andre Miller .75 2.00
FL5 Keith Van Horn .75 2.00
FL6 Allan Houston 1.00 2.50
FL7 Larry Hughes 1.00 2.50
FL8 Jason Williams 1.50 4.00
FL9 Tracy McGrady 2.00 5.00
FL10 Shawn Kemp 1.50 4.00
FL11 Stephon Marbury 1.25 3.00
FL12 Glenn Robinson 1.00 2.50
FL13 Mike Bibby 1.00 2.50
FL14 Baron Davis 1.00 2.50
FL15 Scottie Pippen 2.50 6.00
FL16 David Robinson 2.00 5.00
FL17 Paul Pierce 1.50 4.00
FL18 Wally Szczerbiak .75 2.00
FL19 Jalen Rose .75 2.00
FL20 Lamar Odom 1.00 2.50

2000-01 Upper Deck Hardcourt Game Floor

STATED ODDS 1:15
AHF Anfernee Hardaway 4.00 10.00
AIF Allen Iverson 6.00 15.00
ALF Allan Houston 2.50 6.00
AMF Alonzo Mourning 4.00 10.00
AWF Antoine Walker 2.50 6.00
CWF Chris Webber 3.00 8.00
DRF David Robinson 5.00 12.00
EJF Eddie Jones 2.50 6.00
GHF Grant Hill 4.00 10.00
GPF Gary Payton 4.00 10.00
JKF Jason Kidd 4.00 10.00
KBF Kobe Bryant 40.00 100.00
KGA Kevin Garnett AU/21 150.00 400.00
KGF Kevin Garnett 6.00 15.00
KMA Karl Malone AU/32 150.00 400.00
KMF Karl Malone 5.00 12.00
MCF Antonio McDyess 2.00 5.00
MFF Michael Finley 2.50 6.00
MJA Michael Jordan AU/23 4,000.00 8,000.00
RAF Ray Allen 4.00 10.00
RGF Reggie Miller 5.00 12.00
RMF Ron Mercer 2.00 5.00
RWF Rasheed Wallace 3.00 8.00
SAF Shareef Abdur-Rahim 2.50 6.00
SMF Stephon Marbury 3.00 8.00
SOF Shaquille O'Neal 10.00 25.00
SPF Scottie Pippen 6.00 15.00
THF Tim Hardaway 3.00 8.00

2000-01 Upper Deck Hardcourt Night Court

COMPLETE SET (15) 25.00 60.00
STATED ODDS 1:15
NC1 Kevin Garnett 2.50 6.00
NC2 Tim Duncan 2.50 6.00
NC3 Larry Hughes 1.00 2.50
NC4 Elton Brand 1.00 2.50
NC5 Kobe Bryant 20.00 50.00
NC6 Anfernee Hardaway 1.50 4.00
NC7 Tracy McGrady 2.00 5.00
NC8 Antonio McDyess .75 2.00
NC9 Paul Pierce 1.50 4.00
NC10 Lamar Odom 1.00 2.50
NC11 Chris Webber 1.25 3.00
NC12 Ray Allen 1.50 4.00
NC13 Allan Houston 1.00 2.50
NC14 Wally Szczerbiak .75 2.00
NC15 Alonzo Mourning 1.50 4.00

2000-01 Upper Deck Hardcourt Thriller Instinct

COMPLETE SET (11) 20.00 50.00
STATED ODDS 1:12
TI1 Kevin Garnett 2.50 6.00
TI2 Vince Carter 2.00 5.00
TI3 Shawn Marion 1.00 2.50
TI4 Stephon Marbury 1.25 3.00
TI5 Antawn Jamison 1.00 2.50
TI6 Jason Williams 1.50 4.00
TI7 Michael Finley 1.00 2.50
TI8 Kobe Bryant 15.00 40.00
TI9 Richard Hamilton 1.25 3.00
TI10 Reggie Miller 2.00 5.00
TI11 Elton Brand 1.00 2.50

2000-01 Upper Deck Hardcourt UD Authentics

STATED ODDS 1:100
AH Anfernee Hardaway 60.00 150.00
AI Allen Iverson 100.00 250.00
AM Andre Miller 8.00 20.00
BD Baron Davis 10.00 25.00
DM Darius Miles 10.00 25.00
DS Damon Stoudamire 10.00 25.00
GP Gary Payton 40.00 100.00
JM Jerome Moiso 3.00 8.00
JR Jalen Rose 10.00 25.00
JS Jerry Stackhouse 10.00 25.00
KB Kobe Bryant 1,500.00 3,000.00
KG Kevin Garnett 100.00 250.00
KM Karl Malone 80.00 160.00
LH Larry Hughes 10.00 25.00
MC Antonio McDyess 8.00 20.00
MF Marcus Fizer 8.00 20.00
MF Michael Finley 10.00 25.00
PP Paul Pierce 40.00 100.00
QR Quentin Richardson 8.00 20.00
RA Ray Allen 60.00 150.00
SA Shareef Abdur-Rahim 10.00 25.00
SF Steve Francis 10.00 25.00
TH Tim Hardaway 12.00 30.00
WS Wally Szczerbiak 8.00 20.00

2001-02 Upper Deck Hardcourt

COMP.SET w/o SP's (90) 25.00 50.00
91-100 PRINT RUN 3000 PER PLAYER
91-100 THREE VERSIONS SER.#'d TO 1000
101-110 PRINT RUN 1200 PER PLAYER
101-110 THREE VERSIONS SER.#'d TO 600
111-120 PRINT RUN 900 PER PLAYER
111-120 THREE VERSIONS SER.#'d TO 300
ALL RC VERSIONS SAME VALUE
1 Jason Terry .40 1.00
2 DerMarr Johnson .25 .60
3 Toni Kukoc .50 1.25
4 Antoine Walker .30 .75
5 Paul Pierce .60 1.50
6 Kenny Anderson .30 .75
7 Jamal Mashburn .30 .75
8 Baron Davis .40 1.00
9 David Wesley .25 .60
10 Ron Artest .30 .75
11 Jamal Crawford .40 1.00
12 Ron Mercer .25 .60
13 Andre Miller .30 .75
14 Lamond Murray .25 .60
15 Matt Harpring .25 .60
16 Michael Finley .40 1.00
17 Dirk Nowitzki 1.00 2.50
18 Steve Nash .75 2.00
19 Antonio McDyess .30 .75
20 Nick Van Exel .30 .75
21 James Posey .25 .60
22 Jerry Stackhouse .40 1.00
23 Chucky Atkins .25 .60
24 Mateen Cleaves .25 .60
25 Antawn Jamison .30 .75
26 Larry Hughes .30 .75
27 Marc Jackson .25 .60
28 Steve Francis .40 1.00
29 Maurice Taylor .25 .60
30 Cuttino Mobley .30 .75
31 Reggie Miller .75 2.00
32 Jalen Rose .30 .75
33 Jermaine O'Neal .30 .75
34 Darius Miles .25 .60
35 Lamar Odom .30 .75
36 Elton Brand .30 .75
37 Kobe Bryant 3.00 8.00
38 Shaquille O'Neal 1.50 4.00
39 Derek Fisher .30 .75
40 Robert Horry .40 1.00
41 Alonzo Mourning .60 1.50
42 Eddie Jones .40 1.00
43 Brian Grant .25 .60
44 Anthony Mason .40 1.00
45 Ray Allen .60 1.50
46 Glenn Robinson .40 1.00
47 Tim Thomas .25 .60
48 Kevin Garnett 1.00 2.50
49 Wally Szczerbiak .30 .75
50 Terrell Brandon .30 .75
51 Anthony Peeler .25 .60
52 Jason Kidd .60 1.50
53 Kenyon Martin .30 .75
54 Stephen Jackson .30 .75
55 Latrell Sprewell .50 1.25
56 Allan Houston .40 1.00
57 Glen Rice .40 1.00
58 Tracy McGrady .60 1.50
59 Darrell Armstrong .25 .60
60 Mike Miller .30 .75
61 Allen Iverson 1.00 2.50
62 Dikembe Mutombo .60 1.50
63 Aaron McKie .25 .60
64 Stephon Marbury .50 1.25
65 Shawn Marion .40 1.00
66 Tom Gugliotta .25 .60
67 Rasheed Wallace .50 1.25
68 Scottie Pippen 1.00 2.50
69 Damon Stoudamire .40 1.00
70 Chris Webber .50 1.25
71 Mike Bibby .40 1.00
72 Peja Stojakovic .30 .75
73 Tim Duncan 1.00 2.50
74 David Robinson .75 2.00
75 Derek Anderson .25 .60
76 Gary Payton .60 1.50
77 Rashard Lewis .30 .75
78 Desmond Mason .30 .75
79 Vince Carter .75 2.00
80 Morris Peterson .25 .60
81 Antonio Davis .30 .75
82 Karl Malone .75 2.00
83 John Stockton .75 2.00
84 Donyell Marshall .25 .60
85 Bryant Reeves .25 .60
86 Jason Williams .60 1.50
87 Stromile Swift .25 .60
88 Richard Hamilton .50 1.25
89 Courtney Alexander .25 .60
90 Chris Whitney .25 .60
91A Kenny Satterfield ON RC 1.00 2.50
91B Kenny Satterfield OFF RC 1.00 2.50
91C Kenny Satterfield HI RC 1.00 2.50
92A Jeff Trepagnier ON RC 1.00 2.50
92B Jeff Trepagnier OFF RC 1.00 2.50
92C Jeff Trepagnier HI RC 1.00 2.50
93A Michael Wright ON RC 1.50 4.00
93B Michael Wright OFF RC 1.50 4.00
93C Michael Wright HI RC 1.50 4.00
94A Terence Morris ON RC 1.00 2.50
94B Terence Morris OFF RC 1.00 2.50
94C Terence Morris HI RC 1.00 2.50
95A Omar Cook ON RC 1.50 4.00
95B Omar Cook OFF RC 1.50 4.00
95C Omar Cook HI RC 1.50 4.00
96A Gilbert Arenas ON RC 4.00 10.00
96B Gilbert Arenas OFF RC 4.00 10.00
96C Gilbert Arenas HI RC 4.00 10.00
97A Joseph Forte ON RC 1.00 2.50
97B Joseph Forte OFF RC 1.00 2.50
97C Joseph Forte HI RC 1.00 2.50
98A Jamaal Tinsley ON RC 1.25 3.00
98B Jamaal Tinsley OFF RC 1.25 3.00
98C Jamaal Tinsley HI RC 1.25 3.00
99A Samuel Dalembert ON RC 1.50 4.00
99B Samuel Dalembert OFF RC 1.50 4.00
99C Samuel Dalembert HI RC 1.50 4.00
100A Gerald Wallace ON RC 2.00 5.00
100B Gerald Wallace OFF RC 2.00 5.00
100C Gerald Wallace HI RC 2.00 5.00
101A Brendan Haywood ON RC 1.50 4.00
101B Brendan Haywood OFF RC 1.50 4.00
101C Brendan Haywood HI RC 1.50 4.00
102A Richard Jefferson ON RC 2.50 6.00
102B Richard Jefferson OFF RC 2.50 6.00
102C Richard Jefferson HI RC 2.50 6.00
103A Michael Bradley ON RC 1.25 3.00
103B Michael Bradley OFF RC 1.25 3.00
103C Michael Bradley HI RC 1.25 3.00
104A Loren Woods ON RC 1.25 3.00
104B Loren Woods OFF RC 1.25 3.00
104C Loren Woods HI RC 1.25 3.00
105A Jeryl Sasser ON RC 1.25 3.00
105B Jeryl Sasser OFF RC 1.25 3.00
105C Jeryl Sasser HI RC 1.25 3.00
106A Jason Collins ON RC 1.50 4.00
106B Jason Collins OFF RC 1.50 4.00
106C Jason Collins HI RC 1.50 4.00
107A Kirk Haston ON RC 1.25 3.00
107B Kirk Haston OFF RC 1.25 3.00
107C Kirk Haston HI RC 1.25 3.00
108A Steven Hunter ON RC 1.25 3.00
108B Steven Hunter OFF RC 1.25 3.00
108C Steven Hunter HI RC 1.25 3.00
109A Troy Murphy ON RC 1.50 4.00
109B Troy Murphy OFF RC 1.50 4.00
109C Troy Murphy HI RC 1.50 4.00
110A Vladimir Radmanovic ON RC 1.50 4.00
110B Vladimir Radmanovic OFF RC 1.50 4.00
110C Vladimir Radmanovic HI RC 1.50 4.00
111A Rodney White ON RC 2.50 6.00
111B Rodney White OFF RC 2.50 6.00
111C Rodney White HI RC 2.50 6.00
112A Kedrick Brown ON RC 2.50 6.00
112B Kedrick Brown OFF RC 2.50 6.00
112C Kedrick Brown HI RC 2.50 6.00
113A Joe Johnson ON RC 6.00 15.00
113B Joe Johnson OFF RC 6.00 15.00
113C Joe Johnson HI RC 6.00 15.00
114A Eddie Griffin ON RC 3.00 8.00
114B Eddie Griffin OFF RC 3.00 8.00
114C Eddie Griffin HI RC 3.00 8.00
115A Shane Battier ON RC 8.00 20.00
115B Shane Battier OFF RC 8.00 20.00
115C Shane Battier HI RC 8.00 20.00
116A Eddy Curry ON RC 4.00 10.00
116B Eddy Curry OFF RC 4.00 10.00
116C Eddy Curry HI RC 4.00 10.00
117A Jason Richardson ON RC 6.00 15.00
117B Jason Richardson OFF RC 6.00 15.00
117C Jason Richardson HI RC 6.00 15.00
118A DeSagana Diop ON RC 2.50 6.00
118B DeSagana Diop OFF RC 2.50 6.00
118C DeSagana Diop HI RC 2.50 6.00
119A Tyson Chandler ON RC 6.00 15.00
119B Tyson Chandler OFF RC 6.00 15.00
119C Tyson Chandler HI RC 6.00 15.00
120A Kwame Brown ON RC 4.00 10.00
120B Kwame Brown OFF RC 4.00 10.00
120C Kwame Brown HI RC 4.00 10.00
121 Michael Jordan 6.00 15.00

2001-02 Upper Deck Hardcourt Exclusives

*STARS: 20X TO 50X BASE CARD HI
*ROOKIES 91-100: 3X TO 8X BASE CARD HI
*ROOKIES 101-110: 2.5X TO 6X HI
*ROOKIES 111-120: 1.25X TO 3X HI
PRINT RUN 25 SERIAL #'d SETS

2001-02 Upper Deck Hardcourt Fantastic Floor

PRINT RUN 100 SERIAL #'d SETS
AHLS A.Houston/L.Sprewell 20.00 50.00
AITM A.Iverson/T.McGrady 40.00 100.00
CWPS C.Webber/P.Stojakovic 12.00 30.00
EJTH E.Jones/T.Hardaway 8.00 20.00
GPRLDM Payton/Lewis/Mason 15.00 30.00
JMBD J.Mashburn/B.Davis 8.00 20.00
JSMC J.Stack/M.Cleaves 8.00 20.00
KBAI K.Bryant/A.Iverson 75.00 200.00
KBDM K.Bryant/D.Miles 40.00 100.00
KBKG K.Bryant/K.Garnett 75.00 200.00
KBRL K.Bryant/R.Lewis 40.00 100.00
KBSF K.Bryant/S.Francis 40.00 100.00
KGTBWS Garnett/Brandon/Szcz 15.00 40.00
KMJS K.Malone/J.Stockton 25.00 60.00
MCNV A.McDyess/N.Van Exel 8.00 20.00
MFDNSN Finley/Nowitzki/Nash 25.00 60.00
MJKBKG Jordan/Bryant/KG 200.00 500.00
PPAW P.Pierce/A.Walker 25.00 60.00
RAGR R.Allen/G.Robinson 12.00 30.00
RMJOJB Miller/J.O'Neal/Bender 15.00 40.00
RWSPDS Wallac/Pippn/Stoudm 12.00 30.00
TMMM T.McGrady/M.Miller 12.00 30.00

2001-02 Upper Deck Hardcourt UD Game Film/Floor

STATED ODDS 1:15
AIF Allen Iverson 10.00 25.00
BDF Baron Davis 4.00 10.00
CWF Chris Webber 5.00 12.00
DAF Darius Miles 2.50 6.00
DMF Desmond Mason 3.00 8.00
DRF David Robinson 8.00 20.00
EJF Eddie Jones 4.00 10.00
JMF Jamal Mashburn 3.00 8.00
JSF Jerry Stackhouse 4.00 10.00
JTF Jason Terry 4.00 10.00
KBF Kobe Bryant 40.00 100.00
KEF Kenyon Martin 4.00 10.00
KGF Kevin Garnett 10.00 25.00
KMF Karl Malone 8.00 20.00
LSF Latrell Sprewell 5.00 12.00
MAF Shawn Marion 4.00 10.00
MCF Antonio McDyess 3.00 8.00
MFF Michael Finley 4.00 10.00
MMF Mike Miller 3.00 8.00
MPF Morris Peterson 2.50 6.00
PPF Paul Pierce 6.00 15.00
PSF Peja Stojakovic 3.00 8.00
RAF Ray Allen 6.00 15.00
RMF Reggie Miller 8.00 20.00
SFF Steve Francis 4.00 10.00
SJF Stephen Jackson 3.00 8.00
TMF Tracy McGrady 6.00 15.00

2001-02 Upper Deck Hardcourt UD Game Floor

STATED ODDS 1:15
AI Allen Iverson 6.00 15.00
BD Baron Davis 2.50 6.00
CW Chris Webber 3.00 8.00
DA Darius Miles 1.50 4.00
DM Desmond Mason 2.00 5.00
DR David Robinson 5.00 12.00
EJ Eddie Jones 2.50 6.00
JM Jamal Mashburn 2.00 5.00
JS Jerry Stackhouse 2.50 6.00
JT Jason Terry 2.50 6.00
KB Kobe Bryant 25.00 60.00
KE Kenyon Martin 2.50 6.00
KG Kevin Garnett 6.00 15.00
KM Karl Malone 5.00 12.00
LS Latrell Sprewell 3.00 8.00
MA Shawn Marion 2.50 6.00
MC Antonio McDyess 2.00 5.00
MF Michael Finley 2.50 6.00
MM Mike Miller 2.00 5.00
MP Morris Peterson 1.50 4.00
PP Paul Pierce 4.00 10.00
PS Peja Stojakovic 2.00 5.00
RA Ray Allen 4.00 10.00
RM Reggie Miller 5.00 12.00
SF Steve Francis 2.50 6.00
SJ Stephen Jackson 2.00 5.00
TM Tracy McGrady 4.00 10.00

2001-02 Upper Deck Hardcourt UD Game Floor Autographs

STATED ODDS 1:150
DAA Darius Miles 8.00 20.00
DMA Desmond Mason 8.00 20.00
JMA Jamal Mashburn 8.00 20.00
JSA Jerry Stackhouse 10.00 25.00
KBA Kobe Bryant 1,000.00 2,000.00
KEA Kenyon Martin 10.00 25.00
KGA Kevin Garnett 60.00 150.00
MCA Antonio McDyess 6.00 15.00
MMA Mike Miller 8.00 20.00
MPA Morris Peterson 6.00 15.00
PPA Paul Pierce 25.00 60.00
RAA Ray Allen 20.00 50.00

2002-03 Upper Deck Hardcourt

COMP.SET w/o SP's (90) 20.00 50.00
91-120 PRINT RUN 1999 SER.#'d SETS
121-129 PRINT RUN 1299 SER.#'d SETS
130-135 PRINT RUN 799 SER.#'d SETS
1 Shareef Abdur-Rahim .40 1.00
2 Glenn Robinson .40 1.00
3 Jason Terry .30 .75
4 Antoine Walker .30 .75
5 Paul Pierce .60 1.50
6 Kedrick Brown .25 .60
7 Jalen Rose .30 .75
8 Eddy Curry .25 .60
9 Tyson Chandler .40 1.00
10 Marcus Fizer .25 .60
11 Lamond Murray .25 .60
12 Darius Miles .25 .60
13 Chris Mihm .25 .60
14 Dirk Nowitzki 1.00 2.50
15 Michael Finley .40 1.00
16 Steve Nash .75 2.00
17 James Posey .25 .60
18 Juwan Howard .30 .75
19 Kenny Satterfield .25 .60
20 Jerry Stackhouse .40 1.00
21 Clifford Robinson .40 1.00
22 Ben Wallace .50 1.25
23 Antawn Jamison .30 .75
24 Jason Richardson .40 1.00
25 Gilbert Arenas .40 1.00
26 Steve Francis .40 1.00
27 Cuttino Mobley .25 .60
28 Eddie Griffin .25 .60
29 Reggie Miller .75 2.00
30 Jermaine O'Neal .30 .75
31 Jamaal Tinsley .30 .75
32 Elton Brand .30 .75
33 Andre Miller .30 .75
34 Lamar Odom .40 1.00
35 Kobe Bryant 3.00 8.00
36 Shaquille O'Neal 1.50 4.00
37 Derek Fisher .40 1.00
38 Devean George .25 .60
39 Pau Gasol .60 1.50
40 Jason Williams .50 1.25
41 Shane Battier .40 1.00
42 Alonzo Mourning .60 1.50
43 Eddie Jones .40 1.00
44 Brian Grant .25 .60
45 Ray Allen .60 1.50
46 Tim Thomas .25 .60
47 Sam Cassell .30 .75
48 Kevin Garnett 1.00 2.50
49 Wally Szczerbiak .30 .75
50 Terrell Brandon .25 .60
51 Jason Kidd .60 1.50
52 Richard Jefferson .30 .75
53 Dikembe Mutombo .60 1.50
54 Jamal Mashburn .30 .75
55 Baron Davis .40 1.00
56 David Wesley .25 .60
57 Allan Houston .40 1.00
58 Latrell Sprewell .40 1.00
59 Antonio McDyess .30 .75
60 Tracy McGrady .60 1.50
61 Mike Miller .30 .75
62 Darrell Armstrong .25 .60
63 Allen Iverson 1.00 2.50
64 Keith Van Horn .30 .75
65 Aaron McKie .25 .60
66 Stephon Marbury .50 1.25
67 Shawn Marion .40 1.00
68 Anfernee Hardaway 1.00 2.50
69 Rasheed Wallace .50 1.25
70 Damon Stoudamire .40 1.00
71 Scottie Pippen 1.00 2.50
72 Chris Webber .50 1.25
73 Mike Bibby .40 1.00
74 Peja Stojakovic .30 .75
75 Tim Duncan 1.00 2.50

76 David Robinson .75 2.00
77 Tony Parker .60 1.50
78 Gary Payton .60 1.50
79 Rashard Lewis .30 .75
80 Desmond Mason .30 .75
81 Vince Carter .75 2.00
82 Morris Peterson .30 .75
83 Antonio Davis .30 .75
84 Karl Malone .75 2.00
85 John Stockton .75 2.00
86 Andrei Kirilenko .30 .75
87 Richard Hamilton .50 1.25
88 Michael Jordan 4.00 10.00
89 Chris Whitney .25 .60
90 Kwame Brown .25 .60
91 Efthimios Rentzias RC .75 2.00
92 Marko Jaric 1.25 3.00
93 Jiri Welsch RC 1.00 2.50
94 Carlos Boozer RC 1.25 3.00
95 Fred Jones RC 1.00 2.50
96 Sam Clancy RC 1.00 2.50
97 Predrag Savovic RC 1.00 2.50
98 Frank Williams RC .75 2.00
99 Rod Grizzard RC .75 2.00
100 Casey Jacobsen RC 1.00 2.50
101 Jamal Sampson RC .75 2.00
102 Lonny Baxter RC .75 2.00
103 Darius Songaila RC 1.25 3.00
104 Tito Maddox RC .75 2.00
105 Chris Owens RC .75 2.00
106 Juan Dixon RC 1.00 2.50
107 Chris Jefferies RC .75 2.00
108 Dan Dickau RC .75 2.00
109 Manu Ginobili RC 20.00 50.00
110 Tamar Slay RC .75 2.00
111 Matt Barnes RC 1.50 4.00
112 Vincent Yarbrough RC .75 2.00
113 Bostjan Nachbar RC 1.00 2.50
114 Dan Gadzuric RC 1.00 2.50
115 Robert Archibald RC .75 2.00
116 Ryan Humphrey RC 1.00 2.50
117 Tayshaun Prince RC 2.50 6.00
118 John Salmons RC 1.25 3.00
119 Steve Logan RC 1.25 3.00
120 Melvin Ely RC 1.00 2.50
121 Nikoloz Tskitishvili RC 1.00 2.50
122 Qyntel Woods RC 1.00 2.50
123 Marcus Haislip RC 1.00 2.50
124 Nene Hilario RC 1.50 4.00
125 Amare Stoudemire RC 4.00 10.00
126 Jared Jeffries RC 1.25 3.00
127 Kareem Rush RC 1.25 3.00
128 Chris Wilcox RC 1.25 3.00
129 Curtis Borchardt RC 1.00 2.50
130 Drew Gooden RC 2.00 5.00
131 Mike Dunleavy RC 2.00 5.00
132 DaJuan Wagner RC 1.50 4.00
133 Caron Butler RC 2.00 5.00
134 Yao Ming RC 20.00 50.00
135 Jay Williams RC 1.50 4.00

2002-03 Upper Deck Hardcourt Autographs

STATED ODDS 1:30
AJC Alvin Jones 4.00 10.00
CAC Courtney Alexander 4.00 10.00
GAC Gilbert Arenas 8.00 20.00
HMC Hanno Mottola 4.00 10.00
JMC Jamaal Magloire 4.00 10.00
JRC Jason Richardson 6.00 15.00
JSC Jerry Stackhouse SP 10.00 25.00
JTC Jamaal Tinsley 4.00 10.00
KBC Kobe Bryant SP 125.00 250.00
KGC Kevin Garnett SP 40.00 100.00
KMC Kenyon Martin 6.00 15.00
KSC Kenny Satterfield 4.00 10.00
LHC Larry Hughes 4.00 10.00
LMC Lamond Murray 4.00 10.00
MFC Marcus Fizer SP 4.00 10.00
MJC Michael Jordan/23 2,000.00 5,000.00
MMC Mike Miller 4.00 10.00
QRC Quentin Richardson 4.00 10.00
RWC Rodney White 4.00 10.00
TCC Tyson Chandler 6.00 15.00
WSC Wally Szczerbiak SP 6.00 15.00

2002-03 Upper Deck Hardcourt UD Game Floor

STATED ODDS 1:15
JKF Jason Kidd 2.50 6.00
JSF Jerry Stackhouse 1.50 4.00
KBF Kobe Bryant 12.00 30.00
KGF Kevin Garnett 4.00 10.00
MJF Michael Jordan SP 15.00 40.00
MMF Mike Miller 1.25 3.00
PPF Paul Pierce 2.50 6.00
PSF Peja Stojakovic 1.25 3.00
RLF Rashard Lewis 1.25 3.00
SFF Steve Francis 1.50 4.00
SMF Stephon Marbury 2.00 5.00

2002-03 Upper Deck Hardcourt UD Game Floor Metallics

STATED ODDS 1:150
AIM Allen Iverson 10.00 25.00
AWM Antoine Walker 4.00 10.00
CWM Chris Webber 6.00 15.00
DNM Dirk Nowitzki 12.00 30.00
KBM Kobe Bryant SP 40.00 100.00
KGM Kevin Garnett 12.00 30.00
LSM Latrell Sprewell 5.00 12.00
MFF Michael Finley 5.00 12.00
MJM Michael Jordan SP 100.00 250.00
RAM Ray Allen 8.00 20.00
RLM Rashard Lewis 4.00 10.00
SFM Steve Francis 5.00 12.00
SHM Shawn Marion 5.00 12.00
SMM Stephon Marbury 6.00 15.00
TMN Tracy McGrady 10.00 25.00

2002-03 Upper Deck Hardcourt UD Game Floor/Film

STATED ODDS 1:30
AIFF Allen Iverson 8.00 20.00
CWFF Chris Webber 4.00 10.00
DNFF Dirk Nowitzki 8.00 20.00
JKFF Jason Kidd 5.00 12.00
KBFF Kobe Bryant SP 40.00 100.00
KGFF Kevin Garnett 8.00 20.00
MJFF Michael Jordan SP 30.00 80.00
RLFF Rashard Lewis 2.50 6.00
SFFF Steve Francis 3.00 8.00
TMFF Tracy McGrady 5.00 12.00

2002-03 Upper Deck Hardcourt UD Game Jersey Metallics

STATED ODDS 1:300
AIJ Allen Iverson/75 25.00 60.00
AMJ Andre Miller 5.00 12.00
CWJ Chris Webber/75 25.00 60.00
DMJ Darius Miles 4.00 10.00
EBJ Elton Brand 5.00 12.00
JKJ Jason Kidd 10.00 25.00
KBJ Kobe Bryant/50 60.00 120.00
KGJ Kevin Garnett 15.00 40.00
KMJ Karl Malone 12.00 30.00
MCJ Antonio McDyess 5.00 12.00
MJJ Michael Jordan/23 175.00 350.00
MMJ Mike Miller 5.00 12.00
PPJ Paul Pierce 10.00 25.00
SMJ Stephon Marbury 8.00 20.00
TMJ Tracy McGrady/75 25.00 60.00

2003-04 Upper Deck Hardcourt

COMP.SET w/o SP's (90) 15.00 40.00
91-126 PRINT RUN 1999 SER.#'d SETS
1 Shareef Abdur-Rahim .30 .75
2 Jason Terry .25 .60
3 Glenn Robinson .25 .60
4 Paul Pierce .50 1.25
5 Antoine Walker .30 .75
6 Vin Baker .20 .50
7 Jalen Rose .25 .60
8 Tyson Chandler .25 .60
9 Michael Jordan 3.00 8.00
10 DaJuan Wagner .20 .50
11 Ricky Davis .25 .60
12 Darius Miles .20 .50
13 Dirk Nowitzki .75 2.00
14 Michael Finley .30 .75
15 Steve Nash .60 1.50
16 Nene .25 .60
17 Marcus Camby .25 .60
18 Nikoloz Tskitishvili .20 .50
19 Richard Hamilton .40 1.00
20 Ben Wallace .40 1.00
21 Tayshaun Prince .30 .75
22 Antawn Jamison .30 .75
23 Jason Richardson .30 .75
24 Gilbert Arenas .30 .75
25 Steve Francis .30 .75
26 Yao Ming .75 2.00
27 Eddie Griffin .20 .50
28 Reggie Miller .60 1.50
29 Jamaal Tinsley .20 .50
30 Jermaine O'Neal .30 .75
31 Elton Brand .25 .60
32 Andre Miller .25 .60
33 Lamar Odom .25 .60
34 Kobe Bryant 2.50 6.00
35 Gary Payton .50 1.25
36 Shaquille O'Neal 1.25 3.00
37 Karl Malone .60 1.50
38 Pau Gasol .50 1.25
39 Shane Battier .25 .60
40 Mike Miller .25 .60
41 Eddie Jones .30 .75
42 Rasual Butler .20 .50
43 Caron Butler .25 .60
44 Michael Redd .30 .75
45 Joe Smith .25 .60
46 Desmond Mason .25 .60
47 Kevin Garnett .75 2.00
48 Wally Szczerbiak .25 .60
49 Sam Cassell .25 .60
50 Jason Kidd .50 1.25
51 Richard Jefferson .25 .60
52 Alonzo Mourning .40 1.00
53 Baron Davis .30 .75
54 Jamal Mashburn .25 .60
55 Jamaal Magloire .20 .50
56 Allan Houston .30 .75
57 Antonio McDyess .25 .60
58 Latrell Sprewell .30 .75
59 Tracy McGrady .50 1.25
60 Grant Hill .40 1.00
61 Drew Gooden .25 .60
62 Allen Iverson .75 2.00
63 Keith Van Horn .25 .60
64 Kenny Thomas .20 .50
65 Stephon Marbury .40 1.00
66 Shawn Marion .30 .75
67 Amare Stoudemire .40 1.00
68 Rasheed Wallace .40 1.00
69 Bonzi Wells .20 .50
70 Damon Stoudamire .25 .60
71 Chris Webber .40 1.00
72 Mike Bibby .30 .75
73 Peja Stojakovic .30 .75
74 Bobby Jackson .25 .60
75 Tim Duncan .75 2.00
76 David Robinson .60 1.50
77 Tony Parker .50 1.25
78 Manu Ginobili .60 1.50
79 Ray Allen .50 1.25
80 Rashard Lewis .30 .75
81 Reggie Evans .20 .50
82 Vince Carter .60 1.50
83 Morris Peterson .20 .50
84 Antonio Davis .25 .60
85 Matt Harpring .20 .50
86 John Stockton .60 1.50
87 Andrei Kirilenko .25 .60
88 Jerry Stackhouse .40 1.00
89 Kwame Brown .25 .60
90 Larry Hughes .20 .50
91 Kirk Hinrich RC 2.00 5.00
92 T.J. Ford RC 1.50 4.00
93 Mike Sweetney RC 1.25 3.00
94 Jarvis Hayes RC 1.25 3.00
95 Mickael Pietrus RC 1.50 4.00
96 Nick Collison RC 1.50 4.00
97 Marcus Banks RC 1.25 3.00
98 Luke Ridnour RC 2.00 5.00
99 Reece Gaines RC 1.25 3.00
100 Troy Bell RC 1.25 3.00
101 Zarko Cabarkapa RC 1.25 3.00
102 David West RC 2.50 6.00
103 Aleksandar Pavlovic RC 1.50 4.00
104 Dahntay Jones RC 1.50 4.00
105 Boris Diaw RC 2.00 5.00
106 Zoran Planinic RC 1.25 3.00
107 Travis Outlaw RC 1.50 4.00
108 Brian Cook RC 1.25 3.00
109 Carlos Delfino RC 1.50 4.00
110 Ndudi Ebi RC 1.25 3.00
111 Kendrick Perkins RC 1.50 4.00
112 Leandro Barbosa RC 2.00 5.00
113 Josh Howard RC 2.00 5.00
114 Maciej Lampe RC 1.25 3.00
115 Jason Kapono RC 1.25 3.00
116 Luke Walton RC 2.00 5.00
117 Jerome Beasley RC 1.25 3.00
118 Sofoklis Schortsanitis RC 1.25 3.00
119 Kyle Korver RC 2.50 6.00
120 Travis Hansen RC 1.25 3.00
121 Steve Blake RC 1.50 4.00
122 Slavko Vranes RC 1.25 3.00
123 Zaur Pachulia RC 2.00 5.00
124 Keith Bogans RC 1.25 3.00
125 Matt Bonner RC 2.00 5.00
126 Maurice Williams RC 2.00 5.00
127 Chris Kaman RC 4.00 10.00
128 Dwyane Wade RC 30.00 80.00
129 Chris Bosh RC 12.00 30.00
130 Carmelo Anthony RC 20.00 50.00
131 Darko Milicic RC 3.00 8.00
132 LeBron James RC 400.00 800.00

2003-04 Upper Deck Hardcourt Clear Commemoratives Autographs

STATED ODDS 1:60
BIA Chauncey Billups 20.00 50.00
CBA Carlos Boozer 5.00 12.00
EBA Earl Boykins 5.00 12.00
EGA Eddie Griffin 5.00 12.00
ETA Etan Thomas 5.00 12.00
GAA Gilbert Arenas 5.00 12.00
GWA Gerald Wallace 5.00 12.00
JDA Juan Dixon 5.00 12.00
JMA Jerome Moiso 5.00 12.00
JWA Jay Williams 5.00 12.00
KBA Kobe Bryant SP 6,000.00 12,000.00
LJA LeBron James 8,000.00 15,000.00
MAA Marko Jaric 5.00 12.00
MBA Mike Bibby 5.00 12.00
MJA Michael Jordan SP 8,000.00 15,000.00
MPA Morris Peterson 5.00 12.00
PSA Peja Stojakovic 6.00 15.00
REA Reggie Evans 5.00 12.00
TMA Tracy McGrady 75.00 200.00
TPA Tony Parker 15.00 40.00

2003-04 Upper Deck Hardcourt Floor

STATED ODDS 1:30
AIF Allen Iverson 6.00 15.00
CWF Chris Webber 3.00 8.00
DRF David Robinson 5.00 12.00
GHF Grant Hill 4.00 10.00
GPF Gary Payton 4.00 10.00
GRF Glenn Robinson 2.00 5.00
JKF Jason Kidd 4.00 10.00
JMF Jamal Mashburn 2.00 5.00
JOF Jermaine O'Neal 2.50 6.00
JSF John Stockton 5.00 12.00
JSF Jerry Stackhouse 3.00 8.00
KBF Kobe Bryant 12.00 30.00
KGF Kevin Garnett 6.00 15.00
KMF Karl Malone 5.00 12.00
LJF LeBron James 50.00 120.00
LSF Latrell Sprewell 3.00 8.00
MJF Michael Jordan 25.00 60.00
RAF Ray Allen 4.00 10.00
RMF Reggie Miller 5.00 12.00
RWF Rasheed Wallace 3.00 8.00
SAF Shareef Abdur-Rahim 2.50 6.00
SMF Stephon Marbury 3.00 8.00
SMF Steve Nash 5.00 12.00
SOF Shaquille O'Neal 10.00 25.00
SPF Scottie Pippen 6.00 15.00
TDF Tim Duncan 6.00 15.00
TMF Tracy McGrady 4.00 10.00

2003-04 Upper Deck Hardcourt Floor/Fabric Combos

STATED ODDS 1:60
AIFF Allen Iverson 20.00 50.00
CWFF Chris Webber 10.00 25.00
DRFF David Robinson 15.00 40.00
GHFF Grant Hill 10.00 25.00
GPFF Gary Payton 12.00 30.00
JKFF Jason Kidd 12.00 30.00
JOFF Jermaine O'Neal 8.00 20.00
JSFF John Stockton 15.00 40.00
KBFF Kobe Bryant 20.00 50.00
KMFF Karl Malone 15.00 40.00
LJFF LeBron James 200.00 500.00
LSFF Latrell Sprewell 10.00 25.00
MJFF Michael Jordan 75.00 200.00
RAFF Ray Allen 12.00 30.00
SAFF Shareef Abdur-Rahim 8.00 20.00
SMFF Stephon Marbury 10.00 25.00
SNFF Steve Nash 15.00 40.00
SPFF Scottie Pippen 20.00 50.00
TDFF Tim Duncan 20.00 50.00
TMFF Tracy McGrady 12.00 30.00

2003-04 Upper Deck Hardcourt Hardwood Commemoratives

STATED ODDS 1:300
STATED ODDS FOR DUAL 1:80000
AMAF Antonio McDyess 8.00 20.00
AWAF Antoine Walker 15.00 40.00
CBAF Chauncey Billups 20.00 50.00
DRAF David Robinson 30.00 80.00
DWAF Dominique Wilkins 30.00 80.00
JBAF LeBron James SP 8,000.00 15,000.00
JKAF Jason Kidd 30.00 80.00
JRAF Jalen Rose 15.00 40.00
JSAF Jerry Stackhouse 20.00 50.00
KBAF Kobe Bryant SP 6,000.00 12,000.00
KGAF Kevin Garnett SP 1,000.00 2,000.00
MJAF Michael Jordan SP 8,000.00 15,000.00
TMAF Tracy McGrady SP 75.00 200.00

2003-04 Upper Deck Hardcourt Heart of a Champion

COMPLETE SET (15) 20.00 50.00
COMMON MJ (1-15) 3.00 8.00
1-15 MJ STATED ODDS 1:23
SILVER STATED ODDS 1:60
COMMON GOLD (1-15) 12.00 30.00
GOLD STATED ODDS 1:180

2003-04 Upper Deck Hardcourt LeBron James Floor

COMMON CARD (LB1-LB12) 30.00 80.00
STATED ODDS 1:15

2004-05 Upper Deck Hardcourt

COMP.SET w/o SP's (90) 15.00 40.00
91-96 RC PRINT RUN 999 SER.#'d SETS
105-132 RC PRINT RUN 1999 SER.#'d SETS
1 Boris Diaw .25 .60
2 Antoine Walker .30 .75
3 Al Harrington .25 .60
4 Jiri Welsch .20 .50
5 Paul Pierce .50 1.25
6 Ricky Davis .25 .60
7 Gerald Wallace .25 .60
8 Eddie House .20 .50
9 Jason Kapono .20 .50
10 Tyson Chandler .25 .60
11 Eddy Curry .20 .50
12 Kirk Hinrich .30 .75
13 Jeff McInnis .20 .50
14 DaJuan Wagner .20 .50
15 LeBron James 2.50 6.00
16 Michael Finley .30 .75
17 Dirk Nowitzki .75 2.00
18 Marquis Daniels .20 .50
19 Kenyon Martin .30 .75
20 Carmelo Anthony .60 1.50
21 Nene .25 .60
22 Ben Wallace .40 1.00
23 Richard Hamilton .40 1.00
24 Rasheed Wallace .40 1.00
25 Mike Dunleavy .20 .50
26 Jason Richardson .30 .75
27 Derek Fisher .25 .60
28 Tracy McGrady .50 1.25
29 Tyronn Lue .20 .50
30 Yao Ming .75 2.00
31 Jermaine O'Neal .25 .60
32 Reggie Miller .60 1.50
33 Stephen Jackson .25 .60
34 Corey Maggette .25 .60
35 Elton Brand .25 .60
36 Marko Jaric .20 .50
37 Karl Malone .60 1.50
38 Kobe Bryant 2.50 6.00
39 Lamar Odom .30 .75
40 James Posey .25 .60
41 Mike Miller .25 .60
42 Pau Gasol .50 1.25
43 Dwyane Wade 1.25 3.00
44 Eddie Jones .30 .75
45 Shaquille O'Neal 1.25 3.00
46 Desmond Mason .25 .60
47 Michael Redd .25 .60
48 T.J. Ford .20 .50
49 Kevin Garnett .75 2.00
50 Latrell Sprewell .40 1.00
51 Sam Cassell .25 .60
52 Jason Kidd .50 1.25
53 Aaron Williams .20 .50
54 Richard Jefferson .25 .60
55 Baron Davis .30 .75
56 Jamaal Magloire .20 .50
57 Jamal Mashburn .25 .60
58 Allan Houston .30 .75
59 Jamal Crawford .30 .75
60 Stephon Marbury .40 1.00
61 Hedo Turkoglu .25 .60
62 Steve Francis .30 .75
63 Cuttino Mobley .25 .60
64 Allen Iverson .75 2.00
65 Glenn Robinson .25 .60
66 Kenny Thomas .20 .50
67 Amare Stoudemire .50 1.25
68 Quentin Richardson .20 .50
69 Shawn Marion .30 .75
70 Darius Miles .20 .50
71 Shareef Abdur-Rahim .30 .75
72 Zach Randolph .30 .75
73 Chris Webber .40 1.00
74 Mike Bibby .30 .75
75 Peja Stojakovic .30 .75
76 Manu Ginobili .60 1.50
77 Tim Duncan .75 2.00
78 Tony Parker .50 1.25
79 Rashard Lewis .25 .60
80 Ray Allen .50 1.25
81 Ronald Murray .20 .50
82 Chris Bosh .50 1.25
83 Jalen Rose .25 .60
84 Vince Carter .60 1.50
85 Andrei Kirilenko .25 .60
86 Carlos Arroyo .20 .50
87 Carlos Boozer .25 .60
88 Gilbert Arenas .30 .75
89 Jarvis Hayes .20 .50
90 Antawn Jamison .30 .75
91 Dwight Howard RC 8.00 20.00
92 Emeka Okafor RC 2.00 5.00
93 Ben Gordon RC 2.50 6.00
94 Shaun Livingston RC 2.50 6.00
95 Devin Harris RC 2.00 5.00
96 Josh Childress RC 1.50 4.00
97 Luol Deng RC 2.00 5.00
98 Andre Iguodala RC 3.00 8.00
99 Luke Jackson RC 1.25 3.00
100 Andris Biedrins RC 1.25 3.00
101 Sebastian Telfair RC 1.50 4.00
102 Josh Smith RC 2.00 5.00
103 Rafael Araujo RC 1.25 3.00
104 Robert Swift RC 1.25 3.00
105 Kris Humphries RC 1.50 4.00
106 Al Jefferson RC 2.00 5.00
107 Kirk Snyder RC 1.25 3.00
108 J.R. Smith RC 2.00 5.00
109 Dorell Wright RC 1.50 4.00
110 Jameer Nelson RC 2.00 5.00
111 Pavel Podkolzin RC 1.25 3.00
112 Justin Reed RC 1.25 3.00
113 Sergei Monia RC 1.25 3.00
114 Delonte West RC 1.50 4.00
115 Tony Allen RC 2.00 5.00
116 Kevin Martin RC 2.50 6.00
117 Sasha Vujacic RC 1.50 4.00
118 Beno Udrih RC 1.50 4.00
119 David Harrison RC 1.25 3.00
120 Anderson Varejao RC 1.50 4.00
121 Jackson Vroman RC 1.25 3.00
122 Peter John Ramos RC 1.25 3.00
123 Lionel Chalmers RC 1.50 4.00
124 Donta Smith RC 1.25 3.00
125 Andre Emmett RC 1.25 3.00
126 Antonio Burks RC 1.25 3.00
127 Royal Ivey RC 1.25 3.00
128 Chris Duhon RC 1.50 4.00
129 Trevor Ariza RC 2.00 5.00
130 Ha Seung-Jin RC 2.00 5.00
131 Romain Sato RC 1.25 3.00
132 Rickey Paulding RC 1.25 3.00

2005-06 Upper Deck Hardcourt UD Promos

*PROMOS: .75X TO 2X BASIC

2004-05 Upper Deck Hardcourt Clear Commemorative Autographs

STATED ODDS 1:60
SP INFO PROVIDED BY UPPER DECK
AH Al Harrington 5.00 12.00
AK Andrei Kirilenko 5.00 12.00
AM Andre Miller 5.00 12.00
CH Chauncey Billups 8.00 20.00
CM Corey Maggette 5.00 12.00
DR Dennis Rodman 60.00 150.00
GA Gilbert Arenas 5.00 12.00
JR Jason Richardson 5.00 12.00
KB Kobe Bryant SP 400.00 800.00
KG Kevin Garnett SP 125.00 300.00
LJ LeBron James SP 500.00 1,000.00
LO Lamar Odom 8.00 20.00
MJ Michael Jordan SP 1,500.00 3,000.00
PS Peja Stojakovic 6.00 15.00
RJ Richard Jefferson 5.00 12.00
TM Tracy McGrady SP 25.00 60.00
ZO Alonzo Mourning 25.00 60.00
ZR Zach Randolph 5.00 12.00

2004-05 Upper Deck Hardcourt Engraved Endorsements

STATED ODDS 1:300
SP INFO PROVIDED BY UPPER DECK
AI Andre Iguodala 30.00 80.00
AM Alonzo Mourning 20.00 50.00
AS Amare Stoudemire 15.00 40.00
BD Baron Davis 10.00 25.00
CA Carmelo Anthony 50.00 100.00
CB Carlos Boozer 10.00 25.00
DH Dwight Howard 30.00 80.00
JK Jason Kidd 20.00 50.00
JR Jason Richardson 10.00 25.00
KB Kobe Bryant SP 125.00 300.00
KG Kevin Garnett SP 50.00 120.00
LJ LeBron James SP 1,500.00 3,000.00
LO Lamar Odom 10.00 25.00
MJ Michael Jordan SP 1,500.00 3,000.00
PP Paul Pierce 30.00 80.00
RM Reggie Miller 100.00 200.00
TM Tracy McGrady SP 50.00 100.00
YM Yao Ming 75.00 200.00

2004-05 Upper Deck Hardcourt Hardwood Commemoratives

STATED ODDS 1:60
SP INFO PROVIDED BY UPPER DECK
AJ Antawn Jamison 5.00 12.00
AS Amare Stoudemire 10.00 25.00
BD Baron Davis 5.00 12.00
BO Carlos Boozer 5.00 12.00
CA Carmelo Anthony 25.00 60.00
DA Darius Miles 5.00 12.00
DW Dwyane Wade 30.00 80.00
FJ Fred Jones 5.00 12.00
GW Gerald Wallace 5.00 12.00
JA Jalen Rose 5.00 12.00
JK Jason Kidd 15.00 40.00
JS Jerry Stackhouse 5.00 12.00
KB Kobe Bryant SP 400.00 800.00
KG Kevin Garnett SP 125.00 300.00
LJ LeBron James 500.00 1,000.00
MJ Michael Jordan SP 1,500.00 3,000.00
PG Pau Gasol 8.00 20.00
RH Richard Hamilton 5.00 12.00
RJ Richard Jefferson 5.00 12.00
SA Shareef Abdur-Rahim 5.00 12.00
SC Sam Cassell 5.00 12.00

2004-05 Upper Deck Hardcourt Hardwood Commemoratives Dual

STATED ODDS 1:300
SP INFO PROVIDED BY UPPER DECK
HC2AM C.Anthony/A.Miller SP 25.00 60.00
HC2BH C.Billups/R.Hamilton 20.00 50.00
HC2BS M.Bibby/P.Stojakovic 10.00 25.00
HC2GB P.Gasol/S.Battier 20.00 50.00
HC2GC K.Garnett/S.Cassell SP 60.00 150.00
HC2JA A.Jamison/G.Arenas 10.00 25.00
HC2JB L.James/C.Boozer SP 500.00 1,000.00
HC2JJ L.James/M.Jordan SP 3,000.00 6,000.00
HC2JK J.Kidd/R.Jefferson 10.00 25.00
HC2KS A.Kirilenko/J.Stockton 50.00 120.00
HC2MH R.Miller/A.Harrington 40.00 100.00
HC2MR D.Mason/M.Redd 10.00 25.00
HC2OW L.Odom/D.Wade 25.00 60.00
HC2PR G.Payton/K.Rush 15.00 40.00
HC2RJ J.Rich/F.Jones 10.00 25.00
HC2RM Z.Randolph/S.Abdur-Rahim 10.00 25.00
HC2SH J.Stackhouse/J.Howard 10.00 25.00
HC2SM A.Stoudemire/S.Marion 10.00 25.00

2004-05 Upper Deck Hardcourt Materials

STATED ODDS 1:15
*COMBO SINGLES: .6X TO 1.5X BASE JSY HI
COMBO STATED ODDS 1:15
SP INFO PROVIDED BY UPPER DECK
AI Allen Iverson 6.00 15.00
AJ Antawn Jamison 2.00 5.00
AK Andrei Kirilenko 2.00 5.00
AS Amare Stoudemire 2.50 6.00
BD Baron Davis 2.50 6.00
BW Ben Wallace 3.00 8.00
CA Carmelo Anthony 5.00 12.00
CB Carlos Boozer 2.00 5.00
DN Dirk Nowitzki 6.00 15.00
DW Dwyane Wade 10.00 25.00
EB Elton Brand 2.00 5.00
EG Manu Ginobili 5.00 12.00
GA Gilbert Arenas 2.50 6.00
JC Jamal Crawford 2.50 6.00
JK Jason Kidd 4.00 10.00
JM Jamaal Magloire 1.50 4.00
JO Jermaine O'Neal 2.00 5.00
JR Jason Richardson 2.50 6.00
JT Jason Terry 2.00 5.00
KB Kobe Bryant SP 40.00 100.00
KG Kevin Garnett 6.00 15.00
LJ LeBron James 12.00 30.00
LO Lamar Odom 2.50 6.00
MB Mike Bibby 2.50 6.00
MJ Michael Jordan SP 40.00 100.00
PG Pau Gasol 4.00 10.00
PP Paul Pierce 4.00 10.00
PS Peja Stojakovic 2.00 5.00
RA Ray Allen 4.00 10.00
RJ Richard Jefferson 2.00 5.00
RM Reggie Miller 5.00 12.00
SA Shareef Abdur-Rahim 2.50 6.00
SF Steve Francis 2.50 6.00
SH Shawn Marion 2.50 6.00
SM Stephon Marbury 3.00 8.00
SN Steve Nash 5.00 12.00
SO Shaquille O'Neal 10.00 25.00
TD Tim Duncan 6.00 15.00
TM Tracy McGrady 4.00 10.00
TP Tony Parker 4.00 10.00
YM Yao Ming 6.00 15.00
ZR Zach Randolph 2.50 6.00

2005-06 Upper Deck Hardcourt

COMP.SET w/o SP's (90) 15.00 40.00
91-140 RC PRINT RUN 1750 SER.#'d SETS
1 Tony Delk .20 .50
2 Josh Smith .25 .60
3 Al Harrington .25 .60
4 Antoine Walker .25 .60
5 Gary Payton .50 1.25
6 Paul Pierce .50 1.25
7 Kareem Rush .20 .50
8 Emeka Okafor .25 .60
9 Primoz Brezec .20 .50
10 Eddy Curry .20 .50
11 Kirk Hinrich .25 .60
12 Ben Gordon .25 .60
13 Drew Gooden .25 .60
14 LeBron James 2.50 6.00
15 Zydrunas Ilgauskas .25 .60
16 Dirk Nowitzki .75 2.00
17 Jason Terry .25 .60
18 Jerry Stackhouse .25 .60
19 Carmelo Anthony .50 1.25
20 Kenyon Martin .25 .60
21 Earl Boykins .20 .50
22 Ben Wallace .40 1.00
23 Chauncey Billups .40 1.00
24 Richard Hamilton .40 1.00
25 Troy Murphy .30 .75
26 Jason Richardson .30 .75
27 Baron Davis .30 .75
28 Tracy McGrady .50 1.25
29 Yao Ming .60 1.50
30 Juwan Howard .25 .60
31 Jermaine O'Neal .25 .60
32 Stephen Jackson .25 .60
33 Ron Artest .25 .60
34 Corey Maggette .25 .60
35 Elton Brand .25 .60
36 Bobby Simmons .20 .50
37 Caron Butler .25 .60
38 Kobe Bryant 2.50 6.00
39 Lamar Odom .25 .60
40 Mike Miller .25 .60
41 Jason Williams .50 1.25
42 Pau Gasol .50 1.25
43 Dwyane Wade .60 1.50
44 Eddie Jones .25 .60
45 Shaquille O'Neal 1.00 2.50
46 Desmond Mason .20 .50
47 Maurice Williams .20 .50
48 Michael Redd .25 .60
49 Kevin Garnett .75 2.00
50 Latrell Sprewell .30 .75
51 Sam Cassell .25 .60
52 Vince Carter .60 1.50
53 Jason Kidd .50 1.25
54 Richard Jefferson .25 .60
55 Dan Dickau .20 .50
56 Jamaal Magloire .20 .50
57 J.R. Smith .30 .75
58 Jamal Crawford .30 .75
59 Stephon Marbury .40 1.00
60 Allan Houston .25 .60
61 Dwight Howard .40 1.00
62 Grant Hill .50 1.25
63 Steve Francis .30 .75
64 Allen Iverson .60 1.50
65 Andre Iguodala .30 .75
66 Chris Webber .40 1.00
67 Amare Stoudemire .30 .75
68 Shawn Marion .30 .75
69 Steve Nash .60 1.50
70 Damon Stoudamire .30 .75
71 Shareef Abdur-Rahim .30 .75
72 Zach Randolph .30 .75
73 Mike Bibby .30 .75
74 Peja Stojakovic .30 .75
75 Brad Miller .25 .60
76 Manu Ginobili .60 1.50
77 Tim Duncan .75 2.00
78 Tony Parker .50 1.25
79 Rashard Lewis .30 .75
80 Ray Allen .50 1.25
81 Ronald Murray .20 .50
82 Rafer Alston .25 .60
83 Jalen Rose .25 .60
84 Chris Bosh .40 1.00
85 Andrei Kirilenko .25 .60
86 Carlos Boozer .25 .60
87 Matt Harpring .20 .50
88 Antawn Jamison .25 .60
89 Gilbert Arenas .30 .75
90 Larry Hughes .25 .60
91 Linas Kleiza RC 1.50 4.00
92 Julius Hodge RC 1.25 3.00
93 David Lee RC 2.00 5.00
94 Sarunas Jasikevicius RC 2.00 5.00
95 Jason Maxiell RC 1.50 4.00
96 Luther Head RC 1.25 3.00
97 Brandon Bass RC 1.50 4.00
98 Ricky Sanchez RC 2.00 5.00
99 Ersan Ilyasova RC 1.50 4.00
100 Andray Blatche RC 2.00 5.00
101 Sean May RC 1.25 3.00
102 Ike Diogu RC 1.25 3.00
103 Nate Robinson RC 2.00 5.00
105 Bracey Wright RC 1.25 3.00
106 Daniel Ewing RC 1.50 4.00
107 Salim Stoudamire RC 1.50 4.00
108 Dijon Thompson RC 1.25 3.00
109 Danny Granger RC 2.00 5.00
110 Raymond Felton RC 1.50 4.00
111 Louis Williams RC 5.00 12.00
112 Channing Frye RC 1.50 4.00
113 Francisco Garcia RC 1.25 3.00
114 Ryan Gomes RC 1.50 4.00
115 Travis Diener RC 1.25 3.00
116 Jarrett Jack RC 2.00 5.00
118 Von Wafer RC 1.25 3.00
119 C.J. Miles RC 1.50 4.00
120 Lawrence Roberts RC 1.25 3.00
121 Amir Johnson RC 2.00 5.00
122 Monta Ellis RC 2.50 6.00
123 Martell Webster RC 1.50 4.00
124 Johan Petro RC 1.25 3.00
126 Andrew Bynum RC 1.50 4.00
127 Martynas Andriuskevicius RC 1.25 3.00
128 Charlie Villanueva RC 1.50 4.00
129 Antoine Wright RC 1.50 4.00
130 Joey Graham RC 1.50 4.00
131 Wayne Simien RC 1.25 3.00
132 Hakim Warrick RC 1.50 4.00
133 Gerald Green RC 2.00 5.00
134 Marvin Williams RC 2.00 5.00
135 Deron Williams RC 3.00 8.00
136 Rashad McCants RC 1.25 3.00
137 Yaroslav Korolev RC 1.25 3.00
138 Chris Taft RC 1.25 3.00
139 Chris Paul RC 10.00 25.00
140 Andrew Bogut RC 2.50 6.00

2005-06 Upper Deck Hardcourt Hardwood Signatures

PRINT RUN 25 TO 50 SER.#'d SETS
AB Andrew Bogut/50 10.00 25.00
AK Andrei Kirilenko/50 6.00 15.00
CA Carmelo Anthony/25 75.00 200.00
CF Channing Frye/50 6.00 15.00
CJ C.J. Miles/50 6.00 15.00
CP Chris Paul/50 100.00 200.00
CT Chris Taft/50 5.00 12.00
CV Charlie Villanueva/50 6.00 15.00
DE Daniel Ewing/50 6.00 15.00
DG Danny Granger/50 8.00 20.00
DH Dwight Howard/50 20.00 50.00
DL David Lee/50 8.00 20.00
DT Dijon Thompson/50 5.00 12.00
DW Deron Williams/50 12.00 30.00
FV Fran Vazquez/50 5.00 12.00
GG Gerald Green/50 8.00 20.00
HW Hakim Warrick/50 6.00 15.00
ID Ike Diogu/50 5.00 12.00
JK Jason Kidd/50 30.00 80.00
JR J.R. Smith/50 10.00 25.00
KB Kobe Bryant/25 2,000.00 4,000.00
KH Kirk Hinrich/50 8.00 20.00
KK Kyle Korver/50 8.00 20.00
LH Luther Head/50 5.00 12.00
LJ LeBron James/25 2,000.00 4,000.00
LO Lamar Odom/50 10.00 25.00
MA Martynas Andriuskevicius/50 5.00 12.00
MD Marquis Daniels/50 5.00 12.00
ME Monta Ellis/50 10.00 25.00
MJ Michael Jordan/25 3,000.00 6,000.00
MR Michael Redd/50 15.00 40.00
MW Marvin Williams/50 8.00 20.00
PP Paul Pierce/50 40.00 100.00
RF Raymond Felton/50 6.00 15.00
RM Rashad McCants/50 5.00 12.00
SE Sean May/50 5.00 12.00
SN Steve Nash/25 100.00 200.00
SS Salim Stoudamire/50 6.00 15.00
TA Tony Allen/50 5.00 12.00
WE Martell Webster/50 6.00 15.00
WS Wayne Simien/50 5.00 12.00
YM Yao Ming/50 150.00 400.00

2005-06 Upper Deck Hardcourt Materials

STATED ODDS 1:15
*MAT/WOOD: .6X TO 1.5X BASE MAT HI
MAT/WOOD PRINT RUN 99 SER.#'d SETS
AH Al Harrington 2.50 6.00
AK Andrei Kirilenko 2.50 6.00
AN Andre Iguodala 3.00 8.00
BD Baron Davis 3.00 8.00
BG Ben Gordon 2.50 6.00
BM Brad Miller 2.50 6.00
BW Ben Wallace 4.00 10.00
CB Carlos Boozer 2.50 6.00
CH Chris Bosh 4.00 10.00
CM Corey Maggette 2.50 6.00
DF Derek Fisher 3.00 8.00
DG Drew Gooden 2.50 6.00
DH Dwight Howard 4.00 10.00
DM Desmond Mason 2.00 5.00
GA Gilbert Arenas 3.00 8.00
GP Gary Payton 5.00 12.00
GW Gerald Wallace 2.50 6.00
JC Jamal Crawford 3.00 8.00
JH Josh Howard 2.50 6.00
JK Jason Kidd 5.00 12.00

JM Jamaal Magloire 2.00 5.00
JR Jalen Rose 2.50 6.00
KB Kobe Bryant 40.00 100.00
KD Keyon Dooling 2.00 5.00
KG Kevin Garnett 8.00 20.00
KK Kyle Korver 2.50 6.00
LJ LeBron James 12.00 30.00
MB Mike Bibby 3.00 8.00
MJ Michael Jordan 30.00 80.00
PG Pau Gasol 5.00 12.00
PP Paul Pierce 5.00 12.00
PS Peja Stojakovic 2.50 6.00
QR Quentin Richardson 2.00 5.00
RJ Richard Jefferson 2.50 6.00
RM Ronald Murray 2.00 5.00
SB Shane Battier 2.50 6.00
SF Steve Francis 3.00 8.00
SM Stephon Marbury 4.00 10.00
SN Steve Nash 6.00 15.00
TA Tony Allen 2.00 5.00
TM Tracy McGrady 5.00 12.00
YM Yao Ming 6.00 15.00

2005-06 Upper Deck Hardcourt Materials/Wood Autographs

PRINT RUN 25 TO 50 SER.#'d SETS
AH Al Harrington/50 8.00 20.00
AK Andrei Kirilenko/50 8.00 20.00
AN Andre Iguodala/50 8.00 20.00
BD Baron Davis/50 10.00 25.00
BG Ben Gordon/50 8.00 20.00
BM Brad Miller/50 8.00 20.00
BW Ben Wallace/50 20.00 50.00
CB Carlos Boozer/50 8.00 20.00
CH Chris Bosh/50 10.00 25.00
CM Corey Maggette/50 8.00 20.00
DF Derek Fisher/50 10.00 25.00
DG Drew Gooden/50 8.00 20.00
DH Dwight Howard/50 20.00 50.00
DM Desmond Mason/50 8.00 20.00
GA Gilbert Arenas/50 12.00 30.00
GP Gary Payton/50 15.00 40.00
GW Gerald Wallace/50 8.00 20.00
JH Josh Howard/50 8.00 20.00
JK Jason Kidd/50 15.00 40.00
JM Jamaal Magloire/50 8.00 20.00
JR Jalen Rose/50 8.00 20.00
KD Keyon Dooling/50 8.00 20.00
KG Kevin Garnett/50 75.00 200.00
KK Kyle Korver/50 12.00 30.00
LJ LeBron James/25 1,250.00 2,500.00
MB Mike Bibby/50 8.00 20.00
MJ Michael Jordan/25 1,500.00 3,000.00
PG Pau Gasol/50 12.00 30.00
PP Paul Pierce/50 30.00 80.00
PS Peja Stojakovic/50 10.00 25.00
QR Quentin Richardson/50 8.00 20.00
RJ Richard Jefferson/50 8.00 20.00
RM Ronald Murray/50 8.00 20.00
SB Shane Battier/50 8.00 20.00
SF Steve Francis/50 8.00 20.00
SM Stephon Marbury/50 12.00 30.00
SN Steve Nash/50 25.00 60.00
TA Tony Allen/50 8.00 20.00
TM Tracy McGrady/25 30.00 80.00
YM Yao Ming/25 40.00 100.00

2005-06 Upper Deck Hardcourt Rookie Jerseys

PRINT RUN 99 TO 250 SER.#'d SETS
*JSY/WOOD/250: .6X TO 1.5X BASE JSY HI
*JSY/WOOD/99: .5X TO 1.25X BASE JSY HI
JSY/WOOD PRINT RUN 50 SER.#'d SETS
92J Julius Hodge/250 2.00 5.00
93J David Lee/250 3.00 8.00
95J Jason Maxiell/250 2.50 6.00
96J Luther Head/250 2.00 5.00
97J Brandon Bass/250 2.50 6.00
100J Andray Blatche/250 3.00 8.00
101J Sean May/250 2.00 5.00
103J Nate Robinson/250 3.00 8.00
106J Daniel Ewing/250 2.50 6.00
107J Salim Stoudamire/250 2.50 6.00
109J Danny Granger/250 3.00 8.00
110J Raymond Felton/250 2.50 6.00
111J Louis Williams/250 8.00 20.00
112J Channing Frye/250 2.50 6.00
113J Francisco Garcia/250 2.00 5.00
114J Ryan Gomes/250 2.50 6.00
116J Jarrett Jack/250 3.00 8.00
119J C.J. Miles/250 2.50 6.00
123J Martell Webster/250 2.50 6.00
128J Charlie Villanueva/250 2.50 6.00
129J Antoine Wright/250 2.50 6.00
130J Joey Graham/250 2.50 6.00
131J Wayne Simien/250 2.00 5.00
132J Hakim Warrick/250 2.50 6.00
133J Gerald Green/250 3.00 8.00
134J Marvin Williams/99 3.00 8.00
135J Deron Williams/99 5.00 12.00
136J Rashad McCants/99 2.00 5.00
139J Chris Paul/99 12.00 30.00
140J Andrew Bogut/99 4.00 10.00

2005-06 Upper Deck Hardcourt Signatures

STATED ODDS 1:15
AI Andre Iguodala 6.00 15.00
AK Andrei Kirilenko 4.00 10.00
AM Antonio McDyess 4.00 10.00
AN Andrew Bogut SP 8.00 20.00
AV Anderson Varejao 2.50 6.00
AW Antoine Wright 3.00 8.00
BI Andris Biedrins 2.50 6.00
BU Beno Udrih 2.50 6.00
BY Andrew Bynum 3.00 8.00
CB Chris Bosh SP 10.00 25.00
CD Chris Duhon 2.50 6.00
CF Channing Frye 3.00 8.00
CJ C.J. Miles 2.50 6.00
CM Corey Maggette 3.00 8.00
CP Chris Paul SP 75.00 200.00
CT Chris Taft 2.50 6.00
CU Cuttino Mobley 2.50 6.00
CV Charlie Villanueva 3.00 8.00
DA David Harrison 2.50 6.00
DD Dan Dickau 2.50 6.00
DF Derek Fisher 6.00 15.00
DH Dwight Howard 20.00 50.00
DL David Lee 4.00 10.00
DM Desmond Mason 2.50 6.00
DO Dorell Wright 2.50 6.00
DT Dijon Thompson 2.50 6.00
DW Delonte West 2.50 6.00
FE Raymond Felton 3.00 8.00
FG Francisco Garcia 2.50 6.00
FV Fran Vazquez 2.50 6.00
GA Gilbert Arenas 4.00 10.00
GG Gerald Green 4.00 10.00
GR Danny Granger 4.00 10.00
GW Gerald Wallace 3.00 8.00
HS Ha Seung-Jin 12.00 30.00
HW Hakim Warrick 3.00 8.00
JA Jalen Rose 3.00 8.00
JC Jamal Crawford 4.00 10.00
JM Jamaal Magloire 2.50 6.00
JN Jameer Nelson 2.50 6.00
JO Joey Graham 3.00 8.00
JP Johan Petro 2.50 6.00
JR J.R. Smith 4.00 10.00
JU Justin Reed 2.50 6.00
JW Jason Williams 40.00 100.00
KD Keyon Dooling 2.50 6.00
KH Kirk Hinrich SP 8.00 20.00
KK Kyle Korver 3.00 8.00
KR Kareem Rush 2.50 6.00
KS Kirk Snyder 2.50 6.00
LF Luis Flores 2.50 6.00
LH Luther Head 2.50 6.00
LJ LeBron James 1,500.00 3,000.00
LU Luke Jackson 2.50 6.00
MA Martynas Andriuskevicius 2.50 6.00
MC Rashad McCants 2.50 6.00
ME Monta Ellis 10.00 25.00
MJ Michael Jordan SP 2,500.00 5,000.00
MP Morris Peterson 2.50 6.00
MW Marvin Williams SP 4.00 10.00
NO Andres Nocioni 2.50 6.00
NR Nate Robinson 4.00 10.00
PA Pavel Podkolzin 2.50 6.00
PB Primoz Brezec 2.50 6.00
QR Quentin Richardson 2.50 6.00
RA Rafael Araujo 2.50 6.00
RG Ryan Gomes 3.00 8.00
RO Robert Traylor 2.50 6.00
RT Ronny Turiaf 4.00 10.00
SM Sean May 2.50 6.00
SN Steve Nash SP 75.00 200.00
SS Salim Stoudamire 3.00 8.00
ST Sebastian Telfair 3.00 8.00
TA Trevor Ariza 2.50 6.00
TK Toni Kukoc 8.00 20.00
TM Tracy McGrady SP 150.00 400.00
TO Travis Outlaw 3.00 8.00
UH Udonis Haslem 2.50 6.00
VK Viktor Khryapa 2.50 6.00
WI Maurice Williams 3.00 8.00
WS Wayne Simien 2.50 6.00
YM Yao Ming SP 150.00 400.00
AU Stacey Augmon 3.00 8.00

2006-07 Upper Deck Hardcourt

COMP.SET w/o SP's (100) 15.00 40.00
136-150 AU RC PRINT RUN 399 SER.#'d SETS
1 Joe Johnson .30 .75
2 Salim Stoudamire .20 .50
3 Marvin Williams .20 .50
4 Dan Dickau .20 .50
5 Paul Pierce .50 1.25
6 Wally Szczerbiak .25 .60
7 Raymond Felton .20 .50
8 Emeka Okafor .25 .60
9 Gerald Wallace .25 .60
10 Tyson Chandler .25 .60
11 Luol Deng .25 .60
12 Ben Gordon .25 .60
13 Michael Jordan 2.50 6.00
14 Drew Gooden .25 .60
15 Larry Hughes .25 .60
16 Zydrunas Ilgauskas .25 .60
17 LeBron James 2.50 6.00
18 Erick Dampier .20 .50
19 Devin Harris .20 .50
20 Dirk Nowitzki .75 2.00
21 Jason Terry .25 .60
22 Carmelo Anthony .50 1.25
23 Earl Boykins .20 .50
24 Marcus Camby .25 .60
25 Kenyon Martin .25 .60
26 Chauncey Billups .40 1.00
27 Richard Hamilton .30 .75
28 Antonio McDyess .20 .50
29 Ben Wallace .40 1.00
30 Baron Davis .30 .75
31 Derek Fisher .30 .75
32 Troy Murphy .30 .75
33 Jason Richardson .30 .75
34 Luther Head .20 .50
35 Tracy McGrady .50 1.25
36 Yao Ming .75 2.00
37 Danny Granger .30 .75
38 Jermaine O'Neal .30 .75
39 Peja Stojakovic .25 .60
40 Elton Brand .25 .60
41 Sam Cassell .25 .60
42 Chris Kaman .20 .50
43 Shaun Livingston .25 .60
44 Kwame Brown .20 .50
45 Kobe Bryant 2.50 6.00
46 Andrew Bynum .20 .50
47 Shane Battier .25 .60
48 Pau Gasol .50 1.25
49 Mike Miller .25 .60
50 Hakim Warrick .20 .50
51 Shaquille O'Neal 1.25 3.00
52 Dwyane Wade .60 1.50
53 Jason Williams .40 1.00
54 Andrew Bogut .25 .60
55 T.J. Ford .20 .50
56 Jamaal Magloire .20 .50
57 Michael Redd .25 .60
58 Ricky Davis .25 .60
59 Kevin Garnett .75 2.00
60 Rashad McCants .20 .50
61 Vince Carter .60 1.50
62 Richard Jefferson .25 .60
63 Jason Kidd .50 1.25
64 Desmond Mason .20 .50
65 Chris Paul .60 1.50
66 J.R. Smith .30 .75
67 Jamal Crawford .30 .75
68 Channing Frye .20 .50
69 Stephon Marbury .40 1.00
70 Quentin Richardson .20 .50
71 Dwight Howard .40 1.00
72 Darko Milicic .20 .50
73 Jameer Nelson .20 .50
74 Andre Iguodala .30 .75
75 Allen Iverson .75 2.00
76 Chris Webber .40 1.00
77 Shawn Marion .30 .75
78 Steve Nash .60 1.50
79 Amare Stoudemire .30 .75
80 Zach Randolph .30 .75
81 Sebastian Telfair .20 .50
82 Martell Webster .25 .60
83 Ron Artest .30 .75
84 Mike Bibby .30 .75
85 Brad Miller .25 .60
86 Tim Duncan .75 2.00
87 Manu Ginobili .60 1.50
88 Tony Parker .50 1.25
89 Ray Allen .50 1.25
90 Danny Fortson .20 .50
91 Rashard Lewis .25 .60
92 Chris Bosh .40 1.00
93 Joey Graham .20 .50
94 Charlie Villanueva .20 .50
95 Carlos Boozer .25 .60
96 Andrei Kirilenko .25 .60
97 Deron Williams .25 .60
98 Gilbert Arenas .30 .75
99 Caron Butler .25 .60
100 Antawn Jamison .25 .60
101 Adam Morrison RC 1.25 3.00
102 Randy Foye RC 1.25 3.00
103 Rudy Gay RC 2.00 5.00
104 Patrick O'Bryant RC 1.00 2.50
105 Saer Sene RC 1.00 2.50
106 J.J. Redick RC 3.00 8.00
107 Hilton Armstrong RC 1.00 2.50
108 Thabo Sefolosha RC 1.25 3.00
109 Cedric Simmons RC 1.00 2.50
110 Shawne Williams RC 1.00 2.50
111 Terence Kinsey RC 1.00 2.50
112 Quincy Douby RC 1.00 2.50
113 Renaldo Balkman RC 1.25 3.00
114 Josh Boone RC 1.00 2.50
115 Kyle Lowry RC 5.00 12.00
116 Shannon Brown RC 1.00 2.50
117 Jordan Farmar RC 1.25 3.00
118 Joel Freeland RC 1.00 2.50
119 Paul Davis RC 1.00 2.50
120 P.J. Tucker RC 1.50 4.00
121 Craig Smith RC 1.25 3.00
122 Bobby Jones RC 1.00 2.50
123 David Noel RC 1.00 2.50
124 Denham Brown RC 1.00 2.50
125 James Augustine RC 1.00 2.50
126 Daniel Gibson RC 1.25 3.00
127 Allan Ray RC 1.00 2.50
128 Alexander Johnson RC 1.00 2.50
129 Dee Brown RC 1.00 2.50
130 Paul Millsap RC 2.00 5.00
131 Leon Powe RC 1.00 2.50
132 Ryan Hollins RC 1.00 2.50
133 Mike Gansey RC 1.00 2.50
134 Hassan Adams RC 1.00 2.50
135 Will Blalock RC 1.00 2.50
136 Andrea Bargnani AU RC 3.00 8.00
137 LaMarcus Aldridge AU RC 10.00 25.00
138 Tyrus Thomas AU RC 3.00 8.00
139 Shelden Williams AU RC 2.50 6.00
140 Brandon Roy AU RC 8.00 20.00
141 Ronnie Brewer AU RC 2.50 6.00
142 Rodney Carney AU RC 2.50 6.00
143 Rajon Rondo AU RC 10.00 25.00
144 Marcus Williams AU RC 2.50 6.00
145 Kevin Pittsnogle AU RC 3.00 8.00
146 Maurice Ager AU RC 2.50 6.00
147 Mardy Collins AU RC 2.50 6.00
148 James White AU RC 2.50 6.00
149 Steve Novak AU RC 3.00 8.00
150 Solomon Jones AU RC 2.50 6.00

2006-07 Upper Deck Hardcourt Copper

*1-100 COPPER: 1X TO 2.5X BASE HI
*101-135 COPPER: .6X TO 1.5X BASE HI
*136-150 COPPER: .25X TO .6X BASE HI
COPPER PRINT RUN 199 SER.#'d SETS

2006-07 Upper Deck Hardcourt Silver

*1-100 SILVER: 2.5X TO 6X BASE HI
*101-135 SILVER: 1.25X TO 3X BASE HI
*136-150 SILVER: .5X TO 1.25X BASE HI
PRINT RUN 50 SER.#'d SETS

2006-07 Upper Deck Hardcourt Debut Jerseys

PRINT RUN 199 SER.#'d SETS
AR Allan Ray 2.00 5.00
BA Renaldo Balkman 2.50 6.00
BJ Bobby Jones 2.00 5.00
CS Cedric Simmons 2.00 5.00
DB Dee Brown 2.00 5.00
HA Hilton Armstrong 2.00 5.00
JB Josh Boone 2.00 5.00
JF Jordan Farmar 2.50 6.00
JW James White 2.00 5.00
KL Kyle Lowry 10.00 25.00
MA Maurice Ager 2.00 5.00
MC Mardy Collins 2.00 5.00
MW Marcus Williams 2.00 5.00
PD Paul Davis 2.00 5.00
PO Patrick O'Bryant 2.00 5.00
QD Quincy Douby 2.00 5.00
RB Ronnie Brewer 3.00 8.00
RC Rodney Carney 2.00 5.00
RG Rudy Gay 4.00 10.00
RR Rajon Rondo 8.00 20.00
SB Shannon Brown 2.00 5.00
SJ Solomon Jones 2.00 5.00
SN Steve Novak 2.50 6.00
SW Shawne Williams 2.00 5.00

2006-07 Upper Deck Hardcourt Debut Jerseys 2

PRINT RUN 99 SER.#'d SETS
JR J.J. Redick 8.00 20.00
KP Kevin Pittsnogle 3.00 8.00
LA LaMarcus Aldridge 10.00 25.00
RF Randy Foye 3.00 8.00
TT Tyrus Thomas 3.00 8.00
WS Shelden Williams 2.50 6.00

2006-07 Upper Deck Hardcourt Game Floor

COMMON JORDAN 15.00 40.00
COMMON LEBRON 6.00 15.00
COMMON JORDAN/LEBRON 40.00 100.00
STATED ODDS ONE PER BOX
JORDAN/LEBRON PRINT RUN 99 SER.#'d SETS
AUTO PRINT RUN 23 SER.#'d SETS
1 Michael Jordan 20.00 50.00
25 M.Jordan/L.James 50.00 120.00
26 M.Jordan/L.James 50.00 120.00
27 M.Jordan/L.James 50.00 120.00
28 M.Jordan/L.James AU/23 4,000.00 8,000.00
29 Michael Jordan AU/23 1,500.00 3,000.00
30 LeBron James AU/23 2,000.00 4,000.00

2006-07 Upper Deck Hardcourt Heart of a Champion Autographs

APPROXIMATE ODDS ONE PER BOX
AA Alex Acker 4.00 10.00
AJ Al Jefferson 4.00 10.00
BB Brent Barry 8.00 20.00
BO Bruce Bowen 5.00 12.00
CA Carmelo Anthony SP 12.00 30.00
CB Chauncey Billups 6.00 15.00
CH Chuck Hayes 4.00 10.00
CM Cuttino Mobley 4.00 10.00
CP Chris Paul 75.00 200.00
DJ Dwayne Jones 4.00 10.00
DW Deron Williams 15.00 40.00
GG George Gervin 8.00 20.00
HW Hakim Warrick 6.00 15.00
JA Jarrett Jack 4.00 10.00
JG Joey Graham 4.00 10.00
KA Kareem Abdul-Jabbar SP 50.00 120.00
KD Keyon Dooling 4.00 10.00
ME Maurice Evans 4.00 10.00
NR Nate Robinson 5.00 12.00
QR Quentin Richardson 4.00 10.00
RF Raymond Felton 8.00 20.00
RT Ronny Turiaf 12.00 30.00
RW Robert Whaley 4.00 10.00
SK Steve Kerr 6.00 15.00
SP Sam Perkins 6.00 15.00
TD Travis Diener 4.00 10.00
TF T.J. Ford 4.00 10.00

2006-07 Upper Deck Hardcourt Materials

APPROXIMATE ODDS ONE PER BOX
AI Andre Iguodala 2.50 6.00
AS Amare Stoudemire 2.50 6.00
BR Kwame Brown 1.50 4.00
CA Carmelo Anthony 4.00 10.00
CB Caron Butler 2.00 5.00
CM Corey Maggette 2.00 5.00
CW Chris Webber 3.00 8.00
DG Drew Gooden 2.00 5.00
DH Dwight Howard SP 3.00 8.00
DM Desmond Mason 1.50 4.00
DN Dirk Nowitzki 6.00 15.00
EB Elton Brand 2.00 5.00
EC Eddy Curry 2.00 5.00
FJ Fred Jones 1.50 4.00
GA Gilbert Arenas 2.50 6.00
JM Jeff McInnis 1.50 4.00
JR Jason Richardson 2.50 6.00
JS J.R. Smith 2.50 6.00
KB Kobe Bryant 40.00 100.00
KG Kevin Garnett 6.00 15.00
KH Kirk Hinrich 2.00 5.00
KK Kyle Korver 2.00 5.00
LH Larry Hughes 2.00 5.00
LJ LeBron James 12.00 30.00
LW Luke Walton 1.50 4.00
MG Manu Ginobili 5.00 12.00
MJ Michael Jordan SP 25.00 60.00
MS Mike Sweetney 1.50 4.00
NE Nene 2.00 5.00
PG Pau Gasol 4.00 10.00
PS Peja Stojakovic 2.00 5.00
QR Quentin Richardson 2.00 5.00
RA Ray Allen 4.00 10.00
RH Richard Hamilton 2.50 6.00
RJ Richard Jefferson 2.00 5.00
SD Samuel Dalembert 1.50 4.00
SN Steve Nash 5.00 12.00
SO Shaquille O'Neal 10.00 25.00
TD Tim Duncan 6.00 15.00
TP Tony Parker 4.00 10.00
WS Wally Szczerbiak 2.00 5.00
ZI Zydrunas Ilgauskas 2.00 5.00

2006-07 Upper Deck Hardcourt Materials Dual

PRINT RUN 50 SER.#'d SETS
BG E.Brand/K.Garnett 4.00 10.00
BH C.Bosh/D.Howard 5.00 12.00
BM K.Bryant/T.McGrady 75.00 200.00
DP T.Duncan/T.Parker 10.00 25.00
DR B.Davis/J.Richardson 4.00 10.00
GN K.Garnett/D.Nowitzki 6.00 15.00
GV D.George/S.Vujacic 4.00 10.00
HW R.Hamilton/B.Wallace 4.00 10.00
JA L.James/C.Anthony 25.00 60.00
JJ M.Jordan/L.James 75.00 200.00
KC J.Kidd/V.Carter 6.00 15.00
MM T.McGrady/Y.Ming 8.00 20.00
MO Y.Ming/S.O'Neal 10.00 25.00
MS S.Marion/A.Stoudemire 5.00 12.00
NM S.Nash/S.Marbury 5.00 12.00
SM W.Szczerbiak/J.McInnis 4.00 10.00
SO P.Stojakovic/J.O'Neal 4.00 10.00
WI C.Webber/A.Iguodala 4.00 10.00

2004 Upper Deck Hawaii Trade Conference LeBron James Room Key

NNO LeBron James 12.00 30.00

1999-00 Upper Deck HoloGrFX

COMPLETE SET (90) 20.00 50.00
COMPLETE SET w/o RC (60) 8.00 20.00
61-90 SUBSET STATED ODDS 1:2
1 Dikembe Mutombo .50 1.25
2 Alan Henderson .20 .50
3 Antoine Walker .30 .75
4 Paul Pierce .60 1.50
5 Eddie Jones .30 .75
6 David Wesley .20 .50
7 Dickey Simpkins .20 .50
8 Toni Kukoc .40 1.00
9 Shawn Kemp .50 1.25
10 Zydrunas Ilgauskas .25 .60
11 Michael Finley .30 .75
12 Cedric Ceballos .20 .50
13 Antonio McDyess .25 .60
14 Nick Van Exel .25 .60
15 Grant Hill .50 1.25
16 Bison Dele .20 .50
17 Jerry Stackhouse .30 .75
18 Antawn Jamison .30 .75
19 John Starks .30 .75
20 Scottie Pippen .75 2.00
21 Charles Barkley .75 2.00
22 Hakeem Olajuwon .60 1.50
23 Reggie Miller .60 1.50
24 Rik Smits .25 .60
25 Michael Olowokandi .20 .50
26 Maurice Taylor .20 .50
27 Shaquille O'Neal 1.25 3.00
28 Kobe Bryant 2.50 6.00
29 Tim Hardaway .40 1.00
30 Alonzo Mourning .50 1.25
31 Ray Allen .50 1.25
32 Glenn Robinson .25 .60
33 Kevin Garnett .75 2.00
34 Terrell Brandon .20 .50
35 Stephon Marbury .40 1.00
36 Keith Van Horn .25 .60
37 Allan Houston .25 .60
38 Latrell Sprewell .40 1.00
39 Bo Outlaw .20 .50
40 Darrell Armstrong .20 .50
41 Allen Iverson .75 2.00
42 Larry Hughes .25 .60
43 Jason Kidd .50 1.25
44 Tom Gugliotta .25 .60
45 Damon Stoudamire .30 .75
46 Rasheed Wallace .40 1.00
47 Jason Williams .50 1.25
48 Chris Webber .40 1.00
49 Tim Duncan .75 2.00
50 David Robinson .60 1.50
51 Gary Payton .50 1.25
52 Vin Baker .25 .60
53 Vince Carter .75 2.00
54 Tracy McGrady .50 1.25
55 John Stockton .50 1.25
56 Karl Malone .60 1.50
57 Mike Bibby .30 .75
58 Shareef Abdur-Rahim .30 .75
59 Juwan Howard .25 .60
60 Mitch Richmond .40 1.00
61 Elton Brand RC .75 2.00
62 Lamar Odom RC .75 2.00
63 Kenny Thomas RC .40 1.00
64 Scott Padgett RC .30 .75
65 Trajan Langdon RC .30 .75
66 James Posey RC .40 1.00
67 Shawn Marion RC .75 2.00
68 Chris Herren RC .30 .75
69 Tim James RC .25 .60
70 Evan Eschmeyer RC .30 .75
71 Corey Maggette RC .50 1.25
72 Richard Hamilton RC 1.00 2.50
73 Baron Davis RC 1.00 2.50
74 Galen Young RC .40 1.00
75 Dion Glover RC .25 .60
76 Jumaine Jones RC .25 .60
77 Wally Szczerbiak RC .60 1.50
78 Andre Miller RC .75 2.00
79 Devean George RC .30 .75
80 Obinna Ekezie RC .25 .60
81 Steve Francis RC .75 2.00
82 Jason Terry RC .60 1.50
83 Quincy Lewis RC .25 .60
84 Ryan Robertson RC .25 .60
85 William Avery RC .25 .60
86 A.Radojevic RC .25 .60
87 Jonathan Bender RC .40 1.00
88 Cal Bowdler RC .25 .60
89 Vonteego Cummings RC .25 .60
90 Jeff Foster RC .40 1.00

1999-00 Upper Deck HoloGrFX AUSome

*STARS: 1.5X TO 4X HI COLUMN
*RCs: .75X TO 2X HI
STATED ODDS 1:12

1999-00 Upper Deck HoloGrFX HoloFame

COMPLETE SET (9) 15.00 30.00
STATED ODDS 1:17
*GOLD: 1.5X TO 4X HI COLUMN
GOLD: STATED ODDS 1:210
HF1 Michael Jordan 15.00 40.00
HF2 Julius Erving 2.50 6.00
HF3 Larry Bird 2.50 6.00
HF4 George Gervin 1.00 2.50
HF5 Tim Duncan 2.50 6.00
HF6 Kevin Garnett 2.50 6.00
HF7 Kobe Bryant 8.00 20.00
HF8 Jason Williams 1.50 4.00
HF9 Vince Carter 2.50 6.00

1999-00 Upper Deck HoloGrFX Maximum Jordan

COMPLETE SET (6) 15.00 40.00
COMMON CARD (MJ1-MJ6) 3.00 8.00
STATED ODDS 1:34
COMMON GOLD 25.00 60.00
GOLD: STATED ODDS 1:431

1999-00 Upper Deck HoloGrFX NBA 24-7

COMPLETE SET (15) 4.00 10.00
STATED ODDS 1:3
*GOLD: 2.5X TO 6X HI COLUMN
GOLD: STATED ODDS 1:105
N1 Tim Duncan .75 2.00
N2 Allen Iverson .75 2.00
N3 Vince Carter .75 2.00
N4 Kevin Garnett .75 2.00
N5 Shaquille O'Neal 1.25 3.00
N6 Shareef Abdur-Rahim .30 .75
N7 Jason Williams .50 1.25
N8 Kobe Bryant 2.50 6.00
N9 Grant Hill .50 1.25
N10 Antoine Walker .30 .75
N11 Stephon Marbury .40 1.00
N12 Antonio McDyess .25 .60
N13 Jason Kidd .50 1.25
N14 Keith Van Horn .25 .60
N15 Karl Malone .60 1.50

1999-00 Upper Deck HoloGrFX NBA Shoetime

STATED ODDS 1:431
AIS Allen Iverson 25.00 60.00
BRS Bryon Russell 6.00 15.00
CBS Charles Barkley 30.00 80.00
CWS Chris Webber 30.00 80.00
DMS Dikembe Mutombo 15.00 40.00
DRS David Robinson 10.00 25.00
GHS Grant Hill 20.00 50.00
GPS Gary Payton 15.00 40.00
JKS Jason Kidd 15.00 40.00
JMS Jamal Mashburn 8.00 20.00
JSS John Stockton 15.00 40.00
KBS Kobe Bryant 40.00 100.00
KMA Karl Malone AU/32 300.00 400.00
KMS Karl Malone 20.00 50.00
MJA Michael Jordan AU/23 2,500.00 5,000.00
MJS Michael Jordan 150.00 400.00
PES Patrick Ewing 12.00 30.00
SMS Stephon Marbury 12.00 30.00
SOS Shaquille O'Neal 20.00 50.00
SPS Scottie Pippen 20.00 50.00
THS Tim Hardaway 12.00 30.00

1999-00 Upper Deck HoloGrFX UD Authentics

STATED ODDS 1:431
AJ Antawn Jamison 6.00 15.00
BD Baron Davis 10.00 25.00
BG Brian Grant 4.00 10.00
CM Corey Maggette 5.00 12.00
DA Darrell Armstrong 4.00 10.00
JO Michael Jordan 2,000.00 4,000.00
JS Jerry Stackhouse 6.00 15.00
JT Jason Terry 6.00 15.00
LH Larry Hughes 8.00 20.00
MB Mike Bibby 6.00 15.00
MF Michael Finley 8.00 20.00
MK Mark Jackson 5.00 12.00
MT Maurice Taylor 4.00 10.00
RD Richard Hamilton 10.00 25.00
RH Wally Szczerbiak 6.00 15.00
RL Raef LaFrentz 4.00 10.00
RT Robert Traylor 4.00 10.00
SF Steve Francis 8.00 20.00
SM Sam Mack 4.00 10.00
TG Tom Gugliotta 4.00 10.00
SHM Shawn Marion 8.00 20.00

1993-94 Upper Deck Holojams

COMP. FACT SET (38) 10.00 25.00
H1 Dominique Wilkins .20 .50
H2 Dee Brown .08 .25
H3 Alonzo Mourning .40 1.00
H4A Michael Jordan Hologram on right 8.00 20.00
H4B Michael Jordan Hologram on left 8.00 20.00
H5 Brad Daugherty .08 .25
H6 Jim Jackson .08 .25
H7 Dikembe Mutombo .08 .25
H8 Terry Mills .08 .25
H9 Billy Owens .08 .25
H10 Hakeem Olajuwon .50 1.25
H11 Reggie Miller .15 .40
H12 Ron Harper .08 .25
H13 James Worthy .15 .40
H14 Harold Miner .08 .25
H15 Blue Edwards .08 .25
H16 Doug West .08 .25
H17 Derrick Coleman .08 .25
H18 Patrick Ewing .20 .50
H19 Shaquille O'Neal 2.00 5.00
H20 Clarence Weatherspoon .08 .25
H21 Charles Barkley .50 1.25
H22 Clyde Drexler .20 .50
H23 Walt Williams .08 .25
H24 David Robinson .50 1.25
H25 Shawn Kemp .40 1.00
H26 Karl Malone .75 2.00
H27 Tom Gugliotta .15 .40
H28 Chris Webber 2.50 6.00
H29 Shawn Bradley .15 .40
H30 Anfernee Hardaway 2.00 5.00
H31 Jamal Mashburn .50 1.25
H32 Isaiah Rider .50 1.25
H33 Rodney Rogers .08 .25
H34 Lindsey Hunter .08 .25
H35 Doug Edwards .08 .25
H36 George Lynch .08 .25
NNO Album mail-in card .08 .25
NNO Checklist .08 .25

1997 Upper Deck Holojams

COMPLETE SET (20) 125.00 300.00
COMMON CARD 2.50 6.00
SEMISTARS 3.00 8.00
UNLISTED STARS 4.00 10.00
1 Michael Jordan 60.00 150.00
2 Juwan Howard 3.00 8.00
3 Shaquille O'Neal 12.00 30.00
4 Kevin Garnett 12.00 30.00
5 Allen Iverson 12.00 30.00
6 Glen Rice 4.00 10.00
7 Hakeem Olajuwon 8.00 20.00
8 Patrick Ewing 8.00 20.00
9 Karl Malone 8.00 20.00
10 Reggie Miller 12.00 30.00
11 Shawn Kemp 12.00 30.00
12 Alonzo Mourning 10.00 25.00
13 Grant Hill 8.00 20.00
14 Kobe Bryant 40.00 100.00
15 Stephon Marbury 5.00 12.00
16 Vin Baker 3.00 8.00
17 Latrell Sprewell 6.00 15.00
18 Scottie Pippen 12.00 30.00
19 Shareef Abdur-Rahim 4.00 10.00
20 Anfernee Hardaway 10.00 25.00

2001-02 Upper Deck Honor Roll

COMPLETE SET (130) 125.00 250.00
COMP.SET w/o SP's (90) 12.50 30.00
91-120 PRINT RUN 2499 SER.#'d SETS
121-130 PRINT RUN 1000 SER.#'d SETS
1 Shareef Abdur-Rahim .25 .60
2 Jason Terry .30 .75
3 Dion Glover .20 .50
4 Paul Pierce .50 1.25
5 Antoine Walker .25 .60
6 Kenny Anderson .25 .60
7 Baron Davis .30 .75
8 Jamal Mashburn .25 .60
9 David Wesley .20 .50
10 Ron Mercer .20 .50
11 Brad Miller .30 .75
12 Andre Miller .25 .60
13 Lamond Murray .20 .50
14 Chris Mihm .20 .50
15 Michael Finley .30 .75
16 Dirk Nowitzki .75 2.00
17 Steve Nash .60 1.50
18 Juwan Howard .25 .60
19 Nick Van Exel .30 .75
20 Raef LaFrentz .20 .50
21 Antonio McDyess .25 .60
22 James Posey .20 .50
23 Jerry Stackhouse .30 .75
24 Clifford Robinson .30 .75
25 Ben Wallace .40 1.00
26 Antawn Jamison .25 .60
27 Larry Hughes .25 .60
28 Steve Francis .30 .75
29 Cuttino Mobley .25 .60
30 Glen Rice .30 .75
31 Reggie Miller .60 1.50
32 Jalen Rose .25 .60
33 Jermaine O'Neal .25 .60
34 Darius Miles .20 .50
35 Elton Brand .25 .60
36 Lamar Odom .25 .60
37 Corey Maggette .25 .60
38 Kobe Bryant 2.50 6.00
39 Shaquille O'Neal 1.25 3.00
40 Rick Fox .25 .60
41 Lindsey Hunter .20 .50
42 Stromile Swift .20 .50
43 Jason Williams .50 1.25
44 Alonzo Mourning .50 1.25
45 Eddie Jones .30 .75
46 Anthony Carter .20 .50
47 Brian Grant .20 .50
48 Ray Allen .50 1.25
49 Glenn Robinson .30 .75
50 Sam Cassell .25 .60
51 Kevin Garnett .75 2.00
52 Terrell Brandon .25 .60
53 Wally Szczerbiak .25 .60
54 Joe Smith .25 .60
55 Jason Kidd .50 1.25
56 Kenyon Martin .30 .75
57 Allan Houston .30 .75
58 Latrell Sprewell .40 1.00
59 Marcus Camby .25 .60
60 Mark Jackson .25 .60
61 Tracy McGrady .50 1.25
62 Grant Hill .50 1.25
63 Mike Miller .25 .60
64 Allen Iverson .75 2.00
65 Dikembe Mutombo .50 1.25
66 Aaron McKie .20 .50
67 Stephon Marbury .40 1.00
68 Shawn Marion .30 .75
69 Anfernee Hardaway .75 2.00
70 Tom Gugliotta .20 .50
71 Rasheed Wallace .40 1.00
72 Damon Stoudamire .30 .75
73 Derek Anderson .20 .50
74 Chris Webber .40 1.00
75 Mike Bibby .30 .75
76 Peja Stojakovic .25 .60
77 Tim Duncan .75 2.00
78 David Robinson .60 1.50
79 Steve Smith .25 .60
80 Gary Payton .50 1.25
81 Rashard Lewis .25 .60
82 Desmond Mason .25 .60
83 Vince Carter .60 1.50
84 Morris Peterson .20 .50
85 Antonio Davis .25 .60
86 Karl Malone .60 1.50
87 John Stockton .60 1.50
88 Donyell Marshall .20 .50
89 Richard Hamilton .40 1.00
90 Michael Jordan 2.50 6.00
91 Andrei Kirilenko RC 1.50 4.00
92 Gilbert Arenas RC 2.50 6.00
93 Earl Watson RC .75 2.00
94 Terence Morris RC .60 1.50
95 Kedrick Brown RC .60 1.50
96 Zach Randolph RC 2.00 5.00
97 Joe Johnson RC 1.50 4.00
98 Brandon Armstrong RC .60 1.50
99 DeSagana Diop RC .60 1.50
100 Joseph Forte RC .60 1.50
101 Brendan Haywood RC .75 2.00
102 Samuel Dalembert RC 1.00 2.50
103 Jason Collins RC .75 2.00
104 Michael Bradley RC .60 1.50
105 Gerald Wallace RC 1.25 3.00
106 Tierre Brown RC 1.00 2.50
107 Troy Murphy RC .75 2.00
108 Alton Ford RC 1.00 2.50
109 Vladimir Radmanovic RC .75 2.00

110 Ruben Boumtje-Boumtje RC .75 2.00
111 Bobby Simmons RC 1.00 2.50
112 Oscar Torres RC 1.00 2.50
113 Jeryl Sasser RC .60 1.50
114 Loren Woods RC .60 1.50
115 Shane Battier RC 2.00 5.00
116 Jamison Brewer RC 1.00 2.50
117 Richard Jefferson RC 1.25 3.00
118 Pau Gasol RC 4.00 10.00
119 Damone Brown RC .60 1.50
120 Rodney White RC .60 1.50
121 Kw.Brown RC/Garnett JSY 6.00 15.00
122 Chandler RC/Miles JSY 6.00 15.00
123 Curry RC/Malone JSY 8.00 20.00
124 Richardson RC/Kobe JSY 40.00 100.00
125 Parker RC/Kidd JSY 12.00 30.00
126 Griffin RC/A.Hardaway JSY 5.00 12.00
127 Haston RC/Mash JSY 4.00 10.00
128 Tinsley RC/A.Miller JSY 4.00 10.00
129 Hassell RC/Fizer JSY 4.00 10.00
130 Hunter RC/T-Mac JSY 6.00 15.00

2001-02 Upper Deck Honor Roll All-NBA Authentic Jerseys

STATED ODDS 1:88
1 Kobe Bryant 40.00 100.00
2 Allen Iverson 10.00 25.00
3 Tracy McGrady 6.00 15.00
4 Andre Miller 3.00 8.00
5 Darius Miles 2.50 6.00
6 Baron Davis 4.00 10.00
7 Kevin Garnett 10.00 25.00
8 John Stockton 8.00 20.00
9 Ron Mercer 2.50 6.00
10 Shareef Abdur-Rahim 3.00 8.00
11 Dikembe Mutombo 6.00 15.00
12 Lamar Odom 3.00 8.00
13 Ray Allen 6.00 15.00
14 Mike Miller 3.00 8.00
15 Marcus Fizer 2.50 6.00
16 Toni Kukoc 5.00 12.00
17 Stephon Marbury 5.00 12.00
18 Jason Kidd 6.00 15.00
19 Karl Malone 8.00 20.00

2001-02 Upper Deck Honor Roll All-NBA Authentics Jerseys Combos

STATED ODDS 1:240
1 K.Bryant/K.Garnett 40.00 100.00
2 K.Bryant/A.Iverson 40.00 100.00
3 B.Davis/A.Miller 3.00 8.00
4 J.Kidd/K.Martin 5.00 12.00
5 K.Malone/J.Stockton 6.00 15.00
6 E.Brand/K.Garnett 8.00 20.00
7 G.Hill/M.Miller 5.00 12.00
8 S.Marbury/S.Marion 4.00 10.00
9 S.Abdur-Rahim/J.Terry 3.00 8.00

2001-02 Upper Deck Honor Roll Fab Five All-Stars

COMPLETE SET (10) 15.00 30.00
STATED ODDS 1:24
1 Tim Duncan 2.00 5.00
2 Chris Webber 1.00 2.50
3 Kevin Garnett 2.00 5.00
4 Kobe Bryant 6.00 15.00
5 Shaquille O'Neal 3.00 8.00
6 Vince Carter 1.50 4.00
7 Allen Iverson 2.00 5.00
8 Tracy McGrady 1.25 3.00
9 Latrell Sprewell 1.00 2.50
10 Michael Jordan 6.00 15.00

2001-02 Upper Deck Honor Roll Fab Five Rookies

COMPLETE SET (10) 10.00 25.00
STATED ODDS 1:24
1 Tony Parker 3.00 8.00
2 Jamaal Tinsley .60 1.50
3 Pau Gasol 3.00 8.00
4 Jason Richardson 1.25 3.00
5 Kwame Brown .75 2.00
6 Shane Battier 1.50 4.00
7 Eddie Griffin .60 1.50
8 Eddy Curry .75 2.00
9 Andrei Kirilenko 1.25 3.00
10 Joe Johnson 1.25 3.00

2001-02 Upper Deck Honor Roll Fab Five Scorers

COMPLETE SET (10) 15.00 30.00
STATED ODDS 1:24
F5S1 Michael Jordan 6.00 15.00
F5S2 Kobe Bryant 6.00 15.00
F5S3 Vince Carter 1.50 4.00
F5S4 Shaquille O'Neal 3.00 8.00
F5S5 Dirk Nowitzki 2.00 5.00
F5S6 Tim Duncan 2.00 5.00
F5S7 Kevin Garnett 2.00 5.00
F5S8 Paul Pierce 1.25 3.00
F5S9 Shareef Abdur-Rahim .60 1.50
F5S10 Jerry Stackhouse .75 2.00

2001-02 Upper Deck Honor Roll Fab Floor Autographs

STATED ODDS 1:480
1 Kobe Bryant 1,500.00 3,000.00
2 Michael Jordan 3,000.00 6,000.00
3 Kevin Garnett 100.00 250.00
4 Wally Szczerbiak 6.00 15.00
5 Darius Miles 6.00 15.00
6 Antoine Walker 6.00 15.00
7 Andre Miller 6.00 15.00
8 Jason Kidd 30.00 80.00

2001-02 Upper Deck Honor Roll Fab Floor Duos

STATED ODDS 1:96
1 K.Bryant/M.Jordan 125.00 300.00
2 K.Bryant/K.Garnett 40.00 100.00
3 A.McDyess/S.Marion 4.00 10.00
4 J.Terry/D.Johnson 4.00 10.00
5 K.Garnett/R.Lewis 5.00 12.00
6 K.Garnett/T.Brandon 5.00 12.00
7 K.Garnett/D.Miles 5.00 12.00
8 S.Marbury/S.Marion 4.00 10.00
9 M.Finley/D.Nowitzki 6.00 15.00
10 A.Walker/P.Pierce 6.00 15.00
11 R.Wallace/D.Anderson 4.00 10.00
12 R.Allen/G.Robinson 4.00 10.00
13 J.Stackhouse/R.Wallace 4.00 10.00
14 L.Sprewell/A.Houston 5.00 12.00
15 D.Robinson/D.Mutombo 6.00 15.00
16 B.Davis/J.Mashburn 4.00 10.00
17 G.Payton/D.Mason 4.00 10.00

2001-02 Upper Deck Honor Roll Fab Floor Triples

STATED ODDS 1:240
1 Bryant/Garnett/Jordan 125.00 300.00
2 Bryant/Garnett/Martin 40.00 100.00
3 Garnett/Szcz/Brandon 6.00 15.00
4 G.Robnsn/Allen/Thomas 6.00 15.00
5 R.Miller/J.O'Neal/Bender 6.00 15.00

2002-03 Upper Deck Honor Roll

COMP.SET w/o SP's (90) 12.00 30.00
91-105 PRINT RUN 499 SERIAL #'d SETS
106-135 PRINT RUN 1999 SER.#'d SETS
1 Glenn Robinson .30 .75
2 Shareef Abdur-Rahim .30 .75
3 Jason Terry .25 .60
4 Paul Pierce .50 1.25
5 Antoine Walker .25 .60
6 Tony Delk .20 .50
7 Jalen Rose .25 .60
8 Tyson Chandler .30 .75
9 Eddy Curry .20 .50
10 Darius Miles .20 .50
11 Zydrunas Ilgauskas .25 .60
12 Ricky Davis .25 .60
13 Dirk Nowitzki .75 2.00
14 Michael Finley .30 .75
15 Steve Nash .60 1.50
16 Raef LaFrentz .20 .50
17 Eduardo Najera .20 .50
18 Rodney White .20 .50
19 Juwan Howard .25 .60
20 Chris Whitney .20 .50
21 Ben Wallace .40 1.00
22 Richard Hamilton .40 1.00
23 Chauncey Billups .30 .75
24 Chucky Atkins .20 .50
25 Jason Richardson .30 .75
26 Antawn Jamison .25 .60
27 Gilbert Arenas .30 .75
28 Steve Francis .30 .75
29 Cuttino Mobley .20 .50
30 Jermaine O'Neal .25 .60
31 Reggie Miller .60 1.50
32 Jamaal Tinsley .20 .50
33 Andre Miller .20 .50
34 Elton Brand .25 .60
35 Quentin Richardson .20 .50
36 Shaquille O'Neal 1.25 3.00
37 Kobe Bryant 2.50 6.00
38 Robert Horry .30 .75
39 Shane Battier .30 .75
40 Pau Gasol .50 1.25
41 Stromile Swift .20 .50
42 Eddie Jones .30 .75
43 Brian Grant .20 .50
44 Malik Allen .20 .50
45 Ray Allen .50 1.25
46 Tim Thomas .20 .50
47 Kevin Garnett .75 2.00
48 Wally Szczerbiak .20 .50
49 Jason Kidd .50 1.25
50 Kenyon Martin .30 .75
51 Richard Jefferson .30 .75
52 Baron Davis .30 .75
53 Jamal Mashburn .25 .60
54 David Wesley .20 .50
55 P.J. Brown .20 .50
56 Allan Houston .30 .75
57 Latrell Sprewell .30 .75
58 Kurt Thomas .20 .50
59 Tracy McGrady .50 1.25
60 Grant Hill .50 1.25
61 Mike Miller .25 .60
62 Allen Iverson .50 1.25
63 Keith Van Horn .25 .60
64 Aaron McKie .20 .50
65 Shawn Marion .30 .75
66 Stephon Marbury .40 1.00
67 Rasheed Wallace .40 1.00
68 Derek Anderson .20 .50
69 Bonzi Wells .20 .50
70 Mike Bibby .30 .75
71 Chris Webber .40 1.00
72 Peja Stojakovic .30 .75
73 Hedo Turkoglu .25 .60
74 Tim Duncan .75 2.00
75 David Robinson .60 1.50
76 Tony Parker .50 1.25
77 Gary Payton .50 1.25
78 Rashard Lewis .25 .60
79 Brent Barry .25 .60
80 Desmond Mason .25 .60
81 Vince Carter .60 1.50
82 Antonio Davis .25 .60
83 Morris Peterson .25 .60
84 John Stockton .60 1.50
85 Karl Malone .60 1.50
86 Andrei Kirilenko .25 .60
87 Matt Harpring .30 .75
88 Jerry Stackhouse .30 .75
89 Kwame Brown .20 .50
90 Michael Jordan 3.00 8.00
91 Ryan Humphrey JSY RC 2.50 6.00
92 Juan Dixon JSY RC 2.50 6.00
93 Fred Jones JSY RC 2.50 6.00
94 Marcus Haislip JSY RC 2.00 5.00
95 Melvin Ely JSY RC 2.50 6.00
96 Jared Jeffries JSY RC 2.50 6.00
97 Caron Butler JSY RC 3.00 8.00
98 Amare Stoudemire JSY RC 8.00 20.00
99 Chris Wilcox JSY RC 2.50 6.00
100 Nene Hilario JSY RC 2.50 6.00
101 Dajuan Wagner JSY RC 2.50 6.00
102 Nikoloz Tskitishvili JSY RC 2.00 5.00
103 Drew Gooden JSY RC 3.00 8.00
104 Jay Williams JSY RC 2.50 6.00
105 Yao Ming JSY RC 15.00 40.00
106 Mike Dunleavy RC 1.50 4.00
107 Bostjan Nachbar RC 1.25 3.00
108 Jiri Welsch RC 1.25 3.00
109 Rasual Butler RC 1.25 3.00
110 Kareem Rush RC 1.25 3.00
111 Qyntel Woods RC 1.00 2.50
112 Casey Jacobsen RC 1.25 3.00
113 Tayshaun Prince RC 3.00 8.00
114 Frank Williams RC 1.00 2.50
115 John Salmons RC 1.50 4.00
116 Chris Jefferies RC 1.00 2.50
117 Dan Dickau RC 1.00 2.50
118 Juaquin Hawkins RC 1.00 2.50
119 Roger Mason RC 1.25 3.00
120 Robert Archibald RC 1.00 2.50
121 Vincent Yarbrough RC 1.00 2.50
122 Dan Gadzuric RC 1.25 3.00
123 Carlos Boozer RC 1.50 4.00
124 Tito Maddox RC 1.00 2.50
125 Gordan Giricek RC 1.50 4.00
126 Ronald Murray RC 1.50 4.00
127 Lonny Baxter RC 1.00 2.50
128 Pat Burke RC 1.00 2.50
129 Manu Ginobili RC 8.00 20.00
130 Predrag Savovic RC 1.25 3.00
131 Marko Jaric 1.50 4.00
132 Efthimios Rentzias RC 1.00 2.50
133 J.R. Bremer RC 1.00 2.50
134 Igor Rakocevic RC 1.00 2.50
135 Tamar Slay RC 1.00 2.50

2002-03 Upper Deck Honor Roll Award Performances

COMPLETE SET (14) 10.00 25.00
STATED ODDS 1:12
AP1 Kobe Bryant 5.00 12.00
AP2 Tim Duncan 1.50 4.00
AP3 Eddie Jones .60 1.50
AP4 Steve Francis .60 1.50
AP5 Shareef Abdur-Rahim .60 1.50
AP6 Rasheed Wallace .75 2.00
AP7 Shaquille O'Neal 2.50 6.00
AP8 Rashard Lewis .50 1.25
AP9 Ray Allen 1.00 2.50
AP10 Pau Gasol 1.00 2.50
AP11 Elton Brand .50 1.25
AP12 Ben Wallace .75 2.00
AP13 Andre Miller .50 1.25
AP14 Michael Jordan 6.00 15.00

2002-03 Upper Deck Honor Roll Dual Jerseys

STATED ODDS 1:240
AWPP A.Walker/P.Pierce 6.00 15.00
BDJM B.Davis/J.Mashburn 6.00 15.00
CWMB C.Webber/M.Bibby 6.00 15.00
DNSN D.Nowitzki/S.Nash 8.00 20.00
JKKM J.Kidd/K.Martin 8.00 20.00
JRAJ J.Richardson/A.Jamison 6.00 15.00
KBAI K.Bryant/A.Iverson 75.00 200.00
KMJS K.Malone/J.Stockton 8.00 20.00
MJKB M.Jordan/K.Bryant SP 200.00 500.00
SMSM S.Marbury/S.Marion 6.00 15.00
TMKG T.McGrady/K.Garnett 12.50 30.00
YMJW Y.Ming/J.Williams 10.00 25.00

2002-03 Upper Deck Honor Roll Dual Warm-ups

STATED ODDS 1:48
AWPP A.Walker/P.Pierce 5.00 12.00
BDJM B.Davis/J.Mashburn 4.00 10.00
CWMB C.Webber/M.Bibby 4.00 10.00
DNSN D.Nowitzki/S.Nash 5.00 12.00
DRTP D.Robinson/T.Parker 6.00 15.00
EBAM E.Brand/A.Miller 4.00 10.00
GPRL G.Payton/R.Lewis 4.00 10.00
JKKM J.Kidd/K.Martin 5.00 12.00
JRAJ J.Richardson/A.Jamison 4.00 10.00
KBKG K.Bryant/K.Garnett 75.00 200.00
KGWS K.Garnett/W.Szczerbiak 5.00 12.00
KMJS K.Malone/J.Stockton 5.00 12.00
MJKB M.Jordan/K.Bryant SP 200.00 500.00
SBSS S.Battier/S.Swift 4.00 10.00
SMSM S.Marbury/S.Marion 4.00 10.00
TMMM T.McGrady/M.Miller 5.00 12.00

2002-03 Upper Deck Honor Roll Popular Acclaim

COMPLETE SET (14) 12.50 30.00
STATED ODDS 1:12
PA1 Michael Jordan 6.00 15.00
PA2 Shaquille O'Neal 2.50 6.00
PA3 Shane Battier .60 1.50
PA4 Michael Finley .60 1.50
PA5 Vince Carter 1.25 3.00
PA6 Darius Miles .40 1.00
PA7 Peja Stojakovic .50 1.25
PA8 Kobe Bryant 5.00 12.00
PA9 Yao Ming 3.00 8.00
PA10 Jalen Rose .50 1.25
PA11 Allen Iverson 1.50 4.00
PA12 Jay Williams .50 1.25
PA13 Drew Gooden .60 1.50
PA14 Shawn Marion .60 1.50

2002-03 Upper Deck Honor Roll Principals Autograph Jerseys

STATED ODDS 1:480
AWAJ Antoine Walker 12.00 30.00
CJAJ Chris Jefferies 8.00 20.00
DAAJ Dan Gadzuric 8.00 20.00
DGAJ Drew Gooden 8.00 20.00
DSAJ DeShawn Stevenson 10.00 25.00
JKAJ Jason Kidd 50.00 120.00
JWAJ Jay Williams 10.00 25.00
KBAJO Kobe Bryant/25 3,000.00 6,000.00
KGAJO Kevin Garnett/21 150.00 400.00
KMAJ Kenyon Martin 10.00 25.00
MFAJ Marcus Fizer 8.00 20.00
MJAJ Michael Jordan/23 4,000.00 8,000.00
MMAJ Mike Miller 10.00 25.00
PPAJO Paul Pierce 50.00 120.00
PSAJ Peja Stojakovic 20.00 50.00
SMAJ Shawn Marion 12.00 30.00
TCAJO Tyson Chandler 10.00 25.00
TPAJ Tayshaun Prince 20.00 50.00
YMAJ Yao Ming 150.00 400.00

2002-03 Upper Deck Honor Roll Signature Class

STATED ODDS 1:480
AWS Antoine Walker 12.00 30.00
ETS Etan Thomas 5.00 12.00
JKS Jason Kidd 40.00 100.00
JMS Jerome Moiso 5.00 12.00
KBS Kobe Bryant/25 2,000.00 4,000.00
KMS Kenyon Martin 12.00 30.00
MFS Marcus Fizer 5.00 12.00
MJS Michael Jordan/23 3,000.00 6,000.00
MMS Mike Miller 5.00 12.00
SMS Shawn Marion 8.00 20.00

2002-03 Upper Deck Honor Roll Signature Class Duals

PRINT RUN 25 SERIAL #'d SETS
KBJW K.Bryant/J.Williams 1,000.00 2,000.00
KBKG K.Bryant/K.Garnett 3,000.00 6,000.00
MJKB M.Jordan/K.Bryant 15,000.00 30,000.00
PPAW P.Pierce/A.Walker 75.00 200.00
YMJW Y.Ming/J.Williams 400.00 800.00

2002-03 Upper Deck Honor Roll Superstar Tributes

COMPLETE SET (7) 25.00 60.00
STATED ODDS 1:24
ST1 Kobe Bryant 12.00 30.00
ST2 Michael Jordan 20.00 50.00
ST3 Steve Francis .75 2.00
ST4 Vince Carter 1.50 4.00
ST5 Allen Iverson 2.00 5.00
ST6 Tim Duncan 2.00 5.00
ST7 Shaquille O'Neal 3.00 8.00

2002-03 Upper Deck Honor Roll Tremendous Talents

COMPLETE SET (7) 25.00 60.00
STATED ODDS 1:24
TT1 Jay Williams 1.00 2.50
TT2 Tim Duncan 3.00 8.00
TT3 Kobe Bryant 10.00 25.00
TT4 Yao Ming 6.00 15.00
TT5 Mike Bibby 1.25 3.00
TT6 Vince Carter 2.50 6.00
TT7 Michael Jordan 20.00 50.00

2002-03 Upper Deck Honor Roll Triple Warm-ups

ASTERISK CARDS ARE SP's
STATED ODDS 1:120
1 Miller/Brand/Olowkndi 2.50 6.00
2 Webber/Bryant/Pierce 40.00 100.00
3 Nowitzki/Finley/Nash 8.00 20.00
4 Mash/Davis/Wesley 3.00 8.00
5 Stocktn/Malone/Kirilenko 6.00 15.00
6 Martin/Kidd/Jefferson 5.00 12.00
7 McGrady/Bryant/J-Rich 40.00 100.00
8 Szczerb/Smith/Brandon 2.50 6.00

2003-04 Upper Deck Honor Roll

COMP.SET w/o SP's (90) 15.00 40.00
JSY RC PRINT RUN 999 SER.#'d SETS
1 Shareef Abdur-Rahim .30 .75
2 Dan Dickau .20 .50
3 Jason Terry .25 .60
4 Raef LaFrentz .20 .50
5 Vin Baker .20 .50
6 Paul Pierce .50 1.25
7 Antonio Davis .25 .60
8 Scottie Pippen .75 2.00
9 Jamal Crawford .30 .75
10 Dajuan Wagner .20 .50
11 Ricky Davis .25 .60
12 Darius Miles .25 .60
13 Dirk Nowitzki .75 2.00
14 Antoine Walker .30 .75
15 Steve Nash .60 1.50
16 Michael Finley .30 .75
17 Nikoloz Tskitishvili .20 .50
18 Andre Miller .25 .60
19 Nene .25 .60
20 Chauncey Billups .40 1.00
21 Richard Hamilton .40 1.00
22 Ben Wallace .40 1.00
23 Clifford Robinson .20 .50
24 Jason Richardson .30 .75
25 Mike Dunleavy .25 .60
26 Yao Ming .75 2.00
27 Cuttino Mobley .20 .50
28 Steve Francis .30 .75
29 Jermaine O'Neal .25 .60
30 Reggie Miller .60 1.50
31 Al Harrington .25 .60
32 Elton Brand .25 .60
33 Corey Maggette .25 .60
34 Quentin Richardson .20 .50
35 Kobe Bryant 2.50 6.00
36 Karl Malone .60 1.50
37 Gary Payton .50 1.25
38 Shaquille O'Neal 1.25 3.00
39 Pau Gasol .50 1.25
40 Jason Williams .50 1.25
41 Mike Miller .25 .60
42 Lamar Odom .25 .60
43 Eddie Jones .30 .75
44 Caron Butler .25 .60
45 Michael Redd .30 .75
46 Desmond Mason .25 .60
47 Tim Thomas .20 .50
48 Latrell Sprewell .40 1.00
49 Kevin Garnett .75 2.00
50 Wally Szczerbiak .20 .50
51 Richard Jefferson .25 .60
52 Kenyon Martin .30 .75
53 Jason Kidd .50 1.25
54 Jamal Mashburn .25 .60
55 Baron Davis .30 .75
56 Jamaal Magloire .20 .50
57 Allan Houston .30 .75
58 Antonio McDyess .25 .60
59 Keith Van Horn .25 .60
60 Grant Hill .40 1.00
61 Drew Gooden .25 .60
62 Tracy McGrady .50 1.25
63 Glenn Robinson .25 .60
64 Allen Iverson .75 2.00
65 Eric Snow .20 .50
66 Amare Stoudemire .40 1.00
67 Stephon Marbury .40 1.00
68 Shawn Marion .30 .75
69 Derek Anderson .25 .60
70 Damon Stoudamire .25 .60
71 Rasheed Wallace .40 1.00
72 Peja Stojakovic .25 .60
73 Chris Webber .40 1.00
74 Mike Bibby .30 .75
75 Bobby Jackson .25 .60
76 Tony Parker .50 1.25
77 Tim Duncan .75 2.00
78 Manu Ginobili .60 1.50
79 Vladimir Radmanovic .20 .50
80 Ray Allen .50 1.25
81 Rashard Lewis .25 .60
82 Morris Peterson .20 .50
83 Vince Carter .60 1.50
84 Jalen Rose .25 .60
85 Andrei Kirilenko .25 .60
86 Matt Harpring .20 .50
87 Greg Ostertag .20 .50
88 Gilbert Arenas .30 .75
89 Larry Hughes .25 .60
90 Jerry Stackhouse .40 1.00
91 Kirk Hinrich RC 1.50 4.00
92 T.J. Ford RC 1.25 3.00
93 Nick Collison RC 1.25 3.00
94 Kendrick Perkins RC 1.25 3.00
95 Leandro Barbosa RC 1.25 3.00
96 Josh Howard RC 1.50 4.00
97 Jason Kapono RC 1.00 2.50
98 Jerome Beasley RC 1.00 2.50
99 Travis Hansen RC 1.00 2.50
100 Steve Blake RC 1.25 3.00
101 Willie Green RC 1.50 4.00
102 Zaur Pachulia RC 1.50 4.00
103 Keith Bogans RC 1.00 2.50
104 Kyle Korver RC 2.00 5.00
105 Brandon Hunter RC 1.00 2.50
106 LeBron James JSY RC 500.00 1,000.00
107 Darko Milicic JSY RC 2.50 6.00
108 Carmelo Anthony JSY RC 15.00 40.00
109 Chris Bosh JSY RC 10.00 25.00
110 Dwyane Wade JSY RC 25.00 60.00
111 Chris Kaman JSY RC 3.00 8.00
112 Mike Sweetney JSY RC 2.00 5.00
113 Jarvis Hayes JSY RC 2.00 5.00
114 Mickael Pietrus JSY RC 2.50 6.00
115 Marcus Banks JSY RC 2.00 5.00
116 Luke Ridnour JSY RC 3.00 8.00
117 Reece Gaines JSY RC 2.00 5.00
118 Troy Bell JSY RC 2.00 5.00
119 Z.Cabarkapa JSY RC 2.00 5.00
120 David West JSY RC 4.00 10.00
121 A.Pavlovic JSY RC 2.50 6.00
122 Dahntay Jones JSY RC 2.50 6.00
123 Boris Diaw JSY RC 3.00 8.00
124 Zoran Planinic JSY RC 2.50 6.00
125 Travis Outlaw JSY RC 2.50 6.00
126 Brian Cook JSY RC 2.00 5.00
127 Ndudi Ebi JSY RC 2.00 5.00
128 Maciej Lampe JSY RC 2.00 5.00
129 Slavko Vranes JSY RC 2.00 5.00
130 Luke Walton JSY RC 3.00 8.00

2003-04 Upper Deck Honor Roll Gold

*GOLD 1-90: 4X TO 10X BASE HI
*GOLD 91-105 RCs: 2X TO 5X BASE HI
1-90 PRINT RUN 100 SER.#'d SETS
91-105 PRINT RUN 25 SER.#'d SETS

2003-04 Upper Deck Honor Roll Jersey Autographs Gold

*GOLD: 1.25X TO 3X BASE HI
PRINT RUN 25 SERIAL #'d SETS
106 LeBron James 15,000.00 30,000.00
108 Carmelo Anthony 150.00 400.00
109 Chris Bosh 50.00 120.00
110 Dwyane Wade 500.00 1,000.00

2003-04 Upper Deck Honor Roll Award Performers

COMPLETE SET (14) 10.00 25.00
STATED ODDS 1:12 1.00 2.50
*GOLD SINGLES: 2.5X TO 6X BASE HI
GOLD PRINT RUN 100 SER.#'d SETS
AP1 LeBron James 25.00 60.00
AP2 Peja Stojakovic .30 .75
AP3 Yao Ming 1.00 2.50
AP4 Gilbert Arenas .40 1.00
AP5 Jermaine O'Neal .40 1.00
AP6 Amare Stoudemire .50 1.25
AP7 Kobe Bryant 3.00 8.00
AP8 Jason Kidd .60 1.50
AP9 Vince Carter .75 2.00
AP10 Shaquille O'Neal 1.50 4.00
AP11 Michael Jordan 4.00 10.00
AP12 Caron Butler .30 .75
AP13 Ben Wallace .50 1.25
AP14 Elton Brand .30 .75

2003-04 Upper Deck Honor Roll Dual Warm Ups

STATED ODDS 1:48
*GOLD SINGLES: .6X TO 1.5X BASE HI
GOLD PRINT RUN 100 SER.#'d SETS
1 A.Iverson/E.Snow 5.00 12.00
2 A.Miller/Nene 4.00 10.00
3 D.Milicic/R.Hamilton 4.00 10.00
4 C.Butler/D.Wade 12.00 30.00
5 E.Curry/T.Chandler 4.00 10.00
6 J.Kidd/K.Martin 5.00 12.00
7 B.Davis/J.Magloire 4.00 10.00
8 J.Tinsley/J.O'Neal 4.00 10.00
9 G.Arenas/J.Richardson 4.00 10.00
10 J.Terry/Abdur-Rahim 4.00 10.00
11 K.Bryant/G.Payton 10.00 25.00
12 K.Garnett/Szczerbiak 5.00 12.00
13 K.Malone/D.George 5.00 12.00
14 J.Stockton/M.Jordan 40.00 100.00
15 D.Wagner/D.Miles 4.00 10.00
16 P.Pierce/A.Walker 5.00 12.00
17 M.Bibby/R.Jefferson 4.00 10.00
18 D.Nowitzki/S.Nash 5.00 12.00
19 T.McGrady/D.Gooden 5.00 12.00
20 T.Duncan/T.Parker 5.00 12.00
21 C.Wilcox/S.Francis 4.00 10.00

2003-04 Upper Deck Honor Roll Popular Acclaim

COMPLETE SET (14) 8.00 20.00
STATED ODDS 1:12
*GOLD SINGLES: 2.5X TO 6X BASE HI
GOLD PRINT RUN 50 SER.#'d SETS
PA1 Kobe Bryant 3.00 8.00
PA2 Ray Allen .60 1.50
PA3 Shawn Marion .40 1.00
PA4 Steve Francis .40 1.00
PA5 Dajuan Wagner .25 .60
PA6 Steve Nash .75 2.00
PA7 LeBron James 40.00 100.00
PA8 Carmelo Anthony 2.00 5.00
PA9 Paul Pierce .60 1.50
PA10 Gary Payton .60 1.50
PA11 Richard Jefferson .30 .75
PA12 Michael Jordan 4.00 10.00
PA13 Baron Davis .40 1.00
PA14 Shaquille O'Neal 1.50 4.00

2003-04 Upper Deck Honor Roll Popular Acclaim Gold

*GOLD SINGLES: 2.5X TO 6X BASE HI
PA12 Michael Jordan 30.00 80.00

2003-04 Upper Deck Honor Roll Principals

STATED ODDS 1:480
BA Marcus Banks 5.00 12.00
CA Carmelo Anthony 200.00 500.00
CH Chris Bosh 75.00 200.00
CM Corey Maggette 8.00 20.00
DG Drew Gooden 5.00 12.00
DM Darko Milicic 6.00 15.00
DR David Robinson 75.00 200.00
DW Dajuan Wagner 5.00 12.00
GA Gilbert Arenas 8.00 20.00
JH Jarvis Hayes 5.00 12.00
JK Jason Kidd 25.00 60.00
JM Jerome Moiso 5.00 12.00
LJ LeBron James 6,000.00 12,000.00
MB Mike Bibby 12.00 30.00
MJ Michael Jordan/23 8,000.00 15,000.00
RJ Richard Jefferson 8.00 20.00
SF Steve Francis 10.00 25.00
TO Travis Outlaw 6.00 15.00
WAO Dwyane Wade 500.00 1,000.00
YM Yao Ming 150.00 400.00

2003-04 Upper Deck Honor Roll Signature Class

STATED ODDS 1:480
SC1 Jerome Moiso 4.00 10.00
SC2 Cuttino Mobley 8.00 20.00
SC3 Richard Hamilton 10.00 25.00
SC4 Andre Miller 8.00 20.00
SC5 Mickael Pietrus 6.00 15.00
SC6 Luke Ridnour 4.00 10.00
SC7 Tracy McGrady 50.00 120.00
SC8 Jarvis Hayes 4.00 10.00
SC9 Ndudi Ebi 4.00 10.00
SC10 LeBron James 5,000.00 10,000.00
SC12 Kobe Bryant 500.00 1,000.00

2003-04 Upper Deck Honor Roll Superstar Tributes

COMPLETE SET (7) 10.00 25.00
STATED ODDS 1:24
ST1 Michael Jordan 8.00 20.00
ST2 Dirk Nowitzki 2.00 5.00
ST3 LeBron James 30.00 80.00
ST4 Kobe Bryant 6.00 15.00
ST5 Kevin Garnett 2.00 5.00
ST6 Tracy McGrady 1.25 3.00
ST7 Carmelo Anthony 4.00 10.00

2003-04 Upper Deck Honor Roll Tremendous Talents

COMPLETE SET (7) 8.00 20.00
STATED ODDS 1:24
*GOLD: 3X TO 8X BASE HI
GOLD PRINT RUN 25 SER.#'d SETS
TT1 Tim Duncan 2.00 5.00
TT2 Shaquille O'Neal 3.00 8.00
TT3 Kobe Bryant 6.00 15.00
TT4 Allen Iverson 2.00 5.00
TT5 Vince Carter 1.50 4.00
TT6 Chris Webber 1.00 2.50
TT7 LeBron James 40.00 100.00

2003-04 Upper Deck Honor Roll Triple Warm Ups

STATED ODDS 1:144
*GOLD: .75X TO 2X BASE HI
GOLD PRINT RUN 25 SER.#'d SETS
1 Iverson/McKie/Snow 8.00 20.00
2 Jamison/Arenas/Richardson 6.00 15.00
3 Wagner/Boozer/Miles 6.00 15.00
4 Nowitzki/Finley/Nash 10.00 25.00
5 Wilcox/Brand/Ely 6.00 15.00
6 Curry/Rose/JayWill 6.00 15.00
7 Kobe/Payton/Malone 50.00 120.00
8 A-Rahim/Terry/G.Robinson 6.00 15.00
9 Kidd/Martin/Jefferson 8.00 20.00
10 Haywood/J-Rich/Hughes 6.00 15.00
11 Houston/Vranes/Mutombo 6.00 15.00
12 Amare/Marion/Marbury 6.00 15.00
13 Jordan/Kobe/Stockton 75.00 200.00
14 Odom/Q-Rich/Maggette 6.00 15.00
15 M.Miller/Gasol/Battier 6.00 15.00
16 G.Wallace/Bibby/Peja 6.00 15.00
17 Mason/J.Smith/R.Allen 6.00 15.00
18 Darko/Billups/Hamilton 6.00 15.00
19 Duncan/Parker/Rasho 12.00 30.00
20 Kobe/Garnett/McGrady 50.00 120.00
21 B.Davis/Francis/Marbury 6.00 15.00

2001-02 Upper Deck Inspirations

COMP.SET w/o SP's (90) 15.00 40.00
91-103 PRINT RUN 2249 SER.#'d SETS
104-109 PRINT RUN 275 SER.#'d SETS
110-116 PRINT RUN 1149 SER.#'d SETS
117-124 PRINT RUN 1500 SER.#'d SETS
CARD 118 PRINT RUN 525 SER.#'d SETS
125-134 PRINT RUN 1100 SER.#'d SETS
125-134 BOTH PLAYERS HAVE JSY
135-140 PRINT RUN 275 SER.#'d SETS
135-140 BOTH PLAYERS HAVE JSY
141-152 PRINT RUN 2999 SER.#'d SETS
153-164 PRINT RUN 2699 SER.#'d SETS
165-176 PRINT RUN 1999 SER.#'d SETS
177-182 PRINT RUN 499 SER.#'d SETS
1 Shareef Abdur-Rahim .25 .60
2 Jason Terry .25 .60
3 Dion Glover .20 .50
4 Antoine Walker .25 .60
5 Paul Pierce .50 1.25
6 Larry Bird 1.25 3.00
7 Baron Davis .30 .75
8 Jamal Mashburn .25 .60
9 David Wesley .20 .50
10 Elden Campbell .20 .50
11 Jalen Rose .25 .60
12 Marcus Fizer .20 .50
13 Andre Miller .25 .60
14 Lamond Murray .20 .50
15 Chris Mihm .20 .50
16 Dirk Nowitzki .75 2.00
17 Steve Nash .60 1.50
18 Michael Finley .30 .75
19 Nick Van Exel .30 .75
20 Raef LaFrentz .25 .60
21 Antonio McDyess .25 .60
22 Juwan Howard .25 .60
23 Tim Hardaway .40 1.00
24 James Posey .20 .50
25 Jerry Stackhouse .30 .75
26 Ben Wallace .40 1.00
27 Isiah Thomas .50 1.25
28 Antawn Jamison .25 .60
29 Larry Hughes .25 .60
30 Steve Francis .30 .75
31 Moses Malone .50 1.25
32 Reggie Miller .60 1.50
33 Jermaine O'Neal .25 .60
34 Elton Brand .25 .60
35 Darius Miles .20 .50
36 Lamar Odom .25 .60
37 Quentin Richardson .20 .50
38 Kobe Bryant 2.50 6.00
39 Shaquille O'Neal 1.25 3.00
40 Derek Fisher .25 .60
41 Devean George .25 .60
42 Stromile Swift .20 .50
43 Jason Williams .50 1.25
44 Alonzo Mourning .50 1.25
45 Eddie Jones .30 .75
46 Anthony Carter .20 .50
47 Ray Allen .50 1.25
48 Sam Cassell .25 .60
49 Glenn Robinson .30 .75
50 Tim Thomas .20 .50
51 Oscar Robertson .75 2.00
52 Kevin Garnett .75 2.00
53 Wally Szczerbiak .25 .60
54 Terrell Brandon .25 .60
55 Chauncey Billups .40 1.00
56 Jason Kidd .50 1.25
57 Kenyon Martin .30 .75
58 Latrell Sprewell .40 1.00
59 Allan Houston .25 .60
60 Marcus Camby .25 .60
61 Kurt Thomas .20 .50
62 Grant Hill .50 1.25
63 Mike Miller .25 .60
64 Tracy McGrady .50 1.25
65 Allen Iverson .60 1.50
66 Julius Erving .75 2.00
67 Bobby Jones .25 .60
68 Stephon Marbury .40 1.00
69 Shawn Marion .30 .75
70 Anfernee Hardaway .30 .75
71 Rasheed Wallace .40 1.00
72 Bill Walton .40 1.00
73 Chris Webber .40 1.00
74 Peja Stojakovic .25 .60
75 Mike Bibby .30 .75
76 Tim Duncan .75 2.00
77 David Robinson .60 1.50
78 George Gervin .50 1.25
79 Gary Payton .50 1.25
80 Rashard Lewis .25 .60
81 Desmond Mason .25 .60
82 Vince Carter .60 1.50
83 Morris Peterson .20 .50
84 Antonio Davis .20 .50
85 Hakeem Olajuwon .60 1.50
86 Karl Malone .60 1.50
87 John Stockton .60 1.50
88 Donyell Marshall .20 .50
89 Richard Hamilton .40 1.00
90 Michael Jordan 4.00 10.00
91 Z.Rebraca RC/S.O'Neal 2.00 5.00
92 O.Robertson/O.Torres RC 2.00 5.00
93 R.Miller/J.Brewer RC 2.00 5.00
94 P.Stojak/P.Drobnjak RC 2.00 5.00
95 M.Bateer RC/W.Zhi-Zhi 12.00 30.00
96 J.West/W.Solomon RC 2.00 5.00
97 T.Duncan/M.Allen RC 2.00 5.00
98 W.Frazier/D.Brown RC 2.00 5.00
99 S.Marion/A.Ford RC 2.00 5.00
100 T.Kukoc/A.Fotsis RC 2.00 5.00
101 B.Walton/Z.Randolph RC 5.00 12.00
102 S.Marbury/J.Crispin RC 2.00 5.00
103 W.Unseld/B.Simmons RC 2.00 5.00
104 J.Kidd AU/J.Tinsley RC 8.00 20.00
105 K.Garnett AU/P.Gasol RC 30.00 80.00
106 K.Bryant AU/S.Battier RC 40.00 100.00
107 Carter/J.Trepagnier AU RC 6.00 15.00
108 J.Erving/Kw.Brown AU RC 6.00 15.00
109 T.Duncan/E.Curry AU RC 6.00 15.00
110 Odom AU/E.Griffin AU RC 6.00 15.00
111 Alexndr AU/Watson AU RC 6.00 15.00
112 McPete AU/Arenas AU RC 6.00 15.00
113 Martin AU/Scalabrine AU RC 6.00 15.00
114 Chandler AU RC/Fizer AU 6.00 15.00
115 Mggtte AU/Boumtje AU RC 6.00 15.00
116 Jr.Collins AU RC/Madsen AU 6.00 15.00
117 V.Carter/J.Forte JSY RC 4.00 10.00
118 Jamison/Murphy JSY SP RC 6.00 15.00
119 Martin/Armstrong JSY RC 4.00 10.00
120 Francis/T.Morris JSY RC 4.00 10.00
121 G.Hill/S.Hunter JSY RC 4.00 10.00
122 Mourng/Radmnov JSY RC 4.00 10.00
123 Haywood JSY/Kw.Brown RC 8.00 20.00
124 Dalmbrt JSY RC/M.Malone 6.00 15.00
125 Stojakovic/P.Brezec RC 5.00 12.00
126 P.Stojakovic/M.Bradley RC 5.00 12.00
127 A.Hardaway/J.Johnson RC 8.00 20.00
128 L.Woods RC/T.Ratliff 5.00 12.00
129 C.Webber/G.Wallace RC 6.00 15.00
130 A.Walker/Ke.Brown RC 5.00 12.00

131 B.Davis/J.Brewer RC 5.00 12.00
132 D.Nowitzki/A.Kirilenko RC 10.00 25.00
133 J.Smith/A.Ford RC 5.00 12.00
134 J.Stockton/J.Crispin RC 6.00 15.00
135 K.Malone/R.White RC 6.00 15.00
136 T.McGrady/J.Sasser RC 6.00 15.00
137 E.Brand/Jas.Collins RC 6.00 15.00
138 K.Bryant/R.Jefferson RC 40.00 100.00
139 A.Iverson/T.Parker RC 10.00 25.00
140 Jordan/J.Richardson RC 50.00 120.00
141 Ronald Murray XRC 2.00 5.00
142 Pat Burke XRC 1.50 4.00
143 Manu Ginobili XRC 8.00 20.00
144 Gordan Giricek XRC 2.00 5.00
145 Tito Maddox XRC 1.50 4.00
146 Tamar Slay XRC 1.50 4.00
147 Rasual Butler XRC 2.00 5.00
148 Carlos Boozer XRC 2.50 6.00
149 Dan Gadzuric XRC 2.00 5.00
150 Vincent Yarbrough XRC 1.50 4.00
151 Robert Archibald XRC 1.50 4.00
152 Roger Mason XRC 2.00 5.00
153 Jamal Sampson XRC 1.50 4.00
154 Sam Clancy XRC 2.00 5.00
155 Dan Dickau XRC 2.00 5.00
156 Chris Jefferies XRC 1.50 4.00
157 John Salmons XRC 2.50 6.00
158 Frank Williams XRC 1.50 4.00
159 Lonny Baxter XRC 1.50 4.00
160 Tayshaun Prince XRC 2.50 6.00
161 Casey Jacobsen XRC 2.00 5.00
162 Qyntel Woods XRC 2.00 5.00
163 Kareem Rush XRC 2.00 5.00
164 Ryan Humphrey XRC 2.00 5.00
165 Curtis Borchardt XRC 2.00 5.00
166 Juan Dixon XRC 2.50 6.00
167 Jiri Welsch XRC 2.50 6.00
168 Bostjan Nachbar XRC 2.50 6.00
169 Fred Jones XRC 2.50 6.00
170 Marcus Haislip XRC 2.00 5.00
171 Melvin Ely XRC 2.50 6.00
172 Jared Jeffries XRC 3.00 8.00
173 Caron Butler XRC 3.00 8.00
174 Amare Stoudemire XRC 5.00 12.00
175 Chris Wilcox XRC 2.50 6.00
176 Nene Hilario XRC 3.00 8.00
177 Dajuan Wagner XRC 5.00 12.00
178 Nikoloz Tskitishvili XRC 4.00 10.00
179 Drew Gooden XRC 6.00 15.00
180 Mike Dunleavy XRC 6.00 15.00
181 Jay Williams XRC 6.00 15.00
182 Yao Ming XRC 15.00 40.00

2001-02 Upper Deck Inspirations Hardwood Imagery

COMPLETE SET (21) 75.00 150.00
STATED ODDS 1:47
AI Allen Iverson 6.00 15.00
AM Andre Miller 2.00 5.00
CW Chris Webber 3.00 8.00
DM Darius Miles 1.50 4.00
DN Dirk Nowitzki 6.00 15.00
JK Jason Kidd 4.00 10.00
JS Jerry Stackhouse 2.50 6.00
KB Kobe Bryant 40.00 100.00
KG Kevin Garnett 6.00 15.00
KM Kenyon Martin 2.50 6.00
MF Michael Finley 2.50 6.00
MJ Michael Jordan 20.00 50.00
MM Mike Miller 2.00 5.00
MP Morris Peterson 1.50 4.00
PP Paul Pierce 4.00 10.00
RA Ray Allen 4.00 10.00
SA Shareef Abdur-Rahim 2.00 5.00
SF Steve Francis 2.50 6.00
SH Shawn Marion 2.50 6.00
SM Stephon Marbury 3.00 8.00
TM Tracy McGrady 4.00 10.00

2001-02 Upper Deck Inspirations Hardwood Imagery Combo

COMPLETE SET (21) 150.00 300.00
STATED ODDS 1:47
AH/LS L.Sprewell/A.Houston 5.00 12.00
AI/SF S.Francis/A.Iverson 6.00 15.00
BD/JM J.Mashburn/B.Davis 4.00 10.00
EJ/BG E.Jones/B.Grant 4.00 10.00
JK/KM J.Kidd/K.Martin 5.00 12.00
KB/JK K.Bryant/J.Kidd 40.00 100.00
KB/JS J.Stackhouse/K.Bryant 40.00 100.00
KB/KG K.Bryant/K.Garnett 40.00 100.00
KG/CW K.Garnett/C.Webber 6.00 15.00
KG/WS W.Szczerbiak/K.Garnett 5.00 12.00
KM/JS K.Malone/J.Stockton 10.00 25.00
LO/QR L.Odom/Q.Richardson 4.00 10.00
MF/DN M.Finley/D.Nowitzki 5.00 12.00
MJ/KB M.Jordan/K.Bryant 200.00 500.00
PP/AW A.Walker/P.Pierce 6.00 15.00
RA/GR R.Allen/G.Robinson 4.00 10.00
RM/JO R.Miller/J.O'Neal 4.00 10.00
RW/SP S.Pippen/R.Wallace 6.00 15.00
SA/DJ S.Rahim/D.Johnson 4.00 10.00
SM/SM S.Marbury/S.Marion 4.00 10.00
TM/DM T.McGrady/D.Miles 6.00 15.00

2001-02 Upper Deck Inspirations Like Mike

STATED ODDS 1:576
LBW Bow Wow AU/100 50.00 100.00
LBWAI A.Iverson/Bow Wow JSY 10.00 25.00
LBWCW C.Webb/Bow Wow JSY 10.00 25.00
LBWGP G.Payton/Bow Wow JSY 10.00 25.00
LBWJK J.Kidd/Bow Wow JSY 10.00 25.00

2002-03 Upper Deck Inspirations

COMP.SET w/o SP's (90) 12.50 30.00
91-104 STATED ODDS 1:12
105-110 PRINT RUN 325 SER.#'d SETS
105-110 DUAL JERSEY CARDS
111-127 PRINT RUN 1500 SER.#'d SETS
111-127 DUAL JERSEY CARDS
128-133 PRINT RUN 275 SER.#'d SETS
128-133 DUAL AUTOGRAPH CARDS
134-139 PRINT RUN 1600 SER.#'d SETS
134-139 DUAL AUTOGRAPH CARDS
140-149 PRINT RUN 1600 SER.#'d SETS
140-149 ROOKIE AUTOGRAPH ONLY
156-161 PRINT RUN 499 SER.#'d SETS
162-167 PRINT RUN 799 SER.#'d SETS
168-175 PRINT RUN 1499 SER.#'d SETS
176-197 PRINT RUN 2999 SER.#'d SETS
1 Shareef Abdur-Rahim .30 .75
2 Jason Terry .25 .60
3 Glenn Robinson .30 .75
4 Paul Pierce .50 1.25
5 Antoine Walker .25 .60
6 Bill Russell .50 1.25
7 Vin Baker .25 .60
8 Jalen Rose .25 .60
9 Tyson Chandler .30 .75
10 Eddy Curry .30 .75
11 Ricky Davis .25 .60
12 Zydrunas Ilgauskas .25 .60
13 Darius Miles .20 .50
14 Dirk Nowitzki .75 2.00
15 Michael Finley .30 .75
16 Steve Nash .60 1.50
17 Nick Van Exel .30 .75
18 Rodney White .20 .50
19 Juwan Howard .25 .60
20 Richard Hamilton .40 1.00
21 Ben Wallace .40 1.00
22 Isiah Thomas .50 1.25
23 Antawn Jamison .25 .60
24 Jason Richardson .30 .75
25 Gilbert Arenas .30 .75
26 Steve Francis .30 .75
27 Eddie Griffin .20 .50
28 Cuttino Mobley .20 .50
29 Reggie Miller .60 1.50
30 Jamaal Tinsley .20 .50
31 Jermaine O'Neal .25 .60
32 Elton Brand .25 .60
33 Andre Miller .25 .60
34 Lamar Odom .30 .75
35 Kobe Bryant 2.50 6.00
36 Shaquille O'Neal 1.25 3.00
37 Wilt Chamberlain .60 1.50
38 Derek Fisher .30 .75
39 Pau Gasol .50 1.25
40 Shane Battier .30 .75
41 Stromile Swift .20 .50
42 Eddie Jones .30 .75
43 Alonzo Mourning .50 1.25
44 Travis Best .20 .50
45 Gary Payton .50 1.25
46 Sam Cassell .25 .60
47 Desmond Mason .25 .60
48 Kevin Garnett .75 2.00
49 Wally Szczerbiak .25 .60
50 Joe Smith .25 .60
51 Jason Kidd .50 1.25
52 Richard Jefferson .25 .60
53 Kenyon Martin .30 .75
54 Baron Davis .30 .75
55 Jamal Mashburn .25 .60
56 David Wesley .20 .50
57 Allan Houston .30 .75
58 Antonio McDyess .25 .60
59 Latrell Sprewell .30 .75
60 Tracy McGrady .50 1.25
61 Grant Hill .50 1.25
62 Pat Garrity .20 .50
63 Allen Iverson .75 2.00
64 Julius Erving .50 1.25
65 Stephon Marbury .40 1.00
66 Shawn Marion .30 .75
67 Anfernee Hardaway .75 2.00
68 Rasheed Wallace .40 1.00
69 Derek Anderson .20 .50
70 Scottie Pippen .75 2.00
71 Chris Webber .40 1.00
72 Mike Bibby .30 .75
73 Peja Stojakovic .25 .60
74 Hedo Turkoglu .25 .60
75 Tim Duncan .75 2.00
76 David Robinson .60 1.50
77 Tony Parker .50 1.25
78 Ray Allen .50 1.25
79 Rashard Lewis .25 .60
80 Brent Barry .20 .50
81 Voshon Lenard .20 .50
82 Vince Carter .60 1.50
83 Morris Peterson .25 .60
84 Antonio Davis .25 .60
85 Karl Malone .60 1.50
86 John Stockton .60 1.50
87 Andrei Kirilenko .25 .60
88 Jerry Stackhouse .30 .75
89 Michael Jordan 3.00 8.00
90 Kwame Brown .20 .50
91 Mason RC/Jordan 1.50 4.00
92 Harrington RC/English 1.25 3.00
93 Dunleavy RC/R.Barry 1.50 4.00
94 Archibald RC/Swift 1.25 3.00
95 Maddox RC/Francis 1.25 3.00
96 Hawkins RC/M.Malone 1.25 3.00
97 Batiste RC/Jas.Williams 1.25 3.00
98 K.Johnson/Mourning 1.25 3.00
99 S.Parker RC/D.Miles 1.25 3.00
100 P.Burke RC/S.O'Neal 1.25 3.00
101 R.Lopez RC/J.Stockton 1.25 3.00
102 C.Owens RC/S.Battier 1.25 3.00
103 M.Wilks RC/E.Boykins 1.25 3.00
104 Rigadeau RC/Nowitzki 1.25 3.00
105 Butler JSY RC/Garnett JSY 8.00 20.00
106 Wagner JSY RC/Iversn JSY 6.00 15.00
107 Rush JSY RC/Bryant JSY 50.00 120.00
108 Hilario JSY RC/Duncan JSY 8.00 20.00
109 Ely JSY RC/E.Brand JSY 4.00 10.00
110 Hmphry JSY RC/T-Mac JSY 4.00 10.00
111 M.Jaric JSY/A.Miller JSY 3.00 8.00
112 Jones JSY RC/Miller JSY 3.00 8.00
113 Baxter JSY RC/Smith JSY 3.00 8.00
114 Bremer JSY RC/Pierce JSY 3.00 8.00
115 Boozer JSY RC/Hill JSY 6.00 15.00
116 Savovic JSY RC/Divac JSY 3.00 8.00
117 Okur JSY RC/Turkoglu JSY 4.00 10.00
118 Pargo JSY RC/Fisher JSY 3.00 8.00
119 Trybnski JSY RC/Swift JSY 3.00 8.00
120 Murray JSY RC/Lewis JSY 6.00 15.00
121 Evans JSY RC/Allen JSY 3.00 8.00
122 Butler JSY RC/Jones JSY 3.00 8.00
123 Smpsn JSY RC/A-Rahim JSY 3.00 8.00
124 Rakocv JSY RC/Brndn JSY 3.00 8.00
125 Slay JSY RC/Jefferson JSY 3.00 8.00
126 E.Rentz JSY RC/V.Horn JSY 3.00 8.00
127 Yarbr.JSY RC/Howard JSY 3.00 8.00
128A JayWill AU RC/Kobe AU 75.00 200.00
128B JayWill AU RC/Jordan AU 800.00 1,500.00
129 Gooden AU RC/Garnett AU 30.00 80.00
130 A.Stoud AU RC/Marion AU 20.00 50.00
131 Tskitishv AU RC/Peja AU 10.00 25.00
132 Ming AU RC/Zhizhi AU 500.00 1,200.00
133 Dixon AU RC/Kidd AU 10.00 25.00
134 Jeffries AU RC/Stack AU 6.00 15.00
135 Haislip AU/K-Mart AU 6.00 15.00
136 Welsch AU RC/J-Rich AU 6.00 15.00
137 Salmons AU RC/Wallace AU 6.00 15.00
138 Ginobili AU RC/Parker AU 150.00 400.00
139 Dickau AU RC/Bibby AU 6.00 15.00
140 Clancy AU RC/J.Erving 3.00 8.00
141 Woods AU RC/Wallace 3.00 8.00
142 F.Williams AU RC/Houston 3.00 8.00
143 Jacobsen AU RC/Hardaway 3.00 8.00
144 Nachbar AU RC/Duncan 3.00 8.00
145 Gadzuric AU RC/S.O'Neal 3.00 8.00
146 Giricek AU RC/McGrady 3.00 8.00
147 Borchardt AU RC/Malone 3.00 8.00
148 Prince AU RC/Walker 3.00 8.00
149 Wilcox AU RC/Carter 3.00 8.00
156 LeBron James XRC 800.00 1,500.00
157 Darko Milicic XRC 4.00 10.00
158 Carmelo Anthony XRC 12.00 30.00
159 Chris Bosh XRC 6.00 15.00
160 Dwyane Wade XRC 40.00 100.00
161 Chris Kaman XRC 4.00 10.00
162 Kirk Hinrich XRC 4.00 10.00
163 T.J. Ford XRC 3.00 8.00
164 Mike Sweetney XRC 3.00 8.00
165 Jarvis Hayes XRC 3.00 8.00
166 Mickael Pietrus XRC 3.00 8.00
167 Nick Collison XRC 3.00 8.00
168 Marcus Banks XRC 2.50 6.00
169 Luke Ridnour XRC 2.50 6.00
170 Reece Gaines XRC 2.50 6.00
171 Troy Bell XRC 2.50 6.00
172 Zarko Cabarkapa XRC 2.50 6.00
173 David West XRC 3.00 8.00
174 Aleksandar Pavlovic XRC 2.50 6.00
175 Dahntay Jones XRC 2.50 6.00
176 Boris Diaw XRC 1.50 4.00
177 Zoran Planinic XRC 1.50 4.00
178 Travis Outlaw XRC 1.50 4.00
179 Brian Cook XRC 1.50 4.00
180 Udonis Haslem XRC 1.50 4.00
181 Ndudi Ebi XRC 1.50 4.00
182 Kendrick Perkins XRC 1.50 4.00
183 Leandro Barbosa XRC 1.50 4.00
184 Josh Howard XRC 1.50 4.00
185 Maciej Lampe XRC 1.50 4.00
186 Jason Kapono XRC 1.50 4.00
190 Luke Walton XRC 1.50 4.00
191 Jerome Beasley XRC 1.50 4.00
192 Travis Hansen XRC 1.50 4.00
193 Steve Blake XRC 1.50 4.00
194 Slavko Vranes XRC 1.50 4.00
195 Keith Bogans XRC 1.50 4.00
196 Willie Green XRC 1.50 4.00
197 Zaur Pachulia XRC 1.50 4.00

2002-03 Upper Deck Inspirations Rookie Holofoil

*HOLO 156-161: 1X TO 2.5X BASE HI
*HOLO 162-167: 1.25X TO 3X BASE HI
*HOLO 168-175: 1.5X TO 4X BASE HI
*HOLO 176-197: 2.5X TO 6X BASE HI
PRINT RUN FIRST 50 CARDS OF XRC EXCHANGE
156A LeBron James 8,000.00 12,000.00
160A Dwyane Wade 125.00 300.00
172A Zarko Cabarkapa 10.00 25.00

2002-03 Upper Deck Inspirations UD Promos

*PROMOS: .75X TO 2X BASIC

1991-92 Upper Deck International Award Winner Holograms

COMPLETE SET (9) 8.00 20.00
1 Derrick Coleman .50 1.25
2 Michael Jordan MVP 4.00 10.00
3 Michael Jordan Scoring 4.00 10.00
4 Hakeem Olajuwon 1.25 3.00
5 Alvin Robertson .40 1.00
6 David Robinson 1.25 3.00
7 Dennis Rodman 1.25 3.00
8 Detlef Schrempf .50 .13
9 John Stockton 1.00 2.50

1991-92 Upper Deck International Italian

COMPLETE SET (200) 15.00 40.00
1 Checklist East All-Stars 3.00 8.00
2 Checklist West All-Stars .20 .50
3 Isiah Thomas AS .60 1.50
4 Michael Jordan AS 3.00 8.00
5 Scottie Pippen AS 1.00 2.50
6 Charles Barkley AS .75 2.00
7 Patrick Ewing AS .60 1.50
8 Michael Adams AS .30 .75
9 Dennis Rodman AS .75 2.00
10 Reggie Lewis AS .40 1.00
11 Joe Dumars AS .50 1.25
12 Mark Price AS .40 1.00
13 Brad Daugherty AS .40 1.00
14 Kevin Willis AS .30 .75
15 Clyde Drexler AS .60 1.50
16 Magic Johnson AS 1.25 3.00
17 Chris Mullin AS .50 1.25
18 Karl Malone AS .75 2.00
19 David Robinson AS .75 2.00
20 Tim Hardaway AS .50 1.25
21 Jeff Hornacek AS .30 .75
22 John Stockton AS .75 2.00
23 Dikembe Mutombo AS 1.50 4.00
24 Hakeem Olajuwon AS .75 2.00
25 James Worthy AS .50 1.25
26 Otis Thorpe AS .30 .75
27 Dan Majerle AS .40 1.00
28 Stacey Augmon .40 1.00
29 Dominique Wilkins .60 1.50
30 Rumeal Robinson .25 .60
31 Rick Fox .40 1.00
32 Reggie Lewis .40 1.00
33 Kevin McHale .60 1.50
34 Robert Parish .50 1.25
35 Muggsy Bogues .40 1.00
36 Larry Johnson 1.25 3.00
37 Kendall Gill .40 1.00
38 Michael Jordan 3.00 8.00
39 Scottie Pippen 1.00 2.50
40 Horace Grant .40 1.00
41 Mark Price .40 1.00
42 Brad Daugherty .40 1.00
43 Doug Smith .25 .60
44 Derek Harper .30 .75
45 Dikembe Mutombo 1.50 4.00
46 Reggie Williams .30 .75
47 Isiah Thomas .60 1.50
48 Joe Dumars .50 1.25
49 Bill Laimbeer .40 1.00
50 Dennis Rodman .75 2.00
51 Chris Mullin .50 1.25
52 Tim Hardaway .50 1.25
53 Sarunas Marciulionis .40 1.00
54 Billy Owens .40 1.00
55 Hakeem Olajuwon .75 2.00
56 Otis Thorpe .30 .75
57 Reggie Miller .60 1.50
58 Vern Fleming .30 .75
59 Detlef Schrempf .30 .75
60 Rik Smits .30 .75
61 Danny Manning .30 .75
62 Ron Harper .40 1.00
63 James Worthy .50 1.25
64 Vlade Divac .30 .75
65 Byron Scott .40 1.00
66 Sam Perkins .30 .75
67 Magic Johnson 1.25 3.00
68 Rony Seikaly .30 .75
69 Glen Rice .40 1.00
70 Alvin Robertson .30 .75
71 Moses Malone .60 1.50
72 Doug West .25 .60
73 Felton Spencer .25 .60
74 Derrick Coleman .40 1.00
75 Drazen Petrovic .50 1.25
76 Patrick Ewing .60 1.50
77 Charles Oakley .30 .75
78 Scott Skiles .30 .75
79 Dennis Scott .30 .75
80 Manute Bol .40 1.00
81 Johnny Dawkins .30 .75
82 Hersey Hawkins .30 .75
83 Tom Chambers .40 1.00
84 Kevin Johnson .40 1.00
85 Dan Majerle .40 1.00
86 Clyde Drexler .60 1.50
87 Terry Porter .30 .75
88 Kevin Duckworth .30 .75
89 Mitch Richmond .50 1.25
90 Spud Webb .40 1.00
91 Terry Cummings .40 1.00
92 David Robinson .75 2.00
93 Sean Elliott .30 .75
94 Shawn Kemp .60 1.50
95 Ricky Pierce .30 .75
96 Eddie Johnson .25 .60
97 Gary Payton .60 1.50
98 Karl Malone .75 2.00
99 John Stockton .75 2.00
100 Checklist .20 .50
101 Jeff Malone .30 .75
102 Mark Eaton .40 1.00
103 Michael Adams .30 .75
104 Bernard King .50 1.25
105 Pervis Ellison .25 .60
106 Magic's Moment ART 1.25 3.00
107 Michael Jordan ART 3.00 8.00
108 Stacey Augmon ART .40 1.00
109 Ferdinando Gentile INT .40 1.00
110 Walter Magnifico INT .40 1.00
111 Alberto Rossini INT .40 1.00
112 Carlton Myers INT .40 1.00
113 Riccardo Pittis INT .40 1.00
114 Antonello Riva INT .40 1.00
115 Ario Costa INT .40 1.00
116 Davide Cantarello INT .40 1.00
117 Alberto Vianini INT .40 1.00
118 Claudio Coldebella INT .40 1.00
119 Juan Antonio San SNT .40 1.00
120 Javier Fernandez SNT .40 1.00
121 Jose A. Arcega SNT .40 1.00
122 Juan Antonio SNT .40 1.00
123 Jordi Villacampa SNT .40 1.00
124 Enrique Andreu SNT .40 1.00
125 Jose Antonio Montero SNT .40 1.00
126 Rafael Jofresa SNT .40 1.00
127 Jose Biriukov SNT .40 1.00
128 Santiago Aldama SNT .40 1.00
129 Alberto Herreros SNT .40 1.00
130 Andres Jimenez SNT .40 1.00
131 Hawks Logo .40 1.00
132 Celtics Logo .40 1.00
133 Hornets Logo .40 1.00
134 Bulls Logo .40 1.00
135 Cavaliers Logo .40 1.00
136 Mavericks Logo .40 1.00
137 Nuggets Logo .40 1.00
138 Pistons Logo .40 1.00
139 Warriors Logo .40 1.00
140 Rockets Logo .40 1.00
141 Pacers Logo .40 1.00
142 Clippers Logo .40 1.00
143 Lakers Logo .40 1.00
144 Heat Logo .40 1.00
145 Bucks Logo .40 1.00
146 Timberwolves Logo .40 1.00
147 Nets Logo .40 1.00
148 Knicks Logo .40 1.00
149 Magic Logo .40 1.00
150 76ers Logo .40 1.00
151 Suns Logo .40 1.00
152 Trail Blazers Logo .40 1.00
153 Kings Logo .40 1.00
154 Spurs Logo .40 1.00
155 Supersonics Logo .40 1.00
156 Jazz Logo .40 1.00
157 Bullets Logo .40 1.00
158 Michael Jordan
Rony Seikaly PC 3.00 8.00
159 Kevin McHale
Dale Davis PO .60 1.50
160 Cavaliers
Nets PO .20 .50
161 Patrick Ewing
Joe Dumars PO .60 1.50
162 Kevin Duckworth PO .30 .75
163 John Stockton PO .75 2.00
164 Tim Hardaway
Ricky Pierce PC .50 1.25
165 Kevin Johnson
Sean Elliott PO .40 1.00
166 New York Knicks
Scottie Pippen
Michael Jordan PO 3.00 8.00
167 Brad Daugherty PO .40 1.00
168 Terry Porter
Kevin Johnson PO .40 1.00
169 Shawn Kemp
Karl Malone PC .75 2.00
170 Scottie Pippen
Larry Nance PC 1.00 2.50
171 Clyde Drexler
Jeff Malone PO .60 1.50
172 Michael Jordan FIN 3.00 8.00
173 Clifford Robinson FIN .30 .75
174 Clyde Drexler
Michael Jordan FIN 3.00 8.00
175 Clyde Drexler FIN .60 1.50
176 Michael Jordan FIN 3.00 8.00
177 Michael Jordan FIN 3.00 8.00
178 Michael Jordan COC 3.00 8.00
179 Drazen Petrovic COC .50 1.25
180 Magic Johnson COC 1.25 3.00
181 Michael Jordan COC 3.00 8.00
182 Sarunas Marciulionis COC 1.50 4.00
183 Rik Smits COC .30 .75
184 Rumeal Robinson WS .25 .60
185 Luc Longley WS .60 1.50
186 Vlade Divac WS .30 .75
187 Rik Smits WS .30 .75
188 Drazen Petrovic WS .50 1.25
189 Detlef Schrempf WS .30 .75
190 Dominique Wilkins WS .60 1.50
191 Sarunas Marciulionis WS 1.50 4.00
192 Rick Fox WS .40 1.00
193 Patrick Ewing WS .60 1.50
194 Manute Bol WS .40 1.00
195 Steve Kerr WS .50 1.25
196 Dikembe Mutombo WS 1.50 4.00
197 Hakeem Olajuwon WS .75 2.00
198 Rony Seikaly WS .30 .75
199 Carl Herrera WS .25 .60
200 Checklist Card .20 .50

1991-92 Upper Deck International Spanish

COMPLETE SET (200) 15.00 40.00
SPANISH: SAME VALUE AS ITALIAN

1992-93 Upper Deck International French

COMPLETE SET (255) 15.00 40.00
1 All-Star Checklist .07 .20
2 Scottie Pippen AS .40 1.00
3 Larry Johnson AS .15 .40
4 Shaquille O'Neal AS 1.50 4.00
5 Michael Jordan AS 1.00 2.50
6 Isiah Thomas AS .30 .75
7 Brad Daugherty AS .07 .20
8 Joe Dumars AS .25 .60
9 Patrick Ewing AS .40 1.00
10 Larry Nance AS .08 .25
11 Mark Price AS .08 .25
12 Detlef Schrempf AS .07 .20
13 Dominique Wilkins AS .40 1.00
14 Karl Malone AS .40 1.00
15 Charles Barkley AS .40 1.00
16 David Robinson AS .40 1.00
17 John Stockton AS .40 1.00
18 Clyde Drexler AS .40 1.00
19 Sean Elliott AS .10 .30
20 Tim Hardaway AS .08 .25
21 Shawn Kemp AS .30 .75
22 Dan Majerle AS .20 .50
23 Danny Manning AS .07 .20
24 Hakeem Olajuwon AS .40 1.00
25 Terry Porter AS .07 .20
26 Harold Miner FACE .07 .20
27 David Benoit FACE .07 .20
28 Cedric Ceballos FACE .07 .20
29 Mahmoud Abdul-Rauf FACE .07 .20
30 Tim Perry FACE .07 .20
31 Kenny Smith FACE .08 .25
32 Clarence Weatherspoon FACE .07 .20
33 Michael Jordan FACE 1.00 2.50
34 Dominique Wilkins FACE .40 1.00
35 Shaquille O'Neal AD 1.50 4.00
36 Derrick Coleman AD .07 .20
37 Glen Rice AD .20 .50
38 Reggie Lewis AD .08 .25
39 Kenny Anderson AD .07 .20
40 Brad Daugherty AD .07 .20
41 Dominique Wilkins AD .40 1.00
42 Larry Johnson AD .15 .40
43 Michael Jordan AD 1.00 2.50
44 Mark Price AD .08 .25
45 David Robinson AD .40 1.00
46 Karl Malone AD .40 1.00
47 Sean Elliott AD .10 .30
48 John Stockton AD .40 1.00
49 Derek Harper AD .07 .20
50 Kevin Duckworth AD .25 .60
51 Chris Mullin AD .15 .40
52 Charles Barkley AD .40 1.00
53 Tim Hardaway AD .08 .25
54 Clyde Drexler AD .40 1.00
55 Adam Keefe RS .07 .20
56 Alonzo Mourning RS .60 1.50
57 Sean Rooks RS .07 .20
58 LaPhonso Ellis RS .07 .20
59 Latrell Sprewell RS .40 1.00
60 Robert Horry RS .40 1.00
61 Malik Sealy RS .10 .30
62 Anthony Peeler RS .07 .20
63 Harold Miner RS .07 .20
64 Anthony Avent RS .07 .20
65 Todd Day RS .07 .20
66 Lee Mayberry RS .07 .20
67 Christian Laettner RS .30 .75
68 Tom Gugliotta RS .40 1.00
69 Shaquille O'Neal RS 1.50 4.00
70 Clarence Weatherspoon RS .07 .20
71 Richard Dumas RS .07 .20
72 Walt Williams RS .07 .20
73 Lloyd Daniels RS .07 .20
74 Hubert Davis RS .07 .20
75 Manute Bol FE .07 .20
76 Vlade Divac FE .08 .25
77 Patrick Ewing FE .40 1.00
78 Sarunas Marciulionis FE .10 .30
79 Dikembe Mutombo FE .20 .50
80 Hakeem Olajuwon FE .40 1.00
81 Detlef Schrempf FE .07 .20
82 Rony Seikaly FE .07 .20
83 Rik Smits FE .07 .20
84 Kiki Vandeweghe FE .08 .25
85 Dominique Wilkins FE .40 1.00
86 Michael Jordan FAN 1.00 2.50
87 Larry Bird FAN .50 1.25
88 Karl Malone FAN .40 1.00
89 Dikembe Mutombo FAN .20 .50
90 Michael Jordan FAN
Larry Bird 1.00 2.50
91 Stacey Augmon .07 .20
92 Mookie Blaylock .08 .25
93 Duane Ferrell .07 .20
94 Paul Graham .07 .20
95 Adam Keefe .07 .20
96 Jon Koncak .07 .20
97 Dominique Wilkins .40 1.00
98 Kevin Willis .07 .20
99 Alaa Abdelnaby .07 .20
100 Dee Brown .07 .20
101 Sherman Douglas .07 .20
102 Rick Fox .15 .40
103 Reggie Lewis .08 .25
104 Xavier McDaniel .07 .20
105 Robert Parish .15 .40
106 Ed Pinckney .07 .20
107 Muggsy Bogues .15 .40
108 Dell Curry .07 .20
109 Kenny Gattison .07 .20
110 Kendall Gill .08 .25
111 Larry Johnson .15 .40
112 Alonzo Mourning .75 2.00
113 Johnny Newman .07 .20
114 David Wingate .07 .20
115 B.J. Armstrong .15 .40
116 Bill Cartwright .08 .25
117 Horace Grant .15 .40
118 Michael Jordan 2.00 5.00
119 Stacey King .07 .20
120 John Paxson .15 .40
121 Scottie Pippen .60 1.50
122 Scott Williams .07 .20
123 John Battle .07 .20
124 Terrell Brandon .10 .30
125 Brad Daugherty .07 .20
126 Craig Ehlo .07 .20
127 Larry Nance .15 .40
128 Mark Price .20 .50
129 Gerald Wilkins .07 .20
130 Hot Rod Williams .07 .20
131 Walter Bond .07 .20
132 Terry Davis .07 .20
133 Derek Harper .15 .40
134 Donald Hodge .07 .20
135 Brian Howard .07 .20
136 Jim Jackson .75 2.00
137 Sean Rooks .07 .20
138 Doug Smith .07 .20
139 LaPhonso Ellis .20 .50
140 Mahmoud Abdul-Rauf .07 .20
141 Marcus Liberty .07 .20
142 Todd Lichti .07 .20
143 Mark Macon .07 .20
144 Dikembe Mutombo .25 .60
145 Robert Pack .07 .20
146 Reggie Williams .07 .20
147 Mark Aguirre .08 .25
148 Joe Dumars .25 .60
149 Gerald Glass .07 .20
150 Bill Laimbeer .15 .40
151 Terry Mills .07 .20
152 Olden Polynice .07 .20
153 Dennis Rodman .40 1.00
154 Isiah Thomas .30 .75
155 Victor Alexander .07 .20
156 Chris Gatling .07 .20
157 Tim Hardaway .15 .40
158 Tyrone Hill .07 .20
159 Sarunas Marciulionis .10 .30
160 Chris Mullin .25 .60
161 Billy Owens .07 .20
162 Latrell Sprewell .40 1.00
163 Scott Brooks .07 .20
164 Matt Bullard .07 .20
165 Sleepy Floyd .07 .20
166 Robert Horry .40 1.00
167 Vernon Maxwell .07 .20
168 Hakeem Olajuwon .40 1.00
169 Kenny Smith .08 .25
170 Otis Thorpe .08 .25
171 Dale Davis .07 .20
172 Vern Fleming .07 .20
173 Reggie Miller .30 .75
174 Sam Mitchell .07 .20
175 Pooh Richardson .07 .20
176 Detlef Schrempf .07 .20
177 Malik Sealy .10 .30
178 Rik Smits .08 .25
179 Gary Grant .07 .20
180 Ron Harper .30 .75
181 Mark Jackson .30 .75
182 Danny Manning .08 .25
183 Ken Norman .07 .20
184 Stanley Roberts .07 .20
185 Loy Vaught .07 .20
186 John Williams .07 .20
187 Elden Campbell .07 .20
188 Doug Christie .10 .30
189 Vlade Divac .20 .50
190 A.C. Green .20 .50
191 Anthony Peeler .07 .20
192 Byron Scott .20 .50
193 Sedale Threatt .07 .20
194 James Worthy .30 .75
195 Bimbo Coles .07 .20
196 Kevin Edwards .07 .20
197 Grant Long .07 .20
198 Harold Miner .07 .20
199 Glen Rice .30 .75
200 John Salley .08 .25
201 Rony Seikaly .07 .20
202 Brian Shaw .07 .20
203 Frank Brickowski .07 .20
204 Todd Day .07 .20
205 Blue Edwards .07 .20
206 Eric Murdock .07 .20
207 Christian Laettner .30 .75
208 Luc Longley .08 .25
209 Chuck Person .07 .20
210 Doug West .07 .20
211 Kenny Anderson .08 .25
212 Derrick Coleman .08 .25
213 Chris Morris .07 .20
214 Rumeal Robinson .07 .20
215 Patrick Ewing .40 1.00
216 Charles Oakley .08 .25
217 Doc Rivers .15 .40
218 John Starks .08 .25
219 Nick Anderson .08 .25
220 Shaquille O'Neal 5.00 12.00
221 Scott Skiles .25 .60
222 Manute Bol .07 .20
223 Hersey Hawkins .08 .25
224 Jeff Hornacek .25 .60
225 Danny Ainge .15 .40
226 Charles Barkley .40 1.00
227 Richard Dumas .07 .20
228 Kevin Johnson .15 .40
229 Dan Majerle .20 .50
230 Clyde Drexler .40 1.00
231 Terry Porter .07 .20
232 Clifford Robinson .10 .30
233 Buck Williams .08 .25
234 Mitch Richmond .25 .60
235 Lionel Simmons .07 .20
236 Spud Webb .15 .40
237 Walt Williams .07 .20
238 Antoine Carr .07 .20
239 Vinny Del Negro .07 .20
240 Sean Elliott .15 .40
241 David Robinson .40 1.00
242 Eddie Johnson .07 .20
243 Shawn Kemp .30 .75
244 Derrick McKey .07 .20
245 Gary Payton .07 .20
246 Mark Eaton .07 .20
247 Jeff Malone .07 .20
248 Karl Malone .40 1.00
249 John Stockton .40 1.00
250 Michael Adams .07 .20
251 Rex Chapman .07 .20
252 Pervis Ellison .07 .20
253 Tom Gugliotta .40 1.00
254 Michael Jordan
Checklist 1-128 .40 1.00
255 Michael Jordan
Checklist 129-255 .40 1.00

1992-93 Upper Deck International French Award Winner Holograms

COMPLETE SET (9) 6.00 15.00
1 Michael Jordan
Scoring 3.00 8.00
2 John Stockton
Steals 1.25 3.00
3 Dennis Rodman
Rebounds 1.25 3.00
4 Detlef Schrempf
Sixth Man .20 .50
5 Larry Johnson
Rookie of the Year .40 1.00
6 David Robinson
Blocked Shots .75 2.00
7 David Robinson
Def. Player of Year .75 2.00
8 John Stockton
Assists 1.25 3.00
9 Michael Jordan
Most Valuable Player 3.00 8.00

1992-93 Upper Deck International Italian

COMPLETE SET (255) 15.00 40.00
*ITALIAN: SAME VALUE AS FRENCH

1992-93 Upper Deck International Italian Award Winner Holograms

COMPLETE SET (9) 6.00 15.00
*ITALIAN: SAME VALUE AS FRENCH

1992-93 Upper Deck International Spanish

COMPLETE SET (255) 15.00 40.00
*SPANISH: SAME VALUE AS FRENCH

1992-93 Upper Deck International Spanish Award Winner Holograms

COMPLETE SET (9) 6.00 15.00
*SPANISH: SAME VALUE AS FRENCH

1993-94 Upper Deck International French

COMPLETE SET (194) 12.00 30.00
1 Stacey Augmon .05 .15
2 Chris Mills .08 .25
3 Joe Dumars .30 .75
4 Grant Long .05 .15
5 Robert Horry .20 .50
6 Rod Strickland .08 .25
7 Frank Brickowski .05 .15
8 Ricky Pierce .05 .15
9 Dan Majerle .20 .50
10 Dell Curry .05 .15
11 Derek Harper .08 .25
12 Anthony Avent .05 .15
13 Vern Fleming .05 .15

14 Dee Brown .05 .15
15 Kevin Johnson .20 .50
16 Clifford Robinson .08 .25
17 Doc Rivers .15 .40
18 Doug West .05 .15
19 Michael Adams .05 .15
20 Sherman Douglas .05 .15
21 Harold Miner .05 .15
22 John Williams .05 .15
23 Michael Jordan 2.00 5.00
24 Jim Jackson .20 .50
25 Glen Rice .20 .50
26 Jeff Hornacek .25 .60
27 Derrick Coleman .08 .25
28 Sam Perkins .20 .50
29 Willie Anderson .05 .15
30 Rumeal Robinson .05 .15
31 Blue Edwards .05 .15
32 Sarunas Marciulionis .15 .40
33 Clyde Drexler .50 1.25
34 Shawn Bradley .20 .50
35 Ron Harper .20 .50
36 Chris Morris .05 .15
37 Brad Daugherty .05 .15
38 Duane Ferrell .05 .15
39 Chuck Person .05 .15
40 Todd Day .05 .15
41 Sedale Threatt .05 .15
42 Xavier McDaniel .05 .15
43 Kevin Willis .05 .15
44 Chris Mullin .30 .75
45 Terrell Brandon .08 .25
46 Kenny Smith .15 .40
47 Malik Sealy .08 .25
48 John Starks .08 .25
49 Dino Radja .05 .15
50 David Robinson .60 1.50
51 John Salley .08 .25
52 Danny Ainge .25 .60
53 Sam Cassell .40 1.00
54 Latrell Sprewell .25 .60
55 Dikembe Mutombo .20 .50
56 Doug Edwards .05 .15
57 A.C. Green .20 .50
58 Otis Thorpe .05 .15
59 Antoine Carr .05 .15
60 Tim Legler .05 .15
61 Don MacLean .05 .15
62 Horace Grant .15 .40
63 John Stockton .60 1.50
64 Muggsy Bogues .25 .60
65 Rex Chapman .20 .50
66 Stanley Roberts .05 .15
67 Walt Williams .05 .15
68 Dominique Wilkins .30 .75
69 Brent Price .05 .15
70 Lloyd Daniels .05 .15
71 Mark Price .20 .50
72 Sean Elliott .20 .50
73 Scottie Pippen .60 1.50
74 Rodney Rogers .08 .25
75 Charles Barkley .60 1.50
76 Kevin Gamble .05 .15
77 Lionel Simmons .05 .15
78 Dennis Rodman .40 1.00
79 Jeff Malone .05 .15
80 Larry Johnson .25 .60
81 Armon Gilliam .05 .15
82 Chris Dudley .05 .15
83 Bryant Stith .05 .15
84 Mark Jackson .30 .75
85 Paul Graham .05 .15
86 Calbert Cheaney .08 .25
87 Clarence Weatherspoon .05 .15
88 Isiah Thomas .40 1.00
89 Scott Brooks .05 .15
90 Mitch Richmond .30 .75
91 Kendall Gill .15 .40
92 Robert Parish .20 .50
93 Karl Malone .50 1.25
94 Rik Smits .05 .15
95 Rex Walters .05 .15
96 Oliver Miller .05 .15
97 Hersey Hawkins .15 .40
98 Vinny Del Negro .05 .15
99 Spud Webb .20 .50
100 Chris Webber 1.25 3.00
101 Moses Malone .25 .60
102 Hubert Davis .05 .15
103 Gary Payton .40 1.00
104 Mahmoud Abdul-Rauf .05 .15
105 Larry Nance .15 .40
106 Bobby Hurley .15 .40
107 David Benoit .05 .15
108 Danny Manning .08 .25
109 Pervis Ellison .05 .15
110 Anthony Peeler .05 .15
111 Tim Hardaway .20 .50
112 Detlef Schrempf .15 .40
113 Hakeem Olajuwon .40 1.00
114 Elden Campbell .05 .15
115 Charles Smith .05 .15
116 B.J. Armstrong .15 .40
117 Dennis Scott .05 .15
118 LaPhonso Ellis .05 .15
119 Isaiah Rider .08 .25
120 Tim Perry .05 .15
121 Lindsey Hunter .08 .25
122 Anthony Bowie .05 .15
123 Micheal Williams .05 .15
124 Gerald Wilkins .05 .15
125 Tom Chambers .15 .40
126 Vincent Askew .05 .15
127 Vernon Maxwell .05 .15
128 Nick Van Exel .40 1.00
129 Buck Williams .15 .40
130 Alonzo Mourning .30 .75
131 Loy Vaught .05 .15
132 Shaquille O'Neal 1.00 2.50
133 Derrick McKey .05 .15
134 Kenny Anderson .08 .25
135 Bill Cartwright .15 .40
136 Nick Anderson .05 .15
137 Billy Owens .05 .15
138 Anfernee Hardaway .75 2.00
139 Terry Mills .05 .15
140 John Paxson .15 .40
141 Charles Oakley .05 .15
142 Steve Smith .20 .50
143 Johnny Dawkins .05 .15
144 Thurl Bailey .05 .15
145 Jamal Mashburn .75 2.00
146 Terry Porter .08 .25
147 Duane Causwell .05 .15
148 Reggie Miller .40 1.00
149 Shawn Kemp .20 .50
150 James Worthy .30 .75
151 Scott Skiles .20 .50
152 Donald Hodge .05 .15
153 Christian Laettner .20 .50
154 Vin Baker .15 .40
155 Doug Christie .05 .15
156 Tyrone Corbin .05 .15
157 Toni Kukoc .40 1.00
158 Ken Norman .05 .15
159 Randy White .05 .15
160 Rony Seikaly .05 .15
161 Tom Gugliotta .08 .25
162 Vlade Divac .20 .50
163 Eric Murdock .05 .15
164 Pooh Richardson .05 .15
165 Patrick Ewing .40 1.00
166 Michael Jordan A Steal 2.00 5.00
167 Michael Jordan High Five 2.00 5.00
168 Michael Jordan Finals MVP 2.00 5.00
169 Michael Jordan 35 Points 2.00 5.00
170 Michael Jordan Three-Point King 2.00 5.00
171 Michael Jordan Back-To-Back 2.00 5.00
172 Michael Jordan 55-Point Game 2.00 5.00
173 Michael Jordan Scoring Avg. 2.00 5.00
174 Michael Jordan Third Straight MVP 2.00 5.00
175 Michael Jordan Mr. June Checklist 2.00 5.00
176 Michael Jordan SM 2.00 5.00
177 Shawn Kemp SM .20 .50
178 Karl Malone SM .50 1.25
179 Clyde Drexler SM .40 1.00
180 Tim Hardaway SM .20 .50
181 Charles Barkley FT .40 1.00
182 Cedric Ceballos FT .05 .15
183 Derrick Coleman FT .05 .15
184 Clyde Drexler FT .40 1.00
185 Larry Johnson FT .15 .40
186 Shawn Kemp FT .20 .50
187 Harold Miner FT .05 .15
188 Alonzo Mourning FT .30 .75
189 Shaquille O'Neal FT .50 1.25
190 Scottie Pippen FT .40 1.00
192 Dominique Wilkins FT .30 .75
193 Kenny Anderson Xavier McDaniel CL .05 .15
194 Doug West James Worthy CL .15 .40
195 Reggie Miller Joe Dumars CL .40 1.00

1993-94 Upper Deck International German

COMPLETE SET (195) 12.00 30.00
*GERMAN: SAME VALUE AS FRENCH

1993-94 Upper Deck International German Triple Double

COMPLETE SET (10) 5.00 12.00
*GERMAN: SAME VALUE AS FRENCH

1993-94 Upper Deck International Italian

COMPLETE SET (195) 12.00 30.00
*ITALIAN: SAME VALUE AS FRENCH

1993-94 Upper Deck International Italian Triple Double

COMPLETE SET (10) 5.00 12.00
*ITALIAN: SAME VALUE AS FRENCH

1993-94 Upper Deck International Spanish

COMPLETE SET (195) 12.00 30.00
*SPANISH: SAME VALUE AS FRENCH

1993-94 Upper Deck International Spanish Triple Double

COMPLETE SET (10) 5.00 12.00
*SPANISH: SAME VALUE AS FRENCH

1993-94 Upper Deck International French Triple Double

COMPLETE SET (9) 5.00 12.00
TD1 Charles Barkley 1.00 2.50
TD2 Michael Jordan 3.00 8.00
TD3 Scottie Pippen 1.25 3.00
TD4 Micheal Williams .20 .50
TD5 Mark Jackson .40 1.00
TD6 Kenny Anderson .20 .50
TD7 Larry Johnson .30 .75
TD8 Dikembe Mutombo .30 .75
TD9 Rumeal Robinson .20 .50

1996-97 Upper Deck International Japanese Coast to Coast

COMPLETE SET (3)
CC2 Michael Jordan 40.00 100.00

1996-97 Upper Deck International Japanese Jordan Greater Heights

COMPLETE SET (10)
COMMON JORDAN (1-10)

1996-97 Upper Deck Italian Stickers

COMPLETE SET (186) 15.00 40.00
1 NBA Logo .10 .25
2 Western Conference Logo .10 .25
3 Eastern Conference Logo .10 .25
4 Golden State Warriors Logo .10 .25
5 B.J. Armstrong .12 .30
6 Joe Smith .12 .30
7 Donyell Marshall .10 .25
8 Rony Seikaly .12 .30
9 Chris Mullin .20 .50
10 Los Angeles Clippers Logo .10 .25
11 Rodney Rogers .10 .25
12 Brent Barry .12 .30
13 Lamond Murray .10 .25
14 Pooh Richardson .10 .25
15 Loy Vaught .10 .25
16 Los Angeles Lakers Logo .10 .25
17 Cedric Ceballos .12 .30
18 George Lynch .10 .25
19 Eddie Jones .15 .40
20 Anthony Peeler .10 .25
21 Nick Van Exel .15 .40
22 Phoenix Suns Logo .10 .25
23 Charles Barkley .40 1.00
24 Wayman Tisdale .12 .30
25 Wesley Person .10 .25
26 A.C. Green .12 .30
27 Danny Manning .12 .30
28 Portland Trail Blazers Logo .10 .25
29 Harvey Grant .10 .25
30 Aaron McKie .10 .25
31 Gary Trent .10 .25
32 Buck Williams .15 .40
33 Clifford Robinson .15 .40
34 Sacramento Kings Logo .10 .25
35 Billy Owens .10 .25
36 Brian Grant .12 .30
37 Tyus Edney .10 .25
38 Olden Polynice .10 .25
39 Mitch Richmond .20 .50
40 Seattle Supersonics Logo .10 .25
41 Nate McMillan .10 .25
42 Vincent Askew .10 .25
43 Hersey Hawkins .10 .25
44 Detlef Schrempf .15 .40
45 Shawn Kemp .25 .60
46 Dallas Mavericks Logo .10 .25
47 Tony Dumas .10 .25
48 Jim Jackson .10 .25
49 Loren Meyer .10 .25
50 Jamal Mashburn .15 .40
51 Jason Kidd .25 .60
52 Denver Nuggets Logo .10 .25
53 Mahmoud Abdul-Rauf .12 .30
54 Antonio McDyess .15 .40
55 Tom Hammonds .10 .25
56 Dale Ellis .12 .30
57 LaPhonso Ellis .10 .25
58 Houston Rockets Logo .10 .25
59 Hakeem Olajuwon .30 .75
60 Mario Elie .10 .25
61 Robert Horry .15 .40
62 Chucky Brown .10 .25
63 Clyde Drexler .25 .60
64 Minnesota Timberwolves Logo .10 .25
65 Kevin Garnett .50 1.25
66 Terry Porter .10 .25
67 Sam Mitchell .10 .25
68 Tom Gugliotta .10 .25
69 Isaiah Rider .12 .30
70 San Antonio Spurs Logo .10 .25
71 Avery Johnson .12 .30
72 Vinny Del Negro .10 .25
73 Sean Elliott .15 .40
74 Will Perdue .10 .25
75 David Robinson .30 .75
76 Utah Jazz Logo .10 .25
77 Jeff Hornacek .12 .30
78 Chris Morris .10 .25
79 Antoine Carr .10 .25
80 Karl Malone .30 .75
81 John Stockton .30 .75
82 Vancouver Grizzlies Logo .10 .25
83 Shareef Abdur-Rahim .25 .60
84 Blue Edwards .10 .25
85 Bryant Reeves .10 .25
86 Lawrence Moten .10 .25
87 Greg Anthony .10 .25
88 Michael Jordan Bulls Victory Tour 1.50 4.00
89 Michael Jordan Bulls Victory Tour 1.50 4.00
90 Michael Jordan Bulls Victory Tour 1.50 4.00
91 Michael Jordan Bulls Victory Tour 1.50 4.00
92 Scottie Pippen Bulls Victory Tour .40 1.00
93 Luc Longley Bulls Victory Tour .12 .30
94 Luc Longley Bulls Victory Tour .12 .30
95 Toni Kukoc Bulls Victory Tour .15 .40
96 Toni Kukoc Bulls Victory Tour .15 .40
97 Atlanta Hawks Logo .10 .25
98 Grant Long .10 .25
99 Mookie Blaylock .15 .40
100 Christian Laettner .15 .40
101 Ken Norman .10 .25
102 Stacey Augmon .12 .30
103 Charlotte Hornets Logo .10 .25
104 Dell Curry .15 .40
105 Scott Burrell .10 .25
106 Matt Geiger .10 .25
107 Muggsy Bogues .15 .40
108 Glen Rice .15 .40
109 Chicago Bulls Logo .10 .25
110 Steve Kerr .12 .30
111 Dennis Rodman .40 1.00
112 Scottie Pippen .40 1.00
113 Luc Longley .12 .30
114 Michael Jordan 1.50 4.00
115 Cleveland Cavaliers Logo .10 .25
116 Terrell Brandon .12 .30
117 Bobby Phills .10 .25
118 Tyrone Hill .10 .25
119 Bob Sura .10 .25
120 Danny Ferry .10 .25
121 Detroit Pistons Logo .10 .25
122 Joe Dumars .20 .50
123 Theo Ratliff .10 .25
124 Lindsey Hunter .10 .25
125 Terry Mills .10 .25
126 Grant Hill .25 .60
127 Indiana Pacers Logo .10 .25
128 Derrick McKey .10 .25
129 Eddie Johnson .10 .25
130 Travis Best .10 .25
131 Mark Jackson .12 .30
132 Rik Smits .12 .30
133 Milwaukee Bucks Logo .10 .25
134 Vin Baker .12 .30
135 Shawn Respert .10 .25
136 Sherman Douglas .10 .25
137 Johnny Newman .10 .25
138 Glenn Robinson .15 .40
139 Toronto Raptors Logo .10 .25
140 Sharone Wright .10 .25
141 Zan Tabak .10 .25
142 Doug Christie .10 .25
143 Damon Stoudamire .15 .40
144 Oliver Miller .10 .25
145 Boston Celtics Logo .10 .25
146 Dana Barros .10 .25
147 Rick Fox .10 .25
148 David Wesley .10 .25
149 Eric Williams .10 .25
150 Dee Brown .10 .25
151 Miami Heat Logo .10 .25
152 Rex Chapman .10 .25
153 Kurt Thomas .10 .25
154 Keith Askins .10 .25
155 Walt Williams .10 .25
156 Alonzo Mourning .25 .60
157 New Jersey Nets Logo .10 .25
158 Kendall Gill .15 .40
159 Jayson Williams .10 .25
160 Kevin Edwards .10 .25
161 Shawn Bradley .10 .25
162 Ed O'Bannon .10 .25
163 New York Knicks Logo .10 .25
164 Gary Grant .10 .25
165 J.R. Reid .10 .25
166 Charles Oakley .15 .40
167 John Starks .15 .40
168 Patrick Ewing .25 .60
169 Orlando Magic Logo .10 .25
170 Nick Anderson .10 .25
171 Brian Shaw .10 .25
172 Anfernee Hardaway .40 1.00
173 Dennis Scott .12 .30
174 Shaquille O'Neal .60 1.50
175 Philadelphia 76ers Logo .10 .25
176 Allen Iverson 1.25 3.00
177 Rex Walters .10 .25
178 Clarence Weatherspoon .10 .25
179 Jerry Stackhouse .20 .50
180 Derrick Coleman .12 .30
181 Washington Bullets Logo .10 .25
182 Calbert Cheaney .10 .25
183 Chris Webber .20 .50
184 Tim Legler .10 .25
185 Gheorghe Muresan .10 .25
186 Rasheed Wallace .20 .50
NNO Sticker Album 1.50 4.00

1996-97 Upper Deck Italian Stickers Eurostar

COMPLETE SET (10) 1.50 4.00
ES1 Sasha Danilovic .20 .50
ES2 Vlade Divac .30 .75
ES3 Toni Kukoc .30 .75
ES4 Gheorghe Muresan .20 .50
ES5 Dino Radja .20 .50
ES6 Arvydas Sabonis .30 .75
ES7 Detlef Schrempf .30 .75
ES8 Rik Smits .25 .60
ES9 Zan Tabak .20 .50
ES10 George Zidek .20 .50

1996 Upper Deck Jordan Metal

COMPLETE SET (6) 20.00 50.00
COMMON CARD (1-6) 5.00 12.00
*ORANGE: .5X TO 1.25X BASE HI

1994 Upper Deck Jordan Rare Air

COMPLETE SET (90) 100.00 250.00
1 Michael Jordan (Close-up with white robe) 2.00 5.00
2 Michael Jordan (Close-up profile) 2.00 5.00
3 Michael Jordan (Michael's shooting form) 2.00 5.00
4 Michael Jordan (Close-up of his left hand) 2.00 5.00
5 Michael Jordan (Entering onto court in Orlando) 2.00 5.00
6 Michael Jordan (Lifting weights) 2.00 5.00
7 Michael Jordan (Driving car to Chicago Stadium) 2.00 5.00
8 Michael Jordan (Sitting in visitor's locker room in Miami Arena) 2.00 5.00
9 Michael Jordan (Relaxing on trainer's table) 2.00 5.00
10 Michael Jordan (Listening to pre-game instructions) 2.00 5.00
11 Michael Jordan (Readying himself for action on the floor) 2.00 5.00
12 Michael Jordan (Greeted by teammates during pre-game introductions) 2.00 5.00
13 Michael Jordan (Pre-game huddle with Chicago teammates) 2.00 5.00
14 Michael Jordan (Performing final pre-game rituals) 2.00 5.00
15 Michael Jordan (Close-up look at his feet) 2.00 5.00
16 Michael Jordan (Stealing a pass intended for A.C. Green) 2.00 5.00
17 Michael Jordan (Guarding James Worthy) 2.00 5.00
18 Michael Jordan (Greeted in mid-air by Shaquille O'Neal) 2.00 5.00
19 Michael Jordan (Slaming another one home during a game in Chicago Stadium) 2.00 5.00
20 Michael Jordan (Pippen with hand on Michael's head during playoff game) 2.00 5.00
21 Michael Jordan (Facing reporters in locker room after game) 2.00 5.00
22 Michael Jordan (Heading to locker room after game at Chicago Stadium) 2.00 5.00
23 Michael Jordan (Listening to questions from reporters) 2.00 5.00
24 Michael Jordan (Sleeping on the bus) 2.00 5.00
25 Michael Jordan (Boarding plane after bus ride to airport) 2.00 5.00
26 Michael Jordan (Settling into seat on team's private airplane) 2.00 5.00
27 Michael Jordan (Treating sprained ankle in hotel room) 2.00 5.00
28 Michael Jordan (Getting rest and relaxation on road trip) 2.00 5.00
29 Michael Jordan (Peering out of car window) 2.00 5.00
30 Michael Jordan (Enjoying game of cards) 2.00 5.00
31 Michael Jordan (Shooting pool) 2.00 5.00
32 Michael Jordan (Caring for golf clubs) 2.00 5.00
33 Michael Jordan (Preparing to drive shot onto green) 2.00 5.00
34 Michael Jordan (Sizing up a putt) 2.00 5.00
35 Michael Jordan (Calling home from golf course) 2.00 5.00
36 Michael Jordan (Sitting by window taking time out) 2.00 5.00
37 Michael Jordan (Close-up view, chin resting in hand) 2.00 5.00
38 Michael Jordan (Wearing uniform, enjoying 1993 baseball All-Star Game) 2.00 5.00
39 Michael Jordan (Shaving head) 2.00 5.00
40 Michael Jordan (Wearing warm-ups, standing outside locker room) 2.00 5.00
41 Michael Jordan (Passing to Horace Grant in game against Atlanta) 2.00 5.00
42 Michael Jordan (Preparing to shoot free throw in playoff game against Atlanta) 2.00 5.00
43 Michael Jordan (Driving lane between New York's John Starks and Doc Rivers) 2.00 5.00
44 Michael Jordan (Standing next to Charles Barkley during game) 2.00 5.00
45 Michael Jordan (Celebrating third NBA Championship) 2.00 5.00
46 Michael Jordan (Celebrating third NBA Championship, arms outstretched) 2.00 5.00
47 Michael Jordan (Celebrating with team in locker 2.00 5.00
48 Michael Jordan (Holding up three fingers, representing three NBA titles) 2.00 5.00
49 Michael Jordan (Michael with a special friend) 2.00 5.00
50 Michael Jordan (Close-up shot from back) 2.00 5.00
51 Michael Jordan (Head bowed, hand on brow) 2.00 5.00
52 Michael Jordan (Palming basketball) 2.00 5.00
53 Michael Jordan (Lifting weights with curl bar) 2.00 5.00
54 Michael Jordan (Sitting in weight training room) 2.00 5.00
55 Michael Jordan (Resting on sofa beside telephone) 2.00 5.00
56 Michael Jordan (Signing sports cards) 2.00 5.00
57 Michael Jordan (Boarding team bus) 2.00 5.00
58 Michael Jordan (In black sports car, outside Chicago Stadium) 2.00 5.00
59 Michael Jordan (In locker room before game) 2.00 5.00
60 Michael Jordan (Michael at free throw line, shot from above) 2.00 5.00
61 Michael Jordan (Close-up with ball, orange background) 2.00 5.00
62 Michael Jordan (Winning NBA Slam Dunk Championship) 2.00 5.00
63 Michael Jordan (Cheering on sidelines) 2.00 5.00
64 Michael Jordan (Preparing to shoot free throw) 2.00 5.00
65 Michael Jordan (Defensive posture) 2.00 5.00
66 Michael Jordan Efficient Scorer 2.00 5.00
67 Michael Jordan (In mid-air preparing to dunk) 2.00 5.00
68 Michael Jordan (Signing autographs for fans) 2.00 5.00
69 Michael Jordan (A multi-mirror image) 2.00 5.00
70 Michael Jordan (Playing wheel chair basketball with child) 2.00 5.00
71 Michael Jordan (Watching a game on TV) 2.00 5.00
72 Michael Jordan (Scoring over opponent) 2.00 5.00
73 Michael Jordan (Jordan defended by Mark West and Charles Barkley) 2.00 5.00
74 Michael Jordan (Dunking over Patrick Ewing) 2.00 5.00
75 Michael Jordan (Driving baseline) 2.00 5.00
76 Michael Jordan (Fighting for rebound position) 2.00 5.00
77 Michael Jordan (Shooting over Scott Skiles) 2.00 5.00
78 Michael Jordan (Defending against Orlando Magic player) 2.00 5.00
79 Michael Jordan (Driving past Vlade Divac) 2.00 5.00
80 Michael Jordan (Shooting jump shot over Orlando Magic players) 2.00 5.00
81 Michael Jordan (Shooting lay up around Patrick Ewing) 2.00 5.00
82 Michael Jordan (Shooting jump shot over outstretched arms) 2.00 5.00
83 Michael Jordan (Driving down court) 2.00 5.00
84 Michael Jordan (In mid-air during game against Nets) 2.00 5.00
85 Michael Jordan (Dribbling past New York defender) 2.00 5.00
86 Michael Jordan (Positioning for rebound against Phoenix) 2.00 5.00
87 Michael Jordan (Shooting jump shot over Dan Majerle) 2.00 5.00
88 Michael Jordan (Fingerroll lay up against Phoenix) 2.00 5.00
89 Michael Jordan (Shooting jump shot over Gerald Wilkins and Lyle and Erik Menendez in background) 75.00 200.00
90 Michael Jordan (In warm-ups shot from above) 2.00 5.00
NNO Michael Jordan/60000 Jumbo 5.00 12.00
NNO Michael Jordan/55000 Jumbo 5.00 12.00
NNO Michael Jordan/30000 Promo Jumbo 5.00 12.00
NNO Michael Jordan/30000 Passing Jumbo 5.00 12.00
NNO Michael Jordan/30000 Under Backboard Jumbo 5.00 12.00
NNO Michael Jordan Promo 2.00 5.00

2013 Upper Deck Kansas

COMPLETE SET 20.00 50.00
1 James Naismith .50 1.25
2 Phog Allen .50 1.25
3 W.O. Hamilton .50 1.25
4 Dutch Lonborg .50 1.25
5 Paul Endacott .50 1.25
6 Adolph Rupp .50 1.25
7 Tusten Ackerman .50 1.25
8 Skinny Johnson .50 1.25
9 Howard Engleman .30 .75
10 Ray Evans .50 1.25
11 Max Falkenstien .50 1.25
12 Clyde Lovellette .50 1.25
13 Bob Kenney .50 1.25
14 Bill Lienhard .50 1.25
15 Dean Smith .60 1.50
16 Dean Kelley .50 1.25
17 B.H. Born .50 1.25
18 Wilt Chamberlain 1.00 2.50
19 Wilt Chamberlain 1.00 2.50
20 Ron Loneski .40 1.00
21 Jerry Gardner .40 1.00
22 Butch Ellison .50 1.25
23 Nolen Ellison .30 .75
24 Walt Wesley .30 .75
25 Ted Owens .50 1.25
26 Jo Jo White .40 1.00
27 Dave Robisch .50 1.25
28 Bud Stallworth .50 1.25
29 Roger Brown .30 .75
30 Roger Morningstar .50 1.25
31 John Douglas .30 .75
32 Darnell Valentine .40 1.00
33 Paul Mokeski .30 .75
34 Dave Magley .50 1.25
35 Larry Brown .50 1.25
36 Danny Manning .50 1.25
37 Greg Dreiling .30 .75
38 Calvin Thompson .50 1.25
39 Scooter Barry .50 1.25
40 Kevin Pritchard .30 .75
41 Mark Randall .40 1.00
42 Archie Marshall .40 1.00
43 Jeff Gueldner .50 1.25
44 Chris Piper .40 1.00
45 Lincoln Minor .30 .75
46 Roy Williams .50 1.25
47 Terry Brown .40 1.00
48 Alonzo Jamison .40 1.00
49 Adonis Jordan .40 1.00
50 Mike Maddox .40 1.00
51 Steve Woodberry .30 .75
52 Rex Walters .30 .75
53 Greg Ostertag .30 .75
54 Eric Pauley .30 .75
55 Scot Pollard .30 .75
56 Scot Pollard .50 1.25
57 Jerod Haase .50 1.25
58 Billy Thomas .40 1.00
59 Raef LaFrentz .30 .75
60 Paul Pierce .60 1.50
61 Ryan Robertson .30 .75
62 Eric Chenowith .30 .75
63 Kenny Gregory .50 1.25
64 Jeff Boschee .30 .75
65 Nick Bradford .40 1.00
66 Drew Gooden .40 1.00
67 Nick Collison .30 .75
68 Kirk Hinrich .50 1.25
69 Wayne Simien .50 1.25
70 Keith Langford .40 1.00
71 Mario Chalmers .40 1.00
72 Sherron Collins .30 .75
73 Brady Morningstar .50 1.25
74 Tyrel Reed .40 1.00
75 Tyshawn Taylor .40 1.00
76 Bill Self .50 1.25
77 Rock Chalk Jayhawk MM .40 1.00
78 Rules of Basketball MM .40 1.00
79 1952 NCAA Champions MM .40 1.00
80 Clyde Lovellette MM .50 1.25
81 Phog Allen MM .50 1.25
82 Allen Fieldhouse MM .40 1.00
83 Wilt Chamberlain MM 1.00 2.50
84 1957 NCAA Championship MM .40 1.00
85 Bud Stallworth MM .50 1.25
86 1988 NCAA Champions MM .40 1.00
87 150-95 MM .40 1.00
88 1991 Final Four MM .40 1.00
89 Danny Manning MM .50 1.25
90 Wilt Chamberlain MM 1.00 2.50
91 Perfect 16-0 MM .40 1.00
92 Nick Collison MM .30 .75
93 2003 Final Four MM .40 1.00
94 50 Conference Titles MM .40 1.00
95 2008 Final Four MM .40 1.00
96 2008 NCAA Champions MM .40 1.00
97 2000 Wins MM .40 1.00
98 69 in a row MM .40 1.00
99 Border Showdown MM .40 1.00
100 Beware The Phog MM .40 1.00

2013 Upper Deck Kansas Gold

*GOLD: 5X TO 12X BASIC
OVERALL INSERT ODDS 3:1
STATED PRINT RUN 50 SER.#'d SETS
6 Adolph Rupp 10.00 25.00
17 B.H. Born 10.00 25.00
36 Danny Manning 12.00 30.00

2013 Upper Deck Kansas Autographs

OVERALL AUTO ODDS 1:24
11 Max Falkenstien 4.00 10.00
12 Clyde Lovellette 6.00 15.00
13 Bob Kenney 6.00 15.00
14 Bill Lienhard 6.00 15.00
17 B.H. Born 4.00 10.00
20 Ron Loneski 4.00 10.00
21 Jerry Gardner 5.00 12.00
22 Butch Ellison 4.00 10.00
23 Nolen Ellison 4.00 10.00
24 Walt Wesley 4.00 10.00
25 Ted Owens 6.00 15.00
26 Jo Jo White 25.00 60.00
27 Dave Robisch 6.00 15.00
28 Bud Stallworth 4.00 10.00
29 Roger Brown 4.00 10.00
30 Roger Morningstar 4.00 10.00
31 John Douglas 8.00 20.00
32 Darnell Valentine 4.00 10.00
33 Paul Mokeski 4.00 10.00
34 Dave Magley 6.00 15.00
35 Larry Brown 60.00 150.00
36 Danny Manning 150.00 250.00
37 Greg Dreiling 4.00 10.00
38 Calvin Thompson 6.00 15.00
39 Richard Barry 12.00 30.00
40 Kevin Pritchard 10.00 25.00
41 Mark Randall 4.00 10.00
42 Archie Marshall 4.00 10.00
43 Jeff Gueldner 6.00 15.00
44 Chris Piper 4.00 10.00
45 Lincoln Minor 4.00 10.00
46 Roy Williams 30.00 80.00
47 Terry Brown 4.00 10.00
48 Alonzo Jamison 4.00 10.00
49 Adonis Jordan 4.00 10.00
50 Mike Maddox 5.00 12.00
51 Steve Woodberry 4.00 10.00
52 Rex Walters 4.00 10.00
53 Greg Ostertag 10.00 25.00
54 Eric Pauley 6.00 15.00
56 Scot Pollard 10.00 25.00
57 Jerod Haase 4.00 10.00
58 Billy Thomas 5.00 12.00
59 Raef LaFrentz 10.00 25.00
60 Paul Pierce 25.00 60.00
61 Ryan Robertson 4.00 10.00
62 Eric Chenowith 4.00 10.00
63 Kenny Gregory 6.00 15.00
64 Jeff Boschee 4.00 10.00
65 Nick Bradford 4.00 10.00
66 Drew Gooden 10.00 25.00
67 Nick Collison 10.00 25.00
69 Wayne Simien 8.00 20.00
70 Keith Langford 4.00 10.00
71 Mario Chalmers 15.00 40.00
73 Brady Morningstar 8.00 20.00
74 Tyrel Reed 4.00 10.00
75 Tyshawn Taylor 5.00 12.00
76 Bill Self 30.00 80.00

2013 Upper Deck Kansas Distinguished Numbers

OVERALL INSERT ODDS 3:1
DN1 Ray Evans .75 2.00
DN2 Clyde Lovellette .75 2.00
DN3 B.H. Born .75 2.00
DN4 Wilt Chamberlain 1.50 4.00
DN5 Jo Jo White .60 1.50
DN6 Dave Robisch .75 2.00
DN7 Bud Stallworth .75 2.00
DN8 Darnell Valentine .60 1.50
DN9 Danny Manning .75 2.00
DN10 Bill Lienhard .75 2.00
DN11 Raef LaFrentz .50 1.25
DN12 Paul Pierce 1.00 2.50
DN13 Drew Gooden .60 1.50
DN14 Kirk Hinrich .75 2.00
DN15 Nick Collison .50 1.25

2013 Upper Deck Kansas Final 4 Legacy

OVERALL INSERT ODDS 3:1
F41 Phog Allen .75 2.00
F42 Clyde Lovellette .75 2.00
F43 Wilt Chamberlain 1.50 4.00

F44 Larry Brown .75 2.00
F45 Danny Manning .75 2.00
F46 Roy Williams .75 2.00
F47 Drew Gooden .60 1.50
F48 Kirk Hinrich .75 2.00
F49 Nick Collison .50 1.25
F410 Mario Chalmers .60 1.50

2013 Upper Deck Kansas Final 4 Legacy Duos
OVERALL INSERT ODDS 3:1
F4D1 C.Lovellette/B.Born .75 2.00
F4D2 B.Born/D.Kelley .75 2.00
F4D3 L.Brown/D.Manning .75 2.00
F4D4 N.Collison/K.Hinrich .75 2.00
F4D5 M.Chalmers/B.Self .75 2.00

2013 Upper Deck Kansas Icons
STATED ODDS 1:12
BH B.H. Born 5.00 12.00
BL Bill Lienhard 5.00 12.00
BS Bud Stallworth 5.00 12.00
CL Clyde Lovellette 5.00 12.00
DG Drew Gooden 4.00 10.00
DM Danny Manning 5.00 12.00
DR Dave Robisch 5.00 12.00
DV Darnell Valentine 4.00 10.00
JW Jo Jo White 4.00 10.00
KH Kirk Hinrich 5.00 12.00
LB Larry Brown 5.00 12.00
MC Mario Chalmers 4.00 10.00
NC Nick Collison 3.00 8.00
PA Phog Allen 5.00 12.00
PP Paul Pierce 6.00 15.00
RE Ray Evans 5.00 12.00
RL Raef LaFrentz 3.00 8.00
SC Sherron Collins 3.00 8.00
SJ Skinny Johnson 5.00 12.00
WC Wilt Chamberlain 10.00 25.00
WW Walt Wesley 3.00 8.00

2013 Upper Deck Kansas Jayhawk Legacy
OVERALL INSERT ODDS 3:1
JL1 James Naismith .75 2.00
JL2 Phog Allen .75 2.00
JL3 Dutch Lonborg .75 2.00
JL4 Tusten Ackerman .75 2.00
JL5 Skinny Johnson .75 2.00
JL6 Ray Evans .75 2.00
JL7 Bill Lienhard .75 2.00
JL8 Clyde Lovellette .75 2.00
JL9 B.H. Born .75 2.00
JL10 Wilt Chamberlain 1.50 4.00
JL11 Walt Wesley .50 1.25
JL12 Jo Jo White .60 1.50
JL13 Dave Robisch .75 2.00
JL14 Bud Stallworth .75 2.00
JL15 Darnell Valentine .60 1.50
JL16 Larry Brown .75 2.00
JL17 Danny Manning .75 2.00
JL18 Roy Williams .75 2.00
JL19 Greg Ostertag .50 1.25
JL20 Scot Pollard .50 1.25
JL21 Raef LaFrentz .50 1.25
JL22 Paul Pierce 1.00 2.50
JL23 Drew Gooden .60 1.50
JL24 Nick Collison .50 1.25
JL25 Kirk Hinrich .75 2.00
JL26 Wayne Simien .75 2.00
JL27 Bill Self .75 2.00
JL28 Mario Chalmers .60 1.50
JL29 Sherron Collins .50 1.25
JL30 Tyshawn Taylor .60 1.50

2013 Upper Deck Kansas Jayhawk Legacy Duos
OVERALL INSERT ODDS 3:1
JLD1 P.Allen/J.Naismith .75 2.00
JLD2 J.Naismith/W.Chamberlain 1.50 4.00
JLD3 P.Allen/A.Rupp .75 2.00
JLD4 B.Stallworth/J.White .75 2.00
JLD5 C.Lovellette/D.Manning .75 2.00
JLD6 R.Morningstar/B.Morningstar .75 2.00
JLD7 D.Gooden/N.Collison .60 1.50
JLD8 B.Self/R.Williams .75 2.00
JLD9 M.Chalmers/S.Collins .60 1.50
JLD10 B.Self/T.Taylor .75 2.00

2013 Upper Deck Kansas Jayhawk Legacy Trios
OVERALL INSERT ODDS 3:1
JLT1 Allen/Naismith/Hamilton .75 2.00
JLT2 Lovellette/Chalmers/Manning .75 2.00
JLT3 Williams/Self/Brown .75 2.00
JLT4 Pollard/Pierce/LaFrentz 1.00 2.50
JLT5 Gooden/Collison/Hinrich .75 2.00

2013 Upper Deck Kansas Jayhawk Hall of Fame
OVERALL INSERT ODDS 3:1
HOF1 James Naismith .75 2.00
HOF2 Phog Allen .75 2.00
HOF3 Tusten Ackerman .75 2.00
HOF4 Bob Kenney .75 2.00
HOF5 Skinny Johnson .75 2.00
HOF6 Larry Brown .75 2.00
HOF7 Howard Engleman .50 1.25
HOF8 Bill Lienhard .75 2.00
HOF9 Ray Evans .75 2.00
HOF10 Clyde Lovellette .75 2.00
HOF11 B.H. Born .75 2.00
HOF12 Wilt Chamberlain 1.50 4.00
HOF13 Dutch Lonborg .75 2.00
HOF14 Walt Wesley .50 1.25
HOF15 Jo Jo White .60 1.50
HOF16 Dave Robisch .75 2.00
HOF17 Bud Stallworth .75 2.00
HOF18 Darnell Valentine .60 1.50
HOF19 Dean Smith 1.00 2.50
HOF20 Danny Manning .75 2.00
HOF21 Raef LaFrentz .50 1.25
HOF22 Paul Pierce 1.00 2.50
HOF23 Drew Gooden .60 1.50
HOF24 Nick Collison .50 1.25

1996 Upper Deck Kellogg's Space Jam
3 Michael Jordan 6.00 15.00

2007 Upper Deck Kevin Durant Team Upper Deck
KD1 Kevin Durant
Pictured as Longhorn w/ball 8.00 20.00

2000 Upper Deck Lakers Championship Jumbos
COMP. FACT SET (10) 12.00 30.00
1 Shaquille O'Neal 3.20 8.00
2 Kobe Bryant 4.00 10.00
3 Glen Rice .80 2.00
4 A.C. Green .80 2.00
5 Ron Harper .80 2.00
6 Robert Horry .40 1.00
7 Derek Fisher .40 1.00
8 Rick Fox .40 1.00
9 Kobe Bryant 4.80 12.00
10 Team Photo 4.00 10.00
NNO Kobe Bryant JSY/100 100.00 250.00

2000 Upper Deck Lakers Master Collection
COMPLETE SET (25) 200.00 400.00
STATED PRINT RUN 300 SERIAL #'d SETS
1 Magic Johnson 8.00 20.00
2 Wilt Chamberlain 8.00 20.00
3 Kareem Abdul-Jabbar 8.00 20.00
4 Jerry West 6.00 15.00
5 Elgin Baylor 5.00 12.00
6 James Worthy 4.00 10.00
7 Byron Scott 2.50 6.00
8 Kurt Rambis 2.50 6.00
9 Michael Cooper 2.50 6.00
10 Norm Nixon 2.00 5.00
11 Gail Goodrich 3.00 8.00
12 Jamaal Wilkes 2.50 6.00
13 A.C. Green 2.00 5.00
14 Kobe Bryant 20.00 50.00
15 Shaquille O'Neal 8.00 20.00
16 Glen Rice 4.00 10.00
17 Derek Fisher 4.00 10.00
18 Robert Horry 4.00 10.00
19 Rick Fox 4.00 10.00
20 Ron Harper 4.00 10.00
21 Chick Hearn 10.00 25.00
22 Phil Jackson 6.00 15.00
23 Pat Riley 5.00 12.00
24 Mitch Kupchak 4.00 10.00
25 L.A. Forum 4.00 10.00

2000 Upper Deck Lakers Master Collection Fabulous Forum Floor Cards
STATED PRINT RUN 50 SERIAL #'d SETS
EBJ Elgin Baylor 50.00 100.00
EJF Magic Johnson 150.00 300.00
JWF Jerry West 75.00 150.00
KAF Kareem Abdul-Jabbar 50.00 120.00
WCF Wilt Chamberlain 125.00 250.00
WOJ James Worthy 40.00 80.00

2000 Upper Deck Lakers Master Collection Game Jerseys
COMPLETE SET (10) 250.00 500.00
STATED PRINT RUN 300 SERIAL #'d SETS
AGJ A.C. Green 20.00 50.00
BSJ Byron Scott 12.00 30.00
EJJ Magic Johnson 60.00 150.00
JWJ Jerry West 20.00 50.00
KAJ Kareem Abdul-Jabbar 20.00 50.00
KBJ Kobe Bryant 150.00 400.00
MCJ Michael Cooper 12.00 30.00
RHJ Robert Horry 12.00 30.00
SOJ Shaquille O'Neal 25.00 60.00
WOJ James Worthy 12.00 30.00

2000 Upper Deck Lakers Master Collection Mystery Pack Inserts
SS: SIGNS OF SUCCESS AUTOGRAPHS
ALL ITEMS ARE AUTOGRAPHED
PRINT RUNS LISTED BELOW
EBAF Elgin Baylor FF/22 175.00 350.00
EJAF Magic Johnson FF/32 500.00 1,000.00
EJAJ Magic Johnson JSY/32 500.00 1,000.00
JWAF Jerry West FF/44 125.00 250.00
JWAJ Jerry West JSY/44 250.00 500.00
KAAF K.Abdul-Jabbar FF/33 250.00 500.00
KAAJ K.Abdul-Jabbar JSY/33 250.00 500.00
WOAJ James Worthy JSY/42 75.00 150.00

2000 Upper Deck Lakers Master Collection Warm-Ups
STATED PRINT RUN 300 SERIAL #'d SETS
WCW Wilt Chamberlain 15.00 40.00

2003 Upper Deck LeBron James Box Set
COMPLETE SET (30) 100.00 250.00
COMMON JAMES (1-30) 8.00 20.00
COMMON JUMBO (LJ1-LJ2) 15.00 40.00
EACH SET INCLUDES TWO JUMBOS

2006 Upper Deck LeBron James Game Giveaway
COMPLETE SET (10) 10.00 25.00
COMMON CARD (1-10) 1.25 3.00

2003 Upper Deck LeBron James Jumbo Motion
NNO LeBron James 12.00 30.00

2004 Upper Deck LeBron James Freshman Season
COMPLETE SET (90) 75.00 200.00
COMMON CARD (1-90) 3.00 8.00

2001-02 Upper Deck Legends
COMP.SET w/o SP's (90) 10.00 25.00
91-110 PRINT RUN 3250 SER.#'d SETS
111-125 PRINT RUN 1999 SER.#'d SETS
126-132 PRINT RUN 500 SER.#'d SETS
NOTE CARDS READ 2000-01
1 Michael Jordan 2.00 5.00
2 Wilt Chamberlain .75 2.00
3 Karl Malone .50 1.25
4 Steve Francis .25 .60
5 George McGinnis .15 .40
6 Julius Erving .60 1.50
7 Alonzo Mourning .40 1.00
8 Kobe Bryant 2.00 5.00
9 Glen Rice .25 .60
10 Mitch Kupchak .25 .60
11 Isiah Thomas .40 1.00
12 Rick Barry .20 .50
13 Moses Malone .40 1.00
14 Larry Bird 1.00 2.50
15 Vince Carter .50 1.25
16 Jamaal Wilkes .20 .50
17 John Havlicek .60 1.50
18 Elgin Baylor .50 1.25
19 Dave Bing .25 .60
20 Steve Smith .20 .50
21 Kevin Garnett .60 1.50
22 Hakeem Olajuwon .50 1.25
23 Walt Bellamy .20 .50
24 Kevin McHale .40 1.00
25 Kareem Abdul-Jabbar .75 2.00
26 Chris Webber .30 .75
27 Tom Heinsohn .25 .60
28 Walt Frazier .40 1.00
29 Ron Boone .15 .40
30 Gary Payton .40 1.00
31 Wes Unseld .25 .60
32 Magic Johnson 1.00 2.50
33 David Thompson .20 .50
34 Maurice Lucas .25 .60
35 Paul Pierce .40 1.00
36 Dikembe Mutombo .40 1.00
37 Gail Goodrich .20 .50
38 Bob Lanier .40 1.00
39 Chris Mullin .25 .60
40 Allen Iverson .60 1.50
41 Sam Jones .25 .60
42 James Worthy .40 1.00
43 Cedric Maxwell .15 .40
44 George Gervin .40 1.00
45 Earl Monroe .25 .60
46 Lenny Wilkens .25 .60
47 Tracy McGrady .40 1.00
48 Walter Davis .25 .60
49 Stephon Marbury .30 .75
50 Bob Cousy .30 .75
51 Spencer Haywood .15 .40
52 Dave Cowens .20 .50
53 Scottie Pippen .60 1.50
54 Hal Greer .20 .50
55 Kiki Vandeweghe .20 .50
56 Paul Silas .20 .50
57 Elton Brand .25 .60
58 John Stockton .50 1.25
59 Shareef Abdur-Rahim .20 .50
60 Reggie Miller .50 1.25
61 Nate Thurmond .20 .50
62 Billy Cunningham .25 .60
63 Patrick Ewing .40 1.00
64 Nate Archibald .20 .50
65 Tim Duncan .60 1.50
66 Lafayette Lever .20 .50
67 Willis Reed .40 1.00
68 Ray Allen .40 1.00
69 Jo Jo White .20 .50
70 Pete Maravich .75 2.00
71 Grant Hill .40 1.00
72 Jerry West .60 1.50
73 George Karl .25 .60
74 Bill Sharman .25 .60
75 Dave DeBusschere .25 .60
76 Tim Hardaway .30 .75
77 Bill Walton .30 .75
78 Jerry Lucas .25 .60
79 Antonio McDyess .20 .50
80 Robert Parish .30 .75
81 Shaquille O'Neal 1.00 2.50
82 Bill Russell .75 2.00
83 Clyde Drexler .40 1.00
84 Dolph Schayes .25 .60
85 K.C. Jones .25 .60
86 Bob Pettit .25 .60
87 Jason Kidd .40 1.00
88 Mitch Richmond .30 .75
89 Oscar Robertson .40 1.00
90 David Robinson .50 1.25
91 Bobby Simmons RC 1.50 4.00
92 Jamison Brewer RC 1.50 4.00
93 Earl Watson RC 1.25 3.00
94 Kenny Satterfield RC 1.00 2.50
95 Zeljko Rebraca RC 1.50 4.00
96 Damone Brown RC 1.00 2.50
97 Ruben Boumtje-Boumtje RC 1.25 3.00
98 Brian Scalabrine RC 1.50 4.00
99 Terence Morris RC 1.00 2.50
100 Willie Solomon RC 1.25 3.00
101 Primoz Brezec RC 1.50 4.00
102 Gilbert Arenas RC 4.00 10.00
103 Trenton Hassell RC 1.00 2.50
104 Loren Woods RC 1.00 2.50
105 Tony Parker RC 6.00 15.00
106 Jamaal Tinsley RC 1.25 3.00
107 Samuel Dalembert RC 1.50 4.00
108 Gerald Wallace RC 2.00 5.00
109 Andrei Kirilenko RC 2.50 6.00
110 Brandon Armstrong RC 1.00 2.50
111 Jeryl Sasser RC 2.00 5.00
112 Joseph Forte RC 2.00 5.00
113 Brendan Haywood RC 2.50 6.00
114 Zach Randolph RC 6.00 15.00
115 Jason Collins RC 2.50 6.00
116 Michael Bradley RC 2.00 5.00
117 Kirk Haston RC 2.00 5.00
118 Steven Hunter RC 2.00 5.00
119 Troy Murphy RC 2.50 6.00
120 Richard Jefferson RC 4.00 10.00
121 Vladimir Radmanovic RC 2.50 6.00
122 Kedrick Brown RC 2.00 5.00
123 Joe Johnson RC 5.00 12.00
124 Rodney White RC 2.00 5.00
125 DeSagana Diop RC 2.00 5.00
126 Eddie Griffin RC 3.00 8.00
127 Shane Battier RC 8.00 20.00
128 Jason Richardson RC 6.00 15.00
129 Eddy Curry RC 4.00 10.00
130 Pau Gasol RC 15.00 40.00
131 Tyson Chandler RC 6.00 15.00
132 Kwame Brown RC 4.00 10.00

2001-02 Upper Deck Legends Fiorentino Collection
COMPLETE SET (15) 20.00 50.00
STATED ODDS 1:15
F1 Michael Jordan 6.00 15.00
F2 Larry Bird 3.00 8.00
F3 Magic Johnson 3.00 8.00
F4 Julius Erving 2.00 5.00
F5 Bill Russell 2.50 6.00
F6 Jerry West 2.00 5.00
F7 Oscar Robertson 2.00 5.00
F8 Wilt Chamberlain 2.50 6.00
F9 Kareem Abdul-Jabbar 2.50 6.00
F10 Isiah Thomas 1.25 3.00
F11 George Gervin 1.25 3.00
F12 Elgin Baylor 1.50 4.00
F13 Bob Cousy 2.00 5.00
F14 Pete Maravich 2.50 6.00
F15 John Havlicek 2.00 5.00

2001-02 Upper Deck Legends Fiorentino Collection Autographs
ANNOUNCED PRINT RUNS LISTED IN CL
EB Elgin Baylor/22* 40.00 100.00
GG George Gervin/44* 25.00 60.00
JH John Havlicek/17* 100.00 250.00
JW Jerry West/44* 100.00 250.00
KA Kareem Abdul-Jabbar/33* 125.00 300.00
LB Larry Bird/33* 200.00 500.00
MA Magic Johnson/32* 200.00 500.00

2001-02 Upper Deck Legends Generations
COMPLETE SET (9) 75.00 200.00
STATED ODDS 1:24
G1 M.Jordan/K.Bryant 75.00 200.00
G2 O.Robertson/J.Kidd 3.00 8.00
G3 W.Frazier/R.Allen 3.00 8.00
G4 E.Hayes/K.Garnett 3.00 8.00
G5 M.Malone/T.Duncan 3.00 8.00
G6 B.Lanier/D.Robinson 3.00 8.00
G7 G.Gervin/T.McGrady 3.00 8.00
G8 N.Archibald/S.Francis 2.50 6.00
G9 M.Jordan/V.Carter 12.00 30.00

2001-02 Upper Deck Legends Legendary Floor
STATED ODDS 1:23
AIF Allen Iverson 12.00 30.00
AMF Alonzo Mourning 8.00 20.00
CWF Chris Webber 6.00 15.00
DAF David Robinson 10.00 25.00
DRF Julius Erving 12.00 30.00
GHF Grant Hill 8.00 20.00
HOF Hakeem Olajuwon 10.00 25.00
ITF Isiah Thomas 8.00 20.00
JHF John Havlicek 12.00 30.00
JKF Jason Kidd 8.00 20.00
JSF John Stockton 10.00 25.00
JWF James Worthy 8.00 20.00
KAF Kareem Abdul-Jabbar 15.00 40.00
KBF Kobe Bryant 40.00 100.00
KGF Kevin Garnett 12.00 30.00
KMF Karl Malone 10.00 25.00
LBF Larry Bird 20.00 50.00
MAF Magic Johnson 20.00 50.00
MJF Michael Jordan 75.00 200.00
MMF Moses Malone 8.00 20.00
PEF Patrick Ewing 8.00 20.00
PMF Pete Maravich 60.00 150.00
RMF Reggie Miller 10.00 25.00
SFF Steve Francis 5.00 12.00
SMF Stephon Marbury 6.00 15.00
SPF Scottie Pippen 12.00 30.00
THF Tim Hardaway 6.00 15.00
TMF Tracy McGrady 8.00 20.00
WCF Wilt Chamberlain 60.00 150.00

2001-02 Upper Deck Legends Legendary Floor Autographs
STATED PRINT RUN 23 TO 100 SETS
DRAF Julius Erving/100 125.00 300.00
JHAF John Havlicek/100 125.00 300.00
KAAF Kareem Abdul-Jabbar/100 150.00 400.00
KBAF Kobe Bryant/100 1,500.00 3,000.00
KGAF Kevin Garnett/100 150.00 400.00
LBAF Larry Bird/100 200.00 500.00
MAAF Magic Johnson/100 200.00 500.00
MJAF Michael Jordan/23 3,000.00 6,000.00
MMAF Moses Malone/100 100.00 250.00
SFAF Steve Francis/100 40.00 100.00

2001-02 Upper Deck Legends Legendary Jerseys
STATED ODDS 1:23
AIJ Allen Iverson 20.00 50.00
BRJ Bill Russell 40.00 100.00
BWJ Bill Walton 6.00 15.00
CDJ Clyde Drexler 8.00 20.00
DAJ David Robinson 10.00 25.00
DDJ Dave DeBusschere 8.00 20.00
DRJ Julius Erving 12.00 30.00
EMJ Earl Monroe 6.00 15.00
GGJ George Gervin 6.00 15.00
GHJ Grant Hill 12.00 30.00
ITJ Isiah Thomas 8.00 20.00
JHJ John Havlicek 20.00 50.00
JSJ John Stockton 10.00 25.00
JWJ Jerry West 12.00 30.00
KAJ Kareem Abdul-Jabbar 40.00 100.00
KBJ Kobe Bryant 75.00 200.00
KGJ Kevin Garnett 12.00 30.00
KMJ Karl Malone 10.00 25.00
LBJ Larry Bird 40.00 100.00
MAJ Magic Johnson 40.00 100.00
MCJ Kevin McHale 8.00 20.00
MJJ Michael Jordan 125.00 300.00
MJ/DRJ M.Jordan/J.Erving 150.00 400.00
MJ/KBJ M.Jordan/K.Bryant 400.00 800.00
MJ/LBJ M.Jordan/L.Bird 200.00 500.00
PEJ Patrick Ewing 8.00 20.00
RPJ Robert Parish 6.00 15.00
SPJ Scottie Pippen 20.00 50.00

2001-02 Upper Deck Legends Legendary Jerseys Autographs
STATED PRINT RUN 10 TO 50 SETS
BRAJ Bill Russell/50 1,500.00 3,000.00
DDAJ Dave DeBusschere/50 200.00 500.00
DRAJ Julius Erving/50 400.00 800.00
EMAJ Earl Monroe/50 100.00 250.00
GGAJ George Gervin/50 125.00 300.00
JWAJ Jerry West/50 200.00 500.00
KAAJ Kareem Abdul-Jabbar/50 500.00 1,000.00
KBAJ Kobe Bryant/50 2,500.00 5,000.00
KGAJ Kevin Garnett/50 300.00 600.00
LBAJ Larry Bird/50 500.00 1,000.00
MAAJ Magic Johnson/50 500.00 1,000.00
MJAJ Michael Jordan/23 4,000.00 8,000.00

2001-02 Upper Deck Legends Legendary Signatures
STATED ODDS 1:71
BR Bill Russell 400.00 800.00
BS Bill Sharman 25.00 60.00
DR Julius Erving 125.00 300.00
DT David Thompson 12.00 30.00
EB Elgin Baylor 40.00 100.00
EM Earl Monroe 12.00 30.00
GG George Gervin 20.00 50.00
JH John Havlicek 100.00 250.00
JW Jerry West 75.00 200.00
KA Kareem Abdul-Jabbar 125.00 300.00
KV Kiki Vandeweghe 6.00 15.00
LB Larry Bird SP 200.00 500.00
MA Magic Johnson 200.00 500.00
MM Moses Malone 75.00 200.00
NA Nate Archibald 12.00 30.00
OR Oscar Robertson 40.00 100.00
SF Steve Francis SP 20.00 50.00
WR Willis Reed 40.00 100.00

2001-02 Upper Deck Legends Record Producers
COMPLETE SET (9) 15.00 40.00
STATED ODDS 1:24
RP1 Michael Jordan 12.00 30.00
RP2 John Stockton 1.50 4.00
RP3 Reggie Miller 1.50 4.00
RP4 Oscar Robertson 2.00 5.00
RP5 Hakeem Olajuwon 1.50 4.00
RP6 Elgin Baylor 1.50 4.00
RP7 Karl Malone 1.50 4.00
RP8 Kobe Bryant 6.00 15.00
RP9 Jerry West 2.00 5.00

2001-02 Upper Deck Legends Yearbook
COMPLETE SET (9) 25.00 60.00
STATED ODDS 1:24
Y1 Michael Jordan 20.00 50.00
Y2 Kobe Bryant 10.00 25.00
Y3 Walt Frazier 1.25 3.00
Y4 Pete Maravich 2.50 6.00
Y5 Clyde Drexler 1.25 3.00
Y6 Bob Lanier 1.25 3.00
Y7 Bill Russell 2.50 6.00
Y8 Bill Walton 1.00 2.50
Y9 Kevin Garnett 2.00 5.00

2003-04 Upper Deck Legends
COMP.SET w/o SP's (90) 12.50 30.00
136-150 DRAFT EXCH ODDS 1:24
1 Bob Sura .20 .50
2 Stephen Jackson .25 .60
3 Jason Terry .25 .60
4 Ricky Davis .25 .60
5 Jiri Welsch .20 .50
6 Paul Pierce .50 1.25
7 Eddy Curry .25 .60
8 Jamal Crawford .30 .75
9 Tyson Chandler .25 .60
10 Dajuan Wagner .25 .60
11 Carlos Boozer .25 .60
12 Zydrunas Ilgauskas .25 .60
13 Dirk Nowitzki .75 2.00
14 Antoine Walker .30 .75
15 Steve Nash .60 1.50
16 Michael Finley .30 .75
17 Jon Barry .20 .50
18 Andre Miller .25 .60
19 Nene .25 .60
20 Rasheed Wallace .40 1.00
21 Richard Hamilton .40 1.00
22 Ben Wallace .40 1.00
23 Erick Dampier .25 .60
24 Jason Richardson .30 .75
25 Nick Van Exel .30 .75
26 Yao Ming .75 2.00
27 Cuttino Mobley .20 .50
28 Steve Francis .30 .75
29 Jermaine O'Neal .30 .75
30 Reggie Miller .60 1.50
31 Ron Artest .30 .75
32 Elton Brand .25 .60
33 Corey Maggette .25 .60
34 Quentin Richardson .20 .50
35 Kobe Bryant 2.50 6.00
36 Karl Malone .60 1.50
37 Gary Payton .50 1.25
38 Shaquille O'Neal 1.25 3.00
39 Pau Gasol .50 1.25
40 Bonzi Wells .20 .50
41 Mike Miller .25 .60
42 Lamar Odom .25 .60
43 Eddie Jones .30 .75
44 Caron Butler .25 .60
45 Keith Van Horn .25 .60
46 Desmond Mason .25 .60
47 Michael Redd .30 .75
48 Latrell Sprewell .40 1.00
49 Kevin Garnett .75 2.00
50 Sam Cassell .25 .60
51 Richard Jefferson .25 .60
52 Kenyon Martin .25 .60
53 Jason Kidd .50 1.25
54 Jamal Mashburn .25 .60
55 Baron Davis .25 .60
56 David Wesley .20 .50
57 Allan Houston .25 .60
58 Stephon Marbury .40 1.00
59 Kurt Thomas .20 .50
60 Juwan Howard .25 .60
61 Drew Gooden .25 .60
62 Tracy McGrady .50 1.25
63 Zendon Hamilton RC .30 .75
64 Allen Iverson .75 2.00
65 Eric Snow .20 .50
66 Amare Stoudemire .40 1.00
67 Joe Johnson .25 .60
68 Shawn Marion .30 .75
69 Zach Randolph .30 .75
70 Damon Stoudamire .20 .50
71 Shareef Abdur-Rahim .30 .75
72 Peja Stojakovic .25 .60
73 Chris Webber .40 1.00
74 Mike Bibby .30 .75
75 Brad Miller .25 .60
76 Tony Parker .50 1.25
77 Tim Duncan .75 2.00
78 Manu Ginobili .60 1.50
79 Ronald Murray .20 .50
80 Ray Allen .50 1.25
81 Rashard Lewis .25 .60
82 Donyell Marshall .20 .50
83 Vince Carter .60 1.50
84 Jalen Rose .25 .60
85 Andrei Kirilenko .25 .60
86 Matt Harpring .20 .50
87 Carlos Arroyo .25 .60
88 Gilbert Arenas .30 .75
89 Larry Hughes .25 .60
90 Jerry Stackhouse .40 1.00
91 Devin Brown RC 1.25 3.00
92 Ronald Dupree RC 1.25 3.00
93 Alex Garcia RC 1.25 3.00
94 Udonis Haslem RC 2.50 6.00
95 Maurice Williams RC 2.00 5.00
96 Brandon Hunter RC 1.25 3.00
97 Keith Bogans RC 1.25 3.00
98 Willie Green RC 2.00 5.00
99 Zaza Pachulia RC 2.00 5.00
100 Zarko Cabarkapa RC 1.25 3.00
101 Kyle Korver RC 2.50 6.00
102 Luke Walton RC 2.00 5.00
103 Maciej Lampe RC 1.25 3.00
104 Josh Howard RC 2.00 5.00
105 Kendrick Perkins RC 1.50 4.00
106 Ndudi Ebi RC 1.25 3.00
107 Jerome Beasley RC 1.25 3.00
108 Brian Cook RC 1.25 3.00
109 Travis Outlaw RC 1.50 4.00
110 Zoran Planinic RC 1.25 3.00
111 Boris Diaw RC 2.00 5.00
112 Steve Blake RC 1.50 4.00
113 Aleksandar Pavlovic RC 1.50 4.00
114 David West RC 2.50 6.00
115 Mike Sweetney RC 1.25 3.00
116 Troy Bell RC 1.25 3.00
117 Reece Gaines RC 1.25 3.00
118 Marcus Banks RC 1.25 3.00
119 Dahntay Jones RC 1.50 4.00
120 Chris Kaman RC 2.00 5.00
121 Mickael Pietrus RC 1.50 4.00
122 Luke Ridnour RC 2.00 5.00
123 Jason Kapono RC 1.50 4.00
124 Marquis Daniels RC 1.50 4.00
125 Travis Hansen RC 1.25 3.00
126 Leandro Barbosa RC 2.50 6.00
127 Nick Collison RC 2.00 5.00
128 Kirk Hinrich RC 2.50 6.00
129 T.J. Ford RC 2.00 5.00
130 Jarvis Hayes RC 1.50 4.00
131 Dwyane Wade RC 20.00 50.00
132 Chris Bosh RC 8.00 20.00
133 Carmelo Anthony RC 12.00 30.00
134 Darko Milicic RC 2.00 5.00
135 LeBron James RC 500.00 1,000.00
136 Dwight Howard XRC 10.00 25.00
137 Emeka Okafor XRC 2.50 6.00
138 Ben Gordon XRC 3.00 8.00
139 Shaun Livingston XRC 3.00 8.00
140 Devin Harris XRC 3.00 8.00
141 Josh Childress XRC 2.50 6.00
142 Luol Deng XRC 3.00 8.00
143 Rafael Araujo XRC 2.00 5.00
144 Andre Iguodala XRC 4.00 10.00
145 Luke Jackson XRC 2.00 5.00
146 Andris Biedrins XRC 2.00 5.00
147 Robert Swift XRC 2.00 5.00
148 Sebastian Telfair XRC 2.50 6.00
149 Kris Humphries XRC 2.50 6.00
150 Al Jefferson XRC 3.00 8.00

2003-04 Upper Deck Legends Throwback
COMP.SET w/o SP's 15.00 40.00
*TB 91-125: .5X TO 1.25X BASE HI
*TB 126-135: .4X TO 1X BASE HI
91-135 PRINT RUN 100 SER.#'d SETS
*TB 136-150: 1.25X TO 3X BASE HI
136-150 DRAFT EXCH ODDS 1:380
1 Dominique Wilkins .40 1.00
2 Spud Webb .25 .60
3 Danny Ainge .30 .75
4 Larry Bird .75 2.00
5 John Havlicek .30 .75
6 Bob Cousy .50 1.25
7 Bill Russell .50 1.25
8 Kevin McHale .40 1.00
9 Dave Cowens .25 .60
10 Dennis Johnson .25 .60
11 K.C. Jones .30 .75
12 Robert Parish .40 1.00
13 Nate Archibald .25 .60
14 Michael Jordan 3.00 8.00
15 Dennis Rodman .60 1.50
16 Bill Cartwright .25 .60
17 Spencer Haywood .20 .50
18 World B. Free .25 .60
19 Rolando Blackman .25 .60
20 Walt Bellamy .25 .60
21 Dan Issel .25 .60
22 David Thompson .25 .60
23 Alex English .25 .60
24 Dave Bing .20 .50
25 Isiah Thomas .30 .75
26 Bill Laimbeer .25 .60
27 Bob Lanier .25 .60
28 Vinnie Johnson .25 .60
29 M.L. Carr .30 .75
30 Cazzie Russell .25 .60
31 Rick Barry .25 .60
32 Chris Mullin .40 1.00
33 Nate Thurmond .25 .60
34 Gail Goodrich .25 .60
35 Kenny Smith .25 .60
36 George McGinnis .20 .50
37 Clark Kellogg .30 .75
38 Michael Cage .20 .50
39 Wilt Chamberlain .60 1.50
40 Magic Johnson .75 2.00
41 Kurt Rambis .30 .75
42 James Worthy .40 1.00
43 Jamaal Wilkes .25 .60
44 Kareem Abdul-Jabbar .50 1.25
45 George Mikan .60 1.50
46 Elgin Baylor .30 .75
47 Michael Cooper .25 .60
48 Pat Riley .40 1.00
49 Alonzo Mourning .40 1.00
50 Rony Seikaly .20 .50
51 Ricky Pierce .20 .50
52 Terry Cummings .25 .60
53 Oscar Robertson .30 .75
54 Sidney Moncrief .20 .50
55 Darryl Dawkins .20 .50
56 Otis Birdsong .25 .60
57 Jerry Lucas .30 .75
58 Dave DeBusschere .30 .75
59 Patrick Ewing .40 1.00
60 Willis Reed .50 1.25
61 Walt Frazier .30 .75
62 Earl Monroe .30 .75
63 Donald Royal .30 .75
64 Moses Malone .30 .75
65 Julius Erving .50 1.25
66 Maurice Cheeks .25 .60
67 Billy Cunningham .30 .75
68 Kevin Johnson .30 .75
69 Tom Chambers .25 .60
70 Larry Nance .25 .60
71 Walter Davis .30 .75
72 Maurice Lucas .30 .75
73 Paul Westphal .40 1.00
74 Bill Walton .50 1.25
75 Jim Paxson .30 .75
76 Clyde Drexler .40 1.00
77 Reggie Theus .25 .60
78 Nate McMillan .30 .75
79 David Robinson .60 1.50
80 Artis Gilmore .25 .60
81 George Gervin .50 1.25
82 Fred Brown .20 .50
83 Detlef Schrempf .30 .75
84 Jack Sikma .25 .60
85 Lenny Wilkens .30 .75
86 Pete Maravich .60 1.50
87 John Stockton .60 1.50
88 Darrell Griffith .20 .50
89 Wes Unseld .30 .75
90 Elvin Hayes .30 .75
106 Ndudi Ebi 1.50 4.00
131 Dwyane Wade 15.00 40.00
135 LeBron James 2,000.00 4,000.00

2003-04 Upper Deck Legends Championship Numbers Autographs
PRINT RUNS LISTED BELOW
BL Bill Laimbeer/40 30.00 80.00
BS Bill Sharman/21 40.00 100.00
CD Chuck Daly/80 30.00 80.00
CM Cedric Maxwell/31 15.00 40.00
CO Michael Cooper/21 25.00 60.00
CR Cazzie Russell/33 15.00 40.00
CU Billy Cunningham/80 25.00 60.00
DC Dave Cowens/18 20.00 50.00
DR David Robinson/50 60.00 150.00
GM George Mikan/99 300.00 600.00
JW James Worthy/42 60.00 150.00
KJ K.C. Jones/80 12.00 30.00
KJ K.C. Jones/25 20.00 50.00
KR Kurt Rambis/31 60.00 150.00
LB Larry Bird/33 100.00 250.00
MA Magic Johnson/32 75.00 200.00
MJ Michael Jordan/90 1,500.00 3,000.00
PR Pat Riley/80 50.00 120.00
RO Dennis Rodman/91 50.00 120.00
RP Robert Parish/80 20.00 50.00
WI Jamaal Wilkes/52 30.00 80.00
WR Willis Reed/19 125.00 300.00
WU Wes Unseld/41 12.00 30.00

2003-04 Upper Deck Legends Championship Teammates Dual Autographs
PRINT RUN 25 SER.#'d SETS
BT B.Cousy/T.Heinsohn 60.00 150.00
BW L.Bird/B.Walton 125.00 300.00
CC Cunningham/Cheeks 25.00 60.00
CR B.Cousy/B.Russell 2,500.00 5,000.00
EC J.Erving/M.Cheeks 60.00 150.00
FR W.Frazier/W.Reed 125.00 300.00
JH K.C.Jones/T.Heinsohn 25.00 60.00
JS K.C.Jones/B.Sharman 60.00 150.00
JW M.Johnson/J.Worthy 150.00 400.00
RF C.Russell/W.Frazier 40.00 100.00
RR P.Riley/K.Rambis 30.00 80.00
TL I.Thomas/B.Laimbeer 30.00 80.00
WJ B.Walton/D.Johnson 25.00 60.00
WP B.Walton/R.Parish 40.00 100.00
WR J.Worthy/K.Rambis 60.00 150.00

2003-04 Upper Deck Legends Hall of Fame Induction Ink
COMBINED AUTO ODDS 1:8
DM Dino Meneghin 20.00 50.00
EL Earl Lloyd 25.00 60.00
JW James Worthy 30.00 80.00
LB Leon Barmore 15.00 40.00
ML Meadowlark Lemon 40.00 80.00
RP Robert Parish 10.00 25.00

2003-04 Upper Deck Legends Legendary Inscriptions
PRINT RUN 100 SER.#'d SETS
AG A.Gilmore A-Train 20.00 50.00
BC B.Cousy Cooz 50.00 120.00
BW B.Walton Big Red 25.00 60.00
CM C.Maxwell Cornbread 15.00 40.00
DA D.Robinson Admiral 75.00 150.00
DC D.Cowens Big Red 25.00 60.00
DD Dawkins Chocolate Thunder 20.00 50.00
DD1 D.Dawkins Love Tron 20.00 50.00

DG D.Griffith Dr. Dunkenstein 15.00 40.00
DJ Dennis Johnson DJ 30.00 80.00
DT D.Thompson Skywalker 25.00 60.00
EH E.Hayes The Big E 15.00 40.00
GG G.Gervin The Iceman 25.00 60.00
GM G.Mikan Mr. Basketball 800.00 1,500.00
IT I.Thomas Zeke 40.00 100.00
JA J.Wilkes Silk 25.00 60.00
JE J.Erving Dr. J 50.00 100.00
JS J.Salley Spider 15.00 40.00
JW J.Worthy Big Game James 75.00 200.00
KR K.Rambis Clark Kent 20.00 50.00
MA Magic Johnson Magic 50.00 120.00
MC Michael Cooper Coop 20.00 50.00
MO Maurice Cheeks Mo 15.00 40.00
RP Robert Parish Chief 30.00 80.00
SW Anthony Webb Spud 15.00 40.00
WF Walt Frazier Clyde 30.00 80.00
WR W.Reed The Captain 200.00 500.00
ZO A.Mourning Zo 30.00 80.00

2003-04 Upper Deck Legends Legendary Signatures

COMBINED AUTO ODDS 1:8
AG Artis Gilmore 6.00 15.00
AM Alonzo Mourning 20.00 50.00
BC Bob Cousy 50.00 120.00
BL Bill Laimbeer 6.00 15.00
BR Bill Russell SP 1,000.00 2,000.00
BS Bill Sharman 12.00 30.00
BW Bill Walton 8.00 20.00
CD Chuck Daly 25.00 60.00
CR Cazzie Russell 6.00 15.00
CU Billy Cunningham 50.00 120.00
DA David Robinson SP 100.00 250.00
DC Dave Cowens 8.00 20.00
DD Darryl Dawkins 6.00 15.00
DG Darrell Griffith 6.00 15.00
DJ Dennis Johnson 30.00 80.00
DR Dennis Rodman 40.00 100.00
DT David Thompson 6.00 15.00
EH Elvin Hayes 6.00 15.00
GG George Gervin 6.00 15.00
GM George Mikan 200.00 500.00
IT Isiah Thomas 10.00 25.00
JA Jamaal Wilkes 6.00 15.00
JE Julius Erving SP 100.00 250.00
JS John Stockton SP 100.00 250.00
JW James Worthy 25.00 60.00
KC K.C. Jones 20.00 50.00
KR Kurt Rambis 6.00 15.00
LB Larry Bird SP 100.00 250.00
MA Magic Johnson SP 60.00 150.00
MC Michael Cooper 6.00 15.00
MC1 Michael Coop Cooper 6.00 15.00
MJ Michael Jordan SP 5,000.00 10,000.00
MO Maurice Cheeks 6.00 15.00
PE Patrick Ewing 200.00 400.00
PR Pat Riley 30.00 80.00
RP Robert Parish 6.00 15.00
SW Spud Webb 6.00 15.00
TH Tommy Heinsohn 25.00 60.00
WF Walt Frazier 10.00 25.00
WR Willis Reed 40.00 100.00
WU Wes Unseld 10.00 25.00

2003-04 Upper Deck Legends Rookie Impressions Dual Autographs

PRINT RUN 25 SER.#'d SETS
THROWBACKS: SAME PRICE AS BASIC
AJJH A.Jamison/J.Howard 15.00 40.00
GADA G.Arenas/D.West 10.00 25.00
GPTB G.Payton/T.Bell 20.00 50.00
JDSB J.Dixon/S.Blake 10.00 25.00
JKMB J.Kidd/M.Banks 20.00 50.00
JRMP J.Richardson/M.Pietrus 10.00 25.00
KBDW K.Bryant/D.Wade 800.00 1,500.00
KGCB K.Garnett/C.Bosh 100.00 250.00
LBDM L.Bird/D.Milicic 75.00 200.00
MJLJ M.Jordan/L.James 15,000.00 30,000.00
TMCA T.McGrady/C.Anthony 75.00 200.00
YMCK Y.Ming/C.Kaman 40.00 100.00

2003-04 Upper Deck Legends Signs of a Future Legend

COMBINED AUTO ODDS 1:8
AK Andrei Kirilenko 3.00 8.00
AM Andre Miller 3.00 8.00
AS Amare Stoudemire 5.00 12.00
BC Brian Cook 2.50 6.00
BD Boris Diaw 4.00 10.00
BO Carlos Boozer 3.00 8.00
CA Carmelo Anthony SP 125.00 300.00
CB Chris Bosh SP 12.00 30.00
CH Chauncey Billups 6.00 15.00
DA David West 5.00 12.00
DM Darko Milicic SP 3.00 8.00
DW Dajuan Wagner 2.50 6.00
DY Dwyane Wade 200.00 500.00
EG Manu Ginobili 40.00 100.00
FJ Fred Jones 2.50 6.00
GA Gilbert Arenas 8.00 20.00
GP Gary Payton SP 20.00 50.00
JA Jalen Rose 3.00 8.00
JH Josh Howard 4.00 10.00
JK Jason Kidd SP 20.00 50.00
JR Jason Richardson 4.00 10.00
KB Keith Bogans 2.50 6.00
KG Kevin Garnett SP 125.00 300.00
KK Kyle Korver 5.00 12.00
KR Kareem Rush 2.50 6.00
LB Leandro Barbosa 4.00 10.00
LJ LeBron James SP 5,000.00 10,000.00
LR Luke Ridnour 4.00 10.00
LW Luke Walton 4.00 10.00
ML Maciej Lampe 2.50 6.00
NH Nene 3.00 8.00
RH Richard Hamilton 5.00 12.00
RJ Richard Jefferson 3.00 8.00
SC Sam Cassell 3.00 8.00
TM Tracy McGrady SP 25.00 60.00
YM Yao Ming SP 75.00 200.00

2000 Upper Deck Legends Master Collection

COMPLETE SET (18) 125.00 250.00
STATED PRINT RUN 200 SERIAL #'d SETS
1 Michael Jordan 30.00 80.00
2 Bill Russell 20.00 50.00
3 Magic Johnson 20.00 50.00
4 Larry Bird 20.00 50.00
5 Julius Erving 15.00 40.00
6 Wilt Chamberlain 20.00 50.00
7 Jerry West 15.00 40.00
8 Bill Walton 8.00 20.00
9 Bob Cousy 15.00 40.00
10 John Havlicek 15.00 40.00
11 Elgin Baylor 12.00 30.00
12 Oscar Robertson 12.00 30.00
13 Walt Frazier 10.00 25.00
14 George Gervin 10.00 25.00
15 Pete Maravich 12.00 30.00
16 Isiah Thomas 10.00 25.00
17 Moses Malone 10.00 25.00
18 Rick Barry 8.00 20.00

2000 Upper Deck Legends Master Collection Legendary Floor

COMPLETE SET (2) 100.00 200.00
COMMON CARD (F1-F2) 60.00 120.00
PRINT RUN 100 SERIAL #'d SETS

2000 Upper Deck Legends Master Collection Living Legends Autographs

PRINT RUN 50 SERIAL #'d SETS
BL1 Bill Russell 1,000.00 2,000.00
BL2 Bill Russell 1,000.00 2,000.00
BL3 Bill Russell 1,000.00 2,000.00
BL4 Bill Russell 1,000.00 2,000.00
EL1 Magic Johnson 100.00 250.00
EL2 Magic Johnson 100.00 250.00
EL3 Magic Johnson 100.00 250.00
EL4 Magic Johnson 100.00 250.00
JL1 Julius Erving 75.00 200.00
JL2 Julius Erving 75.00 200.00
JL3 Julius Erving 75.00 200.00
JL4 Julius Erving 75.00 200.00
LL1 Larry Bird 100.00 250.00
LL2 Larry Bird 100.00 250.00
LL3 Larry Bird 100.00 250.00
LL4 Larry Bird 100.00 250.00
ML1 Michael Jordan 2,500.00 5,000.00
ML2 Michael Jordan 2,500.00 5,000.00
ML3 Michael Jordan 2,500.00 5,000.00
ML4 Michael Jordan 2,500.00 5,000.00

2000 Upper Deck Legends Master Collection Mystery Pack Inserts

STATED PRINT RUNS LISTED BELOW
EJA Magic Johnson Floor AU/32 80.00 160.00
DREJ Erving/Johnson Jsy/37 30.00 80.00

2000 Upper Deck Legends Master Collection Warm-Ups

STATED PRINT RUN 200 SERIAL #'d SETS
WC1 Wilt Chamberlain 40.00 80.00

2003 Upper Deck Lego Sports

COMPLETE SET (24) 6.00 15.00
*GOLD: .75X TO 2X BASE HI
1 Ray Allen .40 1.00
2 Shaquille O'Neal .75 2.00
5 Antoine Walker .40 1.00
6 Tony Parker .40 1.00
7 Vince Carter .40 1.00
8 Dirk Nowitzki .50 1.25
10 Kobe Bryant 2.00 5.00
11 Jason Kidd .50 1.25
12 Toni Kukoc .40 1.00
13 Allen Iverson .50 1.25
14 Tracy McGrady .50 1.25
15 Karl Malone .50 1.25
16 Paul Pierce .40 1.00
17 Jerry Stackhouse .40 1.00
18 Steve Nash .50 1.25
19 Kevin Garnett .60 1.50
21 Jalen Rose .40 1.00
22 Chris Webber .40 1.00
23 Steve Francis .40 1.00
24 Allan Houston .40 1.00

2014-15 Upper Deck Lettermen

COMPLETE SET (80)
51-80 PRINT RUN 999 SER.#'d SETS
1 Allan Houston .40 1.00
2 James Worthy .60 1.50
3 Magic Johnson 1.50 4.00
4 Glenn Robinson .30 .75
5 Jerry Lucas .50 1.25
6 Vinny Del Negro .30 .75
7 A.C. Green .40 1.00
8 Elvin Hayes .60 1.50
9 Karl Malone .75 2.00
10 Kendall Gill .40 1.00
11 Bo Outlaw .25 .60
12 Christian Laettner .40 1.00
13 Hakeem Olajuwon .75 2.00
14 David Robinson .75 2.00
15 James Harden .75 2.00
16 Nick Van Exel .40 1.00
17 Sleepy Floyd .30 .75
18 Stephen Curry 3.00 8.00
19 Sean Elliott .40 1.00
20 LeBron James 3.00 8.00
21 Joe Smith .30 .75
22 Derek Harper .30 .75
23 Julius Erving 1.00 2.50
24 Jamal Mashburn .30 .75
25 Larry Bird 1.50 4.00
26 Alex English .50 1.25
27 Reggie Theus .30 .75
28 Shane Battier .30 .75
29 Dave Cowens .50 1.25
30 Brad Daugherty .30 .75
31 Bo Kimble .30 .75
32 John Salley .30 .75
33 Antoine Walker .30 .75
34 Stacey Augmon .25 .60
35 Danny Manning .30 .75
36 Jerry Stackhouse .30 .75
37 Jay Williams .30 .75
38 Shaquille O'Neal 1.50 4.00
39 Fat Lever .40 1.00
40 Antonio McDyess .30 .75
41 Bobby Hurley .40 1.00
42 Pervis Ellison .25 .60
43 Bill Russell 1.25 3.00
44 Michael Jordan 3.00 8.00
45 Bill Walton .60 1.50
46 David Thompson .40 1.00
47 Harold Miner .40 1.00
48 Paul George .60 1.50
49 Keith Smart .40 1.00
50 Jerry West 1.00 2.50
51 Aaron Gordon 6.00 15.00
52 Adreian Payne 1.25 3.00
53 Sean Kilpatrick 1.25 3.00
54 C.J. Wilcox 1.25 3.00
55 Clint Capela 5.00 12.00
56 Alessandro Gentile 1.25 3.00
57 Dario Saric 2.50 6.00
58 Doug McDermott 2.00 5.00
59 Gary Harris 2.00 5.00
60 Glenn Robinson III 1.50 4.00
61 Jordan Adams 1.25 3.00
62 James Michael McAdoo 1.25 3.00
63 James Young 1.25 3.00
64 Thanasis Antetokounmpo 2.50 6.00
65 Kyle Anderson 2.00 5.00
66 Joe Harris 2.00 5.00
67 Josh Huestis 1.25 3.00
68 Elfrid Payton 2.00 5.00
69 Jusuf Nurkic 4.00 10.00
70 Shabazz Napier 1.50 4.00
71 Mitch McGary 1.25 3.00
72 Nik Stauskas 1.25 3.00
73 Nikola Mirotic 2.00 5.00
74 P.J. Hairston 1.25 3.00
75 Patric Young 1.25 3.00
76 Rodney Hood 1.50 4.00
77 T.J. Warren 2.00 5.00
78 DeAndre Daniels 1.25 3.00
79 Cleanthony Early 1.25 3.00
80 Zach LaVine 8.00 20.00

2014-15 Upper Deck Lettermen Blue

*BLUE 1-50: 1.2X TO 3X BASE HI
*BLUE 51-80: .5X TO 1.2X BASE HI
STATED PRINT RUN B/WN 249-499 COPIES PER

2014-15 Upper Deck Lettermen Silver

*SILVER 51-80: .75X TO 2X BASE HI
STATED PRINT RUN B/WN 15-99 COPIES PER

2014-15 Upper Deck Lettermen Autographs Blue

EXCHANGE DEADLINE 11/13/2016
LACK OF PRICING DUE TO MARKET INFO
4 Glenn Robinson 4.00 10.00
5 Jerry Lucas 6.00 15.00
7 A.C. Green 5.00 12.00
9 Karl Malone 20.00 50.00
10 Kendall Gill 6.00 15.00
12 Christian Laettner 10.00 25.00
16 Nick Van Exel 5.00 12.00
19 Sean Elliott 5.00 12.00
20 LeBron James 1,000.00 2,000.00
22 Derek Harper 4.00 10.00
23 Julius Erving 25.00 60.00
24 Jamal Mashburn 4.00 10.00
28 Shane Battier 4.00 10.00
30 Brad Daugherty 8.00 20.00
33 Antoine Walker 4.00 10.00
34 Stacey Augmon 15.00 40.00
40 Antonio McDyess 4.00 10.00
41 Bobby Hurley 8.00 20.00
45 Bill Walton 8.00 20.00
49 Keith Smart 8.00 20.00
50 Jerry West 15.00 40.00
51 Aaron Gordon 15.00 40.00
52 Adreian Payne 3.00 8.00
53 Sean Kilpatrick 3.00 8.00
54 C.J. Wilcox 3.00 8.00
55 Clint Capela 12.00 30.00
56 Alessandro Gentile 3.00 8.00
57 Dario Saric 6.00 15.00
58 Doug McDermott 5.00 12.00
59 Gary Harris 5.00 12.00
60 Glenn Robinson III 4.00 10.00
61 Jordan Adams 3.00 8.00
62 James Michael McAdoo 3.00 8.00
63 James Young 3.00 8.00
64 Thanasis Antetokounmpo 6.00 15.00
65 Kyle Anderson 5.00 12.00
66 Joe Harris 5.00 12.00
67 Josh Huestis 3.00 8.00
68 Elfrid Payton 5.00 12.00
69 Jusuf Nurkic 10.00 25.00
70 Shabazz Napier 4.00 10.00
71 Mitch McGary 3.00 8.00
72 Nik Stauskas 3.00 8.00
73 Nikola Mirotic 5.00 12.00
74 P.J. Hairston 3.00 8.00
75 Patric Young 3.00 8.00
76 Rodney Hood 4.00 10.00
77 T.J. Warren 4.00 10.00
78 DeAndre Daniels 3.00 8.00
79 Cleanthony Early 3.00 8.00
80 Zach LaVine 20.00 50.00

2014-15 Upper Deck Lettermen Championship Banners

STATED PRINT RUN 50 SER.#'d SETS
CBBW Bill Walton 8.00 20.00
CBCL Christian Laettner 5.00 12.00
CBCW Corliss Williamson 3.00 8.00
CBDM Danny Manning 4.00 10.00
CBDT David Thompson 5.00 12.00
CBGH Grant Hill 8.00 20.00
CBHI Grant Hill 8.00 20.00
CBJA LeBron James 40.00 100.00
CBJL Jerry Lucas 6.00 15.00
CBJO Larry Johnson 6.00 15.00
CBJW James Worthy 8.00 20.00
CBKS Keith Smart 5.00 12.00
CBLE LeBron James 15.00 50.00
CBLJ LeBron James 15.00 40.00
CBMJ Michael Jordan 150.00 250.00
CBSN Shabazz Napier 12.00 30.00
CBSP Sam Perkins 4.00 10.00

2014-15 Upper Deck Lettermen Championship Banners Autographs

STATED PRINT RUN B/WN 23-99 COPIES PER
EXCHANGE DEADLINE 11/13/2016
CBBW Bill Walton/99 12.00 30.00
CBCL Christian Laettner/99 15.00 40.00
CBDM Danny Manning/99 6.00 15.00
CBDT David Thompson/99 8.00 20.00
CBGH Grant Hill/99 25.00 60.00
CBHI Grant Hill/99 25.00 60.00
CBJA LeBron James/23 1,500.00 3,000.00
CBJL Jerry Lucas/99 12.00 30.00
CBJO Larry Johnson/99 12.00 30.00
CBJW James Worthy/99 12.00 30.00
CBKS Keith Smart/99 8.00 20.00
CBLE LeBron James/23 1,500.00 3,000.00
CBLJ LeBron James/23 1,500.00 3,000.00
CBMJ Michael Jordan/23 250.00 500.00
CBSN Shabazz Napier/99 6.00 15.00
CBSP Sam Perkins/99 8.00 20.00

2014-15 Upper Deck Lettermen Home Court Stars

HSAG Aaron Gordon 5.00 12.00
HSAH Anfernee Hardaway 4.00 10.00
HSAL Allan Houston 1.50 4.00
HSBW Bill Walton 2.50 6.00
HSDR David Robinson 3.00 8.00
HSGH Grant Hill 2.50 6.00
HSHO Hakeem Olajuwon 3.00 8.00
HSJA LeBron James 12.00 30.00
HSJE Julius Erving 4.00 10.00
HSJO Magic Johnson 6.00 15.00
HSJW James Worthy 2.50 6.00
HSLB Larry Bird 6.00 15.00
HSLJ Larry Johnson 2.00 5.00
HSMJ Michael Jordan 12.00 30.00
HSNS Nik Stauskas 1.00 2.50
HSSF Sleepy Floyd 1.25 3.00
HSSO Shaquille O'Neal 6.00 15.00
HSZL Zach LaVine 6.00 15.00

2014-15 Upper Deck Lettermen Home Court Stars Autographs

LACK OF PRICING DUE TO MARKET INFO
EXCHANGE DEADLINE 11/13/2016
HS-AG Aaron Gordon 12.00 30.00
HSAH Anfernee Hardaway 20.00 50.00
HSAL Allan Houston 6.00 15.00
HSBW Bill Walton 10.00 25.00
HSHO Hakeem Olajuwon 15.00 40.00
HSJA LeBron James 1,000.00 2,000.00
HSNS Nik Stauskas 4.00 10.00
HSSF Sleepy Floyd 5.00 12.00
HSZL Zach LaVine 12.00 30.00

2014-15 Upper Deck Lettermen Legendary Letterman Autographs

STATED PRINT RUN B/WN 9-245 COPIES PER
NO PRICING ON QTY 15 OR LESS
LACK OF PRICING DUE TO MARKET INFO
EXCHANGE DEADLINE 11/13/2016
LLAH Allan Houston/180 10.00 25.00
LLAM Antonio McDyess/175 8.00 20.00
LLCL Christian Laettner/40 25.00 60.00
LLDH Derek Harper/200 8.00 20.00
LLDN Vinny Del Negro/70 8.00 20.00
LLDW Dominique Wilkins/21 15.00 40.00
LLEP Eric Piatkowski/200 6.00 15.00
LLJL Jerry Lucas/27 12.00 30.00
LLJO Michael Jordan/195 300.00 600.00
LLJS Jerry Stackhouse/195 12.00 30.00
LLKS Keith Smart/245 6.00 15.00
LLLJ LeBron James/75 1,500.00 3,000.00
LLLO Lute Olson/35 75.00 200.00
LLRI Doc Rivers/27 12.00 30.00
LLRT Reggie Theus/40 8.00 20.00
LLSA John Salley/33 12.00 30.00
LLSF Sleepy Floyd/100 8.00 20.00
LLSP Sam Perkins/195 15.00 40.00

2014-15 Upper Deck Lettermen Monumental Logo Patches

STATED PRINT RUN B/WN 210-300 COPIES PER
MLAG Aaron Gordon/15 20.00 50.00
MLBR Bill Russell/30 12.00 30.00
MLDR David Robinson/15 12.00 30.00
MLER Julius Erving/30 15.00 40.00
MLGH Grant Hill/15 20.00 50.00
MLHO Hakeem Olajuwon/15 15.00 40.00
MLJH James Harden/15 15.00 40.00
MLJO Michael Jordan/15 40.00 100.00
MLKM Karl Malone/15 20.00 50.00
MLLA Larry Johnson/15 15.00 40.00
MLLB Larry Bird/30 25.00 60.00
MLLJ LeBron James/15 50.00 120.00
MLSO Shaquille O'Neal/15 12.00 30.00
MLWO James Worthy/15 15.00 40.00

2014-15 Upper Deck Lettermen Retired Numbers

STATED PRINT RUN 72 SER.#'d SETS
RNBR Bill Russell 10.00 25.00
RNJA LeBron James 25.00 60.00
RNJE Julius Erving 8.00 20.00
RNJO Michael Jordan 30.00 80.00
RNKM Karl Malone 6.00 15.00
RNLB Larry Bird 12.00 30.00
RNMJ Magic Johnson 12.00 30.00
RNSO Shaquille O'Neal 10.00 25.00
RNWO James Worthy 5.00 12.00

2014-15 Upper Deck Lettermen Rookie Premier Letterman Autographs

STATED PRINT RUN B/WN 120-350 COPIES PER
EXCHANGE DEADLINE 11/13/2016
RLAG Aaron Gordon/25 20.00 50.00
RLAP Adreian Payne/25 15.00 40.00
RLCC Clint Capela/35 20.00 50.00
RLCE Cleanthony Early/25 6.00 15.00
RLCW C.J. Wilcox/35 6.00 15.00
RLDD DeAndre Daniels/65 6.00 15.00
RLDM Doug McDermott/25 20.00 50.00
RLDS Dario Saric/50 30.00 80.00
RLEP Elfrid Payton/10 10.00 25.00
RLGE Alessandro Gentile/50 6.00 15.00
RLGH Gary Harris/10 10.00 25.00
RLGR Glenn Robinson III/35 8.00 20.00
RLHA Joe Harris/50 10.00 25.00
RLJA Jordan Adams/50 6.00 15.00
RLJH Josh Huestis/15 6.00 15.00
RLJM James Michael McAdoo/25 6.00 15.00
RLJN Jusuf Nurkic/35 20.00 50.00
RLJY James Young/35 6.00 15.00
RLKA Kyle Anderson/50 15.00 40.00
RLMC Jordan McRae/35 6.00 15.00
RLMM Mitch McGary/35 6.00 15.00
RLNS Nik Stauskas/35 6.00 15.00
RLPH P.J. Hairston/25 6.00 15.00
RLPY Patric Young/50 6.00 15.00
RLRH Rodney Hood/75 15.00 40.00
RLSK Sean Kilpatrick/35 8.00 20.00
RLSN Shabazz Napier/50 8.00 20.00
RLTA Thanasis Antetokounmpo/50 12.00 30.00
RLTW T.J. Warren/35 10.00 25.00
RLZL Zach LaVine/50 25.00 60.00

2008-09 Upper Deck Lineage

COMP.SET w/o RCs (200) 20.00 40.00
1 Bill Russell 1.00 2.50
2 Sam Jones .40 1.00
3 Oscar Robertson .30 .75
4 Kareem Abdul-Jabbar .50 1.25
5 Julius Erving .75 2.00
6 George Gervin .50 1.25
7 Bill Walton .50 1.25
8 Robert Parish .30 .75
9 Larry Bird 1.00 2.50
10 Magic Johnson 1.00 2.50
11 Isiah Thomas .50 1.25
12 James Worthy .30 .75
13 Dominique Wilkins .50 1.25
14 Clyde Drexler .40 1.00
15 John Stockton .60 1.50
16 Hakeem Olajuwon .60 1.50
17 Michael Jordan 2.50 6.00
18 Tom Chambers .25 .60
19 Adrian Dantley .25 .60
20 David Robinson .60 1.50
21 Shaquille O'Neal 1.00 2.50
22 Alonzo Mourning .40 1.00
23 Jason Kidd .50 1.25
24 Grant Hill .50 1.25
25 Rasheed Wallace .40 1.00
26 Kevin Garnett .75 2.00
27 Bruce Bowen .25 .60
28 Steve Nash .60 1.50
29 Marcus Camby .25 .60
30 Derek Fisher .25 .60
31 Ben Wallace .40 1.00
32 Allen Iverson .60 1.50
33 Ray Allen .50 1.25
34 Brad Miller .25 .60
35 Kobe Bryant 2.50 6.00
36 Jermaine O'Neal .30 .75
37 Tim Duncan .75 2.00
38 Chauncey Billups .50 1.25
39 Tracy McGrady .50 1.25
40 Zydrunas Ilgauskas .25 .60
41 Javaris Crittenton .20 .50
42 Antawn Jamison .50 1.25
43 Vince Carter .60 1.50
44 Peja Stojakovic .30 .75
45 Paul Pierce .50 1.25
46 Mike Bibby .30 .75
47 Dirk Nowitzki .75 2.00
48 Rashard Lewis .25 .60
49 Al Harrington .25 .60
50 Andre Miller .25 .60
51 Wally Szczerbiak .25 .60
52 Jason Terry .25 .60
53 Richard Hamilton .30 .75
54 Shawn Marion .30 .75
55 Elton Brand .25 .60
56 Baron Davis .30 .75
57 Lamar Odom .25 .60
58 Corey Maggette .25 .60
59 Ron Artest .25 .60
60 Morris Peterson .20 .50
61 Desmond Mason .20 .50
62 Kenyon Martin .25 .60
63 Stephen Jackson .25 .60
64 Hedo Turkoglu .25 .60
65 Michael Redd .25 .60
66 Mike Miller .25 .60
67 Jamal Crawford .30 .75
68 Quentin Richardson .25 .60
69 Keyon Dooling .20 .50
70 DeShawn Stevenson .20 .50
71 Jamaal Tinsley .20 .50
72 Shane Battier .25 .60
73 Earl Watson .20 .50
74 Richard Jefferson .25 .60
75 Pau Gasol .40 1.00
76 Jason Richardson .30 .75
77 Andrei Kirilenko .25 .60
78 Joe Johnson .30 .75
79 Zach Randolph .25 .60
80 Gilbert Arenas .30 .75
81 Tony Parker .40 1.00
82 Gerald Wallace .25 .60
83 Tyson Chandler .25 .60
84 Eddy Curry .25 .60
85 Manu Ginobili .60 1.50
86 Marko Jaric .20 .50
87 Mehmet Okur .20 .50
88 John Salmons .20 .50
89 Tayshaun Prince .30 .75
90 Caron Butler .25 .60
91 Yao Ming .75 2.00
92 Mike Dunleavy .20 .50
93 Samuel Dalembert .20 .50
94 Carlos Boozer .25 .60
95 Chris Wilcox .20 .50
96 Nene .20 .50
97 Amare Stoudemire .30 .75
98 Steve Blake .20 .50
99 Luke Walton .25 .60
100 Josh Howard .25 .60
101 Keith Bogans .20 .50
102 Udonis Haslem .20 .50
103 David West .20 .50
104 Kirk Hinrich .25 .60
105 Kyle Korver .25 .60
106 Willie Green .20 .50
107 Dwyane Wade .60 1.50
108 Boris Diaw .25 .60
109 Chris Kaman .20 .50
110 Leandro Barbosa .25 .60
111 Mo Williams .25 .60
112 Chris Bosh .40 1.00
113 Carmelo Anthony .40 1.00
114 Kendrick Perkins .20 .50
115 LeBron James 2.50 6.00
116 Andres Nocioni .20 .50
117 Damien Wilkins .20 .50
118 Jameer Nelson .20 .50
119 Beno Udrih .20 .50
120 Chris Duhon .20 .50
121 Anderson Varejao .20 .50
122 Emeka Okafor .20 .50
123 Kevin Martin .25 .60
124 Devin Harris .20 .50
125 T.J. Ford .20 .50
126 Ben Gordon .25 .60
127 Andre Iguodala .25 .60
128 Sasha Vujacic .20 .50
129 Al Jefferson .20 .50
130 Luol Deng .25 .60
131 J.R. Smith .30 .75
132 Josh Smith .20 .50
133 Dwight Howard .40 1.00
134 Fabricio Oberto .20 .50
135 Jose Calderon .20 .50
136 Francisco Garcia .20 .50
137 Hakim Warrick .20 .50
138 Luther Head .20 .50
139 Jason Maxiell .20 .50
140 Danny Granger .25 .60
141 David Lee .25 .60
142 Chuck Hayes .20 .50
143 Jarrett Jack .25 .60
144 Raymond Felton .20 .50
145 Deron Williams .25 .60
146 Rashad McCants .20 .50
147 Andrew Bogut .25 .60
148 Brandon Bass .20 .50
149 Chris Paul .60 1.50
150 Shaun Livingston .20 .50
151 Monta Ellis .25 .60
152 Marvin Williams .20 .50
153 Louis Williams .25 .60
154 Martell Webster .20 .50
155 Andrew Bynum .25 .60
156 Randy Foye .30 .75
157 Shelden Williams .20 .50
158 Leon Powe .20 .50
159 Rodney Carney .20 .50
160 Jose Barea .40 1.00
161 Brandon Roy .20 .50
162 Josh Boone .20 .50
163 Ronnie Brewer .20 .50
164 LaMarcus Aldridge .25 .60
165 Andrea Bargnani .20 .50
166 Rajon Rondo .40 1.00
167 Daniel Gibson .20 .50
168 Kyle Lowry .20 .50
169 Sergio Rodriguez .20 .50
170 Tyrus Thomas .20 .50
171 Rudy Gay .30 .75
172 Jordan Farmar .20 .50
173 Luis Scola .20 .50
174 Jamario Moon .20 .50
175 Carl Landry .20 .50
176 Al Thornton .20 .50
177 C.J. Watson .20 .50
178 Adam Morrison .20 .50
179 Acie Law .20 .50
180 Morris Almond .20 .50
181 Joakim Noah .30 .75
182 Nick Young .20 .50
183 Arron Afflalo .20 .50
184 Jared Dudley .20 .50
185 Glen Davis .20 .50
186 Corey Brewer .25 .60
187 Marco Belinelli .20 .50
188 Ramon Sessions .20 .50
189 Rodney Stuckey .20 .50
190 Al Horford .30 .75
191 Jeff Green .25 .60
192 Sean Williams .20 .50
193 Daequan Cook .20 .50
194 Julian Wright .30 .75
195 Brandan Wright .20 .50
196 Mike Conley Jr. .25 .60
197 Yi Jianlian .40 1.00
198 Thaddeus Young .25 .60
199 Kevin Durant 1.25 3.00
200 Greg Oden .20 .50
201 Derrick Rose RC 3.00 8.00
202 Michael Beasley RC .75 2.00
203 O.J. Mayo RC .60 1.50
204 Russell Westbrook RC 12.00 30.00
205 Kevin Love RC 1.50 4.00
206 Danilo Gallinari RC 1.25 3.00
207 Eric Gordon RC 1.25 3.00
208 Joe Alexander RC .50 1.25
209 D.J. Augustin RC .75 2.00
210 Brook Lopez RC 1.00 2.50
211 Jerryd Bayless RC .60 1.50
212 Jason Thompson RC .50 1.25
213 Brandon Rush RC .50 1.25
214 Anthony Randolph RC .50 1.25
215 Robin Lopez RC .60 1.50
216 Marreese Speights RC .60 1.50
217 Roy Hibbert RC .60 1.50
218 J.J. Hickson RC .60 1.50
219 Ryan Anderson RC .60 1.50
220 George Hill RC .75 2.00
221 Darrell Arthur RC .50 1.25
222 Donte Greene RC .50 1.25
223 D.J. White RC .50 1.25
224 J.R. Giddens RC .50 1.25
225 Walter Sharpe RC .50 1.25
226 Mario Chalmers RC .75 2.00
227 Sonny Weems RC .50 1.25
228 Chris Douglas-Roberts RC .50 1.25
229 Sean Singletary RC .50 1.25
230 Luc Richard Mbah A Moute RC .60 1.50
231 Bill Walker RC .50 1.25
232 Marc Gasol RC 1.50 4.00
233 Rudy Fernandez RC .60 1.50

2008-09 Upper Deck Lineage SE

*1-200 VETS: 1.25X TO 3X BASE HI
*201-233 ROOKIES: .6X TO 1.5X BASE HI

2008-09 Upper Deck Lineage 15,000 Point Club

COMBINED AUTO ODDS 1:12
15AD Adrian Dantley 6.00 15.00
15AE Alex English 6.00 15.00
15AG Artis Gilmore 6.00 15.00
15BA Rick Barry 10.00 25.00
15GG George Gervin 8.00 20.00
15GR Glen Rice 6.00 15.00
15HO Hakeem Olajuwon 10.00 25.00
15KA Kareem Abdul-Jabbar 40.00 100.00
15KG Kevin Garnett 40.00 75.00
15MJ Michael Jordan 300.00 500.00
15RP Robert Parish 6.00 15.00
15SJ Sam Jones 10.00 25.00
15TC Tom Chambers 6.00 15.00
15VC Vince Carter 30.00 60.00

2008-09 Upper Deck Lineage Collection

COMBINED AUTO ODDS 1:12
LCAD Adrian Dantley 5.00 12.00
LCAM Alonzo Mourning 150.00 300.00
LCBA B.J. Armstrong 6.00 15.00
LCBD Brad Daugherty 6.00 15.00
LCDR David Robinson 40.00 100.00
LCGR Glen Rice 6.00 15.00
LCHG Horace Grant 20.00 50.00
LCHO Hakeem Olajuwon 25.00 60.00
LCIT Isiah Thomas 10.00 25.00
LCJO Michael Jordan 300.00 500.00
LCJS John Stockton 125.00 250.00
LCMB Muggsy Bogues 6.00 15.00
LCME Mark Eaton 5.00 12.00
LCMJ Magic Johnson 30.00 60.00
LCMM Moses Malone 8.00 20.00
LCMP Mark Price 12.00 30.00
LCSA John Salley 6.00 15.00
LCSP Sam Perkins 8.00 20.00
LCSW Spud Webb 6.00 15.00
LCTC Terry Cummings 5.00 12.00
LCTO Tom Chambers 5.00 12.00
LCVD Vlade Divac 6.00 15.00

2008-09 Upper Deck Lineage Flight Team

COMBINED AUTO ODDS 1:12
FTAI Andre Iguodala 6.00 15.00
FTAT Al Thornton 8.00 20.00
FTBD Baron Davis 15.00 30.00
FTDH Dwight Howard 20.00 40.00
FTDM Desmond Mason 5.00 12.00
FTDS DeShawn Stevenson 5.00 12.00
FTGG Gerald Green 5.00 12.00
FTJA Joe Alexander 5.00 12.00
FTJR J.R. Giddens 5.00 12.00
FTKB Kobe Bryant 500.00 1,000.00
FTLJ LeBron James 1,000.00 2,000.00
FTLM Luc Richard Mbah A Moute 5.00 12.00
FTRG Rudy Gay 6.00 15.00
FTRJ Richard Jefferson 5.00 12.00
FTSM J.R. Smith 8.00 20.00
FTSW Sean Williams 5.00 12.00
FTTP Tayshaun Prince 5.00 12.00
FTWE Sonny Weems 5.00 12.00

2008-09 Upper Deck Lineage Mr. June

COMPLETE SET (23) 30.00 60.00
COMMON CARD 1.50 4.00

2008-09 Upper Deck Lineage Rookie Standouts

COMPLETE SET (54) 30.00 60.00
RS1 Derrick Rose 3.00 8.00
RS2 Michael Beasley .75 2.00
RS3 O.J. Mayo .60 1.50
RS4 Russell Westbrook 4.00 10.00
RS5 Kevin Love 1.50 4.00
RS6 Danilo Gallinari 1.25 3.00
RS7 Eric Gordon 1.25 3.00
RS8 Joe Alexander .50 1.25
RS9 D.J. Augustin .75 2.00
RS10 Brook Lopez 1.00 2.50
RS11 Jerryd Bayless .60 1.50
RS12 Jason Thompson .50 1.25
RS13 Brandon Rush .50 1.25
RS14 Anthony Randolph .50 1.25
RS15 Robin Lopez .60 1.50
RS16 Marreese Speights .60 1.50
RS17 Roy Hibbert .60 1.50
RS18 Luc Richard Mbah A Moute .60 1.50
RS19 Mario Chalmers .75 2.00
RS20 Javale McGee .75 2.00
RS21 Anthony Morrow .75 2.00
RS22 Darrell Arthur .60 1.50
RS23 Nicolas Batum 1.00 2.50
RS24 Ryan Anderson .60 1.50
RS25 Bobby Brown .50 1.25
RS26 J.J. Hickson .50 1.25
RS27 Sun Yue 1.00 2.50
RS28 DeMarcus Nelson .50 1.25
RS29 Courtney Lee .60 1.50
RS30 Kosta Koufos .50 1.25
RS31 Donte Greene .50 1.25
RS32 Mike Taylor .50 1.25
RS33 Roko Leni Ukic .75 2.00
RS34 Anthony Tolliver .50 1.25
RS35 Darnell Jackson .50 1.25
RS36 Alexis Ajinca .50 1.25
RS37 Goran Dragic 20.00 50.00
RS38 Chris Douglas-Roberts .50 1.25
RS39 Sean Singletary .50 1.25
RS40 Kyle Weaver .50 1.25
RS41 Bill Walker .50 1.25
RS42 DeAndre Jordan 1.00 2.50
RS43 Rob Kurz .50 1.25
RS44 Rudy Fernandez .60 1.50
RS45 George Hill .75 2.00
RS46 Greg Oden .50 1.25
RS47 Marc Gasol 1.50 4.00
RS48 Louis Amundson .50 1.25
RS49 Nathan Jawai .75 2.00
RS50 Othello Hunter .75 2.00
RS51 Walter Sharpe .50 1.25

RS52 Joey Dorsey .50 1.25
RS53 J.R. Giddens .50 1.25
RS54 Jawad Williams .75 2.00

2008-09 Upper Deck Lineage SE Die Cut Autographs

COMBINED AUTO ODDS 1:12
2 Sam Jones 15.00 40.00
3 Oscar Robertson 50.00 125.00
4 Kareem Abdul-Jabbar 40.00 80.00
5 Julius Erving 50.00 120.00
6 George Gervin 8.00 20.00
8 Robert Parish 6.00 15.00
10 Magic Johnson 30.00 80.00
12 James Worthy 40.00 80.00
13 Dominique Wilkins 40.00 100.00
17 Michael Jordan 1,500.00 3,000.00
18 Tom Chambers 5.00 12.00
19 Adrian Dantley 4.00 10.00
20 David Robinson 50.00 125.00
23 Jason Kidd 20.00 50.00
26 Kevin Garnett 50.00 100.00
27 Bruce Bowen 4.00 10.00
28 Steve Nash 30.00 60.00
30 Derek Fisher 6.00 15.00
33 Ray Allen 20.00 40.00
36 Jermaine O'Neal 12.00 30.00
38 Chauncey Billups 8.00 20.00
41 Javaris Crittenton 4.00 10.00
43 Vince Carter 30.00 60.00
45 Paul Pierce 30.00 60.00
49 Al Harrington 4.00 10.00
57 Lamar Odom 6.00 15.00
58 Corey Maggette 6.00 15.00
59 Ron Artest 6.00 15.00
65 Michael Redd 4.00 10.00
68 Quentin Richardson 4.00 10.00
74 Richard Jefferson 4.00 10.00
78 Joe Johnson 6.00 15.00
84 Eddy Curry 4.00 10.00
89 Tayshaun Prince 4.00 10.00
90 Caron Butler 15.00 40.00
94 Carlos Boozer 5.00 12.00
97 Amare Stoudemire 15.00 30.00
100 Josh Howard 20.00 50.00
103 David West 4.00 10.00
105 Kyle Korver 4.00 10.00
108 Boris Diaw 4.00 10.00
109 Chris Kaman 4.00 10.00
110 Leandro Barbosa 4.00 10.00
112 Chris Bosh 20.00 40.00
115 LeBron James 1,250.00 2,500.00
118 Jameer Nelson 4.00 10.00
119 Beno Udrih 4.00 10.00
120 Chris Duhon 4.00 10.00
121 Anderson Varejao 5.00 12.00
126 Ben Gordon 6.00 15.00
127 Andre Iguodala 6.00 15.00
128 Sasha Vujacic 6.00 15.00
129 Al Jefferson 5.00 12.00
130 Luol Deng 4.00 10.00
131 J.R. Smith 6.00 15.00
133 Dwight Howard 20.00 40.00
136 Francisco Garcia 4.00 10.00
139 Jason Maxiell 4.00 10.00
140 Danny Granger 6.00 15.00
141 David Lee 6.00 15.00
143 Jarrett Jack 4.00 10.00
144 Raymond Felton 4.00 10.00
145 Deron Williams 8.00 20.00
148 Brandon Bass 4.00 10.00
149 Chris Paul 60.00 150.00
150 Shaun Livingston 4.00 10.00
152 Marvin Williams 4.00 10.00
153 Louis Williams 4.00 10.00
155 Andrew Bynum 20.00 40.00
156 Randy Foye 4.00 10.00
157 Shelden Williams 4.00 10.00
161 Brandon Roy 10.00 25.00
162 Josh Boone 4.00 10.00
163 Ronnie Brewer 5.00 12.00
165 Andrea Bargnani 5.00 12.00
166 Rajon Rondo 8.00 20.00
167 Daniel Gibson 6.00 15.00
168 Kyle Lowry 4.00 10.00
170 Tyrus Thomas 8.00 20.00
171 Rudy Gay 5.00 12.00
172 Jordan Farmar 6.00 15.00
173 Luis Scola 4.00 10.00
175 Carl Landry 4.00 10.00
176 Al Thornton 6.00 15.00
180 Morris Almond 4.00 10.00
183 Arron Afflalo 4.00 10.00
184 Jared Dudley 4.00 10.00
185 Glen Davis 6.00 15.00
188 Ramon Sessions 5.00 12.00
189 Rodney Stuckey 6.00 15.00
191 Jeff Green 6.00 15.00
192 Sean Williams 4.00 10.00
193 Daequan Cook 4.00 10.00
194 Julian Wright 4.00 10.00
199 Kevin Durant 100.00 200.00
201 Derrick Rose 100.00 200.00
203 O.J. Mayo 10.00 25.00
204 Russell Westbrook 150.00 400.00
205 Kevin Love 40.00 100.00
206 Danilo Gallinari 10.00 25.00
207 Eric Gordon 15.00 40.00
208 Joe Alexander 3.00 8.00
209 D.J. Augustin 5.00 12.00
210 Brook Lopez 6.00 15.00
211 Jerryd Bayless 4.00 10.00
212 Jason Thompson 3.00 8.00
213 Brandon Rush 3.00 8.00
214 Anthony Randolph 10.00 25.00
215 Robin Lopez 4.00 10.00
216 Marreese Speights 4.00 10.00
217 Roy Hibbert 4.00 10.00
218 J.J. Hickson 3.00 8.00
219 Ryan Anderson 4.00 10.00
220 George Hill 5.00 12.00
221 Darrell Arthur 4.00 10.00
222 Donte Greene 3.00 8.00
223 D.J. White 3.00 8.00
224 J.R. Giddens 3.00 8.00
225 Walter Sharpe 3.00 8.00
226 Mario Chalmers 5.00 12.00
227 Sonny Weems 3.00 8.00
228 Chris Douglas-Roberts 3.00 8.00
229 Sean Singletary 5.00 12.00
230 Luc Richard Mbah A Moute 5.00 12.00
231 Bill Walker 10.00 25.00
233 Rudy Fernandez 10.00 25.00

2014-15 Upper Deck March Madness Collection

STATED SP ODDS 1:1 PACK
AC1 A.C. Green 2.00 5.00
AC2 A.C. Green SP 2.00 5.00
AE1 Alex English SP 2.50 6.00
AG1 Aaron Gordon 6.00 15.00
AH1 Anfernee Hardaway 3.00 8.00
AH2 Anfernee Hardaway SP 3.00 8.00
AI1 Allen Iverson 5.00 12.00
AI2 Allen Iverson 5.00 12.00
AI3 Allen Iverson SP 5.00 12.00
AI4 Allen Iverson SP 5.00 12.00
AM1 Alonzo Mourning 3.00 8.00
AM2 Alonzo Mourning SP 3.00 8.00
AN1 Antonio McDyess 1.50 4.00
AN2 Antonio McDyess 1.50 4.00
AP1 Adreian Payne 1.25 3.00
AW1 Antoine Walker 1.50 4.00
AW2 Antoine Walker SP 1.50 4.00
AW3 Antoine Walker SP 1.50 4.00
BD1 Brad Daugherty 1.50 4.00
BD2 Brad Daugherty 1.50 4.00
BD3 Brad Daugherty SP 1.50 4.00
BD4 Brad Daugherty SP 1.50 4.00
BH1 Bobby Hurley 2.00 5.00
BH2 Bobby Hurley SP 2.00 5.00
BH3 Bobby Hurley SP 2.00 5.00
BK1 Bo Kimble 1.50 4.00
BL1 Bill Laimbeer 2.00 5.00
BL2 Bill Laimbeer SP 2.00 5.00
BO1 Bo Outlaw 1.25 3.00
BR1 Bill Russell SP 6.00 15.00
BR2 Bill Russell SP 6.00 15.00
BU1 Buck Williams 2.00 5.00
BW1 Bill Walton 3.00 8.00
BW2 Bill Walton 3.00 8.00
BW3 Bill Walton SP 3.00 8.00
BW4 Bill Walton SP 3.00 8.00
BY1 Byron Scott 2.00 5.00
CC1 Calbert Cheaney 1.25 3.00
CC2 Calbert Cheaney 1.25 3.00
CC3 Calbert Cheaney SP 1.25 3.00
CE1 Cleanthony Early SP 1.25 3.00
CL1 Christian Laettner 2.00 5.00
CL2 Christian Laettner 2.00 5.00
CL3 Christian Laettner 2.00 5.00
CL4 Christian Laettner SP 2.00 5.00
CL5 Christian Laettner SP 2.00 5.00
CL6 Christian Laettner SP 2.00 5.00
CM1 Cheryl Miller 2.00 5.00
CM2 Cheryl Miller SP 2.00 5.00
CW1 Corliss Williamson 1.25 3.00
CW2 Corliss Williamson SP 1.25 3.00
DC1 Dave Cowens SP 2.50 6.00
DD1 DeAndre Daniels 1.25 3.00
DH1 Derek Harper 1.50 4.00
DH2 Derek Harper SP 1.50 4.00
DM1 Danny Manning 1.50 4.00
DM2 Danny Manning 1.50 4.00
DM3 Danny Manning SP 1.50 4.00
DM4 Danny Manning SP 1.50 4.00
DM5 Danny Manning SP 1.50 4.00
DO1 Doc Rivers SP 2.00 5.00
DR1 David Robinson 4.00 10.00
DR2 David Robinson SP 4.00 10.00
DR3 David Robinson SP 4.00 10.00
DS1 Detlef Schrempf 2.00 5.00
DT1 David Thompson 2.00 5.00
DT2 David Thompson 2.00 5.00
DT3 David Thompson SP 2.00 5.00
EH1 Elvin Hayes 3.00 8.00
EH2 Elvin Hayes 3.00 8.00
EP1 Eric Piatkowski 1.25 3.00
FL1 Fat Lever SP 2.00 5.00
GH1 Grant Hill 3.00 8.00
GH1 Gary Harris SP 2.00 5.00
GH2 Grant Hill 3.00 8.00
GH3 Grant Hill SP 3.00 8.00
GH4 Grant Hill SP 3.00 8.00
GH5 Grant Hill SP 3.00 8.00
GH6 Grant Hill SP 3.00 8.00
GH7 Grant Hill SP 3.00 8.00
GL1 Glenn Robinson 1.50 4.00
GL2 Glenn Robinson SP 1.50 4.00
GN1 Glenn Robinson III SP 1.50 4.00
GR1 Glen Rice 2.00 5.00
GR2 Glen Rice SP 2.00 5.00
GR3 Glen Rice SP 2.00 5.00
HA1 James Harden 4.00 10.00
HG1 Horace Grant SP 2.00 5.00
HM1 Harold Miner 2.00 5.00
HM2 Harold Miner SP 2.00 5.00
JA1 Jordan Adams 1.25 3.00
JH1 John Havlicek 4.00 10.00
JH2 John Havlicek SP 4.00 10.00
JH3 John Havlicek SP 4.00 10.00
JK1 Jason Kidd 3.00 8.00
JK2 Jason Kidd SP 3.00 8.00
JL1 Jerry Lucas 2.50 6.00
JL2 Jerry Lucas 2.50 6.00
JL3 Jerry Lucas SP 2.50 6.00
JM1 Jamal Mashburn 1.50 4.00
JM2 Jamal Mashburn 1.50 4.00
JM3 Jamal Mashburn SP 1.50 4.00
JS1 Jerry Stackhouse 1.50 4.00
JS2 Jerry Stackhouse 1.50 4.00
JS3 Jerry Stackhouse SP 1.50 4.00
JT1 Jerry Tarkanian SP 2.00 5.00
JT2 Jerry Tarkanian SP 2.00 5.00
JV1 Jim Valvano SP 1.50 4.00
JV2 Jim Valvano SP 1.50 4.00
JW1 Jerry West 5.00 12.00
JW2 Jerry West 5.00 12.00
JW3 Jerry West SP 5.00 12.00
JY1 James Young 1.25 3.00
KA1 Kenny Anderson 1.50 4.00
KG1 Kendall Gill 2.00 5.00
KG2 Kendall Gill SP 2.00 5.00
KS1 Keith Smart SP 2.00 5.00
KS2 Keith Smart SP 2.00 5.00
KY1 Kyle Anderson 2.00 5.00
LB1 Larry Bird 3.00 8.00
LB2 Larry Bird 3.00 8.00
LB3 Larry Bird SP 3.00 8.00
LE1 LaPhonso Ellis SP 1.25 3.00
LJ1 Larry Johnson 2.50 6.00
LJ2 Larry Johnson 2.50 6.00
LJ3 Larry Johnson SP 2.50 6.00
LO1 Lute Olson 2.50 6.00
LS1 Lonnie Shelton 1.50 4.00
MA1 Donyell Marshall 1.25 3.00
MA2 Donyell Marshall SP 1.25 3.00
MC1 Doug McDermott SP 2.00 5.00
MG1 Magic Johnson 3.00 8.00
MG2 Magic Johnson 3.00 8.00
MG3 Magic Johnson SP 3.00 8.00
MG4 Magic Johnson SP 3.00 8.00
MJ1 Michael Jordan 3.00 8.00
MJ2 Michael Jordan 3.00 8.00
MJ3 Michael Jordan 3.00 8.00
MJ4 Michael Jordan SP 3.00 8.00
MJ5 Michael Jordan SP 3.00 8.00
MJ6 Michael Jordan SP 3.00 8.00
MJ7 Michael Jordan SP 3.00 8.00
MM1 Mitch McGary SP 1.25 3.00
MR1 Micheal Ray Richardson 1.50 4.00
NA1 Swen Nater SP 1.25 3.00
NE1 Nick Van Exel 2.00 5.00
NE2 Nick Van Exel SP 2.00 5.00
NS1 Nik Stauskas SP 1.25 3.00
PA1 Elfrid Payton SP 2.00 5.00
PE1 Pervis Ellison 1.25 3.00
PE2 Pervis Ellison 1.25 3.00
PE3 Pervis Ellison SP 1.25 3.00
PY1 Patric Young 1.25 3.00
RE1 Bryant Reeves SP 1.25 3.00
RH1 Robert Horry 2.00 5.00
RH2 Robert Horry SP 2.00 5.00
RR1 Rajon Rondo 2.50 6.00
RR2 Rajon Rondo SP 2.50 6.00
RT1 Reggie Theus 1.50 4.00
RT2 Reggie Theus SP 1.50 4.00
SA1 John Salley 1.50 4.00
SA2 John Salley SP 1.50 4.00
SB1 Shane Battier 1.50 4.00
SB2 Shane Battier 1.50 4.00
SB3 Shane Battier SP 1.50 4.00
SB4 Shane Battier SP 1.50 4.00
SB5 Shane Battier SP 1.50 4.00
SC1 Stephen Curry 15.00 40.00
SC2 Stephen Curry SP 15.00 40.00
SE1 Sean Elliott 2.00 5.00
SE2 Sean Elliott SP 2.00 5.00
SE3 Sean Elliott SP 2.00 5.00
SF1 Sleepy Floyd SP 1.50 4.00
SK1 Sean Kilpatrick 1.25 3.00
SM1 Joe Smith 1.50 4.00
SM2 Joe Smith 1.50 4.00
SM3 Joe Smith SP 1.50 4.00
SN1 Shabazz Napier 1.50 4.00
SN2 Shabazz Napier SP 1.50 4.00
SO1 Shaquille O'Neal 2.00 5.00
SO2 Shaquille O'Neal 2.00 5.00
SO3 Shaquille O'Neal SP 2.00 5.00
SP1 Sam Perkins 1.50 4.00
SP2 Sam Perkins SP 1.50 4.00
SP3 Sam Perkins SP 1.50 4.00
ST1 Stacey Augmon 1.25 3.00
ST2 Stacey Augmon 1.25 3.00
ST3 Stacey Augmon SP 1.25 3.00
SW1 Spud Webb 2.00 5.00
TH1 Tim Hardaway 2.50 6.00
TW1 T.J. Warren SP 2.00 5.00
VN1 Vinny Del Negro 1.50 4.00
VN2 Vinny Del Negro SP 1.50 4.00
WI1 Jay Williams 1.50 4.00
WI2 Jay Williams 1.50 4.00
WI3 Jay Williams SP 1.50 4.00
WO1 James Worthy 3.00 8.00
WO2 James Worthy 3.00 8.00
WO3 James Worthy SP 3.00 8.00
ZL1 Zach LaVine SP 8.00 20.00

2014-15 Upper Deck March Madness Collection Sepia

*SEPIA: .8X TO 2X BASE HI
STATED ODDS 1:6 PACKS

2014-15 Upper Deck March Madness Collection Autographs Exclusives

OVERALL ODDS 1:144 PACKS
GROUP A ODDS 1:24,192 PACKS
GROUP B ODDS 1:3,456 PACKS
GROUP C ODDS 1:1,613 PACKS
GROUP D ODDS 1:453 PACKS
GROUP E ODDS 1:233 PACKS
EXCHANGE DEADLINE 1/8/2017
KAA Kenny Anderson E 3.00 8.00
SPA Sam Perkins E 12.00 30.00
STA Stacey Augmon D 3.00 8.00

2014-15 Upper Deck March Madness Collection Bracketology

STATED ODDS 1:4 PACKS
AR Arkansas Razorbacks 3.00 8.00
AW Arizona Wildcats 3.00 10.00
AZ Akron Zips 3.00 8.00
BB Belmont Bruins 3.00 8.00
BE Baylor Bears 3.00 8.00
BF Colorado Buffaloes 3.00 8.00
BI Cornell Big Red 3.00 8.00
BU Butler Bulldogs 3.00 10.00
C4 Charlotte 49ers 3.00 8.00
CB Cincinnati Bearcats 3.00 8.00
CB Creighton Bluejays 3.00 8.00
CH Connecticut Huskies 3.00 10.00
CT Clemson Tigers 3.00 8.00
DD Drexel Dragons 3.00 8.00
DW Davidson Wildcats 3.00 8.00
EC East Carolina Pirates 3.00 8.00
FG Florida Gators 3.00 8.00
GH Georgetown Hoyas 3.00 10.00
GW George Washington Colonials 3.00 8.00
IH Iowa Hawkeyes 3.00 8.00
IH Indiana Hoosiers 3.00 8.00
KJ Kansas Jayhawks 8.00 20.00
KW Kentucky Wildcats 20.00 50.00
LC Louisville Cardinals 3.00 8.00
MH Miami Hurricanes 3.00 8.00
MR Mississippi Rebels 3.00 10.00
MT Memphis Tigers 3.00 8.00
MW Michigan Wolverines 3.00 8.00
ND Notre Dame Fighting Irish 3.00 10.00
NW Northwestern Wildcats 3.00 8.00
OB Ohio Bobcats 3.00 8.00
OD Oregon Ducks 3.00 8.00
OS Oklahoma Sooners 3.00 8.00
PB Purdue Boilermakers 3.00 8.00
PF Providence Friars 3.00 8.00
PP Pittsburgh Panthers 3.00 10.00
RS Richmond Spiders 3.00 8.00
SO Syracuse Orange 3.00 8.00
TL Texas Longhorns 3.00 8.00
TO Temple Owls 3.00 8.00
TV Tennessee Volunteers 3.00 8.00
UB UCLA Bruins 3.00 10.00
UR UNLV Rebels 3.00 10.00
VC Virginia Cavaliers 6.00 15.00
VR VCU Rams 3.00 10.00
VW Villanova Wildcats 6.00 15.00
WB Wisconsin Badgers 10.00 25.00
WC Wildcard 50.00 120.00
WH Washington Huskies 3.00 8.00
ACT Alabama Crimson Tide 3.00 8.00
ASS Arizona State Sun Devils 3.00 8.00
BCE Boston College Eagles 3.00 8.00
BSB Boise State Broncos 3.00 10.00
BYU BYU Cougars 3.00 8.00
CFK Central Florida Knights 3.00 8.00
CGB California Golden Bears 3.00 8.00
DBD Duke Blue Devils 20.00 50.00
FSB Fresno State Bulldogs 3.00 8.00
FSS Florida State Seminoles 3.00 8.00
GB1 Gonzaga Bulldogs 3.00 10.00
GB2 Georgia Bulldogs 3.00 8.00
GMP George Mason Patriots 3.00 8.00
GTY Georgia Tech Yellow Jackets 3.00 8.00
IFI Illinois Fighting Illini 3.00 8.00
ISC Iowa State Cyclones 3.00 10.00
KSW Kansas State Wildcats 3.00 10.00
LSU LSU Tigers 3.00 8.00
MGE Marquette Golden Eagles 3.00 8.00
MGG Minnesota Golden Gophers 3.00 8.00
MSS Michigan State Spartans 3.00 10.00
MTE Maryland Terrapins 3.00 8.00
MTI Missouri Tigers 3.00 8.00
MTS Middle Tennessee State Blue Raiders 3.00 8.00
NCS North Carolina State Wolfpack 3.00 8.00
NCT North Carolina Tar Heels 8.00 20.00
NML New Mexico Lobos 3.00 8.00
NMS New Mexico State Aggies 3.00 8.00
ODM Old Dominion Monarchs 3.00 8.00
OSB Ohio State Buckeyes 3.00 8.00
OSC Oklahoma State Cowboys 3.00 8.00
RIR Rhode Island Rams 3.00 8.00
SCG South Carolina Gamecocks 3.00 8.00
SDS San Diego State Aztecs 3.00 8.00
SJH Saint Joseph's Hawks 3.00 8.00
SJR St. John's Red Storm 3.00 8.00
SLB Saint Louis Billikens 3.00 8.00
SMG Southern Mississippi Golden Eagles 3.00 8.00
TAM Texas A&M Aggies 3.00 8.00
WSS Wichita State Shockers 3.00 10.00
WVM West Virginia Mountaineers 3.00 8.00

2014-15 Upper Deck March Madness Collection Most Outstanding Player Autographs

OVERALL ODDS 1:288 PACKS
GROUP A ODDS 1:5,498 PACKS
GROUP B ODDS 1:2,372 PACKS
GROUP C ODDS 1:1,234 PACKS
GROUP D ODDS 1:806 PACKS
EXCHANGE DEADLINE 1/8/2017
MOP7 Pervis Ellison D 12.00 30.00
MOP8 Keith Smart D 10.00 25.00
MOP11 Christian Laettner C 6.00 15.00
MOP12 Bobby Hurley C 20.00 50.00
MOP14 Shane Battier B 20.00 50.00
MOP15 S.Napier C EXCH 15.00 40.00

2014-15 Upper Deck March Madness Collection Tournament Champions Autographs

OVERALL ODDS 1:288 PACKS
GROUP A ODDS 1:17,280 PACKS
GROUP B ODDS 1:5,760 PACKS
GROUP C ODDS 1:1,592 PACKS
GROUP D ODDS 1:1,712 PACKS
EXCHANGE DEADLINE 1/8/2017
TC7 Sam Perkins E 6.00 15.00
TC13 Christian Laettner B 20.00 50.00
TC15 C.Williamson D EXCH 12.00 30.00
TC19 DeAndre Daniels E 6.00 15.00
TC20 S.Napier C EXCH 6.00 15.00

2014-15 Upper Deck March Madness Collection Tournament Stars Autographs

OVERALL ODDS 1:1,52 PACKS
GROUP A ODDS 1:30,240 PACKS
GROUP B ODDS 1:3,665 PACKS
GROUP C ODDS 1:2,520 PACKS
EXCHANGE DEADLINE 1/8/2017
DANW V.Del Negro/S.Webb C 6.00 15.00
DAWB J.Williams/S.Battier B 15.00 40.00

1999-00 Upper Deck MJ Master Collection

COMMON CARD (1-23) 60.00 150.00
STATED PRINT RUN 500 SERIAL #'d SETS

1999-00 Upper Deck MJ Master Collection Game Jerseys

COMMON CARD (MJGJ1-5) 500.00 1,000.00
STATED PRINT RUN 100 SETS

1999-00 Upper Deck MJ Master Collection Mystery Pack Inserts

PRINT RUNS LISTED BELOW
M1 M.Jordan FLR/54 150.00 300.00
MJGS1 M.Jordan Shoe/223 150.00 300.00
MJGU1 M.Jordan Uniform/200 150.00 300.00

1999-00 Upper Deck MJ Master Collection Signature Performances

COMMON CARD (MJ1-MJ10) 6,000.00 12,000.00
STATED PRINT RUN 50 SERIAL #'d SETS

1998 Upper Deck MJ Sticker Collection

COMPLETE SET (138) 25.00 50.00
COMMON STICKER (1-138) .60 1.50

1998 Upper Deck MJ Sticker Collection Stickers

COMPLETE SET (38) 6.00 15.00
COMMON STICKER (1-38) .60 1.50

1998 Upper Deck MJx

COMPLETE SET (135) 100.00 200.00
COMMON CARD (1-45) .20 .50
COMMON CARD (45-55) 5.00 12.00
COMMON CARD (56-65) 4.00 10.00
COMMON CARD (66-110) .20 .50
COMMON CARD (111-120) 2.50 6.00
COMMON CARD (121-130) .40 1.00
COMMON CARD (131-135) 6.00 15.00
A1 Michael Jordan AU/50 5,000.00 8,000.00
GC1 Michael Jordan Warmups 150.00 400.00
GC2 Michael Jordan Shoes 150.00 400.00

1998 Upper Deck MJx Live

COMMON CARD (1-30) 50.00 125.00

1998 Upper Deck MJx Timepieces Red

COMPLETE SET (90) 200.00 500.00
COMMON CARD 6.00 15.00

1998 Upper Deck MJx Timepieces Bronze

COMMON CARD 25.00 60.00

1998 Upper Deck MJx Timepieces Gold

COMMON CARD 125.00 300.00

1991-92 Upper Deck McDonald's/Paris

COMPLETE SET (11) 3.00 8.00
M1 Elden Campbell .40 1.00
M2 Vlade Divac .40 1.00
M3 A.C. Green .40 1.00
M4 Magic Johnson 2.50 6.00
M5 Sam Perkins .40 1.00
M6 Byron Scott .40 1.00
M7 Tony Smith .20 .50
M8 Terry Teagle .20 .50
M9 James Worthy .60 1.50
M10 Checklist .20 .50
NNO Byron Scott
James Worthy
A.C. Green
Magic Johnson
Sam Perkins
Vlade Divac 4.00 10.00
NNO Hologram Card .20 .50

1992-93 Upper Deck McDonald's

COMPLETE SET (103) 25.00 60.00
COMPLETE FACT.SET (103) 25.00 60.00
COMPLETE NAT.SET (50) 5.00 12.00
COMPLETE BOST SET (10) 3.00 8.00
COMPLETE CHI SET (12) 6.00 15.00
COMPLETE CLE SET (10) 1.50 4.00
COMPLETE LA SET (10) 3.00 8.00
COMPLETE ORL SET (10) 5.00 12.00
P1 Dominique Wilkins .40 1.00
P2 Reggie Lewis .40 1.00
P3 Kevin McHale .40 1.00
P4 Larry Johnson .40 1.00
P5 Michael Jordan 4.00 10.00
P6 Horace Grant .40 1.00
P7 Brad Daugherty .40 1.00
P8 Mark Price .40 1.00
P9 Derek Harper .30 .75
P10 Dikembe Mutombo .40 1.00
P11 Joe Dumars .40 1.00
P12 Isiah Thomas .40 1.00
P13 Tim Hardaway .40 1.00
P14 Chris Mullin .40 1.00
P15 Hakeem Olajuwon .40 1.00
P16 Otis Thorpe .30 .75
P17 Detlef Schrempf .30 .75
P18 Reggie Miller .40 1.00
P19 Ron Harper .40 1.00
P20 Danny Manning .30 .75
P21 James Worthy .40 1.00
P22 Sam Perkins .30 .75
P23 Rony Seikaly .30 .75
P24 Steve Smith .30 .75
P25 Alvin Robertson .30 .75
P26 Derrick Coleman .40 1.00
P27 Drazen Petrovic .40 1.00
P28 Patrick Ewing .40 1.00
P29 Scott Skiles .30 .75
P30 Hersey Hawkins .30 .75
P31 Dan Majerle .40 1.00
P32 Kevin Johnson .40 1.00
P33 Clyde Drexler .40 1.00
P34 Terry Porter .30 .75
P35 Spud Webb .40 1.00
P36 Antoine Carr .20 .50
P37 David Robinson .40 1.00
P38 Shawn Kemp .40 1.00
P39 Ricky Pierce .30 .75
P40 Karl Malone .40 1.00
P41 John Stockton .40 1.00
P42 Michael Adams .20 .50
P43 Shaquille O'Neal 1.50 4.00
P44 Alonzo Mourning .75 2.00
P45 Christian Laettner .40 1.00
P46 LaPhonso Ellis .20 .50
P47 Walt Williams .20 5.00
P48 Todd Day .20 .50
P49 Clarence Weatherspoon .20 .50
P50 Tom Gugliotta .30 .75
BT1 Dee Brown .20 .50
BT2 Sherman Douglas .20 .50
BT3 Rick Fox .25 .60
BT4 Kevin Gamble .20 .50
BT5 Joe Kleine .20 .50
BT6 Reggie Lewis .40 1.00
BT7 Xavier McDaniel .20 .50
BT8 Kevin McHale 1.00 2.50
BT9 Robert Parish .75 2.00
BT10 Ed Pinckney .20 .50
CH1 B.J. Armstrong .20 .50
CH2 Bill Cartwright .20 .50
CH3 Horace Grant .30 .75
CH4 Michael Jordan 5.00 12.00
CH5 Stacey King .20 .50
CH6 Rodney McCray .20 .50
CH7 John Paxson .20 .50
CH8 Will Perdue .20 .50
CH9 Scottie Pippen 1.50 4.00
CH10 Trent Tucker .20 .50
CH11 Corey Williams .20 .50
CH12 Scott Williams .20 .50
CL1 John Battle .20 .50
CL2 Terrell Brandon .40 1.00
CL3 Brad Daugherty .20 .50
CL4 Craig Ehlo .20 .50
CL5 Danny Ferry .20 .50
CL6 Larry Nance .30 .75
CL7 Mark Price .30 .75
CL8 Mike Sanders .20 .50
CL9 Gerald Wilkins .20 .50
CL10 Hot Rod Williams .20 .50
LA1 Elden Campbell .30 .75
LA2 Duane Cooper .20 .50
LA3 Vlade Divac .40 1.00
LA4 James Edwards .20 .50
LA5 A.C. Green .40 1.00
LA6 Anthony Peeler .40 1.00
LA7 Sam Perkins .40 1.00
LA8 Byron Scott .40 1.00
LA9 Sedale Threatt .20 .50
LA10 James Worthy .75 2.00
OR1 Nick Anderson .40 1.00
OR2 Anthony Bowie .20 .50
OR3 Terry Catledge .20 .50
OR4 Greg Kite .20 .50
OR5 Shaquille O'Neal 4.00 10.00
OR6 Jerry Reynolds .20 .50
OR7 Donald Royal .20 .50
OR8 Dennis Scott .40 1.00
OR9 Scott Skiles .30 .75
OR10 Jeff Turner .20 .50
NNO Michael Jordan Holo 5.00 12.00

1999 Upper Deck Michael Jordan Athlete of the Century

COMPLETE SET (90) 40.00 100.00
COMMON CARD (1-90) 3.00 8.00
MC1 Master Collection 3.00 8.00
MJSS1 Michael Jordan AU/23 6,000.00 12,000.00
MJSS2 Michael Jordan AU/23 6,000.00 12,000.00

1999 Upper Deck Michael Jordan Athlete of the Century Gold

COMMON CARD (1-90) 100.00 250.00

1999 Upper Deck Michael Jordan Athlete of the Century Elevation

COMPLETE SET (16) 25.00 60.00
COMMON CARD (EL1-16) 3.00 8.00

1999 Upper Deck Michael Jordan Athlete of the Century Extreme Air

COMPLETE SET (15) 300.00 600.00
COMMON CARD (EA1-15) 25.00 60.00

1999 Upper Deck Michael Jordan Athlete of the Century High Class

COMPLETE SET (6) 12.00 30.00
COMMON CARD (HC1-HC6) 3.00 8.00

1999 Upper Deck Michael Jordan Athlete of the Century MJ Phenomenon

COMPLETE SET (15) 75.00 200.00
COMMON CARD (P1-P15) 8.00 20.00

1999 Upper Deck Michael Jordan Athlete of the Century The Jordan Era

COMPLETE SET (20) 25.00 60.00
COMMON CARD (JE1-20) 3.00 8.00

1999 Upper Deck Michael Jordan Athlete of the Century Total Dominance

COMPLETE SET (20) 75.00 200.00
COMMON CARD (TD1-20) 10.00 25.00

1999 Upper Deck Michael Jordan Athlete of the Century Upper Deck Remembers

COMPLETE SET (10) 25.00 60.00
COMMON CARD (UD1-10) 5.00 12.00

1999 Upper Deck Michael Jordan Career

COMP. FACT SET (60) 20.00 50.00
COMMON CARD (1-60) 1.25 3.00

1998 Upper Deck Michael Jordan Career Collection

COMP.FACT SET (60) 12.00 30.00
COMMON CARD (1-60) .40 1.00
1 Michael Jordan
Rookie Card 15.00 40.00
20 Michael Jordan
Spectacular Stats 90-91 2.00 5.00
21 Michael Jordan
Spectacular Stats 1993 2.00 5.00
22 Michael Jordan
Spectacular Stats 92-93 2.00 5.00
23 Michael Jordan
Spectacular Stats 89-90 2.00 5.00
24 Michael Jordan
Spectacular Stats 1991 2.00 5.00
25 Michael Jordan
Spectacular Stats 88-89 2.00 5.00
26 Michael Jordan
Spectacular Stats 87-88 2.00 5.00
27 Michael Jordan
Spectacular Stats 1988 2.00 5.00
28 Michael Jordan
Spectacular Stats 86-87 2.00 5.00

1997 Upper Deck Michael Jordan Championship Journals

COMP.FACT SET (25) 12.00 30.00
COMMON CARD (1-24) .60 1.50
NNO Michael Jordan
Special Card/5000 2.00 5.00
NNO Michael Jordan
Special Card - AU/50 1,000.00 2,500.00

1998 Upper Deck Michael Jordan Gatorade

COMPLETE SET (12) 12.00 30.00
COMMON CARD (1-12) 2.50 6.00

1999 Upper Deck Michael Jordan Gatorade

COMPLETE SET (6) 12.00 30.00
COMMON CARD (MJ1-MJ6) 3.00 8.00

2008-09 Upper Deck Michael Jordan Legacy Collection

COMMON CARD 2.00 5.00

2008-09 Upper Deck Michael Jordan Legacy Collection Memorabilia

COMMON CARD (1-100) 125.00 300.00
STATED PRINT RUN 23 SER.#'d SETS

2009-10 Upper Deck Michael Jordan Legacy Collection

COMPLETE SET (50) 15.00 40.00
COMP.FAC.SET (51) 20.00 50.00
COMMON CARD (1-50) 1.50 4.00

2009-10 Upper Deck Michael Jordan Legacy Collection Gold

COMPLETE SET (100) 100.00 250.00
COMMON CARD (1-100) 2.00 5.00
97 Michael Jordan
'86-87 Fleer reprint 25.00 60.00

2009-10 Upper Deck Michael Jordan Legacy Collection Oversized

COMPLETE SET (10) 30.00 80.00
COMMON CARD (MJ1-MJ10) 6.00 15.00
ONE PER FACTORY SET

1998 Upper Deck Michael Jordan Living Legend

COMPLETE SET (165) 40.00 100.00
COMMON CARD (1-165) 1.50 4.00
147 Michael Jordan JF
L.A. Lakers 75.00 200.00
MJ1 Michael Jordan AU/50 4,000.00 8,000.00

1998 Upper Deck Michael Jordan Living Legend Cover Story

COMPLETE SET (8) 25.00 60.00
COMMON CARD (C1-C8) 6.00 12.00

1998 Upper Deck Michael Jordan Living Legend Game Action Red

COMPLETE SET (30) 150.00 400.00
COMMON CARD (G1-G30) 12.00 30.00

1998 Upper Deck Michael Jordan Living Legend Game Action Silver

COMMON CARD (G1-G30) 60.00 150.00

1998 Upper Deck Michael Jordan Living Legend Game Action Gold

COMMON CARD (G1-G30) 300.00 800.00

1998 Upper Deck Michael Jordan Living Legend In-Flight

COMPLETE SET (15) 20.00 50.00
COMMON CARD (IF1-IF15) 2.00 5.00

1995 Upper Deck Michael Jordan Milk Caps

COMPLETE SET (54) 30.00 80.00
COMMON POG .75 2.00

1995 Upper Deck Michael Jordan Milk Caps Foil

COMPLETE SET (54) 50.00 120.00
COMMON FOIL (S1-S54) 1.25 3.00

1999 Upper Deck Michael Jordan Retirement

COMP.FACT SET (23) 20.00 50.00
COMMON CARD (1-23) 1.50 4.00

1997 Upper Deck Michael Jordan Tribute

COMPLETE SET (90) 30.00 75.00
COMP.VISIONS SET (30) 10.00 25.00
COMP.IMPRESSIONS SET (30) 10.00 25.00
COMP.REFLECTIONS SET (30) 10.00 25.00
COMMON CARD (1-90) .40 1.00

1996-97 Upper Deck Folz Minis

COMPLETE SET (48) 250.00 500.00
1 Michael Jordan FOIL 30.00 80.00
2 Anfernee Hardaway FOIL 20.00 50.00
3 Shawn Kemp FOIL 12.00 30.00
4 Shaquille O'Neal FOIL 30.00 80.00
5 Grant Hill FOIL 12.00 30.00
6 Hakeem Olajuwon FOIL 15.00 40.00
7 Mookie Blaylock 3.00 8.00
8 Antoine Walker 5.00 12.00
9 Anthony Mason 2.50 6.00
10 Scottie Pippen 8.00 20.00
11 Terrell Brandon 2.50 6.00
12 Samaki Walker 2.50 6.00
13 LaPhonso Ellis 2.00 5.00
14 Joe Dumars 4.00 10.00
15 Latrell Sprewell 3.00 8.00
16 Charles Barkley 8.00 20.00
17 Reggie Miller 6.00 15.00
18 Brent Barry 2.50 6.00
19 Eddie Jones 3.00 8.00
20 Tim Hardaway 4.00 10.00
21 Vin Baker 2.50 6.00
22 Stephon Marbury 10.00 25.00
23 Kendall Gill 3.00 8.00
24 Patrick Ewing 5.00 12.00
25 Horace Grant 3.00 8.00
26 Allen Iverson 25.00 60.00
27 Kevin Johnson 3.00 8.00
28 Kenny Anderson 2.50 6.00
29 Olden Polynice 2.00 5.00
30 Sean Elliott 3.00 8.00
31 Gary Payton 5.00 12.00
32 Marcus Camby 5.00 12.00
33 John Stockton 6.00 15.00
34 Shareef Abdur-Rahim 5.00 12.00
35 Juwan Howard 3.00 8.00
36 Dikembe Mutombo 5.00 12.00
37 Glen Rice 3.00 8.00
38 Dennis Rodman 8.00 20.00

39 Antonio McDyess 3.00 8.00
40 Rik Smits 2.50 6.00
41 Nick Van Exel 3.00 8.00
42 Alonzo Mourning 5.00 12.00
43 Glenn Robinson 3.00 8.00
44 Larry Johnson 4.00 10.00
45 Dennis Scott 2.50 6.00
46 Jerry Stackhouse 4.00 10.00
47 Sam Perkins 2.50 6.00
48 Chris Webber 4.00 10.00

1999-00 Upper Deck MVP
COMPLETE SET (220) 20.00 40.00
1 Dikembe Mutombo .30 .75
2 Steve Smith .15 .40
3 Mookie Blaylock .12 .30
4 Alan Henderson .12 .30
5 LaPhonso Ellis .12 .30
6 Grant Long .12 .30
7 Kenny Anderson .15 .40
8 Antoine Walker .20 .50
9 Ron Mercer .15 .40
10 Paul Pierce .40 1.00
11 Vitaly Potapenko .12 .30
12 Dana Barros .12 .30
13 Elden Campbell .12 .30
14 Eddie Jones .20 .50
15 David Wesley .12 .30
16 Bobby Phills .12 .30
17 Derrick Coleman .15 .40
18 Ricky Davis .20 .50
19 Toni Kukoc .25 .60
20 Brent Barry .15 .40
21 Ron Harper .15 .40
22 Kornell David RC .12 .30
23 Mark Bryant .12 .30
24 Dickey Simpkins .12 .30
25 Shawn Kemp .30 .75
26 Derek Anderson .12 .30
27 Brevin Knight .12 .30
28 Andrew DeClercq .12 .30
29 Zydrunas Ilgauskas .15 .40
30 Cedric Henderson .12 .30
31 Shawn Bradley .12 .30
32 A.C. Green .15 .40
33 Gary Trent .12 .30
34 Michael Finley .20 .50
35 Dirk Nowitzki .60 1.50
36 Steve Nash .40 1.00
37 Antonio McDyess .15 .40
38 Nick Van Exel .15 .40
39 Chauncey Billups .20 .50
40 Danny Fortson .12 .30
41 Eric Washington .12 .30
42 Raef LaFrentz .15 .40
43 Grant Hill .30 .75
44 Bison Dele .12 .30
45 Lindsey Hunter .12 .30
46 Jerry Stackhouse .20 .50
47 Don Reid .12 .30
48 Christian Laettner .15 .40
49 John Starks .20 .50
50 Antawn Jamison .20 .50
51 Erick Dampier .12 .30
52 Donyell Marshall .15 .40
53 Chris Mills .12 .30
54 Bimbo Coles .12 .30
55 Charles Barkley .50 1.25
56 Hakeem Olajuwon .40 1.00
57 Scottie Pippen .50 1.25
58 Othella Harrington .12 .30
59 Bryce Drew .12 .30
60 Michael Dickerson .12 .30
61 Rik Smits .15 .40
62 Reggie Miller .40 1.00
63 Mark Jackson .15 .40
64 Antonio Davis .12 .30
65 Jalen Rose .15 .40
66 Dale Davis .12 .30
67 Chris Mullin .20 .50
68 Maurice Taylor .12 .30
69 Lamond Murray .12 .30
70 Rodney Rogers .12 .30
71 Darrick Martin .12 .30
72 Michael Olowokandi .12 .30
73 Tyrone Nesby RC .12 .30
74 Kobe Bryant 1.50 4.00
75 Shaquille O'Neal .75 2.00
76 Robert Horry .15 .40
77 Glen Rice .20 .50
78 J.R. Reid .12 .30
79 Rick Fox .12 .30
80 Derek Fisher .15 .40
81 Tim Hardaway .25 .60
82 Alonzo Mourning .30 .75
83 Jamal Mashburn .15 .40
84 P.J. Brown .12 .30
85 Terry Porter .12 .30
86 Dan Majerle .20 .50
87 Ray Allen .30 .75
88 Vinny Del Negro .12 .30
89 Glenn Robinson .15 .40
90 Dell Curry .12 .30
91 Sam Cassell .15 .40
92 Robert Traylor .12 .30
93 Kevin Garnett .50 1.25
94 Terrell Brandon .12 .30
95 Joe Smith .15 .40
96 Sam Mitchell .12 .30
97 Anthony Peeler .12 .30
98 Bobby Jackson .15 .40
99 Keith Van Horn .15 .40
100 Stephon Marbury .25 .60
101 Jayson Williams .12 .30
102 Kendall Gill .20 .50
103 Kerry Kittles .15 .40
104 Scott Burrell .12 .30
105 Patrick Ewing .25 .60
106 Allan Houston .15 .40
107 Latrell Sprewell .25 .60
108 Larry Johnson .20 .50
109 Marcus Camby .15 .40
110 Charlie Ward .12 .30
111 Anfernee Hardaway .50 1.25
112 Darrell Armstrong .12 .30
113 Nick Anderson .12 .30
114 Horace Grant .15 .40
115 Isaac Austin .12 .30
116 Matt Harpring .12 .30
117 Michael Doleac .12 .30
118 Allen Iverson .50 1.25
119 Theo Ratliff .15 .40
120 Matt Geiger .12 .30
121 Larry Hughes .15 .40
122 Tyrone Hill .12 .30
123 George Lynch .12 .30
124 Jason Kidd .30 .75
125 Tom Gugliotta .15 .40
126 Rex Chapman .12 .30
127 Clifford Robinson .15 .40
128 Luc Longley .15 .40
129 Danny Manning .15 .40
130 Rasheed Wallace .25 .60
131 Arvydas Sabonis .15 .40
132 Damon Stoudamire .20 .50
133 Brian Grant .12 .30
134 Isaiah Rider .15 .40
135 Walt Williams .12 .30
136 Jim Jackson .12 .30
137 Jason Williams .30 .75
138 Vlade Divac .20 .50
139 Chris Webber .25 .60
140 Corliss Williamson .12 .30
141 Peja Stojakovic .20 .50
142 Tariq Abdul-Wahad .12 .30
143 Tim Duncan .50 1.25
144 Sean Elliott .15 .40
145 David Robinson .40 1.00
146 Mario Elie .12 .30
147 Avery Johnson .15 .40
148 Steve Kerr .15 .40
149 Gary Payton .30 .75
150 Vin Baker .15 .40
151 Detlef Schrempf .15 .40
152 Hersey Hawkins .12 .30
153 Dale Ellis .12 .30
154 Olden Polynice .12 .30
155 Vince Carter .50 1.25
156 John Wallace .12 .30
157 Doug Christie .15 .40
158 Tracy McGrady .30 .75
159 Kevin Willis .12 .30
160 Charles Oakley .20 .50
161 Karl Malone .40 1.00
162 John Stockton .30 .75
163 Jeff Hornacek .15 .40
164 Bryon Russell .12 .30
165 Howard Eisley .12 .30
166 Shandon Anderson .12 .30
167 Shareef Abdur-Rahim .20 .50
168 Mike Bibby .20 .50
169 Bryant Reeves .12 .30
170 Felipe Lopez .12 .30
171 Cherokee Parks .12 .30
172 Michael Smith .12 .30
173 Juwan Howard .15 .40
174 Rod Strickland .15 .40
175 Mitch Richmond .25 .60
176 Otis Thorpe .12 .30
177 Calbert Cheaney .12 .30
178 Tracy Murray .12 .30
179 Michael Jordan 1.00 2.50
180 Michael Jordan 1.00 2.50
181 Michael Jordan 1.00 2.50
182 Michael Jordan 1.00 2.50
183 Michael Jordan 1.00 2.50
184 Michael Jordan 1.00 2.50
185 Michael Jordan 1.00 2.50
186 Michael Jordan 1.00 2.50
187 Michael Jordan 1.00 2.50
188 Michael Jordan 1.00 2.50
189 Michael Jordan 1.00 2.50
190 Michael Jordan 1.00 2.50
191 Michael Jordan 1.00 2.50
192 Michael Jordan 1.00 2.50
193 Michael Jordan 1.00 2.50
194 Michael Jordan 1.00 2.50
195 Michael Jordan 1.00 2.50
196 Michael Jordan 1.00 2.50
197 Michael Jordan 1.00 2.50
198 Michael Jordan 1.00 2.50
199 Michael Jordan 1.00 2.50
200 Michael Jordan 1.00 2.50
201 Michael Jordan 1.00 2.50
202 Michael Jordan 1.00 2.50
203 Michael Jordan 1.00 2.50
204 Michael Jordan 1.00 2.50
205 Michael Jordan 1.00 2.50
206 Michael Jordan 1.00 2.50
207 Michael Jordan 1.00 2.50
208 Michael Jordan 1.00 2.50
209 Elton Brand RC .60 1.50
210 Steve Francis RC .60 1.50
211 Baron Davis RC .75 2.00
212 Wally Szczerbiak RC .50 1.25
213 Richard Hamilton RC .75 2.00
214 Andre Miller RC .60 1.50
215 Jason Terry RC .50 1.25
216 Corey Maggette RC .40 1.00
217 Shawn Marion RC .60 1.50
218 Lamar Odom RC .60 1.50
219 M.Jordan CL 1.00 2.50
220 M.Jordan CL 1.00 2.50
S1 Michael Jordan PROMO 1.25 3.00

1999-00 Upper Deck MVP Silver Script
COMMON MJ (179-208/CL) 2.00 5.00
*STARS: 1.5X TO 4X BASE CARD HI
*RCs: .75X TO 2X BASE HI
STATED ODDS 1:2 HOB/RET
S1 Michael Jordan PROMO 2.00 5.00

1999-00 Upper Deck MVP Gold Script
COMMON MJ (179-208/CL) 25.00 60.00
*STARS: 20X TO 50X BASE CARD HI
*RCs: 6X TO 15X BASE HI
STATED PRINT RUN 100 SERIAL #'d SETS
57 Scottie Pippen 15.00 40.00
143 Tim Duncan 25.00 60.00
149 Gary Payton 20.00 50.00
161 Karl Malone 12.00 30.00

1999-00 Upper Deck MVP Super Script
COMMON MJ (179-208/CL) 60.00 150.00
*STARS: 50X TO 120X BASE CARD HI
*RCs: 15X TO 40X BASE HI
STATED PRINT RUN 25 SERIAL #'d SETS

1999-00 Upper Deck MVP 21st Century NBA
COMPLETE SET (10) 4.00 10.00
STATED ODDS 1:13 HOB/RET
N1 Jason Williams .75 2.00
N2 Paul Pierce 1.00 2.50
N3 Antoine Walker .50 1.25
N4 Keith Van Horn .40 1.00
N5 Allen Iverson 1.25 3.00
N6 Antawn Jamison .50 1.25
N7 Kobe Bryant 4.00 10.00
N8 Shareef Abdur-Rahim .50 1.25
N9 Stephon Marbury .60 1.50
N10 Grant Hill .75 2.00

1999-00 Upper Deck MVP Draw Your Own Trading Card
COMPLETE SET (26) 5.00 12.00
W1 Michael Jordan 1.00 2.50
W2 Grant Hill .15 .40
W3 Kobe Bryant .75 2.00
W4 Michael Jordan 1.00 2.50
W5 Glen Rice .10 .25
W6 Michael Jordan 1.00 2.50
W7 David Robinson .20 .50
W8 Grant Hill .15 .40
W9 Stephon Marbury .12 .30
W10 Michael Jordan 1.00 2.50
W12 Charles Barkley .25 .60
W13 Antoine Walker .10 .25
W14 Shaquille O'Neal .40 1.00
W16 Michael Jordan 1.00 2.50
W17 Stephon Marbury .12 .30
W18 Michael Jordan 1.00 2.50
W20 Allen Iverson .25 .60
W21 Michael Jordan 1.00 2.50
W22 Shareef Abdur-Rahim .10 .25
W23 Reggie Miller .20 .50
W24 Karl Malone .20 .50
W25 Christian Laettner .07 .20
W26 John Stockton .15 .40
W28 Michael Jordan 1.00 2.50
W29 Michael Jordan 1.00 2.50
W30 Michael Jordan 1.00 2.50

1999-00 Upper Deck MVP Dynamics
COMPLETE SET (6) 8.00 20.00
STATED ODDS 1:27 HOB/RET
D1 Michael Jordan 8.00 20.00
D2 Kobe Bryant 6.00 15.00
D3 Grant Hill 1.25 3.00
D4 Shareef Abdur-Rahim .75 2.00
D5 Kevin Garnett 2.00 5.00
D6 Vince Carter 2.00 5.00

1999-00 Upper Deck MVP Electrifying
COMPLETE SET (15) 4.00 10.00
STATED ODDS 1:9 HOB/RET
E1 Shaquille O'Neal 2.00 5.00
E2 Steve Smith .40 1.00
E3 Toni Kukoc .60 1.50
E4 Ron Mercer .40 1.00
E5 Damon Stoudamire .50 1.25
E6 Tim Hardaway .60 1.50
E7 Paul Pierce 1.00 2.50
E8 Jason Kidd .75 2.00
E9 Stephon Marbury .60 1.50
E10 Terrell Brandon .30 .75
E11 Reggie Miller 1.00 2.50
E12 Ray Allen .75 2.00
E13 Maurice Taylor .30 .75
E14 Chris Webber .60 1.50
E15 Charles Barkley 1.25 3.00

1999-00 Upper Deck MVP Game-Used Souvenirs
STATED ODDS 1:131 HOBBY
AHS Anfernee Hardaway 8.00 20.00
AJS Antawn Jamison 4.00 10.00
AMS Antonio McDyess 3.00 8.00
GPS Gary Payton 6.00 15.00
JKS Jason Kidd 6.00 15.00
JWS Jason Williams 10.00 25.00
KBS Kobe Bryant 15.00 40.00
KGS Kevin Garnett 10.00 25.00
KMA Karl Malone AU/32 250.00 500.00
KMS Karl Malone 8.00 20.00
MBS Mike Bibby 4.00 10.00
MFS Michael Finley 4.00 10.00
MOS Michael Olowokandi 2.50 6.00
SOS Shaquille O'Neal 15.00 40.00
SPS Scottie Pippen 10.00 25.00
TDS Tim Duncan 12.00 30.00

1999-00 Upper Deck MVP Jam Time
COMPLETE SET (14) 3.00 8.00
STATED ODDS 1:6 HOB/RET
JT1 Michael Jordan 2.50 6.00
JT2 Alonzo Mourning .40 1.00
JT3 Shawn Kemp .40 1.00
JT4 Juwan Howard .20 .50
JT5 Chris Webber .30 .75
JT6 Tim Duncan .60 1.50
JT7 Keith Van Horn .30 .75
JT8 Eddie Jones .25 .60
JT9 Michael Finley .25 .60
JT10 Anfernee Hardaway .60 1.50
JT11 Antonio McDyess .20 .50
JT12 Charles Barkley .60 1.50
JT13 Latrell Sprewell .30 .75
JT14 Hakeem Olajuwon .50 1.25

1999-00 Upper Deck MVP Jordan MVP Moments
COMMON CARD (MJ1-MJ14) 3.00 8.00
STATED ODDS 1:27 HOB/RET

1999-00 Upper Deck MVP MVP Theatre
COMPLETE SET (15) 5.00 12.00
STATED ODDS 1:9 HOB/RET
M1 Karl Malone 1.00 2.50
M2 Tom Gugliotta .40 1.00
M3 Shaquille O'Neal 2.00 5.00
M4 Mitch Richmond .60 1.50
M5 David Robinson 1.00 2.50
M6 Gary Payton .75 2.00
M7 Allen Iverson 1.25 3.00
M8 Glenn Robinson .40 1.00
M9 Antoine Walker .50 1.25
M10 Hakeem Olajuwon 1.00 2.50
M11 Patrick Ewing .60 1.50
M12 Antonio McDyess .40 1.00
M13 Tim Hardaway .60 1.50
M14 Scottie Pippen 1.25 3.00
M15 Anfernee Hardaway 1.25 3.00

1999-00 Upper Deck MVP ProSign
STATED ODDS 1:144 RETAIL
CH Charlie Ward 8.00 20.00
CW Clarence Weatherspoon 5.00 12.00
DA Darrell Armstrong 5.00 12.00
DF Derek Fisher 8.00 20.00
IA Isaac Austin 5.00 12.00
JJ Jim Jackson 5.00 12.00
JK Jaren Jackson 5.00 12.00
JR Jalen Rose 8.00 20.00
MD Michael Dickerson 5.00 12.00
MJ Michael Jordan/23 8,000.00 15,000.00
NV Nick Van Exel 10.00 25.00
RT Robert Traylor 5.00 12.00
SA Stacey Augmon 5.00 12.00
TC Terry Cummings 5.00 12.00
TR Theo Ratliff 5.00 12.00
VC Vince Carter 100.00 250.00

2000-01 Upper Deck MVP
COMPLETE SET (220) 12.00 30.00
1 Dikembe Mutombo .30 .75
2 Jason Terry .20 .50
3 Jim Jackson .15 .40
4 Alan Henderson .12 .30
5 Roshown McLeod .12 .30
6 Bimbo Coles .12 .30
7 Lorenzen Wright .12 .30
8 Antoine Walker .20 .50
9 Paul Pierce .30 .75
10 Kenny Anderson .15 .40
11 Adrian Griffin .12 .30
12 Vitaly Potapenko .12 .30
13 Dana Barros .12 .30
14 Eric Williams .12 .30
15 Eddie Jones .20 .50
16 Eddie Robinson .12 .30
17 Ricky Davis .15 .40
18 Elden Campbell .12 .30
19 Derrick Coleman .20 .50
20 David Wesley .15 .40
21 Baron Davis .20 .50
22 Elton Brand .20 .50
23 Ron Artest .20 .50
24 Hersey Hawkins .12 .30
25 Chris Carr .12 .30
26 Corey Benjamin .12 .30
27 Will Perdue .12 .30
28 Andre Miller .15 .40
29 Shawn Kemp .30 .75
30 Wesley Person .12 .30
31 Lamond Murray .12 .30
32 Bob Sura .12 .30
33 Andrew DeClercq .12 .30
34 Dirk Nowitzki .50 1.25
35 Michael Finley .20 .50
36 Cedric Ceballos .15 .40
37 Shawn Bradley .12 .30
38 Erick Strickland .12 .30
39 Hubert Davis .12 .30
40 Antonio McDyess .15 .40
41 Raef LaFrentz .15 .40
42 Keon Clark .12 .30
43 Nick Van Exel .20 .50
44 James Posey .12 .30
45 Chris Gatling .12 .30
46 George McCloud .12 .30
47 Grant Hill .30 .75
48 Jerry Stackhouse .20 .50
49 Lindsey Hunter .12 .30
50 Christian Laettner .20 .50
51 Jerome Williams .12 .30
52 Terry Mills .12 .30
53 Antawn Jamison .20 .50
54 Donyell Marshall .15 .40
55 Chris Mills .12 .30
56 Larry Hughes .20 .50
57 Mookie Blaylock .20 .50
58 Vonteego Cummings .12 .30
59 Steve Francis .20 .50
60 Shandon Anderson .12 .30
61 Cuttino Mobley .15 .40
62 Hakeem Olajuwon .40 1.00
63 Walt Williams .12 .30
64 Kelvin Cato .12 .30
65 Reggie Miller .40 1.00
66 Austin Croshere .12 .30
67 Rik Smits .12 .30
68 Jalen Rose .15 .40
69 Dale Davis .15 .40
70 Jonathan Bender .12 .30
71 Michael Olowokandi .12 .30
72 Lamar Odom .20 .50
73 Tyrone Nesby .12 .30
74 Eldrick Bohannon RC .12 .30
75 Eric Piatkowski .12 .30
76 Shaquille O'Neal .75 2.00
77 Kobe Bryant 1.50 4.00
78 Robert Horry .20 .50
79 Ron Harper .20 .50
80 Rick Fox .15 .40
81 Derek Fisher .20 .50
82 Devean George .12 .30
83 Alonzo Mourning .30 .75
84 Clarence Weatherspoon .12 .30
85 Anthony Carter .12 .30
86 P.J. Brown .12 .30
87 Tim Hardaway .25 .60
88 Jamal Mashburn .15 .40
89 Voshon Lenard .12 .30
90 Ray Allen .30 .75
91 Glenn Robinson .20 .50
92 Tim Thomas .12 .30
93 Sam Cassell .15 .40
94 Robert Traylor .12 .30
95 Ervin Johnson .12 .30
96 Danny Manning .12 .30
97 Kevin Garnett .50 1.25
98 Wally Szczerbiak .15 .40
99 Terrell Brandon .15 .40
100 William Avery .12 .30
101 Anthony Peeler .12 .30
102 Radoslav Nesterovic .12 .30
103 Dean Garrett .12 .30
104 Keith Van Horn .15 .40
105 Kerry Kittles .15 .40
106 Stephon Marbury .25 .60
107 Evan Eschmeyer .12 .30
108 Jim McIlvaine .12 .30
109 Lucious Harris .12 .30
110 Jamie Feick .12 .30
111 Allan Houston .20 .50
112 Latrell Sprewell .25 .60
113 Patrick Ewing .30 .75
114 Chris Childs .12 .30
115 Marcus Camby .15 .40
116 Charlie Ward .15 .40
117 Larry Johnson .25 .60
118 Darrell Armstrong .12 .30
119 Corey Maggette .15 .40
120 Ron Mercer .15 .40
121 Pat Garrity .12 .30
122 Chucky Atkins .12 .30
123 Ben Wallace .25 .60
124 Michael Doleac .12 .30
125 Allen Iverson .50 1.25
126 Matt Geiger .12 .30
127 Eric Snow .12 .30
128 Toni Kukoc .25 .60
129 Theo Ratliff .12 .30
130 George Lynch .12 .30
131 Jason Kidd .30 .75
132 Tom Gugliotta .15 .40
133 Rodney Rogers .12 .30
134 Shawn Marion .20 .50
135 Clifford Robinson .20 .50
136 Kevin Johnson .15 .40
137 Anfernee Hardaway .30 .75
138 Scottie Pippen .50 1.25
139 Damon Stoudamire .20 .50
140 Arvydas Sabonis .20 .50
141 Jermaine O'Neal .15 .40
142 Bonzi Wells .12 .30
143 Rasheed Wallace .25 .60
144 Detlef Schrempf .15 .40
145 Chris Webber .25 .60
146 Vlade Divac .20 .50
147 Peja Stojakovic .15 .40
148 Jason Williams .30 .75
149 Corliss Williamson .12 .30
150 Nick Anderson .15 .40
151 Jon Barry .12 .30
152 Tim Duncan .50 1.25
153 David Robinson .40 1.00
154 Avery Johnson .15 .40
155 Terry Porter .12 .30
156 Mario Elie .12 .30
157 Jaren Jackson .12 .30
158 Steve Kerr .12 .30
159 Gary Payton .30 .75
160 Vin Baker .15 .40
161 Brent Barry .15 .40
162 Horace Grant .20 .50
163 Ruben Patterson .12 .30
164 Rashard Lewis .15 .40
165 Tracy McGrady .40 1.00
166 Charles Oakley .20 .50
167 Doug Christie .15 .40
168 Antonio Davis .15 .40
169 Vince Carter .40 1.00
170 Kevin Willis .12 .30
171 Karl Malone .40 1.00
172 John Stockton .40 1.00
173 Bryon Russell .12 .30
174 Quincy Lewis .12 .30
175 Olden Polynice .12 .30
176 Jacque Vaughn .12 .30
177 Shareef Abdur-Rahim .20 .50
178 Michael Dickerson .12 .30
179 Bryant Reeves .12 .30
180 Mike Bibby .20 .50
181 Othella Harrington .12 .30
182 Felipe Lopez .12 .30
183 Mitch Richmond .25 .60
184 Richard Hamilton .25 .60
185 Jahidi White .12 .30
186 Aaron Williams .12 .30
187 Juwan Howard .15 .40
188 Rod Strickland .12 .30
189 Kobe Bryant CL 1.50 4.00
190 Kevin Garnett CL .50 1.25
191 Kenyon Martin RC .40 1.00
192 Marcus Fizer RC .15 .40
193 Chris Mihm RC .12 .30
194 Stromile Swift RC .15 .40
195 Morris Peterson RC .20 .50
196 Quentin Richardson RC .15 .40
197 Courtney Alexander RC .12 .30
198 Scoonie Penn RC .20 .50
199 Mateen Cleaves RC .15 .40
200 Erick Barkley RC .12 .30
201 A.J. Guyton RC .12 .30
202 Darius Miles RC .20 .50
203 DerMarr Johnson RC .12 .30
204 Jerome Moiso RC .12 .30
205 Jamaal Magloire RC .20 .50
206 Hanno Mottola RC .12 .30
207 Mike Miller RC .30 .75
208 Desmond Mason RC .25 .60
209 Chris Carrawell RC .12 .30
210 Eduardo Najera RC .20 .50
211 Speedy Claxton RC .20 .50
212 Joel Przybilla RC .15 .40
213 Mark Madsen RC .20 .50
214 Khalid El-Amin RC .12 .30
215 Etan Thomas RC .15 .40
216 Jason Collier RC .20 .50
217 Jason Hart RC .20 .50
218 Michael Redd RC .50 1.25
219 Keyon Dooling RC .15 .40
220 Mamadou N'Diaye RC .12 .30

2000-01 Upper Deck MVP Silver Script
*STARS: 1.25X TO 3X BASE CARD HI
*RCs: .75X TO 2X BASE HI
STATED ODDS 1:2 HOB/RET

2000-01 Upper Deck MVP Gold Script
*STARS: 12X TO 30X BASE CARD HI
*RCs: 8X TO 20X BASE HI
STATED PRINT RUN 100 SERIAL #'d SETS
77 Kobe Bryant 40.00 100.00
137 Anfernee Hardaway 25.00 60.00
159 Gary Payton 15.00 40.00
189 Kobe Bryant CL 40.00 100.00

2000-01 Upper Deck MVP Super Script
*STARS: 50X TO 120X BASE CARD HI
*RCs: 20X TO 50X BASE HI
STATED PRINT RUN 25 SERIAL #'d SETS

2000-01 Upper Deck MVP Dynamics
COMPLETE SET (20) 15.00 40.00
STATED ODDS 1:28 HOB/RET
D1 Shaquille O'Neal 4.00 10.00
D2 Allen Iverson 2.50 6.00
D3 Paul Pierce 1.50 4.00
D4 Scottie Pippen 2.50 6.00
D5 Lamar Odom 1.00 2.50
D6 Kobe Bryant 8.00 20.00
D7 Gary Payton 1.50 4.00
D8 Antonio McDyess .75 2.00
D9 Stephon Marbury 1.25 3.00
D10 Alonzo Mourning 1.50 4.00
D11 Vince Carter 2.00 5.00
D12 Jason Kidd 1.50 4.00
D13 Michael Finley 1.00 2.50
D14 Chris Webber 1.25 3.00
D15 Anfernee Hardaway 1.50 4.00
D16 Kevin Garnett 2.50 6.00
D17 Jason Williams 1.50 4.00
D18 Allan Houston 1.00 2.50
D19 Elton Brand 1.00 2.50
D20 Karl Malone 2.00 5.00

2000-01 Upper Deck MVP Electrifying
COMPLETE SET (10) 2.00 5.00
STATED ODDS 1:9 HOB/RET
E1 Kevin Garnett .75 2.00
E2 Stephon Marbury .40 1.00
E3 Damon Stoudamire .30 .75
E4 Jalen Rose .25 .60
E5 Eddie Jones .30 .75
E6 Elton Brand .30 .75
E7 Wally Szczerbiak .25 .60
E8 Kobe Bryant 2.50 6.00
E9 Shawn Marion .30 .75
E10 Mike Bibby .30 .75

2000-01 Upper Deck MVP Game-Used Souvenirs
STATED ODDS 1:130 HOBBY
AHS Allan Houston 4.00 10.00
AIS Allen Iverson 10.00 25.00
AJS Antawn Jamison 4.00 10.00
AMS Andre Miller 3.00 8.00
ANS Anfernee Hardaway 6.00 15.00
EJS Eddie Jones 4.00 10.00
GPS Gary Payton 6.00 15.00
JKS Jason Kidd 6.00 15.00
JWS Jason Williams 8.00 20.00
KBS Kobe Bryant 25.00 60.00
KGS Kevin Garnett 10.00 25.00
KMS Karl Malone 8.00 20.00
LHS Larry Hughes 4.00 10.00
MBS Mike Bibby 4.00 10.00
MCS Antonio McDyess 3.00 8.00
MFS Michael Finley 4.00 10.00
PPS Paul Pierce 6.00 15.00
RAS Ron Artest 4.00 10.00
RHS Richard Hamilton 5.00 12.00
RMS Reggie Miller 8.00 20.00
RWS Rasheed Wallace 5.00 12.00
RYS Ray Allen 5.00 12.00
SFS Steve Francis 4.00 10.00
SMS Stephon Marbury 5.00 12.00
SOS Shaquille O'Neal 15.00 40.00
SPS Scottie Pippen 10.00 25.00
TMS Tracy McGrady 8.00 20.00
WSS Wally Szczerbiak 2.50 6.00

2000-01 Upper Deck MVP Game-Used Souvenirs Autographs
STATED PRINT RUN 25 SERIAL #'d SETS
ANA Anfernee Hardaway 1,000.00 2,000.00
KBA Kobe Bryant 20,000.00 40,000.00
KGA Kevin Garnett 2,000.00 4,000.00
KMA Karl Malone 400.00 800.00
LHA Larry Hughes 60.00 150.00
MBA Mike Bibby 75.00 200.00
MCA Antonio McDyess 25.00 60.00
PPA Paul Pierce 400.00 800.00
RHA Richard Hamilton 75.00 200.00
RYA Ray Allen 300.00 600.00
SFA Steve Francis 40.00 100.00
WSA Wally Szczerbiak 25.00 60.00

2000-01 Upper Deck MVP Theatre
COMPLETE SET (10) 3.00 8.00
STATED ODDS 1:14 HOB/RET
M1 Kobe Bryant 3.00 8.00
M2 Alonzo Mourning .60 1.50
M3 Reggie Miller .75 2.00
M4 Chris Webber .50 1.25
M5 John Stockton .75 2.00
M6 Vince Carter .75 2.00
M7 Richard Hamilton .50 1.25
M8 Hakeem Olajuwon .75 2.00
M9 Kevin Garnett 1.00 2.50
M10 David Robinson .75 2.00

2000-01 Upper Deck MVP MVPerformers
COMPLETE SET (11) 5.00 12.00
STATED ODDS 1:28 HOB/RET
P1 Kobe Bryant 5.00 12.00
P2 Antawn Jamison .60 1.50
P3 John Stockton 1.25 3.00
P4 Andre Miller .50 1.25
P5 Latrell Sprewell .75 2.00
P6 Jason Williams 1.00 2.50
P7 Kevin Garnett 1.50 4.00
P8 Lamar Odom .60 1.50
P9 Allan Houston .60 1.50
P10 Keith Van Horn .50 1.25
P11 Antoine Walker .60 1.50

2000-01 Upper Deck MVP ProSign
STATED ODDS 1:216 RETAIL
AH Anfernee Hardaway 30.00 80.00
CB Calvin Booth 4.00 10.00
DA Darrell Armstrong 4.00 10.00
DS Damon Stoudamire 10.00 25.00
GP Gary Payton 12.00 30.00
JR Jalen Rose 10.00 25.00
KA Karl Malone 40.00 80.00
KB Kobe Bryant 150.00 400.00
KG Kevin Garnett 50.00 120.00
LH Larry Hughes 6.00 15.00
MB Mike Bibby 6.00 15.00
MD Antonio McDyess 6.00 15.00
PP Paul Pierce 10.00 25.00
RA Ray Allen 10.00 25.00
SA Shareef Abdur-Rahim 6.00 15.00
SF Steve Francis 6.00 15.00
WS Wally Szczerbiak 5.00 12.00

2000-01 Upper Deck MVP ProSign Gold
*GOLD: .75X TO 2X HI
STATED PRINT RUN 25 SERIAL #'d SETS
KB Kobe Bryant 400.00 800.00
MJ Michael Jordan 5,000.00 8,000.00

2000-01 Upper Deck MVP World Jam
COMPLETE SET (20) 4.00 10.00
STATED ODDS 1:5 HOB/RET
WJ1 Kobe Bryant 2.50 6.00
WJ2 Vince Carter .60 1.50
WJ3 Steve Francis .30 .75
WJ4 Keith Van Horn .25 .60
WJ5 Rasheed Wallace .40 1.00
WJ6 Corey Maggette .25 .60
WJ7 Kevin Garnett .75 2.00
WJ8 Larry Hughes .30 .75
WJ9 Tim Duncan .75 2.00
WJ10 Alonzo Mourning .50 1.25
WJ11 Chris Webber .40 1.00
WJ12 Shareef Abdur-Rahim .30 .75
WJ13 Lamar Odom .30 .75
WJ14 Ron Mercer .25 .60
WJ15 Rashard Lewis .25 .60
WJ16 Michael Dickerson .20 .50
WJ17 Jerry Stackhouse .30 .75
WJ18 Latrell Sprewell .40 1.00
WJ19 Shawn Kemp .50 1.25
WJ20 Elton Brand .30 .75

2001-02 Upper Deck MVP
COMPLETE SET (220) 20.00 40.00
1 Jason Terry .30 .75
2 Alan Henderson .20 .50
3 Toni Kukoc .40 1.00
4 Hanno Mottola .20 .50
5 Theo Ratliff .20 .50
6 DerMarr Johnson .20 .50
7 Paul Pierce .50 1.25
8 Antoine Walker .25 .60
9 Bryant Stith .20 .50
10 Kenny Anderson .25 .60
11 Vitaly Potapenko .20 .50
12 Eric Williams .20 .50
13 Jamal Mashburn .25 .60
14 David Wesley .20 .50
15 Baron Davis .30 .75
16 Elden Campbell .20 .50
17 P.J. Brown .20 .50
18 Jamaal Magloire .20 .50
19 Eddie Robinson .20 .50
20 Elton Brand .25 .60
21 Ron Mercer .20 .50
22 Fred Hoiberg .20 .50
23 Jamal Crawford .30 .75
24 Ron Artest .25 .60
25 Marcus Fizer .20 .50
26 Andre Miller .25 .60
27 Lamond Murray .20 .50
28 Jim Jackson .20 .50
29 Chris Mihm .20 .50
30 Matt Harpring .20 .50
31 Chris Gatling .20 .50
32 Michael Finley .30 .75
33 Steve Nash .60 1.50
34 Dirk Nowitzki .75 2.00
35 Juwan Howard .25 .60
36 Howard Eisley .20 .50
37 Eduardo Najera .20 .50
38 Wang Zhizhi .30 .75
39 Antonio McDyess .25 .60
40 Nick Van Exel .30 .75
41 Raef LaFrentz .20 .50
42 James Posey .20 .50
43 George McCloud .20 .50
44 Voshon Lenard .20 .50
45 Jerry Stackhouse .30 .75
46 Chucky Atkins .20 .50
47 Corliss Williamson .20 .50
48 Joe Smith .25 .60
49 Mateen Cleaves .20 .50
50 Ben Wallace .40 1.00
51 Antawn Jamison .25 .60
52 Marc Jackson .20 .50
53 Larry Hughes .25 .60
54 Bob Sura .20 .50
55 Chris Porter .20 .50
56 Vonteego Cummings .20 .50
57 Steve Francis .30 .75
58 Hakeem Olajuwon .60 1.50
59 Cuttino Mobley .25 .60
60 Maurice Taylor .20 .50
61 Shandon Anderson .20 .50
62 Walt Williams .20 .50
63 Moochie Norris .20 .50

64 Reggie Miller .60 1.50
65 Jalen Rose .25 .60
66 Jermaine O'Neal .25 .60
67 Austin Croshere .20 .50
68 Travis Best .20 .50
69 Al Harrington .25 .60
70 Jonathan Bender .20 .50
71 Darius Miles .20 .50
72 Corey Maggette .25 .60
73 Lamar Odom .25 .60
74 Quentin Richardson .20 .50
75 Keyon Dooling .20 .50
76 Jeff McInnis .20 .50
77 Eric Piatkowski .20 .50
78 Kobe Bryant 2.50 6.00
79 Shaquille O'Neal 1.25 3.00
80 Rick Fox .25 .60
81 Derek Fisher .25 .60
82 Robert Horry .30 .75
83 Ron Harper .25 .60
84 Brian Shaw .20 .50
85 Alonzo Mourning .50 1.25
86 Eddie Jones .30 .75
87 Tim Hardaway .40 1.00
88 Anthony Mason .30 .75
89 Brian Grant .30 .75
90 Anthony Carter .20 .50
91 Bruce Bowen .20 .50
92 Ray Allen .50 1.25
93 Glenn Robinson .30 .75
94 Sam Cassell .25 .60
95 Tim Thomas .20 .50
96 Ervin Johnson .20 .50
97 Joel Przybilla .20 .50
98 Kevin Garnett .75 2.00
99 Terrell Brandon .25 .60
100 Wally Szczerbiak .25 .60
101 Chauncey Billups .40 1.00
102 LaPhonso Ellis .25 .60
103 Anthony Peeler .20 .50
104 Stephon Marbury .40 1.00
105 Keith Van Horn .25 .60
106 Kenyon Martin .30 .75
107 Kendall Gill .20 .50
108 Lucious Harris .20 .50
109 Stephen Jackson .20 .50
110 Latrell Sprewell .40 1.00
111 Allan Houston .30 .75
112 Marcus Camby .25 .60
113 Mark Jackson .25 .60
114 Glen Rice .30 .75
115 Kurt Thomas .25 .60
116 Tracy McGrady .50 1.25
117 Darrell Armstrong .20 .50
118 Mike Miller .25 .60
119 Grant Hill .50 1.25
120 Pat Garrity .20 .50
121 John Amaechi .20 .50
122 Allen Iverson .75 2.00
123 Dikembe Mutombo .50 1.25
124 Aaron McKie .20 .50
125 Tyrone Hill .20 .50
126 George Lynch .20 .50
127 Eric Snow .20 .50
128 Matt Geiger .20 .50
129 Jason Kidd .50 1.25
130 Shawn Marion .30 .75
131 Tony Delk .25 .60
132 Rodney Rogers .20 .50
133 Tom Gugliotta .20 .50
134 Anfernee Hardaway .75 2.00
135 Rasheed Wallace .40 1.00
136 Damon Stoudamire .30 .75
137 Arvydas Sabonis .25 .60
138 Scottie Pippen .75 2.00
139 Steve Smith .25 .60
140 Stacey Augmon .20 .50
141 Bonzi Wells .20 .50
142 Jason Williams .50 1.25
143 Chris Webber .40 1.00
144 Peja Stojakovic .25 .60
145 Doug Christie .20 .50
146 Scot Pollard .20 .50
147 Hedo Turkoglu .25 .60
148 Vlade Divac .25 .60
149 Tim Duncan .75 2.00
150 David Robinson .60 1.50
151 Antonio Daniels .20 .50
152 Sean Elliott .25 .60
153 Derek Anderson .25 .60
154 Avery Johnson .25 .60
155 Malik Rose .20 .50
156 Gary Payton .50 1.25
157 Rashard Lewis .25 .60
158 Patrick Ewing .50 1.25
159 Vin Baker .20 .50
160 Emanual Davis .20 .50
161 Desmond Mason .25 .60
162 Vince Carter .60 1.50
163 Morris Peterson .20 .50
164 Antonio Davis .25 .60
165 Keon Clark .20 .50
166 Chris Childs .20 .50
167 Charles Oakley .25 .60
168 Alvin Williams .20 .50
169 Dell Curry .20 .50
170 Karl Malone .60 1.50
171 John Stockton .60 1.50
172 Donyell Marshall .20 .50
173 John Starks .20 .50
174 Bryon Russell .20 .50
175 David Benoit .20 .50
176 Jacque Vaughn .20 .50
177 Shareef Abdur-Rahim .25 .60
178 Mike Bibby .30 .75
179 Michael Dickerson .20 .50
180 Bryant Reeves .20 .50
181 Grant Long .20 .50
182 Stromile Swift .20 .50
183 Richard Hamilton .40 1.00
184 Tyrone Nesby .20 .50
185 Jahidi White .20 .50
186 Chris Whitney .20 .50
187 Courtney Alexander .20 .50
188 Christian Laettner .25 .60
189 Kobe Bryant CL 2.50 6.00
190 Kevin Garnett CL .75 2.00
191 Vladimir Radmanovic RC .30 .75
192 Alvin Jones RC .25 .60
193 Tyson Chandler RC .60 1.50
194 Omar Cook RC .40 1.00
195 Kedrick Brown RC .25 .60
196 DeSagana Diop RC .25 .60
197 Eddie Griffin RC .30 .75
198 Zach Randolph RC .75 2.00
199 Eddy Curry RC .40 1.00
200 Jeryl Sasser RC .25 .60
201 Gerald Wallace RC .50 1.25
202 Jamaal Tinsley RC .30 .75
203 Kirk Haston RC .25 .60
204 Terence Morris RC .25 .60
205 Jarron Collins RC .40 1.00
206 Joseph Forte RC .25 .60
207 Kenny Satterfield RC .25 .60
208 Michael Wright RC .40 1.00
209 Jason Richardson RC .60 1.50
210 Michael Bradley RC .25 .60
211 Gilbert Arenas RC 1.00 2.50
212 Jeff Trepagnier RC .25 .60
213 Samuel Dalembert RC .40 1.00
214 Troy Murphy RC .30 .75
215 Rodney White RC .25 .60
216 Joe Johnson RC .60 1.50
217 Richard Jefferson RC .50 1.25
218 Kwame Brown RC .40 1.00
219 Jason Collins RC .30 .75
220 Steven Hunter RC .25 .60

2001-02 Upper Deck MVP Airborne

COMPLETE SET (7) 5.00 12.00
STATED ODDS 1:24
A1 Kobe Bryant 5.00 12.00
A2 Vince Carter 1.25 3.00
A3 Baron Davis .60 1.50
A4 Kevin Garnett 1.50 4.00
A5 Tracy McGrady 1.00 2.50
A6 Shaquille O'Neal 2.50 6.00
A7 Desmond Mason .50 1.25

2001-02 Upper Deck MVP Authentic Kobe

COMMON AU (KBA1-KBA2) 100.00 200.00
AU PRINT RUN 100 SERIAL #'d SETS
COMMON FLOOR (KBF1-KBF8) 10.00 25.00
OVERALL ODDS 1:288 H, 1:240 R
KBW Kobe Bryant Warm-up 40.00 100.00
KBSS Kobe Bryant Shirt 40.00 100.00

2001-02 Upper Deck MVP Basketball Diary

COMPLETE SET (14) 6.00 15.00
STATED ODDS 1:12
BD1 Alonzo Mourning .75 2.00
BD2 Wang Zhizhi .50 1.25
BD3 Chris Webber .60 1.50
BD4 Paul Pierce .75 2.00
BD5 Kevin Garnett 1.25 3.00
BD6 Dirk Nowitzki 1.25 3.00
BD7 Marc Jackson .30 .75
BD8 Kobe Bryant 4.00 10.00
BD9 Ray Allen .75 2.00
BD10 Tracy McGrady .75 2.00
BD11 Jerry Stackhouse .50 1.25
BD12 Kenyon Martin .50 1.25
BD13 Rasheed Wallace .60 1.50
BD14 Steve Francis .50 1.25

2001-02 Upper Deck MVP Game Night Gear

STATED ODDS 1:96 H, 1:120 R
AIG Allen Iverson 8.00 20.00
AJG A.J. Guyton 2.00 5.00
BCG Brian Cardinal 2.00 5.00
CMG Chris Mihm 2.00 5.00
COG Corey Maggette 2.50 6.00
DAG Darrell Armstrong 2.00 5.00
DGG Dean Garrett 2.00 5.00
DHG Donnell Harvey 2.00 5.00
IRG Isaiah Rider 2.50 6.00
JAG John Amaechi 2.00 5.00
JSG Jerry Stackhouse 3.00 8.00
KBG Kobe Bryant 40.00 100.00
KGG Kevin Garnett 8.00 20.00
KVG Keith Van Horn 2.50 6.00
LMG Lamond Murray 2.00 5.00
MAG Marcus Camby 2.50 6.00
MCG Antonio McDyess 2.50 6.00
RMG Ron Mercer 2.00 5.00
WSG Wally Szczerbiak 2.50 6.00

2001-02 Upper Deck MVP Game Night Gear Autographs

STATED PRINT RUN 100 SERIAL #'d SETS
CMA Chris Mihm 8.00 20.00
COA Corey Maggette 8.00 20.00
DAA Darrell Armstrong 8.00 20.00
DHA Donnell Harvey 8.00 20.00
JSA Jerry Stackhouse 15.00 40.00
KBA Kobe Bryant 1,500.00 3,000.00
KGA Kevin Garnett 150.00 400.00
LMA Lamond Murray 8.00 20.00
MCA Antonio McDyess 12.00 30.00
WSA Wally Szczerbiak 8.00 20.00

2001-02 Upper Deck MVP Respect the Game

COMPLETE SET (14) 8.00 20.00
STATED ODDS 1:12
RG1 Kobe Bryant 5.00 12.00
RG2 Gary Payton 1.00 2.50
RG3 Tim Duncan 1.50 4.00
RG4 Lamar Odom .50 1.25
RG5 Vince Carter 1.25 3.00
RG6 Eddie Jones .60 1.50
RG7 Kevin Garnett 1.50 4.00
RG8 Jamal Mashburn .50 1.25
RG9 Michael Finley .60 1.50
RG10 Shaquille O'Neal 2.50 6.00
RG11 Latrell Sprewell .75 2.00
RG12 Steve Francis .60 1.50
RG13 Reggie Miller 1.25 3.00
RG14 Ray Allen 1.00 2.50

2001-02 Upper Deck MVP Souvenirs

STATED ODDS 1:96 HOBBY
*GOLD: 1.25X TO 3X SOUVENIR HI
GOLD PRINT RUN 50 SER.#'d SETS
AJ Antawn Jamison 3.00 8.00
AM Andre Miller 3.00 8.00
CW Chris Webber 5.00 12.00
DM Darius Miles 2.50 6.00
DR David Robinson 8.00 20.00
JK Jason Kidd 6.00 15.00
JS Jerry Stackhouse 4.00 10.00
JT Jason Terry 4.00 10.00
KB Kobe Bryant 40.00 100.00
KG Kevin Garnett 10.00 25.00
KM Karl Malone 8.00 20.00
MC Antonio McDyess 3.00 8.00
MF Michael Finley 4.00 10.00
RH Richard Hamilton 5.00 12.00
RM Ron Mercer 2.50 6.00
SF Steve Francis 4.00 10.00
SH Shawn Marion 4.00 10.00
SM Stephon Marbury 5.00 12.00
TB Terrell Brandon 3.00 8.00

2001-02 Upper Deck MVP Souvenirs Combos

STATED ODDS 1:288
*GOLD: 1X TO 2.5X COMBO HI
GOLD PRINT RUN 50 SER.#'d SETS
AWPP A.Walker/P.Pierce 10.00 25.00
BDJM B.Davis/J.Mashburn 8.00 20.00
DMQRCM Miles/Rchrdsn/Mggtte 8.00 20.00
DRDA D.Robinson/D.Anderson 8.00 20.00
JKSM J.Kidd/S.Marion 10.00 25.00
KBDM K.Bryant/D.Miles 40.00 100.00
KBKG K.Bryant/K.Garnett 75.00 200.00
KMJS K.Malone/J.Stockton 15.00 40.00
SMKMKV Mrbury/Mrtn/V.Horn 8.00 20.00

2001-02 Upper Deck MVP Watch

COMPLETE SET (7) 8.00 20.00
STATED ODDS 1:24
M1 Shaquille O'Neal 3.00 8.00
M2 Vince Carter 1.50 4.00
M3 Chris Webber 1.00 2.50
M4 Karl Malone 1.50 4.00
M5 Kevin Garnett 2.00 5.00
M6 Kobe Bryant 6.00 15.00
M7 Tim Duncan 2.00 5.00

2002-03 Upper Deck MVP

COMPLETE SET (220) 20.00 50.00
1 Shareef Abdur-Rahim .20 .50
2 Jason Terry .15 .40
3 Toni Kukoc .20 .50
4 DerMarr Johnson .12 .30
5 Nazr Mohammed .12 .30
6 Theo Ratliff .12 .30
7 Dion Glover .12 .30
8 Paul Pierce .30 .75
9 Antoine Walker .15 .40
10 Kenny Anderson .15 .40
11 Tony Delk .12 .30
12 Eric Williams .12 .30
13 Rodney Rogers .12 .30
14 Jamal Mashburn .15 .40
15 Baron Davis .20 .50
16 David Wesley .12 .30
17 Elden Campbell .12 .30
18 P.J. Brown .12 .30
19 Jamaal Magloire .12 .30
20 Stacey Augmon .12 .30
21 Jalen Rose .15 .40
22 Marcus Fizer .12 .30
23 Tyson Chandler .20 .50
24 Trenton Hassell .12 .30
25 Eddy Curry .12 .30
26 Travis Best .12 .30
27 Andre Miller .15 .40
28 Lamond Murray .12 .30
29 Ricky Davis .15 .40
30 Zydrunas Ilgauskas .15 .40
31 Jumaine Jones .12 .30
32 Chris Mihm .12 .30
33 Dirk Nowitzki .50 1.25
34 Michael Finley .20 .50
35 Steve Nash .40 1.00
36 Nick Van Exel .20 .50
37 Raef LaFrentz .12 .30
38 Adrian Griffin .12 .30
39 Avery Johnson .15 .40
40 Marcus Camby .15 .40
41 Juwan Howard .15 .40
42 James Posey .12 .30
43 Ryan Bowen .12 .30
44 Donnell Harvey .12 .30
45 Voshon Lenard .12 .30
46 Jerry Stackhouse .20 .50
47 Clifford Robinson .20 .50
48 Chucky Atkins .12 .30
49 Ben Wallace .25 .60
50 Jon Barry .12 .30
51 Corliss Williamson .12 .30
52 Antawn Jamison .15 .40
53 Jason Richardson .20 .50
54 Danny Fortson .12 .30
55 Gilbert Arenas .20 .50
56 Bob Sura .12 .30
57 Troy Murphy .15 .40
58 Steve Francis .20 .50
59 Cuttino Mobley .12 .30
60 Eddie Griffin .12 .30
61 Kenny Thomas .12 .30
62 Moochie Norris .12 .30
63 Kelvin Cato .12 .30
64 Glen Rice .15 .40
65 Reggie Miller .40 1.00
66 Jermaine O'Neal .15 .40
67 Ron Mercer .12 .30
68 Jamaal Tinsley .12 .30
69 Al Harrington .15 .40
70 Ron Artest .15 .40
71 Austin Croshere .12 .30
72 Elton Brand .15 .40
73 Darius Miles .15 .40
74 Lamar Odom .20 .50
75 Quentin Richardson .12 .30
76 Corey Maggette .15 .40
77 Jeff McInnis .12 .30
78 Michael Olowokandi .12 .30
79 Kobe Bryant 1.50 4.00
80 Shaquille O'Neal .75 2.00
81 Derek Fisher .20 .50
82 Rick Fox .12 .30
83 Robert Horry .20 .50
84 Devean George .12 .30
85 Samaki Walker .12 .30
86 Pau Gasol .30 .75
87 Jason Williams .25 .60
88 Shane Battier .20 .50
89 Stromile Swift .12 .30
90 Lorenzen Wright .12 .30
91 Tony Massenburg .12 .30
92 Eddie Jones .20 .50
93 Alonzo Mourning .30 .75
94 Brian Grant .12 .30
95 Anthony Carter .12 .30
96 LaPhonso Ellis .15 .40
97 Jim Jackson .12 .30
98 Ray Allen .30 .75
99 Glenn Robinson .20 .50
100 Sam Cassell .15 .40
101 Tim Thomas .12 .30
102 Anthony Mason .15 .40
103 Joel Przybilla .12 .30
104 Ervin Johnson .12 .30
105 Kevin Garnett .50 1.25
106 Wally Szczerbiak .15 .40
107 Chauncey Billups .20 .50
108 Terrell Brandon .12 .30
109 Marc Jackson .12 .30
110 Joe Smith .15 .40
111 Jason Kidd .30 .75
112 Keith Van Horn .15 .40
113 Kenyon Martin .20 .50
114 Kerry Kittles .12 .30
115 Richard Jefferson .15 .40
116 Jason Collins .12 .30
117 Todd MacCulloch .12 .30
118 Allan Houston .20 .50
119 Latrell Sprewell .20 .50
120 Kurt Thomas .12 .30
121 Antonio McDyess .15 .40
122 Othella Harrington .12 .30
123 Clarence Weatherspoon .12 .30
124 Tracy McGrady .30 .75
125 Mike Miller .15 .40
126 Darrell Armstrong .12 .30
127 Grant Hill .30 .75
128 Horace Grant .15 .40
129 Steven Hunter .12 .30
130 Allen Iverson .50 1.25
131 Dikembe Mutombo .30 .75
132 Aaron McKie .12 .30
133 Derrick Coleman .15 .40
134 Eric Snow .12 .30
135 Matt Harpring .15 .40
136 Stephon Marbury .25 .60
137 Shawn Marion .20 .50
138 Joe Johnson .15 .40
139 Anfernee Hardaway .50 1.25
140 Iakovos Tsakalidis .12 .30
141 Tom Gugliotta .12 .30
142 Bo Outlaw .12 .30
143 Rasheed Wallace .25 .60
144 Damon Stoudamire .20 .50
145 Scottie Pippen .50 1.25
146 Ruben Patterson .12 .30
147 Derek Anderson .12 .30
148 Dale Davis .12 .30
149 Bonzi Wells .12 .30
150 Chris Webber .25 .60
151 Peja Stojakovic .15 .40
152 Mike Bibby .20 .50
153 Doug Christie .12 .30
154 Vlade Divac .15 .40
155 Bobby Jackson .12 .30
156 Hedo Turkoglu .15 .40
157 Tim Duncan .50 1.25
158 David Robinson .40 1.00
159 Steve Smith .15 .40
160 Tony Parker .30 .75
161 Antonio Daniels .12 .30
162 Charles Smith .12 .30
163 Bruce Bowen .12 .30
164 Gary Payton .30 .75
165 Rashard Lewis .15 .40
166 Vin Baker .15 .40
167 Brent Barry .15 .40
168 Desmond Mason .15 .40
169 Vladimir Radmanovic .12 .30
170 Vince Carter .40 1.00
171 Morris Peterson .15 .40
172 Antonio Davis .15 .40
173 Hakeem Olajuwon .25 .60
174 Alvin Williams .12 .30
175 Jerome Williams .12 .30
176 Keon Clark .12 .30
177 Karl Malone .40 1.00
178 John Stockton .40 1.00
179 Donyell Marshall .12 .30
180 Andrei Kirilenko .15 .40
181 Bryon Russell .12 .30
182 Jarron Collins .12 .30
183 DeShawn Stevenson .12 .30
184 Michael Jordan 2.00 5.00
185 Richard Hamilton .25 .60
186 Kwame Brown .12 .30
187 Chris Whitney .12 .30
188 Tyronn Lue .12 .30
189 Brendan Haywood .12 .30
190 Jahidi White .12 .30
191 DaJuan Wagner RC .40 1.00
192 Jay Williams RC .40 1.00
193 Yao Ming RC 2.50 6.00
194 Drew Gooden RC .50 1.25
195 Chris Jefferies RC .30 .75
196 Casey Jacobsen RC .40 1.00
197 Juan Dixon RC .40 1.00
198 Melvin Ely RC .40 1.00
199 Curtis Borchardt RC .30 .75
200 John Salmons RC .50 1.25
201 Carlos Boozer RC .50 1.25
202 Fred Jones RC .40 1.00
203 Frank Williams RC .30 .75
204 Jamal Sampson RC .30 .75
205 Dan Dickau RC .30 .75
206 Marcus Haislip RC .30 .75
207 Jared Jeffries RC .40 1.00
208 Amare Stoudemire RC 1.25 3.00
209 Caron Butler RC .50 1.25
210 Qyntel Woods RC .30 .75
211 Kareem Rush RC .40 1.00
212 Ryan Humphrey RC .40 1.00
213 Jiri Welsch RC .40 1.00
214 Mike Dunleavy RC .50 1.25
215 Tayshaun Prince RC 1.00 2.50
216 Nene Hilario RC .50 1.25
217 Nikoloz Tskitishvili RC .30 .75
218 Bostjan Nachbar RC .40 1.00
219 Efthimios Rentzias RC .30 .75
220 Rod Grizzard RC .30 .75

2002-03 Upper Deck MVP Classic

*CLASSIC: .5X TO 1.25X BASE CARD HI
STATED ODDS 1:2

2002-03 Upper Deck MVP Classic Black

*BLACK: 10X TO 25X BASE CARD HI
PRINT RUN 50 SERIAL #'d SETS

2002-03 Upper Deck MVP Gold

*GOLD: 8X TO 20X BASE CARD HI
PRINT RUN 100 SERIAL #'d SETS
79 Kobe Bryant 25.00 60.00

2002-03 Upper Deck MVP Air Apparent

COMPLETE SET (7) 5.00 12.00
STATED ODDS 1:24
1 Kobe Bryant 6.00 15.00
2 Kevin Garnett 2.00 5.00
3 Darius Miles .50 1.25
4 Vince Carter 1.50 4.00
5 Tracy McGrady 1.25 3.00
6 Rashard Lewis .60 1.50
7 Jason Richardson .75 2.00

2002-03 Upper Deck MVP Basketball Diary

COMPLETE SET (14) 8.00 20.00
STATED ODDS 1:12
B1 Michael Jordan 5.00 12.00
2 Kobe Bryant 4.00 10.00
3 Kevin Garnett 1.25 3.00
4 Dirk Nowitzki 1.25 3.00
5 Shaquille O'Neal 2.00 5.00
6 Pau Gasol .75 2.00
7 Stephon Marbury .60 1.50
8 Jerry Stackhouse .50 1.25
9 Steve Francis .50 1.25
10 Jason Richardson .50 1.25
11 Elton Brand .40 1.00
12 Vince Carter 1.00 2.50
13 Jamaal Tinsley .30 .75
14 Tim Duncan 1.25 3.00

2002-03 Upper Deck MVP East Side West Side Shooting Shirt

PRINT RUN 100 SERIAL #'d SETS
BD/SM B.Davis/S.Marbury 15.00 40.00
JK/JS J.Kidd/J.Stockton 40.00 80.00
KW/CW K.Martin/C.Webber 25.00 60.00
MJ/KB M.Jordan/K.Bryant 200.00 500.00
PP/SH P.Pierce/S.Marion 25.00 60.00
RH/PS R.Hamilton/P.Stojakovic 15.00 40.00

2002-03 Upper Deck MVP Materials Combo

STATED ODDS 1:144
1 Chris Webber 5.00 12.00
2 Kobe Bryant 30.00 80.00
3 Kevin Garnett 10.00 25.00
4 Lamar Odom 4.00 10.00
5 Michael Jordan 40.00 80.00
6 Wally Szczerbiak 3.00 8.00

2002-03 Upper Deck MVP Materials Shooting Shirt

STATED ODDS 1:72
AKS Andrei Kirilenko 3.00 8.00
AWS Antoine Walker 3.00 8.00
DJS DerMarr Johnson 2.50 6.00
EBS Elton Brand 3.00 8.00
JSS Jeryl Sasser 2.50 6.00
KBS Kobe Bryant 40.00 100.00
MBS Mike Bibby 4.00 10.00
MJS Michael Jordan 60.00 150.00
MPS Morris Peterson 3.00 8.00
SHS Shawn Marion 4.00 10.00
SMS Stephon Marbury 5.00 12.00

2002-03 Upper Deck MVP Materials Warm Up

STATED ODDS 1:48
ADW Antonio Davis 2.50 6.00
BDW Baron Davis 3.00 8.00
BHW Brendan Haywood 2.00 5.00
DNW Dirk Nowitzki 8.00 20.00
GRW Glenn Robinson 3.00 8.00
KBW Kobe Bryant 40.00 100.00
KGW Kevin Garnett 8.00 20.00
KMW Karl Malone 6.00 15.00
KVW Keith Van Horn 2.50 6.00
MCW Antonio McDyess 2.50 6.00
MJW Michael Jordan 40.00 100.00
SAW Shareef Abdur-Rahim 3.00 8.00

2002-03 Upper Deck MVP Moments

COMPLETE SET (7) 8.00 20.00
STATED ODDS 1:24
1 Shaquille O'Neal 2.50 6.00
2 Jason Kidd 1.00 2.50
3 Allen Iverson 1.50 4.00
4 Tim Duncan 1.50 4.00
5 Michael Jordan 6.00 15.00
6 Kevin Garnett 1.50 4.00
7 Kobe Bryant 5.00 12.00

2002-03 Upper Deck MVP Prosign

STATED ODDS 1:288
1 Brandon Armstrong 5.00 12.00
2 Corey Maggette 6.00 15.00
3 DerMarr Johnson 5.00 12.00
4 Eddie Griffin 5.00 12.00
5 Gilbert Arenas 10.00 25.00
6 Hanno Mottola 5.00 12.00
7 Jeff Trepagnier 5.00 12.00
8 Jamaal Magloire 5.00 12.00
9 Jason Richardson 8.00 20.00
12 Kobe Bryant 125.00 300.00
13 Kenyon Martin 15.00 40.00
17 Michael Bradley 5.00 12.00
18 Marcus Fizer 5.00 12.00
20 Terence Morris 5.00 12.00
21 Paul Pierce 20.00 50.00
22 Richard Jefferson 10.00 25.00
25 Samuel Dalembert 5.00 12.00
26 Tyson Chandler 8.00 20.00

2002-03 Upper Deck MVP Rising to the Occasion

COMPLETE SET (14) 8.00 20.00
STATED ODDS 1:12
1 Kobe Bryant 4.00 10.00
2 Kevin Garnett 1.25 3.00
3 Michael Jordan 5.00 12.00
4 Paul Pierce .75 2.00
5 Shawn Marion .50 1.25
6 Jason Kidd .75 2.00
7 Peja Stojakovic .40 1.00
8 Tim Duncan 1.25 3.00
9 Shaquille O'Neal 2.00 5.00
10 Steve Francis .50 1.25
11 Ray Allen .75 2.00
12 Latrell Sprewell .50 1.25
13 Darius Miles .30 .75
14 Vince Carter 1.00 2.50

2002-03 Upper Deck MVP Triple Dimension

STATED PRINT RUN 25 SERIAL #'d SETS
KGWSTB Garnett/Szcz/Brandon 25.00 60.00
KMJSAK Malone/Stockton/Kirilenko 30.00 80.00
MJKBKG Jordan/Kobe/Garnett 300.00 600.00
TMMMGH McG/M.Miller/Hill 30.00 80.00

2003-04 Upper Deck MVP

COMPLETE SET (230) 75.00 200.00
201-230 STATED ODDS 1:1
1 Shareef Abdur-Rahim .30 .75
2 Jason Terry .25 .60
3 Terrell Brandon .20 .50
4 Alan Henderson .20 .50
5 Dan Dickau .20 .50
6 Theo Ratliff .20 .50
7 Dion Glover .20 .50
8 Paul Pierce .50 1.25
9 Antoine Walker .30 .75
10 Eric Williams .20 .50
11 Tony Delk .25 .60
12 J.R. Bremer .20 .50
13 Vin Baker .20 .50
14 Jalen Rose .25 .60
15 Marcus Fizer .20 .50
16 Tyson Chandler .25 .60
17 Jamal Crawford .30 .75
18 Eddy Curry .20 .50
19 Scottie Pippen .75 2.00
20 Darius Miles .20 .50
21 Dajuan Wagner .20 .50
22 Ricky Davis .25 .60
23 Zydrunas Ilgauskas .25 .60
24 Carlos Boozer .25 .60
25 Chris Mihm .20 .50
26 Dirk Nowitzki .75 2.00
27 Michael Finley .30 .75
28 Steve Nash .60 1.50
29 Nick Van Exel .30 .75
30 Raef LaFrentz .20 .50
31 Eduardo Najera .20 .50
32 Shawn Bradley .20 .50
33 Marcus Camby .25 .60
34 Vincent Yarbrough .20 .50
35 Rodney White .20 .50
36 Nene Hilario .25 .60
37 Nikoloz Tskitishvili .20 .50
38 Shammond Williams .20 .50
39 Richard Hamilton .40 1.00
40 Clifford Robinson .20 .50
41 Chauncey Billups .40 1.00
42 Ben Wallace .40 1.00
43 Elden Campbell .20 .50
44 Corliss Williamson .20 .50
45 Antawn Jamison .30 .75
46 Jason Richardson .30 .75
47 Danny Fortson .20 .50
48 Speedy Claxton .20 .50
49 Mike Dunleavy .25 .60
50 Troy Murphy .20 .50
51 Steve Francis .30 .75
52 Cuttino Mobley .20 .50
53 Eddie Griffin .20 .50
54 Yao Ming .75 2.00
55 Maurice Taylor .20 .50
56 Kelvin Cato .20 .50
57 Glen Rice .20 .50
58 Reggie Miller .60 1.50
59 Jermaine O'Neal .30 .75
60 Scot Pollard .20 .50
61 Jamaal Tinsley .20 .50
62 Al Harrington .25 .60
63 Ron Artest .30 .75
64 Danny Ferry .20 .50
65 Elton Brand .25 .60
66 Andre Miller .25 .60
67 Lamar Odom .25 .60
68 Quentin Richardson .25 .60
69 Corey Maggette .25 .60
70 Chris Wilcox .20 .50
71 Marko Jaric .20 .50
72 Kobe Bryant 2.50 6.00
73 Shaquille O'Neal 1.25 3.00
74 Derek Fisher .30 .75
75 Karl Malone .60 1.50
76 Gary Payton .50 1.25
77 Devean George .20 .50
78 Kareem Rush .20 .50
79 Pau Gasol .50 1.25
80 Jason Williams .50 1.25
81 Shane Battier .25 .60
82 Stromile Swift .20 .50
83 Lorenzen Wright .20 .50
84 Mike Miller .25 .60
85 Eddie Jones .30 .75
86 Ken Johnson .20 .50
87 Brian Grant .20 .50
88 Anthony Carter .20 .50
89 Rasual Butler .20 .50
90 Caron Butler .25 .60
91 Marcus Haislip .20 .50
92 Toni Kukoc .30 .75
93 Joe Smith .25 .60
94 Tim Thomas .20 .50
95 Anthony Mason .20 .50
96 Joel Przybilla .20 .50
97 Desmond Mason .25 .60
98 Kevin Garnett .75 2.00
99 Wally Szczerbiak .25 .60
100 Troy Hudson .20 .50
101 Michael Olowokandi .20 .50
102 Kendall Gill .30 .75
103 Sam Cassell .25 .60
104 Jason Kidd .50 1.25
105 Kenyon Martin .30 .75
106 Alonzo Mourning .40 1.00
107 Kerry Kittles .25 .60
108 Richard Jefferson .25 .60
109 Jason Collins .20 .50
110 Dikembe Mutombo .40 1.00
111 Jamal Mashburn .25 .60
112 Baron Davis .30 .75
113 David Wesley .20 .50
114 Kenny Anderson .25 .60
115 P.J. Brown .20 .50
116 Jamaal Magloire .20 .50
117 George Lynch .20 .50
118 Courtney Alexander .20 .50
119 Allan Houston .30 .75
120 Keith Van Horn .25 .60
121 Kurt Thomas .20 .50
122 Antonio McDyess .25 .60
123 Othella Harrington .20 .50
124 Clarence Weatherspoon .20 .50
125 Tracy McGrady .50 1.25
126 Drew Gooden .25 .60
127 Tyronn Lue .20 .50
128 Pat Garrity .20 .50
129 Grant Hill .40 1.00
130 Gordan Giricek .20 .50
131 Juwan Howard .25 .60
132 Allen Iverson .75 2.00
133 Glenn Robinson .25 .60
134 Aaron McKie .20 .50
135 Derrick Coleman .30 .75
136 Eric Snow .30 .75
137 Kenny Thomas .20 .50
138 Stephon Marbury .40 1.00
139 Shawn Marion .30 .75
140 Joe Johnson .25 .60
141 Anfernee Hardaway .75 2.00
142 Amare Stoudemire .40 1.00
143 Casey Jacobsen .20 .50
144 Tom Gugliotta .20 .50
145 Bo Outlaw .20 .50
146 Rasheed Wallace .40 1.00
147 Damon Stoudamire .25 .60
148 Jeff McInnis .20 .50
149 Ruben Patterson .20 .50
150 Derek Anderson .25 .60
151 Dale Davis .20 .50
152 Bonzi Wells .20 .50
153 Chris Webber .40 1.00
154 Peja Stojakovic .25 .60
155 Mike Bibby .30 .75
156 Doug Christie .25 .60
157 Vlade Divac .30 .75
158 Bobby Jackson .25 .60
159 Brad Miller .25 .60
160 Keon Clark .20 .50
161 Tim Duncan .75 2.00
162 David Robinson .60 1.50
163 Steve Smith .25 .60
164 Tony Parker .50 1.25
165 Hedo Turkoglu .25 .60
166 Radoslav Nesterovic .20 .50
167 Manu Ginobili .60 1.50
168 Ron Mercer .20 .50
169 Ray Allen .50 1.25
170 Rashard Lewis .25 .60
171 Antonio Daniels .20 .50
172 Brent Barry .20 .50
173 Predrag Drobnjak .20 .50
174 Vladimir Radmanovic .20 .50
175 Vince Carter .60 1.50
176 Morris Peterson .20 .50
177 Antonio Davis .25 .60
178 Chris Jefferies .20 .50
179 Lindsey Hunter .20 .50
180 Alvin Williams .20 .50
181 Jerome Williams .20 .50
182 Jerome Moiso .20 .50
183 Greg Ostertag .20 .50
184 John Stockton .60 1.50
185 Matt Harpring .20 .50
186 Andrei Kirilenko .25 .60
187 Calbert Cheaney .20 .50
188 Jarron Collins .20 .50
189 DeShawn Stevenson .20 .50
190 Michael Jordan 3.00 8.00
191 Jerry Stackhouse .40 1.00
192 Kwame Brown .20 .50
193 Larry Hughes .25 .60
194 Gilbert Arenas .30 .75
195 Brendan Haywood .20 .50
196 Juan Dixon .20 .50
197 Jahidi White .20 .50
198 Etan Thomas .20 .50
199 Michael Jordan CL 3.00 8.00
200 Michael Jordan CL 3.00 8.00
201 LeBron James RC 50.00 120.00
202 Darko Milicic RC .50 1.25
203 Carmelo Anthony RC 3.00 8.00
204 Chris Bosh RC 2.00 5.00
205 Dwyane Wade RC 5.00 12.00
206 Chris Kaman RC .60 1.50
207 Kirk Hinrich RC .60 1.50
208 T.J. Ford RC .50 1.25

209 Mike Sweetney RC .40 1.00
210 Jarvis Hayes RC .40 1.00
211 Mickael Pietrus RC .50 1.25
212 Nick Collison RC .50 1.25
213 Marcus Banks RC .40 1.00
214 Luke Ridnour RC .60 1.50
215 Reece Gaines RC .40 1.00
216 Troy Bell RC .40 1.00
217 Zarko Cabarkapa RC .40 1.00
218 David West RC .75 2.00
219 Aleksandar Pavlovic RC .50 1.25
220 Dahntay Jones RC .50 1.25
221 Boris Diaw-Riffiod RC .60 1.50
222 Zoran Planinic RC .40 1.00
223 Travis Outlaw RC .50 1.25
224 Brian Cook RC .40 1.00
225 Carlos Delfino RC .50 1.25
226 Ndudi Ebi RC .40 1.00
227 Kendrick Perkins RC .50 1.25
228 Leandro Barbosa RC .60 1.50
229 Josh Howard RC .60 1.50
230 Maciej Lampe RC .40 1.00

2003-04 Upper Deck MVP Black

*BLACK SINGLES: 15X TO 40X BASE HI
*BLACK RCs: 6X TO 15X BASE HI
PRINT RUN 25 SERIAL #'d SETS
190 Michael Jordan 125.00 300.00
199 Michael Jordan CL 125.00 300.00
200 Michael Jordan CL 125.00 300.00
201 LeBron James 5,000.00 10,000.00
205 Dwyane Wade 800.00 1,500.00

2003-04 Upper Deck MVP Gold

*GOLD SINGLES: 6X TO 15X BASE CARD HI
*GOLD CL: 12X TO 30X BASE CARD HI
*GOLD RCs: 4X TO 10X BASE CARD HI
PRINT RUN 100 SERIAL #'d SETS
201 LeBron James 2,000.00 4,000.00

2003-04 Upper Deck MVP Silver

*SINGLES: .75X TO 2X BASE CARD HI
1-200 STATED ODDS 1:2
201-230 STATED ODDS 1:24
205 Dwyane Wade 40.00 100.00

2003-04 Upper Deck MVP Basketball Diary

COMPLETE SET (14) 10.00 25.00
STATED ODDS 1:12
*PLATINUM: 4X TO 10X BASE HI
PLATINUM PRINT RUN 100 SER.#'d SETS
BD1 Yao Ming 1.00 2.50
BD2 Michael Jordan 4.00 10.00
BD3 Kevin Garnett 1.00 2.50
BD4 Jason Richardson .40 1.00
BD5 Jason Kidd .60 1.50
BD6 Peja Stojakovic .30 .75
BD7 Gilbert Arenas .40 1.00
BD8 Kobe Bryant 3.00 8.00
BD9 Tim Duncan 1.00 2.50
BD10 R.Allen/G.Payton .60 1.50
BD11 Vince Carter .75 2.00
BD12 Amare Stoudemire .50 1.25
BD13 LeBron James 12.00 30.00
BD14 T.Duncan/D.Robinson 1.00 2.50

2003-04 Upper Deck MVP Combo Materials

STATED ODDS 1:144
DMRJ Mutombo/Jefferson SP 5.00 12.00
DRTP D.Robinson/T.Parker 10.00 25.00
JSKM J.Stockton/K.Malone 10.00 25.00
JSRH Stack/R.Hamilton SP 6.00 15.00
JWEC J.Williams/E.Curry 5.00 12.00
KBMJ Bryant/Jordan SP 75.00 200.00
SHSM S.Marion/S.Marbury 5.00 12.00
WSTB W.Szczerb/T.Brandon 5.00 12.00

2003-04 Upper Deck MVP Materials Shirts

STATED ODDS 1:72
AKSS Andrei Kirilenko SP 2.00 5.00
CWSS Chris Webber 3.00 8.00
DASS Darrell Armstrong 2.00 5.00
EBSS Elton Brand 2.00 5.00
GWSS Gerald Wallace 2.00 5.00
JKSS Jason Kidd SP 4.00 10.00
JOSS Jermaine O'Neal 2.50 6.00
KBSS Kobe Bryant SP 8.00 20.00
MJSS Michael Jordan SP 50.00 120.00
RMSS Reggie Miller 5.00 12.00
SASS Shareef Abdur-Rahim 2.50 6.00
TCSS Tyson Chandler 2.00 5.00

2003-04 Upper Deck MVP Materials Warmups

STATED ODDS 1:48
AMWU Antonio McDyess 2.00 5.00
CMWU Corey Maggette 2.00 5.00
GAWU Gilbert Arenas 2.50 6.00
JFWU Joseph Forte 2.00 5.00
JMWU Jamaal Magloire 2.00 5.00
JWWU Jay Williams 2.00 5.00
KBWU Kobe Bryant SP 8.00 20.00
KGWU Kevin Garnett 6.00 15.00
MJWU Michael Jordan SP 40.00 100.00
RAWU Ray Allen 4.00 10.00
TKWU Toni Kukoc 2.50 6.00

2003-04 Upper Deck MVP Monumental Moments

STATED ODDS 1:24
MM1 Kobe Bryant 5.00 12.00
MM2 Michael Jordan 6.00 15.00
MM3 Tim Duncan 1.50 4.00
MM4 Ben Wallace .75 2.00
MM5 Bobby Jackson .50 1.25
MM6 David Robinson 1.25 3.00
MM7 Amare Stoudemire .75 2.00

2003-04 Upper Deck MVP ProSign

STATED ODDS 1:288
AJ Antawn Jamison 8.00 20.00
AS Amare Stoudemire 15.00 40.00
BI Chauncey Billups 6.00 15.00
CB Carlos Boozer 4.00 10.00
CK Chris Kaman SP 10.00 25.00
CM Cuttino Mobley 4.00 10.00
DD Dan Dickau 4.00 10.00
DG Dan Gadzuric 4.00 10.00
DJ DerMarr Johnson 4.00 10.00
DW Dajuan Wagner 4.00 10.00
EB Earl Boykins 4.00 10.00
EG Eddie Griffin 4.00 10.00
ET Etan Thomas 4.00 10.00
GI Manu Ginobili/20 15.00 40.00
GO Drew Gooden 5.00 12.00
HA Richard Hamilton SP 12.50 30.00
JD Juan Dixon 4.00 10.00
JM Jerome Moiso 4.00 10.00
JS Jerry Stackhouse 5.00 12.00
KB Kobe Bryant/25 150.00 400.00
LJ LeBron James/23 5,000.00 10,000.00
MA Corey Maggette 4.00 10.00
MP Morris Peterson 6.00 15.00
PP Paul Pierce/34 12.00 30.00
PS Peja Stojakovic SP 8.00 20.00
RE Reggie Evans 4.00 10.00
RH Ryan Humphrey 4.00 10.00
SB Shane Battier 4.00 10.00
SM Shawn Marion/31 15.00 40.00
TP Tony Parker 12.50 30.00
YM Yao Ming/25 30.00 80.00

2003-04 Upper Deck MVP Rising to the Occasion

COMPLETE SET (14) 10.00 25.00
STATED ODDS 1:12
*GOLD: 1.5X TO 4X BASE HI
GOLD PRINT RUN 250 SER.#'d SETS
RO1 Kobe Bryant 4.00 10.00
RO2 LeBron James 50.00 120.00
RO3 Michael Jordan 5.00 12.00
RO4 Desmond Mason .40 1.00
RO5 Richard Jefferson .40 1.00
RO6 Vince Carter 1.00 2.50
RO7 Shaquille O'Neal 2.00 5.00
RO8 Yao Ming 1.25 3.00
RO9 Tracy McGrady .75 2.00
RO10 Jason Richardson .50 1.25
RO11 Rashard Lewis .40 1.00
RO12 Caron Butler .40 1.00
RO13 Baron Davis .50 1.25
RO14 Amare Stoudemire .60 1.50

2003-04 Upper Deck MVP Rising to the Occasion Gold

*GOLD: 1.5X TO 4X BASE HI
RO2 LeBron James 300.00 600.00

2003-04 Upper Deck MVP Sportsnut Fantasy

COMPLETE SET (90) 20.00 50.00
STATED ODDS 1:3
SN1 Shareef Abdur-Rahim .40 1.00
SN2 Jason Terry .30 .75
SN3 Glenn Robinson .30 .75
SN4 Theo Ratliff .25 .60
SN5 Antoine Walker .40 1.00
SN6 Paul Pierce .60 1.50
SN7 Jalen Rose .30 .75
SN8 Eddy Curry .25 .60
SN9 Tyson Chandler .30 .75
SN10 Dajuan Wagner .25 .60
SN11 Darius Miles .25 .60
SN12 Zydrunas Ilgauskas .30 .75
SN13 Michael Finley .40 1.00
SN14 Steve Nash .75 2.00
SN15 Dirk Nowitzki 1.00 2.50
SN16 Nene Hilario .30 .75
SN17 Juwan Howard .30 .75
SN18 Marcus Camby .30 .75
SN19 Richard Hamilton .50 1.25
SN20 Ben Wallace .50 1.25
SN21 Chauncey Billups .50 1.25
SN22 Danny Fortson .25 .60
SN23 Antawn Jamison .40 1.00
SN24 Jason Richardson .40 1.00
SN25 Gilbert Arenas .40 1.00
SN26 Yao Ming 1.00 2.50
SN27 Steve Francis .40 1.00
SN28 Reggie Miller .75 2.00
SN29 Jermaine O'Neal .40 1.00
SN30 Brad Miller .30 .75
SN31 Elton Brand .30 .75
SN32 Michael Olowokandi .25 .60
SN33 Andre Miller .30 .75
SN34 Kobe Bryant 3.00 8.00
SN35 Shaquille O'Neal 1.50 4.00
SN36 Pau Gasol .60 1.50
SN37 Mike Miller .30 .75
SN38 Lorenzen Wright .25 .60
SN39 Alonzo Mourning .50 1.25
SN40 Eddie Jones .40 1.00
SN41 Caron Butler .30 .75
SN42 Gary Payton .60 1.50
SN43 Dan Gadzuric .25 .60
SN44 Sam Cassell .30 .75
SN45 Kevin Garnett 1.00 2.50
SN46 Radoslav Nesterovic .25 .60
SN47 Jason Kidd .60 1.50
SN48 Kenyon Martin .40 1.00
SN49 Dikembe Mutombo .50 1.25
SN50 Baron Davis .40 1.00
SN51 Jamaal Magloire .25 .60
SN52 Jamal Mashburn .30 .75
SN53 Latrell Sprewell .50 1.25
SN54 Allan Houston .40 1.00
SN55 Kurt Thomas .25 .60
SN56 Tracy McGrady .60 1.50
SN57 Drew Gooden .30 .75
SN58 Grant Hill .50 1.25
SN59 Allen Iverson 1.00 2.50
SN60 Todd MacCulloch .25 .60
SN61 Amare Stoudemire .50 1.25
SN62 Stephon Marbury .50 1.25
SN63 Shawn Marion .40 1.00
SN64 Rasheed Wallace .50 1.25
SN65 Damon Stoudamire .30 .75
SN66 Dale Davis .25 .60
SN67 Vlade Divac .40 1.00
SN68 Mike Bibby .40 1.00
SN69 Peja Stojakovic .30 .75
SN70 Chris Webber .50 1.25
SN71 Tim Duncan 1.00 2.50
SN72 Tony Parker .60 1.50
SN73 Ray Allen .60 1.50
SN74 Vladimir Radmanovic .25 .60
SN75 Rashard Lewis .30 .75
SN76 Vince Carter .75 2.00
SN77 Antonio Davis .30 .75
SN78 Karl Malone .75 2.00
SN79 Andrei Kirilenko .30 .75
SN80 Jerry Stackhouse .50 1.25
SN81 Kwame Brown .25 .60
SN82 Nick Collison .30 .75
SN83 Jarvis Hayes .25 .60
SN84 Mike Sweetney .25 .60
SN85 Dwyane Wade 3.00 8.00
SN86 T.J. Ford .30 .75
SN87 Chris Bosh 1.25 3.00
SN88 Darko Milicic .30 .75
SN89 Carmelo Anthony 2.00 5.00
SN90 LeBron James 15.00 40.00

2003-04 Upper Deck MVP Tribute to Greatness

COMMON CARD (MJ1-MJ7) 2.50 6.00
STATED ODDS 1:24
COMMON PLAT. (MJ1-MJ7) 25.00 60.00
PLATINUM PRINT RUN 50 SER.#'d SETS

2008-09 Upper Deck MVP

COMPLETE SET (258) 30.00 60.00
COMP.SET w/o SPs (200) 10.00 25.00
ROOKIE STATED ODDS 1:1
LEGEND STATED ODDS 1:2
1 Joe Johnson .30 .75
2 Marvin Williams .20 .50
3 Acie Law .25 .60
4 Al Horford .30 .75
5 Mike Bibby .30 .75
6 Josh Smith .20 .50
7 Kendrick Perkins .20 .50
8 Glen Davis .25 .60
9 Rajon Rondo .40 1.00
10 Ray Allen .50 1.25
11 Paul Pierce .50 1.25
12 Kevin Garnett .75 2.00
13 Adam Morrison .20 .50
14 Raymond Felton .20 .50
15 Jason Richardson .30 .75
16 Emeka Okafor .20 .50
17 Gerald Wallace .25 .60
18 Tyrus Thomas .20 .50
19 Andres Nocioni .20 .50
20 Joakim Noah .20 .50
21 Luol Deng .25 .60
22 Kirk Hinrich .25 .60
23 Ben Gordon .25 .60
24 Zydrunas Ilgauskas .25 .60
25 Anderson Varejao .20 .50
26 Ben Wallace .40 1.00
27 Daniel Gibson .20 .50
28 LeBron James 2.50 6.00
29 Wally Szczerbiak .25 .60
30 Dirk Nowitzki .75 2.00
31 Josh Howard .25 .60
32 Jason Kidd .50 1.25
33 Jerry Stackhouse .30 .75
34 Jason Terry .25 .60
35 Brandon Bass .20 .50
36 Allen Iverson .60 1.50
37 Carmelo Anthony .40 1.00
38 Marcus Camby .25 .60
39 Kenyon Martin .25 .60
40 J.R. Smith .30 .75
41 Linas Kleiza .20 .50
42 Chauncey Billups .40 1.00
43 Richard Hamilton .25 .60
44 Tayshaun Prince .30 .75
45 Rasheed Wallace .40 1.00
46 Rodney Stuckey .25 .60
47 Jason Maxiell .20 .50
48 Baron Davis .30 .75
49 Monta Ellis .25 .60
50 Al Harrington .25 .60
51 Stephen Jackson .25 .60
52 Marco Belinelli .20 .50
53 Yao Ming .75 2.00
54 Tracy McGrady .50 1.25
55 Luis Scola .25 .60
56 Rafer Alston .20 .50
57 Shane Battier .25 .60
58 Mike Dunleavy .20 .50
59 Danny Granger .25 .60
60 Jermaine O'Neal .30 .75
61 Jamaal Tinsley .20 .50
62 David Harrison .20 .50
63 Elton Brand .25 .60
64 Chris Kaman .20 .50
65 Corey Maggette .25 .60
66 Al Thornton .20 .50
67 Cuttino Mobley .20 .50
68 Tim Thomas .20 .50
69 Kobe Bryant 2.50 6.00
70 Pau Gasol .40 1.00
71 Andrew Bynum .20 .50
72 Jordan Farmar .20 .50
73 Luke Walton .25 .60
74 Lamar Odom .25 .60
75 Rudy Gay .30 .75
76 Kyle Lowry .30 .75
77 Mike Conley Jr. .25 .60
78 Mike Miller .25 .60
79 Hakim Warrick .20 .50
80 Dwyane Wade .60 1.50
81 Shawn Marion .30 .75
82 Ricky Davis .25 .60
83 Jason Williams .25 .60
84 Daequan Cook .20 .50
85 Michael Redd .25 .60
86 Maurice Williams .25 .60
87 Yi Jianlian .40 1.00
88 Charlie Villanueva .20 .50
89 Andrew Bogut .25 .60
90 Al Jefferson .20 .50
91 Rashad McCants .20 .50
92 Corey Brewer .25 .60
93 Randy Foye .30 .75
94 Ryan Gomes .20 .50
95 Richard Jefferson .25 .60
96 Vince Carter .60 1.50
97 Josh Boone .20 .50
98 Bostjan Nachbar .20 .50
99 Sean Williams .20 .50
100 Chris Paul .60 1.50
101 David West .25 .60
102 Peja Stojakovic .25 .60
103 Tyson Chandler .25 .60
104 Morris Peterson .20 .50
105 Julian Wright .20 .50
106 Jamal Crawford .30 .75
107 Zach Randolph .30 .75
108 Stephon Marbury .30 .75
109 Eddy Curry .20 .50
110 Nate Robinson .20 .50
111 David Lee .20 .50
112 Dwight Howard .40 1.00
113 Hedo Turkoglu .25 .60
114 Rashard Lewis .25 .60
115 Jameer Nelson .20 .50
116 Keith Bogans .20 .50
117 Carlos Arroyo .20 .50
118 Andre Iguodala .25 .60
119 Andre Miller .25 .60
120 Willie Green .20 .50
121 Samuel Dalembert .20 .50
122 Reggie Evans .20 .50
123 Thaddeus Young .25 .60
124 Amare Stoudemire .30 .75
125 Steve Nash .60 1.50
126 Leandro Barbosa .25 .60
127 Shaquille O'Neal 1.00 2.50
128 Grant Hill .50 1.25
129 Raja Bell .25 .60
130 Brandon Roy .25 .60
131 LaMarcus Aldridge .30 .75
132 Travis Outlaw .25 .60
133 Martell Webster .25 .60
134 Greg Oden .20 .50
135 Jarrett Jack .25 .60
136 Kevin Martin .25 .60
137 Ron Artest .30 .75
138 Brad Miller .25 .60
139 John Salmons .25 .60
140 Mikki Moore .20 .50
141 Francisco Garcia .20 .50
142 Manu Ginobili .60 1.50
143 Tim Duncan .75 2.00
144 Tony Parker .40 1.00
145 Michael Finley .30 .75
146 Bruce Bowen .25 .60
147 Damon Stoudamire .25 .60
148 Kevin Durant 1.25 3.00
149 Chris Wilcox .20 .50
150 Jeff Green .25 .60
151 Damien Wilkins .20 .50
152 Earl Watson .20 .50
153 Chris Bosh .40 1.00
154 Jose Calderon .20 .50
155 T.J. Ford .20 .50
156 Andrea Bargnani .25 .60
157 Jamario Moon .20 .50
158 Jason Kapono .20 .50
159 Carlos Boozer .25 .60
160 Deron Williams .25 .60
161 Kyle Korver .25 .60
162 Andrei Kirilenko .25 .60
163 Ronnie Brewer .20 .50
164 Mehmet Okur .20 .50
165 Gilbert Arenas .30 .75
166 Caron Butler .25 .60
167 Antawn Jamison .25 .60
168 DeShawn Stevenson .25 .60
169 Brendan Haywood .20 .50
170 Nick Young .20 .50
171 Joe Johnson .30 .75
172 Kevin Garnett .75 2.00
173 Gerald Wallace .25 .60
174 Luol Deng .25 .60
175 LeBron James 2.50 6.00
176 Dirk Nowitzki .75 2.00
177 Carmelo Anthony .40 1.00
178 Chauncey Billups .40 1.00
179 Monta Ellis .25 .60
180 Tracy McGrady .50 1.25
181 Danny Granger .25 .60
182 Chris Kaman .20 .50
183 Kobe Bryant 2.50 6.00
184 Rudy Gay .30 .75
185 Dwyane Wade .60 1.50
186 Michael Redd .25 .60
187 Al Jefferson .20 .50
188 Vince Carter .60 1.50
189 Chris Paul .60 1.50
190 Zach Randolph .30 .75
191 Dwight Howard .40 1.00
192 Andre Iguodala .25 .60
193 Steve Nash .60 1.50
194 Brandon Roy .25 .60
195 Kevin Martin .25 .60
196 Tim Duncan .75 2.00
197 Kevin Durant 1.25 3.00
198 Chris Bosh .40 1.00
199 Deron Williams .25 .60
200 Antawn Jamison .25 .60
201 Derrick Rose RC 2.50 6.00
202 Michael Beasley RC .60 1.50
203 O.J. Mayo RC .50 1.25
204 Russell Westbrook RC 12.00 30.00
205 Kevin Love RC 1.25 3.00
206 Danilo Gallinari RC 1.00 2.50
207 Eric Gordon RC 1.00 2.50
208 Joe Alexander RC .40 1.00
209 D.J. Augustin RC .60 1.50
210 Brook Lopez RC .75 2.00
211 Jerryd Bayless RC .50 1.25
212 Jason Thompson RC .40 1.00
213 Brandon Rush RC .40 1.00
214 Anthony Randolph RC .40 1.00
215 Robin Lopez RC .50 1.25
216 Marreese Speights RC .50 1.25
217 Roy Hibbert RC .50 1.25
218 Courtney Lee RC .50 1.25
219 J.J. Hickson RC .40 1.00
220 Ryan Anderson RC .50 1.25
221 Kosta Koufos RC .40 1.00
223 Darrell Arthur RC .50 1.25
224 Donte Greene RC .40 1.00
225 D.J. White RC .40 1.00
226 Bill Walker RC .40 1.00
227 James Gist RC .40 1.00
228 Joey Dorsey RC .40 1.00
229 Mario Chalmers RC .60 1.50
230 DeAndre Jordan RC .75 2.00
231 Luc Richard Mbah A Moute RC .50 1.25
232 Kyle Weaver RC .40 1.00
233 Sonny Weems RC .40 1.00
234 Chris Douglas-Roberts RC .40 1.00
235 Sean Singletary RC .40 1.00
236 Patrick Ewing Jr. RC .40 1.00
237 Darnell Jackson RC .40 1.00
238 Maarty Leunen RC .40 1.00
240 Deron Washington RC .40 1.00
241 Spud Webb .75 2.00
242 Larry Bird 3.00 8.00
243 Bill Russell 3.00 8.00
244 Kevin McHale 1.25 3.00
245 Michael Jordan 8.00 20.00
246 Scottie Pippen 1.50 4.00
247 Joe Dumars 1.00 2.50
248 Isiah Thomas 1.50 4.00
249 Hakeem Olajuwon 2.00 5.00
250 Magic Johnson 3.00 8.00
251 Wilt Chamberlain 3.00 8.00
252 Kareem Abdul-Jabbar 1.50 4.00
253 Oscar Robertson 1.00 2.50
254 Pete Maravich 2.50 6.00
255 Patrick Ewing 1.50 4.00
256 Willis Reed 1.50 4.00
257 Julius Erving 2.50 6.00
258 David Robinson 2.00 5.00
259 Karl Malone 1.25 3.00
260 John Stockton 2.00 5.00

2008-09 Upper Deck MVP Gold Script

*GOLD 1-200: 3X TO 8X BASE HI
*GOLD 201-240: 1.25X TO 3X BASE HI
*GOLD 241-260: 1.25X TO 3X BASE
PRINT RUN 100 SER.#'d SET
28 LeBron James 12.00 30.00
69 Kobe Bryant 12.00 30.00
175 LeBron James 12.00 30.00
183 Kobe Bryant 12.00 30.00
204 Russell Westbrook 75.00 200.00
245 Michael Jordan 30.00 80.00

2008-09 Upper Deck MVP Silver Script

*SILVER: .6X TO 1.5X BASE HI
OVERALL PARALLEL ODDS 1:4
245 Michael Jordan 15.00 40.00

2008-09 Upper Deck MVP Game Night Souvenirs

STATED ODDS 1:36
*PATCHES: .75X TO 2X BASE HI
PATCH PRINT RUN 25 SER.#'d SETS
GNAB Andris Biedrins 2.00 5.00
GNAI Allen Iverson 6.00 15.00
GNAK Andrei Kirilenko 2.50 6.00
GNAM Adam Morrison 2.00 5.00
GNAW Antoine Walker 2.50 6.00
GNBB Brent Barry 2.00 5.00
GNBC Brian Cook 2.00 5.00
GNBD Boris Diaw 2.50 6.00
GNBO Andrew Bogut 2.50 6.00
GNCM Corey Maggette 2.50 6.00
GNCS Cedric Simmons 2.50 6.00
GNDG Drew Gooden 2.50 6.00
GNDH Devin Harris 2.00 5.00
GNDM Dikembe Mutombo 3.00 8.00
GNDN Dirk Nowitzki 8.00 20.00
GNDW Delonte West 2.00 5.00
GNEB Elton Brand 2.50 6.00
GNGH Grant Hill 6.00 15.00
GNGW Gerald Wallace 2.50 6.00
GNJH Josh Howard 2.50 6.00
GNJJ Joe Johnson 3.00 8.00
GNJK Jason Kidd 5.00 12.00
GNJN Jameer Nelson 2.00 5.00
GNJO Jermaine O'Neal 3.00 8.00
GNJP Johan Petro 2.00 5.00
GNJR Jason Richardson 3.00 8.00
GNJT Jamaal Tinsley 2.00 5.00
GNKG Kevin Garnett 8.00 20.00
GNKM Kenyon Martin 2.50 6.00
GNLJ LeBron James 15.00 40.00
GNMA Donyell Marshall 2.00 5.00
GNMB Mike Bibby 3.00 8.00
GNMG Manu Ginobili 6.00 15.00
GNMR Michael Redd 2.50 6.00
GNPG Pau Gasol 4.00 10.00
GNPS Peja Stojakovic 2.50 6.00
GNRW Rasheed Wallace 4.00 10.00
GNSO Shaquille O'Neal 10.00 25.00
GNWE David West 2.50 6.00
GNZR Zach Randolph 3.00 8.00

2008-09 Upper Deck MVP Kobe MVP

COMMON CARD (KB1-100) 1.50 4.00
STATED ODDS 1:2
COMMON WHITE (KB1-100) 2.50 6.00
WHITE APPROXIMATELY ONE PER BOX

2008-09 Upper Deck MVP Kobe MVP White

COMMON CARD (1-100) 2.50 6.00
INSERTED APPROXIMATELY ONE PER BOX

2008-09 Upper Deck MVP SE

*STARS: 1X TO 2.5X BASE HI
*RCs: .4X TO 1X BASE HI

2008-09 Upper Deck MVP Signatures Required

STATED ODDS 1:288
SRAO K.Azubuike/P.O'Bryant 4.00 10.00
SRAS A.Afflalo/R.Stuckey 4.00 10.00
SRAT A.Tucker/M.Almond 4.00 10.00
SRAW H.Armstrong/J.Wright 4.00 10.00
SRBA C.Brewer/A.Afflalo 4.00 10.00
SRBJ L.James/K.Bryant 3,000.00 6,000.00
SRBL A.Law/M.Bibby 4.00 10.00
SRBP T.Parker/C.Billups 20.00 50.00
SRCW J.Crittenton/M.West 4.00 10.00
SRDD J.Davidson/J.Dudley 4.00 10.00
SRDG K.Durant/J.Green 100.00 250.00
SRDH A.Horford/K.Durant 100.00 250.00
SRDS K.Durant/L.Scola 100.00 250.00
SRFD J.Dudley/R.Felton 4.00 10.00
SRGS T.Green/D.Strawberry 4.00 10.00
SRHG L.Hughes/A.Gray 4.00 10.00
SRHH D.Howard/A.Horford 12.00 30.00
SRHW M.Williams/A.Horford 6.00 15.00
SRIS J.Smith/A.Iguodala 5.00 12.00
SRJG T.Green/B.Jones 4.00 10.00
SRJL J.Smith/L.Williams 4.00 10.00
SRJW M.Williams/R.Jefferson 4.00 10.00
SRKB R.Brewer/K.Korver 5.00 12.00
SRKW C.Kaman/S.Williams 4.00 10.00
SRLB C.Landry/A.Brooks 4.00 10.00
SRLS C.Landry/L.Scola 4.00 10.00
SRMS T.McGrady/L.Scola 25.00 60.00
SRNC D.Nichols/J.Curry 4.00 10.00
SRNL S.Novak/C.Landry 4.00 10.00
SRNS A.Stoudemire/S.Nash 40.00 100.00
SROW S.Williams/P.O'Bryant 4.00 10.00
SRPW D.Williams/C.Paul 25.00 60.00
SRRP G.Pruitt/R.Rondo 6.00 15.00
SRSS S.Hawes/S.Williams 4.00 10.00
SRSW S.Williams/C.Samb 4.00 10.00
SRTL C.Landry/A.Tucker 4.00 10.00
SRWH L.Williams/H.Hill 4.00 10.00
SRWS R.Sessions/M.Williams 4.00 10.00

2008-09 Upper Deck MVP Star Combos

STATED ODDS 1:84
*PATCH: 1.25X TO 3X BASE HI
PATCH PRINT RUN 25 SER.#'d SETS
SCBJ J.Johnson/M.Bibby 4.00 10.00
SCBM C.Maggette/E.Brand 4.00 10.00
SCCN B.Cook/J.Nelson 4.00 10.00
SCCR Z.Randolph/E.Curry 4.00 10.00
SCGD D.Gooden/L.Deng 4.00 10.00
SCGK A.Kirilenko/K.Garnett 6.00 15.00
SCGN K.Garnett/D.Nowitzki 10.00 25.00
SCHD G.Hill/B.Diaw 8.00 20.00
SCIA A.Iverson/C.Anthony 8.00 20.00
SCJB L.James/K.Bryant 200.00 500.00
SCKH D.Harris/J.Kidd 4.00 10.00
SCKN D.Nowitzki/J.Kidd 8.00 20.00
SCMB D.Mutombo/S.Battier 4.00 10.00
SCMO S.O'Neal/S.Marion 8.00 20.00
SCOG P.Gasol/L.Odom 4.00 10.00
SCRB A.Bogut/M.Redd 4.00 10.00
SCRM A.Morrison/J.Richardson 4.00 10.00
SCTO J.O'Neal/J.Tinsley 4.00 10.00
SCWP R.Wallace/T.Prince 4.00 10.00
SCWS P.Stojakovic/D.West 4.00 10.00

2008-09 Upper Deck MVP Victory

COMPLETE SET (90) 25.00 50.00
*ULTIMATE: .6X TO 1.5X VICTORY HI
ULTIMATE STATED ODDS 1:2 HOBBY
1 Joe Johnson .30 .75
2 Al Horford .30 .75
3 Paul Pierce .50 1.25
4 Kevin Garnett .75 2.00
5 Jason Richardson .30 .75
6 Gerald Wallace .25 .60
7 Luol Deng .25 .60
8 Ben Gordon .25 .60
9 Ben Wallace .40 1.00
10 LeBron James 2.50 6.00
11 Dirk Nowitzki .75 2.00
12 Jason Kidd .50 1.25
13 Allen Iverson .60 1.50
14 Carmelo Anthony .40 1.00
15 Chauncey Billups .40 1.00
16 Richard Hamilton .30 .75
17 Baron Davis .30 .75
18 Stephen Jackson .25 .60
19 Yao Ming .75 2.00
20 Tracy McGrady .50 1.25
21 Danny Granger .25 .60
22 Jermaine O'Neal .30 .75
23 Chris Kaman .20 .50
24 Corey Maggette .25 .60
25 Kobe Bryant 2.50 6.00
26 Pau Gasol .40 1.00
27 Rudy Gay .30 .75
28 Mike Conley Jr. .25 .60
29 Dwyane Wade .60 1.50
30 Shawn Marion .30 .75
31 Michael Redd .25 .60
32 Maurice Williams .25 .60
33 Al Jefferson .20 .50
34 Rashad McCants .20 .50
35 Richard Jefferson .25 .60
36 Vince Carter .60 1.50
37 Chris Paul .60 1.50
38 David West .25 .60
39 Jamal Crawford .30 .75
40 Zach Randolph .30 .75
41 Dwight Howard .40 1.00
42 Rashard Lewis .25 .60
43 Andre Iguodala .25 .60
44 Andre Miller .25 .60
45 Amare Stoudemire .30 .75
46 Steve Nash .60 1.50
47 Brandon Roy .25 .60
48 Greg Oden .20 .50
49 Kevin Martin .25 .60
50 Ron Artest .30 .75
51 Tim Duncan .75 2.00
52 Tony Parker .40 1.00
53 Kevin Durant 1.25 3.00
54 Jeff Green .25 .60
55 Chris Bosh .40 1.00
56 Jose Calderon .20 .50
57 Carlos Boozer .25 .60
58 Deron Williams .25 .60
59 Gilbert Arenas .30 .75
60 Antawn Jamison .25 .60
61 Derrick Rose 2.00 5.00
62 Michael Beasley .50 1.25
63 O.J. Mayo .40 1.00
64 Russell Westbrook 2.50 6.00
65 Kevin Love 1.00 2.50
66 Danilo Gallinari .75 2.00
67 Eric Gordon .75 2.00
68 Joe Alexander .30 .75
69 D.J. Augustin .50 1.25
70 Brook Lopez .60 1.50
71 Jerryd Bayless .40 1.00
72 Jason Thompson .30 .75
73 Brandon Rush .30 .75
74 Anthony Randolph .30 .75
75 Robin Lopez .40 1.00
76 Marreese Speights .40 1.00
77 Roy Hibbert .40 1.00
78 Mario Chalmers .50 1.25
79 J.J. Hickson .30 .75
80 Ryan Anderson .40 1.00
81 Kosta Koufos .30 .75
82 Sonny Weems .30 .75
83 Courtney Lee .40 1.00
84 Darrell Arthur .40 1.00
85 Donte Greene .30 .75
86 D.J. White .30 .75
87 J.R. Giddens .30 .75
88 Darnell Jackson .30 .75
89 Chris Douglas-Roberts .30 .75
90 Patrick Ewing Jr. .30 .75

1992-93 Upper Deck MVP Holograms

COMP. FACT SET (38) 20.00 50.00
1 Dominique Wilkins .15 .40
2 Reggie Lewis .08 .25
3 Larry Johnson .40 1.00
4 Michael Jordan 12.00 30.00
5 Mark Price .08 .25
6 Derek Harper .08 .25
7 Dikembe Mutombo .15 .40
8 Isiah Thomas .15 .40
9 Chris Mullin .15 .40
10 Hakeem Olajuwon .50 1.25
11 Reggie Miller .30 .75
12 Danny Manning .08 .25
13 James Worthy .15 .40
14 Glen Rice .30 .75
15 Alvin Robertson .08 .25
16 Chuck Person .08 .25
17 Derrick Coleman .08 .25
18 Patrick Ewing .30 .75
19 Scott Skiles .08 .25
20 Hersey Hawkins .08 .25
21 Charles Barkley .50 1.25
22 Clyde Drexler .30 .75
23 Mitch Richmond .30 .75
24 David Robinson .50 1.25
25 Shawn Kemp .75 2.00
26 Karl Malone .50 1.25
27 Pervis Ellison .08 .25
28 Lloyd Daniels .08 .25
29 Todd Day .08 .25
30 Tom Gugliotta 1.00 2.50
31 Robert Horry .50 1.25
32 Christian Laettner .75 2.00
33 Harold Miner .08 .25
34 Alonzo Mourning 1.50 4.00
35 Shaquille O'Neal 6.00 15.00
36 Walt Williams .30 .75
NNO Checklist .08 .25
NNO Album Offer Card .08 .25

2000 Upper Deck NBA Card Clips

COMPLETE SET (58) 25.00 50.00
1 Dikembe Mutombo 1.00 2.50
2 Lorenzen Wright .50 1.25
3 Antoine Walker .50 1.25
4 Kenny Anderson .50 1.25
5 Elden Campbell .50 1.25
6 Baron Davis 1.25 3.00
7 Elton Brand 1.00 2.50
8 Ron Mercer .50 1.25
9 Andre Miller .50 1.25
10 Chris Mihm .50 1.25
11 Michael Finley .60 1.50
12 Dirk Nowitzki 2.00 5.00
13 Antonio McDyess .50 1.25
14 Nick Van Exel .50 1.25
15 Jerry Stackhouse .50 1.25
16 Mateen Cleaves .50 1.25
17 Antawn Jamison .50 1.25
18 Larry Hughes .50 1.25
19 Steve Francis .60 1.50
20 Hakeem Olajuwon 1.00 2.50
21 Reggie Miller 1.25 3.00
22 Jalen Rose .50 1.25
23 Michael Olowokandi .50 1.25
24 Lamar Odom 1.00 2.50
25 Shaquille O'Neal 2.50 6.00
26 Kobe Bryant 4.00 10.00
27 Alonzo Mourning 1.00 2.50
28 Tim Hardaway .50 1.25
29 Ray Allen 1.25 3.00
30 Glenn Robinson .50 1.25
31 Kevin Garnett 2.50 6.00
32 Wally Szczerbiak .50 1.25
33 Keith Van Horn .50 1.25
34 Stephon Marbury .60 1.50
35 Allan Houston .50 1.25
36 Latrell Sprewell .50 1.25
37 Grant Hill 1.25 3.00
38 Tracy McGrady 1.50 4.00
39 Allen Iverson 1.50 4.00
40 Toni Kukoc .50 1.25
41 Jason Kidd 1.50 4.00
42 Anfernee Hardaway .50 1.25
43 Scottie Pippen 1.50 4.00
44 Rasheed Wallace 1.00 2.50
45 Chris Webber 1.25 3.00
46 Jason Williams .50 1.25
47 Tim Duncan 2.00 5.00
48 David Robinson 2.00 5.00
49 Gary Payton .50 1.25
50 Vin Baker .50 1.25
51 Charles Oakley .50 1.25
52 Vince Carter 2.00 5.00
53 Karl Malone 1.50 4.00
54 John Stockton 1.50 4.00
55 Shareef Abdur-Rahim .50 1.25
56 Bryant Reeves .50 1.25
57 Mitch Richmond .50 1.25
58 Juwan Howard .50 1.25

2007-08 Upper Deck NBA Rookie Box Set

COMPLETE SET (30) 10.00 25.00
1 Arron Afflalo .40 1.00
2 Morris Almond .30 .75
3 Corey Brewer .40 1.00
4 Aaron Brooks .40 1.00

5 Wilson Chandler .40 1.00
6 Mike Conley Jr. 1.25 3.00
7 Daequan Cook .40 1.00
8 Javaris Crittenton .30 .75
9 Glen Davis .40 1.00
10 Jared Dudley .40 1.00
11 Kevin Durant 5.00 12.00
12 Nick Fazekas .30 .75
13 Jeff Green .40 1.00
14 Taurean Green .30 .75
15 Spencer Hawes .30 .75
16 Al Horford 1.25 3.00
17 Acie Law .30 .75
18 Josh McRoberts .30 .75
19 Joakim Noah .50 1.25
20 Greg Oden .50 1.25
21 Gabe Pruitt .30 .75
22 D.J. Strawberry .30 .75
23 Rodney Stuckey .30 .75
24 Al Thornton .30 .75
25 Alando Tucker .30 .75
26 Sean Williams .30 .75
27 Brandan Wright .40 1.00
28 Julian Wright .30 .75
29 Nick Young .50 1.25
30 Thaddeus Young .50 1.25

2000 Upper Deck National Kobe Bryant

COMPLETE SET (10) 12.00 30.00
COMMON CARD (KB1-KB10) 1.00 2.50

2004 Upper Deck National Convention LeBron James Fan Favorite

STATED PRINT RUN 100 SER.#'d SETS
FF1 LeBron James 10.00 25.00
FF2 LeBron James 10.00 25.00
FF3 LeBron James 10.00 25.00
FF4 LeBron James 10.00 25.00

2004 Upper Deck National Convention VIP

VIP1 LeBron James 6.00 15.00
VIP2 Michael Jordan 8.00 20.00

2006 Upper Deck National NBA

COMPLETE SET (3) 5.00 12.00
PRINT RUN 500 SER.#'d SETS
NBA1 Michael Jordan 3.00 8.00
NBA2 LeBron James 2.50 6.00
NBA3 Chris Paul 1.25 3.00

2006 Upper Deck National NBA VIP

COMPLETE SET (6) 6.00 15.00
1 Michael Jordan 3.00 8.00
2 LeBron James 2.50 6.00
3 Chris Bosh 1.25 3.00
4 Yao Ming 1.25 3.00
5 Tim Duncan 1.25 3.00
6 Chris Paul 1.25 3.00

2011 Upper Deck National Convention VIP

1 Michael Jordan 1.50 4.00
4 LeBron James 1.00 2.50

2012 Upper Deck National Convention VIP

3 LeBron James 2.00 5.00
5 Michael Jordan 4.00 10.00

2013 Upper Deck National Convention

COMPLETE SET (20) 15.00 40.00

2013 Upper Deck National Convention VIP

COMPLETE SET (6) 3.00 8.00

2004 Upper Deck Naxcom LeBron James

NNO LeBron James 10.00 25.00

1997 Upper Deck Nestle Crunch Time

COMPLETE SET (40) 8.00 20.00
CT1 Kenny Anderson .30 .75
CT2 Arvydas Sabonis .30 .75
CT3 Elliot Perry UER Misp. Elliott .25 .60
CT4 Chris Webber .40 1.00
CT5 Michael Jordan 4.00 10.00
CT6 Terrell Brandon .25 .60
CT7 Rick Fox .25 .60
CT8 Brent Barry .30 .75
CT9 Bryant Reeves .25 .60
CT10 Steve Smith .30 .75
CT11 Mookie Blaylock .30 .75
CT12 Christian Laettner .30 .75
CT13 Tim Hardaway .40 1.00
CT14 Voshon Lenard .25 .60
CT15 Dan Majerle .40 1.00
CT16 Glen Rice .40 1.00
CT17 Dell Curry .25 .60
CT18 Karl Malone .75 2.00
CT19 John Stockton .75 2.00
CT20 Mitch Richmond .50 1.25
CT21 Patrick Ewing .60 1.50
CT22 Kobe Bryant 3.00 8.00
CT23 Eddie Jones .40 1.00
CT24 Anfernee Hardaway 1.00 2.50
CT25 Rony Seikaly .30 .75
CT26 Chris Gatling .25 .60
CT27 Kendall Gill .25 .60
CT28 Dale Ellis .25 .60
CT29 Reggie Miller .75 2.00
CT30 Terry Mills .25 .60
CT31 Damon Stoudamire .50 1.25
CT32 Clyde Drexler .50 1.25
CT33 Allen Iverson 1.00 2.50
CT34 Jerry Stackhouse .40 1.00
CT35 Hersey Hawkins .25 .60
CT36 Gary Payton .60 1.50
CT37 Carl Herrera .25 .60
CT38 Rex Chapman .25 .60
CT39 Tom Gugliotta .25 .60
CT40 Latrell Sprewell .50 1.25

1996 Upper Deck Nestle Slam Dunk

COMPLETE SET (40) 8.00 20.00
1 Grant Long .25 .60
2 Scott Burrell .25 .60
3 Ron Harper .30 .75
4 Michael Jordan 4.00 10.00
5 Scottie Pippen .60 1.50
6 Bobby Phills .25 .60
7 Tyrone Hill .25 .60
8 Tony Dumas .25 .60
9 LaPhonso Ellis .25 .60
10 Antonio McDyess .40 1.00
11 Theo Ratliff .30 .75
12 Joe Smith .30 .75
13 Rodney Rogers .25 .60
14 Brent Barry .30 .75
15 Cedric Ceballos .25 .60
16 Eddie Jones .40 1.00
17 Vlade Divac .40 1.00
18 Anthony Peeler .25 .60
19 Kurt Thomas .25 .60
20 Vin Baker .30 .75
21 Kevin Garnett 1.00 2.50
22 Shawn Bradley .25 .60
23 Ed O'Bannon .25 .60
24 Nick Anderson .25 .60
25 Clarence Weatherspoon .25 .60
26 Jerry Stackhouse .50 1.25
27 Charles Barkley .60 1.50
28 Gary Trent .25 .60
29 Brian Grant .30 .75
30 Olden Polynice .25 .60
31 Will Perdue .25 .60
32 Vincent Askew .25 .60
33 Doug Christie .25 .60
34 Chris Morris .25 .60
35 Chris Webber .50 1.25
36 Grant Hill .60 1.50
37 Alonzo Mourning .50 1.25
38 Dee Brown .25 .60
39 Shawn Kemp .40 1.00
40 Rasheed Wallace .50 1.25

1997 Upper Deck Nestle Slam Dunk

COMPLETE SET (40) 8.00 20.00
1 Chris Webber .40 1.00
2 Shawn Kemp .60 1.50
3 Dikembe Mutombo .40 1.00
4 Alonzo Mourning .60 1.50
5 Marcus Camby .40 1.00
6 Otis Thorpe .25 .60
7 Antonio McDyess .30 .75
8 Vin Baker .30 .75
9 Kevin Garnett .75 2.00
10 Patrick Ewing .60 1.50
11 Shareef Abdur-Rahim .60 1.50
12 Antoine Walker .40 1.00
13 Joe Smith .30 .75
14 Glen Rice .40 1.00
15 Juwan Howard .30 .75
16 Eddie Jones .40 1.00
17 Karl Malone .75 2.00
18 Bryant Reeves .25 .60
19 Anfernee Hardaway 1.00 2.50
20 LaPhonso Ellis .25 .60
21 Kerry Kittles .30 .75
22 Michael Jordan 3.00 8.00
23 Latrell Sprewell .50 1.25
24 Olden Polynice .25 .60
25 Rik Smits .25 .60
26 Glenn Robinson .40 1.00
27 Loy Vaught .25 .60
28 Jim Jackson .25 .60
29 Horace Grant .30 .75
30 Allen Iverson 1.00 2.50
31 Clifford Robinson .25 .60
32 Isaiah Rider .30 .75
33 Clyde Drexler .50 1.25
34 Sean Elliott .30 .75
35 Eric Williams .25 .60
36 Larry Johnson .50 1.25
37 Anthony Mason .25 .60
38 Terrell Brandon .25 .60
39 Reggie Miller .75 2.00
40 Kevin Johnson .40 1.00

1997 Upper Deck Nestle Slam Dunk Contestants

COMPLETE SET (6) 25.00 60.00
CC1 Kobe Bryant Champion 25.00 60.00
CC2 Chris Carr 3.00 8.00
CC3 Michael Finley 5.00 12.00
CC4 Darvin Ham 5.00 12.00
CC5 Bob Sura 3.00 8.00
CC6 Ray Allen 6.00 15.00

1994 Upper Deck Nintendo Chaos in the Windy City

NNO Michael Jordan 25.00 60.00

1994 Upper Deck Nothing But Net

COMPLETE SET (15) 5.00 12.00
1 Larry Bird Michael Jordan (I've got an idea) 1.00 2.50
2 Charles Barkley (Can I play) .40 1.00
3 Over the Grand Canyon .20 .50
4 Off your face (Mt. Rushmore) .20 .50
5 Michael Jordan (Through the window off the floor) .75 2.00
6 Larry Bird (Nothing but Net) .75 2.00
7 Michael Jordan Larry Bird (Watch this shot) 1.00 2.50
8 Charles Barkley (Hey, can I play) .30 .75
9 Michael Jordan Larry Bird (No) 1.00 2.50
10 Charles Barkley (The Shark) .30 .75
11 Charles Barkley (Please...Pretty Please) .30 .75
12 Larry Bird Michael Jordan Charles Barkley (No) .75 2.00
13 Michael Jordan (I'm hungry ...) .75 2.00
14 Larry Bird (Play ya to see who buys) .60 1.50
15 McDonald's Logo in Outer Space .08 .25

1998-99 Upper Deck Ovation

COMPLETE SET (80) 25.00 60.00
COMPLETE SET w/o RC (70) 12.00 30.00
1 Steve Smith .30 .75
2 Dikembe Mutombo .60 1.50
3 Antoine Walker .40 1.00
4 Ron Mercer .30 .75
5 Glen Rice .40 1.00
6 Bobby Phills .25 .60
7 Michael Jordan 8.00 20.00
8 Toni Kukoc .40 1.00
9 Dennis Rodman 1.00 2.50
10 Scottie Pippen 1.00 2.50
11 Shawn Kemp .60 1.50
12 Derek Anderson .30 .75
13 Brevin Knight .25 .60
14 Michael Finley .40 1.00
15 Shawn Bradley .25 .60
16 LaPhonso Ellis .25 .60
17 Bobby Jackson .30 .75
18 Grant Hill .60 1.50
19 Jerry Stackhouse .40 1.00
20 Donyell Marshall .25 .60
21 Erick Dampier .25 .60
22 Hakeem Olajuwon .75 2.00
23 Charles Barkley 1.00 2.50
24 Reggie Miller .75 2.00
25 Chris Mullin .50 1.25
26 Rik Smits .30 .75
27 Maurice Taylor .25 .60
28 Lorenzen Wright .25 .60
29 Kobe Bryant 3.00 8.00
30 Eddie Jones .40 1.00
31 Shaquille O'Neal 1.50 4.00
32 Alonzo Mourning .60 1.50
33 Tim Hardaway .50 1.25
34 Jamal Mashburn .40 1.00
35 Ray Allen .60 1.50
36 Terrell Brandon .30 .75
37 Glenn Robinson .40 1.00
38 Kevin Garnett 1.00 2.50
39 Tom Gugliotta .30 .75
40 Stephon Marbury .50 1.25
41 Keith Van Horn .40 1.00
42 Kerry Kittles .30 .75
43 Jayson Williams .25 .60
44 Patrick Ewing .60 1.50
45 Allan Houston .40 1.00
46 Larry Johnson .60 1.50
47 Anfernee Hardaway 1.00 2.50
48 Nick Anderson .25 .60
49 Allen Iverson 1.00 2.50
50 Joe Smith .30 .75
51 Tim Thomas .30 .75
52 Jason Kidd .60 1.50
53 Antonio McDyess .30 .75
54 Damon Stoudamire .40 1.00
55 Isaiah Rider .30 .75
56 Rasheed Wallace .50 1.25
57 Tariq Abdul-Wahad .25 .60
58 Corliss Williamson .25 .60
59 Tim Duncan 1.00 2.50
60 David Robinson .75 2.00
61 Vin Baker .30 .75
62 Gary Payton .60 1.50
63 Chauncey Billups .50 1.25
64 Tracy McGrady .60 1.50
65 Karl Malone .75 2.00
66 John Stockton .75 2.00
67 Shareef Abdur-Rahim .60 1.50
68 Bryant Reeves .25 .60
69 Juwan Howard .30 .75
70 Rod Strickland .30 .75
71 Michael Olowokandi RC 1.00 2.50
72 Mike Bibby RC 1.50 4.00
73 Raef LaFrentz RC 1.00 2.50
74 Antawn Jamison RC 1.25 3.00
75 Vince Carter RC 8.00 20.00
76 Robert Traylor RC .75 2.00
77 Jason Williams RC 2.50 6.00
78 Larry Hughes RC 1.25 3.00
79 Dirk Nowitzki RC 12.00 30.00
80 Paul Pierce RC 6.00 15.00
BK1 Michael Jordan Ball/90 1,000.00 2,000.00

1998-99 Upper Deck Ovation Gold

*STARS: 3X TO 8X BASE CARD HI
*RCs: 1.25X TO 3X BASE HI
STATED PRINT RUN 1000 SERIAL #'d SETS
7 Michael Jordan 75.00 200.00
29 Kobe Bryant 40.00 100.00
75 Vince Carter 40.00 100.00
77 Jason Williams 15.00 40.00
79 Dirk Nowitzki 60.00 150.00
80 Paul Pierce 20.00 50.00

1998-99 Upper Deck Ovation Future Forces

COMPLETE SET (20) 12.00 30.00
STATED ODDS 1:29
F1 Tim Duncan 2.50 6.00
F2 Keith Van Horn 1.00 2.50
F3 Kobe Bryant 8.00 20.00
F4 Tracy McGrady 1.50 4.00
F5 Maurice Taylor .60 1.50
F6 Shareef Abdur-Rahim 1.00 2.50
F7 Kevin Garnett 2.50 6.00
F8 Brevin Knight .60 1.50
F9 Ron Mercer .75 2.00
F10 Tim Thomas .75 2.00
F11 Antoine Walker 1.00 2.50
F12 Michael Finley 1.00 2.50
F13 Grant Hill 1.50 4.00
F14 Jerry Stackhouse 1.00 2.50
F15 Erick Dampier .60 1.50
F16 Lorenzen Wright .60 1.50
F17 Ray Allen 1.50 4.00
F18 Stephon Marbury 1.25 3.00
F19 Allen Iverson 2.50 6.00
F20 Damon Stoudamire 1.00 2.50

1998-99 Upper Deck Ovation Jordan Rules

COMMON CARD (J1-J5) 6.00 15.00
COMMON CARD (J6-J10) 10.00 25.00
COMMON CARD (J11-J15) 12.00 30.00
J1-J5 STATED ODDS 1:23
J6-J10 STATED ODDS 1:45
J11-J15 STATED ODDS 1:99

1998-99 Upper Deck Ovation Superstars of the Court

COMPLETE SET (20) 10.00 25.00
STATED ODDS 1:2
C1 Michael Jordan 4.00 10.00
C2 Tim Duncan 1.00 2.50
C3 Grant Hill .60 1.50
C4 Karl Malone .75 2.00
C5 Dennis Rodman 1.00 2.50
C6 Hakeem Olajuwon .75 2.00
C7 Keith Van Horn .40 1.00
C8 Kobe Bryant 3.00 8.00
C9 Jason Kidd .60 1.50
C10 Stephon Marbury .50 1.25
C11 Reggie Miller .75 2.00
C12 Damon Stoudamire .40 1.00
C13 Tracy McGrady .60 1.50
C14 Scottie Pippen 1.00 2.50
C15 Vin Baker .30 .75
C16 Shaquille O'Neal 1.50 4.00
C17 Anfernee Hardaway 1.00 2.50
C18 Charles Barkley 1.00 2.50
C19 Kevin Garnett 1.00 2.50
C20 Antoine Walker .40 1.00

1999-00 Upper Deck Ovation

COMPLETE SET (90) 30.00 80.00
COMPLETE SET w/o RC (60) 10.00 25.00
61-90 SUBSET: STATED ODDS 1:4
1 Dikembe Mutombo .60 1.50
2 Alan Henderson .25 .60
3 Antoine Walker .40 1.00
4 Paul Pierce .75 2.00
5 David Wesley .25 .60
6 Eddie Jones .40 1.00
7 Toni Kukoc .50 1.25
8 Randy Brown .25 .60
9 Shawn Kemp .60 1.50
10 Zydrunas Ilgauskas .30 .75
11 Michael Finley .40 1.00
12 Dirk Nowitzki 1.25 3.00
13 Nick Van Exel .30 .75
14 Antonio McDyess .30 .75
15 Grant Hill .60 1.50
16 Jerry Stackhouse .40 1.00
17 Antawn Jamison .40 1.00
18 John Starks .40 1.00
19 Hakeem Olajuwon .75 2.00
20 Charles Barkley 1.00 2.50
21 Cuttino Mobley .25 .60
22 Reggie Miller .75 2.00
23 Rik Smits .30 .75
24 Maurice Taylor .25 .60
25 Michael Olowokandi .25 .60
26 Kobe Bryant 3.00 8.00
27 Shaquille O'Neal 1.50 4.00
28 Tim Hardaway .50 1.25
29 Alonzo Mourning .60 1.50
30 Glenn Robinson .30 .75
31 Ray Allen .60 1.50
32 Kevin Garnett 1.00 2.50
33 Joe Smith .30 .75
34 Stephon Marbury .50 1.25
35 Keith Van Horn .30 .75
36 Patrick Ewing .50 1.25
37 Latrell Sprewell .50 1.25
38 Darrell Armstrong .25 .60
39 Bo Outlaw .25 .60
40 Allen Iverson 1.00 2.50
41 Larry Hughes .30 .75
42 Jason Kidd .60 1.50
43 Anfernee Hardaway 1.00 2.50
44 Brian Grant .25 .60
45 Damon Stoudamire .40 1.00
46 Jason Williams .60 1.50
47 Chris Webber .50 1.25
48 Tim Duncan 1.00 2.50
49 David Robinson .75 2.00
50 Sean Elliott .30 .75
51 Gary Payton .60 1.50
52 Vin Baker .30 .75
53 Vince Carter 1.00 2.50
54 Tracy McGrady 1.00 2.50
55 Karl Malone .75 2.00
56 John Stockton .60 1.50
57 Shareef Abdur-Rahim .40 1.00
58 Mike Bibby .40 1.00
59 Juwan Howard .30 .75
60 Mitch Richmond .50 1.25
61 Elton Brand RC 1.25 3.00
62 Steve Francis RC 1.25 3.00
63 Baron Davis RC 1.50 4.00
64 Lamar Odom RC 1.25 3.00
65 Jonathan Bender RC .60 1.50
66 Wally Szczerbiak RC .60 1.50
67 Richard Hamilton RC 1.50 4.00
68 Andre Miller RC .60 1.50
69 Shawn Marion RC 1.25 3.00
70 Jason Terry RC 1.00 2.50
71 Trajan Langdon RC .50 1.25
72 A.Radojevic RC .40 1.00
73 Corey Maggette RC .75 2.00
74 William Avery RC .40 1.00
75 Galen Young RC .60 1.50
76 Chris Herren RC .50 1.25
77 Cal Bowdler RC .40 1.00
78 James Posey RC .60 1.50
79 Quincy Lewis RC .40 1.00
80 Dion Glover RC .40 1.00
81 Jeff Foster RC .60 1.50
82 Kenny Thomas RC .60 1.50
83 Devean George RC .50 1.25
84 Tim James RC .40 1.00
85 Vonteego Cummings RC .40 1.00
86 Jumaine Jones RC .40 1.00
87 Scott Padgett RC .50 1.25
88 Obinna Ekezie RC .40 1.00
89 Ryan Robertson RC .40 1.00
90 Evan Eschmeyer RC .50 1.25
MJS M.Jordan AU/23 2,500.00 5,000.00

1999-00 Upper Deck Ovation Standing Ovation

*STARS: 15X TO 40X BASE CARD HI
*RCs: 4X TO 10X BASE HI
STATED PRINT RUN 50 SERIAL #'d SETS

1999-00 Upper Deck Ovation A Piece of History

STATED ODDS 1:352
STATED PRINT RUN 4560 TOTAL CARDS
AM Andre Miller 6.00 15.00
BD Baron Davis 8.00 20.00
HO Hakeem Olajuwon 20.00 50.00
JB Jonathan Bender 3.00 8.00
JS John Stockton 10.00 25.00
JW Jason Williams 25.00 60.00
KB Kobe Bryant 30.00 80.00
KG Kevin Garnett 15.00 40.00
KM Karl Malone 12.00 30.00
RH Richard Hamilton 8.00 20.00
RM Reggie Miller 30.00 80.00
SF Steve Francis 6.00 15.00
SM Shawn Marion 6.00 15.00
WS Wally Szczerbiak 5.00 12.00

1999-00 Upper Deck Ovation A Piece of History Autographs

PRINT RUN TO PLAYER'S JERSEY #
KGA Kevin Garnett/21 300.00 600.00
KMA Karl Malone/32 300.00 600.00
RHA Richard Hamilton/32 40.00 100.00
SMA Shawn Marion/3 60.00 120.00

1999-00 Upper Deck Ovation Curtain Calls

COMPLETE SET (10) 3.00 8.00
STATED ODDS 1:9
CC1 Hakeem Olajuwon 1.00 2.50
CC2 Karl Malone 1.00 2.50
CC3 Latrell Sprewell .60 1.50
CC4 Allen Iverson 1.25 3.00
CC5 Tim Hardaway .60 1.50
CC6 Shaquille O'Neal 2.00 5.00
CC7 Jason Kidd .75 2.00
CC8 Charles Barkley 1.25 3.00
CC9 Antonio McDyess .40 1.00
CC10 Gary Payton .75 2.00

1999-00 Upper Deck Ovation Lead Performers

COMPLETE SET (10) 5.00 12.00
STATED ODDS 1:9
LP1 Tim Duncan 1.25 3.00
LP2 Kevin Garnett 1.25 3.00
LP3 Keith Van Horn .40 1.00
LP4 Shareef Abdur-Rahim .50 1.25
LP5 Antoine Walker .50 1.25
LP6 Shaquille O'Neal 2.00 5.00
LP7 Grant Hill .75 2.00
LP8 Kobe Bryant 4.00 10.00
LP9 Allen Iverson 1.25 3.00
LP10 Jason Williams .75 2.00

1999-00 Upper Deck Ovation MJ Center Stage

COMMON CARD (CS1-CS5) 2.50 6.00
COMMON CARD (CS6-CS10) 5.00 12.00
COMMON CARD (CS11-CS15) 10.00 25.00
CS1-CS5: STATED ODDS 1:9
CS6-CS10: STATED ODDS 1:39
CS11-CS15: STATED ODDS 1:99

1999-00 Upper Deck Ovation Premiere Performers

COMPLETE SET (10) 4.00 10.00
STATED ODDS 1:19
PP1 Elton Brand .60 1.50
PP2 Steve Francis .60 1.50
PP3 Baron Davis .75 2.00
PP4 Lamar Odom .60 1.50
PP5 Jonathan Bender .30 .75
PP6 Wally Szczerbiak .50 1.25
PP7 Richard Hamilton .75 2.00
PP8 Andre Miller .60 1.50
PP9 Shawn Marion .60 1.50
PP10 Jason Terry .50 1.25

1999-00 Upper Deck Ovation Spotlight

COMPLETE SET (10) 2.50 6.00
STATED ODDS 1:3
OS1 Kevin Garnett .75 2.00
OS2 Antawn Jamison .30 .75
OS3 Kobe Bryant 2.50 6.00
OS4 Shareef Abdur-Rahim .30 .75
OS5 Keith Van Horn .25 .60
OS6 Vince Carter .75 2.00
OS7 Stephon Marbury .40 1.00
OS8 Paul Pierce .60 1.50
OS9 Tim Duncan .75 2.00
OS10 Jason Williams .50 1.25

1999-00 Upper Deck Ovation Superstar Theatre

COMPLETE SET (20) 30.00 60.00
STATED ODDS 1:19
ST1 Michael Jordan 12.00 30.00
ST2 Vince Carter 3.00 8.00
ST3 Kevin Garnett 3.00 8.00
ST4 Paul Pierce 2.50 6.00
ST5 Jason Williams 2.00 5.00
ST6 Tim Duncan 3.00 8.00
ST7 Allen Iverson 3.00 8.00
ST8 Antawn Jamison 1.25 3.00
ST9 Kobe Bryant 10.00 25.00
ST10 Grant Hill 2.00 5.00
ST11 Antoine Walker 1.25 3.00
ST12 Tracy McGrady 2.00 5.00
ST13 Shareef Abdur-Rahim 1.25 3.00
ST14 Stephon Marbury 1.50 4.00
ST15 Jason Kidd 2.00 5.00
ST16 Shaquille O'Neal 5.00 12.00
ST17 Tim Hardaway 1.50 4.00
ST18 Keith Van Horn 1.00 2.50
ST19 Gary Payton 2.00 5.00
ST20 Karl Malone 2.50 6.00

2000-01 Upper Deck Ovation

COMPLETE SET w/o RC (60) 10.00 25.00
RCs: STATED PRINT RUN 2000 SERIAL #'d SETS
1 Dikembe Mutombo .50 1.25
2 Jim Jackson .25 .60
3 Paul Pierce .50 1.25
4 Antoine Walker .30 .75
5 Derrick Coleman .30 .75
6 Baron Davis .30 .75
7 Elton Brand .30 .75
8 Ron Artest .30 .75
9 Lamond Murray .20 .50
10 Andre Miller .25 .60
11 Michael Finley .30 .75
12 Dirk Nowitzki .75 2.00
13 Antonio McDyess .25 .60
14 Nick Van Exel .30 .75
15 Jerry Stackhouse .30 .75
16 Jerome Williams .20 .50
17 Larry Hughes .30 .75
18 Antawn Jamison .30 .75
19 Steve Francis .30 .75
20 Hakeem Olajuwon .60 1.50
21 Reggie Miller .60 1.50
22 Jalen Rose .25 .60
23 Lamar Odom .30 .75
24 Michael Olowokandi .20 .50
25 Shaquille O'Neal 1.25 3.00
26 Kobe Bryant 2.50 6.00
27 Alonzo Mourning .50 1.25
28 Anthony Carter .20 .50
29 Ray Allen .50 1.25
30 Tim Thomas .30 .75
31 Kevin Garnett .75 2.00
32 Wally Szczerbiak .25 .60
33 Stephon Marbury .40 1.00
34 Keith Van Horn .25 .60
35 Allan Houston .30 .75
36 Latrell Sprewell .40 1.00
37 Grant Hill .50 1.25
38 Tracy McGrady .60 1.50
39 Allen Iverson .75 2.00
40 Toni Kukoc .40 1.00
41 Jason Kidd .50 1.25
42 Anfernee Hardaway .50 1.25
43 Rasheed Wallace .40 1.00
44 Scottie Pippen .75 2.00
45 Damon Stoudamire .30 .75
46 Chris Webber .40 1.00
47 Jason Williams .50 1.25
48 Tim Duncan .75 2.00
49 David Robinson .60 1.50
50 Gary Payton .50 1.25
51 Brent Barry .25 .60
52 Rashard Lewis .25 .60
53 Vince Carter .60 1.50
54 Antonio Davis .25 .60
55 Karl Malone .60 1.50
56 John Stockton .60 1.50
57 Shareef Abdur-Rahim .30 .75
58 Mike Bibby .30 .75
59 Mitch Richmond .40 1.00
60 Richard Hamilton .40 1.00
61 Kenyon Martin RC 2.50 6.00
62 Stromile Swift RC 1.00 2.50
63 Darius Miles RC 1.25 3.00
64 Marcus Fizer RC 1.00 2.50
65 Mike Miller RC 2.00 5.00
66 DerMarr Johnson RC .75 2.00
67 Chris Mihm RC .75 2.00
68 Jamal Crawford RC 3.00 8.00
69 Joel Przybilla RC 1.00 2.50
70 Keyon Dooling RC 1.00 2.50
71 Jerome Moiso RC .75 2.00
72 Etan Thomas RC 1.00 2.50
73 Courtney Alexander RC .75 2.00
74 Mateen Cleaves RC 1.00 2.50
75 Jason Collier RC 1.25 3.00
76 Hedo Turkoglu RC 2.00 5.00
77 Desmond Mason RC 1.50 4.00
78 Quentin Richardson RC 1.00 2.50
79 Jamaal Magloire RC 1.25 3.00
80 Speedy Claxton RC 1.25 3.00
81 Morris Peterson RC 1.25 3.00
82 Donnell Harvey RC 1.00 2.50
83 DeShawn Stevenson RC 1.25 3.00
84 Mamadou N'Diaye RC .75 2.00
85 Erick Barkley RC .75 2.00
86 Mark Madsen RC 1.25 3.00
87 A.J. Guyton RC .75 2.00
88 Khalid El-Amin RC .75 2.00
89 Eddie House RC 1.00 2.50
90 Chris Porter RC .75 2.00

2000-01 Upper Deck Ovation Standing Ovation

*STARS: 20X TO 50X BASE CARD HI
*RCs: 1.5X TO 4X BASE HI
STATED PRINT RUN 50 SERIAL #'d SETS

2000-01 Upper Deck Ovation A Piece of History

STATED ODDS 1:120
PIECES ARE GAME BALLS UNLESS NOTED
AHB Anfernee Hardaway 15.00 40.00
AIB Allen Iverson 20.00 50.00
ALB Alonzo Mourning 10.00 25.00
AMB Andre Miller 5.00 12.00
BDB Baron Davis 6.00 15.00
CWS Chris Webber Shoe 12.00 30.00
GPB Gary Payton 10.00 25.00
JSB Jerry Stackhouse 6.00 15.00
JWB Jason Williams 20.00 50.00
KBB Kobe Bryant 100.00 250.00
KBC Kobe Bryant Combo/25 400.00 800.00
KBS Kobe Bryant Shoe 125.00 300.00
KGA Kevin Garnett AU/21 400.00 800.00
KGB Kevin Garnett 40.00 100.00
KGC Kevin Garnett Combo/25 125.00 300.00
KGS Kevin Garnett Shoe 40.00 100.00
KMS Karl Malone Shoe 15.00 40.00
LHB Larry Hughes 6.00 15.00
MFB Michael Finley 6.00 15.00
MJA Michael Jordan AU/23 5,000.00 10,000.00
MJS Michael Jordan Shoe 400.00 800.00
PPB Paul Pierce 20.00 50.00
RAB Ray Allen 15.00 40.00
SAB Shareef Abdur-Rahim 6.00 15.00
SOS Shaquille O'Neal Shoe 75.00 200.00
SPB Scottie Pippen 20.00 50.00
WSB Wally Szczerbiak 5.00 12.00

2000-01 Upper Deck Ovation Center Stage

COMPLETE SET (10) 6.00 15.00
STATED ODDS 1:19
*SILVER: 2X TO 5X BASE CARD HI
SILVER: PRINT RUN 200 SERIAL #'d SETS
*GOLD: 12X TO 30X BASE CARD HI
GOLD: PRINT RUN 25 SERIAL #'d SETS
CS1 Kevin Garnett 1.50 4.00
CS2 Tim Duncan 1.50 4.00
CS3 Lamar Odom .60 1.50
CS4 Jason Kidd 1.00 2.50
CS5 Vince Carter 1.25 3.00
CS6 Alonzo Mourning 1.00 2.50
CS7 Elton Brand .60 1.50
CS8 Chris Webber .75 2.00
CS9 Anfernee Hardaway 1.00 2.50
CS10 Kobe Bryant 5.00 12.00

2000-01 Upper Deck Ovation Lead Performers

COMPLETE SET (11) 6.00 15.00
STATED ODDS 1:12
LP1 Shaquille O'Neal 2.00 5.00
LP2 Vince Carter 1.00 2.50
LP3 Kevin Garnett 1.25 3.00
LP4 Allen Iverson 1.25 3.00
LP5 Jason Kidd .75 2.00
LP6 Elton Brand .50 1.25
LP7 Gary Payton .75 2.00
LP8 Kobe Bryant 4.00 10.00
LP9 Steve Francis .50 1.25
LP10 Stephon Marbury .60 1.50
LP11 Tim Duncan 1.25 3.00

2000-01 Upper Deck Ovation Spotlight

COMPLETE SET (20) 6.00 15.00
STATED ODDS 1:7
OS1 Kobe Bryant 4.00 10.00
OS2 Larry Hughes .50 1.25
OS3 Andre Miller .40 1.00
OS4 Michael Finley .50 1.25
OS5 Ray Allen .75 2.00
OS6 Latrell Sprewell .60 1.50
OS7 Jalen Rose .40 1.00
OS8 Antonio McDyess .40 1.00
OS9 Karl Malone 1.00 2.50
OS10 Paul Pierce .75 2.00
OS11 Shareef Abdur-Rahim .50 1.25
OS12 Chris Webber .60 1.50
OS13 Stephon Marbury .60 1.50
OS14 Scottie Pippen 1.25 3.00
OS15 Lamar Odom .50 1.25
OS16 Alonzo Mourning .75 2.00
OS17 Kevin Garnett 1.25 3.00
OS18 Anfernee Hardaway .75 2.00
OS19 Jason Williams .75 2.00
OS20 Rasheed Wallace .60 1.50

2000-01 Upper Deck Ovation Super Signatures

STATED ODDS 1:200
AH Anfernee Hardaway 75.00 200.00
CA Courtney Alexander 2.50 6.00
CM Chris Mihm 2.50 6.00
DA Darrell Armstrong 2.50 6.00
DM DerMarr Johnson 2.50 6.00
JP Joel Przybilla 3.00 8.00
JR Jalen Rose 3.00 8.00
KB Kobe Bryant 1,000.00 2,000.00
KG Kevin Garnett 300.00 600.00
KY Kenyon Martin 6.00 15.00
LH Larry Hughes 4.00 10.00
MF Marcus Fizer 3.00 8.00
SA Shareef Abdur-Rahim 4.00 10.00
SM Shawn Marion 4.00 10.00
SS Stromile Swift 3.00 8.00

2000-01 Upper Deck Ovation Super Signatures Gold

STATED PRINT RUN ONE TO 31 SETS
KG Kevin Garnett/21 500.00 1,000.00
LH Larry Hughes/20 30.00 80.00

2000-01 Upper Deck Ovation Superstar Theatre

COMPLETE SET (11) 6.00 15.00
STATED ODDS 1:12
S1 Kobe Bryant 4.00 10.00
S2 Vince Carter 1.00 2.50
S3 Jason Kidd .75 2.00
S4 Steve Francis .50 1.25
S5 Reggie Miller 1.00 2.50
S6 Tim Duncan 1.25 3.00
S7 Kevin Garnett 1.25 3.00
S8 Gary Payton .75 2.00
S9 Elton Brand .50 1.25
S10 Allen Iverson 1.25 3.00
S11 Shaquille O'Neal 2.00 5.00

2000-01 Upper Deck Ovation UD Authentics Rookie Exclusives

JP Joel Przybilla 2.50 6.00
MC Mateen Cleaves 2.50 6.00
MP Morris Peterson 3.00 8.00

2001-02 Upper Deck Ovation

COMP.SET w/o SP's (90) 20.00 40.00
91-110 PRINT RUN 1875 PER PLAYER
91-110 THREE VERSIONS SER.#'d TO 625
111-120 PRINT RUN 750 PER PLAYER
111-120 THREE VERSIONS SER.#'d TO 250
1 Jason Terry .30 .75
2 DerMarr Johnson .20 .50
3 Shareef Abdur-Rahim .25 .60
4 Paul Pierce .50 1.25
5 Antoine Walker .25 .60
6 Kenny Anderson .25 .60
7 Jamal Mashburn .25 .60
8 David Wesley .25 .60
9 Baron Davis .30 .75
10 Ron Mercer .20 .50
11 Marcus Fizer .20 .50
12 Ron Artest .25 .60
13 Andre Miller .25 .60

14 Lamond Murray .20 .50
15 Chris Mihm .20 .50
16 Michael Finley .30 .75
17 Steve Nash .60 1.50
18 Dirk Nowitzki .75 2.00
19 Antonio McDyess .25 .60
20 Nick Van Exel .25 .60
21 Raef LaFrentz .20 .50
22 Jerry Stackhouse .30 .75
23 Chucky Atkins .20 .50
24 Corliss Williamson .20 .50
25 Antawn Jamison .25 .60
26 Chris Porter .20 .50
27 Larry Hughes .25 .60
28 Steve Francis .30 .75
29 Cuttino Mobley .25 .60
30 Maurice Taylor .20 .50
31 Reggie Miller .60 1.50
32 Jalen Rose .25 .60
33 Jermaine O'Neal .25 .60
34 Darius Miles .20 .50
35 Corey Maggette .25 .60
36 Lamar Odom .25 .60
37 Elton Brand .25 .60
38 Kobe Bryant 2.50 6.00
39 Shaquille O'Neal 1.25 3.00
40 Rick Fox .25 .60
41 Derek Fisher .25 .60
42 Stromile Swift .20 .50
43 Michael Dickerson .20 .50
44 Jason Williams .50 1.25
45 Alonzo Mourning .50 1.25
46 Eddie Jones .30 .75
47 Anthony Carter .20 .50
48 Ray Allen .50 1.25
49 Glenn Robinson .30 .75
50 Sam Cassell .25 .60
51 Kevin Garnett .75 2.00
52 Terrell Brandon .25 .60
53 Wally Szczerbiak .25 .60
54 Joe Smith .25 .60
55 Kenyon Martin .30 .75
56 Keith Van Horn .25 .60
57 Jason Kidd .50 1.25
58 Latrell Sprewell .40 1.00
59 Allan Houston .30 .75
60 Marcus Camby .25 .60
61 Tracy McGrady .50 1.25
62 Mike Miller .25 .60
63 Grant Hill .50 1.25
64 Allen Iverson .75 2.00
65 Dikembe Mutombo .50 1.25
66 Aaron McKie .20 .50
67 Stephon Marbury .40 1.00
68 Shawn Marion .30 .75
69 Tom Gugliotta .20 .50
70 Rasheed Wallace .40 1.00
71 Damon Stoudamire .30 .75
72 Bonzi Wells .20 .50
73 Chris Webber .40 1.00
74 Peja Stojakovic .25 .60
75 Mike Bibby .30 .75
76 Tim Duncan .75 2.00
77 David Robinson .60 1.50
78 Antonio Daniels .20 .50
79 Gary Payton .50 1.25
80 Rashard Lewis .25 .60
81 Desmond Mason .20 .50
82 Vince Carter .60 1.50
83 Morris Peterson .25 .60
84 Antonio Davis .25 .60
85 Karl Malone .60 1.50
86 John Stockton .60 1.50
87 Donyell Marshall .20 .50
88 Richard Hamilton .40 1.00
89 Courtney Alexander .20 .50
90 Michael Jordan 2.50 6.00
91A Jeff Trepagnier P RC .75 2.00
91B Jeff Trepagnier S RC .75 2.00
91C Jeff Trepagnier SR RC .75 2.00
92A Pau Gasol P RC 5.00 12.00
92B Pau Gasol S RC 5.00 12.00
92C Pau Gasol SR RC 5.00 12.00
93A Will Solomon P RC 1.00 2.50
93B Will Solomon S RC 1.00 2.50
93C Will Solomon SR RC 1.00 2.50
94A Gilbert Arenas P RC 3.00 8.00
94B Gilbert Arenas S RC 3.00 8.00
94C Gilbert Arenas SR RC 3.00 8.00
95A Andrei Kirilenko P RC 2.00 5.00
95B Andrei Kirilenko S RC 2.00 5.00
95C Andrei Kirilenko SR RC 2.00 5.00
96A Jamaal Tinsley P RC 1.00 2.50
96B Jamaal Tinsley S RC 1.00 2.50
96C Jamaal Tinsley SR RC 1.00 2.50
97A Samuel Dalembert P RC 1.25 3.00
97B Samuel Dalembert S RC 1.25 3.00
97C Samuel Dalembert SR RC 1.25 3.00
98A Gerald Wallace P RC 1.50 4.00
98B Gerald Wallace S RC 1.50 4.00
98C Gerald Wallace SR RC 1.50 4.00
99A Brandon Armstrong P RC .75 2.00
99B Brandon Armstrong S RC .75 2.00
99C Brandon Armstrong SR RC .75 2.00
100A Jeryl Sasser P RC .75 2.00
100B Jeryl Sasser S RC .75 2.00
100C Jeryl Sasser SR RC .75 2.00
101A Joseph Forte P RC .75 2.00
101B Joseph Forte S RC .75 2.00
101C Joseph Forte SR RC .75 2.00
102A Brendan Haywood P RC 1.00 2.50
102B Brendan Haywood S RC 1.00 2.50
102C Brendan Haywood SR RC 1.00 2.50
103A Zach Randolph P RC 2.50 6.00
103B Zach Randolph S RC 2.50 6.00
103C Zach Randolph SR RC 2.50 6.00
104A Jason Collins P RC 1.00 2.50
104B Jason Collins S RC 1.00 2.50
104C Jason Collins SR RC 1.00 2.50
105A Michael Bradley P RC .75 2.00
105B Michael Bradley S RC .75 2.00
105C Michael Bradley SR RC .75 2.00
106A Kirk Haston P RC .75 2.00
106B Kirk Haston S RC .75 2.00
106C Kirk Haston SR RC .75 2.00
107A Steven Hunter P RC .75 2.00
107B Steven Hunter S RC .75 2.00
107C Steven Hunter SR RC .75 2.00
108A Troy Murphy P RC 1.00 2.50
108B Troy Murphy S RC 1.00 2.50
108C Troy Murphy SR RC 1.00 2.50
109A Richard Jefferson P RC 1.50 4.00
109B Richard Jefferson S RC 1.50 4.00
109C Richard Jefferson SR RC 1.50 4.00
110A V.Radmanovic P RC 1.00 2.50
110B V.Radmanovic S RC 1.00 2.50
110C V.Radmanovic SR RC 1.00 2.50
111A Kedrick Brown P RC 1.50 4.00
111B Kedrick Brown S RC 1.50 4.00
111C Kedrick Brown SR RC 1.50 4.00
112A Joe Johnson P RC 4.00 10.00
112B Joe Johnson S RC 4.00 10.00
112C Joe Johnson SR RC 4.00 10.00
113A Rodney White P RC 1.50 4.00
113B Rodney White S RC 1.50 4.00
113C Rodney White SR RC 1.50 4.00
114A DeSagana Diop P RC 1.50 4.00
114B DeSagana Diop S RC 1.50 4.00
114C DeSagana Diop SR RC 1.50 4.00
115A Eddie Griffin P RC 2.00 5.00
115B Eddie Griffin S RC 2.00 5.00
115C Eddie Griffin SR RC 2.00 5.00
116A Shane Battier P RC 5.00 12.00
116B Shane Battier S RC 5.00 12.00
116C Shane Battier SR RC 5.00 12.00
117A Jason Richardson P RC 4.00 10.00
117B Jason Richardson S RC 4.00 10.00
117C Jason Richardson SR RC 4.00 10.00
118A Eddy Curry P RC 2.50 6.00
118B Eddy Curry S RC 2.50 6.00
118C Eddy Curry SR RC 2.50 6.00
119A Tyson Chandler P RC 4.00 10.00
119B Tyson Chandler S RC 4.00 10.00
119C Tyson Chandler SR RC 4.00 10.00
120A Kwame Brown P RC 2.50 6.00
120B Kwame Brown S RC 2.50 6.00
120C Kwame Brown SR RC 2.50 6.00

2001-02 Upper Deck Ovation MJ UNC Memorabilia

MJF1 Michael Jordan Floor 40.00 100.00
MJF2 Michael Jordan Floor 40.00 100.00
MJF3 Michael Jordan Floor 40.00 100.00
MJF4 Michael Jordan Floor 40.00 100.00
MJF5 Michael Jordan Floor 40.00 100.00
MJJ1 Michael Jordan JSY/82 200.00 500.00
MJC1 M.Jordan Floor-JSY/82 300.00 600.00
MJFA M.Jordan Floor AU/23 3,000.00 6,000.00
MJJA M.Jordan JSY AU/23 3,000.00 6,000.00
MJCA Jordan Flr-JSY AU/23 4,000.00 8,000.00

2001-02 Upper Deck Ovation Superstar Warm-Ups

STATED ODDS 1:10
AM Andre Miller 2.50 6.00
AW Antoine Walker 2.50 6.00
BD Baron Davis 3.00 8.00
CM Corey Maggette 2.50 6.00
DA Darrell Armstrong 2.00 5.00
DJ DerMarr Johnson 2.00 5.00
DM Darius Miles 2.00 5.00
DN Dirk Nowitzki 8.00 20.00
GH Grant Hill 5.00 12.00
HM Hanno Mottola 2.00 5.00
JA Jamaal Magloire 2.00 5.00
JM Jamal Mashburn 2.50 6.00
JS Joe Smith 2.50 6.00
KB Kobe Bryant 40.00 100.00
KD Keyon Dooling 2.00 5.00
KG Kevin Garnett 8.00 20.00
KM Karl Malone 6.00 15.00
MC Antonio McDyess 2.50 6.00
MF Michael Finley 3.00 8.00
MO Michael Olowokandi 2.00 5.00
MP Morris Peterson 2.00 5.00
PP Paul Pierce 5.00 12.00
QR Quentin Richardson 2.00 5.00
RH Richard Hamilton 4.00 10.00
RM Ron Mercer 2.00 5.00
SM Shawn Marion 3.00 8.00
ST John Stockton 6.00 15.00
TB Terrell Brandon 2.50 6.00
WS Wally Szczerbiak 2.50 6.00

2001-02 Upper Deck Ovation Superstar Warm-Ups Autographs

STATED ODDS 1:240
DAS Darrell Armstrong 5.00 12.00
DMS Darius Miles 5.00 12.00
HMS Hanno Mottola 5.00 12.00
JMS Jamal Mashburn 8.00 20.00
KBS Kobe Bryant 1,000.00 2,000.00
KGS Kevin Garnett 100.00 250.00
MPS Morris Peterson 5.00 12.00
QRS Quentin Richardson 5.00 12.00

2001-02 Upper Deck Ovation Tremendous Trios

STATED ODDS 1:240
AJLHMA Jamison/Hughes/Jckson 8.00 20.00
BDJMDW Davis/Mash/Wesley 8.00 20.00
KGTBWS Garnett/Brandon/Szcz 8.00 20.00
MJKBKG Jordan/Kobe/Garnett 125.00 300.00
RMRAJC Mercer/Artest/Fizer 8.00 20.00
TMGHMM T-Mac/Hill/M.Miller 10.00 25.00

2002-03 Upper Deck Ovation

COMP.SET w/o SP's (90) 20.00 50.00
100-119 PRINT RUN 2999 SER.#'d SETS
120-134 PRINT RUN 1999 SER.#'d SETS
1 Shareef Abdur-Rahim .30 .75
2 Jason Terry .25 .60
3 Glenn Robinson .30 .75
4 Paul Pierce .50 1.25
5 Antoine Walker .25 .60
6 Vin Baker .25 .60
7 Jalen Rose .25 .60
8 Tyson Chandler .30 .75
9 Eddy Curry .20 .50
10 Marcus Fizer .20 .50
11 Darius Miles .20 .50
12 Lamond Murray .20 .50
13 Chris Mihm .20 .50
14 Dirk Nowitzki .75 2.00
15 Michael Finley .30 .75
16 Steve Nash .60 1.50
17 Marcus Camby .25 .60
18 Juwan Howard .25 .60
19 James Posey .20 .50
20 Jerry Stackhouse .30 .75
21 Ben Wallace .40 1.00
22 Clifford Robinson .30 .75
23 Antawn Jamison .25 .60
24 Jason Richardson .30 .75
25 Gilbert Arenas .30 .75
26 Steve Francis .30 .75
27 Eddie Griffin .20 .50
28 Cuttino Mobley .20 .50
29 Jermaine O'Neal .25 .60
30 Reggie Miller .60 1.50
31 Jamaal Tinsley .20 .50
32 Elton Brand .25 .60
33 Andre Miller .25 .60
34 Lamar Odom .30 .75
35 Kobe Bryant 2.50 6.00
36 Shaquille O'Neal 1.25 3.00
37 Derek Fisher .30 .75
38 Devean George .20 .50
39 Pau Gasol .50 1.25
40 Shane Battier .30 .75
41 Jason Williams .40 1.00
42 Alonzo Mourning .50 1.25
43 Eddie Jones .30 .75
44 Brian Grant .20 .50
45 Ray Allen .50 1.25
46 Tim Thomas .20 .50
47 Sam Cassell .25 .60
48 Kevin Garnett .75 2.00
49 Wally Szczerbiak .25 .60
50 Terrell Brandon .20 .50
51 Jason Kidd .50 1.25
52 Kenyon Martin .30 .75
53 Richard Jefferson .25 .60
54 Jamal Mashburn .25 .60
55 Baron Davis .30 .75
56 David Wesley .20 .50
57 Latrell Sprewell .30 .75
58 Allan Houston .30 .75
59 Antonio McDyess .25 .60
60 Tracy McGrady .50 1.25
61 Mike Miller .25 .60
62 Darrell Armstrong .20 .50
63 Allen Iverson .75 2.00
64 Eric Snow .20 .50
65 Aaron McKie .20 .50
66 Stephon Marbury .40 1.00
67 Shawn Marion .30 .75
68 Anfernee Hardaway .75 2.00
69 Rasheed Wallace .40 1.00
70 Bonzi Wells .20 .50
71 Scottie Pippen .75 2.00
72 Chris Webber .40 1.00
73 Mike Bibby .30 .75
74 Peja Stojakovic .25 .60
75 Tim Duncan .75 2.00
76 David Robinson .60 1.50
77 Tony Parker .50 1.25
78 Gary Payton .50 1.25
79 Rashard Lewis .25 .60
80 Desmond Mason .25 .60
81 Vince Carter .60 1.50
82 Morris Peterson .25 .60
83 Antonio Davis .25 .60
84 Karl Malone .60 1.50
85 John Stockton .60 1.50
86 Andrei Kirilenko .25 .60
87 Michael Jordan 3.00 8.00
88 Richard Hamilton .40 1.00
89 Chris Whitney .20 .50
90 Kwame Brown .20 .50
91 Kevin Garnett/2999 3.00 8.00
92 Kevin Garnett/2999 3.00 8.00
93 Kevin Garnett/2999 3.00 8.00
94 Kobe Bryant/1999 8.00 20.00
95 Kobe Bryant/1999 8.00 20.00
96 Kobe Bryant/1999 8.00 20.00
97 Michael Jordan/499 15.00 40.00
98 Michael Jordan/499 15.00 40.00
99 Michael Jordan/499 15.00 40.00
100 Fred Jones RC 2.00 5.00
101 Jamal Sampson RC 1.50 4.00
102 John Salmons RC 2.50 6.00
103 Jiri Welsch RC 2.00 5.00
104 Dan Gadzuric RC 2.00 5.00
105 Vincent Yarbrough RC 1.50 4.00
106 Juan Dixon RC 2.00 5.00
107 Efthimios Rentzias RC 1.50 4.00
108 Predrag Savovic RC 2.00 5.00
109 Rod Grizzard RC 1.50 4.00
110 Bostjan Nachbar RC 2.00 5.00
111 Marko Jaric 2.50 6.00
112 Tayshaun Prince RC 5.00 12.00
113 Chris Jefferies RC 1.50 4.00
114 Casey Jacobsen RC 2.00 5.00
115 Carlos Boozer RC 2.50 6.00
116 Frank Williams RC 1.50 4.00
117 Dan Dickau RC 1.50 4.00
118 Ryan Humphrey RC 2.00 5.00
119 Melvin Ely RC 2.00 5.00
120 Nene Hilario RC 3.00 8.00
121 Nikoloz Tskitishvili RC 2.00 5.00
122 Marcus Haislip RC 2.00 5.00
123 Qyntel Woods RC 2.00 5.00
124 Caron Butler RC 3.00 8.00
125 Amare Stoudemire RC 8.00 20.00
126 Curtis Borchardt RC 2.00 5.00
127 Chris Wilcox RC 2.50 6.00
128 Drew Gooden RC 3.00 8.00
129 Jared Jeffries RC 2.50 6.00
130 Kareem Rush RC 2.50 6.00
131 Mike Dunleavy RC 3.00 8.00
132 Yao Ming RC 15.00 40.00
133 DaJuan Wagner RC 2.50 6.00
134 Jay Williams RC 2.50 6.00

2002-03 Upper Deck Ovation Authentics Shooting Shirt

STATED ODDS 1:144
AIS Allen Iverson 6.00 15.00
CWS Chris Webber 3.00 8.00
DJS DerMarr Johnson 1.50 4.00
ECS Eddy Curry 1.50 4.00
JES Jerry Stackhouse 2.50 6.00
JSS John Stockton 5.00 12.00
KBS Kobe Bryant 40.00 100.00
KGS Kevin Garnett 6.00 15.00
KWS Kwame Brown 1.50 4.00
MBS Mike Bibby 2.50 6.00
PSS Peja Stojakovic 2.00 5.00
SAS Shareef Abdur-Rahim 2.50 6.00
SMS Stephon Marbury 3.00 8.00

2002-03 Upper Deck Ovation Authentics Uniform

STATED ODDS 1:72
*GOLD: 1.25X TO 3X BASE HI
GOLD PRINT RUN 25 SER.#'d SETS
AHU Anfernee Hardaway 8.00 20.00
AIU Allen Iverson 8.00 20.00
BDU Baron Davis 3.00 8.00
CMU Corey Maggette 2.50 6.00
DMU Darius Miles 2.00 5.00
DNU Dirk Nowitzki 8.00 20.00
DSU DeShawn Stevenson 2.00 5.00
KBU Kobe Bryant 40.00 100.00
KEU Kenyon Martin 3.00 8.00
KGU Kevin Garnett 8.00 20.00
KMU Karl Malone 6.00 15.00
RFU Rick Fox 2.00 5.00
RLU Rashard Lewis 2.50 6.00

2002-03 Upper Deck Ovation Authentics Warm-Ups

STATED ODDS 1:24
*GOLD: .75X TO 2X WARM UP HI
GOLD PRINT RUN 100 SER.#'d SETS
AWW Antoine Walker 2.50 6.00
BDW Baron Davis 3.00 8.00
CMW Corey Maggette 2.50 6.00
EBW Elton Brand 2.50 6.00
JKW Jason Kidd 5.00 12.00
JMW Jamal Mashburn 2.50 6.00
KBW Kobe Bryant 40.00 100.00
KGW Kevin Garnett 8.00 20.00
KMW Kenyon Martin 3.00 8.00
KWW Kwame Brown 2.00 5.00
LOW Lamar Odom 3.00 8.00
MAW Karl Malone 6.00 15.00
MBW Mike Bibby 3.00 8.00
MJW Michael Jordan 50.00 120.00
MMW Mike Miller 2.50 6.00
QRW Quentin Richardson 2.00 5.00
RJW Richard Jefferson 2.50 6.00
SMW Stephon Marbury 4.00 10.00

2002-03 Upper Deck Ovation Authentics Warm-Ups Dual

STATED ODDS 1:144
*GOLD: .75X TO 2X WARM UP DUAL HI
GOLD PRINT RUN 50 SER.#'d SETS
AH/LS A.Houston/L.Sprewell 6.00 15.00
AM/LM A.Miller/L.Murray 6.00 15.00
BD/JM B.Davis/J.Mashburn 6.00 15.00
CM/DM C.Maggette/D.Miles 6.00 15.00
CW/PS P.Stojakovic/C.Webber 10.00 25.00
EC/MF E.Curry/M.Fizer 6.00 15.00
KB/KG K.Bryant/K.Garnett 40.00 100.00
KB/MJ K.Bryant/M.Jordan 125.00 300.00
KG/KW K.Garnett/Kw.Brown 10.00 25.00
KG/TB K.Garnett/T.Brandon 10.00 25.00
KG/WS K.Garnett/W.Szczerbiak 10.00 25.00
KM/AK K.Malone/A.Kirilenko 6.00 15.00
KM/RJ K.Martin/R.Jefferson 6.00 15.00
LO/QR L.Odom/Q.Richardson 6.00 15.00
PP/AW P.Pierce/A.Walker 10.00 25.00
SA/JT S.Abdur-Rahim/J.Terry 6.00 15.00
SM/SH S.Marbury/S.Marion 6.00 15.00
WS/TB W.Szczerbiak/T.Brandon 6.00 15.00

2002-03 Upper Deck Ovation Authentics Warm-Ups Triple

STATED ODDS 1:288
*GOLD: .75X TO 2X BASE HI
GOLD PRINT RUN 25 SER.#'d SETS
BGK Kobe/Garnett/Kidd 125.00 300.00
BJG Kobe/Jordan/Garnett 200.00 500.00
CFC Curry/Fizer/Chandler 10.00 25.00
GSB Garnett/Szcz/T.Brndn 15.00 40.00
MBO Miles/Brand/Odom 10.00 25.00
WSB C.Webb/Peja/Bibby 15.00 40.00

2002-03 Upper Deck Ovation Signatures

STATED ODDS 1:96
CA Courtney Alexander 4.00 10.00
CM Chris Mihm 4.00 10.00
DM Darius Miles 4.00 10.00
GA Gilbert Arenas 4.00 10.00
HM Hanno Mottola 4.00 10.00
JP Joel Przybilla 4.00 10.00
JR Jason Richardson 6.00 15.00
JS Jerry Stackhouse 6.00 15.00
KS Kenny Satterfield 4.00 10.00
LW Loren Woods 4.00 10.00
MF Marcus Fizer 4.00 10.00
QR Quentin Richardson 4.00 10.00
TC Tyson Chandler 6.00 15.00
TM Terence Morris 4.00 10.00
ZZ Wang ZhiZhi 30.00 80.00
OS1 M.Jordan/Kobe/KG/25 2,000.00 4,000.00

2006-07 Upper Deck Ovation

COMP.SET w/o SP's (90) 20.00 50.00
91-132 RC PRINT RUN 999 SER.#'d SETS
1 Joe Johnson .40 1.00
2 Marvin Williams .25 .60
3 Paul Pierce .60 1.50
4 Wally Szczerbiak .25 .60
5 Raymond Felton .25 .60
6 Emeka Okafor .30 .75
7 Gerald Wallace .30 .75
8 Tyson Chandler .30 .75
9 Ben Gordon .30 .75
10 Michael Jordan 3.00 8.00
11 Drew Gooden .30 .75
12 Zydrunas Ilgauskas .30 .75
13 LeBron James 3.00 8.00
14 Devin Harris .25 .60
15 Dirk Nowitzki 1.00 2.50
16 Jason Terry .30 .75
17 Carmelo Anthony .60 1.50
18 Marcus Camby .30 .75
19 Kenyon Martin .30 .75
20 Chauncey Billups .50 1.25
21 Richard Hamilton .40 1.00
22 Ben Wallace .50 1.25
23 Baron Davis .40 1.00
24 Jason Richardson .40 1.00
25 Luther Head .25 .60
26 Tracy McGrady .60 1.50
27 Yao Ming 1.00 2.50
28 Austin Croshere .25 .60
29 Jermaine O'Neal .40 1.00
30 Peja Stojakovic .30 .75
31 Elton Brand .30 .75
32 Sam Cassell .30 .75
33 Cuttino Mobley .30 .75
34 Kwame Brown .25 .60
35 Kobe Bryant 3.00 8.00
36 Lamar Odom .30 .75
37 Pau Gasol .60 1.50
38 Mike Miller .30 .75
39 Damon Stoudamire .30 .75
40 Shaquille O'Neal 1.50 4.00
41 Wayne Simien .25 .60
42 Dwyane Wade .75 2.00
43 Andrew Bogut .30 .75
44 T.J. Ford .25 .60
45 Michael Redd .30 .75
46 Ricky Davis .30 .75
47 Kevin Garnett 1.00 2.50
48 Rashad McCants .25 .60
49 Vince Carter .75 2.00
50 Richard Jefferson .30 .75
51 Jason Kidd .60 1.50
52 Desmond Mason .25 .60
53 Chris Paul .75 2.00
54 J.R. Smith .40 1.00
55 Steve Francis .40 1.00
56 Stephon Marbury .40 1.00
57 Nate Robinson .30 .75
58 Dwight Howard .50 1.25
59 Darko Milicic .25 .60
60 Jameer Nelson .25 .60
61 Andre Iguodala .40 1.00
62 Allen Iverson 1.00 2.50
63 Chris Webber .50 1.25
64 Boris Diaw .30 .75
65 Shawn Marion .40 1.00
66 Steve Nash .75 2.00
67 Zach Randolph .40 1.00
68 Sebastian Telfair .25 .60
69 Ron Artest .40 1.00
70 Mike Bibby .40 1.00
71 Bonzi Wells .25 .60
72 Tim Duncan 1.00 2.50
73 Manu Ginobili .75 2.00
74 Tony Parker .60 1.50
75 Ray Allen .60 1.50
76 Rashard Lewis .30 .75
77 Luke Ridnour .30 .75
78 Chris Bosh .50 1.25
79 Joey Graham .25 .60
80 Charlie Villanueva .25 .60
81 Carlos Boozer .30 .75
82 Andrei Kirilenko .30 .75
83 Gilbert Arenas .40 1.00
84 Antawn Jamison .30 .75
85 Josh Childress .25 .60
86 Al Jefferson .25 .60
87 Derek Fisher .40 1.00
88 Juan Dixon .25 .60
89 Deron Williams .30 .75
90 Caron Butler .30 .75
91 Tyrus Thomas RC 1.25 3.00
92 Adam Morrison RC 1.25 3.00
93 LaMarcus Aldridge RC 4.00 10.00
94 Rudy Gay RC 2.00 5.00
95 Andrea Bargnani RC 1.25 3.00
96 Rodney Carney RC 1.00 2.50
97 Will Blalock RC 1.00 2.50
98 Brandon Roy RC 3.00 8.00
99 Patrick O'Bryant RC 1.00 2.50
100 Randy Foye RC 1.25 3.00
101 Ronnie Brewer RC 1.50 4.00
102 Mardy Collins RC 1.00 2.50
103 Shelden Williams RC 1.00 2.50
104 J.J. Redick RC 3.00 8.00
105 Hilton Armstrong RC 1.00 2.50
106 Marcus Williams RC 1.00 2.50
107 Rajon Rondo RC 5.00 12.00
108 Cedric Simmons RC 1.00 2.50
109 Alexander Johnson RC 1.00 2.50
110 Jordan Farmar RC 1.25 3.00
111 Maurice Ager RC 1.00 2.50
112 Renaldo Balkman RC 1.25 3.00
113 Leon Powe RC 1.00 2.50
114 Saer Sene RC 1.00 2.50
115 Paul Millsap RC 2.00 5.00
116 Josh Boone RC 1.00 2.50
117 Steve Novak RC 1.25 3.00
118 Daniel Gibson RC 1.25 3.00
119 Hassan Adams RC 1.00 2.50
120 Kyle Lowry RC 5.00 12.00
121 James White RC 1.00 2.50
122 Dee Brown RC 1.00 2.50
123 Shawne Williams RC 1.00 2.50
124 P.J. Tucker RC 1.50 4.00
125 Craig Smith RC 1.00 2.50
126 Paul Davis RC 1.00 2.50
127 Solomon Jones RC 1.00 2.50
128 Denham Brown RC 1.00 2.50
129 Thabo Sefolosha RC 1.25 3.00
130 Quincy Douby RC 1.00 2.50
131 Joel Freeland RC 1.00 2.50
132 Ryan Hollins RC 1.00 2.50

2006-07 Upper Deck Ovation Gold

*1-90 GOLD: 2X TO 5X BASE HI
*91-132 GOLD NON AU: 1.25X TO 3X BASE HI
PRINT RUN 99 SER.#'d SETS
10 Michael Jordan 50.00 120.00
13 LeBron James 30.00 80.00
91 Tyrus Thomas AU 6.00 15.00
93 LaMarcus Aldridge AU 20.00 50.00
94 Rudy Gay AU 10.00 25.00
95 Andrea Bargnani AU 6.00 15.00
96 Rodney Carney AU 5.00 12.00
98 Brandon Roy AU 15.00 40.00
99 Patrick O'Bryant AU 5.00 12.00
100 Randy Foye AU 6.00 15.00
101 Ronnie Brewer AU 8.00 20.00
102 Mardy Collins AU 5.00 12.00
103 Shelden Williams AU 5.00 12.00
105 Hilton Armstrong AU 5.00 12.00
106 Marcus Williams AU 5.00 12.00
107 Rajon Rondo AU 20.00 50.00
108 Cedric Simmons AU 5.00 12.00
110 Jordan Farmar AU 6.00 15.00
111 Maurice Ager AU 5.00 12.00
112 Renaldo Balkman AU 6.00 15.00
115 Paul Millsap AU 10.00 25.00
116 Josh Boone AU 5.00 12.00
117 Steve Novak AU 6.00 15.00
118 Daniel Gibson AU 6.00 15.00
119 Hassan Adams AU 5.00 12.00
120 Kyle Lowry AU 25.00 60.00
123 Shawne Williams AU 5.00 12.00
124 P.J. Tucker AU 8.00 20.00
125 Craig Smith AU 6.00 15.00
127 Solomon Jones AU 5.00 12.00
128 Denham Brown AU 5.00 12.00
130 Quincy Douby AU 5.00 12.00
132 Ryan Hollins AU 5.00 12.00

2006-07 Upper Deck Ovation Apparel

APPROXIMATE ODDS 1:18
*GOLD: .6X TO 1.5X BASE JSY HI
GOLD PRINT RUN 50 SER.#'d SETS
AB Andrew Bynum 1.50 4.00
AI Andre Iguodala 2.50 6.00
AK Andrei Kirilenko 2.00 5.00
AS Amare Stoudemire 2.50 6.00
BC Brian Cook 2.00 5.00
BD Baron Davis 2.50 6.00
BH Brendan Haywood 2.00 5.00
BU Beno Udrih 2.00 5.00
CW Chris Wilcox 2.00 5.00
DG Drew Gooden 2.00 5.00
DN Dirk Nowitzki 6.00 15.00
EC Eddy Curry 2.00 5.00
GA Gilbert Arenas 2.50 6.00
HO Julius Hodge 2.00 5.00
JH Josh Howard 2.00 5.00
JM Jeff McInnis 2.00 5.00
JO Jermaine O'Neal 2.50 6.00
JR Jason Richardson 2.50 6.00
JT Jamaal Tinsley 2.00 5.00
KB Kobe Bryant SP 40.00 100.00
KG Kevin Garnett 6.00 15.00
KK Kyle Korver 2.00 5.00
LJ LeBron James SP 20.00 50.00
LK Linas Kleiza 2.00 5.00
LW Luke Walton 2.00 5.00
MG Manu Ginobili 5.00 12.00
MJ Michael Jordan SP 50.00 120.00
MS Mike Sweetney 2.00 5.00
PG Pau Gasol 4.00 10.00
RA Ray Allen 4.00 10.00
RH Richard Hamilton SP 2.50 6.00
RL Rashard Lewis 2.50 6.00
SC Sam Cassell 2.00 5.00
SL Shaun Livingston 2.00 5.00
SM Shawn Marion 2.50 6.00
TC Tyson Chandler 2.00 5.00
TD Tim Duncan 6.00 15.00
TP Tony Parker 4.00 10.00
VC Vince Carter 5.00 12.00
WS Wally Szczerbiak 2.00 5.00
ZI Zydrunas Ilgauskas 2.00 5.00

2006-07 Upper Deck Ovation Center Stage

COMPLETE SET (12) 4.00 10.00
APPROXIMATE ODDS 1:9
AS Amare Stoudemire .60 1.50
BM Brad Miller .50 1.25
BW Ben Wallace .75 2.00
CF Channing Frye .40 1.00
CK Chris Kaman .40 1.00
DH Dwight Howard .75 2.00
MC Marcus Camby .40 1.00
MO Mehmet Okur .40 1.00
SO Shaquille O'Neal 2.50 6.00
YM Yao Ming 1.50 4.00
ZI Zydrunas Ilgauskas .50 1.25

2006-07 Upper Deck Ovation Leading Performers

COMPLETE SET (20) 10.00 25.00
APPROXIMATE ODDS 1:9
AI Allen Iverson 1.50 4.00
BG Ben Gordon .50 1.25
CB Chauncey Billups .75 2.00
CP Chris Paul 1.25 3.00
DH Dwight Howard .75 2.00
DN Dirk Nowitzki 1.50 4.00
DW Dwyane Wade 1.25 3.00
EB Elton Brand .50 1.25
EO Emeka Okafor .50 1.25
KB Kobe Bryant 5.00 12.00
KG Kevin Garnett 1.50 4.00
LJ LeBron James 5.00 12.00
MA Shawn Marion .60 1.50
MJ Michael Jordan 5.00 12.00
PP Paul Pierce 1.00 2.50
SM Stephon Marbury .75 2.00
SN Steve Nash 1.25 3.00
SO Shaquille O'Neal 2.50 6.00
TM Tracy McGrady 1.00 2.50
YM Yao Ming 1.50 4.00

2006-07 Upper Deck Ovation Spotlight Signature

APPROXIMATE ODDS 1:18
*GOLD: .75X TO 2X BASE HI
GOLD PRINT RUN 25 SER.#'d SETS
AA Alex Acker 4.00 10.00
AB Andrew Bogut SP 5.00 12.00
AJ Al Jefferson 4.00 10.00
AN Andrea Bargnani SP 10.00 25.00
BA Brent Barry 6.00 15.00
BB Brandon Bass 4.00 10.00
BD Baron Davis 4.00 10.00
BJ Bobby Jackson 4.00 10.00
BK Bernard King 8.00 20.00
BO Bruce Bowen 4.00 10.00
BR Brandon Roy 10.00 25.00
BS Bobby Simmons 4.00 10.00
BW Bill Walton 6.00 15.00
CA Carmelo Anthony 12.50 30.00
CB Carlos Boozer 4.00 10.00
CD Chris Duhon 4.00 10.00
CM Cuttino Mobley 4.00 10.00
CP Chris Paul 75.00 200.00
CS Cedric Simmons 4.00 10.00
CT Chris Taft 4.00 10.00
DJ Dwayne Jones 4.00 10.00
DM Desmond Mason 4.00 10.00
DS DeShawn Stevenson 4.00 10.00
DT Dijon Thompson 4.00 10.00
EI Ersan Ilyasova 4.00 10.00
FO Randy Foye 10.00 25.00
HA Hilton Armstrong 4.00 10.00
HW Hakim Warrick 4.00 10.00
ID Ike Diogu SP 4.00 10.00
JK Jarrett Jack 4.00 10.00
JO Amir Johnson 4.00 10.00
JR Jalen Rose 4.00 10.00
JS J.R. Smith 4.00 10.00
KB Kwame Brown 4.00 10.00
KD Keyon Dooling 4.00 10.00
KH Kirk Hinrich 6.00 15.00
LA LaMarcus Aldridge 10.00 25.00
LJ LeBron James SP 1,250.00 2,500.00
LR Lawrence Roberts 4.00 10.00
MC Mardy Collins 4.00 10.00
MD Marquis Daniels 4.00 10.00
ME Maurice Evans 4.00 10.00
MJ Michael Jordan SP 1,000.00 2,000.00
MW Marvin Williams 4.00 10.00
NR Nate Robinson 4.00 10.00
PO Patrick O'Bryant 4.00 10.00
PP Paul Pierce SP 8.00 20.00
PS Peja Stojakovic 4.00 10.00
QR Quentin Richardson 4.00 10.00
RB Ronnie Brewer 12.00 30.00
RC Rodney Carney 4.00 10.00
RF Raymond Felton 5.00 12.00
RG Rudy Gay 8.00 20.00
RI Luke Ridnour 4.00 10.00
RJ Richard Jefferson 4.00 10.00
RM Rashad McCants 4.00 10.00
RR Rajon Rondo 12.00 30.00
RT Ronny Turiaf 6.00 15.00
SC Speedy Claxton 4.00 10.00
SI James Singleton 4.00 10.00
SK Steve Kerr 4.00 10.00
SL Shaun Livingston 4.00 10.00
SS Stromile Swift 4.00 10.00
SW Shelden Williams 4.00 10.00
TF T.J. Ford 4.00 10.00
TT Tyrus Thomas 5.00 12.00
VC Vince Carter 12.50 30.00
VR Vladimir Radmanovic 4.00 10.00
VW Von Wafer 4.00 10.00
WI Marcus Williams 4.00 10.00
WR Bracey Wright 4.00 10.00
YK Yaroslav Korolev 4.00 10.00
YM Yao Ming SP 12.50 30.00

2006-07 Upper Deck Ovation Superstar Theatre

COMPLETE SET (10) 8.00 20.00
APPROXIMATE ODDS 1:9
BR Bill Russell 2.00 5.00
JE Julius Erving 1.25 3.00
JO Magic Johnson 2.00 5.00
KA Kareem Abdul-Jabbar 2.00 5.00
KB Kobe Bryant 5.00 12.00
LJ LeBron James 5.00 12.00
MJ Michael Jordan 5.00 12.00
SN Steve Nash 1.25 3.00
SO Shaquille O'Neal 2.50 6.00
TM Tracy McGrady 1.00 2.50

2001-02 Upper Deck Playmakers

COMPLETE SET (145) 100.00 250.00
COMP.SET w/o SP's (100) 20.00 50.00
101-130 PRINT RUN 1999 SER.#'d SETS
131-145 PRINT RUN 999 SER.#'d SETS
1 Shareef Abdur-Rahim .30 .75
2 Dion Glover .25 .60
3 Jason Terry .40 1.00
4 Toni Kukoc .50 1.25
5 Theo Ratliff .25 .60
6 Paul Pierce .60 1.50
7 Antoine Walker .30 .75
8 Baron Davis .40 1.00
9 Jamal Mashburn .30 .75
10 Ron Mercer .25 .60
11 Brad Miller .40 1.00
12 Marcus Fizer .30 .75
13 Andre Miller .30 .75
14 Chris Mihm .25 .60
15 Lamond Murray .25 .60
16 Michael Finley .40 1.00
17 Dirk Nowitzki 1.00 2.50
18 Steve Nash .75 2.00
19 Tim Hardaway .50 1.25
20 Antonio McDyess .30 .75
21 Nick Van Exel .40 1.00
22 Raef LaFrentz .25 .60
23 Jerry Stackhouse .40 1.00
24 Clifford Robinson .40 1.00
25 Ben Wallace .50 1.25
26 Antawn Jamison .30 .75
27 Larry Hughes .30 .75
28 Danny Fortson .25 .60
29 Steve Francis .40 1.00
30 Cuttino Mobley .30 .75
31 Kenny Thomas .25 .60
32 Jalen Rose .30 .75
33 Reggie Miller .75 2.00
34 Jermaine O'Neal .30 .75
35 Darius Miles .25 .60
36 Elton Brand .30 .75
37 Corey Maggette .30 .75
38 Quentin Richardson .25 .60
39 Kobe Bryant 3.00 8.00
40 Shaquille O'Neal 1.50 4.00
41 Mitch Richmond .50 1.25
42 Derek Fisher .30 .75
43 Lindsey Hunter .25 .60
44 Stromile Swift .25 .60

45 Jason Williams .60 1.50
46 Michael Dickerson .25 .60
47 Eddie Jones .40 1.00
48 Alonzo Mourning .60 1.50
49 Anthony Carter .25 .60
50 Brian Grant .25 .60
51 Glenn Robinson .40 1.00
52 Ray Allen .60 1.50
53 Sam Cassell .30 .75
54 Tim Thomas .25 .60
55 Anthony Mason .40 1.00
56 Kevin Garnett 1.00 2.50
57 Wally Szczerbiak .30 .75
58 Terrell Brandon .30 .75
59 Joe Smith .30 .75
60 Jason Kidd .60 1.50
61 Kenyon Martin .40 1.00
62 Allan Houston .40 1.00
63 Latrell Sprewell .50 1.25
64 Marcus Camby .30 .75
65 Mark Jackson .30 .75
66 Kurt Thomas .25 .60
67 Tracy McGrady .60 1.50
68 Grant Hill .60 1.50
69 Mike Miller .30 .75
70 Allen Iverson 1.00 2.50
71 Dikembe Mutombo .60 1.50
72 Aaron McKie .25 .60
73 Stephon Marbury .50 1.25
74 Shawn Marion .40 1.00
75 Anfernee Hardaway 1.00 2.50
76 Tom Gugliotta .25 .60
77 Rasheed Wallace .50 1.25
78 Derek Anderson .25 .60
79 Bonzi Wells .25 .60
80 Chris Webber .50 1.25
81 Peja Stojakovic .30 .75
82 Mike Bibby .40 1.00
83 Doug Christie .25 .60
84 Tim Duncan 1.00 2.50
85 David Robinson .75 2.00
86 Antonio Daniels .25 .60
87 Steve Smith .30 .75
88 Gary Payton .60 1.50
89 Rashard Lewis .30 .75
90 Desmond Mason .30 .75
91 Vince Carter .75 2.00
92 Morris Peterson .25 .60
93 Antonio Davis .30 .75
94 Hakeem Olajuwon .75 2.00
95 Karl Malone .75 2.00
96 John Stockton .75 2.00
97 Donyell Marshall .25 .60
98 Michael Jordan 4.00 10.00
99 Courtney Alexander .25 .60
100 Richard Hamilton .50 1.25
101 Jeryl Sasser RC .60 1.50
102 DeSagana Diop RC .60 1.50
103 Alvin Jones RC .60 1.50
104 Gerald Wallace RC 1.25 3.00
105 Kenny Satterfield RC .60 1.50
106 Ruben Boumtje-Boumtje RC .75 2.00
107 Brian Scalabrine RC 1.00 2.50
108 Oscar Torres RC 1.00 2.50
109 Jarron Collins RC 1.00 2.50
110 Jeff Trepagnier RC .60 1.50
111 Brendan Haywood RC .75 2.00
112 Vladimir Radmanovic RC .75 2.00
113 Loren Woods RC .60 1.50
114 Terence Morris RC .60 1.50
115 Kirk Haston RC .60 1.50
116 Earl Watson RC .75 2.00
117 Brandon Armstrong RC .60 1.50
118 Zach Randolph RC 2.00 5.00
119 Bobby Simmons RC 1.00 2.50
120 Alton Ford RC 1.00 2.50
121 Trenton Hassell RC .60 1.50
122 Damone Brown RC .60 1.50
123 Michael Bradley RC .60 1.50
124 Zeljko Rebraca RC 1.00 2.50
125 Jason Collins RC .75 2.00
126 Samuel Dalembert RC 1.00 2.50
127 Gilbert Arenas RC 2.50 6.00
128 Willie Solomon RC .75 2.00
129 Joseph Forte RC .60 1.50
130 Steven Hunter RC .60 1.50
131 Andrei Kirilenko RC 2.50 6.00
132 Eddy Curry RC 1.50 4.00
133 Tony Parker RC 6.00 15.00
134 Troy Murphy RC 1.25 3.00
135 Shane Battier RC 3.00 8.00
136 Kedrick Brown RC 1.00 2.50
137 Tyson Chandler RC 2.50 6.00
138 Jamaal Tinsley RC 1.25 3.00
139 Pau Gasol RC 6.00 15.00
140 Joe Johnson RC 2.50 6.00
141 Jason Richardson RC 2.50 6.00
142 Richard Jefferson RC 2.00 5.00
143 Eddie Griffin RC 1.25 3.00
144 Rodney White RC 1.00 2.50
145 Kwame Brown RC 1.50 4.00

2001-02 Upper Deck Playmakers PC Game Jersey
PRINT RUN 350 SER.#'d SETS
*GOLD: .75X TO 2X BASE JSY HI
GOLD PRINT RUN 100 SER.#'d SETS
AIJ Allen Iverson 10.00 25.00
AJJ Antawn Jamison 2.50 6.00
BDJ Baron Davis 3.00 8.00
CWJ Chris Webber 4.00 10.00
DEJ Desmond Mason 2.50 6.00
DMJ Darius Miles 2.00 5.00
DNJ Dirk Nowitzki 10.00 25.00
ECJ Eddy Curry 3.00 8.00
EGJ Eddie Griffin 2.50 6.00
GWJ Gerald Wallace 4.00 10.00
JJJ Joe Johnson 4.00 10.00
JKJ Jason Kidd 5.00 12.00
JRJ Jason Richardson 5.00 12.00
JSJ John Stockton 6.00 15.00
JTJ Jamaal Tinsley 2.50 6.00
KBJ Kobe Bryant 50.00 120.00
KEJ Kedrick Brown 2.00 5.00
KGJ Kevin Garnett 10.00 25.00
KMJ Karl Malone 6.00 15.00
KWJ Kwame Brown 3.00 8.00
LOJ Lamar Odom 2.50 6.00
MAJ Kenyon Martin 3.00 8.00
MMJ Mike Miller 2.50 6.00
PPJ Paul Pierce 5.00 12.00
SHJ Steven Hunter 2.00 5.00
SMJ Stephon Marbury 4.00 10.00
TMJ Tracy McGrady 10.00 25.00

2001-02 Upper Deck Playmakers PC Shooting Shirt
STATED PRINT RUN 350 SERIAL #'d SETS
*GOLD: .75X TO 2X BASE SHIRT HI
GOLD PRINT RUN 150 SER.#'d SETS
AIS Allen Iverson 10.00 25.00
AKS Andrei Kirilenko 5.00 12.00
DMS Desmond Mason 2.50 6.00
EGS Eddie Griffin 2.50 6.00
JAS Jamaal Magloire 2.00 5.00
JES Jerry Stackhouse 3.00 8.00
JSS Joe Smith 2.50 6.00
JTS Jason Terry 3.00 8.00
KBS Kobe Bryant 50.00 120.00
KDS Keyon Dooling 2.00 5.00
KGS Kevin Garnett 8.00 20.00
KMS Karl Malone 6.00 15.00
KWS Kwame Brown 3.00 8.00
MFS Michael Finley 3.00 8.00
MOS Michael Olowokandi 2.00 5.00
NVS Nick Van Exel 3.00 8.00
PGS Pau Gasol 12.00 30.00
SBS Shane Battier 6.00 15.00
SSS Stromile Swift 2.00 5.00
TBS Terrell Brandon 2.50 6.00
TCS Tyson Chandler 5.00 12.00
TJS Jamaal Tinsley 2.50 6.00
TMS Tracy McGrady 8.00 20.00
VBS Vin Baker 2.50 6.00
WSS Wally Szczerbiak 2.50 6.00
ZRS Zach Randolph 6.00 15.00

2001-02 Upper Deck Playmakers PC Shooting Shirt Autographs
STATED PRINT RUN 25 SERIAL #'d SETS
JEAS Jerry Stackhouse 40.00 100.00
KBAS Kobe Bryant 2,000.00 4,000.00
KGAS Kevin Garnett 150.00 400.00
MJAS Michael Jordan 3,000.00 6,000.00
TCAS Tyson Chandler 25.00 60.00
TIAS Jamaal Tinsley 15.00 40.00
WSAS Wally Szczerbiak 15.00 40.00

2001-02 Upper Deck Playmakers PC Warm Up
STATED PRINT RUN 350 SERIAL #'d SETS
*GOLD: .6X TO 1.5X WARMUP HI
WARMUP PRINT RUN 250 SER.#'d SETS
AHW Allan Houston 3.00 8.00
ALW Al Harrington 2.50 6.00
AMW Andre Miller 2.50 6.00
AWW Antoine Walker 2.50 6.00
CMW Corey Maggette 2.50 6.00
DNW Dirk Nowitzki 8.00 20.00
DRW David Robinson 6.00 15.00
ECW Eddy Curry 3.00 8.00
GHW Grant Hill 5.00 12.00
GPW Gary Payton 5.00 12.00
JAW Jamaal Magloire 2.00 5.00
JBW Jonathan Bender 2.00 5.00
JMW Jamal Mashburn 2.50 6.00
JSW Joe Smith 2.50 6.00
KBW Kobe Bryant 50.00 120.00
KGW Kevin Garnett 8.00 20.00
KMW Kenyon Martin 3.00 8.00
LSW Latrell Sprewell 4.00 10.00
MCW Antonio McDyess 2.50 6.00
MFW Michael Finley 3.00 8.00
MPW Morris Peterson 2.00 5.00
PPW Paul Pierce 5.00 12.00
RYW Ray Allen 5.00 12.00
STW John Stockton 6.00 15.00
TBW Terrell Brandon 2.50 6.00
TCW Tyson Chandler 5.00 12.00
TMW Tracy McGrady 5.00 12.00
WSW Wally Szczerbiak 2.50 6.00

2001-02 Upper Deck Playmakers PC Warm Up Autographs
STATED PRINT RUN 50 SERIAL #'d SETS
AMAW Andre Miller 12.00 30.00
CMAW Corey Maggette 12.00 30.00
JAAW Jamaal Magloire 12.00 30.00
KBAW Kobe Bryant 1,500.00 3,000.00
KGAW Kevin Garnett 75.00 200.00
KMAW Kenyon Martin 12.00 30.00
MPAW Morris Peterson 12.00 30.00
PPAW Paul Pierce 60.00 150.00
TBAW Terrell Brandon 12.00 30.00
WSAW Wally Szczerbiak 12.00 30.00

2001-02 Upper Deck Playmakers Playmaker Dolls
STATED ODDS 1:24
HOME AND AWAY SAME VALUE
APMAIH Allen Iverson H 8.00 20.00
APMAIR Allen Iverson A 8.00 20.00
APMECH Eddy Curry H 6.00 15.00
APMECR Eddy Curry A 6.00 15.00
APMEGH Eddie Griffin H 6.00 15.00
APMEGR Eddie Griffin A 6.00 15.00
APMJEH Julius Erving H 12.00 30.00
APMJER Julius Erving A 12.00 30.00
APMJJH Joe Johnson H 6.00 15.00
APMJJR Joe Johnson A 6.00 15.00
APMJRH Jason Richardson H 6.00 15.00
APMJRR Jason Richardson A 6.00 15.00
APMKBH Kwame Brown H 6.00 15.00
APMKBR Kwame Brown A 6.00 15.00
APMKGH Kevin Garnett H 8.00 20.00
APMKGR Kevin Garnett A 8.00 20.00
APMTCH Tyson Chandler H 6.00 15.00
APMTCR Tyson Chandler A 6.00 15.00
APMTMH Tracy McGrady H 8.00 20.00
APMTMR Tracy McGrady A 8.00 20.00
PMKMH Kenyon Martin H 6.00 15.00
PMKMR Kenyon Martin A 6.00 15.00
PMKOBH Kobe Bryant H 15.00 40.00
PMKOBR Kobe Bryant A 15.00 40.00
PMLSH Latrell Sprewell H 6.00 15.00
PMLSR Latrell Sprewell A 6.00 15.00

2001-02 Upper Deck Playmakers Playmaker Dolls Autographs
STATED ODDS 1:336
HOME VERSIONS SERIALLY #'d BELOW
APMEGR Eddie Griffin 15.00 40.00
APMJJR Joe Johnson 30.00 80.00
APMJRH Jason Richardson/23 60.00 150.00
APMJRR Jason Richardson 25.00 60.00
APMKGA Kevin Garnett 125.00 300.00
APMKMR Kenyon Martin 20.00 50.00
APMKOBR Kobe Bryant 1,000.00 2,000.00
APMTCR Tyson Chandler 20.00 50.00

2001-02 Upper Deck Playmakers Triple Overtime
STATED PRINT RUN 50 SER.#'d SETS
AHOT Anfernee Hardaway 50.00 120.00
CMOT Corey Maggette 15.00 40.00
DMOT Darius Miles 12.00 30.00
ECOT Eddy Curry 20.00 50.00
EGOT Eddie Griffin 15.00 40.00
GWOT Gerald Wallace 25.00 60.00
JAOT Jason Terry 20.00 50.00
JKOT Jason Kidd 30.00 80.00
JSOT Joe Smith 15.00 40.00
KBOT Kobe Bryant 150.00 400.00
KGOT Kevin Garnett 50.00 120.00
KMOT Karl Malone 40.00 100.00
KWOT Kwame Brown 20.00 50.00
MMOT Mike Miller 15.00 40.00
NAOT Steve Nash 20.00 50.00
SAOT Shareef Abdur-Rahim 15.00 40.00
SMOT Stephon Marbury 25.00 60.00
SSOT Stromile Swift 12.00 30.00
TBOT Terrell Brandon 15.00 40.00
TCOT Tyson Chandler 30.00 80.00
WSOT Wally Szczerbiak 15.00 40.00

2003-04 Upper Deck Phenomenal Beginning LeBron James
COMPLETE SET 75.00 200.00
*GOLD: 1.5X TO 4X BASE HI
GOLD: ONE PER BOX
*GOLD 100: 12X TO 30X BASE HI
LJ L.James AU/23 1,000.00 2,000.00

2013 Upper Deck Precious Metal Gems Employee Exclusive
UD2012 Quad Spokesmen MEM
Michael Jordan
LeBron James
Tiger Woods
Wayne Gretzky 125.00 250.00

2007-08 Upper Deck Premier
1-94 PRINT RUN 99 SER.#'d SETS
95-136 RC PRINT RUN 199 SER.#'d SETS
1 Bill Russell 8.00 20.00
2 Larry Bird 10.00 25.00
3 Paul Pierce 4.00 10.00
4 Ray Allen 4.00 10.00
5 Al Harrington 2.00 5.00
6 Baron Davis 2.00 5.00
7 Rick Barry 2.00 5.00
8 Earl Monroe 2.50 6.00
9 Eddy Curry 1.50 4.00
10 Stephon Marbury 3.00 8.00
11 Chauncey Billups 3.00 8.00
12 Dave Bing 2.50 6.00
13 Richard Hamilton 3.00 8.00
14 Kobe Bryant 20.00 50.00
15 Luke Walton 2.00 5.00
16 Magic Johnson 10.00 25.00
17 Kevin Martin 2.00 5.00
18 Mike Bibby 2.50 6.00
19 Ron Artest 2.50 6.00
20 Bob Pettit 2.50 6.00
21 Joe Johnson 2.00 5.00
22 Josh Smith 1.50 4.00
23 Andre Iguodala 2.50 6.00
24 Andre Miller 2.00 5.00
25 Julius Erving 6.00 15.00
26 Elvin Hayes 2.50 6.00
27 Caron Butler 2.00 5.00
28 Gilbert Arenas 2.50 6.00
29 Ben Gordon 2.00 5.00
30 Ben Wallace 3.00 8.00
31 Michael Jordan 20.00 50.00
32 Allen Iverson 6.00 15.00
33 Carmelo Anthony 4.00 10.00
34 Marcus Camby 2.00 5.00
35 Hakeem Olajuwon 5.00 12.00
36 Tracy McGrady 4.00 10.00
37 Yao Ming 6.00 15.00
38 Jamaal Tinsley 1.50 4.00
39 Jermaine O'Neal 2.50 6.00
40 Mike Dunleavy 1.50 4.00
41 Jason Kidd 4.00 10.00
42 Richard Jefferson 2.00 5.00
43 Vince Carter 5.00 12.00
44 Chris Wilcox 1.50 4.00
45 Delonte West 1.50 4.00
46 Detlef Schrempf 2.50 6.00
47 Andrew Bogut 2.00 5.00
48 Michael Redd 2.00 5.00
49 Oscar Robertson 2.50 6.00
50 Amare Stoudemire 2.50 6.00
51 Grant Hill 4.00 10.00
52 Shawn Marion 2.50 6.00
53 Steve Nash 5.00 12.00
54 Brad Daugherty 2.00 5.00
55 Larry Hughes 2.00 5.00
56 LeBron James 20.00 50.00
57 Cuttino Mobley 2.00 5.00
58 Elton Brand 2.00 5.00
59 Sam Cassell 2.00 5.00
60 Brandon Roy 3.00 8.00
61 Clyde Drexler 4.00 10.00
62 LaMarcus Aldridge 2.50 6.00
63 Sean Elliott 2.50 6.00
64 George Gervin 3.00 8.00
65 Tim Duncan 6.00 15.00
66 Tony Parker 4.00 10.00
67 Carlos Boozer 2.00 5.00
68 Deron Williams 2.00 5.00
69 Karl Malone 3.00 8.00
70 Mehmet Okur 1.50 4.00
71 Dirk Nowitzki 6.00 15.00
72 Jason Terry 2.00 5.00
73 Josh Howard 2.00 5.00
74 Alonzo Mourning 4.00 10.00
75 Dwyane Wade 5.00 12.00
76 Shaquille O'Neal 10.00 25.00
77 Chris Paul 5.00 12.00
78 David West 2.00 5.00
79 Tyson Chandler 2.50 6.00
80 Kevin Garnett 6.00 15.00
81 Randy Foye 2.00 5.00
82 Al Jefferson 1.50 4.00
83 Dwight Howard 3.00 8.00
84 Jameer Nelson 1.50 4.00
85 Rashard Lewis 2.00 5.00
86 Darko Milicic 1.50 4.00
87 Mike Miller 2.00 5.00
88 Pau Gasol 4.00 10.00
89 Andrea Bargnani 1.50 4.00
90 Chris Bosh 3.00 8.00
91 T.J. Ford 1.50 4.00
92 Emeka Okafor 2.00 5.00
93 Gerald Wallace 2.00 5.00
94 Jason Richardson 2.50 6.00
95 Yi Jianlian RC 5.00 12.00
96 Marco Belinelli RC 3.00 8.00
97 Greg Oden RC 4.00 10.00
98 Brandan Wright RC 3.00 8.00
99 Nick Young RC 4.00 10.00
100 Thaddeus Young RC 4.00 10.00
101 Kevin Durant JSY AU RC 800.00 1,500.00
102 Al Horford JSY AU RC 15.00 40.00
103 Mike Conley Jr. JSY AU RC 15.00 40.00
104 Jeff Green JSY AU RC 5.00 12.00
105 Corey Brewer JSY AU RC 5.00 12.00
106 Joakim Noah JSY AU RC 6.00 15.00
107 Spencer Hawes JSY AU RC 4.00 10.00
108 Acie Law JSY AU RC 4.00 10.00
109 Julian Wright JSY AU RC 4.00 10.00
110 Al Thornton JSY AU RC 4.00 10.00
111 Rodney Stuckey JSY AU RC 4.00 10.00
112 Sean Williams JSY AU RC 4.00 10.00
113 Javaris Crittenton JSY AU RC 4.00 10.00
114 Jason Smith JSY AU RC 4.00 10.00
115 Daequan Cook JSY AU RC 5.00 12.00
116 Jared Dudley JSY AU RC 5.00 12.00
117 Wilson Chandler JSY AU RC 5.00 12.00
118 Morris Almond JSY AU RC 4.00 10.00
119 Arron Afflalo JSY AU RC 5.00 12.00
120 Alando Tucker JSY AU RC 4.00 10.00
121 Carl Landry JSY AU RC 4.00 10.00
122 Gabe Pruitt JSY AU RC 4.00 10.00
124 Nick Fazekas JSY AU RC 4.00 10.00
125 Glen Davis JSY AU RC 5.00 12.00
126 Jermareo Davidson JSY AU RC 4.00 10.00
127 Josh McRoberts JSY AU RC 4.00 10.00
129 Adam Haluska JSY AU RC 4.00 10.00
131 Stephane Lasme JSY AU RC 4.00 10.00
132 Dominic McGuire JSY AU RC 4.00 10.00
133 Aaron Gray JSY AU RC 4.00 10.00
134 Taurean Green JSY AU RC 4.00 10.00
135 Demetris Nichols JSY AU RC 4.00 10.00
136 D.J. Strawberry JSY AU RC 4.00 10.00
137 Aaron Brooks JSY AU RC 5.00 12.00
138 Herbert Hill JSY AU RC 4.00 10.00
139 Chris Richard JSY AU RC 4.00 10.00

2007-08 Upper Deck Premier Attractions Autographs Jerseys
PRINT RUN 50 SER.#'d SETS
PAAB Andrea Bargnani 6.00 15.00
PAAD Adrian Dantley 8.00 20.00
PAAI Andre Iguodala 10.00 25.00
PAAJ Al Jefferson 6.00 15.00
PAAM Alonzo Mourning 40.00 100.00
PABD Baron Davis 8.00 20.00
PABG Ben Gordon 8.00 20.00
PACM Corey Maggette 8.00 20.00
PACP Chris Paul 75.00 200.00
PADR Dennis Rodman 125.00 300.00
PADW Deron Williams 8.00 20.00
PAEO Emeka Okafor 8.00 20.00
PAHO Hakeem Olajuwon 60.00 150.00
PAJA Antawn Jamison 8.00 20.00
PAJO Michael Jordan 2,500.00 5,000.00
PAJW James Worthy 25.00 60.00
PAKB Kobe Bryant 1,500.00 3,000.00
PALJ LeBron James 1,500.00 3,000.00
PAMB Mike Bibby 10.00 25.00
PAMJ Magic Johnson 150.00 400.00
PAPA Tony Parker 40.00 100.00
PAPR Pat Riley 50.00 120.00
PARG Rudy Gay 8.00 20.00
PASN Steve Nash 125.00 300.00
PATP Tayshaun Prince 10.00 25.00
PAVC Vince Carter 125.00 300.00
PAWE Jerry West 75.00 200.00
PAWF Walt Frazier 40.00 100.00

2007-08 Upper Deck Premier Draft Mates Autographs
PRINT RUN 15 SER.#'d SETS
DMAR B.Roy/L.Aldridge 20.00 50.00
DMBC M.Conley/C.Brewer 12.00 30.00
DMBF C.Bosh/T.Ford 12.00 30.00
DMBN K.Bryant/S.Nash 1,000.00 2,000.00
DMBV R.Barry/D.Van Arsdale 20.00 50.00
DMCB L.Bird/M.Cooper 125.00 300.00
DMCJ V.Carter/A.Jamison 60.00 150.00
DMDG K.Durant/J.Green 300.00 600.00
DMDH K.Durant/A.Horford 300.00 600.00
DMDM A.Miller/B.Davis 12.00 30.00
DMDR B.Daugherty/D.Rodman 50.00 120.00
DMDS A.Dantley/L.Shelton 12.00 30.00
DMGI A.Iguodala/B.Gordon 12.00 30.00
DMHJ D.Howard/A.Jefferson 15.00 40.00
DMHL A.Horford/A.Law 12.00 30.00
DMJA L.James/C.Anthony 1,000.00 2,000.00
DMJM M.Johnson/S.Moncrief 125.00 300.00
DMJO M.Jordan/H.Olajuwon 2,000.00 4,000.00
DMKM S.Kerr/D.Manning 15.00 40.00
DMNH J.Noah/A.Horford 12.00 30.00
DMPH P.Pierce/A.Harrington 25.00 60.00
DMPR Q.Richardson/M.Peterson 12.00 30.00
DMRE S.Elliott/G.Rice 12.00 30.00
DMRF W.Frazier/P.Riley 40.00 100.00
DMRS J.Sikma/T.Rollins 12.00 30.00
DMSB R.Stuckey/M.Belinelli 12.00 30.00
DMTG A.Green/W.Tisdale 15.00 40.00
DMTW J.Wright/A.Thornton 12.00 30.00
DMWJ D.Williams/J.Jack 12.00 30.00
DMWW B.Walton/J.Wilkes 15.00 40.00

2007-08 Upper Deck Premier Exclusivity Autographs
PRINT RUN 25 SER.#'d SETS
EXAH Al Horford 15.00 40.00
EXJG Jeff Green 12.00 30.00
EXJN Joakim Noah 12.00 30.00
EXKB Kobe Bryant 1,500.00 3,000.00
EXKD Kevin Durant 1,000.00 2,000.00
EXKG Kevin Garnett 150.00 400.00
EXLJ LeBron James 1,500.00 3,000.00
EXMC Mike Conley Jr. 12.00 30.00
EXMJ Michael Jordan 3,000.00 6,000.00
EXSN Steve Nash 150.00 400.00

2007-08 Upper Deck Premier First Round Phenoms Autographs
PRINT RUN 6 TO 50 SER.#'d SETS
FPAD Adrian Dantley/50 8.00 20.00
FPAM Andre Miller/50 8.00 20.00
FPBD Baron Davis/50 10.00 25.00
FPBI Larry Bird/33 150.00 400.00
FPBW Bill Walton/50 20.00 50.00
FPCA Carmelo Anthony/50 60.00 150.00
FPCB Chris Bosh/50 15.00 40.00
FPDA Brad Daugherty/50 10.00 25.00
FPHG Horace Grant/50 15.00 40.00
FPHO Hakeem Olajuwon/34 60.00 150.00
FPJO Magic Johnson/32 150.00 400.00
FPJS John Stockton/12 100.00 250.00
FPKB Kobe Bryant/24 1,500.00 3,000.00
FPLB Leandro Barbosa/50 8.00 20.00
FPLJ LeBron James/23 1,500.00 3,000.00
FPMB Mike Bibby/50 12.00 30.00
FPMJ Michael Jordan/23 3,000.00 6,000.00
FPMO Alonzo Mourning/50 50.00 120.00
FPMP Morris Peterson/50 8.00 20.00
FPPA Tony Parker/50 40.00 100.00
FPPP Paul Pierce/50 60.00 150.00
FPSN Steve Nash/50 150.00 400.00
FPTC Tom Chambers/50 8.00 20.00
FPTF T.J. Ford/50 8.00 20.00
FPTM Tracy McGrady/50 125.00 300.00
FPTP Tayshaun Prince/50 12.00 30.00
FPVC Vince Carter/50 150.00 400.00
FPWF Walt Frazier/50 40.00 100.00
FPYM Yao Ming/50 200.00 500.00

2007-08 Upper Deck Premier Franchise Faces Autographs
PRINT RUN 24 TO 50 SER.#'d SETS
FFAI Andre Iguodala/50 15.00 40.00
FFAJ Antawn Jamison/50 10.00 25.00
FFAM Alonzo Mourning/50 50.00 120.00
FFBD Brad Daugherty/50 10.00 25.00
FFBG Ben Gordon/50 10.00 25.00
FFBL Bill Laimbeer/50 20.00 50.00
FFBR Brandon Roy/50 15.00 40.00
FFCA Carmelo Anthony/50 60.00 150.00
FFCB Chris Bosh/50 15.00 40.00
FFDH Dwight Howard/50 20.00 50.00
FFDR David Robinson/50 75.00 200.00
FFDW Deron Williams/50 12.00 30.00
FFHO Hakeem Olajuwon/34 60.00 150.00
FFJE Julius Erving/50 125.00 300.00
FFJO Magic Johnson/32 150.00 400.00
FFJS John Stockton/24 100.00 250.00
FFJW Jerry West/50 75.00 200.00
FFKB Kobe Bryant/24 1,500.00 3,000.00
FFLB Larry Bird/33 150.00 400.00
FFLJ LeBron James/23 1,500.00 3,000.00
FFMJ Michael Jordan/23 3,000.00 6,000.00
FFPA Tony Parker/50 40.00 100.00
FFPP Paul Pierce/50 60.00 150.00
FFRB Rick Barry/50 20.00 50.00
FFSE Sean Elliott/50 10.00 25.00
FFTM Tracy McGrady/50 125.00 300.00
FFTP Tayshaun Prince/50 12.00 30.00
FFWF Walt Frazier/50 40.00 100.00
FFWU Wes Unseld/50 20.00 50.00
FFYM Yao Ming/50 200.00 500.00

2007-08 Upper Deck Premier Impressions
PRINT RUN 50 SER.#'d SETS
*GOLD/25: .5X TO 1.2X BASIC
PIAA Arron Afflalo 5.00 12.00
PIAB Aaron Brooks 5.00 12.00
PIAH Al Horford 15.00 40.00
PIAL Acie Law 4.00 10.00
PIAT Alando Tucker 4.00 10.00
PICB Corey Brewer 5.00 12.00
PICL Carl Landry 4.00 10.00
PIDC Daequan Cook 5.00 12.00
PIDM Dominic McGuire 4.00 10.00
PIGD Glen Davis 5.00 12.00
PIGP Gabe Pruitt 4.00 10.00
PIJA Jared Dudley 5.00 12.00
PIJC Javaris Crittenton 5.00 12.00
PIJD Jermareo Davidson 4.00 10.00
PIJG Jeff Green 5.00 12.00
PIJM Josh McRoberts 6.00 15.00
PIJN Joakim Noah 6.00 15.00
PIJS Jason Smith 4.00 10.00
PIJW Julian Wright 4.00 10.00
PIKD Kevin Durant 400.00 800.00
PILS Luis Scola 6.00 15.00
PIMA Morris Almond 4.00 10.00
PIMB Marco Belinelli 5.00 12.00
PIMC Mike Conley Jr. 15.00 40.00
PINF Nick Fazekas 4.00 10.00
PIRS Rodney Stuckey 4.00 10.00
PISH Spencer Hawes 4.00 10.00
PISW Sean Williams 4.00 10.00
PITH Al Thornton 4.00 10.00
PIWC Wilson Chandler 5.00 12.00

2007-08 Upper Deck Premier Impressions Gold
PRINT RUN 25 SER.#'d SETS

2007-08 Upper Deck Premier Noteworthy
PRINT RUNS LISTED IN CHECKLIST
*GOLD/25: .5X TO 1.2X BASIC
NWAB Andrea Bargnani/23 6.00 15.00
NWAD Adrian Dantley/57 8.00 20.00
NWAE Alex English/54 10.00 25.00
NWAI Andre Iguodala/34 10.00 25.00
NWAJ Antawn Jamison/51 8.00 20.00
NWBG Ben Gordon/48 10.00 25.00
NWBI Larry Bird/60 150.00 400.00
NWBR Brandon Roy/29 15.00 40.00
NWCB Chris Bosh/41 15.00 40.00
NWCP Chris Paul/35 75.00 200.00
NWCU Terry Cummings/52 8.00 20.00
NWDH Dwight Howard/35 15.00 40.00
NWDR David Robinson/71 50.00 120.00
NWDT David Thompson/73 8.00 20.00
NWDW Dominique Wilkins/57 25.00 60.00
NWEB Elgin Baylor/71 40.00 100.00
NWGR Glen Rice/56 10.00 25.00
NWHO Hakeem Olajuwon/51 50.00 120.00
NWJE Al Jefferson/32 6.00 15.00
NWJW Jerry West/63 30.00 80.00
NWKB Kobe Bryant/81 1,000.00 2,000.00
NWLA LaMarcus Aldridge/30 12.00 30.00
NWLB Leandro Barbosa/32 6.00 15.00
NWLH Larry Hughes/44 10.00 25.00
NWLJ LeBron James/56 1,500.00 3,000.00
NWMB Mike Bibby/44 12.00 30.00
NWMJ Michael Jordan/69 3,000.00 6,000.00
NWPM Paul Millsap/20 6.00 15.00
NWPP Paul Pierce/50 50.00 120.00
NWPR Tayshaun Prince/33 10.00 25.00
NWRB Rick Barry/64 12.00 30.00
NWRG Rudy Gay/31 8.00 20.00
NWSN Steve Nash/42 75.00 200.00
NWTC Tom Chambers/60 8.00 20.00
NWTF T.J. Ford/34 6.00 15.00
NWTM Tracy McGrady/62 100.00 250.00
NWTP Tony Parker/38 40.00 100.00
NWTT Tyrus Thomas/27 6.00 15.00
NWVC Vince Carter/51 125.00 300.00
NWWI Deron Williams/33 8.00 20.00

2007-08 Upper Deck Premier Noteworthy Gold
PRINT RUN 25 SER.#'d SETS
NWBI Larry Bird 200.00 500.00
NWBR Brandon Roy 20.00 50.00
NWCP Chris Paul 100.00 250.00
NWDR David Robinson 60.00 150.00
NWDT David Thompson 10.00 25.00
NWEB Elgin Baylor 50.00 120.00
NWHO Hakeem Olajuwon 60.00 150.00
NWJW Jerry West 40.00 100.00
NWKB Kobe Bryant 1,250.00 2,500.00
NWLJ LeBron James 2,000.00 4,000.00
NWMJ Michael Jordan 4,000.00 8,000.00
NWPP Paul Pierce 60.00 150.00
NWRG Rudy Gay 10.00 25.00
NWSN Steve Nash 100.00 250.00
NWTM Tracy McGrady 125.00 300.00
NWTP Tony Parker 50.00 120.00
NWVC Vince Carter 150.00 400.00

2007-08 Upper Deck Premier Opening Night Autographs Jerseys
PRINT RUN 25 SER.#'d SETS
ONAD K.Durant/C.Anthony 500.00 1,000.00
ONAJ A.Jefferson/C.Anthony 60.00 150.00
ONBI C.Bosh/A.Iguodala 20.00 50.00
ONBM K.Bryant/T.McGrady 1,000.00 2,000.00
ONBP M.Bibby/C.Paul 60.00 150.00
ONBS J.Smith/A.Bargnani 10.00 25.00
ONBW M.Bibby/J.Wright 10.00 25.00
ONCG M.Collins/D.Gibson 10.00 25.00
ONCT V.Carter/T.Thomas 60.00 150.00
ONDM B.Davis/C.Maggette 12.00 30.00
ONDW B.Davis/D.Williams 12.00 30.00
ONFB N.Fazekas/S.Brown 10.00 25.00
ONFH A.Horford/N.Fazekas 10.00 25.00
ONGJ K.Garnett/A.Jamison 75.00 200.00
ONHN D.Howard/D.Noel 20.00 50.00
ONHT A.Thornton/A.Harrington 10.00 25.00
ONJF L.James/N.Fazekas 300.00 600.00
ONKH K.Hinrich/J.Kidd 20.00 50.00
ONMB B.Bowen/J.McRoberts 10.00 25.00
ONMC Y.Ming/J.Crittenton 100.00 250.00
ONMF A.Miller/T.Ford 10.00 25.00
ONML P.Millsap/S.Lasme 10.00 25.00
ONND K.Durant/S.Nash 500.00 1,000.00
ONNW J.Noah/S.Williams 10.00 25.00
ONPC T.Parker/M.Conley 25.00 60.00
ONPR T.Parker/B.Roy 25.00 60.00
ONRD M.Redd/J.Dudley 10.00 25.00
ONSC R.Stuckey/D.Cook 10.00 25.00
ONWM D.McGuire/S.Williams 10.00 25.00
ONWT D.Wilkins/A.Tucker 10.00 25.00

2007-08 Upper Deck Premier Pairings Autographs
PRINT RUN 20 SER.#'d SETS
PPAJ A.Bargnani/J.Garbajosa 12.00 30.00
PPAR B.Roy/L.Aldridge 25.00 60.00
PPAS R.Stuckey/A.Afflalo 12.00 30.00
PPBD B.Davis/M.Belinelli 12.00 30.00
PPBF C.Bosh/T.Ford 15.00 40.00
PPBG M.Bibby/F.Garcia 12.00 30.00
PPBJ L.James/K.Bryant 4,000.00 8,000.00
PPBL B.Diaw/L.Barbosa 12.00 30.00
PPBM M.Bibby/B.Miller 12.00 30.00
PPBN S.Nash/K.Bryant 1,000.00 2,000.00
PPCG J.Green/M.Conley 15.00 40.00
PPCJ A.Jamison/V.Carter 75.00 200.00
PPCM V.Carter/T.McGrady 150.00 400.00
PPCW J.Wright/T.Chandler 12.00 30.00
PPDB B.Davis/R.Barry 12.00 30.00
PPDP M.Price/B.Daugherty 20.00 50.00
PPFD W.Frazier/L.Dampier 25.00 60.00
PPFS R.Foye/C.Smith 12.00 30.00
PPGB D.Gibson/S.Brown 12.00 30.00
PPGC A.Gray/J.Curry 12.00 30.00
PPGH D.Howard/H.Grant 20.00 50.00
PPGL R.Gay/K.Lowry 15.00 40.00
PPGN B.Gordon/J.Noah 15.00 40.00
PPHB A.Horford/C.Brewer 12.00 30.00
PPHC T.Chandler/A.Harrington 12.00 30.00
PPHG D.Howard/B.Gordon 20.00 50.00
PPIS J.Smith/A.Iguodala 12.00 30.00
PPJB L.Bird/M.Johnson 300.00 600.00
PPJC R.Carney/A.Jefferson 12.00 30.00
PPJE M.Jordan/J.Erving 3,000.00 6,000.00
PPJJ M.Jordan/L.James 6,000.00 12,000.00
PPJP A.Jefferson/P.Pierce 40.00 100.00
PPKA B.Armstrong/S.Kerr 20.00 50.00
PPKB J.Boone/J.Kidd 20.00 50.00
PPKC J.Kidd/V.Carter 100.00 250.00
PPLC M.Conley/K.Lowry 15.00 40.00
PPMD P.Davis/C.Mihm 12.00 30.00
PPMG D.Gibson/D.Marshall 12.00 30.00
PPML T.McGrady/C.Landry 75.00 200.00
PPMN D.Noel/S.May 12.00 30.00
PPMO H.Olajuwon/Y.Ming 200.00 500.00
PPMP Y.Ming/T.Prince 125.00 300.00
PPND K.Durant/J.Noah 300.00 600.00
PPNM P.Millsap/D.Noel 12.00 30.00
PPOM H.Olajuwon/A.Mourning 100.00 250.00
PPPD P.Davis/M.Peterson 12.00 30.00
PPPP M.Peterson/C.Paul 40.00 100.00
PPPR R.Rondo/L.Powe 12.00 30.00
PPPW T.Parker/D.Williams 20.00 50.00
PPRG B.Roy/T.Green 12.00 30.00
PPRP G.Pruitt/R.Rondo 12.00 30.00
PPRR D.Rodman/D.Robinson 125.00 300.00
PPRS Q.Richardson/D.Stevenson 12.00 30.00
PPTB T.Thomas/A.Bargnani 12.00 30.00
PPTN T.Thomas/J.Noah 12.00 30.00
PPWA J.Wright/H.Armstrong 12.00 30.00
PPWB D.Williams/R.Brewer 12.00 30.00
PPWH A.Horford/D.Wilkins 25.00 60.00
PPWP B.Walton/R.Parish 20.00 50.00
PPWW S.Williams/S.Williams 12.00 30.00

2007-08 Upper Deck Premier Patches Dual Gold
PRINT RUN 9 TO 50 SER.#'d SETS
AA Arron Afflalo/25 5.00 12.00
AB Aaron Brooks/25 5.00 12.00
AJ Antawn Jamison/25 5.00 12.00
AM Andre Miller/25 5.00 12.00
AT Al Thornton/25 4.00 10.00
BD Boris Diaw/25 5.00 12.00
BI Mike Bibby/25 6.00 15.00
BJ Bobby Jackson/25 4.00 10.00
BM Brad Miller/25 5.00 12.00
CA Carmelo Anthony/25 20.00 50.00
CM Corey Maggette/25 5.00 12.00
CP Chris Paul/25 25.00 60.00
DC Daequan Cook/25 5.00 12.00
DE Deron Williams/25 5.00 12.00
DM Donyell Marshall/25 4.00 10.00
DN David Noel/25 4.00 10.00
DR David Robinson/25 25.00 60.00
DS DeShawn Stevenson/25 4.00 10.00
DW Damien Wilkins/25 4.00 10.00
FG Francisco Garcia/25 4.00 10.00
HA Hilton Armstrong/25 4.00 10.00
JC Javaris Crittenton/25 4.00 10.00
JD Jared Dudley/9 5.00 12.00
JE Julius Erving/25 40.00 100.00
JG Joey Graham/25 4.00 10.00
JS Jason Smith/25 4.00 10.00
JW Jerry West/25 25.00 60.00
KB Kobe Bryant/25 125.00 300.00
KD Keyon Dooling/25 4.00 10.00
LH Larry Hughes/25 5.00 12.00
LJ LeBron James/25 125.00 300.00
MB Marco Belinelli/25 5.00 12.00
MC Mardy Collins/25 4.00 10.00
MJ Mike James/25 4.00 10.00
MP Morris Peterson/12 4.00 10.00
PA Tony Parker/25 20.00 50.00
PD Paul Davis/25 4.00 10.00
PP Paul Pierce/25 20.00 50.00
RC Rodney Carney/13 4.00 10.00
SB Shannon Brown/25 4.00 10.00
SL Shaun Livingston/25 5.00 12.00
SM Sean May/25 4.00 10.00
SN Steve Nash/25 40.00 100.00
ST John Stockton/25 25.00 60.00
SW Sean Williams/25 4.00 10.00
TC Tom Chambers/25 6.00 15.00
TP Tayshaun Prince/25 6.00 15.00
TS Thabo Sefolosha/25 4.00 10.00
VC Vince Carter/25 25.00 60.00
WC Wilson Chandler/25 5.00 12.00

2007-08 Upper Deck Premier Patches Dual Silver
STATED PRINT RUN ONE TO 52 SER.#'d SETS

2007-08 Upper Deck Premier Patches Dual Silver Spectrum
PRINT RUN 15 SER.#'d SETS
AA Arron Afflalo 6.00 15.00
CA Carmelo Anthony 12.00 30.00
DE Deron Williams 6.00 15.00
DR David Robinson 15.00 40.00
JC Javaris Crittenton 5.00 12.00
JS Jason Smith 5.00 12.00
JW Jerry West 20.00 40.00
KB Kobe Bryant 150.00 400.00
LJ LeBron James 25.00 60.00
SB Shannon Brown 5.00 12.00
SN Steve Nash 15.00 40.00
ST John Stockton 15.00 40.00
SW Sean Williams 5.00 12.00
TC Tom Chambers 8.00 20.00
VC Vince Carter 15.00 40.00

2007-08 Upper Deck Premier Patches Triple Silver
PRINT RUN 35 SER.#'d SETS
AH Al Horford 15.00 40.00
AJ Antawn Jamison 5.00 12.00
AL Acie Law 4.00 10.00
AM Andre Miller 5.00 12.00
BD Boris Diaw 5.00 12.00
BJ Bobby Jackson 4.00 10.00
BM Brad Miller 5.00 12.00
CA Carmelo Anthony 20.00 50.00
CB Corey Brewer 5.00 12.00
CM Corey Maggette 5.00 12.00
CO Mardy Collins 4.00 10.00
CP Chris Paul 25.00 60.00
DM Donyell Marshall 4.00 10.00
DN David Noel 4.00 10.00
DR David Robinson 25.00 60.00
DS DeShawn Stevenson 4.00 10.00
DU Kevin Durant 100.00 250.00
DW Damien Wilkins 4.00 10.00

FG Francisco Garcia 4.00 10.00
GR Jeff Green 5.00 12.00
HA Hilton Armstrong 4.00 10.00
JE Julius Erving 40.00 100.00
JG Joey Graham 4.00 10.00
JN Joakim Noah 6.00 15.00
JS John Stockton 25.00 60.00
JW Julian Wright 4.00 10.00
KB Kobe Bryant 125.00 300.00
KD Keyon Dooling 4.00 10.00
KG Kevin Garnett 25.00 60.00
LH Larry Hughes 5.00 12.00
LJ LeBron James 125.00 300.00
MB Mike Bibby 6.00 15.00
MC Mike Conley Jr. 15.00 40.00
MJ Mike James 4.00 10.00
MP Morris Peterson 4.00 10.00
PD Paul Davis 4.00 10.00
PP Paul Pierce 20.00 50.00
PR Tayshaun Prince 6.00 15.00
RC Rodney Carney 4.00 10.00
RS Rodney Stuckey 4.00 10.00
SB Shannon Brown 4.00 10.00
SH Spencer Hawes 4.00 10.00
SL Shaun Livingston 5.00 12.00
SM Sean May 4.00 10.00
SN Steve Nash 40.00 100.00
TC Tom Chambers 6.00 15.00
TP Tony Parker 20.00 50.00
TS Thabo Sefolosha 4.00 10.00
VC Vince Carter 25.00 60.00
WE Jerry West 25.00 60.00

2007-08 Upper Deck Premier Penmanship Autographs

PRINT RUN 50 SER.#'d SETS
AH Al Horford 25.00 60.00
AJ Antawn Jamison 8.00 20.00
AL Acie Law 6.00 15.00
AM Alonzo Mourning 40.00 100.00
AT Al Thornton 6.00 15.00
BA B.J. Armstrong 10.00 25.00
BR Brandon Roy 12.00 30.00
BW Bill Walton 40.00 100.00
CA Carmelo Anthony 125.00 300.00
CH Connie Hawkins 12.00 30.00
CL Clyde Lovellette 10.00 25.00
CM Chris Mullin 12.00 30.00
CO Corey Brewer 8.00 20.00
CP Chris Paul 75.00 200.00
CS Craig Smith 6.00 15.00
CU Terry Cummings 8.00 20.00
DG Daniel Gibson 6.00 15.00
DI Boris Diaw 15.00 40.00
DM Danny Manning 8.00 20.00
DN David Noel 6.00 15.00
DO Donyell Marshall 6.00 15.00
DR Dennis Rodman 100.00 250.00
DW Deron Williams 8.00 20.00
EO Emeka Okafor 8.00 20.00
GR Glen Rice 10.00 25.00
HA Al Harrington 8.00 20.00
HG Hal Greer 12.00 30.00
HO Horace Grant 20.00 50.00
JA James Augustine 6.00 15.00
JB Josh Boone 6.00 15.00
JC Javaris Crittenton 6.00 15.00
JE Al Jefferson 6.00 15.00
JG Jeff Green 8.00 20.00
JJ Jarrett Jack 8.00 20.00
JK Jason Kidd 20.00 50.00
JM Mike James 6.00 15.00
JN Joakim Noah 10.00 25.00
JO Magic Johnson 150.00 400.00
JW Julian Wright 6.00 15.00
KB Kobe Bryant 1,500.00 3,000.00
KD Kevin Durant 500.00 1,000.00
KL Kyle Lowry 12.00 30.00
KV Kiki Vandeweghe 8.00 20.00
LA LaMarcus Aldridge 10.00 25.00
LB Larry Bird 150.00 400.00
LE Leandro Barbosa 8.00 20.00
LH Larry Hughes 8.00 20.00
LJ LeBron James 1,500.00 3,000.00
LP Leon Powe 6.00 15.00
MA Mardy Collins 6.00 15.00
MB Marco Belinelli 8.00 20.00
MC Mike Conley Jr. 25.00 60.00
MD Marquis Daniels 6.00 15.00
MI Michael Cooper 10.00 25.00
MJ Michael Jordan 6,000.00 12,000.00
OL Hakeem Olajuwon 60.00 150.00
PA Tony Parker 40.00 100.00
PM Paul Millsap 8.00 20.00
PP Paul Pierce 50.00 120.00
PR Pat Riley 40.00 100.00
RC Rodney Carney 6.00 15.00
RF Randy Foye 8.00 20.00
RG Rudy Gay 8.00 20.00
RO David Robinson 40.00 100.00
RR Rajon Rondo 30.00 80.00
RS Rodney Stuckey 6.00 15.00
RU Bill Russell 500.00 1,000.00
SB Shannon Brown 6.00 15.00
SE Sean Elliott 8.00 20.00
SH Spencer Hawes 6.00 15.00
SI Cedric Simmons 6.00 15.00
SJ Solomon Jones 6.00 15.00
SK Steve Kerr 25.00 60.00
SM Sean May 6.00 15.00
SP Sam Perkins 8.00 20.00
SW Shelden Williams 6.00 15.00
TC Tom Chambers 10.00 25.00
TF T.J. Ford 6.00 15.00
TM Tracy McGrady 100.00 250.00
TP Tayshaun Prince 10.00 25.00
TT Tyrus Thomas 6.00 15.00
TY Tyson Chandler 10.00 25.00
VC Vince Carter 125.00 300.00
WD Damien Wilkins 6.00 15.00
WE Jerry West 40.00 100.00
WF Walt Frazier 20.00 50.00
WI Dominique Wilkins 20.00 50.00
WO James Worthy 20.00 50.00
WS Shawne Williams 6.00 15.00
WT Wayman Tisdale 12.00 30.00
WU Wes Unseld 12.00 30.00
YM Yao Ming 150.00 400.00

2007-08 Upper Deck Premier Penmanship Autographs Gold

PRINT RUNS LISTED IN CHECKLIST
AH Al Horford/15 20.00 50.00
AM Alonzo Mourning/33 50.00 120.00
CA Carmelo Anthony/15 50.00 120.00
CO Corey Brewer/22 8.00 20.00
DN David Noel/34 6.00 15.00
DO Donyell Marshall/24 6.00 15.00
FG Francisco Garcia/32 6.00 15.00
HO Horace Grant/54 20.00 50.00
JO Magic Johnson/32 200.00 500.00
KB Kobe Bryant/24 1,250.00 2,500.00
KD Kevin Durant/35 600.00 1,200.00
KV Kiki Vandeweghe/55 6.00 15.00
LB Larry Bird/33 200.00 500.00
LJ LeBron James/23 2,000.00 4,000.00
MA Mardy Collins/25 6.00 15.00
MC Mike Conley Jr./11 25.00 60.00
MI Michael Cooper/21 10.00 25.00
MJ Michael Jordan/23 4,000.00 8,000.00
OL Hakeem Olajuwon/34 75.00 200.00
PM Paul Millsap/24 8.00 20.00
PP Paul Pierce/34 60.00 150.00
RC Rodney Carney/25 6.00 15.00
RG Rudy Gay/22 8.00 20.00
RO David Robinson/50 50.00 120.00
SH Spencer Hawes/31 6.00 15.00
SI Cedric Simmons/22 6.00 15.00
SJ Solomon Jones/44 6.00 15.00
SK Steve Kerr/25 30.00 80.00
SM Sean May/42 6.00 15.00
SW Shelden Williams/33 6.00 15.00
TC Tom Chambers/24 10.00 25.00
VC Vince Carter/15 150.00 400.00
WE Jerry West/44 50.00 120.00
WO James Worthy/42 25.00 60.00

2007-08 Upper Deck Premier Preeminence

COMMON CARD 5.00 12.00
SEMISTARS 6.00 15.00
UNLISTED STARS 8.00 20.00
PRINT RUN 50 SER.#'d SETS
GOLD/25 1.2X BASE
PEAB Andrea Bargnani 5.00 12.00
PEAH Al Harrington 6.00 15.00
PEAI Andre Iguodala 8.00 20.00
PEAJ Antawn Jamison 6.00 15.00
PEBA B.J. Armstrong 8.00 20.00
PEBD Baron Davis 6.00 15.00
PEBR Brandon Roy 10.00 25.00
PECH Tom Chambers 8.00 20.00
PECP Chris Paul 75.00 200.00
PECU Terry Cummings 6.00 15.00
PEDG Daniel Gibson 5.00 12.00
PEDH Dwight Howard 15.00 40.00
PEDW Deron Williams 6.00 15.00
PEJE Al Jefferson 5.00 12.00
PEKB Kobe Bryant 1,000.00 2,000.00
PELA LaMarcus Aldridge 8.00 20.00
PELB Leandro Barbosa 6.00 15.00
PELH Larry Hughes 6.00 15.00
PEMJ Magic Johnson 150.00 400.00
PEMP Morris Peterson 5.00 12.00
PEPM Paul Millsap 6.00 15.00
PERG Rudy Gay 6.00 15.00
PESK Steve Kerr 20.00 50.00
PESW Shelden Williams 5.00 12.00
PETC Tyson Chandler 8.00 20.00
PETP Tayshaun Prince 8.00 20.00
PETT Tyrus Thomas 5.00 12.00
PEVC Vince Carter 125.00 300.00
PEWT Wayman Tisdale 12.00 30.00
PEYM Yao Ming 150.00 400.00

2007-08 Upper Deck Premier Preeminence Gold

PRINT RUN 25 SER.#'d SETS

2007-08 Upper Deck Premier Rare Patches Dual Gold

PRINT RUN 15 SER.#'d SETS
*SILVER PATCH: .4X TO 1X BASE HI
SILVER PRINT RUN 25 SER.#'d SETS
AC A.Horford/C.Brewer 8.00 20.00
AG R.Allen/K.Garnett 25.00 50.00
AH R.Allen/R.Hamilton 8.00 20.00
AS A.Afflalo/R.Stuckey 8.00 20.00
BB S.Battier/C.Boozer 10.00 25.00
BJ K.Bryant/L.James 1,000.00 2,000.00
BM D.Mason/A.Bogut 8.00 20.00
BN K.Bryant/S.Nash 200.00 500.00
DG K.Durant/J.Green 75.00 200.00
DJ J.Stockton/D.Williams 15.00 30.00
DM T.Duncan/Y.Ming 15.00 30.00
DR C.Drexler/D.Robinson 20.00 40.00
GI B.Gordon/A.Iguodala 8.00 20.00
GJ K.Garnett/A.Jefferson 20.00 40.00
GN A.Gray/J.Noah 8.00 20.00
HB R.Hamilton/C.Billups 8.00 20.00
HL A.Horford/A.Law 10.00 25.00
IA A.Iverson/C.Anthony 20.00 40.00
IN A.Iverson/D.Nowitzki 15.00 30.00
JB M.Johnson/L.Bird 20.00 40.00
JD L.James/K.Durant 300.00 600.00
JJ M.Jordan/L.James 100.00 250.00
JW A.Jamison/L.Walton 8.00 20.00
KM J.Kidd/S.Marbury 10.00 25.00
PD G.Pruitt/G.Davis 8.00 20.00
PH P.Pierce/K.Hinrich 8.00 20.00
PR C.Paul/B.Roy 10.00 25.00
PW C.Paul/J.Wright 10.00 25.00
SH A.Stoudemire/D.Howard 8.00 20.00
WD G.Wallace/J.Dudley 8.00 20.00
WN B.Wallace/J.Noah 8.00 20.00
WW R.Wallace/B.Wallace 8.00 20.00
YS T.Young/J.Smith 8.00 20.00

2007-08 Upper Deck Premier Rare Patches Triple Silver

PRINT RUN 15 SER.#'d SETS
ASH Afflalo/Stuckey/Hamilton 12.50 30.00
BFC Crittenton/Bryant/Farmar 75.00 200.00
BGJ Bryant/Garnett/James 200.00 500.00
BNI Iverson/Bryant/Nash 100.00 250.00
BPW Paul/Billups/Williams 20.00 50.00
DGC Conley/Durant/Green 40.00 75.00
DGO O'Neal/Garnett/Duncan 25.00 50.00
DPG Parker/Ginobili/Duncan 20.00 50.00
JJB Bird/Jordan/Johnson 100.00 200.00
MRL Lee/Randolph/Marbury 12.50 30.00
NHB Horford/Brewer/Noah 25.00 50.00
NHH Nowitzki/Howard/Harris 15.00 40.00
OGR Robinson/KG/Olajuwon 25.00 50.00
PAG Garnett/Allen/Pierce 50.00 100.00
WSD Stockton/West/Drexler 40.00 100.00

2007-08 Upper Deck Premier Rare Remnants Quad

PRINT RUN 50 SER.#'d SETS
ABWB Artest/Bowen/Wllce/Butler 6.00 15.00
AGDG Durant/Green/Allen/KG 15.00 40.00
AGPD Davis/KG/Pruitt/Allen 8.00 20.00
ARPA Aldridge/Roy/Hilton/Paul 8.00 20.00
BHWR Brand/Hill/Wallace/ZBo 8.00 20.00
BMMO O'Neal/Mllr/Darko/Brown 6.00 15.00
CNCI Camby/Tysn/Ilgausk/Dirk 8.00 20.00
DNSA Dirk/Duncan/Melo/Amare 10.00 25.00
GCMM KG/Carter/TMac/Marion 15.00 40.00
GJGB LJ/Gibsn/Goodn/Brwn 15.00 40.00
GRJF KG/BigAl/Randolph/Frye 8.00 20.00
HARS Redd/Arenas/Stojak/Rip 6.00 15.00
HDGT Gordon/Kirk/Deng/Tyrus 6.00 15.00
JABW James/Melo/Bosh/Wade 50.00 120.00
JEJB Bird/Magic/Jordan/Erving 60.00 150.00
KCJW RJeff/Vince/Kidd/Williams 8.00 20.00
KFD Kirilenko/Davis/Nene/Frye 6.00 15.00
KJHO LJ/Shaq/Howard/Kidd 25.00 60.00
LHBW Lewis/Hrringtn/Wltn/Battier 6.00 15.00
MCPD Douby/Steph/Paul/Cssll 6.00 15.00
MWOC Shaq/Wade/Cook/Zo 10.00 25.00
NGHB Noah/Horford/Brewer/Green 6.00 15.00
OGMV May/Odom/Villva/Goodn 6.00 15.00
SDRR DRob/Worm/Stock/Glide 20.00 50.00
SPRH QRich/Szczer/Kirk/MoPete 6.00 15.00
TJRR Jet/Ridnour/James/Redick 6.00 15.00
TWHW Deron/Tinsley/Harris/West 6.00 15.00
WGAB Deron/Aldrdg/Brwn/Grngr 6.00 15.00
WJIG Iggy/Wallce/Green/Jhnsn 6.00 15.00
YHSI Young/Smith/Iguodala/Hill 6.00 15.00

2007-08 Upper Deck Premier Rare Remnants Quad Gold

PRINT RUN 25 SER.#'d SETS
AGDG Durant/Green/Allen/KG 20.00 50.00
ARPA Aldridge/Roy/Hilton/Paul 10.00 25.00
DNSA Dirk/Duncan/Melo/Amare 15.00 30.00
GCMM KG/Vince/TMac/Marion 15.00 40.00
GJGB LJ/Gibsn/Goodn/Brwn 20.00 40.00
HDGT Gordo/Hinrich/Deng/Tyrus 10.00 25.00
JABW James/Melo/Bosh/Wade 50.00 120.00
KJHO LJ/Shaq/Howard/Kidd 25.00 60.00
MWOC Shaq/Wade/Cook/Zo 20.00 50.00
YHSI Young/Smith/Iguodala/Hill 10.00 25.00

2007-08 Upper Deck Premier Rare Remnants Triple

PRINT RUN 99 SER.#'d SETS
ASB Afflalo/Stuckey/Billups 4.00 10.00
BAH Artest/Hawes/Bibby 4.00 10.00
BGJ Bryant/Garnett/James 125.00 300.00
BMA Bryant/McGrady/Anthony 60.00 150.00
BNI Iverson/Bryant/Nash 60.00 150.00
BPW Paul/Billups/Williams 6.00 15.00
CBH Carter/Bosh/Howard 6.00 15.00
DGO O'Neal/Garnett/Duncan 8.00 20.00
JAB James/Anthony/Bosh 10.00 25.00
JCS Smith/Johnson/Childress 5.00 12.00
JDM James/Durant/McGrady 20.00 50.00
JEB Jordan/Bird/Erving 30.00 80.00
JHB Harrington/Jamison/Boozer 4.00 10.00
JJJ James/Jordan/Johnson 75.00 200.00
KWS Stockton/Kirilenko/Williams 8.00 20.00
MMB McGrady/Ming/Brooks 6.00 15.00
MNW Williams/Nowitzki/McGrady 6.00 15.00
MSO O'Neal/Stoudemire/Ming 10.00 25.00
NHB Noah/Horford/Brewer 6.00 15.00
NMS Nash/Stoudemire/Marion 6.00 15.00
OGR Robinson/Olajuwon/Garnett 8.00 20.00
TAB Bargnani/Thomas/Aldridge 4.00 10.00

2007-08 Upper Deck Premier Rare Remnants Triple Gold

*GOLD: .5X TO 1.25X HI COLUMN
PRINT RUN 50 SER.#'d SETS

2007-08 Upper Deck Premier Rare Remnants Triple Silver Spectrum

*SILVER SPECT: .6X TO 1.5X TRIPLE HI
PRINT RUN 25 SER.#'d SETS
JAB James/Anthony/Bosh 20.00 50.00

2007-08 Upper Deck Premier Remnants Quad

STATED PRINT RUN ONE TO 99 SER.#'d SETS
DR David Robinson/89 8.00 20.00
JE Julius Erving/76 10.00 25.00
JS John Stockton/84 8.00 20.00
KB Kobe Bryant/96 75.00 200.00
KG Kevin Garnett/95 10.00 25.00
SN Steve Nash/96 8.00 20.00
TC Tom Chambers/81 4.00 10.00
VC Vince Carter/98 8.00 20.00
WE Jerry West/60 8.00 20.00

2007-08 Upper Deck Premier Remnants Quad Autographs

PRINT RUN 25 SER.#'d SETS
AH Al Horford 15.00 40.00
AL Acie Law 8.00 20.00
AM Andre Miller 8.00 20.00
BD Boris Diaw 8.00 20.00
CA Carmelo Anthony 25.00 60.00
CB Corey Brewer 12.00 30.00
CO Mardy Collins 8.00 20.00
CP Chris Paul 60.00 150.00
DM Donyell Marshall 8.00 20.00
DN David Noel 8.00 20.00
DS DeShawn Stevenson 8.00 20.00
DU Kevin Durant 2,000.00 4,000.00
DW Damien Wilkins 8.00 20.00
FG Francisco Garcia 8.00 20.00
HA Hilton Armstrong 8.00 20.00
JE Julius Erving 50.00 100.00
JG Joey Graham 8.00 20.00
JN Joakim Noah 25.00 60.00
JS John Stockton 50.00 100.00
JW Julian Wright 8.00 20.00
KB Kobe Bryant 1,500.00 3,000.00
KD Keyon Dooling 8.00 20.00
LJ LeBron James 1,500.00 3,000.00
MB Mike Bibby 8.00 20.00
MC Mike Conley Jr. 12.00 30.00
MJ Mike James 8.00 20.00
MP Morris Peterson 8.00 20.00
PD Paul Davis 8.00 20.00
PP Paul Pierce 20.00 50.00
RS Rodney Stuckey 8.00 20.00
SN Steve Nash 30.00 80.00
VC Vince Carter 25.00 50.00
WE Jerry West 40.00 80.00

2007-08 Upper Deck Premier Remnants Quad Gold

PRINT RUN 50 SER.#'d SETS
CA Carmelo Anthony 8.00 20.00
CP Chris Paul 10.00 25.00
DR David Robinson 10.00 25.00
DU Kevin Durant 60.00 150.00
GR Jeff Green 4.00 10.00
JE Julius Erving 12.00 30.00
JN Joakim Noah 5.00 12.00
JS John Stockton 10.00 25.00
JW Julian Wright 3.00 8.00
KB Kobe Bryant 100.00 250.00
LJ LeBron James 15.00 40.00
MC Mike Conley Jr. 12.00 30.00
TC Tom Chambers 5.00 12.00
TP Tony Parker 10.00 25.00
VC Vince Carter 10.00 25.00
WE Jerry West 8.00 20.00

2007-08 Upper Deck Premier Remnants Triple

PRINT RUN 99 SER.#'d SETS
*GOLD: .5X TO 1.25X BASE HI
GOLD PRINT RUN 50 SER.#'d SETS
*SILVER SPEC: .6X TO 1.5X BASE HI
SILVER SPEC.PRINT RUN 25 SETS
AT Al Thornton 2.00 5.00
CP Chris Paul 6.00 15.00
DC Daequan Cook 2.50 6.00
DE Deron Williams 2.50 6.00
JE Julius Erving 8.00 20.00
KB Kobe Bryant 60.00 150.00
LJ LeBron James 12.00 30.00
SN Steve Nash 6.00 15.00
SW Sean Williams 2.00 5.00
TP Tayshaun Prince 3.00 8.00
VC Vince Carter 6.00 15.00

2007-08 Upper Deck Premier Remnants Triple Autographs

PRINT RUN 50 SER.#'d SETS
AA Arron Afflalo 6.00 15.00
AB Aaron Brooks 6.00 15.00
AM Andre Miller 6.00 15.00
BD Boris Diaw 6.00 15.00
CA Carmelo Anthony 25.00 60.00
CM Corey Maggette 6.00 15.00
CP Chris Paul 50.00 120.00
DC Daequan Cook 6.00 15.00
DE Deron Williams 10.00 25.00
DR David Robinson 30.00 60.00
JE Julius Erving 40.00 80.00
JW Jerry West 30.00 80.00
KB Kobe Bryant 1,500.00 3,000.00
LJ LeBron James 1,250.00 2,500.00
PA Tony Parker 15.00 40.00
PP Paul Pierce 12.00 30.00
SN Steve Nash 25.00 60.00
ST John Stockton 40.00 75.00
SW Sean Williams 6.00 15.00
TP Tayshaun Prince 6.00 15.00
VC Vince Carter 20.00 40.00
WC Wilson Chandler 10.00 25.00

2007-08 Upper Deck Premier Rookies Autographs Jerseys Copper

PRINT RUN 99 SER.#'d SETS
*BLUE: .6X TO 1.5X COPPER HI
BLUE PRINT RUN 25 SER.#'d SETS
*GREEN: .5X TO 1.25X COPPER
GREEN PRINT RUN 49 SER.#'d SETS
101 Kevin Durant 1,000.00 2,000.00
102 Al Horford 15.00 40.00
103 Mike Conley Jr. 12.00 30.00
104 Jeff Green 5.00 12.00
105 Corey Brewer 5.00 12.00
106 Joakim Noah 15.00 40.00
107 Spencer Hawes 4.00 10.00
108 Acie Law 4.00 10.00
109 Julian Wright 4.00 10.00
110 Al Thornton 4.00 10.00
111 Rodney Stuckey 6.00 15.00
112 Sean Williams 4.00 10.00
113 Javaris Crittenton 4.00 10.00
114 Jason Smith 4.00 10.00
115 Daequan Cook 5.00 12.00
116 Jared Dudley 5.00 12.00
117 Wilson Chandler 5.00 12.00
118 Morris Almond 4.00 10.00
119 Arron Afflalo 5.00 12.00
120 Alando Tucker 4.00 10.00
121 Carl Landry 4.00 10.00
122 Gabe Pruitt 4.00 10.00
125 Glen Davis 5.00 12.00
126 Jermareo Davidson 4.00 10.00
129 Adam Haluska 4.00 10.00
133 Aaron Gray 4.00 10.00
134 Taurean Green 4.00 10.00
135 Demetris Nichols 4.00 10.00
136 D.J. Strawberry 4.00 10.00
137 Aaron Brooks 5.00 12.00
138 Herbert Hill 4.00 10.00
139 Chris Richard 4.00 10.00

2007-08 Upper Deck Premier Stitchings Patches

PRINT RUN 50 SER.#'d SETS
STITCHINGS PATCH FEATURE TEAM LOGO
*ALT LOGO: .4X TO 1X BASE HI
ALT LOGO PRINT RUN 50 SETS
*GOLD: .4X TO 1X BASE HI
GOLD PRINT RUN 25 SETS
*GOLD ALT: .4X TO 1X BASE HI
GOLD ALT PRINT RUN 25 SETS
PSAB Aaron Brooks 8.00 20.00
PSAH Al Horford 8.00 20.00
PSAI Allen Iverson 10.00 25.00
PSAN Carmelo Anthony 10.00 25.00
PSAS Amare Stoudemire 10.00 25.00
PSAT Al Thornton 8.00 20.00
PSBA Andrea Bargnani 8.00 20.00
PSBB Bill Bradley 8.00 20.00
PSBG Ben Gordon 8.00 20.00
PSBM Bob McAdoo 10.00 25.00
PSBO Chris Bosh 8.00 20.00
PSBR Bill Russell 12.50 30.00
PSBW Bill Walton 8.00 20.00
PSCA Carlos Arroyo 10.00 25.00
PSCB Carlos Boozer 8.00 20.00
PSCD Clyde Drexler 8.00 20.00
PSCH Wilt Chamberlain 10.00 25.00
PSCO Corey Brewer 8.00 20.00
PSCP Chris Paul 10.00 25.00
PSDC Daequan Cook 8.00 20.00
PSDE Dennis Rodman 20.00 40.00
PSDH Dwight Howard 10.00 25.00
PSDN Dirk Nowitzki 10.00 25.00
PSDR David Robinson 12.50 30.00
PSDW Deron Williams 8.00 20.00
PSEJ Magic Johnson 12.50 30.00
PSEM Earl Monroe 8.00 20.00
PSEO Emeka Okafor 8.00 20.00
PSGG George Gervin 10.00 25.00
PSGO Greg Oden 6.00 15.00
PSGR Gerald Green 8.00 20.00
PSHO Hakeem Olajuwon 10.00 25.00
PSIT Isiah Thomas 10.00 25.00
PSJD Jared Dudley 8.00 20.00
PSJG Jeff Green 8.00 20.00
PSJH John Havlicek 10.00 25.00
PSJK Jason Kidd 10.00 25.00
PSJO Jermaine O'Neal 8.00 20.00
PSJS Jason Smith 8.00 20.00
PSJW Jerry West 12.50 30.00
PSKB Kobe Bryant 75.00 200.00
PSKD Kevin Durant 15.00 40.00
PSKG Kevin Garnett 12.50 30.00
PSKH Kirk Hinrich 8.00 20.00
PSKM Karl Malone 8.00 20.00
PSLA LaMarcus Aldridge 8.00 20.00
PSLB Larry Bird 15.00 40.00
PSLD Luol Deng 8.00 20.00
PSLJ LeBron James 15.00 40.00
PSMB Marco Belinelli 8.00 20.00
PSMC Kevin McHale 8.00 20.00
PSMG Manu Ginobili 10.00 25.00
PSMJ Michael Jordan 75.00 200.00
PSMM Moses Malone 8.00 20.00
PSNO Joakim Noah 8.00 20.00
PSNY Nick Young 8.00 20.00
PSOR Oscar Robertson 10.00 25.00
PSPA Tony Parker 12.00 30.00
PSPP Paul Pierce 8.00 20.00
PSPS Peja Stojakovic 8.00 20.00
PSPW Paul Westphal 8.00 20.00
PSRE Willis Reed 20.00 50.00
PSRF Randy Foye 8.00 20.00
PSRG Rudy Gay 8.00 20.00
PSRO Brandon Roy 8.00 20.00
PSRP Robert Parish 10.00 25.00
PSRR Rajon Rondo 10.00 25.00
PSRS Rodney Stuckey 8.00 20.00
PSSH Spencer Hawes 8.00 20.00
PSSN Steve Nash 10.00 25.00
PSSO Shaquille O'Neal 12.50 30.00
PSST John Stockton 10.00 25.00
PSTD Tim Duncan 12.50 30.00
PSTM Tracy McGrady 8.00 20.00
PSTT Tyrus Thomas 8.00 20.00
PSTU Alando Tucker 8.00 20.00
PSTY Thaddeus Young 8.00 20.00
PSVC Vince Carter 10.00 25.00
PSWA Dwyane Wade 12.50 30.00
PSWC Wilson Chandler 8.00 20.00
PSWF Walt Frazier 10.00 25.00
PSWI Dominique Wilkins 10.00 25.00
PSWR Brandan Wright 8.00 20.00
PSYM Yao Ming 10.00 25.00

2007-08 Upper Deck Premier Trios Autographs

PRINT RUN 15 SER.#'d SETS
CAW Wright/Chandler/Armstrong 15.00 40.00
DHO O'Bryant/Davis/Harrington 15.00 40.00
FIR Roy/Iguodala/Ford 20.00 50.00
GLC Conley/Gay/Lowry 25.00 60.00
HGB Brown/Gibson/Hughes 15.00 40.00
HGN Hinrich/Noah/Gordon 20.00 50.00
JFB Foye/Jefferson/Brewer 15.00 40.00
JJJ Jordan/James/Johnson 3,000.00 6,000.00
JSM McGuire/Jamison/Stevenson 15.00 40.00
KCW Williams/Kidd/Carter 100.00 250.00
MGH Hawes/Miller/Garcia 15.00 40.00
MLB Landry/Brooks/McGrady 40.00 100.00
OHJ Jefferson/Okafor/Howard 25.00 60.00
PAG Garnett/Pierce/Allen 300.00 600.00
RFD Riley/Frazier/Dampier 75.00 200.00
SAS Stuckey/Samb/Afflalo 15.00 40.00
SDG Durant/Green/Shelton 100.00 250.00
TAG Thomas/Aldridge/Gay 25.00 60.00
WHL Horford/Law/Williams 25.00 60.00
WMB Brewer/Williams/Millsap 15.00 40.00

2008-09 Upper Deck Premier

1-94 PRINT RUN 99 SER.#'d SETS
95-100 PRINT RUN 99 SER.#'d SETS
95-130 PRINT RUN 199 SER.#'d SETS
1 Kevin Garnett 5.00 12.00
2 Paul Pierce 3.00 8.00
3 Ray Allen 3.00 8.00
4 Larry Bird 6.00 15.00
5 Stephen Jackson 1.50 4.00
6 Monta Ellis 1.50 4.00
7 Mitch Richmond 2.00 5.00
8 Stephon Marbury 2.00 5.00
9 Jamal Crawford 2.00 5.00
10 Patrick Ewing 3.00 8.00
11 Chauncey Billups 2.50 6.00
12 Rasheed Wallace 2.50 6.00
13 Isiah Thomas 3.00 8.00
14 Kobe Bryant 15.00 40.00
15 Pau Gasol 2.50 6.00
16 Magic Johnson 6.00 15.00
17 Elgin Baylor 3.00 8.00
18 Kevin Martin 1.50 4.00
19 Beno Udrih 1.25 3.00
20 Oscar Robertson 2.00 5.00
21 Joe Johnson 2.00 5.00
22 Al Horford 2.00 5.00
23 Dominique Wilkins 3.00 8.00
24 Andre Iguodala 1.50 4.00
25 Elton Brand 1.50 4.00
26 Julius Erving 5.00 12.00
27 Wilt Chamberlain 6.00 15.00
28 Gilbert Arenas 2.00 5.00
29 Antawn Jamison 1.50 4.00
30 Elvin Hayes 2.00 5.00
31 Ben Gordon 1.50 4.00
32 Luol Deng 1.50 4.00
33 Michael Jordan 40.00 100.00
34 Scottie Pippen 3.00 8.00
35 Allen Iverson 4.00 10.00
36 Carmelo Anthony 2.50 6.00
37 Alex English 2.50 6.00
38 Tracy McGrady 3.00 8.00
39 Yao Ming 5.00 12.00
40 Hakeem Olajuwon 4.00 10.00
41 T.J. Ford 1.25 3.00
42 Danny Granger 1.50 4.00
43 Mike Dunleavy 1.25 3.00
44 Yi Jianlian 2.50 6.00
45 Vince Carter 4.00 10.00
46 Buck Williams 1.25 3.00
47 Kevin Durant 8.00 20.00
48 Jeff Green 1.50 4.00
49 Detlef Schrempf 2.00 5.00
50 Richard Jefferson 1.50 4.00
51 Andrew Bogut 1.50 4.00
52 Kareem Abdul-Jabbar 3.00 8.00
53 Steve Nash 4.00 10.00
54 Shaquille O'Neal 6.00 15.00
55 Kevin Johnson 2.00 5.00
56 LeBron James 15.00 40.00
57 Daniel Gibson 1.25 3.00
58 Mark Price 3.00 8.00
59 Baron Davis 2.00 5.00
60 Chris Kaman 1.25 3.00
61 World B. Free 1.50 4.00
62 Brandon Roy 1.50 4.00
63 LaMarcus Aldridge 2.00 5.00
64 Clyde Drexler 2.50 6.00
65 Tim Duncan 5.00 12.00
66 Tony Parker 2.50 6.00
67 David Robinson 4.00 10.00
68 Deron Williams 1.50 4.00
69 Carlos Boozer 1.50 4.00
70 Karl Malone 2.50 6.00
71 John Stockton 4.00 10.00
72 Dirk Nowitzki 5.00 12.00
73 Jason Kidd 3.00 8.00
74 Rolando Blackman 1.50 4.00
75 Dwyane Wade 4.00 10.00
76 Alonzo Mourning 2.50 6.00
77 Tim Hardaway 2.50 6.00
78 Chris Paul 4.00 10.00
79 David West 1.50 4.00
80 Larry Johnson 2.00 5.00
81 Al Jefferson 1.25 3.00
82 Corey Brewer 1.50 4.00
83 Dwight Howard 2.50 6.00
84 Hedo Turkoglu 1.50 4.00
85 Nick Anderson 1.50 4.00
86 Rudy Gay 2.00 5.00
87 Hakim Warrick 1.25 3.00
88 Mike Conley Jr. 1.50 4.00
89 Chris Bosh 2.50 6.00
90 Jermaine O'Neal 2.00 5.00
91 Jose Calderon 1.25 3.00
92 Emeka Okafor 1.25 3.00
93 Gerald Wallace 1.50 4.00
94 Raymond Felton 1.25 3.00
95 Courtney Lee RC 2.00 5.00
96 Chris Douglas-Roberts RC 1.50 4.00
97 Patrick Ewing Jr. RC 1.50 4.00
98 Alexis Ajinca RC 1.50 4.00
99 Bill Walker RC 1.50 4.00
100 Sonny Weems RC 1.50 4.00
101 Derrick Rose JSY AU RC 40.00 100.00
102 Michael Beasley JSY AU RC 5.00 12.00
103 O.J. Mayo JSY AU RC 4.00 10.00
104 R.Westbrook JSY AU RC 150.00 400.00
105 Kevin Love JSY AU RC 30.00 80.00
106 Patrick Ewing Jr. JSY AU RC 3.00 8.00
107 Eric Gordon JSY AU RC 8.00 20.00
108 Joe Alexander JSY AU RC 3.00 8.00
109 D. J. Augustin JSY AU RC 5.00 12.00
110 Brook Lopez JSY AU RC 6.00 15.00
111 Jerryd Bayless JSY AU RC 4.00 10.00
112 Jason Thompson JSY AU RC 3.00 8.00
113 Brandon Rush JSY AU RC 3.00 8.00
114 A.Randolph JSY AU RC 3.00 8.00
115 Robin Lopez JSY AU RC 4.00 10.00
116 Marreese Speights JSY AU RC 4.00 10.00
117 C.Douglas-Roberts JSY AU RC 3.00 8.00
118 Javale McGee JSY AU RC 5.00 12.00
119 J.J. Hickson JSY AU RC 3.00 8.00
120 Ryan Anderson JSY AU RC 4.00 10.00
121 Kosta Koufos JSY AU RC 3.00 8.00
122 George Hill JSY AU RC 5.00 12.00
123 Darrell Arthur JSY AU RC 4.00 10.00
124 Donte Greene JSY AU RC 3.00 8.00
125 Sonny Weems JSY AU RC 3.00 8.00
126 J.R. Giddens JSY AU RC 3.00 8.00
127 Walter Sharpe JSY AU RC 3.00 8.00
128 Joey Dorsey JSY AU RC 3.00 8.00
129 Mario Chalmers JSY AU RC 5.00 12.00
130 DeAndre Jordan JSY AU RC 12.00 30.00

2008-09 Upper Deck Premier Attractions Autographs Jerseys

STATED PRINT RUN 50 SER.#'d SETS
ATAD Adrian Dantley 5.00 12.00
ATAH Al Horford 6.00 15.00
ATAJ Al Jefferson 4.00 10.00
ATAM Louis Amundson 4.00 10.00
ATAZ Kelenna Azubuike 4.00 10.00
ATBG Ben Gordon 5.00 12.00
ATBR Brandon Roy 5.00 12.00
ATBY Andrew Bynum 4.00 10.00
ATCB Carlos Boozer 5.00 12.00
ATCL Carl Landry 4.00 10.00
ATJA Antawn Jamison 5.00 12.00
ATJB Josh Boone 4.00 10.00
ATJE Julius Erving 50.00 120.00
ATJF Jordan Farmar 4.00 10.00
ATJO Michael Jordan 2,000.00 4,000.00
ATKB Kobe Bryant 1,500.00 3,000.00
ATKD Kevin Durant 125.00 300.00
ATLA LaMarcus Aldridge 10.00 25.00
ATLB Larry Bird 75.00 200.00
ATLJ LeBron James 2,500.00 5,000.00
ATMP Mark Price 15.00 40.00
ATMR Micheal Ray Richardson 5.00 12.00
ATPP Paul Pierce 60.00 150.00
ATRB Renaldo Balkman 4.00 10.00
ATRG Rudy Gay 6.00 15.00
ATRJ Richard Jefferson 5.00 12.00
ATRP Robert Parish 10.00 25.00
ATSA Stacey Augmon 4.00 10.00
ATSV Sasha Vujacic 4.00 10.00
ATSW Sean Williams 4.00 10.00
ATTC Tom Chambers 5.00 12.00
ATWE Spud Webb 12.00 30.00

2008-09 Upper Deck Premier Classmates Autographs

STATED PRINT RUN 50 SER.#'d SETS
CLASS01 T.Parker/Jefferson 15.00 30.00
CLASS03 D.West/L.Walton 8.00 20.00
CLASS04 D.Howard/Okafor 10.00 25.00
CLASS07 K.Durant/Horford 50.00 120.00
CLASS70 Lanier/Tomjanovich 10.00 25.00
CLASS86 J.Salley/M.Price 25.00 50.00
CLASS87 K.Smith/M.Bogues 15.00 30.00
CLASS88 T.Horford/S.Kerr 8.00 20.00

2008-09 Upper Deck Premier Consumate Masters Autographs

STATED PRINT RUN 15 SER.#'d SETS
CMBP Bob Pettit 20.00 40.00
CMBR Bill Russell 1,000.00 2,000.00
CMCA Adrian Dantley 12.00 30.00
CMCP Chris Paul 60.00 150.00
CMDH Dwight Howard 30.00 60.00
CMDR Dennis Rodman 40.00 100.00
CMGR Glen Rice 12.00 30.00
CMHO Hakeem Olajuwon 30.00 60.00
CMJK Jason Kidd 30.00 60.00
CMJO Michael Jordan 450.00 650.00
CMJS John Stockton 50.00 125.00
CMKB Kobe Bryant 1,000.00 2,000.00
CMLJ LeBron James 2,500.00 5,000.00
CMMB Muggsy Bogues 12.00 30.00
CMMJ Magic Johnson 50.00 100.00
CMMR Micheal Ray Richardson 12.00 30.00
CMRP Robert Parish 15.00 40.00

2008-09 Upper Deck Premier Foursome Autographs

STATED PRINT RUN 10 SER.#'d SETS
P4BOJA Kobe/Odm/Magic/KAJ 600.00 1,200.00
P4BWWH Bib/Webb/Wlkns/Hrfrd 100.00 200.00
P4PGBP Pierce/KG/Bird/RP 200.00 400.00
P4WBPJ West/Bges/Paul/LJ 150.00 400.00

2008-09 Upper Deck Premier Franchise Faces Autographs

STATED PRINT RUN 25 TO 50 SER.#'d SETS
FFAD Adrian Dantley/50 8.00 20.00
FFAH Al Horford/25 6.00 15.00
FFAM Alonzo Mourning/25 30.00 60.00
FFCW Chet Walker/25 6.00 15.00
FFGI Artis Gilmore/50 8.00 20.00
FFJO Michael Jordan/25 300.00 450.00
FFKB Kobe Bryant/25 500.00 1,000.00
FFKD Kevin Durant/25 125.00 250.00
FFKG Kevin Garnett/25 75.00 150.00
FFLJ LeBron James/25 2,000.00 4,000.00
FFSW Spud Webb/25 6.00 15.00
FFTP Tony Parker/25 8.00 20.00
FFWF Walt Frazier/25 10.00 25.00

2008-09 Upper Deck Premier Head to Head Autographs Jerseys

STATED PRINT RUN 25 SER.#'d SETS
H2HBG J.Green/C.Boozer 12.00 30.00
H2HBJ L.James/K.Bryant 3,000.00 6,000.00
H2HBK A.Bynum/C.Kaman 12.00 30.00
H2HGB R.Gay/S.Battier 12.00 30.00
H2HHH D.Howard/A.Horford 15.00 40.00
H2HJA A.Jefferson/L.Aldridge 15.00 40.00
H2HKF R.Foye/J.Kidd 15.00 40.00
H2HMC T.Chandler/B.Miller 12.00 30.00
H2HWB L.Walton/B.Bowen 12.00 30.00
H2HWR B.Roy/D.Williams 12.00 30.00

2008-09 Upper Deck Premier Impressions Autographs

STATED PRINT RUN 50 SER.#'d SETS
PIAA Alexis Ajinca 3.00 8.00
PIAR Anthony Randolph 3.00 8.00
PIBL Brook Lopez 6.00 15.00
PIBR Brandon Rush 3.00 8.00
PIDG Danilo Gallinari 12.50 30.00
PIDW D.J. White 3.00 8.00
PIGH George Hill 5.00 12.00
PIJA Joe Alexander 3.00 8.00
PIJB Jerryd Bayless 4.00 10.00
PIJH J.J. Hickson 3.00 8.00
PIJM Javale McGee 5.00 12.00
PIJT Jason Thompson 3.00 8.00
PIMC Mario Chalmers 5.00 12.00
PIMS Marreese Speights 4.00 10.00
PIRA Ryan Anderson 4.00 10.00
PIRH Roy Hibbert 12.50 30.00
PIRL Robin Lopez 4.00 10.00
PIRW Russell Westbrook 200.00 500.00

2008-09 Upper Deck Premier Pairings Autographs

STATED PRINT RUN 25 SER.#'d SETS
P2AR L.Aldridge/B.Roy 15.00 40.00
P2DJ L.James/K.Durant 2,500.00 5,000.00
P2FR W.Frazier/M.Richardson 15.00 40.00
P2GB K.Bryant/K.Garnett 1,000.00 2,000.00
P2GC R.Gay/M.Conley 15.00 40.00

P2HH A.Horford/T.Horford 10.00 25.00
P2JJ M.Jordan/L.James 10,000.00 15,000.00
P2JW A.Jamison/D.West 10.00 25.00
P2ML M.Bogues/L.Johnson 50.00 120.00
P2PA R.Allen/P.Pierce 150.00 400.00
P2PS J.Salley/T.Prince 12.00 30.00
P2SB R.Sessions/A.Brooks 10.00 25.00
P2SD K.Smith/C.Drexler 20.00 50.00
P2SV J.Smith/S.Vujacic 10.00 25.00

2008-09 Upper Deck Premier Penmanship Autographs

STATED PRINT RUN 50 SER.#'d SETS
PENAE Alex English 5.00 12.00
PENAH Al Harrington 5.00 12.00
PENBD Bob Dandridge 8.00 20.00
PENBL Bob Lanier 6.00 15.00
PENBM Brad Miller 5.00 12.00
PENCH Cliff Hagan 8.00 20.00
PENCK Chris Kaman 5.00 12.00
PENDA Brad Daugherty 5.00 12.00
PENDF Derek Fisher 6.00 15.00
PENDO Don Ohl 8.00 20.00
PENDR Dennis Rodman 75.00 200.00
PENDV Dick Van Arsdale 6.00 15.00
PENEM Ed Macauley 6.00 15.00
PENGI Artis Gilmore 10.00 25.00
PENGR Glen Rice 20.00 40.00
PENHO Tito Horford 5.00 12.00
PENJP Jim Paxson 6.00 15.00
PENKB Kobe Bryant 1,500.00 3,000.00
PENLH Lou Hudson 5.00 12.00
PENPA John Paxson 10.00 25.00
PENPF Phil Ford 6.00 15.00
PENRG Richie Guerin 15.00 40.00
PENRH Rod Hundley 25.00 50.00
PENRS Ralph Sampson 6.00 15.00
PENSJ Sam Jones 15.00 30.00
PENSM Slater Martin 30.00 80.00
PENTC Terry Cummings 6.00 15.00
PENTD Terry Dischinger 8.00 20.00
PENTR Tree Rollins 6.00 15.00

2008-09 Upper Deck Premier Preeminence Autographs

STATED PRINT RUN 25 SER.#'d SETS
PEAB Andrew Bynum 6.00 15.00
PEAD Adrian Dantley 6.00 15.00
PEAG Artis Gilmore 8.00 20.00
PEAH Al Horford 6.00 15.00
PEAJ Al Jefferson 6.00 15.00
PEAL Joe Alexander 6.00 15.00
PEAT Al Thornton 6.00 15.00
PEBA B.J. Armstrong 8.00 20.00
PEBR Brandon Roy 8.00 20.00
PECW Chet Walker 6.00 15.00
PEDC Daequan Cook 6.00 15.00
PEDW David West 6.00 15.00
PEEG Eric Gordon 15.00 40.00
PEJA Antawn Jamison 6.00 15.00
PEJO Michael Jordan 6,000.00 12,000.00
PEKB Kobe Bryant 4,000.00 8,000.00
PEKD Kevin Durant 1,000.00 2,000.00
PEKG Kevin Garnett 800.00 1,500.00
PELE LeBron James 5,000.00 10,000.00
PELJ Larry Johnson 25.00 60.00
PELW Luke Walton 10.00 25.00
PEMP Mark Price 20.00 50.00
PEMR Micheal Ray Richardson 6.00 15.00
PEPM Paul Millsap 6.00 15.00
PERG Rudy Gay 6.00 15.00
PERJ Richard Jefferson 6.00 15.00
PERS Ramon Sessions 6.00 15.00
PERU Brandon Rush 6.00 15.00
PESK Steve Kerr 15.00 40.00
PESV Sasha Vujacic 6.00 15.00
PESW Spud Webb 8.00 20.00
PETK Toni Kukoc 20.00 40.00
PETP Tayshaun Prince 8.00 20.00

2008-09 Upper Deck Premier Rare Patch Dual

STATED PRINT RUN 15 TO 50 SER.#'d SETS
RP2AW L.James/Anthony/50 60.00 150.00
RP2BD K.Bryant/Durant/50 300.00 600.00
RP2BJ L.James/Bryant/50 500.00 1,000.00
RP2CM Martin/V.Carter/40 10.00 25.00
RP2DO O'Neal/Duncan/50 10.00 25.00
RP2EW B.Wright/Ellis/50 8.00 20.00
RP2GG Garnett/P.Gasol/50 15.00 40.00
RP2GN Nowitzki/Garnett/50 15.00 40.00
RP2GT Gordon/Thomas/50 8.00 20.00
RP2HW G.Hill/L.Walton/50 25.00 60.00
RP2IA Iverson/Anthony/50 12.00 30.00
RP2IB Iguodala/Brewer/50 8.00 20.00
RP2JA Aldridge/Jefferson/50 8.00 20.00
RP2JD K.Durant/L.James/50 100.00 250.00
RP2LM R.Lewis/S.Marion/15 12.00 30.00
RP2MB A.Bogut/D.Mason/50 8.00 20.00
RP2MP P.Gasol/Ginobili/50 10.00 25.00
RP2MS Zo/Stoudemire/50 15.00 30.00
RP2NG J.Green/J.Noah/50 8.00 20.00
RP2NP S.Nash/C.Paul/30 20.00 40.00
RP2PA P.Pierce/R.Allen/50 15.00 30.00
RP2RB A.Bogut/M.Redd/50 8.00 20.00
RP2RC Q.Rich/E.Curry/50 8.00 20.00
RP2SH Stoudemire/Howard/50 15.00 30.00
RP2TH J.Terry/J.Howard/50 8.00 20.00
RP2WJ Garnett/L.James/50 60.00 150.00
RP2WR B.Roy/D.Williams/50 8.00 20.00
RP2YW B.Wright/T.Young/50 8.00 20.00

2008-09 Upper Deck Premier Rare Patch Rookies Dual

STATED PRINT RUN 25 SER.#'d SETS
R2RAG E.Gordon/D.Augustin 10.00 25.00
R2RAK K.Koufos/D.Arthur 6.00 15.00
R2RAL R.Anderson/C.Lee 15.00 40.00
R2RBL M.Beasley/K.Love 10.00 25.00
R2RBR D.Rose/M.Beasley 25.00 50.00
R2RDS W.Sharpe/J.Dorsey 6.00 15.00
R2RDW K.Weaver/C.D.Roberts 8.00 20.00
R2RGB E.Gordon/J.Bayless 8.00 20.00
R2RGH G.Hill/D.Greene 8.00 20.00
R2RJE D.Jordan/P.Ewing Jr. 6.00 15.00
R2RLL B.Lopez/R.Lopez 10.00 25.00
R2RMR D.Rose/O.Mayo 20.00 50.00
R2RRT J.Thompson/Randolph 10.00 25.00

2008-09 Upper Deck Premier Rare Patch Rookies Triple

STATED PRINT RUN 15 SER.#'d SETS
R3RABJ Beasley/Augustin/Jordan 20.00 40.00
R3RABM Beasley/Augustin/McGee 10.00 25.00
R3RARB Augustin/Bayless/Rush 8.00 20.00
R3RBLK Love/Bayless/Koufos 8.00 20.00
R3RBWW Bayless/Weaver/Weems 8.00 20.00
R3RGEA Alexander/Greene/Ewing Jr. 8.00 20.00
R3RGGT Thompson/Gordon/Greene 8.00 20.00
R3RGLA Love/Gordon/Alexander 15.00 40.00
R3RHAS Alexander/Hickson/Sharpe 8.00 20.00
R3RLDA Lopez/Anderson/
Douglas-Roberts 8.00 20.00
R3RMBL Mayo/Love/Bayless 10.00 25.00
R3RMBR Rose/Beasley/Mayo 30.00 60.00
R3RMEH Mayo/Hill/Ewing Jr. 10.00 25.00
R3RRAC Rush/Arthur/Chalmers 10.00 25.00
R3RRDD Rose/Dorsey/D-Roberts 25.00 50.00
R3RRDS Rose/Sharpe/Dorsey 20.00 40.00
R3RRLT Lopez/Thmpsn/Rndlph 15.00 40.00
R3RRWS Speight/Rndlph/Weems 15.00 30.00
R3RWAL Lopez/Anderson/Weaver 10.00 25.00

2008-09 Upper Deck Premier Rare Patch Triple

STATED PRINT RUN 10 TO 25 SER.#'d SETS
RPTBGJ James/Bryant/Garnett 200.00 500.00
RPTBOG Bryant/Gasol/Odom 125.00 300.00
RPTDGR Duncan/Gnbli/D.Rob 60.00 150.00
RPTDLT Thomas/Lmbr/Dmrs 30.00 80.00
RPTHDG Hinrich/Deng/Gordon 15.00 40.00
RPTHMS Stcktn/Malone/Hrnck 40.00 100.00
RPTIMA Ivrsn/Anthony/Martin 20.00 50.00
RPTJAW Bosh/Anthony/LJ/10 50.00 120.00
RPTJBJ James/Jordan/Bryant 500.00 1,000.00
RPTJPR MJ/Pippen/Rodman 150.00 400.00
RPTKNH Nwtzki/Howard/Kidd 20.00 50.00
RPTMMS Ming/McGrady/Scola 30.00 80.00
RPTNDH Durant/Horford/Noah 20.00 50.00
RPTNSO Stdmre/O'Neal/Nash 50.00 120.00
RPTPAG Allen/Garnett/Pierce 60.00 150.00
RPTPWR Williams/Paul/Roy 20.00 50.00
RPTWJG Ilgskas/James/Gibson 40.00 100.00
RPTWMW Wilkins/Webb/Malone 20.00 50.00

2008-09 Upper Deck Premier Rare Remnants Quad Patch

STATED PRINT RUN 5 TO 25 SER.#'d SETS
RR4AJ L.James/Anthony/25 25.00 50.00
RR4BD K.Bryant/Durant/25 400.00 800.00
RR4BF C.Boozer/Frye/25 8.00 20.00
RR4BJ L.James/Bryant/25 600.00 1,200.00
RR4BK Kirilenko/Battier/25 6.00 15.00
RR4CM K.Martin/V.Carter/25 15.00 30.00
RR4DD Davidson/Dudley/25 6.00 15.00
RR4GG Garnett/P.Gasol/25 15.00 40.00
RR4GN Nowitzki/Garnett/25 30.00 60.00
RR4GT Gordon/Thomas/25 8.00 20.00
RR4HD Hinrich/L.Deng/25 8.00 20.00
RR4HW G.Hill/L.Walton/15 60.00 120.00
RR4IA Iverson/Anthony/25 15.00 30.00
RR4IB Iguodala/Brewer/25 6.00 15.00
RR4JD Durant/L.James/25 25.00 60.00
RR4JS J.Johnson/J.Smith/25 8.00 20.00
RR4KP T.Parker/J.Kidd/25 10.00 25.00
RR4LM R.Lewis/Marion/25 10.00 25.00
RR4MB Bogut/D.Mason/25 6.00 15.00
RR4MH Mutombo/Howard/25 12.00 30.00
RR4MS Zo/Stoudemire/25 20.00 40.00
RR4MW Maggette/Wright/25 6.00 15.00
RR4NP S.Nash/C.Paul/25 20.00 40.00
RR4NS J.Smith/J.Noah/25 10.00 25.00
RR4PA Pierce/R.Allen/25 15.00 30.00
RR4PM P.Gasol/Ginobili/25 15.00 30.00
RR4RC Q.Rich/E.Curry/25 6.00 15.00
RR4TH J.Terry/J.Howard/25 6.00 15.00
RR4WM Martin/R.Wallace/25 6.00 15.00
RR4YW B.Wright/T.Young/25 6.00 15.00

2008-09 Upper Deck Premier Rare Remnants Triple Patch

STATED PRINT RUN 35 TO 50 SER.#'d SETS
RR3AI Allen Iverson 12.00 30.00
RR3AJ Al Jefferson 4.00 10.00
RR3AK Andrei Kirilenko 5.00 12.00
RR3BG Ben Gordon 5.00 12.00
RR3BR Brandon Roy 5.00 12.00
RR3BU Caron Butler 5.00 12.00
RR3BW Brandan Wright 4.00 10.00
RR3CB Carlos Boozer/35 5.00 12.00
RR3CM Corey Maggette 5.00 12.00
RR3DG Danny Granger 5.00 12.00
RR3DM Dikembe Mutombo 6.00 15.00
RR3DN Dirk Nowitzki 15.00 40.00
RR3EB Elton Brand 5.00 12.00
RR3GH Grant Hill 10.00 25.00
RR3IG Andre Iguodala 5.00 12.00
RR3JA Antawn Jamison 5.00 12.00
RR3JK Jason Kidd 10.00 25.00
RR3JN Joakim Noah 4.00 10.00
RR3JT Jason Terry 5.00 12.00
RR3KA Kelenna Azubuike 4.00 10.00
RR3KB Kobe Bryant 75.00 200.00
RR3KD Kevin Durant 20.00 50.00
RR3KG Kevin Garnett 15.00 40.00
RR3KH Kirk Hinrich 5.00 12.00
RR3KK Kyle Korver 5.00 12.00
RR3KM Kenyon Martin 5.00 12.00
RR3LD Luol Deng 5.00 12.00
RR3LJ LeBron James 40.00 100.00
RR3LW Luke Walton 5.00 12.00
RR3MA Kevin Martin 5.00 12.00
RR3MC Mike Conley Jr. 5.00 12.00
RR3MG Manu Ginobili 12.00 30.00
RR3MR Michael Redd 5.00 12.00
RR3PG Pau Gasol 8.00 20.00
RR3PS Peja Stojakovic 5.00 12.00
RR3RA Ray Allen 8.00 20.00
RR3RL Rashard Lewis 5.00 12.00
RR3RW Rasheed Wallace 8.00 20.00
RR3SM Shawn Marion 6.00 15.00
RR3SN Steve Nash 12.00 30.00
RR3SO Shaquille O'Neal 20.00 50.00
RR3TD Tim Duncan 15.00 40.00
RR3TM Tracy McGrady 10.00 25.00
RR3VC Vince Carter 12.00 30.00

2008-09 Upper Deck Premier Rare Remnants Triple Patch NBA Logo

*NBA LOGO: .5X TO 1.25X BASE HI
STATED PRINT RUN 25 SER.#'d SETS
RR3AB Andrea Bargnani 6.00 15.00
RR3AH Al Harrington 6.00 15.00
RR3AS Amare Stoudemire 8.00 20.00
RR3CA Carmelo Anthony 10.00 25.00
RR3DH Dwight Howard 10.00 25.00
RR3GH Grant Hill 40.00 80.00
RR3GI Daniel Gibson 5.00 12.00
RR3JH Josh Howard 6.00 15.00
RR3JJ Joe Johnson 8.00 20.00
RR3JR Jason Richardson 8.00 20.00
RR3PP Paul Pierce 10.00 25.00
RR3SB Shane Battier 6.00 15.00
RR3TT Tyrus Thomas 5.00 12.00

2008-09 Upper Deck Premier Remnants Quad

STATED PRINT RUN 50 SER.#'d SETS
*CONFERENCE: .4X TO 1X BASE HI
CONFERENCE PRINT RUN 25 SETS
PR4AR A.Bogut/R.Jefferson 4.00 10.00
PR4BD K.Bryant/K.Durant 150.00 400.00
PR4BF C.Boozer/C.Frye 4.00 10.00
PR4BJ L.James/K.Bryant 200.00 500.00
PR4BP C.Billups/C.Paul 6.00 15.00
PR4BW J.Boone/S.Williams 4.00 10.00
PR4DB B.Davis/C.Billups 4.00 10.00
PR4DD J.Davidson/J.Dudley 4.00 10.00
PR4EC V.Carter/J.Erving 10.00 25.00
PR4FB A.Bynum/J.Farmar 10.00 25.00
PR4FR W.Frazier/M.Richardson 5.00 12.00
PR4GC R.Gay/M.Conley 4.00 10.00
PR4GT B.Gordon/T.Thomas 4.00 10.00
PR4HD D.Howard/A.Horford 5.00 12.00
PR4HL A.Law/A.Horford 4.00 10.00
PR4IB A.Iguodala/C.Brewer 4.00 10.00
PR4JA L.Aldridge/A.Jefferson 4.00 10.00
PR4JB M.Jordan/K.Bryant 400.00 800.00
PR4JD K.Durant/L.James 25.00 60.00
PR4JH A.Jamison/A.Harrington 4.00 10.00
PR4JR O.Robertson/M.Jordan 25.00 60.00
PR4KW B.Walton/C.Kaman 4.00 10.00
PR4LB C.Landry/A.Brooks 6.00 15.00
PR4LM R.Lewis/S.Marion 4.00 10.00
PR4MA T.McGrady/C.Anthony 6.00 15.00
PR4MG C.Mullin/D.Gibson 4.00 10.00
PR4ML M.Johnson/L.Bird 25.00 60.00
PR4MO Y.Ming/E.Okafor 5.00 12.00
PR4MS A.Mourning/Amare 8.00 20.00
PR4MT C.Maggette/A.Thornton 4.00 10.00
PR4ND G.Davis/J.Noah 6.00 15.00
PR4NK S.Nash/J.Kidd 10.00 25.00
PR4NP S.Nash/C.Paul 10.00 25.00
PR4PA P.Pierce/R.Allen 10.00 25.00
PR4RC Q.Richardson/E.Curry 4.00 10.00
PR4RJ O.Robertson/L.James 25.00 60.00
PR4RM D.Rodman/M.Malone 6.00 15.00
PR4WG D.Griffith/D.Williams 4.00 10.00
PR4WR B.Roy/D.Williams 6.00 15.00

2008-09 Upper Deck Premier Remnants Triple

STATED PRINT RUN 99 SER.#'d SETS
PR3AB Andrew Bynum 2.00 5.00
PR3AM Alonzo Mourning 6.00 15.00
PR3AS Amare Stoudemire 3.00 8.00
PR3AT Al Thornton 2.00 5.00
PR3BD Baron Davis 3.00 8.00
PR3BR Brandon Roy 2.50 6.00
PR3CA Carmelo Anthony 4.00 10.00
PR3CB Chauncey Billups 4.00 10.00
PR3CM Corey Maggette 2.50 6.00
PR3CP Chris Paul 6.00 15.00
PR3DG Darrell Griffith 2.00 5.00
PR3DH Dwight Howard 4.00 10.00
PR3DR Dennis Rodman 8.00 20.00
PR3DW Deron Williams 2.50 6.00
PR3HO Hakeem Olajuwon 6.00 15.00
PR3JE Julius Erving 8.00 20.00
PR3JK Jason Kidd 5.00 12.00
PR3JO Michael Jordan 75.00 200.00
PR3KB Kobe Bryant 50.00 120.00
PR3KD Kevin Durant 12.00 30.00
PR3KG Kevin Garnett 8.00 20.00
PR3LB Larry Bird/89 10.00 25.00
PR3LJ LeBron James 30.00 80.00
PR3MJ Magic Johnson 10.00 25.00
PR3MU Chris Mullin 3.00 8.00
PR3ON Jermaine O'Neal 3.00 8.00
PR3OR Oscar Robertson 6.00 15.00
PR3PE Patrick Ewing 6.00 15.00
PR3PP Paul Pierce 5.00 12.00
PR3RA Ray Allen 5.00 12.00
PR3RJ Richard Jefferson 2.50 6.00
PR3RR Rajon Rondo 4.00 10.00
PR3SM Shawn Marion 3.00 8.00
PR3SN Steve Nash 6.00 15.00
PR3TM Tracy McGrady 5.00 12.00
PR3VC Vince Carter 6.00 15.00
PR3WF Walt Frazier 3.00 8.00
PR3YM Yao Ming 8.00 20.00

2008-09 Upper Deck Premier Remnants Triple City

STATED PRINT RUN 50 SER.#'d SETS
PR3AB Andrew Bynum 2.50 6.00
PR3AH Al Horford 4.00 10.00
PR3AI Andre Iguodala 3.00 8.00
PR3AJ Antawn Jamison 3.00 8.00
PR3AL Acie Law 3.00 8.00
PR3AM Alonzo Mourning 8.00 20.00
PR3AS Amare Stoudemire 4.00 10.00
PR3AT Al Thornton 2.50 6.00
PR3BD Baron Davis 4.00 10.00
PR3BG Ben Gordon 3.00 8.00
PR3BO Carlos Boozer 3.00 8.00
PR3BR Brandon Roy 3.00 8.00
PR3CA Carmelo Anthony 5.00 12.00
PR3CB Chauncey Billups 5.00 12.00
PR3CL Carl Landry 2.50 6.00
PR3CM Corey Maggette 3.00 8.00
PR3CP Chris Paul 8.00 20.00
PR3DG Darrell Griffith 2.50 6.00
PR3DH Dwight Howard 5.00 12.00
PR3DR Dennis Rodman 10.00 25.00
PR3DW Deron Williams 3.00 8.00
PR3HO Hakeem Olajuwon 8.00 20.00
PR3JE Julius Erving 10.00 25.00
PR3JF Al Jefferson 2.50 6.00
PR3JK Jason Kidd 6.00 15.00
PR3JO Michael Jordan 40.00 100.00
PR3KB Kobe Bryant 60.00 150.00
PR3KD Kevin Durant 20.00 50.00
PR3KG Kevin Garnett 10.00 25.00
PR3LA LaMarcus Aldridge 4.00 10.00
PR3LB Larry Bird 12.00 30.00
PR3LJ LeBron James 30.00 80.00
PR3MC Mike Conley Jr. 3.00 8.00
PR3MJ Magic Johnson 12.00 30.00
PR3MU Chris Mullin 4.00 10.00
PR3ON Jermaine O'Neal 4.00 10.00
PR3OR Oscar Robertson 8.00 20.00
PR3PE Patrick Ewing 8.00 20.00
PR3PP Paul Pierce 6.00 15.00
PR3QR Quentin Richardson 2.50 6.00
PR3RA Ray Allen 5.00 12.00
PR3RG Rudy Gay 4.00 10.00
PR3RJ Richard Jefferson 3.00 8.00
PR3RR Rajon Rondo 5.00 12.00
PR3SM Shawn Marion 4.00 10.00
PR3SN Steve Nash 8.00 20.00
PR3TM Tracy McGrady 6.00 15.00
PR3VC Vince Carter 8.00 20.00
PR3WF Walt Frazier 4.00 10.00
PR3YM Yao Ming 10.00 25.00

2008-09 Upper Deck Premier Remnants Triple Position

PRINT RUN 25 SER.#'d SETS
PR3AB Andrew Bynum 3.00 8.00
PR3AH Al Horford 5.00 12.00
PR3AI Andre Iguodala 4.00 10.00
PR3AJ Antawn Jamison 4.00 10.00
PR3AL Acie Law 4.00 10.00
PR3AM Alonzo Mourning 15.00 30.00
PR3AS Amare Stoudemire 5.00 12.00
PR3AT Al Thornton 3.00 8.00
PR3BD Baron Davis 5.00 12.00
PR3BG Ben Gordon 4.00 10.00
PR3BO Carlos Boozer 4.00 10.00
PR3BR Brandon Roy 4.00 10.00
PR3CA Carmelo Anthony 6.00 15.00
PR3CB Chauncey Billups 6.00 15.00
PR3CL Carl Landry 3.00 8.00
PR3CM Corey Maggette 4.00 10.00
PR3CP Chris Paul 10.00 25.00
PR3DG Darrell Griffith 3.00 8.00
PR3DH Dwight Howard 6.00 15.00
PR3DR Dennis Rodman 12.00 30.00
PR3DW Deron Williams 4.00 10.00
PR3HO Hakeem Olajuwon 10.00 25.00
PR3JE Julius Erving 12.00 30.00
PR3JF Al Jefferson 3.00 8.00
PR3JK Jason Kidd 8.00 20.00
PR3JO Michael Jordan 60.00 150.00
PR3KB Kobe Bryant 75.00 200.00
PR3KD Kevin Durant 20.00 50.00
PR3KG Kevin Garnett 12.00 30.00
PR3LA LaMarcus Aldridge 5.00 12.00
PR3LB Larry Bird 15.00 40.00
PR3LJ LeBron James 40.00 100.00
PR3MC Mike Conley Jr. 3.00 8.00
PR3MJ Magic Johnson 15.00 40.00
PR3MU Chris Mullin 5.00 12.00
PR3ON Jermaine O'Neal 5.00 12.00
PR3OR Oscar Robertson 10.00 25.00
PR3PE Patrick Ewing 10.00 25.00
PR3PP Paul Pierce 8.00 20.00
PR3QR Quentin Richardson 3.00 8.00
PR3RA Ray Allen 8.00 20.00
PR3RG Rudy Gay 5.00 12.00
PR3RJ Richard Jefferson 4.00 10.00
PR3RR Rajon Rondo 6.00 15.00
PR3SM Shawn Marion 5.00 12.00
PR3SN Steve Nash 10.00 25.00
PR3TM Tracy McGrady 8.00 20.00
PR3VC Vince Carter 10.00 25.00
PR3WF Walt Frazier 5.00 12.00
PR3YM Yao Ming 12.00 30.00

2008-09 Upper Deck Premier Rookies Autographs Jerseys 75

STATED PRINT RUN 75 SER.#'d SETS
101 Derrick Rose 60.00 150.00
102 Michael Beasley 5.00 12.00
103 O.J. Mayo 4.00 10.00
104 Russell Westbrook 200.00 500.00
105 Kevin Love 50.00 120.00
106 Patrick Ewing Jr. 3.00 8.00
107 Eric Gordon 10.00 25.00
108 Joe Alexander 3.00 8.00
109 D.J. Augustin 3.00 8.00
110 Brook Lopez 6.00 15.00
111 Jerryd Bayless 4.00 10.00
112 Jason Thompson 3.00 8.00
113 Brandon Rush 3.00 8.00
114 Anthony Randolph 3.00 8.00
115 Robin Lopez 4.00 10.00
116 Marreese Speights 4.00 10.00
117 Chris Douglas-Roberts 3.00 8.00
118 Javale McGee 5.00 12.00
119 J.J. Hickson 3.00 8.00
120 Ryan Anderson 4.00 10.00
121 Kosta Koufos 3.00 8.00
122 George Hill 6.00 15.00
123 Darrell Arthur 4.00 10.00
124 Donte Greene 3.00 8.00
125 Sonny Weems 3.00 8.00
126 J.R. Giddens 3.00 8.00
127 Walter Sharpe 3.00 8.00
128 Joey Dorsey 3.00 8.00
129 Mario Chalmers 5.00 12.00
130 DeAndre Jordan 6.00 15.00

2008-09 Upper Deck Premier Stitchings

STATED PRINT RUN 50 SER.#'d SETS
*STITCH 25: .5X TO 1.25X BASE
PSAC Austin Carr 6.00 15.00
PSAH Al Horford 6.00 15.00
PSAI Allen Iverson 15.00 40.00
PSAM Alonzo Mourning 15.00 40.00
PSAS Amare Stoudemire 6.00 15.00
PSAT Al Thornton 6.00 15.00
PSBB Bill Bradley 6.00 15.00
PSBC Billy Cunningham 6.00 15.00
PSBP Bob Pettit 6.00 15.00
PSBR Bill Russell 15.00 40.00
PSBS Bill Sharman 12.00 30.00
PSBW Bill Walton 8.00 20.00
PSCA Carmelo Anthony 6.00 15.00
PSCD Clyde Drexler 10.00 25.00
PSCM Calvin Murphy 6.00 15.00
PSCO Bob Cousy 15.00 40.00
PSCP Chris Paul 8.00 20.00
PSDA D.J. Augustin 6.00 15.00
PSDB Dave Bing 10.00 25.00
PSDC Dave Cowens 10.00 25.00
PSDD Dave DeBusschere 6.00 15.00
PSDE Dennis Rodman 20.00 50.00
PSDG Darrell Griffith 6.00 15.00
PSDH Dwight Howard 8.00 20.00
PSDN Dirk Nowitzki 12.00 30.00
PSDR David Robinson 10.00 25.00
PSDS Dolph Schayes 6.00 15.00
PSDT David Thompson 6.00 15.00
PSDW Dominique Wilkins 8.00 20.00
PSEB Elgin Baylor 8.00 20.00
PSEG Eric Gordon 6.00 15.00
PSEH Elvin Hayes 6.00 15.00
PSEM Earl Monroe 6.00 15.00
PSGA Danilo Gallinari 6.00 15.00
PSGG George Gervin 6.00 15.00
PSGH Grant Hill 20.00 50.00
PSGM George Mikan 15.00 40.00
PSGO Greg Oden 6.00 15.00
PSHG Hal Greer 6.00 15.00
PSHO Hakeem Olajuwon 8.00 20.00
PSIT Isiah Thomas 8.00 20.00
PSJA LeBron James 40.00 100.00
PSJB Jerryd Bayless 6.00 15.00
PSJD Joe Dumars 8.00 20.00
PSJE Julius Erving 15.00 40.00
PSJH John Havlicek 8.00 20.00
PSJK Jason Kidd 8.00 20.00
PSJL Jerry Lucas 6.00 15.00
PSJO Michael Jordan 60.00 150.00
PSJS John Stockton 12.00 30.00
PSJW James Worthy 6.00 15.00
PSKA Kareem Abdul-Jabbar 10.00 25.00
PSKB Kobe Bryant 60.00 150.00
PSKD Kevin Durant 12.00 30.00
PSKG Kevin Garnett 12.00 30.00
PSKL Kevin Love 8.00 20.00
PSKM Karl Malone 8.00 20.00
PSLB Larry Bird 15.00 40.00
PSLJ Larry Johnson 10.00 25.00
PSLW Lenny Wilkens 6.00 15.00
PSMB Michael Beasley 6.00 15.00
PSMC Kevin McHale 10.00 25.00
PSMJ Magic Johnson 15.00 40.00
PSMM Moses Malone 6.00 15.00
PSMU Chris Mullin 6.00 15.00
PSNA Nate Archibald 6.00 15.00
PSNT Nate Thurmond 8.00 20.00
PSOA Charles Oakley 6.00 15.00
PSOM O.J. Mayo 6.00 15.00
PSOR Oscar Robertson 8.00 20.00
PSPE Patrick Ewing 10.00 25.00
PSPG Pau Gasol 10.00 25.00
PSPM Pete Maravich 25.00 60.00
PSPP Paul Pierce 15.00 30.00
PSPR Pat Riley 8.00 20.00
PSRA Ray Allen 10.00 25.00
PSRB Rick Barry 6.00 15.00
PSRD Derrick Rose 20.00 50.00
PSRO Brandon Roy 6.00 15.00
PSRP Robert Parish 8.00 20.00
PSRS Ralph Sampson 6.00 15.00
PSRW Russell Westbrook 50.00 120.00
PSSJ Sam Jones 10.00 25.00
PSSN Steve Nash 10.00 25.00
PSSO Shaquille O'Neal 12.00 30.00
PSSP Scottie Pippen 15.00 40.00
PSTD Tim Duncan 10.00 25.00
PSTM Tracy McGrady 6.00 15.00
PSVC Vince Carter 10.00 25.00
PSWA Dwyane Wade 8.00 20.00
PSWC Wilt Chamberlain 12.00 30.00
PSWE Jerry West 12.00 30.00
PSWF Walt Frazier 6.00 15.00
PSWR Willis Reed 6.00 15.00
PSWU Wes Unseld 6.00 15.00
PSR08 Rose/Beasley/Mayo 8.00 20.00
PSBBOY Thms/Rod/Lmbr/Dms 8.00 20.00
PSBSTN Bird/Russ/Hav/Csy 15.00 40.00
PSSHOW Magic/KAJ/Wrty/Coop 12.00 30.00

2008-09 Upper Deck Premier Trios Autographs

STATED PRINT RUN 15 SER.#'d SETS
P3TD Westbrk/Drn/White 400.00 800.00
P3BLA Beasley/Love/Alxndr 12.00 30.00
P3BVB Brynt/Bynm/Vujacic 200.00 500.00
P3HDS Durant/Hrfrd/Scola 75.00 200.00
P3IND Rush/Granger/Hibbrt 10.00 25.00
P3JJJ MJ/Magic/James 3,000.00 6,000.00
P3LRD Laimbr/Rdmn/Dntley 50.00 120.00
P3MEM Rose/Dorsey/D.Rbrts 30.00 80.00
P3MTW Brewer/Love/Jffrsn 12.00 30.00
P3PAG Allen/Garnett/Pierce 200.00 500.00
P3RBM Rose/Beasley/Mayo 30.00 80.00
P3SHJ Amare/Hwrd/Jffrsn 12.00 30.00
P3WGA Westbrk/Grdn/D.J. 60.00 150.00
P3BLAZ Byless/Roy/Aldrdg 15.00 40.00
P3GRIZ Conley/Mayo/Gay 12.00 30.00
P3HEAT Beasly/Chlmrs/Cook 10.00 25.00
P3UCLA Wstbrk/Love/Mbah 150.00 400.00

2004-05 Upper Deck Pro Sigs

COMP.SET w/o SP's 8.00 20.00
91-120 STATED ODDS 1:6
1 Antoine Walker .25 .60
2 Al Harrington .20 .50
3 Boris Diaw .20 .50
4 Paul Pierce .40 1.00
5 Ricky Davis .20 .50
6 Gary Payton .40 1.00
7 Jahidi White .15 .40
8 Jason Kapono .15 .40
9 Gerald Wallace .20 .50
10 Eddy Curry .15 .40
11 Kirk Hinrich .25 .60
12 Tyson Chandler .20 .50
13 LeBron James 2.00 5.00
14 Dajuan Wagner .15 .40
15 Drew Gooden .15 .40
16 Dirk Nowitzki .60 1.50
17 Michael Finley .25 .60
18 Jerry Stackhouse .25 .60
19 Carmelo Anthony .50 1.25
20 Andre Miller .20 .50
21 Kenyon Martin .25 .60
22 Chauncey Billups .30 .75
23 Rasheed Wallace .30 .75
24 Ben Wallace .30 .75
25 Derek Fisher .20 .50
26 Jason Richardson .25 .60
27 Mike Dunleavy .15 .40
28 Yao Ming .60 1.50
29 Jim Jackson .20 .50
30 Tracy McGrady .40 1.00
31 Jermaine O'Neal .20 .50
32 Reggie Miller .50 1.25
33 Ron Artest .25 .60
34 Elton Brand .20 .50
35 Corey Maggette .20 .50
36 Kerry Kittles .20 .50
37 Kobe Bryant 2.00 5.00
38 Chris Mihm .15 .40
39 Lamar Odom .25 .60
40 Pau Gasol .40 1.00
41 Jason Williams .20 .50
42 Bonzi Wells .15 .40
43 Shaquille O'Neal 1.00 2.50
44 Dwyane Wade 1.00 2.50
45 Eddie Jones .25 .60
46 Michael Redd .20 .50
47 Desmond Mason .20 .50
48 T.J. Ford .15 .40
49 Latrell Sprewell .30 .75
50 Kevin Garnett .60 1.50
51 Sam Cassell .20 .50
52 Richard Jefferson .20 .50
53 Aaron Williams .15 .40
54 Jason Kidd .40 1.00
55 Jamal Mashburn .20 .50
56 Baron Davis .25 .60
57 Jamaal Magloire .15 .40
58 Allan Houston .25 .60
59 Jamal Crawford .25 .60
60 Stephon Marbury .30 .75
61 Cuttino Mobley .20 .50
62 Kelvin Cato .15 .40
63 Steve Francis .25 .60
64 Glenn Robinson .20 .50
65 Allen Iverson .60 1.50
66 Samuel Dalembert .15 .40
67 Amare Stoudemire .25 .60
68 Steve Nash .50 1.25
69 Shawn Marion .25 .60
70 Shareef Abdur-Rahim .25 .60
71 Damon Stoudamire .25 .60
72 Zach Randolph .25 .60
73 Peja Stojakovic .25 .60
74 Chris Webber .30 .75
75 Mike Bibby .25 .60
76 Tony Parker .40 1.00
77 Tim Duncan .60 1.50
78 Manu Ginobili .50 1.25
79 Ronald Murray .15 .40
80 Ray Allen .40 1.00
81 Rashard Lewis .25 .60
82 Chris Bosh .40 1.00
83 Vince Carter .50 1.25
84 Jalen Rose .20 .50
85 Andrei Kirilenko .20 .50
86 Carlos Boozer .20 .50
87 Carlos Arroyo .15 .40
88 Gilbert Arenas .25 .60
89 Jarvis Hayes .15 .40
90 Antawn Jamison .20 .50
91 Dwight Howard RC 3.00 8.00
92 Emeka Okafor RC .75 2.00
93 Ben Gordon RC 1.00 2.50
94 Shaun Livingston RC 1.00 2.50
95 Devin Harris RC .75 2.00
96 Josh Childress RC .60 1.50
97 Luol Deng RC 1.00 2.50
98 Rafael Araujo RC .60 1.50
99 Andre Iguodala RC 1.50 4.00
100 Luke Jackson RC .60 1.50
101 Andris Biedrins RC .60 1.50
102 Robert Swift RC .60 1.50
103 Sebastian Telfair RC .75 2.00
104 Kris Humphries RC .75 2.00
105 Al Jefferson RC 1.50 4.00
106 Kirk Snyder RC .60 1.50
107 Josh Smith RC 1.00 2.50
108 J.R. Smith RC 1.00 2.50
109 Dorell Wright RC .75 2.00
110 Jameer Nelson RC 1.00 2.50
111 Pavel Podkolzin RC .60 1.50
112 Viktor Khryapa RC .60 1.50
113 Sergei Monia RC .60 1.50
114 Delonte West RC .75 2.00
115 Tony Allen RC 1.00 2.50
116 Kevin Martin RC 1.25 3.00
117 Sasha Vujacic RC .75 2.00
118 Beno Udrih RC .75 2.00
119 David Harrison RC .60 1.50
120 Lionel Chalmers RC .75 2.00

2004-05 Upper Deck Pro Sigs Gold

*1-90 GOLD SINGLES: 2X TO 5X BASE HI
1-90 STATED ODDS 1:24
*91-120 GOLD RC's: 1.25X TO 3X BASE HI
91-120 PRINT RUN 100 SER.#'d SETS

2004-05 Upper Deck Pro Sigs Silver

*1-90 SILVER SINGLES: .75X TO 2X BASE HI
1-90 STATED ODDS 1:8
*91-120 SILVER RC's: .6X TO 1.5X BASE HI
91-120 RC STATED ODDS 1:24

2004-05 Upper Deck Pro Sigs Pro Signs

STATED ODDS 1:170
SP INFO PROVIDED BY UPPER DECK
AB Antonio Burks 3.00 8.00
AH Al Harrington 4.00 10.00
AK Andrei Kirilenko 4.00 10.00
AN Antonio McDyess SP 6.00 15.00
BB Brent Barry 5.00 12.00
BH Brandon Hunter 3.00 8.00
CE Cedric Maxwell 6.00 15.00
CL Clyde Drexler SP 20.00 50.00
CM Corey Maggette 4.00 10.00
CR Jamal Crawford 15.00 40.00
DD Dan Dickau 3.00 8.00
DJ Dahntay Jones 3.00 8.00
DM Desmond Mason 4.00 10.00
DY Dwyane Wade SP 50.00 100.00
FE Francisco Elson 3.00 8.00
GA Gilbert Arenas SP 8.00 20.00
GG Gordan Giricek 3.00 8.00
GR Glenn Robinson 4.00 10.00
GW Gerald Wallace 4.00 10.00
JA Jalen Rose 4.00 10.00
JB Jerome Beasley SP 3.00 8.00
JD Juan Dixon 3.00 8.00
JH Josh Howard 4.00 10.00
JJ James Jones 3.00 8.00
JK Jason Kapono SP 3.00 8.00
JM Jerome Moiso 3.00 8.00
JO Jon Barry 4.00 10.00
JS John Salley 6.00 15.00
JW Jamaal Wilkes 4.00 10.00
KB Kobe Bryant SP 100.00 250.00
KK Kyle Korver 5.00 12.00
KR Kareem Rush 3.00 8.00
LJ LeBron James SP 1,000.00 2,000.00
LO Lamar Odom SP 10.00 25.00
LR Luke Ridnour 4.00 10.00
MB Marcus Banks 3.00 8.00
MD Marquis Daniels 3.00 8.00
MI Darko Milicic SP 3.00 8.00
MP Mickael Pietrus 3.00 8.00
MS Mike Sweetney 3.00 8.00
MW Maurice Williams 4.00 10.00
NH Nene 4.00 10.00
PB Primoz Brezec 3.00 8.00
RG Reece Gaines 3.00 8.00
RH Richard Hamilton 8.00 20.00
RM Reggie Miller SP 75.00 200.00
SB Steve Blake 3.00 8.00
TO Travis Outlaw 4.00 10.00
TS Theron Smith 3.00 8.00
WG Willie Green 5.00 12.00
WZ Wang Zhizhi 30.00 80.00
ZC Zarko Cabarkapa 3.00 8.00
ZO Zoran Planinic 3.00 8.00
ZP Zaza Pachulia 3.00 8.00

2004-05 Upper Deck Pro Sigs Pro Signs Gold

PRINT RUNS LISTED IN CHECKLIST
AB Antonio Burks/25 5.00 12.00
AK Andrei Kirilenko/47 5.00 12.00
BB Brent Barry/32 20.00 50.00
BH Brandon Hunter/56 5.00 12.00
CL Clyde Drexler/22 40.00 100.00
DJ Dahntay Jones/30 5.00 12.00
DM Desmond Mason/24 8.00 20.00
FE Francisco Elson/56 5.00 12.00
GR Glenn Robinson/31 6.00 15.00
JB Jerome Beasley/24 5.00 12.00
JB2 Jon Barry/20 5.00 12.00
JJ James Jones/33 5.00 12.00
JK Jason Kapono/25 5.00 12.00
JS John Salley/22 10.00 25.00
JU Justin Reed/25 5.00 12.00
JW Jamaal Wilkes/52 6.00 15.00
KG Kevin Garnett/21 100.00 250.00
KK Kyle Korver/26 12.00 30.00
KR Kareem Rush/21 5.00 12.00
LJ LeBron James/23 1,500.00 3,000.00
MA Magic Johnson/32 75.00 150.00
MJ Michael Jordan/23 2,000.00 4,000.00
MS Mike Sweetney/25 5.00 12.00
MW Maurice Williams/25 5.00 12.00
NH Nene/31 8.00 20.00
PB Primoz Brezec/27 5.00 12.00
RH Richard Hamilton/32 12.00 30.00
RM Reggie Miller/31 150.00 400.00
TO Travis Outlaw/25 5.00 12.00
WG Willie Green/33 5.00 12.00
ZP Zaza Pachulia/27 5.00 12.00

2004-05 Upper Deck Pro Sigs Pro Signs Rookies

STATED ODDS 1:30
*GOLD: 1.25X TO 3X BASE HI
GOLD PRINT RUN 25 SER.#'d SETS
AE Andre Emmett 2.50 6.00
AI Andre Iguodala 6.00 15.00
AL Al Jefferson Big Al 4.00 10.00
AV Anderson Varejao 3.00 8.00
BG Ben Gordon 4.00 10.00
BI Andris Biedrins 2.50 6.00
BS Blake Stepp 4.00 10.00
BU Antonio Burks 2.50 6.00
CD Chris Duhon 3.00 8.00
DA David Harrison 2.50 6.00
DE Delonte West 3.00 8.00
DH Devin Harris 3.00 8.00
DH Dwight Howard 12.00 30.00
DO Dorell Wright 3.00 8.00
DS Donta Smith 2.50 6.00
HS Ha Seung-Jin 4.00 10.00
JC Josh Childress 2.50 6.00
JN Jameer Nelson 4.00 10.00
JR J.R. Smith 4.00 10.00
JR2 Justin Reed 2.50 6.00
JV Jackson Vroman 2.50 6.00
KH Kris Humphries 3.00 8.00
KM Kevin Martin 5.00 12.00
KS Kirk Snyder 2.50 6.00
LC Lionel Chalmers 3.00 8.00
LD Luol Deng 4.00 10.00
LU Luke Jackson 2.50 6.00
MF Matt Freije 2.50 6.00
PP Pavel Podkolzin 2.50 6.00
PR Peter John Ramos 2.50 6.00
PS Pape Sow 2.50 6.00

RA Rafael Araujo 2.50 6.00
RI Royal Ivey 2.50 6.00
RS Robert Swift 2.50 6.00
SL Shaun Livingston 4.00 10.00
ST Sebastian Telfair 3.00 8.00
SV Sasha Vujacic 3.00 8.00
TA Tony Allen 4.00 10.00
TP Tim Pickett 3.00 8.00
TR Trevor Ariza 4.00 10.00
UD Beno Udrih 3.00 8.00
VK Viktor Khryapa 2.50 6.00

2000-01 Upper Deck Pros and Prospects

COMPLETE SET (120) 40.00 80.00
COMP.SET w/o RC (90) 10.00 25.00
RCs: PRINT RUN 999 SERIAL #'d SETS
1 Dikembe Mutombo .50 1.25
2 Alan Henderson .20 .50
3 Jim Jackson .25 .60
4 Paul Pierce .50 1.25
5 Kenny Anderson .25 .60
6 Antoine Walker .30 .75
7 Baron Davis .30 .75
8 Derrick Coleman .30 .75
9 David Wesley .25 .60
10 Elton Brand .30 .75
11 Ron Artest .30 .75
12 Hersey Hawkins .20 .50
13 Andre Miller .25 .60
14 Lamond Murray .20 .50
15 Shawn Kemp .50 1.25
16 Michael Finley .30 .75
17 Dirk Nowitzki .75 2.00
18 Cedric Ceballos .25 .60
19 Antonio McDyess .25 .60
20 Nick Van Exel .30 .75
21 Raef LaFrentz .25 .60
22 Christian Laettner .30 .75
23 Jerry Stackhouse .30 .75
24 Lindsey Hunter .20 .50
25 Antawn Jamison .30 .75
26 Larry Hughes .30 .75
27 Chris Mills .20 .50
28 Steve Francis .30 .75
29 Hakeem Olajuwon .60 1.50
30 Shandon Anderson .20 .50
31 Reggie Miller .60 1.50
32 Jonathan Bender .20 .50
33 Jalen Rose .25 .60
34 Lamar Odom .30 .75
35 Michael Olowokandi .20 .50
36 Tyrone Nesby .20 .50
37 Kobe Bryant 2.50 6.00
38 Shaquille O'Neal 1.25 3.00
39 Ron Harper .30 .75
40 Robert Horry .30 .75
41 Alonzo Mourning .50 1.25
42 P.J. Brown .20 .50
43 Jamal Mashburn .25 .60
44 Ray Allen .50 1.25
45 Glenn Robinson .30 .75
46 Sam Cassell .25 .60
47 Kevin Garnett .75 2.00
48 Wally Szczerbiak .25 .60
49 Terrell Brandon .25 .60
50 William Avery .20 .50
51 Stephon Marbury .40 1.00
52 Keith Van Horn .25 .60
53 Kerry Kittles .25 .60
54 Latrell Sprewell .40 1.00
55 Allan Houston .30 .75
56 Patrick Ewing .50 1.25
57 Darrell Armstrong .20 .50
58 Pat Garrity .20 .50
59 Michael Doleac .20 .50
60 Allen Iverson .75 2.00
61 Theo Ratliff .20 .50
62 Tyrone Hill .20 .50
63 Jason Kidd .50 1.25
64 Anfernee Hardaway .50 1.25
65 Shawn Marion .30 .75
66 Scottie Pippen .75 2.00
67 Rasheed Wallace .40 1.00
68 Damon Stoudamire .30 .75
69 Bonzi Wells .20 .50
70 Chris Webber .40 1.00
71 Peja Stojakovic .25 .60
72 Jason Williams .50 1.25
73 Tim Duncan .75 2.00
74 David Robinson .60 1.50
75 Terry Porter .20 .50
76 Gary Payton .50 1.25
77 Rashard Lewis .25 .60
78 Vin Baker .25 .60
79 Vince Carter .60 1.50
80 Doug Christie .25 .60
81 Antonio Davis .20 .50
82 Karl Malone .60 1.50
83 John Stockton .60 1.50
84 Bryon Russell .20 .50
85 Shareef Abdur-Rahim .30 .75
86 Mike Bibby .30 .75
87 Michael Dickerson .20 .50
88 Mitch Richmond .40 1.00
89 Richard Hamilton .40 1.00
90 Juwan Howard .25 .60
91 Kenyon Martin JSY RC 12.00 30.00
92 Stromile Swift RC 1.50 4.00
93 Darius Miles RC 2.00 5.00
94 Marcus Fizer JSY RC 4.00 10.00
95 Mike Miller RC 3.00 8.00
96 DerMarr Johnson RC 1.25 3.00
97 Chris Mihm RC 1.25 3.00
98 Chris Porter RC 1.25 3.00
99 Joel Przybilla RC 1.50 4.00
100 Keyon Dooling RC 1.50 4.00
101 Jerome Moiso RC 1.25 3.00
102 Etan Thomas RC 1.50 4.00
103 Courtney Alexander RC 1.25 3.00
104 Mateen Cleaves RC 1.50 4.00
105 Jason Collier RC 2.00 5.00
106 Dan Langhi RC 1.25 3.00
107 Desmond Mason RC 2.50 6.00
108 Quentin Richardson RC 1.50 4.00
109 Jamaal Magloire RC 2.00 5.00
110 Speedy Claxton RC 2.00 5.00
111 Morris Peterson RC 2.00 5.00
112 Donnell Harvey RC 1.50 4.00
113 Hanno Mottola RC 1.25 3.00
114 Mamadou N'Diaye RC 1.25 3.00
115 Erick Barkley RC 1.25 3.00
116 Mark Madsen RC 2.00 5.00
117 A.J. Guyton RC 1.25 3.00
118 Khalid El-Amin RC 1.25 3.00
119 Lavor Postell RC 1.25 3.00
120 Eddie House RC 1.50 4.00

2000-01 Upper Deck Pros and Prospects ProActive

COMPLETE SET (10) 3.00 8.00
STATED ODDS 1:6
PA1 Kobe Bryant 2.50 6.00
PA2 Kevin Garnett .75 2.00
PA3 Vince Carter .60 1.50
PA4 Jason Kidd .50 1.25
PA5 Steve Francis .30 .75
PA6 Chris Webber .40 1.00
PA7 Shaquille O'Neal 1.25 3.00
PA8 Larry Hughes .30 .75
PA9 Gary Payton .50 1.25
PA10 Allen Iverson .75 2.00

2000-01 Upper Deck Pros and Prospects ProMotion

COMPLETE SET (10) 2.50 6.00
STATED ODDS 1:6
PM1 Darius Miles .40 1.00
PM2 Stromile Swift .30 .75
PM3 Marcus Fizer .30 .75
PM4 Kenyon Martin .75 2.00
PM5 Courtney Alexander .25 .60
PM6 Keyon Dooling .30 .75
PM7 DerMarr Johnson .25 .60
PM8 Chris Mihm .25 .60
PM9 Chris Porter .25 .60
PM10 Mike Miller .60 1.50

2000-01 Upper Deck Pros and Prospects Signature Jerseys

STATED ODDS 1:96
AH Anfernee Hardaway 40.00 100.00
AW Antoine Walker 12.00 30.00
BD Baron Davis 12.00 30.00
CM Corey Maggette 6.00 15.00
DS Damon Stoudamire 12.00 30.00
GP Gary Payton 30.00 80.00
GR Glenn Robinson 6.00 15.00
KB Kobe Bryant 2,000.00 4,000.00
KG Kevin Garnett 150.00 400.00
KM Karl Malone 75.00 200.00
MB Mike Bibby 8.00 20.00
MF Michael Finley 25.00 60.00
PP Paul Pierce 60.00 150.00
SA Shareef Abdur-Rahim 12.00 30.00
TB Terrell Brandon 6.00 15.00
VB Vin Baker 6.00 15.00
WA William Avery 6.00 15.00
WS Wally Szczerbiak 6.00 15.00

2000-01 Upper Deck Pros and Prospects Signature Jerseys Level 2

PRINT RUNS TO PLAYERS JERSEY NUMBER
CM2 Corey Maggette/50 20.00 50.00
KG2 Kevin Garnett/21 2,000.00 4,000.00
KM2 Karl Malone/32 800.00 1,500.00
MJ2 Michael Jordan/23 20,000.00 40,000.00

2000-01 Upper Deck Pros and Prospects Star Command

COMPLETE SET (12) 8.00 20.00
STATED ODDS 1:12
SC1 Kobe Bryant 5.00 12.00
SC2 Vince Carter 1.25 3.00
SC3 Allen Iverson 1.50 4.00
SC4 Shaquille O'Neal 2.50 6.00
SC5 Chris Webber .75 2.00
SC6 Karl Malone 1.25 3.00
SC7 Lamar Odom .60 1.50
SC8 Jason Kidd 1.00 2.50
SC9 Steve Francis .60 1.50
SC10 Kevin Garnett 1.50 4.00
SC11 Larry Hughes .60 1.50
SC12 Gary Payton 1.00 2.50

2000-01 Upper Deck Pros and Prospects Star Futures

COMPLETE SET (10) 5.00 12.00
STATED ODDS 1:12
SF1 Kenyon Martin 1.25 3.00
SF2 Keyon Dooling .50 1.25
SF3 Chris Porter .40 1.00
SF4 Courtney Alexander .40 1.00
SF5 Darius Miles .60 1.50
SF6 Mike Miller 1.00 2.50
SF7 Mateen Cleaves .50 1.25
SF8 Stromile Swift .50 1.25
SF9 Marcus Fizer .50 1.25
SF10 DerMarr Johnson .40 1.00

2000-01 Upper Deck Pros and Prospects UD Authentics Rookie Exclusives

STATED PRINT RUN 200 SETS
CM Chris Mihm 3.00 8.00
ET Etan Thomas 4.00 10.00
JP Joel Przybilla 4.00 10.00

2001-02 Upper Deck Pros and Prospects

COMP.SET w/o SP's (90) 10.00 25.00
91-125 PRINT RUN 1000 SERIAL #'d SETS
126-131 PRINT RUN 350 SERIAL #'d SETS
1 Jason Terry .30 .75
2 Toni Kukoc .40 1.00
3 DerMarr Johnson .20 .50
4 Paul Pierce .50 1.25
5 Antoine Walker .25 .60
6 Kenny Anderson .25 .60
7 Jamal Mashburn .25 .60
8 Baron Davis .30 .75
9 David Wesley .20 .50
10 Elton Brand .25 .60
11 Ron Mercer .20 .50
12 Jamal Crawford .30 .75
13 Andre Miller .25 .60
14 Lamond Murray .20 .50
15 Chris Mihm .20 .50
16 Michael Finley .30 .75
17 Wang ZhiZhi .30 .75
18 Dirk Nowitzki .75 2.00
19 Antonio McDyess .25 .60
20 Nick Van Exel .30 .75
21 Raef LaFrentz .25 .60
22 Jerry Stackhouse .30 .75
23 Joe Smith .25 .60
24 Mateen Cleaves .20 .50
25 Antawn Jamison .25 .60
26 Marc Jackson .25 .60
27 Larry Hughes .25 .60
28 Steve Francis .30 .75
29 Maurice Taylor .20 .50
30 Hakeem Olajuwon .60 1.50
31 Reggie Miller .60 1.50
32 Jermaine O'Neal .25 .60
33 Jalen Rose .25 .60
34 Lamar Odom .25 .60
35 Darius Miles .25 .60
36 Quentin Richardson .25 .60
37 Kobe Bryant 2.50 6.00
38 Shaquille O'Neal 1.25 3.00
39 Derek Fisher .25 .60
40 Rick Fox .25 .60
41 Alonzo Mourning .50 1.25
42 Eddie Jones .30 .75
43 Tim Hardaway .40 1.00
44 Brian Grant .20 .50
45 Ray Allen .50 1.25
46 Glenn Robinson .30 .75
47 Tim Thomas .20 .50
48 Kevin Garnett .75 2.00
49 Terrell Brandon .25 .60
50 Wally Szczerbiak .25 .60
51 Chauncey Billups .40 1.00
52 Stephon Marbury .40 1.00
53 Kenyon Martin .30 .75
54 Keith Van Horn .25 .60
55 Allan Houston .30 .75
56 Latrell Sprewell .40 1.00
57 Glen Rice .30 .75
58 Tracy McGrady .50 1.25
59 Mike Miller .25 .60
60 Darrell Armstrong .20 .50
61 Allen Iverson .75 2.00
62 Dikembe Mutombo .50 1.25
63 Aaron McKie .20 .50
64 Jason Kidd .50 1.25
65 Shawn Marion .30 .75
66 Tom Gugliotta .20 .50
67 Rasheed Wallace .40 1.00
68 Damon Stoudamire .30 .75
69 Scottie Pippen .75 2.00
70 Peja Stojakovic .25 .60
71 Jason Williams .50 1.25
72 Chris Webber .40 1.00
73 Tim Duncan .75 2.00
74 Derek Anderson .20 .50
75 David Robinson .60 1.50
76 Gary Payton .50 1.25
77 Rashard Lewis .25 .60
78 Desmond Mason .25 .60
79 Vince Carter .60 1.50
80 Morris Peterson .20 .50
81 Antonio Davis .25 .60
82 Karl Malone .60 1.50
83 John Stockton .60 1.50
84 Donyell Marshall .20 .50
85 Shareef Abdur-Rahim .25 .60
86 Mike Bibby .30 .75
87 Stromile Swift .30 .75
88 Richard Hamilton .40 1.00
89 Courtney Alexander .20 .50
90 Chris Whitney .20 .50
91 Ruben Boumtje-Boumtje RC 1.50 4.00
92 Sean Lampley RC 2.00 5.00
93 Ken Johnson RC 1.25 3.00
94 Earl Watson RC 1.50 4.00
95 Jamaal Tinsley RC 1.50 4.00
96 Damone Brown RC 1.25 3.00
97 Michael Wright RC 2.00 5.00
98 Alvin Jones RC 1.25 3.00
99 Omar Cook RC 2.00 5.00
100 Jarron Collins RC 2.00 5.00
101 Brian Scalabrine RC 2.00 5.00
102 Jeryl Sasser RC 1.25 3.00
103 Samuel Dalembert RC 2.00 5.00
104 Terence Morris RC 1.25 3.00
105 Will Solomon RC 1.50 4.00
106 Kirk Haston RC 1.25 3.00
107 Richard Jefferson RC 2.50 6.00
108 Jason Collins RC 1.50 4.00
109 Troy Murphy RC 1.50 4.00
110 Gerald Wallace RC 2.50 6.00
111 Shane Battier RC 4.00 10.00
112 Jeff Trepagnier RC 1.25 3.00
113 Brandon Armstrong RC 1.25 3.00
114 Loren Woods RC 1.25 3.00
115 Joseph Forte RC 1.25 3.00
116 Michael Bradley RC 1.25 3.00
117 Joe Johnson RC 3.00 8.00
118 Gilbert Arenas RC 5.00 12.00
119 Ousmane Cisse RC 1.25 3.00
120 Kenny Satterfield RC 1.25 3.00
121 Vladimir Radmanovic RC 1.50 4.00
122 DeSagana Diop RC 1.25 3.00
123 Kedrick Brown RC 1.25 3.00
124 Trenton Hassell RC 1.25 3.00
125 Steven Hunter RC 1.25 3.00
126 Rodney White RC 2.50 6.00
127 Eddy Curry RC 4.00 10.00
128 Jason Richardson RC 6.00 15.00
129 Tyson Chandler RC 6.00 15.00
130 Eddie Griffin RC 3.00 8.00
131 Kwame Brown RC 4.00 10.00

2001-02 Upper Deck Pros and Prospects Rookie Memorabilia

STATED PRINT RUN 350 SERIAL #'d SETS
126 Rodney White Shoe 3.00 8.00
127 Eddy Curry Shoe 5.00 12.00
128 Jason Richardson Shoe 8.00 20.00
129 Tyson Chandler Shoe 8.00 20.00
130 Eddie Griffin Shoe 4.00 10.00
131 Kwame Brown Shoe 5.00 12.00

2001-02 Upper Deck Pros and Prospects Alley-Oop Team-Ups

STATED PRINT RUN 100 SERIAL #'d SETS
*GOLD: 1.25X TO 3X BASE HI
GOLD PRINT RUN 25 SER.#'d SETS
BDJM B.Davis/J.Mashburn 8.00 20.00
CPAJ C.Porter/A.Jamison 8.00 20.00
DATM D.Armstrong/T.McGrady 10.00 25.00
GPRL G.Payton/R.Lewis 10.00 25.00
JSKM J.Stockton/K.Malone 30.00 80.00
KGKB K.Garnett/K.Bryant 75.00 200.00
NVAM N.Van Exel/A.McDyess 8.00 20.00
PPAW P.Pierce/A.Walker 10.00 25.00
QRDM Q.Richardson/D.Miles 8.00 20.00
TBKG T.Brandon/K.Garnett 10.00 25.00

2001-02 Upper Deck Pros and Prospects All-Star Team-Ups

STATED ODDS 1:192
*GOLD: 1.25X TO 3X BASE HI
GOLD PRINT RUN 25 SER.#'d SETS
ADDM A.Davis/D.Mutombo 8.00 20.00
AHLS A.Houston/L.Sprewell 12.50 30.00
AIKB A.Iverson/K.Bryant 100.00 250.00
CWAM C.Webber/A.McDyess 10.00 25.00
DRKG D.Robinson/K.Garnett 10.00 25.00
JKGP J.Kidd/G.Payton 8.00 20.00
JSRW J.Stackhouse/R.Wallace 8.00 20.00
KMMF K.Malone/M.Finley 8.00 20.00
RAGR R.Allen/G.Robinson 8.00 20.00
TMSM T.McGrady/S.Marbury 10.00 25.00

2001-02 Upper Deck Pros and Prospects Game Jerseys

STATED ODDS 1:24
*GOLD: 1X TO 2.5X JSY HI
GOLD PRINT RUN 75 SER.#'d SETS
AI Allen Iverson 10.00 25.00
AJ Antawn Jamison 3.00 8.00
AW Antoine Walker 3.00 8.00
CM Chris Mihm 2.50 6.00
CO Corey Maggette 3.00 8.00
DA Darrell Armstrong 2.50 6.00
DC Derrick Coleman 3.00 8.00
DM Darius Miles 2.50 6.00
GR Glen Rice 4.00 10.00
HM Hanno Mottola 2.50 6.00
JC Jamal Crawford 4.00 10.00
JM Jerome Moiso 2.50 6.00
JS John Stockton 8.00 20.00
KA Kenny Anderson 3.00 8.00
KB Kobe Bryant 75.00 200.00
KG Kevin Garnett 10.00 25.00
KV Keith Van Horn 3.00 8.00
LM Lamond Murray 2.50 6.00
MA Desmond Mason 3.00 8.00
MO Michael Olowokandi 2.50 6.00
MP Morris Peterson 2.50 6.00
RL Raef LaFrentz 2.50 6.00
RM Ron Mercer 2.50 6.00
SS Stromile Swift 2.50 6.00
TB Terrell Brandon 3.00 8.00
WA William Avery 2.50 6.00

2001-02 Upper Deck Pros and Prospects Game Jerseys Autographs

STATED ODDS 1:192
*GOLD: .6X TO 1.5X BASE AU HI
GOLD PRINT RUN 50 SER.#'d SETS
AWA Antoine Walker 8.00 20.00
CMA Chris Mihm 6.00 15.00
COA Corey Maggette 8.00 20.00
DAA Darrell Armstrong 6.00 15.00
DMA Darius Miles 6.00 15.00
KBA Kobe Bryant 1,500.00 3,000.00
LMA Lamond Murray 6.00 15.00
MPA Morris Peterson 6.00 15.00
SSA Stromile Swift 6.00 15.00
TBA Terrell Brandon 6.00 15.00
KGA Kevin Garnett 75.00 200.00

2001-02 Upper Deck Pros and Prospects ProActive

COMPLETE SET (10) 8.00 20.00
STATED ODDS 1:23
PA1 Kobe Bryant 8.00 20.00
PA2 Vince Carter 1.50 4.00
PA3 Tim Duncan 2.00 5.00
PA4 Ray Allen 1.25 3.00
PA5 Michael Finley .75 2.00
PA6 Paul Pierce 1.25 3.00
PA7 Latrell Sprewell 1.00 2.50
PA8 Steve Francis .75 2.00
PA9 Kevin Garnett 2.00 5.00
PA10 Eddie Jones .75 2.00

2001-02 Upper Deck Pros and Prospects ProMotion

COMPLETE SET (12) 10.00 25.00
STATED ODDS 1:18
PM1 Kevin Garnett 2.00 5.00
PM2 Chris Webber 1.00 2.50
PM3 Michael Finley .75 2.00
PM4 Tim Duncan 2.00 5.00
PM5 Ray Allen 1.25 3.00
PM6 Jamal Mashburn .60 1.50
PM7 Antonio McDyess .60 1.50
PM8 Kobe Bryant 6.00 15.00
PM9 Latrell Sprewell 1.00 2.50
PM10 Vince Carter 1.50 4.00
PM11 Shaquille O'Neal 3.00 8.00
PM12 Karl Malone 1.50 4.00

2001-02 Upper Deck Pros and Prospects Star Command

COMPLETE SET (10) 12.00 30.00
STATED ODDS 1:23
SC1 Allen Iverson 2.00 5.00
SC2 Steve Francis .75 2.00
SC3 Kevin Garnett 2.00 5.00
SC4 Vince Carter 1.50 4.00
SC5 Kobe Bryant 10.00 25.00
SC6 Tim Duncan 2.00 5.00
SC7 Chris Webber 1.00 2.50
SC8 Tracy McGrady 1.25 3.00
SC9 Darius Miles .50 1.25
SC10 Shaquille O'Neal 3.00 8.00

2001-02 Upper Deck Pros and Prospects Star Futures

COMPLETE SET (10) 12.00 30.00
STATED ODDS 1:23
SF1 Eddy Curry 1.25 3.00
SF2 Rodney White .75 2.00
SF3 Tyson Chandler 2.00 5.00
SF4 Steven Hunter .75 2.00
SF5 Eddie Griffin 1.00 2.50
SF6 Kwame Brown 1.25 3.00
SF7 DeSagana Diop .75 2.00
SF8 Troy Murphy 1.00 2.50
SF9 Joe Johnson 2.00 5.00
SF10 Jason Richardson 2.00 5.00

1993-94 Upper Deck Pro View

COMPLETE SET (110) 15.00 30.00
1 Karl Malone .40 1.00
2 Chuck Person .10 .30
3 Latrell Sprewell .40 1.00
4 Dominique Wilkins .15 .40
5 Reggie Miller .15 .40
6 Vlade Divac .12 .30
7 Otis Thorpe .12 .30
8 Patrick Ewing .12 .30
9 Ron Harper .12 .30
10 Brad Daugherty .12 .30
11 Robert Parish .12 .30
12 Glen Rice .12 .30
13 Kevin Johnson .12 .30
14 Christian Laettner .12 .30
15 Ricky Pierce .12 .30
16 Joe Dumars .15 .40
17 James Worthy .20 .50
18 John Stockton .25 .60
19 Robert Horry .12 .30
20 John Starks .12 .30
21 Danny Manning .12 .30
22 Alonzo Mourning .20 .50
23 Michael Jordan 2.00 5.00
24 Hakeem Olajuwon .25 .60
25 Scott Skiles .12 .30
26 Stacey Augmon .12 .30
27 Mitch Richmond .15 .40
28 Derrick Coleman .12 .30
29 Jeff Malone .12 .30
30 Larry Johnson .15 .40
31 Sam Perkins .12 .30
32 Shaquille O'Neal .75 2.00
33 Walt Williams .12 .30
34 Doug West .12 .30
35 Mark Price .12 .30
36 Rony Seikaly .12 .30
37 Michael Adams .12 .30
38 Anthony Peeler .12 .30
39 Larry Nance .12 .30
40 Shawn Kemp .15 .40
41 Terry Porter .12 .30
42 Dan Majerle .12 .30
43 Dennis Rodman .20 .50
44 Isiah Thomas .15 .40
45 Spud Webb .12 .30
46 Pooh Richardson .12 .30
47 Tim Hardaway .15 .40
48 Derek Harper .12 .30
49 Pervis Ellison .12 .30
50 Xavier McDaniel .12 .30
51 Jeff Hornacek .12 .30
52 Ken Norman .12 .30
53 LaPhonso Ellis .12 .30
54 Charles Barkley .25 .60
55 Tom Gugliotta .15 .40
56 Clifford Robinson .12 .30
57 Mark Jackson .12 .30
58 Mahmoud Abdul-Rauf .12 .30
59 Todd Day .12 .30
60 Kenny Anderson .12 .30
61 Jim Jackson .12 .30
62 Chris Mullin .15 .40
63 Scottie Pippen .50 1.25
64 Dikembe Mutombo .12 .30
65 Sean Elliott .12 .30
66 Clarence Weatherspoon .12 .30
67 Chris Morris .12 .30
68 Clyde Drexler .20 .50
69 Dennis Scott .12 .30
70 David Robinson .25 .60
71 Larry Johnson PL .12 .30
72 Chris Webber PL .75 2.00
73 Alonzo Mourning PL .12 .30
74 Lloyd Daniels PL .12 .30
75 Derrick Coleman PL .12 .30
76 Tim Hardaway PL .12 .30
77 Isiah Thomas PL .12 .30
78 Chris Mullin PL .12 .30
79 Shaquille O'Neal PL .40 1.00
80 Shawn Bradley PL .12 .30
81 Chris Webber RC 1.25 3.00
82 Jamal Mashburn RC .30 .75
83 Anfernee Hardaway RC 1.25 3.00
84 Calbert Cheaney RC .12 .30
85 Vin Baker RC .30 .75
86 Isaiah Rider RC .20 .50
87 Lindsey Hunter RC .12 .30
88 Bobby Hurley RC .12 .30
89 Dominique Wilkins 3DJ .12 .30
90 Charles Barkley 3DJ .12 .30
91 Michael Jordan 3DJ 1.00 2.50
92 Derrick Coleman 3DJ .12 .30
93 Scottie Pippen 3DJ .12 .30
94 Karl Malone 3DJ .15 .40
95 Larry Johnson 3DJ .12 .30
96 Cedric Ceballos 3DJ .12 .30
97 David Robinson 3DJ .15 .40
98 Patrick Ewing 3DJ .12 .30
99 Clarence Weatherspoon 3DJ .12 .30
100 Alonzo Mourning 3DJ .12 .30
101 Stacey Augmon 3DJ .12 .30
102 Shaquille O'Neal 3DJ .40 1.00
103 Clyde Drexler 3DJ .12 .30
104 Shawn Kemp 3DJ .12 .30
105 Harold Miner 3DJ .12 .30
106 Chris Webber 3DJ .75 2.00
107 Dikembe Mutombo 3DJ .12 .30
108 Doug West 3DJ .12 .30
109 Michael Jordan CL .12 .30
110 Michael Jordan CL .12 .30

2004-05 Upper Deck R-Class

COMPLETE SET (132) 15.00 40.00
COMP.SET w/o RC's (90) 8.00 20.00
91-132 STATED ODDS 2:1
1 Antoine Walker .25 .60
2 Al Harrington .20 .50
3 Boris Diaw .20 .50
4 Paul Pierce .40 1.00
5 Gary Payton .40 1.00
6 Jiri Welsch .15 .40
7 Gerald Wallace .20 .50
8 Jason Kapono .15 .40
9 Brandon Hunter .15 .40
10 Eddy Curry .15 .40
11 Kirk Hinrich .25 .60
12 Tyson Chandler .20 .50
13 LeBron James 2.00 5.00
14 Dajuan Wagner .15 .40
15 Zydrunas Ilgauskas .20 .50
16 Dirk Nowitzki .60 1.50
17 Michael Finley .25 .60
18 Jason Terry .20 .50
19 Andre Miller .20 .50
20 Carmelo Anthony .50 1.25
21 Kenyon Martin .25 .60
22 Chauncey Billups .30 .75
23 Rasheed Wallace .30 .75
24 Ben Wallace .30 .75
25 Speedy Claxton .15 .40
26 Jason Richardson .25 .60
27 Mike Dunleavy .15 .40
28 Yao Ming .60 1.50
29 Tracy McGrady .40 1.00
30 Juwan Howard .20 .50
31 Jermaine O'Neal .20 .50
32 Reggie Miller .50 1.25
33 Ron Artest .25 .60
34 Elton Brand .20 .50
35 Corey Maggette .20 .50
36 Marko Jaric .15 .40
37 Kobe Bryant 2.00 5.00
38 Devean George .15 .40
39 Lamar Odom .25 .60
40 Pau Gasol .40 1.00
41 Jason Williams .20 .50
42 Bonzi Wells .15 .40
43 Shaquille O'Neal 1.00 2.50
44 Dwyane Wade 1.00 2.50
45 Eddie Jones .25 .60
46 Michael Redd .25 .60
47 Desmond Mason .20 .50
48 T.J. Ford .15 .40
49 Latrell Sprewell .30 .75
50 Kevin Garnett .60 1.50
51 Sam Cassell .20 .50
52 Richard Jefferson .20 .50
53 Aaron Williams .15 .40
54 Jason Kidd .40 1.00
55 Jamal Mashburn .20 .50
56 Baron Davis .25 .60
57 Jamaal Magloire .15 .40
58 Allan Houston .25 .60
59 Jamal Crawford .20 .50
60 Stephon Marbury .30 .75
61 Steve Francis .25 .60
62 Kelvin Cato .15 .40
63 Cuttino Mobley .20 .50
64 Glenn Robinson .20 .50
65 Allen Iverson .60 1.50
66 Willie Green .20 .50
67 Amare Stoudemire .25 .60
68 Quentin Richardson .15 .40
69 Steve Nash .50 1.25
70 Shareef Abdur-Rahim .25 .60
71 Damon Stoudamire .25 .60
72 Zach Randolph .25 .60
73 Peja Stojakovic .20 .50
74 Chris Webber .30 .75
75 Mike Bibby .25 .60
76 Tony Parker .40 1.00
77 Tim Duncan .60 1.50
78 Manu Ginobili .50 1.25
79 Ronald Murray .15 .40
80 Ray Allen .40 1.00
81 Rashard Lewis .20 .50
82 Chris Bosh .40 1.00
83 Vince Carter .50 1.25
84 Jalen Rose .20 .50
85 Andrei Kirilenko .20 .50
86 Carlos Boozer .20 .50
87 Carlos Arroyo .15 .40
88 Gilbert Arenas .25 .60
89 Jarvis Hayes .15 .40
90 Antawn Jamison .20 .50
91 Dwight Howard RC 2.00 5.00
92 Emeka Okafor RC .50 1.25
93 Ben Gordon RC .60 1.50
94 Shaun Livingston RC .60 1.50
95 Devin Harris RC .60 1.50
96 Josh Childress RC .40 1.00
97 Luol Deng RC .60 1.50
98 Andre Iguodala RC 1.00 2.50
99 Luke Jackson RC .40 1.00
100 Andris Biedrins RC .40 1.00
101 Sebastian Telfair RC .50 1.25
102 Josh Smith RC .60 1.50
103 Rafael Araujo RC .40 1.00
104 Robert Swift RC .40 1.00
105 Kris Humphries RC .50 1.25
106 Al Jefferson RC .60 1.50
107 Kirk Snyder RC .40 1.00
108 J.R. Smith RC .60 1.50
109 Dorell Wright RC .60 1.50
110 Jameer Nelson RC .40 1.00
111 Pavel Podkolzin RC .40 1.00
112 Bernard Robinson RC .40 1.00
113 Yuta Tabuse RC .60 1.50
114 Delonte West RC .50 1.25
115 Tony Allen RC .60 1.50
116 Kevin Martin RC .75 2.00
117 Sasha Vujacic RC .50 1.25
118 Beno Udrih RC .50 1.25
119 David Harrison RC .40 1.00
120 Anderson Varejao RC .50 1.25
121 Jackson Vroman RC .40 1.00
122 Peter John Ramos RC .40 1.00
123 Lionel Chalmers RC .50 1.25
124 Donta Smith RC .40 1.00
125 Andre Emmett RC .40 1.00
126 Antonio Burks RC .40 1.00
127 Royal Ivey RC .40 1.00
128 Chris Duhon RC .50 1.25
129 Trevor Ariza RC .60 1.50
130 Tim Pickett RC .50 1.25
131 Romain Sato RC .40 1.00
132 Nenad Krstic RC .50 1.25

2004-05 Upper Deck R-Class Gold

*1-90 GOLD: 2X TO 5X BASE HI
1-90 PRINT RUN 150 SER.#'d SETS
*91-132 GOLD: 2.5X TO 6X BASE RC HI
91-132 PRINT RUN 50 SER.#'d SETS

2004-05 Upper Deck R-Class Platinum

*1-90 PLATINUM: 8X TO 20X BASE HI
1-90 PRINT RUN 25 SER.#'d SETS

2004-05 Upper Deck R-Class R-Tifacts

STATED ODDS 1:18
SP INFO PROVIDED BY UPPER DECK
AH Allan Houston 2.50 6.00
AK Andrei Kirilenko 2.00 5.00
AS Amare Stoudemire 2.50 6.00
BC Brian Cook 2.00 5.00
BD Baron Davis 2.50 6.00
BI Chauncey Billups 3.00 8.00
BM Brad Miller 2.00 5.00
BO Carlos Boozer 2.00 5.00
CA Carmelo Anthony 5.00 12.00
CB Caron Butler 2.00 5.00
CM Corey Maggette 2.00 5.00
DG Drew Gooden 1.50 4.00
DN Dirk Nowitzki 6.00 15.00
DW Dajuan Wagner 2.00 5.00
EC Eddy Curry 1.50 4.00
EG Manu Ginobili 5.00 12.00
ES Eric Snow 2.00 5.00
GA Gilbert Arenas 2.50 6.00
GP Gary Payton 4.00 10.00
JC Jamal Crawford 2.50 6.00
JM Jamaal Magloire 2.00 5.00
JO Jermaine O'Neal 2.00 5.00
JT Jason Terry 2.00 5.00
KB Kobe Bryant 40.00 100.00
KG Kevin Garnett 6.00 15.00
KM Karl Malone 5.00 12.00
LJ LeBron James 6.00 15.00
MF Michael Finley 2.50 6.00
MJ Michael Jordan SP 25.00 60.00
MP Morris Peterson 1.50 4.00
PP Paul Pierce 4.00 10.00
QR Quentin Richardson 1.50 4.00
RJ Richard Jefferson 2.00 5.00
RM Reggie Miller 5.00 12.00
SD Samuel Dalembert 2.00 5.00
SM Shawn Marion 2.50 6.00
SS Steve Smith 2.00 5.00
ST Stephon Marbury 3.00 8.00
TC Tyson Chandler 2.00 5.00
TM Tracy McGrady 4.00 10.00
VD Vlade Divac 2.50 6.00
WS Wally Szczerbiak 2.00 5.00

2004-05 Upper Deck R-Class R-Tifacts Dual

STATED ODDS 1:36
SP INFO PROVIDED BY UPPER DECK
AH G.Arenas/B.Haywood 4.00 10.00
AM C.Anthony/A.Miller 5.00 12.00
BJ K.Bryant/L.James SP 125.00 300.00
BM E.Brand/C.Maggette 4.00 10.00
CC E.Curry/T.Chandler 4.00 10.00
CW B.Cook/L.Walton 4.00 10.00
DG T.Duncan/M.Ginobili 10.00 25.00
DM B.Davis/J.Magloire 4.00 10.00
FM S.Francis/C.Mobley 4.00 10.00
GM P.Gasol/M.Miller 4.00 10.00
GS K.Garnett/W.Szczerbiak 6.00 15.00
HB D.Harrison/C.Billups 4.00 10.00
HW A.Harrington/A.Walker 4.00 10.00
JJ L.James/M.Jordan SP 60.00 150.00
KB A.Kirilenko/C.Boozer 4.00 10.00
KJ N.Krstic/R.Jefferson 4.00 10.00
KK K.Bryant/K.Malone 8.00 20.00
MF T.McGrady/S.Francis 6.00 15.00
ML R.Murray/R.Lewis 4.00 10.00
MR S.Marion/Q.Richardson 4.00 10.00
MS S.Marbury/M.Sweetney 4.00 10.00
NF D.Nowitzki/M.Finley 5.00 12.00
OH S.O'Neal/U.Haslem 6.00 15.00
PP P.Pierce/G.Payton 5.00 12.00
PR M.Peterson/J.Richardson 4.00 10.00
RF J.Richardson/D.Fisher 4.00 10.00
RM Q.Richardson/D.Miles 4.00 10.00
SJ A.Stoudemire/J.Johnson 5.00 12.00
TO J.Tinsley/J.O'Neal 4.00 10.00
WS C.Webber/P.Stojakovic 5.00 12.00

2004-05 Upper Deck R-Class R-Tifacts Triple

PRINT RUN 25 SER.#'d SETS
JJB LeBron/Jordan/Kobe 500.00 1,000.00
MGB McGrady/Garnett/Kobe 150.00 400.00

2004-05 Upper Deck R-Class R-Tifacts Signatures

PRINT RUN 50 SER.#'d SETS
AB Andris Biedrins 5.00 12.00
AI Andre Iguodala 12.00 30.00
AJ Al Jefferson 8.00 20.00
AV Anderson Varejao 6.00 15.00
BG Ben Gordon 8.00 20.00
DA David Harrison 5.00 12.00
DE Devin Harris 6.00 15.00
DF Derek Fisher 8.00 20.00
DH Dwight Howard 100.00 200.00
DO Dorell Wright 6.00 15.00
DW Delonte West 6.00 15.00
JA Jamal Crawford 10.00 25.00
JN Jameer Nelson 8.00 20.00
JR J.R. Smith 8.00 20.00
JS Josh Smith 8.00 20.00
KB Kobe Bryant 500.00 1,000.00
KH Kris Humphries 6.00 15.00

KM Kevin Martin 10.00 25.00
KS Kirk Snyder 5.00 12.00
LC Lionel Chalmers 6.00 15.00
LJ LeBron James 1,000.00 2,000.00
LU Luke Jackson 5.00 12.00
MJ Michael Jordan 1,500.00 3,000.00
NK Nenad Krstic 6.00 15.00
RA Rafael Araujo 5.00 12.00
ST Sebastian Telfair 6.00 15.00
TA Tony Allen 8.00 20.00
YT Yuta Tabuse 8.00 20.00

2004-05 Upper Deck R-Class Signatures

STATED ODDS 1:480
SP INFO PROVIDED BY UPPER DECK
AI Andre Iguodala 10.00 25.00
JR J.R. Smith 6.00 15.00
KG Kevin Garnett SP 25.00 60.00
LJ LeBron James SP 2,000.00 4,000.00

2008-09 Upper Deck Radiance

COMP.SET w/o RCs (90) 800.00 1,500.00
1-90 PRINT RUN 299 SER.#'d SETS
91-110 RC PRINT RUN 299 SER.#'d SETS
101-120 RC PRINT RUN 99 SER.#'d SETS
1 LaMarcus Aldridge 2.50 6.00
2 Ray Allen 4.00 10.00
3 Carmelo Anthony 3.00 8.00
4 Ron Artest 2.50 6.00
5 Brandon Bass 1.50 4.00
6 Chauncey Billups 3.00 8.00
7 Carlos Boozer 2.00 5.00
8 Chris Bosh 3.00 8.00
9 Elton Brand 2.00 5.00
10 Kobe Bryant 300.00 600.00
11 Caron Butler 2.00 5.00
12 Andrew Bynum 1.50 4.00
13 Jose Calderon 1.50 4.00
14 Marcus Camby 2.00 5.00
15 Vince Carter 5.00 12.00
16 Tyson Chandler 2.00 5.00
17 Wilson Chandler 2.00 5.00
18 Mike Conley Jr. 2.00 5.00
19 Jamal Crawford 2.50 6.00
20 Eddy Curry 1.50 4.00
21 Baron Davis 2.50 6.00
22 Luol Deng 2.00 5.00
23 Michael Jordan 400.00 800.00
24 Tim Duncan 6.00 15.00
25 Kevin Durant 10.00 25.00
26 Monta Ellis 2.00 5.00
27 T.J. Ford 1.50 4.00
28 Francisco Garcia 1.50 4.00
29 Kevin Garnett 6.00 15.00
30 Rudy Gay 2.50 6.00
31 Manu Ginobili 5.00 12.00
32 Ben Gordon 2.00 5.00
33 Danny Granger 2.00 5.00
34 Devin Harris 1.50 4.00
35 Al Horford 2.50 6.00
36 Dwight Howard 3.00 8.00
37 Andre Iguodala 2.00 5.00
38 Allen Iverson 5.00 12.00
39 Stephen Jackson 2.00 5.00
40 LeBron James 300.00 600.00
41 Antawn Jamison 2.00 5.00
42 Al Jefferson 1.50 4.00
43 Richard Jefferson 2.00 5.00
44 Yi Jianlian 3.00 8.00
45 Jason Kidd 4.00 10.00
46 Andrei Kirilenko 2.00 5.00
47 David Lee 1.50 4.00
48 Corey Maggette 2.00 5.00
49 Shawn Marion 2.50 6.00
50 Kenyon Martin 2.00 5.00
51 Kevin Martin 2.00 5.00
52 Desmond Mason 1.50 4.00
53 Tracy McGrady 4.00 10.00
54 Brad Miller 2.00 5.00
55 Mike Miller 2.00 5.00
56 Yao Ming 6.00 15.00
57 Jamario Moon 1.50 4.00
58 Alonzo Mourning 3.00 8.00
59 Steve Nash 5.00 12.00
60 Joakim Noah 1.50 4.00
61 Dirk Nowitzki 6.00 15.00
62 Shaquille O'Neal 8.00 20.00
63 Greg Oden 1.50 4.00
64 Lamar Odom 2.00 5.00
65 Tony Parker 3.00 8.00
66 Chris Paul 5.00 12.00
67 Paul Pierce 4.00 10.00
68 Tayshaun Prince 2.50 6.00
69 Michael Redd 2.00 5.00
70 Jason Richardson 2.50 6.00
71 Brandon Roy 2.50 6.00
72 Luis Scola 2.00 5.00
73 Ramon Sessions 1.50 4.00
74 Josh Smith 1.50 4.00
75 Amare Stoudemire 2.50 6.00
76 Rodney Stuckey 1.50 4.00
77 Al Thornton 1.50 4.00
78 Hedo Turkoglu 2.00 5.00
79 Dwyane Wade 5.00 12.00
80 Ben Wallace 3.00 8.00
81 Gerald Wallace 2.00 5.00
82 Rasheed Wallace 3.00 8.00
83 David West 2.00 5.00
84 Chris Wilcox 1.50 4.00
85 Deron Williams 2.00 5.00
86 Louis Williams 2.00 5.00
87 Marvin Williams 1.50 4.00
88 Mo Williams 2.00 5.00
89 Brandan Wright 1.50 4.00
90 Thaddeus Young 2.00 5.00
91 Joe Alexander AU RC 3.00 8.00
92 Mario Chalmers AU RC 5.00 12.00
93 Joey Dorsey AU RC 3.00 8.00
94 Darrell Arthur AU RC 4.00 10.00
95 Rudy Fernandez AU RC 4.00 10.00
96 Marc Gasol AU RC 10.00 25.00
97 J.R. Giddens AU RC 3.00 8.00
98 Donte Greene AU RC 3.00 8.00
99 Roy Hibbert AU RC 4.00 10.00
100 J.J. Hickson AU RC 3.00 8.00
101 George Hill AU RC 5.00 12.00
102 Robin Lopez AU RC 4.00 10.00
103 A.Randolph AU RC 3.00 8.00
104 Brandon Rush AU RC 3.00 8.00
105 Walter Sharpe AU RC 3.00 8.00
106 Marreese Speights AU RC 4.00 10.00
107 Jason Thompson AU RC 3.00 8.00
108 Kyle Weaver AU RC 3.00 8.00
109 Sonny Weems AU RC 3.00 8.00
110 D.J. White AU RC 3.00 8.00
81RC D.J. Augustin AU RC 10.00 25.00
82RC Jerryd Bayless AU RC 8.00 20.00
83RC Michael Beasley AU RC 10.00 25.00
84RC Danilo Gallinari AU RC 15.00 40.00
85RC Eric Gordon AU RC 15.00 40.00
86RC Brook Lopez AU RC 12.00 30.00
87RC Kevin Love AU RC 20.00 50.00
88RC O.J. Mayo AU RC 8.00 20.00
89RC Derrick Rose AU RC 75.00 200.00
90RC Russell Westbrook AU RC 150.00 400.00

2008-09 Upper Deck Radiance AU Standard

STATED PRINT RUN 10 TO 25 SER.#'d SETS
AUAD Adrian Dantley/25 6.00 15.00
AUAG Artis Gilmore/25 12.00 30.00
AUAH Al Horford/25 12.00 30.00
AUBR Brandon Roy/25 10.00 25.00
AUCL Carl Landry/25 6.00 15.00
AUCP Chris Paul/25 125.00 300.00
AUDA D.J. Augustin/25 6.00 15.00
AUDH Dwight Howard/25 40.00 100.00
AUDR Derrick Rose/25 200.00 500.00
AUEG Eric Gordon/25 10.00 25.00
AUGG George Gervin/25 15.00 40.00
AUJA Joe Alexander/25 6.00 15.00
AUJB Jerryd Bayless/25 6.00 15.00
AUJG J.R. Giddens/25 6.00 15.00
AULJ LeBron James/23 2,000.00 4,000.00
AULW Luke Walton/25 8.00 20.00
AUMA Morris Almond/25 6.00 15.00
AUMB Michael Beasley/25 8.00 20.00
AUMJ Michael Jordan/23 3,000.00 6,000.00
AUOM O.J. Mayo/25 8.00 20.00
AUPP Paul Pierce/25 40.00 100.00
AURF Rudy Fernandez/25 8.00 20.00
AURR Rajon Rondo/25 20.00 50.00
AURW Russell Westbrook/25 300.00 600.00
AUSW Sonny Weems/25 6.00 15.00
AUTC Tom Chambers/25 6.00 15.00
AUYM Yao Ming/25 400.00 800.00

2008-09 Upper Deck Radiance Auto Focus

APPROXIMATE ODDS 1:6
AFBE Marco Belinelli 6.00 15.00
AFCL Carl Landry 6.00 15.00
AFDH Dwight Howard SP 12.00 30.00
AFDR Derrick Rose SP 150.00 400.00
AFDW Deron Williams 6.00 15.00
AFGH George Hill 6.00 15.00
AFJF Jordan Farmar 6.00 15.00
AFJG J.R. Giddens 6.00 15.00
AFKB Kobe Bryant SP 500.00 1,000.00
AFKG Kevin Garnett SP 75.00 200.00
AFLJ LeBron James SP 2,000.00 4,000.00
AFMB Michael Beasley 8.00 20.00
AFMC Mario Chalmers 6.00 15.00
AFMJ Michael Jordan 800.00 1,500.00
AFOM O.J. Mayo SP 8.00 20.00
AFRF Rudy Fernandez 6.00 15.00
AFRR Rajon Rondo 12.00 30.00

2008-09 Upper Deck Radiance Auto Focus Dual

STATED PRINT RUN 10 TO 25 SER.#'d SETS
AFDBF Farmar/Bynum/25 15.00 40.00
AFDCC Cook/Chalmers/25 15.00 40.00
AFDDH Durant/Horford/25 400.00 800.00
AFDJB Bird/M.Johnson/25 1,000.00 2,000.00
AFDJE M.Jordan/Erving/25 1,500.00 3,000.00
AFDMB O.J.Mayo/Beasley/25 15.00 40.00
AFDPG K.Garnett/Pierce/25 500.00 1,000.00
AFDRH Rush/Hibbert/25 15.00 40.00

2008-09 Upper Deck Radiance Diplomatic Autographs

APPROXIMATE ODDS 1:3
DIAD Adrian Dantley 5.00 12.00
DICD Clyde Drexler 20.00 50.00
DIDG Donte Greene 5.00 12.00
DIDH Dwight Howard SP 20.00 50.00
DIDR David Robinson SP 30.00 80.00
DIDW D.J. White 5.00 12.00
DIJC Javaris Crittenton 5.00 12.00
DIJK Jason Kidd SP 30.00 80.00
DIJO Magic Johnson 75.00 200.00
DIKB Kobe Bryant SP 1,500.00 3,000.00
DIKG Kevin Garnett 125.00 300.00
DILJ LeBron James 1,500.00 3,000.00
DIMB Michael Beasley SP 12.00 30.00
DIMJ Michael Jordan 2,500.00 5,000.00
DIMP Mark Price 15.00 40.00
DIRF Randy Foye 5.00 12.00
DIRH Richard Hendrix 5.00 12.00
DIRJ Richard Jefferson 5.00 12.00
DITP Tayshaun Prince 8.00 20.00
DIVC Vince Carter 40.00 100.00

2008-09 Upper Deck Radiance Inked

STATED PRINT RUN 10 TO 99 SER.#'d SETS
IAL Acie Law/99 4.00 10.00
IBE Michael Beasley/99 4.00 10.00
ICW C.J. Watson/99 4.00 10.00
IDE Deron Williams/99 4.00 10.00
IDG Donte Greene/99 4.00 10.00
IEC Eddy Curry/99 4.00 10.00
IGH George Hill/99 4.00 10.00
IJF Jordan Farmar/99 4.00 10.00
IJS Josh Smith/99 4.00 10.00
ILA LaMarcus Aldridge/99 10.00 25.00
ILJ LeBron James/23 1,500.00 3,000.00
IMB Mike Bibby/99 10.00 25.00
IMW Mo Williams/99 4.00 10.00
IQR Quentin Richardson/99 4.00 10.00
IRB Ronnie Brewer/99 4.00 10.00
ISM J.R. Smith/99 4.00 10.00
ITT Tyrus Thomas/99 4.00 10.00
IWE David West/99 4.00 10.00

2008-09 Upper Deck Radiance Marks Dual

STATED PRINT RUN 10 TO 50 SER.#'d SETS
DMBW D.Williams/Boozer/50 8.00 20.00
DMCB D.Cook/Beasley/50 8.00 20.00
DMGF Fernandez/Gasol/50 15.00 40.00
DMGM O.J. Mayo/R.Gay/50 10.00 25.00
DMGR Gordon/D.Rose/50 75.00 200.00
DMPG K.Garnett/Pierce/50 400.00 800.00
DMSA W.Sharpe/Afflalo/50 8.00 20.00
DMSW J.R.Smith/Weems/50 8.00 20.00

2008-09 Upper Deck Radiance Name Tag Autographs

APPROXIMATE ODDS 1:3
NTAA Alexis Ajinca 4.00 10.00
NTBW Bill Walker 4.00 10.00
NTDA D.J. Augustin SP 8.00 20.00
NTDG Danilo Gallinari 6.00 15.00
NTDR Derrick Rose SP 125.00 300.00
NTDW D.J. White 4.00 10.00
NTGH George Hill 5.00 12.00
NTGR Donte Greene 4.00 10.00
NTJA Joe Alexander 4.00 10.00
NTJB Jerryd Bayless SP 6.00 15.00
NTJJ J.J. Hickson 4.00 10.00
NTJM Javale McGee 5.00 12.00
NTJT Jason Thompson 4.00 10.00
NTKL Kevin Love SP 25.00 60.00
NTLM Luc Richard Mbah A Moute 4.00 10.00
NTMB Michael Beasley 6.00 15.00
NTMC Mario Chalmers 5.00 12.00
NTMT Mike Taylor 4.00 10.00
NTOM O.J. Mayo SP 20.00 40.00
NTRF Rudy Fernandez 4.00 10.00
NTRH Roy Hibbert 4.00 10.00
NTRW Russell Westbrook SP 200.00 500.00
NTSS Sean Singletary 4.00 10.00
NTSW Sonny Weems 4.00 10.00
NTWS Walter Sharpe 4.00 10.00

2008-09 Upper Deck Radiance Signature Flight

APPROXIMATE ODDS 1:3
SFAB Aaron Brooks 4.00 10.00
SFAT Al Thornton SP 4.00 10.00
SFDH Dwight Howard SP 20.00 50.00
SFDT David Thompson 6.00 15.00
SFDW Dominique Wilkins SP 20.00 50.00
SFJF Jordan Farmar SP 4.00 10.00
SFJG J.R. Giddens 4.00 10.00
SFKB Kobe Bryant SP 1,000.00 2,000.00
SFLJ LeBron James 1,000.00 2,000.00
SFMJ Michael Jordan 2,000.00 4,000.00
SFQR Quentin Richardson SP 4.00 10.00
SFRB Ronnie Brewer 4.00 10.00
SFSS Stromile Swift SP 4.00 10.00
SFSW Sonny Weems 4.00 10.00
SFTM Tracy McGrady 20.00 50.00
SFTP Tayshaun Prince SP 8.00 20.00
SFWE Spud Webb SP 12.00 30.00

2008-09 Upper Deck Radiance Sweet Shot Autographs

APPROXIMATE ODDS 1:6
SSAA Arron Afflalo 4.00 10.00
SSBB Bruce Bowen 12.00 30.00
SSBG Ben Gordon SP 6.00 15.00
SSBM Brad Miller 4.00 10.00
SSBO Andrew Bogut 6.00 15.00
SSCB Carlos Boozer 8.00 20.00
SSCM Corey Maggette SP 6.00 15.00
SSCP Chris Paul 75.00 200.00
SSCS Cedric Simmons 4.00 10.00
SSDG Danny Granger 4.00 10.00
SSDH Dwight Howard SP 25.00 60.00
SSGD Glen Davis 4.00 10.00
SSGI Daniel Gibson SP 4.00 10.00
SSGP Gabe Pruitt 4.00 10.00
SSHA Devin Harris 4.00 10.00
SSJB Josh Boone 4.00 10.00
SSKV Kiki Vandeweghe SP 6.00 15.00
SSLA LaMarcus Aldridge SP 12.00 30.00
SSMA Morris Almond 4.00 10.00
SSMW Marvin Williams 4.00 10.00
SSNR Nate Robinson 4.00 10.00
SSRB Ronnie Brewer SP 4.00 10.00
SSSB Shannon Brown 4.00 10.00
SSSK Steve Kerr 25.00 60.00
SSTP Tony Parker 20.00 50.00

2008-09 Upper Deck Radiance Writing Samples

STATED PRINT RUN 50 SER.#'d SETS
WSAB A.Afflalo/M.Belinelli 10.00 25.00
WSBH S.Battier/D.Howard 20.00 50.00
WSDA K.Durant/D.J.Augustin 150.00 400.00
WSGR G.Hill/R.Hibbert 10.00 25.00
WSGS G.Gervin/R.Stuckey 10.00 25.00
WSJD G.Davis/L.Johnson 15.00 40.00
WSLL B.Lopez/R.Lopez 10.00 25.00
WSLP B.Laimbeer/T.Prince 12.00 30.00
WSLW R.Westbrook/K.Love 100.00 250.00
WSPG K.Garnett/P.Pierce 125.00 300.00
WSRC B.Rush/M.Chalmers 10.00 25.00
WSWR J.Wilkes/D.Rodman 40.00 100.00

1999-00 Upper Deck Retro

COMPLETE SET (110) 20.00 40.00
1 Michael Jordan 2.50 6.00
2 John Havlicek .30 .75
3 Antawn Jamison .25 .60
4 Chris Webber .30 .75
5 Maurice Taylor .15 .40
6 Kevin Garnett .60 1.50
7 Walter Davis .25 .60
8 Kobe Bryant 2.00 5.00
9 Tim Duncan .60 1.50
10 Karl Malone .60 1.50
11 Larry Bird .60 1.50
12 Juwan Howard .20 .50
13 Bill Walton .25 .60
14 Bob Cousy .40 1.00
15 Dave DeBusschere .25 .60
16 Toni Kukoc .30 .75
17 Allan Houston .20 .50
18 Grant Hill .40 1.00
19 Rik Smits .20 .50
20 Glenn Robinson .20 .50
21 Dave Cowens .20 .50
22 Isaac Austin .15 .40
23 Derek Anderson .15 .40
24 Tracy McGrady .40 1.00
25 Nate Thurmond .20 .50
26 Dikembe Mutombo .40 1.00
27 Oscar Robertson .30 .75
28 Antonio McDyess .20 .50
29 Jamaal Wilkes .20 .50
30 Eddie Jones .25 .60
31 Nick Van Exel .20 .50
32 Reggie Miller .50 1.25
33 David Thompson .20 .50
34 Ray Allen .40 1.00
35 Anfernee Hardaway .60 1.50
36 Brian Grant .15 .40
37 Allen Iverson .60 1.50
38 Vince Carter .60 1.50
39 Mitch Richmond .30 .75
40 Kareem Abdul-Jabbar .40 1.00
41 Alonzo Mourning .40 1.00
42 Jonathan Bender RC .30 .75
43 Scottie Pippen .60 1.50
44 George Gervin .25 .60
45 Shawn Kemp .40 1.00
46 Dave Bing .25 .60
47 John Starks .25 .60
48 Earl Monroe .25 .60
49 Stephon Marbury .30 .75
50 Cedric Maxwell .15 .40
51 Tom Gugliotta .20 .50
52 David Robinson .50 1.25
53 Shareef Abdur-Rahim .25 .60
54 Elvin Hayes .25 .60
55 Wilt Chamberlain .50 1.25
56 Willis Reed .40 1.00
57 Kevin McHale .30 .75
58 Elden Campbell .15 .40
59 Steve Smith .20 .50
60 Brent Barry .20 .50
61 Jerry Stackhouse .25 .60
62 Otis Birdsong .20 .50
63 Michael Olowokandi .15 .40
64 Joe Smith .20 .50
65 Tim Thomas .20 .50
66 Rick Barry .25 .60
67 Jason Williams .40 1.00
68 Julius Erving .60 1.50
69 John Stockton .40 1.00
70 Cal Bowdler RC .20 .50
71 Nate Archibald .20 .50
72 Elgin Baylor .25 .60
73 Ron Mercer .20 .50
74 Damon Stoudamire .25 .60
75 Jerry West .40 1.00
76 Michael Finley .25 .60
77 Charles Barkley .60 1.50
78 Shaquille O'Neal 1.00 2.50
79 Paul Pierce .50 1.25
80 Keith Van Horn .20 .50
81 Jason Kidd .40 1.00
82 Gary Payton .40 1.00
83 James Worthy .30 .75
84 Mike Bibby .25 .60
85 Bill Russell .40 1.00
86 Wes Unseld .25 .60
87 Robert Parish .25 .60
88 Walt Frazier .25 .60
89 Antoine Walker .25 .60
90 Steve Nash .50 1.25
91 Moses Malone .25 .60
92 Hakeem Olajuwon .50 1.25
93 Tim Hardaway .30 .75
94 Patrick Ewing .30 .75
95 Vin Baker .20 .50
96 Trajan Langdon RC .30 .75
97 Ron Artest RC .75 2.00
98 James Posey RC .30 .75
99 Shawn Marion RC .60 1.50
100 Jumaine Jones RC .20 .50
101 William Avery RC .20 .50
102 Corey Maggette RC .40 1.00
103 Andre Miller RC .60 1.50
104 Jason Terry RC .50 1.25
105 Wally Szczerbiak RC .50 1.25
106 Richard Hamilton RC .75 2.00
107 Elton Brand RC .60 1.50
108 Baron Davis RC .75 2.00
109 Steve Francis RC .60 1.50
110 Lamar Odom RC .60 1.50

1999-00 Upper Deck Retro Gold

*STARS: 6X TO 15X BASE CARD HI
*RCs: 3X TO 8X BASE HI
STATED PRINT RUN 250 SERIAL #'d SETS

1999-00 Upper Deck Retro Distant Replay

COMPLETE SET (10) 12.50 25.00
STATED ODDS 1:11
*PARALLEL: 2.5X TO 6X HI COLUMN
PARALLEL: PRINT RUN 100 SERIAL #'d SETS
D1 Michael Jordan 8.00 20.00
D2 Kareem Abdul-Jabbar 1.25 3.00
D3 Bill Russell 1.25 3.00
D4 Julius Erving 2.00 5.00
D5 George Gervin .75 2.00
D6 Moses Malone .75 2.00
D7 Larry Bird 2.00 5.00
D8 Jerry West 1.25 3.00
D9 Oscar Robertson 1.00 2.50
D10 Elgin Baylor .75 2.00

1999-00 Upper Deck Retro Epic Jordan

COMPLETE SET (10) 12.00 30.00
COMMON CARD (J1-J10) 2.50 6.00
STATED ODDS 1:23

1999-00 Upper Deck Retro Epic Jordan Parallel

COMMON CARD (J1-J10) 60.00 150.00
STATED PRINT RUN 50 SERIAL #'d SETS

1999-00 Upper Deck Retro Fast Forward

COMPLETE SET (15) 15.00 40.00
STATED ODDS 1:23
F1 Kevin Garnett 2.50 6.00
F2 Kobe Bryant 8.00 20.00
F3 Keith Van Horn .75 2.00
F4 Allen Iverson 2.50 6.00
F5 Vince Carter 2.50 6.00
F6 Paul Pierce 2.00 5.00
F7 Shareef Abdur-Rahim 1.00 2.50
F8 Jason Williams 1.50 4.00
F9 Tim Duncan 2.50 6.00
F10 Shaquille O'Neal 4.00 10.00
F11 Scottie Pippen 2.50 6.00
F12 Anfernee Hardaway 2.50 6.00
F13 Antawn Jamison 1.00 2.50
F14 Antonio McDyess .75 2.00
F15 Stephon Marbury 1.25 3.00

1999-00 Upper Deck Retro Inkredible

STATED ODDS 1:23
AH Anfernee Hardaway 75.00 200.00
AJ Antawn Jamison 6.00 15.00
BC Bob Cousy 75.00 200.00
BG Brian Grant 10.00 25.00
BR Bill Russell 4,000.00 8,000.00
CA Cory Alexander 5.00 12.00
DA Darrell Armstrong 5.00 12.00
EH Elvin Hayes 10.00 25.00
ES Eric Snow 5.00 12.00
GG George Gervin 25.00 60.00
GR Glen Rice 25.00 60.00
JH John Havlicek 60.00 150.00
JR Jalen Rose 10.00 25.00
JW Jerry West 100.00 250.00
MB Mookie Blaylock 12.00 30.00
MJ Mark Jackson 5.00 12.00
MT Maurice Taylor 5.00 12.00
NA Nate Archibald 12.00 30.00
RL Raef LaFrentz 8.00 20.00
RT Robert Traylor 15.00 40.00
TK Toni Kukoc 30.00 80.00
VC Vince Carter 100.00 250.00
WC Wilt Chamberlain 6,000.00 12,000.00
WF Walt Frazier 40.00 100.00

1999-00 Upper Deck Retro Inkredible Level 2

PRINT RUN TO PLAYER'S JERSEY #
BG Brian Grant/44 20.00 50.00
ES Eric Snow/20 20.00 50.00
GG George Gervin/44 50.00 120.00
GR Glen Rice/41 50.00 120.00
JH John Havlicek/17 125.00 300.00
JW Jerry West/44 125.00 300.00
MJ Michael Jordan/23 25,000.00 50,000.00
MT Maurice Taylor/23 12.00 30.00
RL Raef LaFrentz/45 20.00 50.00
RT Robert Traylor/54 30.00 80.00
VC Vince Carter/15 200.00 500.00

1999-00 Upper Deck Retro Lunchboxes

1 Larry Bird 6.00 15.00
2 Julius Erving 6.00 15.00
3 J.Erving/L.Bird 6.00 15.00
4 Michael Jordan #1 6.00 15.00
5 Michael Jordan #2 6.00 15.00
6 Michael Jordan #3 6.00 15.00
7 M.Jordan/L.Bird 6.00 15.00
8 M.Jordan/J.Erving 6.00 15.00
9 M.Jordan #1
M.Jordan #2 6.00 15.00
10 M.Jordan #1
M.Jordan #3 6.00 15.00
11 M.Jordan #2
M.Jordan #3 6.00 15.00

1999-00 Upper Deck Retro Old School/New School

COMPLETE SET (30) 12.50 30.00
STATED ODDS 1:3
*PARALLEL: 2X TO 5X HI COLUMN
PARALLEL: PRINT RUN 500 SERIAL #'d SETS
S1 Michael Jordan 4.00 10.00
S2 Wilt Chamberlain .75 2.00
S3 Oscar Robertson .50 1.25
S4 Julius Erving 1.00 2.50
S5 George Gervin .40 1.00
S6 John Havlicek .50 1.25
S7 Elgin Baylor .40 1.00
S8 Earl Monroe .40 1.00
S9 Jerry West .60 1.50
S10 Larry Bird 1.00 2.50
S11 Elvin Hayes .40 1.00
S12 Moses Malone .40 1.00
S13 Bill Walton .40 1.00
S14 Kareem Abdul-Jabbar .60 1.50
S15 Bill Russell .60 1.50
S16 Kobe Bryant 3.00 8.00
S17 Allen Iverson 1.00 2.50
S18 Stephon Marbury .50 1.25
S19 Shaquille O'Neal 1.50 4.00
S20 Kevin Garnett 1.00 2.50
S21 Keith Van Horn .30 .75
S22 Jason Williams .60 1.50
S23 Paul Pierce .75 2.00
S24 Vince Carter 1.00 2.50
S25 Tim Duncan 1.00 2.50
S26 Antoine Walker .40 1.00
S27 Shareef Abdur-Rahim .40 1.00
S28 Ray Allen .60 1.50
S29 Anfernee Hardaway 1.00 2.50
S30 Grant Hill .60 1.50

2004-05 Upper Deck Rivals Box Set

COMPLETE SET (30) 8.00 20.00
COMMON LEBRON (1-13) .60 1.50
COMMON CARMELO (14-26) .30 .75
COMMON DUAL (27-30) .40 1.00
KCLJ LeBron James Jumbo 1.25 3.00

2004-05 Upper Deck Rivals Box Set Gold

*GOLD SINGLES: 1.25X TO 3X BASE HI

2004-05 Upper Deck Rivals Box Set Platinum

LEBRON PRINT RUN 23 SER.#'d SETS
CARMELO PRINT RUN 15 SER.#'d SETS
COMMON COMBO (27-30) 40.00 100.00
COMBO PRINT RUN 38 SER.#'d SETS

2005-06 Upper Deck Rookie Debut

COMPLETE SET (150) 40.00 80.00
COMP.SET w/o RC's (100) 15.00 40.00
1 Tony Delk .15 .40
2 Josh Smith .20 .50
3 Al Harrington .20 .50
4 Antoine Walker .20 .50
5 Ricky Davis .20 .50
6 Paul Pierce .40 1.00
7 Kareem Rush .15 .40
8 Emeka Okafor .20 .50
9 Primoz Brezec .15 .40
10 Eddy Curry .15 .40
11 Kirk Hinrich .20 .50
12 Ben Gordon .20 .50
13 Luol Deng .20 .50
14 Drew Gooden .20 .50
15 LeBron James 2.00 5.00
16 Zydrunas Ilgauskas .20 .50
17 Dirk Nowitzki .60 1.50
18 Jason Terry .20 .50
19 Josh Howard .20 .50
20 Michael Finley .25 .60
21 Carmelo Anthony .40 1.00
22 Kenyon Martin .20 .50
23 Andre Miller .20 .50
24 Earl Boykins .15 .40
25 Ben Wallace .30 .75
26 Chauncey Billups .30 .75
27 Richard Hamilton .30 .75
28 Tayshaun Prince .25 .60
29 Troy Murphy .15 .40
30 Jason Richardson .25 .60
31 Baron Davis .25 .60
32 Tracy McGrady .40 1.00
33 Yao Ming .50 1.25
34 Juwan Howard .20 .50
35 Jermaine O'Neal .20 .50
36 Stephen Jackson .20 .50
37 Ron Artest .20 .50
38 Corey Maggette .20 .50
39 Elton Brand .20 .50
40 Bobby Simmons .15 .40
41 Caron Butler .20 .50
42 Kobe Bryant 2.00 5.00
43 Lamar Odom .20 .50
44 Mike Miller .20 .50
45 Jason Williams .40 1.00
46 Pau Gasol .40 1.00
47 Stromile Swift .15 .40
48 Dwyane Wade .50 1.25
49 Eddie Jones .20 .50
50 Shaquille O'Neal .75 2.00
51 Desmond Mason .15 .40
52 Maurice Williams .20 .50
53 Michael Redd .20 .50
54 Kevin Garnett .60 1.50
55 Latrell Sprewell .25 .60
56 Sam Cassell .20 .50
57 Vince Carter .50 1.25
58 Jason Kidd .40 1.00
59 Richard Jefferson .20 .50
60 Dan Dickau .15 .40
61 Jamaal Magloire .15 .40
62 J.R. Smith .25 .60
63 Jamal Crawford .25 .60
64 Stephon Marbury .30 .75
65 Allan Houston .20 .50
66 Dwight Howard .30 .75
67 Grant Hill .40 1.00
68 Steve Francis .25 .60
69 Allen Iverson .50 1.25
70 Andre Iguodala .25 .60
71 Chris Webber .30 .75
72 Kyle Korver .20 .50
73 Amare Stoudemire .25 .60
74 Shawn Marion .25 .60
75 Steve Nash .50 1.25
76 Quentin Richardson .15 .40
77 Damon Stoudamire .25 .60
78 Shareef Abdur-Rahim .25 .60
79 Zach Randolph .25 .60
80 Brad Miller .25 .60
81 Mike Bibby .25 .60
82 Peja Stojakovic .25 .60
83 Cuttino Mobley .15 .40
84 Manu Ginobili .50 1.25
85 Tim Duncan .60 1.50
86 Tony Parker .40 1.00
87 Rashard Lewis .20 .50
88 Ray Allen .40 1.00
89 Luke Ridnour .20 .50
90 Vladimir Radmanovic .15 .40
91 Rafer Alston .20 .50
92 Jalen Rose .20 .50
93 Chris Bosh .30 .75
94 Andrei Kirilenko .25 .60
95 Carlos Boozer .20 .50
96 Matt Harpring .15 .40
97 Antawn Jamison .20 .50
98 Gilbert Arenas .25 .60
99 Larry Hughes .20 .50
100 Jarvis Hayes .15 .40
101 Andrew Bogut RC 1.00 2.50
102 Chris Taft RC .50 1.25
103 Chris Paul RC 4.00 10.00
104 Martynas Andriuskevicius RC .50 1.25
105 Amir Johnson RC .75 2.00
106 Andrew Bynum RC .60 1.50
107 Gerald Green RC .75 2.00
108 Rashad McCants RC .50 1.25
109 Fran Vazquez RC .50 1.25
110 Ike Diogu RC .50 1.25
111 Raymond Felton RC .60 1.50
112 Hakim Warrick RC .60 1.50
113 Deron Williams RC 1.25 3.00
114 Daniel Ewing RC .50 1.25
115 Sean May RC .50 1.25
116 Johan Petro RC .50 1.25
117 Erazem Lorbek RC .75 2.00
118 Joey Graham RC .60 1.50
119 Antoine Wright RC .60 1.50
120 Ronny Turiaf RC .75 2.00
121 Linas Kleiza RC .60 1.50
122 Alex Acker RC .50 1.25
123 Jarrett Jack RC .75 2.00
124 Danny Granger RC .75 2.00
125 Francisco Garcia RC .50 1.25
126 Ryan Gomes RC .60 1.50
127 Wayne Simien RC .50 1.25
128 Robert Whaley RC .50 1.25
129 Dijon Thompson RC .50 1.25
130 Nate Robinson RC .75 2.00
131 Brandon Bass RC .60 1.50
132 Andray Blatche RC .75 2.00
133 Channing Frye RC .60 1.50
134 Salim Stoudamire RC .60 1.50
135 Luther Head RC .50 1.25
136 Julius Hodge RC .50 1.25
137 David Lee RC .75 2.00
138 Travis Diener RC .50 1.25
139 Marvin Williams RC .75 2.00
140 Lawrence Roberts RC .50 1.25
141 C.J. Miles RC .60 1.50
142 Ricky Sanchez RC .75 2.00
143 Bracey Wright RC .50 1.25
144 Jason Maxiell RC .60 1.50
145 Uros Slokar RC .75 2.00
146 Martell Webster RC .60 1.50
147 Orien Greene RC .60 1.50
148 Charlie Villanueva RC .60 1.50
149 Monta Ellis RC 1.00 2.50
150 Von Wafer RC .50 1.25

2005-06 Upper Deck Rookie Debut Blue

*1-100 BLUE: 2X TO 5X BASE HI
*101-150 RC BLUE: .6X TO 1.5X BASE HI
BLUE PRINT RUN 150 SER.#'d SETS

2005-06 Upper Deck Rookie Debut Gold

*1-100 GOLD: 5X TO 12X BASE HI
*101-150 RC GOLD: 1.5X TO 4X BASE HI
PRINT RUN 50 SER.#'d SETS

2005-06 Upper Deck Rookie Debut Silver

*1-100 SILVER: 3X TO 8X BASE HI
*101-150 RC SILVER: 1X TO 2.5X BASE HI
PRINT RUN 100 SER.#'d SETS

2005-06 Upper Deck Rookie Debut Spectrum

*1-100 SPEC: 8X TO 20X BASE HI
101-150 SPEC: 3X TO 6X BASE HI
PRINT RUN 25 SER.#'d SETS

2005-06 Upper Deck Rookie Debut Draft Duos

PRINT RUN 25 TO 75 SER.#'d SETS
AP Andriuskevicius/Petro/75 6.00 15.00
BT A.Bogut/C.Taft/75 10.00 25.00
EB A.Emmett/A.Burks/75 6.00 15.00
EM M.Ellis/C.J.Miles/75 10.00 25.00
FM R.Felton/R.McCants/75 8.00 20.00
FS C.Frye/S.Stoudamire/75 8.00 20.00
GG R.Gomes/D.Granger/75 10.00 25.00
GM G.Green/C.J.Miles/75 10.00 25.00
HN D.Howard/J.Nelson/75 15.00 40.00
JA LeBron/Carmelo/25 1,250.00 2,500.00
JG R.Jefferson/P.Gasol/75 15.00 40.00
LG D.Lee/F.Garcia/75 10.00 25.00
PU P.Podkolzin/B.Udrih/75 6.00 15.00
PW C.Paul/D.Williams/75 40.00 80.00
RD K.Rush/D.Dickau/75 6.00 15.00
RW J.Reed/Del.West/75 6.00 15.00
SP H.Seung-Jin/P.Podkolzin/75 6.00 15.00
TH Thompson/J.Hodge/75 6.00 15.00
TS R.Turiaf/W.Simien/75 10.00 25.00
VD F.Vazquez/T.Diener/75 6.00 15.00
WM M.Williams/S.May/75 6.00 15.00
WV H.Warrick/C.Villanueva/75 8.00 20.00
WW A.Wright/M.Webster/75 8.00 20.00

2005-06 Upper Deck Rookie Debut Hotagraphs

SIX AUTO's PER HOT PACK
HOT PACK STATED ODDS 1:336
ABA Andrew Bogut SP 8.00 20.00
ANA Andres Nocioni 5.00 12.00
AWA Antoine Wright 4.00 10.00
CDA Chris Duhon 3.00 8.00
CFA Channing Frye SP 4.00 10.00
CPA Chris Paul SP 50.00 120.00
CTA Chris Taft 3.00 8.00
CVA Charlie Villanueva 4.00 10.00
DEA Daniel Ewing 4.00 10.00
DHA Dwight Howard 8.00 20.00
DWA Deron Williams SP 8.00 20.00
FVA Fran Vazquez 3.00 8.00
GGA Gerald Green SP 5.00 12.00
HWA Hakim Warrick 4.00 10.00
JGA Joey Graham 4.00 10.00
JHA Julius Hodge 3.00 8.00
JNA Jameer Nelson 3.00 8.00
JRA J.R. Smith 5.00 12.00
LHA Luther Head 3.00 8.00
LJA LeBron James SP 2,000.00 4,000.00
MAA Martell Webster 4.00 10.00
MWA Marvin Williams SP 5.00 12.00
RFA Raymond Felton 4.00 10.00
RGA Ryan Gomes 4.00 10.00
RMA Rashad McCants 3.00 8.00
RTA Ronny Turiaf 5.00 12.00
SMA Sean May SP 4.00 10.00
SSA Salim Stoudamire 4.00 10.00

2005-06 Upper Deck Rookie Debut Ink

STATED ODDS 1:14
AB Andrew Bogut SP 6.00 15.00
AE Andre Emmett 3.00 8.00
AJ Al Jefferson 3.00 8.00
AN Antonio Burks 3.00 8.00
AV Anderson Varejao 3.00 8.00
AW Antoine Wright 4.00 10.00
BI Andris Biedrins 3.00 8.00
BL Andray Blatche 5.00 12.00
BR Bernard Robinson 3.00 8.00
BU Beno Udrih 3.00 8.00
BW Bracey Wright 3.00 8.00
BY Andrew Bynum 4.00 10.00
CB Chauncey Billups SP 6.00 15.00
CD Chris Duhon 3.00 8.00
CF Channing Frye 4.00 10.00

CJ C.J. Miles 4.00 10.00
CP Chris Paul SP 40.00 100.00
CT Chris Taft 3.00 8.00
CV Charlie Villanueva 4.00 10.00
DA Danny Granger 5.00 12.00
DD Dan Dickau 3.00 8.00
DE Daniel Ewing 4.00 10.00
DH Dwight Howard 8.00 20.00
DL David Lee 5.00 12.00
DT Dijon Thompson 3.00 8.00
DW Deron Williams SP 8.00 20.00
ED Erik Daniels 3.00 8.00
FG Francisco Garcia 3.00 8.00
FV Fran Vazquez 3.00 8.00
GG Gerald Green 5.00 12.00
HS Ha Seung-Jin 3.00 8.00
HW Hakim Warrick 4.00 10.00
ID Ike Diogu 3.00 8.00
JE John Edwards 3.00 8.00
JH Julius Hodge 3.00 8.00
JJ Jarrett Jack 5.00 12.00
JM Jason Maxiell 4.00 10.00
JN Jameer Nelson 3.00 8.00
JP Johan Petro 3.00 8.00
JR J.R. Smith 5.00 12.00
JU Justin Reed 3.00 8.00
JW Jawad Williams 3.00 8.00
KD Keyon Dooling 3.00 8.00
KS Kirk Snyder 3.00 8.00
LC Lionel Chalmers 3.00 8.00
LF Luis Flores 3.00 8.00
LH Luther Head 3.00 8.00
LJ LeBron James SP 1,000.00 2,000.00
MA Martynas Andriuskevicius 3.00 8.00
MD Marquis Daniels 3.00 8.00
ME Monta Ellis 6.00 15.00
MG Mickael Gelabale 5.00 12.00
ML Martell Webster 4.00 10.00
MR Michael Redd SP 8.00 20.00
MW Marvin Williams SP 5.00 12.00
NO Andres Nocioni 3.00 8.00
NR Nate Robinson 5.00 12.00
PP Pavel Podkolzin 3.00 8.00
RA Rafael Araujo 3.00 8.00
RF Raymond Felton 4.00 10.00
RG Ryan Gomes 4.00 10.00
RI Royal Ivey 3.00 8.00
RM Rashad McCants 3.00 8.00
RT Ronny Turiaf 5.00 12.00
SM Sean May 3.00 8.00
SS Salim Stoudamire 4.00 10.00
ST Sebastian Telfair 4.00 10.00
TD Travis Diener 3.00 8.00
UH Udonis Haslem 3.00 8.00
VK Viktor Khryapa 3.00 8.00
WE Delonte West 3.00 8.00
WI Maurice Williams 3.00 8.00
WS Wayne Simien 3.00 8.00

2005-06 Upper Deck Rookie Debut Sizzling Swatches

FOUR PER MEMORABILIA HOT PACK
HOT PACKS STATED ODDS 1:168
AI Allen Iverson 5.00 12.00
AJ Antawn Jamison 2.00 5.00
AS Amare Stoudemire 2.50 6.00
BG Ben Gordon 2.00 5.00
BW Ben Wallace 3.00 8.00
CA Carmelo Anthony 4.00 10.00
CB Chris Bosh 3.00 8.00
CW Chris Webber 3.00 8.00
DE Devin Harris 1.50 4.00
DH Dwight Howard 3.00 8.00
DN Dirk Nowitzki 6.00 15.00
GA Gilbert Arenas 2.50 6.00
GP Gary Payton 4.00 10.00
IG Andre Iguodala 2.50 6.00
JA Jason Richardson 2.50 6.00
JC Josh Childress 1.50 4.00
JK Jason Kidd 4.00 10.00
JR J.R. Smith 2.50 6.00
JS Josh Smith 2.00 5.00
KB Kobe Bryant 40.00 100.00
KG Kevin Garnett 6.00 15.00
LD Luol Deng 2.00 5.00
LJ LeBron James 20.00 50.00
MF Michael Finley 2.50 6.00
MG Manu Ginobili 5.00 12.00
MJ Michael Jordan 40.00 100.00
PG Pau Gasol 4.00 10.00
PP Paul Pierce 4.00 10.00
PS Peja Stojakovic 2.00 5.00
RA Ray Allen 4.00 10.00
RH Richard Hamilton 3.00 8.00
RJ Richard Jefferson 2.00 5.00
RL Rashard Lewis 2.00 5.00
SF Steve Francis 2.50 6.00
SM Shawn Marion 2.00 5.00
SN Steve Nash 5.00 12.00
SO Shaquille O'Neal 8.00 20.00
ST Stephon Marbury 3.00 8.00
TD Tim Duncan 6.00 15.00
TM Tracy McGrady 4.00 10.00
TP Tony Parker 4.00 10.00
YM Yao Ming 5.00 12.00

2005-06 Upper Deck Rookie Debut Threads

STATED ODDS 1:28
AH Allan Houston 2.00 5.00
AI Allen Iverson 5.00 12.00
AK Andrei Kirilenko 2.00 5.00
AL Rafer Alston 2.00 5.00
AM Andre Miller 2.00 5.00
AN Antonio McDyess 2.00 5.00
AR Ron Artest 2.00 5.00
AS Amare Stoudemire 2.50 6.00
AW Antoine Walker 2.00 5.00
BC Brian Cook 2.00 5.00
BD Baron Davis 2.50 6.00
BM Brad Miller 2.00 5.00
BO Chris Bosh 3.00 8.00
BU Caron Butler 2.00 5.00
BW Ben Wallace 3.00 8.00
CA Carmelo Anthony 4.00 10.00
CB Carlos Boozer 2.00 5.00
CH Chauncey Billups 3.00 8.00
CK Chris Kaman 2.00 5.00
CM Corey Maggette 2.00 5.00
CU Cuttino Mobley 1.50 4.00
CW Chris Webber 3.00 8.00
DD Dan Dickau 2.00 5.00
DF Derek Fisher 2.50 6.00
DG Devean George 2.00 5.00
DM Darko Milicic 2.00 5.00
DN Dirk Nowitzki 6.00 15.00
DO Donyell Marshall 2.00 5.00
DR Drew Gooden 2.00 5.00
DS Damon Stoudamire 2.50 6.00
EB Elton Brand 2.00 5.00
EC Eddy Curry 1.50 4.00
GA Gilbert Arenas 2.50 6.00
GH Grant Hill 4.00 10.00
GP Gary Payton 4.00 10.00
GR Glenn Robinson 2.00 5.00
GW Gerald Wallace 2.00 5.00
HA Anfernee Hardaway 6.00 15.00
HO Josh Howard 2.00 5.00
HT Hedo Turkoglu 2.00 5.00
IG Andre Iguodala 2.50 6.00
JA Jason Richardson 2.50 6.00
JC Jamal Crawford 2.50 6.00
JH Jarvis Hayes 2.00 5.00
JJ Joe Johnson 2.00 5.00
JK Jason Kidd 4.00 10.00
JO Jermaine O'Neal 2.00 5.00
JR Jalen Rose 2.00 5.00
JT Jamaal Tinsley 2.00 5.00
KB Kobe Bryant 40.00 100.00
KG Kevin Garnett 6.00 15.00
KK Kyle Korver 2.00 5.00
KM Kenyon Martin 2.00 5.00
KR Kareem Rush 2.00 5.00
KT Kurt Thomas 2.00 5.00
KW Kwame Brown 2.00 5.00
LJ LeBron James 10.00 25.00
LO Lamar Odom 2.00 5.00
LW Luke Walton 2.00 5.00
MA Marko Jaric 2.00 5.00
MB Mike Bibby 2.50 6.00
MF Michael Finley 2.50 6.00
MG Manu Ginobili 5.00 12.00
MJ Michael Jordan 40.00 100.00
MO Morris Peterson 1.50 4.00
MP Mickael Pietrus 1.50 4.00
MR Michael Redd 2.00 5.00
NH Nene 2.00 5.00
NV Nick Van Exel 2.50 6.00
PG Pau Gasol 4.00 10.00
PP Paul Pierce 4.00 10.00
PS Peja Stojakovic 2.00 5.00
QR Quentin Richardson 1.50 4.00
RA Ray Allen 4.00 10.00
RH Richard Hamilton 3.00 8.00
RJ Richard Jefferson 2.00 5.00
RL Rashard Lewis 2.00 5.00
RW Rasheed Wallace 2.50 6.00
SF Steve Francis 2.50 6.00
SM Shawn Marion 2.00 5.00
SN Steve Nash 5.00 12.00
SO Shaquille O'Neal 8.00 20.00
ST Stephon Marbury 3.00 8.00
TC Tyson Chandler 2.00 5.00
TD Tim Duncan 6.00 15.00
TE Jason Terry 2.00 5.00
TM Tracy McGrady 4.00 10.00
TP Tony Parker 4.00 10.00
WE Bonzi Wells 2.00 5.00
WI Chris Wilcox 2.00 5.00

2006-07 Upper Deck Rookie Debut

COMPLETE SET (146) 40.00 80.00
COMP.SET w/o SP's (100) 12.50 30.00
1 Josh Childress .15 .40
2 Joe Johnson .25 .60
3 Marvin Williams .15 .40
4 Gerald Green .20 .50
5 Al Jefferson .15 .40
6 Paul Pierce .40 1.00
7 Raymond Felton .15 .40
8 Emeka Okafor .20 .50
9 Gerald Wallace .20 .50
10 Tyson Chandler .20 .50
11 Luol Deng .20 .50
12 Ben Gordon .20 .50
13 Larry Hughes .20 .50
14 Zydrunas Ilgauskas .20 .50
15 LeBron James 2.00 5.00
16 Devin Harris .15 .40
17 Josh Howard .20 .50
18 Dirk Nowitzki .60 1.50
19 Jason Terry .20 .50
20 Carmelo Anthony .40 1.00
21 Marcus Camby .20 .50
22 Kenyon Martin .20 .50
23 Chauncey Billups .30 .75
24 Richard Hamilton .25 .60
25 Tayshaun Prince .25 .60
26 Ben Wallace .30 .75
27 Baron Davis .25 .60
28 Troy Murphy .15 .40
29 Jason Richardson .25 .60
30 Rafer Alston .20 .50
31 Tracy McGrady .40 1.00
32 Stromile Swift .15 .40
33 Yao Ming .60 1.50
34 Jermaine O'Neal .25 .60
35 Peja Stojakovic .20 .50
36 Jamaal Tinsley .15 .40
37 Elton Brand .20 .50
38 Sam Cassell .20 .50
39 Chris Kaman .15 .40
40 Kobe Bryant 2.00 5.00
41 Devean George .15 .40
42 Ronny Turiaf .20 .50
43 Pau Gasol .40 1.00
44 Mike Miller .20 .50
45 Damon Stoudamire .20 .50
46 Shaquille O'Neal 1.00 2.50
47 Gary Payton .30 .75
48 Dwyane Wade .50 1.25
49 Andrew Bogut .20 .50
50 T.J. Ford .15 .40
51 Jamaal Magloire .15 .40
52 Michael Redd .20 .50
53 Ricky Davis .20 .50
54 Kevin Garnett .60 1.50
55 Rashad McCants .15 .40
56 Vince Carter .50 1.25
57 Richard Jefferson .20 .50
58 Jason Kidd .40 1.00
59 P.J. Brown .15 .40
60 Desmond Mason .15 .40
61 Chris Paul .50 1.25
62 J.R. Smith .25 .60
63 Steve Francis .25 .60
64 Channing Frye .15 .40
65 Stephon Marbury .30 .75
66 Nate Robinson .20 .50
67 Grant Hill .40 1.00
68 Dwight Howard .30 .75
69 Jameer Nelson .15 .40
70 Darko Milicic .15 .40
71 Andre Iguodala .25 .60
72 Allen Iverson .60 1.50
73 Kyle Korver .20 .50
74 Chris Webber .30 .75
75 Boris Diaw .20 .50
76 Shawn Marion .25 .60
77 Steve Nash .50 1.25
78 Amare Stoudemire .25 .60
79 Juan Dixon .15 .40
80 Joel Przybilla .15 .40
81 Sebastian Telfair .15 .40
82 Shareef Abdur-Rahim .25 .60
83 Ron Artest .25 .60
84 Mike Bibby .25 .60
85 Tim Duncan .60 1.50
86 Manu Ginobili .50 1.25
87 Robert Horry .25 .60
88 Tony Parker .40 1.00
89 Ray Allen .40 1.00
90 Rashard Lewis .20 .50
91 Luke Ridnour .20 .50
92 Chris Bosh .30 .75
93 Jose Calderon .15 .40
94 Charlie Villanueva .15 .40
95 Carlos Boozer .20 .50
96 Andrei Kirilenko .20 .50
97 Deron Williams .25 .60
98 Gilbert Arenas .25 .60
99 Antawn Jamison .25 .60
100 Caron Butler .20 .50
101 Tyrus Thomas RC .50 1.25
102 Adam Morrison RC .50 1.25
103 LaMarcus Aldridge RC 1.50 4.00
104 Rudy Gay RC .75 2.00
105 Andrea Bargnani RC .50 1.25
106 Rodney Carney RC .40 1.00
107 Mike Gansey RC .40 1.00
108 Brandon Roy RC 1.25 3.00
109 Patrick O'Bryant RC .40 1.00
110 Randy Foye RC .50 1.25
111 Ronnie Brewer RC .60 1.50
112 Mardy Collins RC .40 1.00
113 Shelden Williams RC .40 1.00
114 J.J. Redick RC 1.25 3.00
115 Hilton Armstrong RC .40 1.00
116 Marcus Williams RC .40 1.00
117 Rajon Rondo RC 2.00 5.00
118 Cedric Simmons RC .40 1.00
119 Ryan Hollins RC .40 1.00
120 Jordan Farmar RC .50 1.25
121 Maurice Ager RC .40 1.00
122 Renaldo Balkman RC .50 1.25
123 Leon Powe RC .40 1.00
124 Solomon Jones RC .40 1.00
125 Bobby Jones RC .40 1.00
126 Josh Boone RC .40 1.00
127 Saer Sene RC .40 1.00
128 Daniel Gibson RC .50 1.25
129 Hassan Adams RC .40 1.00
130 Kyle Lowry RC 2.00 5.00
131 Shannon Brown RC .40 1.00
132 Dee Brown RC .40 1.00
133 Shawne Williams RC .40 1.00
134 P.J. Tucker RC .60 1.50
135 Craig Smith RC .50 1.25
136 Paul Davis RC .40 1.00
137 Allan Ray RC .40 1.00
138 Denham Brown RC .40 1.00
139 Chris Quinn RC .40 1.00
140 Joel Freeland RC .40 1.00
141 James Augustine RC .40 1.00
142 Thabo Sefolosha RC .50 1.25
143 Quincy Douby RC .40 1.00
144 James White RC .40 1.00
145 David Noel RC .40 1.00
146 Steve Novak RC .50 1.25

2006-07 Upper Deck Rookie Debut Bronze

*1-100 BRONZE: 2.5X TO 6X BASE HI
*101-146 BRONZE: 1.25X TO 3X BASE HI
BRONZE PRINT RUN 100 SER.#'d SETS

2006-07 Upper Deck Rookie Debut Gold

*1-100 GOLD: 10X TO 25X BASE HI
*101-146 GOLD: 6X TO 15X BASE HI
GOLD PRINT RUN 10 SER.#'d SETS

2006-07 Upper Deck Rookie Debut Platinum

*1-100 PLATINUM: 2X TO 5X BASE HI
*101-146 PLATINUM: 1X TO 2.5X BASE HI
STATED PRINT RUN 150 SER.#'d SETS

2006-07 Upper Deck Rookie Debut Silver

*1-100 SILVER: 3X TO 8X BASE HI
*101-146 SILVER: 2X TO 5X BASE HI
SILVER PRINT RUN 50 SER.#'d SETS

2006-07 Upper Deck Rookie Debut Draft Duos

COMPLETE SET (25) 20.00 50.00
APPROXIMATE ODDS 1:20
BA E.Brand/R.Artest 1.50 4.00
BH M.Bibby/L.Hughes 1.50 4.00
BJ C.Billups/B.Jackson 1.50 4.00
BP C.Boozer/T.Prince 1.50 4.00
BW A.Bogut/Mv.Williams 1.50 4.00
CB T.Chandler/Kw.Brown 1.50 4.00
DH B.Davis/R.Hamilton 1.50 4.00
DS K.Dooling/D.Stevenson 1.50 4.00
EK D.Ewing/Y.Korolev 1.50 4.00
FM R.Felton/S.May 1.50 4.00
FV C.Frye/C.Villanueva 1.50 4.00
GD B.Gordon/C.Duhon 1.50 4.00
IC A.Iguodala/J.Childress 2.00 5.00
JA L.James/C.Anthony 4.00 10.00
JJ J.Johnson/R.Jefferson 1.50 4.00
KH K.Korver/K.Hinrich 1.50 4.00
LS S.Livingston/J.R.Smith 1.50 4.00
NJ J.Nelson/A.Jefferson 1.50 4.00
OH E.Okafor/D.Howard 2.00 5.00
PC P.Pierce/V.Carter 2.50 6.00
PW C.Paul/D.Williams 3.00 8.00
RH L.Ridnour/K.Hinrich 1.50 4.00
RS V.Radmanovic/B.Simmons 1.50 4.00
SR Q.Richardson/S.Swift 1.50 4.00
WH H.Warrick/L.Head 1.50 4.00

2006-07 Upper Deck Rookie Debut Draft Duos Autographs

STATED PRINT RUN 5 TO 25 SER.#'d SETS
BH M.Bibby/L.Hughes/25 12.00 30.00
BW A.Bogut/Mv.Williams/25 12.00 30.00
CB T.Chandler/Kw.Brown/25 10.00 25.00
DS K.Dooling/D.Stevenson/25 10.00 25.00
EK D.Ewing/Y.Korolev/25 10.00 25.00
FM R.Felton/S.May/25 12.00 30.00
JJ J.Johnson/R.Jefferson/25 10.00 25.00
KH K.Korver/K.Hinrich/25 10.00 25.00
LS S.Livingston/J.R.Smith/25 10.00 25.00
PW C.Paul/D.Williams/25 40.00 100.00
RS Radmanovic/Simmons/25 10.00 25.00
SR Q.Richardson/S.Swift/25 10.00 25.00

2006-07 Upper Deck Rookie Debut Ink

APPROXIMATE ODDS 1:20
*GOLD: .75X TO 2X BASE HI
GOLD PRINT RUN 25 SER.#'d SETS
AB Andrea Bargnani 3.00 8.00
AD Hassan Adams 2.50 6.00
BJ Bobby Jones 2.50 6.00
BR Brandon Roy 8.00 20.00
CS Cedric Simmons 2.50 6.00
DB Dee Brown 2.50 6.00
DE Denham Brown 2.50 6.00
DG Daniel Gibson 3.00 8.00
DN David Noel 2.50 6.00
HA Hilton Armstrong 2.50 6.00
JA James Augustine 2.50 6.00
JB Josh Boone 2.50 6.00
JF Jordan Farmar 3.00 8.00
JW James White 2.50 6.00
KL Kyle Lowry 8.00 20.00
LA LaMarcus Aldridge 10.00 25.00
MA Maurice Ager 2.50 6.00
MC Mardy Collins 2.50 6.00
MW Marcus Williams 2.50 6.00
PD Paul Davis 2.50 6.00
PO Patrick O'Bryant 2.50 6.00
PT P.J. Tucker 4.00 10.00
QD Quincy Douby 2.50 6.00
RB Ronnie Brewer 4.00 10.00
RC Rodney Carney 2.50 6.00
RF Randy Foye 3.00 8.00
RG Rudy Gay 5.00 12.00
RH Ryan Hollins 2.50 6.00
RR Rajon Rondo 20.00 50.00
SJ Solomon Jones 2.50 6.00
SN Steve Novak 3.00 8.00
SW Shelden Williams 2.50 6.00
TS Thabo Sefolosha 3.00 8.00
TT Tyrus Thomas 3.00 8.00

2006-07 Upper Deck Rookie Debut Materialization

APPROXIMATE ODDS 1:12
AB Andrew Bynum 1.50 4.00
AI Andre Iguodala 2.50 6.00
AS Amare Stoudemire 2.50 6.00
BL Andray Blatche 2.00 5.00
BO Andrew Bogut 2.00 5.00
BR Kobe Bryant 50.00 120.00
CA Carmelo Anthony SP 4.00 10.00
CB Chris Bosh 3.00 8.00
CM Corey Maggette 2.00 5.00
CP Chris Paul 5.00 12.00
CV Charlie Villanueva 1.50 4.00
CW Chris Webber 3.00 8.00
DG Danny Granger 1.50 4.00
DH Dwight Howard 3.00 8.00
DM Donyell Marshall 2.00 5.00
DN Dirk Nowitzki 6.00 15.00
DS Damon Stoudamire 2.00 5.00
EB Elton Brand 2.00 5.00
FG Francisco Garcia 1.50 4.00
GE Devean George 2.00 5.00
GW Gerald Wallace SP 2.00 5.00
HO Julius Hodge 2.00 5.00
ID Ike Diogu 2.00 5.00
JG Joey Graham 2.00 5.00
JJ Joe Johnson 2.50 6.00
JK Jason Kidd 4.00 10.00
JM Jamaal Magloire 2.00 5.00
JO Jermaine O'Neal 2.50 6.00
JP Johan Petro 2.00 5.00
KB Kwame Brown 2.00 5.00
KG Kevin Garnett 6.00 15.00
KM Kenyon Martin 2.00 5.00
KT Kurt Thomas 2.00 5.00
LH Larry Hughes 2.00 5.00
LJ LeBron James 10.00 25.00
MA Desmond Mason 2.00 5.00
MC Jeff McInnis 2.00 5.00
MJ Michael Jordan SP 30.00 80.00
MR Michael Redd 2.00 5.00
MS Mike Sweetney 2.00 5.00
MW Martell Webster 2.00 5.00
PG Pau Gasol 4.00 10.00
PP Paul Pierce 4.00 10.00
PS Peja Stojakovic 2.00 5.00
RJ Richard Jefferson 2.00 5.00
RM Rashad McCants 2.00 5.00
SD Samuel Dalembert 2.00 5.00
SF Steve Francis 2.50 6.00
SH Shawn Marion 2.50 6.00
SM Sean May 1.50 4.00
SO Shaquille O'Neal 10.00 25.00
SS Stromile Swift 2.00 5.00
TC Tyson Chandler 2.00 5.00
TD Tim Duncan 6.00 15.00
TM Tracy McGrady SP 4.00 10.00
TP Tony Parker 4.00 10.00
VC Vince Carter 5.00 12.00
WS Wally Szczerbiak 2.00 5.00
YM Yao Ming 6.00 15.00
ZI Zydrunas Ilgauskas 2.00 5.00

2003-04 Upper Deck Rookie Exclusives

COMPLETE SET (60) 30.00 80.00
1 LeBron James RC 60.00 150.00
2 Darko Milicic RC .30 .75
3 Carmelo Anthony RC 2.00 5.00
4 Chris Bosh RC 1.25 3.00
5 Dwyane Wade RC 3.00 8.00
6 Chris Kaman RC .40 1.00
7 Jarvis Hayes RC .25 .60
8 Mickael Pietrus RC .30 .75
9 Marcus Banks RC .25 .60
10 Luke Ridnour RC .40 1.00
11 Reece Gaines RC .25 .60
12 Troy Bell RC .25 .60
13 Zarko Cabarkapa RC .25 .60
14 David West RC .50 1.25
15 Aleksandar Pavlovic RC .30 .75
16 Dahntay Jones RC .30 .75
17 Boris Diaw RC .40 1.00
18 Zoran Planinic RC .25 .60
19 Travis Outlaw RC .25 .60
20 Brian Cook RC .25 .60
21 Ndudi Ebi RC .25 .60
22 Kendrick Perkins RC .30 .75
23 Leandro Barbosa RC .40 1.00
24 Josh Howard RC .40 1.00
25 Maciej Lampe RC .25 .60
26 Jason Kapono RC .25 .60
27 Luke Walton RC .40 1.00
28 Travis Hansen RC .25 .60
29 Steve Blake RC .30 .75
30 Slavko Vranes RC .25 .60
31 Darius Miles .25 .60
32 Tony Parker .60 1.50
33 Chauncey Billups .50 1.25
34 Carlos Boozer .30 .75
35 Richard Hamilton .50 1.25
36 Jamaal Tinsley .25 .60
37 Tracy McGrady .60 1.50
38 Manu Ginobili .75 2.00
39 Andre Miller .30 .75
40 Richard Jefferson .30 .75
41 Paul Pierce .60 1.50
42 Peja Stojakovic .30 .75
43 Jason Richardson .40 1.00
44 Shawn Marion .40 1.00
45 Antawn Jamison .40 1.00
46 Reggie Evans .25 .60
47 Earl Boykins .25 .60
48 Corey Maggette .30 .75
49 Cuttino Mobley .25 .60
50 Shane Battier .25 .60
51 Shareef Abdur-Rahim .40 1.00
52 Chris Wilcox .25 .60
53 Steve Francis .40 1.00
54 Mike Bibby .40 1.00
55 Morris Peterson .25 .60
56 Nene .30 .75
57 Juan Dixon .25 .60
58 Yao Ming 1.00 2.50
59 Kobe Bryant 5.00 12.00
60 Michael Jordan 6.00 15.00

2003-04 Upper Deck Rookie Exclusives Gold

*1-60: 4X TO 10X BASE CARD HI
GOLD PRINT RUN 100 SER.#'d SETS
3 Carmelo Anthony 30.00 80.00
5 Dwyane Wade 150.00 400.00
59 Kobe Bryant 100.00 250.00
60 Michael Jordan 125.00 300.00

2003-04 Upper Deck Rookie Exclusives Variation

*1-30 RCs: 1X TO 2.5X BASE CARD HI
CHECKLIST 31-60 DIFFERENT FROM BASE
1 LeBron James 300.00 600.00
31 Allen Iverson 1.25 3.00
32 Dirk Nowitzki 1.25 3.00
33 Steve Nash 1.00 2.50
34 Richard Hamilton .60 1.50
35 Shaquille O'Neal 2.00 5.00
36 Jamaal Tinsley .30 .75
37 Tim Duncan 1.25 3.00
38 Stephon Marbury .60 1.50
39 Caron Butler .40 1.00
40 Paul Pierce .75 2.00
41 Amare Stoudemire .75 2.00
42 Gary Payton .75 2.00
43 Karl Malone 1.00 2.50
44 Ben Wallace .60 1.50
45 Antoine Walker .50 1.25
46 Kenyon Martin .50 1.25
47 Latrell Sprewell .60 1.50
48 Rasheed Wallace .60 1.50
49 Chris Webber .60 1.50
50 Ray Allen .75 2.00
51 Jermaine O'Neal .50 1.25
52 Chris Wilcox .30 .75
53 Kevin Garnett 1.25 3.00
54 Pau Gasol .75 2.00
55 Jason Kidd .75 2.00
56 Jason Terry .40 1.00
57 Dajuan Wagner .30 .75
58 Yao Ming 1.25 3.00
59 Kobe Bryant 4.00 10.00
60 Michael Jordan 5.00 12.00

2003-04 Upper Deck Rookie Exclusives Autographs

AU STATED ODDS 1:28 H, 1:1000 R
A1 LeBron James SP 5,000.00 10,000.00
A2 Darko Milicic 3.00 8.00
A3 Carmelo Anthony SP 30.00 80.00
A4 Chris Bosh 15.00 40.00
A5 Dwyane Wade 300.00 600.00
A6 Chris Kaman 4.00 10.00
A7 Jarvis Hayes 2.50 6.00
A8 Mickael Pietrus 3.00 8.00
A9 Marcus Banks 2.50 6.00
A10 Luke Ridnour 4.00 10.00
A11 Reece Gaines 2.50 6.00
A12 Troy Bell 2.50 6.00
A13 Zarko Cabarkapa 2.50 6.00
A14 David West 5.00 12.00
A15 Aleksandar Pavlovic 3.00 8.00
A16 Dahntay Jones 3.00 8.00
A17 Boris Diaw 4.00 10.00
A18 Zoran Planinic 2.50 6.00
A19 Travis Outlaw 3.00 8.00
A20 Brian Cook 2.50 6.00
A21 Ndudi Ebi 2.50 6.00
A22 Kendrick Perkins 3.00 8.00
A23 Leandro Barbosa 4.00 10.00
A24 Josh Howard 4.00 10.00
A25 Maciej Lampe 2.50 6.00
A26 Jason Kapono 2.50 6.00
A27 Luke Walton 4.00 10.00
A28 Travis Hansen 2.50 6.00
A29 Steve Blake 3.00 8.00
A30 Slavko Vranes 2.50 6.00
A31 Darius Miles 4.00 10.00
A32 Tony Parker 15.00 40.00
A33 Chauncey Billups 6.00 15.00
A34 Carlos Boozer 5.00 12.00
A35 Richard Hamilton 6.00 15.00
A37 Tracy McGrady 20.00 50.00
A38 Manu Ginobili 25.00 60.00
A39 Andre Miller 4.00 10.00
A40 Richard Jefferson 4.00 10.00
A41 Paul Pierce 12.00 30.00
A42 Peja Stojakovic 8.00 20.00
A43 Jason Richardson 6.00 15.00
A44 Shawn Marion 6.00 15.00
A45 Antawn Jamison 4.00 10.00
A46 Reggie Evans 4.00 10.00
A47 Earl Boykins 4.00 10.00
A48 Corey Maggette 4.00 10.00
A49 Cuttino Mobley 4.00 10.00
A50 Shane Battier 5.00 12.00
A51 Shareef Abdur-Rahim 4.00 10.00
A52 Chris Wilcox 4.00 10.00
A53 Steve Francis 6.00 15.00
A54 Mike Bibby 4.00 10.00
A55 Morris Peterson 4.00 10.00
A56 Nene 4.00 10.00
A57 Juan Dixon 4.00 10.00
A58 Yao Ming 60.00 150.00
A59 Kobe Bryant 400.00 800.00
A60 Michael Jordan 800.00 1,500.00

2003-04 Upper Deck Rookie Exclusives Jerseys

ALL JSY STATED ODDS 1:28 H, 1:14 R
J1 LeBron James 300.00 600.00
J2 Darko Milicic 2.00 5.00
J3 Carmelo Anthony 12.00 30.00
J4 Chris Bosh 8.00 20.00
J5 Dwyane Wade 20.00 50.00
J6 Chris Kaman 2.50 6.00
J7 Jarvis Hayes 1.50 4.00
J8 Mickael Pietrus 2.00 5.00
J9 Marcus Banks 1.50 4.00
J10 Luke Ridnour 2.50 6.00
J11 Reece Gaines 1.50 4.00
J12 Troy Bell 1.50 4.00
J13 Zarko Cabarkapa 1.50 4.00
J14 David West 3.00 8.00
J15 Aleksandar Pavlovic 2.00 5.00
J16 Dahntay Jones 2.00 5.00
J17 Boris Diaw 2.50 6.00
J18 Zoran Planinic 1.50 4.00
J19 Travis Outlaw 2.00 5.00
J20 Brian Cook 1.50 4.00
J21 Ndudi Ebi 1.50 4.00
J22 Kendrick Perkins 2.00 5.00
J23 Leandro Barbosa 2.50 6.00
J24 Josh Howard 2.50 6.00
J25 Maciej Lampe 1.50 4.00
J26 Jason Kapono 1.50 4.00
J27 Luke Walton 2.50 6.00
J28 Travis Hansen 1.50 4.00
J29 Steve Blake 2.00 5.00
J30 Slavko Vranes 1.50 4.00
J31 Darius Miles 1.50 4.00
J32 Tony Parker 4.00 10.00
J33 Chauncey Billups 3.00 8.00
J34 Carlos Boozer SP 4.00 10.00
J35 Richard Hamilton 3.00 8.00
J36 Jamaal Tinsley 1.50 4.00
J37 Tracy McGrady 4.00 10.00
J38 Manu Ginobili 5.00 12.00
J39 Andre Miller 1.50 4.00
J40 Richard Jefferson 2.00 5.00
J41 Paul Pierce 4.00 10.00
J42 Peja Stojakovic 2.00 5.00
J43 Jason Richardson 2.50 6.00
J44 Shawn Marion 2.50 6.00
J45 Antawn Jamison 2.50 6.00
J46 Reggie Evans 1.50 4.00
J47 Earl Boykins 1.50 4.00
J48 Corey Maggette 2.00 5.00
J49 Cuttino Mobley SP 4.00 10.00
J50 Shane Battier 2.00 5.00
J51 Shareef Abdur-Rahim 2.50 6.00
J52 Chris Wilcox 1.50 4.00
J53 Steve Francis 2.50 6.00
J54 Mike Bibby 2.50 6.00
J55 Morris Peterson 1.50 4.00
J56 Nene 2.00 5.00
J57 Juan Dixon 1.50 4.00
J58 Yao Ming 6.00 15.00
J59 Kobe Bryant 20.00 50.00
J60 Michael Jordan 50.00 120.00

2003-04 Upper Deck Rookie Exclusives Jerseys Variation

ALL JSY STATED ODDS 1:28 H, 1:14 R
J24 Mike Sweetney 1.50 4.00
J31 Allen Iverson 6.00 15.00
J32 Dirk Nowitzki 6.00 15.00
J33 Steve Nash 5.00 12.00
J35 Shaquille O'Neal 10.00 25.00
J37 Tim Duncan 6.00 15.00
J38 Stephon Marbury 3.00 8.00
J39 Caron Butler 2.00 5.00
J41 Amare Stoudemire 3.00 8.00
J42 Gary Payton 4.00 10.00
J43 Karl Malone 5.00 12.00
J44 Ben Wallace 3.00 8.00
J45 Antoine Walker SP 2.50 6.00
J46 Kenyon Martin 2.50 6.00
J47 Latrell Sprewell 3.00 8.00
J48 Rasheed Wallace SP 3.00 8.00
J49 Chris Webber 3.00 8.00
J50 Ray Allen SP 4.00 10.00
J51 Jermaine O'Neal 2.50 6.00
J53 Kevin Garnett 6.00 15.00
J54 Pau Gasol 4.00 10.00
J55 Jason Kidd 4.00 10.00
J56 Jason Terry 2.00 5.00
J57 Dajuan Wagner 2.00 5.00

2003-04 Upper Deck Rookie Exclusives Superstar Exclusives

PRINT RUN 100 SER.#'d SETS
EX1 Tracy McGrady 5.00 12.00
EX2 Dajuan Wagner 2.00 5.00
EX3 Allen Iverson 8.00 20.00
EX4 Caron Butler 2.50 6.00
EX5 Jason Kidd 5.00 12.00
EX6 Kenyon Martin 3.00 8.00
EX7 Lamar Odom 2.50 6.00
EX8 Kobe Bryant 25.00 60.00
EX9 T.J. Ford 2.50 6.00
EX10 Wally Szczerbiak 2.50 6.00
EX11 Yao Ming 8.00 20.00
EX12 Kirk Hinrich 3.00 8.00
EX13 Steve Nash 6.00 15.00
EX14 Baron Davis 3.00 8.00
EX15 Carmelo Anthony 15.00 40.00
EX16 Pau Gasol 5.00 12.00
EX17 Amare Stoudemire 4.00 10.00
EX18 Reggie Miller 6.00 15.00
EX19 Sam Cassell 2.50 6.00
EX20 Gary Payton 5.00 12.00
EX21 Kevin Garnett 8.00 20.00
EX22 Reece Gaines 2.00 5.00
EX23 LeBron James 500.00 1,000.00
EX24 Andre Miller 2.50 6.00
EX25 Rasheed Wallace 4.00 10.00
EX26 Darius Miles 2.00 5.00
EX27 Peja Stojakovic 2.50 6.00
EX28 Paul Pierce 5.00 12.00
EX29 Nick Collison 2.50 6.00
EX30 Dahntay Jones 2.50 6.00
EX31 Darko Milicic 2.50 6.00
EX32 Richard Hamilton 4.00 10.00
EX33 Scottie Pippen 8.00 20.00
EX34 Shaquille O'Neal 12.00 30.00
EX35 Jarvis Hayes 2.00 5.00
EX36 Tony Parker 5.00 12.00
EX37 Nick Van Exel 3.00 8.00
EX38 Maciej Lampe 2.00 5.00
EX39 Jalen Rose 2.50 6.00
EX40 Ray Allen 5.00 12.00
EX41 Dirk Nowitzki 8.00 20.00
EX42 Elton Brand 2.50 6.00
EX43 Jermaine O'Neal 3.00 8.00
EX44 Brian Grant 2.00 5.00
EX45 Jason Richardson 3.00 8.00
EX46 Allan Houston 3.00 8.00
EX47 Tim Thomas 2.00 5.00
EX48 Glenn Robinson 2.50 6.00
EX49 Nene 2.50 6.00
EX50 Corey Maggette 2.50 6.00
EX51 Richard Jefferson 2.50 6.00
EX52 Mickael Pietrus 2.50 6.00
EX53 Stephon Marbury 4.00 10.00
EX54 Mike Miller 2.50 6.00
EX55 Bonzi Wells 2.00 5.00
EX56 Boris Diaw 3.00 8.00
EX57 Manu Ginobili 6.00 15.00
EX58 Steve Francis 3.00 8.00
EX59 Jamal Mashburn 2.50 6.00
EX60 Mike Bibby 3.00 8.00
EX61 Tony Delk 2.50 6.00
EX62 Troy Bell 2.00 5.00
EX63 Dwyane Wade 25.00 60.00
EX64 Karl Malone 6.00 15.00
EX65 Desmond Mason 2.50 6.00
EX66 Antawn Jamison 2.50 6.00
EX67 Vince Carter 6.00 15.00
EX68 Eddie Jones 3.00 8.00
EX69 Gordan Giricek 2.00 5.00
EX70 Ben Wallace 4.00 10.00
EX71 Latrell Sprewell 4.00 10.00
EX72 Leandro Barbosa 3.00 8.00
EX73 Jamaal Tinsley 2.00 5.00
EX74 Travis Outlaw 2.50 6.00
EX75 Jason Terry 2.50 6.00
EX76 Quentin Richardson 2.00 5.00
EX77 Morris Peterson 2.00 5.00
EX78 Cuttino Mobley 2.00 5.00
EX79 Rashard Lewis 2.50 6.00
EX80 Jerry Stackhouse 4.00 10.00
EX81 Michael Finley 3.00 8.00
EX82 Antoine Walker 3.00 8.00
EX83 Shawn Marion 3.00 8.00
EX84 Gilbert Arenas 3.00 8.00
EX85 Marcus Banks 2.00 5.00
EX86 Tim Duncan 8.00 20.00
EX87 Brian Cook 2.00 5.00
EX88 Chauncey Billups 4.00 10.00
EX89 Andrei Kirilenko 2.50 6.00
EX90 Shareef Abdur-Rahim 3.00 8.00
EX91 Antonio McDyess 2.50 6.00
EX92 Chris Bosh 10.00 25.00
EX93 Ron Artest 3.00 8.00
EX94 David West 4.00 10.00
EX95 Chris Webber 3.00 8.00
EX96 Ricky Davis 2.50 6.00
EX97 Vladimir Radmanovic 2.00 5.00
EX98 Nikoloz Tskitishvili 2.00 5.00
EX99 Drew Gooden 2.50 6.00
EX100 Zach Randolph 3.00 8.00

1993-94 Upper Deck SE
COMPLETE SET (225) 12.00 30.00
JK1/MJR1: STATED ODDS 1:72
1 Scottie Pippen 1.00 2.50
2 Todd Day .25 .60
3 Detlef Schrempf .40 1.00
4 Chris Webber RC 2.00 5.00
5 Michael Adams .30 .75
6 Loy Vaught .25 .60
7 Doug West .25 .60
8 A.C. Green .30 .75
9 Anthony Mason .30 .75
10 Clyde Drexler .60 1.50
11 Popeye Jones RC .40 1.00
12 Vlade Divac .40 1.00
13 Armon Gilliam .25 .60
14 Hersey Hawkins .30 .75
15 Dennis Scott .25 .60
16 Bimbo Coles .25 .60
17 Blue Edwards .25 .60
18 Negele Knight .25 .60
19 Dale Davis .30 .75
20 Isiah Thomas .60 1.50
21 Latrell Sprewell .60 1.50
22 Kenny Smith .30 .75
23 Bryant Stith .25 .60
24 Terry Porter .30 .75
25 Spud Webb .30 .75
26 John Battle .25 .60
27 Jeff Malone .30 .75
28 Olden Polynice .25 .60
29 Kevin Willis .30 .75
30 Robert Parish .50 1.25
31 Kevin Johnson .40 1.00
32 Shaquille O'Neal 2.00 5.00
33 Willie Anderson .25 .60
34 Micheal Williams .25 .60
35 Steve Smith .30 .75
36 Rik Smits .30 .75
37 Pete Myers .25 .60
38 Oliver Miller .25 .60
39 Eddie Johnson .25 .60
40 Calbert Cheaney RC .40 1.00
41 Vernon Maxwell .30 .75
42 James Worthy .50 1.25
43 Dino Radja RC .40 1.00
44 Derrick Coleman .40 1.00
45 Reggie Williams .25 .60
46 Dale Ellis .25 .60
47 Clifford Robinson .40 1.00
48 Doug Christie .30 .75
49 Ricky Pierce .30 .75
50 Sean Elliott .40 1.00
51 Anfernee Hardaway RC 2.00 5.00
52 Dana Barros .25 .60
53 Reggie Miller .75 2.00
54 Brian Williams .25 .60
55 Otis Thorpe .40 1.00
56 Jerome Kersey .30 .75
57 Larry Johnson .50 1.25
58 Rex Chapman .25 .60
59 Kevin Edwards .25 .60
60 Nate McMillan .30 .75
61 Chris Mullin .50 1.25
62 Bill Cartwright .25 .60
63 Dennis Rodman 1.00 2.50
64 Pooh Richardson .30 .75
65 Tyrone Hill .25 .60
66 Scott Brooks .25 .60
67 Brad Daugherty .30 .75
68 Joe Dumars .50 1.25
69 Vin Baker RC .60 1.50
70 Rod Strickland .30 .75
71 Tom Chambers .40 1.00
72 Charles Oakley .40 1.00
73 Craig Ehlo .25 .60
74 LaPhonso Ellis .30 .75
75 Kevin Gamble .25 .60
76 Shawn Bradley RC .40 1.00
77 Kendall Gill .30 .75
78 Hakeem Olajuwon .75 2.00
79 Nick Anderson .30 .75
80 Anthony Peeler .25 .60
81 Wayman Tisdale .30 .75
82 Danny Manning .30 .75
83 John Starks .40 1.00
84 Jeff Hornacek .30 .75
85 Victor Alexander .25 .60
86 Mitch Richmond .50 1.25
87 Mookie Blaylock .40 1.00
88 Harvey Grant .30 .75
89 Doug Smith .25 .60
90 John Stockton .75 2.00
91 Charles Barkley 1.00 2.50
92 Gerald Wilkins .30 .75
93 Mario Elie .30 .75
94 Ken Norman .25 .60
95 B.J. Armstrong .40 1.00
96 John Williams .25 .60
97 Rony Seikaly .30 .75
98 Sean Rooks .25 .60
99 Shawn Kemp .60 1.50
100 Danny Ainge .40 1.00
101 Terry Mills .25 .60
102 Doc Rivers .30 .75
103 Chuck Person .30 .75
104 Sam Cassell RC .75 2.00
105 Kevin Duckworth .25 .60
106 Dan Majerle .40 1.00
107 Mark Jackson .30 .75
108 Steve Kerr .30 .75
109 Sam Perkins .30 .75
110 Clarence Weatherspoon .25 .60
111 Felton Spencer .25 .60
112 Greg Anthony .25 .60
113 Pete Chilcutt .25 .60
114 Malik Sealy .25 .60
115 Horace Grant .40 1.00
116 Chris Morris .25 .60
117 Xavier McDaniel .40 1.00
118 Lionel Simmons .25 .60
119 Dell Curry .40 1.00
120 Moses Malone .60 1.50
121 Lindsey Hunter RC .40 1.00
122 Buck Williams .30 .75
123 Mahmoud Abdul-Rauf .30 .75
124 Rumeal Robinson .25 .60
125 Chris Mills RC .40 1.00
126 Scott Skiles .25 .60
127 Derrick McKey .30 .75
128 Avery Johnson .30 .75
129 Harold Miner .30 .75
130 Frank Brickowski .25 .60
131 Gary Payton .50 1.25
132 Don MacLean .25 .60
133 Thurl Bailey .25 .60
134 Nick Van Exel RC 1.00 2.50
135 Matt Geiger .25 .60
136 Stacey Augmon .30 .75
137 Sedale Threatt .25 .60
138 Patrick Ewing .60 1.50
139 Tyrone Corbin .25 .60
140 Jim Jackson .30 .75
141 Christian Laettner .40 1.00
142 Robert Horry .40 1.00
143 J.R. Reid .30 .75
144 Eric Murdock .25 .60
145 Alonzo Mourning .60 1.50
146 Sherman Douglas .25 .60
147 Tom Gugliotta .30 .75
148 Glen Rice .40 1.00
149 Mark Price .40 1.00
150 Dikembe Mutombo .60 1.50
151 Derek Harper .30 .75
152 Karl Malone .75 2.00
153 Byron Scott .40 1.00
155 Dominique Wilkins .60 1.50
156 Bobby Hurley RC .40 1.00
157 Ron Harper .40 1.00
158 Bryon Russell RC .40 1.00
159 Frank Johnson .25 .60
160 Toni Kukoc RC 1.00 2.50
161 Lloyd Daniels .25 .60
162 Jeff Turner .25 .60
163 Muggsy Bogues .40 1.00
164 Chris Gatling .25 .60
165 Kenny Anderson .30 .75
166 Stanley Roberts .25 .60
167 Jamal Mashburn RC .75 2.00
168 Tim Perry .25 .60
169 Antonio Davis RC .50 1.25
170 Isaiah Rider RC .60 1.50
171 Dee Brown .30 .75
172 Walt Williams .40 1.00
173 Elden Campbell .25 .60
174 Benoit Benjamin .25 .60
175 Billy Owens .30 .75
176 Andrew Lang .25 .60
177 David Robinson .75 2.00
178 Checklist 1 .20 .50
179 Checklist 2 .20 .50
180 Checklist 3 .20 .50
181 Shawn Bradley ASW .40 1.00
182 Calbert Cheaney ASW .40 1.00
183 Toni Kukoc ASW 1.00 2.50
184 Popeye Jones ASW .40 1.00
185 Lindsey Hunter ASW .40 1.00
186 Chris Webber ASW 2.00 5.00
187 Bryon Russell ASW .40 1.00
188 A.Hardaway ASW 2.00 5.00
189 Nick Van Exel ASW 1.00 2.50
190 P.J.Brown ASW .40 1.00
191 Isaiah Rider ASW .60 1.50
192 Chris Mills ASW .40 1.00
193 Antonio Davis ASW .50 1.25
194 Jamal Mashburn ASW .75 2.00
195 Dino Radja ASW .40 1.00
196 Sam Cassell ASW .75 2.00
197 Isaiah Rider ASW SD .60 1.50
198 Mark Price LDS .40 1.00
199 Stacey Augmon TH .30 .75
200 Celtics Team TH .20 .50
201 Eddie Johnson TH .25 .60
202 Scottie Pippen TH 1.00 2.50
203 Brad Daugherty TH .30 .75
204 Jamal Mashburn TH .75 2.00
205 Dikembe Mutombo TH .60 1.50
206 Lindsey Hunter TH .40 1.00
207 Chris Webber TH 2.00 5.00
208 Rockets Team TH .20 .50
209 Derrick McKey TH .30 .75
210 Danny Manning TH .30 .75
211 Doug Christie TH .30 .75
212 Glen Rice TH .40 1.00
213 Day/Norman/Barry/Baker T .60 1.50
214 Isaiah Rider TH .60 1.50
215 Kenny Anderson TH .30 .75
216 Patrick Ewing TH .60 1.50
217 Anfernee Hardaway TH 2.00 5.00
218 Moses Malone TH .60 1.50
219 Kevin Johnson TH .40 1.00
220 Clifford Robinson TH .40 1.00
221 Wayman Tisdale TH .30 .75
222 David Robinson TH .75 2.00
223 Sonics Team TH .20 .50
224 John Stockton TH .75 2.00
225 Don MacLean TH .25 .60
JK1 Johnny Kilroy 8.00 20.00
MJR1 M.Jordan Retirement 4.00 10.00

1993-94 Upper Deck SE Electric Court
COMPLETE SET (225) 25.00 50.00
*STARS: .75X TO 2X BASE CARD HI
*RCs: .6X TO 1.5X BASE HI
ONE PER PACK

1993-94 Upper Deck SE Electric Court Gold
*STARS: 8X TO 20X BASE CARD HI
*RCs: 5X TO 12X BASE HI
STATED ODDS 1:36 HOB/RET

1993-94 Upper Deck SE Behind the Glass
COMPLETE SET (15) 40.00 100.00
STATED ODDS 1:30 RETAIL
BHG TRADE: STATED ODDS 1:360 HOBBY
G1 Shawn Kemp 1.50 4.00
G2 Patrick Ewing 1.50 4.00
G3 Dikembe Mutombo 1.50 4.00
G4 Charles Barkley 2.50 6.00
G5 Hakeem Olajuwon 2.00 5.00
G6 Larry Johnson 1.25 3.00
G7 Chris Webber 5.00 12.00
G8 John Starks 1.00 2.50
G9 Kevin Willis .75 2.00
G10 Scottie Pippen 2.50 6.00
G11 Michael Jordan 40.00 100.00
G12 Alonzo Mourning 1.50 4.00
G13 Shaquille O'Neal 5.00 12.00
G14 Shawn Bradley 1.00 2.50
G15 Ron Harper 1.00 2.50
NNO Expired BHG Trade .60 1.50
NNO Redeemed BHG Trade .08 .25

1993-94 Upper Deck SE Die Cut All-Stars
COMPLETE SET (30) 100.00 250.00
COMP.EAST SET (15) 50.00 125.00
COMP.WEST SET (15) 50.00 125.00
STATED ODDS 1:30 HOBBY
E1 Dominique Wilkins 5.00 10.00
E2 Alonzo Mourning 5.00 12.00
E3 B.J. Armstrong 2.50 6.00
E4 Scottie Pippen 12.00 30.00
E5 Mark Price 2.50 6.00
E6 Isiah Thomas 4.00 10.00
E7 Harold Miner 2.00 5.00
E8 Vin Baker 2.00 5.00
E9 Kenny Anderson 2.50 6.00
E10 Derrick Coleman 2.50 6.00
E11 Patrick Ewing 6.00 15.00
E12 Anfernee Hardaway 20.00 50.00
E13 Shaquille O'Neal 20.00 50.00
E14 Shawn Bradley 4.00 10.00
E15 Calbert Cheaney 2.50 6.00
W1 Jim Jackson 3.00 8.00
W2 Jamal Mashburn 8.00 20.00
W3 Dikembe Mutombo 6.00 15.00
W4 Latrell Sprewell 12.00 30.00
W5 Chris Webber 15.00 40.00
W6 Hakeem Olajuwon 10.00 25.00
W7 Danny Manning 4.00 10.00
W8 Nick Van Exel 6.00 15.00
W9 Isaiah Rider 8.00 20.00
W10 Charles Barkley 10.00 25.00
W11 Clyde Drexler 8.00 20.00
W12 Mitch Richmond 5.00 12.00
W13 David Robinson 10.00 25.00
W14 Shawn Kemp 8.00 20.00
W15 Karl Malone 10.00 25.00

1993-94 Upper Deck SE USA Trade
COMPLETE SET (24) 20.00 50.00
TRADE CARD: STATED ODDS 1:360 HOB/RET
1 Charles Barkley 2.50 6.00
2 Larry Bird 4.00 10.00
3 Clyde Drexler 1.50 4.00
4 Patrick Ewing 1.50 4.00
5 Michael Jordan 10.00 25.00
6 Christian Laettner 1.00 2.50
7 Karl Malone 2.00 5.00
8 Chris Mullin 1.25 3.00
9 Scottie Pippen 2.50 6.00
10 David Robinson 2.00 5.00
11 John Stockton 2.00 5.00
12 Dominique Wilkins 1.50 4.00
13 Isiah Thomas 1.50 4.00
14 Dan Majerle 1.00 2.50
15 Steve Smith .75 2.00
16 Alonzo Mourning 1.50 4.00
17 Shawn Kemp 1.50 4.00
18 Larry Johnson 1.25 3.00
19 Tim Hardaway 1.25 3.00
20 Joe Dumars 1.25 3.00
21 Mark Price 1.00 2.50
22 Derrick Coleman 1.00 2.50
23 Reggie Miller 2.00 5.00
24 Shaquille O'Neal 5.00 12.00
NNO Expired USA Trade Card .40 1.00
NNO Red. USA Trade Card .20 .50

1991-92 Upper Deck Sheets
COMPLETE SET (14) 60.00 150.00
1 Number 1 Draft Choices
June 26, 1991 (12,000)
Number One Picks
Patrick Ewing
Brad Daugherty
David Robinson
Danny Manning
Pervis Ellison
Derrick Coleman 4.00 10.00
2 12th National Sports
Collectors Convention
July 4, 1991 (65,000)
Brad Daugherty
David Robinson
Danny Manning
Pervis Ellison
Derrick Coleman 2.00 5.00
3 Philadelphia Sports
Heroes *
Oct. 17, 1991 (21,500)
Charles Barkley
Mike Schmidt
Rick Tocchet
Reggie White 4.00 10.00
4 McDonald's Open
Paris, France
Oct. 18-19, 1991 (59,000)
James Worthy
Byron Scott
A.C. Green
Magic Johnson
Sam Perkins
Vlade Divac 4.00 10.00
5 Detroit Pistons vs.
Nov. 27, 1991 (38,500)
Joe Dumars
Dennis Rodman
Mark Aguirre
Bill Laimbeer
John Salley
Isiah Thomas 3.00 8.00
6 All-Star Weekend
Orlando, Florida
Feb. 7-9, 1992 (22,000) 8.00 20.00
7 1971-72 World Champion
Feb. 26, 1992 (22,000)(20th Anniversary)
Wilt Chamberlain
Bill Sharman CO
Jerry West
Pat Riley
Jim McMillian
Gail Goodrich 8.00 20.00
8 New York Knicks
vs. Minnesota Timberwolves
Feb. 29, 1992 (19,000)
Kiki Vandeweghe
Patrick Ewing
Charles Oakley
Gerald Wilkins
John Starks
Anthony Mason
Xavier McDaniel
Mark Jackson 3.00 8.00
9 Detroit Pistons
vs. Los Angeles Clippers
March 31, 1992 (38,500)
Bill Laimbeer
John Salley
Isiah Thomas
Orlando Woolridge
Dennis Rodman
Joe Dumars 3.00 8.00
10 1992 NCAA Final Four
Championship Coaches
April 4-6, 1992 (68,000)
John Wooden
Dean Smith
Adolph Rupp
Bob Knight 8.00 20.00
11 Hoop It Up
San Jose, California
June 6-7, 1992 (158,000)
Sarunas Marciulonis
Billy Owens
Tim Hardaway
Victor Alexander
Chris Gatling
Chris Mullin 4.00 10.00
12 Battle of the
Basketball Stars
Undated (10,000)
Reportedly issued 6/20/92
Charles Smith
Dominique Wilkins
Pervis Ellison
Kenny Smith
Isiah Thomas
Mitch Richmond
Pooh Richardson
Tim Hardaway 4.00 10.00
13 Upper Deck Commemorates
the NBA Draft
June 24, 1992 (15,000)
Larry Johnson
Kenny Anderson
Billy Owens
Dikembe Mutombo
Steve Smith
Doug Smith
Luc Longley
Mark Macon 6.00 15.00
14 1992 USA Basketball
Team/(80,000)
Issued June 1992 8.00 20.00

1992-93 Upper Deck Sheets
COMPLETE SET (10) 50.00 125.00
1 Utah Jazz
Stay in School
Undated (67,000)
Issued Oct. 1992
David Benoit
Karl Malone
Mark Eaton
Jeff Malone
Mike Brown
John Stockton
Jay Humphries
Tyrone Corbin 4.00 10.00
2 Cleveland Cavaliers
Jan. 12, 1993 (30,000)
Larry Nance
Hot Rod Williams
Mark Price
Brad Daugherty
Craig Ehlo
John Battle 3.00 8.00
3 Larry Bird Salute
(Retirement Ceremony,
Boston Garden)
Feb. 4, 1993 (25,000)
(Alan Studt artwork) 10.00 25.00
4 All-Star Weekend
Autograph Sheet/Upper Deck Trading Card
and Memorabilia Show
Feb. 19-21, 1993 (75,000)
(Picture of Salt Lake
City with mountains in
background) 1.25 3.00
5 All-Star Heroes
Feb. 19-21, 1993 (10,000)
Jerry West
John Havlicek
Elgin Baylor
Dave Cowens 8.00 20.00
6 Milwaukee Bucks
25th Anniversary
Undated (13,000)
Reportedly issued 3/3/93
Jon McGlocklin
Sidney Moncrief
Oscar Robertson
Kareem Abdul-Jabbar
Bob Lanier
Brian Winters
Junior Bridgeman 6.00 15.00
7 Atlanta Hawks
Undated (10,000)
Reportedly issued
March 25, 1993
Stacey Augmon
Mookie Blaylock
Duane Ferrell
Adam Keefe
Dominique Wilkins
Kevin Willis 6.00 15.00
8 Upper Deck Salutes
April 20, 1993 (22,500)
Bill Cartwright
Michael Jordan
John Paxson
Scottie Pippen
B.J. Armstrong
Horace Grant 10.00 25.00
9 AT and T Long Distance
Shootout
Undated (22,500)
Reportedly issued 6/93
Dan Majerle
Mark Price
Terry Porter
Dana Barros
Kenny Smith
B.J. Armstrong
Reggie Miller 5.00 12.00
10 Upper Deck Commemorates
the NBA Draft/(1992 Top Draft Choices)
June 30, 1993 (22,000)
Shaquille O'Neal
Alonzo Mourning
Christian Laettner
Jim Jackson
LaPhonso Ellis
Tom Gugliotta
Walt Williams
Todd Day 8.00 20.00

1993-94 Upper Deck Sheets
COMPLETE SET (8) 25.00 60.00
1 1993 National Conv.
Chicago, Illinois
July 20-25, 1993
Michael Jordan 4.00 10.00
2 1993 McDonald's Open
October 21, 1993
Danny Ainge
Dan Majerle
Oliver Miller
Charles Barkley
Kevin Johnson
Mark West
Negele Knight
Cedric Ceballos 4.00 10.00
3 Chicago Bulls
Nov. 13, 1993 (22,000)
John Paxson
B.J. Armstrong
Corie Blount
Scottie Pippen
Bill Cartwright
Horace Grant 6.00 15.00
4 Upper Deck Salutes
NBA Standouts
All-Star Weekend
Undated (30,000)
Issued Feb. 1994
Harold Miner
Patrick Ewing
Hakeem Olajuwon
Alonzo Mourning
Jim Jackson
Derrick Coleman 4.00 10.00
5 Upper Deck All-Star
Autograph Sheet
All-Star Weekend
Undated (20,000)
Issued Feb. 1994 1.25 3.00
6 SE Preview
Undated (16,000)
Issued March 1994
Shawn Bradley
Shaquille O'Neal
LaPhonso Ellis
Jamal Mashburn
Chris Webber
Calbert Cheaney 5.00 12.00
7 1994 NBA All-Rookie
Team
No Date (40,000)
Chris Webber
Isaiah Rider
Jamal Mashburn
Vin Baker
Anfernee Hardaway 4.00 10.00
8 Upper Deck Salutes
NBA Draft Picks
June 29, 1994 (25,000)
Chris Webber
Shawn Bradley
Anfernee Hardaway
Jamal Mashburn
Isaiah Rider
Calbert Cheaney 5.00 12.00

1994-95 Upper Deck Sheets
COMPLETE SET (4) 12.00 30.00
1 Series Two NBA
Basketball Cards/(Promo sheet)
Shawn Kemp (Predictor)
Scottie Pippen
Shaquille O'Neal
Shawn Kemp (Slam Dunk)
Bobby Hurley
Jason Kidd 3.00 8.00
2 Upper Deck Predictor
Series Cards
No date (12,000)
Shawn Kemp
Patrick Ewing
Kevin Willis
Mookie Blaylock
Tim Hardaway
Glenn Robinson 4.00 10.00
3 Upper Deck Salutes
Michael Jordan
Jewel
No date (50,000) 4.00 10.00
4 1995 NBA Draft
Grant Hill
Juwan Howard
Jason Kidd
Donyell Marshall
Glenn Robinson
Sharone Wright
No date(5,000 issued) 5.00 12.00

1995-96 Upper Deck Sheets
COMPLETE SET (2) 8.00 20.00
1 1996 NBA Draft
Kevin Garnett
Antonio McDyess
Bryant Reeves
Joe Smith
Jerry Stackhouse
Rasheed Wallace 6.00 15.00
2 1996 NBA Champions
Randy Brown
Toni Kukoc
Dickey Simpkins
Ron Harper
Luc Longley
John Salley
Michael Jordan
Steve Kerr
Jud Buechler
Scottie Pippen
Bill Wennington
Jason Caffey
James Edwards
Jack Haley
Dennis Rodman 6.00 15.00

2000-01 Upper Deck Slam
COMPLETE SET w/o RC (60) 8.00 20.00
RCs: PRINT RUN 90 TO 2500 SERIAL SETS
1 Dikembe Mutombo .50 1.25
2 Jim Jackson .25 .60
3 Paul Pierce .50 1.25
4 Antoine Walker .30 .75
5 Eddie Jones .30 .75
6 Baron Davis .30 .75
7 Derrick Coleman .30 .75
8 Elton Brand .30 .75
9 Ron Artest .30 .75
10 Andre Miller .25 .60
11 Shawn Kemp .50 1.25
12 Michael Finley .30 .75
13 Dirk Nowitzki .75 2.00
14 Antonio McDyess .25 .60
15 James Posey .20 .50
16 Jerry Stackhouse .30 .75
17 Jerome Williams .20 .50
18 Larry Hughes .30 .75
19 Antawn Jamison .30 .75
20 Steve Francis .30 .75
21 Hakeem Olajuwon .60 1.50
22 Reggie Miller .60 1.50
23 Jalen Rose .25 .60
24 Lamar Odom .30 .75
25 Michael Olowokandi .20 .50
26 Shaquille O'Neal 1.25 3.00
27 Kobe Bryant 12.00 30.00
28 Alonzo Mourning .50 1.25
29 Jamal Mashburn .25 .60
30 Ray Allen .50 1.25
31 Glenn Robinson .30 .75
32 Kevin Garnett .75 2.00
33 Wally Szczerbiak .25 .60
34 Stephon Marbury .40 1.00
35 Keith Van Horn .25 .60
36 Latrell Sprewell .40 1.00
37 Allan Houston .30 .75
38 Darrell Armstrong .20 .50
39 Ron Mercer .25 .60
40 Allen Iverson .75 2.00
41 Toni Kukoc .40 1.00
42 Jason Kidd .50 1.25
43 Anfernee Hardaway .50 1.25
44 Shawn Marion .30 .75
45 Scottie Pippen .75 2.00
46 Rasheed Wallace .40 1.00
47 Chris Webber .40 1.00
48 Vlade Divac .30 .75
49 Tim Duncan .75 2.00
50 David Robinson .60 1.50
51 Gary Payton .50 1.25
52 Rashard Lewis .30 .75
53 Vince Carter .60 1.50
54 Doug Christie .25 .60
55 Karl Malone .60 1.50
56 Bryon Russell .20 .50
57 Shareef Abdur-Rahim .30 .75
58 Michael Dickerson .20 .50
59 Juwan Howard .25 .60
60 Richard Hamilton .40 1.00
61 Jerome Moiso/2500 RC .60 1.50
62 Etan Thomas/2500 RC .75 2.00
63 Courtney Alexander/2500 RC .60 1.50
64 Mateen Cleaves/2500 RC .75 2.00
65 Jason Collier/2500 RC 1.00 2.50
66 Hedo Turkoglu/900 RC 3.00 8.00
67 Desmond Mason/2500 RC 1.25 3.00
68 Quentin Richardson/2500 RC .75 2.00
69 Jamaal Magloire/2500 RC 1.00 2.50
70 Speedy Claxton/2500 RC 1.00 2.50
71 Morris Peterson/2500 RC 1.00 2.50
72 Donnell Harvey/2500 RC .75 2.00
73 Ira Newble/2500 RC .75 2.00
74 Mamadou N'Diaye/2500 RC .60 1.50
75 Erick Barkley/2500 RC .60 1.50
76 Mark Madsen/2500 RC 1.00 2.50
77 Dan Langhi/2500 RC .60 1.50
78 A.J. Guyton/2500 RC .60 1.50
79 Olumide Oyedeji/900 RC 1.25 3.00
80 Eddie House/900 RC 1.50 4.00
81 Eduardo Najera/900 RC 2.00 5.00
82 Lavor Postell/900 RC 1.25 3.00
83 Hanno Mottola/900 RC 1.25 3.00
84 Chris Carrawell/2500 RC .60 1.50
85 Michael Redd/900 RC 5.00 12.00
86 Jabari Smith/900 RC 1.25 3.00
87 Jason Hart/900 RC 2.00 5.00
88 Corey Hightower/2500 RC 1.00 2.50
89 Chris Porter/2500 RC .60 1.50
90 Justin Love/900 RC 2.00 5.00
91 Kenyon Martin/2500 RC 2.00 5.00
92 Stromile Swift/2500 RC .75 2.00
93 Darius Miles/2500 RC 1.00 2.50
94 Marcus Fizer/2500 RC .75 2.00
95 Mike Miller/2500 RC 1.50 4.00
96 DerMarr Johnson/2500 RC .60 1.50
97 Chris Mihm/2500 RC .60 1.50
98 Jamal Crawford/2500 RC 2.50 6.00
99 Joel Przybilla/2500 RC .75 2.00
100 Keyon Dooling/2500 RC .75 2.00
P21 Kevin Garnett 1.00 2.50

2000-01 Upper Deck Slam Extra Strength Silver
*STARS: 3X TO 8X BASE CARD HI
*RCs/2500: .5X TO 1.25X BASE CARD HI
*RCs/900: .25X TO .6X BASE CARD HI
STATED PRINT RUN 500 SERIAL #'d SETS
27 Kobe Bryant 150.00 400.00

2000-01 Upper Deck Slam Extra Strength Gold
*STARS: 25X TO 60X BASE CARD HI
*RCs/2500: 4X TO 10X BASE CARD HI
*RCs/900: 2X TO 5X BASE CARD HI
STATED PRINT RUN 25 SERIAL #'d SETS
27 Kobe Bryant 1,000.00 2,000.00

2000-01 Upper Deck Slam Air Styles
COMPLETE SET (9) 25.00 60.00
STATED ODDS 1:9
AS1 Kevin Garnett 2.50 6.00
AS2 Vince Carter 2.00 5.00
AS3 Gary Payton 1.50 4.00
AS4 Steve Francis 1.00 2.50
AS5 Shareef Abdur-Rahim 1.00 2.50
AS6 Allen Iverson 2.50 6.00
AS7 Elton Brand 1.00 2.50
AS8 Kobe Bryant 20.00 50.00
AS9 Scottie Pippen 2.50 6.00

2000-01 Upper Deck Slam Air Supremacy
COMPLETE SET (6) 20.00 50.00
STATED ODDS 1:18
S1 Kobe Bryant 15.00 40.00
S2 Vince Carter 2.00 5.00
S3 Shaquille O'Neal 4.00 10.00
S4 Allen Iverson 2.50 6.00
S5 Steve Francis 1.00 2.50
S6 Kevin Garnett 2.50 6.00

2000-01 Upper Deck Slam Flight Gear
STATED ODDS 1:108
KB2G Kobe Bryant 100.00 250.00
KG2G Kevin Garnett 10.00 25.00
AIG Allen Iverson 10.00 25.00
AMG Alonzo Mourning 6.00 15.00
DRG David Robinson 8.00 20.00
GPG Gary Payton 6.00 15.00
KBG Kobe Bryant 100.00 250.00
KGA Kevin Garnett AU/21 100.00 250.00
KGG Kevin Garnett 10.00 25.00
KMG Karl Malone 8.00 20.00
MJG Michael Jordan/23 500.00 1,000.00
SAG Shareef Abdur-Rahim 4.00 10.00
SOG Shaquille O'Neal 15.00 40.00
THG Tim Hardaway 5.00 12.00
WSG Wally Szczerbiak 3.00 8.00

2000-01 Upper Deck Slam Power Windows
COMPLETE SET (6) 5.00 12.00
STATED ODDS 1:18
PW1 Shaquille O'Neal 2.50 6.00
PW2 Kevin Garnett 1.50 4.00
PW3 Karl Malone 1.25 3.00
PW4 Kobe Bryant 15.00 40.00
PW5 Elton Brand .60 1.50
PW6 Vince Carter 1.25 3.00

2000-01 Upper Deck Slam Signature Slams
STATED ODDS 1:108
AH Anfernee Hardaway 25.00 60.00
AJ Antawn Jamison 6.00 15.00
AM Andre Miller 6.00 15.00
BD Baron Davis 6.00 15.00
KB Kobe Bryant 2,000.00 4,000.00
KG Kevin Garnett 60.00 150.00
RA Ray Allen 15.00 40.00
TM Tracy McGrady 15.00 40.00
WS Wally Szczerbiak 6.00 15.00

2000-01 Upper Deck Slam Slam Exam
COMPLETE SET (9) 3.00 8.00
STATED ODDS 1:6
SE1 Kobe Bryant 15.00 40.00
SE2 Kevin Garnett 1.00 2.50
SE3 Anfernee Hardaway .60 1.50
SE4 Lamar Odom .40 1.00
SE5 Michael Finley .40 1.00
SE6 Latrell Sprewell .50 1.25
SE7 Larry Hughes .40 1.00
SE8 Chris Webber .50 1.25
SE9 Antonio McDyess .30 .75

2000-01 Upper Deck Slam UD Authentics
DH Donnell Harvey 3.00 8.00
JM Jamaal Magloire 4.00 10.00
MN Mamadou N'Diaye 2.50 6.00

2005-06 Upper Deck Slam
COMPLETE SET (120) 20.00 50.00
COMP.SET w/o SP's 8.00 20.00
91-120 RC STATED ODDS 1:1
1 Tony Delk .20 .50
2 Josh Smith .25 .60
3 Al Harrington .25 .60
4 Antoine Walker .25 .60
5 Gary Payton .50 1.25
6 Paul Pierce .50 1.25
7 Kareem Rush .20 .50
8 Emeka Okafor .25 .60
9 Primoz Brezec .20 .50
10 Eddy Curry .20 .50
11 Kirk Hinrich .25 .60
12 Ben Gordon .25 .60
13 Drew Gooden .25 .60
14 LeBron James 2.50 6.00
15 Zydrunas Ilgauskas .25 .60
16 Dirk Nowitzki .75 2.00
17 Jason Terry .25 .60

18 Michael Finley .30 .75
19 Carmelo Anthony .50 1.25
20 Kenyon Martin .25 .60
21 Earl Boykins .20 .50
22 Ben Wallace .40 1.00
23 Chauncey Billups .40 1.00
24 Richard Hamilton .40 1.00
25 Troy Murphy .20 .50
26 Jason Richardson .30 .75
27 Baron Davis .30 .75
28 Tracy McGrady .50 1.25
29 Yao Ming .60 1.50
30 Juwan Howard .25 .60
31 Jermaine O'Neal .25 .60
32 Stephen Jackson .25 .60
33 Ron Artest .25 .60
34 Corey Maggette .25 .60
35 Elton Brand .25 .60
36 Bobby Simmons .20 .50
37 Caron Butler .25 .60
38 Kobe Bryant 2.50 6.00
39 Lamar Odom .25 .60
40 Mike Miller .25 .60
41 Jason Williams .50 1.25
42 Pau Gasol .50 1.25
43 Dwyane Wade .60 1.50
44 Eddie Jones .25 .60
45 Shaquille O'Neal 1.00 2.50
46 Desmond Mason .20 .50
47 Maurice Williams .25 .60
48 Michael Redd .25 .60
49 Kevin Garnett .75 2.00
50 Latrell Sprewell .30 .75
51 Sam Cassell .25 .60
52 Vince Carter .60 1.50
53 Jason Kidd .50 1.25
54 Richard Jefferson .25 .60
55 Dan Dickau .20 .50
56 Jamaal Magloire .20 .50
57 J.R. Smith .30 .75
58 Jamal Crawford .30 .75
59 Stephon Marbury .40 1.00
60 Allan Houston .25 .60
61 Dwight Howard .40 1.00
62 Grant Hill .50 1.25
63 Steve Francis .30 .75
64 Allen Iverson .60 1.50
65 Andre Iguodala .30 .75
66 Chris Webber .40 1.00
67 Amare Stoudemire .30 .75
68 Shawn Marion .25 .60
69 Steve Nash .60 1.50
70 Damon Stoudamire .30 .75
71 Shareef Abdur-Rahim .30 .75
72 Zach Randolph .30 .75
73 Mike Bibby .30 .75
74 Peja Stojakovic .25 .60
75 Brad Miller .25 .60
76 Manu Ginobili .60 1.50
77 Tim Duncan .75 2.00
78 Tony Parker .50 1.25
79 Rashard Lewis .25 .60
80 Ray Allen .50 1.25
81 Ronald Murray .20 .50
82 Rafer Alston .25 .60
83 Jalen Rose .25 .60
84 Chris Bosh .40 1.00
85 Andrei Kirilenko .25 .60
86 Carlos Boozer .25 .60
87 Matt Harpring .20 .50
88 Antawn Jamison .25 .60
89 Gilbert Arenas .30 .75
90 Larry Hughes .25 .60
91 Andrew Bogut RC .75 2.00
92 Martynas Andriuskevicius RC .40 1.00
93 Chris Paul RC 3.00 8.00
94 Deron Williams RC 1.00 2.50
95 Luther Head RC .40 1.00
96 Chris Taft RC .40 1.00
97 David Lee RC .60 1.50
98 Gerald Green RC .60 1.50
99 Andrew Bynum RC .50 1.25
100 Rashad McCants RC .40 1.00
101 Raymond Felton RC .50 1.25
102 Danny Granger RC .60 1.50
103 Johan Petro RC .40 1.00
104 Antoine Wright RC .50 1.25
105 Channing Frye RC .50 1.25
106 Joey Graham RC .50 1.25
107 Wayne Simien RC .40 1.00
108 Monta Ellis RC .75 2.00
109 Charlie Villanueva RC .50 1.25
110 Martell Webster RC .50 1.25
111 C.J. Miles RC .50 1.25
112 Hakim Warrick RC .50 1.25
113 Ike Diogu RC .40 1.00
114 Jarrett Jack RC .40 1.00
115 Nate Robinson RC .60 1.50
116 Francisco Garcia RC .40 1.00
117 Sarunas Jasikevicius RC .60 1.50
118 Salim Stoudamire RC .50 1.25
119 Marvin Williams RC .60 1.50
120 Sean May RC .40 1.00

2005-06 Upper Deck Slam Dunk Swatches

STATED ODDS 1:24
AK Andrei Kirilenko 2.00 5.00
BB Bruce Bowen 2.00 5.00
BR Bryon Russell 2.00 5.00
CB Carlos Boozer 2.00 5.00
CH Chris Bosh 3.00 8.00
DG Devean George 2.00 5.00
DN Dirk Nowitzki 6.00 15.00
DW Dajuan Wagner 2.00 5.00
JK Jason Kidd 4.00 10.00
JO Jermaine O'Neal 2.00 5.00
JR Jason Richardson 2.50 6.00
KB Kobe Bryant 40.00 100.00
KG Kevin Garnett 6.00 15.00
KR Kareem Rush 2.00 5.00
KT Kurt Thomas 2.00 5.00
LJ LeBron James 8.00 20.00
ME Stanislav Medvedenko 2.00 5.00
MJ Michael Jordan SP 25.00 60.00
MR Malik Rose 2.00 5.00
RJ Richard Jefferson 2.00 5.00
SF Steve Francis 2.50 6.00
SM Shawn Marion 2.00 5.00
SN Steve Nash 5.00 12.00
SO Shaquille O'Neal 8.00 20.00
ST Stephon Marbury 3.00 8.00
TD Tim Duncan 6.00 15.00
TM Tracy McGrady 4.00 10.00
UH Udonis Haslem 1.50 4.00
WS Wally Szczerbiak 2.00 5.00
YM Yao Ming 5.00 12.00

2005-06 Upper Deck Slam Signature Slams

STATED ODDS 1:480
SP INFO PROVIDED BY UPPER DECK
AI Andre Iguodala 8.00 20.00
AJ Antawn Jamison 5.00 12.00
BM Brad Miller 5.00 12.00
BU Beno Udrih 5.00 12.00
CD Chris Duhon 5.00 12.00
CW Chris Wilcox 5.00 12.00
DM Desmond Mason 5.00 12.00
DW Dorell Wright 5.00 12.00
JR J.R. Smith 5.00 12.00
JW Jason Williams 40.00 100.00
LJ LeBron James 1,250.00 2,500.00
MJ Michael Jordan SP 2,000.00 4,000.00
MP Morris Peterson 5.00 12.00
PP Paul Pierce SP 40.00 100.00
RJ Richard Jefferson 5.00 12.00
SN Steve Nash SP 50.00 120.00

2005-06 Upper Deck Slam Target Jerseys

HC21 Austin Croshere 1.50 4.00
HC22 Brendan Haywood 1.50 4.00
HC23 Darius Songaila 1.50 4.00
HC24 Grant Hill 4.00 10.00
HC25 Jameer Nelson 1.50 4.00
HC26 Jason Richardson 2.50 6.00
HC27 Jason Terry 2.00 5.00
HC28 Josh Howard 2.00 5.00
HC29 Kelvin Cato 1.50 4.00
HC30 Kevin Martin 2.00 5.00
HC31 Lamar Odom 2.00 5.00
HC32 LeBron James 20.00 50.00
HC33 Malik Rose 1.50 4.00
HC34 Marcus Camby 2.00 5.00
HC35 Mike Sweetney 1.50 4.00
HC36 Peja Stojakovic 2.00 5.00
HC37 Reggie Miller 4.00 10.00
HC38 Tayshaun Prince 2.50 6.00
HC39 Yao Ming 5.00 12.00
HC40 Zydrunas Ilgauskas 2.00 5.00

2005 Upper Deck Sportsfest

COMPLETE SET (6) 8.00 20.00
NBA1 LeBron James 2.50 6.00
NBA2 Kobe Bryant 2.50 6.00
NBA3 Michael Jordan 5.00 12.00
NBA4 Kevin Garnett 1.50 4.00
NBA5 Yao Ming 1.25 3.00
NBA6 Steve Nash 1.25 3.00

2006 Upper Deck Sportsfest

COMPLETE SET (3) 7.50 15.00
NBA1 Michael Jordan 4.00 10.00
NBA2 LeBron James 3.00 8.00
NBA3 Chris Paul 2.00 5.00

2007 Upper Deck Sportsfest

SF7 Kevin Durant 10.00 25.00
SF8 Michael Jordan 2.50 6.00
SF9 LeBron James 2.00 5.00

2003-04 Upper Deck Standing O

COMP.SET w/o SP's 15.00 40.00
85-126 STATED ODDS 1:4
1 Shareef Abdur-Rahim .30 .75
2 Jason Terry .25 .60
3 Theo Ratliff .20 .50
4 Paul Pierce .50 1.25
5 Antoine Walker .40 1.00
6 Vin Baker .20 .50
7 Jalen Rose .25 .60
8 Tyson Chandler .25 .60
9 Michael Jordan 8.00 20.00
10 Dajuan Wagner .20 .50
11 Zydrunas Ilgauskas .25 .60
12 Darius Miles .20 .50
13 Dirk Nowitzki .75 2.00
14 Michael Finley .30 .75
15 Steve Nash .60 1.50
16 Nene .20 .50
17 Rodney White .20 .50
18 Richard Hamilton .40 1.00
19 Ben Wallace .40 1.00
20 Chauncey Billups .40 1.00
21 Nick Van Exel .30 .75
22 Jason Richardson .30 .75
23 Mike Dunleavy .25 .60
24 Steve Francis .30 .75
25 Yao Ming .75 2.00
26 Cuttino Mobley .20 .50
27 Reggie Miller .60 1.50
28 Jamaal Tinsley .20 .50
29 Jermaine O'Neal .30 .75
30 Elton Brand .25 .60
31 Corey Maggette .25 .60
32 Quentin Richardson .20 .50
33 Kobe Bryant 2.50 6.00
34 Shaquille O'Neal 1.25 3.00
35 Gary Payton .30 .75
36 Karl Malone .60 1.50
37 Pau Gasol .50 1.25
38 Mike Miller .25 .60
39 Eddie Jones .30 .75
40 Brian Grant .20 .50
41 Caron Butler .25 .60
42 Michael Redd .25 .60
43 Joe Smith .25 .60
44 Desmond Mason .20 .50
45 Kevin Garnett .75 2.00
46 Latrell Sprewell .40 1.00
47 Sam Cassell .25 .60
48 Jason Kidd .50 1.25
49 Richard Jefferson .25 .60
50 Alonzo Mourning .40 1.00
51 Baron Davis .30 .75
52 Jamal Mashburn .25 .60
53 Jamaal Magloire .20 .50
54 Allan Houston .30 .75
55 Antonio McDyess .25 .60
56 Keith Van Horn .25 .60
57 Tracy McGrady .50 1.25
58 Juwan Howard .25 .60
59 Drew Gooden .25 .60
60 Allen Iverson .75 2.00
61 Glenn Robinson .25 .60
62 Stephon Marbury .40 1.00
63 Shawn Marion .30 .75
64 Amare Stoudemire .40 1.00
65 Rasheed Wallace .40 1.00
66 Bonzi Wells .20 .50
67 Chris Webber .40 1.00
68 Mike Bibby .30 .75
69 Peja Stojakovic .25 .60
70 Tim Duncan .75 2.00
71 David Robinson .60 1.50
72 Tony Parker .50 1.25
73 Ray Allen .50 1.25
74 Rashard Lewis .25 .60
75 Reggie Evans .20 .50
76 Vince Carter .60 1.50
77 Morris Peterson .20 .50
78 Antonio Davis .25 .60
79 Jarron Collins .20 .50
80 John Stockton .60 1.50
81 Andrei Kirilenko .25 .60
82 Jerry Stackhouse .40 1.00
83 Gilbert Arenas .30 .75
84 Larry Hughes .25 .60
85 LeBron James RC 50.00 120.00
86 Darko Milicic RC 1.00 2.50
87 Carmelo Anthony RC 6.00 15.00
88 Chris Bosh RC 4.00 10.00
89 Dwyane Wade RC 10.00 25.00
90 Chris Kaman RC 1.25 3.00
91 Kirk Hinrich RC 1.25 3.00
92 T.J. Ford RC 1.00 2.50
93 Mike Sweetney RC .75 2.00
94 Jarvis Hayes RC .75 2.00
95 Mickael Pietrus RC 1.00 2.50
96 Nick Collison RC 1.00 2.50
97 Marcus Banks RC .75 2.00
98 Luke Ridnour RC 1.25 3.00
99 Reece Gaines RC .75 2.00
100 Troy Bell RC .75 2.00
101 Zarko Cabarkapa RC .75 2.00
102 David West RC 1.50 4.00
103 Aleksandar Pavlovic RC 1.00 2.50
104 Dahntay Jones RC 1.00 2.50
105 Boris Diaw RC 1.25 3.00
106 Zoran Planinic RC .75 2.00
107 Travis Outlaw RC .75 2.00
108 Brian Cook RC .75 2.00
109 Carlos Delfino RC 1.00 2.50
110 Ndudi Ebi RC .75 2.00
111 Kendrick Perkins RC 1.00 2.50
112 Leandro Barbosa RC 1.25 3.00
113 Josh Howard RC 1.25 3.00
114 Maciej Lampe RC .75 2.00
115 Jason Kapono RC .75 2.00
116 Luke Walton RC 1.25 3.00
117 Jerome Beasley RC .75 2.00
118 Willie Green RC .75 2.00
119 Kyle Korver RC 1.50 4.00
120 Travis Hansen RC .75 2.00
121 Steve Blake RC 1.00 2.50
122 Slavko Vranes RC .75 2.00
123 Zaur Pachulia RC .75 2.00
124 Keith Bogans RC .75 2.00
125 Theron Smith RC .75 2.00
126 Brandon Hunter RC .75 2.00

2003-04 Upper Deck Standing O Die Cuts/Embossed

*SINGLES: .75X TO 2X BASE CARD HI
1-84 STATED ODDS 1:1
*RCs: .4X TO 1X BASE CARD HI
85-126 RC STATED ODDS 1:24
ROOKIES ARE EMBOSSED

2003-04 Upper Deck Standing O Graphs

AVAILABLE VIA REDEMPTION CARDS
BI Chauncey Billups SP 10.00 25.00
BO Carlos Boozer 8.00 20.00
DJ DerMarr Johnson 4.00 10.00
ET Etan Thomas 4.00 10.00
GA Gilbert Arenas SP 12.00 30.00
KB Kobe Bryant SP 125.00 300.00
LJ LeBron James SP 5,000.00 10,000.00
MJ Michael Jordan/23 2,000.00 4,000.00
MP Morris Peterson 4.00 10.00
RE Reggie Evans SP 4.00 10.00
RL Rashard Lewis 6.00 15.00
TM Tracy McGrady/25 20.00 50.00

2003-04 Upper Deck Standing O Swatches

AVAILABLE VIA REDEMPTION CARDS
AIPH Allen Iverson 8.00 20.00
CBPH Caron Butler 2.50 6.00
CWPH Chris Webber 4.00 10.00
DNPH Dirk Nowitzki 8.00 20.00
GHPH Grant Hill 5.00 12.00
JKPH Jason Kidd 5.00 12.00
JOPH Jermaine O'Neal 3.00 8.00
JSPH John Stockton 6.00 15.00
KBPH Kobe Bryant 12.50 30.00
KGPH Kevin Garnett 8.00 20.00
KMPH Kenyon Martin 3.00 8.00
LSPH Latrell Sprewell 4.00 10.00
MJPH Michael Jordan 60.00 120.00
PPPH Paul Pierce 5.00 12.00
SAPH Amare Stoudemire 4.00 10.00
SMPH Stephon Marbury 4.00 10.00
SNPH Steve Nash 6.00 15.00
SPPH Scottie Pippen 8.00 20.00
TDPH Tim Duncan 8.00 20.00
TMPH Tracy McGrady 5.00 12.00
YMPH Yao Ming 8.00 20.00

1991-92 Upper Deck Stay in School Sheets

COMPLETE SET (10) 15.00 40.00
1 Boston Celtics 2.50 6.00
2 Charlotte Hornets 2.50 6.00
3 Chicago Bulls 2.50 6.00
4 Detroit Pistons 2.50 6.00
5 Houston Rockets 2.50 6.00
6 Miami Heat 2.50 6.00
7 New Jersey Nets 2.50 6.00
8 Orlando Magic DP .75 2.00
9 Portland Trail Blazers 2.50 6.00
10 San Antonio Spurs 2.50 6.00

2003 Upper Deck Superstars LeBron James

COMPLETE SET (6) 20.00 50.00
COMMON CARD (1-6) 5.00 12.00

2013 Upper Deck Tiger Woods Master Collection Legendary Duos Dual Autographs

STATED PRINT RUN 1 SER.#'d SET

2003 Upper Deck Top Prospects LeBron James Promos

COMPLETE SET (3) 12.00 30.00
COMMON CARD (P1-P3) 6.00 15.00

1999 Upper Deck Tribute to Michael Jordan

COMP. FACT SET (30) 25.00 60.00
COMMON CARD (1-30) 1.50 4.00

2004-05 Upper Deck Trilogy

COMP.SET w/o SP's (100) 30.00 60.00
141-150 RC PRINT RUN 499 SER.#'d SETS
1 Antoine Walker .75 2.00
2 Al Harrington .60 1.50
3 Boris Diaw .60 1.50
4 Paul Pierce 1.25 3.00
5 Ricky Davis .60 1.50
6 Gary Payton 1.25 3.00
7 Gerald Wallace .60 1.50
8 Emeka Okafor RC .60 1.50
9 Keith Bogans .50 1.25
10 Eddy Curry .50 1.25
11 Kirk Hinrich .75 2.00
12 Michael Jordan 6.00 15.00
13 LeBron James 6.00 15.00
14 Dajuan Wagner .50 1.25
15 Jeff McInnis .50 1.25
16 Drew Gooden .50 1.25
17 Dirk Nowitzki 2.00 5.00
18 Michael Finley .75 2.00
19 Jerry Stackhouse .75 2.00
20 Jason Terry .60 1.50
21 Kenyon Martin .75 2.00
22 Andre Miller .60 1.50
23 Carmelo Anthony 1.50 4.00
24 Nene .60 1.50
25 Chauncey Billups 1.00 2.50
26 Rasheed Wallace 1.00 2.50
27 Ben Wallace 1.00 2.50
28 Richard Hamilton 1.00 2.50
29 Derek Fisher .60 1.50
30 Jason Richardson .75 2.00
31 Mike Dunleavy .50 1.25
32 Yao Ming 2.00 5.00
33 Tracy McGrady 1.25 3.00
34 Juwan Howard .60 1.50
35 Jermaine O'Neal .60 1.50
36 Reggie Miller 1.50 4.00
37 Ron Artest .75 2.00
38 Jamaal Tinsley .75 2.00
39 Elton Brand .60 1.50
40 Corey Maggette .60 1.50
41 Marko Jaric .50 1.25
42 Kerry Kittles .60 1.50
43 Kobe Bryant 6.00 15.00
44 Caron Butler .60 1.50
45 Lamar Odom .75 2.00
46 Brian Cook .50 1.25
47 Pau Gasol 1.25 3.00
48 Jason Williams .60 1.50
49 Bonzi Wells .50 1.25
50 Shaquille O'Neal 3.00 8.00
51 Dwyane Wade 3.00 8.00
52 Eddie Jones .75 2.00
53 Michael Redd .60 1.50
54 Desmond Mason .60 1.50
55 Maurice Williams .60 1.50
56 Latrell Sprewell 1.00 2.50
57 Kevin Garnett 2.00 5.00
58 Sam Cassell .60 1.50
59 Troy Hudson .50 1.25
60 Vince Carter 1.50 4.00
61 Richard Jefferson .60 1.50
62 Jason Kidd 1.25 3.00
63 P.J. Brown .50 1.25
64 Baron Davis .75 2.00
65 Jamaal Magloire .50 1.25
66 Allan Houston .75 2.00
67 Jamal Crawford .75 2.00
68 Stephon Marbury 1.00 2.50
69 Grant Hill 1.00 2.50
70 Cuttino Mobley .60 1.50
71 Steve Francis .75 2.00
72 Glenn Robinson .60 1.50
73 Allen Iverson 2.00 5.00
74 Willie Green .60 1.50
75 Amare Stoudemire .75 2.00
76 Steve Nash 1.50 4.00
77 Quentin Richardson .50 1.25
78 Shawn Marion .75 2.00
79 Shareef Abdur-Rahim .75 2.00
80 Damon Stoudamire .75 2.00
81 Zach Randolph .75 2.00
82 Darius Miles .50 1.25
83 Peja Stojakovic .60 1.50
84 Chris Webber 1.00 2.50
85 Mike Bibby .75 2.00
86 Tony Parker 1.25 3.00
87 Tim Duncan 2.00 5.00
88 Manu Ginobili 1.50 4.00
89 Ronald Murray .50 1.25
90 Ray Allen 1.25 3.00
91 Rashard Lewis .60 1.50
92 Chris Bosh 1.25 3.00
93 Rafer Alston .60 1.50
94 Jalen Rose .60 1.50
95 Andrei Kirilenko .60 1.50
96 Carlos Arroyo .50 1.25
97 Carlos Boozer .60 1.50
98 Gilbert Arenas .75 2.00
99 Jarvis Hayes .50 1.25
100 Antawn Jamison .60 1.50
101 Rafael Araujo RC 2.00 5.00
102 Luke Jackson RC 2.00 5.00
103 Andris Biedrins RC 2.00 5.00
104 Robert Swift RC 2.00 5.00
105 Kris Humphries RC 2.50 6.00
106 Al Jefferson RC 3.00 8.00
107 Kirk Snyder RC 2.00 5.00
108 Josh Smith RC 3.00 8.00
109 Dorell Wright RC 2.50 6.00
110 Jameer Nelson RC 3.00 8.00
111 Pavel Podkolzin RC 2.00 5.00
112 Andres Nocioni RC 3.00 8.00
113 Luis Flores RC 2.50 6.00
114 Delonte West RC 2.50 6.00
115 Tony Allen RC 3.00 8.00
116 Kevin Martin RC 4.00 10.00
117 Sasha Vujacic RC 2.50 6.00
118 Beno Udrih RC 2.50 6.00
119 David Harrison RC 2.00 5.00
120 Anderson Varejao RC 2.50 6.00
121 Jackson Vroman RC 2.00 5.00
122 Peter John Ramos RC 2.00 5.00
123 Lionel Chalmers RC 2.50 6.00
124 Donta Smith RC 2.00 5.00
125 Andre Emmett RC 2.00 5.00
126 Antonio Burks RC 2.00 5.00
127 Royal Ivey RC 2.00 5.00
128 Chris Duhon RC 2.50 6.00
129 Nenad Krstic RC 2.50 6.00
130 Justin Reed RC 2.00 5.00
131 Pape Sow RC 2.00 5.00
132 Trevor Ariza RC 3.00 8.00
133 Tim Pickett RC 2.50 6.00
134 Bernard Robinson RC 2.00 5.00
135 John Edwards RC 2.00 5.00
136 Damien Wilkins RC 2.50 6.00
137 Romain Sato RC 2.00 5.00
138 Matt Freije RC 2.00 5.00
139 D.J. Mbenga RC 2.00 5.00
140 Yuta Tabuse RC 3.00 8.00
141 Dwight Howard RC 12.00 30.00
142 Emeka Okafor 3.00 8.00
143 Ben Gordon RC 4.00 10.00
144 Shaun Livingston RC 4.00 10.00
145 Devin Harris RC 3.00 8.00
146 Josh Childress RC 2.50 6.00
147 Luol Deng RC 4.00 10.00
148 Andre Iguodala RC 6.00 15.00
149 Sebastian Telfair RC 3.00 8.00
150 J.R. Smith RC 4.00 10.00
P23 Carmelo Anthony PROMO 2.00 5.00

2004-05 Upper Deck Trilogy Gold

*GOLD SINGLES: 1.25X TO 3X BASE HI
GOLD PRINT RUN 100 SER.#'d SETS
12 Michael Jordan 40.00 100.00

2004-05 Upper Deck Trilogy UD Promos

*PROMOS: .6X TO 1.5X BASIC

2004-05 Upper Deck Trilogy Rookie Premiere Crystal

*101-140 RCs: 1X TO 2.5X BASE HI
*141-150 RCs: .75X TO 2X BASE HI
PRINT RUN 25 SER.#'d SETS

2004-05 Upper Deck Trilogy Auto Focus

STATED ODDS 1:9
AI Andre Iguodala 8.00 20.00
AJ Al Jefferson 5.00 12.00
AK Andrei Kirilenko 4.00 10.00
AL Ray Allen 20.00 50.00
AS Amare Stoudemire 5.00 12.00
BD Baron Davis 6.00 15.00
BG Ben Gordon 5.00 12.00
CA Carmelo Anthony SP 20.00 40.00
DE Devin Harris 4.00 10.00
DH Dwight Howard SP 12.00 30.00
DW Dorell Wright 4.00 10.00
JC Josh Childress 3.00 8.00
JK Jason Kidd SP 15.00 30.00
JN Jameer Nelson 4.00 10.00
JR J.R. Smith 5.00 12.00
JS Josh Smith 5.00 12.00
KB Kobe Bryant SP 150.00 400.00
KG Kevin Garnett SP 40.00 100.00
KH Kris Humphries 4.00 10.00
KI Kirk Hinrich 5.00 12.00
KS Kirk Snyder 3.00 8.00
LD Luol Deng 5.00 12.00
LJ LeBron James SP 1,000.00 2,000.00
LU Luke Jackson 3.00 8.00
MB Mike Bibby 5.00 12.00
MJ Michael Jordan SP 1,500.00 3,000.00
PG Pau Gasol 8.00 20.00
PP Paul Pierce 10.00 25.00
PS Peja Stojakovic 6.00 15.00
RA Rafael Araujo 3.00 8.00
RH Richard Hamilton 6.00 15.00
RS Robert Swift 3.00 8.00
SH Shawn Marion 6.00 15.00
SL Shaun Livingston 5.00 12.00
SM Stephon Marbury SP 12.00 30.00
ST Sebastian Telfair 4.00 10.00
TA Tony Allen 5.00 12.00
TM Tracy McGrady SP 12.00 30.00
WE Delonte West 4.00 10.00
YM Yao Ming 30.00 80.00

2004-05 Upper Deck Trilogy Auto Focus Crystal

*CRYSTAL: 1X TO 2.5X BASE HI
PRINT RUN 25 SER.#'d SETS
TM Tracy McGrady 25.00 60.00
YM Yao Ming 50.00 120.00

2004-05 Upper Deck Trilogy One Two Combo Clearcut Autographs

PRINT RUN 25 SER.#'d SETS
AM C.Anthony/A.Miller 30.00 80.00
CS J.Childress/Josh Smith 20.00 50.00
DG L.Deng/B.Gordon 20.00 50.00
DS B.Davis/J.R.Smith 20.00 50.00
HJ D.Howard/L.James 1,000.00 2,000.00
HN D.Howard/J.Nelson 60.00 150.00
JB L.James/K.Bryant 3,000.00 5,000.00
JJ M.Jordan/L.James 3,000.00 6,000.00
KH A.Kirilenko/K.Humphries 20.00 50.00
KJ J.Kidd/R.Jefferson 40.00 100.00
MC S.Marbury/J.Crawford 25.00 60.00
MM Y.Ming/T.McGrady 100.00 250.00
PB P.Pierce/L.Bird 100.00 250.00
SM A.Stoudemire/S.Marion 40.00 100.00

2004-05 Upper Deck Trilogy Signature Swatches

PRINT RUN 25 SER.#'d SETS
AI Andre Iguodala 20.00 50.00
AJ Al Jefferson 12.00 30.00
AK Andrei Kirilenko 15.00 40.00
AS Amare Stoudemire 30.00 80.00
BD Baron Davis 12.00 30.00
BG Ben Gordon 12.00 30.00
CA Carmelo Anthony 40.00 100.00
DE Devin Harris 10.00 25.00
DH Dwight Howard 125.00 250.00
JC Josh Childress 8.00 20.00
JK Jason Kidd 25.00 60.00
JN Jameer Nelson 12.00 30.00
JR J.R. Smith 12.00 30.00
JS Josh Smith 12.00 30.00
KB Kobe Bryant 1,000.00 2,000.00
KG Kevin Garnett 125.00 250.00
KH Kris Humphries 10.00 25.00
KS Kirk Snyder 8.00 20.00
LD Luol Deng 12.00 30.00
LJ LeBron James 175.00 350.00
LO Lamar Odom 12.00 30.00
LU Luke Jackson 8.00 20.00
MB Mike Bibby 12.00 30.00
MJ Michael Jordan 2,000.00 4,000.00
PG Pau Gasol 12.00 30.00
PP Paul Pierce 25.00 60.00
SL Shaun Livingston 12.00 30.00
SM Stephon Marbury 25.00 60.00
ST Sebastian Telfair 10.00 25.00
TM Tracy McGrady 40.00 100.00

2004-05 Upper Deck Trilogy Signs of Stardom

STATED ODDS 1:3
AE Andre Emmett 2.50 6.00
AI Andre Iguodala 6.00 15.00
AJ Al Jefferson 4.00 10.00
AK Andrei Kirilenko 4.00 10.00
AL Ray Allen 15.00 40.00
AS Amare Stoudemire 4.00 10.00
AV Anderson Varejao 3.00 8.00
BD Baron Davis 4.00 10.00
BG Ben Gordon 4.00 10.00
BM Brad Miller 3.00 8.00
BU Beno Udrih 3.00 8.00
CA Carmelo Anthony SP 20.00 50.00
CD Chris Duhon 3.00 8.00
DA David Harrison 2.50 6.00
DE Devin Harris 3.00 8.00
DH Dwight Howard SP 12.00 30.00
DW Dorell Wright 3.00 8.00
JC Josh Childress 2.50 6.00
JK Jason Kidd SP 12.00 30.00
JM Jamaal Magloire 2.50 6.00
JN Jameer Nelson 4.00 10.00
JR J.R. Smith 4.00 10.00
JS Josh Smith 4.00 10.00
JV Jackson Vroman 2.50 6.00
KB Kobe Bryant SP 400.00 800.00
KG Kevin Garnett SP 125.00 300.00
KH Kris Humphries 3.00 8.00
KI Kirk Hinrich 4.00 10.00
KM Kevin Martin 5.00 12.00
KS Kirk Snyder 2.50 6.00
LC Lionel Chalmers 3.00 8.00
LD Luol Deng 4.00 10.00
LJ LeBron James SP 1,000.00 3,000.00
LO Lamar Odom 4.00 10.00
LU Luke Jackson 2.50 6.00
MB Mike Bibby 4.00 10.00
MJ Michael Jordan SP 3,000.00 5,000.00
PG Pau Gasol 6.00 15.00
PP Paul Pierce 20.00 50.00
RA Rafael Araujo 2.50 6.00
RH Richard Hamilton 6.00 15.00
SH Shawn Marion 6.00 15.00
SL Shaun Livingston 4.00 10.00
SM Stephon Marbury 10.00 25.00
ST Sebastian Telfair 3.00 8.00
SV Sasha Vujacic 3.00 8.00
TA Tony Allen 3.00 8.00
TM Tracy McGrady SP 20.00 50.00
TR Trevor Ariza 4.00 10.00
WE Delonte West 3.00 8.00

2004-05 Upper Deck Trilogy Swatches of Stardom

PRINT RUN 50 SER.#'d SETS
AI Allen Iverson 12.00 30.00
AK Andrei Kirilenko 4.00 10.00
AS Amare Stoudemire 5.00 12.00
BD Baron Davis 5.00 12.00
BG Ben Gordon 5.00 12.00
BK Bernard King 6.00 15.00
BR Bill Russell 20.00 50.00
BW Ben Wallace 6.00 15.00
CA Carmelo Anthony 10.00 25.00
DE Devin Harris 4.00 10.00
DH Dwight Howard 15.00 40.00
DN Dirk Nowitzki 12.00 30.00
EB Elton Brand 4.00 10.00
JC Josh Childress 3.00 8.00
JE Julius Erving 20.00 50.00
JK Jason Kidd 8.00 20.00
JN Jameer Nelson 5.00 12.00
JO Jermaine O'Neal 4.00 10.00
JR J.R. Smith 5.00 12.00
JS Josh Smith 5.00 12.00
KB Kobe Bryant 75.00 200.00
KG Kevin Garnett 12.00 30.00
LB Larry Bird 25.00 60.00
LD Luol Deng 5.00 12.00
LJ LeBron James 100.00 250.00
MA Magic Johnson 20.00 50.00
MJ Michael Jordan 150.00 400.00
PG Pau Gasol 8.00 20.00
PP Paul Pierce 8.00 20.00
PS Peja Stojakovic 4.00 10.00
RM Reggie Miller 10.00 25.00
SF Steve Francis 5.00 12.00
SH Shawn Marion 5.00 12.00
SL Shaun Livingston 5.00 12.00
SM Stephon Marbury 6.00 15.00
SN Steve Nash 10.00 25.00
SO Shaquille O'Neal 15.00 40.00
ST Sebastian Telfair 4.00 10.00
TD Tim Duncan 12.00 30.00
TM Tracy McGrady 8.00 20.00
WF Walt Frazier 6.00 15.00
YM Yao Ming 12.00 30.00

2004-05 Upper Deck Trilogy The Cutting Edge

STATED ODDS 1:3
AE Andre Emmett 1.50 4.00
AI Allen Iverson 6.00 15.00
AJ Al Jefferson 2.50 6.00
AN Andre Iguodala 4.00 10.00
AS Amare Stoudemire 2.50 6.00
BD Baron Davis SP 2.50 6.00
BG Ben Gordon 2.50 6.00
CA Carmelo Anthony 5.00 12.00
CD Chris Duhon 2.00 5.00
DE Devin Harris 2.00 5.00
DH Dwight Howard 8.00 20.00
DN Dirk Nowitzki 6.00 15.00
JA Jason Richardson 2.50 6.00
JC Josh Childress 1.50 4.00
JK Jason Kidd 4.00 10.00
JN Jameer Nelson 2.50 6.00
JR J.R. Smith 2.50 6.00
JS Josh Smith 2.50 6.00
KB Kobe Bryant SP 40.00 100.00
KG Kevin Garnett SP 6.00 15.00
KH Kris Humphries 2.00 5.00
KM Kevin Martin 3.00 8.00
KS Kirk Snyder 1.50 4.00
LD Luol Deng 2.50 6.00
LJ LeBron James SP 75.00 150.00
LU Luke Jackson 1.50 4.00
MB Mike Bibby 2.50 6.00
MJ Michael Jordan SP 40.00 100.00
PP Paul Pierce 4.00 10.00
PS Peja Stojakovic 2.00 5.00
RA Ray Allen 4.00 10.00
RJ Richard Jefferson 2.00 5.00
SA Shareef Abdur-Rahim 2.50 6.00
SL Shaun Livingston 2.50 6.00
SM Stephon Marbury 3.00 8.00
SO Shaquille O'Neal SP 10.00 25.00
ST Sebastian Telfair 2.00 5.00
TA Tony Allen 2.50 6.00
TD Tim Duncan 6.00 15.00
TM Tracy McGrady 4.00 10.00
WE Delonte West 2.00 5.00
YM Yao Ming 6.00 15.00

2004-05 Upper Deck Trilogy TriMarks I

PRINT RUN 35 SER.#'d SETS
CARDS WITH ASTERISK ISSUED AS EXCH
AMS R.Allen/Murray/R.Swift* 20.00 50.00
ART Abdur-Rah/Z-BO/Telfair* 20.00 50.00
BMM Bibby/B.Miller/Kv.Martin* 20.00 50.00
BOR Bryant/Odom/Rush 125.00 300.00
CSI Childress/JoshSmith/Ivey* 20.00 50.00
DWK B.Davis/J.Williams/Kidd 125.00 225.00
GDH Gordon/Deng/Hinrich* 20.00 50.00
GEB Gasol/Emmett/Burks 20.00 50.00
HCS Harrington/Childress/Smith 20.00 50.00
HGL Howard/Gordon/Livingston 25.00 60.00
HHD J.Howard/Harris/Daniels 20.00 50.00
HJB Howard/LeBron/Kobe 3,000.00 6,000.00
HMB Rip/Chauncey/Darko* 20.00 50.00
IBJ Iguodala/Bibby/Jefferson* 20.00 50.00
JAR Jamison/Arenas/Ramos 20.00 50.00
JJV James/L.Jackson/Varejao* 500.00 1,000.00
JWA A.Jefferson/West/T.Allen* 20.00 50.00
KHS AK-47/Humphries/Snyder* 20.00 50.00
MCA Marbury/Crawford/Ariza* 20.00 50.00
MLC Magg/Livingstn/Chalmers* 20.00 50.00
MSP Magloire/J.R.Smith/Pickett 20.00 50.00
NTL Nelson/Telfair/Livingston* 20.00 50.00
OVR Odom/Vujacic/Rush 20.00 50.00
PUS Parker/Udrih/Sato 25.00 60.00
RFB J-Rich/Fisher/Biedrins 20.00 50.00
RMK Redd/Mason/Kukoc* 25.00 60.00
RPA Rose/MoPete/Araujo* 20.00 50.00
SBM Peja/Bibby/B.Miller* 30.00 80.00
SMV Amare/Marion/Vroman* 25.00 60.00

2005-06 Upper Deck Trilogy

COMP.SET w/o SP's (90) 25.00 60.00
91-130 RC PRINT RUN 999 SER.#'d SETS
131-140 RC PRINT RUN 599 SER.#'d SETS
1 Josh Smith .75 2.00
2 Josh Childress .60 1.50
3 Al Harrington .75 2.00
4 Paul Pierce 1.50 4.00
5 Ricky Davis .75 2.00
6 Al Jefferson .60 1.50
7 Emeka Okafor .75 2.00
8 Gerald Wallace .75 2.00
9 Kareem Rush .60 1.50
10 Michael Jordan 8.00 20.00
11 Luol Deng .75 2.00
12 Ben Gordon .75 2.00
13 LeBron James 8.00 20.00
14 Larry Hughes .75 2.00
15 Donyell Marshall .60 1.50
16 Dirk Nowitzki 2.50 6.00
17 Josh Howard .75 2.00
18 Jason Terry .75 2.00
19 Carmelo Anthony 1.50 4.00
20 Kenyon Martin .75 2.00
21 Andre Miller .75 2.00
22 Chauncey Billups 1.25 3.00
23 Richard Hamilton 1.25 3.00
24 Ben Wallace 1.25 3.00
25 Jason Richardson 1.00 2.50
26 Baron Davis 1.00 2.50
27 Troy Murphy .60 1.50
28 Yao Ming 2.00 5.00
29 Tracy McGrady 1.50 4.00

30 Stromile Swift .60 1.50
31 Ron Artest .75 2.00
32 Jermaine O'Neal .75 2.00
33 Fred Jones .60 1.50
34 Elton Brand .75 2.00
35 Shaun Livingston .75 2.00
36 Corey Maggette .75 2.00
37 Kobe Bryant 8.00 20.00
38 Kwame Brown .60 1.50
39 Lamar Odom .75 2.00
40 Pau Gasol 1.50 4.00
41 Shane Battier .75 2.00
42 Mike Miller .75 2.00
43 Shaquille O'Neal 3.00 8.00
44 Dwyane Wade 2.00 5.00
45 Udonis Haslem .60 1.50
46 Michael Redd .75 2.00
47 Maurice Williams .75 2.00
48 Desmond Mason .60 1.50
49 Kevin Garnett 2.50 6.00
50 Wally Szczerbiak .75 2.00
51 Marko Jaric .60 1.50
52 Jason Kidd 1.50 4.00
53 Vince Carter 2.00 5.00
54 Richard Jefferson .75 2.00
55 Jamaal Magloire .60 1.50
56 J.R. Smith 1.00 2.50
57 Speedy Claxton .60 1.50
58 Stephon Marbury 1.25 3.00
59 Jamal Crawford 1.00 2.50
60 Quentin Richardson .60 1.50
61 Steve Francis 1.00 2.50
62 Dwight Howard 1.25 3.00
63 Grant Hill 1.50 4.00
64 Allen Iverson 2.00 5.00
65 Kyle Korver .75 2.00
66 Chris Webber 1.25 3.00
67 Steve Nash 2.00 5.00
68 Amare Stoudemire 1.00 2.50
69 Shawn Marion .75 2.00
70 Sebastian Telfair .75 2.00
71 Zach Randolph 1.00 2.50
72 Travis Outlaw .75 2.00
73 Peja Stojakovic .75 2.00
74 Mike Bibby 1.00 2.50
75 Brad Miller .75 2.00
76 Tim Duncan 2.50 6.00
77 Manu Ginobili 2.00 5.00
78 Tony Parker 1.50 4.00
79 Ray Allen 1.50 4.00
80 Rashard Lewis .75 2.00
81 Luke Ridnour .75 2.00
82 Chris Bosh 1.25 3.00
83 Morris Peterson .60 1.50
84 Jalen Rose .75 2.00
85 Carlos Boozer .75 2.00
86 Matt Harpring .60 1.50
87 Andrei Kirilenko .75 2.00
88 Antawn Jamison .75 2.00
89 Gilbert Arenas 1.00 2.50
90 Caron Butler .75 2.00
91 Sarunas Jasikevicius RC 2.50 6.00
92 Alex Acker RC 1.50 4.00
93 Amir Johnson RC 2.50 6.00
94 Lawrence Roberts RC 1.50 4.00
95 Dijon Thompson RC 1.50 4.00
96 Orien Greene RC 2.00 5.00
97 Robert Whaley RC 1.50 4.00
98 Ryan Gomes RC 2.00 5.00
99 Andray Blatche RC 2.50 6.00
100 Yaroslav Korolev RC 1.50 4.00
101 Bracey Wright RC 1.50 4.00
102 Louis Williams RC 6.00 15.00
103 Martynas Andriuskevicius RC 1.50 4.00
104 Chris Taft RC 1.50 4.00
105 Monta Ellis RC 3.00 8.00
106 Von Wafer RC 1.50 4.00
107 Travis Diener RC 1.50 4.00
108 Ersan Ilyasova RC 2.00 5.00
109 Arvydas Macijauskas RC 1.50 4.00
110 C.J. Miles RC 2.00 5.00
111 Brandon Bass RC 2.00 5.00
112 Daniel Ewing RC 2.00 5.00
113 Salim Stoudamire RC 2.00 5.00
114 David Lee RC 2.50 6.00
115 Wayne Simien RC 1.50 4.00
116 Jason Maxiell RC 2.00 5.00
117 Johan Petro RC 1.50 4.00
118 Luther Head RC 1.50 4.00
119 Francisco Garcia RC 1.50 4.00
120 Jarrett Jack RC 2.50 6.00
121 Nate Robinson RC 2.50 6.00
122 Julius Hodge RC 1.50 4.00
123 Hakim Warrick RC 2.00 5.00
124 Gerald Green RC 2.50 6.00
125 Danny Granger RC 2.50 6.00
126 Joey Graham RC 2.00 5.00
127 Antoine Wright RC 2.00 5.00
128 Rashad McCants RC 1.50 4.00
129 Sean May RC 1.50 4.00
130 Linas Kleiza RC 2.00 5.00
131 Andrew Bynum RC 2.50 6.00
132 Ike Diogu RC 2.00 5.00
133 Channing Frye RC 2.50 6.00
134 Charlie Villanueva RC 2.50 6.00
135 Martell Webster RC 2.50 6.00
136 Raymond Felton RC 2.50 6.00
137 Chris Paul RC 15.00 40.00
138 Deron Williams RC 5.00 12.00
139 Marvin Williams RC 3.00 8.00
140 Andrew Bogut RC 4.00 10.00

2005-06 Upper Deck Trilogy Auto Focus
APPROXIMATELY ONE PER BOX
AB Andrew Bogut 6.00 15.00
AN Andrew Bynum 4.00 10.00
AW Antoine Wright 4.00 10.00
BG Ben Gordon 4.00 10.00
CF Channing Frye 4.00 10.00
CP Chris Paul 100.00 250.00
DG Danny Granger 5.00 12.00
DH Dwight Howard 30.00 80.00
EO Emeka Okafor 4.00 10.00
FG Francisco Garcia 3.00 8.00
GG George Gervin 15.00 40.00
HO Hakeem Olajuwon SP 75.00 200.00
ID Ike Diogu 3.00 8.00
IT Isiah Thomas 30.00 80.00
JA Jarrett Jack 5.00 12.00
JJ Joe Johnson 12.00 30.00
JP Johan Petro 3.00 8.00
JR J.R. Smith SP 20.00 50.00
KB Kwame Brown 3.00 8.00
KD Keyon Dooling 3.00 8.00
LA Larry Bird SP 150.00 400.00
LB LeBron James 2,500.00 5,000.00
MA Magic Johnson SP 150.00 400.00
MJ Michael Jordan SP 3,000.00 6,000.00
MR Michael Redd 10.00 25.00
MW Marvin Williams 5.00 12.00
NR Nate Robinson 5.00 12.00
PP Paul Pierce 60.00 150.00
RF Raymond Felton 4.00 10.00
RH Richard Hamilton 15.00 40.00
RM Rashad McCants 3.00 8.00
SE Sean May 3.00 8.00
SJ Sarunas Jasikevicius 5.00 12.00
SM Stephon Marbury 20.00 50.00
SP Scottie Pippen SP 125.00 300.00
TM Tracy McGrady SP 100.00 250.00
VR Vladimir Radmanovic 3.00 8.00
WF Walt Frazier 25.00 60.00
WS Wayne Simien 3.00 8.00
YM Yao Ming SP 150.00 400.00

2005-06 Upper Deck Trilogy DuoMarks
PRINT RUN 25 TO 75 SER.#'d SETS
AW C.Anthony/Warrick/25 40.00 100.00
BF A.Bogut/C.Frye/25 10.00 25.00
BP A.Bynum/J.Petro/75 6.00 15.00
BS B.King/S.Marbury/75 30.00 80.00
CD Cabarkapa/Diogu/75 5.00 12.00
CK V.Carter/J.Kidd/75 100.00 250.00
DR Daniels/Q.Richardson/75 5.00 12.00
GH B.Gordon/Hinrich/75 6.00 15.00
GW D.Granger/Warrick/75 8.00 20.00
HE L.Head/D.Ewing/75 6.00 15.00
HS K.Hinrich/Simien/75 6.00 15.00
HW D.Howard/M.Williams/75 10.00 25.00
IW Iguodala/L.Williams/75 20.00 50.00
JA M.Johnson/Kareem/25 1,000.00 2,000.00
JC J.Johnson/Childress/75 6.00 15.00
JG A.Jefferson/O.Greene/75 6.00 15.00
JJ M.Jordan/L.James/25 6,000.00 12,000.00
KH L.Kleiza/J.Hodge/75 6.00 15.00
KM J.Kidd/S.Marbury/25 40.00 100.00
LB D.Lee/B.Bass/75 8.00 20.00
LE Livingston/D.Ewing/75 6.00 15.00
MM S.May/R.McCants/75 5.00 12.00
MS J.Maxiell/W.Simien/75 6.00 15.00
MY T.McGrady/Y.Ming/25 200.00 500.00
NB S.Nash/C.Billups/25 100.00 250.00
ND J.Nelson/T.Diener/75 5.00 12.00
PB T.Prince/C.Billups/75 25.00 60.00
PG P.Pierce/G.Green/75 40.00 100.00
PR S.Pippen/Rodman/25 200.00 500.00
PW C.Paul/M.Williams/25 75.00 200.00
RG D.Robinson/Gervin/25 100.00 250.00
RJ N.Robinson/J.Jack/75 8.00 20.00
SM Jasikevicius/Andriuskevicius/75 8.00 20.00
SP J.Smith/C.Paul/75 100.00 250.00
SS D.Stoudamire/S.Stoudamire/75 8.00 20.00
SW J.Stockton/D.Williams/25 60.00 150.00
VG C.Villanueva/J.Graham/75 6.00 15.00
WF D.Williams/R.Felton/75 12.00 30.00
WG M.Webster/G.Green/75 8.00 20.00
WH A.Wright/J.Hodge/75 6.00 15.00
WJ M.Webster/J.Jack/75 8.00 20.00

2005-06 Upper Deck Trilogy One Two Combo Clearcut Autographs
PRINT RUN 50 SER.#'d SETS
BP L.Bird/R.Parish 200.00 500.00
BV C.Bosh/C.Villanueva 50.00 120.00
BW A.Bogut/M.Williams 25.00 60.00
FM R.Felton/S.May 15.00 40.00
GH B.Gordon/K.Hinrich 25.00 60.00
GW P.Gasol/H.Warrick 40.00 100.00
HB R.Hamilton/C.Billups 75.00 200.00
HJ D.Howard/A.Jefferson 40.00 100.00
JJ L.James/M.Jordan 6,000.00 12,000.00
JP A.Jefferson/P.Pierce 60.00 150.00
KW J.Kidd/A.Wright 40.00 100.00
MH T.McGrady/L.Head 75.00 200.00
PW C.Paul/D.Williams 100.00 250.00
RB M.Redd/A.Bogut 30.00 80.00
RM Q.Richardson/S.Marbury 40.00 100.00
SP J.Smith/C.Paul 75.00 200.00
TB I.Thomas/C.Billups 100.00 250.00
TJ S.Telfair/J.Jack 15.00 40.00
VG C.Villanueva/J.Graham 15.00 40.00
WF D.Williams/R.Felton 25.00 60.00

2005-06 Upper Deck Trilogy Signature Swatches
PRINT RUN 25 SER.#'d SETS
AB Andrew Bogut 20.00 50.00
AW Antoine Wright 12.00 30.00
BG Ben Gordon 12.00 30.00
CF Channing Frye 12.00 30.00
CP Chris Paul 150.00 400.00
CV Charlie Villanueva 12.00 30.00
DG Danny Granger 15.00 40.00
DH Dwight Howard 40.00 100.00
DW Deron Williams 25.00 60.00
FG Francisco Garcia 10.00 25.00
HW Hakim Warrick 12.00 30.00
ID Ike Diogu 10.00 25.00
JG Joey Graham 10.00 25.00
JH Julius Hodge 10.00 25.00
JJ Jarrett Jack 15.00 40.00
JK Jason Kidd 60.00 150.00
JM Jason Maxiell 12.00 30.00
LB LeBron James 2,500.00 5,000.00
LH Luther Head 10.00 25.00
MA Martell Webster 12.00 30.00
MJ Michael Jordan 3,000.00 6,000.00
MW Marvin Williams 15.00 40.00
NR Nate Robinson 15.00 40.00
PG Pau Gasol 30.00 80.00
PP Paul Pierce 60.00 150.00
RF Raymond Felton 12.00 30.00
RM Rashad McCants 10.00 25.00
SM Sean May 10.00 25.00
TM Tracy McGrady 125.00 300.00
YM Yao Ming 200.00 500.00

2005-06 Upper Deck Trilogy Signs of Stardom
APPROXIMATELY TWO PER BOX
AB Andrew Bogut 6.00 15.00
AJ Antawn Jamison 4.00 10.00
AL Al Jefferson 3.00 8.00
AN Andrew Bynum 4.00 10.00
AW Antoine Wright 4.00 10.00
BD Baron Davis 8.00 20.00
BJ Bobby Jackson 4.00 10.00
BM Brad Miller 4.00 10.00
BS Bobby Simmons 3.00 8.00
CA Carmelo Anthony SP 75.00 200.00
CF Channing Frye 4.00 10.00
CH Chauncey Billups 20.00 50.00
CJ C.J. Miles 4.00 10.00
CP Chris Paul 125.00 300.00
CT Chris Taft SP 3.00 8.00
DE Daniel Ewing 4.00 10.00
DG Danny Granger 5.00 12.00
DH Dwight Howard 20.00 50.00
DL David Lee 5.00 12.00
DM Donyell Marshall 3.00 8.00
FG Francisco Garcia 3.00 8.00
GG Gerald Green 5.00 12.00
ID Ike Diogu 3.00 8.00
JA Jamaal Magloire 3.00 8.00
JG Joey Graham 4.00 10.00
JH Julius Hodge 3.00 8.00
JJ Jarrett Jack 5.00 12.00
JK Jason Kidd SP 40.00 100.00
JM Jason Maxiell 4.00 10.00
JP Johan Petro 3.00 8.00
JR J.R. Smith 12.00 30.00
LH Luther Head 3.00 8.00
LJ LeBron James SP 2,500.00 5,000.00
LK Linas Kleiza 4.00 10.00
LO Lamar Odom 4.00 10.00
MJ Michael Jordan SP 3,000.00 6,000.00
MR Michael Redd 4.00 10.00
MW Marvin Williams 5.00 12.00
NR Nate Robinson 5.00 12.00
PP Paul Pierce 40.00 100.00
RF Raymond Felton 4.00 10.00
RH Richard Hamilton 15.00 40.00
RM Rashad McCants 3.00 8.00
SE Sean May 3.00 8.00
SM Stephon Marbury SP 20.00 50.00
SP Speedy Claxton 3.00 8.00
SS Salim Stoudamire 4.00 10.00
ST Stromile Swift 3.00 8.00
TC Tyson Chandler 4.00 10.00
TM Tracy McGrady 125.00 300.00
TP Tayshaun Prince 5.00 12.00
WS Wayne Simien 3.00 8.00
YK Yaroslav Korolev 3.00 8.00

2005-06 Upper Deck Trilogy Swatches of Stardom
PRINT RUN 50 SER.#'d SETS
AB Andrew Bogut 5.00 12.00
AW Antoine Wright 3.00 8.00
BK Bernard King 5.00 12.00
CD Clyde Drexler 15.00 40.00
CF Channing Frye 3.00 8.00
CP Chris Paul 20.00 50.00
CV Charlie Villanueva 3.00 8.00
DG Danny Granger 4.00 10.00
DH Dwight Howard 5.00 12.00
DW Deron Williams 6.00 15.00
FG Francisco Garcia 2.50 6.00
GG Gerald Green 4.00 10.00
HK Hakeem Olajuwon 15.00 40.00
HW Hakim Warrick 3.00 8.00
ID Ike Diogu 2.50 6.00
IT Isiah Thomas 6.00 15.00
JG Joey Graham 3.00 8.00
JH Julius Hodge 2.50 6.00
JJ Jarrett Jack 4.00 10.00
JM Jason Maxiell 3.00 8.00
JO John Stockton 15.00 40.00
JP Sarunas Jasikevicius 4.00 10.00
JS Jamal Sampson 2.50 6.00
JW James Worthy 15.00 40.00
KB Kobe Bryant 125.00 300.00
KG Kevin Garnett 15.00 40.00
KM Kevin McHale 10.00 25.00
LB Larry Bird 30.00 80.00
LH Luther Head 2.50 6.00
LJ LeBron James 125.00 300.00
MA Magic Johnson 30.00 80.00
MJ Michael Jordan 200.00 500.00
MW Marvin Williams 4.00 10.00
NR Nate Robinson 4.00 10.00
PM Pete Maravich 75.00 200.00
RF Raymond Felton 3.00 8.00
RM Rashad McCants 2.50 6.00
SM Sean May 2.50 6.00
TM Tracy McGrady 15.00 40.00
WE Martell Webster 3.00 8.00
WS Wayne Simien 2.50 6.00
YM Yao Ming 15.00 40.00

2005-06 Upper Deck Trilogy The Cutting Edge
APPROXIMATELY TWO PER BOX
AB Andrew Bogut 4.00 10.00
AI Andre Iguodala 3.00 8.00
AJ Antawn Jamison 2.50 6.00
AS Amare Stoudemire 3.00 8.00
AW Antoine Wright 2.50 6.00
BW Ben Wallace 4.00 10.00
CA Carmelo Anthony 5.00 12.00
CF Channing Frye 2.50 6.00
CP Chris Paul 15.00 40.00
CV Charlie Villanueva 2.50 6.00
CW Chris Webber 4.00 10.00
DE Deron Williams 5.00 12.00
DG Danny Granger 3.00 8.00
DH Dwight Howard 4.00 10.00
DN Dirk Nowitzki 8.00 20.00
EB Elton Brand 2.50 6.00
GA Gilbert Arenas SP 3.00 8.00
ID Ike Diogu 2.00 5.00
JG Joey Graham 2.50 6.00
JK Jason Kidd SP 5.00 12.00
JO Jermaine O'Neal 2.50 6.00
JR Jason Richardson 3.00 8.00
JS J.R. Smith 3.00 8.00
KB Kobe Bryant 50.00 120.00
KG Kevin Garnett 8.00 20.00
KM Kenyon Martin 2.50 6.00
LJ LeBron James 50.00 120.00
MA Martell Webster 2.50 6.00
MJ Michael Jordan SP 75.00 200.00
MW Marvin Williams 3.00 8.00
PP Paul Pierce 5.00 12.00
RF Raymond Felton 2.50 6.00
RJ Richard Jefferson SP 2.50 6.00
RM Rashad McCants 2.50 6.00
SE Sean May 2.00 5.00
SF Steve Francis 3.00 8.00
SH Shawn Marion 2.50 6.00
SM Stephon Marbury 4.00 10.00
SO Shaquille O'Neal 10.00 25.00
TD Tim Duncan 8.00 20.00
TM Tracy McGrady 5.00 12.00
YM Yao Ming 6.00 15.00

2005-06 Upper Deck Trilogy TriMarks
PRINT RUN 10 TO 40 SER.#'d SETS
AGJ Allen/Green/Jefferson 8.00 20.00
BGV Bosh/Graham/Villanueva* 8.00 20.00
DBT I.Diogu/A.Biedrins/C.Taft* 8.00 20.00
DDT B.Davis/I.Diogu/C.Taft 8.00 20.00
DEB C.Duhon/D.Ewing/C.Boozer* 8.00 20.00
FFK W.Frazier/C.Frye/B.King 30.00 80.00
FLR C.Frye/D.Lee/N.Robinson 8.00 20.00
GJA Granger/Sarunas/Artest* 10.00 25.00
GJW Gasol/B.Jackson/Warrick* 12.00 30.00
GOV Gordon/Okafor/Villanueva* 8.00 20.00
HGC K.Hinrich/B.Gordon/E.Curry 8.00 20.00
JBM J.Jack/C.Bosh/S.Marbury* 20.00 50.00
KJW Kidd/R.Jefferson/Wright 20.00 50.00
MME Maggette/Mobley/D.Ewing* 8.00 20.00
MMF McCants/S.May/Felton 8.00 20.00
MRR Marbury/N.Rob/Q-Rich 20.00 50.00
OBW L.Odom/A.Bynum/V.Wafer* 10.00 25.00
OMF E.Okafor/S.May/R.Felton 8.00 20.00
PSB C.Paul/J.Smith/B.Bass* 100.00 250.00
RSM Redd/Simmons/Mason 8.00 20.00
TRL Isiah/Rodman/Laimbeer* 100.00 250.00
WBG Webster/Bynum/Green* 8.00 20.00
WBP B.Wallace/Billups/Prince 60.00 150.00
WPM Walton/Parish/Maxwell* 40.00 100.00

2006-07 Upper Deck Trilogy
COMP.SET w/o SP's (90) 20.00 50.00
91-98 PRINT RUN 299 SER.#'d SETS
99-140 PRINT RUN 499 SER.#'d SETS
1 Joe Johnson .75 2.00
2 Marvin Williams .50 1.25
3 Paul Pierce 1.25 3.00
4 Wally Szczerbiak .60 1.50
5 Emeka Okafor .60 1.50
6 Raymond Felton .50 1.25
7 Ben Wallace 1.00 2.50
8 Kirk Hinrich .60 1.50
9 Ben Gordon .60 1.50
10 LeBron James 6.00 15.00
11 Larry Hughes .60 1.50
12 Dirk Nowitzki 1.50 4.00
13 Jason Terry .60 1.50
14 Carmelo Anthony 1.25 3.00
15 Andre Miller .60 1.50
16 Chauncey Billups 1.00 2.50
17 Richard Hamilton .75 2.00
18 Jason Richardson .75 2.00
19 Baron Davis .75 2.00
20 Yao Ming 2.00 5.00
21 Tracy McGrady 1.25 3.00
22 Jermaine O'Neal .75 2.00
23 Al Harrington .60 1.50
24 Elton Brand .60 1.50
25 Sam Cassell .60 1.50
26 Kobe Bryant 6.00 15.00
27 Lamar Odom .60 1.50
28 Pau Gasol 1.25 3.00
29 Dwyane Wade 1.50 4.00
30 Shaquille O'Neal 3.00 8.00
31 Michael Redd .60 1.50
32 Andrew Bogut .60 1.50
33 Kevin Garnett 2.00 5.00
34 Mike James .50 1.25
35 Vince Carter 1.50 4.00
36 Jason Kidd 1.25 3.00
37 Richard Jefferson .60 1.50
38 Chris Paul 1.50 4.00
39 David West .60 1.50
40 Stephon Marbury 1.00 2.50
41 Steve Francis .75 2.00
42 Dwight Howard 1.00 2.50
43 Jameer Nelson .50 1.25
44 Allen Iverson 2.00 5.00
45 Chris Webber 1.00 2.50
46 Steve Nash 1.50 4.00
47 Shawn Marion .75 2.00
48 Zach Randolph .75 2.00
49 Mike Bibby .75 2.00
50 Ron Artest .75 2.00
51 Tim Duncan 2.00 5.00
52 Tony Parker 1.25 3.00
53 Ray Allen 1.25 3.00
54 Rashard Lewis .60 1.50
55 Chris Bosh 1.00 2.50
56 T.J. Ford .50 1.25
57 Mehmet Okur .50 1.25
58 Andrei Kirilenko .60 1.50
59 Gilbert Arenas .75 2.00
60 Antawn Jamison .60 1.50
61 Childress/Claxton/Smith .75 2.00
62 Jefferson/West/Telfair .75 2.00
63 Wallace/Brezec/Knight .75 2.00
64 Nocioni/Deng/Brown 1.25 3.00
65 Gooden/Ilgauskas/Marshall .75 2.00
66 Howard/Stackhouse/Harris 1.25 3.00
67 Martin/Camby/Smith 1.25 3.00
68 Wallace/Prince/Mohammed 1.25 3.00
69 Murphy/Dunleavy/Diogu .75 2.00
70 Alston/Battier/Wells .75 2.00
71 Granger/Tinsley/Dunleavy .75 2.00
72 Kaman/Maggette/Livingston .75 2.00
73 Parker/Radmanovic/Brown 1.25 3.00
74 Miller/Stoudamire/Warrick .75 2.00
75 Walker/Haslem/Williams 1.25 3.00
76 Villanueva/Patterson/Williams .75 2.00
77 Davis/Hassell/Blount .75 2.00
78 Krstic/Collins/Robinson .75 2.00
79 Chandler/Stojakovic/Mason .75 2.00
80 Curry/Crawford/Frye .75 2.00
81 Milicic/Turkoglu/Hill 1.00 2.50
82 Iguodala/Korver/Dalembert .75 2.00
83 Stoudemire/Diaw/Bell 1.25 3.00
84 Jack/Randolph/Webster .75 2.00
85 Miller/Abdur-Rahim/Martin 1.00 2.50
86 Ginobili/Finley/Bowen 1.50 4.00
87 Ridnour/Wilcox/Collison .75 2.00
88 Peterson/Graham/Calderon .75 2.00
89 Boozer/Williams/Giricek 1.25 3.00
90 Butler/Thomas/Stevenson .75 2.00
91 Shelden Williams RC 2.00 5.00
92 Tyrus Thomas RC 2.50 6.00
93 Rudy Gay RC 4.00 10.00
94 Randy Foye RC 2.50 6.00
95 Rodney Carney RC 1.50 4.00
96 LaMarcus Aldridge RC 8.00 20.00
97 Brandon Roy RC 6.00 15.00
98 Andrea Bargnani RC 2.50 6.00
99 Solomon Jones RC 1.25 3.00
100 Rajon Rondo RC 6.00 15.00
101 Allan Ray RC 1.25 3.00
102 Thabo Sefolosha RC 1.50 4.00
103 Shannon Brown RC 1.25 3.00
104 Maurice Ager RC 1.25 3.00
105 Patrick O'Bryant RC 1.25 3.00
106 Steve Novak RC 1.50 4.00
107 Shawne Williams RC 1.25 3.00
108 Paul Davis RC 1.25 3.00
109 Jordan Farmar RC 1.50 4.00
110 Kyle Lowry RC 6.00 15.00
111 David Noel RC 1.25 3.00
112 Craig Smith RC 1.50 4.00
113 Marcus Williams RC 1.25 3.00
114 Josh Boone RC 1.25 3.00
115 Hilton Armstrong RC 1.25 3.00
116 Cedric Simmons RC 1.25 3.00
117 Renaldo Balkman RC 1.50 4.00
118 Mardy Collins RC 1.25 3.00
119 Bobby Jones RC 1.25 3.00
120 Quincy Douby RC 1.25 3.00
121 Saer Sene RC 1.25 3.00
122 P.J. Tucker RC 2.00 5.00
123 Jorge Garbajosa RC 1.50 4.00
124 Ronnie Brewer RC 2.00 5.00
125 Dee Brown RC 1.25 3.00
126 Leon Powe RC 1.25 3.00
127 Ryan Hollins RC 1.25 3.00
128 Adam Morrison RC 1.50 4.00
129 Daniel Gibson RC 1.50 4.00
130 Pops Mensah-Bonsu RC 1.25 3.00
131 Yakhouba Diawara RC 1.25 3.00
132 Will Blalock RC 1.25 3.00
133 Alexander Johnson RC 1.25 3.00
134 Damir Markota RC 1.25 3.00
135 Hassan Adams RC 1.25 3.00
136 Marcus Vinicius RC 1.25 3.00
137 James Augustine RC 1.25 3.00
138 J.J. Redick RC 4.00 10.00
139 Sergio Rodriguez RC 1.50 4.00
140 Paul Millsap RC 2.50 6.00

2006-07 Upper Deck Trilogy Blue
*1-60 BLUE: .75X TO 2X BASE HI
1-60 BLUE PRINT RUN 66 SER.#'d SETS
*61-90 BLUE: 1.25X TO 3X BASE HI
*91-98 BLUE: .75X TO 2X BASE HI
*99-140 BLUE: 1.25X TO 3X BASE HI
61-140 BLUE PRINT RUN 33 SER.#'d SETS

2006-07 Upper Deck Trilogy Auto Focus
APPROXIMATE ODDS ONE PER BOX
AFAB Andrea Bargnani 4.00 10.00
AFAI Andre Iguodala 6.00 15.00
AFBG Ben Gordon 4.00 10.00
AFBO Chris Bosh 6.00 15.00
AFBR Brandon Roy 10.00 25.00
AFCA Carmelo Anthony 15.00 40.00
AFCP Chris Paul 20.00 50.00
AFCS Cedric Simmons 3.00 8.00
AFJB Josh Boone 3.00 8.00
AFJF Jordan Farmar 4.00 10.00
AFJK Jason Kidd 10.00 25.00
AFJW James White 3.00 8.00
AFLA LaMarcus Aldridge 20.00 50.00
AFLJ LeBron James SP 2,500.00 5,000.00
AFMB Mike Bibby 5.00 12.00
AFMC Mardy Collins 3.00 8.00
AFMJ Michael Jordan SP 300.00 600.00
AFMW Marcus Williams 3.00 8.00
AFPP Paul Pierce 12.00 30.00
AFQD Quincy Douby 3.00 8.00
AFRB Renaldo Balkman 4.00 10.00
AFRC Rodney Carney 3.00 8.00
AFRF Randy Foye 4.00 10.00
AFRG Rudy Gay 6.00 15.00
AFRH Richard Hamilton 6.00 15.00
AFRJ Richard Jefferson 5.00 12.00
AFRO Ronnie Brewer 5.00 12.00
AFRR Rajon Rondo 15.00 40.00
AFSB Shannon Brown 3.00 8.00
AFSN Steve Nash SP 60.00 120.00
AFSR Sergio Rodriguez 4.00 10.00
AFSS Saer Sene 3.00 8.00
AFSW Shawne Williams 3.00 8.00
AFTS Thabo Sefolosha 4.00 10.00
AFTT Tyrus Thomas 4.00 10.00
AFWI Shelden Williams 3.00 8.00
AFYM Yao Ming 20.00 50.00

2006-07 Upper Deck Trilogy Generations Future Memorabilia
APPROXIMATE ODDS ONE PER BOX
*PATCHES: .6X TO 1.5X BASE HI
PATCH PRINT RUN 50 SER.#'d SETS
FMAB Andrea Bargnani 2.00 5.00
FMAR Allan Ray 1.50 4.00
FMBJ Bobby Jones 1.50 4.00
FMBR Ronnie Brewer 2.50 6.00
FMCS Cedric Simmons 1.50 4.00
FMHA Hilton Armstrong 1.50 4.00
FMJB Josh Boone 1.50 4.00
FMJG Jorge Garbajosa 2.00 5.00
FMJR J.J. Redick 5.00 12.00
FMJW James White 1.50 4.00
FMKL Kyle Lowry 8.00 20.00
FMLA LaMarcus Aldridge 1.50 4.00
FMMC Mardy Collins 1.50 4.00
FMMW Marcus Williams 1.50 4.00
FMPD Paul Davis 1.50 4.00
FMPO Patrick O'Bryant 1.50 4.00
FMPT P.J. Tucker 2.50 6.00
FMQD Quincy Douby 1.50 4.00
FMRB Renaldo Balkman 2.00 5.00
FMRC Rodney Carney 1.50 4.00
FMRF Randy Foye 2.00 5.00
FMRG Rudy Gay 3.00 8.00
FMRO Brandon Roy 5.00 12.00
FMSB Shannon Brown 1.50 4.00
FMSJ Solomon Jones 1.50 4.00
FMSS Saer Sene 1.50 4.00
FMSW Shawne Williams 1.50 4.00
FMTT Tyrus Thomas 2.00 5.00
FMWB Will Blalock 1.50 4.00
FMWI Shelden Williams 1.50 4.00

2006-07 Upper Deck Trilogy Generations Future Signatures
APPROXIMATE ODDS ONE PER BOX
FSAB Andrea Bargnani 3.00 8.00
FSAR Allan Ray 2.50 6.00
FSBR Brandon Roy 8.00 20.00
FSCS Cedric Simmons 2.50 6.00
FSDN David Noel 2.50 6.00
FSHA Hilton Armstrong 2.50 6.00
FSJB Josh Boone 2.50 6.00
FSJF Jordan Farmar 3.00 8.00
FSKL Kyle Lowry 12.00 30.00
FSLA LaMarcus Aldridge 10.00 25.00
FSMA Maurice Ager 2.50 6.00
FSMC Mardy Collins 2.50 6.00
FSMW Marcus Williams 2.50 6.00
FSPD Paul Davis 2.50 6.00
FSPO Patrick O'Bryant 2.50 6.00
FSQD Quincy Douby 2.50 6.00
FSRB Renaldo Balkman 3.00 8.00
FSRC Rodney Carney 2.50 6.00
FSRF Randy Foye 3.00 8.00
FSRG Rudy Gay 5.00 12.00
FSRO Ronnie Brewer 4.00 10.00
FSRR Rajon Rondo 10.00 25.00
FSSB Shannon Brown 2.50 6.00
FSSM Craig Smith 3.00 8.00
FSSN Steve Novak 3.00 8.00
FSSS Saer Sene 2.50 6.00
FSSW Shawne Williams 2.50 6.00
FSTS Thabo Sefolosha 3.00 8.00
FSTT Tyrus Thomas 3.00 8.00
FSWI Shelden Williams 2.50 6.00

2006-07 Upper Deck Trilogy Generations Past and Future Memorabilia
PRINT RUN 50 SER.#'d SETS
PFMBB L.Bird/A.Bargnani 10.00 25.00
PFMBE M.Eaton/R.Brewer 5.00 12.00
PFMCN T.Chambers/S.Novak 5.00 12.00
PFMDA A.Dantley/M.Ager 5.00 12.00
PFMDB C.Drexler/S.Brown 8.00 20.00
PFMDC D.Dawkins/R.Carney 5.00 12.00
PFMEB M.Eaton/J.Boone 5.00 12.00
PFMEW J.Erving/S.Williams 8.00 20.00
PFMFB W.Frazier/R.Balkman 5.00 12.00
PFMGW G.Gervin/J.White 5.00 12.00
PFMJA J.White/A.Ray 5.00 12.00
PFMJW M.Johnson/M.Williams 8.00 20.00
PFMKB B.King/R.Brewer 5.00 12.00
PFMKC K.Malone/C.Simmons 6.00 15.00
PFMMD K.McHale/P.Davis 5.00 12.00
PFMMF E.Monroe/R.Foye 5.00 12.00
PFMMJ M.Malone/S.Jones 5.00 12.00
PFMMN J.Worthy/D.Noel 6.00 15.00
PFMMR C.Mullin/J.Redick 8.00 20.00
PFMMS K.Malone/C.Smith 6.00 15.00
PFMMT P.Maravich/T.Thomas 30.00 80.00
PFMON H.Olajuwon/S.Novak 5.00 12.00
PFMRJ D.Robinson/S.Jones 6.00 15.00
PFMRS D.Rodman/T.Sefolosha 10.00 25.00
PFMSB J.Stockton/D.Brown 8.00 20.00
PFMTD R.Theus/Q.Douby 5.00 12.00
PFMWE S.Elliott/J.White 5.00 12.00
PFMWF J.West/J.Farmar 10.00 25.00
PFMWG J.Worthy/R.Gay 6.00 15.00
PFMWL S.Webb/K.Lowry 5.00 12.00

2006-07 Upper Deck Trilogy Generations Past and Future Signatures
PRINT RUN 33 SER.#'d SETS
PFSAL N.Archibald/K.Lowry 8.00 20.00
PFSAR A.Robertson/R.Brewer 8.00 20.00
PFSBR D.Brown/R.Rondo 8.00 20.00
PFSDB D.Dawkins/J.Boone 8.00 20.00
PFSEB M.Eaton/R.Brewer 8.00 20.00
PFSEH M.Eaton/R.Hollins 8.00 20.00
PFSEW W.Tisdale/S.Williams 8.00 20.00
PFSFF W.Frazier/R.Foye 8.00 20.00
PFSGG G.Gervin/R.Gay 10.00 25.00
PFSHA E.Hayes/L.Aldridge 15.00 30.00
PFSJA A.Johnson/M.Ager 8.00 20.00
PFSJC B.Jones/R.Carney 8.00 20.00
PFSJR C.Drexler/B.Roy 10.00 25.00
PFSKA S.Kerr/H.Adams 10.00 25.00
PFSMA A.Dantley/P.Millsap 8.00 20.00
PFSMN B.McAdoo/D.Noel 8.00 20.00
PFSMR M.Richardson/R.Balkman 8.00 20.00
PFSMS X.McDaniel/S.Sene 8.00 20.00
PFSPA R.Parish/H.Armstrong 8.00 20.00
PFSPB D.Robinson/A.Bargnani 20.00 50.00
PFSRM A.Robertson/D.Markota 8.00 20.00
PFSRT D.Rodman/T.Thomas 25.00 60.00
PFSRW M.Richardson/M.Williams 8.00 20.00
PFSSF B.Scott/J.Farmar 8.00 20.00
PFSSN R.Sampson/S.Novak 8.00 20.00
PFSTD R.Theus/Q.Douby 8.00 20.00
PFSTO N.Thurmond/P.O'Bryant 8.00 20.00
PFSTS W.Tisdale/C.Simmons 8.00 20.00
PFSWR B.Walton/B.Roy 8.00 20.00
PFSWW S.Webb/S.Williams 8.00 20.00

2006-07 Upper Deck Trilogy Generations Past and Present Memorabilia
PRINT RUN 50 SER.#'d SETS
PPMAM E.Monroe/C.Anthony 6.00 15.00
PPMBP L.Bird/P.Pierce 15.00 40.00
PPMCM T.Chambers/S.Marion 6.00 15.00
PPMCO W.Chamberlain/S.O'Neal 15.00 40.00
PPMDM C.Drexler/T.McGrady 15.00 40.00
PPMDR A.Dantley/M.Redd 5.00 12.00
PPMEK M.Eaton/A.Kirilenko 6.00 15.00
PPMFH W.Frazier/R.Hamilton 8.00 20.00
PPMJB M.Johnson/K.Bryant 75.00 200.00
PPMJJ M.Jordan/L.James 75.00 200.00
PPMKA B.King/G.Arenas 5.00 12.00
PPMKE K.McHale/E.Brand 5.00 12.00
PPMKJ S.Kerr/R.Jefferson 5.00 12.00
PPMMA C.Mullin/R.Artest 10.00 25.00
PPMMB K.Malone/C.Boozer 8.00 20.00
PPMMH M.Malone/D.Howard 6.00 15.00
PPMMI P.Maravich/A.Iverson 40.00 80.00
PPMMN P.Maravich/S.Nash 30.00 80.00
PPMOM H.Olajuwon/Y.Ming 6.00 15.00
PPMRB O.Robertson/A.Bogut 12.00 30.00
PPMRD D.Robinson/T.Duncan 20.00 50.00
PPMRK O.Robertson/J.Kidd 15.00 40.00
PPMRO P.Riley/L.Odom 8.00 20.00
PPMRW D.Rodman/B.Wallace 10.00 25.00
PPMTB R.Theus/M.Bibby 5.00 12.00
PPMTG R.Theus/B.Gordon 5.00 12.00
PPMWA J.West/R.Allen 20.00 50.00
PPMWH J.White/K.Hinrich 5.00 12.00
PPMWP S.Webb/C.Paul 8.00 20.00

2006-07 Upper Deck Trilogy Generations Past and Present Signatures
PRINT RUN 33 SER.#'d SETS
PPSAA N.Archibald/G.Arenas 10.00 25.00
PPSAC A.Robertson/C.Bell 8.00 20.00
PPSAG B.Armstrong/B.Gordon 8.00 20.00
PPSBA D.Brown/T.Allen 8.00 20.00
PPSBC M.Cooper/A.Bynum 8.00 20.00
PPSBP M.Bogues/C.Paul 75.00 200.00
PPSDC D.Rodman/C.Billups 30.00 80.00
PPSDH B.Daugherty/L.Hughes 8.00 20.00
PPSDO D.Dawkins/J.O'Neal 12.00 30.00
PPSEB M.Eaton/C.Boozer 8.00 20.00
PPSEJ S.Elliott/R.Jefferson 8.00 20.00
PPSEK M.Eaton/C.Kaman 8.00 20.00
PPSHK C.Hawkins/K.Korver 15.00 40.00
PPSJA M.Jordan/C.Anthony 800.00 1,500.00
PPSJM M.Richardson/C.Frye 6.00 20.00
PPSJW B.Jones/M.Williams 8.00 20.00
PPSKB S.Kerr/B.Barry 30.00 80.00
PPSLP B.Laimbeer/T.Prince 15.00 40.00
PPSME B.McAdoo/D.Ewing 8.00 20.00
PPSMR X.McDaniel/L.Ridnour 8.00 20.00
PPSMT R.Theus/B.Miller 8.00 20.00
PPSMW X.McDaniel/D.Wilkins 8.00 20.00
PPSPP R.Parish/P.Pierce 25.00 60.00
PPSSM R.Sampson/Y.Ming 30.00 80.00
PPSSV K.Vandeweghe/J.Smith 8.00 20.00
PPSTB R.Theus/M.Bibby 8.00 20.00
PPSTM W.Tisdale/B.Miller 8.00 20.00
PPSWC S.Webb/J.Childress 8.00 20.00
PPSWW S.Webb/M.Williams 8.00 20.00

2006-07 Upper Deck Trilogy Generations Past Memorabilia
APPROXIMATE ODDS ONE PER BOX
*PATCHES: .75X TO 2X BASE HI
PATCH PRINT RUN 50 SER.#'d SETS
PMAD Adrian Dantley 3.00 8.00
PMBK Bernard King 3.00 8.00
PMBL Bill Laimbeer 3.00 8.00
PMCD Clyde Drexler 5.00 12.00
PMCM Chris Mullin 4.00 10.00
PMDR Dennis Rodman 8.00 20.00
PMGG George Gervin 6.00 15.00
PMHO Hakeem Olajuwon 8.00 20.00
PMJE Julius Erving 8.00 20.00
PMJH Jeff Hornacek 3.00 8.00
PMJO Magic Johnson 12.00 30.00
PMJS John Stockton 6.00 15.00
PMKA Kareem Abdul-Jabbar 8.00 20.00
PMKM Kevin McHale 5.00 12.00
PMLB Larry Bird 12.00 30.00
PMME Mark Eaton 2.50 6.00
PMMJ Michael Jordan 40.00 100.00
PMMM Moses Malone 6.00 15.00
PMOR Oscar Robertson 6.00 15.00
PMPR Pat Riley 5.00 12.00
PMRO David Robinson 6.00 15.00
PMRT Reggie Theus 3.00 8.00
PMSK Steve Kerr 4.00 10.00
PMSW Spud Webb 3.00 8.00
PMTC Tom Chambers 3.00 8.00
PMWE Jerry West 8.00 20.00
PMWF Walt Frazier 5.00 12.00
PMWH Jo Jo White 3.00 8.00

2006-07 Upper Deck Trilogy Generations Past Present and Future Memorabilia
PRINT RUN 33 SER.#'d SETS
PPFMBAG Bird/Anthony/Gay 15.00 40.00
PPFMCWS Chmbrs/Wkns/Sene 6.00 15.00
PPFMDIC Dwkns/Igdala/Crny 6.00 15.00
PPFMDMB Drxlr/McGrady/Brwn 15.00 40.00
PPFMDMJ Dwkns/Miller/Jones 6.00 15.00
PPFMDNA Dntly/Nwzki/Ager 10.00 25.00
PPFMGJS Gervin/LJ/Sefsha 12.00 30.00
PPFMGLT Gervin/Lewis/Tckr 6.00 15.00
PPFMJBF Magic/Bryant/Farmar 50.00 120.00
PPFMKGS Kerr/Grdn/Sefsha 10.00 25.00
PPFMKMC King/Mrbry/Collins 6.00 15.00
PPFMLOB Laimbr/Okfr/Boone 6.00 15.00
PPFMMBA Mlne/Bosh/Armstng 6.00 15.00
PPFMMDO Mullin/Davis/O'Bryant 6.00 15.00
PPFMMDS McHale/Dncn/Smith 10.00 25.00
PPFMMHW Malone/Hwrd/Williams 6.00 15.00
PPFMMIR Monroe/Iverson/Roy 15.00 30.00
PPFMMOT Mrvch/Shaq/Thomas 60.00 150.00
PPFMOMN Olajuwon/Yao/Novak 8.00 20.00
PPFMRGA Robinson/KG/Aldridge 20.00 50.00

PPFMRNR Rbrtsn/Nash/Rondo 15.00 40.00
PPFMRWT Rdmn/Wallace/Thomas 10.00 25.00
PPFMSWB Stock/Williams/Brown 8.00 20.00
PPFMWAR West/Allen/Roy 20.00 50.00
PPFMWBB Walton/Bogut/Brgni 6.00 15.00
PPFMWCN Worthy/Carter/Noel 10.00 25.00
PPFMWJW Wrthy/Jffrsn/Williams 6.00 15.00
PPFMWPL Webb/Paul/Lowry 10.00 25.00
PPFMWPR White/Pierce/Rondo 8.00 20.00

2006-07 Upper Deck Trilogy Generations Past Signatures

APPROXIMATE ODDS ONE PER BOX
PSAD Adrian Dantley 5.00 12.00
PSAJ Avery Johnson 5.00 12.00
PSAR Alvin Robertson 5.00 12.00
PSBA B.J. Armstrong 5.00 12.00
PSBJ Bobby Jones 6.00 15.00
PSBL Bill Laimbeer 10.00 25.00
PSBM Bob McAdoo 10.00 25.00
PSBS Byron Scott 6.00 15.00
PSCH Connie Hawkins 6.00 15.00
PSDB Dee Brown 5.00 12.00
PSDD Darryl Dawkins 10.00 25.00
PSEH Elvin Hayes 8.00 20.00
PSGG George Gervin 10.00 25.00
PSKV Kiki Vandeweghe 5.00 12.00
PSMB Muggsy Bogues 10.00 25.00
PSME Mark Eaton 5.00 12.00
PSMJ Michael Jordan 500.00 1,000.00
PSML Maurice Lucas 5.00 12.00
PSMR Michael Ray Richardson 5.00 12.00
PSNA Nate Archibald 5.00 12.00
PSRP Robert Parish 10.00 25.00
PSRS Ralph Sampson 5.00 12.00
PSRT Reggie Theus 5.00 12.00
PSSW Spud Webb 6.00 15.00
PSWT Wayman Tisdale 5.00 12.00
PSXM Xavier McDaniel 5.00 12.00

2006-07 Upper Deck Trilogy Generations Present and Future Memorabilia

PRINT RUN 50 SER.#'d SETS
PRFMAR R.Allen/A.Ray 4.00 10.00
PRFMBD E.Brand/P.Davis 4.00 10.00
PRFMBF A.Bynum/J.Farmar 4.00 10.00
PRFMBG C.Bosh/J.Garbajosa 4.00 10.00
PRFMBN S.Battier/S.Novak 4.00 10.00
PRFMBT C.Bosh/P.Tucker 5.00 12.00
PRFMDF R.Davis/R.Foye 4.00 10.00
PRFMFB C.Frye/R.Balkman 4.00 10.00
PRFMGS K.Garnett/C.Smith 5.00 12.00
PRFMIJ A.Iguodala/B.Jones 4.00 10.00
PRFMJN A.Jamison/D.Noel 4.00 10.00
PRFMKB A.Kirilenko/R.Brewer 4.00 10.00
PRFMKW J.Kidd/M.Williams 6.00 15.00
PRFMLS R.Lewis/S.Sene 4.00 10.00
PRFMMC S.Marbury/M.Collins 4.00 10.00
PRFMMQ M.Bibby/Q.Douby 4.00 10.00
PRFMNA D.Nowitzki/M.Ager 6.00 15.00
PRFMNR J.Nelson/J.Redick 4.00 10.00
PRFMOA E.Okafor/H.Armstrong 4.00 10.00
PRFMPJ P.Gasol/J.Garbajosa 5.00 12.00
PRFMPR P.Pierce/R.Rondo 8.00 20.00
PRFMPS C.Paul/C.Simmons 5.00 12.00
PRFMPW T.Parker/J.White 5.00 12.00
PRFMRA Z.Randolph/L.Aldridge 5.00 12.00
PRFMRO J.Richardson/P.O'Bryant 4.00 10.00
PRFMWB D.Williams/D.Brown 4.00 10.00
PRFMWT B.Wallace/T.Thomas 4.00 10.00
PRFMWW M.Williams/S.Williams 4.00 10.00

2006-07 Upper Deck Trilogy Generations Present and Future Signatures

PRINT RUN 33 SER.#'d SETS
PRFSAR T.Allen/A.Ray 6.00 15.00
PRFSBB C.Billups/W.Blalock 6.00 15.00
PRFSBD M.Bibby/Q.Douby 6.00 15.00
PRFSBM C.Bell/D.Markota 6.00 15.00
PRFSBS R.Balkman/W.Simien 6.00 15.00
PRFSCA C.Bosh/A.Bargnani 6.00 15.00
PRFSCJ J.Childress/S.Jones 6.00 15.00
PRFSFA L.Aldridge/T.Ford 15.00 40.00
PRFSGS B.Gordon/T.Sefolosha 6.00 15.00
PRFSGT B.Gordon/T.Thomas 6.00 15.00
PRFSHW A.Harrington/S.Williams 6.00 15.00
PRFSIC A.Iguodala/R.Carney 6.00 15.00
PRFSJA R.Jefferson/H.Adams 6.00 15.00
PRFSJF M.James/R.Foye 6.00 15.00
PRFSJR I.Udoka/B.Roy 15.00 40.00
PRFSKD C.Kaman/P.Davis 6.00 15.00
PRFSKW J.Kidd/M.Williams 10.00 25.00
PRFSMB B.Miller/J.Boone 6.00 15.00
PRFSMF C.Mihm/J.Farmar 6.00 15.00
PRFSMN Y.Ming/S.Novak 20.00 50.00
PRFSMS R.McCants/C.Smith 6.00 15.00
PRFSOO J.O'Neal/P.O'Bryant 6.00 15.00
PRFSPA M.Peterson/M.Ager 6.00 15.00
PRFSPG M.Peterson/J.Garbajosa 6.00 15.00
PRFSPR P.Pierce/R.Rondo 25.00 60.00
PRFSRS L.Ridnour/S.Sene 6.00 15.00
PRFSSS P.Stojakovic/C.Simmons 8.00 20.00
PRFSWA D.Williams/J.Augustine 6.00 15.00
PRFSWG H.Warrick/R.Gay 6.00 15.00
PRFSWW M.Williams/S.Williams 6.00 15.00

2006-07 Upper Deck Trilogy Generations Present Memorabilia

APPROXIMATE ODDS ONE PER BOX
*PATCHES: 1X TO 2.5X BASE HI
PATCH PRINT RUN 50 SER.#'d SETS
PRMAI Andre Iguodala 2.50 6.00
PRMAJ Antawn Jamison 2.00 5.00
PRMAK Andrei Kirilenko 2.00 5.00
PRMBD Baron Davis 2.50 6.00
PRMCB Chauncey Billups 3.00 8.00
PRMDH Dwight Howard 3.00 8.00
PRMDN Dirk Nowitzki 6.00 15.00
PRMEO Emeka Okafor 2.00 5.00
PRMGA Gilbert Arenas 2.50 6.00
PRMJK Jason Kidd 4.00 10.00
PRMKB Kobe Bryant 40.00 100.00
PRMKG Kevin Garnett 6.00 15.00
PRMLH Larry Hughes 2.00 5.00
PRMLJ LeBron James 20.00 50.00
PRMLO Lamar Odom 2.00 5.00
PRMMB Mike Bibby 2.50 6.00
PRMMP Morris Peterson 1.50 4.00
PRMMR Michael Redd 2.00 5.00
PRMPG Pau Gasol 4.00 10.00
PRMRH Richard Hamilton 2.50 6.00
PRMRL Rashard Lewis 2.00 5.00
PRMSL Shaun Livingston 2.00 5.00
PRMSM Shawn Marion 2.50 6.00
PRMSN Steve Nash 5.00 12.00
PRMSO Shaquille O'Neal 10.00 25.00
PRMTD Tim Duncan 6.00 15.00
PRMTM Tracy McGrady 4.00 10.00
PRMTP Tayshaun Prince 2.50 6.00
PRMVC Vince Carter 5.00 12.00
PRMYM Yao Ming 6.00 15.00

2006-07 Upper Deck Trilogy Generations Present Signatures

APPROXIMATE ODDS ONE PER BOX
PRSAH Al Harrington 4.00 10.00
PRSAM Andre Miller 4.00 10.00
PRSBG Ben Gordon 4.00 10.00
PRSBI Chauncey Billups 6.00 15.00
PRSBJ Bobby Jackson 3.00 8.00
PRSBM Brad Miller 4.00 10.00
PRSBS Bobby Simmons 3.00 8.00
PRSCD Chris Duhon 3.00 8.00
PRSCF Channing Frye 3.00 8.00
PRSCK Chris Kaman 3.00 8.00
PRSCM Chris Mihm 3.00 8.00
PRSDW Damien Wilkins 3.00 8.00
PRSGG Gerald Green 4.00 10.00
PRSGW Gerald Wallace 4.00 10.00
PRSHW Hakim Warrick 3.00 8.00
PRSJC Josh Childress 3.00 8.00
PRSJH Julius Hodge 3.00 8.00
PRSJJ Jarrett Jack 4.00 10.00
PRSJS James Singleton 3.00 8.00
PRSLJ LeBron James 1,000.00 2,000.00
PRSLR Luke Ridnour 4.00 10.00
PRSMJ Mike James 3.00 8.00
PRSMP Morris Peterson 3.00 8.00
PRSMW Marvin Williams 3.00 8.00
PRSRJ Richard Jefferson 4.00 10.00
PRSRM Rashad McCants 3.00 8.00
PRSSL Shaun Livingston 4.00 10.00
PRSTA Tony Allen 3.00 8.00
PRSTP Tayshaun Prince 5.00 12.00
PRSWE Delonte West 3.00 8.00

2006-07 Upper Deck Trilogy Signs of Stardom Dual

PRINT RUN 33 SER.#'d SETS
SOSAA M.Ager/H.Adams 8.00 20.00
SOSAR L.Aldridge/B.Roy 20.00 50.00
SOSBB A.Bargnani/C.Bosh 10.00 25.00
SOSBC R.Balkman/M.Collins 8.00 20.00
SOSBD E.Brand/P.Davis 8.00 20.00
SOSCB R.Carney/S.Brown 8.00 20.00
SOSCM T.McGrady/V.Carter 75.00 200.00
SOSDR S.Rodriguez/Q.Douby 8.00 20.00
SOSFH J.Farmar/R.Hollins 8.00 20.00
SOSFO R.Felton/E.Okafor 8.00 20.00
SOSGL R.Gay/K.Lowry 12.00 30.00
SOSHB C.Billups/R.Hamilton 20.00 50.00
SOSHG B.Gordon/K.Hinrich 8.00 20.00
SOSJJ M.Jordan/L.James 4,000.00 8,000.00
SOSJP R.Jefferson/T.Prince 8.00 20.00
SOSKI A.Iguodala/K.Korver 10.00 25.00
SOSNK J.Kidd/S.Nash 75.00 200.00
SOSOM P.O'Bryant/P.Millsap 8.00 20.00
SOSPA P.Pierce/C.Anthony 30.00 80.00
SOSRD R.Brewer/D.Brown 8.00 20.00
SOSRR R.Rondo/A.Ray 12.00 30.00
SOSSA H.Armstrong/C.Simmons 8.00 20.00
SOSSF C.Smith/R.Foye 8.00 20.00
SOSSP C.Paul/P.Stojakovic 100.00 250.00
SOSSS S.Sene/S.Rodriguez 8.00 20.00
SOSTN P.Tucker/S.Novak 8.00 20.00
SOSTS T.Thomas/T.Sefolosha 8.00 20.00
SOSWB M.Williams/J.Boone 8.00 20.00
SOSWJ S.Williams/S.Jones 8.00 20.00
SOSWW S.Williams/J.White 8.00 20.00

2003-04 Upper Deck Triple Dimensions

COMP.SET w/o SP's (90) 12.50 30.00
91-126 PRINT RUN 1999 SER.#'d SETS
127-132 PRINT RUN 999 SER.#'d SETS
1 Jason Terry .25 .60
2 Theo Ratliff .20 .50
3 Shareef Abdur-Rahim .30 .75
4 Raef LaFrentz .20 .50
5 Vin Baker .20 .50
6 Paul Pierce .50 1.25
7 Eddy Curry .20 .50
8 Tyson Chandler .25 .60
9 Antonio Davis .25 .60
10 Dajuan Wagner .20 .50
11 Zydrunas Ilgauskas .25 .60
12 Carlos Boozer .25 .60
13 Steve Nash .60 1.50
14 Antoine Walker .30 .75
15 Dirk Nowitzki .75 2.00
16 Michael Finley .30 .75
17 Andre Miller .25 .60
18 Nene .25 .60
19 Earl Boykins .20 .50
20 Ben Wallace .40 1.00
21 Chauncey Billups .40 1.00
22 Richard Hamilton .40 1.00
23 Mike Dunleavy .25 .60
24 Jason Richardson .30 .75
25 Nick Van Exel .30 .75
26 Cuttino Mobley .30 .75
27 Yao Ming .75 2.00
28 Steve Francis .30 .75
29 Reggie Miller .60 1.50
30 Jamaal Tinsley .30 .75
31 Jermaine O'Neal .30 .75
32 Corey Maggette .25 .60
33 Elton Brand .25 .60
34 Quentin Richardson .20 .50
35 Shaquille O'Neal 1.25 3.00
36 Kobe Bryant 2.50 6.00
37 Karl Malone .60 1.50
38 Gary Payton .50 1.25
39 Mike Miller .25 .60
40 Pau Gasol .50 1.25
41 Shane Battier .25 .60
42 Eddie Jones .30 .75
43 Caron Butler .25 .60
44 Lamar Odom .25 .60
45 Desmond Mason .25 .60
46 Tim Thomas .20 .50
47 Michael Redd .30 .75
48 Latrell Sprewell .40 1.00
49 Kevin Garnett .75 2.00
50 Wally Szczerbiak .25 .60
51 Kenyon Martin .30 .75
52 Jason Kidd .50 1.25
53 Richard Jefferson .25 .60
54 Jamal Mashburn .25 .60
55 Baron Davis .30 .75
56 Jamaal Magloire .20 .50
57 Stephon Marbury .40 1.00
58 Allan Houston .30 .75
59 Keith Van Horn .30 .75
60 Drew Gooden .25 .60
61 Tracy McGrady .50 1.25
62 Gordan Giricek .20 .50
63 Glenn Robinson .25 .60
64 Allen Iverson .75 2.00
65 Eric Snow .20 .50
66 Antonio McDyess .25 .60
67 Amare Stoudemire .40 1.00
68 Shawn Marion .30 .75
69 Zach Randolph .30 .75
70 Rasheed Wallace .40 1.00
71 Damon Stoudamire .25 .60
72 Mike Bibby .30 .75
73 Chris Webber .40 1.00
74 Peja Stojakovic .25 .60
75 Brad Miller .25 .60
76 Tony Parker .50 1.25
77 Tim Duncan .75 2.00
78 Manu Ginobili .60 1.50
79 Rashard Lewis .25 .60
80 Ray Allen .50 1.25
81 Vladimir Radmanovic .20 .50
82 Morris Peterson .20 .50
83 Vince Carter .60 1.50
84 Jalen Rose .25 .60
85 Andrei Kirilenko .25 .60
86 Matt Harpring .25 .60
87 Carlos Arroyo .25 .60
88 Jerry Stackhouse .40 1.00
89 Gilbert Arenas .30 .75
90 Larry Hughes .25 .60
91 Udonis Haslem RC 2.50 6.00
92 Brandon Hunter RC 1.25 3.00
93 Maurice Williams RC 2.00 5.00
94 Keith Bogans RC 1.25 3.00
95 Zaur Pachulia RC 2.00 5.00
96 Willie Green RC 2.00 5.00
97 Kyle Korver RC 2.50 6.00
98 James Jones RC 1.25 3.00
99 Steve Blake RC 1.50 4.00
100 Travis Hansen RC 1.25 3.00
101 Jerome Beasley RC 1.25 3.00
102 Luke Walton RC 2.00 5.00
103 Jason Kapono RC 1.25 3.00
104 Maciej Lampe RC 1.25 3.00
105 Josh Howard RC 2.00 5.00
106 Leandro Barbosa RC 2.00 5.00
107 Kendrick Perkins RC 1.50 4.00
108 Ndudi Ebi RC 1.25 3.00
109 Brian Cook RC 1.25 3.00
110 Travis Outlaw RC 1.50 4.00
111 Zoran Planinic RC 1.25 3.00
112 Boris Diaw RC 2.00 5.00
113 Dahntay Jones RC 1.25 3.00
114 Aleksandar Pavlovic RC 1.50 4.00
115 David West RC 2.50 6.00
116 Zarko Cabarkapa RC 1.25 3.00
117 Troy Bell RC 1.25 3.00
118 Reece Gaines RC 1.25 3.00
119 Luke Ridnour RC 2.00 5.00
120 Marcus Banks RC 1.25 3.00
121 Nick Collison RC 1.50 4.00
122 Mickael Pietrus RC 1.50 4.00
123 Mike Sweetney RC 1.25 3.00
124 Chris Kaman RC 2.00 5.00
125 T.J. Ford RC 1.50 4.00
126 Kirk Hinrich RC 2.00 5.00
127 Jarvis Hayes RC 1.50 4.00
128 Dwyane Wade RC 20.00 50.00
129 Chris Bosh RC 8.00 20.00
130 Carmelo Anthony RC 12.00 30.00
131 Darko Milicic RC 2.00 5.00
132 LeBron James RC 400.00 800.00

2003-04 Upper Deck Triple Dimensions Slam Hologram

*91-132 SLAM HOLO: .75X TO 2X BASE HI
91-132 SLAM HOLO FIRST 100 SER.#'d COPIES

2003-04 Upper Deck Triple Dimensions UD Promos

*PROMOS: .75X TO 2X BASIC

2003-04 Upper Deck Triple Dimensions 3-D Jerseys

PRINT RUN 120 TO 249 SER.#'d SETS
*PATCH: 2X TO 5X BASE HI
PATCH PRINT RUN 25 SER.#'d SETS
J1 Ray Allen 5.00 12.00
J2 Allen Iverson 8.00 20.00
J3 Jason Richardson 3.00 8.00
J4 Shareef Abdur-Rahim 3.00 8.00
J5 Jason Kidd 5.00 12.00
J6 Steve Nash 6.00 15.00
J7 Richard Jefferson 2.50 6.00
J8 Manu Ginobili 6.00 15.00
J9 Shaquille O'Neal 12.00 30.00
J10 Shawn Marion 3.00 8.00
J11 Kenyon Martin 3.00 8.00
J12 Gilbert Arenas 3.00 8.00
J13 LeBron James 300.00 600.00
J14 Richard Hamilton 4.00 10.00
J15 Dajuan Wagner 2.00 5.00
J16 Kobe Bryant 10.00 25.00
J17 Tracy McGrady 5.00 12.00
J18 Andrei Kirilenko 2.50 6.00
J19 Reggie Miller 6.00 15.00
J20 Steve Francis 3.00 8.00
J21 Carmelo Anthony 15.00 40.00
J22 Lamar Odom 2.50 6.00
J23 Tim Duncan/120 8.00 20.00
J24 Stephon Marbury 4.00 10.00
J25 Yao Ming 8.00 20.00
J26 Chauncey Billups 4.00 10.00
J27 Chris Webber 4.00 10.00
J28 Baron Davis 3.00 8.00
J29 Elton Brand 2.50 6.00
J30 Bonzi Wells 2.00 5.00
J31 Caron Butler 2.50 6.00
J32 Jermaine O'Neal 3.00 8.00
J33 Paul Pierce 5.00 12.00
J34 Wally Szczerbiak 2.50 6.00
J35 Gary Payton 5.00 12.00
J36 Michael Jordan 50.00 120.00
J37 Tony Parker 5.00 12.00
J38 Michael Finley 3.00 8.00
J39 Rashard Lewis 2.50 6.00
J40 Amare Stoudemire 4.00 10.00
J41 Dirk Nowitzki 8.00 20.00
J42 Kevin Garnett 8.00 20.00

2003-04 Upper Deck Triple Dimensions 3-D Warmups

PRINT RUN 999 SER.#'d SETS
*SHOOT.SHIRTS: .5X TO 1.25X WARM HI
SHIRTS PRINT RUN 499 SER.#'d SETS
W1 Ray Allen 4.00 10.00
W2 Allen Iverson 6.00 15.00
W3 Jason Richardson 2.50 6.00
W4 Shareef Abdur-Rahim 2.50 6.00
W5 Jason Kidd 4.00 10.00
W6 Steve Nash 5.00 12.00
W7 Richard Jefferson 2.00 5.00
W8 Manu Ginobili 5.00 12.00
W9 Shaquille O'Neal 10.00 25.00
W10 Shawn Marion 2.50 6.00
W11 Kenyon Martin 2.50 6.00
W12 Gilbert Arenas 2.50 6.00
W13 LeBron James 150.00 400.00
W14 Richard Hamilton 3.00 8.00
W15 Dajuan Wagner 2.00 5.00
W16 Kobe Bryant 8.00 20.00
W17 Tracy McGrady 4.00 10.00
W18 Andrei Kirilenko 2.00 5.00
W19 Reggie Miller 5.00 12.00
W20 Steve Francis 2.50 6.00
W22 Lamar Odom 2.50 6.00
W23 Tim Duncan 6.00 15.00
W24 Stephon Marbury 3.00 8.00
W25 Yao Ming 6.00 15.00
W26 Chauncey Billups 3.00 8.00
W27 Chris Webber 3.00 8.00
W28 Baron Davis 2.50 6.00
W29 Elton Brand 2.00 5.00
W30 Jamal Mashburn 2.00 5.00
W31 Caron Butler 2.00 5.00
W32 Jermaine O'Neal 2.50 6.00
W33 Paul Pierce 4.00 10.00
W34 Wally Szczerbiak 2.00 5.00
W35 Gary Payton 4.00 10.00
W36 Michael Jordan 30.00 80.00
W37 Tony Parker 4.00 10.00
W38 Michael Finley 2.50 6.00
W39 Rashard Lewis 2.00 5.00
W40 Amare Stoudemire 3.00 8.00
W41 Dirk Nowitzki 6.00 15.00
W42 Kevin Garnett 6.00 15.00
W43 Jason Terry 2.00 5.00
W44 Eddy Curry 1.50 4.00
W45 Corey Maggette 2.00 5.00
W46 Quentin Richardson 1.50 4.00
W47 Karl Malone 5.00 12.00
W48 Peja Stojakovic 2.00 5.00

2003-04 Upper Deck Triple Dimensions Reflections

ONE PER PACK
*AMETHYST: 1.5X TO 4X BASE REF.HI
AMETH.PRINT RUN 300 SER.#'d SETS
*EMERALD: 2.5X TO 6X BASE REF.HI
EMERALD PRINT RUN 100 SER.#'d SETS
*RUBY: 1X TO 2.5X BASE REF.HI
RUBY PRINT RUN 500 SER.#'d SETS
1 Rasheed Wallace .60 1.50
2 Jason Terry .40 1.00
3 Paul Pierce .75 2.00
4 Ricky Davis .40 1.00
5 Michael Jordan 10.00 25.00
6 Eddy Curry .30 .75
7 Kirk Hinrich .50 1.25
8 Jamal Crawford .50 1.25
9 Scottie Pippen 1.25 3.00
10 LeBron James 60.00 150.00
11 Carlos Boozer .40 1.00
12 Dajuan Wagner .30 .75
13 Dirk Nowitzki 1.25 3.00
14 Steve Nash 1.00 2.50
15 Antoine Walker .50 1.25
16 Josh Howard .50 1.25
17 Carmelo Anthony 1.50 4.00
18 Andre Miller .40 1.00
19 Nene .40 1.00
20 Ben Wallace .60 1.50
21 Darko Milicic .40 1.00
22 Chauncey Billups .60 1.50
23 Jason Richardson .50 1.25
24 Nick Van Exel .50 1.25
25 Steve Francis .50 1.25
26 Yao Ming 1.25 3.00
27 Cuttino Mobley .50 1.25
28 Jermaine O'Neal .50 1.25
29 Al Harrington .40 1.00
30 Reggie Miller 1.00 2.50
31 Kobe Bryant 4.00 10.00
32 Shaquille O'Neal 2.00 5.00
33 Gary Payton .75 2.00
34 Karl Malone 1.00 2.50
35 Elton Brand .50 1.25
36 Chris Kaman .50 1.25
37 Corey Maggette .40 1.00
38 Pau Gasol .75 2.00
39 Troy Bell .30 .75
40 Jason Williams .75 2.00
41 Dwyane Wade 10.00 25.00
42 Lamar Odom .40 1.00
43 Eddie Jones .50 1.25
44 T.J. Ford .40 1.00
45 Michael Redd .50 1.25
46 Desmond Mason .40 1.00
47 Kevin Garnett 1.25 3.00
48 Latrell Sprewell .60 1.50
49 Ndudi Ebi .30 .75
50 Kenyon Martin .50 1.25
51 Jason Kidd .75 2.00
52 Richard Jefferson .40 1.00
53 Baron Davis .50 1.25
54 David West .60 1.50
55 Stephon Marbury .60 1.50
56 Allan Houston .50 1.25
57 Kurt Thomas .30 .75
58 Tracy McGrady .75 2.00
59 Keith Bogans .30 .75
60 Drew Gooden .40 1.00
61 Allen Iverson 1.25 3.00
62 Glenn Robinson .40 1.00
63 Leandro Barbosa .50 1.25
64 Amare Stoudemire .60 1.50
65 Shawn Marion .50 1.25
66 Shareef Abdur-Rahim .50 1.25
67 Zach Randolph .50 1.25
68 Travis Outlaw .40 1.00
69 Darius Miles .30 .75
70 Peja Stojakovic .40 1.00
71 Chris Webber .60 1.50
72 Brad Miller .40 1.00
73 Mike Bibby .50 1.25
74 Bobby Jackson .40 1.00
75 Tim Duncan 1.25 3.00
76 Tony Parker .75 2.00
77 Manu Ginobili 1.00 2.50
78 Ray Allen .75 2.00
79 Nick Collison .40 1.00
80 Luke Ridnour .50 1.25
81 Chris Bosh 1.50 4.00
82 Vince Carter 1.00 2.50
83 Jalen Rose .40 1.00
84 Donyell Marshall .30 .75
85 Andrei Kirilenko .40 1.00
86 Carlos Arroyo .40 1.00
87 Jarvis Hayes .30 .75
88 Jerry Stackhouse .60 1.50
89 Gilbert Arenas .50 1.25
90 Larry Hughes .40 1.00

2003-04 Upper Deck Triple Dimensions Reflections Gold

*GOLD SINGLES: 4X TO 10X BASE REF.HI
PRINT RUN 50 SER.#'d SETS
5 Michael Jordan 200.00 500.00
9 Scottie Pippen 15.00 40.00
10 LeBron James 4,000.00 8,000.00
17 Carmelo Anthony 25.00 60.00
31 Kobe Bryant 100.00 250.00
41 Dwyane Wade 150.00 400.00
81 Chris Bosh 15.00 40.00

2003-04 Upper Deck Triple Dimensions Standout Sigs

PRINT RUN 25 TO 100 SER.#'d SETS
1 Kobe Bryant/25 300.00 600.00
2 Kevin Garnett/25 200.00 500.00
3 LeBron James/25 15,000.00 30,000.00
4 Carmelo Anthony/25 75.00 200.00
5 Michael Jordan/25 2,500.00 5,000.00
6 Patrick Ewing/25 200.00 500.00
7 Tracy McGrady/25 75.00 200.00
8 Amare Stoudemire/25 25.00 60.00
9 Darko Milicic/25 6.00 15.00
12 Luke Walton 6.00 15.00
13 Reggie Evans 4.00 10.00
14 Lamar Odom 10.00 25.00
15 Reggie Miller 75.00 200.00
16 Gerald Wallace 6.00 15.00
17 Dahntay Jones 5.00 12.00
18 Boris Diaw 6.00 15.00
19 Wang ZhiZhi 100.00 250.00
20 Jalen Rose 6.00 15.00
22 Alonzo Mourning 20.00 50.00
23 Dan Dickau 4.00 10.00
24 Antawn Jamison 6.00 15.00
25 Brent Barry 6.00 15.00
26 Cuttino Mobley 4.00 10.00
27 Luke Ridnour 6.00 15.00
28 Chris Wilcox 4.00 10.00
29 Carlos Boozer 6.00 15.00
30 Gordan Giricek 6.00 15.00
31 Chris Kaman 6.00 15.00
32 Josh Howard 6.00 15.00
33 Leandro Barbosa 6.00 15.00
34 Jon Barry 6.00 15.00
35 Shawn Marion 5.00 12.00
36 Kendrick Perkins 5.00 12.00
37 Chris Bosh 20.00 50.00
38 Travis Outlaw 5.00 12.00
39 Antonio McDyess 6.00 15.00
40 Drew Gooden 6.00 15.00
41 Peja Stojakovic 6.00 15.00
42 Chauncey Billups 10.00 25.00
43 Darius Miles 4.00 10.00
44 Marko Jaric 4.00 10.00
45 Corey Maggette 5.00 12.00
46 Dajuan Wagner 6.00 15.00
47 Andre Miller 6.00 15.00
48 Shane Battier 6.00 15.00
49 Reece Gaines 4.00 10.00
50 Troy Bell 4.00 10.00
51 Morris Peterson 6.00 15.00
52 Richard Hamilton 6.00 15.00
53 Mike Sweetney 4.00 10.00
54 Mickael Pietrus 5.00 12.00
55 Tony Parker 20.00 50.00
56 Marcus Banks 4.00 10.00
57 Eddy Curry 4.00 10.00
58 Brian Cook 4.00 10.00
59 Maciej Lampe 4.00 10.00
60 Zoran Planinic 4.00 10.00
61 Paul Pierce 20.00 50.00
62 Jason Kidd 15.00 40.00
63 Richard Jefferson 5.00 12.00
64 Mike Bibby 6.00 15.00
65 Gilbert Arenas 8.00 20.00
66 Earl Boykins 6.00 15.00
67 Dwyane Wade 200.00 500.00
68 David West 8.00 20.00
69 Desmond Mason 6.00 15.00
70 Jerry Stackhouse 8.00 20.00

1996 Upper Deck U.S. Olympic

COMPLETE SET (135) 8.00 20.00
11 Michael Jordan 1.25 3.00
12 Larry Bird .40 1.00
93 Anfernee Hardaway .30 .75
134 Jordan/Hardaway .60 1.50

1996 Upper Deck U.S. Olympic Reflections of Gold

COMPLETE SET (10) 8.00 20.00
STATED ODDS 1:5
RG1 Michael Jordan 6.00 15.00

1996 Upper Deck U.S. Olympic Reflections of Gold Signatures

COMPLETE SET (9) 3,000.00 5,000.00
STATED ODDS 1:79
RG1 Michael Jordan 2,500.00 5,000.00

1996 Upper Deck U.S. Olympic Reign of Gold Holograms

COMPLETE SET (5) 6.00 15.00
STATED ODDS 1:17
RN1 Michael Jordan 6.00 15.00

1994 Upper Deck USA

COMPLETE SET (90) 10.00 25.00
1 Derrick Coleman .15 .40
2 Derrick Coleman .15 .40
3 Derrick Coleman .15 .40
4 Derrick Coleman .15 .40
5 Derrick Coleman .15 .40
6 Derrick Coleman .15 .40
7 Joe Dumars .20 .50
8 Joe Dumars .20 .50
9 Joe Dumars .20 .50
10 Joe Dumars .20 .50
11 Joe Dumars .20 .50
12 Joe Dumars .20 .50
13 Tim Hardaway .20 .50
14 Tim Hardaway .20 .50
15 Tim Hardaway .20 .50
16 Tim Hardaway .20 .50
17 Tim Hardaway .20 .50
18 Tim Hardaway .20 .50
19 Larry Johnson .20 .50
20 Larry Johnson .20 .50
21 Larry Johnson .20 .50
22 Larry Johnson .20 .50
23 Larry Johnson .20 .50
24 Larry Johnson .20 .50
25 Shawn Kemp .20 .50
26 Shawn Kemp .20 .50
27 Shawn Kemp .20 .50
28 Shawn Kemp .20 .50
29 Shawn Kemp .20 .50
30 Shawn Kemp .20 .50
31 Dan Majerle .15 .40
32 Dan Majerle .15 .40
33 Dan Majerle .15 .40
34 Dan Majerle .15 .40
35 Dan Majerle .15 .40
36 Dan Majerle .15 .40
37 Reggie Miller .25 .60
38 Reggie Miller .25 .60
39 Reggie Miller .25 .60
40 Reggie Miller .25 .60
41 Reggie Miller .25 .60
42 Reggie Miller .25 .60
43 Alonzo Mourning .20 .50
44 Alonzo Mourning .20 .50
45 Alonzo Mourning .20 .50
46 Alonzo Mourning .20 .50
47 Alonzo Mourning .20 .50
48 Alonzo Mourning .20 .50
49 Shaquille O'Neal .50 1.25
50 Shaquille O'Neal .50 1.25
51 Shaquille O'Neal .50 1.25
52 Shaquille O'Neal .50 1.25
53 Shaquille O'Neal .50 1.25
54 Shaquille O'Neal .50 1.25
55 Mark Price .15 .40
56 Mark Price .15 .40
57 Mark Price .15 .40
58 Mark Price .15 .40
59 Mark Price .15 .40
60 Mark Price .15 .40
61 Steve Smith .12 .30
62 Steve Smith .12 .30
63 Steve Smith .12 .30
64 Steve Smith .12 .30
65 Steve Smith .12 .30
66 Steve Smith .12 .30
67 Isiah Thomas .25 .60
68 Isiah Thomas .25 .60
69 Isiah Thomas .25 .60
70 Isiah Thomas .25 .60
71 Isiah Thomas .25 .60
72 Isiah Thomas .25 .60
73 Dominique Wilkins .25 .60
74 Dominique Wilkins .25 .60
75 Dominique Wilkins .25 .60
76 Dominique Wilkins .25 .60
77 Dominique Wilkins .25 .60
78 Dominique Wilkins .25 .60
79 Jennifer Azzi 1.25 3.00
80 Daedra Charles .60 1.50
81 Lisa Leslie 1.50 4.00
82 Katrina McClain .60 1.50
83 Dawn Staley 1.25 3.00
84 Sheryl Swoopes 1.50 4.00
85 Michael Jordan ATG 85 1.25 3.00
86 Larry Bird ATG 86 .40 1.00
87 Jerry West ATG 87 .25 .60
88 Adrian Dantley ATG 88 .12 .30
89 Cheryl Miller ATG 89 1.50 4.00
90 Henry Iba ATG 90 .12 .30
CK1 Checklist 1 .12 .30
CK2 Checklist 2 .12 .30

1994 Upper Deck USA Gold Medal

COMPLETE SET (90) 20.00 50.00
*STARS: .75X TO 2X HI COLUMN

1994 Upper Deck USA Chalk Talk

COMPLETE SET (14) 6.00 15.00
CT1 Derrick Coleman .75 2.00
CT2 Joe Dumars 1.00 2.50
CT3 Tim Hardaway 1.00 2.50
CT4 Larry Johnson 1.00 2.50
CT5 Shawn Kemp 1.00 2.50
CT6 Dan Majerle .75 2.00
CT7 Reggie Miller 1.25 3.00
CT8 Alonzo Mourning 1.00 2.50
CT9 Shaquille O'Neal 2.50 6.00
CT10 Mark Price .75 2.00
CT11 Steve Smith .60 1.50
CT12 Isiah Thomas 1.25 3.00
CT13 Dominique Wilkins 1.25 3.00
CT14 Kevin Johnson .75 2.00

1994 Upper Deck USA Follow Your Dreams Assists

COMPLETE SET (14) 6.00 15.00
*REBOUNDS/SCORING: EQUAL VALUE
*EXCHANGE SETS: .5X TO 1.25X HI COLUMN
1 Derrick Coleman .75 2.00
2 Joe Dumars 1.00 2.50
3 Tim Hardaway 1.00 2.50
4 Kevin Johnson .75 2.00
5 Larry Johnson 1.00 2.50
6 Shawn Kemp 1.00 2.50
7 Dan Majerle .75 2.00
8 Reggie Miller 1.25 3.00
9 Alonzo Mourning 1.00 2.50
10 Shaquille O'Neal 2.50 6.00
11 Mark Price .75 2.00
12 Steve Smith .60 1.50
13 Isiah Thomas 1.25 3.00
14 Dominique Wilkins 1.25 3.00

1994 Upper Deck USA Jordan's Highlights

COMPLETE SET (5) 15.00 40.00
COMMON JORDAN (JH1-JH5) 5.00 12.00

1996 Upper Deck USA

COMPLETE SET (62) 8.00 20.00
1 Anfernee Hardaway .15 .40
2 Anfernee Hardaway .15 .40
3 Anfernee Hardaway .15 .40
4 Anfernee Hardaway .15 .40
5 Grant Hill .15 .40
6 Grant Hill .15 .40
7 Grant Hill .15 .40
8 Grant Hill .15 .40
9 Karl Malone .12 .30
10 Karl Malone .12 .30
11 Karl Malone .12 .30
12 Karl Malone .12 .30
13 Reggie Miller .15 .40
14 Reggie Miller .15 .40
15 Reggie Miller .15 .40
16 Reggie Miller .15 .40
17 Shaquille O'Neal .25 .60
18 Shaquille O'Neal .25 .60
19 Shaquille O'Neal .25 .60
20 Shaquille O'Neal .25 .60
21 Hakeem Olajuwon .12 .30
22 Hakeem Olajuwon .12 .30
23 Hakeem Olajuwon .12 .30
24 Hakeem Olajuwon .12 .30
25 Scottie Pippen .15 .40
26 Scottie Pippen .15 .40
27 Scottie Pippen .15 .40
28 Scottie Pippen .15 .40
29 David Robinson .15 .40
30 David Robinson .15 .40
31 David Robinson .15 .40
32 David Robinson .15 .40
33 Glenn Robinson .07 .20
34 Glenn Robinson .07 .20
35 Glenn Robinson .07 .20
36 Glenn Robinson .07 .20
37 John Stockton .12 .30
38 John Stockton .12 .30
39 John Stockton .12 .30
40 John Stockton .12 .30
49 Anfernee Hardaway .15 .40
50 Grant Hill .15 .40
51 Karl Malone .12 .30
52 Reggie Miller .15 .40
53 Shaquille O'Neal .25 .60
54 Hakeem Olajuwon .12 .30
55 Scottie Pippen .15 .40
56 David Robinson .15 .40
57 Glenn Robinson .07 .20
58 John Stockton .12 .30
61 Jennifer Azzi 1.00 2.50
62 Ruthie Bolton-Holifield 1.00 2.50
63 Teresa Edwards .75 2.00
64 Lisa Leslie 1.50 4.00
65 Rebecca Lobo 1.25 3.00
66 Katrina McClain .40 1.00
67 Nikki McCray 1.00 2.50
68 Carla McGhee .40 1.00
69 Dawn Staley 1.00 2.50
70 Katy Steding .40 1.00
71 Sheryl Swoopes 2.00 5.00
72 Tara VanDerveer CO .40 1.00
NNO USA Trade Card Expired .08 .25

1996 Upper Deck USA Exchange Set

COMPLETE SET (10) .75 2.00
41 Charles Barkley .15 .40
42 Charles Barkley .15 .40
43 Charles Barkley .15 .40
44 Charles Barkley .15 .40
45 Mitch Richmond .10 .25
46 Mitch Richmond .10 .25
47 Mitch Richmond .10 .25
48 Mitch Richmond .10 .25
59 Charles Barkley .15 .40
60 Mitch Richmond .10 .25

1996 Upper Deck USA Follow Your Dreams

COMPLETE SET (11) 5.00 12.00
F1 Anfernee Hardaway 1.00 2.50
F2 Grant Hill 1.00 2.50
F3 Karl Malone .75 2.00
F4 Reggie Miller W 1.00 2.50
F5 Shaquille O'Neal 1.50 4.00
F6 Hakeem Olajuwon .75 2.00

F7 Scottie Pippen 1.00 2.50
F8 David Robinson W 1.00 2.50
F9 Glenn Robinson .50 1.25
F10 John Stockton .75 2.00
F11 Field Card .20 .50

1996 Upper Deck USA Follow Your Dreams Exchange Set

COMPLETE SET (12) 8.00 20.00
FD1 Charles Barkley 1.25 3.00
FD2 David Robinson 1.25 3.00
FD3 Reggie Miller 1.25 3.00
FD4 Scottie Pippen 1.25 3.00
FD5 Grant Hill 1.25 3.00
FD6 Mitch Richmond .75 2.00
FD7 Shaquille O'Neal 2.00 5.00
FD8 Anfernee Hardaway 1.25 3.00
FD9 Karl Malone 1.00 2.50
FD10 Gary Payton .75 2.00
FD11 Hakeem Olajuwon 1.00 2.50
FD12 John Stockton 1.00 2.50

1996 Upper Deck USA Anfernee Hardaway American Made

COMPLETE SET (4) 10.00 25.00
COMMON CARD (A1-A4) 3.00 8.00

1996 Upper Deck USA Michael Jordan American Made

COMPLETE SET (4) 20.00 50.00
COMMON CARD (M1-M4) 10.00 25.00

1996 Upper Deck USA SP Career Statistics

COMPLETE SET (10) 2.50 6.00
*GOLD: 3X TO 8X HI COLUMN
GOLD STATED ODDS 1:27 PACKS
S1 Anfernee Hardaway .60 1.50
S2 Grant Hill .60 1.50
S3 Karl Malone .50 1.25
S4 Reggie Miller .60 1.50
S5 Shaquille O'Neal 1.00 2.50
S6 Hakeem Olajuwon .50 1.25
S7 Scottie Pippen .60 1.50
S8 David Robinson .60 1.50
S9 Glenn Robinson .30 .75
S10 John Stockton .50 1.25
S11 Charles Barkley .60 1.50
S12 Mitch Richmond .40 1.00

1999-00 Upper Deck Victory

COMPLETE SET (440) 30.00 80.00
SUBSET CARDS SAME VALUE AS BASE
1 Dikembe Mutombo CL .50 1.25
2 Steve Smith .25 .60
3 Dikembe Mutombo .50 1.25
4 Ed Gray .20 .50
5 Alan Henderson .20 .50
6 LaPhonso Ellis .20 .50
7 Roshown McLeod .20 .50
8 Bimbo Coles .20 .50
9 Chris Crawford .20 .50
10 Anthony Johnson .20 .50
11 Antoine Walker CL .30 .75
12 Kenny Anderson .25 .60
13 Antoine Walker .30 .75
14 Greg Minor .20 .50
15 Tony Battie .20 .50
16 Ron Mercer .25 .60
17 Paul Pierce .60 1.50
18 Vitaly Potapenko .20 .50
19 Dana Barros .20 .50
20 Walter McCarty .20 .50
21 Elden Campbell CL .20 .50
22 Elden Campbell .20 .50
23 Eddie Jones .30 .75
24 David Wesley .20 .50
25 Bobby Phills .20 .50
26 Derrick Coleman .25 .60
27 Anthony Mason .30 .75
28 Brad Miller .25 .60
29 Eldridge Recasner .20 .50
30 Ricky Davis .30 .75
31 Toni Kukoc CL .40 1.00
32 Michael Jordan 3.00 8.00
33 Brent Barry .25 .60
34 Randy Brown .20 .50
35 Keith Booth .20 .50
36 Kornel David RC .20 .50
37 Mark Bryant .20 .50
38 Toni Kukoc .40 1.00
39 Rusty LaRue .20 .50
40 Brevin Knight CL .20 .50
41 Shawn Kemp .50 1.25
42 Wesley Person .20 .50
43 Johnny Newman .20 .50
44 Derek Anderson .20 .50
45 Brevin Knight .20 .50
46 Bob Sura .20 .50
47 Andrew DeClercq .20 .50
48 Zydrunas Ilgauskas .25 .60
49 Danny Ferry .20 .50
50 Steve Nash CL .60 1.50
51 Michael Finley .30 .75
52 Robert Pack .20 .50
53 Shawn Bradley .20 .50
54 John Williams .20 .50
55 Hubert Davis .20 .50
56 Dirk Nowitzki 1.00 2.50
57 Steve Nash .60 1.50
58 Chris Anstey .20 .50
59 Erick Strickland .20 .50
60 Nick Van Exel CL .25 .60
61 Antonio McDyess .25 .60
62 Nick Van Exel .25 .60
63 Bryant Stith .20 .50
64 Chauncey Billups .30 .75
65 Danny Fortson .20 .50
66 Eric Williams .20 .50
67 Eric Washington .20 .50
68 Raef LaFrentz .25 .60
69 Johnny Taylor .20 .50
70 Jerry Stackhouse CL .30 .75
71 Grant Hill .50 1.25
72 Lindsey Hunter .20 .50
73 Bison Dele .20 .50
74 Loy Vaught .20 .50
75 Jerome Williams .20 .50
76 Jerry Stackhouse .30 .75
77 Christian Laettner .25 .60
78 Jud Buechler .20 .50
79 Don Reid .20 .50
80 Antawn Jamison CL .30 .75
81 John Starks .30 .75
82 Antawn Jamison .30 .75
83 Adonal Foyle .20 .50
84 Jason Caffey .20 .50
85 Donyell Marshall .25 .60
86 Chris Mills .20 .50
87 Tony Delk .20 .50
88 Mookie Blaylock .20 .50
89 Charles Barkley CL .75 2.00
90 Hakeem Olajuwon .60 1.50
91 Scottie Pippen .75 2.00
92 Charles Barkley .75 2.00
93 Bryce Drew .20 .50
94 Cuttino Mobley .20 .50
95 Othella Harrington .20 .50
96 Matt Maloney .20 .50
97 Michael Dickerson .20 .50
98 Matt Bullard .20 .50
99 Jalen Rose CL .20 .50
100 Reggie Miller .60 1.50
101 Rik Smits .25 .60
102 Jalen Rose .25 .60
103 Antonio Davis .20 .50
104 Mark Jackson .25 .60
105 Sam Perkins .20 .50
106 Travis Best .20 .50
107 Dale Davis .20 .50
108 Chris Mullin .30 .75
109 Michael Olowokandi CL .20 .50
110 Maurice Taylor .20 .50
111 Tyrone Nesby RC .20 .50
112 Lamond Murray .20 .50
113 Darrick Martin .20 .50
114 Michael Olowokandi .20 .50
115 Rodney Rogers .20 .50
116 Eric Piatkowski .20 .50
117 Lorenzen Wright .20 .50
118 Brian Skinner .20 .50
119 Kobe Bryant CL 2.50 6.00
120 Kobe Bryant 2.50 6.00
121 Shaquille O'Neal 1.25 3.00
122 Derek Fisher .25 .60
123 Tyronn Lue .20 .50
124 Travis Knight .20 .50
125 Glen Rice .30 .75
126 Derek Harper .25 .60
127 Robert Horry .25 .60
128 Rick Fox .25 .60
129 Tim Hardaway CL .40 1.00
130 Tim Hardaway .40 1.00
131 Alonzo Mourning .50 1.25
132 Keith Askins .20 .50
133 Jamal Mashburn .20 .50
134 P.J. Brown .20 .50
135 Clarence Weatherspoon .20 .50
136 Terry Porter .20 .50
137 Dan Majerle .30 .75
138 Voshon Lenard .20 .50
139 Ray Allen CL .50 1.25
140 Ray Allen .50 1.25
141 Vinny Del Negro .20 .50
142 Glenn Robinson .25 .60
143 Dell Curry .20 .50
144 Sam Cassell .25 .60
145 Haywoode Workman .20 .50
146 Armon Gilliam .20 .50
147 Robert Traylor .20 .50
148 Chris Gatling .20 .50
149 Kevin Garnett CL .75 2.00
150 Kevin Garnett .75 2.00
151 Malik Sealy .20 .50
152 Radoslav Nesterovic .30 .75
153 Joe Smith .25 .60
154 Sam Mitchell .20 .50
155 Dean Garrett .20 .50
156 Anthony Peeler .20 .50
157 Tom Hammonds .20 .50
158 Bobby Jackson .25 .60
159 Jayson Williams CL .20 .50
160 Keith Van Horn .25 .60
161 Stephon Marbury .40 1.00
162 Jayson Williams .20 .50
163 Kendall Gill .30 .75
164 Kerry Kittles .20 .50
165 Jamie Feick RC .20 .50
166 Scott Burrell .20 .50
167 Lucious Harris .20 .50
168 Marcus Camby CL .25 .60
169 Patrick Ewing .40 1.00
170 Allan Houston .25 .60
171 Latrell Sprewell .40 1.00
172 Kurt Thomas .20 .50
173 Larry Johnson .30 .75
174 Chris Childs .20 .50
175 Marcus Camby .25 .60
176 Charlie Ward .20 .50
177 Chris Dudley .20 .50
178 Bo Outlaw CL .20 .50
179 Anfernee Hardaway .75 2.00
180 Darrell Armstrong .20 .50
181 Nick Anderson .20 .50
182 Horace Grant .25 .60
183 Isaac Austin .20 .50
184 Matt Harpring .20 .50
185 Michael Doleac .20 .50
186 Bo Outlaw .20 .50
187 Allen Iverson CL .75 2.00
188 Allen Iverson .75 2.00
189 Theo Ratliff .25 .60
190 Matt Geiger .20 .50
191 Larry Hughes .25 .60
192 Tyrone Hill .20 .50
193 George Lynch .20 .50
194 Eric Snow .25 .60
195 Aaron McKie .20 .50
196 Harvey Grant .20 .50
197 Jason Kidd CL .50 1.25
198 Jason Kidd .50 1.25
199 Tom Gugliotta .25 .60
200 Rex Chapman .20 .50
201 Clifford Robinson .25 .60
202 Luc Longley .25 .60
203 Danny Manning .25 .60
204 Pat Garrity .20 .50
205 George McCloud .20 .50
206 Toby Bailey .20 .50
207 Brian Grant CL .20 .50
208 Rasheed Wallace .40 1.00
209 Arvydas Sabonis .25 .60
210 Damon Stoudamire .30 .75
211 Brian Grant .20 .50
212 Isaiah Rider .25 .60
213 Walt Williams .20 .50
214 Jim Jackson .20 .50
215 Greg Anthony .20 .50
216 Stacey Augmon .25 .60
217 Vlade Divac CL .30 .75
218 Jason Williams .50 1.25
219 Vlade Divac .30 .75
220 Chris Webber .40 1.00
221 Nick Anderson .20 .50
222 Peja Stojakovic .30 .75
223 Tariq Abdul-Wahad .20 .50
224 Vernon Maxwell .20 .50
225 Lawrence Funderburke .20 .50
226 Jon Barry .20 .50
227 David Robinson CL .60 1.50
228 Tim Duncan .75 2.00
229 Sean Elliott .25 .60
230 David Robinson .60 1.50
231 Mario Elie .20 .50
232 Avery Johnson .20 .50
233 Steve Kerr .25 .60
234 Malik Rose .20 .50
235 Jaren Jackson .20 .50
236 Vin Baker CL .25 .60
237 Gary Payton .50 1.25
238 Vin Baker .25 .60
239 Detlef Schrempf .25 .60
240 Hersey Hawkins .20 .50
241 Dale Ellis .20 .50
242 Rashard Lewis .25 .60
243 Billy Owens .20 .50
244 Aaron Williams .20 .50
245 Vince Carter CL .75 2.00
246 Vince Carter .75 2.00
247 John Wallace .20 .50
248 Doug Christie .25 .60
249 Tracy McGrady .50 1.25
250 Kevin Willis .20 .50
251 Michael Stewart .20 .50
252 Dee Brown .20 .50
253 John Thomas .20 .50
254 Alvin Williams .20 .50
255 Karl Malone CL .60 1.50
256 Karl Malone .60 1.50
257 John Stockton .50 1.25
258 Jacque Vaughn .20 .50
259 Bryon Russell .20 .50
260 Howard Eisley .20 .50
261 Greg Ostertag .20 .50
262 Adam Keefe .20 .50
263 Todd Fuller .20 .50
264 Mike Bibby CL .30 .75
265 Shareef Abdur-Rahim .30 .75
266 Mike Bibby .30 .75
267 Bryant Reeves .20 .50
268 Felipe Lopez .20 .50
269 Cherokee Parks .20 .50
270 Michael Smith .20 .50
271 Tony Massenburg .20 .50
272 Rodrick Rhodes .20 .50
273 Juwan Howard CL .25 .60
274 Juwan Howard .25 .60
275 Rod Strickland .20 .50
276 Mitch Richmond .40 1.00
277 Otis Thorpe .20 .50
278 Calbert Cheaney .20 .50
279 Tracy Murray .20 .50
280 Ben Wallace .30 .75
281 Terry Davis .20 .50
282 Michael Jordan RF 3.00 8.00
283 Reggie Miller RF .60 1.50
284 Dikembe Mutombo RF .50 1.25
285 Patrick Ewing RF .40 1.00
286 Allan Houston RF .25 .60
287 Danny Manning RF .25 .60
288 Jalen Rose RF .25 .60
289 Rasheed Wallace RF .40 1.00
290 Jerry Stackhouse RF .30 .75
291 Damon Stoudamire RF .30 .75
292 Kenny Anderson RF .25 .60
293 Shawn Kemp RF .50 1.25
294 Vlade Divac RF .30 .75
295 Larry Johnson RF .30 .75
296 Jamal Mashburn RF .25 .60
297 Ron Harper RF .25 .60
298 Steve Smith RF .25 .60
299 Kendall Gill RF .30 .75
300 Chris Mullin RF .30 .75
301 Robert Horry RF .25 .60
302 Dikembe Mutombo DD .50 1.25
303 Ron Mercer DD .25 .60
304 Eddie Jones DD .30 .75
305 Toni Kukoc DD .40 1.00
306 Derek Anderson DD .20 .50
307 Shawn Bradley DD .20 .50
308 Danny Fortson DD .20 .50
309 Bison Dele DD .20 .50
310 Antawn Jamison DD .30 .75
311 Scottie Pippen DD .75 2.00
312 Reggie Miller DD .60 1.50
313 Maurice Taylor DD .20 .50
314 Glen Rice DD .30 .75
315 Alonzo Mourning DD .50 1.25
316 Glenn Robinson DD .25 .60
317 Anthony Peeler DD .20 .50
318 Kerry Kittles DD .20 .50
319 Latrell Sprewell DD .40 1.00
320 Darrell Armstrong DD .20 .50
321 Larry Hughes DD .25 .60
322 Tom Gugliotta DD .25 .60
323 Brian Grant DD .20 .50
324 Chris Webber DD .40 1.00
325 David Robinson DD .60 1.50
326 Vin Baker DD .25 .60
327 Vince Carter DD .75 2.00
328 Bryon Russell DD .20 .50
329 Felipe Lopez DD .20 .50
330 Juwan Howard DD .25 .60
331 Michael Jordan DD 3.00 8.00
332 Jason Kidd CC .50 1.25
333 Rod Strickland CC .25 .60
334 Stephon Marbury CC .40 1.00
335 Gary Payton CC .50 1.25
336 Mark Jackson CC .25 .60
337 John Stockton CC .50 1.25
338 Brevin Knight CC .20 .50
339 Bobby Jackson CC .25 .60
340 Nick Van Exel CC .25 .60
341 Tim Hardaway CC .40 1.00
342 Darrell Armstrong CC .20 .50
343 Avery Johnson CC .25 .60
344 Mike Bibby CC .30 .75
345 Damon Stoudamire CC .30 .75
346 Jason Williams CC .50 1.25
347 Allen Iverson PC .75 2.00
348 Kobe Bryant PC 2.50 6.00
349 Karl Malone PC .60 1.50
350 Keith Van Horn PC .25 .60
351 Kevin Garnett PC .75 2.00
352 Antoine Walker PC .30 .75
353 Tim Duncan PC .75 2.00
354 Scottie Pippen PC .75 2.00
355 Paul Pierce PC .60 1.50
356 Michael Finley PC .30 .75
357 Shaquille O'Neal PC 1.25 3.00
358 Grant Hill PC .50 1.25
359 Jason Williams PC .50 1.25
360 Antonio McDyess PC .25 .60
361 Shareef Abdur-Rahim PC .30 .75
362 Allen Iverson SC .75 2.00
363 Shaquille O'Neal SC 1.25 3.00
364 Karl Malone SC .60 1.50
365 Shareef Abdur-Rahim SC .30 .75
366 Keith Van Horn SC .25 .60
367 Tim Duncan SC .75 2.00
368 Gary Payton SC .50 1.25
369 Stephon Marbury SC .40 1.00
370 Antonio McDyess SC .25 .60
371 Grant Hill SC .50 1.25
372 Kevin Garnett SC .75 2.00
373 Shawn Kemp SC .50 1.25
374 Kobe Bryant SC 2.50 6.00
375 Michael Finley SC .30 .75
376 Vince Carter SC .75 2.00
377 Checklist .10 .25
378 Checklist .10 .25
379 Checklist .10 .25
380 Checklist .10 .25
431 Elton Brand RC .60 1.50
432 Steve Francis RC .60 1.50
433 Baron Davis RC .75 2.00
434 Lamar Odom RC .60 1.50
435 Wally Szczerbiak RC .50 1.25
436 Richard Hamilton RC .75 2.00
437 Andre Miller RC .60 1.50
438 Shawn Marion RC .60 1.50
439 Jason Terry RC .60 1.50
440 Corey Maggette RC .40 1.00
NNO Michael Jordan Jsy Entry .75 2.00

2000-01 Upper Deck Victory

COMPLETE SET (330) 25 60.00
FLY2K CARDS INSERTED
ONE PER PACK .75 2.00
1 Dikembe Mutombo .50 1.25
2 Jim Jackson .25 .60
3 Jason Terry .30 .75
4 Roshown McLeod .20 .50
5 Alan Henderson .20 .50
6 Bimbo Coles .20 .50
7 Dion Glover .20 .50
8 Lorenzen Wright .20 .50
9 Paul Pierce .50 1.25
10 Kenny Anderson .25 .60
11 Antoine Walker .30 .75
12 Adrian Griffin .20 .50
13 Vitaly Potapenko .20 .50
14 Dana Barros .20 .50
15 Eric Williams .20 .50
16 Calbert Cheaney .20 .50
17 Derrick Coleman .20 .50
18 Eddie Jones .30 .75
19 Anthony Mason .30 .75
20 Elden Campbell .20 .50
21 Eddie Robinson .20 .50
22 David Wesley .25 .60
23 Baron Davis .30 .75
24 Ricky Davis .25 .60
25 Elton Brand .30 .75
26 Ron Artest .30 .75
27 Chris Carr .20 .50
28 Fred Hoiberg .20 .50
29 Hersey Hawkins .20 .50
30 Dickey Simpkins .30 .75
31 Corey Benjamin .20 .50
32 Matt Maloney .20 .50
33 Shawn Kemp .50 1.25
34 Lamond Murray .20 .50
35 Wesley Person .20 .50
36 Andre Miller .25 .60
37 Bob Sura .20 .50
38 Andrew DeClercq .20 .50
39 Brevin Knight .20 .50
40 Earl Boykins RC 1.00 2.50
41 Michael Finley .30 .75
42 Dirk Nowitzki .75 2.00
43 Cedric Ceballos .25 .60
44 Robert Pack .20 .50
45 Erick Strickland .20 .50
46 Sean Rooks .20 .50
47 Shawn Bradley .20 .50
48 Steve Nash .50 1.25
49 Antonio McDyess .25 .60
50 Nick Van Exel .30 .75
51 Keon Clark .20 .50
52 Raef LaFrentz .25 .60
53 James Posey .20 .50
54 Chris Gatling .20 .50
55 George McCloud .20 .50
56 Bryant Stith .20 .50
57 Jerry Stackhouse .30 .75
58 Lindsey Hunter .20 .50
59 Christian Laettner .30 .75
60 Jerome Williams .20 .50
61 Michael Curry .20 .50
62 Loy Vaught .20 .50
63 Eric Montross .20 .50
64 Grant Hill .50 1.25
65 Antawn Jamison .30 .75
66 Chris Mills .20 .50
67 Vonteego Cummings .20 .50
68 Larry Hughes .30 .75
69 Donyell Marshall .25 .60
70 Mookie Blaylock .30 .75
71 Erick Dampier .20 .50
72 Jason Caffey .20 .50
73 Steve Francis .30 .75
74 Shandon Anderson .20 .50
75 Hakeem Olajuwon .60 1.50
76 Walt Williams .20 .50
77 Kenny Thomas .20 .50
78 Carlos Rogers .20 .50
79 Bryce Drew .20 .50
80 Kelvin Cato .20 .50
81 Reggie Miller .60 1.50
82 Austin Croshere .20 .50
83 Rik Smits .20 .50
84 Jalen Rose .25 .60
85 Dale Davis .25 .60
86 Jonathan Bender .20 .50
87 Travis Best .20 .50
88 Chris Mullin .40 1.00
89 Lamar Odom .30 .75
90 Tyrone Nesby .20 .50
91 Michael Olowokandi .20 .50
92 Eric Piatkowski .20 .50
93 Jeff McInnis .20 .50
94 Brian Skinner .20 .50
95 Pete Chilcutt .20 .50
96 Eric Murdock .20 .50
97 Shaquille O'Neal 1.25 3.00
98 Kobe Bryant 2.50 6.00
99 Ron Harper .30 .75
100 Robert Horry .30 .75
101 Rick Fox .25 .60
102 Derek Fisher .30 .75
103 Tyronn Lue .20 .50
104 Devean George .20 .50
105 Alonzo Mourning .50 1.25
106 Jamal Mashburn .25 .60
107 Anthony Carter .20 .50
108 P.J. Brown .20 .50
109 Clarence Weatherspoon .20 .50
110 Otis Thorpe .25 .60
111 Voshon Lenard .20 .50
112 Tim Hardaway .40 1.00
113 Ray Allen .50 1.25
114 Glenn Robinson .30 .75
115 Sam Cassell .25 .60
116 Robert Traylor .20 .50
117 Ervin Johnson .20 .50
118 Scott Williams .20 .50
119 Tim Thomas .20 .50
120 Vinny Del Negro .20 .50
121 Kevin Garnett .75 2.00
122 Wally Szczerbiak .25 .60
123 Terrell Brandon .20 .50
124 Dean Garrett .20 .50
125 William Avery .20 .50
126 Sam Mitchell .20 .50
127 Radoslav Nesterovic .20 .50
128 Anthony Peeler .20 .50
129 Stephon Marbury .40 1.00
130 Keith Van Horn .25 .60
131 Kerry Kittles .25 .60
132 Lucious Harris .20 .50
133 Evan Eschmeyer .20 .50
134 Jamie Feick .20 .50
135 Jim McIlvaine .20 .50
136 Kendall Gill .30 .75
137 Allan Houston .30 .75
138 Marcus Camby .25 .60
139 Latrell Sprewell .40 1.00
140 Patrick Ewing .50 1.25
141 Larry Johnson .40 1.00
142 Charlie Ward .25 .60
143 Chris Childs .20 .50
144 John Wallace .20 .50
145 Darrell Armstrong .20 .50
146 Corey Maggette .25 .60
147 Pat Garrity .20 .50
148 John Amaechi .20 .50
149 Matt Harpring .20 .50
150 Michael Doleac .20 .50
151 Ron Mercer .20 .50
152 Chucky Atkins .20 .50
153 Allen Iverson .75 2.00
154 Matt Geiger .20 .50
155 Eric Snow .20 .50
156 Tyrone Hill .20 .50
157 Theo Ratliff .20 .50
158 George Lynch .20 .50
159 Kevin Ollie .20 .50
160 Toni Kukoc .40 1.00
161 Jason Kidd .50 1.25
162 Anfernee Hardaway .50 1.25
163 Rodney Rogers .20 .50
164 Shawn Marion .30 .75
165 Clifford Robinson .20 .50
166 Tom Gugliotta .20 .50
167 Luc Longley .25 .60
168 Randy Livingston .20 .50
169 Scottie Pippen .75 2.00
170 Steve Smith .30 .75
171 Damon Stoudamire .30 .75
172 Bonzi Wells .20 .50
173 Jermaine O'Neal .25 .60
174 Arvydas Sabonis .30 .75
175 Rasheed Wallace .40 1.00
176 Detlef Schrempf .25 .60
177 Jason Williams .50 1.25
178 Chris Webber .40 1.00
179 Peja Stojakovic .25 .60
180 Vlade Divac .30 .75
181 Lawrence Funderburke .20 .50
182 Tony Delk .20 .50
183 Jon Barry .20 .50
184 Tim Duncan .75 2.00
185 Sean Elliott .25 .60
186 Terry Porter .20 .50
187 David Robinson .60 1.50
188 Samaki Walker .20 .50
189 Malik Rose .20 .50
190 Jaren Jackson .20 .50
191 Steve Kerr .25 .60
192 Gary Payton .50 1.25
193 Brent Barry .25 .60
194 Vin Baker .25 .60
195 Horace Grant .30 .75
196 Ruben Patterson .20 .50
197 Vernon Maxwell .20 .50
198 Shammond Williams .20 .50
199 Rashard Lewis .25 .60
200 Tracy McGrady .60 1.50
201 Charles Oakley .30 .75
202 Doug Christie .25 .60
203 Antonio Davis .20 .50
204 Vince Carter .60 1.50
205 Kevin Willis .20 .50
206 Dell Curry .20 .50
207 Dee Brown .20 .50
208 Karl Malone .60 1.50
209 John Stockton .60 1.50
210 Bryon Russell .20 .50
211 Olden Polynice .20 .50
212 Jacque Vaughn .20 .50
213 Greg Ostertag .20 .50
214 Quincy Lewis .20 .50
215 Armon Gilliam .20 .50
216 Shareef Abdur-Rahim .30 .75
217 Michael Dickerson .20 .50
218 Mike Bibby .30 .75
219 Bryant Reeves .20 .50
220 Othella Harrington .20 .50
221 Grant Long .20 .50
222 Felipe Lopez .20 .50
223 Obinna Ekezie .20 .50
224 Mitch Richmond .40 1.00
225 Richard Hamilton .40 1.00
226 Tracy Murray .20 .50
227 Jahidi White .20 .50
228 Aaron Williams .20 .50
229 Juwan Howard .25 .60
230 Rod Strickland .20 .50
231 Isaac Austin .20 .50
232 Dikembe Mutombo VL .50 1.25
233 Antoine Walker VL .30 .75
234 Derrick Coleman VL .20 .50
235 Elton Brand VL .30 .75
236 Shawn Kemp VL .50 1.25
237 Michael Finley VL .30 .75
238 Antonio McDyess VL .25 .60
239 Grant Hill VL .50 1.25
240 Antawn Jamison VL .30 .75
241 Steve Francis VL .30 .75
242 Jalen Rose VL .25 .60
243 Lamar Odom VL .30 .75
244 Shaquille O'Neal VL 1.25 3.00
245 Alonzo Mourning VL .50 1.25
246 Ray Allen VL .50 1.25
247 Kevin Garnett VL .75 2.00
248 Stephon Marbury VL .40 1.00
249 Allan Houston VL .30 .75
250 Darrell Armstrong VL .20 .50
251 Allen Iverson VL .75 2.00
252 Jason Kidd VL .50 1.25
253 Rasheed Wallace VL .40 1.00
254 Chris Webber VL .40 1.00
255 Tim Duncan VL .75 2.00
256 Gary Payton VL .50 1.25
257 Vince Carter VL .60 1.50
258 Karl Malone VL .60 1.50
259 Shareef Abdur-Rahim VL .30 .75
260 Mitch Richmond VL .40 1.00
261 Kenyon Martin RC .60 1.50
262 Marcus Fizer RC .25 .60
263 Chris Mihm RC .20 .50
264 Stromile Swift RC .25 .60
265 Keyon Dooling RC .25 .60
266 Morris Peterson RC .30 .75
267 Quentin Richardson RC .25 .60
268 Courtney Alexander RC .20 .50
269 Desmond Mason RC .40 1.00
270 Mateen Cleaves RC .25 .60
271 Erick Barkley RC .20 .50
272 A.J. Guyton RC .20 .50
273 Darius Miles RC .30 .75
274 DerMarr Johnson RC .20 .50
275 Joel Przybilla RC .25 .60
276 Hanno Mottola RC .20 .50
277 Mike Miller RC .50 1.25
278 Donnell Harvey RC .20 .50
279 Speedy Claxton RC .25 .60
280 Khalid El-Amin RC .20 .50

2003-04 Upper Deck Victory

COMP.SET w/o SP's (100) 6.00 15.00
134-161 AS STATED ODDS 1:8
162-181 CS STATED ODDS 1:10
182-201 POD STATED ODDS 1:10
202-211 AKA STATED ODDS 1:20
212-221 MJ STATED ODDS 1:20
222-226 HR STATED ODDS 1:35
1 Shareef Abdur-Rahim .30 .75
2 Jason Terry .25 .60
3 Glenn Robinson .25 .60
4 Paul Pierce .50 1.25
5 Antoine Walker .30 .75
6 J.R.Bremer .20 .50
7 Vin Baker .20 .50
8 Jalen Rose .25 .60
9 Tyson Chandler .25 .60
10 Eddy Curry .20 .50
11 Jay Williams .20 .50
12 DaJuan Wagner .20 .50
13 Ricky Davis .25 .60
14 Zydrunas Ilgauskas .25 .60
15 Darius Miles .25 .60
16 Dirk Nowitzki .75 2.00
17A Michael Finley .30 .75
17B Jermaine O'Neal .30 .75
18 Steve Nash .60 1.50
19 Nick Van Exel .30 .75
20 Rodney White .20 .50
21 Juwan Howard .25 .60
22 Marcus Camby .25 .60
23 Nene Hilario .25 .60
24 Richard Hamilton .40 1.00
25 Ben Wallace .40 1.00
26 Cliff Robinson .25 .60
27 Antawn Jamison .30 .75
28 Jason Richardson .30 .75
29 Gilbert Arenas .30 .75
30 Mike Dunleavy .25 .60
31 Steve Francis .30 .75
32 Eddie Griffin .20 .50
33 Cuttino Mobley .20 .50
34 Yao Ming .75 2.00
35 Reggie Miller .60 1.50
36 Jamaal Tinsley .25 .60
38 Elton Brand .25 .60
39 Andre Miller .25 .60
40 Lamar Odom .25 .60
41 Kobe Bryant 2.50 6.00
42 Shaquille O'Neal 1.25 3.00
43 Derek Fisher .30 .75
44 Pau Gasol .50 1.25
45 Shane Battier .25 .60
46 Mike Miller .25 .60
47 Eddie Jones .30 .75
48 Alonzo Mourning .40 1.00
49 Caron Butler .25 .60
50 Gary Payton .50 1.25
51 Desmond Mason .25 .60
52 Sam Cassell .25 .60
53 Toni Kukoc .30 .75
54 Kevin Garnett .75 2.00
55 Wally Szczerbiak .25 .60
56 Joe Smith .25 .60
57 Jason Kidd .50 1.25
58 Richard Jefferson .25 .60
59 Kenyon Martin .30 .75
60 Baron Davis .30 .75
61 Jamal Mashburn .25 .60
62 Jamaal Magloire .20 .50
63 Allan Houston .30 .75
64 Antonio McDyess .25 .60
65 Latrell Sprewell .40 1.00
66 Tracy McGrady .50 1.25
67 Grant Hill .40 1.00
68 Drew Gooden .25 .60
69 Gordan Giricek .20 .50
70 Allen Iverson .75 2.00
71 Keith Van Horn .25 .60
72 Aaron McKie .20 .50
73 Stephon Marbury .40 1.00
74 Shawn Marion .30 .75
75 Anfernee Hardaway .75 2.00
76 Amare Stoudemire .40 1.00
77 Rasheed Wallace .40 1.00
78 Derek Anderson .25 .60
79 Scottie Pippen .75 2.00
80 Chris Webber .40 1.00
81 Mike Bibby .30 .75
82 Peja Stojakovic .25 .60
83 Hedo Turkoglu .25 .60
84 Tim Duncan .75 2.00
85 David Robinson .60 1.50
86 Tony Parker .50 1.25
87 Manu Ginobili .60 1.50
88 Ray Allen .50 1.25
89 Rashard Lewis .25 .60
90 Reggie Evans .20 .50
91 Alvin Williams .20 .50
92 Vince Carter .60 1.50
93 Morris Peterson .20 .50
94 Antonio Davis .25 .60
95 Karl Malone .60 1.50
96 John Stockton .60 1.50
97 Andrei Kirilenko .25 .60
98 Jerry Stackhouse .40 1.00
99 Kwame Brown .20 .50
100 Michael Jordan 3.00 8.00
101 Lebron James SP RC 20.00 50.00
102 Darko Milicic RC .40 1.00
103 Carmelo Anthony RC 2.50 6.00
104 Chris Bosh RC 1.50 4.00
105 Dwyane Wade RC 4.00 10.00
106 Chris Kaman RC .50 1.25
107 Kirk Hinrich RC .50 1.25
108 T.J. Ford RC .40 1.00
109 Mike Sweetney RC .30 .75
110 Jarvis Hayes RC .30 .75
111 Mickael Pietrus RC .40 1.00
112 Nick Collison RC .40 1.00
113 Marcus Banks RC .30 .75
114 Luke Ridnour RC .50 1.25
115 Reece Gaines RC .30 .75
116 Troy Bell RC .30 .75
117 Zarko Cabarkapa RC .30 .75
118 David West RC .60 1.50
119 Aleksandar Pavlovic RC .40 1.00
120 Dahntay Jones RC .40 1.00
121 Boris Diaw RC .50 1.25
122 Zoran Planinic RC .30 .75
123 Travis Outlaw RC .40 1.00
124 Brian Cook RC .30 .75
125 Carlos Delfino RC .40 1.00
126 Ndudi Ebi RC .30 .75
127 Kendrick Perkins RC .40 1.00
128 Leandro Barbosa RC .50 1.25
129 Josh Howard RC .50 1.25
130 Maciej Lampe RC .30 .75
134 Michael Jordan AS 6.00 15.00
135 Kobe Bryant AS 5.00 12.00
136 Kevin Garnett AS 1.50 4.00
137 Yao Ming AS 1.50 4.00
138 Vince Carter AS 1.25 3.00
139 Dirk Nowitzki AS 1.50 4.00
140 Antoine Walker AS .60 1.50
141 Chris Webber AS .75 2.00
142 Ben Wallace AS .75 2.00
143 Tracy McGrady AS 1.00 2.50
144 Jason Kidd AS 1.00 2.50
145 Steve Francis AS .60 1.50
146 Gary Payton AS 1.00 2.50
147 Peja Stojakovic AS .50 1.25
148 Brad Miller AS .50 1.25
149 Shawn Marion AS .60 1.50
150 Zydrunas Ilgauskas AS .50 1.25
151 Stephon Marbury AS .75 2.00
152 Jermaine O'Neal AS .60 1.50

153 Desmond Mason AS .50 1.25
154 Jeson Richardson AS .60 1.50
155 Tony Parker AS 1.00 2.50
156 Tim Duncan AS 1.50 4.00
157 Jamal Mashburn AS .50 1.25
158 Allen Iverson AS 1.50 4.00
159 Shaquille O'Neal AS 2.50 6.00
160 Paul Pierce AS 1.00 2.50
161 Steve Nash AS 1.25 3.00
162 Michael Jordan CS 6.00 15.00
163 Mike Bibby CS .60 1.50
164 Jay Williams CS .40 1.00
165 Richard Hamilton CS .75 2.00
166 Jerry Stackhouse CS .75 2.00
167 Peja Stojakovic CS .50 1.25
168 Reggie Miller CS 1.25 3.00
169 Robert Horry CS .60 1.50
170 Tim Duncan CS 1.50 4.00
171 Jalen Rose CS .50 1.25
172 Jason Richardson CS .60 1.50
173 Allen Iverson CS 1.50 4.00
174 Tracy McGrady CS 1.00 2.50
175 Paul Pierce CS 1.00 2.50
176 Dirk Nowitzki CS 1.50 4.00
177 Baron Davis CS .60 1.50
178 Latrell Sprewell CS .75 2.00
179 John Stockton CS 1.25 3.00
180 Ray Allen CS 1.00 2.50
181 Kobe Bryant CS 5.00 12.00
182 Mike Bibby POD .60 1.50
183 Earl Boykins POD .40 1.00
184 John Stockton POD 1.25 3.00
185 Alvin Williams POD .40 1.00
186 Darrell Armstrong POD .40 1.00
187 Tony Parker POD 1.00 2.50
188 Gary Payton POD 1.00 2.50
189 Jalen Rose POD .50 1.25
190 Jason Williams POD 1.00 2.50
191 Derek Fisher POD .60 1.50
192 Steve Nash POD 1.25 3.00
193 Jamaal Tinsley POD .40 1.00
194 Andre Miller POD .50 1.25
195 Baron Davis POD .60 1.50
196 Steve Francis POD .60 1.50
197 DaJuan Wagner POD .40 1.00
198 Stephon Marbury POD .75 2.00
199 Jason Kidd POD 1.00 2.50
200 Chauncey Billups POD .75 2.00
201 Jay Williams POD .40 1.00
202 Allen Iverson AKA 2.50 6.00
203 Steve Francis AKA 1.00 2.50
204 Kenyon Martin AKA 1.00 2.50
205 Vince Carter AKA 2.00 5.00
206 Lebron James AKA 10.00 25.00
207 Julius Erving AKA 1.50 4.00
208 Tracy McGrady AKA 1.50 4.00
209 Jason Richardson AKA 1.00 2.50
210 Earvin Johnson AKA 2.50 6.00
211 Michael Jordan AKA 10.00 25.00
212 Michael Jordan MJ 10.00 25.00
213 Kobe Bryant MJ 8.00 20.00
214 Richard Jefferson MJ .75 2.00
215 Desmond Mason MJ .75 2.00
216 Vince Carter MJ 2.00 5.00
217 Amare Stoudemire MJ 1.25 3.00
218 Yao Ming MJ 2.50 6.00
219 Elton Brand MJ .75 2.00
220 Kevin Garnett MJ 2.50 6.00
221 Shaquille O'Neal MJ 4.00 10.00
222 Lebron James HR 10.00 25.00
223 Kobe Bryant HR 8.00 20.00
224 Richard Jefferson HR .75 2.00
225 Yao Ming HR 2.50 6.00
226 Amare Stoudemire HR 1.25 3.00
227 Michael Jordan HR 8.00 20.00
228 Michael Jordan FL 8.00 20.00
229 Michael Jordan FL 8.00 20.00
230 Michael Jordan FL 8.00 20.00
231 Michael Jordan FL 8.00 20.00
232 Michael Jordan FL 8.00 20.00
233 Michael Jordan FL 8.00 20.00
300 Michael Jordan
Promotional Card 4.00 10.00

2003-04 Upper Deck Victory Parallel

*101-133 RCs: 6X TO 15X BASE HI
*134-201 SINGLES: 2.5X TO 6X BASE HI
*202-226 SINGLES: 1.5X TO 4X BASE HI
COMMON JORDAN (227-233) 40.00 100.00
134-226 PRINT RUN 100 SER.#'d SETS
101 Lebron James 1,000.00 2,000.00

1993-94 Upper Deck Wal-mart Jumbos

COMPLETE SET (28) 30.00 75.00
32 Shawn Kemp 1.00 2.50
48 Ron Harper .30 .75
64 Mitch Richmond .75 2.00
154 Glen Rice .75 2.00
195 Reggie Miller .75 2.00
243 Kenny Anderson .30 .75
361 Isaiah Rider 1.00 2.50
382 Anfernee Hardaway 4.00 10.00
391 LaPhonso Ellis .40 1.00
483 Chris Webber 5.00 12.00
485 Shawn Bradley .75 2.00
486 Jamal Mashburn 2.00 5.00
487 Calbert Cheaney .60 1.50
490 Vin Baker 2.50 6.00
492 Lindsey Hunter .60 1.50
497 Nick Van Exel 2.50 6.00
AN5 Mark Price .30 .75
AN8 Patrick Ewing .75 2.00
FT2 Charles Barkley 1.25 3.00
FT4 Dee Brown .20 .50
FT7 Clyde Drexler .75 2.00
FT13 Karl Malone 2.00 5.00
FT15 Alonzo Mourning .60 1.50
LT3 Shaquille O'Neal 3.00 8.00
TM1 Dominique Wilkins .30 .75
TM4 Scottie Pippen 2.50 6.00
TM10 Hakeem Olajuwon 1.25 3.00
TM24 David Robinson 1.25 3.00

2010 Upper Deck World of Sports

COMPLETE SET (375) 100.00 150.00
COMP.SET w/o SPs (300) 30.00 60.00
1 LeBron James 1.50 4.00
2 Yao Ming .25 .60
3 Brandon Roy .15 .40
4 Russell Westbrook .25 .60
5 Derrick Rose .40 1.00
6 Bill Russell .25 .60
7 Bobby Hurley .15 .40
8 Christian Laettner .15 .40
9 Danny Ferry .15 .40
10 Bill Walton .15 .40
11 Jerry West .25 .60
12 Rick Barry .15 .40
13 Steve Alford .15 .40
14 Calbert Cheaney .15 .40
15 Larry Johnson .15 .40
16 John Havlicek .25 .60
17 Tim Hardaway .15 .40
18 Dennis Rodman .25 .60
19 Bill Laimbeer .15 .40
20 Mateen Cleaves .15 .40
21 Magic Johnson .25 .60
22 Larry Bird .40 1.00
23 Michael Jordan 2.00 5.00
24 Craig Brackins .15 .40
25 Gani Lawal .15 .40
26 James Anderson .15 .40
27 Sherron Collins .15 .40
28 Stanley Robinson .15 .40
29 Trevor Booker .15 .40
30 Devin Ebanks .15 .40
31 Aubrey Coleman .15 .40
32 Ekpe Udoh .25 .60
33 Solomon Alabi .15 .40
34 Jarvis Varnado .15 .40
35 Jerome Jordan .15 .40
36 Luke Babbitt .15 .40
37 Terrico White .15 .40
38 DeMarcus Cousins .75 2.00
39 Hassan Whiteside .15 .40
40 Da'Sean Butler .15 .40
41 Derrick Favors .40 1.00
42 Damion James .15 .40
43 Gordon Hayward .25 .60
44 Paul George .25 .60
45 Dexter Pittman .15 .40
46 Luke Harangody .15 .40
47 Jordan Crawford .15 .40
48 Manny Harris .25 .60
49 Quincy Pondexter .15 .40
50 Scottie Reynolds .15 .40
51 Elliot Williams .15 .40
52 Brian Zoubek .15 .40
53 Xavier Henry .25 .60
54 A.J. Ogilvy .15 .40
55 Armon Johnson .15 .40
56 Cole Aldrich .25 .60
57 Deon Thompson .15 .40
58 Donald Williams .15 .40
59 Sam Cassell .15 .40
60 Toni Kukoc .15 .40
331 Xavier Henry SP 2.00 5.00
332 DeMarcus Cousins SP 1.00 2.50
333 Derrick Favors SP 1.00 2.50
334 Damion James SP 1.00 2.50
335 Luke Harangody SP 1.00 2.50
336 LeBron James SP 2.00 5.00
337 Michael Jordan SP 3.00 8.00
338 Larry Bird SP 1.50 4.00
339 Magic Johnson SP 1.00 2.50
340 Dennis Rodman SP 1.00 2.50
345 Tubby Smith SP 1.00 2.50
346 Gary Williams SP 1.00 2.50
347 Matt Painter SP 1.00 2.50
348 Jamie Dixon SP 1.00 2.50
349 Mark Few SP 1.00 2.50
350 Steve Alford SP 1.00 2.50
351 Bruce Pearl SP 2.00 5.00
352 Mike Montgomery SP 1.00 2.50
353 Steve Fisher SP 1.00 2.50
354 Bo Ryan SP 1.00 2.50
355 Jeff Capel III SP 1.00 2.50
356 Bobby Cremins SP 1.00 2.50
357 Rick Majerus SP 1.00 2.50
358 Sean Miller SP 1.00 2.50
359 Jim Boeheim SP 1.00 2.50
360 Dana Altman SP 1.00 2.50
361 Tom Crean SP 1.00 2.50
362 Roy Williams SP 1.00 2.50
363 Jim Calhoun SP 1.00 2.50
364 Tom Izzo SP 1.00 2.50
365 Ben Howland SP 1.00 2.50
366 Billy Donovan SP 1.00 2.50
367 Bill Self SP 1.00 2.50
368 Thad Matta SP 1.00 2.50
369 Bob Huggins SP 1.00 2.50
370 John Beilein SP 1.00 2.50
371 Homer Drew SP 1.00 2.50
372 Jay Wright SP 1.00 2.50
373 Bruce Weber SP 1.00 2.50
374 Mike Brey SP 1.00 2.50
375 Seth Greenberg SP 1.00 2.50

2010 Upper Deck World of Sports All-Sport Apparel Memorabilia

STATED ODDS ONE PER BOX
ASA1 LeBron James 8.00 20.00
ASA2 Michael Jordan 25.00 50.00
ASA3 Yao Ming 5.00 12.00
ASA4 Brandon Roy 4.00 10.00
ASA5 Russell Westbrook 5.00 12.00
ASA6 Derrick Rose 6.00 15.00
ASA8 Hakeem Olajuwon 6.00 15.00
ASA9 Julius Erving 5.00 12.00
ASA10 Magic Johnson 6.00 15.00
ASA11 Alonzo Mourning 5.00 12.00
ASA12 Bill Walton 4.00 10.00
ASA13 David Robinson 5.00 12.00
ASA14 Xavier Henry 4.00 10.00

2010 Upper Deck World of Sports All-Sport Apparel Memorabilia Autographs

OVERALL AUTO ODDS TWO PER BOX
STATED PRINT RUN 25 SER.#'d SETS
ASA1 LeBron James 125.00 250.00
ASA2 Michael Jordan 300.00 600.00
ASA3 Yao Ming 20.00 50.00
ASA4 Brandon Roy 12.00 30.00
ASA5 Russell Westbrook 60.00 150.00
ASA6 Derrick Rose 75.00 150.00
ASA7 Clyde Drexler 20.00 50.00
ASA8 Hakeem Olajuwon 25.00 60.00
ASA9 Julius Erving 40.00 80.00
ASA11 Alonzo Mourning 25.00 60.00
ASA13 David Robinson 40.00 100.00
ASA15 Greg Monroe 12.00 30.00

2010 Upper Deck World of Sports Autographs

OVERALL AUTO ODDS TWO PER BOX
1 LeBron James 600.00 1,200.00
2 Yao Ming 20.00 50.00
3 Brandon Roy 6.00 15.00
4 Russell Westbrook 40.00 100.00
5 Derrick Rose 40.00 100.00
6 Bill Russell 100.00 250.00
7 Bobby Hurley 5.00 12.00
9 Danny Ferry 5.00 12.00
10 Bill Walton 12.00 30.00
11 Jerry West 25.00 60.00
12 Rick Barry 10.00 25.00
13 Steve Alford 6.00 15.00
14 Calbert Cheaney 5.00 12.00
17 Tim Hardaway 6.00 15.00
18 Dennis Rodman 15.00 40.00
19 Bill Laimbeer 5.00 12.00
20 Mateen Cleaves 5.00 12.00
22 Larry Bird 30.00 80.00
23 Michael Jordan 1,000.00 2,000.00
24 Craig Brackins 5.00 12.00
25 Gani Lawal 5.00 12.00
26 James Anderson 6.00 15.00
27 Sherron Collins 10.00 25.00
28 Stanley Robinson 5.00 12.00
29 Trevor Booker 5.00 12.00
32 Ekpe Udoh 5.00 12.00
33 Solomon Alabi 5.00 12.00
35 Jerome Jordan 5.00 12.00
36 Luke Babbitt 5.00 12.00
38 DeMarcus Cousins 8.00 20.00
39 Hassan Whiteside 5.00 12.00
40 Da'Sean Butler 6.00 15.00
41 Derrick Favors 6.00 15.00
43 Gordon Hayward 10.00 25.00
44 Paul George 6.00 15.00
45 Dexter Pittman 5.00 12.00
46 Luke Harangody 5.00 12.00
47 Jordan Crawford 5.00 12.00
49 Quincy Pondexter 6.00 15.00
50 Scottie Reynolds 5.00 12.00
51 Elliot Williams 5.00 12.00
52 Brian Zoubek 5.00 12.00
53 Xavier Henry 5.00 12.00
54 A.J. Ogilvy 5.00 12.00
55 Armon Johnson 5.00 12.00
56 Cole Aldrich 5.00 12.00
58 Donald Williams 5.00 12.00
59 Sam Cassell 6.00 15.00
331 Xavier Henry 5.00 12.00
332 DeMarcus Cousins 8.00 20.00
333 Derrick Favors 6.00 15.00
335 Luke Harangody 5.00 12.00
336 LeBron James 125.00 300.00
337 Michael Jordan 300.00 800.00
338 Larry Bird 30.00 80.00
340 Dennis Rodman 12.00 30.00
345 Tubby Smith 10.00 25.00
346 Gary Williams 30.00 60.00
347 Matt Painter 8.00 20.00
348 Jamie Dixon 10.00 25.00
349 Mark Few 10.00 25.00
350 Steve Alford 6.00 15.00
351 Bruce Pearl 30.00 80.00
352 Mike Montgomery 6.00 15.00
353 Steve Fisher 6.00 15.00
354 Bo Ryan 12.00 30.00
355 Jeff Capel III 6.00 15.00
356 Bobby Cremins 8.00 20.00
358 Sean Miller 6.00 15.00
359 Jim Boeheim 10.00 25.00
360 Dana Altman 8.00 20.00
361 Tom Crean 8.00 20.00
362 Roy Williams 25.00 50.00
363 Jim Calhoun 15.00 40.00
364 Tom Izzo 15.00 40.00
365 Ben Howland 6.00 15.00
366 Billy Donovan 10.00 25.00
367 Bill Self 10.00 25.00
368 Thad Matta 10.00 25.00
369 Bob Huggins 15.00 40.00
370 John Beilein 12.00 30.00
371 Homer Drew 6.00 15.00
372 Jay Wright 15.00 40.00
373 Bruce Weber 6.00 15.00
374 Mike Brey 10.00 25.00
375 Seth Greenberg 6.00 15.00

2010 Upper Deck World of Sports Clear Competitors

STATED ODDS ONE PER BOX
STATED PRINT RUN 550 SER.#'d SETS
CC1 LeBron James 6.00 15.00
CC2 Yao Ming 3.00 8.00
CC3 Magic Johnson 4.00 10.00
CC4 Larry Bird 5.00 12.00
CC5 Derrick Rose 5.00 12.00
CC6 DeMarcus Cousins 5.00 12.00
CC7 Derrick Favors 3.00 8.00
CC8 Xavier Henry 4.00 10.00
CC9 Anfernee Hardaway 4.00 10.00
CC10 Tom Izzo 3.00 8.00
CC11 Roy Williams 5.00 12.00
CC12 Jim Boeheim 3.00 8.00

2011 Upper Deck World of Sports Evolution Video Cards

EVO1 Michael Jordan 150.00 250.00
EVO2 Chris Paul 15.00 40.00
EVO3 Alonzo Mourning 50.00 100.00

2001-02 USBL

COMPLETE SET (44) 6.00 15.00
1 Kwan Johnson .15 .40
2 Mark Blount .15 .40
3 Sean Colson .15 .40
4 Chudney Gray .15 .40
5 Tariq Kirksay .15 .40
6 Larry Abney .15 .40
7 Tyson Patterson .15 .40
8 Steve Smith .15 .40
9 Bryan Gates .15 .40
10 Darryl Dawkins .30 .75
11 Kent Davison .15 .40
12 Rick Barry .30 .75
13 K'Zell Wesson .15 .40
14 Tunji Awojobi .15 .40
15 Artie Griffin .15 .40
16 Bryant Basemore .15 .40
17 Andre Perry .15 .40
18 Willie Burton .15 .40
19 Raphael Edwards .15 .40
20 Kelvin Price .15 .40
21 Ira Newbie .15 .40
22 Alvin Jefferson .15 .40
23 LaMarr Greer .15 .40
24 David Harrison .15 .40
25 Reggie Slater .15 .40
26 Michael Lewis .15 .40
27 Doug Gottlieb .15 .40
28 Chianti Roberts .15 .40
29 Mike Lloyd .15 .40
30 Wayne Copeland .15 .40
31 Franklin Paul .15 .40
32 Tom Wideman .15 .40
33 Marshall Phillips .15 .40
34 Terrell Baker .15 .40
35 Jerrod West .15 .40
36 Billy Thomas .15 .40
37 Brian Green .15 .40
38 Martin Lewis .15 .40
39 Duane Woodward .15 .40
40 Rashon Turner .15 .40
41 Fred Herzog .15 .40
42 Reggie Bassette .15 .40
43 Adrian Peterson .15 .40
44 Checklist Card .15 .40

2001-02 USBL Chase Cards

COMPLETE SET (6) 1.00 2.50
C1 Sean Colson .20 .50
C2 Artie Griffin .20 .50
C3 Denny Price .20 .50
C4 Chudney Gray .20 .50
C5 Lloyd Daniels .20 .50
C6 USBL Champions .20 .50

1988-89 Warriors Smokey

COMPLETE SET (4) 12.00 30.00
1 Winston Garland 2.00 5.00
2 Chris Mullin 10.00 20.00
3 Ralph Sampson 3.00 8.00
4 Larry Smith 2.00 5.00

1971-72 Warriors Team Issue

COMPLETE SET (13) 40.00 80.00
1 Odis Allison 1.50 4.00
2 Al Attles 5.00 10.00
3 Jim Barnett 2.00 5.00
4 Vic Bartolome 1.50 4.00
5 Joe Ellis 2.00 5.00
6 Nick Jones 1.50 4.00
7 Clyde Lee 2.00 5.00
8 Jeff Mullins 5.00 10.00
9 Bob Portman 1.50 4.00
10 Cazzie Russell 6.00 12.00
11 Nate Thurmond 10.00 20.00
12 Bill Turner 1.50 4.00
13 Ron(Fritz) Williams 2.00 5.00

1993-94 Warriors Topps/Safeway

COMPLETE SET (16) 3.00 8.00
1 Chris Mullin .60 1.50
2 Byron Houston .08 .25
3 Chris Gatling .20 .50
4 Don Nelson CO .20 .50
5 Nate Thurmond LEGEND .40 1.00
6 Chris Webber 1.50 4.00
7 Latrell Sprewell .60 1.50
8 Jeff Grayer .08 .25
9 Al Attles LEGEND .20 .50
10 Tim Hardaway .60 1.50
11 Jud Buechler .08 .25
12 Victor Alexander .08 .25
13 Keith Jennings .08 .25
14 Sarunas Marciulionis .30 .75
15 Billy Owens .20 .50
16 Avery Johnson .30 .75

1994-95 Warriors Topps/Safeway

COMPLETE SET (12) 3.00 8.00
GS1 Tim Hardaway .50 1.25
GS2 Victor Alexander .25 .60
GS3 Latrell Sprewell
(Numbered GS13 on back) .50 1.25
GS5 Chris Mullin .50 1.25
GS6 Clifford Rozier .25 .60
GS7 Chris Gatling .25 .60
GS8 Keith Jennings .25 .60
GS9 Rony Seikaly .25 .60
GS10 Carlos Rogers .30 .75
GS11 Ricky Pierce
(Numbered 267 on back) .25 .60
GS12 Bob Lanier CO .50 1.25

1995-96 Warriors Topps/Safeway

COMPLETE SET (15) 2.00 5.00
GS1 Chris Gatling .08 .25
GS2 Donyell Marshall .20 .50
GS3 Tim Hardaway .50 1.25
GS4 Rick Adelman CO .20 .50
GS5 B.J. Armstrong .15 .40
GS6 Jon Barry .15 .40
GS7 Latrell Sprewell .40 1.00
GS8 Joe Smith .75 2.00
GS9 Jerome Kersey .08 .25
GS10 Rony Seikaly .08 .25
GS11 Chris Mullin .50 1.25
GS12 Clifford Rozier .08 .25
NNO Kodak Ad Card .08 .25
NNO Kellogg's Ad Card 2 .08 .25
NNO Kellogg's Ad Card 1 .08 .25

1996-98 Worldcom Calling Cards

1 Michael Jordan 10 minutes
Black Uniform 2.50 6.00
2 Michael Jordan 10 minutes
Red Uniform 2.50 6.00
3 Michael Jordan 30 minutes
Black Uniform 4.00 10.00
4 Michael Jordan 10 minutes
Rayovac 2.50 6.00
5 Michael Jordan 5 minutes
Red Uniform 2.00 5.00
6 Michael Jordan 5 minutes
Cologne Ad 2.00 5.00
7 Michael Jordan 60 minutes
Black Uniform 4.00 10.00
10 Michael Jordan 5 dollars
Limited Edition 4.00 10.00

2005 WNBA Promo Sheet

NNO Promo Sheet 4.00 10.00

2005 WNBA

COMPLETE SET (110) 20.00 50.00
1 Seattle Storm TC 1.25 3.00
2 LaToya Thomas .40 1.00
3 Crystal Robinson .40 1.00
4 Chasity Melvin .40 1.00
5 Dawn Staley 2.50 6.00
6 Svetlana Abrosimova .40 1.00
7 Houston Comets TC .60 1.50
8 Wendy Palmer-Daniel 1.00 2.50
9 Betty Lennox .75 2.00
10 Lisa Leslie 2.00 5.00
11 Margo Dydek .60 1.50
12 Vickie Johnson .60 1.50
13 Charlotte Sting TC .60 1.50
14 Ayana Walker .40 1.00
15 Shannon Johnson .40 1.00
16 Tangela Smith .40 1.00
17 Michelle Snow .50 1.25
18 Chandi Jones .40 1.00
19 Adrienne Goodson .40 1.00
20 Lauren Jackson 2.00 5.00
21 Elaine Powell .40 1.00
22 Minnesota Lynx TC .60 1.50
23 La'Keshia Frett .40 1.00
24 Allison Feaster .50 1.25
25 Lindsay Whalen 1.00 2.50
26 DeMya Walker .40 1.00
27 Tamecka Dixon .60 1.50
28 Kelly Miller .40 1.00
29 San Antonio Silver Stars TC .60 1.50
30 Tina Thompson 1.25 3.00
31 Tamika Williams .50 1.25
32 Doneeka Hodges RC .60 1.50
33 Kelly Mazzante .60 1.50
34 Shameka Christon .40 1.00
35 Sheryl Swoopes 2.50 6.00
36 Nicole Powell .50 1.25
37 Indiana Fever TC .60 1.50
38 Alicia Thompson .60 1.50
39 Kristen Rasmussen .40 1.00
40 Diana Taurasi 2.50 6.00
41 Elena Baranova 1.00 2.50
42 Taj McWilliams-Franklin .40 1.00
43 Nakia Sanford RC .75 2.00
44 Tamika Whitmore .40 1.00
45 Katie Smith 1.25 3.00
46 Phoenix Mercury TC .60 1.50
47 Tully Bevilaqua .60 1.50
48 Tari Phillips .40 1.00
49 Charlotte Smith-Taylor .40 1.00
50 Sue Bird 2.50 6.00
51 Natalie Williams .75 2.00
52 Connecticut Sun TC .75 2.00
53 Bernadette Ngoyisa RC .75 2.00
54 Anna DeForge .40 1.00
55 Becky Hammon 2.50 6.00
56 Sacramento Monarchs TC .60 1.50
57 Mwadi Mabika .40 1.00
58 Asjha Jones .50 1.25
59 Kamila Vodichkova .40 1.00
60 Yolanda Griffith 1.25 3.00
61 Deanna Jackson .40 1.00
62 Le'Coe Willingham RC .60 1.50
63 Gwen Jackson .40 1.00
64 Erin Buescher .40 1.00
65 Alana Beard .50 1.25
66 New York Liberty TC .60 1.50
67 Helen Darling .40 1.00
68 Dominique Canty .60 1.50
69 Marie Ferdinand .40 1.00
70 Tamika Catchings .60 1.50
71 Kara Lawson .75 2.00
72 Vanessa Hayden .40 1.00
73 Nikki McCray 1.00 2.50
74 Washington Mystics TC .60 1.50
75 Ruth Riley .60 1.50
76 Penny Taylor .60 1.50
77 Ticha Penicheiro 1.00 2.50
78 Katie Douglas .60 1.50
79 Janeth Arcain .40 1.00
80 Swin Cash .60 1.50
81 Kelly Schumacher .40 1.00
82 Detroit Shock TC .60 1.50
83 Plenette Pierson .60 1.50
84 Sheri Sam .40 1.00
85 Chamique Holdsclaw 2.50 6.00
86 Delisha Milton-Jones .40 1.00
87 Nicole Ohlde .40 1.00
88 Edna Campbell .50 1.25
89 Tammy Sutton-Brown .40 1.00
90 Nikki Teasley .40 1.00
91 Ann Wauters .50 1.25
92 Janell Burse .60 1.50
93 Kristi Harrower .40 1.00
94 Murriel Page .50 1.25
95 Cheryl Ford .60 1.50
96 Christi Thomas .40 1.00
97 Brooke Wyckoff .60 1.50
98 Barbara Farris .40 1.00
99 Mandisa Stevenson RC .75 2.00
100 Nykesha Sales .75 2.00
101 Jurgita Streimikyte .40 1.00
102 Amber Jacobs RC .60 1.50
103 Coco Miller .40 1.00
104 Iziane Castro Marques .40 1.00
105 Deanna Nolan .40 1.00
106 Los Angeles Sparks TC .60 1.50
107 Rebekkah Brunson .40 1.00
108 Checklist 1 2.50 6.00
109 Checklist 2 .15 .40
110 Checklist 3 1.25 3.00
P1 Diana Taurasi PROMO 2.50 6.00
P1A Becky Hammon Binder 4.00 10.00

2005 WNBA Autographs

STATED ODDS 1:20
AB Adia Barnes Trophy 12.00 30.00
AB1 Alana Beard Posed 8.00 20.00
AB2 Alana Beard Action 8.00 20.00
AD Anne Donovan CO 15.00 40.00
AT Alicia Thompson Trophy 5.00 12.00
BH1 Becky Hammon Posed 60.00 150.00
BH2 Becky Hammon Action 60.00 150.00
BH3 Becky Hammon Dress 60.00 150.00
BL Betty Lennox Trophy 6.00 15.00
CC1 Cynthia Cooper 15.00 40.00
DA1 L.Jackson/S.Bird AU 150.00 400.00
DS1 Dawn Staley Posed 40.00 100.00
DS2 Dawn Staley Action 40.00 100.00
DT1 Diana Taurasi Posed 75.00 200.00
DT2 Diana Taurasi Action 75.00 200.00
DT3 Diana Taurasi Dress 75.00 200.00
JB Janell Burse Trophy 5.00 12.00
KS1 Katie Smith Posed 10.00 25.00
KS2 Katie Smith Action 10.00 25.00
KS3 Katie Smith Dress 10.00 25.00
KV Kamila Vodichkova Trophy 5.00 12.00
LJ1 Lauren Jackson Trophy 25.00 60.00
LJ2 Lauren Jackson Action 25.00 60.00
LL1 Lisa Leslie Yellow 30.00 80.00
LL2 Lisa Leslie Black 30.00 80.00
LL3 Lisa Leslie Dress 30.00 80.00
NS1 Nykesha Sales Action 6.00 15.00
NS2 Nykesha Sales Dress 6.00 15.00
NT1 Nikki Teasley Posed 5.00 12.00
NT2 Nikki Teasley Action 5.00 12.00
NT3 Nikki Teasley Dress 5.00 12.00
SB1 Sue Bird Trophy 75.00 200.00
SB2 Sue Bird Posed 75.00 200.00
SB3 Sue Bird Action 75.00 200.00
SB4 Sue Bird Posed in Uni 75.00 200.00
SC1 Swin Cash Posed 20.00 50.00
SC2 Swin Cash Action 20.00 50.00
SC3 Swin Cash Dress 20.00 50.00
SE Simone Edwards Trophy 6.00 15.00
SJ1 Shannon Johnson Action 6.00 15.00
SJ2 Shannon Johnson Dress 6.00 12.00
SS Sheri Sam Trophy 8.00 20.00
TB Tully Bevilaqua Trophy 10.00 25.00
TC1 Tamika Catchings Posed 20.00 50.00
TC2 Tamika Catchings Action 20.00 50.00
TC3 Tamika Catchings Dress 20.00 50.00
YG1 Yolanda Griffith Press 12.00 30.00
YG2 Yolanda Griffith Action 12.00 30.00

2005 WNBA Jerseys

STATED ODDS 1:80
R1 Lisa Leslie 10.00 25.00
R2 Lauren Jackson 20.00 50.00
R3 Tina Thompson 4.00 10.00
R4 Diana Taurasi 15.00 40.00
R5 Sue Bird 20.00 50.00
R6 Yolanda Griffith 4.00 10.00
R7 Tamika Catchings 4.00 10.00
R8 Swin Cash 6.00 15.00
R9 Nikki Teasley 6.00 15.00
R10 Nykesha Sales 4.00 10.00
AR1 Lisa Leslie AU/299 30.00 80.00
AR2 Diana Taurasi AU/99 300.00 600.00
DR1 S.Bird/L.Jackson Topper 40.00 100.00
NNO Becky Hammon Archives 12.00 30.00

2005 WNBA League Leaders

COMPLETE SET (8) 8.00 20.00
STATED ODDS 1:20
LL1 Jackson/Thompson/Leslie 2.00 5.00
LL2 Teasley/Bird/Staley 2.50 6.00
LL3 Leslie/Ford/Snow 2.00 5.00
LL4 Griffith/Sales/Beard 1.25 3.00
LL5 Leslie/Sutton-Brown/Jackson 2.00 5.00
LL6 Smith/Johnson/Miller 1.25 3.00
LL7 Smith-T/Baranova/Jackson 1.00 2.50
LL8 Williams/Griffith/Leslie 2.00 5.00

2005 WNBA Playoffs

STATED ODDS 1:7
P1 Conn. def. Wash 2-1 1.25 3.00
P2 NY def. LA 2-1 .75 2.00
P3 Sacram. def. LA 2-1 .75 2.00
P4 Seattle def. Minn. 2-0 .75 2.00
P5 Conn. def. NY 2-0 .75 2.00
P6 Seattle def. Sacram 2-1 1.25 3.00
P7 Conn. Win Game 1 .75 2.00
P8 Seattle Ties it Up 2.50 6.00
P9 Seattle Reigns 3.00 8.00

2005 WNBA Rookies

COMPLETE SET (33) 250.00 450.00
STATED PRINT RUN 333 SER.#'d SETS
RC1 Janel McCarville 8.00 20.00
RC2 Tan White 10.00 25.00
RC3 Sandora Irvin 10.00 25.00
RC4 Kendra Wecker 10.00 25.00
RC5 Sancho Lyttle 8.00 20.00
RC6 Temeka Johnson 8.00 20.00
RC7 Kara Braxton 10.00 25.00
RC8 Katie Feenstra 10.00 25.00
RC9 Kristin Haynie 15.00 40.00
RC10 Loree Moore 8.00 20.00
RC11 Kristen Mann 8.00 20.00
RC12 Tanisha Wright 12.00 30.00
RC13 Shyra Ely 10.00 25.00
RC14 Roneeka Hodges 8.00 20.00
RC15 Yolanda Paige 10.00 25.00
RC16 Jacqueline Batteast 10.00 25.00
RC17 Angelina Williams 8.00 20.00
RC18 Chelsea Newton 12.00 30.00
RC19 Jessica Moore 10.00 25.00
RC20 Ashley Battle 10.00 25.00
RC21 Belinda Snell 8.00 20.00
RC22 Laurie Koehn 8.00 20.00
RC23 Caity Matter 8.00 20.00
RC24 Cathrine Kraayeveld 8.00 20.00
RC25 Edwige Lawson 8.00 20.00
RC26 Francesca Zara 8.00 20.00
RC27 Jamie Carey 8.00 20.00
RC28 Jenni Benningfield 8.00 20.00
RC29 Laura Summerton 8.00 20.00
RC30 Miao Li Jie 8.00 20.00
RC31 Natalia Vodopyanova 8.00 20.00
RC32 Sui Fei Fei 8.00 20.00
RC33 Suzy Batkovic 8.00 20.00

2005 WNBA Team Leaders

COMPLETE SET (13) 8.00 20.00
STATED ODDS 1:8
TL1 Feaster/Staley/Sutton-Brn 2.00 5.00
TL2 Sales/Whalen/McWilliams-F .75 2.00
TL3 Cash/Powell/Ford .50 1.25
TL4 Thompson/Swoopes/Snow 2.00 5.00
TL5 Tamika Catchings .50 1.25
TL6 Leslie/Teasley/Leslie 1.50 4.00
TL7 Smith/Darling/Williams 1.00 2.50
TL8 Hammon/Hammon/Baranova 2.00 5.00
TL9 Taurasi/Taurasi/Taylor 2.00 5.00
TL10 Griffith/Penicheiro/Griffith 1.00 2.50
TL11 Thomas/Johnson/Goodson .30 .75
TL12 Jackson/Bird/Jackson 2.00 5.00
TL13 Holdsclaw/Beard/Holdsclaw 2.00 5.00

2006 WNBA

COMPLETE SET (1-110) 20.00 50.00
1 Sacramento Monarchs TC .60 1.50
2 Lindsay Whalen 1.00 2.50
3 Tamika Whitmore .40 1.00
4 Tangela Smith .40 1.00
5 Alana Beard .50 1.25
6 Chicago Sky TC .60 1.50
7 Vickie Johnson .60 1.50
8 Kelly Schumacher .40 1.00
9 Plenette Pierson .60 1.50
10 Sheryl Swoopes 2.50 6.00
11 Los Angeles Sparks TC 1.00 2.50
12 Katie Douglas .60 1.50
13 Nicole Ohlde .40 1.00
14 Anna DeForge .40 1.00
15 Swin Cash .60 1.50
16 Kelly Miller .40 1.00
17 Kara Lawson .75 2.00
18 Shameka Christon .40 1.00
19 Dominique Canty .60 1.50
20 Sue Bird 2.50 6.00
21 Detroit Shock TC .75 2.00
22 Margo Dydek .60 1.50
23 Shannon Johnson .40 1.00
24 Chandi Jones .40 1.00
25 Cheryl Ford .60 1.50
26 Katie Feenstra .50 1.25
27 Ashley Battle .50 1.25
28 Tammy Sutton-Brown .40 1.00
29 Deanna Jackson .40 1.00
30 Yolanda Griffith 1.25 3.00
31 Minnesota Lynx TC .60 1.50
32 Asjha Jones .50 1.25
33 Nicole Powell .50 1.25
34 Sancho Lyttle .50 1.25
35 Nykesha Sales .60 1.50
36 LaToya Thomas .40 1.00
37 Nikki Teasley .40 1.00
38 Kara Braxton .60 1.50
39 Rebekkah Brunson .40 1.00
40 Lauren Jackson 2.00 5.00
41 Phoenix Mercury TC .75 2.00
42 Brooke Wyckoff .60 1.50
43 Betty Lennox .75 2.00
44 Tan White .40 1.00
45 Dawn Staley 1.00 2.50
46 Washington Mystics TC .60 1.50
47 Svetlana Abrosimova .40 1.00
48 Mandisa Stevenson .40 1.00
49 Chantelle Anderson .40 1.00
50 Deanna Nolan .60 1.50
51 Indiana Fever TC .60 1.50
52 Le'coe Willingham .40 1.00
53 Stacey Dales .60 1.50
54 Tully Bevilaqua .40 1.00
55 Ruth Riley .60 1.50
56 Janell Burse .40 1.00
57 Doneeka Hodges .40 1.00
58 Stacey Lovelace .60 1.50
59 Hamchetou Maiga-Ba .40 1.00
60 Tamika Catchings 1.00 2.50
61 New York Liberty TC 1.00 2.50
62 Jamie Carey .40 1.00
63 Delisha Milton-Jones .40 1.00
64 Elaine Powell .40 1.00
65 Laurie Koehn .40 1.00
66 Allison Feaster .50 1.25
67 Shyra Ely .50 1.25
68 Ticha Penicheiro 1.00 2.50
69 Laura Summerton .40 1.00
70 Diana Taurasi 2.50 6.00
71 Seattle Storm TC 1.25 3.00
72 Kristin Haynie .60 1.50
73 Iziane Castro Marques .50 1.25
74 Tamika Williams .50 1.25
75 Marie Ferdinand .40 1.00
76 Belinda Snell .40 1.00
77 Mwadi Mabika .40 1.00
78 Loree Moore .40 1.00
79 Crystal Robinson .40 1.00
80 Taj McWilliams-Franklin .40 1.00
81 Houston Comets TC .60 1.50
82 Kendra Wecker .50 1.25
83 Janel McCarville .40 1.00
84 Kristen Mann .40 1.00
85 Chamique Holdsclaw 2.50 6.00
86 Tanisha Wright .50 1.25
87 Kamila Vodichkova .40 1.00
88 Christi Thomas .40 1.00
89 Chasity Melvin .40 1.00
90 Lisa Leslie 2.00 5.00
91 Tina Thompson 1.25 3.00
92 Connecticut Sun TC .75 2.00
93 Erin Buescher .40 1.00
94 Chelsea Newton .60 1.50
95 Katie Smith 1.25 3.00
96 Temeka Johnson .40 1.00
97 Sheri Sam .40 1.00
98 Wendy Palmer 1.00 2.50
99 DeMya Walker .40 1.00
100 Becky Hammon 2.50 6.00
101 Charlotte Sting TC .60 1.50
102 Charlotte Smith .40 1.00
103 Cathrine Kraayeveld .40 1.00
104 Tamecka Dixon .60 1.50

2006 WNBA

105 Michelle Snow .50 1.25
106 Vanessa Hayden .40 1.00
107 San Antonio Silver Stars TC .60 1.50
108 Checklist 1 2.00 5.00
109 Checklist 2 .15 .40
110 Checklist 3 .15 .40

2006 WNBA All-Star Jerseys

APPROXIMATELY ONE PER BOX
RE1 Alana Beard 2.50 6.00
RE2 Swin Cash 3.00 8.00
RE3 Tamika Catchings 5.00 12.00
RE4 Cheryl Ford 3.00 8.00
RE5 Becky Hammon 12.00 30.00
RE6 Taj McWilliams-Franklin 2.00 5.00
RE7 Deanna Nolan 3.00 8.00
RE8 Ruth Riley 3.00 8.00
RE9 Nykesha Sales 3.00 8.00
RW1 Sue Bird 12.00 30.00
RW2 Marie Ferdinand 2.00 5.00
RW3 Yolanda Griffith 6.00 15.00
RW4 Chamique Holdsclaw 12.00 30.00
RW5 Lauren Jackson 10.00 25.00
RW6 Lisa Leslie 10.00 25.00
RW7 Katie Smith 6.00 15.00
RW8 Michelle Snow 2.50 6.00
RW9 Sheryl Swoopes 12.00 30.00
RE10 Dawn Staley 5.00 12.00
RE11 Ann Wauters 3.00 8.00
RW10 Diana Taurasi 12.00 30.00
RW11 DeMya Walker 2.00 5.00

2006 WNBA Autographs

APPROXIMATELY TWO PER BOX
NNO Svetlana Abrosimova 5.00 12.00
NNO Sue Bird Action 75.00 200.00
NNO Sue Bird Assists 75.00 200.00
NNO Sue Bird Glamour 75.00 200.00
NNO Kara Braxton 5.00 12.00
NNO Rebekkah Brunson 6.00 15.00
NNO Erin Buescher 5.00 12.00
NNO Tamika Catchings 2nd Team 12.00 30.00
NNO Tamika Catchings Defensive 12.00 30.00
NNO Tamika Catchings Glamour 12.00 30.00
NNO Anna DeForge Action 5.00 12.00
NNO Anna DeForge Glamour 5.00 12.00
NNO Katie Feenstra Action 5.00 12.00
NNO Katie Feenstra Close Up 5.00 12.00
NNO Marie Ferdinand Action 5.00 12.00
NNO Marie Ferdinand Glamour 5.00 12.00
NNO Cheryl Ford Action 6.00 15.00
NNO Cheryl Ford Glamour 6.00 15.00
NNO Yolanda Griffith Champs 8.00 20.00
NNO Yolanda Griffith MVP 8.00 20.00
NNO Becky Hammon Action 30.00 80.00
NNO Becky Hammon Career 30.00 80.00
NNO Becky Hammon Glamour 30.00 80.00
NNO Kristin Haynie 5.00 12.00
NNO Chamique Holdsclaw Glamour 8.00 20.00
NNO Chamique Holdsclaw Portrait 8.00 20.00
NNO Temeka Johnson Action 5.00 12.00
NNO Temeka Johnson ROY 5.00 12.00
NNO Kara Lawson 6.00 15.00
NNO Hamchetou Maiga 5.00 12.00
NNO Janel McCarville 5.00 12.00
NNO Taj McWilliams Action 5.00 12.00
NNO Taj McWilliams Award 5.00 12.00
NNO Taj McWilliams Glamour 5.00 12.00
NNO Chelsea Newton 5.00 12.00
NNO Chelsea Newton 5.00 12.00
NNO Deanna Nolan Action 5.00 12.00
NNO Deanna Nolan Glamour 5.00 12.00
NNO Nicole Ohlde 5.00 12.00
NNO Ticha Penicheiro 8.00 20.00
NNO Nicole Powell 5.00 12.00
NNO Ruth Riley Action 8.00 20.00
NNO Ruth Riley Glamour 8.00 20.00
NNO Olympia Scott-Richardson 5.00 12.00
NNO Michelle Snow Action 5.00 12.00
NNO Michelle Snow Glamour 5.00 12.00
NNO S.Swoopes AS MVP 15.00 40.00
NNO Sheryl Swoopes Glamour 15.00 40.00
NNO Sheryl Swoopes MVP 15.00 40.00
NNO S.Swoopes WNBA 1st Team 15.00 40.00
NNO Diana Taurasi Action 75.00 200.00
NNO Diana Taurasi Glamour 75.00 200.00
NNO DeMya Walker 5.00 12.00
NNO Lindsey Whalen Album 12.00 30.00
NNO John Whisenant 5.00 12.00
NNO Tan White 5.00 12.00

2006 WNBA League Leaders

COMPLETE SET (9) 8.00 20.00
APPROXIMATELY TWO PER BOX
LL1 Swoopes/Jackson/Hldsclw 2.00 5.00
LL2 Bird/Johnson/Whalen 2.00 5.00
LL3 Ford/Jackson/Catchings 1.50 4.00
LL4 Catch/Swoopes/Leslie 2.00 5.00
LL5 Dydek/Layden/Leslie 1.50 4.00
LL6 Hammon/Arcain/Lennx 2.00 5.00
LL7 Koehn/Hodges/Lawson .60 1.50
LL8 Snow/Wauters/Walker .50 1.25
LL9 Ford/Jackson 1.50 4.00

2006 WNBA Patches

PRINT RUN 250 SER.#'d SETS
P1 Sheryl Swoopes 30.00 80.00
P2 Sue Bird 30.00 80.00
P3 Yolanda Griffith 10.00 25.00
P4 Lauren Jackson 30.00 80.00
P5 Deanna Nolan 8.00 20.00
P6 Tamika Catchings 15.00 40.00
P7 Diana Taurasi 30.00 80.00
P8 Taj McWilliams-Franklin 8.00 20.00
P9 Lisa Leslie 30.00 80.00
P10 Becky Hammon 30.00 80.00

2006 WNBA Playoffs

COMPLETE SET (10) 5.00 12.00
APPROXIMATELY SIX PER BOX
P1 Eastern Semi-Finals .75 2.00
P2 Eastern Semi-Finals .75 2.00
P3 Western Semi-Finals .75 2.00
P4 Western Semi-Finals .75 2.00
P5 Eastern Finals .75 2.00
P6 Western Finals .75 2.00
P7 WNBA Finals .75 2.00
P8 WNBA Finals .75 2.00
P9 WNBA Finals .75 2.00
P10 WNBA Finals .75 2.00

2006 WNBA Rookies

PRINT RUN 333 SER.#'d SETS
RC1 Seimone Augustus 150.00 400.00
RC2 Cappie Pondexter 75.00 200.00
RC3 Monique Currie 12.00 30.00
RC4 Sophia Young 12.00 30.00
RC5 Lisa Willis 8.00 20.00
RC6 Candice Dupree 15.00 40.00
RC7 Shona Thorburn 8.00 20.00
RC8 Tamara James 8.00 20.00
RC9 La'Tangela Atkinson 8.00 20.00
RC10 Tye'sha Fluker 8.00 20.00
RC11 Barbara Turner 12.00 30.00
RC12 Sherill Baker 8.00 20.00
RC13 Kim Smith 8.00 20.00
RC14 Ann Strother 20.00 50.00
RC15 Shanna Zolman 20.00 50.00
RC16 Ambrosia Anderson 8.00 20.00
RC17 Liz Shimek 8.00 20.00
RC18 Nikki Blue 10.00 25.00
RC19 Mistie Williams 10.00 25.00
RC20 LaToya Bond 8.00 20.00
RC21 Erin Phillips 8.00 20.00
RC22 Megan Mahoney 25.00 60.00
RC23 Scholanda Dorrell 8.00 20.00
RC24 Jennifer Lacy 8.00 20.00
RC25 Megan Duffy 10.00 25.00
RC26 Crystal Smith 8.00 20.00
RC27 Anastasia Hostaki 8.00 20.00
RC28 Emmeline Ndongue 8.00 20.00
RC29 Yelena Leuchanka 8.00 20.00
RC30 Kasha Terry 8.00 20.00
RC31 Brandi Davis 8.00 20.00
RC32 Christelle N'Garsanet 8.00 20.00
RC33 Brittany Wilkins 8.00 20.00
RC34 Zane Teilane 8.00 20.00

2006 WNBA Team Leaders

COMPLETE SET (13) 5.00 12.00
APPROXIMATELY FIVE PER BOX
L1 Smith/Staley/Sutton .50 1.25
L2 Sales/Whalen/Taj .50 1.25
L3 D.Nolan/C.Ford .30 .75
L4 S.Swoopes/M.Snow 1.25 3.00
L5 Tamika Catchings .50 1.25
L6 Holdsclaw/Tsly/Leslie 1.25 3.00
L7 Smith/Harrower/Ohlde .60 1.50
L8 B.Hammon/E.Baranova 1.25 3.00
L9 D.Taurasi/Vodichkova 1.25 3.00
L10 Walker/Pnchro/Griffith .60 1.50
L11 Ferdinand/Jhnsn/Palmer .50 1.25
L12 L.Jackson/S.Bird 1.25 3.00
L13 Beard/Johnson/Melvin .25 .60

2006 WNBA Toppers

AR6 S.Bird JSY AU/175 150.00 400.00
AR4 T.Johnson JSY AU/150 8.00 20.00
AR3 Y.Griffith JSY AU/333 12.00 30.00
AR5 S.Swoops JSY AU/150 20.00 50.00
NNO White JSY/Feenstra JSY 6.00 15.00

2007 WNBA

COMPLETE SET (90) 20.00 50.00
1 Diana Taurasi 2.00 5.00
2 Marie Ferdinand-Harris .60 1.50
3 Megan Mahoney 1.00 2.50
4 Chasity Melvin .60 1.50
5 Lauren Jackson 2.00 5.00
6 Tammy Sutton-Brown .60 1.50
7 Nicole Ohlde .60 1.50
8 Dominique Canty .60 1.50
9 Alana Beard .50 1.25
10 Tina Thompson 1.25 3.00
11 Janell Burse .60 1.50
12 Asjha Jones .50 1.25
13 Kelly Miller .50 1.25
14 Tamika Catchings .60 1.50
15 Kara Braxton .60 1.50
16 Erika DeSouza RC .60 1.50
17 Erin Thorn RC .60 1.50
18 Tamika Whitmore .50 1.25
19 Seimone Augustus 1.25 3.00
20 Erin Buescher .50 1.25
21 Nicole Powell .50 1.25
22 Mwadi Mabika .50 1.25
23 Cappie Pondexter .60 1.50
24 Stacey Dales .60 1.50
25 Temeka Johnson .60 1.50
26 Nikki Teasley .60 1.50
27 Katie Douglas .60 1.50
28 Sheryl Swoopes 2.50 6.00
29 Anna DeForge .60 1.50
30 Monique Currie .50 1.25
31 Kelly Schumacher .60 1.50
32 Becky Hammon 2.50 6.00
33 Tangela Smith .60 1.50
34 Jia Perkins RC .50 1.25
35 DeMya Walker .50 1.25
36 DeLisha Milton-Jones .50 1.25
37 Chamique Holdsclaw 2.50 6.00
38 Kelly Mazzante .60 1.50
39 Tan White .60 1.50
40 Penny Taylor .60 1.50
41 Cheryl Ford .60 1.50
42 Ebony Hoffman .50 1.25
43 Vickie Johnson .60 1.50
44 Loree Moore .50 1.25
45 Candice Dupree .60 1.50
46 Deanna Nolan .60 1.50
47 Nakia Sanford .50 1.25
48 Cathrine Kraayeveld .50 1.25
49 Hamchetou Maiga-Ba .50 1.25
50 Nykesha Sales .60 1.50
51 Amber Jacobs .60 1.50
52 Kara Lawson .75 2.00
53 Shannon Johnson .60 1.50
54 Taj McWilliams-Franklin .60 1.50
55 Sue Bird 2.50 6.00
56 Laurie Koehn .60 1.50
57 Barbara Farris .60 1.50
58 Tari Phillips .60 1.50
59 Swin Cash .60 1.50
60 Jamie Carey .60 1.50
61 Kristen Mann .60 1.50
62 Sherill Baker .60 1.50
63 Lindsay Whalen 1.00 2.50
64 Yolanda Griffith 1.25 3.00
65 Shanna Zolman Crossley .75 2.00
66 Tully Bevilaqua .60 1.50
67 Chelsea Newton .60 1.50
68 Katie Smith 1.25 3.00
69 K.B. Sharp .60 1.50
70 Iziane Castro Marques .60 1.50
71 Rebekkah Brunson .60 1.50
72 Sophia Young .50 1.25
73 Shameka Christon .60 1.50
74 Christi Thomas .60 1.50
75 Coco Miller .60 1.50
76 Plenette Pierson .60 1.50
77 Ruth Riley .60 1.50
78 Scholanda Robinson RC .60 1.50
79 Murriel Page .50 1.25
80 Ashley Battle .50 1.25
81 Michelle Snow .50 1.25
82 Betty Lennox .75 2.00
83 LaToya Thomas .60 1.50
84 Katie Feenstra .60 1.50
85 Kendra Wecker .60 1.50
86 Margo Dydek .60 1.50
87 Ticha Penicheiro 1.00 2.50
88 Kayte Christensen .60 1.50
89 Lecoe Willingham .60 1.50
90 Lisa Leslie 2.00 5.00

2007 WNBA Parallel

*PARALLEL: 2X TO 5X BASE HI
PRINT RUN 333 SER.#'d SETS

2007 WNBA 3-Case Incentive

1 N.Lieberman/A.Meyers AU 20.00 50.00

2007 WNBA All-WNBA Team

PRINT RUN 100 SER.#'d SETS
T01 Lisa Leslie 25.00 60.00
T02 Tamika Catchings 8.00 20.00
T03 Diana Taurasi 25.00 60.00
T04 Lauren Jackson 25.00 60.00
T05 Katie Douglas 8.00 20.00
T06 Alana Beard 6.00 15.00
T07 Cheryl Ford 8.00 20.00
T08 Taj McWilliams-Franklin 8.00 20.00
T09 Seimone Augustus 15.00 40.00
T10 Sheryl Swoopes 30.00 80.00

2007 WNBA Autographs

APPROXIMATE ODDS THREE PER BOX
1 Seimone Augustus 12.00 30.00
2 Cheryl Ford 6.00 15.00
3 Plenette Pierson 6.00 15.00
4 Kara Braxton 5.00 12.00
5 Angelina Williams 4.00 10.00
6 Jacqueline Batteast 5.00 12.00
7 Bill Laimbeer 12.00 30.00
8 Cheryl Miller 15.00 40.00
9 Ann Meyers 10.00 25.00
10 Sherill Baker 6.00 15.00
11 Shanna Zolman Crossley 8.00 20.00
12 Cappie Pondexter 6.00 15.00
13 Barbara Turner 6.00 15.00
14 Scholanda Robinson 6.00 15.00
15 Jennifer Lacy 4.00 10.00
17 Brooke Wyckoff 6.00 15.00
18 Katie Douglas 6.00 15.00
19 Asjha Jones 6.00 15.00
20 Le'coe Willingham 6.00 15.00
21 Margo Dydek 6.00 15.00
22 Tamika Whitmore 5.00 12.00
23 Sophia Young 5.00 12.00
24 Kristen Mann 6.00 15.00
25 Amber Jacobs 6.00 15.00
26 Shameka Christon 6.00 15.00
27 Cathrine Kraayeveld 6.00 15.00
28 Kelly Schumacher 6.00 15.00
29 Kendra Wecker 6.00 15.00
30 Chasity Melvin 6.00 15.00
31 Nakia Sanford 5.00 12.00
32 Jia Perkins 5.00 12.00
33 Dominique Canty 6.00 15.00
34 Candice Dupree 6.00 15.00
35 Mwadi Mabika 5.00 12.00
36 Katie Smith 10.00 25.00
37 Swin Cash 6.00 15.00
38 Ruth Riley 6.00 15.00
39 Elaine Powell 4.00 10.00
40 Deanna Nolan 6.00 15.00
MC Monique Currie 6.00 15.00
MT Mike Thibault 6.00 15.00
DMJ DeLisha Milton-Jones 5.00 12.00

2007 WNBA Highlights

COMPLETE SET (9) 10.00 25.00
H1 L.Leslie 5,000th Point 2.50 6.00
H2 2006 All-Star Game .75 2.00
H3 D.Taurasi 47 Points 2.50 6.00
H4 D.Taurasi Scoring Mark 2.50 6.00
H5 S.Augustus RC Scoring 1.50 4.00
H6 C.Ford Rebound Total .75 2.00
H7 V.Chancellor 200 Wins .75 2.00
H8 Detroit Shock WNBA Title .75 2.00
H9 L.Leslie Ties MVP 2.50 6.00

2007 WNBA League Leaders

COMPLETE SET (9) 8.00 20.00
LL1 Taurasi/Agstus/Leslie 1.50 4.00
LL2 Teasley/Temeka/Bird 2.00 5.00
LL3 Ford/Taj/Leslie 1.50 4.00
LL4 Catchings/Tully/Swoopes 2.00 5.00
LL5 Dydek/Suttn-Bwn/Jkson 1.50 4.00
LL6 Hammon/Smith/Whalen 2.00 5.00
LL7 Hoffman/DeLisha/Staley .50 1.25
LL8 Bschr/Jackson/Ngoyisa 1.50 4.00
LL9 Ford/Leslie/Taj 1.50 4.00

2007 WNBA Rookies

PRINT RUN 444 SER.#'d SETS
RC01 Lindsey Harding 4.00 10.00
RC02 Jessica Davenport 4.00 10.00
RC03 Armintie Price 4.00 10.00
RC04 Noelle Quinn 3.00 8.00
RC05 Tiffany Jackson 6.00 15.00
RC06 Bernice Mosby 5.00 12.00
RC07 Katie Gearlds 6.00 15.00
RC08 Ashley Shields 3.00 8.00
RC09 Alison Bales 6.00 15.00
RC10 Carla Thomas 4.00 10.00
RC11 Ivory Latta 4.00 10.00
RC12 Kamesha Hairston 3.00 8.00
RC13 Dee Davis 3.00 8.00
RC14 Eshaya Murphy 4.00 10.00
RC15 Shay Doron 8.00 20.00
RC16 Camille Little 5.00 12.00
RC17 Stephanie Raymond 3.00 8.00
RC18 Amy Sanders 3.00 8.00
RC19 Kathrin Ress 4.00 10.00
RC20 Sidney Spencer 10.00 25.00
RC21 Cori Chambers 4.00 10.00
RC22 Martina Weber 3.00 8.00
RC23 Gillian Goring 3.00 8.00
RC24 Claire Coggins 5.00 12.00
RC25 Navonda Moore 4.00 10.00
RC26 Marta Fernandez 3.00 8.00
RC27 Lindsay Bowen 3.00 8.00

2008 WNBA

COMPLETE SET (90) 40.00 100.00
COMP.ARCHIVE BOX SET 400.00 800.00
1 Lauren Jackson 2.00 5.00
2 Jia Perkins .50 1.25
3 Swin Cash .60 1.50
4 Tina Thompson 1.25 3.00
5 Katie Douglas .60 1.50
6 Taj McWilliams-Franklin .40 1.00
7 Nicole Ohlde .40 1.00
8 Shameka Christon .40 1.00
9 Nicole Powell .50 1.25
10 Diana Taurasi 2.50 6.00
11 Yolanda Griffith 1.25 3.00
12 Nikki Blue .50 1.25
13 Cathrine Kraayeveld .40 1.00
14 Jamie Carey .40 1.00
15 Deanna Nolan .40 1.00
16 Sidney Spencer 1.00 2.50
17 Rebekkah Brunson .40 1.00
18 Tamecka Dixon .60 1.50
19 Becky Hammon 2.50 6.00
20 Tamika Catchings .60 1.50
21 Alana Beard .50 1.25
22 Betty Lennox .75 2.00
23 Tangela Smith .60 1.50
24 Asjha Jones .50 1.25
25 Temeka Johnson .40 1.00
26 Elaine Powell .40 1.00
27 Michelle Snow .50 1.25
28 Marie Ferdinand-Harris .40 1.00
29 Noelle Quinn .40 1.00
30 Candice Dupree .60 1.50
31 Kelly Miller .40 1.00
32 Kara Lawson .75 2.00
33 Monique Currie .50 1.25
34 Barbara Turner .50 1.25
35 Katie Smith 1.25 3.00
36 Janel McCarville .40 1.00
37 Katie Feenstra .50 1.25
38 Tan White .50 1.25
39 Tiffany Jackson .60 1.50
40 Stacey Lovelace .60 1.50
41 Kristen Rasmussen .40 1.00
42 Nakia Sanford .50 1.25
43 Murriel Page .50 1.25
44 Helen Darling .40 1.00
45 Seimone Augustus 1.00 2.50
46 Brooke Wyckoff .60 1.50
47 Tammy Sutton-Brown .40 1.00
48 Iziane Castro .40 1.00
49 Ticha Penicheiro 1.00 2.50
50 Cappie Pondexter .60 1.50
51 Mwadi Mabika .40 1.00
52 Erin Thorn .40 1.00
53 Kim Smith .40 1.00
54 Keisha Brown RC .60 1.50
55 Lindsay Whalen 1.00 2.50
56 Alison Bales .75 2.00
57 Tamika Whitmore .40 1.00
58 Sancho Lyttle .50 1.25
59 Chasity Melvin .40 1.00
60 Cheryl Ford .60 1.50
61 Loree Moore .40 1.00
62 Camille Little .50 1.25
63 Le'coe Willingham .40 1.00
64 Jessica Davenport .50 1.25
65 DeLisha Milton-Jones .60 1.50
66 Katie Gearlds .75 2.00
67 Shanna Crossley RC .60 1.50
68 Tamika Raymond RC .60 1.50
69 Kara Braxton .50 1.25
70 Sheryl Swoopes 2.50 6.00
71 Erika DeSouza .40 1.00
72 Coco Miller .40 1.00
73 Ivory Latta .40 1.00
74 Ruth Riley .50 1.25
75 Armintie Price .50 1.25
76 Erin Buescher .40 1.00
77 Plenette Pierson .60 1.50
78 Chelsea Newton .40 1.00
79 Vickie Johnson .60 1.50
80 Lisa Leslie 2.00 5.00
81 Tully Bevilaqua .40 1.00
82 Nykesha Sales .60 1.50
83 Lindsey Harding .50 1.25
84 Sophia Young .50 1.25
85 Adrian Williams-Strong .40 1.00
86 Shannon Johnson .40 1.00
87 Dominique Canty .60 1.50
88 Anna DeForge .40 1.00
89 Kelly Mazzante .60 1.50
90 Sue Bird 2.50 6.00
P1 All-Star Team Promo 2.00 5.00
P2 Candace Parker Promo 25.00 60.00

2008 WNBA 3-Case Incentive

TP Taurasi AU/Pondexter AU 75.00 200.00

2008 WNBA Autographs

APPROXIMATE ODDS 1:12
AM Ann Meyers-Drysdale 10.00 25.00
AP Armintie Price 5.00 12.00
AS Ann Strother 8.00 20.00
BH Becky Hammon 30.00 80.00
CL Crystal Langhorne 8.00 20.00
CL Camille Little 5.00 12.00
CP Cappie Pondexter 6.00 15.00
CP Candace Parker 200.00 500.00
CW Candice Wiggins 15.00 40.00
DT Diana Taurasi 75.00 200.00
ET Erin Thorn 4.00 10.00
JD Jessica Davenport 5.00 12.00
JD Jennifer Derevjanik 4.00 10.00
JL Jennifer Lacy 4.00 10.00
KM Kelly Miller 6.00 15.00
KM Kelly Mazzante 6.00 15.00
KS Kelly Schumacher 6.00 15.00
LH Lindsey Harding 5.00 12.00
LH Laura Harper 6.00 15.00
LJ Lauren Jackson 40.00 100.00
LM Loree Moore 4.00 10.00
LW Lindsay Whalen 10.00 25.00
NL Nancy Lieberman 12.00 30.00
NQ Noelle Quinn 4.00 10.00
OS Olympia Scott 4.00 10.00
SF Sylvia Fowles 15.00 40.00
SS Sidney Spencer 10.00 25.00
TJ Tiffany Jackson 6.00 15.00
TS Tangela Smith 6.00 15.00

2008 WNBA Case Topper

BALL PRINT RUN 250 SER.#'d SETS
2Q 2006 AS 2Q Ball/250 15.00 40.00
3Q 2006 AS 3Q Ball/250 15.00 40.00
NNO Monique Currie AU 6.00 15.00
NNO Kendra Wecker AU 6.00 15.00

2008 WNBA Relics

PRINT RUN 444 SER.#'d SETS
AS1 Cheryl Ford 3.00 8.00
AS2 Tamika Catchings 3.00 8.00
AS3 Anna DeForge 2.00 5.00
AS4 Deanna Nolan 2.00 5.00
AS5 Kara Braxton 2.50 6.00
AS6 Katie Douglas 3.00 8.00
AS7 Asjha Jones 2.50 6.00
AS8 Alana Beard 2.50 6.00
AS9 DeLisha Milton-Jones 3.00 8.00
AS10 Candice Dupree 3.00 8.00
AS11 Tammy Sutton-Brown 2.00 5.00
AS12 Diana Taurasi 12.00 30.00
AS13 Becky Hammon 12.00 30.00
AS14 Tina Thompson 6.00 15.00
AS15 Lauren Jackson 10.00 25.00
AS16 Yolanda Griffith 6.00 15.00
AS17 Taj McWilliams-Franklin 2.00 5.00
AS18 Seimone Augustus 5.00 12.00
AS19 Penny Taylor 3.00 8.00
AS20 Sophia Young 2.50 6.00
AS21 Cappie Pondexter 3.00 8.00
AS22 Kara Lawson 4.00 10.00
PM1 Cappie Pondexter 5.00 12.00
PM2 Diana Taurasi 20.00 50.00
PM3 Penny Taylor 5.00 12.00
PM4 Tangela Smith 5.00 12.00
PM5 Kelly Miller 5.00 12.00
PM6 Kelly Schumacher 5.00 12.00
PM7 Kelly Mazzante 5.00 12.00
PM8 Belinda Snell 3.00 8.00
RR1 Candace Parker 12.00 30.00
RR2 Sylvia Fowles 10.00 25.00
RR3 Candice Wiggins 8.00 20.00

2008 WNBA Rookies

PRINT RUN 444 SER.#'d SETS
R01 Candace Parker 300.00 600.00
R02 Sylvia Fowles 40.00 100.00
R03 Candice Wiggins 10.00 25.00
R04 Alexis Hornbuckle 10.00 25.00
R05 Matee Ajavon 5.00 12.00
R06 Crystal Langhorne 5.00 12.00
R07 Essence Carson 6.00 15.00
R08 Tamera Young 6.00 15.00
R09 Amber Holt 6.00 15.00
R10 Laura Harper 4.00 10.00
R11 Tasha Humphrey 4.00 10.00
R12 Ketia Swanier 4.00 10.00
R13 LaToya Pringle 4.00 10.00
R14 Erlana Larkins 6.00 15.00
R15 Charde Houston 6.00 15.00
R16 Nicky Anosike 10.00 25.00
R17 Jolene Anderson 6.00 15.00
R18 Khadijah Whittington 4.00 10.00
R19 Crystal Kelly 4.00 10.00
R20 Sandrine Gruda 4.00 10.00
R21 Shannon Bobbitt 4.00 10.00
R22 Brooke Smith 4.00 10.00
R23 Leilani Mitchell 4.00 10.00
R24 Erica White 4.00 10.00
R25 Kerri Gardin 4.00 10.00
R26 Olayinka Sanni 4.00 10.00
R27 Quianna Chaney 4.00 10.00
R28 Morenike Atunrase 4.00 10.00
R29 A'Quonesia Franklin 4.00 10.00

2008 WNBA USAB Womens National Team

STATED PRINT RUN 66 SER.#'d SETS
STATED PRINT RUN 44 SER.#'d SETS
G1 Seimone Augustus 4.00 10.00
G2 Sue Bird 10.00 25.00
G3 Tamika Catchings 2.50 6.00
G4 Sylvia Fowles 8.00 20.00
G5 Kara Lawson 3.00 8.00
G6 Lisa Leslie 8.00 20.00
G7 DeLisha Milton-Jones 2.50 6.00
G8 Candace Parker 20.00 50.00
G9 Cappie Pondexter 2.50 6.00
G10 Katie Smith 5.00 12.00
G11 Diana Taurasi 10.00 25.00
G12 Tina Thompson 5.00 12.00
USAB1 Parker/Fowles/Wiggins 20.00 50.00
USAB2 Taurasi/Bird/Cash 20.00 50.00
USAB3 Snow/Catch/Lawson 3.00 8.00
USAB4 Augustus/Ford/Swoopes 10.00 25.00
USAB5 Smith/Davenport/Douglas 5.00 12.00
USAB6 Beard/Milton-Jones/Moore 2.50 6.00
USAB7 McCarville/Jones/Whalen 4.00 10.00
USAB8 Leslie/Thomp/McW-Frank 8.00 20.00
USAB9 Brundon/Harding/Pondexter 2.50 6.00

2009 WNBA 1

COMPLETE BOX SET (17) 45.00 90.00
STATED PRINT RUN 399 SER.#'d SETS
1 Phoenix Mercury 4.00 10.00
4 Atlanta Dream 1.25 3.00
7 Detroit Shock 2.00 5.00
10 Los Angeles Sparks 4.00 10.00
13 Chicago Sky 1.50 4.00
16 Connecticut Sun 1.50 4.00
19 Seattle Storm 5.00 12.00
22 Washington Mystics 1.25 3.00
25 Indiana Fever 1.50 4.00
28 New York Liberty 1.25 3.00
31 Sacramento Monarchs 1.25 3.00
34 Minnesota Lynx 2.00 5.00
37 San Antonio Silver Stars 4.00 10.00
NNO Parker/Leslie Header 4.00 10.00

2009 WNBA 1 Autographs

INSERTED IN SERIES 1 BOX SET
CP Candace Parker 25.00 60.00
MA Matee Ajavon 4.00 10.00
NA Nicky Anosike 4.00 10.00

2009 WNBA 2 Rookies

COMPLETE BOX SET 45.00 90.00
PRINT RUN 499 SER.#'d SETS
BOX SET INCLUDES FIVE AUTOS
1 Angel McCoughtry 6.00 15.00
2 Marissa Coleman 5.00 12.00
3 Kristi Toliver 6.00 15.00
4 Renee Montgomery 5.00 12.00
5 DeWanna Bonner 8.00 20.00
6 Briann January 3.00 8.00
7 Courtney Paris 2.50 6.00
8 Kia Vaughn 3.00 8.00
9 Quanitra Holligsworth 3.00 8.00
10 Chante Black 3.00 8.00
11 Shavonte Zellous 5.00 12.00
12 Ashley Walker 3.00 8.00
13 Lindsay Wisdom-Hylton 4.00 10.00

2009 WNBA 2 Rookies Autographs

INSERTED IN SERIES 2 BOX SET
AM Angel McCoughtry 6.00 15.00
CP Courtney Paris 2.50 6.00
KT Kristi Toliver 6.00 15.00
MC Marissa Coleman 5.00 12.00
RM Renee Montgomery 5.00 12.00

2009 WNBA 3 All-Stars

COMPLETE BOX SET 60.00 120.00
BOX SET INCL. 4 RCs AND 5 AUTOS
AS1 S.Bird/K.Douglas 5.00 12.00
AS2 B.Hammon/A.Beard 5.00 12.00
AS3 T.Thompson/S.Fowles 2.50 6.00
AS4 S.Cash/C.Dupree 1.25 3.00
AS5 L.Jackson/T.Catchings 3.00 8.00
AS6 D.Taurasi/A.Jones 4.00 10.00
AS7 N.Anosike/K.Smith 2.00 5.00
AS8 C.Pondexter/E.DeSouza 1.25 3.00
AS9 N.Powell/S.Christon 1.25 3.00
AS10 S.Young/J.Perkins 1.25 3.00
AS11 C.Houston/S.Lyttle 1.25 3.00

2009 WNBA 3 Rookies

PRINT RUN 499 SER.#'d SETS
RC14 Megan Frazee 4.00 10.00
RC15 Anete Jekabsone 3.00 8.00
RC16 Rashanda McCants 4.00 10.00
RC17 Shalee Lehning 6.00 15.00

2009 WNBA 3 Rookies Autographs

INSERTED IN SERIES 3 BOX SET
BJ Briann January 4.00 10.00
CB Chante Black 4.00 10.00
DB DeWanna Bonner 10.00 25.00
MF Megan Frazee 5.00 12.00
QH Quanitra Hollingsworth 4.00 10.00
SZ Shavonte Zellous 6.00 15.00

2009 WNBA Autographs Three-Set Incentive

ANNOUNCED PRINT RUN 133 SETS
CP Candace Parker MVP 30.00 80.00

2010 WNBA

COMPLETE SET (36) 15.00 40.00
COMPLETE FACT.BOX 45.00 90.00
ANNOUNCED PRINT RUN 675 SETS
1 A.McCoughtry/I.Castro-Marques 1.00 2.50
2 S.Lyttle/A.Bales 1.25 3.00
3 E.deSouza/A.Price .75 2.00
4 S.Christon/D.Canty 1.00 2.50
5 S.Fowles/J.Perkins 1.25 3.00
6 C.Kraayeveld/E.Thorn .60 1.50
7 A.Jones/T.White .75 2.00
8 K.Lawson/S.Gruda 1.25 3.00
9 R.Montgomery/A.Jekabsone-Zogota .60 1.50
10 T.Catchings/E.Hoffman 1.50 4.00
11 K.Douglas/T.Sutton-Brown 1.00 2.50
12 B.January/E.Murphy .75 2.00
13 C.Parker/T.Thompson 4.00 10.00
14 D.Milton-Jones/B.Lennox 1.25 3.00
15 N.Quinn/K.Toliver 1.00 2.50
16 S.Augustus/N.Anosike 2.00 5.00
17 C.Houston/C.Wiggins 2.00 5.00
18 L.Whalen/R.McCants 1.50 4.00
19 C.Pondexter/J.McCarville 1.25 3.00
20 E.Carson/McWilliams-Franklin 1.00 2.50
21 N.Powell/L.Mitchell .75 2.00
22 D.Taurasi/T.Smith 4.00 10.00
23 C.Dupree/P.Taylor 1.00 2.50
24 D.Bonner/T.Johnson .60 1.50
25 S.Young/M.Snow .75 2.00
26 B.Hammon/R.Riley 4.00 10.00
27 E.Lawson-Wade/C.Holdsclaw 4.00 10.00
28 S.Bird/S.Cash 5.00 12.00
29 L.Jackson/T.Wright 3.00 8.00
30 C.Little/L.Willingham .60 1.50
31 K.Braxton/S.Crossley 1.25 3.00
32 C.Black/S.Robinson .60 1.50
33 A.Holt/A.Hornbuckle 1.25 3.00
34 K.Smith/L.Harding 2.00 5.00
35 C.Langhorne/M.Coleman 1.00 2.50
36 M.Currie/N.Sanford .75 2.00

2010 WNBA Autographs

AH Ashley Houts 4.00 10.00
DM Danielle McCray 4.00 10.00
MW Monica Wright 6.00 15.00
TC Tina Charles 12.00 30.00

2010 WNBA Diana Taurasi MVP Bonus

NNO Diana Taurasi MVP/250 10.00 25.00

2010 WNBA Rookies

COMPLETE SET (12) 60.00 120.00
PRINT RUN 250 SER.#'d SETS
R1 Tina Charles 15.00 40.00
R2 Monica Wright 8.00 20.00
R3 Kelsey Griffin 8.00 20.00
R4 Epiphanny Prince 6.00 15.00
R6 Jacinta Monroe 5.00 12.00
R7 Andrea Riley 5.00 12.00
R8 Alison Lacey 5.00 12.00
R9 Jene Morris 6.00 15.00
R10 Natasha Lacy 6.00 15.00
R11 Kalana Greene 6.00 15.00
R12 Marion Jones 10.00 25.00

2011 WNBA

STATED PRINT RUN 225 SER.#'d SETS
1 Diana Taurasi 12.00 30.00
2 Cappie Pondexter 4.00 10.00
3 Angel McCoughtry 5.00 12.00
4 Candace Parker 10.00 25.00
5 Lauren Jackson 12.00 30.00
6 Tamika Catchings 4.00 10.00
7 Sylvia Fowles 6.00 15.00
8 Iziane Castro-Marques 2.50 6.00
9 Seimone Augustus 4.00 10.00
10 Tina Thompson 8.00 20.00
11 Crystal Langhorne 3.00 8.00
12 Penny Taylor 5.00 12.00
13 Candice Dupree 4.00 10.00
14 Tina Charles 8.00 20.00
15 DeLisha Milton-Jones 2.50 6.00
16 Sophia Young 3.00 8.00
17 Becky Hammon 15.00 40.00
18 Monique Currie 3.00 8.00
19 Swin Cash 4.00 10.00
20 Candice Wiggins 8.00 20.00
21 Katie Douglas 4.00 10.00
22 Renee Montgomery 3.00 8.00
23 Sancho Lyttle 3.00 8.00
24 Lindsay Whalen 6.00 15.00
25 Ivory Latta 3.00 8.00
26 Erika DeSouza 2.50 6.00
27 Lindsey Harding 3.00 8.00
28 DeWanna Bonner 5.00 12.00
29 Scholanda Robinson 2.50 6.00
30 Charde Houston 4.00 10.00
31 Matee Ajavon 3.00 8.00
32 Rebekkah Brunson 2.50 6.00
33 Monica Wright 4.00 10.00
34 Sue Bird 15.00 40.00
35 Asjha Jones 3.00 8.00
36 Jia Perkins 3.00 8.00
37 Taj McWilliams-Franklin 3.00 8.00
38 Michelle Snow 3.00 8.00
39 Noelle Quinn 2.50 6.00
40 Camille Little 3.00 8.00
41 Tan White 3.00 8.00
42 Kara Braxton 3.00 8.00
43 Epiphanny Prince 3.00 8.00
44 Plenette Pierson 4.00 10.00
45 Kelsey Griffin 4.00 10.00
46 Katie Smith 8.00 20.00
47 Leilani Mitchell 2.50 6.00
48 Nicole Powell 3.00 8.00
49 Tangela Smith 2.50 6.00
50 Temeka Johnson 2.50 6.00
51 Tanisha Wright 3.00 8.00
52 Nicky Anosike 4.00 10.00
53 Dominique Canty 4.00 10.00
54 Marie Ferdinand-Harris 2.50 6.00
55 Essence Carson 3.00 8.00
56 Amber Holt 4.00 10.00
57 Kristi Toliver 4.00 10.00
58 Kelly Miller 2.50 6.00
59 Kara Lawson 5.00 12.00
60 Tammy Sutton-Brown 2.50 6.00
61 Ebony Hoffman 3.00 8.00
62 Ticha Penicheiro 6.00 15.00
63 Sheryl Swoopes 15.00 40.00

2011 WNBA 3-Box Incentive Autographs

NNO Tina Charles/55 40.00 100.00

2011 WNBA Autographs

STATED ODDS THREE PER PACK
NNO CARDS LISTED BY INITIALS
AH Amber Harris 3.00 8.00
AM Angel McCoughtry 6.00 15.00
CP Cappie Pondexter 3.00 8.00
CV Courtney Vandersloot 125.00 300.00
DR Danielle Robinson 4.00 10.00
DT Diana Taurasi 40.00 100.00
JM1 Jene Morris 3.00 8.00
JM2 Jacinta Monroe 3.00 8.00
JP Jeanette Pohlen 5.00 12.00
JT Jasmine Thomas 3.00 8.00
KG1 Kelsey Griffin 6.00 15.00
KG2 Kalana Greene 3.00 8.00
KP Kayla Pedersen 4.00 10.00
MM1 Maya Moore 400.00 800.00
MM2 M.Moore VAR Hold Jsy 400.00 800.00
PT Penny Taylor 10.00 25.00
TP Ta'Shia Phillips 3.00 8.00
VD Victoria Dunlap 3.00 8.00

2011 WNBA Rookies

STATED PRINT RUN 225 SER.#'d SETS
R1 Maya Moore 500.00 1,000.00
R2 Elizabeth Cambage 8.00 20.00
R3 Courtney Vandersloot 75.00 200.00
R4 Amber Harris 6.00 15.00
R5 Jantel Lavender 8.00 20.00
R6 Danielle Robinson 6.00 15.00
R7 Kayla Pedersen 6.00 15.00
R8 Ta'Shia Phillips 5.00 12.00

R9 Jeanette Pohlen 6.00 15.00
R10 Victoria Dunlap 5.00 12.00
R11 Jasmine Thomas 10.00 25.00
R12 Danielle Adams 6.00 15.00

2012 WNBA
COMPLETE FACT.SET (111) 200.00 500.00
COMPLETE SET (96) 100.00 250.00
ANNOUNCED PRINT RUN 400 SETS
1 Angel McCoughtry 5.00 12.00
2 Armintie Price 3.00 8.00
3 Cathrine Kraayeveld 2.50 6.00
4 Ketia Swanier 2.50 6.00
5 Lindsey Harding 3.00 8.00
6 Sancho Lyttle 3.00 8.00
7 Yelena Leuchanka 2.50 6.00
8 Courtney Vandersloot 8.00 20.00
9 Epiphanny Prince 3.00 8.00
10 Eshaya Murphy 3.00 8.00
11 Le'coe Willingham 2.50 6.00
12 Ruth Riley 4.00 10.00
13 Swin Cash 4.00 10.00
14 Sylvia Fowles 4.00 10.00
15 Tamera Young 3.00 8.00
16 Ticha Penicheiro 6.00 15.00
17 Allison Hightower RC 4.00 10.00
18 Asjha Jones 3.00 8.00
19 Danielle McCray 2.50 6.00
20 Kalana Greene 3.00 8.00
21 Kara Lawson 5.00 12.00
22 Mistie Mims RC 4.00 10.00
23 Renee Montgomery 3.00 8.00
24 Tan White 3.00 8.00
25 Tina Charles 8.00 20.00
26 Briann January 2.50 6.00
27 Erin Phillips 2.50 6.00
28 Jeanette Pohlen 3.00 8.00
29 Jessica Davenport 3.00 8.00
30 Katie Douglas 4.00 10.00
31 Shavonte Zellous 3.00 8.00
32 Tamika Catchings 4.00 10.00
33 Tammy Sutton-Brown 2.50 6.00
34 Alana Beard 3.00 8.00
35 Candace Parker 10.00 25.00
36 Delisha Milton-Jones 2.50 6.00
37 Ebony Hoffman 3.00 8.00
38 Jantel Lavender 3.00 8.00
39 Kristi Toliver 4.00 10.00
40 Marissa Coleman 3.00 8.00
41 Candice Wiggins 8.00 20.00
42 Jessica Adair RC 4.00 10.00
43 Lindsay Whalen 6.00 15.00
44 Maya Moore 12.00 30.00
45 Monica Wright 4.00 10.00
46 Rebekkah Brunson 2.50 6.00
47 Seimone Augustus 4.00 10.00
48 Taj McWilliams-Franklin 4.00 10.00
49 Cappie Pondexter 4.00 10.00
50 DeMya Walker 2.50 6.00
51 Essence Carson 3.00 8.00
52 Kara Braxton 3.00 8.00
53 Kelly Miller 2.50 6.00
54 Kia Vaughn 2.50 6.00
55 Leilani Mitchell 2.50 6.00
56 Nicole Powell 3.00 8.00
57 Plenette Pierson 4.00 10.00
58 Alexis Gray-Lawson RC 4.00 10.00
59 Alexis Hornbuckle 5.00 12.00
60 Candice Dupree 4.00 10.00
61 Charde Houston 4.00 10.00
62 DeWanna Bonner 5.00 12.00
63 Diana Taurasi 12.00 30.00
64 Nakia Sanford 3.00 8.00
65 Becky Hammon 15.00 40.00
66 Danielle Adams 3.00 8.00
67 Danielle Robinson 3.00 8.00
69 Jia Perkins 3.00 8.00
70 Shameka Christon 2.50 6.00
71 Sophia Young 3.00 8.00
72 Tangela Smith 2.50 6.00
73 Ann Wauters 4.00 10.00
74 Camille Little 3.00 8.00
75 Ewelina Kobryn RC 4.00 10.00
76 Katie Smith 8.00 20.00
77 Lauren Jackson 12.00 30.00
78 Sue Bird 15.00 40.00
79 Tanisha Wright 3.00 8.00
80 Tina Thompson 8.00 20.00
81 Chante Black 2.50 6.00
82 Ivory Latta 3.00 8.00
83 Courtney Paris 3.00 8.00
84 Jennifer Lacy 2.50 6.00
85 Kayla Pedersen 3.00 8.00
86 Liz Cambage 4.00 10.00
87 Scholanda Dorrell 2.50 6.00
88 Temeka Johnson 2.50 6.00
89 Ashley Robinson 2.50 6.00
90 Crystal Langhorne 3.00 8.00
91 Shannon Bobbitt 2.50 6.00
92 Jasmine Thomas 4.00 10.00
93 Matee Ajavon 3.00 8.00
94 Michelle Snow 3.00 8.00
95 Monique Currie 3.00 8.00
96 Noelle Quinn 2.50 6.00
NNO N.Ogwumike AU 60.00 150.00

2012 WNBA Rookies
COMPLETE SET (14) 75.00 200.00
ANNOUNCED PRINT RUN 400 SETS
R1 Nnemkadi Ogwumike 75.00 200.00
R2 Shekinna Stricklen 6.00 15.00
R3 Devereaux Peters 6.00 15.00
R4 Glory Johnson 8.00 20.00
R5 Shenise Johnson 6.00 15.00
R6 Samantha Prahalis 10.00 25.00
R7 Kelley Cain 6.00 15.00
R8 Natalie Novosel 8.00 20.00
R9 Sasha Goodlett 4.00 10.00
R10 Riquna Williams 4.00 10.00
R11 Avery Warley 4.00 10.00
R12 Tiffany Hayes 8.00 20.00
R13 Aneika Henry 4.00 10.00
R14 April Sykes 4.00 10.00

2013 WNBA
COMP.FACT.SET (102) 60.00 150.00
COMP.SET w/o AU's (100) 40.00 100.00
ANNOUNCED PRINT RUN 500 SETS
1 Alex Bentley RC 2.00 5.00
2 Aneika Henry .75 2.00
3 Angel McCoughtry 1.50 4.00
4 Armintie Herrington .75 2.00
5 Erika de Souza .75 2.00
6 Jasmine Thomas 1.25 3.00
7 Sancho Lyttle 1.00 2.50
8 Tiffany Hayes 1.25 3.00
9 Allie Quigley RC 12.00 30.00
10 Carolyn Swords RC 2.00 5.00
11 Courtney Vandersloot 2.50 6.00
12 Elena Delle Donne RC 100.00 250.00
13 Epiphanny Prince 1.00 2.50
14 Swin Cash 1.25 3.00
15 Sylvia Fowles 1.25 3.00
16 Tamera Young 1.00 2.50
17 Allison Hightower .75 2.00
18 Kalana Greene 1.00 2.50
19 Kara Lawson 1.50 4.00
20 Kelsey Griffin 1.00 2.50
21 Mistie Bass .75 2.00
22 Renee Montgomery 1.00 2.50
23 Tan White .75 2.00
24 Tina Charles 2.50 6.00
25 Briann January .75 2.00
26 Erlana Larkins 1.00 2.50
27 Jessica Breland .75 2.00
28 Karima Christmas 1.25 3.00
29 Katie Douglas 1.25 3.00
30 Layshia Clarendon RC 2.00 5.00
31 Shavonte Zellous 1.00 2.50
32 Tamika Catchings 1.25 3.00
33 Alana Beard 1.25 3.00
34 Candace Parker 3.00 8.00
35 Ebony Hoffman 1.25 3.00
36 Farhiya Abdi RC 2.00 5.00
37 Jantel Lavender 1.25 3.00
38 Kristi Toliver 1.25 3.00
39 Lindsey Harding 1.00 2.50
40 Marissa Coleman 1.00 2.50
41 Nneka Ogwumike 2.00 5.00
42 Amber Harris .75 2.00
43 Devereaux Peters 1.00 2.50
44 Janel McCarville .75 2.00
45 Lindsay Whalen 2.00 5.00
46 Maya Moore 4.00 10.00
47 Monica Wright 1.25 3.00
48 Rebekkah Brunson .75 2.00
49 Seimone Augustus 1.25 3.00
50 Alex Montgomery .75 2.00
51 Cappie Pondexter 1.25 3.00
52 Essence Carson 1.00 2.50
53 Kamiko Williams RC 2.00 5.00
54 Kara Braxton .75 2.00
55 Katie Smith 2.50 6.00
56 Kelsey Bone RC 2.00 5.00
57 Leilani Mitchell .75 2.00
58 Plenette Pierson 1.25 3.00
59 Toni Young RC 2.00 5.00
60 Briana Gilbreath .75 2.00
61 Brittney Griner RC 60.00 150.00
62 Candice Dupree 1.25 3.00
63 Charde Houston 1.25 3.00
64 DeWanna Bonner 1.50 4.00
65 Diana Taurasi 4.00 10.00
66 Lynetta Kizer .75 2.00
67 Penny Taylor 1.25 3.00
68 Becky Hammon 5.00 12.00
69 Danielle Adams 1.00 2.50
70 Danielle Robinson 1.00 2.50
71 Davellyn Whyte RC 2.00 5.00
72 Delisha Milton-Jones .75 2.00
74 Jia Perkins 1.00 2.50
75 Shameka Christon .75 2.00
76 Shenise Johnson 1.00 2.50
77 Alysha Clark RC 50.00 120.00
78 Camille Little .75 2.00
79 Noelle Quinn .75 2.00
80 Shekinna Stricklen .75 2.00
81 Sue Bird 4.00 10.00
82 Tanisha Wright 1.00 2.50
83 Temeka Johnson .75 2.00
84 Tina Thompson 2.50 6.00
85 Angel Goodrich RC 2.00 5.00
86 Candice Wiggins 2.50 6.00
87 Glory Johnson 1.25 3.00
88 Liz Cambage 1.25 3.00
89 Nicole Powell 1.00 2.50
90 Riquna Williams .75 2.00
91 Roneeka Hodges .75 2.00
92 Skylar Diggins RC 75.00 200.00
93 Crystal Langhorne 1.00 2.50
94 Ivory Latta 1.00 2.50
95 Kia Vaughn .75 2.00
96 Matee Ajavon 1.00 2.50
97 Michelle Snow 1.00 2.50
98 Monique Currie 1.00 2.50
99 Tayler Hill RC 4.00 10.00
100 Tierra Ruffin-Pratt RC 2.50 6.00

2013 WNBA Autographs
ANNOUNCED PRINT RUN 500 SETS
BG Brittney Griner 20.00 50.00
EDD Elena Delle Donne 40.00 100.00

2014 WNBA
COMP.FACT.SET (104) 300.00 600.00
COMP.SET w/o AU's (100) 150.00 400.00
ANNOUNCED PRINT RUN 500 SETS
1 Aneika Henry 1.25 3.00
2 Angel McCoughtry 2.50 6.00
3 Erika de Souza 1.25 3.00
4 Jasmine Thomas 1.25 3.00
5 Matee Ajavon 1.50 4.00
6 Sancho Lyttle 1.50 4.00
7 Shoni Schimmel RC 8.00 20.00
8 Tiffany Hayes 2.00 5.00
9 Allie Quigley 1.50 4.00
10 Courtney Vandersloot 4.00 10.00
11 Elena Delle Donne 20.00 50.00
12 Jamierra Faulkner RC 3.00 8.00
13 Jessica Breland 1.50 4.00
14 Markeisha Gatling 1.25 3.00
15 Sasha Goodlett 1.25 3.00
16 Sylvia Fowles 3.00 8.00
17 Tamera Young 1.50 4.00
18 Alex Bentley 2.00 5.00
19 Allison Hightower 1.25 3.00
20 Alyssa Thomas RC 75.00 200.00
21 Chiney Ogwumike RC 40.00 100.00
22 Katie Douglas 2.00 5.00
23 Kelsey Bone 1.25 3.00
24 Kelsey Griffin 1.50 4.00
25 Renee Montgomery 1.50 4.00
26 Briann January 1.25 3.00
27 Erlana Larkins 1.50 4.00
28 Karima Christmas 2.00 5.00
29 Maggie Lucas RC 3.00 8.00
30 Marissa Coleman 1.50 4.00
31 Natasha Howard RC 3.00 8.00
32 Shavonte Zellous 1.50 4.00
33 Tamika Catchings 2.00 5.00
34 Alana Beard 1.50 4.00
35 Armintie Herrington 1.25 3.00
36 Candice Wiggins 4.00 10.00
37 Candace Parker 6.00 15.00
38 Jantel Lavender 1.50 4.00
39 Kristi Toliver 2.00 5.00
40 Lindsey Harding 1.50 4.00
41 Nneka Ogwumike 3.00 8.00
42 Asia Taylor RC 2.00 5.00
43 Damiris Dantas RC 2.00 5.00
44 Janel McCarville 1.25 3.00
45 Lindsay Whalen 3.00 8.00
46 Lindsey Moore 6.00 15.00
47 Maya Moore 6.00 15.00
48 Seimone Augustus 2.00 5.00
49 Tan White 1.50 4.00
50 Anna Cruz RC 2.00 5.00
51 Alex Montgomery 1.25 3.00
52 Cappie Pondexter 2.00 5.00
53 Delisha Milton-Jones 1.25 3.00
54 Essence Carson 1.50 4.00
55 Plenette Pierson 2.00 5.00
56 Sugar Rodgers RC 3.00 8.00
57 Tina Charles 4.00 10.00
58 Anete Jekabsone-Zogota 1.25 3.00
59 Brittney Griner 8.00 20.00
60 Candice Dupree 2.00 5.00
61 DeWanna Bonner 2.50 6.00
62 Diana Taurasi 6.00 15.00
63 Erin Phillips 1.25 3.00
64 Mistie Bass 1.25 3.00
65 Penny Taylor 2.00 5.00
66 Becky Hammon 8.00 20.00
67 Danielle Adams 1.50 4.00
68 Danielle Robinson 1.50 4.00
70 Jia Perkins 1.50 4.00
71 Kayla McBride RC 4.00 10.00
72 Shameka Christon 1.25 3.00
73 Shenise Johnson 1.50 4.00
74 Sophia Young-Malcolm 1.50 4.00
75 Alysha Clark 1.50 4.00
76 Angel Robinson RC 1.25 3.00
77 Camille Little 1.50 4.00
78 Crystal Langhorne 1.50 4.00
79 Jenna O'Hea 1.25 3.00
80 Noelle Quinn 1.25 3.00
81 Shekinna Stricklen 1.25 3.00
82 Sue Bird 8.00 20.00
83 Tanisha Wright 1.50 4.00
84 Temeka Johnson 1.25 3.00
85 Courtney Paris 1.50 4.00
86 Glory Johnson 2.00 5.00
87 Jordan Hooper RC 2.00 5.00
88 Odyssey Sims RC 4.00 10.00
89 Riquna Williams 1.25 3.00
90 Roneeka Hodges 1.25 3.00
91 Skylar Diggins 6.00 15.00
92 Bria Hartley RC 2.50 6.00
93 Emma Meesseman RC 40.00 100.00
94 Ivory Latta 1.50 4.00
95 Jelena Milovanovic RC 1.25 3.00
96 Kara Lawson 2.50 6.00
97 Kia Vaughn 1.25 3.00
98 Monique Currie 1.50 4.00
99 Stefanie Dolson RC 3.00 8.00
100 Tierra Ruffin-Pratt 1.50 4.00

2014 WNBA Autographs
FOUR AUTOS PER FACTORY SET
ANNCD PRINT RUN OF 500 FACTORY SETS
BH Bria Hartley 8.00 20.00
CO Chiney Ogwumike 20.00 50.00
NO Nneka Ogwumike 12.00 30.00
SD Stefanie Dolson 10.00 25.00

2014 WNBA Dual Autographs
THREE SET PURCHASE INCENTIVE
CNO C.Ogwumike/N.Ogwumike 30.00 80.00

2015 WNBA
COMP.FACT.SET (103) 100.00 150.00
COMP.SET w/o AU's (100) 40.00 100.00
ANNOUNCED PRINT RUN 500 SETS
1 Aneika Henry .75 2.00
2 Angel McCoughtry 1.50 4.00
3 Erica Wheeler RC 3.00 8.00
4 Erika de Souza .75 2.00
5 Matee Ajavon 1.00 2.50
6 Sancho Lyttle 1.00 2.50
7 Shoni Schimmel 3.00 8.00
8 Tiffany Hayes 1.25 3.00
9 Allie Quigley 1.00 2.50
10 Betnijah Laney RC 4.00 10.00
11 Cappie Pondexter 1.25 3.00
12 Courtney Vandersloot 8.00 20.00
13 Elena Delle Donne 8.00 20.00
14 Jessica Breland 1.00 2.50
15 Sasha Goodlett .75 2.00
16 Tamera Young 1.00 2.50
17 Alex Bentley 1.25 3.00
18 Alyssa Thomas 1.25 3.00
19 Camille Little 1.00 2.50
20 Chelsea Gray RC 2.00 5.00
21 Chiney Ogwumike 1.25 3.00
22 Elizabeth Williams RC 3.00 8.00
23 Jasmine Thomas 1.25 3.00
24 Kelsey Bone .75 2.00
25 Shekinna Stricklen .75 2.00
26 Briann January 1.00 2.50
27 Layshia Clarendon 1.00 2.50
28 Lynetta Kizer 1.00 2.50
29 Maggie Lucas 1.25 3.00
30 Marissa Coleman 1.00 2.50
31 Natalie Achonwa RC 4.00 10.00
32 Shavonte Zellous 1.00 2.50
33 Tamika Catchings 1.25 3.00
34 Alana Beard 1.00 2.50
35 Erin Phillips .75 2.00
36 Farhiya Abdi 1.00 2.50
37 Jantel Lavender 1.00 2.50
38 Jennifer Lacy 1.00 2.50
39 Candace Parker 3.00 8.00
40 Marianna Tolo RC 3.00 8.00
41 Nneka Ogwumike 1.50 4.00
42 Asjha Jones 1.25 3.00
43 Damiris Dantas 1.25 3.00
44 Jennifer O'Neill RC 3.00 8.00
45 Lindsay Whalen 2.00 5.00
46 Maya Moore 4.00 10.00
47 Rebekkah Brunson 1.25 3.00
48 Seimone Augustus 1.25 3.00
49 Tricia Liston 1.00 2.50
50 Brittany Boyd RC 2.50 6.00
51 Candice Wiggins 2.50 6.00
52 Carolyn Swords .75 2.00
53 Essence Carson 1.00 2.50
54 Kiah Stokes RC 3.00 8.00
55 Sugar Rodgers 1.25 3.00
56 Swin Cash 1.25 3.00
57 Tanisha Wright 1.00 2.50
58 Tina Charles 2.50 6.00
59 Alex Harden RC 3.00 8.00
60 Brittney Griner 4.00 10.00
61 Candice Dupree 1.25 3.00
62 Cayla Francis RC 3.00 8.00
63 DeWanna Bonner 1.50 4.00
64 Leilani Mitchell .75 2.00
65 Mistie Bass .75 2.00
66 Monique Currie 1.00 2.50
67 Danielle Robinson 1.00 2.50
68 Dearica Hamby RC 2.50 6.00
70 Jia Perkins 1.00 2.50
71 Kayla Alexander RC 2.50 6.00
72 Kayla McBride 1.50 4.00
73 Sophia Young-Malcolm 1.25 3.00
74 Sydney Colson RC 2.00 5.00
75 Abby Bishop 1.25 3.00
76 Alysha Clark 1.00 2.50
77 Crystal Langhorne 1.00 2.50
78 Jenna O'Hea .75 2.00
79 Jewell Loyd RC 5.00 12.00
80 Kaleena Mosqueda-Lewis RC 2.00 5.00
81 Quanitra Hollingsworth .75 2.00
82 Ramu Tokashiki RC 2.00 5.00
83 Renee Montgomery 1.00 2.50
84 Sue Bird 4.00 10.00
85 Amanda Zahui B. RC 2.50 6.00
86 Courtney Paris 1.00 2.50
87 Jordan Hooper .75 2.00
88 Karima Christmas 1.25 3.00
89 Odyssey Sims 1.25 3.00
90 Plenette Pierson 1.25 3.00
91 Riquna Williams .75 2.00
92 Skylar Diggins 2.50 6.00
93 Armintie Herrington .75 2.00
94 Emma Meesseman 2.50 6.00
95 Ivory Latta 1.00 2.50
96 Kara Lawson 1.50 4.00
97 Natasha Cloud RC 2.00 5.00
98 Stefanie Dolson 3.00 8.00
99 Tayler Hill 1.50 4.00
100 Tierra Ruffin-Pratt 1.00 2.50

2015 WNBA Autographs
THREE AUTOS PER FACTORY SET
ANNCD PRINT RUN OF 500 FACTORY SETS
AZ Amanda Zahui B. 8.00 20.00
JL Jewell Loyd 8.00 20.00
KM Kaleena Mosqueda-Lewis 8.00 20.00

2016 WNBA
COMP.FACT.SET (102) 2,000.00 4,000.00
COMP.SET w/o AU's (100) 1,000.00 2,000.00
ANNOUNCED PRINT RUN 500 SETS
1 Angel McCoughtry 2.00 5.00
2 Bria Holmes RC 2.00 5.00
3 Carla Cortijo 1.00 2.50
4 Elizabeth Williams 1.50 4.00
5 Layshia Clarendon 1.50 4.00
6 Meighan Simmons RC 2.00 5.00
7 Rachel Hollivay RC 2.00 5.00
8 Reshanda Gray 1.00 2.50
9 Sancho Lyttle 1.50 4.00
10 Tiffany Hayes 1.50 4.00
11 Allie Quigley 1.25 3.00
12 Cappie Pondexter 1.50 4.00
13 Courtney Vandersloot 2.50 6.00
14 Elena Delle Donne 6.00 15.00
15 Erika de Souza 1.00 2.50
16 Imani Boyette RC 2.00 5.00
17 Jamierra Faulkner 1.25 3.00
18 Jessica Breland 1.25 3.00
19 Tamera Young 1.25 3.00
20 Alex Bentley 1.50 4.00
21 Alyssa Thomas 1.50 4.00
22 Camille Little 1.25 3.00
23 Chiney Ogwumike 1.50 4.00
24 Jasmine Thomas 1.25 3.00
25 Jonquel Jones RC 100.00 250.00
26 Kelsey Bone 1.25 3.00
27 Morgan Tuck RC 5.00 12.00
28 Rachel Banham RC 4.00 10.00
29 Aerial Powers RC 3.00 8.00
30 Courtney Paris 1.25 3.00
31 Erin Phillips 1.00 2.50
32 Glory Johnson 1.50 4.00
33 Jordan Hooper 1.00 2.50
34 Karima Christmas 1.50 4.00
35 Odyssey Sims 1.50 4.00
36 Plenette Pierson 1.50 4.00
37 Skylar Diggins 3.00 8.00
38 Theresa Plaisance RC 1.25 3.00
39 Briann January 1.25 3.00
40 Devereaux Peters 1.25 3.00
41 Erica Wheeler 1.25 3.00
42 Erlana Larkins 1.25 3.00
43 Lynetta Kizer 1.25 3.00
44 Maggie Lucas 1.50 4.00
45 Marissa Coleman 1.25 3.00
46 Shenise Johnson 1.25 3.00
47 Tamika Catchings 1.50 4.00
48 Tiffany Mitchell RC 5.00 12.00
49 Alana Beard 1.25 3.00
50 Ana Dabovic RC 1.00 2.50
51 Candace Parker 4.00 10.00
52 Chelsea Gray 1.00 2.50
53 Essence Carson 1.25 3.00
54 Evgeniia Belyakova RC 1.50 4.00
55 Jantel Lavender 1.25 3.00
56 Kristi Toliver 1.50 4.00
57 Nneka Ogwumike 2.50 6.00
58 Janel McCarville 1.00 2.50
59 Jia Perkins 1.25 3.00
60 Lindsay Whalen 3.00 8.00
61 Maya Moore 5.00 12.00
62 Natasha Howard 1.25 3.00
63 Rebekkah Brunson 1.25 3.00
64 Renee Montgomery 1.25 3.00
65 Seimone Augustus 1.25 3.00
66 Sylvia Fowles 1.50 4.00
67 Brittany Boyd 1.00 2.50
68 Carolyn Swords 1.50 4.00
69 Kiah Stokes 1.25 3.00
70 Amanda Zahui B 1.25 3.00
71 Shavonte Zellous 1.25 3.00
72 Sugar Rodgers 1.50 4.00
73 Swin Cash 1.50 4.00
74 Tanisha Wright 1.25 3.00
75 Tina Charles 3.00 8.00
76 Brittney Griner 5.00 12.00
77 Candice Dupree 1.50 4.00
78 DeWanna Bonner 2.00 5.00
79 Diana Taurasi 6.00 15.00
80 Isabelle Harrison RC 1.50 4.00
81 Mistie Bass 1.00 2.50
82 Noelle Quinn 1.00 2.50
83 Penny Taylor 1.50 4.00
84 Sonja Petrovic RC 1.25 3.00
85 Alex Montgomery 1.00 2.50
86 Dearica Hamby 2.00 5.00
87 Haley Peters RC 1.50 4.00
88 Jayne Appel-Marinelli 1.25 3.00
89 Kayla Alexander 1.25 3.00
90 Kayla McBride 2.00 5.00
91 Monique Currie 1.25 3.00
92 Moriah Jefferson RC 5.00 12.00
93 Sydney Colson 1.00 2.50
94 Alysha Clark 1.25 3.00
95 Breanna Stewart RC 800.00 1,500.00
96 Crystal Langhorne 1.25 3.00
97 Jenna O'Hea RC 1.25 3.00
98 Jewell Loyd 2.50 6.00
99 Kaleena Mosqueda-Lewis 1.00 2.50
100 Ramu Tokashiki 1.00 2.50
101 Sue Bird 6.00 15.00
102 Bria Hartley 1.25 3.00
103 Emma Meesseman 3.00 8.00
104 Ivory Latta 1.25 3.00
105 Kahleah Copper RC 40.00 100.00
106 Kia Vaughn 1.00 2.50
107 Stefanie Dolson 1.50 4.00
108 Tayler Hill 2.00 5.00
109 Tierra Ruffin-Pratt 1.25 3.00
110 Natasha Cloud 1.00 2.50

2016 WNBA Autographs
TWO AUTOS PER FACTORY SET
BS1 Stewart Action 800.00 1,500.00
BS2 Stewart Draft 800.00 1,500.00
BS3 Stewart Posed 800.00 1,500.00
MT1 Tuck Action 8.00 20.00
MT2 Tuck Draft 8.00 20.00
MT3 Tuck Posed 8.00 20.00

2017 WNBA
COMP.FACT.SET (110) 200.00 500.00
COMP.SET w/o AU's
ANNOUNCED PRINT RUN 500 SETS
1 Bria Holmes 1.25 3.00
2 Brittney Sykes RC 6.00 15.00
3 Damiris Dantas 1.50 4.00
4 Elizabeth Williams 1.50 4.00
5 Layshia Clarendon 1.50 4.00
6 Sancho Lyttle 1.25 3.00
7 Tiffany Hayes 1.50 4.00
8 Allie Quigley 1.50 4.00
9 Cappie Pondexter 1.50 4.00
10 Cheyenne Parker RC 2.00 5.00
11 Courtney Vandersloot 3.00 8.00
12 Imani Boyette 1.25 3.00
13 Jessica Breland 1.25 3.00
14 Kahleah Copper 3.00 8.00
15 Stefanie Dolson 1.50 4.00
16 Tamera Young 1.25 3.00
17 Alex Bentley 1.50 4.00
18 Alyssa Thomas 3.00 8.00
19 Courtney Williams RC 3.00 8.00
20 Jasmine Thomas 1.25 3.00
21 Jonquel Jones 4.00 10.00
22 Lynetta Kizer 1.25 3.00
23 Morgan Tuck 2.00 5.00
24 Rachel Banham 2.00 5.00
25 Shekinna Stricklen 1.00 2.50
26 Allisha Gray RC 4.00 10.00
27 Glory Johnson 1.25 3.00
28 Kaela Davis RC 2.00 5.00
29 Karima Christmas-Kelly 1.50 4.00
30 Kayla Thornton RC 3.00 8.00
31 Saniya Chong RC 2.00 5.00
32 Skylar Diggins-Smith 3.00 8.00
33 Theresa Plaisance 1.25 3.00
34 Briann January 1.25 3.00
35 Candice Dupree 1.50 4.00
36 Erica Wheeler 1.25 3.00
37 Erlana Larkins 1.25 3.00
38 Jazmon Gwathmey RC 1.25 3.00
39 Jeanette Pohlen-Mavunga 1.25 3.00
40 Marissa Coleman 1.25 3.00
41 Natalie Achonwa 1.50 4.00
42 Shenise Johnson 1.25 3.00
43 Tiffany Mitchell 2.00 5.00
44 Alana Beard 1.25 3.00
45 Candace Parker 5.00 12.00
46 Chelsea Gray 2.50 6.00
47 Essence Carson 1.25 3.00
48 Jantel Lavender 1.25 3.00
49 Nneka Ogwumike 2.00 5.00
50 Odyssey Sims 1.50 4.00
51 Riquna Williams 1.00 2.50
52 Sydney Wiese RC 1.50 4.00
53 Jia Perkins 1.25 3.00
54 Lindsay Whalen 3.00 8.00
55 Maya Moore 5.00 12.00
56 Natasha Howard 1.25 3.00
57 Plenette Pierson 1.50 4.00
58 Rebekkah Brunson 1.25 3.00
59 Renee Montgomery 1.25 3.00
60 Seimone Augustus 1.50 4.00
61 Sylvia Fowles 1.50 4.00
62 Bria Hartley 1.25 3.00
63 Brittany Boyd 1.00 2.50
64 Epiphanny Prince 1.25 3.00
65 Kia Vaughn 1.00 2.50
66 Kiah Stokes 1.25 3.00
67 Nayo Raincock-Ekunwe RC 1.25 3.00
68 Shavonte Zellous 1.25 3.00
69 Sugar Rodgers 1.50 4.00
70 Tina Charles 3.00 8.00
71 Brittney Griner 5.00 12.00
72 Camille Little 1.25 3.00
73 Cayla George 1.25 3.00
74 Danielle Robinson 1.25 3.00
75 Diana Taurasi 6.00 15.00
76 Emma Cannon RC 1.25 3.00
77 Leilani Mitchell 1.00 2.50
78 Monique Currie 1.25 3.00
79 Stephanie Talbot RC 2.00 5.00
80 Yvonne Turner RC 1.50 4.00
81 Alex Montgomery 1.00 2.50
82 Dearica Hamby 2.00 5.00
83 Erika de Souza 1.00 2.50
84 Isabelle Harrison 1.00 2.50
85 Kayla Alexander 1.25 3.00
86 Kayla McBride 2.00 5.00
87 Kelsey Plum RC 125.00 300.00
88 Moriah Jefferson 2.00 5.00
89 Nia Coffey RC 2.00 5.00
90 Sequoia Holmes RC 1.25 3.00
91 Shay Murphy 1.25 3.00
92 Alysha Clark 1.25 3.00
93 Breanna Stewart 20.00 50.00
94 Carolyn Swords 1.00 2.50
95 Crystal Langhorne 1.25 3.00
96 Jewell Loyd 3.00 8.00
97 Kaleena Mosqueda-Lewis 1.00 2.50
98 Noelle Quinn 1.00 2.50
99 Ramu Tokashiki 1.00 2.50
100 Sami Whitcomb RC 1.50 4.00
101 Sue Bird 12.00 30.00
102 Elena Delle Donne 4.00 10.00
103 Emma Meesseman 3.00 8.00
104 Ivory Latta 1.25 3.00
105 Kristi Toliver 1.50 4.00
106 Krystal Thomas RC 1.25 3.00
107 Natasha Cloud 1.00 2.50
108 Tayler Hill 2.00 5.00
109 Tianna Hawkins RC 1.25 3.00
110 Tierra Ruffin-Pratt 1.25 3.00

2017 WNBA Autographs
TWO AUTOS PER FACTORY SET
ALL VERSIONS EQUALLY PRICED
1 Kelsey Plum 300.00 600.00
2 Kelsey Plum
Street Clothes 300.00 600.00
3 Kelsey Plum
Uniform 300.00 600.00
4 Maya Moore 75.00 200.00
5 Maya Moore
Game Action
3x WNBA Champ 75.00 200.00
6 Maya Moore
Game Action
2014 MVP 75.00 200.00
7 Maya Moore
Game Action
Go Huskies! 75.00 200.00
8 Maya Moore
Game Action
Go UCONN! 75.00 200.00
9 Maya Moore
Street Clothes
Go Lynx! 75.00 200.00
10 Maya Moore
Street Clothes
3x WNBA Champ 75.00 200.00
11 Maya Moore
Street Clothes
2014 MVP 75.00 200.00
12 Maya Moore
Street Clothes
Go Huskies! 75.00 200.00
13 Maya Moore
Street Clothes
Go UCONN! 75.00 200.00
14 Maya Moore
Uniform
Go Lynx! 75.00 200.00
15 Maya Moore
Uniform
3x WNBA Champs 75.00 200.00
16 Maya Moore
Uniform
2014 MVP 75.00 200.00
17 Maya Moore
Uniform
Go Huskies! 75.00 200.00
18 Maya Moore
Uniform
Go UCONN! 75.00 200.00
19 Sue Bird 75.00 200.00
20 Sue Bird
Game Action
Go Huskies 75.00 200.00
21 Sue Bird
Game Action
Go Storm 75.00 200.00
22 Sue Bird
Game Action
4x Olympian 75.00 200.00
23 Sue Bird
Game Action
2X WNBA Champ 75.00 200.00
24 Sue Bird
Game Action
Go UCONN! 75.00 200.00
25 Sue Bird
Street Clothes
10x All Star 75.00 200.00
26 Sue Bird
Street Clothes
Go Huskies! 75.00 200.00
27 Sue Bird
Street Clothes
Go Storm! 75.00 200.00
28 Sue Bird
Street Clothes
4x Olympian 75.00 200.00
29 Sue Bird
Street Clothes
2x WNBA Champ 75.00 200.00
30 Sue Bird
Street Clothes
Go UCONN! 75.00 200.00
31 Sue Bird
Uniform
10x All Star 75.00 200.00
32 Sue Bird
Uniform
Go Huskies 75.00 200.00
33 Sue Bird
Uniform
Go Storm! 75.00 200.00
34 Sue Bird
Uniform
4x Olympic Gold! 75.00 200.00
35 Sue Bird
Uniform
2x WNBA Champ 75.00 200.00
36 Sue Bird
Uniform
Go UCONN 75.00 200.00

2018 WNBA
COMP.FACT.SET (110) 2,000.00 4,000.00
COMP.SET w/o AU's
COMMON CARD (1-110) 1.25 3.00
SEMISTARS 1.50 4.00
UNLISTED STARS 2.00 5.00
COMMON RC (1-110) 2.00 5.00
RC SEMIS 2.50 6.00
RC UNLISTED 3.00 8.00
ANNOUNCED PRINT RUN 500 SETS
1 Angel McCoughtry 2.50 6.00
2 Brittney Sykes 4.00 10.00
3 Elizabeth Williams 2.00 5.00
4 Jessica Breland 1.50 4.00
5 Layshia Clarendon 2.00 5.00
6 Monique Billings RC 3.00 8.00
7 Renee Montgomery 1.50 4.00
8 Tiffany Hayes 2.00 5.00
9 Alaina Coates RC 3.00 8.00
10 Allie Quigley 2.00 5.00
11 Astou Ndour RC 3.00 8.00
12 Cheyenne Parker 2.00 5.00
13 Courtney Vandersloot 3.00 8.00
14 Diamond DeShields RC 4.00 10.00
15 Gabby Williams RC 20.00 50.00
16 Jamierra Faulkner 2.00 5.00
17 Kahleah Copper 3.00 8.00
18 Stefanie Dolson 2.00 5.00
19 Alex Bentley 2.00 5.00
20 Alyssa Thomas 3.00 8.00
21 Brionna Jones RC 12.00 30.00
22 Chiney Ogwumike 2.00 5.00
23 Courtney Williams 2.50 6.00
24 Jasmine Thomas 2.00 5.00
25 Jonquel Jones 4.00 10.00
26 Lexie Brown RC 3.00 8.00
27 Morgan Tuck 2.00 5.00
28 Rachel Banham 2.00 5.00
29 Shekinna Stricklen 2.00 5.00
30 Allisha Gray 2.50 6.00
31 Azura Stevens RC 5.00 12.00
32 Glory Johnson 2.00 5.00
33 Kaela Davis RC 2.00 5.00
34 Karima Christmas-Kelly 2.00 5.00
35 Kayla Thornton 2.00 5.00
36 Liz Cambage 2.00 5.00
37 Skylar Diggins-Smith 6.00 15.00
38 Candice Dupree 2.00 5.00
39 Cappie Pondexter 2.00 5.00
40 Erica McCall 2.00 5.00
41 Erica Wheeler 2.00 5.00
42 Kayla Alexander 2.00 5.00
43 Kelsey Mitchell RC 100.00 250.00
44 Natalie Achonwa 2.00 5.00
45 Stephanie Mavunga RC 3.00 8.00
46 Tiffany Mitchell 2.00 5.00
47 Victoria Vivians RC 3.00 8.00
48 A'ja Wilson RC 800.00 1,500.00
49 Dearica Hamby 2.50 6.00
50 Jaime Nared RC 3.00 8.00
51 Ji-Su Park RC 5.00 12.00
52 Kayla McBride 2.00 5.00
53 Kelsey Bone 2.00 5.00
54 Kelsey Plum 5.00 12.00
55 Lindsay Allen 2.00 5.00
56 Nia Coffey 2.00 5.00
57 Tamera Young 2.00 5.00
58 Alana Beard 2.00 5.00
59 Candace Parker 8.00 20.00
60 Chelsea Gray 3.00 8.00
61 Essence Carson 2.00 5.00

62 Jantel Lavender 2.00 5.00
63 Nneka Ogwumike 2.50 6.00
64 Odyssey Sims 2.00 5.00
65 Riquna Williams 2.00 5.00
66 Alexis Jones 2.00 5.00
67 Cecilia Zandalasini RC 3.00 8.00
68 Danielle Robinson 2.00 5.00
69 Lindsay Whalen 4.00 10.00
70 Maya Moore 6.00 15.00
71 Rebekkah Brunson 2.00 5.00
72 Seimone Augustus 2.00 5.00
73 Sylvia Fowles 2.50 6.00
74 Tanisha Wright 2.00 5.00
75 Amanda Zahui B 2.00 5.00
76 Bria Hartley 2.00 5.00
77 Epiphanny Prince 2.00 5.00
78 Kia Nurse RC 4.00 10.00
79 Kia Vaughn 2.00 5.00
80 Marissa Coleman 2.00 5.00
81 Shavonte Zellous 2.00 5.00
82 Sugar Rodgers 2.00 5.00
83 Tina Charles 4.00 10.00
84 Brianna January 2.00 5.00
85 Brittney Griner 8.00 20.00
86 Camille Little 2.00 5.00
87 DeWanna Bonner 2.50 6.00
88 Diana Taurasi 8.00 20.00
89 Leilani Mitchell 2.00 5.00
90 Marie Gulich RC 3.00 8.00
91 Sancho Lyttle 2.00 5.00
92 Alysha Clark 2.00 5.00
93 Breanna Stewart 20.00 50.00
94 Courtney Paris 2.00 5.00
95 Jewell Loyd 3.00 8.00
96 Jordin Canada RC 4.00 10.00
97 Kaleena Mosqueda-Lewis 2.00 5.00
98 Natasha Howard 2.50 6.00
99 Sue Bird 12.00 30.00
100 Ariel Atkins RC 10.00 25.00
101 Elena Delle Donne 5.00 12.00
102 Kristi Toliver 2.00 5.00
103 Krystal Thomas 2.00 5.00
104 LaToya Sanders 2.00 5.00
105 Monique Currie 2.00 5.00
106 Myisha Hines-Allen RC 4.00 10.00
107 Natasha Cloud 2.00 5.00
108 Shatori Walker-Kimbrough RC 10.00 25.00
109 Tianna Hawkins 2.00 5.00
110 Tierra Ruffin-Pratt 2.00 5.00

2018 WNBA Autographs

AW1 A'ja Wilson Street Clothes 600.00 1,200.00
AW2 A'ja Wilson Uniform 600.00 1,200.00
AW3 A'ja Wilson Game Action 600.00 1,200.00
SA1 Seimone Augustus Legends 40.00 100.00
SA2 Seimone Augustus Uniform 40.00 100.00
SA3 Seimone Augustus Game Action 40.00 100.00
EDD1 Elena Delle Donne Legends 60.00 150.00
EDD2 Elena Delle Donne Uniform 60.00 150.00
EDD3 Elena Delle Donne Game Action 60.00 150.00

1995 Women's Basketball Association

COMPLETE SET (27) 4.00 10.00
1 Checklist .20 .50
2 Lightning Mitchell DIR .20 .50
3 Sarah Campbell .20 .50
4 Lisa Carlsen .20 .50
5 Joy Champ .20 .50
6 Cledella Evans .20 .50
7 Crystal Flint .20 .50
8 Robbie Garcia .20 .50
9 Kay Kay Hart .20 .50
10 Petra Jackson .20 .50
11 Patrice Marshall .20 .50
12 Evette Ott .20 .50
13 Lynn Page .20 .50
14 Lisa Sandbothe .20 .50
15 Danielle Shareef .20 .50
16 Lisa Tate .20 .50
17 Diana Vines .20 .50
18 Tammy Williams .20 .50
19 Cynthia Wilson .20 .50
L1 Kansas City Mustangs .08 .25
L2 Chicago Twisters .08 .25
L3 St. Louis River Queens .08 .25
L4 Kentucky Marauders .08 .25
L5 Memphis Blues .08 .25
L6 Minnesota Stars .08 .25
L7 Nebraska Express .08 .25
L8 Oklahoma Flames .08 .25

1993 World University Games

COMPLETE SET (10) 1.20 3.00
2 Basketball .10 .25

1993 XXV Jogos Olimpicos

COMPLETE SET (84) 25.00 60.00
77 Scottie Pippen 3.00 8.00
78 Magic Johnson 5.00 12.00

1996-97 Z-Force

COMPLETE SET (200) 30.00 80.00
COMPLETE SERIES 1 (100) 10.00 20.00
COMPLETE SERIES 2 (100) 25.00 60.00
SUBSET CARDS SAME VALUE AS BASE CARDS
HILL Z: SER.2 STATED ODDS 1:900 HOB/RET
1 Mookie Blaylock .40 1.00
2 Alan Henderson .25 .60
3 Christian Laettner .40 1.00
4 Steve Smith .30 .75
5 Rick Fox .25 .60
6 Dino Radja .25 .60
7 Eric Williams .25 .60
8 Muggsy Bogues .40 1.00
9 Larry Johnson .50 1.25
10 Glen Rice .40 1.00
11 Michael Jordan 4.00 10.00
12 Toni Kukoc .40 1.00
13 Scottie Pippen 1.00 2.50
14 Dennis Rodman 1.00 2.50
15 Terrell Brandon .30 .75
16 Bobby Phills .25 .60
17 Bob Sura .25 .60
18 Jim Jackson .25 .60
19 Jason Kidd .60 1.50
20 Jamal Mashburn .30 .75
21 George McCloud .25 .60
22 Mahmoud Abdul-Rauf .25 .60
23 Antonio McDyess .40 1.00
24 Dikembe Mutombo .60 1.50
25 Joe Dumars .50 1.25
26 Grant Hill .60 1.50
27 Allan Houston .40 1.00
28 Otis Thorpe .30 .75
29 Chris Mullin .50 1.25
30 Joe Smith .30 .75
31 Latrell Sprewell .40 1.00
32 Sam Cassell .30 .75
33 Clyde Drexler .60 1.50
34 Robert Horry .40 1.00
35 Hakeem Olajuwon .75 2.00
36 Travis Best .25 .60
37 Dale Davis .25 .60
38 Reggie Miller .75 2.00
39 Rik Smits .30 .75
40 Brent Barry .30 .75
41 Loy Vaught .25 .60
42 Brian Williams .25 .60
43 Cedric Ceballos .30 .75
44 Eddie Jones .40 1.00
45 Nick Van Exel .40 1.00
46 Tim Hardaway .50 1.25
47 Alonzo Mourning .60 1.50
48 Kurt Thomas .25 .60
49 Walt Williams .25 .60
50 Vin Baker .30 .75
51 Glenn Robinson .40 1.00
52 Kevin Garnett 1.25 3.00
53 Tom Gugliotta .25 .60
54 Isaiah Rider .30 .75
55 Shawn Bradley .25 .60
56 Chris Childs .25 .60
57 Jayson Williams .25 .60
58 Patrick Ewing .60 1.50
59 Anthony Mason .30 .75
60 Charles Oakley .40 1.00
61 Nick Anderson .25 .60
62 Horace Grant .40 1.00
63 Anfernee Hardaway 1.00 2.50
64 Shaquille O'Neal 1.50 4.00
65 Dennis Scott .30 .75
66 Jerry Stackhouse .50 1.25
67 Clarence Weatherspoon .25 .60
68 Charles Barkley 1.00 2.50
69 Michael Finley .40 1.00
70 Kevin Johnson .40 1.00
71 Clifford Robinson .40 1.00
72 Arvydas Sabonis .40 1.00
73 Rod Strickland .40 1.00
74 Tyus Edney .25 .60
75 Brian Grant .30 .75
76 Billy Owens .25 .60
77 Mitch Richmond .50 1.25
78 Vinny Del Negro .25 .60
79 Sean Elliott .40 1.00
80 Avery Johnson .30 .75
81 David Robinson .75 2.00
82 Hersey Hawkins .60 1.50
83 Shawn Kemp .60 1.50
84 Gary Payton .60 1.50
85 Detlef Schrempf .40 1.00
86 Doug Christie .25 .60
87 Damon Stoudamire .40 1.00
88 Sharone Wright .25 .60
89 Jeff Hornacek .30 .75
90 Karl Malone .75 2.00
91 John Stockton .75 2.00
92 Greg Anthony .25 .60
93 Bryant Reeves .25 .60
94 Byron Scott .40 1.00
95 Juwan Howard .40 1.00
96 Gheorghe Muresan .25 .60
97 Rasheed Wallace .50 1.25
98 Chris Webber .50 1.25
99 Checklist .12 .30
100 Checklist .12 .30
101 Dikembe Mutombo .60 1.50
102 Dee Brown .25 .60
103 Dell Curry .40 1.00
104 Vlade Divac .40 1.00
105 Anthony Mason .30 .75
106 Robert Parish .50 1.25
107 Oliver Miller .25 .60
108 Eric Montross .25 .60
109 Ervin Johnson .25 .60
110 Stacey Augmon .30 .75
111 Charles Barkley 1.00 2.50
112 Jalen Rose .30 .75
113 Rodney Rogers .30 .75
114 Shaquille O'Neal 1.50 4.00
115 Dan Majerle .40 1.00
116 Kendall Gill .40 1.00
117 Khalid Reeves .25 .60
118 Allan Houston .40 1.00
119 Larry Johnson .50 1.25
120 John Starks .40 1.00
121 Rony Seikaly .30 .75
122 Gerald Wilkins .25 .60
123 Michael Cage .25 .60
124 Derrick Coleman .30 .75
125 Sam Cassell .30 .75
126 Danny Manning .30 .75
127 Robert Horry .40 1.00
128 Kenny Anderson .30 .75
129 Isaiah Rider .30 .75
130 Rasheed Wallace .50 1.25
131 Mahmoud Abdul-Rauf .30 .75
132 Vernon Maxwell .25 .60
133 Dominique Wilkins .60 1.50
134 Hubert Davis .25 .60
135 Popeye Jones .25 .60
136 Anthony Peeler .25 .60
137 Tracy Murray .25 .60
138 Rod Strickland .40 1.00
139 Shareef Abdur-Rahim RC .60 1.50
140 Ray Allen RC 2.00 5.00
141 Shandon Anderson RC .30 .75
142 Kobe Bryant RC 20.00 50.00
143 Marcus Camby RC .60 1.50
144 Erick Dampier RC .40 1.00
145 Emanual Davis RC .30 .75
146 Tony Delk RC .40 1.00
147 Todd Fuller RC .25 .60
148 Darvin Ham RC .75 2.00
149 Othella Harrington RC .30 .75
150 Shane Heal RC .40 1.00
151 Allen Iverson RC 3.00 8.00
152 Dontae' Jones RC .30 .75
153 Kerry Kittles RC .40 1.00
154 Priest Lauderdale RC .25 .60
155 Matt Maloney RC .30 .75
156 Stephon Marbury RC 1.25 3.00
157 Walter McCarty RC .40 1.00
158 Steve Nash RC 2.50 6.00
159 Jermaine O'Neal RC .60 1.50
160 Ray Owes RC .30 .75
161 Vitaly Potapenko RC .30 .75
162 Roy Rogers RC .30 .75
163 Antoine Walker RC .60 1.50
164 Samaki Walker RC .30 .75
165 Ben Wallace RC 2.00 5.00
166 John Wallace RC .30 .75
167 Jerome Williams RC .30 .75
168 Lorenzen Wright RC .30 .75
169 Vin Baker ZUP .30 .75
170 Charles Barkley ZUP 1.00 2.50
171 Patrick Ewing ZUP .60 1.50
172 Michael Finley ZUP .40 1.00
173 Kevin Garnett ZUP 1.25 3.00
174 Anfernee Hardaway ZUP 1.00 2.50
175 Grant Hill ZUP .60 1.50
176 Juwan Howard ZUP .40 1.00
177 Jim Jackson ZUP .25 .60
178 Eddie Jones ZUP .40 1.00
179 Michael Jordan ZUP 4.00 10.00
180 Shawn Kemp ZUP .60 1.50
181 Jason Kidd ZUP .60 1.50
182 Karl Malone ZUP .75 2.00
183 Antonio McDyess ZUP .40 1.00
184 Reggie Miller ZUP .75 2.00
185 Alonzo Mourning ZUP .60 1.50
186 Hakeem Olajuwon ZUP .75 2.00
187 Shaquille O'Neal ZUP 1.50 4.00
188 Gary Payton ZUP .60 1.50
189 Mitch Richmond ZUP .50 1.25
190 Clifford Robinson ZUP .40 1.00
191 David Robinson ZUP .75 2.00
192 Glenn Robinson ZUP .40 1.00
193 Dennis Rodman ZUP 1.00 2.50
194 Joe Smith ZUP .30 .75
195 Jerry Stackhouse ZUP .50 1.25
196 John Stockton ZUP .75 2.00
197 Damon Stoudamire ZUP .40 1.00
198 Chris Webber ZUP .50 1.25
199 Checklist (101-157) .12 .30
200 Checklist (158-200/ins.) .12 .30
NNO Grant Hill PROMO .75 2.00
NNO Grant Hill Total Z 8.00 20.00
NNO Grant Hill Jerry Stackhouse PROMO .75 2.00

1996-97 Z-Force Z-Cling

COMPLETE SET (100) 15.00 40.00
*Z-CLING: .75X TO 2X BASIC
R1 Ray Allen 4.00 10.00
R2 Stephon Marbury 2.50 6.00
R3 Shareef Abdur-Rahim 1.25 3.00

1996-97 Z-Force Big Men on the Court

COMPLETE SET (10) 2,500.00 5,000.00
SER.2 STATED ODDS 1:240 HOBBY/RETAIL
*Z-PEAT: .75X TO 2X BASE
1 Charles Barkley 75.00 200.00
2 Anfernee Hardaway 75.00 200.00
3 Grant Hill 60.00 60.00
4 Michael Jordan 2,000.00 4,000.00
5 Shawn Kemp 40.00 100.00
6 Alonzo Mourning 40.00 100.00
7 Hakeem Olajuwon 60.00 150.00
8 Shaquille O'Neal 125.00 300.00
9 Scottie Pippen 75.00 200.00
10 David Robinson 60.00 150.00

1996-97 Z-Force Little Big Men

COMPLETE SET (10) 25.00 60.00
SER.2 STATED ODDS 1:36 RETAIL
1 Kenny Anderson 2.50 6.00
2 Mookie Blaylock 3.00 8.00
3 Muggsy Bogues 12.00 30.00
4 Terrell Brandon 2.50 6.00
5 Allen Iverson 25.00 60.00
6 Avery Johnson 2.50 6.00
7 Kevin Johnson 3.00 8.00
8 Stephon Marbury 10.00 25.00
9 Gary Payton 5.00 12.00
10 Nick Van Exel 3.00 8.00

1996-97 Z-Force Slam Cam

COMPLETE SET (9) 2,000.00 4,000.00
SER.1 STATED ODDS 1:240 HOBBY/RETAIL
SC1 Clyde Drexler 25.00 60.00
SC2 Michael Finley 15.00 40.00
SC3 Anfernee Hardaway 50.00 120.00
SC4 Grant Hill 40.00 100.00
SC5 Michael Jordan 1,500.00 3,000.00
SC6 Shawn Kemp 30.00 80.00
SC7 Karl Malone 25.00 60.00
SC8 Antonio McDyess 15.00 40.00
SC9 Shaquille O'Neal 100.00 250.00

1996-97 Z-Force Swat Team

COMPLETE SET (9) 50.00 120.00
SER.1 STATED ODDS 1:72 HOBBY
ST1 Patrick Ewing 8.00 20.00
ST2 Kevin Garnett 15.00 40.00
ST3 Alonzo Mourning 8.00 20.00
ST4 Dikembe Mutombo 8.00 20.00
ST5 Hakeem Olajuwon 10.00 25.00
ST6 Shaquille O'Neal 20.00 50.00
ST7 David Robinson 10.00 25.00
ST8 Dennis Rodman 12.00 30.00
ST9 Joe Smith 4.00 10.00

1996-97 Z-Force Vortex

COMPLETE SET (15) 200.00 500.00
SER.1 STATED ODDS 1:36 RETAIL
V1 Charles Barkley 12.00 30.00
V2 Anfernee Hardaway 12.00 30.00
V3 Grant Hill 8.00 20.00
V4 Juwan Howard 5.00 12.00
V5 Michael Jordan 200.00 500.00
V6 Jason Kidd 8.00 20.00
V7 Reggie Miller 10.00 25.00
V8 Gary Payton 8.00 20.00
V9 Scottie Pippen 12.00 30.00
V10 Mitch Richmond 6.00 15.00
V11 Glenn Robinson 5.00 12.00
V12 Arvydas Sabonis 5.00 12.00
V13 Jerry Stackhouse 6.00 15.00
V14 John Stockton 10.00 25.00
V15 Damon Stoudamire 5.00 12.00

1996-97 Z-Force Zebut

COMPLETE SET (20) 300.00 600.00
SER.2 STATED ODDS 1:24 HOBBY
*ZPEAT: 1.5X TO 4X BASE HI
1 Shareef Abdur-Rahim 4.00 10.00
2 Ray Allen 12.00 30.00
3 Kobe Bryant 200.00 500.00
4 Marcus Camby 4.00 10.00
5 Erick Dampier 2.50 6.00
6 Todd Fuller 1.50 4.00
7 Othella Harrington 2.00 5.00
8 Allen Iverson 40.00 100.00
9 Kerry Kittles 2.50 6.00
10 Priest Lauderdale 1.50 4.00
11 Stephon Marbury 8.00 20.00
12 Steve Nash 15.00 40.00
13 Jermaine O'Neal 4.00 10.00
14 Ray Owes 2.00 5.00
15 Vitaly Potapenko 2.00 5.00
16 Roy Rogers 2.00 5.00
17 Antoine Walker 4.00 10.00
18 Samaki Walker 2.00 5.00
19 John Wallace 2.00 5.00
20 Lorenzen Wright 2.00 5.00

1996-97 Z-Force Zensations

COMPLETE SET (20) 10.00 25.00
SER.2 STATED ODDS 1:6 HOBBY/RETAIL
1 Shareef Abdur-Rahim 1.25 3.00
2 Ray Allen 4.00 10.00
3 Nick Anderson .50 1.25
4 Vin Baker .60 1.50
5 Mookie Blaylock .75 2.00
6 Calbert Cheaney .50 1.25
7 Kevin Garnett 2.50 6.00
8 Horace Grant .75 2.00
9 Tim Hardaway 1.00 2.50
10 Allen Iverson 6.00 15.00
11 Avery Johnson .60 1.50
12 Kevin Johnson .75 2.00
13 Danny Manning .60 1.50
14 Stephon Marbury 2.50 6.00
15 Jamal Mashburn .75 2.00
16 Glen Rice .75 2.00
17 Isaiah Rider .60 1.50
18 Latrell Sprewell .75 2.00
19 Rod Strickland .75 2.00
20 Nick Van Exel .75 2.00

1997-98 Z-Force

COMPLETE SET (210) 20.00 50.00
COMPLETE SERIES 1 (110) 8.00 20.00
COMPLETE SERIES 2 (100) 12.00 30.00
CARD NUMBER 143 DOES NOT EXIST
BAKER AND MCGRADY BOTH #'d 172
SUBSET CARDS SAME VALUE AS BASE
1 Anfernee Hardaway 1.00 2.50
2 Mitch Richmond .50 1.25
3 Stephon Marbury .50 1.25
4 Charles Barkley 1.00 2.50
5 Juwan Howard .30 .75
6 Avery Johnson .30 .75
7 Rex Chapman .25 .60
8 Antoine Walker .40 1.00
9 Nick Van Exel .40 1.00
10 Tim Hardaway .50 1.25
11 Clarence Weatherspoon .25 .60
12 John Stockton .75 2.00
13 Glenn Robinson .40 1.00
14 Anthony Mason .30 .75
15 Latrell Sprewell .50 1.25
16 Kendall Gill .25 .60
17 Terry Mills .25 .60
18 Mookie Blaylock .40 1.00
19 Michael Finley .40 1.00
20 Gary Payton .60 1.50
21 Kevin Garnett 1.00 2.50
22 Clyde Drexler .60 1.50
23 Michael Jordan 4.00 10.00
24 Antonio McDyess .40 1.00
25 Nick Anderson .30 .75
26 Patrick Ewing .60 1.50
27 Anthony Peeler .25 .60
28 Doug Christie .25 .60
29 Bobby Phills .30 .75
30 Kerry Kittles .30 .75
31 Reggie Miller .75 2.00
32 Karl Malone .75 2.00
33 Grant Hill .60 1.50
34 Shaquille O'Neal 1.25 3.00
35 Loy Vaught .30 .75
36 Kenny Anderson .30 .75
37 Wesley Person .30 .75
38 Jamal Mashburn .30 .75
39 Christian Laettner .40 1.00
40 Shawn Kemp .60 1.50
41 Glen Rice .40 1.00
42 Vin Baker .30 .75
43 Popeye Jones .25 .60
44 Derrick Coleman .40 1.00
45 Rik Smits .30 .75
46 Dale Ellis .30 .75
47 Rod Strickland .30 .75
48 Mark Price .40 1.00
49 Toni Kukoc .50 1.25
50 David Robinson .75 2.00
51 John Wallace .25 .60
52 Samaki Walker .25 .60
53 Shareef Abdur-Rahim .40 1.00
54 Rodney Rogers .30 .75
55 Dikembe Mutombo .60 1.50
56 Rony Seikaly .30 .75
57 Matt Maloney .25 .60
58 Chris Webber .50 1.25
59 Robert Horry .40 1.00
60 Rasheed Wallace .50 1.25
61 Jeff Hornacek .40 1.00
62 Walt Williams .30 .75
63 Detlef Schrempf .40 1.00
64 Dan Majerle .40 1.00
65 Dell Curry .30 .75
66 Scottie Pippen 1.00 2.50
67 Greg Anthony .30 .75
68 Mahmoud Abdul-Rauf .25 .60
69 Cedric Ceballos .30 .75
70 Terrell Brandon .30 .75
71 Arvydas Sabonis .50 1.25
72 Malik Sealy .30 .75
73 Dean Garrett .25 .60
74 Joe Dumars .50 1.25
75 Joe Smith .30 .75
76 Shawn Bradley .25 .60
77 Gheorghe Muresan .25 .60
78 Dale Davis .30 .75
79 Bryant Stith .25 .60
80 Lorenzen Wright .25 .60
81 Chris Childs .25 .60
82 Bryon Russell .25 .60
83 Steve Smith .30 .75
84 Jerry Stackhouse .40 1.00
85 Hersey Hawkins .30 .75
86 Ray Allen .75 2.00
87 Dominique Wilkins .50 1.25
88 Kobe Bryant 4.00 10.00
89 Tom Gugliotta .30 .75
90 Dennis Scott .30 .75
91 Dennis Rodman 1.00 2.50
92 Bryant Reeves .25 .60
93 Vlade Divac .40 1.00
94 Jason Kidd .60 1.50
95 Mario Elie .25 .60
96 Lindsey Hunter .25 .60
97 Olden Polynice .25 .60
98 Allan Houston .40 1.00
99 Alonzo Mourning .60 1.50
100 Allen Iverson 1.25 3.00
101 LaPhonso Ellis .30 .75
102 Bob Sura .25 .60
103 Chris Mullin .50 1.25
104 Sam Cassell .30 .75
105 Eric Williams .25 .60
106 Antonio Davis .30 .75
107 Marcus Camby .40 1.00
108 Isaiah Rider .30 .75
109 Checklist .25 .60
110 Checklist .25 .60
111 Tim Duncan RC 2.50 6.00
112 Joe Smith .30 .75
113 Shawn Kemp .60 1.50
114 Terry Mills .25 .60
115 Jacque Vaughn RC .30 .75
116 Ron Mercer RC .50 1.25
117 Brian Williams .30 .75
118 Rik Smits .30 .75
119 Eric Williams .25 .60
120 Tim Thomas RC .50 1.25
121 Damon Stoudamire .40 1.00
122 God Shammgod RC .40 1.00
123 Tyrone Hill .30 .75
124 Elden Campbell .30 .75
125 Keith Van Horn RC .60 1.50
126 Brian Grant .30 .75
127 Antonio McDyess .40 1.00
128 Darrell Armstrong .25 .60
129 Sam Perkins .30 .75
130 Chris Mills .25 .60
131 Reggie Miller .75 2.00
132 Chris Gatling .25 .60
133 Ed Gray RC .40 1.00
134 Hakeem Olajuwon .75 2.00
135 Chris Webber .50 1.25
136 Kendall Gill .30 .75
137 Wesley Person .30 .75
138 Derrick Coleman .40 1.00
139 Dana Barros .25 .60
140 Dennis Scott .25 .60
141 Paul Grant RC .25 .60
142 Scott Burrell .25 .60
144 Austin Croshere RC .30 .75
145 Maurice Taylor RC .30 .75
146 Kevin Johnson .40 1.00
147 Tony Battie RC .40 1.00
148 Tariq Abdul-Wahad RC .30 .75
149 Johnny Taylor RC .25 .60
150 Allen Iverson 1.25 3.00
151 Terrell Brandon .30 .75
152 Derek Anderson RC .40 1.00
153 Calbert Cheaney .30 .75
154 Jayson Williams .25 .60
155 Rick Fox .30 .75
156 John Thomas RC .25 .60
157 David Wesley .30 .75
158 Bobby Jackson RC .50 1.25
159 Kelvin Cato RC .30 .75
160 Vinny Del Negro .30 .75
161 Adonal Foyle RC .30 .75
162 Larry Johnson .50 1.25
163 Brevin Knight RC .40 1.00
164 Rod Strickland .30 .75
165 Rodrick Rhodes RC .30 .75
166 Scot Pollard RC .30 .75
167 Sam Cassell .30 .75
168 Jerry Stackhouse .40 1.00
169 Mark Jackson .30 .75
170 John Wallace .25 .60
171 Horace Grant .40 1.00
172A Vin Baker .30 .75
172B Tracy McGrady ERR RC 2.00 5.00
173 Eddie Jones .40 1.00
174 Kerry Kittles .30 .75
175 Antonio Daniels RC .40 1.00
176 Alan Henderson .25 .60
177 Sean Elliott .30 .75
178 John Starks .40 1.00
179 Chauncey Billups RC 1.25 3.00
180 Juwan Howard .30 .75
181 Bobby Phills .30 .75
182 Latrell Sprewell .50 1.25
183 Jim Jackson .30 .75
184 Danny Fortson RC .40 1.00
185 Zydrunas Ilgauskas .40 1.00
186 Clifford Robinson .30 .75
187 Chris Mullin .50 1.25
188 Greg Ostertag .25 .60
189 Antoine Walker ZUP .40 1.00
190 Michael Jordan ZUP 4.00 10.00
191 Scottie Pippen ZUP 1.00 2.50
192 Dennis Rodman ZUP 1.00 2.50
193 Grant Hill ZUP .60 1.50
194 Clyde Drexler ZUP .60 1.50
195 Kobe Bryant ZUP 4.00 10.00
196 Shaquille O'Neal ZUP 1.25 3.00
197 Alonzo Mourning ZUP .60 1.50
198 Ray Allen ZUP .75 2.00
199 Kevin Garnett ZUP 1.00 2.50
200 Stephon Marbury ZUP .50 1.25
201 Anfernee Hardaway ZUP 1.00 2.50
202 Jason Kidd ZUP .60 1.50
203 David Robinson ZUP .75 2.00
204 Gary Payton ZUP .60 1.50
205 Marcus Camby ZUP .40 1.00
206 Karl Malone ZUP .75 2.00
207 John Stockton ZUP .75 2.00
208 Shareef Abdur-Rahim ZUP .40 1.00
209 Charles Barkley CL 1.00 2.50
210 Gary Payton CL .60 1.50

1997-98 Z-Force Rave

*RAVE: 15X TO 40X BASE CARD HI
STATED PRINT RUN 399 SERIAL #'d SETS
23 Michael Jordan 1,500.00 3,000.00
88 Kobe Bryant 1,000.00 2,000.00
100 Allen Iverson 150.00 400.00
111 Tim Duncan 200.00 500.00
190 Michael Jordan ZUP 1,500.00 3,000.00
195 Kobe Bryant ZUP 1,000.00 2,000.00

1997-98 Z-Force Super Rave

*SUPER RAVE: 40X TO 100X BASE HI
STATED PRINT RUN 50 SERIAL #'d SETS
111 Tim Duncan 600.00 1,200.00
190 Michael Jordan ZUP 15,000.00 30,000.00
195 Kobe Bryant ZUP 5,000.00 10,000.00

1997-98 Z-Force Big Men on Court

COMPLETE SET (15) 3,000.00 6,000.00
SER.2 STATED ODDS 1:288 HOB/RET
1 Shareef Abdur-Rahim 40.00 100.00
2 Kobe Bryant 800.00 1,500.00
3 Marcus Camby 40.00 100.00
4 Tim Duncan 200.00 500.00
5 Kevin Garnett 150.00 400.00
6 Anfernee Hardaway 150.00 400.00
7 Grant Hill 150.00 400.00
8 Allen Iverson 300.00 600.00
9 Michael Jordan 2,000.00 4,000.00
10 Shawn Kemp 125.00 300.00
11 Stephon Marbury 60.00 150.00
12 Shaquille O'Neal 150.00 400.00
13 Scottie Pippen 125.00 300.00
14 Dennis Rodman 150.00 400.00
15 Antoine Walker 30.00 80.00

1997-98 Z-Force Boss

COMPLETE SET (20) 50.00 120.00
SER.1 STATED ODDS 1:6 HOBBY/RETAIL
*SUPER BOSS: 1X TO 2.5X BASE BOSS
SUPER BOSS: SER.1 STATED ODDS 1:36 H/R
1 Shareef Abdur-Rahim .60 1.50
2 Ray Allen 1.25 3.00
3 Kobe Bryant 15.00 40.00
4 Marcus Camby .60 1.50
5 Kevin Garnett 1.50 4.00
6 Anfernee Hardaway 1.50 4.00
7 Grant Hill 1.00 2.50
8 Allen Iverson 2.00 5.00
9 Eddie Jones .60 1.50
10 Michael Jordan 30.00 80.00
11 Shawn Kemp 1.00 2.50
12 Kerry Kittles .50 1.25
13 Stephon Marbury .75 2.00
14 Shaquille O'Neal 2.00 5.00
15 Hakeem Olajuwon 1.25 3.00
16 Scottie Pippen 1.50 4.00
17 Dennis Rodman 1.50 4.00
18 Joe Smith .50 1.25
19 Damon Stoudamire .60 1.50
20 Antoine Walker .60 1.50

1997-98 Z-Force Fast Track

COMPLETE SET (12) 15.00 40.00
SER.1 STATED ODDS 1:24 HOBBY/RETAIL
1 Ray Allen 3.00 8.00
2 Kobe Bryant 15.00 40.00
3 Marcus Camby 1.50 4.00
4 Juwan Howard 1.25 3.00
5 Eddie Jones 1.50 4.00
6 Kerry Kittles 1.25 3.00
7 Antonio McDyess 1.50 4.00
8 Joe Smith 1.25 3.00
9 Jerry Stackhouse 1.50 4.00
10 Damon Stoudamire 1.50 4.00
11 Antoine Walker 1.50 4.00
12 Chris Webber 2.00 5.00

1997-98 Z-Force Limited Access

COMPLETE SET (10) 30.00 80.00
SER.1 STATED ODDS 1:18 RETAIL
1 Shareef Abdur-Rahim 1.00 2.50
2 Ray Allen 2.00 5.00
3 Charles Barkley 2.50 6.00
4 Anfernee Hardaway 2.50 6.00
5 Juwan Howard .75 2.00
6 Michael Jordan 25.00 60.00
7 Stephon Marbury 1.25 3.00
8 Shaquille O'Neal 3.00 8.00
9 Dennis Rodman 2.50 6.00
10 Antoine Walker 1.00 2.50

1997-98 Z-Force Quick Strike

COMPLETE SET (12) 600.00 1,200.00
SER.2 STATED ODDS 1:96 HOB/RET
1 Shareef Abdur-Rahim 10.00 25.00
2 Anfernee Hardaway 25.00 60.00
3 Grant Hill 15.00 40.00
4 Allen Iverson 50.00 120.00
5 Michael Jordan 500.00 1,000.00
6 Stephon Marbury 12.00 30.00
7 Hakeem Olajuwon 20.00 50.00
8 Scottie Pippen 25.00 60.00
9 Damon Stoudamire 10.00 25.00
10 Keith Van Horn 15.00 40.00
11 Antoine Walker 10.00 25.00
12 Chris Webber 12.00 30.00

1997-98 Z-Force Rave Reviews

COMPLETE SET (12) 400.00 800.00
SER.1 STATED ODDS 1:288 HOBBY/RETAIL
1 Shareef Abdur-Rahim 25.00 60.00
2 Kevin Garnett 60.00 150.00
3 Anfernee Hardaway 40.00 100.00
4 Grant Hill 40.00 100.00
5 Allen Iverson 75.00 200.00
6 Michael Jordan 1,500.00 3,000.00
7 Shawn Kemp 40.00 100.00
8 Stephon Marbury 40.00 100.00
9 Shaquille O'Neal 60.00 150.00
10 Hakeem Olajuwon 40.00 100.00
11 Scottie Pippen 60.00 150.00
12 Dennis Rodman 60.00 150.00

1997-98 Z-Force Slam Cam

COMPLETE SET (12) 200.00 500.00
SER.2 STATED ODDS 1:36 HOB/RET
1 Kobe Bryant 75.00 200.00
2 Marcus Camby 2.00 5.00
3 Tim Duncan 12.00 30.00
4 Kevin Garnett 5.00 12.00
5 Michael Jordan 125.00 300.00
6 Shawn Kemp 3.00 8.00
7 Karl Malone 4.00 10.00
8 Antonio McDyess 2.00 5.00
9 Shaquille O'Neal 6.00 15.00
10 Joe Smith 1.50 4.00
11 Jerry Stackhouse 2.00 5.00
12 Chris Webber 2.50 6.00

1997-98 Z-Force Star Gazing

COMPLETE SET (15) 60.00 150.00
SER.2 STATED ODDS 1:18 RETAIL
1 Shareef Abdur-Rahim 2.00 5.00
2 Kobe Bryant 50.00 120.00
3 Marcus Camby 2.00 5.00
4 Kevin Garnett 5.00 12.00
5 Anfernee Hardaway 5.00 12.00
6 Grant Hill 3.00 8.00
7 Allen Iverson 6.00 15.00
8 Stephon Marbury 2.50 6.00
9 Hakeem Olajuwon 4.00 10.00
10 Shaquille O'Neal 6.00 15.00
11 Scottie Pippen 5.00 12.00
12 Dennis Rodman 5.00 12.00
13 Damon Stoudamire 2.00 5.00
14 Keith Van Horn 3.00 8.00
15 Antoine Walker 2.00 5.00

1997-98 Z-Force Total Impact

COMPLETE SET (12) 20.00 50.00
SER.1 STATED ODDS 1:48 HOBBY/RETAIL
1 Kobe Bryant 40.00 100.00
2 Marcus Camby 2.50 6.00
3 Kevin Garnett 6.00 15.00
4 Grant Hill 4.00 10.00
5 Allen Iverson 8.00 20.00
6 Eddie Jones 2.50 6.00
7 Shawn Kemp 4.00 10.00
8 Kerry Kittles 2.00 5.00
9 Hakeem Olajuwon 5.00 12.00
10 Scottie Pippen 6.00 15.00
11 Joe Smith 2.00 5.00
12 Chris Webber 3.00 8.00

1997-98 Z-Force Zebut

COMPLETE SET (12) 8.00 20.00
SER.2 STATED ODDS 1:24 HOB/RET
1 Derek Anderson .50 1.25
2 Tony Battie .50 1.25
3 Chauncey Billups 1.50 4.00
4 Austin Croshere .40 1.00
5 Antonio Daniels .50 1.25
6 Tim Duncan 3.00 8.00
7 Danny Fortson .50 1.25
8 Tracy McGrady 2.50 6.00
9 Ron Mercer .60 1.50
10 Tariq Abdul-Wahad .40 1.00
11 Tim Thomas .60 1.50
12 Keith Van Horn .75 2.00

1997-98 Z-Force Zensations

COMPLETE SET (25) 10.00 25.00
SER.2 STATED ODDS 1:6 HOB/RET
1 Ray Allen 1.25 3.00
2 Vin Baker .50 1.25
3 Charles Barkley 1.50 4.00
4 Clyde Drexler 1.00 2.50
5 Patrick Ewing 1.00 2.50
6 Juwan Howard .50 1.25
7 Eddie Jones .60 1.50
8 Shawn Kemp 1.00 2.50
9 Jason Kidd 1.00 2.50
10 Kerry Kittles .50 1.25
11 Karl Malone 1.25 3.00
12 Antonio McDyess .60 1.50
13 Hakeem Olajuwon 1.25 3.00
14 Gary Payton 1.00 2.50
15 Glen Rice .60 1.50
16 Mitch Richmond .75 2.00
17 David Robinson 1.25 3.00
18 Dennis Rodman 1.50 4.00
19 Joe Smith .50 1.25
20 Latrell Sprewell .75 2.00
21 Jerry Stackhouse .60 1.50
22 John Stockton 1.25 3.00
23 Damon Stoudamire .60 1.50
24 Rasheed Wallace .75 2.00
25 Chris Webber .75 2.00